WEBSTER'S
NEW
STUDENTS
DICTIONARY

A Merriam-Webster ®

G. & C. MERRIAM COMPANY, *Publishers*
SPRINGFIELD, MASSACHUSETTS, U.S.A.

CONTENTS

ISBN 0-87779-180-5

The phrase "akin to" indicates a word which is a cognate of the entry word.

Words cited in an etymology from a language which does not use the Roman alphabet are transliterated:

pter·o·dac·tyl . . . *n* [Gk *pteron* wing . . . +*daktylos* finger]

Words cited from a tone language show small superscript figures which indicate the tone of the word or syllable they follow:

¹kow·tow . . . *n* [Chin (Pek) *k'o¹ t'ou²* . . .]

No etymology is given for an entry word if it is a compound, if it is closely related to a word whose etymology is shown, or if its origin is unknown.

USAGE

Three types of status labels—temporal, regional, and stylistic—are used in this dictionary to signal that a word or a sense of a word is not part of the standard English vocabulary.

The temporal label *obs* ("obsolete") means that there is no evidence of the use of the word since 1755. The temporal label *archaic* means that a word once in common use is found today only sporadically or in special contexts:

³post *n* . . . **1** *obs*
thorp . . . *n* . . . *archaic*

A word or sense limited in use to a specific region of the U.S. or to one of the other countries of the English-speaking world has an appropriate regional label:

²wash *n* . . . **3** . . . **d** *West*
pi·az·za . . . *n* . . . **2** . . . **b** *chiefly North & Midland*
sun·down·er . . . *n, Austral*
bon·net . . . *n* . . . **4** *Brit*
ma·vour·neen *also* **ma·vour·nin** . . . *n, Irish*

The label *dial* ("dialect") indicates a complex pattern of use that usually includes several regional varieties of American English or of American and British English:

lar·rup . . . *vt, dial*

The stylistic label *slang* is used with words that are especially appropriate in contexts of extreme informality:

¹bug·house . . . *n, slang*

No satisfactory objective test for *slang* has been devised, however, and no word is invariably slang.

Many standard words, in fact, can be given slang application.

Definitions are sometimes followed by verbal illustrations that show a typical use of the word in context. These illustrations are enclosed in angle brackets, and the word being illustrated is printed in italics:

²old *n* . . . ⟨days of *old*⟩

Definitions are sometimes followed by usage notes that give supplementary information about such matters as idiom, syntax, and semantic relationship:

¹but . . . *conj* **1** . . . **c** . . . — used after a negative
²nuptial *n* . . . — usu. used in pl.
²sire *vt* **1** . . . — used esp. of domestic animals

And occasionally a usage note is used in place of a definition (as for conjunctions, prepositions, and interjections):

hi . . . *interj* — used esp. as a greeting

A usage note is introduced by a lightface dash.

SENSE DIVISION

A boldface colon is used in this dictionary to introduce a definition; it is also used to separate two or more definitions of a single sense:

Af·ro . . . *adj* . . . **:** having the hair shaped into a round bushy mass
²content *vt* **:** to appease the desires of **:** SATISFY

Boldface Arabic numerals separate the senses of a word that has more than one sense, and boldface lowercase letters separate the subsenses of a word:

¹sim·ple . . . *adj* . . . **1 :** free from guile or vanity **2 a :** of humble origin **b :** deficient in education, experience, or intelligence

A particular semantic relationship between senses is sometimes suggested by the use of one of the two italic sense dividers *esp* or *also*:

¹track . . . *n* . . . **5 :** track-and-field sports; *esp* **:** those performed on a racing track
²robe *vb* . . . **2 :** to put on a robe; *also* **:** DRESS

The sense divider *esp* ("especially") is used to introduce the most common meaning subsumed in the more general preceding definition. The sense divider *also* is used to introduce a meaning related to the preceding sense by an easily understood extension of that sense.

When an italicized label follows a boldface numeral, the label applies only to that specific numbered sense and its subsenses:

²com·mune . . . *n* . . . **3** *cap* **a** . . . **b**

When an italicized label follows a boldface letter, the label applies only to that specific lettered sense:

¹thun·der ... *n* ... **1** ... **b** *archaic*

The order of senses is historical: the sense known to have been first used in English is entered first. This is not to be taken to mean, however, that each sense of a word having several senses developed from the immediately preceding sense. It is altogether possible that sense 2 and sense 3 of a word developed independently of one another from sense 1.

CROSS-REFERENCE

Four different kinds of cross-references are used in this dictionary: directional, synonymous, cognate, and inflectional. In each instance the cross=reference is readily recognized by the lightface small capitals in which it is printed.

A cross-reference following a lightface dash and beginning with *compare* or *see* is a directional cross=reference. It directs the dictionary user to look elsewhere for further information:

knit stitch *n* ... — compare PURL STITCH
Ve·nus ... *n* ... **2** ... — see PLANET table

A cross-reference following a boldface colon is a synonymous cross-reference. It may stand alone, it may follow an analytical definition, or it may be one of two or more synonymous cross-references separated by commas:

vapor trail *n* : CONTRAIL
va·por·ous ... *adj* ... **2** : containing or obscured by vapors : MISTY **3** : UNSUBSTANTIAL, VAGUE

A synonymous cross-reference indicates that a definition at the entry cross-referred to can be substituted as a definition for the entry or the sense in which the cross-reference appears.

A cross-reference following an italic *var of* ("variant of") is a cognate cross-reference:

rou·ble *var of* RUBLE

A cross-reference following an italic label that identifies an entry as an inflected form (as of a noun or verb) is an inflectional cross-reference:

won *past of* WIN

Cognate and inflectional cross-references direct the user to another entry for further information.

COMBINING FORMS, PREFIXES, & SUFFIXES

An entry that begins or ends with a hyphen is a word element that forms part of an English compound; for example, *self-*, *inter-*, and *-ness*. Combining forms, prefixes, and suffixes are entered in this dictionary to make understandable the meaning of many undefined run-ons and to make recognizable the meaningful elements of new words that have not yet achieved dictionary entry.

LISTS OF UNDEFINED WORDS

Lists of undefined words occur at the bottom of the pages after the entries *anti-*, *non-*, *over-*, *re-*, *sub-*, *super-*, and *un-*. These words are not defined because they are self-explanatory: their meanings are the sum of a meaning of the prefix and a meaning of the root word.

PREFACE

Webster's New Students Dictionary is a new work in the Merriam-Webster series of dictionaries. It is a school dictionary edited for use either as the third dictionary in a three-dictionary progression, being preceded by Webster's New Elementary Dictionary and Webster's Intermediate Dictionary, or as the second of a two-dictionary progression, being preceded by Webster's Intermediate Dictionary.

The vocabulary entries in Webster's New Students Dictionary have been selected chiefly on the basis of their occurrence in textbooks and supplementary reading in all subjects of the school curriculum. The definers have had before them this firsthand evidence as well as the millions of examples of usage that underlie Webster's Third New International Dictionary. This method of editing ensures the coverage of today's school vocabulary, especially in mathematics, science, and social studies, and at the same time makes certain that the current literary and general vocabulary is not neglected.

This dictionary includes several features found in more advanced Merriam-Webster dictionaries. The etymologies, enclosed in square brackets, give students a substantial basis for the fascinating study of word origins. The synonym paragraphs, printed at the end of definitions, clarify commonly confused words (as *imply* and *infer*) and discriminate between closely related terms (as *danger, peril,* and *hazard*). There are more than 500 pictorial illustrations, and a dozen useful tables (as at *Bible* and *planet*). The back matter following the A–Z vocabulary includes a section of abbreviations widely used in writing and printing and a section devoted to signs and symbols. The pages immediately preceding the A-Z vocabulary are given over to a series of explanatory notes that should be read carefully by all users of the dictionary.

Webster's New Students Dictionary is the product of a company that began publishing dictionaries in 1847. It is offered to students with pride and confidence, and with the hope that they will derive pleasure and satisfaction from its use.

G. & C. Merriam Co.

ENTRIES

A boldface letter or a combination of such letters set flush with the left-hand margin of each column of type is a main entry. The main entry may consist of letters set solid, of letters joined by a hyphen, or of letters separated by one or more spaces:

old·ish . . . *adj*
old-line . . . *adj*
old maid *n*

The main entries follow one another in alphabetical order letter by letter: *man-o'-war bird* follows *manor house*. Those containing an Arabic numeral are alphabetized as if the numeral were spelled out: *carbon 14* comes between *carbon disulfide* and *carbonic*.

A pair of guide words is printed at the top of each page. They are usually the alphabetically first and the alphabetically last entries on the page, and thus they indicate at a glance the alphabetical spread of entries on the page:

full-blown   **fungicidal**

Any boldface word—a main entry with definition, a variant, an inflected form, a defined or undefined run-on, an entry in a list of self-explanatory words —may be used as a guide word.

Centered periods within entry words indicate division points at which a hyphen may be put at the end of a line of print or writing. Thus the noun *rec·i·ta·tion* may be ended on one line and continued on the next in three ways:

rec-
itation
   reci-
   tation
      recita-
      tion

Centered periods are not shown after a single initial letter or before a single final letter because printers seldom divide a word in such a place:

idol . . . *n*
heavy . . . *adj*

There are, in fact, acceptable alternative end-of-line divisions just as there are acceptable variant spellings and pronunciations, but no alternative divisions are shown for any entry in this dictionary.

A double hyphen at the end of a line in this dictionary (as in the definition of **¹coif**) stands for a hyphen that belongs at that point in a hyphened word and that is retained when the word is written on one line.

When one main entry has exactly the same written form as another, the two are distinguished by superscript numerals preceding each entry:

¹play . . . *n*
²play *vb*

Centered periods are usually shown only at the first homograph:

¹me·an·der . . . *n*
²meander *vi*

When a main entry is followed by the word *or* and another spelling, the two spellings are equal variants. Both are standard, and either one may be used according to personal inclination:

the·a·ter *or* **the·a·tre** . . . *n*

If two variants joined by *or* are out of alphabetical order, the one printed first is somewhat more common than the second:

judg·ment *or* **judge·ment** . . . *n*

They are, however, considered equal variants. When another spelling is joined to the main entry by the word *also*, the spelling after *also* is a secondary variant and occurs much less frequently than the first:

ko·peck *also* **ko·pek** . . . *n*

Secondary variants belong to standard usage, however, and may be used according to personal inclination.

A main entry may be followed by one or more derivatives or by a homograph with a different functional label:

nudge . . . *vt* . . . — **nudge** *n* — **nudg·er** *n*

These are run-on entries, which are not defined because their meanings are readily derivable from the meaning of the root word. A main entry may also be followed by one or more phrases containing the entry word or one of its inflected forms:

hilt . . . *n* . . . — **to the hilt**

These are likewise run-on entries, but they are defined since their meanings are more than the sum of the meanings of their elements.

PRONUNCIATION

The matter between a pair of reversed virgules \ \ following a boldface entry indicates the pronunciation. The symbols are explained in the chart printed inside the front and back covers, and in a simplified key along the bottom of the page in the A-Z vocabulary section.

A high-set mark ' indicates major (primary) stress or accent; a low-set mark ˌ indicates minor (secondary) stress or accent; a syllable with neither a high-set nor a low-set mark is unstressed:

dead·line \'ded-ˌlīn\ *n*
em·bryo \'em-brē-ˌō\ *n*

A stress mark stands at the beginning of the syllable that receives the stress.

Hyphens used in the pronunciation indicate syllabic division. Sometimes these hyphens coincide with the centered periods in the boldface entry which indicate end-of-line divisions; sometimes they do not:

hip·ster \'hip-stər\ *n*
boil·er \'bȯi-lər\ *n*

The placement of syllabic divisions is based solely on phonetic considerations.

Symbols in the pronunciation enclosed by parentheses represent elements that are present in the pronunciation of some speakers but are absent from the pronunciation of other speakers, elements that are present in some but absent from other utterances of the same speaker, or elements whose presence or absence is uncertain:

rec·to·ry \'rek-t(ə-)rē\ *n*
ab·sence \'ab-sən(t)s\ *n*

The presence of variant pronunciations indicates that not all educated speakers pronounce words the same way. A second-place variant is not to be regarded as less acceptable than the pronunciation given first. It may, in fact, be used by as many educated speakers as the first variant. One comes before the other simply because of the requirements of the printed page:

bat·tery \'bat-ə-rē, 'ba-trē\ *n*
era \'ir-ə, 'er-ə, 'ē-rə\ *n*

When a main entry has an incomplete pronunciation, the missing part (indicated by one or more hyphens) is to be supplied from a pronunciation in another entry:

conn·ing tower \'kän-iŋ-\ *n*
res·o·na·tor \-ˌāt-ər\ *n*

When part of a second or other variant pronunciation is missing, it is to be supplied from a preceding variant pronunciation within the same pair of reversed virgules:

¹proc·ess \'präs-ˌes, 'prōs-, -əs\ *n*

FUNCTIONAL LABELS

An italic label indicating one of the eight traditional parts of speech or some other functional classification follows the pronunciation or, if no pronunciation is given, the main entry:

uni·sex . . . *adj*　　　　**¹it** . . . *pron*
high·ly . . . *adv*　　　　**²rap** *vb*
²why *conj*　　　　　　　**¹ought** . . . *auxiliary verb*
ouch . . . *interj*　　　　**multi-** *comb form*
voice·print . . . *n*　　　**demi-** *prefix*
at . . . *prep*　　　　　　**-ize** . . . *vb suffix*

INFLECTED FORMS

The plurals of nouns are shown in this dictionary when suffixation brings about a change of final -*y* to -*i*-, when the noun ends in -*o* or in -*ey*, when the noun has an irregular plural or a zero plural or a foreign plural, when the noun is a compound that pluralizes any element but the last, when the noun has variant plurals, and when it is believed that the dictionary user might have reasonable doubts about the spelling of the plural or when the plural is spelled in a way contrary to what is expected:

²cry *n, pl* **cries**
ego . . . *n, pl* **egos**
sur·rey . . . *n, pl* **surreys**
¹mouse . . . *n, pl* **mice**
sheep . . . *n, pl* **sheep**
hi·lum . . . *n, pl* **hi·la**
jack-of-all-trades . . . *n, pl* **jacks-of-all-trades**
ru·men . . . *n, pl* **ru·mi·na** . . . *or* **rumens**
¹pi . . . *n, pl* **pis**
³dry . . . *n, pl* **drys**

Plural forms are usually cut back when the noun has three or more syllables:

ca·su·al·ty . . . *n, pl* **-ties**

Some plural nouns like *environs* and *mores* are regularly followed by a plural verb; others like *genetics* and *news* are regularly followed by a singular verb. Still others may take either a singular or a plural verb, and they are appropriately labeled:

ath·let·ics . . . *n sing or pl*

The principal parts of verbs are shown when suffixation brings about a doubling of a final consonant or a change of final -*y* to -*i*-, when final -*c* changes to -*ck*- in suffixation, when the verb ends in -*ee* or -*ey*, when the inflection is irregular, when there are variant inflected forms, and when it is believed that the dictionary user might have reasonable doubts about the spelling of an inflected form or when the inflected form is spelled in a way contrary to what is expected:

²rap *vb* **rapped; rap·ping**
³rally *vt* **ral·lied; ral·ly·ing**
¹frol·ic ... *vi* **frol·icked; frol·ick·ing**
²decree *vb* **de·creed; de·cree·ing**
¹sur·vey ... *vt* **sur·veyed; sur·vey·ing**
¹see ... *vb* **saw** ...; **seen** ...; **see·ing**
²burn *vb* **burned** ... *or* **burnt** ...; **burn·ing**
²visa *vt* **vi·saed** ...; **vi·sa·ing**
²chagrin *vt* **cha·grined** ...; **cha·grin·ing**

The principal parts of regularly inflected verbs are shown when it is desirable to indicate the pronunciation of one of the inflected forms:

²sober *vb* **so·bered; so·ber·ing**\-b(ə-)riŋ\

Principal parts are often cut back when the verb has three or more syllables, when it is a disyllable that ends in -*l* and has variant spellings, and when it is a compound whose second element is readily recognized as an irregular verb:

scar·i·fy ... *vt* **-fied; -fy·ing**
²jewel *vt* **-eled** *or* **-elled; -el·ing** *or* **-el·ling**
¹re·take ... *vt* **-took** ...;**-tak·en**

The comparative and superlative forms of adjectives and adverbs are shown in this dictionary when suffixation brings about a doubling of a final consonant or a change of final -*y* to -*i*-, when the word ends in -*ey*, when the inflection is irregular, and when there are variant inflected forms:

³squat *adj* **squat·ter; squat·test**
cloudy ... *adj* **cloud·i·er; -est**
glu·ey ... *adj* **glu·i·er; -est**
¹good ... *adj* **bet·ter** ...; **best**
³well *adv* **bet·ter** ...; **best**
sly ... *adj* **sli·er** *also* **sly·er** ...; **sli·est** *also* **sly·est**

The superlative forms of adjectives and adverbs of two or more syllables are usually cut back:

scanty ... *adj* **scant·i·er; -est**

The comparative and superlative forms of regularly inflected adjectives and adverbs are shown when it is desirable to indicate the pronunciation of the inflected forms:

¹long ... *adj* **long·er** \'lȯŋ-gər\; **long·est** \'lȯŋ-gəst\

Notwithstanding the inclusion of forms in -*er* and -*est*, the comparative and superlative degrees of many of these adjectives and adverbs (especially ones whose base form is of two or more syllables) may also be expressed with *more* and *most*: *windier* or *more windy*; *windiest* or *most windy*.

Inflected forms are not shown at undefined run-ons.

Irregular inflected forms are entered at their own alphabetical places if they fall alphabetically more than a column away from the main entry:

men *pl of* MAN
taught *past of* TEACH

CAPITALIZATION

Most entries in this dictionary begin with a lowercase letter. Some of them have an italicized label *often cap* which indicates that the word is as likely to be capitalized as not. Some entries begin with an uppercase letter which indicates that the word is usually capitalized. The absence of an initial capital or of an *often cap* label indicates that the word is not ordinarily capitalized:

girl ... *n*
ant·arc·tic ... *adj, often cap*
Pla·to·nism ... *n*

The capitalization of entries that are open or hyphened compounds is indicated by the form of the entry or by an italicized label:

North Star *n*
neo·im·pres·sion·ism ... *n, often cap N&I*
plaster of par·is ... *often cap 2d P*

Words capitalized in some senses and lowercase in others show variations from the form of the main entry by the use of italicized labels at the appropriate senses:

com·mon·wealth ... *n* ... **5** *often cap* ... **6** *often cap*

ETYMOLOGY

The etymology of a vocabulary entry is given in boldface square brackets just before the definition. The etymology traces the history of the entry word as far back as possible in English, tells from what language and in what form it came into English, and traces the pre-English source as far as possible. The words which are the ancestors of the entry word are italicized; their meanings are given in roman type:

¹clock ... *n* [MD *clocke* bell, clock, fr. ML *clocca* bell]

If the form of a source word does not follow the language abbreviation in an etymology, its form is the same as that of its immediate descendant. If the meaning of a source word does not follow the word, its meaning is the same as that of its immediate descendant:

lan·guage ... *n* [ME, fr. OF, fr. *langue* tongue, language, fr. L *lingua*]

ABBREVIATIONS IN THIS WORK

ab ....about
abbr ....abbreviation
abl ....ablative
acc, accus ..accusative
A.D. ....anno Domini
adj ....adjective
adv ....adverb
AF ....Anglo-French
Afrik ......Afrikaans
alter ......alteration
a.m. ....ante meridiem
Am ....American
AmerF .....American
　　　　 French
AmerInd ...American
　　　　 Indian
AmerSp ....American
　　　　 Spanish
anc ....ancient
Ar ....Arabic
Aram ......Aramaic
Arm........Armenian
aug ....augmentative
Austral .....Australia,
　　　　 Australian
AV ....Authorized
　　　　 Version

b ....born
B.C. ....before Christ
Belg ....Belgian
Bib ....biblical
Bret........Breton
Brit ....British
bro ....brother
bros ....brothers

C ....centigrade
Canad .....Canada
CanF ......Canadian
　　　　 French
Cant ....Cantonese
cap ....capitalized
Capt ......Captain
Catal ......Catalan
caus ......causative
Celt ....Celtic
cen ....central
cent ....century
cgs ....centimeter-
　　　　 gram-second
Chin ....Chinese
comb .....combining
compar .....comparative
conj ....conjunction
contr .....contraction
Corn ......Cornish

d ....died
D ....Dutch
Dan ....Danish
dat ....dative
dau ....daughter
dial ....dialect
dim ....diminutive
Dr ....Doctor
Du ....Dutch
DV ....Douay Version

E ....east, eastern,
　　　　 English

Egypt ......Egyptian
ENE ......east-northeast
Eng ....English
ESE ....east-southeast
Esk ....Eskimo
esp ....especially

F ....Fahrenheit,
　　　　 French
fem ......feminine
Finn ......Finnish
fl ....flourished
Flem .....Flemish
fr ....from
Fr ....French
freq ......frequentative
ft ....feet
fut ....future

G ....German
gen ......genitive
Ger ....German
Gk ....Greek
Gmc ......Germanic
Goth ......Gothic

Heb ....Hebrew
Hung ......Hungarian

I ....island
Icel ....Icelandic
i.e. ....id est (L, that
　　　　 is)
imper ......imperative
incho ......inchoative
indic ......indicative
infin ......infinitive
intens ......intensive
interj ......interjection
IrGael .....Irish Gaelic
irreg ......irregular
It, Ital .....Italian

Jap ....Japanese
Jav ....Javanese

L ....Latin
LaF ....Louisiana
　　　　 French
lat ....latitude
LG ....Low German
LGk ......Late Greek
LHeb .....Late Hebrew
lit ....literally
LL ....Late Latin
long ....longitude

m ....miles
masc ......masculine
MD ....Middle Dutch
ME ....Middle English
Mex ....Mexican
MexSp ....Mexican
　　　　 Spanish
MF ....Middle French
MGk ......Middle Greek
MHG ......Middle High
　　　　 German
MIr ....Middle Irish
mks ....meter-
　　　　 kilogram-
　　　　 second

ML ....Medieval Latin
MLG ......Middle Low
　　　　 German
mm ....millimeter
modif ......modification
MSS ....manuscripts
Mt ....Mount

n ....noun
N ....north, northern
NATO .....North Atlantic
　　　　 Treaty Orga-
　　　　 nization
naut ....nautical
NCE ......New Catholic
　　　　 Edition
NE ....northeast,
　　　　 northeastern
neut ......neuter
NewEng ....New England
NGk ....New Greek
NHeb .....New Hebrew
NL ....New Latin
NNE ......north-
　　　　 northeast
NNW .....north-
　　　　 northwest
no ....number
No ....North
nom ....nominative
nonstand ...nonstandard
Norw .....Norwegian
n pl ....noun plural
NW ....northwest,
　　　　 northwestern

obs ....obsolete
occas .....occasionally
OE ....Old English
OF ....Old French
OHG ......Old High
　　　　 German
OIr ....Old Irish
OIt ....Old Italian
ON ....Old Norse
ONF ......Old North
　　　　 French
OPer ......Old Persian
OProv .....Old Provençal
orig ....originally

PaG ....Pennsylvania
　　　　 German
part ......participle
pass ......passive
Pek ....Pekingese
Per ....Persian
perf ......perfect
perh ......perhaps
pers ......person
Pg ....Portuguese
pl ....plural
p.m. ....post meridiem
Pol ....Polish
Port ......Portuguese
pp ....past participle
prep ......preposition
pres ......present
prob ......probably
pron ......pronoun

Prov ....Provençal
prp ....present
　　　　 participle
pseud .....pseudonym

R.C. ....Roman
　　　　 Catholic
refl ....reflexive
Rom ....Roman
RSV ....Revised Stan-
　　　　 dard Version
Russ ....Russian

S ....south, southern
Sc ....Scots
Scand .....Scandinavian
ScGael ....Scottish Gaelic
Scot ....Scottish
SE ....southeast,
　　　　 southeastern
Sem ....Semitic
Serb ....Serbian
sing ....singular
Skt ....Sanskrit
Slav ....Slavic
So ....South
Sp, Span ...Spanish
SSE ....south-
　　　　 southeast
SSW ......south-
　　　　 southwest
St ....Saint
subj ....subjunctive
substand ....substandard
superl ......superlative
Sw ....Swedish
SW ....southwest,
　　　　 southwestern
Swed ......Swedish
syll ....syllable
syn ....synonymy

Tag ....Tagalog
trans ......translation
Turk ......Turkish

U ....University
U.A.R. ....United Arab
　　　　 Republic
UN ....United
　　　　 Nations
U.S. ....United States
U.S.S.R. ...Union of
　　　　 Soviet Social-
　　　　 ist Republics
usu ....usually

var ....variant
vars ......variants
vb ....verb
vi ....verb intransi-
　　　　 tive
VL ....Vulgar Latin
voc ....vocative
vt ....verb transitive

W ....Welsh, west,
　　　　 western
WNW .....west-northwest
WSW .....west-southwest

9a

PRONUNCIATION SYMBOLS

ə .....banana, collect, abut; in stressed syllables as in humdrum, abut

ə......immediately preceding \l\, \n\, \m\, \ŋ\, as in battle, mitten, eaten, and sometimes cap and bells \-ᵊm-\, lock and key \-ᵊŋ-\; immediately following \l\, \m\, \r\, as often in French table, prisme, titre

ər ....operation, around, other; in stressed syllables as in fur, urge, urgent, furry, hurry

a ......mat, map, mad, gag, snap, patch

ā .....day, fade, date, aorta, drape, cape

ä .....bother, cot, and, with most American speakers, father, cart

à .....vowel between \a\ and \ä\, as in some pronunciations of aunt, half, can't and as in French patte

aù ....now, loud, out

b .....baby, rib

ch ....chin, nature \'nā-chər\ (actually, this sound is \t\ + \sh\)

d .....did, adder

e .....bet, bed, peck

ē .....beat, nosebleed, easy; in unstressed syllables as in create and in the last syllable of easy, mealy

f ......fifty, cuff, phone

g .....go, big, gift

h .....hat, ahead

hw ...whale

i ......tip, banish, active

ī .....site, side, buy, tripe (actually, this sound is \ä\ + \i\, or \à\ + \i\)

j .....job, gem, edge, join, judge (actually, this sound is \d\ + \zh\)

k .....kin, cook, ache

k̲ .....German ich, Buch

l̲ ......lily, pool

m ....murmur, dim, nymph

n .....no, own

ⁿ .....indicates that a preceding vowel or diphthong is pronounced with the nasal passages open, as in French un bon vin blanc \œⁿ-bōⁿ-vaⁿ-bläⁿ\

ŋ .....sing \'siŋ\, singer \'siŋ-ər\, finger \'fiŋ-gər\, ink \'iŋk\, thing \'thiŋ\

ō .....bone, know, beau

ȯ .....saw, all, gnaw

œ ....French bœuf, German Hölle

ō̅e̅ ....French feu, German Höhle

ȯi ....coin, destroy, sawing

p .....pepper, lip

r .....rarity

s .....source, less

sh ....with nothing between, as in shy, mission, machine, special (actually, this is a single sound, not two); with a hyphen between, two sounds as in death's-head \'deths-,hed\

t ......tie, attack

th ....with nothing between, as in thin, ether (actually, this is a single sound, not two); with a hyphen between, two sounds as in knighthood \'nīt-,hùd\

t̲h̲ ....then, either, this (actually, this is a single sound, not two)

ü .....rule, youth, union \'yü-nyən\, few \'fyü\

ù .....pull, wood, book, curable \'kyùr-ə-bəl\

ᵫ ....German füllen, hübsch

ᵫ̅ ....French rue, German fühlen

v .....vivid, give

w.....we, away, strenuous \'stren-yə-wəs\

y .....yard, young, cue \'kyü\, union \'yü-nyən\

ʸ......indicates that during the articulation of the sound represented by the preceding character the front of the tongue has substantially the position it has for the articulation of the first sound of yard, as in French digne \dēnʸ\, Italian gli \lʸē\

yü ....youth, union, cue, few, mute

yù ....curable, fury

z .....zone, raise

zh ....with nothing between, as in vision, azure \'azh-ər\ (actually, this is a single sound, not two); with a hyphen between, two sounds as in jew's-harp \'jüz-,härp\

\ .....slant line used in pairs to mark the beginning and end of a transcription \'pen\

' ......mark preceding a syllable with primary (strongest) stress: \'pen-mən-,ship\

, ...mark preceding a syllable with secondary (next-strongest) stress: \'pen-mən-,ship\

- ......mark of syllable division

( ) ....indicate that what is symbolized between is present in some utterances but not in others: at factory, \'fak-t(ə-)rē\ = \'fak-tə-rē, 'fak-trē\ or \'fak-trē, 'fak-tə-rē\

A
DICTIONARY
OF
THE ENGLISH LANGUAGE

¹a \'ā\ *n, often cap* **1 :** the 1st letter of the English alphabet **2 :** the musical tone A **3 :** a grade rating a student's work as superior

²a \ə, (')ā\ *indefinite article* [ME *an, a,* fr. OE *ān* one] **1 :** some one unspecified ⟨*a* man overboard⟩ ⟨*a* dozen⟩ **2 :** ONE **:** the same ⟨two of *a* kind⟩ ⟨birds of *a* feather⟩ **3 :** ANY ⟨*a* man who is sick can't work⟩ **4** [OE *an, on, a-* on, in] **:** in each **:** to each **:** for each ⟨twice *a* week⟩ — used in all senses before words beginning with a consonant sound; compare ¹AN

³a \ə\ *prep* [OE *an, on, a-*] *chiefly dial* **:** ON, IN, AT

¹a- \ə\ *prefix* [OE *an, on, a-*] **1 :** on **:** in **:** at ⟨abed⟩ **2 :** in (such) a state or condition ⟨afire⟩ **3 :** in (such) a manner ⟨aloud⟩ **4 :** in the act or process of ⟨gone *a*-hunting⟩

²a- *prefix* [Gk; akin to E *un-*] **:** not **:** without ⟨asexual⟩ — *a-* before consonants other than *h* and sometimes even before *h, an-* before vowels and usu. before *h* ⟨anastigmatic⟩ ⟨anhydrate⟩

aard·vark \'ärd-,värk\ *n* [Afrikaans, lit., earth pig] **:** a large African mammal that burrows in the ground and lives on ants which it catches with its long sticky tongue

Aar·on \'ar-ən, 'er-\ *n* **:** the first high priest of the Hebrews and a brother of Moses

Aa·ron·ic \a-'rän-ik, e-\ *adj* **:** of or relating to the lower order of the Mormon priesthood

ab- *prefix* [L *ab-, abs-, a-*; akin to E *off*] **:** from **:** away **:** off ⟨abaxial⟩

ab·a·ca \,ab-ə-'kä\ *n* **:** a strong fiber obtained from the leafstalk of a Philippine banana

aback \ə-'bak\ *adv* **1** *archaic* **:** BACK, BACKWARD **2 :** by surprise **:** UNAWARES ⟨taken *aback* by the turn of events⟩

ab·a·cus \'ab-ə-kəs\ *n, pl* **-ci** \-,sī, -,kē\ *or* **-cus·es** \-kə-səz\ [L, fr. Gk *abak-, abax* board, slab] **1 :** a slab that forms the uppermost part of the capital of a column **2 :** an instrument for making calculations by sliding counters along rods or in grooves

abaft \ə-'baft\ *adv* [¹*a-* + obs. *baft* behind] **:** toward the stern **:** at the stern **:** AFT

²abaft *prep* **:** to the rear of; *esp* **:** toward the stern from

ab·a·lo·ne \,ab-ə-'lō-nē\ *n* [AmerSp *abulón*] **:** a mollusk with a flattened slightly spiral shell perforated along the edge and lined with mother-of-pearl

¹aban·don \ə-'ban-dən\ *vt* [MF *abandoner,* fr. *a bandon* in one's power] **1 :** to give up completely **2 :** to withdraw from often in the face of danger ⟨*abandon* ship⟩ **3 :** to withdraw protection, support, or help from **:** DESERT **4 :** to give (oneself) over to a feeling or emotion without restraint — **aban·don·er** *n* — **aban·don·ment** \-dən-mənt\ *n*

syn ABANDON, DESERT, FORSAKE mean to leave or go away from. ABANDON may stress withdrawing protection or care from ⟨*abandon* a property⟩ DESERT implies leaving in violation of a duty or promise ⟨*desert* a sentry post⟩ ⟨*deserted* his wife and family⟩ FORSAKE implies breaking ties with something familiar or cherished

²abandon *n* **1 :** a thorough yielding to natural impulses **2 :** ENTHUSIASM, EXUBERANCE

aban·doned \ə-'ban-dənd\ *adj* **1 :** DESERTED, FORSAKEN ⟨an *abandoned* house⟩ **2 :** wholly given up to wickedness or vice ⟨an *abandoned* criminal⟩

abase \ə-'bās\ *vt* [MF *abaisser*] **:** to lower in rank or position **:** HUMBLE, DEGRADE — **abase·ment** \-mənt\ *n*

abash \ə-'bash\ *vt* [MF *esbaiss-, esbair* to be astonished] **:** to destroy the self-possession or self-confidence of **:** DISCONCERT **syn** see EMBARRASS — **abash·ment** \-mənt\ *n*

abate \ə-'bāt\ *vb* [OF *abattre* to beat down] **:** to reduce or decrease in degree, amount, or intensity **:** DIMINISH, LESSEN — **abat·er** *n*

abate·ment \ə-'bāt-mənt\ *n* **1 :** the act or process of abating **:** the state of being abated **2 :** an amount abated; *esp* **:** a deduction from the full amount of a tax

ab·a·tis \'ab-ə-,tē, 'ab-ət-əs\ *n, pl* **-tis** \-ə-,tēz\ *or* **-tis·es** \-ət-ə-səz\ [F] **:** a defensive obstacle formed by cut-down trees with sharpened branches facing the enemy

ab·at·toir \'ab-ə-,twär\ *n* [F, fr. *abattre* to beat down] **:** SLAUGHTERHOUSE

ab·ax·i·al \(')ab-'ak-sē-əl\ *adj* **:** situated out of or directed away from the axis

ab·ba·cy \'ab-ə-sē\ *n, pl* **-cies :** the office, term of office, position, or jurisdiction of an abbot

ab·ba·tial \ə-'bā-shəl\ *adj* **:** of or relating to an abbot, abbess, or abbey

ab·bé \a-'bā, 'ab-,ā\ *n* [F, fr. LL *abbat-, abbas* abbot] **:** a French cleric not in a religious order — used as a title

ab·bess \'ab-əs\ *n* **:** a woman who is the superior of a convent of nuns

ab·bey \'ab-ē\ *n, pl* **abbeys** [OF *abaïe,* fr. LL *abbatia,* fr. *abbat-, abbas* abbot] **1 a :** a monastery governed by an abbot **b :** a convent governed by an abbess **2 :** a church that once belonged to an abbey ⟨Westminster *Abbey*⟩

ab·bot \'ab-ət\ *n* [OE *abbod,* fr. LL *abbat-, abbas,* fr. LGk *abbas,* fr. Aram *abbā* father] **:** the superior of a monastery esp. under a Benedictine rule

ab·bre·vi·ate \ə-'brē-vē-,āt\ *vt* [LL *abbreviare,* fr. L *ad-* + *brevis* short, brief] **:** to make briefer **:** SHORTEN; *esp* **:** to reduce (as a word or phrase) to a shorter form intended to stand for the whole **syn** see SHORTEN — **ab·bre·vi·a·tor** \-,āt-ər\ *n*

ab·bre·vi·a·tion \ə-,brē-vē-'ā-shən\ *n* **1 :** the act or result of abbreviating **:** ABRIDGMENT **2 :** a shortened form of a word or phrase used for brevity esp. in writing in place of the whole

ABC \,ā-(,)bē-'sē\ *n* **1 :** ALPHABET — usu. used in pl. **2 a :** the rudiments of reading, writing, and spelling — usu. used in pl. **b :** the rudiments of any subject

ab·di·cate \'ab-di-,kāt\ *vb* [L *abdicare,* fr. *ab-* + *dicare* to proclaim] **1 :** to relinquish (as sovereign power)

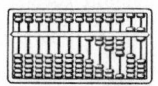

acabus

formally **:** RENOUNCE **2 :** to renounce a throne, high office, dignity, or function — **ab·di·ca·tion** \ˌab-di-'kā-shən\ *n* — **ab·di·ca·tor** \'ab-di-ˌkāt-ər\ *n*

ab·do·men \'ab-də-mən, ab-'dō-mən\ *n* [L *abdomin-, abdomen*] **1 :** the part of the body between the chest and the pelvis; *also* **:** the body cavity containing the chief digestive organs **2 :** the hind portion of the body behind the thorax in an arthropod — see INSECT illustration — **ab·dom·i·nal** \ab-'däm-ən-ᵊl\ *adj* — **ab·dom·i·nal·ly** \-ᵊl-ē\ *adv*

ab·duce \ab-'d(y)üs\ *vt* **:** ABDUCT

ab·du·cens \ab-'d(y)ü-ˌsenz\ *n* **:** either of the 6th pair of cranial nerves supplying muscles of the eyes

ab·duct \ab-'dəkt\ *vt* [L *abduct-, abducere*, lit., to lead away, fr. *ab-* + *ducere* to lead] **1 :** to carry (a person) off by force **2 :** to draw (a part of the body) away from the median axis of the body; *also* **:** to move (similar parts) apart — **ab·duc·tion** \-'dək-shən\ *n*

ab·duc·tor \-'dək-tər\ *n* **:** one that abducts; *esp* **:** a muscle that draws a body part away from the median axis — compare ADDUCTOR, EXTENSOR, RETRACTOR

abeam \ə-'bēm\ *adv (or adj)* **:** on a line at right angles to a ship's keel

abe·ce·dar·i·an \ˌā-bē-(ˌ)sē-'der-ē-ən\ *n* **:** one learning the rudiments of something (as the alphabet)

abed \ə-'bed\ *adv (or adj)* **:** in bed

Abel \'ā-bəl\ *n* **:** a son of Adam and Eve killed by his brother Cain

Ab·er·deen An·gus \ˌab-ər-ˌdēn-'aŋ-gəs\ *n* [*Aberdeen & Angus*, counties in Scotland] **:** any of a breed of black hornless beef cattle originating in Scotland

ab·er·rance \a-'ber-ən(t)s\ *or* **ab·er·ran·cy** \-ən-sē\ *n, pl* **ab·er·ranc·es** *or* **aberrancies : DEVIATION**

ab·er·rant \a-'ber-ənt\ *adj* [L *aberrare* to wander away] **1 :** straying from the right or normal way **2 :** deviating from the usual or natural type — **ab·er·rant·ly** *adv*

ab·er·ra·tion \ˌab-ə-'rā-shən\ *n* **1 :** the act of deviating esp. from a moral standard or normal state **2 :** failure of a mirror or lens to produce exact point-to-point correspondence between an object and its image **3 :** unsoundness or disorder of the mind **4 :** a small periodic change of apparent position in heavenly bodies due to the combined effect of the motion of light and the motion of the observer — **ab·er·ra·tion·al** \-shnəl, -shən-ᵊl\ *adj*

abet \ə-'bet\ *vt* **abet·ted; abet·ting** [MF *abeter*, fr. *a-* *ad-* + *beter* to bait] **1 :** to instigate, encourage, or aid in doing wrong **2 :** to assist in the achievement of a purpose — **abet·ment** \-mənt\ *n* — **abet·tor** *or* **abet·ter** \-'bet-ər\ *n*

abey·ance \ə-'bā-ən(t)s\ *n* [AF, fr. OF *abaer, abeer* to desire, hope for] **:** a state of suspension or temporary inactivity (plans held in *abeyance*) — **abey·ant** \-ənt\ *adj*

ab·hor \ab-'hȯ(ə)r, əb-\ *vt* **ab·horred; ab·hor·ring** [L *abhorrēre*, fr. *ab-* + *horrēre* to shudder] **1 :** to feel extreme repugnance toward **:** LOATHE **2 :** to turn aside or shrink from in scorn or disgust **:** REJECT *syn* see HATE — **ab·hor·rence** \-'hȯr-ən(t)s, -'här-\ *n* — **ab·hor·rer** \-'hȯr-ər\ *n*

ab·hor·rent \-'hȯr-ənt, -'här-\ *adj* **1 :** feeling or showing abhorrence **2 :** not agreeable (conclusions *abhorrent* to their philosophy) **3 :** DETESTABLE *syn* see REPUGNANT — **ab·hor·rent·ly** *adv*

abid·ance \ə-'bīd-ᵊn(t)s\ *n* **1 :** CONTINUANCE **2 :** COMPLIANCE

abide \ə-'bīd\ *vb* **abode** \-'bōd\ *or* **abid·ed; abid·ing** [OE *ābīdan*, fr. *ā-*, prefix denoting completion + *bīdan* to bide] **1** *archaic* **:** to wait for **:** AWAIT **2 a :** to endure without yielding **:** WITHSTAND **b :** to bear patiently **:** TOLERATE **3 :** to accept without objection (*abide* the court's decision) **4 :** to remain stable or fixed in a state **5 :** to reside or continue in a place **:** DWELL *syn* see STAY — **abid·er** *n* — **abide by :** to accept the terms of **:** be obedient to (*abide by* the rules of the club)

abid·ing *adj* **:** ENDURING, LASTING, PERMANENT — **abid·ing·ly** \-iŋ-lē\ *adv*

ab·i·gail \'ab-ə-ˌgāl\ *n* **:** a lady's waiting maid

abil·i·ty \ə-'bil-ət-ē\ *n, pl* **-ties** **1 a :** the quality or state of being able; *esp* **:** physical, mental, or legal power to do something **b :** competence in doing **:** SKILL **2 :** natural talent or acquired proficiency **:** APTITUDE

-abil·i·ty *also* **-ibil·i·ty** \ə-'bil-ət-ē\ *n suffix, pl* **-ties** [L

-*abilitas, -ibilitas,* fr. -*abilis, -ibilis* -able] **:** capacity, fitness, or tendency to act or be acted on in a (specified) way (read*ability*)

abio·gen·e·sis \ˌā-ˌbi-ō-'jen-ə-səs\ *n, pl* **-gen·e·ses** \-'jen-ə-ˌsēz\ **:** the origination of living from lifeless matter — **abio·ge·net·ic** \-ō-jə-'net-ik\ *adj* — **abio·ge·net·i·cal·ly** \-'net-i-k(ə-)lē\ *adv* — **abi·og·e·nist** \ˌā-bī-'äj-ə-nəst\ *n*

ab·ject \'ab-ˌjekt, ab-'\ *adj* [L *abjectus*, fr. pp. of *abicere* to cast off, fr. *ab-* + *jacere* to throw] **1 :** sunk to a low condition **2 a :** having no pride or spirit **:** SERVILE **b :** showing utter resignation **:** HOPELESS — **ab·ject·ly** *adv* — **ab·ject·ness** *n*

ab·jure \ab-'ju̇(ə)r\ *vt* [L *abjurare*, fr. *ab-* + *jurare* to swear] **1 a :** to renounce upon oath (*abjure* allegiance) **b :** to reject solemnly **:** REPUDIATE **2 :** to abstain from **:** AVOID — **ab·ju·ra·tion** \ˌab-jə-'rā-shən\ *n* — **ab·jur·er** *n*

ab·late \a-'blāt\ *vb* **1 :** to remove by cutting, melting, evaporation, or vaporization **2 :** to undergo ablation

ab·la·tion \a-'blā-shən\ *n* **:** the process of ablating: as **a :** surgical removal **b :** the vaporization of an outer covering (as of a spacecraft) to keep an inner part cool

ab·la·tive \'ab-lət-iv\ *adj* [L *ablat-*, used as stem of *auferre* to carry away, remove, fr. *au-* away + *ferre* to carry] **:** of, relating to, or constituting a grammatical case expressing typically the relations of separation and source and also frequently such relations as cause or instrument — **ablative** *n*

ablative absolute *n* **:** a construction in Latin that consists of a noun or pronoun and its adjunct both in the ablative case and together forming an adverbial phrase expressing generally the time, cause, or an attendant circumstance of an action

ablaze \ə-'blāz\ *adj* **1 :** being on fire **2 :** radiant with light or bright color

able \'ā-bəl\ *adj* **abler** \-b(ə-)lər\; **ablest** \-b(ə-)ləst\ [MF, fr. L *habilis* handy, apt, fr. *habēre* to have, hold] **1 a :** having sufficient power, skill, or resources to do something (*able* to swim) **b :** free from restrictions preventing an action (*able* to vote) **2 :** marked by intelligence, knowledge, skill, or competence (an *able* news editor)

  syn ABLE, CAPABLE, COMPETENT mean having power to do or accomplish. ABLE may further imply skill that is above average and proved by performance (an *able* trial lawyer) CAPABLE stresses having necessary qualities or skill for a specified function or action (a *capable* nurse) COMPETENT suggests having necessary training, experience, or special knowledge (a *competent* judge of figure skating)

-a·ble *also* **-i·ble** \ə-bəl\ *adj suffix* [L -*abilis, -ibilis*] **1 :** capable of, fit for, or worthy of (being so acted upon or toward) — chiefly in adjectives derived from verbs (break*able*) (collect*ible*) **2 :** tending, given, or liable to (knowledge*able*) (perish*able*)

able-bod·ied \ˌā-bəl-'bäd-ēd\ *adj* **:** having a sound strong body **:** physically fit

able-bodied seaman *n* **:** an experienced deck-department seaman qualified to perform routine duties at sea — called also *able seaman*

abloom \ə-'blüm\ *adj* **:** BLOOMING

ab·lu·tion \a-'blü-shən, ə-'blü-\ *n* [L *abluere* to wash away, fr. *ab-* + *lavere* to wash] **:** the washing of one's body or part of it esp. as a religious rite

ably \'ā-blē\ *adv* **:** in an able manner

ABM \ˌā-(ˌ)bē-'em\ *n* **:** ANTIBALLISTIC MISSILE

ab·ne·gate \'ab-ni-ˌgāt\ *vt* **1 :** to give up or surrender (as a right or privilege) **:** RELINQUISH **2 :** to deny to or reject for oneself **:** RENOUNCE — **ab·ne·ga·tion** \ˌab-ni-'gā-shən\ *n* — **ab·ne·ga·tor** \'ab-ni-ˌgāt-ər\ *n*

ab·nor·mal \(')ab-'nȯr-məl\ *adj* **:** differing from the normal or average; *esp* **:** markedly irregular — **ab·nor·mal·ly** \-mə-lē\ *adv*

ab·nor·mal·i·ty \ˌab-nȯr-'mal-ət-ē\ *n, pl* **-ties** **1 :** the quality or state of being abnormal **2 :** something abnormal

¹aboard \ə-'bȯrd, -'bȯrd\ *adv* **1 :** on, onto, or within a ship, a railway car, or a passenger vehicle **2 :** ALONGSIDE

²aboard *prep* **:** on or into esp. for passage (go *aboard* ship)

abode \ə-'bōd\ *n* **:** the place where one abides **:** dwelling place **:** RESIDENCE, HOME

abol·ish \ə-'bäl-ish\ *vt* [MF *aboliss-, abolir*, fr. L *abolēre*] **:** to do away with wholly **:** put an end to — **abol·ish·a·ble**

\-ə-bəl\ *adj* — **abol·ish·er** — **abol·ish·ment** \-mənt\ *n*

ab·o·li·tion \,ab-ə-'lish-ən\ *n* : the act of abolishing : the state of being abolished; *esp* : the abolishing of slavery — **ab·o·li·tion·ary** \-'lish-ə-,ner-ē\ *adj*

ab·o·li·tion·ist \-'lish-(ə-)nəst\ *n* : a person who is in favor of abolition; *esp* : one favoring the abolition of Negro slavery — **ab·o·li·tion·ism** \-'lish-ə-,niz-əm\ *n*

ab·oma·sum \,ab-ō-'mā-səm\ *n, pl* **-sa** \-sə\ : the fourth or true digestive stomach of a ruminant (as a cow) — **ab·oma·sal** \-səl\ *adj*

A–bomb \'ā-,bäm\ *n* : ATOM BOMB — **A–bomb** *vb*

abom·i·na·ble \ə-'bäm-(ə-)nə-bəl\ *adj* **1** : deserving or causing loathing or hatred : DETESTABLE **2** : quite disagreeable or unpleasant ⟨*abominable* weather⟩ — **abom·i·na·bly** \-blē\ *adv*

abominable snow·man \-'snō-mən, -,man\ *n, often cap A & S* : a creature thought to exist in the Himalayas and held to be a subhuman, an ape, or more commonly a bear

abom·i·nate \ə-'bäm-ə-,nāt\ *vt* [L *abominari*, lit., to deprecate as an ill omen, fr. *ab-* + *omin-, omen* omen] : to hate or loathe intensely : ABHOR — **abom·i·na·tor** \-,nāt-ər\ *n*

abom·i·na·tion \ə-,bäm-ə-'nā-shən\ *n* **1** : something abominable **2** : extreme disgust and hatred : LOATHING

ab·oral \(')ab-'ȯr-əl, -'ȯr-\ *adj* : situated opposite to or away from the mouth — **ab·oral·ly** \-ə-lē\ *adv*

ab·o·rig·i·nal \,ab-ə-'rij-nəl, -ən-ᵊl\ *adj* **1** : INDIGENOUS, ORIGINAL, PRIMITIVE **2** : of or relating to aborigines **syn** see NATIVE — **ab·o·rig·i·nal·ly** \-ē\ *adv*

ab·o·rig·i·ne \,ab-ə-'rij-ə-(,)nē\ *n* [L *aborigines*, pl., fr. *ab origine* from the beginning] : an indigenous inhabitant esp. as contrasted with an invading or colonizing people

aborn·ing \ə-'bȯr-niŋ\ *adv* : while being born or produced

abort \ə-'bȯrt\ *vb* **1** : to bring forth premature or stillborn offspring **2** : to become checked in development **3** : to terminate prematurely ⟨*abort* a project⟩

abor·tion \ə-'bȯr-shən\ *n* [L *abort-, aboriri* to miscarry, fr. *ab-* + *oriri* to rise, be born] **1** : a premature birth occurring before the fetus can survive — compare MISCARRIAGE **2** : failure to reach full development; *also* : a result of such failure

abor·tion·ist \-sh(ə-)nəst\ *n* : a producer of illegal abortions

abor·tive \ə-'bȯrt-iv\ *adj* **1** : failing to achieve the desired end : UNSUCCESSFUL ⟨an *abortive* attempt⟩ **2** : imperfectly formed or developed : RUDIMENTARY — **abor·tive·ly** *adv* — **abor·tive·ness** *n*

abound \ə-'baund\ *vi* [MF *abonder*, fr. L *abundare*, fr. *ab-* + *unda* wave] **1** : to be present in large numbers or in great quantity **2** : to become copiously supplied ⟨a stream *abounding* in fish⟩

¹about \ə-'baut\ *adv* [OE *abūtan*, fr. *¹a-* + *būtan* outside, fr. *be* by + *ūtan* outside, fr. *ūt* out] **1** : on all or various sides : AROUND ⟨wander *about*⟩ ⟨people standing *about*⟩ **2 a** : APPROXIMATELY ⟨*about* three years⟩ **b** : ALMOST ⟨*about* starved⟩ **3** : in succession : ALTERNATELY ⟨turn *about* is fair play⟩ **4 a** : in the opposite direction ⟨face *about*⟩ **b** : in reverse order ⟨the other way *about*⟩

²about *prep* **1** : on every side of : AROUND **2 a** : in the immediate neighborhood of : NEAR **b** : on or near the person of **c** : in the makeup of ⟨something strange *about* him⟩ **d** : at the command of ⟨has his wits *about* him⟩ **3 a** : engaged in ⟨do it thoroughly while you're *about* it⟩ **b** : on the verge of ⟨*about* to join the army⟩ **4** : with regard to : CONCERNING ⟨told me *about* it⟩ **5** : over or in different parts of ⟨traveled *about* the country⟩

about–face \ə-'baut-'fās\ *n* **1** : a reversal of direction **2** : a reversal of attitude or point of view — **about–face** *vi*

¹above \ə-'bəv\ *adv* [OE *abufan*, fr. *¹a-* + *bufan* above, fr. *be* by + *ufan* above, over] **1** : in or to a higher place : OVERHEAD **2** : higher on the same page or on a preceding page **3** : in or to a higher rank or number

²above *prep* **1** : in or to a higher place than : OVER **2 a** : superior to (as in rank, quality, or degree) ⟨a captain is *above* a lieutenant⟩ **b** : out of reach of ⟨*above* criticism⟩ **c** : too proud or honorable to stoop to ⟨*above* such petty tricks⟩ **3** : exceeding in number, quantity, or size ⟨*above* the average⟩

³above *n* : something that is above

⁴above *adj* : written higher on the same page or on a preceding page

above·board \ə-'bəv-,bōrd, -,bȯrd\ *adv* (*or adj*) : in open sight : in a straightforward manner : without concealment or deceit

ab·ra·ca·dab·ra \,ab-rə-kə-'dab-rə\ *n* **1** : a magical charm or incantation against calamity **2** : unintelligible language : JARGON

abrad·ant \ə-'brād-ᵊnt\ *n* : ABRASIVE

abrade \ə-'brād\ *vb* [L *abradere* to scrape off, fr. *ab-* + *radere* to scrape] **1 a** : to rub or wear away esp. by friction : ERODE **b** : to irritate or roughen by rubbing **2** : to undergo abrasion — **abrad·er** *n*

Abra·ham \'ā-brə-,ham\ *n* : an Old Testament patriarch and the founder of the Hebrew people

abra·sion \ə-'brā-zhən\ *n* [L *abras-, abradere* to abrade] **1** : a rubbing or wearing away ⟨protect the surface from *abrasion*⟩ **2** : a place where the surface has been rubbed or scraped off ⟨had an *abrasion* on his knee⟩

¹abra·sive \ə-'brā-siv, -ziv\ *adj* : having the effect of abrading

²abrasive *n* : a substance (as emery, pumice, fine sand) used for grinding, smoothing, or polishing

abreast \ə-'brest\ *adv* (*or adj*) **1** : side by side with bodies in line **2** : up to a standard or level esp. of knowledge ⟨keep *abreast* of the times⟩

abridge \ə-'brij\ *vt* [MF *abregier*, fr. LL *abbreviare* to abbreviate] **1 a** *archaic* : DEPRIVE **b** : to make less : DIMINISH, CURTAIL ⟨forbidden to *abridge* the rights of citizens⟩ **2** : to shorten in duration or extent **3** : to shorten by omission of words while retaining the substance : CONDENSE — **abridg·er** *n*

abridg·ment *or* **abridge·ment** \ə-'brij-mənt\ *n* **1 a** : the action of abridging **b** : the state of being abridged **2** : a shortened form of a work retaining the general sense and unity of the original

abroad \ə-'brȯd\ *adv* (*or adj*) **1** : over a wide area : WIDELY **2** : outside of an implied place; *esp* : in the open ⟨doesn't go *abroad* for days at a time⟩ **3** : in or to foreign countries ⟨travel *abroad*⟩ **4** : in wide circulation : going about ⟨disturbing rumors were *abroad*⟩

ab·ro·gate \'ab-rə-,gāt\ *vt* [L *abrogare*, fr. *ab-* + *rogare* to ask, propose] **1** : to annul or repeal by authoritative action ⟨*abrogate* a law⟩ **2** : to do away with — **ab·ro·ga·tion** \,ab-rə-'gā-shən\ *n*

abrupt \ə-'brəpt\ *adj* [L *abruptus*, fr. pp. of *abrumpere* to break off, fr. *ab-* + *rumpere* to break] **1** : broken off; *also* : suddenly terminating as if cut or broken off ⟨*abrupt* plant filaments⟩ **2 a** : SUDDEN ⟨*abrupt* change in the weather⟩ **b** : unceremoniously curt ⟨*abrupt* manner⟩ **c** : DISCONNECTED ⟨an *abrupt* style of speaking⟩ **3** : rising or dropping sharply : PRECIPITOUS, STEEP — **abrupt·ly** *adv* — **abrupt·ness** \ə-'brəp(t)-nəs\ *n*

ab·scess \'ab-,ses\ *n* [L *abscessus*, lit., departure, fr. *abscess-, abscedere* to go away, fr. *ab-, abs-* + *cedere* to go] : a localized collection of pus surrounded by inflamed tissue — **ab·scessed** \-,sest\ *adj*

ab·scis·sa \ab-'sis-ə\ *n* [L, fr. fem. of *abscissus*, pp. of *abscindere* to cut off, fr. *ab-* + *scindere* to cut] **1** : the distance of a point on a graph to the right or to the left of the axis conventionally labeled *y* **2** : the horizontal coordinate in a plane coordinate system

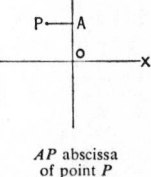

AP abscissa of point *P*

ab·scis·sion \ab-'sizh-ən\ *n* **1** : the act or process of cutting off **2** : the natural separation of flowers, fruit, or leaves from plants at a special separation layer

ab·scond \ab-'skänd\ *vi* [L *abscondere* to hide away, fr. *ab-, abs-* + *condere* to store up, conceal, fr. *com-* + *-dere* to put] : to depart secretly and hide oneself — **ab·scond·er** *n*

ab·sence \'ab-sən(t)s\ *n* **1** : the state of being absent **2** : WANT, LACK **3** : inattention to things present

¹ab·sent \'ab-sənt\ *adj* [L *absent-, absens*, fr. prp. of *abesse* to be away, fr. *ab-* + *esse* to be] **1** : not present or attending : MISSING **2** : not existing : LACKING **3** : INATTENTIVE — **ab·sent·ly** *adv*

²ab·sent \ab-'sent\ *vt* : to keep (oneself) away

ab·sen·tee \,ab-sən-'tē\ *n* **1** : a person who is absent or who absents himself **2** : a proprietor that lives away from his estate or business — **absentee** *adj*

---

j joke; ŋ sing; ō flow; ȯ flaw; ȯi coin; th thin; th this; ü loot; u̇ foot; y yet; yü few; yu̇ furious; zh vision

absentee ballot *n* : a ballot for use by a voter who because of illness or necessary absence from his voting district is permitted to vote in advance by mail

ab·sen·tee·ism \,ab-sən-'tē-,iz-əm\ *n* **1** : protracted absence of an owner from his property **2** : chronic absence from work or other duty

ab·sent·mind·ed \,ab-sənt-'mīn-dəd\ *adj* : lost in thought and unaware of one's surroundings or action; *also* : given to absence of mind — **ab·sent·mind·ed·ly** *adv* — **ab·sent·mind·ed·ness** *n*

ab·sinthe *or* **ab·sinth** \'ab-,sin(t)th\ *n* [F *absinthe*, fr. L *absinthium* wormwood, fr. Gk *apsinthion*] : a green liqueur flavored with aromatics (as wormwood and anise)

ab·so·lute \'ab-sə-,lüt\ *adj* [L *absolutus*, fr. pp. of *absolvere* to set free, absolve] **1 a** : free from imperfection : PERFECT **b** : free or relatively free from mixture : PURE ⟨*absolute* alcohol⟩ **2** : completely free from constitutional or other restraint or limitation ⟨*absolute* power⟩ ⟨an *absolute* monarch⟩ **3 a** : lacking grammatical connection with any other word in a sentence ⟨the *absolute* construction *this being the case* in "this being the case, let us go"⟩ **b** : standing alone without a modified substantive ⟨the *absolute* adjective *blind* in "help the blind"⟩ ⟨the *absolute* possessive pronoun *ours* in "your work and ours"⟩ **c** : having no object in the particular construction under consideration though normally transitive ⟨*kill* in "if looks could kill" is an *absolute* verb⟩ **4** : having no restriction, exception, or qualification ⟨an *absolute* requirement⟩ ⟨*absolute* freedom⟩ **5** : free from doubt : CERTAIN, UNQUESTIONABLE ⟨*absolute* proof⟩ **6 a** : independent of standards of measurement : ACTUAL ⟨*absolute* brightness of a star⟩ ⟨*absolute* motion⟩ **b** : relating to or derived from the fundamental units of length, mass, and time ⟨*absolute* electric units⟩ **c** : relating to the absolute-temperature scale ⟨10° *absolute*⟩ **7** : FUNDAMENTAL, ULTIMATE **8** : perfectly embodying the nature of a thing — **absolute** *n* — **ab·so·lute·ly** \'ab-sə-,lüt-lē, ,ab-sə-'\ *adv* — **ab·so·lute·ness** \-,lüt-nəs, -'lüt-\ *n*

absolute majority *n* **1** : more than half of those qualified to vote whether actually voting or not **2** : more than half of a total of votes cast — compare PLURALITY

absolute pitch *n* **1** : the position of a tone in a standard scale independently determined by its rate of vibration **2** : the ability to sing or name a note asked for or heard

absolute temperature *n* : temperature measured on a scale that has absolute zero as the zero point

absolute value *n* **1** : the numerical value of a real number without regard to its sign **2** : the positive square root of the sum of the squares of the real and imaginary parts of a complex number

absolute zero *n* : a hypothetical temperature characterized by complete absence of heat and equivalent to approximately −273.16°C or −459.69°F

ab·so·lu·tion \,ab-sə-'lü-shən\ *n* : the act of absolving; *esp* : a forgiving of sins by a confessor in the sacrament of penance

ab·so·lut·ism \'ab-sə-,lüt-,iz-əm\ *n* **1 a** : a political theory that absolute power should be vested in one or more rulers **b** : government by an absolute ruler or authority **2** : advocacy of absolute standards or principles — **ab·so·lut·ist** \-,lüt-əst\ *n or adj* — **ab·so·lu·tis·tic** \,ab-sə-,lü-'tis-tik\ *adj*

ab·solve \əb-'sälv, -'zälv, -'sólv, -'zólv\ *vt* [L *absolvere*, fr. *ab-* + *solvere* to loosen] **1** : to set free from an obligation or from the consequences of guilt **2** : to forgive (a sin) by absolution — **ab·solv·er** *n*

ab·sorb \əb-'sórb, -'zórb\ *vt* [L *absorbēre*, fr. *ab-* + *sorbēre* to suck up] **1** : to take in or swallow up : INCORPORATE ⟨the corporation *absorbed* three small companies⟩ **2** : to suck or take up or in ⟨a sponge *absorbs* water⟩ — compare ADSORB **3** : to engage or engross wholly ⟨*absorbed* in thought⟩ **4** : to receive without recoil or echo ⟨a sound-absorbing surface⟩ — **ab·sorb·a·bil·i·ty** \əb-,sór-bə-'bil-ət-ē, -,zór-\ *n* — **ab·sorb·a·ble** \əb-'sór-bə-bəl, -'zór-\ *adj* — **ab·sorb·er** *n*

syn ABSORB, ASSIMILATE mean to take in. ABSORB may imply that matter or energy enters a body and is retained without essential change to itself or to the receiving body ⟨dark colors *absorb* light⟩ ASSIMILATE may apply to an active process of incorporating substance into the substance of the receiving body ⟨*assimilate* nourishment⟩

ab·sorbed \-'sórbd, -'zórbd\ *adj* : wholly occupied or interested in a thought or activity : ENGROSSED — **ab·sorb·ed·ly** \-'sór-bəd-lē, -'zór-\ *adv*

ab·sorb·en·cy \əb-'sór-bən-sē, -'zór-\ *n, pl* **-cies** : the quality or state of being absorbent

ab·sorb·ent \-bənt\ *adj* : able to absorb ⟨*absorbent* cotton⟩ — **absorbent** *n*

ab·sorb·ing *adj* : fully taking attention : ENGROSSING — **ab·sorb·ing·ly** \-biŋ-lē\ *adv*

ab·sorp·tion \əb-'sórp-shən, -'zórp-\ *n* **1** : the process of absorbing or being absorbed: as **a** : the passing of digested food through the intestinal wall into the blood or lymph **b** : interception esp. of light or sound waves **2** : entire occupation of the mind — **ab·sorp·tive** \-'sórp-tiv, -'zórp-\ *adj*

ab·stain \əb-'stān\ *vi* [MF *abstenir*, fr. L *abstinēre*, fr. *ab-*, *abs-* + *tenēre* to hold] : to refrain voluntarily esp. from an action ⟨*abstain* from voting⟩ **syn** see REFRAIN — **ab·stain·er** *n*

ab·ste·mi·ous \ab-'stē-mē-əs\ *adj* [L *abstemius*] **1** : sparing esp. in eating and drinking **2** : sparingly used or indulged in ⟨*abstemious* diet⟩ — **ab·ste·mi·ous·ly** *adv*

ab·sten·tion \əb-'sten-chən\ *n* [L *abstent-*, *abstinēre* to abstain] : the act or practice of abstaining; *esp* : a usu. formal refusal to vote ⟨3 ayes, 5 nays, and 2 *abstentions*⟩ — **ab·sten·tious** \-chəs\ *adj*

ab·sti·nence \'ab-stə-nən(t)s\ *n* [L *abstinēre* to abstain] **1** : a restraining of oneself from indulgence of appetite or from eating certain foods **2** : an abstaining from drinking alcoholic liquors — **ab·sti·nent** \-nənt\ *adj* — **ab·sti·nent·ly** *adv*

¹ab·stract \'ab-,strakt, ab-'\ *adj* [L *abstractus*, pp. of *abstrahere* to draw off, fr. *ab-*, *abs-* + *trahere* to draw] **1 a** : considered apart from application to any specific instance or particular object ⟨whiteness and triangularity are *abstract* qualities⟩ **b** : existing as a concept and not in any particular object or specific instance ⟨the *abstract* ideas of patriotism and honesty⟩ ⟨problems of an *abstract* nature⟩ **c** : IDEAL ⟨*abstract* justice⟩ **d** : existing in theory and not in practice : purely formal ⟨possessed only an *abstract* right⟩ **2** : standing for an abstract quality or idea ⟨an *abstract* noun⟩ **3** : difficult to understand : ABSTRUSE ⟨*abstract* problems⟩ **4** : dealing with a subject in purely abstract terms ⟨*abstract* algebra⟩ : THEORETICAL **5** : having only intrinsic form with little or no attempt at pictorial representation ⟨*abstract* painting⟩ — **ab·stract·ly** *adv* — **ab·stract·ness** \-,strakt(t)-nəs, -'strakt(t)-\ *n*

²abstract \'ab-,strakt, *in sense 2 also* ab-'\ *n* **1** : a brief statement of the main points or facts : SUMMARY ⟨an *abstract* of a book⟩ **2** : an abstract thing or state **3** : ABSTRACTION 4

³ab·stract \ab-'strakt, 'ab-,, *in sense 3 usu* 'ab-,\ *vt* **1** : REMOVE, SEPARATE **2** : to consider apart from application to a particular instance **3** : to make an abstract of **5** : SUMMARIZE **4** : to draw away the attention of **5** : to take away secretly or dishonestly — **ab·strac·tor** *or* **ab·stract·er** *n*

ab·stract·ed \ab-'strak-təd, 'ab-,\ *adj* : PREOCCUPIED, ABSENTMINDED — **ab·stract·ed·ly** *adv* — **ab·stract·ed·ness** *n*

ab·strac·tion \ab-'strak-shən\ *n* **1 a** : the act or process of abstracting : the state of being abstracted **b** : an abstract idea or term **c** : a purely imaginary or visionary idea **2** : a state of not paying attention to nearby persons or things : ABSENTMINDEDNESS **3** : abstract quality or character **4** : a composition or creation esp. in the art of painting or sculpture characterized by designs not recognizably representing objects in actual existence or by designs not precisely representing concrete objects or figures but with recognizable elements — **ab·strac·tive** \-'strak-tiv\ *adj*

ab·strac·tion·ism \ab-'strak-shə-,niz-əm\ *n* **1** : the creation of abstractions in art **2** : the principles or ideals of abstract art — **ab·strac·tion·ist** \-sh(ə-)nəst\ *adj or n*

ab·struse \ab-'strüs, əb-\ *adj* [L *abstrusus*, fr. pp. of *abstrudere* to conceal, fr. *ab-*, *abs-* + *trudere* to push] : hard to understand : RECONDITE — **ab·struse·ly** *adv* — **ab·struse·ness** *n*

ab·surd \əb-'sərd, -'zərd\ *adj* [L *absurdus*, fr. *ab-* + *surdus* dull sounding, deaf] **:** ridiculously unreasonable, unsound, or incongruous — **ab·surd·ly** *adv* — **ab·surd·ness** *n*

ab·sur·di·ty \ab-'sərd-ət-ē, -'zərd-\ *n, pl* **-ties 1 :** the state of being absurd **2 :** something that is absurd

abun·dance \ə-'bən-dən(t)s\ *n* **1 :** an ample or over-flowing quantity **:** PROFUSION **2 :** AFFLUENCE, WEALTH **3 :** relative degree of plentifulness

abun·dant \-dənt\ *adj* [L *abundare* to abound] **:** existing in or possessing abundance **:** ABOUNDING **syn** see PLENTI-FUL — **abun·dant·ly** *adv*

¹abuse \ə-'byüz\ *vt* [L *abus-, abuti* to misuse, fr. *ab-* + *uti* to use] **1 :** to attack in words **:** REVILE **2 :** to treat cruelly **:** MISTREAT ⟨*abuse* a dog⟩ **3 :** to put to a wrong or improper use **:** MISUSE ⟨*abuse* a privilege⟩ **4 :** to use so as to injure or damage **:** MALTREAT ⟨*abuse* a machine⟩ — **abus·er** *n*

²abuse \ə-'byüs\ *n* **1 :** a corrupt practice or custom **2 :** improper use or treatment **:** MISUSE ⟨*abuse* of privileges⟩ **3 :** abusive language **4 :** physical maltreatment
syn ABUSE, INVECTIVE, VITUPERATION mean vigorous con-demnation. ABUSE stresses the offensive character of the language used; INVECTIVE may add additional suggestion of logical effectiveness and serious purpose in directing abuse; VITUPERATION suggests an unrestrained torrent of abuse

abu·sive \ə-'byü-siv, -ziv\ *adj* **1 :** using or characterized by harsh insulting language **:** serving to abuse ⟨*abusive* language⟩ **2 :** physically injurious — **abu·sive·ly** *adv* — **abu·sive·ness** *n*

abut \ə-'bət\ *vb* **abut·ted; abut·ting** [OF *abouter*, fr. *a* to + *bout* end] **1 :** to touch along a border or with a projecting part **:** BORDER ⟨the farm *abuts* on the road⟩ ⟨stores *abut* the sidewalk⟩ **2 a :** to terminate at a point of contact **b :** to lean for support — **abut·ter** *n*

abut·ment \ə-'bət-mənt\ *n* **1 :** the action or place of abutting **2 :** something against which another thing rests its weight or pushes with force ⟨*abut-ments* that support a bridge⟩

abut·tals \ə-'bət-ᵊlz\ *n pl* **:** the boundaries of lands with respect to other contiguous lands or high-ways by which they are bounded

a, a, abutments of a bridge

abysm \ə-'biz-əm\ *n* [OF *abisme*, modif. of LL *abyssus*] **:** ABYSS

abys·mal \ə-'biz-məl\ *adj* **1 :** having the character of an abyss **:** immeasurably deep **:** BOTTOMLESS **2 :** of or relating to the lowest depths of the ocean — **abys·mal·ly** \-mə-lē\ *adv*
syn ABYSMAL, ABYSSAL mean unfathomable by ordinary means. ABYSMAL applies chiefly to figurative depths that seem to be without a lower limit ⟨*abysmal* ignorance⟩ ⟨*abysmal* poverty⟩ ABYSSAL refers to the ocean bottom at great depths ⟨fauna in the *abyssal* zone⟩ ⟨*abyssal* sedi-ments⟩

abyss \ə-'bis\ *n* [LL *abyssus*, fr. Gk *abyssos*] **1 :** the bottomless gulf, pit, or chaos of the old descriptions of the origins of the universe **2 :** an immeasurably deep gulf or great space

abys·sal \ə-'bis-əl\ *adj* **1 :** UNFATHOMABLE **2 :** of or re-lating to the bottom waters of the ocean depths **syn** see ABYSMAL

Ab·ys·sin·i·an cat \,ab-ə-,sin-ē-ən-, -,sin-yən-\ *n* **:** any of a breed of small slender cats of African origin with short brownish hair ticked with darker color

ac- — see AD-

aca·cia \ə-'kā-shə\ *n* **1 :** any of numerous woody plants of the legume family with ball-shaped white or yellow flower clusters and often pinnate leaves **2 :** GUM ARABIC

ac·a·deme \'ak-ə-,dēm\ *n* **1 a :** SCHOOL **b :** academic environment **2 :** PEDANT

ac·a·dem·ic \,ak-ə-'dem-ik\ *adj* **1 :** of, relating to, or associated with an academy or school esp. of higher learn-ing ⟨*academic* costume⟩ **2 :** of or relating to liberal arts rather than technical or professional studies ⟨took the *academic* course⟩ **3 :** conforming to the traditions or rules of a school (as of literature or art) or an official academy **:** CONVENTIONAL ⟨*academic* verse⟩ **4 :** having no immediate or practical significance **:** THEORETICAL ⟨an *academic* question⟩ — **ac·a·dem·i·cal·ly** \-'dem-i-k(ə-)lē\ *adv*

academic freedom *n* **:** freedom to teach or to learn with-out interference (as by government officials)

ac·a·de·mi·cian \,ak-əd-ə-'mish-ən, ə-,kad-ə-\ *n* **:** a mem-ber of an academy for promoting science, art, or literature

ac·a·dem·i·cism \,ak-ə-'dem-ə,siz-əm\ *also* **acad·e·mism** \ə-'kad-ə-,miz-əm\ *n* **:** academic manner, style, or content **:** FORMALISM

acad·e·my \ə-'kad-ə-mē\ *n, pl* **-mies** [Gk *Akadēmeia*, gymnasium in the suburbs of Athens where Plato estab-lished his school] **1** *cap* **:** the school of philosophy founded by Plato **2 a :** a private high school **b :** an institution for training in special subjects or skills **3 :** a society of learned persons united to advance art, science, or literature

Aca·di·an \ə-'kād-ē-ən\ *n* **:** an inhabitant of the 17th and 18th century French colony of Acadia; *esp* **:** one of the colonists deported by the British in 1755 some of whom eventually settled in Louisiana

acan·tho·ceph·a·lan \ə-,kan(t)-thə-'sef-ə-lən\ *n* [Gk *akan-tha* thorn + *kephalē* head] **:** any of a group (Acantho-cephala) of intestinal worms with a hooked proboscis — **acanthocephalan** *adj*

ac·an·thop·ter·yg·i·an \,ak-ən-,thäp-tə-'rij-ē-ən, ə-,kan(t)-thō-tə-\ *n* **:** any of a group (Acanthopterygii) of fishes including most spiny-finned and some soft-finned fishes — **acanthopterygian** *adj*

acan·thus \ə-'kan(t)-thəs\ *n, pl* **acan-thus·es** *also* **acan·thi** \-'kan-,thī\ **1 :** any of a genus of prickly herbs of the Mediterranean region **2 :** an ornamentation representing the leaves of the acanthus

acanthus 2

a cap·pel·la *also* **a ca·pel·la** \,äk-ə-'pel-ə\ *adv (or adj)* [It *a cappella* in chapel style] **:** without instrumental accompaniment

acar·pous \(')ā-'kär-pəs\ *adj* [Gk *a-* ²*a-* + *karpos* fruit] **:** not producing fruit **:** STERILE

acau·les·cent \,ā-kȯ-'les-ᵊnt\ *or* **acau·line** \(')ā-'kȯ-,lin\ *adj* [²*a-* + L *caulis* stem] **:** having no stem or appear-ing to have none

ac·cede \ak-'sēd\ *vi* [L *accedere* to go to, fr. *ad-* + *cedere* to go] **1 a :** to adhere to an agreement **b :** to give consent **:** AGREE ⟨*accede* to a proposed plan⟩ **2 :** to enter upon an office or dignity ⟨*acceded* to the throne in 1838⟩

ac·ce·le·ran·do \(,)ä-,chel-ə-'rän-dō\ *adv (or adj)* [It] **:** gradually faster — used as a direction in music

ac·cel·er·ate \ik-'sel-ə-,rāt, ak-\ *vb* [L *accelerare*, fr. *ad-* + *celer* swift] **1 :** to bring about at an earlier point of time ⟨*accelerated* his departure⟩ **2 a :** to hasten the ordi-nary progress or development of **b :** to speed up (a course of study) **3 a :** to add to the speed of **b :** to cause to undergo acceleration; *esp* **:** to increase the velocity of **4 :** to move or progress faster — **ac·cel·er·a·tive** \-,rāt-iv\ *adj*

ac·cel·er·a·tion \ik-,sel-ə-'rā-shən, (,)ak-\ *n* **1 :** the act or process of accelerating **:** the state of being accelerated **2 :** change of velocity or the time rate of such change

acceleration of gravity : the acceleration of a freely falling body under the influence of gravity expressed as the rate of increase of velocity per unit of time with the value being about 980.616 centimeters per second per second

ac·cel·er·a·tor \ik-'sel-ə-,rāt-ər, ak-\ *n* **:** one that acceler-ates: **a :** a pedal in an automobile used for varying the supply of fuel-air mixture to the combustion chamber and so controlling the speed of the motor **b :** an apparatus for imparting high velocities to charged particles (as electrons and protons)

ac·cel·er·om·e·ter \ik-,sel-ə-'räm-ət-ər, ak-\ *n* **:** an instru-ment for measuring acceleration and vibrations

¹ac·cent \'ak-,sent\ *n* [L *accentus*, fr. *ad-* + *cantus* song, chant] **1 :** a peculiar or characteristic manner of speech ⟨foreign *accent*⟩ ⟨southern *accent*⟩ **2 :** special prominence given to one syllable of a word or group of words in speaking esp. by increase of stress or change of pitch ⟨*before* has the *accent* on the last syllable⟩ **3 :** rhythmically significant stress on the syllables of a verse usu. at regular intervals **4** *archaic* **:** UTTERANCE **5 a :** a mark (as ˊ, ˋ, ˆ) used chiefly to indicate a specific sound value, stress, or pitch — compare ACUTE, CIRCUMFLEX, GRAVE **b :** a mark (as ˈ or ˌ) identifying a syllable that is accented in speaking

6 a : greater stress given to one musical tone than to its neighbors; *also* : a mark indicating this **b :** the principle of regularly recurring stresses which serve to distribute a succession of pulses into measures **7 a :** EMPHASIS **b :** a small detail in sharp contrast with its surroundings **8 :** a mark placed to the right of a letter or number and usu. slightly above it: **a** (1) : a double prime (2) : PRIME **b :** a mark used singly and doubly with numbers to denote respectively minutes and seconds of time or of an angle or arc or to denote respectively feet and inches

²**ac·cent** \ak-'sent, 'ak-\ *vt* **1 a :** to utter with accent : STRESS ⟨*accent* the first syllable of *after*⟩ **b :** to mark with a written or printed accent **2 :** to give prominence to or increase the prominence of

accent mark *n* **1 :** ACCENT 5 **2 :** one of several symbols used to indicate musical stress

ac·cen·tu·al \ak-'sench-(ə-)wəl\ *adj* **1 :** of, relating to, or characterized by accent **2 :** of, relating to, or constituting a type of verse based upon accent rather than upon quantity or syllabic recurrence — **ac·cen·tu·al·ly** \-ē\ *adv*

ac·cen·tu·ate \ak-'sen-chə-ˌwāt\ *vt* **1 :** to pronounce or mark with an accent **2 :** EMPHASIZE — **ac·cen·tu·a·tion** \(ˌ)ak-ˌsen-chə-'wā-shən\ *n*

ac·cept \ik-'sept, ak-\ *vb* [L *acceptare*, freq. of *accipere* to receive, fr. *ad-* + *capere* to take] **1 :** to receive with consent or approval ⟨*accept* a gift⟩ ⟨*accepted* him as a member⟩ **2 :** to agree or assent to: as **a :** to receive as true **b :** to regard as proper, normal, or inevitable **c :** to take without protest : TOLERATE **3 a :** to make an affirmative or favorable response to ⟨*accept* an offer⟩ **b :** to undertake the responsibility of **4 :** to assume an obligation to pay ⟨*accept* a bill of exchange⟩ **5 :** to receive officially ⟨the Senate *accepted* the committee report⟩ **syn** see RECEIVE — **ac·cept·er** *or* **ac·cep·tor** \-'sep-tər\ *n*

ac·cept·a·ble \ik-'sep-tə-bəl, ak-\ *adj* **1 :** capable or worthy of being accepted : SATISFACTORY ⟨an *acceptable* excuse⟩ **2 :** barely adequate ⟨plays an *acceptable* game⟩ — **ac·cept·a·bil·i·ty** \-ˌsep-tə-'bil-ət-ē\ *n* — **ac·cept·a·ble·ness** \-'sep-tə-bəl-nəs\ *n* — **ac·cept·a·bly** \-blē\ *adv*

ac·cept·ance \ik-'sep-tən(t)s, ak-\ *n* **1 :** the act of accepting **2 :** the quality or state of being accepted or acceptable **syn** ACCEPTATION: ACCEPTANCE is used of the act of accepting or receiving favorably or agreeing to ⟨*acceptance* of the terms of a contract⟩ ⟨*acceptance* of responsibility⟩ ACCEPTATION is used of a sense of a word or phrase as regularly understood by most users

ac·cep·ta·tion \ˌak-ˌsep-'tā-shən\ *n* **1 :** ACCEPTANCE **2 :** the generally accepted meaning of a word or expression **syn** see ACCEPTANCE

ac·cess \'ak-ˌses\ *n* [L *accessus*, fr. *access-, accedere* to go to, fr. *ad-* + *cedere* to go] **1 :** a fit of intense feeling : OUTBURST **2 a :** permission, liberty, or ability to enter, approach, communicate with, pass to and from, or make use of ⟨*access* to the president⟩ **b :** a way or means of approach ⟨a nation's *access* to the sea⟩ **3 :** an increase by addition ⟨a sudden *access* of wealth⟩

ac·ces·si·ble \ak-'ses-ə-bəl, ik-\ *adj* **1 :** easy of access ⟨*accessible* by train or car⟩ **2 :** open to influence ⟨a mind *accessible* to reason⟩ **3 :** OBTAINABLE ⟨*accessible* information⟩ — **ac·ces·si·bil·i·ty** \(ˌ)ak-ˌses-ə-'bil-ət-ē, ik-\ *n* — **ac·ces·si·ble·ness** \ak-'ses-ə-bəl-nəs, ik-\ *n* — **ac·ces·si·bly** \-blē\ *adv*

ac·ces·sion \ak-'sesh-ən, ik-\ *n* **1 :** something added : ACQUISITION **2 :** ADHERENCE ⟨*accession* to a treaty⟩ **3 a :** increase by something added **b :** acquisition of additional property by growth, increase, or other addition to existing property **4 :** the act of assenting or agreeing ⟨*accession* to a proposal⟩ **5 :** the act of coming to high office or a position of honor or power ⟨the *accession* of a king⟩ **6 :** ACCESS 1 — **ac·ces·sion·al** \-'sesh-nəl, -ən-ᵊl\ *adj*

¹**ac·ces·so·ry** *also* **ac·ces·sa·ry** \ak-'ses-(ə-)rē, ik-\ *n, pl* **-ries** **1 a :** a thing of secondary or subordinate importance : ADJUNCT **b :** an object or device not essential in itself but adding to the beauty, convenience, or effectiveness of something else **2 :** a person who aids or encourages another in the commission of a crime or who aids an offender in an attempt to escape justice

²**accessory** *adj* : aiding or contributing in a secondary way : SUPPLEMENTARY

accessory fruit *n* : a fruit (as the strawberry) of which a conspicuous part consists of tissue other than that of the ripened ovary

ac·ci·dence \'ak-səd-ən(t)s, -sə-ˌden(t)s\ *n* : the part of grammar that deals with inflections

ac·ci·dent \'ak-səd-ənt, -sə-ˌdent\ *n* [L *accidere* to happen, befall, fr. *ad-* + *cadere* to fall] **1 a :** an event occurring by chance or from unknown causes **b :** lack of intention or necessity : CHANCE **2 :** an unintended and usu. sudden and unexpected happening or change occurring through carelessness or ignorance or from unavoidable causes and resulting usu. in loss or injury ⟨an automobile *accident*⟩ **3 a :** a nonessential property : ATTRIBUTE **b :** a chance circumstance ⟨the *accident* of noble birth⟩

¹**ac·ci·den·tal** \ˌak-sə-'dent-ᵊl\ *adj* **1 :** arising from extrinsic causes : NONESSENTIAL **2 a :** occurring unexpectedly or by chance ⟨an *accidental* discovery of oil⟩ **b :** happening without intent or from carelessness often with unfortunate results ⟨an *accidental* shooting⟩ — **ac·ci·den·tal·ly** \-'dent-lē, -'dent-ᵊl-ē\ *adv* — **ac·ci·den·tal·ness** \-'dent-ᵊl-nəs\ *n*

syn ACCIDENTAL, FORTUITOUS, INCIDENTAL mean not foreseen or intended. ACCIDENTAL implies an absence of immediate intention ⟨an *accidental* discovery⟩ or reasonably foreseeable probability ⟨*accidental* death⟩ FORTUITOUS stresses chance so strongly that it often connotes entire absence of cause ⟨*fortuitous* presence of a witness⟩ INCIDENTAL implies a secondary or nonessential character ⟨*incidental* advantages of college training⟩

²**accidental** *n* : a chromatically altered note (as a sharp or flat) foreign to a key indicated by a signature

ac·cip·i·ter \ak-'sip-ət-ər\ *n* [L, hawk] : any of various hawks that have short wings and long legs and that dart in and out among trees — **ac·cip·i·trine** \-'sip-ə-ˌtrīn\ *adj or n*

¹**ac·claim** \ə-'klām\ *vb* [L *acclamare*, fr. *ad-* + *clamare* to shout] **1 :** to welcome with applause or great praise ⟨a novel *acclaimed* by the critics⟩ **2 :** to declare or proclaim by or as if by acclamation — **ac·claim·er** *n*

²**acclaim** *n* **1 :** the act of acclaiming **2 :** APPLAUSE, PRAISE

ac·cla·ma·tion \ˌak-lə-'mā-shən\ *n* **1 :** a loud eager expression of approval, praise, or assent **2 :** an overwhelming affirmative vote by cheers, shouts, or applause rather than by ballot ⟨elected by *acclamation*⟩

ac·cli·mate \ə-'klī-mət, 'ak-lə-ˌmāt\ *vt* : ACCLIMATIZE — **ac·cli·ma·tion** \ˌak-ˌlī-'mā-shən, ˌak-lə-\ *n*

ac·cli·ma·tize \ə-'klī-mə-ˌtīz\ *vb* : to adapt to a new temperature, altitude, climate, environment, or situation — **ac·cli·ma·ti·za·tion** \ə-ˌklī-mət-ə-'zā-shən\ *n*

ac·cliv·i·ty \ə-'kliv-ət-ē\ *n, pl* **-ties** [L *ad-* + *clivus* slope] : a slope that ascends

ac·co·lade \'ak-ə-ˌlād\ *n* [F, fr. *accoler* to fall on the neck of, embrace, fr. L *ad-* + *collum* neck] **1 :** a ceremonial embrace **2 :** a formal salute (as a tap on the shoulder with the blade of a sword) that marks the conferring of knighthood **3 a :** a mark of recognition of merit : COMMENDATION **b :** AWARD

ac·com·mo·date \ə-'käm-ə-ˌdāt\ *vb* [L *accommodare*, fr. *ad-* + *commodus* convenient, suitable, fr. *com-* + *modus* measure, mode] **1 a :** to make fit or suitable : ADAPT **b :** to adapt oneself; *esp* : to undergo accommodation **2 :** to furnish with something desired: as **a :** to provide with lodgings **b :** to make room for **c :** to hold without crowding **syn** see ADAPT, CONTAIN — **ac·com·mo·da·tive** \-ˌdāt-iv\ *adj* — **ac·com·mo·da·tive·ness** *n*

ac·com·mo·dat·ing *adj* : disposed to be helpful or obliging — **ac·com·mo·dat·ing·ly** \-ˌdāt-iŋ-lē\ *adv*

ac·com·mo·da·tion \ə-ˌkäm-ə-'dā-shən\ *n* **1 a :** something supplied for convenience or to satisfy a need **b** *pl* : hotel lodging and services **2 :** the act of accommodating : the state of being accommodated: as **a :** the provision of what is needed or desired for convenience **b :** ADAPTATION, ADJUSTMENT **c :** the automatic adjustment of the eye for seeing at different distances **d :** an adjustment of differences : SETTLEMENT — **ac·com·mo·da·tion·al** \-shnəl, -shən-ᵊl\ *adj*

ac·com·pa·ni·ment \ə-'kəmp-(ə-)nē-mənt\ *n* **1 :** a subordinate instrumental or vocal part designed to support or complement a principal voice or instrument **2 :** an accompanying object, situation, or occurrence

---

ə abut; ᵊ kitten; ər further; a back; ā bake; ä cot, cart; aù out; ch chin; e less; ē easy; g gift; i trip; ī life

ac·com·pa·nist \ə-'kəmp-(ə-)nəst\ *also* **ac·com·pa·ny·ist** \-'kəmp-(ə-)nē-əst\ *n* : one (as a pianist) that plays an accompaniment

ac·com·pa·ny \ə-'kəmp-(ə-)nē\ *vb* **-nied; -ny·ing** **1** : to go with or attend as an associate or companion **2** : to perform an accompaniment to or for **3** : to occur at the same time as or along with

syn ACCOMPANY stresses closeness of association ⟨rain *accompanied* by wind⟩ and equality of status ⟨*accompany* a friend⟩ ESCORT adds the implication of protection often as a courtesy or mark of honor ⟨troops *escorted* the visitors to the palace⟩

ac·com·plice \ə-'käm-pləs, -'kəm-\ *n* [alter. of archaic *complice* associate, fr. L *complic-, complex*, fr. *com-* + *plicare* to fold] : one associated with another in wrongdoing

ac·com·plish \ə-'käm-plish, -'kəm-\ *vt* [MF *acompliss-, acomplir*, fr. *a-* ad- + L *comple e* to complete] **1** : to execute fully : PERFORM **2 a** : FULFILL **b** : TRAVERSE, COVER **3** : PERFECT — **ac·com·plish·a·ble** \-ə-bəl\ *adj*

ac·com·plished *adj* **1** : COMPLETED, EFFECTED **2 a** : complete in skills or acquirements as the result of practice or training : EXPERT ⟨an *accomplished* pianist⟩ **b** : having many accomplishments ⟨a very *accomplished* young lady⟩

ac·com·plish·ment \ə-'käm-plish-mənt, -'kəm-\ *n* **1** : the act of accomplishing : COMPLETION **2** : something accomplished : ACHIEVEMENT **3** : an ability, a social quality, or a special skill acquired by training or practice

¹ac·cord \ə-'kȯ(ə)rd\ *vb* [L *ad-* + *cord-, cor* heart] **1** : to bring into agreement : RECONCILE ⟨*accorded* their differing views⟩ **2** : to grant as suitable or proper ⟨*accords* the right of appeal⟩ **3** : to be in harmony : AGREE ⟨the decision *accords* with our sense of justice⟩

²accord *n* **1 a** : AGREEMENT, HARMONY **b** : an agreement between parties ⟨the disputants reached an *accord*⟩ **2** : voluntary or spontaneous impulse to act : WILLINGNESS ⟨everyone went of his own *accord*⟩

ac·cord·ance \ə-'kȯ d-ᵊn(t)s\ *n* : AGREEMENT, CONFORMITY ⟨in *accordance* with a rule⟩

ac·cord·ant \-'kȯrd-ᵊnt\ *adj* **1** : AGREEING **2** : HARMONIOUS — **ac·cord·ant·ly** *adv*

ac·cord·ing as *conj* **1** : in accord with the way in which **2 a** : depending on how **b** : depending on whether : IF

ac·cord·ing·ly \ə-'kȯrd-iŋ-lē\ *adv* **1** : in accordance : CORRESPONDINGLY **2** : CONSEQUENTLY, SO

according to *prep* **1** : in agreement or conformity with **2** : as stated by **3** : depending on

¹ac·cor·di·on \ə-'kȯrd-ē-ən\ *n* [G *akkordion*] : a portable keyboard wind instrument in which the wind is forced past metallic reeds by means of a hand-operated bellows — **ac·cor·di·on·ist** \-ē-ə-nəst\ *n*

accordion

²accordion *adj* : folding or creased or hinged to fold like an accordion

ac·cost \ə-'kȯst\ *vt* [L *ad* to + *costa* rib, side] : to approach and speak first to : ADDRESS

¹ac·count \ə-'kaȯnt\ *n* [MF *acompte* reckoning, fr. *acompter* to reckon, fr. *a-* ad- + *compter* to count] **1** : a chronological record of debits and credits covering transactions involving a particular item, person, or concern **2** : a collection of items to be balanced **3** : an explanation of one's conduct **4 a** : a periodically rendered reckoning listing charged purchases and credits **b** : the transactions between a business and an individual customer **5 a** : VALUE **b** : ESTEEM **6** : PROFIT, ADVANTAGE **7 a** : a statement of reasons, causes, or motives **b** : a reason giving rise to an action or other result **c** : careful thought : CONSIDERATION **8** : a statement of facts or events : RELATION **9** : HEARSAY, REPORT **10** : a sum of money deposited in a bank and subject to withdrawal by the depositor — **on account of** : for the sake of : by reason of : because of

²account *vb* **1** : to think of as ⟨*accounts* himself lucky⟩ **2** : to furnish a detailed analysis or a justifying explanation ⟨*account* for his expenditures⟩ **3 a** : to be the sole or primary factor ⟨poor diet *accounts* for the high mortality rate⟩ **b** : to bring about the capture or destruction of something ⟨*accounted* for two rabbits⟩

ac·count·a·ble \ə-'kaȯnt-ə-bəl\ *adj* **1** : responsible for

giving an account (as of one's acts) : ANSWERABLE ⟨*accountable* to his superiors⟩ **2** : capable of being accounted for : EXPLAINABLE — **ac·count·a·bil·i·ty** \-,kaȯnt-ə-'bil-ət-ē\ *n* — **ac·count·a·ble·ness** \-'kaȯnt-ə-bəl-nəs\ *n* — **ac·count·a·bly** \-blē\ *adv*

ac·count·an·cy \ə-'kaȯnt-ᵊn-sē\ *n* : ACCOUNTING

ac·count·ant \ə-'kaȯnt-ᵊnt\ *n* : a person professionally trained in the practice of accounting **syn** see BOOKKEEPER

ac·count·ing \ə-'kaȯnt-iŋ\ *n* **1** : the skill, system, or practice of recording and analyzing money transactions of a person or business **2** : the action of giving an account ⟨management is required to make *accounting* to the stockholders⟩

ac·cou·ter *or* **ac·cou·tre** \ə-'küt-ər\ *vt* **-cou·tered** *or* **-cou·tred; -cou·ter·ing** *or* **-cou·tring** \-'küt-ə-riŋ, -'kü-triŋ\ [F *accoutrer*] : to provide with equipment or furnishings : OUTFIT

ac·cou·ter·ment *or* **ac·cou·tre·ment** \ə-'küt-ər-mənt, -'kü-trə-mənt\ *n* **1** : the act of accoutering : the state of being accoutered **2** : EQUIPMENT; *esp* : a soldier's outfit usu. not including clothes and weapons

ac·cred·it \ə-'kred-ət\ *vt* **1** : to give official authorization or approval to: **a** : to send with credentials and authority to act as an official representative ⟨*accredit* an ambassador to France⟩ **b** : to vouch for as in conformity with a standard **c** : to recognize (an educational institution) as maintaining standards that qualify the graduates for admission to higher or more specialized institutions or for professional practice **2** : CREDIT — **ac·cred·i·ta·tion** \ə-,kred-ə-'tā-shən\ *n*

ac·cre·tion \ə-'krē-shən\ *n* [L *accret-, accrescere* to increase, fr. *ad-* + *crescere* to grow] **1** : the process of growth or enlargement; *esp* : increase by external addition or accumulation **2** : a product or result of accretion — **ac·cre·tion·ary** \-shə-,ner-ē\ *adj* — **ac·cre·tive** \ə-'krēt-iv\ *adj*

ac·cru·al \ə-'krü-əl\ *n* **1** : the action or process of accruing **2** : something that accrues or has accrued

ac·crue \ə-'krü\ *vb* [MF *acrue* increase, fr. *acreistre* to increase, fr. L *accrescere*] **1** : to come by way of increase or addition ⟨benefits *accrue* to society from free education⟩ **2** : to accumulate over a period of time ⟨*accrued* interest⟩ — **ac·crue·ment** \-mənt\ *n*

ac·cul·tur·a·tion \ə-,kəl-chə-'rā-shən\ *n* : a process of intercultural borrowing between diverse peoples resulting in new and blended patterns — **ac·cul·tur·ate** \-'kəl-chə-,rāt\ *vb* — **ac·cul·tur·a·tion·al** \-,kəl-chə-'rā-shnəl, -shən-ᵊl\ *adj* — **ac·cul·tur·a·tive** \-'kəl-chə-,rāt-iv\ *adj*

ac·cu·mu·late \ə-'kyü-myə-,lāt\ *vb* [L *accumulare*, fr. *ad-* + *cumulus* heap, pile] **1** : to pile up ⟨*accumulate* a fortune⟩ **2** : COLLECT, GATHER ⟨*accumulates* friends easily⟩ **3** : to increase in quantity, number, or amount ⟨rubbish *accumulates* quickly⟩

syn ACCUMULATE, AMASS mean to collect so as to form a large quantity. ACCUMULATE implies building up by successive small increases ⟨*accumulated* heaps of slag⟩ AMASS suggests a more vigorous action during a limited time and applies esp. to a putting together of something valuable ⟨*amass* a fortune⟩

ac·cu·mu·la·tion \ə-,kyü-myə-'lā-shən\ *n* **1** : a collecting together : AMASSING **2** : increase or growth by addition esp. when continuous or repeated ⟨*accumulation* of interest⟩ **3** : something that has accumulated or has been accumulated

ac·cu·mu·la·tive \ə-'kyü-myə-,lāt-iv, -lət-\ *adj* : CUMULATIVE — **ac·cu·mu·la·tive·ly** *adv* — **ac·cu·mu·la·tive·ness** *n*

ac·cu·mu·la·tor \-,lāt-ər\ *n* **1** : one that accumulates **2** *Brit* : STORAGE CELL

ac·cu·ra·cy \'ak-yə-rə-sē\ *n, pl* **-cies** **1** : freedom from mistake or error : CORRECTNESS **2 a** : conformity to a standard : EXACTNESS **b** : degree of conformity of a measure to a standard or a true value

ac·cu·rate \'ak-yə-rət\ *adj* [L *accuratus*, fr. pp. of *accurare* to apply care to, fr. *ad-* + *cura* care] **1** : free from mistakes esp. as the result of care **2** : conforming exactly to truth or to a standard : EXACT **syn** see CORRECT — **ac·cu·rate·ly** \-yə-rət-lē, -yərt-\ *adv* — **ac·cu·rate·ness** \-nəs\ *n*

ac·cursed \ə-'kər-səd, -'kərst\ *or* **ac·curst** \ə-'kərst\ *adj* **1** : being under a curse **2** : DAMNABLE, DETESTABLE —

---

j joke; **ŋ** sing; **ō** flow; **ȯ** flaw; **ȯi** coin; **th** thin; **t̲h̲** this; **ü** loot; **u̇** foot; **y** yet; **yü** few; **yu̇** furious; **zh** vision

ac·curs·ed·ly \-'kər-səd-lē\ *adv* — **ac·curs·ed·ness** \-'kər-səd-nəs\ *n*

ac·cus·al \ə-'kyü-zəl\ *n* : ACCUSATION

ac·cu·sa·tion \,ak-yə-'zā-shən\ *n* **1** : the act of accusing : the state or fact of being accused **2** : a charge of wrong-doing

ac·cu·sa·tive \ə-'kyü-zət-iv\ *adj* **1** : of, relating to, or constituting the grammatical case that marks the direct object of a verb or the object of any of several prepositions — compare OBJECTIVE **2** : ACCUSATORY — **accusative** *n* — **ac·cu·sa·tive·ly** *adv*

ac·cu·sa·to·ry \ə-'kyü-zə-,tōr-ē, -,tor-\ *adj* : expressing accusation

ac·cuse \ə-'kyüz\ *vb* [L *accusare,* fr. *ad-* + *causa* cause, lawsuit] : to charge with a fault or wrong or esp. with a criminal offense — **ac·cus·er** *n* — **ac·cus·ing·ly** \-'kyü-ziŋ-lē\ *adv*

ac·cused \ə-'kyüzd\ *n, pl* **accused** : one charged with an offense; *esp* : the defendant in a criminal case

ac·cus·tom \ə-'kəs-təm\ *vt* : to make familiar through use or experience : HABITUATE

ac·cus·tomed *adj* : familiar through use or long experience: **a** : CUSTOMARY, USUAL ⟨*accustomed* lunch hour⟩ **b** : USED, WONT ⟨*accustomed* to hard luck⟩ **syn** see USUAL

¹ace \'ās\ *n* [ME *as,* fr. OF, fr. L, unit, unity] **1 a** : a dice face or domino end marked with one spot **b** : a playing card bearing in its center one large pip **2** : a very small amount or degree ⟨came within an *ace* of winning⟩ **3** : a point scored on a stroke (as in tennis) that an opponent fails to touch **4** : a golf hole made in one stroke **5** : a combat pilot who has brought down at least five enemy airplanes **6** : one that excels at something

²ace *vt* : to score an ace against (as a tennis opponent)

³ace *adj* : of first or high rank or quality

acel·lu·lar \(')ā-'sel-yə-lər\ *adj* : not made up of cells

-a·ceous \'ā-shəs\ *adj suffix* [L *-aceus*] **1 a** : characterized by : full of ⟨set*aceous*⟩ **b** : consisting of ⟨carbon*aceous*⟩ : having the nature or form of ⟨sapon*aceous*⟩ **2** : of or relating to a group of animals typified by (such) a form ⟨cet*aceous*⟩ or characterized by (such) a feature ⟨crus*taceous*⟩

ac·er·ate \'as-ə-,rāt\ *or* **ac·er·ose** \-,rōs\ *adj* [L *acer* sharp] : having the form of or a tip like the point of a needle

acerb \ə-'sərb\ *adj* : ACID

acer·bi·ty \ə-'sər-bət-ē\ *n, pl* **-ties** : acidity of temper, manner, or tone

ace·tab·u·lum \,as-ə-'tab-yə-ləm\ *n, pl* **-lums** *or* **-la** \-lə\ : a cup-shaped socket (as in the hipbone) — **ace·tab·u·lar** \-lər\ *adj*

ac·et·al·de·hyde \,as-ə-'tal-də-,hīd\ *n* : a colorless volatile water-soluble liquid compound CH_3CHO used chiefly in making organic chemicals

ac·et·an·i·lide *or* **ac·et·an·i·lid** \,as-ə-'tan-ᵊl-,īd, -ᵊl-əd\ *n* : a white crystalline compound C_8H_9NO used esp. to check pain or fever

ac·e·tate \'as-ə-,tāt\ *n* **1** : a salt or ester of acetic acid **2** : a textile fiber made from cellulose acetate and characterized by fast drying property; *also* : a fabric made of this fiber **3** : a plastic made from cellulose acetate and used for wrapping film and phonograph records; *also* : a phonograph recording disk made of this plastic

ace·tic \ə-'sēt-ik\ *adj* [L *acetum* vinegar] : of, relating to, or producing acetic acid or vinegar

acetic acid *n* : a colorless pungent liquid acid CH_3COOH that is the chief acid of vinegar and that is used esp. in synthesis (as of plastics)

ace·ti·fy \ə-'sēt-ə-,fī\ *vb* **-fied; -fy·ing** : to turn into acetic acid or vinegar — **ace·ti·fi·ca·tion** \ə-,sēt-ə-fə-'kā-shən\ *n*

ac·e·tone \'as-ə-,tōn\ *n* : a volatile fragrant flammable liquid compound CH_3COCH_3 used chiefly as a solvent and in organic synthesis

ace·tyl \ə-'sēt-ᵊl\ *n* : the radical CH_3CO — of acetic acid

ace·tyl·cho·line \ə-,sēt-ᵊl-'kō-,lēn\ *n* : a compound $C_7H_{17}NO_3$ released at autonomic nerve endings that is held to function in the transmission of the nerve impulse

acet·y·lene \ə-'set-ᵊl-ən, -ᵊl-,ēn\ *n* : a colorless gas C_2H_2 made esp. by the action of water on calcium carbide and used chiefly in welding and soldering and in organic synthesis

ace·tyl·sal·i·cyl·ic acid \ə-,sēt-ᵊl-,sal-ə-,sil-ik-\ *n* : AS-PIRIN 1

¹Achae·an \ə-'kē-ən\ *adj* : of or relating to a group of city-states in the southern part of ancient Greece forming a political confederation about 280 B.C.

²Achaean *n* **1** : one of a Greek people dominant on the Greek mainland from 1600 to 1100 B.C. **2** : a Greek of the Homeric period

¹ache \'āk\ *vi* [OE *acan*] **1** : to suffer a usu. dull persistent pain **2** : to become filled with painful yearning

²ache *n* : a usu. dull persistent pain — **achy** \'ā-kē\ *adj*

achene \ā-'kēn\ *n* : a small dry one-seeded fruit (as of the buttercup) that ripens without bursting its sheath — **ache·ni·al** \ə-'kē-nē-əl\ *adj*

Ach·er·on \'ak-ə-,rän\ *n* : a river in Hades

achieve \ə-'chēv\ *vb* [MF *achever,* fr. *a* to + *chief* head] **1** : to bring to a successful conclusion : ACCOMPLISH ⟨*achieved* his purpose⟩ **2** : to get as the result of exertion : WIN ⟨*achieve* greatness⟩ — **achiev·a·ble** \-'chē-və-bəl\ *adj*

achieve·ment \-mənt\ *n* **1** : the act of achieving **2** : something achieved; *esp* : something accomplished by great effort or persistence ⟨heroic *achievements* by the early settlers⟩ **syn** see FEAT

Achil·les \ə-'kil-ēz\ *n* : a Greek warrior and hero of Homer's *Iliad*

Achil·les' heel \-,kil-ēz-'hēl\ *n* [fr. the legend that Achilles was vulnerable only in the heel] : a vulnerable point

Achilles tendon *n* : the strong tendon joining the muscles in the calf of the leg to the bone of the heel

ach·la·myd·e·ous \,ak-lə-'mid-ē-əs, ,ā-klə-\ *adj* : lacking both calyx and corolla

achon·dro·pla·sia \ā-,kän-drə-'plā-zh(ē-)ə\ *n* : failure of normal development of cartilage resulting in dwarfism — **achon·dro·plas·tic** \-'plas-tik\ *adj*

ach·ro·mat·ic \,ak-rə-'mat-ik\ *adj* [Gk *achrōmatos* colorless] **1** : giving an image practically free from colors not in the object ⟨*achromatic* lens⟩ **2** : being black, gray, or white : COLORLESS

¹ac·id \'as-əd\ *adj* [L *acidus;* akin to E *edge*] **1** : sour, sharp, or biting to the taste : resembling vinegar in taste **2** : sour in temper : CROSS ⟨make *acid* remarks⟩ **3** : of, relating to, or having the characteristics of an acid **4** : rich in silica ⟨*acid* rocks⟩ **syn** see SOUR — **ac·id·ly** *adv* — **ac·id·ness** *n*

²acid *n* **1** : a sour substance **2** : any of various typically water-soluble and sour compounds that are capable of reacting with a base to form a salt, that redden litmus, that evolve hydrogen on reaction with various metals, that in water solution yield hydrogen ions, and that have hydrogen-containing molecules or ions able to give up a proton to a base or that are substances able to accept an unshared pair of electrons from a base **3** : LSD

ac·id–fast \'as-əd-,fast\ *adj* : not easily decolorized by acids

acid·ic \ə-'sid-ik\ *adj* **1** : acid-forming **2** : ACID

acid·i·fy \ə-'sid-ə-,fī\ *vb* **-fied; -fy·ing** **1** : to make or become acid **2** : to change into an acid — **acid·i·fi·ca·tion** \ə-,sid-ə-fə-'kā-shən\ *n*

acid·i·ty \ə-'sid-ət-ē\ *n, pl* **-ties** **1** : the quality, state, or degree of being acid : TARTNESS **2** : HYPERACIDITY

ac·i·do·sis \,as-ə-'dō-səs\ *n* : an abnormal state of reduced alkalinity of the blood and of the body tissues — **ac·i·dot·ic** \-'dät-ik\ *adj*

acid test *n* : a severe or crucial test

acid·u·late \ə-'sij-ə-,lāt\ *vt* : to make acid or slightly acid — **acid·u·la·tion** \ə-,sij-ə-'lā-shən\ *n*

acid·u·lous \ə-'sij-ə-ləs\ *adj* : acid in taste or manner : HARSH

ac·i·nus \'as-ə-nəs\ *n, pl* **-ni** \-,nī\ [L, berry] : one of the small sacs in a racemose gland lined with secreting cells — **ac·i·nous** \-nəs\ *adj*

ack–ack \'ak-,ak\ *n* : an antiaircraft gun; *also* : antiaircraft fire

ac·knowl·edge \ik-'näl-ij, ak-\ *vt* [*ac-* (as in *accord*) + *knowledge*] **1** : to own or admit the truth or existence of ⟨*acknowledged* his mistake⟩ **2** : to recognize the rights, authority, or status of **3 a** : to take notice of **b** : to make known the receipt of ⟨*acknowledge* a letter⟩ — **ac·knowl·edge·a·ble** \-ij-ə-bəl\ *adj*

syn ACKNOWLEDGE, ADMIT, CONFESS mean to disclose against one's will or inclination. ACKNOWLEDGE implies disclosing what has been or might be denied or concealed; ADMIN implies some degree of reluctance in disclosing or conceding; CONFESS implies admitting a weakness, failure, or guilt usu. under compulsion

ac·knowl·edged \-ijd\ *adj* : generally recognized or accepted ⟨the *acknowledged* leader of the group⟩ — **ac·knowl·edged·ly** \-ij(-ǝ)d-lē\ *adv*

ac·knowl·edg·ment *also* **ac·knowl·edge·ment** \ik-'näl-ij-mǝnt, ak-\ *n* **1 a** : the act of acknowledging **b** : recognition or favorable notice of an act or achievement **2** : a thing done or given in recognition of something received

ac·me \'ak-mē\ *n* [Gk *akmē*; akin to E *edge*] : the highest point : PEAK ⟨the *acme* of his ambition⟩

ac·ne \'ak-nē\ *n* : a disorder of the skin caused by inflammation of skin glands and hair follicles and marked by pimples esp. on the face

acoe·lom·ate \(')ā-'sē-lǝ-mǝt, -,māt\ *n* : a lowly animal that has no true body cavity

ac·o·lyte \'ak-ǝ-,līt\ *n* [Gk *akolouthos* follower, attendant] **1** : a man or boy who assists the clergyman in a liturgical service **2** : one who attends or assists : FOLLOWER

ac·o·nite \'ak-ǝ-,nīt\ *n* [Gk *akoniton*] **1** : any of a genus of poisonous usu. blue-flowered or purple-flowered plants related to the buttercups — compare MONKSHOOD **2** : a drug obtained from the common Old World monkshood

acorn \'ā-,kȯrn, -kǝrn\ *n* [OE *æcern*] : the nut of the oak tree

acorn worm *n* : HEMICHORDATE

acous·tic \ǝ-'kü-stik\ *adj* [Gk *akous-, akouein* to hear; akin to E *hear*] : of or relating to the sense or organs of hearing, to sound, or to the science of sounds: as **a** : deadening sound **b** : operated by or utilizing sound waves — **acous·ti·cal** \-sti-kǝl\ *adj* — **acous·ti·cal·ly** \-sti-k(ǝ-)lē\ *adv*

acorns of
white oak

acous·ti·cian \ǝ-,kü-'stish-ǝn, ǝ-,kü-\ *n* : a specialist in acoustics

acous·tics \ǝ-'kü-stiks\ *n sing or pl* **1** : the science dealing with sound **2** *also* **acous·tic** \-stik\ : the qualities in a room or hall that make it easy or hard for a person in it to hear distinctly ⟨the *acoustics* of the hall permitted the faintest sound to be heard⟩

ac·quaint \ǝ-'kwānt\ *vt* [OF *acointier*, fr. LL *accognitus*, pp. of *accognoscere* to know perfectly, fr. L *ad-* + *cognoscere* to know] **1** : to cause to know socially ⟨became *acquainted* through mutual friends⟩ **2** : to cause to know firsthand : INFORM ⟨*acquaint* him with his duties⟩

ac·quaint·ance \ǝ-'kwānt-ǝn(t)s\ *n* **1** : knowledge gained by personal observation, contact, or experience ⟨had some *acquaintance* with the subject⟩ **2** : a person one knows but not familiarly or intimately — **ac·quaint·ance·ship** \-,ship\ *n*

ac·qui·esce \,ak-wē-'es\ *vi* [L *acquiescere*, fr. *ad-* + *quiescere* to be quiet] : to accept, agree, or give implied consent by keeping silent or by not raising objections — **ac·qui·es·cence** \-'es-ᵊn(t)s\ *n*

ac·qui·es·cent \-'es-ᵊnt\ *adj* : acquiescing or disposed to acquiesce — **ac·qui·es·cent·ly** *adv*

ac·quire \ǝ-'kwī(ǝ)r\ *vt* [L *acquirere*, fr. *ad-* + *quaerere* to seek] **1** : to come into possession of esp. by one's own efforts : GAIN ⟨*acquired* great wealth⟩ **2 a** : to come to have as a characteristic, trait, or ability often by sustained effort ⟨the milk *acquired* a sour taste⟩ ⟨*acquired* study skills⟩ **b** : to develop after birth usu. as a result of environmental forces ⟨an *acquired* disease⟩ — compare CONGENITAL, HEREDITARY — **ac·quir·a·ble** \-'kwī-rǝ-bǝl\ *adj*

ac·quire·ment \-'kwī(ǝ)r-mǝnt\ *n* **1** : the act of acquiring **2** : an attainment of mind or body usu. resulting from continued endeavor ⟨the *acquirements* expected of a high school graduate⟩

ac·qui·si·tion \,ak-wǝ-'zish-ǝn\ *n* [L *acquisit-, acquirere* to acquire] **1** : the act of acquiring ⟨the *acquisition* of property⟩ **2** : something acquired or gained ⟨the book was a recent *acquisition*⟩

ac·quis·i·tive \ǝ-'kwiz-ǝt-iv\ *adj* : strongly desirous of acquiring : GRASPING — **ac·quis·i·tive·ly** *adv* — **ac·quis·i·tive·ness** *n*

ac·quit \ǝ-'kwit\ *vt* **-quit·ted; -quit·ting** [OF *acquiter* fr. *a-* ad- + *quite* quit, free] **1** : to set free or discharge

completely (as from an obligation or accusation) ⟨the court *acquitted* the prisoner⟩ **2** : to conduct (oneself) usu. satisfactorily ⟨the recruits *acquitted* themselves like veterans⟩ — **ac·quit·ter** *n*

ac·quit·tal \ǝ-'kwit-ᵊl\ *n* : the setting free of a person from the charge of an offense by verdict, sentence, or other legal process

ac·quit·tance \-ᵊn(t)s\ *n* : a writing (as a receipt) evidencing a discharge from an obligation

acr- *or* **acro-** *comb form* [Gk *akros* topmost, extreme] **1 a** : beginning : end ⟨*acronym*⟩ **b** : extremity ⟨*acromegaly*⟩ **2** : peak : height ⟨*acrophobia*⟩

acre \'ā-kǝr\ *n* [OE *æcer*] **1** *pl* : LANDS, ESTATE **2** : a unit of area equal to 160 square rods — see MEASURE table **3** : a broad expanse or great quantity

acre·age \'ā-k(ǝ-)rij\ *n* : area in acres : ACRES

ac·rid \'ak-rǝd\ *adj* [L *acr-, acer* sharp; akin to E *edge*] **1** : sharp and harsh or unpleasantly pungent in taste or odor : IRRITATING, CORROSIVE **2** : bitterly irritating to the feelings ⟨an *acrid* remark⟩ — **acrid·i·ty** \ǝ-'krid-ǝt-ē, ǝ-\ *n* — **ac·rid·ly** \'ak-rǝd-lē\ *adv* — **ac·rid·ness** *n*

ac·ri·mo·ni·ous \,ak-rǝ-'mō-nē-ǝs\ *adj* : marked by acrimony : BITTER, RANCOROUS ⟨an *acrimonious* dispute⟩ — **ac·ri·mo·ni·ous·ly** *adv* — **ac·ri·mo·ni·ous·ness** *n*

ac·ri·mo·ny \'ak-rǝ-,mō-nē\ *n, pl* **-nies** [L *acrimonia*, fr. *acr-, acer* sharp] : harsh or biting sharpness esp. of words, manner, or disposition

ac·ro·bat \'ak-rǝ-,bat\ *n* [Gk *akrobates*, fr. *akros* topmost, extreme + *bainein* to step, go] **1** : one that performs gymnastic feats requiring skillful control of the body **2** : one adept at swiftly changing his position — **ac·ro·bat·ic** \,ak-rǝ-'bat-ik\ *adj* — **ac·ro·bat·i·cal·ly** \-'bat-i-k(ǝ-)lē\ *adv*

ac·ro·bat·ics \,ak-rǝ-'bat-iks\ *n sing or pl* **1** : the art or performance of an acrobat **2** : a striking performance involving great agility or maneuverability ⟨airplane *acrobatics*⟩

ac·ro·meg·a·ly \,ak-rō-'meg-ǝ-lē\ *n* : a disorder caused by excessive secretion of the pituitary gland and marked by progressive enlargement of hands, feet, and face — **ac·ro·me·gal·ic** \-mi-'gal-ik\ *adj*

ac·ro·nym \'ak-rǝ-,nim\ *n* : a word (as *radar*) formed from the initial letter or letters of each of the successive parts or major parts of a compound term

ac·ro·pho·bia \,ak-rǝ-'fō-bē-ǝ\ *n* : abnormal dread of being at a great height

acrop·o·lis \ǝ-'kräp-ǝ-lǝs\ *n* [Gk *akropolis*, fr. *akros* topmost + *polis* city] **1** : the upper fortified part of an ancient Greek city **2** *cap* : the acropolis at Athens

¹across \ǝ-'krȯs\ *adv* **1** : so as to reach or pass from one side to the other ⟨boards sawed directly *across*⟩ **2** : to or on the opposite side ⟨got *across* in a boat⟩

²across *prep* **1** : to or on the opposite side of ⟨*across* the street⟩ **2** : so as to intersect or pass at an angle ⟨lay one stick *across* another⟩ **3** : into an accidental or transitory meeting or contact with ⟨ran *across* an old friend⟩

across–the–board *adj* **1** : placed in combination to win, place, or show ⟨an *across-the-board* bet⟩ **2** : including all classes or categories ⟨an *across-the-board* wage increase⟩

acros·tic \ǝ-'krȯ-stik\ *n* [Gk *akrostichis*, fr. *akros* extreme + *stichos* line] **1** : a composition usu. in verse in which sets of letters (as the initial or final letters of the lines) taken in order form a word or phrase or a regular sequence of letters of the alphabet **2** : ACRONYM **3** : a series of words of equal length arranged to read the same horizontally or vertically — **acrostic** *adj* — **acros·ti·cal·ly** \-sti-k(ǝ-)lē\ *adv*

ac·ry·late resin \,ak-rǝ-,lāt-\ *or* **acryl·ic resin** \ǝ-,kril-ik-\ *n* : a glassy synthetic organic plastic used for cast and molded parts or as coatings and adhesives

¹act \'akt\ *n* [partly fr. L *actum* thing done (fr. neut. of *actus*, pp. of *agere* to do) & partly fr. L *actus* action, fr. *act-, agere* to do] **1** : something that is done : DEED ⟨an *act* of kindness⟩ **2** : the doing of something ⟨caught in the *act* of stealing⟩ **3** : a law made by a governing body (as a legislature) ⟨an *act* of Congress⟩ **4 a** : one of the main divisions of a play or opera **b** : one of the successive parts of a variety show or circus **syn** see ACTION

²act *vb* **1** : to perform by action esp. on the stage **2** : to play the part of ⟨*act* the man of the world⟩ **3 a** : to behave in a manner suitable to ⟨*act* your age⟩ **b** : to conduct

oneself ⟨*act* like a fool⟩ **4 :** PRETEND **5 :** to take action
: MOVE ⟨think before you *act*⟩ **6 a :** to perform a specified
function **:** discharge the duties of a specified office
: SERVE **b :** to produce an effect **:** WORK ⟨wait for a
medicine to *act*⟩ **7 :** to make a decision — **act·a·bil·i·ty**
\ˌak-tə-'bil-ət-ē\ *n* — **act·a·ble** \'ak-tə-bəl\ *adj*

ac·tin \'ak-tən\ *n* [L *actus* action] **:** a protein of muscle
that is active in muscular contraction

actin- *or* **actini-** *or* **actino-** *comb form* [Gk *aktin-, aktis*
ray] **:** having a radiate form ⟨*actinoid*⟩

¹act·ing \'ak-tiŋ\ *adj* **:** serving temporarily or in place of
another ⟨*acting* chairman⟩

²acting *n* **:** the art or practice of representing a character
on a stage or before cameras

ac·ti·nide \'ak-tə-ˌnīd\ *n* **:** a heavy radioactive metallic
element in the series of increasing atomic number beginning with actinium and ending with element of atomic
number 103

ac·ti·nism \'ak-tə-ˌniz-əm\ *n* **:** the property of radiant
energy by which chemical changes are produced — **ac·
tin·ic** \ak-'tin-ik\ *adj*

ac·tin·i·um \ak-'tin-ē-əm\ *n* **:** a radioactive metallic element found esp. in pitchblende — see ELEMENT table

ac·ti·no·mor·phic \ˌak-tə-nō-'mȯr-fik\ *also* **ac·ti·no·
mor·phous** \-fəs\ *adj* **:** radially symmetrical and capable
of division into essentially symmetrical halves by any
longitudinal plane passing through the axis — **ac·ti·no·
mor·phy** \'ak-tə-nō-ˌmȯr-fē\ *n*

ac·ti·no·my·cete \ˌak-tə-nō-'mī-ˌsēt, -mī-'sēt\ *n* **:** any of
an order (Actinomycetales) of filamentous or rod-shaped
bacteria including soil saprophytes and disease producers
— **ac·ti·no·my·ce·tous** \-mī-'sēt-əs\ *adj*

ac·ti·no·my·co·sis \ˌak-tə-nō-mī-'kō-səs\ *n, pl* **-co·ses**
\-'kō-ˌsēz\ **:** infection with or disease caused by actinomycetes — **ac·ti·no·my·cot·ic** \-'kät-ik\ *adj*

ac·tion \'ak-shən\ *n* **1 :** a proceeding in a court of justice
by which one demands or enforces one's right or the
redress or punishment of a wrong **2 :** the bringing about
of an alteration by force or through a natural agency ⟨the
action of acids on metals⟩ **3 :** the process or manner of
acting or functioning **:** PERFORMANCE **4 a :** a thing done
: DEED **b** *pl* **:** BEHAVIOR, CONDUCT **5 :** combat in war
: BATTLE **6 :** the unfolding of the events of a drama or
work of fiction **:** PLOT **7 :** an operating mechanism;
also **:** the way it operates

syn ACT, DEED: ACTION may apply to a process that
involves more than one step, or is continuous, or is
capable of repetition ⟨the *action* of water is wearing away
rock⟩ ACT suggests a single accomplishment complete in
itself and essentially unique ⟨a traitorous *act*⟩ DEED applies
to a remarkable or illustrious act ⟨*deeds* of famous heroes⟩

ac·tion·a·ble \'ak-sh(ə-)nə-bəl\ *adj* **:** subject to or affording ground for an action or suit at law — **ac·tion·a·bly**
\-blē\ *adv*

ac·ti·vate \'ak-tə-ˌvāt\ *vt* **:** to make active or more active:
as **a :** to make (as molecules) reactive **b :** to make (a
substance) radioactive **c :** to treat (as carbon or alumina)
so as to improve adsorptive properties **d :** to aerate
(sewage) so as to favor the growth of organisms that
cause decomposition — **ac·ti·va·tion** \ˌak-tə-'vā-shən\ *n*
— **ac·ti·va·tor** \'ak-tə-ˌvāt-ər\ *n*

ac·tive \'ak-tiv\ *adj* **1 :** characterized by action rather
than contemplation **2 :** productive of or involving action
or movement ⟨an *active* sport⟩ **3 :** of, relating to, or
constituting a verb form or voice indicating that the person
or thing represented by the grammatical subject performs
the action represented by the verb ⟨*hits* in "he hits the ball"
is *active*⟩ **4 :** quick in physical movement **:** LIVELY
5 a : disposed to action **:** ENERGETIC ⟨*active* interest⟩
b : engaged in an action or activity **:** PARTICIPATING ⟨an
active club member⟩ **6 :** engaged in full-time service esp.
in the armed forces ⟨*active* duty⟩ **7 :** marked by present
action, operation, movement, or use ⟨*active* account⟩
⟨*active* titles in a publisher's catalog⟩ ⟨a student's *active*
vocabulary⟩ **8 a :** capable of acting or reacting **b :** tending to progress or increase ⟨*active* tuberculosis⟩ — **ac·
tive·ly** *adv* — **ac·tive·ness** *n*

active immunity *n* **:** immunity produced by the individual
when exposed to an antigen — compare PASSIVE IM-
MUNITY

ac·tiv·ism \'ak-ti-ˌviz-əm\ *n* **:** a doctrine or practice that

emphasizes vigorous action and esp. the use of force for
political ends — **ac·tiv·ist** \-vəst\ *n or adj*

ac·tiv·i·ty \ak-'tiv-ət-ē\ *n, pl* **-ties 1 :** the quality or
state of being active **2 :** vigorous or energetic action
: LIVELINESS **3 a :** natural or normal function **b** (1) **:** a
process that an organism carries on or participates in by
virtue of being alive (2) **:** a similar process actually
or potentially involving mental function **4 :** an educational procedure designed to stimulate learning by firsthand experience **5 :** an active force **6 a :** PURSUIT 2
b : a form of organized, supervised, often extracurricular
recreation **c :** the work or duties of a government unit
or agency organized for a specific function

act of God : an extraordinary interruption by a natural
cause (as a flood or earthquake) of the usual course of
events that experience, prescience, or care cannot reasonably foresee or prevent

ac·to·my·o·sin \ˌak-tə-'mī-ə-sən\ *n* **:** a viscous contractile complex of actin and myosin held to function
together with adenosine triphosphate in muscular
contraction

ac·tor \'ak-tər\ *n* **1 a :** one that acts **:** DOER **b :** one that
acts a part; *esp* **:** a theatrical performer **2 :** PARTICIPANT
— **ac·tress** \'ak-trəs\ *n*

Acts \'ak(t)s\ *n* — see BIBLE table

ac·tu·al \'ak-ch(ə-w)əl, 'aksh-wəl\ *adj* **1 a :** existing in
act and not merely potentially **b :** existing in fact or
reality as distinguished from being ideal or nominal ⟨*actual*
and imagined conditions⟩ ⟨*actual* costs⟩ **c :** not false
: REAL **2 :** present or active at the time **:** CURRENT
syn see REAL

ac·tu·al·i·ty \ˌak-chə-'wal-ət-ē\ *n, pl* **-ties 1 :** the quality
or state of being actual **2 :** something that is actual ⟨face
the *actualities* of the situation⟩

ac·tu·al·ize \'ak-ch(ə-w)ə-ˌlīz, 'aksh-wə-\ *vb* **:** to make or
become actual — **ac·tu·al·i·za·tion** \ˌak-ch(ə-w)ə-lə-
'zā-shən, ˌaksh-wə-\ *n*

ac·tu·al·ly \'ak-ch(ə-w)ə-lē, 'aksh-wə-; 'aksh-lē\ *adv* **:** in
act or in fact **:** REALLY

ac·tu·ary \'ak-chə-ˌwer-ē\ *n, pl* **-ar·ies** [L *actuarius* one
who keeps accounts, fr. *actum* thing done, record] **:** one
who calculates insurance premiums and dividends — **ac·
tu·ar·i·al** \ˌak-chə-'wer-ē-əl\ *adj* — **ac·tu·ar·i·al·ly**
\-ē-ə-lē\ *adv*

ac·tu·ate \'ak-chə-ˌwāt\ *vt* **1 :** to put into action ⟨the
windmill *actuates* the pump⟩ **2 :** to move to action **:** arouse
to activity ⟨the students were *actuated* by the hope of
winning prizes⟩ **syn** see MOVE — **ac·tu·a·tion** \ˌak-chə-
'wā-shən\ *n*

act up *vi* **:** to act in an unruly, abnormal, or annoying way

acu·ity \ə-'kyü-ət-ē\ *n* [L *acutus* sharp] **:** keenness of
perception **:** SHARPNESS

acu·le·ate \ə-'kyü-lē-ət\ *adj* **:** having a sting **:** furnished
with spines or prickles

acu·men \ə-'kyü-mən\ *n* [L *acumin-, acumen,* lit., point, fr.
acuere to make sharp] **:** keenness of insight esp. in practical
matters **:** SHREWDNESS

acu·mi·nate \ə-'kyü-mə-nət\ *adj* **:** tapering to a slender
point **:** POINTED

acute \ə-'kyüt\ *adj* [L *acutus,* fr. pp. of *acuere* to sharpen,
fr. *acus* needle; akin to E *edge*] **1 a :** measuring less
than a right angle ⟨*acute* angle⟩ — see ANGLE illustration
b : composed of acute angles **2 a :** marked by keen discernment or intellectual perception esp. of subtle distinctions **:** PENETRATING **b :** responsive to slight impressions
or stimuli ⟨*acute* observer⟩ **3 :** marked by sharpness or
severity ⟨an *acute* pain⟩ **4 :** HIGH, SHRILL ⟨an *acute* sound⟩
5 a : having a sudden onset and short duration ⟨*acute*
disease⟩ **b :** being at or near a turning point **:** URGENT,
CRITICAL ⟨an *acute* situation that may lead to war⟩ **6 :** of,
marked by, or being an accent mark having the form ´
syn see SHARP — **acute·ly** *adv* — **acute·ness** *n*

ad \'ad\ *n* **1 :** ADVERTISEMENT 2

ad- *or* **ac-** *or* **ag-** *or* **al-** *or* **ap-** *or* **as-** *or* **at-** *prefix* [L; akin
to E *at*] **1 :** to **:** toward — usu. *ac-* before *c, k,* or *q*
⟨*acculturation*⟩ and *ag-* before *g* ⟨*aggrade*⟩ and *al-* before *l*
⟨*alliteration*⟩ and *ap-* before *p* ⟨*approximal*⟩ and *as-* before
s ⟨*assuasive*⟩ and *at-* before *t* ⟨*attune*⟩ and *ad-* before other
sounds but sometimes *ad-* even before one of the listed
consonants ⟨*adsorb*⟩ **2 :** near **:** adjacent to — in this
sense always in the form *ad-* ⟨*adrenal*⟩

-ad \,ad, əd\ *adv suffix* [L *ad* to] **:** in the direction of **:** toward ⟨cephal*ad*⟩

ad·age \'ad-ij\ *n* [L *adagium*] **:** a saying embodying common observation often in metaphorical form

¹ada·gio \ə-'däj-ō, -'däj-ē-,ō, -'däzh-\ *adv* (*or adj*) [It] **:** in an easy graceful manner **:** SLOWLY — used chiefly as a direction in music

²adagio *n* **1 :** a musical composition or movement in adagio tempo **2 :** a ballet duet by a man and woman or a mixed trio displaying difficult feats of balance, lifting, or spinning

¹Ad·am \'ad-əm\ *n* **1 :** the first man and progenitor of the human race **2 :** the unregenerate nature of man

²Adam *adj* **:** of or relating to an 18th century style of furniture characterized by straight lines, surface decoration, and conventional designs (as festooned garlands and medallions)

¹ad·a·mant \'ad-ə-mənt, -,mant\ *n* [Gk *adamant-, adamas*, a very hard metal] **1 :** a stone believed to be of impenetrable hardness **2 :** an extremely hard substance

²adamant *adj* **:** unshakable or immovable esp. in opposition **:** UNYIELDING **syn** see INFLEXIBLE — **ad·a·mant·ly** *adv*

ad·a·man·tine \,ad-ə-'man-,tēn, -,tīn\ *adj* **1 :** made of or having the quality of adamant **2 :** rigidly firm **:** UNYIELDING **3 :** resembling the diamond in hardness or luster

Ad·am's apple \,ad-əmz-\ *n* **:** the projection in the front of the neck formed by the largest cartilage of the larynx

adapt \ə-'dapt\ *vb* **:** to make or become suitable; *esp* **:** to change so as to fit a new or specific use or situation ⟨*adapt* to life in a new school⟩⟨*adapt* the novel for children⟩ — **adapt·a·bil·i·ty** \-,dap-tə-'bil-ət-ē\ *n* — **adapt·a·ble** \-'dap-tə-bəl\ *adj*

syn ADAPT, ADJUST, ACCOMMODATE, CONFORM mean to bring one into correspondence with another. ADAPT implies suiting or fitting by modification and may suggest pliability or readiness; ADJUST implies bringing into close or exact correspondence; ACCOMMODATE implies adapting or adjusting to by yielding or stretching; CONFORM implies bringing or coming into accord with a pattern or principle

ad·ap·ta·tion \,ad-,ap-'tā-shən\ *n* **1 a :** the act or process of adapting **b :** the state of being adapted **2 :** adjustment to environmental conditions: as **a :** adjustment of a sense organ to the intensity or quality of stimulation **b :** modification of an organism or its parts that fits it better for the conditions of its environment; *also* **:** a change or structure resulting from such modification **3 :** something that is adapted; *esp* **:** a composition rewritten into a new form — **ad·ap·ta·tion·al** \-shnəl, -shən-ᵊl\ *adj* — **ad·ap·ta·tion·al·ly** \-ē\ *adv*

adapt·ed \ə-'dap-təd\ *adj* **:** SUITABLE

adapt·er *also* **adap·tor** \ə-'dap-tər\ *n* **1 :** one that adapts **2 a :** a device for connecting two parts (as of different diameters) of an apparatus **b :** an attachment for adapting apparatus for uses not originally intended

adap·tive \ə-'dap-tiv\ *adj* **:** showing or having a capacity for or tendency toward adaptation — **adap·tive·ly** *adv*

ad·ax·i·al \(')ad-'ak-sē-əl\ *adj* **:** situated on the same side as or facing the axis (as of an organ)

add \'ad\ *vb* [L *addere*, fr. *ad-* + *-dere* to put; akin to E *do*] **1 a :** to join or unite to a thing so as to enlarge, increase, or enhance it ⟨*add* a wing to the house⟩ **b :** to unite in a single whole ⟨it all *adds* up⟩ **2 :** to put or say something more ⟨*add* one cup of sugar⟩⟨*add* to his remarks⟩ **3 :** to combine numbers into a single sum — **add·a·ble** *or* **add·i·ble** \'ad-ə-bəl\ *adj*

ad·dax \'ad-,aks\ *n* [L] **:** a large light-colored antelope of No. Africa, Arabia, and Syria

ad·dend \'ad-,end\ *n* [short for *addendum*] **:** a number that is to be added to another number

ad·den·dum \ə-'den-dəm\ *n, pl* **-den·da** \-'den-də\ [L, thing to be added, fr. *addere* to add] **1 :** a thing added **:** ADDITION **2 :** a supplement to a book **:** APPENDIX

¹ad·der \'ad-ər\ *n* [ME *nadder* (the phrase *a nadder* being understood as *an adder*), fr. OE *nǣdre*] **1 :** a poisonous European viper; *also* **:** any of several related snakes **2 :** any of several harmless No. American snakes (as the hognose snakes)

²add·er \'ad-ər\ *n* **:** one that adds

ad·der's-tongue \'ad-ərz-,təŋ\ *n* **1 :** a fern whose fruiting spike resembles a serpent's tongue **2 :** DOGTOOTH VIOLET

¹ad·dict \ə-'dikt\ *vt* [L *addict-, addicere* to award, devote, fr. *ad-* + *dicere* to say] **:** to devote or surrender (oneself) to something habitually or obsessively

²ad·dict \'ad-(,)ikt\ *n* **:** one who is addicted (as to a drug)

ad·dic·tion \ə-'dik-shən\ *n* **:** the quality or state of being addicted; *esp* **:** compulsive use of habit-forming drugs

ad·dic·tive \ə-'dik-tiv\ *adj* **:** causing or characterized by addiction

Ad·di·son's disease \'ad-ə-sənz-\ *n* **:** a destructive disease marked by deficient secretion of the adrenal cortical hormone

ad·di·tion \ə-'dish-ən\ *n* **1 :** the result of adding **:** INCREASE **2 :** the act or process of adding **3 :** the operation of adding numbers to obtain their sum **4 :** a part added (as to a building or residential section) **5 :** direct chemical combination of substances into a single product — **in addition :** BESIDES — **in addition to :** over and above

ad·di·tion·al \ə-'dish-nəl, -'dish-ən-ᵊl\ *adj* **:** ADDED, EXTRA ⟨an *additional* charge⟩ — **ad·di·tion·al·ly** \-ē-\ *adv*

¹ad·di·tive \'ad-ət-iv\ *adj* **:** relating to or produced by addition — **ad·di·tive·ly** *adv*

²additive *n* **:** a substance added to another in relatively small amounts to impart or improve desirable properties or suppress undesirable properties ⟨a gasoline *additive* intended to improve engine performance⟩

additive inverse *n* **:** a number of opposite sign with respect to a given number so that addition of the two numbers gives zero ⟨the *additive inverse* of 4 is −4⟩

ad·dle \'ad-ᵊl\ *vb* **ad·dled**; **ad·dling** \'ad-liŋ, -ᵊl-iŋ\ [fr. earlier *addle* rotten, empty] **1 :** to make or become confused **2 :** to become rotten

¹ad·dress \ə-'dres\ *vt* [MF *adresser*, fr. *a-* ad- + *dresser* to arrange, dress] **1 :** to direct the attention of (oneself) ⟨*addressed* himself to his work⟩ **2 a :** to communicate directly to a person or group ⟨*address* a petition to the governor⟩ **b :** to deliver a formal speech to ⟨*address* the convention⟩ **3 :** to mark directions for delivery on ⟨*address* a letter⟩ **4 :** to greet by a prescribed form — **ad·dress·er** *n*

²ad·dress \ə-'dres, 'ad-,res\ *n* **1 a :** BEARING, DEPORTMENT **b :** the manner of speaking or singing **:** DELIVERY **2 :** dutiful attention esp. in courtship — usu. used in pl. **3 a :** a formal usu. prepared speech **b :** PETITION **4 a :** a place where a person or organization may be communicated with **b :** directions for delivery on the outside of an object (as a letter or package) **c :** the designation of place of delivery above the salutation on a business letter **5 :** a unit where particular information is stored (as in a computer)

ad·dress·ee \,ad-,res-'ē, ə-,dres-'ē\ *n* **:** one to whom something is addressed

ad·duce \ə-'d(y)üs\ *vt* [L *adduct-, adducere*, lit., to lead to, fr. *ad-* + *ducere* to lead] **:** to offer as example, reason, or proof in discussion or analysis — **ad·duc·er** *n*

ad·duct \ə-'dəkt\ *vt* **:** to draw (a part of the body) toward or past the median axis of the body; *also* **:** to bring (similar parts) together — **ad·duc·tive** \-'dək-tiv\ *adj*

ad·duc·tion \ə-'dək-shən\ *n* **1 :** the action of adducting **:** the state of being adducted **2 :** the act or action of adducing or bringing forward

ad·duc·tor \ə-'dək-tər\ *n* **:** a muscle that draws a body part toward the median axis — compare ABDUCTOR, EXTENSOR, RETRACTOR

-ade \'ād, ,ād\ *n suffix* [MF, fr. Old Provençal *-ada*, fr. L *-ata*, feminine of past participle in *-atus*] **1 :** act **:** action ⟨block*ade*⟩ **2 :** product; *esp* **:** sweet drink ⟨lim*eade*⟩

ad·e·nine \'ad-ᵊn-,ēn\ *n* **:** a purine base regularly present in the polynucleotide chain of deoxyribonucleic acid and ribonucleic acid

¹ad·e·noid \'ad-ᵊn-,ȯid, 'ad-,nȯid\ *or* **ad·e·noi·dal** \,ad-ᵊn-'ȯid-ᵊl\ *adj* [Gk *adenoeidēs*, fr. *adēn* gland] **1 :** of, relating to, or resembling glands or glandular or lymphoid tissue **2 :** of or relating to adenoids or adenoid disorder

²adenoid *n* **:** an enlarged mass of lymphoid tissue at the back of the pharynx characteristically obstructing breathing — usu. used in pl.

aden·o·sine \ə-'den-ə-,sēn\ *n* [blend of *adenine* & *ribose*] **:** a compound $C_{10}H_{13}N_5O_4$ that is a constituent of ribonucleic acid and yields adenine and ribose on hydrolysis

adenosine di·phos·phate \-dī-'fäs-,fāt\ *n* **:** a derivative of adenosine that is formed in living cells and reacts in muscle tissue to produce adenosine triphosphate — abbr. *ADP*

adenosine tri·phos·phate \-trī-'fäs-ˌfāt\ *n* : a derivative of adenosine that occurs widely in tissue and serves as a source of energy (as in muscles) — abbr. *ATP*

¹**ad·ept** \'ad-ˌept\ *n* [NL *adeptus* alchemist who has attained the knowledge of how to change base metals to gold, fr. L, pp. of *adipisci* to attain, fr. *ad-* + *apisci* to reach] : a highly skilled or well-trained individual : EXPERT

²**adept** \ə-'dept\ *adj* : thoroughly proficient : EXPERT **syn** see PROFICIENT — **adept·ly** *adv* — **adept·ness** \-'dep(t)-nəs\ *n*

ad·e·qua·cy \'ad-i-kwə-sē\ *n* : the quality or state of being adequate

ad·e·quate \'ad-i-kwət\ *adj* [L *adaequatus*, pp. of *adaequare* to make equal, fr. *ad-* + *aequus* equal] **1** : suitable or fully sufficient for a specific requirement **2** : barely sufficient or satisfactory **syn** see SUFFICIENT — **ad·e·quate·ly** *adv* — **ad·e·quate·ness** *n*

ad·here \ad-'hi(ə)r, əd-\ *vi* [L *adhaerēre* to stick to, fr. *ad-* + *haerēre* to stick] **1** : to give support or maintain loyalty (as to a cause or belief) **2** : to hold fast or stick by or as if by gluing : CLING **3** : to agree to accept as binding ⟨*adhere* to a treaty⟩ **syn** see STICK

ad·her·ence \-'hir-ən(t)s\ *n* **1** : the action or quality of adhering **2** : steady or faithful attachment : FIDELITY ⟨*adherence* to a cause⟩

  syn ADHERENCE, ADHESION mean a sticking to or sticking together. ADHERENCE is applied chiefly to mental or moral attachment ⟨strict *adherence* to principles⟩ ADHESION is commonly restricted to physical attachment ⟨*adhesion* of iron filings to a magnet⟩

¹**ad·her·ent** \-'hir-ənt\ *adj* **1** : able or tending to adhere **2** : connected or associated with something — **ad·her·ent·ly** *adv*

²**adherent** *n* : one that adheres: as **a** : a follower of a leader or party **b** : a believer in or advocate of something (as an idea, church, or doctrine)

ad·he·sion \ad-'hē-zhən, əd-\ *n* [L *adhaes-, adhaerēre* to adhere] **1** : steady or firm attachment : ADHERENCE **2** : the action or state of adhering **3** : tissues abnormally united by fibrous tissue following inflammation (as after surgery) **4** : the molecular attraction exerted between the surfaces of bodies in contact **syn** see ADHERENCE — **ad·he·sion·al** \-'hēzh-nəl, -'hē-zhən-ᵊl\ *adj*

¹**ad·he·sive** \ad-'hē-siv, -ziv\ *adj* **1** : tending to remain in association or memory **2** : tending to adhere : prepared for adhering : STICKY — **ad·he·sive·ly** *adv* — **ad·he·sive·ness** *n*

²**adhesive** *n* : an adhesive substance (as glue or cement)

adhesive plaster *n* : material (as textile or plastic) coated on one side with an adhesive mixture and used esp. for fixing or covering bandages or supporting injuries

ad hoc \(')ad-'häk\ *adv (or adj)* [L, for this] : for the particular purpose or case at hand ⟨a decision made *ad hoc*⟩

ad ho·mi·nem \(')ad-'häm-ə-ˌnem\ *adj* [NL, lit., to the man] : appealing to a person's feelings or prejudices rather than his intellect ⟨an *ad hominem* argument⟩

ad·i·a·bat·ic \ˌad-ē-ə-'bat-ik, ˌā-ˌdī-ə-\ *adj* [Gk *adiabatos* impassable, fr. *a-* ²*a-* + *dia-* + *bainein* to go] : occurring without loss or gain of heat ⟨*adiabatic* expansion⟩ — **ad·i·a·bat·i·cal·ly** \-'bat-i-k(ə-)lē\ *adv*

adieu \ə-'d(y)ü\ *n, pl* **adieus** *or* **adieux** \-'d(y)üz\ [MF, fr. *a Dieu* to God] : FAREWELL — often used interjectionally

ad in·fi·ni·tum \ˌad-ˌin-fə-'nīt-əm\ *adv (or adj)* [L] : without end or limit

¹**ad in·ter·im** \(')ad-'in-tə-rəm\ *adv* : for the intervening time : TEMPORARILY ⟨serving *ad interim*⟩

²**ad interim** *adj* : made or serving ad interim ⟨an *ad interim* appointment⟩

adi·os \ˌad-ē-'ōs, ˌäd-\ *interj* [Sp *adios*, fr. *a Dios* to God] — used to express farewell

ad·i·pose \'ad-ə-ˌpōs\ *adj* [L *adip-, adeps* fat, n.] : of or relating to animal fat : FATTY — **ad·i·pos·i·ty** \ˌad-ə-'päs-ət-ē\ *n*

ad·ja·cent \ə-'jās-ᵊnt\ *adj* [L *adjacent-, adjacens*, prp. of *adjacēre* to lie near, fr. *ad-* + *jacēre* to lie] **1** : lying next or near : having a common border ⟨a field *adjacent* to the road⟩ **2** : having a common vertex and side ⟨*adjacent* angles⟩ — **ad·ja·cen·cy** \-ᵊn-sē\ *n* — **ad·ja·cent·ly** *adv*

ad·jec·ti·val \ˌaj-ik-'tī-vəl\ *adj* : ADJECTIVE — **ad·jec·ti·val·ly** \-və-lē\ *adv*

¹**ad·jec·tive** \'aj-ik-tiv\ *adj* [L *adject-, adicere* to add, fr. *ad-* + *jacere* to throw] **1** : of, relating to, or functioning as an adjective ⟨*adjective* clause⟩ **2** : not standing by itself : DEPENDENT — **ad·jec·tive·ly** *adv*

²**adjective** *n* : a word typically serving as a modifier of a noun to denote a quality of the thing named, to indicate its quantity or extent, or to specify a thing as distinct from something else

ad·join \ə-'jóin\ *vt* **1** : to add or attach by joining **2** : to lie next to or in contact with

ad·join·ing *adj* : touching or bounding at a point or line

ad·journ \ə-'jərn\ *vb* [MF *ajourner*, fr. *a* to + *jour* day] : to suspend further proceedings or business for an indefinite or stated period of time ⟨Congress *adjourned*⟩ ⟨*adjourn* a meeting⟩ — **ad·journ·ment** \-mənt\ *n*

ad·judge \ə-'jəj\ *vt* **1** : ADJUDICATE **2** : to hold or pronounce to be : DEEM

ad·ju·di·cate \ə-'jüd-i-ˌkāt\ *vt* [L *adjudicare*, fr. *ad-* + *judicare* to judge] : to decide, award, or sentence judicially ⟨*adjudicate* a claim⟩ — **ad·ju·di·ca·tive** \-ˌkāt-iv\ *adj* — **ad·ju·di·ca·tor** \-ˌkāt-ər\ *n*

ad·ju·di·ca·tion \-ˌjüd-i-'kā-shən\ *n* **1** : the act or process of adjudicating **2** : a judicial decision — **ad·ju·di·ca·to·ry** \-'jüd-i-kə-ˌtōr-ē, -ˌtór-\ *adj*

¹**ad·junct** \'aj-ˌəŋ(k)t\ *n* [L *adjunctum*, fr. neut. of *adjunctus*, pp. of *adjungere* to join to, fr. *ad-* + *jungere* to join] **1** : something joined or added to another thing but not essentially a part of it **2** : a word or word group that qualifies or completes the meaning of another word or other words and is not itself one of the principal structural elements in its sentence **3** : a person associated with or assisting another — **ad·junc·tive** \ə-'jəŋ(k)-tiv\ *adj*

²**adjunct** *adj* **1** : added or joined as an accompanying object or circumstance **2** : attached in a subordinate or temporary capacity to a staff — **ad·junct·ly** \'aj-ˌəŋ(k)t-lē\ *adv*

ad·jure \ə-'ju̇(ə)r\ *vt* [L *adjurare*, fr. *ad-* + *jurare* to swear] **1** : to charge or command solemnly under or as if under oath or penalty of a curse **2** : to entreat earnestly : CHARGE — **ad·ju·ra·tion** \ˌaj-ə-'rā-shən\ *n* — **ad·jur·a·to·ry** \ə-'ju̇r-ə-ˌtōr-ē, -ˌtór-\ *adj*

ad·just \ə-'jəst\ *vb* [F *ajuster*, fr. *a-* + *juste* exact, just] **1** : to bring to a more satisfactory state: **a** : SETTLE, RESOLVE ⟨*adjust* conflicts⟩ **b** : RECTIFY ⟨*adjust* the error⟩ **2** : to move the parts of an instrument or a piece of machinery until they fit together in the best working order : REGULATE ⟨*adjust* a watch⟩ ⟨*adjust* the brakes on an automobile⟩ **3** : to determine the amount of an insurance claim **4** : to adapt or accommodate oneself to external conditions **syn** see ADAPT — **ad·just·a·ble** \-'jəs-tə-bəl\ *adj* — **ad·just·er** *also* **ad·jus·tor** \-'jəs-tər\ *n*

ad·just·ment \ə-'jəs(t)-mənt\ *n* **1** : the act or process of adjusting **2** : a settlement of a claim or debt **3** : the state of being adjusted **4** : a means of adjusting one part (as in a machine) to another ⟨an *adjustment* for focusing a microscope⟩ **5** : a correction or modification to reflect actual conditions — **ad·just·ment·al** \ˌə-ˌjəs(t)-'ment-ᵊl\ *adj*

ad·ju·tan·cy \'aj-ət-ən-sē\ *n* : the office or rank of an adjutant

ad·ju·tant \'aj-ət-ənt\ *n* [L *adjutare* to aid] **1** : a staff officer (as in the army) assisting the commanding officer and responsible esp. for correspondence **2** : one who helps : ASSISTANT

adjutant bird *n* : any of several large upright tropical storks having the head and neck bare

adjutant general *n, pl* **adjutants general** : the chief administrative officer of an army or of one of its major units (as a division or corps)

ad·ju·vant \'aj-ə-vənt\ *n* : something that enhances the effectiveness of medical treatment

ad lib \(')ad-'lib\ *adv* [NL *ad libitum*] : without restraint or limit

¹**ad-lib** \(')ad-'lib\ *adj* : spoken, composed, or performed without preparation

²**ad-lib** *vb* **ad-libbed; ad-lib·bing 1** : to deliver spontaneously **2** : to improvise lines or a speech

ad li·bi·tum \(')ad-'lib-ət-əm\ *adv* [NL]

adjutant
bird

: freely in accordance with one's wishes — used as a direction in music

ad·man \'ad-,man\ *n* : one who writes, solicits, or places advertisements

ad·min·is·ter \əd-'min-ə-stər\ *vb* **ad·min·is·tered; ad·min·is·ter·ing** \-st(ə-)riŋ\ **1 a** : to superintend the execution, use, or conduct of ⟨*administer* an examination⟩ **b** : to manage or direct the affairs of ⟨*administer* a government⟩ **c** : SETTLE 7a ⟨*administer* an estate⟩ **2 a** : to mete out : DISPENSE ⟨*administer* justice⟩ **b** : to give ritually **c** : to give remedially **3** : to furnish a benefit : MINISTER — **ad·min·is·tra·ble** \-strə-bəl\ *adj* — **ad·min·is·trant** \-strənt\ *n*

ad·min·is·tra·tion \əd-,min-ə-'strā-shən, (,)ad-\ *n* **1** : the act or process of administering **2** : performance of executive duties : MANAGEMENT **3** : the execution of public affairs as distinguished from policy making **4 a** : a body of persons who administer **b** *cap* : a group constituting the political executive in a presidential government **c** : a governmental agency or board **5** : the term of office of an administrative officer or body

ad·min·is·tra·tive \əd-'min-ə-,strāt-iv\ *adj* : of or relating to administration ⟨an *administrative* position⟩

administrative county *n* : a British local administrative unit that may or may not be identical with an older geographical county

ad·min·is·tra·tor \əd-'min-ə-,strāt-ər\ *n* **1** : one that administers; *esp* : a person legally vested with the right of administration of an estate **2** : a priest appointed to administer temporarily a diocese or parish — **ad·min·is·tra·trix** \əd-,min-ə-'strā-triks\ *n*

ad·mi·ra·ble \'ad-mə-rə-bəl, -mrə-bəl\ *adj* : deserving to be admired : EXCELLENT — **ad·mi·ra·ble·ness** *n* — **ad·mi·ra·bly** \-blē\ *adv*

ad·mi·ral \'ad-mə-rəl, -mrəl\ *n* [MF *amiral* & ML *admirallus*, fr. Ar *amīr-al-bahr* commander of the sea] **1 a** : a naval officer of flag rank **b** : a commissioned officer in the navy ranking above a vice admiral and below a fleet admiral **2** : any of several brightly colored butterflies

admiral of the fleet : the highest ranking officer of the British navy

ad·mi·ral·ty \'ad-mə-rəl-tē, -mrəl-\ *adj* : of, relating to, or having jurisdiction over maritime affairs ⟨*admiralty* court⟩ ⟨*admiralty* law⟩

Admiralty *n* : the body of officials having jurisdiction over the British navy

ad·mi·ra·tion \,ad-mə-'rā-shən\ *n* **1** : an object of admiring esteem **2** : delighted or astonished approval

ad·mire \əd-'mī(ə)r\ *vt* [L *admirari*, fr. *ad-* + *mirari* to wonder] **1** *archaic* : to marvel at **2** : to regard with admiration ⟨*admired* his courage⟩ **3** : to esteem highly syn see REGARD — **ad·mir·er** \-'mīr-ər\ *n*

ad·mis·si·ble \əd-'mis-ə-bəl\ *adj* : that can be or is worthy to be admitted or allowed : ALLOWABLE ⟨*admissible* evidence⟩ — **ad·mis·si·bil·i·ty** \-,mis-ə-'bil-ət-ē\ *n* — **ad·mis·si·bly** \-'mis-ə-blē\ *adv*

ad·mis·sion \əd-'mish-ən\ *n* **1** : the act of admitting **2** : the right or permission to enter ⟨standards of *admission* to a school⟩ **3** : the price of entrance to a place **4** : a granting of something that has not been fully proved ⟨an *admission* of guilt⟩ syn see ADMITTANCE — **ad·mis·sive** \-'mis-iv\ *adj*

ad·mit \əd-'mit\ *vb* **ad·mit·ted; ad·mit·ting** [L *admiss-*, *admittere* to allow entry, permit, fr. *ad-* + *mittere* to send, let go] **1** : to allow scope for : PERMIT **2** : to allow entry : let in ⟨*admit* a state to the Union⟩ **3** : to confess to : make acknowledgment ⟨*admit* guilt⟩ syn see ACKNOWLEDGE — **ad·mit·ted·ly** \-'mit-əd-lē\ *adv*

ad·mit·tance \əd-'mit-ⁿ(t)s\ *n* : permission to enter a place : ENTRANCE
syn ADMITTANCE, ADMISSION mean permitted entrance. ADMITTANCE applies usu. to mere physical entrance into a building or locality; ADMISSION implies formal acceptance that carries with it rights, privileges, or membership

ad·mix \ad-'miks\ *vt* [back-formation fr. obs. *admixt*, mingled with, fr. L *admixtus*] : MINGLE, MIX ⟨*admix* soil and gravel⟩

ad·mix·ture \ad-'miks-chər\ *n* **1 a** : the act or process of mixing ⟨made by *admixture* of chemicals⟩ **b** : the fact of being mixed **2** : something formed by mixing : MIXTURE **3** : something added to another thing in mixing

ad·mon·ish \ad-'män-ish\ *vt* [MF *admonester*, fr. L *ad-* + *monēre* to warn, remind] **1 a** : to indicate duties or obligations to **b** : to reprove gently but seriously : warn of a fault **2** : to give friendly earnest advice or encouragement to — **ad·mon·ish·er** *n* — **ad·mon·ish·ing·ly** \-'män-i-shiŋ-lē\ *adv* — **ad·mon·ish·ment** \-'män-ish-mənt\ *n*

ad·mo·ni·tion \,ad-mə-'nish-ən\ *n* [L *admonit-*, *admonēre* to suggest, admonish, fr. *ad-* + *monēre* to warn, remind] **1** : gentle or friendly reproof **2** : counsel or warning against fault or oversight

ad·mon·i·to·ry \ad-'män-ə-,tōr-ē, -,tȯr-\ *adj* : expressing admonition : WARNING

ad·nate \'ad-,nāt\ *adj* [L *adgnat-*, *adgnasci* to grow on, fr. *ad-* + *gnasci* to be born] : grown to in a usu. unlike part esp. along a margin ⟨an *adnate* antler⟩ — **ad·na·tion** \ad-'nā-shən\ *n*

ad nau·se·am \ad-'nȯ-zē-əm\ *adv* [L] : to a sickening degree

ado \ə-'dü\ *n* : FUSS, TROUBLE ⟨much *ado* about nothing⟩

ado·be \ə-'dō-bē\ *n* [Sp, fr. Ar *aṭ-ṭub* the brick] **1** : a brick made of clayey mud dried in the sun **2** : a building made of adobe bricks

ad·o·les·cence \,ad-ⁿl-'es-ⁿn(t)s\ *n* : the state or process of growing up; *also* : the period of life from puberty to maturity

¹ad·o·les·cent \-ⁿnt\ *n* [L *adolescent-*, *adolescens*, fr. prp. of *adolescere* to grow up] : one that is in the state of adolescence : a person not fully mature

²adolescent *adj* : of, relating to, or being in adolescence — **ad·o·les·cent·ly** *adv*

Adon·is \ə-'dän-əs, -'dō-nəs\ *n* : a beautiful youth loved by Aphrodite

adopt \ə-'däpt\ *vt* [L *adoptare*, fr. *ad-* + *optare* to choose] **1** : to take by choice into a relationship; *esp* : to take (a child of other parents) voluntarily and usu. by formal legal act as one's own child **2** : to take up and practice as one's own **3** : to accept formally and put into effect ⟨the assembly *adopted* a constitution⟩ **4** : to choose (a textbook) for required study in a course — **adopt·a·bil·i·ty** \ə-,däp-tə-'bil-ət-ē\ *n* — **adopt·a·ble** \ə-'däp-tə-bəl\ *adj* — **adopt·er** *n*

adop·tion \ə-'däp-shən\ *n* : the act of adopting : the state of being adopted ⟨a son by *adoption*⟩ ⟨*adoption* of a resolution⟩

adop·tive \ə-'däp-tiv\ *adj* : made or acquired by adoption ⟨*adoptive* father⟩ — **adop·tive·ly** *adv*

ador·a·ble \ə-'dȯr-ə-bəl, -'dȯr-\ *adj* **1** : deserving to be adored **2** : CHARMING, LOVELY ⟨an *adorable* child⟩ — **ador·a·bil·i·ty** \ə-,dȯr-ə-'bil-ət-ē, -,dȯr-\ *n* — **ador·a·ble·ness** *n* — **ador·a·bly** \ə-'dȯr-ə-blē, -'dȯr-\ *adv*

ad·o·ra·tion \,ad-ə-'rā-shən\ *n* : the act of adoring : the state of being adored

adore \ə-'dō(ə)r, -'dȯ(ə)r\ *vt* [L *adorare*, fr *ad-* + *orare* to speak, pray] **1** : WORSHIP **2** : to be extremely fond of — **ador·er** *n*

adorn \ə-'dȯrn\ *vt* [L *adornare*, fr. *ad-* + *ornare* to furnish, ornament] : to decorate with ornaments : BEAUTIFY
syn DECORATE, EMBELLISH: ADORN implies enhancing appearance by adding something beautiful in itself ⟨*adorned* with jewels⟩ DECORATE suggests relieving plainness or monotony by adding color or design ⟨*decorate* a lampshade with painted scenes⟩ EMBELLISH often stresses the adding of superfluous ornament ⟨*embellish* a page with floral borders⟩

adorn·ment \-mənt\ *n* **1** : the action of adorning : the state of being adorned **2** : something that adorns

ad rem \ad-'rem\ *adv* [L] : to the point : RELEVANTLY

¹adre·nal \ə-'drēn-ⁿl\ *adj* [L *ad* to, at, near + *renes* kidneys] **1** : adjacent to the kidneys **2** : of, relating to, or derived from adrenal glands or secretion

²adrenal *n* : ADRENAL GLAND

adrenal gland *n* : either of a pair of complex endocrine organs occurring one near each kidney and consisting of a mesodermal cortex that produces steroid hormones and an ectodermal medulla that produces adrenaline

Adren·a·lin \ə-'dren-ⁿl-ən\ *trademark* — used for a preparation of adrenaline

adren·a·line \-ⁿl-ən\ *n* : a hormone of the adrenal gland acting esp. on smooth muscle, causing narrowing of blood vessels, and raising blood pressure

---

j joke; ŋ sing; ō flow; ȯ flaw; ȯi coin; th thin; th̲ this; ü loot;   u̇ foot; y yet; yü few; yu̇ furious; zh vision

ad·ren·er·gic \ad-rə-'nər-jik\ *adj* : liberating or activated by adrenaline or a substance like adrenaline ⟨an *adrenergic* nerve⟩

adre·nin \ə-'drēn-ən, -'dren-\ *n* : ADRENALINE

adre·no·cor·ti·cal \ə-,drē-nō-'kort-i-kəl\ *adj* : of, relating to, or derived from the cortex of the adrenal glands

adre·no·cor·ti·co·trop·ic hormone \ə-,drē-nō-,kort-i-kō-,träp-ik-\ *n* : a protein hormone of the anterior lobe of the pituitary gland that stimulates the cortex of the adrenal gland — abbr. *ACTH*

adrift \ə-'drift\ *adv (or adj)* **1** : without motive power, anchor, or mooring ⟨a damaged ship *adrift* in the storm⟩ **2** : without guidance or purpose

adroit \ə-'droit\ *adj* [F, fr. *à droit* on the right] **1** : dexterous in the use of the hands **2** : showing shrewdness, craft, or resourcefulness in coping with difficulty or danger **syn** see DEXTEROUS — **adroit·ly** *adv* — **adroit·ness** *n*

ad·sorb \ad-'sorb, -'zorb\ *vt* [*ad-* + *-sorb* (as in *absorb*)] : to take up and hold by adsorption — **ad·sorb·ent** \-'sor-bənt, -'zor-\ *adj or n*

ad·sorp·tion \-'sorp-shən, -'zorp-\ *n* : the adhesion in an extremely thin layer of molecules (as of gases, solutes, or liquids) to the surfaces of solid bodies or liquids with which they are in contact — compare ABSORPTION — **ad·sorp·tive** \-'sorp-tiv, -'zorp-\ *adj*

ad·u·late \'aj-ə-,lāt\ *vt* [L *adulari* to flatter] : to flatter or admire excessively or slavishly — **ad·u·la·tion** \,aj-ə-'lā-shən\ *n* — **ad·u·la·tor** \'aj-ə-,lāt-ər\ *n* — **ad·u·la·to·ry** \'aj-ə-lə-,tōr-ē, -,tor-\ *adj*

¹adult \ə-'dəlt, 'ad-,əlt\ *adj* [L *adultus*, fr. pp. of *adolescere* to grow up] **1** : fully developed and mature : GROWN-UP **2** : of, relating to, or characteristic of adults — **adult·hood** \ə-'dəlt-,hud\ *n* — **adult·ness** \ə-'dəlt-nəs, 'ad-,əlt-\ *n*

²adult *n* **1** : a fully grown person, animal, or plant **2** : a person having attained legal majority

adul·ter·ant \ə-'dəl-tə-rənt\ *n* : something used to adulterate another thing

adul·ter·ate \ə-'dəl-tə-,rāt\ *vt* [L *adulterare*, fr. *ad-* + *alter* other] : to make impure or weaker by adding a foreign or inferior substance; *esp* : to prepare for sale by using in whole or in part a substance that reduces quality or strength — **adul·ter·a·tion** \ə-,dəl-tə-'rā-shən\ *n* — **adul·ter·a·tor** \ə-'dəl-tə-,rāt-ər\ *n*

adul·tery \ə-'dəl-t(ə-)rē\ *n, pl* **-ter·ies** : voluntary sexual intercourse between a married person and someone other than his or her spouse — **adul·ter·er** \-tər-ər\ *n* — **adul·ter·ess** \-t(ə-)rəs\ *n* — **adul·ter·ous** \-t(ə-)rəs\ *adj* — **adul·ter·ous·ly** *adv*

ad·um·brate \ad-əm-,brāt\ *vt* [L *ad-* + *umbra* shadow] **1** : to foreshadow vaguely : INTIMATE **2** : to suggest or disclose partially **3** : SHADE, OBSCURE — **ad·um·bra·tion** \,ad-(,)əm-'brā-shən\ *n* — **ad·um·bra·tive** \ə-'dəm-brət-iv\ *adj* — **ad·um·bra·tive·ly** *adv*

ad va·lo·rem \,ad-və-'lōr-əm, -'lor-\ *adj* [NL, according to value] : based on a percentage of the monetary value of the goods imported ⟨an *ad valorem* tariff⟩

¹ad·vance \əd-'van(t)s\ *vb* [OF *avancier*, fr. L *abante* before, fr. *ab* from + *ante* before] **1** : to move forward ⟨*advance* a few yards⟩ **2** : to further the progress of ⟨sacrifices that *advance* the cause of freedom⟩ **3** : to raise to a higher rank or position : PROMOTE ⟨was *advanced* from clerk to assistant manager⟩ **4** : to supply or furnish in expectation of repayment ⟨*advanced* him a loan⟩ **5** : to bring forward : PROPOSE ⟨*advance* a new plan⟩ **6** : to raise or rise in rate or price : INCREASE ⟨gasoline *advanced* another two cents⟩ — **ad·vanc·er** *n*

syn ADVANCE, PROCEED, PROGRESS mean to move forward in space or time or toward an objective. ADVANCE may imply no more than this; PROCEED implies movement from one point to another and often suggests continuing or renewing a movement already begun; PROGRESS implies advance of a definite character such as through a process, cycle, or evolution

²advance *n* **1** : a forward movement **2** : progress in development : IMPROVEMENT **3** : a rise in price, value, or amount **4** : a first step or approach made : OFFER **5 a** : a provision of something (as money or goods) before a return is received ⟨asked for an *advance* on his salary⟩ **b** : the money or goods supplied — **in advance** : BEFORE, BEFOREHAND ⟨knew of the change two weeks *in advance*⟩ — **in advance of** : ahead of

³advance *adj* **1** : made, sent, or furnished ahead of time ⟨an *advance* payment⟩ **2** : going or situated before

ad·vanced \əd-'van(t)st\ *adj* **1** : far on in time or course ⟨an *advanced* case of tuberculosis⟩ **2 a** : being beyond the elementary or introductory ⟨*advanced* mathematics⟩ **b** : being beyond others in progress or development ⟨an *advanced* civilization⟩

ad·vance·ment \əd-'van(t)s-mənt\ *n* **1** : the action of advancing : the state of being advanced: **a** : promotion or elevation to a higher rank or position **b** : progression to a higher stage of development **2** : money or property given in advance

ad·van·tage \əd-'vant-ij\ *n* [MF *avantage*, fr. *avant* before, fr. L *abante*] **1** : superiority of position or condition **2** : BENEFIT, GAIN; *esp* : benefit resulting from some course of action **3** : the 1st point won in tennis after deuce — **to advantage** : so as to produce a favorable impression or effect

ad·van·ta·geous \,ad-vən-'tā-jəs, -,van-\ *adj* : giving an advantage : HELPFUL, FAVORABLE **syn** see BENEFICIAL — **ad·van·ta·geous·ly** *adv* — **ad·van·ta·geous·ness** *n*

Ad·vent \'ad-,vent\ *n* [ML *adventus*, fr. L, arrival, fr. *advent-*, *advenire* to arrive, happen, fr. *ad-* + *venire* to come] **1** : a penitential season beginning four Sundays before Christmas **2** : the coming of Christ at the incarnation or as judge on the last day **3** *not cap* : COMING, ARRIVAL ⟨*advent* of spring⟩

Ad·vent·ist \-,vent-əst\ *n* **1** : one who believes Christ's second coming near at hand **2** : SEVENTH-DAY ADVENTIST — **Ad·vent·ism** \-,vent-,iz-əm\ *n* — **Adventist** *adj*

ad·ven·ti·tia \,ad-vən-'tish-(ē-)ə\ *n* : an external chiefly connective-tissue covering of an organ (as a blood vessel) — **ad·ven·ti·tial** \-'tish-əl\ *adj*

ad·ven·ti·tious \,ad-vən-'tish-əs\ *adj* [L *adventicius* coming from outside, fr. *advent-*, *advenire* to arrive] **1** : added externally and not becoming an essential part : ACCIDENTAL **2** : appearing out of the usual or normal place ⟨*adventitious* buds⟩ — **ad·ven·ti·tious·ly** *adv* — **ad·ven·ti·tious·ness** *n*

Advent Sunday *n* : the first Sunday in Advent

¹ad·ven·ture \əd-'ven-chər\ *n* [OF *aventure*, fr. L *advent-*, *advenire* to arrive, happen, fr. *ad-* + *venire* to come] **1 a** : an undertaking involving unknown dangers and risks **b** : the encountering of risks **2** : an unusual experience

²adventure *vb* **-ven·tured; -ven·tur·ing** \-'vench-(ə-)riŋ\ **1** : RISK, VENTURE ⟨*adventure* their capital in foreign trade⟩ **2** : to proceed despite danger or risk

ad·ven·tur·er \-'ven-chər-ər\ *n* **1** : one that adventures: as **a** : SOLDIER OF FORTUNE **b** : one that engages in risky commercial enterprises for profit **2** : one that seeks position or wealth by sharp practice and dubious methods

ad·ven·ture·some \-'ven-chər-səm\ *adj* : inclined to take risks : DARING

ad·ven·tur·ess \-'vench-(ə-)rəs\ *n* : a female adventurer

ad·ven·tur·ous \əd-'vench-ə-)rəs\ *adj* **1** : ready to seek adventure or to cope with the new and unknown **2** : characterized by unknown dangers and risks — **ad·ven·tur·ous·ly** *adv* — **ad·ven·tur·ous·ness** *n*

syn VENTURESOME, DARING: ADVENTUROUS stresses a willingness to try the unknown regardless of possible or probable danger; VENTURESOME may stress the tendency to take chances; DARING heightens the implication of fearlessness in accepting risks that could be avoided

ad·verb \'ad-,vərb\ *n* [L *adverbium*, fr. *ad-* + *verbum* word, verb] : a word used to modify a verb, an adjective, another adverb, a preposition, a phrase, a clause, or a sentence and often used to show degree, manner, place, or time — **adverb** *adj*

ad·ver·bi·al \ad-'vər-bē-əl\ *adj* : of, relating to, or having the function of an adverb ⟨*adverbial* phrase⟩ — **ad·ver·bi·al·ly** \-bē-ə-lē\ *adv*

ad·ver·sary \'ad-və(r)-,ser-ē\ *n, pl* **-sar·ies** : one that contends with, opposes, or resists **syn** see OPPONENT

ad·ver·sa·tive \əd-'vər-sət-iv\ *adj* : expressing opposition or adverse circumstance ⟨the *adversative* conjunction *but*⟩ — **ad·ver·sa·tive·ly** *adv*

ad·verse \ad-'vərs, 'ad-,vərs\ *adj* [L *adversus* facing, opposite, adverse, fr. pp. of *advertere* to turn toward, fr. *ad-* + *vertere* to turn] **1** : acting in a contrary direction ⟨*adverse* winds⟩ **2** : actively opposed : ANTAGONISTIC ⟨a mind *adverse* to compromise⟩ **3** : having a harmful or hindering effect **:** UNFAVORABLE ⟨*adverse* circumstances⟩ — **ad·verse·ly** *adv* — **ad·verse·ness** *n*

ad·ver·si·ty \ad-'vər-sət-ē\ *n, pl* **-ties :** a condition or experience of serious or continued misfortune esp. following good fortune

ad·vert \ad-'vərt\ *vb* **:** to direct attention (as in speaking or writing) **:** REFER ⟨*advert* to a remark made by a previous speaker⟩

ad·ver·tise \'ad-vər-,tīz\ *vb* [MF *advertiss-, avertir* to inform, fr. L *advertere* to turn toward] **1 :** to announce publicly esp. by a printed notice or a broadcast ⟨*advertise* a sale⟩ **2 :** to call public attention to esp. by emphasizing desirable qualities so as to arouse a desire to buy or patronize ⟨*advertise* a breakfast food⟩ **3 :** to issue or sponsor advertising ⟨*advertise* for a lost dog⟩ — **ad·ver·tis·er** *n*

ad·ver·tise·ment \,ad-vər-'tīz-mənt, əd-'vərt-əz-\ *n* **1 :** the act or process of advertising **2 :** a public notice; *esp* **:** one published or broadcast

ad·ver·tis·ing \'ad-vər-,tī-ziŋ\ *n* **1 :** the action of calling something to the attention of the public esp. by paid announcements **2 :** ADVERTISEMENTS **3 :** the business of preparing advertisements for publication or broadcast

ad·vice \əd-'vīs\ *n* [OF *avis* opinion] **1 :** recommendation regarding a decision or course of conduct **:** COUNSEL **2 :** information or notice given **:** INTELLIGENCE — usu. used in pl.

syn COUNSEL: ADVICE implies real or pretended special knowledge on the part of the one advising; COUNSEL stresses the fruit of wisdom or deliberation and may suggest a weighty occasion or imply authority or personal concern on the part of the one counseling

ad·vis·a·ble \əd-'vī-zə-bəl\ *adj* **:** reasonable or proper under the circumstances **:** WISE, PRUDENT ⟨it is not *advisable* to swim just after a meal⟩ **syn** see EXPEDIENT — **ad·vis·a·bil·i·ty** \əd-,vī-zə-'bil-ət-ē\ *n* — **ad·vis·a·bly** \əd-'vī-zə-blē\ *adv*

ad·vise \əd-'vīz\ *vb* **1 a :** to give advice to **:** COUNSEL **b :** RECOMMEND **2 :** to give information or notice to **:** INFORM **3 :** to take counsel **:** CONSULT — **ad·vis·er** or **ad·vi·sor** \-'vī-zər\ *n*

ad·vised \-'vīzd\ *adj* **:** thought out **:** CONSIDERED ⟨well *advised* conduct⟩ — **ad·vis·ed·ly** \-'vī-zəd-lē\ *adv*

ad·vise·ment \əd-'vīz-mənt\ *n* **:** careful consideration ⟨take a matter under *advisement*⟩

ad·vi·so·ry \əd-'vīz-(ə-)rē\ *adj* **1 :** having the power or right to advise ⟨an *advisory* committee⟩ **2 :** giving or containing advice ⟨an *advisory* opinion⟩

ad·vo·ca·cy \'ad-və-kə-sē\ *n* **:** the act of advocating **:** public support ⟨*advocacy* of a proposal⟩

¹ad·vo·cate \'ad-və-kət, -,kāt\ *n* [L *advocatus*, fr. pp. of *advocare* to summon, fr. *ad-* + *vocare* to call] **1 :** one that pleads the cause of another esp. before a judicial tribunal **2 :** one that argues for, recommends, or supports a cause or policy

²ad·vo·cate \-,kāt\ *vt* **:** to speak in favor of **:** support or recommend openly ⟨*advocate* a new plan⟩

adz *or* **adze** \'adz\ *n* [OE *adesa*] **:** a cutting tool that has a thin arched blade set at right angles to the handle and is used for shaping wood

ae \'ā\ *adj, chiefly Scot* **:** ONE

ae·cio·spore \'ē-sē-ə-,spō(ə)r, -,spò(ə)r\ *n* **:** a spore formed in an aecium

ae·ci·um \'ē-s(h)ē-əm\ *n, pl* **-cia** \-s(h)ē-ə\ **:** a fruiting body of a rust fungus in which the first binucleate spores are formed — **ae·cial** \'ē-sh(ē-)əl, 'ē-sē-əl\ *adj*

aë·des \ā-'ēd-ēz\ *n, pl* **aëdes** [Gk *aēdēs* unpleasant, fr. *a-* ²*a-* + *ēdos* pleasure] **:** any of a genus of mosquitoes including carriers of disease (as yellow fever)

ae·dile \'ē-,dīl\ *n* [L *aedilis*, fr. *aedes* temple] **:** an official in ancient Rome in charge of public works and games, police, and the grain supply

Ae·ge·an \i-'jē-ən\ *adj* **:** of or relating to a chiefly Bronze Age civilization of the Aegean islands and adjacent areas (3000–1100 B.C.) — **Aegean** *n*

ae·gis \'ē-jəs\ *n* [Gk *aigis* shield of goatskin] **1 :** a

shield or breastplate emblematic of majesty associated chiefly with Zeus and Athena **2 :** PROTECTION, DEFENSE **3 :** PATRONAGE, SPONSORSHIP

-ae·mia — see -EMIA

Ae·ne·as \i-'nē-əs\ *n* **:** a defender of Troy and hero of Vergil's *Aeneid*

ae·o·li·an \ē-'ō-lē-ən\ *var of* EOLIAN

Aeolian \ē-'ō-lē-ən\ *n* **:** one of a group of ancient Greeks colonizing Lesbos and the adjacent coast of Asia Minor

aeolian harp *n* **:** a box-shaped musical instrument having stretched strings usu. tuned in unison on which the wind produces varying harmonics over the same fundamental tone

Ae·o·lus \'ē-ə-ləs\ *n* **:** the god of the winds in classical mythology

ae·on \'ē-ən, 'ē-,än\ *n* [Gk *aiōn*] **:** an immeasurably or indefinitely long period of time **:** AGE

aer- *or* **aero-** *comb form* [Gk *aēr*] **1 a :** air **:** atmosphere ⟨*aerate*⟩ ⟨*aerobiology*⟩ **b :** aerial and ⟨*aeromarine*⟩ **2 :** gas ⟨*aerosol*⟩ **3 :** aviation ⟨*aerodrome*⟩

aer·ate \'a(ə)r-,āt, 'e(ə)r-\ *vt* **1 :** to supply (blood) with oxygen by respiration **2 :** to supply or impregnate with air **3 :** to combine or charge with gas — **aer·a·tion** \,a(ə)r-'ā-shən, ,e(ə)r-\ *n* — **aer·a·tor** \'a(ə)r-,āt-ər, 'e(ə)r-\ *n*

¹ae·ri·al \'ar-ē-əl, 'er-; ā-'ir-ē-əl\ *adj* **1 a :** of, relating to, or occurring in the air or atmosphere **b :** living or growing in the air rather than on the ground or in water **c :** operating or operated overhead on elevated cables or rails **2 a :** lacking substance **:** THIN **b :** IMAGINARY, ETHEREAL **3 a :** of or relating to aircraft **b :** designed for use in, taken from, or operating from or against aircraft — **ae·ri·al·ly** \-ē-ə-lē\ *adv*

²aer·i·al \'ar-ē-əl, 'er-\ *n* **1 :** ANTENNA 2 **2 :** FORWARD PASS

ae·ri·al·ist \'ar-ē-ə-ləst, 'er-, ā-'ir-\ *n* **:** a performer of feats above the ground esp. on a flying trapeze

aerial root *n* **:** a root (as for clinging to a wall) that does not enter the soil and usu. arises adventitiously

ae·rie \'a(ə)r-ē, 'e(ə)r-, 'i(ə)r-\ *n* [ML *aerea*, fr. OF *aire*, fr. L *area* area, barnyard] **1 :** the nest of a bird on a cliff or a mountaintop **2 :** a dwelling on a height

aero \'a(ə)r-ō, 'e(ə)r-\ *adj* **1 :** of or relating to aircraft **2 :** designed for aerial use

aer·o·bat·ics \,a-(ə)-'bat-iks, ,er-\ *n sing or pl* [*aer-* + *-batics* (as in *acrobatics*)] **:** performance of stunts in an airplane or glider

aer·o·bic \,a-(ə-)'rō-bik, ,e-\ *adj* **1 :** living or active only in the presence of oxygen **2 :** of, relating to, or caused by aerobic organisms — **aer·o·bi·cal·ly** \,a-(ə-)'rō-bi-k(ə-)lē, ,e-\ *adv*

aer·o·drome \'ar-ə-,drōm, 'er-\ *n, Brit* **:** AIRFIELD, AIRPORT

aer·o·dy·nam·ics \,ar-ō-dī-'nam-iks, ,er-\ *n* **:** a science that deals with the motion of gaseous fluids (as air) and with the forces acting on bodies that move through such fluids or bodies past which such fluids flow — **aer·o·dy·nam·ic** \-ik\ *adj* — **aer·o·dy·nam·i·cal·ly** \-i-k(ə-)lē\ *adv*

aer·ol·o·gy \,a-(ə-)'räl-ə-jē, ,e-\ *n* **1 :** METEOROLOGY **2 :** a branch of meteorology that deals esp. with the air at some distance above the earth — **aer·o·log·i·cal** \,ar-ə-'läj-i-kəl, ,er-\ *adj* — **aer·ol·o·gist** \,a-(ə-)'räl-ə-jəst, ,e-\ *n*

aero·med·i·cine \,ar-ō-'med-ə-sən, ,er-\ *n* **:** a branch of medicine that deals with the diseases and disturbances arising from flying and the associated physiologic and psychologic problems — **aero·med·i·cal** \-'med-i-kəl\ *adj*

aer·o·naut \'ar-ə-,nòt, 'er-\ *n* [Gk *aēr* air + *nautēs* sailor] **:** one that operates or travels in an airship or balloon

aer·o·nau·tics \,ar-ə-'nòt-iks, ,er-\ *n* **:** a science dealing with the operation of aircraft or with aircraft design and manufacture — **aer·o·nau·tic** \-'nòt-ik\ *adj* — **aer·o·nau·ti·cal** \-'nòt-i-kəl\ *adj* — **aer·o·nau·ti·cal·ly** \-i-k(ə-)lē\ *adv*

aero·pause \'ar-ō-,pòz, 'er-\ *n* **:** the level above the earth's surface where the atmosphere becomes ineffective for human and aircraft functions

aero·plane \'ar-ə-,plān, 'er-\ *chiefly Brit var of* AIRPLANE

aero·sol \-,sòl, -,säl\ *n* [*aer-* + ³*sol*] **:** a suspension of fine solid or liquid particles (as of smoke, fog, or an insecticide) in gas

1 2 3

adzes: *1* carpenter's with flat head, *2* ship carpenter's with spur, *3* cooper's

---

j joke; **ŋ** sing; **ō** flow; **ò** flaw; **òi** coin; **th** thin; **th** this; **ü** loot; **ú** foot; **y** yet; **yü** few; **yù** furious; **zh** vision

aero·space \'ar-ō-,spās, 'er-\ *n* : the earth's atmosphere and the space beyond

aery \'a(ə)r-ē, 'e(ə)r-\ *adj* **aer·i·er; -est** : having an aerial quality : ETHEREAL

Aes·cu·la·pi·us \,es-kyə-'lā-pē-əs\ *n* : the Roman god of medicine

Ae·so·pi·an \ē-'sō-pē-ən\ *adj* : conveying an innocent meaning to an outsider but a concealed meaning to an informed member of a conspiracy or underground movement ⟨*Aesopian* language⟩

aes·thete \'es-,thēt\ *n* : one having or affecting sensitivity to the beautiful esp. in art

aes·thet·ic \es-'thet-ik\ *adj* [Gk aisthē-, aisthanesthai to perceive] **1** : having to do with beauty or with what is beautiful esp. as distinguished from what is useful ⟨an *aesthetic* interest in antique furniture⟩ **2** : appreciative of or responsive to what is beautiful ⟨an *aesthetic* person⟩ **syn** see ARTISTIC — **aes·thet·i·cal·ly** \-'thet-i-k(ə)-lē\ *adv*

aes·thet·i·cism \es-'thet-ə-,siz-əm\ *n* : devotion to or emphasis on beauty or the cultivation of the arts

aes·thet·ics \es-'thet-iks\ *n* **1** : a branch of philosophy that studies and explains the principles and forms of beauty esp. in art and literature **2** : description and explanation of artistic phenomena and aesthetic experience by means of other sciences (as psychology, sociology, ethnology, or history)

aes·ti·vate \'es-tə-,vāt\ *vi* [L aestivare to spend the summer, fr. *aestivus* of summer, fr. *aestas* summer] : to pass the summer in a state of torpor

aes·ti·va·tion \,es-tə-'vā-shən\ *n* **1** : the state of one that aestivates **2** : the disposition or method of arrangement of floral parts in a bud

ae·ther \'ē-thər\ *var of* ETHER

afar \ə-'fär\ *adv* : to or at a great distance

afeard *or* **afeared** \ə-'fi(ə)rd\ *adj, dial* : AFRAID

af·fa·ble \'af-ə-bəl\ *adj* [L affabilis, fr. *affari* to speak to, fr. *ad-* + *fari* to speak] **1** : being pleasant and at ease in talking to others **2** : characterized by ease and friendliness — **af·fa·bil·i·ty** \,af-ə-'bil-ət-ē\ *n* — **af·fa·bly** \'af-ə-blē\ *adv*

af·fair \ə-'fa(ə)r, -'fe(ə)r\ *n* [MF *affaire*, fr. *a faire* to do] **1 a** *pl* : commercial, professional, or public business ⟨government *affairs*⟩ **b** : MATTER, CONCERN ⟨not your *affair* at all⟩ **2 a** : EVENT, ACTIVITY ⟨attended a social *affair*⟩ **b** : PRODUCT, THING ⟨a flimsy *affair* of ropes bridging the river⟩ **3 a** *also* **af·faire** : a romantic or passionate attachment typically of limited duration **b** : a matter occasioning public anxiety, controversy, or scandal : CASE

¹af·fect \ə-'fekt, a-\ *vt* [L affectare to aim at, fr. *affect-, afficere* to act on, influence] **1** : to be given to : FANCY ⟨*affect* flashy clothes⟩ **2** : to make a display of liking or using : CULTIVATE ⟨*affect* a worldly manner⟩ **3** : to put on a pretense of : FEIGN ⟨*affect* indifference, though deeply hurt⟩

²affect *vt* [L affect-, afficere to act on, influence, fr. *ad-* + *facere* to do] **1** : to attack or act on as a disease does ⟨thought that night air *affected* the lungs⟩ **2** : to have an effect upon : INFLUENCE ⟨the coach's criticism *affected* the players strongly⟩

syn AFFECT, EFFECT are often confused because both verbs take the same word *effect* as the corresponding noun. AFFECT applies to the action of an agency in causing a change in or alteration of something ⟨moisture *affects* steel⟩ ⟨the climate *affected* his health⟩ EFFECT applies to the producing of a result by an intelligent agent ⟨asked how the prisoner *effected* his escape⟩ **syn** see in addition INFLUENCE

af·fec·ta·tion \,af-,ek-'tā-shən\ *n* **1** : an assuming or displaying of an attitude or kind of behavior not natural or not genuine **2** : unnatural speech or conduct

syn MANNERISM: AFFECTATION applies to a specific trick of speech or behavior that impresses others as being deliberately assumed and insincere; MANNERISM designates a peculiarity or eccentricity in behavior that is not deliberately assumed but results from unconscious, accidentally acquired habit

af·fect·ed *adj* : not natural or genuine ⟨an *affected* interest in music⟩ ⟨a man with *affected* manners⟩ — **af·fect·ed·ly** *adv* — **af·fect·ed·ness** *n*

af·fect·ing *adj* : arousing pity, sympathy, or sorrow ⟨an *affecting* story⟩ — **af·fect·ing·ly** \ə-'fek-tiŋ-lē, a-\ *adv*

¹af·fec·tion \ə-'fek-shən\ *n* **1** : a feeling of attachment : FONDNESS **2** : PROPENSITY, DISPOSITION

²af·fec·tion *n* : DISEASE, DISORDER ⟨an *affection* of the brain⟩

af·fec·tion·ate \ə-'fek-sh(ə)-nət\ *adj* : feeling or showing a great liking for a person or thing : TENDER — **af·fec·tion·ate·ly** *adv*

af·fer·ent \'af-ə-rənt, 'af-,er-ənt\ *adj* [L afferre to bring to, fr. *ad-* + *ferre* to carry] : bearing or conducting inward; *esp* : conveying impulses toward a nerve center — compare EFFERENT — **af·fer·ent·ly** *adv*

af·fi·ance \ə-'fī-ən(t)s\ *vt* : to solemnly promise (oneself or another) in marriage : BETROTH ⟨the *affianced* couple⟩

af·fi·da·vit \,af-ə-'dā-vət\ *n* [ML, he has made an oath, fr. *affidare* to give surety, fr. L *ad-* + *fides* faith] : a sworn written statement; *esp* : one made under oath before an authorized official

¹af·fil·i·ate \ə-'fil-ē-,āt\ *vb* [ML affiliare to adopt as a son, fr. L *ad-* + *filius* son] : to connect closely often as a member, branch, or associate ⟨*affiliated* himself with a political party⟩ ⟨a school *affiliated* with the university⟩ — **af·fil·i·a·tion** \ə-,fil-ē-'ā-shən\ *n*

²af·fil·i·ate \ə-'fil-ē-ət\ *n* : an affiliated person or organization

af·fin·i·ty \ə-'fin-ət-ē\ *n, pl* **-ties** [L affinis bordering on, related by marriage, fr. *ad-* + *finis* end, border] **1** : relationship by marriage **2 a** : RELATIONSHIP, KINSHIP **b** : ATTRACTION; *esp* : an attractive force between substances or particles that causes them to enter into and remain in chemical combination **3** : a relation between biological groups indicating community of origin

af·firm \ə-'fərm\ *vb* [L affirmare, fr. *ad-* + *firmus* firm] **1 a** : CONFIRM, RATIFY ⟨*affirm* a contract⟩ **b** : to state positively or with confidence : declare to be true **2** : to make a solemn and formal declaration or assertion in place of an oath **syn** see ASSERT — **af·fir·ma·tion** \,af-ər-'mā-shən\ *n*

¹af·firm·a·tive \ə-'fər-mət-iv\ *adj* **1** : asserting a predicate of a subject **2** : asserting that the fact is so **3** : POSITIVE ⟨*affirmative* approach⟩ **4** : favoring or supporting a proposition or motion — **af·firm·a·tive·ly** *adv*

²affirmative *n* **1** : an expression (as the word *yes*) of affirmation or assent **2** : an affirmative proposition **3** : the affirmative side in a debate or vote

¹af·fix \ə-'fiks\ *vt* **1** : to attach physically : FASTEN ⟨*affix* a stamp to a letter⟩ **2** : to add as an associated part (as to a document) ⟨*affixed* his signature⟩ — **af·fix·a·tion** \,af-,ik-'sā-shən\ *n*

²af·fix \'af-,iks\ *n* : one or more sounds or letters attached to the beginning or end of a word and serving to produce a derivative word or an inflectional form — **af·fix·al** \-,ik-səl\ *or* **af·fix·i·al** \a-'fik-sē-əl\ *adj*

af·fla·tus \ə-'flāt-əs\ *n* : a divine imparting of knowledge or power : INSPIRATION

af·flict \ə-'flikt\ *vt* [L afflict-, affligere to cast down, fr. *ad-* + *fligere* to strike] **1** : to distress severely so as to cause continued suffering **2** : TROUBLE, INJURE

syn TORMENT, TORTURE: AFFLICT is general and applies to the causing of pain, annoyance, or distress; TORMENT suggests persecution or the repeated inflicting of suffering or annoyance; TORTURE adds the implication of causing to writhe with unbearable pain

af·flic·tion \ə-'flik-shən\ *n* **1** : the state of being afflicted **2** : the cause of continued pain or distress

af·flic·tive \ə-'flik-tiv\ *adj* : causing affliction : DISTRESSING — **af·flic·tive·ly** *adv*

af·flu·ence \'af-,lü-ən(t)s\ *n* **1** : an abundant flow or supply **2** : abundance of wealth or property

¹af·flu·ent \-ənt\ *adj* [L affluere to flow to, fr. *ad-* + *fluere* to flow] **1 a** : flowing in abundance : COPIOUS **b** : having an abundance of material possessions : WEALTHY, RICH **2** : flowing toward — **af·flu·ent·ly** *adv*

²affluent *n* : a tributary stream

af·ford \ə-'fōrd, -'förd\ *vt* [ME aforthen, fr. OE geforthian to carry out, fr. *ge-*, prefix denoting completion + *forth* forth] **1** : to have resources enough to pay for ⟨unable to *afford* a new car⟩ **2** : to be able to do or to bear without serious harm ⟨no one can *afford* to waste his strength⟩ **3** : PROVIDE, FURNISH ⟨playing tennis *affords* healthful exercise⟩

af·fray \ə-'frā\ *n* [MF *effray*] : a noisy quarrel or fight : BRAWL

¹af·fright \ə-'frīt\ *vt* : FRIGHTEN, ALARM

²affright *n* : sudden and great fear : TERROR

¹af·front \ə-'frənt\ *vt* [MF *afronter* to shame, fr. *a* to + *front* forehead] **1** : to insult esp. to the face : OFFEND **2** : to face in defiance : CONFRONT **syn** see OFFEND

²affront *n* **1** : a deliberately offensive act or utterance **2** : an offense to one's self-respect : INSULT
syn INSULT, INDIGNITY: AFFRONT implies an open, deliberate act of disrespect; INSULT implies an attack intended to humiliate and degrade; INDIGNITY suggests an outrageous offense to one's personal dignity

Af·ghan \'af-gən, -,gan\ *n* **1** : a native or inhabitant of Afghanistan **2** : PASHTO **3** *not cap* : a blanket or shawl of colored wool knitted or crocheted in strips or squares — **Afghan** *adj*

Afghan hound *n* : a tall slim swift hunting dog native to the Near East with a coat of silky thick hair and a long silky topknot

afi·ci·o·na·do \ə-,fis-ē-ə-'näd-ō\ *n, pl* **-dos** [Sp] : DEVOTEE, FAN

afield \ə-'fēld\ *adv* **1** : to, in, or on the field **2** : away from home **3** : out of one's regular course : ASTRAY

afire \ə-'fī(ə)r\ *adj* : on fire : BURNING

aflame \ə-'flām\ *adj* : FLAMING, GLOWING

afloat \ə-'flōt\ *adv (or adj)* **1 a** : borne on or as if on the water **b** : at sea **2** : free of difficulties : SELF-SUFFICIENT **3 a** : circulating about : RUMORED **b** : ADRIFT **4** : flooded with or submerged under water : AWASH

aflut·ter \ə-'flət-ər\ *adj* **1** : FLUTTERING **2** : nervously excited

afoot \ə-'fut\ *adv (or adj)* **1** : on foot ⟨travels *afoot*⟩ **2 a** : on the move : ASTIR ⟨trouble *afoot*⟩ **b** : in progress ⟨projects *afoot*⟩

afore \ə-'fō(ə)r, -'fò(ə)r\ *adv or conj or prep, chiefly dial* : BEFORE

afore·men·tioned \-,men-chənd\ *adj* : mentioned previously

afore·said \-,sed\ *adj* : said or named previously

afore·thought \-,thòt\ *adj* : thought of, deliberated, or planned beforehand ⟨with malice *aforethought*⟩

a for·ti·o·ri \,ä-,fòrt-ē-'ōr-ē, -'òr-\ *adv* [NL, lit., from the stronger (argument)] : with greater reason or more convincing force — used in drawing a conclusion that is inferred to be even more certain than another

afoul \ə-'faùl\ *adj* : FOULED, TANGLED

afoul of *prep* **1** : in or into collision or entanglement with **2** : in or into conflict with

Afr- *or* **Afro-** *comb form* : African ⟨*Afr*american⟩: African and ⟨*Afro*-Asiatic⟩

afraid \ə-'frād, *South also* -'fre(ə)d\ *adj* [ME *affraied*, fr. pp. of *affraien* to frighten] **1** : filled with fear or apprehension ⟨*afraid* of snakes⟩ **2** : filled with concern or regret over an unwanted contingency ⟨*afraid* that he might be late⟩ **3** : DISINCLINED, RELUCTANT ⟨*afraid* of hard work⟩

afresh \ə-'fresh\ *adv* : from a new start : AGAIN

Af·ri·can \'af-ri-kən\ *n* **1** : a native or inhabitant of Africa **2** : a person of African descent; *esp* : NEGRO — **African** *adj*

African sleeping sickness *n* : SLEEPING SICKNESS 1

African violet *n* : a tropical African plant related to the gloxinias and widely grown as a house plant for its velvety fleshy leaves and showy purple, pink, or white flowers

Af·ri·kaans \,af-ri-'kän(t)s, -'känz\ *n* : a language developed from 17th century Dutch that is one of the official languages of the Republic of South Africa

Af·ri·ka·ner \-'kän-ər\ *n* : a native South African of European descent; *esp* : an Afrikaans-speaking descendant of the 17th century Dutch settlers

Af·ro \'af-(,)rō\ *adj* [prob. fr. *Afro-American*] : having the hair shaped into a round bushy mass — **Afro** *n*

Af·ro-Amer·i·can \,af-rō-ə-'mer-ə-kən\ *or* **Af·ra·mer·i·can** \,af-rə-'mer-ə-kən\ *adj* : of or relating to Americans of African and esp. of negroid descent — **Afro-American** *n*

Af·ro-Asi·at·ic languages \,af-rō-,ā-zhē-,at-ik-\ *n pl* : a family of languages widely distributed over southwestern Asia and northern Africa comprising the Semitic, Egyptian, Berber, Cushitic, and Chad subfamilies

aft \'aft\ *adv* [OE *æftan* from behind, behind] : near, toward, or in the stern of a ship or the tail of an aircraft

¹af·ter \'af-tər\ *adv* [OE *æfter*] : following in time or place : AFTERWARD, BEHIND

²after *prep* **1 a** : behind in place ⟨following *after* him⟩ **b** : later in time than ⟨*after* dinner⟩ **c** : following in rank or order ⟨the next highest mountain *after* Everest⟩ **d** (1) : later than and in consequence of ⟨*after* such an eloquent appeal he is sure to agree⟩ (2) : later than and in spite of ⟨*after* all our objections he went ahead with his original plan⟩ **2** — used as a function word to introduce an object or goal ⟨go *after* gold⟩ ⟨thirsting *after* fame⟩ **3 a** : in accordance with ⟨*after* an old custom⟩ **b** : with the name of or a name derived from that of ⟨named Pauline *after* her father Paul⟩ **c** : in imitation or resemblance of ⟨patterned *after* a Gothic cathedral⟩

³after *conj* : later than the time when

⁴after *adj* **1** : later in time : SUBSEQUENT **2** : located toward the stern of a ship or tail of an aircraft : HINDER

af·ter·birth \'af-tər-,bərth\ *n* : the placenta and fetal membranes that are expelled after delivery

af·ter·brain \-,brān\ *n* : the posterior subdivision of the hindbrain

af·ter·burn·er \-,bər-nər\ *n* : an auxiliary burner attached to the tail pipe of a turbojet engine for injecting fuel into the hot exhaust gases and burning it to provide extra thrust

af·ter·care \-,ke(ə)r, -,ka(ə)r\ *n* : the care, nursing, or treatment of a convalescent patient

af·ter·deck \-,dek\ *n* : the rear half of the deck of a ship

af·ter·ef·fect \-ə-,fekt\ *n* **1** : an effect that follows its cause after some time has passed **2** : a secondary effect coming on after the first or immediate effect has subsided ⟨a medicine with no noticeable *aftereffects*⟩

af·ter·glow \-,glō\ *n* **1** : a glow remaining (as in the sky after sunset) where a light has disappeared **2** : a reflection of past splendor, success, or emotion

af·ter·im·age \-,im-ij\ *n* : a usu. visual sensation continuing after the stimulus causing it has ended

af·ter·life \-,līf\ *n* **1** : an existence after death **2** : a later period in one's life

af·ter·math \'af-tər-,math\ *n* [OE *mæth* mowing, fr. *māwan* to mow] **1** : a second-growth crop esp. of hay **2** : CONSEQUENCE, RESULT

af·ter·most \-,mōst\ *adj* : nearest the stern of a ship

af·ter·noon \,af-tər-'nün\ *n* : the part of day between noon and sunset — **afternoon** *adj*

af·ter·noons \-'nünz\ *adv* : in the afternoon repeatedly

af·ter·taste \'af-tər-,tāst\ *n* : a sensation (as of flavor) continuing after the stimulus causing it has ended

af·ter·thought \-,thòt\ *n* : a later thought about something one has done or said

af·ter·ward \'af-tə(r)-wərd\ *or* **af·ter·wards** \-wərdz\ *adv* : at a later time

af·ter·world \'af-tər-,wərld\ *n* : a future world : a world after death

ag- — see AD-

again \ə-'gen\ *adv* [ME, opposite, again, fr. OE *ongēan* opposite, back, fr. *on* + *gēan* still, again] **1** : in return ⟨bring us word *again*⟩ **2** : another time : ANEW ⟨come see us *again*⟩ **3** : in addition ⟨half as much *again*⟩ **4** : on the other hand ⟨he may, and *again* he may not⟩ **5** : FURTHER, MOREOVER ⟨*again*, there is another matter to consider⟩

against \ə-'gen(t)st\ *prep* **1** : directly opposite : FACING ⟨over *against* the park⟩ **2 a** : in opposition or hostility to ⟨campaign *against* the enemy⟩ **b** : as a defense or protection from ⟨a shield *against* aggression⟩ **3** : in preparation or provision for ⟨storing food *against* the winter⟩ **4 a** : in the direction of and into contact with ⟨ran *against* a tree⟩ **b** : in contact with ⟨leaning *against* the wall⟩ **5** : in a direction opposite to the motion or course of ⟨*against* the wind⟩ **6** : before the background of ⟨green trees *against* the blue sky⟩ **7** : as a basis for disapproval of ⟨I have nothing *against* him⟩ **8** : in exchange for ⟨lend money *against* a promissory note⟩

Ag·a·mem·non \,ag-ə-'mem-,nän\ *n* : the leader of the Greeks in the Trojan War

agam·ic \(')ā-'gam-ik\ *adj* [Gk *a-* ²*a-* + *gamos* marriage] : ASEXUAL, PARTHENOGENETIC — **agam·i·cal·ly** \-'gam-i-k(ə-)lē\ *adv*

aga·mo·gen·e·sis \,ā-,gam-ə-'jen-ə-səs, ,ag-ə-mō-'jen-\ *n, pl* **-gen·e·ses** \-ə-,sēz\ [Gk *a-* ²*a-* + *gamos* marriage + L *genesis*] **1** : PARTHENOGENESIS **2** : asexual reproduction — **aga·mo·ge·net·ic** \-ə-'net-ik\ *adj* — **aga·mo·ge·net·i·cal·ly** \-'net-i-k(ə-)lē\ *adv*

---

j joke; ŋ sing; ō flow; ò flaw; òi coin; th thin; th this; ü loot; ù foot; y yet; yü few; yù furious; zh vision

¹**agape** \ə-'gāp, ə-'gap\ *adj* : having the mouth open in wonder or surprise : GAPING

²**aga·pe** \ä-'gäp-,ā, 'äg-ə-,pā\ *n* [Gk *agapē*] **1** : LOVE 3a **2** : LOVE FEAST

agar \'äg-,är\ *or* **agar-agar** \,äg-,är-'äg-,är\ *n* [Malay *agar-agar*] **1** : a gelatinous colloidal extractive of a red alga used esp. in culture media or as a stabilizing agent in foods **2** : a culture medium containing agar

ag·a·ric \'ag-ə-rik, ə-'gar-ik\ *n* [Gk *agarikon*, a fungus] **1** : any of several corky fungi used esp. in the preparation of punk **2** : any of a family of gill fungi including the common brown-spored edible meadow mushroom

ag·ate \'ag-ət\ *n* [MF, fr. L *achates*, fr. Gk *achatēs*] **1** : a fine-grained variegated quartz having its colors arranged in stripes, blended in clouds, or showing mosslike forms **2** : a child's playing marble of agate or of glass resembling it **3** : a size of type approximately 5½ point

ag·ate·ware \-,wa(ə)r, -,we(ə)r\ *n* **1** : pottery veined and mottled to resemble agate **2** : an enameled iron or steel ware for household utensils

aga·ve \ə-'gäv-ē\ *n* [Gk *Agauē*, a daughter of Cadmus] : any of a genus of plants of the amaryllis family having spiny-edged leaves and flowers in tall branched clusters and including some cultivated for fiber or for ornament

agave

¹**age** \'āj\ *n* [OF *aage*, fr. L *ætat-*, *ætas*] **1 a** : the time from birth to a specified date ⟨a boy six years of *age*⟩ **b** : the time of life when a person attains some right or capacity ⟨*age* of reason⟩; *esp* : MAJORITY **c** : normal lifetime **d** : the later part of life **2** : a period of time in history or in the development of man or in the history of the earth; *esp* : one characterized by some distinguishing feature ⟨machine *age*⟩ ⟨*Age* of Discovery⟩ ⟨*Age* of Reptiles⟩ **3** : a long period of time ⟨it happened *ages* ago⟩ **syn** see PERIOD

²**age** *vb* **aged; ag·ing** *or* **age·ing** **1** : to become old : show the effects or the characteristics of increasing age **2** : to become or cause to become mellow or mature : RIPEN **3** : to cause to seem or appear old esp. prematurely (as by strain or suffering)

-age \ij\ *n suffix* [OF, fr. L *-aticum*] **1** : aggregate : collection ⟨track*age*⟩ **2 a** : action : process ⟨haul*age*⟩ **b** : cumulative result of ⟨break*age*⟩ **c** : rate of ⟨dos*age*⟩ **3** : house or place of ⟨orphan*age*⟩ **4** : state : rank ⟨vassal*age*⟩ **5** : fee : charge ⟨post*age*⟩

aged \'ā-jəd, *in senses* 1b *and* 2b 'ājd\ *adj* **1** : grown old : as **a** : of an advanced age **b** : having attained a specified age ⟨a man *aged* forty years⟩ **2 a** : typical of old age **b** : having acquired a desired quality with age ⟨*aged* whiskey⟩ — **aged·ness** *n*

age·less \'āj-ləs\ *adj* **1** : not growing old or showing the effects of age **2** : TIMELESS, ETERNAL ⟨an *ageless* story⟩ — **age·less·ly** *adv*

age·long \'āj-,lȯŋ\ *adj* : lasting for an age : EVERLASTING

agen·cy \'ā-jən-sē\ *n, pl* **-cies** **1** : the capacity, condition, or state of acting or of exerting power : OPERATION **2** : a person or thing through which power is exerted or an end is achieved **3 a** : the office or function of an agent **b** : the relationship between a principal and his agent **4** : an establishment doing business under a franchise from another ⟨automobile *agency*⟩ **5** : an administrative division (as of a government) ⟨Central Intelligence *Agency*⟩

agen·da \ə-'jen-də\ *n* [L, things to be done, fr. *agere* to do] : a list of the items of business to be considered (as at a meeting)

agen·e·sis \(')ā-'jen-ə-səs\ *n, pl* **agen·e·ses** \-ə-,sēz\ : lack or failure of development (as of a body part)

agent \'ā-jənt\ *n* [ML *agent-*, *agens*, fr. L, prp. of *agere* to drive, lead, act, do] **1 a** : something that produces an effect : an active or efficient cause ⟨a cleansing *agent*⟩ **b** : a chemically, physically, or biologically active principle **2** : one that acts or exerts power **3** : MEANS, INSTRUMENT **4** : one who acts for or in the place of another and by his authority ⟨government *agent*⟩ ⟨real estate *agent*⟩

agent pro·vo·ca·teur \,äzh-,äⁿ-prō-,väk-ə-'tər, ,ā-jənt-\ *n, pl* **agents provocateurs** \,äzh-,äⁿ-prō-,väk-ə-'tər, ,ā-**

jənⁿ(t)s-prō-\ [F, lit., provoking agent] : a person paid to associate with members of a suspected group and to pretend sympathy with their aims so as to incite them to a legally punishable act

age-old \'āj-'ōld\ *adj* : having existed for ages : ANCIENT

ag·er·a·tum \,aj-ə-'rāt-əm\ *n* : any of a large genus of tropical American composite herbs often cultivated for their small showy heads of blue or white flowers

¹**ag·glom·er·ate** \ə-'gläm-ə-,rāt\ *vb* [L *ad-* + *glomer-*, *glomus* ball] : to gather into a ball, mass, or cluster

²**ag·glom·er·ate** \-rət\ *n* **1** : a jumbled mass or collection **2** : a rock composed of volcanic fragments of various sizes

ag·glom·er·a·tion \ə-,gläm-ə-'rā-shən\ *n* **1** : the action or process of collecting in a mass **2** : a heap or cluster of dissimilar elements — **ag·glom·er·a·tive** \ə-'gläm-ə-,rāt-iv\ *adj*

ag·glu·ti·nate \ə-'glüt-ᵊn-,āt\ *vb* [L *agglutinare*, fr. *ad-* + *glutin-*, *gluten* glue] **1** : to cause to adhere : FASTEN **2** : to cause to clump or undergo agglutination **3** : to unite into a group or gather into a mass **4** : to form words by agglutination

ag·glu·ti·na·tion \ə-,glüt-ᵊn-'ā-shən\ *n* **1** : the action or process of agglutinating **2** : a mass or group formed by the union of separate elements **3** : the formation of derivative or compound words by putting together constituents of which each expresses a single definite meaning **4** : a reaction in which particles (as red blood cells or bacteria) suspended in a liquid collect into clumps usu. as a response to a specific antibody — **ag·glu·ti·na·tive** \ə-'glüt-ᵊn-,āt-iv\ *adj*

ag·glu·ti·nin \ə-'glüt-ᵊn-ən\ *n* : an antibody causing agglutination

ag·glu·tin·o·gen \,ag-lü-'tin-ə-jən\ *n* : an antigen whose presence results in the formation of an agglutinin

ag·gran·dize \ə-'gran-,dīz, 'ag-rən-\ *vt* : to make great or greater (as in power, rank, size, or resources) — **ag·gran·dize·ment** \ə-'gran-dəz-mənt, -,dīz-,; ,ag-rən-'dīz-mənt\ *n* — **ag·gran·diz·er** *n*

ag·gra·vate \'ag-rə-,vāt\ *vt* [L *aggravare* to make heavier, fr *ad-* + *gravis* heavy, grave] **1** : to make worse, more serious, or more severe **2** : EXASPERATE, ANNOY **syn** see IRRITATE

ag·gra·va·tion \,ag-rə-'vā-shən\ *n* **1** : the act of making something worse or more severe : an increase in severity ⟨the treatment caused an *aggravation* of the pain⟩ **2** : something that makes a thing worse or more severe ⟨the cold winter was an *aggravation* of their misery⟩ **3** : IRRITATION, PROVOCATION

¹**ag·gre·gate** \'ag-ri-gət\ *adj* [L *aggregatus*, pp. of *aggregare* to add to, fr. *ad-* + *greg-*, *grex* flock] **1** : formed by the collection of units or particles into a body, mass, or amount : COLLECTIVE ⟨*aggregate* expenses for a party of tourists⟩ **2** : clustered in a dense mass or head ⟨an *aggregate* flower⟩ — **ag·gre·gate·ly** *adv* — **ag·gre·gate·ness** *n*

²**ag·gre·gate** \-,gāt\ *vt* **1** : to collect or gather into a mass or whole **2** : to amount to in the aggregate to **syn** AGGREGATE, SEGREGATE involve grouping or herding together. AGGREGATE implies the gathering of single or scattered units into one mass; SEGREGATE may apply to the drawing off of a portion of an aggregation, or some of its members, to form an isolated or excluded group

³**ag·gre·gate** \-gət\ *n* **1** : a mass or body of units or parts somewhat loosely associated with one another **2** : the whole sum or amount : SUM TOTAL **3 a** : any of several hard inert materials used for mixing with a cementing material to form concrete, mortar, or plaster **b** : a clustered mass of individual soil particles considered the basic structural unit of soil **syn** see SUM

aggregate fruit *n* : a compound fruit (as a raspberry) made up of the several separate ripened ovaries of a single flower

ag·gre·ga·tion \,ag-ri-'gā-shən\ *n* **1** : the collecting of units or parts into a mass or whole **2** : a group, body, or mass composed of many distinct parts : ASSEMBLAGE

ag·gres·sion \ə-'gresh-ən\ *n* [L *aggress-*, *aggredi* to attack, fr. *ad-* + *gradi* to step, go] **1** : a forceful action or procedure; *esp* : an unprovoked attack **2** : the practice of making attacks or encroachments; *esp* : unprovoked violation by one country of the territorial integrity of another **3** : hostile, injurious, or destructive behavior or outlook esp. when caused by frustration

---

ə abut; ᵊ kitten; ər further; a back; ā bake; ä cot, cart; aù out; ch chin; e less; ē easy; g gift; i trip; ī life

ag·gres·sive \ə-'gres-iv\ *adj* **1 a** : showing a readiness to attack others ⟨an *aggressive* dog⟩ **b** : practicing or marked by aggression ⟨*aggressive* nation⟩ **2 a** : ENERGETIC, FORCEFUL ⟨an *aggressive* fund-raising campaign⟩ **b** : obtrusively self-assertive — **ag·gres·sive·ly** *adv* — **ag·gres·sive·ness** *n*

ag·gres·sor \ə-'gres-ər\ *n* : one that makes an unprovoked attack; *esp* : a country that commits aggression

ag·grieved \ə-'grēvd\ *adj* **1** : troubled or distressed in spirit **2** : having a grievance; *esp* : suffering from injury or loss

aghast \ə-'gast\ *adj* [ME *agast*, fr. pp. of *agasten* to frighten, fr. *gast, gost* ghost] : struck with terror, amazement, or horror : SHOCKED

ag·ile \'aj-əl\ *adj* [L *agilis*, fr. *agere* to act, do] **1** : able to move quickly and easily : readily active : NIMBLE **2** : mentally quick ⟨an *agile* thinker⟩ — **ag·ile·ly** \-ə(l)-lē\ *adv*

agil·i·ty \ə-'jil-ət-ē\ *n* : the quality or state of being agile ⟨the grace and *agility* of a gymnast⟩

aging *pres part of* AGE

ag·i·tate \'aj-ə-ˌtāt\ *vb* [L *agitare*, freq. of *agere* to drive, do] **1** : to shake jerkily : set in violent irregular motion ⟨water *agitated* by wind⟩ **2** : to stir up : EXCITE, DISTURB ⟨*agitated* by bad news⟩ **3** : to attempt to arouse or influence public interest in something esp. by discussion or appeals ⟨*agitate* for better schools⟩ **syn** see SHAKE — **ag·i·tat·ed·ly** \-ˌtāt-əd-lē\ *adv* — **ag·i·ta·tion** \ˌaj-ə-'tā-shən\ *n*

agi·ta·to \ˌaj-ə-'tät-ō\ *adv (or adj)* [It] : in a restless hurried manner — used as a direction in music

ag·i·ta·tor \'aj-ə-ˌtāt-ər\ *n* : one that agitates: as **a** : one who stirs up public feeling on a controversial issue **b** : a device for stirring or shaking

Agla·ia \ə-'glā-(y)ə\ *n* : one of the three Graces

agleam \ə-'glēm\ *adj* : GLEAMING

agley \ə-'glā, -'glē\ *adv* [Sc, fr. [1]*a-* + *gley* to squint] *chiefly Scot* : AWRY, WRONG

aglit·ter \ə-'glit-ər\ *adj* : GLITTERING

aglow \ə-'glō\ *adj* : GLOWING

ag·nath \'ag-ˌnath\ *n* : CYCLOSTOME

ag·nos·tic \ag-'näs-tik, əg-\ *n* [Gk *agnōstos* unknown, unknowable, fr. *a-* [2]*a-* + *gnōs-, gignōskein* to know; akin to E *know*] : a person who does not deny the possible existence of God but holds that this existence and the origin of the universe are not known and probably cannot be known **syn** see ATHEIST — **agnostic** *adj* — **ag·nos·ti·cism** \-'näs-tə-ˌsiz-əm\ *n*

Ag·nus Dei \ˌäg-ˌnús-'dā(-ˌē), ˌän-ˌyüs-; ˌag-nəs-'dē-ˌī\ *n* [LL, lamb of God; fr. its opening words] **1** : a liturgical prayer said or sung to Christ as Savior **2** : an image of a lamb often with a halo and a banner and cross as a symbol of Christ

ago \ə-'gō\ *adj (or adv)* [ME *agon, ago*, fr. pp. of *agon* to pass away, fr. OE *āgān*, fr. *ā-*, prefix denoting completion + *gān* to go] : earlier than the present time ⟨a week *ago*⟩

agog \ə-'gäg\ *adj* [MF *en gogues* in mirth] : full of intense interest or excitement : EAGER

ag·o·nal \'ag-ən-ᵊl\ *adj* : of, relating to, or associated with agony and esp. the death agony

ag·o·nist \'ag-ə-nəst\ *n* : a muscle whose action is checked and controlled by the simultaneous contraction of another muscle

ag·o·nize \'ag-ə-ˌnīz\ *vb* **1** : to suffer or cause to suffer extreme pain or anguish of body or mind **2** : to strive desperately : STRUGGLE — **ag·o·niz·ing·ly** \-ˌnī-ziŋ-lē\ *adv*

ag·o·ny \'ag-ə-nē\ *n, pl* **-nies** [Gk *agōnia*, fr. *agōn* assembly, gathering to hold contests for athletic and artistic prizes, contest, struggle] **1 a** : intense pain of mind or body : ANGUISH, TORTURE **b** : the throes of death **2** : a strong sudden display (as of joy or delight) : OUTBURST

ag·o·ra \'ag-ə-rə\ *n, pl* **agoras** *or* **ag·o·rae** \-ˌrē, -ˌrī\ [Gk] : the marketplace or place of assembly in an ancient Greek city

ag·o·ra·pho·bia \ˌag-ə-rə-'fō-bē-ə\ *n* : abnormal fear of crossing or of being in open spaces — **ag·o·ra·pho·bic** \-'fō-bik, -'fäb-ik\ *adj*

agou·ti \ə-'güt-ē\ *n* [F, fr. Sp *agutí*, of AmerInd origin] **1** : a tropical American rodent about the size of a rabbit **2** : a grizzled color of fur resulting from the barring of each hair in several alternate dark and light bands

[1]**agrar·i·an** \ə-'grer-ē-ən\ *adj* [L *agr-, ager* field] **1** : of or relating to the land or its ownership ⟨*agrarian* reforms⟩ **2** : of, relating to, or concerned with farmers or peasants or farming interests ⟨an *agrarian* political party⟩ **3** : AGRICULTURAL 2 ⟨an *agrarian* country⟩

[2]**agrarian** *n* : a member of an agrarian party or movement

agrar·i·an·ism \-ē-ə-ˌniz-əm\ *n* : a social or political movement designed chiefly to improve the economic status of the farmer or peasant

agree \ə-'grē\ *vb* **agreed; agree·ing** [MF *agreer*, fr. *a* to, at + *gré* pleasure, fr. L *gratus* pleasant, agreeable] **1** : to give one's approval : CONSENT ⟨*agree* to a plan⟩ **2** : ADMIT, CONCEDE **3** : to be alike : CORRESPOND **4** : to get on well together **5** : to come to a harmonious understanding ⟨*agree* on a price⟩ **6** : to be fitting, pleasing, or healthful : SUIT ⟨climate *agrees* with him⟩ **7** : to be alike or correspond grammatically in gender, number, case, or person

agree·a·ble \ə-'grē-ə-bəl\ *adj* **1** : pleasing to the mind or senses : PLEASANT **2** : ready or willing to agree **3** : being in harmony : CONSONANT — **agree·a·ble·ness** *n* — **agree·a·bly** \-blē\ *adv*

agreed \ə-'grēd\ *adj* : settled by agreement ⟨a previously *agreed* price⟩

agree·ment \ə-'grē-mənt\ *n* **1 a** : the act of agreeing **b** : harmony of opinion, action, or character : CONCORD **2 a** : a mutual arrangement or understanding (as a contract or treaty) between two or more parties about some course of action **b** : a written record of such an agreement **3** : the fact of agreeing grammatically

ag·ri·cul·tur·al \ˌag-ri-'kəlch-(ə-)rəl\ *adj* **1** : of, relating to, or used in agriculture **2** : engaged in or concerned with agriculture ⟨an *agricultural* society⟩ — **ag·ri·cul·tur·al·ly** \-ē\ *adv*

ag·ri·cul·ture \'ag-ri-ˌkəl-chər\ *n* [L *agr-, ager* field; akin to E *acre*] : the science, art, or occupation of cultivating the soil, producing crops, and raising livestock : FARMING — **ag·ri·cul·tur·ist** \ˌag-ri-'kəlch-(ə-)rəst\ *or* **ag·ri·cul·tur·al·ist** \-(ə-)rə-ləst\ *n*

ag·ri·mo·ny \'ag-rə-ˌmō-nē\ *n, pl* **-nies** : a common yellow-flowered herb of the rose family having toothed leaves and fruits like burs

ag·ro·bi·ol·o·gy \ˌag-rō-bī-'äl-ə-jē\ *n* : the study of plant nutrition and growth and crop production in relation to soil management — **ag·ro·bi·o·log·ic** \-ˌbī-ə-'läj-ik\ *or* **ag·ro·bi·o·log·i·cal** \-'läj-i-kəl\ *adj* — **ag·ro·bi·o·log·i·cal·ly** \-i-k(ə-)lē\ *adv*

agrol·o·gy \ə-'gräl-ə-jē\ *n* : a branch of agriculture dealing with soils esp. in relation to crops — **ag·ro·log·ic** \ˌag-rə-'läj-ik\ *or* **ag·ro·log·i·cal** \-'läj-i-kəl\ *adj* — **agrol·o·gist** \ə-'gräl-ə-jəst\ *n*

agron·o·my \ə-'grän-ə-mē\ *n* [Gk *agros* field (akin to E *acre*) + *nomos* law] : a branch of agriculture that deals with the raising of crops and the care of the soil — **ag·ro·nom·ic** \ˌag-rə-'näm-ik\ *adj* — **ag·ro·nom·i·cal·ly** \-'näm-i-k(ə-)lē\ *adv* — **agron·o·mist** \ə-'grän-ə-məst\ *n*

aground \ə-'graůnd\ *adv (or adj)* **1** : on or onto the shore or the bottom of a body of water : STRANDED **2** : on the ground

ague \'ā-gyü\ *n* [MF *aguë*, fr. ML *febris acuta*, lit., sharp fever] **1** : a fever (as malaria) marked by outbreaks of chills, fever, and sweating that recur at regular intervals **2** : a fit of shivering : CHILL

ah \'ä\ *interj* — used to express delight, relief, regret, or contempt

aha \ä-'hä\ *interj* — used to express surprise, triumph, or derision

ahead \ə-'hed\ *adv* **1 a** : in a forward direction or position : FORWARD ⟨go *ahead*⟩ **b** : in front ⟨the man *ahead*⟩ **2** : in, into, or for the future ⟨think *ahead*⟩ **3** : in or toward a more advantageous position **4** : in advance ⟨make payments *ahead*⟩ — **ahead** *adj*

ahead of *prep* **1** : in front or advance of **2** : in excess of : ABOVE

ahoy \ə-'hȯi\ *interj* — used in hailing ⟨ship *ahoy*⟩

agitators b

Ahu·ra–Maz·da \ə-,hůr-ə-'maz-də, ä-,hůr-\ *n* : the god of goodness and light in Zoroastrianism

¹aid \'ād\ *vb* [MF *aider*, fr. L *adjutare*, freq. of *adjuvare* to help, fr. *ad-* + *juvare* to help] **1** : to provide with what is useful or necessary in achieving an end : ASSIST **2** : to give assistance — **aid·er** *n*

²aid *n* **1** : the act of helping or the help given : ASSISTANCE **2 a** : an assisting person or group **b** : an auxiliary device

aide \'ād\ *n* [short for *aide-de-camp*] **1** : a military or naval officer acting as assistant to a superior **2** : a person who acts as an assistant or helper : AID

aide–de–camp \,ād-di-'kamp, -'käⁿ\ *n, pl* **aides–de–camp** \,ādz-di-\ [F *aide de camp*, lit., camp assistant] : AIDE 1

ai·grette \ā-'gret, 'ā-,\ *n* [F] : a plume or decorative tuft for the head

ail \'āl\ *vb* [OE *eglan*] **1** : to be the matter with : TROUBLE ⟨what *ails* you?⟩ **2** : to have something the matter; *esp* : to suffer ill health

ai·lan·thus \ā-'lan(t)-thəs\ *n* : a widely grown quick-growing Asiatic tree with pinnate leaves and terminal clusters of ill-scented greenish flowers

ai·le·ron \'ā-lə-,rän\ *n* [F, fr. dim. of *aile* wing, fr. L *ala*] : a movable portion of an airplane wing or a movable airfoil external to the wing for imparting a rolling motion and thus providing lateral control

ail·ment \'āl-mənt\ *n* : a bodily disorder : SICKNESS

¹aim \'ām\ *vb* [ME *aimen* to estimate, aim, fr. MF *aesmer*, fr. *a-* ad- + *esmer* to estimate, fr. L *aestimare*] **1 a** : to direct a course **b** : to point a weapon **2** : ASPIRE, INTEND **3 a** : POINT **b** : to direct to or toward a specified object or goal

²aim *n* **1** : the directing of a weapon or a missile at a mark **2** : GOAL, PURPOSE **syn** see INTENTION

aim·less \'ām-ləs\ *adj* : lacking aim or purpose ⟨*aimless* wandering⟩ — **aim·less·ly** *adv* — **aim·less·ness** *n*

ain't \(')ānt\ **1 a** : are not **b** : is not **c** : am not — though disapproved by many and more common in less educated speech, used orally in most parts of the U. S. by many educated speakers esp. in the phrase *ain't I* **2** *substand* **a** : have not **b** : has not

Ai·nu \'ī-nü\ *n* **1** : a member of an indigenous Caucasoid people of Japan living chiefly in the northern islands **2** : the language of the Ainu people

¹air \'a(ə)r, 'e(ə)r\ *n* [OF, fr. L *aer*, fr. Gk *aēr*] **1 a** : the invisible mixture of odorless tasteless gases (as nitrogen and oxygen) that surrounds the earth **b** : a light breeze **2** : COMPRESSED AIR ⟨*air* sprayer⟩ **3 a** : a field of operation for aircraft ⟨transport by *air*⟩ **b** : AIRCRAFT ⟨*air* attack⟩ ⟨*air* mechanic⟩ ⟨*air* patrol⟩ **c** : AVIATION ⟨*air* safety⟩ ⟨*air* rights⟩ **d** : AIR FORCE ⟨*air* headquarters⟩ **e** : the medium of transmission of radio waves; *also* : RADIO, TELEVISION ⟨went on the *air*⟩ **4 a** : outward appearance : apparent nature **b** *pl* : an artificial or affected manner : HAUGHTINESS ⟨put on *airs*⟩ **c** : a surrounding or pervading influence : ATMOSPHERE ⟨an *air* of mystery⟩ **5** : TUNE, MELODY

²air *vt* **1** : to place in the air for cooling, refreshing, or cleansing ⟨*air* blankets⟩ **2** : to make known in public

air base *n* : a base of operations for military aircraft

air bladder *n* : a sac in a fish containing gas and esp. air and serving as a hydrostatic organ or assisting respiration

air·borne \-,bōrn, -,bȯrn\ *adj* : supported or transported by air

air brake *n* **1** : a brake operated by a piston driven by compressed air **2** : a surface that may be projected into the air for lowering the speed of an airplane

air·brush \-,brəsh\ *n* : an atomizer for applying by compressed air a fine spray (as of paint or a protective coating) — **airbrush** *vt*

air-con·di·tion \,a(ə)r-kən-'dish-ən, ,e(ə)r-\ *vt* : to equip with an apparatus for washing air and controlling its humidity and temperature; *also* : to subject (air) to these processes — **air-con·di·tion·er** \-'dish-(ə-)nər\ *n*

air-cool \'a(ə)r-,kül, 'e(ə)r-\ *vt* : to cool the cylinders of (an internal-combustion engine) by air without the use of any intermediate medium

air·craft \'a(ə)r-,kraft, 'e(ə)r-\ *n, pl* **aircraft** : a weight-carrying machine for navigation of the air that is supported either by its own buoyancy or by the action of the air against its surfaces

aircraft carrier *n* : a warship with a deck on which airplanes can be launched and landed

air·crew \'a(ə)r-,krü, 'e(ə)r-\ *n* : the crew manning an airplane

air·drome \-,drōm\ *n* : AIRPORT

air·drop \-,dräp\ *n* : delivery of cargo or personnel by parachute from an airplane in flight — **air-drop** \-,dräp\ *vt*

Aire·dale \'a(ə)r-,dāl, 'e(ə)r-\ *n* : any of a breed of large terriers with a hard wiry coat that is dark on back and sides and tan elsewhere — see TERRIER illustration

air express *n* : package transport by airlines

air·field \'a(ə)r-,fēld, 'e(ə)r-\ *n* **1** : the landing field of an airport **2** : AIRPORT

air·foil \-,fȯil\ *n* : an airplane surface (as a wing or rudder) designed to produce reaction from the air through which it moves

air force *n* : the military organization of a nation for air warfare

air·frame \-,frām\ *n* : the structure of an airplane or rocket without the power plant

air gun *n* **1** : a pistol-shaped hand tool that works by compressed air **2** : AIRBRUSH

air hole *n* **1 a** : a hole to admit or discharge air **b** : a spot not frozen over in ice **2** : AIR POCKET

air lane *n* : an airway that is customarily followed by airplanes

air·less \'a(ə)r-ləs, 'e(ə)r-\ *adj* : lacking air, fresh air, or movement of air

air letter *n* **1** : an airmail letter **2** : a sheet of paper designed for folding and sealing so as to form an envelope for a message written on the inside and sometimes bearing a stamp for airmail delivery

air·lift \'a(ə)r-,lift, 'e(ə)r-\ *n* : a supply line operated by aircraft — **airlift** *vt*

air line *n* **1** : BEELINE **2 air·line** *a* : an established system of transportation by airplanes, its equipment, or the organization owning or operating it **b** : a regular route followed in transportation by air

air·lin·er \-,lī-nər\ *n* : a large passenger airplane operating over an airline

air lock *n* : an air space with two airtight doors for permitting movement between two spaces with different pressures or different atmospheres

air·mail \'a(ə)r-'māl, 'e(ə)r-, -,māl\ *n* : the system of transporting mail by airplanes; *also* : the mail transported — **airmail** *vt*

air·man \-mən\ *n* **1** : an enlisted man in the air force; *esp* : one of any of four ranks below a staff sergeant **2** : a civilian or military pilot or aviator

airman basic *n* : an enlisted man of the lowest rank in the air force

air mass *n* : a body of air extending hundreds or thousands of miles horizontally and sometimes as high as the stratosphere and maintaining as it travels nearly uniform conditions of temperature and humidity at any given level

air mile *n* : a mile in air navigation; *esp* : a unit of length equal to 6076.1154 feet

air·mind·ed \'a(ə)r-'mīn-dəd, 'e(ə)r-\ *adj* : interested in aviation or in air travel — **air·mind·ed·ness** *n*

air·plane \-,plān\ *n* [alter. of *aeroplane*, fr. Gk *aēr* air + *planos* wandering, fr. *planasthai* to wander] : a fixed-wing aircraft heavier than air that is driven by a screw propeller or by a rearward jet and supported by the reaction of the air against its wings

air plant *n* **1** : EPIPHYTE **2** : BRYOPHYLLUM

air pocket *n* : a condition of the atmosphere that causes an airplane to drop suddenly

air police *n* : the military police of an air force

air·port \'a(ə)r-,pōrt, 'e(ə)r-, -,pȯrt\ *n* : a tract of land or water that is maintained for the landing and takeoff of airplanes and for receiving and discharging passengers and cargo and that usu. has facilities for the shelter, supply, and repair of planes

air·post \-'pōst\ *n* : AIRMAIL

air pump *n* : a pump for exhausting air from a closed space or for compressing air or forcing it through other apparatus

air raid *n* : an attack by armed airplanes (as with bombs) on a surface target

air sac *n* **1** : one of the air-filled spaces connected with the lungs of a bird **2** : one of the thin-walled microscopic pouches in which gases are exchanged in the lungs

ə abut; ᵊ kitten; ər further; a back; ā bake; ä cot, cart; au̇ out; ch chin; e less; ē easy; g gift; i trip; ī life

air·ship \'a(ə)r-,ship, 'e(ə)r-\ *n* : a lighter-than-air aircraft having propulsion and steering systems

air·sick \-,sik\ *adj* : affected with motion sickness associated with flying — **air·sick·ness** *n*

air·space \-,spās\ *n* : the space lying above a nation and coming under its jurisdiction

air·speed \-,spēd\ *n* : the speed of an airplane with relation to the air as distinguished from its speed relative to the earth

air·strip \-,strip\ *n* : a runway without normal air base or airport facilities

air·tight \-'tīt\ *adj* **1** : so tightly sealed that no air can get in or out **2** : leaving no opening for attack ⟨*airtight* defenses⟩ ⟨an *airtight* argument⟩ — **air·tight·ness** *n*

air·wave \-,wāv\ *n* : the medium of radio and television transmission — usu. used in pl.

air·way \-,wā\ *n* **1** : a passage for a current of air **2** : a regular route for airplanes from airport to airport; *esp* : such a route equipped with navigational aids **3** : AIR LINE 2a

air·wor·thy \-,wər-thē\ *adj* : fit or safe for operation in the air ⟨a very *airworthy* plane⟩ — **air·wor·thi·ness** *n*

airy \'a(ə)r-ē, 'e(ə)r-\ *adj* **air·i·er; -est** **1** : of, relating to, or living in the air : AERIAL ⟨*airy* spirits⟩ **2** : open to the air : BREEZY ⟨an *airy* room⟩ **3** : resembling air in lightness : DELICATE, GRACEFUL, ETHEREAL **4** : lacking a sound or solid basis — **air·i·ly** \'ar-ə-lē, 'er-\ *adv* — **air·i·ness** \'ar-ē-nəs, 'er-\ *n*

aisle \'īl\ *n* [MF *aile* wing, fr. L *ala*] **1** : the side of a church separated by piers from the nave — see BASILICA illustration **2** : a passage between sections of seats

¹ajar \ə-'jär\ *adv (or adj)* [ME *on char*, fr. *on* + *char* turn, fr. OE *cierr*] : slightly open ⟨the door was *ajar*⟩

²ajar *adj* [¹*a-* + *jar*] : DISCORDANT

Ajax \'ā-,jaks\ *n* **1** : a Greek hero in the Trojan War who kills himself because the armor of Achilles is awarded to Odysseus **2** : a fleet-footed Greek hero in the Trojan War — called also *Ajax the Less*

akim·bo \ə-'kim-bō\ *adv (or adj)* [ME *in kenebowe*] : with the hand on the hip and the elbow turned outward

akin \ə-'kin\ *adj* **1** : related by blood : descended from a common ancestor or prototype **2** : essentially similar or related : ALIKE

Ak·ka·di·an \ə-'kād-ē-ən\ *n* **1** : one of a Semitic people invading and settling central Mesopotamia north of the Sumerians (3000–1900 B.C.) **2** : an ancient Semitic language of Mesopotamia used from about the 28th to the 1st century B.C. — **Akkadian** *adj*

al- — see AD-

¹-al \əl, ²l\ *adj suffix* [L *-alis*] : of, relating to, or characterized by ⟨direction*al*⟩ ⟨fiction*al*⟩

²-al *n suffix* [OF *-aille*, fr. L *-alia*, neut. pl. of *-alis*] : action : process ⟨rehears*al*⟩

a la *or* **à la** \,al-ə, ,äl-ə\ [F *à la*, short for *à la mode*] : in the manner of

ala \'ā-lə\ *n, pl* **alae** \-,lē\ [L] : a wing-shaped anatomic process or part : WING — **alar** \'ā-lər\ *adj* — **ala·ry** \-lə-rē\ *adj*

al·a·bas·ter \'al-ə-,bas-tər\ *n* [L *alabaster* vase of alabaster, fr. Gk *alabastros*] **1** : a compact fine-textured usu. white and translucent gypsum that is carved into objects (as vases) **2** : a hard translucent calcite that is translucent and sometimes banded

a la carte \,al-ə-'kärt, ,äl-\ *adv (or adj)* [F *à la carte* by the bill of fare] : with a separate price for each item on the menu — compare TABLE D'HÔTE

alack \ə-'lak\ *interj, archaic* — used to express sorrow, regret, or reproach

alac·ri·ty \ə-'lak-rət-ē\ *n* [L *alacr-, alacer* lively, eager] : a cheerful readiness to do something : BRISKNESS, LIVELINESS **syn** see CELERITY — **alac·ri·tous** \-rət-əs\ *adj*

Alad·din \ə-'lad-²n\ *n* : a youth in the *Arabian Nights' Entertainments* who comes into possession of a magic lamp and ring

a la mode \,al-ə-'mōd, ,äl-\ *adj* [F *à la mode* according to the fashion] **1** : FASHIONABLE, STYLISH **2** : topped with ice cream

al·a·nine \'al-ə-,nēn\ *n* : amino acid $C_3H_7NO_2$ formed esp. by the hydrolysis of proteins

¹alarm \ə-'lärm\ *also* **alar·um** \ə-'lar-əm\ *n* [It *all' arme* to arms] **1** *usu alarum, obs* : a call to arms **2 a** : a sound or

signal giving notice of danger or calling attention to some event or condition **b** : a device that warns or signals (as by a bell) **3** : the fear caused by a sudden sense of danger

²alarm *also* **alarum** *vt* **1** : to notify of danger **2** : to arouse to a sense of danger : FRIGHTEN, DISTURB — **alarm·ing·ly** \-'lär-miŋ-lē\ *adv*

alarm clock *n* : a clock that can be set to sound an alarm at any desired time

alarm·ist \ə-'lär-məst\ *n* : a person who is given to alarming others esp. needlessly — **alarm·ism** \-,miz-əm\ *n*

alas \ə-'las\ *interj* — used to express unhappiness, pity, or concern

Alas·kan malamute \ə-,las-kən-\ *n* : any of a breed of powerful heavy-coated deep-chested dogs of Alaskan origin with erect ears, heavily cushioned feet, and plumy tail

Alas·ka standard time \ə-'las-kə-\ *n* : the time of the 10th time zone west of Greenwich that includes central Alaska and the Hawaiian islands : HAWAII STANDARD TIME

alate \'ā-,lāt\ *also* **alat·ed** \-,lāt-əd\ *adj* : having wings or a winglike part — **ala·tion** \ā-'lā-shən\ *n*

alb \'alb\ *n* [OE, fr. ML *alba*, fr. L, fem. of *albus* white] : a basic full-length white linen vestment with close sleeves worn at the Eucharist

al·ba·core \'al-bə-,kō(ə)r, -,kò(ə)r\ *n, pl* **-core** *or* **-cores** : a large pelagic tuna with long pectoral fins that is the source of most canned tuna; *also* : any of several tunas

Al·ba·ni·an \al-'bā-nē-ən, -nyən\ *n* **1** : a native or inhabitant of Albania **2** : the Indo-European language of the Albanian people — **Albanian** *adj*

al·ba·tross \'al-bə-,trós, -,träs\ *n, pl* **-tross** *or* **-tross·es** : any of various large web-footed seabirds that are related to the petrels and include the largest birds of the sea

albatross

al·be·it \al-'bē-ət, òl-\ *conj* : even though : ALTHOUGH

al·bi·no \al-'bī-nō\ *n, pl* **-nos** [Sp, fr. *albo* white, fr. L *albus*] : an organism deficient in coloring matter; *esp* : a human being or lower animal that is congenitally deficient in pigment and usu. has a milky or translucent skin, white or colorless hair, and eyes with pink or blue iris and deep red pupil — **al·bin·ic** \al-'bin-ik\ *adj* — **al·bi·nism** \'al-bə-,niz-əm, al-'bī-\ *n* — **al·bi·nis·tic** \,al-bə-'nis-tik\ *adj* — **albino** *adj* — **al·bi·not·ic** \,al-bə-'nät-ik, -,bī-\ *adj*

Al·bi·on \'al-bē-ən\ *n* **1** : the island of Great Britain **2** : the country of England

al·bite \'al-,bīt\ *n* : a usu. white feldspar containing sodium

al·bum \'al-bəm\ *n* [L, white tablet, fr. neut. of *albus* white] **1 a** : a book with blank pages for autographs, stamps, or photographs **b** : a container with envelopes for phonograph records **c** : one or more phonograph records or tape recordings carrying a major musical work or a group of related selections **2** : a collection usu. in book form of literary selections, musical compositions, or pictures : ANTHOLOGY

al·bu·men \al-'byü-mən\ *n* [L *albumin-, albumen*, fr. *albus* white] **1** : the white of an egg **2** : ALBUMIN

al·bu·min \al-'byü-mən\ *n* : any of numerous heat-coagulable water-soluble proteins found esp. in blood, the whites of eggs, and various animal and plant tissues

al·bu·min·ous \al-'byü-mə-nəs\ *adj* : relating to, containing, or having the properties of albumen or albumin

al·bur·num \al-'bər-nəm\ *n* : SAPWOOD

al·ca·zar \al-'kaz-ər\ *n* [Sp *alcázar*, fr. Ar *al- qaşr* the castle] : a Spanish fortress or palace

al·che·mist \'al-kə-məst\ *n* : one who studies or practices alchemy

al·che·my \'al-kə-mē\ *n* [ML *alchimia*, fr. Arabic *al- kīmiyā'* the alchemy] **1** : a medieval chemical science and philosophy aiming to achieve the conversion of the base metals into gold, the discovery of a universal cure for disease, and the discovery of a means of indefinitely prolonging life **2** : a power or process of transforming something common into something precious — **al·chem·i·cal** \al-'kem-i-kəl\ *adj* — **al·chem·i·cal·ly** \-k(ə-)lē\ *adv*

al·co·hol \'al-kə-,hòl\ *n* [Ar *al-kuḥul* the powdered antimony] **1 a** : a colorless volatile flammable liquid C_2H_5OH

---

j joke; ŋ sing; ō flow; ò flaw; òi coin; th thin; th̶ this; ü loot; u̇ foot; y yet; yü few; yu̇ furious; zh vision

that is the intoxicating agent in fermented and distilled liquors (as beer, wine, whiskey) — called also *ethyl alcohol* **b** : any of various carbon compounds that are similar to ethyl alcohol in having at least one hydroxyl group **2** : a liquor (as beer, wine, or whiskey) containing alcohol; *also* : LIQUORS

¹al·co·hol·ic \,al-kə-'hȯl-ik, -'häl-\ *adj* **1** : of, relating to, caused by, or containing alcohol **2** : affected with alcoholism — **al·co·hol·i·cal·ly** \-i-k(ə-)lē\ *adv*

²alcoholic *n* : one affected with alcoholism

al·co·hol·ism \'al-kə-,hȯl,iz-əm\ *n* : continued excessive and usu. uncontrollable use of alcoholic drinks; *also* : the abnormal state associated with such use

Al·co·ran \,al-kə-'ran\ *n, archaic* : KORAN

al·cove \'al-,kōv\ *n* [Sp *alcoba,* fr. Ar *al-qubbah* the arch] **1 a** : a nook or small recess opening off a larger room **b** : a niche or arched opening (as in a wall) **2** : SUMMERHOUSE

Al·cy·o·ne \al-'sī-ə-(,)nē\ *n* : the brightest star in the Pleiades

Al·deb·a·ran \al-'deb-ə-rən\ *n* [Ar *al-dabarān,* lit., the follower] : a red star of the first magnitude that is seen in the eye of Taurus

al·de·hyde \'al-də-,hīd\ *n* [NL *al. dehyd.,* abbr. of *alcohol dehydrogenatum* dehydrogenated alcohol] **1** : ACETALDEHYDE **2** : any of various highly reactive organic compounds typified by acetaldehyde and characterized by the group —CHO

al·der \'ȯl-dər\ *n* [OE *alor*] : any of a genus of toothed-leaved trees or shrubs related to the birches and found esp. in moist ground

al·der·fly \-,flī\ *n* : any of several winged insects closely related to the dobsonflies

al·der·man \'ȯl-dər-mən\ *n* [OE *ealdorman,* fr. *ealdor* elder, parent] **1** : a high Anglo-Saxon government official **2** : a specially chosen member of a British county or borough council **3** : a member of a municipal legislative body in a U.S. city — **al·der·man·ic** \,ȯl-dər-'man-ik\ *adj*

al·drin \'ȯl-drən\ *n* : a long-acting insecticide that is a chlorinated derivative of naphthalene

ale \'āl\ *n* [OE *ealu*] **1** : an alcoholic drink made from malt and flavored with hops; *esp* : one that is brewed by rapid fermentation and is heavier bodied and more bitter than beer **2** : an English country festival at which ale is the chief beverage

alee \ə-'lē\ *adv (or adj)* : on or toward the lee

ale·house \'āl-,haůs\ *n* : a place where ale is sold to be drunk on the premises

alem·bic \ə-'lem-bik\ *n* [ML *alembicum,* fr. Ar *al-anbīq* the still] : an apparatus formerly used in distillation

¹alert \ə-'lərt\ *adj* [It *all' erta* on the ascent] **1 a** : being watchful and prompt to meet danger **b** : quick to perceive and act **2** : ACTIVE, BRISK **syn** see WATCHFUL — **alert·ly** *adv* — **alert·ness** *n*

²alert *n* **1** : a signal (as an alarm) of danger **2** : the period during which an alert is in effect — **on the alert** : on the lookout for danger

³alert *vt* : to call to a state of readiness : WARN ⟨sirens to *alert* the public in case of attack⟩

al·eu·rone \'al-yə-,rōn\ *n* [Gk *aleuron* flour] : granular protein matter in the endosperm of a seed — **al·eu·ron·ic** \,al-yə-'rän-ik\ *adj*

Aleut \ə-'lüt\ *n* **1** : a member of a people of the Aleutian and Shumagin islands and the western part of Alaska peninsula **2** : the language of the Aleuts

¹ale·wife \'āl-,wīf\ *n* : a woman who keeps an alehouse

²alewife *n* : a food fish of the herring family abundant on the Atlantic coast

Al·ex·an·dri·an \,al-ig-'zan-drē-ən, ,el-\ *adj* [fr. the prominence of Alexandria, Egypt, in the intellectual and cultural life of the Hellenistic period] : HELLENISTIC

al·ex·an·drine \-'zan-drən\ *n, often cap* [MF *vers alexandrin,* lit., verse of Alexander; so called fr. its use in a poem on Alexander the Great] : a line consisting of six iambic feet

al·fal·fa \al-'fal-fə\ *n* [Sp, of Ar origin] : a deep-rooted European leguminous plant with purple flowers and leaves like clover that is widely grown for hay and forage

al·fil·a·ria \(,)al-,fil-ə-'rē-ə\ *n* : a European herb of the geranium family grown for forage in western America

al·fres·co \al-'fres-kō\ *adv (or adj)* [It *al fresco*] : in the open air

al·ga \'al-gə\ *n, pl* **al·gae** \'al-(,)jē\ [L] : any plant of a group (Algae) that forms the lowest division of the plant kingdom and includes seaweeds and related forms mostly growing in water, lacking a vascular system, and having chlorophyll often masked by brown or red coloring matter — **al·gal** \'al-gəl\ *adj*

al·ge·bra \'al-jə-brə\ *n* [Ar *al-jabr,* lit., the reduction] : a branch of mathematics in which symbols (as letters and numbers) representing various entities are combined according to special rules of operation

al·ge·bra·ic \,al-jə-'brā-ik\ *adj* **1** : of or relating to algebra ⟨*algebraic* expression⟩ **2** : involving only a finite number of algebraic operations — **al·ge·bra·i·cal·ly** \-'brā-ə-k(ə-)lē\ *adv*

-al·gia \'al-j(ē-)ə\ *n comb form* [Gk, fr. *algos*] : pain ⟨neur*algia*⟩

al·gin \'al-jən\ *n* : any of various colloidal substances from brown algae including some used esp. as stabilizers or emulsifiers

Al·gol \'al-,gäl, -,gȯl\ *n* [Ar *al-ghūl,* lit., the ghoul] : a binary star in the constellation Perseus whose larger component revolves about and eclipses the smaller brighter star causing periodic variation in brightness

Al·gon·qui·an \al-'gäŋ-kwē-ən, -'gäŋ-\ *or* **Al·gon·ki·an** \-'gäŋ-kē-ən\ *n* **1** : a stock of Indian languages spoken from Labrador to the Carolinas and westward to the Great Plains **2** : a member of any of the peoples speaking Algonquian languages — **Algonquian** *adj*

Al·gon·quin \al-'gäŋ-kwən, -'gäŋ-\ *n* : an Indian people of the Ottawa river valley — **Algonquin** *adj*

al·go·rithm \'al-gə-,rith-əm\ *n* : a rule of procedure for solving a recurrent mathematical problem (as of finding the greatest common divisor of two numbers)

¹ali·as \'ā-lē-əs, 'āl-yəs\ *adv* [L, otherwise, fr. *alius* other] : otherwise called : otherwise known as ⟨John Doe *alias* Richard Roe⟩

²alias *n* : an assumed name

¹al·i·bi \'al-ə-,bī\ *n, pl* **-bis** \-,bīz\ [L, elsewhere, fr. *alius* other] **1** : the plea made by a person accused of a crime that he was at another place when the crime occurred **2** : a plausible excuse

²alibi *vb* **-bied; -bi·ing** **1** : to offer an excuse **2** : to make an excuse for

¹alien \'ā-lē-ən, 'āl-yən\ *adj* [L *alienus,* fr. *alius* other; akin to E *else*] **1** : belonging or relating to another person or place : STRANGE **2 a** : relating or belonging to another country ⟨*alien* property custodian⟩ **b** : owing allegiance to a foreign country ⟨*alien* residents⟩ **3** : wholly different in nature or character

²alien *n* **1** : a person of another family, race, or nation **2** : a foreign-born resident who has not been naturalized and is still a subject or citizen of a foreign country

alien·able \'āl-yə-nə-bəl, 'ā-lē-ə-nə-\ *adj* : transferable to the ownership of another ⟨*alienable* property⟩ — **alien·a·bil·i·ty** \,āl-yə-nə-'bil-ət-ē, ,ā-lē-ə-nə-\ *n*

alien·ate \'ā-lē-ə-,nāt, 'āl-yə-,nāt\ *vt* **1** : to convey or transfer (as a title, property, or right) to another **2** : to cause to lose former feelings of love, loyalty, attachment, or a sense of filling a useful and respected position in a society : ESTRANGE ⟨an intellectual *alienated* by new class relationships⟩ **3** : to cause to be withdrawn or diverted — **alien·a·tion** \,ā-lē-ə-'nā-shən, ,āl-yə-'nā-\ *n* — **alien·a·tor** \'ā-lē-ə-,nāt-ər, 'āl-yə-,nāt-\ *n*

alien·ist \'ā-lē-ə-nəst, 'āl-yə-nəst\ *n* : PSYCHIATRIST; *esp* : one who testifies in a legal proceeding

¹alight \ə-'līt\ *vi* **alight·ed** \-'līt-əd\ *also* **alit** \ə-'lit\; **alight·ing** **1** : to get down : DISMOUNT **2** : to descend from the air and settle : LAND

²alight *adj* : LIGHTED, AFLAME

align *also* **aline** \ə-'līn\ *vb* **1** : to bring into line or alignment **2** : to array on the side of or against a party or cause **3** : to be in or come into alignment — **align·er** *n*

align·ment *also* **aline·ment** \ə-'līn-mənt\ *n* **1 a** : the act of aligning : the state of being aligned **b** : the proper positioning of parts in relation to each other **c** : the proper state of adjustment of electronic parts for best performance of an apparatus **2** : an arrangement of groups or forces in relation to one another ⟨a new *alignment* in national politics⟩

ə abut; ° kitten; ər further; a back; ā bake; ä cot, cart; aů out; ch chin; e less; ē easy; g gift; i trip; ī life

¹alike \ə-'līk\ *adj* : LIKE — **alike·ness** *n*

²alike *adv* : in the same manner, form, or degree : EQUALLY

al·i·ment \'al-ə-mənt\ *n* : FOOD, NUTRIMENT; *also* : SUSTENANCE — **al·i·men·tal** \,al-ə-'ment-ᵊl\ *adj* — **al·i·men·tal·ly** \-ᵊl-ē\ *adv*

al·i·men·ta·ry \,al-ə-'ment-ə-rē, -'men-trē\ *adj* [L *alimentum* nourishment, fr. *alere* to nourish] : of or relating to nourishment or nutrition

alimentary canal *n* : the tube that extends from mouth to anus and functions in direction and absorption of food and in elimination of residual waste

al·i·mo·ny \'al-ə-,mō-nē\ *n* [L *alimonia* support, fr. *alere* to nourish] : an allowance of money made by a man to a woman for her support during or after her divorce or legal separation from him

Al·i·oth \'al-ē-,äth, -,ōth\ *n* : a star of the 2d magnitude in the handle of the Big Dipper

al·i·phat·ic \,al-ə-'fat-ik\ *adj* : belonging to a group of organic compounds whose structure is in the form of a chain whose ends are not joined

al·i·quot \'al-ə-,kwät, -kwət\ *adj* [ML *aliquotus*, fr. L *aliquot* some, several] **1** : contained an exact number of times in another **2** : FRACTIONAL

alive \ə-'līv\ *adj* **1 a** : having life : not dead or inanimate **b** : LIVING ⟨proudest boy *alive*⟩ **2** : still in existence, force, or operation : ACTIVE ⟨kept hope *alive*⟩ **3** : knowingly aware or conscious : SENSITIVE ⟨was *alive* to the danger⟩ **4** : marked by much life, animation, or activity : SWARMING ⟨blossoms *alive* with bees⟩ — **alive·ness** *n*

aliz·a·rin \ə-'liz-ə-rən\ *n* : an orange or red crystalline compound $C_{14}H_8O_4$ made synthetically and used as a red dye and in making red pigments

al·ka·li \'al-kə-,lī\ *n, pl* **-lies** *or* **-lis** [Ar *al-qili* the soda ash] **1** : a substance (as a hydroxide or carbonate of an alkali metal) having marked basic properties **2** : ALKALI METAL **3** : a soluble salt or a mixture of soluble salts present in some soils of arid regions

alkali metal *n* : any of the mostly basic metals of the group lithium, sodium, potassium, rubidium, cesium, and francium

al·ka·line \'al-kə-,līn, -lən\ *adj* : of, relating to, or having the properties of an alkali — **al·ka·lin·i·ty** \,al-kə-'lin-ət-ē\ *n*

alkaline earth *n* **1** : an oxide of any of several strongly basic metals comprising calcium, strontium, and barium and sometimes also magnesium, radium, or less often beryllium **2** : ALKALINE-EARTH METAL

alkaline–earth metal *n* : any of the metals whose oxides are the alkaline earths

al·ka·lin·ize \'al-kə-lə-,nīz\ *also* **al·ka·lize** \'al-kə-,līz\ *vt* : to make alkaline — **al·ka·lin·i·za·tion** \,al-kə-,lin-ə-'zā-shən\ *n*

al·ka·loid \'al-kə-,lȯid\ *n* : any of numerous usu. colorless, complex, and bitter organic basic compounds containing nitrogen and usu. oxygen that occur esp. in seed plants — **al·ka·loi·dal** \,al-kə-'lȯid-ᵊl\ *adj*

al·kyd \'al-kəd\ *n* : any of numerous synthetic resins made by heating alcohols with acids or their anhydrides and used esp. for protective coatings

¹all \'ȯl\ *adj* [OE *eall*] **1 a** : the whole of ⟨sat up *all* night⟩ **b** : as much as possible ⟨told in *all* seriousness⟩ **2** : every member or individual component of ⟨*all* men will go⟩ **3** : the whole number or sum of ⟨*all* the angles of a triangle are equal to two right angles⟩ **4** : EVERY ⟨*all* manner of hardship⟩ **5** : any whatever ⟨beyond *all* doubt⟩ **6** : nothing but : ONLY ⟨*all* ears⟩ **7** : being more than one person or thing ⟨who *all* was there⟩

²all *adv* **1** : WHOLLY, ALTOGETHER ⟨sat *all* alone⟩ — often used as an intensive ⟨*all* across the country⟩ **2** *obs* : EXCLUSIVELY, ONLY **3** *archaic* : JUST **4** : so much ⟨*all* the better for it⟩ **5** : for each side : APIECE ⟨the score is two *all*⟩

³all *pron* **1** : the whole number, quantity, or amount ⟨*all* that I have⟩ ⟨*all* of us⟩ **2** : EVERYBODY, EVERYTHING ⟨sacrificed *all* for love⟩ ⟨known to *all*⟩

all- *or* **allo-** *comb form* [Gk *allos*; akin to E *else*] : other : different : atypical ⟨*allogamous*⟩

¹al·la breve \,al-ə-'brev, ,äl-ə-'brev-,ā\ *adv* (*or adj*) [It, lit., according to the breve] : in duple or quadruple time with the beat represented by the half note instead of the quarter note

²alla breve *n* : the sign ₵ marking a piece or passage to be played alla breve; *also* : a passage so marked

Al·lah \'al-ə\ *n* [Ar *Allāh*] : the Supreme Being of the Muslims

all–Amer·i·can \,ȯl-ə-'mer-ə-kən\ *adj* **1** : composed wholly of American elements **2** : representative of the U.S. as a whole; *esp* : selected as the best in the U.S.

al·lan·to·is \ə-'lant-ə-wəs\ *n, pl* **al·lan·to·ides** \,al-ən-'tō-ə-,dēz\ : a vascular fetal membrane of higher vertebrates formed as a pouch from the hindgut and associated with the chorion in formation of the placenta in mammals — **al·lan·to·ic** \,al-ən-'tō-ik\ *adj*

al·lar·gan·do \,äl-,är-'gän-dō\ *adv* (*or adj*) [It, lit., widening] : gradually slower with crescendo — used as a direction in music

all–around \,ȯl-ə-'raùnd\ *adj* **1** : competent in many fields **2** : having general utility

al·lay \ə-'lā\ *vt* **-layed**; **-lay·ing** [OE *ālecgan*, fr. *ā-*, prefix denoting completion + *lecgan* to lay] **1** : to make less severe : RELIEVE ⟨*allay* pain⟩ **2** : to make quiet : CALM ⟨*allay* anxiety⟩

all but *adv* : very nearly : ALMOST

all clear *n* : a signal that a danger has passed

al·le·ga·tion \,al-i-'gā-shən\ *n* **1** : the act of alleging **2** : something alleged : **a** : a positive assertion **b** : a statement by a party to a legal action of what he undertakes to prove **c** : an assertion unsupported by proof or evidence

al·lege \ə-'lej\ *vt* [OF *alleguer*, fr. L *allegare* to dispatch, cite, fr. *ad-* + *legare* to depute] **1** : to state positively but without proof or before attempting to prove : DECLARE ⟨*allege* a person's guilt⟩ **2** : to offer as a reason or an excuse ⟨*allege* illness in order to avoid work⟩ — **al·leg·ed·ly** \ə-'lej-əd-lē\ *adv*

al·le·giance \ə-'lē-jən(t)s\ *n* [ME *allegeaunce*, modif. of MF *ligeance*, fr. *liege, lige* liege] **1** : the obligation of fidelity and obedience owed by a subject or citizen to his sovereign or government **2** : devotion or loyalty to a person, group, or cause **syn** see FIDELITY

al·le·gor·i·cal \,al-ə-'gȯr-i-kəl, -'gär-\ *adj* : consisting of or containing allegory : having the characteristics of allegory ⟨an *allegorical* tale⟩ — **al·le·gor·i·cal·ly** \-i-k(ə-)lē\ *adv* — **al·le·gor·i·cal·ness** \-kəl-nəs\ *n*

al·le·go·rist \'al-ə-,gȯr-əst, -,gȯr-\ *n* : a writer of allegory

al·le·go·rize \'al-ə-,gȯr-,īz, -,gȯr-; -gə-,rīz\ *vt* **1** : to make into allegory **2** : to treat or explain as allegory — **al·le·go·ri·za·tion** \,al-ə-,gȯr-ə-'zā-shən, -,gȯr-\ *n* — **al·le·go·riz·er** *n*

al·le·go·ry \'al-ə-,gȯr-ē, -,gȯr-\ *n, pl* **-ries** [Gk *allēgoria*, fr. *allēgorein* to speak figuratively, fr. *allos* other + *-agorein* to speak, fr. *agora* public assembly] : a story in which the characters and events are symbols expressing truths about human life

al·le·gret·to \,al-ə-'gret-ō\ *adv* (*or adj*) : faster than andante but not so fast as allegro — used as a direction in music

¹al·le·gro \ə-'leg-rō, -'lā-grō\ *adv* (*or adj*) [It, lit., merry] : in a brisk lively manner — used as a direction in music

²allegro *n, pl* **-gros** : a piece or movement in allegro tempo

al·lele \ə-'lēl\ *n* [G *allel*, short for *allelomorph*, fr. Gk *allēlōn* of one another + *morphē* form] **1** : either of a pair of characters inherited alternatively — compare MENDEL'S LAW **2** : a gene that is the vehicle of an allele — **al·le·lic** \-'lē-lik, -'lel-ik\ *adj* — **al·lel·ism** \-'lēl-,iz-əm\ *n*

al·le·lo·morph \ə-'lel-ə-,mȯrf, -'lē-lə-\ *n* : ALLELE — **al·le·lo·mor·phic** \ə-,lel-ə-'mȯr-fik, -,lē-lə-\ *adj* — **al·le·lo·mor·phism** \ə-'lel-ə-,mȯr-,fiz-əm, -'lē-lə-\ *n*

al·le·lu·ia \,al-ə-'lü-yə\ *interj* : HALLELUJAH

al·le·mande \,al-ə-'mand\ *n, often cap* [F, fr. fem. of *allemand* German] **1 a** : a 17th and 18th century court dance developed in France from a German folk dance **b** : a step with arms interlaced **2** : music for the allemande

al·ler·gen \'al-ər-jən\ *n* : a substance that induces allergy — **al·ler·gen·ic** \,al-ər-'jen-ik\ *adj*

al·ler·gic \ə-'lər-jik\ *adj* **1** : of, relating to, or inducing allergy **2** : disagreeably sensitive : ANTIPATHETIC

al·ler·gist \'al-ər-jəst\ *n* : a specialist in allergy

al·ler·gy \'al-ər-jē\ *n, pl* **-gies** [G *allergie*, fr. Gk *allos* other + *ergon* work] **1 a** : altered bodily reactivity (as to antigens) **b** : exaggerated or abnormal reaction (as by sneezing, itching, or rashes) to substances, situations, or physical states that are harmless to most people **2 :** a feeling of dislike

al·le·vi·ate \ə-'lē-vē-,āt\ *vt* [L *levis* light] **1 :** to make easier to be endured **:** RELIEVE 〈*alleviate* pain〉 **2 :** to remove or correct in part **:** lessen the presence of 〈*alleviate* a labor shortage〉 **syn** see RELIEVE — **al·le·vi·a·tion** \ə-,lē-vē-'ā-shən\ *n*

¹**al·ley** \'al-ē\ *n, pl* **al·leys** [MF *alee,* fr. *aler* to go, modif. of L *ambulare* to walk] **1 :** a garden or park walk bordered by trees or bushes **2 :** a place for bowling or skittles; *esp* **:** a hardwood lane for bowling **3 :** a narrow street or passageway between buildings; *esp* **:** one giving access to the rear of buildings

²**alley** *n, pl* **al·leys** [by shortening and alter. fr. *alabaster*] **:** a superior playing marble

al·ley·way \'al-ē-,wā\ *n* **1 :** a narrow passageway **2 :** ALLEY 3

All Fools' Day *n* **:** APRIL FOOLS' DAY

all fours *n pl* **:** all four legs of a quadruped or the two legs and two arms of a biped

all hail *interj* — used to express greeting, welcome, or acclamation

All·hal·lows \ȯl-'hal-ōz, -əz\ *n* **:** ALL SAINTS' DAY

al·li·ance \ə-'lī-ən(t)s\ *n* **1 a :** the state of being allied **:** the action of allying **b :** a union or connection between families, parties, or individuals **2 a :** an association to further the common interests of the members; *esp* **:** one formed by two or more nations usu. by treaty and often for their mutual assistance and protection **b :** a treaty of alliance **3 :** union by relationship in qualities **:** AFFINITY

al·lied \ə-'līd, 'al-,īd\ *adj* **1 :** JOINED, CONNECTED **2 a :** joined in alliance esp. by treaty 〈*allied* nations〉 **b** *cap* **:** of or relating to the nations united against the Central European powers in World War I or those united against the Axis powers in World War II **3 :** related esp. by common properties, characteristics, or ancestry

al·li·ga·tor \'al-ə-,gāt-ər\ *n* [Sp *el lagarto* the lizard] **1 :** either of two large short-legged reptiles resembling crocodiles but having a shorter and broader snout **2 :** leather made from alligator's hide

alligator pear *n* **:** AVOCADO

al·lit·er·ate \ə-'lit-ə-,rāt\ *vb* **1 :** to form an alliteration **2 :** to arrange so as to make alliteration

al·lit·er·a·tion \ə-,lit-ə-'rā-shən\ *n* [*ad-* + L *littera, litera* letter] **:** the repetition of a sound at the beginning of two or more neighboring words (as in *wild and woolly* or *a babbling brook*) — **al·lit·er·a·tive** \ə-'lit-ə-,rāt-iv\ *adj* — **al·lit·er·a·tive·ly** *adv*

allo- — see ALL-

al·lo·cate \'al-ə-,kāt\ *vt* **1 :** to apportion for a specific purpose or among particular persons or things **:** DISTRIBUTE 〈*allocate* funds among charities〉 **2 :** to set apart and designate **:** ASSIGN 〈*allocate* materials for a project〉 — **al·lo·ca·tion** \,al-ə-'kā-shən\ *n*

al·log·a·mous \ə-'läg-ə-məs\ *adj* **:** reproducing by cross-fertilization — **al·log·a·my** \-mē\ *n*

al·lom·e·try \ə-'läm-ə-trē\ *n* **:** relative growth of a part in relation to an entire organism; *also* **:** the measure and study of such growth — **al·lo·met·ric** \,al-ə-'me-trik\ *adj*

al·lo·pat·ric \,al-ə-'pa-trik\ *adj* **:** occurring in different areas or in isolation 〈*allopatric* speciation〉 — **al·lo·pat·ri·cal·ly** \-tri-k(ə-)lē\ *adv* — **al·lop·a·try** \ə-'läp-ə-trē\ *n*

al·lo·phone \'al-ə-,fōn\ *n* **:** one of two or more variants of the same phoneme 〈the /t/ of *tip* and the /t/ of *pit* are *allophones* of the phoneme *t*〉 — **al·lo·phon·ic** \,al-ə-'fän-ik\ *adj*

all-or-none \,ȯl-ər-'nən\ *adj* **:** marked either by entire or complete operation or effect or by none at all

al·lot \ə-'lät\ *vt* **al·lot·ted; al·lot·ting** **1 :** to assign as a share or portion **:** ALLOCATE 〈*allot* rooms in a dormitory〉 **2 :** to distribute by or as if by lot

syn APPORTION, ASSIGN **:** ALLOT may imply haphazard or arbitrary distribution; ASSIGN may stress an authoritative and fixed allotting without implying an even division; APPORTION implies a dividing according to some regular principle

al·lot·ment \ə-'lät-mənt\ *n* **1 :** the act of allotting **2 :** something that is allotted

al·lot·ro·py \ə-'lä-trə-pē\ *n* [Gk *tropos* way, manner] **:** the

existence of a chemical element in two or more different forms 〈diamond and graphite show the *allotropy* of carbon〉 — **al·lo·trope** \'al-ə-,trōp\ *n* — **al·lo·trop·ic** \,al-ə-'träp-ik\ *adj*

all out *adv* **:** with maximum effort

all-out \'ȯl-'aȯt\ *adj* **:** made with maximum effort **:** EXTREME

all over *adv* **:** EVERYWHERE

¹**all-over** \'ȯl-,ō-vər\ *adj* **:** covering the whole extent or surface

²**allover** *n* **1 :** an embroidered, printed, or lace fabric with a design covering most of the surface **2 :** a pattern or design repeated so as to cover the surface

al·low \ə-'laȯ\ *vb* [MF *alouer* to assign, allocate (fr. ML *allocare*) & *allouer* to approve, fr. L *allaudare,* fr. *ad-* + *laudare* to praise] **1 a :** to assign as a share or suitable amount (as of time or money) **b :** to allot as a deduction or an addition 〈*allow* a gallon for leakage〉 **2 :** ADMIT, CONCEDE **3 a :** PERMIT 〈gaps *allow* passage〉 〈refused to *allow* smoking〉 **b :** to neglect to restrain or prevent 〈*allow* the meat to burn〉 **4 :** to make allowance 〈*allow* for growth〉 **5** *dial* **:** SUPPOSE, CONSIDER

al·low·a·ble \ə-'laȯ-ə-bəl\ *adj* **:** not forbidden **:** not unlawful or improper **:** PERMISSIBLE 〈an *allowable* tax deduction〉 — **al·low·a·bly** \-blē\ *adv*

al·low·ance \ə-'laȯ-ən(t)s\ *n* **1 a :** a share or portion allotted or granted **b :** a sum granted as a reimbursement or bounty or for expenses **2 :** HANDICAP **3 :** an allowed dimensional difference between mating parts of a machine **4 :** the act of allowing **:** PERMISSION **5 :** the taking into account of things that may partly excuse an offense or mistake 〈make *allowances* for inexperience〉

¹**al·loy** \'al-,ȯi, ə-'lȯi\ *n* [MF *aloi,* fr. *alier, aloier* to ally, combine] **1 :** a substance composed of two or more metals or of a metal and a nonmetal united usu. by being melted together **2 :** a metal mixed with a more valuable metal to give a desired quality (as durability)

²**al·loy** \ə-'lȯi, 'al-,ȯi\ *vt* **1 :** to reduce the purity of by mixing with a less valuable metal **2 :** to mix so as to form an alloy **3 :** to debase by admixture

¹**all right** *adv* **1 :** SATISFACTORILY **2 :** very well **:** YES **3 :** beyond doubt **:** CERTAINLY

²**all right** *adj* **1 :** SATISFACTORY, CORRECT **2 :** SAFE, WELL **3** *slang* **:** GOOD, HONEST

all-round \'ȯl-'raȯnd\ *var of* ALL-AROUND

All Saints' Day *n* **:** November 1 observed as a church festival in honor of the saints

All Souls' Day *n* **:** November 2 observed in some churches as a day of prayer for the souls in purgatory

all·spice \'ȯl-,spīs\ *n* **:** the berry of a West Indian tree of the myrtle family or a mildly pungent and aromatic spice prepared from it

all told *adv* **:** with everything counted **:** in all

al·lude \ə-'lüd\ *vi* [L *allus-, alludere* to play on or with, fr. *ad-* + *ludere* to play] **:** to make indirect reference 〈*alluding* to a recent scandal〉 **syn** see REFER

¹**al·lure** \ə-'lu̇(ə)r\ *vt* **:** to entice by charm or attraction

²**allure** *n* **:** ATTRACTION, CHARM

al·lure·ment \ə-'lu̇(ə)r-mənt\ *n* **1 :** the action of alluring **:** FASCINATION **2 :** something that allures **:** ATTRACTION

al·lu·sion \ə-'lü-zhən\ *n* **1 :** the act of alluding or hinting **2 :** an implied or indirect reference — **al·lu·sive** \ə-'lü-siv, -ziv\ *adj* — **al·lu·sive·ly** *adv* — **al·lu·sive·ness** *n*

al·lu·vi·al \ə-'lü-vē-əl\ *adj* **:** relating to, composed of, or found in alluvium

al·lu·vi·um \-vē-əm\ *n, pl* **-vi·ums** *or* **-via** \-vē-ə\ [LL, neut. of *alluvius* alluvial, fr. L *alluere* to wash against, fr. *ad-* + *lavere* to wash] **:** soil material (as clay, silt, sand, or gravel) deposited by running water

¹**al·ly** \ə-'lī, 'al-,ī\ *vb* **al·lied; al·ly·ing** [OF *alier,* fr. L *alligare* to bind to, fr. *ad-* + *ligare* to bind] **1 :** to form (as by marriage or treaty) a connection between **:** join in an alliance **:** UNITE **2 :** to form (as by likeness or compatibility) a relation between

²**al·ly** \'al-,ī, ə-'lī\ *n, pl* **al·lies** **1 :** a plant or animal linked to another by genetic or evolutionary relationship **2 a :** one associated or united with another for some common purpose; *esp* **:** a nation that has joined an alliance **b** *pl, cap* **:** the Allied nations in World War I or World War II

ə abut; ᵊ kitten; ər further; a back; ā bake; ä cot, cart; aȯ out; ch chin; e less; ē easy; g gift; i trip; ī life

-al·ly \(-ə-)lē\ *adv suffix* [¹-*al* + -*ly*] : ²-LY ⟨terrifi*cally*⟩ — in adverbs formed from adjectives in -*ic* with no alternative form in -*ical*

al·ma ma·ter \ˌal-mə-'mät-ər\ *n* [L, fostering mother] : a school, college, or university that one has attended

al·ma·nac \'ȯl-mə-ˌnak, 'al-\ *n* [ML *almanach*, of Arabic origin] **1** : a publication containing astronomical and meteorological data arranged according to the days, weeks, and months of the year and often including a miscellany of other information **2** : a publication containing statistical, tabular, and general information

al·man·dine \'al-mən-ˌdēn\ *n* : ALMANDITE

al·man·dite \-ˌdīt\ *n* : a deep red garnet containing iron and aluminum

al·mighty \ȯl-'mīt-ē\ *adj* **1** *often cap* : having absolute power over all ⟨*Almighty* God⟩ **2** : relatively unlimited in power

Almighty *n* : ²GOD — used with *the*

al·mond \'äm-ənd, 'am-; 'al-mənd\ *n* [OF *almande*, fr. LL *amandula*, alteration of L *amygdala*, fr. Gk *amygdalē*] : a small tree of the rose family having flowers like those of a peach tree; *also* : the edible kernel of its fruit used as a nut

almond eye *n* : a somewhat triangular obliquely set eye — **al·mond-eyed** \-'īd\ *adj*

al·mo·ner \'al-mə-nər, 'äm-ə-\ *n* : a person who distributes alms for someone else ⟨the king's *almoner*⟩

al·most \'ȯl-ˌmōst, ȯl-'\ *adv* : only a little less than : NEARLY

alms \'ämz, 'älmz\ *n, pl* **alms** [OE *ælmesse*, fr. LL *eleēmosyna*, fr. Gk *eleēmosynē* mercy, alms, fr. *eleein* to have mercy] : something and esp. money given freely to help the poor — **alms·giv·er** \-ˌgiv-ər\ *n* — **alms·giv·ing** \-ˌgiv-iŋ\ *n*

alms·house \-ˌhaús\ *n* **1** *Brit* : a privately endowed home for the poor **2** : POORHOUSE

al·ni·co \'al-ni-ˌkō\ *n* : a powerful permanent-magnet alloy containing iron, nickel, aluminum, and one or more of the elements cobalt, copper, and titanium

al·oe \'al-ō\ *n* : any of a large genus of succulent chiefly southern African plants of the lily family with spikes of often showy flowers; *also* : the dried bitter juice of the leaves of an aloe used as a purgative and tonic — usu. used in pl. but sing. in constr.

aloft \ə-'lȯft\ *adv* (*or adj*) [ON *ā lopt*, fr. *ā* in + *lopt* air] **1** : at or to a great height **2** : in the air; *esp* : in flight **3** : at, on, or to the masthead or the higher rigging

alo·ha \ə-'lō-ə, ä-'lō-ˌhä\ *interj* [Hawaiian, lit., love] — used to express greeting or farewell

¹alone \ə-'lōn\ *adj* [ME, fr. *al* all + *one* one] **1** : separated from others : ISOLATED **2** : exclusive of anyone or anything else

syn LONELY, LONESOME: ALONE stresses the objective fact of being entirely by oneself; LONELY adds the suggestion of longing for companionship; LONESOME may add an appearance of being deserted or desolate

²alone *adv* **1** : SOLELY, EXCLUSIVELY **2** : without company, aid, or support

¹along \ə-'lȯŋ\ *prep* [OE *andlang*, fr. *and-* against + *lang* long] **1** : lengthwise of : parallel with the length and direction of ⟨walk *along* the beach⟩ ⟨lined up *along* the wall⟩ **2** : in accordance with : IN ⟨research *along* several lines⟩

²along *adv* **1** : FORWARD, ON ⟨move *along*⟩ **2** : as a companion or associate ⟨brought his wife *along*⟩ ⟨work *along* with colleagues⟩ **3 a** : at or to an advanced point ⟨plans are far *along*⟩ **b** : throughout the time ⟨knew the truth all *along*⟩ **4** : at or on hand ⟨had his gun *along*⟩

along·shore \-ˌshō(ə)r, -ˌshó(ə)r\ *adv* (*or adj*) : along the shore or coast

¹along·side \-ˌsīd\ *adv* : along or close at the side : in parallel position

²alongside *prep* : side by side with; *esp* : parallel to

¹aloof \ə-'lüf\ *adv* [obs. *aloof* to windward] : at a distance : out of involvement ⟨stood *aloof* from their quarrels⟩

²aloof *adj* : removed or distant in interest or feeling : RESERVED ⟨a shy, *aloof* manner⟩ — **aloof·ly** *adv* — **aloof·ness** *n*

aloud \ə-'laúd\ *adv* **1** *archaic* : LOUDLY **2** : with the speaking voice

alp \'alp\ *n* **1** : a high rugged mountain **2** : a mountain pasture

al·paca \al-'pak-ə\ *n* [Sp, of AmerInd origin] **1** : a mammal with fine long woolly hair domesticated in Peru and related to the llama **2** : wool of the alpaca or a thin cloth made of it; *also* : a rayon or cotton imitation of this cloth

al·pen·horn \'al-pən-ˌhȯrn\ *or* **alp·horn** \'alp-ˌhȯrn\ *n* [G] : a long wooden horn used by Swiss herdsmen

al·pen·stock \'al-pən-ˌstäk\ *n* : a long iron-pointed staff used in mountain climbing

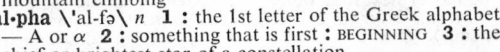

alpaca

al·pha \'al-fə\ *n* **1** : the 1st letter of the Greek alphabet — A or α **2** : something that is first : BEGINNING **3** : the chief or brightest star of a constellation

al·pha·bet \'al-fə-ˌbet, -bət\ *n* [Gk *alphabētos*, fr. *alpha* + *bēta* beta] **1** : the characters (as letters) of a written language arranged in their customary order **2** : a system of signs or signals that serve as equivalents for letters

al·pha·bet·ic \ˌal-fə-'bet-ik\ *adj* **1** : of, relating to, or employing an alphabet **2** : arranged in the order of the letters of the alphabet — **al·pha·bet·i·cal** \-'bet-i-kəl\ *adj* — **al·pha·bet·i·cal·ly** \-i-k(ə-)lē\ *adv*

al·pha·bet·ize \'al-fə-bə-ˌtīz\ *vt* : to arrange in alphabetic order — **al·pha·bet·i·za·tion** \ˌal-fə-ˌbet-ə-'zā-shən\ *n* — **al·pha·bet·iz·er** \'al-fə-bə-ˌtī-zər\ *n*

alpha particle *n* : a positively charged particle that is identical with the nucleus of a helium atom, consists of 2 protons and 2 neutrons, and is ejected at high speed in various radioactive transformations

alpha ray *n* **1** : an alpha particle moving at high speed **2** : a stream of alpha particles — called also *alpha radiation*

al·pine \'al-ˌpīn\ *n* : a plant native to alpine or boreal regions

Alpine *adj* **1** *often not cap* **a** : relating to or resembling the Alps or any mountains **b** : of, relating to, or growing on upland slopes above timberline **2** : of or relating to a central and southeastern European human Caucasoid stock marked by broad heads, stocky build, medium height, and brown hair and eyes

al·ready \ȯl-'red-ē, 'ȯl-ˌ\ *adv* **1** : before a stated or implied time : PREVIOUSLY ⟨when the firemen arrived the fire was *already* out⟩ **2** : so soon ⟨surprised to find it done *already*⟩

al·right \ȯl-'rīt\ *adv* (*or adj*) : all right

Al·sa·tian \al-'sā-shən\ *n* : GERMAN SHEPHERD

al·sike clover \'al-ˌsak-, -ˌsīk-\ *n* : a European perennial clover widely grown as a forage plant

al·so \'ȯl-sō\ *adv* **1** : LIKEWISE **2** : in addition : TOO

al·so-ran \-ˌran\ *n* **1** : a horse or dog that finishes out of the money in a race **2** : a contestant that does not win

Al·ta·ic \al-'tā-ik\ *n* [*Altai* mountains, Asia] : a language family comprising the Turkic, Tungusic, and Mongolic subfamilies — **Altaic** *adj*

Al·tair \al-'tī(ə)r\ *n* [Ar *al-ṭā'ir*, lit., the flier] : the first-magnitude star in Aquila

al·tar \'ȯl-tər\ *n* [OE, fr. L *altare*] **1** : a usu. raised structure or place on which sacrifices are offered or incense is burned in worship — see BASILICA illustration **2** : a usu. enclosed table used in consecrating the eucharistic elements or as a center of worship or ritual

altar boy *n* : ACOLYTE 1

altar call *n* : an appeal by an evangelist to worshipers to come forward and commit their lives to Christ

altar of repose *often cap A&R* : REPOSITORY 2

al·tar·piece \'ȯl-tər-ˌpēs\ *n* : a work of art to decorate the space above and behind the altar

altar rail *n* : a railing in front of an altar separating the chancel from the body of the church

altar stone *n* : a consecrated stone fixed in or forming the top of an altar or used as a portable altar

al·ter \'ȯl-tər\ *vb* [L *alterare*, fr. *alter* the other of two; akin to E *else*] **1** : to change partly but not completely : make or become different in some details ⟨*alter* a dress⟩ ⟨my opinion on that question has never *altered*⟩ **2** : CASTRATE, SPAY **syn** see CHANGE — **al·ter·a·bil·i·ty** \ˌȯl-tə-rə-'bil-ət-ē\ *n* — **al·ter·a·ble** \'ȯl-tə-rə-bəl\ *adj* — **al·ter·a·bly** \-blē\ *adv*

al·ter·ation \ˌȯl-tə-'rā-shən\ *n* **1 a** : the act or process of altering **b** : the state of being altered **2** : the result of altering : MODIFICATION

al·ter·ca·tion \ˌȯl-tər-'kā-shən\ *n* [L *altercari* to wrangle, fr. *alter* the other] : a noisy or angry dispute : WRANGLE

al·ter ego \ˌȯl-tər-'ē-gō, -'eg-ō\ *n* [L, lit., second I] : a second self; *esp* : a trusted friend

¹al·ter·nate \ˌȯl-tər-nət, 'al-\ *adj* [L *alternatus*, pp. of *alternare* to alternate, fr. *alternus* alternate, fr. *alter* the other] **1** : occurring or succeeding by turns ⟨*alternate* sunshine and rain⟩ **2 a** : occurring first on one side and then on the other at different levels along an axis ⟨leaves *alternate*⟩ — compare OPPOSITE **b** : arranged one above, beside, or next to another in regularly recurring sequence ⟨*alternate* layers of cake and filling⟩ ⟨*alternate* stamens and petals⟩ **3** : every other : every second ⟨delivery on *alternate* days⟩ **4** : ALTERNATIVE, SUBSTITUTE — **al·ter·nate·ly** *adv*

²al·ter·nate \-ˌnāt\ *vb* **1** : to do, occur, or act by turns **2** : to cause to alternate

³al·ter·nate \-nət\ *n* **1** : ALTERNATIVE **2** : one that alternates with another; *esp* : a person named to take the place of another whenever necessary ⟨delegates and *alternates* at a convention⟩

alternate angle *n* : either of a pair of angles that are on opposite sides of a transversal at its intersections with two other lines and that are either both within or both without the two intersected lines

a, a′, and *b, b′,* alternate interior angles; *c, c′,* and *d, d′,* alternate exterior angles

alternating current *n* : an electric current that reverses its direction at regular intervals — abbr. *AC*

al·ter·na·tion \ˌȯl-tər-'nā-shən, ˌal-\ *n* **1** : the act or process of alternating **2** : alternate position or occurrence : SUCCESSION **3** : regular reversal in direction of flow ⟨an *alternation* of an electric current⟩

alternation of generations : the alternate occurrence of two or more forms and esp. of a sexual and an asexual generation in the life cycle of a plant or animal

¹al·ter·na·tive \ȯl-'tər-nət-iv, al-\ *adj* **1** : offering or expressing a choice ⟨*alternative* plans⟩ **2** : ALTERNATE — **al·ter·na·tive·ly** *adv* — **al·ter·na·tive·ness** *n*

²alternative *n* **1** : a chance to choose between two things ⟨the *alternative* of going by train or by automobile⟩ **2** : one of the two or sometimes more things between which a choice is to be made **syn** see CHOICE

al·ter·na·tor \'ȯl-tər-ˌnāt-ər, 'al-\ *n* : an electric generator for producing alternating current

alt·horn \'alt-ˌhȯrn\ *n* [G, fr. *alt* alto + *horn* horn] : the alto member of the saxhorn family used chiefly in bands where it often replaces the French horn

al·though *also* **al·tho** \ȯl-'t͟hō\ *conj* : in spite of the fact that : THOUGH

al·tim·e·ter \al-'tim-ət-ər, 'al-tə-ˌmēt-ər\ *n* : an instrument for measuring altitude; *esp* : an aneroid barometer that registers changes in atmospheric pressure accompanying changes in altitude

al·ti·tude \'al-tə-ˌt(y)üd\ *n* [L *altitudo* height, fr. *altus* high; akin to E *old*] **1 a** : the angular height of a celestial object above the horizon **b** : the vertical distance of an object above sea level **c** : the perpendicular distance from the base of a geometric figure to the vertex or to the side parallel to the base **2 a** : vertical distance or extent **b** : position at a height **c** : an elevated region : EMINENCE — usu. used in pl. **syn** see HEIGHT — **al·ti·tu·di·nal** \ˌal-tə-'t(y)üd-nəl, -ᵊn-əl\ *adj*

al·to \'al-tō\ *n, pl* **altos** [It, lit., high, fr. L *altus*] **1 a** : CONTRALTO **b** : the second highest of the four voice parts of the mixed chorus **2** : the second highest member of a family of musical instruments; *esp* : ALTHORN

al·to·cu·mu·lus \ˌal-tō-'kyü-myə-ləs\ *n* : a fleecy cloud formation consisting of large whitish globular cloudlets with shaded portions

al·to·geth·er \ˌȯl-tə-'geth-ər\ *adv* **1** : WHOLLY, THOROUGHLY **2** : on the whole

al·to·stra·tus \ˌal-tō-'strāt-əs, -'strat-\ *n* : a cloud formation similar to cirrostratus but darker and at a lower level

al·tri·cial \al-'trish-əl\ *adj* [L *altric-, altrix* nurse, fr. *alere* to nourish] : having the young hatched in a very immature and helpless condition so as to require care for some time — compare PRECOCIAL

al·tru·ism \'al-trü-ˌiz-əm\ *n* [F *altruisme*, fr. *autrui* other people, fr. OF, oblique case form of *autre* other, fr. L *alter* the other] : unselfish interest in or care for the welfare of others — **al·tru·ist** \-trü-əst\ *n* — **al·tru·is·tic** \ˌal-trü-'is-tik\ *adj* — **al·tru·is·ti·cal·ly** \-'is-ti-k(ə-)lē\ *adv*

al·um \'al-əm\ *n* [MF, fr. L *alumin-, alumen*] **1** : either of two colorless crystalline compounds containing aluminum KAl(SO₄)₂.12H₂O or NH₄Al(SO₄)₂.12H₂O that have a sweetish-sourish taste and a puckering effect on the mouth and are used in medicine (as to check local sweating or to stop bleeding) **2** : an aluminum compound Al₂(SO₄)₃ made from bauxite and used in paper manufacture, dyeing, and sewage treatment

alu·mi·na \ə-'lü-mə-nə\ *n* : the oxide of aluminum Al₂O₃ that occurs native as corundum and in bauxite and is used as a source of aluminum, as an abrasive, and as an absorbent

al·u·min·i·um \ˌal-yə-'min-ē-əm\ *n, chiefly Brit* : ALUMINUM

alu·mi·nize \ə-'lü-mə-ˌnīz\ *vt* : to treat or coat with aluminum

alu·mi·num \ə-'lü-mə-nəm\ *n* : a silver-white malleable ductile light metallic element with good electrical and thermal conductivity and resistance to oxidation that is the most abundant metal in the earth's crust — see ELEMENT table

aluminum hydroxide *n* : a compound Al(OH)₃ that is a hydrated form of alumina, acts as both an acid and a base, and is used as a mordant

aluminum oxide *n* : ALUMINA

alum·na \ə-'ləm-nə\ *n, pl* **-nae** \-(ˌ)nē\ : a girl or woman who has attended or has graduated from a particular school, college, or university

alum·nus \ə-'ləm-nəs\ *n, pl* **-ni** \-ˌnī\ [L, foster son, pupil, fr. *alere* to nourish] : one that has attended or graduated from a particular school, college, or university

al·ve·o·lar \al-'vē-ə-lər\ *adj* **1** : of, relating to, resembling, or having alveoli **2** : pronounced with the tip of the tongue touching or near the teethridge — **al·ve·o·lar·ly** *adv*

al·ve·o·lus \al-'vē-ə-ləs\ *n, pl* **-li** \-ˌlī, -(ˌ)lē\ [L, dim. of *alveus* cavity, fr. *alvus* belly] **1** : a small cavity or pit: as **a** : a socket for a tooth **b** : an air cell of the lungs **c** : a group of secretory cells about a central space in a compound gland **d** : a cell of a honeycomb **2** : TEETHRIDGE

al·way \'ȯl-ˌwā\ *adv, archaic* : ALWAYS

al·ways \'ȯl-wēz, -wəz, -ˌwāz\ *adv* **1** : at all times : INVARIABLY **2** : FOREVER, PERPETUALLY

alys·sum \ə-'lis-əm\ *n* [Gk *alysson*, plant believed to cure rabies, fr. *a-* ²a- + *lyssa* rabies] **1** : any of a genus of Old World herbs of the mustard family with small yellow flowers **2** : SWEET ALYSSUM

am [OE *eom; akin to E is*] *pres 1st sing of* BE

amah \'äm-ə, 'äm-ˌä\ *n* [Pg *ama* nurse] : an Oriental female servant; *esp* : a Chinese nurse

amain \ə-'mān\ *adv* **1** : with all one's might **2 a** : at full speed **b** : in great haste

amal·gam \ə-'mal-gəm\ *n* [ML *amalgama*] **1** : an alloy of mercury with some other metal or metals that is used for tooth filling **2** : a combination or mixture of different elements

amal·ga·mate \ə-'mal-gə-ˌmāt\ *vb* : to unite in or as if in an amalgam; *esp* : to combine into a single body — **amal·ga·ma·tor** \-ˌmāt-ər\ *n*

amal·ga·ma·tion \ə-ˌmal-gə-'mā-shən\ *n* **1 a** : the act or process of amalgamating ⟨made by the *amalgamation* of mercury with silver⟩ **b** : the state of being amalgamated **2** : the result of amalgamating; *esp* : a combination of different elements (as races or business corporations) into a single body — **amal·ga·ma·tive** \-'mal-gə-ˌmāt-iv\ *adj*

am·a·ni·ta \ˌam-ə-'nīt-ə, -'nēt-\ *n* : any of various mostly poisonous white-spored fungi with a bulbous sac about the base of the stem

aman·u·en·sis \ə-ˌman-yə-'wen(t)-səs\ *n, pl* **aman·u·en·ses** \-'wen(t)-ˌsēz\ [L, fr. *servus a manu* slave with secretarial duties] : a person employed to write from dictation or to copy manuscript : SECRETARY

ə abut; ᵊ kitten; ər further; a back; ā bake; ä cot, cart; au̇ out; ch chin; e less; ē easy; g gift; i trip; ī life

am·a·ranth \'am-ə-,ran(t)th\ *n* [Gk *amaranton*, a flower, fr. *a-* ²a- + *marainein* to wither, fade] **1** : an imaginary flower that never fades **2** : any of a large genus of coarse herbs including pigweeds and various forms cultivated for their showy flowers or for color

am·a·ran·thine \,am-ə-'ran(t)-thən, -'ran-,thīn\ *adj* : relating to or resembling amaranth : UNFADING, UNDYING

am·a·ryl·lis \,am-ə-'ril-əs\ *n* : any of various plants of a family related to the lily family; *esp* : any of several African bulbous herbs grown for their umbels of large showy flowers

amass \ə-'mas\ *vt* **1** : to collect for oneself : ACCUMULATE **2** : to pile up into a mass ⟨*amass* statistics from many sources⟩ **syn** see ACCUMULATE — **amass·er** *n*

am·a·teur \'am-ə-,tər, -ət-ər, -ə-,t(y)ú(ə)r\ *n* [F, lit., lover, fr. L *amator*, fr. *amare* to love] **1** : a person who takes part in sports or occupations for pleasure and not for pay **2** : a person who engages in something without experience or competence ⟨mistakes that would only be made by an *amateur*⟩ — **amateur** *adj* — **am·a·teur·ish** \,am-ə-'tər-ish, -'t(y)ú(ə)r-ish\ *adj* — **am·a·teur·ish·ly** *adv* — **am·a·teur·ish·ness** *n* — **am·a·teur·ism** \'am-ə-,tər-,iz-əm, -ət-ər-, -ə-,t(y)ú(ə)r-\ *n*

am·a·to·ry \'am-ə-,tōr-ē, -,tòr-\ *adj* : of, relating to, or expressing sexual love

amaze \ə-'māz\ *vt* [OE *āmasian*] : to surprise or astonish greatly : fill with wonder : ASTOUND

amaze·ment \ə-'māz-mənt\ *n* : great surprise or astonishment

amaz·ing *adj* : causing amazement or wonder — **amaz·ing·ly** \-'mā-ziŋ-lē\ *adv*

am·a·zon \'am-ə-,zän, -ə-zən\ *n* **1** *cap* : a member of a race of female warriors repeatedly warring with the ancient Greeks of mythology **2** : a tall strong masculine woman

Am·a·zo·ni·an \,am-ə-'zō-nē-ən, -,zō-nyən\ *adj* **1 a** : of, relating to, or resembling an Amazon **b** *not cap* : MASCULINE, WARLIKE ⟨*amazonian* women⟩ **2** : of or relating to the Amazon river or its valley

am·a·zon·ite \'am-ə-zə-,nīt\ *or* **am·a·zon·stone** \-zən-,stōn\ *n* : a green microcline

am·bas·sa·dor \am-'bas-əd-ər\ *n* [MF *ambassadeur*, of Gmc origin] **1** : an official envoy; *esp* : a diplomatic agent of the highest rank accredited to a foreign sovereign or government as the resident representative of his own sovereign or government or appointed for a special and often temporary diplomatic assignment **2** : an authorized representative or messenger — **am·bas·sa·do·ri·al** \(,)am-,bas-ə-'dōr-ē-əl, -'dòr-\ *adj* — **am·bas·sa·dor·ship** \am-'bas-əd-ər-,ship\ *n*

am·bas·sa·dress \-'bas-ə-drəs\ *n* : a female ambassador

¹am·ber \'am-bər\ *n* [MF *ambre*, fr. ML *ambra*, fr. Ar 'anbar *ambergris*] **1** : a hard yellowish to brownish translucent resin from trees long dead that takes a fine polish and is used in making ornamental objects (as beads) **2** : a variable color averaging a dark orange yellow

²amber *adj* **1** : consisting of amber **2** : having the color amber

am·ber·gris \'am-bər-,gris, -,grēs\ *n* [MF *ambre gris*, lit., gray amber] : a waxy substance from the sperm whale used in the manufacture of perfumes

ambi- *prefix* [L, both, around; akin to E *by*] : both ⟨*ambivalent*⟩

am·bi·dex·trous \,am-bi-'dek-strəs\ *adj* [L *ambi-* + *dextera* right hand] **1** : using both hands with equal ease **2** : unusually skillful : VERSATILE **3** : characterized by duplicity : DOUBLE-DEALING — **am·bi·dex·trous·ly** *adv*

am·bi·ence *or* **am·bi·ance** \äⁿ-byäⁿs, 'am-bē-ən(t)s\ *n* : a surrounding or pervading atmosphere : ENVIRONMENT

am·bi·ent \'am-bē-ənt\ *adj* : surrounding on all sides : ENCOMPASSING

am·bi·gu·i·ty \,am-bə-'gyü-ət-ē\ *n, pl* **-ties** **1** : uncertainty or confusion of meaning (as of a word or phrase) **2** : an ambiguous word or passage

am·big·u·ous \am-'big-yə-wəs\ *adj* [L *ambigere* to wander about, fr. *ambi-* around + *agere* to lead, drive] : not clear in meaning because able to be understood in more than one way : EQUIVOCAL — **am·big·u·ous·ly** *adv* — **am·big·u·ous·ness** *n*

am·bi·tion \am-'bish-ən\ *n* [L *ambition-, ambitio* canvass for votes, lit., going around, fr. *ambire* to go around, fr.

ambi- around + *ire* to go] **1 a** : an ardent desire for rank, fame, or power **b** : desire to achieve a particular end : ASPIRATION **2** : the object of ambition **syn** ASPIRATION: AMBITION implies a strong desire for personal advancement and may apply either to a praiseworthy or an inordinate and ruthless desire; ASPIRATION implies a striving after something higher than oneself or one's status which may be admirable and ennobling or idle and presumptuous

am·bi·tious \am-'bish-əs\ *adj* **1** : stirred by or possessing ambition ⟨*ambitious* to be captain of the team⟩ **2** : showing ambition ⟨an *ambitious* plan⟩ — **am·bi·tious·ly** *adv*

am·biv·a·lence \am-'biv-ə-lən(t)s\ *n* : simultaneous attraction toward and repulsion from something or someone — **am·biv·a·lent** \-lənt\ *adj* — **am·biv·a·lent·ly** *adv*

am·bi·vert \'am-bi-,vərt\ *n* : a person having characteristics of both extrovert and introvert — **am·bi·ver·sion** \,am-bi-'vər-zhən\ *n* — **am·bi·ver·sive** \-'vər-siv, -ziv\ *adj*

¹am·ble \'am-bəl\ *vi* **am·bled**; **am·bling** \-b(ə-)liŋ\ [L *ambulare* to walk, fr. *ambi-* around] : to go at an amble : SAUNTER — **am·bler** \-b(ə-)lər\ *n*

²amble *n* **1** : an easy gait of a horse in which the legs on the same side of the body move together **2** : a gentle easy gait

am·bro·sia \am-'brō-zh(ē-)ə\ *n* [Gk, lit., immortality, fr. *ambrotos* immortal, fr. *a-* ²a- + *-mbrotos* mortal; akin to E *murder*] **1** : the food of the Greek and Roman gods **2** : something extremely pleasing to taste or smell — **am·bro·sial** \-zh(ē-)əl\ *adj* — **am·bro·sial·ly** \-ē-\ *adv*

am·bu·lance \'am-byə-lən(t)s\ *n* : a vehicle equipped for transporting the injured or the sick

am·bu·lant \'am-byə-lənt\ *adj* : moving about : AMBULATORY

¹am·bu·la·to·ry \'am-byə-lə-,tōr-ē, -,tòr-\ *adj* **1** : of, relating to, or adapted to walking **2** : able to walk about ⟨*ambulatory* patients in a hospital⟩

²ambulatory *n, pl* **-ries** : a sheltered place (as a cloister) for walking

am·bus·cade \'am-bə-,skäd\ *n* : AMBUSH — **ambuscade** *vb* — **am·bus·cad·er** *n*

¹am·bush \'am-,bùsh\ *vt* [OF *embuschier*, fr. *en* in + *busche* firewood] **1** : to station in ambush **2** : to attack from an ambush : WAYLAY

²ambush *n* : a trap in which concealed persons lie in wait to attack by surprise; *also* : the persons so concealed or their position

am·bys·to·ma \am-'bis-tə-mə\ *n* : TIGER SALAMANDER

ame·ba, ame·ban, ame·bic, ame·boid *var of* AMOEBA, AMOEBAN, AMOEBIC, AMOEBOID

am·e·bi·a·sis \,am-i-'bī-ə-səs\ *n, pl* **-bi·a·ses** \-'bī-ə-,sēz\ : infection with or disease caused by amoebas

amebic dysentery *n* : acute intestinal amebiasis of man marked by dysentery, griping pain, and injury to the intestinal wall

ame·lio·rate \ə-'mēl-yə-,rāt\ *vb* [F *améliorer*, fr. *a-* ad- + L *melior* better] : to make or grow better or more tolerable — **ame·lio·ra·tion** \-,mēl-yə-'rā-shən\ *n* — **ame·lio·ra·tive** \-'mēl-yə-,rāt-iv\ *adj* — **ame·lio·ra·tor** \-,rāt-ər\ *n* — **ame·lio·ra·to·ry** \-rə-,tōr-ē, -,tòr-\ *adj*

amen \(')ā-'men, (')ä-; *in singing*, 'ä-\ *interj* [Heb *āmēn*] — used to express solemn agreement or hearty approval

ame·na·ble \ə-'mē-nə-bəl, -'men-ə-\ *adj* [MF *amener* to lead to, fr. *a-* ad- + *mener* to lead, fr. L *minare* to drive] **1** : subject to some authority and therefore liable to be called to account by it ⟨*amenable* to the law⟩ **2** : easily influenced or managed : RESPONSIVE ⟨amenable to discipline⟩ — **ame·na·bil·i·ty** \-,mē-nə-'bil-ət-ē, -,men-ə-\ *n* — **ame·na·bly** \-'mē-nə-blē, -'men-ə-\ *adv*

amen corner \,ā-,men-\ *n* : a conspicuous corner in a church occupied by fervent worshipers

amend \ə-'mend\ *vb* [OF *amender*, modification of L *emendare* to emend, fr. *ex-, e-* + *menda* fault] **1** : to put right; *esp* : to make emendations in **2 a** : to change for the better : IMPROVE **b** : to alter esp. in phraseology; *esp* : to alter formally by modification, deletion, or addition ⟨*amend* a legislative bill⟩ **syn** see CORRECT — **amend·a·ble** \-'men-də-bəl\ *adj* — **amen·da·to·ry** \-'men-də-,tōr-ē, -,tòr-\ *adj* — **amend·er** *n*

---

amend·ment \ə-'men(d)-mənt\ n 1 : the act or process of amending esp. for the better 2 : a modification, addition, or deletion (as to a law, bill, or motion) made or proposed ⟨a constitutional *amendment*⟩

amends \ə-'men(d)z\ n sing or pl : something done or given by a person to make up for a loss or injury he has caused ⟨make *amends* for an unkindness⟩

amen·i·ty \ə-'men-ət-ē, -'mē-nət-\ n, pl -ties [L amoenus pleasant] 1 : the quality of being pleasant or agreeable 2 : something (as a conventional social gesture) that adds to material comfort or convenience or to smoothness of social intercourse — usu. used in pl.

am·ent \'am-ənt, 'ā-mənt\ n : a flower cluster in which flowers all of one sex and without petals grow in close circular rows on a slender stalk (as in the alder, willow, birch, and poplar) : CATKIN — **am·en·ta·ceous** \,am-ən-'tā-shəs, ,ā-mən-\ adj — **am·en·tif·er·ous** \-'tif-(ə-)rəs\ adj

amerce \ə-'mərs\ vt [OF a merci at (one's) mercy] : to punish by a fine fixed in amount by the court — **amerce·ment** \-'mərs-mənt\ n — **amer·cia·ble** \-'mər-sē-ə-bəl, -'mər-shə-bəl\ adj

¹Amer·i·can \ə-'mer-ə-kən\ n : a native or inhabitant of No. America or So. America; esp : a citizen of the U.S.

²American adj 1 : of or relating to America or its inhabitants ⟨*American* coastline⟩ 2 : of or relating to the U.S., its possessions, original territory, or inhabitants

Amer·i·ca·na \ə-,mer-ə-'kan-ə, -'kän-ə, -'kā-nə\ n pl : materials concerning America, its civilization, or its culture; also : a collection of such materials

American chameleon n : a long-tailed lizard of the southeastern U.S. that can change its color

American Indian n : INDIAN 2a

Amer·i·can·ism \ə-'mer-ə-kə-,niz-əm\ n 1 : a characteristic feature of English as used in the U.S. 2 : attachment or loyalty to the traditions, interests, or ideals of the U.S. 3 : a custom or trait peculiar to the U.S. or to Americans

amer·i·can·ize \-kə-,nīz\ vb, often cap : to make or become American (as in customs, habits, dress, or speech) — **amer·i·can·i·za·tion** \ə-,mer-ə-kə-nə-'zā-shən\ n, often cap

American plan n : a hotel rate whereby guests are charged a fixed sum for room and meals combined — compare EUROPEAN PLAN

American Standard Version n : an American revision of the Authorized Version of the Bible published in 1901 — called also *American Revised Version*

am·er·i·ci·um \,am-ə-'ris(h)-ē-əm\ n : a radioactive metallic chemical element produced by bombardment of uranium with high-energy helium nuclei — see ELEMENT table

am·e·thyst \'am-ə-thəst\ n [Gk a- ²a- + methyein to be drunk; so called from its supposed efficacy as a remedy against drunkenness] 1 : a clear purple or bluish violet variety of crystallized quartz used as a jeweler's stone 2 : a variable color averaging a moderate purple

ami·a·ble \'ā-mē-ə-bəl\ adj [MF, fr. LL amicabilis friendly, fr. L amicus friend, fr. amare to love] : generally agreeable : having a friendly, sociable, and congenial disposition — **ami·a·bil·i·ty** \,ā-mē-ə-'bil-ət-ē\ n — **ami·a·ble·ness** n — **ami·a·bly** \-blē\ adv

am·i·ca·ble \'am-i-kə-bəl\ adj : characterized by friendship and goodwill : PEACEABLE ⟨an *amicable* settlement of differences⟩ — **am·i·ca·bil·i·ty** \,am-i-kə-'bil-ət-ē\ n — **am·i·ca·ble·ness** n — **am·i·ca·bly** \'am-i-kə-blē\ adv

am·ice \'am-əs\ n : a white linen cloth worn about the neck and shoulders under other vestments

amid \ə-'mid\ or **amidst** \-'midst\ prep : in or into the middle of : AMONG

am·ide \'am-,īd, -əd\ n [ammonia + -ide] : a compound resulting from replacement of an atom of hydrogen in ammonia by an element or radical or of one or more atoms of hydrogen in ammonia by univalent acid radicals

amid·ships \ə-'mid-,ships\ adv : in or near the middle of a ship

amine \ə-'mēn, 'am-ən\ n : any of various compounds derived from ammonia by replacement of hydrogen by one or more univalent hydrocarbon radicals

ami·no \ə-'mē-nō, 'am-ə-,nō\ adj : relating to or containing the group NH_2 united to a radical

amino acid n : any of numerous organic acids that contain the amino group NH_2 and include some which are the building blocks of proteins and are synthesized by living cells or are obtained as essential components of the diet

amir \ə-'mi(ə)r, ä-\ var of EMIR

Amish \'äm-ish, 'am-\ adj : of or relating to a strict Mennonite sect that settled in America — **Amish** n — **Amish·man** \-ish-mən\ n

¹amiss \ə-'mis\ adv 1 : WRONGLY, FAULTILY 2 : ASTRAY

²amiss adj : WRONG, FAULTY, IMPROPER ⟨something seems to be *amiss* here⟩

ami·to·sis \,ā-mī-'tō-səs\ n, pl -to·ses \-'tō-,sēz\ [²a- + mitosis] : cell division in which simple cleavage of the nucleus is followed by the division of the cytoplasm — **ami·tot·ic** \-'tät-ik\ adj — **ami·tot·i·cal·ly** \-'tät-i-k(ə-)lē\ adv

am·i·ty \'am-ət-ē\ n, pl -ties [MF amité, fr. ami friend, fr. L amicus] : FRIENDSHIP; esp : friendly relations between nations

am·me·ter \'am-,ēt-ər\ n : an instrument for measuring electric current in amperes

am·mo \'am-ō\ n, pl **ammos** : AMMUNITION

am·mo·nia \ə-'mō-nyə\ n [L sal ammoniacus sal ammoniac, lit., salt of Ammon; so called from its discovery near a temple of Ammon (Amon)] 1 : a colorless gas NH_3 that is a compound of nitrogen and hydrogen, has a sharp smell and taste, is very soluble in water, can be easily liquefied by cold and pressure, and is used in the manufacture of ice, fertilizers, and explosives 2 : a solution of ammonia in water — called also *ammonia water* — **am·mo·ni·a·cal** \,am-ə-'nī-ə-kəl\ adj

am·mo·ni·fi·ca·tion \ə-,mō-nə-fə-'kā-shən\ n : decomposition with production of ammonia or ammonium compounds esp. by the action of bacteria on nitrogenous organic matter — **am·mo·ni·fi·er** \ə-'mō-nə-,fī(-ə)r\ n — **am·mo·ni·fy** \-,fī\ vb

am·mo·nite \'am-ə-,nīt\ n [L cornu Ammonis, lit., horn of Ammon (Amon)] : any of numerous flat spiral fossil shells of mollusks esp. abundant in the Mesozoic — **am·mo·nit·ic** \,am-ə-'nit-ik\ adj

Am·mon·ite \'am-ə-,nīt\ n : a member of a Semitic people living in Old Testament times east of the Jordan between the Jabbok and the Arnon — **Ammonite** adj

am·mo·ni·um \ə-'mō-nē-əm\ n : an ion NH_4^+ or radical NH_4 derived from ammonia by combination with a hydrogen ion or atom and known in compounds (as ammonium chloride)

ammonium chloride n : a white crystalline volatile salt NH_4Cl used in dry cells and as an expectorant — called also *sal ammoniac*

ammonium hydroxide n : a compound NH_4OH that is formed when ammonia dissolves in water and that exists only in solution

ammonium nitrate n : a colorless crystalline salt NH_4NO_3 used in explosives and fertilizers

ammonium sulfate n : a colorless crystalline salt $(NH_4)_2SO_4$ used chiefly as a fertilizer

am·mo·noid \'am-ə-,nȯid\ n : AMMONITE

am·mu·ni·tion \,am-yə-'nish-ən\ n [obs. F amunition, alter. of munition] 1 : something that can be hurled at a target; esp : something (as a bullet, shell, grenade, or bomb) propelled by or containing explosives 2 : material that may be used (as in a controversy) in attack or defense

am·ne·sia \am-'nē-zhə\ n [Gk a- ²a- + mnēs-, mimnēskesthai to remember] : loss of memory due usu. to brain injury, shock, fatigue, repression, or illness — **am·ne·si·ac** \-z(h)ē-,ak\ or **am·ne·sic** \-zik, -sik\ adj or n

am·nes·ty \'am-nə-stē\ n, pl -ties [Gk amnēstia, lit., forgetting, fr. a- ²a- + mnēs-, mimnēskesthai to remember] : a general pardon granted by a ruler or government to a large group of persons guilty of a political offense (as treason or rebellion)

am·ni·on \'am-nē-,än, -ən\ n, pl **amnions** or **am·nia** \-nē-ə\ : a thin membrane forming a closed sac about the embryo of a reptile, bird, or mammal and containing a serous fluid in which the embryo is immersed — **am·ni·ote** \-nē-,ōt\ adj or n — **am·ni·ot·ic** \,am-nē-'ät-ik\ adj

---

ə abut; ᵊ kitten; ər further; a back; ā bake; ä cot, cart; aù out; ch chin; e less; ē easy; g gift; i trip; ī life

amoe·ba \ə-'mē-bə\ *n, pl* **amoebas** *or* **amoe·bae** \-(,)bē\ [Gk *amoibē* change] : any of numerous naked protozoans (group Rhizopoda) that have lobed and separate pseudopodia and no permanent cell organs or supporting structures and are widespread in fresh and salt water and in moist soils — **amoe·bic** \-bik\ *also* **amoe·ban** \-bən\ *adj*

amoe·boid \-,bȯid\ *adj* : resembling an amoeba esp. in moving or changing in shape by means of protoplasmic flow

amoeba: *1* nucleus, *2* contractile vacuole, *3* food vacuole

amok \ə-'mək, -'mäk\ *adv* [Malay] : in a murderously frenzied state or violently raging manner 〈run *amok*〉 — **amok** *adj*

Amon \'äm-ən\ *n* : a god of ancient Egypt worshiped in Thebes as a local deity and in the empire as a supreme deity identified with the sun-god Ra

among \ə-'məŋ\ *also* **amongst** \-'məŋ(k)st\ *prep* [OE *on gemonge* in the crowd] **1** : in or through the midst of 〈*among* the crowd〉 **2** : in company or association with 〈living *among* artists〉 **3** : by or through the whole or a large part of 〈discontent *among* the poor〉 **4** : in the number or class of 〈wittiest *among* poets〉 **5** : in shares to each of 〈divided *among* the heirs〉 **6** : through the reciprocal or joint action of 〈quarrel *among* themselves〉〈made a fortune *among* themselves〉 **syn** see BETWEEN

amon·til·la·do \ə-,män-tə-'läd-ō\ *n, pl* **-dos** [Sp, fr. *a* to + *montilla*, a sherry from Montilla, Spain] : a pale dry sherry

amor·al \(')ā-'mȯr-əl, (')a-, -'mär-\ *adj* [²a- + *moral*] : neither moral nor immoral; *esp* : outside the sphere to which moral judgments apply — **amor·al·ly** \-ə-lē\ *adv*

Am·o·rite \'am-ə-,rīt\ *n* : a member of one of various Semitic peoples living in Mesopotamia, Syria, and Palestine during the 3d and 2d millenniums B.C.; *esp* : one of the group founding the first Babylonian empire — **Amorite** *adj*

am·o·rous \'am-(ə-)rəs\ *adj* [L *amor* love, fr. *amare* to love] **1 a** : inclined to love : easily falling in love 〈of *amorous* nature〉 **b** : being in love : ENAMORED **2** : of, relating to, or caused by love 〈an *amorous* glance〉 — **am·o·rous·ly** *adv* — **am·o·rous·ness** *n*

amor·phous \ə-'mȯr-fəs\ *adj* [Gk *a-* ²a- + *morphē* form] : having no determinate form : SHAPELESS : as **a** : lacking complex bodily organization **b** : UNCRYSTALLIZED — **amor·phous·ly** *adv* — **amor·phous·ness** *n*

am·or·tize \'am-ər-,tīz, ə-'mȯr-,tīz\ *vt* : to extinguish (as a mortgage) usu. by payment on the principle at the time of each periodic interest payment — **am·or·ti·za·tion** \,am-ərt-ə-'zā-shən, ə-,mȯrt-ə-\ *n*

Amos \'ā-məs\ *n* **1** : a Hebrew prophet of the 8th century B.C. **2** — see BIBLE table

¹amount \ə-'maȯnt\ *vi* [OF *amonter*, fr. *amont* upward, fr. L *ad montem* to the mountain] **1** : to add up (the bill *amounted* to 10 dollars) **2** : to be equivalent 〈acts that *amount* to treason〉

²amount *n* **1** : the total number or quantity : AGGREGATE **2** : the whole effect, significance, or import **3** : a principal sum and the interest on it

syn NUMBER, QUANTITY: AMOUNT applies to what cannot be counted individually 〈*amount* of time〉〈*amount* of energy〉 NUMBER applies to what can be counted as members or units of an amount 〈*number* of hours worked〉〈*number* of stars〉 QUANTITY is used chiefly of things usually measured in bulk even though they may be counted; it may also refer to anything measurable in extent, duration, intensity, or value and suggests more precision than AMOUNT **syn** see in addition SUM

amour \ə-'mú(ə)r, a-, ä-\ *n* [F, love, fr. L *amor*] : a love affair; *esp* : a secret love affair

amour pro·pre \,am-,úr-'prōprᵊ\ *n* [F] : SELF-ESTEEM

am·per·age \'am-pə-rij, -,pi(ə)r-ij\ *n* : the strength of a current of electricity expressed in amperes

am·pere \'am-,pi(ə)r\ *n* [after André M. *Ampère d*1836 F physicist] : a unit of electric current that is equivalent to a flow of one coulomb per second or to the steady current produced by one volt applied across a resistance of one ohm

am·per·sand \'am-pər-,sand\ *n* [*and* (&) *per se and*, lit., (the character) & by itself (is the word) *and*] : a character & standing for the word *and*

am·phet·amine \am-'fet-ə-,mēn, -mən\ *n* : a compound $C_9H_{13}N$ used esp. as an inhalant and in solution as a spray in head colds and hay fever

amphi- *or* **amph-** *prefix* [Gk, around, on both sides; akin to E *by*] : on both sides : of both kinds : both 〈*amphi*biotic〉

am·phib·ia \am-'fib-ē-ə\ *n pl* : AMPHIBIANS

am·phib·i·an \-ē-ən\ *n* **1** : an amphibious organism; *esp* : any of a class (Amphibia) of cold-blooded vertebrate animals (as frogs and newts) intermediate in many respects between fishes and reptiles **2** : an airplane designed to take off from and land on either land or water **3** : a flat-bottomed vehicle that moves on tracks having finlike extensions by means of which it is propelled on land or water — **amphibian** *adj*

am·phib·i·ous \-ē-əs\ *adj* [Gk *amphi-* + *bios* life] **1** : able to live both on land and in water 〈*amphibious* plants〉 **2 a** : relating to or adapted for both land and water 〈*amphibious* vehicles〉 **b** : executed by coordinated action of land, sea, and air forces organized for invasion from the sea; *also* : trained or organized for such action 〈*amphibious* forces〉 — **am·phib·i·ous·ly** *adv* — **am·phib·i·ous·ness** *n*

am·phi·bole \'am(p)-fə-,bōl\ *n* : any of a group of white, gray, green, or black rock-forming minerals that are complex hydrous silicates and contain calcium, magnesium, iron, aluminum, and sodium

am·phi·mic·tic \,am(p)-fi-'mik-tik\ *adj* : capable of interbreeding freely and of producing fertile offspring — **am·phi·mic·ti·cal·ly** \-ti-k(ə-)lē\ *adv*

am·phi·mix·is \-'mik-səs\ *n, pl* **-mix·es** \-'mik-,sēz\ **1** : the union of germ cells in sexual reproduction **2** : INTERBREEDING

am·phi·ox·us \,am(p)-fē-'äk-səs\ *n, pl* **-oxi** \-'äk-,sī\ *or* **-ox·us·es** : LANCELET

am·phi·pod \'am(p)-fə-,päd\ *n* : any of a large group (Amphipoda) of crustaceans comprising the sand fleas and related forms — **amphipod** *adj*

am·phi·the·a·ter \'am(p)-fə-,thē-ət-ər\ *n* **1** : a round or oval building with seats rising in curved rows around an open space on which games and plays take place **2** : something resembling an amphitheater (as a piece of level ground surrounded by hills)

am·pho·ra \'am(p)-fə-rə\ *n, pl* **-pho·rae** \-,rē, -,rī\ *or* **-phoras** [L, fr. Gk *amphoreus*, fr. *amphi-* + *pherein* to carry] : an ancient Greek jar or vase with two handles that rise almost to the level of the mouth

am·pho·ter·ic \,am(p)-fə-'ter-ik\ *adj* [Gk *amphoteros* each of two, fr. *amphō* both] : capable of reacting chemically either as an acid or as a base

am·ple \'am-pəl\ *adj* [L *amplus*] **1** : generous or more than adequate in size, scope, or capacity : COPIOUS **2** : enough to satisfy : ABUNDANT **syn** see PLENTIFUL — **am·ple·ness** *n* — **am·ply** \-plē\ *adv*

am·pli·fi·ca·tion \,am-plə-fə-'kā-shən\ *n* **1** : an act, example, or product of amplifying **2 a** : matter by which a statement is expanded **b** : an expanded statement

am·pli·fi·er \'am-plə-,fī(-ə)r\ *n* : one that amplifies; *esp* : a device usu. employing vacuum tubes or transistors to obtain amplification of voltage, current, or power

am·pli·fy \'am-plə-,fī\ *vt* **-fied; -fy·ing 1** : ENLARGE; *esp* : to expand by clarifying details or illustration 〈*amplify* a statement〉 **2** : to increase (voltage, current, or power) in magnitude or strength (as by use of a vacuum tube) **3** : to make louder 〈*amplify* the voice by using a megaphone〉

am·pli·tude \'am-plə-,t(y)üd\ *n* **1** : the quality or state of being ample : FULLNESS **2** : the extent or range of a quality, property, process, or phenomenon: as **a** : the extent of a vibratory movement (as of a pendulum) measured from the mean position to an extreme **b** : the absolute value of the maximum departure of an alternating current or wave or of a periodic function from the average value **3** : the angle that determines the final position of the radius vector in polar coordinates

amplitude modulation *n* : modulation of the amplitude of a radio carrier wave in accordance with the strength of the audio or other signal; *also* : a broadcasting system using such modulation — abbr. *AM*

am·pul *or* **am·poule** \'am-,p(y)ül\ *n* [L *ampulla* vial] : a small sealed bulbous glass vessel used to hold a solution for hypodermic injection

am·pul·la \am-'pùl-ə, -'pəl-\ *n, pl* **-lae** \-(,)ē, -,ī\ **1 :** a globular vessel; *esp* **:** one used to hold consecrated oil for a coronation ceremony **2 :** an anatomic sac or pouch — **am·pul·lar** \-ər\ *adj*

am·pu·tate \'am-pyə-,tāt\ *vt* [L *amputare*, fr. *ambi-* + *putare* to cut, prune] **:** to cut or lop off **:** PRUNE; *esp* **:** to cut (as a limb) from the body — **am·pu·ta·tion** \,am-pyə-'tā-shən\ *n* — **am·pu·ta·tor** \'am-pyə-,tāt-ər\ *n*

am·pu·tee \,am-pyə-'tē\ *n* **:** one that has had a limb amputated

amuck \ə-'mək\ *var of* AMOK

am·u·let \'am-yə-lət\ *n* **:** a small object worn as a charm against evil

amuse \ə-'myüz\ *vt* [MF *amuser*] **1 :** to occupy with something pleasant **:** DIVERT ⟨*amuse* a child with a toy⟩ **2 :** to please or delight the sense of humor of ⟨his story *amused* everyone⟩ — **amus·ing·ly** \-'myü-ziŋ-lē\ *adv*

syn ENTERTAIN, DIVERT: AMUSE implies engaging the attention so as to keep one interested usu. lightly or frivolously; ENTERTAIN suggests supplying amusement by specially prepared activity or performance; DIVERT stresses distracting the attention from worry or routine concern esp. with something causing laughter or gaiety

amuse·ment \ə-'myüz-mənt\ *n* **1 :** the condition of being amused **2 :** pleasant diversion **3 :** something that amuses or entertains

amusement park *n* **:** a commercially operated park with various devices (as a merry-go-round or roller coaster) for entertainment

amyg·da·loid \ə-'mig-də-,lóid\ *or* **amyg·da·loi·dal** \-,mig-də-'lói-dəl\ *adj* **:** almond-shaped

am·yl alcohol \,am-əl-\ *n* **:** either of two commercially produced mixtures of alcohols $C_5H_{11}OH$ used esp. as solvents

am·y·lase \'am-ə-,lās\ *n* [Gk *amylon* starch] **:** an enzyme that accelerates the hydrolysis of starch or glycogen

am·y·lol·y·sis \,am-ə-'läl-ə-səs\ *n* **:** the conversion of starch into soluble products (as dextrins and sugars) esp. by enzymes — **am·y·lo·lyt·ic** \-lō-'lit-ik\ *adj*

am·y·lop·sin \,am-ə-'läp-sən\ *n* **:** the amylase of the pancreatic juice

¹an \ən, (')an\ *indefinite article* [OE *ān* one] **: ²A** — in standard speech and writing used (1) invariably before words beginning with a vowel letter and sound ⟨*an* oak⟩; (2) invariably before *h*-initial words in which the *h* is silent ⟨*an* honor⟩; (3) frequently before *h*-initial words which have in an initial unstressed syllable an \h\ sound often lost after the *an* ⟨*an* historian⟩; (4) sometimes esp. in England before words like *union* and *European* whose initial letter is a vowel and whose initial sounds are \yü\ or \yü\

²an *or* **an'** *conj* **1** *see* AND\ *substand* **:** AND **2** \(')an\ *archaic* **:** IF

an- — see A-

¹-an *or* **-ian** *also* **-ean** *n suffix* [L *-anus*, *-ianus*, adj. & n. suffix] **1 :** one that belongs to ⟨American⟩ ⟨Boston*ian*⟩ ⟨crustac*ean*⟩ **2 :** one skilled in or specializing in ⟨phoneti*cian*⟩

²-an *or* **-ian** *also* **-ean** *adj suffix* **1 :** of or belonging to ⟨American⟩ ⟨Florid*ian*⟩ **2 :** characteristic of **:** resembling ⟨Mozart*ean*⟩

³-an *n suffix* [alter. of *-ane*] **1 :** unsaturated carbon compound **2 :** anhydride of a carbohydrate ⟨pentos*an*⟩

ana- *or* **an-** *prefix* [Gk, up, back, again; akin to E *on*] **:** up **:** upward ⟨*anabolism*⟩

-a·na \'an-ə, 'än-ə, 'ā-nə\ *or* **-i·a·na** \ē-'\ *n pl suffix* [L, neut. pl. of *-anus*, *-ianus* -an] **:** collected items of information esp. anecdotal or bibliographical concerning ⟨American*a*⟩ ⟨Johnson*iana*⟩

an·a·bae·na \,an-ə-'bē-nə\ *n* **:** a common filamentous freshwater blue-green alga

Ana·bap·tist \,an-ə-'bap-təst\ *n* [LGk *anabaptizein* to rebaptize] **:** a Protestant of one of several 16th century sects rejecting infant baptism — **Anabaptist** *adj*

anab·o·lism \ə-'nab-ə-,liz-əm\ *n* **:** the part of metabolism concerned with the building up of the substance of plants and animals — **an·a·bol·ic** \,an-ə-'bäl-ik\ *adj*

anach·ro·nism \ə-'nak-rə-,niz-əm\ *n* **1 :** an error in chronology; *esp* **:** a chronological misplacing of persons, events, objects, or customs in regard to each other **2 :** a person or a thing that is chronologically out of place;

esp **:** something from a former age incongruous in the present — **anach·ro·nis·tic** \ə-,nak-rə-'nis-tik\ *adj* — **anach·ro·nis·ti·cal·ly** \-ti-k(ə-)lē\ *adv*

an·a·co·lu·thon \,an-ə-kə-'lü-,thän\ *n, pl* **-tha** \-thə\ *or* **-thons** [Gk *a-* + *akolouthos* following] **:** lack of connection between the parts of one continuous stretch of speech or writing esp. as the result of a shift from one construction to another in the middle of a sentence (as in "you really ought — well, do it your own way")

an·a·con·da \,an-ə-'kän-də\ *n* **:** a large So. American snake of the boa family that crushes its prey in its coils; *also* **:** a large constricting snake

an·a·dem \'an-ə-,dem\ *n* **:** GARLAND, CHAPLET

anad·ro·mous \ə-'nad-rə-məs\ *adj* [Gk *anadromos* running upward] **:** ascending rivers from the sea for breeding ⟨shad are *anadromous*⟩

anae·mia *var of* ANEMIA

an·aer·o·bic \,an-ə-'rō-bik\; ,an-,a-(ə-)'rō-, -,e-(ə-)'rō-\ *adj* **:** living, active, or occurring in the absence of free oxygen — **an·aer·obe** \(')an-'a(-ə)r-,ōb, -'e(-ə)r-\ *n* — **an·aer·o·bi·cal·ly** *adv*

anaerobic respiration *n* **:** FERMENTATION

an·aes·the·sia, an·aes·thet·ic *var of* ANESTHESIA, ANESTHETIC

ana·gram \'an-ə-,gram\ *n* [Gk *anagrammatizein* to transpose letters, fr. *ana-* + *grammat-*, *gramma* letter] **:** a word or phrase made out of another by changing the order of the letters ⟨*rebate* is an *anagram* of *beater*⟩

anal \'ān-°l\ *adj* **:** of, relating to, or situated near the anus — **anal·ly** \-°l-ē\ *adv*

anal fin *n* **:** an unpaired median fin located behind the vent of a fish

an·al·ge·sia \,an-°l-'jē-zhə\ *n* [Gk *algos* pain] **:** insensibility to pain without loss of consciousness — **an·al·ge·sic** \-'jē-zik, -sik\ *adj or n* — **an·al·get·ic** \-'jet-ik\ *adj or n*

an·a·log·i·cal \,an-°l-'äj-i-kəl\ *adj* **1 :** of, relating to, or based on analogy **2 :** expressing or implying analogy — **an·a·log·i·cal·ly** \-k(ə-)lē\ *adv*

anal·o·gous \ə-'nal-ə-gəs\ *adj* [Gk *analogos*, lit., in proportion, fr. *ana* up, in accordance with + *logos* reason, ratio] **1 :** showing an analogy or a likeness permitting one to draw an analogy **2 :** being or related to as an analogue syn see SIMILAR — **anal·o·gous·ly** *adv* — **anal·o·gous·ness** *n*

an·a·logue *or* **an·a·log** \'an-°l-,óg\ *n* **1 :** something that is analogous or similar to something else **2 :** an organ similar in function to an organ of another animal or plant but different in structure and origin

analogue computer *n* **:** a calculating machine that operates with numbers represented by directly measurable quantities (as voltages, resistances, or rotations) — compare DIGITAL COMPUTER

anal·o·gy \ə-'nal-ə-jē\ *n, pl* **-gies** **1 :** an inference that if two or more things agree with one another in some respects they will prob. agree in others **2 :** resemblance in some particulars between things otherwise unlike **:** SIMILARITY **3 :** correspondence in function between anatomical parts of different structure and origin — compare HOMOLOGY

an·a·lyse *chiefly Brit var of* ANALYZE

anal·y·sis \ə-'nal-ə-səs\ *n, pl* **anal·y·ses** \-'nal-ə-,sēz\ [Gk, fr. *analyein* to break up, fr. *ana-* + *lyein* to loosen] **1 :** separation of a whole into its component parts **2 a :** an examination of a whole to discover its elements and their relations **b :** a statement of such an analysis **c :** an examination and interpretation of the nature and significance of something (as news events or business conditions) **3 :** the use of function words instead of inflectional forms as a characteristic device of a language **4 :** the identification or separation of ingredients of a substance **5 :** proof of a proposition by assuming the result and deducing a valid statement by a series of reversible steps **6 :** PSYCHOANALYSIS

an·a·lyst \'an-°l-əst\ *n* **1 :** a person who analyzes or who is skilled in analysis ⟨news *analyst*⟩ **2 :** PSYCHOANALYST

an·a·lyt·ic \,an-°l-'it-ik\ *adj* **1 a :** of or relating to analysis; *esp* **:** separating something into component parts or constituent elements **b :** skilled in or using analysis ⟨a keenly *analytic* man⟩ **2 :** involving or applying the methods of algebra and calculus rather than geometry

⟨*analytic* trigonometry⟩ — **an·a·lyt·i·cal** \-i-kəl\ *adj* — **an·a·lyt·i·cal·ly** \-k(ə-)lē\ *adv*

analytic geometry *n* : the study of geometric properties by means of algebraic symbols representing parts or relations of figures in a coordinate system — called also *coordinate geometry*

an·a·lyze \'an-ᵊl-,īz\ *vt* : to make an analysis of; *esp* : to study or determine the nature and relationship of the parts of by analysis ⟨*analyze* a traffic pattern⟩ — **an·a·lyz·a·ble** \-,ī-zə-bəl\ *adj* — **an·a·ly·za·tion** \,an-ᵊl-ə-'zā-shən\ *n* — **an·a·lyz·er** \'an-ᵊl-,ī-zər\ *n*

An·a·ni·as \,an-ə-'nī-əs\ *n* **1** : an early Christian struck dead for lying **2** : LIAR

an·a·pest \'an-ə-,pest\ *n* [Gk *anapaistos* foot of two short syllables followed by one long, lit., struck back, fr. *ana-* + *paiein* to strike; so called fr. its being a dactyl reversed] : a metrical foot consisting of two unaccented syllables followed by one accented syllable (as in *the accused*) — **an·a·pes·tic** \,an-ə-'pes-tik\ *adj*

ana·phase \'an-ə-,fāz\ *n* : the stage of mitosis in which the chromosome halves move toward the poles of the spindle — **ana·pha·sic** \,an-ə-'fā-zik\ *adj*

ana·phy·lax·is \,an-ə-fə-'lak-səs\ *n* : hypersensitivity (as to a drug) resulting from sensitization during an earlier exposure to the causative agent — **ana·phy·lac·tic** \-'lak-tik\ *adj* — **ana·phy·lac·ti·cal·ly** \-ti-k(ə-)lē\ *adv* — **ana·phy·lac·toid** \-'lak-,tȯid\ *adj*

an·ar·chic \a-'när-kik\ *adj* : of, relating to, or tending toward anarchy : LAWLESS — **an·ar·chi·cal** \-ki-kəl\ *adj* — **an·ar·chi·cal·ly** \-k(ə-)lē\ *adv*

an·ar·chism \'an-ər-,kiz-əm\ *n* **1** : a political theory holding all governmental authority to be unnecessary and undesirable and advocating a society based on the voluntary cooperation of individuals and groups **2** : the advocacy or practice of anarchistic principles

an·ar·chist \'an-ər-kəst\ *n* **1** : one who rebels against any authority, established order, or ruling power **2** : one who believes in, advocates, or promotes anarchism; *esp* : one who uses violent means to overthrow the established order — **anarchist** *or* **an·ar·chis·tic** \,an-ər-'kis-tik\ *adj*

an·ar·cho-syn·di·cal·ism \a-,när-kō-'sin-di-kə-,liz-əm, ,an-ər-kō-\ *n* : SYNDICALISM

an·ar·chy \'an-ər-kē\ *n* [Gk *anarchia*, fr. *a-* ²a- + *archein* to rule] **1** : the condition of a society without a government **2** : a state of lawlessness, confusion, or disorder **3** : an ideal society having no government and made up of individuals who enjoy complete freedom

syn ANARCHY, CHAOS mean absence, suspension, or breakdown of government, law, and order. ANARCHY stresses the absence of government; CHAOS implies the utter absence of order

an·astig·mat·ic \,an-ə-stig-'mat-ik, ,an-,as-tig-\ *adj* : not astigmatic — used esp. of lenses that are able to form approximately point images of object points — **an·as·tig·mat** \a-'nas-tig-,mat, ,an-ə-'stig-\ *n*

anas·to·mose \ə-'nas-tə-,mōz, -,mōs\ *vb* : to connect or communicate by anastomosis

anas·to·mo·sis \ə-,nas-tə-'mō-səs\ *n, pl* **-mo·ses** \-'mō-,sēz\ [Gk *stoma* mouth, outlet] : the union of parts or branches (as of streams or blood vessels) so as to intercommunicate; *also* : NETWORK, MESH — **anas·to·mot·ic** \-'mät-ik\ *adj*

anath·e·ma \ə-'nath-ə-mə\ *n* [Gk] **1 a** : a curse solemnly pronounced by ecclesiastical authority and accompanied by excommunication **b** : a vigorous denunciation : CURSE **2** : a person or thing that is cursed or intensely disliked or loathed

anath·e·ma·tize \-,tīz\ *vt* : to pronounce an anathema upon

anat·o·mize \ə-'nat-ə-,mīz\ *vt* **1** : to dissect so as to show or to examine the structure and use of the parts **2** : ANALYZE

anat·o·my \ə-'nat-ə-mē\ *n, pl* **-mies** [Gk *anatemnein* to dissect, fr. *ana-* + *temnein* to cut] **1** : a branch of knowledge that deals with the structure of organisms; *also* : a writing on bodily structure **2** : structural makeup esp. of an organism or any of its parts **3** : a separating into parts for examination : ANALYSIS — **an·a·tom·ic** \,an-ə-'täm-ik\ *or* **an·a·tom·i·cal** \-'täm-i-kəl\ *adj* — **an·a·tom·i·cal·ly** \-k(ə-)lē\ *adv* — **anat·o·mist** \ə-'nat-ə-məst\ *n*

-ance \ən(t)s, ᵊn(t)s\ *n suffix* [OF, fr. L *-antia*, fr. *-ant-*, *-ans* -ant] **1** : action or process ⟨further*ance*⟩ : instance of an action or process ⟨perform*ance*⟩ **2** : quality or state : instance of a quality or state ⟨protuber*ance*⟩ **3** : amount or degree ⟨conduct*ance*⟩

an·ces·tor \'an-,ses-tər\ *n* [MF *ancestre*, fr. L *antecessor*, fr. *antecess-*, *antecedere* to go before] **1** : one from whom an individual or kind of individual is descended and who is usu. more remote in the line of descent than a grandparent **2** : FORERUNNER, PROTOTYPE — **an·ces·tress** \-trəs\ *n*

an·ces·tral \an-'ses-trəl\ *adj* : of, relating to, or derived from an ancestor ⟨*ancestral* home⟩ ⟨*ancestral* portraits⟩ — **an·ces·tral·ly** \-trə-lē\ *adv*

an·ces·try \'an-,ses-trē\ *n* **1** : line of descent : LINEAGE **2** : individuals initiating or comprising a line of descent : ANCESTORS

An·chi·ses \an-'kī-(,)sēz, aŋ-\ *n* : the father of Aeneas

¹an·chor \'aŋ-kər\ *n* [L *anchora*, fr. Gk *ankyra*] **1** : a heavy iron or steel device attached to a boat or ship by a cable or chain and so made that when thrown overboard it digs into the earth and holds the boat or ship in place **2** : something that secures or steadies or that gives a feeling of stability ⟨the *anchor* of a bridge⟩ **3** : one who competes or is placed last — called also *anchor man*

²anchor *vb* **an·chored; an·chor·ing** \-k(ə-)riŋ\ **1** : to hold in place by means of an anchor ⟨*anchor* a ship⟩ **2** : to fasten securely to a firm foundation ⟨*anchor* the cables of a bridge⟩ **3** : to drop anchor : become anchored ⟨the boat *anchored* in the harbor⟩

anchor: *1* ring, *2* stock, *3* shank, *4* bill, *5* fluke, *6* arm, *7* throat, *8* crown

an·chor·age \'aŋ-k(ə-)rij\ *n* **1** : a place where boats may be anchored **2** : a secure hold to resist a strong pull **3** : a means of security : REFUGE **4** : a charge made for the right to anchor in a place

an·cho·rite \'aŋ-kə-,rīt\ *n* [ML *anchorita*, fr. Gk *anachōrētēs*, lit., one that withdraws] : a person who gives up worldly things and lives in solitude usu. for religious reasons

an·cho·vy \'an-,chō-vē, an-'\ *n, pl* **-vies** *or* **-vy** [Sp *anchova*] : any of numerous small fishes resembling herrings; *esp* : a common Mediterranean fish used esp. for sauces and relishes

an·cien ré·gime \ä°s-yaⁿ-rā-zhēm\ *n* [F, lit., old regime] **1** : the political and social system of France before the Revolution of 1789 **2** : a system or mode no longer prevailing

¹an·cient \'ān-shənt, -chənt; 'āŋ(k)-shənt\ *adj* [MF *ancien*, fr. L *ante* before] **1** : having existed for many years : very old ⟨*ancient* customs⟩ **2** : of or relating to a period of time long past or to those living in such a period; *esp* : of or relating to the historical period from the earliest civilizations to the fall of the western Roman Empire A.D. 476 **3** : having the qualities of age or long existence : **a** : VENERABLE **b** : OLD-FASHIONED, ANTIQUE *syn* see OLD — **an·cient·ness** *n*

²ancient *n* **1** : an aged person **2** *pl* : the civilized peoples of ancient times and esp. of Greece and Rome

an·cient·ly \-lē\ *adv* : in ancient times

an·cil·lary \'an(t)-sə-,ler-ē, an-'sil-ə-rē\ *adj* [L *ancilla* female servant] **1** : SUBORDINATE, SUBSIDIARY **2** : AUXILIARY, SUPPLEMENTARY

-an·cy \ən-sē, ᵊn-\ *n suffix, pl* **-ancies** [L *-antia* -ance] : quality or state ⟨piquanc*y*⟩

and \ən(d), (')an(d), *usu* ᵊn(d) *after* t, d, s *or* z, *often* ᵊn(d) *after* p *or* b, *sometimes* ᵊŋ *after* k *or* g\ *conj* [OE] — used as a function word to join words or word groups of the same grammatical rank or function (as two nouns that are subjects of the same verb, two relative clauses modifying the same noun, or an adverb and a prepositional phrase modifying the same verb) and to express connection or addition

¹an·dan·te \än-'dän-,tā, an-'dant-ē\ *adv (or adj)* [It, lit., going] : moderately slow — used as a direction in music

²andante *n* : a musical piece or movement in andante tempo

---

an·dan·ti·no \ˌän-ˌdän-'tē-nō\ *adv (or adj)* [It, dim. of *andante*] **:** somewhat quicker in tempo than andante — used as a direction in music

and·iron \'an-ˌdī-(ə)rn\ *n* [modif. of OF *andier*] **:** one of a pair of metal supports for firewood in a fireplace

and/or \'an-'ȯ(ə)r\ *conj* — used as a function word to indicate that either *and* or *or* may apply ⟨men *and/or* women means men *and* women or men *or* women⟩

an·dra·dite \an-'dräd-ˌīt\ *n* **:** a garnet ranging from yellow and green to brown and black and containing calcium and iron

An·dro·cles \'an-drə-ˌklēz\ *n* **:** a Roman slave held to have been spared in the arena by a lion from whose foot he had years before extracted a thorn

an·droe·ci·um \an-'drē-s(h)ē-əm\ *n, pl* **-cia** \-s(h)ē-ə\ [Gk *andr-, anēr* man, male + *oikion* house] **:** the stamens of a flower

an·dro·gen \'an-drə-jən\ *n* [Gk *andr-, anēr* male] **:** a male sex hormone — **an·dro·gen·ic** \ˌan-drə-'jen-ik\ *adj*

an·drog·y·nous \an-'dräj-ə-nəs\ *adj* [Gk *andr-, anēr* man, male + *gynē* woman] **1 :** HERMAPHRODITIC **2 :** bearing both staminate and pistillate flowers in the same cluster — **an·drog·y·ny** \-nē\ *n*

An·drom·a·che \an-'dräm-ə-(ˌ)kē\ *n* **:** the wife of Hector

An·drom·e·da \an-'dräm-əd-ə\ *n* **1 :** an Ethiopian princess rescued from a monster by Perseus who marries her **2 :** a northern constellation directly south of Cassiopeia between Pegasus and Perseus

-ane \ˌān\ *n suffix* [alter. of *-ene, -ine*] **:** saturated or completely hydrogenated carbon compound (as a hydrocarbon) ⟨meth*ane*⟩

an·ec·dote \'an-ik-ˌdōt\ *n* [Gk *anekdotos* unpublished, fr. *a-* ²*a-* + *ekdo-, ekdidonai* to publish, fr. *ex-* + *didonai* to give] **:** a short narrative of an interesting, amusing, or biographical incident — **an·ec·dot·al** \ˌan-ik-'dōt-ᵊl\ *adj* — **an·ec·dot·al·ly** \-ᵊl-ē\ *adv*

ane·mia \ə-'nē-mē-ə\ *n* [Gk *a-* ²*a-* + *haima* blood] **1 :** a condition in which the blood is deficient in red blood cells, in hemoglobin, or in total volume and which is usu. marked by pale skin, shortness of breath, and irregular heart action **2 :** lack of vitality — **ane·mic** \-mik\ *adj* — **ane·mi·cal·ly** \-mi-k(ə-)lē\ *adv*

an·e·mom·e·ter \ˌan-ə-'mäm-ət-ər\ *n* [Gk *anemos* wind] **:** an instrument for measuring the force or speed of the wind

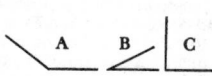
anemometer

anem·o·ne \ə-'nem-ə-nē\ *n* **1 :** any of a large genus of herbs related to the buttercups that have showy flowers without petals but with conspicuous often colored sepals **2 :** SEA ANEMONE

anent \ə-'nent\ *prep* [OE *onemn* together, alongside, fr. *on* + *efen* even] **:** ABOUT, CONCERNING

an·er·oid barometer \ˌan-ə-ˌrȯid-\ *n* [F *anéroïde* without liquid, fr. *a-* ²*a-* + LGk *nēron* water] **:** an instrument in which the atmospheric pressure in bending a metallic surface (as of a box from which part of the air has been removed) is made to move a pointer

an·es·the·sia \ˌan-əs-'thē-zhə\ *n* [Gk *a-* ²*a-* + *aisthē-, aisthanesthai* to perceive] **:** loss of bodily sensation with or without loss of consciousness

¹an·es·thet·ic \ˌan-əs-'thet-ik\ *adj* **:** of, relating to, or capable of producing anesthesia — **an·es·thet·i·cal·ly** \-'thet-i-k(ə-)lē\ *adv*

²anesthetic *n* **:** a substance that produces either local or general anesthesia

anes·the·tist \ə-'nes-thət-əst\ *n* **:** one who administers anesthetics

anes·the·tize \ə-'nes-thə-ˌtīz\ *vt* **:** to make insensible to pain esp. by the use of an anesthetic

an·eu·rysm *also* **an·eu·rism** \'an-yə-ˌriz-əm\ *n* [Gk *aneurynein* to dilate, fr. *ana-* + *eurys* wide] **:** a permanent abnormal blood-filled dilatation of a blood vessel resulting from disease of the vessel wall — **an·eu·rys·mal** \ˌan-yə-'riz-məl\ *adj*

anew \ə-'n(y)ü\ *adv* **1 :** over again **:** for an additional time **:** AFRESH ⟨begin *anew*⟩ **2 :** in a new or different form

an·gel \'ān-jəl\ *n* [ME, fr. LL *angelus*, fr. Gk *angelos*, lit., messenger] **1 a :** a spiritual being serving God esp. as a

messenger or as a guardian of men; *esp* **:** one in the lowest rank **b :** a white-robed winged figure of human form in fine art representing an angel **2 :** an attendant spirit or guardian **3 :** MESSENGER, HARBINGER ⟨*angel* of death⟩ **4 :** a person felt to resemble (as in virtue, innocence or beauty) an angel **5 :** a financial backer of a theatrical venture or other enterprise — **an·gel·ic** \an-'jel-ik\ *or* **an·gel·i·cal** \-i-kəl\ *adj* — **an·gel·i·cal·ly** \-i-k(ə-)lē\ *adv*

an·gel·fish \'ān-jəl-ˌfish\ *n* **1 :** any of several compressed bright-colored bony fishes of warm seas **2 :** SCALARE

an·gel·i·ca \an-'jel-i-kə\ *n* **:** a biennial herb of the carrot family whose roots and fruit furnish a flavoring oil

An·ge·lus \'an-jə-ləs\ *n* [LL, angel, the first word of the opening versicle] **1 :** a Roman Catholic devotion that commemorates the Incarnation and is said morning, noon, and evening **2 :** a bell announcing the time for the Angelus

¹an·ger \'an-gər\ *n* [ME, affliction, anger, fr. ON *angr* grief] **:** a strong feeling of displeasure and usu. of antagonism

syn RAGE, WRATH, FURY: ANGER is the general term for emotional reaction of anger in any degree of intensity; RAGE implies loss of self-control from violence of emotion; WRATH implies usu. righteous rage with a desire to avenge or punish; FURY suggests a violence of emotion amounting to temporary madness

²anger *vt* **an·gered; an·ger·ing** \-g(ə)riŋ\ **:** to make angry

An·ge·vin \'an-jə-vən\ *adj* **:** of, relating to, or characteristic of Anjou or the Plantagenets — **Angevin** *n*

an·gi·na \an-'jī-nə\ *n* [L, fr. *angere* to choke] **:** a disorder marked by spasmodic attacks of intense pain: as **a :** a severe inflammatory condition of the mouth or throat **b :** ANGINA PECTORIS — **an·gi·nal** \-'jīn-ᵊl\ *adj*

angina pec·to·ris \an-ˌjī-nə-'pek-t(ə-)rəs\ *n* [NL, lit., angina of the chest] **:** a heart disorder marked by brief recurrent attacks of intense chest pain

an·gio·sperm \'an-jē-ə-ˌspərm\ *n* [Gk *angeion* vessel + *sperma* seed] **:** any of a class (Angiospermae) of vascular plants with the seeds in a closed ovary **:** FLOWERING PLANT — **an·gio·sper·mous** \ˌan-jē-ə-'spər-məs\ *adj*

¹an·gle \'an-gəl\ *n* [L *angulus* corner, angle; akin to E *ankle*] **1 :** the figure formed by two lines extending from the same point or by two surfaces diverging from the same line **2 :** a measure of the amount of turning that would be required to cause one line of an angle to coincide with the other at all points **3 :** a sharp projecting corner **4 a :** POINT OF VIEW, ASPECT ⟨consider a problem from a new *angle*⟩ **b :** a special approach or technique for accomplishing an objective **5 :** a course or direction abruptly diverging from the one orig. pursued — **an·gled** \-gəld\ *adj*

angles 1: obtuse, *A;* acute, *B;* right, *C*

²angle *vb* **an·gled; an·gling** \-g(ə-)liŋ\ **1 :** to turn, move, or direct at an angle **2 :** to present (as a news story or speech) from a particular often biased point of view **:** SLANT

³angle *vi* **an·gled; an·gling** \-g(ə-)liŋ\ [ME *angelen*, fr. *angel* fishhook, fr. OE] **1 :** to fish with hook and line **2 :** to use artful means to attain an objective

An·gle \'aŋ-gəl\ *n* **:** a member of a Germanic people conquering England with the Saxons and Jutes in the 5th century A.D. and merging with them to form the Anglo-Saxon people

angle bracket *n* **:** BRACKET 3b

angle of incidence : the angle that a line (as a ray of light) falling on a surface makes with a perpendicular to the surface at the point of incidence

angle of reflection : the angle between a reflected ray and the perpendicular to a reflecting surface drawn at the point of incidence

an·gler \'aŋ-glər\ *n* **1 :** FISHERMAN; *esp* **:** one who fishes for sport **2 :** a sea fish having a large flat head with projections that attract other fish within reach of its broad mouth

an·gle·worm \'aŋ-gəl-ˌwərm\ *n* **:** EARTHWORM

An·gli·can \'aŋ-gli-kən\ *n* [ML *anglicus* English, fr. L *Angli* Angles] **:** a member of the established Church of

ə abut; ᵊ kitten; ər further; a back; ā bake; ä cot, cart; aú out; ch chin; e less; ē easy; g gift; i trip; ī life

England or of one of the related churches in communion with it — **Anglican** *adj*

An·gli·can·ism \-kə-ˌniz-əm\ *n* **1** : the faith or worship of Anglicans **2** : the churches of Anglican communion

an·gli·cism \'aŋ-glə-ˌsiz-əm\ *n, often cap* **1** : a characteristic feature of English occurring in another language **2** : adherence or attachment to English customs or ideas

an·gli·cize \'aŋ-glə-ˌsīz\ *vt, often cap* **1** : to make English (as in habits, speech, character, or outlook) **2** : to borrow (a foreign word or phrase) into English without changing form or spelling and sometimes without changing pronunciation — **an·gli·ci·za·tion** \ˌaŋ-glə-sə-'zā-shən\ *n, often cap*

an·gling \'aŋ-gliŋ\ *n* : the act of fishing with hook and line usu. for sport

Anglo- *comb form* [LL *Angli* Englishmen, fr. L, Angles] **1** : English ⟨*Anglo*-Norman⟩ **2** : English and ⟨*Anglo*-Japanese⟩

An·glo–Cath·o·lic \ˌaŋ-glō-'kath-(ə-)lik\ *adj* : of or relating to a High Church movement in Anglicanism emphasizing its continuity with historic Catholicism and fostering Catholic dogmatic and liturgical traditions — **Anglo-Catholic** *n* — **An·glo–Ca·thol·i·cism** \-kə-'thäl-ə-ˌsiz-əm\ *n*

An·glo–French \ˌaŋ-glō-'french\ *n* : the French language used in medieval England

An·glo–Nor·man \-'nȯr-mən\ *n* **1** : one of the Normans living in England after the Norman conquest **2** : the form of Anglo-French used by Anglo-Normans

an·glo·phile \'aŋ-glə-ˌfīl\ *n, often cap* : one who greatly admires England and things English

an·glo·phobe \-ˌfōb\ *n, often cap* : one who is averse to England and things English

An·glo–Sax·on \ˌaŋ-glō-'sak-sən\ *n* **1** : a member of the Germanic people conquering England in the 5th century A.D. and forming the ruling class until the Norman conquest — compare ANGLE, JUTE, SAXON **2** : ENGLISHMAN **3 a** : a person of English ancestry **b** : a white person whose native tongue is English **4 a** : OLD ENGLISH **b** : direct plain English — **Anglo-Saxon** *adj*

an·go·ra \aŋ-'gȯr-ə, an-, -'gȯr-\ *n* : yarn or cloth made from the hair of the Angora goat or the Angora rabbit

Angora cat *n* [*Angora* (Ankara), Turkey] : a long-haired domestic cat

Angora goat *n* : any of a breed or variety of the domestic goat raised for its long silky hair which is the true mohair

Angora rabbit *n* : a usu. white rabbit raised for its long fine soft hair

an·gry \'aŋ-grē\ *adj* **an·gri·er; -est 1 a** : stirred by anger : ENRAGED, WRATHFUL ⟨become *angry* at the slightest provocation⟩ **b** : showing or arising from anger ⟨*angry* words⟩ **c** : threatening as if in anger ⟨an *angry* sky⟩ **2** : painfully inflamed ⟨an *angry* rash⟩ — **an·gri·ly** \-grə-lē\ *adv* — **an·gri·ness** \-grē-nəs\ *n*

angst \'äŋ(k)st\ *n* [G] : a feeling of anxiety : DREAD

ang·strom \'aŋ-strəm\ *n* [Anders J. *Ångström* d1874 Swedish physicist] : a unit of length used esp. of wavelengths (as of light) and equal to one ten-billionth of a meter — abbr. *A*

an·guish \'aŋ-gwish\ *n* [OF *angoisse*, fr. L *angustiae*, pl., straits, distress, fr. *angustus* narrow] : extreme pain or distress of body or mind **syn** see SORROW

an·guished \'aŋ-gwisht\ *adj* : full of anguish : TORMENTED ⟨an *anguished* call for help⟩

an·gu·lar \'aŋ-gyə-lər\ *adj* **1 a** : having one or more angles **b** : forming an angle : sharp-cornered : POINTED ⟨an *angular* mountain peak⟩ **2** : measured by an angle ⟨*angular* distance⟩ **3** : being lean and bony ⟨his *angular* figure⟩ — **an·gu·lar·i·ty** \ˌaŋ-gyə-'lar-ət-ē\ *n* — **an·gu·lar·ly** *adv*

an·gu·late \'aŋ-gyə-lət, -ˌlāt\ *adj* : formed with corners ⟨*angulate* leaves⟩ — **an·gu·late·ly** *adv*

An·gus \'aŋ-gəs\ *n* : ABERDEEN ANGUS

an·hy·dride \(')an-'hī-ˌdrīd\ *n* : a compound derived from another (as an acid) by removal of the elements of water

an·hy·drite \-'hī-ˌdrīt\ *n* : a mineral CaSO₄ consisting of an anhydrous calcium sulfate

an·hy·drous \-'hī-drəs\ *adj* : free from water

an·i·line \'an-ᵊl-ən\ *n* [G *anil* indigo, fr. Ar *an-nīl* the indigo plant, fr. Skt *nīlī*, fr. *nīla* dark blue] : an oily liquid

poisonous amine $C_6H_5NH_2$ made esp. from nitrobenzene and used chiefly in organic synthesis (as of dyes)

an·i·mad·ver·sion \ˌan-ə-ˌmad-'vər-zhən\ *n* **1** : a critical remark or comment **2** : hostile criticism

an·i·mad·vert \-'vərt\ *vi* [L *animadvers-*, *animadvertere*, lit., to take notice of, fr. *animum advertere* to turn the attention to] : to make a critical remark : comment unfavorably ⟨to *animadvert* on a display of bad manners⟩

¹an·i·mal \'an-ə-məl\ *n* [L, fr. *animalis* animate, fr. *anima* breath, soul] **1** : any of a kingdom (Animalia) of living beings typically differing from plants in capacity for active movement, in rapid response to stimulation, and in lack of cellulose cell walls **2 a** : one of the lower animals as distinguished from man **b** : MAMMAL

²animal *adj* **1** : of, relating to, or derived from animals **2** : of or relating to the physical nature of a person as contrasted with the intellectual; *esp* : SENSUOUS ⟨man's *animal* appetites⟩

an·i·mal·cule \ˌan-ə-'mal-kyül\ *n* [NL *animalculum*, dim. of L *animal*] : a very small animal that is invisible or nearly invisible to the naked eye — **an·i·mal·cu·lar** \-'mal-kyə-lər\ *adj*

animal heat *n* : heat produced in the body of a living animal by its chemical and physical activity

an·i·mal·ism \'an-ə-mə-ˌliz-əm\ *n* **1** : qualities typical of animals **2** : preoccupation with the satisfaction of physical drives or wants — **an·i·mal·ist** \-mə-ləst\ *n* — **an·i·mal·is·tic** \ˌan-ə-mə-'lis-tik\ *adj*

¹an·i·mate \'an-ə-mət\ *adj* **1** : having life : ALIVE **2** : ANIMATED, LIVELY — **an·i·mate·ly** *adv* — **an·i·mate·ness** *n*

²an·i·mate \'an-ə-ˌmāt\ *vt* **1** : to give life to : make alive ⟨belief that the soul *animates* the body⟩ **2** : to give spirit and vigor to : ENLIVEN ⟨the speaker's arguments *animated* the discussion⟩ **3** : to give the appearance of life to; *esp* : to make appear to move ⟨*animate* a cartoon⟩

an·i·mat·ed \-ˌmāt-əd\ *adj* **1 a** : ALIVE, LIVING **b** : full of movement and activity **c** : full of vigor and spirit : VIVACIOUS **2** : having the appearance or movement of something alive **syn** see LIVELY — **an·i·mat·ed·ly** *adv*

animated cartoon *n* : a motion picture made from a series of drawings simulating motion by means of slight progressive changes

an·i·ma·tion \ˌan-ə-'mā-shən\ *n* **1** : SPIRIT, LIVELINESS ⟨the topic was discussed with increasing *animation*⟩ **2 a** : ANIMATED CARTOON **b** : the preparation of animated cartoons

an·i·ma·to \ˌan-ə-'mät-ō\ *adv (or adj)* : with animation — used as a direction in music

an·i·mism \'an-ə-ˌmiz-əm\ *n* : attribution of conscious life to nature as a whole or to inanimate objects — **an·i·mist** \-məst\ *n* — **an·i·mis·tic** \ˌan-ə-'mis-tik\ *adj*

an·i·mos·i·ty \ˌan-ə-'mäs-ət-ē\ *n, pl* **-ties** : ill will or resentment tending toward active hostility **syn** see ENMITY

an·i·mus \'an-ə-məs\ *n* [L, mind, spirit, anger] **1** : basic attitude : DISPOSITION, INTENTION **2** : deep-seated hostility : ANTAGONISM

an·ion \'an-ˌī-ən, -ˌī-ˌän\ *n* [Gk, neut. of *aniōn*, prp. of *anienai* to go up, fr. *ana-* + *ienai* to go] **1** : the ion in an electrolyzed solution that migrates to the anode **2** : a negatively charged ion — **an·ion·ic** \ˌan-ī-'än-ik\ *adj*

an·ise \'an-əs\ *n* [Gk *anison*] : an herb of the carrot family with aromatic seeds; *also* : ANISEED

ani·seed \'an-ə(s)-ˌsēd\ *n* : the seed of anise often used as a flavoring in cordials and in cooking

an·isog·a·mous \ˌan-ī-'säg-ə-məs\ *also* **an·iso·gam·ic** \-ˌī-sə-'gam-ik\ *adj* : involving unlike gametes ⟨*anisogamous* reproduction⟩ — **an·isog·a·my** \-ī-'säg-ə-mē\ *n*

ankh \'aŋk\ *n* : a cross having a loop for its upper vertical arm and serving esp. in ancient Egypt as an emblem of life

an·kle \'aŋ-kəl\ *n* [OE *anclēow*] : the joint between the foot and the leg; *also* : the region of this joint

an·kle·bone \-'bōn, -ˌbōn\ *n* : TALUS 1

an·klet \'aŋ-klət\ *n* **1** : something (as an ornament) worn around the ankle **2** : a short sock reaching slightly above the ankle

an·ky·lo·sis \ˌaŋ-ki-'lō-səs\ *n, pl* **-lo·ses** \-'lō-ˌsēz\ [Gk *ankylos* crooked] : a growing together of parts (as bones) into a rigid whole; *also* : stiffness of a joint resulting from such growth — **an·ky·lose** \'aŋ-ki-ˌlōs, -ˌlōz\ *vb* — **an·ky·lot·ic** \ˌaŋ-ki-'lät-ik\ *adj*

---

an·na \'än-ə\ *n* **1** : a former monetary unit of Burma, India, and Pakistan equal to ¹⁄₁₆ rupee **2** : a coin representing one anna

an·nal·ist \'an-ᵊl-əst\ *n* : a writer of annals : HISTORIAN — **an·nal·is·tic** \ˌan-ᵊl-'is-tik\ *adj*

an·nals \'an-ᵊlz\ *n pl* [L *annales,* fr. pl. of *annalis* yearly, fr. *annus* year] **1** : a record of events arranged in yearly sequence **2** : historical records : CHRONICLES **3** : records of the activities of an organization

An·nam·ese \ˌan-ə-'mēz, -'mēs\ *n, pl* **Annamese 1 a** : a Mongolian people of Vietnam **b** *or* **An·nam·ite** \'an-ə-ˌmīt\ : a member of this people **2** : the language of the Annamese people : VIETNAMESE — **Annamese** *adj*

an·nat·to \ə-'nät-ō\ *n, pl* **-tos** : a yellowish red dyestuff made from the pulp around the seeds of a tropical tree

an·neal \ə-'nēl\ *vt* [ME *anelen* to set on fire, fr. OE *onǣlan,* fr. *on* + *ǣlan* to burn] **1** : to heat and then cool (as steel or glass) for softening and making less brittle **2** : STRENGTHEN, TOUGHEN ⟨*annealed* by hardship⟩

an·ne·lid \'an-ᵊl-əd\ *n* [L *annellus* little ring, dim. of *annulus* ring] : any of a phylum (Annelida) of long segmented invertebrate animals having a body cavity and including the earthworms, leeches, and related forms — **annelid** *adj* — **an·nel·i·dan** \ə-'nel-əd-ᵊn\ *adj or n*

¹an·nex \ə-'neks, 'an-ˌeks\ *vt* [L *annex-, annectere* to bind to, fr. *ad-* + *nectere* to bind] **1** : to add as a subsidiary part : APPEND ⟨a protocol *annexed* to the treaty⟩ **2** : to incorporate (a country or other territory) within one's own domain ⟨the United States *annexed* Texas in 1845⟩ — **an·nex·a·tion** \ˌan-ˌek-'sā-shən\ *n* — **an·nex·a·tion·al** \-shnəl, -shən-ᵊl\ *adj* — **an·nex·a·tion·ist** \-sh(ə-)nəst\ *n*

²an·nex \'an-ˌeks, 'an-iks\ *n* : something annexed or appended: as **a** : an added stipulation or statement : APPENDIX **b** : an added part of a building : WING **c** : a subsidiary district

an·ni·hi·late \ə-'nī-ə-ˌlāt\ *vt* [L *ad* + *nihil* nothing] : to destroy entirely : put completely out of existence : SHATTER ⟨*annihilate* an entire army⟩ **syn** see DESTROY — **an·ni·hi·la·tion** \-ˌnī-ə-'lā-shən\ *n* — **an·ni·hi·la·tor** \-'nī-ə-ˌlāt-ər\ *n*

an·ni·ver·sa·ry \ˌan-ə-'vərs-(ə-)rē\ *n, pl* **-ries** [L *annus* year + *vers-, vertere* to turn] **1** : the annual recurrence of a date marking a notable event **2** : the celebration of an anniversary

an·no Do·mi·ni \ˌan-ō-'däm-ə-nē, -'dō-mə-, -ˌnī\ *adv, often cap A* [ML, in the year of the Lord] — used to indicate that a time division falls within the Christian era

an·no·tate \'an-ə-ˌtāt\ *vb* : to make or furnish critical or explanatory notes or comment — **an·no·ta·tor** \-ˌtāt-ər\ *n*

an·no·ta·tion \ˌan-ə-'tā-shən\ *n* **1** : the act of annotating **2** : a note added by way of comment or explanation

an·nounce \ə-'naún(t)s\ *vb* [MF *annoncer,* fr. L *annuntiare,* fr. *ad-* + *nuntiare* to report, fr. *nuntius* messenger] **1** : to make known publicly : PROCLAIM **2 a** : to give notice of the arrival, presence, or readiness of **b** : to indicate beforehand : FORETELL **3** : to serve as an announcer **syn** see DECLARE

an·nounce·ment \ə-'naún(t)s-mənt\ *n* **1** : the act of announcing **2** : a public notice announcing something

an·nounc·er \ə-'naún(t)s-ər\ *n* : one that announces; *esp* : one that introduces television or radio programs, makes announcements, and gives the news and station identification

an·noy \ə-'nói\ *vb* [ME *anoien,* fr. OF *enuier,* fr. LL *inodiare* to make hateful, fr. L *in* + *odium* hatred] : to disturb or irritate esp. by repeated disagreeable acts : VEX — **an·noy·er** *n* — **an·noy·ing·ly** \-iŋ-lē\ *adv*
syn WORRY, HARASS: ANNOY implies disturbing one's composure or peace of mind by intrusion, interference or petty attacks; WORRY suggests incessant attacks intending to drive one to desperation or defeat; HARASS implies petty persecutions or burdensome demands that exhaust one's nervous or mental power

an·noy·ance \ə-'nói-ən(t)s\ *n* **1 a** : the act of annoying or of being annoyed **b** : the state or feeling of being annoyed : VEXATION **2** : a source of vexation or irritation : NUISANCE

¹an·nu·al \'an-y(ə-w)əl\ *adj* [L *annualis,* fr. *annus* year] **1** : covering the period of a year **2** : occurring or performed once a year : YEARLY **3** : completing the life cycle in one growing season — **an·nu·al·ly** \-ē\ *adv*

²annual *n* **1** : a publication appearing yearly **2** : an event that occurs yearly **3** : an annual plant

annual ring *n* : the layer of wood produced by a single year's growth of a woody plant

an·nu·i·tant \ə-'n(y)ü-ət-ənt\ *n* : a beneficiary of an annuity

an·nu·i·ty \ə-'n(y)ü-ət-ē\ *n, pl* **-ties** [L *annuus* yearly, fr. *annus* year] **1** : a sum of money paid at regular intervals (as every year) **2** : an insurance contract providing for the payment of an annuity ⟨buy an *annuity*⟩

an·nul \ə-'nəl\ *vt* **an·nulled; an·nul·ling** [L *ad* to + *nullus* not any] **1** : to reduce to nothing : OBLITERATE **2** : to make ineffective or inoperative : NEUTRALIZE, CANCEL ⟨*annul* the drug's effect⟩ **3** : to declare or make legally void ⟨*annul* a marriage⟩ **syn** see NULLIFY

an·nu·lar \'an-yə-lər\ *adj* [L *annulus* ring] : of, relating to, or forming a ring — **an·nu·lar·i·ty** \ˌan-yə-'lar-ət-ē\ *n* — **an·nu·lar·ly** \'an-yə-lər-lē\ *adv*

annular eclipse *n* : an eclipse in which a thin outer ring of the sun's disk is not covered by the apparently smaller dark disk of the moon

an·nu·late \'an-yə-lət, -ˌlāt\ *or* **an·nu·lat·ed** \-ˌlāt-əd\ *adj* : furnished with or composed of rings : RINGED

an·nu·la·tion \ˌan-yə-'lā-shən\ *n* : formation of rings; *also* : RING

an·nul·ment \ə-'nəl-mənt\ *n* : the act of annulling or of being annulled; *esp* : a legal declaration that a marriage is invalid

an·nu·lus \'an-yə-ləs\ *n, pl* **-li** \-ˌlī, -ˌlē\ *also* **-lus·es** [L] : RING; *esp* : a part, structure, or marking resembling a ring

an·nun·ci·ate \ə-'nən(t)-sē-ˌāt\ *vt* : ANNOUNCE — **an·nun·ci·a·tor** \-ˌāt-ər\ *n* — **an·nun·ci·a·to·ry** \-sē-ə-ˌtōr-ē, -ˌtór-\ *adj*

an·nun·ci·a·tion \ə-ˌnən(t)-sē-'ā-shən\ *n* : the act of announcing : ANNOUNCEMENT

Annunciation *n* : March 25 observed as a church festival in commemoration of the announcement of the Incarnation of the Virgin Mary

an·ode \'an-ˌōd\ *n* [Gk *anodos* way up, fr. *ana-* + *hodos* way] **1** : the positive electrode of an electrolytic cell to which the negative ions are attracted — compare CATHODE **2** : the negative terminal of a primary cell or of a storage battery that is delivering current **3** : the electron-collecting electrode of an electron tube — **an·od·ic** \a-'näd-ik\ *adj*

an·o·dize \'an-ə-ˌdīz\ *vt* : to subject (a metal) to electrolytic action as the anode of a cell in order to coat with a protective or decorative film

¹an·o·dyne \'an-ə-ˌdīn\ *adj* [Gk *a-* ²*a-* + *odynē* pain] : serving to assuage pain : SOOTHING

²anodyne *n* : an anodyne drug or agent — **an·o·dyn·ic** \ˌan-ə-'din-ik\ *adj*

anoint \ə-'nóint\ *vt* [MF *enoint,* pp. of *enoindre,* fr. L *inunguere,* fr. *in-* + *unguere* to smear] **1** : to rub over with oil or an oily substance **2 a** : to apply oil to as a sacred rite **b** : to consecrate with or as if with oil — **anoint·er** *n* — **anoint·ment** \-'nóint-mənt\ *n*

anom·a·lous \ə-'näm-ə-ləs\ *adj* [Gk *anōmalos,* lit., uneven, fr. *a-* + *homalos* even, fr. *homos* same] **1** : deviating from a general rule, method, or analogy or from accepted notions of fitness or order : ABNORMAL ⟨an *anomalous* procedure⟩ **2** : being not what would naturally be expected — **anom·a·lous·ly** *adv* — **anom·a·lous·ness** *n*

anom·a·ly \ə-'näm-ə-lē\ *n, pl* **-lies 1** : deviation from the common rule **2** : something anomalous

anon \ə-'nän\ *adv* [OE *on ān,* fr. *on* in + *ān* one] **1** *archaic* : at once : IMMEDIATELY **2** : SOON, PRESENTLY; *also* : LATER

an·o·nym·i·ty \ˌan-ə-'nim-ət-ē\ *n, pl* **-ties** : the quality or state of being anonymous

anon·y·mous \ə-'nän-ə-məs\ *adj* [Gk *a-* ²*a-* + *onyma, onoma* name] **1** : having or giving no name ⟨*anonymous* author⟩ **2** : of unknown or unnamed source or origin ⟨*anonymous* gifts⟩⟨an *anonymous* letter⟩ — **anon·y·mous·ly** *adv* — **anon·y·mous·ness** *n*

anoph·e·les \ə-'näf-ə-ˌlēz\ *n* [Gk *anōphelēs* useless] : any of a genus of mosquitoes that includes all mosquitoes which transmit malaria to man — **anoph·e·line** \-ˌlīn\ *adj or n*

an·or·thite \ə-'nȯr-ˌthīt\ *n* : a white, grayish, or reddish calcium-containing feldspar

¹an·oth·er \ə-'nəth-ər\ *adj* **1** : different or distinct from the one considered ⟨from *another* angle⟩ **2** : some other : LATER ⟨at *another* time⟩ **3** : being one more in addition : NEW ⟨bring *another* cup⟩

²another *pron* **1** : an additional one **2** : one that is different from the first or present one

an·ox·ia \a-'näk-sē-ə\ *n* : a condition in which insufficient oxygen (as at high altitudes) reaches the tissues — **an·ox·ic** \-sik\ *adj*

¹an·swer \'an(t)-sər\ *n* [OE *andswaru*] **1 a** : something spoken or written in reply esp. to a question **b** : a correct response **2** : a reply to a charge or accusation : DEFENSE **3** : an act done in response **4** : a solution of a problem

²answer *vb* **an·swered; an·swer·ing** \'an(t)s-(ə-)riŋ\ **1** : to speak or write in or by way of reply **2 a** : to be or make oneself responsible or accountable **b** : to make amends : ATONE **3** : CONFORM, CORRESPOND ⟨*answered* to the description⟩ **4** : to act in response ⟨the ship *answers* to the helm⟩ **5** : to be adequate : SERVE ⟨*answer* the purpose⟩ **6** : to offer a solution for; esp : SOLVE — **an·swer·er** \'an(t)-sər-ər\ *n*

an·swer·a·ble \'an(t)s-(ə-)rə-bəl\ *adj* **1** : subject to be called to account : RESPONSIBLE ⟨*answerable* for one's actions⟩ ⟨*answerable* for a debt⟩ **2** : capable of being answered; esp : capable of being proved wrong ⟨an *answerable* argument⟩

ant \'ant\ *n* [ME *emete*, *ante*, fr. OE *æmette*] : any of a family of colonial insects that are related to the wasps and bees and have a complex social organization with various castes performing special duties

ant- — see ANTI-

¹-ant \ənt, °nt\ *n suffix* [OF, fr. *-ant*, prp. suffix, fr. L *-ant-, -ans*, prp. suffix of some verbs] **1** : one that performs or promotes (a specified action) ⟨cool*ant*⟩ ⟨expector*ant*⟩ **2** : thing that is acted upon (in a specified manner) ⟨inhal*ant*⟩

²-ant *adj suffix* **1** : performing (a specified action) or being (in a specified condition) ⟨propell*ant*⟩ **2** : promoting (a specified action or process) ⟨expector*ant*⟩

ant·ac·id \(')ant-'as-əd\ *adj* : counteractive of acidity — **antacid** *n*

an·tag·o·nism \an-'tag-ə-ˌniz-əm\ *n* **1 a** : active opposition, hostility, or antipathy **b** : opposition between two conflicting forces, tendencies, or principles **2** : opposition in physiological action (as of two drugs or muscles)

an·tag·o·nist \-nəst\ *n* [Gk *anti-* + *agōn* contest, struggle] **1** : one that opposes another esp. in combat : ADVERSARY **2** : an agent of physiological antagonism; esp : a muscle that contracts with and limits the action of an agonist with which it is paired **syn** see OPPONENT

an·tag·o·nis·tic \(ˌ)an-ˌtag-ə-'nis-tik\ *adj* : characterized by or resulting from antagonism : OPPOSING — **an·tag·o·nis·ti·cal·ly** \-ti-k(ə-)lē\ *adv*

an·tag·o·nize \an-'tag-ə-ˌnīz\ *vt* **1** : to act in opposition to : COUNTERACT **2** : to incur or provoke the hostility of

ant·arc·tic \(')ant-'ärk-tik, -'ärt-ik\ *adj, often cap* [Gk *antarktikos*, fr. *anti-* + *arktikos* arctic] : of or relating to the south pole or to the region near it

antarctic circle *n, often cap A&C* : a small circle of the earth parallel to its equator approximately 23° 27′ from the south pole — see ZONE illustration

An·tar·es \an-'ta(ə)r-(ˌ)ēz, -'te(ə)r-\ *n* [Gk *Antarēs*] : a giant red star of very low density that is the brightest star in Scorpius

ant bear *n* : a large So. American anteater with shaggy gray fur, a black band across the breast, and a white shoulder stripe

ant cow *n* : an aphid from which ants obtain honeydew

¹an·te \'ant-ē\ *n* [*ante-*] : a poker stake usu. put up before the deal to build the pot

²ante *vt* **an·ted; an·te·ing** : to put up (an ante); *also* : PAY, PRODUCE

ante- *prefix* [L; akin to E *end*] **1** : prior : earlier ⟨*ante*nuptial⟩ ⟨*ante*date⟩ **2** : anterior : in front of ⟨*ante*room⟩

ant·eat·er \'ant-ˌēt-ər\ *n* : any of several mammals (as

anteater

an echidna or aardvark) that feed largely or entirely on ants; *esp* : an edentate with a long narrow snout and very long extensible tongue

an·te·bel·lum \ˌant-i-'bel-əm\ *adj* [L *ante bellum* before the war] : existing before a war; *esp* : existing before the Civil War

¹an·te·ce·dent \ˌant-ə-'sēd-°nt\ *n* **1** : a noun, pronoun, phrase, or clause referred to by a personal or relative pronoun ⟨in "the house that Jack built", *house* is the *antecedent* of *that*⟩ **2** : the first term of a mathematical ratio **3** : a preceding event, condition, or cause **4 a** : a predecessor in a series; *esp* : a model or stimulus for later developments **b** *pl* : ANCESTORS, PARENTS

²antecedent *adj* [L *antecedere* to go before, fr. *ante-* + *cedere* to go] **1** : coming earlier in time or order : existing or occurring before **2** : causally or logically prior **syn** see PRECEDING — **an·te·ce·dent·ly** *adv*

an·te·cham·ber \'ant-i-ˌchām-bər\ *n* : an outer room leading to another usu. more important room

an·te·choir \'ant-i-ˌkwī(ə)r\ *n* : a space enclosed or reserved for the clergy and choristers at the entrance to a choir

an·te·date \'ant-i-ˌdāt\ *vt* **1** : to date with a date prior to that of execution or occurrence **2** : to precede in time ⟨automobiles *antedate* airplanes⟩

an·te·di·lu·vi·an \ˌant-i-də-'lü-vē-ən, -dī-\ *adj* [*ante-* + L *diluvium* flood] **1** : of or relating to the period before the Flood described in the Bible **2** : made, evolved, or developed a long time ago : ANTIQUATED — **antediluvian** *n*

an·te·lope \'ant-°l-ˌōp\ *n, pl* **-lope** *or* **-lopes** [LGk *antholop-*, *antholops*, a fabulous animal] **1 a** : any of various Old World ruminant mammals that are related to the goats and oxen but differ from the true oxen esp. in lighter racier build and horns directed upward and backward **b** : PRONGHORN **2** : leather from antelope hide

an·te me·ri·di·em \ˌant-i-mə-'rid-ē-əm\ *adj* [L, before noon] : being before noon

an·te·mor·tem \ˌant-i-'mȯrt-əm\ *adj* [L *ante mortem*] : preceding death

antelope

an·te·na·tal \ˌant-i-'nāt-°l\ *adj* **1** : of or relating to an unborn child **2** : occurring during pregnancy

an·ten·na \an-'ten-ə\ *n, pl* **-ten·nae** \-'ten-(ˌ)ē\ *or* **-tennas** [L, sail yard] **1** : any of one or two pairs of long slender segmented sensory organs on the head of an arthropod (as an insect or a crab) — see INSECT illustration **2** *pl usu* **antennas** : a usu. metallic device (as a rod or wire) for radiating or receiving radio waves

an·ten·nule \an-'ten-yül\ *n* : a small antenna (as of a crayfish)

an·te·pen·di·um \ˌant-i-'pen-dē-əm\ *n, pl* **-di·ums** *or* **-dia** \-dē-ə\ [L *ante-* + *pendēre* to hang] : a hanging for the front of an altar, pulpit, or lectern

an·te·pe·nult \ˌant-i-'pē-ˌnəlt\ *n* : the 3d syllable of a word counting from the end ⟨*-cu-* is the *antepenult* in *accumulate*⟩ — **an·te·pen·ul·ti·mate** \-pi-'nəl-tə-mət\ *adj or n*

an·te·ri·or \an-'tir-ē-ər\ *adj* [L, compar. of *ante* before] **1 a** : situated before or toward the front **b** : ABAXIAL **2** : coming before in time : ANTECEDENT — **an·te·ri·or·ly** *adv*

an·te·room \'ant-i-ˌrüm, -ˌrùm\ *n* : a room used as an entrance to another : WAITING ROOM

an·them \'an(t)-thəm\ *n* [OE *antefn* antiphon, fr. LL *antiphona*] **1 a** : a psalm or hymn sung antiphonally or responsively **b** : a sacred vocal composition with words usu. from the Scriptures **2** : a song or hymn of praise or gladness

an·ther \'an(t)-thər\ *n* [Gk *anthos* flower] : the part of a stamen that produces and contains pollen and is usu. borne on a stalk — see FLOWER illustration — **an·ther·al** \-thə-rəl\ *adj*

an·ther·id·i·um \ˌan(t)-thə-'rid-ē-əm\ *n, pl* **-ia** \-ē-ə\ : the male reproductive organ of a cryptogamous plant — **an·ther·id·i·al** \-ē-əl\ *adj*

an·ther·o·zo·id \ˌan(t)-thə-rə-'zō-əd\ *n* : SPERMATOZOID

---

j joke; ŋ sing; ō flow; ȯ flaw; ȯi coin; th thin; t͟h this; ü loot; ù foot; y yet; yü few; yù furious; zh vision

an·the·sis \an-'thē-səs\ *n, pl* **-the·ses** \-'thē-,sēz\ : the action or period of opening of a flower

ant·hill \'ant-,hil\ *n* : a mound thrown up by ants or termites in digging their nest

an·tho·cy·a·nin \,an(t)-thə-'sī-ə-nən\ *n* [Gk *anthos* flower + *kyanos* dark blue] : any of various soluble pigments producing blue to red coloring in flowers and plants

an·thol·o·gy \an-'thäl-ə-jē\ *n, pl* **-gies** [Gk *anthologia* gathering of flowers, fr. *anthos* flower + *legein* to gather] : a collection of selected literary pieces or passages — **an·thol·o·gist** \-jəst\ *n*

an·tho·zo·an \,an(t)-thə-'zō-ən\ *n* [Gk *anthos* flower + *zōion* animal] : any of a class (Anthozoa) of marine coelenterates (as the corals and sea anemones) having polyps with radial partitions — **anthozoan** *adj*

an·thra·cene \'an(t)-thrə-,sēn\ *n* : a crystalline hydrocarbon $C_{14}H_{10}$ obtained from coal-tar distillation

an·thra·cite \'an(t)-thrə-,sīt\ *n* [Gk *anthrakitis*, fr. *anthrak-, anthrax* coal, carbuncle] : a hard glossy coal that burns without much smoke or flame — **an·thra·cit·ic** \,an(t)-thrə-'sit-ik\ *adj*

an·thrax \'an-,thraks\ *n* : an infectious and usu. fatal bacterial disease of warm-blooded animals (as cattle and sheep)

anthrop- *or* **anthropo-** *comb form* [Gk *anthrōpos*] : human being ⟨*anthropogenesis*⟩

an·thro·po·cen·tric \,an(t)-thrə-pə-'sen-trik\ *adj* : interpreting or regarding the world in terms of human values and experiences

¹an·thro·poid \'an(t)-thrə-,pȯid\ *adj* **1** : resembling man **2** : resembling an ape ⟨*anthropoid* mobsters⟩

²anthropoid *n* : any of several large tailless semierect apes

an·thro·pol·o·gy \,an(t)-thrə-'päl-ə-jē\ *n* : a science that collects and studies the facts about man and esp. about his physical characteristics, the origin and distribution of races, human environment and social relations, and culture — **an·thro·po·log·i·cal** \-pə-'läj-i-kəl\ *adj* — **an·thro·po·log·i·cal·ly** \-'läj-i-k(ə-)lē\ *adv* — **an·thro·pol·o·gist** \-'päl-ə-jəst\ *n*

an·thro·pom·e·try \,an(t)-thrə-'päm-ə-trē\ *n* : the study of human body measurements — **an·thro·po·met·ric** \-pə-'me-trik\ *adj* — **an·thro·po·met·ri·cal** \-tri-kəl\ *adj* — **an·thro·po·met·ri·cal·ly** \-tri-k(ə-)lē\ *adv*

an·thro·po·mor·phic \,an(t)-thrə-pə-'mȯr-fik\ *adj* [Gk *morphē* form] **1** : described or thought of as having a human form or human attributes ⟨*anthropomorphic* deities⟩ **2** : ascribing human characteristics to nonhuman things — **an·thro·po·mor·phi·cal·ly** \-fi-k(ə-)lē\ *adv* — **an·thro·po·mor·phism** \-,fiz-əm\ *n*

an·thro·po·mor·phize \-'mȯr-,fīz\ *vt* : to attribute human form or personality to

an·thro·poph·a·gous \,an(t)-thrə-'päf-ə-gəs\ *adj* : feeding on human flesh — **an·thro·poph·a·gy** \-'päf-ə-jē\ *n*

¹an·ti \'an-,tī, 'ant-ē\ *n* [*anti-*] : one who is opposed

²anti *prep* : opposed to : AGAINST

anti- \,ant-i, ,ant-ē, ,an-,tī\ *or* **ant-** *or* **anth-** *prefix* [Gk, opposite, against, instead; akin to E *end*] **1** : opposite in kind, position, or action ⟨*anticline*⟩ ⟨*anti*histamine⟩ **2** : hostile toward ⟨*anti*-Communist⟩ ⟨*anti*slavery⟩

an·ti·air·craft \,ant-ē-'a(ə)r-,kraft, -'e(ə)r-\ *adj* : designed or used for defense against aircraft ⟨an *antiaircraft* gun⟩ — **antiaircraft** *n*

an·ti·bac·te·ri·al \,ant-ē-,bak-'tir-ē-əl, ,an-,tī-,bak-\ *adj* : directed or effective against bacteria

an·ti·bal·lis·tic missile \,ant-i-bə-,lis-tik-, ,an-,tī-\ *n* : a missile for intercepting and destroying ballistic missiles

an·ti·bi·o·sis \,ant-i-(,)bī-'ō-səs, ,an-,tī-, -bē-\ *n* : antagonistic association between organisms to the detriment of one of them or between one organism and a metabolic product of another

an·ti·bi·ot·ic \-'ät-ik\ *n* : a substance produced by an organism and usu. by a fungus or bacterium that in dilute solution inhibits or kills a harmful microorganism — **antibiotic** *adj* — **an·ti·bi·ot·i·cal·ly** \-'ät-i-k(ə-)lē\ *adv*

an·ti·body \'ant-i-,bäd-ē\ *n* : an immune substance of the body that interacts with a corresponding antigen and counteracts the effects of a disease-producing microorganism or its poisons

¹an·tic \'ant-ik\ *n* **1** : a grotesquely ludicrous act or action : CAPER **2** *archaic* : CLOWN, BUFFOON

²antic *adj* [It *antico* ancient, fr. L *antiquus*] **1** *archaic* : GROTESQUE, BIZARRE **2** : whimsically gay : FROLICSOME

an·ti·cho·lin·er·gic \,an-ti-,kō-lə-'nər-jik, ,an-,tī-, -,käl-ə-\ *adj* : opposing or annulling the physiologic action of acetylcholine — **anticholinergic** *n*

an·ti·christ \'ant-i-,krīst\ *n* **1** : one who denies or opposes Christ; *esp, cap* : a great antagonist expected to fill the world with wickedness but to be conquered forever by Christ at his second coming **2** : a false Christ

an·tic·i·pate \an-'tis-ə-,pāt\ *vb* [L *ante-* + *capere* to take] **1 a** : to do something before the appointed time **b** : to take up, use, or introduce ahead of time ⟨*anticipate* an opponent's argument⟩ **2** : to be before in doing or acting : FORESTALL **3** : to see and perform beforehand ⟨*anticipate* a person's wishes⟩ **4** : to experience beforehand : look forward to : EXPECT ⟨*anticipate* the pleasure of a visit⟩ *syn* see FORESEE — **an·tic·i·pa·tor** \-,pāt-ər\ *n*

an·tic·i·pa·tion \(,)an-,tis-ə-'pā-shən\ *n* **1 a** : a prior action that takes into account or forestalls a later action **b** : the act of looking forward; *esp* : pleasurable expectation **2** : a picturing beforehand of a future event or state — **an·tic·i·pa·to·ry** \an-'tis-ə-pə-,tōr-ē, -,tȯr-\ *adj*

an·ti·cler·i·cal \,ant-i-'kler-i-kəl, ,an-,tī-\ *adj* : opposed to the influence of the clergy in secular affairs — **anticlerical** *n* — **an·ti·cler·i·cal·ism** \-'kler-i-kə-,liz-əm\ *n*

an·ti·cli·max \,ant-i-'klī-,maks\ *n* **1** : the usu. sudden transition in writing or speaking from a significant idea to a trivial or ludicrous idea; *also* : an instance of such transition **2** : an event esp. closing a series that is strikingly less important than what has preceded it — **an·ti·cli·mac·tic** \-klī-'mak-tik\ *adj*

an·ti·cline \'ant-i-,klīn\ *n* [Gk *klinein* to lean] : an arch of stratified rock in which the layers bend downward in opposite directions from the crest — compare SYNCLINE

an·ti·clock·wise \,ant-i-'kläk-,wīz\ *adj or adv* : COUNTERCLOCKWISE

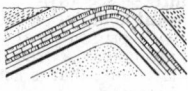
cross section of strata showing anticline

an·ti·co·ag·u·lant \,ant-i-kō-'ag-yə-lənt, ,an-,tī-\ *n* : a substance that hinders clotting of blood — **anticoagulant** *adj*

an·ti·cy·clone \,ant-i-'sī-,klōn\ *n* : a system of winds that rotates about a center of high atmospheric pressure clockwise in the northern hemisphere, that usu. advances at 20 to 30 miles per hour, and that usu. has a diameter of 1500 to 2500 miles — **an·ti·cy·clon·ic** \-sī-'klän-ik\ *adj*

an·ti·dote \'ant-i-,dōt\ *n* [Gk *antidotos*, fr. *anti-* + *didonai* to give] **1** : a remedy to counteract the effects of poison **2** : something that relieves, prevents, or counteracts — **an·ti·dot·al** \,ant-i-'dōt-ᵊl\ *adj*

an·ti–fed·er·al·ist \,ant-i-'fed-(ə-)rə-ləst, ,an-,tī-\ *n, often cap A & F* : one opposing in 1787–88 the adoption of the U.S. Constitution

an·ti·fer·til·i·ty \-fər-'til-ət-ē\ *adj* : intended to control excess or unwanted fertility : CONTRACEPTIVE

an·ti·freeze \'ant-i-,frēz\ *n* : a substance added to the liquid in an automobile radiator to prevent its freezing

an·ti·fric·tion \,ant-i-'frik-shən, ,an-,tī-\ *adj* : reducing friction

an·ti·gen \'ant-i-jən\ *n* : a substance (as a toxin or enzyme) that when introduced into the body stimulates the production of an antibody — **an·ti·gen·ic** \,ant-i-'jen-ik\ *adj* — **an·ti·gen·i·cal·ly** \-'jen-i-k(ə-)lē\ *adv* — **an·ti·ge·nic·i·ty** \-jə-'nis-ət-ē\ *n*

an·ti·his·ta·mine \,ant-i-'his-tə-,mēn, -mən\ *n* : any of various drugs used for treating allergic reactions and cold symptoms presumably by inactivating histamine

an·ti–in·tel·lec·tu·al·ism \,ant-i-,int-ᵊl-'ek-chə-wə-,liz-əm, ,an-,tī-, -chə,liz-\ *n* : hostility toward or suspicion of intellectuals or intellectual traits and activities

an·ti·knock \,ant-ē-'näk\ *n* : a substance that when added to the fuel of an internal-combustion engine helps to prevent knocking

an·ti·log·a·rithm \,ant-i-'lȯg-ə-,rith-əm, ,an-,tī-, -'läg-\ : the number corresponding to a given logarithm

---

See *anti-* and 2d element

anticapitalist	anti-Communism	antidiabetic	anti-imperialism
anti-American	anti-Catholic	anti-Communist	antifascist	anti-imperialist
anti-Americanism	anticolonial	anticorrosion	antigravity	antilabor

---

ə abut; ᵊ kitten; ər further; a back; ā bake; ä cot, cart; aú out; ch chin; e less; ē easy; g gift; i trip; ī life

an·ti·ma·cas·sar \,ant-i-mə-'kas-ər\ *n* [*anti-* + *Macassar oil*, a hair dressing] : a cover to protect the back or arms of furniture

an·ti·mag·net·ic \,ant-i-mag-'net-ik, ,an-,tī-\ *adj* : having a balance unit composed of alloys that will not remain magnetized ⟨an *antimagnetic* watch⟩

an·ti·ma·lar·i·al \-mə-'ler-ē-əl\ *adj* : serving to prevent, check, or cure malaria — **antimalarial** *n*

An·ti·Ma·son \,ant-i-'mās-ᵊn, ,an-,tī-\ *n* : a member of a minor U.S. political party opposing Freemasonry from 1826 to 1835 — **An·ti·Ma·son·ic** \-mə-'sän-ik\ *adj*

an·ti·mat·ter \'ant-i-,mat-ər\ *n* : matter held to be composed of the counterparts of ordinary matter

an·ti·mere \'ant-i-,mi(ə)r\ *n* : one of the comparable segments (as an arm of a starfish) of a radially symmetrical animal

an·ti·mi·cro·bi·al \,ant-i-mī-'krō-bē-əl\ *adj* : inhibiting or destructive to microbes — **antimicrobial** *n*

an·ti·mis·sile missile \,ant-i-'mis-əl-, ,an-,tī-\ *n* : a missile for intercepting another missile in flight; *esp* : ANTIBALLISTIC MISSILE

an·ti·mo·ny \'ant-ə-,mō-nē\ *n* [ML *antimonium*] : a metallic silvery white crystalline and brittle element that is used esp. as a constituent of alloys and in medicine — see ELEMENT table — **an·ti·mo·ni·al** \,ant-ə-'mō-nē-əl\ *adj*

an·ti·ox·i·dant \,ant-ē-'äk-səd-ənt, ,an-,tī-\ *n* : a substance that opposes oxidation or inhibits reactions promoted by oxygen

an·ti·pas·to \,ant-i-'pas-tō, -'päs-\ *n* [It] : HORS D'OEUVRE

an·tip·a·thy \an-'tip-ə-thē\ *n, pl* **-thies** [Gk *anti-* + *path-*, *paschein* to suffer, feel] **1** : strong feeling against someone or something **2** : a person or thing that arouses strong dislike — **an·ti·pa·thet·ic** \,ant-i-pə-'thet-ik\ *adj*

an·ti·per·son·nel \,ant-i-,pərs-ᵊn-'el, ,an-,tī-\ *adj* : designed for use against military personnel

an·ti·per·spi·rant \-'pər-spə-rənt\ *n* : a cosmetic preparation used to check excessive perspiration

an·ti·phon \'ant-ə-fən, -,fän\ *n* [LL *antiphona*, fr. Gk *antiphōnos* responsive, fr. *anti-* + *phōnē* sound] **1** : a psalm, anthem, or verse sung antiphonally **2** : a verse usu. from Scripture said or sung liturgically before and after a canticle, psalm, or psalm verse

an·tiph·o·nal \an-'tif-ən-ᵊl\ *adj* : performed by two alternating groups : ANSWERING — **an·tiph·o·nal·ly** \-ᵊl-ē\ *adv*

an·tip·o·dal \an-'tip-əd-ᵊl\ *adj* **1** : of or relating to the antipodes; *esp* : situated at the opposite side of the earth **2** : diametrically opposite **3** : OPPOSED

an·ti·pode \'ant-ə-,pōd\ *n, pl* **an·tip·o·des** \an-'tip-ə-,dēz\ [Gk *antipod-*, *antipous* with feet opposite, fr. *anti-* + *pous* foot] **1** : the parts of the earth diametrically opposite — usu. used in pl. **2** : the exact opposite or contrary — **an·tip·o·de·an** \(,)an-,tip-ə-'dē-ən\ *adj*

an·ti·pope \'ant-i-,pōp\ *n* [MF *antipape*, fr. ML *antipapa*, fr. *anti-* + *papa* pope] : one elected or claiming to be pope in opposition to the pope canonically chosen

an·ti·py·ret·ic \,ant-i-pī-'ret-ik\ *n* [Gk *pyretos* fever, fr. *pyr* fire] : an agent that reduces fever

¹an·ti·quar·i·an \,ant-ə-'kwer-ē-ən\ *n* : ANTIQUARY

²antiquarian *adj* : of or relating to antiquaries or antiquities

an·ti·quary \'ant-ə-,kwer-ē\ *n, pl* **-quar·ies** : a person who collects or studies antiquities

an·ti·quate \'ant-ə-,kwāt\ *vt* : to make old or obsolete

an·ti·quat·ed *adj* **1** : OLD-FASHIONED, OUTMODED **2** : advanced in age

¹an·tique \an-'tēk\ *adj* [L *antiquus*, fr. *ante* before, earlier] **1 a** : belonging to antiquity **b** : being among the oldest of its class **2** : belonging to earlier periods : ANCIENT **3** : belonging to or resembling a former style or fashion : OLD-FASHIONED ⟨silver of an *antique* design⟩ **syn** see OLD — **an·tique·ly** *adv* — **an·tique·ness** *n*

²antique *n* : an object of an earlier period; *esp* : a work of art, piece of furniture, or decorative object made at an earlier period

an·tiq·ui·ty \an-'tik-wət-ē\ *n, pl* **-ties** **1** : ancient times; *esp* : those before the Middle Ages **2** : the quality of being ancient **3** *pl a* : relics or monuments of ancient times **b** : matters relating to the life or culture of ancient times

an·ti·scor·bu·tic \,ant-i-skȯr-'byüt-ik\ *adj* : tending to prevent or relieve scurvy

an·ti·Sem·ite \,ant-i-'sem-,īt, ,an-,tī-\ *n* : one who is hostile to or discriminates against Jews — **anti-Se·mit·ic** \-sə-'mit-ik\ *adj* — **anti-Sem·i·tism** \-'sem-ə-,tiz-əm\ *n*

an·ti·sep·tic \,ant-ə-'sep-tik\ *adj* [Gk *anti-* + *sēpein* to putrefy] **1** : preventing or arresting the growth of germs that cause disease or decay **2** : relating to or characterized by the use of antiseptics **3 a** : protecting or protected from what is undesirable ⟨lives in *antiseptic* seclusion⟩ **b** : marked by cleanliness, orderliness, and neatness; *esp* : neat to the point of being bare or uninteresting **c** : COLD, IMPERSONAL ⟨an *antiseptic* greeting⟩ — **antiseptic** *n* — **an·ti·sep·ti·cal·ly** \-ti-k(ə-)lē\ *adv*

an·ti·se·rum \'ant-i-,sir-əm, 'an-,tī-\ *n* : a serum containing antibodies

an·ti·so·cial \,ant-i-'sō-shəl, ,an-,tī-\ *adj* **1** : contrary or hostile to the well-being of society ⟨crime is *antisocial*⟩ **2** : disliking the society of others : MISANTHROPIC

an·ti·tank \,ant-i-'taŋk\ *adj* : designed to destroy or check tanks

an·tith·e·sis \an-'tith-ə-səs\ *n, pl* **-tith·e·ses** \-'tith-ə-,sēz\ [Gk, fr. *antitithenai* to place opposite, oppose, fr. *anti-* + *the-*, *tithenai* to put] **1** : the rhetorical contrast of ideas by means of parallel arrangements of words, clauses, or sentences **2 a** : OPPOSITION, CONTRAST **b** : the second of two contrasted things **3** : the direct opposite : CONTRARY **4** : the second stage of a dialectic process that denies or is diametrically opposed to the thesis — **an·ti·thet·ic** \,ant-ə-'thet-ik\ *adj* — **an·ti·thet·i·cal** \-'thet-i-kəl\ *adj* — **an·ti·thet·i·cal·ly** \-i-k(ə-)lē\ *adv*

an·ti·tox·in \,ant-i-'täk-sən\ *n* : an antibody capable of neutralizing a particular toxin that is formed when the toxin is introduced into the body and is produced commercially in lower animals for use in treating human diseases (as diphtheria) in which such a toxin is present — **an·ti·tox·ic** \-sik\ *adj*

an·ti·trades \'ant-i-,trādz\ *n pl* **1** : the prevailing westerly winds of middle latitudes **2** : the westerly winds above the trade winds

an·ti·trust \,ant-i-'trəst, ,an-,tī-\ *adj* : opposing or designed to restrict the power of trusts and similar business combinations ⟨*antitrust* laws⟩

an·ti·ven·in \,ant-i-'ven-ən, ,an-,tī-\ *n* : a serum containing an antitoxin to a venom (as of a snake)

ant·ler \'ant-lər\ *n* [MF *antoillier*, fr. L *ante-* + *oculus* eye] : the solid deciduous horn of an animal of the deer family or a branch of such horn — **ant·lered** \-lərd\ *adj*

ant lion *n* : the long-jawed larva of various 4-winged insects that digs a conical pit in which it lies in wait to catch insects (as ants) on which it feeds

an·to·nym \'an-tə-,nim\ *n* [Gk *anti-* + *onyma*, *onoma* name] : a word of opposite meaning ⟨*hot* and *cold* are *antonyms*⟩ — **an·ton·y·mous** \an-'tän-ə-məs\ *adj*

an·trum \'an-trəm\ *n, pl* **an·tra** \-trə\ [Gk *antron* cave] : the cavity of a hollow organ or a sinus

an·uran \ə-'n(y)ùr-ən, a-\ *adj or n* [Gk *a-* ²a + *oura* tail] : SALIENTIAN

anus \'ā-nəs\ *n* [L] : the posterior opening of the alimentary canal

an·vil \'an-vəl\ *n* [OE *anfilt*] **1** : a heavy usu. steel-faced iron block on which metal is shaped **2** : INCUS

anx·i·e·ty \aŋ-'zī-ət-ē\ *n, pl* **-ties** **1** : painful or apprehensive uneasiness of mind usu. over an impending or anticipated ill **2** : solicitous concern or interest

anx·ious \'aŋ(k)-shəs\ *adj* [L *anxius*, fr. *angere* to choke] **1** : fearful of what may happen : WORRIED ⟨*anxious* about her son's health⟩ **2** : desiring earnestly ⟨a boy *anxious* to make good⟩ **syn** see EAGER — **anx·ious·ly** *adv* — **anx·ious·ness** *n*

¹any \'en-ē\ *adj* [OE *ǣnig*; akin to E *one*] **1 a** : one taken at random ⟨*any* man you meet⟩ **b** : EVERY — used to indicate one selected without restriction ⟨*any* child would know that⟩ **2** : one, some, or all indiscriminately of whatever quantity ⟨I can't find *any* book⟩ ⟨have you *any* money⟩ ⟨give me *any* letters you find⟩ ⟨needs *any* help he can get⟩ **3** : unmeasured or unlimited in amount, number, or extent ⟨*any* quantity you desire⟩

²any *pron* **1** : any person or persons **2 a** : any thing or things **b** : any part, quantity, or number

³any *adv* : to any extent or degree : at all ⟨can't go *any* farther⟩ ⟨you're not helping *any*⟩

See *anti-* and 2d element | antislavery | antispasmodic | antisubmarine

---

any·body \'en-ē-,bäd-ē\ *pron* : ANYONE
any·how \'en-ē-,haú\ *adv* **1** : in any way, manner, or order **2** : at any rate : in any case
any·more \,en-ē-'mō(ə)r, -'mó(ə)r\ *adv* : at the present time : NOWADAYS ⟨we never see him *anymore*⟩
any·one \'en-ē-(,)wən\ *pron* : any person at all
any·place \'en-ē-,plās\ *adv* : in any place : ANYWHERE
any·thing \'en-ē-,thiŋ\ *pron* : any thing at all
any·way \'en-ē-,wā\ *adv* : ANYHOW
any·ways \-,wāz\ *adv, chiefly dial* : in any case
any·where \'en-ē-,hwe(ə)r, -,hwa(ə)r\ *adv* : in, at, or to any place
any·wise \'en-ē-,wīz\ *adv* : in any way whatever : at all
An·zac \'an-,zak\ *n* [*A*ustralian and *N*ew *Z*ealand *A*rmy *C*orps] : a soldier from Australia or New Zealand
A1 \'ā-'wən\ *adj* : of the finest quality : FIRST-RATE
ao·rist \'ā-ə-rəst, 'e-ə-\ *n* [Gk *aoristos* undefined, fr. *a-* + *horizein* to define] : a form or set of forms of a verb expressing simple occurrence of an action without reference to its completeness, duration, or repetition — **aorist** *adj*
aor·ta \ā-'ôrt-ə\ *n, pl* **aortas** *or* **aor·tae** \-'ôr-,tē\ [Gk *aortē*, fr. *aeirein* to lift] : the main artery that carries blood from the heart to be distributed by branch arteries through the body — **aor·tal** \-'ôrt-ᵊl\ *adj* — **aor·tic** \-'ôrt-ik\ *adj*
aou·dad \'aú-,dad\ *n* [F, fr. Berber *audad*] : a wild sheep of No. Africa
¹ap- — see AD-
²ap- — see APO-
apace \ə-'pās\ *adv* : at a quick pace : SWIFTLY
Apache \ə-'pach-ē, *in sense 2* ə-'pash\ *n, pl* **Apache** *or* **Apach·es** \-'pach-ēz, -'pash-əz\ **1** : a member of an Indian people of the American Southwest **2** *not cap* [F, fr. *Apache* Apache Indian] **a** : a member of a gang of criminals esp. in Paris **b** : RUFFIAN
ap·a·nage *var of* APPANAGE
¹apart \ə-'pärt\ *adv* **1** : at a distance in space or time ⟨two towns five miles *apart*⟩ **2** : as a separate unit : INDEPENDENTLY ⟨considered *apart* from other points⟩ **3** : ASIDE **4** : into two or more parts : to pieces ⟨tear a book *apart*⟩
²apart *adj* **1** : SEPARATE, ISOLATED **2** : DIVIDED — **apart·ness** *n*
apart·heid \ə-'pär-,tāt, -,tīt\ *n* [Afrik., lit., separateness] : a policy of racial segregation practiced in the Republic of So. Africa
apart·ment \ə-'pärt-mənt\ *n* **1** : a room or set of rooms used as a dwelling **2** : APARTMENT BUILDING
apartment building *n* : a building divided into individual dwelling units — called also *apartment house*
ap·a·thet·ic \,ap-ə-'thet-ik\ *adj* **1** : having or showing little or no feeling or emotion : SPIRITLESS **2** : having little or no interest or concern : INDIFFERENT **syn** see IMPASSIVE — **ap·a·thet·i·cal·ly** \-'thet-i-k(ə-)lē\ *adv*
ap·a·thy \'ap-ə-thē\ *n, pl* **-thies** [Gk *a-* ²*a-* + *path-, paschein* to suffer, feel] **1** : lack of feeling or emotion **2** : lack of interest or concern : INDIFFERENCE
ap·a·tite \'ap-ə-,tīt\ *n* [G *apatit*, fr. Gk *apatē* deceit] : any of a group of minerals of variable color that are phosphates of calcium usu. with some fluorine and that are used as a source of phosphorus and its compounds
¹ape \'āp\ *n* [OE *apa*] **1 a** : MONKEY; *esp* : one of the larger tailless forms **b** : any of a family of large semierect primates (as the chimpanzee or gorilla) **2 a** : MIMIC **b** : a large uncouth person
²ape *vt* : COPY, MIMIC **syn** see IMITATE — **ap·er** *n*
apeak \ə-'pēk\ *adv* (*or adj*) : in a vertical position ⟨oars *apeak*⟩
ape·man \'āp-'man\ *n* : a primate (as pithecanthropus) intermediate in character between true man and the higher apes
ape·ri·ent \ə-'pir-ē-ənt\ *adj* [L *aperire* to open] : gently moving the bowels : LAXATIVE — **aperient** *n*
aper·i·tif \,ap-,er-ə-'tēf\ *n* : an alcoholic drink taken before a meal as an appetizer
ap·er·ture \'ap-ə-(r)-,chù(ə)r, -chər\ *n* : an opening or open space : HOLE
apet·al·ous \(')ā-'pet-ᵊl-əs\ *adj* : having no petals — **apet·aly** \-ᵊl-ē\ *n*
apex \'ā-,peks\ *n, pl* **apex·es** *or* **api·ces** \'ā-pə-,sēz, 'ap-ə-\

[L *apic-, apex*] **1 a** : the uppermost point : VERTEX **b** : the narrowed or pointed end : TIP **2** : the highest or culminating point **syn** see SUMMIT
aphaer·e·sis *or* **apher·e·sis** \ə-'fer-ə-səs\ *n* : the loss of one or more sounds or letters at the beginning of a word (as in *coon* for *raccoon*) — **aph·ae·ret·ic** \,af-ə-'ret-ik\ *adj*
apha·sia \ə-'fā-zh(ē-)ə\ *n* [Gk a- ²*a-* + *phanai* to say] : loss or impairment of the power to use and understand words — **apha·si·ac** \-zē-,ak\ *adj* — **apha·sic** \-zik\ *n or adj*
aph·elion \a-'fēl-yən\ *n, pl* **aph·elia** [*apo-* + Gk *hēlios* sun] : the point of a planet's or comet's orbit most distant from the sun
aph·e·sis \'af-ə-səs\ *n* : aphaeresis consisting of the loss of a short unaccented vowel (as in *lone* for *alone*) — **aphet·ic** \ə-'fet-ik\ *adj* — **aphet·i·cal·ly** \-'fet-i-k(ə-)lē\ *adv*
aphid \'ā-fəd, 'af-əd\ *n* : any of numerous small sluggish insects that suck the juices of plants
aphis \'ā-fəs, 'af-əs\ *n, pl* **aphi·des** \'ā-fə-,dēz, 'af-ə-\ : APHID
aphis lion *n* : any of several insect larvae (as a lacewing or ladybug larva) that feed on aphids
aph·o·rism \'af-ə-,riz-əm\ *n* [Gk *aphorizein* to define, fr. *apo-* + *horizein* to bound] : a short sentence stating a general truth or practical observation — **aph·o·ris·tic** \,af-ə-'ris-tik\ *adj* — **aph·o·ris·ti·cal·ly** \-ti-k(ə-)lē\ *adv*
aph·ro·dis·i·ac \,af-rə-'diz-ē-,ak\ *adj* [Gk *aphrodisios* of Aphrodite] : exciting sexual desire — **aphrodisiac** *n* — **aph·ro·di·si·a·cal** \,af-rəd-ə-'zī-ə-kəl, -'sī-\ *adj*
Aph·ro·di·te \,af-rə-'dīt-ē\ *n* **1** : the Greek goddess of love and beauty **2** : a brown black-spotted butterfly of the U.S.
api·ary \'ā-pē-,er-ē\ *n, pl* **-ar·ies** [L *apis* bee] : a place where bees are kept; *esp* : a collection of hives of bees — **api·ar·i·an** \,ā-pē-'er-ē-ən\ *adj* — **api·a·rist** \'ā-pē-ə-rəst\ *n*
ap·i·cal \'ap-i-kəl, 'ā-pi-\ *adj* : of, relating to, or situated at an apex — **ap·i·cal·ly** \-k(ə-)lē\ *adv*
api·cul·ture \'ā-pə-,kəl-chər\ *n* : beekeeping esp. on a large scale — **api·cul·tur·al** \,ā-pə-'kəlch-(ə-)rəl\ *adj* — **api·cul·tur·ist** \-'kəlch-(ə-)rəst\ *n*
apiece \ə-'pēs\ *adv* : for each one : INDIVIDUALLY ⟨selling for ten cents *apiece*⟩
ap·ish \'ā-pish\ *adj* **1** : given to slavish imitation **2** : extremely silly or affected — **ap·ish·ly** *adv* — **ap·ish·ness** *n*
aplomb \ə-'pläm, -'pləm\ *n* [F, lit., perpendicularity, fr. *à plomb* according to the plummet] : complete composure or self-assurance : POISE
apo- *or* **ap-** *prefix* [Gk, away, off, un-; akin to E *of, off*] **1** : away from : off ⟨*aphelion*⟩ **2** : detached : separate ⟨*apocarpous*⟩ **3** : formed from : related to ⟨*apomorphine*⟩
apoc·a·lypse \ə-'päk-ə-,lips\ *n* [Gk *apokalypsis*, lit., uncovering, fr. *apo-* + *kalyptein* to cover] **1** : a Jewish or early Christian symbolic writing about a final cataclysm destroying the powers of evil and ushering in the kingdom of God; *esp* : the biblical book of Revelation **2** : a prophetic revelation **3** : a writing envisaging a world cataclysm **4** : CATACLYSM — **apoc·a·lyp·tic** \ə-,päk-ə-'lip-tik\ *adj* — **apoc·a·lyp·ti·cal·ly** \-'lip-ti-k(ə-)lē\ *adv*
apoc·o·pe \ə-'päk-ə-(,)pē\ *n* : the loss of one or more sounds or letters at the end of a word (as in *sing* from Old English *singan*)
apoc·ry·pha \ə-'päk-rə-fə\ *n sing or pl* [LL *apocryphus* not canonical, fr. Gk *apokryphos* obscure, fr. *apokryph-, apokryptein* to hide away, fr. *apo-* + *kryptein* to hide] **1** : writings or statements of dubious authenticity **2** *cap a* : books included in the Septuagint and Vulgate but excluded from the Jewish and Protestant canons of the Old Testament — see BIBLE table **b** : early Christian writings not included in the New Testament
apoc·ry·phal \-fəl\ *adj* **1** *often cap* : of or resembling the Apocrypha **2** : not canonical : SPURIOUS — **apoc·ry·phal·ly** \-fə-lē\ *adv* — **apoc·ry·phal·ness** *n*
ap·o·dal \'ap-əd-ᵊl\ *or* **ap·o·dous** \-əd-əs\ *adj* : having no feet or analogous appendages ⟨eels are *apodal*⟩
apo·gee \'ap-ə-(,)jē\ *n* [Gk *apo-* + *gaia, gē* earth] **1** : the point in the orbit of a satellite of the earth or of a vehicle orbiting the earth that is at the greatest distance from the center of the earth; *also* : the point farthest from a planet

or a satellite (as the moon) reached by any object orbiting it — compare PERIGEE **2** : the farthest or highest point : CULMINATION ⟨the *apogee* of Aegean civilization⟩

Apol·lo \ə-'päl-ō\ *n* : the Greek god of the sun and of music and poetry

Apol·lyon \ə-'päl-yən, -'päl-ē-ən\ *n* : the angel of hell

apol·o·get·ic \ə-,päl-ə-'jet-ik\ *adj* **1** : offered by way of excuse or apology **2** : expressing or seeming to express apology ⟨an *apologetic* face⟩ — **apol·o·get·i·cal·ly** \-'jet-i-k(ə-)lē\ *adv*

apol·o·get·ics \-'jet-iks\ *n* : systematic argument in defense esp. of the divine origin and authority of Christianity

apo·lo·gia \,ap-ə-'lō-j(ē-)ə\ *n* : APOLOGY; *esp* : DEFENSE 3b

apol·o·gist \ə-'päl-ə-jəst\ *n* : one who speaks or writes in defense of a faith, a cause, or an institution

apol·o·gize \ə-'päl-ə-,jīz\ *vi* : to make an apology : express regret for something one has done — **apol·o·giz·er** *n*

apol·o·gy \-jē\ *n, pl* **-gies** [Gk *apo-* + *log-, legein* to speak] **1** : a formal justification or defense **2** : an admission of error or discourtesy accompanied by an expression of regret **3** : a poor substitute

syn EXCUSE: APOLOGY implies that one has been actually or apparently in the wrong; it may offer an explanation or it may simply acknowledge error and express regret; EXCUSE implies an intent to remove blame or censure for a wrong, mistake, or failure

apoph·y·sis \ə-'päf-ə-səs\ *n, pl* **apoph·y·ses** \-'päf-ə-,sēz\ [Gk *apo-* + *phyein* to bring forth] : an expanded or projecting part esp. of an organism

ap·o·plec·tic \,ap-ə-'plek-tik\ *adj* **1** : of, relating to, or caused by apoplexy ⟨*apoplectic* symptoms⟩ **2 a** : affected with or inclined to apoplexy ⟨*apoplectic* patients⟩ **b** : highly excited or excitable — **ap·o·plec·ti·cal·ly** \-ti-k(ə-)lē\ *adv*

ap·o·plexy \'ap-ə-,plek-sē\ *n, pl* **-plex·ies** [Gk *apoplēssein* to cripple by a stroke, fr. *apo-* + *plēssein* to strike] : sudden weakening or loss of consciousness, sensation, and voluntary motion caused by rupture or obstruction of an artery of the brain (as by a clot)

aport \ə-'pōrt, -'port\ *adv* (*or adj*) : on or toward the left side of a ship

apos·ta·sy \ə-'päs-tə-sē\ *n, pl* **-sies** [Gk *apo-* + *sta-, histasthai* to stand] **1** : renunciation of a religious faith **2** : abandonment of a previous loyalty : DEFECTION

apos·tate \ə-'päs-,tāt, -tət\ *n* : one who commits apostasy — **apostate** *adj*

a pos·te·ri·o·ri \,ä-pō-,stir-ē-'ōr-ē, -'ōr-\ *adj* [L, from the latter] : of or relating to reasoning from known or observed facts to a conclusion — **a posteriori** *adv*

apos·tle \ə-'päs-əl\ *n* [Gk *apostolos*, lit., one sent forth, fr. *apo-* + *stellein* to send] **1** : one sent on a religious mission: as **a** : one of an authoritative New Testament group made up esp. of Christ's twelve original disciples and Paul **b** : the first Christian missionary to a region **c** *cap* : PAUL **2** : ADVOCATE, PROPAGANDIST; *esp* : one who first advocates a viewpoint — **apos·tle·ship** \-əl-,ship\ *n*

Apostles' Creed *n* : a Christian creed anciently ascribed to the Twelve Apostles that begins "I believe in God the Father Almighty"

apos·to·late \ə-'päs-tə-,lāt, -lət\ *n* : the office or mission of an apostle

ap·os·tol·ic \,ap-ə-'stäl-ik\ *adj* **1 a** : of or relating to an apostle **b** : of or relating to the New Testament apostles or their times **2 a** : of or forming a succession of spiritual authority from the apostles held in Catholic tradition to be perpetuated by successive ordinations of bishops and orders **b** : PAPAL — **apos·to·lic·i·ty** \ə-,päs-tə-'lis-ət-ē\ *n*

apostolic delegate *n* : a diplomatic representative with full powers from the Holy See to a country with which it has no formal diplomatic relations

¹apos·tro·phe \ə-'päs-trə-(,)fē\ *n* [Gk *apo-* + *stroph-, strephein* to turn] : the rhetorical addressing of an absent person as if present or of an abstract idea or inanimate object as if capable of understanding (as in "O grave, where is thy victory?")

²apostrophe *n* : a mark ' or ' used to show the omission of letters or figures (as in *can't* for *cannot* or *'76* for *1776*),

the possessive case (as in *James's*), or the plural of letters or figures (as in *cross your t's, six 7's*)

apos·tro·phize \ə-'päs-trə-,fīz\ *vb* **1** : to address by or in apostrophe **2** : to make use of apostrophe

apothecaries' measure *n* — see MEASURE table

apothecaries' weight *n* — see MEASURE table

apoth·e·cary \ə-'päth-ə-,ker-ē\ *n, pl* **-car·ies** [LL *apothecarius* shopkeeper, fr. *apotheca* storehouse, fr. Gk *apothēkē*, fr. *apo-* + *thē-, tithenai* to put] : DRUGGIST

apo·thegm \'ap-ə-,them\ *n* [Gk *apo-* + *phthengesthai* to utter] : a short, pithy, and instructive saying or formulation : APHORISM

apo·them \'ap-ə-,them\ *n* [Gk *apo-* + *thema* something laid down, theme] : the perpendicular from the center to one of the sides of a regular polygon

apo·the·o·sis \ə-,päth-ē-'ō-səs, ,ap-ə-'thē-ə-səs\ *n, pl* **-o·ses** \-'ō-,sēz, -ə-,sēz\ [Gk *apotheoun* to deify, fr. *apo-* + *theos* god] **1** : elevation to divine status : DEIFICATION **2** : a perfect example — **ap·o·the·o·size** \,ap-ə-'thē-ə-,sīz, ə-'päth-ē-ə-\ *vt*

ap·pall *also* **ap·pal** \ə-'pól\ *vt* **ap·palled; ap·pal·ling** [MF *apalir* to make pale, fr. *a-* ad- + *pale* pale] : to overcome with fear or dread

ap·pall·ing *adj* : inspiring horror or dismay : SHOCKING — **ap·pall·ing·ly** \-'pò-liŋ-lē\ *adv*

Ap·pa·loo·sa \,ap-ə-'lü-sə\ *n* [prob. fr. *Palouse*, an Indian people of Wash. and Idaho] : a rugged American saddle horse that has a mottled skin and a blotched or dotted patch of white hair over the rump and loins

ap·pa·nage \'ap-ə-nij\ *n* [F *apanage*, fr. OProv *apanar* to support, fr. L *ad-* + *panis* bread] **1 a** : a grant (as of land or revenue) made by a sovereign or a legislative body to a member of the royal family or a nobleman **b** : a customary or rightful possession or privilege **2** : a natural accompaniment or endowment

ap·pa·rat \'ap-ə-,rat\ *n* : APPARATUS 2

ap·pa·ra·tchik \,äp-ə-'räch-ik\ *n, pl* **-ratchiks** *or* **-ratchi·ki** \-'räch-ə-(,)kē\ [Russ] : a member of a Communist apparatus

ap·pa·ra·tus \,ap-ə-'rat-əs, -'rāt-\ *n, pl* **-us·es** *or* **-us** [L, fr. *apparare* to prepare, fr. *ad-* + *parare* to prepare] **1 a** : the equipment used to do a particular kind of work **b** : an instrument or appliance for a specific operation **2** : the system of persons and agencies through which an organization functions; *esp* : the administrative machinery of a Communist party

¹ap·par·el \ə-'par-əl\ *vt* **-eled** *or* **-elled; -el·ing** *or* **-el·ling** [OF *apareillier* to prepare, irreg. fr. L *apparare*] **1** : CLOTHE, DRESS **2** : ADORN, EMBELLISH

²apparel *n* : personal attire : CLOTHING

ap·par·ent \ə-'par-ənt, -'per-\ *adj* [L *apparēre* to appear] **1** : open to view : VISIBLE **2** : clear to the understanding ⟨it was *apparent* that the road was little used⟩ **3** : appearing as actual to the eye or mind **4** : appearing to be reasonably true — **ap·par·ent·ly** *adv* — **ap·par·ent·ness** *n*

syn APPARENT, EVIDENT mean readily perceived or apprehended. APPARENT implies having outward signs that may prove on deeper analysis to be misleading ⟨the *apparent* size of the sun⟩ EVIDENT suggests an appearance unmistakably corresponding with reality ⟨her *evident* delight at his gift⟩

ap·pa·ri·tion \,ap-ə-'rish-ən\ *n* [L *apparit-, apparēre* to appear] **1 a** : an unusual or unexpected sight : PHENOMENON **b** : a ghostly figure : GHOST **2** : APPEARANCE — **ap·pa·ri·tion·al** \-'rish-nəl, -ən-°l\ *adj*

¹ap·peal \ə-'pēl\ *n* [OF *apel*, fr. *apeler* to call, accuse, appeal, fr. L *appellare*] **1 a** : a legal proceeding by which a case is brought from a lower to a higher court for a reexamination **b** : a request for a review of a decision by a higher authority **2** : an earnest request : PLEA **3** : the power of arousing a sympathetic response : ATTRACTION

²appeal *vb* **1** : to charge with a crime : ACCUSE **2** : to take action to have a case or decision reviewed by a higher court or authority **3** : to call upon another for corroboration or vindication **4** : to make an earnest request **5** : to arouse a sympathetic response — **ap·peal·a·ble** \ə-'pē-lə-bəl\ *adj*

ap·peal·ing *adj* : arousing interest esp. by beauty or charm : ATTRACTIVE — **ap·peal·ing·ly** \-'pē-liŋ-lē\ *adv*

ap·pear \ə-'pi(ə)r\ *vi* [L *apparēre*, fr. *ad-* + *parēre* to show oneself, obey] **1** : to come into sight : become evident

: SHOW ⟨stars *appeared* in the sky⟩ **2** : to present oneself formally (as to answer a charge, give testimony, or plead a cause) ⟨*appear* in court⟩ **3** : to become clear to the mind **4 a** : to come out in printed form ⟨a book scheduled to *appear* next month⟩ **b** : to come before the public on stage or screen ⟨*appears* on television⟩ **5** : SEEM, LOOK ⟨*appear* to be tired⟩

ap·pear·ance \ə-'pir-ən(t)s\ *n* **1** : the act, action, or process of appearing **2 a** : outward aspect : LOOK **b** : external show : SEMBLANCE **c** *pl* : outward indications ⟨guilty to all *appearances*⟩ **3 a** : something that appears : PHENOMENON **b** : an instance of appearing ⟨a personal *appearance*⟩

ap·pease \ə-'pēz\ *vt* [OF *apaisier,* fr. *a-* ad- + *pais* peace] **1** : to make calm or quiet : ALLAY **2** : to make concessions to (a potential aggressor) usu. at the sacrifice of principles in order to avoid war : CONCILIATE **syn** see PACIFY — **ap·pease·ment** \-mənt\ *n* — **ap·peas·er** *n*

¹ap·pel·lant \ə-'pel-ənt\ *adj* : making an appeal

²appellant *n* : one that appeals; *esp* : one that appeals from a judicial decision or decree

ap·pel·late \ə-'pel-ət\ *adj* : of or relating to appeals ⟨*appellate* jurisdiction⟩; *esp* : having the power to review the decisions of a lower court ⟨an *appellate* court⟩

ap·pel·la·tion \,ap-ə-'lā-shən\ *n* : identifying or descriptive name or title : DESIGNATION

ap·pel·lee \,ap-ə-'lē\ *n* : one against whom an appeal is taken

ap·pend \ə-'pend\ *vt* [LL *appendere,* fr. L *ad-* + *pendere* hang] **1** : ATTACH, AFFIX **2** : to add as a supplement or appendix

ap·pend·age \ə-'pen-dij\ *n* **1** : something attached to a larger or more important thing **2** : a subordinate or derivative body part; *esp* : a limb or an analogous part

ap·pen·dec·to·my \,ap-ən-'dek-tə-mē\ *n, pl* **-mies** : surgical removal of the human appendix

ap·pen·di·ci·tis \ə-,pen-də-'sīt-əs\ *n* : inflammation of the appendix

ap·pen·dic·u·lar \,ap-ən-'dik-yə-lər\ *adj* : of or relating to an appendage and esp. a limb ⟨the *appendicular* skeleton⟩

ap·pen·dix \ə-'pen-diks\ *n, pl* **-dix·es** *or* **-di·ces** \-də-,sēz\ [L *appendic-, appendix* addition, fr. *appendere* to append] **1** : supplementary material usu. attached at the end of a piece of writing **2** : a bodily outgrowth or process; *esp* : a small tubular outgrowth from the cecum of the intestine

ap·per·ceive \,ap-ər-'sēv\ *vt* : PERCEIVE, APPREHEND

ap·per·cep·tion \,ap-ər-'sep-shən\ *n* **1** : introspective self-consciousness **2** : the process of understanding something perceived in terms of previous experience — **ap·per·cep·tive** \-'sep-tiv\ *adj*

ap·per·tain \,ap-ər-'tān\ *vi* [MF *apartenir,* fr. L *appertinēre,* fr. *ad-* + *pertinēre* to pertain] : to belong or be connected as a possession, part, or right : PERTAIN ⟨duties that *appertain* to the office of governor⟩

ap·pe·tite \'ap-ə-,tīt\ *n* [L *appetitus,* fr. *appetit-, appetere* to seek after, fr. *ad-* + *petere* to seek] **1** : one of the instinctive desires necessary to keep up organic life; *esp* : the desire to eat **2 a** : an inherent craving **b** : TASTE, PREFERENCE

ap·pe·tiz·er \-,tī-zər\ *n* : a food or drink that stimulates the appetite and is usu. served before a meal

ap·pe·tiz·ing \-,tī-ziŋ\ *adj* : appealing to the appetite — **ap·pe·tiz·ing·ly** \-ziŋ-lē\ *adv*

ap·plaud \ə-'plȯd\ *vb* [L *applaudere,* fr. *ad-* + *plaudere* to clap] **1** : PRAISE, APPROVE **2** : to show approval esp. by clapping the hands — **ap·plaud·a·ble** \-ə-bəl\ *adj* — **ap·plaud·a·bly** \-blē\ *adv* — **ap·plaud·er** *n*

ap·plause \ə-'plȯz\ *n* [ML *applausus,* fr. L *applaus-, applaudere* to applaud] : approval publicly expressed (as by clapping the hands) : ACCLAIM

ap·ple \'ap-əl\ *n* [OE *æppel*] : a rounded fruit with a red, yellow, or green skin, firm white flesh, a seedy core, and usu. a tart taste; *also* : the tree of the rose family that bears this fruit

ap·ple·jack \'ap-əl-,jak\ *n* : brandy distilled from cider

ap·pli·ance \ə-'plī-ən(t)s\ *n* **1** : a piece of equipment for adapting a tool or machine to a special purpose : ATTACHMENT **2** : an instrument or device designed for a particular use ⟨a fire-fighting *appliance*⟩ ⟨a mechanical *appliance*⟩ ⟨an *appliance* serving as an artificial arm⟩ **3** : a piece (as a stove, toaster, refrigerator, or vacuum cleaner) of house-

hold or office equipment that is operated by gas, electricity, or a small electric motor

ap·pli·ca·ble \'ap-li-kə-bəl, ə-'plik-ə-\ *adj* : capable of being or suitable to be applied : APPROPRIATE — **ap·pli·ca·bil·i·ty** \,ap-li-kə-'bil-ət-ē, ə-,plik-ə-\ *n*

ap·pli·cant \'ap-li-kənt\ *n* : one who applies for something ⟨an *applicant* for work⟩ ⟨*applicants* for admission⟩

ap·pli·ca·tion \,ap-lə-'kā-shən\ *n* **1** : the act or an instance of applying ⟨*application* of paint to a house⟩ **2** : something put or spread on a surface ⟨hot *applications* on a sprained ankle⟩ **3** : ability to fix one's attention on a task **4 a** : PETITION ⟨an *application* for aid⟩ **b** : a request made personally or in writing ⟨an *application* for a job⟩; *also* : a form used in making such a request **5** : capacity for practical use

ap·pli·ca·tor \'ap-lə-,kāt-ər\ *n* : one that applies; *esp* : a device for applying a substance (as medicine or polish)

ap·plied \ə-'plīd\ *adj* : put to practical use; *esp* : applying general principles to solve definite problems ⟨*applied* sciences⟩

¹ap·pli·qué \,ap-lə-'kā\ *n* : a cutout decoration fastened to a larger piece of material

²appliqué *vt* **-quéd; -qué·ing** : to apply (as a decoration or ornament) to a larger surface

ap·ply \ə-'plī\ *vb* **ap·plied; ap·ply·ing** [MF *aplier,* fr. L *applicare,* fr. *ad-* + *plicare* to fold] **1 a** : to put to use esp. for some practical or specific purpose ⟨*apply* a rule⟩ ⟨*apply* knowledge⟩ **b** : to bring into action ⟨*apply* the brakes⟩ **c** : to lay or spread on **d** : to place in contact ⟨*apply* heat⟩ **e** : to put into operation or effect ⟨*apply* a law⟩ **2** : to employ diligently or with close attention **3** : to have relevance or a valid connection ⟨this law *applies* to everyone⟩ **4** : to make an appeal or request esp. in the form of a written application ⟨*apply* for a job⟩ — **ap·pli·er** \-'plī(-ə)r\ *n*

ap·pog·gia·tu·ra \ə-,päj-ə-'tùr-ə\ *n* [It, lit., act of leaning] : an embellishing note or tone preceding an essential melodic note or tone and usu. written as a note of smaller size

appoggiatura

ap·point \ə-'pȯint\ *vt* [MF *apointier,* fr. *a-* ad- + *point*] **1** : to fix or set officially ⟨*appoint* a day for a meeting⟩ **2** : to name officially esp. to an office or position ⟨the president *appoints* the members of his cabinet⟩

ap·point·ed *adj* : FURNISHED, EQUIPPED ⟨a well-*appointed* house⟩

ap·poin·tee \ə-,pȯin-'tē, ,a-,pȯin-\ *n* : a person appointed to a position or an office

ap·point·ive \ə-'pȯint-iv\ *adj* : of, relating to, or filled by appointment ⟨an *appointive* office⟩

ap·point·ment \ə-'pȯint-mənt\ *n* **1** : the act or an instance of appointing : DESIGNATION ⟨holds office by *appointment*⟩ **2** : a position or office to which a person is named but not elected ⟨received an *appointment* from the president⟩ **3** : an agreement to meet at a fixed time ⟨a two-o'clock *appointment* with the dentist⟩ **4** : EQUIPMENT, FURNISHINGS — usu. used in pl.

ap·por·tion \ə-'pōr-shən, -'pȯr-\ *vt* **-tioned; -tion·ing** \-sh(ə-)niŋ\ : to divide and distribute proportionately ⟨his time was carefully *apportioned* among his various studies⟩ **syn** see ALLOT

ap·por·tion·ment \-shən-mənt\ *n* : the act or result of apportioning; *esp* : the apportioning of representatives or taxes among states or districts according to population

ap·pose \a-'pōz\ *vt* [MF *aposer,* fr. *a-* ad- + *poser* to place, pose] : to place near or in close relationship

ap·po·site \'ap-ə-zət\ *adj* [L *appositus,* fr. pp. of *apponere* to apply, add, fr. *ad-* + *ponere* to place] : highly pertinent or appropriate : APT — **ap·po·site·ly** *adv* — **ap·po·siteness** *n*

ap·po·si·tion \,ap-ə-'zish-ən\ *n* **1 a** : a grammatical construction in which a noun or noun equivalent is followed by another that explains it ⟨as *the poet* and *Burns* in "a biography of the poet Burns"⟩ **b** : the relation of one of such a pair of nouns or noun equivalents to the other **2 a** : an act or instance of apposing; *esp* : the deposition of new layers upon those already present **b** : the state of being apposed — **ap·po·si·tion·al** \-'zishnəl, -ən-ᵊl\ *adj* — **ap·po·si·tion·al·ly** \-ē\ *adv*

¹ap·pos·i·tive \ə-'päz-ət-iv\ *adj* : of, relating to, or standing in grammatical apposition — **ap·pos·i·tive·ly** *adv*

²appositive *n* : the second of a pair of nouns or noun equivalents in apposition

ap·prais·al \ə-'prā-zəl\ *n* **1** : an act or instance of appraising **2** : a determination of the value of property by an appraiser; *also* : the value so determined

ap·praise \ə-'prāz\ *vt* [ME *appreisen*, fr. MF *aprisier*, fr. *a-* ad- + *prisier* to prize, value] : to set a value on; *esp* : to determine the money value of ⟨a house *appraised* at $9,000⟩ **syn** see ESTIMATE — **ap·praise·ment** \-mənt\ *n*

ap·prais·er \ə-'prā-zər\ *n* : one that appraises; *esp* : an official who appraises real estate and personal property for purposes of taxation

ap·pre·cia·ble \ə-'prē-shə-bəl\ *adj* : large enough to be recognized and measured or to be felt ⟨an *appreciable* difference in temperature⟩ — **ap·pre·cia·bly** \-blē\ *adv*

ap·pre·ci·ate \ə-'prē-shē-,āt\ *vb* [LL *appretiare*, fr. L *ad- + pretium* price] **1 a** : to evaluate the worth, quality, or significance of **b** : to admire greatly **c** : to judge with heightened perception or understanding : be fully aware of **d** : to recognize with gratitude **2** : to increase in number or value **syn** see ESTEEM — **ap·pre·ci·a·tor** \-,āt-ər\ *n* — **ap·pre·cia·to·ry** \-shə-,tōr-ē, -,tȯr-\ *adj*

ap·pre·ci·a·tion \ə-,prē-shē-'ā-shən\ *n* **1** : the act of appreciating **2** : awareness or understanding of worth or value **3** : a rise in value

ap·pre·cia·tive \ə-'prē-shət-iv, -shē-,āt-iv\ *adj* : having or showing appreciation ⟨an *appreciative* audience⟩ — **ap·pre·cia·tive·ly** *adv* — **ap·pre·cia·tive·ness** *n*

ap·pre·hend \,ap-ri-'hend\ *vb* [L *apprehendere*, fr. *ad- + prehendere* to seize, grasp] **1** : ARREST, SEIZE ⟨*apprehend* a suspect⟩ **2 a** : to become aware of : PERCEIVE **b** : to anticipate esp. with anxiety, dread, or fear **3** : to grasp with the understanding : UNDERSTAND — **ap·pre·hen·si·ble** \-'hen(t)-sə-bəl\ *adj* — **ap·pre·hen·si·bly** \-blē\ *adv*

ap·pre·hen·sion \,ap-ri-'hen-chən\ *n* [L *apprehens-, apprehendere* to seize] **1** : CAPTURE, ARREST ⟨*apprehension* of a burglar⟩ **2** : UNDERSTANDING, COMPREHENSION **3** : fear of what may be coming : dread of the future

ap·pre·hen·sive \,ap-ri-'hen(t)-siv\ *adj* : feeling apprehension : fearful of what may be coming — **ap·pre·hen·sive·ly** *adv* — **ap·pre·hen·sive·ness** *n*

¹ap·pren·tice \ə-'prent-əs\ *n* [MF *aprentis*, fr. *aprendre* to learn, fr. L *apprehendere* to apprehend] **1** : one legally bound to serve a master for a term in consideration of instruction in an art or trade and formerly usu. of maintenance **2** : one who is learning a trade, art, or calling by practical experience under skilled workers — **ap·pren·tice·ship** \-ə(sh)-,ship, -əs-,ship\ *n*

²apprentice *vt* : to bind or set at work as an apprentice

ap·pressed \a-'prest\ *adj* : pressed close to or lying flat against something

ap·prise *also* **ap·prize** \ə-'prīz\ *vt* [F *appris*, pp. of *apprendre* to learn, fr. L *apprehendere* to apprehend] : to give notice to : INFORM

¹ap·proach \ə-'prōch\ *vb* [OF *aprochier*, fr. LL *appropiare*, fr. L *ad- + prope* near] **1 a** : to draw close : come near or nearer : NEAR **b** : APPROXIMATE **2** : to take preliminary steps toward

²approach *n* **1 a** : an act or instance of approaching **b** : APPROXIMATION **2 a** : a preliminary step **b** : manner of advance **3** : a means of access : AVENUE

ap·proach·a·ble \ə-'prō-chə-bəl\ *adj* : capable of being approached : ACCESSIBLE; *esp* : easy to meet or deal with — **ap·proach·a·bil·i·ty** \-,prō-chə-'bil-ət-ē\ *n*

ap·pro·ba·tion \,ap-rə-'bā-shən\ *n* [L *approbare* to approve] **1** : the act of approving formally or officially **2** : COMMENDATION, PRAISE

¹ap·pro·pri·ate \ə-'prō-prē-,āt\ *vt* [LL *appropriare*, fr. L *ad- + proprius* one's own] **1** : to take exclusive possession of : ANNEX **2** : to set apart for a particular purpose or use ⟨Congress *appropriated* funds for naval research⟩ **3** : to take without permission — **ap·pro·pri·a·tor** \-,āt-ər\ *n*

²ap·pro·pri·ate \-prē-ət\ *adj* : especially suitable or fitting : PROPER **syn** see FIT — **ap·pro·pri·ate·ly** *adv* — **ap·pro·pri·ate·ness** *n*

ap·pro·pri·a·tion \ə-,prō-prē-'ā-shən\ *n* **1** : an act or instance of appropriating **2** : something that has been appropriated; *esp* : a sum of money formally set aside for a specific use

ap·prov·al \ə-'prü-vəl\ *n* **1** : an act or instance of ap-

proving : APPROBATION **2** *pl* : postage stamps for collectors sent on approval to prospective purchasers — **on approval** : subject to a prospective buyer's acceptance or refusal ⟨goods sent *on approval*⟩

ap·prove \ə-'prüv\ *vb* [OF *aprover*, fr. L *approbare*, fr. *ad- + probare* to prove] **1** : to have or express a favorable judgment : take a favorable view **2 a** : to accept as satisfactory **b** : to give formal or official sanction to — **ap·prov·ing·ly** \-'prü-viŋ-lē\ *adv*

syn APPROVE, ENDORSE, SANCTION mean to have or express a favorable opinion of. APPROVE may imply no more than this or it may suggest some degree of admiration; ENDORSE adds the implication of backing with an explicit statement; SANCTION implies both approving and authorizing

¹ap·prox·i·mate \ə-'präk-sə-mət\ *adj* [LL *approximatus*, pp. of *approximare* to approach, fr. L *ad- + proximus* nearest, next] : nearly correct or exact ⟨the *approximate* cost⟩ — **ap·prox·i·mate·ly** *adv*

²ap·prox·i·mate \-,māt\ *vt* **1 a** : to bring near or close **b** : to bring together **2** : to come near : APPROACH

ap·prox·i·ma·tion \ə-,präk-sə-'mā-shən\ *n* **1** : the act or process of approximating **2** : the quality or state of being close esp. in value **3** : something that is approximate; *esp* : a nearly exact estimate of a value — **ap·prox·i·ma·tive** \ə-'präk-sə-,māt-iv\ *adj* — **ap·prox·i·ma·tive·ly** *adv*

ap·pur·te·nance \ə-'pərt-nən(t)s, -ᵊn-ən(t)s\ *n* [AF *apurtenance*, fr. OF *apartenir* to appertain] : something (as a right or fixture) that belongs to or goes along with another usu. larger and more important thing ⟨a house for sale with its furniture and all other *appurtenances*⟩ — **ap·pur·te·nant** \-'pərt-nənt, -ᵊn-ənt\ *adj*

ap·ri·cot \'ap-rə-,kät, 'ā-prə-\ *n* [Ar *al-birqūq* the apricot] : an oval orange-colored fruit resembling the related peach and plum in flavor; *also* : a tree that bears apricots

April \'ā-prəl\ *n* [L *Aprilis*] : the 4th month of the year

April fool *n* : one who is tricked on April Fools' Day

April Fools' Day *n* : April 1 characteristically marked by the playing of practical jokes

a pri·o·ri \,ä-prē-'ȯr-ē, -'ȯr-\ *adj* [L, from the former] **1** : of or relating to reasoning from self-evident propositions **2** : estimated from available facts without close examination : PRESUMPTIVE ⟨*a priori* probability⟩ — **a priori** *adv*

apron \'ā-prən, -pərn\ *n* [ME *napron*, the phrase *a napron* being understood as *an apron*] **1** : a garment worn on the front of the body to protect the clothing **2** : something resembling an apron in shape, position, or use: as **a** : the part of the stage in front of the proscenium arch **b** : a shield (as of concrete, planking, or brushwood) along the bank of a river to prevent erosion **c** : the extensive paved part of an airport immediately adjacent to the terminal area or hangars

¹ap·ro·pos \,ap-rə-'pō, 'ap-rə-,\ *adv* [F *à propos*, lit., to the purpose] **1** : at the right time : SEASONABLY **2** : by the way

²apropos *adj* : being to the point : PERTINENT

apropos of *prep* : with regard to : CONCERNING

apse \'aps\ *n* [ML *apsis*, fr. L, arch, orbit, fr. Gk *hapsis*, fr. *haptein* to fasten] : a vaulted semicircular or polygonal projection on the end of a church or other building — see BASILICA illustration — **ap·si·dal** \'ap-səd-ᵊl\ *adj*

apt \'apt\ *adj* [L *aptus*, fr. pp. of *apere* to fasten, fit] **1** : FITTING, SUITABLE ⟨an *apt* quotation⟩ **2** : having an habitual tendency or inclination : LIKELY ⟨he is *apt* to become angry over trifles⟩ **3** : quick to learn ⟨a pupil *apt* in arithmetic⟩ — **apt·ly** *adv* — **apt·ness** \'ap(t)-nəs\ *n*

syn APT, LIKELY, LIABLE, PRONE: APT implies an inherent or habitual tendency and may apply to the past or present as well as the future ⟨children are *apt* to imitate their parents⟩ LIKELY stresses probability and is used in predictions ⟨it is *likely* to rain tomorrow⟩ LIABLE implies exposure to a risk or danger and suggests chance rather than probability ⟨cars are *liable* to skid on wet roads⟩ PRONE is close to APT but is used chiefly of unfavorable tendencies or predispositions ⟨*prone* to yield to selfish impulse⟩

ap·ter·ous \'ap-tə-rəs\ *adj* [Gk *a-* ²a- + *pteron* wing] : lacking wings

ap·ter·yx \'ap-tə-riks\ *n* [Gk *pteryx* wing] : KIWI

ap·ti·tude \'ap-tə-,t(y)üd\ *n* **1** : capacity for learning

: APTNESS **2 a :** INCLINATION, TENDENCY **b :** a natural ability **:** TALENT ⟨has an *aptitude* for mathematics⟩ **3 :** general suitability **:** APPROPRIATENESS — **ap·ti·tu·di·nal** \,ap-tə-'t(y)üd-°n-əl\ *adj* — **ap·ti·tu·di·nal·ly** \-ē\ *adv*

aq·ua·cade \'ak-wə-,kād, 'äk-\ *n* [L *aqua* water + E *-cade* (as in *cavalcade*)] **:** an elaborate water spectacle consisting of exhibitions of swimming, diving, and acrobatics accompanied by music

aq·ua·for·tis \,ak-wə-'fórt-əs, ,äk-\ *n* [NL *aqua fortis*, lit., strong water] **:** NITRIC ACID

aq·ua·ma·rine \,ak-wə-mə-'rēn, ,äk-\ *n* **1 :** a transparent semiprecious bluish or greenish stone that is a variety of beryl **2 :** a pale blue to light greenish blue

aq·ua·plane \'ak-wə-,plān, 'äk-\ *n* **:** a board towed behind a speeding motorboat and ridden by a person standing on it — **aquaplane** *vi* — **aqua·plan·er** *n*

aq·ua re·gia \,ak-wə-'rē-j(ē-)ə, ,äk-\ *n* [NL, lit., royal water] **:** a mixture of nitric and hydrochloric acids that dissolves gold or platinum

aq·ua·relle \,ak-wə-'rel, ,äk-\ *n* **:** a drawing in water-color and esp. transparent watercolor — **aq·ua·rell·ist** \-'rel-əst\ *n*

aquar·ist \ə-'kwer-əst, -'kwar-\ *n* **:** one who keeps an aquarium

aquar·i·um \ə-'kwer-ē-əm, -'kwar-\ *n, pl* **-i·ums** *or* **-ia** \-ē-ə\ [L *aqua* water] **:** a container (as a glass tank) in which living water animals or plants are kept; *also* **:** an establishment where such aquatic collections are kept and shown

Aquar·i·us \ə-'kwar-ē-əs, -'kwer-\ *n* [L, lit., water carrier] **1 :** a constellation south of Pegasus pictured as a man pouring water **2 :** the 11th sign of the zodiac — see ZODIAC table

¹aquat·ic \ə-'kwät-ik, -'kwat-\ *adj* **1 :** growing or living in or frequenting water **2 :** performed in or on water — **aquat·i·cal·ly** \-i-k(ə-)lē\ *adv*

²aquatic *n* **1 :** an aquatic animal or plant **2** *pl* **:** water sports

aq·ua·tint \'ak-wə-,tint, 'äk-\ *n* **:** an etching in which spaces are eaten in with nitric acid to produce an effect resembling a drawing in watercolors or india ink — **aquatint** *vt*

aq·ue·duct \'ak-wə-,dəkt\ *n* [L *aquaeductus*, fr. *aquae ductus* conduit for water] **1 :** an artificial channel for carrying flowing water from place to place; *esp* **:** a structure that carries the water of a canal across a river or hollow **2 :** a canal or passage in a body part or organ

aque·ous \'ā-kwē-əs, 'ak-wē-\ *adj* **1 a :** of, relating to, or resembling water **b :** made of, by, or with water ⟨an *aqueous* solution⟩ **2 :** of or relating to the aqueous humor

aqueous humor *n* **:** a clear fluid between the lens and the cornea of the eye

aq·ui·fer \'ak-wə-fər, 'äk-\ *n* **:** a water-bearing stratum of permeable rock, sand, or gravel — **aquif·er·ous** \ə-'kwif-(ə-)rəs, ä-\ *adj*

Aq·ui·la \'ak-wə-lə\ *n* [L, lit., eagle] **:** a northern constellation in the Milky Way southerly from Lyra and Cygnus

aq·ui·le·gia \,ak-wə-'lē-j(ē-)ə\ *n* **:** COLUMBINE

aq·ui·line \'ak-wə-,līn, -lən\ *adj* [L *aquila* eagle] **1 :** of, relating to, or resembling an eagle **2 :** curving like an eagle's beak ⟨an *aquiline* nose⟩ — **aq·ui·lin·i·ty** \,ak-wə-'lin-ət-ē\ *n*

-ar \ər\ *adj suffix* [L *-aris*, alter. of *-alis* -al] **:** of or relating to ⟨molecular⟩; being ⟨spectacular⟩; resembling ⟨oracular⟩

Ar·ab \'ar-əb, in sense 2 often '\ā-,rab\ *n* **1 a :** a member of the Semitic people of the Arabian peninsula **b :** a member of an Arabic-speaking people **2** *not cap* **:** STREET ARAB **3 :** a horse of the stock used by the natives of Arabia and adjacent regions; *esp* **:** one of a breed noted for graceful build, speed, intelligence, and spirit — **Arab** *adj*

ar·a·besque \,ar-ə-'besk\ *n* [F, fr. It *arabesco* in Arabian style] **:** an ornament or a style of decoration consisting of interlacing lines and figures usu. of flowers, foliage, or fruit — **arabesque** *adj*

¹Ara·bi·an \ə-'rā-bē-ən\ *adj* **:** of or relating to Arabia or the Arabs

²Arabian *n* **:** a native or inhabitant of Arabia **:** ARAB

¹Ar·a·bic \'ar-ə-bik\ *adj* **:** ARABIAN, ARAB

²Arabic *n* **:** a Semitic language of Arabia spoken also in

Jordan, Lebanon, Syria, Iraq, Egypt, and parts of northern Africa

arabic numeral *n, often cap A* **:** one of the number symbols 1, 2, 3, 4, 5, 6, 7, 8, 9, and 0 — see NUMBER table

ar·a·ble \'ar-ə-bəl\ *adj* [L *arabilis*, fr. *arare* to plow] **:** fit for or cultivated by plowing or tillage **:** suitable for producing crops — **ar·a·bil·i·ty** \,ar-ə-'bil-ət-ē\ *n* — **arable** *n*

Ar·a·by \'ar-ə-bē\ *n* **:** Arabia

Arach·ne \ə-'rak-nē\ *n* **:** a Lydian girl transformed into a spider for challenging Athena to a contest in weaving

arach·nid \ə-'rak-nəd\ *n* [Gk *arachnē* spider] **:** any of a class (Arachnida) of arthropods including the spiders, scorpions, mites, and ticks and having a segmented body divided into two regions of which the anterior bears four pairs of legs but no antennae — **arachnid** *adj* — **arach·ni·dan** \-nəd-ən\ *adj or n* — **arach·noid** \-,nóid\ *adj*

arach·noid \-,nóid\ *n* [Gk *arachnē* spider web] **:** a thin membrane of the brain and spinal cord that lies between the dura mater and the pia mater — **arachnoid** *adj*

arag·o·nite \ə-'rag-ə-,nīt, 'ar-ə-gə-\ *n* **:** a mineral that is chemically the same as calcite but is denser and takes a different crystalline form

Ar·a·mae·an \,ar-ə-'mē-ən\ *n* **1 :** a member of a Semitic people of the 2d millennium B.C. in Syria and Upper Mesopotamia **2 :** ARAMAIC — **Aramaean** *adj*

Ar·a·ma·ic \,ar-ə-'mā-ik\ *n* **:** a Semitic language of the Aramaeans later used extensively in southwest Asia (as by the Jews after the Babylonian exile)

ara·ne·id \ə-'rā-nē-əd\ *n* [L *aranea* spider] **:** SPIDER 1 — **ar·a·ne·i·dal** \,ar-ə-'nē-əd-°l\ *adj* — **ar·a·ne·i·dan** \-əd-°n\ *adj or n*

Arap·a·ho *or* **Arap·a·hoe** \ə-'rap-ə-,hō\ *n* **1 :** an Algonquian people of the plains region of the U.S. and Canada **2 :** a member of the Arapaho people

Arau·ca·ni·an \ə-,raù-'kän-ē-ən\ *n* **:** a member of a group of Indian peoples of Chile and Argentina — **Araucanian** *adj*

Ar·a·wak \'ar-ə-,wäk\ *n* **:** a member of an Indian people chiefly of British Guiana

ar·ba·lest *or* **ar·ba·list** \'är-bə-ləst\ *n* [OF *arbaleste*, fr. LL *arcuballista*, fr. L *arcus* bow + *ballista* machine for hurling missiles] **:** a medieval military weapon with a steel bow used to throw balls, stones, and quarrels

ar·bi·ter \'är-bət-ər\ *n* [L] **1 :** a person delegated to decide a dispute **:** ARBITRATOR, UMPIRE **2 :** a person having absolute authority to judge and decide what is right or proper ⟨an *arbiter* of taste⟩

ar·bi·tra·ment \är-'bi-trə-mənt\ *n* **1 :** the settling of a dispute by an arbiter **:** ARBITRATION **2 :** a decision or award made by an arbiter

ar·bi·trary \'är-bə-,trer-ē\ *adj* **1 :** depending on choice or discretion **2 :** arising from or guided by ungoverned will, impulse, caprice, or judgment ⟨an *arbitrary* decision⟩ ⟨an *arbitrary* ruler⟩ **3 :** selected at random or without reason — **ar·bi·trar·i·ly** \,är-bə-'trer-ə-lē\ *adv* — **ar·bi·trar·i·ness** \'är-bə-,trer-ē-nəs\ *n*

ar·bi·trate \'är-bə-,trāt\ *vb* **1 :** to settle a dispute after hearing and considering the arguments of both sides **:** hear and decide as an arbiter ⟨a committee appointed to *arbitrate* between the company and the union⟩ **2 :** to refer a dispute to others for settlement **:** submit to arbitration ⟨agreed to *arbitrate* their differences⟩ — **ar·bi·tra·ble** \-bə-trə-bəl\ *adj* — **ar·bi·tra·tive** \-,trāt-iv\ *adj*

ar·bi·tra·tion \,är-bə-'trā-shən\ *n* **:** the act of arbitrating; *esp* **:** the settling of a dispute in which both parties agree beforehand to abide by the decision of an arbitrator or body of arbitrators — **ar·bi·tra·tion·al** \-shnəl, -shən-°l\ *adj*

ar·bi·tra·tor \'är-bə-,trāt-ər\ *n* **:** a person chosen to settle differences between two parties in controversy **:** ARBITER

¹ar·bor \'är-bər\ *n* [ME *erber*, fr. OF *herbier* plot of grass, fr. *herbe* herb, grass] **:** a bower of vines or branches or of latticework covered with climbing shrubs or vines

²arbor *n* [L, tree, shaft] **:** a shaft on which a revolving cutting tool is mounted or on which the work is mounted for turning

Arbor Day *n* **:** a day appointed for planting trees

ar·bo·re·al \är-'bōr-ē-əl, -'bór-\ *adj* [L *arboreus*, fr. *arbor* tree] **1 :** of, relating to, or resembling a tree **2 :** living in or frequenting trees — **ar·bo·re·al·ly** \-ē-ə-lē\ *adv*

---

ar·bo·res·cent \,är-bə-'res-ᵊnt\ *adj* : resembling a tree in growth, structure, or appearance; *esp* : branching repeatedly like a tree — **ar·bo·res·cence** \-ᵊn(t)s\ *n* — **ar·bo·res·cent·ly** *adv*

ar·bo·re·tum \,är-bə-'rēt-əm\ *n, pl* **-retums** *or* **-re·ta** \-'rēt-ə\ : a place where trees and plants are grown for scientific and educational purposes

ar·bo·rize \'är-bə-,rīz\ *vi* : to branch freely and repeatedly

ar·bor·vi·tae \,är-bər-'vīt-ē\ *n* [NL *arbor vitae*, lit., tree of life] : any of various evergreen trees of the pine family with closely overlapping scale leaves that are often grown for ornament and hedges

ar·bu·tus \är-'byüt-əs\ *n* [L, strawberry tree] : any of a genus of shrubs and trees of the heath family with white or pink flowers and scarlet berries; *also* : a related trailing plant of eastern No. America with fragrant pinkish flowers borne in early spring

¹arc \'ärk\ *n* [L *arcus* bow, arch, arc] 1 : something arched or curved; *esp* : a sustained luminous discharge of electricity across a gap in a circuit or between electrodes 2 : a continuous portion of a circle or other curve — see CIRCLE illustration

²arc *vi* 1 : to form an electric arc 2 : to follow an arc≠shaped course

ar·cade \är-'kād\ *n* 1 : a row of arches with the columns that support them 2 : an arched or covered passageway; *esp* : one lined with shops — **ar·cad·ed** \-'kād-əd\ *adj*

ar·ca·dia \är-'kād-ē-ə\ *n, often cap* [*Arcadia*, region of ancient Greece frequently chosen as setting for pastoral poetry] : a region or scene of simple pleasure and quiet — **ar·ca·di·an** \-ē-ən\ *adj or n, often cap*

Ar·ca·dy \'är-kəd-ē\ *n* : ARCADIA

ar·cane \är-'kān\ *adj* [L *arcanus*, fr. *arca* chest for valuables] : SECRET, MYSTERIOUS

ar·ca·num \är-'kā-nəm\ *n, pl* **-na** \-nə\ : mysterious knowledge known only to the initiate

ar·cel·la \är-'sel-ə\ *n* : any of a genus of shelled protozoans related to the amoebas

¹arch \'ärch\ *n* [OF *arche*, modification of L *arcus* bow, arch] 1 : a usu. curved structural member spanning an opening and serving as a support (as for the wall above the opening) 2 : something resembling an arch in form or function: as **a** : either of two vaulted portions of the bony structure of the foot that impart elasticity to it **b** : a curved element having the form of an arch 3 : ARCHWAY

arches: *1* round, *2* lancet, *3* trefoil, *4* ogee

²arch *vb* 1 : to cover or provide with an arch 2 : to form or bend into an arch 3 : to move in an arch : ARC

³arch \'ärch\ *adj* [arch-] 1 : PRINCIPAL, CHIEF ⟨an arch≠villain⟩ 2 **a** : cleverly sly and alert **b** : playfully saucy : ROGUISH

arch- *prefix* [Gk *archi-*, *arch-*, fr. *archein* to begin, rule] 1 : chief : principal ⟨archenemy⟩ 2 : most remarkable or outstanding ⟨archrogue⟩

archaeo- *also* **archeo-** *comb form* [Gk *archaios*, fr. *archē* beginning] : ancient : primitive ⟨Archeozoic⟩

ar·chae·ol·o·gy *or* **ar·che·ol·o·gy** \,är-kē-'äl-ə-jē\ *n* : the science that deals with past human life and activities as shown by fossil relics and the monuments and artifacts left by ancient peoples — **ar·chae·o·log·i·cal** \-kē-ə-'läj-i-kəl\ *adj* — **ar·chae·ol·o·gist** \-kē-'äl-ə-jəst\ *n*

ar·chae·op·ter·yx \,är-kē-'äp-tə-riks\ *n* [Gk *pteryx* wing] : a primitive extinct Mesozoic European bird with reptilian characteristics

ar·chae·or·nis \,är-kē-'ȯr-nəs\ *n* [Gk *ornis* bird] : any of several extinct Mesozoic toothed birds

ar·cha·ic \är-'kā-ik\ *adj* [Gk *archaïkos*, fr. *archē* beginning] 1 : of, relating to, or characteristic of an earlier or more primitive time : ANTIQUATED 2 : having the characteristics of the language of the past and surviving chiefly in specialized uses ⟨the *archaic* words *methinks* and *saith*⟩ 3 : surviving from an earlier period ⟨an *archaic* plant⟩ **syn** see OLD

ar·cha·ism \'är-kē-,iz-əm, -kā-\ *n* 1 : the use of archaic words 2 : an archaic word or expression

arch·an·gel \'ärk-,ān-jəl\ *n* : an angel of high rank — **arch·an·gel·ic** \,ärk-,an-'jel-ik\ *adj*

arch·bish·op \(')ärch-'bish-əp\ *n* : the bishop of highest rank in a group of dioceses — **arch·bish·op·ric** \-'bish-ə-(,)prik\ *n*

arch·dea·con \(')ärch-'dē-kən\ *n* 1 : an ecclesiastical dignitary usu. ranking below a bishop 2 : an Anglican priest who supervises a part of a diocese or the missionary work of a diocese — **arch·dea·con·ate** \-kə-nət\ *n* — **arch·dea·con·ry** \-kən-rē\ *n*

arch·di·o·cese \(')ärch-'dī-ə-səs, -,sēz, -,sēs\ *n* : the diocese of an archbishop — **arch·di·oc·e·san** \,ärch-dī-'äs-ə-sən\ *adj*

arch·du·cal \(')ärch-'d(y)ü-kəl\ *adj* : of or relating to an archduke or archduchy

arch·duch·ess \(')ärch-'dəch-əs\ *n* 1 : the wife or widow of an archduke 2 : a woman having in her own right the rank of archduke

arch·duchy \-'dəch-ē\ *n* : the territory of an archduke or archduchess

arch·duke \-'d(y)ük\ *n* : a sovereign prince; *esp* : a prince of the imperial family of Austria — **arch·duke·dom** \-dəm\ *n*

ar·che·go·ni·um \,är-ki-'gō-nē-əm\ *n, pl* **-nia** \-nē-ə\ : a flask-shaped female sex organ found esp. in mosses and ferns — **ar·che·go·ni·al** \-nē-əl\ *adj*

arch·en·e·my \(')ärch-'en-ə-mē\ *n* : a principal enemy

arch·en·ter·on \är-'kent-ə-,rän, -rən\ *n* : the cavity of the gastrula of an embryo

Ar·cheo·zo·ic \,är-kē-ə-'zō-ik\ *n* : the earliest of the five eras of geological history; *also* : the corresponding system of rocks — see GEOLOGIC TIME table — **Archeozoic** *adj*

ar·cher \'är-chər\ *n* [OF, fr. LL *arcarius*, fr. L *arcus* bow] : one who uses a bow and arrow — called also *bowman*

ar·chery \'ärch-(ə-)rē\ *n* 1 : the art, practice, or skill of shooting with bow and arrow 2 : a body of archers

ar·che·type \'är-ki-,tīp\ *n* [Gk *archetypon*, fr. *archein* to begin + *typos* type] : the original pattern or model of a work or the model from which others are copied — **ar·che·typ·al** \,är-ki-'tī-pəl\ *or* **ar·che·typ·i·cal** \-'tip-i-kəl\ *adj*

arch·fiend \(')ärch-'fēnd\ *n* : a chief fiend; *esp* : SATAN

ar·chi·epis·co·pal \,är-kē-ə-'pis-kə-pəl\ *adj* [Gk *archiepiskopos* archbishop, fr. *archi-* arch- + *episkopos* bishop] : of or relating to an archbishop

Ar·chi·me·de·an \,är-kə-'mēd-ē-ən, -mi-'dē-ən\ *adj* : of, relating to, or invented by Archimedes

ar·chi·pel·a·go \,är-kə-'pel-ə-,gō, ,är-chə-\ *n, pl* **-goes** *or* **-gos** [*Archipelago* Aegean sea, fr. It *Arcipelago*, lit., chief sea, fr. Gk *archi-* arch- + *pelagos* sea] : a sea or other expanse of water with many scattered islands; *also* : a group of islands in such a body of water — **ar·chi·pe·lag·ic** \-pə-'laj-ik\ *adj*

ar·chi·tect \'är-kə-,tekt\ *n* [Gk *architektōn* master builder, fr. *archi-* arch- + *tektōn* builder, carpenter] : a person who designs buildings and oversees their construction

ar·chi·tec·ton·ic \,är-kə-,tek-'tän-ik\ *adj* : of, relating to, or according with the principles of architecture : ARCHITECTURAL — **ar·chi·tec·ton·i·cal·ly** \-'tän-i-k(ə-)lē\ *adv*

ar·chi·tec·ton·ics \-'tän-iks\ *n sing or pl* : structural design : STRUCTURE, ORDER, PLAN

ar·chi·tec·tur·al \,är-kə-'tek-chə-rəl, -'tek-shrəl\ *adj* : of, relating to, or conforming to the rules of architecture — **ar·chi·tec·tur·al·ly** \-ē\ *adv*

ar·chi·tec·ture \'är-kə-,tek-chər\ *n* 1 : the art of making plans for buildings 2 : the style of building that architects produce or imitate ⟨a church of modern *architecture*⟩ 3 : architectural work : BUILDINGS

ar·chi·trave \'är-kə-,trāv\ *n* [It, fr. Gk *archi-* arch- + It *trave* beam, fr. L *trabs*] : the lowest division of an entablature resting immediately on the capital of the column in an ancient Greek or Roman building — see ORDER illustration

ar·chive \'är-,kīv\ *n* [L *archivum*, fr. Gk *archeia* government documents, fr. *archē* beginning, rule, government] : a place in which public records or historical documents are preserved; *also* : the material preserved — usu. used in pl. — **ar·chi·val** \är-'kī-vəl\ *adj*

ar·chi·vist \'är-kə-vəst, -,kī-\ *n* : a person in charge of archives

---

j joke; **ŋ** sing; **ō** flow; **ȯ** flaw; **ȯi** coin; **th** thin; **th̲** this; **ü** loot; **u̇** foot; **y** yet; **yü** few; **yu̇** furious; **zh** vision

arch·ly \'ärch-lē\ *adv* **:** in an arch manner **:** ROGUISHLY, MISCHIEVOUSLY

arch·ness *n* **:** the quality of being arch

ar·chon \'är-ˌkän, -kən\ *n* [Gk *archōn*, fr. prp. of *archein* to rule] **:** one of the chief magistrates in ancient Athens

arch·way \'ärch-ˌwā\ *n* **:** a way or passage under an arch; *also* **:** an arch over a passage

-ar·chy \ˌär-kē, *in some words also* ər-kē\ *n comb form, pl* **-archies** [Gk *-archia*, fr. *archein* to rule] **:** rule **:** government ⟨squire*archy*⟩

arc lamp *n* **:** a lamp whose light is produced when an electric current passes between two hot electrodes surrounded by gas — called also *arc light*

¹**arc·tic** \'ärk-tik, 'ärt-ik\ *adj* [Gk *arktikos*, fr. *arktos* bear, Ursa Major, north] **1** *often cap* **:** of or relating to the north pole or the region around it **2 :** very cold **:** FRIGID

²**arc·tic** \'ärt-ik, 'ärk-tik\ *n* **:** a rubber overshoe reaching to the ankle or above

arctic circle *n, often cap A&C* **:** a small circle of the earth parallel to its equator approximately 23° 27′ from the north pole — see ZONE illustration

Arc·tu·rus \ärk-'t(y)ùr-əs\ *n* [Gk *Arktouros*, lit., bear watcher] **:** a giant fixed star of the first magnitude in Boötes

ar·dent \'ärd-ᵊnt\ *adj* [L *ardēre* to burn] **1 a :** characterized by warmth of feeling **:** PASSIONATE **b :** ZEALOUS, DEVOTED **2 :** FIERY, HOT **3 :** GLOWING, SHINING — **ar·den·cy** \-ᵊn-sē\ *n* — **ar·dent·ly** *adv*

arctic

ar·dor \'ärd-ər\ *n* **1 a :** a warmth of feeling or sentiment **b :** extreme vigor or energy **:** INTENSITY **2 :** ZEAL, EAGERNESS **syn** see PASSION

ar·du·ous \'ärj-(ə-)wəs\ *adj* [L *arduus* steep, high, difficult] **:** extremely difficult ⟨an *arduous* climb⟩ — **ar·du·ous·ly** *adv* — **ar·du·ous·ness** *n*

¹**are** [OE *earun*, pres. pl.; akin to E *is*] *pres 2d sing or pres pl of* BE

²**are** \'a(ə)r, 'e(ə)r, 'är\ *n* [F, fr. L *area* level space] — see METRIC SYSTEM table

ar·ea \'ar-ē-ə, 'er-\ *n* **1 :** a flat surface or space; *esp* **:** a level piece of ground **2 :** the amount of surface included within a closed figure; *also* **:** the number of unit squares equal in measure to the surface **3 a :** REGION ⟨a farming *area*⟩ **b :** a field of activity — **ar·e·al** \-ē-əl\ *adj* — **ar·e·al·ly** \-ē-ə-lē\ *adv*

area·way \-ē-ə-ˌwā\ *n* **:** a sunken space affording access, air, and light to a basement

are·na \ə-'rē-nə\ *n* [L, lit., sand] **1 :** an area in a Roman amphitheater for gladiatorial combats **2 a :** an enclosed area used for public entertainment **b :** a building containing an arena **3 :** a sphere of interest or activity

arena theater *n* **:** a theater having the acting area in the center of the auditorium with the audience seated on all sides of the stage

aren't \(')ärnt, 'är-ənt\ **:** are not

are·o·la \ə-'rē-ə-lə\ *n, pl* **-lae** \-ˌlē\ *or* **-las** [L, small open space, dim. of *area*] **:** a colored ring (as about the nipple) — **are·o·lar** \-lər\ *adj*

Ar·e·op·a·gus \ˌar-ē-'äp-ə-gəs\ *n* **:** the supreme tribunal of Athens

Ares \'a(ə)r-(ˌ)ēz, 'e(ə)r-; 'ā-ˌrēz\ *n* **:** the Greek god of war

arête \ə-'rāt\ *n* [F, lit., fish bone] **:** a sharp-crested ridge in rugged mountains

Ar·e·thu·sa \ˌar-ə-'th(y)ü-zə\ *n* **:** a wood nymph transformed by Artemis into a stream running under the sea and emerging in Sicily as a fountain

ar·gent \'är-jənt\ *adj* [L *argentum*, n., silver] **:** of or resembling silver **:** SILVERY, WHITE, SHINING

ar·gen·tite \'är-jən-ˌtīt\ *n* **:** a dark gray mineral Ag₂S that is a silver sulfide and constitutes an ore of silver

ar·gil·la·ceous \ˌär-jə-'lā-shəs\ *adj* [L *argilla* clay] **:** of, relating to, or containing clay or the minerals of clay

ar·gi·nine \'är-jə-ˌnēn\ *n* **:** an amino acid $C_6H_{14}O_2N_4$ that is found in various proteins and is essential in the diet of rats

Ar·give \'är-ˌjīv, -ˌgīv\ *adj* **:** of or relating to the Greeks or Greece and esp. to the Achaean city of Argos or the surrounding territory of Argolis — **Argive** *n*

Ar·go \'är-ˌgō\ *n* [Gk *Argō*] **:** a large constellation in the

southern hemisphere lying principally between Canis Major and the Southern Cross

ar·gon \'är-ˌgän\ *n* [Gk. neut. of *argos* idle, fr. *a-* ²*a-* + *ergon* work] **:** a colorless odorless inert gaseous chemical element found in the air and in volcanic gases and used esp. as a filler for electric bulbs — see ELEMENT table

ar·go·naut \'är-gə-ˌnòt\ *n* **:** NAUTILUS 2

Argonaut *n* [Gk *Argonautēs*, fr. *Argō*, name of Jason's ship + *nautēs* sailor] **:** one of a band of heroes sailing with Jason in quest of the Golden Fleece

ar·go·sy \'är-gə-sē\ *n, pl* **-sies** [modif. of It *ragusea* vessel of Ragusa (now Dubrovnik, Yugoslavia)] **1 :** a large ship; *esp* **:** a large merchant ship **2 :** a fleet of ships

ar·got \'är-gət, -ˌgō\ *n* [F] **:** the language of a particular group or class esp. of the underworld

ar·gu·a·ble \'är-gyə-wə-bəl\ *adj* **:** open to argument, dispute, or question — **ar·gu·a·bly** \-blē\ *adv*

ar·gue \'är-(ˌ)gyü\ *vb* [L *arguere* to make clear, accuse & MF *arguer* to reason, fr. L *argutare* to orate, fr. *argutus* clear, noisy, fr. pp. of *arguere*] **1 :** to give reasons for or against ⟨*argue* in favor of lowering taxes⟩ **2 :** to debate or discuss some matter **:** DISPUTE ⟨*argue* about politics⟩ **3 :** to persuade by giving reasons ⟨tried to *argue* his father into getting a new car⟩ **4 :** INDICATE ⟨the boy's manner *argued* his guilt⟩ **syn** see DISCUSS — **ar·gu·er** *n*

ar·gu·ment \'är-gyə-mənt\ *n* **1 a :** a reason for or against something **b :** a discussion in which arguments are presented **:** DISPUTE, DEBATE **2 :** a heated dispute **:** QUARREL **3 :** the subject matter or topic (as of a book) or a summary of such subject matter

ar·gu·men·ta·tion \ˌär-gyə-mən-'tā-shən, -ˌmen-\ *n* **1 :** the act or process of forming reasons and of drawing conclusions and applying them to a case under discussion **2 :** DEBATE, DISCUSSION

ar·gu·men·ta·tive \ˌär-gyə-'ment-ət-iv\ *adj* **:** marked by or given to argument **:** DISPUTATIOUS — **ar·gu·men·ta·tive·ly** *adv*

Ar·gus \'är-gəs\ *n* **:** a hundred-eyed monster of Greek legend

Ar·gus-eyed \ˌär-gəs-'īd\ *adj* **:** vigilantly observant

ar·gyle \'är-ˌgīl\ *n* **:** a geometric knitting pattern of varicolored diamonds on a single background color; *also* **:** a sock knit in this pattern

aria \'är-ē-ə\ *n* [It, lit., atmospheric air, modif. of L *aer*, fr. Gk *aēr*] **:** AIR, MELODY, TUNE; *esp* **:** an accompanied elaborate melody sung (as in an opera) by a single voice

Ar·i·ad·ne \ˌar-ē-'ad-nē\ *n* **:** a daughter of Minos who gives Theseus the thread whereby he escapes from the labyrinth

Ar·i·an \'ar-ē-ən, 'er-\ *adj* **:** of or relating to Arius or his doctrines esp. that the Son is not of the same substance as the Father but was created as an agent for creating the world — **Arian** *n* — **Ar·i·an·ism** \-ē-ə-ˌniz-əm\ *n*

-ar·i·an \'er-ē-ən, 'ar-\ *n suffix* [L *-arius* -ary] **:** believer ⟨Unit*arian*⟩ **:** advocate ⟨latitudin*arian*⟩ ⟨disciplin*arian*⟩

ar·id \'ar-əd\ *adj* [L *aridus*] **1 :** excessively dry; *esp* **:** having insufficient rainfall to support agriculture **2 :** lacking in interest and life **:** DULL — **arid·i·ty** \ə-'rid-ət-ē, a-\ *n*

Ar·i·es \'ar-ē-ˌēz, 'er-\ *n* [L, lit., ram] **1 :** a constellation between Pisces and Taurus pictured as a ram **2 :** the 1st sign of the zodiac — see ZODIAC table

aright \ə-'rīt\ *adv* **:** RIGHTLY, CORRECTLY ⟨done *aright*⟩

ar·il \'ar-əl\ *n* **:** an outer covering or appendage of some seeds that develops after fertilization — **ar·il·late** \'ar-ə-ˌlāt\ *adj*

arise \ə-'rīz\ *vi* **arose** \-'rōz\; **aris·en** \-'riz-ᵊn\; **aris·ing** \-'rī-ziŋ\ [OE *ārisan*, fr. *ā-*, prefix denoting completion + *rīsan* to rise] **1 :** to move upward **:** ASCEND **2 :** to get up from sleep or after lying down **3 :** to come into existence from or as if from a source **:** spring up **:** OCCUR ⟨a dispute *arose* between the leaders⟩

ar·is·toc·ra·cy \ˌar-ə-'stäk-rə-sē\ *n, pl* **-cies** [Gk *aristos* best] **1 :** government by the best individuals or by a small privileged class **2 a :** a government in which power is exercised by a minority esp. of those felt to be best qualified **b :** a state with such a government **3 a :** a governing body or upper class usu. made up of an hereditary nobility **b :** a group felt to be superior (as in wealth, culture, or intelligence)

ə abut; ᵊ kitten; ər further; a back; ā bake; ä cot, cart; aù out; ch chin; e less; ē easy; g gift; i trip; ī life

aris·to·crat \ə-'ris-tə-ˌkrat\ *n* **1** : a member of an aristocracy; *esp* : NOBLE **2** : one who has habits and viewpoints (as snobbishness) that are typical of the aristocracy — **aris·to·crat·ic** \ə-ˌris-tə-'krat-ik\ *adj* — **aris·to·crat·i·cal·ly** \-'krat-i-k(ə-)lē\ *adv*

Ar·is·to·te·lian *or* **Ar·is·to·te·lean** \ˌar-ə-stə-'tēl-yən\ *adj* : of, relating to, or characteristic of Aristotle or his philosophy — **Ar·is·to·te·lian·ism** \-yə-ˌniz-əm\ *n*

arith·me·tic \ə-'rith-mə-ˌtik\ *n* [Gk *arithmētikē*, fr. *arithmein* to number, fr. *arithmos* number] **1** : a branch of mathematics that deals with real numbers and computations with them **2** : an act or method of computing : CALCULATION — **ar·ith·met·ic** \ˌar-ith-'met-ik\ *or* **ith·met·i·cal** \-'met-i-kəl\ *adj* — **ar·ith·met·i·cal·ly** \-k(ə-)lē\ *adv* — **arith·me·ti·cian** \ə-ˌrith-mə-'tish-ən\ *n*

arithmetical discount \ ... \ *n* : TRUE DISCOUNT

arithmetic mean \ˌar-ith-ˌmet-ik-\ *n* : a value that is computed by dividing the sum of a set of terms by the number of terms

arithmetic progression \ˌar-ith-ˌmet-ik-\ *n* : a progression in which each term is greater than its predecessor by a constant

-ar·i·um \'ar-ē-əm, 'er-\ *n suffix, pl* **-ar·i·ums** *or* **-ar·ia** \-ē-ə\ [L, fr. neut. of -*arius* -ary] : thing or place relating to ⟨planet*arium*⟩

ark \'ärk\ *n* [OE *arc*, fr. L *arca* chest] **1 a** : the ship in which Noah and his family were preserved from the Deluge **b** : a clumsy boat or ship **2 a** : a sacred chest in which the ancient Hebrews kept the two tablets of the Law **b** : a repository traditionally in or against the wall of a synagogue for the scrolls of the Torah

¹arm \'ärm\ *n* [OE *earm*] **1 a** : a human upper limb; *esp* : the part between the shoulder and wrist **b** : a corresponding limb of a lower vertebrate **2** : something resembling an arm: as **a** : a lateral branch of a tree **b** : an inlet of water (as from the sea) **c** : a slender usu. functional projecting part (as of a machine) **3** : POWER, MIGHT ⟨the *arm* of the law⟩ **4** : a support (as on a chair) for the elbow and forearm **5** : SLEEVE **6** : a division of an organization — **armed** \'ärmd\ *adj* — **arm·less** \'ärm-ləs\ *adj*

²arm *vb* [L *armare*, fr. *arma* tools, weapons] **1** : to provide with weapons ⟨*arm* and equip a new regiment⟩ **2** : to provide with a means of defense ⟨*arm* oneself with facts⟩ **3** : to provide oneself with arms and armament ⟨the country *armed* for war⟩ **4** : to equip or ready for action or operation ⟨*arm* a bomb⟩

³arm *n* **1 a** : a means of offense or defense : WEAPON; *esp* : FIREARM **b** : a branch of an army (as the infantry or artillery) that actually fights **c** : a branch of the military forces (as the navy) **2** *pl* : the heraldic devices of a family or a government **3 a** *pl* : active hostilities : WARFARE **b** *pl* : military service

ar·ma·da \är-'mäd-ə, -'mād-\ *n* [Sp, fr. ML *armata* armed force, fleet] **1** : a large fleet of warships **2** *cap* : the fleet sent by Spain against England in 1588 **3** : a large force of moving objects (as vehicles)

ar·ma·dil·lo \ˌär-mə-'dil-ō\ *n, pl* **-los** [Sp, fr. dim. of *armado* armed one, fr. L *armatus*, pp. of *armare* to arm] : any of several small burrowing chiefly nocturnal mammals of warm parts of the Americas having body and head encased in an armor of small bony plates

Ar·ma·ged·don \ˌär-mə-'ged-ᵊn\ *n* [Gk *Armageddōn*, scene of the battle foretold in Revelation 16:14–16] **1 a** : a final and conclusive battle between the forces of good and evil **b** : the site or time of Armageddon **2** : a vast decisive conflict

ar·ma·ment \'är-mə-mənt\ *n* **1** : the whole military strength and equipment of a nation **2** : the total supply of weapons, ammunition, and related equipment of a ship, fort, military unit, or system of defense **3** : means of protection or defense : ARMOR **4** : the process of preparing for war

ar·ma·ture \'är-mə-chər, -ˌchu̇(ə)r\ *n* [L *armatura*, fr. *armare* to arm] **1** : a protective or defensive mechanism or covering (as the spines of a cactus) **2** : the part of an electric generator that consists of coils of wire around an iron core and that induces an electric current when it is rotated in a magnetic field **3** : the part of an electric motor that consists of coils of wire around an iron core and that is caused to rotate in a magnetic field when an electric current is passed through the coils **4** : the movable part of an electromagnetic device (as an electric bell) **5** : a framework used by a sculptor to support a figure being modeled (as in clay)

¹arm·chair \'ärm-ˌche(ə)r, -ˌcha(ə)r, 'ärm-'\ *n* : a chair with arms

²armchair *adj* **1** : remote from direct dealing with problems ⟨*armchair* strategist⟩ **2** : sharing vicariously in another's experiences ⟨*armchair* traveler⟩

armed forces *n pl* : the combined military, naval, and air forces of a nation

Ar·me·ni·an \är-'mē-nē-ən, -nyən\ *n* **1** : a member of a people dwelling chiefly in Armenia **2** : the Indo-European language of the Armenians — **Armenian** *adj*

arm·ful \'ärm-ˌfu̇l\ *n, pl* **arm·fuls** \-ˌfu̇lz\ *or* **arms·ful** \'ärmz-ˌfu̇l\ : as much as a person's arm can hold ⟨carrying an *armful* of books⟩

arm·hole \'ärm-ˌhōl\ *n* : an opening for the arm in a garment

Ar·min·i·an \är-'min-ē-ən\ *adj* : of or relating to Arminius or his doctrines opposing the absolute predestination of strict Calvinism and maintaining the possibility of salvation for all — **Arminian** *n* — **Ar·min·i·an·ism** \-ē-ə-ˌniz-əm\ *n*

ar·mi·stice \'är-mə-stəs\ *n* [NL *armistitium*, fr. L *arma* arms + -*stitium* (as in *solstitium* solstice] : temporary suspension of fighting brought about by agreement between the two sides : TRUCE

Armistice Day *n* [so called because it commemorates the armistice which ended World War I on Nov. 11, 1918] : VETERANS DAY

arm·let \'ärm-lət\ *n* : a bracelet or band for the upper arm

ar·mor \'är-mər\ *n* [OF *armure*, fr. L *armatura*, fr. *armare* to arm] **1** : defensive covering for the body; *esp* : covering (as of metal) used in combat **2** : something that affords protection **3** : a protective covering (as the steel plates of a battleship or a sheathing for wire) **4** : armored forces and vehicles (as tanks)

ar·mored \'-mərd\ *adj* **1** : protected by armor ⟨an *armored* car⟩ ⟨*armored* reptiles⟩ **2** : supplied with armored equipment ⟨an *armored* force⟩

armored scale *n* : any of numerous scale insects having a firm covering of wax

armor: *1* plate, *2* chain

ar·mor·er \'är-mər-ər\ *n* **1** : one that makes armor or arms **2** : one that repairs, assembles, and tests firearms or that services and loads aircraft armament including bombs

ar·mo·ri·al \är-'mōr-ē-əl, -'mȯr-\ *adj* : of, relating to, or bearing heraldic arms

ar·mo·ry \'ärm-(ə-)rē\ *n, pl* **-ries** **1** : a supply of arms **2** : a place where arms are stored; *esp* : one used for training military reserve personnel **3** : a place where arms are manufactured

ar·mour \'är-mər\ *chiefly Brit var of* ARMOR

arm·pit \'ärm-ˌpit\ *n* : the hollow beneath the junction of the arm and shoulder

arm·rest \-ˌrest\ *n* : a support for the arm

ar·my \'är-mē\ *n, pl* **ar·mies** [MF *armee*, fr. ML *armata* armed force, army, fleet, fr. L, fem. of *armatus*, pp. of *armare* to arm] **1 a** : a large organized body of men armed and trained for land warfare **b** : a military unit capable of independent action and consisting usu. of a headquarters, two or more corps, and auxiliary troops **c** *often cap* : the complete military organization of a nation for land warfare **2** : a great multitude **3** : a body of persons organized to advance a cause

ar·my·worm \-ˌwərm\ *n* : any of numerous larval moths that travel in multitudes from field to field destroying crops (as grass or grain)

ar·ni·ca \'är-ni-kə\ *n* : dried flower heads of a mountain herb related to the daisies and used esp. in the form of a tincture as a liniment; *also* : this tincture

aro·ma \ə-'rō-mə\ *n* [Gk *arōmat-, arōma*] **1** : a distinctive, pleasing, and usu. penetrating odor ⟨the *aroma* of fresh coffee⟩ — compare FRAGRANCE **2** : a distinctive but faint quality : FLAVOR **syn** see SMELL

ar·o·mat·ic \ˌar-ə-'mat-ik\ *adj* **1** : of, relating to, or having aroma **2** : of, relating to, or characterized by the presence of at least one benzene ring — used of hydrocarbons and their derivatives — **aromatic** *n*

arose *past of* ARISE

¹around \ə-'raůnd\ *adv* **1 a** : in circumference ⟨a tree five feet *around*⟩ **b** : in, along, or through a curving or roundabout course ⟨the road goes *around* by the lake⟩ **2 a** : on all or various sides ⟨papers lying *around*⟩ **b** : NEARBY ⟨stick *around*⟩ **3 a** : here and there in various places ⟨traveled *around* from state to state⟩ **b** : to a particular place ⟨come *around* for dinner⟩ **4 a** : in rotation or succession ⟨pass the candy *around*⟩ **b** : from beginning to end ⟨mild the year *around*⟩ **c** : to a customary or improved condition ⟨the medicine brought him *around*⟩ **5** : in or to an opposite direction or position ⟨turned *around* and waved goodbye⟩ **6** : APPROXIMATELY ⟨a price of *around* $20⟩

²around *prep* **1 a** : on all or various sides of ⟨yard with a fence *around* it⟩ ⟨fields *around* the village⟩ **b** : so as to encircle or enclose ⟨people seated *around* the table⟩ **c** : on or to another side of ⟨voyage *around* Cape Horn⟩ **2** : here and there in or throughout ⟨traveling *around* the country⟩ **3** : not far from in number or amount ⟨selling at prices *around* $20⟩

arouse \ə-'raůz\ *vb* [*a-* (as in *arise*) + *rouse*] **1** : to awaken from sleep **2** : to rouse to action : EXCITE

ar·peg·gio \är-'pej-ō, -'pej-ē-,ō\ *n, pl* **-gios** [It, fr. *arpeggiare* to play on the harp, fr. *arpa* harp] **1** : production of the tones of a chord in succession and not simultaneously **2** : a chord played in arpeggio

ar·que·bus \'är-\ *var of* HARQUEBUS

ar·raign \ə-'rān\ *vt* **1** : to call before a court to answer to an indictment : CHARGE **2** : ACCUSE, DENOUNCE — **ar·raign·ment** \-mənt\ *n*

ar·range \ə-'rānj\ *vb* [MF *arangier*, fr. *a-* ad- + *rang* rank] **1** : to put in order; *esp* : to put in a particular order ⟨*arrange* books on shelves⟩ **2** : to make plans for : PREPARE ⟨*arrange* a meeting⟩ **3** : ADJUST, SETTLE ⟨*arrange* one's affairs to have the weekend free⟩ **4 a** : to adapt a musical composition for voices or instruments other than those orig. intended **b** : ORCHESTRATE — **ar·rang·er** *n*

ar·range·ment \ə-'rānj-mənt\ *n* **1** : a putting in order : the order in which things are put ⟨the *arrangement* of furniture in a room⟩ **2** : PREPARATION, PLAN ⟨make *arrangements* for a trip⟩ **3** : something made by arranging ⟨a flower *arrangement*⟩ **4 a** : ADAPTATION; *esp* : an adaptation of a piece of music to voices or instruments other than those orig. intended **b** : ORCHESTRATION

ar·rant \'ar-ənt\ *adj* [alter. of *errant*] : THOROUGHGOING, CONFIRMED ⟨an *arrant* knave⟩ — **ar·rant·ly** *adv*

ar·ras \'ar-əs\ *n, pl* **arras** [*Arras*, France] **1** : a tapestry of Flemish origin used esp. for wall hangings and curtains **2** : a wall hanging or screen of tapestry

¹ar·ray \ə-'rā\ *vt* [OF *arayer*, of Gmc origin; akin to E *ready*] **1** : to set in order : draw up : MARSHAL **2** : to clothe or dress esp. in splendid or impressive attire : ADORN — **ar·ray·er** *n*

²array *n* **1** : regular order or arrangement; *also* : persons (as troops) in array **2 a** : CLOTHING, ATTIRE **b** : rich or beautiful apparel : FINERY **3** : an imposing group : large number **4** : a group of mathematical elements (as numbers or letters) arranged in rows and columns

ar·rears \ə-'ri(ə)rz\ *n pl* [MF *arrere* behind, backward, fr. L *ad* to + *retro* backward] **1** : the state of being behind in the discharge of debts owed ⟨two months in *arrears* on his payments⟩ **2** : an unpaid and overdue debt

¹ar·rest \ə-'rest\ *vt* [MF *arester*, fr. L *ad-* + *restare* to rest] **1** : to stop the progress or movement of : CHECK, SLOW ⟨an *arrested* motion picture⟩ ⟨*arrest* a disease⟩ **2** : SEIZE, CAPTURE; *esp* : to take or keep in custody by authority of law ⟨*arrested* him on suspicion of robbery⟩ **3** : to attract and hold the attention of ⟨colors that *arrest* the eye⟩

²arrest *n* **1 a** : the act of stopping : CHECK **b** : the state of being stopped **2** : the act of taking or holding in custody by authority of law

ar·rest·ing *adj* : STRIKING, IMPRESSIVE

ar·riv·al \ə-'rī-vəl\ *n* **1** : the act of arriving ⟨await the *arrival* of guests⟩ **2** : a person or thing that has arrived ⟨late *arrivals* at a concert⟩

ar·rive \ə-'rīv\ *vi* [OF *ariver*, fr. L *ad* to + *ripa* shore, bank] **1** : to reach a place and esp. one's destination ⟨*arrive* home at six o'clock⟩ **2** : to gain an end or object ⟨*arrive* at a decision⟩ **3** : COME ⟨the time *arrived* to begin⟩ **4** : to be successful

ar·ro·gance \'ar-ə-gən(t)s\ *n* : a sense of one's own superiority that shows itself in an offensively proud manner : HAUGHTINESS

ar·ro·gant \-gənt\ *adj* [L *arrogare* to claim, fr. *ad-* + *rogare* to ask] **1** : exaggerating one's own worth or importance in an overbearing manner **2** : marked by arrogance ⟨*arrogant* remarks⟩ — **ar·ro·gant·ly** *adv*

ar·ro·gate \'ar-ə-,gāt\ *vt* **1** : to take or claim for one's own without right or in a haughty manner ⟨the dictator *arrogated* to himself the powers of parliament⟩ **2** : to ascribe to another esp. unduly or without right ⟨*arrogate* to a rival intentions he never had⟩ — **ar·ro·ga·tion** \,ar-ə-'gā-shən\ *n*

ar·ron·disse·ment \ə-'rän-dəs-mənt\ *n* [F] **1** : the largest division of a French department **2** : an administrative district of some large French cities

ar·row \'ar-ō\ *n* [OE *arwe*] **1** : a missile weapon shot from a bow and usu. having a slender shaft, a pointed head, and feathers at the butt **2** : a mark (as on a map or signboard) to indicate direction

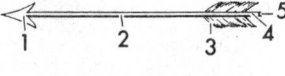

arrow: *1* head, *2* shaft, *3* feather, *4* butt, *5* nock

ar·row·head \-,hed\ *n* **1** : the usu. separate wedge-shaped striking end of an arrow **2** : something (as a wedge-shaped mark) resembling an arrowhead

ar·row·root \-,rüt, -,růt\ *n* : any of several tropical American plants with starchy tuberous roots; *also* : an edible starch from these roots

arrow worm *n* : any of a small phylum (Chaetognatha) of transparent tapering sea worms

ar·royo \ə-'rói-ō, -'rói-ə\ *n, pl* **-roy·os** [Sp] **1** : a watercourse (as a creek or stream) in a dry region **2** : an often dry gully or channel carved by water

ar·se·nal \'ärs-nəl, -ᵊn-əl\ *n* [It *arsenale*, fr. Ar *dār ṣinā'ah* house of manufacture] **1 a** : a place for the manufacture or storage of arms **b** : a collection of weapons **2** : STORE, STOREHOUSE, REPERTORY

ar·se·nate \'ärs-ᵊn-ət, -ᵊn-,āt\ *n* : a salt or ester of an arsenic acid

ar·se·nic \'ärs-nik, -ᵊn-ik\ *n* [Gk *arsenikon* yellow orpiment] **1** : a solid poisonous chemical element commonly metallic steel-gray, crystalline, and brittle — see ELEMENT table **2** : ARSENIC TRIOXIDE

arsenic acid *n* : a white crystalline poisonous acid $H_3AsO_4 \cdot \frac{1}{2}H_2O$ that consists of hydrogen, arsenic, and oxygen and is used in making chemicals

ar·sen·i·cal \är-'sen-i-kəl\ *adj* : of, relating to, or containing arsenic — **arsenical** *n*

arsenic trioxide *n* : a white or transparent extremely poisonous chemical compound As_2O_3 or As_4O_6 used in making glass and insecticides — called also *white arsenic*

ar·se·no·py·rite \,ärs-ᵊn-ō-'pī-,rīt\ *n* : a hard tin-white mineral FeAsS consisting of iron, arsenic, and sulfur

ar·sine \är-'sēn, 'är-,\ *n* : a colorless flammable extremely poisonous gas AsH₃ with an odor like garlic

ar·son \'ärs-ᵊn\ *n* [OF, fr. L *ars-, ardēre* to burn] : the malicious burning of a building or property (as a dwelling house) — **ar·son·ist** \-ᵊn-əst, -ᵊn-ᵊst\ *n*

ars·phen·a·mine \ärs-'fen-ə-,mēn\ *n* [*arsenic* + *phen-* + *amine*] : an arsenic-containing substance formerly used in the treatment of spirochetal diseases

¹art \(')ärt, ərt\ [OE *eart*; akin to E *is*] *archaic pres 2d sing of* BE

²art \'ärt\ *n* [L *art-, ars*] **1** : the power of doing something easily and skillfully : skill in performance : KNACK ⟨the *art* of making friends⟩ **2** : an occupation that requires a natural skill in addition to training and practice ⟨the *art* of cookery⟩ **3** : the rules or ideas that a person must know in order to follow a profession or craft ⟨the *art* of medicine⟩ ⟨the theater *arts*⟩ **4** : a branch of learning; *esp* **:** one of the nonscientific branches of learning (as history, philosophy, or literature) — usu. used in pl. ⟨a bachelor's degree in *arts*⟩ **5 :** the study of drawing, painting, and sculpture **6 :** the works produced by artists (as painters, sculptors, or writers) **:** a product of creative imagination

syn SKILL, CRAFT: ART may be distinct from the other two in implying personal, unanalyzable creative or imaginative power and resource; SKILL stresses technical knowledge and proficiency gained through practice and experience; CRAFT implies expertness in workmanship

Ar·te·mis \'ärt-ə-məs\ *n* **:** the Greek goddess of the moon, wild animals, and hunting

¹ar·te·ri·al \är-'tir-ē-əl\ *adj* **1 a :** of or relating to an artery **b :** being the bright red oxygen-rich blood present in most arteries **2 :** of, relating to, or constituting through≈ traffic facilities — **ar·te·ri·al·ly** \-ē-ə-lē\ *adv*

²arterial *n* **:** a through street or arterial highway

arterio- *comb form* **1 :** artery ⟨*arterio*logy⟩ **2 :** arterial and ⟨*arterio*venous⟩

ar·te·ri·ole \är-'tir-ē-,ōl\ *n* **:** a very small artery connecting a larger artery with capillaries — **ar·te·ri·o·lar** \(,)är-,tir-ē-'ō-lər, är-'tir-ē-ə-lər\ *adj*

ar·te·rio·scle·ro·sis \är-,tir-ē-ō-sklə-'rō-səs\ *n* **:** a chronic disease characterized by abnormal thickening and hardening of the arterial walls — **ar·te·rio·scle·rot·ic** \-'rät-ik\ *adj or n*

ar·te·rio·ve·nous \är-,tir-ē-ō-'vē-nəs\ *adj* **:** of, relating to, or connecting the arteries and veins

ar·tery \'ärt-ə-rē\ *n, pl* **-ter·ies** [Gk *artēria*] **1 :** one of the tubular branching muscular-walled and elastic-walled vessels that carry blood from the heart through the body **2 :** a channel (as a river or highway) of communication

ar·te·sian well \är-,tē-zhən-\ *n* [F *artésien* of Artois, region of France where such wells were common] **1 :** a bored well from which water flows up like a fountain **2 :** a deep-bored well

art·ful \'ärt-fəl\ *adj* **1 :** performed with or showing art or skill **2 :** ARTIFICIAL **3 :** skillful or ingenious in gaining an end; *also* **:** CRAFTY, WILY — **art·ful·ly** \-fə-lē\ *adv* — **art·ful·ness** *n*

arthr- *or* **arthro-** *comb form* [Gk *arthron*] **:** joint ⟨*arthral*gia⟩ ⟨*arthro*pathy⟩

ar·thri·tis \är-'thrīt-əs\ *n* **:** inflammation of the joints — **ar·thrit·ic** \-'thrit-ik\ *adj or n* — **ar·thrit·i·cal·ly** \-'thrit-i-k(ə-)lē\ *adv*

ar·thro·pod \'är-thrə-,päd\ *n* [Gk *arthron* joint + *pod-*, *pous* foot] **:** any of a phylum (Arthropoda) of invertebrate animals (as insects, arachnids, and crustaceans) with body and limbs segmented — **arthropod** *adj* — **ar·throp·o·dal** \är-'thräp-əd-ºl\ *or* **ar·throp·o·dan** \-əd-ən\ *or* **ar·throp·o·dous** \-əd-əs\ *adj*

Ar·thur \'är-thər\ *n* **:** a semilegendary 6th century king of the Britons — **Ar·thu·ri·an** \är-'th(y)ùr-ē-ən\ *adj*

ar·ti·choke \'ärt-ə-,chōk\ *n* [It dial. *articiocco*, fr. Ar *al-khurshûf* the artichoke] **:** a tall composite herb like a thistle with coarse pinnately incised leaves; *also* **:** its edible flower head which is cooked as a vegetable

¹ar·ti·cle \'ärt-i-kəl\ *n* [L *articulus* joint, division, dim. of *artus* joint] **1 :** a distinct part of a document (as a constitution, contract, or treaty) dealing with a single subject **2 :** a nonfictional prose composition forming an independent part of a publication and usu. dealing with a single topic ⟨an *article* on winter sports⟩ **3 :** any of a small set of words (as *a, an,* or *the*) used with nouns to limit or give definiteness to their application **4 :** a member of a class of things; *esp* **:** COMMODITY ⟨*articles* of commerce⟩

²article *vt* **-cled; -cling** \-k(ə-)liŋ\ **:** to bind by the articles of a contract ⟨an *articled* apprentice⟩

ar·tic·u·lar \är-'tik-yə-lər\ *adj* **:** of or relating to a joint

¹ar·tic·u·late \är-'tik-yə-lət\ *adj* **1 a :** divided clearly into words and syllables **:** INTELLIGIBLE **b :** able to speak; *esp* **:** able to express oneself effectively **2 :** consisting of segments united by joints **:** JOINTED ⟨*articulate* animals⟩ — **ar·tic·u·late·ly** *adv* — **ar·tic·u·late·ness** *n*

²ar·tic·u·late \-,lāt\ *vb* **1 a :** to make articulate sounds **b :** to speak in distinct syllables or words **:** express clearly and distinctly ⟨*articulate* every shade of meaning⟩ **2 :** to unite or become united or connected by or as if by a joint — **ar·tic·u·la·tor** \-,lāt-ər\ *n*

ar·tic·u·la·tion \(,)är-,tik-yə-'lā-shən\ *n* **1 :** the making

of articulate sounds (as in pronunciation) ⟨his *articulation* was distinct⟩ **2 a :** a joint between rigid parts of an animal; *esp* **:** one between bones or cartilages **b :** a joint between plant parts; *also* **:** a node or internode of a stem — **ar·tic·u·la·to·ry** \är-'tik-yə-lə-,tōr-ē, -,tór-\ *adj*

ar·ti·fact *or* **ar·te·fact** \'ärt-ə-,fakt\ *n* [L *arte factus* made by art] **:** a usu. simple object (as a tool or ornament) showing human workmanship or modification — **ar·ti·fac·tu·al** \,ärt-ə-'fak-chə-wəl, -chəl\ *adj*

ar·ti·fice \'ärt-ə-fəs\ *n* [L *artificium*, lit., handicraft, fr. *artific-, artifex* artisan, fr. *art-, ars* art + *facere* to make] **1 :** SKILL, INGENUITY **2 a :** a clever or esp. a crafty device **:** a cunning trick **b :** GUILE, TRICKERY

ar·tif·i·cer \är-'tif-ə-sər, 'ärt-ə-fə-sər\ *n* **:** a skilled or artistic workman **:** CRAFTSMAN

ar·ti·fi·cial \,ärt-ə-'fish-əl\ *adj* [L *artificium* handicraft, artifice] **1 :** not natural **:** produced by a human agency ⟨an *artificial* lake⟩ **2 :** made or changed to resemble something natural ⟨*artificial* flowers⟩ **3 :** not genuine or sincere **:** FORCED ⟨*artificial* gaiety⟩ — **ar·ti·fi·ci·al·i·ty** \-,fish-ē-'al-ət-ē\ *n* — **ar·ti·fi·cial·ly** \-'fish-(ə-)lē\ *adv* — **ar·ti·fi·cial·ness** \-'fish-əl-nəs\ *n*

syn SYNTHETIC: ARTIFICIAL may apply to anything that is not the result of natural process or conditions ⟨the state is an *artificial* society⟩ but esp. to something that has a natural counterpart ⟨*artificial* teeth⟩ SYNTHETIC applies esp. to a manufactured substance or to a natural substance that is treated to resemble and substitute for another; both terms may suggest a lack of naturalness and spontaneity in personal feeling or behavior

artificial respiration *n* **:** the rhythmic forcing of air into and out of the lungs of one whose breathing has stopped

ar·til·ler·ist \är-'til-ə-rəst\ *n* **:** ARTILLERYMAN

ar·til·lery \är-'til-(ə-)rē\ *n* [MF *artillerie*] **1 :** large caliber crew-served mounted firearms (as guns, howitzers, rockets) **:** ORDNANCE **2 :** a branch of an army armed with artillery — **ar·til·lery·man** \-mən\ *n*

ar·tio·dac·tyl \,ärt-ē-ō-'dak-tºl\ *n* [Gk *artios* even in number + *daktylos* finger, toe] **:** any of an order (Artiodactyla) of hoofed mammals (as the camel or ox) with an even number of functional toes on each foot — **artiodactyl** *or* **ar·tio·dac·ty·lous** \-tə-ləs\ *adj*

ar·ti·san \'ärt-ə-zən\ *n* [MF, fr. It *artigiano*, fr. *arte* art, fr. L *art-, ars*] **:** a person (as a carpenter) trained to have manual dexterity or skill in a trade

art·ist \'ärt-əst\ *n* **1 :** a person skilled in one of the arts (as painting, sculpture, music, or writing); *esp* **:** PAINTER **2 :** a person showing unusual ability in an occupation requiring skill

ar·tiste \är-'tēst\ *n* **:** a skilled adept performer; *esp* **:** a musical or theatrical entertainer

art·is·tic \är-'tis-tik\ *adj* **1 :** relating to or characteristic of art or artists **2 :** showing taste in arrangement or execution — **ar·tis·ti·cal·ly** \-'tis-ti-k(ə-)lē\ *adv*

syn AESTHETIC: ARTISTIC implies the point of view of one who produces art and thinks in terms of creating beautiful forms; AESTHETIC stresses the point of view of one who analyzes and reflects upon the effect a work of art has on him; either term may suggest a contrast with the practical, the functional, or the moral aspects of anything

art·ist·ry \'ärt-ə-strē\ *n* **1 :** artistic quality of effect or workmanship **2 :** artistic ability

art·less \'ärt-ləs\ *adj* **1 :** lacking art, knowledge, or skill **:** UNCULTURED **2 a :** made without skill **:** RUDE **b :** being simple and sincere **:** NATURAL ⟨*artless* grace⟩ **3 :** free from deceit — **art·less·ly** *adv* — **art·less·ness** *n*

art song *n* **:** a song whose melody and accompaniment are of artistic rather than popular or traditional origin and character

arty \'ärt-ē\ *adj* **art·i·er; -est 1 :** showily imitative of art **2 :** aspiring to be artistic **:** DILETTANTE — **art·i·ly** \'ärt-ºl-ē\ *adv* — **art·i·ness** \'ärt-ē-nəs\ *n*

ar·um \'ar-əm, 'er-\ *n* [L, fr. Gk *aron*] **:** any of a family of plants (as the jack-in-the-pulpit or the skunk cabbage) having heart-shaped or sword-shaped leaves and flowers in a fleshy spike enclosed in a leafy sheath

¹-ary *n suffix, pl* **-aries** [L *-arius, -aria, -arium,* fr. *-arius* ²-*ary*] **:** thing or person belonging to or connected with ⟨*ovary*⟩ ⟨function*ary*⟩

²-ary *adj suffix* [L *-arius*] **:** of, relating to, or connected with ⟨budget*ary*⟩

---

j joke; ŋ sing; ō flow; ó flaw; ói coin; th thin; th̲ this; ü loot; ù foot; y yet; yü few; yù furious; zh vision

¹**Ary·an** \'ar-ē-ən, 'er-\ *adj* **1** : INDO-EUROPEAN **2** : of or relating to the Aryans **3** : of or relating to a hypothetical ethnic type represented by early speakers of Indo-European languages

²**Aryan** *n* **1** : a member of the Indo-European-speaking people occupying the Iranian plateau and later entering India and conquering the non-Indo-European inhabitants **2 a** : a member of the people speaking the language from which the Indo-European languages are derived **b** : a member of any of the peoples speaking an Indo-European language **c** : NORDIC **d** : GENTILE

¹**as** \əz, (,)az\ *adv* [OE *eallswā* just so, just as, fr. *eall* all + *swā* so] **1** : to the same degree or extent ⟨as deaf as a post⟩ **2** : for instance ⟨various trees, *as* oak or pine⟩

²**as** *conj* **1** : in or to the same degree that ⟨deaf *as* a post⟩ **2** : in the way or manner that ⟨do *as* I do⟩ **3** : WHILE, WHEN ⟨spilled the milk *as* she got up⟩ **4** : regardless of the degree to which : THOUGH ⟨improbable *as* it seems, it's true⟩ **5** : for the reason that ⟨stayed home *as* she had no car⟩ **6** : that the result is — used after *so* or *such* ⟨so clearly guilty *as* to leave no doubt⟩

³**as** *pron* **1** : THAT, WHO, WHICH — used in standard English after *same* or *such* ⟨the same school *as* his father attended⟩ **2** : a fact that ⟨is a foreigner, *as* is evident from his accent⟩

⁴**as** *prep* **1** : LIKE 2 ⟨all rose *as* one man⟩ **2** : in the character or position of ⟨working *as* an editor⟩

⁵**as** \'as\ *n, pl* **as·ses** \'as-,ēz, 'as-əz\ [L] **1** : an ancient Roman unit of value **2** : a bronze coin representing one as

as- — see AD-

as·a·fet·i·da or **as·a·foe·ti·da** \,as-ə-'fit-əd-ē, -'fet-əd-ə\ *n* [ML, fr. Per *azā* mastic + L *foetidus* fetid] : a gum resin that has an unpleasant smell and taste and comes from several oriental plants of the carrot family formerly used in medicine

as·bes·tos \as-'bes-təs, az-\ *n* [Gk, quick-lime, fr. *asbestos* inextinguishable] : a non-combustible and heat-resistant grayish mineral that readily separates into long flexible fibers and is used in making various fireproof, nonconducting, and chemically resistant materials

as (showing head of Janus)

as·ca·rid \'as-kə-rəd\ *n* [Gk *askarid-, askaris*] : any of a family of roundworms that includes the common large roundworm parasitic in the human intestine

as·ca·ris \'as-kə-rəs\ *n, pl* **as·car·i·des** \a-'skar-ə-,dēz\ : ASCARID

as·cend \ə-'send\ *vb* [L *ascens-, ascendere*, fr, *ad-* + *scandere* to climb] : to go up : slope upward : CLIMB, RISE ⟨*ascend* a hill⟩ ⟨smoke *ascends*⟩ — **as·cend·a·ble** or **as·cend·i·ble** \-'sen-də-bəl\ *adj*

  syn ASCEND, MOUNT, CLIMB, SCALE mean to move upward or toward the top. ASCEND implies no more than this; MOUNT implies reaching the top ⟨*mount* a ladder⟩ CLIMB suggests effort and often the use of hands and feet; SCALE implies the use of a ladder or rope in climbing vertically

as·cend·an·cy \ə-'sen-dən-sē\ or **as·cend·ance** \-dən(t)s\ *n* : governing or controlling influence : DOMINATION **syn** see SUPREMACY

¹**as·cend·ant** \ə-'sen-dənt\ *n* **1** : the point of the ecliptic or degree of the zodiac that rises above the eastern horizon at any moment **2** : a state or position of dominant power

²**ascendant** *adj* **1** : moving upward : RISING **2 a** : SUPERIOR **b** : DOMINANT

as·cen·sion \ə-'sen-chən\ *n* : the act or process of ascending

Ascension Day *n* : the Thursday 40 days after Easter observed in some churches in commemoration of Christ's ascension into heaven

as·cent \ə-'sent\ *n* **1** : the act of rising or mounting upward : CLIMB **2** : an upward slope : RISE

as·cer·tain \,as-ər-'tān\ *vt* [MF *acertainer*, fr. *a-* ad- + *certain*] : to learn with certainty : find out ⟨*ascertain* the date of the concert⟩ — **as·cer·tain·a·ble** \-'tā-nə-bəl\ *adj* — **as·cer·tain·ment** \-'tān-mənt\ *n*

as·cet·ic \ə-'set-ik\ *adj* [Gk *askein* to practice, exercise] **1** : practicing strict self-denial esp. as a means of religious discipline ⟨*ascetic* in his way of life⟩ **2** : AUSTERE ⟨*ascetic* surroundings⟩ — **ascetic** *n* — **as·cet·i·cism** \ə-'set-ə-,siz-əm\ *n*

as·cid·i·an \ə-'sid-ē-ən\ *n* : any of various simple or compound tunicates

As·cle·pi·us \ə-'sklē-pē-əs\ *n* : the Greek god of medicine

as·co·carp \'as-kə-,kärp\ *n* : the fruiting body of an ascomycetous fungus — **as·co·car·pous** \,as-kə-'kär-pəs\ *adj*

as·co·my·cete \,as-kō-'mī-,sēt, -mī-'sēt\ *n* : any of a class (Ascomycetes) of higher fungi (as yeasts, molds) with septate hyphae and spores formed in asci — **as·co·my·ce·tous** \-mī-'sēt-əs\ *adj*

ascor·bic acid \ə-,skór-bik-\ *n* [²a- + NL *scorbutus* scurvy] : VITAMIN C

as·co·spore \'as-kə-,spō(ə)r, -,spó(ə)r\ *n* : a spore produced in an ascus — **as·co·spor·ic** \,as-kə-'spōr-ik, -'spór-\ or **as·co·spo·rous** \,as-kə-'spōr-əs, -'spór-; a-'skäs-pə-rəs\ *adj*

as·cot \'as-kət, -,kät\ *n* [*Ascot* Heath, English racetrack] : a broad neck scarf that is looped under the chin and sometimes pinned

as·cribe \ə-'skrīb\ *vt* [L *ascript-, ascribere*, fr. *ad-* + *scribere* to write] : to refer to a supposed cause, source, or author : ATTRIBUTE — **as·crib·a·ble** \-'skrī-bə-bəl\ *adj*

  syn ATTRIBUTE, IMPUTE: ASCRIBE suggests inferring or conjecturing the cause, source, or author of something; ATTRIBUTE implies more definiteness or stronger evidence for ascribing; IMPUTE suggests ascribing something that brings discredit by way of accusation or blame

as·crip·tion \ə-'skrip-shən\ *n* : the act of ascribing : ATTRIBUTION

as·cus \'as-kəs\ *n, pl* **as·ci** \'as-,(k)ī, -,kē\ [NL, fr. Gk *askos* wineskin, bladder] : a membranous oval or tubular spore sac of an ascomycete usu. bearing eight spores

as·dic \'az-(,)dik\ *n* : SONAR

-ase \,ās\ *n suffix* [F, fr. *diastase*] : enzyme ⟨malt*ase*⟩

asep·sis \(')ā-'sep-səs, ə-\ *n* : the condition of being aseptic; *also* : the methods of making or keeping aseptic

asep·tic \-'sep-tik\ *adj* **1** : preventing infection; *also* : free or freed from disease-causing microorganisms **2 a** : lacking life, emotion, or warmth ⟨*aseptic* essays⟩ ⟨*aseptic* apartments⟩ **b** : DETACHED, OBJECTIVE ⟨an *aseptic* view of civilization⟩ — **asep·ti·cal·ly** \-ti-k(ə-)lē\ *adv*

asex·u·al \(')ā-'sek-sh(ə-w)əl\ *adj* **1** : lacking sex ⟨*asexual* organisms⟩ **2** : occurring or formed without sexual action ⟨*asexual* reproduction⟩ ⟨*asexual* spores⟩ — **asex·u·al·ly** \-ē\ *adv*

as for *prep* : with regard to : CONCERNING ⟨*as for* me⟩

as good as *adv* : in effect : for all practical purposes ⟨*as good as* new⟩

¹**ash** \'ash\ *n* [OE *æsc*] : any of a genus of trees of the olive family with thin furrowed bark and winged seeds; *also* : its tough elastic wood

²**ash** *n* [OE *asce*] **1 a** : the solid residue left when material is thoroughly burned or is oxidized by chemical means **b** : fine particles of mineral matter from a volcanic vent **2** *pl a* : a collection of ash left after something has been burned **b** : the remains of the dead human body esp. after cremation **c** : ruins or last traces **3** *pl* : something that symbolizes grief, repentance, or humiliation **4** *pl* : deathly pallor

ashamed \ə-'shāmd\ *adj* **1** : feeling shame, guilt, or disgrace ⟨*ashamed* of his behavior⟩ **2** : kept back by anticipation of shame ⟨*ashamed* to beg⟩ — **asham·ed·ly** \-'shā-məd-lē\ *adv*

¹**ash·en** \'ash-ən\ *adj* : of or relating to ash trees or wood : made of ash

²**ashen** *adj* **1** : of the color of ashes **2** : deadly pale : BLANCHED

Ash·ke·nazi \,ash-kə-'naz-ē\ *n, pl* **-naz·im** \-'naz-əm\ : a member of one of the two great divisions of Jews comprising the eastern European Yiddish-speaking Jews — **Ash·ke·naz·ic** \-'naz-ik\ *adj*

ash·lar \'ash-lər\ *n* [MF *aisselier* traverse beam] : hewn or squared stone; *also* : masonry of hewn or squared stone

ashore \ə-'shō(ə)r, -'shó(ə)r\ *adv (or adj)* : on or to the shore

Ashur \'äsh-,ù(ə)r\ *n* : the chief god of Assyria

Ash Wednesday *n* : the first day of Lent

ashy \'ash-ē\ *adj* **ash·i·er; -est** **1** : of, relating to, or resembling ashes **2** : deadly pale

Asian \'ā-zhən, 'ā-shən\ *n* **1** : a native or inhabitant of Asia **2** : a person of Asian descent — **Asian** *adj*

Asi·at·ic \,ā-zhē-'at-ik\ *adj* : ASIAN — often taken to be offensive — **Asiatic** *n*

ə abut; ə kitten; ər further; a back; ā bake; ä cot, cart; aù out; ch chin; e less; ē easy; g gift; i trip; ī life

Asiatic cholera *n* : a destructive bacterial disease of Asiatic origin marked by violent vomiting and purging

¹aside \ə-'sīd\ *adv* **1** : to or toward the side ⟨stepped *aside*⟩ **2** : out of the way : AWAY **3** : away from one's thought : APART ⟨jesting *aside*⟩

²aside *n* **1** : words meant to be inaudible to someone; *esp* : an actor's words supposedly not heard by others on the stage **2** : DIGRESSION

aside from *prep* **1** : in addition to : BESIDES **2** : except for

as if *conj* **1** : as it would be if ⟨it was *as if* he had lost his last friend⟩ **2** : as one would do if ⟨he ran *as if* ghosts were chasing him⟩ **3** : THAT ⟨it seemed *as if* the day would never end⟩

as·i·nine \'as-ᵊn-,īn\ *adj* [L *asinus* ass] : of, relating to, or resembling an ass esp. in stupidity or obstinacy — **as·i·nine·ly** *adv* — **as·i·nin·i·ty** \,as-ᵊn-'in-ət-ē\ *n*

ask \'ask\ *vb* [OE *āscian*] **1** : to seek information : put a question to someone or about something : INQUIRE **2** : to make a request ⟨*ask* for help⟩ **3** : to set as a price : DEMAND ⟨*ask* twenty dollars for a bicycle⟩ **4** : INVITE ⟨be *asked* to a party⟩ **5** : LOOK ⟨he is *asking* for trouble⟩ — **ask·er** *n*

syn ASK, REQUEST mean to try to obtain by making known one's wants. ASK implies simply the statement of the desire; REQUEST suggests some formality or courtesy in asking and implies an expectation of an affirmative response

askance \ə-'skan(t)s\ *also* **askant** \-'skant\ *adv* **1** : with a side glance : OBLIQUELY **2** : with distrust, suspicion, or disapproval

askew \ə-'skyü\ *adv (or adj)* : out of line : AWRY, AMISS **syn** see CROOKED

¹aslant \ə-'slant\ *adv* : in a slanting direction

²aslant *prep* : over or across in a slanting direction

¹asleep \ə-'slēp\ *adj* **1** : SLEEPING **2** : lacking sensation : NUMB **3** : INACTIVE, SLUGGISH

²asleep *adv* : into a state of sleep

as long as *conj* **1** : PROVIDED ⟨can do as they like *as long as* they have a B average⟩ **2** : inasmuch as : SINCE ⟨*as long as* you're going, I'll go too⟩

aso·cial \(')ā-'sō-shəl\ *adj* **1** : inconsiderate of others : SELFISH **2** : SOLITARY, WITHDRAWN

as of *prep* : ON, AT, DURING, FROM ⟨takes effect *as of* July 1⟩

asp \'asp\ *n* [Gk *aspis*] : a small venomous snake of Egypt

as·par·a·gus \ə-'spar-ə-gəs\ *n* [Gk *asparagos*] : a tall branching perennial herb of the lily family widely grown for its thick edible young shoots

as·par·tic acid \ə-,spärt-ik-\ *n* : a crystalline amino acid $C_4H_7NO_4$ found esp. in plants

as·pect \'as-,pekt\ *n* [L *aspectus*, fr. *aspect-*, *aspicere* to look at, fr. *ad-* + *specere* to look] **1 a** : the position of planets or stars with respect to one another held by astrologers to influence human affairs **b** : a position facing a particular direction : EXPOSURE **2** : a particular status or phase in which something appears or may be regarded ⟨studied every *aspect* of the question⟩ **3** : MIEN — **as·pec·tu·al** \a-'spek-chə(-wə)l\ *adj*

as·pen \'as-pən\ *n* [OE *æspe*] : any of several poplars with leaves that flutter in the lightest breeze

as·per·i·ty \a-'sper-ət-ē, ə-'sper-\ *n, pl* **-ties** [L *asper* rough] **1** : RIGOR, SEVERITY **2** : roughness of surface : UNEVENNESS **3** : harshness of temper, manner, or tone

as·perse \ə-'spərs, a-\ *vt* [L *aspers-*, *aspergere*, lit., to sprinkle, fr. *ad-* + *spargere* to scatter] : to utter damaging charges or implications against ⟨*asperse* a man's character⟩

as·per·sion \ə-'spər-zhən\ *n* : an injurious or offensive charge or implication ⟨cast *aspersions* on a person⟩

¹as·phalt \'as-,fólt\ *or* **as·phal·tum** \as-'fól-təm\ *n* [ME *aspalt*, fr. LL *aspaltus*, fr. Gk *asphaltos*] **1** : a brown to black substance that is found in natural beds or obtained as a residue in petroleum or coal-tar refining and that consists chiefly of hydrocarbons **2** : any of various compositions of asphalt having diverse uses (as for pavement or for waterproof cement or paint) — **as·phal·tic** \as-'fól-tik\ *adj*

²asphalt *vt* : to cover or impregnate with asphalt

as·pho·del \'as-fə-,del\ *n* : any of several herbs of the lily family with white or yellow flowers in long erect spikes

as·phyx·ia \as-'fik-sē-ə\ *n* [Gk, stopping of the pulse, fr. *a-* + *sphyzein* to throb] : a lack of oxygen or excess of carbon dioxide in the body usu. caused by interruption of breathing and resulting in unconsciousness

as·phyx·i·ate \as-'fik-sē-,āt\ *vt* : to cause asphyxia in; *also* : to kill or make unconscious by interference with the normal oxygen intake — **as·phyx·i·a·tion** \(,)as-,fik-sē-'ā-shən\ *n* — **as·phyx·i·a·tor** \as-'fik-sē-,āt-ər\ *n*

as·pic \'as-pik\ *n* : a savory jelly of fish or meat stock used cold esp. to make a mold of meat, fish, or vegetables

as·pi·dis·tra \,as-pə-'dis-trə\ *n* [NL, irreg. fr. Gk *aspid-*, *aspis* shield] : an Asiatic plant of the lily family with large basal leaves that is often grown as a house plant

as·pi·rant \'as-p(ə-)rənt, ə-'spī-rənt\ *n* : one who aspires

¹as·pi·rate \'as-pə-,rāt\ *vt* [L *aspirare* to breathe on, aspire] **1** : to pronounce with an initial *h*-sound ⟨we do not *aspirate* the word *hour*⟩ **2** : to draw or remove by suction

²as·pi·rate \'as-p(ə-)rət\ *n* **1** : an independent sound \h\ or a character (as the letter *h*) representing it **2** : a consonant having as its final element an *h*-like sound in the same syllable ⟨\t\ in English *toe* is an *aspirate*⟩

as·pi·ra·tion \,as-pə-'rā-shən\ *n* **1 a (1)** : pronunciation with an aspirate ⟨*aspiration* of the word *herb*⟩ **(2)** : pronunciation as an aspirate ⟨occasional *aspiration* of the final \t\ in *hot*⟩ **b** : an independent sound \h\ or its symbol **2** : a drawing of something in, out, up, or through by or as if by suction **3 a** : a strong desire to achieve something high or great **b** : an object of such desire **syn** see AMBITION

as·pi·ra·tor \'as-pə-,rāt-ər\ *n* : an apparatus for producing suction or moving or collecting materials by suction

as·pire \ə-'spī(ə)r\ *vb* [L *aspirare* to breathe on, favor, aspire, fr. *ad-* + *spirare* to breathe] **1** : to seek to attain something high or great : desire eagerly ⟨*aspired* to the presidency⟩ **2** : ASCEND, SOAR — **as·pir·er** *n*

as·pi·rin \'as-p(ə-)rən\ *n* **1** : a white crystalline drug $C_9H_8O_4$ used as a remedy for pain and fever **2** : a tablet of aspirin

as regards *or* **as respects** *prep* : in regard to : with respect to

ass \'as\ *n* [OE *assa*] **1** : an animal resembling but smaller than the related horse and having a shorter mane, shorter hair on the tail, and longer ears : DONKEY **2** : a stupid, obstinate, or perverse person

as·sa·fet·i·da *or* **as·sa·foe·ti·da** *var of* ASAFETIDA

as·sail \ə-'sāl\ *vt* [ME *assailen*, fr. OF *asaillir*, fr. L *ad-* + *salire* to leap] : to attack violently with blows or words **syn** see ATTACK — **as·sail·a·ble** \-'sā-lə-bəl\ *adj* — **as·sail·ant** \-'sā-lənt\ *n*

as·sas·sin \ə-'sas-ᵊn\ *n* [Ar *ḥashshāshīn*, pl. of *ḥashshāsh* one addicted to hashish] : a person who kills another by a surprise or secret attack; *esp* : a hired murderer of a prominent person

as·sas·si·nate \ə-'sas-ᵊn-,āt\ *vt* : to murder (a usu. prominent person) by a surprise or secret attack esp. for pay **syn** see KILL — **as·sas·si·na·tion** \ə-,sas-ᵊn-'ā-shən\ *n*

¹as·sault \ə-'sólt\ *n* [OF *assaut*, fr. L *ad-* + *saltus* leap, fr. *salire* to leap] **1** : a violent or sudden attack : ONSLAUGHT **2** : an apparent attempt or a threat to do harm to another — compare BATTERY 1b

²assault *vt* : to make an assault upon **syn** see ATTACK

¹as·say \'as-,ā, a-'sā\ *n* [OF *essai*, *assai* test, essay, effort] **1** *archaic* : TRIAL, ATTEMPT **2** : examination or analysis (as of an ore, a metal, or a drug) for the purpose of determining composition, measure, or quality or of determining the quantity of one or more components

²as·say \a-'sā, 'as-,ā\ *vb* **1** : TRY, ATTEMPT **2 a** : to analyze (as an ore) for one or more valuable components **b** : ESTIMATE **3** : to prove up in an assay — **as·say·er** *n*

as·se·gai *or* **as·sa·gai** \'as-i-,gī\ *n* : a slender hardwood usu. iron-tipped spear used in southern Africa

as·sem·blage \ə-'sem-blij\ *n* **1** : a collection of persons or things : GATHERING **2** : the act of assembling : the state of being assembled

assegai

as·sem·ble \ə-'sem-bəl\ *vb* **-bled; -bling** \-b(ə-)liŋ\ [OF *assembler*, fr. L *ad-* + *simul* together] **1** : to collect into one place or group ⟨*assembled* the crew⟩ **2** : to fit together the parts of ⟨*assemble* a machine gun⟩ **3** : to meet together : CONVENE ⟨the right to *assemble* peacefully⟩ **syn** see GATHER — **as·sem·bler** \-b(ə-)lər\ *n*

as·sem·bly \ə-'sem-blē\ *n, pl* **-blies** **1** : a body of persons gathered together (as for deliberation, worship, or entertainment) **2** *cap* : a legislative body; *esp* : the lower house of a legislature **3** : ASSEMBLAGE **4** : a signal given (as by drum or bugle) for troops to assemble or fall in **5** : a collection of parts that go to make up a complete unit ⟨the tail *assembly* of an airplane⟩

assembly line *n* : an arrangement of machines, equipment, and workers in which work passes from operation to operation in direct line until the product is assembled

as·sem·bly·man \ə-'sem-blē-mən\ *n* : a member of a legislative assembly

¹as·sent \ə-'sent\ *vi* [L *assentire*, fr. *ad-* + *sentire* to feel] : AGREE, CONCUR

syn ASSENT, CONSENT mean to agree with what someone else has proposed. ASSENT implies the action of the understanding or judgment toward propositions or opinions; CONSENT involves the will or the feelings and indicates acceptance or approval of or compliance with what is desired or requested

²assent *n* : an act of assenting : ACQUIESCENCE, AGREEMENT

as·sert \ə-'sərt\ *vt* [L *assert-*, *asserere* to annex, claim, assert, fr. *ad-* + *serere* to join] **1** : to state clearly and strongly : declare positively ⟨*assert* an opinion in a loud voice⟩ **2** : MAINTAIN, DEFEND ⟨*assert* one's rights⟩

syn DECLARE, AFFIRM: ASSERT implies stating confidently without need for proof or evidence; DECLARE often adds to ASSERT an implication of open or public statement; AFFIRM implies conviction of truth and willingness to stand by one's statement **syn** see in addition MAINTAIN — **assert oneself** : to demand and insist that others recognize one's rights

as·ser·tion \ə-'sər-shən\ *n* : the act of asserting; *also* : something asserted : DECLARATION

as·sert·ive \ə-'sərt-iv\ *adj* : disposed to bold or confident assertion — **as·sert·ive·ly** *adv* — **as·sert·ive·ness** *n*

asses *pl of* AS *or of* ASS

as·sess \ə-'ses\ *vt* [prob. fr. ML *assess-*, *assidēre*, fr. L, to sit beside, assist in giving judgment, fr. *ad-* + *sedēre* to sit] **1** : to determine the rate or amount of ⟨the jury *assessed* damages of $5000⟩ **2** : to set a value on (as property) for purposes of taxation ⟨a house *assessed* at $6300⟩ **3** : to lay a tax or charge on ⟨the city *assessed* all car owners five dollars⟩ **4** : to determine the importance, size, or value of **syn** see ESTIMATE — **as·sess·a·ble** \ə-'ses-ə-bəl\ *adj*

as·sess·ment \ə-'ses-mənt\ *n* **1** : the act of assessing : APPRAISAL **2** : the amount or value assessed ⟨a special *assessment* for new sewers⟩

as·ses·sor \ə-'ses-ər\ *n* : an official who assesses property for purposes of taxation

as·set \'as-ˌet\ *n* [back-formation fr. obs. *assets*, sing., sufficient property to pay debts and legacies, fr. OF *assez* enough, fr. L *ad* to + *satis* enough] **1** *pl* : all the property (as cash, securities, real property, goods, accounts receivable) of a person, corporation, or estate that may be used in payment of debts **2** : ADVANTAGE, RESOURCE

as·sev·er·ate \ə-'sev-ə-ˌrāt\ *vt* [L *asseverare*, fr. *ad-* + *severus* severe] : to declare positively or earnestly : AVER — **as·sev·er·a·tion** \ə-ˌsev-ə-'rā-shən\ *n*

as·si·du·i·ty \ˌas-ə-'d(y)ü-ət-ē\ *n* : the quality or state of being assiduous : DILIGENCE

as·sid·u·ous \ə-'sij-(ə-)wəs\ *adj* [L *assiduus*, fr. *assidēre* to sit beside, fr. *ad-* + *sedēre* to sit] : steadily attentive : DILIGENT — **as·sid·u·ous·ly** *adv* — **as·sid·u·ous·ness** *n*

as·sign \ə-'sīn\ *vt* [L *assignare*, fr. *ad-* + *signare* to mark, designate, fr. *signum* mark, sign] **1** : to transfer to another ⟨*assign* a patent to his son⟩ **2 a** : to appoint to a post or duty **b** : PRESCRIBE ⟨*assign* the lesson⟩ **3** : to fix authoritatively : SPECIFY ⟨*assign* a limit⟩ **4** : ASCRIBE, REFER **syn** see ALLOT — **as·sign·a·ble** \ə-'sī-nə-bəl\ *adj* — **as·sign·er** \ə-'sī-nər\ *or* **as·sign·or** \ə-'sī-nər; ə-ˌsī-'nò(ə)r, ˌas-ˌī-; ˌas-ə-'nò(ə)r\ *n*

as·sig·nat \ˌas-ig-'nä, 'as-ig-ˌnat\ *n* : a bill issued as currency by the French Revolutionary government (1790–95) on the security of lands seized by the state

as·sig·na·tion \ˌas-ig-'nä-shən\ *n* **1** : ASSIGNMENT **2** : a usu. clandestine or illicit meeting esp. for lovemaking; *also* : an appointment for such a meeting

as·sign·ee \ə-ˌsī-'nē, ˌas-ˌī-; ˌas-ə-'nē\ *n* : a person to whom an assignment is made

as·sign·ment \ə-'sīn-mənt\ *n* **1** : the act of assigning ⟨*assignment* of seats⟩ **2** : something assigned : an assigned task ⟨an *assignment* in arithmetic⟩ **syn** see TASK

as·sim·i·late \ə-'sim-ə-ˌlāt\ *vb* [L *assimulare* to make like, fr. *ad-* + *similis* like, similar] **1 a** : to take something in and make it part of and like the thing it has joined ⟨*assimilate* nutrients into the body⟩⟨the nation *assimilated* millions of immigrants⟩ **b** : to comprehend thoroughly : ABSORB **2 a** : to make similar **b** : to alter by assimilation **syn** see ABSORB — **as·sim·i·la·bil·i·ty** \-ˌsim-ə-lə-'bil-ət-ē\ *n* — **as·sim·i·la·ble** \-'sim-ə-lə-bəl\ *adj* — **as·sim·i·la·tor** \-'sim-ə-ˌlāt-ər\ *n*

as·sim·i·la·tion \ə-ˌsim-ə-'lā-shən\ *n* **1** : the act or process of assimilating; *esp* : the conversion of nutrients (as digested food) into protoplasm **2** : change of a sound so that it becomes identical with or similar to a neighboring sound ⟨in the word *impractical* the \n\ of the prefix *in-* has undergone *assimilation*⟩ — **as·sim·i·la·tive** \-'sim-ə-ˌlāt-iv\ *adj*

¹as·sist \ə-'sist\ *vb* [L *assistere* to stand by, assist in court, fr. *ad-* + *sistere* to stand; akin to E *stand*] : to give support or aid : HELP

²assist *n* **1** : an act of assistance : AID **2** : the act of a player who by handling the ball (as in baseball) or passing the puck (as in hockey) enables a teammate to make a putout or score a goal

as·sist·ance \ə-'sis-tən(t)s\ *n* : the act of assisting or the aid supplied : SUPPORT

as·sist·ant \ə-'sis-tənt\ *n* : one who assists : HELPER; *also* : one who serves in a subordinate capacity — **assistant** *adj*

as·size \ə-'sīz\ *n* : a session of an English superior court held for the trial of civil and criminal cases three or four times a year in most counties by judges traveling on circuit — usu. used in pl.

¹as·so·ci·ate \ə-'sō-s(h)ē-ˌāt\ *vb* [L *associare* to bring together, fr. *ad-* + *socius* companion, ally] **1** : to join or come together as partners, friends, or companions **2** : to connect or bring (as ideas) together **3** : to combine or join with other parts : UNITE

²as·so·ci·ate \ə-'sō-s(h)ē-ət, -shət, -s(h)ē-ˌāt\ *n* **1** : a fellow worker : PARTNER, COLLEAGUE **2** : COMPANION **3** *often cap* : a degree conferred esp. by a junior college ⟨*associate* in arts⟩ — **associate** *adj*

as·so·ci·a·tion \ə-ˌsō-sē-'ā-shən, -ˌsō-shē-\ *n* **1** : the act of associating : the state of being associated **2** : an organization of persons having a common interest : SOCIETY **3** : something linked mentally (as with a thing or person); *also* : the process of forming such links **4** : the formation of polymers by linkage through hydrogen bonds **5** : a major ecological unit characterized by essential uniformity — **as·so·ci·a·tion·al** \-shnəl, -shən-ᵊl\ *adj*

association football *n* : SOCCER

as·so·ci·a·tive \ə-'sō-s(h)ē-ˌāt-iv, -shət-iv\ *adj* **1** : of, relating to, or involved in association and esp. mental association ⟨*associative* neurons⟩ **2** : dependent on or acquired by association or learning **3** : combining elements in such a manner that the result is independent of the original grouping of the elements ⟨addition is an *associative* operation⟩ — **as·so·ci·a·tive·ly** *adv* — **as·so·cia·tiv·i·ty** \ə-ˌsō-s(h)ē-ə-'tiv-ət-ē, -ˌsō-shə-'tiv-\ *n*

as·soil \ə-'sòil\ *vt* [OF *assoldre*, fr. L *absolvere*] *archaic* : ABSOLVE

as·so·nance \'as-ə-nən(t)s\ *n* [L *assonare* to answer with the same sound, fr. *ad-* + *sonus* sound] **1** : resemblance of sound in words or syllables **2** : repetition of vowels without repetition of consonants (as in *story* and *holy*) used as an alternative to rhyme in verse — **as·so·nant** \-nənt\ *adj or n*

as soon as *conj* : immediately at or just after the time that ⟨left *as soon as* the meeting was over⟩

as·sort \ə-'sòrt\ *vb* [MF *assortir*, fr. *a-* ad- + *sorte* sort] **1** : to distribute into groups of a like kind : CLASSIFY **2** : to agree in kind : HARMONIZE ⟨the dress *assorted* well with her complexion⟩ — **as·sort·a·tive** \ə-'sòrt-ət-iv\ *adj* — **as·sort·er** *n*

as·sort·ed \ə-'sòrt-əd\ *adj* **1** : consisting of various kinds **2** : MATCHED, SUITED ⟨an ill-*assorted* pair⟩

as·sort·ment \ə-'sòrt-mənt\ *n* **1 a** : arrangement in classes **b** : VARIETY **2** : a collection containing a variety of sorts

as·suage \ə-'swāj\ vt [OF assouagier, fr. L ad- + suavis sweet, pleasant] **1** : to lessen the intensity of (as pain) : EASE, QUIET **2** : SATISFY, QUENCH — **as·suage·ment** \-mənt\ n

as·sume \ə-'süm\ vb [L assumere, fr. ad- + sumere to take up, take, fr. sub- up + emere to take, buy] **1** : to take up or in : RECEIVE **2 a** : to take to or upon oneself : UNDERTAKE **b** : to put on (clothing) : DON **3** : SEIZE, USURP **4** : to put on in appearance only : FEIGN **5** : to take for granted : SUPPOSE

syn ASSUME, PRESUME mean to suppose to be true or real. ASSUME may imply either reasonable grounds for supposing or a deliberate purpose in taking as definite something not actually settled or determined; PRESUME implies greater confidence in supposing without proof or justification

as·sum·ing adj : PRETENTIOUS, PRESUMPTUOUS

as·sump·tion \ə-'səm(p)-shən\ n [L assumpt-, assumere to take up, assume] **1** cap : August 15 observed as a church festival in commemoration of the taking up of the Virgin Mary into heaven **2** : a taking to or upon oneself **3** : the act of laying claim to or taking possession of **4 a** : the supposition that something is true **b** : a fact or statement taken for granted

As·sur \'äs-,ú(ə)r\ n : ASHUR

as·sur·ance \ə-'shúr-ən(t)s\ n **1** : the act of assuring : PLEDGE **2** : the state of being sure or certain **3** : SECURITY, SAFETY **4** chiefly Brit : INSURANCE **5** : SELF-CONFIDENCE, SELF-RELIANCE **6** : AUDACITY, PRESUMPTION

as·sure \ə-'shú(ə)r\ vt [MF assurer, fr. ML assecurare, fr. L ad- + securus secure] **1** : INSURE **2** : REASSURE **3** : to make sure or certain ⟨assure the success of the enterprise⟩ **4** : to inform positively ⟨can assure you of his dependability⟩

¹as·sured \ə-'shú(ə)rd\ adj **1** : made sure or certain: as **a** : SAFE **b** : UNQUESTIONABLE **c** : GUARANTEED **2 a** : CONFIDENT **b** : COMPLACENT **3** : CONVINCED — **as·sur·ed·ly** \-'shúr-əd-lē\ adv — **as·sur·ed·ness** \-əd-nəs\ n

²assured n : a person whose life or property is insured

As·syr·i·an \ə-'sir-ē-ən\ n **1** : a member of an ancient Semitic race forming the Assyrian nation **2** : the Semitic language of the Assyrians

astar·board \ə-'stär-bərd\ adv : toward or on the starboard side of a ship

As·tar·te \ə-'stärt-ē\ n : the Phoenician goddess of love and fertility

as·ta·tine \'as-tə-,tēn\ n [Gk astatos unsteady, fr. a- + sta-, histanai to stand] : a radioactive chemical element discovered by bombarding bismuth with helium nuclei — see ELEMENT table

as·ter \'as-tər\ n [Gk astēr, lit., star; akin to E star] **1** : any of various mostly fall-blooming leafy-stemmed composite herbs usu. with showy white, pink, purple, or yellow flower heads **2** : a system of radiating fibers about a centrosome of a cell

as·ter·isk \'as-tə-,risk\ n [Gk asteriskos, lit., little star, fr. astēr star] : a character * used as a reference mark or to show the omission of letters or words — **asterisk** vt

as·ter·ism \'as-tə-,riz-əm\ n : a star-shaped figure exhibited by some crystals

astern \ə-'stərn\ adv **1** : behind a ship or airplane : in the rear **2** : at or toward the stern of a ship or aircraft **3** : BACKWARD

as·ter·oid \'as-tə-,róid\ n [Gk asteroeidēs starlike, fr. astēr star] : one of thousands of small planets between Mars and Jupiter with diameters from a fraction of a mile to nearly 500 miles

as·the·nia \as-'thē-nē-ə\ n [Gk astheneia, fr. asthenēs weak, fr. a- + sthenos strength] : lack or loss of strength : DEBILITY

as·then·ic \-'then-ik\ adj **1** : of, relating to, or exhibiting asthenia : WEAK **2** : characterized by slender build and slight muscular development : ECTOMORPHIC

asth·ma \'az-mə\ n [Gk asthmat-, asthma] : a condition often of allergic origin that is marked by labored breathing with wheezing, a feeling of tightness in the chest, and coughing — **asth·mat·ic** \az-'mat-ik\ adj or n — **asth·mat·i·cal·ly** \-'mat-i-k(ə-)lē\ adv

as though conj : as if

astig·ma·tism \ə-'stig-mə-,tiz-əm\ n [²a- + Gk stigmat-, stigma mark] : a defect of an optical system (as of the eye) that prevents light from focusing accurately and results in a blurred image or indistinct vision — **as·tig·mat·ic** \,as-tig-'mat-ik\ adj — **as·tig·mat·i·cal·ly** \-'mat-i-k(ə-)lē\ adv

astir \ə-'stər\ adj **1** : being in a state of activity : STIRRING **2** : out of bed : UP

as to prep **1** : with regard or reference to : as for : ABOUT ⟨at a loss as to how to explain the mistake⟩ **2** : according to : BY ⟨graded as to size and color⟩

as·ton·ish \ə-'stän-ish\ vt [ME astonen, astonien, fr. OF estoner, fr. L ex- + tonare to thunder] : to strike with sudden wonder : surprise greatly : AMAZE syn see SURPRISE

as·ton·ish·ing adj : causing astonishment : SURPRISING — **as·ton·ish·ing·ly** \-'stän-i-shin-lē\ adv

as·ton·ish·ment \ə-'stän-ish-mənt\ n **1** : the state of being astonished; also : CONSTERNATION **2** : a cause of amazement or wonder

as·tound \ə-'staúnd\ vb [ME astoned astonished, fr. pp. of astonen to astonish] : to fill with bewildered wonder syn see SURPRISE

¹astrad·dle \ə-'strad-ªl\ adv : on or above and extending onto both sides : ASTRIDE

²astraddle prep : with one leg on each side of : ASTRIDE

as·trag·a·lus \ə-'strag-ə-ləs\ n, pl -li \-,lī, -,lē\ : a proximal bone of the tarsus

as·tra·khan or **as·tra·chan** \'as-trə-kən, -,kan\ n, often cap **1** : karakul of Russian origin **2** : a cloth with a usu. wool, curled, and looped pile resembling karakul

as·tral \'as-trəl\ adj [L astrum star, fr. Gk astron] **1** : of or relating to the stars : STARRY **2** : of or relating to a cell aster **3** : of or consisting of a substance imperceptible by the senses that is held in theosophy to be next above the tangible world in refinement **4** : VISIONARY; also : EXALTED — **as·tral·ly** \-trə-lē\ adv

astray \ə-'strā\ adv (or adj) **1** : off the right path or route : STRAYING **2** : into error : MISTAKEN

¹astride \ə-'strīd\ adv : with one leg on each side

²astride prep : on or above and with one leg on each side of

¹as·trin·gent \ə-'strin-jənt\ adj [L astringere to contract, fr. ad- + stringere to bind tight] **1** : able or tending to shrink body tissues : CONTRACTING, PUCKERY ⟨astringent lotions⟩ ⟨an astringent fruit⟩ **2** : STERN, AUSTERE ⟨an astringent manner⟩ — **as·trin·gen·cy** \-jən-sē\ n — **as·trin·gent·ly** adv

²astringent n : an astringent agent or substance

astro- comb form [Gk astron star; akin to E star] : star : heavens : astronomical ⟨astrophysics⟩

as·tro·gate \'as-trə-,gāt\ vb [astro- + -gate (as in navigate)] : to navigate in interplanetary space — **as·tro·ga·tion** \,as-trə-'gā-shən\ n — **as·tro·ga·tor** \'as-trə-,gāt-ər\ n

as·tro·labe \'as-trə-,lāb\ n : a compact instrument for observing the positions of celestial bodies that is superseded by the sextant

as·trol·o·ger \ə-'sträl-ə-jər\ n : one who practices astrology

as·trol·o·gy \-jē\ n : the divination of the supposed influences of the stars upon human affairs by their positions and aspects — **as·tro·log·i·cal** \,as-trə-'läj-i-kəl\ adj — **as·tro·log·i·cal·ly** \-'läj-i-k(ə-)lē\ adv

as·tro·naut \'as-trə-,nót\ n [astro- + -naut (as in aeronaut)] : a traveler in a spacecraft — **as·tro·nau·ti·cal** \,as-trə-'nót-i-kəl\ adj — **as·tro·nau·ti·cal·ly** \-'nót-i-k(ə-)lē\ adv

as·tro·nau·tics \-'nót-iks\ n **1** : the science of the construction and operation of spacecraft **2** : ASTROGATION

as·tron·o·mer \ə-'strän-ə-mər\ n : one who is skilled in astronomy or who makes observations of celestial phenomena

as·tro·nom·i·cal \,as-trə-'näm-i-kəl\ or **as·tro·nom·ic** \-'näm-ik\ adj **1** : of or relating to astronomy **2** : extremely or unimaginably large ⟨an astronomical amount of money⟩ — **as·tro·nom·i·cal·ly** \-'näm-i-k(ə-)lē\ adv

astronomical unit n : a unit of length used in astronomy equal to the mean distance of the earth from the sun or about 93 million miles

---

j joke; ŋ sing; ō flow; ȯ flaw; ȯi coin; th thin; th this; ü loot; u̇ foot; y yet; yü few; yu̇ furious; zh vision

as·tron·o·my \ə-'strän-ə-mē\ *n, pl* **-mies** [Gk *astronomia*, fr. *astron* star + *nom-, nemein* to distribute, control] **1** : the science of the celestial bodies and of their magnitudes, motions, and constitution **2** : a treatise on astronomy

as·tro·phys·ics \ˌas-trə-'fiz-iks\ *n* : a branch of astronomy dealing with the physical and chemical constitution of the celestial bodies — **as·tro·phys·i·cal** \-'fiz-i-kəl\ *adj* — **as·tro·phys·i·cist** \-'fiz-ə-səst\ *n*

as·tute \ə-'st(y)üt, a-\ *adj* [L *astutus*, fr. *astus* craft] : CLEVER, SAGACIOUS; *also* : WILY **syn** see SHREWD — **as·tute·ly** *adv* — **as·tute·ness** *n*

asun·der \ə-'sən-dər\ *adv (or adj)* **1** : into parts ⟨torn *asunder*⟩ **2** : APART

as well as *prep* : in addition to : BESIDES ⟨a scholar *as well as* a gentleman⟩

as yet *adv* : up to the present time : YET

asy·lum \ə-'sī-ləm\ *n* [L, fr. Gk *asylon*] **1** : an inviolable place of refuge and protection giving shelter to criminals and debtors — SANCTUARY **2** : a place of retreat and security : SHELTER **3** : protection or inviolability afforded by or as if by an asylum : REFUGE ⟨a political refugee given *asylum* in the embassy⟩ **4** : an institution for the relief or care of the destitute or afflicted and esp. the insane

asym·met·ric \ˌā-sə-'me-trik\ *adj* : not symmetrical — **asym·met·ri·cal** \-tri-kəl\ *adj* — **asym·met·ri·cal·ly** \-tri-k(ə-)lē\ *adv* — **asym·me·try** \(')ā-'sim-ə-trē\ *n*

as·ymp·tote \'as-əm(p)-ˌtōt\ *n* [Gk *asymptōtos* not meeting, fr. *a-* + *symptō-, sympiptein* to meet, fr. *syn-* + *piptein* to fall] : a straight line that is approached more and more closely by a curve that never coincides with it no matter how far the curve is extended — **as·ymp·tot·ic** \ˌas-əm(p)-'tät-ik\ *adj*

asyn·de·ton \ə-'sin-də-ˌtän\ *n, pl* **-tons** *or* **-ta** \-ˌdət-ə\ [Gk *asyndetos* unconnected, fr. *a-* + *syndein* to bind together, fr. *syn-* + *dein* to bind] : omission of the connectives ordinarily expected (as in *I came, I saw, I conquered*) — **as·yn·det·ic** \ˌas-°n-'det-ik\ *adj* — **as·yn·det·i·cal·ly** \-'det-i-k(ə-)lē\ *adv*

at \ət, (')at\ *prep* [OE *æt*] — used as a function word to introduce an expression indicating (1) a place or location ⟨staying *at* a hotel⟩ ⟨sick *at* heart⟩, (2) a goal of action or motion ⟨aim *at* the target⟩ ⟨laugh *at* him⟩, (3) that with which one is occupied or employed ⟨*at* work⟩ ⟨expert *at* chess⟩, (4) a condition ⟨*at* liberty⟩ ⟨*at* rest⟩, (5) a means, cause, or manner ⟨sold *at* auction⟩ ⟨laughed *at* his joke⟩ ⟨act *at* your own discretion⟩, or (6) a rate, degree, or position in a scale or series ⟨the temperature *at* 90⟩ ⟨retire *at* 65⟩ ⟨awoke *at* midnight⟩

at- — see AD-

At·a·brine \'at-ə-brən, -ˌbrēn\ *trademark* — used for a synthetic antimalarial drug

At·a·lan·ta \ˌat-°l-'ant-ə\ *n* : a beautiful and fleet-footed heroine of Greek legend who challenges her suitors to a race and is defeated when she stops to pick up three golden apples dropped by one of the suitors

at all \ət-'ol *also esp for 2* ə-'tol\ *adv* **1** : in all ways : INDISCRIMINATELY ⟨will go anywhere *at all*⟩ **2** : in any way or respect : to the least extent or degree : under any circumstances ⟨not *at all* likely⟩

at·a·rac·tic \ˌat-ə-'rak-tik\ *or* **at·a·rax·ic** \-'rak-sik\ *n* [Gk *a-* ²*a-* + *tarach-, tarassein* to disturb] : a tranquilizer drug — **ataractic** *adj*

at·a·vism \'at-ə-ˌviz-əm\ *n* [L *atavus* ancestor] **1** : recurrence in an organism of a character typical of ancestors more remote than the parents usu. due to recombination of ancestral genes **2** : an individual or character manifesting atavism — **at·a·vis·tic** \ˌat-ə-'vis-tik\ *adj* — **at·a·vis·ti·cal·ly** \-'vis-ti-k(ə-)lē\ *adv*

atax·ia \ə-'tak-sē-ə\ *n* [Gk, confusion, fr. *a-* ²*a-* + *tag-, tassein* to put in order] : inability to coordinate voluntary muscular movements — **atax·ic** \-sik\ *adj*

ate *past of* EAT

Ate \'ät-ē, 'āt-; 'ä-ˌtā, 'ā-ˌtē\ *n* : a Greek goddess held to lead gods and men to rash actions

¹-ate \ət, ˌāt\ *n suffix* [L *-atus, -atum,* masc. & neut. *-atus,* pp. ending of certain verbs] **1** : one acted upon (in a specified way) ⟨distill*ate*⟩ **2** [NL *-atum,* fr. L] : chemical compound derived from a (specified) compound or element; *esp* : salt or ester of an acid with a name ending in *-ic* ⟨borate⟩

²-ate *n suffix* [L *-atus*] : office : function : rank : group of persons holding a (specified) office or rank ⟨professor*ate*⟩

³-ate *adj suffix* [ME *-at,* fr. L *-atus,* fr. pp. ending of certain verbs] **1** : acted on (in a specified way) : brought into or being in a (specified) state ⟨temper*ate*⟩ **2** : marked by having ⟨chord*ate*⟩

⁴-ate \ˌāt\ *vb suffix* [ME *-aten,* fr. L *-atus,* pp. ending] : cause to be modified or affected by ⟨camphor*ate*⟩ : cause to become ⟨activ*ate*⟩ : furnish with ⟨aer*ate*⟩

ate·lier \ˌat-°l-'yā\ *n* [F] **1** : an artist's studio **2** : WORKSHOP

a tem·po \ä-'tem-pō\ *adv (or adj)* [It] : in time — used as a direction in music to return to the original rate of speed

Ath·a·na·sian Creed \ˌath-ə-ˌnā-zhən-, -ˌnā-shən-\ *n* [*Athanasius d*373 bishop of Alexandria] : a Christian creed originating in Europe about A.D. 400 and relating esp. to the Trinity and Incarnation

athe·ism \'ā-thē-ˌiz-əm\ *n* [Gk *atheos* godless, fr. *a-* ²*a-* + *theos* god] : the belief that there is no God : denial of the existence of a supreme being

athe·ist \-thē-əst\ *n* : a person who believes there is no God — **athe·is·tic** \ˌā-thē-'is-tik\ *adj* — **athe·is·ti·cal·ly** \-'is-ti-k(ə-)lē\ *adv*

syn AGNOSTIC, FREETHINKER: an ATHEIST denies the existence of God and rejects all religious faith and practice; an AGNOSTIC withholds belief because he is unwilling to accept the evidence of revelation and spiritual experience; a FREETHINKER is one who has lost or rejected traditional faith and believes only in what is rational and credible

ath·e·ling \'ath-ə-liŋ\ *n* [OE *ætheling*] : an Anglo-Saxon prince or nobleman

Athe·na \ə-'thē-nə\ *or* **Athe·ne** \-(ˌ)nē\ *n* : the Greek goddess of wisdom

ath·e·nae·um *or* **ath·e·ne·um** \ˌath-ə-'nē-əm\ *n* [Gk *Athēnaion* temple of Athena] **1** : a literary or scientific association **2** : a building or room in which books, periodicals, and newspapers are kept for use

ath·ero·scle·ro·sis \ˌath-ə-rō-sklə-'rō-səs\ *n* : an arteriosclerosis in which fatty substances are deposited in the inner layer of the arteries — **ath·ero·scle·rot·ic** \-sklə-'rät-ik\ *adj*

athirst \ə-'thərst\ *adj* [OE *ofthyrst,* pp. of *ofthyrstan* to suffer from thirst, fr. *of* off, from + *thyrstan* to thirst] **1** : THIRSTY **2** : EAGER, LONGING

ath·lete \'ath-ˌlēt\ *n* [Gk *athlētēs,* fr. *athlein* to contend for a prize, fr. *athlon* prize, contest] : a person who is trained in or good at games and exercises that require physical skill, endurance, and strength

athlete's foot *n* : ringworm of the feet

ath·let·ic \ath-'let-ik\ *adj* **1** : of, relating to, or characteristic of athletes or athletics **2** : VIGOROUS, ACTIVE **3** : characterized by heavy frame, large chest, and powerful muscular development **4** : used by athletes — **ath·let·i·cal·ly** \-'let-i-k(ə-)lē\ *adv*

ath·let·ics \ath-'let-iks\ *n sing or pl* : games, sports, and exercises requiring strength and skill

¹athwart \ə-'thwort, *naut often* -'thort\ *adv* : ACROSS : obliquely across

²athwart *prep* **1** : ACROSS **2** : in opposition to

atilt \ə-'tilt\ *adj (or adv)* **1** : TILTED **2** : with lance in hand

-a·tion \'ā-shən\ *n suffix* [L *-ation-, -atio,* fr. verbs in *-are*] **1** : action or process ⟨flirt*ation*⟩ **2** : something connected with an action or process ⟨discolor*ation*⟩

-a·tive \ˌāt-iv, ət-\ *adj suffix* [L *-ativus,* fr. verbs in *-are*] **1** : of, relating to, or connected with ⟨authorit*ative*⟩ **2** : tending to ⟨talk*ative*⟩

At·lan·tic standard time \ət-'lant-ik-\ *n* : the time of the 4th time zone west of Greenwich that includes the Canadian Maritime provinces

At·lan·tis \ət-'lant-əs\ *n* : an island sunk according to the ancients beneath the ocean west of the Strait of Gibraltar

at·las \'at-ləs\ *n* **1** *cap* : a Titan forced to bear the heavens on his shoulders **2 a** : a book of maps often including descriptive text **b** : a book of tables, charts, or illustrations ⟨an *atlas* of anatomy⟩ **3** : the first vertebra of the neck

at·mo·sphere \'at-mə-ˌsfi(ə)r\ *n* [Gk *atmos* vapor + *sphaira* sphere] **1 a** : the whole mass of air surrounding the earth **b** : a gaseous mass surrounding a celestial body (as a planet) **2 :** the air in a particular place ⟨the stuffy *atmosphere* of this room⟩ **3 :** any surrounding influence or set of conditions **:** ENVIRONMENT ⟨the home *atmosphere*⟩ **4 :** a unit of pressure equal to the pressure of the air at sea level or approximately 14.7 pounds to the square inch

at·mo·spher·ic \,at-mə-'sfi(ə)r-ik, -'sfer-\ *adj* **:** of or relating to the atmosphere ⟨*atmospheric* pressure⟩ — **at·mo·spher·i·cal·ly** \-i-k(ə-)lē\ *adv*

at·mo·spher·ics \-iks\ *n pl* **:** disturbances produced in radio receiving apparatus by atmospheric electrical phenomena; *also* **:** the electrical phenomena causing such disturbances

atoll \'a-,tȯl, -,täl, -,tōl, 'ä-\ *n* [of Austronesian origin] **:** a ring-shaped coral island or string of islands consisting of a coral reef surrounding a lagoon

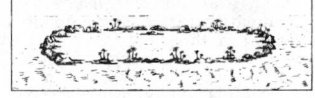

atoll

at·om \'at-əm\ *n* [Gk *atomos*, fr. *atomos* indivisible, fr. *a-* ²*a-* + *tom-*, *temnein* to cut] **1 :** a tiny particle **:** BIT **2 a :** the smallest particle of an element that can exist either alone or in combination ⟨an *atom* of hydrogen⟩ ⟨an *atom* of iron⟩ **b :** an atom that is a source of vast potential energy

atom bomb *n* **1 :** a bomb whose violent explosive power is due to the sudden release of atomic energy resulting from the splitting of nuclei of a heavy chemical element (as plutonium or uranium) by neutrons in a very rapid chain reaction — called also *fission bomb* **2 :** FUSION BOMB — **at·om–bomb** \,at-əm-'bäm\ *vt*

atom·ic \ə-'täm-ik\ *adj* **1 :** of, relating to, or concerned with atoms, atomic energy, or atomic bombs **2 :** extremely small **:** MINUTE **3 :** existing in the state of separate atoms ⟨*atomic* hydrogen⟩ — **atom·i·cal·ly** \-i-k(ə-)lē\ *adv*

atomic age *n* **:** the period of history characterized by the use of atomic energy

atomic bomb *n* **:** ATOM BOMB

atomic energy *n* **:** energy that can be liberated by changes (as by fission of a heavy nucleus or fusion of light nuclei into heavier ones with accompanying loss of mass) in the nucleus of an atom

at·o·mic·i·ty \,at-ə-'mis-ət-ē\ *n* **:** the state of consisting of atoms

atomic mass *n* **:** the mass of any species of atom usu. expressed in atomic mass units

atomic mass unit *n* **:** a unit of mass for expressing masses of atoms, molecules, or nuclear particles equal to ¹⁄₁₂ of the atomic mass of the most abundant kind of carbon

atomic number *n* **:** a number that is characteristic of a chemical element and represents the number of protons in the nucleus

atomic pile *n* **:** REACTOR 2b

atom·ics \ə-'täm-iks\ *n* **:** the science of atoms esp. when involving atomic energy

atomic theory *n* **1 :** a theory of the nature of matter: all material substances are composed of minute particles or atoms of a comparatively small number of kinds and all the atoms of the same kind are uniform in size, weight, and other properties **2 :** any of several theories of the structure of the atom; *esp* **:** one holding that the atom is composed essentially of a small positively charged comparatively heavy nucleus surrounded by a comparatively large arrangement of electrons

atomic weight *n* **:** the relative weight of an atom of a chemical element in comparison with that of an oxygen atom assigned a relative weight of 16 or a carbon atom assigned a relative weight of 12 taken as a standard

at·om·ize \'at-ə-,mīz\ *vt* **1 :** to reduce to minute particles or to a fine spray **2 :** to treat as made up of many discrete units **3 :** to subject to atomic bombing — **at·om·i·za·tion** \,at-ə-mə-'zā-shən\ *n*

at·om·iz·er \'at-ə-,mī-zər\ *n* **:** a device for spraying a liquid (as a perfume or disinfectant)

atom smasher *n* **:** ACCELERATOR b

aton·al \(')ā-'tōn-ᵊl, (')a-\ *adj* **:** characterized by avoidance of traditional musical tonality — **ato·nal·i·ty** \,ā-tō-'nal-ət-ē\ *n* — **aton·al·ly** \(')ā-'tōn-ᵊl-ē, (')a-\ *adv*

atone \ə-'tōn\ *vb* [ME *atonen* to become reconciled, fr.

atone in agreement, fr. *at* + *one*] **:** to do something to make up for a wrong done **:** make amends **:** EXPIATE

atone·ment \-mənt\ *n* **1 :** the reconciliation of God and man through the death of Jesus Christ **2 :** reparation for an offense or injury **:** SATISFACTION

¹**atop** \ə-'täp\ *prep* **:** on top of

²**atop** *adv* (*or adj*), *archaic* **:** on, to, or at the top

atrio·ven·tric·u·lar \,ā-trē-ō-ven-'trik-yə-lər\ *adj* **:** of, relating to, or located between an atrium and ventricle of the heart

atri·um \'ā-trē-əm\ *n, pl* **atria** \-trē-ə\ *also* **atri·ums** [L] **1 :** the central hall of a Roman house **2 :** an anatomical cavity or passage; *esp* **:** the main chamber of an auricle of the heart or the entire auricle

atro·cious \ə-'trō-shəs\ *adj* [L *atroc-, atrox*] **1 :** extremely wicked, brutal, or cruel **2 :** savagely fierce **:** MURDEROUS **3 :** APPALLING, TERRIBLE **4 :** very bad **:** ABOMINABLE **syn** see OUTRAGEOUS — **atro·cious·ly** *adv* — **atro·cious·ness** *n*

atroc·i·ty \ə-'träs-ət-ē\ *n, pl* **-ties 1 :** the quality or state of being atrocious **2 :** an atrocious act, object, or situation

¹**at·ro·phy** \'a-trə-fē\ *n, pl* **-phies** [Gk *atrophia*, fr. *a-* ²*a-* + *troph-, trephein* to nourish] **:** decrease in size or wasting away of a body part or tissue — **atroph·ic** \ə-'träf-ik\ *adj*

²**atrophy** *vi* **-phied; -phy·ing :** to undergo atrophy

at·ro·pine \'a-trə-,pēn, -pən\ *n* [NL *Atropa*, genus name of belladonna, fr. Gk *Atropos*, the Fate] **:** a poisonous white crystalline compound $C_{17}H_{23}NO_3$ from belladonna and related plants used esp. to relieve spasms and to dilate the pupil of the eye

At·ro·pos \'a-trə-,päs, -pəs\ *n* **:** the one of the three Fates in classical mythology who cuts off the thread of life

at·tach \ə-'tach\ *vb* [MF *attacher*, alter. of OF *estachier*, fr. *estache* stake, of Gmc origin; akin to E *stake*] **1 :** to take money or property by legal authority esp. to secure payment of a debt ⟨*attach* a man's salary⟩ **2 :** to fasten or join one thing to another **:** TIE ⟨*attach* a bell to a bicycle⟩ **3 :** to tie or bind by feelings of affection ⟨the boy was *attached* to his dog⟩ **4 :** to assign by authority **:** APPOINT ⟨*attach* an officer to a headquarters⟩ **5 :** to think of as belonging to something **:** ATTRIBUTE ⟨*attach* no importance to a remark⟩ **6 :** to be associated or connected ⟨the interest that naturally *attaches* to a statement by the president⟩ — **at·tach·a·ble** \-ə-bəl\ *adj*

at·ta·ché \,at-ə-'shā, ,a-,ta-, ə-,ta-\ *n* [F, fr. pp. of *attacher*] **:** a technical expert on the diplomatic staff of his country at a foreign capital ⟨military *attaché*⟩

attaché case \ə-'tash-ē-\ *n* **:** a small suitcase used esp. for carrying papers and documents

at·tach·ment \ə-'tach-mənt\ *n* **1 :** a seizure by legal process or the writ commanding such seizure **2 :** the state of being personally attached **:** FIDELITY, FONDNESS **3 :** a device attached to a machine or implement ⟨*attach-ments* for a vacuum cleaner⟩ **4 :** the physical connection by which one thing is attached to another **5 :** the process of physically attaching

¹**at·tack** \ə-'tak\ *vb* [MF *attaquer*, fr. It *attaccare* to attach, attack, of Gmc origin; akin to E *stake*] **1 :** to set upon forcefully **2 :** to threaten (a piece in chess) with immediate capture **3 :** to use unfriendly or bitter words against **4 :** to begin to affect or to act upon injuriously **5 :** to set to work upon — **at·tack·er** *n*

syn ASSAIL, ASSAULT, STORM: ATTACK implies taking the initiative in a struggle; ASSAIL implies trying to break down resistance by repeated blows or shots; ASSAULT suggests a direct attempt to overpower by suddenness and violence; STORM implies trying to overrun or capture a defended position by the irresistible weight of rapidly advancing numbers

²**attack** *n* **1 :** the act of attacking **:** ASSAULT **2 :** the beginning of destructive action (as by a chemical agent) **3 :** a setting to work **:** START **4 :** a fit of sickness; *esp* **:** an active episode of a chronic or recurrent disease

at·tain \ə-'tān\ *vb* [OF *ataindre*, modif. of L *attingere*, fr. *ad-* + *tangere* to touch] **1 :** ACHIEVE, ACCOMPLISH **2 :** to come into possession of **:** OBTAIN **3 :** to arrive at **:** ARRIVE, REACH ⟨*attain* the top of the mountain⟩ ⟨*attain* to maturity⟩ — **at·tain·a·bil·i·ty** \ə-,tā-nə-'bil-ət-ē\ *n* — **at·tain·a·ble** \-'tā-nə-bəl\ *adj* — **at·tain·a·ble·ness** *n*

at·tain·der \ə-'tān-dər\ n [MF *ataindre* to attain, accuse] : the taking away of a person's civil rights when he has been declared an outlaw or sentenced to death

at·tain·ment \ə-'tān-mənt\ n 1 : the act of attaining : the state of being attained 2 : something attained : ACCOMPLISHMENT

at·tar \'at-ər, 'a-,tär\ n [Per *'aṭir* perfumed] : a fragrant essential oil (as from rose petals)

¹at·tempt \ə-'tem(p)t\ vt [L *attemptare,* fr. *ad-* + *temptare* to try, tempt] 1 : to try to do or perform : make an effort to accomplish ⟨*attempt* an escape⟩ 2 : to try to take by force : ATTACK ⟨*attempt* a man's life⟩ 3 : ENDEAVOR ⟨*attempted* to solve the problem⟩ syn see TRY

²attempt n : the act or an instance of attempting; *esp* : an unsuccessful effort

at·tend \ə-'tend\ vb [L *attendere,* fr. *ad-* + *tendere* to stretch, strain] 1 : to care for : look after : take charge of ⟨*attend* to taking out the rubbish⟩ 2 : to wait on : SERVE ⟨nurses *attend* the sick⟩ 3 : to go or stay with as a servant or companion ⟨a king *attended* by his court⟩ 4 : to be present at ⟨*attend* a party⟩ 5 : to be present with : ACCOMPANY ⟨illness *attended* by fever⟩ 6 : to pay attention ⟨*attend* to his remarks⟩

at·tend·ance \ə-'ten-dən(t)s\ n 1 : the act of attending 2 a : the persons or number of persons attending b : the number of times a person attends

¹at·tend·ant \ə-'ten-dənt\ adj : accompanying or following as a consequence

²attendant n : one who attends another to perform a service; *esp* : an employee who waits on customers

at·ten·tion \ə-'ten-chən\ n [L *attent-, attendere* to attend] 1 : the act or the power of fixing one's mind upon something : careful listening or watching 2 : careful consideration of something with a view to taking action on it ⟨a matter requiring *attention*⟩ 3 : an act of kindness, care, or courtesy 4 : a military position of readiness to act on the next command — **at·ten·tion·al** \ə-'tench-nəl, -'ten-chən-ᵊl\ adj

at·ten·tive \ə-'tent-iv\ adj 1 : paying attention : HEEDFUL, OBSERVANT 2 : heedful of the comfort of others : COURTEOUS — **at·ten·tive·ly** adv — **at·ten·tive·ness** n

¹at·ten·u·ate \ə-'ten-yə-,wāt\ vb [L *attenuare,* fr. *ad-* + *tenuis* thin] 1 : to make thin or slender 2 : to make less in amount, force, value, virulence, vitality, or density : WEAKEN, RAREFY 3 : to become thin, fine, or less — **at·ten·u·a·tion** \ə-,ten-yə-'wā-shən\ n

²at·ten·u·ate \ə-'ten-yə-wət\ adj : tapering gradually usu. to a long slender point ⟨*attenuate* leaves⟩

at·test \ə-'test\ vb [L *attestari,* fr. *ad-* + *testis* witness] : to give proof of : testify to : CERTIFY ⟨his conduct *attests* his innocence⟩ ⟨*attest* the truth of a statement⟩ ⟨an *attested* document⟩ — **at·tes·ta·tion** \,a-,tes-'tā-shən\ n — **at·test·er** \ə-'tes-tər\ n

at·tic \'at-ik\ n [F *attique,* fr. *attique* Attic, having square pilasters] 1 : a low story or wall at the top of a classical facade 2 : a room or a space immediately below the roof of a building

At·tic \'at-ik\ adj [Gk *attikos* of Attica, Athenian] 1 : ATHENIAN 2 : marked by simplicity, purity, and refinement

¹at·tire \ə-'tī(ə)r\ vt [OF *atirier,* fr. *a-* ad- + *tire* order, rank] 1 : DRESS, ARRAY 2 : to clothe with rich garments

²attire n : DRESS, CLOTHES; *esp* : fine clothing

at·ti·tude \'at-ə-,t(y)üd\ n [F, fr. It *attitudine,* fr. *attitudine* aptitude, fr. L *aptitudo*] 1 : the arrangement of the body or figure : POSTURE 2 : a mental position or feeling regarding a fact or state 3 : the position of something in relation to something else (as a line or plane) that serves as a reference

at·ti·tu·di·nize \,at-ə-'t(y)üd-ᵊn-,īz\ vi : to assume an affected mental attitude : POSE

at·tor·ney \ə-'tər-nē\ n, pl **-neys** [MF *atorné,* pp. of *atorner* to transfer homage or service, fr. *a-* ad- + *torner* to turn] : one who is legally appointed by another to transact business for him; *esp* : a legal agent qualified to act for suitors and defendants in legal proceedings

attorney general n, pl **attorneys general** or **attorney generals** : the chief law officer of a nation or state who represents the government in legal matters and serves as its principal legal advisor

at·tract \ə-'trakt\ vb [L *attract-, attrahere,* fr. *ad-* + *trahere* to draw] 1 : to draw to or toward oneself or itself : cause to approach or adhere ⟨a magnet *attracts* iron⟩ 2 : to draw by appealing to interest or feeling ⟨*attract* attention⟩

at·trac·tion \ə-'trak-shən\ n 1 : the act, process, or power of attracting; *esp* : personal charm or beauty 2 : an attractive quality, object, or feature 3 : a force acting mutually between particles of matter, tending to draw them together, and resisting their separation

at·trac·tive \ə-'trak-tiv\ adj : having the power or quality of attracting; *esp* : CHARMING, PLEASING ⟨an *attractive* smile⟩ — **at·trac·tive·ly** adv — **at·trac·tive·ness** n

¹at·tri·bute \'a-trə-,byüt\ n [L *attributus,* pp. of *attribuere* to attribute, fr. *ad-* + *tribuere* to bestow] 1 : an inherent characteristic : a quality belonging to a particular person or thing 2 : an object closely associated with a specific person, thing, or office ⟨crown and scepter are *attributes* of royalty⟩ 3 : a word ascribing a quality; *esp* : ADJECTIVE syn see QUALITY

²at·trib·ute \ə-'trib-yət\ vt 1 : to explain by way of cause ⟨*attributes* his success to hard work⟩ 2 a : to regard as a characteristic of a person or thing ⟨*attributed* the worst motives to him⟩ b : to reckon as made or originated in an indicated fashion syn see ASCRIBE — **at·trib·ut·a·ble** \-yət-ə-bəl\ adj — **at·trib·ut·er** n

at·tri·bu·tion \,a-trə-'byü-shən\ n : the act of attributing; *also* : an ascribed quality, character, or right

at·trib·u·tive \ə-'trib-yət-iv\ adj : relating to or of the nature of an attribute; *esp* : joined directly to a modified noun without a copulative verb ⟨*red* in *red hair* is an *attributive* adjective⟩ — compare PREDICATE — **attributive** n — **at·trib·u·tive·ly** adv

at·tri·tion \ə-'trish-ən\ n [L *attrit-, atterere* to rub against, fr. *ad-* + *terere* to rub] 1 : the act of wearing or grinding down by friction 2 : the act of weakening or exhausting by constant harassment or abuse — **at·tri·tion·al** \-'trish-nəl, -ən-ᵊl\ adj

at·tune \ə-'t(y)ün\ vt [ad- + tune] : to bring into harmony : TUNE — **at·tune·ment** \-mənt\ n

atyp·i·cal \(')ā-'tip-i-kəl\ adj : not typical : IRREGULAR — **atyp·i·cal·ly** \-k(ə-)lē\ adv

¹au·burn \'ȯ-bərn\ adj [MF *auborne* blond, fr. ML *alburnus* whitish, fr. L *albus* white] 1 : of the color auburn 2 : of a reddish brown color ⟨*auburn* hair⟩

²auburn n : a moderate brown

au cou·rant \ō-kü-'räⁿ\ adj [F, lit., in the current] : fully informed : UP-TO-DATE

¹auc·tion \'ȯk-shən\ n [L *auction-, auctio,* lit., increase, fr. *auct-, augēre* to increase] : a public sale in which persons bid on property to be sold and the property is sold to the highest bidder

²auction vt **auc·tioned**; **auc·tion·ing** \-sh(ə-)niŋ\ : to sell at auction

auction bridge n : a bridge game differing from contract bridge in that tricks made in excess of the contract are scored toward game

auc·tion·eer \,ȯk-shə-'ni(ə)r\ n : an agent who sells goods for another at auction — **auctioneer** vt

auc·to·ri·al \ȯk-'tōr-ē-əl, -'tȯr-\ adj : of or relating to an author

au·da·cious \ȯ-'dā-shəs\ adj [L *audac-, audax,* fr. *audēre* to dare, fr. *avidus* eager, avid] 1 a : intrepidly daring : ADVENTUROUS b : recklessly bold : RASH 2 : INSOLENT, IMPUDENT — **au·da·cious·ly** adv — **au·da·cious·ness** n

au·dac·i·ty \ȯ-'das-ət-ē\ n, pl **-ties** 1 : BOLDNESS, DARING 2 : IMPUDENCE syn see TEMERITY

audi- or **audio-** comb form [L *audire* to hear] 1 : hearing ⟨*audiometer*⟩ 2 : sound ⟨*audiophile*⟩ 3 : auditory and ⟨*audiovisual*⟩

au·di·ble \'ȯd-ə-bəl\ adj [L *audire* to hear] : loud enough to be heard ⟨the sound was barely *audible*⟩ — **au·di·bil·i·ty** \,ȯd-ə-'bil-ət-ē\ n — **au·di·bly** \'ȯd-ə-blē\ adv

au·di·ence \'ȯd-ē-ən(t)s\ n [L *audientia,* fr. *audient-, audiens,* prp. of *audire* to hear] 1 : the act or state of hearing ⟨gave *audience* to his words⟩ 2 : an assembled group that listens or watches (as at a play, concert, or sports event) 3 : an opportunity of being heard; *esp* : a formal interview with a person of very high rank 4 : those of the general public who give attention to something said, done, or written ⟨the radio *audience*⟩ ⟨the *audience* for a new novel⟩

ə **abut**; ᵊ **kitten**; ər **further**; a **back**; ā **bake**; ä **cot, cart**; aù **out**; ch **chin**; e **less**; ē **easy**; g **gift**; i **trip**; ī **life**

¹**au·dio** \'ȯd-ē-ˌō\ *adj* **1** : of or relating to electrical or other vibrational frequencies corresponding to normally audible sound waves which are of frequencies approximately from 15 to 20,000 cycles per second **2 a** : of or relating to sound or its reproduction and esp. high-fidelity reproduction **b** : relating to or used in the transmission or reception of sound — compare VIDEO

²**audio** *n* **1** : the transmission, reception, or reproduction of sound **2** : the section of television equipment that deals with sound

au·di·om·e·ter \ˌȯd-ē-'äm-ət-ər\ *n* : an instrument used in measuring acuteness of hearing — **au·di·o·met·ric** \ˌȯd-ē-ə-'me-trik\ *adj* — **au·di·om·e·try** \ˌȯd-ē-'äm-ə-trē\ *n*

au·dio·phile \'ȯd-ē-ə-ˌfīl\ *n* : one who is enthusiastic about high-fidelity sound reproduction

au·dio·vi·su·al \ˌȯd-ē-ō-'vizh-(ə-)wəl, -'vizh-əl\ *adj* : of, relating to, or making use of both hearing and sight ⟨*audiovisual* teaching aids⟩

¹**au·dit** \'ȯd-ət\ *n* [L *auditus* a hearing, fr. *audire* to hear] : a searching examination and verification of accounts and account books esp. of a business or society; *also* : the final report of such an examination

²**audit** *vt* : to make an audit of ⟨*audit* accounts⟩

¹**au·di·tion** \ȯ-'dish-ən\ *n* **1** : the power or sense of hearing **2** : a critical hearing; *esp* : a trial performance to appraise an entertainer's merits

²**audition** *vb* **-di·tioned; -di·tion·ing** \-'dish-(ə-)niŋ\ **1** : to test in an audition ⟨*audition* a new trumpeter⟩ **2** : to give a trial performance ⟨the singers *auditioned* for the choirmaster⟩

au·di·tor \'ȯd-ət-ər\ *n* **1** : one that hears or listens **2** : a person authorized to examine and verify accounts

au·di·to·ri·um \ˌȯd-ə-'tōr-ē-əm, -'tȯr-\ *n* **1** : the part of a public building where an audience sits **2** : a room, hall, or building used for public gatherings

au·di·to·ry \'ȯd-ə-ˌtōr-ē, -ˌtȯr-\ *adj* : of or relating to hearing or to the sense or organs of hearing ⟨*auditory* canal⟩ ⟨*auditory* sensation⟩

auditory nerve *n* : a nerve connecting the inner ear with the brain and transmitting impulses concerned with hearing and balance

auf Wie·der·seh·en \ˌaůf-'vēd-ər-ˌzā-(ə)n\ *interj* [G, lit., till seeing again] — used to express farewell

Au·ge·an stables \ȯ-ˌjē-ən-\ *n pl* : the stables of Augeas king of Elis that sheltered 3000 oxen and were not cleaned for 30 years until Hercules cleaned them in a day by diverting 2 rivers through them

au·ger \'ȯ-gər\ *n* [ME *nauger* (the phrase *a nauger* being understood as *an auger*), fr. OE *nafogār*, lit., nave spear; so called fr. its use for boring holes in the naves of wheels] **1** : a tool for boring holes in wood consisting of a shank with a crosswise handle for turning and a central tapered feed screw **2** : any of various instruments made like an auger and used for boring (as in soil)

augers

¹**aught** \'ȯt, 'ät\ *pron* [OE *āwiht*, fr. *ā* ever + *wiht* creature, thing] **1** : *archaic* : ANYTHING **2** : ALL ⟨for *aught* I care, he can stay home⟩

²**aught** *n* [²*naught*, the phrase *a naught* being understood as *an aught*] : ZERO, CIPHER

aug·ment \ȯg-'ment\ *vb* [LL *augmentare*, fr. *augmentum* increase, fr. L *augēre* to increase; akin to E *eke*] **1** : to enlarge or increase esp. in size, amount, or degree **2** : to become augmented : INCREASE — **aug·ment·a·ble** \-ə-bəl\ *adj* — **aug·ment·er** *n*

aug·men·ta·tion \ˌȯg-mən-'tā-shən, -ˌmen-\ *n* **1** : the act of augmenting **2** : something that augments : INCREASE, ENLARGEMENT

¹**aug·men·ta·tive** \ȯg-'ment-ət-iv\ *adj* **1** : capable of augmenting or serving to augment **2** : indicating large size and sometimes awkwardness or unattractiveness — used of words and affixes; compare DIMINUTIVE

²**augmentative** *n* : an augmentative word or affix

aug·ment·ed \ȯg-'ment-əd\ *adj* : made greater by one half step than a major or perfect interval ⟨an *augmented* interval⟩

au gra·tin \ō-'grät-ᵊn, ȯ-, -'grat-\ *adj* [F] : covered with bread crumbs, butter, and cheese and browned

¹**au·gur** \'ȯ-gər\ *n* [L] **1** : an official diviner of ancient Rome **2** : SOOTHSAYER, DIVINER

²**augur** *vb* **1** : to predict or foretell esp. from signs or omens **2** : to serve as a sign : INDICATE ⟨today's report *augurs* well for our success⟩

au·gu·ry \'ȯ-gyə-rē, -gə-\ *n, pl* **-ries 1** : divination from omens or portents or from chance events (as the fall of lots) **2** : an indication of the future : OMEN

au·gust \ȯ-'gəst\ *adj* [L *augustus*] : marked by majestic dignity or grandeur — **au·gust·ly** *adv* — **au·gust·ness** *n*

Au·gust \'ȯ-gəst\ *n* [L *Augustus*, fr. *Augustus* Caesar] : the 8th month of the year

Au·gus·tan \ȯ-'gəs-tən\ *adj* **1** : of, relating to, or characteristic of Augustus Caesar or his age **2** : of, relating to, or characteristic of the neoclassical period in England — Augustan *n*

¹**Au·gus·tin·i·an** \ˌȯ-gə-'stin-ē-ən\ *adj* **1** : of or relating to St. Augustine or his doctrines **2** : of or relating to any of several orders under a rule ascribed to St. Augustine — **Au·gus·tin·i·an·ism** \-ē-ə-ˌniz-əm\ *n*

²**Augustinian** *n* **1** : a follower of St. Augustine **2** : a member of an Augustinian order; *esp* : a friar of the Hermits of St. Augustine founded in 1256 and devoted to educational, missionary, and parish work

auk \'ȯk\ *n* [ON *ālka*] : any of several thickset black-and-white short-necked diving seabirds that breed in colder parts of the northern hemisphere

auk·let \'ȯ-klət\ *n* : any of several small auks of the No. Pacific coasts

au lait \ō-'lā\ *adj* [F] : containing milk

auld \'ȯl(d), 'äl(d)\ *adj, chiefly Scot* : OLD

auld lang syne \ˌōl-,(d)aŋ-'zīn, ,ōl-,(d)laŋ-, ,ȯl-, -'sīn\ *n* [Sc, lit., old long ago] : the good old times

aunt \'ant, 'änt\ *n* [OF *ante*, fr. L *amita*] **1** : the sister of one's father or mother **2** : the wife of one's uncle

au·ra \'ȯr-ə\ *n* [L, air, breeze, fr. Gk] **1 a** : a subtle sensory stimulus (as an aroma) **b** : a distinctive atmosphere or impression surrounding a person or thing ⟨an *aura* of sanctity⟩ ⟨an *aura* of respectability⟩ **2** : a luminous radiation : NIMBUS

au·ral \'ȯr-əl\ *adj* [L *auris* ear; akin to E *ear*] : of or relating to the ear or sense of hearing — **au·ral·ly** \-ə-lē\ *adv*

au·re·ate \'ȯr-ē-ət\ *adj* [ML *aureatus* adorned with gold, fr. L *aureus* golden, fr. *aurum* gold] **1** : of a golden color or brilliance **2** : RESPLENDENT, ORNATE, GRANDILOQUENT ⟨*aureate* rhetoric⟩

au·re·lia \ȯ-'rēl-yə\ *n* : any of a genus of large jellyfishes

au·re·ole \'ȯr-ē-ˌōl\ *or* **au·re·o·la** \ȯ-'rē-ə-lə\ *n* [ML *aureola*, fr. L, fem. of *aureolus* golden, fr. *aurum* gold] **1** : a radiant light around the head or body of a representation of a sacred personage **2** : a bright area surrounding a bright light (as the sun) when seen through thin cloud or mist

Au·reo·my·cin \ˌȯr-ē-ō-'mīs-ᵊn\ *trademark* — used for an antibiotic produced by a soil bacterium and effective against various infectious diseases

au re·voir \ˌȯr-əv-'wär, ˌȯr-\ *n* [F, lit., till seeing again] : GOOD-BYE

au·ric \'ȯr-ik\ *adj* [L *aurum* gold] : of, relating to, or derived from gold esp. when trivalent

au·ri·cle \'ȯr-i-kəl\ *n* [L *auricula*, fr. dim. of *auris* ear] **1** : PINNA 3 **2** : the chamber or either of the chambers of the heart that receives blood from the veins

au·ric·u·lar \ȯ-'rik-yə-lər\ *adj* [L *auricula*, dim. of *auris* ear] **1** : of or relating to the ear or the sense of hearing **2** : told privately **3** : known by the sense of hearing **4** : of or relating to an auricle

au·ric·u·lo·ven·tric·u·lar \ȯ-ˌrik-yə-ˌlō-ven-'trik-yə-lər\ *adj* : ATRIOVENTRICULAR

au·rif·er·ous \ȯ-'rif-(ə-)rəs\ *adj* : gold-bearing

Au·ri·ga \ȯ-'rī-gə\ *n* [L, lit., charioteer] : a constellation between Perseus and Gemini

Au·ri·gna·cian \ˌȯr-ēn-'yā-shən\ *adj* : of or relating to an Upper Paleolithic culture with finely made stone and bone tools, paintings, and engravings

au·rochs \'aů(ə)r-ˌäks, 'ȯ(ə)r-\ *n, pl* **aurochs** *also* **au·rochs·es 1** : URUS **2** : WISENT

au·ro·ra \ə-'rōr-ə, ȯ-'rōr-, -'rȯr-\ *n* [L; akin to E *east*] **1** : the rising light of morning : DAWN **2** : AURORA BOREALIS **3** : AURORA AUSTRALIS — **au·ro·ral** \-əl\ *adj*

---

j joke; **ŋ** sing; **ō** flow; **ȯ** flaw; **ȯi** coin; **th** thin; **th̲** this; **ü** loot; **ů** foot; **y** yet; **yü** few; **yů** furious; **zh** vision

aurora aus·tra·lis \-ȯ-'strā-ləs, -ä-\ *n* [NL, lit., southern aurora] : a display of light in the southern hemisphere corresponding to the aurora borealis

aurora bo·re·al·is \-,bōr-ē-'al-əs, -,bȯr-\ *n* [NL, lit., northern aurora] : streamers or arches of light in the sky at night that are held to be of electrical origin and appear to best advantage in the arctic regions

au·rous \'ȯr-əs\ *adj* : of, relating to, or containing gold esp. when univalent

aus·cul·ta·tion \,ȯ-skəl-'tā-shən\ *n* [L *auscultare* to listen] : the act of listening to sounds arising within organs as an aid to diagnosis and treatment — **aus·cul·tate** \'ȯ-skəl-,tāt\ *vt* — **aus·cul·ta·to·ry** \ȯ-'skəl-tə-,tōr-ē, -,tȯr-\ *adj*

aus·pice \'ȯ-spəs\ *n, pl* **aus·pic·es** \-spə-səz, -,sēz\ [L *auspicium*, fr. *avis* bird + *specere* to look at] **1** : observation in augury esp. of the flight and feeding of birds **2** : a prophetic sign : AUGURY; *esp* : a favorable sign **3** *pl* : kindly patronage and guidance : PROTECTION ⟨a concert given under the *auspices* of the school⟩

aus·pi·cious \ȯ-'spish-əs\ *adj* **1** : promising success : FAVORABLE ⟨an *auspicious* beginning⟩ **2** : PROSPEROUS, FORTUNATE ⟨an *auspicious* year⟩ — **aus·pi·cious·ly** *adv* — **aus·pi·cious·ness** *n*

aus·tere \ȯ-'sti(ə)r\ *adj* [Gk *austēros* harsh, severe] **1 a** : stern and forbidding in appearance and manner **b** : SOMBER, GRAVE **2** : rigidly abstemious : ASCETIC **3** : UNADORNED, SIMPLE **syn** see SEVERE — **aus·tere·ly** *adv* — **aus·tere·ness** *n*

aus·ter·i·ty \ȯ-'ster-ət-ē\ *n, pl* **-ties 1** : the quality or state of being austere **2 a** : an austere act, manner, or attitude **b** : an ascetic practice **3** : enforced or extreme economy

Austr- *or* **Austro-** *comb form* [L *Austr-*, *Auster* south wind] **1** : south : southern ⟨*Austro*asiatic⟩ **2** : Australian and ⟨*Austro*-Malayan⟩

aus·tral \'ȯs-trəl, 'äs-\ *adj* : SOUTHERN

Aus·tra·lian ballot \ȯ-,strāl-yən-, ä-\ *n* : an official ballot printed at public expense containing the names of all candidates and all proposals, distributed only at the polling place, and marked in secret

Aus·tra·loid \'ȯs-trə-,lȯid, 'äs-\ *adj* : of or relating to an ethnic group including the Australian aborigines and related peoples — **Australoid** *n*

aus·tra·lo·pith·e·cine \ȯ-,strā-lō-'pith-ə-,sīn, ä-,strā-\ *adj* : of or relating to a group of extinct southern African apes with near-human dentition — **australopithecine** *n*

Aus·tral·orp \'ȯs-trə-,lȯrp, 'äs-\ *n* : a usu. black domestic fowl developed in Australia and valued for egg production

Aus·tro·ne·sian \,ȯs-trə-'nē-zhən, ,äs-, -shən\ *adj* : of, relating to, or constituting a family of agglutinative languages spoken in the Malay peninsula and archipelago and the islands of the Pacific and Indian oceans — **Austronesian** *n*

aut- *or* **auto-** *comb form* [Gk *autos* same, -self, self] **1** : self : same one ⟨*auto*biography⟩ **2** : automatic : self‑ acting ⟨*auto*-rifle⟩

au·tar·ky \'ȯ-,tär-kē\ *n* [Gk *autarkeia* self-sufficiency] : a policy of establishing national economic self-sufficiency — **au·tar·kic** \ȯ-'tär-kik\ *adj* — **au·tar·ki·cal** \-ki-kəl\ *adj*

aut·ecol·o·gy \,ȯt-i-'käl-ə-jē\ *n* : ecology dealing with individual organisms or individual kinds of organisms

au·then·tic \ə-'thent-ik, ȯ-\ *adj* [Gk *authentikos*, fr. *authentēs* perpetrator, author] **1** : being really what it seems to be : GENUINE ⟨an *authentic* signature of George Washington⟩ **2** : TRUE, CORRECT ⟨a report *authentic* in every detail⟩ — **au·then·ti·cal·ly** \-'thent-i-k(ə-)lē\ *adv* — **au·then·tic·i·ty** \,ȯ-,then-'tis-ət-ē, -thən-\ *n*

syn GENUINE: AUTHENTIC implies being fully trustworthy as according with fact or actuality ⟨*authentic* record of the campaign⟩ GENUINE implies accordance with an original or an accepted type without counterfeiting, admixture, or adulteration ⟨*genuine* maple syrup⟩

au·then·ti·cate \ȯ-'thent-i-,kāt, ə-\ *vt* : to prove, establish, or attest the authenticity of **syn** see CONFIRM — **au·then·ti·ca·tion** \ə-,thent-i-'kā-shən, (,)ȯ-\ *n* — **au·then·ti·ca·tor** \ə-'thent-i-,kāt-ər, ȯ-\ *n*

au·thor \'ȯ-thər\ *n* [OF *auctour*, fr. L *auctor* promoter, originator, author, fr. *auct-*, *augēre* to increase] **1** : one that writes or composes a literary work (as a book)

2 : one that originates or makes : CREATOR; *esp* : GOD — **author** *vt* — **au·thor·ess** \'ȯ-th(ə-)rəs\ *n* — **au·tho·ri·al** \ȯ-'thōr-ē-əl, -'thȯr-\ *adj*

au·thor·i·tar·i·an \ə-,thȯr-ə-'ter-ē-ən, ȯ-, -,thär-\ *adj* : relating to, advocating, or demanding total submission to authority as concentrated in a leader or an elite not constitutionally responsible to the people ⟨an *authoritarian* dictator⟩ — **authoritarian** *n* — **au·thor·i·tar·i·an·ism** \-ē-ə-,niz-əm\ *n*

au·thor·i·ta·tive \ə-'thȯr-ə-,tāt-iv, ȯ-, -'thär-\ *adj* **1** : having authority : coming from or based on authority ⟨*authoritative* teachings⟩ **2** : entitled to obedience or acceptance ⟨an *authoritative* order⟩ **3** : having an air of authority : POSITIVE ⟨an *authoritative* manner⟩ ⟨*authoritative* tones⟩ — **au·thor·i·ta·tive·ly** *adv* — **au·thor·i·ta·tive·ness** *n*

au·thor·i·ty \ə-'thȯr-ət-ē, ȯ-, -'thär-\ *n, pl* **-ties 1 a** : a fact or statement used to support a position; *also* : a person, text, or prior decision that is the source of such a fact or statement **b** : a person appealed to as an expert **2 a** : the right to give commands and the power to enforce obedience ⟨parental *authority*⟩ **b** : delegated power **3 a** : a person or persons having powers of government ⟨turned the prisoner over to local *authorities*⟩ **b** : a government agency or corporation that administers a revenue-producing public enterprise ⟨turnpike *authority*⟩ ⟨Tennessee Valley *Authority*⟩ **syn** see INFLUENCE

au·tho·rize \'ȯ-thə-,rīz\ *vt* **1** : to give authority to : EMPOWER ⟨*authorize* a son to act for his father⟩ **2** : to give legal or official approval or permission to ⟨*authorize* a loan⟩ ⟨an *authorized* abridgment⟩ **3** : to establish by or as if by authority : SANCTION, APPROVE ⟨customs *authorized* by time⟩ — **au·tho·ri·za·tion** \,ȯ-th(ə-)rə-'zā-shən\ *n* — **au·tho·riz·er** \'ȯ-thə-,rī-zər\ *n*

Authorized Version *n* : a revision of the English Bible carried out under James I, published in 1611, and widely used by Protestants — see BIBLE table

au·thor·ship \'ȯ-thər-,ship\ *n* **1** : the profession of writing **2 a** : the origin of a literary production ⟨a novel of unknown *authorship*⟩ **b** : the state or act of creating or causing

au·to \'ȯt-ō, 'ät-\ *n* : AUTOMOBILE

au·to·bahn \'aut-ō-,bän\ *n* [G] : a German expressway

au·to·bi·og·ra·phy \,ȯt-ə-bī-'äg-rə-fē, -bē-\ *n* : the biography of a person narrated by himself — **au·to·bi·og·ra·pher** \-rə-fər\ *n* — **au·to·bio·graph·ic** \-,bī-ə-'graf-ik\ *or* **au·to·bio·graph·i·cal** \-'graf-i-kəl\ *adj* — **au·to·bio·graph·i·cal·ly** \-i-k(ə-)lē\ *adv*

au·toch·tho·nous \ȯ-'täk-thə-nəs\ *adj* : INDIGENOUS, NATIVE — **au·toch·tho·nous·ly** *adv*

au·to·clave \'ȯt-ō-,klāv\ *n* : an apparatus (as for sterilizing) using superheated steam under pressure — **autoclave** *vt*

au·toc·ra·cy \ȯ-'täk-rə-sē\ *n, pl* **-cies 1** : government in which one person possesses unlimited power **2** : the authority or rule of an autocrat **3** : a community or state governed by autocracy

au·to·crat \'ȯt-ə-,krat\ *n* : a person (as a monarch) ruling with unlimited authority

au·to·crat·ic \,ȯt-ə-'krat-ik\ *adj* : of, relating to, characteristic of, or resembling autocracy or an autocrat : DESPOTIC ⟨*autocratic* rule⟩ — **au·to·crat·i·cal·ly** \-'krat-i-k(ə-)lē\ *adv*

au·to·da·fé \,aut-ō-də-'fā, ,ȯt-\ *n, pl* **au·tos·da·fé** \-ōz-də-\ [Pg *auto da fé*, lit., act of the faith] : the ceremony accompanying the pronouncement of judgment by the Inquisition and followed by the execution of sentence by the secular authorities; *also* : the burning of a heretic

au·to·erot·i·cism \,ȯt-ō-i-'rät-ə-,siz-əm\ *n* : sexual gratification obtained solely through one's own organism — **au·to·erot·ic** \-'rät-ik\ *adj* — **au·to·erot·i·cal·ly** \-'rät-i-k(ə-)lē\ *adv*

au·tog·a·my \ȯ-'täg-ə-mē\ *n, pl* **-mies** : SELF-FERTILIZATION; *esp* : pollination of a flower by its own pollen — compare ENDOGAMY — **au·tog·a·mous** \-məs\ *adj*

au·tog·e·nous \ȯ-'täj-ə-nəs\ *or* **au·to·gen·ic** \,ȯt-ə-'jen-ik\ *adj* : originating within or derived from the same individual ⟨an *autogenous* graft⟩ — **au·tog·e·nous·ly** *adv*

¹au·to·graph \'ȯt-ə-,graf\ *n* : something written with one's own hand; *esp* : a person's handwritten signature

²autograph *vt* : to write one's signature in or on

au·to·in·tox·i·ca·tion \ˌȯt-ō-in-ˌtäk-sə-'kā-shən\ *n* : a state of being poisoned by substances produced within the body

au·to·mat \'ȯt-ə-ˌmat\ *n* : a cafeteria in which food is delivered to patrons from coin-operated compartments

au·to·mate \'ȯt-ə-ˌmāt\ *vt* **1** : to operate by automation **2** : to convert to automatic operation

¹au·to·mat·ic \ˌȯt-ə-'mat-ik\ *adj* [Gk *automatos* self-acting] **1 a** : largely or wholly involuntary; *esp* : REFLEX 4 **b** : acting or done spontaneously or unconsciously; *also* : resembling an automaton : MECHANICAL **2** : having a self-acting or self-regulating mechanism ⟨*automatic* pistol⟩ ⟨*automatic* washer⟩ **syn** see SPONTANEOUS — **au·to·mat·i·cal·ly** \-'mat-i-k(ə-)lē\ *adv*

²automatic *n* : an automatic machine or apparatus; *esp* : an automatic firearm

au·to·ma·tion \ˌȯt-ə-'mā-shən\ *n* **1** : the method of making an apparatus, a process, or a system operate automatically **2** : the state of being operated automatically **3** : automatic operation of an apparatus, process, or system by mechanical or electronic devices that take the place of human operators

au·tom·a·tism \ȯ-'täm-ə-ˌtiz-əm\ *n* **1** : the quality or state of being automatic **2** : an automatic action — **au·tom·a·tist** \-'täm-ət-əst\ *n*

au·tom·a·tize \ȯ-'täm-ə-ˌtīz\ *vt* : to make automatic — **au·tom·a·ti·za·tion** \ȯ-ˌtäm-ət-ə-'zā-shən\ *n*

au·tom·a·ton \ȯ-'täm-ət-ən, -'täm-ə-ˌtän\ *n, pl* **-atons** *or* **-a·ta** \-ət-ə\ **1** : a machine that can move by itself; *esp* : one made to imitate the motions of a man or an animal **2** : a person who acts in a mechanical fashion

¹au·to·mo·bile \ˌȯt-ə-mō-'bēl, -'mō-ˌbēl\ *adj* : AUTOMOTIVE

²automobile *n* : a usu. four-wheeled automotive vehicle designed for passenger transportation on streets and roadways and commonly propelled by an internal-combustion engine — **automobile** *vi* — **au·to·mo·bil·ist** \-mo-'bē-ləst\ *n*

au·to·mo·tive \ˌȯt-ə-'mōt-iv\ *adj* **1** : SELF-PROPELLED **2** : of, relating to, or concerned with automotive vehicles and esp. automobiles and motorcycles

au·to·nom·ic \ˌȯt-ə-'näm-ik\ *adj* : of, relating to, controlled by, or being the part of the nervous system that regulates activity (as of glands or smooth muscle) not under voluntary control — **au·to·nom·i·cal·ly** \-'näm-i-k(ə-)lē\ *adv*

au·ton·o·mous \ȯ-'tän-ə-məs\ *adj* [Gk *autonomos*, fr. *autos* self + *nomos* law] **1** : relating to, marked by, or possessing autonomy; *esp* : independent of outside control : SELF-GOVERNING **2** : existing, responding, reacting, or developing independently of the whole ⟨an *autonomous* growth⟩ ⟨*autonomous* zooids⟩ — **au·ton·o·mous·ly** *adv*

au·ton·o·my \-mē\ *n, pl* **-mies** : the quality or state of being self-governing; *also* : the power or right of self-government

au·top·sy \'ȯ-ˌtäp-sē, 'ȯt-əp-\ *n, pl* **-sies** [Gk *autopsia* seeing for oneself, fr. *autos* self + *op-*, used as stem of *horan* to see] : POSTMORTEM EXAMINATION — **autopsy** *vt*

au·to·ra·dio·graph \ˌȯt-ō-'rād-ē-ə-ˌgraf\ *or* **au·to·ra·dio·gram** \-ˌgram\ *n* : an image produced on a photographic film or plate by the radiations from a radioactive substance in an object

au·to·some \'ȯt-ə-ˌsōm\ *n* : a chromosome other than a sex chromosome — **au·to·so·mal** \ˌȯt-ə-'sō-məl\ *adj*

au·to·sug·ges·tion \ˌȯt-ō-sə(g)-'jes(h)-chən\ *n* : an influencing of one's own attitudes, behavior, or physical condition by mental processes other than conscious thought

au·tot·o·my \ȯ-'tät-ə-mē\ *n, pl* **-mies** : reflex separation of a part from the body : division of the body into two or more pieces — **au·to·tom·ic** \ˌȯt-ə-'täm-ik\ *or* **au·tot·o·mous** \ȯ-'tät-ə-məs\ *adj*

au·to·troph·ic \ˌȯt-ə-'träf-ik\ *adj* : able to live and grow on carbon from carbon dioxide or carbonates and nitrogen from a simple inorganic compound — **au·to·troph** \'ȯt-ə-ˌträf\ *n* — **au·to·troph·i·cal·ly** \ˌȯt-ə-'träf-i-k(ə-)lē\ *adv* — **au·tot·ro·phism** \ȯ-'tä-trə-ˌfiz-əm\ *or* **au·tot·ro·phy** \-trə-fē\ *n*

au·tumn \'ȯt-əm\ *n* [L *autumnus*] **1** : the season between summer and winter comprising in the northern hemisphere usu. the months of September, October, and November or as reckoned astronomically extending from the September equinox to the December solstice — called also *fall* **2** : a time or season of maturity or decline — **au·tum·nal** \ȯ-'təm-nəl\ *adj*

autumn crocus *n* : MEADOW SAFFRON

¹aux·il·ia·ry \ȯg-'zil-yə-rē\ *adj* [L *auxilium* help, reinforcement; akin to E ³*wax*] **1 a** : offering or providing help **b** : functioning in a subsidiary capacity : SUPPLEMENTARY, RESERVE ⟨an *auxiliary* engine⟩ **2** : being a verb that accompanies another verb and typically expresses such things as person, number, mood, or tense

²auxiliary *n, pl* **-ries** **1** : an auxiliary person, group, or device ⟨a women's *auxiliary* of a veteran's organization⟩; *esp* : a member of a foreign force serving a nation at war **2** : an auxiliary verb

aux·in \'ȯk-sən\ *n* : a plant hormone that stimulates shoot elongation and plays a role in water metabolism in the plant; *also* : PLANT HORMONE

¹avail \ə-'vāl\ *vb* [ME *vailen, availen*, fr. OF *vail-, valoir* to be of worth, fr. L *valēre* to be strong] : to be of use or advantage : HELP, BENEFIT

²avail *n* : help or benefit toward attainment of a goal : USE ⟨effort was of little *avail*⟩

avail·a·bil·i·ty \ə-ˌvā-lə-'bil-ət-ē\ *n, pl* **-ties** **1** : the quality or state of being available **2** : an available person or thing

avail·a·ble \ə-'vā-lə-bəl\ *adj* **1 a** : such as may be availed of : USABLE **b** : ACCESSIBLE, OBTAINABLE **2 a** : having qualifications regarded as likely to win votes in an election **b** : willing to accept nomination or election — **avail·a·ble·ness** *n* — **avail·a·bly** \-blē\ *adv*

av·a·lanche \'av-ə-ˌlanch\ *n* [F] **1** : a large mass of snow and ice or of earth and rock sliding down a mountainside or over a steep cliff **2** : a sudden overwhelming rush of something seeming to descend like an avalanche ⟨an *avalanche* of words⟩

Av·a·lon \'av-ə-ˌlän\ *n* : an island in the western seas held esp. in Arthurian legend to be an earthly paradise

avant-garde \ˌäv-ˌän(t)-'gärd, ˌäv-ˌä°-\ *n* [F, vanguard] : those in the arts who create or apply new or highly experimental ideas — **avant-garde** *adj* — **avant-gard·ism** \-'gärd-ˌiz-əm\ *n* — **avant-gard·ist** \-'gärd-əst\ *n*

av·a·rice \'av-(ə-)rəs\ *n* [L *avaritia*, fr. *avarus* greedy] : excessive or insatiable desire for wealth or gain : GREED

av·a·ri·cious \ˌav-ə-'rish-əs\ *adj* : greedy of gain : GRASPING **syn** see COVETOUS — **av·a·ri·cious·ly** *adv* — **av·a·ri·cious·ness** *n*

avast \ə-'vast\ *imperative verb* — a nautical command to stop or cease

av·a·tar \'av-ə-ˌtär\ *n* [Skt *avatāra* descent, incarnation of a deity] : an embodiment (as of a concept, philosophy, or tradition) usu. in human form

avaunt \ə-'vȯnt, ə-'vänt\ *adv* [MF *avant* before, forward, fr. L *abante*, fr. *ab* from + *ante* before] *archaic* : AWAY, HENCE

ave \'äv-ˌā\ *n* [L, hail!] : an expression of greeting or parting : HAIL, FAREWELL

Ave Ma·ria \ˌäv-ˌā-mə-'rē-ə\ *n* : a salutation to the Virgin Mary combined with a prayer to her as mother of God

avenge \ə-'venj\ *vt* [ME *vengen, avengen*, fr. OF *vengier*, fr. L *vindicare*] **1** : to take vengeance for or on behalf of **2** : to exact satisfaction for (a wrong) by punishing the wrongdoer ⟨*avenge* an insult⟩ — **aveng·er** *n*

syn REVENGE: AVENGE implies inflicting deserved punishment esp. on one who has injured someone other than oneself; REVENGE implies getting even or paying back in kind or degree

av·ens \'av-ənz\ *n, pl* **avens** : any of a genus of perennial herbs of the rose family with white, purple, or yellow flowers in loose clusters

av·e·nue \'av-ə-ˌn(y)ü\ *n* [MF, fr. fem. of *avenu*, pp. of *avenir* to come to, fr. L *advenire*, fr. *ad-* + *venire* to come] **1** : an opening or passageway to a place **2** : a way or means to an end **3** : a street esp. when broad and attractive

aver \ə-'vər\ *vt* **averred; aver·ring** [MF *averer* to verify, fr. L *ad-* + *verus* true] : to declare positively : ASSERT, ALLEGE

¹av·er·age \'av-(ə-)rij\ *n* [E *average* distribution of costs of damage to ship or cargo, fr. MF *avarie* damage to ship or cargo, fr. It *avaria*, fr. Ar '*awārīyah* damaged merchandise] **1 :** a single value representative of a set of other values; *esp :* ARITHMETIC MEAN **2 :** something typical of a group, class, or series **3 :** a ratio (as a rate per thousand) of successful tries to total tries ⟨batting *average*⟩

syn MEAN, MEDIAN: AVERAGE is the result obtained by dividing the sum total of a set of figures by the number of figures; MEAN may be the average or it may be the value midway between two extremes ⟨a high of 70° and a low of 50° give a *mean* of 60°⟩ MEDIAN applies to the value that represents the point at which there are as many instances above as there are below ⟨the *average* of a group of persons earning 3, 4, 5, 8, and 10 dollars a day is 6 dollars a day, but the *median* is 5 dollars⟩

²**average** *adj* **1 :** equaling or approximating an arithmetic mean **2 a :** being about midway between extremes **b :** being not out of the ordinary : COMMON ⟨the *average* man⟩ — **av·er·age·ly** *adv* — **av·er·age·ness** *n*

³**average** *vb* **1 :** to be at or come to an average ⟨the gain *averaged* out to be 20 percent⟩ **2 :** to amount to on the average : be usually ⟨those children *average* four feet in height⟩ **3 :** to find the average of **4 :** to bring toward an average **5 :** to divide among a number proportionally

aver·ment \ə-'vər-mənt\ *n* : AFFIRMATION

Aver·nus \ə-'vər-nəs\ *n* : the infernal regions

averse \ə-'vərs\ *adj* [L *aversus*, pp. of *avertere* to turn away, avert] : having an active feeling of repugnance or distaste ⟨*averse* to strenuous exercise⟩ — **averse·ly** *adv* — **averse·ness** *n*

aver·sion \ə-'vər-zhən\ *n* **1 :** a feeling of repugnance toward something with a desire to avoid or turn from it **2 :** a settled dislike : ANTIPATHY

avert \ə-'vərt\ *vt* [L *avertere*, fr. *ab-* + *vertere* to turn] **1 :** to turn away ⟨*avert* one's eyes⟩ **2 :** to prevent from happening : ward off ⟨narrowly *averted* an accident by a quick stop⟩ **syn** see PREVENT

Aves·ta \ə-'ves-tə\ *n* : the sacred books of Zoroastrianism

avi·an \'ā-vē-ən\ *adj* [L *avis* bird] : of, relating to, or derived from birds

avi·ary \'ā-vē-,er-ē\ *n*, *pl* -**ar·ies** : a place (as a large cage or a building) where many live birds are kept usu. for exhibition — **avi·a·rist** \-vē-ə-rəst\ *n*

avi·a·tion \,ā-vē-'ā-shən, ,av-ē-\ *n* [F, fr. L *avis* bird] **1 :** the operation of heavier-than-air aircraft **2 :** military airplanes — **aviation** *adj*

aviation cadet *n* : a student officer in the air force

avi·a·tor \'ā-vē-,āt-ər, 'av-ē-\ *n* : the pilot of a heavier-than-air aircraft

avi·a·trix \,ā-vē-'ā-triks, ,av-ē-\ *n* : a woman aviator — called also *aviatress*

avi·cul·ture \'ā-və-,kəl-chər, 'av-ə-\ *n* : the raising and care of birds and esp. of wild birds in captivity — **avi·cul·tur·ist** \,ā-və-'kəlch-(ə-)rəst, ,av-ə-\ *n*

av·id \'av-əd\ *adj* [F or L; F *avide*, fr. L *avidus*, fr. *avēre* to long for] **1 :** craving eagerly : GREEDY **2 :** marked by eagerness and enthusiasm — **avid·i·ty** \ə-'vid-ət-ē, a-\ *n* — **av·id·ly** \'av-əd-lē\ *adv* — **av·id·ness** *n*

avi·on·ics \,ā-vē-'än-iks, ,av-ē-\ *n* : the development and production of electrical and electronic devices for use in aviation, missilery, and astronautics — **avi·on·ic** \-ik\ *adj*

avi·ta·min·osis \,ā-,vīt-ə-mə-'nō-səs\ *n*, *pl* -**min·oses** \-'nō-,sēz\ : disease resulting from a deficiency of one or more vitamins — **avi·ta·min·ot·ic** \-mə-'nät-ik\ *adj*

av·o·ca·do \,av-ə-'käd-ō\ *n*, *pl* -**dos** [Sp *aguacate*, fr. Nahuatl *ahuacatl*] : the usu. green pulpy pear-shaped or egg-shaped oily edible fruit of a tropical American tree; *also :* the tree that bears this fruit

av·o·ca·tion \,av-ə-'kā-shən, 'av-ə-,\ *n* [L *avocare* to call away, fr. *ab-* + *vocare* to call] **1** *archaic :* DIVERSION, DISTRACTION **2 :** a subordinate occupation pursued in addition to one's vocation esp. for enjoyment : HOBBY **syn** see VOCATION — **av·o·ca·tion·al** \-shnəl,-shən-°l\ *adj*

av·o·cet \'av-ə-,set\ *n* [F *avocette*, fr. It *avocetta*] : any of several rather large long-legged shorebirds with webbed feet and slender upward-curving bill

avoid \ə-'vȯid\ *vt* [ME *avoiden* to empty out, fr. OF *esvuidier*, fr. *es-* ex- + *vuide* empty, void] **1 :** to make legally void : ANNUL ⟨*avoid* a contract⟩ **2 a :** to keep away from : SHUN ⟨*avoid* accidents⟩ **b :** to refrain from — **avoid·a·ble** \-ə-bəl\ *adj* — **avoid·a·bly** \-blē\ *adv*

avoid·ance \ə-'vȯid-°n(t)s\ *n* **1 :** the act of annulling **2 :** the act of keeping away from or clear of

avoiding reaction *n* : a negative tropism or taxis

av·oir·du·pois \,av-ərd-ə-'pȯiz\ *n* [ME *avoir de pois* goods sold by weight, fr. OF, lit., goods of weight] **1 :** AVOIRDUPOIS WEIGHT **2 :** WEIGHT, HEAVINESS

avoirdupois weight *n* : the series of units of weight based on the pound of 16 ounces and the ounce of 16 drams — see MEASURE table

avouch \ə-'vaůch\ *vt* [ME *avouchen* to cite, appeal to, fr. MF *avochier*, fr. L *advocare*, fr. *ad-* + *vocare* to call] **1 :** to declare positively : AFFIRM **2 :** to vouch for : GUARANTEE — **avouch·ment** \-mənt\ *n*

avow \ə-'vaů\ *vt* [OF *avouer* to appeal to, fr. L *advocare*, fr. *ad-* + *vocare* to call] : to declare or acknowledge openly and frankly

avow·al \ə-'vaů(-ə)l\ *n* : an open declaration or acknowledgment

avowed \ə-'vaůd\ *adj* : openly acknowledged or declared : ADMITTED — **avowed·ly** \-'vaů(-ə)d-lē\ *adv*

avun·cu·lar \ə-'vəŋ-kyə-lər\ *adj* [L *avunculus* maternal uncle] : of, relating to, or characteristic of an uncle

await \ə-'wāt\ *vb* **1 :** to wait for : stay for : EXPECT ⟨*await* a train⟩ **2 :** to be ready or waiting for ⟨a reward *awaits* him⟩

¹**awake** \ə-'wāk\ *vb* **awoke** \-'wōk\ *or* **awaked** \-'wākt\; **awak·ing** **1 :** to cease sleeping **2 :** to become conscious or aware of something ⟨*awoke* to their danger⟩ **3 :** to arouse from sleep **4 :** to make or become active : STIR

²**awake** *adj* : roused from sleep : ALERT

awak·en \ə-'wā-kən\ *vb* **awak·ened**; **awak·en·ing** \-'wāk-(ə-)niŋ\ : AWAKE — **awak·en·er** \-(ə-)nər\ *n*

¹**award** \ə-'wȯrd\ *vt* [ONF *eswarder* to examine, decide, fr. *es-* ex- + *warder* to watch, ward] **1 :** to give by judicial decision (as after a lawsuit) : ADJUDGE ⟨*award* damages⟩ **2 :** to give or grant as a reward ⟨*award* a prize to the best speaker⟩ — **award·a·ble** \-ə-bəl\ *adj* — **award·er** *n*

²**award** *n* **1 :** JUDGMENT, DECISION; *esp :* the decision of arbitrators in a case submitted to them **2 :** something that is conferred or bestowed : PRIZE

aware \ə-'wa(ə)r, -'we(ə)r\ *adj* [ME *iwar*, fr. OE *gewær*, fr. *ge-*, prefix denoting completion + *wær* wary] : having or showing realization, perception, or knowledge : CONSCIOUS — **aware·ness** *n*

awash \ə-'wȯsh, -'wäsh\ *adv* (*or adj*) **1 :** washed by waves or tide **2 :** washing about : AFLOAT **3 :** overflowed by water

¹**away** \ə-'wā\ *adv* [OE *aweg*, fr. ¹*a-* + *weg* way] **1 :** on the way : ALONG ⟨get *away* early⟩ **2 :** from this or that place : HENCE, THENCE ⟨go *away*⟩ **3 a :** in another place **b :** in another direction ⟨turn *away*⟩ **4 :** out of existence : to an end ⟨echoes dying *away*⟩ **5 :** from one's possession ⟨gave *away* a fortune⟩ **6 a :** UNINTERRUPTEDLY, ON ⟨clocks ticking *away*⟩ **b :** without hesitation or delay ⟨talk *away*⟩ **7 :** by a long distance or interval : FAR ⟨*away* back in 1910⟩

²**away** *adj* **1 :** absent from a place : GONE ⟨be *away* from home⟩ **2 :** DISTANT ⟨a lake 10 miles *away*⟩

¹**awe** \'ȯ\ *n* [ME, terror, awe, fr. ON *agi* terror] **1 :** a profoundly humble and reverential attitude in the presence of deity **2 :** abashed fear inspired by authority or power **3 :** veneration inspired by something sacred, mysterious, or sublime

²**awe** *vt* **1 :** to inspire with awe **2 :** to control or check by inspiring with awe

awea·ry \ə-'wi(ə)r-ē\ *adj* : WEARIED

aweigh \ə-'wā\ *adj* : just clear of the bottom and hanging perpendicularly ⟨anchors *aweigh*⟩

awe·some \'ȯ-səm\ *adj* **1 :** expressive of awe **2 :** inspiring awe — **awe·some·ly** *adv* — **awe·some·ness** *n*

awe-strick·en \'ȯ-,strik-ən\ *or* **awe-struck** \-,strək\ *adj* : filled with awe

¹**aw·ful** \'ȯ-fəl\ *adj* **1 :** inspiring awe **2 :** extremely disagreeable or objectionable **3 :** exceedingly great — used as an intensive ⟨took an *awful* chance⟩ — **aw·ful·ness** *n*

²**awful** *adv* : AWFULLY, VERY, EXTREMELY

aw·ful·ly \usu 'ȯ-fə-lē in sense 1, 'ȯ-flē in senses 2 & 3\ *adv* **1 :** in a manner to inspire awe **2 :** in a disagreeable or objectionable manner **3 :** EXCEEDINGLY, EXTREMELY ⟨an *awfully* hard rain⟩

---

awhile \ə-'hwīl\ *adv* : for a while : for a short time ⟨sit and rest *awhile*⟩

awhirl \ə-'hwərl\ *adv (or adj)* : in a whirl : WHIRLING

awk·ward \'ȯ-kwərd\ *adj* [ME *awke* turned the wrong way, fr. ON *öfugr*] **1** : lacking dexterity or skill esp. in the use of the hands or of instruments : CLUMSY **2 a** : lacking ease or grace of movement or expression **b** : appearing ill-proportioned, outsize, or poorly fitted together : UNGAINLY **3** : causing embarrassment **4** : poorly adapted for use or handling — **awk·ward·ly** *adv* — **awk·ward·ness** *n*

   syn CLUMSY, GAUCHE: AWKWARD is widely applicable and may suggest unhandiness or inconvenience of things, lack of muscular coordination or grace of movement, lack of tact, embarrassment of circumstances or situation; CLUMSY implies stiffness and heaviness and so connotes unwieldiness or lack of ordinary skill; GAUCHE implies the effects of shyness or inexperience

awl \'ȯl\ *n* [OE *alr*] : a pointed tool for making small holes (as in leather or wood)

awn \'ȯn\ *n* [OE *agen*, fr. ON *ögn*] : one of the slender bristles that terminate the glumes in some cereal and other grasses — **awned** \'ȯnd\ *adj* — **awn·less** \'ȯn-ləs\ *adj*

awl

aw·ning \'ȯn-iŋ, 'än-\ *n* : a cover esp. of canvas resembling a roof and extended over or in front of something to provide shade or shelter

awoke *past of* AWAKE

AWOL \'ā-,wȯl, ,ā-,dəb-əl-yü-,ō-'el\ *n* [absent *w*ithout *l*eave] : a person who is absent without permission — **AWOL** *adv (or adj)*

awry \ə-'rī\ *adv (or adj)* **1** : turned or twisted toward one side : ASKEW **2** : out of the right course : AMISS **syn** see CROOKED

ax *or* **axe** \'aks\ *n* [OE *æcx*] : a cutting tool that consists of a heavy edged head fixed to a handle and is used for chopping and splitting wood

ax·i·al \'ak-sē-əl\ *or* **ax·al** \-səl\ *adj* **1** : of, relating to, or functioning as an axis **2** : situated around, in the direction of, on, or along an axis — **ax·i·al·ly** \-sē-ə-lē\ *adv*

axes

axial skeleton *n* : the skeleton of the trunk and head

ax·il \'ak-səl, -,sil\ *n* [L *axilla* armpit] : the angle between a branch or leaf and the stem from which it arises

ax·il·la \ak-'sil-ə\ *n, pl* **ax·il·lae** \-'sil-(,)ē, -,ī\ *or* **axillas** [L] : ARMPIT

ax·il·lar \ak-'sil-ər, 'ak-sə-lər\ *n* : an axillary part (as a vein, nerve, or feather)

ax·il·lary \'ak-sə-,ler-ē\ *adj* **1** : of, relating to, or located near the axilla **2** : situated in or growing from an axil ⟨an *axillary* bud⟩ — **axillary** *n*

ax·i·om \'ak-sē-əm\ *n* [Gk *axiōma*, fr. *axioun* to think proper, demand, fr. *axios* worthy] **1** : a maxim widely accepted on its intrinsic merit **2 a** : a proposition regarded as a self-evident truth **b** : POSTULATE 1 — **ax·i·om·at·ic** \,ak-sē-ə-'mat-ik\ *adj* : of, relating to, or having the nature of an axiom : SELF-EVIDENT — **ax·i·om·at·i·cal·ly** \-'mat-i-k(ə-)lē\ *adv*

ax·is \'ak-səs\ *n, pl* **ax·es** \'ak-,sēz\ [L, axle, axis] **1 a** : a straight line about which a body or a geometric figure rotates or may be supposed to rotate **b** : a straight line with respect to which a body or figure is symmetrical **c** : one of the reference lines of a coordinate system **d** : a line used as the basis of measurements or reference in an architectural or other working drawing or an artistic composition **e** : one of several imaginary lines assumed in describing the positions of the planes by which a crystal is bounded **2 a** : the second vertebra of the neck on which the head turns as on a pivot **b** : an anatomical structure that is an axis of symmetry ⟨the cerebrospinal *axis*⟩; *esp* : the main stem of a plant from which leaves and branches arise **3** : a main line of direction, motion, growth, or extension **4** : a central, crucial, or fundamental part : PIVOT **5** : PARTNERSHIP, ALLIANCE

Axis *adj* : of or relating to the three powers Germany,

Italy, and Japan engaged against the western Allies in World War II

ax·le \'ak-səl\ *n* [ON *öxull* axis] **1** : a pin or shaft on or with which a wheel or pair of wheels revolves **2** : AXLETREE

axle·tree \-(,)trē\ *n* : a fixed bar with bearings at its ends on which wheels (as of a cart) revolve

Ax·min·ster \'ak-,smin(t)-stər\ *n* : a machine-woven carpet with pile tufts inserted mechanically in a variety of textures and patterns

ax·o·lotl \'ak-sə-,lät-ᵊl\ *n* : any of several salamanders of mountain lakes of Mexico and the western U.S. that ordinarily live and breed without metamorphosing

ax·on \'ak-,sän\ *also* **ax·one** \-,sōn\ *n* : a usu. long and single nerve-cell process that as a rule conducts impulses away from the cell body — **ax·o·nal** \'ak-sən-ᵊl\ *or* **ax·on·ic** \ak-'sän-ik\ *adj*

ayah \'ī-ə\ *n* [Hindi *āyā*, fr. Pg *aia*, fr. L *avia* grandmother] : a native nurse or maid in India

¹aye *also* **ay** \'ā\ *adv* [ON *ei*] : FOREVER, ALWAYS, CONTINUALLY

²aye *also* **ay** \'ī\ *adv* : YES

³aye *also* **ay** \'ī\ *n, pl* **ayes** : an affirmative vote or voter

aye-aye \'ī-,ī\ *n* : a nocturnal lemur of Madagascar

Ayr·shire \'a(ə)r-,shi(ə)r, 'e(ə)r-, -shər\ *n* : any of a breed of hardy dairy cattle originated in Ayr that vary in color from white to red or brown

aza·lea \ə-'zāl-yə\ *n* : any of numerous rhododendrons with funnel-shaped flowers and usu. deciduous leaves including many grown as ornamentals

az·i·muth \'az-(ə-)məth\ *n* [Ar *as-sumūt* the azimuth, fr. pl. of *as-samt* the way] **1** : an arc of the horizon measured between a fixed point (as true north) and the vertical circle passing through the center of an object **2** : horizontal direction

azo \'az-ō\ *adj* [*azo-*, fr. F *azote* nitrogen] : relating to or containing the group of nitrogen atoms −N=N− united at both ends to carbon ⟨an *azo* dye⟩

azo·ic \(')ā-'zō-ik, ə-\ *adj* : having no life; *esp* : of or relating to the part of geologic time that antedates life

azon·al \(')ā-'zōn-ᵊl\ *adj* : of, relating to, or being a soil or a major soil group lacking well-developed horizons — compare INTRAZONAL, ZONAL

Az·tec \'az-,tek\ *n* **1** : a member of a Nahuatl people that founded the Mexican empire and were conquered by Cortes in 1519 **2** : a member of any people under Aztec influence — **Az·tec·an** \-ən\ *adj*

azure \'azh-ər\ *n* [OF *azur*, fr. Ar *lāzaward*] : the blue color of the clear sky — **azure** *adj*

azur·ite \'azh-ə-,rīt\ *n* : a blue mineral $Cu_3(OH)_2(CO_3)_2$ consisting of carbonate of copper, occurring in crystals, in mass, and in earthy form, and constituting an ore of copper

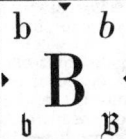

b \'bē\ *n, often cap* **1** : the 2d letter of the English alphabet **2** : the musical tone B **3** : a grade rating a student's work as good

baa *or* **ba** \'ba, 'bä\ *n* : the bleat of a sheep — **baa** *vi*

Baal \'bā-(ə)l\ *n, pl* **Baals** *or* **Baa·lim** \'bā-(ə-)ləm\ [Heb *ba'al* lord] : one of the local fertility gods of ancient Canaan

Bab·bitt \'bab-ət\ *n* [after George F. *Babbitt*, character of the novel *Babbitt* (1922) by Sinclair Lewis] : a business or professional man who conforms unthinkingly to prevailing middle-class standards — **Bab·bitt·ry** \'bab-ə-trē\ *n*

bab·bitt metal \'bab-ət-\ *n* [Isaac *Babbitt* d1862 American inventor] : an alloy used for lining bearings; *esp* : one containing tin, copper, and antimony

bab·ble \'bab-əl\ *vb* **bab·bled; bab·bling** \'bab-(ə-)liŋ\ [ME *babelen*] **1 a** : to utter meaningless sounds **b** : to talk foolishly : PRATTLE **c** : to talk excessively : CHATTER **2** : to make sounds as though babbling ⟨a *babbling* brook⟩ **3** : to reveal by too free talk — **babble** *n* — **bab·bler** \'bab-(ə-)lər\ *n*

ȷ joke; ŋ sing; ō flow; ȯ flaw; ȯi coin; th thin; th this; ü loot; u̇ foot; y yet; yü few; yu̇ furious; zh vision

babe \'bāb\ *n* : INFANT, BABY

Ba·bel \'bā-bəl, 'bab-əl\ *n* **1** : a city in Shinar where the building of a tower is said in the Book of Genesis to have been interrupted by the confusion of tongues **2** *often not cap* **a** : a confusion of sounds or voices **b** : a scene of noise or confusion

ba·boon \ba-'bün\ *n* [MF *babouin*, fr. *baboue* grimace] : any of several large African and Asiatic apes having doglike muzzles and short tails — **ba·boon·ish** \-'bü-nish\ *adj*

ba·bush·ka \bə-'büsh-kə\ *n* [Russian, grandmother] : a kerchief for the head usu. folded triangularly

¹ba·by \'bā-bē\ *n, pl* **ba·bies** [ME] **1 a** : an extremely young child; *esp* : INFANT **b** : the youngest of a group **2** : a childish person — **ba·by·hood** \-‚hüd\ *n* — **ba·by·ish** \-ish\ *adj*

²baby *vt* **ba·bied; ba·by·ing 1** : to treat as a baby : FONDLE, PET **2** : to operate or treat with care

Bab·y·lon \'bab-ə-lən, -‚län\ *n* : a large city held to resemble the ancient capital of Babylonia in being full of luxury and vice

baby's breath *n* **1** : GYPSOPHILA **2** : any of several plants (as a grape hyacinth) with delicate scented flowers

ba·by-sit \'bā-bē-‚sit\ *vi* [back-formation fr. *baby-sitter*] : to care for children usu. during a short absence of the parents — **ba·by-sit·ter** *n*

bac·ca·lau·re·ate \‚bak-ə-'lȯr-ē-ət, -'lär-\ *n* [ML *baccalaureatus*, fr. *baccalaureus* bachelor] **1** : the degree of bachelor conferred by universities and colleges **2** : a sermon to a graduating class or the service at which such a sermon is delivered

bac·ca·rat \‚bäk-ə-'rä, ‚bak-\ *n* : a card game played in European casinos

bac·cate \'bak-‚āt\ *adj* [L *bacca* berry] : resembling a berry : bearing berries

Bac·chae \'bak-‚ē, -‚ī\ *n pl* [Gk *Bakchai*] : the female attendants or priestesses of Bacchus

¹bac·cha·nal \'bak-ən-ᵊl\ *adj* : BACCHANALIAN

²bac·cha·nal \'bak-ən-ᵊl; ‚bak-ə-'nal, -'näl\ *n* **1 a** : a devotee of Bacchus; *esp* : one who celebrates the Bacchanalia **b** : REVELER **2** : BACCHANALIA

bac·cha·na·lia \‚bak-ə-'nāl-yə\ *n, pl* **bacchanalia** [L] **1** *pl, cap* : a Roman festival of Bacchus celebrated with dancing, song, and revelry **2** : a drunken feast : ORGY — **bac·cha·na·lian** \-'nāl-yən\ *adj or n*

bac·chant \bə-'kant, -'känt; 'bak-ənt\ *n, pl* **bacchants** *or* **bacchantes** \bə-'kants, -'känts, -'kant-ēz, -'känt-ēz\ : BACCHANAL — **bacchant** *adj* — **bac·chan·tic** \bə-'kant-ik, -'känt-\ *adj*

bac·chante \bə-'kant(-ē), -'känt(-ē)\ *n* : a priestess or female follower of Bacchus

bac·chic \'bak-ik\ *adj* **1** : of or relating to Bacchus **2** : BACCHANALIAN

Bac·chus \'bak-əs\ *n* : the god of wine in classical mythology

bach·e·lor \'bach-(ə-)lər\ *n* [OF *bacheler*, fr. ML *baccalarius, baccalaureus*, of Celtic origin] **1** : a young knight who fights under the banner of another **2** : a person who has received the lowest degree conferred by a college, university, or professional school ⟨*bachelor* of arts⟩ **3 a** : an unmarried man **b** : an unmated male animal — **bach·e·lor·hood** \-‚hüd\ *n*

bachelor's button *n* : any of numerous plants with flowers or flower heads that suggest buttons; *esp* : CORNFLOWER

bac·il·la·ry \'bas-ə-‚ler-ē, bə-'sil-ə-rē\ *or* **ba·cil·lar** \bə-'sil-ər, 'bas-ə-lər\ *adj* **1** : shaped like a rod; *also* : consisting of small rods **2** : of, relating to, or produced by bacilli

ba·cil·lus \bə-'sil-əs\ *n, pl* **-cil·li** \-'sil-‚ī, -'sil-ē\ [NL, dim. of L *baculus* staff, rod] : any of numerous straight aerobic rod-shaped bacteria usu. producing endospores; *also* : a disease-producing bacterium

¹back \'bak\ *n* [OE *bæc*] **1 a** : the rear part of the human body esp. from the neck to the end of the spine **b** : the corresponding part of a quadruped or other lower animal **2 a** : the hinder part : REAR; *also* : the farther or reverse side **b** : something at or on the back for support ⟨*back* of a chair⟩ **3** : a position in some games behind the front line of players; *also* : a player in this position — **backed** \'bakt\ *adj* — **back·less** \'bak-ləs\ *adj*

²back *adv* **1 a** : to, toward, or at the rear **b** : in or into the past : AGO **c** : in or into a reclining position **d** : under

restraint ⟨held *back*⟩ **2 a** : to, toward, or in a place or state from which a person or thing came ⟨go *back*⟩ **b** : in return or reply ⟨write *back*⟩

³back *adj* **1 a** : being at or in the back ⟨*back* door⟩ **b** : distant from a central or main area : REMOTE **c** : pronounced with closure or narrowing at or toward the back of the oral passage ⟨the *back* vowels \ä\ and \ü\⟩ **2** : being in arrears : OVERDUE ⟨*back* rent⟩ **3** : moving or operating backward **4** : not current ⟨*back* number of a magazine⟩

⁴back *vb* **1 a** : to give aid or support to : ASSIST ⟨*backed* the new enterprise by investing in it⟩ **b** : SUBSTANTIATE **2** : to move or cause to move back, backward, or in reverse **3 a** : to furnish with a back **b** : to be or be at the back of — **back·er** *n*

back·ache \'bak-‚āk\ *n* : pain in the back; *esp* : dull persistent pain in the lower back

back-bench·er \-'ben-chər\ *n* : a rank-and-file member of a British legislature

back·bite \-‚bīt\ *vb* : to say mean or spiteful things about someone who is absent : SLANDER — **back·bit·er** *n*

back·board \-‚bȯrd, -‚bȯrd\ *n* : a board or construction placed at the back or serving as a back; *esp* : one rising vertically behind the basket on a basketball court

back·bone \-'bōn, -‚bōn\ *n* **1** : SPINAL COLUMN **2** : the foundation or sturdiest part of something **3** : firm and resolute character — **back·boned** \-'bōnd, -‚bōnd\ *adj*

back·cross \'bak-‚krȯs\ *vt* : to cross (a first-generation hybrid) with or as if with one parent — **backcross** *n*

back·drop \'bak-‚dräp\ *n* : a painted cloth hung across the rear of a stage

back·field \-‚fēld\ *n* : the football players who line up behind the line of scrimmage

¹back·fire \-‚fī(ə)r\ *n* **1** : a fire started to check an advancing fire by clearing an area **2** : an improperly timed explosion of fuel mixture in the cylinder of an internal-combustion engine

²backfire *vi* **1** : to make or undergo a backfire **2** : to have an effect that is the reverse of the one desired or expected

back-formation *n* **1** : a word formed by subtraction of a real or supposed affix from an already existing longer word (as *pea* from *pease*) **2** : the formation of a back-formation

back·gam·mon \'bak-‚gam-ən\ *n* : a game played by two persons on a double board with 12 spaces on each side in which each player has 15 men whose movements are determined by throwing dice

back·ground \-‚graund\ *n* **1** : the scenery, ground, or surface behind an object seen or represented (as in a painting) **2** : an inconspicuous position ⟨keeps in the *background*⟩ **3 a** : the setting within which something takes place **b** (1) : the situation or events leading up to a phenomenon or development (2) : information essential to understanding a problem or situation **c** : the total of a person's experience, knowledge, and education **4** : sound that interferes with received or recorded electronic signals

¹back·hand \'bak-‚hand\ *n* **1** : a stroke made with the back of the hand turned in the direction of movement **2** : handwriting whose strokes slant downward from left to right

²backhand *adj* : using or made with a backhand

³backhand *vt* : to do, hit, or catch with a backhand

⁴backhand *or* **back·hand·ed** \-‚han-dəd\ *adv* : with a backhand

back·hand·ed \-‚han-dəd\ *adj* **1** : BACKHAND **2** : INDIRECT, DEVIOUS; *esp* : SARCASTIC ⟨a *backhanded* compliment⟩ **3** : written in backhand

backhand

back·ing \-iŋ\ *n* **1** : something forming a back **2 a** : SUPPORT, AID **b** : ENDORSEMENT, APPROVAL **3** : those who support a person or enterprise ⟨a candidate with a wide *backing*⟩

back·lash \'bak-‚lash\ *n* : a sudden violent backward movement or reaction

back·log \-‚lȯg, -‚läg\ *n* **1** : a large log at the back of a hearth fire **2** : a reserve esp. of unfilled orders **3** : an accumulation of unperformed tasks

back of *prep* : BEHIND

back·rest \'bak-ˌrest\ *n* : a rest at or for the back
back·side \'bak-ˈsīd\ *n* : BUTTOCKS
back·slap \-ˌslap\ *vb* : to display excessive cordiality —
back·slap·per *n* — **back·slap·ping** *n*
back·slide \-ˌslīd\ *vi* **-slid** \-ˌslid\; **-slid** *or* **-slid·den**
\-ˌslid-ᵊn\; **-slid·ing** \-ˌslīd-iŋ\ : to lapse morally or in
the practice of religion — **back·slid·er** \-ˌslīd-ər\ *n*
back·spin \-ˌspin\ *n* : a backward rotary motion of a ball
¹back·stage \'bak-ˈstāj\ *adv* **1** : in or to a backstage
area **2** : SECRETLY, PRIVATELY
²backstage *adj* : of, relating to, or occurring in the area
behind the proscenium and esp. in the dressing rooms
back·stay \-ˌstā\ *n* **1** : a stay extending from the mast-
heads to the side of a ship and slanting aft **2** : a strengthening or supporting device at the back
back·stop \-ˌstäp\ *n* **1** : something serving as a stop behind something else; *esp* : a screen or fence used in baseball or other games to keep a ball from leaving the field of
play **2** : a baseball catcher
back·stretch \-ˌstrech, -'strech\ *n* : the side opposite the
homestretch on a racecourse
back·stroke \-ˌstrōk\ *n* : a swimming stroke executed by
a swimmer lying on his back
back·swept \-ˌswept\ *adj* : swept or slanting backward
back swimmer *n* : a water bug that swims on its back
back talk *n* : an insolent or argumentative reply
back·track \'bak-ˌtrak\ *vi* **1** : to retrace one's course
2 : to reverse a position or stand
¹back·ward \-wərd\ *or* **back·wards** \-wərdz\ *adv*
1 a : toward the back ⟨look *backward*⟩ **b** : with the back
foremost ⟨ride *backward*⟩ **2 a** : in a reverse or contrary
direction or way ⟨count *backward*⟩ **b** : toward the past
c : toward a worse state
²backward *adj* **1 a** : directed or turned backward ⟨a
backward glance⟩ **b** : done or executed backward **2** : DIF-
FIDENT, SHY **3** : retarded in development ⟨*backward*
nations⟩ — **back·ward·ly** *adv* — **back·ward·ness** *n*
back·wash \-ˌwȯsh, -ˌwäsh\ *n* **1** : backward movement
(as of water or air) produced by motion of oars or other
propelling force **2** : a consequence or by-product of an
event : AFTERMATH
back·wa·ter \'bak-ˌwȯt-ər, -ˌwät-\ *n* **1** : water held,
pushed, or turned back from its course **2** : a backward
stagnant place or condition
back·woods \-'wu̇dz, -ˌwu̇dz\ *n pl* **1** : wooded or partly
cleared areas on the frontier **2** : a remote culturally
backward area — **back·woods·man** \-mən\ *n*
ba·con \'bā-kən\ *n* [MF, of Gmc origin; akin to E *back*]
: salted and smoked meat from the sides and sometimes
the back of a pig
Ba·co·ni·an \bā-ˈkō-nē-ən\ *adj* : of, relating to, or characteristic of Francis Bacon or his doctrines
bacteria *pl of* BACTERIUM
bac·te·ri·cid·al \ˌbak-ˌtir-ə-ˈsīd-ᵊl\ *adj* : destroying bacteria — **bac·te·ri·cid·al·ly** \-ᵊl-ē\ *adv* — **bac·te·ri·cide**
\-'tir-ə-ˌsīd\ *n*
bac·te·ri·ol·o·gy \bak-ˌtir-ē-ˈäl-ə-jē\ *n* **1** : a science that
deals with bacteria and their relations to medicine, industry, and agriculture **2** : bacterial life and phenomena
— **bac·te·ri·o·log·ic** \-ē-ə-ˈläj-ik\ *or* **bac·te·ri·o·log-
i·cal** \-'läj-i-kəl\ *adj* — **bac·te·ri·o·log·i·cal·ly** \-'läj-i-
k(ə-)lē\ *adv* — **bac·te·ri·ol·o·gist** \-ē-ˈäl-ə-jəst\ *n*
bac·te·rio·phage \bak-'tir-ē-ə-ˌfāj, -ˌfäzh\ *n* : any of
various viruses that specifically attack bacteria
bac·te·rio·sta·sis \bak-ˌtir-ē-ō-ˈstā-səs\ *n* : inhibition of
the growth of bacteria without destruction — **bac·te-
rio·stat** \-'tir-ē-ō-ˌstat\ *n* — **bac·te·rio·stat·ic** \-ˌtir-ē-
ō-ˈstat-ik\ *adj* — **bac·te·rio·stat·i·cal·ly** \-ˈstat-i-
k(ə-)lē\ *adv*
bac·te·ri·um \bak-'tir-ē-əm\ *n, pl* **-ria** \-ē-ə\ [NL, fr.
Gk *baktērion* small staff] : any of a class of microscopic
plants living in soil, water, organic matter, or the bodies
of plants and animals and being important to man because
of their chemical effects and as causers of disease — **bac-
te·ri·al** \-ē-əl\ *adj*
¹bad \'bad\ *adj* **worse** \'wərs\; **worst** \'wərst\ [ME]
1 a : below standard : POOR **b** : UNFAVORABLE ⟨*bad* im-
pression⟩ **c** : DECAYED, SPOILED **2 a** : morally evil
b : MISCHIEVOUS, DISOBEDIENT **3** : INADEQUATE ⟨*bad*
lighting⟩ **4** : DISAGREEABLE, UNPLEASANT ⟨*bad* news⟩
5 a : INJURIOUS, HARMFUL **b** : SEVERE ⟨*bad* cold⟩ **6** : IN-

CORRECT, FAULTY ⟨*bad* spelling⟩ **7** : ILL, SICK ⟨feel *bad*⟩
8 : SORROWFUL, SORRY **9** : INVALID, VOID — **bad** *adv*
— **bad·ly** *adv* — **bad·ness** *n*
²bad *n* **1** : something that is bad **2** : an evil or unhappy
state
bad blood *n* : ill feeling : BITTERNESS ⟨*bad blood* existed
between the two branches of the family⟩
bade *past of* BID
badge \'baj\ *n* [ME *bagge*] **1** : a mark or sign worn to
show that a person belongs to a certain group, class, or
rank ⟨a policeman's *badge*⟩ **2** : an outward sign **3** : an
emblem awarded for some achievement ⟨a scout's merit
badge⟩
¹badg·er \'baj-ər\ *n* : any of several sturdy burrowing
mammals widely distributed in the northern hemisphere;
also : the pelt or fur of a badger
²badger *vt* **badg·ered; badg·er·ing** \'baj-(ə-)riŋ\ [fr. the
practice of baiting badgers] : to harass or annoy
persistently
bad·i·nage \ˌbad-ᵊn-ˈäzh\ *n* [F] : playful talk back and
forth : BANTER
bad·land \'bad-ˌland\ *n* : a region where erosion has
formed the soft rocks into sharp and intricate shapes and
where plant life is scarce ⟨the *badlands* of So. Dakota⟩
— often used in pl.
bad·min·ton \'bad-ˌmint-ᵊn\ *n* [after *Badminton*, the
residence of the Duke of Beaufort, where it was first
played in England] : a court game played with a light
racket and a shuttlecock volleyed over a net
¹baf·fle \'baf-əl\ *vt* **baf·fled; baf·fling** \'baf-(ə-)liŋ\
1 : to defeat or check by confusing : PERPLEX **2 a** : to
check or turn the flow of by or as if by a baffle **b** : to
prevent (sound waves) from interfering with each other
(as by a baffle) **syn** see FRUSTRATE — **baf·fle·ment**
\-əl-mənt\ *n* — **baf·fler** \-(ə-)lər\ *n*
²baffle *n* : a plate, wall, screen, or other device to deflect,
check, or regulate flow
¹bag \'bag\ *n* [ON *baggi*] **1 a** : a flexible usu. closed
container for holding, storing, or carrying something
b : PURSE; *esp* : HANDBAG **c** : TRAVELING BAG, SUITCASE
2 : something resembling a bag: as **a** : a pouched or
pendulous bodily part or organ; *esp* : UDDER **b** : a
puffed-out sag or bulge in cloth **c** : a square white
canvas container to mark a base in baseball **3** : the
amount contained in a bag **4** : a quantity of game
taken or permitted to be taken **5** *slang* : a slovenly unattractive woman — **in the bag** : SURE, CERTAIN
²bag *vb* **bagged; bag·ging** **1 a** : to swell out : BULGE
b : to hang loosely **2** : to put into a bag **3 a** : to take
(animals) as game **b** : CAPTURE, SEIZE; *also* : to shoot
down : DESTROY
ba·gasse \bə-ˈgas\ *n* [F] : plant residue (as of sugarcane)
left after a product (as juice) has been extracted
bag·a·telle \ˌbag-ə-ˈtel\ *n* [F, fr. It *bagattella*] **1** : TRIFLE
2 : a game played with a ball and balls on an oblong table
having cups or cups and arches at one end
ba·gel \'bā-gəl\ *n* [Yiddish *beygel*, fr. OHG *boug* ring]
: a hard glazed doughnut-shaped roll
bag·gage \'bag-ij\ *n* [MF *bagage*, fr. *bague* bundle]
1 : the traveling bags and personal belongings of a traveler
: LUGGAGE **2** : the equipment carried with a military force
3 : unnecessary or unwanted things or circumstances or
ideas **4** : a worthless saucy woman or girl
bag·ging \'bag-iŋ\ *n* : material (as cloth) for
bags
bag·gy \'bag-ē\ *adj* **bag·gi·er; -est** : loose,
puffed out, or hanging like a bag ⟨*baggy*
trousers⟩ — **bag·gi·ly** \'bag-ə-lē\ *adv* —
bag·gi·ness \'bag-ē-nəs\ *n*
ba·gnio \'ban-yō\ *n, pl* **bagnios** : BROTHEL
bag·pipe \'bag-ˌpīp\ *n* : a wind instrument
consisting of a leather bag, a valve-stopped
tube, and three or four sounding pipes —
often used in pl. — **bag·pip·er** \-ˌpī-pər\ *n*
ba·guette \ba-ˈget\ *n* [F, rod] : a gem having
the shape of a long narrow rectangle
bag·worm \'bag-ˌwərm\ *n* : a destructive
larval moth living in a silk case covered with
plant debris and feeding on foliage
bah \'bä, 'ba\ *interj* — used to express disdain or contempt

bagpipe
(and
Scottish
Highlander)

¹bail \'bāl\ *n* [MF, custody, fr. *baillier* to have in charge, fr. L *bajulare* to carry a burden, fr. *bajulus* porter] **1** : security given to guarantee the appearance of a prisoner when legally required in order to obtain his release from prison until that time **2** : the temporary release of a prisoner upon security **3** : one who provides bail

²bail *vt* **1** : to entrust (personal property) to another for a specific purpose and for a limited period **2 a** : to release under bail **b** : to gain the release of by giving bail **3** : to help from a predicament usu. by financial aid

³bail *n* [MF *baille* bucket, fr. ML *bajula*, fr. L, fem. of *bajulus* porter] : a container used to remove water from a boat

⁴bail *vt* : to clear (water) from a boat by dipping and throwing over the side

⁵bail *n* **1 a** : a supporting half hoop **b** : a hinged bar for holding paper against the platen of a typewriter **2** : the arched handle of a kettle or pail

bail·ee \bā-'lē\ *n* : the person to whom property is bailed

bai·ley \'bā-lē\ *n* [OF *baille, balie*] : an outer wall of a castle or the space within it

bai·liff \'bā-ləf\ *n* [OF *baillif*, fr. *bail* custody] **1 a** : an official employed by a British sheriff to serve writs and make arrests and executions **b** : a minor officer of some U.S. courts usu. serving as a messenger or doorkeeper **2** *chiefly Brit* : one who manages an estate or farm — **bail·iff·ship** \-,ship\ *n*

bai·li·wick \'bā-li-,wik\ *n* [ME *baillif* bailiff + *wik* dwelling place] **1** : the office or jurisdiction of a bailiff or a sheriff **2** : one's special province or domain

bail·or \bā-'lò(ə)r, 'bā-lər\ *or* **bail·er** \'bā-lər\ *n* : one who entrusts personal property to another

bail out *vi* : to jump with a parachute from an airplane in flight

bails·man \'bālz-mən\ *n* : one who gives bail for another

bairn \'ba(ə)rn, 'be(ə)rn\ *n, chiefly Scot* : CHILD

¹bait \'bāt\ *vt* [ON *beita*] **1 a** : to persecute or exasperate by repeated attacks **b** : NAG, TEASE **2 a** : to harass with dogs usu. for sport **b** : to attack by biting and tearing **3 a** : to furnish (as a hook) with bait **b** : ENTICE, LURE **4** : to give food and drink to (an animal) esp. on the road — **bait·er** *n*

²bait *n* **1** : something used in luring esp. to a hook or trap; *also* : a poisonous material distributed in food to kill pests **2** : LURE, TEMPTATION

baize \'bāz\ *n* : a coarse woolen or cotton fabric napped to imitate felt

¹bake \'bāk\ *vb* [OE *bacan*] **1** : to cook or become cooked in a dry heat esp. in an oven **2** : to dry or harden by heat (*bake* bricks) **3** : to prepare baked foods — **bak·er** *n*

²bake *n* **1** : the act or process of baking **2** : a social gathering at which a baked food is served

Ba·ke·lite \'bā-kə-,līt, -,klīt\ *trademark* — used for any of various synthetic resins and plastics

baker's dozen *n* : THIRTEEN

bakers' yeast *n* : a yeast used or suitable for use as leaven — compare BREWER'S YEAST

bak·ery \'bā-k(ə-)rē\ *n, pl* **-er·ies** : a place where bread, cakes, and pastry are made or sold

bake·shop \'bāk-,shäp\ *n* : BAKERY

baking powder *n* : a powder that consists of a carbonate, an acid, and a starch and that makes the dough rise and become light in baking cakes and biscuits

baking soda *n* : SODIUM BICARBONATE

bak·sheesh \'bak-,shēsh, bak-'\ *n, pl* **baksheesh** [Per *bakhshīsh*] : a gift of money esp. in the Near East : GRATUITY

bal·a·lai·ka \,bal-ə-'lī-kə\ *n* [Russ] : a triangular wooden instrument of the guitar kind used esp. in the U.S.S.R.

¹bal·ance \'bal-ən(t)s\ *n* [OF, fr. L *bi-* + *lanc-, lanx* plate] **1** : an instrument for weighing; *esp* : a beam that is supported freely in the center and has two pans of equal weight suspended from its ends **2** : a means of judging or deciding **3** : a counterbalancing weight, force, or influence **4** : a vibrating wheel operating with a hairspring to regulate the

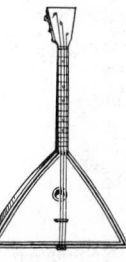

balalaika

movement of a timepiece **5 a** : equipoise between contrasting or interacting elements ⟨reaching a sane *balance* between right and need⟩⟨the *balance* of nature⟩ **b** : equality between the totals of the two sides of an account **6** : an aesthetically pleasing integration of elements : HARMONY **7** : something left over : REMAINDER; *esp* : the amount by which one side of an account is greater than the other ⟨a *balance* of $10 on the credit side⟩ **8** : mental and emotional steadiness

syn BALANCE, REMAINDER, REST mean that which is left after subtraction or removal of a part. BALANCE strictly involves a comparison of two amounts, where one falls short of the other and must be equalized ⟨a bank *balance* is the amount left in an account after withdrawals and other deductions⟩ REMAINDER refers to what remains after a major or significant part of a group or mass has been taken away or accounted for ⟨a few went ahead, but the *remainder* of the party turned back⟩ REST and REMAINDER are interchangeable although REST often suggests a less precisely measured REMAINDER ⟨U.S. and the *rest* of the free world⟩

²balance *vb* **1 a** (1) : to compute the difference between the debits and credits of an account (2) : to pay the amount due on : SETTLE **b** : to make two parts exactly equal ⟨*balance* equations⟩ **c** : to complete (a chemical equation) so that the same number of atoms of each kind appears on each side **2 a** : COUNTERBALANCE, OFFSET **b** : to equal or equalize in weight, number, or proportion **3** : to compare the weight of in or as if in a balance **4 a** : to bring or come to a state or position of equipoise **b** : to poise in or as if in balance **c** : to bring into harmony or proportion; *also* : to so plan and prepare that all needed elements will be present ⟨*balance* a diet⟩ ⟨a *balanced* aquarium⟩ **5** : to move with a swaying or swinging motion **syn** see COMPENSATE — **bal·anc·er** *n*

balance of power **1** : an equilibrium of power between two or more nations sufficient to prevent any one nation or group of nations from becoming strong enough to make war or otherwise attempt to impose its will upon another **2** : the power or influence of a third group or force sufficient when exerted to decide a conflict in favor of one of two equally powerful opponents ⟨the Liberals held the *balance of power* between Conservatives and Labour⟩

balance of trade : the difference in value over a period of time between a country's imports and exports

balance sheet *n* : a statement of the financial condition of an enterprise at a given date

balance wheel *n* : a wheel that regulates or stabilizes the motion of a mechanism (as a timepiece or a sewing machine)

ba·la·ta \bə-'lät-ə\ *n* : a substance like gutta-percha that is the dried juice of tropical American trees related to the sapodilla and is used esp. in belting and golf balls; *also* : a tree yielding balata

bal·boa \bal-'bō-ə\ *n* [Sp, fr. Vasco Núñez de *Balboa* d1517 Spanish explorer] **1** : the basic monetary unit of Panama **2** : a silver coin representing one balboa

bal·brig·gan \bal-'brig-ən\ *n* : a knitted cotton fabric used esp. for underwear or hosiery

bal·co·ny \'bal-kə-nē\ *n, pl* **-nies** [It *balcone*] **1** : a platform enclosed by a low wall or a railing and built out from the side of a building **2** : a gallery inside a building (as a theater or auditorium)

bald \'bòld\ *adj* [ME *balled*] **1** : lacking a natural or usual covering (as of hair) **2** : UNADORNED, PLAIN, SIMPLE ⟨a *bald* summary of the debate⟩⟨the *bald* facts⟩ — **bald·ly** *adv* — **bald·ness** \'bòl(d)-nəs\ *n*

bal·da·chin \'bòl-də-kən, 'bal-\ *or* **bal·da·chi·no** \,bal-də-'kē-nō\ *n* [It *baldacchino*, fr. *Baldacco* Baghdad, Iraq] : a canopylike structure over an altar

bald eagle *n* : the common eagle of No. America which is wholly dark when young but has white head and neck feathers when mature — see EAGLE illustration

bal·der·dash \'bòl-dər-,dash\ *n* : NONSENSE

bald·pate \'bòl(d)-,pāt\ *n* **1** : a bald-headed person **2** : a white-crowned No. American widgeon

bal·dric \'bòl-drik\ *n* [ME *baudrik*] : an often ornamented belt worn over one shoulder to support a sword or bugle

¹bale \'bāl\ *n* [OE *bealu*] **1** : great evil **2** : WOE, SORROW

²bale *n* [OF, of Gmc origin] : a large bundle of goods; *esp*

: a large closely pressed package of merchandise bound and usu. wrapped

³bale *vt* **:** to make up into a bale — **bal·er** *n*

ba·leen \bə-'lēn\ *n* [L *ballaena* whale] **:** WHALEBONE

bale·ful \'bāl-fəl\ *adj* **1 :** deadly or harmful in influence **2 :** foreboding evil **:** OMINOUS — **bale·ful·ly** \-fə-lē\ *adv* — **bale·ful·ness** *n*

¹balk \'bȯk\ *n* [OE *balca*] **1 :** a ridge of land left unplowed or missed in plowing **2 :** BEAM, RAFTER **3 :** HINDRANCE, CHECK **4 :** failure of a player to complete a motion begun; *esp* **:** an illegal motion of a baseball pitcher while in position

²balk *vb* **1** *archaic* **:** to pass over **:** fail to grasp **2 :** to check or stop by or as if by an obstacle **:** BLOCK **3 :** to stop short and refuse to go **:** refuse abruptly ⟨horse *balked* at the steep hill⟩ **4 :** to commit a balk in sports — **balk·er** *n*

bal·kan·ize \'bȯl-kə-,nīz\ *vt, often cap* [*Balkan* peninsula] **:** to break up (as a region) into smaller and often hostile units — **bal·kan·i·za·tion** \,bȯl-kə-nə-'zā-shən\ *n, often cap*

balky \'bȯ-kē\ *adj* **balk·i·er; -est :** likely to balk **:** BALKING

¹ball \'bȯl\ *n* [ON *bǫllr*] **1 :** a round or roundish body or mass: as **a :** a spherical or ovoid body used in a game or sport **b :** EARTH, GLOBE **c :** a usu. round solid shot for a firearm **d :** the rounded bulge at the base of the thumb or great toe **2 :** a game in which a ball is thrown, kicked, or struck; *esp* **:** BASEBALL **3 :** a pitched baseball not struck at by the batter that fails to pass through the strike zone

²ball *vb* **:** to form or gather into a ball

³ball *n* [F *bal*, fr. LL *ballare* to dance, fr. Gk *ballizein*] **:** a large formal gathering for social dancing

bal·lad \'bal-əd\ *n* [OProv *balada* dance, dancing song, fr. LL *ballare* to dance] **1 :** a simple song **2 :** a narrative poem usu. in stanzas of two or four lines and suitable for singing; *esp* **:** one of unknown authorship handed down orally from generation to generation **3 :** a popular song; *esp* **:** a slow romantic or sentimental dance song — **bal·lad·ry** \-ə-drē\ *n*

ball-and-socket joint *n* **:** a joint (as in the hip) in which a rounded part moves within a socket so as to allow movements in many directions

¹bal·last \'bal-əst\ *n* **1 :** something heavy carried in a ship to steady it **2 :** something heavy put into the car of a balloon to steady it or to control its ascent **3 :** gravel, cinders, or crushed stone used in making a roadbed (as of a railroad) or in making concrete

²ballast *vt* **:** to provide with ballast

ball bearing *n* **1 :** a bearing in which the revolving part turns on steel balls that roll easily in a groove **2 :** one of the balls in a ball bearing

ball·car·ri·er \'bȯl-,kar-ē-ər\ *n* **:** the football player carrying the ball in an offensive play

bal·le·ri·na \,bal-ə-'rē-nə\ *n* **:** a female ballet dancer

bal·let \'bal-ā, ba-'lā\ *n* [F, fr. It *balletto*, dim. of *ballo* dance, fr. *ballare* to dance, fr. LL] **1 a :** dancing in which conventional poses and steps are combined with light flowing figures and movements **b :** a theatrical art form using ballet dancing to convey a story, theme, or atmosphere **2 :** music for a ballet **3 :** a group that performs ballets

bal·let·o·mane \ba-'let-ə-,mān\ *n* **:** a devotee of ballet

bal·lis·tic \bə-'lis-tik\ *adj* [L *ballista* machine for hurling missiles, fr. Gk *ballein* to throw] **:** of or relating to ballistics or to a body in motion according to the laws of ballistics

ballistic missile *n* **:** a self-propelled missile that is guided during the ascent of a high-arch path and that falls freely in the descent

bal·lis·tics \bə-'lis-tiks\ *n sing or pl* **1 a :** the science that deals with the motion of projectiles (as bullets) **b :** the flight characteristics of a projectile **2 :** the firing characteristics of a firearm or cartridge

¹bal·loon \bə-'lün\ *n* [F *ballon*, fr. It dial. *ballone*, aug. of *balla* ball, of Gmc origin] **1 :** an airtight bag filled with heated air or with a gas lighter than air so as to rise and float above the ground **2 :** a toy consisting of a rubber bag that can be inflated with air or gas — **bal·loon·ist** \-'lü-nəst\ *n*

²balloon *vb* **1 :** to ascend or travel in a balloon **2 :** to swell or puff out **3 :** to increase rapidly

¹bal·lot \'bal-ət\ *n* [It *ballotta*, fr. dim. of *balla* ball]

1 a : a small ball used in secret voting **b :** a sheet of paper used to cast a vote **2 a :** the action or system of voting **b :** the right to vote **3 :** the number of votes cast

²ballot *vi* **:** to vote or decide by ballot — **bal·lot·er** *n*

ball park *n* **:** a park or enclosed ground in which ball and esp. baseball is played

ball-point pen *n* **:** a pen having as the writing point a small rotating steel ball that inks itself by contact with an inner magazine

ball·room \'bȯl-,rüm, -,rùm\ *n* **:** a large room for dances

bal·ly·hoo \'bal-ē-,hü\ *n, pl* **-hoos 1 :** a noisy attention-getting demonstration or talk **2 :** grossly exaggerated or sensational advertising or propaganda — **ballyhoo** *vt*

balm \'bäm, 'bälm\ *n* [OF *baume*, fr. L *balsamum* balsam] **1 :** a balsamic resin; *esp* **:** one from small tropical evergreen trees **2 :** a fragrant healing or soothing preparation (as an ointment) **3 :** something that comforts or refreshes ⟨sleep is *balm* to a tired body⟩ **4 :** any of several spicy fragrant herbs **5 :** a spicy aromatic odor

balm of Gil·e·ad \-'gil-ē-əd\ **1 a :** a small African and Asiatic tree with aromatic evergreen leaves; *also* **:** its fragrant oleoresin **b :** any of several aromatic plants **2 :** an agency that soothes, relieves, or heals

balmy \'bäm-ē, 'bäl-mē\ *adj* **balm·i·er; -est 1 a :** having the qualities of balm **:** SOOTHING **b :** MILD **2 :** FOOLISH, INSANE — **balm·i·ly** \'bäm-ə-lē, 'bäl-mə-\ *adv* — **balm·i·ness** \'bäm-ē-nəs, 'bäl-mē-\ *n*

bal·sa \'bȯl-sə\ *n* [Sp] **1 :** a tropical American tree with extremely light strong wood used esp. for floats; *also* **:** its wood **2 :** a raft made of bundles of grass or reeds lashed together **3 :** a life raft made of two cylinders of metal or wood joined by a framework and often used for landing through surf

bal·sam \'bȯl-səm\ *n* [L *balsamum*, fr. Gk *balsamon*] **1 a :** an aromatic and usu. oily and resinous substance flowing from various plants **b :** a preparation containing or smelling like balsam **2 a :** a balsam-yielding tree **b :** IMPATIENS; *esp* **:** one grown as an ornamental **3 :** BALM 2 — **bal·sam·ic** \bȯl-'sam-ik\ *adj*

balsam fir *n* **:** a resinous American evergreen tree of the pine family widely used for pulpwood and as a Christmas tree — see FIR illustration

balsam of Pe·ru \-pə-'rü\ **:** a balsam from a tropical American leguminous tree used in perfumery and medicine

Bal·tic \'bȯl-tik\ *adj* **1 :** of or relating to the Baltic sea or to the states of Lithuania, Latvia, and Estonia **2 :** of or relating to a branch of the Indo-European languages containing Latvian, Lithuanian, and Old Prussian

bal·us·ter \'bal-ə-stər\ *n* [F *balustre*, fr. It *balaustro*, fr. *balaustra* pomegranate flower] **:** an upright rounded, square, or vase-shaped support of a rail (as in the railing of a staircase or balcony)

bal·us·trade \'bal-ə-,strād\ *n* **1 :** a row of balusters topped by a rail to serve as an open barrier (as along the edge of a terrace or a balcony) **2 :** a stair rail; *esp* **:** a wide rail having heavy supports

bam·bi·no \bam-'bē-nō\ *n, pl* **bambinos** *or* **bam·bi·ni** \-(,)nē\ [It] **1 :** CHILD, BABY **2** *pl usu* **bambini :** a representation of the infant Christ

bam·boo \bam-'bü\ *n, pl* **bamboos** [Malay *bambu*] **:** any of various chiefly tropical tall woody grasses including some with strong hollow stems used for building, furniture, or utensils — **bamboo** *adj*

bamboo curtain *n* **:** an iron curtain surrounding and isolating areas under Chinese Communist control

bam·boo·zle \bam-'bü-zəl\ *vt* **-boo·zled; -boo·zling** \-'büz-(ə-)liŋ\ **:** to deceive by trickery **:** HOODWINK — **bam·boo·zle·ment** \-'büz-əl-mənt\ *n*

¹ban \'ban\ *vb* **banned; ban·ning** [OE *bannan* to summon] **1** *archaic* **:** CURSE **2 :** to prohibit esp. by legal means or social pressure

²ban *n* **1 :** ANATHEMA, EXCOMMUNICATION **2 :** MALEDICTION, CURSE **3 :** an official prohibition **4 :** censure or condemnation esp. through public opinion

ba·nal \bə-'näl, -'nal; 'bān-ᵊl\ *adj* [F, fr. MF, of feudal service, possessed in common, fr. *ban* summons to feudal service, of Gmc origin] **:** wanting originality, freshness, or novelty **:** TRITE, COMMONPLACE, ORDINARY — **ba·nal·i·ty** \bā-'nal-ət-ē, bə-\ *n* — **ba·nal·ly** \bə-'näl-lē, -'nal-; 'bān-ᵊl-(l)ē\ *adv*

---

j joke; **ŋ** sing; **ō** flow; **ȯ** flaw; **ȯi** coin; **th** thin; **th̲** this; **ü** loot; **ù** foot; **y** yet; **yü** few; **yù** furious; **zh** vision

ba·nana \bə-'nan-ə\ *n* [of African origin] : a treelike tropical plant with large leaves and flower clusters that develop into a bunch of finger-shaped fruit which are yellow or red when ripe; *also* : its fruit

banana oil *n* : a colorless liquid acetate that has a pleasant fruity odor and is used as a solvent

¹**band** \'band\ *n* [partly fr. ON, something that constricts (akin to E *bind, bond*) & partly fr. MF *bende, bande* strip, of Gmc origin (akin to E *bind*)] **1** : something (as a fetter or shackle) that confines or constricts **2** : something that binds or restrains legally, morally, or spiritually **3** : a strip serving to join or hold things together **4** : a thin encircling strip that confines, supports, or protects ⟨protect the baby's navel with a soft *band*⟩ **5 a** : a strip distinguishable by some characteristic (as color, texture, or composition) from adjacent matter ⟨a *band* of nerve fibers⟩ **b** : a range of wavelengths or frequencies between two specified limits **c** : a narrow strip serving chiefly as decoration **d** *pl* : a pair of strips hanging at the front of the neck as part of a clerical, legal, or academic dress **e** : a strip of grooves on a phonographic record containing a single piece or a section of a long piece — **band·ed** \'ban-dəd\ *adj*

²**band** *vb* **1** : to put a band on or tie up with a band **2** : to finish with a band **3 a** : to attach (oneself) to a group **b** : to gather together or summon for a purpose **c** : to unite in a company or confederacy or for a common purpose — **band·er** *n*

³**band** *n* [MF *bande* troop] : a group of persons, animals, or things; *esp* : a group of musicians organized for playing together

¹**ban·dage** \'ban-dij\ *n* : a strip of fabric used esp. to dress and bind up wounds

²**bandage** *vt* : to bind, dress, or cover with a bandage — **ban·dag·er** *n*

ban·dan·na *or* **ban·dana** \ban-'dan-ə\ *n* [Hindi *bādhnū* cloth dyed by knotting portions so as to leave them undyed] : a large figured handkerchief with usu. a red or blue background

band·box \'ban(d)-,bäks\ *n* : a usu. cylindrical box of pasteboard or thin wood for holding light articles of attire

ban·deau \ban-'dō\ *n, pl* **ban·deaux** \-'dōz\ **1** : a fillet or band esp. for the hair **2** : BRASSIERE

ban·de·role *or* **ban·de·rol** \'ban-də-,rōl\ *n* : a long narrow forked flag or streamer

ban·di·coot \'ban-di-,küt\ *n* : any of various small insect-eating and plant-eating marsupial mammals esp. of Australia

ban·dit \'ban-dət\ *n, pl* **bandits** [It *bandito,* fr. pp. of *bandire* to banish, of Gmc origin; akin to E *ban*] **1** *pl also* **ban·dit·ti** \ban-'dit-ē\ : OUTLAW, BRIGAND **2** : one who steals, profiteers, or kills : GANGSTER, CRIMINAL — **ban·dit·ry** \'ban-də-trē\ *n*

band·mas·ter \'ban(d)-,mas-tər\ *n* : a conductor of a musical band

ban·dog \'ban-,dȯg\ *n* : a fierce dog formerly kept tied as a watchdog

ban·do·lier *or* **ban·do·leer** \,ban-də-'li(ə)r\ *n* : a belt worn over the shoulder and across the breast to carry something (as cartridges) or as part of an official or ceremonial dress

band saw *n* : a saw in the form of an endless steel belt running over pulleys

band shell *n* : a bandstand having at the rear a sounding board shaped like a huge concave seashell

bands·man \'ban(d)z-mən\ *n* : a member of a musical band

band·stand \'ban(d)-,stand\ *n* : a usu. roofed outdoor stand or platform on which a band or orchestra performs

band·wag·on \'ban(d)-,wag-ən\ *n* **1** : a wagon carrying musicians in a parade **2** : a candidate, side, or movement that attracts open support or approval because it seems to be winning or gaining popularity — used in phrases like *climb on the bandwagon*

¹**ban·dy** \'ban-dē\ *vb* **ban·died; ban·dy·ing 1** : to bat (as a tennis ball) to and fro **2 a** : to toss from side to side or from one to another **b** : EXCHANGE; *esp* : to exchange (words) argumentatively **c** : to discuss lightly or banteringly or as a subject of gossip **3** *archaic* : to band together

²**bandy** *adj* : curved esp. outward : BOWED ⟨*bandy* legs⟩

ban·dy–legged \,ban-dē-'leg(-ə)d\ *adj* : having bandy legs : BOWLEGGED

bane \'bān\ *n* [OE *bana* murderer] **1** : something that destroys life; *esp* : deadly poison **2** : a source of injury, harm, ruin, or woe : a destructive influence

bane·ful \'bān-fəl\ *adj* **1** *archaic* : POISONOUS, NOXIOUS **2** : creating destruction or woe : RUINOUS — **bane·ful·ly** \-fə-lē\ *adv*

¹**bang** \'baŋ\ *vb* **1** : to strike against : BUMP **2** : to strike with a sharp noise **3** : to produce a sharp often metallic explosive or percussive noise or series of noises

²**bang** *n* **1** : a resounding blow **2** : a sudden loud noise **3 a** : a sudden striking effect **b** : a quick burst of energy **c** : THRILL

³**bang** *adv* : RIGHT, DIRECTLY ⟨*bang* in the middle⟩

⁴**bang** *n* : a fringe of banged hair

⁵**bang** *vt* : to cut (as front hair) short and squarely across

ban·gle \'baŋ-gəl\ *n* [Hindi *baṅglī*] **1** : a stiff usu. ornamental bracelet or anklet slipped or clasped on **2** : a small ornament hanging (as from a bracelet) loosely

bang·tail \'baŋ-,tāl\ *n* **1** : RACEHORSE **2** : a wild horse

bang–up \'baŋ-,əp\ *adj* : FIRST-RATE, EXCELLENT ⟨had a *bang-up* time⟩ ⟨a *bang-up* job⟩

ban·ish \'ban-ish\ *vt* [MF *baniss-, banir,* of Gmc origin; akin to E *ban*] **1** : to compel by authority to leave a country ⟨the king *banished* the traitors⟩ **2** : to drive out from or as if from a home : EXPEL ⟨*banish* fears⟩ — **ban·ish·er** *n* — **ban·ish·ment** \-ish-mənt\ *n*

ban·is·ter \'ban-ə-stər\ *n* [alter. of *baluster*] **1** : one of the slender posts used to support the handrail of a staircase **2** : a stair rail and its supporting posts — usu. used in pl. **3** : the handrail of a staircase

ban·jo \'ban-,jō\ *n, pl* **banjos** *also* **banjoes** : a musical instrument of the guitar class with a long narrow fretted neck and small drum-shaped body — **ban·jo·ist** \-,jō-əst\ *n*

¹**bank** \'baŋk\ *n* [ME, prob. of Scand origin; akin to E *bench*] **1** : a mound, pile, or ridge esp. of earth **2** : a piled up mass of cloud or fog **3** : an undersea elevation rising esp. from the continental shelf : SHOAL **4** : the rising ground bordering a lake, river, or sea or forming the edge of a hollow (as a cut) **5** : a steep slope (as of a hill) **6** : the inward tilt of a surface along a curve or of a vehicle (as an airplane) when taking a curve

²**bank** *vb* **1** : to raise a bank about **2** : to heap or pile in a bank **3** : to line or form a bank **4** : to cover (a fire) with fresh fuel so as to reduce the speed of burning **5** : to build (a curve) with the roadbed or track inclined laterally upward from the inside edge **6** : to incline an airplane laterally when turning ⟨the airplane was *banking*⟩ **7** : to form or group in a tier

³**bank** *n* [OF *banc* bench, of Gmc origin; akin to E *bench*] **1** : a bench for the rowers of a galley **2** : a group or series of objects arranged near together in a row or a tier: as **a** : a row of keys on a typewriter **b** : a set of two or more elevators

⁴**bank** *n* [It *banca, banco,* lit., bench, of Gmc origin; akin to E *bench*] **1** : a place of business that receives, lends, issues, exchanges, and takes care of money, extends credit, and provides ways of sending money and credit quickly from place to place **2** : a small container in which coins or bills are saved **3** : a supply of something held in reserve: as **a** : the fund of the banker or dealer in a gambling game **b** : a fund of pieces belonging to a game (as dominoes) from which the players draw **4** : a storage place for a reserve supply ⟨eye *bank*⟩

⁵**bank** *vb* **1** : to keep a bank **2** : act as a banker **2** : to have an account in a bank **3** : to deposit in a bank ⟨*banks* $10 every week⟩ — **bank on** *or* **bank upon** : to depend upon

bank·book \'baŋk-,bȯok\ *n* : the depositor's book in which a bank enters his deposits and withdrawals — called also *passbook*

bank discount *n* : the interest discounted in advance on a note and computed on the face value of the note — compare TRUE DISCOUNT

bank·er \'baŋ-kər\ *n* **1** : one that engages in the business of banking **2** : the player who keeps the bank in a gambling game

bank holiday *n, Brit* : LEGAL HOLIDAY

bank·ing *n* : the business of a bank or a banker

bank note *n* : a promissory note issued by a bank payable to bearer on demand without interest and acceptable as money

bank·roll \'baŋk-,rōl\ *n* : supply of money : FUNDS

¹bank·rupt \'baŋ-(,)krəpt\ *n* [modif. of It *bancarotta* bankruptcy, lit., broken bank] : a person who becomes unable to pay his debts; *esp* : one whose property by court order is turned over to a trustee to be administered for the benefit of his creditors

²bankrupt *vt* : to reduce to bankruptcy

³bankrupt *adj* **1 a** : fallen into a state of financial ruin : IMPOVERISHED **b** : legally declared a bankrupt **2 a** : BROKEN, RUINED **b** : DEPLETED, STERILE **c** : DESTITUTE

bank·rupt·cy \'baŋ-(,)krəp-(t)sē\ *n, pl* **-cies** : the condition of being bankrupt

¹ban·ner \'ban-ər\ *n* [OF *banere*, of Gmc origin] **1 a** : a piece of cloth attached by one edge to a staff and used as a standard **b** : ⁴FLAG **c** : an ensign displaying a distinctive or symbolic device or legend **2** : a headline in large type running across a newspaper page **3** : a strip of cloth on which a sign is painted

²banner *adj* : distinguished from all others esp. in excellence ⟨a *banner* year for apple growers⟩

ban·nock \'ban-ək\ *n* : an often unleavened bread of oat or barley flour baked in flat loaves

banns \'banz\ *n pl* : public announcement esp. in church of a proposed marriage

¹ban·quet \'baŋ-kwət, 'ban-, -,kwet\ *n* [MF, fr. OIt *banchetto*, fr. dim. of *banco* bench, bank] : an elaborate often ceremonious meal for numerous people sometimes in celebration of a special occasion

²banquet *vb* **1** : to treat with a banquet : FEAST **2** : to partake of a banquet — **ban·quet·er** *n*

ban·quette \baŋ-'ket, ban-\ *n* **1** : a raised way along the inside of a parapet or trench for gunners or guns **2** : a long upholstered seat esp. along a wall

ban·shee \'ban-(,)shē\ *n* [ScGael *bean-sīth*, lit., woman of fairyland] : a female spirit in Gaelic folklore whose wailing warns of approaching death

¹ban·tam \'bant-əm\ *n* [*Bantam*, Java] **1** : any of numerous small domestic fowls that are often miniatures of members of the standard breeds **2** : a person of diminutive stature and often combative disposition

²bantam *adj* **1** : SMALL, DIMINUTIVE **2** : PERT, SAUCY

ban·tam·weight \-,wāt\ *n* : a boxer weighing more than 112 but not over 118 pounds

¹ban·ter \'bant-ər\ *vb* **1** : to speak to in a witty and teasing manner : RALLY **2** : to talk or act in a humorous way — **ban·ter·er** \-ər-ər\ *n* — **ban·ter·ing·ly** \'bant-ə-riŋ-lē\ *adv*

²banter *n* : good-natured teasing or joking

bant·ling \'bant-liŋ\ *n* : a very young child

Ban·tu \'ban-,tü\ *n* **1** : a member of a family of negroid peoples occupying equatorial and southern Africa **2** : a group of African languages spoken generally south of a line from Cameroons to Kenya — **Bantu** *adj*

Ban·tu·stan \,ban-tü-'stan, ,bän-tü-'stän\ *n* [*Bantu* + *-stan* land (as in *Hindustan*)] : an all-black enclave in the Republic of So. Africa with a limited degree of self-government

ban·yan \'ban-yən\ *n* : a large East Indian tree from whose branches aerial roots grow downward into the ground and form new supporting trunks

ban·zai \(')bän-'zī\ *n* : a Japanese cheer or cry of triumph

bao·bab \'baù-,bab, 'bā-ə-,bab\ *n* : an Old World tropical tree with a broad trunk and an edible acid fruit resembling a gourd

bap·tism \'bap-,tiz-əm\ *n* **1** : a Christian sacrament signifying spiritual rebirth and admitting the recipient to the Christian community through the ritual use of water **2** : an act or ceremony of naming or dedicating in a manner suggestive of baptism **3** : an act, experience, or ordeal that is like baptism in purifying or in initiating into a new life ⟨a soldier's *baptism* of fire⟩ — **bap·tis·mal** \bap-'tiz-məl\ *adj* — **bap·tis·mal·ly** \-mə-lē\ *adv*

Bap·tist \'bap-təst\ *n* **1** : John the baptizer and forerunner of Christ **2** : a Protestant of an evangelical denomination practicing congregational government and baptism by immersion for believers — **Baptist** *adj*

bap·tis·tery *or* **bap·tis·try** \'bap-tə-strē\ *n, pl* **-ter·ies** *or*

-tries : a part of a church or formerly a separate building used for baptism

bap·tize \bap-'tīz, 'bap-,\ *vt* [Gk *baptizein* to dip, baptize] **1** : to administer baptism to **2 a** : to purify spiritually esp. by a cleansing experience or ordeal **b** : INITIATE **3** : to give a name to (as at baptism) : CHRISTEN — **bap·tiz·er** *n*

¹bar \'bär\ *n* [OF *barre*] **1 a** : a rigid piece (as of wood or metal) that is longer than it is wide and has various uses (as for a lever, barrier, or fastening) **b** : a usu. rectangular solid piece or block of material considerably longer than it is wide **2** : something that obstructs or prevents passage, progress, or action : IMPEDIMENT: as **a** : any intangible or nonphysical impediment **b** : a submerged or partly submerged bank along a shore or in a river **3 a** : the railing in a courtroom that encloses the place where the business of the court is transacted **b** : a court or system of courts **c** : an authority or tribunal that renders judgment ⟨before the *bar* of public opinion⟩ **d** : the body of lawyers qualified to practice in a jurisdiction ⟨the New York *bar*⟩; *also* : the profession of lawyer **4** : a straight stripe, band, or line much longer than it is wide **5 a** : a counter for serving food or esp. alcoholic beverages **b** : BARROOM **6 a** : a vertical line across the musical staff before the initial measure accent **b** : MEASURE

bars 6a: *1, 2* bars, *3* double bar

²bar *vt* **barred**; **bar·ring** **1 a** : to fasten with a bar **b** : to place bars across to prevent passage **2** : to mark with bars : STRIPE **3** : to block off : OBSTRUCT **4 a** : to set aside : rule out **b** : to keep out : EXCLUDE **c** : PREVENT, FORBID

³bar *prep* : with the exception of ⟨*bar* none⟩

Ba·rab·bas \bə-'rab-əs\ *n* : a prisoner released instead of Jesus at the demand of the multitude

¹barb \'bärb\ *n* [MF *barbe*, lit., beard, fr. L *barba*] **1 a** : a sharp projection extending backward (as from the point of an arrow or fishhook) and preventing easy extraction **b** : any of various natural objects (as a hooked plant hair or a lateral filament of a feather) resembling a barb **2** : a biting or pointedly critical remark or comment

²barb *vt* : to furnish with a barb

³barb *n* [F *barbe*, fr. It *barbero*, fr. *barbero* of Barbary] : a horse of a breed related to the Arab and introduced into Spain by the Moors

bar·bar·i·an \bär-'ber-ē-ən, bär-'bar-\ *adj* [L *barbarus*, fr. Gk *barbaros* not Greek, uncultured] **1** : of, relating to, or being a land, culture, or people alien to one's own and usu. believed to be inferior to one's own **2** : lacking refinement, learning, or artistic or literary culture — **barbarian** *n* — **bar·bar·i·an·ism** \-ē-ə-,niz-əm\ *n*

syn BARBARIAN, BARBAROUS, BARBARIC, SAVAGE mean characteristic of uncivilized man. BARBARIAN often implies a state somewhere between tribal savagery and full civilization; BARBAROUS tends to stress the harsher or more brutal side of uncivilized life; BARBARIC suggests crudeness of taste and fondness for gorgeous and unrestrained display; SAVAGE suggests more primitive culture than BARBARIAN and greater harshness or fierceness than BARBAROUS

bar·bar·ic \bär-'bar-ik\ *adj* **1** : of, relating to, or characteristic of barbarians **2 a** : marked by a lack of restraint **b** : having a bizarre, primitive, or unsophisticated quality ⟨*barbaric* splendor⟩ **syn** see BARBARIAN

bar·ba·rism \'bär-bə-,riz-əm\ *n* **1** : a word or expression not accepted as belonging to the standard language **2 a** : a barbarian state of social or intellectual development **b** : the practice or display of barbarian acts, attitudes, or ideas

bar·bar·i·ty \bär-'bar-ət-ē\ *n, pl* **-ties** **1** : BARBARISM **2 a** : barbarous cruelty : INHUMANITY **b** : an act or instance of barbarous cruelty

bar·ba·rize \'bär-bə-,rīz\ *vb* : to make or become barbarian or barbarous — **bar·ba·ri·za·tion** \,bär-b(ə-)rə-'zā-shən\ *n*

bar·ba·rous \'bär-b(ə-)rəs\ *adj* **1** : characterized by the use of barbarisms in speech or writing **2 a** : UNCIVILIZED **b** : lacking culture or refinement **3** : mercilessly harsh or cruel **syn** see BARBARIAN — **bar·ba·rous·ly** *adv* — **bar·ba·rous·ness** *n*

Bar·ba·ry ape \ˌbär-b(ə-)rē-\ *n* : a tailless monkey of No. Africa and Gibraltar

¹bar·be·cue \ˈbär-bi-ˌkyü\ *n* [AmerSp *barbacoa*] **1** : a large animal (as a hog or steer) roasted or broiled whole or split over an open fire or bed of hot coals **2** : a social gathering esp. in the open air at which barbecued food is eaten

²barbecue *vt* **1** : to roast or broil on a rack over hot coals or on a revolving spit before or over a source of heat **2** : to cook in a highly seasoned vinegar sauce

barbed \ˈbärbd\ *adj* : having a barb

barbed wire \ˈbä(r)b(d)-ˈwī(ə)r\ *n* : twisted wires armed with barbs or sharp points — called also *barbwire*

bar·bel \ˈbär-bəl\ *n* [MF, fr. L *barbus*, fr. *barba* beard] **1** : a European freshwater fish of the carp family with four barbels on its upper jaw **2** : a slender tactile process on the lips of a fish

bar·bell \ˈbär-ˌbel\ *n* : a bar with adjustable weighted disks attached to each end used for exercise and in weight lifting

¹bar·ber \ˈbär-bər\ *n* [MF *barbeor*, fr. *barbe* beard, fr. L *barba*; akin to E *beard*] : one whose business is cutting and dressing hair, shaving and trimming beards, and performing related services

²barber *vb* **bar·bered; bar·ber·ing** \-b(ə-)riŋ\ : to perform the services of a barber

bar·ber·ry \ˈbär-ˌber-ē\ *n* [Ar *barbārīs*] : any of a genus of spiny yellow-flowered shrubs often grown for hedges or ornament

bar·ber·shop \ˈbär-bər-ˌshäp\ *n* : a barber's place of business

barber's itch *n* : ringworm of the face and neck

bar·bette \bär-ˈbet\ *n* **1** : a mound of earth or a protected platform from which guns fire over a parapet **2** : a cylinder of armor protecting a gun turret on a warship

bar·bi·can \ˈbär-bi-kən\ *n* [ML *barbacana*] : an outer defensive work; *esp* : a tower at a gate or bridge

bar·bi·tal \ˈbär-bə-ˌtol\ *n* : a white habit-forming hypnotic drug often administered in the form of its soluble sodium salt

bar·bi·tu·rate \bär-ˈbich-ə-rət\ *n* **1** : a salt or ester of barbituric acid **2** : any of various derivatives of barbituric acid used esp. as sedatives or hypnotics

bar·bi·tu·ric acid \ˌbär-bə-ˌt(y)ùr-ik-\ *n* [G *barbitur*säure, irreg. fr. the name *Barbara* + NL *urea*] : a crystalline acid C₄H₄N₂O₃ used in making plastics and drugs

bar·bule \ˈbär-byül\ *n* : a minute barb; *esp* : one of the processes that fringe the barbs of a feather

bar·ca·role *or* **bar·ca·rolle** \ˈbär-kə-ˌrōl\ *n* [F *barcarolle*, fr. It *barcarola*, fr. *barca* bark] **1** : a Venetian boat song characterized by a beat suggesting a rowing rhythm **2** : a piece of music imitating a barcarole

bar chart *n* : a graphic means of comparing numbers by rectangles whose lengths are proportional to the numbers represented — called also *bar graph*

bard \ˈbärd\ *n* [MIr] **1** : a tribal poet-singer gifted in composing and reciting verses on heroes and their deeds **2** : POET — **bard·ic** \ˈbärd-ik\ *adj*

¹bare \ˈba(ə)r, ˈbe(ə)r\ *adj* [OE *bær*] **1 a** : lacking its natural, usual, or appropriate covering **b** : lacking clothing **2** : open to view : EXPOSED **3 a** : completely unfurnished or only scantily supplied **b** : DESTITUTE ⟨*bare* of all safeguards⟩ **4 a** : having nothing left over or added : MERE **b** : not adorned or expanded : PLAIN ⟨the *bare* facts⟩ — **bare·ly** *adv* — **bare·ness** *n*

²bare *vt* : to make or lay bare : UNCOVER, REVEAL

³bare *archaic past of* BEAR

bare·back \-ˌbak\ *or* **bare·backed** \-ˈbakt\ *adv (or adj)* : on the bare back of a horse : without a saddle

bare·faced \-ˈfāst\ *adj* : SHAMELESS, BOLD ⟨a *barefaced* lie⟩

bare·foot \-ˌfüt\ *or* **bare·foot·ed** \-ˈfüt-əd\ *adv (or adj)* : with the feet bare : UNSHOD

bare·hand·ed \-ˈhan-dəd\ *adv (or adj)* **1** : with the hands bare : without gloves or mittens **2** : without tools or weapons

bare·head·ed \-ˈhed-əd\ *adv (or adj)* : with the head bare : without a hat

¹bar·gain \ˈbär-gən\ *n* [MF *bargaigne*, fr. *bargaignier* to bargain, of Gmc origin; akin to E *borrow*] **1** : an agreement between parties settling what each is to give or receive in a transaction **2** : something gained by or as if

by bargaining; *esp* : an advantageous purchase ⟨at 35 percent off, the suit was a real *bargain*⟩ **3** : a situation or event with important good or bad results ⟨got the worst of a bad *bargain*⟩

²bargain *vb* **1** : to talk over the terms of a purchase, agreement, or contract; *esp* : to try to win advantageous terms from the other party to a proposed bargain **2** : to come to terms : AGREE **3** : to sell or dispose of by bargaining : BARTER — **bar·gain·er** *n* — **bargain for** : to count on in advance : EXPECT ⟨more trouble than he bargained for⟩

¹barge \ˈbärj\ *n* [OF, fr. LL *barca*] **1** : a broad flat-bottomed boat used chiefly in harbors and on rivers and canals **2** : a ship's boat for the use of a naval officer ranking above a captain

²barge *vb* **1** : to carry by barge **2** : to move or thrust oneself clumsily or rudely ⟨he *barged* right in without being invited⟩

barge·man \-mən\ *n* : the master or a deckhand of a barge

bar·ite \ˈba(ə)r-ˌīt, ˈbe(ə)r-\ *n* : a white, yellow, or colorless mineral BaSO₄ consisting of barium sulfate and occurring in crystals or as a mass

bar·i·tone \ˈbar-ə-ˌtōn\ *n* [Gk *barys* heavy + *tonos* tone] **1 a** : a male singing voice of medium compass between bass and tenor **b** : a man having such a voice **2** : the saxhorn intermediate in size between althorn and tuba

bar·i·um \ˈbar-ē-əm, ˈber-\ *n* [NL, fr. Gk *barys* heavy] : a silver-white malleable toxic bivalent metallic chemical element that occurs only in combination — see ELEMENT table

barium hydroxide *n* : a strong chemical base Ba(OH)₂.-8H₂O used in making lubricating greases and as a reagent

barium sulfate *n* : a colorless crystalline insoluble compound BaSO₄ that is used as a pigment, as a filler, and as a substance that can be x-rayed in medical photography of the alimentary canal

¹bark \ˈbärk\ *vb* [OE *beorcan*] **1** : to make the characteristic short loud cry of a dog or a similar noise **2** : to speak or utter in a curt usu. angry tone ⟨*bark* out an order⟩ **3** : to work as a barker

²bark *n* : the sound made by a barking dog or a similar sound

³bark *n* [ON *bark-, börkr*] : the tough largely corky exterior covering of a woody root or stem

⁴bark *vt* **1** : to strip the bark from **2** : to rub off or abrade the skin of

⁵bark *or* **barque** *n* [MF *barque*, fr. OProv *barca*, fr. LL] **1 a** : a small sailing ship **b** : a 3-masted ship with foremast and mainmast square-rigged and mizzenmast fore-and-aft rigged **2** : a craft propelled by sails or oars

bar·keep·er \ˈbär-ˌkē-pər\ *or* **bar·keep** \-ˌkēp\ *n* : one that keeps or tends a bar for the sale of liquors

bar·ken·tine *or* **bar·quen·tine** \ˈbär-kən-ˌtēn\ *n* : a 3-masted ship having the foremast square-rigged and the mainmast and mizzenmast fore-and-aft rigged

bark·er \ˈbär-kər\ *n* : a person who stands at the entrance to a show or a store and tries to attract customers to it ⟨a sideshow *barker*⟩

barky \ˈbär-kē\ *adj* **bark·i·er; -est** : covered with or resembling bark

bar·ley \ˈbär-lē\ *n* [OE *bærlic* of barley] : a cereal grass with flowers in dense long-awned spikes with three spikelets at each joint; *also* : its seed used in malt beverages and as food or stock feed

bar·ley·corn \-ˌkorn\ *n* : a grain of barley

barm \ˈbärm\ *n* [OE *beorma*] : yeast formed on fermenting malt liquors

bar magnet *n* : a magnet in the shape of a bar

bar·maid \ˈbär-ˌmād\ *n*, *chiefly Brit* : a female bartender

bar·man \-mən\ *n* : BARTENDER

Bar·me·cid·al \ˌbär-mə-ˈsīd-ᵊl\ *or* **Bar·me·cide** \ˈbär-mə-ˌsīd\ *adj* [*Barmecide*, a wealthy Persian, who, in a tale of *The Arabian Nights*, invited a beggar to a feast of imaginary food] : providing only an apparent abundance ⟨a *Barmecidal* feast⟩

bar mitz·vah \bär-ˈmits-və\ *n*, *often cap B&M* [LHeb *bar miswāh*, lit., son of the law] **1** : a Jewish boy who reaches his 13th birthday and attains the age of religious duty and responsibility **2** : the initiatory ceremony recognizing ⟨ boy as a bar mitzvah

barn \ˈbärn\ *n* [OE *bereærn*, fr. *bere* barley + *ærn* place]

: a building used chiefly for storing grain and hay and for housing farm animals (as cows and horses)

bar·na·cle \'bär-ni-kəl\ *n* [alter. of ME *bernake*, a goose believed to be produced from barnacles] : any of numerous marine crustaceans (order Cirripedia) that are free-swimming as larvae but fixed (as to rocks or pilings) as adults — **bar·na·cled** \-kəld\ *adj*

barn·storm \'bärn-ˌstorm\ *vi* **1** : to tour through rural districts staging theatrical performances usu. in one-night stands **2** : to travel from place to place making brief stops (as in political campaigning) **3** : to pilot an airplane in sight-seeing flights with passengers or in exhibition stunts in an unscheduled course esp. in rural districts — **barn·storm·er** *n*

barn·yard \-ˌyärd\ *n* : a usu. fenced area adjoining a barn

baro- *comb form* [Gk *baros* weight] : weight : pressure ⟨*barometer*⟩

baro·graph \'bar-ə-ˌgraf\ *n* : a self-registering barometer

ba·rom·e·ter \bə-'räm-ət-ər\ *n* **1** : an instrument for determining the pressure of the atmosphere and hence for assisting in judgment as to probable weather changes and for determining the height of an ascent **2** : something that registers changes (as in public opinion) — **bar·o·met·ric** \ˌbar-ə-'me-trik\ *adj*

bar·on \'bar-ən\ *n* [OF, of Gmc origin] **1 a** : a tenant holding his rights and title usu. by military service directly from a feudal superior (as a king) **b** : NOBLEMAN, PEER **2** : a member of the lowest grade of the British peerage **3** : a man of great or excessive power or influence in some field ⟨cattle *baron*⟩

barometer

bar·on·age \-ə-nij\ *n* : the whole body of barons or peers

bar·on·ess \-ə-nəs\ *n* **1** : the wife or widow of a baron **2** : a woman who holds a baronial title in her own right

bar·on·et \'bar-ə-nət\ *n* : a man holding a rank of honor below a baron but above a knight

ba·ro·ni·al \bə-'rō-nē-əl\ *adj* : of, relating to, or suitable for a baron or the baronage (lives in *baronial* splendor)

bar·ony \'bar-ə-nē\ *n, pl* **bar·on·ies** : the domain, rank, or dignity of a baron

ba·roque \bə-'rōk, ba-, -'räk\ *adj* [F, fr. It *barocco*] : of or relating to a style of artistic expression esp. of the 17th century marked by elaborate and sometimes grotesque ornamentation and the use of curved and exaggerated figures in art and architecture, by improvisation, contrast, and tension in music, and by complex form and bizarre, ingenious, and often ambiguous imagery in literature — **baroque** *n*

ba·rouche \bə-'rüsh\ *n* : a four-wheeled carriage with a driver's seat high in front, 2 double seats inside facing each other, and a folding top

bar·racks \'bar-əks, -iks\ *n sing or pl* [F *baraque* hut] **1** : a building or group of buildings in which soldiers are quartered **2** : a plain large building

bar·ra·cou·ta \ˌbar-ə-'küt-ə\ *n* **1** : a large marine food fish **2** : BARRACUDA

bar·ra·cu·da \ˌbar-ə-'küd-ə\ *n, pl* **-da** *or* **-das** [AmerSp] : any of several large gluttonous and fierce marine fishes of warm seas related to the gray mullets

bar·rage \bə-'räzh, -'räj\ *n* **1** : a barrier formed by continuous artillery or machine-gun fire directed upon a narrow strip of ground **2** : a rapid or concentrated delivery or outpouring (as of speech or writing)

bar·ra·try \'bar-ə-trē\ *n, pl* **-tries** **1** : the purchase or sale of office or preferment in church or state **2** : a fraudulent breach of duty by the master or crew of a ship intended to harm the owner or cargo **3** : the practice of inciting lawsuits or quarrels

barred \'bärd\ *adj* : having alternate bands of different color

¹bar·rel \'bar-əl\ *n* [MF *baril*] **1** : a round bulging container that is longer than it is wide and has flat ends **2 a** : the amount held by a barrel **b** : a great quantity **3** : a cylindrical or tubular part (gun *barrel*) **4** : the trunk of a quadruped — **bar·reled** \-əld\ *adj*

²barrel *vb* **-reled** *or* **-relled**; **-rel·ing** *or* **-rel·ling** **1** : to put or pack in a barrel **2** : to travel at a high speed

bar·rel·ful \'bar-əl-ˌful\ *n, pl* **bar·rel·fuls** \-əl-ˌfulz\ *or* **bar·rels·ful** \-əlz-ˌful\ : BARREL 2a

barrel organ *n* : a musical instrument consisting of a revolving cylinder studded with pegs that open a series of valves to admit air from a bellows to a set of pipes

¹bar·ren \'bar-ən\ *adj* [OF *barain*] **1** : not reproducing: as **a** : incapable of producing offspring ⟨a *barren* woman⟩ **b** : habitually failing to fruit **2 a** : producing inferior or scanty vegetation ⟨*barren* soils⟩ **b** : unproductive of results or gain : FRUITLESS ⟨a *barren* scheme⟩ **3** : lacking interest, information, or charm **syn** see STERILE — **bar·ren·ly** *adv* — **bar·ren·ness** \-ən-nəs\ *n*

²barren *n* **1** : a tract of barren land **2** *pl* : a wide usu. level tract with stunted or scrub trees or little vegetation

bar·rette \bä-'ret, bə-\ *n* : a clip or bar for holding a woman's hair in place

¹bar·ri·cade \'bar-ə-ˌkād, ˌbar-ə-'\ *vt* **1** : to block off or stop up with a barricade **2** : to prevent access to by means of a barricade

²barricade *n* : an obstruction or rampart thrown up across a way or passage to check an advance or block passage

bar·ri·er \'bar-ē-ər\ *n* **1 a** : a material object or set of objects that separates or marks off or serves as a barricade **b** : an extension of the antarctic continental ice sheet into the sea resting partly on the bottom **2** : something immaterial that separates ⟨language *barriers* between peoples⟩ **3** : a material or immaterial factor that keeps organisms from interbreeding or spreading into new territory

barrier reef *n* : a coral reef roughly parallel to a shore and separated from it by a lagoon

bar·ring \'bär-iŋ\ *prep* **1** : with the exception of ⟨*barring* none⟩ **2** : apart from the possibility of ⟨will be there on time, *barring* accidents⟩

bar·ris·ter \'bar-ə-stər\ *n* [irreg. fr. ¹*bar*] : a lawyer who is permitted to plead cases in any English court — compare SOLICITOR

bar·room \'bär-ˌrüm, -ˌrum\ *n* : a room or establishment whose main feature is a bar for the sale of liquor

¹bar·row \'bar-ō\ *n* [OE *beorg* mountain, barrow] **1** : MOUND — used only in the names of hills in England **2** : a large burial mound of earth or stones

²barrow *n* [OE *bearg*] : a male hog castrated before sexual maturity

³barrow *n* [OE *bearwe;* akin to E ²*bear*] **1** : a framework that has handles and sometimes a wheel and is used for carrying things **2** : a cart with a shallow box body, two wheels, and shafts for pushing it : PUSHCART

bar·tend·er \'bär-ˌten-dər\ *n* : one that serves alcoholic beverages at a bar

¹bar·ter \'bärt-ər\ *vb* [MF *barater*] : to trade one commodity directly for another without the use of money ⟨*bartered* for furs with tobacco and rum⟩ — **bar·ter·er** \'bärt-ər-ər\ *n*

²barter *n* : the exchange of goods without the use of money; *also* : something given in such an exchange

Bar·tho·lin's gland \ˌbärt-ʰl-ənz-, ˌbär-thə-lənz-\ *n* [after Kaspar *Bartholin* d1738 Dan physician] : either of two oval racemose glands lying one to each side of the lower part of the vagina and secreting a lubricating mucus

bar·ti·zan \'bärt-ə-zən\ *n* : a small overhanging or projecting structure for lookout or defense

bar·yte \'ba(ə)r-ˌīt, 'be(ə)r-\ *or* **ba·ry·tes** \bə-'rīt-ēz\ *var of* BARITE

bary·tone \'bar-ə-ˌtōn\ *var of* BARITONE

bas·al \'bā-səl\ *adj* **1** : relating to, situated at, or forming the base **2** : of, relating to, or constituting a foundation or basis : FUNDAMENTAL — **bas·al·ly** \-ə-lē\ *adv*

basal metabolic rate *n* : the rate at which heat is given off by an organism at complete rest

basal metabolism *n* : the energy turnover in a fasting and resting organism in which energy is being used solely to maintain vital cellular activity, respiration, and circulation

ba·salt \bə-'solt, 'bā-\ *n* [L *basaltes*] : a dark gray to black dense to fine-grained igneous rock — **ba·sal·tic** \bə-'sol-tik\ *adj*

bas·cule \'bas-ˌkyül\ *n* [F, seesaw] : an apparatus or structure in which one end is counterbalanced by the other on the principle of the seesaw or by weights ⟨a *bascule* bridge⟩

¹base \'bās\ *n, pl* **bas·es** \'bā-səz\ [L *basis*, fr. Gk. *bainein* to step, go] **1** : the bottom of something that serves as its support : FOUNDATION **2 a** : a main ingredient **b** : a supporting or carrying ingredient (as of a medicine) **3 a :** the fundamental part of something **: GROUNDWORK b :** the economic factors upon which in Marxist theory all legal, social, and political relations are formed **4 a :** the point or line from which a start is made in an action or undertaking **b :** the locality or installations from which a military force operates **c :** the number with reference to which a system of numbers or a mathematical table is constructed **d :** ROOT 5 **5 a :** the starting place or goal in various games **b :** any of the four stations a runner in baseball must touch in order to score **6 :** any of various compounds (as lime) that are capable of reacting with an acid to form a salt, that when dissolved in water have a strong somewhat salty taste, that turn litmus blue, and yield hydroxyl ions, that have a molecule or ion which can take up a proton from an acid, or that are substances able to give up to an acid an unshared pair of electrons — **based** \'bāst\ *adj*

²base *vt* **1 :** to make, form, or serve as a base for **2 :** to use as a base or basis for **:** ESTABLISH

³base *adj* **:** constituting or serving as a base

⁴base *adj* [MF *bas* low, fr. ML *bassus*] **1** *archaic* **:** of humble birth **:** LOWLY **2 a :** of inferior quality; *esp* **:** alloyed with or made of inferior metal **b :** of comparatively little value; *esp* **:** of comparatively low value and relatively inferior in certain properties 〈*base* metals〉 **3 :** morally low **:** MEAN, CONTEMPTIBLE 〈*base* conduct〉 — **base·ly** *adv* — **base·ness** *n*

base·ball \'bās-,bȯl\ *n* **:** a game played with a bat and ball between two teams of nine players each on a field with four bases that mark the course a runner must take to score; *also* **:** the ball used in this game

base·board \-,bȯrd, -,bȯrd\ *n* **:** a line of boards or molding covering the joint of a wall and the adjoining floor

base·born \-'bȯrn\ *adj* **1 :** of humble birth **:** LOWLY **2 :** of illegitimate birth **:** BASTARD

base hit *n* **:** a hit in baseball that enables the batter to reach base safely with no error made and no base runner forced out

base·less \'bās-ləs\ *adj* **:** having no basis or reason **:** GROUNDLESS 〈a *baseless* accusation〉

base line *n* **1 :** a line taken as or representing a base **2 :** the area within which a baseball player must keep when running between bases

base·man \'bās-mən\ *n* **:** a baseball player stationed at a base

base·ment \'bās-mənt\ *n* **1 :** the part of a building that is wholly or partly below ground level **2 :** the lowest or fundamental part of something

basement membrane *n* **:** a thin vascular connective tissue layer supporting a sheet of epithelium

ba·sen·ji \bə-'sen-jē\ *n* **:** any of an African breed of small compact curly-tailed chestnut-brown dogs that rarely bark

base on balls *n* **:** an advance to first base given to a baseball player who receives four balls

base path *n* **:** the area marked between the bases of a baseball field and used by a base runner

base runner *n* **:** a baseball player of the team at bat who is on base or is attempting to reach a base — **base·run·ning** \'bās-,rən-iŋ\ *n*

base word *n* **:** a word to which a prefix or a suffix can be added to form a new word

bash \'bash\ *vb* **1 :** to strike violently **:** BEAT **2 :** to smash by a blow **3 :** CRASH

bash·ful \'bash-fəl\ *adj* [ME *bashen* to abash, be abashed] **1 :** inclined to shrink from public attention **:** SHY, DIFFIDENT **2 :** characterized by or resulting from extreme sensitiveness or self-consciousness **syn** see SHY — **bash·ful·ly** \-fə-lē\ *adv* — **bash·ful·ness** *n*

bashi·ba·zouk \,bash-ē-bə-'zük\ *n* **:** a member of an irregular ill-disciplined auxiliary of the Ottoman Empire

¹ba·sic \'bā-sik\ *adj* **1 :** of, relating to, or forming the base or foundation **:** FUNDAMENTAL 〈*basic* industries〉 〈the *basic* facts〉 **2 :** constituting or serving as a base or starting point 〈*basic* course in school〉 **3 :** of, relating to, containing, or having the character of a base; *also* **:** having an alkaline reaction **4 :** containing relatively little silica 〈*basic* rocks〉 — **ba·si·cal·ly** \-si-k(ə-)lē\ *adv*

²basic *n* **:** something that is basic **:** FUNDAMENTAL 〈the *basics* of education〉

ba·sic·i·ty \bā-'sis-ət-ē\ *n, pl* **-ties :** the quality or degree of being a base

ba·sid·io·carp \bə-'sid-ē-ə-,kärp\ *n* **:** the fruiting body of a basidiomycete

ba·sid·io·my·cete \bə-,sid-ē-ō-'mī-,sēt, -mī-'sēt\ *n* **:** any of a large class (Basidiomycetes) of higher fungi (as rusts, smuts, or puffballs) having septate hyphae and spores borne on a basidium — **ba·sid·io·my·ce·tous** \-ō-mī-'sēt-əs\ *adj*

ba·sid·io·spore \bə-'sid-ē-ə-,spō(ə)r-, ,spó(ə)r\ *n* **:** a spore produced by a basidium — **ba·sid·io·spo·rous** \-,sid-ē-ə-'spōr-əs, -'spór-; -ē-'äs-pə-rəs\ *adj*

ba·sid·i·um \bə-'sid-ē-əm\ *n, pl* **-ia** \-ē-ə\ **:** a specialized cell of a basidiomycete bearing usu. four basidiospores — **ba·sid·i·al** \-ē-əl\ *adj*

bas·il \'baz-əl, 'bās-, 'bas-, 'bāz-\ *n* **:** any of several plants of the mint family; *esp* **:** either of two plants with aromatic leaves used in cookery

bas·i·lar \'bas-ə-lər\ *also* **bas·i·lary** \-,ler-ē\ *adj* **:** of, relating to, or situated at a base

ba·sil·i·ca \bə-'sil-i-kə, -'zil-\ *n* [L, fr. Gk *basilikē*, lit., royal (hall), fr. *basileus* king] **1 :** an oblong public building of ancient Rome ending in an apse **2 :** an early Christian church building consisting of nave and aisles with clerestory and apse **3 :** a Roman Catholic church with ceremonial privileges — used as a canonical title — **ba·sil·i·can** \-kən\ *adj*

bas·i·lisk \'bas-ə-,lisk, 'baz-\ *n* **1 :** a legendary reptile with fatal breath and glance **2 :** any of several crested tropical American lizards related to the iguanas

ba·sin \'bās-ⁿn\ *n* [OF *bacin*, fr. LL *bacchinon*] **1 a :** a wide shallow usu. round dish or bowl with sloping or curving sides for holding liquid (as water) **b :** the amount that a basin holds **2 a :** a natural or artificial hollow, depression, or enclosure containing water; *esp* **:** a partly enclosed water area for anchoring ships **3 :** an area of land drained by a river and its branches

ba·sip·e·tal \bā-'sip-ət-ⁿl\ *adj* **:** proceeding from the apex toward the base or from above downward — **ba·sip·e·tal·ly** \-ⁿl-ē\ *adv*

ba·sis \'bā-səs\ *n, pl* **ba·ses** \'bā-,sēz\ [L, base] **1 :** the base, foundation, or chief supporting part **2 :** the principal component of something **3 a :** something on which something else is constructed or established **b :** BASE 3b **4 :** the basic principle

bask \'bask\ *vi* [ON *bathask* to bathe oneself; akin to E *bath*] **:** to lie in or expose oneself to a pleasant warmth or atmosphere 〈*basked* in an air of good fellowship〉

bas·ket \'bas-kət\ *n* [ME] **1 a :** a container made by weaving together the constituent material (as twigs, straw, cane, or strips of wood) **b :** the contents of a basket **2 :** something that resembles a basket in shape or use **3 a :** a net open at the bottom and suspended from a metal ring that constitutes the goal in basketball **b :** a field goal in basketball — **bas·ket·work** \-,wərk\ *n*

bas·ket·ball \-,bȯl\ *n* **:** a usu. indoor court game in which each of two teams tries to toss an inflated ball through a raised goal; *also* **:** the ball used in this game

basket-of-gold *n* **:** a European perennial herb widely cultivated for its grayish foliage and yellow flowers

bas·ket·ry \'bas-kə-trē\ *n* **1 :** the art or craft of making baskets or objects woven like baskets **2 :** objects produced by basketry

basket weave *n* **:** a textile weave resembling the checkered pattern of a plaited basket

bas mitz·vah \bäs-'mits-və\ *n, often cap B&M* **1 :** a Jewish girl who at about 13 years of age assumes religious responsibilities **2 :** the initiatory ceremony recognizing a girl as a bas mitzvah

ba·so·phil \'bā-sə-,fil\ *or* **ba·so·phile** \-,fīl\ *n* **:** a basophilic substance or structure; *esp* **:** a white blood cell with basophilic granules

ba·so·phil·ic \,bā-sə-'fil-ik\ *adj* **:** staining readily with basic dyes

Basque \'bask\ *n* **1 :** a member of a people inhabiting a region bordering on the Bay of Biscay in northern

basilica 2: *1* narthex, *2* nave, *3* aisle, *4* altar, *5* bema, *6* apse, *7* transept

Spain and southwestern France **2** : the language of the Basque people — **Basque** adj

bas·re·lief \,bä-ri-'lēf\ n [F, fr. bas low + relief] : a sculpture in relief in which the design is raised very slightly from the background

¹bass \'bas\ n, pl bass or bass·es [OE bærs] **1** : any of several spiny-finned freshwater sport and food fishes of eastern No. America **2** : any of several saltwater fishes resembling the perch

²bass \'bās\ n [MF bas low, fr. ML bassus] **1** : a deep or low-pitched tone : a low-pitched sound **2 a** (1) : the lowest part in polyphonic or harmonic music (2) : the lower half of the whole vocal or instrumental tonal range **b** (1) : the lowest male singing voice (2) : a person having such a voice **c** : the lowest member in range of a family of instruments — **bass** adj

bass clef n **1** : a clef placing the F below middle C on the 4th line of the staff — see CLEF illustration **2** : the bass staff

bass drum n : a large drum having two heads and giving a booming sound of low indefinite pitch

bas·set \'bas-ət\ n : any of an old French breed of short-legged slow-moving hunting dogs with very long ears and crooked front legs

bass horn n : TUBA

bas·si·net \,bas-ə-'net\ n : an infant's bed with sides of various materials (as wickerwork or plastic) often with a hood over one end

bas·so \'bas-ō, 'bäs-\ n, pl bassos [It, fr. ML bassus, fr. bassus low] : a bass singer; esp : an operatic bass

bas·soon \ba-'sün, bə-\ n [F basson, fr. It bassone, fr. basso] : a tenor or bass double-reed woodwind instrument having a long doubled conical wooden body connected to the mouthpiece by a thin metal tube — **bas·soon·ist** \-'sü-nəst\ n

bass viol n : DOUBLE BASS

bass·wood \'bas-,wùd\ n [bass bast, alter. of bast] **1** : any of several trees of the linden family; also : TULIP TREE **2** : the pale straight-grained wood of a basswood

bast \'bast\ n [OE bæst] **1** : PHLOEM **2** : a strong woody fiber obtained chiefly from the phloem of plants and used esp. in cordage and matting

¹bas·tard \'bas-tərd\ n [OF] **1** : an illegitimate child **2** : something that is spurious, irregular, inferior, or of questionable origin — **bas·tard·ly** \-lē\ adj

²bastard adj **1** : ILLEGITIMATE **2** : of an inferior or atypical kind, stock, or form **3** : not genuine or authoritative : SPURIOUS — **bastardy** n

¹baste \'bāst\ vt [MF bastir, of Gmc origin] : to sew with long loose stitches in order to hold the work temporarily in place — **bast·er** n

²baste \'bāst\ vt : to moisten (as roasting meat) with melted butter or fat — **bast·er** n

Bas·tille \ba-'stēl\ n : a medieval fortress in Paris used as a prison until stormed by mobs on July 14, 1789 and destroyed

Bastille Day n : July 14 observed in France as a national holiday in commemoration of the fall of the Bastille in 1789

bas·ti·na·do \,bas-tə-'nād-ō, -'näd-\ n, pl -does [Sp bastonada, fr. bastón stick, fr. LL bastum] **1** : a blow with a stick or cudgel **2** : a punishment consisting of beating the soles of the feet with a stick — **bastinado** vt

bast·ing \'bā-stiŋ\ n : the thread used in loose stitching or the stitching made by this thread

bas·tion \'bas-chən\ n [MF bastillon, bastion, fr. bastide, bastille fort, fr. OProv bastida, fr. bastir to build, of Gmc origin] **1** : a projecting part of a fortification **2** : a fortified area or position **3** : STRONGHOLD, BULWARK

¹bat \'bat\ n [OE batt] **1** : a stout solid stick : CLUB **2** : a sharp blow **3 a** : a wooden implement used for hitting the ball in various games **b** : a racket used in various games (as squash) **4** : a turn at batting **5** or **batt** : BATTING 2 — usu. used in pl. **6** : BINGE

²bat vb bat·ted; bat·ting **1** : to strike or hit with or as if with a bat **2 a** : to advance (a base runner) by batting **b** : to have a batting average of **3** : to take one's turn at bat in baseball

³bat n [alter. of ME bakke] : any of an order (Chiroptera)

of nocturnal flying mammals with the forelimbs modified to form wings

⁴bat vt bat·ted; bat·ting : to wink esp. in surprise or emotion ⟨never batted an eye⟩

batch \'bach\ n [ME bache] **1** : a quantity baked at one time ⟨the first batch of cookies⟩ **2** : a quantity of any material for use at one time or produced at one operation ⟨a batch of dough⟩ ⟨a batch of cement⟩ **3** : a group of persons or things : LOT ⟨a batch of letters⟩

bate \'bāt\ vt [ME baten, short for abaten to abate] **1** : to reduce the force or intensity of ⟨listen with bated breath⟩ **2** : to take away : DEDUCT ⟨refuses to bate a jot of his claim⟩

ba·teau also **bat·teau** \ba-'tō\ n, pl ba·teaux \-'tō(z)\ [F bateau, fr. OE bāt boat] : any of various small craft; esp : a flat-bottomed boat with raked bow and stern and flaring sides

bath \'bath, 'båth\ n, pl baths \'bathz, 'baths, 'båthz, 'båths\ [OE bæth] **1** : a washing or soaking (as in water or steam) of all or part of the body **2 a** : water used for bathing ⟨drew his bath⟩ **b** : a liquid in which objects are placed so that it can act upon them ⟨a dyeing bath⟩; also : the container holding such a liquid **c** : a contained medium for regulating the temperature of something ⟨a hot water bath⟩ **3 a** : BATHROOM ⟨house with two baths⟩ **b** : a building containing rooms designed for bathing **c** : SPA — usu. used in pl.

bathe \'bāth\ vb **1** : to take a bath **2** : to go swimming **3 a** : to wash in a liquid (as water) **b** : MOISTEN, WET **4** : to apply water or a liquid medicament to **5** : to flow along the edge of : LAVE **6** : SUFFUSE, OVERSPREAD — **bath·er** \'bā-thər\ n — **bath·ing** \-thiŋ\ n

ba·thet·ic \bə-'thet-ik\ adj : characterized by bathos — **ba·thet·i·cal·ly** \-i-k(ə-)lē\ adv

bath·house \'bath-,haùs, 'båth-\ n **1** : a building equipped for bathing **2** : a building containing dressing rooms for bathers

batho·lith \'bath-ə-,lith\ n : a great mass of igneous rock that forced its way into or between other rocks and that stopped in its rise a considerable distance below the surface

ba·thos \'bā-,thäs\ n [Gk, lit., depth] **1 a** : the sudden appearance of the commonplace in otherwise elevated matter or style **b** : ANTICLIMAX **2** : FLATNESS, TRITENESS **3** : insincere or overdone pathos

bath·room \'bath-,rüm, 'båth-, -,rùm\ n : a room containing a bathtub or shower and usu. a washbowl and toilet

bath·tub \-,təb\ n : a usu. fixed tub for bathing

bathy·al \'bath-ē-əl\ adj : DEEP-SEA

bathy·scaphe \'bath-i-,skaf, -,skåf\ n [Gk bathys deep + skaphē light boat] : a navigable submersible ship for deep-sea exploration having a spherical watertight cabin attached to its underside

bathy·sphere \'bath-i-,sfi(ə)r\ n : a strongly built steel diving sphere for deep-sea observation

ba·tik \bə-'tēk, 'bat-ik\ n [Malay] **1 a** : an Indonesian method of hand-printing textiles by coating with wax the parts not to be dyed **b** : a design so executed **2** : a fabric printed by batik

bat·ing \'bāt-iŋ\ prep : with the exception of

ba·tiste \bə-'tēst, ba-\ n [F] : a fine soft sheer fabric of plain weave made of various fibers

bat·man \'bat-mən\ n : an orderly of a British military officer

ba·ton \ba-'tän, bə-\ n [F bâton stick, fr. OF baston, fr. LL bastum] **1** : a staff borne as a symbol of office **2** : a stick or wand with which a leader directs a band or orchestra **3** : a hollow cylinder carried by each member of a relay team and passed to the succeeding runner **4** : a smooth staff with a ball at one end carried by a drum major or baton twirler

ba·tra·chi·an \bə-'trā-kē-ən\ n [Gk batrachos frog] : FROG, TOAD, SALIENTIAN — **batrachian** adj

bats·man \'bats-mən\ n : ³BATTER

bat·tal·ion \bə-'tal-yən\ n **1** : a large organized body of troops : ARMY **2** : a military unit composed of a headquarters and two or more companies, batteries, or subunits **3** : a large body of persons organized to act together ⟨labor battalions⟩

¹bat·ten \'bat-ᵊn\ vb bat·tened; bat·ten·ing \'bat-niŋ, -ᵊn-iŋ\ [prob. fr. ON batna to improve] **1 a** : to grow

bassoon

fat **b :** to feed gluttonously **2 :** to grow prosperous **: THRIVE 3 :** to make fat **: FATTEN**
²**batten** n [F *bâton* stick] **1 :** a thin narrow strip of lumber used esp. to seal or reinforce a joint **2 :** a strip, bar, or support resembling or used similarly to a batten
³**batten** vt **:** to furnish or fasten with battens
¹**bat·ter** \'bat-ər\ vb [ME *bateren*, prob. freq. of *batten* to bat] **1 :** to beat with successive violent, heavy, or shattering blows ⟨*batter* down the door⟩ **2 :** to wear or damage by blows or hard usage ⟨a *battered* old hat⟩
²**batter** n **:** a mixture that consists chiefly of flour and liquid and is thin enough to pour or drop from a spoon
³**batter** n **:** one that bats; *esp* **:** the baseball player at bat
battering ram n **1 :** a military siege engine consisting of a large wooden beam with a head of iron used in ancient times to beat down the walls of a besieged place **2 :** a heavy metal bar with handles used to batter down doors and walls
bat·tery \'bat-ə-rē, 'ba-trē\ n, pl **-ter·ies 1 a :** the act of battering or beating **b :** the unlawful beating or use of force upon a person without his consent — compare ASSAULT 2 **2 a :** a tactical grouping of artillery pieces **b :** the guns of a warship **3 :** an artillery unit in the army equivalent to a company **4 :** a group of two or more electric cells connected together for furnishing electric current; *also* **:** a single electric cell ⟨a flashlight *battery*⟩ **5 :** a number of machines or devices grouped together or forming a unit ⟨a *battery* of lights or of cameras⟩ **6 :** the pitcher and catcher of a baseball team
battery jar n **:** a round, square, or rectangular glass container that has straight sides and is open at the top
bat·ting \'bat-iŋ\ n **1 a :** the act of one who bats **b :** the use of or ability with a bat **2 :** layers or sheets of raw cotton or wool used for lining quilts or for stuffing or packaging
¹**bat·tle** \'bat-ʰl\ n [OF *bataille*, fr. LL *battalia* combat, fr. L *battuere* to beat] **1 :** a general encounter between armies, ships of war, or airplanes **2 :** a combat between two persons ⟨trial by *battle*⟩ **3** archaic **: BATTALION 4 :** an extended contest, struggle, or controversy ⟨a *battle* of wits⟩
²**battle** vb **bat·tled; bat·tling** \'bat-liŋ, -ʰl-iŋ\ **1 :** to engage in battle **: FIGHT** ⟨armies *battling* for a city⟩ **2 :** to contend with full strength, craft, or resources **: STRUGGLE** ⟨*battle* for a cause⟩ **3 :** to fight against ⟨*battle* a storm⟩ ⟨*battling* a forest fire⟩
bat·tle-ax or **bat·tle-axe** \'bat-ʰl-,aks\ n **:** a broadax formerly used as a weapon of war
battle cruiser n **:** a warship of battleship size and of the highest speed and heaviest battery but without the heavy armor protection of the battleship
bat·tle·dore \'bat-ʰl-,dō(ə)r, -,dȯ(ə)r\ n [ME *batyldore* bat used in washing clothes] **:** a light flat bat or racket used in striking a shuttlecock
bat·tle·field \-,fēld\ n **:** a place where a battle is fought — called also **bat·tle·ground** \-,graȯnd\
battle group n **:** a military unit normally made up of five companies
bat·tle·ment \'bat-ʰl-mənt\ n **:** a parapet with open spaces that surmounts a wall and is used for defense or decoration — **bat·tle·ment·ed** \-,ment-əd\ adj
battle royal n, pl **battles royal** or **battle royals 1 a :** a fight participated in by more than two combatants; *esp* **:** such a contest in which the last man in the ring or on his feet is declared the winner **b :** a violent struggle **2 :** a heated dispute

battlements

bat·tle·ship \'bat-ʰl-,ship\ n [short for *line-of-battle ship*] **:** a warship of the largest and most heavily armed and armored class
bat·tle·wag·on \-,wag-ən\ n **: BATTLESHIP**
bat·ty \'bat-ē\ adj **bat·ti·er; -est** [³*bat*] slang **:** mentally unstable **: CRAZY**
bat·wing \'bat-,wiŋ\ adj **:** shaped like the wing of a bat
bau·ble \'bȯ-bəl, 'bäb-əl\ n [MF *babel*] **1 : TRINKET 2 :** a fool's scepter **3 : TRIFLE**
baux·ite \'bȯk-,sīt, 'bäk-\ n **:** a mineral that consists of an impure mixture of earthy hydrous aluminum oxides and hydroxides and is the principal ore of aluminum

baw·bee or **bau·bee** \'bȯ-(,)bē\ n **1 : HALFPENNY 2 : TRIFLE**
bawd \'bȯd\ n [ME *bawde*] **1** obs **: PANDER 2 a :** one who keeps a house of prostitution **b : PROSTITUTE**
bawd·ry \'bȯ-drē\ n, pl **bawdries 1** obs **: UNCHASTITY 2 :** offensively suggestive or obscene language **: BAWDINESS**
bawdy \'bȯd-ē\ adj **bawd·i·er; -est : OBSCENE, LEWD — bawd·i·ly** \'bȯd-ʰl-ē-\ adv **— bawd·i·ness** \'bȯd-ē-nəs\ n
¹**bawl** \'bȯl\ vb [ME *baulen*] **1 :** to cry out loudly and unrestrainedly **: YELL 2 : WAIL 3 :** to reprimand loudly or severely — used with *out* — **bawl·er** n
²**bawl** n **:** a loud prolonged cry **: OUTCRY**
¹**bay** \'bā\ adj [MF *bai*, fr. L *badius*] **:** of the color bay
²**bay** n **1 :** a horse with a bay-colored body and black mane, tail, and points — compare CHESTNUT 3 **2 :** a reddish brown
³**bay** n [MF *baie* berry, fr. L *baca*] **1 a : LAUREL 1 b :** any of several shrubs or trees resembling the laurel **2 :** a wreath esp. of laurel given as a prize for victory or excellence — usu. used in pl. ⟨a poet's garland of *bays*⟩
⁴**bay** n [MF *baee* opening, fr. *baer* to gape] **1 :** a section of a building set off from other parts (as by pillars or beams) **2 :** a compartment in a barn for storing fodder (as hay) **3 : BAY WINDOW 4 a :** the forward part of a ship on each side between decks often used as a ship's hospital **b :** any of several compartments in the fuselage of an airplane **5 :** a vertical support for electronic equipment
⁵**bay** vb [OF *abaiier*] **1 :** to bark with long deep tones **2 a :** to bark at ⟨wolves *baying* the moon⟩ **b :** to utter with bays ⟨*bay* a welcome⟩ **3 :** to bring to bay
⁶**bay** n **1 :** the position of one unable to retreat and forced to face danger ⟨the stag at *bay* turned on his pursuers⟩ **2 :** the position of one checked ⟨kept the hounds at *bay*⟩ **3 :** the baying of a dog **:** a deep bark
⁷**bay** n [MF *baie*] **:** an inlet or indentation of a body of water (as the sea) syn see GULF
bay·ber·ry \'bā-,ber-ē\ n **1 :** a West Indian tree of the myrtle family yielding a yellow aromatic oil **2 : WAX MYRTLE**; *also* **:** its fruit used esp. in making candles
bay leaf n **:** the dried leaf of the European laurel used in cooking
¹**bay·o·net** \'bā-ə-nət, ,bā-ə-'net\ n [F *baïonette*, fr. *Bayonne*, France] **:** a steel blade made to be attached at the muzzle end of a shoulder arm and used in hand-to-hand combat
²**bayonet** vb **-net·ed** also **-net·ted; -net·ing** also **-net·ting 1 :** to stab with a bayonet **2 :** to compel or drive by or as if by the bayonet
bay·ou \'bī-ō, 'bī-ü\ n [LaF, fr. Choctaw *bayuk*] **:** a usu. marshy or sluggish body of water (as a stream on a delta or an offshoot of a river)
bay rum n **:** a fragrant cosmetic and medicinal liquid prepared from essential oils, alcohol, and water
bay window n **:** a window or a set of windows in a compartment that projects outward from the wall of a building
ba·zaar \bə-'zär\ n [Per *bāzār*] **1 :** an Oriental market consisting of rows of shops or stalls selling miscellaneous goods **2 a :** a place for the sale of goods **b : DEPARTMENT STORE 3 :** a fair for the sale of articles esp. for charitable purposes
ba·zoo·ka \bə-'zü-kə\ n **:** a light portable shoulder weapon that consists of a tube open at both ends and shoots an explosive rocket able to pierce armor
BB \'bē-,bē\ n **1 :** a round shot pellet 0.18 inch in diameter for use in a shotgun cartridge **2 :** a round shot pellet 0.175 inch in diameter for use in a gun that propels the shot by compressed air produced by a plunger operated by a spring
B complex n **: VITAMIN B COMPLEX**
be \(')bē\ vb, past 1st & 3d sing **was** \(')wəz, 'wäz\; 2d sing **were** \(')wər\; pl **were**; past subjunctive **were**; past part **been** \(')bin, chiefly Brit (')bēn\; pres part **be·ing** \'bē-iŋ\; pres 1st sing **am** \(ə)m, (')am\; 2d sing **are** \ər, (')är\; 3d sing **is** \(')iz, (ə)z\; pl **are**; pres subjunctive **be** [OE *bēon*] **1 a :** to have the same meaning as **:** serve as a sign for ⟨January *is* the first month⟩⟨let *x be* 10⟩ **b :** to have identity with ⟨the first person I met *was* my brother⟩ **c :** to constitute the same class as **d :** to have a specified qualification or characterization ⟨the leaves *are* green⟩ **e :** to belong to the class of ⟨the fish *is* a trout⟩⟨apes *are* mammals⟩ — used regularly in senses 1a through 1e

as the copula of simple predication **2 a** : to have reality : EXIST, LIVE ⟨I think, therefore I *am*⟩ ⟨once there *was* a knight⟩ **b** : to have, keep, or occupy a place, situation, or position ⟨the book *is* on the table⟩ **c** : to remain unmolested, undisturbed, or uninterrupted — used only in infinitive form ⟨let him *be*⟩ **d** : OCCUR : take place ⟨the concert *was* last night⟩ **3** — used with the past participle of transitive verbs as a passive-voice auxiliary ⟨the money *was* found⟩ ⟨the house is *being* built⟩ **4** — used as the auxiliary of the present participle in progressive tenses expressing continuous action ⟨he *is* reading⟩ ⟨I have *been* sleeping⟩ **5** — used with the past participle of some intransitive verbs as an auxiliary forming archaic perfect tenses **6** — used with the infinitive with *to* to express futurity, arrangement in advance, or obligation ⟨I *am* to interview him today⟩ ⟨he *was* to become famous⟩

be- *prefix* [OE *bi-*, *be-*; akin to E *by*] **1** : on : around : over ⟨*be*daub⟩ ⟨*be*smear⟩ **2** : excessively : ostentatiously ⟨*be*jewel⟩ ⟨*be*ribboned⟩ **3** : about : to : upon ⟨*be*stride⟩ ⟨*be*speak⟩ **4** : make : cause to be ⟨*be*little⟩⟨*be*fool⟩ **5** : provide with or cover with esp. excessively ⟨*be*whiskered⟩ ⟨*be*fog⟩

¹beach \'bēch\ *n* : a shore of an ocean, sea, or lake or the bank of a river covered by sand, gravel, or larger rock fragments : STRAND

²beach *vt* : to run or drive ashore ⟨*beach* a boat⟩

beach·comb·er \'bēch-,kō-mər\ *n* **1** : a drifter, loafer, or casual worker along the seacoast **2** : one who searches along a shore for useful or salable flotsam and refuse

beach flea *n* : any of numerous small leaping crustaceans common on sea beaches

beach·head \'bēch-,hed\ *n* **1** : an area on an enemy-held shore occupied by an advance attacking force to protect the later landing of troops or supplies **2** : FOOTHOLD

beach plum *n* : a shrubby plum with showy white flowers that grows along the Atlantic shores of the northern U.S. and Canada; *also* : its dark purple fruit often used in preserves

beach wagon *n* : STATION WAGON

¹bea·con \'bē-kən\ *n* [OE *bēacen* sign] **1** : a signal fire commonly on a hill, tower, or pole **2 a** : a signal (as a lighthouse) for guidance **b** : a radio transmitter emitting signals for guidance of airplanes

²beacon *vb* **1** : to furnish or light up with a beacon **2** : to shine as a beacon

¹bead \'bēd\ *n* [ME *bede* prayer, prayer bead, fr. OE *bed* prayer; akin to E *bid*] **1** *pl* : a series of prayers and meditations made with a rosary **2** : a small piece of material pierced for threading on a string or wire **3** : a small ball-shaped body: as **a** : a bubble formed in or on a beverage **b** : a small metal knob on a firearm used as a front sight **4** : a projecting rim, band, or molding

²bead *vb* **1** : to adorn or cover with beads or beading **2** : to string together like beads **3** : to form into a bead

bead·ing *n* **1** : material or a part or a piece consisting of a bead **2** : a beaded molding **3** : an openwork trimming **4** : BEADWORK

bea·dle \'bēd-ᵊl\ *n* [OE *bydel*] : a minor parish official whose duties include ushering and keeping order in church and sometimes at civic functions

bead·roll \'bēd-,rōl\ *n* [so called fr. the reading in church of a list of names of persons for whom prayers are to be said] **1** : a list of names : CATALOG **2** : ROSARY

beads·man \'bēdz-mən\ *n*, *archaic* : one who prays for another

bead·work \'bēd-,wərk\ *n* **1** : ornamental work in beads **2** : joinery beading

beady \'bēd-ē\ *adj* **bead·i·er; -est 1** : resembling beads; *esp* : small, round, and shiny with interest or greed ⟨*beady* eyes⟩ **2** : marked by beads

bea·gle \'bē-gəl\ *n* : a small short-legged smooth-coated hound

beak \'bēk\ *n* [OF *bec*] **1 a** : the bill of a bird; *esp* : the bill of a bird of prey adapted for striking and tearing **b** : any of various rigid projecting mouth structures (as of a turtle); *also* : the long sucking mouth of some insects **c** : the human nose **2** : a pointed structure or formation: **a** : a pointed beam projecting from the bow of an ancient galley for piercing an enemy ship **b** : the spout of a vessel — **beaked** \'bēkt\ *adj*

syn BEAK, BILL mean the horny bipartite projection that

serves a bird for jaws. In popular usage BEAK is applied esp. to the strong triangular pointed or hooked shape associated with striking, tearing, or crushing ⟨an eagle's *beak*⟩ BILL may apply to the mouths of all birds ⟨a duck's *bill*⟩

bea·ker \'bē-kər\ *n* [ON *bikarr*] **1** : a large widemouthed drinking cup **2** : a deep thin vessel having a wide mouth and often a projecting lip that is used esp. by chemists and pharmacists

¹beam \'bēm\ *n* [OE *bēam* tree, beam] **1 a** : a long heavy piece of timber used esp. as a main horizontal support of a building or a ship **b** : a wood or metal cylinder in a loom on which the warp is wound **2** : the bar of a balance from which the scales hang **3** : the width of a ship at its widest part **4 a** : a ray or shaft of light **b** : a collection of nearly parallel rays (as X rays) or particles (as electrons) **5** : a constant directional radio signal sent out for the guidance of pilots along a particular course; *also* : the course indicated by this signal — **on the beam 1** : on a true course **2** : operating well

²beam *vb* **1** : to emit in beams or as a beam **2 a** : to aim (a broadcast) by directional antennas **b** : to direct to a particular audience **3** : to send out beams of light **4** : to smile with joy

bean \'bēn\ *n* [OE *bēan*] **1 a** : BROAD BEAN **b** : the seed or pod of any of various erect or climbing leguminous plants **c** : a plant bearing beans **2 a** : a valueless item **b** *pl* : a small amount **3** : a seed or fruit like a bean ⟨coffee *beans*⟩ **4** : HEAD, BRAIN

bean·ie \'bē-nē\ *n* : a small round tight-fitting skullcap worn esp. by schoolboys and collegians

¹bear \'ba(ə)r, 'be(ə)r\ *n*, *pl* **bear** *or* **bears** [OE *bera*] **1** : any of a family (order Carnivora) of large heavy mammals having long shaggy hair and rudimentary tail, walking on the soles of its feet, and feeding largely on fruit and insects as well as on flesh **2** : a surly, uncouth, or shambling person **3** : one that sells securities or commodities in expectation of a price decline — compare BULL

²bear *vb* **bore** \'bō(ə)r, 'bȯ(ə)r\; **borne** \'bōrn, 'bȯrn\ *also* **born** \'bȯrn\; **bear·ing** [OE *beran*] **1 a** : to move while holding up : CARRY ⟨arrived *bearing* gifts⟩ **b** : to be furnished with ⟨entitled to *bear* arms⟩ **c** : to have as a feature or characteristic ⟨*bears* a good reputation⟩ : POSSESS ⟨*bears* a resemblance to his uncle⟩ **d** : to hold in the mind : HARBOR ⟨has *borne* a grudge for years⟩ **e** : DISSEMINATE ⟨constantly *bearing* tales⟩ **f** : to bring forward in testifying ⟨*bears* false witness⟩ **g** : BEHAVE, CONDUCT ⟨*bore* himself like a gentleman⟩ **2 a** : to give birth to ⟨has *borne* many children⟩ ⟨a son *born* to her⟩ ⟨he was *born* last year⟩ **b** : PRODUCE, YIELD **3 a** : to support the weight of : hold up ⟨a colonnade *bore* the roof⟩ **b** : to support a burden or strain ⟨*bears* up well in his grief⟩ **c** : ENDURE **d** : ASSUME, ACCEPT ⟨*bore* all the costs⟩ ⟨had to *bear* the blame⟩ **e** : to admit of : ALLOW ⟨can hardly *bear* scrutiny⟩ **4** : THRUST, PRESS ⟨*borne* along by the crowd⟩ ⟨*bears* down on her pencil⟩ **5 a** : to move, extend, or incline in an indicated direction ⟨five ships *bearing* off the cape⟩ ⟨*bear* right at the next fork⟩ **b** : to become directed ⟨brought the guns to *bear* on the target⟩ **6 a** : APPLY, PERTAIN ⟨facts *bearing* on the question⟩ **b** : to exert influence or force ⟨brings pressure to *bear* to win votes⟩

bear·a·ble \'bar-ə-bəl, 'ber-\ *adj* : capable of being borne : TOLERABLE

bear·ber·ry \'ba(ə)r-,ber-ē, 'be(ə)r-\ *n* : a trailing evergreen plant of the heath family with glossy red berries; *also* : any of several related plants (as a cranberry)

¹beard \'bi(ə)rd\ *n* [OE] **1** : the hair that grows on a man's face often excluding the moustache **2** : a hairy or bristly growth or tuft (as on the chin of a goat or on a head of rye) — **beard·ed** \-əd\ *adj* — **beard·less** \-ləs\ *adj*

²beard *vt* : to confront and oppose daringly : DEFY

bear·er \'bar-ər, 'ber-\ *n* : one that bears: as **a** : PORTER **b** : a plant yielding fruit **c** : a person holding a check, draft, or order for payment

bear·ing \'ba(ə)r-iŋ, 'be(ə)r-\ *n* **1** : the manner in which one bears or comports oneself : CARRIAGE, BEHAVIOR **2 a** : the act, power, or time of bringing forth offspring or fruit **b** : a product of bearing : CROP **3 a** : PRESSURE, THRUST **b** : ENDURANCE **4 a** : an object, surface, or point that supports something **b** : a machine part in which one part (as a journal or pin) turns **5** : a charge in a coat of arms ⟨armorial *bearings*⟩ **6 a** : the position or direction of one point with respect to another or to the compass **b** : a determination of position ⟨to take a *bearing*⟩ **c** *pl* : comprehension of one's position, environment, or situation ⟨lose one's *bearings*⟩ **d** : RELATION, CONNECTION; *also* : PURPORT

bear·ish \-ish\ *adj* **1** : resembling a bear in roughness, gruffness, or surliness **2** : marked by, tending to, or expecting a decline in stock prices — **bear·ish·ly** *adv* — **bear·ish·ness** *n*

bear·skin \'ba(ə)r-ˌskin, 'be(ə)r-\ *n* : an article made of the skin of a bear; *esp* : a military hat made of the skin of a bear

beast \'bēst\ *n* [L *bestia*] **1 a** : ANIMAL 1; *esp* : a lower mammal as distinguished on the one hand from man and on the other from lower vertebrate and invertebrate animals **b** : a domesticated mammal ⟨the care of a farmer for his *beasts*⟩; *esp* : a draft animal **2** : a contemptible person

¹**beast·ly** \'bēst-lē\ *adj* **beast·li·er; -est 1** : of, relating to, or resembling a beast **2** : relating to or characteristic of man's animal nature : BESTIAL **3** : ABOMINABLE, DISGUSTING — **beast·li·ness** *n*

²**beastly** *adv* : VERY ⟨a *beastly* cold day⟩

¹**beat** \'bēt\ *vb* **beat; beat·en** \'bēt-ᵊn\ *or* **beat; beat·ing** [OE *bēatan*] **1** : to strike repeatedly : **a** : to hit repeatedly so as to inflict pain **b** : to dash against ⟨rain *beating* on the roof⟩ **c** : to thrash at vigorously : FLAP **d** : to range over in or as if in quest of game **e** : to mix by stirring : WHIP **f** : to strike repeatedly to produce music or a signal ⟨*beat* a drum⟩ **2 a** : to drive or force by blows ⟨*beat* off the intruder⟩ **b** : to make by repeated treading or driving over ⟨a *beaten* path⟩ **c** : to shape by repeated blows ⟨*beat* swords into plowshares⟩; *esp* : to flatten thin by blows **d** : to sound or express by drumbeat or sound **3** : to cause to strike or flap repeatedly **4 a** : OVERCOME, DEFEAT; *also* : SURPASS **b** : to prevail despite ⟨*beat* the odds⟩ **c** : BEWILDER, BAFFLE **d** : EXHAUST, DISPIRIT **e** : CHEAT **5 a** (1) : to act ahead of usu. so as to forestall (2) : to report a news item in advance of **b** : to come or arrive before **c** : CIRCUMVENT ⟨*beat* the system⟩ **6** : to indicate by beats ⟨*beat* the tempo⟩ **7 a** : DASH **b** : to glare or strike with oppressive intensity **8 a** : PULSATE **b** : TICK **c** : to sound upon being struck **9** : to progress with much tacking or with difficulty

²**beat** *n* **1 a** : a single stroke or blow esp. in a series; *also* : PULSATION, TICK **b** : a sound produced by or as if by beating ⟨the *beat* of waves against the rock⟩ **c** : a driving impact or force : each of the pulsations of amplitude produced by the union of sound or radio waves or electric currents having different frequencies **3 a** : a metrical or rhythmic stress in poetry or music or the rhythmic effect of these stresses **b** : the tempo indicated to a musical performer **4** : a regularly traversed round ⟨a policeman's *beat*⟩ **5 a** : something that excels **b** : the reporting of a news story ahead of competitors **6** : DEADBEAT

³**beat** *adj* **1** : EXHAUSTED **2** : sapped of resolution or morale **3** : of or relating to beatniks

beat·er \'bēt-ər\ *n* **1** : one that beats **2** : one that beats up game in hunting

be·a·tif·ic \ˌbē-ə-'tif-ik\ *adj* : giving or expressing great joy or blessedness : BLISSFUL ⟨a *beatific* experience⟩ ⟨his *beatific* countenance⟩ — **be·a·tif·i·cal·ly** \-'tif-i-k(ə-)lē\ *adv*

beatific vision *n* : the direct knowledge of God enjoyed by the blessed in heaven

be·at·i·fy \bē-'at-ə-ˌfī\ *vt* **-fied; -fy·ing** [LL *beatificare*, fr. L *beatus* blessed, happy] **1** : to make supremely happy **2** : to declare to have attained the blessedness of heaven and authorize the title "Blessed" and limited public religious honor for — **be·at·i·fi·ca·tion** \-ˌat-ə-fə-'kā-shən\ *n*

be·at·i·tude \bē-'at-ə-ˌt(y)üd\ *n* **1** : supreme bliss **2** : a declaration made in the Sermon on the Mount (Matthew 5:3–12) beginning "Blessed are"

beat·nik \'bēt-nik\ *n* [³*beat*] : a person who behaves and dresses unconventionally and is inclined to exotic philosophizing and extreme self-expression

beau \'bō\ *n, pl* **beaux** \'bōz\ *or* **beaus** \'bōz\ [F, fr.

egg-beater

beau beautiful, fr. L *bellus* pretty] **1** : a man who dresses very carefully in the latest fashion : DANDY **2 a** : a man who is courting : LOVER, ADMIRER **b** : ESCORT

Beau Brum·mell \ˌbō-'brəm-əl\ *n* [nickname of G. B. *Brummell* d1840 English dandy] : DANDY

Beau·fort scale \ˌbō-fərt-\ *n* : a scale in which the force of the wind is indicated by numbers from 0 to 17

beau geste \bō-'zhest\ *n, pl* **beaux gestes** *or* **beau gestes** \bō-'zhest\ [F, beautiful gesture] **1** : a graceful or magnanimous gesture **2** : an insubstantial conciliatory gesture

beau ide·al \ˌbō-ˌī-'dē-(-ə)l\ *n, pl* **beau ideals** [F *beau idéal* ideal beauty] : the perfect type or model

beau monde \bō-'mänd\ *n, pl* **beau mondes** *or* **beaux mondes** \bō-'män(d)z\ [F, lit., fine world] : the world of high society and fashion

beau·te·ous \'byüt-ē-əs\ *adj* : BEAUTIFUL — **beau·te·ous·ly** *adv* — **beau·te·ous·ness** *n*

beau·ti·cian \byü-'tish-ən\ *n* : COSMETOLOGIST

beau·ti·ful \'byüt-i-fəl\ *adj* : having qualities of beauty : exciting aesthetic pleasure — **beau·ti·ful·ly** \-f(ə-)lē\ *adv* — **beau·ti·ful·ness** \-fəl-nəs\ *n*

syn LOVELY, FAIR : BEAUTIFUL applies to whatever excites the keenest pleasure in the mind and senses and stirs emotion by its suggestion of perfection or the ideal ⟨a *beautiful* scene⟩ ⟨a *beautiful* thought⟩ LOVELY is close to BEAUTIFUL but applies to a narrower range of emotional excitation in suggesting the graceful, delicate, or exquisite ⟨a *lovely* melody⟩ FAIR suggests beauty because of purity, flawlessness, or freshness ⟨*fair* skies⟩ ⟨a *fair* face⟩

beau·ti·fy \'byüt-ə-ˌfī\ *vt* **-fied; -fy·ing** : to make beautiful or add beauty to : EMBELLISH — **beau·ti·fi·ca·tion** \ˌbyüt-ə-fə-'kā-shən\ *n* — **beau·ti·fi·er** \'byüt-ə-ˌfī-(-ə)r\ *n*

beau·ty \'byüt-ē\ *n, pl* **beauties** [OF *biauté*, fr. *biau* beautiful, fr. L *bellus* pretty] **1** : the qualities of a person or a thing that give pleasure to the senses : LOVELINESS **2** : a lovely person or thing; *esp* : a lovely woman

beauty shop *n* : an establishment or department where hairdressing, facials, and manicures are done — called also *beauty parlor*

beaux arts \bō-'zär\ *n pl* [F] : FINE ARTS

¹**bea·ver** \'bē-vər\ *n, pl* **beaver** *or* **beavers** [OE *beofor*] **1** : a large fur-bearing mammal with webbed hind feet and a broad flat tail that builds dams and underwater houses of mud and branches; *also* : its fur **2** : a hat made of beaver fur or of a fabric imitating it

²**beaver** *n* [MF *baviere*] **1** : a piece of armor protecting the lower part of the face **2** : a helmet visor

be·calm \bi-'käm, -'kälm\ *vt* **1** : to bring to a stop or keep motionless by lack of wind **2** : to make calm : SOOTHE

be·cause \bi-'kòz\ *conj* : for the reason that

syn FOR, SINCE : BECAUSE assigns a reason immediately and definitely ⟨I hid myself *because* I was afraid⟩ FOR is less immediate and regards the statement to which it is added as relatively independent ⟨I hid myself *for* [I may add as explanation] I was afraid⟩ SINCE is less formal, more casual than BECAUSE, and may suggest concurrence rather than direct cause ⟨*since* I was afraid, I hid myself⟩

because of *prep* : by reason of

be·chance \bi-'chan(t)s\ *vb, archaic* : BEFALL

bêche–de–mer \ˌbäsh-də-'me(ə)r\ *n, pl* **bêche–de–mer** *or* **bêches–de–mer** \ˌbäsh-(əz-)də-\ [F] : TREPANG

beck \'bek\ *n* **1** : a beckoning gesture **2** : BIDDING, SUMMONS

beck·et \'bek-ət\ *n* : a device for holding something in place; *esp* : a loop of rope with a knot at one end

beck·on \'bek-ən\ *vb* **beck·oned; beck·on·ing** \'bek-(ə-)niŋ\ [OE *bīecnan*, fr. *bēacen* sign] **1** : to summon or signal to a person by gesture (as a wave or nod) **2** : to appear inviting : ATTRACT

be·cloud \bi-'klaùd\ *vt* : to obscure with or as if with a cloud

be·come \bi-'kəm\ *vb* **-came** \-'kām\; **-come; -com·ing 1** : to come or grow to be ⟨a tadpole *becomes* a frog⟩ ⟨the days *become* shorter as summer ends⟩ **2** : to suit or be suitable ⟨her dress *becomes* her⟩ — **become of** : to happen to : be the state of ⟨whatever *became of* him⟩

be·com·ing \bi-'kəm-iŋ\ *adj* : SUITABLE, FITTING; *esp* : attractively suitable ⟨a *becoming* dress⟩ — **be·com·ing·ly** \-iŋ-lē\ *adv*

¹bed \'bed\ *n* [OE *bedd*] **1 a** : a piece of furniture on or in which one may lie and sleep **b** : a place or time for sleeping **2** : a flat or level surface: as **a** : a plot of ground prepared for plants **b** : the bottom of a body of water **3** : a supporting surface or structure : FOUNDATION **4** : LAYER ⟨a *bed* of sandstone⟩
²bed *vb* **bed·ded; bed·ding 1 a** : to furnish with a bed or bedding **b** : to put or go to bed **2 a** : to fix in a foundation : EMBED ⟨*bedded* on rock⟩ **b** : to plant or arrange in beds **3** : to lay flat or in a layer **4** : to form a layer
be·daub \bi-'dȯb, -'däb\ *vt* : to daub over : SMEAR
be·daz·zle \bi-'daz-əl\ *vt* : to confuse by or as if by a strong light : DAZZLE — **be·daz·zle·ment** \-əl-mənt\ *n*
bed·bug \'bed-,bəg\ *n* : a wingless bloodsucking bug sometimes infesting houses and esp. beds
bed·clothes \'bed-,klō(th)z\ *n pl* : the covering (as sheets and blankets) used on a bed
bed·ding \'bed-iŋ\ *n* **1** : BEDCLOTHES **2** : a bottom layer : FOUNDATION **3** : material to provide a bed for livestock **4** : the arrangement of rock in layers
be·deck \bi-'dek\ *vt* : to deck out : ADORN
be·dev·il \bi-'dev-əl\ *vt* : to drive frantic : confuse utterly : HARASS — **be·dev·il·ment** \-mənt\ *n*
be·dew \bi-'d(y)ü\ *vt* : to wet with or as if with dew
bed·fast \'bed-,fast\ *adj* : BEDRIDDEN
bed·fel·low \'bed-,fel-ō\ *n* : one who shares a bed with another
be·dight \bi-'dīt\ *adj* [ME *dighten* to adorn, fr. OE *dihtan* to arrange, compose, fr. L *dictare* to dictate, compose] *archaic* : ADORNED, DECORATED
be·dim \bi-'dim\ *vt* : to make dim or obscure
Bed·i·vere \'bed-ə-,vi(ə)r\ *n* : a knight of the Round Table present at the departure of the dying Arthur for Avalon
be·di·zen \bi-'dīz-ⁿn, -'diz-\ *vt* : to dress or adorn in a showy way esp. with gaudy finery — **be·di·zen·ment** \-mənt\ *n*
bed·lam \'bed-ləm\ *n* [*Bedlam*, popular name for the Hospital of St. Mary of Bethlehem, London, an insane asylum, fr. ME *Bedlem* Bethlehem] **1** *archaic* : a lunatic asylum **2** : a place or scene of uproar and confusion
bed·lam·ite \'bed-lə-,mīt\ *n* : MADMAN, LUNATIC
Bed·ling·ton terrier \,bed-liŋ-tən-\ *n* : a swift rough≠coated terrier of light build
bed·ou·in \'bed-ə-wən\ *n, pl* **bedouin** *or* **bedouins** *often cap* [F *bédouin*, fr. Ar *bidwān*, pl. of *badawi* desert dweller] : a nomadic Arab of the Arabian, Syrian, or No. African deserts
bed·pan \'bed-,pan\ *n* : a shallow pan for use as a toilet by a person confined to bed
be·drag·gle \bi-'drag-əl\ *vt* : to wet and usu. soil thoroughly (as by rain or mud)
bed·rid·den \'bed-,rid-ⁿn\ *adj* [OE *bedreda* one confined to bed, lit., bed rider] : confined to bed by illness or weakness
bed·rock \'bed-'räk, -,räk\ *n* **1** : the solid rock underlying surface materials (as soil) **2** : a solid foundation
bed·roll \'bed-,rōl\ *n* : bedding rolled up for carrying
bed·room \-,rüm, -,rùm\ *n* : a room furnished with a bed and used for sleeping
bed·side \'bed-,sīd\ *n* : the side of a bed or the place beside a bed esp. of a sick or dying person
bed·sore \-,sōr, -,sȯr\ *n* : a sore caused by constant pressure against a bed (as in a prolonged illness)
bed·spread \-,spred\ *n* : a usu. decorative cloth cover for a bed
bed·spring \-,spriŋ\ *n* : a spring supporting a mattress
bed·stead \-,sted\ *n* : the framework of a bed usu. including head, foot, and side rails
bed·straw \-,strȯ\ *n* [so called fr. its former use for mattresses] : an herb of the madder family with angled stems, opposite or whorled leaves, and small flowers
bed·time \'bed-,tīm\ *n* : time to go to bed
bee \'bē\ *n* [OE *bēo*] **1** : a social colonial 4-winged insect often kept in hives for the honey that it produces; *also* : any of numerous related insects that differ from the wasps esp. in the heavier hairier body and in having sucking as well as chewing mouthparts **2** : an eccentric notion : FANCY **3** : a gathering of people for a specific purpose ⟨quilting *bee*⟩

bee balm *n* : any of several mints (as monarda) attractive to bees
bee·bread \'bē-,bred\ *n* : a bitter yellowish brown pollen mixture stored in honeycomb cells and used with honey by bees as food
beech \'bēch\ *n, pl* **beech·es** *or* **beech** [OE *bēce*] : any of a genus of hardwood trees with smooth gray bark and small edible nuts; *also* : its wood — **beech·en** \'bē-chən\ *adj* — **beech·wood** \'bēch-,wùd\ *n*
beef \'bēf\ *n, pl* **beeves** \'bēvz\ *or* **beefs** [OF *buef*, fr. L *bov-, bos* head of cattle; akin to E *cow*] **1** : the flesh of a steer, cow, or bull; *also* : the dressed carcass of a beef animal **2** : a steer, cow, or bull esp. when fattened for food **3** : muscular flesh : BRAWN
beef cattle *n pl* : cattle developed primarily for the efficient production of meat and marked by capacity for rapid growth, heavy well-fleshed body, and stocky build
beef·eat·er \'bēf-,ēt-ər\ *n* : a yeoman of the guard of an English monarch
beef·steak \'bēf-,stāk\ *n* : a slice of beef suitable for broiling or frying
beef up *vt* : to add strength or power to ⟨*beef up* the army with new men and equipment⟩
beefy \'bē-fē\ *adj* **beef·i·er; -est** : BRAWNY, THICKSET
¹bee·hive \'bē-,hīv\ *n* **1** : a hive for bees **2** : something resembling a hive for bees; *esp* : a scene of crowded activity
²beehive *adj* : resembling a dome-shaped or conical beehive
bee·keep·er \-,kē-pər\ *n* : one that raises bees — **bee·keep·ing** *n*
bee·line \'bē-,līn\ *n* [so called fr. the belief that nectar≠laden bees return to their hives in a direct line] : a straight direct course
Beel·ze·bub \bē-'el-zi-,bəb, 'bēl-zi-, 'bel-\ *n* [Gk *Beelzeboub*, fr. Heb *Ba'al zĕbhūbh*, a Philistine god, lit., lord of flies] : DEVIL
been *past part of* BE
beer \'bi(ə)r\ *n* [OE *bēor*] **1** : an alcoholic drink made from malt and flavored with hops **2** : a nonalcoholic drink made from roots or other parts of plants ⟨ginger *beer*⟩
beery \'bi(ə)r-ē\ *adj* **1** : affected or caused by beer **2** : smelling or tasting of beer
bees·wax \'bēz-,waks\ *n* : WAX 1
beet \'bēt\ *n* [OE *bēte*, fr. L *beta*] : a biennial garden plant of the goosefoot family with thick long-stalked edible leaves and a swollen root used as a vegetable, as a source of sugar, or for forage; *also* : this root
¹bee·tle \'bēt-ⁿl\ *n* [OE *bitula*, fr. *bītan* to bite] **1** : any of an order (Coleoptera) of insects having four wings of which the outer pair are modified into stiff cases that protect the inner pair when at rest **2** : any of various insects resembling a beetle
²beetle *n* [OE *bīetel*; akin to E *¹beat*] : a heavy tool usu. with a wooden head used for hammering
³beetle *adj* [ME *bitel-browed* having overhanging brows] : being prominent and overhanging ⟨*beetle* brows⟩
⁴beetle *vi* **bee·tled; bee·tling** \'bēt-liŋ, -ⁿl-iŋ\ : PROJECT, JUT
be·fall \bi-'fȯl\ *vb* **-fell** \-'fel\; **-fall·en** \-'fȯ-lən\; **-fall·ing 1** : to come to pass : HAPPEN **2** : to happen to
be·fit \bi-'fit\ *vt* : to be suitable to or proper for ⟨clothes *befitting* the occasion⟩
be·fog \bi-'fȯg, -'fäg\ *vt* **1** : to make foggy : OBSCURE **2** : CONFUSE
be·fool \bi-'fül\ *vt* : DECEIVE
¹be·fore \bi-'fō(ə)r, -'fȯ(ə)r\ *adv* [OE *beforan*, fr. *be-* + *foran* before] **1** : in advance : AHEAD ⟨go on *before*⟩ **2** : EARLIER, PREVIOUSLY ⟨has been here *before*⟩ ⟨tomorrow and not *before*⟩
²before *prep* **1 a (1)** : in front of ⟨*before* one's eyes⟩ **(2)** : in the presence of ⟨stood *before* the judge⟩ **b** : under the consideration of ⟨the case *before* the court⟩ **c** : in store for ⟨many years of life still *before* him⟩ **2** : earlier than : previously to ⟨come *before* six o'clock⟩ **3** : in a higher or more important position than ⟨put quantity *before* quality⟩
³before *conj* **1** : earlier than the time when ⟨think *before* you speak⟩ **2** : more willingly than ⟨he will starve *before* he will steal⟩

be·fore·hand \-,hand\ *adv* : in advance : ahead of time ⟨think out *beforehand* what you are going to say⟩
be·foul \bi-'faul\ *vt* : to make dirty : SOIL
be·friend \bi-'frend\ *vt* : to act as a friend to
be·fud·dle \bi-'fəd-°l\ *vt* 1 : to muddle the senses of : STUPEFY 2 : CONFUSE, PERPLEX — **be·fud·dle·ment** \-°l-mənt\ *n*
beg \'beg\ *vb* **begged; beg·ging** [ME *beggen*] 1 : to ask for money, food, or help as a charity ⟨*beg* in the streets⟩ 2 : to ask earnestly or politely ⟨*beg* a favor⟩ ⟨*beg* to be taken to the circus⟩
syn BEG, BESEECH, IMPLORE mean to ask urgently: BEG suggests earnestness or insistence esp. in asking for a favor; BESEECH implies great eagerness or anxiety; IMPLORE adds a suggestion of greater urgency or anguished appeal
— **beg the question** : to assume as true or take for granted the thing that is the subject of the argument
be·gat \bi-'gat\ *archaic past of* BEGET
be·get \bi-'get\ *vt* **-got** \-'gät\; **-got·ten** \-'gät-°n\ *or* **-got; -get·ting** 1 : to become the father of : SIRE 2 : CAUSE — **be·get·ter** *n*
¹beg·gar \'beg-ər\ *n* 1 : one that begs; *esp* : one that lives by asking for gifts 2 : PAUPER 3 : FELLOW
²beggar *vt* 1 : to reduce to beggary 2 : to exceed the resources or capacity of ⟨*beggars* description⟩
beg·gar·ly \'beg-ər-lē\ *adj* 1 : befitting or resembling a beggar; *esp* : marked by extreme poverty 2 : MEAN — **beg·gar·li·ness** *n*
beg·gar's-lice \'beg-ərz-,līs\ *or* **beg·gar-lice** \-ər-,līs\ *n sing or pl* : any of several plants with prickly or adhesive fruits; *also* : one of these fruits
beg·gar–ticks *or* **beg·gar's–ticks** \-,tiks\ *n sing or pl* 1 : BUR MARIGOLD; *also* : its prickly fruits 2 : BEGGAR'S‑LICE
beg·gary \'beg-ə-rē\ *n* : extreme poverty or want
be·gin \bi-'gin\ *vb* **be·gan** \-'gan\; **be·gun** \-'gən\; **be·gin·ning** [OE *beginnan*] 1 a : to do the first part of an action **b** : to undertake or undergo initial steps : COMMENCE 2 a : to come into existence : ARISE **b** : to have a starting point ⟨the road *begins* there⟩ 3 : to do or succeed in the least degree ⟨does not *begin* to fill our needs⟩ 4 : FOUND, ORIGINATE, INVENT ⟨*begin* a dynasty⟩ 5 : to come first in ⟨the letter *A begins* the alphabet⟩
be·gin·ner \bi-'gin-ər\ *n* : one that is beginning something or doing something for the first time : an inexperienced person
be·gin·ning \bi-'gin-iŋ\ *n* 1 : the point at which something begins 2 : the first part 3 : ORIGIN, SOURCE 4 a : a first stage or early period **b** : something undeveloped or incomplete
be·gone \bi-'gón, -'gän\ *vi* : to go away : DEPART — used esp. in the imperative
be·go·nia \bi-'gō-nyə\ *n* [NL, after Michel *Bégon d*1710 French governor of Santo Domingo] : any of a large genus of tropical herbs often grown for their shining leaves and bright waxy flowers
be·grime \bi-'grīm\ *vt* : to make dirty with grime
be·grudge \bi-'grəj\ *vt* 1 : to give, do, or concede reluctantly ⟨*begrudge* a person a favor⟩ 2 : to grumble at or be annoyed by 3 : to envy a person's possession or enjoyment of — **be·grudg·ing·ly** \-iŋ-lē\ *adv*
be·guile \bi-'gīl\ *vt* 1 : to deceive by means of flattery or by a trick or lie 2 : to draw notice or interest by wiles or charm ⟨a *beguiling* manner⟩ 3 : to cause time to pass pleasantly : while away ⟨*beguile* the hour by telling stories⟩ — **be·guile·ment** \-mənt\ *n* — **be·guil·er** *n*
be·guine \bi-'gēn\ *n* : a vigorous popular dance of the islands of Saint Lucia and Martinique
be·gum \'bē-gəm\ *n* [Hindi *begam*] : a Muslim woman of high rank
be·half \bi-'haf, -'hàf\ *n* [ME, fr. *by* + *half* half, side] : INTEREST, BENEFIT; *also* : SUPPORT, DEFENSE — used esp. in the phrase *in behalf of* or *on behalf of*
be·have \bi-'hāv\ *vb* 1 : to bear or comport oneself in a particular way 2 : to conduct oneself in a proper manner 3 : to act, function, or react in a particular way : exhibit reaction (as to an environment)
be·hav·ior \bi-'hā-vyər\ *n* 1 : the manner in which a person conducts himself 2 : the way in which something (as an organism, machine, or substance) behaves — **be·hav·ior·al** \-vyə-rəl\ *adj* — **be·hav·ior·al·ly** \-rə-lē\ *adv*

be·head \bi-'hed\ *vt* : to cut off the head of
be·he·moth \bi-'hē-məth, 'bē-ə-,möth\ *n* [Heb *běhēmōth*] 1 *often cap* : an animal described in Job 40:15–24 that is prob. the hippopotamus 2 : something of oppressive or monstrous size or power
be·hest \bi-'hest\ *n* [OE *behæs* promise] : COMMAND, ORDER
¹be·hind \bi-'hīnd\ *adv* 1 a : in a place, situation, or time that is being or has been departed from ⟨stay *behind*⟩ ⟨leaving his years of poverty *behind*⟩ **b** : at, to, or toward the back ⟨look *behind*⟩ 2 a : in a secondary or inferior position ⟨lag *behind* in competition⟩ **b** : in a state of failing to keep up to schedule ⟨*behind* in his payments⟩
²behind *prep* 1 a : in a place, situation, or time left by ⟨the staff stayed *behind* the troops⟩ **b** : at, to, or toward the back of ⟨look *behind* you⟩ ⟨a garden *behind* the house⟩ 2 : inferior to ⟨sales *behind* those of last year⟩ 3 : retarded in relation to ⟨*behind* his class in school⟩ 4 a : MOTIVATING ⟨the conditions *behind* the strike⟩ **b** : SUPPORTING ⟨an argument with experience *behind* it⟩
³behind *n* : BUTTOCKS
be·hind·hand \bi-'hīnd-,hand\ *adv (or adj)* : not keeping up : LATE, BACKWARD, BEHIND ⟨*behindhand* with the rent⟩
be·hold \bi-'hōld\ *vb* 1 : SEE 2 : to gaze upon : OBSERVE 3 — used in the imperative esp. to call attention — **be·hold·er** *n*
be·hold·en \bi-'hōl-dən\ *adj* : being under obligation for a favor or gift : INDEBTED
be·hoof \bi-'hüf\ *n* [OE *behōf*] : PROFIT, ADVANTAGE, BENEFIT
be·hoove \bi-'hüv\ *or* **be·hove** \-'hōv\ *vt* : to be necessary for as a matter of duty or obligation : be fitting or proper for ⟨an example which it would *behoove* any ambitious boy to follow⟩ ⟨it *behooves* a soldier to obey orders⟩
beige \'bāzh\ *n* [F] 1 : cloth made of natural undyed wool 2 a : a variable color averaging light grayish yellowish brown **b** : a pale to grayish yellow — **beige** *adj*
be·ing \'bē-iŋ\ *n* 1 a : EXISTENCE **b** : LIFE 2 : the totality of existing things 3 : a living thing; *esp* : PERSON
bel \'bel\ *n* [Alexander Graham *Bell d*1922 Scottish-American inventor of the telephone] : ten decibels
be·la·bor \bi-'lā-bər\ *vt* 1 : to work on or at to absurd lengths ⟨*belabor* the obvious⟩ 2 : ASSAIL, ATTACK
be·lat·ed \bi-'lāt-əd\ *adj* [pp. of *belate* to make late] 1 : delayed beyond the usual time 2 : existing or appearing past the normal time — **be·lat·ed·ly** *adv* — **be·lat·ed·ness** *n*
be·lay \bi-'lā\ *vb* [OE *belecgan* to beset, fr. *be-* + *lecgan* to lay] 1 a : to secure (as a rope) by turns around a cleat or pin **b** : to make fast 2 : STOP
belch \'belch\ *vb* [OE *bealcian*] 1 : to expel gas suddenly from the stomach through the mouth 2 : to eject, emit, or issue forth violently — **belch** *n*
bel·dam *or* **bel·dame** \'bel-dəm\ *n* : an old woman; *esp* : HAG
be·lea·guer \bi-'lē-gər\ *vt* **-guered; -guer·ing** \-g(ə-)riŋ\ [D *belegeren*] 1 : to surround with an army so as to prevent escape : BESIEGE 2 : BESET, HARASS
bel·em·nite \'bel-əm-,nīt\ *n* : a conical fossil shell of an extinct cephalopod — **bel·em·nit·ic** \,bel-əm-'nit-ik\ *adj* — **bel·em·noid** \'bel-əm-,nòid\ *adj or n*
bel·fry \'bel-frē\ *n, pl* **belfries** [MF *berfrei*, of Gmc origin] : a tower or a room in a tower for a bell or set of bells
Bel·gae \'bel-,gī, -,jē\ *n pl* : a people occupying northern France and Belgium in Caesar's time — **Bel·gic** \-jik\ *adj*
Bel·gian \'bel-jən\ *n* 1 : a native or inhabitant of Belgium 2 : any of a Belgian breed of heavy usu. roan or chestnut draft horses — **Belgian** *adj*
Belgian hare *n* : any of a breed of slender dark red domestic rabbits
Belgian sheepdog *n* : any of a breed of hardy black or gray dogs developed in Belgium esp. for herding sheep
Be·li·al \'bē-lē-əl\ *n* : SATAN
be·lie \bi-'lī\ *vt* **-lied; -ly·ing** 1 : MISREPRESENT ⟨words that *belie* one's feelings⟩ 2 : to be false or unfaithful to ⟨*belied* his principles⟩ 3 : to show to be false ⟨the man's actions *belie* his promise⟩ — **be·li·er** *n*
be·lief \bə-'lēf\ *n* [ME *beleave*] 1 : confidence that a person or thing exists or is true or trustworthy : FAITH,

TRUST ⟨a child's *belief* in his parents⟩ ⟨a *belief* in the democratic way of government⟩ **2** : religious faith; *esp* : CREED **3** : the thing that is believed : CONVICTION, OPINION ⟨political *beliefs*⟩

syn BELIEF, FAITH mean the assent to the truth of something offered for acceptance and are often used interchangeably. BELIEF may or may not imply certitude in the believer, whereas FAITH always does and implies trust and confidence even when there is no evidence or proof; FAITH may also suggest credulity **syn** see in addition OPINION

be·lieve \bə-'lēv\ *vb* [OE *belēfan*, fr. *be-* + *lēfan* to allow, believe] **1** : to have a firm religious faith **2** : to have a firm conviction as to the reality or goodness of something **3** : to take as true or honest ⟨*believe* the reports⟩ **4** : to hold as an opinion ⟨*believe* the reports⟩ **4** : to hold as an opinion : THINK, SUPPOSE — **be·liev·a·ble** \-'lē-və-bəl\ *adj* — **be·liev·a·bly** \-və-blē\ *adv* — **be·liev·er** *n*

be·like \bi-'līk\ *adv, archaic* : most likely : PROBABLY

be·lit·tle \bi-'lit-ᵊl\ *vt* **-lit·tled; -lit·tling** \-'lit-liŋ, -'lit-ᵊl-iŋ\ : to make (a person or a thing) seem little or unimportant : speak of in a slighting way ⟨*belittle* the success of a rival⟩ — **be·lit·tle·ment** \-ᵊl-mənt\ *n* — **be·lit·tler** \-'lit-lər, -ᵊl-ər\ *n*

¹bell \'bel\ *n* [OE *belle*] **1** : a hollow usu. cup-shaped metallic device that makes a ringing sound when struck **2** : the stroke or sound of a bell that tells the hour esp. on shipboard **3 a** : the time indicated by the stroke of a bell **b** : a half hour on board ship **4** : something (as a flower or the flaring mouth of a trumpet) shaped like a bell

SHIP'S BELLS

No. of Bells	Hour (A.M. or P.M.)		
1	12:30	4:30	8:30
2	1:00	5:00	9:00
3	1:30	5:30	9:30
4	2:00	6:00	10:00
5	2:30	6:30	10:30
6	3:00	7:00	11:00
7	3:30	7:30	11:30
8	4:00	8:00	12:00

²bell *vb* **1** : to provide with a bell **2** : to take the form of a bell : FLARE

bel·la·don·na \,bel-ə-'dän-ə\ *n* [It, lit., beautiful lady] : a European poisonous herb of the nightshade family with reddish bell-shaped flowers, shining black berries, and root and leaves that yield atropine; *also* : a drug or extract from this plant

bell·bird \'bel-,bərd\ *n* : any of several birds whose notes are likened to the sound of a bell

bell·boy \-,bói\ *n* : a hotel or club employee who escorts guests to rooms, assists them with luggage, and runs errands

belle \'bel\ *n* [F, fr. fem. of *beau* beautiful] : a popular attractive girl or woman

belles let·tres \bel-'letr'\ *n pl* [F, lit., fine letters] : literature that is an end in itself and not practical or purely informative — **bel·le·tris·tic** \,bel-ə-'tris-tik\ *adj*

bell·flow·er \'bel-,flau(-ə)r\ *n* : CAMPANULA

bell·hop \'bel-,häp\ *n* : BELLBOY

bel·li·cose \'bel-ə-,kōs\ *adj* [L *bellicosus*, fr. *bellum* war] : inclined to quarrel or fight : WARLIKE — **bel·li·cos·i·ty** \,bel-ə-'käs-ət-ē\ *n*

bel·lig·er·ence \bə-'lij-(ə-)rən(t)s\ *n* : an aggressive or truculent attitude, atmosphere, or disposition

bel·lig·er·en·cy \-(ə-)rən-sē\ *n* **1** : the status of a nation that is at war **2** : WARFARE

bel·lig·er·ent \bə-'lij-(ə-)rənt\ *adj* [L *belligerare* to wage war, fr. *bellum* war + *gerere* to wage] **1** : waging war; *esp* : belonging to or recognized as a power at war and protected by and subject to the laws of war **2** : inclined to or exhibiting assertiveness or combativeness — **belligerent** *n* — **bel·lig·er·ent·ly** *adv*

bell jar *n* : a bell-shaped usu. glass vessel designed to cover objects or to contain gases or a vacuum

bell·man \'bel-mən\ *n* : BELLBOY

bel·low \'bel-ō\ *vb* **1** : to make the loud deep hollow sound characteristic of a bull **2** : to shout in a deep voice : BAWL — **bellow** *n*

bel·lows \'bel-ōz, -əz\ *n sing or pl* [ME *bely, below* belly, bellows] **1** : a device (as for blowing fires or operating an organ) that by alternate expansion and contraction of a closed box draws in air through a valve and expels it forcibly through a tube; *also* : any of various blowers or various enclosures of variable volume **2** : the pleated expansible part of some cameras

hand bellows

bell·pull \'bel-,púl\ *n* : a handle or knob attached to a cord or wire by which one rings a bell; *also* : the cord itself

bell·weth·er \'bel-'weth-ər\ *n* **1** : a belled usu. wether sheep that runs with and identifies the location of a flock **2** : one that takes the lead or initiative : LEADER

¹bel·ly \'bel-ē\ *n, pl* **bellies** [ME *bely*, bellows, belly, fr. OE *belg* bag] **1 a** : ABDOMEN 1 **b** : the undersurface of an animal's body; *also* : hide from this part **c** : UTERUS **d** : STOMACH 1a **2** : the internal cavity : INTERIOR **3** : a surface or object curved or rounded like a human belly ⟨the *belly* of an airplane⟩ **4 a** : the part of a sail that swells out when filled with wind **b** : the enlarged fleshy body of a muscle

²belly *vb* **bel·lied; bel·ly·ing** : to swell or bulge out

¹bel·ly·ache \'bel-ē-,āk\ *n* : pain in the abdomen and esp. in the bowels : COLIC

²bel·ly·ache *vi* : to complain esp. in a whining or peevish way

bel·ly·band \'bel-ē-,band\ *n* : a band around or across the belly: as **a** : GIRTH **b** : BAND 4

belly button *n* : NAVEL 1

bel·ly·land \'bel-ē-,land\ *vb* : to land an airplane without use of landing gear — **belly landing** *n*

be·long \bə-'lóŋ\ *vi* [ME *belongen*, fr. *be-* + *longen* to be suitable] **1 a** : to be suitable, appropriate, or advantageous **b** : to be in a proper situation ⟨this book *belongs* on the top shelf⟩ **2 a** : to be the property of a person or thing — used with *to* ⟨this book *belongs* to me⟩ **b** : to become attached or bound by birth, allegiance, or dependency **3** : to be an attribute, part, adjunct, or function of a person or thing ⟨parts *belonging* to a watch⟩ **4** : to be properly classified ⟨whales *belong* among the mammals⟩

be·long·ings \bə-'lóŋ-iŋz\ *n pl* : the things that belong to a person : POSSESSIONS

be·loved \bi-'ləv-(-ə)d\ *adj* : dearly loved — **beloved** *n*

¹be·low \bə-'lō\ *adv* **1** : in or to a lower place **2 a** : on earth **b** : in or to Hades or hell **3** : on or to a lower floor or deck **4** : lower on the same page or on a following page

²below *prep* : lower than in place, rank, or value ⟨*below* average⟩

syn UNDER, BENEATH: BELOW is opposed to *above* and implies only that one thing is on a lower level than another ⟨ten degrees *below* zero⟩ UNDER is opposed to *over* and implies a relation between two things such as contact, support, subjection, inferiority ⟨his legs doubled *under* him⟩ ⟨held the cup *under* the spout⟩ ⟨men *under* his command⟩ BENEATH is chiefly poetical for UNDER or BELOW except when expressing moral or social inferiority ⟨actions *beneath* contempt⟩ ⟨thought housekeeping *beneath* her⟩

¹belt \'belt\ *n* [OE, fr. L *balteus*] **1** : a strip of flexible material (as leather or cloth) worn around a person's body for holding in or supporting clothing or weapons or for ornament **2** : something resembling a belt : BAND, CIRCLE ⟨a *belt* of trees⟩ **3** : a flexible endless band running around wheels or pulleys and used for moving or carrying something ⟨a fan *belt* on an automobile⟩ **4** : a natural area characterized by some distinctive feature (as of habitation, geology, weather, or life forms); *esp* : one suited to a particular crop ⟨the corn *belt*⟩ — **belt·ed** \'bel-təd\ *adj* — **below the belt** : UNFAIRLY

²belt *vt* **1** : to put a belt on or around **2** : to beat with or as if with a belt : THRASH, STRIKE **3** : to mark with a band

³belt *n* : a jarring blow

belt highway *n* : a highway skirting an urban area — called also *beltway*

belt·ing \'bel-tiŋ\ *n* **1** : BELTS **2** : material for belt

be·lu·ga \bə-'lü-gə\ *n* [Russ, fr. *belyĭ* white] **1** : a white sturgeon esp. of the Black and Caspian seas **2** [Russ

---

j joke; ŋ sing; ō flow; ó flaw; ói coin; th thin; th this; ü loot; ú foot; y yet; yü few; yú furious; zh vision

belukha, fr. belyĭ] **:** a mammal of the dolphin family becoming about 10 feet long and white when adult

bel·ve·dere \'bel-və-ˌdi(ə)r\ *n* [It, lit., beautiful view] **:** a structure (as a summerhouse) designed to command a view

be·ma \'bē-mə\ *n* [LGk *bēma*, fr. Gk, step, tribunal, fr. *bainein* to step, go] **:** the part of an Eastern church containing the altar **:** SANCTUARY — see BASILICA illustration

be·mire \bi-'mī(ə)r\ *vt* **:** to cover or soil with or sink in mire

be·moan \bi-'mōn\ *vt* **1 :** to express grief over **:** LAMENT **2 :** to look upon with regret, displeasure, or disapproval

be·muse \bi-'myüz\ *vt* **:** to make confused **:** BEWILDER

¹bench \'bench\ *n* [OE *benc*] **1 :** a long seat for two or more persons **2 :** a long table for holding work and tools (as of a carpenter or a shoemaker) **3 a :** the seat where a judge sits in a court of law **b :** the position or rank of a judge **c :** a person sitting as a judge or the persons who sit as judges taken together **4 :** a seat where the members of a team wait for an opportunity to play

²bench *vt* **1 :** to furnish with benches **2 :** to seat on a bench **3 :** to remove from or keep out of a game

bench mark *n* **:** a mark on a permanent object indicating elevation and serving as a reference in geological surveys

¹bend \'bend\ *n* [MF *bende, bande* strip, band] **1 :** a diagonal band in heraldry **2** [OE *bend* fetter; akin to E *bind*] **:** a knot by which one rope is fastened to another or to some object

²bend *vb* **bent** \'bent\; **bend·ing** [OE *bendan;* akin to E *bind*] **1 :** to pull taut or tense ⟨*bend* a bow⟩ **2 :** to curve or cause a change of shape ⟨*bend* a wire into a circle and then *bend* it straight again⟩ **3 :** to turn in a certain direction **:** DIRECT ⟨*bent* his steps toward town⟩ **4 :** to force to yield ⟨*bent* his family to his will⟩ **5 a :** to apply closely ⟨*bend* your energy to the task⟩ **b :** to apply oneself closely or vigorously **6 :** to curve out of line ⟨the road *bends* to the left⟩ **7 :** to curve downward **:** STOOP **8 :** YIELD, SUBMIT

³bend *n* **1 :** the act or process of bending **:** the state of being bent **2 :** something that is bent; *esp* **:** a curved part of a stream **3** *pl* **:** CAISSON DISEASE

bend·er \'ben-dər\ *n* **1 :** one that bends **2 :** SPREE

¹be·neath \bi-'nēth\ *adv* [OE *beneothan*, fr. *be-* + *neothan* below; akin to E *nether*] **1 :** in or to a lower position **2 :** directly under

²beneath *prep* **1 a :** in or to a lower position than **b :** directly under ⟨the ground *beneath* one's feet⟩ **2 :** unworthy of ⟨*beneath* his dignity⟩ **syn** see BELOW

ben·e·dict \'ben-ə-ˌdikt\ *n* [alter. of *Benedick*, character in Shakespeare's *Much Ado about Nothing*] **:** a newly married man who has long been a bachelor

Ben·e·dic·tine \ˌben-ə-'dik-tən, -ˌtēn\ *n* **:** a monk or a nun of a religious order following the rule of St. Benedict and devoted esp. to scholarship and liturgical worship — **Benedictine** *adj*

ben·e·dic·tion \ˌben-ə-'dik-shən\ *n* [LL *benedicere* to bless, fr. L, to speak well of, fr. *bene* well + *dicere* to say] **1 :** the invocation of a blessing; *esp* **:** the short blessing with which public worship is concluded **2** *often cap* **: a** Roman Catholic or Anglo-Catholic devotion including the exposition of the eucharistic Host in the monstrance and the blessing of the people with it **3 :** a prayer or scripture passage pronounced to dismiss a meeting (as of a fraternal organization) — **ben·e·dic·to·ry** \-'dik-t(ə-)rē\ *adj*

Ben·e·dic·tus \-'dik-təs\ *n* [LL, blessed, its first word] **1 :** a canticle from Matthew 21:9 beginning "Blessed is he that cometh in the name of the Lord" **2 :** a canticle from Luke 1:68 beginning "Blessed be the Lord God of Israel"

ben·e·fac·tion \ˌben-ə-,fak-shən, ˌben-ə-'\ *n* [L *bene fact-, bene facere* to do good] **1 :** the action of benefiting **2 : a** benefit conferred; *esp* **:** a charitable donation

ben·e·fac·tor \'ben-ə-,fak-tər\ *n* **:** one that confers a benefit; *esp* **:** one that makes a gift or bequest — **ben·e·fac·tress** \-,fak-trəs\ *n*

ben·e·fice \'ben-ə-fəs\ *n* [ML *beneficium*, fr. L, benefit, favor, promotion] **:** a post conferred upon a clergyman that gives him the right to use certain property and to receive income from stated sources — **benefice** *vt*

be·nef·i·cence \bə-'nef-ə-sən(t)s\ *n* **1 :** the quality or state of being beneficent **2 :** BENEFACTION

be·nef·i·cent \-sənt\ *adj* **1 :** doing or producing good; *esp* **:** performing acts of kindness and charity **2 :** productive of benefit — **be·nef·i·cent·ly** *adv*

ben·e·fi·cial \ˌben-ə-'fish-əl\ *adj* [L *beneficium* kindness, benefit, fr. *beneficus* conferring benefits, fr. *bene* well + *facere* to do] **:** conferring benefits **:** ADVANTAGEOUS — **ben·e·fi·cial·ly** \-'fish-ə-lē\ *adv* — **ben·e·fi·cial·ness** *n*

syn ADVANTAGEOUS, PROFITABLE: BENEFICIAL implies promoting health or well-being; ADVANTAGEOUS stresses a choice or preference that brings superiority or greater success in attaining an end; PROFITABLE implies the yielding of useful or lucrative returns

ben·e·fi·ci·ary \ˌben-ə-'fish-ē-ˌer-ē, -'fish-(ə-)rē\ *n, pl* **-ar·ies :** a person who benefits or is expected to benefit from something; *esp* **:** the person named in a life insurance policy to receive the insurance on the death of the assured

¹ben·e·fit \'ben-ə-,fit\ *n* [ME, fr. AF *benfet* good deed, kindness, fr. L *bene factum*, lit., thing well done] **1 a :** something that promotes well-being **:** ADVANTAGE **b :** useful aid **:** HELP **2 :** assistance (as money) provided for under an annuity, pension plan, or insurance policy ⟨unemployment *benefits*⟩ **3 :** an entertainment or social event to raise funds for a person or cause

²benefit *vb* **-fit·ed** *or* **-fit·ted; -fit·ing** *or* **-fit·ting 1 :** to be useful or profitable to **2 :** to receive benefit

benefit of clergy 1 : clerical exemption from trial in a civil court **2 :** the ministration or sanction of the church

be·nev·o·lence \bə-'nev-(ə-)lən(t)s\ *n* **1 :** disposition to do good **2 a :** an act of kindness **b :** a generous gift **3 :** a tax levied by some English kings under an asserted claim of prerogative

be·nev·o·lent \-(ə-)lənt\ *adj* [L *bene* well + *volent-, volens*, prp. of *velle* to wish] **1 :** having or showing good will to others **:** KINDLY **2 :** freely or generously giving to charity **3 :** existing or operated for the purpose of doing good to others and not for profit ⟨*benevolent* institutions⟩ — **be·nev·o·lent·ly** *adv* — **be·nev·o·lent·ness** *n*

Ben·gali \ben-'gȯ-lē, beŋ-\ *n* **1 :** a native or inhabitant of Bengal **2 :** the modern Indic language of Bengal — **Bengali** *adj*

ben·ga·line \'beŋ-gə-ˌlēn\ *n* **:** fabric with a crosswise rib made from the major textile fibers or a combination of these

be·night·ed \bi-'nīt-əd\ *adj* **1 :** overtaken by night or darkness **2 :** IGNORANT

be·nign \bi-'nīn\ *adj* [L *benignus*, lit., good-natured, fr. *bene* well + *gigni* to be born] **1 :** of a gentle disposition **:** GRACIOUS **2 a :** manifesting kindness and gentleness **b :** FAVORABLE **3 :** of a mild character; *esp* **:** not malignant ⟨*benign* tumor⟩ — **be·nig·ni·ty** \-'nig-nət-ē\ *n* — **be·nign·ly** \-'nīn-lē\ *adv*

syn BENIGN, BENIGNANT both mean kindly or favorable in appearance, but BENIGN suggests actual effect given by action or appearance ⟨the weather remained *benign*⟩ ⟨a frown on his usually *benign* face⟩ BENIGNANT tends to suggest conscious feeling or intention of kindliness ⟨giving out candy with a *benignant* smile for each child⟩

be·nig·nant \bi-'nig-nənt\ *adj* **1 :** KINDLY, GENTLE **2 :** FAVORABLE, BENEFICIAL **syn** see BENIGN — **be·nig·nant·ly** *adv*

ben·i·son \'ben-ə-sən, -zən\ *n* [OF *beneiçon*, fr. LL *benediction-, benedictio*] **:** BLESSING, BENEDICTION

Ben·ja·min \'benj-(ə-)mən\ *n* **:** the youngest of Jacob's 12 sons

¹bent \'bent\ *n* [ME] **:** any of a genus of mostly perennial and rhizomatous pasture and lawn grasses with fine velvety or wiry herbage

²bent *n* [irreg. fr. ²*bend*] **1 a :** strong inclination or interest **b :** a natural capacity **:** TALENT **2 :** capacity of endurance

ben·thic \'ben(t)-thik\ *or* **ben·thon·ic** \ben-'thän-ik\ *adj* [Gk *benthos* depths of the sea] **:** of, relating to, or occurring in the depths of a body of water (as the ocean)

ben·thos \'ben-ˌthäs\ *n* **:** the benthic region or the organisms that live there

ben·ton·ite \'bent-ᵊn-ˌīt\ *n* **:** an absorptive and colloidal clay used esp. as a filler (as in paper)

be·numb \bi-'nəm\ *vt* **:** to make numb esp. by cold

Ben·ze·drine \'ben-zə-ˌdrēn\ *trademark* — used for amphetamine

ben·zene \'ben-ˌzēn, ben-'\ *n* [alter. of *benzine*] **:** a colorless volatile flammable liquid C_6H_6 that is obtained chiefly in the distillation of coal and that is used as a solvent and in making other chemicals (as dyes and drugs) — called also *benzol*

benzene ring *n* : an arrangement of atoms held to exist in benzene and other aromatic compounds and marked by six carbon atoms linked by alternate single and double bonds in a hexagon

ben·zine \'ben-ˌzēn, ben-'\ *n* [*benzoic acid*] **1** : BENZENE **2** : any of various volatile flammable petroleum distillates used esp. as solvents for fatty substances or as motor fuels

ben·zo·ate of soda \ˌben-zə-ˌwāt-\ : SODIUM BENZOATE

ben·zo·ic acid \(ˌ)ben-ˌzō-ik-\ *n* [*benzoin*] : a white crystalline acid $C_7H_6O_2$ found naturally (as in cranberries) or made synthetically and used esp. as a preservative and as an antiseptic

ben·zo·in \'ben-zə-wən, -ˌzóin\ *n* [MF *benjoin*, fr. Catal *benjuí*, fr. Ar *lubān jāwi*, lit., frankincense of Java] : a hard fragrant yellowish balsamic resin from trees of southeastern Asia used esp. in medicine, as a fixative in perfumes, and as incense

ben·zol \'ben-ˌzól, -ˌzōl\ *n* : BENZENE

Be·o·wulf \'bā-ə-ˌwùlf\ *n* : a Geatish warrior and hero of the Old English poem *Beowulf*

be·queath \bi-'kwēth, -'kwēth\ *vt* [OE *becwethan*, fr. *be-* + *cwethan* to say] **1** : to give or leave esp. personal property by will — compare DEVISE **2** : to hand down — **be·queath·al** \-əl\ *n*

be·quest \bi-'kwest\ *n* **1** : the action of bequeathing **2** : something bequeathed : LEGACY

be·rate \bi-'rāt\ *vt* : to scold violently

Ber·ber \'bər-bər\ *n* **1** : a member of a Caucasoid people of northwestern Africa **2** : any of a group of languages spoken in northwestern Africa — **Berber** *adj*

ber·ceuse \ber-'sə(r)z\ *n, pl* **ber·ceuses** \-'sə(r)z(-əz)\ [F, fr. *bercer* to rock] **1** : LULLABY **2** : a musical composition of a tranquil nature

be·reave \bi-'rēv\ *vt* **be·reaved** \-'rēvd\ *or* **be·reft** \-'reft\; **be·reav·ing** : to deprive of something cherished esp. by death : STRIP, DISPOSSESS — **be·reave·ment** \-'rēv-mənt\ *n*

be·ret \bə-'rā\ *n* [F *béret*, fr. Prov *berret*] : a soft flat visorless wool cap

berg \'bərg\ *n* : ICEBERG

ber·ga·mot \'bər-gə-ˌmät\ *n* **1** : a pear-shaped orange whose rind yields an oil used in perfumery **2** : any of several mints (as Oswego tea)

ber·i·beri \ˌber-ē-'ber-ē\ *n* [Sinhalese *bæri-bæri*] : a deficiency disease marked by weakness, wasting, and damage to nerves and caused by a dietary lack of or inability to assimilate thiamine

Be·ring standard time \'bi(ə)r-iŋ-, 'be(ə)r-\ *n* : the time of the 11th time zone west of Greenwich that includes western Alaska and the Aleutian islands

berke·li·um \'bər-klē-əm, (ˌ)bər-'kē-lē-əm\ *n* [NL, fr. *Berkeley*, Calif.] : an artificially prepared radioactive chemical element — see ELEMENT table

Ber·mu·da shorts \bər-'myüd-ə-\ *n pl* : knee-length walking shorts

¹ber·ry \'ber-ē\ *n, pl* **berries** [OE *berie*] **1 a** : a small pulpy and usu. edible fruit (as a strawberry or raspberry) **b** : a simple fruit (as a currant, grape, tomato, or banana) with the wall of the ripened ovary pulpy or fleshy **c** : the dry seed of some plants (as coffee) **2** : an egg of a fish or lobster

²berry *vi* **ber·ried**; **ber·ry·ing** **1** : to bear or produce berries ⟨*berrying* wheat⟩ **2** : to gather or seek berries ⟨go *berrying* every summer⟩

¹ber·serk \bə(r)-'sərk, -'zərk, 'bər-,\ *or* **ber·serk·er** \-ər\ *n* [ON *berserkr*, fr. *björn* bear + *serkr* shirt] : an ancient Scandinavian warrior frenzied in battle and held to be invulnerable

²berserk *adj* : FRENZIED, CRAZED — **berserk** *adv*

¹berth \'bərth\ *n* [prob. fr. ²*bear* + *-th*] **1** : distance sufficient to maneuver a ship **2** : a place where a ship lies at anchor or at a wharf **3** : a place to sit or sleep on a ship or vehicle : ACCOMMODATION **4 a** : a billet on a ship **b** : JOB, POSITION

²berth *vb* **1** : to bring or come into a berth **2** : to allot a berth to

ber·tha \'bər-thə\ *n* : a wide round collar covering the shoulders

ber·yl \'ber-əl\ *n* [Gk *bēryllos*, of Indic origin] : a mineral $Be_3Al_2Si_6O_{18}$ consisting of a silicate of beryllium and aluminum of great hardness and occurring in green, bluish green, yellow, pink, or white prisms

be·ryl·li·um \bə-'ril-ē-əm\ *n* : a steel-gray light strong brittle metallic element — see ELEMENT table

be·seech \bi-'sēch\ *vb* **be·sought** \-'sót\ *or* **be·seeched**; **be·seech·ing** [ME *besechen*, fr. *be-* + *sechen* to seek] : to ask earnestly for : IMPLORE **syn** see BEG

be·seem \bi-'sēm\ *vb* **1** *archaic* : to be fitting or becoming **2** *archaic* : to be suitable to : BEFIT

be·set \bi-'set\ *vt* **-set**; **-set·ting** **1** : to stud with ornaments **2** : TROUBLE, HARASS **3 a** : to set upon : ASSAIL **b** : to hem in : SURROUND

be·set·ting *adj* : constantly present or attacking : OBSESSIVE ⟨a *besetting* danger⟩

be·shrew \bi-'shrü\ *vt, archaic* : CURSE

¹be·side \bi-'sīd\ *adv, archaic* : BESIDES

²beside *prep* **1 a** : by the side of ⟨walk *beside* me⟩ **b** : in comparison with ⟨she looks like a midget *beside* him⟩ **2** : BESIDES **3** : not relevant to ⟨*beside* the point⟩ — **beside oneself** : out of one's wits

¹be·sides \bi-'sīdz\ *adv* : in addition — ALSO ⟨the play is excellent, and *besides* the tickets cost very little⟩

²besides *prep* **1** : in addition to ⟨how many were there *besides* you?⟩ **2** : other than ⟨no news *besides* what I have already told you⟩

be·siege \bi-'sēj\ *vt* **1** : to surround with armed forces : lay siege to **2** : to crowd around : BESET — **be·sieg·er** *n*

be·smear \bi-'smi(ə)r\ *vt* : SMEAR

be·smirch \bi-'smərch\ *vt* : SULLY, SOIL

be·som \'bē-zəm\ *n* [OE *besma*] : a broom made of twigs

be·sot \bi-'sät\ *vt* **be·sot·ted**; **be·sot·ting** : to make dull or stupid : STUPEFY; *esp* : to muddle with drink

be·spat·ter \bi-'spat-ər\ *vt* : SPATTER

be·speak \bi-'spēk\ *vt* **-spoke** \-'spōk\; **-spo·ken** \-'spō-kən\; **-speak·ing** **1 a** : to ask or arrange for beforehand **b** : REQUEST **2 a** : INDICATE, SIGNIFY **b** : to show beforehand : FORETELL

be·sprent \bi-'sprent\ *adj, archaic* : sprinkled over

be·sprin·kle \bi-'spriŋ-kəl\ *vt* : SPRINKLE

Bes·se·mer converter \ˌbes-ə-mər-\ *n* [Sir Henry *Bessemer d*1898 English engineer] : the furnace used in the Bessemer process

Bessemer process *n* : a process of making steel from pig iron by burning out impurities (as carbon) by means of a blast of air forced through the molten metal

¹best \'best\ *adj, superlative of* GOOD [OE *betst*] **1** : good or useful in the highest degree : most excellent **2** : MOST, LARGEST ⟨the *best* part of a week⟩

²best *adv, superlative of* WELL **1** : in the best way **2** : to the highest degree : MOST ⟨*best* able to do the work⟩

³best *n* **1** : the best state or part **2** : one that is best ⟨the *best* falls short⟩ **3** : one's maximum effort ⟨do your *best*⟩ **4** : best clothes ⟨put on your Sunday *best*⟩

⁴best *vt* : to get the better of : OUTDO

be·stead \bi-'sted\ *adj, archaic* : BESET

bes·tial \'bes-chəl\ *adj* [L *bestia* beast] **1 a** : of or relating to beasts **b** : resembling a beast **2 a** : lacking intelligence or reason **b** : VICIOUS, BRUTAL — **bes·tial·ly** \-chə-lē\ *adv*

bes·ti·al·i·ty \ˌbes-chē-'al-ət-ē\ *n* **1** : the condition or status of a lower animal **2** : display or gratification of bestial traits or impulses

bes·ti·ary \'bes-chē-ˌer-ē\ *n, pl* **-ar·ies** : a medieval allegorical or moralizing work on the appearance and habits of animals

be·stir \bi-'stər\ *vt* : to stir up : rouse to action

best man *n* : the principal groomsman at a wedding

be·stow \bi-'stō\ *vt* **1** : USE, APPLY **2** *archaic* : QUARTER, LODGE **3** : to present as a gift : CONFER — **be·stow·al** \-'stō-əl\ *n*

be·strew \bi-'strü\ *vt* **-strewed**; **-strewed** *or* **-strewn** \-'strün\; **-strew·ing** **1** : STREW **2** : to lie scattered over

be·stride \bi-'strīd\ *vt* **-strode** \-'strōd\; **-strid·den** \-'strid-ᵊn\; **-strid·ing** **1** : to ride, sit, or stand astride

beret

: STRADDLE **2** : to tower over : DOMINATE **3** *archaic* : to stride across

best seller *n* : an article (as a book) whose sales are among the highest of its class

¹**bet** \'bet\ *n* **1 a** : an agreement requiring the person whose guess about the result of a contest or the outcome of an event proves wrong to give something to a person whose guess proves right **b** : the making of such an agreement : WAGER **2** : the money or thing risked ⟨a *bet* of 10 cents⟩

²**bet** *vb* **bet** *or* **bet·ted; bet·ting 1** : to stake on the outcome of an issue **2** : to make a bet with **3** : to lay a bet

be·ta \'bāt-ə\ *n* **1** : the 2d letter of the Greek alphabet — B or β **2** : the second brightest star of a constellation

be·take \bi-'tāk\ *vt* : to cause (oneself) to go

beta particle *n* : an electron or positron ejected from the nucleus of an atom during radioactive decay

beta ray *n* **1** : BETA PARTICLE **2** : a stream of beta particles

be·ta·tron \'bāt-ə-,trän\ *n* : a device that accelerates electrons by the inductive action of a rapidly varying magnetic field

be·tel \'bēt-ᵊl\ *n* [Pg., fr. Tamil *verrilai*] : a climbing pepper whose dried leaves are chewed together with betel nut and lime as a stimulant esp. by southeastern Asians

Be·tel·geuse \'bet-ᵊl-,jüz, 'bēt-, -,jə(r)z\ *n* [F *Bételgeuse,* fr. Ar *bayt al-jawzā'* Gemini, lit., the house of the twins (confused with Orion)] : a variable red giant star of the first magnitude near one shoulder of Orion

betel nut *n* : the astringent seed of an Asiatic palm

bête noire \,bāt-nə-'wär, bāt-'nwär\ *n, pl* **bêtes noires** \-'wär(z), -'nwär(z)\ [F, lit., black beast] : a person or thing strongly detested or avoided : BUGBEAR

beth·el \'beth-əl\ *n* [Heb *bēthēl* house of God] : a place of worship esp. for seamen

be·think \bi-'think\ *vt* **-thought** \-'thȯt\; **-think·ing 1 a** : REMEMBER, RECALL **b** : to cause (oneself) to be reminded **2** : to cause (oneself) to consider

be·tide \bi-'tīd\ *vb* : to happen or happen to : BEFALL

be·times \bi-'tīmz\ *adv* : in time : EARLY

be·to·ken \bi-'tō-kən\ *vt* : to be a sign of : INDICATE

be·tray \bi-'trā\ *vt* [ME *betrayen,* fr. *be-* + F *traïr* to betray, fr. L *tradere* to hand over, betray, fr. *trans-* + *dare* to give] **1** : to give over to an enemy by treachery or fraud **2** : to be unfaithful or treacherous to : FAIL ⟨*betrayed* his trust⟩ **3** : to lead into error, sin, or danger : DECEIVE, SEDUCE **4** : to reveal unintentionally ⟨*betray* his ignorance⟩ **5** : to tell in violation of a trust — **be·tray·al** \-'trā(-ə)l\ *n* — **be·tray·er** \-'trā-ər\ *n*

be·troth \bi-'trȯth, -'träth, -'trōth\ *vt* : to promise to marry or give in marriage

be·troth·al \-əl\ *n* **1** : an engagement to be married **2** : the act or ceremony of becoming engaged to be married

be·trothed *n* : the person to whom one is betrothed

bet·ta \'bet-ə\ *n* : any of a genus of small brilliantly colored long-finned freshwater fishes of southeastern Asia

¹**bet·ter** \'bet-ər\ *adj, comparative of* GOOD [OE *betera*] **1** : more than half ⟨the *better* part of a week⟩ **2** : improved in health **3** : of higher quality

²**better** *adv, comparative of* WELL **1** : in a more excellent manner **2 a** : to a higher or greater degree **b** : MORE

³**better** *n* **1 a** : something better **b** : a superior esp. in merit or rank **2** : ADVANTAGE, VICTORY ⟨get the *better* of him⟩

⁴**better** *vt* **1** : to make better **2** : to surpass in excellence : EXCEL

bet·ter·ment \'bet-ər-mənt\ *n* : IMPROVEMENT

bet·tor *or* **bet·ter** \'bet-ər\ *n* : one that bets

¹**be·tween** \bi-'twēn\ *prep* [OE *betwēonum,* adv. & prep., fr. *be-* + *-twēonum* (dat. pl.) two; akin to E *two*] **1** : by the common action of : in common to ⟨ate six *between* them⟩ **2** : in the time, space, or interval that separates ⟨*between* nine and ten o'clock⟩ ⟨*between* the desk and the wall⟩ **3** : DISTINGUISHING ⟨the difference *between* soccer and football⟩ **4** : by comparison of ⟨choose *between* the two coats⟩ **5** : from one to the other or another of ⟨the bond *between* friends⟩

  syn AMONG: BETWEEN indicates a relation of two objects in position, distribution, participation, or communication ⟨*between* two fires⟩ ⟨lost it *between* school and home⟩ but may be used of more than two if it brings them in-

dividually into the expressed relation ⟨the four boys had only seven dollars *between* them⟩ ⟨a treaty *between* three countries⟩ AMONG always implies more than two objects which it brings less definitely or individually into the relationship ⟨scattered the corn *among* the chickens⟩ ⟨it was whispered *among* his friends that he was bankrupt⟩

²**between** *adv* : in an intermediate space or interval — **be·tween·nes** \-'twēn-nəs\ *n*

be·tween·brain \-,brān\ *n* : DIENCEPHALON

be·twixt \bi-'twikst\ *adv or prep* [OE *betwux*] *archaic* : BETWEEN

¹**bev·el** \'bev-əl\ *adj* [(assumed) MF, n., bevel] : OBLIQUE, BEVELED

²**bevel** *n* **1 a** : the angle that one surface or line makes with another when they are not at right angles **b** : the slant or inclination of such a surface or line **2** : an instrument consisting of two rules or arms jointed together and opening to any angle for drawing angles or adjusting surfaces to be given a bevel

³**bevel** *vb* **bev·eled** *or* **bev·elled; bev·el·ing** *or* **bev·el·ling** \'bev-(ə-)lin\ **1** : to cut or shape (as an edge or surface) to a bevel **2** : INCLINE, SLANT

bev·er·age \'bev-(ə-)rij\ *n* [MF *bevrage,* fr. *beivre* to drink, fr. L *bibere*] : a liquid for drinking; *esp* : such liquid other than water

bevy \'bev-ē\ *n, pl* **bev·ies** : GROUP, CLUSTER, COLLECTION ⟨a *bevy* of girls⟩

be·wail \bi-'wāl\ *vt* **1** : to wail over **2** : to express deep regret for

be·ware \bi-'wa(ə)r, -'we(ə)r\ *vb* [ME *been war,* fr. *been* to be + *ware* aware, wary] **1** : to be on one's guard ⟨*beware* of the dog⟩ **2** : to be wary of

be·wil·der \bi-'wil-dər\ *vt* **-dered; -der·ing** \-d(ə-)rin\ **1** : to cause to lose one's bearings **2** : to perplex or confuse esp. by a complex variety or large number of objects or possibilities — **be·wil·der·ment** \-dər-mənt\ *n*

be·witch \bi-'wich\ *vt* **1** : to gain an influence over by means of magic or witchcraft : put under a spell **2** : CHARM, FASCINATE — **be·witch·ery** \-ə-rē\ *n* — **be·witch·ment** \-mənt\ *n*

be·wray \bi-'rā\ *vt* [ME *bewreyen,* fr. *be-* + *wreyen* to accuse, fr. OE *wrēgan*] *archaic* : DIVULGE, BETRAY, REVEAL

bey \'bā\ *n* [Turk, gentleman, chief] **1 a** : a provincial governor in the Ottoman Empire **2** : the former native ruler of Tunis **2** — formerly used as a courtesy title in Turkey and Egypt

¹**be·yond** \bē-'änd\ *adv* [OE *begeondan,* fr. *be-* + *geond* yond] : on or to the farther side ⟨extending to the river and somewhat *beyond*⟩

²**beyond** *prep* **1** : on or to the farther side of ⟨*beyond* that tree⟩ **2** : out of the reach or sphere of ⟨*beyond* help⟩ ⟨beautiful *beyond* expression⟩

³**beyond** *n* : HEREAFTER

bez·ant \'bez-ᵊnt, bə-'zant\ *n* : SOLIDUS 1

bez·el \'bez-əl\ *n* **1** : a sloping edge or face esp. on a cutting tool **2 a** : the top part of a ring setting that holds a stone or ornament; *also* : the top including the stone **b** : the oblique side or face of a cut gem; *esp* : the upper faceted portion of a brilliant projecting from the setting **3** : the grooved rim that holds the crystal on a watch; *also* : a rim that holds a covering (as on a clock dial or headlight)

be·zique \bə-'zēk\ *n* : a card game similar to pinochle that is played with a pack of 64 cards

be·zoar \'bē-,zō(ə)r, -,zȯ(ə)r\ *n* [Sp, fr. Ar *bāzahr*] : a concretion of the alimentary organs of a ruminant formerly believed to possess magical properties

bhang \'baŋ\ *n* [Hindi *bhāg*] **1** : a narcotic product of hemp **2** : the leaves and flowering tips of hemp or a narcotic and intoxicant product from this

bi- *prefix* [L; akin to E *two*] **1 a** : two ⟨biracial⟩ **b** : coming or occurring every two ⟨bimonthly⟩ — compare SEMI- **c** : into two parts ⟨bisect⟩ **2** : twice : doubly : on both sides ⟨biconvex⟩ ⟨biserrate⟩

bi·an·nu·al \(')bī-'an-yə(-wə)l\ *adj* : occurring twice a year — **bi·an·nu·al·ly** \-ē\ *adv*

¹**bi·as** \'bī-əs\ *n* [MF *biais*] **1** : a line diagonal to the grain of a fabric often utilized in the cutting of garments for smoother fit **2** : an inclination of temperament or outlook; *esp* : such an inclination marked by strong prejudice **3** : the tendency of a bowl to swerve on the

---

ə abut; ᵊ kitten; ər further; a back; ā bake; ä cot, cart; au̇ out; ch chin; e less; ē easy; g gift; i trip; ī life

green; *also* : the lopsidedness of the bowl or the impulse causing this tendency **4** : the direct-current voltage in the grid circuit of an electron tube **syn** see PREJUDICE

²bias *adj* : DIAGONAL, SLANTING — used chiefly of fabrics and their cut

³bias *vt* **bi·ased** *or* **bi·assed**; **bi·as·ing** *or* **bi·as·sing** : to give a bias to : PREJUDICE

bib \'bib\ *n* **1** : a cloth or plastic shield tied under a child's chin to protect the clothes **2** : the part of an apron or of overalls extending above the waist in front

bib and tuck·er \,bib-ən-'tək-ər\ *n* : an outfit of clothing

bib·ber \'bib-ər\ *n* [*bib* to tipple] : TIPPLER — **bib·bery** \-ə-rē\ *n*

bi·be·lot \,bib-(ə-)'lō, ,bēb-\ *n* [F] : a small household ornament or decorative object

Bi·ble \'bī-bəl\ *n* [ML *biblia*, fr. Gk, pl. of *biblion* book, dim. of *byblos* papyrus, book, fr. *Byblos*, ancient Phoenician city from which papyrus was exported] **1** : the sacred scriptures of Christians comprising the Old Testament and the New Testament **2** : the sacred scriptures of Judaism or of some other religion **3** *not cap* : a publication that is preeminent esp. in authoritativeness

THE BOOKS OF THE OLD TESTAMENT

DOUAY VERSION	AUTHORIZED VERSION
Genesis	Genesis
Exodus	Exodus
Leviticus	Leviticus
Numbers	Numbers
Deuteronomy	Deuteronomy
Josue	Joshua
Judges	Judges
Ruth	Ruth
1 & 2 Kings	1 & 2 Samuel
3 & 4 Kings	1 & 2 Kings
1 & 2 Paralipomenon	1 & 2 Chronicles
1 Esdras	Ezra
2 Esdras	Nehemiah
Tobias	
Judith	
Esther	Esther
Wisdom	
Ecclesiasticus	
Isaias	Isaiah
Jeremias	Jeremiah
Lamentations	Lamentations
Baruch	
Ezechiel	Ezekiel
Daniel	Daniel
Osee	Hosea
Joel	Joel
Amos	Amos
Abdias	Obadiah
Jonas	Jonah
Micheas	Micah
Nahum	Nahum
Habacuc	Habakkuk
Sophonias	Zephaniah
Job	Job
Psalms	Psalms
Proverbs	Proverbs
Ecclesiastes	Ecclesiastes
Canticle of Canticles	Song of Solomon
Aggeus	Haggai
Zacharias	Zechariah
Malachias	Malachi
1 & 2 Machabees	

THE BOOKS OF THE NEW TESTAMENT

(*DV* and *AV* names the same)

Matthew
Mark
Luke
John
Acts of the Apostles
Romans
1 & 2 Corinthians
Galatians
Ephesians
Philippians
Colossians
1 & 2 Thessalonians
1 & 2 Timothy
Titus
Philemon
Hebrews
James
1 & 2 Peter
1, 2, 3 John
Jude
Revelation (*DV*: Apocalypse)

PROTESTANT APOCRYPHA

1 & 2 Esdras¹
Tobit
Judith
part of Esther²
Wisdom of Solomon
Ecclesiasticus or the Wisdom of Jesus Son of Sirach
Baruch
Prayer of Azariah and the Song of the Three Holy Children³
Susanna⁴
Bel and the Dragon⁵
The Prayer of Manasses⁶
1 & 2 Maccabees

¹not the same as 1 & 2 Esdras in *DV*
²ch. 11–16 in *DV*
³from ch. 3 of *DV* Daniel
⁴ch. 13 of *DV* Daniel
⁵ch. 14 of *DV* Daniel
⁶not in *DV*

bib·li·cal \'bib-li-kəl\ *adj* **1** : of, relating to, or in accord with the Bible **2** : suggestive of the Bible or Bible times — **bib·li·cal·ly** \-k(ə-)lē\ *adv*

biblio- *comb form* [Gk *biblion*] : book ⟨*biblio*film⟩

bib·lio·film \'bib-lē-ō-,film\ *n* : a microfilm used esp. for photographing pages of books

bib·li·og·ra·pher \,bib-lē-'äg-rə-fər\ *n* **1** : an expert in bibliography **2** : a compiler of bibliography

bib·li·og·ra·phy \,bib-lē-'äg-rə-fē\ *n, pl* **-phies** **1** : the history, identification, or description of writings or publications **2** : a list often with descriptive or critical notes of writings relating to a particular subject, period, or author; *also* : a list of works written by an author or printed by a publishing house **3** : a list of the works referred to in a text or consulted by the author in its production — **bib·li·o·graph·ic** \,bib-lē-ə-'graf-ik\ *or* **bib·li·o·graph·i·cal** \-'graf-i-kəl\ *adj* — **bib·li·o·graph·i·cal·ly** \-'graf-i-k(ə-)lē\ *adv*

bib·lio·phile \'bib-lē-ə-,fīl\ *n* : a lover of books esp. for qualities of format; *also* : a book collector

bib·u·lous \'bib-yə-ləs\ *adj* [L *bibulus*, fr. *bibere* to drink] **1** : highly absorbent **2 a** : inclined to drink **b** : of or relating to drink or drinking — **bib·u·lous·ly** *adv* — **bib·u·lous·ness** *n*

bi·cam·er·al \(')bī-'kam-(ə-)rəl\ *adj* [L *camera* room, chamber] : having, consisting of, or based upon two legislative chambers ⟨*bicameral* legislature⟩ — **bi·cam·er·al·ism** \-rə-,liz-əm\ *n*

bi·car·bon·ate \(')bī-'kär-bə-,nāt, -nət\ *n* : an acid carbonate

bicarbonate of soda : SODIUM BICARBONATE

bi·cen·te·na·ry \,bī-sen-'ten-ə-rē, (')bī-'sent-°n-,er-ē\ *adj* : BICENTENNIAL — **bicentenary** *n*

bi·cen·ten·ni·al \,bī-sen-'ten-ē-əl\ *adj* : relating to a 200th anniversary — **bicentennial** *n*

bi·ceps \'bī-,seps\ *n* [NL *bicipit-*, *biceps*, fr. L, two-headed, fr. *bi-* + *capit-*, *caput* head] : a muscle having two heads; *esp* : a large flexor muscle of the front of the upper arm

bi·chlo·ride \(')bī-'klōr-,īd, -'klòr-\ *n* **1** : DICHLORIDE **2** *or* **bichloride of mercury** : MERCURIC CHLORIDE

bi·chro·mate \(')bī-'krō-,māt\ *n* : DICHROMATE

bick·er \'bik-ər\ *vi* **bick·ered**; **bick·er·ing** \'bik-(ə-)riŋ\ [ME *bikeren*] : to quarrel petulantly or pettily : WRANGLE — **bicker** *n*

bi·col·or \'bī-,kəl-ər\ *adj* : two-colored — **bicolor** *n* — **bi·col·ored** \-'kəl-ərd\ *adj*

bicolor lespedeza *n* : a purple-flowered Asiatic leguminous shrub widely used as an ornamental, as a source of wild≈ bird food, and in erosion control

bi·con·cave \,bī-(,)kän-'kāv, (')bī-'kän-,\ *adj* : concave on both sides — **bi·con·cav·i·ty** \,bī-(,)kän-'kav-ət-ē\ *n*

bi·con·vex \,bī-(,)kän-'veks, (')bī-'kän-,\ *adj* : convex on both sides — **bi·con·vex·i·ty** \,bī-(,)kän-'vek-sət-ē\ *n*

bi·cor·nu·ate \(')bī-'kòr-nyə-wət\ *adj* [*bi-* + L *cornu* horn] : having two horns or horn-shaped processes

¹bi·cus·pid \(')bī-'kəs-pəd\ *also* **bi·cus·pi·date** \-pə-,dāt\ *adj* [*bi-* + L *cuspid-*, *cuspis* point, cusp] : having or ending in two points

²bicuspid *n* : a human premolar tooth — see DENTITION illustration, TOOTH illustration

bicuspid valve *n* : a valve guarding the opening between the left auricle and ventricle of the heart and consisting of two triangular flaps — called also *mitral valve*

¹bi·cy·cle \'bī-,sik-əl\ *n* [Gk *kyklos* wheel] : a vehicle with two wheels tandem, a steering handle, a saddle seat, and pedals by which it is propelled — **bi·cy·clist** \-,sik-(ə-)ləst\ *n*

²bicycle *vi* **bi·cy·cled**; **bi·cy·cling** \-,sik-(ə-)liŋ\ : to ride a bicycle — **bi·cy·cler** \-,sik-(ə-)lər\ *n*

bi·cy·clic \(')bī-'sī-klik, -'sik-lik\ *adj* : consisting of or arranged in two cycles

¹bid \'bid\ *vb* **bade** \'bad, 'bād\ *or* **bid**; **bid·den** \'bid-°n\ *or* **bid** *also* **bade**; **bid·ding** [partly fr. OE *biddan* to ask, pray; partly fr. OE *bēodan* to offer, command] **1 a** : to issue an order to : TELL ⟨did as he was **bidden**⟩ **b** : to request to come : INVITE **2** : to give expression to ⟨*bade* me a tearful farewell⟩ **3** *past bid* **a** : to offer (a price) for something (as at an auction) **b** : to make a bid of in a card game — **bid·der** *n* — **bid fair** : to seem likely — **bid up** : to raise the price of by bids at an auction

²bid *n* **1** : an offer to pay a certain sum for something or to perform certain work at a stated fee; *also* : the price or fee offered **2** : an opportunity or turn to bid **3** : INVITATION **4 a** : an announcement of what a card player

---

j joke; ŋ sing; ō flow; ò flaw; òi coin; th thin; th̲ this; ü loot; u̇ foot; y yet; yü few; yu̇ furious; zh vision

proposes to undertake **b** : the amount of such a bid **5** : an attempt or effort to win, achieve, or attract

bid·da·ble \'bid-ə-bəl\ *adj* **1** : OBEDIENT, DOCILE **2** : capable of being bid — **bid·da·bly** \-blē\ *adv*

bide \'bīd\ *vb* **bode** \'bōd\ *or* **bid·ed; bid·ed; bid·ing** [OE *bīdan*] **1** : to continue in a state or condition : WAIT ⟨*bide* a while⟩ **2** : to wait for ⟨*bided* his time before acting⟩ — **bid·er** *n*

bi·en·ni·al \(')bī-'en-ē-əl\ *adj* **1** : occurring every two years **2 a** : continuing or lasting for two years **b** : growing vegetatively during the first year and fruiting and dying during the second — **biennial** *n* — **bi·en·ni·al·ly** \-ē-ə-lē\ *adv*

bi·en·ni·um \bī-'en-ē-əm\ *n* [L, fr. *bi-* + *annus* year] : a period of two years

bier \'bi(ə)r\ *n* [OE *bēr;* akin to E [2]*bear*] : a stand on which a corpse or coffin is placed; *also* : a coffin together with its stand

bi·fa·cial·ly \(')bī-'fā-shə-lē\ *adv* : on two and usu. opposite sides ⟨*bifacially* flattened⟩

bi·fid \'bī-,fid, -fəd\ *adj* [L *bifidus,* fr. *bi-* + *findere* to split] : divided into two equal lobes or parts by a median cleft ⟨a *bifid* leaf⟩ — **bi·fid·i·ty** \bī-'fid-ət-ē\ *n* — **bi·fid·ly** *adv*

[1]**bi·fo·cal** \(')bī-'fō-kəl\ *adj* : having two focal lengths

[2]**bifocal** *n* **1** : a bifocal glass or lens **2** *pl* : eyeglasses with bifocal lenses

bi·fur·cate \'bī-fər-,kāt, bī-'fər-\ *vb* [L *furca* fork] : to divide into two branches or parts — **bi·fur·cate** \(')bī-'fər-kət, -,kāt; 'bī-fər-,kāt\ *adj* — **bi·fur·cate·ly** *adv* — **bi·fur·ca·tion** \,bī-(,)fər-'kā-shən\ *n*

[1]**big** \'big\ *adj* **big·ger; big·gest** [ME] **1** : of great force ⟨a *big* storm⟩ **2 a** : large in size, bulk, or extent ⟨a *big* house⟩ ⟨a *big* herd⟩ **b** : conducted on a large scale ⟨*big* government⟩ **c** : PREGNANT **b** : full to bursting : SWELLING **c** : being full and resonant ⟨a *big* voice⟩ **4 a** : CHIEF, PREEMINENT **b** : of great importance or significance ⟨the *big* moment⟩ **c** : IMPOSING, PRETENTIOUS; *also* : BOASTFUL ⟨*big* talk⟩ **d** : MAGNANIMOUS **syn** see LARGE — **big·ness** *n*

[2]**big** *adv* **1** : to a large amount or extent **2 a** : in an outstanding manner **b** : POMPOUSLY, PRETENTIOUSLY **c** : MAGNANIMOUSLY

big·a·mist \'big-ə-məst\ *n* : one who practices bigamy

big·a·my \'big-ə-mē\ *n* [Gk *gamos* marriage] : the act of marrying one person while still legally married to another — **big·a·mous** \-məs\ *adj* — **big·a·mous·ly** *adv*

big bang theory *n* : a theory in astronomy: the universe originated billions of years ago from the explosion of a single mass of material so that the pieces are still flying apart — compare STEADY STATE THEORY

Big Bear *n* : URSA MAJOR

big business *n* : large-scale industries or grouped enterprises often favoring monopoly

Big Dipper *n* : DIPPER 2a

bi·ge·ner·ic \,bī-jə-'ner-ik\ *adj* : of, relating to, or involving two genera ⟨a *bigeneric* hybrid⟩

big·eye \'big-,ī\ *n* : either of two small widely distributed marine reddish to silvery food fishes related to the perches

big·gish \'big-ish\ *adj* : somewhat big : comparatively big

big·horn \'big-,hörn\ *n, pl* **bighorn** *or* **bighorns** : a usu. grayish brown wild sheep of mountainous western No. America

bight \'bīt\ *n* [OE *byht* bend] **1** : the slack middle part of a rope when it is fastened at both ends : a loop or double part of a bent rope **2** : a bend or curve esp. in a river **3** : a bend in a coast or the bay it forms

big·ot \'big-ət\ *n* [MF] : a person obstinately or intolerantly devoted to his own group, beliefs, or opinions

bighorn

big·ot·ed \'big-ət-əd\ *adj* : obstinately attached to a belief, opinion, or practice and intolerant of the ideas and opinions of others

big·ot·ry \'big-ə-trē\ *n, pl* **-ries** : the state of mind of a bigot; *also* : behavior or beliefs arising from such a state of mind

big shot *n* : an important person

big stick *n* : coercive use or threat of military or political intervention

big time *n* **1** : a high-paying vaudeville circuit requiring only two performances a day **2** : the top rank

big toe *n* : the innermost and largest digit of the foot

big top *n* **1** : the main tent of a circus **2** : CIRCUS 2

big tree \-,trē\ *n* : a California evergreen of the pine family that often exceeds 300 feet in height — compare SEQUOIA

big·wig \'big-,wig\ *n* : an important person

bike \'bīk\ *n or vi* : BICYCLE — **bik·er** *n*

bi·ki·ni \bə-'kē-nē\ *n* [F, fr. *Bikini,* atoll of the Marshall islands] : a woman's abbreviated two-piece bathing suit

bi·la·bi·al \(')bī-'lā-bē-əl\ *adj* : of, relating to, or produced with both lips ⟨a *bilabial* consonant⟩

bi·la·bi·ate \-bē-ət\ *adj* : having two lips ⟨a *bilabiate* corolla of a mint⟩

bi·lat·er·al \(')bī-'lat-ə-rəl, -'la-trəl\ *adj* **1** : having or involving two sides; *esp* : affecting reciprocally two sides or parties ⟨a *bilateral* treaty⟩ **2** : bilaterally symmetrical — **bi·lat·er·al·ism** \-,iz-əm\ *n* — **bi·lat·er·al·ly** \-ē\ *adv* — **bi·lat·er·al·ness** *n*

bilateral symmetry *n* : a pattern of animal symmetry in which similar parts are arranged on opposite sides of a median axis so that one and only one plane can divide the individual into essentially identical halves — compare RADIAL SYMMETRY

bil·ber·ry \'bil-,ber-ē\ *n* : any of several blueberries with flowers and fruit borne in leaf axils; *also* : the sweet edible bluish fruit

bil·bo *or* **bil·boa** \'bil-,bō\ *n* : a finely tempered sword

bile \'bīl\ *n* [L *bilis*] **1** : a thick bitter yellow or greenish fluid secreted by the liver and used in the duodenum to aid in the digestion and absorption of fats **2** : proneness to anger : SPLEEN

bile duct *n* : a canal by which bile passes from the liver or gall bladder to the duodenum

[1]**bilge** \'bilj\ *n* **1** : the bulging part of a cask or barrel **2 a** : the part of a ship's hull between the flat of the bottom and the vertical topsides **b** : the lowest point of a ship's inner hull **3** : stale or worthless remarks or ideas

[2]**bilge** *vi* : to undergo damage (as a fracture) in the bilge

bilge water *n* : water that collects in the bilge of a ship

bil·i·ary \'bil-ē-,er-ē, 'bil-yə-rē\ *adj* : of, relating to, or conveying bile

bi·lin·gual \(')bī-'liŋ-gwəl\ *adj* [L *lingua* tongue, language] **1** : of, containing, or expressed in two languages ⟨a *bilingual* dictionary⟩ **2** : using or able to use two languages esp. with the fluency characteristic of a native speaker

bil·ious \'bil-yəs\ *adj* **1 a** : of or relating to bile **b** : marked by or suffering from disordered liver function **2** : of a peevish ill-natured disposition : CHOLERIC — **bil·ious·ly** *adv* — **bil·ious·ness** *n*

bil·i·ru·bin \,bil-ə-'rü-bən, ,bī-lə-\ *n* [L *ruber* red] : a reddish yellow pigment occurring in bile, blood, urine, and gallstones

bil·i·ver·din \-'vərd-ᵊn\ *n* [obs. F *verd* green] : a green pigment occurring in bile

bilk \'bilk\ *vt* : to cheat out of what is due : SWINDLE

[1]**bill** \'bil\ *n* [OE *bile*] **1** : the jaws of a bird together with their horny covering — see BIRD illustration **2** : a beak (as of a turtle) or mouth structure resembling a bird's bill **3** : a projection of land like a beak **4** : the visor of a cap *syn* see BEAK — **billed** \'bild\ *adj*

[2]**bill** *vi* **1** : to touch bill to bill **2** : to caress affectionately ⟨lovers *billing* and cooing⟩

[3]**bill** *n* [OE] : a weapon used up to the 18th century that consists of a long staff terminating in a hook-shaped blade

[4]**bill** *n* [ML *billa* formal document, alter. of *bulla* seal, sealed document, fr. L, bubble, boss] **1** : a draft of a law presented to a legislature for enactment **2** : a written declaration of a wrong one person has suffered from another or of a breach of law by some person **3** : a written list or statement of particulars **4** : an itemized account of the cost of goods sold, services rendered, or work done : INVOICE **5 a** : a written or printed advertisement posted or distributed to announce an event (as a theatrical entertainment) of interest to the public **b** : a programmed presentation : the entertainment presented on a given program **6** : NOTE 2f(1); *esp* : a piece of paper money

[5]**bill** *vt* **1 a** : to enter in a book of accounts : make a bill ⟨of charges⟩ ⟨*bill* the goods to my account⟩ **b** : to submit a bill of charges to ⟨*bill* a customer⟩ **2 a** : to advertise esp. by posters or placards **b** : to arrange for the presentation of ⟨*billed* the play for three weeks⟩ — **bill·er** *n*

bill·board \'bil-,bōrd, -,bȯrd\ *n* : a flat surface on which bills are posted; *esp* : a large panel designed to carry outdoor advertising

bill·bug \-,bəg\ *n* : a usu. small dark weevil with larvae that eat the roots of grasses

¹bil·let \'bil-ət\ *n* [MF *billette* note, letter, alter. of *bullette*, dim. of *bulle* document, fr. ML *bulla*] **1** : an official order directing that a soldier be lodged (as in a private home) **2** : quarters assigned by or as if by a billet **3** : BERTH, POSITION ⟨a soft *billet*⟩

²billet *vb* **1** : to assign lodging to by a billet : QUARTER **2** : to have quarters : LODGE

³billet *n* [MF *billette*, dim. of *bille* log, of Celt origin] **1** : a chunky piece of wood (as for firewood) **2** : a bar of metal; *esp* : one of iron or steel

bil·let-doux \,bil-(,)ā-'dü\ *n, pl* **bil·lets-doux** \-(,)ā-'dü(z)\ [F *billet doux*, lit., sweet note] : a love letter

bill·fold \'bil-,fōld\ *n* **1** : a folding pocketbook for paper money **2** : WALLET 2b

bill·head \-,hed\ *n* : a printed form usu. headed with a business address and used for billing charges

bil·liard \'bil-yərd\ *n* **1** : CAROM 1 — used as an attributive form of *billiards* ⟨*billiard* ball⟩

bil·liards \-yərdz\ *n* [MF *billard* billiard cue, billiards, fr. *bille* log] : any of several games played on an oblong table by driving small balls against one another or into pockets with a cue; *esp* : a game in which one scores by causing a cue ball to hit in succession two object balls

bil·lings·gate \'bil-iŋz-,gāt\ *n* [*Billingsgate*, a fish market, London, England] : coarsely abusive language

bil·lion \'bil-yən\ *n* [F, fr. *bi-* + *-llion* (as in *million*)] **1** — see NUMBER table **2** : a very large or indefinitely large number ⟨*billions* of dollars⟩ — **billion** *adj* — **bil·lionth** \-yən(t)th\ *adj* — **billionth** *n*

bil·lion·aire \,bil-yə-'na(ə)r, -'ne(ə)r, 'bil-yə-,\ *n* : one whose wealth is a billion or more

bill of exchange : a written order from one person to another to pay a specified sum of money to a designated person : DRAFT 11a

bill of fare : MENU

bill of health : a certificate of the state of health of a ship's company and of a port with regard to infectious diseases given to the ship's master at the time of leaving

bill of lad·ing \-'lād-iŋ\ : a receipt listing goods shipped that is signed by the agent of the owner of a ship or issued by a common carrier

bill of rights *often cap B&R* : a statement of fundamental rights and privileges guaranteed to a people against violation by the state; *esp* : the first 10 amendments to the U.S. Constitution

bill of sale : a formal document for conveyance or transfer of title to goods and chattels

¹bil·low \'bil-ō\ *n* **1** : WAVE; *esp* : a great wave or surge of water **2** : a rolling mass (as of flame or smoke) like a high wave

²billow *vb* **1** : to rise or roll in waves or surges ⟨the *billowing* ocean⟩ **2** : to bulge or swell out (as through action of the wind) ⟨sails *billowing* in the breeze⟩ ⟨the wind *billowed* her skirt⟩

bil·lowy \'bil-ə-wē\ *adj* **bil·low·i·er**; **-est** : characterized by billows

bil·ly \'bil-ē\ *n, pl* **billies** : a heavy usu. wooden club; *esp* : a policeman's club

billy goat \'bil-ē-\ *n* : a male goat

bi·lo·bate \(')bī-'lō-,bāt\ *also* **bi·lo·bat·ed** \-,bāt-əd\ *adj* : divided into two lobes

bi·lobed \'bī-'lōbd\ *adj* : BILOBATE

bi·loc·u·lar \(')bī-'läk-yə-lər\ *or* **bi·loc·u·late** \-lət\ *adj* [*bi-* + NL *loculus*] : divided into two cells or compartments

bi·met·al \'bī-,met-ªl\ *adj* : BIMETALLIC

bi·me·tal·lic \,bī-mə-'tal-ik\ *adj* **1** : of or relating to bimetallism **2** : composed of two different metals — often used of devices having a part in which two metals that expand differently are bonded together — **bimetallic** *n*

bi·met·al·lism \(')bī-'met-ªl-,iz-əm\ *n* : the use of two metals (as gold and silver) jointly as a monetary standard with both constituting legal tender at a legally fixed ratio — **bi·met·al·list** \-ªl-əst\ *n* — **bi·met·al·lis·tic** \,bī-,met-ªl-'is-tik\ *adj*

¹bi·month·ly \(')bī-'mən(t)th-lē\ *adj* **1** : occurring every two months **2** : occurring twice a month : SEMIMONTHLY

²bimonthly *n* : a bimonthly publication

³bimonthly *adv* **1** : once every two months **2** : twice a month

bin \'bin\ *n* [OE *binn*] : a box, frame, crib, or enclosed place used for storage

¹bi·na·ry \'bī-nə-rē\ *adj* [L *bini* two each; akin to E *two*] **1** : compounded or consisting of or characterized by two often similar things or parts ⟨*binary* fission of the cell⟩ **2** : relating to, being, or belonging to a system of numbers having two as its base ⟨*binary* digit⟩

²binary *n, pl* **-ries** : something constituted of two things or parts

binary star *n* : a system of two stars that revolve around each other under their mutual gravitation

bin·au·ral \(')bī-'nȯr-əl\ *adj* [L *bini* two each + *auris* ear] **1** : of, relating to, or used with two or both ears **2** : of, relating to, or characterized by the placement of sound sources (as in sound transmission and recording) to achieve in sound reproduction an effect of hearing the sound sources in their original positions — **bin·au·ral·ly** \-ə-lē\ *adv*

¹bind \'bīnd\ *vb* **bound** \'baund\; **bind·ing** [OE *bindan*] **1 a** : to make secure by tying **b** : to confine, restrain, or restrict as if with bonds **c** : to put under an obligation ⟨*bound* himself with an oath⟩ **2 a** : to wrap around with something so as to enclose, encircle, or cover **b** : BANDAGE **3** : to tie or fasten together ⟨*bind* the stalks into sheaves⟩ **4 a** : to stick together **b** : to form a cohesive mass **c** : to take up and hold by chemical forces **5** : CONSTIPATE **6** : to make firm or sure ⟨a deposit *binds* the sale⟩ **7 a** : to protect, strengthen, or decorate by a band or binding **b** : to apply the parts of the cover to (a book) **8** : INDENTURE, APPRENTICE **9** : to cause to be attached (as by gratitude)

²bind *n* : something that binds

bind·er \'bīn-dər\ *n* **1** : a person that binds something (as books) **2 a** : something used in binding **b** : a detachable cover or device for holding together sheets of paper or similar material **c** : a harvesting machine that cuts grain and ties it in bundles **d** : a band applied (as about the abdomen) for support **3** : something (as tar or cement) that produces or promotes cohesion in loosely assembled substances

bind·ery \'bīn-d(ə-)rē\ *n, pl* **-er·ies** : a place where books are bound

bind·ing \'bīn-diŋ\ *n* **1** : the action of one that binds **2** : a material or device used to bind: as **a** : the cover and fastenings of a book **b** : a narrow fabric used to finish raw edges

binding energy *n* : the energy required to break up a molecule, atom, or atomic nucleus completely into its constituent particles

bind·weed \'bīnd-,wēd\ *n* : any of various twining plants esp. of the morning-glory family that mat or interlace with plants among which they grow

bine \'bīn\ *n* [alter. of ²*bind*] : a twining stem or flexible shoot (as of the hop)

binge \'binj\ *n* **1** : CAROUSAL, SPREE **2** : an unrestrained indulgence ⟨a buying *binge*⟩

bin·na·cle \'bin-i-kəl\ *n* [alter. of ME *bitakille*, fr. L *habitaculum* habitation, fr. *habitare* to dwell] : a case, box, or stand containing a ship's compass and a lamp

¹bin·oc·u·lar \bī-'näk-yə-lər, bə-\ *adj* [L *bini* two each + *oculus* eye] : of, relating to, using, or adapted to the use of both eyes ⟨*binocular* vision⟩ — **bin·oc·u·lar·ly** *adv*

²bin·oc·u·lar \bə-'näk-yə-lər, bī-\ *n* **1** : a binocular optical instrument **2** : FIELD GLASS — usu. used in pl.

bi·no·mi·al \bī-'nō-mē-əl\ *n* [NL *binomium*, fr. L *bi-* + *nomen* name, term] **1** : a mathematical expression consisting of two terms connected by a plus sign or minus sign **2** : a biological species name consisting of two terms — **binomial** *adj* — **bi·no·mi·al·ly** \-mē-ə-lē\ *adv*

binomial nomenclature *n* : a system of nomenclature in which each species of animal or plant receives a binomial name of which the first term identifies the genus to which it belongs and the second the species itself

binomial theorem *n* : a theorem by means of which a binomial may be raised to any power by formula

bi·nu·cle·ar \(')bī-'n(y)ü-klē-ər\ *or* **bi·nu·cle·ate**

---

j joke; ŋ sing; ō flow; ȯ flaw; ȯi coin; th thin; th̲ this; ü loot; u̇ foot; y yet; yü few; yu̇ furious; zh vision

\-klē-ət\ *or* **bi·nu·cle·at·ed** \-klē-ˌāt-əd\ *adj* : having two nuclei

bio- *comb form* [Gk *bios* life, mode of life; akin to E *quick*] **1** : life ⟨bio*sphere*⟩ **2** : living organisms or tissue ⟨*bio*luminescence⟩

bio·as·say \ˌbī-ō-'as-ˌā, -a-'sā\ *n* : determination of relative strength (as of a drug) by comparison of effect on a test organism with that of a standard preparation — **bio·as·say** \-a-'sā, -'as-ˌā\ *vt*

bio·chem·i·cal \ˌbī-ō-'kem-i-kəl\ *adj* : of or relating to biochemistry — **bio·chem·i·cal·ly** \-k(ə-)lē\ *adv*

bio·chem·is·try \-'kem-ə-strē\ *n* : chemistry that deals with the chemical compounds and processes occurring in organisms — **bio·chem·ist** \-'kem-əst\ *n*

bio·de·grad·able \-di-'grād-ə-bəl\ *adj* : capable of being broken down esp. into innocuous products by the action of living beings (as microorganisms) — **bio·de·grad·abil·i·ty** \-ˌgrād-ə-'bil-ət-ē\ *n* — **bio·de·grade** \-di-'grād\ *vt*

bio·ecol·o·gy \ˌbī-ō-i-'käl-ə-jē\ *n* : ecology dealing with the interrelation of plants and animals with their common environment

bio·fla·vo·noid \ˌbī-ō-'flā-və-ˌnòid\ *n* : any of several related chemical compounds that occur in plants and have an important effect on the functioning of minute blood vessels in mammals — called also *vitamin P*

bio·gen·e·sis \ˌbī-ō-'jen-ə-səs\ *n, pl* **-gen·e·ses** \-'jen-ə-ˌsēz\ **1** : the development of life from preexisting life **2** : an assumed tendency for stages in the evolutionary history of a race to briefly recur during the development and differentiation of an individual of that race — **bio·ge·net·ic** \-jə-'net-ik\ *adj* — **bio·ge·net·i·cal·ly** \-'net-i-k(ə-)lē\ *adv*

bio·ge·og·ra·phy \ˌbī-ō-jē-'äg-rə-fē\ *n* : a branch of biology that deals with the geographical distribution of animals and plants — **bio·ge·og·ra·pher** \-jē-'äg-rə-fər\ *n* — **bio·geo·graph·ic** \-ˌjē-ə-'graf-ik\ *or* **bio·geo·graph·i·cal** \-'graf-i-kəl\ *adj*

bi·og·ra·pher \bī-'äg-rə-fər, bē-\ *n* : a writer of a biography

bio·graph·i·cal \ˌbī-ə-'graf-i-kəl\ *or* **bio·graph·ic** \-'graf-ik\ *adj* **1** : of, relating to, or constituting biography ⟨*biographical* sketch⟩ **2** : consisting of biographies ⟨*biographical* dictionary⟩ — **bio·graph·i·cal·ly** \-'graf-i-k(ə-)lē\ *adv*

bi·og·ra·phy \bī-'äg-rə-fē, bē-\ *n, pl* **-phies** **1** : a usu. written history of a person's life **2** : biographical writings in general **3** : a life history ⟨*biography* of a building⟩

¹**bi·o·log·i·cal** \ˌbī-ə-'läj-i-kəl\ *or* **bi·o·log·ic** \-'läj-ik\ *adj* : of or relating to biology or to life and living processes ⟨*biological* supplies⟩⟨*biological* forces⟩ — **bi·o·log·i·cal·ly** \-'läj-i-k(ə-)lē\ *adv*

²**biological** *or* **biologic** *n* : a medicinal product of biological origin

biological clock *n* : an inherent timing mechanism in a living being responsible for various cyclical physiological and behavioral responses

biological control *n* : attack upon pests (as vermin) by interference with their ecology

bi·ol·o·gy \bī-'äl-ə-jē\ *n* **1 a** : a branch of knowledge that deals with living organisms and life processes **b** : ECOLOGY **2 a** : the plant and animal life of a region or environment **b** : the laws and phenomena relating to an organism or group — **bi·ol·o·gist** \-jəst\ *n*

bio·lu·mi·nes·cence \ˌbī-ō-ˌlü-mə-'nes-ᵊn(t)s\ *n* : the emission of light by living organisms — **bio·lu·mi·nes·cent** \-ᵊnt\ *adj*

bi·ome \'bī-ˌōm\ *n* : a major ecological community type

bi·o·nom·ic \ˌbī-ə-'näm-ik\ *adj* [F *bionomie* ecology, fr. *bio-* + Gk *nomos* law] : ECOLOGICAL — **bi·o·nom·i·cal** \-i-kəl\ *adj* — **bi·o·nom·i·cal·ly** \-'näm-i-k(ə-)lē\ *adv*

bio·phys·ics \'bī-ō-ˌfiz-iks\ *n* : a branch of knowledge concerned with the application of physical principles and methods to biological problems — **bio·phys·i·cal** \ˌbī-ō-'fiz-i-kəl\ *adj* — **bio·phys·i·cist** \-'fiz-ə-səst\ *n*

bi·op·sy \'bī-ˌäp-sē\ *n, pl* **-sies** [Gk *bios* life + E *-opsy* (as in *autopsy*)] : the removal and examination of tissue, cells, or fluids from the living body

bio·sphere \'bī-ə-ˌsfi(ə)r\ *n* : the part of the world in which life can exist

bio·syn·the·sis \ˌbī-ō-'sin(t)-thə-səs\ *n* : the production

of a chemical compound by a living organism — **bio·syn·thet·ic** \-sin-'thet-ik\ *adj*

bi·o·ta \bī-'ōt-ə\ *n* [NL, fr. Gk *biotē* life] : the flora and fauna of a region

bi·ot·ic \bī-'ät-ik\ *adj* [Gk *biōtikos*, fr. *bioun* to live, fr. *bios* life] : of or relating to life; *esp* : caused by living beings

biotic potential *n* : the inherent capacity of an organism or species to reproduce and survive

bi·o·tin \'bī-ə-tən\ *n* [Gk *biotos* life, sustenance; akin to Gk *bios*] : a colorless crystalline growth vitamin of the vitamin B complex found esp. in yeast, liver, and egg yolk

bi·o·tite \'bī-ə-ˌtīt\ *n* [Jean B. *Biot* d1862 French mathematician] : a generally black or dark green mica containing iron, magnesium, potassium, and aluminum

bio·type \'bī-ə-ˌtīp\ *n* : organisms with a common genotype; *also* : their genotype or its distinguishing peculiarity

bi·pa·ren·tal \ˌbī-pə-'rent-ᵊl\ *adj* : involving or derived from two parents ⟨*biparental* reproduction⟩

bi·par·ti·san \(')bī-'pärt-ə-zən\ *adj* : representing, composed of, or formulated by members of two parties ⟨a *bipartisan* foreign policy⟩ — **bi·par·ti·san·ism** \-zə-ˌniz-əm\ *n* — **bi·par·ti·san·ship** \-zən-ˌship\ *n*

bi·par·tite \(')bī-'pär-ˌtīt\ *adj* **1** : being in two parts **2** : shared by two ⟨*bipartite* treaty⟩ — **bi·par·tite·ly** *adv* — **bi·par·ti·tion** \ˌbī-ˌpär-'tish-ən\ *n*

bi·ped \'bī-ˌped\ *n* [L *bi-* + *ped-, pes* foot] : a 2-footed animal — **biped** *or* **bi·ped·al** \(')bī-'ped-ᵊl\ *adj*

bi·plane \'bī-ˌplān\ *n* : an airplane with two main supporting surfaces usu. placed one above the other

bi·po·lar \(')bī-'pō-lər\ *adj* **1** : having or involving two poles **2** : having or marked by two mutually repellent forces or diametrically opposed natures or views — **bi·po·lar·i·ty** \ˌbī-pō-'lar-ət-ē\ *n*

bi·ra·cial \(')bī-'rā-shəl\ *adj* : of, relating to, or involving members of two races — **bi·ra·cial·ism** \-shə-ˌliz-əm\ *n*

bi·ra·di·al \(')bī-'rād-ē-əl\ *adj* : having both bilateral and radial symmetry — **bi·ra·di·al·ly** \-ē-ə-lē\ *adv*

bi·ra·mous \(')bī-'rā-məs\ *adj* : having two branches

¹**birch** \'bərch\ *n* [OE *beorc*] **1** : any of a genus of deciduous usu. short-lived trees or shrubs with simple petioled leaves and typically a layered membranous outer bark that peels readily; *also* : its hard pale close-grained wood **2** : a birch rod or bundle of twigs for flogging — **birch** *or* **birch·en** \'bər-chən\ *adj*

²**birch** *vt* : to beat with or as if with a birch : WHIP

¹**bird** \'bərd\ *n* [OE *bridd*] **1** : any of a class (Aves) of warm-blooded egg-laying vertebrate animals with the body covered with feathers and the forelimbs modified as wings **2** *slang* : FELLOW; *esp* : a peculiar person

²**bird** *vi* : to observe or identify wild birds in their natural environment — **bird·er** *n*

bird·bath \'bərd-ˌbath, -ˌbȧth\ *n* : a usu. ornamental basin set up for birds to bathe in

bird·brain \-ˌbrān\ *n* : a stupid or a flighty thoughtless person

bird dog *n* : a dog trained to hunt or retrieve birds

bird·house \'bərd-ˌhaús\ *n* : an artificial nesting place for birds; *also* : AVIARY

¹**bird·ie** \'bərd-ē\ *n* : a golf score of one stroke less than par on a hole

²**birdie** *vt* : to shoot (a hole in golf) in one stroke under par

bird·lime \'bərd-ˌlīm\ *n* : a sticky substance smeared on twigs to catch and hold small birds

bird louse *n* : any of numerous wingless insects (order Mallophaga) that are mostly parasitic on birds

bird·man \'bərd-mən\ *n* **1** : one who deals with birds **2** : AVIATOR

bird of paradise : any of numerous brilliantly colored plumed birds related to the crows and found in the New Guinea area

bird of passage : a migratory bird

bird of prey : a carnivorous bird that feeds wholly or chiefly on meat taken by hunting

bird (waxwing): *1* bill, *2* forehead, *3* crown, *4* crest, *5* auricular region, *6* throat, *7* breast, *8* abdomen, *9* under tail coverts, *10* tail, *11* primaries, *12* secondaries, *13* upper wing coverts, *14* scapulars

ə abut; ᵊ kitten; ər further; a back; ā bake; ä cot, cart; au̇ out; ch chin; e less; ē easy; g gift; i trip; ī life

bird·seed \'bərd-ˌsēd\ n : a mixture of small seeds (as of hemp or millet) used chiefly for feeding cage birds

bird's-eye \'bərd-ˌzī\ adj 1 a : seen from above as if by a flying bird ⟨bird's-eye view⟩ b : CURSORY 2 : marked with spots resembling birds' eyes ⟨bird's-eye maple⟩; also : made of bird's-eye wood

bird's-foot trefoil \ˌbərdz-ˌfüt-\ n : a European legume with claw-shaped pods that is widely used as a forage and fodder plant

bi·rec·tan·gu·lar \ˌbī-ˌrek-'taŋ-gyə-lər\ adj : having two right angles ⟨a birectangular spherical triangle⟩

bi·reme \'bī-ˌrēm\ n [L remus oar] : a galley with two banks of oars

bi·ret·ta \bə-'ret-ə\ n [It berretta, fr. OProv berret cap] : a square cap with three upright projecting pieces extending from the center of the top to the edges worn ceremonially by clergymen esp. of the Roman Catholic Church

birth \'bərth\ n [ON byrth; akin to E ²bear] 1 a : the emergence of a new individual from the body of its parent b : the act or process of bringing forth young from the womb 2 : LINEAGE, EXTRACTION ⟨a man of noble birth⟩ 3 : BEGINNING, ORIGIN ⟨birth of an idea⟩

birth·day \-ˌdā\ n 1 : the day or anniversary of one's birth 2 : the day or anniversary of a beginning

birth·mark \-ˌmärk\ n : an unusual mark or blemish on the skin at birth — **birthmark** vt

birth·place \-ˌplās\ n : place of birth or origin

birth·rate \-ˌrāt\ n : the number of births for every hundred or every thousand persons in a given area or group during a given time

birth·right \-ˌrīt\ n : a right, privilege, or possession to which a person is entitled by birth

birth·stone \-ˌstōn\ n : a precious stone associated symbolically with the month of one's birth

Bi·sa·yan \bə-'sī-ən\ n : a member of any of several peoples of the Visayan islands, Philippines

bis·cuit \'bis-kət\ n, pl biscuits also biscuit [MF bescuit, fr. bescuit twice-cooked] 1 : a crisp flat cake; esp, Brit : CRACKER 2 2 : earthenware or porcelain after the first firing and before glazing 3 : a small quick bread made from dough that has been rolled and cut or dropped from a spoon

bi·sect \'bī-ˌsekt, bī-'\ vb [bi- + L sect-, secare to cut] : to divide into two usu. equal parts : SEPARATE; also : CROSS, INTERSECT — **bi·sec·tion** \'bī-ˌsek-shən, bī-'\ — **bi·sec·tion·al** \-shnəl, -shən-ᵊl\ adj — **bi·sec·tion·al·ly** \-ē\ adv

bi·sec·tor \'bī-ˌsek-tər, bī-'\ n : one that bisects; esp : a straight line that bisects an angle or a line segment

bi·sex·u·al \(')bī-'sek-sh(ə-w)əl\ adj 1 : possessing characters of or sexually oriented toward both sexes 2 : of, relating to, or involving two sexes — **bisexual** n — **bi·sex·u·al·i·ty** \ˌbī-ˌsek-shə-'wal-ət-ē\ n — **bi·sex·u·al·ly** \(')bī-'sek-sh(ə-w)ə-lē\ adv

bish·op \'bish-əp\ n [OE bisceop, fr. LL episcopus, fr. Gk episkopos, lit., overseer, fr. epi- + skop-, skeptesthai to look at] 1 a : a clergyman ranking above a priest, having authority to ordain and confirm, and typically governing a diocese b : a clergyman who oversees a church district 2 : a chess piece that can move diagonally across any number of unoccupied squares

bish·op·ric \'bish-ə-(ˌ)prik\ n [OE bisceoprīce, fr. bisceop bishop + rīce realm] 1 : DIOCESE 2 : the office of bishop 3 : a bishop's seat or residence

bis·muth \'biz-məth\ n [G wismut, bismut] : a heavy brittle grayish white metallic element that is chemically like arsenic and antimony and is used in alloys and medicine — see ELEMENT table

bi·son \'bīs-ᵊn, 'bīz-\ n, pl bison [L, of Gmc origin] : any of several large shaggy-maned usu. gregarious recent or extinct mammals of the ox family with a large head, short horns, and heavy forequarters surmounted by a large fleshy hump: as a : WISENT b : BUFFALO b — **bi·son·tine** \-ᵊn-ˌtīn\ adj

bisque \'bisk\ n [F] 1 : a thick cream soup made of shellfish, meat, or vegetables 2 : ice cream containing powdered nuts or macaroons

bis·ter or **bis·tre** \'bis-tər\ n : a grayish to yellowish brown

bis·tro \'bis-ˌtrō\ n, pl bistros [F] 1 : a small or un-

pretentious European wineshop or restaurant 2 a : BAR b : NIGHTCLUB

bi·sul·fate \(')bī-'səl-ˌfāt\ n : an acid sulfate

bi·sul·fide \-ˌfīd\ n : DISULFIDE

bi·sul·fite \-ˌfīt\ n : an acid sulfite

¹bit \'bit\ n [ME bitt, fr. OE bite action of biting] 1 : the part of a bridle inserted in the mouth of a horse 2 : the biting or cutting edge or part of a tool; also : a replaceable part of a compound tool that actually performs the function (as drilling or boring) for which the whole tool (as a brace or drilling machine) is designed 3 : something that curbs or restrains

²bit vt bit·ted; bit·ting 1 : to put a bit in the mouth of (a horse) 2 : to control as if with a bit : CURB

³bit n [OE bita piece bitten off] 1 a : a small piece ⟨a bit of cheese⟩ b : AMOUNT, QUANTITY ⟨a little bit of luck⟩; esp : a small amount or quantity ⟨with a bit of luck⟩ 2 : a short time : WHILE ⟨rest a bit⟩ 3 : SOMEWHAT ⟨a bit of a fool⟩

⁴bit n [binary digit] 1 : a unit of information equivalent to the result of a choice between two equally probable alternatives 2 : a unit of computer memory corresponding to the ability to store the result of a choice between two alternatives

bitch \'bich\ n [OE bicce] : the female of the dog

¹bite \'bīt\ vb bit \'bit\; bit·ten \'bit-ᵊn\; bit·ing \'bīt-iŋ\ [OE bītan] 1 : to seize, grip, or cut into with or as if with teeth ⟨bite an apple⟩ ⟨steam shovel bites into the earth⟩ 2 : to wound or pierce with or as if with fangs ⟨bitten by a snake⟩ 3 : to make a gash or cut ⟨the sword bit into his arm⟩ 4 : to cause to smart : STING ⟨pepper bites the mouth⟩ 5 : to eat into : CORRODE ⟨acid bites metal⟩ 6 : to respond to a lure : take a bait ⟨the fish are really biting⟩ — **bit·er** n — **bite the dust** : to fall dead esp. in battle

²bite n 1 : a seizing of something by biting; also : the grip taken in biting 2 a : the amount of food taken at a bite b : a light informal meal : SNACK 3 : a wound made by biting 4 : a keen incisive quality or sharp penetrating effect

bit·ing \'bīt-iŋ\ adj : SHARP, CUTTING ⟨biting remarks⟩ ⟨a biting wind⟩

bitt \'bit\ n : a single or double post on the deck of a ship for securing mooring lines

¹bit·ter \'bit-ər\ adj [OE biter; akin to E bite] 1 : having or being a disagreeable acrid taste that is one of the four basic taste sensations ⟨bitter as quinine⟩ 2 : marked by intensity or severity: a : hard to bear : PAINFUL ⟨bitter disappointment⟩ b : VEHEMENT, RELENTLESS ⟨bitter partisan⟩ c : sharp and resentful ⟨a bitter answer⟩ d : intensely unpleasant esp. in coldness or rawness ⟨a bitter wind⟩ 3 : expressive of severe pain, grief, or regret ⟨bitter tears⟩ — **bit·ter·ish** \'bit-ə-rish\ adj — **bit·ter·ly** \-ər-lē\ adv — **bit·ter·ness** n

²bitter adv : BITTERLY ⟨it's bitter cold⟩

bit·tern \'bit-ərn\ n [MF butor] : any of various small or medium-sized nocturnal herons with a characteristic booming cry

bit·ters \'bit-ərz\ n sing or pl : a usu. alcoholic solution of bitter and often aromatic plant products used in mixing drinks and as a mild tonic

¹bit·ter·sweet \'bit-ər-ˌswēt\ n 1 : something that is bittersweet 2 a : a sprawling poisonous weedy nightshade with purple flowers and oval reddish orange berries b : a No. American woody climbing plant with yellow capsules that open when ripe and disclose the scarlet seed covers

²bittersweet adj 1 : being both bitter and sweet 2 : of or relating to a prepared chocolate containing little sugar

bit·ty or **bit·tie** \'bit-ē\ adj, dial : SMALL, TINY ⟨a little bitty dog⟩

bi·tu·men \bə-'t(y)ü-mən, bī-\ n [L bitumin-, bitumen asphalt] : any of various mixtures of hydrocarbons (as asphalt, crude petroleum, or tar)

bi·tu·mi·nous \-mə-nəs\ adj 1 : resembling, containing, or impregnated with bitumen 2 : of or relating to bituminous coal

bituminous coal n : a coal that when heated yields considerable volatile bituminous matter — called also soft coal

bi·va·lence \(')bī-'vā-lən(t)s\ or **bi·va·len·cy** \-lən-sē\ n : the quality or state of being bivalent

¹**bi·va·lent** \-lənt\ *adj* **1** : having a valence of two **2** : associated in pairs in synapsis

²**bivalent** *n* : a pair of synaptic chromosomes

¹**bi·valve** \'bī-ˌvalv\ *also* **bi·valved** \-ˌvalvd\ *adj* **1** : having a shell composed of two movable valves **2** : having or consisting of two corresponding movable pieces

²**bivalve** *n* : an animal (as a clam) with a bivalve shell

¹**biv·ouac** \'biv-ˌwak, -ə-ˌwak\ *n* [F, fr. LG *biwake*, fr. *bi* by, at + *wake* guard] **1** : an encampment under little or no shelter usu. for a short time **2** : a camping out for a night; *also* : a temporary shelter or settlement

²**bivouac** *vi* **biv·ouacked**; **biv·ouack·ing** : to encamp with little or no shelter

¹**bi·week·ly** \(')bī-'wē-klē\ *adj* **1** : occurring, done, or produced every two weeks : FORTNIGHTLY **2** : occurring, done, or produced twice a week — **biweekly** *adv*

²**biweekly** *n* : a biweekly publication

bi·year·ly \(')bī-'yi(ə)r-lē\ *adj* **1** : BIENNIAL **2** : BIANNUAL

bi·zarre \bə-'zär\ *adj* [F, fr. It *bizarro*] : strikingly unusual or odd in appearance (as in fashion, design, or color) ⟨*bizarre* costumes of gypsies⟩ **syn** see FANTASTIC — **bi·zarre·ly** *adv* — **bi·zarre·ness** *n*

¹**blab** \'blab\ *n* **1** : TATTLETALE **2** : idle or excessive talk : CHATTER — **blab·by** \'blab-ē\ *adj*

²**blab** *vb* **blabbed**; **blab·bing** **1** : to reveal esp. by talking without reserve or discretion : TATTLE **2** : PRATTLE

¹**blab·ber** \'blab-ər\ *vb* **blab·bered**; **blab·ber·ing** \'blab-(ə-)riŋ\ : BABBLE, CHATTER

²**blabber** *n* : idle talk : BABBLE

³**blabber** *n* : one that blabs

blab·ber·mouth \'blab-ər-ˌmaüth\ *n* : one who talks too much; *esp* : TATTLETALE

¹**black** \'blak\ *adj* [OE *blæc*] **1 a** : of the color black **b** : very dark **2** : having dark skin, hair, and eyes : SWARTHY; *esp* : NEGROID **3 a** : EVIL, WICKED ⟨a *black* deed⟩ **b** : invoking evil supernatural powers ⟨*black* curse⟩ **4 a** : GLOOMY, CALAMITOUS ⟨the outlook was *black*⟩; *esp* : DISASTROUS **b** : SULLEN, HOSTILE — **black·ish** \-ish\ *adj* — **black·ly** *adv* — **black·ness** *n*

²**black** *n* **1** : a black pigment or dye; *esp* : one consisting largely of carbon **2** : the characteristic color of soot or coal **3** : something that is black; *esp* : black clothing **4** : a person belonging to a dark-skinned race **5** : absence of light : DARKNESS ⟨the *black* of night⟩ **6** : the condition of making a profit ⟨in the *black*⟩

³**black** *vb* : BLACKEN

black·a·moor \'blak-ə-ˌmü(ə)r\ *n* : a dark-skinned person; *esp* : NEGRO

black-and-blue \ˌblak-ən-'blü\ *adj* : darkly discolored (as from a bruise)

Black and Tan *n* **1** : a member of a faction of the Republican party favoring proportional representation of Negroes and whites in politics — compare LILY-WHITE **2** : one recruited in England in 1920–21 into the Royal Irish Constabulary to suppress the Irish revolution

black art *n* : magic practiced by conjurers and witches

black-a-vised \'blak-ə-ˌvīst\ *adj* : dark-complexioned

¹**black·ball** \'blak-ˌbȯl\ *n* **1** : a small black ball used to cast a negative vote **2** : an adverse vote; *esp* : one against admitting someone to membership in an organization

²**blackball** *vt* : to vote against; *esp* : to exclude from membership by casting a negative vote

black bass *n* : any of several highly prized freshwater sunfishes native to eastern and central No. America

black bear *n* : the common usu. largely black-furred bear of No. America

black belt *n* : an area inhabited by large numbers of Negroes

black·ber·ry \'blak-ˌber-ē\ *n* **1** : the usu. black or dark purple juicy but seedy edible fruit of various brambles **2** : a plant that bears blackberries

black·bird \'blak-ˌbərd\ *n* : any of various birds of which the males are largely or entirely black: as **a** : a common and familiar British thrush **b** : any of several American birds related to the bobolink

black·board \'blak-ˌbȯrd, -ˌbȯrd\ *n* : a hard smooth usu. dark surface used for writing or drawing on with chalk

black·body \'blak-'bäd-ē\ *n* : a body or surface that completely absorbs all radiant energy falling upon it with no reflection

black book *n* : a book containing a blacklist

black·cap \'blak-ˌkap\ *n* **1** : any of several black-crowned birds (as the chickadee) **2** : a black-fruited raspberry of eastern No. America — **black–capped** \-'kapt\ *adj*

black·cock \-ˌkäk\ *n* : BLACK GROUSE; *esp* : the male black grouse

black code *n* : a set of laws adopted in a southern state of the U.S. after the Civil War limiting the civil rights of Negroes

black crappie *n* : a silvery black-mottled sunfish of the central and eastern U.S.

black death *n* : a form of epidemic plague present in Europe and Asia in the 14th century

black·en \'blak-ən\ *vb* **black·ened**; **black·en·ing** \'blak-(ə-)niŋ\ **1** : to make or become black **2** : SOIL, DIRTY **3** : to injure the reputation of — **black·en·er** \-(ə-)nər\ *n*

black eye *n* : a puffy darkening of the area about an eye caused by bruising (as from a blow)

black-eyed pea \ˌblak-ˌīd-\ *n* : COWPEA

black-eyed Su·san \-'süz-ᵊn\ *n* : an American daisy with deep yellow or orange petals and a dark center

black·face \-ˌfās\ *n* : makeup for a Negro role esp. in a minstrel show

black·fish \-ˌfish\ *n* **1** : any of numerous dark-colored fishes; *esp* : a small food fish of Alaska and Siberia that is esp. resistant to cold **2** : any of several small toothed whales related to the dolphins

black flag *n* : a pirate's flag usu. bearing a skull and cross-bones

black·fly \'blak-ˌflī\ *n* : any of several small dark-colored insects; *esp* : a two-winged biting fly whose larvae live in flowing streams

Black·foot \-ˌfüt\ *n*, *pl* **Black·feet** \-ˌfēt\ *or* **Blackfoot** : a member of a people belonging to an Indian confederacy of Montana, Alberta, and Saskatchewan

black grouse *n* : a large grouse of Europe and western Asia of which the male is black with white wing patches and the female is barred and mottled

¹**black·guard** \'blag-ərd, -ˌärd; 'blak-ˌgärd\ *n* : a rude or unscrupulous person — **black·guard·ly** \-lē\ *adj or adv*

²**blackguard** *vt* : to abuse with bad language : REVILE

black gum *n* : an important timber tree of the southeastern U.S. with light and soft but tough wood

black hand *n*, *often cap* **B&H** : a Sicilian or Italian-American secret society engaged in crime (as terrorism or extortion) — **black–hand·er** *n*

black·head \'blak-ˌhed\ *n* : a small oily plug blocking the duct of a sebaceous gland

black·ing \'blak-iŋ\ *n* : a substance that is applied to an object to make it black; *esp* : a paste or liquid used in shining black shoes

black·jack \'blak-ˌjak\ *n* **1** : a small leather-covered club with a flexible handle **2** : a common often scrubby oak of the southern U.S. with black bark **3** : TWENTY-ONE

black lead \-'led\ *n* : GRAPHITE

black·leg \'blak-ˌleg\ *n*, *chiefly Brit* : SCAB 3b

black light *n* : invisible ultraviolet or infrared light

black·list \-ˌlist\ *n* : a list of persons who are disapproved of and are to be punished (as by refusal of jobs or a boycott) — **blacklist** *vt*

black lung *n* : a disease of the lungs caused by habitual inhalation of coal dust

black magic *n* : WITCHCRAFT

black·mail \-ˌmāl\ *n* [Sc *mail* payment, fr. OE *māl* agreement, pay, fr. ON, agreement] : extortion of money from a person by a threat to reveal some secret information that will bring trouble and disgrace upon him; *also* : the money extorted — **blackmail** *vt* — **black·mail·er** *n*

black mark *n* : a mark placed beside or as if beside a person's name to record a fault

black market *n* : trade in violation of government controls (as price controls, rationing regulations, or official currency exchange rates) or illegal trade in government property; *also* : a place where such activity is carried on — **black mar·ket·er** \-'mär-kət-ər\ *or* **black mar·ke·teer** \-ˌmär-kə-'ti(ə)r\ *n*

¹**black out** \(')blak-'aut\ *vb* **1** : to undergo a temporary loss of vision, consciousness, or memory **2** : to extinguish or screen all lights for protection esp. against air attack **3** : to cause to black out

²**black·out** \'blak-ˌaut\ *n* **1** : a period of darkness en-

forced as a precaution against air raids in wartime **2 : a** transient dulling or loss of vision or consciousness

black power *n* : the mobilization of the political and economic power of black Americans esp. to further racial equality

black sheep *n* : a discreditable member of an otherwise respectable group ⟨the *black sheep* of the family⟩

Black·shirt \'blak-,shərt\ *n* : a member of a fascist organization having a black shirt as a distinctive part of its uniform; *esp* : a member of the Italian Fascist party

black·smith \'blak-,smith\ *n* [fr. his working with iron, known as black metal] : a workman who shapes iron by heating it and then hammering it on an iron block — **black·smith·ing** *n*

black·snake \-,snāk\ *n* **1** : any of several snakes largely black or dark in color; *esp* : either of two large harmless snakes of the U.S. **2** : a long tapering braided whip

black studies *n pl* : studies (as history and literature) relating to the culture of black Americans

black·thorn \'blak-,thȯrn\ *n* **1** : a European spiny plum with hard wood and small white flowers **2** : any of several American hawthorns

black tie *n* : semiformal evening dress for men

black·top \'blak-,täp\ *n* : a bituminous material used esp. for surfacing roads — **blacktop** *vt*

black walnut *n* : a walnut of eastern No. America with hard strong heavy dark brown wood and oily edible nuts; *also* : its wood or nut

black widow *n* : a poisonous New World spider having the female black with an hourglass-shaped red mark on the underside of the abdomen

blad·der \'blad-ər\ *n* [OE *blǣdre*] **1** : a membranous sac in an animal in which a liquid or gas is stored; *esp* : one in a vertebrate into which urine passes from the kidneys **2** : something resembling a bladder; *esp* : an inflatable bag or container — **blad·der·like** \-,līk\ *adj*

bladder worm *n* : a bladderlike larval tapeworm

blad·der·wort \'blad-ər-,wərt, -,wȯrt\ *n* : any of several slender plants growing in water or on wet shores and having insect-catching bladders on the stem, scalelike leaves, and irregular yellow or purple flowers

blade \'blād\ *n* [OE *blæd*] **1 a** : a leaf of a plant and esp. of a grass   **b** : the broad flat part of a leaf as distinguished from its stalk — see LEAF illustration **2** : something resembling the blade of a leaf: as **a** : the broad flattened part of a paddle   **b** : an arm of a propeller, electric fan, or steam turbine   **c** : the upper flat part of the tongue immediately behind the tip **3 a** : the cutting part of an implement   **b** (1) : SWORD (2) : SWORDSMAN (3) : a jaunty rakish fellow ⟨gay *blade*⟩   **c** : the runner of an ice skate — **blad·ed** \'blād-əd\ *adj*

blain \'blān\ *n* : an inflammatory swelling or sore

¹blame \'blām\ *vt* [OF *blamer*, fr. LL *blasphemare* to blaspheme] **1** : to find fault with : CENSURE **2 a** : to hold responsible ⟨*blame* him for everything⟩   **b** : to place responsibility for ⟨*blames* it on me⟩ — **blam·a·ble** \'blā-mə-bəl\ *adj* — **blam·a·bly** \-ə-blē\ *adv* — **blam·er** *n*   **syn** CENSURE, CONDEMN: BLAME may imply simply the opposite of *praise* but often suggests an accusation or the placing of responsibility for something bad or unfortunate; CENSURE carries a stronger suggestion of authority and reprimanding than BLAME; CONDEMN usu. suggests an unqualified and final unfavorable judgment

²blame *n* **1** : expression of disapproval **2** : responsibility for something that fails : FAULT

blame·less \'blām-ləs\ *adj* : free from blame or fault — **blame·less·ly** *adv* — **blame·less·ness** *n*

blame·wor·thy \'blām-,wər-,thē\ *adj* : deserving blame — **blame·wor·thi·ness** *n*

blanch \'blanch\ *vb* [MF *blanchir*, fr. *blanc* white] **1** : to take the color out of: **a** : to bleach by excluding light ⟨*blanch* celery⟩   **b** : to scald in order to remove the skin from or whiten ⟨*blanch* almonds⟩ ⟨*blanch* kidney⟩ **2** : to become white or pale **syn** see WHITEN — **blanch·er** *n*

blanc·mange \blə-'mänj\ *n* [MF *blanc manger*, lit., white food] : a dessert made from gelatin or a starchy substance and milk usu. sweetened and flavored

bland \'bland\ *adj* [L *blandus*] **1** : smooth and soothing in manner : GENTLE ⟨a *bland* smile⟩ **2** : having soft and soothing qualities : not irritating ⟨*bland* diet⟩ **syn** see SUAVE — **bland·ly** *adv* — **bland·ness** \'blan(d)-nəs\ *n*

blan·dish \'blan-dish\ *vt* [MF *blandiss-*, *blandir*, fr. L *blandiri*, fr. *blandus* bland] : to coax with flattery : CAJOLE — **blan·dish·er** *n* — **blan·dish·ment** \-mənt\ *n*

¹blank \'blaŋk\ *adj* [MF *blanc* white, of Gmc origin] **1** : being without writing, printing, or marks ⟨*blank* sheet of paper⟩ **2** : having empty spaces to be filled in ⟨a *blank* form⟩ **3** : appearing dazed or confused : EXPRESSIONLESS ⟨*blank* look⟩ **4** : lacking variety, change, or accomplishment : EMPTY ⟨a *blank* day⟩ **5** : lacking lively expression or interest ⟨a *blank* face⟩ **6** : ABSOLUTE, UNQUALIFIED ⟨*blank* refusal⟩ **7** : not shaped into finished form ⟨*blank* key⟩ **syn** see EMPTY — **blank·ly** *adv* — **blank·ness** *n*

²blank *n* **1 a** : an empty space (as on a paper) **b** : a paper with spaces for the entry of data **2** : an empty space or period **3** : the bull's-eye of a target **4 a** : a piece of material prepared to be made into something **b** : a cartridge loaded with powder but no bullet **5** : VOID 4

³blank *vt* **1 a** : OBSCURE, OBLITERATE **b** : to stop up : SEAL **2** : to keep from scoring ⟨*blanked* for eight innings⟩

blank check *n* **1** : a signed check with the amount unspecified **2** : complete freedom of action

¹blan·ket \'blaŋ-kət\ *n* [OF *blankete*, fr. *blanc* white] **1** : a heavy woven often woolen covering used for beds **2** : a covering of any kind ⟨a *blanket* of snow⟩

²blanket *vt* : to cover with or as if with a blanket

³blanket *adj* : covering all instances or members of a group or class ⟨*blanket* approval⟩ ⟨a *blanket* insurance policy⟩

blank verse *n* : unrhymed verse; *esp* : unrhymed iambic pentameter verse

¹blare \'bla(ə)r, 'ble(ə)r\ *vb* [ME *bleren*] **1** : to sound loud and harsh **2** : to utter or proclaim in a harsh noisy manner ⟨loudspeakers *blaring* advertisements⟩

²blare *n* : a loud strident noise ⟨the *blare* of trumpets⟩

blar·ney \'blär-nē\ *n* [*Blarney stone*] : skillful flattery : BLANDISHMENT — **blarney** *vb*

Blarney stone *n* : a stone in Blarney Castle near Cork, Ireland, held to make those who kiss it skilled in flattery

bla·sé \blä-'zā\ *adj* [F] : not responsive to pleasure or excitement as a result of excessive indulgence; *also* : SOPHISTICATED

blas·pheme \blas-'fēm, 'blas-,\ *vb* [LL *blasphemare*, fr. Gk *blasphēmein*] **1 a** : to speak of or address with irreverence   **b** : to utter blasphemy **2** : REVILE, ABUSE — **blas·phem·er** *n*

blas·phe·my \'blas-fə-mē\ *n, pl* **-mies** : great disrespect shown to God or to sacred persons or things — **blas·phe·mous** \-məs\ *adj* — **blas·phe·mous·ly** *adv* — **blas·phe·mous·ness** *n*   **syn** PROFANITY: BLASPHEMY applies in strict use to an utterance defying or offering indignity to God; PROFANITY includes all irreverent reference to holy persons or things

¹blast \'blast\ *n* [OE *blǣst*; akin to E *blow*] **1** : a strong gust of wind **2** : a current of air or gas forced through an opening (as in an organ or furnace) **3** : the blowing that a charge of ore or metal receives in a blast furnace **4** : the sound made by a wind instrument (as a horn) or by a whistle **5 a** : EXPLOSION; *esp* : an explosion (as of dynamite) for shattering rock   **b** : an explosive charge for this purpose   **c** : the sudden air pressure produced in the vicinity of an explosion that has the effect of a violent wind **6** : a sudden harmful effect from or as if from a hot wind; *esp* : a withering blight of plants

²blast *vb* **1** : to produce a strident sound **2 a** : to use an explosive   **b** : SHOOT **3** : to injure by or as if by the action of wind : BLIGHT **4 a** : to shatter by or as if by an explosive : DEMOLISH   **b** : to strike with explosive force — **blast·er** *n*

blast furnace *n* : a furnace in which combustion is forced by a current of air under pressure; *esp* : one for the reduction of iron ore

blas·to·coel *or* **blas·to·coele** \'blas-tə-,sēl\ *n* : the cavity of a blastula — **blas·to·coe·lic** \,blas-tə-'sē-lik\ *adj*

blas·to·cyst \'blas-tə-,sist\ *n* : the modified blastula of a placental mammal

blas·to·derm \-tə-,dərm\ *n* : a discoidal blastula formed esp. in an egg with much yolk — **blas·to·der·mat·ic** \,blas-tə-,der-'mat-ik\ *or* **blas·to·der·mic** \-'dər-mik\ *adj*

blast off \(')blas-'tȯf\ *vi* : to take off — used of rocket-propelled missiles and vehicles — **blast-off** \'blas-,tȯf\ *n*

blas·to·mere \'blas-tə-,mi(ə)r\ *n* [Gk *blastos* bud, embyro + *meros* part] **:** a cell produced during cleavage of an egg — **blas·to·mer·ic** \,blas-tə-'mi(ə)r-ik, -'mer-\ *adj*

blas·to·pore \'blas-tə-,pō(ə)r, -,pȯ(ə)r\ *n* **:** the opening of the archenteron — **blas·to·por·al** \,blas-tə-'pōr-əl, -'pȯr-\ *or* **blas·to·por·ic** \-'pōr-ik, -'pȯr-\ *adj*

blas·tu·la \'blas-chə-lə\ *n, pl* **-las** *or* **-lae** \-,lē, -,lī\ [NL, fr. Gk *blastos* bud, embryo] **:** an early metazoan embryo typically having the form of a hollow fluid-filled rounded cavity bounded by a single layer of cells — compare GASTRULA, MORULA — **blas·tu·lar** \-lər\ *adj* — **blas·tu·la·tion** \,blas-chə-'lā-shən\ *n*

blat \'blat\ *vi* **blat·ted; blat·ting :** to cry like a calf or sheep — **blat** *n*

bla·tant \'blāt-ᵊnt\ *adj* **1 :** noisy esp. in a vulgar or offensive manner **:** CLAMOROUS **2 :** OBTRUSIVE, BRAZEN —**bla·tan·cy** \-ᵊn-sē\ *n* — **bla·tant·ly** *adv*

blath·er \'blath-ər\ *vi* **blath·ered; blath·er·ing** \-(ə-)riŋ\ [ON *blathra*] **:** to talk foolishly — **blather** *n* — **blath·er·er** \-ər-ər\ *n*

blath·er·skite \'blath-ər-,skīt\ *n* **:** a blustering talkative person

¹blaze \'blāz\ *n* [OE *blæse*] **1 a :** an intensely burning fire **b :** intense direct light often accompanied by heat **c :** a sudden outburst of flame **2 a :** a dazzling display **b :** a sudden outburst

²blaze *vi* **1 a :** to burn brightly **b :** to flare up **:** FLAME **2 :** to be conspicuously brilliant **3 :** to shoot rapidly and repeatedly ⟨*blaze* away⟩

³blaze *vt* [MD *blāsen* to blow; akin to E *blast*] **:** to make public **:** PROCLAIM ⟨*blaze* the news abroad⟩

⁴blaze *n* [G *blas*] **1 :** a white mark usu. running lengthwise on the face of an animal **2 :** a mark made on a tree by chipping off a piece of the bark usu. to leave a trail

⁵blaze *vt* **:** to mark (as a trail) with blazes

blaz·er \'blā-zər\ *n* [²*blaze*] **:** a single-breasted sports jacket in bright stripes or solid color

blazing star *n* **:** any of several plants having conspicuous flower clusters

¹bla·zon \'blāz-ᵊn\ *n* [MF *blason*] **1 a :** COAT OF ARMS **b :** the proper description of a coat of arms **2 :** ostentatious display **:** SHOW

²blazon *vt* **bla·zoned; bla·zon·ing** \'blāz-niŋ, -ᵊn-iŋ\ **1 a :** to describe (heraldic or armorial bearings) in technical terms **b :** to represent (armorial bearings) in a drawing or engraving **2 :** to depict in colors **3 :** DECK, ADORN — **bla·zon·er** \'blāz-nər, -ᵊn-ər\ *n*

bla·zon·ry \'blāz-ᵊn-rē\ *n* **:** BLAZON

¹bleach \'blēch\ *vb* [OE *blǣcean*] **1 :** to remove color or stains from **2 :** to make whiter or lighter **3 :** to grow white **:** lose color **syn** see WHITEN

²bleach *n* **1 :** the act or process of bleaching **2 :** a preparation used in bleaching

bleach·er \'blē-chər\ *n* **1 :** one that bleaches or is used in bleaching **2 :** a usu. uncovered stand of tiered planks providing seats for spectators — usu. used in pl.

bleaching powder *n* **:** a mixture of calcium hydroxide, chloride, and hypochlorite used as a bleach, disinfectant, or deodorant

bleak \'blēk\ *adj* [ME *bleke* pale] **1 :** exposed to wind or weather ⟨a *bleak* coast⟩ **2 :** DREARY, CHEERLESS **3 :** COLD, RAW **4 :** severely simple — **bleak·ly** *adv* — **bleak·ness** *n*

¹blear \'bli(ə)r\ *vt* [ME *bleren*] **1 :** to make (the eyes) sore or watery **2 :** DIM, BLUR ⟨*bleared* sight⟩

²blear *adj* **1 :** dim with water or tears **2 :** DULL, DIM — **blear-eyed** \-'īd\ *adj*

bleary \'bli(ə)r-ē\ *adj* **1 :** dull or dimmed esp. from fatigue or sleep ⟨*bleary* eyes⟩ **2 :** poorly outlined or defined **:** DIM

¹bleat \'blēt\ *vb* [OE *blǣtan*] **1 :** to utter the natural cry of a sheep or goat **2 :** to utter in a bleating manner

²bleat *n* **:** the cry of a sheep or goat or a sound resembling this cry

bleb \'bleb\ *n* **:** a small blister — **bleb·by** \-ē\ *adj*

bleed \'blēd\ *vb* **bled** \'bled\; **bleed·ing** [OE *blēdan*, fr. *blōd* blood] **1 :** to lose or shed blood ⟨a cut finger *bleeds*⟩ **2 :** to be wounded ⟨*bleed* for one's country⟩ **3 :** to feel pain or deep sympathy ⟨my heart *bleeds* for him⟩ **4 :** to run out from a wounded surface **5 :** to draw liquid (as blood or sap) from ⟨*bleed* a patient⟩ ⟨*bleed* a carburetor⟩ **6 :** to extort money from

bleed·er \'blēd-ər\ *n* **:** one that bleeds; *esp* **:** HEMOPHILIAC

bleeding heart *n* **:** a garden plant of the poppy family with drooping spikes of deep pink heart-shaped flowers

¹blem·ish \'blem-ish\ *vt* [MF *blemiss-, blemir* to make pale, wound, of Gmc origin] **:** to spoil by a flaw **:** MAR

²blemish *n* **:** a noticeable imperfection; *esp* **:** one that impairs appearance but not utility

syn BLEMISH, DEFECT, FLAW mean an imperfection. BLEMISH suggests something, as a spot or stain, that mars the surface or appearance; DEFECT implies a lack, often hidden, of something essential to completeness ⟨a *defect* in the organs of vision⟩ FLAW suggests a defect in continuity or cohesion, as a crack, break, or fissure

¹blench \'blench\ *vi* [OE *blencan* to deceive] **:** to shrink back out of fear **:** FLINCH

²blench *vb* [alter. of *blanch*] **:** to grow or make pale **:** BLANCH

¹blend \'blend\ *vb* [ON *blanda*] **1 :** to mix thoroughly so that the separate things mixed cannot be distinguished **2 :** to shade into each other **:** MERGE, HARMONIZE ⟨furniture that *blends* with the draperies⟩ **syn** see MIX — **blend·er** *n*

²blend *n* **1 :** thorough mixture **2 :** a product (as coffee) prepared by blending **3 :** a word produced by combining parts of other words in an unusual way (as *motel* from *motor* and *hotel*)

blend·ing inheritance *n* **:** inheritance of characters intermediate between those of the parents due to incomplete genetic dominance

blen·ny \'blen-ē\ *n, pl* **blennies** [L *blennius*, fr. Gk *blennos*] **:** any of numerous usu. small and elongated and often scaleless fishes living about rocky seashores

bless \'bles\ *vt* **blessed** \'blest\ *also* **blest** \'blest\; **bless·ing** [OE *blētsian*, fr. *blōd* blood; fr. the use of blood in consecration] **1 :** to hallow or consecrate by religious rite or word **2 :** to make the sign of the cross upon or over **3 :** to invoke divine care or protection for **4 :** PRAISE, GLORIFY **5 :** to make prosperous or happy

blessed \'bles-əd, 'blest\ *or* **blest** \'blest\ *adj* **1 :** HOLY ⟨the *blessed* Trinity⟩ **2 :** of or enjoying happiness; *esp* **:** enjoying the bliss of heaven — used as a title for a beatified person — **bless·ed·ly** \'bles-əd-lē\ *adv* — **bless·ed·ness** \'bles-əd-nəs\ *n*

Blessed Sacrament \,bles-əd-\ *n* **1 :** EUCHARIST **2 :** the consecrated Host

bless·ing *n* **1 a :** the act of one that blesses **b :** APPROVAL **2 :** a thing conducive to happiness or welfare **3 :** grace said at a meal

blew *past of* BLOW

¹blight \'blīt\ *n* **1 a :** a disease or disorder of plants resulting in withering and death without rotting **b :** an organism that causes blight **2 a :** something that impairs or destroys **b :** an impaired or deteriorated condition

²blight *vb* **1 :** to affect with blight **2 :** to cause to deteriorate ⟨slums and *blighted* areas⟩ **3 :** to suffer from or become affected with blight

blimp \'blimp\ *n* **:** a small balloon-shaped airship

¹blind \'blīnd\ *adj* [OE] **1 :** sightless or grossly defective in power to see **2 :** lacking in judgment or understanding **3 a :** closed at one end ⟨a *blind* street⟩ **b :** having no opening ⟨a *blind* wall⟩ **4 :** made or done without the aid of sight; *esp* **:** performed solely by the aid of instruments within an airplane ⟨a *blind* landing⟩ — **blind·ly** *adv* — **blind·ness** \'blīn(d)-nəs\ *n*

²blind *vt* **1 :** to make blind **2 :** to make temporarily blind **:** DAZZLE ⟨*blinded* by oncoming headlights⟩ **3 :** to make dim by comparison **4 :** to deprive of judgment or understanding ⟨love may *blind* parents to a child's faults⟩

³blind *n* **1 :** a device (as a window shade) to hinder sight or keep out light **2 :** a place of concealment esp. for hunters **3 a :** something intended to mislead **:** SUBTERFUGE **b :** a person acting for another who remains hidden

⁴blind *adv* **1 :** BLINDLY; *esp* **:** to the point of insensibility **2 :** without seeing outside of an airplane ⟨fly *blind* with the aid of instruments⟩

blind date *n* **1 :** a date between two persons of opposite sex who have not previously met **2 :** either participant in a blind date

blind·er \'blīn-dər\ *n* **:** either of two flaps on a horse's bridle to prevent sight of objects at his sides

¹blind·fold \'blīn(d)-,fōld\ *vt* [ME *blindfellen*, lit., to

ə abut; ᵊ kitten; ər further; a back; ā bake; ä cot, cart; au̇ out; ch chin; e less; ē easy; g gift; i trip; ī life

strike blind, fr. *blind* + *fellen* to fell] **:** to cover the eyes of with or as if with a bandage — **blindfold** *adj*

²**blindfold** *n* **:** a bandage for covering the eyes

blind·man's buff \,blin(d)-,manz-'bəf\ *n* **:** a group game in which a blindfolded player tries to catch and identify another player

blind spot *n* **1 :** a point in the retina through which the optic nerve enters and which is insensitive to light **2 :** an area of weakness (as in judgment or discrimination) **3 :** a locality in which radio reception is poor

blind·worm \'blīnd-,wərm\ *n* **:** a small burrowing limbless lizard with minute eyes

¹**blink** \'bliŋk\ *vb* [ME *blinken* to open one's eyes] **1 :** to look with half-shut winking eyes **2 :** to wink quickly ⟨*blink* back tears⟩ **3 :** TWINKLE **4 :** to shine with a light that goes or seems to go on and off ⟨street lights *blinking* through rain⟩ **5 :** to shut one's eyes to **:** IGNORE ⟨*blink* the facts⟩ **6 :** to look with surprise or dismay **syn** see WINK

²**blink** *n* **1 :** GLIMMER, SPARKLE **2 :** a usu. involuntary shutting and opening of the eye — **on the blink :** not functioning properly **:** DISABLED

blink·er \'bliŋ-kər\ *n* **:** one that blinks; *esp* **:** a light that can be flashed on and off in a sequence of coded intervals for signaling

blin·tze \'blin(t)s-sə\ *or* **blintz** \'blin(t)s\ *n* [Yiddish *blintse*, fr. Russ *blinets*] **:** a thin rolled pancake with a filling usu. of cream cheese

blip \'blip\ *n* **:** an image on a radar screen

bliss \'blis\ *n* [OE; akin to E *blithe*] **:** great happiness **:** JOY — **bliss·ful** \-fəl\ *adj* — **bliss·ful·ly** \-fə-lē\ *adv* — **bliss·ful·ness** *n*

¹**blis·ter** \'blis-tər\ *n* [MD *bluyster* blister] **1 :** a raised area of the outer skin containing watery liquid **2 :** a raised spot (as in paint) resembling a blister **3 :** an agent that causes blistering **4 :** any of various structures that bulge out (as a gunner's compartment on an airplane) — **blis·tery** \-t(ə-)rē\ *adj*

²**blister** *vb* **blis·tered; blis·ter·ing** \-t(ə-)riŋ\ **1 :** to develop a blister **:** rise in blisters **2 :** to raise a blister on

blister beetle *n* **:** any of a family of soft-bodied beetles including some whose dried bodies are used medicinally to blister the skin

blister copper *n* **:** metallic copper that has a black blistered surface, is the product of converting a crude smelted sulfur-containing ore, and is about 98.5 to 99.5 percent pure

blister rust *n* **:** any of several diseases of pines caused by rust fungi and marked by external blisters

blithe \'blīth, 'blīth\ *adj* [OE *blīthe*] **1 :** of a happy lighthearted character or disposition **2 :** HEEDLESS **syn** see MERRY — **blithe·ly** *adv*

blithe·some \'blīth-səm, 'blīth-\ *adj* **:** GAY, MERRY — **blithe·some·ly** *adv*

blitz \'blits\ *n* [short for *blitzkrieg*] **1 :** an intensive series of air raids; *also* **:** AIR RAID **2 :** a fast intensive campaign — **blitz** *vt*

blitz·krieg \'blits-,krēg\ *n* [G, lit., lightning war] **:** a violent swift surprise offensive by coordinated air and ground forces — **blitzkrieg** *vt*

bliz·zard \'bliz-ərd\ *n* **1 :** a long severe snowstorm **2 :** an intensely strong cold wind filled with fine snow

¹**bloat** \'blōt\ *vb* **:** to swell by filling with or as if with water or air **:** puff up

²**bloat** *n* **:** a disorder of cattle marked by abdominal bloating

bloat·er \'blōt-ər\ *n* [obs. *bloat* to cure] **:** a large fat herring or mackerel lightly salted and briefly smoked

blob \'bläb\ *n* [ME] **:** a small lump or drop of something (as paste or paint) of a thick consistency

bloc \'bläk\ *n* [F] **1 a :** a temporary combination of parties in a legislative assembly **b :** a group of legislators who act together on some issues regardless of party lines ⟨the farm *bloc* in Congress⟩ **2 :** a combination of persons, groups, or nations united by treaty, agreement, or common interest ⟨the Soviet *bloc*⟩

¹**block** \'bläk\ *n* [MF *bloc*, fr. MD *blok*] **1 a :** a solid piece of material (as stone or wood) usu. with one or more flat sides ⟨building *blocks*⟩; *also* **:** a hollow rectangular building unit (as of glass) **b :** a piece of wood on which condemned persons are beheaded **c :** a stand for

something to be sold at auction **d :** a mold or form on which something is shaped ⟨a hat *block*⟩

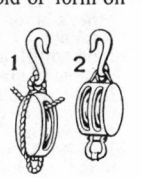

2 a : OBSTACLE **b :** an obstruction of an opponent's play in sports **c :** interruption of normal function of body or mind ⟨heart *block*⟩ **3 :** a wooden or metal case enclosing one or more pulleys **4 :** a number of things thought of as forming a group or unit ⟨a *block* of seats⟩ **5 a :** a large building divided into separate houses or shops **:** a number of houses or shops joined ⟨an apartment *block*⟩ ⟨a business *block*⟩ **b :** a space enclosed by streets **c :** the length of one of the sides of such a block ⟨three *blocks* south⟩ **d :** a part of a building or set of buildings devoted to a specific use **6 :** a section of railroad track controlled by block signals **7 :** a piece of material having on its surface a hand-cut design from which impressions are to be printed

blocks 3: *1* single, *2* double

²**block** *vt* **1 a :** to stop up or close off **:** OBSTRUCT **b :** to hinder the progress or advance of; *esp* **:** to interfere with an opponent (as in football) **c :** to prevent normal functioning of **2 :** to mark the chief lines of ⟨*block* out a sketch⟩ **3 :** to shape on, with, or as if with a block **4 :** to make (lines of writing or type) flush at the left or at both left and right **5 :** to secure, support, or provide with a block — **block·er** *n*

block·ade \blä-'kād\ *n* **:** the isolation by a nation at war of a particular enemy area by means of troops or warships to prevent passage of persons or supplies in or out; *also* **:** any similar measure designed to obstruct commerce of an unfriendly nation — **blockade** *vt* — **block·ad·er** *n*

block·ade-run·ner \-,rən-ər\ *n* **:** a ship or person that attempts to sail through a blockade — **block·ade-run·ning** \-,rən-iŋ\ *n*

block and tackle *n* **:** pulley blocks with associated rope or cable for hoisting or hauling

block·bust·er \'bläk-,bəs-tər\ *n* **:** a very large high-explosive demolition bomb

block·head \'bläk-,hed\ *n* **:** a stupid person

block·house \-,haůs\ *n* **1 :** a building of heavy timbers or of concrete built with holes in its sides through which persons inside may fire out at an enemy **2 :** a building serving as an observation point for an operation likely to be accompanied by heat, blast, or radiation hazard

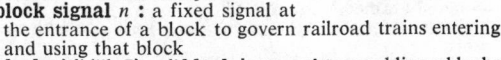

blockhouse

block·ish \'bläk-ish\ *adj* **:** DULL, STUPID — **block·ish·ly** *adv*

block signal *n* **:** a fixed signal at the entrance of a block to govern railroad trains entering and using that block

blocky \'bläk-ē\ *adj* **block·i·er; -est :** resembling a block; *esp* **:** solidly built ⟨a *blocky* physique⟩

bloke \'blōk\ *n*, *chiefly Brit* **:** MAN, FELLOW

¹**blond** *also* **blonde** \'bländ\ *adj* [F] **1 a :** of a flaxen, golden, light auburn, or pale yellowish brown color ⟨*blond* hair⟩ **b :** of a pale white or rosy white color ⟨*blond* skin⟩ **2 a :** of a light color **b :** of the color blond — **blond·ness** \'blän(d)-nəs\ *n*

²**blond** *or* **blonde** *n* **1 :** a blond person **2 :** a light yellowish brown to dark grayish yellow

¹**blood** \'bləd\ *n* [OE *blōd*] **1 :** the red fluid that circulates in the heart, arteries, capillaries, and veins of a vertebrate animal carrying nourishment and oxygen to and bringing away waste products from all parts of the body; *also* **:** a fluid resembling this **2 a :** LINEAGE, DESCENT; *esp* **:** royal lineage ⟨a prince of the *blood*⟩ **b :** relationship by descent from a common ancestor **:** KINSHIP; *also* **:** KINDRED **c :** descent from parents of superior status or breeding **3 a :** EMOTIONS, TEMPER **b :** ANGER **4 :** a foppish man **:** RAKE

²**blood** *vt* **:** to give experience to ⟨troops already *blooded* in battle⟩

blood bank *n* **:** a reserve supply of blood or plasma or the place where it is stored

blood·bath \-,bath, -,båth\ *n* **:** a great slaughter **:** MASSACRE

blood brother *n* **1 :** a brother by birth **2 :** one that is bound in ceremonial blood brotherhood

blood brotherhood *n* **:** a solemn friendship established between usu. unrelated men by a ceremonial use of each other's blood

blood cell *n* : a cell normally present in blood

blood count *n* : the counting of the blood cells in a definite volume of blood; *also* : the number of cells so determined

blood·cur·dling \'bləd-,kərd-liŋ\ *adj* : seeming to have the effect of congealing the blood through fear or horror : TERRIFYING, HORRIBLE ⟨bloodcurdling screams⟩

blood·ed \'bləd-əd\ *adj* 1 : entirely or largely of pure blood or stock ⟨blooded horses⟩ 2 : having blood of a specified kind ⟨warm-blooded⟩

blood feud *n* : a feud between different clans or families

blood fluke *n* : a flatworm (as a schistosome) parasitic in blood vessels

blood group *n* : one of the classes into which human beings can be separated on the basis of the presence or absence in their blood of specific antigens — called also *blood type* — **blood grouping** *n*

blood·hound \'bləd-,haund\ *n* : a large powerful hound of a breed of European origin remarkable for keenness of smell

blood·less \'bləd-ləs\ *adj* 1 : deficient in blood 2 : not accompanied by loss of blood or by bloodshed or slaughter ⟨a bloodless revolution⟩ 3 : lacking in spirit or feeling — **blood·less·ly** *adv* — **blood·less·ness** *n*

blood·let·ting \-,let-iŋ\ *n* 1 : PHLEBOTOMY 2 : BLOODSHED

blood·line \-,līn\ *n* : a sequence of direct ancestors esp. in a pedigree; *also* : FAMILY, STRAIN

blood·mo·bile \'bləd-mō-,bēl\ *n* [*blood* + auto*mobile*] : an automobile staffed and equipped for collecting blood from donors

blood money *n* 1 : money obtained at the cost of another's life 2 : money paid to the next of kin of a slain person by the slayer or his relatives

blood platelet *n* : one of the minute protoplasmic disks of vertebrate blood that assist in blood clotting

blood poisoning *n* : SEPTICEMIA

blood pressure *n* : pressure of the blood on the walls of blood vessels and esp. arteries varying with physical condition and age

blood·red \'bləd-'red\ *adj* : having the color of blood

blood·root \-,rüt, -,rüt\ *n* : a plant of the poppy family having a red root and sap and bearing a single lobed leaf and white flower in early spring

blood·shed \'bləd-,shed\ *n* 1 : the shedding of blood 2 : the taking of life : SLAUGHTER

blood·shot \-,shät\ *adj* : inflamed to redness ⟨bloodshot eyes⟩

blood·stain \-,stān\ *n* : a discoloration caused by blood — **blood·stained** \-,stānd\ *adj*

blood·stone \-,stōn\ *n* : a green quartz sprinkled with red spots

blood·stream \-,strēm\ *n* : the flowing blood in a circulatory system

blood·suck·er \-,sək-ər\ *n* 1 : an animal that sucks blood; *esp* : LEECH 2 : a person who sponges or preys on another — **blood·suck·ing** \-,sək-iŋ\ *adj*

blood test *n* : a test of the blood; *esp* : a serologic test for syphilis

blood·thirsty \'bləd-,thər-stē\ *adj* : eager to shed blood : CRUEL — **blood·thirst·i·ly** \-stə-lē\ *adv* — **blood·thirst·i·ness** \-stē-nəs\ *n*

blood type *n* : BLOOD GROUP — **blood-type** *vt*

blood vessel *n* : a vessel in which blood circulates in an animal

blood·worm \'bləd-,wərm\ *n* : any of various reddish annelid worms often used as bait

bloody \'bləd-ē\ *adj* **blood·i·er**; **-est** 1 : smeared or stained with blood ⟨a bloody handkerchief⟩; *also* : BLEEDING ⟨a bloody nose⟩ 2 : causing or accompanied by bloodshed ⟨a bloody battle⟩ 3 : BLOODTHIRSTY, MURDEROUS — **blood·i·ly** \'bləd-ᵊl-ē\ *adv* — **blood·i·ness** \'bləd-ē-nəs\ *n* — **bloody** *vt*

¹bloom \'blüm\ *n* [OE *blōma*] 1 : a mass of wrought iron from a forge or puddling furnace 2 : a bar of iron or steel hammered or rolled from an ingot

²bloom *n* [ON *blōm*; akin to E *³blow*] 1 a : FLOWER b : flowers or amount of flowers (as of a plant) c : the period or state of flowering 2 : a state or time of beauty, freshness, and vigor 3 : a surface coating or appearance:

as a : a delicate powdery coating on some fruits and leaves b : a rosy appearance of the cheeks; *also* : an outward evidence of freshness or healthy vigor 4 : the bouquet of a wine — **bloomy** \'blü-mē\ *adj*

syn BLOOM, BLOSSOM mean flower, but BLOOM suggests the full achievement or perfection of development ⟨roses in full *bloom*⟩ BLOSSOM stresses the promise of fruit to come ⟨cherry trees in *blossom*⟩

³bloom *vi* 1 : to produce or yield flowers 2 a : to be in a state of youthful beauty or freshness : FLOURISH b : SHINE, GLOW 3 : to appear unexpectedly in large quantities — **bloom·er** *n*

bloo·mers \'blü-mərz\ *n pl* [after Amelia *Bloomer* d1894 American pioneer in feminism] : full loose trousers gathered at the knee formerly worn by women (as for athletics); *also* : underpants of similar design worn chiefly by girls

bloop·er \'blü-pər\ *n* : an embarrassing blunder made in public

¹blos·som \'bläs-əm\ *n* [OE *blōstm;* akin to E *³blow*] 1 a : the flower of a seed plant ⟨apple *blossoms*⟩ b : the period or state of flowering 2 : a period or stage of development suggesting the unfolding of a flower **syn** see BLOOM — **blos·somy** \-ə-mē\ *adj*

²blossom *vi* 1 : BLOOM 2 : to unfold like a blossom: as a : to flourish and prosper markedly b : DEVELOP, EXPAND c : to come into being

¹blot \'blät\ *n* [ME] 1 : SPOT, STAIN 2 : DISGRACE, BLEMISH

²blot *vb* **blot·ted**; **blot·ting** 1 a : SPOT, STAIN b : SPATTER 2 : OBSCURE, DIM 3 : DISGRACE 4 a : to dry with blotting paper or other absorbing agent b : to remove by blotting the surface 5 : to become marked with a blot

blotch \'bläch\ *n* 1 : IMPERFECTION, BLEMISH 2 : a spot or mark (as of color or ink) esp. when large or irregular — **blotch** *vt* — **blotched** \'blächt\ *adj* — **blotchy** \'bläch-ē\ *adj*

blot out *vt* 1 : to make obscure or invisible : HIDE 2 : DESTROY, KILL

blot·ter \'blät-ər\ *n* 1 : a piece of blotting paper 2 : a book in which entries are made temporarily pending their transfer to permanent record books ⟨a police *blotter*⟩

blotting paper *n* : a soft spongy paper used to absorb wet ink

blouse \'blaus, 'blauz; *some say* 'blaus *but* 'blau-zəz\ *n* [F] 1 : a loose overgarment like a shirt or smock varying from hip-length to calf-length 2 : the upper outer garment of a uniform 3 : a usu. loose-fitting garment covering the body from the neck to the waist

¹blow \'blō\ *vb* **blew** \'blü\; **blown** \'blōn\; **blow·ing** [OE *blāwan*] 1 : to move or become moved esp. rapidly or with power ⟨wind *blowing* from the north⟩ 2 : to send forth a strong current of air (as from the mouth) ⟨*blow* on one's hands⟩ 3 : to drive or become driven by a current of air ⟨a tree *blown* down in a storm⟩ 4 : to make a sound or cause to sound by blowing ⟨*blow* a horn⟩⟨*blow* a whistle⟩ 5 : PANT, GASP 6 a : to melt when overloaded ⟨the lights went out when a fuse *blew*⟩ b : to cause (a fuse) to blow 7 a : to release suddenly the contained air through a rupture ⟨the tire *blew* out⟩ b : to rupture by too much pressure ⟨*blew* a gasket⟩ 8 : to clear of contents by forcing air through 9 a : to swell with or as if with gas b : to produce or shape by the action of blown or injected air ⟨*blow* bubbles⟩ ⟨*blow* glass⟩ 10 : to shatter or destroy by explosion 11 a : to put out of breath with exertion b : to let (as a horse) pause to catch the breath 12 a : to spend (money) recklessly ⟨*blew* all his money in one day⟩ b : TREAT ⟨I'll *blow* you to a steak⟩

²blow *n* 1 : a blowing of wind esp. when violent : GALE 2 : a forcing of air from the mouth or nose or through some instrument

³blow *vi* **blew** \'blü\; **blown** \'blōn\; **blow·ing** [OE *blōwan*] : FLOWER, BLOOM

⁴blow *n* 1 : a display of flowers 2 : *²*BLOOM 1c

⁵blow *n* [ME *blaw*] 1 : a forcible stroke delivered with a part of the body or with an instrument 2 : a hostile act : COMBAT ⟨come to *blows*⟩ 3 : a forcible or sudden act or effort : ASSAULT 4 : a severe and sudden calamity ⟨a heavy *blow* to the nation⟩

syn STROKE: BLOW implies violence or force; STROKE suggests suddenness or definiteness or precision

blow–by–blow \-bī-, -bə-\ *adj* : minutely detailed ⟨*blow-by-blow* account⟩

blow·er \'blō-(ə)r\ *n* **1** : one that blows **2** : a device for producing a current of air or gas

blow·fly \'blō-,flī\ *n* : any of various two-winged flies (as a bluebottle) that deposit their eggs or maggots on meat or in wounds

blow·gun \-,gən\ *n* : a tube from which an arrow or a dart may be shot by the force of the breath

blow·hard \-,härd\ *n* : BRAGGART

blow·hole \-,hōl\ *n* **1** : a hole for the escape of air or gas **2** : a nostril in the top of the head of a whale or related animal **3** : a hole in the ice to which aquatic mammals (as seals) come to breathe

blown \'blōn\ *adj* **1** : SWOLLEN; *esp* : afflicted with bloat **2** : FLYBLOWN **3** : out of breath

blow out \(')blō-'aut\ *vb* **1** : to extinguish or become extinguished by a gust **2** : to dissipate (itself) by blowing — used of a storm

blow·out \'blō-,aut\ *n* **1** *slang* : a big social affair **2** : a bursting of a container (as a tire) by pressure of the contents on a weak spot; *also* : a hole made in a container by such bursting

blow·pipe \'blō-,pīp\ *n* **1** : a small round tube for blowing a jet of gas (as air) into a flame so as to concentrate and increase the heat **2** : BLOWGUN

blow·sy *also* **blow·zy** \'blau-zē\ *adj* [E dial. *blowse* wench] : DISHEVELED, SLOVENLY; *also* : COARSE

blow·torch \'blō-,tȯrch\ *n* : a small portable burner that intensifies combustion by means of a blast of air or oxygen and that usu. includes a fuel tank pressurized by a hand pump

blow up \(')blō-'əp\ *vb* **1** : to expand or become expanded to unreasonable proportions **2** : to make an enlargement of ⟨*blow up* a photograph⟩ **3 a** : EXPLODE **b** : to become violently angry

blow·up \'blō-,əp\ *n* **1** : EXPLOSION **2** : an outburst of temper **3** : a photographic enlargement

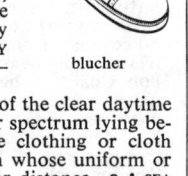
blowtorch

blowy \'blō-ē\ *adj* **blow·i·er**; **-est** : WINDY

¹**blub·ber** \'bləb-ər\ *n* [ME *bluber* bubble, foam] **1 a** : the fat of large sea mammals (as whales) **b** : excessive fat on the body **2** : the action of blubbering

²**blubber** *vb* **blub·bered**; **blub·ber·ing** \-(ə-)riŋ\ **1** : to weep noisily and childishly or so as to swell or disfigure one's face **2** : to utter while weeping

³**blub·ber** \-ər\ *or* **blub·bery** \-(ə-)rē\ *adj* : puffed out : THICK ⟨*blubber* lips⟩

blu·cher \'blü-chər, -kər\ *n* [after G. L. von *Blücher* d1819 Prussian field marshal] : a shoe having the tongue and vamp cut in one piece and the quarters lapped over the vamp and laced

bludg·eon \'bləj-ən\ *n* : a short club with one end thicker and heavier than the other — **bludgeon** *vt*

¹**blue** \'blü\ *adj* [ME *bleu*, fr. OF *blou*, of Gmc origin] **1** : of the color blue **2 a** : BLUISH **b** : LIVID **c** : bluish gray **3 a** : low in spirits : MELANCHOLY **b** : DEPRESSING **4** : PURITANICAL — **blue·ly** *adv* — **blue·ness** *n*

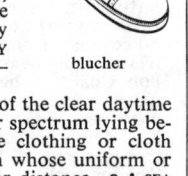
blucher

²**blue** *n* **1** : a color whose hue is that of the clear daytime sky or that of the portion of the color spectrum lying between green and violet **2 a** : blue clothing or cloth **b** : one belonging to an organization whose uniform or badge is blue **3 a** : SKY **b** : the far distance **c** : SEA

³**blue** *vt* **blued**; **blue·ing** *or* **blu·ing** **1** : to make blue **2** : to add bluing to so as to make white ⟨*blue* the sheets⟩

blue baby *n* : an infant with a bluish tint usu. from a congenital defect of the heart

blue·beard \'blü-,bi(ə)rd\ *n* [after *Bluebeard*, a character in a fairy tale] : a man who marries and kills one woman after another

blue·bell \-,bel\ *n* : any of various plants (as a grape hyacinth) with blue bell-shaped flowers; *esp* : HAREBELL

blue·ber·ry \'blü-,ber-ē, -b(ə)rē\ *n* : the edible blue or blackish small-seeded berry of any of several plants of the heath family; *also* : a low or tall shrub producing these berries — compare HUCKLEBERRY

blue·bird \-,bərd\ *n* : any of several small No. American songbirds related to the robin but more or less blue above

blue blood *n* **1** \'blü-'bləd\ : ARISTOCRACY **2** \-,bləd\ : a member of a noble or socially prominent family — **blue–blood·ed** \-'bləd-əd\ *adj*

blue–bon·net \'blü-,bän-ət\ *n* **1** : CORNFLOWER **2** : a low-growing annual lupine of Texas with silky foliage and blue flowers

blue–bot·tle \-,bät-ʰl\ *n* : any of several blowflies with the abdomen or the whole body iridescent blue in color

blue cat *n* : a large bluish catfish of the Mississippi valley

blue chip *n* [so called because in games of chance blue chips have the highest value of all counters] : a stock issue that commands a high price as a result of public confidence in its stability

blue·coat \'blü-,kōt\ *n* : POLICEMAN

blue–col·lar *adj* : of, relating to, or constituting the wage-earning class

blue crab *n* : a largely blue edible swimming crab of the Atlantic and Gulf coasts

blue·fin \'blü-,fin\ *n* : a very large tuna

blue·fish \-,fish\ *n* : an active greedy saltwater food and sport fish that is related to the pompanos and is bluish above and silvery below; *also* : any of several bluish food fishes

blue flag *n* : a blue-flowered iris; *esp* : a common iris of the eastern U.S. with a root formerly used medicinally

blue·gill \'blü-,gil\ *n* : a common food and sport sunfish of the eastern and central U.S.

blue·grass \-,gras\ *n* : a valuable pasture and lawn grass with bluish green stems

blue–green alga \,blü-,grēn-\ *n* : any of a class (Myxophyceae) of algae having the chlorophyll masked by bluish green pigments

blue·jack·et \'blü-,jak-ət\ *n* : an enlisted man in the navy : SAILOR

blue jay \-,jā\ *n* : any of several crested and largely blue American jays

blue jeans *n pl* : work pants or overalls usu. made of blue denim

blue law *n* **1** : one of many extremely strict laws regulating morals and conduct in colonial New England **2** : a statute limiting work, commerce, and amusements on Sundays or holidays

blue mold *n* : a fungus and esp. a penicillium that produces blue or blue-green surface growths

blue moon *n* : a very long period of time ⟨once in a *blue moon*⟩

blue·nose \'blü-,nōz\ *n* : one who advocates a rigorous moral code

blue note *n* : a minor interval occurring in a melody or harmony where a major would be expected

blue plate \-,plāt\ *n* [fr. its being traditionally served on a plate with a blue design] : a main course (as of meat and vegetable) served as a single menu item

blue·point \-,point\ *n* [*Blue Point*, Long Island] : a small oyster typically from the south shore of Long Island

¹**blue·print** \-,print\ *n* **1** : a photographic print in white on a bright blue ground used esp. for copying mechanical drawings and architects' plans **2** : a detailed plan or program of action

²**blue·print** *vt* : to make a blueprint of or for

blue racer *n* : a blacksnake of a bluish green variety occurring from Ohio to Texas

blue ribbon *n* **1** : a blue ribbon awarded the first-place winner in a competition **2** : an honor or award gained for preeminence

blues \'blüz\ *n pl* **1** : low spirits : MELANCHOLY **2** : a song sung or composed in a style originating among the American Negroes, expressing melancholy, and exhibiting continual occurrence of blue notes in melody and harmony **3** : a blue uniform

blue–sky law *n* [fr. *blue-sky stock* worthless stock; so called in allusion to the emptiness of the sky] : a law providing for the regulation of the sale of securities (as stocks)

blue·stem \'blü-,stem\ *n* : either of two important hay and forage grasses of the western U.S. with smooth bluish leaf sheaths

blue·stock·ing \-,stäk-iŋ\ *n* [fr. the *Bluestocking Ladies*, so called fr. their support of informal dress at 18th cent. literary gatherings] : a woman having intellectual or literary interests

blu·et \'blü-ət\ *n* : a low American herb with dainty solitary bluish flowers

blue vitriol *n* : a hydrated copper sulfate $CuSO_4.5H_2O$

blue whale *n* : a whale held to reach a weight of 100 tons and a length of 100 feet and generally considered the largest living animal

¹bluff \'bləf\ *adj* [obs. D *blaf* flat] **1** : rising steeply with a broad front (as from a plain or shore) ⟨a *bluff* coastline⟩ **2** : frank and outspoken in a rough but good-natured manner — **bluff·ly** *adv* — **bluff·ness** *n*

²bluff *n* : a high steep bank : CLIFF

³bluff *vb* [prob. fr. D *bluffen* to boast] : to deceive or frighten by pretending to have strength or confidence that one does not really have — **bluff·er** *n*

⁴bluff *n* **1 a** : an act or instance of bluffing **b** : the practice of bluffing **2** : one who bluffs

blu·ing *or* **blue·ing** \'blü-iŋ\ *n* : a preparation of blue or violet dyes used in laundering to counteract yellowing of white fabrics

blu·ish *or* **blue·ish** \'blü-ish\ *adj* : somewhat blue

¹blun·der \'blən-dər\ *vb* **blun·dered**; **blun·der·ing** \-d(ə-)riŋ\ [ME *blundren*] **1** : to move unsteadily or confusedly **2** : to make a mistake through stupidity, ignorance, confusion, or carelessness **3** : to say stupidly or thoughtlessly : BLURT **4** : BUNGLE — **blun·der·er** \-dər-ər\ *n*

²blunder *n* : a gross error or mistake resulting from stupidity, ignorance, confusion, or carelessness **syn** see ERROR

blun·der·buss \'blən-dər-,bəs\ *n* [modif. of obs. D *donderbus*, lit., thunder gun] **1** : an obsolete short firearm having a large bore and usu. a flaring muzzle for use at close range without taking precise aim **2** : a blundering person

blunderbuss

¹blunt \'blənt\ *adj* [ME] **1 a** : slow or deficient in feeling : INSENSITIVE **b** : obtuse in understanding or discernment : DULL **2** : having an edge or point that is not sharp **3** : lacking refinement or tact : ABRUPT — **blunt·ly** *adv* — **blunt·ness** *n*

syn DULL, OBTUSE: BLUNT suggests an innate or inherent lack of sharpness or quickness of feeling or perception ⟨*blunt* refusal⟩ DULL suggests lack or loss of keenness, zest, pungency; OBTUSE implies bluntness or insensitivity in perception or imagination ⟨an *obtuse* audience⟩

²blunt *vb* : to make or become blunt

¹blur \'blər\ *n* **1** : a smear or stain that obscures but does not efface **2** : something vague or lacking definite outline ⟨saw through his tears only a *blur* of words⟩ — **blur·ry** \-ē\ *adj*

²blur *vb* **blurred**; **blur·ring** **1** : to obscure or blemish by smearing **2** : to make indistinct or confused **3** : to become vague, indistinct, or indefinite

blurb \'blərb\ *n* [coined by Gelett Burgess] : a brief notice esp. in advertising praising a product extravagantly

blurt \'blərt\ *vt* : to utter suddenly and without thinking ⟨*blurt* out a secret⟩

¹blush \'bləsh\ *vi* [OE *blyscan* to redden, fr. *blysa* flame] **1** : to become red in the face esp. from shame, modesty, or confusion **2** : to feel shame or embarrassment **3** : to have a rosy or fresh color : BLOOM — **blush·er** *n*

²blush *n* **1** : APPEARANCE, VIEW ⟨at first *blush*⟩ **2** : a reddening of the face esp. from shame, modesty, or confusion **3** : a red or rosy tint — **blush·ful** \-fəl\ *adj*

¹blus·ter \'bləs-tər\ *vb* **blus·tered**; **blus·ter·ing** \-t(ə-)riŋ\ [ME *blustren*] **1** : to blow violently and noisily **2** : to talk or act in a noisy boastful way : SWAGGER, RAGE — **blus·ter·er** \-tər-ər\ *n*

²bluster *n* **1** : a violent noisy blowing **2** : violent commotion **3** : boisterous action **4** : boastful empty speech — **blus·tery** \-t(ə-)rē\ *adj*

boa \'bō-ə\ *n* [L, a water snake] **1** : a large snake (as the boa constrictor, anaconda, or python) that crushes its prey **2** : a long fluffy scarf of fur, feathers, or delicate fabric

boa con·stric·tor \-kən-'strik-tər\ *n* : a mottled brown tropical American boa

boar \'bō(ə)r, 'bȯ(ə)r\ *n* [OE *bār*] **1** : a male swine; *also* : the male of any of several mammals **2** : the Old World wild hog from which most domestic swine derive — **boar·ish** \-ish\ *adj*

¹board \'bōrd, 'bȯrd\ *n* [OE *bord*] **1** : the side of a ship — often used in combination ⟨star*board*⟩ ⟨over*board*⟩ **2 a** : a thin flat relatively long piece of sawed lumber **b** *pl* : STAGE 2a ⟨trod the *boards* for 40 years⟩ **3 a** : a dining table **b** : daily meals esp. when furnished for pay ⟨room and *board*⟩ **c** : a group of persons having managerial, supervisory, or investigatory powers and functions ⟨*board* of directors⟩ ⟨school *board*⟩ ⟨*board* of examiners⟩ **4 a** : a flat usu. rectangular piece of material designed for a special purpose **b** : a surface, frame, or device for posting notices or listing market quotations **5 a** : any of various wood pulps or composition materials formed into flat rectangular sheets **b** : the stiff foundation piece for the side of a book cover — **by the board** **1** : over the side of a ship **2** : into a state of discard, neglect, or ruin ⟨all our plans went *by the board* when the building was sold⟩ — **on board** : ABOARD

²board *vb* **1** : to go aboard : get on ⟨*boarded* just before the ship sailed⟩ ⟨*boarded* the plane in New York⟩ **2** : to cover with boards ⟨*boarded* up a window⟩ **3** : to provide or be provided with regular meals and often lodging usu. for pay

board·er \'bōrd-ər, 'bȯrd-\ *n* : one that boards; *esp* : one who receives meals and sometimes lodging at another's house for pay

board foot *n* : a unit of quantity for lumber equal to the volume of a board 12 x 12 x 1 inches

board·ing·house \'bōrd-iŋ-,haůs, 'bȯrd-\ *n* : a house at which persons are boarded

boarding school *n* : a school in which pupils are boarded and lodged as well as taught

board measure *n* : measurement in board feet

Board of Trade : a British governmental department concerned with commerce and industry

board·walk \'bōrd-,wȯk, 'bȯrd-\ *n* **1** : a walk constructed of planking **2** : a promenade orig. of planking along a beach

¹boast \'bōst\ *n* [ME *boost*] **1** : the act of boasting : BRAG **2** : a cause for pride — **boast·ful** \'bōst-fəl\ *adj* — **boast·ful·ly** \-fə-lē\ *adv* — **boast·ful·ness** *n*

²boast *vb* **1** : to praise oneself ⟨*boasts* of his ability⟩ **2** : to tell with extreme pride : BRAG ⟨*boasting* about his money⟩ ⟨*boasted* that they'd win easily⟩ **3** : to possess or display proudly ⟨band *boasting* new uniforms⟩ — **boast·er** *n*

¹boat \'bōt\ *n* [OE *bāt*] **1** : a small vessel propelled by oars or paddles or by sail or power **2** : SHIP **3** : a boat-shaped utensil or device ⟨gravy *boat*⟩

²boat *vb* **1** : to place in or bring into a boat **2** : to travel by boat — **boat·er** *n*

boat hook *n* : a hook with a point or knob on the back fixed to a pole and used esp. to pull or push a boat into place

boat·house \'bōt-,haůs\ *n* : a house or shelter for boats

boat·man \'bōt-mən\ *n* : a man who manages, works on, or deals in boats — **boat·man·ship** \-,ship\ *n*

boat·swain \'bōs-ᵊn\ *n* [ME *bootswein*, fr. *boot* boat + *swein* servant] : a warrant officer on a warship or a petty officer on a merchant ship in charge of the hull and all related equipment

¹bob \'bäb\ *vb* **bobbed**; **bob·bing** [ME *boben*] **1 a** : to move or cause to move up and down in a short quick movement ⟨*bob* the head⟩ ⟨a cork *bobbing* in the water⟩ **b** : to emerge, arise, or appear suddenly or unexpectedly ⟨*bob* up again⟩ **2** : to grasp or make a grab with the teeth ⟨*bob* for apples⟩

²bob *n* : a short jerky motion ⟨a *bob* of the head⟩

³bob *n* [ME *bobbe* bunch, cluster] **1** : a woman's or child's short haircut **2** : a ball or weight hanging from a rod or line **3** : a device (as a cork) for buoying up the baited end of a fishing line

⁴bob *vt* **bobbed**; **bob·bing** **1** : to cut shorter : CROP **2** : to cut (hair) in the style of a bob

⁵bob *n* : BOBSLED

⁶bob *n*, *pl* **bob** *slang* : SHILLING

bob·ber \'bäb-ər\ *n* : one that bobs

bob·bin \'bäb-ən\ *n* **1** : a cylinder or spindle on which yarn or thread is wound (as in a sewing machine) **2** : a coil of insulated wire or the reel it is wound on

bob·bi·net \ˌbäb-ə-'net\ *n* [blend of *bobbin* and *net*] : a machine-made net of cotton, silk, or nylon usu. with hexagonal mesh

bob·ble \'bäb-əl\ *vb* **bob·bled**; **bob·bling** \'bäb-(ə-)liŋ\ [freq. of ¹*bob*] **1** : ¹BOB **2** : FUMBLE — **bobble** *n*

bob·by \'bäb-ē\ *n, pl* **bobbies** [*Bobby*, nickname for *Robert*, after Sir *Robert* Peel, who organized the London police force] *Brit* : POLICEMAN

bob·by pin \'bäb-ē-\ *n* : a flat wire hairpin with prongs that press close together

bobby socks *or* **bobby sox** *n pl* : girls' socks reaching above the ankle

bob·by-sox·er \'bäb-ē-ˌsäk-sər\ *or* **bob·by-sock·er** \-ˌsäk-ər\ *n* : an adolescent girl

bob·cat \'bäb-ˌkat\ *n* [³*bob*; fr. the stubby tail] : a common usu. rusty-colored No. American lynx

bob·o·link \'bäb-ə-ˌliŋk\ *n* [imit.] : an American migratory songbird related to the blackbirds

bob·sled \'bäb-ˌsled\ *n* **1** : a short sled usu. used as one of a joined pair **2** : a compound sled formed of two bobsleds and a coupling — **bobsled** *vi*

bob·stay \'bäb-ˌstā\ *n* : a stay to hold a ship's bowsprit down

bob·tail \'bäb-ˌtāl\ *n* **1 a** : a bobbed tail **b** : a horse or dog with a bobbed tail **2** : something curtailed or abbreviated — **bobtail** \-ˌtāl\ *or* **bob·tailed** \-ˌtāld\ *adj*

bob·white \(')bäb-'hwīt\ *n* [imit.] : any of several American quails; *esp* : a favorite gray, white, and reddish game bird of the eastern and central U.S. — called also *partridge*

boc·cie *or* **boc·ci** *or* **boc·ce** \'bäch-ē\ *n* [It *bocce* balls] : lawn bowls played in a long narrow court

bock \'bäk\ *n* [G] : a heavy dark rich beer usu. sold in the early spring

¹bode \'bōd\ *vt* [OE *bodian*] : to indicate (as a future event) by signs : PRESAGE — **bode·ment** \-mənt\ *n*

²bode *past of* BIDE

bod·ice \'bäd-əs\ *n* [alter. of *bodies*, pl. of *body*] : the upper part of a woman's dress

bod·ied \'bäd-ēd\ *adj* : having a body or such a body ⟨long-*bodied*⟩

bod·i·less \'bäd-i-ləs, -ᵊl-əs\ *adj* : having no body : INCORPOREAL

¹bod·i·ly \'bäd-ᵊl-ē\ *adj* **1** : having a body **2** : of or relating to the body ⟨*bodily* comfort⟩ ⟨*bodily* organs⟩

²bodily *adv* **1** : in the flesh **2** : as a whole : ENTIRELY

bod·ing \'bōd-iŋ\ *n* : FOREBODING

bod·kin \'bäd-kən\ *n* [ME] **1 a** : DAGGER, STILETTO **b** : a sharp slender instrument for making holes in cloth **2** : a blunt needle with a large eye for drawing tape or ribbon through a loop or hem

body \'bäd-ē\ *n, pl* **bod·ies** [OE *bodig*] **1 a** : the physical whole of a living or dead organism **b** : the trunk or main part of an organism as distinguished from the head and appendages **c** : a human being : PERSON **2** : the main or central part: as **a** : the box of a vehicle on or in which the load is placed **b** : the main part of a document **3** : the part of a garment covering the body or trunk **4** : a mass or portion of matter distinct from other masses ⟨a *body* of water⟩ ⟨a *body* of cold air⟩ **5 a** : a group of individuals united for some purpose ⟨a legislative *body*⟩ **b** : a unit formed of a number of persons or things : a collective whole ⟨a *body* of laws⟩ **6 a** : VISCOSITY ⟨paint with a good *body*⟩ **b** : richness of flavor (as of wine)

body·guard \'bäd-ē-ˌgärd\ *n* : a man or group of men whose duty it is to protect a person

body louse *n* : a sucking louse that lives in the clothing and feeds on the body of man

body politic *n* : a group of persons politically organized under a single government; *esp* : STATE

body snatcher *n* : one that steals corpses from graves usu. for dissection

Boer \'bō(ə)r, 'bȯ(ə)r, 'bü(ə)r\ *n* [D, lit., farmer] : a South African of Dutch or Huguenot descent

¹bog \'bäg, 'bȯg\ *n* [of Celtic origin] : wet spongy ground; *esp* : poorly drained acid soil that adjoins a body of water and is usu. grown over by sedges, heaths, and sphagnum — **bog·gy** \-ē\ *adj*

²bog *vb* **bogged**; **bog·ging** : to sink into or as if into a bog : MIRE

¹bo·gey *or* **bo·gy** *or* **bo·gie** *n, pl* **bogeys** *or* **bogies** [prob. alter. of E dial. *bogle* terrifying apparition] **1** \'bůg-ē, 'bō-gē, 'bü-gē, 'bůg-ər\ : SPECTER, PHANTOM **2** \'bō-gē *also* 'bůg-ē *or* 'bü-gē\ : a source of annoyance, perplexity, or harassment **3** \'bō-gē\ : one golf stroke over par on a hole

²bo·gey \'bō-gē\ *vt* **bo·geyed**; **bo·gey·ing** : to shoot (a hole in golf) in one over par

bo·gey·man \'bůg-ē-ˌman, 'bō-gē-, 'bü-gē-, 'bůg-ər-\ *n* : a terrifying person or thing; *esp* : a monstrous imaginary figure used in threatening children

bog·gle \'bäg-əl\ *vb* **bog·gled**; **bog·gling** \'bäg-(ə-)liŋ\ **1** : to start with fright or amazement **2** : to hesitate because of doubt, fear, or scruples **3** : BUNGLE — **boggle** *n*

bo·gie *also* **bo·gey** *or* **bo·gy** \'bō-gē\ *n, pl* **bogies** *also* **bogeys** **1** : a low strongly built cart **2** : the driving-wheel assembly consisting of the rear four wheels of a 6-wheel automotive truck

bo·gus \'bō-gəs\ *adj* [fr. *bogus*, a machine for making counterfeit money] : not genuine : SPURIOUS, SHAM

bo·he·mia \bō-'hē-mē-ə\ *n, often cap* : a community of bohemians : the world of bohemians

Bo·he·mi·an \bō-'hē-mē-ən\ *n* **1 a** : a native or inhabitant of Bohemia **b** : the group of Czech dialects used in Bohemia **2** *often not cap* **a** : VAGABOND, WANDERER; *esp* : GYPSY **b** : a writer or artist living an unconventional life — **bohemian** *adj, often cap* — **bo·he·mi·an·ism** \-mē-ə-ˌniz-əm\ *n, often cap*

¹boil \'bȯil\ *n* [alter. of OE *bȳl*] : a painful swollen inflamed area in the skin resulting from infection and usu. ending with the discharge of pus and a hardened core — compare CARBUNCLE

²boil *vb* [OF *boillir*, fr. L *bullire* to bubble, fr. *bulla* bubble] **1 a** : to generate bubbles of vapor when heated ⟨the water is *boiling*⟩ **b** : to come or bring to the boiling point ⟨the coffee *boiled*⟩ **2** : to become agitated like boiling water : SEETHE ⟨*boiling* flood waters⟩ **3** : to be excited or stirred up ⟨*boiling* with anger⟩ **4** : to undergo or cause to undergo the action of a boiling liquid ⟨*boil* the eggs⟩

³boil *n* : the act or state of boiling

boil·er \'bȯi-lər\ *n* **1** : a container in which something is boiled **2** : a tank holding hot water **3** : a strong metal container used in making steam for heating buildings or for driving engines

boil·er·mak·er \-ˌmā-kər\ *n* : a workman who makes, assembles, or repairs boilers

boiling point *n* : the temperature at which a liquid boils

bois·ter·ous \'bȯi-st(ə-)rəs\ *adj* [ME *boistous* rough] **1 a** : noisily turbulent : ROWDY ⟨a *boisterous* crowd⟩ **b** : marked by exuberance and high spirits ⟨*boisterous* laughter⟩ **2** : STORMY, TUMULTUOUS ⟨*boisterous* winds⟩ — **bois·ter·ous·ly** *adv* — **bois·ter·ous·ness** *n*

bo·la \'bō-lə\ *or* **bo·las** \-ləs\ *n, pl* **bo·las** \-ləz\ [AmerSp *bolas*, lit., balls] : a weapon consisting of two or more stone or iron balls attached to the ends of a cord for hurling at and entangling an animal

bold \'bōld\ *adj* [OE *beald*] **1 a** : fearless before danger : INTREPID **b** : showing or reflecting a courageous daring spirit and contempt of danger ⟨a *bold* plan⟩ **2** : IMPUDENT, PRESUMPTUOUS **3** : SHEER, STEEP ⟨*bold* cliffs⟩ **4** : ADVENTUROUS, DARING ⟨a *bold* thinker⟩ **5** : standing out prominently : CONSPICUOUS ⟨a dress with *bold* stripes⟩ — **bold·ly** *adv* — **bold·ness** \'bōl(d)-nəs\ *n*

bold·face \'bōl(d)-ˌfās\ *n* : a heavy-faced type; *also* : printing in boldface

bold-faced \-'fāst\ *adj* **1** : bold in manner or conduct : IMPUDENT **2** : set in boldface

bole \'bōl\ *n* [ON *bolr*] : the trunk of a tree

bo·le·ro \bə-'le(ə)r-ō\ *n, pl* **-ros** [Sp] **1** : a Spanish dance in ¾ time; *also* : the music for it **2** : a loose waist-length jacket open at the front

bo·le·tus \bə-'lēt-əs\ *n, pl* **-le·tus·es** *or* **-le·ti** \-'lē-ˌtī\ : any of a genus of pore fungi some of which are edible

bo·li·var \bə-'lē-ˌvär, 'bäl-ə-vər\ *n, pl* **bo·li·vars** *or* **bo·li·va·res** \ˌbäl-ə-'vär-ˌās, -li-\ [AmerSp *bolívar*, fr. Simón *Bolívar* d1830 So. American liberator] **1** : the basic monetary unit of Venezuela **2** : a silver coin representing one bolívar

bo·li·vi·a·no \bə-ˌliv-ē-'än-ō\ *n, pl* **-nos** **1** : the basic monetary unit of Bolivia **2** : a coin or note representing one boliviano

boll \'bōl\ *n* [ME] : a seedpod or capsule of a plant (as cotton)

bol·lard \'bäl-ərd\ *n* **1** : a post on a wharf around which to fasten mooring lines **2** : BITT

boll weevil *n* : a small grayish weevil with a larva that lives in and feeds on the buds and bolls of the cotton plant

bo·lo \'bō-lō\ *n*, *pl* **bolos** [Sp] : a long heavy single-edged knife used in the Philippines

bo·lo·gna \bə-'lō-nē *also* -n(y)ə\ *n* [fr. *Bologna*, Italy] : a large smoked sausage of beef, veal, and pork

bo·lom·e·ter \bə-'läm-ət-ər\ *n* : a very sensitive thermometer based on varying electrical resistance and used in the detection and measurement of feeble thermal radiation

Bol·she·vik \'bōl-shə-,vik\ *n*, *pl* **Bolsheviks** *or* **Bolshe·vi·ki** \,bōl-shə-'vik-ē\ [Russ *bol'shevik*, fr. *bol'she* larger; fr. their forming the majority group in the party in 1903] **1** : a member of the extremist wing of the Russian Social Democratic party favoring the overthrow of capitalism by force and seizing supreme power in Russia by the revolution of November 1917 **2** : COMMUNIST — **Bolshevik** *adj*

Bol·she·vism \'bōl-shə-,viz-əm\ *n* : the theories and practices of Bolsheviks — **Bol·she·vist** \-vəst\ *n or adj* — **Bol·she·vis·tic** \,bōl-shə-'vis-tik\ *adj*

¹bol·ster \'bōl-stər\ *n* [OE] **1** : a long pillow or cushion extending the full width of a bed **2** : a structural part designed to eliminate friction or provide support

²bolster *vt* **bol·stered**; **bol·ster·ing** \-st(ə-)riŋ\ : to support with or as if with a bolster; *also* : REINFORCE — **bol·ster·er** \-stər-ər\ *n*

¹bolt \'bōlt\ *n* [OE] **1 a** : a shaft or missile for a crossbow or catapult **b** : a lightning stroke : THUNDERBOLT **2** : a sliding bar used to fasten a door **3** : the part of a lock worked by a key **4** : a metal pin or rod usu. with a head at one end and a screw thread at the other that is used to hold something in place **5** : a roll of cloth or wallpaper of a specified length **6** : the breech closure of a breech-loading rifle

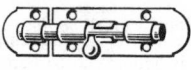

bolt 2

²bolt *vb* **1** : to move suddenly or nervously **2** : to move rapidly : DASH ⟨reporters *bolted* for the door⟩ **3** : to run away ⟨his horse shied and *bolted*⟩ **4** : to break away from or oppose one's political party **5** : to say impulsively : BLURT **6** : to fasten with a bolt **7** : to swallow hastily or without chewing ⟨*bolted* down his dinner and rushed out⟩ — **bolt·er** *n*

³bolt *n* : an act of bolting

⁴bolt *vt* [OF *buleter*, of Gmc origin] : to sift (as flour) usu. through fine-meshed cloth — **bolt·er** *n*

bo·lus \'bō-ləs\ *n* [Gk *bōlos* lump] : a rounded mass: as **a** : a large pill **b** : a soft mass of chewed food

¹bomb \'bäm\ *n* [It *bomba*] **1** : a hollow case or shell containing explosive material and variously made to be dropped from an airplane, thrown by hand, or set off by a fuse **2** : a container in which a substance (as an insecticide) is stored under pressure and from which it is released in the form of a fine spray

²bomb *vb* : to attack with bombs

¹bom·bard \'bäm-,bärd\ *n* : a cannon used in late medieval times chiefly to hurl large stones

²bom·bard \bäm-'bärd, bəm-\ *vt* **1** : to attack with artillery **2** : to assail vigorously or persistently (as with questions) **3** : to subject to the impact of rapidly moving particles (as electrons or alpha rays) — **bom·bard·ment** \-mənt\ *n*

bom·bar·dier \,bäm-bə(r)-'di(ə)r\ *n* : a bomber-crew member who releases the bombs

bom·bast \'bäm-,bast\ *n* [obs. *bombast* padding, fr. MF *bombace* cotton] : pretentious inflated speech or writing — **bom·bas·tic** \bäm-'bas-tik\ *adj* — **bom·bas·ti·cal·ly** \-ti-k(ə-)lē\ *adv*

bom·ba·zine \,bäm-bə-'zēn\ *n* **1** : a silk fabric in twill weave dyed black **2** : a twilled fabric with silk warp and worsted filling

bomb bay *n* : a bomb-carrying compartment in the underside of a combat airplane

bomb·er \'bäm-ər\ *n* : one that bombs; *esp* : an airplane designed for dropping bombs

bom·bi·nate \'bäm-bə-,nāt\ *vi* : BUZZ, DRONE — **bom·bi·na·tion** \,bäm-bə-'nā-shən\ *n*

bomb·proof \'bäm-'prüf\ *adj* : safe against the explosive force of bombs

bomb·shell \'bäm-,shel\ *n* **1** : BOMB 1 **2** : a devastating surprise

bomb·sight \-,sīt\ *n* : a sighting device on an airplane for aiming bombs

bo·na fide \'bō-nə-,fīd, ,bō-nə-'fīd-ē\ *adj* [L, in good faith] **1 a** : made or carried out in good faith without fraud or deceit ⟨*bona fide* offer⟩ **b** : acting in good faith without fraud or deceit ⟨*bona fide* purchaser⟩ **2** : GENUINE ⟨he is a *bona fide* cowboy⟩

bo·nan·za \bə-'nan-zə\ *n* [Sp, lit., fair weather, fr. ML *bonacia*, alter. of L *malacia* calm at sea, fr. Gk *malakia*, lit., softness, fr. *malakos* soft] **1** : a rich mass of ore in a mine **2** : something that brings a rich return

bon·bon \'bän-,bän\ *n* [F] : a candy with chocolate or fondant coating and fondant center with fruits and nuts sometimes added

¹bond \'bänd\ *n* [ME *band*, *bond* band, fr. ON *band*] **1** : something that restrains : FETTER **2** : a binding agreement : COVENANT **3 a** : a material or device for binding **b** : a mechanism by means of which atoms, ions, or groups of atoms are held together in a molecule or crystal **c** : a cementing material that combines, unites, or strengthens **4** : a tie of loyalty, sentiment, or friendship **5 a** : a pledge to do a specified act or pay a sum on or before a set date under penalty of forfeit of a sum deposited; *also* : the sum deposited **b** : one who gives bail or acts as surety **c** : a certificate bearing interest and promising payment of a certain sum on or before a stated day and issued by a government or corporation as an evidence of indebtedness **d** : insurance taken out by a party (as a contractor) to insure another against his failure to perform an obligation **6** : a binding or connection made by overlapping parts of a structure (as in laying brick) **7** : the state of goods manufactured, stored, or transported under the care of bonded agencies until taxes on them are paid

²bond *vb* **1** : to protect or secure by or operate under a bond ⟨*bonded* locksmiths⟩; *esp* : to secure payment of taxes on (goods) by giving a bond **2 a** : to cause to adhere firmly **b** : to embed in a cementing material **c** : to hold together or solidify by or as if by means of a bond or binder : COHERE — **bond·a·ble** \'bän-də-bəl\ *adj* — **bond·er** *n*

bond·age \'bän-dij\ *n* [ME *bonde* peasant, serf, fr. OE *bōnda* householder, fr. ON *bōndi*] : involuntary personal servitude (as serfdom or slavery)

bond·hold·er \'bänd-,hōl-dər\ *n* : one that owns a government or corporation bond

bond·man \'bän(d)-mən\ *n* : SLAVE, SERF — **bond·wom·an** \'bänd-,wùm-ən\ *n*

bond paper *n* : a strong durable paper used esp. for documents

bond servant *n* : a person bound to service without wages; *also* : SLAVE

¹bonds·man \'bän(d)z-mən\ *n* : BONDMAN

²bondsman *n* : SURETY

¹bone \'bōn\ *n* [OE *bān*] **1 a** : the hard largely calcareous connective tissue of which the skeleton of most vertebrate animals is formed; *also* : one of the hard pieces in which this tissue occurs ⟨break a *bone*⟩ **b** : a similar hard animal substance (as whalebone or ivory) **2 a** *pl* : something usu. or orig. made from bone (as dice or clappers) **b** : STAY 1b **3** *pl* : an end man in a minstrel show — **bone·less** \-ləs\ *adj*

²bone *vb* **1** : to remove the bones from ⟨*bone* a fish⟩ **2** : to provide (a garment) with stays **3** : to study hard ⟨*bone* up on math⟩

bone black *n* : the black chiefly carbon residue of bones heated in a closed vessel that is used esp. as a pigment or a decolorizing material — called also *bone char*

bone·fish \'bōn-,fish\ *n* **1** : a slender silvery small-scaled fish that is a notable sport and food fish of warm seas **2** : TENPOUNDER

bone·head \-,hed\ *n* : a stupid person : NUMSKULL

bone meal *n* : fertilizer or feed made of crushed or ground bone

bon·er \'bō-nər\ *n* **1** : one that bones **2** : BLUNDER, HOWLER

bon·fire \'bän-ˌfī(ə)r\ n [ME bonefire fire of bones] : a large fire built in the open air

bong \'bäŋ, 'böŋ\ n : a deep resonant sound (as of a bell) — **bong** vb

bon·go \'bäŋ-gō\ n, pl **bongos** also **bongoes** [AmerSp bongó] : one of a pair of small tuned drums played with the hands

bon·ho·mie also **bon·hom·mie** \ˌbän-ə-'mē, ˌbō-nə-\ n [F bonhomie, fr. bonhomme good-natured man, fr. bon good + homme man] : good-natured easy friendliness : GENIALITY

bon·i·face \'bän-ə-fəs, -ˌfās\ n [after Boniface, innkeeper in The Beaux' Stratagem, play by George Farquhar] : the proprietor of a hotel, nightclub, or restaurant

bo·ni·to \bə-'nēt-ō\ n, pl **bonitos** or **bonito** [Sp, fr. bonito pretty, fr. L bonus good] : any of various medium-sized tunas

bon mot \bōⁿ-'mō\ n, pl **bons mots** \bōⁿ-'mō(z)\ or **bon mots** \-'mō(z)\ [F, lit., good word] : a clever remark : WITTICISM

bon·net \'bän-ət\ n [MF bonet] 1 : a head covering often tied under the chin by ribbons or strings and worn by women and small children 2 : a soft woolen cap worn by men in Scotland 3 : the headdress of an American Indian 4 Brit : an automobile hood

bon·ny also **bon·nie** \'bän-ē\ adj, chiefly Brit : HANDSOME, ATTRACTIVE, FINE — **bon·ni·ly** \'bän-ᵊl-ē\ adv

bon·sai \bōn-'sī\ n, pl **bonsai** [Jap] : a potted plant (as a tree) dwarfed by special methods of culture

bon·spiel \'bän-ˌspēl\ n : a match or tournament between curling clubs

bon ton \(')bän-'tän\ n [F, lit., good tone] 1 : fashionable manner or style 2 : the fashionable or proper thing

bo·nus \'bō-nəs\ n [L, good] : something given in addition to what is usual or what is strictly due; esp : money given in addition to an agreed salary or wages

bon vi·vant \ˌbän-vē-'vänt, ˌbōⁿ-vē-'väⁿ\ n, pl **bons vivants** \ˌbän-vē-'vänts, ˌbōⁿ-vē-'väⁿ(z)\ or **bon vivants** \same\ [F, lit., good liver] : a person having cultivated or refined tastes esp. in food and drink

bon voy·age \ˌbōⁿv-, wī-'äzh, -ˌwä-'yäzh\ n [F] : a good trip : FAREWELL — often used interjectionally

bony \'bō-nē\ adj **bon·i·er**; **-est** 1 : of or relating to bone ⟨the bony structure of the body⟩ 2 : full of bones 3 : resembling bone esp. in hardness ⟨a bony substance⟩ 4 : having large or prominent bones ⟨a rugged bony face⟩; also : SKINNY, SCRAWNY ⟨bony underfed children⟩

bony fish n : any of a class (Teleostomi) comprising higher fishes with usu. well-developed bony skeletons

¹**boo** \'bü\ interj — used to express contempt or disapproval or to startle or frighten

²**boo** n : a shout of disapproval or contempt — **boo** vb

boob \'büb\ n [short for booby] : SIMPLETON; also : BOOR

boo·by \'bü-bē\ n, pl **boobies** [modif. of Sp bobo, fr. L balbus stammering] 1 : a foolish person : DOPE 2 a : any of several small tropical gannets b : any of several American ducks

booby trap n : a trap for a careless or unwary person; esp : a concealed explosive device set to go off when some harmless-looking object is touched — **boo·by-trap** \'bü-bē-ˌtrap\ vt

boo·dle \'büd-ᵊl\ n 1 : a collection of persons : CROWD 2 : bribe money; esp : political graft

boo·gie-woo·gie \ˌbug-ē-'wug-ē\ n : a percussive style of playing blues on the piano characterized by a persistent rhythmic bass and complex improvised formations built up on a simple melody

¹**book** \'bük\ n [OE bōc; akin to E beech; prob. fr. the early Germanic practice of carving runic characters on beech wood tablets] 1 a : a set of written, printed, or blank sheets of paper bound together into a volume b : a long written or printed literary composition c : a major division of a literary work d : a volume of business records (as accounts) 2 cap : BIBLE 3 : something felt to be a source of enlightenment or instruction 4 : all the charges that can be made against a person ⟨threw the book at him⟩ 5 a : LIBRETTO b : the script of a play 6 : a packet of commodities bound together ⟨a book of matches⟩ 7 : the bets registered by a bookmaker 8 : the tricks a cardplayer must win before scoring — **one for the book** : an act or occurrence worth noting

²**book** vb 1 a : to engage transportation or reserve lodgings b : to schedule engagements for ⟨book an entertainer⟩ 2 : to enter charges against in a police register — **book·er** n

³**book** adj 1 : derived from books ⟨book learning⟩ 2 : shown by books of account ⟨book value⟩

book·bind·ing \'bük-ˌbīn-diŋ\ n 1 : the binding of a book 2 : the art or trade of binding books — **book·bind·er** n

book·case \'bük-ˌkās\ n : a piece of furniture consisting of shelves to hold books

book·end \'bük-ˌend\ n : a support placed at the end of a row of books to hold them up

book·ie \'bük-ē\ n : BOOKMAKER

book·ish \'bük-ish\ adj 1 : fond of books and reading 2 : inclined to rely on knowledge from books rather than practical experience 3 : resembling or derived from the language of books : FORMAL — **book·ish·ly** adv — **book·ish·ness** n

book·keep·er \'bük-ˌkē-pər\ n : a person who keeps accounts (as of a business) — **book·keep·ing** \-piŋ\ n
syn ACCOUNTANT: a BOOKKEEPER keeps regular, concise, accurate records of business transactions by entering them in account books; an ACCOUNTANT is an expert bookkeeper who may be employed to organize or set up a system of records or to investigate or report upon the financial condition of an organization

book·let \'bük-lət\ n : a little book; esp : PAMPHLET

book louse n : any of several minute wingless insects (order Corrodentia) injurious esp. to books

book lung n : a specialized breathing organ of spiders and related animals

book·mak·er \'bük-ˌmā-kər\ n : one who determines odds and receives and pays off bets — **book·mak·ing** \-kiŋ\ n

book·mark \'bük-ˌmärk\ n : a marker for finding a place in a book

book–match \'bük-ˌmach\ vt : to match the grains of (as two sheets of veneer) so that one sheet seems to be the mirrored image of the other

book·mo·bile \'bük-mō-ˌbēl\ n [book + automobile] : a truck that serves as a traveling library

Book of Common Prayer : the service book of the Anglican Communion

book·plate \'bük-ˌplāt\ n : a label placed in a book showing who owns it

book review n : a critical estimate of a new book

book·sell·er \'bük-ˌsel-ər\ n : the proprietor of a bookstore

book·worm \-ˌwərm\ n 1 : any of various insect larvae that feed on the binding and paste of books 2 : a person unusually devoted to reading or study

Bool·ean algebra \ˌbü-lē-ən-\ n [George Boole d1860 English mathematician] : a mathematical set together with its subsets and axioms for combining the subsets

¹**boom** \'büm\ n [D, tree, beam, boom; akin to E beam] 1 : a long pole; esp : one for stretching the bottom of a sail 2 a : a long beam projecting from the mast of a derrick to support or guide the thing that is being lifted b : a long movable arm used to manipulate a microphone 3 : a line of connected floating timbers to hold logs together in a river

²**boom** vi 1 : to make a deep hollow sound 2 a : to increase in esteem or importance b : to experience a sudden rapid growth and expansion ⟨business was booming⟩ c : to develop rapidly in population and importance

³**boom** n 1 : a booming sound or cry 2 : a rapid expansion or increase: as a : a general movement in support of a candidate for office b : rapid settlement and development of a town or district c : a rapid widespread expansion of economic activity

¹**boo·mer·ang** \'bü-mə-ˌraŋ\ n 1 : a curved club or stick usu. somewhat flat that can be thrown so as to return to the thrower 2 : an act or utterance that reacts with harm to its maker or doer

²**boomerang** vi : to return in the manner of a boomerang; esp : to injure the originator instead of an intended target

boom·town \'büm-ˌtaün\ n : a town undergoing a sudden growth in economic activity and population

boomerangs

¹boon \'bün\ *n* [ON *bōn* petition] **1** : BENEFIT, FAVOR; *esp* : one given in answer to a request **2** : a timely benefit : BLESSING

²boon *adj* [MF *bon* good, fr. L *bonus*] **1** : BOUNTEOUS, KIND **2** : MERRY, JOVIAL; *also* : INTIMATE ⟨a *boon* companion⟩

boon·dog·gling \'bün-,dóg-(ə-)lin̩, -,däg-\ *n* : a trivial, useless, or wasteful activity

boor \'bu̇(ə)r\ *n* [D *boer*] **1** : PEASANT; *esp* : a rough clownish rustic : YOKEL **2** : a rude or insensitive person

boor·ish \'bu̇(ə)r-ish\ *adj* : resembling a boor : RUDE — **boor·ish·ly** *adv* — **boor·ish·ness** *n*

¹boost \'büst\ *vt* **1** : to push or shove up from below **2** : to increase in force, power, or amount ⟨*boost* airplane production⟩ ⟨*boost* prices⟩; *also* : RAISE, PROMOTE ⟨*boost* morale⟩ **3** : to promote enthusiastically the cause or interests of

²boost *n* **1** : a push upwards **2** : an increase in amount ⟨a *boost* in production⟩ **3** : an act giving needed help or encouragement

boost·er \'bü-stər\ *n* **1** : one that boosts **2** : an enthusiastic supporter **3** : a supplementary dose of an immunizing agent given to maintain or revive a previously established immunity **4** : a device for strengthening radio or television signals in areas where reception is weak **5** : the first stage of a multistage rocket providing thrust for the launching and the initial part of the flight

¹boot \'büt\ *n* [OE *bōt* profit, advantage; akin to E *better*] *chiefly dial* : something to equalize a trade — **to boot** : BESIDES

²boot *vb, archaic* : AVAIL, PROFIT

³boot *n* [MF *bote*] **1 a** : a covering (as of leather or rubber) for the foot and leg **b** *Brit* : a shoe reaching to the ankle **2** : a protective sheath or casing **3** : a patch for the inside of a tire casing **4** *Brit* : an automobile trunk **5** : a blow delivered by the foot : KICK; *also* : a rude discharge or dismissal **6** : a navy or marine recruit undergoing basic training

⁴boot *vt* **1** : to put boots on **2 a** : KICK **b** : to discharge rudely

boot·black \'büt-,blak\ *n* : a person who shines boots and shoes

boot camp *n* : a camp for the basic training of navy or marine recruits

boot·ee *or* **boot·ie** \'büt-ē\ *n* : an infant's knitted or crocheted sock

Bo·ö·tes \bō-'ōt-ēz\ *n* [L, fr. Gk *Boōtēs*, lit., plowman, fr. *bous* ox, cow] : a northern constellation containing the bright star Arcturus

booth \'büth\ *n, pl* **booths** \'büt͟hz, 'büths\ [ME *bothe*, of Scand origin] **1** : a temporary shelter **2 a** : a stall or stand for the sale or exhibition of goods (as at a fair, market, or exhibition) **b** (1) : a small enclosure affording privacy for one person at a time ⟨voting *booth*⟩ ⟨telephone *booth*⟩ (2) : a small enclosure used to separate its occupant from customers or patrons ⟨information *booth*⟩ **c** : a restaurant accommodation consisting of a table between two backed benches

boot·jack \'büt-,jak\ *n* : a V-shaped device for use in pulling off one's boots

¹boot·leg \'büt-,leg\ *vb* [fr. the carrying of illicit liquor concealed in the leg of a boot] **1** : to make or transport for sale alcoholic liquor contrary to law **2 a** : to produce or sell illicitly **b** : SMUGGLE — **boot·leg·ger** \-,leg-ər\ *n*

²bootleg *n* : something bootlegged; *esp* : MOONSHINE — **bootleg** *adj*

boot·less \'büt-ləs\ *adj* : USELESS, UNPROFITABLE — **boot·less·ly** *adv* — **boot·less·ness** *n*

boots \'büts\ *n sing or pl, Brit* : a servant esp. in a hotel who shines shoes

boo·ty \'büt-ē\ *n* [modif. of MF *butin*] **1** : SPOILS; *esp* : goods seized from the enemy in war **2** : a rich gain or prize

¹booze \'büz\ *vi* [MD *būsen*] : to drink intoxicating liquor to excess — **booz·er** \'bü-zər\ *n* — **boozy** \'bü-zē\ *adj*

²booze *n* : intoxicating liquor

bo·rac·ic acid \bə-,ras-ik-\ *n* : BORIC ACID

bor·age \'bór-ij, 'bär-\ *n* [MF *bourage*] : a rough-hairy blue-flowered European herb used medicinally and in salads

bo·rate \'bō(ə)r-,āt, 'bó(ə)r-\ *n* : a salt or ester of a boric acid

bo·rax \'bō(ə)r-,aks, 'bó(ə)r-\ *n* [ML *borac-, borax*, fr. Ar *būraq*, fr. Per *būrah*] : a crystalline slightly alkaline compound $Na_2B_4O_7.10H_2O$ that is a borate of sodium, occurs as a mineral, and is used as a flux, cleansing agent, and antiseptic

bo·ra·zon \'bór-ə-,zän, 'bór-\ *n* : a crystalline compound BN of boron and nitrogen as hard as diamond but more resistant to high temperature

bor·deaux mixture \bór-'dō-\ *n, often cap B* : a fungicide made by reaction of copper sulfate, lime, and water

¹bor·der \'bórd-ər\ *n* [MF *bordure*, fr. OF, fr. *border* to border, fr. *bort* border, of Gmc origin] **1** : an outer part or edge **2** : BOUNDARY, FRONTIER **3** : a narrow bed of planted ground along the edge of a garden or walk **4** : an ornamental design at the edge of a fabric or rug — **bor·dered** \-ərd\ *adj*

syn BORDER, EDGE, MARGIN mean a line or narrow space marking the limit or outermost bound of something. A BORDER is that part of a surface lying along its boundary line; EDGE denotes specif. the terminating line made by two converging surfaces as of a blade or a box; MARGIN suggests a border of definite width or distinctive character ⟨sandy *margin* of the sea⟩

²border *vb* **bor·dered; bor·der·ing** \'bórd-(ə-)rin̩\ **1** : to put a border on **2** : to touch at the edge or boundary : BOUND **3** : to lie on the border **4** : to approach the nature of a specified thing : VERGE ⟨*borders* on the ridiculous⟩ — **bor·der·er** \-ər-ər\ *n*

bor·der·land \'bórd-ər-,land\ *n* **1** : territory at or near a border : FRONTIER **2** : an outlying or intermediate region often not clearly defined ⟨the *borderland* between sleeping and waking⟩

bor·der·line \-,līn\ *adj* **1** : situated at or near a border or boundary **2** : having characteristics of a state or condition without clearly being in it : UNCERTAIN ⟨a *borderline* case of mental illness⟩ **3** : having characteristics of two states or conditions without clearly belonging to either : INTERMEDIATE

¹bore \'bō(ə)r, 'bó(ə)r\ *vb* [OE *borian*] **1** : to make a hole in esp. with a tool that turns round : PIERCE ⟨*bore* a piece of wood⟩ **2** : to make by piercing or drilling ⟨*bore* a hole⟩ ⟨*bore* a well⟩ **3 a** : to make a hole by boring **b** : to sink a mine shaft or well

²bore *n* **1** : a hole made by or as if by boring **2 a** : an interior lengthwise cylindrical cavity **b** : the interior tube of a gun **3 a** : the diameter of a hole or tube; *esp* : the interior diameter of a gun barrel **b** : the diameter of an engine cylinder

³bore *past of* BEAR

⁴bore *n* [ON *bāra* wave] : a tidal flood with a high abrupt front usu. due to a rapidly narrowing inlet

⁵bore *n* : one that causes boredom

⁶bore *vt* : to weary by being dull or monotonous

bo·re·al \'bōr-ē-əl, 'bór-\ *adj* [Gk *Boreas* north wind, north] : of, relating to, or located or growing in northern or mountainous regions

Bo·re·as \-ē-əs\ *n* **1** : the god of the north wind in Greek mythology **2** : the north wind personified

bore·dom \'bórd-əm, 'bórd-\ *n* : the state of being bored

bor·er \'bōr-ər, 'bór-\ *n* : one that bores: as **a** : a tool used for boring **b** (1) : SHIPWORM (2) : an insect that as larva or adult bores in the woody parts of plants

Bor·gia \'bór-(,)jä, -jə\ *n* : a member of an Italian family powerful in Italian and papal politics during the 15th and 16th centuries and notorious for cruelty and vice

bo·ric acid \,bōr-ik-, ,bór-\ *n* : a white crystalline weak acid H_3BO_3 that contains boron, occurs naturally in solution, and is used as a mild antiseptic

bor·ing \'bōr-in̩, 'bór-\ *n* : a hole made by boring

born \'bórn\ *adj* [OE *boren*, pp. of *beran* to bear] **1 a** : brought into life by birth **b** : NATIVE ⟨American-*born*⟩ **2** : having special natural abilities or character from birth ⟨a *born* leader⟩

borne *past part of* BEAR

born·ite \'bó(ə)r-,nīt\ *n* : a brittle metallic-looking mineral Cu_5FeS_4 consisting of a sulfide of copper and iron and constituting a valuable ore of copper

bo·ron \'bō(ə)r-,än, 'bó(ə)r-\ *n* [*borax* + *-on* (as in *carbon*)] : a metalloid element found in nature only in combination (as in borax) — see ELEMENT table

bor·ough \'bər-ō\ *n* [OE *burg* fortified town] **1 a** : a town

---

ə **abut**; ᵊ **kitten**; ər **further**; a **back**; ā **bake**; ä **cot, cart**; aú **out**; ch **chin**; e **less**; ē **easy**; g **gift**; i **trip**; ī **life**

or urban constituency in Great Britain that sends one or more members to Parliament **b :** a self-governing incorporated urban area in Great Britain **2 a :** a municipal corporation in some states corresponding to the incorporated town or village of the other states **b :** one of the five constituent political divisions of New York City

bor·row \'bär-ō\ vb [OE borgian] **1 :** to take or receive something with the promise or intention of returning it **2 a :** to take for one's own use **b :** COPY, IMITATE **c :** ADOPT 〈borrow an idea〉 **3 :** to take 1 from a figure of the minuend in subtraction and add it as 10 to the next lower denomination — **bor·row·er** \'bär-ə-wər\ n

Bors \'bórz\ n : a knight of the Round Table and nephew of Lancelot

borscht or **borsch** \'bórsh(t)\ n [Russ borshch] : a soup made primarily of beets and served hot or cold

bor·zoi \'bór-,zói\ n [Russ borzoǐ, fr. borzoǐ swift] : any of a breed of large long-haired dogs of greyhound type developed in Russia esp. for pursuing wolves

bosh \'bäsh\ n [Turk boş empty] : foolish talk : NONSENSE

Bos·kop man \,bäs-,käp-\ n : a late Pleistocene southern African man prob. ancestral to modern Bushmen and Hottentots — **bos·kop·oid** \'bäs-kə-,póid\ adj

bosky \'bäs-kē\ adj : covered with trees or shrubs

bo·s'n or **bo'·s'n** or **bo·sun** or **bo'·sun** \'bōs-ʰn\ var of BOATSWAIN

¹bos·om \'bùz-əm\ n [OE bōsm] **1 :** the front of the human chest; esp : the female breasts **2 a :** the center of secret thoughts and feelings **b :** close relationship : EMBRACE 〈in the bosom of her family〉 **3 :** the part of a garment covering the breast — **bos·omed** \-əmd\ adj

²bosom adj : CLOSE, INTIMATE 〈bosom friends〉

¹boss \'bós, 'bäs\ n [OF boce] : a rounded projecting part; esp : an ornament (as on a shield or a ceiling) resembling a knob : STUD

²boss vt : to ornament with bosses : EMBOSS

³boss \'bós\ n [D baas master] **1 :** one who exercises control or authority; esp : one who directs or supervises workers **2 a :** a politician who controls votes or dictates appointments or legislative measures **b :** an official having dictatorial authority over an organization — **boss** adj — **boss·ism** \-,iz-əm\ n

⁴boss \'bós\ vt **1 :** DIRECT, SUPERVISE **2 :** ORDER

¹bossy \'bó-sē, 'bäs-ē\ adj : ornamented with bosses : STUDDED

²bossy \'bó-sē\ n, pl **boss·ies** [E dialect, young cow] : COW, CALF

³bossy \'bó-sē\ adj **boss·i·er; -est** : inclined to domineer : DICTATORIAL — **boss·i·ness** n

Bos·ton fern \,bó-stən-\ n : a fern widely grown for its often drooping much-divided fronds

Boston ivy n : a woody Asiatic vine of the grape family with 3-lobed leaves often grown over walls

Boston terrier n : any of a breed of small smooth-coated brindle or black terriers with white markings — called also Boston bull

bot \'bät\ n : the larva of a botfly

¹bo·tan·i·cal \bə-'tan-i-kəl\ or **bo·tan·ic** \-ik\ adj **1 :** of or relating to plants or botany **2 :** derived from plants **3 :** SPECIES — **bo·tan·i·cal·ly** \-i-k(ə-)lē\ adv

²botanical n : a vegetable drug esp. in the crude state

bot·a·nize \'bät-ʰn-,īz\ vi : to collect and study plants

bot·a·ny \'bät-ʰn-ē, 'bät-nē\ n [Gk botanē pasture, herb, fr. boskein to graze] **1 :** a branch of biology dealing with plant life **2 a :** plant life **b :** the laws and phenomena relating to a plant or plant group — **bot·a·nist** \'bät-ʰn-əst, 'bät-nəst\ n

¹botch \'bäch\ vt [ME bocchen] **1 :** REPAIR; esp : to patch clumsily **2 :** BUNGLE

²botch n : a botched job : BUNGLE, MESS — **botchy** \-ē\ adj

bot·fly \'bät-,flī\ n : any of various stout two-winged flies whose larvae are parasitic in cavities or tissues of various mammals

¹both \'bōth\ adj [ON bāthir] : the two : the one and the other 〈both feet〉

²both pron : the one as well as the other 〈both of us〉 〈we are both well〉

³both conj — used as a function word to indicate and stress the inclusion of each of two or more things specified by coordinated words, phrases, or clauses 〈both New York and London〉

¹both·er \'bäth-ər\ vb **both·ered; both·er·ing** \-(ə-)riŋ\ **1 a :** ANNOY, IRK **b :** PESTER **2 a :** to cause to be anxious or concerned : TROUBLE **b :** to feel concern or anxiety **3 :** to take pains : make an effort 〈don't bother to knock〉

²bother n **1 a :** a state of petty annoyance **b :** something that causes petty annoyance **2 :** FUSS, DISTURBANCE

both·er·some \'bäth-ər-səm\ adj : causing bother : VEXING

bot·ry·oi·dal \,bä-trē-'óid-ʰl\ also **bot·ry·oid** \'bä-trē-,óid\ adj : having the form of a bunch of grapes

¹bot·tle \'bät-ʰl\ n [MF bouteille, fr. ML butticula, dim. of LL buttis cask] **1 a :** a container typically of glass or plastic with a narrow neck and mouth and no handle **b :** a bag made of skin **2 :** the quantity held by a bottle — **bot·tle·ful** \-,fúl\ n

²bottle vt **bot·tled; bot·tling** \'bät-liŋ, -ʰl-iŋ\ **1 :** to put into a bottle **2 :** to confine as if in a bottle — usu. used with up — **bot·tler** \'bät-lər, -ʰl-ər\ n

bottled gas n : gas under pressure in portable cylinders

bot·tle·neck \'bät-ʰl-,nek\ n **1 :** a narrow passageway **2 :** a place, condition, or point where progress is held up 〈a bottleneck for traffic〉

¹bot·tom \'bät-əm\ n [OE botm] **1 a :** the under surface of something **b :** a supporting surface or part : BASE **c :** BUTTOCKS, RUMP **2 :** the bed of a body of water **3 a :** the part of a ship's hull lying below the water **b :** BOAT, SHIP **4 :** the lowest part, place, or point **5 :** low land along a river 〈the Mississippi river bottoms〉 **6** pl : the trousers of pajamas **7 :** the main plowing mechanism of a plow — **bot·tomed** \-əmd\ adj — **at bottom :** BASICALLY, REALLY

²bottom vb : to rest on, bring to, or reach the bottom

bot·tom·less \'bät-əm-ləs\ adj **1 :** having no bottom **2 :** very deep 〈a bottomless pit〉 — **bot·tom·less·ly** adv — **bot·tom·less·ness** n

bot·u·lism \'bäch-ə-,liz-əm\ n [fr. Clostridium botulinum, a species of bacterium] : an acute food poisoning caused by bacterial toxin formed by clostridia in food

bou·clé or **bou·cle** \bü-'klā\ n [F bouclé curly, fr. boucle buckle, curl] : a fabric of yarn looped at intervals

bou·doir \'büd-,wär, 'bùd-, -,wòr\ n [F, fr. bouder to pout] : a woman's dressing room, bedroom, or private sitting room

bouf·fant \bü-'fänt, -'fä"\ adj : puffed out 〈bouffant hairdos〉

bough \'baù\ n [OE bōg shoulder, bough] : a branch of a tree; esp : a main branch — **boughed** \'baùd\ adj

bought past of BUY

bought·en \'bót-ʰn\ chiefly dial past part of BUY

bouil·la·baisse \,bü-yə-'bās\ n [F] : a highly seasoned fish stew made of at least two kinds of fish

bouil·lon \'bü-,yän; 'bùl-,yän, -,yən\ n [F, fr. bouillir to boil] : a clear seasoned soup made usu. from lean beef

boul·der \'bōl-dər\ n [of Scand origin] : a detached and rounded or much-worn mass of rock — **boul·dery** \-d(ə-)rē\ adj

bou·le·vard \'bùl-ə-,värd, 'bül-\ n [F, modif. of MD bolwerc bulwark; so called because the first boulevards followed the lines of old city fortifications] : a broad often landscaped thoroughfare

boulle \'bül\ n [after André Charles Boulle d1732 French cabinetmaker] : inlaid decoration of tortoiseshell, yellow metal, and white metal in cabinetwork

¹bounce \'baùn(t)s\ vb [ME bounsen] **1 a :** to cause to rebound 〈bounce a ball〉 **b :** to spring backward after striking **2 a :** DISMISS, FIRE **b :** to throw out violently from a place **3 :** to recover quickly from a blow or defeat — usu. used with back **4 :** to be returned by a bank as no good 〈his checks bounce〉 **5 :** to leap suddenly : BOUND

²bounce n **1 a :** a sudden leap or bound **b :** a bouncing back : REBOUND **2 :** LIVELINESS, VERVE

bounc·er \'baùn(t)-sər\ n : one that bounces; esp : a man employed in a public place to remove disorderly persons

bounc·ing \-siŋ\ adj : HEALTHY, ROBUST 〈a bouncing baby〉 — **bounc·ing·ly** \-siŋ-lē\ adv

bouncing bet \,baùn(t)-siŋ-'bet\ n, often cap 2d B : SOAPWORT — called also bouncing bess

¹bound \'baùnd\ adj [ME boun, fr. ON būinn ready, fr. pp. of būa to dwell, prepare] : going or intending to go 〈bound for home〉

²bound n [OF bodne] **1 :** a boundary line (as of a piece of property) **2 :** a point or a line beyond which one cannot go **:** LIMIT ⟨out of bounds⟩ **3 :** the land within specific bounds — usu. used in pl.

³bound vt **1 :** to set limits to **:** CONFINE **2 :** to form the boundary of **:** ENCLOSE; also **:** ADJOIN **3 :** to name the boundaries of

⁴bound adj [fr. pp. of bind] **1 a :** fastened by or as if by a band **:** CONFINED ⟨desk-bound⟩ **b :** CERTAIN, SURE ⟨bound to rain soon⟩ **2 a :** OBLIGED ⟨duty-bound⟩ **b :** RESOLVED, DETERMINED **3 :** always occurring in combination with another linguistic form (as un- in unknown, -er in speaker) — compare FREE

⁵bound n [MF bond, fr. bondir to leap] **1 :** LEAP, JUMP **2 :** BOUNCE, REBOUND

⁶bound vi **1 :** to move by leaping **2 :** REBOUND, BOUNCE

bound·a·ry \'baùn-d(ə-)rē\ n, pl **-ries :** something that marks or shows a limit or end (as of a region or a piece of land) **:** a dividing line

bound·en \'baùn-dən\ adj **:** OBLIGATORY, BINDING ⟨our bounden duty⟩

bound·er \'baùn-dər\ n **1 :** one that bounds **2** chiefly Brit **:** CAD, BOOR

bound·less \'baùnd-ləs\ adj **:** having no boundaries; also **:** immeasurably large **:** VAST — **bound·less·ly** adv — **bound·less·ness** n

boun·te·ous \'baùnt-ē-əs\ adj **1 :** GENEROUS **2 :** given plentifully ⟨bounteous gifts⟩ — **boun·te·ous·ly** adv — **boun·te·ous·ness** n

boun·ti·ful \'baùnt-i-fəl\ adj **1 :** giving in abundance **:** GENEROUS ⟨a bountiful host⟩ **2 :** PLENTIFUL, ABUNDANT ⟨bountiful supply⟩ syn see GENEROUS — **boun·ti·ful·ly** \-f(ə-)lē\ adv — **boun·ti·ful·ness** \-fəl-nəs\ n

boun·ty \'baùnt-ē\ n, pl **bounties** [OF bonté goodness, fr. L bonitat-, bonitas, fr. bonus good] **1 a :** GENEROSITY **b :** something given generously **2 :** money given as a reward or inducement (as for the killing of vermin)

bou·quet \bō-'kā, bü-\ n [F, fr. MF, thicket] **1 :** a bunch of flowers **2 :** FRAGRANCE, AROMA

bour·bon \'bü(ə)r-bən, usu 'bər- in sense 3\ n **1** cap **:** a member of a French family to which belong many kings of France, Spain, Naples, and the kingdom of the Two Sicilies **2** often cap **:** a person who clings obstinately to social and political ideas of the old order of things; esp **:** an extreme Southern conservative of the U.S. **3** [fr. Bourbon county, Kentucky] **:** a whiskey distilled from corn mash; one distilled from a mash of corn, malt, and rye — **bour·bon·ism** \-bə-,niz-əm\ n, often cap

¹bour·geois \'bü(ə)rzh-,wä, bùrzh-'\ n, pl **bour·geois** \-,wä(z), -'wä(z)\ [F, fr. bourg town, fr. LL burgus fortified place, fr. Gmc origin; akin to E borough] **1 :** BURGHER **2 :** a person whose social behavior and political views are held to be influenced by his interest in private property; esp **:** CAPITALIST **3** pl **:** BOURGEOISIE

²bourgeois adj **1 :** of, relating to, or characteristic of townsmen or of the middle class **2 :** marked by a concern for material interests and respectability and a tendency toward mediocrity **3 :** dominated by commercial and industrial interests **:** CAPITALISTIC

bour·geoi·sie \,bùrzh-,wä-'zē\ n, pl **bourgeoisie 1 :** the class of bourgeois **2 :** a social order dominated by bourgeois

¹bourn or **bourne** \'bōrn, 'bórn, 'bü(ə)rn\ n **:** STREAM, BROOK

²bourn or **bourne** n [MF bourne, alter. of OF bodne] **1** archaic **:** BOUNDARY, LIMIT **2** archaic **:** GOAL, DESTINATION

bour·rée \bù-'rā\ n [F] **:** a lively 17th century French dance

bourse \'bù(ə)rs\ n [F, lit., purse, fr. ML bursa] **:** EXCHANGE 5a; esp **:** a European stock exchange

bout \'baùt\ n [E dial., a trip going and returning in plowing, fr. ME bought bend] **:** a spell of activity: as **a :** an athletic match (as of boxing) **b :** OUTBREAK, ATTACK ⟨a bout of measles⟩ **c :** SESSION

bou·tique \bü-'tēk\ n [F] **:** a small retail store; esp **:** a fashionable specialty shop for women

bou·ton·niere \,büt-ᵊn-'i(ə)r, ,bü-tən-'ye(ə)r\ n [F boutonnière buttonhole, fr. bouton button] **:** a flower or bouquet worn in a buttonhole

¹bo·vine \'bō-,vīn, -,vēn\ adj [LL bovinus, fr. L bov-, bos

ox, cow; akin to E cow] **1 :** of, relating to, or resembling the ox or cow **2 :** sluggish or patient like an ox or cow

²bovine n **:** a bovine animal

¹bow \'baù\ vb [OE būgan to bend, bow] **1 :** to bend the head, body, or knee in greeting, reverence, respect, or submission **2 :** SUBMIT, YIELD ⟨bow to authority⟩ **3 :** BEND ⟨bowed with age⟩ **4 :** to express by bowing ⟨bow one's thanks⟩

²bow n **:** a bending of the head or body in respect, submission, assent, or greeting

³bow \'bō\ n [OE boga; akin to E ¹bow] **1 :** RAINBOW **2 :** a weapon for shooting arrows that is made of a strip of elastic material (as wood) bent by a cord connecting the two ends **3 :** something shaped in a curve like a bow **:** BEND **4 :** a wooden rod with horsehairs stretched from end to end used for playing a violin or similar instrument **5 :** a knot formed by doubling a ribbon or string into one or two loops

⁴bow \'bō\ vb **1 :** to bend into a curve **2 :** to play a stringed musical instrument with a bow

⁵bow \'baù\ n **:** the forward part of a ship

bowd·ler·ize \'bōd-lə-,rīz, 'baùd-\ vt [Thomas Bowdler d1825 English editor of Shakespeare] **:** to expurgate (as a book) by omitting or modifying parts considered indelicate — **bowd·ler·i·za·tion** \,bōd-lə-rə-'zā-shən, ,baùd-\ n

bow·el \'baù(-ə)l\ n [OF boel, fr. ML botellus, fr. L, dim. of botulus sausage] **1 a :** INTESTINE, GUT — usu. used in pl. **b :** a division of the intestine **2** archaic **:** the seat of pity or tenderness — usu. used in pl. **3** pl **:** the interior parts ⟨the bowels of the earth⟩

bow·er \'baù(-ə)r\ n [OE būr dwelling] **1 :** a place for rest **:** RETREAT **2 :** a shelter (as in a garden) made with tree boughs or vines twined together **:** ARBOR — **bow·ery** \-ē\ adj

bow·er·bird \'baù(-ə)r-,bərd\ n **:** any of various mostly Australian birds that build chambers or passages arched over with twigs and grasses

bow·fin \'bō-,fin\ n **:** a gluttonous dull green iridescent American freshwater fish related to the sturgeons

bow·ie knife \'bü-ē-, 'bō-ē-\ n [after James Bowie d1836 American soldier who first used one] **:** a stout straight single-edged hunting knife

bow·knot \'bō-,nät, -'nät\ n **:** a knot with decorative loops

¹bowl \'bōl\ n [OE bolla] **1 :** a rounded hollow dish generally deeper than a basin and larger than a cup **2 :** the contents of a bowl **3 :** the bowl-shaped part of something (as a spoon or a tobacco pipe) **4 :** a bowl-shaped amphitheater — **bowled** \'bōld\ adj

²bowl n [MF boule ball, fr. L bulla bubble] **1 a :** a ball weighted or shaped to give it a bias when rolled **b** pl **:** a game played on a green in which bowls are rolled at a jack **2 :** a cast of the ball in bowling or bowls

³bowl vb **1 :** to participate or roll a ball in bowling or bowls **2 :** to travel smoothly and rapidly **3 a :** to strike with a swiftly moving object **b :** to overwhelm with surprise ⟨the news bowled him over⟩

bowlder var of BOULDER

bow·leg \'bō-,leg, -'leg\ n **:** a leg bowed outward at or below the knee — **bow·legged** \'bō-'leg(-ə)d\ adj

¹bowl·er \'bō-lər\ n **:** one that bowls

²bowl·er \'bō-lər\ n **:** DERBY 3

bowl game n **:** a football game played after the regular season between specially invited teams

bow·line \'bō-lən, -,līn\ n **1 :** a rope used to keep the weather edge of a square sail pulled forward **2 :** a knot used for making a loop that will not slip

bowl·ing \'bō-liŋ\ n **1 :** a game played by rolling balls so as to knock down wooden pins set up at the far end of an alley **:** ninepins or tenpins **2 :** BOWLS

bow·man \'bō-mən\ n **:** ARCHER

Bow·man's capsule \,bō-mənz-\ n **:** a membranous capsule enclosing each glomerulus of a kidney

bow·sprit \'baù-,sprit, 'bō-\ n **:** a large spar projecting forward from the bow of a ship

bow·string \'bō-,striŋ\ n **:** the cord connecting the two ends of a bow

bows 2: 1 ancient Greek, 2 African, 3 South American

bow tie \'bō-\ *n* : a short necktie tied in a bowknot

bow window \'bō-\ *n* : a curved bay window

bow·yer \'bō-yər\ *n* : one that makes shooting bows

¹box \'bäks\ *n, pl* **box** *or* **box·es** [OE, fr. L *buxus*, fr. Gk *pyxos*] : an evergreen shrub or small tree used esp. for hedges

²box *n* [OE, fr. LL *buxis*, fr. Gk *pyxis*, fr. *pyxos* box tree, boxwood] **1 a** : a receptacle usu. having four sides, a bottom, and a cover **b** : the amount held by a box **2** : a small compartment for a group of spectators in a theater **3** : BOX STALL **4** : the driver's seat on a carriage **5** : a shed that protects ⟨sentry *box*⟩ **6** : a receptacle (as for a bearing) resembling a box **7** : printed matter enclosed by rules or white space **8** : a space on a baseball diamond where a batter, coach, pitcher, or catcher stands

³box *vt* **1** : to enclose in or as if in a box **2** : to mix (paint) by pouring back and forth between two containers — **box the compass 1** : to name the 32 points of the compass in their order **2** : to make a complete reversal

⁴box *n* [ME] : a punch or slap esp. on the ear

⁵box *vb* **1** : to strike with the hand **2** : to engage in boxing : fight with the fists

box·car \'bäks-ˌkär\ *n* : a roofed freight car usu. with sliding doors in the sides

box elder *n* : a No. American maple with compound leaves

¹box·er \'bäk-sər\ *n* : one that engages in the sport of boxing

²boxer *n* : a compact medium-sized short-haired usu. fawn or brindle dog of a breed originating in Germany

Box·er \'bäk-sər\ *n* : a member of a Chinese secret society that in 1900 attempted by violence to drive foreigners out of China and to force native converts to renounce Christianity

box·ing *n* : the art of attack and defense with the fists practiced as a sport

Box·ing Day \'bäk-siŋ-\ *n* : the first weekday after Christmas observed as a legal holiday in parts of the British Commonwealth and marked by the giving of Christmas boxes (as to postmen)

boxing glove *n* : one of a pair of padded leather mittens worn in boxing

box kite *n* : a tailless kite consisting of two or more open-ended connected boxes

box·like \'bäks-ˌlīk\ *adj* : resembling a box esp. in shape

box office *n* : an office in a public place (as a theater or stadium) where tickets of admission are sold

box pleat *n* : a pleat made by forming two folded edges one facing right and the other left

box score *n* : the complete score of a baseball game giving the names and positions of the players and a record of the play arranged in tabular form

box spring *n* : a bedspring that consists of spiral springs attached to a foundation and enclosed in a cloth-covered frame

box stall *n* : an individual enclosure for an animal

box turtle *n* : any of several No. American land tortoises able to withdraw completely into the shell

box·wood \'bäks-ˌwùd\ *n* : the close-grained tough hard wood of the box; *also* : the box tree

boy \'bòi\ *n* [ME] **1** : a male child from birth to young manhood **2** : SON **3** : a male servant; *esp* : a native man-servant (as in the Far East) — **boy·hood** \-ˌhùd\ *n* — **boy·ish** \-ish\ *adj* — **boy·ish·ly** *adv* — **boy·ish·ness** *n*

bo·yar \bō-'yär\ *n* [Russ *boyarin*] : a member of a Russian aristocratic order next in rank below the ruling princes until its abolition by Peter the Great

¹boy·cott \'bòi-ˌkät\ *vt* [Charles C. *Boycott* d1897 English land agent in Ireland who was ostracized for refusing to reduce rents] : to engage in a joint refusal to have dealings with a person, organization, or country usu. as an expression of disapproval or to force acceptance of terms

²boycott *n* : the process or an instance of boycotting

boy·friend \'bòi-ˌfrend\ *n* : a regular male companion of a girl or woman

boy scout *n* : a member of the Boy Scouts of America

boy·sen·ber·ry \'bòiz-ᵊn-ˌber-ē, 'bòis-\ *n* [after Rudolph *Boysen* fl1923 American horticulturist] : a very large bramble fruit with a raspberry flavor; *also* : the trailing hybrid bramble of this fruit developed by crossing several blackberries and raspberries

bra \'brä\ *n* : BRASSIERE

¹brace \'brās\ *n, pl* **brac·es** *or* **brace** [ME, pair, clasp, fr. MF, two arms, fr. L *bracchia*, pl. of *bracchium* arm] **1** : two of a kind ⟨several *brace* of quail⟩ **2** : something (as a clasp) that connects or fastens **3** : a crank-shaped instrument for turning a wood-boring bit **4 a** : something that transmits, directs, resists, or supports weight or pressure; *esp* : an inclined timber used as a support **b** *pl* : SUSPENDERS **c** : a device for supporting a body part (as the shoulders) **d** : a dental appliance worn on the teeth to correct irregularities of growth and position **5 a** : a mark { or } — used to connect words or items to be considered together **b** : this mark connecting two or more musical staffs the parts on which are to be performed simultaneously; *also* : the group of staffs so connected **6** : a cord or rod for producing or maintaining tightness

²brace *vb* **1 a** : to make firm or taut ⟨*brace* a drum⟩ **b** : to get ready or set : STEEL ⟨*braced* himself for the test⟩ **2 a** : to furnish or support with a brace : prop up : REINFORCE **b** : INVIGORATE, FRESHEN **3 a** : to make rigid : STIFFEN **b** : to plant firmly ⟨*bracing* his feet in the stirrups⟩ **4** : to take heart : buck up ⟨*brace* up, all is not lost⟩

brace·let \'brā-slət\ *n* [MF, fr. dim. of *bras* arm, fr. L *bracchium*] : an ornamental band or chain worn around the wrist

bra·cer \'brā-sər\ *n* : an arm or wrist protector

brace root *n* : PROP ROOT

brach·i·al \'brak-ē-əl, 'brā-kē-\ *adj* [L *bracchium*, *brachium* arm] : of or relating to the arm or a comparable process

brachial plexus *n* : a network of nerves lying mostly in the armpit and supplying nerves to the chest, shoulder, and arm

brach·i·ate \'brak-ē-ˌāt, 'brā-kē-\ *vi* : to progress by swinging from one hold to another by the arms ⟨*brachiating* gibbon⟩ — **brach·i·a·tion** \ˌbrak-ē-'ā-shən, ˌbrāk-ē-\ *n*

brach·io·pod \'brak-ē-ə-ˌpäd\ *n* [L *bracchium* arm + Gk *pod-*, *pous* foot] : any of a phylum (Brachiopoda) of marine invertebrate animals with bivalve shells and a pair of arms bearing tentacles — **brachiopod** *adj*

brachy- *comb form* [Gk *brachys*] : short ⟨*brachy*cranial⟩

brachy·ce·phal·ic \ˌbrak-i-sə-'fal-ik\ *adj* : short-headed or broad-headed with a cephalic index of over 80 — **brachy·ceph·a·ly** \-i-'sef-ə-lē\ *n*

brack·en \'brak-ən\ *n* [ME *braken*] : a large coarse branching fern; *also* : a growth of such ferns

¹brack·et \'brak-ət\ *n* [MF *braguette* projecting part on breeches, fr. dim. of *brague* breeches, fr. L *braca*, fr. Gaulish, of Gmc origin; akin to E *breeches*] **1** : an overhanging member or fixture that projects from a structure (as a wall) and is usu. designed to support a vertical load or to strengthen an angle **2** : a short wall shelf **3 a** : one of a pair of marks [ ] used to enclose matter or in mathematics as signs of aggregation — called also *square bracket* **b** : one of a pair of marks ⟨ ⟩ used to enclose matter — called also *angle bracket* **4** : a section of a continuously numbered or graded series; *esp* : one of a series of groups graded by income

²bracket *vt* **1** : to place within or as if within brackets **2** : to put into the same class : ASSOCIATE **3** : to get the range on (a target) by firing over and short ⟨*bracketed* the position with artillery fire⟩

bracket fungus *n* : a basidiomycete that forms shelflike fruiting bodies

brack·ish \'brak-ish\ *adj* [D *brac* salty] : somewhat salty

bract \'brakt\ *n* [L *bractea* thin metal plate] **1** : a leaf from the axil of which a flower or inflorescence arises **2** : a leaf that grows on a flower-bearing stem — see COMPOSITE illustration, CORYMB illustration — **bract·ed** \'brak-təd\ *adj*

brad \'brad\ *n* [ON *broddr* spike] : a slender wire nail with a small deep round head

brady·car·dia \ˌbrad-i-'kärd-ē-ə\ *n* : a slow heart rate

brae \'brā\ *n, chiefly Scot* : a hillside esp. along a river

¹brag \'brag\ *n* [ME] **1** : a pompous or boastful statement **2** : arrogant talk or manner : COCKINESS **3** : BRAGGART

²brag *vb* **bragged**; **brag·ging** : to talk or assert boastfully — **brag·ger** \'brag-ər\ *n*

brag·ga·do·cio \ˌbrag-ə-'dō-s(h)ē-ˌō, -shō\ *n, pl* **-cios** [fr. *Braggadochio*, personification of boasting in *Faerie Queene*] by Edmund Spenser] **1** : BRAGGART, BOASTER **2 a** : empty boasting **b** : COCKINESS

brag·gart \'brag-ərt\ *n* : a loud arrogant boaster — **braggart** *adj*

Brah·ma \'bräm-ə\ *n* **1** : the ultimate ground of all being in Hinduism **2** : the creator god of the Hindu sacred triad — compare SIVA, VISHNU

Brah·man *or* **Brah·min** \'bräm-ən\ *n* [Skt *brāhmaṇa*, fr. *brahman* prayer, sacred lore] **1** : a Hindu of the highest and traditionally the priestly caste **2** : BRAHMA 1 — **Brahman** *or* **Brah·man·ic** \brä-'man-ik\ *adj*

Brah·man·ism \'bräm-ə-ˌniz-əm\ *n* : orthodox Hinduism adhering to the pantheism of the Vedas and to the ancient sacrifices and family ceremonies

Brah·min \'bräm-ən\ *n* : an aloof intellectually and socially cultivated person; *esp* : such a person from one of the older New England families — **Brah·min·i·cal** \brä-'min-i-kəl\ *adj* — **Brah·min·ism** \'bräm-ə-ˌniz-əm\ *n*

¹braid \'brād\ *vt* [OE *bregdan* to move suddenly] **1** : to form (three or more strands) into a braid ⟨*braided* the girl's hair⟩ **2** : to ornament esp. with ribbon or braid — **braid·er** *n*

²braid *n* **1** : a cord or ribbon having usu. three or more component strands forming a regular diagonal pattern down its length; *esp* : a narrow fabric of intertwined threads used esp. for trimming **2** : a length of braided hair

braid·ing \'brād-iŋ\ *n* : something made of braided material

brail \'brāl\ *n* **1** : a rope fastened to the leech of a sail for hauling the sail up or in **2** : a dip net for hauling fish aboard a boat — **brail** *vt*

braille \'brāl\ *n, often cap* [after Louis *Braille* d1852

a	b	c	d	e	f	g	h	i	j
1	2	3	4	5	6	7	8	9	0

k	l	m	n	o	p	q	r	s	t

| u | v | x | y | z | w | Capital Sign | Numeral Sign |

braille alphabet: the first ten letters serve also as numerals and each letter serves also, when standing alone, as a common word

French teacher of the blind, who invented it] : a system of writing for the blind that uses characters made up of raised dots

¹brain \'brān\ *n* [OE *brægen*] **1 a** : the portion of the vertebrate central nervous system that is the organ of thought and nervous coordination, is made up of neurons and supporting and nutritive structures, is enclosed within the skull, and is continuous with the spinal cord **b** : a major nervous center in an invertebrate animal **2 a** : INTELLECT, INTELLIGENCE — often used in pl. **b** : a very intelligent or intellectual person

²brain *vt* **1** : to kill by smashing the skull **2** : to hit on the head

brain·case \-ˌkās\ *n* : the cranium enclosing the brain

brain·child \-ˌchīld\ *n* : a product of one's creative imagination

brain·less \'brān-ləs\ *adj* : UNINTELLIGENT, SILLY — **brain·less·ly** *adv* — **brain·less·ness** *n*

brain stem *n* : the posterior and lower part of the brain including the midbrain and medulla oblongata

brain·storm \'brān-ˌstorm\ *n* **1** : a temporary but violent mental upset or disturbance **2** : a sudden burst of inspiration : a startling idea

brain trust *n* : a group of expert advisers esp. on planning and strategy who often lack official status — **brain trust·er** \-ˌtrəs-tər\ *n*

brain·wash·ing \'brān-ˌwòsh-iŋ, -ˌwäsh-\ *n* : a forcible attempt by indoctrination to induce someone to give up his basic political, social, or religious beliefs and attitudes and to accept contrasting regimented ideas

brain wave *n* : rhythmic fluctuations of voltage between parts of the brain that alter in abnormal states

brainy \'brā-nē\ *adj* **brain·i·er**; **-est** : INTELLIGENT, INTELLECTUAL — **brain·i·ness** *n*

braise \'brāz\ *vt* [F *braiser*] : to cook slowly in fat and little moisture in a closed pot

¹brake \'brāk\ *archaic past of* BREAK

²brake *n* [ME] : a coarse fern often growing several feet high : BRACKEN

³brake *n* [MLG; akin to E *break*] **1** : a toothed instrument or machine for separating out the fiber of flax or hemp **2** : a machine for bending sheet metal

⁴brake *n* [ME] : a device for slowing up or stopping motion (as of a wheel, vehicle, or engine) esp. by friction

⁵brake *vb* **1** : to retard or stop by or as if by a brake **2** : to operate a brake esp. on a vehicle

⁶brake *n* [ME *-brake*] : rough or marshy land thickly overgrown usu. with one kind of plant — **braky** \'brā-kē\ *adj*

brake·man \'brāk-mən\ *n* : a freight or passenger train crew member whose duties include inspecting the train and assisting the conductor

bram·ble \'bram-bəl\ *n* [OE *brēmel*] : any of a large genus of usu. prickly shrubs of the rose family including the raspberries and blackberries — **bram·bly** \-b(ə-)lē\ *adj*

bran \'bran\ *n* [OF] : the broken coat of the seed of cereal grain separated from the flour or meal by sifting or bolting

¹branch \'branch\ *n* [OF *branche*] **1** : a natural subdivision (as a bough arising from a trunk or a twig from a bough) of a plant stem **2** : something (as a tributary of a river or a secondary road) forming a part of a larger whole in a manner suggesting the relation of a branch to a tree ⟨a *branch* of an antler⟩⟨the *branches* of an artery⟩: as **a** : a division of a family descending from a particular ancestor **b** : a division of an organization ⟨executive *branch* of the government⟩ **c** : a subordinate office or part of a central system ⟨a *branch* of a bank⟩ — **branched** \'brancht\ *adj* — **branch·less** \'branch-ləs\ *adj* — **branchy** \'bran-chē\ *adj*

²branch *vi* **1** : to put forth branches : spread or separate into branches ⟨a great elm *branches* over the yard⟩ **2** : to spring out (as from a main stem) : DIVERGE ⟨streets *branching* off the highway⟩ **3** : to extend activities ⟨the business is *branching* out all over the state⟩

bran·chi·al \'braŋ-kē-əl\ *adj* [L *branchia* gill, fr. Gk, pl. of *branchion* gill] : of, relating to, or situated near the gills

¹brand \'brand\ *n* [OE, torch, sword; akin to E *burn*] **1** : a charred or burning piece of wood **2** : SWORD **3 a** : a mark made by burning (as on cattle) to show ownership or origin **b** : a mark made with a stamp or stencil for similar purposes : TRADEMARK **c** : a mark put on criminals with a hot iron **d** : a mark of disgrace : STIGMA **4 a** : a class of goods identified as the product of a single firm or manufacturer : MAKE **b** : a characteristic or distinctive kind : VARIETY

²brand *vt* **1** : to mark with or as if with a brand **2** : to mark or expose as bad or infamous : STIGMATIZE — **brand·er** *n*

bran·dish \'bran-dish\ *vt* [MF *brandiss-, brandir*, fr. *brand* sword, of Gmc origin; akin to E *brand*] **1** : to shake or wave (as a weapon) threateningly **2** : to display in a showy or aggressive manner — **brandish** *n*

brand–new \'bran-'n(y)ü\ *adj* : conspicuously new and unused

¹bran·dy \'bran-dē\ *n, pl* **-dies** [short for *brandywine*, fr. D *brandewijn*, fr. MD *brant* distilled + *wijn* wine] : an alcoholic liquor distilled from wine or fermented fruit juice

²brandy *vt* **bran·died**; **bran·dy·ing** : to flavor, blend, or preserve with brandy ⟨*brandied* cherries⟩

brant \'brant\ *n, pl* **brant** *or* **brants** : a wild goose; *esp* : any of several small dark geese that breed in the Arctic

brash \'brash\ *adj* **1** : IMPETUOUS, RASH ⟨a *brash* attack⟩ **2 a** : aggressively self-assertive : IMPUDENT ⟨a *brash* youth⟩ **b** : HARSH, BLATANT — **brash·ly** *adv* — **brash·ness** *n*

brass \'bras\ *n* [OE *bræs*] **1** : an alloy consisting essentially of copper and zinc; *also* : the reddish yellow color of this alloy **2 a** : brass musical instruments — often used in pl. **b** : a usu. brass memorial tablet **c** : bright metal fittings or utensils **3** : brazen self-assurance : GALL **4** : BRASS HATS — **brass** *adj*

bras·sard \brə-'särd, 'bras-,ärd\ *also* **bras·sart** \-'sär(t), -,är(t)\ *n* : a cloth band worn around the upper arm usu. bearing an identifying mark

brass·bound \'bras-,baúnd, -'baúnd\ *adj* 1 : having trim made of brass ⟨*brassbound* trunk⟩ 2 : uncompromisingly bound by tradition : INFLEXIBLE

brass hat *n* : a person (as a military officer) in a high-ranking position

brass·ie \'bras-ē\ *n* : a wooden-headed golf club with more loft than a driver — called also *number two wood*

bras·siere \brə-'zi(ə)r, ,bras-ē-'e(ə)r\ *n* [obs. F *brassière* bodice, fr. OF *braciere* arm protector, fr. *bras* arm] : a woman's close-fitting undergarment having cups for bust support

brass tacks *n pl* : details of immediate practical importance ⟨get down to *brass tacks*⟩

brassy \'bras-ē\ *adj* **brass·i·er; -est** 1 : BRAZEN, OBSTREPEROUS 2 : resembling brass esp. in color 3 : resembling the sound of a brass instrument — **brass·i·ly** \'bras-ə-lē\ *adv* — **brass·i·ness** \'bras-ē-nəs\ *n*

brat \'brat\ *n* : CHILD; *esp* : an ill-mannered annoying child — **brat·tish** \'brat-ish\ *adj* — **brat·ty** \'brat-ē\ *adj*

bra·va·do \brə-'väd-ō\ *n, pl* **-does** *or* **-dos** [MF *bravade*, fr. OIt *bravata*, fr. *bravo* courageous] 1 : blustering swaggering conduct 2 : show of bravery

¹**brave** \'brāv\ *adj* [MF, fr. It & Sp *bravo* wild, courageous, fr. L *barbarus* barbarous] 1 : COURAGEOUS 2 : making a fine show : SPLENDID — **brave·ly** *adv*

²**brave** *vt* : to face or endure with courage ⟨*braved* the taunts of the mob⟩

³**brave** *n* : one who is brave; *esp* : a No. American Indian warrior

brav·ery \'brāv-(ə-)rē\ *n, pl* **-er·ies** 1 a : fine clothes b : showy display 2 : the quality or state of being brave : FEARLESSNESS **syn** see COURAGE

¹**bra·vo** \'bräv-ō\ *n, pl* **bravos** *or* **bravoes** [It, fr. *bravo* wild, courageous] : VILLAIN, DESPERADO; *esp* : a hired assassin

²**bra·vo** \'bräv-ō, brä-'vō\ *n, pl* **bravos** : a shout of approval — often used interjectionally in applauding a performance

bra·vu·ra \brə-'v(y)ùr-ə\ *n* 1 : a florid brilliant musical style 2 : self-assured brilliant performance

braw \'brò\ *adj* [modif. of MF *brave*] *chiefly Scot* : GOOD, FINE; *also* : well dressed

¹**brawl** \'bròl\ *vi* [ME *brawlen*] 1 : to quarrel noisily : WRANGLE 2 : to make a loud confused noise — **brawl·er** *n*

²**brawl** *n* : a noisy quarrel or fight

brawn \'bròn\ *n* [MF *braon* muscle, of Gmc origin] 1 : full strong muscles esp. of the arm or leg 2 : muscular strength

brawny \'brò-nē\ *adj* **brawn·i·er; -est** : MUSCULAR, STRONG — **brawn·i·ness** *n*

bray \'brā\ *vb* 1 : to utter the characteristic loud harsh cry of a donkey 2 : to utter or play loudly, harshly, or discordantly — **bray** *n*

bray·er \'brā-ər\ *n* [ME *brayen* to crush to powder, fr. MF *broiier*] : a printer's hand inking roller

braze \'brāz\ *vb* : to solder with a relatively infusible alloy (as brass)

¹**bra·zen** \'brāz-ⁿn\ *adj* [OE *bræsen*, fr. *bræs* brass] 1 : made of brass 2 a : sounding harsh and loud like struck brass b : of the color of polished brass 3 : IMPUDENT, SHAMELESS — **bra·zen-faced** \,brāz-ⁿn-'fāst\ *adj* — **bra·zen·ly** *adv* — **bra·zen·ness** \'brāz-ⁿn-(n)əs\ *n*

²**brazen** *vt* **bra·zened; bra·zen·ing** \'brāz-niŋ, -ⁿn-iŋ\ : to face with defiance or impudence

¹**bra·zier** \'brā-zhər\ *n* : one that works in brass

²**brazier** *n* [F *brasier*, fr. OF, fire of hot coals, fr. *brese* hot coals] 1 : a pan for holding burning coals 2 : a utensil on which food is exposed to heat (as from burning charcoal) through a wire grill

Bra·zil nut \brə-,zil-\ *n* : one of the 3-sided oily edible nuts that occur packed inside the round fruit of a large Brazilian tree

¹**breach** \'brēch\ *n* [OE *bryce*] 1 : violation of a law, duty, or tie ⟨a *breach* of trust⟩ 2 a : a broken, ruptured, or torn condition or area b : a gap (as in a wall) made by battering 3 a : a break in accustomed friendly relations b : HIATUS

²**breach** *vb* 1 : to make a breach in 2 : BREAK, VIOLATE 3 : to leap out of water ⟨an otter *breaching*⟩

breach of promise : violation of a promise esp. to marry

¹**bread** \'bred\ *n* [OE *brēad*; akin to E *brew*] 1 : a baked food made of a mixture whose basic constituent is flour or meal 2 : a portion of bread 3 : FOOD, SUSTENANCE

²**bread** *vt* : to cover with bread crumbs ⟨*breaded* veal cutlet⟩

bread–and–but·ter \,bred-ⁿn-'bət-ər\ *adj* 1 : of or relating to a means of livelihood 2 : sent or given as thanks for hospitality ⟨a *bread-and-butter* letter⟩

bread·bas·ket \'bred-,bas-kət\ *n* : a major cereal-producing region

bread·fruit \-,früt\ *n* : a round usu. seedless fruit that resembles bread in color and texture when baked; *also* : a tall tropical tree of the mulberry family that bears this fruit

bread·stuff \-,stəf\ *n* 1 : GRAIN, FLOUR 2 : BREAD

breadth \'bredth\ *n* [OE *brǣdu*, fr. *brād* broad] 1 : distance from side to side : WIDTH 2 a : something of full width b : a wide expanse 3 : COMPREHENSIVENESS, SCOPE

bread·win·ner \'bred-,win-ər\ *n* : a member of a family whose wages supply its livelihood

¹**break** \'brāk\ *vb* **broke** \'brōk\; **bro·ken** \'brō-kən\; **break·ing** [OE *brecan*] 1 a : to separate into parts with suddenness or violence : SHATTER ⟨*break* a dish⟩ ⟨the glass *broke* in his hand⟩⟨*break* up rocks⟩ b : MAIM c : RUPTURE d : to curl over and fall apart in surf or foam ⟨waves *breaking* against the shore⟩ 2 : VIOLATE, TRANSGRESS ⟨*broke* the law⟩⟨*break* a promise⟩ 3 a : to force a way into, out of, or through ⟨the burglars *broke* into the old house⟩ ⟨*break* jail⟩ b : to escape with sudden forceful effort ⟨*broke* away from his captors⟩ c : to develop, appear, or burst forth with suddenness or force ⟨day *breaks* in the east⟩ ⟨the storm *broke* with a thunderclap⟩ ⟨*broke* into laughter⟩ d : to become fair ⟨waited for the weather to *break*⟩ e : to make a sudden dash ⟨*break* for cover⟩ f : to make or effect by cutting, forcing, or pressing ⟨*break* open a package⟩ ⟨*break* a trail⟩ g : PENETRATE, PIERCE 4 : LOOSEN, SUNDER ⟨*break* a hold⟩ 5 : to cut into and turn over the surface of : PLOW ⟨*break* ground for a new school⟩ 6 a : to disrupt the order, compactness, or uniformity of ⟨*break* ranks⟩ b : to end by or as if by dispersing ⟨police *broke* up the mob⟩⟨*break* up a corporation⟩ c : to give way in disorderly retreat ⟨the soldiers *broke* under fire⟩ d : to decline suddenly and sharply in price or value e : to end a relationship or accord 7 a : to subdue completely ⟨*broke* the revolt⟩ b : to lose or cause to lose health, strength, or spirit ⟨*broke* under the strain⟩ ⟨*broken* by grief⟩ c : to become inoperative because of damage, wear, or strain ⟨the TV set is *broken*⟩⟨the car has *broken* down⟩ d : to ruin financially e : to reduce in rank ⟨*broke* him from sergeant to private⟩ f : to force (a strike) to end by measures outside bargaining practices g : to ruin the prospects of 8 a : to stop or bring to an end suddenly ⟨*break* a deadlock⟩ ⟨*broke* the silence⟩ b : INTERRUPT, SUSPEND ⟨*broke* in with a comment⟩⟨broke their tour for a rest⟩ 9 a : to make (an animal) fit for use (as by training) b : to accustom to an activity or occurrence ⟨*break* in a new worker⟩ 10 : to make known ⟨*break* the news to mother⟩ 11 : to turn aside or lessen the force or intensity of ⟨an awning *broke* his fall⟩ 12 : EXCEED, SURPASS ⟨*broke* all records⟩ 13 : OPEN ⟨*break* an electric circuit⟩ 14 : to split the surface of ⟨fish *breaking* water⟩ 15 : to cause to discontinue a habit ⟨*broke* the child of thumb-sucking⟩ 16 : SOLVE ⟨*broke* the enemy code⟩ 17 a : to alter course sharply ⟨the fox *broke* to the left⟩ b : to curve, drop, or rise sharply ⟨the pitch *broke* over the plate for a strike⟩ c : to alter sharply in tone, pitch, or intensity d : to shift abruptly from one register to another 18 : HAPPEN, DEVELOP ⟨everything *broke* right for him⟩ — **break·a·ble** \'brā-kə-bəl\ *adj* — **break the ice** 1 : to make a beginning 2 : to get through the first difficulties in starting a conversation or discussion — **break wind** : to expel gas from the intestine

²**break** *n* 1 a : an act or action of breaking b : the opening shot in a game of pool or billiards 2 a : a condition produced by breaking b : a gap in an electric circuit interrupting the flow of current 3 : an interruption in continuity: as a : a respite from work or duty b : a planned interruption in a radio or television program c : a noticeable change (as in a surface, course, movement,

or direction) **d** : a notable variation in vocal pitch, intensity, or tone   **e** : an abrupt run : DASH   **f** : the act of separating after a boxing or wrestling clinch   **4** : a rupture in previously friendly relations   **5** : a place or situation at which a break occurs: as   **a** : the point where one musical register changes to another   **b** : the place at which a word is divided   **c** : CAESURA   **6** : an awkward social blunder   **7** : a stroke of good luck

break·age \'brā-kij\ *n* **1 a** : the action of breaking   **b** : a quantity broken   **2** : an allowance for things broken

break down \(')brāk-'daůn\ *vb* **1 a** : to cause to fall or collapse by breaking or shattering   **b** : to make ineffective   **2 a** : to separate (as a protein) into simpler substances : DECOMPOSE   **b** : to undergo decomposition   **3** : to be susceptible to analysis or subdivision

break·down \'brāk-,daůn\ *n* : the action or result of breaking down: as   **a** : a failure to function properly   **b** : a physical, mental, or nervous collapse   **c** : failure to progress or have effect : DISINTEGRATION   **d** : DECOMPOSITION   **e** : division into categories : CLASSIFICATION

break·er \'brā-kər\ *n* **1** : one that breaks   **2** : a wave breaking into foam against the shore

break even *vi* : to emerge (as from a business transaction) with gains and losses balanced

break·fast \'brek-fəst\ *n* : the first meal of the day — **breakfast** *vb*

break·neck \'brāk-,nek\ *adj* : extremely dangerous ⟨*breakneck* speed⟩

break out \(')brāk-'aůt\ *vb* **1** : to be affected with a skin eruption   **2** : to take from stowage preparatory to using

break·out \'brāk-,aůt\ *n* : a violent or forceful break from restraint; *esp* : a military attack to break from encirclement

break·through \'brāk-,thrü\ *n* **1** : an act or point of breaking through an obstruction or defensive line   **2** : a sudden advance in knowledge or technique

break·wa·ter \'brāk-,wȯt-ər, -,wät-\ *n* : a structure (as a wall) to protect a harbor or beach from the force of waves

bream \'brim\ *n, pl* **bream** *or* **breams** [MF *breme*] : any of various mostly freshwater spiny-finned fishes; *esp* : any of several sunfishes (as a bluegill)

¹breast \'brest\ *n* [OE *brēost*] **1** : either of two protuberant milk-producing glandular organs situated on the front of the chest in the human female and some other mammals; *also* : any mammary gland   **2** : the fore or ventral part of the body between the neck and the abdomen   **3** : the seat of emotion and thought : BOSOM   **4** : something resembling a breast — **breast·ed** \'brestəd\ *adj*

²breast *vt* **1** : FACE, CONFRONT ⟨*breasted* the waves⟩   **2** : to struggle against courageously ⟨*breast* a storm⟩

breast·bone \'bres(t)-'bōn, -,bōn\ *n* : STERNUM

breast·plate \'bres(t)-,plāt\ *n* : a metal plate worn as defensive armor for the breast

breast·stroke \'bres(t)-,strōk\ *n* : a swimming stroke executed by extending the arms in front of the head while drawing the knees forward and outward and then sweeping the arms back with palms out while kicking backward and outward

breast·work \'brest-,wərk\ *n* : an improvised or temporary fortification

breath \'breth\ *n* [OE *brēth*] **1 a** : air charged with a fragrance or odor   **b** : a slight indication : SUGGESTION   **2 a** : the faculty of breathing   **b** : an act of breathing   **c** : RESPITE   **3** : a slight breeze   **4 a** : air inhaled and exhaled in breathing   **b** : something (as moisture on a cold surface) produced by breathing   **5** : a spoken sound : UTTERANCE   **6** : expiration of air with the glottis wide open in the formation of speech sounds — **out of breath** : breathing very rapidly (as from strenuous exercise)

breathe \'brēth\ *vb* **1** : to draw air into and expel it from the lungs : RESPIRE   **3** : to pause and rest before continuing   **4** : to blow softly   **5 a** : to send out by exhaling   **b** : to instill by or as if by breathing ⟨*breathe* new life into the movement⟩   **6 a** : UTTER, EXPRESS ⟨never *breathed* a word of it⟩   **b** : to make or become manifest   **7** : to allow to rest after exertion ⟨*breathe* a horse⟩   **8** : to take in in breathing — **breath·a·ble** \'brē-thə-bəl\ *adj*

breathed \'bretht\ *adj* : VOICELESS 2

breath·er \'brē-thər\ *n* **1** : one that breathes   **2** : a break in activity for rest

breath·ing \'brē-thiŋ\ *n* : either of the marks ' and ' used in writing Greek to indicate an initial *h*-sound or its absence

breath·less \'breth-ləs\ *adj* **1 a** : not breathing   **b** : DEAD   **2 a** : panting or gasping for breath   **b** : leaving one breathless — **breath·less·ly** *adv* — **breath·less·ness** *n*

breath·tak·ing \'breth-,tā-kiŋ\ *adj* **1** : making one out of breath ⟨a *breathtaking* climb⟩   **2** : EXCITING, THRILLING ⟨*breathtaking* beauty⟩ — **breath·tak·ing·ly** \-kiŋ-lē\ *adv*

breathy \'breth-ē\ *adj* : marked by the audible passage of breath — **breath·i·ness** *n*

brec·cia \'brech-(ē-)ə\ *n* [It] : a rock consisting of sharp fragments embedded in a fine-grained material

brede \'brēd\ *n* [alter. of *braid*] *archaic* : EMBROIDERY

breech \'brēch; "breeches" (*garment*) *is usu* 'brich-əz\ *n* [OE *brēc* breeches, pl. of *brōc* leg covering] **1** *pl a* : short trousers fitting snugly at the lower edges at or just below the knee   **b** : PANTS   **2** : BUTTOCKS   **3** : the back part of a cannon or gun behind the bore

breech·es buoy \'brē-chəz-, 'brich-əz-\ *n* : a canvas sling in the form of a pair of short-legged breeches hung from a life buoy running along a rope stretched from ship to shore or from one ship to another that is used to take persons off a ship esp. in rescue operations

breech·load·er \'brēch-,lōd-ər\ *n* : a firearm receiving its ammunition at the breech

¹breed \'brēd\ *vb* **bred** \'bred\; **breed·ing** [OE *brēdan*] **1 a** : BEGET 1   **b** : PRODUCE, ORIGINATE   **2** : to propagate (plants or animals) sexually and usu. under controlled conditions (as for the development of improved forms)   **3 a** : to bring up : NURTURE   **b** : to inculcate by training   **4** : to mate with : MATE   **5** : to produce offspring sexually — **breed·er** *n*

²breed *n* **1** : a group of presumably related animals or plants visibly similar in most characters; *esp* : one differentiated from the wild type under the influence of man   **2** : a number of persons of the same stock   **3** : CLASS, KIND

breed·ing *n* **1** : ANCESTRY   **2** : training or education esp. in manners   **3** : the sexual propagation of plants or animals

¹breeze \'brēz\ *n* [ME *brise*] **1** : a gentle wind; *esp* : one of from 4 to 31 miles per hour   **2** : something easily done : CINCH

²breeze *vi* : to proceed quickly and easily ⟨*breezed* through the report⟩

breeze·way \'brēz-,wā\ *n* : a roofed open passage connecting two buildings (as a house and garage) or halves of a building

breezy \'brē-zē\ *adj* **breez·i·er; -est** **1** : swept by breezes   **2** : BRISK, LIVELY — **breez·i·ly** \-zə-lē\ *adv* — **breez·i·ness** \-zē-nəs\ *n*

brethren *pl of* BROTHER — used chiefly in formal or solemn address

Bret·on \'bret-ᵊn\ *n* **1** : a native or inhabitant of Brittany   **2** : the Celtic language of the Bretons — **Breton** *adj*

breve \'brēv, 'brev\ *n* [L, neut. of *brevis* brief] **1** : a mark ˘ placed over a vowel to show that the vowel is short   **2** : a note equivalent to four half notes

¹bre·vet \brə-'vet\ *n* : a commission giving a military officer higher nominal rank than that for which he receives pay

²brevet *vt* **bre·vet·ted** *or* **bre·vet·ed; bre·vet·ting** *or* **bre·vet·ing** : to confer rank upon by brevet

bre·via·ry \'brē-v(y)ə-rē, -vē-,er-ē\ *n, pl* **-ries** [L *breviarium*, fr. *brevis* brief] **1** : MANUAL, HANDBOOK   **2 a** : a book containing the prayers, hymns, and readings prescribed esp. for priests for each day of the year   **b** : the prescribed prayers for a day

brev·i·ty \'brev-ət-ē\ *n* **1** : shortness of duration   **2** : expression in few words : CONCISENESS

¹brew \'brü\ *vb* [OE *brēowan*] **1** : to prepare (as beer or ale) by steeping, boiling, and fermentation or by infusion and fermentation   **2** : to bring about as if by brewing magical potions : CONTRIVE, PLOT   **3** : to prepare (as tea) by infusion in hot water   **4** : to be forming ⟨a storm is *brewing*⟩ — **brew·er** \'brü-ər, 'brů-(ə)r\ *n*

²brew *n* **1** : a brewed beverage   **2** : a product of brewing

brewer's yeast *n* : a yeast used or suitable for use in brewing; *also* : the dried pulverized cells of such a yeast used as a source of B-complex vitamins — compare BAKERS' YEAST

brew·ery \'brü-ə-rē, 'brù(-ə)r-ē\ n, pl **-er·ies** : a plant where malt liquors are manufactured

bri·ar var of BRIER

¹**bribe** \'brīb\ n [ME, something stolen, fr. MF, bread given to a beggar] **1** : money or favor given or promised to a person in a position of trust to influence dishonestly his judgment or conduct **2** : something that serves to induce or influence

²**bribe** vb : to induce or influence by or as if by giving bribes — **brib·a·ble** \'brī-bə-bəl\ adj — **brib·er** n

brib·ery \'brī-b(ə-)rē\ n, pl **-er·ies** : the act or practice of bribing

bric-a-brac \'brik-ə-,brak\ n [F bric-à-brac] : small ornamental articles : KNICKKNACKS, CURIOS

¹**brick** \'brik\ n [MF brique, fr. MD bricke] **1 a** : a building or paving material made from clay molded into blocks and hardened in the sun or baked **b** : a rectangular block made of brick **2** : a brick-shaped mass ⟨a brick of ice cream⟩

²**brick** vt : to close, face, or pave with bricks

brick·bat \'brik-,bat\ n **1** : a piece of a broken brick; esp : one thrown as a missile **2** : an uncomplimentary remark

brick·lay·er \'brik-,lā-ər, -,le(-ə)r\ n : a person who builds or paves with bricks — **brick·lay·ing** \-,lā-iŋ\ n

brick·work \'brik-,wərk\ n : work of or with brick

brick·yard \-,yärd\ n : a place where bricks are made

¹**brid·al** \'brīd-ᵊl\ n [OE brȳdealu, fr. brȳd bride + ealu ale, festival] : a wedding festival or ceremony : MARRIAGE

²**bridal** adj : of or relating to a bride or a wedding : NUPTIAL

bridal wreath n : a spirea widely grown for its slender drooping branches and clusters of small white flowers borne in spring

bride \'brīd\ n [OE brȳd] : a woman newly married or about to be married

bride·groom \-,grüm, -,grùm\ n [OE brȳdguma, fr. brȳd bride + guma man] : a man just married or about to be married

brides·maid \'brīdz-,mād\ n : a woman who attends a bride at her wedding

¹**bridge** \'brij\ n [OE brycg] **1** : a structure built over a

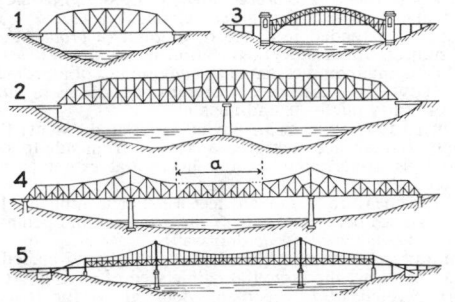

bridges: 1 simple truss, 2 continuous truss, 3 steel arch, 4 cantilever (a suspended span), 5 suspension

depression or an obstacle (as a river or a railroad) for use as a passageway **2** : a platform above and across the deck of a ship for the captain or officer in charge **3** : something resembling a bridge in form or function: as **a** : the upper bony part of the nose **b** : an arch serving to raise the strings of a musical instrument **4** : something (as a partial denture anchored to adjacent teeth) that fills a gap

²**bridge** vt : to make a bridge over or across ⟨bridge a gap⟩ — **bridge·a·ble** \-ə-bəl\ adj

³**bridge** n : any of various card games for four players developed from whist; esp : CONTRACT BRIDGE

bridge·head \-,hed\ n **1** : a fortified position protecting a bridge **2** : an advanced position seized in enemy territory as a foothold for further advance

bridge·work \-,wərk\ n : the dental bridges in a mouth

¹**bri·dle** \'brīd-ᵊl\ n [OE brīdel] **1** : the headgear with which a horse is controlled consisting of a headstall, a bit, and reins **2** : CURB, RESTRAINT

²**bridle** vb **bri·dled; bri·dling** \'brīd-liŋ, -ᵊl-iŋ\ **1** : to put a bridle upon **2** : to restrain with or as if with a bridle **3** : to show hostility or resentment esp. by drawing back the head and chin

bridle path n : a path suitable for or open only to horseback riders

¹**brief** \'brēf\ adj [MF, fr. L brevis] **1** : short in duration or extent ⟨a brief visit⟩ **2 a** : CONCISE **b** : CURT, ABRUPT — **brief·ly** adv — **brief·ness** n

²**brief** n **1 a** : a brief summary of an argument, set of facts, or document **b** : a concise statement of a client's case for the instruction of counsel in a trial at law **c** : a formal outline of the pleadings and the main contentions with supporting evidence and of the court's decision in a court of law **2** pl : short snug underpants

³**brief** vt **1** : to make an abstract or abridgment of **2 a** : to give final precise instructions to ⟨brief a bombing crew⟩ **b** : to give essential information to ⟨brief reporters⟩

brief·case \-,kās\ n : a flat flexible case usu. of leather for carrying papers

¹**bri·er** \'brī(-ə)r\ n [OE brēr] : a plant (as the blackberry or the wild rose) with a thorny or prickly woody stem — **bri·ery** \'brī(-ə)r-ē\ adj

²**brier** n [F bruyère] : a heath of southern Europe the root of which is used for making tobacco pipes

¹**brig** \'brig\ n [short for brigantine] : a 2-masted square-rigged ship

²**brig** n : a place (as on a ship) for temporary confinement of offenders in the U.S. Navy

bri·gade \brig-'ād\ n [F] **1** : a military unit composed of a headquarters, one or more units of infantry or armor, and supporting units **2** : a group of people organized for special activity ⟨fire brigade⟩ ⟨labor brigade⟩

brig·a·dier \,brig-ə-'di(ə)r\ n : BRIGADIER GENERAL

brig

brigadier general n : a commissioned officer (as in the army) ranking above a colonel and below a major general

brig·and \'brig-ənd\ n [MF, fr. It brigante, fr. brigare to fight] : a lawless person who lives by plunder usu. as a member of a band : BANDIT — **brig·and·age** \-ən-dij\ n — **brig·and·ism** \-,diz-əm\ n

brig·an·tine \'brig-ən-,tēn\ n [MF brigantin, fr. It brigantino, fr. brigante brigand] : a 2-masted square-rigged ship differing from a brig in not carrying a square mainsail

bright \'brīt\ adj [OE beorht] **1** : shedding much light : SHINING, GLOWING ⟨a bright fire⟩ ⟨a bright day⟩ **2** : very clear or vivid in color : of high saturation or brilliance ⟨a bright red⟩ **3** : CLEVER, INTELLIGENT **4** : LIVELY, CHEERFUL **5** : PROMISING ⟨a bright future⟩ — **bright** adv — **bright·ly** adv — **bright·ness** n

bright·en \'brīt-ᵊn\ vb **bright·ened; bright·en·ing** \'brīt-niŋ, -ᵊn-iŋ\ : to make or become bright or brighter

Bright's disease \'brīts-\ n : kidney disease in which albumin appears in the urine

brill \'bril\ n, pl **brill** : a European flatfish related to the turbot

¹**bril·liant** \'bril-yənt\ adj [F brillant, prp. of briller to shine, fr. L beryllus beryl] **1 a** : very bright : GLITTERING **b** : being light and strong : high in saturation and lightness ⟨a brilliant blue⟩ **2 a** : STRIKING, DISTINGUISHED **b** : unusually keen or alert in mind — **bril·liance** \-yən(t)s\ or **bril·lian·cy** \-yən-sē\ n — **bril·liant·ly** adv — **bril·liant·ness** n

²**brilliant** n : a gem (as a diamond) cut with numerous facets so as to have especial brilliance

bril·lian·tine \'bril-yən-,tēn\ n **1** : a preparation for making hair glossy **2** : a light lustrous fabric similar to alpaca usu. of cotton and mohair or worsted

¹**brim** \'brim\ n [ME brimme] **1 a** : the rim esp. of a cup, bowl, or depression ⟨the brim of the crater⟩ **b** : BRINK, VERGE **2** : the projecting rim of a hat **syn** see RIM — **brim·ful** \-'fùl\ adj

²**brim** vb **brimmed; brim·ming 1** : to fill or become full to the brim **2** : to reach or overflow a brim

brim·stone \'brim-,stōn\ n [ME brinston, prob. fr. brinnen to burn + ston stone] : SULFUR

brin·dle \'brin-d°l\ *n* : a brindled color or animal

brin·dled \-d°l\ *or* **brin·dle** \-d°l\ *adj* : having faint dark streaks or flecks on a gray or tawny ground

brine \'brīn\ *n* [OE brȳne] **1** : water containing a great deal of common salt **2 a** : OCEAN **b** : the water of an ocean, sea, or salt lake

bring \'briŋ\ *vt* **brought** \'brȯt\; **bring·ing** \'briŋ-iŋ\ [OE bringan] **1 a** : to convey, lead, carry, or cause to come along with one **b** : to cause to be, act, or move in a special way: as (1) : ATTRACT (2) : PERSUADE, INDUCE (3) : FORCE, COMPEL (4) : to cause to come into a particular state or condition **2** : to cause to exist or occur: as **a** : PRODUCE ⟨winter will *bring* snow⟩ **b** : INSTITUTE ⟨*bring* legal action⟩ **3** : to procure in exchange : sell for ⟨apples will *bring* a good price this year⟩

syn BRING, TAKE may denote identical action performed in opposite directions in relation to the speaker. BRING implies carrying, leading, transporting *toward* a point where the speaker is or will be; TAKE implies the same action *away* from the speaker ⟨*take* this message to the foreman and *bring* back an answer⟩

— **bring up the rear** : to come last or behind

bring about *vt* : to cause to take place : EFFECT

bring forth *vt* : to bear or give birth to : PRODUCE

bring out *vb* : to present to the public⟨*bring out* a new book⟩

bring to *vt* : to restore to consciousness

bring up *vb* **1** : REAR, EDUCATE **2** : to stop suddenly **3** : to bring to attention : INTRODUCE **4** : VOMIT

brink \'briŋk\ *n* [ME] **1** : EDGE; *esp* : the edge at the top of a steep place **2** : the point of onset : VERGE ⟨*brink* of war⟩

brink·man·ship \-mən-,ship\ *n* : the practice of pushing a dangerous situation to the limit of safety before stopping

briny \'brī-nē\ *adj* **brin·i·er; -est** : of or resembling brine : SALTY — **brin·i·ness** *n*

brio \'brē-ō\ *n* [It] : VIVACITY, SPIRIT

bri·oche \brē-'ōsh\ *n* [F] : a roll baked from light yeast dough rich with eggs and butter

bri·quette *or* **bri·quet** \brik-'et\ *n* [F briquette, dim. of brique brick] : a compacted often brick-shaped mass of usu. fine material

¹brisk \'brisk\ *adj* **1** : very active or alert : LIVELY **2** : INVIGORATING, REFRESHING ⟨*brisk* autumn weather⟩ **3** : ENERGETIC, QUICK ⟨a *brisk* pace⟩ — **brisk·ly** *adv* — **brisk·ness** *n*

²brisk *vb* : to make or become brisk

bris·ket \'bris-kət\ *n* [ME brusket; akin to E breast] : the breast or lower chest of a quadruped animal

bris·ling *or* **bris·tling** \'briz-liŋ, 'bris-\ *n* [Norw brisling] : a small herring that resembles and is processed like a sardine

¹bris·tle \'bris-əl\ *n* [ME brust, fr. OE byrst] : a short stiff coarse hair or filament — **bris·tled** \-əld\ *adj* — **bris·tly** \'bris-(ə-)lē\ *adj*

²bristle *vi* **bris·tled; bris·tling** \'bris-(ə-)liŋ\ **1** : to rise up and stand stiffly erect ⟨quills *bristling* in all directions⟩ **2** : to show signs of anger or defiance ⟨the boy *bristled* when he was criticized⟩ **3** : to appear as if covered with bristles ⟨a harbor *bristling* with the masts of ships⟩ — **bris·tly** \'bris-(ə-)lē\ *adj*

bris·tle·cone pine \,bris-əl-,kōn-\ *n* : a pine of the western U.S. of which some specimens are held to be nearly 5000 years old

bris·tle·tail \'bris-əl-,tāl\ *n* : any of various wingless insects (orders Thysanura and Entotrophi) with two projecting tail bristles

bris·tol \'brist-°l\ *n* [fr. Bristol, England] : cardboard with a smooth surface suitable for writing or printing

brit *or* **britt** \'brit\ *n* : tiny sea animals important as fish food

bri·tan·nia metal \bri-,tan-yə-\ *n* : a silver-white alloy similar to pewter composed largely of tin, antimony, and copper

Bri·tan·nic \bri-'tan-ik\ *adj* : BRITISH

britch·es \'brich-əz\ *n pl* [by alter.] : BREECHES

Brit·i·cism \'brit-ə-,siz-əm\ *n* [British + -icism (as in gallicism)] : a characteristic feature of British English

¹Brit·ish \'brit-ish\ *n* **1 British** *pl* : the people of Great Britain or their descendants **b** : ENGLISH

²British *adj* **1** : of, relating to, or characteristic of the original inhabitants of Britain **2 a** : of, relating to, or

characteristic of Great Britain, the British Commonwealth, or the British **b** : ENGLISH

Brit·ish·er \'brit-i-shər\ *n* : BRITON 2

British thermal unit *n* : the quantity of heat required to raise the temperature of one pound of water one degree Fahrenheit at or near 39.2°F — abbr. *Btu*

Brit·on \'brit-°n\ *n* **1** : a member of one of the peoples inhabiting Britain previous to the Anglo-Saxon invasions **2** : a native or subject of Great Britain; *esp* : ENGLISHMAN

Brit·ta·ny spaniel \,brit-°n-ē-\ *n* : a large active spaniel of a French breed developed by interbreeding pointers with spaniels of Brittany

brit·tle \'brit-°l\ *adj* [ME britil] **1 a** : being hard but not tough : easily broken, cracked, or snapped ⟨*brittle* clay⟩ ⟨*brittle* glass⟩ **b** : FRAIL **2** : PERISHABLE, MORTAL **3** : lacking warmth, depth, or generosity of spirit : COLD — **brit·tle·ness** *n*

syn BRITTLE, CRISP, FRIABLE, FRAGILE mean tending to break easily. BRITTLE implies hardness without toughness or elasticity and susceptibility to snapping or fracture; CRISP suggests the light firmness and brittleness desirable in some foods as opposed to limpness or sogginess ⟨*crisp* lettuce⟩ ⟨*crisp* crackers⟩ FRIABLE is applied to substances that are readily crumbled or pulverized ⟨*friable* soil⟩ FRAGILE is applicable to anything that must be handled with care and implies delicacy of material or structure

brittle star *n* : any of a group (Ophiuroidea) of sea animals similar to the related starfishes but having slender flexible arms

¹broach \'brōch\ *n* [MF broche, fr. L broccus projecting] **1** : any of various pointed or tapered tools, implements, or parts: as **a** : a spit for roasting meat **b** : a tool for tapping casks **c** : a cutting tool with a series of teeth in a straight line used esp. for shaping a hole already bored **2** : BROOCH

²broach *vb* **1** : to pierce (as a cask) in order to draw the contents : TAP **2** : to shape or enlarge (a hole) with a broach **3** : to introduce or make known for the first time ⟨*broach* a subject for discussion⟩ **4** : to break the surface from below — **broach·er** *n*

broad \'brȯd\ *adj* [OE brād] **1** : not narrow : WIDE ⟨a *broad* highway⟩ **2** : extending far and wide : SPACIOUS ⟨*broad* prairies⟩ **3** : CLEAR, FULL ⟨*broad* daylight⟩ **4** : PLAIN, OBVIOUS ⟨a *broad* hint⟩ **5** : COARSE, INDELICATE **6** : liberal in thought ⟨*broad* religious views⟩ **7** : not limited : extended in range or amount ⟨a *broad* choice of subjects for a story⟩ ⟨education in its *broadest* sense⟩ **8** : being main and essential ⟨*broad* outlines of a problem⟩ **9** : ³LOW 12 — used specif. of *a* pronounced as in *father* — **broad·ly** *adv* — **broad·ness** *n*

syn BROAD, WIDE mean having horizontal extent; they apply to a surface measured or viewed from side to side. BROAD is preferred when full horizontal extent is considered ⟨*broad* shoulders⟩ WIDE is commonly used with units of measure ⟨rugs eight feet *wide*⟩ or is applied when the distance between limits or the extent of an opening is in mind ⟨*wide* view⟩ ⟨*wide* doorway⟩

broad·ax *or* **broad·axe** \'brȯd-,aks\ *n* : a broad-bladed ax

broad bean *n* : the large flat edible seed of an Old World upright vetch; *also* : this plant widely grown for its seeds and as fodder

¹broad·cast \'brȯd-,kast\ *adj* **1** : cast or scattered in all directions **2** : made public by means of radio or television — **broadcast** *adv*

²broadcast *n* **1** : the act of transmitting sound or images by radio or television **2** : a single radio or television program

³broadcast *vb* **broadcast** *also* **broad·cast·ed; broad·cast·ing** **1** : to scatter or sow (seed) broadcast **2** : to make widely known **3 a** : to send out a broadcast from a radio or television transmitting station **b** : to speak or perform on a broadcast program — **broad·cast·er** *n*

Broad Church *adj* : of or relating to a liberal party in the Anglican Communion esp. in the later 19th century — **Broad Churchman** *n*

broad·cloth \'brȯd-,klȯth\ *n* **1** : a fine woolen or worsted fabric made compact and glossy in finishing **2** : a fine cloth usu. of cotton, silk, or rayon made in plain and ribbed weaves

broad·en \'brȯd-°n\ *vb* **broad·ened; broad·en·ing** \'brȯd-niŋ, -°n-iŋ\ : to make or become broad or broader

broad jump *n* : a jump for distance in a track-and-field contest — **broad jumper** *n*

broad·leaf \'brȯd-,lēf\ *adj* : BROAD-LEAVED

broad–leaved \-'lēvd\ *or* **broad–leafed** \-'lēft\ *adj* : having broad leaves; *esp* : having leaves that are not needles ⟨*broad-leaved* evergreens⟩

broad·loom \-,lüm\ *adj* : woven on a wide loom; *also* : so woven in solid color ⟨*broadloom* carpeting⟩ — **broadloom** *n*

broad–mind·ed \-'mīn-dəd\ *adj* **1** : tolerant of varied views **2** : inclined to condone minor departures from orthodox behavior — **broad–mind·ed·ly** *adv* — **broad–mind·ed·ness** *n*

¹**broad·side** \'brȯd-,sīd\ *n* **1** : the part of a ship's side above the waterline **2 a** : all the guns that can be fired from the same side of a ship **b** : a discharge of all these guns together **3** : a storm of abuse : a strongly worded attack **4** : a sheet of paper printed on one side (as for advertising)

²**broadside** *adv* **1** : with the broadside toward a given object or point **2** : in one volley **3** : at random — **broadside** *adj*

broad–spectrum *adj* : effective against various micro-organisms ⟨*broad-spectrum* antibiotics⟩

broad·sword \'brȯd-,sȯrd, -,sȯrd\ *n* : a broad-bladed sword for cutting rather than thrusting

broad·tail \-,tāl\ *n* : the fur or skin of a very young or premature karakul lamb having a flat and wavy appearance resembling moiré silk — compare PERSIAN LAMB

bro·cade \brō-'kād\ *n* [Sp *brocado*, fr. It *broccare* to brocade, fr. *brocco* small nail, fr. L *broccus* projecting] : a rich fabric with raised patterns often in gold or silver thread — **bro·cad·ed** \-'kād-əd\ *adj*

broc·co·li \'bräk-(ə-)lē\ *n* [It, fr. *brocco* small nail, sprout, fr. L *broccus* projecting] : an open branching form of cauliflower whose young flowering shoots are used as a vegetable

bro·chette \brō-'shet\ *n* : a small spit : SKEWER

bro·chure \brō-'shu̇(ə)r\ *n* [F] : PAMPHLET

brock \'bräk\ *n* : BADGER

bro·gan \'brō-gən, brō-'gan\ *n* : a heavy shoe; *esp* : a coarse work shoe reaching to the ankle

¹**brogue** \'brōg\ *n* [Gaelic *brōg*, fr. MIr *brōc*, fr. ON *brōk* leg covering; akin to E *breeches*] : a heavy shoe often with a hobnailed sole : BROGAN

²**brogue** *n* : a marked dialect or regional pronunciation; *esp* : an Irish accent

broi·der \'brȯid-ər\ *vt* : EMBROIDER — **broi·dery** \'brȯid-(ə-)rē\ *n*

¹**broil** \'brȯil\ *vb* [MF *bruler* to burn, modif. of L *ustulare* to singe, fr. *ustus*, pp. of *urere* to burn] **1** : to cook or become cooked by direct exposure to fire or flame **2** : to make or become extremely hot ⟨a *broiling* sun⟩

²**broil** *vi* [MF *brouiller* to mix, broil] : BRAWL

³**broil** *n* : a confused or noisy disturbance; *esp* : a loud quarrel

broil·er \'brȯi-lər\ *n* **1** : a rack and pan or an oven equipped with a rack and pan for broiling meats **2** : a young chicken suitable for broiling

¹**broke** \'brōk\ *adj* [ME, broken] : having no money : PENNILESS

²**broke** *past of* BREAK

bro·ken \'brō-kən\ *adj* [OE *brocen*, fr. pp. of *brecan* to break] **1** : shattered into pieces ⟨*broken* glass⟩ **2 a** : ROUGH, UNEVEN ⟨*broken* country⟩ **b** : having gaps or breaks ⟨a *broken* line⟩ **3** : not kept ⟨a *broken* promise⟩ **4** : SUBDUED, CRUSHED ⟨*broken* spirit⟩ **5** : imperfectly spoken ⟨*broken* English⟩ **6 a** : FRACTURED ⟨a *broken* leg⟩ **b** : cut off : DISCONNECTED — **bro·ken·ly** *adv* — **bro·ken·ness** \-kən-nəs\ *n*

bro·ken–heart·ed \,brō-kən-'härt-əd\ *adj* : crushed by grief or despair

bro·ker \'brō-kər\ *n* [ME, negotiator] : a person who acts as an agent for others in the purchase and sale of property

bro·ker·age \'brō-k(ə-)rij\ *n* **1** : the business of a broker **2** : the fee or commission charged by a broker

bro·mide \'brō-,mīd\ *n* **1** : any of various compounds of bromine with another element or a radical including some (as potassium bromide) used as sedatives **2** : a commonplace or hackneyed statement or notion

bro·mid·ic \brō-'mid-ik\ *adj* : DULL, TIRESOME ⟨*bromidic* remarks⟩

bro·mine \'brō-,mēn\ *n* [F *brome* bromine, fr. Gk *brōmos* bad smell] : a chemical element that is normally a deep red corrosive liquid giving off an irritating reddish brown vapor of disagreeable odor — see ELEMENT table

bronc \'bräŋk\ *n* : BRONCO

bron·chi·al \'bräŋ-kē-əl\ *adj* : of, relating to, or involving the bronchi or their branches — **bron·chi·al·ly** \-ə-lē\ *adv*

bronchial tube *n* : a primary bronchus or any of its branches

bron·chi·ole \'bräŋ-kē-,ōl\ *n* : a tiny thin-walled branch of a bronchial tube

bron·chi·tis \brän-'kīt-əs, bräŋ-\ *n* : acute or chronic inflammation of the bronchial tubes or a disease marked by this — **bron·chit·ic** \-'kit-ik\ *adj*

bron·cho·pneu·mo·nia \,bräŋ-kō-n(y)u̇-'mō-nyə, ,brän-\ *n* : pneumonia involving many relatively small areas of lung tissue — called also *bronchial pneumonia*

bron·chus \'bräŋ-kəs\ *n, pl* **bron·chi** \'brän-,kī, 'bräŋ-, -,kē\ [NL, fr. Gk *bronchos* windpipe] : either of the main divisions of the trachea each leading to a lung

bron·co \'bräŋ-kō, 'brän-\ *n, pl* **broncos** [MexSp, fr. Sp, rough, wild] : an unbroken or partly broken range horse of western No. America; *also* : MUSTANG

bron·to·sau·rus \,bränt-ə-'sȯr-əs\ *also* **bron·to·saur** \'bränt-ə-,sȯr\ *n* [Gk *brontē* thunder + *sauros* lizard] : any of several very large four-footed and prob. herbivorous dinosaurs — called also *thunder lizard*

Bronx cheer \'bräŋ(k)s-\ *n* : RASPBERRY 2

¹**bronze** \'bränz\ *vt* [F *bronzer*, fr. *bronze*, n., fr. It *bronzo*] : to give the appearance of bronze to

²**bronze** *n* **1** : an alloy of copper and tin and sometimes other elements (as zinc) **2** : a work of art (as a statue, bust, or medallion) made of bronze **3** : a moderate yellowish brown — **bronzy** \'brän-zē\ *adj*

Bronze Age *n* : a period of human culture characterized by the use of bronze tools and held to begin in Europe about 3500 B.C. and in western Asia and Egypt somewhat earlier

brooch \'brōch, 'brüch\ *n* : an ornament to be worn at or near the neck of a dress and held by a pin or clasp

¹**brood** \'brüd\ *n* [OE *brōd*] **1** : a family of young animals or children; *esp* : the young (as of a bird) hatched or cared for at one time **2** : a group resembling (as in similarity of form or nature) a brood of young

²**brood** *vb* **1** : to sit on eggs in order to hatch them **2** : to cover young with the wings **3** : to think anxiously or moodily upon a subject : PONDER **4** : to hover over : LOOM — **brood·ing·ly** \-iŋ-lē\ *adv*

³**brood** *adj* : kept for breeding ⟨*brood* mare⟩ ⟨*brood* flock⟩

brood·er \'brüd-ər\ *n* **1** : a person or animal that broods **2** : a heated structure used for raising young fowl

broody \'brüd-ē\ *adj* **1** : physiologically ready to brood **2** : CONTEMPLATIVE, MOODY — **brood·i·ness** *n*

¹**brook** \'bru̇k\ *vt* [OE *brūcan* to use, enjoy] : to put up with : BEAR, TOLERATE ⟨*brooks* no interference⟩

²**brook** *n* [OE *brōc*] : CREEK 2

brook·let \'bru̇k-lət\ *n* : a small brook

brook trout *n* : a common speckled cold-water char of eastern No. America

broom \'brüm, 'bru̇m\ *n* [OE *brōm*] **1** : a plant of the pea family with long slender branches along which grow many drooping yellow flowers **2** : a long-handled brush used for sweeping and orig. made from twigs of broom

broom·corn \-,kȯrn\ *n* : a tall cultivated sorghum whose stiff branched flower cluster is used in brooms and brushes

broom·stick \-,stik\ *n* : the handle of a broom

broth \'brȯth\ *n, pl* **broths** \'brȯths, 'brȯthz\ [OE] : liquid in which meat, fish, cereal grains, or vegetables have been cooked

broth·el \'bräth-əl, 'brȯth-\ *n* : an establishment in which prostitutes are available

broth·er \'brəth-ər\ *n, pl* **brothers** *or* **breth·ren** \'breth-(ə-)rən, 'breth-ərn\ [OE *brōthor*] **1** : a male who has

brooms

one or both parents in common with another **2** : KINS-MAN **3** : a fellow member — used as a title for ministers in some evangelical denominations **4** : one related to another by common ties or interests **5** *often cap* : a man who is a religious but not a priest ⟨a lay *brother*⟩

broth·er·hood \'brəth-ər-,húd\ *n* **1** : the state of being brothers or a brother **2** : an association (as a labor union) for a particular purpose **3** : the whole body of persons engaged in a business or profession

broth·er-in-law \'brəth-(ə-)rən-,ló, 'brəth-ərn-,ló\ *n, pl* **broth·ers-in-law** \'brəth-ər-zən-\ **1** : the brother of one's spouse **2** : the husband of one's sister

broth·er·ly \'brəth-ər-lē\ *adj* **1** : of or relating to brothers **2** : natural or becoming to brothers : AFFEC-TIONATE ⟨*brotherly* love⟩ — **broth·er·li·ness** *n*

brougham \'brü-(ə)m, 'brō-əm\ *n* **1** : a light closed carriage with seats inside for two or four **2** : a 2-door sedan; *esp* : one electrically driven

brought *past of* BRING

brou·ha·ha \brü-'hä-hä\ *n* : HUBBUB, FURORE

brow \'braú\ *n* [OE *brū*] **1 a** : EYEBROW **b** : the ridge on which the eyebrow grows **c** : FOREHEAD **2** : the edge or projecting upper part of a steep slope ⟨on the *brow* of a hill⟩

brow·beat \'braú-,bēt\ *vt* **-beat; -beat·en** \-,bēt-°n\; **-beat·ing** : to frighten by a stern manner or threatening speech : BULLY, ABUSE

¹brown \'braún\ *adj* [OE *brūn*] : of the color brown; *esp* : of dark or tanned complexion

²brown *n* : any of a group of colors between red and yellow in hue, of medium to low lightness, and of moderate to low saturation — **brown·ish** \'braú-nish\ *adj*

³brown *vb* : to make or become brown

brown alga *n* : any of a division (Phaeophyta) of mostly marine algae with chlorophyll masked by brown pigment

brown coal *n* : LIGNITE

Brown·i·an movement \,braú-nē-ən-\ *n* : a random movement of microscopic particles suspended in liquids or gases resulting from the impact of molecules of the fluid surrounding the particle — called also *Brownian motion*

brown·ie \'braú-nē\ *n* **1** : a good-natured goblin who performs helpful services at night **2** : a member of the Girl Scouts of the United States of America program for girls of the age range 7–9 **3** : a small square or rectangle of rich usu. chocolate cake containing nuts

brown·stone \'braún-,stōn\ *n* **1** : a reddish brown sandstone used for building **2** : a dwelling faced with brownstone

brown study *n* : a state of serious absorption or abstraction

brown sugar *n* : a somewhat moist cane sugar that is brown and contains some of the solids removed in refining white sugar

brown-tail moth *n* : a tussock moth whose larvae feed on foliage and are irritating to the skin

brown trout *n* : a speckled European trout widely introduced as a game fish

¹browse \'braúz\ *n* **1** : tender shoots, twigs, and leaves of trees and shrubs fit for food for cattle **2** : an act or instance of browsing

²browse *vb* **1** : to nibble or feed on leaves and shoots : GRAZE **2 a** : to skim a book reading random passages **b** : to look over books esp. in order to select one to read syn see GRAZE — **brows·er** *n*

bru·in \'brü-ən\ *n* [D, name of the bear in the beast epic *Reynard the Fox*] : BEAR

¹bruise \'brüz\ *vb* [partly fr. MF *bruisier* to break, of Celtic origin; partly fr. OE *brȳsan* to bruise] **1** : to inflict a bruise on **2** : to break down (as leaves or berries) by pounding : CRUSH **3** : to wound or hurt the feelings of **4** : to become bruised or show the effects of bruises

²bruise *n* : an injury (as from a blow) in which the skin is not broken but is discolored from the rupture of small underlying blood vessels : CONTUSION

bruis·er \'brü-zər\ *n* **1** *slang* : a professional boxer : PUGILIST **2** : a big husky man

¹bruit \'brüt\ *n* [MF, fr. OF, noise] *archaic* : REPORT, RUMOR

²bruit *vt* : to noise abroad : REPORT

¹brum·ma·gem \'brəm-i-jəm\ *adj* [alter. of *Birmingham*,

England, the source in the 17th cent. of counterfeit groats] : being showy and cheap

²brummagem *n* : something cheap or inferior : TINSEL

brunch \'brənch\ *n* : a late breakfast, an early lunch, or a combination of the two

bru·net *or* **bru·nette** \brü-'net\ *adj* [F, fr. *brun* brown, of Gmc origin; akin to E *brown*] : of dark or relatively dark pigmentation; *esp* : having brown or black hair and eyes — **brunet** *n*

brunt \'brənt\ *n* [ME] : the main force of a blow or an attack : the heaviest shock, stress, or strain ⟨coastal towns bore the *brunt* of the storm⟩

¹brush \'brəsh\ *n* [MF *brosse* brushwood] **1** : BRUSH-WOOD **2 a** : scrub vegetation **b** : land covered with scrub vegetation

²brush *n* [MF *brosse*, fr. *brosse* brushwood] **1** : a device composed of bristles set into a handle and used esp. for sweeping, scrubbing, or painting **2** : a bushy tail (as of a fox or squirrel) **3** : a conductor for an electric current between a moving and a nonmoving part of an electric motor or generator **4 a** : an act of brushing **b** : a quick light touch or momentary contact

³brush *vb* **1 a** : to apply a brush to **b** : to apply with a brush **2 a** : to remove with or as if with a brush **b** : to dispose of in an offhand way : DISMISS ⟨*brushed* his protest aside⟩ **3** : to pass lightly across : touch gently against in passing **4** : to move so as to graze something gently ⟨*brushed* past the doorman⟩ — **brush·er** *n*

⁴brush *n* : a brief encounter or skirmish

brush-off \'brəsh-,óf\ *n* : an abrupt or offhand dismissal

brush up *vb* : to refresh one's memory of : renew one's skill or knowledge

brush·wood \'brəsh-,wùd\ *n* **1** : small branches cut from trees or shrubs **2** : a thicket of shrubs and small trees

¹brushy \'brəsh-ē\ *adj* **brush·i·er; -est** : SHAGGY, ROUGH

²brushy *adj* **brush·i·er; -est** : covered with or abounding in brush or brushwood

brusque \'brəsk\ *adj* [F, fr. It *brusco*, fr. ML *bruscus*, a plant with stiff branches] : markedly abrupt in manner or speech : being sharp and often harsh — **brusque·ly** *adv* — **brusque·ness** *n*

brus·sels sprout \,brəs-əlz-\ *n, often cap B* : one of the edible small green heads borne on the stem of a plant related to the cabbage; *also* : this plant

bru·tal \'brüt-°l\ *adj* : ruthlessly violent : CRUEL, IN-HUMAN, SAVAGE ⟨a *brutal* attack⟩ — **bru·tal·ly** \-°l-ē\ *adv*
syn BRUTE, BRUTISH: BRUTAL applies only to human behavior, stresses lack of humanity, and always implies moral condemnation; BRUTE stresses crude force or strength in contrast with skill or intelligence; BRUTISH stresses lack of refinement and sensitivity and often suggests stupidity rather than cruelty

bru·tal·i·ty \brü-'tal-ət-ē\ *n, pl* **-ties** **1** : the quality or state of being brutal **2** : a brutal act or course of action

bru·tal·ize \'brüt-°l-,īz\ *vt* **1** : to make brutal, unfeeling, or inhuman **2** : to treat brutally — **bru·tal·i·za·tion** \,brüt-°l-ə-'zā-shən\ *n*

¹brute \'brüt\ *adj* [MF *brut*, fr. L *brutus* stupid] **1** : of, relating to, or typical of beasts **2** : having neither mind nor soul **3** : resembling an animal in quality, action, or instinct: as **a** : CRUEL, SAVAGE **b** : grossly sensual **c** : UNREASONING **4** : CRUDE syn see BRUTAL

²brute *n* **1** : BEAST **2** : a brutal person

brut·ish \'brüt-ish\ *adj* **1** : of or resembling a beast **2 a** : grossly sensual : INSENSITIVE **b** : UNREASONING, IRRATIONAL syn see BRUTAL — **brut·ish·ly** *adv* — **brut·ish·ness** *n*

bry·ol·o·gy \brī-'äl-ə-jē\ *n* [Gk *bryon* moss] : a branch of botany that deals with mosses and liverworts

bry·o·ny \'brī-ə-nē\ *n, pl* **-nies** [Gk *bryōnia*] : any of a genus of tendril-bearing vines of the gourd family with large leaves, red or black fruit, and a cathartic root

bry·o·phyl·lum \,brī-ə-'fil-əm\ *n* : a kalanchoe often grown as a foliage plant esp. from leaf cuttings — called also *air plant, life plant*

bry·o·phyte \'brī-ə-,fīt\ *n* [Gk *bryon* moss + *phyton* plant] : any of a division (Bryophyta) of nonflowering green plants comprising the mosses and liverworts — **bry·o·phyt·ic** \,brī-ə-'fit-ik\ *adj*

bry·o·zo·an \,brī-ə-'zō-ən\ *n* [NL *Bryozoa*, class name, fr. Gk *bryon* + NL *-zoa*] : any of a phylum or class (Bryozoa)

ə abut; ⁹ kitten; ər further; a back; ā bake; ä cot, cart; aú out; ch chin; e less; ē easy; g gift; i trip; ī life

of colonial aquatic invertebrate animals that reproduce by budding — **bryozoan** *adj*

¹bub·ble \'bəb-əl\ *vb* **bub·bled; bub·bling** \'bəb-(ə-)liŋ\ [ME *bublen*] **1 :** to form or produce bubbles **2 :** to flow out with a gurgling sound **3 :** to seem to give off bubbles **:** EFFERVESCE **4 a :** to cause to bubble **b :** BURP

²bubble *n* **1 :** a small typically hollow and light globule: as **a :** a small body of gas within a liquid **b :** a thin film of liquid inflated with air or gas **c :** a globule in a transparent solid **2 a :** something that lacks firmness, solidity, or reality **b :** a delusive scheme **3 :** a sound like that of bubbling

bubble chamber *n* **:** a chamber of heated liquid in which the path of an ionizing particle is made visible by a string of vapor bubbles

bubble gum *n* **:** a chewing gum that can be blown into large bubbles

bub·bler \'bəb-(ə-)lər\ *n* **:** a drinking fountain from which a stream of water bubbles upward

bub·bly \'bəb-(ə-)lē\ *adj* **1 :** full of bubbles **:** EFFERVESCENT **2 :** resembling a bubble

bu·bo \'b(y)ü-bō\ *n, pl* **buboes** [ML *bubon-, bubo,* fr. Gk *boubōn*] **:** an inflammatory swelling of a lymph gland esp. in the groin — **bu·bon·ic** \b(y)ü-'bän-ik\ *adj*

bubonic plague *n* **:** plague in which the formation of buboes is a prominent feature

buc·cal \'bək-əl\ *adj* [L *bucca* cheek] **:** of, relating to, or involving the cheeks or the cavity of the mouth

buc·ca·neer \,bək-ə-'ni(ə)r\ *n* [F *boucanier*] **:** PIRATE; *esp* **:** a pirate preying upon Spanish ships and settlements in the West Indies in the 17th century — **buccaneer** *vi*

Bu·ceph·a·lus \byü-'sef-ə-ləs\ *n* **:** the war-horse of Alexander the Great

¹buck \'bək\ *n, pl* **buck** *or* **bucks** [OE *bucca* stag, he-goat] **1 :** a male animal; *esp* **:** a male deer or antelope **2 a :** a male human being **:** MAN **b :** DANDY **3 a :** BUCKSKIN; *also* **:** an article made of buckskin **b** *slang* **:** DOLLAR **3b 4 a :** a supporting rack or frame **b :** a short thick leather-covered block for gymnastic vaulting

²buck *vb* **1 a :** to spring with a quick plunging leap ⟨*bucking* horse⟩ **b :** to throw (as a rider) by bucking **2 a :** to charge against something as if butting **b :** to charge into (the opposing line) in football **c :** OPPOSE, RESIST ⟨tried to *buck* the prevailing fashion⟩ **3 :** to start, move, or react jerkily **4 :** to strive for advancement or promotion ⟨was *bucking* for sergeant⟩ — **buck·er** *n*

³buck *n* **:** an act or instance of bucking; *esp* **:** a charge by a ballcarrier into an opposing line in football

⁴buck *adj* **:** of the lowest grade within a military category ⟨*buck* private⟩

buck·a·roo *or* **buck·er·oo** \,bək-ə-'rü\ *n, pl* **-aroos** *or* **-eroos** [modif. of Sp *vaquero,* fr. *vaca* cow, fr. L *vacca*] **:** COWBOY

buck·board \'bək-,bōrd, -,bórd\ *n* [obs. E *buck* body of a wagon] **:** a four-wheeled vehicle with a springy platform carrying the seat

¹buck·et \'bək-ət\ *n* [AF *buket,* fr. OE *būc* pitcher] **1 :** a typically round vessel for catching, holding, or carrying liquids or solids **2 :** an object resembling a bucket in collecting, scooping, or carrying something: as **a :** the scoop of an excavating machine **b :** one of the vanes of a turbine rotor **3 a :** BUCKETFUL **b :** a large quantity

²bucket *vb* **1 :** to draw or lift in or as if in buckets **2 :** HUSTLE, HURRY **3 a :** to move about haphazardly or irresponsibly **b :** to move roughly or jerkily

bucket brigade *n* **:** a chain of persons acting to put out a fire by passing buckets of water from hand to hand

buck·et·ful \'bək-ət-,fùl\ *n, pl* **buck·et·fuls** \-ət-,fùlz\ *or* **buck·ets·ful** \-əts-,fùl\ **:** the amount held by a bucket

bucket seat *n* **:** a low separate seat for one person used chiefly in automobiles and airplanes

buck·eye \'bək-,ī\ *n* **:** a shrub or tree of the horse-chestnut family; *also* **:** its large nutlike seed

buck fever *n* **:** nervous excitement of an inexperienced hunter at the sight of game

buck·hound \'bək-,haùnd\ *n* **:** a dog used for coursing deer

¹buck·le \'bək-əl\ *n* [MF *boucle* boss of a shield, buckle, fr. L *buccula,* dim. of *bucca* cheek] **1 :** a fastening for two loose ends that is attached to one and holds the other

by a catch **2 :** an ornamental device that suggests a buckle

²buckle *vb* **buck·led; buck·ling** \'bək-(ə-)liŋ\ **1 :** to fasten with a buckle **2 :** to apply oneself with vigor ⟨*buckles* down to the job⟩ **3 :** to bend, warp, or kink usu. under the influence of some external agency ⟨the pavement *buckled* in the heat⟩ ⟨knees *buckled* from the weight on his shoulders⟩ **4 :** to become distorted by buckling; *also* **:** COLLAPSE **5 :** to give way **:** YIELD

³buckle *n* **:** a product of buckling **:** BEND

buck·ler \'bək-lər\ *n* **1 a :** a small round shield held by a handle at arm's length **b :** a shield worn on the left arm **2 :** one that shields and protects

buck passer *n* **:** a person that habitually evades responsibility — **buck–pass·ing** \'bək-,pas-iŋ\ *n*

buck·ram \'bək-rəm\ *n* [OF *boquerant,* fr. OProv *bocaran,* fr. *Bokhara,* city of central Asia] **:** a stiff-finished heavily sized fabric of cotton or linen used in garments, millinery, and bookbindings — **buckram** *adj*

buck·saw \'bək-,sò\ *n* **:** a saw set in a usu. H-shaped frame that is used for sawing wood on a sawbuck — see SAW illustration

buck·shot \-,shät\ *n* **:** a coarse lead shot used in shotgun shells

buck·skin \-,skin\ *n* **1 a :** the skin of a buck **b :** a soft pliable usu. suede-finished leather **2** *pl* **:** buckskin breeches **3 :** a horse of a light yellowish dun color usu. with dark mane and tail

buck·thorn \-,thórn\ *n* **:** any of a genus of often thorny trees or shrubs some of which yield purgatives or pigments

buck·tooth \-'tüth\ *n* **:** a large projecting front tooth — **buck–toothed** \-'tütht\ *adj*

buck up *vb* **1 :** to become encouraged **:** cheer up **2 :** to raise the morale of **:** give a lift to

buck·wheat \'bək-,hwēt\ *n* **:** any of several herbs with pinkish white flowers and triangular seeds; *also* **:** the seeds used as a cereal grain

¹bu·col·ic \byü-'käl-ik\ *adj* [L *bucolicus,* fr. Gk *boukolikos,* fr. *boukolos* cowherd, fr. *bous* cow + *-kolos* herd; akin to E *cow*] **1 :** of or relating to shepherds or herdsmen **:** PASTORAL **2 :** RUSTIC — **bu·col·i·cal·ly** \-i-k(ə-)lē\ *adv*

²bucolic *n* **:** a pastoral poem **:** ECLOGUE

¹bud \'bəd\ *n* [ME *budde*] **1 :** a small growth at the tip or on the side of a plant stem that later develops into a flower, leaf, or new shoot **2 :** a flower that has not fully opened **3 :** a part that grows out from the body of an organism and develops into a new organism **:** GEMMA **4 :** a stage of development in which something is not yet fully developed **:** an early stage or condition ⟨trees in *bud*⟩ ⟨a plan still in the *bud*⟩

²bud *vb* **bud·ded; bud·ding** **1 a :** to set or put forth buds **b :** to reproduce asexually by forming and developing buds **2 :** to be or develop like a bud (as in freshness and promise of growth) ⟨a *budding* diplomat⟩ **3 :** to insert a bud from one plant into an opening cut in the bark of (another plant) in order to propagate a desired variety — **bud·der** *n*

Bud·dha \'büd-ə, 'bùd-\ *n* [Skt, enlightened] **1 :** a person who has attained the perfect spiritual fulfillment sought in Buddhism **2 :** a representation of Gautama Buddha ⟨a little bronze *Buddha*⟩

Bud·dhism \'bü-,diz-əm, 'bùd-,iz-\ *n* **:** a religion of eastern and central Asia growing out of the teaching of Gautama Buddha that suffering is inherent in life and that one can be liberated from it by mental and moral self-purification — **Bud·dhist** \'büd-əst, 'bùd-\ *n or adj* — **Bud·dhis·tic** \bü-'dis-tik, bù-\ *adj*

bud·dy \'bəd-ē\ *n, pl* **buddies :** COMPANION, PARTNER, PAL

budge \'bəj\ *vb* [MF *bouger*] **:** MOVE, SHIFT; *esp* **:** YIELD

bud·ger·i·gar \'bəj-(ə-)rē-,gär\ *n* **:** a small Australian parrot usu. light green with black and yellow markings in the wild but bred under domestication in many colors

¹bud·get \'bəj-ət\ *n* [MF *bougette,* dim. of *bouge* leather bag, fr. L *bulga,* fr. Gaulish] **1 :** STOCK, SUPPLY **2 a :** a statement of the estimated expenditures (as of a nation) during a period and of proposals to finance them **b :** a plan for using resources to finance expenditures **c :** the amount of money available for or assigned to some purpose ⟨a low-*budget* operation⟩

²budget *vb* **1 :** to include or assign in or as if in a budget

⟨*budget* $5,000,000 for highway construction⟩ **2 :** to provide a budget or detailed plan for ⟨*budget* a trip abroad⟩ ⟨*budget* one's time⟩ **3 :** to draw up and operate under a budget ⟨*budget* for a new car⟩

bud·get·ar·y \'bəj-ə-,ter-ē\ *adj* **:** of or relating to a budget

bud·gie \'bəj-ē\ *n* **:** BUDGERIGAR

bud scale *n* **:** one of the leaves resembling scales that form the sheath of a plant bud

¹buff \'bəf\ *n* [MF *buffle* wild ox, fr. It *bufalo*] **1 :** a garment (as a uniform) made of buff leather **2 :** the bare skin **3 a :** a moderate orange yellow **b :** a light to moderate yellow **4 :** a device (as a stick or wheel) with a soft absorbent surface for applying polishing material **5** [earlier *buff* one enthusiastic about going to fires; fr. the buff overcoats worn by volunteer firemen in New York City ab1820] **:** FAN, ENTHUSIAST

²buff *adj* **:** of the color buff

³buff *vt* **:** to polish with or as if with a buff

¹buf·fa·lo \'bəf-ə-,lō\ *n, pl* **-lo** *or* **-loes** [It *bufalo* & Sp *búfalo*] **:** any of several wild oxen: as **a :** WATER BUFFALO **b :** any of a genus of wild oxen (as the wisent) of the northern hemisphere; *esp* **:** a large shaggy-maned No. American wild ox with short horns and heavy forequarters bearing a large muscular hump

²buffalo *vt* **1 :** BEWILDER, BAFFLE **2 :** OVERAWE

buffalo bug *n* **:** CARPET BEETLE

buffalo grass *n* **:** a low-growing native fodder grass of the American plains and prairies

¹buff·er \'bəf-ər\ *n* **:** one that buffs

²buf·fer \'bəf-ər\ *n* [Sc *buff* to beat] **1 :** a device or material for reducing shock due to contact **2 a :** BUFFER STATE **b :** a person who shields another esp. from annoying routine matters **3 :** a substance capable in solution of neutralizing both acids and bases and thereby maintaining the original hydrogen-ion concentration of the solution

³buf·fer *vt* **:** to treat or prepare (a solution) with a buffer

buffer state *n* **:** a small neutral state lying between two larger potentially rival powers

¹buf·fet \'bəf-ət\ *n* **1 :** a blow esp. with the hand **2 :** something having the effect of a blow

²buffet *vb* **1 :** STRIKE, SLAP **2 a :** to pound repeatedly **:** BATTER ⟨was *buffeted* by the crowd⟩ **b :** to contend against ⟨*buffet* a storm⟩ **3 a :** CONTEND, STRUGGLE **b :** to make one's way by fighting or struggling

³buf·fet \(,)bə-'fā, bü-\ *n* [F] **1 :** a sideboard often without a mirror **2 :** a cupboard or set of shelves for the display of tableware **3 a :** a counter for refreshments **b** *chiefly Brit* **:** a restaurant operated as a public convenience (as in a railway station) **c :** a meal set out on a buffet or table to be eaten without formal service

buff leather *n* **:** a strong supple oil-tanned leather produced chiefly from cattle hides

buf·fle·head \'bəf-əl-,hed\ *n* **:** a small No. American diving duck

buf·foon \(,)bə-'fün\ *n* [MF *bouffon*, fr. It *buffone*] **1 :** a person who amuses others by tricks, jokes, and antics **:** CLOWN **2 :** a coarse clownish person — **buf·foon·ish** \-'fü-nish\ *adj*

buf·foon·ery \-'fün-(ə-)rē\ *n, pl* **-er·ies :** the art or the conduct of a buffoon; *esp* **:** coarse loutish behavior

¹bug \'bəg\ *n* [ME *bugge* scarecrow] **1 a :** an insect or other creeping or crawling invertebrate; *esp* **:** an obnoxious insect (as a bedbug or head louse) **b :** any of an order (Hemiptera) of insects with sucking mouthparts and incomplete metamorphosis that includes many destructive plant pests — called also *true bug* **2 :** an unexpected defect, fault, flaw, or imperfection **3 :** a disease-producing germ or a disease caused by it **4 a :** FAD, ENTHUSIASM **b :** ENTHUSIAST, HOBBYIST

²bug *vt* **bugged; bug·ging :** to plant a concealed microphone in

bug·a·boo \'bəg-ə-,bü\ *n, pl* **-boos :** BUGBEAR, BOGEY

bug·bear \'bəg-,ba(ə)r, -,be(ə)r\ *n* **1 :** an imaginary goblin or specter used to excite fear **2 :** an object or source of dread

¹bug·gy \'bəg-ē\ *adj* **bug·gi·er; -est** **1 :** infested with bugs **2** *slang* **:** SILLY, CRAZY

²bug·gy \'bəg-ē\ *n, pl* **buggies :** a light single-seated carriage usu. drawn by one horse

¹bug·house \'bəg-,haůs\ *n, slang* **:** an insane asylum

²bughouse *adj, slang* **:** mentally deranged **:** CRAZY

¹bu·gle \'byü-gəl\ *n* [OF, fr. LL *bugula*] **:** a European annual mint with spikes of blue flowers that is naturalized in the U.S.

²bugle *n* [OF, buffalo, instrument made fr. a buffalo horn, bugle, fr. L *buculus*, dim. of *bos* head of cattle] **:** a brass instrument with a cupped mouthpiece like the trumpet but having a shorter and more conical tube

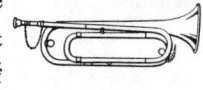
bugle

³bugle *vb* **bu·gled; bu·gling** \-g(ə-)liŋ\ **1 :** to sound or summon by or as if by a bugle call **2 :** to sound a bugle — **bu·gler** \-glər\ *n*

bu·gloss \'byü-,gläs, -,glòs\ *n* **:** any of a genus of rough-hairy herbs of the borage family

buhl \'bül, 'byül\ *var of* BOULLE

buhr·stone \'bər-,stōn\ *n* **:** a siliceous rock used for millstones; *also* **:** a millstone of this rock

¹build \'bild\ *vb* **built** \'bilt\; **build·ing** [OE *byldan*] **1 :** to make by putting together parts or materials **:** CONSTRUCT ⟨*build* a house⟩ ⟨*build* a bridge⟩ **2 :** to produce or create gradually esp. by effort ⟨*build* a winning team⟩ ⟨*build* a reputation⟩ **3 :** to cause to be constructed **4 :** to engage in building **5 :** INCREASE, ENLARGE **6 :** to progress toward a peak ⟨tension *building* up⟩

²build *n* **:** form or mode of structure **:** MAKE; *esp* **:** PHYSIQUE

build·ed *archaic past of* BUILD

build·er \'bil-dər\ *n* **:** one that builds; *esp* **:** a person whose business is the building of houses and similar structures

build in *vt* **:** to construct as an integral part of something ⟨*build in* a bookcase⟩

build·ing \'bil-diŋ\ *n* **1 :** a usu. roofed and walled structure built for permanent use (as for a dwelling) **2 :** the art, work, or business of assembling materials into a structure ⟨bridge *building*⟩

built-in \'bilt-'in\ *adj* **1 :** forming an integral part of a structure; *esp* **:** constructed as or in a recess in a wall ⟨*built-in* bookcases⟩ **2 :** INHERENT

bulb \'bəlb\ *n* [L *bulbus*, fr. Gk *bolbos* bulbous plant] **1 a :** a plant underground resting stage consisting of a short stem base bearing one or more buds enclosed in thickened storage leaves — compare CORM, TUBER **b :** a fleshy structure (as a tuber or corm) resembling a bulb in appearance or function **c :** a plant having or developing from a bulb **2 :** a bulb-shaped object or part: as **a :** an incandescent lamp of rounded shape; *also* **:** a small electric lamp (as a fluorescent lamp) **b :** a rounded or swollen anatomical structure — **bul·ba·ceous** \,bəl-'bā-shəs\ *adj* — **bulbed** \'bəlbd\ *adj*

bul·bar \'bəl-bər\ *adj* **:** of or relating to a bulb; *also* **:** involving the medulla oblongata

bul·bil \'bəl-bəl, -,bil\ *n* **:** a small or secondary plant bulb; *esp* **:** one produced in a leaf axil or replacing the flowers

bul·bous \'bəl-bəs\ *adj* **1 :** having a bulb **:** growing from or bearing bulbs **2 :** resembling a bulb **:** ROUNDED, SWOLLEN — **bul·bous·ly** *adv*

bul·bul \'bùl-,bùl\ *n* [Per, fr. Ar] **1 :** a Persian songbird that is prob. a nightingale **2 :** any of various social songbirds of Asia and Africa

Bul·gar \'bəl-,gär, 'bùl-\ *n* **:** BULGARIAN

Bul·gar·i·an \,bəl-'gar-ē-ən, bùl-, -'ger-\ *n* **1 :** a native or inhabitant of Bulgaria **2 :** the Slavic language of the Bulgarians — **Bulgarian** *adj*

¹bulge \'bəlj\ *n* [MF *boulge* leather bag, fr. L *bulga*] **:** a swelling or protuberant part **:** a part that has an outward bend ⟨a *bulge* in a line⟩

²bulge *vb* **:** to swell or bend outward **:** become or cause to become protuberant

bulgy \'bəl-jē\ *adj* **bulg·i·er; -est :** BULGED, BULGING

¹bulk \'bəlk\ *n* [ON *bulki* heap] **1 :** greatness of size or extent **:** MAGNITUDE, VOLUME **2 :** a large body or mass **3 :** the main or greater part

syn BULK, MASS, VOLUME mean the aggregate that forms a body or unit with reference to its size or amount. BULK implies an aggregate that is large, heavy, or unwieldy; MASS suggests an aggregate made by piling together things of the same kind; VOLUME applies to an aggregate without shape or outline and capable of flowing or fluctuating ⟨*volume* of water⟩⟨*volume* of traffic⟩

— **in bulk** : in a mass : not divided into parts or packaged in separate units

²**bulk** vb **1** : to swell or bulge or cause to swell or bulge : EXPAND **2 a** : to have a bulky appearance : LOOM **b** : to be weighty or impressive **3** : to form into a cohesive mass

bulk·head \'bəlk-,hed\ n **1** : an upright partition separating compartments on a ship **2** : a structure or partition to resist pressure or to shut off water, fire, or gas **3** : a projecting framework with a sloping door giving access to a cellar stairway

bulky \'bəl-kē\ adj **bulk·i·er; -est** : having bulk: as **a** : large of its kind; esp : being large and unwieldy **b** : having great volume in proportion to weight — **bulk·i·ly** \-kə-lē\ adv — **bulk·i·ness** \-kē-nəs\ n

¹**bull** \'bul\ n [OE bula] **1 a** : an adult male bovine animal; also : a usu. adult male of various large animals **b** : ELEPHANT **2** : a person who buys something (as stocks) in expectation of a price rise or who acts to bring about such a rise — compare BEAR 3 **3** : one that resembles a bull **4** : BULLDOG **5** slang : POLICEMAN, DETECTIVE

²**bull** adj **1 a** : MALE **b** : of, relating to, or resembling a bull **2** : large of its kind **3** : RISING ⟨a bull market⟩

³**bull** vb : to act or act on with the violence of a bull : FORCE ⟨bulling his way ahead⟩

⁴**bull** n [ML bulla papal seal, bull, fr. L, bubble, amulet] : a papal pronouncement of the most formal and important kind

⁵**bull** n **1** : a grotesque blunder in language **2** slang **a** : empty boastful talk **b** : NONSENSE

¹**bull·dog** \'bul-,dog\ n : a compact muscular short-haired dog of English origin with forelegs set widely apart and an undershot lower jaw

²**bulldog** adj : resembling a bulldog : STUBBORN ⟨bulldog courage⟩

³**bulldog** vt : to throw (a steer) by seizing the horns and twisting the neck

bull·doze \'bul-,dōz\ vt **1** : BULLY **2** : to move, clear, gouge out, or level off with a bulldozer **3** : to force as if by using a bulldozer

bull·doz·er \-,dō-zər\ n **1** : one that bulldozes **2** : a tractor-driven machine having a broad horizontal blade or ram for pushing (as in clearing land or road building)

bul·let \'bul-ət\ n [MF boulet, dim. of boule ball] **1** : a shaped piece of metal made to be shot from a firearm **2** : something suggesting a bullet (as in form or vigor of action)

bul·le·tin \'bul-ət-ᵊn\ n **1** : a brief public notice issuing usu. from an authoritative source ⟨weather bulletin⟩ ⟨special news bulletin⟩ **2** : a periodical publication; esp : the organ of an institution or association

bulletin board n : a board for posting notices

bul·let·proof \,bul-ət-'prüf\ adj : so made as to prevent the passing through of bullets ⟨bulletproof glass⟩ ⟨wore a bulletproof vest⟩

bull fiddle n : DOUBLE BASS — **bull fiddler** n

bull·fight \'bul-,fīt\ n : a spectacle in which men ceremonially excite, fight with, and usu. kill bulls in an arena for public amusement — **bull·fight·er** n

bull·finch \-,finch\ n : a thick-billed red-breasted European songbird often kept as a cage bird

bull·frog \-,frog, -,fräg\ n : FROG; esp : a large heavy frog that makes a booming or bellowing sound

bull·head \-,hed\ n : any of various large-headed fishes; esp : any of several common freshwater catfishes of the U.S.

bull·head·ed \'bul-'hed-əd\ adj : stupidly stubborn : HEADSTRONG — **bull·head·ed·ly** adv — **bull·head·ed·ness** n

bul·lion \'bul-yən\ n [AF, mint] : gold or silver metal; esp : gold or silver in bars or ingots

bull·ish \'bul-ish\ adj **1** : suggestive of a bull **2 a** : marked by, tending to cause, or hopeful of rising prices (as in a stock market) **b** : OPTIMISTIC — **bull·ish·ly** adv

bull mastiff n : a large powerful dog of a breed developed by crossing bulldogs with mastiffs

Bull Moose \'bul-'müs\ n [fr. the bull moose, emblem of the Progressive party of 1912] : a follower of Theodore Roosevelt in the U.S. presidential campaign of 1912

bull neck n : a thick short powerful neck — **bull-necked** \'bul-'nekt\ adj

bull·ock \'bul-ək\ n **1** : a young bull **2** : a castrated bull : STEER — **bull·ocky** \-ə-kē\ adj

bull·pen \'bul-,pen\ n : a place on a baseball field where relief pitchers warm up during a game

bull·ring \'bul-,riŋ\ n : an arena for bullfights

bull session n : an informal discursive group discussion

bull's-eye \'bul-,zī\ n **1** : a small thick disk of glass inserted (as in a deck) to let in light **2 a** : a very hard globular candy **3 a** : the center of a target; also : something central or crucial **b** : a shot that hits a bull's-eye : a complete success **4** : a simple lens for concentrating rays of light

bull snake n : any of several large harmless No. American snakes feeding chiefly on rodents

bull·ter·ri·er \'bul-'ter-ē-ər\ n : a short-haired terrier of a breed originated in England by crossing the bulldog with terriers

bull·whip \'bul-,hwip\ n : a rawhide whip with plaited lash 15 to 25 feet long

¹**bul·ly** \'bul-ē\ n, pl **bullies** : a blustering browbeating fellow; esp : one habitually cruel to others weaker than himself

²**bully** adj : EXCELLENT, FIRST-RATE — often used interjectionally

³**bully** vb **bul·lied; bul·ly·ing** **1** : BROWBEAT, INTIMIDATE, DOMINEER **2** : to act like a bully : BLUSTER

bul·ly·rag \'bul-ē-,rag\ vt **1** : to intimidate by bullying **2** : to vex by teasing : BADGER

bul·rush \'bul-,rəsh\ n : any of several large sedges growing in wet land or water

¹**bul·wark** \'bul-(,)wərk, -,work; 'bəl-(,)wərk\ n [MD bolwerc, lit., plank work] **1 a** : a solid wall-like structure raised for defense : RAMPART **b** : BREAKWATER, SEAWALL **2** : a strong support or protection in danger **3** : the side of a ship above the upper deck — usu. used in pl.

²**bulwark** vt : to fortify or safeguard with a bulwark : PROTECT

¹**bum** \'bəm\ vb **bummed; bum·ming** **1** : to go around in the manner of a bum: **a** : LOAF **b** : to wander like a tramp **2** : to obtain by begging

²**bum** n **1** : a person who avoids work and tries to live off others **2** : TRAMP, HOBO

³**bum** adj **1** : INFERIOR, WORTHLESS **2** : DISABLED ⟨a bum knee⟩

bum·ble·bee \'bəm-bəl-,bē\ n : any of numerous large robust hairy social bees

bum·boat \'bəm-,bōt\ n : a boat that brings provisions and commodities for sale to ships in port or offshore

¹**bump** \'bəmp\ vb **1** : to strike or knock against something with force or violence **2** : to collide with **3** : to proceed in a series of bumps : JOLT — **bump into** : to encounter esp. by chance

²**bump** n **1** : a sudden forceful blow, impact, or jolt **2 a** : a rounded projection or protuberance; esp : a swelling (as from a blow or sting) of tissue **b** : an irregularity in a road surface likely to cause a jolt

¹**bump·er** \'bəm-pər\ n : a cup or glass filled to the brim

²**bumper** adj : unusually large or fine ⟨a bumper crop of wheat⟩

³**bumper** n : a device for absorbing shock or preventing damage (as in collision); esp : a metal bar at the end of an automobile

bump·kin \'bəm(p)-kən\ n : an awkward and unsophisticated rustic

bump·tious \'bəm(p)-shəs\ adj [¹bump + -tious (as in fractious)] : obtusely and often noisily self-assertive : PRESUMPTUOUS — **bump·tious·ly** adv — **bump·tious·ness** n

bumpy \'bəm-pē\ adj **bump·i·er; -est** **1** : having or covered with bumps **2** : causing or marked by bumps or jolts ⟨a bumpy ride⟩ — **bump·i·ly** \-pə-lē\ adv — **bump·i·ness** \-pē-nəs\ n

bun \'bən\ n [ME bunne] **1** : a sweet or plain small bread; esp : a round roll **2** : a knot of hair shaped like a bun

¹**bunch** \'bənch\ n [ME bunche] **1** : PROTUBERANCE, SWELLING **2 a** : a number of things of the same kind : CLUSTER ⟨a bunch of grapes⟩ **b** : GROUP, COLLECTION ⟨a bunch of his friends⟩ — **bunch·i·ly** \'bən-chə-lē\ adv — **bunchy** \-chē\ adj

²**bunch** vb : to form in or gather into a group or cluster

bun·co *or* **bun·ko** \'bəŋ-kō\ *n, pl* **buncos** *or* **bunkos** : a swindling game or scheme — **bunco** *vt*

bund \'bủnd, 'bənd\ *n, often cap* [G, league] : a political association; *esp* : a pro-Nazi German-American organization of the 1930s — **bund·ist** \-əst\ *n, often cap*

¹**bun·dle** \'bən-d²l\ *n* [MD *bundel;* akin to E *bind*] **1 a** : a group of things tied together **b** : PACKAGE, PARCEL **2 a** : a small band of mostly parallel fibers (as of nerve) **b** : VASCULAR BUNDLE

²**bundle** *vb* **bun·dled; bun·dling** \'bən-dliŋ, -d²l-iŋ\ **1** : to make into a bundle : WRAP **2** : to hurry off unceremoniously : HUSTLE **3** : to practice bundling — **bun·dler** \-dlər, -d²l-ər\ *n*

bundle up *vb* : to dress warmly

bun·dling \'bən-dliŋ, -d²l-iŋ\ *n* : a former custom in which a couple during courtship would occupy the same bed without undressing

¹**bung** \'bəŋ\ *n* [MD *bonghe,* fr. LL *puncta* puncture, fr. L *punct-, pungere* to prick] **1** : the stopper in the bunghole of a cask; *also* : BUNGHOLE **2** : the cecum or anus esp. of a slaughter animal

²**bung** *vt* **1** : to plug with or as if with a bung **2** : BATTER, BRUISE ⟨badly *bunged* up⟩

bun·ga·low \'bəŋ-gə-‚lō\ *n* [Hindi *baṅglā,* lit., (house) in the Bengal style] : a usu. one-storied house characterized by low sweeping lines and a wide veranda

bung·hole \'bəŋ-‚hōl\ *n* : a hole for emptying or filling a cask

bun·gle \'bəŋ-gəl\ *vb* **bun·gled; bun·gling** \-g(ə-)liŋ\ : to act, do, make, or work in a clumsy manner — **bungle** *n* — **bun·gler** \-g(ə-)lər\ *n*

bun·ion \'bən-yən\ *n* : an inflamed swelling on the first joint of the big toe

¹**bunk** \'bəŋk\ *n* **1** : a built-in bed (as on a ship) that is often one of a tier **2** : a sleeping place

²**bunk** *vb* **1** : to occupy a bunk **2** : to provide with a bunk

³**bunk** *n* [short for *bunkum*] : NONSENSE

bun·ker \'bəŋ-kər\ *n* [Sc *bonker* chest, box] **1** : a bin or compartment for storage (as for coal or oil on a ship) **2 a** : a protective embankment or dugout *esp* : a fortified chamber mostly below ground **b** : a sand trap or embankment constituting a hazard on a golf course

bunk·house \'bəŋk-‚hau̇s\ *n* : a rough simple building providing sleeping quarters (as for construction workers)

bun·kum *or* **bun·combe** \'bəŋ-kəm\ *n* [fr. *Buncombe* County, N.C.; fr. the statement by its congressional representative in defending a seemingly irrelevant speech that he was speaking to Buncombe] : insincere or foolish talk : NONSENSE

bun·ny \'bən-ē\ *n, pl* **bunnies** [E dial. *bun* rabbit] : RABBIT

Bun·sen burner \‚bən(t)-sən-\ *n* [after Robert W. *Bunsen* *d*1899 German chemist] : a gas burner consisting typically of a tube with small holes at the bottom where air enters and mixes with the gas to produce a very hot blue flame

¹**bunt** \'bənt\ *n* : the middle part of a square sail

²**bunt** *n* : a destructive smut of wheat in which the grains are replaced by greasy masses of dark ill-smelling spores

³**bunt** *vb* [alter. of ¹*butt*] **1** : to strike or push with or as if with the head : BUTT **2** : to push or tap a baseball lightly without swinging the bat — **bunt·er** *n*

⁴**bunt** *n* **1** : an act or instance of bunting **2** : a bunted ball

¹**bun·ting** \'bənt-iŋ\ *n* [ME] : any of various stout-billed finches of the size and habits of a sparrow

²**bunting** *n* **1** : a thin fabric used chiefly for making flags and patriotic decorations **2** : flags or decorations made of bunting

bunt·line \'bənt-‚līn, -lən\ *n* : one of the ropes attached to the foot of a square sail to haul the sail up to the yard for furling

¹**buoy** \'bü-ē, 'bȯi\ *n* [ME *boye,* fr. (assumed) MF *boie,* of Gmc origin; akin to E *beacon*] **1** : a floating object anchored in a body of water to mark a channel or warn of danger **2** : LIFE BUOY

²**buoy** *vt* **1** : to mark by or as if by a buoy **2 a** : to keep afloat **b** : to raise the spirits of : SUSTAIN

buoy·an·cy \'bȯi-ən-sē, 'bü-

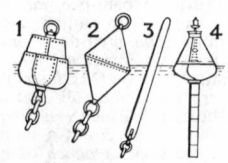

buoys 1: *1* can, 2 nun,
3 spar, 4 whistling

yən-\ *n* **1 a** : the tendency of a body to float or to rise when submerged in a fluid ⟨the *buoyancy* of a cork in water⟩ **b** : the power of a fluid to exert an upward force on a body placed in it ⟨the *buoyancy* of seawater⟩ **2** : natural lightness of spirit : LIGHTHEARTEDNESS

buoy·ant \'bȯi-ənt, 'bü-yənt\ *adj* **1** : able to rise and float in the air or on the surface of a liquid **2** : able to keep a body afloat ⟨gliding in *buoyant* currents of air⟩ **3** : LIGHTHEARTED, CHEERFUL **syn** *see* ELASTIC — **buoy·ant·ly** *adv*

bur *var of* BURR

bur·ble \'bər-bəl\ *vi* **bur·bled; bur·bling** \'bər-b(ə-)liŋ\ : BABBLE, PRATTLE — **burble** *n* — **bur·bler** \-b(ə-)lər\ *n* — **bur·bly** \-b(ə-)lē\ *adv*

bur·bot \'bər-bət\ *n, pl* **burbot** *also* **burbots** [MF *bourbotte,* fr. *bourbe* mud] : a northern freshwater fish related to the cod but somewhat resembling an eel

¹**bur·den** \'bərd-²n\ *n* [OE *byrthen;* akin to E ²*bear*] **1 a** : something that is carried : LOAD **b** : something borne as a duty, obligation, or responsibility often with labor or difficulty ⟨tax *burdens*⟩ **c** : the duty of doing or providing something ⟨*burden* of proof⟩ **2** : something hard to bear : ENCUMBRANCE **3 a** : CARGO, LADING ⟨beast of *burden*⟩ **b** : capacity for carrying cargo ⟨a ship of 100 tons *burden*⟩

²**burden** *vt* **bur·dened; bur·den·ing** \'bərd-niŋ, -²n-iŋ\ : LOAD, OPPRESS

³**burden** *n* [ME *burdoun* bass part, fr. MF *bourdon* bass horn, of imit. origin] **1** : the refrain or chorus of a song **2** : a main or recurring theme : central idea : GIST

bur·den·some \'bərd-²n-səm\ *adj* : difficult or distressing to bear : OPPRESSIVE — **bur·den·some·ly** *adv* — **bur·den·some·ness** *n*

bur·dock \'bər-‚däk\ *n* [*bur* + *dock*] : any of a genus of coarse herbs related to the daisy that have globular flower heads with prickly bracts

bu·reau \'byu̇(ə)r-ō\ *n, pl* **bu·reaus** *also* **bu·reaux** \-ōz\ [F, cloth covering for desks, desk, fr. OF *burel* woolen cloth, fr. LL *burra* shaggy cloth] **1 a** *Brit* : DESK; *esp* : one with drawers and a slant top **b** : a low chest of drawers with a mirror for use in a bedroom **2 a** : a specialized administrative unit; *esp* : a subdivision of a governmental department ⟨Weather *Bureau*⟩ ⟨*Bureau* of the Budget⟩ **b** : a commercial agency providing services for the public or for other businesses ⟨travel *bureau*⟩ ⟨credit *bureau*⟩ **3** : a political executive committee

bu·reau·cra·cy \byu̇-'räk-rə-sē\ *n, pl* **-cies** **1** : a body of officials; *esp* : the whole body of appointed or hired rather than elected government officials **2 a** : a system of administration characterized by specialization of functions, adherence to fixed rules, and a hierarchy of authority **b** : a system of administration marked by constant strivings for increased functions and power, by lack of initiative and flexibility, by indifference to human needs or public opinion, and by a tendency to defer decisions to superiors or to impede action with red tape

bu·reau·crat \'byu̇r-ə-‚krat\ *n* : a member of a bureaucracy; *esp* : a government official who carries out his duties in a narrow routine way

bu·reau·crat·ic \‚byu̇r-ə-'krat-ik\ *adj* : of, relating to, or having the characteristics of a bureaucracy or a bureaucrat ⟨*bureaucratic* government⟩ — **bu·reau·crat·i·cal·ly** \-'krat-i-k(ə-)lē\ *adv*

bu·rette *or* **bu·ret** \byu̇-'ret\ *n* [F *burette*] : a graduated glass tube usu. with a small aperture and stopcock for delivering measured quantities of liquid or for measuring the liquid gas received or discharged

burg \'bərg\ *n* [OE] **1** : a medieval fortress or walled town **2** : CITY, TOWN

bur·gee \‚bər-'jē\ *n* : a swallow-tailed flag used esp. by ships for signals or identification

bur·geon \'bər-jən\ *vi* [ME *burjon* bud, fr. OF] **1 a** : to put forth new growth (as buds) **b** : BLOSSOM, BLOOM **2** : EXPAND, FLOURISH

bur·gess \'bər-jəs\ *n* [ME *burgeis* burgher, fr. OF *bourgeois*] **1** : a citizen of a British borough **2 a** : a representative in the lower house of the legislature of colonial Virginia

burgh \'bər-ō, 'bə-rō\ *n* [ME, fr. OE *burg, burh* fortified town] : BOROUGH; *esp* : a Scottish town with certain local lawmaking rights

ə abut; ᵊ kitten; ər further; a back; ā bake; ä cot, cart; au̇ out; ch chin; e less; ē easy; g gift; i trip; ī life

bur·gher \'bər-gər\ *n* : an inhabitant of a borough or a town; *esp* : a prosperous solid citizen

bur·glar \'bər-glər\ *n* [AF *burgler*, fr. ML *burgator, burglator*, fr. *burgare* to commit burglary, fr. L *burgus* fortified place] : one who commits burglary : THIEF

bur·glar·ize \'bər-glə-,rīz\ *vt* : to break into and steal from

bur·gla·ry \'bər-glə-rē\ *n, pl* -ries : the act of breaking into a building (as a house) esp. at night and with the intent of committing a crime (as stealing)

bur·go·mas·ter \'bər-gə-,mas-tər\ *n* [modif. of D *burgemeester*] : the chief magistrate of a town in some European countries : MAYOR

Bur·gun·di·an \(,)bər-'gən-dē-ən\ *n* **1** : one of a Germanic people invading Gaul early in the 5th century A.D. **2** : a native or inhabitant of Burgundy

Bur·gun·dy \'bər-gən-dē\ *n* : a red or white table wine from parts of Burgundy; *also* : a similar wine made elsewhere

buri·al \'ber-ē-əl\ *n* : the act of burying

bu·rin \'byùr-ən, 'bər-\ *n* [F] : a pointed steel cutting tool used by engravers

¹burl \'bərl\ *n* **1** : a knot or lump in thread or cloth **2** : a gnarled woody outgrowth on a tree; *also* : veneer cut from this

²burl *vt* : to finish (cloth) esp. by repairing burls — **burl·er** *n*

bur·lap \'bər-,lap\ *n* : a coarse fabric made usu. from jute or hemp and used for bags and wrappings and also for curtains and couch covers

¹bur·lesque \(,)bər-'lesk\ *n* [F, comical, fr. It *burlesco*, fr. *burla* joke, fr. Sp] **1 a** : mockery usu. by caricature or travesty **b** : a witty or derisive literary or dramatic imitation **2** : theatrical entertainment consisting of low comedy skits and dance routines **syn** see CARICATURE — **bur·lesque** *adj*

²bur·lesque *vt* : to mock or ridicule through burlesque : imitate in such a way as to make ridiculous — **bur·lesqu·er** *n*

bur·ley \'bər-lē\ *n, often cap* [prob. fr. the name *Burley*] : an air-cured tobacco grown mainly in Kentucky

bur·ly \'bər-lē\ *adj* **bur·li·er; -est** [ME] : strongly and heavily built : HUSKY — **bur·li·ness** *n*

bur marigold *n* : any of a genus of coarse herbs related to the daisies whose burs adhere to clothing

Bur·mese \,bər-'mēz, -'mēs\ *n, pl* **Burmese 1** : a native or inhabitant of Burma **2** : the language of the Burmese people — **Burmese** *adj*

¹burn \'bərn\ *n* [OE] *Brit* : BROOK, RIVULET

²burn *vb* **burned** \'bərnd\ *or* **burnt** \'bərnt\; **burn·ing** [OE *byrnan* (v.i.) & *bærnan* (v.t.)] **1 a** : BLAZE **b** : to undergo combustion **2 a** : to feel hot **b** : to become altered by or as if by the action of fire or heat; *esp* : SCORCH **c** : to appear as if on fire : GLOW **d** : to cause to undergo combustion; *esp* : to destroy by fire ⟨*burn* trash⟩ **e** : to use as fuel ⟨this furnace *burns* gas⟩ **3** : to produce by the action of fire or heat **4** : to injure or alter by or as if by fire or heat ⟨*burn* out a bearing⟩ — **burn·a·ble** \'bər-nə-bəl\ *adj* — **burn·ing·ly** \-niŋ-lē\ *adv*

³burn *n* : injury, damage, or effect produced by or as if by burning

burn·er \'bər-nər\ *n* : one that burns; *esp* : the part of a stove or furnace, of an oil or gas lamp, or of an engine where the flame is produced

burning glass *n* : a convex lens for producing an intense heat by focusing the rays of the sun through it

¹bur·nish \'bər-nish\ *vt* [MF *bruniss-, brunir*, lit., to make brown, fr. *brun* brown] : to make shiny or lustrous esp. by rubbing with a hard smooth tool — **bur·nish·er** *n* **syn** BURNISH, POLISH mean to smooth or brighten by rubbing. BURNISH applies chiefly to metals that are rubbed until they become lustrous; POLISH implies friction and usu. the application of a substance (as wax) that gives a smooth and glossy surface

²burnish *n* : LUSTER, GLOSS

bur·noose *or* **bur·nous** \(,)bər-'nüs\ *n* [F *burnous*, fr. Ar *burnus*] : a hooded cloak worn by Arabs and Moors

burn·sides \'bərn-,sīdz\ *n pl* [Ambrose E. *Burnside* d1881 American general] : SIDE-WHISKERS; *esp* : full muttonchop whiskers

¹burp \'bərp\ *n* : BELCH

²burp *vb* **1** : BELCH **2** : to help (a baby) expel gas from the stomach esp. by patting or rubbing the back

burp gun *n* : a small submachine gun

¹burr \'bər\ *n* [ME *burre*] **1** *usu* **bur a** : a rough or prickly envelope of a fruit **b** : a plant that bears burs **2 a** : a small rotary cutting tool **b** *usu* **bur** : a bit used on a dental drill **3** : BURL **2 4** : a roughness left (as in drilling or engraving) by a tool in cutting or shaping metal **5 a** : a trilled uvular *r* as used by some speakers of English esp. in northern England and in Scotland **b** : a tongue-point trill that is the usual Scottish *r* **6** : a rough humming sound : WHIR — **burred** \'bərd\ *adj*

²burr *vb* **1** : to speak or pronounce with a burr **2** : to make a whirring sound **3 a** : to form into a rough edge **b** : to remove burrs from — **burr·er** \'bər-ər\ *n*

bur·ro \'bər-ō, 'bùr-; 'bə-rō\ *n, pl* **burros** : DONKEY; *esp* : a small one used as a pack animal

¹bur·row \'bər-ō, 'bə-rō\ *n* [ME *borow*] : a hole in the ground made by an animal (as a rabbit) for shelter and habitation

²burrow *vb* **1** : to construct by tunneling ⟨*burrow* a passage through the hill⟩ **2** : to conceal oneself in or as if in a burrow **3 a** : to make a burrow **b** : to progress by or as if by digging **4** : to make a thorough search : DELVE ⟨*burrowed* through his files⟩ **5** : to enter by stealth ⟨spies *burrowed* into the organization⟩ — **bur·row·er** *n*

bur·ry \'bər-ē\ *adj* **1** : containing burs **2** : resembling a bur : PRICKLY

bur·sa \'bər-sə\ *n, pl* **bur·sas** *or* **bur·sae** \-,sē, -,sī\ [NL, fr. ML, bag, purse, fr. LL, animal skin, fr. Gk *byrsa*] : a bodily pouch or sac; *esp* : a small serous sac between a tendon and a bone — **bur·sal** \-səl\ *adj*

bur·sar \'bər-sər, -,sär\ *n* [ML *bursarius*, fr. *bursa* bag, purse] : a treasurer esp. of a college or monastery

bur·sa·ry \'bərs-(ə-)rē\ *n, pl* -ries **1** : the treasury of a college or monastery **2** : a monetary grant to a needy college student

burse \'bərs\ *n* [ML *bursa* purse] : a square cloth case for carrying the corporal used in the Eucharist

bur·si·tis \(,)bər-'sīt-əs\ *n* : inflammation of a bursa esp. of the shoulder or elbow

¹burst \'bərst\ *vb* **burst; burst·ing** [OE *berstan*] **1 a** : to break open, apart, or into pieces from or as if from impact or from or as if from pressure within ⟨buds ready to *burst* open⟩ ⟨bombs *bursting* in the air⟩ **b** : to cause to burst **2 a** : to give way from an excess of emotion ⟨his heart *burst* with grief⟩ **b** : to give vent suddenly to an emotion ⟨*burst* into tears⟩ **3 a** : to emerge or spring suddenly ⟨*burst* out of a house⟩ **b** : LAUNCH, PLUNGE ⟨*burst* into song⟩ **4** : to be filled to the breaking point

²burst *n* **1 a** : a sudden outbreak or outburst ⟨a *burst* of laughter⟩ **b** : a sudden intense effort or exertion ⟨a *burst* of speed⟩ **c** : a short quick volley of shots ⟨fire a machine gun in *bursts*⟩ **2** : an act of bursting **3** : a result of bursting; *esp* : a visible puff accompanying the explosion of a shell **4** : a sudden increase in the strength of a received radio signal

bur·then \'bər-thən\ *archaic var of* BURDEN

bur·weed \'bər-,wēd\ *n* : any of various plants with burry fruit

bury \'ber-ē\ *vt* **bur·ied; bury·ing** [OE *byrgan*] **1** : to deposit (a dead body) in or as if in the earth; *esp* : to inter with funeral ceremonies **2** : to place in the ground and cover over ⟨*buried* treasure⟩ **3** : CONCEAL, HIDE ⟨*bury* her face in her hands⟩ **4** : to remove from the world of action ⟨*bury* oneself in a book⟩ — **buri·er** *n*

¹bus \'bəs\ *n, pl* **bus·es** *or* **bus·ses** [short for *omnibus*] **1 a** : a large motor-driven passenger vehicle **b** *slang* : AUTOMOBILE **2** : a usu. uninsulated bar or tube used as an electrical conductor at a circuit junction — called also *bus bar*

²bus *vb* **bussed; bus·sing** : to travel or transport by bus

bus·boy \'bəs-,bòi\ *n* : a man or boy employed in a restaurant to help (as by removing soiled dishes and resetting tables after use)

bus·by \'bəz-bē\ *n, pl* **busbies 1** : a military full-dress fur hat with a bag hanging down on one side **2** : the bearskin worn by British guardsmen

busby

bush \'bush\ *n* [ME] **1** : SHRUB; *esp* : a low densely branched shrub **2** : a large uncleared or sparsely settled area (as in Australia) **3** : a bushy tuft or mass; *esp* : BRUSH 2

bush baby *n* : any of several small African lemurs

bush·el \'bush-əl\ *n* [OF *boissel*] **1** : any of various units of dry capacity — see MEASURE table **2** : a container holding a bushel **3** : a large quantity : LOTS

Bu·shi·do \,bü-shē-'dō\ *n* [Jap *bushidō*] : a Japanese code of feudal chivalry emphasizing loyalty and valuing honor above life

bush·ing \'bush-iŋ\ *n* [D *bus* box, bushing] **1** : a usu. removable cylindrical lining in an opening of a mechanical part to limit the size of the opening, resist wear (as in a bearing for an axle), or serve as a guide **2** : an electrically insulating lining for a hole to protect a conductor

bush·man \'bush-mən\ *n* : a member of a nomadic hunting people of southern Africa

bush·mas·ter \-,mas-tər\ *n* : a tropical American pit viper that is the largest New World venomous snake

bush pilot *n* : a pilot who flies a small plane over uncleared or sparsely settled country esp. off regular commercial air routes

bush·whack \'bush-,hwak\ *vb* **1** : to live or hide out in the woods **2** : AMBUSH — **bush·whack·er** *n* — **bush·whack·ing** *n*

bushy \'bush-ē\ *adj* **bush·i·er; -est** **1** : full of or overgrown with bushes **2** : resembling a bush esp. in thick spreading form or growth — **bush·i·ness** *n*

busi·ness \'biz-nəs, -nəz\ *n* [ME *bisinesse*, fr. *bisy* busy] **1 a** : an activity that takes a major part of the time, attention, or effort of a person or group; *esp* : OCCUPATION **b** : a commercial or mercantile activity engaged in as a means of livelihood **2** : an immediate task or objective : MISSION ⟨state your *business* promptly⟩ **3 a** : a commercial or industrial enterprise **b** : the area of economic activity that usu. includes trade, commerce, finance, and industry **c** : transactions of any sort; *esp* : PATRONAGE **4** : AFFAIR, MATTER ⟨a strange *business*⟩

syn BUSINESS, COMMERCE, TRADE mean activity in supplying commodities. BUSINESS may be an inclusive term but specif. applies to the activities of all engaged in the sale and purchase of commodities or in related financial transactions; COMMERCE and TRADE apply to the exchange and transportation of commodities

business cycle *n* : a recurring succession of increases and decreases of economic activity from prosperity to recession to recovery

busi·ness·like \'biz-nəs-,līk, -nəz-\ *adj* **1** : having or showing qualities desirable in business : EFFICIENT, PRACTICAL **2** : SERIOUS, PURPOSEFUL

busi·ness·man \-,man\ *n* : a man engaged in a commercial or industrial enterprise esp. on an executive level

bus·kin \'bəs-kən\ *n* **1** : a boot reaching halfway to the knee **2 a** : a high boot worn by actors in Greek tragedy **b** : TRAGEDY; *esp* : ancient Greek tragedy

bus·man's holiday \,bəs-mənz-\ *n* : a holiday spent in following or observing the practice of one's usual occupation

buss \'bəs\ *n* : KISS — **buss** *vt*

¹bust \'bəst\ *n* [F *buste*, fr. It *busto*, fr. L *bustum* tomb] **1** : a piece of sculpture representing the upper part of the human figure including the head and neck **2** : the upper portion of the human torso between neck and waist; *esp* : the breasts of a woman

²bust *vb* **bust·ed** *also* **bust; bust·ing** [alter. of *burst*] **1** : HIT, PUNCH **2 a** : BREAK; *esp* : to break up or apart ⟨*bust* trusts⟩ **b** : to ruin financially **3** : to demote esp. in military rank **4** : BURST — **bust·er** *n*

³bust *n* **1** *slang* : ²PUNCH 2 **2 a** : a complete failure **b** : a severe business depression or recession **3** : SPREE

bus·tard \'bəs-tərd\ *n* [MF *bistarde*, fr. It *bistarda*, fr. L *avis tarda*, lit., slow bird] : any of various Old World and Australian game birds

¹bus·tle \'bəs-əl\ *vi* **bus·tled; bus·tling** \'bəs-(ə-)liŋ\ **1** : to move about with fussy or noisy activity **2** : to be busily astir

²bustle *n* : noisy or energetic activity

³bustle *n* : a pad or a light frame formerly worn by women just below the back waistline to give fullness to the skirt

¹busy \'biz-ē\ *adj* **bus·i·er; -est** [ME *bisy*, *busy*, fr. OE

bisig] **1 a** : engaged in action : OCCUPIED ⟨too *busy* to eat⟩ **b** : being in use ⟨a *busy* telephone⟩ **2** : full of activity : BUSTLING ⟨a *busy* street⟩ **3** : OFFICIOUS, MEDDLING **4** : full of distracting detail ⟨a *busy* design⟩ — **bus·i·ly** \'biz-ə-lē\ *adv*

²busy *vb* **bus·ied; busy·ing** **1** : to make or keep busy : OCCUPY **2** : to be busy

busy·body \'biz-ē-,bäd-ē\ *n* : a person who meddles in the affairs of others

busy·ness \'biz-ē-nəs\ *n* : the quality or state of being busy

¹but \(')bət\ *conj* **1 a** (1) : if not : UNLESS (2) : without the consequence or accompanying circumstance that ⟨it never rains *but* it pours⟩ **b** : that not ⟨not so stupid *but* he could learn⟩ **c** : THAT — used after a negative ⟨there is no doubt *but* he won⟩ **2 a** (1) : on the contrary ⟨not peace *but* a sword⟩ (2) : despite that fact ⟨he tried *but* he failed⟩ **b** : with this exception, namely ⟨no one *but* he may enter⟩

syn HOWEVER, STILL, NEVERTHELESS: BUT marks opposition without emphasizing it ⟨winter is over, *but* it is almost as cold⟩ HOWEVER is weaker and often suggests a parenthetical opposition ⟨winter is over; it is, *however*, almost as cold⟩ STILL states the opposing conclusion more strongly but implies a concession in what precedes ⟨winter is over; *still*, it is just as cold⟩ NEVERTHELESS implies that the concession has no decisive bearing on the question ⟨of course it is no longer winter; *nevertheless*, it is quite cold⟩

²but *prep* [OE *būtan* outside, except, except that; akin to E *by* & E *out*] **1** : with the exception of ⟨no one there *but* me⟩ **2** : other than ⟨this letter is nothing *but* an insult⟩

³but *adv* **1** : ONLY, MERELY ⟨he is *but* a child⟩ **2** : to the contrary ⟨who knows *but* that he may succeed⟩

bu·ta·di·ene \,byüt-ə-'dī-,ēn, -,dī-'\ *n* : a flammable gaseous hydrocarbon C_4H_6 used in making synthetic rubbers

bu·tane \'byü-,tān\ *n* [*butyric* + *-ane*] : either of two flammable gaseous hydrocarbons C_4H_{10} obtained usu. from petroleum or natural gas

¹butch·er \'büch-ər\ *n* [OF *bouchier*, fr. *bouc* he-goat] **1 a** : one who slaughters animals or dresses their flesh **b** : a dealer in meat **2** : one that kills ruthlessly or brutally **3** : a vendor esp. on trains or in theaters

²butcher *vt* **butch·ered; butch·er·ing** \-(ə-)riŋ\ **1** : to slaughter and dress for meat ⟨*butchered* hogs last week⟩ **2** : to kill in a barbarous manner **3** : to make a mess of : BOTCH — **butch·er·er** \-ər-ər\ *n*

butch·er·bird \'büch-ər-,bərd\ *n* : any of various shrikes that impale their prey upon thorns

butch·ery \'büch-(ə-)rē\ *n*, *pl* **-er·ies** **1** *chiefly Brit* : SLAUGHTERHOUSE **2** : the business of a butcher **3** : brutal murder : great slaughter

bu·teo \'byüt-ē-,ō\ *n*, *pl* **-te·os** [L *buteon-*, *buteo*] : any of various hawks with broad rounded wings and soaring flight — **bu·te·o·nine** \-'tē-ə-,nīn\ *adj or n*

but·ler \'bət-lər\ *n* [OF *bouteillier* servant in charge of wine, fr. *bouteille* bottle] : the chief male servant of a household

butler's pantry *n* : a service room between kitchen and dining room

¹butt \'bət\ *vb* [OF *boter* to strike, thrust, of Gmc origin; akin to E *beat*] : to strike with the head or horns

²butt *n* : a blow or thrust usu. with the head or horns

³butt *n* [MF *but* target, end & *bute* backstop] **1 a** : a mound, bank, or structure for stopping missiles shot at a target **b** : TARGET **c** *pl* : RANGE 5b **2** : a target of abuse or ridicule ⟨the *butt* of a joke⟩

⁴butt *vb* **1** : ABUT **2** : to place end to end without overlapping

⁵butt *n* **1** : the large or thicker end of something; *esp* : the thicker or handle end of a tool or weapon **2** : an unused remainder

⁶butt *n* [MF *botte*, fr. LL *buttis*] **1** : a large cask esp. for wine, beer, or water **2** : any of various units of liquid capacity; *esp* : a measure equal to 108 imperial gallons

butte \'byüt\ *n* [F] : an isolated hill with steep sides usu. having a smaller summit area than a mesa

¹but·ter \'bət-ər\ *n* [OE *butere*, fr. L *butyrum*, fr. Gk *boutyron*, fr. *bous* cow + *tyros* cheese] **1** : a solid yellow emulsion of fat, air, and water made by churning milk

ə abut; ᵊ kitten; ər further; a back; ā bake; ä cot, cart; aú out; ch chin; e less; ē easy; g gift; i trip; ī life

or cream and used as food **2** : a substance resembling butter in appearance, texture, or use ⟨apple *butter*⟩ ⟨cocoa *butter*⟩

²butter *vt* : to spread with or as if with butter

but·ter-and-eggs \ˌbət-ər-ən-'egz\ *n sing or pl* : any of several plants (as toadflax) having flowers of two shades of yellow

butter bean *n* **1** : WAX BEAN **2** : LIMA BEAN **3** : a green shell bean esp. as opposed to a snap bean

but·ter·cup \'bət-ər-ˌkəp\ *n* : any of a genus of yellow-flowered herbs with usu. five petals and sepals and fruits that are achenes

but·ter·fat \-ˌfat\ *n* : the natural fat of milk and chief constituent of butter

but·ter·fin·gered \'bət-ər-ˌfiŋ-gərd\ *adj* : likely to let things fall or slip through the fingers

but·ter·fish \-ˌfish\ *n* : any of numerous fishes with a slippery coating of mucus

but·ter·fly \'bət-ər-ˌflī\ *n* **1** : any of numerous slender-bodied day-flying insects (order Lepidoptera) with large broad usu. brightly colored wings — compare MOTH **2** : a person who dresses gaudily or who is chiefly occupied in the pursuit of pleasure

butterfly fish *n* : any of various fishes having variegated colors, broad expanded fins, or both

butterfly weed *n* : a showy orange-flowered milkweed of eastern No. America

but·ter·milk \'bət-ər-ˌmilk\ *n* **1** : the liquid left after the butterfat has been churned from milk or cream **2** : cultured milk made by the addition of certain organisms to sweet milk

but·ter·nut \-ˌnət\ *n* : the edible oily nut of an American tree of the walnut family; *also* : this tree

but·ter·scotch \-ˌskäch\ *n* : a candy made from sugar, corn syrup, and water; *also* : the flavor of such candy — **butterscotch** *adj*

¹but·tery \'bət-ə-rē, 'bə-trē\ *n, pl* **-ter·ies** [ME *boterie* storeroom for liquors, fr. MF, fr. *botte* cask, butt] *chiefly dial* : PANTRY

²but·tery \'bət-ə-rē\ *adj* **1** : having the qualities, consistency, or appearance of butter **2** : spread with butter **3** : FLATTERING

butt hinge *n* : a hinge usu. set flush into the edge of a door

butt joint *n* : a joint made by fastening the parts together end-to-end without overlap and often with reinforcement

but·tock \'bət-ək\ *n* **1** : the back of the hip which forms one of the fleshy parts on which a person sits **2** *pl a* : the seat of the body **b** : RUMP

¹but·ton \'bət-ᵊn\ *n* [MF *boton*, fr. *boter* to butt, thrust] **1** : a small knob or disk (as of shell, leather, or plastic) used for holding parts of a garment together or as an ornament **2** : something that resembles a button

²button *vb* **but·toned**; **but·ton·ing** \'bət-niŋ, -ᵊn-iŋ\ **1** : to close or fasten with buttons **2** : to have buttons for fastening — **but·ton·er** \'bət-nər, -ᵊn-ər\ *n*

¹but·ton·hole \'bət-ᵊn-ˌhōl\ *n* : a slit or loop for fastening a button

²buttonhole *vt* **1** : to furnish with buttonholes **2** : to work with buttonhole stitch

³buttonhole *vt* : to detain in conversation by or as if by holding on to the outer garments of — **but·ton·hol·er** *n*

buttonhole stitch *n* : a closely worked loop stitch used to make a firm edge (as on a buttonhole)

but·ton·hook \'bət-ᵊn-ˌhůk\ *n* : a hook for drawing small buttons through buttonholes

but·ton·wood \'bət-ᵊn-ˌwůd\ *n* : ²PLANE

¹but·tress \'bə-trəs\ *n* [MF *bouterez*, fr. *bouter* to thrust] **1** : a projecting structure of masonry or wood for supporting or giving stability to a wall or building **2** : something that supports, props, or strengthens

²buttress *vt* : to support with or as if with a buttress : PROP, BRACE

bu·tyl alcohol \ˌbyüt-ᵊl-\ *n* : any of four flammable alcohols C_4H_9OH derived from butanes and used in organic synthesis and as solvents

bu·tyr·ic acid \byü-ˌtir-ik-\ *n* [L *butyrum* butter] : an acid $C_4H_8O_2$ of unpleasant odor found in rancid butter

bux·om \'bək-səm\ *adj* [ME *buxsum* obedient, tractable; akin to E ¹*bow*] : vigorously or healthily plump; *esp* : full-bosomed — **bux·om·ly** *adv* — **bux·om·ness** *n*

¹buy \'bī\ *vt* **bought** \'bot\; **buy·ing** [OE *bycgan*]

1 : to get possession or ownership of by giving or agreeing to give money in exchange : PURCHASE **2** : to obtain by sacrificing something ⟨*buy* fame at the cost of honor⟩ **3** : to secure decisive control over by bribery ⟨*buy* votes⟩ **4** : to be sufficient to purchase ⟨$500 will *buy* this land⟩

²buy *n* : something sold or for sale at a price favorable to the purchaser : BARGAIN

buy·er \'bī(-ə)r\ *n* : one that buys; *esp* : a person who purchases goods to be sold in a retail store

¹buzz \'bəz\ *vb* **1** : to make a low continuous humming sound like that of a bee **2** : to be filled with a confused murmur ⟨the room *buzzed* with excitement⟩ **3** : to summon or signal with a buzzer **4** : to fly low and fast over ⟨planes *buzzed* the crowd⟩

²buzz *n* **1** : a persistent sound produced by or as if by fast pulsations (as of the wings of a bee) **2** : a confused murmur or flurry of activity **3 a** : a signal conveyed by buzzer **b** *slang* : a call on the telephone

buz·zard \'bəz-ərd\ *n* [OF *busard*, modif. of *buison*, fr. L *buteon-*, *buteo*] : any of various usu. large slow-flying birds of prey (as a short-winged hawk) — compare TURKEY BUZZARD

buzz·er \'bəz-ər\ *n* : an electric signaling device that makes a buzzing sound

buzz saw *n* : a circular saw having teeth on its periphery and revolving upon a spindle

¹by \(')bī, *esp before consonants* bə\ *prep* [OE *be*, *bī*] **1** : close to : NEAR ⟨*by* the sea⟩ **2 a** : ALONG, THROUGH ⟨*by* a different route⟩ ⟨enter *by* the door⟩ **b** : PAST ⟨went right *by* him⟩ **3 a** : during the course of ⟨studied *by* night⟩ **b** : not later than ⟨be there *by* 2 p.m.⟩ **4** : through the agency or instrumentality of ⟨*by* force⟩ **5** : with the witness or sanction of ⟨swear *by* all that is holy⟩ **6 a** : in conformity with ⟨*by* the rules⟩ **b** : according to ⟨called *by* a different name⟩ ⟨sold *by* the pound⟩ **7** : with respect to ⟨a doctor *by* profession⟩ **8** : in or to the amount or extent of ⟨win *by* a nose⟩ **9** : in successive units of ⟨walk two *by* two⟩ **10** — used as a function word in multiplication and in measurements ⟨2 *by* 4⟩

syn BY, THROUGH, WITH are used in explaining or accounting for an action or effect. BY names the immediate agent or causative agency ⟨a novel *by* Dickens⟩ ⟨destroyed *by* fire⟩ THROUGH implies intermediateness and names a means or medium ⟨express feelings *through* music⟩ ⟨money lost *through* carelessness⟩ WITH designates an instrument or instrumentality used in or accompanying the action ⟨wrote *with* a pen⟩ ⟨amused them *with* his jokes⟩

²by \'bī\ *adv* **1 a** : close at hand : NEAR ⟨standing *by*⟩ **b** : at or to another's home ⟨stop *by* for a chat⟩ **2** : PAST ⟨saw the parade go *by*⟩ **3** : ASIDE, AWAY ⟨putting some money *by*⟩

³by *or* **bye** \'bī\ *adj* **1** : off the main route : SIDE **2** : INCIDENTAL

⁴by *or* **bye** \'bī\ *n, pl* **byes** \'bīz\ : something of secondary importance : a side issue — **by the by** : by the way : INCIDENTALLY

by and by \ˌbī-ən-'bī\ *adv* : before long : SOON

by-and-by \ˌbī-ən-'bī\ *n* : a future time or occasion

by and large \ˌbī-ən-'lärj\ *adv* : on the whole : in general

bye \'bī\ *n* : a position of a participant in a tournament who has no opponent after pairs are drawn and advances to the next round without playing

by-elec·tion \'bī-ə-ˌlek-shən\ *n* : a special election held between regular elections in order to fill a vacancy

by·gone \'bī-ˌgón, -ˌgän\ *adj* : gone by : PAST — **bygone** *n*

by·law \'bī-ˌlo\ *n* [ME *bilawe*, of Scand origin] : a rule adopted by an organization (as a club or municipality) chiefly for the government of its members and the regulation of its affairs

by·line \'bī-ˌlīn\ *n* : a line at the head of a newspaper or magazine article giving the writer's name

¹by·pass \'bī-ˌpas\ *n* **1** : a passage to one side; *esp* : an alternate route around a congested area **2** : a channel carrying a fluid around a part and back to the main stream

²bypass *vt* : to make a detour or circuit around : avoid by means of a bypass ⟨*bypass* a city⟩

by·path \'bī-ˌpath, -ˌpàth\ *n* : BYWAY

by·play \-ˌplā\ *n* : action engaged in at the side of a stage while the main action proceeds

by-prod·uct \'bī-ˌpräd-(ˌ)əkt\ *n* **1** : something produced (as in manufacturing) in addition to the principal product **2 :** a secondary and often unexpected or unintended result

byre \'bī(ə)r\ *n* [OE *byre* hut, byre; akin to E *bower*] *chiefly Brit* **:** a cow barn

by·road \'bī-,rōd\ *n* **:** BYWAY

By·ron·ic \bī-'rän-ik\ *adj* **:** of, relating to, or having the characteristics of the poet Byron or his writings — **By·ron·i·cal·ly** \-'rän-i-k(ə-)lē\ *adv* — **By·ron·ism** \'bī-rə-,niz-əm\ *n*

bys·sus \'bis-əs\ *n* [Gk *byssos* flax] **:** a tuft of long tough filaments by which some mollusks (as mussels) make themselves fast — **bys·sal** \'bis-əl\ *adj*

by·stand·er \'bī-,stan-dər\ *n* **:** a person present or standing near but taking no part in something going on

by·street \'bī-,strēt\ *n* **:** a street off a main thoroughfare **:** a side street

by the way *adv* **:** in passing **:** INCIDENTALLY

by·way \'bī-,wā\ *n* **1 :** a side road; *esp* **:** one that is little traveled **2 :** a secondary or little known aspect or field

by·word \'bī-,wərd\ *n* **1 :** a proverbial saying **2 :** a person or thing that is typical esp. of some bad class or quality **:** an object of scorn or contempt

¹Byz·an·tine \'biz-°n-,tēn, bə-'zan-, 'bīz-°n-; 'biz-°n-,tīn\ *n* **:** a native or inhabitant of Byzantium or of the Byzantine Empire

²Byzantine *adj* **1 a :** of, relating to, or characteristic of the ancient city of Byzantium **b :** of or relating to the Eastern Roman Empire flourishing from the 5th century A.D. to the capture of Constantinople by the Turks in 1453 **2 :** of or relating to a style of architecture developed in the Byzantine Empire esp. in the 5th and 6th centuries characterized by a central dome over a square space and by much use of mosaics **3 :** of or relating to the Eastern Orthodox Church or the rite characteristic of it

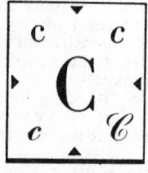

c \'sē\ *n, often cap* **1 :** the 3d letter of the English alphabet **2 :** the roman numeral 100 **3 :** the musical tone C **4 :** a grade rating a student's work as fair or mediocre

cab \'kab\ *n* **1 a :** CABRIOLET **b :** a light closed carriage (as a hansom) **c :** a carriage for hire **2 :** TAXICAB **3 a :** the part of a locomotive that houses the engineer and operating controls **b :** a comparable shelter on a truck, tractor, or crane

ca·bal \kə-'bal\ *n* [F *cabale*, fr. ML *cabbala* cabala, fr. Heb *qabbālāh*] **:** a small group of persons working together to promote their own plans or interests esp. by intrigue

ca·ba·la *or* **cab·ba·la** *or* **cab·ba·lah** \'kab-ə-lə, kə-'bäl-ə\ *n, often cap* **1 :** a system of Jewish theosophy, mysticism, and magic using a cipher method of interpreting Scripture **2 :** an esoteric doctrine or mysterious art — **cab·a·lism** \'kab-ə-,liz-əm\ *n* — **cab·a·list** \-ləst\ *adj* — **cab·a·lis·tic** \,kab-ə-'lis-tik\ *adj*

ca·bal·le·ro \,kab-ə-'le(ə)r-ō, -ə(l)-'ye(ə)r-\ *n, pl* **-leros** [Sp] *chiefly Southwest* **:** HORSEMAN

ca·ba·na \kə-'ban-(y)ə\ *n* [Sp *cabaña*, lit., hut] **:** a beach shelter resembling a cabin usu. with an open side facing the sea

cab·a·ret \,kab-ə-'rā\ *n* [F] **:** a restaurant serving liquor and providing entertainment (as by singers or dancers)

cab·bage \'kab-ij\ *n* [ME *caboche*, fr. ONF, head] **:** a garden plant related to the turnip but lacking a swollen root and having a dense globular head of leaves used as a vegetable

cab·by *or* **cab·bie** \'kab-ē\ *n, pl* **cabbies :** a driver of a cab

cab·driv·er \'kab-,drī-vər\ *n* **:** a driver of a cab

cab·in \'kab-ən\ *n* [MF *cabane*, fr. ML *capanna* hut] **1 a :** a private room on a ship for one or a few persons **b :** a compartment below deck on a small boat for pas-

sengers or crew **c :** an airplane or airship compartment for cargo, crew, or passengers **2 :** a small one-story dwelling usu. of simple construction

cabin boy *n* **:** a boy acting as servant on a ship

cabin class *n* **:** a class of accommodations on a passenger ship superior to tourist class and inferior to first class

cab·i·net \'kab-(ə-)nət\ *n* [MF, small room] **1 a :** a case or cupboard usu. having doors and shelves **b :** an upright case housing a radio or television **:** CONSOLE **2** *archaic* **:** a small room providing seclusion **3 a :** a group of ministers acting as advisers to a monarch or chief of state but constituting the real political executive in a cabinet government ⟨the British *cabinet*⟩ **b :** a body of advisers to the president of the U.S. consisting chiefly of the heads of the executive departments

cabinet government *n* **:** a government in which the real executive and policy-making power is held by a cabinet of ministers who are responsible to the legislature

cab·i·net·mak·er \-,mā-kər\ *n* **:** a skilled woodworker who makes fine furniture — **cab·i·net·mak·ing** \-kiŋ\ *n*

cab·i·net·work \-,wərk\ *n* **:** the finished work of a cabinetmaker

¹ca·ble \'kā-bəl\ *n* [ONF, fr. ML *capulum* lasso, fr. L *capere* to take] **1 a :** a strong rope esp. of 10 or more inches in circumference **b :** a wire rope or metal chain of great strength **c :** a wire or wire rope by which force is exerted to operate a mechanism **2 :** CABLE LENGTH **3 a :** a bundle of electrical conductors insulated from each other but held together usu. by being twisted around a central core **b :** CABLEGRAM

²cable *vb* **ca·bled; ca·bling** \'kā-b(ə-)liŋ\ **1 :** to fasten or provide with a cable **2 :** to telegraph by submarine cable

cable car *n* **:** a car moved on a railway by an endless cable or along an overhead cableway

ca·ble·gram \'kā-bəl-,gram\ *n* **:** a message sent by submarine cable

cable length *n* **:** a maritime unit of length variously reckoned as 100 fathoms, 120 fathoms, or 608 feet

ca·ble·way \'kā-bəl-,wā\ *n* **:** a suspended cable used as a track along which carriers can be pulled

cab·o·chon \'kab-ə-,shän\ *n* [MF, aug. of ONF *caboche* head] **:** a gem or bead cut in convex form and highly polished but not faceted — **cabochon** *adv*

ca·boose \kə-'büs\ *n* [prob. fr. D *kabuis* ship's galley] **:** a freight-train car attached usu. to the rear mainly for the use of the train crew and railroad workmen

cab·ri·o·let \,kab-rē-ə-'lā\ *n* [F, fr. dim. of *cabriole* caper] **1 :** a light 2-wheeled one-horse carriage with a folding leather hood and upward-curving shafts **2 :** a convertible coupe

cab·stand \'kab-,stand\ *n* **:** a place for cabs to park while waiting for passengers

ca·cao \kə-'kaù, kə-'kā-ō\ *n, pl* **ca·caos** [Sp, fr. Nahuatl *cacahuatl* cacao beans] **:** a So. American tree with small yellowish flowers followed by fleshy yellow pods with many seeds; *also* **:** its dried partly fermented fatty seeds from which cocoa and chocolate are made

cach·a·lot \'kash-ə-,lät, -,lō\ *n* **:** SPERM WHALE

¹cache \'kash\ *n* [F, fr. *cacher* to hide] **1 :** a place for hiding, storing, or safeguarding treasure, food, or other supplies **2 :** the material hidden or stored in a cache

²cache *vt* **:** to place, hide, or store in a cache

ca·chet \ka-'shā\ *n* [MF, fr. *cacher* to press, hide] **1 :** a seal esp. of official approval **2 :** a characteristic feature or quality conferring prestige **3 :** a commemorative device

ca·chex·ia \ka-'kek-sē-ə\ *n* [Gk *kachexia* bad condition] **:** general physical wasting and malnutrition usu. associated with chronic disease — **ca·chec·tic** \-'kek-tik\ *adj*

ca·cique \kə-'sēk\ *n* [Sp, of AmerInd origin] **:** an Indian chief in Latin America

cack·le \'kak-əl\ *vi* **cack·led; cack·ling** \-(ə-)liŋ\ **1 :** to make the sharp broken noise or cry characteristic of a hen esp. after laying **2 :** to laugh or chatter noisily — **cackle** *n* — **cack·ler** \-(ə-)lər\ *n*

cac·o·e·thes \,kak-ə-'wē-,thēz\ *n* **:** an insatiable desire **:** MANIA

caco·gen·e·sis \,kak-ə-'jen-ə-səs\ *n* **:** racial deterioration esp. when due to the retention of inferior breeding stock — **caco·gen·ic** \-'jen-ik\ *adj*

ca·coph·o·ny \kȧ-'käf-ə-nē\ *n, pl* **-nies** [Gk *kakophōnia*, fr. *kakos* bad + *phōnē* sound] **:** harsh or discordant sound **:** DISSONANCE — **ca·coph·o·nous** \-nəs\ *adj*

cac·tus \'kak-təs\ *n, pl* **cac·tus·es** *or* **cac·ti** \-,tī, -(,)tē\ [Gk *kaktos*] **:** any of a large family of flowering plants able to live in dry regions and having fleshy stems and branches that bear scales or prickles instead of leaves

cad \'kad\ *n* [E dial., unskilled assistant] **:** a person who behaves esp. deliberately in an ungentlemanly way

ca·dav·er \kə-'dav-ər\ *n* [L, fr. *cadere* to fall] **:** a dead body esp. of a human being **:** CORPSE — **ca·dav·er·ic** \-'dav-ə-rik\ *adj*

ca·dav·er·ous \kə-'dav-(ə-)rəs\ *adj* **:** of, relating to, or having the look of a cadaver: as **a :** PALE, GHASTLY **b :** THIN, HAGGARD — **ca·dav·er·ous·ly** *adv*

cactus

¹**cad·die** *or* **cad·dy** \'kad-ē\ *n, pl* **caddies :** a person who carries a golfer's clubs

²**caddie** *or* **caddy** *vi* **-died; -dy·ing :** to work as a caddie

cad·dis *or* **cad·dice** \'kad-əs\ *n* **:** CADDISWORM

caddis fly *n* **:** any of an order (Trichoptera) of 4-winged insects with aquatic larvae — compare CADDISWORM

cad·dish \'kad-ish\ *adj* **:** resembling a cad or the behavior of a cad — **cad·dish·ly** *adv* — **cad·dish·ness** *n*

cad·dis·worm \'kad-əs-,wərm\ *n* **:** a larval caddis fly that lives in and carries around a silken case covered with bits of debris

cad·dy \'kad-ē\ *n, pl* **caddies** [Malay *kati*] **:** a small box, can, or chest; *esp* **:** one to keep tea in

ca·delle \kə-'del\ *n* **:** a small cosmopolitan black beetle destructive to stored grain

ca·dence \'kād-ᵊn(t)s\ *n* [It *cadenza*, fr. *cadere* to fall, fr. L] **1 a :** rhythmic flow of sounds in language **b :** the beat, time, or measure of rhythmical motion or activity **2 :** a concluding and usu. falling strain; *esp* **:** a musical chord sequence moving to a harmonic close or point of rest — **ca·denced** \-ᵊn(t)st\ *adj*

ca·den·za \kə-'den-zə\ *n* [It, cadence, cadenza] **1 :** an added flourish in a solo piece (as an aria) commonly just before the end **2 :** a technically brilliant sometimes improvised solo passage toward the close of a movement of a concerto

ca·det \kə-'det\ *n* [F, fr. F dial. *capdet* chief, fr. LL *capitellum*, dim. of L *caput* head] **1 a :** a younger brother or son **b :** a younger branch of a family or a member of it **2 :** one in training for a military commission; *esp* **:** a student in a service academy **3 :** a student at a military school **4 :** a boy or girl in any of various organizations usu. associated with an adult group organized on military lines — **ca·det·ship** \-,ship\ *n*

cadge \'kaj\ *vb* **:** BEG, SPONGE — **cadg·er** *n*

cad·mi·um \'kad-mē-əm\ *n* [L *cadmia* calamine; fr. the occurrence of its ores together with calamine] **:** a grayish white malleable ductile metallic element used esp. in protective platings and in bearing metals — see ELEMENT table

Cad·mus \'kad-məs\ *n* **:** a Phoenician prince held in Greek legend to have killed a dragon and sown its teeth from which sprang armed men who fought together until only five survived who with Cadmus founded Thebes

cad·re \'kad-rē\ *n* [F, frame, framework, fr. It *quadro*, fr. L *quadrum* square] **1 :** a nucleus of trained personnel capable of assuming leadership and control and of training others **2 :** a member of a cadre

ca·du·ce·us \kə-'d(y)ü-sē-əs\ *n, pl* **-cei** \-sē-,ī\ [L, modif. of Gk *karykeion*, fr. *karyk-, karyx, kēryx* herald] **1 :** the staff of a herald; *esp* **:** a representation of a staff with two entwined snakes and two wings at the top **2 :** an insignia bearing a caduceus and symbolizing a physician — **ca·du·ce·an** \-sē-ən\ *adj*

ca·du·cous \kə-'d(y)ü-kəs\ *adj* [L *caducus*, fr. *cadere* to fall] **:** falling off easily or before the usual time — used esp. of floral organs

cae·cal, cae·cum *var of* CECAL, CECUM

cae·ci·lian \si-'sil-yən, -'sēl-\ *n* [L *caecilia*, a lizard] **:** any of an order (Gymnophiona) of chiefly tropical burrowing amphibians resembling worms — **caecilian** *adj*

Cae·sar \'sē-zər\ *n* [[L, fr. cognomen of the emperor Augustus] **1 :** any of the Roman emperors succeeding

Augustus Caesar — used as a title **2 a** *often not cap* **:** a powerful ruler: (1) **:** EMPEROR (2) **:** AUTOCRAT, DICTATOR **b** [fr. the reference in Matthew 22:21] **:** the civil power **:** a temporal ruler — **Cae·sar·e·an** *or* **Cae·sar·i·an** \si-'zar-ē-ən, -'zer-\ *adj*

cae·sar·e·an *var of* CESAREAN

cae·si·um *var of* CESIUM

caes·pi·tose \'ses-pə-,tōs\ *adj* **1 :** forming a dense turf or sod **2 :** growing in clusters or tufts

cae·su·ra \si-'z(h)ùr-ə\ *n, pl* **-su·ras** *or* **-su·rae** \-'z(h)ù(ə)r-(,)ē\ [L, cutting, fr. *caes-, caedere* to cut] **:** a break in the flow of sound usu. in the middle of a line of verse — **cae·su·ral** \-'z(h)ùr-əl\ *adj*

ca·fé *also* **ca·fe** \ka-'fā, kə-\ *n* [F *café* coffee, café, fr. Turk *kahve*] **1 :** COFFEEHOUSE **2 :** BARROOM, SALOON **3 :** RESTAURANT; *also* **:** NIGHTCLUB

ca·fé au lait \(,)ka-,fā-ō-'lā\ *n* [F, lit., coffee with milk] **:** coffee with usu. hot milk in about equal parts

caf·e·te·ria \,kaf-ə-'tir-ē-ə\ *n* [AmerSp *cafetería* coffee store, fr. Sp *café* coffee, fr. F] **:** a restaurant in which the customers serve themselves or are served at a counter but take the food to tables to eat

caf·feine \ka-'fēn, 'kaf-ē-ən\ *n* [G *kaffein*, fr. *kaffee* coffee, fr. F *café*] **:** a bitter stimulating compound $C_8H_{10}N_4O_2$ found esp. in coffee, tea, and kola nuts

caf·tan \kaf-'tan\ *n* **:** an ankle-length garment with long sleeves worn in the Levant

¹**cage** \'kāj\ *n* [OF, fr. L *cavea*, fr. *cavus* hollow] **1 :** a largely openwork enclosure for confining or carrying an animal (as a bird) **2 :** an enclosure like a cage in form or purpose **3 :** a goal structure consisting of posts or a frame with a net attached (as in ice hockey) **4 :** a large building with unobstructed interior for practicing outdoor sports

²**cage** *vt* **:** to confine or keep in or as if in a cage

cage·ling \'kāj-liŋ\ *n* **:** a caged bird

ca·gey *also* **ca·gy** \'kā-jē\ *adj* **ca·gi·er; -est :** wary of being trapped or deceived **:** SHREWD, CAUTIOUS — **ca·gi·ly** \-jə-lē\ *adv* — **ca·gi·ness** \-jē-nəs\ *n*

ca·hier \kä-'yā\ *n* [F] **:** a statement of local grievances and proposals for reform brought by each delegate to the French States General in 1789

ca·hoot \kə-'hüt\ *n* **:** PARTNERSHIP, LEAGUE — usu. used in pl. ⟨in *cahoots* with the devil⟩

cai·man \kā-'man, kī-; 'kā-mən\ *n* **:** any of several Central and So. American reptiles basically similar to alligators but often superficially resembling crocodiles

Cain \'kān\ *n* **:** the brother and murderer of Abel

ca·ique \kä-'ēk\ *n* **1 :** a light skiff used on the Bosporus **2 :** a Greek fishing and passenger boat with one mast and an auxiliary engine

cairn \'ka(ə)rn, 'ke(ə)rn\ *n* [ScGael *carn*] **:** a heap of stones piled up as a landmark or as a memorial

cairn·gorm \-,górm\ *n* **:** a yellow or smoky brown crystalline quartz

cairn terrier *n* [fr. its use in hunting in rock piles] **:** a small compactly built hard-coated terrier of Scottish origin

cais·son \'kā-,sän, 'kās-ᵊn\ *n* [F, aug. of *caisse* box, case] **1 a :** a chest for ammunition **b :** a 2-wheeled vehicle for artillery ammunition **2 a :** a watertight chamber used in construction work under water or as a foundation **b :** a float for raising a sunken vessel

caisson disease *n* **:** a severe disorder marked by pain (as in joints and limbs), distress in breathing, and often collapse and caused by release of gas bubbles in the tissues upon too rapid decrease in air pressure after a stay in a compressed atmosphere

cai·tiff \'kāt-əf\ *adj* [ONF *caitif*, lit., captive, fr. L *captivus*] **:** being base, cowardly, or despicable — **caitiff** *n*

ca·jole \kə-'jōl\ *vt* [F *cajoler*] **:** to coax or persuade esp. by flattery or false promises **:** WHEEDLE — **ca·jol·ery** \-'jōl-(ə-)rē\ *n*

Ca·jun \'kā-jən\ *n* [alter. of *Acadian*] **:** a Louisianian descended from French-speaking immigrants from Acadia

¹**cake** \'kāk\ *n* [ON *kaka*] **1 :** a small mass of food (as dough or batter, meat, or fish) baked or fried **2 :** a baked food made from a mixture of flour, sugar, eggs, and flavoring **3 :** a substance hardened or molded into a solid mass ⟨a *cake* of soap⟩

²**cake** *vb* **1 :** ENCRUST **2 :** to form or harden into a mass

cal·a·bash \'kal-ə-,bash\ *n* **1 :** GOURD; *esp* **:** one whose hard shell is used for a utensil (as a bottle) **2** : a tropical American tree related to the trumpet creeper; *also* : its hard round fruit **3** : a utensil made from the shell of a calabash

cal·a·boose \'kal-ə-ˌbüs\ *n* [Sp *calabozo* dungeon] *dial* : JAIL

ca·la·di·um \kə-'lād-ē-əm\ *n* [Malay *kĕladi*] : any of a genus of tropical American herbs related to the arums and often grown for their showy brightly colored leaves

cal·a·mine \'kal-ə-ˌmīn, -mən\ *n* [F, ore of zinc, fr. ML *calamina*, alter. of L *cadmia*, fr. Gk *kadmeia*] : a mixture of zinc oxide and a small amount of ferric oxide used in lotions, liniments, and ointments in skin treatment

cal·a·mite \'kal-ə-ˌmīt\ *n* : a Paleozoic fossil plant resembling a giant horsetail

ca·lam·i·tous \kə-'lam-ət-əs\ *adj* : causing or accompanied by calamity : DISASTROUS — **ca·lam·i·tous·ly** *adv* — **ca·lam·i·tous·ness** *n*

ca·lam·i·ty \kə-'lam-ət-ē\ *n, pl* **-ties** [L *calamitas*] **1** : a state of deep distress or misery caused by major misfortune or loss **2** : an extraordinarily grave event marked by great loss and lasting distress and affliction *syn* see DISASTER

cal·a·mus \'kal-ə-məs\ *n, pl* **-mi** \-ˌmī, -ˌmē\ **1** : the sweet flag or its aromatic root **2** : QUILL 2a

ca·lash \kə-'lash\ *n* **1** : a light small-wheeled 4-passenger carriage with a folding top **2** : a large hood on a hoop frame worn by women in the 18th century

cal·ca·ne·um \kal-'kā-nē-əm\ *n, pl* **-nea** \-nē-ə\ : CALCANEUS

cal·ca·ne·us \-nē-əs\ *n, pl* **-nei** \-nē-ˌī\ : a tarsal bone that in man is the great bone of the heel — **cal·ca·ne·al** \-nē-əl\ *adj*

cal·car \'kal-ˌkär\ *n, pl* **cal·car·ia** \kal-'kar-ē-ə, -'ker-\ : a spurred prominence

cal·car·e·ous \kal-'kar-ē-əs, -'ker-\ *adj* **1** : resembling calcite or calcium carbonate esp. in hardness **2** : consisting of or containing calcium carbonate; *also* : containing calcium — **cal·car·e·ous·ly** *adv* — **cal·car·e·ous·ness** *n*

cal·ce·o·lar·ia \ˌkal-sē-ə-'lar-ē-ə, -'ler-\ *n* : any of a genus of tropical American plants of the figwort family widely grown for their showy pouch-shaped flowers

calces *pl of* CALX

cal·ci·cole \'kal-sə-ˌkōl\ *n* : a plant normally growing on calcareous soils — **cal·cic·o·lous** \kal-'sik-ə-ləs\ *adj*

cal·cif·er·ol \kal-'sif-ə-ˌrȯl, -ˌrōl\ *n* : a vitamin D prepared by irradiation of ergosterol

cal·cif·er·ous \kal-'sif-(ə-)rəs\ *adj* : producing or containing calcium carbonate and esp. calcite

cal·ci·fi·ca·tion \ˌkal-sə-fə-'kā-shən\ *n* **1** : the process of calcifying; *esp* : deposition of insoluble lime salts (as in tissue) ⟨bone formation by *calcification* of cartilage⟩ **2** : a calcified structure

cal·ci·fuge \'kal-sə-ˌfyüj\ *n* : a plant not normally growing on calcareous soils — **cal·cif·u·gous** \kal-'sif-yə-gəs\ *adj*

cal·ci·fy \'kal-sə-ˌfī\ *vb* **-fied; -fy·ing** **1** : to make calcareous by deposit of calcium salts **2** : to become calcareous

cal·ci·mine \'kal-sə-ˌmīn\ *n* : a white or tinted wash of glue, whiting or zinc white, and water used esp. on plastered surfaces — **calcimine** *vt*

cal·cine \kal-'sīn\ *vt* : to heat to a high temperature but without fusing in order to drive off volatile matter (as carbon dioxide from limestone) and thus to disintegrate (as bone) or in order to produce an oxide of a metal — **cal·ci·na·tion** \ˌkal-sə-'nā-shən\ *n*

cal·cite \'kal-ˌsīt\ *n* : a crystalline mineral substance composed of calcium carbonate and found in numerous forms including limestone, chalk, and marble — **cal·cit·ic** \kal-'sit-ik\ *adj*

cal·ci·um \'kal-sē-əm\ *n* [NL, fr. L *calc-, calx* lime] : a silver-white bivalent soft metallic chemical element that is found only in combination with other chemical elements (as in limestone) and that is one of the essential parts of the bodies of most plants and animals — see ELEMENT table

calcium carbide *n* : a usu. dark gray crystalline compound CaC_2 used for the generation of acetylene

calcium carbonate *n* : a solid substance $CaCO_3$ found in

nature as limestone and marble and in plant ashes, bones, and shells

calcium chloride *n* : a salt $CaCl_2$ that absorbs moisture from the air and that is used as a drying agent and in a hydrated state to lay dust

calcium hydroxide *n* : a strongly alkaline substance $Ca(OH)_2$ commonly sold as a white powder or in water solution

calcium oxide *n* : a white caustic solid CaO that is the chief ingredient of lime

calcium phosphate *n* : any of various phosphates of calcium: as **a** : the phosphate $Ca_3(PO_4)_2$ used as a fertilizer **b** : a naturally occurring phosphate containing other elements (as fluorine) and occurring as the chief constituent of phosphate rock, bones, and teeth

calcium sulfate *n* : a white compound of calcium with sulfur and oxygen $CaSO_4$ best known in the hydrated forms gypsum and plaster of paris but also found as the anhydrous mineral anhydrite

cal·cu·late \'kal-kyə-ˌlāt\ *vb* [L *calculare*, fr. *calculus* pebble, stone used in reckoning, fr. dim. of *calc-, calx* lime, stone] **1 a** : to determine by mathematical processes **b** : to reckon by an informed guess : ESTIMATE **2** : to make a calculation **3** : to plan by careful thought ⟨a plan *calculated* to succeed⟩ **4** : RELY, DEPEND — **cal·cu·la·ble** \-kyə-lə-bəl\ *adj* — **cal·cu·la·bly** \-blē\ *adv*

cal·cu·lat·ed \-ˌlāt-əd\ *adj* : undertaken after estimating the probability of success or failure ⟨a *calculated* risk⟩ — **cal·cu·lat·ed·ly** *adv*

cal·cu·lat·ing \-ˌlāt-iŋ\ *adj* **1** : designed to make calculations ⟨*calculating* machine⟩ **2** : marked by shrewd analysis of one's own self-interest : SCHEMING — **cal·cu·lat·ing·ly** \-iŋ-lē\ *adv*

cal·cu·la·tion \ˌkal-kyə-'lā-shən\ *n* **1 a** : the process or an act of calculating **b** : the result of an act of calculating **2** : studied care in analyzing or planning : CAUTION — **cal·cu·la·tive** \'kal-kyə-ˌlāt-iv\ *adj*

cal·cu·la·tor \'kal-kyə-ˌlāt-ər\ *n* **1** : one that calculates **2** : a machine for performing mathematical operations mechanically

cal·cu·lous \'kal-kyə-ləs\ *adj* : caused or marked by the presence of calculi ⟨*calculous* jaundice⟩

cal·cu·lus \'kal-kyə-ləs\ *n, pl* **-li** \-ˌlī, -ˌlē\ *also* **-lus·es** [L, pebble, stone] **1** : a mass usu. of mineral salts deposited in or around organic material in a hollow organ or bodily duct **2 a** : a method of computation or calculation in a special symbolic notation **b** : the mathematical methods comprising differential and integral calculus

cal·dron \'kȯl-drən\ *n* [ONF *cauderon*, fr. LL *caldaria*, fr. L *calidus* warm] : a large kettle or boiler

¹cal·en·dar \'kal-ən-dər\ *n* [ML *kalendarium*, fr. L *kalendae* calends] **1 a** : an arrangement of time into days, weeks, months, and years **b** : a sheet, folder, or book containing a record of such an arrangement for a certain period usu. a year **2** : an orderly list: as **a** : a list of cases to be tried in court **b** : a list of bills to be considered by a legislative assembly **c** : a schedule of coming events

²calendar *vt* : to enter in a calendar

¹cal·en·der \'kal-ən-dər\ *vt* [MF *calandrer*, fr. *calandre* calender, fr. Gk *kylindros* cylinder] : to press (as cloth or paper) between rollers or plates in order to smooth and glaze or thin into sheets — **cal·en·der·er** *n*

²calender *n* : a machine for calendering cloth or paper

cal·ends \'kal-ən(d)z\ *n pl* : the first day of the ancient Roman month

ca·len·du·la \kə-'len-jə-lə\ *n* : any of a small genus of yellow-rayed herbs related to the daisies — compare POT MARIGOLD

¹calf \'kaf, 'kȧf\ *n, pl* **calves** \'kavz, 'kȧvz\ [OE *cealf*] **1 a** : the young of the domestic cow **b** : the young of various large animals (as the elephant or whale) **2** *pl* **calfs** : CALFSKIN **3** : an awkward or silly boy or youth

²calf *n, pl* **calves** [ON *kalfi*] : the fleshy back part of the leg below the knee

calf·skin \'kaf-ˌskin, 'kȧf-\ *n* : leather made of the skin of a calf

cal·i·ber *or* **cal·i·bre** \'kal-ə-bər\ *n* [MF *calibre*, fr. It *calibro*, fr. Ar *qālib* shoemaker's last] **1** : the diameter of a projectile **2** : the diameter of the bore of a gun usu.

expressed in hundredths or thousandths of an inch and as a decimal fraction ⟨.32 *caliber*⟩ **3 a :** mental ability or moral quality **b :** degree of excellence **:** QUALITY

cal·i·brate \'kal-ə-,brāt\ *vt* **1 :** to measure the caliber of **2 :** to determine, correct, or put the measuring marks on (as a thermometer tube) — **cal·i·bra·tion** \,kal-ə-'brā-shən\ *n* — **cal·i·bra·tor** \'kal-ə-,brāt-ər\ *n*

cal·i·co \'kal-i-,kō\ *n, pl* **-coes** *or* **-cos** [fr. *Calicut*, city of India] **1 :** cotton cloth; *esp* **:** cotton cloth with a colored pattern printed on one side **2 :** a blotched or spotted animal (as a piebald horse) — **calico** *adj*

Cal·i·for·nia current \,kal-ə-,fȯr-nyə-\ *n* **:** a cold current of the north Pacific flowing southeast along the west coast of No. America from about 50°N lat. to about 20°N lat.

California poppy *n* **:** any of a genus of herbs of the poppy family including one widely grown for its pale yellow to red flowers

cal·i·for·ni·um \,kal-ə-'fȯr-nē-əm\ *n* **:** an artificially prepared radioactive chemical element — see ELEMENT table

cal·i·per *or* **cal·li·per** \'kal-ə-pər\ *n* [alter. of *caliber*] **:** a measuring instrument with two legs or jaws that can be adjusted to determine thickness, diameter, and distance between surfaces — usu. used in pl. ⟨a pair of *calipers*⟩

calipers

ca·liph *or* **ca·lif** \'kā-ləf, 'kal-əf\ *n* [MF *calife*, fr. Ar *khalīfah* successor] **:** a successor of Muhammad as temporal and spiritual head of Islam — used as a title — **ca·liph·ate** \-,āt\ *n*

cal·is·then·ics \,kal-əs-'then-iks\ *n sing or pl* [Gk *kalos* beautiful + *sthenos* strength] **1 :** systematic bodily exercises without apparatus or with light hand apparatus **2 :** the art or practice of calisthenics — **cal·is·then·ic** \-ik\ *adj*

¹calk \'kȯk\ *var of* CAULK

²calk *n* **:** a tapered piece projecting downward from a shoe (as of a horse) to prevent slipping

³calk *vt* **1 :** to furnish with calks **2 :** to wound with a calk

¹call \'kȯl\ *vb* [prob. fr. ON *kalla*] **1 :** to speak in a loud distinct voice so as to be heard at a distance **:** CRY, SHOUT **2 :** to utter in a loud clear voice ⟨*call* a roll⟩ ⟨*call* out a command⟩ **3 :** to announce with authority **:** PROCLAIM **4 a :** to summon with a shout ⟨*call* someone to dinner⟩ **b :** to cause to come ⟨*call* to mind an old saying⟩ **5 :** to bring into action or discussion ⟨*call* up reserves⟩ ⟨*call* a strike⟩ **6 :** to make an appeal, request, or demand ⟨*call* on a person's sense of decency⟩ **7 :** to get in touch with by telephone **:** make a telephone call **8 :** SUMMON, CONVOKE ⟨*call* a meeting⟩ **9 :** to make a brief visit **10 :** to give a name to **:** address by name **11 :** to regard as being of a certain kind **12 :** to estimate as being ⟨*call* the distance 10 miles⟩ **13 a** *of an animal* **:** to utter a characteristic note or cry **b :** to attract (as game) by imitating the characteristic cry **14 :** to make a demand in card games (as for a particular card or for a show of hands) **15 :** to halt (as a baseball game) because of unsuitable conditions **16 :** SUSPEND ⟨time was *called* while the field was cleared⟩ — **call·a·ble** \'kȯ-lə-bəl\ *adj* — **call·er** *n*

²call *n* **1 a :** an act of calling with the voice **:** SHOUT **b :** a cry of an animal (as a bird); *also* **:** an imitation of this or a device used (as in calling game) to make such an imitation **2 a :** a request or command to assemble **b :** a signal on a drum or bugle **c :** an invitation to become the minister of a church or to accept a professional appointment **d :** a divine or inner prompting to a course of action **e :** the attraction or appeal of a particular activity, condition, or place ⟨the *call* of the wild⟩ **3 a :** DEMAND, CLAIM **b :** NEED, JUSTIFICATION **c :** REQUEST ⟨many *calls* for Christmas stories⟩ **4 :** a short visit **5 :** a name or thing called ⟨the *call* was heads⟩ **6 :** the act of calling in a card game **7 :** the act of calling on the telephone **8 :** a direction or set of directions for a square dance rhythmically called to the dancers **9 :** a decision or ruling made by an official of a sports contest

cal·la \'kal-ə\ *n* **:** a plant of the arum family often grown for its white showy spathe surrounding a fleshy spike of yellow florets

call-board \'kȯl-,bȯrd, -,bȯrd\ *n* **:** BULLETIN BOARD

call down *vt* **:** REPRIMAND

cal·lig·ra·phy \kə-'lig-rə-fē\ *n* [Gk *kalli-* beautiful (fr. *kallos* beauty) + *graphein* to write] **1 :** beautiful or elegant handwriting or the art of producing such writing **2 :** PENMANSHIP — **cal·lig·ra·pher** \-fər\ *n* — **cal·li·graph·ic** \,kal-ə-'graf-ik\ *adj* — **cal·li·graph·i·cal·ly** \-'graf-i-k(ə-)lē\ *adv*

call·ing \'kȯ-liŋ\ *n* **1 :** a strong inner impulse; *esp* **:** one toward the ministry or priesthood accompanied by conviction of divine influence **2 :** one's customary vocation or profession

cal·li·o·pe \kə-'lī-ə-(,)pē, 'kal-ē-,ōp\ *n* **:** a musical instrument consisting of a series of whistles played by keys arranged as in an organ

Cal·li·o·pe \kə-'lī-ə-(,)pē\ *n* **:** the Greek muse of eloquence and heroic poetry

cal·li·op·sis \,kal-ē-'äp-səs\ *n* **:** COREOPSIS — used esp. of annual forms

call number *n* **:** a combination of characters assigned to a library book to indicate its place on a shelf

call off *vt* **1 :** to draw away **:** DIVERT **2 :** CANCEL ⟨*call off* a meeting⟩

cal·lose \'kal-,ōs\ *n* **:** a carbohydrate component of plant cell walls

cal·los·i·ty \ka-'läs-ət-ē, kə-\ *n, pl* **-ties** **1 :** the quality or state of being callous **2 :** CALLUS 1

¹cal·lous \'kal-əs\ *adj* [L *callosus*, fr. *callus* + *-osus* -ous] **1 :** so thickened and usu. hardened as to form callus or a callus **2 :** deficient in emotional response **:** UNFEELING ⟨a *callous* disregard for human rights⟩ — **cal·lous·ly** *adv* — **cal·lous·ness** *n*

²callous *vt* **:** to make callous

cal·low \'kal-ō\ *adj* [OE *calu* bald] **:** lacking adult sophistication **:** IMMATURE — **cal·low·ness** *n*

call-up \'kȯl-,əp\ *n* **:** an order to report for military service

¹cal·lus \'kal-əs\ *n* [L] **1 :** a thickening of or a hard thickened area on skin or bark **2 :** a mass of exudate and connective tissue that surrounds a break in a bone and is converted into bone in the healing of the break **3 :** tissue that forms over an injured plant surface

²callus *vi* **:** to form callus

¹calm \'käm, 'kälm\ *n* [It *calma*, fr. Gk *kauma* heat] **1 :** a period or condition of freedom from storm, wind, or rough activity of water **2 :** a state of repose and freedom from turmoil or agitation **:** QUIET, PEACEFULNESS

²calm *adj* **1 :** marked by calm **:** STILL **2 :** free from agitation, excitement, or disturbance — **calm·ly** *adv* — **calm·ness** *n*

syn CALM, SERENE, PLACID mean free from turbulence or excitement. CALM implies a contrast with a foregoing or nearby state of agitation or violence; SERENE stresses an unclouded and lofty tranquillity; PLACID suggests an undisturbed appearance and often implies a degree of complacency

³calm *vb* **1 :** to become calm **2 :** to make calm

cal·o·mel \'kal-ə-məl, -,mel\ *n* [Gk *kalos* beautiful + *melas* black] **:** a white tasteless substance Hg_2Cl_2 that occurs as a mineral or is made chemically and that is used as a cathartic, fungicide, and insecticide — called also *mercurous chloride*

¹ca·lor·ic \kə-'lȯr-ik, -'lōr-, -'lär-\ *n* **:** a supposed form of matter formerly held responsible for the phenomena of heat and combustion

²caloric *adj* **1 :** of or relating to heat **2 :** of or relating to calories — **ca·lor·i·cal·ly** \-i-k(ə-)lē\ *adv*

cal·o·rie *or* **cal·o·ry** \'kal-(ə-)rē\ *n, pl* **-ries** [F *calorie*, fr. L *calor* heat] **1 :** a unit of heat: **a :** the heat required to raise the temperature of one gram of water one degree centigrade — called also *small calorie*; abbr. *cal* **b :** 1000 small calories — used esp. to indicate the heat and energy producing value of foods; called also *large calorie*; abbr. *Cal* **2 :** the amount of food producing one large calorie

cal·o·rif·ic \,kal-ə-'rif-ik\ *adj* **:** CALORIC

cal·o·rim·e·ter \,kal-ə-'rim-ət-ər\ *n* **:** an apparatus for measuring quantities of absorbed or evolved heat or for determining specific heats — **cal·o·ri·met·ric** \,kal-ə-rə-'me-trik\ *adj* — **cal·o·ri·met·ri·cal·ly** \-'me-tri-k(ə-)lē\ *adv* — **cal·o·rim·e·try** \-'rim-ə-trē\ *n*

cal·u·met \'kal-yə-,met, -mət\ *n* **:** an ornamented ceremonial pipe of the American Indians

ca·lum·ni·ate \kə-'ləm-nē-ˌāt\ *vt* : to accuse falsely and maliciously : SLANDER — **ca·lum·ni·a·tion** \-ˌləm-nē-'ā-shən\ *n* — **ca·lum·ni·a·tor** \-'ləm-nē-ˌāt-er\ *n*

cal·um·ny \'kal-əm-nē\ *n, pl* **-nies** [L *calumnia*] : a false accusation made to injure another person's character; *also* : the uttering of such charges — **ca·lum·ni·ous** \kə-'ləm-nē-əs\ *adj* — **ca·lum·ni·ous·ly** *adv*

calve \'kav, 'kàv\ *vi* : to give birth to a calf; *also* : to produce offspring

calves *pl of* CALF

Cal·vin·ism \'kal-və-ˌniz-əm\ *n* : the system of theological teachings and practices of John Calvin and his followers emphasizing the absolute power of God, the total depravity of man, and election — **Cal·vin·ist** \-və-nəst\ *n or adj* — **Cal·vin·is·tic** \ˌkal-və-'nis-tik\ *adj*

calx \'kalks\ *n, pl* **calx·es** *or* **cal·ces** \'kal-ˌsēz\ : the crumbly residue left when a metal or mineral has been subjected to calcination or combustion

ca·lyp·so \kə-'lip-sō\ *n, pl* **-sos** : an improvised ballad usu. satirizing current events in a rhythmic style originating in the West Indies — **ca·lyp·so·ni·an** \kə-ˌlip-'sō-nē-ən, ˌkal-ip-\ *adj or n*

ca·lyp·tra \kə-'lip-trə\ *n* [Gk *kalyptra* veil] : a covering of a plant reproductive structure suggestive of a cap or hood — **ca·lyp·trate** \kə-'lip-ˌtrāt, 'kal-əp-\ *adj*

ca·lyx \'kā-liks, 'kal-iks\ *n, pl* **ca·lyx·es** *or* **ca·ly·ces** \'kā-lə-ˌsēz, 'kal-ə-\ [Gk *kalyk-, kalyx*] **1** : the external usu. green or leafy part of a flower consisting of sepals **2** : a cuplike animal structure — **ca·ly·ce·al** \ˌkā-lə-'sē-əl, ˌkal-ə-\ *adj*

cam \'kam\ *n* : a device that consists of a plate or cylinder on a revolving shaft and that transmits motion by means of its edge or a groove to another mechanical part (as a rod or lever) so that circular motion may be transformed into intermittent or back-and-forth motion

ca·ma·ra·de·rie \ˌkam-(ə-)'rad-ə-rē, ˌkäm-(ə-)'räd-\ *n* [F] : good feeling existing between comrades

cam·as *or* **cam·ass** \'kam-əs\ *n* : any of a genus of plants of the lily family of the western U.S. with edible bulbs — compare DEATH CAMAS

¹cam·ber \'kam-bər\ *vb* **cam·bered; cam·ber·ing** \-b(ə-)riŋ\ : to curve upward in the middle : arch slightly

²camber *n* **1** : a slight convexity, arching, or curvature (as of a beam, deck, or road) **2** : a setting of the wheels of an automotive vehicle closer together at the bottom than at the top

cam·bi·um \'kam-bē-əm\ *n, pl* **-bi·ums** *or* **-bia** \-bē-ə\ [ML, exchange, fr. L *cambiare* to exchange] : a thin cell layer between the xylem and phloem of most vascular plants from which new cells (as of wood and bark) develop — **cam·bi·al** \-bē-əl\ *adj*

Cam·bri·an \'kam-brē-ən\ *n* : the earliest period of the Paleozoic era marked by fossils of every great animal type except the vertebrate and by scarcely recognizable plant fossils; *also* : the corresponding system of rocks — **Cambrian** *adj*

cam·bric \'kām-brik\ *n* : a fine thin white linen fabric; *also* : a similar cotton fabric

came *past of* COME

cam·el \'kam-əl\ *n* [OE, fr. L *camelus*, fr. Gk *kamēlos*, of Sem origin] : either of two large cud-chewing mammals used as draft and saddle animals in desert regions esp. of Africa and Asia: **a** : a single-humped camel of southwestern Asia and Africa — called also *Arabian camel* **b** : a two-humped camel of central Asian origin — called also *Bactrian camel*

cam·el·back \-ˌbak\ *n* : an uncured compound chiefly of reclaimed or synthetic rubber used for retreading or recapping pneumatic tires

cam·el·eer \ˌkam-ə-'li(ə)r\ *n* : a camel driver

ca·mel·lia *also* **ca·me·lia** \kə-'mēl-yə\ *n* [fr. *Camellus* (Georg Josef Kamel) *d*1706 Moravian Jesuit missionary] : any of several shrubs or trees of the tea family; *esp* : a greenhouse shrub with glossy evergreen leaves and showy roselike flowers

ca·mel·o·pard \kə-'mel-ə-ˌpärd\ *n* [Gk *kamēlopardalis*, fr. *kamēlos* camel + *pardalis* leopard] : GIRAFFE

camel b

Cam·e·lot \'kam-ə-ˌlät\ *n* : the site of King Arthur's palace and court in Arthurian legend

camel's hair *n* : a fabric made of the hair of camels or of a mixture of this hair with wool

Cam·em·bert \'kam-əm-ˌbe(ə)r\ *n* : a soft unpressed cheese with an odor and flavor produced by a blue mold

cam·eo \'kam-ē-ˌō\ *n, pl* **-eos** [It] : a gem carved in such a way that the design is higher than its background

cam·era \'kam-(ə-)rə\ *n* **1** [LL, room] : a judge's private office ⟨hearings held in *camera*⟩ **2** [NL *camera obscura*, lit., dark chamber] : a lighttight box fitted with a lens through the opening of which the image of an object is recorded on a material that is sensitive to light **3** : the part of a television transmitting apparatus in which the image to be televised is formed for change into electrical impulses

cam·era·man \-ˌman, -mən\ *n* : one that operates a camera

camera tube *n* : an electron tube in a television camera that converts the optical image into electrical impulses

cam·i·sole \'kam-ə-ˌsōl\ *n* [F] : a short sleeveless undergarment for women

camomile *var of* CHAMOMILE

cam·ou·flage \'kam-ə-ˌfläzh, -ˌfläj\ *n* [F, fr. *camoufler* to disguise, fr. It *camuffare*] **1 a** : the disguising of military equipment or installations with paint, nets, or foliage **b** : the disguise so applied **2 a** : concealment by means of disguise **b** : behavior or a trick intended to deceive or hide — **camouflage** *vt*

¹camp \'kamp\ *n* [L *campus* plain, field] **1 a** : ground on which temporary shelters are erected **b** : a group of tents or buildings erected on the ground **c** : TENT, CABIN, SHELTER **d** : an open-air location where persons camp **e** : a new lumbering or mining town **2 a** : a body of persons encamped **b** (1) : a body of persons holding a theory or doctrine (2) : an ideological position **3** : military service or life

²camp *vb* **1** : to make or occupy a camp **2** : to live in a camp or outdoors

cam·paign \kam-'pān\ *n* **1** : a series of military operations forming a distinct phase of a war **2** : a connected series of operations designed to bring about a particular result ⟨an election *campaign*⟩ — **campaign** *vi* — **cam·paign·er** *n*

cam·pa·ni·le \ˌkam-pə-'nē-lē\ *n* [It, fr. *campana* bell, fr. LL] : a bell tower; *esp* : one built separate from another building

cam·pa·nol·o·gy \ˌkam-pə-'näl-ə-jē\ *n* : the art of bell ringing — **cam·pa·nol·o·gist** \-jəst\ *n*

cam·pan·u·la \kam-'pan-yə-lə\ *n* [LL *campana* bell] : any of a large genus of herbs with regular bell-shaped flowers including several grown as ornamentals

cam·pan·u·late \-lət, -ˌlāt\ *adj* : shaped like a bell

camp·er \'kam-pər\ *n* **1** : one that camps **2** : a portable dwelling (as a specially equipped automotive vehicle) for use during casual travel and camping

cam·pes·tral \kam-'pes-trəl\ *adj* : of or relating to fields or open country : RURAL

camp fire girl *n* : a member of a national organization for girls from 7 to 18

cam·phor \'kam(p)-fər\ *n* [ML *camphora*, fr. Ar *kāfūr*, fr. Malay *kāpūr*] : a tough gummy volatile fragrant crystalline compound $C_{10}H_{16}O$ obtained esp. from the wood and bark of the camphor tree and used as a stimulant, as a plasticizer, and as an insect repellent

cam·phor·ate \'kam(p)-fə-ˌrāt\ *vt* : to impregnate with camphor ⟨*camphorated* oil⟩

camphor tree *n* : a large evergreen Asiatic tree of the laurel family

cam·pi·on \'kam-pē-ən\ *n* : any of various plants of the pink family

camp meeting *n* : a series of evangelistic meetings held outdoors or in a tent and attended by families who often camp nearby

camp·o·ree \ˌkam-pə-'rē\ *n* [*camp* + jam*boree*] : a gathering of boy or girl scouts from a given area

camp·stool \'kamp-ˌstül\ *n* : a folding stool

cam·pus \'kam-pəs\ *n* [L, field, plain] : the grounds and buildings of a college or a school

cam·shaft \'kam-ˌshaft\ *n* : a shaft to which a cam is fastened

¹can \kən, (')kan\ *auxiliary verb, past* **could** \kəd, (')kud\; *pres sing & pl* **can** [OE, know, knows, am able, is able; akin to E *know*] **1 a :** to know how to ⟨he *can* read⟩ **b :** be physically or mentally able to ⟨he *can* lift 200 pounds⟩ **c :** be permitted by conscience or feeling ⟨you *can* hardly blame him⟩ **d :** be inherently able or designed to ⟨everything that money *can* buy⟩ **e :** be enabled by law, agreement, or custom to **2 :** have permission to ⟨you *can* go now if you like⟩

   syn MAY: CAN primarily implies physical or mental ability ⟨he *can* run very fast⟩ or circumstantial possibility ⟨we *can* take an earlier train⟩ MAY expresses primarily permission or sanction, not capability ⟨you *may* leave when you wish⟩ but CAN is frequently used in asking permission ⟨*can* I help you⟩ and normally used in denying it ⟨you *cannot* smoke here⟩

²can \'kan\ *n* [OE *canne*] **1 :** a usu. cylindrical receptacle: **a :** a vessel for holding liquids; *esp :* a drinking vessel **b :** a receptacle (as for milk, oil, or ashes) usu. with an open top and often with a cover **c :** a tinplate container in which a perishable product (as food) is hermetically sealed **d :** a jar for packing or preserving a fruit or vegetable **2 :** the contents of a can

³can \'kan\ *vt* **canned; can·ning :** to put in a can; *esp :* to preserve by sealing in an airtight can or jar

Ca·na \'kā-nə\ *adj :* of or constituting a Roman Catholic movement sponsoring conferences on marriage and family life

Can·a·da balsam \,kan-əd-ə-\ *n :* a viscid yellowish to greenish resin exuded by the balsam fir that solidifies to a transparent mass and is used as a transparent cement esp. in microscopy

Canada goose *n :* the common wild goose of No. America that is mostly gray and brownish in color with black head and neck

ca·naille \kə-'nāl, -'nī\ *n* [F, fr. It *canaglia*, fr. *cane* dog, fr. L *canis*] : RABBLE, RIFFRAFF

ca·nal \kə-'nal\ *n* [L *canalis* pipe, channel, fr. *canna* reed, cane] **1 :** a tubular anatomical passage or channel : DUCT **2 :** an artificial waterway for navigation or for draining or irrigating land

ca·nal·boat \-,bōt\ *n :* a boat for use on a canal

can·a·lic·u·lus \,kan-ᵊl-'ik-yə-ləs\ *n, pl* **-u·li** \-yə-,lī, -,lē\ *:* a minute bodily canal (as in bone)

can·al·i·za·tion \kə-,nal-ə-'zā-shən\ *n* **1 :** an act or instance of canalizing **2 :** a system of channels

can·al·ize \kə-'nal-,īz\ *vt* **1 :** to provide with a canal **2 :** to make into or like a canal

can·a·pé \'kan-ə-pē\ *n* [F, lit., sofa] : an appetizer consisting of a piece of bread or toast or a cracker topped with a spread (as of fish or cheese)

ca·nard \kə-'närd\ *n* [F, lit., duck, fr. MF *vendre des canards à moitié* to cheat, lit., to half-sell ducks] : a false or unfounded report or story; *esp :* one deliberately made up

ca·nary \kə-'ne(ə)r-ē\ *n, pl* **-nar·ies** **1 :** a sweet wine made in the Canary islands **2 :** a small usu. yellow or greenish finch native to the Canary islands that is kept as a cage bird

canary yellow *n :* a light to a moderate or vivid yellow

ca·nas·ta \kə-'nas-tə\ *n* [Sp, lit., basket] **1 :** rummy using two decks plus four jokers **2 :** a combination of seven cards of the same rank in canasta

can·can \'kan-,kan\ *n* [F] : a woman's dance of French origin characterized by high kicking

¹can·cel \'kan-səl\ *vb* **-celed** *or* **-celled; -cel·ing** *or* **-cel·ling** \-s(ə-)liŋ\ [LL *cancellare*, fr. L, to make like a lattice, fr. *cancelli* latticework, grating] **1 a :** to mark or strike out for deletion **b :** OMIT, DELETE **2 a :** to destroy the force, effectiveness, or validity of : ANNUL **b :** to match in force or effect : OFFSET **3 a :** to remove (a common divisor) from numerator and denominator **b :** to remove (equivalents) on opposite sides of an equation or account **4 :** to deface (a postage or revenue stamp) esp. with a set of parallel lines so as to invalidate for reuse **syn** see ERASE — **can·cel·er** *or* **can·cel·ler** \-s(ə-)lər\ *n*

²cancel *n* : CANCELLATION

can·cel·la·tion \,kan(t)-sə-'lā-shən\ *n* **1 :** an act of canceling ⟨*cancellation* of a game because of bad weather⟩ **2 :** a mark made to cancel something ⟨a *cancellation* on a postage stamp⟩

can·cel·lous \'kan(t)-sə-ləs\ *adj :* having a porous structure ⟨*cancellous* bone⟩

can·cer \'kan(t)-sər\ *n* [L, crab, Cancer, cancer] **1** *cap* **a :** a northern zodiacal constellation between Gemini and Leo **b :** the 4th sign of the zodiac — see ZODIAC table **2 :** a malignant tumor that tends to spread locally and to other parts of the body; *also :* an abnormal state marked by such tumors **3 :** a dangerous evil that eats away slowly but fatally — **can·cer·ous** \'kan(t)s-(ə-)rəs\ *adj*

can·de·la·bra \,kan-də-'läb-rə, -'lab-, -'lāb-\ *n :* CANDELABRUM

can·de·la·brum \-rəm\ *n, pl* **-bra** \-rə\ *or* **-brums :** a candlestick that has several branches for holding more than one candle

can·des·cent \kan-'des-ᵊnt\ *adj :* glowing or dazzling esp. from great heat — **can·des·cence** \-ᵊn(t)s\ *n*

can·did \'kan-dəd\ *adj* [F *candide*, fr. L *candidus* shining, white, fr. *candēre* to shine] **1 :** free from bias, prejudice, or malice : FAIR **2 a :** marked by honest sincere expression **b :** showing sincere honesty and absence of deception **3 :** relating to photography of subjects acting naturally or spontaneously without being posed ⟨*candid* picture⟩ **syn** see FRANK — **can·did·ly** *adv* — **can·did·ness** *n*

can·di·da·cy \'kan-dəd-ə-sē\ *n, pl* **-cies :** the state of being a candidate ⟨announce one's *candidacy* for office⟩

can·di·date \'kan-də-,dāt, -dət\ *n* [L *candidatus*, lit., one clothed in white, fr. *candidus* white; so called fr. the white toga worn by candidates for office in ancient Rome] : one who offers himself or is proposed by others for an office, membership, right, or honor ⟨a gubernatorial *candidate*⟩

can·di·da·ture \'kan-dəd-ə-,chu̇(ə)r, -chər\ *n, chiefly Brit* : CANDIDACY

candid camera *n :* a small camera with a fast lens for taking photographs of unposed subjects often without their knowledge

can·died \'kan-dēd\ *adj* **1 :** encrusted or coated with sugar **2 :** baked with sugar or syrup until translucent

¹can·dle \'kan-dᵊl\ *n* [OE *candel*, fr. L *candela*, fr. *candēre* to shine] **1 :** a long slender cylindrical mass of tallow or wax containing a loosely twisted linen or cotton wick that is burned to give light **2 :** a unit of luminous intensity equal to one sixtieth of the luminous intensity of one square centimeter of a blackbody surface at the solidification temperature of platinum — called also *candela*

²candle *vt* **can·dled; can·dling** \'kan-dliŋ, -dᵊl-iŋ\ *:* to examine (an egg) by holding between the eye and a light — **can·dler** \-dlər, -dᵊl-ər\ *n*

can·dle·light \'kan-dᵊl-,(l)īt\ *n* **1 a :** the light of a candle **b :** a soft artificial light **2 :** the time when candles are lit : TWILIGHT

can·dle·lit \-dᵊl-,(l)it\ *adj :* illuminated by candlelight

Can·dle·mas \'kan-dᵊl-məs\ *n :* February 2 observed as a church festival in commemoration of the presentation of Christ in the temple and the purification of the Virgin Mary

can·dle·pin \'kan-dᵊl-,pin\ *n* **1 :** a slender bowling pin tapering toward top and bottom **2** *pl :* a bowling game using candlepins and a smaller ball than that used in tenpins

can·dle·pow·er \-,pau̇(-ə)r\ *n :* luminous intensity expressed in candles

can·dle·stick \-,stik\ *n :* a holder with a socket for a candle

can·dor \'kan-dər\ *n* [L, lit., whiteness, fr. *candēre* to shine] **1 :** freedom from prejudice **2 :** FRANKNESS

¹can·dy \'kan-dē\ *n, pl* **-dies** [MF *sucre candi* candied sugar, fr. *sucre* sugar + Ar *qandī* candied, fr. *qand* cane sugar] **1 :** crystallized sugar formed by boiling down sugar syrup **2 a :** a confection made of sugar often with flavoring and filling **b :** a piece of such confection

²candy *vb* **can·died; can·dy·ing** **1 :** to coat or become coated with sugar often by cooking **2 :** to make seem attractive : SWEETEN **3 :** to crystallize into sugar

can·dy·tuft \'kan-dē-,təft\ *n :* any of a genus of plants related to the mustards and grown for their white, pink, or purple flowers

¹cane \'kān\ *n* [L *canna*] **1 a :** a hollow or pithy and usu. slender, flexible, and jointed stem (as of a reed or bramble) **b :** any of various tall woody grasses or reeds; *esp :* SUGAR-

CANE **2 a :** WALKING STICK; *esp* **:** a cane walking stick **b :** a rod for flogging **c :** RATTAN; *esp* **:** split rattan for wickerwork or basketry

²cane *vt* **1 :** to beat with a cane **2 :** to make or repair with cane ⟨*cane* the seat of a chair⟩

cane·brake \-,brāk\ *n* **:** a thicket of cane

cane sugar *n* **:** sugar from sugarcane commonly used at the dining table and in cooking

¹ca·nine \'kā-,nīn\ *adj* [L *caninus*, fr. *canis* dog; akin to E *hound*] **1 :** of or relating to dogs or to the family that includes the dogs, wolves, jackals, and foxes **2 :** of, relating to, or resembling a dog

²canine *n* **1 :** a conical pointed tooth; *esp* **:** one situated between the outer incisor and the first premolar — see DENTITION illustration, TOOTH illustration **2 :** DOG

Ca·nis Ma·jor \,kā-nəs-'mā-jər, ,kan-əs-\ *n* [L, lit., greater dog] **:** a constellation to the southeast of Orion containing Sirius

Canis Mi·nor \-'mī-nər\ *n* [L, lit., lesser dog] **:** a constellation to the east of Orion containing Procyon

can·is·ter \'kan-ə-stər\ *n* [L *canistrum* basket] **1 :** a small box or can for holding a dry product (as tea, coffee, flour, or sugar) **2 :** a shell for close-range artillery fire consisting of a number of bullets enclosed in a lightweight case that is burst by the firing charge **3 :** a perforated box that contains material to absorb, filter, or make harmless a poisonous or irritating substance in the air and is used esp. with a gas mask

¹can·ker \'kaŋ-kər\ *n* [ONF *cancre*, fr. L *cancer* crab, cancer] **1 a :** a spreading sore that eats into the tissue **b :** a disorder in a plant or animal marked by chronic inflammatory changes **2 :** a source of corruption or destruction — **can·ker·ous** \'kaŋ-k(ə-)rəs\ *adj*

²canker *vb* **can·kered; can·ker·ing** \'kaŋ-k(ə-)riŋ\ **:** to corrupt malignantly or undergo corruption

canker sore *n* **:** a small painful ulcer esp. of the mouth

can·ker·worm \'kaŋ-kər-,wərm\ *n* **:** an insect larva (as a looper) that injures plants esp. by feeding on buds and foliage

can·na \'kan-ə\ *n* [L, reed] **:** a tall tropical herb with large leaves and an unbranched stem bearing bright-colored flowers at the end

can·na·bis \'kan-ə-bəs\ *n* **:** the dried flowering spikes of the pistillate plants of the hemp

canned \'kand\ *adj* **1 :** preserved in a sealed can or jar **2 :** transcribed for radio or television reproduction

can·nel coal \,kan-ᵊl\ *n* **:** a bituminous coal containing much volatile matter that burns brightly

can·ner \'kan-ər\ *n* **:** a person whose business or occupation is canning food

can·nery \'kan-(ə-)rē\ *n, pl* **-ner·ies :** a factory for the canning of food

can·ni·bal \'kan-ə-bəl\ *n* [Sp *Caníbal* Carib, fr. Arawakan *Caniba, Carib*] **1 :** a human being who eats human flesh **2 :** an animal that eats its own kind — **cannibal** *adj* — **can·ni·bal·ism** \-bə-,liz-əm\ *n* — **can·ni·bal·is·tic** \,kan-ə-bə-'lis-tik\ *adj*

can·ni·bal·ize \'kan-ə-bə-,līz\ *vb* **:** to dismantle a machine for parts to be used as replacements in other machines

can·non \'kan-ən\ *n, pl* **cannons** *or* **cannon** [It *cannone*, lit., large tube, fr. *canna* reed, tube, fr. L, reed, cane] **1 a :** a heavy gun mounted on a carriage and fired from that position **:** a piece of artillery **b :** a heavy-caliber automatic gun on an airplane **2 :** the part of the leg in which the cannon bone is found

¹can·non·ade \,kan-ə-'nād\ *n* **:** a heavy firing of artillery

²cannonade *vb* **:** to attack with artillery

can·non·ball \'kan-ən-,bol\ *n* **:** a round solid missile made for firing from a cannon

cannon bone *n* **:** a bone in hoofed mammals that supports the leg from the hock joint to the fetlock

can·non·eer \,kan-ə-'ni(ə)r\ *n* **:** an artilleryman who tends and fires cannon : GUNNER

can·not \'kan-(,)ät; kə-'nät, ka-'\ **:** can not — **cannot but** **:** to be bound to : MUST

can·ny \'kan-ē\ *adj* **can·ni·er; -est** [¹*can*] **:** being cautious and shrewd **:** watchful of one's own interests ⟨a *canny* man with money⟩ — **can·ni·ly** \'kan-ᵊl-ē\ *adv* — **can·ni·ness** \'kan-ē-nəs\ *n*

¹ca·noe \kə-'nü\ *n* [Sp *canoa*, of AmerInd origin] **:** a long light narrow boat with sharp ends and curved sides that is usu. paddled by hand

²canoe *vb* **ca·noed; ca·noe·ing :** to travel or transport in a canoe — **ca·noe·ist** *n*

¹can·on \'kan-ən\ *n* [OE, fr. L, rule, standard, fr. Gk *kanōn*] **1 :** a church law or doctrinal decree **2 :** the fundamental and unvarying part of the Mass including the consecration of the bread and wine **3 :** an official or authoritative list (as of the saints or of the books of the Bible) **4 :** an accepted principle or rule ⟨the *canons* of good taste⟩ **5 :** a contrapuntal musical composition in two or more voice parts in which the melody is imitated exactly and completely by the successive voices

²canon *n* **1 :** one of the clergy of a medieval cathedral or large church living in community under a rule **2 :** a clergyman on the staff of a cathedral **3 :** CANON REGULAR

³ca·ñon \'kan-yən\ *var of* CANYON

ca·non·i·cal \kə-'nän-i-kəl\ *adj* **1 :** of, relating to, or complying with church law **2 :** accepted as authoritative or genuine — **ca·non·i·cal·ly** \-k(ə-)lē\ *adv*

canonical hour *n* **1 :** a time of day canonically appointed for an office of devotion **2 :** one of the daily offices in the breviary including matins with lauds, prime, terce, sext, none, vespers, and compline

ca·non·i·cals \kə-'nän-i-kəlz\ *n pl* **:** the vestments prescribed by canon for an officiating clergyman

can·on·ic·i·ty \,kan-ə-'nis-ət-ē\ *n* **:** the quality or state of being canonical

can·on·ize \'kan-ə-,nīz\ *vt* **1 :** to declare (a beatified person) to be a saint and worthy of public veneration throughout the church **2 :** GLORIFY, EXALT — **can·on·i·za·tion** \,kan-ə-nə-'zā-shən\ *n*

canon law *n* **:** the body of laws governing a church (as the Roman Catholic Church)

canon regular *n, pl* **canons regular :** a member of one of several Roman Catholic religious institutes of regular priests living in community

Ca·no·pus \kə-'nō-pəs\ *n* [Gk *Kanōpos*] **:** a star of the first magnitude in the constellation Argo not visible north of 37° latitude

¹can·o·py \'kan-ə-pē\ *n, pl* **-pies** [ML *canopeum* mosquito net, modif. of Gk *kōnōpion*, fr. *kōnōps* mosquito] **1 a :** a covering suspended over a bed, throne, or shrine or carried on poles over a person of high rank or over some sacred object **b :** AWNING, MARQUEE **2 :** an overhanging shade or shelter ⟨a *canopy* of chestnut trees⟩ **3 a :** the transparent enclosure over an airplane cockpit **b :** the lifting or supporting surface of a parachute — **can·o·py·like** \-,līk\ *adj*

²canopy *vt* **-pied; -py·ing :** to cover with or as if with a canopy

canst \kən(t)st, (')kan(t)st\ *archaic pres 2d sing of* CAN

¹cant \'kant\ *n* [ONF, edge, corner, fr. L *canthus* iron tire] **1 :** a slanting surface (as of a buttress or bank of earth) **2 :** TILT, SLOPE, INCLINE ⟨the steep *cant* of the road⟩

²cant *vt* **1 :** to give a cant or oblique edge to **2 :** to set at an angle : TIP

³cant *vi* [L *cantare* to sing, recite] **1 :** BEG **2 :** to talk hypocritically

⁴cant *n* **1 a :** ARGOT **b :** JARGON **2 :** insincere speech; *esp* **:** pious words or statements

can't \'kant, 'känt, *esp South* 'kānt\ **:** can not

can·ta·bi·le \kän-'täb-ə-,lä\ *adv (or adj)* [It] **:** in a singing smoothly flowing manner — used as a direction in music

Can·ta·bri·gian \,kant-ə-'brij-(ē-)ən\ *n* [ML *Cantabrigia* Cambridge] **:** a student or graduate of Cambridge University — **Cantabrigian** *adj*

can·ta·loupe \'kant-ᵊl-,ōp\ *n* [*Cantalupo*, former papal villa near Rome, where the true cantaloupe was first grown in Europe] **:** MUSKMELON; *esp* **:** a muskmelon with a hard ridged or warty rind and reddish orange flesh

can·tan·ker·ous \kan-'taŋ-k(ə-)rəs\ *adj* **:** ILL-NATURED, QUARRELSOME — **can·tan·ker·ous·ly** *adv* — **can·tan·ker·ous·ness** *n*

can·ta·ta \kən-'tät-ə\ *n* [It, fr. fem. of *cantato*, pp. of *cantare* to sing, fr. L] **:** a poem or narrative set to music to be sung by a chorus and soloists

can·teen \kan-'tēn\ *n* [F *cantine* bottle case, sutler's shop] **1 :** a store (as in a camp or a factory) in which food, drinks, and small supplies are sold **2 :** a place of recrea-

ə abut; ə kitten; ər further; a back; ā bake; ä cot, cart; aù out; ch chin; e less; ē easy; g gift; i trip; ī life

tion and entertainment for servicemen **3 :** a small container used for carrying liquid (as drinking water)

¹can·ter \'kant-ər\ *vb* [short for obs. *canterbury*, fr. *Canterbury*, England; fr. the supposed gait of pilgrims to Canterbury] **:** to move or cause to move at or as if at a canter **:** LOPE

²canter *n* **:** a 3-beat gait (as of a horse) resembling but smoother and slower than the gallop

Can·ter·bury bell \,kant-ə(r)-,ber-ē-\ *n* **:** a cultivated campanula

cant hook *n* **:** a stout wooden lever used esp. in handling logs that has a blunt usu. metal-clad end and a movable metal arm with a sharp spike

can·ti·cle \'kant-i-kəl\ *n* [L *canticulum*, dim. of *canticum* song, fr. *cant-*, *canere* to sing] **1 :** SONG **2 :** one of several liturgical songs taken from the Bible

¹can·ti·le·ver \'kant-ºl-,ē-vər, -,ev-ər\ *n* **1 :** a projecting beam or similar structure fastened (as by being built into a wall or pier) only at one end **2 :** either of two beams or structures that project from piers toward each other and when joined form a span in a bridge — see BRIDGE illustration

²cantilever *vt* **:** to build or project in the form of a cantilever

can·tle \'kant-ºl\ *n* **:** the upwardly projecting rear part of a saddle

can·to \'kan-,tō\ *n*, *pl* **cantos** [It, fr. L *cantus* song, fr. *cant-*, *canere* to sing] **:** one of the major divisions of a long poem

¹can·ton \'kant-ºn, 'kan-,tän\ *n* [MF, fr. It *cantone*, fr. *canto* corner, fr. L *canthus* iron tire] **1 :** a small territorial division of a country; *esp* **:** one of the states of the Swiss confederation **2 :** the top inner quarter of a flag — **can·ton·al** \'kant-ºn-əl, kan-'tän-ºl\ *adj*

²can·ton \'kant-ºn, 'kan-,tän, in sense 2 usu kan-'tōn or -'tän\ *vt* **1 :** to divide into parts; *esp* **:** to divide into cantons **2 :** to allot quarters to (troops)

Can·ton·ese \,kant-ºn-'ēz, -'ēs\ *n*, *pl* **Cantonese** **1 :** a native or inhabitant of Canton, China **2 :** the dialect of Chinese spoken in and around Canton — **Cantonese** *adj*

can·ton flannel \,kan-,tän-\ *n*, *often cap C* **:** FLANNEL 1b

can·ton·ment \kan-'tōn-mənt, -'tän-\ *n* **:** a group of temporary structures for housing troops

can·tor \'kant-ər\ *n* [L, singer, fr. *cant-*, *canere* to sing] **1 :** a choir leader **2 :** a synagogue official who sings or chants the liturgy and leads the congregation in prayer

Ca·nuck \kə-'nək\ *n* [prob. alter. of *Canadian*] **1 :** CANADIAN **2** *chiefly Canad* **:** FRENCH CANADIAN

can·vas \'kan-vəs\ *n* [ONF *canevas*, fr. L *cannabis* hemp] **1 :** a strong cloth of hemp, flax, or cotton that is used for making tents and sails and as the material on which oil paintings are made **2 :** something made of canvas or on canvas; *esp* **:** OIL PAINTING **3 :** the floor of a boxing or wrestling ring

can·vas·back \-,bak\ *n* **:** a No. American wild duck with reddish head and grayish back

can·vass \'kan-vəs\ *vb* [obs. *canvass* to toss in a canvas sheet, beat thoroughly] **1 a :** to examine in detail; *esp* **:** to investigate officially ⟨*canvass* election returns⟩ **b :** DISCUSS, DEBATE ⟨*canvass* a question⟩ **2 a :** to go through (an area) soliciting something (as information, contributions, or votes) ⟨*canvasses* every precinct before an election⟩ **b :** to ask for information, money, or votes ⟨*canvassed* for her favorite charity⟩ ⟨*canvass* faculty members for opinions⟩ — **canvass** *n* — **can·vass·er** *n*

can·yon \'kan-yən\ *n* [AmerSp *cañón*] **:** a deep valley with high steep slopes and often with a stream flowing through it

caou·tchouc \kaù-'chük\ *n* **:** RUBBER 2a

¹cap \'kap\ *n* [OE *cæppe*, fr. LL *cappa* head covering, cloak] **1 :** a head covering; *esp* **:** one for men and boys that has a visor and no brim **2 :** something like a cap in appearance, position, or function ⟨a bottle *cap*⟩ ⟨the *cap* of a fountain pen⟩ **3 :** a natural cover or top: as **a :** the umbrella-shaped part that bears the spores of a mushroom **b :** the top of a bird's head **4 :** a paper or metal container holding an explosive charge (as for a toy pistol)

²cap *vt* **capped; cap·ping** **1 :** to provide with a cap **2 :** to match with something equal or better ⟨*cap* one story with another⟩

ca·pa·bil·i·ty \,kā-pə-'bil-ət-ē\ *n*, *pl* **-ties** **1 :** the quality

or state of being capable **2 :** a feature or faculty capable of development **:** POTENTIALITY **3 :** the capacity for an indicated use or development ⟨the *capability* of a metal to be fused⟩

ca·pa·ble \'kā-pə-bəl\ *adj* [LL *capabilis*, fr. L *capere* to take] **1 :** having the ability, capacity, or power to do something ⟨a room *capable* of holding 50 people⟩ **2 :** of such a nature as to permit **:** SUSCEPTIBLE ⟨a remark *capable* of being misunderstood⟩ **3 :** EFFICIENT, COMPETENT ⟨a capable salesman⟩ **syn** see ABLE — **ca·pa·bly** \-blē\ *adv*

ca·pa·cious \kə-'pā-shəs\ *adj* [L *capac-*, *capax*, fr. *capere* to take] **:** able to contain a great deal **:** not narrow ⟨*capacious* pockets⟩ ⟨men with *capacious* minds⟩ — **ca·pa·cious·ly** *adv* — **ca·pa·cious·ness** *n*

ca·pac·i·tance \kə-'pas-ət-ən(t)s\ *n* **:** the property of a system of conductors and dielectrics that permits the storage of electrical energy; *also* **:** a measure of this property — **ca·pac·i·tive** \-ət-iv\ *adj*

ca·pac·i·tate \kə-'pas-ə-,tāt\ *vt* **:** to make capable **:** QUALIFY

ca·pac·i·tor \kə-'pas-ət-ər\ *n* **:** a device giving capacitance and usu. consisting of conducting plates separated by layers of dielectric with the plates on opposite sides of the dielectric layers oppositely charged by a source of voltage — called also *condenser*

ca·pac·i·ty \kə-'pas-ət-ē, -'pas-tē\ *n*, *pl* **-ties** [L *capac-*, *capax* capacious] **1 a :** the ability to hold or accommodate ⟨the seating *capacity* of a room⟩ **b :** a measure of content **:** VOLUME ⟨a jug with a *capacity* of one gallon⟩ **c :** productive ability or potential ⟨a plant with a *capacity* of 50 tons a month⟩ **d** (1) **:** CAPACITANCE (2) **:** the quantity of electricity that a battery can deliver under specified conditions **2 :** legal competence **3 :** ABILITY, CALIBER ⟨a man of unknown *capacity*⟩ **4 :** a position or character assigned or assumed ⟨in his *capacity* as a judge⟩

cap-a-pie *or* **cap-à-pie** \,kap-ə-'pē\ *adv* [MF (de) *cap a pé* from head to foot] **:** from head to foot **:** at all points

ca·par·i·son \kə-'par-ə-sən\ *n* **1 a :** an ornamental covering for a horse **b :** decorative trappings and harness **2 :** rich clothing **:** ADORNMENT — **caparison** *vt*

¹cape \'kāp\ *n* [MF *cap*, fr. OProv, fr. L *caput* head] **:** a point or extension of land jutting out into water either as a peninsula or as a projecting point

²cape *n* [prob. alter. of Sp *capa*, fr. LL *cappa* head covering, cloak] **:** a sleeveless outer garment or part of a garment that fits closely at the neck and hangs loosely from the shoulders

cap·e·lin \'kap-(ə-)lən\ *n* **:** a small northern sea fish related to the smelts and often used as cod bait

Ca·pel·la \kə-'pel-ə\ *n* [L, lit., she-goat, fr. fem. dim. of *caper* he-goat] **:** a star of the first magnitude in Auriga

¹ca·per \'kā-pər\ *n* [L *capparis*, fr. Gk *kapparis*] **1 :** any of a genus of low prickly shrubs of the Mediterranean region; *esp* **:** one cultivated for its buds **2 :** one of the flower buds or young berries of the caper pickled for use as a relish

²caper *vi* **ca·pered; ca·per·ing** \-p(ə-)riŋ\ **:** to leap about in a gay frolicsome way

³caper *n* **1 :** a gay bounding leap **2 :** PRANK, TRICK

cap·er·cail·lie \,kap-ər-'kāl-(y)ē\ *or* **cap·er·cail·zie** \-'kāl-zē\ *n* [ScGael *capalcoille*, lit., horse of the woods] **:** the largest Old World grouse

cape·skin \'kāp-,skin\ *n* [*Cape* of Good Hope] **:** a light flexible leather made from sheepskins with the natural grain retained

Ca·pe·tian \kə-'pē-shən\ *adj* **:** of or relating to the French dynasty founded in A.D. 987 by Hugh Capet — **Capetian** *n*

cap·il·lar·i·ty \,kap-ə-'lar-ət-ē\ *n* **:** the action by which the surface of a liquid where (as in a slender tube) it is in contact with a solid is raised or lowered depending upon the relative attraction of the molecules of the liquid for each other and for those of the solid

¹cap·il·lary \'kap-ə-,ler-ē\ *adj* [L *capillaris*, fr. *capillus* hair] **1 :** resembling a hair in having a slender elongated form; *esp* **:** having a very small bore ⟨a *capillary* tube⟩ **2 :** of or relating to capillaries or capillarity

²capillary *n*, *pl* **-lar·ies** **:** a capillary tube; *esp* **:** any of the tiny blood vessels connecting arterioles with venules and forming networks throughout the body

¹cap·i·tal \'kap-ət-ºl\ *adj* [L *capitalis*, fr. *capit-*, *caput* head; akin to E *head*] **1 a :** punishable by death ⟨a *capital* crime⟩ **b :** resulting in death ⟨*capital* punishment⟩ **2 :** being a letter that belongs to or conforms to the series A, B, C, etc. rather than a, b, c, etc. **3 a :** first in importance or influence **:** CHIEF **b :** being the seat of government ⟨the *capital* city of a country⟩ **4 :** of or relating to capital ⟨*capital* investment⟩ **5 :** EXCELLENT ⟨a *capital* performance⟩

²**capital** *n* [It *capitale,* fr. *capitale,* adj., chief, principal, fr. L *capitalis* capital] **1 a :** accumulated goods on hand at a specified time in contrast to income received over a specified period and carried in a separate account **b :** the excess of assets over liabilities **:** net assets **2 a :** capital goods and invested savings used in the process of production **b :** possessions (as money) used to bring in income **c :** persons owning or investing capital **:** INVESTORS, CAPITALISTS **d :** CAPITAL STOCK **3 :** ADVANTAGE, GAIN ⟨make *capital* out of another's weakness⟩ **4 :** a capital letter ⟨begin each sentence with a *capital*⟩ **5 :** a capital city ⟨what is the *capital* of Vermont⟩

³**capital** *n* [LL *capitellum,* fr. dim. of L *capit-, caput* head] **:** the top part or piece of an architectural column

capital goods *n pl* **:** machinery, tools, factories, and commodities used in the production of goods

capitals: *1* Doric,
2 Ionic, *3* Corinthian

cap·i·tal·ism \'kap-ət-ᵊl-,iz-əm\ *n* **:** an economic system in which natural resources and means of production are privately owned, investments are determined by private decision rather than by state control, and prices, production, and the distribution of goods are determined mainly by competition in a free market — **cap·i·tal·ist** \-ᵊl-əst\ *or* **cap·i·tal·is·tic** \,kap-ət-ᵊl-'is-tik\ *adj* — **cap·i·tal·is·ti·cal·ly** \-ti-k(ə-)lē\ *adv*

cap·i·tal·ist \'kap-ət-ᵊl-əst\ *n* **1 :** a person who has capital; *esp* **:** one who has or controls a great amount of business capital **2 :** a person who favors capitalism

cap·i·tal·i·za·tion \,kap-ət-ᵊl-ə-'zā-shən\ *n* **1 :** the act or process of capitalizing **2 :** the amount of money used as capital in a business

cap·i·tal·ize \'kap-ət-ᵊl-,īz\ *vb* **1 :** to write or print with an initial capital or in capitals **2 a :** to charge (an expenditure) to a capital account **b** (1) **:** to supply capital for ⟨*capitalize* an enterprise at $50,000⟩ (2) **:** to use as capital ⟨*capitalize* reserve funds⟩ — often used with *on* ⟨*capitalize* on a new demand⟩ **3 :** to act profitably ⟨*capitalize* on an opponent's mistake⟩

cap·i·tal·ly \'kap-ət-ᵊl-ē\ *adv* **:** in a capital manner **:** EXCELLENTLY ⟨got along *capitally* in school⟩

capital ship *n* **:** a warship (as a battleship or aircraft carrier) of the greatest size or offensive power

capital stock *n* **:** the total amount invested by stockholders in a corporation that constitutes them the owners of the corporation; *also* **:** the shares of stock held by these stockholders

cap·i·tate \'kap-ə-,tāt\ *adj* [L *capit-, caput* head] **:** forming or ending in a head or knob

cap·i·ta·tion \,kap-ə-'tā-shən\ *n* **:** a direct uniform tax imposed upon each head or person **:** POLL TAX

cap·i·tol \'kap-ət-ᵊl\ *n* [L *Capitolium,* chief temple of Jupiter in Rome] **1 :** a building in which a state legislative body meets **2** *cap* **:** the building in which the U.S. Congress meets in Washington

Cap·i·to·line \'kap-ət-ᵊl-,īn\ *adj* **:** of or relating to the smallest of the seven hills of ancient Rome, the temple on it, or the gods worshiped there

ca·pit·u·late \kə-'pich-ə-,lāt\ *vi* [ML *capitulare* to draw up under chapters, negotiate, fr. LL *capitulum* chapter, fr. L, dim. of *capit-, caput* head] **:** to surrender usu. on terms agreed upon in advance

ca·pit·u·la·tion \kə-,pich-ə-'lā-shən\ *n* **1 :** a set of terms or articles constituting an agreement between governments **2 :** an act of capitulating **:** a surrender on stipulated terms

ca·pit·u·lum \kə-'pich-ə-ləm\ *n, pl* **-la** \-lə\ **1 :** a rounded knob (as on a bone) **2 :** an inflorescence (as of a dandelion or daisy) in the form of a rounded or flattened cluster of sessile flowers — see INFLORESCENCE illustration

ca·pon \'kā-,pän, -pən\ *n* [OE *capūn,* prob. fr. ONF

capon, fr. L *capon-, capo*] **:** a castrated male chicken — **ca·pon·ize** \'kā-pə-,nīz\ *vt*

ca·pric·cio \kə-'prē-chō, -chē-,ō\ *n, pl* **-cios** [It] **:** an instrumental piece in free form usu. lively in tempo and brilliant in style

ca·price \kə-'prēs\ *n* [F, fr. It *capriccio* shudder, whim] **1 :** a sudden unpredictable turn or change **2 :** a disposition to change one's mind impulsively **3 :** CAPRICCIO

syn CAPRICE, WHIM, VAGARY mean an irrational or unpredictable idea or desire. CAPRICE stresses lack of apparent motivation and suggests a degree of willfulness; WHIM implies a fantastic, capricious turn or inclination; VAGARY stresses the erratic, irresponsible character of the notion or desire

ca·pri·cious \kə-'prish-əs, -'prē-shəs\ *adj* **:** moved or controlled by caprice **:** apt to change suddenly **:** FICKLE, CHANGEABLE ⟨a *capricious* child⟩ ⟨*capricious* weather⟩ — **ca·pri·cious·ly** *adv* — **ca·pri·cious·ness** *n*

Cap·ri·corn \'kap-rə-,kȯrn\ *also* **Cap·ri·cor·nus** \,kap-rə-'kȯr-nəs\ *n* [L *Capricornus,* fr. *caper* goat + *cornu* horn] **1 :** a southern zodiacal constellation between Sagittarius and Aquarius **2 :** the 10th sign of the zodiac — see ZODIAC table

cap·rine \'kap-,rīn\ *adj* **:** of, relating to, or being a goat

cap·ri·ole \'kap-rē-,ōl\ *n* **:** CAPER; *esp* **:** an upward leap of a horse without forward motion — **capriole** *vi*

cap·si·cum \'kap-si-kəm\ *n* **:** any of a genus of tropical herbs and shrubs of the nightshade family widely cultivated for their many-seeded usu. fleshy-walled berries — called also *pepper*

cap·size \'kap-,sīz, kap-'\ *vb* **:** to turn over **:** UPSET ⟨canoes *capsize* easily⟩ ⟨wind *capsized* the sailboat⟩

cap·stan \'kap-stən\ *n* [ME] **:** a mechanical device that consists of an upright revolving drum to which a rope is fastened, is used on ships for moving or raising weights and for exerting pulling force, and is rotated manually or by steam or electric power

cap·su·lar \'kap-sə-lər\ *adj* **:** of, relating to, or resembling a capsule

cap·su·late \-,lāt, -lət\ *or* **cap·su·lat·ed** \-,lāt-əd\ *adj* **:** enclosed in a capsule

¹**cap·sule** \'kap-səl, -sül\ *n* [L *capsula,* dim. of *capsa* case, box] **1 :** an enveloping cover ⟨the *capsule* of a joint⟩: as **a :** a case bearing spores or seeds; *esp* **:** a dry dehiscent fruit made up of two or more united carpels **b :** an edible shell (as of gelatin) enclosing medicine **2 :** an extremely brief condensation **3 :** a small pressurized compartment for an aviator or astronaut for flight or emergency escape

²**capsule** *adj* **1 :** extremely brief ⟨a *capsule* review of the news⟩ **2 :** being small and very compact ⟨a *capsule* submarine⟩

¹**cap·tain** \'kap-tən\ *n* [MF *capitain,* fr. LL *capitaneus* chief, fr. L *capit-, caput* head] **1 :** a leader of a group **:** one in command ⟨the *captain* of a team⟩ **2 a :** a commissioned officer in the navy ranking above a commander and below a rear admiral **b :** a commissioned officer (as in the army) ranking above a first lieutenant and below a major **3 :** the commanding officer of a ship **4 :** a fire or police department officer usu. ranking between a chief and a lieutenant — **cap·tain·ship** \-,ship\ *n*

²**captain** *vt* **:** to be captain of **:** LEAD

cap·tain·cy \'kap-tən-sē\ *n, pl* **-cies :** a captain's rank or position

¹**cap·tion** \'kap-shən\ *n* [L *caption-, captio* act of taking, fr. *capt-, capere* to take] **1 :** the heading esp. of an article or document **2 :** the explanatory comment or designation accompanying a pictorial illustration **3 :** a motion-picture subtitle

²**caption** *vt* **:** to furnish with a caption **:** ENTITLE

cap·tious \'kap-shəs\ *adj* [L *captiosus* designed to entrap, fr. *capt-, capere* to take, catch] **:** quick to find fault esp. over trifles — **cap·tious·ly** *adv* — **cap·tious·ness** *n*

cap·ti·vate \'kap-tə-,vāt\ *vb* **:** to attract with appeal and win over **:** CHARM, FASCINATE ⟨music that *captivated* everybody who heard it⟩ — **cap·ti·va·tion** \,kap-tə-'vā-shən\ *n* — **cap·ti·va·tor** \'kap-tə-,vāt-ər\ *n*

¹**cap·tive** \'kap-tiv\ *adj* [L *captivus,* fr. *capere* to take, capture] **1 a :** taken and held prisoner esp. in war **b :** held or confined so as to prevent escape ⟨*captive*

capstan

capsule

balloon⟩ **c** : owned or controlled by another for its own interest ⟨a *captive* coal mine⟩ **2** : of or relating to captivity

²captive *n* : one that is captive : PRISONER

cap·tiv·i·ty \kap-'tiv-ət-ē\ *n, pl* **-ties** : the state of being captive

cap·tor \'kap-tər\ *n* : one that has captured a person or thing

¹cap·ture \'kap-chər\ *n* [L *captura,* fr. *capt-, capere* to take] **1** : the act of catching or gaining control by force, stratagem, or guile **2** : one that has been taken captive

²capture *vt* **cap·tured; cap·tur·ing** \'kap-chə-riṇ, 'kap-shriṇ\ **1 a** : to take captive : WIN, GAIN ⟨*capture* a city⟩ **b** : to preserve in a relatively permanent form ⟨*captured* her smile on film⟩ **2** : to take according to rules of a game *syn* see CATCH

cap·u·chin \'kap-yə-shən, kə-'p(y)ü-\ *n* [It *cappuccino,* fr. *cappuccio* hood, fr. *cappa* cloak, fr. LL; fr. his cowl] **1** *cap* : a member of an austere branch of the first order of St. Francis of Assisi engaged in missionary work and preaching **2** : a So. American monkey with the forehead bare and bordered by a fringe of dark hair

cap·y·bara \,kap-i-'bar-ə\ *n* : a tailless largely aquatic So. American rodent often exceeding four feet in length

car \'kär\ *n* [ONF *carre,* fr. L *carrus*] **1** : a vehicle (as a railroad coach or an automobile) moved on wheels **2** : the cage of an elevator **3** : the part of a balloon or an airship in which passengers or equipment are carried

ca·ra·bao \,kar-ə-'baù, ,kär-\ *n, pl* **-baos** : WATER BUFFALO

car·a·bi·neer *or* **car·a·bi·nier** \,kar-ə-bə-'ni(ə)r\ *n* : a soldier armed with a carbine

ca·ra·ca·ra \,kar-ə-'kar-ə, -ə-kə-'rä\ *n* : any of various large long-legged mostly So. American hawks like vultures in habits

car·a·cole \'kar-ə-,kōl\ *n* [F] : a half turn to right or left executed by a mounted horse — **caracole** *vb*

car·a·cul \'kar-ə-kəl\ *n* [alter. of *karakul*] : the pelt of a karakul lamb after the curl begins to loosen

ca·rafe \kə-'raf\ *n* [F, fr. It *caraffa,* fr. Ar *gharrāfah*] : a bottle with a wide base and flaring lip used to hold water or beverages

car·a·ga·na \,kar-ə-'gän-ə\ *n* : any of a genus of Asiatic leguminous shrubs or small trees much used in dry areas esp. for hedges

car·a·mel \'kar-ə-məl, 'kär-məl\ *n* [Sp *caramelo,* fr. Pg, icicle, caramel, fr. LL *calamellus* dim. of *calamus* reed] **1** : a brittle brown and somewhat bitter substance obtained by heating sugar and used as a coloring and flavoring agent **2** : a firm chewy candy usu. in small blocks

car·a·mel·ize \-mə-,līz\ *vb* : to turn into caramel — **car·a·mel·i·za·tion** \,kar-ə-mə-lə-'zā-shən, ,kär-mə-\ *n*

car·a·pace \'kar-ə-,pās\ *n* [F, fr. Sp *carapacho*] : a bony or chitinous case or shield covering all or part of the back of an animal (as a turtle)

¹carat *var of* KARAT

²car·at \'kar-ət\ *n* [Ar *qīrāṭ,* a small weight, fr. Gk *keration,* fr. dim. of *kerat-, keras* horn] : a unit of weight for precious stones (as diamonds) equal to 200 milligrams

car·a·van \'kar-ə-,van\ *n* [It *caravana,* fr. Per *kārwān*] **1 a** : a company of travelers on a journey through desert or hostile regions **b** : a train of pack animals or of vehicles traveling together **2** : a covered vehicle: as **a** : one equipped as traveling living quarters **b** *Brit* : TRAILER 2b

car·a·van·sa·ry \,kar-ə-'van(t)-sə-rē\ *n, pl* **-ries** [Per *kārwānsarāī,* fr. *kārwān* caravan + *sarāī* palace, inn] **1** : an inn in eastern countries where caravans rest at night **2** : HOTEL, INN

car·a·vel \'kar-ə-,vel, -vəl\ *n* [MF *caravelle,* fr. Pg *caravela*] : a small 15th and 16th century ship with broad bows, high narrow poop, and lateen sails

car·a·way \'kar-ə-,wā\ *n* [Ar *karawyā*] : a usu. white-flowered aromatic herb of the carrot family with pungent fruits used in seasoning and medicine

carb- *or* **carbo-** *comb form* : carbon : carbonic : carbonyl : carboxyl ⟨*carbide*⟩ ⟨*carbohydrate*⟩

car·bide \'kär-,bīd\ *n* : a compound of carbon with another element; *esp* : CALCIUM CARBIDE

car·bine \'kär-,bīn, -,bēn\ *n* [F *carabine*] : a short light rifle

car·bo·hy·drase \,kär-bō-'hī-,drās\ *n* : an enzyme that promotes a decomposing or synthesizing of carbohydrate

car·bo·hy·drate \-,drāt\ *n* : any of various neutral compounds of carbon, hydrogen, and oxygen (as sugars, starches, or celluloses)

car·bo·lat·ed \'kär-bə-,lāt-əd\ *adj* : impregnated with carbolic acid

car·bol·ic acid \,kär-,bäl-ik-\ *n* [*carb-* + L *oleum* oil] : PHENOL 1

car·bon \'kär-bən\ *n* [L *carbon-, carbo* ember, charcoal] **1** : a nonmetallic chiefly tetravalent chemical element found native (as in the diamond and graphite) or as a constituent of coal, petroleum, and asphalt, of limestone and other carbonates, and of organic compounds or obtained artificially — see ELEMENT table **2 a** : a sheet of carbon paper **b** : a copy made with carbon paper **3** : a carbon rod used in an arc lamp

car·bo·na·ceous \,kär-bə-'nā-shəs\ *adj* : relating to, containing, or composed of carbon

car·bo·na·do \,kär-bə-'nād-ō, -'näd-\ *n, pl* **-nados** : an impure opaque dark-colored fine-grained aggregate of diamond particles valuable for its superior toughness

carbon arc *n* : an arc lamp having carbon electrodes

¹car·bon·ate \'kär-bə-,nāt, -nət\ *n* : a salt or ester of carbonic acid

²car·bon·ate \-,nāt\ *vt* **1** : to convert into a carbonate **2** : to impregnate with carbon dioxide ⟨a *carbonated* beverage⟩ — **car·bon·a·tion** \,kär-bə-'nā-shən\ *n*

carbon black *n* : any of various colloidal black substances consisting wholly or principally of carbon obtained as soot and used esp. as pigments

carbon copy *n* **1** : a copy made by carbon paper **2** : DUPLICATE

carbon cycle *n* : the cycle of carbon in living beings in which carbon dioxide fixed by photosynthesis to form organic nutrients is ultimately restored to the inorganic state by respiration and decay

carbon dioxide *n* : a heavy colorless gas CO_2 that does not support combustion, dissolves in water to form carbonic acid, is formed esp. by the combustion and decomposition of organic substances, is absorbed from the air by plants in photosynthesis, and is used in the carbonation of beverages

carbon disulfide *n* : a colorless flammable poisonous liquid CS_2 used as a solvent for rubber and as an insecticide — called also *carbon bisulfide*

carbon 14 *n* : a heavy radioactive form of carbon that has mass number 14, is formed esp. by the action of cosmic rays on nitrogen in the atmosphere, and is used as a tracer or for determining the age of very old specimens of formerly living materials (as bones or charcoal)

car·bon·ic \kär-'bän-ik\ *adj* : of, relating to, or derived from carbon, carbonic acid, or carbon dioxide

carbonic acid *n* : a weak acid H_2CO_3 that decomposes readily into water and carbon dioxide

car·bon·if·er·ous \,kär-bə-'nif-(ə-)rəs\ *adj* **1** : producing or containing carbon or coal **2** *cap* : of, relating to, or being the period of the Paleozoic era between the Devonian and the Permian or the corresponding system of rocks that include coal beds — **Carboniferous** *n*

car·bon·ize \'kär-bə-,nīz\ *vb* : to convert or become converted into carbon — **car·bon·i·za·tion** \,kär-bə-nə-'zā-shən\ *n*

carbon monoxide *n* : a colorless odorless very poisonous gas CO formed by the incomplete burning of carbon

carbon paper *n* : a thin paper faced with a waxy pigmented coating so that when placed between two sheets of paper the pressure of writing or typing on the top sheet causes transfer of pigment to the bottom sheet

carbon tetrachloride *n* : a colorless nonflammable poisonous liquid CCl_4 that has an odor resembling that of chloroform and is used as a solvent esp. of grease and as a fire extinguisher

car·bon·yl \'kär-bə-,nil\ *n* : a bivalent radical CO occurring in aldehydes, ketones, esters, and amides

Car·bo·run·dum \,kär-bə-'rən-dəm\ *trademark* — used for various abrasives

car·box·yl \kär-'bäk-səl\ *n* : a univalent radical —COOH typical of organic acids — **car·box·yl·ic** \,kär-bäk-'sil-ik\ *adj*

car·box·yl·ase \kär-'bäk-sə-,lās\ *n* : an enzyme that catalyzes the addition or removal of carboxyl or carbon dioxide

---

j joke; **ŋ** sing; **ō** flow; **ȯ** flaw; **ȯi** coin; **th** thin; **th̲** this; **ü** loot; **u̇** foot; **y** yet; **yü** few; **yu̇** furious; **zh** vision

car·box·yl·ic acid *n* : an organic acid (as acetic acid) containing one or more carboxyl groups

car·boy \'kär-,bȯi\ *n* [Per *qarāba*] : a large bottle cushioned in a special container ⟨a 5-gallon *carboy*⟩

car·bun·cle \'kär-,bəŋ-kəl\ *n* [L *carbunculus*, fr. dim. of *carbon-*, *carbo* ember] **1** : a garnet cut cabochon **2** : a painful inflammation of the skin and deeper tissues that discharges pus from several openings — compare BOIL — **car·bun·cled** \-kəld\ *adj* — **car·bun·cu·lar** \kär-'bəŋ-kyə-lər\ *adj*

car·bu·ret·or \'kär-b(y)ə-,rāt-ər\ *n* [*carburet* to combine with carbon, fr. obs. *carburet* carbide] : an apparatus for supplying an internal-combustion engine with vaporized fuel mixed with air in an explosive mixture

car·ca·jou \'kär-kə-,jü, -,zhü\ *n* : WOLVERINE

car·case \'kär-kəs\ *Brit var of* CARCASS

car·cass \'kär-kəs\ *n* [MF *carcasse*] **1** : a dead body; *esp* : the dressed body of a meat animal **2** : the living body **3** : the foundation structure of something (as a tire)

car·cin·o·gen \kär-'sin-ə-jən, 'kärs-ᵊn-ə-,jen\ *n* [Gk *karkinos* crab, cancer] : a substance or agent producing or inciting cancer — **car·ci·no·gen·ic** \,kärs-ᵊn-ō-'jen-ik\ *adj* — **car·ci·no·ge·nic·i·ty** \-jə-'nis-ət-ē\ *n*

car·ci·no·ma \,kärs-ᵊn-'ō-mə\ *n, pl* **-mas** *or* **-ma·ta** \-mət-ə\ : a malignant tumor originating in epithelium — **car·ci·nom·a·tous** \,kärs-ᵊn-'äm-ət-əs, -'ō-mət-\ *adj*

¹card \'kärd\ *vt* [MF *carder*] : to cleanse and untangle (fibers) by combing with a card before spinning — **card·er** *n*

²card *n* [MF *carde*, fr. L *carduus* thistle] : an instrument usu. having bent wire teeth for combing fibers (as wool or cotton)

³card *n* [MF *carte*, fr. L *charta* piece of papyrus, document] **1** : PLAYING CARD **2** *pl* **a** : a game played with cards **b** : card playing **3** : a clownishly amusing person : WAG **4 a** : a flat stiff usu. small and rectangular piece of paper or thin paperboard (as a postcard) **b** : a sports program ⟨racing *card*⟩ **c** (1) : a wine list (2) : MENU

car·da·mom \'kärd-ə-məm, -,mäm\ *n* [Gk *kardamōmon*] : the aromatic capsular fruit of an East Indian herb of the ginger family with seeds used as a condiment and in medicine; *also* : this plant

card·board \'kärd-,bȯrd, -,bȯrd\ *n* : a stiff moderately thick paperboard

cardi- *or* **cardio-** *comb form* [Gk *kardia*] : heart ⟨*cardiogram*⟩

¹car·di·ac \'kärd-ē-,ak\ *adj* [Gk *kardiakos*, fr. *kardia* heart; akin to E *heart*] **1** : of, relating to, situated near, or acting on the heart **2** : of, relating to, or being the part of the stomach into which the esophagus opens

²cardiac *n* : a person with heart disease

cardiac muscle *n* : striated muscle tissue that is found in the heart, is made up of cells united into a continuous mass, and is not under voluntary control

car·di·gan \'kärd-i-gən\ *n* [after the 7th earl of *Cardigan* d1868] : a sweater usu. without a collar and opening the full length of the front

Cardigan *n* [*Cardigan*, county in Wales] : a Welsh corgi with rounded ears, slightly bowed forelegs, and long tail

¹car·di·nal \'kärd-nəl, -ᵊn-əl\ *adj* [LL *cardinalis*, fr. L *cardin-*, *cardo* hinge] : of basic importance : MAIN, CHIEF, PRIMARY — **car·di·nal·ly** \-ē\ *adv*

²cardinal *n* **1** : one of the dignitaries of the Roman Catholic Church who rank next below the pope and who form his advisory and administrative council and elect his successor **2** : CARDINAL NUMBER **3** [fr. its color, resembling that of the cardinal's robes] : any of several American finches of which the male is bright red with a black face and pointed crest

car·di·nal·ate \-ət, -,āt\ *n* **1** : the office, rank, or dignity of a cardinal **2** : CARDINALS

cardinal flower *n* : the brilliant red flower of a No. American lobelia; *also* : this plant

car·di·nal·i·ty \,kärd-ᵊn-'al-ət-ē\ *n, pl* **-ties** : the number of elements in a given mathematical set

cardinal number *n* : a number (as 1, 5, 15) that is used in simple counting and that indicates how many elements there are in a collection — see NUMBER table

cardinal point *n* : one of the four principal points of the compass: north, south, east, west

car·dio·gram \'kärd-ē-ə-,gram\ *n* : the curve or tracing made by a cardiograph

car·dio·graph \-,graf\ *n* : an instrument that records graphically the duration and character of the heart movements — **car·dio·graph·ic** \,kärd-ē-ə-'graf-ik\ *adj*

car·di·ol·o·gy \,kärd-ē-'äl-ə-jē\ *n* : the study of the heart and its action and diseases — **car·di·o·lo·gist** \-jəst\ *n*

car·dio·re·spi·ra·to·ry \,kärd-ē-ō-'res-p(ə-)rə-,tōr-ē, -ri-'spī-rə-, -,tȯr-\ *adj* : of or relating to the heart and lungs

car·dio·vas·cu·lar \-'vas-kyə-lər\ *adj* : of, relating to, or involving the heart and blood vessels

car·doon \kär-'dün\ *n* [LL *cardon-*, *cardo* thistle] : a large perennial plant related to the artichoke and sometimes grown for its edible root and leafstalks

card-play·er \'kärd-,plā-ər\ *n* : one that plays cards

¹care \'ke(ə)r, 'ka(ə)r\ *n* [OE *caru*] **1** : a heavy sense of responsibility : WORRY, ANXIETY, CONCERN **2** : serious attention : HEED ⟨take *care* in crossing streets⟩ **3** : SUPERVISION ⟨under a doctor's *care*⟩ **4** : a person or thing that is an object of one's watchful attention

²care *vb* **1 a** : to feel trouble or anxiety **b** : to feel interest or concern ⟨*care* about freedom⟩ **2** : to give care ⟨*care* for the sick⟩ **3 a** : to have a liking, fondness, or taste ⟨don't *care* for her⟩ **b** : to have an inclination ⟨would you *care* for some pie⟩ — **car·er** *n*

ca·reen \kə-'rēn\ *vb* [MF *carène* keel, fr. L *carina*] **1** : to cause a boat to lean or tilt over on one side for cleaning, caulking, or repairing **2** : to sway from side to side : LURCH

¹ca·reer \kə-'ri(ə)r\ *n* [MF *carrière*, fr. OProv *carriera* street, fr. ML *carraria* road for vehicles, fr. L *carrus* car] **1 a** : COURSE, PROGRESS **b** : full speed or exercise of activity ⟨in full *career*⟩ **2** : a course of continued progress or activity **3** : a profession for which one trains and which is undertaken as a permanent calling

²career *vi* : to go at top speed esp. in a headlong manner

care·free \'ke(ə)r-,frē, 'ka(ə)r-\ *adj* : free from care

care·ful \-fəl\ *adj* **1** : using care : taking care : WATCHFUL, CAUTIOUS ⟨a *careful* driver⟩ **2** : made, done, or said with care ⟨*careful* examination⟩ — **care·ful·ly** \-f(ə-)lē\ *adv* — **care·ful·ness** \-fəl-nəs\ *n*

syn METICULOUS, SCRUPULOUS: CAREFUL implies attentiveness and cautiousness in avoiding mistakes ⟨*careful* workman⟩ ⟨*careful* nurse⟩ METICULOUS may imply either commendable extreme carefulness or a hampering finicky caution over small points; SCRUPULOUS applies to what is proper or fitting or ethical ⟨*scrupulous* honesty⟩

care·less \'ke(ə)r-ləs, 'ka(ə)r-\ *adj* **1** : CAREFREE **2** : not taking proper care : HEEDLESS ⟨*careless* of danger⟩ **3** : done, made, or said without due care ⟨a *careless* mistake⟩ — **care·less·ly** *adv* — **care·less·ness** *n*

¹ca·ress \kə-'res\ *n* [F *caresse*, fr. It *carezza*, fr. *caro* dear, fr. L *carus*] : a tender or loving touch or embrace — **ca·res·sive** \-'res-iv\ *adj* — **ca·res·sive·ly** *adv*

²caress *vt* : to touch or stroke lightly in a loving or endearing manner — **ca·ress·er** *n*

car·et \'kar-ət\ *n* [L, there is lacking, fr. *carēre* to lack] : a mark ∧ used to show where something is to be inserted

care·tak·er \'ke(ə)r-,tā-kər, 'ka(ə)r-\ *n* : one that takes care of buildings or land often for an absent owner

care·worn \-,wȯrn, -,wȯrn\ *adj* : showing the effect of grief or anxiety

car·fare \'kär-,fa(ə)r, -,fe(ə)r\ *n* : the fare charged for carrying a passenger on a car (as a streetcar)

car·go \'kär-,gō\ *n, pl* **cargoes** *or* **cargos** [Sp, fr. *cargar* to load, charge, fr. LL *carricare*] : the goods or merchandise conveyed in a ship, airplane, or vehicle : FREIGHT

car·hop \'kär-,häp\ *n* : one who serves customers at a drive-in restaurant

Car·ib \'kar-əb\ *n* **1** : a member of an Indian people of northern So. America and the Lesser Antilles **2** : the language of the Caribs

ca·ri·be \kə-'rē-bē\ *n* [AmerSp, fr. Sp, Carib, cannibal] : a small voracious So. American freshwater fish that may attack swimmers

car·i·bou \'kar-ə-,bü\ *n, pl* **-bou** *or* **-bous** [CanF, of Algonquian origin] : any of several large deer of northern No. America closely related to the reindeer

car·i·ca·ture \'kar-i-kə-,chù(ə)r\ *n* [It *caricatura*, lit., act of loading, fr. *caricare* to load, fr. LL *carricare*] **1** : exaggeration by means of ludicrous distortion of parts or

characteristics **2** : a representation esp. in literature or art that has the qualities of caricature — **caricature** *vt* — **car·i·ca·tur·ist** \-əst\ *n*
syn BURLESQUE, PARODY, TRAVESTY mean a comic or grotesque imitation. CARICATURE implies ludicrous exaggeration of the characteristic features of a subject; BURLESQUE implies the ridiculous effect resulting either from treating a trivial subject in a mock-heroic style or from giving a serious or lofty subject a frivolous treatment; PARODY applies to treatment of a trivial or ludicrous subject in the exactly imitated style of a particular author or work; TRAVESTY implies that the subject remains unaltered but that the style and effect is extravagant or absurd

car·ies \'ka(ə)r-ēz, 'ke(ə)r-\ *n, pl* **caries** [L, decay] : a progressive destruction of bone or tooth; *esp* : tooth decay — **car·i·ous** \'kar-ē-əs, 'ker-\ *adj*

car·il·lon \'kar-ə-,län\ *n* [F, alter. of OF *quarregnon*, fr. LL *quaternion-, quaternio* set of four] **1** : a set of fixed bells sounded by hammers controlled by a keyboard **2** : a composition for the carillon

car·il·lon·neur \,kar-ə-lä-'nər\ *n* : a carillon player

ca·ri·na \kə-'rī-nə, -'rē-\ *n, pl* **-rinas** *or* **-ri·nae** \-'rī-,nē, -'rē-,nī\ [NL, fr. L, keel] : a keel-shaped anatomical part, ridge, or process — **ca·ri·nal** \kə-'rīn-ᵊl\ *adj* — **car·i·nate** \'kar-ə-,nāt\ *adj*

car·i·ole \'kar-ē-,ōl\ *n* : a toboggan drawn by a horse or dogs

car·load \'kär-'lōd\ *n* : a load that fills a car

Car·mel·ite \'kär-mə-,līt\ *n* : a friar or nun of the Roman Catholic Order of Our Lady of Mount Carmel founded in the 12th century — **Carmelite** *adj*

car·min·a·tive \kär-'min-ət-iv\ *adj* [L *carminare* to card, comb out knots in] : expelling gas from the alimentary canal — **carminative** *n*

car·mine \'kär-mən, -,mīn\ *n* [ML *carminium*, fr. Ar *qirmiz* kermes + L *minium* red lead] **1** : a rich crimson or scarlet coloring matter made from cochineal **2** : a vivid red

car·nage \'kär-nij\ *n* : great destruction of life (as in battle) : SLAUGHTER

car·nal \'kärn-ᵊl\ *adj* [L *carn-, caro* flesh] **1** : of or relating to the body **2** : not spiritual : CORPOREAL **3** : SENSUAL — **car·nal·i·ty** \kär-'nal-ət-ē\ *n* — **car·nal·ly** \'kärn-ᵊl-ē\ *adv*

car·nas·si·al \kär-'nas-ē-əl\ *adj* : of, relating to, or being teeth of a carnivore adapted for cutting rather than tearing — **carnassial** *n*

car·na·tion \kär-'nā-shən\ *n* **1 a** : the variable color of human flesh **b** : a moderate red **2** : any of the numerous cultivated usu. double-flowered pinks derived from the common gillyflower

car·nau·ba \kär-'nȯ-bə, ,kär-nə-'ü-bə\ *n* [Pg] : a Brazilian palm that yields a brittle yellowish wax used esp. in polishes; *also* : this wax

car·ne·lian \kär-'nēl-yən\ *n* [ME *corneline*, fr. MF] : a hard tough reddish quartz used as a gem

car·ni·val \'kär-nə-vəl\ *n* [It *carnevale*, alter. of earlier *carnelevare*, lit., removal of meat] **1** : a season of merrymaking before Lent **2** : a merrymaking, feasting, or masquerading **3 a** : a traveling enterprise offering amusements **b** : an organized program of entertainment or exhibition

car·niv·o·ra \kär-'niv-(ə-)rə\ *n pl* [NL] : carnivorous mammals

car·ni·vore \'kär-nə-,vō(ə)r, -,vȯ(ə)r\ *n* **1** : a flesh-eating animal; *esp* : any of an order (Carnivora) of flesh-eating mammals **2** : an insectivorous plant

car·niv·o·rous \kär-'niv-(ə-)rəs\ *adj* [L *carnivorus*, fr. *carn-, caro* flesh + *vorare* to devour] **1** : subsisting or feeding on animal tissues **2** : of or relating to the carnivores — **car·niv·o·rous·ly** *adv* — **car·niv·o·rous·ness** *n*

car·no·tite \'kär-nə-,tīt\ *n* : a mineral consisting of a radioactive compound of potassium, uranium, vanadium, and oxygen

¹car·ol \'kar-əl\ *n* [OF *carole*, modif. of LL *choraula* choral song, fr. Gk *choros* chorus + *aulein* to play a reed instrument, fr. *aulos*, a reed instrument] **1** : an old round dance with singing **2** : a song of joy or mirth **3** : a popular song of religious joy ⟨Christmas *carol*⟩

²carol *vb* **-oled** *or* **-olled**; **-ol·ing** *or* **-ol·ling** **1** : to sing esp. in a joyful manner **2** : to sing carols — **car·ol·er** *or* **car·ol·ler** *n*

Car·o·line \'kar-ə-,līn, -lən\ *adj* [ML *Carolus* Charles] : of or relating to Charles I or Charles II of England

Car·o·lin·gian \,kar-ə-'lin-j(ē-)ən\ *adj* : of or relating to a Frankish dynasty dating from about A.D. 613 and ruling France from 751 to 987, Germany from 752 to 911, and Italy from 774 to 961 — **Carolingian** *n*

¹car·om \'kar-əm\ *n* [Sp *carambola*] **1** : a shot in billiards in which the cue ball strikes each of two object balls **2** : a rebounding esp. at an angle

²carom *vi* **1** : to make a carom **2** : to strike and rebound at an angle : GLANCE

car·o·tene \'kar-ə-,tēn\ *or* **car·o·tin** \'kar-ət-ᵊn\ *n* [LL *carota* carrot] : any of several orange or red hydrocarbon pigments (as $C_{40}H_{56}$) that occur in plants and in the fatty tissues of plant-eating animals and are convertible to vitamin A

ca·rot·enoid \kə-'rät-ᵊn-,ȯid\ *n* : any of various usu. yellow to red pigments (as carotenes) found widely in plants and animals and characterized chemically by a long chain of carbon atoms — **carotenoid** *adj*

ca·rot·id \kə-'rät-əd\ *adj* [Gk *karōtides* carotid arteries] : of, relating to, or being the chief artery or pair of arteries that pass up each side of the neck and supply the head — **carotid** *n*

ca·rous·al \kə-'rau̇-zəl\ *n* : CAROUSE

¹ca·rouse \kə-'rau̇z\ *n* [MF *carousse*, fr. *boire carous* to empty the cup, fr. *boire* to drink + G *garaus* all out] : a drunken revel

²carouse *vi* **1** : to drink liquor freely **2** : to take part in a carouse — **ca·rous·er** *n*

¹carp \'kärp\ *vi* [of Scand origin] : to find fault : complain fretfully — **carp·er** *n*

²carp *n, pl* **carp** *or* **carps** [LL *carpa*] : a large variable Old World soft-finned freshwater fish noted for its longevity and often raised for food; *also* : any of various related or similar fishes

-carp \,kärp\ *n comb form* [NL *-carpium*, fr. Gk *karpos* fruit; akin to E *harvest*] : part of a fruit ⟨mesocarp⟩ : fruit ⟨schizocarp⟩

¹car·pal \'kär-pəl\ *adj* : relating to the wrist or carpus

²carpal *n* : a carpal bone or cartilage

car·pel \'kär-pəl\ *n* [NL *carpellum*, fr. Gk *karpos* fruit] : one of the structures of the innermost whorl of a flower that together form the ovary of a seed plant — **car·pel·lary** \-pə-,ler-ē\ *adj* — **car·pel·late** \-,lāt\ *adj*

car·pen·ter \'kär-pən-tər\ *n* [ONF *carpentier*, fr. L *carpentarius* carriage maker, fr. *carpentum* carriage] : a workman who builds or repairs wooden structures — **carpenter** *vb* — **car·pen·try** \-trē\ *n*

car·pet \'kär-pət\ *n* [MF *carpite*, fr. It *carpita*, fr. *carpire* to pluck, fr. L *carpere*] : a heavy woven or felted fabric used as a floor covering; *also* : a floor covering made of this fabric — **carpet** *vt*

¹car·pet·bag \-,bag\ *n* : a traveling bag made of carpeting common in the 19th century

²carpetbag *adj* : of, relating to, or characteristic of carpetbaggers

car·pet·bag·ger \-,bag-ər\ *n* : a Northerner in the South during the reconstruction period seeking private gain by taking advantage of unsettled conditions and political corruption — **car·pet·bag·gery** \-,bag-ə-rē\ *n*

carpet beetle *n* : a small beetle whose larva damages woolen goods

car·pet·ing \'kär-pət-iŋ\ *n* : material for carpets; *also* : CARPETS

carp·ing *adj* : likely to carp — **carp·ing·ly** \'kär-piŋ-lē\ *adv*

car·po·go·ni·um \,kär-pə-'gō-nē-əm\ *n, pl* **-nia** \-nē-ə\ : the flask-shaped egg-bearing organ of some thallophytes — **car·po·go·ni·al** \-nē-əl\ *adj*

car·poph·a·gous \kär-'päf-ə-gəs\ *adj* : feeding on fruits

car·port \'kär-,pōrt, -,pȯrt\ *n* : an open-sided automobile shelter usu. formed by extension of a roof from the side of a building

-car·pous \'kär-pəs\ *adj comb form* [Gk *karpos* fruit]

flower with part removed to show: *1* petal, *2* stamen, *3* carpel, *4* sepal

: having (such) fruit or (so many) fruits 〈poly*carpous*〉 — **-car·py** \,kär-pē\ *n comb form*

car·pus \'kär-pəs\ *n, pl* **car·pi** \-,pī, -,pē\ [NL, fr. Gk *karpos* wrist] **:** the wrist or its bones

car·rack \'kar-ək\ *n* **:** GALLEON

car·rel \'kar-əl\ *n* [earlier *carrell* enclosure for study in a cloister, alter. of ME *carol* ring, carol] **:** a table with bookshelves often partitioned or enclosed for individual study in a library

car·riage \'kar-ij\ *n* **1 a :** the act of carrying **b :** manner of bearing the body **:** POSTURE **2 :** the price or expense of carrying **3 a :** a wheeled vehicle; *esp* **:** a horse-drawn vehicle designed for private use and comfort **b** *Brit* **:** a railway passenger coach **4 :** a wheeled support carrying a load 〈a gun *carriage*〉 **5 :** a movable part of a machine for supporting or carrying some other movable object or part

carriage trade *n* **:** trade from well-to-do or upper-class people

car·ri·er \'kar-ē-ər\ *n* **1 :** one that carries **2 a :** a person or firm engaged in transporting passengers or goods **b :** a postal employee who delivers or collects mail **c :** one that delivers newspapers **3 :** a bearer and transmitter of disease germs; *esp* **:** one who carries in his system germs of a disease (as typhoid fever) to which he is immune **4 :** an electric wave or alternating current whose modulations are used as signals in radio, telephonic, or telegraphic transmission

car·ri·on \'kar-ē-ən\ *n* **:** dead and decaying flesh

car·rot \'kar-ət\ *n* [LL *carota*, fr. Gk *karōton*] **:** a biennial herb with a usu. orange spindle-shaped edible root; *also* **:** its root

car·roty \-ət-ē\ *adj* **:** resembling carrots in color

car·rou·sel *or* **car·ou·sel** \,kar-ə-'sel, -'zel\ *n* **:** MERRY-GO-ROUND

¹car·ry \'kar-ē\ *vb* **car·ried; car·ry·ing** [ONF *carier* to transport in a vehicle, fr. *car* car, fr. L *carrus*] **1 a :** to support and take from one place to another **:** TRANSPORT, CONVEY 〈*carry* a package〉 **b :** to act as a bearer **2 :** to influence by mental or emotional appeal 〈the speaker *carried* his audience〉 **3 :** to get possession or control of **:** CAPTURE **4 :** to transfer from one place to another 〈*carry* a number in addition〉 **5 :** to contain and direct the course of **:** CONDUCT 〈a pipe *carries* water〉 **6 a :** to wear or have on one's person 〈*carries* a gun〉 **b :** to bear upon or within one 〈*carries* a scar〉 **c :** IMPLY, INVOLVE 〈the crime *carries* a penalty〉 **7 :** to conduct oneself **8 :** to sustain the weight of 〈pillars *carry* an arch〉 **9 :** to sing in correct pitch 〈*carry* a tune〉 **10 :** to keep in stock for sale 〈*carries* three brands of tires〉 **11 :** to provide sustenance for 〈land *carrying* 10 head of cattle〉 **12 :** to maintain on a list or record 〈*carry* him on the payroll〉 **13 :** MAINTAIN, SUPPORT **14 :** to prolong in space, time, or degree 〈*carry* the war into the enemy's homeland〉 **15 a** (1) **:** to gain victory for; *esp* **:** to secure the adoption or passage of 〈*carry* a bill〉 (2) **:** to win adoption 〈the bill *carried*〉 **b** (1) **:** to succeed in (an election) (2) **:** to win a majority of votes in 〈*carry* a state〉 **16 :** PUBLISH 〈the paper *carries* weather reports〉 **17 a :** to bear the charges of holding (as merchandise) **b :** to keep on one's books as a debtor **18 :** to penetrate to a distance 〈a voice that *carries* well〉

²carry *n, pl* **carries** **1 :** the range of a gun or projectile or of a struck or thrown ball **2 a :** the act or method of carrying 〈fireman's *carry*〉 **b :** PORTAGE

car·ry·all \'kar-ē-,ȯl\ *n* **1 :** a light covered carriage for four or more persons **2 :** a passenger automobile similar to a station wagon but with a higher body often on a truck chassis **3 :** a capacious bag or case

carry away *vt* **:** to arouse to a high and often excessive degree of emotion or enthusiasm

carrying charge *n* **1 :** expense incident to ownership or use of property **2 :** a charge added to the price of merchandise sold on the installment plan

carry on *vb* **1 :** CONDUCT, MANAGE 〈*carries* on a dry-cleaning business〉 **2 :** to behave in a foolish, excited, or improper manner 〈embarrassed at the way he *carried on*〉 **3 :** to continue in spite of hindrance or discouragement 〈still *carrying on*〉

carry out *vt* **1 :** to put into execution 〈*carry out* a plan〉 **2 :** to bring to a successful conclusion

car·sick \'kär-,sik\ *adj* **:** affected with motion sickness associated with riding in a car — **car sickness** *n*

¹cart \'kärt\ *n* [ME] **1 :** a heavy usu. horse-drawn 2-wheeled vehicle used for haulage **2 :** a light usu. 2-wheeled vehicle 〈a garden *cart*〉 〈pony *carts*〉

²cart *vt* **:** to convey in or as if in a cart — **cart·er** *n*

cart·age \'kärt-ij\ *n* **:** the act of or rate charged for carting

carte blanche \'kärt-'bläⁿsh, -'blänch\ *n, pl* **cartes blanches** *same*\ [F, lit., white paper, blank paper] **:** full discretionary power

car·tel \kär-'tel\ *n* **:** a combination of independent commercial enterprises often international in scope designed to limit competition **syn** see MONOPOLY

Car·te·sian \kär-'tē-zhən\ *adj* [NL *Cartesius* Descartes] **:** of or relating to René Descartes, his philosophy, or his mathematical methods

Cartesian coordinate system *n* **:** a system of locating geometrical coordinates in terms of two straight-line axes usu. at right angles to each other

Car·thu·sian \kär-'th(y)ü-zhən\ *n* **:** a member of an austere contemplative religious order founded in 1084 — **Carthusian** *adj*

car·ti·lage \'kärt-ˀl-ij\ *n* [L *cartilagin-, cartilago*] **1 :** a translucent elastic tissue that composes most of the skeleton of the embryonic and very young vertebrates and becomes for the most part converted into bone in the higher vertebrates **2 :** a part or structure composed of cartilage

car·ti·lag·i·nous \,kärt-ˀl-'aj-ə-nəs\ *adj* **1 :** of, relating to, or resembling cartilage **2 :** having a skeleton mostly of cartilage 〈*cartilaginous* fishes〉

car·tog·ra·phy \kär-'täg-rə-fē\ *n* [F *cartographie*, fr. *carte* card, map] **:** the making of maps — **car·tog·ra·pher** \-fər\ *n* — **car·to·graph·ic** \,kärt-ə-'graf-ik\ *adj*

car·ton \'kärt-ˀn\ *n* [F, fr. It *cartone* pasteboard] **:** a paperboard box or container

car·toon \kär-'tün\ *n* [It *cartone* pasteboard, cartoon, fr. L *charta* piece of papyrus] **1 :** a preparatory design, drawing, or painting **2 a :** a drawing intended as humor, caricature, or satire and comment on public affairs **b :** COMIC STRIP **3 :** ANIMATED CARTOON — **cartoon** *vb* — **car·toon·ist** \-'tü-nəst\ *n*

car·tridge \'kär-trij\ *n* [modif. of F *cartouche* scroll, cartridge, fr. It *cartoccio*, fr. *carta* paper, fr. L *charta* leaf of papyrus] **1 a :** a tube of metal or paper containing a complete charge for a firearm **b :** a case containing an explosive charge for blasting **2 :** an often cylindrical container of material for insertion into a larger mechanism or apparatus **3 a :** a phonograph pickup that translates stylus motion into electrical voltage **b :** a case of magnetic tape for use without threading

cart·wheel \'kärt-,hwēl\ *n* **1 :** a large coin (as a silver dollar) **2 :** a lateral handspring with arms and legs extended

car·un·cle \'kar-,ən-kəl, kə-'rəŋ-\ *n* [L *caruncula*, dim. of *caro* flesh] **:** a fleshy outgrowth (as on a seed) — **ca·run·cu·lat·ed** \kə-'rəŋ-kyə-,lāt-əd\ *adj*

carve \'kärv\ *vb* [OE *ceorfan*] **1 :** to cut with care or precision esp. artistically 〈*carve* friezes〉 **2 :** to make or get by cutting **3 :** to cut into pieces or slices **4 :** to cut up and serve meat

carv·en \'kär-vən\ *adj* **:** CARVED

carv·er \'kär-vər\ *n* **1 :** one that carves **2 :** a large knife for carving meat

carv·ing \'kär-viŋ\ *n* **1 :** the act or art of one who carves **2 :** a carved object, design, or figure

cary·at·id \,kar-ē-'at-əd\ *n, pl* **-at·ids** *or* **-at·i·des** \-'at-ə-,dēz\ **:** a sculptured figure of a woman in flowing robes used as an architectural column

cary·op·sis \,kar-ē-'äp-səs\ *n, pl* **-op·ses** \-'äp-,sēz\ *or* **-op·si·des** \-'äp-sə-,dēz\ **:** a small one-seeded dry indehiscent fruit in which the fruit and seed fuse in a single grain

ca·sa·ba \kə-'säb-ə\ *n* [*Kasaba* (now Turgutlu), Turkey] **:** any of several winter melons with yellow rind and sweet flesh

¹cas·cade \kas-'kād\ *n* [F, fr. It *cascata*, fr. *cascare* to fall] **1 :** a steep usu. small fall of water; *esp* **:** one of a series **2 :** something

caryatid

---

arranged in a series or in a succession of stages so that each stage derives from or acts upon the product of the preceding **3** : something falling or rushing forth in quantity
²**cascade** *vi* : to fall in a cascade
cas·cara \kas-'kar-ə\ *n* [Sp *cáscara* bark] : the dried laxative bark of a buckthorn tree that grows along the Pacific coast of the U.S. — called also *cascara sa·gra·da* \-sə-'gräd-ə\
¹**case** \'kās\ *n* [L *casus* fall, chance, grammatical case, fr. *cas-, cadere* to fall] **1** : a special set of circumstances or conditions **2 a** : a situation requiring investigation or action (as by the police) **b** : an object of investigation or consideration **3 a** : an inflectional form of a noun, pronoun, or adjective indicating its grammatical relation to other words (the word *boy's* in "the boy's shirt" is in the possessive *case*) **b** : such a relation whether indicated by inflection or not (the subject of a verb is in the nominative *case*) **4** : what actually exists or happens : FACT **5 a** : a suit or action in law or equity **b** (1) : the evidence supporting a conclusion or judgment (2) : ARGUMENT; *esp* : a convincing argument **6 a** : an instance of disease or injury; *also* : PATIENT **b** : INSTANCE, EXAMPLE **syn** see INSTANCE — **in case 1** : IF **2** : as a precaution **3** : as a precaution against the event that
²**case** *n* [ONF *casse*, fr. L *capsa*, fr. *capere* to take] **1 a** : a box or receptacle to contain something **b** : a box with its contents **c** : SET; *esp* : PAIR **2** : an outer covering or housing **3** : a shallow divided tray for holding printing type **4** : the frame of a door or window : CASING
³**case** *vt* : to enclose in or cover with a case : ENCASE
case hard·en \'kās-,härd-ᵊn\ *vt* : to harden (an iron alloy) so that the surface layer is harder than the interior — **case–hard·ened** *adj*
case history *n* : a record of history, environment, and relevant details (as of individual behavior or condition) esp. for use in analysis or illustration
ca·sein \kā-'sēn, 'kā-sē-ən\ *n* [L *caseus* cheese] **1** : a phosphorus-containing protein that is precipitated from milk by heating with an acid or by lactic acid in souring and that is used in making paints and adhesives **2** : a phosphorus-containing protein that is produced when milk is curdled by rennet, that is one of the chief constituents of cheese, and that is used in making plastics
case knife *n* **1** : SHEATH KNIFE **2** : a table knife
case·mate \'kās-,māt\ *n* : a fortified position or enclosure from which guns are fired through embrasures
case·ment \'kās-mənt\ *n* : a window sash opening on hinges like a door; *also* : a window with such a sash
ca·se·ous \'kā-sē-əs\ *adj* : CHEESY
case·work \'kās-,wərk\ *n* : intensive sociological study of the history and environment of a maladjusted individual or family for diagnosis and treatment — **case·work·er** *n*
¹**cash** \'kash\ *n* [MF *casse* money box, fr. It *cassa*, fr. L *capsa* case, chest] **1** : ready money **2** : money or its equivalent paid promptly after purchasing
²**cash** *vt* : to pay or obtain cash for (*cash* a check)
³**cash** *n, pl* **cash** [Pg *caixa*, fr. Tamil *kācu*, a small coin] : any of various coins of small value in China and India; *esp* : a Chinese coin of copper alloy with a square hole in the center
cash–and–carry \,kash-ən-'kar-ē\ *n* : the policy of selling for cash and without delivery service
cash·book \'kash-,bùk\ *n* : a book in which record is kept of all cash receipts and disbursements
cash·ew \'kash-ü, kə-'shü\ *n* [Pg *acajú, cajú,* of AmerInd origin] : a tropical American tree of the sumac family grown for its edible kidney-shaped nut and receptacle and for the gum it yields; *also* : its nut
¹**cash·ier** \ka-'shi(ə)r\ *n* **1** : a high officer of a bank responsible for all money received and paid out **2** : an employee of a store or restaurant who receives and records payments made by customers
²**cashier** *vt* [D *casseren*] : DISCHARGE; *esp* : to discharge in disgrace from a position of responsibility or trust
cashier's check *n* : a check drawn by a bank upon its own funds and signed by its cashier
cash·mere \'kazh-,mi(ə)r, 'kash-\ *n* [*Cashmere* Kashmir] : fine wool from the undercoat of Kashmir goats or a yarn of this wool; *also* : a soft twilled fabric orig. from this wool
cash register *n* : a business machine usu. with a money

drawer that records the amount of money received and exhibits the amount of each sale
cas·ing \'kā-siŋ\ *n* **1** : something that encases : material for encasing: as **a** : an enclosing frame esp. around a door or window opening **b** : TIRE 2b **c** : a membranous case for processed meat **2** : a space formed between two parallel lines of stitching through at least two layers of cloth into which something (as a rod or string) may be inserted
ca·si·no \kə-'sē-nō\ *n, pl* **-nos** [It, fr. *casa* house, fr. L, cabin] **1** : a building or room used for social amusements; *esp* : a building or room for gambling **2** *or* **cas·si·no** : a card game
cask \'kask\ *n* [MF *casque* helmet] **1** : a barrel-shaped container usu. for liquids **2** : the quantity contained in a cask
cas·ket \'kas-kət\ *n* **1** : a small chest or box (as for jewels) **2** : a usu. ornamented and lined coffin
casque \'kask\ *n* [MF, fr. Sp *casco*] **1** : a piece of armor for the head : HELMET **2** : an anatomic structure suggestive of a helmet
cas·sa·ba *var of* CASABA
Cas·san·dra \kə-'san-drə\ *n* : a daughter of Priam endowed with the gift of prophecy but fated never to be believed
cas·sa·va \kə-'säv-ə\ *n* : any of several plants of the spurge family grown in the tropics for their fleshy rootstocks which yield a nutritious starch; *also* : the rootstock or its starch — compare TAPIOCA
cas·se·role \'kas-ə-,rōl\ *n* [F] **1** : a covered dish in which food can be baked and served **2** : the food cooked and served in a casserole
cas·sette \kə-'set\ *n* : a lightproof container for holding film or plates for use in a camera
cas·sia \'kash-ə\ *n* **1** : a coarse cinnamon bark **2** : any of a genus of leguminous herbs, shrubs, and trees of warm regions some of which yield senna
cas·si·mere \'kaz-ə-,mi(ə)r, 'kas-\ *n* : a smooth twilled usu. wool fabric
Cas·si·o·pe·ia \,kas-ē-ə-'pē-(y)ə\ *n* : a northern constellation between Andromeda and Cepheus
Cassiopeia's Chair *n* : a group of stars in the constellation Cassiopeia resembling a chair
cas·sit·er·ite \kə-'sit-ə-,rīt\ *n* [Gk *kassiteros* tin] : a brown or black mineral SnO₂ that consists of tin dioxide and is the chief source of tin
cas·sock \'kas-ək\ *n* [MF *casaque*, fr. Per *kazhāghand* padded jacket] : a close-fitting ankle-length gown worn esp. in Roman Catholic and Anglican churches by the clergy and by laymen assisting in divine services
cas·so·wary \'kas-ə-,wer-ē\ *n, pl* **-war·ies** [Malay *kĕsuari*] : any of several tall swift-running birds of New Guinea and Australia closely related to the emu
¹**cast** \'kast\ *vb* **cast·ing** [ON *kasta*] **1 a** (1) : THROW, FLING, TOSS (*cast* a stone) (2) : to throw out a lure with a fishing rod **b** : DIRECT (*cast* a glance) (*cast* doubt on his integrity) **c** : to deposit (a ballot) formally **d** : to throw off, out, or away (the horse *cast* a shoe): as (1) : EMIT (2) : DISCARD (3) : SHED, MOLT (a snake *casts* its skin) **2 a** : ADD, COMPUTE **b** : to calculate by astrology (*cast* a horoscope) **3 a** : to assign the parts of to actors (*cast* a play) **b** : to assign (an actor) to a part **4 a** : to give shape to (a substance) by pouring in liquid or plastic form into a mold and letting harden without pressure (*cast* steel) **b** : to form by this process (*cast* machine parts) — **cast about** : to search here and there — **cast lots** : to draw lots to determine a matter by chance
²**cast** *n* **1 a** : an act of casting **b** : something that happens as a result of chance **2 a** : the form in which a thing is constructed **b** : the characters or the actors in a play or narrative **3** : the distance to which a thing can be thrown **4** : a turning of the eye; *also* : EXPRESSION **5** : something thrown or the quantity thrown **6 a** : something formed by casting in a mold or form : CASTING (a bronze *cast* of a statue) **b** : an impression taken from an object with a liquid or plastic substance : MOLD **c** : a rigid structure of gauze impregnated with plaster of paris for immobilizing a diseased or broken part **7** : FORECAST **8** : an overspread of a color : SHADE **9 a** : SHAPE, APPEARANCE **b** : characteristic quality **10** : something

thrown out or off, shed, or ejected; *esp* : the excrement of an earthworm **11** : a ranging (as by a dog) in search of a trail

cas·ta·net \‚kas-tə-'net\ *n* [Sp *castañeta*, fr. *castaña* chestnut, fr. L *castanea*] : a rhythm instrument used esp. by dancers that consists of two small ivory, wood, or plastic shells fastened to the thumb and clicked together by the fingers — usu. used in pl.

castanets

cast·away \'kas-tə-‚wā\ *adj* **1** : thrown away : REJECTED **2** : cast adrift or ashore as a survivor of a shipwreck — **castaway** *n*

caste \'kast\ *n* [Pg *casta* race, breed, fr. *casto* pure, chaste, fr. L *castus*] **1** : one of the hereditary classes formerly dividing Hindu society **2 a** : a division of society based upon differences of wealth, inherited rank, or occupation **b** : the position conferred by caste standing : PRESTIGE **3** : a specialized form that carries out a particular function in the colony of a social insect (as the honeybee) ⟨the worker *caste*⟩

cas·tel·lat·ed \'kas-tə-‚lāt-əd\ *adj* : having battlements like a castle

cast·er \'kas-tər\ *n* **1** : one that casts **2** : a small container (as for salt) with a perforated top **3** : a small tray for cruets and other containers **4** *or* **cas·tor** \'kas-tər\ : a wheel or set of wheels mounted in a swivel frame used for supporting furniture, trucks, and portable machines

cas·ti·gate \'kas-tə-‚gāt\ *vt* [L *castigare*, lit., to correct, fr. *castus* pure, chaste] : to punish, reprove, or criticize severely — **cas·ti·ga·tion** \‚kas-tə-'gā-shən\ *n* — **cas·ti·ga·tor** \'kas-tə-‚gāt-ər\ *n*

cas·tile soap \‚kas-‚tēl-\ *n, often cap C* : a fine hard bland soap made from olive oil and sodium hydroxide

Cas·til·ian \ka-'stil-yən\ *n* **1 a** : a native or inhabitant of Castile **b** : SPANIARD **2** : the official and literary language of Spain based on the dialect of Castile — **Castilian** *adj*

cast·ing *n* **1** : the act of one that casts **2** : something cast in a mold ⟨a bronze *casting*⟩ **3** : something that is cast out or off

casting vote *n* : a deciding vote cast by a presiding officer in case of a tied vote

cast iron *n* : a hard brittle alloy of iron, carbon, and silicon shaped by being poured into a mold while it is molten and being allowed to harden

¹cas·tle \'kas-əl\ *n* [OE *castel*, fr. L *castellum*, dim. of *castrum* fortified place] **1 a** : a large fortified building or set of buildings **b** : a massive or imposing house **2** : ³ROOK

²castle *vb* **cas·tled**; **cas·tling** \'kas-(ə-)liŋ\ **1** : to establish in a castle **2** : to move the king two squares toward a rook and the rook to the square next past the king

cast–off \'kast-‚óf\ *adj* : thrown away as no longer wanted : DISCARDED — **castoff** *n*

cas·tor \'kas-tər\ *n* [Gk *kastōr* beaver, castor] **1** : a bitter strong-smelling creamy orange-brown substance obtained from the beaver and used esp. by perfumers **2** : a beaver hat

Cas·tor \'kas-tər\ *n* **1** : the mortal twin of Pollux — compare DIOSCURI **2** : the more northern of the two bright stars in Gemini

castor bean *n* : the very poisonous seed of the castor-oil plant; *also* : this plant

castor oil *n* : a thick yellowish oil extracted from castor beans and used as a lubricant, in soap, and as a cathartic

castor–oil plant *n* : a tropical Old World herb widely grown as an ornamental or for its oil-rich castor beans

¹cas·trate \'kas-‚trāt\ *vt* [L *castrare*] : to deprive of the sex glands and esp. the testes — **cas·tra·tion** \ka-'strā-shən\ *n*

²castrate *n* : a castrated individual

ca·su·al \'kazh-(ə-)wəl, 'kazh-əl\ *adj* [L *casus* fall, chance, fr. *cas-*, *cadere* to fall] **1** : subject to or occurring by chance **2** : occurring without regularity : OCCASIONAL **3 a** : feeling or showing little concern : NONCHALANT **b** : INFORMAL, NATURAL — **ca·su·al·ly** \-ē\ *adv* — **ca·su·al·ness** *n*

ca·su·al·ty \'kazh-əl-tē, 'kazh-(ə-)wəl-\ *n, pl* **-ties** **1** : serious or fatal accident : DISASTER **2 a** : a military

person lost (as by death or capture) during warfare **b** : a person or thing injured, lost, or destroyed **3** : injury or death from accident ⟨*casualty* insurance⟩

ca·su·ist·ry \'kazh-(ə-)wə-strē\ *n, pl* **-ries** **1** : the study or resolution of questions of right and wrong in conduct **2** : false reasoning or application of principles esp. with regard to morals — **ca·su·ist** \'kazh-(ə-)wəst\ *n* — **ca·su·is·tic** \‚kazh-ə-'wis-tik\ *or* **ca·su·is·ti·cal** \-'wis-ti-kəl\ *adj*

¹cat \'kat\ *n* [OE *catt*] **1 a** : a small carnivorous mammal long domesticated and kept by man as a pet or for catching rats and mice **b** : an animal of the cat family including the lion, tiger, leopard, jaguar, cougar, wildcat, lynx, and cheetah **2** : a malicious woman **3** : a strong tackle used to hoist an anchor to the cathead of a ship **4** : CAT‑O'‑NINE‑TAILS **5** : CATFISH

²cat *vt* **cat·ted**; **cat·ting** : to bring (an anchor) up to the cathead

Cat \'kat\ *trademark* — used for a Caterpillar tractor

cata- *or* **cat-** *prefix* [Gk *kata-*, *kat-*] : down

ca·tab·o·lism \kə-'tab-ə-‚liz-əm\ *n* : the part of metabolism concerned with the destruction of the substance of plants and animals — **cat·a·bol·ic** \‚kat-ə-'bäl-ik\ *adj*

cat·a·clysm \'kat-ə-‚kliz-əm\ *n* [Gk *kataklysmos*, fr. *kataklyzein* to wash down, inundate] **1** : a great flood : DELUGE **2** : a violent and destructive upheaval (as an earthquake) of nature **3** : a violent social or political upheaval **syn** see DISASTER — **cat·a·clys·mal** \‚kat-ə-'kliz-məl\ *adj* — **cat·a·clys·mic** \-'kliz-mik\ *adj*

cat·a·comb \'kat-ə-‚kōm\ *n* : an underground place of burial; *esp* : one that has passages with hollowed places in the sides for tombs

ca·tad·ro·mous \kə-'tad-rə-məs\ *adj* [Gk *katadrom-*, *katadramein* to run down] : living in fresh water and going to the sea to spawn

cat·a·falque \'kat-ə-‚falk, -‚fó(l)k\ *n* [It *catafalco*] : an ornamental structure sometimes used in solemn funerals to hold the body

Cat·a·lan \'kat-ə-lən, -‚an\ *n* **1** : a native or inhabitant of Catalonia **2** : the Romance language of Catalonia, Valencia, and the Balearic islands — **Catalan** *adj*

cat·a·lase \'kat-ə-‚lās, -‚āz\ *n* : an enzyme that catalyzes the decomposition of hydrogen peroxide into water and oxygen and the oxidation by hydrogen peroxide of alcohols to aldehydes

cat·a·lep·sy \'kat-ə-‚lep-sē\ *n* [Gk *katalēpsis*, fr. *kataleb-*, *katalambanein* to seize, fr. *kata-* cata- + *lambanein* to take] : a condition of suspended animation and loss of voluntary motion in which the limbs hold any position they are placed in — **cat·a·lep·tic** \‚kat-ə-'lep-tik\ *adj or n*

¹cat·a·log *or* **cat·a·logue** \'kat-ə-‚óg\ *n* [Gk *katalogos*, fr. *katalegein* to list, fr. *kata-* cata- + *legein* to gather, speak] : a list of names, titles, or articles arranged according to a system; *also* : a book or a file containing such a list or the items listed

²catalog *or* **catalogue** *vt* **1** : to make a catalog of **2** : to enter in a catalog; *esp* : to classify (library contents) descriptively — **cat·a·log·er** *or* **cat·a·logu·er** *n*

ca·tal·pa \kə-'tal-pə, -'tól-\ *n* [Creek *kutuhlpa*] : a small tree of America and Asia with broad oval leaves, flowers brightly striped inside and spotted outside, and long narrow pods

ca·tal·y·sis \kə-'tal-ə-səs\ *n* [Gk *katalysis* dissolution, fr. *katalyein* to dissolve, fr. *kata-* cata- + *lyein* to loosen, dissolve] : the change and esp. increase in the rate of a chemical reaction brought about by a catalyst — **cat·a·lyt·ic** \‚kat-ə-'lit-ik\ *adj* — **cat·a·lyt·i·cal·ly** \-'it-i-k(ə-)lē\ *adv*

cat·a·lyst \'kat-ə-ləst\ *n* : a substance that changes the rate of a chemical reaction but is itself unchanged at the end of the process; *esp* : such a substance that speeds up a reaction or enables it to proceed under milder conditions than otherwise possible

cat·a·lyze \'kat-ə-‚līz\ *vt* : to bring about or produce by chemical catalysis — **cat·a·lyz·er** *n*

cat·a·ma·ran \‚kat-ə-mə-'ran\ *n* [Tamil *kattumaram*, fr. *kattu* to tie + *maram* tree] **1** : a raft propelled by paddles or sails **2** : a boat with twin hulls

cat·a·mount \'kat-ə-‚maunt\ *n* [ME *cat of the mountain*] : any of various wild cats: as **a** : COUGAR **b** : LYNX

ə abut; ᵊ kitten; ər further; a back; ā bake; ä cot, cart; au̇ out; ch chin; e less; ē easy; g gift; i trip; ī life

¹**cat·a·pult** \'kat-ə-ˌpəlt, -ˌpu̇lt\ *n* [L *catapulta*, fr. Gk *katapaltēs*, fr. *kata-* cata- + *pallein* to hurl] **1 :** an ancient military device for hurling missiles **2 :** a device for launching an airplane at flying speed (as from the deck of a ship)

²**catapult** *vb* **1 :** to throw or launch by or as if by a catapult **2 :** to become catapulted

cat·a·ract \'kat-ə-ˌrakt\ *n* [L *cataracta* waterfall, portcullis, fr. Gk *kataraktēs*, fr. *katarassein* to dash down] **1 :** a clouding of the lens of the eye or of its capsule obstructing the passage of light **2 a :** WATERFALL; *esp* **:** a large one over a precipice **b :** steep rapids in a river **c :** DOWNPOUR, FLOOD — **cat·a·rac·tal** \ˌkat-ə-'rak-tᵊl\ *adj*

ca·tarrh \kə-'tär\ *n* [Gk *katarrhous*, fr. *katarrhein* to flow down + *kata-* cata- + *rhein* to flow] **:** inflammation of a mucous membrane; *esp* **:** one chronically affecting the human nose and air passages — **ca·tarrh·al** \-'tär-əl\ *adj* — **ca·tarrh·al·ly** \-ə-lē\ *adv*

ca·tas·tro·phe \kə-'tas-trə-(ˌ)fē\ *n* [Gk *katastrophē*, fr. *katastrephein* to overturn, fr. *kata-* cata- + *strephein* to turn, twist] **1 :** the final event of the dramatic action esp. of a tragedy **2 :** a momentous tragic event **3 :** a violent and sudden change in a feature of the earth **4 :** utter failure or ruin **:** FIASCO **syn** see DISASTER — **cat·a·stroph·ic** \ˌkat-ə-'sträf-ik\ *adj* — **cat·a·stroph·i·cal·ly** \-'sträf-i-k(ə-)lē\ *adv*

cat·bird \'kat-ˌbərd\ *n* **:** a dark gray American songbird with black cap and reddish under tail coverts

cat·boat \-ˌbōt\ *n* **:** a sailboat with a single mast set far forward and a single large sail extended by a long boom

catboat

cat·call \-ˌkȯl\ *n* **:** a sound like the cry of a cat or a noise made to express disapproval (as at a sports event) — **catcall** *vb*

¹**catch** \'kach, 'kech\ *vb* **caught** \'kȯt\; **catch·ing** [ONF *cachier* to hunt, fr. L *captare* to seek to take, fr. *capt-, capere* to take] **1 a :** to capture or seize something in flight or motion **b :** TRAP, ENSNARE **2 a :** to discover unexpectedly **:** come upon suddenly ⟨*caught* in the act⟩ **b :** to check suddenly or momentarily **3 :** to take hold of **:** SNATCH **4 a :** to get entangled ⟨*catch* a sleeve on a nail⟩ **b :** to engage firmly ⟨this lock will not *catch*⟩ **c :** FASTEN **5 :** to become affected by ⟨*catch* fire⟩ ⟨*catch* pneumonia⟩ **6 :** to take or get momentarily or quickly ⟨*catch* a glimpse of a friend⟩ **7 a :** OVERTAKE **b :** to get aboard in time ⟨*catch* the bus⟩ **8 :** to grasp by the senses or the mind **:** APPREHEND ⟨didn't *catch* what he said⟩ **9 :** to play ball as a catcher

syn CAPTURE, SNARE, TRAP: CATCH implies the simple fact of seizing something in motion or in flight or in hiding; CAPTURE adds an implication of overcoming resistance or difficulty; SNARE and TRAP imply using a device that catches by surprise and holds at the mercy of the captor; SNARE may stress the wiliness of the captor; TRAP may suggest some lack of caution in the victim

— **catch one's breath :** to pause or rest long enough to regain normal breathing

²**catch** *n* **1 :** something caught; *esp* **:** the total quantity caught at one time **2 a :** the act of catching **b :** a game in which a ball is thrown and caught **3 :** something that checks or holds immovable **4 :** one worth catching esp. as a spouse **5 :** a round for three or more voices **6 :** FRAGMENT, SNATCH **7 :** a concealed difficulty

catch·all \'kach-ˌȯl, 'kech-\ *n* **:** something to hold a variety of odds and ends

catch·er \'kach-ər, 'kech-\ *n* **:** one that catches; *esp* **:** a baseball player stationed behind home plate

catch·ing *adj* **1 :** INFECTIOUS, CONTAGIOUS **2 :** ALLURING, CATCHY

catch·ment \'kach-mənt, 'kech-\ *n* **1 :** the action of catching water **2 :** something that catches water

catch·pen·ny \'kach-ˌpen-ē, 'kech-\ *adj* **:** designed esp. to get small sums of money from the ignorant

catch·up \'kech-əp, 'kach-; 'kat-səp\ *var of* CATSUP

catch·word \'kach-ˌwərd, 'kech-\ *n* **1 :** either of the terms to right and left of the head of a page of an alpha-

betical reference work (as a dictionary) indicating the first and last entries on the page **2 :** SLOGAN

catchy \'kach-ē, 'kech-ē\ *adj* **catch·i·er**, **-est** **1 :** likely to attract ⟨*catchy* music⟩ **2 :** apt to entangle one **:** TRICKY ⟨a *catchy* question⟩

cate \'kāt\ *n* **:** a dainty or choice food

cat·e·chet·i·cal \ˌkat-ə-'ket-i-kəl\ *adj* **:** of or relating to instruction in religious doctrine

cat·e·chism \'kat-ə-ˌkiz-əm\ *n* **1 :** a summary of religious doctrine often in the form of questions and answers **2 :** a set of formal questions put as a test — **cat·e·chis·mal** \ˌkat-ə-'kiz-məl\ *adj* — **cat·e·chis·tic** \-'kis-tik\ *adj*

cat·e·chist \'kat-ə-ˌkist, -i-kəst\ *n* **:** one that catechizes

cat·e·chize \'kat-ə-ˌkīz\ *vt* [LL *catechizare*, fr. Gk *katēchein* to teach, lit., to din into, fr. *kata-* cata- + *ēchein* to resound] **1 :** to instruct systematically esp. by questions, answers, and explanations and corrections; *esp* **:** to give religious instruction in this manner **2 :** to question systematically or searchingly — **cat·e·chiz·er** *n*

cat·e·chu·men \ˌkat-ə-'kyü-mən\ *n* [Gk *katēchoumenos*, pres. pass. part. of *katēchein* to catechize] **1 :** a convert to Christianity receiving training in doctrine and discipline before baptism **2 :** one receiving instruction in the basic doctrines of Christianity before admission to communicant membership in a church

cat·e·gor·i·cal \ˌkat-ə-'gȯr-i-kəl, -'gär-\ *also* **cat·e·gor·ic** \-ik\ *adj* [Gk *katēgorikos* characterized by assertion, fr. *katēgoria* assertion] **1 :** being without qualification or reservation **:** ABSOLUTE ⟨a *categorical* denial⟩ **2 :** of, relating to, or constituting a category — **cat·e·gor·i·cal·ly** \-i-k(ə-)lē\ *adv*

cat·e·go·rize \'kat-i-gə-ˌrīz\ *vt* **:** to put into a category **:** CLASSIFY — **cat·e·go·ri·za·tion** \ˌkat-i-gə-rə-'zā-shən\ *n*

cat·e·go·ry \'kat-ə-ˌgȯr-ē, -ˌgȯr-\ *n, pl* **-ries** [Gk *katēgoria* assertion, predication, category, fr. *katēgorein* to accuse, assert, fr. *kata-* cata- + *agora* public assembly] **1 :** one of the divisions or groupings used in a system of classification ⟨"species" and "genus" are botanical and zoological *categories*⟩ **2 :** CLASS, VARIETY, KIND

ca·ter \'kāt-ər\ *vi* [ME *acatour, catour* buyer of provisions, fr. ONF *acater* to buy] **1 :** to provide a supply of food **2 :** to supply what is required or desired esp. by a special group

cat·er·cor·ner \ˌkat-ē-'kȯr-nər, ˌkat-ə-, ˌkit-ē-\ *or* **cat·er·cor·nered** \-nərd\ *adv (or adj)* **:** in a diagonal or oblique position **:** on a diagonal or oblique line

ca·ter·er \'kāt-ər-ər\ *n* **:** one that caters; *esp* **:** one who provides food and service for a social affair — **ca·ter·ess** \'kāt-ə-rəs\ *n*

cat·er·pil·lar \'kat-ə(r)-ˌpil-ər\ *n* [ONF *catepelose*, lit., hairy cat] **:** the long wormlike larva of a butterfly or moth; *also* **:** any of various similar insect larvae (as of a sawfly)

Caterpillar *trademark* — used for a tractor for use on rough or soft ground that travels on two endless belts

cat·er·waul \'kat-ər-ˌwȯl\ *vi* **:** to make the characteristic harsh cry of a rutting cat — **caterwaul** *n*

cat·fish \'kat-ˌfish\ *n* **:** any of numerous usu. stout‑bodied large-headed gluttonous fishes (order Ostariophysi) with long sensory barbels

cat·gut \-ˌgət\ *n* **:** a tough cord made usu. from sheep intestines and used for strings of musical instruments and rackets and for sewing in surgery

ca·thar·sis \kə-'thär-səs\ *n, pl* **-thar·ses** \-'thär-ˌsēz\ [Gk *katharsis*, fr. *kathairein* to purge, fr. *katharos* pure] **1 :** PURGATION **2 :** a purification that brings about spiritual renewal or release from tension

¹**ca·thar·tic** \-'thärt-ik\ *adj* **:** of or relating to catharsis or to a cathartic

²**cathartic** *n* **:** PURGATIVE

cat·head \'kat-ˌhed\ *n* **:** a projecting piece of timber or iron near the bow of a ship to which the anchor is hoisted and secured

¹**ca·the·dral** \kə-'thē-drəl\ *adj* [LL *cathedra* chair, throne, fr. Gk *kathedra*, fr. *kata-* cata- + *hed-, hezesthai* to sit] **1 :** of, relating to, or containing a bishop's throne **2 :** of or relating to a cathedral

²**cathedral** *n* **:** a church that contains a bishop's throne and is the principal church of a diocese

ca·thep·sin \kə-'thep-sən\ *n* **:** a proteinase that functions inside the body cells

cath·e·ter \'kath-ət-ər\ *n* [Gk *kathetēr*, fr. *kathienai* to send down] : a slender tube for insertion (as for medication or removal of contents) into a bodily passage or cavity

cath·ode \'kath-,ōd\ *n* [Gk *kathodos* way down, fr. *kata-* cata- + *hodos* way] **1** : the negative electrode of an electrolytic cell to which the positive ions are attracted — compare ANODE **2** : the positive terminal of a primary cell or of a storage battery that is delivering current **3** : the electron-emitting electrode of an electron tube — **ca·thod·ic** \ka-'thäd-ik\ *adj*

cathode ray *n* **1** : one of the high-speed electrons projected in a stream from the heated cathode of a vacuum tube under the propulsion of a strong electric field **2** : a stream of cathode-ray electrons

cathode–ray tube *n* : a vacuum tube in which cathode rays. in the form of a slender beam are projected upon a fluorescent screen and produce a luminous spot

cath·o·lic \'kath-(ə-)lik\ *adj* [LL *catholicus*, fr. Gk *katholikos*, fr. *kath' holou*, *katholou* on the whole, in general] **1** : COMPREHENSIVE, UNIVERSAL; *esp* : broad in sympathies, tastes, or interests **2** *cap* **a** : of, relating to, or forming the church universal **b** : emphasizing historical continuity from apostolic times of doctrinal and liturgical traditions and of the succession of bishops **c** : of or relating to the church of which the pope is head : Roman Catholic — **ca·thol·i·cal·ly** \kə-'thäl-i-k(ə-)le\ *adv* — **Ca·thol·i·cism** \kə-'thäl-ə-,siz-əm\ *n* — **ca·thol·i·cize** \kə-'thäl-ə-,sīz\ *vb*

Catholic *n* **1** : a person who belongs to the universal Christian church **2** : a member of a Catholic church; *esp* : ROMAN CATHOLIC

cath·o·lic·i·ty \,kath-ə-'lis-ət-ē\ *n* **1** *cap* : the character of being in conformity with a Catholic church **2 a** : liberality of sentiments or views **b** : comprehensive range

cat·ion \'kat-,ī-ən\ *n* [Gk *kation*, neut. of *katiōn*, prp. of *katienai* to go down, fr. *kata-* cata- + *ienai* to go] : the ion in an electrolyzed solution that migrates to the cathode; *also* : a positively charged ion

cat·kin \'kat-kən\ *n* : a flower cluster that is a usu. long ament densely crowded with bracts

cat·like \'kat-,līk\ *adj* : resembling a cat; *esp* : STEALTHY

cat·nap \-,nap\ *n* : a very short light nap — **catnap** *vi*

cat·nip \-,nip\ *n* [*cat* + ME *nep* catnip, fr. OE *nepte*, fr. L *nepeta*] : a common strong-scented mint of which cats are especially fond

cat-o'-nine-tails \,kat-ə-'nīn-,tālz\ *n, pl* **cat-o'-nine-tails** : a whip used in flogging and made of nine knotted cords fastened to a handle

cat's cradle *n* : a game played with a string looped on the fingers in such a way as to resemble a small cradle

cat's-eye \'kats-,ī\ *n* : any of various gems (as a chrysoberyl or a chalcedony) exhibiting opalescent reflections from within suggestive of reflections from the eye of a cat

cat-o'-nine-tails

cat's-paw \'kats-,pȯ\ *n* **1** : a light breeze that ruffles the surface of the water in patches **2** : a person used by another person for his own ends

cat·sup \'kech-əp, 'kach-; 'kat-səp\ *n* [Malay *kĕchap* spiced fish sauce] : a seasoned sauce of puree consistency usu. of tomatoes

cat·tail \'kat-,tāl\ *n* : a tall reedy marsh plant with brown furry spikes of very tiny flowers

cat·ta·lo \'kat-ᵊl-,ō\ *n, pl* **-loes** *or* **-los** : a hybrid between the American buffalo and domestic cattle

cat·tle \'kat-ᵊl\ *n, pl* **cattle** [ME *catel*, fr. ONF, personal property, fr. ML *capitale*, fr. L, neut. of *capitalis* of the head, capital] **1** : domesticated quadrupeds held as property or raised for use; *esp* : bovine animals kept on a farm or ranch **2** : contemptible persons

cat·tle·man \-mən, -,man\ *n* : a man who tends or raises cattle

cat·ty \'kat-ē\ *adj* **cat·ti·er; -est** : resembling or held to resemble a cat; *esp* : slyly spiteful : MALICIOUS — **cat·ti·ly** \'kat-ᵊl-ē\ *adv* — **cat·ti·ness** \'kat-ē-nəs\ *n*

cat·ty-cor·ner *or* **cat·ty-cor·nered** *var of* CATERCORNER

cat·walk \'kat-,wȯk\ *n* : a narrow walk or way (as along a bridge or over or around a large machine or tank)

Cau·ca·sian \kȯ-'kā-zhən, -'kazh-ən\ *adj* **1** : of or re-

lating to the Caucasus or its inhabitants **2 a** : of or relating to the white race of mankind as classified according to physical features **b** : of or relating to the white race as defined by law specif. as composed of persons of European, No. African, or southwest Asian ancestry — **Caucasian** *n* — **Cau·ca·soid** \'kȯ-kə-,sȯid\ *adj or n*

1cau·cus \'kȯ-kəs\ *n* : a closed meeting of members of the same political party or faction usu. to select candidates or decide policy

2caucus *vi* : to meet in caucus

cau·dad \'kȯ-,dad\ *adv* [L *cauda*] : toward the tail or posterior end

cau·dal \'kȯd-ᵊl\ *adj* [L *cauda* tail] **1** : of, relating to, or being a tail — see FIN illustration **2** : situated in or directed toward the hind part of the body — **cau·dal·ly** \-ᵊl-ē\ *adv*

caudal fin *n* : the impaired fin at the posterior end of the body of a fish

cau·date \'kȯ-,dāt\ *also* **cau·dat·ed** \-,dāt-əd\ *adj* : having a tail or a taillike appendage : TAILED

cau·dex \'kȯ-,deks\ *n, pl* **cau·di·ces** \'kȯd-ə-,sēz\ *or* **cau·dex·es** : the woody base of a perennial plant

cau·dil·lo \kau̇-'thē-(y)ō, -'thēl-yō\ *n, pl* **-dil·los** [Sp, fr. LL *capitellum* small head, fr. L, dim. of *capit-, caput* head] : a Spanish or Latin-American military dictator

cau·dle \'kȯd-ᵊl\ *n* : a drink (as for invalids) usu. of warm ale or wine mixed with bread or gruel, eggs, sugar, and spices

caught *past of* CATCH

caul \'kȯl\ *n* [MF *cale*] : an enveloping membrane; *esp* : the large fatty omentum covering the intestines

cauldron *var of* CALDRON

cau·li·flow·er \'kȯ-li-,flau̇(-ə)r\ *n* [modif. of It *cavolfiore*, fr. *cavolo* cabbage (fr. L *caulis* stem, cabbage) + *fiore* flower, fr. L *flor-, flos*] : a garden plant closely related to the cabbage and grown for its compact edible head of usu. white undeveloped flowers

cauliflower ear *n* : an ear deformed from injury and excessive growth of scar tissue

1caulk \'kȯk\ *vt* [ONF *cauquer* to trample, fr. L *calcare*, fr. *calc-, calx* heel] **1** : to stop up and make watertight the seams of by filling with a waterproofing compound or material **2** : to stop up and make tight against leakage — **caulk·er** *n*

2caulk *var of* CALK

caus·al \'kȯ-zəl\ *adj* **1** : expressing or indicating cause : CAUSATIVE **2** : of, relating to, or constituting a cause **3** : involving causation or a cause **4** : arising from a cause — **caus·al·ly** \-zə-lē\ *adv*

cau·sal·i·ty \kȯ-'zal-ət-ē\ *n, pl* **-ties** **1** : a causal quality or agency **2** : the relation between a cause and its effect or between regularly correlated events or phenomena

cau·sa·tion \kȯ-'zā-shən\ *n* **1 a** : the act or process of causing **b** : the act or agency by which an effect is produced **2** : CAUSALITY

caus·a·tive \'kȯ-zət-iv\ *adj* **1** : effective or operating as a cause or agent **2** : expressing causation — **caus·a·tive·ly** *adv*

1cause \'kȯz\ *n* [L *causa*] **1** : something or someone that brings about or effects a result : a person or thing that is the occasion of an action or state **2** : a good or adequate reason ⟨a *cause* for anxiety⟩ **3 a** : a ground of legal action **b** : CASE 5a **c** : a matter or question to be decided **4** : a principle or movement militantly defended or supported — **cause·less** \-ləs\ *adj*

syn REASON, MOTIVE: CAUSE applies to any event, circumstance, or condition that brings about or helps bring about a result ⟨an icy road was the *cause* of the accident⟩ REASON applies to a traceable or explainable cause of a known effect or action ⟨the *reason* he was late was that his car would not start⟩ MOTIVE applies only to the cause of voluntary action ⟨revenge was the killer's chief *motive*⟩

2cause *vt* **1** : to serve as cause or occasion of ⟨fire *caused* the damage⟩ **2** : to effect by command, authority, or force ⟨*caused* all offenders to appear⟩ — **caus·er** *n*

cause cé·lè·bre \,kȯz-sā-'lebrᵊ, ,kȯz-\ *n, pl* **causes cé·lè·bres** *same*\ [F, celebrated case] : a notorious incident or episode

cau·se·rie \,kȯz-(ə-)'rē\ *n* : a short informal composition

cause·way \'kȯz-,wā\ *n* [ME *cauciwey*, fr. *cauci* causeway + *wey* way] : a raised way esp. across wet ground or water

¹**caus·tic** \'kȯ-stik\ *adj* [Gk *kau-, kaus-, kaiein* to burn] **1** : capable of destroying or eating away by chemical action : CORROSIVE **2** : INCISIVE, BITING ⟨*caustic* wit⟩ — **caus·ti·cal·ly** \-sti-k(ə-)lē\ *adv*

²**caustic** *n* : a caustic substance (as caustic soda)

caustic potash *n* : POTASSIUM HYDROXIDE

caustic soda *n* : SODIUM HYDROXIDE

cau·ter·ize \'kȯt-ə-,rīz\ *vb* [Gk *kau-, kaiein* to burn] : to burn with a hot iron or a caustic substance usu. to destroy infected tissue ⟨*cauterize* a wound⟩ — **cau·ter·i·za·tion** \,kȯt-ə-rə-'zā-shən\ *n*

¹**cau·tion** \'kȯ-shən\ *n* [L *caution-, cautio* precaution, fr. *caut-, cavēre* to be on one's guard] **1** : WARNING **2** : prudent forethought to minimize risk

²**caution** *vt* **cau·tioned**; **cau·tion·ing** \'kȯ-sh(ə-)niŋ\ : to advise caution to **syn** see WARN

cau·tion·ary \'kȯ-shə-,ner-ē\ *adj* : serving as or offering a warning ⟨a *cautionary* tale⟩

cau·tious \'kȯ-shəs\ *adj* : marked by or given to caution ⟨a *cautious* reply⟩ ⟨a *cautious* driver⟩ — **cau·tious·ly** *adv* — **cau·tious·ness** *n*

cav·al·cade \,kav-əl-'kād, 'kav-əl-,\ *n* [MF, horseback ride, fr. It *cavalcata*, fr. *cavalcare* to go on horseback, fr. L *caballus* horse] **1 a** : a procession of riders or carriages **b** : a procession of vehicles or ships **2** : a sequence of dramatic scenes : PAGEANT ⟨a *cavalcade* of American history⟩

¹**cav·a·lier** \,kav-ə-'li(ə)r\ *n* [It *cavaliere*, fr. LL *caballarius* horseman, fr. L *caballus* horse] **1** : a gentleman trained in arms and horsemanship **2** : a mounted soldier : KNIGHT **3** *cap* : an adherent of Charles I of England **4** : GALLANT

²**cavalier** *adj* **1** : DEBONAIR **2** : marked by lofty disregard of others' interests or offhand dismissal of important matters : DISDAINFUL **3 a** *cap* : of or relating to the party of Charles I of England in his struggles with the Puritans and Parliament **b** : ARISTOCRATIC — **cav·a·lier·ly** *adv* — **cav·a·lier·ness** *n*

cav·al·ry \'kav-əl-rē\ *n, pl* **-ries** [It *cavalleria*, cavalry, chivalry, fr. *cavaliere* cavalier] **1** : HORSEMEN **2** : a highly mobile army component mounted on horseback or moving in motor vehicles — **cav·al·ry·man** \-rē-mən, -,man\ *n*

¹**cave** \'kāv\ *n* [OF, fr. L *cavus*, adj., hollow] : a hollowed-out place in the earth or in the side of a hill or cliff; *esp* : a large natural underground cavity with an opening to the surface : CAVERN

²**cave** *vb* **1** : to fall or cause to fall in or down esp. from being undermined : COLLAPSE ⟨the retaining wall *caved* in⟩ **2** : to cease to resist : SUBMIT ⟨the defenders *caved* in and surrendered⟩

ca·ve·at \'kā-vē-,at\ *n* [L, let him beware, fr. *cavēre* to be on one's guard] : WARNING

caveat emp·tor \-'em(p)-tər, -,tȯ(ə)r\ *n* [NL, let the buyer beware] : a warning that without a warranty the buyer of goods takes the risk of their quality upon himself

cave–in \'kāv-,in\ *n* **1** : the action of caving in **2** : a place where earth has caved in

cave·man \'kāv-,man\ *n* **1** : one who lives in a cave; *esp* : a man of the Stone Age — called also *cave dweller* **2** : a man who acts with rough or violent directness esp. toward women

cav·ern \'kav-ərn\ *n* [L *caverna*, fr. *cavus* hollow] : an underground chamber often of large or indefinite extent : CAVE

cav·ern·ous \-ər-nəs\ *adj* **1** : having caverns or cavities **2** : constituting or suggesting a cavern **3** : composed largely of vascular spaces and capable of filling with blood to bring about the enlargement of a body part — **cav·ern·ous·ly** *adv*

cav·i·ar *or* **cav·i·are** \'kav-ē-,är\ *n* [obs. It *caviaro*, fr. Turk *havyar*] : processed salted roe of a large fish (as the sturgeon) prepared as an appetizer

cav·il \'kav-əl\ *vb* **-iled** *or* **-illed**; **-il·ing** *or* **-il·ling** \-(ə-)liŋ\ [L *cavillari*] : to raise trivial and frivolous objections : QUIBBLE — **cavil** *n* — **cav·il·er** *or* **cav·il·ler** \-(ə-)lər\ *n*

cav·i·ty \'kav-ət-ē\ *n, pl* **-ties** : an unfilled space within a mass : a hollow place : HOLE ⟨a *cavity* in a tooth⟩

ca·vort \kə-'vȯrt\ *vi* : to bound or frisk about : CAPER, PRANCE

ca·vy \'kā-vē\ *n, pl* **cavies** : any of several short-tailed rough-haired So. American rodents; *esp* : GUINEA PIG

caw \'kȯ\ *vi* : to utter the harsh raucous natural call of the crow or a similar cry — **caw** *n*

cay \'kē, 'kā\ *n* : a small low island or emergent reef of sand or coral : ISLET, KEY

cay·enne pepper \,kī-,en-, ,kā-\ *n* [modif. of Tupi *kyinha*] : a pungent condiment consisting of the ground dried fruits or seeds of hot peppers; *also* : a plant bearing such fruits

cay·man *var of* CAIMAN

Ca·yu·ga \kē-'ü-gə, kā-'(y)ü-\ *n* : a member of an Iroquoian people of western New York

cay·use \'kī-,(y)üs, kī-'\ *n* **1** *cap* : a member of an Indian people of Washington and Oregon **2** : a native range horse of the western U.S.

C clef *n* : a movable clef indicating middle C by its placement on one of the lines of the staff

¹**cease** \'sēs\ *vb* [OF *cesser*, fr. L *cessare* to loiter, delay, freq. of *cedere* to withdraw, cede] : to come or bring to an end : leave off : DISCONTINUE ⟨the storm *ceased* as abruptly as it began⟩ ⟨ordered the soldiers to *cease* firing⟩ **syn** see STOP

²**cease** *n* : CESSATION — usu. used with *without*

cease–fire \'sēs-'fī(ə)r\ *n* **1** : a military order to cease firing **2** : a suspension of active hostilities

cease·less \'sēs-ləs\ *adj* : CONSTANT, CONTINUAL — **cease·less·ly** *adv* — **cease·less·ness** *n*

ce·cro·pia moth \si-,krō-pē-ə-\ *n* [Gk *Kekrops* Cecrops, legendary first king of Athens] : a large silkworm moth that is the largest moth of the eastern U.S.

ce·cum \'sē-kəm\ *n, pl* **ce·ca** \-kə\ [L *caecum*, neut. of *caecus* blind] : a cavity open at one end; *esp* : the blind pouch in which the large intestine begins and into which the ileum opens from one side — **ce·cal** \-kəl\ *adj* — **ce·cal·ly** \-kə-lē\ *adv*

ce·dar \'sēd-ər\ *n* [L *cedrus*, fr. Gk *kedros*] **1 a** : any of a genus of usu. tall trees of the pine family noted for their fragrant durable wood **b** : any of numerous coniferous trees (as some junipers or arborvitaes) resembling the true cedars esp. in the fragrance and durability of their wood **2** : the wood of a cedar

cede \'sēd\ *vt* [L *cedere* to go, withdraw, yield] **1** : to yield or grant typically by treaty **2** : ASSIGN, TRANSFER — **ced·er** *n*

ce·dil·la \si-'dil-ə\ *n* [Sp, the obs. letter ç (actually a medieval form of the letter z), cedilla, fr. dim. of *ceda, zeda* the letter z, fr. L *zeta*, fr. Gk *zēta*] : a mark placed under the letter c (as ç) to show that the c is to be pronounced like s

cei·ba \'sā-bə\ *n* : a massive tropical tree related to the silk-cotton tree that bears large pods containing a silky floss which yields the fiber kapok

ceil·ing \'sē-liŋ\ *n* [ME *celen* to furnish with a ceiling] **1** : the overhead inside lining of a room **2** : something that overhangs like a shelter **3 a** : the greatest height at which an airplane can maintain level flight or operate efficiently **b** : the height above the ground of the base of the lowest layer of clouds when over half of the sky is obscured **4** : an upper usu. prescribed limit ⟨price *ceiling*⟩

cel·an·dine \'sel-ən-,dīn, -,dēn\ *n* **1** : a yellow-flowered biennial herb related to the poppy **2** : a perennial tuber-forming buttercup — called also *lesser celandine*

cel·e·brant \'sel-ə-brənt\ *n* : one who celebrates; *esp* : the priest officiating at the Eucharist

cel·e·brate \'sel-ə-,brāt\ *vb* [L *celebrare* to frequent, celebrate, fr. *celeber* much frequented, famous] **1** : to perform publicly and according to rule or form : officiate at ⟨*celebrate* a mass⟩ ⟨*celebrate* a marriage⟩ **2** : to observe in some special way (as by merrymaking or by staying away from business) ⟨*celebrate* one's birthday with a party⟩ **3** : to praise or make known publicly **4** : to observe a special day or event (as a holiday or anniversary) with festivities **syn** see KEEP — **cel·e·bra·tion** \,sel-ə-'brā-shən\ *n* — **cel·e·bra·tor** \'sel-ə-,brāt-ər\ *n*

cel·e·brat·ed *adj* : widely known and often referred to : RENOWNED **syn** see FAMOUS — **cel·e·brat·ed·ness** *n*

ce·leb·ri·ty \sə-'leb-rət-ē\ *n, pl* **-ties** **1** : the state of being celebrated : FAME **2** : a celebrated person ⟨met government *celebrities*⟩

ce·le·ri·ac \sə-'ler-ē-,ak, -'lir-\ *n* : a celery grown for its thickened edible root

---

j joke; ŋ sing; ō flow; ȯ flaw; ȯi coin; th thin; t͟h this; ü loot; u̇ foot; y yet; yü few; yu̇ furious; zh vision

ce·ler·i·ty \sə-'ler-ət-ē\ *n, pl* **-ties** [L *celeritas,* fr. *celer* swift] **:** rapidity of motion **:** SWIFTNESS
　syn CELERITY, ALACRITY mean quickness of movement or action. CELERITY stresses speed in moving esp. so as to accomplish work ⟨she got dinner ready with remarkable *celerity*⟩ ALACRITY stresses promptness in responding and often suggests readiness or eagerness ⟨the soldiers volunteered with surprising *alacrity*⟩

cel·ery \'sel-(ə-)rē\ *n* [It dial. *seleri,* pl. of *selero,* modif. of Gk *selinon*] **:** a European herb of the carrot family widely grown for its thick edible leafstalks

ce·les·ta \sə-'les-tə\ *n* **:** a keyboard instrument with hammers that strike steel plates producing a tone similar to that of a glockenspiel

ce·les·tial \sə-'les-chəl\ *adj* [L *caelestis,* fr. *caelum* sky, heaven] **1 :** of, relating to, or suggesting the spiritual heaven **:** HEAVENLY ⟨*celestial* beings⟩ **2 :** of or relating to the sky or heavens ⟨a star is a *celestial* body⟩ — **ce·les·tial·ly** \-chə-lē\ *adv*

celestial navigation *n* **:** navigation by observation of the positions of celestial bodies

celestial sphere *n* **:** an imaginary sphere of infinite radius against which the celestial bodies appear to be projected

ce·li·ac \'sē-lē-,ak\ *var of* COELIAC

celiac disease *n* **:** a chronic nutritional disorder in young children in which fats are not normally digested and used

cel·i·ba·cy \'sel-ə-bə-sē\ *n* **1 :** the state of not being married **2 :** the single life esp. of one bound by vow not to marry

cel·i·bate \'sel-ə-bət\ *n* [L *caelibatus,* fr. *caelib-, caelebs* unmarried] **:** one who lives in celibacy — **celibate** *adj*

cell \'sel\ *n* [L *cella* small room] **1 a :** a one-room dwelling occupied by a solitary person (as a hermit) **b :** a single room (as in a convent or prison) usu. for one person **2 :** a small compartment (as in a honeycomb), receptacle (as for a polyp), cavity (as in a plant ovary), or bounded space (as in an insect wing) **3 :** a tiny mass of protoplasm that includes a nucleus and is enclosed by a semipermeable membrane and that is the fundamental unit of living matter and the basic structural element of plant and animal tissues **4 a :** a receptacle (as a jar) containing electrodes and an electrolyte either for generating electricity by chemical action or for use in electrolysis **b :** a single unit in a device for converting radiant energy into electrical energy or for varying the intensity of an electric current in accordance with radiation **5 :** the basic and usu. smallest unit of an organization or movement; *esp* **:** the primary unit of a Communist organization — **celled** \'seld\ *adj*

cel·lar \'sel-ər\ *n* [L *cellarium* storeroom, fr. *cella* room] **1 :** BASEMENT **2 :** a stock of wines

cel·lar·age \'sel-ə-rij\ *n* **1 :** a cellar esp. for storage **2 :** charge for storage in a cellar

cel·list \'chel-əst\ *n* **:** one that plays the cello

cell membrane *n* **1 :** PLASMA MEMBRANE **2 :** CELL WALL

cel·lo \'chel-ō\ *n, pl* **cellos** [short for *violoncello*] **:** the bass member of the violin family tuned an octave below the viola

cel·loi·din \se-'lòid-ᵊn\ *n* **:** a purified pyroxylin used chiefly in microscopy

cel·lo·phane \'sel-ə-,fān\ *n* **:** a thin transparent usu. waterproof material made from cellulose and used esp. as a wrapping

cell plate *n* **:** the rudiment of a new cell wall that forms between dividing plant cells

cell sap *n* **:** the liquid consisting of a watery solution of nutrients and wastes that fills the vacuole of most plant cells

cell theory *n* **:** a generally accepted theory in biology according to which all living things are or are made up of cells each of which has come from a previously existing cell

cel·lu·lar \'sel-yə-lər\ *adj* **1 :** of, relating to, or consisting of cells **2 :** containing cavities **:** having a porous texture — **cel·lu·lar·i·ty** \,sel-yə-'lar-ət-ē\ *n* — **cel·lu·lar·ly** \'sel-yə-lər-lē\ *adv*

cellular respiration *n* **1 :** INTERNAL RESPIRATION **2 :** the metabolic oxidations of the cell

cel·lu·lase \'sel-yə-,lās\ *n* **:** an enzyme that hydrolyzes cellulose

cel·lu·loid \'sel-(y)ə-,lòid\ *n* **:** motion-picture film

Cel·lu·loid *trademark* — used for a tough flammable plastic composed essentially of cellulose nitrate and camphor

cel·lu·lose \'sel-yə-,lōs\ *n* **:** a complex carbohydrate constituting the chief part of the cell walls of plants, yielding many fibrous products, and being commonly obtained as a white fibrous substance from vegetable matter (as wood or cotton) that is used in making various products (as rayon and cellophane)

cellulose acetate *n* **:** any of several compounds formed esp. by the action of acetic acid, anhydride of acetic acid, and sulfuric acid on cellulose and used for making textile fibers, packaging sheets, photographic films, and varnishes

cellulose nitrate *n* **:** a compound formed by the action of nitric acid on cellulose in the presence of sulfuric acid and used for making explosives, plastics, rayon, and varnishes

cel·lu·los·ic \,sel-yə-'lō-sik\ *adj* **:** of, relating to, or made from cellulose ⟨*cellulosic* fibers⟩ — **cellulosic** *n*

cell wall *n* **:** the firm nonliving and usu. chiefly cellulose wall that encloses and supports most plant cells

Cel·si·us \'sel-sē-əs, 'sel-shəs\ *adj* [after Anders *Celsius* d1744 Swedish astronomer] **:** CENTIGRADE ⟨10° *Celsius*⟩

Celt \'selt, 'kelt\ *n* **1 :** a member of a division of the early Indo-European peoples distributed from the British Isles and Spain to Asia Minor **2 :** a modern Gael, Highland Scot, Irishman, Welshman, Cornishman, or Breton

¹Celt·ic \'sel-tik, 'kel-\ *adj* **:** of, relating to, or characteristic of the Celts or their languages

²Celtic *n* **:** a group of languages now confined to Brittany, Wales, western Ireland, and the Scottish Highlands

celt·tuce \'sel-təs\ *n* **:** a vegetable related to lettuce but grown for its leafstalks that combine the flavor of celery and lettuce

cem·ba·lo \'chem-bə-,lō\ *n, pl* **-los** *or* **-li** \-,lē\ **:** HARPSICHORD

¹ce·ment \si-'ment\ *n* [L *caementum* stone chips used in making mortar, fr. *caedere* to cut] **1 :** a powder of alumina, silica, lime, iron oxide, and magnesia burned together in a kiln and finely pulverized and used as an ingredient of mortar and concrete; *also* **:** CONCRETE, MORTAR **2 :** a binding element or agency: as **a :** a substance to make objects adhere to each other **b :** a notion or feeling serving to unite firmly **3 :** CEMENTUM

²cement *vb* **1 :** to unite by or as if by cement **2 :** to overlay with concrete — **ce·ment·er** *n*

ce·men·ta·tion \,sē-,men-'tā-shən\ *n* **:** the act or process of cementing

ce·ment·ite \si-'ment-,īt\ *n* **:** a hard brittle carbide of iron Fe_3C in steel, cast iron, and iron-carbon alloys

ce·men·tum \si-'ment-əm\ *n* **:** a specialized external bony layer of the part of a tooth normally within the gum

cem·e·tery \'sem-ə-,ter-ē\ *n, pl* **-ter·ies** [Gk *koimētērion,* lit., sleeping place, fr. *koiman* to put to sleep; akin to E *home*] **:** a burial ground

cen- *or* **ceno-** *comb form* [Gk *kainos*] **:** new **:** recent ⟨*Cenozoic*⟩

-cene \,sēn\ *adj comb form* **:** recent — in names of geologic periods ⟨*Eocene*⟩

cen·o·bite \'sen-ə-,bīt\ *n* [LL *coenobita,* fr. *coenobium* monastery, fr. LGk *koinobion,* fr. Gk *koinos* common + *bios* life] **:** a member of a religious group living together — **cen·o·bit·ic** \,sen-ə-'bit-ik\ *or* **cen·o·bit·i·cal** \-'bit-i-kəl\ *adj*

cen·o·taph \'sen-ə-,taf\ *n* [Gk *kenotaphion,* fr. *kenos* empty + *taphos* tomb] **:** a tomb or a monument erected in honor of a person whose body is elsewhere

Ce·no·zo·ic \,sē-nə-'zō-ik, ,sen-ə-\ *n* **:** the most recent of the five eras of geological history that extends to the present time and is marked by a rapid evolution of mammals and birds and of grasses, shrubs, and various flowering plants; *also* **:** the corresponding system of rocks — see GEOLOGIC TIME table — **Cenozoic** *adj*

cen·ser \'sen(t)-sər\ *n* **:** a vessel for burning incense; *esp* **:** a covered incense burner swung on chains in a religious ritual

¹cen·sor \'sen(t)-sər\ *n* [L, fr. *censēre* to assess, tax] **1 :** one of two magistrates of ancient Rome acting as census takers,

censer

assessors, and inspectors of morals and conduct **2** : an official who examines publications or communications for objectionable matter **3** *archaic* : a faultfinding critic —
cen·so·ri·al \sen-'sōr-ē-əl, -'sòr-\ *adj*
²**censor** *vt* **cen·sored**; **cen·sor·ing** \'sen(t)s-(ə-)riŋ\ : to examine in order to suppress or delete anything thought to be harmful or dangerous
syn CENSOR, CENSURE are not actually synonymous but are easily confused. CENSOR denotes examining officially in order to suppress or alter anything thought morally or politically objectionable; CENSURE denotes criticizing adversely and usu. publicly or officially
cen·so·ri·ous \sen-'sōr-ē-əs, -'sòr-\ *adj* : marked by or given to censure : sternly critical — **cen·so·ri·ous·ly** *adv* — **cen·so·ri·ous·ness** *n*
cen·sor·ship \'sen(t)-sər-ˌship\ *n* : the institution, system, or practice of censoring or censors
¹**cen·sure** \'sen-chər\ *n* **1** : the act of blaming or condemning sternly **2** : an official reprimand
²**censure** *vt* **cen·sured**; **cen·sur·ing** \'sench-(ə-)riŋ\ : to find fault with : criticize as blameworthy **syn** see BLAME, CENSOR — **cen·sur·a·ble** \'sench-(ə-)rə-bəl\ *adj* — **cen·sur·er** \'sen-chər-ər\ *n*
cen·sus \'sen(t)-səs\ *n* [L, fr. *censēre* to tax, rate, estimate] **1** : a periodic governmental counting of population and usu. gathering of related statistics **2** : COUNT, TALLY
cent \'sent\ *n* [L *centum* hundred; akin to E *hundred*] **1** : a unit of value equal to ¹⁄₁₀₀ part of a basic monetary unit (as in the U.S. and Canada ¹⁄₁₀₀ dollar) **2** : a coin, token, or note representing one cent
cent·are \'sen-ˌta(ə)r, -ˌte(ə)r, -ˌtär\ *or* **cen·ti·are** \'sent-ē-ˌa(ə)r, -ˌe(ə)r, -ˌär\ *n* — see METRIC SYSTEM table
cen·taur \'sen-ˌtòr\ *n* : one of a race in Greek mythology fabled to be half man and half horse
¹**cen·ta·vo** \sen-'täv-ō\ *n, pl* **-vos** **1** : a unit of value equal to ¹⁄₁₀₀ part of any of several basic monetary units (as the peso or rupee) **2** : a coin representing one centavo
²**cen·ta·vo** \-'täv-ü, -'täv-ō\ *n, pl* **-vos** **1** : a unit of value equal to ¹⁄₁₀₀ cruzeiro or escudo **2** : a coin representing one centavo
cen·te·nar·i·an \ˌsent-ᵊn-'er-ē-ən\ *n* : one that is 100 years old or older — **centenarian** *adj*
cen·ten·a·ry \sen-'ten-ə-rē, 'sent-ᵊn-ˌer-ē\ *adj or n* [L *centenarius* of a hundred, fr. *centeni* a hundred each, fr. *centum* hundred] : CENTENNIAL
cen·ten·ni·al \sen-'ten-ē-əl\ *n* [L *centum* + E *-ennial* (as in *biennial*)] : a 100th anniversary or its celebration — **centennial** *adj* — **cen·ten·ni·al·ly** \-ē-ə-lē\ *adv*
¹**cen·ter** \'sent-ər\ *n* [L *centrum*, fr. Gk *kentron*, lit., sharp point] **1** : the point at an equal distance or at the average distance from the exterior points of a geometric figure (as a circle or sphere) **2 a** : a place in or around which an activity concentrates or from which something originates ⟨*center* of government⟩ **b** : a group of nerve cells having a common function ⟨respiratory *center*⟩ **c** : a region of concentrated population **3 a** : a middle part (as of an army or stage) **b** *often cap* (1) : individuals holding moderate political views esp. between those of conservatives and liberals (2) : the views of such individuals **4** : a player occupying a middle position on a team; *esp* : a football lineman who lines up between the guards and snaps the ball **5 a** : one of two tapered rods which support work in a lathe or grinding machine and about or with which the work revolves **b** : a conical recess in the end of work (as a shaft) for receiving such a center
²**center** *vb* **cen·tered**; **cen·ter·ing** \'sent-ə-riŋ, 'sen-triŋ\ **1** : to place or fix at or around a center or central area or position ⟨*center* a title on the page⟩ **2** : to gather to a center : CONCENTRATE ⟨the discussion *centered* on finances⟩ **3** : to adjust (as lenses) so that the axes coincide **4** : to have a center ⟨the search *centered* on one building⟩ **5 a** : to pass (a ball or puck) from either side to or toward the middle of a playing area **b** : to snap (the ball) in football
cen·ter·board \'sent-ər-ˌbōrd, -ˌbòrd\ *n* : a retractable keel used esp. in sailboats
center field *n* **1** : the part of the baseball outfield between right and left field **2** : the position of the player defending center field — **center fielder** *n*
center of gravity : the point at which the entire weight of

a body may be considered as concentrated so that if supported at this point the body would remain in equilibrium in any position
cen·ter·piece \'sent-ər-ˌpēs\ *n* : an object occupying a central position; *esp* : an adornment in the center of a table
cen·tes·i·mal \sen-'tes-ə-məl\ *adj* [L *centesimus* hundredth, fr. *centum* hundred] : marked by or relating to division into hundredths
¹**cen·tes·i·mo** \chen-'tez-ə-mō\ *n, pl* **-mi** \-(ˌ)mē\ **1** : a unit of value equal to ¹⁄₁₀₀ lira **2** : a coin representing one centesimo
²**cen·tes·i·mo** \sen-'tes-ə-ˌmō\ *n, pl* **-mi** **1** : a unit of value equal to ¹⁄₁₀₀ part of any of several basic monetary units (as the balboa) **2** : a coin representing one centesimo
centi- *comb form* [F, fr. L *centum* hundred] : hundredth part ⟨*centimeter*⟩ — used in terms of the metric system
cen·ti·grade \'sent-ə-ˌgrād, 'sänt-\ *adj* [F, fr. L *centum* hundred + *gradus* step, degree] : relating to, conforming to, or having a thermometer scale on which the interval between the freezing point and the boiling point of water is divided into 100 degrees with 0° representing the freezing point and 100° the boiling point — abbr. *C*
cen·ti·gram \-ˌgram\ *n* — see METRIC SYSTEM table
cen·ti·li·ter \-ˌlēt-ər\ *n* — see METRIC SYSTEM table
cen·time \'sän-ˌtēm, 'sen-\ *n* **1** : a unit of value equal to ¹⁄₁₀₀ franc **2** : a coin representing one centime
cen·ti·me·ter \'sent-ə-ˌmēt-ər, 'sänt-\ *n* — see MEASURE table, METRIC SYSTEM table
centimeter–gram–second *adj* : of, relating to, or being a system of units based upon the centimeter as the unit of length, the gram as the unit of mass, and the second as the unit of time — abbr. *cgs*
cen·ti·mo \'sent-ə-ˌmō\ *n, pl* **-mos** **1** : a unit of value equal to ¹⁄₁₀₀ part of any of several basic monetary units (as the peseta) **2** : a coin representing one centimo
cen·ti·pede \'sent-ə-ˌpēd\ *n* [L *centipeda*, fr. *centum* hundred + *ped-, pes* foot] : any of a class (Chilopoda) of long flattened many-segmented arthropods with each segment bearing one pair of legs of which the foremost pair is modified into poison fangs — compare MILLIPEDE
centr- *or* **centro-** *comb form* [Gk *kentron*] : center ⟨*centroid*⟩
¹**cen·tral** \'sen-trəl\ *adj* **1** : containing or constituting a center **2** : ESSENTIAL, PRINCIPAL **3** : situated at, in, or near the center **4** : controlling or directing local or branch activities **5** : holding to a middle between extremes : MODERATE **6** : of, relating to, or comprising the brain and spinal cord; *also* : originating within the central nervous system ⟨*central* deafness⟩ — **cen·tral·i·ty** \sen-'tral-ət-ē\ *n* — **cen·tral·ly** \'sen-trə-lē\ *adv*
²**central** *n* : a telephone exchange or operator
central angle *n* : an angle with a vertex at the center of a circle and with sides that are radii of the circle
central committee *n* : a large central executive body of a Communist party that is elected to function between party congresses and that elects in turn from its own membership a powerful executive presidium
cen·tral·ism \'sen-trə-ˌliz-əm\ *n* : the concentration of power and control in the central authority esp. of a nation — compare FEDERALISM — **cen·tral·ist** \-ləst\ *n or adj* — **cen·tral·is·tic** \ˌsen-trə-'lis-tik\ *adj*
cen·tral·ize \'sen-trə-ˌlīz\ *vt* : to concentrate (as authority) in a center or central organization — **cen·tral·i·za·tion** \ˌsen-trə-lə-'zā-shən\ *n* — **cen·tral·iz·er** \'sen-trə-ˌlīz-ər\ *n*
Central Powers *n* : a coalition of nations in World War I consisting of Germany and Austria-Hungary and their allies Bulgaria and Turkey
Central standard time *n* : the time of the 6th time zone west of Greenwich that includes the central U.S.
cen·tre \'sent-ər\ *chiefly Brit var of* CENTER
cen·tric \'sen-trik\ *adj* : concentrated about or directed to a center — **cen·tri·cal·ly** \-tri-k(ə-)lē\ *adv* — **cen·tric·i·ty** \sen-'tris-ət-ē\ *n*
-cen·tric \'sen-trik\ *adj comb form* [L *centrum* center] : having (such) a center or (such or so many) centers ⟨*polycentric*⟩ : having (something specified) as its center ⟨*heliocentric*⟩
¹**cen·trif·u·gal** \sen-'trif-yə-gəl, -'trif-i-gəl\ *adj* [L *centrum* center + *fugere* to flee] **1** : proceeding or acting

in a direction away from a center or axis **2 :** using or acting by centrifugal force ⟨a *centrifugal* pump⟩ — **cen·trif·u·gal·ly** \-gə-lē\ *adv*

²centrifugal *n* **:** a centrifugal machine or a drum in such a machine

centrifugal force *n* **:** the force that tends to impel a thing or parts of a thing outward from a center of rotation

¹cen·tri·fuge \'sen-trə-ˌfyüj, 'sän-\ *n* **:** a machine using centrifugal force for separating substances of different densities, for removing moisture, or for simulating gravitational effects — compare SEPARATOR

²centrifuge *vt* **:** to subject to centrifugal action esp. in a centrifuge — **cen·trif·u·ga·tion** \(ˌ)sen-ˌtrif-(y)ə-'gā-shən, (ˌ)sän-\ *n*

cen·tri·ole \'sen-trē-ˌōl\ *n* **1 :** a minute body forming the center of a centrosome **2 :** CENTROSOME

cen·trip·e·tal \sen-'trip-ət-ᵊl\ *adj* [L *centrum* center + *petere* to seek] **:** proceeding or acting in a direction toward a center or axis — **cen·trip·e·tal·ly** \-ᵊl-ē\ *adv*

centripetal force *n* **:** the force that tends to impel a thing or parts of a thing inward toward a center of rotation

cen·troid \'sen-ˌtroid\ *n* **:** the point of intersection of the medians of a triangle

cen·tro·mere \'sen-trə-ˌmi(ə)r\ *n* **:** the point on a chromosome by which it appears to attach to the spindle in mitosis — **cen·tro·mer·ic** \ˌsen-trə-'mer-ik, -'mi(ə)r-\ *adj*

cen·tro·some \'sen-trə-ˌsōm\ *n* **:** a minute body in the cell cytoplasm which divides at the beginning of mitosis and from which the spindle appears to rise — **cen·tro·so·mic** \ˌsen-trə-'sō-mik\ *adj*

cen·trum \'sen-trəm\ *n, pl* **centrums** *or* **cen·tra** \-trə\ **:** the body of a vertebra

cen·tu·ri·on \sen-'t(y)ur-ē-ən\ *n* **:** an officer commanding a Roman century

cen·tu·ry \'sench-(ə-)rē\ *n, pl* **-ries** [L *centuria*, fr. *centum* hundred] **1 :** a subdivision of the Roman legion **2 :** a group, sequence, or series of 100 like things **3 :** a Roman voting unit based on property qualifications **4 :** a period of 100 years; *esp* **:** one of the 100-year divisions of the Christian era or of the preceding period

century plant *n* **:** a Mexican agave maturing and flowering only once in many years and then dying

ceorl \'chā-ˌorl\ *n* [OE] **:** a freeman of the lowest rank in Anglo-Saxon England

cephal- *or* **cephalo-** *comb form* [Gk *kephalē*] **:** head ⟨*cephal*ad⟩

ce·phal·ic \sə-'fal-ik\ *adj* **1 :** of or relating to the head **2 :** directed toward or situated on or in or near the head — **ce·phal·i·cal·ly** \-i-k(ə-)lē\ *adv*

cephalic index *n* **:** the ratio multiplied by 100 of the maximum breadth of the head to its maximum length

ceph·a·lo·pod \'sef-ə-lə-ˌpäd\ *n* **:** any of a class (Cephalopoda) of mollusks including the squids, cuttlefishes, and octopuses having a group of muscular sucker-bearing arms, highly developed eyes, and usu. a bag of inky fluid which they can eject — **cephalopod** *adj* — **ceph·a·lop·o·dan** \ˌsef-ə-'läp-əd-ən\ *adj or n*

ceph·a·lo·tho·rax \ˌsef-ə-lō-'thō(ə)r-ˌaks, -'thò(ə)r-\ *n* **:** a united head and thorax (as of a spider or crustacean) — **ceph·a·lo·tho·rac·ic** \-thə-'ras-ik\ *adj*

Ce·phe·id \'sē-fē-əd\ *n* **:** one of a class of pulsating stars whose light variations are very regular

Ce·pheus \'sē-ˌfyüs, -fē-əs\ *n* [Gk *Kēpheus*] **:** a constellation between Cygnus and the north pole

ce·ra·ceous \sə-'rā-shəs\ *adj* **:** resembling wax

¹ce·ram·ic \sə-'ram-ik\ *adj* [Gk *keramos* pottery] **:** of or relating to a product (as earthenware, porcelain, or brick) made essentially from a nonmetallic mineral by firing at high temperatures

²ceramic *n* **1** *pl* **:** the art of making ceramic articles **2 :** a product of ceramic manufacture

ce·ram·ist \sə-'ram-əst\ *or* **ce·ram·i·cist** \-'ram-ə-səst\ *n* **:** one who engages in ceramics

Cer·ber·us \'sər-b(ə-)rəs\ *n* **:** a 3-headed dog held in classical mythology to guard the entrance to Hades

cer·car·ia \(ˌ)sər-'kar-ē-ə, -'ker-\ *n, pl* **-i·ae** \-ē-ˌē\ *also* **-i·as** [Gk *kerkos* tail] **:** a usu. tadpole-shaped larval trematode worm produced in a molluscan host by a redia — **cer·car·i·al** \-ē-əl\ *adj*

cer·cus \'sər-kəs\ *n, pl* **cer·ci** \'sər-ˌsī\ **:** a many-jointed posterior appendage of an insect

¹ce·re·al \'sir-ē-əl\ *adj* [L *cerealis*, lit., of Ceres] **:** relating to grain or to the plants that produce it; *also* **:** made of grain

²cereal *n* **1 :** a plant (as a grass) yielding farinaceous grain suitable for food; *also* **:** its grain **2 :** a prepared foodstuff of grain

cer·e·bel·lum \ˌser-ə-'bel-əm\ *n, pl* **-bel·lums** *or* **-bel·la** \-'bel-ə\ [ML, fr. L, dim. of *cerebrum*] **:** a large part of the brain esp. concerned with the coordination of muscles and the maintenance of bodily equilibrium and situated in front of and above the medulla which it partly overlaps — **cer·e·bel·lar** \-'bel-ər\ *adj*

ce·re·bral \sə-'rē-brəl, 'ser-ə-\ *adj* **1 a :** of or relating to the brain or the intellect **b :** of, relating to, or being the cerebrum **2 :** appealing to the intellect ⟨*cerebral* drama⟩ — **ce·re·bral·ly** \-brə-lē\ *adv*

cerebral accident *n* **:** a sudden damaging occurrence (as of hemorrhage) within the cerebrum — compare APOPLEXY

cerebral hemisphere *n* **:** either of the two hollow convoluted lateral halves of the cerebrum

cerebral palsy *n* **:** a disability resulting from damage to the brain usu. before or during birth and outwardly manifested by muscular incoordination and speech disturbances

cer·e·brate \'ser-ə-ˌbrāt\ *vi* see THINK — **cer·e·bra·tion** \ˌser-ə-'brā-shən\ *n*

ce·re·bro·spi·nal \sə-ˌrē-brō-'spīn-ᵊl, ˌser-ə-brō-\ *adj* **:** of or relating to the brain and spinal cord or to these together with the cranial and spinal nerves that innervate voluntary muscles

cerebrospinal fluid *n* **:** a liquid comparable to serum that occupies the cavities of the brain and spinal cord and the space between these and the meninges

ce·re·brum \sə-'rē-brəm, 'ser-ə-brəm\ *n, pl* **-brums** *or* **-bra** \-brə\ [L] **1 :** BRAIN 1a **2 :** an enlarged anterior or upper part of the brain; *esp* **:** the expanded anterior portion of the brain that consists of cerebral hemispheres and connecting structures and is held to be the seat of conscious mental processes — called also *tel·en·ceph·a·lon* \ˌtel-ˌen-'sef-ə-ˌlän\

cere·cloth \'si(ə)r-ˌklòth\ *n* [L *cera* wax] **:** cloth treated with melted wax or gummy matter and formerly used esp. for wrapping a dead body

cer·e·ment \'ser-ə-mənt, 'si(ə)r-mənt\ *n* **:** a shroud for the dead; *esp* **:** CERECLOTH — usu. used in pl.

¹cer·e·mo·ni·al \ˌser-ə-'mō-nē-əl\ *adj* **:** of, relating to, or forming a ceremony — **cer·e·mo·ni·al·ism** \-nē-ə-ˌliz-əm\ *n* — **cer·e·mo·ni·al·ist** \-ləst\ *n* — **cer·e·mo·ni·al·ly** \-nē-ə-lē\ *adv* — **cer·e·mo·ni·al·ness** *n*

syn CEREMONIOUS: CEREMONIAL applies to things that are themselves ceremonies or an essential part of them ⟨*ceremonial* offering⟩ ⟨*ceremonial* gown⟩ CEREMONIOUS applies to a person careful to observe formalities or to acts performed elaborately or pompously ⟨took *ceremonious* leave⟩

²ceremonial *n* **:** a ceremonial act, action, or system

cer·e·mo·ni·ous \ˌser-ə-'mō-nē-əs\ *adj* **1 :** of, relating to, or constituting a ceremony **2 :** devoted to forms and ceremony **:** PUNCTILIOUS **3 :** according to formal usage or prescribed procedures **syn** see CEREMONIAL — **cer·e·mo·ni·ous·ly** *adv* — **cer·e·mo·ni·ous·ness** *n*

cer·e·mo·ny \'ser-ə-ˌmō-nē\ *n, pl* **-nies** [L *caerimonia*] **1 :** a formal act or series of acts prescribed by ritual or custom ⟨graduation *ceremonies*⟩ **2 :** a conventional act of politeness or etiquette ⟨went through the *ceremony* of introductions⟩ **3 :** the social behavior required by strict etiquette **:** FORMALITY ⟨dined without *ceremony*⟩

Ce·res \'si(ə)r-(ˌ)ēz\ *n* **1 :** the Roman goddess of agriculture **2 :** the largest asteroid and the one first discovered

ce·re·us \'sir-ē-əs\ *n* **:** any of various cacti of the western U.S. and tropical America often with showy flowers

ce·rise \sə-'rēs, -'rēz\ *n* [F, lit., cherry] **:** a moderate red

ce·ri·um \'sir-ē-əm\ *n* **:** a malleable ductile metallic element — see ELEMENT table

cer·met \'sər-ˌmet\ *n* **:** a strong alloy of a heat-resistant compound (as carbide of titanium) and a metal (as nickel) used esp. for turbine blades — called also *ceramal*

cer·nu·ous \'sər-nyə-wəs\ *adj* **:** NODDING, PENDULOUS

cer·tain \'sərt-ᵊn\ *adj* [OF, fr. L *certus*, fr. pp. of *cernere* to sift, decide] **1 a :** FIXED, SETTLED **b :** proved to be true

2 : implied as being specific but not named **:** PARTICULAR **3 a :** DEPENDABLE, RELIABLE **b :** INDISPUTABLE **4 a :** IN-EVITABLE **b :** incapable of failing **:** DESTINED **5 :** assured in mind or action **syn** see SURE — **cer·tain·ly** adv

cer·tain·ty \-tē\ n, pl **-ties 1 :** something that is certain **2 :** the quality or state of being certain

syn CERTAINTY, CERTITUDE, CONVICTION mean a state of being free from doubt. CERTAINTY and CERTITUDE are frequently interchangeable but CERTAINTY may stress objective proof or evidence supporting a belief ⟨scientific *certainty*⟩ CERTITUDE stressing rather the strength of inner belief in something not needing or not capable of proof; CONVICTION applies esp. to a strong individual belief concerned with moral or spiritual rather than merely factual matters

¹**cer·tif·i·cate** \(ˌ)sər-ˈtif-i-kət\ n **1 :** a document containing a certified statement esp. as to the truth of something; *esp* **:** one certifying that a person has fulfilled the requirements of a school or profession ⟨teaching *certificate*⟩ **2 :** a document evidencing ownership or debt ⟨stock *certificate*⟩

²**cer·tif·i·cate** \-ˈtif-ə-ˌkāt\ vt **:** to testify to, furnish with, or authorize by a certificate — **cer·tif·i·ca·to·ry** \-ˈtif-i-kə-ˌtōr-ē, -ˌtȯr-\ adj

cer·ti·fi·ca·tion \ˌsərt-ə-fə-ˈkā-shən\ n **1 :** the act of certifying **:** the state of being certified **2 :** a certified statement

certified check n **:** a check certified to be good by the bank upon which it is drawn

certified mail n **:** first class mail for which proof of delivery is secured but no indemnity value is claimed

certified milk n **:** milk of high quality produced under the rules and regulations of an authorized medical milk commission

certified public accountant n **:** an accountant who has met the requirements of a state law and has been granted a state certificate

cer·ti·fy \ˈsərt-ə-ˌfī\ vt **-fied; -fy·ing** [LL *certificare*, fr. L *certus* certain] **1 :** to attest authoritatively; *esp* **:** to guarantee to be true or valid or as represented or meeting a standard **2 :** to inform with certainty **3 :** CERTIFICATE, LICENSE — **cer·ti·fi·a·ble** \-ˌfī-ə-bəl\ adj — **cer·ti·fi·er** \-ˌfī(-ə)r\ n

cer·ti·tude \ˈsərt-ə-ˌt(y)üd\ n **1 :** the state of being or feeling certain **:** CONFIDENCE **2 :** unfailingness of act or event **syn** see CERTAINTY

ce·ru·le·an \sə-ˈrü-lē-ən\ adj [L *caeruleus* dark blue] **:** somewhat resembling the blue of the sky

ce·ru·men \sə-ˈrü-mən\ n **:** the yellow waxy secretion from the glands of the external ear — called also *earwax* — **ce·ru·mi·nous** \-mə-nəs\ adj

cer·vi·cal \ˈsər-vi-kəl\ adj **:** of or relating to a neck or cervix

cer·vine \ˈsər-ˌvīn\ adj **:** of, relating to, or resembling deer

cer·vix \ˈsər-viks\ n, pl **cer·vi·ces** \ˈsər-və-ˌsēz\ or **cer·vix·es** [L *cervic-, cervix*] **:** a constricted portion of an organ or part; *esp* **:** the narrow outer end of the uterus

ce·sar·e·an or **ce·sar·i·an** \si-ˈzar-ē-ən, -ˈzer-\ n [fr. the belief that Julius Caesar was born this way] **:** surgical incision of the walls of the abdomen and uterus for delivery of offspring — **cesarean** or **cesarian** adj

ce·si·um \ˈsē-zē-əm\ n **:** a silver-white soft ductile element used in electron tubes — see ELEMENT table

ces·sa·tion \se-ˈsā-shən\ n [L *cessare* to delay, be idle] **:** a temporary or final ceasing (as of action) **:** STOP

ces·sion \ˈsesh-ən\ n **:** a yielding (as of territory or rights) to another

cess·pool \ˈses-ˌpül\ n [ME *suspiral* vent, cesspool, fr. MF *souspirail* ventilator] **:** an underground pit or tank for liquid waste (as household sewage)

ces·tode \ˈses-ˌtōd\ n [Gk *kestos* girdle] **:** any of a group (Cestoda) of internally parasitic flatworms comprising the tapeworms — **cestode** adj

cesura var of CAESURA

ce·ta·cean \si-ˈtā-shən\ n **:** any of an order (Cetacea) of aquatic mammals including the whales, dolphins, porpoises, and related forms — **cetacean** adj — **ce·ta·ceous** \-shəs\ adj

Ce·tus \ˈsēt-əs\ n [L, lit., whale] **:** an equatorial constellation south of Pisces and Aries

Chad \ˈchad\ n **:** a branch of the Afro-Asiatic language family comprising numerous languages of northern Nigeria and Cameroons

chae·tog·nath \ˈkēt-ˌäg-ˌnath, -əg-\ n **:** any of a class (Chaetognatha) of small free-swimming marine worms with movable curved bristles on each side of the mouth — **chaetognath** adj — **chae·tog·na·than** \kē-ˈtäg-nə-thən\ adj or n

¹**chafe** \ˈchāf\ vb [ME *chaufen* to warm, fr. MF *chaufer*, fr. L *calefacere*, fr. *calēre* to be warm + *facere* to make] **1 a :** IRRITATE, VEX **b :** to feel irritation or discontent **:** FRET **2 :** to warm by rubbing **3 a :** to rub so as to wear away **:** ABRADE **b :** to make sore by or as if by rubbing ⟨the tight collar *chafed* his neck⟩

²**chafe** n **1 :** a state of vexation **:** RAGE **2 :** injury or wear caused by friction; *also* **:** RUBBING, FRICTION

cha·fer \ˈchā-fər\ n **:** any of various large beetles

¹**chaff** \ˈchaf\ n [OE *ceaf*] **1 :** the debris (as seed coverings) separated from the seed in threshing grain **2 :** something light and worthless — **chaffy** \-ē\ adj

²**chaff** n **:** light jesting talk **:** BANTER

³**chaff** vb **:** to tease good-naturedly **:** BANTER

chaf·fer \ˈchaf-ər\ vb **:** to dispute about a price **:** BARGAIN — **chaf·fer·er** n

chaf·finch \ˈchaf-(ˌ)inch\ n **:** a European finch of which the male has a reddish breast plumage and a cheerful song

chaf·ing dish \ˈchā-fing-\ n [ME *chaufen, chafen* to warm, chafe] **:** a utensil for cooking or warming food at the table

¹**cha·grin** \shə-ˈgrin\ n [F, fr. *chagrin* sad] **:** a feeling of annoyance caused by failure or disappointment

²**chagrin** vt **cha·grined** \-ˈgrind\; **cha·grin·ing** \-ˈgrin-iŋ\ **:** to cause to feel chagrin

¹**chain** \ˈchān\ n [OF *chaeine*, fr. L *catena*] **1 a :** a series of connected usu. metal links or rings **b** (1) **:** a measuring instrument of 100 links used in surveying (2) **:** a unit of length equal to 66 feet **2 :** something that confines or restrains **3 a :** a series of things linked, connected, or associated together **b :** a number of atoms united like links in a chain

²**chain** vt **:** to fasten, bind, or connect with or as if with a chain

chain gang n **:** a gang of convicts chained together

chain mail n **:** flexible armor of interlinked metal rings — called also *chain armor;* see ARMOR illustration

chain–re·act \ˌchān-rē-ˈakt\ vi **:** to take part in or undergo chain reaction

chain reaction n **1 :** a series of events so related to each other that each one initiates the succeeding one **2 :** a chemical or nuclear reaction yielding energy or products that cause further reactions of the same kind and so becoming self-sustaining (as in the splitting of a uranium atom by a neutron whereby more neutrons are released that cause further splittings and so on)

chain saw n **:** a portable power saw that has teeth linked together to form an endless chain

chain stitch n **:** an ornamental stitch like the links of a chain

chain store n **:** one of numerous usu. retail stores under the same ownership and general management and selling the same lines of goods

chair \ˈche(ə)r, ˈcha(ə)r\ n [OF *chaiere*, fr. L *cathedra*, fr. Gk *kathedra*, fr. *kata-* cata- + *hed-, hezesthai* to sit; akin to E *sit*] **1 :** a seat with legs and a back for use by one person **2 a :** an official seat or a seat of authority or dignity **b :** an office or position of authority or dignity **c :** CHAIRMAN **3 :** any of various supporting devices

chair·man \-mən\ n **:** the presiding officer of a meeting or an organization or committee — **chair·man·ship** \-ˌship\ n

chaise \ˈshāz\ n [F, chair, chaise, alter. of OF *chaiere* chair] **1 :** a 2-wheeled carriage with a folding top **2 :** a light carriage or pleasure cart

chaise longue \ˈshāz-ˈlȯŋ\ n, pl **chaise longues** also **chaises longues** \ˈshāz-ˈlȯŋz\ [F, lit., long chair] **:** a long reclining chair — called also *chaise lounge* \-ˈlaȯnj\

Chal·ce·do·ni·an \ˌkal-sə-ˈdō-nē-ən\ adj **:** of or relating to Chalcedon or the ecumenical council held there in A.D. 451 declaring heretical the doctrine that the human and divine in Christ constitute only one nature — **Chalcedonian** n

chal·ced·o·ny \kal-ˈsed-ə-nē\ n, pl **-nies :** a translucent

---

j joke; **ŋ** sing; **ō** flow; **ȯ** flaw; **ȯi** coin; **th** thin; **t̲h̲** this; **ü** loot; **u̇** foot; **y** yet; **yü** few; **yu̇** furious; **zh** vision

quartz commonly pale blue or gray with nearly waxy luster

chal·cid \'kal-səd\ *n* **:** any of a large group of mostly tiny insects related to the bees and ants and parasitic in the larval state on the larvae or pupae of other insects — **chalcid** *adj*

chal·co·cite \'kal-kə-,sīt\ *n* **:** a black or gray mineral Cu₂S of metallic luster consisting of a sulfide of sulfur

chal·co·py·rite \,kal-kə-'pī(ə)r-,īt\ *n* **:** a yellow mineral CuFeS₂ consisting of copper-iron sulfide and constituting an important ore of copper

Chal·de·an \kal-'dē-ən\ *n* **1 :** one of an ancient Semitic people founding the second Babylonian Empire in the 7th century B.C. — called also *Chal·dee* \'kal-,dē\ **2 :** the Semitic language of the Chaldeans — **Chal·da·ic** \kal-'dā-ik\ *adj or n* — **Chaldean** *adj*

cha·let \sha-'lā\ *n* [F] **1 :** a remote herdsman's hut in the Alps **2 a :** a Swiss dwelling with a wide roof overhang **b :** a cottage in chalet style

chal·ice \'chal-əs\ *n* [AF, fr. L *calic-, calix*] **1 :** a drinking cup **:** GOBLET; *esp* **:** the eucharistic cup **2 :** a flower cup

¹chalk \'chȯk\ *n* [OE *cealc,* fr. L *calc-, calx* lime, limestone, pebble] **1 :** a soft white, gray, or buff limestone chiefly composed of the shells of foraminifers `2 :** chalk or a chalky material esp. when used in the form of a crayon — **chalky** \'chȯ-kē\ *adj*

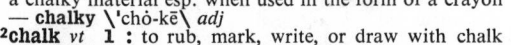
chalet 2a

²chalk *vt* **1 :** to rub, mark, write, or draw with chalk **2 a :** to delineate roughly **:** SKETCH **b :** to record or add up with or as if with chalk **:** TOT

chalk·board \-,bȯrd, -,bȯrd\ *n* **:** BLACKBOARD

chalk up *vt* **1 :** ASCRIBE, CREDIT ⟨*chalk* success *up* to hard work⟩ **2 :** ATTAIN, ACHIEVE ⟨*chalk up* a victory⟩

¹chal·lenge \'chal-ənj\ *vb* [OF *chalengier* to accuse, fr. L *calumniari* to accuse falsely, fr. *calumnia* calumny] **1 :** to claim as due or deserved ⟨an act that *challenged* everyone's admiration⟩ **2 :** to question and demand the countersign from **3 a :** to take exceptions to **:** object to **:** DISPUTE ⟨*challenge* a juror⟩ **b :** to question the legality or legal qualifications of ⟨*challenge* a vote⟩ **4 :** to issue an invitation to compete against one esp. in single combat **:** DARE, DEFY — **chal·leng·er** *n*

²challenge *n* **1 :** an exception taken to something as not being true, genuine, accurate, valid, or justified or to a person as not being qualified or acceptable **2 :** a sentry's command to halt and prove identity **3 :** an often threatening or provocative summons or invitation to compete; *esp* **:** a summons to single combat **4 :** a test of immunity by exposure to virulent infective material after specific immunization

chal·lis \'shal-ē\ *n, pl* **chal·lises** \-ēz\ **:** a lightweight soft clothing fabric esp. of cotton or wool

cha·lyb·e·ate \kə-'lib-ē-ət, -'lē-bē-\ *adj* [Gk *chalyb-, chalyps* steel] **:** impregnated with salts of iron ⟨*chalybeate* springs⟩

cham \'kam\ *var of* KHAN

¹cham·ber \'chām-bər\ *n* [OF *chambre,* fr. LL *camera,* fr. L, vault, fr. Gk *kamara*] **1 :** ROOM; *esp* **:** BEDROOM **2 :** an enclosed space or compartment **3 a :** a meeting hall of a deliberative, legislative, or judicial body **b :** a room where a judge transacts business out of court **c :** the reception room of a person of rank or authority **4 a :** a legislative or judicial body; *esp* **:** either of the houses of a bicameral legislature **b :** a voluntary board or council (as of businessmen) **5 :** a compartment in the cartridge cylinder of a revolver — **cham·bered** \-bərd\ *adj*

²chamber *vt* **:** to place or hold in or as if in a chamber **:** HOUSE

³chamber *adj* **:** intended for performance by a few musicians for a small audience ⟨*chamber* music⟩

cham·ber·lain \'chām-bər-lən\ *n* **1 :** a chief officer in the household of a king or nobleman **2 :** TREASURER **3 :** an often honorary papal attendant

cham·ber·maid \'chām-bər-,mād\ *n* **:** a maid who makes beds and does general cleaning of bedrooms (as in a hotel)

chamber of commerce : an association of businessmen to promote commercial and industrial interests

chamber pot *n* **:** a portable bedroom vessel for urination and defecation

cham·bray \'sham-,brā, -brē\ *n* **:** a lightweight clothing fabric with colored and white yarns

cha·me·leon \kə-'mēl-yən\ *n* [Gk *chamaileōn,* fr. *chamai* on the ground + *leōn* lion] **:** a lizard that has the ability to vary the color of its skin

¹cham·fer \'cham(p)-fər\ *n* **:** a beveled edge

²chamfer *vt* **1 :** to cut a furrow in (as a column) **:** GROOVE **2 :** to make a chamfer on **:** BEVEL

cham·ois \'sham-ē\ *n, pl* **cham·ois** *also* **cham·oix** \'sham-ēz\ [MF, fr. LL *camox*] **1 :** a small goatlike mountain antelope of Europe and the Caucasus **2** *also* **cham·my** \'sham-ē\ **:** a soft pliant leather prepared from the skin of the chamois or from sheepskin

chamois

cham·o·mile \'kam-ə-,mīl, -,mēl\ *n* **:** any of a genus of strong-scented herbs related to the daisies with flower heads that contain a bitter medicinal principle

¹champ \'champ\ *vb* **1 :** to bite and chew noisily ⟨a horse *champing* his bit⟩ **2 :** to show restive impatience

²champ *n* **:** CHAMPION

cham·pagne \sham-'pān\ *n* **:** a white sparkling wine made in Champagne, France; *also* **:** a similar wine made elsewhere

cham·paign \sham-'pān\ *n* [MF *champagne,* fr. LL *campania,* fr. L *campus* field, plain] **:** an expanse of level open country **:** PLAIN

¹cham·pi·on \'cham-pē-ən\ *n* [OF, warrior, fr. ML *campion-, campio,* of Gmc origin] **1 :** a militant advocate or defender **2 :** one that fights for another's rights or honor **3 a :** a person formally acknowledged as better than all others in a sport or in a game of skill **b :** the winner of first place in a competition

²champion *vt* **:** to protect or fight for as a champion

cham·pi·on·ship \-,ship\ *n* **1 :** the act of defending as a champion ⟨known for his *championship* of states' rights⟩ **2 a :** the position or title of champion **b :** a contest held to determine a champion

¹chance \'chan(t)s\ *n* [OF, lit., act of falling, fr. *cheoir* to fall, fr. L *cadere*] **1 :** the way in which things take place **:** the happening of events **:** FORTUNE ⟨occurred by *chance*⟩ **2 :** OPPORTUNITY ⟨had a *chance* to travel⟩ **3 :** RISK, GAMBLE ⟨take *chances*⟩ **4 a :** the possibility of an indicated or a favorable outcome in an uncertain situation **b :** the degree of likelihood of such an outcome **5 :** a ticket in a raffle — **chance** *adj*

²chance *vb* **1 a :** to take place or come about by chance **:** HAPPEN **b :** to be found by chance **c :** to have the good or bad luck ⟨*chanced* to miss his train⟩ **2 :** to come casually and unexpectedly — used with *upon* **3 :** to accept the hazard of **:** RISK **syn** see HAPPEN

chan·cel \'chan(t)-səl\ *n* [MF, fr. L *cancelli* lattice; so called fr. the latticework enclosing it] **:** the part of a church containing the altar and seats for the clergy and choir

chan·cel·lery *or* **chan·cel·lory** \'chan(t)-s(ə-)lə-rē\ *n, pl* **-ler·ies** *or* **-lor·ies 1 a :** the position or department of a chancellor **b :** the building or room where a chancellor has his office **2 :** the office or staff of an embassy or consulate

chan·cel·lor \'chan(t)-s(ə-)lər\ *n* [OF *chancelier,* fr. LL *cancellarius* doorkeeper, secretary, fr. *cancelli* lattice] **1 a** *obs* **:** the secretary of a nobleman, prince, or king **b :** the lord chancellor of Great Britain **c :** a Roman Catholic priest heading the office in which diocesan business is transacted and recorded **2 :** the head of a university **3 :** a judge in a court of chancery or equity **4 :** the chief minister of state in some European countries — **chan·cel·lor·ship** \-,ship\ *n*

chancellor of the exchequer : a member of the British cabinet in charge of the public income and expenditure

chan·cery \'chan(t)s-(ə-)rē\ *n, pl* **-cer·ies 1 :** a court having jurisdiction in equity; *also* **:** the principles and practices of judicial equity **2 :** a record office for public or for ecclesiastical, legal, or diplomatic archives **3 :** CHANCELLERY — **in chancery :** in litigation in a court

---

ə abut; ə kitten; ər further; a back; ā bake; ä cot, cart; aù out; ch chin; e less; ē easy; g gift; i trip; ī life

of chancery; *also* **:** under the superintendence of the lord chancellor ⟨a ward *in chancery*⟩

chan·cre \'shaŋ-kər\ *n* [F, fr. L *cancer* crab, cancer] **:** a primary sore or ulcer at the site of entry of an infective agent (as of syphilis) — **chan·crous** \-k(ə-)rəs\ *adj*

chancy \'chan(t)-sē\ *adj* **chanc·i·er; -est** **:** uncertain in outcome or prospect **:** RISKY

chan·de·lier \ˌshan-də-'li(ə)r\ *n* [F, modif. of L *candelabrum*] **:** a branched often ornate lighting fixture usu. suspended from a ceiling

chan·dler \'chan-dlər\ *n* [MF *chandelier*, fr. *chandelle* candle, fr. L *candela*] **1 :** a maker or seller of candles **2 :** a dealer in provisions and supplies or equipment esp. for ships — **chan·dlery** \-dlə-rē\ *n*

¹change \'chānj\ *vb* [OF *changier*, fr. L *cambiare* to exchange] **1 :** to make or become different **:** MODIFY, TRANSFORM **2 a :** to give a different position, course, or direction to **b :** REVERSE ⟨*change* one's vote⟩ **3 :** to replace with another; *also* **:** SWITCH **4 :** to put fresh clothes or covering on ⟨*change* a bed⟩ **5 :** to shift one's means of conveyance **:** TRANSFER **6 :** to undergo transformation, transition, or substitution **7 :** to put on different clothes **8 :** to give up one thing for something else in return **:** EXCHANGE ⟨*change* places⟩ ⟨*change* a dollar bill⟩ — **chang·er** *n*

syn ALTER, MODIFY, VARY **:** CHANGE implies making either an essential difference amounting to loss of original identity or a substitution of one thing for another; ALTER implies a difference in some respect without loss of identity; MODIFY suggests a difference that limits, restricts, or adapts to a new purpose; VARY stresses a breaking away from exact repetition

— **change hands :** to pass from the possession of one person to that of another

²change *n* **1 :** the act, process, or result of changing: as **a :** ALTERATION **b :** TRANSFORMATION **c :** SUBSTITUTION **2 :** a fresh set of clothes **3 a :** money in small denominations received in exchange for an equivalent sum in larger denominations **b :** money returned when a payment exceeds the amount due **c :** COINS **2 :** an order in which a set of bells is struck in change ringing

change·a·ble \'chān-jə-bəl\ *adj* **1 :** capable of or given to change **:** VARIABLE, ALTERABLE ⟨*changeable* weather⟩ **2 :** appearing different (as in color) from different points of view — **change·a·bil·i·ty** \ˌchān-jə-'bil-ət-ē\ *n* — **change·a·ble·ness** *n* — **change·a·bly** \'chān-jə-blē\ *adv*

change·ful \'chānj-fəl\ *adj* **:** full of or given to change **:** UNCERTAIN — **change·ful·ly** \-fə-lē\ *adv* — **change·ful·ness** *n*

change·less \'chānj-ləs\ *adj* **:** UNCHANGING, CONSTANT — **change·less·ly** *adv* — **change·less·ness** *n*

change·ling \'chānj-liŋ\ *n* **:** a child secretly exchanged for another in infancy by fairies or elves

change of life : MENOPAUSE

change ringing *n* **:** the art or practice of ringing a set of tuned bells in continually varying order

¹chan·nel \'chan-ᵊl\ *n* [OF *chanel*, fr. L *canalis* pipe, channel, canal] **1 :** the bed of a stream **2 :** the deeper part of a river, harbor, or strait **:** a strait or a narrow sea between two close land masses ⟨the English *Channel*⟩ **4 :** a closed course (as a tube) through which something flows **:** PASSAGEWAY ⟨*channels* of trade⟩ **5 :** a long gutter, groove, or furrow **6 :** a means of passage or transmission **7 :** a range of frequencies of sufficient width for a single radio or television transmission

²channel *vt* **-neled** *or* **-nelled; -nel·ing** *or* **-nel·ling** **1 a :** to form, cut, or wear a channel in **b :** GROOVE ⟨*channel* a chair leg⟩ **2 :** to direct into or through a channel

chan·nel·ize \'chan-ᵊl-ˌīz\ *vt* **:** CHANNEL — **chan·nel·i·za·tion** \ˌchan-ᵊl-ə-'zā-shən\ *n*

chan·son \shäⁿ-sōⁿ\ *n, pl* **chan·sons** \-sōⁿ(z)\ [F] **:** SONG; *esp* **:** a French song

¹chant \'chant\ *vb* [MF *chanter*, fr. L *cantare*, freq. of *canere* to sing] **1 :** SING; *esp* **:** to sing a chant **2 :** to recite in a monotonous repetitive tone

²chant *n* **1 :** a melody in which several words or syllables are sung on one tone **2 :** SONG, SINGING **3 :** a rhythmic monotonous utterance

chan·te·relle \ˌshant-ə-'rel, ˌshänt-\ *n* [F] **:** an edible mushroom of rich yellow color and pleasant aroma

chan·teuse \shäⁿ-'tə(r)z, shan-'tüz\ *n* [F, fr. *chanter* to sing] **:** a female concert or nightclub singer

chan·tey *or* **chan·ty** \'shant-ē, 'chant-\ *n, pl* **chanteys** *or* **chanties** [F *chanter* to sing, chant] **:** a song sung by sailors in rhythm with their work

chan·ti·cleer \ˌchant-ə-'kli(ə)r, ˌshant-\ *n* [OF *Chantecler*, rooster in the beast epic *Reynard the Fox*] **:** ¹COCK 1

cha·os \'kā-ˌäs\ *n* [L, fr. Gk] **:** complete confusion and disorder ⟨a *chaos* of wind, spray, foam, and swirling water⟩ **syn** see ANARCHY — **cha·ot·ic** \kā-'ät-ik\ *adj* — **cha·ot·i·cal·ly** \-i-k(ə-)lē\ *adv*

¹chap \'chap\ *n* [short for *chapman*] **:** FELLOW

²chap *vb* **chapped; chap·ping** [ME *chappen*] **:** to open in slits **:** CRACK ⟨*chapped* lips⟩

³chap. *n* **:** a crack or a sore roughening of the skin from exposure

⁴chap \'chäp, 'chap\ *n* **:** JAW **:** the fleshy covering of a jaw; *also* **:** the forepart of the face — usu. used in pl.

chap·ar·ral \ˌshap-ə-'ral, -'rel\ *n* **:** a thicket of dwarf evergreen oaks; *also* **:** a dense impenetrable thicket

chap·book \'chap-ˌbuk\ *n* **:** a small book containing ballads, tales, or tracts

cha·peau \sha-'pō\ *n, pl* **cha·peaus** *or* **cha·peaux** \-'pōz\ **:** HAT

chap·el \'chap-əl\ *n* [OF *chapele*, fr. ML *cappella*, fr. dim. of LL *cappa* cloak; so called fr. the preservation of the cloak of St. Martin of Tours in a chapel built for the purpose] **1 :** a place of worship in a residence or institution **2 :** a building or a room or recess esp. in a church for prayer or special religious services **3 :** a service of worship or an assembly in a school or college **4 :** a place of worship used by British Nonconformists

¹chap·er·on *or* **chap·er·one** \'shap-ə-ˌrōn\ *n* [F *chaperon*, lit., hood] **:** a person and esp. a married woman who accompanies and is responsible for (as at a dance) a young woman or a group of young people

²chaperon *or* **chaperone** *vb* **:** to act as a chaperon **:** ESCORT — **chap·er·on·age** \-ˌrō-nij\ *n*

chap·fall·en \'chap-ˌfȯ-lən, 'chäp-\ *adj* **1 :** having the lower jaw hanging loosely **2 :** DEJECTED, DEPRESSED

chap·lain \'chap-lən\ *n* [OF *chapelain* clergyman in charge of a chapel, fr. ML *cappellanus*, fr. *cappella* chapel] **1 :** a clergyman appointed to serve a dignitary, institution, or military force **2 :** a person chosen to conduct religious exercises for an organization — **chap·lain·cy** \-sē\ *n* — **chap·lain·ship** \-ˌship\ *n*

chap·let \'chap-lət\ *n* **1 :** a wreath worn on the head **2 a :** a string of beads **b :** a five-decade part of the rosary devoted to one group of sacred mysteries

chap·man \'chap-mən\ *n* [OE *cēapman*, fr. *cēap* trade + *man*] *Brit* **:** an itinerant merchant

chaps \'shaps\ *n pl* **:** leather leggings resembling trousers without a seat that are worn esp. by western ranch hands

chap·ter \'chap-tər\ *n* [OF *chapitre*, fr. LL *capitulum*, fr. L, dim. of *capit-, caput* head] **1 :** a main division of a book or of a law code **2 a :** a regular meeting of the canons of a cathedral or collegiate church or of the members of a religious house **b :** the body of canons of a cathedral or collegiate church **3 :** a local branch of a society or fraternity

¹char \'chär\ *n, pl* **char** *or* **chars** **:** any of a genus of small-scaled trouts including the common brook trout

²char *vb* **charred; char·ring** [back-formation fr. *charcoal*] **1 :** to change to charcoal by burning **2 :** to burn slightly **:** SCORCH **3 :** to burn to a cinder

³char *n* **:** a charred substance

⁴char *vi* **charred; char·ring** **:** to work as a charwoman

char·a·banc \'shar-ə-ˌbaŋ\ *n* [F *char à bancs*, lit., wagon with benches] *Brit* **:** a sight-seeing motor coach

char·a·cin \'kar-ə-sən\ *n* **:** any of a family of usu. small brightly colored tropical fishes — **characin** *adj*

char·ac·ter \'kar-ik-tər\ *n* [Gk *charaktēr* mark, distinctive quality, fr. *charassein* to scratch, engrave] **1 a :** a conventional marking indicating origin or ownership **b :** a mark or symbol (as a hieroglyph or a letter of an alphabet) used in writing or printing **c :** WRITING, PRINTING **2 a** (1) **:** a distinguishing feature of a person or thing **:** CHARACTERISTIC (2) **:** the sum total of the distinguishing qualities of a person, group, or thing **:** NATURE **b :** the detectable result of the action of a gene or group of genes **3 :** POSITION, STATUS ⟨his *character* as a son⟩ **4 :** REFERENCE

4b **5 :** a person having notable traits or characteristics; *esp* **:** an odd or peculiar person **6 :** a person in a story, novel, or play **7 :** REPUTATION **8 :** moral excellence and strength — **char·ac·ter·less** \-ləs\ *adj*

¹**char·ac·ter·is·tic** \,kar-ik-tə-'ris-tik\ *adj* **:** serving to mark the distinctive character of an individual, group, or class **:** TYPICAL — **char·ac·ter·is·ti·cal·ly** \-ti-k(ə-)lē\ *adv*

syn CHARACTERISTIC, INDIVIDUAL, DISTINCTIVE mean indicating a special quality or identity. CHARACTERISTIC applies to something that marks a person or thing or class; INDIVIDUAL stresses qualities that distinguish one from all other members of the same kind or class; DISTINCTIVE indicates qualities that are distinguishing and uncommon and often superior or praiseworthy

²**characteristic** *n* **1 :** a distinguishing trait, quality, or property **2 :** the integral part of a common logarithm

char·ac·ter·i·za·tion \,kar-ik-tə-rə-'zā-shən\ *n* **1 :** the act of characterizing **:** description by a statement of characteristics **2 :** the creation of characters in fiction or drama **:** the artistic representation of fictitious persons

char·ac·ter·ize \'kar-ik-tə-,rīz\ *vt* **1 :** to indicate the character or characteristics of **:** DESCRIBE **2 :** to be characteristic of

character sketch *n* **:** a usu. short piece of writing dealing with a character of strongly marked individuality

char·ac·tery \'kar-ik-t(ə-)rē\ *n* **:** written letters or symbols

cha·rades \shə-'rādz\ *n pl* [F] **:** a game in which each syllable of a word to be guessed is acted out by some of the persons playing the game while the others try to guess the word

char·coal \'chär-,kōl\ *n* [ME *charcole*] **1 :** a dark or black porous carbon prepared from vegetable or animal substances (as from wood by charring in a kiln from which air is excluded) **2 a :** a piece or pencil of fine charcoal used in drawing **b :** a charcoal drawing

chard \'chärd\ *n* **:** a beet that lacks a swollen root and forms large leaves and succulent stalks often cooked as a vegetable — called also *Swiss chard*

chare \'cha(ə)r, 'che(ə)r\ *n* **:** CHORE

¹**charge** \'chärj\ *vb* [OF *chargier*, fr. LL *carricare*, fr. L *carrus* vehicle, car] **1 a :** to place a charge (as of powder) in ⟨*charge* the magazine with three rounds⟩ **b :** to load or fill to capacity **c** (1) **:** to impart an electric charge to (2) **:** to restore the active materials in (a storage battery) by the passage of a direct current through in the opposite direction to that of discharge **2 a :** to impose a task or responsibility on **b :** to command, instruct, or exhort with right or authority **c :** to give a charge to (a jury) **3 a :** ACCUSE, BLAME **b :** to impute blame or guilt for **4 :** to rush against or bear down upon a place **:** ASSAULT, ATTACK **5 a :** to impose a monetary charge upon a person ⟨*charged* him $50 for the goods⟩ ⟨*charge* debts to an estate⟩ **b :** to fix or ask as fee or payment ⟨*charge* $2.50 for a ticket⟩ **c :** to ask or set a price ⟨*charges* too much⟩ — **charge·a·ble** \'chär-jə-bəl\ *adj* — **charge·a·ble·ness** *n*

²**charge** *n* **1 :** a figure borne on a heraldic field **2 a :** the quantity (as of powder) that an apparatus (as a gun) is intended to receive and fitted to hold **b :** a store or accumulation of force **c :** ELECTRIC CHARGE **3 a :** OBLIGATION, REQUIREMENT **b :** MANAGEMENT, SUPERVISION; *also* **:** CARE, CUSTODY **c :** a person or thing committed to the care of another **4 a :** INSTRUCTION, COMMAND **b :** an instruction in points of law given by a court to a jury **5 a :** EXPENSE, COST **b :** PRICE **c :** a debit to an account **6 a :** ACCUSATION, INDICTMENT **b :** a complaint of error, failure, or wrong **7 :** a rush to attack an enemy **:** ASSAULT

syn INDICTMENT: in criminal law CHARGE applies to any formal complaint, information, accusation, or indictment; INDICTMENT applies to a written charge approved and presented by a grand jury and in general use commonly implies greater precision and detailedness and often less emotion than CHARGE

char·gé d'af·faires \'shär-,zhād-ə-'fa(ə)r, -'fe(ə)r\ *n, pl* **char·gés d'af·faires** \-,zhād-ə-, -,zhäz-də-\ [F] **1 :** a diplomat who substitutes for an absent ambassador or minister **2 :** a diplomat of inferior rank

¹**char·ger** \'chär-jər\ *n, archaic* **:** a large flat platter for carrying meat

²**charg·er** \'chär-jər\ *n* **1 :** a cavalry horse **2 :** a device for charging storage batteries

char·i·ot \'char-ē-ət\ *n* [MF, fr. *char* car, fr. L *carrus*] **1 :** a 2-wheeled horse-drawn battle car of ancient times used also in processions and races

char·i·o·teer \,char-ē-ə-'ti(ə)r\ *n* **1 :** a driver of a chariot **2** *cap* **:** the constellation Auriga

chariot

cha·ris·ma \kə-'riz-mə\ *n, pl* **-ma·ta** \-mət-ə\ [Gk, favor, gift, fr. *charis* grace] **:** an extraordinary power (as of healing) given a Christian by the Holy Spirit for the good of the church

char·is·mat·ic \,kar-əz-'mat-ik\ *adj* **:** having or showing a personal quality of leadership that arouses special popular loyalty or enthusiasm

char·i·ta·ble \'char-ət-ə-bəl\ *adj* **1 :** liberal with money or help for poor and needy persons **:** GENEROUS **2 :** given for the needy **:** of service to the needy ⟨*charitable* funds⟩ ⟨a *charitable* institution⟩ **3 :** generous and kindly in judging other people **:** FORGIVING, LENIENT — **char·i·ta·bly** \-blē\ *adv*

char·i·ty \'char-ət-ē\ *n, pl* **-ties** [OF *charité*, fr. L *caritat-*, *caritas* dearness, fr. *carus* dear] **1 :** love for one's fellowmen **2 :** kindliness in judging others **3 a :** the giving of aid to the poor and suffering **b :** public aid for the poor **c :** an institution or fund for aiding the needy

char·la·tan \'shär-lə-tən\ *n* [It *ciarlatano*, alter. of *cerretano*, lit., inhabitant of Cerreto, village in Italy] **:** a person who pretends to have knowledge or ability he does not have **:** QUACK — **char·la·tan·ism** \-tə-,niz-əm\ *n* — **char·la·tan·ry** \-tən-rē\ *n*

Charles·ton \'chärl-stən\ *n* **:** a ballroom dance in which the knees are twisted in and out and the heels are swung sharply outward on each step

char·ley horse \'chär-lē-,hȯrs\ *n* **:** pain and stiffness from muscular strain esp. in a leg

char·lotte russe \,shär-lət-'rüs\ *n* [F, fr. *charlotte*, a kind of dessert + *russe* Russian] **:** a dessert made with sponge cake or ladyfingers and a whipped-cream or custard-gelatin filling

¹**charm** \'chärm\ *n* [OF *charme*, fr. L *carmen* song, charm, fr. *canere* to sing] **1 :** a word, action, or thing believed to have magic powers **2 :** something worn or carried to keep away evil and bring good luck **3 :** a small decorative object worn on a chain or bracelet **4 :** a quality that attracts and pleases; *also* **:** physical grace or attractiveness

²**charm** *vt* **1 :** to affect or influence by or as if by magic **:** COMPEL; *also* **:** DELIGHT **2 :** to protect by or as if by a charm ⟨a *charmed* life⟩ **3 :** to control (an animal) by charms (as the playing of music) ⟨*charm* a snake⟩ **4 :** to attract by grace or beauty — **charm·er** *n*

char·nel \'chärn-ᵊl\ *n* [MF, fr. ML *carnale*, fr. LL *carnalis* carnal] **:** a building or chamber in which dead bodies or bones are deposited — **charnel** *adj*

Char·on \'kar-ən, 'ker-\ *n* **:** a son of Erebus held in Greek mythology to ferry the souls of the dead over the Styx

charr *var of* CHAR

¹**chart** \'chärt\ *n* [MF *charte*, fr. L *charta* piece of papyrus, document, fr. Gk *chartēs* piece of papyrus] **1 :** MAP: as **a :** an outline map exhibiting something (as climatic or magnetic variations) in its geographical aspects **b :** a map for the use of navigators **2 :** a sheet giving information in the form of a table or of lists or by means of diagrams or graphs; *also* **:** GRAPH **3 :** a sheet of paper ruled and graduated for use in a recording instrument

²**chart** *vt* **1 :** to make a map or chart of ⟨set out to *chart* the eastern coast⟩ **2 :** to lay out a plan for ⟨*charting* campaign strategy⟩

¹**char·ter** \'chärt-ər\ *n* [MF *chartre*, fr. ML *chartula*, fr. L, dim. of *charta* document] **1 a :** an instrument in writing issued by the sovereign power of a state, country, or authority (as a union) granting, guaranteeing, or defining the rights and duties of the body (as a municipality, corporation, or a local society) to which it is issued **b :** CONSTITUTION ⟨United Nations *Charter*⟩ **2 :** a special privilege or immunity **3 :** a contract by which the owners of a ship lease it to others — called also *charter party*

²**charter** *vt* **1** : to grant a charter to **2** : to hire (as a ship or a bus) for one's own use — **char·ter·er** \'chärt-ər-ər\ *n*

Char·tism \'chärt-ˌiz-əm\ *n* : the principles and practices of a body of 19th century English political reformers advocating better social and industrial conditions for the working classes — **Char·tist** \'chärt-əst\ *adj or n*

char·treuse \shär-'trüz, -'trüs\ *n* **1** : a usu. green or yellow liqueur **2** : a variable color averaging a brilliant yellow green

char·wom·an \'chär-ˌwùm-ən\ *n* [ME *char* chore] **1** *Brit* : a woman hired to do household work (as cleaning) **2** : a cleaning woman usu. in a large building

chary \'cha(ə)r-ē, 'che(ə)r-\ *adj* **char·i·er; -est** [OE *cearig* sorrowful] **1** : cautiously sparing or frugal ⟨*chary* of giving praise⟩ **2** : cautiously watchful esp. in preserving something ⟨*chary* of one's reputation⟩ — **char·i·ly** \'char-ə-lē, 'cher-\ *adv* — **char·i·ness** \'char-ē-nəs, 'cher-\ *n*

Cha·ryb·dis \kə-'rib-dəs\ *n* : a whirlpool off the coast of Sicily personified by the ancients as a female monster — compare SCYLLA

¹**chase** \'chās\ *vb* [MF *chasser*, fr. L *captare* to seek to take, fr. *capt-*, *capere* to take] **1 a** : to follow rapidly : PURSUE **b** : HUNT **2** : to seek out **3** : to drive away or out ⟨*chase* a dog off the lawn⟩ ⟨*chased* the pitcher with four hits in the 6th inning⟩
syn PURSUE, FOLLOW, TRAIL: CHASE implies going swiftly after and trying to overtake something running or fleeing usu. in full view ⟨a dog *chasing* a cat⟩ PURSUE may add the suggestion of a continuing effort to overtake ⟨*pursue* a fox⟩ FOLLOW puts less emphasis upon speed and may not imply intent to overtake ⟨a stray dog *followed* him home⟩ TRAIL applies to a following of tracks or traces rather than a visible object ⟨*trail* a deer through the snow⟩

²**chase** *n* **1 a** : the act of chasing : PURSUIT **b** : HUNTING — used with *the* **2** : something pursued **3** : a tract of unenclosed land used as a game preserve

³**chase** *vt* : to ornament (metal) by embossing or engraving ⟨*chased* bronze⟩

⁴**chase** *n* **1** : GROOVE **2** : TRENCH **3** : a channel (as in a wall) for something to lie in or pass through

⁵**chase** *n* : a rectangular steel or iron frame into which letterpress matter is locked for printing or plating — compare FORM

chas·er \'chā-sər\ *n* **1** : one that chases **2** : a mild drink (as water or beer) taken after hard liquor

Cha·sid \'has-əd\ *n, pl* **Cha·si·dim** \'has-əd-əm\ *var of* HASID

chasm \'kaz-əm\ *n* [Gk *chasma*, fr. *chainein* to yawn; akin to E *yawn*] **1** : a deep cleft in the earth : GORGE **2** : GULF

chas·seur \sha-'sər\ *n* : one of a body of light cavalry or infantry trained for rapid maneuvering

chas·sis \'shas-ē, 'chas-ē\ *n, pl* **chas·sis** \-ēz\ [F *châssis*] : a supporting framework (as that bearing the body of an automobile or airplane or the parts of a radio or television receiving set)

chaste \'chāst\ *adj* [OF, fr. L *castus* pure, chaste] **1** : innocent of unlawful sexual intercourse **2** : CELIBATE **3** : pure in thought and act : MODEST **4** : pure or severe in design and expression — **chaste·ly** *adv* — **chaste·ness** \'chās(t)-nəs\ *n*
syn PURE, MODEST: CHASTE implies a refraining from acts, thoughts, or desires that are not virginal or not sanctioned in marriage; it may suggest avoidance of anything that cheapens or debases; PURE implies innocence and absence of temptation; MODEST applies esp. to behavior and dress as outward signs of chastity or purity

chas·ten \'chās-ᵊn\ *vt* **chas·tened; chas·ten·ing** \'chās-niŋ, -ᵊn-iŋ\ **1** : to correct by punishment or suffering : DISCIPLINE; *also* : PURIFY **2** : to prune of excess, pretense, or falsity : REFINE — **chas·ten·er** \'chās-nər, -ᵊn-ər\ *n*

chas·tise \chas-'tīz\ *vt* [ME *chastisen*, alter. of *chasten*] **1** : to inflict (as by whipping) punishment on **2** : to censure severely : CASTIGATE **syn** see PUNISH — **chas·tise·ment** \chas-'tīz-mənt, 'chas-təz-\ *n* — **chas·tis·er** \chas-'tīz-ər\ *n*

chas·ti·ty \'chas-tət-ē\ *n, pl* **-ties** : the quality or state of being chaste; *esp* : personal purity and modesty

cha·su·ble \'chaz(h)-ə-bəl, 'chas-ə-\ *n* : a sleeveless outer vestment worn by the officiating priest at mass

¹**chat** \'chat\ *vi* **chat·ted; chat·ting** **1** : CHATTER, PRATTLE **2** : to talk in a light, informal, or familiar manner

²**chat** *n* **1 a** : light familiar talk **b** : an informal conversation **2** : any of several songbirds with a chattering call

châ·teau \sha-'tō\ *n, pl* **châ·teaus** \-'tōz\ *or* **châ·teaux** \-'tō(z)\ [F, fr. L *castellum* castle] **1** : a feudal castle in France **2** : a large country house **3** : a French vineyard estate

chasuble
(Gothic)

chat·e·laine \'shat-ᵊl-ˌān\ *n* **1** : the mistress of a château or a household **2** : an ornamental clasp or hook for a watch, purse, or bunch of keys

chat·tel \'chat-ᵊl\ *n* [OF *chatel* property, fr. ML *capitale*, fr. L, neut. of *capitalis* of the head, capital] **1** : SLAVE, BONDMAN **2** : an item of property (as animals, furniture, money, or goods) other than real estate : a piece of personal property

chat·ter \'chat-ər\ *vb* **1** : to utter rapidly succeeding sounds suggesting speech but lacking meaning ⟨squirrels *chattered* angrily⟩ **2** : to speak idly, incessantly, or rapidly : JABBER **3 a** : to click repeatedly or uncontrollably ⟨*chattering* teeth⟩ **b** : to vibrate rapidly in cutting ⟨a *chattering* tool⟩ — **chatter** *n* — **chat·ter·er** \'chat-ər-ər\ *n*

chat·ter·box \'chat-ər-ˌbäks\ *n* : a person who talks unceasingly : a constant chatterer

chat·ty \'chat-ē\ *adj* **chat·ti·er; -est** **1** : fond of chatting : TALKATIVE **2** : having the style and manner of light familiar conversation ⟨a *chatty* letter⟩ — **chat·ti·ly** \'chat-ᵊl-ē\ *adv* — **chat·ti·ness** \'chat-ē-nəs\ *n*

¹**chauf·feur** \'shō-fər, shō-'\ *n* [F, lit., stoker, fr. *chauffer* to heat] : a person employed to drive an automobile

²**chauffeur** *vb* **1** : to do the work of a chauffeur **2** : to operate as chauffeur

chau·tau·qua \shə-'tò-kwə\ *n* [fr. *Chautauqua*, N.Y., where it originated] : an institution of the late 19th and early 20th centuries offering educational entertainment (as lectures) in circuit performances often in a tent

chau·vin·ism \'shō-və-ˌniz-əm\ *n* [after Nicolas *Chauvin*, 19th cent. French soldier excessively devoted to Napoleon and his regime] : excessive or blind patriotism — compare JINGOISM — **chau·vin·ist** \-və-nəst\ *n* — **chau·vin·is·tic** \ˌshō-və-'nis-tik\ *adj* — **chau·vin·is·ti·cal·ly** \-ti-k(ə-)lē\ *adv*

cheap \'chēp\ *adj* [obs. *cheap* bargain, fr. OE *cēap* trade, fr. L *caupo* tradesman] **1** : of low cost or price ⟨a *cheap* watch⟩ **2** : worth little : of inferior quality ⟨*cheap* material wears out quickly⟩ **3 a** : gained with little effort **b** : not worth gaining ⟨*cheap* applause⟩ **4** : lowered in one's own opinion : ABASHED ⟨feel *cheap*⟩ **5 a** : charging low prices : dealing in inferior goods **6 a** : depreciated in value or purchasing power (as by inflation) ⟨*cheap* dollars⟩ **b** : obtainable at a low rate of interest ⟨*cheap* money⟩ **syn** see CONTEMPTIBLE — **cheap** *adv* — **cheap·ly** *adv* — **cheap·ness** *n*

cheap·en \'chē-pən\ *vb* **cheap·ened; cheap·en·ing** \'chēp-(ə-)niŋ\ : to make or become cheap or cheaper

cheap–jack \'chēp-ˌjak\ *n* : a hawker of or dealer in cheap and usu. inferior or worthless merchandise

cheap·skate \-ˌskāt\ *n* : a shabby or miserly person

¹**cheat** \'chēt\ *n* [ME *chete* forfeited property, short for *eschete* escheat] **1** : an act of cheating : DECEPTION, FRAUD **2** : one that cheats : DECEIVER

²**cheat** *vb* **1** : to rob by deceit or fraud ⟨*cheated* him out of a large sum⟩ **2** : to influence or lead astray by deceit, trick, or artifice **3** : to defeat in an expectation or purpose by deceit and trickery **4 a** : to practice fraud or trickery **b** : to violate rules dishonestly (as at cards)
syn CHEAT, DEFRAUD, SWINDLE mean to get something from another by deception or dishonesty. CHEAT suggests using trickery that escapes observation; DEFRAUD stresses depriving one of his rights and connotes deliberate lying or deception; SWINDLE implies cheating usu. on a large scale by abuse of confidence

¹**check** \'chek\ *n* [OF *eschec*, fr. *eschec*, interj. announcing check, fr. Ar *shāh*, fr. Per, lit., king] **1** : exposure of

a chess king to an attack **2** : a stoppage of progress : ARREST, PAUSE **3** : something that arrests, limits, or restrains : RESTRAINT ⟨constitutional *checks* and balances⟩ **4 a** : a standard for testing and evaluation : CRITERION **b** : EXAMINATION, INVESTIGATION, VERIFICATION; *also* : the sample used for testing **5** : an order directing a bank to pay out money in accordance with instructions written thereon **6 a** : a ticket or token that shows that the bearer has a claim to property ⟨baggage *check*⟩ or has made payment for a previous performance that did not take place ⟨rain *check*⟩ **b** : a slip indicating the amount due : BILL **7** [ME *chek*, short for *cheker* chessboard] **a** : a pattern in squares that resembles a checkerboard **b** : a fabric with such a design **8** : a mark √ placed beside an item to show it has been noted **9** : CRACK, BREAK ⟨a *check* in wood or steel⟩ — **in check** : under restraint or control

²**check** *vb* **1** : to put (a chess king) in check **2 a** : to bring to a sudden pause : STOP **b** : to halt through caution, uncertainty, or fear : STOP **3** : RESTRAIN, CURB **4 a** : to make sure of the correctness or satisfactoriness of **b** : to mark printing or writing with a check to show that something has been specially noted **5** : to mark with squares or checks ⟨a *checked* suit⟩ **6** : to leave or accept for safekeeping in a checkroom or for shipment as baggage **7** : to investigate conditions ⟨*check* up on things⟩ **8** : to correspond point for point : TALLY **9** : to develop small cracks

check·book \'chek-ˌbùk\ *n* : a book containing blank checks to be drawn on a bank

¹**check·er** \'chek-ər\ *n* [ME *cheker* chessboard, fr. OF *eschequier*, fr. *eschec* check] **1** : a square or spot resembling the markings on a checkerboard **2** : a man in checkers

²**checker** *vt* **check·ered; check·er·ing** \'chek-(ə-)riŋ\ **1** : to mark with squares or spots of different colors ⟨a *checkered* tablecloth⟩ **2** : to subject to frequent changes (as of fortune) ⟨a *checkered* career⟩

³**checker** *n* : one that checks; *esp* : an employee who checks out purchases in a supermarket

check·er·ber·ry \'chek-ə(r)ˌber-ē\ *n* : the spicy red fruit of an American wintergreen; *also* : this plant

check·er·board \-ə(r)-ˌbȯrd, -ˌbȯrd\ *n* : a board used in games (as checkers) and marked with 64 squares in 2 alternating colors

check·ers \'chek-ərz\ *n* : a game played on a checkerboard by two persons each having 12 men

check·ing account \'chek-iŋ-\ *n* : an account in a bank from which the depositor can draw money by writing checks — compare SAVINGS ACCOUNT

check·list \'chek-ˌlist\ *n* : a list of items that may easily be referred to

¹**check·mate** \'chek-ˌmāt\ *vt* [ME *chekmate*, interj. announcing checkmate, fr. MF *eschec mat*, fr. Ar *shāh māt*, fr. Per, lit., the king is left unable to escape] **1** : to arrest or frustrate completely **2** : to check (a chess opponent's king) so that escape is impossible

²**checkmate** *n* **1 a** : the act of checkmating **b** : the situation of a checkmated king **2** : a complete check

check·off \'chek-ˌȯf\ *n* : the deduction of union dues from a worker's paycheck by the employer

check out *vb* : to total or have totaled the cost of purchases in a self-service store (as a supermarket) and make or receive payment for them

check·point \'chek-ˌpȯint\ *n* : a point at which vehicular traffic is halted for inspection or clearance

check·rein \-ˌrān\ *n* : a short rein fastened so that it prevents a horse from lowering its head

check·room \-ˌrüm, -ˌrùm\ *n* : a room at which baggage, parcels, or clothing is checked

check·up \'chek-ˌəp\ *n* : EXAMINATION; *esp* : a general physical examination

ched·dar \'ched-ər\ *n, often cap* [*Cheddar*, England] : a hard pressed cheese of smooth texture

cheek \'chēk\ *n* [OE *cēace*] **1** : the fleshy side of the face below the eye and above and to the side of the mouth **2 a** : something suggestive of the human cheek in position or form **b** : SIDE **3** : saucy speech or behavior : IM-PUDENCE — **cheek by jowl** : in close proximity

cheek·bone \-'bōn, -ˌbōn\ *n* : the bone or the bony prominence below the eye

cheeky \'chē-kē\ *adj* **cheek·i·er; -est** : SAUCY, IMPUDENT — **cheek·i·ness** *n*

cheep \'chēp\ *vb* : to utter faint shrill sounds : PEEP, CHIRP — **cheep** *n*

¹**cheer** \'chi(ə)r\ *n* [ME *chere* face, cheer, fr. OF, face] **1** : state of mind or heart : SPIRIT ⟨be of good *cheer*⟩ **2** : ANIMATION, GAIETY **3** : food and drink for a feast : FARE **4** : something that gladdens **5** : a shout of applause or encouragement

²**cheer** *vb* **1** : to give hope to or make happier : COMFORT ⟨*cheer* a sick person⟩ **2** : to urge on esp. with shouts or cheers ⟨*cheer* one's team to victory⟩ **3** : to shout with joy, approval, or enthusiasm ⟨the students *cheered* loudly at the end of the speech⟩ **4** : to grow or be cheerful : REJOICE — usu. used with *up*

cheer·ful \'chi(ə)r-fəl\ *adj* **1 a** : full of good spirits : GAY **b** : UNGRUDGING ⟨*cheerful* obedience⟩ **2** : pleasantly bright : likely to dispel gloom or worry ⟨sunny *cheerful* room⟩ — **cheer·ful·ly** \-f(ə-)lē\ *adv* — **cheer·ful·ness** \-fəl-nəs\ *n*

syn CHEERY : CHEERFUL implies an inner contentment that may or may not be shown or expressed outwardly ⟨*cheerful* acceptance of responsibility⟩ CHEERY stresses the brightening or enlivening effect of behavior on others ⟨*cheery* welcome⟩ ⟨*cheery* laughter⟩

cheer·lead·er \'chi(ə)r-ˌlēd-ər\ *n* : a person who directs organized cheering esp. at a sports event

cheer·less \'chi(ə)r-ləs\ *adj* : lacking in warmth or kindliness : DEPRESSING, GLOOMY — **cheer·less·ly** *adv* — **cheer·less·ness** *n*

cheery \'chi(ə)r-ē\ *adj* **cheer·i·er; -est** : causing or suggesting cheerfulness : gay in manner or effect **syn** see CHEERFUL — **cheer·i·ly** \'chir-ə-lē\ *adv* — **cheer·i·ness** \'chir-ē-nəs\ *n*

cheese \'chēz\ *n* [OE *cēse*, fr. L *caseus*] : the curd of milk pressed and used as food

cheese·bur·ger \-ˌbər-gər\ *n* : a hamburger with a slice of toasted cheese

cheese·cake \-ˌkāk\ *n* **1** : a cake made by baking a mixture of cottage cheese, eggs, and sugar in a pastry shell or a mold **2** : photographs of attractive usu. scantily clothed girls

cheese·cloth \-ˌklȯth\ *n* : a thin loose-woven cotton cloth

cheesy \'chē-zē\ *adj* : resembling or suggesting cheese (as in texture or odor)

chee·tah \'chēt-ə\ *n* [Hindi *cītā*] : a long-legged spotted swift-moving African and formerly Asiatic cat about the size of a small leopard that is often trained to run down game

chef \'shef\ *n* [F, short for *chef de cuisine* head of the kitchen] : COOK; *esp* : a head cook

chef d'oeu·vre \shā-dœvr°\ *n, pl* **chefs d'oeuvre** *same*\ [F, lit., leading work] : a masterpiece esp. in art or literature

Che·ka \'chā-kə\ *n* : the secret police in Soviet Russia from 1918 to 1922

che·la \'kē-lə\ *n, pl* **che·lae** \-(ˌ)lē\ [NL, fr. Gk *chēlē* claw] : a pincerlike organ or claw on a limb of a crustacean or arachnid

che·late \'kē-ˌlāt\ *adj* : resembling or having chelae — chelated *n*

che·lic·era \ki-'lis-ə-rə\ *n, pl* **-er·as** *or* **-er·ae** \-ˌrē\ : either of the front pair of appendages of an arachnid often specialized as fangs — **che·lic·er·al** \-ə-rəl\ *adj*

che·li·ped \'kē-lə-ˌped\ *n* : either of the pair of legs of a crustacean that bear chelae

che·lo·ni·an \ki-'lō-nē-ən\ *adj* : of, relating to, or being a tortoise or turtle — **chelonian** *n*

chem- *or* **chemo-** *also* **chemi-** *comb form* : chemical : chemistry ⟨*chemotaxis*⟩

chem·ic \'kem-ik\ *adj* : CHEMICAL

¹**chem·i·cal** \'kem-i-kəl\ *adj* [NL *chimicus* alchemist, short for ML *alchimicus*, fr. *alchimia* alchemy] **1** : of, relating to, used in, or produced by chemistry **2** : acting or operated or produced by chemicals — **chem·i·cal·ly** \-i-k(ə-)lē\ *adv*

²**chemical** *n* **1** : a substance formed when two or more other substances act upon one another to cause a permanent change ⟨sulfuric acid is a manufactured *chemical*⟩ **2 a** : a substance that is prepared for use in the manufacture of another substance ⟨a *chemical* used in making

ə abut; ° kitten; ər further; a back; ā bake; ä cot, cart; au̇ out; ch chin; e less; ē easy; g gift; i trip; ī life

plastics⟩ **b :** a substance that acts upon something else to cause a permanent change ⟨a *chemical* that turns starch blue⟩

che·mise \shə-'mēz\ *n* [OF, shirt, fr. LL *camisia*] **1 :** a woman's one-piece undergarment **2 :** a loose straight‑hanging dress

chem·ist \'kem-əst\ *n* **1 :** one trained or engaged in chemistry **2** *Brit* **:** PHARMACIST

chem·is·try \'kem-ə-strē\ *n* **1 :** a science that deals with the composition, structure, and properties of elementary substances and compound substances and of the changes that they undergo **2 :** chemical composition, properties, or processes ⟨the *chemistry* of gasoline⟩ ⟨the *chemistry* of iron⟩⟨the *chemistry* of blood⟩

che·mo·re·cep·tion \,kē-mō-ri-'sep-shən\ *n* **:** the physiological reception of chemical stimuli — **che·mo·re·cep·tive** \-'sep-tiv\ *adj* — **che·mo·re·cep·tor** \-'sep-tər\ *n*

che·mo·syn·the·sis \-'sin(t)-thə-səs\ *n* **:** formation of organic compounds (as in living cells) using energy derived from chemical reactions — **che·mo·syn·the·siz·er** \-'sin(t)-thə-,sī-zər\ *n* — **che·mo·syn·thet·ic** \-sin-'thet-ik\ *adj*

che·mo·tax·is \-'tak-səs\ *n* **:** orientation or movement in relation to chemical agents — **che·mo·tac·tic** \-'tak-tik\ *adj*

che·mo·ther·a·peu·tic \-,ther-ə-'pyüt-ik\ *adj* **:** of or relating to chemotherapy — **che·mo·ther·a·peu·ti·cal·ly** \-'pyüt-i-k(ə-)lē\ *adv*

che·mo·ther·a·py \-'ther-ə-pē\ *n* **:** the use of chemical agents in the treatment or control of disease

che·mot·ro·pism \ki-'mä-trə-,piz-əm\ *n* **:** orientation of cells or organisms in relation to chemical stimuli — **che·mo·trop·ic** \,kē-mō-'träp-ik\ *adj*

chem·ur·gy \'kem-(,)ər-jē, kə-'mər-\ *n* **:** chemistry that deals with industrial utilization of organic raw materials esp. from farm products — **chem·ur·gic** \kə-'mər-jik, ke-\ *adj* — **chem·ur·gi·cal·ly** \-ji-k(ə-)lē\ *adv*

che·nille \shə-'nēl\ *n* [F, lit., caterpillar, fr. L *canicula*, dim. of *canis* dog] **:** a fabric with a deep fuzzy pile used for bedspreads and rugs

cheque \'chek\ *chiefly Brit var of* CHECK 5

cher·ish \'cher-ish\ *vt* [MF *cheriss-, cherir*, fr. *cher* dear, fr. L *carus*] **1 a :** to hold dear **:** feel or show affection for **b :** to keep with care and affection **:** NURTURE **2 :** to harbor in the mind ⟨*cherish* a hope⟩

Cher·o·kee \'cher-ə-,kē\ *n* **:** a member of an Iroquoian people orig. of the Appalachian mountains of Tennessee and No. Carolina

che·root \shə-'rüt, chə-\ *n* **:** a cigar cut square at both ends

cher·ry \'cher-ē\ *n, pl* **cherries** [ONF *cherise* fruit of the cherry (understood as pl.), fr. LL *ceresia*, fr. L *cerasus* cherry tree, fr. Gk *kerasos*] **1 a :** any of numerous trees and shrubs of the rose family with rather small pale yellow to deep blackish red smooth-skinned fruits including several grown for their fruits or showy flowers **b :** the fruit or wood of a cherry **2 :** a variable color averaging a moderate red — **cherry** *adj*

chert \'chərt, 'chat\ *n* **:** a rock resembling flint and consisting essentially of fine crystalline quartz or fibrous chalcedony — **cherty** \-ē\ *adj*

cher·ub \'cher-əb\ *n* [Gk *cheroub*, fr. Heb *kĕrūbh*] **1** *pl* **cher·u·bim** \'cher-(y)ə-,bim\ **:** an angel of high rank **2** *pl* **cher·ubs** \'cher-əbz\ **a :** a painting or drawing of a beautiful child usu. with wings **b :** a chubby rosy child — **che·ru·bic** \chə-'rü-bik\ *adj*

cher·vil \'chər-vəl\ *n* [OE *cerfille*, fr. L *cerefolium*] **:** an aromatic herb of the carrot family with finely divided leaves often used in soups and salads

Ches·a·peake Bay retriever \,ches-(ə-),pēk-,bā-\ *n* **:** a large powerful sporting dog developed in Maryland by crossing Newfoundlands with native retrievers

Chesh·ire cat \,chesh-ər-\ *n* **:** a cat with a broad grin in Lewis Carroll's *Alice's Adventures in Wonderland*

Cheshire cheese *n* **:** a cheese similar to cheddar made chiefly in Cheshire, England

chess \'ches\ *n* [OF *esches*, pl. of *eschec* check] **:** a game for 2 players played with 16 pieces on a checkerboard — **chess·board** \-,bōrd, -,bȯrd\ *n* — **chess·man** \-,man, -mən\ *n*

chest \'chest\ *n* [OE *cest*, fr. L *cista*] **1 :** a container for storage or shipping; *esp* **:** a box with a lid esp. for safe-

keeping of belongings **2 :** a public fund accumulated for some purpose **3 :** the part of the body enclosed by the ribs and breastbone — **chest·ed** \'ches-təd\ *adj*

ches·ter·field \'ches-tər-,fēld\ *n* **:** an overcoat with a velvet collar

Ches·ter White \,ches-tər-\ *n* **:** any of a breed of large white swine

¹chest·nut \'ches-(,)nət\ *n* [ME *chesten* chestnut tree, fr. MF *chastaigne*, fr. L *castanea*, fr. Gk *kastanea*] **1 :** an edible nut from several trees or shrubs of the beech family; *also* **:** a plant bearing chestnuts or its wood **2 :** HORSE CHESTNUT **3 :** a horse with the body colored pure or reddish brown and the mane, tail, and points of the same or a lighter shade — compare ²BAY 1, SORREL **4 :** a callosity on the inner side of the leg of the horse **5 :** an often repeated old joke or story

²chestnut *adj* **:** of a grayish to reddish brown color

chestnut blight *n* **:** a destructive fungous disease of the American chestnut

che·val–de–frise \shə-,val-də-'frēz\ *n, pl* **che·vaux–de–frise** \shə-,vōd-ə-\ [F, lit., horse from Friesland] **:** a defense consisting of a timber or barrel covered with projecting spikes

che·val glass \shə-'val-\ *n* **:** a full-length mirror that may be tilted in a frame

chev·a·lier \,shev-ə-'li(ə)r, *esp for 2 also* shə-'val-,yā\ *n* [MF, fr. LL *caballarius* horseman] **1 :** CAVALIER 2 **2 :** a member of any of various orders of knighthood or of merit (as the French Legion of Honor)

chev·i·ot \'shev-ē-ət, 'chev-\ *n* [*Cheviot* hills, England and Scotland] **1 :** any of a breed of hardy hornless medium‑wooled meat-type British sheep **2 a :** a heavy rough napped woolen or worsted fabric **b :** a sturdy cotton shirting

chev·ron \'shev-rən\ *n* [MF, rafter, chevron] **1 :** a figure resembling an upside‑down V **2 :** a sleeve badge usu. indicating the wearer's rank or service (as in the armed forces)

¹chew \'chü\ *vb* [OE *cēowan*] **:** to crush or grind (as food) with the teeth **:** MASTICATE — **chew·a·ble** \-ə-bəl\ *adj* — **chew·er** *n* — **chewy** \'chü-ē\ *adj*

²chew *n* **1 :** the act of chewing **2 :** something for chewing

chevrons 2: *1* marine staff sergeant, *2* air force sergeant, *3* army staff sergeant

chewing gum *n* **:** gum usu. of sweetened and flavored chicle prepared for chewing

che·wink \chi-'wiŋk\ *n* **:** a common towhee of eastern No. America

Chey·enne \shī-'an, -'en\ *n* **:** a member of an Indian people of the western plains

chi \'kī\ *n* **:** the 22d letter of the Greek alphabet — X or χ

Chi·an·ti \kē-'änt-ē\ *n* **:** a still dry usu. red table wine

chiar·oscu·ro \kē-,är-ə-'sk(y)ù(ə)r-ō\ *n* [It, fr. *chiaro* clear, light + *oscuro* obscure, dark] **1 :** pictorial representation in terms of light and shade without regard to color **2 :** the arrangement or treatment of light and dark parts in a pictorial work of art — **chiar·oscu·rist** \-'sk(y)ùr-əst\ *n*

¹chic \'shēk\ *n* [F] **:** STYLISHNESS

²chic *adj* **:** cleverly stylish **:** SMART

chi·cane \shik-'ān\ *n* [F] **:** CHICANERY

chi·ca·nery \-'ān-(ə-)rē\ *n, pl* **-ner·ies :** TRICKERY, DECEIT

Chi·ca·no \chi-'kän-(,)ō\ *n, pl* **-nos** [modif. of Sp *mejicano* Mexican] **:** an American of Mexican descent — **Chicano** *adj*

chi·chi \'shē-(,)shē, 'chē-(,)chē\ *adj* **1 :** elaborately ornamented **2 :** ARTY **3 :** FASHIONABLE, CHIC ⟨*chichi* nightclubs⟩ — **chichi** *n*

chick \'chik\ *n* **1 a :** CHICKEN; *esp* **:** one newly hatched **b :** the young of any bird **2 :** CHILD **3** *slang* **:** a young woman

chick·a·dee \'chik-əd-(,)ē\ *n* **:** any of several crestless American titmice usu. with the crown of the head darker than the body

chick·a·ree \'chik-ə-,rē\ *n* **:** a common American red squirrel

Chick·a·saw \'chik-ə-,sò\ *n* **:** a member of an Indian people of northern Mississippi and Alabama

chick·en \'chik-ən\ *n* [OE *cicen*; akin to E *cock*] **1 :** the common domestic fowl esp. when young; *also* **:** its flesh used as food **2 :** any of various birds or their young

chicken hawk *n* **:** a hawk that preys or is reputed to prey on chickens

chick·en·heart·ed \,chik-ən-'härt-əd\ *adj* **:** TIMID, COWARDLY

chicken pox *n* **:** a contagious virus disease esp. of children marked by low fever and watery blisters on the skin

chicken snake *n* **:** any of various large harmless No. American snakes — called also *rat snake*

chick-pea \'chik-,pē\ *n* **:** an Asiatic leguminous herb cultivated for its short pods with one or two edible seeds; *also* **:** its seed

chick·weed \'chik-,wēd\ *n* **:** any of several low-growing small-leaved weedy plants of the pink family

chi·cle \'chik-əl\ *n* [Sp, fr. Nahuatl *chictli*] **:** a gum from the latex of the sapodilla used as the chief ingredient of chewing gum

chic·o·ry \'chik-(ə-)rē\ *n, pl* **-ries** [MF *cichorée, chicorée,* fr. L *cichoreum,* fr. Gk *kichoreia*] **:** a thick-rooted usu. blue-flowered European perennial herb related to the daisies and grown for its roots and as a salad plant; *also* **:** its dried ground roasted root used to flavor or adulterate coffee

chide \'chīd\ *vb* **chid** \'chid\ *or* **chid·ed** \'chīd-əd\; **chid** *or* **chid·den** \'chid-ᵊn\ *or* **chided**; **chid·ing** \'chīd-iŋ\ [OE *cīdan*] **:** to voice disapproval to **:** SCOLD, REBUKE

¹chief \'chēf\ *n* [OF, lit., head, fr. L *caput*] **1 :** the upper part of an heraldic field **2 :** the head of a body or organization **:** LEADER ⟨an Indian *chief*⟩ ⟨*chief* of police⟩ **3 :** the principal part — **in chief 1 :** held or holding rights or title directly from a paramount feudal lord ⟨tenure *in chief*⟩ **2 :** in the chief position or place ⟨editor *in chief*⟩

²chief *adj* **1 :** highest in rank, office, or authority ⟨*chief* executive⟩ **2 :** of greatest importance, significance, or influence ⟨his *chief* claim to fame⟩

chief justice *n* **:** the presiding or principal judge of a court of justice

¹chief·ly \'chē-flē\ *adv* **1 :** most importantly **:** PRINCIPALLY, ESPECIALLY **2 :** for the most part **:** MOSTLY, MAINLY

²chiefly *adj* **:** of or relating to a chief ⟨*chiefly* family⟩

chief master sergeant *n* **:** a noncommissioned officer in the air force of the highest enlisted rank

chief of staff 1 : the ranking officer of a military staff and principal adviser to the commander **2 :** the ranking office of the army or air force

chief of state : the formal head of a national state as distinguished from the head of the government

chief petty officer *n* **:** a petty officer in the navy ranking above a petty officer and below a senior chief petty officer

chief·tain \'chēf-tən\ *n* [MF *chevetain,* fr. LL *capitaneus* chief].**:** a chief esp. of a band, tribe, or clan — **chief·tain·cy** \-sē\ *n* — **chief·tain·ship** \-,ship\ *n*

chief warrant officer *n* **:** a warrant officer (as in the army) of senior rank

chif·fon \shif-'än, 'shif-,\ *n* [F, lit., rag] **:** a sheer silk fabric

chif·fo·nier \,shif-ə-'ni(ə)r\ *n* **:** a high narrow chest of drawers often with a mirror

chig·ger \'chig-ər, 'jig-\ *n* [of African origin] **1 :** CHIGOE 1 **2 :** a 6-legged larval mite that sucks the blood of vertebrates and causes intense irritation

chi·gnon \'shēn-,yän\ *n* [F] **:** a knot of hair worn at the back of the head

chig·oe \'chig-ō, 'chē-gō\ *n* **1 :** a tropical flea of which the fertile female burrows under the skin causing great discomfort — called also *chigger* **2 :** CHIGGER 2

Chi·hua·hua \chə-'wä-,wä, shə-, -wə\ *n* **:** a very small round-headed large-eared short-coated dog held to antedate Aztec civilization

chil·blain \'chil-,blān\ *n* **:** an inflammatory swelling or sore caused by exposure (as of the feet or hands) to cold

child \'chīld\ *n, pl* **chil·dren** \'chil-drən, -dərn\ [OE *cild*] **1 :** an unborn or recently born person **2 a :** a young person of either sex esp. between infancy and youth **b :** a childlike or childish person **c :** a person not yet of legal age **3** *usu* **childe** \'chīld\ *archaic* **:** a youth of noble birth **4 a :** a son or daughter of human parents **b :** DESCENDANT **5 :** one strongly influenced by another

or by a place or state of affairs ⟨a *child* of his times⟩ — **child·less** \'chīl(d)-ləs\ *adj* — **with child :** PREGNANT

child·bear·ing \'chīl(d)-,bar-iŋ, -,ber-\ *n* **:** the act of giving birth to children **:** PARTURITION — **childbearing** *adj*

child·bed fever \,chīl(d)-,bed-\ *n* **:** puerperal fever

child·birth \'chīl(d)-,bərth\ *n* **:** PARTURITION

child·hood \'chīld-,hud\ *n* **:** the state or time of being a child

child·ish \'chīl-dish\ *adj* **1 :** of, resembling, or suitable to a child ⟨*childish* games⟩ **2 :** FOOLISH, SILLY **syn** see CHILDLIKE — **child·ish·ly** *adv* — **child·ish·ness** *n*

child·like \'chīl(d)-,līk\ *adj* **:** of, relating to, or resembling a child or childhood; *esp* **:** marked by simplicity, innocence, and trust — **child·like·ness** *n*

syn CHILDISH: CHILDLIKE suggests admirable and attractive qualities of children such as innocence, trust, directness; CHILDISH implies having such qualities as fretful impatience or undeveloped taste and judgment that are appropriate to children but deplorable in adults; both terms may apply to any age

Chile saltpeter \'chil-ē-\ *n* **:** sodium nitrate esp. occurring naturally

chili *or* **chile** *or* **chil·li** \'chil-ē\ *n, pl* **chil·ies** *or* **chil·es** *or* **chil·lies** [Sp *chile,* fr. Nahuatl *chilli*] **1 a :** HOT PEPPER 1 **b** *usu* **chilli,** *chiefly Brit* **:** a pepper whether hot or sweet **2 :** HOT PEPPER 2 **3 :** CHILI CON CARNE

chili con car·ne \,chil-ē-,kän-'kär-nē, -ē-kən-\ *n* [Sp *chile con carne* chili with meat] **:** a stew of ground beef, chilies or chili powder, and usu. beans

¹chill \'chil\ *vb* [ME *chillen,* fr. *chile* cold, frost, fr. OE *cele;* akin to E *cold*] **1 :** to become cold **2 :** to make cold or chilly **3 :** to harden the surface of (metal) by sudden cooling — **chill·er** *n* — **chill·ing·ly** \-iŋ-lē\ *adv*

²chill *adj* **1 a :** moderately cold **b :** COLD, RAW **2 :** affected by cold **3 :** not cordial **:** DISTANT, FORMAL ⟨a *chill* greeting⟩ — **chill·ness** *n*

³chill *n* **1 :** a sensation of cold accompanied by shivering **2 :** a moderate but disagreeable degree of cold **3 :** a check to enthusiasm or warmth of feeling

chilly \'chil-ē\ *adj* **chill·i·er; -est 1 :** noticeably cold **:** CHILLING **2 :** unpleasantly affected by cold **3 :** lacking warmth of feeling — **chill·i·ly** \'chil-ə-lē\ *adv* — **chill·i·ness** \'chil-ē-nəs\ *n*

¹chime \'chīm\ *n* [ME, cymbal, fr. OF *chimbe,* fr. L *cymbalum*] **1 :** a musically tuned set of bells **2 a :** the sound of a set of bells — usu. used in pl. **b :** a musical sound suggesting that of bells

²chime *vb* **1 a :** to make a musical esp. harmonious sound **b :** to make the sounds of a chime **c :** to cause to chime **2 :** to be or act in accord **3 :** to call or indicate by chiming ⟨clock *chiming* midnight⟩ **4 :** to utter repetitively **:** DIN — **chim·er** *n*

chime in *vb* **:** to break into or join in a conversation or discussion

chi·me·ra *or* **chi·mae·ra** \kī-'mir-ə, kə-\ *n* [Gk *chimaira* she-goat, chimera] **1** *cap* **:** a she-monster in Greek mythology usu. with a lion's head vomiting flames, a goat's body, and a serpent's tail **2 :** an often grotesque creation of the imagination **3 :** an individual, organ, or part with tissues of diverse genetic constitution

chi·mer·i·cal \kī-'mer-i-kəl, kə-, -'mir-\ *or* **chi·mer·ic** \-ik\ *adj* **1 :** existing only in the imagination **:** FANCIFUL, FANTASTIC **2 :** inclined to favor fantastic ideas or schemes — **chi·mer·i·cal·ly** \-i-k(ə-)lē\ *adv*

chim·ney \'chim-nē\ *n, pl* **chimneys** [MF *cheminée,* fr. LL *caminata,* fr. L *caminus* furnace, fireplace, fr. Gk *kaminos*] **1 :** a passage for smoke; *esp* **:** an upright structure of brick or stone extending above the roof of a building **2 :** a glass tube around a lamp flame

chimney piece *n* **:** a decorative construction over a fireplace

chimney pot *n* **:** a usu. earthenware pipe at the top of a chimney to increase draft and carry off smoke

chimney sweep *n* **:** a person who cleans soot from chimneys

chimney swift *n* **:** a small sooty-gray bird with long narrow wings that often attaches its nest to the inside of an unused chimney

chimp \'chimp, 'shimp\ *n* **:** CHIMPANZEE

chim·pan·zee \,chim-,pan-'zē, ,shim-; chim-'pan-zē, shim-\ *n* [Kongo dial. *chimpenzi*] **:** an African anthropoid ape that is smaller, more arboreal, and less fierce than the gorilla

¹chin \'chin\ *n* [OE *cinn*] : the lower portion of the face lying below the lower lip and including the prominence of the lower jaw

²chin *vb* **chinned; chin·ning** **1** : to raise (oneself) while hanging by the hands until the chin is level with the support **2** *slang* : to talk idly : CHATTER

chi·na \'chī-nə\ *n* [Per *chīnī* Chinese porcelain] **1** : vitreous porcelain ware orig. from the Orient; *also* : pottery (as dishes) for domestic use **2** : PORCELAIN

chi·na·ber·ry \'chī-nə-,ber-ē\ *n* **1** : a soapberry of the southern U.S. and Mexico **2** : a small Asiatic tree of the mahogany family naturalized in the southern U.S. where it is widely planted for shade or ornament

Chi·na·man \'chī-nə-mən\ *n* : CHINESE — often taken to be offensive

Chi·na·town \-,taùn\ *n* : the Chinese quarter of a city

China tree *n* : CHINABERRY

chi·na·ware \'chī-nə-,wa(ə)r, -,we(ə)r\ *n* : CHINA

chinch \'chinch\ *n* [Sp *chinche*, fr. L *cimic-, cimex*] : BEDBUG

chinch bug *n* : a small black-and-white bug very destructive to cereal grasses

chin·chil·la \chin-'chil-ə\ *n* [Sp] **1** : a So. American rodent the size of a large squirrel widely bred in captivity for its very soft fur of a pearly gray color; *also* : its fur **2** : a heavy twilled woolen coating

chine \'chīn\ *n* [MF *eschine*] **1** : BACKBONE, SPINE; *also* : a cut of meat or fish including the backbone or part of it and the surrounding flesh **2** : RIDGE, CREST

Chi·nese \chī-'nēz, -'nēs\ *n, pl* **Chinese** **1 a** : a native or inhabitant of China **b** : a person of Chinese descent **2 a** : a group of related languages used by the people of China that are often mutually unintelligible in their spoken form but share a single system of writing **b** : MANDARIN — **Chinese** *adj*

Chinese cabbage *n* : either of two Asiatic plants related to common cabbage and widely used as greens

Chinese lantern *n* : a collapsible lantern of thin colored paper

Chinese puzzle *n* **1** : an intricate or ingenious puzzle **2** : something intricate and hard to solve

Ching *or* **Ch'ing** \'chiŋ\ *n* : a Manchu dynasty in China dated 1644–1912 and the last imperial dynasty

¹chink \'chiŋk\ *n* : a narrow slit or crack (as in a wall)

²chink *vt* : to fill the chinks of (as by caulking) : stop up

³chink *n* : a short sharp sound

⁴chink *vb* : to make or cause to make a short sharp sound

chi·no \'chē-nō, 'shē-\ *n, pl* **-nos** **1** : a usu. khaki cotton twill fabric **2** : an article of clothing made of chino — usu. used in pl.

Chi·nook \shə-'nùk, chə-\ *n* **1** : a member of an Indian people of the north shore of the Columbia river at its mouth **2** *not cap* **a** : a warm moist southwest wind of the coast from Oregon northward **b** : a warm dry wind that descends the eastern slopes of the Rocky mountains

chin·qua·pin \'chiŋ-ki-,pin\ *n* [of Algonquian origin] : an American dwarf chestnut; *also* : its edible nut

chintz \'chin(t)s\ *n* [earlier *chints*, pl. of *chint*, fr. Hindi *chīṭ*] **1** : a printed calico from India **2** : a usu. glazed printed cotton fabric

chintzy \'chin(t)-sē\ *adj* **1** : decorated with or as if with chintz **2** : GAUDY

¹chip \'chip\ *n* [ME] **1 a** : a small piece (as of wood, stone, or glass) broken off by a sharp blow : FLAKE **b** (1) : a thin crisp slice of potato (2) : FRENCH FRY **2 a** : a counter used in poker **b** *pl, slang* : MONEY **3** : a piece of dried dung ⟨cow *chip*⟩ **4** : a flaw left after a small piece has been broken off ⟨a cup with a *chip* in it⟩ — **chip off the old block** : a child that resembles his parent — **chip on one's shoulder** : a challenging or belligerent attitude

²chip *vb* **chipped; chip·ping** **1 a** : to cut or hew with an edged tool ⟨*chip* ice from a sidewalk⟩ **b** (1) : to cut or break (a small piece) from something (2) : to cut or break a chip from ⟨*chip* a cup⟩ **2** : to break off in small pieces

chip in *vb* : CONTRIBUTE ⟨everyone *chipped in* to buy him a farewell gift⟩

chip·munk \'chip-,məŋk\ *n* [of Algonquian origin] : any of numerous small striped largely terrestrial American squirrels

chipped beef \'chip(t)-\ *n* : smoked dried beef sliced thin

Chip·pen·dale \'chip-ən-,dāl\ *adj* [after Thomas *Chippendale* d1779 English cabinetmaker] : of or relating to a late 18th century English furniture style characterized by graceful outline and often ornate rococo ornamentation

chipmunk

chip·per \'chip-ər\ *adj* : GAY, SPRIGHTLY ⟨looks bright and *chipper* every morning⟩

Chip·pe·wa \'chip-ə-,wo, -,wä, -,wā\ *n* : OJIBWA

chip·ping sparrow \'chip-iŋ-\ *n* : a small eastern No. American sparrow whose song is a weak monotonous trill

chiro- *comb form* [Gk *cheir*] : hand ⟨*chiro*mancy⟩

chi·rog·ra·phy \kī-'räg-rə-fē\ *n* **1** : HANDWRITING, PENMANSHIP **2** : CALLIGRAPHY **1** — **chi·rog·ra·pher** \-fər\ *n* — **chi·ro·graph·ic** \,kī-rə-'graf-ik\ *adj*

chi·rop·o·dy \kə-'räp-əd-ē\ *n* [Gk *cheir* hand + *pod-, pous* foot] : professional care and treatment of the human foot in health and disease — **chi·rop·o·dist** \-əd-əst\ *n*

chi·ro·prac·tic \'kī-rə-,prak-tik\ *n* : a system of healing based on manipulation and specific adjustment of body structures (as the spinal column) — **chi·ro·prac·tor** \-tər\ *n*

chi·rop·ter \kī-'räp-tər\ *n* : ³BAT — **chi·rop·ter·an** \-tə-rən\ *adj or n*

chirp \'chərp\ *n* : a short sharp sound characteristic of a small bird or cricket — **chirp** *vb*

chirr \'chər\ *n* : a vibrant or trilled sound characteristic of a cicada — **chirr** *vi*

chir·rup \'chər-əp, 'chir-\ *n* : CHIRP — **chirrup** *vb*

chi·rur·geon \kī-'rər-jən\ *n, archaic* : SURGEON

¹chis·el \'chiz-əl\ *n* [ONF, fr. L *caes-, caedere* to cut] : a metal tool with a cutting edge at the end of a blade used to shape or chip away stone, wood, or metal

²chisel *vb* **-eled** *or* **-elled; -el·ing** *or* **-el·ling** \'chiz-(ə-)liŋ\ **1** : to cut or work with or as if with a chisel **2 a** : to use shrewd sometimes unfair practices **b** : CHEAT — **chis·el·er** \'chiz-(ə-)lər\ *n*

chis·eled *or* **chis·elled** \'chiz-əld\ *adj* **1** : cut or shaped with a chisel **2** : appearing as if shaped with a chisel : finely cut ⟨sharply *chiseled* features⟩

¹chit \'chit\ *n* **1** : CHILD **2** : a pert young woman

²chit *n* [Hindi *ciṭṭhī*] : a short letter or note; *esp* : a signed voucher of a small debt (as for food)

chit·chat \'chit-,chat\ *n* : SMALL TALK, GOSSIP

chi·tin \'kīt-°n\ *n* [F *chitine*, fr. Gk *chitōn* tunic] : an amorphous horny substance that forms part of the hard outer integument of some invertebrates (as insects and crustaceans) — **chi·tin·ous** \-əs\ *adj*

chi·ton \'kīt-°n, 'kī-,tän\ *n* [Gk *chitōn* tunic] **1** : any of a class (Amphineura) of bilaterally symmetrical marine mollusks with a dorsal shell of calcareous plates **2 a** : tunic worn in ancient Greece

chit·ter \'chit-ər\ *vi* : TWITTER, CHIRP; *also* : CHATTER

chit·ter·lings *or* **chit·lings** *or* **chit·lins** \'chit-lənz\ *n pl* : the intestines of hogs esp. prepared as food

chi·val·ric \shə-'val-rik\ *adj* : of or relating to chivalry : CHIVALROUS

chiv·al·rous \'shiv-əl-rəs\ *adj* **1** : VALIANT **2** : of or relating to chivalry **3** : having or displaying the qualities of an ideal knight of the age of chivalry: as **a** : marked by honor, generosity, and courtesy **b** : marked by especial courtesy and consideration to women — **chiv·al·rous·ly** *adv* — **chiv·al·rous·ness** *n*

chiv·al·ry \-rē\ *n* [OF *chevalerie*, fr. *chevalier*] **1** : a body of knights ⟨the *chivalry* of France⟩ **2** : the system, spirit, ways, or customs of medieval knighthood **3** : the qualities (as bravery, honor, protection of the weak, and generous treatment of foes) held to characterize an ideal knight : chivalrous conduct

chive \'chīv\ *n* [ONF, fr. L *cepa* onion] : a perennial herb related to the onion and used for flavoring

chlam·y·dom·o·nas \,klam-ə-'däm-ə-nəs\ *n* : any of a genus of single-celled algae with an eyespot and two flagella that are abundant in fresh water and damp soil

---

j joke; **ŋ** sing; **ō** flow; **ȯ** flaw; **ȯi** coin; **th** thin; **t̲h̲** this; **ü** loot; **ù** foot; **y** yet; **yü** few; **yù** furious; **zh** vision

chla·mydo·spore \klə-'mid-ə-ˌspō(ə)r, -ˌspȯ(ə)r\ *n* : a thick-walled usu. resting spore — **chla·mydo·spor·ic** \klə-ˌmid-ə-'spȯr-ik, -'spȯr-\ *adj*

chla·mys \'klam-əs, 'klām-\ *n, pl* **chla·mys·es** *or* **chla·my·des** \-ə-ˌdēz\ [Gk *chlamyd-, chlamys*] : a short mantle worn by young men of ancient Greece

chlor- *or* **chloro-** *comb form* [Gk *chlōros* greenish yellow; akin to E *yellow*] **1** : green ⟨*chlor*ine⟩ ⟨*chlor*osis⟩ **2** : chlorine ⟨*chlor*ic⟩

chlo·ral \'klōr-əl, 'klȯr-\ *n* : a bitter white crystalline drug C₂H₃Cl₃O₂ used to bring sleep — called also *chloral hydrate*

chlo·rate \'klōr-ˌāt, 'klȯr-\ *n* : a salt of chloric acid

chlor·dane \'klōr-ˌdān\ *or* **chlor·dan** \-ˌdan\ *n* : a viscous volatile liquid insecticide C₁₀H₆Cl₈

chlo·rel·la \klə-'rel-ə\ *n* : any of a genus of unicellular green algae potentially a cheap source of high-grade protein and B-complex vitamins

chlo·ric acid \ˌklōr-ik-, ˌklȯr-\ *n* : a strong acid HClO₃ like nitric acid in oxidizing properties but far less stable

chlo·ride \'klōr-ˌīd, 'klȯr-\ *n* : a chemical compound of chlorine with another element or radical; *esp* : a salt or ester of hydrochloric acid

chloride of lime *n* : BLEACHING POWDER

chlo·rin·ate \'klōr-ə-ˌnāt, 'klȯr-\ *vt* : to treat or cause to combine with chlorine esp. for purifying — **chlo·rin·a·tion** \ˌklōr-ə-'nā-shən, ˌklȯr-\ *n* — **chlo·rin·a·tor** \'klōr-ə-ˌnāt-ər, 'klȯr-\ *n*

chlorinated lime *n* : BLEACHING POWDER

chlo·rine \'klōr-ˌēn, 'klȯr-, -ən\ *n* : a chemical element that is a heavy greenish yellow irritating gas of pungent odor used esp. as a bleach, oxidizing agent, and disinfectant in water purification — see ELEMENT table

chlorine water *n* : a yellowish aqueous solution of chlorine in water used for bleaching

chlo·rite \'klōr-ˌīt, 'klȯr-\ *n* : any of a group of usu. green minerals associated with and resembling the micas

¹chlo·ro·form \'klōr-ə-ˌfȯrm, 'klȯr-\ *n* [*chlorine* + *formic* acid] : a colorless volatile heavy poisonous liquid CHCl₃ that smells like ether and is used esp. as a solvent or as a general anesthetic

²chloroform *vt* : to treat with chloroform esp. so as to produce anesthesia or death

Chlo·ro·my·ce·tin \ˌklōr-ō-mī-'sēt-ʲn, ˌklȯr-\ *trademark* — used for an antibiotic obtained from a soil microorganism or prepared synthetically

chlo·ro·phyll *also* **chlo·ro·phyl** \'klōr-ə-ˌfil, 'klȯr-\ *n* [Gk *chlōros* greenish yellow + *phyllon* leaf] : the green magnesium-containing photosynthetic coloring matter of pants found in chloroplasts — **chlo·ro·phyl·lose** \ˌlklōr-ə-'fil-ˌōs, ˌklȯr-\ *adj* — **chlo·ro·phyl·lous** \-'fil-əs\ *adj*

chlo·ro·plast \'klōr-ə-ˌplast, 'klȯr-\ *n* : a plastid that contains chlorophyll and is the seat of photosynthesis and starch formation in a plant cell

chlo·ro·sis \klə-'rō-səs\ *n, pl* **-ro·ses** \-'rō-ˌsēz\ **1** : an anemia in which the skin is greenish **2** : a disorder of green plants marked by yellowing or blanching — **chlo·rot·ic** \-'rät-ik\ *adj* — **chlo·rot·i·cal·ly** \-'rät-i-k(ə-)lē\ *adv*

chlo·rous acid \ˌklōr-əs-, ˌklȯr-\ *n* : a strongly oxidizing acid HClO₂ known only in solution and in the form of its salts

chlor·tet·ra·cy·cline \ˌklōr-ˌte-trə-'sī-ˌklēn, ˌklȯr-\ *n* : a yellow crystalline antibiotic C₂₂H₂₃ClN₂O₈ produced by a soil actinomycete, used in the treatment of diseases, and added to animal feeds for stimulating growth

¹chock \'chäk\ *n* **1** : a wedge or block for steadying a body (as a cask) and holding it motionless, for filling in an unwanted space, or for blocking the movement of a wheel **2** : a metal casting with two short arms curving inward between which ropes may pass for mooring or towing

²chock *vt* : to stop or make fast with or as if with chocks

chock·a·block \'chäk-ə-ˌbläk\ *adj* : very full : CROWDED

chock–full \'chäk-'fùl\ *adj* : full to the limit

choc·o·late \'chäk-(ə-)lət, 'chȯk-\ *n* [Sp, fr. Nahuatl *xocoatl*] **1** : a food prepared from ground roasted cacao beans **2** : a beverage of chocolate in water or milk **3** : a candy with a chocolate coating **4** : a variable color averaging a brownish gray — **chocolate** *adj*

Choc·taw \'chäk-ˌtȯ\ *n* : a member of an Indian people of Mississippi, Alabama, and Louisiana

¹choice \'chȯis\ *n* [OF *chois*, fr. *choisir* to choose, of Gmc origin; akin to E *choose*] **1** : the act of choosing : SELECTION **2** : power of choosing : OPTION **3 a** : a person or thing chosen **b** : the best part : CREAM **4** : a sufficient number and variety for wide or free selection
syn OPTION, ALTERNATIVE: CHOICE suggests the opportunity or privilege of choosing freely; OPTION implies a power to choose that is specifically granted or guaranteed; ALTERNATIVE implies a necessity to choose one and reject another possibility

²choice *adj* **1** : very fine : better than most ⟨a supply of *choice* fruits⟩ **2** : of a grade between prime and good ⟨*choice* meat⟩ — **choice·ly** *adv* — **choice·ness** *n*

¹choir \'kwī(ə)r\ *n* [OF *cuer*, fr. L *chorus*] **1** : an organized group of singers esp. in a church **2** : the part of a church between the sanctuary and the nave **3** : a division of angels **4** : a group of instruments of the same class

²choir *adj* : of the class in a religious order bound to recite the Divine Office and devoted chiefly to the order's special work

choir·boy \-ˌbȯi\ *n* : a boy member of a church choir

choir loft *n* : a gallery occupied by the choir

choir·mas·ter \-ˌmas-tər\ *n* : the director of a choir (as in a church)

¹choke \'chōk\ *vb* [OE *acēocian*] **1** : to hinder normal breathing by cutting off the supply of air ⟨thick smoke *choked* the firemen⟩ **2** : to have the windpipe stopped entirely or partly ⟨*choke* on a bone⟩ **3** : to check the growth or action of : SUPPRESS, SMOTHER ⟨*choke* a fire⟩ ⟨*choke* back tears⟩ **4** : to obstruct by clogging ⟨leaves *choked* the sewer⟩ **5** : to fill to the limit ⟨the store was *choked* with customers⟩ **6** : to decrease or shut off the air intake of the carburetor of a gasoline engine in order to make the fuel mixture richer

²choke *n* : something that chokes: as **a** : a valve for choking a gasoline engine **b** : a narrowing toward the muzzle in the bore of a gun **c** : a coil of wire that provides inductance in an electric circuit and is used to impede the flow of current, to block surges of current, or to filter out unwanted frequencies — called also *choke coil*

choke·cher·ry \-ˌcher-ē, -'cher-\ *n* : any of several American wild cherries with bitter or astringent fruit; *also* : this fruit

choke·damp \'chōk-ˌdamp\ *n* : a heavy nonexplosive mine gas that consists chiefly of carbon dioxide and will not support life

choky \'chō-kē\ *adj* **chok·i·er; -est** **1** : having the power to choke ⟨a *choky* gas⟩ **2** : inclined to choke : having a tendency to choke ⟨grow *choky* with fear⟩

chol- *or* **chole-** *comb form* [Gk *cholē*; akin to E *gall*] : bile : gall ⟨*choli*ne⟩ ⟨*chole*sterol⟩

cho·le·cys·ti·tis \ˌkō-lə-ˌsis-'tīt-əs, ˌkäl-ə-\ *n* : inflammation of the gallbladder

chol·er \'käl-ər, 'kō-lər\ *n* [LL *cholera* bile, fr. Gk, cholera] : IRASCIBILITY, TEMPER

chol·era \'käl-ə-rə\ *n* [Gk, fr. *cholē* bile] : any of several diseases usu. marked by severe vomiting and dysentery; *esp* : ASIATIC CHOLERA — **chol·e·ra·ic** \ˌkäl-ə-'rā-ik\ *adj*

chol·er·ic \'käl-ə-rik, kə-'ler-ik\ *adj* **1** : easily moved to anger : hot-tempered **2** : ANGRY, IRATE **syn** *see* IRASCIBLE

cho·les·ter·ol \kə-'les-tə-ˌrȯl, -ˌrōl\ *n* : a physiologically important waxy substance C₂₇H₄₅OH present in animal cells and tissues and when deposited in arterial walls held to be a factor in their abnormal thickening and hardening

cho·line \'kō-ˌlēn, 'käl-ˌēn\ *n* : a basic substance C₅H₁₅NO₂ that is widely distributed in animal and plant products and is a vitamin of the B complex essential to the liver function

cho·lin·er·gic \ˌkō-lə-'nər-jik, ˌkäl-ə-\ *adj* : liberating or activated by acetylcholine ⟨a *cholinergic* nerve fiber⟩

cho·lin·es·ter·ase \ˌkō-lə-'nes-tə-ˌrās, ˌkäl-ə-\ *n* : an enzyme that hydrolyzes choline esters

chon·drio·some \'kän-drē-ə-ˌsōm\ *n* [Gk *chondrion*, dim. of *chondros* granule] : any of the minute apparently self-perpetuating bodies in cytoplasm held to function in cellular metabolism and secretion

choose \'chüz\ *vb* **chose** \'chōz\; **cho·sen** \'chōz-ʲn\;

choos·ing \'chü-ziŋ\ [OE *cēosan*] **1** : to select esp. freely and after consideration ⟨*choose* a leader⟩ **2 a** : DE-CIDE ⟨*chose* to go by train⟩ **b** : PREFER **3** : to see fit : IN-CLINE ⟨take them if you *choose*⟩ — **choos·er** *n*

choosy *or* **choos·ey** \'chü-zē\ *adj* **choos·i·er; choos·i·est** : fastidiously selective : PARTICULAR

¹chop \'chäp\ *vb* **chopped; chop·ping** [ME *chappen, choppen* to chop, crack] **1** : to cut by striking esp. repeatedly with something sharp ⟨*chop* down a tree⟩ **2** : to cut into small pieces : MINCE **3** : to strike quickly or repeatedly (as with an ax) — **chop·per** *n*

²chop *n* **1 a** : a forceful sudden stroke with a sharp instrument **b** : a sharp downward blow **2** : a small cut of meat often including a part of a rib **3** : a short quick motion (as of a wave)

³chop *vi* **chopped; chop·ping** [OE *cēapian* to barter] **1** : to change direction **2** : to veer with or as if with the wind

chop·fall·en \'chäp-,fȯ-lən\ *var of* CHAPFALLEN

chop·house \'chäp-,haùs\ *n* : RESTAURANT

chop·pi·ness \'chäp-ē-nəs\ *n* : the quality or state of being choppy

¹choppy \'chäp-ē\ *adj* **chop·pi·er; -est** : CHANGEABLE, VARIABLE ⟨*choppy* wind⟩

²choppy *adj* **chop·pi·er; -est** **1** : rough with small waves **2** : JERKY, DISCONNECTED

chops \'chäps\ *n pl* : the fleshy covering of the jaws

chop·stick \'chäp-,stik\ *n* [pidgin E, fr. *chop* fast] : one of a pair of slender sticks used chiefly in oriental countries to lift food to the mouth

chop su·ey \chäp-'sü-ē\ *n* [Chin (Cant) *shap sui* miscellaneous bits] : a dish pre-pared chiefly from bean sprouts, bamboo shoots, water chestnuts, onions, mush-rooms, and meat or fish

chopsticks

cho·ral \'kōr-əl, 'kȯr-\ *adj* : of, relating to, or performed by a chorus or choir or in chorus — **cho·ral·ly** \-ə-lē\ *adv*

cho·rale *also* **cho·ral** \kə-'ral, -'räl\ *n* **1** : a hymn or psalm sung to a traditional or composed melody in church; *also* : a hymn tune or a harmonization of a traditional melody **2** : CHORUS, CHOIR

¹chord \'kȯrd\ *n* [ME *cord*, short for *accord*] : a combination of tones that blend harmoniously when sounded to-gether — **chord·al** \-ᵊl\ *adj*

²chord *vb* **1** : ACCORD, HARMONIZE **2** : to play chords on a stringed instrument

³chord *n* [alter. of ¹*cord*] **1** : CORD 3a **2** : a straight line joining two points on a curve — see CIRCLE illustration **3** : an individual emotion or disposition ⟨strike a familiar *chord*⟩ **4** : a straight line joining the leading and trailing edges of an airfoil

chor·da·mes·o·derm \,kȯrd-ə-'mez-ə-,dərm, -'mes-\ : the portion of the embryonic mesoderm that forms notochord and related structures and serves as an inductor of neural structures — **chor·da·mes·o·der·mal** \-,mez-ə-'dər-məl, -,mes-\ *adj*

chor·date \'kȯrd-ət, 'kȯr-,dāt\ *n* : any of a phylum or other major group (Chordata) of animals having at least at some stage of development a notochord and a dorsally situated central nervous system and including the verte-brates, lancelets, and tunicates — compare HEMICHORDATE — **chordate** *adj*

chore \'chō(ə)r, 'chȯ(ə)r\ *n* [alter. of ME *char*, lit., turn, fr. OE *cierr*] **1** *pl* : the regular light work of a household or farm **2** : a routine task or job **3** : a difficult or dis-agreeable task

cho·rea \kə-'rē-ə\ *n* [Gk *choreia* dance] : a nervous dis-order (as of man or dogs) marked by spasmodic move-ments and lack of coordination

cho·re·og·ra·phy \,kōr-ē-'äg-rə-fē, ,kȯr-\ *n* [Gk *choreia* dance, fr. *choros* chorus] : the art of dancing or of arrang-ing dances and esp. ballets — **cho·re·og·ra·pher** \-fər\ *n* — **cho·re·o·graph·ic** \-ē-ə-'graf-ik\ *adj* — **cho·re·o·graph·i·cal·ly** \-'graf-i-k(ə-)lē\ *adv*

cho·ric \'kōr-ik, 'kȯr-, 'kär-\ *adj* : of, relating to, or being in the style of a chorus and esp. a Greek chorus

cho·ri·on \'kōr-ē-,än, 'kȯr-\ *n* [Gk] : the highly vascular outer embryonic membrane of higher vertebrates that in placental mammals joins the allantois in the formation of the placenta — **cho·ri·on·ic** \,kōr-ē-'än-ik, ,kȯr-\ *adj*

cho·ris·ter \'kȯr-ə-stər, 'kȯr-, 'kär-\ *n* : a singer in a choir

cho·roid \'kōr-,ȯid, 'kȯr-\ *also* **cho·ri·oid** \-ē-,ȯid\ *adj* [Gk *chorioeidēs*, fr. *chorion*] : of, relating to, or being the vascular pigmented middle layer of the vertebrate eye lying between the sclera and the retina — **choroid** *n*

choroid coat *n* : CHOROID

chor·tle \'chȯrt-ᵊl\ *vi* **chor·tled; chor·tling** \'chȯrt-liŋ, -ᵊl-iŋ\ [blend of *chuckle* and *snort*] : to laugh or chuckle esp. in satisfaction or exultation — **chortle** *n* — **chor·tler** \'chȯrt-lər, -ᵊl-ər\ *n*

¹cho·rus \'kōr-əs, 'kȯr-\ *n* [Gk *choros*] **1 a** : a group of singers and dancers in Greek drama participating in or commenting on the action **b** : a character in Elizabethan drama who speaks the prologue and epilogue and com-ments on the action **c** : an organized group of singers : CHOIR; *esp* : a body of singers who sing the choral parts of a work (as in opera) **d** : a group of supporting dancers and singers in a musical comedy or revue **2 a** : a recurring part of a song or hymn **b** : the part of a drama sung or spoken by the chorus **c** : a composition to be sung by a chorus **d** : the main part of a popular song **3** : something uttered simultaneously by a number of persons ⟨a *chorus* of boos⟩ — **in chorus** : in unison

²chorus *vb* : to sing or utter in chorus

chorus girl *n* : a young woman who sings or dances in a chorus (as of a musical comedy) — called also *cho·rine* \'kōr-,ēn, 'kȯr-\

chose *past of* CHOOSE

cho·sen \'chōz-ᵊn\ *adj* [ME, fr. pp. of *chosen* to choose] **1** : selected or marked for favor or special privilege ⟨privileges granted to a *chosen* few⟩ **2** : selected by God ⟨a *chosen* people⟩

Chou \'jō\ *n* : a Chinese dynasty traditionally dated 1122 to about 256 B.C. and marked by the development of the philosophical schools of Confucius and Lao-tzu

chough \'chəf\ *n* : an Old World black red-legged bird related to the crows

¹chow \'chaù\ *n* : a thick-coated straight-legged muscular dog with a blue-black tongue and a short tail curled close to the back — called also *chow chow* \'chaù-,chaù\

²chow \'chaù\ *n, slang* : FOOD, VICTUALS

chow-chow \'chaù-,chaù\ *n* : chopped mixed pickles in mustard sauce

chow·der \'chaùd-ər\ *n* [F *chaudière* kettle, fr. LL *caldaria*, fr. L *calidus* warm] : a soup or stew made of fish, clams, or a vegetable usu. stewed in milk

chow mein \'chaù-'mān\ *n* [Chin (Pek) *ch'ao³ mien⁴*] **1** : fried noodles **2** : a thick stew of shredded meat, mushrooms, and vegetables served with fried noodles

chrism \'kriz-əm\ *n* [Gk *chrisma* ointment, fr. *chriein* to anoint] : consecrated oil used esp. in baptism, confirma-tion, and ordination

Christ \'krīst\ *n* [L *Christus*, fr. Gk *Christos*, lit., anointed] **1** : MESSIAH **2** : JESUS **3** : an ideal type of humanity

chris·ten \'kris-ᵊn\ *vt* **chris·tened; chris·ten·ing** \'kris-niŋ, -ᵊn-iŋ\ [OE *cristnian*, fr. *cristen* Christian, fr. L *christianus*] **1 a** : BAPTIZE **b** : to name at baptism **2** : to name or dedicate (as a ship) by a ceremony suggestive of baptism

Chris·ten·dom \'kris-ᵊn-dəm\ *n* **1** : the entire body of Christians **2** : all the countries or peoples that are pre-dominantly Christian

chris·ten·ing *n* : the ceremony of baptizing and naming a child

¹Chris·tian \'kris-chən\ *n* **1** : a person who believes in Jesus Christ and follows his teachings **2** : a member of a Christian church **3** : a member of a group (as the Dis-ciples of Christ or the Churches of Christ) seeking a return to New Testament Christianity

²Christian *adj* **1** : of or relating to Jesus Christ or the religion deriving from him **2** : of or relating to Christians ⟨a *Christian* nation⟩ **3** : befitting a Christian : KIND, DECENT

Christian Brother *n* : a member of the Roman Catholic institute of Brothers of the Christian Schools founded in France in 1680 and devoted to primary and secondary education

Christian era *n* : the era used in Christian countries for numbering the years since the birth of Christ

chris·ti·an·ia \,kris-chē-'an-ē-ə\ *n, often cap* : a skiing turn executed usu. at high speed by shifting body weight

---

j joke;   ŋ sing;   ō flow;   ȯ flaw;   ȯi coin;   th thin;   th this;   ü loot;   ù foot;   y yet;   yü few;   yù furious;   zh vision

forward and skidding into a turn — called also *chris·tie*, *chris·ty* \'kris-tē\

Chris·ti·an·i·ty \‚kris-chē-'an-ət-ē\ n 1 : the religion deriving from Jesus Christ 2 : Christian belief or practice

Chris·tian·ize \'kris-chə-‚nīz\ vt : to make Christian — **Chris·tian·i·za·tion** \‚kris-chə-nə-'zā-shən\ n — **Chris·tian·iz·er** n

christian name n, *often cap* C : the name given to a person at birth or christening as distinct from the family name

Christian Science n : a religion and system of healing founded by Mary Baker Eddy and taught by the Church of Christ, Scientist — **Christian Scientist** n

Christ·like \'krīst-‚līk\ adj : resembling Christ in character or spirit

Christ·mas \'kris-məs\ n [OE *Cristes mæsse*, lit., Christ's mass] 1 : December 25 celebrated as a church festival in commemoration of the birth of Christ and observed as a legal holiday 2 : CHRISTMASTIDE

Christmas club n : a savings account in which regular deposits are made throughout the year to provide money for Christmas shopping in December

Christmas fern n : a No. American evergreen fern often used for winter decorations

Christ·mas·tide \'kris-məs-‚tīd\ n : the season of Christmas

Christmas tree n : a usu. evergreen tree decorated at Christmas

chrom- *or* **chromo-** *comb form* [Gk *chrōma* color] : color : colored ⟨*chromosphere*⟩

chro·ma \'krō-mə\ n [Gk *chrōma*] : SATURATION 3a

chromat- *or* **chromato-** *comb form* [Gk *chrōmat-, chrōma*] 1 : color ⟨*chromatin*⟩ 2 : chromatin ⟨*chromatolysis*⟩

¹chro·mat·ic \krō-'mat-ik\ adj 1 : of or relating to color or color phenomena; *esp* : being a shade other than black, gray, or white ⟨*chromatic* colors like green, red, blue⟩ 2 : of, relating to, or giving all the tones of the chromatic scale — **chro·mat·i·cal·ly** \-'mat-i-k(ə-)lē\ adv

²chromatic n : ACCIDENTAL 2

chromatic aberration n : aberration caused by the differences in refraction of the colored rays of the spectrum

chromatic scale n : a musical scale that consists wholly of half steps

chro·ma·tid \'krō-mə-təd\ n : one of the paired longitudinal strands of a chromosome

chro·ma·tin \-tən\ n : a material present in chromosomes that contains nucleic acid, stains deeply with basic dyes, and is held to be the actual carrier of the genes — **chro·ma·tin·ic** \‚krō-mə-'tin-ik\ adj

chro·ma·tog·ra·phy \‚krō-mə-'täg-rə-fē\ n : a separating esp. of closely related compounds by allowing a solution or mixture of them to seep through an adsorbent (as clay or paper) so that each compound becomes adsorbed in a separate often colored layer — **chro·mato·graph·ic** \krō-‚mat-ə-'graf-ik\ adj

chro·mato·phore \krō-'mat-ə-‚fō(ə)r, -‚fȯ(ə)r\ n : a pigment-bearing cell — **chro·mato·phor·ic** \krō-‚mat-ə-'fōr-ik, -'fär-\ adj — **chro·ma·toph·o·rous** \‚krō-mə-'täf-(ə-)rəs\ adj

chrome \'krōm\ n 1 a : CHROMIUM b : a chromium pigment 2 : something plated with an alloy of chromium

-chrome \‚krōm\ n comb form or adj comb form 1 : colored thing : colored 2 : coloring matter

chrome green n : any of various brilliant green pigments containing or consisting of chromium compounds

chrome yellow n : any of various bright yellow pigments consisting essentially of a compound $PbCrO_4$ of lead, chromium, and oxygen

chro·mic \'krō-mik\ adj : of, relating to, or derived from chromium

chro·mite \'krō-‚mīt\ n : a mineral $FeCr_2O_4$ that consists of an oxide of iron and chromium and is an important ore of chromium

chro·mi·um \'krō-mē-əm\ n [NL, fr. F *chrome*, fr. Gk *chrōma* color] : a blue-white metallic element found naturally only in combination and used esp. in alloys, as a lustrous rust-resisting plating, and in its compounds in paints and in electroplating — see ELEMENT table

chro·mo \'krō-mō\ n, pl chromos : a colored picture printed from lithographic surfaces

chro·mo·mere \'krō-mə-‚mi(ə)r\ n : one of the enlargements of the chromonema at which nucleoproteins appear

to be concentrated — **chro·mo·mer·ic** \‚krō-mə-'mer-ik, -'mi(ə)r-\ adj

chro·mo·ne·ma \‚krō-mə-'nē-mə\ n, pl **-ne·ma·ta** \-'nē-mət-ə\ : the coiled filamentous core of a chromatid held to be the actual carrier of the genes — **chro·mo·ne·mal** \-'nē-məl\ *or* **chro·mo·ne·mat·ic** \-ni-'mat-ik\ *or* **chro·mo·ne·mic** \-'nē-mik\ adj

chro·mo·phil \'krō-mə-‚fil\ *or* **chro·mato·phil** \krō-'mat-ə-‚fil\ adj : staining readily with dyes

chro·mo·phobe \'krō-mə-‚fōb\ adj : resisting staining with dyes

chro·mo·phore \-‚fō(ə)r, -‚fȯ(ə)r\ n : a group of atoms that gives rise to color in a molecule

chro·mo·plast \-‚plast\ n : a colored plastid usu. containing red or yellow pigment

chro·mo·some \'krō-mə-‚sōm\ n : one of the usu. elongated chromatin-containing bodies of a cell nucleus made up of chromatids, usu. constant in number in any one kind of plant or animal, and seen esp. during mitosis — **chro·mo·som·al** \‚krō-mə-'sō-məl\ *or* **chro·mo·so·mic** \-'sō-mik\ adj

chro·mo·sphere \'krō-mə-‚sfi(ə)r\ n : the lower part of the atmosphere of the sun composed chiefly of hydrogen

chron- *or* **chrono-** *comb form* [Gk *chronos*] : time

chron·ic \'krän-ik\ adj 1 a : marked by long duration or frequent recurrence : not acute b : suffering from a chronic disease 2 a : constantly present or frequently recurring ⟨a *chronic* financial predicament⟩ b : HABITUAL, ACCUSTOMED ⟨a *chronic* complainer⟩ — **chron·i·cal·ly** \-i-k(ə)lē\ adv — **chro·nic·i·ty** \krä-'nis-ət-ē\ n

¹chron·i·cle \'krän-i-kəl\ n 1 : an historical account of events arranged in order of time without analysis or interpretation 2 : HISTORY, NARRATIVE

²chronicle vt **chron·i·cled**; **chron·i·cling** \-k(ə-)liŋ\ : to record in or as if in a chronicle : tell the story of — **chron·i·cler** \-k(ə-)lər\ n

Chron·i·cles \'krän-i-kəlz\ n — see BIBLE table

chro·no·graph \'krän-ə-‚graf, 'krō-nə-\ n : an instrument for measuring and recording time intervals with accuracy: as a : an instrument having a revolving drum on which a stylus makes marks b : a watch with a seconds-indicating hand mounted so that it can be read on the same dial as the minute hand — **chron·o·graph·ic** \‚krän-ə-'graf-ik, ‚krō-nə-\ adj — **chro·nog·ra·phy** \krə-'näg-rə-fē\ n

chron·o·log·i·cal \‚krän-ᵊl-'äj-i-kəl, ‚krōn-\ adj : arranged in or according to the order of time ⟨*chronological* tables of American history⟩ — **chron·o·log·i·cal·ly** \-'äj-i-k(ə)lē\ adv

chro·nol·o·gy \krə-'näl-ə-jē\ n, pl **-gies** 1 : the science that deals with measuring time by regular divisions and that assigns to events their proper dates 2 : a chronological table or list 3 : an arrangement (as of events) in order of occurrence — **chro·nol·o·gist** \-jəst\ n

chro·nom·e·ter \krə-'näm-ət-ər\ n : an instrument for measuring time; *esp* : one intended to keep time with great accuracy — **chron·o·met·ric** \‚krän-ə-'me-trik, ‚krō-nə-\ adj

chro·no·scope \'krän-ə-‚skōp, 'krō-nə-\ n : an instrument for precise measurement of small time intervals

chrys·a·lid \'kris-ə-ləd\ n : CHRYSALIS — **chrysalid** adj

chrys·a·lis \'kris-ə-ləs\ n, pl **chry·sal·i·des** \kri-'sal-ə-‚dēz\ *or* **chrys·a·lis·es** \'kris-ə-lə-səz\ [Gk *chrysallid-, chrysallis*, fr. *chrysos* gold] : the pupa of insects (as butterflies) that pass the pupal stage in a quiescent condition enclosed in a firm case

chry·san·the·mum \kris-'an(t)-thə-məm\ n [L, fr. Gk *chrysanthemon*, fr. *chrysos* gold + *anthemon* flower] 1 : any of a genus of plants related to the daisies that include weeds, ornamentals grown for their brightly colored often double flower heads, and important sources of medicinals and insecticides 2 : a flower head of an ornamental chrysanthemum

chrys·o·phyte \'kris-ə-‚fīt\ n : any of a major group (Chrysophyta) of algae (as diatoms) with yellowish green to golden brown pigments — **chry·soph·y·tan** \kris-'äf-ət-ᵊn, ‚kris-ə-'fīt-ᵊn\ adj

chrys·o·prase \'kris-ə-‚prāz\ n : an apple-green chalcedony valued as a gem

chrys·o·tile \'kris-ə-‚tīl\ n [Gk *chrysos* gold + *tilos* plucked hair, fr. *tillein* to pluck] : a fibrous silky serpentine that is one kind of asbestos

---

ə abut; ᵊ kitten; ər further; a back; ā bake; ä cot, cart; au̇ out; ch chin; e less; ē easy; g gift; i trip; ī life

chub \'chəb\ *n, pl* **chub** *or* **chubs** : any of several small freshwater fishes related to the carp

chub·by \'chəb-ē\ *adj* **chub·bi·er; -est** : PLUMP ⟨a chubby boy⟩ — **chub·bi·ness** *n*

¹chuck \'chək\ *vt* **1** : to give a pat or a tap ⟨chuck a person under the chin⟩ **2** : to throw easily or carelessly : TOSS ⟨chuck a ball back and forth⟩

²chuck *n* **1** : a pat or nudge under the chin **2** : TOSS, JERK

³chuck *n* **1** : a portion of a side of dressed beef including most of the neck and the parts about the shoulder blade and the first three ribs **2** : a device for holding work or a tool in a machine and esp. in a lathe

chuck-full \'chək-'ful\ *var of* CHOCK-FULL

chuck·hole \'chək-ˌhōl, 'chəg-\ *n* : a hole or rut in a road

chuck·le \'chək-əl\ *vi* **chuck·led; chuck·ling** \'chək-(ə-)liŋ\ : to laugh inwardly or quietly — **chuckle** *n*

chuck·le·head \'chək-əl-ˌhed\ *n* : BLOCKHEAD — **chuck·le·head·ed** \ˌchək-əl-'hed-əd\ *adj*

chuck wagon \-ˌchək-\ *n* : a wagon carrying a stove and provisions for cooking (as on a ranch)

chuck·wal·la \'chək-ˌwäl-ə\ *n* [MexSp *chacahuala*, of AmerInd origin] : a large but harmless lizard of the desert regions of the southwestern U.S.

chuck-will's-wid·ow \ˌchək-ˌwilz-'wid-ō\ *n* : a goatsucker of the southern U.S.

¹chug \'chəg\ *n* : a dull explosive sound made by or as if by a laboring engine

²chug *vi* **chugged; chug·ging** : to move or go with chugs ⟨a locomotive chugging along⟩

chuk·ka \'chək-ə\ *n* : a short usu. ankle-length leather boot with two pairs of eyelets

chuk·ker *or* **chuk·kar** \'chək-ər\ *or* **chuk·ka** \'chək-ə\ *n* [Hindi *cakkar* circular course, fr. Skt *cakra* wheel; akin to E *wheel*] : a playing period of a polo game

¹chum \'chəm\ *n* : a steady companion : a close friend : PAL

²chum *vi* **chummed; chum·ming** : to go about with a person : be on terms of close friendship

chum·my \'chəm-ē\ *adj* **chum·mi·er; -est** : INTIMATE, SOCIABLE — **chum·mi·ly** \'chəm-ə-lē\ *adv* — **chum·mi·ness** \'chəm-ē-nəs\ *n*

chump \'chəmp\ *n* : FOOL, DUPE

chunk \'chəŋk\ *n* : a short thick piece or lump (as of wood or coal) : HUNK

chunky \'chəŋ-kē\ *adj* **chunk·i·er; -est** : STOCKY

¹church \'chərch\ *n* [OE *cirice*, fr. LGk *kyriakon*, fr. neut. of *kyriakos* of the Lord, fr. Gk *kyrios* lord] **1** : a building for public worship esp. by a Christian parish or congregation **2** : a body or organization of religious believers **3** : public worship esp. in a church — **church·ly** \-lē\ *adj*

²church *vt* : to bring to church to receive one of its rites

church·go·er \-ˌgō(-)ər\ *n* : one that goes to church esp. habitually — **church·go·ing** \-ˌgō-iŋ\ *adj or n*

church·less \-ləs\ *adj* : not affiliated with a church

church·man \-mən\ *n* **1** : CLERGYMAN **2** : a church member

Church of England : the established episcopal church of England

church·yard \'chərch-ˌyärd\ *n* : a yard that belongs to a church and is often used as a burial ground

churl \'chərl\ *n* [ME, fr. OE *ceorl* man, churl] **1** : an Anglo-Saxon freeman of the lowest rank **2** : a medieval peasant **3** : RUSTIC, COUNTRYMAN **4 a** : a rude ill-bred person **b** : a surly person

churl·ish \'chər-lish\ *adj* : SURLY, RUDE, ILL-MANNERED — **churl·ish·ly** *adv* — **churl·ish·ness** *n*

¹churn \'chərn\ *n* [OE *cyrin*] : a vessel in which cream is agitated to separate the butterfat from the other constituents

²churn *vb* **1** : to agitate cream in a churn in making butter **2 a** : to stir or agitate violently **b** : to make (as foam) by stirring **3** : to be in violent agitation **4** : to proceed by means of rotating devices (as wheels or propellers)

churr \'chər\ *vi* : to make a vibrant or whirring noise like that of a partridge — **churr** *n*

chute \'shüt\ *n* [F, fall, fr. OF, fr. *cheoir* to fall, fr. L *cadere*] **1** : a quick drop (as of water in a river) **2** : an inclined plane, trough, or passage down or through which things may pass ⟨a coal chute⟩ ⟨a mail chute⟩ **3** : PARACHUTE

chut·ney \'chət-nē\ *n, pl* **chutneys** [Hindi *caṭnī*] : a condiment of acid fruits with raisins, dates, and onions

chyle \'kīl\ *n* [Gk *chylos* juice, chyle, fr. *chein* to pour] : lymph milky from emulsified fats that is seen esp. in the lacteals during intestinal absorption of fats — **chy·lous** \'kī-ləs\ *adj*

chyme \'kīm\ *n* [Gk *chymos* juice, fr. *chein* to pour] : the semifluid mass of partly digested food that passes from the stomach into the duodenum — **chy·mous** \'kī-məs\ *adj*

chy·mo·tryp·sin \ˌkī-mə-'trip-sən\ *n* : a pancreatic enzyme that acts on proteins by breaking internal peptide bonds

ci·bo·ri·um \sə-'bōr-ē-əm, -'bȯr-\ *n, pl* **-ria** \-ē-ə\ *or* **-ri·ums** **1** : a covered goblet-shaped vessel for holding eucharistic bread **2** : a vaulted canopy supported by four columns over a high altar

ci·ca·da \sə-'kād-ə, -'käd-\ *n* [L] : any of a family of stout-bodied insects that are related to the bugs and have a wide blunt head and large transparent wings

cic·a·trix \'sik-ə-(ˌ)triks, sə-'kā-triks\ *n, pl* **cic·a·tri·ces** \ˌsik-ə-'trī-(ˌ)sēz, sə-'kā-trə-ˌsēz\ [L *cicatric-, cicatrix*] **1** : a scar resulting from formation and contraction of fibrous tissue in a flesh wound **2** : a scar marking the previous point of attachment of a part or organ (as a leaf or seed) — **cic·a·tri·cial** \ˌsik-ə-'trish-əl\ *adj*

cic·a·trize \'sik-ə-ˌtrīz\ *vi* : to heal by forming a scar

cic·e·ly \'sis-(ə-)lē\ *n, pl* **-lies** : any of several herbs of the carrot family with white flowers and aromatic root

ci·ce·ro·ne \ˌsis-ə-'rō-nē, ˌchich-ə-\ *n, pl* **-ro·ni** \-(ˌ)nē\ : a guide who conducts sightseers

Cic·er·o·ni·an \ˌsis-ə-'rō-nē-ən\ *adj* : of, relating to, or characteristic of Cicero or his writings

-cide \ˌsīd\ *n comb form* [L *-cida*, fr. *caedere* to cut, kill] **1** : killer ⟨insecticide⟩ **2** [L *-cidium*, fr. *caedere* to cut, kill] : killing ⟨genocide⟩

ci·der \'sīd-ər\ *n* [OF *sidre*, fr. LL *sicera* strong drink, fr. Gk *sikera*, fr. Heb *shēkhār*] : the expressed juice of fruit (as apples) used as a beverage or for making other products (as vinegar)

ci·gar \sig-'är\ *n* [Sp *cigarro*] : a roll of tobacco for smoking usu. consisting of a core bound together by a leaf and encased in another leaf of smooth even texture

cig·a·rette *also* **cig·a·ret** \ˌsig-ə-'ret, 'sig-ə-ˌ\ *n* : a small roll of cut tobacco wrapped in paper for smoking

cil·i·ary \'sil-ē-ˌer-ē\ *adj* **1** : of or relating to cilia **2** : of, relating to, or being the muscular body supporting the lens of the eye

¹cil·i·ate \'sil-ē-ət, -ˌāt\ *or* **cil·i·at·ed** \-ˌāt-əd\ *adj* : provided with cilia — **cil·i·ate·ly** *adv*

²ciliate *n* : any of a group (Ciliophora) of ciliate protozoans

cil·i·um \'sil-ē-əm\ *n, pl* **cil·ia** \-ē-ə\ [L, eyelid] **1** : EYELASH **2** : one of the tiny filaments of many cells that are capable of lashing movement

Cim·me·ri·an \sə-'mir-ē-ən\ *adj* [fr. *Cimmerians*, a mythical people in Homer dwelling in eternal gloom] : very dark or gloomy : STYGIAN

¹cinch \'sinch\ *n* [Sp *cincha*, fr. L *cingula* girdle, girth, fr. *cingere* to gird] **1** : a strong girth for a pack or saddle **2** : a tight grip **3 a** : a thing done with ease **b** : a certainty to happen : sure thing

²cinch *vt* **1** : to put a cinch on **2** : to make certain : ASSURE

cin·cho·na \siŋ-'kō-nə, sin-'chō-\ *n* **1** : any of a genus of So. American trees and shrubs **2** : the dried bark of a cinchona containing alkaloids (as quinine) and having use as a specific in malaria — **cin·chon·ic** \siŋ-'kän-ik, sin-'chän-\ *adj*

cinc·ture \'siŋ(k)-chər\ *n* **1** : the act of encircling; *also* : an encircled area **2** : GIRDLE, BELT

cin·der \'sin-dər\ *n* [OE *sinder*] **1** : waste matter from the smelting of metal ores : SLAG **2 a** : a piece of partly burned coal or wood in which fire is extinct **b** : a hot coal without flame **3** *pl* : ASHES — **cin·dery** \-d(ə-)rē\ *adj*

cinder block *n* : a building block made of concrete using coal cinders as aggregate

Cin·der·el·la \ˌsin-də-'rel-ə\ *n* : the heroine of a fairy tale who is mistreated by her stepmother but elevated to happiness and wealth through a fairy godmother

cine- *comb form* : motion picture ⟨cinefilm⟩

cin·e·ma \'sin-ə-mə\ *n* [short for *cinematograph*, fr. Gk *kinēmat-, kinēma* motion, fr. *kinein* to move] **1** *chiefly Brit* **a** : MOTION PICTURE **b** : a motion-picture theater

2 : MOVIES — **cin·e·mat·ic** \,sin-ə-'mat-ik\ *adj* — **cin·e·mat·i·cal·ly** \-'mat-i-k(ə-)lē\ *adv*

cin·e·mat·o·graph \,sin-ə-'mat-ə-,graf\ *n, chiefly Brit* : a motion-picture camera, projector, theater, or show

cin·e·ma·tog·ra·phy \,sin-ə-mə-'täg-rə-fē\ *n* : the art or science of motion-picture photography — **cin·e·mat·o·graph·ic** \-,mat-ə-'graf-ik\ *adj*

cin·er·ar·ia \,sin-ə-'rer-ē-ə, -'rar-\ *n* : a pot plant related to the daisies that has heart-shaped leaves and clusters of bright flower heads

cin·er·ar·i·um \-ē-əm\ *n, pl* **-ar·ia** \-ē-ə\ [L, fr. *ciner-, cinis* ashes] : a place to receive the ashes of the cremated dead — **cin·er·ary** \'sin-ə-,rer-ē\ *adj*

cin·gu·lum \'siŋ-gyə-ləm\ *n, pl* **-la** \-lə\ : a differentiated band or girdle (as of color) — **cin·gu·late** \-lət\ *adj*

cin·na·bar \'sin-ə-,bär\ *n* : a red mineral HgS that consists of a sulfide of mercury and is the only important ore of mercury

cin·na·mon \'sin-ə-mən\ *n* [Gk *kinnamon*, of Semitic origin] **1 a** : the highly aromatic bark of any of several trees of the laurel family used as a spice **b** : a tree that yields cinnamon **2** : a light yellowish brown — **cin·na·mon·ic** \,sin-ə-'män-ik\ *adj*

cinque·foil \'siŋk-,foil, 'saŋk-\ *n* [MF *cincfoille*, fr. L *quinquefolium*, fr. *quinque* five + *folium* leaf] **1** : any of a genus of plants of the rose family with 5-lobed leaves **2** : a design enclosed by five joined foils

ci·on *var of* SCION

¹ci·pher \'sī-fər\ *n* [ML *cifra*, fr. Ar *ṣifr*, fr. *ṣifr* empty] **1 a** : the symbol 0 denoting the absence of all magnitude or quantity : ZERO — see NUMBER table **b** : an insignificant individual : NONENTITY **2 a** : a method of transforming a text in order to conceal its meaning — compare CODE 4 **b** : a message in code **3** : an arabic numeral **4** : a combination of symbolic letters; *esp* : the interwoven initials of a name

²cipher *vb* **ci·phered; ci·pher·ing** \-f(ə-)riŋ\ **1** : to use figures in a mathematical process **2** : to compute arithmetically **3** : ENCIPHER

cir·ca \'sər-kə, 'ki(ə)r-(,)kä\ *prep* [L, fr. *circum* around] : at, in, or of approximately — used with numerals and esp. with dates (born *circa* 1600)

Cir·cas·sian walnut \(,)sər-,kash-ən-\ *n* : the light brown irregularly black-veined wood of the English walnut much used for veneer and cabinetwork

Cir·ce \'sər-(,)sē\ *n* : an island sorceress in the *Odyssey* who turned her victims into beasts

cir·ci·nate \'sərs-ᵊn-,āt\ *adj* : COILED, ROUNDED; *esp* : rolled up on the axis with the apex as a center — **cir·ci·nate·ly** *adv*

¹cir·cle \'sər-kəl\ *n* [L *circulus*, dim. of *circus* circle, circus] **1 a** : RING, HALO **b** : a closed plane curve every point of which is equidistant from a fixed point within the curve **c** : the plane surface bounded by such a curve **2** : something in the form of a circle or section of a circle: as **a** : CIRCLET, DIADEM **b** : a balcony or tier of seats in a theater **c** : a circle on the surface of a sphere (as the earth) — compare GREAT CIRCLE, SMALL CIRCLE **d** : ROTARY **3** : an area of action or influence : REALM **4** : CYCLE, ROUND **5** : a group bound by a common tie; *esp* : COTERIE

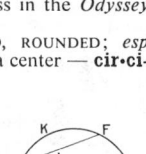

circle 1b: diameter, *AB*; center, *C*; radii, *CD, CA, CB*; arc, *EKF*, on chord, *EF*; segment(area)*EKFL* on chord, *EF*; sector (area) *ACD*; secant, *GH*; tangent, *TPM*, at point, *P*; circumference, *EKFBPDA*

²circle *vb* **cir·cled; cir·cling** \-k(ə-)liŋ\ **1** : to enclose in or as if in a circle **2** : to move or revolve around **3** : to move in or as if in a circle — **cir·cler** \-k(ə-)lər\ *n*

circle graph *n* : PIE CHART

cir·clet \'sər-klət\ *n* : a little circle; *esp* : an ornament for the person in the form of a circle

¹cir·cuit \'sər-kət\ *n* [L *circuitus*, fr. *circuire* to go around, fr. *circum-* + *ire* to go] **1** : a boundary around an enclosed space; *also* : the space enclosed **2** : a moving or revolving around (as in a circle or orbit) : CIRCLING (the *circuit* of the earth around the sun) **3 a** : a regular tour (as by a judge or preacher) around an assigned territory **b** : the route traveled **4 a** : an association of similar

groups : LEAGUE **b** : a group of establishments offering similar entertainment or presenting a series of contests; *esp* : a chain of theaters at which productions are successively presented **5** : the complete path of an electric current or any part of this path **6** : a radio or television hookup **7** : a closed path followed by a fluid in a mechanical system — **cir·cuit·al** \-kət-ᵊl\ *adj*

²circuit *vb* : to make a circuit about something

circuit breaker *n* : a switch that automatically interrupts an electric circuit under an abnormal condition

circuit court *n* **1** : a court whose judges travel from one place to another in a judicial district to hold sessions **2** : a U.S. federal court intermediate between the Supreme Court and the district courts until abolished in 1912

cir·cu·i·tous \(,)sər-'kyü-ət-əs\ *adj* : marked by a circular or winding course (a *circuitous* route) **2** : marked by roundabout or indirect procedure — **cir·cu·i·tous·ly** *adv* — **cir·cu·i·tous·ness** *n*

cir·cuit·ry \'sər-kə-trē\ *n* : the plan or the components of an electric circuit

cir·cu·i·ty \(,)sər-'kyü-ət-ē\ *n* : INDIRECTION

¹cir·cu·lar \'sər-kyə-lər\ *adj* **1** : having the form of a circle : bounded by a circle : ROUND (a *circular* driveway) **2** : moving in or describing a circle or spiral **3** : CIRCUITOUS, ROUNDABOUT (a *circular* explanation) **4** : sent around to a number of persons (a *circular* letter) — **cir·cu·lar·i·ty** \,sər-kyə-'lar-ət-ē\ *n* — **cir·cu·lar·ly** \'sər-kyə-lər-lē\ *adv* — **cir·cu·lar·ness** *n*

²circular *n* : a paper (as a leaflet containing an advertisement) intended for wide distribution

cir·cu·lar·ize \'sər-kyə-lə-,rīz\ *vt* **1 a** : to send circulars to **b** : to poll by questionnaire **2** : PUBLICIZE — **cir·cu·lar·i·za·tion** \,sər-kyə-lə-rə-'zā-shən\ *n*

circular mil *n* : a unit of area equal to the area of a circle having a diameter of one mil

cir·cu·late \'sər-kyə-,lāt\ *vb* **1** : to move or cause to move in a circle, circuit, or orbit; *esp* : to follow a course that returns to the starting point (blood *circulates* through the body) **2** : to pass from person to person or place to place: as **a** : to flow without obstruction **b** : to become or cause to become well known or widespread (*circulate* a rumor) **c** : to come into the hands of readers (a magazine that *circulated* widely) — **cir·cu·la·tor** \-,lāt-ər\ *n*

cir·cu·la·tion \,sər-kyə-'lā-shən\ *n* **1** : FLOW **2** : orderly movement through a circuit; *esp* : the movement of blood through the vessels of the body caused by the pumping action of the heart **3 a** : passage or transmission from person to person or place to place; *esp* : the interchange of currency (coins in *circulation*) **b** : the extent of dissemination (as of copies of a publication sold over a given period) — **cir·cu·la·tive** \-kyə-,lāt-iv\ *adj*

cir·cu·la·to·ry \'sər-kyə-lə-,tōr-ē, -,tȯr-\ *adj* : of or relating to circulation (as of the blood) (the *circulatory* system)

circum- *prefix* [L, fr. *circus* circle] : around : about (*circum*polar)

cir·cum·am·bi·ent \,sər-kəm-'am-bē-ənt\ *adj* : SURROUNDING, ENCOMPASSING

cir·cum·am·bu·late \-'am-byə-,lāt\ *vb* : to circle on foot esp. ritualistically

cir·cum·cen·ter \'sər-kəm-,sent-ər\ *n* : the point at which the perpendicular bisectors of the sides of a triangle intersect

cir·cum·cise \'sər-kəm-,sīz\ *vt* [L *circumcis-, circumcidere,* fr. *circum-* + *caedere* to cut] : to cut off the foreskin of

cir·cum·ci·sion \,sər-kəm-'sizh-ən\ *n* **1** : the act of circumcising or being circumcised; *esp* : a Jewish rite performed on male infants as a sign of inclusion in the covenant between God and Abraham **2** *cap* : January 1 observed as a church festival in commemoration of the circumcision of Christ

cir·cum·fer·ence \sə(r)-'kəm(p)-fərn(t)s, -f(ə-)rən(t)s\ *n* [L *circumferentia,* fr. *circumferre* to carry around, fr. *circum-* + *ferre* to carry] **1** : the perimeter of a circle — see CIRCLE illustration **2** : the external boundary or surface of a figure or object : PERIPHERY — **cir·cum·fer·en·tial** \-,kəm(p)-fə-'ren-chəl\ *adj*

¹cir·cum·flex \'sər-kəm-,fleks\ *adj* **1 a** : having the kind of sound indicated by a circumflex **b** : marked with a circumflex **c** : being a circumflex (*circumflex* accent) **2** : bending around (a *circumflex* artery)

²circumflex *n* [L *circumflexus* bent around, fr. pp. of

circumflectere to bend around, fr. *circum-* + *flectere* to bend] **:** a mark ˆ, ˇ, or ˜ used chiefly to indicate length, contraction, or a specific vowel quality

cir·cum·flu·ent \(ˌ)sər-'kəm-flə-wənt\ *adj* **:** flowing round or surrounding in the manner of a fluid

cir·cum·fuse \ˌsər-kəm-'fyüz\ *vt* **:** SURROUND, ENVELOP — **cir·cum·fu·sion** \-'fyü-zhən\ *n*

cir·cum·lo·cu·tion \ˌsər-kəm-lō-'kyü-shən\ *n* [L *circum-locution-, circumlocutio,* fr. *circum-* + *locutio* speech, fr. *loqui* to speak] **1 :** the use of an unnecessary large number of words to express an idea **2 :** evasion in speech — **cir·cum·loc·u·to·ry** \-'läk-yə-ˌtōr-ē, -ˌtòr-\ *adj*

cir·cum·lu·nar \ˌsər-kəm-'lü-nər\ *adj* **:** revolving about or surrounding the moon

cir·cum·nav·i·gate \-'nav-ə-ˌgāt\ *vt* **:** to go completely around (as the earth) esp. by water — **cir·cum·nav·i·ga·tion** \-ˌnav-ə-'gā-shən\ *n* — **cir·cum·nav·i·ga·tor** \-'nav-ə-ˌgāt-ər\ *n*

cir·cum·po·lar \ˌsər-kəm-'pō-lər\ *adj* **1 :** continually visible above the horizon ⟨a *circumpolar* star⟩ **2 :** surrounding or found in the vicinity of the north pole or south pole

cir·cum·scribe \'sər-kəm-ˌskrīb\ *vt* [L *circumscribere,* fr. *circum-* + *scribere* to write, draw] **1 a :** to draw a line around **b :** to surround by a boundary **2 a :** to limit esp. narrowly the range or activity of **b :** to define or mark off carefully **3 :** to construct or be constructed around (a geometrical figure) so as to touch at as many points as possible

cir·cum·scrip·tion \ˌsər-kəm-'skrip-shən\ *n* [L *circum-script-, circumscribere* to circumscribe] **1 :** something that circumscribes: as **a :** BOUNDARY **b :** RESTRICTION **c :** an outline or inscription around something **2 :** the act of circumscribing **:** the state of being circumscribed **3 :** a circumscribed area

cir·cum·spect \'sər-kəm-ˌspekt\ *adj* [L *circumspectus,* fr. pp. of *circumspicere* to look around, fr. *circum-* + *specere* to look] **:** careful to consider all circumstances and possible consequences **:** PRUDENT — **cir·cum·spect·ly** *adv*

cir·cum·spec·tion \ˌsər-kəm-'spek-shən\ *n* **:** circumspect action or behavior **:** CAUTION, PRUDENCE

cir·cum·stance \'sər-kəm-ˌstan(t)s\ *n* [L *circumstantia,* fr. *circumstare* to surround, fr. *circum-* + *stare* to stand] **1 :** a fact or event that must be considered along with another fact or event **2** *pl* **:** surrounding conditions ⟨impossible under the *circumstances*⟩ **3** *pl* **:** condition or situation with respect to wealth ⟨in easy *circumstances*⟩ **4 :** formality accompanying an event **:** CEREMONY ⟨with pomp and *circumstance*⟩ **5 :** a happening or fact in a chain of events **:** DETAIL **6 :** CHANCE, FATE ⟨a victim of *circumstance*⟩

cir·cum·stanced \-ˌstan(t)st\ *adj* **:** placed in particular circumstances esp. in regard to property or income

cir·cum·stan·tial \ˌsər-kəm-'stan-chəl\ *adj* **1 :** consisting of or relating to circumstances **:** dependent on circumstances ⟨*circumstantial* evidence⟩ **2 :** relating to a matter but not essential to it **:** INCIDENTAL **3 :** containing full details ⟨a *circumstantial* account of what happened⟩ — **cir·cum·stan·tial·ly** \-'stanch-(ə-)lē\ *adv*

syn PARTICULAR, MINUTE: CIRCUMSTANTIAL implies fullness of details that fixes something described in time and space ⟨a *circumstantial* account of her visit⟩ PARTICULAR implies a precise attention to every detail ⟨a *particular* description of the scene of the crime⟩ MINUTE implies searching, close attention to the smallest details ⟨a *minute* examination of a fossil⟩

¹cir·cum·val·late \ˌsər-kəm-'val-ˌāt, -'val-ət\ *adj* **:** surrounded by or as if by a rampart; *esp* **:** enclosed by a ridge of tissue ⟨*circumvallate* papilla⟩

²cir·cum·val·late \-'val-ˌāt\ *vt* **:** to surround by or as if by a rampart — **cir·cum·val·la·tion** \-ˌval-'ā-shən\ *n*

cir·cum·vent \ˌsər-kəm-'vent\ *vt* [L *circumvent-, circumvenire,* fr. *circum-* + *venire* to come] **1 :** to hem in **2 :** to go around **:** make a circuit of **3 :** to check or defeat esp. by ingenuity or stratagem — **cir·cum·ven·tion** \-'ven-chən\ *n*

cir·cus \'sər-kəs\ *n* [L, lit., circle, ring] **1 a :** a large arena enclosed by tiers of seats and used for spectacles (as athletic contests or exhibitions of horsemanship) **b :** a public spectacle **2 a :** an arena often covered by a tent and used for variety shows usu. including feats of physical skill and daring, wild animal acts, and performances by jugglers and clowns **b :** a circus performance **c :** the physical plant, livestock, and personnel of such a circus **3** *Brit* **:** a usu. circular area at an intersection of streets ⟨Piccadilly *Circus*⟩

cirque \'sərk\ *n* **1 :** CIRCLE, CIRCLET **2 :** a deep steep-walled hollow on a mountain shaped like half a bowl

cir·rate \'sir-ˌāt\ *adj* **:** bearing or curled like a cirrus ⟨a *cirrate* leaf⟩

cir·rho·sis \sə-'rō-səs\ *n* [Gk *kirrhos* orange-colored] **:** fibrosis and hardening esp. of the liver — **cir·rhot·ic** \-'rät-ik\ *adj or n*

cir·ri·ped \'sir-ə-ˌped\ *or* **cir·ri·pede** \-ˌpēd\ *n* **:** BARNACLE — **cirriped** *adj*

cir·ro·cu·mu·lus \ˌsir-ō-'kyü-myə-ləs\ *n* **:** a cloud form of small white rounded masses at a high altitude usu. in regular groupings

cir·ro·stra·tus \-'strāt-əs, -'strat-\ *n* **:** a fairly uniform layer of high stratus darker than cirrus

cir·rus \'sir-əs\ *n, pl* **cir·ri** \'sir-ˌī\ [L, curl] **1 a :** TENDRIL **b :** a slender usu. flexible animal appendage **2 :** a wispy white cloud usu. of minute ice crystals formed at altitudes of 20,000 to 40,000 feet

cis- *prefix* [L] **:** on this side ⟨*cis*alpine⟩

cis·co \'sis-kō\ *n, pl* **ciscoes** **:** any of various whitefishes including important food fishes of the Great Lakes region

cis·lu·nar \(ˈ)sis-'lü-nər\ *adj* **:** lying between the earth and the moon or the moon's orbit

Cis·ter·cian \sis-'tər-shən\ *n* **:** a member of a monastic order founded at Cîteaux, France in 1098 under an austere rule — **Cistercian** *adj*

cis·tern \'sis-tərn\ *n* [L *cisterna,* fr. *cista* box, chest] **1 :** an often underground artificial reservoir or tank for storing water and esp. rainwater **2 :** a fluid-containing sac or cavity in an organism

cit·a·del \'sit-əd-ˀl, -ə-ˌdel\ *n* [It *cittadella,* dim. of *cittade* city, fr. L *civitat-, civitas* state, city] **1 :** a fortress that commands a city **2 :** STRONGHOLD

ci·ta·tion \sī-'tā-shən\ *n* **1 :** an official summons to appear (as before a court) **2 a :** an act or instance of quoting **b :** a word or passage quoted **:** EXCERPT **3 :** MENTION: as **a :** a formal statement of the achievements of a person receiving an award (as an honorary degree) **b :** specific reference in a military dispatch to meritorious performance of duty

cite \'sīt\ *vt* [L *citare* to rouse, summon, freq. of *ciēre* to stir, move] **1 :** to summon to appear before a court **2 :** to quote as an example, authority, or proof **3 a :** to refer to; *esp* **:** to mention formally in commendation or praise **b :** to name in a citation

cith·a·ra \'sith-ə-rə, 'kith-\ *n* [Gk *kithara*] **:** an ancient Greek stringed instrument of the lyre class with a wooden sounding board

cit·i·fy \'sit-i-ˌfī\ *vt* **-fied; -fy·ing :** to stamp with or accustom to urban ways

cit·i·zen \'sit-ə-zən\ *n* [AF *citezein,* alter. of OF *citeien,* fr. *cité* city] **1 :** an inhabitant of a city or town; *esp* **:** one entitled to the rights and privileges of a freeman **2 a :** a member of a state **b :** a person who by birth or naturalization owes allegiance to a government and is entitled to protection from it **3 :** CIVILIAN — **cit·i·zen·ly** \-lē\ *adj*

syn CITIZEN, SUBJECT, NATIONAL mean a person owing allegiance to and entitled to the protection of a sovereign state. CITIZEN is preferred for one owing allegiance to a state in which sovereign power is retained by the people and sharing in the political rights of those people; SUBJECT implies allegiance to a personal sovereign such as a monarch; NATIONAL designates one who may claim the protection of a state whether or not he is an actual citizen or subject and applies esp. to one living or traveling outside that state

cit·i·zen·ess \-zə-nəs\ *n* **:** a female citizen

cit·i·zen·ry \-zən-rē\ *n* **:** the whole body of citizens

cit·i·zen·ship \-zən-ˌship\ *n* **1 :** the status of being a citizen **:** possession of the rights and privileges of a citizen **2 :** the quality of an individual's response to membership in a community

cit·rate \'si-ˌtrāt *also* 'sī-\ *n* **:** a salt or ester of citric acid

cit·ric acid \ˌsi-trik-\ *n* **:** a pleasantly sour-tasting acid

$C_6H_8O_7$ obtained esp. from lemon and lime juices or by fermentation of sugars and used as a flavoring

citric acid cycle *n* : KREBS CYCLE

cit·ri·cul·ture \'si-tro-,kol-chor\ *n* : the cultivation of citrus fruits — **cit·ri·cul·tur·ist** \-,kolch-(ə)-rəst\ *n*

cit·rine \'si-,trīn\ *adj* : resembling a citron or lemon esp. in color

cit·ron \'si-trən\ *n* [OProv. modif. of L *citrus* citron tree] **1 a** : a fruit like the lemon in appearance and structure but larger; *also* : the citrus tree producing this fruit **b** : the preserved rind of the citron used esp. in fruitcake **2** : a small hard-fleshed watermelon used esp. in pickles and preserves

cit·ro·nel·la \,si-trə-'nel-ə\ *n* : a fragrant grass of southern Asia that yields an oil used in perfumery and as an insect repellent

cit·rus \'si-trəs\ *n, pl* **citrus** *or* **cit·rus·es** [L, citron tree] : any of a genus of often thorny trees and shrubs of the rue family grown in warm regions for their fruits (as orange, grapefruit, or lemon) with firm usu. thick rind and juicy pulp

city \'sit-ē\ *n, pl* **cit·ies** [OF *cité*, fr. L *civitat-*, *civitas* state, city, lit., citizenship, fr. *civis* citizen; akin to E *home*] **1 a** : an inhabited place of greater size or importance than a town **b** : an incorporated British town usu. of major size or importance and having the status of an episcopal see **c** : a usu. large or important municipality in the U.S. governed under a charter granted by the state **d** : an incorporated municipal unit of the highest class in Canada **2** : CITY-STATE **3** : the people of a city

city hall *n* : the chief administrative building of a city

city manager *n* : an official employed by an elected council to direct the administration of a city government

city–state \'sit-ē-'stāt, -,stāt\ *n* : a self-governing state (as of ancient Greece) consisting of a city and surrounding territory

civ·et \'siv-ət\ *n* [MF *civette*, fr. It *zibetto*, fr. Ar *zabād*] : a thick yellowish musky-odored substance obtained from the civet cat and used in perfume

civet cat *n* **1** : a long-bodied short-legged African mammal that produces most of the civet of commerce **2** : any of the small spotted skunks of western No. America

civ·ic \'siv-ik\ *adj* [L *civicus*, fr. *civis* citizen] : of or relating to a citizen, a city, citizenship, or civil affairs ⟨*civic* pride⟩ ⟨*civic* duty⟩ — **civ·i·cal·ly** \'siv-i-k(ə-)lē\ *adv*

civ·ics \'siv-iks\ *n* : a social science dealing with the rights and duties of citizens

civ·il \'siv-əl\ *adj* [L *civilis*, fr. *civis* citizen] **1** : of or relating to citizens or their rights ⟨*civil* responsibilities⟩ **2** : of or relating to the state as an organized political body ⟨*civil* institutions⟩ **3** : of or relating to the general population as distinguished from military or religious personnel or organizations ⟨*civil* affairs⟩ **4** : marked by courtesy or politeness ⟨give a *civil* answer⟩ **5 a** : relating to legal proceedings in connection with private rights and obligations distinct from criminal proceedings ⟨the *civil* code⟩ ⟨a *civil* suit⟩ **b** : of or relating to the civil law

syn POLITE, COURTEOUS: CIVIL implies no more than barely meeting the requirements of good breeding and the avoidance of roughness or unpleasantness; POLITE implies showing good manners and thoughtfulness but may often suggest lack of warmth or cordiality; COURTEOUS implies more actively considerate or dignified politeness

civil defense *n* : protective measures and emergency relief activities carried on by civilians in case of hostile attack or sabotage or natural disaster

civil engineering *n* : engineering that deals with the designing and construction of public works (as roads or harbors) and of various private works — **civil engineer** *n*

ci·vil·ian \sə-'vil-yən\ *n* : one not on active duty in a military, police, or fire-fighting force — **civilian** *adj*

ci·vil·i·ty \sə-'vil-ət-ē\ *n, pl* **-ties** **1** : POLITENESS, COURTESY **2** : a polite act or expression

civ·i·li·za·tion \,siv-ə-lə-'zā-shən\ *n* **1 a** : a relatively high level of cultural and technological development; *esp* : the stage of cultural development at which writing is attained **b** : the special culture of a people or a period ⟨Greek *civilization*⟩ ⟨18th century *civilization*⟩ **2** : the process of becoming civilized **3 a** : refinement of thought, manners, or taste **b** : a situation of urban comfort

civ·i·lize \'siv-ə-,līz\ *vt* **1** : to raise out of a savage state;

esp : to bring to an advanced and ordered stage of cultural development **2** : REFINE — **civ·i·lized** *adj*

civil law *n, often cap C & L* **1** : Roman law or the body of private law developed from it that is used in Louisiana and in many countries outside the English-speaking world **2** : the law of civil or private rights

civil liberty *n* : freedom from governmental interference with rights (as of free speech) esp. as guaranteed by a bill of rights

civ·il·ly \'siv-ə(l)-lē\ *adv* **1** : in a civil manner : POLITELY **2** : in terms of civil rights, matters, or law ⟨*civilly* dead⟩

civil marriage *n* : a marriage performed by a civil magistrate

civil rights *n pl* : the nonpolitical rights of a citizen; *esp* : the rights of personal liberty guaranteed to U.S. citizens by the 13th and 14th amendments to the Constitution and by acts of Congress

civil servant *n* : a member of a civil service

civil service *n* : the administrative service of a government exclusive of the armed forces; *esp* : one in which appointments are determined by competitive examination

civil war *n* : a war between opposing groups of citizens of the same country or nation

clab·ber \'klab-ər\ *n, chiefly dial* : sour milk that has thickened or curdled

¹clack \'klak\ *vb* [ME *clacken*] **1** : CHATTER, PRATTLE **2** : to make or cause to make a clatter — **clack·er** *n*

²clack *n* **1** : rapid continuous talk : CHATTER ⟨the *clack* of voices⟩ **2** : a sound of clacking ⟨the *clack* of a typewriter⟩

clad \'klad\ *adj* [fr. pp. of *clothe*] : CLOTHED, COVERED

clado·phyll \'klad-ə-,fil\ *n* [Gk *klados* branch + *phyllon* leaf] : a modified branch resembling an ordinary foliage leaf

¹claim \'klām\ *vt* [OF *clamer*, fr. L *clamare* to cry out] **1 a** : to ask for as rightfully belonging to oneself ⟨*claiming* the inheritance⟩ **b** : to take as the rightful owner ⟨*claimed* his bags an hour ago⟩ **c** : to call for : REQUIRE ⟨this matter *claims* our attention⟩ **2 a** : to state as a fact : MAINTAIN ⟨*claimed* that he'd been cheated⟩ **b** : PROFESS ⟨*claimed* to know nothing of the matter⟩ — **claim·a·ble** \'klā-mə-bəl\ *adj* — **claim·er** *n*

²claim *n* **1** : a demand for something due or believed to be due ⟨insurance *claim*⟩ **2 a** : a right to something; *esp* : a title to something in the possession of another **b** : an assertion open to challenge ⟨a *claim* of authenticity⟩ **3** : something claimed; *esp* : a tract of land marked out by a settler or prospector

claim·ant \'klā-mənt\ *n* : a person who claims or asserts his right to something

clair·voy·ance \kla(ə)r-'vȯi-ən(t)s, kle(ə)r-\ *n* **1** : the professed power of seeing or knowing about things that are not present to the senses **2** : keenness of perception : PENETRATION

¹clair·voy·ant \-ənt\ *adj* [F, fr. *clair* clear + *voyant*, prp. of *voir* to see] **1** : unusually perceptive : DISCERNING **2** : of or relating to clairvoyance — **clair·voy·ant·ly** *adv*

²clairvoyant *n* : a person held to have the power of clairvoyance

¹clam \'klam\ *n* [fr. earlier *clam* clamp; fr. the clamping action of the shells] **1** : any of numerous edible marine bivalve mollusks living in sand or mud **2** : a freshwater mussel **3** : the flesh of a clam used as food

²clam *vi* **clammed**; **clam·ming** : to gather clams esp. by digging

clam·a·to·ri·al \,klam-ə-'tōr-ē-əl, -'tȯr-\ *adj* : of or relating to a large group (Clamatores) of passerine birds with little singing ability

clam·bake \'klam-,bāk\ *n* : a party or gathering (as at the seashore) at which food (as clams, potatoes) is cooked usu. on heated rocks covered by seaweed

clam·ber \'klam-bər\ *vb* **clam·bered**; **clam·ber·ing** \'klam-b(ə-)riŋ\ [ME *clambren*; akin to E *climb*] : to climb awkwardly (as by scrambling) ⟨*clamber* over steep rocks⟩ — **clam·ber·er** \-bər-ər\ *n*

clam·my \'klam-ē\ *adj* **clam·mi·er**; **-est** [ME, prob. fr. *clammen* to smear, stick, fr. OE *clǣman*] **1** : being damp, soft, sticky, and usu. cool **2** : causing clamminess ⟨*clammy* fear⟩ — **clam·mi·ly** \'klam-ə-lē\ *adv* — **clam·mi·ness** \'klam-ē-nəs\ *n*

¹clam·or \'klam-ər\ *n* [L, fr. *clamare* to cry out] **1 a** : noisy shouting **b** : a loud continuous noise **2** : vigorous and insistent protest or demand ⟨a great *clamor* against price controls⟩ ⟨public *clamor* for a tax cut⟩

²**clamor** *vb* **clam·ored; clam·or·ing** \'klam-(ə-)riŋ\ **1 :** to make a clamor ⟨*clamoring* about his appointment⟩ **2 :** to express in a clamor ⟨*clamoring* that they had been misunderstood⟩

clam·or·ous \'klam-(ə-)rəs\ *adj* **:** full of clamor **:** NOISY ⟨a *clamorous* mob⟩ — **clam·or·ous·ly** *adv* — **clam·or·ous·ness** *n*

¹**clamp** \'klamp\ *n* **:** a device that holds or presses two or more parts together firmly

²**clamp** *vb* **1 :** to fasten with or as if with a clamp ⟨*clamp* two boards together⟩ ⟨a pipe *clamped* between his teeth⟩ **2 :** to impose forcibly or authoritatively ⟨*clamped* on a curfew after the riots⟩

clamp down *vt* **:** to impose harsh penalties and restrictions ⟨*clamping down* on speeders⟩

clam·shell \'klam-,shel\ *n* **:** a bucket or grapple (as on a dredge) having two hinged jaws

clam up *vi, slang* **:** to become silent; *esp* **:** to refuse to talk further

clamp

clam worm *n* **:** any of several large burrowing annelid worms often used as bait

clan \'klan\ *n* [ScGael *clann* offspring, clan, fr. OIr *cland* plant, offspring, fr. L *planta* plant] **1 :** a group (as in the Scottish Highlands) made up of households whose heads claim descent from a common ancestor **2 :** a group of persons united by a common interest ⟨the whole *clan* of actors⟩

clan·des·tine \klan-'des-tən\ *adj* [L *clandestinus*, irreg. fr. *clam* secretly] **:** managed with planned secrecy **:** UNDERHAND ⟨a *clandestine* meeting⟩ **syn** see SECRET — **clan·des·tine·ly** *adv* — **clan·des·tine·ness** *n*

¹**clang** \'klaŋ\ *vb* [L *clangere*] **:** to make or cause to make a clang

²**clang** *n* **:** a loud ringing sound like that made by pieces of metal striking each other ⟨the *clang* of a fire alarm⟩

clang·or \'klaŋ-ər, -gər\ *n* **:** a resounding clang or medley of clangs — **clang·or** *vi* — **clang·or·ous** \-(g)ə-rəs\ *adj* — **clang·or·ous·ly** *adv*

¹**clank** \'klaŋk\ *vb* **1 :** to make or cause to make a clank or series of clanks ⟨the radiator hissed and *clanked*⟩ **2 :** to move with a clank ⟨tanks *clanking* through the streets⟩ — **clank·ing·ly** \'klaŋ-kiŋ-lē\ *adv*

²**clank** *n* **:** a sharp brief metallic ringing sound

clan·nish \'klan-ish\ *adj* **1 :** of or relating to a clan **2 :** tending to associate only with a group of similar background or status ⟨*clannish* immigrants⟩ — **clan·nish·ly** *adv* — **clan·nish·ness** *n*

clans·man \'klanz-mən\ *n* **:** a member of a clan

¹**clap** \'klap\ *vb* **clapped; clap·ping** [OE *clæppan*] **1 :** to strike noisily **:** SLAM, BANG ⟨*clap* two boards together⟩ ⟨the door *clapped* shut⟩ **2 :** to strike the hands together repeatedly in applause **:** APPLAUD **3 :** to strike with the open hand ⟨*clapped* his friend on the shoulder⟩ **4 :** to put hastily ⟨*clapped* him in jail⟩ ⟨*clapped* on his hat and left⟩

²**clap** *n* **1 :** a loud noisy crash made by or as if by the striking together of two hard surfaces ⟨a *clap* of thunder⟩ **2 :** a hard slap ⟨a *clap* on the shoulder⟩ **3 :** the sound made by clapping the hands together **:** APPLAUSE

³**clap** *n* [MF *clapoir* bubo] **:** GONORRHEA

clap·board \'klab-ərd; 'kla(p)-,bōrd, -,bȯrd\ *n* [D *klaphout* stave wood] **:** a narrow board thicker at one edge than at the other used horizontally for covering the outside of wooden buildings — **clapboard** *vt*

clap·per \'klap-ər\ *n* **:** one that makes a clapping sound: as **a :** the tongue of a bell **b :** one of a pair of flat sticks held between the fingers and used to produce musical rhythms **c :** a person who applauds

clap·trap \'klap-,trap\ *n* [¹*clap*] **:** pretentious nonsense **:** TRASH

claque \'klak\ *n* [F, fr. *claquer* to clap] **1 :** a group hired to applaud at a performance **2 :** a group of toadies

clar·et \'klar-ət\ *n* [MF *vin claret* clear wine] **1 :** a dry red table wine **2 :** a dark purplish red — **claret** *adj*

clar·i·fi·ca·tion \,klar-ə-fə-'kā-shən\ *n* **:** the act or process of clarifying

clar·i·fy \'klar-ə-,fī\ *vb* **-fied; -fy·ing** [MF *clarifier*, fr. LL *clarificare*, fr. L *clarus* clear] **1 :** to make or become pure or clear ⟨*clarify* a liquid⟩ **2 :** to make or become more

readily understandable ⟨*clarify* one's meaning⟩ — **clar·i·fi·er** \-,fī(-ə)r\ *n*

clar·i·net \,klar-ə-'net, 'klar-ə-,net\ *n* [F *clarinette*] **:** a single-reed woodwind instrument in the form of a cylindrical tube with moderately flaring end

clar·i·net·ist *or* **clar·i·net·tist** \,klar-ə-'net-əst\ *n* **:** a person who plays a clarinet

¹**clar·i·on** \'klar-ē-ən\ *n* [ML *clarion-, clario*, fr. L *clarus* clear] **:** a trumpet having very clear and shrill tones

²**clarion** *adj* **:** brilliantly clear ⟨a *clarion* call to action⟩

clar·i·ty \'klar-ət-ē\ *n* **:** CLEARNESS

clary \'kla(ə)r-ē\ *n, pl* **clar·ies** [ME *clarie*, fr. MF *sclaree*, fr. ML *sclareia*] **:** an aromatic mint of southern Europe grown as a potherb and ornamental

clar·inet

¹**clash** \'klash\ *vb* **1 :** to make a clash ⟨*clashing* cymbals⟩ **2 a :** to come into conflict ⟨rebels *clashed* with the police⟩ **b :** to be sharply out of harmony ⟨some colors *clash* when placed side by side⟩ **3 :** to cause to clash ⟨the deer rushed together, *clashing* their horns⟩ — **clash·er** *n*

²**clash** *n* **1 :** a noisy usu. metallic sound of collision ⟨the *clash* of swords⟩ **2 a :** a hostile encounter ⟨a *clash* between two armies⟩ **b :** a sharp conflict ⟨a *clash* of opinion⟩

¹**clasp** \'klasp\ *n* [ME *claspe*] **1 :** a device for holding together two objects or two parts of something ⟨a belt *clasp*⟩ ⟨the *clasp* of a necklace⟩ **2 :** EMBRACE, GRASP ⟨the warm *clasp* of his hand⟩

²**clasp** *vt* **1 :** to fasten with or as if with a clasp **2 :** to enclose and hold with or as if with the arms; *esp* **:** EMBRACE **3 :** to seize with or as if with the hand **:** GRASP — **clasp·er** *n*

clasp knife *n* **:** POCKETKNIFE; *esp* **:** one having a clasp for holding the blade open

¹**class** \'klas\ *n* [L *classis* group called to arms, class of citizens] **1 a :** a group of persons of the same general economic or social status or level ⟨the working *class*⟩ **b** *pl* **:** persons of high social or economic status ⟨the *classes* as opposed to the masses⟩ **c :** social rank or level ⟨an awareness of *class*⟩ **d :** high quality ⟨the team was competent but lacked *class*⟩ **2 a :** a course of instruction ⟨a *class* in arithmetic⟩ **b :** the group of pupils meeting regularly in a course ⟨a big *class* this year⟩ **c :** the period during which a study group meets **d :** a group of students or alumni whose graduation date is the same ⟨*class* of '68⟩ **3 a :** a group or set alike in some way; *esp* **:** a major category in biological taxonomy ranking above the order and below the phylum or division **b :** a division or rating based on grade or quality ⟨a *class* A movie⟩ — **class·less** \-ləs\ *adj*

²**class** *vt* **:** CLASSIFY

class-con·scious \'klas-,kän-chəs\ *adj* **1 :** aware of one's common status with others in an economic or social class **2 :** believing in and actively aware of class struggle — **class consciousness** *n*

¹**clas·sic** \'klas-ik\ *adj* [L *classicus* of the highest class of Roman citizens, first-rate, fr. *classis* class] **1 a :** serving as a standard of excellence **b :** TRADITIONAL, ENDURING ⟨a *classic* heritage⟩ **c :** characterized by simple tailored lines in fashion year after year ⟨*classic* apparel⟩ **2 :** of or relating to the ancient Greeks and Romans or their culture **:** CLASSICAL **3 a :** notable as the best or most typical instance ⟨the *classic* study of American politics⟩ ⟨the *classic* example of a dictator⟩ **b :** AUTHENTIC ⟨a *classic* folk dance⟩

²**classic** *n* **1 :** a literary work of ancient Greece or Rome **2 :** a work of enduring excellence; *also* **:** its author **3 :** something regarded as perfect of its kind **4 :** a traditional event ⟨a football *classic*⟩

clas·si·cal \'klas-i-kəl\ *adj* **1 :** CLASSIC; *esp* **:** of the highest class or degree of excellence **2 :** of or relating to the classics of literature or art; *esp* **:** of or relating to the ancient Greek and Roman classics ⟨*classical* studies⟩ ⟨a *classical* scholar⟩ **3 a :** TRADITIONAL, AUTHENTIC **b :** of or relating to the first developed form or system of a science, art, or discipline ⟨the *classical* economists⟩ ⟨*classical* physics⟩ **c :** conforming to a pattern of usage sanctioned by a body of literature rather than by everyday speech ⟨*classical* Latin⟩ **4 :** concerned with a general study of the arts and sciences and not specializing in technical studies ⟨a *classical* high school⟩ **5 :** composed in accordance with a long-established musical form : appealing to a highly developed musical taste ⟨*classical music*⟩

clas·si·cal·ly \'klas-i-k(ə-)lē\ *adv* : in a classic or classical manner

clas·si·cism \'klas-ə-,siz-əm\ *n* **1 a** : the principles or style embodied in the literature, art, or architecture of ancient Greece and Rome **b** : classical scholarship **c** : a classical idiom or expression **2** : adherence to traditional standards (as of simplicity, restraint, proportion) universally and enduringly valid

clas·si·cist \-səst\ *n* **1** : an advocate or follower of classicism **2** : a classical scholar — **clas·si·cis·tic** \,klas-ə-'sis-tik\ *adj*

clas·si·fi·ca·tion \,klas-ə-fə-'kā-shən\ *n* **1** : the act or process of classifying **2 a** : systematic arrangement in groups or categories according to established criteria; *esp* : TAXONOMY **b** : CLASS, CATEGORY — **clas·si·fi·ca·to·ry** \'klas-(ə-)fə-kə-,tōr-ē, -,tór-\ *adj*

clas·si·fied \'klas-ə-,fīd\ *adj* **1** : divided into classes or placed in a class **2** : withheld from general circulation for reasons of national security ⟨*classified* information⟩

clas·si·fy \'klas-ə-,fī\ *vt* **-fied; -fy·ing** : to arrange in or assign to classes ⟨*classify* books according to subject matter⟩ — **clas·si·fi·a·ble** \-,fī-ə-bəl\ *adj* — **clas·si·fi·er** \-,fī(-ə)r\ *n*

class·mate \'klas-,māt\ *n* : a member of the same class in a school or college

class·room \-,rüm, -,rùm\ *n* : a room in a school or college in which classes meet

class struggle *n* : a basic conflict between the proletariat and bourgeoisie in Marxian theory — called also *class war*

¹clat·ter \'klat-ər\ *vb* **1** : to make or cause to make a rattling sound ⟨*clattering* the dishes⟩ **2** : to move or go with a clatter ⟨*clatter* down the stairs⟩ — **clat·ter·er** \-ər-ər\ *n* — **clat·ter·ing·ly** \'klat-ə-riŋ-lē\ *adv*

²clatter *n* **1** : a rattling sound (as of hard bodies striking together) **2** : COMMOTION **3** : noisy chatter — **clat·tery** \'klat-ə-rē\ *adj*

clau·di·ca·tion \,klód-ə-'kā-shən\ *n* : LAMENESS, LIMPING

clause \'klóz\ *n* [ML *clausa* close of a rhetorical period, fr. L *claus-, claudere* to close] **1** : a separate distinct part of an article or document ⟨a *clause* in a will⟩ **2** : a group of words having its own subject and predicate but forming only part of a compound or complex sentence (as "when it rained" or "they went inside" in the sentence "when it rained, they went inside") — **claus·al** \'kló-zəl\ *adj*

claus·tro·pho·bia \,kló-strə-'fō-bē-ə\ *n* [L *claustrum* bar, bolt, fr. *claudere* to close] : abnormal dread of being in closed or narrow spaces — **claus·tro·pho·bic** \-bik\ *adj*

cla·vate \'klā-,vāt\ *adj* [L *clava* club, fr. *clavus* nail, knot in wood] : gradually narrowing near the distal end — **cla·vate·ly** *adv* — **cla·va·tion** \klā-'vā-shən\ *n*

clave *past of* CLEAVE

clav·i·chord \'klav-ə-,kórd\ *n* [L *clavis* key + *chorda* string] : an early keyboard instrument in use before the piano — **clav·i·chord·ist** \-əst\ *n*

clav·i·cle \'klav-i-kəl\ *n* [L *clavicula*, dim. of *clavis* key] : a bone of the shoulder that joins the breastbone and the shoulder blade — called also *collarbone* — **cla·vic·u·lar** \kla-'vik-yə-lər\ *adj*

clav·i·corn \'klav-ə-,kórn\ *adj* : having club-shaped antennae ⟨*clavicorn* beetles⟩

cla·vier \klə-'vi(ə)r; 'klāv-ē-ər, 'klav-\ *n* **1** : the keyboard of a musical instrument **2** : an early keyboard instrument — **cla·vier·ist** \-əst\ *n*

¹claw \'kló\ *n* [OE *clawu* hoof, claw] **1 a** : a sharp usu. slender and curved nail on the toe of an animal **b** : a sharp curved process esp. if at the end of a limb (as of an insect); *also* : one of the pincerlike organs terminating some limbs of arthropods (as a lobster or scorpion) **2** : something (as the forked end of a hammer) that resembles a claw in shape or use — **clawed** \'klód\ *adj*

²claw *vb* : to rake, seize, or dig with or as if with claws

clay \'klā\ *n* [OE *clæg*] **1 a** : an earthy material that is plastic when moist but hard when fired, is composed chiefly of silicates of aluminum and water, and is used for brick, tile, and earthenware; *also* : soil composed chiefly of this material having particles less than a specified size **b** : EARTH, MUD **2 a** : a plastic substance used for modeling **b** : the mortal human body — **clay·ish** \'klā-ish\ *adj*

clay·ey \'klā-ē\ *adj* **clay·i·er; -est** : resembling clay or containing much clay ⟨a *clayey* soil⟩

clay loam *n* : a loam consisting of from 20 to 30 percent clay

clay·more \'klā-,mō(ə)r, -,mó(ə)r\ *n* : a large 2-edged sword formerly used by Scottish Highlanders

clay pigeon *n* : a saucer-shaped target thrown from a trap in skeet and trapshooting

¹clean \'klēn\ *adj* [OE *clǣne*] **1 a** : free from dirt, foreign matter, or leavings ⟨*clean* clothes⟩ ⟨bring a *clean* plate⟩ **b** : free from contamination or disease **2** : free from admixture : PURE **3 a** : characterized by moral integrity : HONORABLE ⟨a candidate with a *clean* record⟩ **b** : ceremonially or spiritually pure **4 a** : THOROUGH, COMPLETE ⟨made a *clean* sweep⟩ **b** : SKILLFUL ⟨a good *clean* job⟩ **5 a** : being trim and well-formed ⟨a ship with *clean* lines⟩ **b** : EVEN, SMOOTH ⟨a sharp knife makes a *clean* cut⟩ **6** : habitually neat — **clean·ness** \'klēn-nəs\ *n*

²clean *adv* **1 a** : so as to clean ⟨a new broom sweeps *clean*⟩ **b** : in a clean manner ⟨fight *clean*⟩ **2** : all the way : COMPLETELY ⟨bullet went *clean* through his arm⟩ ⟨*clean* out of his head⟩

³clean *vb* **1** : to make or become clean ⟨*clean* this room⟩ ⟨*cleaned* up for supper⟩ **2** : to remove or exhaust the contents or resources of ⟨tourists *cleaned* out the shops⟩ ⟨the job *cleaned* the treasury⟩ **3** : SETTLE ⟨*clean* up some bills⟩ — **clean·er** *n*

syn CLEAN, CLEANSE mean to remove dirt or impurities from. CLEAN applies to any removing of dirt, litter, dust; CLEANSE applies chiefly to washing with water or a solvent; it may also apply to figurative purification ⟨*cleansed* from sin⟩

clean–cut \'klēn-'kət\ *adj* **1** : cut so that the surface or edge is smooth and even **2** : sharply defined or outlined ⟨*clean-cut* decision⟩ **3** : giving an effect of wholesomeness ⟨a *clean-cut* young man⟩

clean–limbed \-'limd\ *adj* : well proportioned : TRIM ⟨a *clean-limbed* youth⟩

clean·li·ness \'klen-lē-nəs\ *n* : the quality or state of being cleanly

¹clean·ly \'klen-lē\ *adj* **clean·li·er; -est** **1** : careful to keep clean ⟨a *cleanly* animal⟩ **2** : habitually kept clean ⟨*cleanly* surroundings⟩

²clean·ly \'klēn-lē\ *adv* : in a clean manner ⟨hit a ball *cleanly*⟩

cleanse \'klenz\ *vt* [OE *clǣnsian* to purify, fr. *clǣn* clean] : to make clean **syn** see CLEAN

cleans·er \'klen-zər\ *n* : a preparation (as a scouring powder) used for cleaning

clean up *vi* **1** : to make a lot of money ⟨*cleaned up* at the races⟩ **2** : to inflict punishment or defeat ⟨*cleaned up* on him after school⟩

¹clear \'kli(ə)r\ *adj* [OF *cler*, fr. L *clarus*] **1 a** : BRIGHT, LUMINOUS ⟨*clear* sunlight⟩ **b** : free from clouds, haze, or mist ⟨a *clear* day⟩ **c** : UNTROUBLED, SERENE ⟨a *clear* gaze⟩ **2** : CLEAN, PURE: as **a** : free of blemishes ⟨a *clear* complexion⟩ **b** : easily seen through : TRANSPARENT ⟨*clear* glass⟩ **3 a** : easily heard ⟨the sound was quite *clear*⟩ **b** : easily visible : PLAIN **c** : easily understandable : UNMISTAKABLE ⟨his meaning was *clear*⟩ **4** : free from doubt : SURE ⟨a *clear* understanding of the issue⟩ **5** : free from guile or guilt : INNOCENT ⟨a *clear* conscience⟩ **6** : unhampered by restriction or limitation: as **a** : unencumbered by debts or charges : NET ⟨a *clear* profit⟩ **b** : UNQUALIFIED, ABSOLUTE ⟨*clear* case of treason⟩ **d** : free from obstruction or entanglement ⟨the coast is *clear*⟩ — **clear·ly** *adv* — **clear·ness** *n*

syn TRANSPARENT, TRANSLUCENT: CLEAR implies absence of cloudiness, haziness, or muddiness ⟨*clear* sky⟩ TRANSPARENT implies being so clear that objects can be seen distinctly ⟨*transparent* film of varnish⟩ TRANSLUCENT usu. implies permitting the passage of light but not vision ⟨*translucent* frosted glass⟩

²clear *adv* **1** : in a clear manner ⟨shout loud and *clear*⟩ **2** : all the way : COMPLETELY ⟨can see *clear* to the mountains on a day like this⟩

³clear *vb* **1 a** : to make or become clear or translucent ⟨*clear* the water by filtering⟩ ⟨has the sky *cleared*⟩ **b** : to go away : DISPERSE ⟨clouds *cleared* away after the rain⟩ ⟨the crowds finally *cleared*⟩ **2 a** : to free from accusation or blame ⟨*cleared* his name⟩ **b** : to certify as trustworthy

⟨*cleared* for defense work⟩ **3** : EXPLAIN ⟨*cleared* the matter up for me⟩ **4** : to get free from obstruction: as **a** : to submit for approval ⟨*clear* this with the boss⟩ **b** : AUTHORIZE **c** : to gain official approval and status ⟨all bills must be *cleared* with the committee first⟩ **5** : SETTLE ⟨*clear* an account⟩ **6** : to go through (customs) **7** : NET ⟨*cleared* a profit⟩ **8** : to get rid of : REMOVE ⟨*clear* away that trash⟩ **9 a** : to jump or go by without touching ⟨*cleared* the fence⟩ **b** : PASS ⟨the bill *cleared* the legislature⟩ — **clear·a·ble** \'klir-ə-bəl\ *adj* — **clear·er** *n*

⁴clear *n* : a clear space or part — **in the clear 1** : in inside measurement **2** : free of resistance or obstruction ⟨some nice blocking got him *in the clear*⟩ **3** : free of suspicion **4** : not in code or cipher ⟨sent the message *in the clear*⟩

clear·ance \'klir-ən(t)s\ *n* **1** : an act or process of clearing: as **a** : the act of clearing a ship at the customhouse; *also* : the papers showing that a ship has cleared **b** : the passage of checks and claims among banks through a clearinghouse **c** : a certification as clear of prohibition, suspicion, or doubt ⟨was given a security *clearance*⟩ **d** : an offering of goods for quick sale usu. at reduced prices **2** : the distance by which one object clears another or the clear space between them

clear–cut \'kli(ə)r-'kət\ *adj* **1** : sharply outlined : DISTINCT ⟨a *clear-cut* pattern⟩ **2** : DEFINITE, UNEQUIVOCAL ⟨*clear-cut* victory⟩

clear·head·ed \-'hed-əd\ *adj* : having a clear understanding : PERCEPTIVE — **clear·head·ed·ly** *adv* — **clear·head·ed·ness** *n*

clear·ing \'kli(ə)r-iŋ\ *n* **1** : the act or process of making or becoming clear **2** : a tract of land cleared of wood and brush **3 a** : CLEARANCE 1b **b** *pl* : the gross amount of balances adjusted by clearance

clear·ing·house \-,haús\ *n* **1** : an institution established and maintained by banks for making an exchange of checks and claims held by each bank against other banks **2** : a central agency for collection, classification, and distribution esp. of information

clear–sight·ed \'kli(ə)r-'sīt-əd\ *adj* **1** : having clear vision **2** : DISCERNING — **clear–sight·ed·ly** *adv* — **clear–sight·ed·ness** *n*

¹cleat \'klēt\ *n* [ME *clete*] **1** : a wedge-shaped piece fastened to something and used as a support or check (as for a rope on the spar of a ship) **2** : a wooden or metal device usu. with two projecting parts around which a rope may be made fast **3** : a strip or projecting piece fastened on or across something to give strength, to provide a grip, or to prevent slipping

²cleat *vt* **1** : to fasten to or by a cleat **2** : to provide with a cleat

cleav·a·ble \'klē-və-bəl\ *adj* : capable of being split

cleav·age \'klē-vij\ *n* **1** : the quality possessed by a crystallized substance or rock of splitting along definite planes **2** : the action of cleaving : the state of being cleft **3** : cell division; *esp* : the series of mitotic divisions of the egg that changes the single-celled zygote into a multicellular embryo

¹cleave \'klēv\ *vi* **cleaved** \'klēvd\ *or* **clove** \'klōv\ *also* **clave** \'klāv\; **cleav·ing** [ME *clevien*, fr. OE *clifian*] : ADHERE, CLING

²cleave *vb* **cleaved** \'klēvd\ *also* **cleft** \'kleft\ *or* **clove** \'klōv\; **cleaved** *also* **cleft** *or* **clo·ven** \'klō-vən\; **cleav·ing** [ME *cleven*, fr. OE *clēofan*] **1 a** : to split by or as if by a cutting blow ⟨*cleaved* the pole with one swing⟩ ⟨some woods cleave along the grain easily⟩ **b** : DIVIDE, SEPARATE ⟨the controversy *cleaved* the group into two camps⟩ **2** : PENETRATE ⟨a ship's bow *cleaving* the waves⟩

cleav·er \'klē-vər\ *n* : one that cleaves; *esp* : a heavy butcher's knife for cutting up meat

cleav·ers \'klē-vərz\ *n sing or pl* [alter. of OE *clife* burdock, cleavers] : any of several plants of the madder family with weak prickly stems

cleek \'klēk\ *n* : a wooden-headed golf club with more loft than a spoon — called also *number four wood*

clef \'klef\ *n* [F, key, fr. L *clavis*] : a sign placed on the staff in music to show what pitch is represented by each line and space

¹cleft \'kleft\ *n* [OE *geclyft*] **1** : a

space or opening made by splitting : FISSURE **2** : a usu. V-shaped indentation resembling a cleft

²cleft *adj* **1** : partially split or divided **2** : divided about halfway to the midrib ⟨a *cleft* leaf⟩

cleft palate *n* : congenital fissure of the roof of the mouth

clem·a·tis \'klem-ət-əs, kli-'mat-əs\ *n* [Gk *klēmatis* brushwood, clematis] : a vine or herb related to the buttercups that has leaves with three leaflets and is widely grown for its showy usu. white or purple flowers

clem·en·cy \'klem-ən-sē\ *n, pl* **-cies 1 a** : disposition to be merciful **b** : an act or instance of leniency **2** : mildness of weather **syn** see MERCY

clem·ent \'klem-ənt\ *adj* [L *clement-, clemens*] **1** : inclined to be merciful : LENIENT ⟨a *clement* judge⟩ **2** : TEMPERATE, MILD ⟨*clement* weather for November⟩ — **clem·ent·ly** *adv*

¹clench \'klench\ *vb* [OE *-clencan*] **1** : CLINCH 1 **2** : to hold fast : CLUTCH **3** : to set or close tightly ⟨*clenched* his teeth⟩ ⟨her hands *clenched* in her pockets⟩

²clench *n* **1** : the end of a nail that is turned back in clinching it **2** : an act or instance of clenching

clep·sy·dra \'klep-sə-drə\ *n, pl* **-dras** *or* **-drae** \-,drē, -,drī\ : WATER CLOCK

clere·sto·ry *or* **clear·sto·ry** \'kli(ə)r-,stōr-ē, -,stòr-\ *n, pl* **-ries** : an outside wall of a room or building that rises above an adjoining roof and contains windows

cler·gy \'klər-jē\ *n, pl* **clergies** [OF *clergie* condition of a cleric, scholarship, fr. *clerc* cleric, clerk] **1** : the body of men ordained for service in the Christian church **2** : the official or priestly class of a religion

cler·gy·man \-ji-mən\ *n* : a member of the clergy

cler·ic \'kler-ik\ *n* [LL *clericus*] **1** : CLERGYMAN **2** : a man in one of the orders preparatory to the priesthood

cler·i·cal \'kler-i-kəl\ *adj* **1** : of, relating to, or characteristic of the clergy, a clergyman, or a cleric **2** : of or relating to a clerk or office worker — **cler·i·cal·ly** \'kler-i-k(ə-)lē\ *adv*

clerical collar *n* : a narrow stiffly upright white collar buttoned at the back of the neck and worn by clergymen

cler·i·cal·ism \'kler-i-kə-,liz-əm\ *n* : a policy of maintaining or increasing the power of a religious hierarchy — **cler·i·cal·ist** \-kə-ləst\ *n*

¹clerk \'klərk\ *n* [ME & OF *clerc*, fr. LL *clericus*, fr. LGk *klērikos*, fr. Gk *klēros* lot, inheritance; so called fr. the statement in Deuteronomy 18:2 that the Lord is the inheritance of the Levite priests] **1** : CLERIC **2 a** : an official responsible for correspondence, records, and accounts ⟨town *clerk*⟩ **b** : one employed to keep records or accounts or to perform general office work **c** : a salesman in a store

²clerk *vi* : to act or work as a clerk

clerk·ly \'klər-klē\ *adj* : of, relating to, or characteristic of a clerk

clerk regular *n* : a religious combining monastic vows with the ministry of a diocesan priest

clerk·ship \'klərk-,ship\ *n* : the office or business of a clerk

clev·er \'klev-ər\ *adj* [ME *cliver*] **1 a** : showing skill or resourcefulness often with physical dexterity **b** : quick in learning **2** : marked by wit or ingenuity — **clev·er·ish** \'klev-(ə-)rish\ *adj* — **clev·er·ly** \-ər-lē\ *adv* — **clev·er·ness** \-ər-nəs\ *n*

syn INTELLIGENT, SMART: CLEVER stresses quickness, deftness, or great aptitude; INTELLIGENT implies success in understanding and coping with new situations and solving problems; SMART suggests alertness and quickness to learn, or it may imply pungency of wit tending often toward impudence

clev·is \'klev-əs\ *n* : a usu. U-shaped metal shackle with the ends drilled to receive a pin or bolt used for attaching or suspending parts

¹clew *or* **clue** \'klü\ *n* [OE *cliewen*] **1** : a ball of thread, yarn, or cord **2** *usu* **clue** : something that guides through an intricate procedure or maze of difficulties; *esp* : a piece of evidence guiding one to the solution of a problem **3** : a metal loop attached to the lower corner of a sail

²clew *or* **clue** *vt* **clewed** *or* **clued**; **clew·ing** *or* **clue·ing** *or* **clu·ing 1** : to roll into a ball **2** *usu* **clue** : to provide with a clue **3** : to haul (a sail) up or down by ropes through the clews

cli·che \kli-'shā\ *n* [F, lit., stereotype] **1** : a trite phrase

G, or Treble, Clef

F, or Bass, Clef

clef

or expression; *also* : the idea expressed by it **2** : a hackneyed theme or situation — **cliché** *adj*

¹click \'klik\ *n* : a slight sharp noise

²click *vb* **1 a** : to make or cause to make a click ⟨a Geiger counter *clicking* away⟩⟨*clicked* his tongue⟩ **b** : to move or strike with a click ⟨*clicked* off the safety on the gun⟩⟨his heels *clicked* together smartly⟩ **2 a** : to fit or work together smoothly **b** : SUCCEED ⟨his idea *clicked*⟩

click beetle *n* : any of a family of beetles able to spring over with a click when turned on its back

cli·ent \'klī-ənt\ *n* [L *client-, cliens*] **1** : a person under the protection of another : DEPENDENT **2 a** : a person who engages the professional services of another **b** : PATRON, CUSTOMER — **cli·ent·age** \-ən-tij\ *n* — **cli·en·tal** \klī-'ent-ᵊl\ *adj*

cli·en·tele \ˌklī-ən-'tel\ *n* : a body of clients and esp. of customers ⟨a store that caters to an exclusive *clientele*⟩

cliff \'klif\ *n* [OE *clif*] : a high steep face of rock

cliff dweller *n*, *often cap C & D* : one of the people of the American Southwest who erected their dwellings on rock ledges or in the recesses of canyon walls and cliffs — **cliff dwelling** *n*

cliff-hang·er \'klif-ˌhaŋ-ər\ *n* **1** : an adventure serial or melodrama; *esp* : one presented in installments each ending in suspense **2** : a contest whose outcome is in doubt up to the very end

¹cli·mac·ter·ic \klī-'mak-tə-rik\ *adj* [Gk *klimaktēr* critical point, lit., rung of a ladder, fr. *klimak-, klimax* ladder] **1** : constituting or relating to a critical period (as of life) **2** : CRITICAL, CRUCIAL

²climacteric *n* **1** : a major turning point or critical stage **2** : MENOPAUSE

cli·mac·tic \klī-'mak-tik\ *adj* : of, relating to, or constituting a climax — **cli·mac·ti·cal·ly** \-ti-k(ə-)lē\ *adv*

cli·mate \'klī-mət\ *n* [LL *climat-, clima*, fr. Gk *klimat-, klima* inclination, latitude, zone, fr. *klinein* to lean] **1 a** : a region with specified weather conditions **b** : the average weather conditions of a particular place or region over a period of years **2** : the prevailing temper or environmental conditions of a group or period ⟨a favorable financial *climate*⟩ ⟨a *climate* of fear⟩ — **cli·mat·ic** \klī-'mat-ik\ *adj* — **cli·mat·i·cal·ly** \-'mat-i-k(ə-)lē\ *adv*

cli·ma·tol·o·gy \ˌklī-mə-'täl-ə-jē\ *n* : the science that deals with climates — **cli·ma·to·log·i·cal** \ˌklī-mət-ᵊl-'äj-i-kəl\ *adj* — **cli·ma·tol·o·gist** \ˌklī-mə-'täl-ə-jəst\ *n*

¹cli·max \'klī-ˌmaks\ *n* [L, fr. Gk *klimax* ladder, fr. *klinein* to lean] **1 a** : a series of ideas or statements so arranged that they increase in force and power from the first to the last **b** : the highest or most forceful in a series **c** : the highest point : CULMINATION ⟨the storm had reached its *climax*⟩ **2** : ORGASM **3** : a relatively stable ecological stage or community

²climax *vb* : to come or bring to a climax

¹climb \'klīm\ *vb* [OE *climban*] **1 a** : to go up or down by grasping or clinging with hands and feet ⟨*climb* a flagpole⟩ ⟨*climb* down a ladder⟩ **b** : to ascend in growth (as by twining) ⟨a *climbing* vine⟩ **2** : to rise gradually to a higher point ⟨*climb* from poverty to wealth⟩ **3** : to slope upward ⟨the road *climbs* steeply to the summit⟩ syn see ASCEND — **climb·a·ble** \'klī-mə-bəl\ *adj* — **climb·er** \'klī-mər\ *n*

²climb *n* **1** : a place where climbing is necessary **2** : the act of climbing : ascent by climbing

climbing iron *n* : a steel framework with spikes attached that may be affixed to one's boots for climbing

clime \'klīm\ *n* **1** : CLIMATE ⟨travel to warmer *climes*⟩

¹clinch \'klinch\ *vb* [prob. alter. of ¹*clench*] **1 a** : to turn over or flatten the protruding end of (as a driven nail) **b** : to fasten by clinching **2** : CLENCH 2 **3** : to make final or irrefutable : SETTLE **4** : to seize or grasp one another : GRAPPLE

²clinch *n* **1 a** : a fastening by means of a clinched nail, rivet, or bolt **b** : the clinched part of a nail, bolt, or rivet **2** : an act or instance of clinching in boxing

clinch·er \'klin-chər\ *n* : one that clinches; *esp* : a decisive fact, argument, act, or remark

cline \'klīn\ *n* : a graded series of differences exhibited by a group of related organisms usu. along a line of environmental or geographic transition

cling \'kliŋ\ *vi* **clung** \'kləŋ\; **cling·ing** \'kliŋ-iŋ\ [OE *clingan*] **1 a** : to adhere as if glued cohesively and firmly : STICK ⟨needle *clinging* to a magnet⟩⟨the shirt *clung* to his

back⟩ **b** : to hold or hold on tightly or tenaciously ⟨*clung* desperately to the ladder⟩ ⟨*clings* to her family⟩ **2** : to have a strong emotional attachment or dependence ⟨*clings* to her family⟩

cling·stone \'kliŋ-ˌstōn\ *n* : a fruit (as a peach) whose flesh adheres strongly to the pit

clin·ic \'klin-ik\ *n* [Gk *klinikē* medical practice at the sickbed, fr. *klinē* bed, fr. *klinein* to lean; akin to E ¹*lean*] **1 a** : a class of medical instruction in which patients are examined and discussed **b** : a facility (as of a hospital) in which persons not bedridden are diagnosed or treated **2** : a class meeting devoted to the analysis and treatment of cases in some special field ⟨a writing *clinic* for poor students⟩

-clin·ic \'klin-ik\ *adj comb form* [Gk *klinein* to lean] **1** : inclining : dipping ⟨isoclinic⟩ **2** : having (so many) oblique intersections of the axes ⟨monoclinic⟩ ⟨triclinic⟩

clin·i·cal \'klin-i-kəl\ *adj* **1 a** : of, relating to, or conducted in or as if in a clinic ⟨*clinical* examination⟩ **b** : involving or based on direct observation of the patient ⟨*clinical* studies⟩ **2** : being analytical, detached, or coolly dispassionate ⟨a *clinical* analysis of the program⟩ — **clin·i·cal·ly** \'klin-i-k(ə-)lē\ *adv*

clinical thermometer *n* : a self-registering thermometer for measuring body temperature

cli·ni·cian \klin-'ish-ən\ *n* : one qualified in clinical practice (as of medicine) as distinguished from a specialist in laboratory or research techniques

¹clink \'kliŋk\ *vb* : to make or cause to make a slight sharp short metallic sound ⟨glasses *clinked*⟩

²clink *n* : a clinking sound

clin·ker \'kliŋ-kər\ *n* : a mass of stony matter fused together by fire (as in a furnace from impurities in the coal) : SLAG

clin·ker-built \-ˌbilt\ *adj* : having the external planks or plates overlapping like clapboards on a house ⟨a *clinker-built* boat⟩

cli·nom·e·ter \klī-'näm-ət-ər\ *n* : an instrument for measuring angles of elevation or inclination

Clio \'klī-ō\ *n* : the Greek Muse of history

¹clip \'klip\ *vb* **clipped**; **clip·ping** [OE *clyppan*] **1** : to clasp or fasten with a clip ⟨*clip* the papers together⟩ **2** : to block (an opposing player in football other than the ballcarrier) by hitting with the body from behind

²clip *n* **1** : a device that grips, clasps, or hooks **2** : a device to hold cartridges for charging the magazine of a rifle **3** : a piece of jewelry held in position by a spring clip

³clip *vb* **clipped**; **clip·ping** [ON *klippa*] **1 a** : to cut or cut off with shears ⟨*clip* a dog's hair⟩ ⟨*clipping* out news items⟩ **b** : to cut off the distal or outer part of **2 a** : CURTAIL, DIMINISH ⟨*clipped* his influence⟩ **b** : to abbreviate in speech or writing **3** : HIT, PUNCH ⟨*clipped* him on the chin⟩

⁴clip *n* **1** : a 2-bladed instrument for cutting esp. the nails **2** : something that is clipped: as **a** : the sheared fleece of a sheep; *also* : a crop of wool **b** : a section of filmed material **3** : an act of clipping **4** : a sharp blow **5** : a rapid pace ⟨move along at a good clip⟩

clip·board \'klip-ˌbōrd, -ˌbȯrd\ *n* : a small writing board with a spring clip at the top for holding papers

clip·per \'klip-ər\ *n* **1** : one that clips **2** *pl* : an implement for clipping esp. hair, fingernails, or toenails **3** : a fast sailing vessel with an overhanging bow, tall masts, and a large sail area

clip·ping \'klip-iŋ\ *n* **1** : a cutting or shearing of something **2** : a piece clipped or cut out or off of something ⟨a newspaper *clipping*⟩ ⟨hedge *clippings*⟩

clip-sheet \'klip-ˌshēt\ *n* : a sheet of newspaper material issued by an organization and usu. printed on only one side to facilitate clipping and reprinting

clique \'klēk, 'klik\ *n* [F] : a small exclusive group or set of people : COTERIE — **cliqu·ey** *or* **cliquy** \-ē\ *adj* — **cliqu·ish** \-ish\ *adj* — **cliqu·ish·ness** *n*

cli·tel·lum \klə-'tel-əm, klī-\ *n* [L *clitellae* packsaddle] : a thickened glandular band about the body of an earthworm that secretes a sticky sac in which the eggs are deposited — **cli·tel·lar** \-'tel-ər\ *adj*

clit·o·ris \'klit-ə-rəs, 'klīt-\ *n* [Gk *kleitoris*] : a small structure in the female mammal homologous to the male penis — **clit·o·ral** \-rəl\ *adj*

clo·a·ca \klō-'ā-kə\ *n, pl* **clo·a·cae** \-ˌkē, -ˌsē\ [L] **1** : ²SEWER **2** : a chamber into which the intestinal, urinary, and reproductive canals discharge in birds, reptiles, amphibians, and many fishes; *also* : a comparable chamber of an invertebrate — **clo·a·cal** \-ˈā-kəl\ *adj*

¹cloak \ˈklōk\ *n* [ME *cloke*, fr. ONF *cloque*, lit., bell, fr. ML *clocca*] **1** : a loose outer garment usu. longer than a cape **2** : something that conceals or covers ⟨under the *cloak* of darkness⟩ **syn** see DISGUISE

²cloak *vt* : to cover or hide with a cloak

cloak-and-dag·ger \ˌklōk-ən-ˈdag-ər\ *adj* : of or relating to intrigue and espionage

clob·ber \ˈkläb-ər\ *vt* **1** *slang* : to pound mercilessly **2** *slang* : to defeat overwhelmingly

cloche \ˈklōsh\ *n* [F, lit., bell, fr. ML *clocca*] : a woman's small helmetlike hat

¹clock \ˈkläk\ *n* [MD *clocke* bell, clock, fr. ML *clocca* bell] **1** : a device for measuring or telling the time; *esp* : one not intended to be worn or carried about by a person **2** : a registering device (as a dial) attached to something (as a machine) to measure or record its performance **3** : TIME CLOCK

²clock *vt* **1** : to time with a stopwatch or by an electric device **2** : to register on a mechanical recording device

³clock *n* : an ornamental figure on a stocking or sock

clock·wise \-ˌwīz\ *adv* : in the direction in which the hands of a clock rotate — **clockwise** *adj*

clock·work \-ˌwərk\ *n* : machinery (as in a mechanical toy or a bomb-actuating device) containing a train of wheels of small size

clod \ˈkläd\ *n* [ME, alter. of *clot*] **1** : a lump or mass esp. of earth or clay **2** : a dull or insensitive person : OAF — **clod·dish** \-ish\ *adj* — **clod·dish·ness** *n* — **clod·dy** \ˈkläd-ē\ *adj*

clod·hop·per \ˈkläd-ˌhäp-ər\ *n* **1** : a clumsy and uncouth rustic **2** : a large heavy shoe

¹clog \ˈkläg\ *n* [ME *clogge* log] **1 a** : a weight attached to a man or an animal to hinder motion **b** : something that hinders or restrains **2** : a shoe having a thick typically wooden sole

²clog *vb* **clogged**; **clog·ging 1** : to impede with a clog : HINDER **2** : to obstruct passage through : fill beyond capacity : OVERLOAD ⟨heavy traffic *clogged* the roads⟩ **3** : to become filled with extraneous matter ⟨the gutters *clogged* quickly⟩ **4** : CLOT **5** : to dance a clog dance

clog dance *n* : a dance in which the performer wears clogs and beats out a clattering rhythm upon the floor — **clog dancer** *n* — **clog dancing** *n*

cloi·son·né \ˌkloiz-ᵊn-ˈā\ *n* [F] : a colored decoration made of enamels poured into the divided areas in a design outlined with bent wire or metal strips

¹clois·ter \ˈkloi-stər\ *n* [OF *cloistre*, fr. ML *claustrum*, fr. L, bar, bolt, fr. *claudere* to close] **1 a** : a monastic establishment **b** : monastic life **2** : a covered passage on the side of or around a court usu. having one side walled and the other an open arcade or colonnade — **clois·tral** \-strəl\ *adj*

cloister 2

²cloister *vt* **1** : to shut away from the world in or as if in a cloister **2** : to surround with a cloister ⟨*cloistered* gardens⟩

clone \ˈklōn\ *n* : the whole asexual progeny of an individual (as a plant increased by grafting) — **clon·al** \ˈklōn-ᵊl\ *adj* — **clon·al·ly** \-ᵊl-ē\ *adv*

clop \ˈkläp\ *n* : a sound made by or as if by a hoof or wooden shoe against pavement

¹close \ˈklōz\ *vb* [OF *clos-*, *clore*, fr. L *claudere*] **1 a** : to move so as to bar passage through something ⟨*close* the gate⟩ **b** : to block against entry or passage ⟨*close* a street⟩ **2** : to suspend or stop the operations of ⟨*close* school⟩ **3** : to bring or come to an end or period : TERMINATE **4 a** : to bring or bind together the parts or edges of ⟨a *closed* fist⟩ **b** : to fill or stop up **5** : to fold, swing, or slide so as to leave no opening **6 a** : to draw near **b** : to engage in a struggle at close quarters : GRAPPLE ⟨*close* with the enemy⟩ **7** : to enter into or complete an agreement ⟨*close* a bargain⟩ — **clos·a·ble** *or* **close·a·ble** \ˈklō-zə-bəl\ *adj* — **clos·er** *n*

syn CONCLUDE, TERMINATE, END: CLOSE implies shutting off from outside forces that could cause further develop-

ment or change ⟨*close* an account⟩ CONCLUDE adds a suggestion of formality; TERMINATE implies setting a limit with or without completing; END stresses finality and usu. implies an achievement of progress or concluding of a sequence ⟨an armistice *ended* hostilities⟩ ⟨the years *ending* the colonial period⟩

²close \ˈklōz\ *n* **1 a** : a coming or bringing to a conclusion **b** : CESSATION **2** : the concluding passage (as of a speech or play)

³close \ˈklōs\ *n* **1** : an enclosed area **2** *Brit* : the precinct of a cathedral

⁴close \ˈklōs\ *adj* **1** : having no openings : CLOSED **2** : confined or confining strictly **3** : restricted to a privileged class **4 a** : SECLUDED, SECRET **b** : SECRETIVE **5** : STRICT, RIGOROUS ⟨keep close watch⟩ **6** : SULTRY, STUFFY **7** : STINGY, TIGHTFISTED **8** : having little space between items or units **9 a** : fitting tightly or exactly **b** : very short or near to the surface ⟨*close* haircut⟩ **c** : matching or blending without gap **10** : being near in time, space, effect, or degree **11** : INTIMATE, FAMILIAR ⟨*close* friend⟩ **12 a** : ACCURATE, PRECISE **b** : marked by fidelity to an original **13** : decided by a narrow margin **syn** see NEAR — **close·ly** *adv* — **close·ness** *n*

⁵close \ˈklōs\ *adv* : in a close position or manner : NEAR

closed \ˈklōzd\ *adj* **1** : not open : ENCLOSED **2 a** : forming a self-contained unit ⟨*closed* association⟩ **b** : traced by a moving point that returns to an arbitrary starting point ⟨*closed* curve⟩ **c** : having elements that when subjected to an operation produce only elements of the same set **3** : confined to a few ⟨*closed* membership⟩ **4** : ending in a consonant ⟨*closed* syllable⟩

closed circuit *n* : a television installation in which the signal is transmitted by wire to a limited number of receivers

closed shop *n* : an establishment in which the employer by agreement hires only union members in good standing

close-fist·ed \ˈklōs-ˈfis-təd\ *adj* : STINGY, TIGHTFISTED

close-grained \-ˈgrānd\ *adj* **1** : having a compact smooth structure **2** : careful and precise esp. in order and articulation

close-hauled \-ˈhold\ *adj* : having the sails set for sailing as nearly against the wind as the ship will go

close-mouthed \-ˈmau̇thd, -ˈmau̇tht\ *adj* : cautious in speaking : UNCOMMUNICATIVE

close quarters *n pl* : immediate contact or close range ⟨fought at *close quarters*⟩

¹clos·et \ˈkläz-ət\ *n* [MF, dim. of *clos* enclosure, fr. *clos-*, *clore* to close] **1** : an apartment or small room for privacy **2** : a cabinet or recess for china, household utensils, or clothing **3** : WATER CLOSET

²closet *vt* **1** : to shut up in or as if in a closet **2** : to take into a private room for an interview ⟨*closeted* for an hour with the governor⟩

closet drama *n* : drama suited primarily for reading

close-up \ˈklōs-ˌəp\ *n* **1** : a photograph or movie shot taken at close range **2** : an intimate view or examination of something

clos·ing \ˈklō-ziŋ\ *n* **1** : a concluding part (as of a speech) **2** : a closable gap (as in an article of wear)

clos·trid·i·um \kläs-ˈtrid-ē-əm\ *n, pl* **-ia** \-ē-ə\ : any of various spore-forming mostly anaerobic soil or intestinal bacteria including some that produce virulent toxins — compare BOTULISM, TETANUS — **clos·trid·i·al** \-ē-əl\ *adj*

clo·sure \ˈklō-zhər\ *n* **1** : an act of closing : the condition of being closed **2** : something that closes **3** : CLOTURE

¹clot \ˈklät\ *n* [ME, fr. OE *clott*] : a mass or lump made by a portion of a liquid substance thickening and sticking together ⟨a *clot* of blood⟩

²clot *vb* **clot·ted**; **clot·ting 1** : to become or cause to become a clot : form clots **2** : to undergo a sequence of chemical and physical changes that convert fluid blood into a coagulated mass

cloth \ˈklȯth\ *n, pl* **cloths** \ˈklȯthz, ˈklȯths\ [OE *clāth*] **1** : a pliable fabric made usu. by weaving, felting, or knitting natural or synthetic fibers and filaments **2** : a piece of cloth adapted for a particular purpose; *esp* : TABLECLOTH **3** : distinctive dress of a profession or calling and esp. of the clergy; *also* : CLERGY

clothe \ˈklōth\ *vt* **clothed** *or* **clad** \ˈklad\; **cloth·ing 1 a** : to cover with or as if with cloth or clothing : DRESS **b** : to provide with clothes **2** : to express or enhance by suitably significant language : COUCH ⟨learned to *clothe* his thought effectively⟩

clothes \'klō(th)z\ *n pl* **1** : CLOTHING **2** : BEDCLOTHES

clothes-horse \-,hòrs\ *n* **1** : a frame on which to hang clothes **2** : a conspicuously dressy person

clothes moth *n* : any of several small yellowish moths whose larvae eat wool, fur, or feathers

clothes-pin \-,pin\ *n* : a forked piece of wood or plastic or a small spring clamp used for fastening clothes on a line

clothes-press \-,pres\ *n* : a receptacle for clothes

clothes tree *n* : an upright post-shaped stand with hooks or pegs around the top on which to hang clothes

cloth-ier \'klōth-yər, 'klō-thē-ər\ *n* : one who makes or sells cloth or clothing

cloth-ing \'klō-thiŋ\ *n* : garments in general; *also* : COVERING

Clo-tho \'klō-thō\ *n* : the one of the three Fates in classical mythology who spins the thread of life

clo-ture \'klō-chər\ *n* : the closing or limitation (as by calling for a vote) of debate in a legislative body — **cloture** *vt*

¹cloud \'klaùd\ *n* [OE *clūd* rock, hill] **1** : a visible mass of particles of water or ice in the form of fog, mist, or haze suspended usu. at a considerable height in the air **2** : a visible mass of minute particles in the air or a mass of obscuring matter in interstellar space **3** : a great crowd or multitude massed together : SWARM ⟨a *cloud* of mosquitoes⟩ **4** : something that has a dark, lowering, or threatening aspect **5** : something that obscures or blemishes **6** : a dark vein or spot (as in marble)

²cloud *vb* **1** : to grow cloudy **2** : to make or become gloomy or ominous **3** : to darken, envelop, or hide with a cloud or as if by a cloud **4** : to make unclear : OBSCURE **5** : TAINT, SULLY

cloud-burst \-,bərst\ *n* : a sudden heavy rainfall

cloud chamber *n* : a vessel containing saturated water vapor whose sudden expansion reveals the passage of an ionizing particle (as an electron) by a trail of visible drop-lets

cloud-less \'klaùd-ləs\ *adj* : free from any cloud : CLEAR — **cloud-less-ly** *adv* — **cloud-less-ness** *n*

cloud-let \-lət\ *n* : a small cloud

cloudy \'klaùd-ē\ *adj* **cloud-i-er; -est** **1** : of, relating to, or resembling cloud **2** : darkened by gloom or anxiety **3 a** : overcast with clouds; *esp* : six tenths to nine tenths covered with clouds **b** : having a cloudy sky **4** : obscure in meaning **5** : dimmed or dulled as if by clouds : not clear : MURKY **6** : marked with veins or spots — **cloud-i-ly** \'klaùd-ᵊl-ē\ *adv* — **cloud-i-ness** \'klaùd-ē-nəs\ *n*

¹clout \'klaùt\ *n* [OE *clūt*] **1** *dial chiefly Brit* : CLOTH, RAG **2** : a blow esp. with the hand; *also* : a hard hit **3** : a white cloth on a stake or frame used as a target in archery

²clout *vt* : to hit forcefully

¹clove \'klōv\ *n* [OE *clufu*] : one of the small bulbs developed in the axils of the scales of a large bulb

²clove *past of* CLEAVE

³clove *n* [ME *clowe*, fr. OF *clou*, lit., nail, fr. L *clavus*] : the dried flower bud of a tropical tree of the myrtle family used as a spice and as the source of an oil used in perfumery and medicine; *also* : this tree

clo-ven \'klō-vən\ *past part of* CLEAVE

cloven foot *n* : a foot (as of a sheep) divided into two parts at its outer extremity — called also *cloven hoof* **2** [fr. the traditional representation of Satan as cloven-footed] : the sign of devilish character — **clo-ven-foot-ed** \,klō-vən-'füt-əd\ *adj*

clo-ver \'klō-vər\ *n* [OE *clāfre*] : any of a genus of leguminous herbs having leaves with three leaflets and flowers in dense heads and including many valuable forage and bee plants; *also* : any of various related plants

clo-ver-leaf \-,lēf\ *n* : a road plan that in shape resembles a four-leaf clover and that is used for passing one highway over another and routing traffic for turns by way of connecting turnoffs that branch only to the right and lead around to enter the other highway from the right and thus merge traffic without left-hand turns or direct crossings

¹clown \'klaùn\ *n* **1** : a rude ill-bred person : BOOR **2 a** : a fool, jester, or comedian in an entertainment (as a play); *esp* : a grotesquely dressed comedy performer in a circus **b** : JOKER

²clown *vi* : to act as or like a clown

clown-ish \'klaù-nish\ *adj* : of or resembling a clown : RUDE — **clown-ish-ly** *adv* — **clown-ish-ness** *n*

cloy \'klòi\ *vb* [ME *acloien* to block, clog, fr. MF *encloer* to drive in a nail, fr. ML *inclavare*, fr. L *in-* + *clavus* nail] **1** : to disgust or nauseate with an excess usu. of something orig. pleasing : SURFEIT **2** : to cause surfeit — **cloy-ing-ly** \-iŋ-lē\ *adv*

¹club \'kləb\ *n* [ON *klubba*] **1 a** : a heavy usu. tapering staff esp. of wood wielded as a weapon **b** : a stick or bat used for hitting a ball in a game **c** : a black figure resembling a clover leaf used to distinguish a suit of playing cards; *also* : a card of the suit bearing clubs **2 a** : an association of persons for some common object **b** : the meeting place of a club

²club *vb* **clubbed; club-bing** **1 a** : to beat or strike with or as if with a club **b** : to gather or form into a club-shaped mass **c** : to hold like a club **2** : to unite or combine for a common cause — often used *with together*

club-foot \'kləb-,füt\ *n* : a misshapen foot twisted out of position from birth; *also* : this deformity — **club-foot-ed** \-əd\ *adj*

club fungus *n* : BASIDIOMYCETE

club-house \-,haùs\ *n* **1** : a house occupied by a club or used for club activities **2** : locker rooms used by an athletic team

club moss *n* : any of an order (Lycopodiales) of low often trailing evergreen vascular plants (as the ground pine) having branching stems covered with small mosslike leaves and reproducing by spores usu. borne in club-shaped cones

club steak *n* : a small steak cut from the end of the short loin

¹cluck \'klək\ *vb* : to make or call with a cluck

²cluck *n* **1** : the characteristic sound made by a hen esp. in calling her chicks; *also* : a sound like a hen's cluck **2** : a broody fowl

clue *var of* CLEW

clum-ber spaniel \,kləm-bər-\ *n, often cap C & S* : a large massive heavyset spaniel with a dense silky largely white coat

¹clump \'kləmp\ *n* **1** : a group of things clustered together **2** : a compact mass : LUMP **3** : a heavy tramping sound — **clumpy** \'kləm-pē\ *adj*

²clump *vb* **1** : to tread clumsily and noisily **2** : to form or cause to form clumps

clum-sy \'kləm-zē\ *adj* **clum-si-er; -est** [prob. fr. obs. E *clumse* benumbed with cold] **1 a** : lacking dexterity, nimbleness, or grace ⟨*clumsy* fingers⟩ **b** : lacking tact or subtlety ⟨a *clumsy* joke⟩ **2** : awkwardly or poorly made : UNWIELDY **syn** see AWKWARD — **clum-si-ly** \-zə-lē\ *adv* — **clum-si-ness** \-zē-nəs\ *n*

clung *past of* CLING

¹clus-ter \'kləs-tər\ *n* [OE] **1** : a number of similar things growing, collected, or grouped closely together : BUNCH **2** : two or more consecutive consonants or vowels in a segment of speech

²cluster *vb* **clus-tered; clus-ter-ing** \-t(ə-)riŋ\ : to grow, collect, or assemble in a cluster

¹clutch \'kləch\ *vb* [OE *clyccan*] **1** : to grasp or hold with or as if with the hand or claws usu. strongly, tightly, or suddenly **2** : to seek to grasp and hold ⟨*clutch* at a swinging rope⟩

²clutch *n* **1 a** : the claws or a hand in the act of grasping or seizing firmly **b** : CONTROL, POWER **2** : a device for gripping an object **3 a** : a coupling used to connect and disconnect a driving and a driven part of a mechanism **b** : a lever operating a clutch **4** : a tight or critical situation : PINCH

³clutch *n* : a nest or batch of eggs or a brood of chicks

¹clut-ter \'klət-ər\ *vt* [ME *clotteren* to clot, clutter, fr. *clot*] : to fill or cover with scattered things that impede movement or reduce effectiveness ⟨*clutter* up a room⟩ ⟨*cluttered* up his mind with trifles⟩

²clutter *n* : a crowded or confused mass or collection : LITTER, DISORDER

clyp-e-us \'klip-ē-əs\ *n, pl* **-ei** \-ē-,ī, -ē-,ē\ : a plate on the anterior median aspect of an insect's head — **clyp-e-ate** \-ē-ət\ *adj*

clys-ter \'klis-tər\ *n* : ENEMA

Cly-tem-nes-tra \,klīt-əm-'nes-trə\ *n* : the wife of Agamemnon

---

c–mitosis *n* : an artificially induced abortive nuclear division in which the chromosome number is doubled — **c–mitotic** *adj*

co- *prefix* [L, fr. *com-*] **1** : with : together : joint : jointly ⟨co*exist*⟩⟨co*heir*⟩ **2** : in or to the same degree ⟨co*extensive*⟩ **3** : fellow : partner ⟨co*author*⟩⟨co*-worker*⟩

co·ac·er·vate \kō-'as-ər-,vāt\ *n* : an aggregate of colloidal droplets held together by electrostatic forces — **co·ac·er·va·tion** \(,)kō-,as-ər-'vā-shən\ *n*

¹coach \'kōch\ *n* [MF *coche*, fr. G *kutsche*] **1 a** : a large usu. closed four-wheeled carriage having doors in the sides and an elevated seat in front for the driver **b** : a railroad passenger car intended primarily for day travel **c** : BUS 1a **d** : an automobile body esp. of a closed model; *also* : a closed 2-door automobile for 4 or 5 passengers **e** : a class of passenger air transportation at a lower fare than first class **2** [fr. the concept that the tutor conveys the student through his examinations] **a** : a private tutor **b** : one who instructs or trains a performer or a team of performers; *esp* : one who instructs players in the fundamentals of a competitive sport and directs team strategy

²coach *vb* **1** : to instruct, direct, or prompt as a coach **2** : to go in a horse-drawn coach — **coach·er** *n*

coach dog *n* : DALMATIAN

coach·man \'kōch-mən\ *n* : a man whose business is driving a coach or carriage

co·ac·tion \kō-'ak-shən\ *n* : joint action

co·ad·ju·tor \,kō-ə-'jüt-ər, kō-'aj-ət-ər\ *n* **1** : one who works together with another : ASSISTANT **2** : a bishop assisting a diocesan bishop and having the right of succession — **coadjutor** *adj*

co·ag·u·la·ble \kō-'ag-yə-lə-bəl\ *adj* : capable of being coagulated — **co·ag·u·la·bil·i·ty** \-,ag-yə-lə-'bil-ət-ē\ *n*

co·ag·u·lant \-'ag-yə-lənt\ *n* : something that produces coagulation

co·ag·u·lase \-,lās\ *n* : an enzyme that promotes coagulation

co·ag·u·late \-,lāt\ *vb* [L *coagulare*, fr. *coagulum* curdling agent, fr. *co-* + *agere* to drive] : to become or cause to become viscous or thickened into a coherent mass : CLOT — **co·ag·u·la·tion** \(,)kō-,ag-yə-'lā-shən\ *n*

¹coal \'kōl\ *n* [OE *col*] **1** : a piece of glowing or charred wood : EMBER **2** : a black solid mineral that is formed by the partial decay of vegetable matter under the influence of moisture and often increased pressure and temperature within the earth and that is mined for use as a fuel

²coal *vb* **1** : to supply with coal **2** : to take in coal

coal·er \'kō-lər\ *n* : something employed in transporting or supplying coal

co·a·lesce \,kō-ə-'les\ *vi* [L *coalescere*, fr. *co-* + *alescere* to grow] **1** : to grow together **2** : to unite into a whole : FUSE **syn** see MIX — **co·a·les·cence** \-'les-ᵊn(t)s\ *n* — **co·a·les·cent** \-ᵊnt\ *adj*

coal·field \'kōl-,fēld\ *n* : a region where deposits of coal occur

coal gas *n* : gas from coal; *esp* : gas made by distilling bituminous coal and used for heating

co·a·li·tion \,kō-ə-'lish-ən\ *n* **1** : UNION, COMBINATION; *esp* : a temporary union of persons, parties, or countries for a common purpose — **co·a·li·tion·ist** \-'lish-(ə-)nəst\ *n*

coal measures *n pl* : beds of coal with the associated rocks

coal oil *n* **1** : a refined oil prepared from petroleum : PETROLEUM **2** : KEROSENE

coal tar *n* : tar obtained by distilling bituminous coal and used in making drugs, dyes, and explosives

co·arc·tate \kō-'ärk-,tāt\ *adj* : CONSTRICTED; *esp* : enclosed in a rigid case — **co·arc·ta·tion** \(,)kō-,ärk-'tā-shən\ *n*

coarse \'kōrs, 'kȯrs\ *adj* [ME *cors*, fr. *course*, *cors* course] **1** : of ordinary or inferior quality or appearance : COMMON **2 a** : composed of relatively large parts or particles ⟨*coarse* sand⟩ **b** : loose or rough in texture ⟨*coarse* skin⟩ **c** : designed for heavy, fast, or less delicate work **d** : not precise or detailed with respect to adjustment or discrimination **3** : crude in taste, manners, or language **4** : harsh or rough in tone — **coarse·ly** *adv* — **coarse·ness** *n*

  syn RIBALD, OBSCENE: COARSE implies roughness, rudeness, or crudeness of spirit, behavior, or language; RIBALD applies to what is amusingly or picturesquely vulgar or irreverent or mildly indecent; OBSCENE may apply to whatever strongly offends the sense of decency or propriety but esp. implies flagrant violation of taboo in sexual matters

coarse–grained \-'grānd\ *adj* **1** : having a coarse grain **2** : not refined : CRUDE

coars·en \'kōrs-ᵊn, 'kȯrs-\ *vb* **coars·ened**; **coars·en·ing** \'kōrs-niŋ, 'kȯrs-, -ᵊn-iŋ\ : to make or become coarse ⟨hands *coarsened* by hard labor⟩

¹coast \'kōst\ *n* [MF *coste*, fr. L *costa* rib, side] **1** : the land near a shore : SEASHORE **2** : a slope suited to sliding (as on a sled) downhill; *also* : a slide down such a slope

²coast *vb* **1 a** : to sail along the shore of **b** : to sail along the coast **2 a** : to slide, run, or glide (as over snow on a sled) downhill by the force of gravity **b** : to move along (as on a bicycle when not pedaling) without application of power

coast·al \'kōst-ᵊl\ *adj* : relating to a coast : located on, near, or along a coast ⟨*coastal* trade⟩

coastal plain *n* : a plain extending inland from a seashore

coast·er \'kō-stər\ *n* **1** : one that coasts; *esp* : a ship engaged in coastal trade between ports of the same country **2 a** : a round tray usu. of silver and often on wheels that is used for circulating a decanter after a meal **b** : a shallow container or a plate or mat to protect a surface **c** : a small vehicle (as a sled or wagon) used in coasting

coaster brake *n* : a brake in the hub of the rear wheel of a bicycle operated by reverse pressure on the pedals

coast guard *n* **1** : a military force employed in guarding or patrolling a coast **2** : a member of a coast guard — **coast·guards·man** \'kōs(t)-,gärdz-mən\ *or* **coast·guard·man** \-,gärd-mən\ *n*

coast·line \'kōst-,līn\ *n* : the outline or shape of a coast

coast·ward \'kōs-twərd\ *or* **coast·wards** \-twərdz\ *adv* : toward the coast — **coastward** *adj*

coast·wise \'kōst-,wīz\ *adv* : by way of or along the coast — **coastwise** *adj*

¹coat \'kōt\ *n* [OF *cote*, of Gmc origin] **1 a** : an outer garment varying in length and style according to fashion and use **b** : something resembling a coat **2** : the external growth (as of fur) on an animal **3** : a layer of one substance covering another ⟨a *coat* of paint⟩ — **coat·ed** \-əd\ *adj*

²coat *vt* : to cover with a coat and esp. a finishing or protecting one

co·a·ti \kə-'wät-ē, ,kō-ə-'tē\ *n* [Pg *coatí*, fr. Tupi] : a tropical American mammal related to the raccoon but with a longer body and tail and a long flexible snout

coat·ing \'kōt-iŋ\ *n* **1** : COAT, COVERING ⟨a thin *coating* of ice on the surface of a pond⟩ **2** : cloth for coats

coat of arms : the particular heraldic bearings (as of a person) usu. depicted on an escutcheon; *also* : a similar symbolic emblem

coat of mail : a garment of metal scales or rings worn as armor

co·au·thor \(')kō-'ȯ-thər\ *n* : a joint or associate author

coax \'kōks\ *vb* [obs. *cokes* simpleton] **1** : to influence by gentle urging, caressing, or flattering : WHEEDLE **2** : to draw or gain by means of gentle urging or flattery ⟨*coaxed* a dollar from her father⟩ — **coax·er** *n*

co·ax·i·al \(')kō-'ak-sē-əl\ *adj* **1** : having coincident axes **2** : mounted on concentric shafts — **co·ax·i·al·ly** \-sē-ə-lē\ *adv*

coaxial cable *n* : a cable that consists of a tube of electrically conducting material surrounding a central conductor and is used to transmit telegraph, telephone, and television signals

cob \'käb\ *n* [ME *cobbe* leader] **1** : a male swan **2** : CORNCOB 1 **3** : a short-legged stocky horse usu. with an artificially high stylish action

co·balt \'kō-,bȯlt\ *n* [G *kobalt*, alter. of *kobold* goblin, kobold] : a tough shiny silver-white magnetic metallic element that occurs with iron and nickel — see ELEMENT table — **co·bal·tic** \kō-'bȯl-tik\ *adj* — **co·bal·tous** \-təs\ *adj*

co·balt·ite \'kō-,bȯl-,tīt\ *or* **co·balt·ine** \-,tēn\ *n* : a grayish to silver-white mineral CoAsS that consists of cobalt, arsenic, and sulfur and is an important ore of cobalt

cobalt 60 *n* : a heavy radioactive isotope of cobalt of the mass number 60 produced in nuclear reactors and used as a source of gamma rays

¹**cob·ble** \'käb-əl\ *vt* **cob·bled; cob·bling** \-(ə-)liŋ\ [ME *coblen*] **:** to make or put together roughly or hastily ⟨a shed *cobbled* up out of scraps⟩

²**cobble** *n* [back-formation fr. *cobblestone*] **:** a naturally rounded stone larger than a pebble and smaller than a boulder; *esp* **:** such a stone used in paving a street

³**cobble** *vt* **:** to pave with cobblestones

cob·bler \'käb-lər\ *n* [ME *cobelere*] **1 :** a mender or maker of shoes **2** *archaic* **:** a clumsy workman **3 :** a deep-dish fruit pie with a thick top crust

cob·ble·stone \'käb-əl-,stōn\ *n* [ME] **:** COBBLE

co·bra \'kō-brə\ *n* [Portuguese *cobra de capello*, lit., serpent with a hood] **:** any of several venomous Asiatic and African snakes that when excited expand the skin of the neck into a hood; *also* **:** any of several related African snakes

cob·web \'käb-,web\ *n* [ME *coppeweb*, fr. *coppe* spider (fr. OE *-coppe*) + *web*] **1 :** the network spread by a spider; *also* **:** a single thread spun by a spider or insect larva **2 :** something resembling a spider web — **cob·webbed** \-,webd\ *adj* — **cob·web·by** \-,web-ē\ *adj*

co·ca \'kō-kə\ *n* [Sp, fr. Quechua *kúka*] **:** a So. American shrub with leaves resembling tea that are chewed by the natives to impart endurance and are the source of cocaine; *also* **:** its dried leaves

co·caine \kō-'kān\ *n* **:** a bitter addictive drug obtained from coca leaves and used as a narcotic and local anesthetic

coc·cid \'käk-səd\ *n* **:** SCALE INSECT, MEALYBUG

coc·coid \'käk-,öid\ *adj* **:** related to or resembling a coccus **:** GLOBOSE

coc·cus \'käk-əs\ *n, pl* **coc·ci** \'käk-,(s)ī, 'käk-(,)(s)ē\ [Gk *kokkos* grain] **:** a spherical bacterium — **coc·cal** \'käk-əl\ *adj*

coc·cyx \'käk-siks\ *n, pl* **coc·cy·ges** \'käk-sə-,jēz\ *also* **coc·cyx·es** [Gk *kokkyg-, kokkyx*, lit., cuckoo; fr. its resemblance to a cuckoo's beak] **:** the end of the vertebral column beyond the sacrum in man and tailless apes consisting of four reduced fused vertebrae — **coc·cyg·eal** \käk-'sij-(ē-)əl\ *adj*

coch·i·neal \'käch-ə-,nēl, 'kō-chə-\ *n* **:** a red dyestuff consisting of the dried bodies of female cochineal insects used *esp.* as a biological stain

cochineal insect *n* **:** a small bright red insect that is related to and resembles the mealybug, feeds on cactus, and yields cochineal

coch·lea \'käk-lē-ə\ *n, pl* **-le·ae** \-lē-,ē, -lē-,ī\ *or* **-le·as** [L, snail, fr. Gk *kochlias*, fr. *kochlos* land snail] **:** a part of the inner ear of higher vertebrates that is usu. coiled like a snail shell and is the seat of the hearing organ — **coch·le·ar** \-lē-ər\ *adj*

¹**cock** \'käk\ *n* [OE *cocc*] **1 :** the adult male of a bird and esp. the domestic fowl **2 :** a device (as a faucet or valve) for regulating the flow of a liquid **3 a :** a domineering person **:** LEADER **b :** SWAGGERER **4 :** the cocked position of the hammer of a firearm

²**cock** *vt* **1 a :** to draw the hammer of (a firearm) back and set for firing **b :** to draw or bend back in preparation to throw or hit **2 a :** to set erect **b :** to turn, tip, or tilt usu. to one side **3 :** to turn up (as a hat brim)

³**cock** *n* **:** TILT, SLANT

⁴**cock** *n* [ME *cok*, of Scand origin] **:** a small pile (as of hay)

⁵**cock** *vt* **:** to put (as hay) into cocks

cock·ade \kä-'kād\ *n* **:** a rosette or a similar ornament worn on the hat as a badge

Cock·aigne \kä-'kān\ *n* **:** an imaginary land of extreme luxury and ease

cock-and-bull story \,käk-ən-'bùl-\ *n* **:** an extravagant incredible story told as true

cock·a·tiel \,käk-ə-'tēl\ *n* **:** a small crested gray Australian parrot with a yellow head

cock·a·too \'käk-ə-,tü\ *n, pl* **-toos** [Malay *kakatua*, fr. *kakak* elder sibling + *tua* old] **:** any of numerous large noisy usu. showy and crested chiefly Australasian parrots

cock·a·trice \'käk-ə-trəs, -,trīs\ *n* **:** a legendary serpent with deadly glance hatched by a reptile from a cock's egg on a dunghill

cock·cha·fer \'käk-,chā-fər\ *n* **:** a large European beetle destructive to vegetation; *also* **:** any of various related beetles

cock·crow \'käk-,krō\ *n* **:** the time of day at which cocks first crow **:** early morning

cocked hat \'käkt-\ *n* **:** a hat with brim turned up to give a 3-cornered appearance

cock·er·el \'käk-(ə-)rəl\ *n* **:** a young male domestic fowl

cock·er spaniel \,käk-ər-\ *n* [fr. *cocking* woodcock hunting] **:** a small spaniel with long ears, square muzzle, and silky coat

cock·eye \'käk-'ī, -,ī\ *n* **:** a squinting eye

cock·eyed \'käk-'īd\ *adj* **1 :** having a cockeye **2** *slang* **a :** ASKEW, AWRY **b :** slightly crazy **c :** DRUNK

cock·fight \'käk-,fīt\ *n* **:** a contest of gamecocks usu. fitted with metal spurs — **cock·fight·ing** \-iŋ\ *adj or n*

cock·horse \'käk-,hórs\ *n* **:** ROCKING HORSE

¹**cock·le** \'käk-əl\ *n* [OE *coccel*] **:** any of several grainfield weeds; *esp* **:** CORN COCKLE

²**cockle** *n* [MF *coquille* shell, fr. Gk *konchylion*, fr. *konchē* conch] **1 :** an edible shellfish with a heart-shaped 2-valved shell **2 :** COCKLESHELL

cock·le·bur \'käk-əl-,bər, 'kak-\ *n* **:** any of a genus of prickly-fruited plants related to the thistles; *also* **:** one of its fruits

cock·le·shell \'käk-əl-,shel\ *n* **1 a :** a shell or shell valve of a cockle **b :** a shell (as a scallop) suggesting a cockleshell **2 :** a light flimsy boat

cock·les of the heart \,käk-əlz-\ **:** the core of one's being

cock·ney \'käk-nē\ *n, pl* **cockneys** *often cap* [ME *cokeney* spoiled child, lit., cock's egg] **1 :** a native of London and esp. of the East End of London **2 :** the dialect of London or of the East End of London — **cockney** *adj*

cock·pit \'käk-,pit\ *n* **1 :** a pit for cockfights **2 a :** an open space aft of a decked area from which a small boat is steered **b :** a space in the fuselage of an airplane for the pilot or the pilot and passengers or in large passenger planes the pilot and crew

cock·roach \'käk-,rōch\ *n* [Sp *cucaracha*] **:** any of an order (Blattaria) of mostly nocturnal insects some of which are domestic pests

cocks·comb \'käks-,kōm\ *n* **1 :** COXCOMB **2 :** a garden plant of the amaranth family grown for its showy flower clusters

cock·sure \'käk-'shù(ə)r\ *adj* **1 :** perfectly sure **:** CERTAIN **2 :** marked by overconfidence **:** COCKY

cocktail *n* **1 :** an iced drink of distilled liquor mixed with flavoring ingredients **2 :** an appetizer (as tomato juice) served as a first course at a meal

cocky \'käk-ē\ *adj* **cock·i·er; -est :** PERT, CONCEITED — **cock·i·ly** \'käk-ə-lē\ *adv* — **cock·i·ness** \'käk-ē-nəs\ *n*

¹**co·co** \'kō-kō\ *n, pl* **cocos** [Sp, fr. Pg *côco*, lit., bogeyman] **:** the coconut palm or its fruit

²**coco** *adj* **:** made from the fibrous husk of the coconut

co·coa \'kō-kō\ *n* [modif. of Sp *cacao*] **1 :** a cacao tree **2 a :** chocolate freed of some of its fat and ground **b :** a beverage prepared by cooking cocoa powder with water or milk

cocoa butter *n* **:** a pale fat with a low melting point obtained from cacao beans

co·co·nut *also* **co·coa·nut** \'kō-kə-(,)nət\ *n* **:** the fruit of the coconut palm with an outer fibrous husk yielding coir and a nut containing thick edible meat and coconut milk

coconut oil *n* **:** a nearly colorless oil or soft white fat extracted from coconuts or copra and used in soaps and foods

coconut palm *n* **:** a tall pinnate-leaved tropical palm prob. of American origin

co·coon \kə-'kün\ *n* [F *cocon*, fr. L *coccum* excrescence on a tree, fr. Gk *kokkos* kermes] **1 a :** a usu. largely silken envelope which an insect larva (as a caterpillar) forms about itself and in which it passes the pupa stage **b :** any of various other protective coverings produced by animals **2 :** a covering suggesting a cocoon

Co·cy·tus \kə-'sīt-əs\ *n* **:** a river tributary to the Acheron in Hades

cod \'käd\ *n, pl* **cod** *also* **cods** [ME] **:** a soft-finned fish of the colder parts of the No. Atlantic that is a major food fish; *also* **:** any of several related fishes

co·da \'kōd-ə\ *n* [It, lit., tail, fr. L *cauda*] **:** a closing section in a musical composition that is formally distinct from the main structure

cod·dle \'käd-əl\ *vt* **cod·dled; cod·dling** \'käd-liŋ, -ᵊl-iŋ\

cockroach

1 : to cook slowly in water below the boiling point ⟨coddle eggs⟩ **2** : to treat as a little child or a pet : PAMPER

¹code \'kōd\ *n* [MF, fr. L *codex* wax writing tablet, codex] **1** : a systematic statement of a body of law; *esp* : one having the force of statute ⟨criminal *code*⟩ **2** : a system of principles or rules ⟨moral *code*⟩ **3** : a system of signals for communicating **4** : a system of letters or symbols used (as in secret communications or in a computing machine) with special meanings

²code *vt* : to put in or into the form or symbols of a code — **cod·er** *n*

co·deine *or* **co·dein** \'kō-,dēn, 'kōd-ē-ən\ *n* [F *codéine*, fr. Gk *kōdeia* poppy capsule] : a drug that is obtained from opium, is feebler than morphine, and is used in cough remedies

co·dex \'kō-,deks\ *n, pl* **co·di·ces** \'kōd-ə-,sēz, 'käd-\ [L *codic-, codex*] : a manuscript book (as of the Scriptures)

cod·fish \'käd-,fish\ *n* : COD; *also* : its flesh used as food

cod·ger \'käj-ər\ *n* : an odd or cranky fellow

cod·i·cil \'käd-ə-səl, -,sil\ *n* [L *codicillus*, dim. of *codic-, codex* writing tablet] : a legal instrument modifying an earlier will

cod·i·fy \'käd-ə-,fī, 'kōd-\ *vt* **-fied; -fy·ing** : to arrange (as a collection of laws) in a systematic form — **cod·i·fi·ca·tion** \,käd-ə-fə-'kā-shən, ,kōd-\ *n*

¹cod·ling \'käd-liŋ\ *n* **1** : a young cod **2** : HAKE

²cod·ling \'käd-liŋ\ *or* **cod·lin** \-lən\ *n* : a small immature apple; *also* : any of several elongated greenish English cooking apples

codling moth *n* : a small stocky moth whose larva lives in apples, pears, quinces, and English walnuts

cod–liver oil *n* : an oil obtained from the liver of the cod and closely related fishes and used as a source of vitamins A and D

¹co–ed \'kō-,ed\ *n* : a female student in a coeducational institution

²co–ed *adj* **1** : COEDUCATIONAL **2** : of or relating to a co-ed

co·ed·u·ca·tion \,(,)kō-,ej-ə-'kā-shən\ *n* : the education of male and female students at the same school or college — **co·ed·u·ca·tion·al** \-'kā-shnəl, -shən-ᵊl\ *adj*

co·ef·fi·cient \,kō-ə-'fish-ənt\ *n* **1** : any of the factors of a product considered in relation to a specific factor **2** : a number that serves as a measure of some property or characteristic (as of a substance or device)

coe·la·canth \'sē-lə-,kan(t)th\ *n* : a fish or fossil of a family of mostly extinct fishes — compare LATIMERIA — **coelacanth** *adj*

-coele *or* **-coel** \,sēl\ *n comb form* [Gk *koilos*, adj., hollow] : cavity : chamber ⟨blastocoel⟩ ⟨enterocoele⟩

coe·len·ter·ate \si-'lent-ə-,rāt, -rət\ *n* [Gk *koilos* hollow + *enteron* intestine] : any of a phylum (Coelenterata) of invertebrate animals that include the corals, sea anemones, jellyfishes, and hydroids and have a radial body symmetry — **coelenterate** *adj*

coe·li·ac \'sē-lē-,ak\ *adj* : of or relating to the abdominal cavity

coe·lom \'sē-ləm\ *n, pl* **coe·loms** *or* **coe·lo·ma·ta** \si-'lō-mət-ə\ : the usu. epithelium-lined body cavity of animals above the lower worms — **coe·lo·mate** \'sē-lə-,māt\ *adj or n* — **coe·lo·mic** \si-'läm-ik, -'lō-mik\ *adj*

coen- *or* **coeno-** *comb form* [Gk *koinos*] : common : general ⟨coenocyte⟩

coe·no·bite \'sē-nə-,bīt\ *var of* CENOBITE

coe·no·cyt·ic \,sē-nə-'sit-ik\ *adj* : containing several or many nuclei ⟨a *coenocytic* cell⟩

coe·nu·rus \si-'n(y)ùr-əs\ *n, pl* **-nu·ri** \-'n(y)ù(ə)r-,ī\ : a complex tapeworm larva consisting of a sac from the inner wall of which numerous scolices develop

co·en·zyme \(')kō-'en-,zīm\ *n* : a substance (as a vitamin) intimately associated with an enzyme and essential for its normal function

co·equal \(')kō-'ē-kwəl\ *adj* : equal esp. in rank or status — **co·equal·i·ty** \,kō-ē-'kwäl-ət-ē\ *n* — **co·equal·ly** \(')kō-'ē-kwə-lē\ *adv*

co·erce \kō-'ərs\ *vt* [L *coercēre*, fr. *co-* + *arcēre* to shut up] **1** : to restrain or dominate by nullifying individual will **2** : to compel to an act or a choice **3** : to enforce by force or threat **syn** *see* FORCE — **co·erc·i·ble** \-'ər-sə-bəl\ *adj*

co·er·cion \kō-'ər-zhən, -shən\ *n* : the act, process, or power of coercing

co·er·cive \-'ər-siv\ *adj* : serving or intended to coerce — **co·er·cive·ly** *adv* — **co·er·cive·ness** *n*

co·eval \kō-'ē-vəl\ *adj* [L *coaevus*, fr. *co-* + *aevum* age] : of the same or equal age, antiquity, or duration — **coeval** *n*

co·ex·ist \,kō-ig-'zist\ *vi* **1** : to exist together or at the same time **2** : to live in peace with each other esp. as a matter of policy — **co·ex·ist·ence** \-'zis-tən(t)s\ *n* — **co·ex·ist·ent** \-tənt\ *adj*

co·ex·ten·sive \,kō-ik-'sten(t)-siv\ *adj* : having the same scope or extent in space or time — **co·ex·ten·sive·ly** *adv*

cof·fee \'kò-fē, 'käf-ē\ *n* [It & Turk; It *caffè*, fr. Turk *kahve*, fr. Ar *qahwah*] **1** : a drink made from the roasted and ground or pounded seeds of a tropical tree or shrub of the madder family; *also* : these seeds or a plant producing them **2** : a cup of coffee ⟨two *coffees*⟩

cof·fee·house \-,haùs\ *n* : a place where refreshments (as coffee) are sold

cof·fee·pot \-,pät\ *n* : a covered utensil for preparing or serving coffee

coffee shop *n* : a small restaurant esp. for light refreshments

coffee table *n* : a low table placed in front of a sofa

cof·fer \'kò-fər, 'käf-ər\ *n* [OF *cofre*, fr. L *cophinus* basket, fr. Gk *kophinos*] **1** : CHEST, BOX; *esp* : a strongbox for valuables **2** : TREASURY, EXCHEQUER — usu. used in pl. **3** : COFFERDAM **4** : a recessed panel in a vault or ceiling

cof·fer·dam \-,dam\ *n* : a watertight enclosure from which water is pumped to expose the bottom of a body of water and permit construction

cof·fin \'kò-fən\ *n* [ME, basket, receptacle, fr. MF *cofin*, fr. L *cophinus*] : a box or chest for a corpse to be buried in

coffin bone *n* : the bone enclosed within the hoof of the horse

co·func·tion \(')kō-'fəŋ(k)-shən, 'kō-,\ *n* : the trigonometric function of the complement of an angle

cog \'käg\ *n* [of Scand origin] : a tooth on the rim of a wheel adjusted to fit the notches in a receiving wheel or bar and to give or receive motion

co·gent \'kō-jənt\ *adj* [L *cogere* to drive together, compel, fr. *co-* + *agere* to drive] : having power to compel or constrain; *esp* : appealing forcibly to the mind or reason : CONVINCING **syn** *see* VALID — **co·gen·cy** \-jən-sē\ *n* — **co·gent·ly** *adv*

cog·i·tate \'käj-ə-,tāt\ *vb* [L *cogitare*, fr. *co-* + *agitare* to agitate] **1** : to think over intently or deeply : PONDER **2** : PLAN, PLOT — **cog·i·ta·tion** \,käj-ə-'tā-shən\ *n* — **cog·i·ta·tive** \'käj-ə-,tāt-iv\ *adj*

co·gnac \'kōn-,yak\ *n* [Cognac, district in France] : a French brandy

cog·nate \'käg-,nāt\ *adj* [L *cognatus* related by birth, fr. *co-* + *gnatus, natus*, pp. of *nasci* to be born] **1** : related by descent from the same ancestral language ⟨Spanish and French are *cognate* languages⟩ ⟨Spanish *madre* meaning "mother" and French *mère* meaning "mother" are *cognate* words⟩ **2 a** : related by processes of derivation within a single language ⟨English *boyish* and *boyhood* are *cognate* words⟩ **b** : related by adoption from one source language into two or more other languages ⟨English *tobacco* and French *tabac* are *cognate* words⟩ **3** : being a substantive that is related usu. in derivation to the verb of which it is the object ⟨*song* in "sang the song" is a *cognate* object⟩ **4** : of the same or similar nature — **cognate** *n* — **cog·nate·ly** *adv*

cog·ni·tion \käg-'nish-ən\ *n* [L *cognit-, cognoscere* to know, fr. *co-* + *gnoscere, noscere* to know] : the act or process of knowing including both awareness and judgment; *also* : something known by this process — **cog·ni·tion·al** \-'nish-nəl, -ən-ᵊl\ *adj* — **cog·ni·tive** \'käg-nət-iv\ *adj* — **cog·ni·tive·ly** *adv*

cog·ni·zance \'käg-nə-zən(t)s\ *n* [OF *conoissance*, fr. *conoistre* to know, fr. L *cognoscere*] **1 a** : KNOWLEDGE **b** : NOTICE, HEED ⟨take *cognizance* of what is happening⟩ **c** : AWARENESS **2 a** : the right and power to hear and decide controversies **b** : the judicial hearing of a matter — **cog·ni·zant** \-zənt\ *adj* : having cognizance

cog·no·men \käg-'nō-mən\ *n, pl* **-nomens** *or* **-no·mi·na** \-'näm-ə-nə, -nō-mə-\ [L, irreg. fr. *co-* + *nomen* name] **1** : SURNAME; *esp* : the third of usu. three names of a person among the ancient Romans **2** : NAME; *esp* : NICKNAME

co·gno·scen·te \ˌkän-yō-'shent-ē\ n, pl **co·gno·scen·ti** \-'shent-ē\ [obs. It, fr. L cognoscent-, cognoscens, prp. of cognoscere to know] : CONNOISSEUR

cog·wheel \'käg-ˌhwēl\ n : a wheel with cogs on the rim

co·hab·it \kō-'hab-ət\ vi : to live together as husband and wife — **co·hab·i·ta·tion** \(ˌ)kō-ˌhab-ə-'tā-shən\ n

co·here \kō-'hi(ə)r\ vi [L cohaes-, cohaerēre, fr. co- + haerēre to stick] **1 a** : to hold together firmly as parts of the same mass **b** : ADHERE **2** : to consist of parts that cohere **3 a** : to become united in principles, relationships, or interests **b** : to be logically or aesthetically consistent syn see STICK — **co·her·ence** \-'hir-ən(t)s, -'her-\ or **co·her·en·cy** \-ən-sē\ n

cogwheel

co·her·ent \kō-'hir-ənt, -'her-\ adj **1** : having the quality of cohering **2** : logically consistent — **co·her·ent·ly** adv

co·he·sion \kō-'hē-zhən\ n **1** : the action of sticking together tightly **2** : union between similar plant parts or organs **3** : molecular attraction by which the particles of a body are united throughout the mass

co·he·sive \kō-'hē-siv, -ziv\ adj : exhibiting or producing cohesion — **co·he·sive·ly** adv — **co·he·sive·ness** n

co·ho \'kō-(ˌ)hō\ n, pl **cohos** or **coho** : a small salmon with light-colored flesh

co·hort \'kō-ˌhȯrt\ n [L cohort-, cohors enclosure, throng, cohort] **1 a** : one of 10 divisions of an ancient Roman legion **b** : a group of warriors or followers **2** : COMPANION, ACCOMPLICE

¹coif \'kȯif, in sense 2 usu 'kwäf\ n [MF coife] **1** : a close-fitting cap **2** : COIFFURE

²coif \'kȯif, 'kwäf\ or **coiffe** \'kwäf\ vt **coiffed** or **coifed**; **coiff·ing** or **coif·ing** : to provide with a coif

coif·fure \kwä-'fyu̇(ə)r\ n : a manner of arranging the hair

coign of van·tage \ˌkȯin-ə-'vant-ij\ [ME coyn, coigne projecting corner, coin] : an advantageous position

¹coil \'kȯil\ n **1** : TUMULT **2** : TROUBLE

²coil vb [MF coillir to collect, fr. L colligere] **1** : to wind into rings or spirals **2** : to move in a circular, spiral, or winding course **3** : to form or lie in a coil

³coil n **1 a** : a series of loops : SPIRAL **b** : a single loop of a coil **2** : a number of turns of wire esp. in spiral form usu. for electromagnetic effect or for providing electrical resistance **3** : a series of connected pipes (as in water-heating apparatus) in rows, layers, or windings

¹coin \'kȯin\ n [ME coyn, coigne wedge, corner, coin, fr. MF coing, coin wedge, corner, coin die, fr. L cuneus wedge] **1** : a piece of metal issued by governmental authority as money **2** : metal money

²coin vt **1 a** : to make (a coin) esp. by stamping : MINT **b** : to convert (metal) into coins **2** : CREATE, INVENT ⟨coin a phrase⟩ — **coin·er** n

coin·age \'kȯi-nij\ n **1** : the act or process of coining **2 a** : COINS **b** : something (as a word) made up or invented

co·in·cide \ˌkō-ən-'sīd\ vi [ML coincidere, fr. L co- + incidere to fall on, occur, fr. in- + cadere to fall] **1** : to occupy the same place in space or time ⟨his birthday coincides with Christmas⟩ **2** : to be the same shape and cover the same area **3** : to correspond or agree exactly ⟨an opinion that coincides with my own⟩

co·in·ci·dence \kō-'in(t)-səd-ən(t)s\ n **1** : the act or condition of coinciding (as in space, time, or opinion) **2** : two things that happen at the same time by accident but seem to have some connection; also : either one of these happenings

co·in·ci·dent \-səd-ənt\ adj **1** : occupying the same space or time ⟨coincident events⟩ **2** : of similar nature : HARMONIOUS ⟨a theory coincident with the facts⟩ syn see CONTEMPORARY — **co·in·ci·dent·ly** adv

co·in·ci·den·tal \(ˌ)kō-ˌin(t)-sə-'dent-ᵊl\ adj **1** : resulting from a coincidence **2** : occurring or existing at the same time — **co·in·ci·den·tal·ly** \-'dent-ᵊl-ē, -'dent-lē\ adv

coir \'kȯi(ə)r\ n [Tamil kayïṟu rope] : a stiff coarse fiber from the outer husk of the coconut

co·i·tus \'kō-ət-əs\ n [L, fr. coire to go together] : sexual intercourse

¹coke \'kōk\ n : gray porous lumps of fuel made by heating soft coal in a closed chamber until some of its gases have passed off

²coke vt : to change into coke

col- — see COM-

co·la \'kō-lə\ n [fr. Coca-Cola, a trademark] : a carbonated soft drink flavored with extract from coca leaves, kola nut, sugar, caramel, and acid and aromatic substances

col·an·der \'kəl-ən-dər, 'käl-\ n [L colare to strain, fr. colum strainer] : a perforated utensil for draining food

col·chi·cine \'käl-chə-ˌsēn, 'käl-kə-\ n : a poisonous substance from the corms or seeds of the meadow saffron used to induce polyploidy in plants and to treat gout

col·chi·cum \'käl-chi-kəm, 'käl-ki\ n : MEADOW SAFFRON; also : its dried corm or dried ripe seeds containing colchicine

¹cold \'kōld\ adj [OE ceald; akin to E cool] **1** : having a low temperature or one decidedly below normal ⟨a cold day⟩ ⟨a cold drink⟩ **2** : lacking warmth of feeling : UNFRIENDLY ⟨a cold welcome⟩ **3** : suffering or uncomfortable from lack of warmth ⟨feel cold⟩ — **cold·ly** adv — **cold·ness** \'kōl(d)-nəs\ n — **in cold blood** : with premeditation : DELIBERATELY

²cold n **1 a** : a condition of low temperature **b** : cold weather **2** : bodily sensation produced by loss or lack of heat : CHILL **3** : a bodily disorder popularly associated with chilling; esp : COMMON COLD

cold–blood·ed \'kōl(d)-'bləd-əd\ adj **1** : lacking or showing a lack of natural human feelings : not moved by sympathy ⟨a cold-blooded criminal⟩ **2** : having cold blood; esp : having a body temperature approximating that of the environment **3** or **cold·blood** \-'bləd\ : of mixed or inferior breeding **4** : sensitive to cold — **cold–blood·ed·ly** adv — **cold–blood·ed·ness** n

cold chisel n : a strong steel chisel for chipping and cutting cold metal

cold cream n : a creamy preparation for cleansing, softening, and soothing the skin

cold cuts n pl : sliced assorted cold meats

cold frame n : a usu. glass-covered frame without artificial heat used to protect plants and seedlings

cold front n : the boundary between an advancing mass of cold or cool air and a mass of warmer air

cold shoulder n : intentionally cold or unsympathetic treatment — **cold–shoulder** vt

cold sore n : a group of blisters about or within the mouth caused by a common virus

cold sweat n : concurrent perspiration and chill usu. associated with fear, pain, or shock

cold war n : a conflict carried on by methods short of sustained overt military action and usu. without breaking off diplomatic relations

cold wave n : a period of unusually cold weather

cole \'kōl\ n [OE cāl, fr. L caulis stem, cabbage] : any of a genus of herbaceous plants that includes the cabbage and turnip

cole·man·ite \'kōl-mə-ˌnīt\ n : a mineral $Ca_2B_6O_{11}.5H_2O$ consisting of a hydrous borate of calcium occurring in brilliant colorless or white massive crystals

co·le·op·tera \ˌkō-lē-'äp-tə-rə\ n pl : insects that are beetles — **co·le·op·ter·ist** \-tə-rəst\ n — **co·le·op·ter·ous** \-tə-rəs\ adj

co·le·op·ter·an \-tə-rən\ n : ¹BEETLE **1** — **coleopteran** adj

co·le·op·tile \-'äp-tᵊl\ n : the first leaf of a monocot seedling forming a protective sheath about the plumule

cole·slaw \'kōl-ˌslȯ\ n [D koolsla, fr. kool cabbage + sla salad] : a salad made of sliced or chopped raw cabbage

co·le·us \'kō-lē-əs\ n [fr. Gk koleos, koleon sheath] : any of a large genus of herbs of the mint family often grown for their varicolored leaves

col·ic \'käl-ik\ n [MF colique, fr. Gk kōlikos colicky, irreg. fr. kolon colon] : sharp sudden pain in the abdomen — **col·icky** \'käl-i-kē\ adj

col·i·form \'kō-lə-ˌfȯrm\ adj : relating to, resembling, or being the colon bacillus — **coliform** n

col·i·se·um \ˌkäl-ə-'sē-əm\ n [ML Colosseum, Coliseum the Colosseum] : a large building, amphitheater, or stadium for athletic contests or public entertainments

co·li·tis \kō-'līt-əs\ n : inflammation of the colon

col·lab·o·rate \kə-'lab-ə-ˌrāt\ vi **1** : to work jointly with others (as in writing a book) **2** : to cooperate with or assist an enemy force occupying one's country — **col·lab·o·ra·tion** \-ˌlab-ə-'rā-shən\ n — **col·lab·o·ra·tion·ist** \-sh(ə)nəst\ n — **col·lab·o·ra·tor** \-'lab-ə-ˌrāt-ər\ n

col·lage \kə-'läzh\ *n* [F, lit., gluing, fr. *coller* to glue, fr. *colle* glue, fr. Gk *kolla*] **1 :** an artistic composition of fragments of materials (as printed matter) pasted on a picture surface **2 :** the art of making collages

col·la·gen \'käl-ə-jən\ *n* [Gk *kolla* glue] **:** an insoluble fibrous protein that is the chief constituent of connective tissue fibrils and yields gelatin and glue on prolonged heating with water — **col·lag·e·nous** \kə-'laj-ə-nəs\ *adj*

¹col·lapse \kə-'laps\ *vb* [L *collaps-*, *collabi*, fr. *com-* + *labi* to slip, fall] **1 :** to break down completely **:** DISINTEGRATE **2 :** to fall or shrink together abruptly and completely **3 :** to fall in ; give way **4 :** to suddenly lose value or effectiveness ⟨the country's currency *collapsed*⟩ **5 :** to break down physically or mentally through exhaustion or disease; *esp* **:** to fall helpless or unconscious **6 :** to fold down into a more compact shape ⟨*collapse* a card table⟩ — **col·laps·i·ble** \-'lap-sə-bəl\ *adj*

²collapse *n* **:** the act or an instance of collapsing **:** BREAKDOWN

¹col·lar \'käl-ər\ *n* [L *collare*, fr. *collum* neck] **1 a :** a band, strip, or chain worn around the neck or the neckline of a garment **b :** a part of the harness of draft animals fitted over the shoulders and taking strain when a load is drawn **2 :** something resembling a collar (as a ring or round flange to restrain motion or hold something in place) — **col·lar·less** \-ər-ləs\ *adj*

²collar *vt* **1 a :** to seize by the collar **b :** CAPTURE, GRAB **2 :** to put a collar on

col·lar·bone \,käl-ər-'bōn, 'käl-ər-,\ *n* **:** CLAVICLE

collar cell *n* **:** a flagellated cell (as of a sponge) with a protoplasmic collar about the base of its flagellum

col·lard \'käl-ərd\ *n* [alter. of *colewort* cole, kale] **:** a stalked smooth-leaved kale — usu. used in pl.

col·late \kə-'lāt, 'käl-,āt\ *vt* [back-formation fr. *collation*] **:** to collect and compare carefully in order to verify and often to integrate or arrange in order — **col·la·tor** \kə-'lāt-ər, 'käl-,āt-\ *n*

¹col·lat·er·al \kə-'lat-ə-rəl, -'la-trəl\ *adj* [ML *collateralis*, fr. L *com-* + *later-*, *latus* side] **1 :** associated but of secondary or merely supporting importance ⟨a main question and *collateral* questions⟩ **2 :** descended from the same ancestors but not in the same line ⟨cousins are *collateral* relatives⟩ **3 a :** of, relating to, or being collateral used as security **b :** secured by collateral — **col·lat·er·al·ly** \-ē\ *adv*

²collateral *n* **1 :** property (as stocks, bonds, or a mortgage) handed over or pledged as security for the repayment of a loan **2 :** a branch of a bodily part (as a vein)

col·la·tion \kə-'lā-shən, kä-\ *n* [L *collat-*, used as stem of *conferre* to bring together, compare, fr. *com-* + *ferre* to carry] **1 :** a light meal **2 :** the act, process, or result of collating

col·league \'käl-,ēg\ *n* [MF *collegue*, fr. L *collega*, fr. *com-* + *legare* to appoint, depute] **:** an associate in a profession or office; *also* **:** a fellow worker

¹col·lect \'käl-ikt, -,ekt\ *n* [ML *collecta*, short for *oratio ad collectam* prayer upon assembly] **:** a short prayer comprising an invocation, petition, and conclusion; *esp*, *often cap* **:** one preceding the eucharistic Epistle

²col·lect \kə-'lekt\ *vb* [L *collect-*, *colligere*, fr. *com-* + *legere* to gather] **1 a :** to bring together into one body or place **b :** to gather or exact from a number of sources ⟨*collect* taxes⟩ **2 :** to gain or regain control of ⟨*collect* his thoughts⟩ **3 :** to gather as due and receive payment for **4 a :** ASSEMBLE **b :** ACCUMULATE **syn** see GATHER — **col·lect·i·ble** *or* **col·lect·a·ble** \-'lek-tə-bəl\ *adj*

³col·lect \kə-'lekt\ *adv* (*or adj*) **:** to be paid for by the receiver ⟨he telephoned *collect*⟩

col·lect·ed \kə-'lek-təd\ *adj* **:** SELF-POSSESSED, CALM — **col·lect·ed·ly** *adv* — **col·lect·ed·ness** *n*

col·lec·tion \kə-'lek-shən\ *n* **1 :** the act or process of collecting **2 :** something collected **:** ASSEMBLAGE; *esp* **:** an accumulation of objects gathered for study, comparison, or exhibition **3 :** a gathering of money (as for charitable purposes) ⟨take up a *collection* in church⟩

¹col·lec·tive \kə-'lek-tiv\ *adj* **1 :** denoting a number of persons or things considered as one group ⟨*flock* is a *collective* noun⟩ **2 :** formed by collecting **:** AGGREGATED **3 :** of or relating to a group of individuals as a whole ⟨*collective* needs⟩ **4 :** marked by similarity among or with the members of a group **5 :** collectivized or characterized

by collectivism **6 :** shared or assumed by all members of the group ⟨*collective* leadership⟩ — **col·lec·tive·ly** *adv*

²collective *n* **1 :** a collective body **:** GROUP **2 :** a cooperative unit or organization; *esp* **:** COLLECTIVE FARM

collective bargaining *n* **:** negotiation between an employer and union representatives usu. on wages, hours, and working conditions

collective farm *n* **:** a farm in a communist country formed from many small holdings collected into a single unit for joint operation under governmental supervision

collective fruit *n* **:** MULTIPLE FRUIT

collective security *n* **:** the maintenance by common action of the security of all members of an association of nations

col·lec·tiv·ism \kə-'lek-ti-,viz-əm\ *n* **:** a political or economic theory advocating collective control esp. over production and distribution or a system marked by such control — **col·lec·tiv·ist** \-vəst\ *adj or n* — **col·lec·tiv·is·tic** \-,lek-ti-'vis-tik\ *adj*

col·lec·tiv·i·ty \,käl-,ek-'tiv-ət-ē, kə-,lek-\ *n, pl* **-ties :** a collective whole

col·lec·tiv·ize \kə-'lek-ti-,vīz\ *vt* **:** to organize under collective control — **col·lec·tiv·i·za·tion** \-,lek-ti-və-'zā-shən\ *n*

col·lec·tor \kə-'lek-tər\ *n* **:** one that collects: as **a :** an official or agent who collects funds or money due ⟨tax *collector*⟩ ⟨bill *collector*⟩ **b :** one that makes a collection ⟨stamp *collector*⟩ **c :** an object or device that collects — **col·lec·tor·ship** \-,ship\ *n*

col·leen \'käl-,ēn, kä-'lēn\ *n* [IrGael *cailín* young girl] **:** an Irish girl

col·lege \'käl-ij\ *n* [L *collegium* group of colleagues, fr. *collega* colleague] **1 :** a building used for an educational or religious purpose **2 a :** a self-governing constituent body of a university **b :** an independent institution of higher learning offering courses in the sciences and humanities leading to a bachelor's degree **c :** a part of a university offering a specialized group of courses **d :** an institution offering instruction usu. in a professional, vocational, or technical field ⟨teachers *college*⟩ ⟨barber *college*⟩ **3 :** an organized body of persons having common interests or duties ⟨*college* of cardinals⟩

col·le·gian \kə-'lē-j(ē-)ən\ *n* **:** a student or recent graduate of a college

col·le·giate \kə-'lē-j(ē-)ət\ *adj* **1 :** of or relating to a college **2 :** of, relating to, or characteristic of college students ⟨*collegiate* clothes⟩

collegiate church *n* **1 :** a church other than a cathedral that has a chapter of canons **2 :** a church or corporate group of churches under the joint pastorate of two or more ministers

col·le·gium \kə-'lē-j(ē-)əm\ *n* **:** a governing group (as in a Communist country) in which each member has approximately equal power and authority — **col·le·gial** \-j(ē-)əl\ *adj*

col·lem·bo·lan \kə-'lem-bə-lən\ *n* **:** SPRINGTAIL — **col·lembolan** *or* **col·lem·bo·lous** \-ləs\ *adj*

col·len·chy·ma \kə-'leŋ-kə-mə\ *n* **:** a plant tissue of living usu. elongated cells with thickened walls — compare SCLERENCHYMA — **col·len·chym·a·tous** \,käl-ən-'kim-ət-əs\ *adj*

col·lide \kə-'līd\ *vi* [L *collis-*, *collidere*, fr. *com-* + *laedere* to injure by striking] **1 :** to come together with solid impact **2 :** CLASH

col·lie \'käl-ē\ *n* **:** a large usu. long-coated dog of a Scottish breed used in herding sheep

col·lier \'käl-yər\ *n* [ME *colier*, fr. *col* coal] **1 :** a coal miner **2 :** a ship for carrying coal

col·liery \'käl-yə-rē\ *n, pl* **-lier·ies :** a coal mine and the buildings connected with it

col·li·mate \'käl-ə-,māt\ *vt* **:** to make (as rays of light) parallel — **col·li·ma·tor** \-,māt-ər\ *n*

col·lin·e·ar \kə-'lin-ē-ər, kä-\ *adj* **:** lying on the same straight line

col·li·sion \kə-'lizh-ən\ *n* **:** an act or instance of colliding **:** CRASH, CLASH

col·lo·ca·tion \,käl-ə-'kā-shən\ *n* **:** a placing together or side by side or the result of such placing

col·lo·di·on \kə-'lōd-ē-ən\ *n* **:** a viscous solution of pyroxylin used esp. as a coating for wounds or for photographic films

col·loid \'käl-,ȯid\ *n* [Gk *kolla* glue] **:** a substance in a fine state of division with particles that are not visible in an ordinary microscope but that when in suspension in a liquid or gas are made visible by a beam of light and do not settle out; *also* : a system consisting of such a substance together with the gaseous, liquid, or solid substance in which it is dispersed — **col·loi·dal** \kə-'loid-ᵊl, kä-\ *adj* — **col·loi·dal·ly** \-ᵊl-ē\ *adv*

col·lo·qui·al \kə-'lō-kwē-əl\ *adj* 1 : CONVERSATIONAL 2 : used in or characteristic of familiar and informal conversation 3 : using conversational style — **col·lo·qui·al·ly** \-kwē-ə-lē\ *adv*

col·lo·qui·al·ism \-kwē-ə-,liz-əm\ *n* 1 : a colloquial expression 2 : colloquial style

col·lo·qui·um \kə-'lō-kwē-əm\ *n, pl* **col·lo·qui·ums** *or* **col·lo·quia** \-kwē-ə\ : CONFERENCE; *esp* : a seminar that several lecturers take turns in leading

col·lo·quy \'käl-ə-kwē\ *n, pl* **-quies** [L *colloquium,* fr. *colloqui* to converse, fr. *com-* + *loqui* to speak] : CONVERSATION; *esp* : a formal conversation or conference

col·lude \kə-'lüd\ *vi* [L *collus-, colludere,* fr. *com-* + *ludere* to play] : CONSPIRE, PLOT

col·lu·sion \kə-'lü-zhən\ *n* : secret agreement or cooperation for a fraudulent or deceitful purpose — **col·lu·sive** \-'lü-siv, -ziv\ *adj* — **col·lu·sive·ly** *adv*

co·log·a·rithm \(')kō-'lòg-ə-,rith-əm, -'läg-\ *n* : the logarithm of the reciprocal of a number

co·logne \kə-'lōn\ *n* [*Cologne,* Germany, where it was first manufactured] : a perfumed toilet water composed of alcohol and certain aromatic oils

¹co·lon \'kō-lən\ *n* [Gk *kolon*] : the part of the large intestine that extends from the cecum to the rectum — **co·lon·ic** \kō-'län-ik\ *adj*

²colon *n* [Gk *kōlon* limb, member, clause] : a punctuation mark : used chiefly to direct attention to what follows (as a list, explanation, or quotation)

³co·lon \kə-'lōn\ *n, pl* **co·lo·nes** \-'lō-,näs\ [Sp *colón*] 1 : the basic monetary unit of Costa Rica and El Salvador 2 : a coin or note representing one colon

colon bacillus *n* : a bacillus regularly present in the intestine and used as an index of fecal contamination (as of water)

col·o·nel \'kərn-ᵊl\ *n* [alter. of earlier *coronel,* fr. MF, modif. of It *colonnello,* fr. *colonna* column, fr. L *columna*] : a commissioned officer (as in the army) ranking above a lieutenant colonel and below a brigadier general — **col·o·nel·cy** \-ᵊl-sē\ *n*

¹co·lo·ni·al \kə-'lō-nē-əl, -nyəl\ *adj* 1 : of, relating to, or characteristic of a colony 2 *often cap* : of or relating to the original 13 colonies forming the United States 3 : possessing, forming, or composed of colonies ⟨a *colonial* nation and its *colonial* empire⟩ — **co·lo·ni·al·ly** \-ē\ *adv* — **co·lo·ni·al·ness** *n*

²colonial *n* : a member or inhabitant of a colony

co·lo·ni·al·ism \-nē-ə-,liz-əm, -nyə-,liz-\ *n* : control by one power over a dependent area or people; *also* : a policy advocating or based on such control — **co·lo·ni·al·ist** \-ləst\ *n or adj*

col·o·nist \'käl-ə-nəst\ *n* 1 : an inhabitant or member of a colony 2 : a person who takes part in founding a colony

col·o·nize \'käl-ə-,nīz\ *vb* 1 : to establish a colony in or on ⟨England *colonized* Australia⟩ 2 : to establish in a colony 3 : to make or establish a colony : SETTLE — **col·o·ni·za·tion** \,käl-ə-nə-'zā-shən\ *n* — **col·o·niz·er** *n*

col·on·nade \,käl-ə-'nād\ *n* [F, fr. It *colonnata,* fr. *colonna* column, fr. L *columna*] : a row of columns set at regular intervals along one or more sides of a building and usu. supporting the base of the roof structure — **col·on·nad·ed** \-'nād-əd\ *adj*

col·o·ny \'käl-ə-nē\ *n, pl* **-nies** [L *colonia,* fr. *colonus* farmer, colonist, fr. *colere* to cultivate] 1 a : a body of people sent out by a state to a new territory b : the territory inhabited by people sent to new territory c : a distant territory belonging to or under the control of a nation 2 a : a distinguishable localized population within a species ⟨*colony* of termites⟩ b : a circumscribed mass of microorganisms usu. growing in or on a solid medium c : the aggregation of zooids of a compound animal 3 : a group of individuals with common characteristics or interests situated in close association; *also* : the section occupied by such a group

col·o·phon \'käl-ə-fən, -,fän\ *n* [Gk *kolophōn* summit,

finishing touch] 1 : an inscription placed at the end of a book with facts relative to its production 2 : an identifying device used by a printer or a publisher

¹col·or \'kəl-ər\ *n* [L *color*] 1 a : a phenomenon of light (as red, brown, pink, gray) or visual perception that enables one to differentiate otherwise identical objects b : the aspect of objects and light sources that may be described in terms of hue, lightness, and saturation for objects and hue, brightness, and saturation for light sources — used in this sense as the psychological basis for definitions of color in this dictionary c : a hue as contrasted with black, white, or gray 2 a : an outward often deceptive show : APPEARANCE ⟨his story has the *color* of truth⟩ b : an appearance of authenticity : PLAUSIBILITY 3 : complexion tint : a : the tint characteristic of good health b : BLUSH 4 : vividness or variety of effects of language 5 : a distinctively colored badge or device or distinctively colored clothing — usu. used in pl. 6 : the use or combination of colors 7 *pl* a : an identifying flag, ensign, or pennant b : service in the armed forces ⟨a call to the *colors*⟩ 8 : VITALITY, INTEREST 9 : something used to give color : PIGMENT 10 : skin pigmentation other than white characteristic of race

syn HUE, TINT, SHADE: COLOR is the general term for any distinguishable quality of light but specif. implies the property of things seen as red, yellow, blue, and so on as distinguished from white, black, or gray; HUE usu. implies some modification of or a finer discrimination of a primary color ⟨a reddish orange *hue*⟩ TINT applies esp. to a color modified toward white; SHADE to one modified toward black; but all four terms are frequently interchangeable

²color *vb* 1 a : to give color to ⟨a blush *colored* the girl's cheeks⟩ b : to change the color of : PAINT 2 : to change as if by dyeing or painting; *esp* : MISREPRESENT, DISTORT ⟨his story is *colored* by his prejudices⟩ 3 : to take on or change color; *esp* : BLUSH ⟨she *colored* at his glance⟩ — **col·or·er** \'kəl-ər-ər\ *n*

Col·o·ra·do potato beetle \,käl-ə-'rad-ō-, -'räd-\ *n* : a black-and-yellow striped beetle that feeds on the leaves of the potato

col·or·a·tion \,kəl-ə-'rā-shən\ *n* : use or arrangement of colors or shades : COLORING ⟨study the *coloration* of a flower⟩

col·or·a·tu·ra \,kəl-ə-rə-'t(y)ùr-ə\ *n* [It, coloring, fr. LL, fr. L *colorare* to color] 1 : florid ornamentation in vocal music 2 : a soprano specializing in coloratura

col·or·blind \'kəl-ər-,blīnd\ *adj* : affected with partial or total inability to distinguish one or more chromatic colors — **color blindness** *n*

col·or·cast \-,kast\ *n* : a television broadcast in color — **col·or·cast·ing** *n*

col·ored \'kəl-ərd\ *adj* 1 : having color ⟨*colored* pictures⟩ 2 : SLANTED, BIASED 3 a : of a race other than the white; *esp* : NEGRO b : of or relating to colored persons

col·or·fast \'kəl-ər-,fast\ *adj* : having color that does not fade or run — **col·or·fast·ness** \-,fas(t)-nəs\ *n*

color film *n* : a photographic film for making color pictures

color filter *n* : a usu. glass filter that absorbs light of certain colors and is used for modifying the light that reaches a sensitized photographic material

col·or·ful \'kəl-ər-fəl\ *adj* 1 : having striking colors 2 : full of variety or interest — **col·or·ful·ly** \-f(ə-)lē\ *adv* — **col·or·ful·ness** \-fəl-nəs\ *n*

color guard *n* : a guard of honor for the colors of an organization

col·or·im·e·ter \,kəl-ə-'rim-ət-ər\ *n* : a device for determining colors; *esp* : one used for chemical analysis by comparison of a liquid's color with standard colors — **col·or·i·met·ric** \,kəl-ə-rə-'me-trik\ *adj* — **col·or·i·met·ri·cal·ly** \-tri-k(ə-)lē\ *adv* — **col·or·im·e·try** \,kəl-ə-'rim-ə-trē\ *n*

col·or·ing \'kəl-ə-riŋ\ *n* 1 : the act of applying colors 2 : something that produces color 3 a : the effect produced by applying or combining colors b : natural color c : COMPLEXION, COLORATION 4 : change of appearance (as by adding color)

col·or·less \'kəl-ər-ləs\ *adj* 1 : lacking color 2 : PALLID, BLANCHED 3 : DULL, UNINTERESTING — **col·or·less·ly** *adv* — **col·or·less·ness** *n*

co·los·sal \kə-'läs-əl\ *adj* 1 : of, relating to, or resembling a colossus; *esp* **:** of very great size **2 :** EXCEPTIONAL, ASTONISHING ⟨*colossal* growth⟩ — **co·los·sal·ly** \-ə-lē\ *adv*

col·os·se·um \,käl-ə-'sē-əm\ *n* [ML, fr. L, neut. of *colosseus* colossal, fr. *colossus*] **1** *cap* **:** an amphitheater built in Rome in the first century A.D. **2 :** COLISEUM

Co·los·sians \kə-'läsh-ənz, -'läs-ē-ənz\ *n* — see BIBLE table

co·los·sus \kə-'läs-əs\ *n, pl* **-los·sus·es** *or* **-los·si** \-'läs-,ī, -,(,)ē\ [Gk *kolossos*] **1 :** a statue of gigantic size and proportions **2 :** one resembling a colossus in size or scope

co·los·trum \kə-'läs-trəm\ *n* **:** milk secreted for a few days after parturition and characterized by high protein and immune body content

col·our \'kəl-ər\ *chiefly Brit var of* COLOR

-c·o·lous \k-ə-ləs\ *adj comb form* [L *colere* to inhabit] **:** living or growing in or on

col·por·teur \'käl-,pōrt-ər, -,pȯrt-\ *n* **:** a peddler of religious books

colt \'kōlt\ *n* [OE] **1 a :** FOAL **b :** a young male horse **2 :** a young untried person

col·ter \'kōl-tər\ *n* [OE *culter* & OF *coltre*, both fr. L *culter* plowshare] **:** a cutter on a plow to cut the turf

colt·ish \'kōl-tish\ *adj* **1 :** FRISKY, PLAYFUL **2 :** of, relating to, or resembling a colt — **colt·ish·ly** *adv*

Co·lum·bia \kə-'ləm-bē-ə\ *n* [NL, fr. Christopher *Columbus*] **:** the United States

col·um·bine \'käl-əm-,bīn\ *n* [ML *columbina*, fr. L *columba* dove] **:** any of a genus of plants related to the buttercups that have showy flowers with usu. five spurred petals

Col·um·bine \'käl-əm-,bīn, -,bēn\ *n* **:** the saucy sweetheart of Harlequin in comedy and pantomime

co·lum·bi·um \kə-'ləm-bē-əm\ *n* [NL, fr. *Columbia*] **:** NIOBIUM

Co·lum·bus Day \kə-'ləm-bəs\ *n* **:** October 12 observed as a legal holiday in many states of the U.S. in commemoration of the landing of Columbus in the Bahamas in 1492

col·u·mel·la \,käl-(y)ə-'mel-ə\ *n, pl* **-mel·lae** \-'mel-(,)ē, -,ī\ **:** any of various plant or animal parts resembling a column — **col·u·mel·lar** \-'mel-ər\ *adj* — **col·u·mel·late** \-'mel-ət\ *adj*

col·umn \'käl-əm\ *n* [L *columna*] **1 a :** one of two or more vertical sections of a printed page separated by a rule or blank space **b :** a special department in a newspaper or periodical **2 :** a supporting pillar; *esp* **:** one consisting of a usu. round shaft, a capital, and a base — see ORDER illustration **3 :** something resembling a column in form, position, or function ⟨a *column* of water⟩ **4 :** a long row (as of soldiers) — **co·lum·nar** \kə-'ləm-nər\ *adj* — **col·umned** \'käl-əmd\ *adj*

col·um·nist \'käl-əm-(n)əst\ *n* **:** a person who writes a newspaper column

col·za \'käl-zə, 'kōl-\ *n* **:** a cole (as rape) producing seed used as a source of oil

com- *or* **col-** *or* **con-** *prefix* [L, with, together, thoroughly] **:** with **:** together **:** jointly — usu. *com-* before *b*, *p*, or *m* ⟨*commingle*⟩, *col-* before *l* ⟨*collinear*⟩, and *con-* before other sounds ⟨*concentrate*⟩

¹co·ma \'kō-mə\ *n* [Gk *kōma* deep sleep] **:** a state of profound unconsciousness caused by disease, injury, or poison — **co·ma·tose** \-,tōs\ *adj*

²coma *n, pl* **co·mae** \-,mē, -,mī\ [L, hair, fr. Gk *komē*] **1 :** a tufted bunch (as of hairs) **2 :** the head of a comet usu. containing a nucleus

Co·ma Ber·e·ni·ces \'kō-mə-,ber-ə-'nī-(,)sēz\ *n* [L, lit., Berenice's hair] **:** a constellation north of Virgo and between Boötes and Leo

Co·man·che \kə-'man-chē\ *n* [Sp, of AmerInd origin] **:** a member of an Indian people ranging from Wyoming and Nebraska south into New Mexico and northwestern Texas

Co·man·che·an \-chē-ən\ *n* [*Comanche*, Texas] **:** the period of the Mesozoic era between the Jurassic and the Upper Cretaceous; *also* **:** the corresponding system of rocks — **Comanchean** *adj*

co·mat·u·lid \kə-'mach-ə-ləd\ *n* **:** a free-swimming stalkless crinoid

¹comb \'kōm\ *n* [OE *camb*] **1 a :** a toothed implement to smooth and arrange the hair or worn in the hair to hold it in place **b :** a toothed instrument for separating fibers (as

of wool or flax) **2 a :** a fleshy crest on the head of the domestic fowl and some related birds **b :** something resembling the comb of a cock **3 :** HONEYCOMB — **combed** \'kōmd\ *adj*

²comb *vb* **1 :** to smooth, arrange, or untangle with a comb ⟨*comb* one's hair⟩ ⟨*comb* wool⟩ **2 :** to go over or through carefully in search of something **:** search thoroughly ⟨*comb* an area a mile square⟩

comb 2a

¹com·bat \kəm-'bat, 'käm-\ *vb* **-bat·ed** *or* **-bat·ted**; **-bat·ing** *or* **-bat·ting** [MF *combattre*, fr. L *com-* + *battuere* to beat] **1 :** to fight with **:** BATTLE **2 :** to struggle against; *esp* **:** to strive to reduce or eliminate ⟨*combat* disease⟩

²com·bat \'käm-,bat\ *n* **1 :** a fight or contest between individuals or groups ⟨a fierce *combat* of antlered stags⟩ **2 :** CONFLICT, CONTROVERSY ⟨a long parliamentary *combat*⟩ **3 :** active fighting in a war **:** ACTION ⟨soldiers experienced in *combat*⟩

com·bat·ant \kəm-'bat-°nt, 'käm-bət-ənt\ *adj* **:** engaging in or ready to engage in combat — **combatant** *n*

combat fatigue *n* **:** a neurotic or psychotic reaction occurring under conditions (as wartime combat) causing intense stress

com·bat·ive \kəm-'bat-iv\ *adj* **:** eager to fight **:** PUGNACIOUS — **com·bat·ive·ly** *adv* — **com·bat·ive·ness** *n*

comb·er \'kō-mər\ *n* **1 :** one that combs fibers (as of wool or flax) **2 :** a long curling wave rolling in from the ocean

com·bi·na·tion \,käm-bə-'nā-shən\ *n* **1 :** a result or product of combining; *esp* **:** an alliance of persons or groups to achieve some end **2 a :** a sequence of letters or numbers chosen in setting a lock; *also* **:** the mechanism operating or moved by the sequence **b :** any of the different possible groupings of a number of individuals without regard to order within the group **3 :** a one-piece undergarment for the upper and lower parts of the body **4 :** an instrument designed to perform two or more tasks **5 a :** the act or process of combining; *esp* **:** that of uniting to form a chemical compound **b :** the quality or state of being combined — **com·bi·na·tion·al** \-'nā-shnəl, -shən-°l\ *adj*

¹com·bine \kəm-'bīn\ *vb* [LL *combinare*, fr. L *com-* + *bini* two each] **1 a :** to bring into close relationship **:** UNIFY **b :** to cause to unite into a chemical compound **2 :** INTERMIX, BLEND **3 a :** to become one **b :** to unite to form a chemical compound **c :** to act together **syn** see JOIN — **com·bin·a·ble** \-'bī-nə-bəl\ *adj* — **com·bin·er** *n*

²com·bine \'käm-,bīn\ *n* **1 :** a combination to gain an often illicit end **2 :** a harvesting machine that harvests, threshes, and cleans grain while moving over a field

³com·bine \'käm-,bīn\ *vt* **:** to harvest with a combine

comb·ings \'kō-miŋz\ *n pl* **:** loose hairs or fibers removed by a comb

combining form \kəm-,bī-niŋ-\ *n* **:** a linguistic form that occurs only in compounds or derivatives (as *cephal-* in *cephalic*, *electro-* in *electromagnetic*, or *mal-* in *malodorous*)

comb jelly *n* **:** any of a phylum (Ctenophora) of marine animals superficially resembling jellyfishes but having eight bands of ciliated swimming plates

com·bo \'käm-,bō\ *n, pl* **combos** [alter. of *combination*] **:** a small jazz or dance band

com·bust \kəm-'bəst\ *vb* **:** BURN

com·bus·ti·ble \kəm-'bəs-tə-bəl\ *adj* **1 :** capable of being burned **2 :** easily excited — **com·bus·ti·bil·i·ty** \-,bəs-tə-'bil-ət-ē\ *n* — **combustible** *n* — **com·bus·ti·bly** \-'bəs-tə-blē\ *adv*

com·bus·tion \kəm-'bəs-chən\ *n* [L *combust-, comburere* to burn up, irreg. fr. *com-* + *urere* to burn] **1 :** the process of burning **2 :** a chemical process in which substances combine with oxygen — **com·bus·tive** \-'bəs-tiv\ *adj*

com·bus·tor \-'bəs-tər\ *n* **:** a chamber (as in a jet engine) in which combustion occurs

come \(')kəm\ *vi* **came** \'kām\; **come**; **com·ing** \'kəm-iŋ\ [OE *cuman*] **1 :** to move toward something **:** APPROACH ⟨*come* here⟩ **2 :** to move toward or enter a scene of action or into a field of interest ⟨the police *came* to our rescue⟩ **3 a :** to reach the point of being or becoming ⟨the rope *came* untied⟩ **b :** AMOUNT ⟨the bill *came* to 10 dollars⟩ **4 a :** to take place **:** have a place (as in a series) ⟨the holiday *came* on Thursday⟩ **b :** to proceed as a consequence, effect, or conclusion ⟨his plans *came* to naught⟩ **5 :** ORIGINATE, ARISE ⟨*comes* from sturdy stock⟩ **6 :** to be obtainable ⟨an article that *comes* in three sizes⟩ **7 :** to be attainable ⟨success *came* after hard work⟩ **8 :** EXTEND, REACH ⟨a coat that *comes* to the knees⟩ **9 a :** to arrive at a particular place, end, result, or conclusion ⟨*came* to his senses⟩ **b :** HAPPEN, OCCUR ⟨no harm will *come* to you⟩ **10 :** to fall within a scope ⟨*comes* under the terms of the treaty⟩ **11 :** BECOME ⟨things will *come* clear if we are patient⟩ — **come across :** to meet or find by chance — **come at :** to reach a mastery of : ATTAIN — **come by :** ACQUIRE — **come into :** to acquire as an inheritance — **come into one's own 1 :** to get what is rightfully one's own **2 :** to approach or reach one's appropriate level of importance, skill, or recognition — **come to be :** to arrive at or attain to being : BECOME — **come to pass :** HAPPEN — used with *it*

come about *vi* **1 :** to come to pass : HAPPEN **2 :** to change direction ⟨the wind has *come about* into the north⟩

come around *vi* **:** to come round

come·back \'kəm-ˌbak\ *n* **1 :** RETORT **2 :** a return to a former position or condition (as of health, power, popularity, or prosperity) : RECOVERY

co·me·di·an \kə-'mēd-ē-ən\ *n* **1 :** an actor who plays in comedy **2 :** a comical individual; *esp* **:** a professional entertainer who tells jokes or who performs comical body movements and finds himself in comical situations

co·me·di·enne \kə-ˌmēd-ē-'en\ *n* **:** a female comedian

com·e·do \'käm-ə-ˌdō\ *n, pl* **com·e·do·nes** \ˌkäm-ə-'dō-(ˌ)nēz\ **:** BLACKHEAD

come down \(ˌ)kəm-'daün\ *vi* **:** to fall sick

come·down \'kəm-ˌdaün\ *n* **:** a descent in rank or dignity

com·e·dy \'käm-əd-ē\ *n, pl* **-dies** [L *comoedia,* fr. Gk *kōmōidia,* fr. *kōmos* revel + *ōid-, aidein* to sing] **1 a :** a drama of light and amusing character typically with a happy ending **b :** dramatic literature dealing with the comic or with the serious in a light or satirical manner **2 a :** a medieval narrative that ends happily ⟨Dante's Divine *Comedy*⟩ **b :** a literary work written in a comic style or treating a comic theme **3 :** an amusing or ludicrous event

come in *vi* **1 :** to be the recipient ⟨*came in* for criticism⟩ **2 :** to attain maturity, fruitfulness, or production

come·ly \'kəm-lē\ *adj* **come·li·er; -est** [ME *comly,* alter. of OE *cȳmlic* glorious] **:** pleasing to the sight **:** good-looking ⟨a *comely* girl⟩ — **come·li·ness** *n*

come-on \'kəm-ˌon, -ˌän\ *n* **:** INDUCEMENT, LURE

come out *vi* **1 a :** to come into view : EMERGE **b :** to make one's debut **2 :** to turn out ⟨the cake *came out* splendidly⟩ **3 :** to declare oneself ⟨*come out* for a candidate⟩ **4 :** UTTER — usu. used with *with* ⟨*came out* with the truth⟩

com·er \'kəm-ər\ *n* **1 :** one that comes ⟨all *comers*⟩ **2 :** a promising newcomer

come round *vi* **1 :** to come to **2 :** to change direction or opinion

¹co·mes·ti·ble \kə-'mes-tə-bəl\ *adj* [L *comest-, comedere* to eat up, fr. *com-* + *edere* to eat] **:** EDIBLE

²comestible *n* **:** FOOD — usu. used in pl.

com·et \'käm-ət\ *n* [OE *cometa,* fr. L, fr. Gk *komētēs,* lit., long-haired one, fr. *komē* hair] **:** a celestial body that consists of a fuzzy head usu. surrounding a bright nucleus, that often when in the part of its orbit near the sun develops a long tail which points away from the sun, and that has a nearly round or an elongated orbit

come to *vi* **:** to recover consciousness

come·up·pance \(ˌ)kə-'məp-ən(t)s\ *n* **:** a deserved rebuke or penalty : DESERTS

com·fit \'kəm(p)-fət, 'käm(p)-\ *n* [MF *confit,* fr. pp. of *confire* to prepare, fr. L *conficere,* fr. *com-* + *facere* to make] **:** a confection consisting of a piece of fruit, a root, or a seed coated and preserved with sugar

¹com·fort \'kəm(p)-fərt\ *n* **1 :** acts or words that comfort **2 :** the feeling of the one that is comforted ⟨find *comfort* in a mother's love⟩ **3 :** something that makes a person comfortable ⟨the *comforts* of home⟩ — **com·fort·less** \-ləs\ *adj*

²comfort *vt* [LL *confortare* to strengthen, fr. L *com-* + *fortis* strong, brave] **1 :** to give strength and hope to : CHEER **2 :** to ease the grief or trouble of : CONSOLE

syn CONSOLE, SOLACE: COMFORT implies giving cheer,

strength, or encouragement as well as lessening pain; CONSOLE stresses the lessening of grief or sense of loss rather than giving relief or pleasure; SOLACE may suggest relieving loneliness or despondency as well as pain or grief

com·fort·a·ble \'kəm(p)(f)-tə-bəl, 'kəm(p)-fərt-ə-bəl\ *adj* **1 :** giving comfort; *esp* **:** providing physical comfort **2 :** more than adequate ⟨*comfortable* income⟩ **3 a :** physically at ease **b :** PLACID, UNDISTURBED — **com·fort·a·ble·ness** *n* — **com·fort·a·bly** \-blē\ *adv*

com·fort·er \'kəm(p)-fə(r)t-ər\ *n* **1 a :** one that gives comfort **b** *cap* **:** HOLY SPIRIT **2 a :** a long narrow neck scarf **b :** QUILT, PUFF

com·fy \'kəm(p)-fē\ *adj* **com·fi·er; -est** [by shortening & alter.] **:** COMFORTABLE

¹com·ic \'käm-ik\ *adj* [Gk *kōmikos,* fr. *kōmos* revel] **1 a :** of, relating to, or marked by comedy **b :** composing or acting in comedies **2 :** causing laughter or amusement **:** FUNNY **3 :** of or relating to comic strips

syn COMIC, COMICAL mean causing laughter. COMIC applies esp. to what arouses thoughtful amusement ⟨a *comic* masterpiece of wit and satire⟩ COMICAL suggests the provoking of unrestrained spontaneous hilarity ⟨*comical* frustrations of a circus clown⟩

²comic *n* **1 :** COMEDIAN **2 a :** COMIC STRIP **b** *pl* **:** the part of a newspaper devoted to comic strips

com·i·cal \'käm-i-kəl\ *adj* **:** amusingly whimsical **:** DROLL, LAUGHABLE **syn** see COMIC — **com·i·cal·i·ty** \ˌkäm-i-'kal-ət-ē\ *n* — **com·i·cal·ly** \'käm-i-k(ə-)lē\ *adv*

comic book *n* **:** a magazine made up of a series of comic strips

comic opera *n* **:** a musical dramatic work with spoken dialogue and usu. of light and amusing character

comic strip *n* **:** a sequence of cartoons that tell a story or part of a story

com·ing \'kəm-iŋ\ *adj* **1 :** APPROACHING, NEXT ⟨the *coming* year⟩ **2 :** gaining importance ⟨recognized as a *coming* young star⟩

Com·in·tern \'käm-ən-ˌtərn\ *n* [*Communist Intern*ational] **:** the Communist International established in 1919 in an attempt to supersede the Second International of Socialist organizations

com·i·ty \'käm-ət-ē\ *n, pl* **-ties** [L *comitas,* fr. *comis* courteous] **:** courteous behavior : CIVILITY

comity of nations : the code of courtesy and friendship by which nations get along together; *also* **:** the group of nations observing such a code

com·ma \'käm-ə\ *n* [Gk *komma* segment, fr. *koptein* to cut] **:** a punctuation mark , used chiefly to show separation of words or word groups within a sentence

comma bacillus *n* **:** the bacterium that causes Asiatic cholera

comma fault *n* **:** the careless or unjustified use of a comma between coordinate main clauses not connected by a conjunction — called also *comma splice*

¹com·mand \kə-'mand\ *vb* [OF *comander,* fr. L *commendare* to commend] **1 a :** to direct authoritatively **:** ORDER, GOVERN **b :** to have authority and control of a military force or post **:** be commander of **2 a :** to have at one's disposal **b :** to demand as one's due : EXACT ⟨*commands* a high fee⟩ **c :** to overlook from a strategic position ⟨the hill *commands* the town⟩

²command *n* **1 :** the act of commanding ⟨march on *command*⟩ **2 :** an order given **3 a :** the ability to control **:** MASTERY ⟨has *command* of the subject⟩ **b :** the authority or right to command **c :** the power to dominate **d :** facility in using ⟨a good *command* of French⟩ **4 :** the personnel, area, or unit under a commander **5 :** a position from which military operations are directed — called also *command post*

³command *adj* **:** done on command or request ⟨*command* performance⟩

com·man·dant \'käm-ən-ˌdant, -ˌdänt\ *n* **:** COMMANDING OFFICER

com·man·deer \ˌkäm-ən-'di(ə)r\ *vt* **:** to take arbitrary or forcible possession of esp. for military purposes

com·mand·er \kə-'man-dər\ *n* **1 :** one in official command; *esp* **:** COMMANDING OFFICER **2 :** a commissioned officer in the navy ranking above a lieutenant commander and below a captain — **com·mand·er·ship** \-ˌship\ *n*

commander in chief : one who holds the supreme command of an armed force

commanding officer *n* : a military or naval officer in command of a unit or post

com·mand·ment \kə-'man(d)-mənt\ *n* : something commanded; *esp* : one of the biblical Ten Commandments

command module *n* : a space vehicle module designed to carry the crew, the chief communication equipment, and the equipment for reentry

com·man·do \kə-'man-dō\ *n*, *pl* **-dos** *or* **-does** [Afrik *kommando*, fr. D *commando* command, fr. F *commander* to command] **1** : a military unit trained and organized for surprise raids into enemy territory **2** : a member of a specialized raiding unit

comme il faut \ˌkəm-ˌēl-'fō\ *adj* [F, lit., as it should be] : conforming to accepted standards : PROPER

com·mem·o·rate \kə-'mem-ə-ˌrāt\ *vt* [L *commemorare*, fr. *com-* + *memor* mindful] **1** : to call to remembrance **2** : to mark by a ceremony : OBSERVE **3** : to be a memorial of — **com·mem·o·ra·tor** \-ˌrāt-ər\ *n*

com·mem·o·ra·tion \kə-ˌmem-ə-'rā-shən\ *n* **1** : the act of commemorating **2** : something that commemorates

com·mem·o·ra·tive \kə-'mem-ə-ˌrāt-iv, -rət-\ *adj* : intended to commemorate an event — **commemorative** *n* — **com·mem·o·ra·tive·ly** *adv*

com·mence \kə-'men(t)s\ *vb* [MF *comencer*, fr. L *com-* + *initiare* to initiate] : BEGIN, START — **com·menc·er** *n*

com·mence·ment \-'men(t)s-mənt\ *n* **1** : an act, instance, or time of commencing **2 a** : the ceremonies or the day for conferring degrees or diplomas upon graduates of a school or college **b** : the period of activities at this time

com·mend \kə-'mend\ *vb* [L *commendare*, fr. *com-* + *mandare* to entrust] **1** : to give into another's care : ENTRUST **2** : to speak of someone or something with approval : PRAISE — **com·mend·a·ble** \-'men-də-bəl\ *adj* — **com·mend·a·bly** \-də-blē\ *adv*

com·men·da·tion \ˌkäm-ən-'dā-shən, -,en-\ *n* **1** : an act of commending **2** : something that commends — **com·men·da·to·ry** \kə-'men-də-ˌtōr-ē, -ˌtōr-\ *adj*

com·men·sal \kə-'men(t)-səl\ *adj* [L *com-* + *mensa* table] : relating to or living in a state of commensalism — **commensal** *n* — **com·men·sal·ly** \-sə-lē\ *adv*

com·men·sal·ism \-sə-ˌliz-əm\ *n* : a relation between two kinds of organisms in which one obtains a benefit (as food) from the other without either damaging or benefiting it

com·men·su·ra·ble \kə-'men(t)s-(ə-)rə-bəl, -'mench-(ə-)rə-\ *adj* : having a common measure; *esp* : divisible by a common unit an integral number of times — **com·men·su·ra·bly** \-blē\ *adv*

com·men·su·rate \kə-'men(t)s-(ə-)rət, -'mench-(ə-)rət\ *adj* **1** : equal in measure or extent **2** : CORRESPONDING, PROPORTIONATE ⟨an income *commensurate* with one's needs⟩ — **com·men·su·rate·ly** *adv* — **com·men·su·ra·tion** \-ˌmen(t)-sə-'rā-shən, -ˌmench-ə-'rā-\ *n*

¹com·ment \'käm-ˌent\ *n* [LL *commentum*, fr. L, neut. of pp. of *comminisci* to invent] **1** : an expression of opinion either in speech or writing **2 a** : REMARK **b** : a critical remark

²comment *vi* : to make a comment : REMARK

com·men·tary \'käm-ən-ˌter-ē\ *n*, *pl* **-tar·ies** **1** : an explanatory or narrative treatise — often used in pl. ⟨Caesar's *Commentaries* on the Gallic Wars⟩ **2** : a series of oral comments or written notes

com·men·tate \'käm-ən-ˌtāt\ *vb* : to give a commentary on : act as a commentator

com·men·ta·tor \-ˌtāt-ər\ *n* : one who gives a commentary; *esp* : one who reports and discusses news on radio or television

com·merce \'käm-(ˌ)ərs\ *n* [L *commercium*, fr. *com-* + *merc-*, *merx* merchandise] **1** : interchange of ideas, opinions, or sentiments **2** : the exchange or buying and selling of commodities on a large scale involving transportation from place to place **syn** see BUSINESS

¹com·mer·cial \kə-'mər-shəl\ *adj* **1 a** : of, relating to, or suitable for commerce **b** : engaged in commerce ⟨a *commercial* city⟩ **2 a** : viewed with regard to profit ⟨a *commercial* success⟩ **b** : designed for profit; *esp* : designed for mass appeal ⟨the *commercial* theater⟩ **3** : emphasizing skills and subjects useful in business ⟨*commercial* high school⟩ **4** : paid for by advertisers ⟨*commercial* TV⟩ — **com·mer·cial·ly** \-'mərsh-(ə-)lē\ *adv*

²commercial *n* : an advertisement broadcast on radio or television

commercial bank *n* : a bank that accepts checking accounts and makes short-term loans and investments

com·mer·cial·ism \kə-'mər-shə-ˌliz-əm\ *n* : a spirit, method, or practice characteristic of business — **com·mer·cial·is·tic** \-ˌmər-shə-'lis-tik\ *adj*

com·mer·cial·ize \kə-'mər-shə-ˌlīz\ *vt* **1** : to manage on a business basis for profit **2** : to exploit for profit ⟨*commercialize* Christmas⟩ — **com·mer·cial·i·za·tion** \-ˌmər-shə-lə-'zā-shən\ *n*

commercial paper *n* : short-term negotiable instruments arising out of commercial transactions

commercial traveler *n* : TRAVELING SALESMAN

com·mie \'käm-ē\ *n*, *often cap* [by alter.] : COMMUNIST

com·mi·na·tion \ˌkäm-ə-'nā-shən\ *n* [L *comminari* to threaten] : DENUNCIATION — **com·mi·na·to·ry** \'käm-ə-nə-ˌtōr-ē, -ˌtór-\ *adj*

com·min·gle \kə-'miŋ-gəl\ *vb* : MIX, MINGLE ⟨*commingle* two liquids⟩

com·mi·nute \'käm-ə-ˌn(y)üt\ *vt* [L *comminuere*, fr. *com-* + *minuere* to lessen] : to reduce to minute particles : PULVERIZE — **com·mi·nu·tion** \ˌkäm-ə-'n(y)ü-shən\ *n*

com·mis·er·ate \kə-'miz-ə-ˌrāt\ *vb* [L *commiserari*, fr. *com-* + *miserari* to pity, fr. *miser* wretched] **1** : to feel or express sorrow or compassion for **2** : CONDOLE, SYMPATHIZE — **com·mis·er·a·tion** \-ˌmiz-ə-'rā-shən\ *n* — **com·mis·er·a·tive** \-'miz-ə-ˌrāt-iv\ *adj*

com·mis·sar \'käm-ə-ˌsär\ *n* [Russ *komissar*] **1** : the head of a government department in the U.S.S.R. from 1917 to 1946 **2** : a Communist party official assigned to a military unit to teach party principles and policies and to ensure party loyalty

com·mis·sar·i·at \ˌkäm-ə-'ser-ē-ət\ *n* **1** : a system for supplying an army with food **2** : a government department in the U.S.S.R. from 1917 to 1946

com·mis·sary \'käm-ə-ˌser-ē\ *n*, *pl* **-sar·ies** [ML *commissarius*, fr. L *commiss-*, *committere* to commit] **1** : a person to whom a duty or office is entrusted by a superior **2** : a store supplying provisions; *esp* : one supplying provisions to military personnel and dependents **3** : a lunchroom in a motion-picture studio

¹com·mis·sion \kə-'mish-ən\ *n* [L *commiss-*, *committere* to commit] **1 a** : a formal order granting the power to perform various acts or duties **b** : a certificate conferring military rank and authority or the rank and authority so conferred **2** : an authorization or command to act in a prescribed manner or to perform prescribed acts : CHARGE **3 a** : authority to act as agent for another **b** : a task or matter entrusted to an agent **4 a** : a group of persons directed to perform some duty **b** : a government agency having administrative, legislative, or judicial powers **c** : a city council having legislative and executive functions **5** : an act of committing (as a crime) **6** : a fee (as a percentage of money received) paid to an agent or employee for transacting a piece of business or performing a service ⟨brokerage *commission*⟩ — **in commission** **1** *of a ship* : ready for active service **2** : in use or ready for use — **out of commission** **1** : out of service or use **2** : out of working order

²commission *vt* **-mis·sioned**; **-mis·sion·ing** \-'mish-(ə-)niŋ\ **1** : to confer a commission on **2** : to order to be made **3** : to put (a ship) in commission

com·mis·sion·aire \kə-ˌmish-ə-'na(ə)r, -'ne(ə)r\ *n*, *chiefly Brit* : a uniformed attendant

commissioned officer *n* : a military or naval officer holding by a commission a rank of second lieutenant or ensign or a higher rank

com·mis·sion·er \kə-'mish-(ə-)nər\ *n* **1** : a member of a commission **2** : an official in charge of a government department ⟨*Commissioner* of Public Safety⟩

commission merchant *n* : one who buys or sells another's goods for a commission

com·mis·sure \'käm-ə-ˌshù(ə)r\ *n* : a connecting band of nerve tissue in the brain or spinal cord — **com·mis·sur·al** \ˌkäm-ə-'shùr-əl\ *adj*

com·mit \kə-'mit\ *vt* **com·mit·ted**; **com·mit·ting** [L *committere*, lit., to put together, fr. *com-* + *mittere* to send] **1 a** : to put into charge or trust : ENTRUST **b** : to place in a prison or mental institution **c** : to consign for preservation, disposal, or safekeeping ⟨*commit* a poem to memory⟩ **d :** to refer (as a legislative bill) to a committee for consideration and report **2 :** to bring about **:** PERFORM ⟨*commit* a crime⟩ **3 a :** OBLIGATE, BIND **b :** to pledge or assign to some particular course or use — **com·mit·ta·ble** \-'mit-ə-bəl\ *adj*

com·mit·ment \kə-'mit-mənt\ *n* **1 :** an act of committing to a charge or trust: as **a :** a consignment to a penal or mental institution **b :** an act of referring a matter to a legislative committee **2 a :** an agreement or pledge to do something in the future **b :** something pledged ⟨financial *commitments*⟩

com·mit·tal \kə-'mit-ᵊl\ *n* **:** COMMITMENT 1a

com·mit·tee \kə-'mit-ē\ *n* **1 :** a body of persons delegated to consider or take action on some matter; *esp* **:** a body of members chosen by a legislative body to consider legislative matters **2 :** a self-constituted organization for the promotion of some common object

com·mit·tee·man \-mən, -ˌman\ *n* **1 :** a member of a committee **2 :** a party leader of a ward or precinct — **com·mit·tee·wom·an** \-ˌwu̇m-ən\ *n*

committee of the whole : the whole membership of a legislative house sitting as a committee and operating under informal rules

com·mix \kä-'miks, kä-\ *vb* **:** MIX

com·mix·ture \-chər\ *n* **:** COMPOUND, MIXTURE

com·mode \kə-'mōd\ *n* [F, suitable, convenient, fr. L *commodus*, fr. *com-* + *modus* measure] **1 :** a woman's ornate cap popular around 1700 **2 a :** a low chest of drawers **b :** a movable washstand with a cupboard underneath **c :** TOILET 2b

com·mo·di·ous \kə-'mōd-ē-əs\ *adj* [ML *commodiosus*, fr. L *commodum* convenience, fr. *commodus* convenient] **1** *archaic* **:** HANDY, SERVICEABLE **2 :** comfortably or conveniently spacious **:** ROOMY — **com·mo·di·ous·ly** *adv* — **com·mo·di·ous·ness** *n*

com·mod·i·ty \kə-'mäd-ət-ē\ *n, pl* **-ties** [L *commoditas*, fr. *commodus* convenient] **:** an economic good: as **a :** a product of agriculture or mining **b :** an article exchanged in commerce

commode 1

com·mo·dore \'käm-ə-ˌdō(ə)r, -ˌdȯ(ə)r\ *n* [prob. modif. of D *komandeur* commander] **1 :** a commissioned officer in the navy ranking above a captain and below a rear admiral **2 :** the chief officer of a yacht club **3 :** the senior captain of a line of merchant ships

¹com·mon \'käm-ən\ *adj* [L *communis*] **1 :** having to do with, belonging to, or used by everybody **:** PUBLIC ⟨work for the *common* good⟩ **2 :** belonging to or shared by two or more individuals or by the members of a group ⟨a *common* ancestor⟩ **3 :** widely or generally known, met, or seen ⟨facts of *common* knowledge⟩ **4 :** FREQUENT, FAMILIAR ⟨a *common* sight⟩ **5 :** not above the average in rank, merit, or social position ⟨a *common* soldier⟩ ⟨the *common* people⟩ **6 :** PLAIN, PRACTICAL ⟨*common* sense⟩ **7 a :** falling below ordinary standards **:** SECOND-RATE **b :** lacking refinement **:** VULGAR **8 a :** being either masculine or feminine ⟨*common* gender⟩ **b :** being a noun that designates any of a class of beings or things **c :** being a grammatical case used both for the subject and the object ⟨the word *man* in "the man is tall", "watch the man", and "with the man" is in the *common* case⟩ **syn** see RECIPROCAL — **com·mon·ly** *adv* — **com·mon·ness** \-ən-nəs\ *n*

²common *n* **1** *pl* **:** the common people **2** *pl* **:** a dining hall **3** *pl, often cap* **a :** the political group or estate comprising the commoners **b :** the parliamentary representatives of the commoners **c :** HOUSE OF COMMONS **4 :** a piece of land subject to common use esp. for pasture — often used in pl. **5 a :** a religious service suitable for a festival **b :** the ordinary of the mass — **in common :** shared together

com·mon·al·i·ty \ˌkäm-ə-'nal-ət-ē\ *or* **com·mon·al·ty** \'käm-ə-nəl-tē\ *n, pl* **-ties :** the common people

common carrier *n* **:** an individual or corporation undertaking to transport for compensation persons, goods, or messages

common cold *n* **:** an acute virus disease of the upper respiratory tract marked by congestion and inflammation of mucous membranes and usu. accompanied by excessive secretion of mucus and coughing and sneezing

common denominator *n* **1 :** a common multiple of the denominators of a number of fractions **2 :** a common trait or theme

common divisor *n* **:** a number or expression that divides two or more numbers or expressions without remainder — called also *common factor*

com·mon·er \'käm-ə-nər\ *n* **:** one of the common people **:** one who is not of noble rank

common fraction *n* **:** a fraction in which both numerator and denominator are expressed

common law *n* **:** the body of law developed in England primarily from judicial decisions based on custom and precedent, unwritten in statute or code, and constituting the basis of the legal system in most jurisdictions of the U.S. and parts of the world under British control or influence

common-law marriage *n* **:** a marriage relationship created by agreement and usu. cohabitation between a man and a woman without ecclesiastical or civil ceremony

common logarithm *n* **:** a logarithm whose base is 10

Common Market *n* **:** an economic unit initially formed by France, West Germany, Italy, Belgium, the Netherlands, and Luxembourg for the elimination of trade barriers among members

common multiple *n* **:** a multiple of each of two or more numbers or expressions

common noun *n* **:** a noun (as *chair* or *fear*) that names a class of persons or things or any individual of a class

¹com·mon·place \'käm-ən-ˌplās\ *n* **:** an obvious or trite remark or observation

²commonplace *adj* **:** ORDINARY, UNREMARKABLE

common room *n* **1 :** a lounge available to all members of a residential community **2 :** a room in a college for the use of the faculty

common salt *n* **:** SALT 1a

common school *n* **:** a free public elementary school

common sense *n* **1 :** sound prudent judgment **2 :** the opinions of ordinary men who are not experts in a field

common stock *n* **:** capital stock other than preferred stock

common time *n* **:** four beats to a measure in music

common touch *n* **:** the gift of appealing to or arousing the sympathetic interest of the generality of man

com·mon·weal \'käm-ən-ˌwēl\ *n* **1 :** the general welfare **2** *archaic* **:** COMMONWEALTH

com·mon·wealth \-ˌwelth\ *n* **1 :** a political unit whose aim is the common good of all the people **2** *cap* **:** the English state from the death of Charles I in 1649 to the Restoration in 1660 **3 :** a state of the U.S. — used officially of Kentucky, Massachusetts, Pennsylvania, and Virginia **4** *cap* **:** a federal union of constituent states —used officially of Australia **5** *often cap* **:** an association of self-governing states having a common political and cultural background and united by a common allegiance ⟨the British *Commonwealth*⟩ **6** *often cap* **:** a political unit having local autonomy but voluntarily united with the U.S. — used officially of Puerto Rico

common year *n* **:** a calendar year of 365 days

com·mo·tion \kə-'mō-shən\ *n* **1 :** disturbed or violent motion **:** AGITATION **2 a :** noisy excitement and confusion **b :** a confused noisy disturbance **:** TUMULT

com·mu·nal \kə-'myün-ᵊl, 'käm-yən-ᵊl\ *adj* **1 :** of or relating to a commune or community **2 a :** characterized by collective ownership and use of property **b :** shared, participated in, or used in common by members of a group or community

Com·mu·nard \ˌkäm-yu̇-'närd\ *n* **:** one who supported or participated in the Commune of Paris in 1871

¹com·mune \kə-'myün\ *vi* **1 :** to receive Communion **2 :** to communicate intimately ⟨*commune* with nature⟩

²com·mune \'käm-ˌyün, kə-'myün\ *n* [F, fr. MF *comugne*, fr. ML *communia*, fr. L *communis* common] **1 :** the smallest administrative district of many countries esp. in Europe **2 a :** a medieval municipality **b :** a rural community (as the Russian *mir*) organized on a communal basis **3** *cap* **a :** the French government elected by representatives of the communes in 1792 **b :** a revolutionary government in Paris from March 18 to May 28, 1871 **4 :** a large collectivized farm in the People's Republic of China characterized by totally regimented work and living conditions

com·mu·ni·ca·ble \kə-'myü-ni-kə-bəl\ *adj* **:** capable of being communicated **:** TRANSMITTABLE ⟨*communicable* diseases⟩ — **com·mu·ni·ca·bil·i·ty** \-,myü-ni-kə-'bil-ət-ē\ n — **com·mu·ni·ca·ble·ness** \-'myü-ni-kə-bəl-nəs\ n — **com·mu·ni·ca·bly** \-blē\ adv

com·mu·ni·cant \kə-'myü-ni-kənt\ n 1 : a person who partakes of Communion : a church member 2 : a person who communicates — **communicant** adj

com·mu·ni·cate \kə-'myü-nə-,kāt\ vb [L communicare, fr. communis common] 1 a : to make known ⟨communicate the news⟩ b : TRANSFER, TRANSMIT ⟨communicate a disease⟩ 2 : to receive Communion 3 : to be in communication 4 : JOIN, CONNECT ⟨the rooms communicate⟩ — **com·mu·ni·ca·tor** \-,kāt-ər\ n

com·mu·ni·ca·tion \kə-,myü-nə-'kā-shən\ n 1 : an act or instance of transmitting 2 a : information communicated b : MESSAGE 3 : an exchange of information 4 pl a : a system (as of telephones) for communicating b : a system of routes for moving troops, supplies, and vehicles 5 pl : the business or technology of the transmission of information

com·mu·ni·ca·tive \kə-'myü-nə-,kāt-iv, -ni-kət-\ adj 1 : tending to communicate : TALKATIVE 2 : of or relating to communication — **com·mu·ni·ca·tive·ly** adv — **com·mu·ni·ca·tive·ness** n

com·mu·nion \kə-'myü-nyən\ n [L communis common] 1 : an act or instance of sharing 2 a cap : a Christian sacrament in which bread and wine are partaken of as a commemoration of the death of Christ b : the act of receiving the sacrament c cap : the part of the Mass in which the sacrament is received 3 : COMMUNICATION, INTERCOURSE 4 : a body of Christians having a common faith and discipline

com·mu·ni·qué \kə-'myü-nə-,kā, -,myü-nə-'\ n [F] : an official communication : BULLETIN

com·mu·nism \'käm-yə-,niz-əm\ n 1 : a social system in which property and goods are owned in common; also : a theory advocating such a system 2 cap a : a doctrine based upon revolutionary Marxian socialism and Marxism-Leninism that is the official ideology of the U.S.S.R., the Chinese People's Republic, and several satellite nations b : a totalitarian system of government in which a single authoritarian party controls state-owned means of production with the professed aim of establishing a stateless society c : a final stage of society in Marxist theory in which the state has withered away and economic goods are distributed equally

com·mu·nist \'käm-yə-nəst\ n 1 : an adherent or advocate of communism 2 cap : a member or adherent of a Communist party or movement — **communist** adj, often cap — **com·mu·nis·tic** \,käm-yə-'nis-tik\ adj, often cap — **com·mu·nis·ti·cal·ly** \-ti-k(ə-)lē\ adv

com·mu·ni·ty \kə-'myü-nət-ē\ n, pl -ties 1 a : the people living in an area; also : the area itself b : an interacting population of various kinds of individuals (as species) in a common location c : a group of people with common interests living together within a larger society ⟨the Christian community⟩ d : a body of persons or nations having a history or social, economic, or political interests or policies in common ⟨European Coal and Steel Community⟩ 2 a : joint ownership or participation ⟨community property of husband and wife⟩ b : LIKENESS c : FELLOWSHIP d : a social state or condition

community center n : a building or group of buildings for a community's educational and recreational activities

community chest n : a general fund made up of individual subscriptions in a community to provide public aid

com·mu·nize \'käm-yə-,nīz\ vb 1 : to place under common ownership 2 : to organize according to Communist principles — **com·mu·ni·za·tion** \,käm-yə-nə-'zā-shən\ n

com·mu·ta·tion \,käm-yə-'tā-shən\ n 1 : EXCHANGE, REPLACEMENT; esp : a substitution of one form of payment for another 2 : a reduction of a legal penalty 3 : an act of commuting 4 : the process of reversing the direction of an electric circuit

commutation ticket n : a transportation ticket sold at a reduced rate for a fixed number of trips over the same route during a limited period

com·mu·ta·tive \'käm-yə-,tāt-iv, kə-'myüt-ət-\ adj : combining elements to produce a result independent of the order in which the elements are taken ⟨addition is commutative⟩ — **com·mu·ta·tiv·i·ty** \kə-,myüt-ə-'tiv-ət-ē\ n

com·mu·ta·tor \'käm-yə-,tāt-ər\ n : a device for reversing the direction of an electric current so that the alternating currents generated in the armature of a dynamo are converted to direct current

com·mute \kə-'myüt\ vb [L commutare, fr. com- + mutare to change] 1 a : EXCHANGE, INTERCHANGE, SUBSTITUTE b : CHANGE, ALTER 2 : to substitute one form of obligation for another 3 : to substitute a less severe penalty for a greater one ⟨commute a death sentence to life imprisonment⟩ 4 a : to travel by use of a commutation ticket b : to travel back and forth regularly — **com·mut·a·ble** \-'myüt-ə-bəl\ adj — **com·mut·er** n

¹com·pact \kəm-'pakt, 'käm-\ adj [L compactus, fr. pp. of compingere to put together, fr. com- + pangere to fasten] 1 : closely united, collected, or packed : not loose or straggling 2 : SOLID : FIRM 2 : arranged so as to save space ⟨a compact house⟩ 3 : not wordy : BRIEF 4 : not gangling or lanky in appearance ⟨a compact body⟩ — **com·pact·ly** adv — **com·pact·ness** \-'pak(t)-nəs, -,pak(t)-\ n

²compact vb 1 a : COMBINE, CONSOLIDATE b : COMPRESS 2 : to make up by connecting or combining : COMPOSE 3 : to become compacted — **com·pac·tor** or **com·pact·er** n

³com·pact \'käm-,pakt\ n 1 : a small cosmetic case 2 : a relatively small automobile

⁴com·pact \'käm-,pakt\ n [L compactum, fr. neut. of pp. of compacisci to make an agreement, fr. com- + pacisci to contract] : an agreement or covenant between two or more parties

com·pac·tion \kəm-'pak-shən\ n : the act or process of compacting : the state of being compacted

¹com·pan·ion \kəm-'pan-yən\ n [LL companion-, companio, fr. L com- + panis bread] 1 : one much in the company of another : COMRADE 2 a : one of a pair of matching things b : one employed to live with and serve another

²companion n [by folk etymology fr. D kampanje poop deck] 1 : a covering at the top of a companionway 2 : COMPANIONWAY

com·pan·ion·a·ble \kəm-'pan-yə-nə-bəl\ adj : fitted to be a companion : SOCIABLE — **com·pan·ion·a·bly** \-blē\ adv

companion cell n : a living nucleated cell adjacent to a sieve tube of a vascular plant

com·pan·ion·ship \kəm-'pan-yən-,ship\ n : FELLOWSHIP

com·pan·ion·way \-,wā\ n : a ship's stairway from one deck to another

com·pa·ny \'kəmp-(ə-)nē\ n, pl -nies [OF compagnie, fr. compain companion, fr. LL companio] 1 a : association with another : FELLOWSHIP b : COMPANIONS, ASSOCIATES c : VISITORS, GUESTS 2 a : a group of persons or things b : a body of soldiers; esp : a unit esp. of infantry consisting usu. of a headquarters and two or more platoons c : an organization of musical or dramatic performers ⟨opera company⟩ d : the officers and men of a ship e : a fire-fighting unit 3 a : a medieval trade guild b : a commercial organization under royal charter ⟨Hudson's Bay Company⟩ c : an association of persons carrying on a commercial or industrial enterprise d : those members of a partnership whose names do not appear in the firm name ⟨John Doe and Company⟩

company union n : an unaffiliated labor union of the employees of a single firm; esp : one dominated by the employer

com·pa·ra·ble \'käm-p-(ə-)rə-bəl\ adj 1 : capable of being compared 2 : worthy of being compared ⟨cloth comparable to the best⟩ — **com·pa·ra·bly** \-blē\ adv

¹com·par·a·tive \kəm-'par-ət-iv\ adj 1 : of, relating to, or constituting the degree of grammatical comparison that denotes increase in the quality, quantity, or relation expressed by an adjective or adverb 2 a : measured by comparison : RELATIVE ⟨comparative stranger⟩ b : involving systematic study of comparable elements ⟨comparative literature⟩ ⟨comparative anatomy⟩ — **com·par·a·tive·ly** adv — **com·par·a·tive·ness** n

²comparative n : the comparative degree or a comparative form in a language

com·par·a·tor \kəm-'par-ət-ər, 'käm-pə-,rāt-\ n : an instrument for comparing something with a like thing or with a standard measure

¹com·pare \kəm-'pa(ə)r, -'pe(ə)r\ vb [L comparare, fr. compar like, fr. com- + par equal] 1 : to represent as similar : LIKEN ⟨compare an anthill to a town⟩ 2 : to examine in order to discover likenesses or differences ⟨*compare* two bicycles⟩ **3** : to be worthy of comparison : be like ⟨roller skating does not *compare* with ice skating⟩ **4** : to inflect or modify (an adjective or adverb) according to the degrees of comparison

syn COMPARE, CONTRAST mean to set side by side in order to show differences and likenesses. COMPARE implies an aim of showing relative values and stresses similarities; CONTRAST implies an emphasis on differences or esp. opposite qualities

²compare *n* : COMPARISON ⟨beauty beyond *compare*⟩
com·par·i·son \kəm-'par-ə-sən\ *n* **1** : the act of comparing : the state of being compared **2** : an examination of two or more objects to find the likenesses and differences between them **3** : change in the form of an adjective or an adverb (as by having *-er* or *-est* added or *more* or *most* prefixed) to show different levels of quality, quantity, or relation
com·part·ment \kəm-'pärt-mənt\ *n* **1** : one of the parts into which an enclosed space is divided **2** : a separate division or section — **com·part·ment·ed** \-,ment-əd\ *adj*
com·part·men·tal·ize \kəm-,pärt-'ment-ʰl-,īz\ *vt* : to separate into compartments — **com·part·men·tal·i·za·tion** \-,ment-ʰl-ə-'zā-shən\ *n*
¹com·pass \'kəm-pəs, 'käm-\ *vt* [OF *compasser* to measure, arrange, contrive, fr. L *com-* + *passus* pace] **1** : CONTRIVE, PLOT **2 a** : ENCOMPASS **b** : to travel entirely around **3 a** : ACHIEVE, ACCOMPLISH; *also* : OBTAIN **b** : COMPREHEND
²compass *n* **1 a** : BOUNDARY, CIRCUMFERENCE **b** : an enclosed space **c** : RANGE, SCOPE **2 a** : a device for determining directions by means of a magnetic needle turning freely on a pivot and pointing to the magnetic north **b** : any of various nonmagnetic devices that indicate direction **c** : an instrument for describing circles or transferring measurements that consists of two pointed branches joined at the top by a pivot — usu. used in pl.; called also *pair of compasses*
compass card *n* : the circular card attached to the needles of a mariner's compass on which are marked 32 points of the compass and the 360° of the circle
com·pas·sion \kəm-'pash-ən\ *n* [L *com-*, *compati* to sympathize, fr. *com-* + *pati* to suffer] : sorrow or pity aroused by the suffering or misfortune of another : SYMPATHY, MERCY
com·pas·sion·ate \kəm-'pash-(ə-)nət\ *adj* : having or showing compassion : SYMPATHETIC — **com·pas·sion·ate·ly** *adv*

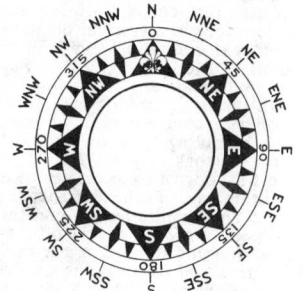

compass card

com·pat·i·ble \kəm-'pat-ə-bəl\ *adj* [ML *compatibilis*, fr. L *compati* to sympathize] : capable of existing together in harmony ⟨*compatible* colors⟩ ⟨friends who were very *compatible*⟩: as **a** : able to cross-fertilize freely ⟨*compatible* plants⟩ **b** : free from untoward or unwanted effect when present together ⟨*compatible* drugs⟩ ⟨*compatible* bloods⟩ —**com·pat·i·bil·i·ty** \-,pat-ə-'bil-ət-ē\ *n* — **com·pat·i·bly** \-'pat-ə-blē\ *adv*
com·pa·tri·ot \kəm-'pā-trē-ət, -,ät\ *n* **1** : a fellow countryman **2** : COLLEAGUE, COMPANION
com·peer \'käm-,pi(ə)r, käm-'\ *n* **1** [OF *compere*, lit., godfather, fr. ML *compater*, fr. L *com-* + *pater* father] : COMPANION **2** [L *compar*, fr. *compar* like, fr. *com-* + *par* equal] : EQUAL, PEER
com·pel \kəm-'pel\ *vt* **com·pelled**; **com·pel·ling** [L *compellere*, fr. *com-* + *pellere* to drive] **1** : to drive or urge with physical force, moral or social pressure, or logical necessity : CONSTRAIN **2** : EXACT, EXTORT ⟨*compel* silence at the point of a gun⟩ **syn** see FORCE — **com·pel·ler** *n*
com·pend \'käm-,pend\ *n* : COMPENDIUM
com·pen·di·ous \kəm-'pen-dē-əs\ *adj* : marked by brief

expression of a comprehensive matter : CONCISE — **com·pen·di·ous·ly** *adv* — **com·pen·di·ous·ness** *n*
com·pen·di·um \-dē-əm\ *n*, *pl* **-di·ums** *or* **-dia** \-dē-ə\ [L, saving, shortcut, fr. *compendere* to weigh together, fr. *com-* + *pendere* to weigh] : a brief summary of a larger work or of a field of knowledge : ABSTRACT
com·pen·sate \'käm-pən-,sāt\ *vb* [L *compensare*, fr. *compens-*, *compendere* to weigh together] **1** : to be equivalent to in value or effect : make up for : COUNTERBALANCE **2** : to make amends ⟨nothing can *compensate* for the loss of reputation⟩ **3** : to make equal return to : REMUNERATE, PAY ⟨*compensate* a workman for his labor⟩ — **com·pen·sa·tive** \'käm-pən-,sāt-iv, kəm-'pent)-sət-\ *adj* — **com·pen·sa·tor** \'käm-pən-,sāt-ər\ *n* — **com·pen·sa·to·ry** \kəm-'pen(t)-sə-,tōr-ē, -,tòr-\ *adj*
syn COMPENSATE, BALANCE, OFFSET mean to make up in one thing what is deficient or excessive in another. COMPENSATE implies making up a lack or making amends for loss or injury; BALANCE suggests the equalizing or adjusting of two things so that neither outweighs the other in effect; OFFSET implies neutralizing one thing's good or bad effect by something exerting an opposite effect **syn** see in addition PAY
com·pen·sa·tion \,käm-pən-'sā-shən\ *n* **1** : the act of compensating : the state of being compensated **2 a** : something that constitutes an equivalent or recompense; *esp* : payment to an unemployed or injured worker or his dependents **b** : SALARY, WAGES — **com·pen·sa·tion·al** \-shnəl, -shən-ʰl\ *adj*
com·pete \kəm-'pēt\ *vi* [LL *competere*, fr. L *com-* + *petere* to seek] : to vie with another for or as if for a prize : contend in rivalry : CONTEST
com·pe·tence \'käm-pət-ən(t)s\ *n* **1** : means sufficient for the necessities of life **2** : the quality or state of being competent
com·pe·ten·cy \-ən-sē\ *n* : COMPETENCE
com·pe·tent \'käm-pət-ənt\ *adj* [L *competent-*, *competens*, fr. prp. of *competere* to come together, be suitable, fr. *com-* + *petere* to seek] **1** : having requisite ability or qualities : FIT **2** : rightfully belonging : PROPER **3** : legally qualified **syn** see ABLE — **com·pe·tent·ly** *adv*
com·pe·ti·tion \,käm-pə-'tish-ən\ *n* **1** : the act or process of competing **2** : a contest between rivals; *also* : the person competing ⟨first-rate *competition*⟩ **3** : the effort of two or more persons or firms acting independently to secure business by offering the most favorable terms — **com·pet·i·to·ry** \kəm-'pet-ə-,tōr-ē, -,tòr-\ *adj*
com·pet·i·tive \kəm-'pet-ət-iv\ *adj* : relating to, characterized by, or based on competition ⟨*competitive* sports⟩ ⟨*competitive* bidding⟩ — **com·pet·i·tive·ly** *adv* — **com·pet·i·tive·ness** *n*
com·pet·i·tor \kəm-'pet-ət-ər\ *n* : one that competes esp. in the selling of goods or services : RIVAL
com·pi·la·tion \,käm-pə-'lā-shən\ *n* **1** : the act or process of compiling **2** : something compiled; *esp* : a book composed of materials gathered from other books or documents
com·pile \kəm-'pīl\ *vt* [L *compilare* to plunder, ransack] **1** : to collect into a volume **2** : to put together in a new form out of materials already existing; *esp* : to compose out of materials from other documents ⟨*compile* a history of India⟩ **3** : LIST, ENUMERATE — **com·pil·er** *n*
com·pla·cence \kəm-'plās-ʰn(t)s\ *n* : calm or secure satisfaction with one's self or lot : SELF-SATISFACTION
com·pla·cen·cy \-ʰn-sē\ *n* : COMPLACENCE
com·pla·cent \kəm-'plās-ʰnt\ *adj* [L *complacēre* to please greatly, fr. *com-* + *placēre* to please] **1** : SATISFIED; *esp* : SELF-SATISFIED **2** : feeling or showing complaisance — **com·pla·cent·ly** *adv*
com·plain \kəm-'plān\ *vi* [MF *complaindre*, fr. L *com-* + *plangere* to lament] **1** : to express grief, pain, or discontent **2** : to make a formal accusation or charge — **com·plain·er** *n* — **com·plain·ing·ly** \-'plā-niŋ-lē\ *adv*
com·plain·ant \kəm-'plā-nənt\ *n* : the party who makes a complaint in a legal action or proceeding
com·plaint \kəm-'plānt\ *n* **1** : expression of grief, pain, or resentment **2 a** : that concerning which one complains **b** : a bodily ailment or disease **3** : a formal charge against a person
com·plai·sance \kəm-'plās-ʰn(t)s, 'käm-plā-,zan(t)s\ *n* : disposition to please or oblige

com·plai·sant \kəm-'plās-ᵊnt, 'käm-plā-ˌzant\ *adj* [F, fr. MF, fr. prp. of *complaire* to gratify, acquiesce, fr. L *complacēre* to please greatly] **1 :** marked by an inclination to please or oblige **2 :** tending to consent to others' wishes — **com·plai·sant·ly** *adv*

com·plect·ed \kəm-'plek-təd\ *adj* [irreg. fr. *complexion*] **:** COMPLEXIONED ⟨dark-*complected*⟩

¹**com·ple·ment** \'käm-plə-mənt\ *n* [L *complementum*, fr. *complēre* to complete] **1 :** something that fills up, completes, or makes perfect **:** a quantity necessary to make a thing complete or one of two parts necessary to make a complete whole **2 :** full quantity, number, or amount ⟨a ship's *complement* of officers and men⟩ **3 :** the amount of angle or arc by which a given angle or arc falls short of 90 degrees **4 :** an added word or group of words by which the predicate of a sentence is made complete ⟨*president* in "they elected him president", *with water* in "he filled it with water", and *good* in "that is good" are different kinds of *complements*⟩ **5 :** a heat-sensitive substance in normal blood that in combination with antibodies destroys antigens (as bacteria and foreign blood corpuscles) **6 :** the set of all elements not included in a given set

syn COMPLEMENT, COMPLIMENT are not synonyms but are easily confused. COMPLEMENT applies to a thing, quantity, or part required to make something complete or full; COMPLIMENT is an often formal expression of approval, praise, or greeting

²**com·ple·ment** \-ˌment\ *vt* **:** to be complementary to **:** form or serve as a complement to

com·ple·men·tal \ˌkäm-plə-'ment-ᵊl\ *adj* **:** relating to or being a complement

com·ple·men·ta·ry \ˌkäm-plə-'ment-ə-rē, -'men-trē\ *adj* **:** forming or serving as a complement **:** COMPLEMENTAL — **complementary** *n*

complementary angles *n pl* **:** two angles whose sum is 90 degrees

complementary colors *n pl* **:** a pair of colors that when mixed in proper proportions give white light

¹**com·plete** \kəm-'plēt\ *adj* [L *completus*, fr. pp. of *complēre* to complete, fr. com- + plēre to fill; akin to E *full*] **1 a :** possessing all necessary parts **:** ENTIRE **b :** having all four sets of floral organs **2 :** brought to an end **:** CONCLUDED **3 :** highly proficient ⟨a *complete* artist⟩ **4 :** fully carried out **:** THOROUGH — **com·plete·ly** *adv* — **com·plete·ness** *n*

²**complete** *vt* **1 :** to bring to an end **:** accomplish or achieve fully **2 :** to make whole or perfect; *esp* **:** to provide with all lacking parts syn see FINISH

com·ple·tion \kəm-'plē-shən\ *n* **:** the act or process of completing **:** the state of being complete ⟨a job near *completion*⟩

¹**com·plex** \käm-'pleks, kəm-', 'käm-ˌ\ *adj* [L *complexus*, pp. of *complecti* to embrace, comprise, fr. com- + plectere to braid] **1 :** composed of two or more parts ⟨a *complex* mixture⟩: as **a :** consisting of a main clause and one or more subordinate clauses ⟨*complex* sentence⟩ **b :** formed by union of simpler substances ⟨a *complex* protein⟩ **2 :** hard to separate, analyze, or solve ⟨a *complex* problem⟩ **3 :** of or relating to complex numbers ⟨*complex* plane⟩ — **com·plex·ly** *adv* — **com·plex·ness** *n*

syn COMPLEX, COMPLICATED, INTRICATE, INVOLVED mean having confusingly interrelated parts. COMPLEX suggests an unavoidable and necessary lack of simplicity and does not imply a fault or failure in designing or arranging; COMPLICATED applies to what offers difficulty in understanding, explaining, or solving; INTRICATE implies an interlacing of parts that can scarcely be grasped or traced separately; INVOLVED implies extreme complication and often suggests disorder

²**com·plex** \'käm-ˌpleks\ *n* **1 :** a whole made up of complicated or interrelated parts **2 a :** a group of culture traits usu. associated with a particular activity or process **b :** a system of repressed desires and memories that exerts a dominating influence upon the personality; *also* **:** an exaggerated reaction to a subject or situation **c :** a group of obviously related units of which the degree and nature of the relationship is imperfectly known **3 :** a complex substance in which the constituents are more intimately associated than in a simple mixture

complex fraction *n* **:** a fraction with a fraction or mixed

number in the numerator or denominator or both — compare SIMPLE FRACTION

com·plex·ion \kəm-'plek-shən\ *n* **1 :** natural disposition **:** TEMPERAMENT **2 :** the hue or appearance of the skin and esp. of the face **3 :** general appearance or impression **:** CHARACTER ⟨information that changes the whole *complexion* of a situation⟩ — **com·plex·ioned** \-shənd\ *adj*

com·plex·i·ty \kəm-'plek-sət-ē, käm-\ *n, pl* -ties **1 :** the quality or state of being complex **2 :** something complex ⟨the *complexities* of the English language⟩

complex number *n* **:** a number (as $3 + 4\sqrt{-1}$) formed by adding a real number to the product of a real number and the square root of minus one

com·pli·ance \kəm-'plī-ən(t)s\ *n* **1 :** the act or process of complying to a desire, demand, or proposal or to coercion **2 :** a readiness or disposition to yield to others — **in compliance with :** in accordance with **:** in obedience to ⟨*in compliance with* rules of etiquette⟩

com·pli·an·cy \-ən-sē\ *n* **:** COMPLIANCE

com·pli·ant \-ənt\ *adj* **:** ready or disposed to comply **:** SUBMISSIVE — **com·pli·ant·ly** *adv*

com·pli·cate \'käm-plə-ˌkāt\ *vb* [L *complicare* to fold together, fr. com- + plicare to fold] **1 :** to combine esp. in an involved or inextricable manner **2 :** to make or become complex, intricate, or difficult

com·pli·cat·ed *adj* **1 :** consisting of parts intricately combined **2 :** difficult to analyze, understand, or explain — syn see COMPLEX — **com·pli·cat·ed·ly** *adv* — **com·pli·cat·ed·ness** *n*

com·pli·ca·tion \ˌkäm-plə-'kā-shən\ *n* **1 a :** a situation or a detail of character complicating the main thread of a plot **b :** a making difficult, involved, or intricate **c :** a complex or intricate feature or element **d :** something that makes a situation more complicated or difficult **2 :** a secondary disease or condition developing in the course of a primary disease

com·plic·i·ty \kəm-'plis-ət-ē\ *n, pl* -ties [LL complic-, *complex*, adj., associate, fr. L com- + plicare to fold] **:** association or participation in a wrongful act

¹**com·pli·ment** \'käm-plə-mənt\ *n* [F, fr. It *complimento*, fr. Sp *cumplimiento*, fr. *cumplir* to comply, be courteous] **1 :** a formal expression of esteem, respect, affection, or admiration; *esp* **:** a flattering remark **2** *pl* **:** best wishes **:** REGARDS syn see COMPLEMENT

²**com·pli·ment** \-ˌment\ *vt* **:** to pay a compliment to

com·pli·men·ta·ry \ˌkäm-plə-'ment-ə-rē, -'men-trē\ *adj* **1 :** expressing or containing a compliment **2 :** given free as a courtesy or favor ⟨*complimentary* ticket⟩ — **com·pli·men·tar·i·ly** \-ˌmen-'ter-ə-lē\ *adv*

com·pline \'käm-plən, -ˌplīn\ *n, often cap* [OF *complie*, modif. of LL *completa*, fr. L *completus* complete] **:** the last of the canonical hours

com·ply \kəm-'plī\ *vi* com·plied; com·ply·ing [It *complire*, fr. Sp *cumplir* to perform what is due, comply, fr. L *complēre* to complete] **:** to conform or adapt one's actions to another's wishes, to a rule, or to necessity ⟨*comply* with a request⟩ — **com·pli·er** \-'plī-(ə)r\ *n*

¹**com·po·nent** \kəm-'pō-nənt, 'käm-ˌ, käm-'\ *n* [L *componere* to put together, fr. com- + ponere to put] **1 a :** a constituent part ⟨the *components* of an electric circuit⟩ **:** INGREDIENT ⟨the *components* of a solution⟩ **2 :** any one of the vector terms added to form a vector sum or resultant syn see ELEMENT — **com·po·nen·tial** \ˌkäm-pə-'nen-chəl\ *adj*

²**component** *adj* **:** being or forming a part **:** CONSTITUENT ⟨the *component* parts of a machine⟩

com·port \kəm-'pōrt, -'pòrt\ *vb* [L *comportare* to bring together, fr. com- + portare to carry] **1 :** ACCORD, SUIT ⟨acts that *comport* with ideals⟩ **2 :** CONDUCT ⟨*comports* himself with dignity⟩

com·port·ment \kəm-'pōrt-mənt, -'pòrt-\ *n* **:** BEHAVIOR, BEARING

com·pose \kəm-'pōz\ *vb* [MF *composer*, irreg. fr. L *componere*, fr. com- + ponere to put] **1 a :** to form by putting together **:** FASHION **b :** to make up **:** CONSTITUTE ⟨a cake *composed* of many ingredients⟩ **c :** to arrange (type) in order for printing **:** SET **2 a :** to create by mental or artistic labor **b :** to compose music for ⟨*compose* a song⟩ **3 :** to reduce to a minimum ⟨*compose* their differences⟩ **4 :** to arrange in proper form **5 :** to free from agitation **:** CALM ⟨try to *compose* their feelings⟩

com·posed \-'pōzd\ *adj* : free from agitation : CALM; *esp* : SELF-POSSESSED — **com·pos·ed·ly** \-'pō-zəd-lē\ *adv* — **com·pos·ed·ness** \-'pō-zəd-nəs\ *n*

com·pos·er \kəm-'pō-zər\ *n* : one that composes; *esp* : a person who writes music

¹**com·pos·ite** \käm-'päz-ət, kəm-\ *adj* [L *compositus*, pp. of *componere* to compose] **1** : made up of various distinct parts or elements : COMPOUNDED ⟨a *composite* photograph⟩ ⟨*composite* racial type⟩ **2** : of or relating to a very large family (Compositae) of dicotyledonous herbs, shrubs, and trees often held to be the most highly evolved plants and characterized by florets arranged in dense heads that resemble single flowers ⟨the daisy and other *composite* plants⟩ — **com·pos·ite·ly** *adv*

²**composite** *n* **1** : something that is made up of different parts : COMPOUND **2** : a composite plant

composite number *n* : a product of two or more whole numbers each greater than 1

com·po·si·tion \,käm-pə-'zish-ən\ *n* **1** : a composing: as **a** : a putting words together to make sentences : the art or practice of writing **b** : the work of a compositor **2** : the manner in which the parts of a thing are put together esp. to form a harmonious whole ⟨a picture famous for its beautiful *composition*⟩; *also* : personal constitution : MAKEUP **3** : the makeup of a compound or mixture ⟨the *composition* of rubber⟩ **4** : mutual settlement or agreement ⟨a *composition* of differences⟩; *also* : something given in settlement **5** : a product of combining various ingredients : COMBINATION ⟨a *composition* made of several different metals⟩ **6** : a literary, musical, or artistic production; *esp* : a short piece of writing done as an educational exercise ⟨must write one *composition* each week⟩ — **com·po·si·tion·al** \-'zish-nəl, -ən-ʰl\ *adj*

com·pos·i·tor \kəm-'päz-ət-ər\ *n* : one who sets type

com·pos men·tis \,käm-pəs-'ment-əs\ *adj* [L, lit., having mastery of one's mind] : of sound mind, memory, and understanding

¹**com·post** \'käm-,pōst\ *n* [ML *compostum*, fr. L, neut. of pp. of *componere* to put together] : a mixture largely of decayed organic matter used for fertilizing and conditioning land

²**compost** *vt* : to convert (as plant debris) to compost

com·po·sure \kəm-'pō-zhər\ *n* : calmness or repose esp. of mind, bearing, or appearance : SELF-POSSESSION

com·pote \'käm-,pōt\ *n* [F, fr. OF *composte*, fr. L *composta*, fem. of pp. of *componere* to compose] **1** : fruits cooked in syrup **2** : a bowl of glass, porcelain, or metal usu. with a base and stem and sometimes a cover from which compotes, fruits, nuts, or sweets are served

¹**com·pound** \käm-'paůnd, kəm-', 'käm-,\ *vb* [MF *compondre*, fr. L *componere* to compose] **1** : to put together or be joined to form a whole : COMBINE **2** : to form by combining parts ⟨*compound* a medicine⟩ **3** : to settle peaceably : COMPROMISE **4 a** : to increase by geometric progression or by an increment that itself increases ⟨*compound* interest quarterly⟩ **b** : to add to **5** : to agree for a consideration not to prosecute (an offense) ⟨*compound* a felony⟩ — **com·pound·a·ble** \-ə-bəl\ *adj* — **com·pound·er** *n*

²**com·pound** \'käm-,paůnd, käm-', kəm-'\ *adj* **1** : composed of or resulting from union of separate elements, ingredients, or parts ⟨a *compound* substance⟩; *also* : composed of united similar elements esp. of a kind usu. independent ⟨*compound* fruit⟩ **2** : involving or used in a combination : COMPOSITE **3 a** : being a word that is a compound ⟨the *compound* noun *steamboat*⟩ **b** : consisting of two or more main clauses ⟨*compound* sentence⟩

³**com·pound** \'käm-,paůnd\ *n* **1 a** : a word consisting of components that are words ⟨*rowboat, high school*, and *light-year* are *compounds*⟩ **b** : a word consisting of any of various combinations of words, word elements, or affixes ⟨*anthropology, kilocycle*, and *builder* are *compounds*⟩ **2** : something formed by a union of elements, ingredients, or parts; *esp* : a distinct substance formed by the union of two or more chemical elements in definite proportion by weight

⁴**com·pound** \'käm-,paůnd\ *n* [Malay *kampong* group of

buildings, village] **1** : an enclosure of European residences and commercial buildings esp. in the Orient **2** : a large fenced or walled-in area

compound–complex *adj* : having two or more main clauses and one or more subordinate clauses ⟨*compound-complex* sentence⟩

compound eye *n* : an eye (as of an insect) made up of many separate visual units — compare MOSAIC VISION

compound fracture *n* : a breaking of a bone in such a way as to produce an open wound through which bone fragments stick out

compound interest *n* : interest paid or to be paid both on the principal and on accumulated unpaid interest

compound leaf *n* : a leaf in which the blade is divided to the midrib forming two or more leaflets on a common axis

compound microscope *n* : a microscope consisting of an objective and an eyepiece mounted in a drawtube

com·pre·hend \,käm-pri-'hend\ *vt* [L *comprehens-, comprehendere*, fr. *com-* + *prehendere* to grasp] **1** : to grasp the meaning of mentally **2** : to take in : EMBRACE see INCLUDE — **com·pre·hend·i·ble** \-'hen-də-bəl\ *adj*

com·pre·hen·si·ble \-'hen(t)-sə-bəl\ *adj* : capable of being comprehended : INTELLIGIBLE — **com·pre·hen·si·bil·i·ty** \-,hen(t)-sə-'bil-ət-ē\ *n* — **com·pre·hen·si·bly** \-'hen(t)-sə-blē\ *adv*

com·pre·hen·sion \,käm-pri-'hen-chən\ *n* **1 a** : the act or process of including or comprising **b** : COMPREHENSIVENESS **2 a** : the act or action of grasping with the intellect **b** : knowledge gained by comprehending **c** : the capacity for understanding

com·pre·hen·sive \-'hen(t)-siv\ *adj* **1** : covering largely or completely : INCLUSIVE ⟨*comprehensive* insurance⟩ ⟨a *comprehensive* examination⟩ **2** : having wide mental comprehension — **com·pre·hen·sive·ly** *adv* — **com·pre·hen·sive·ness** *n*

¹**com·press** \kəm-'pres\ *vb* [L *compress-, comprimere*, fr. *com-* + *premere* to press] : to press or become pressed together : reduce the volume of by pressure syn see CONDENSE

²**com·press** \'käm-,pres\ *n* **1** : a folded cloth or pad applied so as to press upon a body part ⟨a cold *compress*⟩ **2** : a machine for compressing cotton into bales

com·pressed \kəm-'prest, 'käm-,\ *adj* : flattened as though subjected to compression: **a** : flattened laterally ⟨petioles *compressed*⟩ **b** : narrow from side to side and deep in a dorsoventral direction

compressed air *n* : air under pressure greater than that of the atmosphere

com·press·i·ble \kəm-'pres-ə-bəl\ *adj* : capable of being compressed — **com·press·i·bil·i·ty** \-,pres-ə-'bil-ət-ē\ *n*

com·pres·sion \kəm-'presh-ən\ *n* **1** : the act or process of compressing : the state of being compressed **2** : the process of compressing the fuel mixture in the cylinders of an internal-combustion engine (as of an automobile) — **com·pres·sion·al** \-'presh-nəl, -ən-ʰl\ *adj*

com·pres·sive \kəm-'pres-iv\ *adj* : of or relating to compression

com·pres·sor \-'pres-ər\ *n* **1** : one that compresses **2** : a machine that compresses gases and esp. air

com·prise \kəm-'prīz\ *vt* [MF *compris*, pp. of *comprendre*, fr. L *comprehendere*] **1** : to include esp. within a particular scope : CONTAIN **2** : to be made up of **3** : to make up : CONSTITUTE

syn COMPRISE, INCLUDE mean to take in or embrace within one unit or boundary. COMPRISE implies that the list of parts or members is complete ⟨New York City *comprises* the boroughs Manhattan, Brooklyn, Queens, Richmond, and the Bronx⟩ INCLUDE does not imply that other constituent members are presently specified ⟨the United States now *includes* Alaska and Hawaii⟩

¹**com·pro·mise** \'käm-prə-,mīz\ *n* [MF *compromis*, fr. L *compromissum*, fr. neut. of pp. of *compromittere* to promise mutually, fr. *com-* + *promittere* to promise] **1** : a settlement of a dispute by mutual concessions : a giving up to something objectionable or dangerous : SURRENDER ⟨a *compromise* of one's principles⟩ **3** : the thing agreed upon as a result of concessions ⟨Missouri *Compromise*⟩

²**compromise** *vb* **1** : to adjust or settle differences by mutual concessions **2** : to expose to discredit, suspicion, or danger **3** : to make unworthy concessions — **com·pro·mis·er** *n*

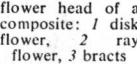

flower head of a composite: *1* disk flower, *2* ray flower, *3* bracts

comp·trol·ler \kən-'trō-lər, 'käm(p)-,\ *n* : a public official who audits government accounts and sometimes certifies expenditures — **comp·trol·ler·ship** \-,ship\ *n*

com·pul·sion \kəm-'pəl-shən\ *n* [L *compuls-*, *compellere* to compel] **1 a** : an act of compelling : the state of being compelled **b** : a force or agency that compels **2** : an irresistible impulse to perform an irrational act

com·pul·sive \-'pəl-siv\ *adj* **1** : having power to compel **2** : of, relating to, or caused by psychological compulsion — **com·pul·sive·ly** *adv* — **com·pul·sive·ness** *n*

com·pul·so·ry \-'pəls-(ə-)rē\ *adj* **1** : ENFORCED, REQUIRED **2** : having the power of compelling

com·punc·tion \kəm-'pəŋ(k)-shən\ *n* [L *compunct-*, *compungere* to prick hard, fr. *com-* + *pungere* to prick] **1** : sharp uneasiness caused by a sense of guilt : REMORSE **2** : a passing feeling of regret for some slight wrong **syn** see QUALM — **com·punc·tious** \-shəs\ *adj*

com·pu·ta·tion \,käm-pyu-'tā-shən\ *n* **1** : the act or action of computing : CALCULATION **2** : a system of reckoning **3** : an amount computed — **com·pu·ta·tion·al** \-shnəl, -shən-ᵊl\ *adj*

com·pute \kəm-'pyüt\ *vb* [L *computare*, fr. *com-* + *putare* to consider] : to determine or calculate esp. by mathematical means — **com·put·a·ble** \-'pyüt-ə-bəl\ *adj*

com·put·er \-'pyüt-ər\ *n* : one that computes; *esp* : an automatic electronic machine for performing calculations

com·put·er·ize \-ə-,rīz\ *vt* **1** : to carry out, control, or conduct by means of a computer **2** : to equip with computers — **com·put·er·iza·tion** \-,pyüt-ə-rə-'zā-shən\ *n*

com·rade \'käm-,rad, -rəd\ *n* [MF *camarade* group of roommates, companion, fr. Sp *camarada*, fr. *cámara* room, fr. L *camera*] **1 a** : an intimate friend or associate : COMPANION **b** : a fellow soldier **2** [fr. its use as a form of address by Communists] : COMMUNIST

com·rade·ship \-,ship\ *n* : association as comrades : FELLOWSHIP, FRIENDSHIP

¹con \'kän\ *vt* **conned**; **con·ning** [ME *connen* to know, study, alter. of *cunnen* to know, infin. of *can*] **1** : to study or examine closely : PERUSE **2** : to commit to memory

²con *adv* [ME, short for *contra*] : on the negative side : in opposition

³con *n* **1** : an argument or evidence in opposition **2** : the negative position or one holding it

⁴con *vt* **conned**; **con·ning** **1** : SWINDLE **2** : CAJOLE

⁵con *n* [short for *consumption*] *slang* : a destructive disease of the lungs; *esp* : TUBERCULOSIS

con- — see COM-

con amo·re \,kän-ə-'mōr-ē, ,kō-nə-\ *adv* [It] **1** : with love, devotion, or zest **2** : TENDERLY — used as a direction in music

con·cat·e·nate \kän-'kat-ə-,nāt\ *vt* : to link together in a series or chain — **con·cat·e·na·tion** \(,)kän-,kat-ə-'nā-shən\ *n*

con·cave \kän-'kāv, 'kän-,\ *adj* [L *concavus*, fr. *com-* + *cavus* hollow] : hollowed or rounded inward like the inside of a bowl — **con·cave·ly** *adv* — **con·cave·ness** *n*

con·cav·i·ty \kän-'kav-ət-ē\ *n*, *pl* **-ties** **1** : a concave surface or space : HOLLOW **2** : the quality or state of being concave

con·cavo–con·vex \kän-,kā-vō-\ *adj* **1** : concave on one side and convex on the other **2** : having the concave side of greater curvature than the convex

con·ceal \kən-'sēl\ *vt* [L *concelare*, fr. *com-* + *celare* to hide] **1** : to hide from sight **2** : to keep secret — **con·ceal·a·ble** \-ə-bəl\ *adj*

con·ceal·ment \-mənt\ *n* **1** : the act of hiding : the state of being hidden **2** : a hiding place

con·cede \kən-'sēd\ *vb* [L *concedere*, fr. *com-* + *cedere* to cede] **1** : to grant as a right or privilege **2** : to acknowledge or admit grudgingly : YIELD **syn** see GRANT — **con·ced·ed·ly** \-'sēd-əd-lē\ *adv* — **con·ced·er** *n*

¹con·ceit \kən-'sēt\ *n* [ME, judgment, fr. *conceiven* to conceive] **1** : excessive appreciation of one's own worth or virtue **2 a** : a fanciful idea **b** : an elaborate metaphor

²conceit *vt*, *obs* : CONCEIVE, IMAGINE

con·ceit·ed \-'sēt-əd\ *adj* : having an excessively high opinion of oneself — **con·ceit·ed·ly** *adv* — **con·ceit·ed·ness** *n*

con·ceiv·a·ble \kən-'sē-və-bəl\ *adj* : capable of being conceived : IMAGINABLE — **con·ceiv·a·bly** \-blē\ *adv*

con·ceive \kən-'sēv\ *vb* [ME *conceiven*, fr. OF *conceivre*, fr. L *concipere*, fr. *com-* + *capere* to take] **1** : to become pregnant ⟨unable to *conceive*⟩ ⟨*conceived* a son⟩ **2 a** : to take into the mind ⟨*conceived* a liking for the man⟩ ⟨*conceive* a prejudice⟩ **b** : to form an idea of : IMAGINE ⟨*conceive* a new system⟩ **3** : to have an opinion : THINK ⟨*conceived* of him as a genius⟩ — **con·ceiv·er** *n*

¹con·cen·trate \'kän(t)-sən-,trāt\ *vb* [L *com-* + *centrum* center] **1 a** : to bring or direct toward a common center or objective **b** : to gather into one body, mass, or force **2** : to make stronger by removing the diluting or admixing material ⟨*concentrate* syrup⟩ ⟨*concentrate* ore⟩ **3** : to draw toward or meet in a common center **4** : to fix one's powers, efforts, or attention on one thing ⟨*concentrate* on a problem⟩ **syn** see CONDENSE — **con·cen·tra·tor** \-,trāt-ər\ *n*

²concentrate *n* : something concentrated

con·cen·tra·tion \,kän(t)-sən-'trā-shən\ *n* **1** : the act or process of concentrating : the state of being concentrated; *esp* : direction of attention on a single object **2** : a concentrated mass **3** : the relative content of a component : STRENGTH ⟨the *concentration* of salt in a solution⟩

concentration camp *n* : a camp where persons (as prisoners of war, political prisoners, or refugees) are detained or confined

con·cen·tric \kən-'sen-trik, (')kän-\ *adj* [L *com-* + *centrum* center] **1** : having a common center ⟨*concentric* circles⟩ **2** : COAXIAL — **con·cen·tri·cal·ly** \-tri-k(ə-)lē\ *adv* — **con·cen·tric·i·ty** \,kän-,sen-'tris-ət-ē\ *n*

con·cept \'kän-,sept\ *n* [L *conceptum*, neut. of pp. of *concipere* to conceive] **1** : something conceived in the mind : THOUGHT, NOTION **2** : an abstract idea generalized from particular instances **syn** see IDEA

con·cep·ta·cle \kən-'sep-ti-kəl\ *n* : an external cavity containing reproductive cells in some algae

con·cep·tion \kən-'sep-shən\ *n* **1 a** (1) : the act of becoming pregnant (2) : the state of being brought into being as an embryo (3) : EMBRYO, FETUS **b** : BEGINNING **2 a** : the function or process of forming or understanding ideas or abstractions or their symbols **b** : a general idea : CONCEPT **3** : the originating of something in the mind **syn** see IDEA — **con·cep·tion·al** \-shnəl, -shən-ᵊl\ *adj* — **con·cep·tive** \-'sep-tiv\ *adj*

con·cep·tu·al \kən-'sep-chə(-wə)l\ *adj* : of, relating to, or consisting of concepts — **con·cep·tu·al·ly** \-ē\ *adv*

¹con·cern \kən-'sərn\ *vt* [ML *concernere*, fr. LL, to sift together, fr. L *com-* + *cernere* to sift, distinguish] **1** : to relate to : be about ⟨the novel *concerns* three soldiers⟩ **2** : to be the business or affair of : AFFECT ⟨the problem *concerns* us all⟩ **3** : to be a care, trouble, or distress to ⟨his mother's illness *concerns* him⟩ **4** : ENGAGE, OCCUPY ⟨*concerned* himself in the matter⟩

²concern *n* **1** : something that relates to or involves one : AFFAIR ⟨the usual *concerns* of the day⟩ **2 a** : marked regard or care usu. arising through a personal tie or relationship ⟨showed deep *concern* for his friend's welfare⟩ **b** : a state of uncertainty and apprehension ⟨public *concern* over the war danger⟩ **3** : a business or manufacturing establishment

con·cerned \-'sərnd\ *adj* : DISTURBED, ANXIOUS ⟨*concerned* for his health⟩

con·cern·ing \-'sər-niŋ\ *prep* : relating to ⟨news *concerning* friends⟩

con·cern·ment \-'sərn-mənt\ *n* **1** : something in which one is concerned **2** : IMPORTANCE, CONSEQUENCE

¹con·cert \kən-'sərt\ *vb* [LL *concertare*, fr. L, to contend, fr. *com-* + *certare* to strive] : to plan or arrange together : settle by agreement ⟨the allies *concerted* their tactics⟩

²con·cert \'kän(t)-(,)sərt\ *n* **1** : agreement in design or plan ⟨work in *concert*⟩ **2** : musical harmony : CONCORD **3** : a musical performance of some length by several voices or instruments or both

con·cert·ed \kən-'sərt-əd\ *adj* **1 a** : mutually contrived or agreed ⟨*concerted* effort⟩ **b** : performed in unison ⟨*concerted* artillery fire⟩ **2** : arranged in parts for several voices ⟨*concerted* music⟩

con·cer·ti·na \,kän(t)-sər-'tē-nə\ *n* : a musical instrument of the accordion family

concertina

con·cer·ti·no \,kän-chər-'tē-nō\ *n, pl* **-nos** : a little concerto

con·cert·mas·ter \'kän(t)-sərt-,mas-tər\ *or* **con·cert·meis·ter** \-,mī-stər\ *n* : the leader of the first violins and assistant conductor

con·cer·to \kən-'chert-ō\ *n, pl* **-tos** *or* **-ti** \-(,)ē\ [It, fr. *concerto* concert] : a piece for one or more soloists and orchestra usu. in symphonic form with three contrasting movements

concerto gros·so \kən-,chert-ō-'grō-sō\ *n, pl* **concerti gros·si** \-,chert-ē-'grō-(,)sē\ [It, lit., big concerto] : a baroque orchestral composition with a small group of solo instruments contrasting with the full orchestra

con·ces·sion \kən-'sesh-ən\ *n* [L *concess-, concedere* to concede] **1** : the act or an instance of conceding **2** : something conceded: **a** : ACKNOWLEDGMENT, ADMISSION **b** : a grant of property or of a right by a government ⟨mining *concession*⟩ **c** : a lease of a part of premises for some purpose ⟨a soft-drink *concession*⟩; *also* : the part leased or the activities carried on

con·ces·sion·aire \kən-,sesh-ə-'na(ə)r, -'ne(ə)r\ *n* : the recipient or operator of a concession

con·ces·sive \kən-'ses-iv\ *adj* : tending toward, expressing, or being a concession — **con·ces·sive·ly** *adv*

conch \'käŋk, 'känch\ *n, pl* **conchs** \'käŋks\ *or* **conch·es** \'kän-chəz\ [L *concha* mussel, mussel shell, fr. Gk *konchē*] **1** : a large spiral-shelled marine gastropod mollusk; *also* : its shell used esp. for cameos **2** : CONCHA

con·cha \'käŋ-kə\ *n, pl* **con·chae** \-,kē, -,kī\ [L, shell] : the largest and deepest concavity of the external ear

con·chol·o·gy \käŋ-'käl-ə-jē\ *n* : a branch of zoology that deals with shells

con·cierge \kōⁿ-'syerzh\ *n* [F, modif. of L *conservus* fellow slave, fr. *com- + servus* slave] : an attendant at the entrance of a building esp. in France who oversees ingress and egress, handles mail, and acts as a janitor or porter

conch

con·cil·i·ate \kən-'sil-ē-,āt\ *vt* [L *conciliare* to assemble, unite, win over, fr. *concilium* assembly, council] **1** : to bring into agreement or compatibility : RECONCILE **2** : to gain the goodwill or favor of ⟨*conciliate* the opposition⟩ — con·cil·i·a·tion \-,sil-ē-'ā-shən\ *n* — **con·cil·i·a·tor** \-'sil-ē-,āt-ər\ *n* — **con·cil·i·a·to·ry** \-'sil-yə-,tōr-ē, -'sil-ē-ə-, -,tor-\ *adj*

con·cise \kən-'sīs\ *adj* [L *concisus*, fr. pp. of *concidere* to cut up, fr. *com- + caedere* to cut] : marked by brevity and compactness of expression or statement ⟨a *concise* review of the year's work⟩ — **con·cise·ly** *adv* — **con·cise·ness** *n*

con·clave \'kän-,klāv\ *n* [ML, fr. L, room that can be locked up, fr. *com- + clavis* key] **1** : a private meeting or secret assembly; *esp* : a meeting of Roman Catholic cardinals secluded continuously while choosing a pope **2** : ASSEMBLY, CONVENTION — **con·clav·ist** \-,klā-vəst\ *n*

con·clude \kən-'klüd\ *vb* [L *conclus-, concludere* to shut up, end, infer, fr. *com- + claudere* to shut] **1** : to bring or come to an end : FINISH ⟨*conclude* a speech⟩⟨*conclude* with a word of warning⟩ **2** : to form an opinion : decide by reasoning ⟨*conclude* that a statement is true⟩ **3** : to bring about as a result : ARRANGE ⟨*conclude* an agreement⟩ **syn** see CLOSE — **con·clud·er** *n*

con·clu·sion \kən-'klü-zhən\ *n* **1 a** : a reasoned judgment : INFERENCE **b** : the necessary consequence of two or more propositions taken as premises **2** : TERMINATION, END: AS **a** : RESULT, OUTCOME **b** : a final summing up **3** : an act or instance of concluding

con·clu·sive \kən-'klü-siv, -ziv\ *adj* : DECISIVE, CONVINCING, FINAL ⟨*conclusive* proof⟩ — **con·clu·sive·ly** *adv* — **con·clu·sive·ness** *n*

con·coct \kən-'käkt, kän-\ *vt* [L *concoct-, concoquere* to cook together, fr. *com- + coquere* to cook] **1** : to prepare by combining various ingredients ⟨*concocted* a strange dish⟩ **2** : DEVISE, FABRICATE ⟨*concocts* a likely story⟩ — **con·coct·er** *n* — **con·coc·tion** \-'käk-shən\ *n* — **con·coc·tive** \-'käk-tiv\ *adj*

con·com·i·tant \kən-'käm-ət-ənt, kän-\ *adj* [L *concomitari* to accompany, fr. *com- + comit-, comes* companion] : accompanying esp. in a subordinate or incidental way — **concomitant** *n* — **con·com·i·tant·ly** *adv*

con·cord \'kän-,kord, 'käŋ-\ *n* [L *concordia*, fr. *com- + cord-, cor* heart] **1 a** : a state of agreement : HARMONY **b** : a harmonious combination of tones simultaneously heard **2** : agreement by covenant or treaty

con·cord·ance \kən-'kord-ⁿ(t)s\ *n* **1** : an alphabetical index of the principal words in a book or in the works of an author with their immediate contexts **2** : CONCORD, AGREEMENT

con·cord·ant \-ⁿnt\ *adj* : AGREEING, CONSONANT — **con·cord·ant·ly** *adv*

con·cor·dat \kən-'kor-,dat\ *n* : COMPACT, COVENANT; *esp* : an agreement between a pope and a government about church affairs

con·course \'kän-,kōrs, -,kors\ *n* [MF *concours*, fr. L *concursus*, fr. *concurs-, concurrere* to run together, concur] **1** : a flocking together : GATHERING ⟨a great *concourse* of people⟩ **2** : a place (as a boulevard, open area, or hall) where many people pass or congregate ⟨met in the *concourse* of the bus terminal⟩

con·cres·cence \kən-'kres-ⁿ(t)s, kän-\ *n* : a growing together : COALESCENCE — **con·cres·cent** \-ⁿnt\ *adj*

¹con·crete \'kän-,krēt, 'kän-, \ *adj* [L *concretus*, fr. pp. of *concrescere* to grow together, fr. *com- + crescere* to grow] **1** : naming a real thing or class of things : not abstract ⟨a *concrete* noun⟩ **2 a** : belonging to or derived from actual experience ⟨*concrete* examples⟩ **b** : REAL, TANGIBLE ⟨*concrete* evidence⟩ **3** \'kän-,, kän-'\ : relating to or made of concrete ⟨*concrete* mixer⟩ ⟨*concrete* bridge abutments⟩ — **con·crete·ly** *adv* — **con·crete·ness** *n*

²con·crete \'kän-,krēt, kän-'\ *n* : a hard strong building material made by mixing cement, sand, and gravel or broken rock with sufficient water to cause the cement to set and bind the entire mass

³con·crete \'kän-,krēt, kän-'\ *vb* **1** : to form into a solid mass : SOLIDIFY **2** : to cover with, form of, or set in concrete

con·cre·tion \kän-'krē-shən\ *n* **1** : the act or process of concreting or solidifying **2** : something concreted; *esp* : a hard usu. inorganic mass formed in a living body — **con·cre·tion·ary** \-shə-,ner-ē\ *adj*

con·cu·bine \'käŋ-kyə-,bīn, 'kän-\ *n* [L *concubina*, fr. *com- + cubare* to lie] : a woman who lives with a man and among some peoples has a legally recognized position in his household less than that of a wife — **con·cu·bi·nage** \kän-'kyü-bə-nij\ *n*

con·cu·pis·cence \kän-'kyü-pə-sən(t)s\ *n* [L *concupiscere* to desire ardently, fr. *com- + cupere* to desire] : ardent desire; *esp* : sexual desire : LUST — **con·cu·pis·cent** \-sənt\ *adj*

con·cur \kən-'kər\ *vi* **con·curred; con·cur·ring** [L *concurrere*, fr. *com- + currere* to run] **1** : to happen together : COINCIDE **2** : to act together to a common end or single effect ⟨several mishaps *concurred* to spoil the occasion⟩ **3** : to be in agreement : ACCORD ⟨four justices *concurred* in the decision⟩

con·cur·rence \kən-'kər-ən(t)s, -'kə-rən(t)s\ *n* **1 a** : agreement in action, opinion, or intent : COOPERATION **b** : CONSENT **2** : a coming together : CONJUNCTION

con·cur·rent \-'kər-ənt, -'kə-rənt\ *adj* **1 a** : CONVERGING **b** : running parallel **2** : operating at the same time ⟨*current* expeditions to the Antarctic⟩ **3** : acting in conjunction **4** : exercised over the same matter or area by two different authorities ⟨*concurrent* jurisdiction⟩ **syn** see CONTEMPORARY — **concurrent** *n* — **con·cur·rent·ly** *adv*

concurrent resolution *n* : a resolution passed by both houses of a legislative body that lacks the force of law

con·cuss \kən-'kəs\ *vt* : to affect with concussion

con·cus·sion \kən-'kəsh-ən\ *n* [L *concuss-, concutere* to shake violently, fr. *com- + quatere* to shake] **1** : SHAKING, AGITATION **2** : a smart or hard blow or collision **3** : bodily injury esp. of the brain resulting from a sudden sharp jar (as from a blow) — **con·cus·sive** \-'kəs-iv\ *adj*

con·demn \kən-'dem\ *vt* [L *condemnare*, fr. *com- + damnare* to damn] **1** : to declare to be wrong : CENSURE **2 a** : to pronounce guilty : CONVICT **b** : SENTENCE **3** : to adjudge unfit for use or consumption **4** : to take for public use under the right of eminent domain **syn** see BLAME — **con·demn·a·ble** \-'dem-(n)ə-bəl\ *adj* — **con·demn·er** *or* **con·demn·or** \-'dem-ər\ *n*

con·dem·na·tion \,kän-,dem-'nā-shən, -dəm-\ *n* **1** : CENSURE, BLAME **2** : the act of judicially condemning **3** : the state of being condemned — **con·dem·na·to·ry** \kən-'dem-nə-ˌtōr-ē, -ˌtor-\ adj

con·den·sa·tion \ˌkän-ˌden-'sā-shən, -dən-\ n **1** : the act or process of condensing **2** : a chemical reaction involving union between atoms in the same or different molecules often with elimination of a simple molecule (as water) to form a new and more complex compound **3** : the quality or state of being condensed **4** : a product of condensing; esp : an abridgment of a literary work — **con·den·sa·tion·al** \-shnəl, -shən-ᵊl\ adj

con·dense \kən-'den(t)s\ vb [L condensare, fr. com- + densus dense] **1** : to make or become more close, compact, concise, or dense : CONCENTRATE, COMPRESS ⟨condense a paragraph into a sentence⟩ **2** : to change from a less dense to a denser form ⟨steam condenses into water⟩ **3** : to subject to or undergo condensation ⟨a chemical that condenses to form a plastic⟩

syn CONDENSE, CONCENTRATE, COMPRESS mean to decrease in bulk or volume. CONDENSE implies reduction to greater compactness usu. of material all of the same kind ⟨condense gas into liquid⟩ CONCENTRATE implies reduction either by massing about a single point ⟨concentrate rifle fire⟩ or by removing all except essential elements ⟨concentrate an acid solution⟩ COMPRESS implies reduction by pressure from without ⟨compress a bale of cotton⟩

condensed milk n : evaporated milk with sugar added

con·dens·er \kən-'den(t)-sər\ n **1** : one that condenses; esp : an apparatus in which gas or vapor is condensed **2** : CAPACITOR

con·de·scend \ˌkän-di-'send\ vi [LL condescendere, fr. L com- + descendere to descend] **1** : to descend in manner or behavior to a level considered less dignified or humbler than one's own **2** : to grant favors with a superior air syn see STOOP

con·de·scend·ing adj : showing or characterized by condescension : PATRONIZING — **con·de·scend·ing·ly** \-'sen-diŋ-lē\ adv

con·de·scen·sion \ˌkän-di-'sen-chən\ n : a patronizing attitude

con·dign \kən-'dīn, 'kän-ˌ\ adj [L condignus very worthy, fr. com- + dignus worthy] : DESERVED, APPROPRIATE ⟨condign punishment⟩ — **con·dign·ly** adv

con·di·ment \'kän-də-mənt\ n [L condire to pickle, season] : something used to give an appetizing taste to food; esp : a pungent seasoning

¹con·di·tion \kən-'dish-ən\ n [L condicion-, condicio terms of agreement, condition, fr. condicere to agree, fr. com- + dicere to say] **1** : a provision upon which the fulfillment of an agreement depends : STIPULATION ⟨conditions of employment⟩ **2** : something essential to another : PREREQUISITE **3 a** : a restricting factor : QUALIFICATION **b** : an unsatisfactory academic grade that may be raised by doing additional work **4 a** : a state of being **b** : social status : RANK **c** pl : attendant circumstances **5** : state of health or fitness

²condition vt **-di·tioned**; **-di·tion·ing** \-'dish-(ə-)niŋ\ **1** : to put into a proper or desired condition **2** : to give a conditional grade to **3** : to adapt, modify, or mold to respond in a particular way — **con·di·tion·er** \-'dish-(ə-)nər\ n

con·di·tion·al \kən-'dish-nəl, -ən-ᵊl\ adj **1** : subject to, implying, or dependent upon a condition ⟨a conditional sale⟩ **2** : expressing, containing, or implying a supposition ⟨conditional clause⟩ — **con·di·tion·al·ly** \-ē\ adv

con·di·tioned adj **1** : CONDITIONAL **2** : brought or put into a specified state **3** : determined or established by conditioning ⟨a conditioned response to a stimulus⟩

conditioned reflex n : a learned reflex reaction caused by repeated exposure to one stimulus in association with another for which the first comes to be a substitute ⟨a flow of saliva occurring in a dog when a bell is rung after the dog has learned to associate the sound with food is a classic conditioned reflex⟩

con·dole \kən-'dōl\ vi [LL condolēre to suffer with, fr. L com- + dolēre to feel pain] : to express sympathetic sorrow ⟨condole with a widow in her grief⟩

con·do·lence \kən-'dō-lən(t)s, 'kän-də-\ n : expression of sympathy with another in sorrow or grief ⟨sent our condolences to the family⟩

con·do·min·i·um \ˌkän-də-'min-ē-əm\ n [L com- + dominium domain] **1** : joint sovereignty by two or more

nations **2** : a politically dependent territory under condominium **3** : individual ownership of a unit in a multi-unit structure (as an apartment building); also : a unit so owned

con·done \kən-'dōn\ vt [L condonare, fr. com- + donare to give] : to pardon or overlook voluntarily ⟨condones his friend's faults⟩ syn see EXCUSE — **con·do·na·tion** \ˌkän-dō-'nā-shən, -də-\ n — **con·don·er** \kən-'dō-nər\ n

con·dor \'kän-dər, -ˌdor\ n [Sp cóndor, fr. Quechua kúntur] : a very large American vulture having the head and neck bare and the plumage dull black with a downy white neck ruff

con·duce \kən-'d(y)üs\ vi [L conducere, fr. com- + ducere to lead] : to lead or tend to a usu. desirable result

con·du·cive \kən-'d(y)ü-siv\ adj : tending to promote or aid : CONTRIBUTING ⟨action conducive to success⟩ — **con·du·cive·ness** n

¹con·duct \'kän-(ˌ)dəkt\ n [ML conductus act of leading, fr. L conduct-, conducere to conduct, conduce] **1** : the act, manner, or process of carrying on : MANAGEMENT ⟨the conduct of foreign affairs⟩ **2** : personal behavior ⟨marked down for bad conduct⟩

²con·duct \kən-'dəkt\ vb **1** : GUIDE, ESCORT **2** : LEAD, DIRECT ⟨conduct a business⟩ **3 a** : to convey in a channel **b** : to act as a medium for conveying ⟨copper conducts electricity⟩ **4** : BEHAVE ⟨conducted himself well at the party⟩ **5** : to act as leader or director **6** : to have the quality of transmitting light, heat, sound, or electricity — **con·duct·i·bil·i·ty** \-ˌdək-tə-'bil-ət-ē\ n — **con·duct·i·ble** \-'dək-tə-bəl\ adj

syn MANAGE, CONTROL, DIRECT: CONDUCT implies guiding or leading in person ⟨conduct an orchestra⟩ ⟨selected to conduct negotiations⟩ MANAGE implies handling of details and maneuvering toward a desired result; CONTROL implies a regulating or restraining so as to keep on a desired course; DIRECT implies constant guidance and suggests the issuance of orders ⟨direct a campaign⟩

con·duct·ance \kən-'dək-tən(t)s\ n **1** : conducting power **2** : the readiness with which a conductor transmits an electric current : the reciprocal of electrical resistance

con·duc·tion \kən-'dək-shən\ n **1** : the act of conducting or conveying **2** : transmission through a conductor; also : CONDUCTIVITY **3** : the transmission of excitation through living and esp. nervous tissue

con·duc·tive \kən-'dək-tiv\ adj : having conductivity

con·duc·tiv·i·ty \ˌkän-ˌdək-'tiv-ət-ē\ n, pl **-ties** : the quality or power of conducting or transmitting

con·duc·tor \kən-'dək-tər\ n : one that conducts: as **a** : a person in charge of a public conveyance (as a bus or railroad train) **b** : the leader of a musical ensemble **c** : a substance or body capable of transmitting electricity, heat, or sound — **con·duc·to·ri·al** \ˌkän-ˌdək-'tōr-ē-əl, -'tor-\ adj — **con·duc·tress** \kən-'dək-trəs\ n

con·duit \'kän-ˌd(y)ü-ət, -dət\ n [MF, fr. ML conductus act of leading] **1** : a natural or artificial channel through which water or other fluid is conveyed **2** archaic : FOUNTAIN **3** : a pipe, tube, or tile for protecting electric wires or cables

con·du·pli·cate \(')kän-'d(y)ü-pli-kət\ adj : folded lengthwise ⟨conduplicate leaves⟩ — **con·du·pli·ca·tion** \ˌkän-ˌd(y)ü-pli-'kā-shən\ n

con·dy·larth \'kän-də-ˌlärth\ n : any of an order (Condylarthra) of primitive extinct ungulate mammals

con·dyle \'kän-ˌdīl, -dᵊl\ n [L condylus knuckle, fr. Gk kondylos] : an articular prominence on a bone; esp : one of a pair like knuckles — **con·dy·lar** \-də-lər\ adj — **con·dy·loid** \-də-ˌloid\ adj

cone \'kōn\ n [Gk kōnos] **1** : a mass of overlapping woody scales that esp. in trees of the pine family are arranged on an axis and bear seeds between them; also : any of several flower or fruit clusters resembling such cones **2 a** : a solid generated by rotating a right triangle about one of its legs — called also right circular cone **b** : a solid figure tapering evenly to a point from a circular base **3** : something that resembles a cone in shape: as **a** : a sensory end organ of the retina usu. held to function in color vision **b** : an ice-cream holder

cone 2b

cone·nose \'kōn-ˌnōz\ n : any of various large blood-sucking bugs

Con·es·to·ga \ˌkän-ə-'stō-gə\ n [fr. *Conestoga,* Pa.] : a broad-wheeled covered wagon usu. drawn by six horses and formerly used esp. for transporting freight across the prairies — called also *Conestoga wagon*

co·ney \'kō-nē\ n [OF *conil,* fr. L *cuniculus*] **1 a** (1) : RABBIT; *esp* : the common European rabbit (2) : PIKA **b** : HYRAX **c** : rabbit fur **2** : any of several fishes; *esp* : a dusky reddish-finned grouper of the tropical Atlantic

con·fab \kən-'fab, 'kän-,\ vi **con·fabbed; con·fab·bing** : CONFABULATE — **con·fab** \'kän-,fab, kən-'\ n

con·fab·u·late \kən-'fab-yə-,lāt\ vi [L *confabulari,* fr. *com-* + *fabula* story] **1** : CHAT **2** : POWWOW — **con·fab·u·la·tion** \-,fab-yə-'lā-shən\ n — **con·fab·u·la·tor** \-'fab-yə-,lāt-ər\ n

con·fect \kən-'fekt\ vt : CONCOCT, COMPOUND

con·fec·tion \kən-'fek-shən\ n [L *confect-, conficere* to prepare, fr. *com-* + *facere* to make] **1** : the act or process of confecting **2** : something confected: as **a** : a fancy dish or sweetmeat **b** : a piece of fine craftsmanship

con·fec·tion·er \-sh(ə-)nər\ n : a manufacturer of or dealer in confections

con·fec·tion·ery \-shə-,ner-ē\ n, pl **-er·ies 1** : sweet edibles (as candy) **2** : the confectioner's art or business **3** : a confectioner's shop

con·fed·er·a·cy \kən-'fed-(ə-)rə-sē\ n, pl **-cies 1** : a loose league of persons, parties, or states : ALLIANCE, CONFEDERATION **2** : a group united in a league; *esp, cap* : the Confederate States of America composed of the 11 southern states that seceded from the U.S. in 1860 and 1861 — **con·fed·er·al** \-'fed-(ə-)rəl\ adj

¹con·fed·er·ate \kən-'fed-(ə-)rət\ adj [L *com-* + *foeder-, foedus* compact] **1** : united in a league : ALLIED **2** cap : of or relating to the Confederate States of America

²confederate n **1** : ALLY, ACCOMPLICE **2** cap : a soldier, citizen, or adherent of the Confederate States of America or their cause

³con·fed·er·ate \-'fed-ə-,rāt\ vb : to unite in a confederacy

Confederate Memorial Day n : any of several days appointed for the commemoration of servicemen of the Confederacy: **a** : April 26 in Alabama, Florida, Georgia, and Mississippi **b** : May 10 in No. and So. Carolina **c** : May 30 in Virginia **d** : June 3 in Kentucky, Louisiana, and Texas

con·fed·er·a·tion \kən-,fed-ə-'rā-shən\ n **1** : an act of confederating **:** a state of being confederated : ALLIANCE **2** : LEAGUE

con·fer \kən-'fər\ vb **con·ferred; con·fer·ring** [L *conferre* to bring together, fr. *com-* + *ferre* to carry; akin to E *bear*] **1** : to give or grant publicly 〈*confer* knighthood on him〉 **2** : to compare views : CONSULT 〈*confer* with the committee〉 — **con·fer·ral** \-'fər-əl\ n — **con·fer·rer** \-'fər-ər\ n

con·fer·ee or **con·fer·ree** \ˌkän-fə-'rē\ n **1** : one conferred with **2** : one on whom something is conferred

con·fer·ence \'kän-f(ə-)rən(t)s, -fərn(t)s\ n **1** : a meeting for formal discussion or exchange of opinions; *also* : the discussion itself **2** : a meeting of committees of two branches of a legislature to adjust differences esp. concerning laws in process of adoption **3** : an association of athletic teams representing educational institutions

con·fess \kən-'fes\ vb [L *confess-, confiteri,* fr. *com-* + *fateri* to confess] **1** : to make acknowledgment of : ADMIT 〈*confess* one's guilt〉 **2 a** : to acknowledge one's sins to God or to a priest **b** : to act as confessor for 〈the priest *confessed* the penitents〉 **3** : to declare faith in : PROFESS **syn** see ACKNOWLEDGE

con·fess·ed·ly \-'fes-əd-lē, -'fest-lē\ adv : by confession **:** ADMITTEDLY

con·fes·sion \kən-'fesh-ən\ n **1** : an act of confessing; *esp* : a disclosure of one's sins in the sacrament of penance **2** : a statement of something confessed: as **a** : acknowledgment of guilt by a party accused of an offense **b** : a formal statement of religious beliefs : CREED **3** : an organized religious body having a common creed

¹con·fes·sion·al \-'fesh-nəl, -ən-²l\ n **1** : the enclosed place in which a priest sits and hears confessions **2** : the practice of confessing to a priest

²confessional adj : of or relating to a confession esp. of faith

con·fes·sor \kən-'fes-ər\ n **1** : one that confesses **2** : one

who gives heroic evidence of faith but does not suffer martyrdom **3** : a priest who hears confessions

con·fet·ti \kən-'fet-ē\ n [It, confections, fr. L *confectus,* pp. of *conficere* to prepare] : small bits of brightly colored paper made for throwing (as at weddings)

con·fi·dant \'kän-fə-,dant, -,dänt\ n : one to whom secrets are entrusted; *esp* : INTIMATE

con·fi·dante \'kän-fə-,dant, -,dänt\ n : a female confidant

con·fide \kən-'fīd\ vb [L *confidere,* fr. *com-* + *fidere* to trust] **1** : to have confidence : TRUST 〈*confide* in a doctor's skill〉 **2** : to show confidence by imparting secrets 〈*confided* in her mother〉 **3** : to tell confidentially 〈*confide* a secret to a friend〉 **4** : ENTRUST 〈*confide* one's safety to the police〉 — **con·fid·er** n

con·fi·dence \'kän-fəd-ən(t)s, -fə-,den(t)s\ n **1** : FAITH, TRUST 〈had *confidence* in his coach〉 **2** : consciousness of feeling sure : ASSURANCE 〈spoke with great *confidence*〉 **3 a** : reliance on another's discretion 〈told a girl friend in *confidence*〉 **b** : legislative support 〈vote of *confidence*〉 **4** : a communication made in confidence : SECRET 〈*confidences* between lawyer and client〉

confidence game n : a swindle in which the swindler takes advantage of the trust he has persuaded the victim to place in him — called also *con game* \'kän-\

confidence man n : a swindler in a confidence game — called also *con man* \'kän-,man\

con·fi·dent \'kän-fəd-ənt, -fə-,dent\ adj : having or showing confidence : SURE, SELF-ASSURED 〈*confident* of winning〉 〈a *confident* manner〉 — **con·fi·dent·ly** adv

con·fi·den·tial \ˌkän-fə-'den-chəl\ adj **1** : SECRET, PRIVATE 〈*confidential* information〉 **2** : INTIMATE, FAMILIAR 〈a *confidential* tone of voice〉 **3** : trusted with secret matters 〈a *confidential* secretary〉 — **con·fi·den·tial·ly** \-'dench-(ə-)lē\ adv — **con·fi·den·tial·ness** \-'den-chəl-nəs\ n

con·fid·ing \kən-'fīd-iŋ\ adj : tending to confide : TRUSTFUL — **con·fid·ing·ly** \-iŋ-lē\ adv

con·fig·u·ra·tion \kən-,fig-(y)ə-'rā-shən\ n [L *configurare* to form from or after, fr. *com-* + *figurare* to form, fr. *figura* figure] : relative arrangement of parts; *also* : the figure, contour, or pattern produced by such arrangement 〈the *configuration* of the atoms of a chemical compound〉 — **con·fig·u·ra·tion·al** \-shnəl, -shən-²l\ adj — **con·fig·u·ra·tion·al·ly** \-ē\ adv — **con·fig·u·ra·tive** \-'fig-(y)ə-,rāt-iv, -rət-\ adj

¹con·fine \'kän-,fīn\ n [L *confine* border, fr. *confinis* adjacent, fr. *com-* + *finis* end] : BOUNDARY, LIMIT 〈the *confines* of a city〉

²con·fine \kən-'fīn\ vt **1** : to keep within limits : RESTRICT 〈*confined* to quarters〉 **2 a** : to shut up : IMPRISON 〈*confined* for life〉 **b** : to keep indoors 〈*confined* with a cold〉 — **con·fin·er** n

con·fine·ment \kən-'fīn-mənt\ n : an act of confining **:** the state of being confined; *esp* : restraint within doors usu. during illness or childbirth

con·firm \kən-'fərm\ vt [L *confirmare,* fr. *com-* + *firmus* firm] **1** : to make firm or firmer (as in a habit, in faith, or in intention) : STRENGTHEN **2** : to make sure of the truth of : VERIFY 〈*confirm* a suspicion by careful investigation〉 **3** : APPROVE, RATIFY 〈*confirm* a treaty〉 **4** : to administer the rite of confirmation to — **con·firm·a·ble** \-'fər-mə-bəl\ adj

syn CONFIRM, CORROBORATE, AUTHENTICATE mean to support the truth or validity of something. CONFIRM implies removing doubts by an authoritative statement or an indisputable fact; CORROBORATE suggests the strengthening of what is already partly established; AUTHENTICATE implies establishing genuineness by showing legal or official documents or adducing expert opinion

con·fir·ma·tion \ˌkän-fər-'mā-shən\ n **1** : an act or process of confirming 〈*confirmation* of an appointment〉: as **a** : a Christian rite or sacrament admitting a baptized person to full church privileges **b** : a ceremony confirming Jewish youths in their ancestral faith **2** : something that confirms : CORROBORATION — **con·fir·ma·to·ry** \kən-'fər-mə-,tōr-ē, -,tòr-\ adj

con·firmed \kən-'fərmd\ adj **1 a** : made firm : STRENGTHENED **b** : deeply ingrained 〈*confirmed* distrust of change〉 **c** : HABITUAL, CHRONIC 〈a *confirmed* drunkard〉 **2** : having received the rite of confirmation — **con·firm·ed·ly** \-'fər-məd-lē\ adv

---

ə abut; ⁰ kitten; ər further; a back; ā bake; ä cot, cart; aú out; ch chin; e less; ē easy; g gift; i trip; ī life

con·fis·cate \'kän-fə-ˌskāt\ vt [L confiscare, fr. com- + fiscus public treasury] : to seize by or as if by public authority for public use or as a penalty ⟨smuggled goods may be confiscated⟩ — **con·fis·ca·tion** \ˌkän-fə-'skā-shən\ n — **con·fis·ca·tor** \'kän-fə-ˌskāt-ər\ n — **con·fis·ca·to·ry** \kən-'fis-kə-ˌtōr-ē, -ˌtȯr-\ adj

Con·fi·te·or \kən-'fēt-ē-ə-ˌr\ n [L, I confess, fr. confitēri to confess] : a confession of sinfulness near the beginning of the Mass

con·fla·gra·tion \ˌkän-flə-'grā-shən\ n [L conflagrare to burn up, fr. com- + flagrare to burn] : FIRE; esp : a large disastrous fire

¹con·flict \'kän-ˌflikt\ n [L conflictus clash, fr. conflict-, confligere to strike together, fr. com- + fligere to strike] 1 : FIGHT, BATTLE, STRUGGLE; esp : a prolonged struggle 2 : a clashing or sharp disagreement (as between ideas, interests, or purposes)

²con·flict \kən-'flikt, 'kän-\ vi : to be in opposition : CLASH ⟨duty and desire often conflict⟩ ⟨conflicting opinions⟩

con·flu·ence \'kän-ˌflü-ən(t)s\ n [L confluere to flow together, fr. com- + fluere to flow] 1 a : a flocking together to one place b : CROWD 2 : a flowing together or place of meeting and esp. of two or more streams

con·flu·ent \'kän-ˌflü-ənt, kən-'\ adj : flowing or coming together ⟨confluent rivers⟩; also : run together ⟨confluent pustules⟩

con·form \kən-'fȯrm\ vb [L conformare, fr. com- + forma form] 1 : to bring into harmony ⟨conforms his behavior to the circumstances⟩ 2 : to be similar or identical ⟨the data conform to the pattern⟩ 3 : to be obedient or compliant; esp : to adapt oneself to prevailing standards or customs ⟨found it easier to conform than rebel⟩ syn see ADAPT — **con·form·er** n — **con·form·ism** \-'fȯr-ˌmiz-əm\ n — **con·form·ist** \-məst\ n

con·form·a·ble \kən-'fȯr-mə-bəl\ adj· 1 : corresponding in form or character ⟨conformable to established practice⟩ 2 : SUBMISSIVE, COMPLIANT — **con·form·a·bly** \-blē\ adv

con·for·mal \kən-'fȯr-məl, (')kän-\ adj 1 : leaving the size of the angle between corresponding curves unchanged 2 : representing small areas in their true shape ⟨a conformal map⟩

con·form·ance \kən-'fȯr-mən(t)s\ n : CONFORMITY

con·for·ma·tion \ˌkän-(ˌ)fȯr-mā-shən, -fər-\ n 1 : the act of conforming or producing conformity : ADAPTATION 2 : formation of anything by symmetrical arrangement of its parts 3 a : STRUCTURE b : the proportionate shape or contour esp. of an animal

con·for·mi·ty \kən-'fȯr-mət-ē\ n, pl -ties 1 : correspondence in form, manner, or character : AGREEMENT ⟨behaved in conformity with his beliefs⟩ 2 : action in accordance with some specified or generally accepted standard or authority : OBEDIENCE ⟨conformity to social custom⟩

con·found \kən-'faünd, kän-\ vt [OF confondre, fr. L confundere to pour together, confuse, fr. com- + fundere to pour] 1 archaic : RUIN, DEFEAT 2 : to put to shame : DISCOMFIT 3 : DAMN 4 : to throw into disorder : mix up : CONFUSE — **con·found·er** n

con·found·ed \kən-'faün-dəd, (')kän-'faün-\ adj 1 : CONFUSED, PERPLEXED 2 : DAMNED — **con·found·ed·ly** adv

con·fra·ter·ni·ty \ˌkän-frə-'tər-nət-ē\ n, pl -ties : a society devoted to a religious or charitable cause

con·frere \'kōⁿ-ˌfre(ə)r, 'kän-\ n [MF, trans. of ML confrater] : COLLEAGUE, COMRADE

con·front \kən-'frənt\ vt [MF confronter to border on, confront, fr. L com- + front-, frons forehead, front] 1 : to face esp. in challenge : OPPOSE ⟨confront an enemy⟩ 2 : to bring face-to-face : cause to meet ⟨confront a person with his accuser⟩ ⟨confronted with difficulties⟩ — **con·fron·ta·tion** \ˌkän-(ˌ)frən-'tā-shən\ n

Con·fu·cian \kən-'fyü-shən\ adj : of or relating to the Chinese philosopher Confucius or his teachings or followers — **Confucian** n — **Con·fu·cian·ism** \-shə-ˌniz-əm\ n — **Con·fu·cian·ist** \-shə-nəst\ n or adj

con·fuse \kən-'fyüz\ vt [L confus-, confundere to confuse, confound] 1 a : to make mentally unclear or uncertain : PERPLEX ⟨a complicated problem confuses him⟩ b : DISCONCERT ⟨heckling confused the speaker⟩ 2 : to make indistinct : BLUR ⟨stop confusing the issue⟩ 3 : to mix up : JUMBLE ⟨his motives were hopelessly confused⟩ 4 : to

fail to distinguish between ⟨teachers always confused the twins⟩ — **con·fused·ly** \-'fyüz(-ə)d-lē\ adv — **con·fus·ing·ly** \-'fyü-ziŋ-lē\ adv

con·fu·sion \kən-'fyü-zhən\ n 1 : an act or instance of confusing 2 : the quality or state of being confused — **con·fu·sion·al** \-'fyüzh-nəl, -'fyü-zhən-ᵊl\ adj

con·fute \kən-'fyüt\ vt [L confutare] : to overwhelm by argument : refute conclusively — **con·fu·ta·tion** \ˌkän-fyü-'tā-shən\ n — **con·fu·ta·tive** \kən-'fyüt-ət-iv\ adj — **con·fut·er** \kən-'fyüt-ər\ n

con·ga \'käŋ-gə\ n [AmerSp, fr. Congo, region in Africa] 1 : a Cuban dance of African origin performed by a group usu. in single file 2 : a tall narrow bass drum beaten with the hands

con·gé \kōⁿ-'zhā\ n 1 : DISMISSAL 2 : FAREWELL

con·geal \kən-'jēl\ vb [MF congeler, fr. L congelare, fr. com- + gelare to freeze] 1 : to change from a fluid to a solid state by or as if by cold 2 : to make or become viscid or curdled : COAGULATE 3 : to make or become rigid or inflexible — **con·geal·ment** \-mənt\ n

con·ge·ner \'kän-jə-nər, kən-'jē-\ n : one related to another: as a : a member of the same taxonomic genus as another plant or animal b : a person or thing resembling another in nature or action — **con·ge·ner·ic** \ˌkän-jə-'ner-ik\ adj — **con·ge·ner·ous** \kən-'jē-nə-rəs, -'jen-ə-\ adj

con·ge·nial \kən-'jē-nyəl\ adj [com- + genius] 1 : having the same nature, disposition, or tastes 2 a : existing together harmoniously b : PLEASANT; esp : agreeably suited to one's nature, tastes, or outlook c : SOCIABLE, GENIAL ⟨the innkeeper was a most congenial host⟩ — **con·ge·nial·ly** \-nyə-lē\ adv

con·ge·ni·al·i·ty \-ˌjē-nē-'al-ət-ē, -ˌjen-'yal-\ n : the quality or state of being congenial

con·gen·i·tal \kən-'jen-ə-tᵊl\ adj [L congenitus, fr. com- + genitus, pp. of gignere to beget, produce] 1 : existing at or dating from birth but usu. not hereditary ⟨congenital disease⟩ 2 : being such by nature : INHERENT, INTRINSIC ⟨a congenital liar⟩ ⟨congenital fears⟩ — **con·gen·i·tal·ly** \-tᵊl-ē\ adv

con·ger eel \ˌkäŋ-gər-\ n [OF congre, fr. L conger, fr. Gk gongros] : a scaleless saltwater eel that sometimes grows to a length of eight feet and is an important food fish of Europe

con·ge·ries \'kän-jə-(ˌ)rēz\ n, pl **congeries** \same\ : AGGREGATION, COLLECTION

con·gest \kən-'jest\ vb [L congest-, congerere to bring together, fr. com- + gerere to carry] 1 : to cause an excessive fullness of the blood vessels of (as an organ) 2 : CLOG, OVERCROWD ⟨congested streets⟩ 3 : to concentrate in a small or narrow space — **con·ges·tion** \-'jes-chən\ n — **con·ges·tive** \-'jes-tiv\ adj

¹con·glom·er·ate \kən-'gläm-(ə-)rət\ adj [L conglomeratus, pp. of conglomerare to roll together, fr. com- + glomer-, glomus ball] 1 : made up of parts from various sources or of various kinds 2 : densely clustered ⟨conglomerate flowers⟩

²con·glom·er·ate \-'gläm-ə-ˌrāt\ vb : to collect or form into a mass

³con·glom·er·ate \-(ə-)rət\ n : a composite mass or mixture; esp : rock composed of rounded fragments varying from small pebbles to large boulders in a cement (as of hardened clay)

con·glom·er·a·tion \kən-ˌgläm-ə-'rā-shən, ˌkän-\ n 1 : a conglomerating or the state of being conglomerated 2 : a conglomerate mass

conglomerate

Con·go red \ˌkäŋ-ˌgō-\ n : an azo dye red in alkaline and blue in acid solution

con·go snake \'käŋ-ˌgō-\ n : a long bluish black amphibian of the southeastern U.S. that has two pairs of very short limbs — called also congo eel

con·grat·u·late \kən-'grach-ə-ˌlāt\ vt [L congratulari to wish joy, fr. com- + gratus pleasing] : to express sympathetic pleasure to on account of success or good fortune : FELICITATE ⟨congratulated the winner⟩

con·grat·u·la·tion \-ˌgrach-ə-'lā-shən\ n 1 : the act of congratulating 2 : an expression of pleasure at another's success, happiness, or good fortune : FELICITATION — usu. used in pl.

---

con·grat·u·la·to·ry \-'grach-ə-lə-,tōr-ē, -,tor-\ *adj* : expressing congratulations ⟨a *congratulatory* smile⟩

con·gre·gate \'käŋ-gri-,gāt\ *vb* [L *congregare,* fr. *com-* + *greg-, grex* flock] : to collect into a group or crowd : ASSEMBLE — **con·gre·ga·tor** \-,gāt-ər\ *n*

con·gre·ga·tion \,käŋ-gri-'gā-shən\ *n* **1** : the action of congregating : the state of being congregated; *also* : a collection of separate things **2** : an assembly of persons; *esp* : one gathered for religious worship **3** : the membership of a church or synagogue **4** : a Roman Catholic religious society under a rule but not under solemn vows **5** : a body of cardinals and officials forming an administrative division of the papal curia

con·gre·ga·tion·al \-'gā-shnəl, -shən-ᵊl\ *adj* **1** : of or relating to a congregation **2** *cap* : of or relating to a body of Protestant churches affirming the essential importance and the autonomy of the local congregation **3** : of or relating to church government placing final authority in the assembly of the local congregation — **con·gre·ga·tion·al·ism** \-,iz-əm\ *n, often cap* — **con·gre·ga·tion·al·ist** \-əst\ *n or adj, often cap*

con·gress \'käŋ-grəs\ *n* [L *congressus,* fr. *congress-, congredi* to come together, fr. *com-* + *gradi* to step, go] **1 a** : the act or action of coming together and meeting **b** : COITUS **2** : a formal meeting of delegates for discussion and action **3** : the supreme legislative body of a nation and esp. of a republic **4** : an association of constituent organizations **5** : a single meeting or session of a group — **con·gres·sion·al** \kən-'gresh-nəl, -ən-ᵊl\ *adj* — **con·gres·sion·al·ly** \-ē\ *adv*

con·gress·man \'käŋ-grəs-mən\ *n* : a member of a congress; *esp* : a member of the U.S. House of Representatives

con·gress·wom·an \-,wùm-ən\ *n* : a female member of a congress; *esp* : a female member of the U.S. House of Representatives

con·gru·ence \kən-'grü-ən(t)s, 'käŋ-grə-wən(t)s\ *n* : the quality or state of according or coinciding

con·gru·en·cy \-ən-sē, -wən-sē\ *n* : CONGRUENCE

con·gru·ent \kən-'grü-ənt, 'käŋ-grə-wənt\ *adj* [L *congruere* to come together, agree] **1** : SUITABLE, AGREEING, CORRESPONDING ⟨the report proved to be *congruent* with the facts⟩ **2** : capable of being placed over another figure so that all points of the one correspond to all points of the other : having the same size and shape ⟨*congruent* triangles⟩ — **con·gru·ent·ly** *adv*

con·gru·i·ty \kən-'grü-ət-ē, kän-\ *n* **1** : the quality or state of being congruent or congruous : AGREEMENT, HARMONY **2** : a point of agreement

con·gru·ous \'käŋ-grə-wəs\ *adj* **1 a** : being in agreement, harmony, or correspondence **b** : SUITABLE, APPROPRIATE **2** : marked by harmony among parts — **con·gru·ous·ly** *adv* — **con·gru·ous·ness** *n*

con·ic \'kän-ik\ *adj* **1** : CONICAL **2** : of or relating to a cone

con·i·cal \'kän-i-kəl\ *adj* : resembling a cone esp. in shape ⟨*conical* roots⟩ — **con·i·cal·ly** \-i-k(ə-)lē\ *adv* — **con·i·cal·ness** \-kəl-nəs\ *n*

conic section *n* **1** : a plane section of a cone **2** : a curve generated by a point which always moves so that the ratio of its distance from a fixed point to its distance from a fixed line is constant

co·nid·i·al \kə-'nid-ē-əl\ *adj* : of, relating to, or resembling conidia

conic sections: *1* straight lines, *2* circle, *3* ellipse, *4* parabola, *5* hyperbola

co·nid·io·phore \kə-'nid-ē-ə-,fōr, -,for\ *n* : a plant structure (as a special hypha) that bears conidia — **co·nid·i·oph·o·rous** \kə-,nid-ē-'äf-(ə-)rəs\ *adj*

co·nid·i·um \kə-'nid-ē-əm\ *n, pl* **-ia** \-ē-ə\ [Gk *konis* dust] : an asexual spore produced on a conidiophore

con·i·fer \'kän-ə-fər, 'kō-nə-\ *n* [L *conifer* cone-bearing, fr. *conus* cone] : any of an order (Coniferales) of mostly evergreen gymnospermous trees and shrubs including forms (as pines) with true cones — **co·nif·er·ous** \kō-'nif-(ə-)rəs, kə-\ *adj*

con·jec·tur·al \kən-'jek-chə-rəl, -'jeksh-rəl\ *adj* **1** : of

the nature of, involving, or based on conjecture **2** : given to conjectures — **con·jec·tur·al·ly** \-ē\ *adv*

¹con·jec·ture \kən-'jek-chər\ *n* [L *conjectura,* fr. *conject-, conicere* to throw together, conjecture, fr. *com-* + *jacere* to throw] **1** : inference from inadequate evidence **2** : a conclusion reached by surmise or guesswork ⟨a mistaken *conjecture*⟩

²conjecture *vb* **-jec·tured; -jec·tur·ing** \-'jek-chə-riŋ, 'jek-shriŋ\ **1** : to arrive at by conjecture **2** : to make conjectures as to : SURMISE — **con·jec·tur·er** \-'jek-chər-ər\ *n*

syn SURMISE, GUESS: CONJECTURE implies forming an opinion on what is recognized as insufficient evidence; SURMISE implies even slighter evidence and suggests the influence of suspicion or imagination; GUESS stresses hitting on a conclusion at random or from very uncertain evidence

con·join \kən-'join, kän-\ *vb* [MF *conjoindre,* fr. L *conjungere,* fr. *com-* + *jungere* to join] : to join together for a common purpose

con·joint \-'joint\ *adj* [MF, pp. of *conjoindre* to conjoin] **1** : UNITED, CONJOINED **2** : related to, made up of, or carried on by two or more in combination : JOINT — **con·joint·ly** *adv*

con·ju·gal \'kän-ji-gəl, kən-'jü-\ *adj* [L *conjug-, conjux* spouse, fr. *conjungere* to conjoin] : of or relating to marriage, the married state, or matrimonial relations *syn* see MATRIMONIAL — **con·ju·gal·ly** *adv*

con·ju·gant \'kän-ji-gənt\ *n* : either of a pair of conjugating gametes or organisms

¹con·ju·gate \'kän-ji-gət, -jə-,gāt\ *adj* [L *conjugatus,* pp. of *conjugare* to unite, fr. *com-* + *jugum* yoke] **1 a** : joined together esp. in pairs : COUPLED **b** : acting or operating as if joined **2** : having features in common but opposite or inverse in some particular — **con·ju·gate·ly** *adv* — **con·ju·gate·ness** *n*

²con·ju·gate \'kän-jə-,gāt\ *vb* **1** : to give the various inflectional forms of (a verb) in a prescribed order **2** : to join together : COUPLE **3** : to unite chemically so that the product is easily broken down into the original compounds **4 a** : to pair and fuse in conjugation **b** : to pair in synapsis

³conjugate *like* ¹CONJUGATE\ *n* : something conjugate : a product of conjugating

conjugated protein *n* : a compound of a protein with a nonprotein

con·ju·ga·tion \,kän-jə-'gā-shən\ *n* **1** : the act of conjugating : the state of being conjugated **2 a** : an orderly arrangement of the inflectional forms of a verb **b** : verb inflection **c** : a class of verbs having the same type of inflectional forms ⟨the weak *conjugation*⟩ **3 a** : fusion of usu. similar gametes that among lower thallophytes replaces typical fertilization **b** : temporary cytoplasmic union with exchange of nuclear material that is the usual sexual process in ciliated protozoans **c** : SYNAPSIS — **con·ju·ga·tion·al** \-shnəl, -shən-ᵊl\ *adj* — **con·ju·ga·tion·al·ly** \-ē\ *adv* — **con·ju·ga·tive** \'kän-jə-,gāt-iv\ *adj*

con·junct \kən-'jəŋ(k)t, kän-\ *adj* : JOINED, UNITED

con·junc·tion \kən-'jəŋ(k)-shən\ *n* [L *conjunct-, conjungere* to conjoin] **1** : the act or instance of conjoining : the state of being conjoined **2** : occurrence together in time or space : CONCURRENCE **3** : the apparent meeting or passing of two or more celestial bodies in the same degree of the zodiac **4** : an uninflected word or expression that joins together words or word groups **5** : a compound statement that is true only if all its components are true — **con·junc·tion·al** \-shnəl, -shən-ᵊl\ *adj* — **con·junc·tion·al·ly** \-ē\ *adv*

con·junc·ti·va \,kän-,jəŋk-'tī-və, -'tē-\ *n, pl* **-tivas** or **-ti·vae** \-'tī(,)vē, -'tē-,vī\ : the mucous membrane that lines the inner surface of the eyelids and is continued over the front part of the eyeball — **con·junc·ti·val** \-vəl\ *adj*

con·junc·tive \kən-'jəŋ(k)-tiv\ *adj* **1** : CONNECTIVE **2** : done or existing in conjunction : CONJUNCT **3** : being or functioning like a conjunction ⟨*conjunctive* adverbs such as *hence, however,* and *therefore*⟩ — **conjunctive** *n* — **con·junc·tive·ly** *adv*

con·junc·ti·vi·tis \kən-,jəŋ(k)-ti-'vīt-əs\ *n* : inflammation of the conjunctiva

con·junc·ture \kən-'jəŋ(k)-chər\ *n* **1** : CONJUNCTION,

UNION   **2** : a combination of circumstances or events esp. producing a crisis : JUNCTURE

con·ju·ra·tion \,kän-jə-'rā-shən ,kən-\ *n* **1** : the act of conjuring : INCANTATION **2** : an expression or trick used in conjuring

con·jure \'kän-jər, 'kən-; *in sense 1* kən-'jü(ə)r\ *vb* [OF *conjurer*, fr. L *conjurare* to swear together, fr. *com-* + *jurare* to swear] **1** : to entreat earnestly or solemnly : BESEECH, IMPLORE **2 a** : to summon by invocation or incantation **b** : to affect or effect by or as if by magic : create or bring about as if by magic ⟨*conjure* up a scheme⟩ ⟨*conjure* up an image⟩ **3 a** : to practice magical arts **b** : to use a conjurer's tricks

con·jur·er *or* **con·ju·ror** \'kän-jər-ər, 'kən-\ *n* **1** : one that practices magic arts : WIZARD **2** : one that performs feats of legerdemain and illusion : MAGICIAN, JUGGLER

¹conk \'käŋk, 'koŋk\ *n* : the visible fruiting body of a tree fungus; *also* : decay caused by such a fungus — **conky** \-ē\ *adj*

²conk *vi* : to break down; *esp* : STALL ⟨the motor *conked* out⟩

con·nate \kä-'nāt, 'kän-,āt\ *adj* [LL *connatus*, pp. of *connasci* to be born together, fr. L *com-* + *nasci* to be born] **1** : INNATE **2** : AKIN **3** : born or originated together **4** : congenitally united — **con·nate·ly** *adv*

con·nect \kə-'nekt\ *vb* [L *connectere*, fr. *com-* + *nectere* to bind] **1** : to join or link together directly or by something coming between ⟨*connect* two wires⟩ ⟨towns *connected* by a railroad⟩ **2** : to attach by personal relationship or association ⟨*connected* by marriage⟩ **3** : to associate in the mind ⟨*connect* two ideas⟩ **4** : to be related causally, logically, or spatially ⟨an event *connected* with his death⟩ **5** : to meet at a time and place suitable for transferring passengers or freight ⟨*connecting* trains⟩ **syn** see JOIN — **con·nec·tor** *or* **con·nect·er** \-'nek-tər\ *n*

con·nect·ed·ly *adv* : in a connected manner : COHERENTLY

connecting rod *n* : a rod that transmits power from one rotating part of a machine to another in reciprocating motion

con·nec·tion \kə-'nek-shən\ *n* **1** : the act of connecting **2** : the fact or condition of being connected : RELATIONSHIP ⟨the close *connection* between dirt and disease⟩ ⟨the *connection* between two ideas⟩ **3** : a thing that connects : a means by which two things are connected : BOND, LINK ⟨a loose *connection* in a radio⟩ ⟨get a *connection* on the telephone⟩ **4 a** : a person connected with others esp. by marriage or kinship ⟨an uncle and several distant *connections* lived in the city⟩ **b** : a social, professional, or commercial relationship ⟨had important business *connections* in the city⟩ **5** : a means of continuing a journey by transferring to another conveyance ⟨make a *connection* for San Francisco at Chicago⟩ **6** : a set of persons associated together: as **a** : DENOMINATION **b** : CLAN — **con·nec·tion·al** \-shnəl, -shən-ᵊl\ *adj*

¹con·nec·tive \kə-'nek-tiv\ *adj* : connecting or tending to connect — **con·nec·tive·ly** *adv* — **con·nec·tiv·i·ty** \,kä-,nek-'tiv-ət-ē\ *n*

²connective *n* : something that connects; *esp* : a word or expression (as a conjunction or a relative pronoun) that connects words or word groups

connective tissue *n* : a tissue of mesodermal origin with much intercellular substance or many interlacing processes that forms a supporting framework (as of bone, cartilage, and fibrous tissue) for the body and its parts

conn·ing tower \'kän-iŋ-\ *n* [fr. *conn* to give sailing directions to the helmsman] **1** : an armored pilothouse (as on a battleship) **2** : a raised structure on the deck of a submarine used as an observation post and often as an entrance to the vessel

con·nip·tion \kə-'nip-shən\ *n* : a fit of rage, hysteria, or alarm

con·niv·ance \kə-'nī-vən(t)s\ *n* : the act of conniving; *esp* : pretended ignorance of wrongdoing or secret cooperation with wrongdoers

con·nive \kə-'nīv\ *vi* [L *conivēre*, lit., to shut the eyes] **1** : to pretend ignorance of something that one ought to oppose or stop **2** : to cooperate secretly or have a secret understanding — **con·niv·er** *n*

con·nois·seur \,kän-ə-'sər, -'sü(ə)r\ *n* [obs. F, fr. OF *connoistre* to know, fr. L *cognoscere*, fr. *com-* + *gnoscere*, *noscere* to know] : a person competent to act as a judge

in matters involving taste and appreciation : EXPERT ⟨a *connoisseur* of rare books⟩ ⟨a *connoisseur* of French painting⟩ — **con·nois·seur·ship** \-,ship\ *n*

con·no·ta·tion \,kän-ə-'tā-shən\ *n* **1** : CONNOTING, IMPLICATION **2** : a meaning or significance suggested by a word or an expression apart from and in addition to its denotation ⟨the word *home* with all its heart-warming *connotations*⟩ — **con·no·ta·tion·al** \-shnəl, -shən-ᵊl\ *adj*

con·no·ta·tive \'kän-ə-,tāt-iv, kə-'nōt-ət-iv\ *adj* **1** : connoting or tending to connote **2** : relating to connotation — **con·no·ta·tive·ly** *adv*

con·note \kə-'nōt\ *vt* [ML *connotare*, fr. L *com-* + *notare* to note] **1** : to suggest or mean along with or in addition to the exact explicit meaning or indication : have the additional meaning of ⟨the word *cell* means a small compartment but it may *connote* imprisonment⟩ **2** : to be associated with as a consequence or concomitant ⟨guilt usu. *connotes* suffering⟩ **syn** see DENOTE

con·nu·bi·al \kə-'n(y)ü-bē-əl\ *adj* [L *connubium* marriage, fr. *com-* + *nubere* to marry] : of or relating to marriage or the marriage state : CONJUGAL — **con·nu·bi·al·ly** \-bē-ə-lē\ *adv*

co·noid \'kō-,noid\ *or* **co·noi·dal** \kō-'noid-ᵊl\ *adj* : shaped like or nearly like a cone — **conoid** *n*

con·quer \'käŋ-kər\ *vb* **con·quered; con·quer·ing** \-k(ə-)riŋ\ [OF *conquerre*, fr. L *com-* + *quaest-, quaerere* to seek, ask] **1** : to gain or acquire by force of arms : SUBJUGATE ⟨*conquer* a country⟩ **2** : to overcome by force of arms : VANQUISH ⟨*conquered* all his enemies⟩ **3** : to gain or win by overcoming obstacles or opposition **4** : to be victorious

syn SUBDUE, SUBJUGATE: CONQUER implies gaining mastery of after a prolonged effort and with more or less permanent result; SUBDUE implies overpowering and suppressing; SUBJUGATE stresses a bringing under oppressive or humiliating rule or control

con·quer·or \'käŋ-kər-ər\ *n* : one that conquers : VICTOR

con·quest \'kän-,kwest, 'käŋ-\ *n* **1** : the act or process of conquering **2 a** : something conquered; *esp* : territory appropriated in war **b** : a person whose affections have been won **syn** see VICTORY

con·quis·ta·dor \kōn-'kēs-tə-,dor; kän-'k(w)is-\ *n, pl* **con·quis·ta·do·res** \kōn,kēs-tə-'dor-ēz, -'dōr-, kän-,k(w)is-\ *or* **con·quis·ta·dors** [Sp, fr. *conquista* conquest] : CONQUEROR; *esp* : a leader in the Spanish conquest of America and esp. of Mexico and Peru in the 16th century

con·san·guin·e·ous \,kän-,san-'gwin-ē-əs, -,saŋ-\ *adj* : of the same blood or origin; *esp* : descended from the same ancestor — **con·san·guin·e·ous·ly** *adv* — **con·san·guin·i·ty** \-'gwin-ət-ē\ *n*

con·science \'kän-chən(t)s\ *n* [L *conscire* to be conscious, be conscious of guilt, fr. *com-* + *scire* to know] : the sense or consciousness of the moral goodness or blameworthiness of one's own conduct, intentions, or character together with a feeling of obligation to do right or be good — **in all conscience** *or* **in conscience 1** : in all fairness **2** : beyond a doubt : to be sure

conscience money *n* : money paid to relieve the conscience by restoring what has been wrongfully acquired

con·sci·en·tious \,kän-chē-'en-chəs\ *adj* **1** : governed by or in accordance with one's conscience : SCRUPULOUS **2** : METICULOUS, CAREFUL — **con·sci·en·tious·ly** *adv* — **con·sci·en·tious·ness** *n*

conscientious objector *n* : a person who refuses to serve in the armed forces or to bear arms as contrary to his moral or religious principles

con·scious \'kän-chəs\ *adj* [L *conscius*, fr. *conscire* to be conscious, fr. *com-* + *scire* to know] **1** : perceiving or noticing with a degree of controlled thought or observation **2** : known or felt by one's inner self ⟨*conscious* guilt⟩ **3** : capable of or marked by thought, will, design, or perception **4** : SELF-CONSCIOUS **5** : having mental faculties undulled by sleep, faint, or stupor : AWAKE **6** : done or acting with critical awareness — **con·scious·ly** *adv*

con·scious·ness \'kän-chəs-nəs\ *n* **1** : awareness of something ⟨*consciousness* of evil⟩ **2** : the condition of having ability to feel, think, and react : MIND **3** : the normal state of conscious life as distinguished from sleep or insensibility **4** : the upper level of mental life as contrasted with unconscious processes

---

j joke;   ŋ sing;   ō flow;   ȯ flaw;   ȯi coin;   th thin;   t͟h this;   ü loot;   u̇ foot;   y yet;   yü few;   yu̇ furious;   zh vision

¹**con·script** \'kän-ˌskript\ *adj* [L *conscriptus*, pp. of *conscribere* to enroll, fr. *com-* + *scribere* to write] **1 :** CONSCRIPTED, DRAFTED **2 :** made up of conscripted persons ⟨a *conscript* army⟩

²**conscript** *n* **:** a conscripted person (as a military recruit)

³**con·script** \kən-'skript\ *vt* **:** to enroll into service (as military) by compulsion **:** DRAFT

con·scrip·tion \kən-'skrip-shən\ *n* **1 :** compulsory enrollment of persons esp. for military service **:** DRAFT **2 :** a forced contribution (as of money) imposed by a government in time of emergency (as war)

¹**con·se·crate** \'kän(t)-sə-ˌkrāt\ *adj* **:** CONSECRATED, HALLOWED

²**consecrate** *vb* [L *consecrare*, fr. *com-* + *sacrare* to hallow, fr. *sacer* sacred] **1 :** to set apart to the service of God; *esp* **:** to ordain to the office of bishop **2 :** to devote to a purpose with deep solemnity or dedication **3 :** to make inviolate or venerable ⟨rules *consecrated* by time⟩ — **con·se·cra·tor** \-ˌkrāt-ər\ *n*

con·se·cra·tion \ˌkän(t)-sə-'krā-shən\ *n* **1 :** the act or ceremony of consecrating **2 :** the state of being consecrated **3** *cap* **:** the part of the Mass in which the elements are consecrated

con·sec·u·tive \kən-'sek-(y)ət-iv\ *adj* [L *consecut-*, *consequi* to follow along] **:** following one after the other in order without gaps **:** CONTINUOUS — **con·sec·u·tive·ly** *adv* — **con·sec·u·tive·ness** *n*

syn CONSECUTIVE, SUCCESSIVE mean following one after the other. CONSECUTIVE stresses immediacy in following and implies that no interruption or interval occurs in the series ⟨three *consecutive* terms in office⟩ SUCCESSIVE may apply to things of the same kind following at intervals ⟨rained on three *successive* weekends⟩

con·sen·sus \kən-'sen(t)-səs\ *n* [L, fr. *consens-*, *consentire* to agree in feeling] **1 :** general agreement (as in opinion or testimony) **:** ACCORD **2 :** the trend of opinion

¹**con·sent** \kən-'sent\ *vi* [L *consentire* to agree in feeling, fr. *com-* + *sentire* to feel] **:** to give assent or approval **:** AGREE **syn** see ASSENT — **con·sent·er** *n*

²**consent** *n* **1 :** compliance in or approval of what is asked or proposed **:** ACQUIESCENCE **2 :** agreement as to action or opinion

con·se·quence \'kän(t)-sə-ˌkwen(t)s, -si-kwən(t)s\ *n* **1 :** something produced by a cause or necessarily following from a set of conditions **2 :** a conclusion that results from reason or argument **3 a :** importance with respect to power to produce an effect **:** MOMENT **b :** social importance **syn** see EFFECT

¹**con·se·quent** \-si-kwənt, -sə-ˌkwent\ *n* **:** the second term of a ratio

²**consequent** *adj* [L *consequi* to follow along, fr. *com-* + *sequi* to follow] **1 :** following as a result or effect **2 :** observing logical sequence **:** RATIONAL

con·se·quen·tial \ˌkän(t)-sə-'kwen-chəl\ *adj* **1 :** of the nature of a consequence or result **:** following as a consequence **2 :** having significant consequences **:** IMPORTANT **3 :** SELF-IMPORTANT ⟨a *consequential* manner⟩ — **con·se·quen·tial·ly** \-'kwench-(ə-)lē\ *adv* — **con·se·quen·tial·ness** \-'kwen-chəl-nəs\ *n*

con·se·quent·ly \'kän(t)-sə-ˌkwent-lē, -si-kwənt-\ *adv* **:** as a result **:** ACCORDINGLY

con·ser·van·cy \kən-'sər-vən-sē\ *n, pl* **-cies :** an organization or area designated to conserve and protect natural resources

con·ser·va·tion \ˌkän(t)-sər-'vā-shən\ *n* **:** a careful preservation and protection of something; *esp* **:** planned management of a natural resource to prevent exploitation, destruction, or neglect — **con·ser·va·tion·al** \-shnəl, -shən-ᵊl\ *adj*

con·ser·va·tion·ist \-'vā-sh(ə-)nəst\ *n* **:** one who advocates conservation esp. of natural resources

conservation of energy : a principle in physics: the total energy of an isolated system remains constant irrespective of whatever internal changes may take place

conservation of mass : a principle in physics: the total mass of any material system is neither increased nor diminished by reactions between the parts — called also *conservation of matter*

con·ser·va·tism \kən-'sər-və-ˌtiz-əm\ *n* **1 a :** disposition in politics to preserve what is established **b :** a political philosophy supporting tradition, social stability, and

established institutions, and preferring gradual development to abrupt change **2 :** tendency to prefer an existing situation and to be suspicious of change

¹**con·ser·va·tive** \kən-'sər-vət-iv\ *adj* **1 :** tending to conserve or preserve **2 a :** of or relating to conservatism **b** *cap* **:** of or constituting a political party professing conservatism **3 a :** tending or disposed to maintain existing views, conditions, or institutions **:** TRADITIONAL **b :** MODERATE, CAUTIOUS ⟨a *conservative* investment⟩ ⟨*conservative* estimate⟩ **c :** marked by traditional standards of taste, elegance, or manners **4** *cap* **:** of or relating to a movement in Judaism that holds sacred the Torah and the religious traditions but accepts some liturgical and ritual change — **con·ser·va·tive·ly** *adv* — **con·ser·va·tive·ness** *n*

²**conservative** *n* **1 a :** an adherent or advocate of conservatism **b** *cap* **:** a member or supporter of a conservative political party **2 :** a cautious or discreet person

con·ser·va·toire \kən-'sər-və-ˌtwär\ *n* [F] **:** CONSERVATORY

con·ser·va·tor \kən-'sər-vət-ər, 'kän(t)-sər-ˌvāt-ər\ *n* **1 :** one that preserves or guards **:** PROTECTOR **2 :** one designated to take over and protect the interests of an incompetent **3** *Brit* **:** an official charged with the protection of something affecting public welfare and interests

con·ser·va·to·ry \kən-'sər-və-ˌtōr-ē, -ˌtȯr-\ *n, pl* **-ries 1 :** a greenhouse for growing or displaying plants **2 :** a school specializing in one of the fine arts

¹**con·serve** \kən-'sərv\ *vt* [L *conservare*, fr. *com-* + *servare* to guard, save] **1 :** to keep in a safe or sound state **:** PRESERVE **2 :** to preserve with sugar — **con·serv·er** *n*

²**con·serve** \'kän-ˌsərv\ *n* **1 :** CONFECTION; *esp* **:** a candied fruit **2 :** PRESERVE; *esp* **:** one prepared from a mixture of fruits

con·sid·er \kən-'sid-ər\ *vb* **-sid·ered; -sid·er·ing** \-'sid-(ə-)riŋ\ [L *considerare*, lit., to observe the stars, fr. *com-* + *sider-*, *sidus* star] **1 :** to think over carefully **:** PONDER, REFLECT **2 :** to regard highly **:** ESTEEM **3 :** to think of in a certain way **:** regard as being ⟨*consider* the price too high⟩

con·sid·er·a·ble \kən-'sid-ər-(ə-)bəl, -'sid-rə-bəl\ *adj* **1 :** deserving consideration **:** IMPORTANT **2 :** large in extent, amount, or quantity ⟨a *considerable* area⟩ ⟨a *considerable* number⟩ — **con·sid·er·a·bly** \-blē\ *adv*

con·sid·er·ate \kən-'sid-(ə-)rət\ *adj* **1 :** marked by or given to careful consideration **:** CIRCUMSPECT **2 :** thoughtful of the rights and feelings of others **syn** see THOUGHTFUL — **con·sid·er·ate·ly** *adv* — **con·sid·er·ate·ness** *n*

con·sid·er·a·tion \kən-ˌsid-ə-'rā-shən\ *n* **1 :** careful thought **:** DELIBERATION **2 :** thoughtfulness for other people **3 :** MOTIVE, REASON **4 :** RESPECT, REGARD **5 a :** a payment made in return for something **:** COMPENSATION **b :** something (as a payment or promise) given to induce another to enter into a contract

con·sid·er·ing *prep* **:** in view of **:** taking into account

con·sign \kən-'sīn\ *vt* [L *consignare* to seal, sign, fr. *com-* + *signum* mark, seal] **1 :** to give over to another's care **:** ENTRUST **2 :** to give, transfer, or deliver formally ⟨*consign* a body to the grave⟩ **3 :** to send or address to an agent to be cared for or sold — **con·sign·a·ble** \-'sī-nə-bəl\ *adj* — **con·sign·ee** \kən-ˌsī-'nē, ˌkän-ˌsī-, ˌkän(t)-sə-\ *n* — **con·sign·or** \kən-'sī-nər; kən-ˌsī-'nȯ(ə)r, ˌkän-ˌsī-, ˌkän(t)-sə-\ *n*

con·sign·ment \kən-'sīn-mənt\ *n* **1 :** the act or process of consigning **2 :** something consigned; *esp* **:** a single shipment of goods delivered to an agent for sale

con·sist \kən-'sist\ *vi* [L *consistere*, lit., to stand firm, fr. *com-* + *sistere* to stand] **1 :** to be contained **:** LIE, RESIDE — used with *in* ⟨bravery *consists* in knowing when to fight and when to run⟩ **2 :** to be made up or composed — used with *of* ⟨breakfast *consisted* of cereal, milk, and fruit⟩

con·sis·tence \kən-'sis-tən(t)s\ *n* **:** CONSISTENCY

con·sis·ten·cy \kən-'sis-tən-sē\ *n, pl* **-cies 1 a :** the condition of adhering together **:** FIRMNESS **b :** the degree of density, firmness, viscosity, or resistance to movement or separation of constituent particles **2 a :** agreement or harmony of parts or features to one another or a whole **b :** harmony with past performance or with stated aims

con·sis·tent \kən-'sis-tənt\ *adj* **1 :** possessing firmness or coherence **2 a :** AGREEING, HARMONIOUS, COMPATIBLE ⟨*consistent* statements⟩ **b :** uniform throughout **3 :** living or acting conformably to one's own belief, professions, or character — **con·sis·tent·ly** adv

con·sis·to·ry \kən-'sis-t(ə-)rē\ n, pl **-ries** [ML consistorium church tribunal, fr. L consistere to stand together, consist] : a solemn meeting of Roman Catholic cardinals presided over by the pope — **con·sis·to·ri·al** \‚kän-‚sis-'tōr-ē-əl, -'tòr-\ adj

con·so·ci·a·tion \kən-‚sō-sē-'ā-shən, -‚sō-shē-\ n : an ecological community with a single dominant — **con·so·ci·a·tion·al** \-shnəl, -shən-ᵊl\ adj

con·so·la·tion \‚kän(t)-sə-'lā-shən\ n **1** : the act or an instance of consoling : the state of being consoled : COMFORT **2** : something (as a contest held for those who have lost early in a tournament) that consoles — **con·sol·a·to·ry** \kən-'säl-ə-‚tōr-ē, -'sō-lə-, -‚tòr-\ adj

¹con·sole \kən-'sōl\ vt [L consolari, fr. com- + solari to give solace to] : to comfort in times of grief or distress : lessen the suffering and raise the spirits of ⟨not easy to console a child who has lost a pet⟩ **syn** see COMFORT — **con·sol·a·ble** \-'sō-lə-bəl\ adj

²con·sole \'kän-‚sōl\ n [F, fr. MF, short for consolateur bracket in human shape, lit., consoler, fr. L consolari to console] **1** : an architectural bracket used for ornament or support **2 a** : the desk from which an organ is played and which contains the keyboards, pedal board, and controls **b** : a panel or cabinet on which are mounted dials and switches used in controlling electrical or mechanical devices **3** : a cabinet (as for a radio or television set) designed to rest directly on the floor

console table \'kän-‚sōl-\ n **1** : a table fixed to a wall with its top supported by brackets or bracket-shaped legs **2** : a table designed to fit against a wall

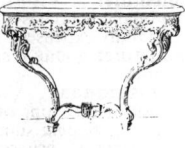

console table 2

con·sol·i·date \kən-'säl-ə-‚dāt\ vb [L consolidare to make solid, fr. com- + solidus solid] **1** : to join together into one whole : UNITE **2** : to make firm or secure : STRENGTHEN ⟨consolidate the beachhead⟩ **3** : to form into a compact mass **4** : to become consolidated; esp : MERGE ⟨the banks consolidated⟩

consolidated school n : a public school usu. elementary and in a rural district that is formed by merging other schools

con·sol·i·da·tion \kən-‚säl-ə-'dā-shən\ n **1** : the act or process of consolidating : the state of being consolidated **2** : the merger of two or more corporations into one

con·som·mé \‚kän(t)-sə-'mā\ n [F] : a clear soup chiefly of meat stock

con·so·nance \'kän(t)-s(ə-)nən(t)s\ n **1** : harmony or agreement among components **2** : an agreeable combination or correspondence of musical tones or speech sounds

¹con·so·nant \'kän(t)-s(ə-)nənt\ n [L consonant-, consonans, fr. prp. of consonare to sound together, agree, fr. com- + sonare to sound] **1** : a speech sound (as \p\, \n\, or \s\) characterized by narrowing or stoppage at one or more points in the breath channel **2** : a letter representing a consonant; esp : any letter of the English alphabet except a, e, i, o, and u

²consonant adj **1** : being in agreement or harmony ⟨consonant with the truth⟩ **2** : marked by musical consonances **3** : having like sounds ⟨consonant words⟩ — **con·so·nant·ly** adv

con·so·nan·tal \‚kän(t)-sə-'nant-ᵊl\ adj : relating to, being, or marked by a consonant or group of consonants

¹con·sort \'kän-‚sòrt\ n [L consort-, consors, fr. com- + sort-, sors lot, share] **1** : a wife or husband : SPOUSE **2** : a ship sailing in company with another ship

²con·sort \kən-'sòrt\ vb **1** : to keep company : ASSOCIATE **2** : ACCORD, HARMONIZE

con·sor·tium \kən-'sòr-sh(ē-)əm\ n, pl **-tia** \-sh(ē-)ə\ [L, fellowship, fr. consort-, consors consort] : an international business or banking agreement or combination

con·spe·cif·ic \‚kän(t)-spi-'sif-ik\ adj : of the same species

con·spec·tus \kən-'spek-təs\ n [L, sight, fr. conspect-, conspicere to get sight of] **1** : a brief survey or summary **2** : OUTLINE, SYNOPSIS

con·spic·u·ous \kən-'spik-yə-wəs\ adj [L conspicuus, fr. conspicere to get sight of, fr. com- + specere to look] **1** : obvious to the eye or mind **2** : attracting attention

: STRIKING **3** : noticeably violating good taste — **con·spic·u·ous·ly** adv — **con·spic·u·ous·ness** n

con·spir·a·cy \kən-'spir-ə-sē\ n, pl **-cies** **1** : the act of conspiring together **2 a** : an agreement among conspirators **b** : a group of conspirators **syn** see PLOT

con·spir·a·tor \kən-'spir-ət-ər\ n : one that conspires : PLOTTER

con·spir·a·to·ri·al \kən-‚spir-ə-'tōr-ē-əl, -'tòr-\ adj : of, relating to, or characteristic of a conspiracy — **con·spir·a·to·ri·al·ly** \-ē\ adv

con·spire \kən-'spī(ə)r\ vb [L conspirare, lit., to breathe together, fr. com- + spirare to breathe] **1** : PLOT, CONTRIVE ⟨conspire to overthrow the government⟩ **2** : to agree secretly to do an unlawful or wrongful act or to use such means to accomplish a lawful end **3** : to act in harmony

con·sta·ble \'kän(t)-stə-bəl, 'kən(t)-\ n [OF conestable, fr. LL comes stabuli, lit., officer of the stable] **1** : a high officer of a medieval royal or noble household **2** : the warden of a royal castle or a fortified town **3 a** : a public officer responsible for keeping the peace **b** : a British policeman

con·stab·u·lary \kən-'stab-yə-‚ler-ē\ n, pl **-lar·ies** **1** : the organized body of constables of a particular district or country **2** : an armed police force organized on military lines but distinct from the regular army

con·stan·cy \'kän(t)-stən-sē\ n **1 a** : firmness in one's beliefs : STEADFASTNESS **b** : FIDELITY, LOYALTY **2** : freedom from change

¹con·stant \'kän(t)-stənt\ adj [L constant-, constans, fr. prp. of constare to stand firm, fr. com- + stare to stand] **1** : STEADFAST, RESOLUTE; also : marked by fidelity **2** : INVARIABLE, UNIFORM **3** : continually recurring : REGULAR **syn** see FAITHFUL — **con·stant·ly** adv

²constant n : something invariable or unchanging: as **a** : a number that has a fixed value (as the velocity of light) in a given situation or universally or that is a characteristic (as the refractive index of glass) of some substance or instrument **b** : a number whose value does not change in a given mathematical discussion

con·stan·tan \'kän-stən-‚tan\ n : an alloy of copper and nickel used for electrical resistors and in thermocouples

con·stel·la·tion \‚kän(t)-stə-'lā-shən\ n [L com- + stella star] : any of 88 groups of stars forming patterns (as the Big Dipper) or an area of the heavens covering one of these groups

con·ster·nate \'kän(t)-stər-‚nāt\ vt : to fill with consternation

con·ster·na·tion \‚kän(t)-stər-'nā-shən\ n [L consternare to bewilder, alarm] : amazement or dismay that hinders or throws into confusion

con·sti·pate \'kän(t)-stə-‚pāt\ vt [ML constipare, fr. L, to crowd together, fr. com- + stipare to pack, press] : to cause constipation in

con·sti·pa·tion \‚kän(t)-stə-'pā-shən\ n : abnormally delayed or infrequent passage of dry hardened feces

con·stit·u·en·cy \kən-'stich-(ə-)wən-sē\ n, pl **-cies** **1** : a body of citizens entitled to elect a representative to a legislative or other public body **2** : the residents in an electoral district **3** : an electoral district

¹con·stit·u·ent \kən-'stich-(ə-)wənt\ n [L constituere to set up, constitute, fr. com- + statuere to set, fix, fr. status standing, status] **1** : one of the parts of which a thing is made up : COMPONENT, ELEMENT ⟨flour is the chief constituent of bread⟩ **2 a** : one of a group who elects another to represent him in a public office **b** : a voter or resident in a constituency **syn** see ELEMENT

²constituent adj **1** : serving to form, compose, or make up a unit or whole : COMPONENT ⟨a constituent republic⟩ **2** : having the power to create a government or frame or amend a constitution ⟨a constituent assembly⟩ — **con·stit·u·ent·ly** adv

con·sti·tute \'kän(t)-stə-‚t(y)üt\ vt **1** : to appoint to an office or duty ⟨a duly constituted representative⟩ **2** : to set up : ESTABLISH, FIX ⟨a fund was constituted to help needy students⟩ **3** : to make up : FORM ⟨twelve months constitute a year⟩

con·sti·tu·tion \‚kän(t)-stə-'t(y)ü-shən\ n **1** : the act of establishing, making, or setting up **2 a** : the physical makeup of the individual : PHYSIQUE **b** : the structure, composition, or nature of something **3** : the mode in which a state or society is organized; esp : the manner in

---

j joke; **ŋ** sing; **ō** flow; **ò** flaw; **òi** coin; **th** thin; **th** this; **ü** loot; **ù** foot; **y** yet; **yü** few; **yù** furious; **zh** vision

which sovereign power is distributed **4 a :** the basic principles and laws of a nation, state, or social group that determine the powers and duties of the government and guarantee certain rights to the people in it **b :** a written instrument embodying the rules of a political or social organization

¹con·sti·tu·tion·al \-shnəl, -shən-ᵊl\ *adj* **1 :** relating to, inherent in, or affecting the constitution of body or mind **2 :** of, relating to, or entering into the fundamental makeup of something **:** ESSENTIAL **3 a :** of, relating to, or in accordance with the constitution of a nation or state ⟨a *constitutional* amendment⟩ ⟨*constitutional* rights⟩ **b :** loyal to or supporting an established constitution or form of government — **con·sti·tu·tion·al·ly** \-ē\ *adv*

²constitutional *n* **:** a walk or other exercise taken for one's health

con·sti·tu·tion·al·ism \-,iz-əm\ *n* **:** adherence to or government according to constitutional principles — **con·sti·tu·tion·al·ist** \-əst\ *n*

con·sti·tu·tion·al·i·ty \,kän(t)-stə-,t(y)ü-shə-'nal-ət-ē\ *n* **:** the quality or state of being constitutional; *esp* **:** accordance with the provisions of a constitution

con·sti·tu·tive \'kän(t)-stə-,t(y)üt-iv, kən-'stich-ət-iv\ *adj* **:** forming part of the structure of a thing **:** CONSTITUENT, ESSENTIAL — **con·sti·tu·tive·ly** *adv*

con·strain \kən-'strān\ *vt* [MF *constraindre*, fr. L *constringere* to constrict, constrain, fr. *com-* + *stringere* to draw tight] **1 :** COMPEL **2 :** to force or produce in an unnatural or strained manner ⟨a *constrained* smile⟩ **3 :** to secure by or as if by bond **:** CONFINE **4 :** to hold back by force **:** RESTRAIN — **con·strained·ly** \-'strān-(ə-)dlē\ *adv*

con·straint \kən-'strānt\ *n* **1 a :** the act of constraining **:** the state of being constrained **:** COMPULSION; *also* **:** RESTRAINT **b :** a constraining agency or force **:** CHECK **2 :** repression of one's feelings, behavior, or actions **:** EMBARRASSMENT

con·strict \kən-'strikt\ *vb* [L *constrict-, constringere*] **1 a :** to draw together **b :** COMPRESS, SQUEEZE ⟨snakes that kill by *constricting* their prey⟩ **2 :** INHIBIT, CONSTRAIN **3 :** to become narrower or smaller ⟨the pupil of the eye *constricts* in bright light⟩ — **con·stric·tive** \-'strik-tiv\ *adj*

con·stric·tion \kən-'strik-shən\ *n* **1 :** an act of constricting **:** the state of being constricted **:** TIGHTENING ⟨the *constriction* of a snake's coils⟩ **2 :** something that constricts **:** a part that is constricted

con·stric·tor \kən-'strik-tər\ *n* **1 :** one that constricts **2 :** a snake that kills prey by compression in its coils

con·struct \kən-'strəkt\ *vt* [L *construct-, construere*, fr. *com-* + *struere* to build] **1 :** to make or form by combining parts **2 :** to draw (a geometrical figure) with suitable instruments and under specified conditions — **con·struct·i·ble** \-'strək-tə-bəl\ *adj* — **con·struc·tor** \-'strək-tər\ *n*

con·struc·tion \kən-'strək-shən\ *n* **1 :** the arrangement and connection of words or groups of words in a sentence **2 :** the process, art, or manner of constructing; *also* **:** a thing constructed **:** STRUCTURE **3 :** an interpretation or explanation of a statement or a fact ⟨put the wrong *construction* on a remark⟩ — **con·struc·tion·al** \-shnəl, -shən-ᵊl\ *adj* — **con·struc·tion·al·ly** \-ē\ *adv*

con·struc·tion·ist \kən-'strək-sh(ə-)nəst\ *n* **:** one who construes an instrument (as the U.S. Constitution) in a specific way ⟨a strict *constructionist*⟩

con·struc·tive \kən-'strək-tiv\ *adj* **1 :** declared such by judicial construction or interpretation ⟨*constructive* fraud⟩ **2 :** fitted for or given to constructing ⟨Edison was a great *constructive* genius⟩ **3 :** helping to develop or improve something ⟨*constructive* suggestions⟩ — **con·struc·tive·ly** *adv* — **con·struc·tive·ness** *n*

con·strue \kən-'strü\ *vb* [LL *construere*, fr. L, to construct] **1 :** to explain the grammatical relationships of the words in a sentence, clause, or phrase **2 :** to understand or explain the sense or intention of **:** INTERPRET — **con·stru·a·ble** \-'strü-ə-bəl\ *adj*

con·sul \'kän(t)-səl\ *n* [L, fr. *consulere* to take counsel, consult] **1 a :** either of two joint annually elected chief magistrates of the Roman republic **b :** one of three chief magistrates of the French republic from 1799 to 1804 **2 :** an official appointed by a government to reside in a foreign country to represent the commercial interests of citizens of the appointing country — **con·sul·ar** \-s(ə-)lər\ *adj* — **con·sul·ship** \-səl-,ship\ *n*

con·sul·ate \'kän(t)-s(ə-)lət\ *n* **1 :** a government by consuls **2 :** the office, term of office, or jurisdiction of a consul **3 :** the residence or official premises of a consul

con·sult \kən-'səlt\ *vb* [L *consultare*, freq. of *consulere* to take counsel, consult] **1 :** to seek the opinion or advice of ⟨*consult* a doctor⟩ **2 :** to seek information from ⟨*consult* an encyclopedia⟩ **3 :** to have regard to **:** CONSIDER ⟨*consult* one's best interests⟩ **4 :** to engage in deliberation **:** CONFER — **con·sult·er** *n*

con·sult·ant \kən-'səlt-ᵊnt\ *n* **1 :** one who consults another **2 :** one who gives professional advice or services

con·sul·ta·tion \,kän(t)-səl-'tā-shən\ *n* **1 :** COUNCIL, CONFERENCE; *esp* **:** a deliberation between physicians on a case or its treatment **2 :** the act of consulting or conferring

con·sul·ta·tive \kən-'səl-tət-iv\ *adj* **:** of, relating to, or intended for consultation **:** ADVISORY

con·sul·tor \kən-'səl-tər\ *n* **:** one that consults or advises; *esp* **:** a member of a Roman Catholic diocesan advisory council

con·sume \kən-'süm\ *vb* [L *consumere*, fr. *com-* + *sumere* to take] **1 a :** to destroy by or as if by fire **b :** to become destroyed by or as if by fire **2 :** to use up **:** EXPEND **3 :** to eat or drink up **4 :** to take up one's attention **:** engage one's interest — **con·sum·a·ble** \-'sü-mə-bəl\ *adj*

con·sum·er \kən-'sü-mər\ *n* **:** one that consumes: as **a :** one that utilizes economic goods **b :** an organism requiring complex organic compounds for food which it obtains by preying on other organisms or by eating particles of organic matter

consumer credit *n* **:** credit granted to an individual esp. to finance purchase of consumer goods or defray personal or family expenses

consumer goods *n pl* **:** goods that directly satisfy human wants

¹con·sum·mate \kən-'səm-ət, 'kän(t)-sə-mət\ *adj* [L *consummatus*, pp. of *consummare* to sum up, finish, fr. *com-* + *summa* sum] **:** of the highest degree or quality **:** COMPLETE, PERFECT ⟨*consummate* skill⟩ — **con·sum·mate·ly** *adv*

²con·sum·mate \'kän(t)-sə-,māt\ *vt* **1 :** to make perfect **:** FINISH, COMPLETE **2 :** to make (marital union) complete by sexual intercourse ⟨*consummate* a marriage⟩ — **con·sum·ma·tion** \,kän(t)-sə-'mā-shən\ *n*

con·sump·tion \kən-'səm(p)-shən\ *n* [L *consumpt-, consumere* to consume] **1 :** the act or process of consuming; *esp* **:** the utilization of economic goods and their destruction, deterioration, or transformation ⟨*consumption* of fuel⟩ **2 a :** a progressive wasting away of the body esp. from pulmonary tuberculosis **b :** TUBERCULOSIS

¹con·sump·tive \kən-'səm(p)-tiv\ *adj* **1 :** tending to consume **:** DESTRUCTIVE **2 :** of, relating to, or affected with consumption — **con·sump·tive·ly** *adv*

²consumptive *n* **:** a person affected with consumption

¹con·tact \'kän-,takt\ *n* [L *contactus*, fr. *contact-, contingere* to have contact with, fr. *com-* + *tangere* to touch] **1 a :** union or junction of surfaces **b** (1) **:** the junction of two electrical conductors through which a current passes (2) **:** a special part made for such a junction or connection **2 a :** ASSOCIATION, RELATIONSHIP **b :** CONNECTION, COMMUNICATION **c :** direct visual observation of the earth's surface made from an airplane esp. as an aid to navigation **d :** an establishing of communication with someone or an observing or receiving of a significant signal from a person or object

²con·tact \'kän-,takt, kən-'\ *vb* **1 :** to bring into contact **2 a :** to enter into or be in contact with ⟨*contact* your local dealer⟩ **b :** to make contact

³con·tact \'kän-,takt\ *adj* **:** maintaining, involving, or caused by contact

contact lens *n* **:** a thin lens designed to fit over the cornea

contact print *n* **:** a photographic print made with the negative in contact with the sensitized paper

con·ta·gion \kən-'tā-jən\ *n* [L *contagion-, contagio*, fr. *contingere* to have contact with] **1 :** the passing of a disease from one individual to another by direct or indirect contact **2 :** a contagious disease or its causative agent (as a virus) **3 :** transmission of an influence to the mind of others or the influence transmitted

con·ta·gious \kən-'tā-jəs\ *adj* **:** communicable by contact **:** CATCHING; *also* **:** relating to contagion or contagious diseases — **con·ta·gious·ly** *adv* — **con·ta·gious·ness** *n*

ə abut; ᵊ kitten; ər further; a back; ā bake; ä cot, cart; aú out; ch chin; e less; ē easy; g gift; i trip; ī life

con·tain \kən-'tān\ *vt* [OF *contenir*, fr. L *continēre* to hold together, contain, fr. *com-* + *tenēre* to hold] **1 :** to keep within limits **:** hold back **:** RESTRAIN **2 a :** to have within **:** HOLD **b :** COMPRISE, INCLUDE **3 a :** to be divisible by esp. without a remainder **b :** ENCLOSE, BOUND — **con·tain·a·ble** \-'tā-nə-bəl\ *adj*
syn HOLD, ACCOMMODATE: CONTAIN implies the actual presence of a specified substance or quantity within something; HOLD may imply only the capacity or usual function of containing or keeping; ACCOMMODATE stresses capacity to hold without crowding or inconvenience
con·tain·er \kən-'tā-nər\ *n* **:** one that contains; *esp* **:** RECEPTACLE
con·tain·ment \kən-'tān-mənt\ *n* **1 :** the act or process of containing **2 :** the policy, process, or result of preventing the expansion of a hostile power or ideology
con·tam·i·nant \kən-'tam-ə-nənt\ *n* **:** something that contaminates
con·tam·i·nate \kən-'tam-ə-,nāt\ *vt* [L *contaminare*] **1 :** to soil, stain, or infect by contact or association **2 :** to make unfit for use by introduction of unwholesome or undesirable elements — **con·tam·i·na·tion** \-,tam-ə-'nā-shən\ *n* — **con·tam·i·na·tive** \-,nāt-iv\ *adj* — **con·tam·i·na·tor** \-'tam-ə-,nāt-ər\ *n*
con·temn \kən-'tem\ *vt* [L *contemnere*, fr. *com-* + *temnere* to despise] **:** to view or treat with contempt **:** DISDAIN, SCORN — **con·tem·ner** \-'tem-ər, -'tem-nər\ *n*
con·tem·plate \'känt-əm-,plāt, 'kän-,tem-\ *vb* [L *contemplari*, fr. *com-* + *templum* temple, space marked out for observation of auguries] **1 :** to consider carefully and for a long time **:** MEDITATE **2 :** to look forward to **:** have in mind **:** INTEND — **con·tem·pla·tor** \-,plāt-ər\ *n*
con·tem·pla·tion \,känt-əm-'plā-shən, ,kän-,tem-\ *n* **1 :** concentration on spiritual things as a form of private devotion **2 :** an act of considering with attention **:** STUDY **3 :** the act of regarding steadily **4 :** INTENTION, EXPECTATION
con·tem·pla·tive \kən-'tem-plət-iv; 'känt-əm-,plāt-, 'kän-,tem-\ *adj* **:** marked by or given to contemplation; *esp* **:** of or relating to a religious order devoted to prayer and penance — **con·tem·pla·tive·ly** *adv* — **con·tem·pla·tive·ness** *n*
con·tem·po·ra·ne·ous \kən-,tem-pə-'rā-nē-əs\ *adj* **:** existing, occurring, or originating during the same time — **con·tem·po·ra·ne·ous·ly** *adv* — **con·tem·po·ra·ne·ous·ness** *n*
¹con·tem·po·rary \kən-'tem-pə-,rer-ē\ *adj* [L *com-* + *tempor-, tempus* time] **1 :** living or occurring at the same period of time **:** CONTEMPORANEOUS ⟨*contemporary* events in different countries⟩ **2 :** of the same age **3 :** of the present time **:** LIVING, MODERN ⟨our *contemporary* writers⟩
syn CONTEMPORARY, SIMULTANEOUS, CONCURRENT, COINCIDENT mean existing or occurring at the same time. CONTEMPORARY applies chiefly to people and what relates to them and suggests indefinite lengths of time ⟨playwrights *contemporary* with Shakespeare⟩ SIMULTANEOUS implies correspondence in instant of time ⟨the two shots were almost *simultaneous*⟩ CONCURRENT implies beginning and ending together ⟨*concurrent* prison sentences⟩ COINCIDENT stresses simultaneousness of events and may emphasize lack of causal relation ⟨found that their birthdays were *coincident*⟩
²contemporary *n, pl* **-rar·ies 1 :** one that is contemporary with another **2 :** one of about the same age as another
con·tempt \kən-'tem(p)t\ *n* [L *contemptus*, fr. *contempt-, contemnere* to contemn] **1 :** the act of despising **:** the state of mind of one who despises **:** DISDAIN **2 :** the state of being despised **3 :** disobedience or disrespect to a court, judge, or legislative body
con·tempt·i·ble \kən-'tem(p)-tə-bəl\ *adj* **:** deserving contempt ⟨a *contemptible* lie⟩ — **con·tempt·i·bly** \-blē\ *adv*
syn DESPICABLE, PITIFUL: CONTEMPTIBLE may apply to whatever is worthy of contempt; DESPICABLE implies arousing scornful often indignant moral disapproval; PITIFUL suggests feebleness, insignificance, or gross inadequacy
con·temp·tu·ous \kən-'tem(p)-chə-wəs\ *adj* **:** feeling or showing contempt **:** SCORNFUL ⟨a *contemptuous* sneer⟩ — **con·temp·tu·ous·ly** *adv* — **con·temp·tu·ous·ness** *n*
con·tend \kən-'tend\ *vb* [L *contendere*, fr. *com-* + *tendere* to stretch, strain] **1 :** to compete with another in opposi-

tion or in rivalry **2 :** STRIVE, STRUGGLE ⟨*contend* against difficulties⟩ **3 :** ARGUE, MAINTAIN ⟨*contends* that his opinion is right⟩ — **con·tend·er** *n*
¹con·tent \kən-'tent\ *adj* [L *contentus*, fr. pp. of *continēre* to hold in, contain] **:** SATISFIED, CONTENTED
²content *vt* **:** to appease the desires of **:** SATISFY
³content *n* **:** CONTENTMENT; *esp* **:** freedom from care or discomfort
⁴con·tent \'kän-,tent\ *n* [L *contentus*, pp. of *continēre* to contain] **1 :** something contained — usu. used in pl. ⟨the *contents* of a jar⟩ **2 :** the subject matter or topics treated (as in a book) ⟨table of *contents*⟩ **3 :** the significant part (as of a book or a speech) **:** essential meaning **4 a :** CAPACITY **b :** the amount contained **:** PROPORTION
con·tent·ed \kən-'tent-əd\ *adj* **:** satisfied or showing satisfaction with one's possessions, status, or situation ⟨a *contented* smile⟩ — **con·tent·ed·ly** *adv* — **con·tent·ed·ness** *n*
con·ten·tion \kən-'ten-chən\ *n* [L *content-, contendere* to contend] **1 :** an act or instance of contending **:** STRIFE, DISPUTE **2 :** a point advanced or maintained in a debate or argument
con·ten·tious \kən-'ten-chəs\ *adj* **:** inclined to find or seek reasons for contention often over unimportant matters **:** QUARRELSOME — **con·ten·tious·ly** *adv* — **con·ten·tious·ness** *n*
con·tent·ment \kən-'tent-mənt\ *n* **:** the state of being contented **:** peaceful satisfaction
con·ter·mi·nous \kən-'tər-mə-nəs, kän-\ *adj* [L *com-* + *terminus* boundary] **:** having the same or a common boundary — **con·ter·mi·nous·ly** *adv*
¹con·test \kən-'test, 'kän-\ *vb* [L *contestari* to call to witness, contest (a lawsuit), fr. *com-* + *testis* witness] **1 :** DISPUTE, CHALLENGE ⟨*contest* a divorce⟩ **2 :** to struggle over or for ⟨a *contested* territory⟩ **3 :** STRIVE, VIE — **con·test·a·ble** \-ə-bəl\ *adj* — **con·test·er** *n*
²con·test \'kän-,test\ *n* **1 :** a struggle for victory or superiority (as in strength, skill, or knowledge) **:** COMPETITION **2 :** OPPOSITION, RIVALRY ⟨meet in friendly *contest*⟩
con·test·ant \kən-'tes-tənt, 'kän-,tes-\ *n* **:** one who contests; *esp* **:** one who takes part in a contest ⟨a *contestant* in a spelling bee⟩
con·text \'kän-,tekst\ *n* [L *contextus*, fr. *context-, contexere* to weave together, fr. *com-* + *texere* to weave] **:** the parts of a written or spoken passage that are near a certain word or group of words and that help to explain its meaning — **con·tex·tu·al** \kän-'teks-chə(-wə)l\ *adj* — **con·tex·tu·al·ly** \-ē\ *adv*
con·ti·gu·i·ty \,känt-ə-'gyü-ət-ē\ *n* **:** the state of being contiguous
con·tig·u·ous \kən-'tig-yə-wəs\ *adj* [L *contiguus*, fr. *contingere* to have contact with] **1 :** being in contact **2 :** very near though not in actual contact **:** TOUCHING **2 :** very near though not in actual contact **:** NEIGHBORING — **con·tig·u·ous·ly** *adv* — **con·tig·u·ous·ness** *n*
con·ti·nence \'känt-ᵊn-ən(t)s\ *n* **1 :** SELF-RESTRAINT **2 :** ability to refrain from a bodily activity
¹con·ti·nent \'känt-ᵊn-ənt\ *adj* [L *continent-, continens*, fr. prp. of *continēre* to hold together, hold in, contain] **:** exercising continence — **con·ti·nent·ly** *adv*
²con·ti·nent \'känt-ᵊn-ənt, 'känt-nənt\ *n* **1 :** MAINLAND **2 a :** one of the great divisions of land (as North America, South America, Europe, Asia, Africa, Australia, or Antarctica) on the globe **b** *cap* **:** the continent of Europe ⟨spent the summer on the *Continent*⟩
¹con·ti·nen·tal \,känt-ᵊn-'ent-ᵊl\ *adj* **1 :** of, relating to, or characteristic of a continent ⟨*continental* waters⟩; *esp* **:** of or relating to the continent of Europe as distinguished from the British Isles **2** *often cap* **:** of or relating to the colonies later forming the U.S. ⟨*Continental* Congress⟩ — **con·ti·nen·tal·ly** \-ᵊl-ē\ *adv*
²continental *n* **1 a** *often cap* **:** an American soldier of the Revolution in the Continental army **b :** a piece of paper currency issued by the Continental Congress at the time of the American Revolution **c :** an inhabitant of a continent and esp. the continent of Europe **2** [so called fr. the dubious value of Continental currency] **:** the least bit ⟨not worth a *continental*⟩
continental shelf *n* **:** a shallow submarine plain of varying width forming a border to a continent and typically ending in a steep slope to the depths of the ocean

con·tin·gen·cy \kən-'tin-jən-sē\ *n, pl* **-cies** **1 :** the state of being contingent **2 :** a chance happening or event **3 :** a possible event or one foreseen as possible if another occurs ⟨prepared for every *contingency*⟩
¹con·tin·gent \-jənt\ *adj* [L *contingere* to have contact with, happen to] **1 :** likely but not certain to happen **:** POSSIBLE **2 a :** happening by chance or unforeseen causes **b :** intended for use in circumstances not completely foreseen ⟨*contingent* funds⟩ **3 :** dependent on or conditioned by something else ⟨plans *contingent* on the weather⟩ — **con·tin·gent·ly** *adv*
²contingent *n* **1 :** a chance occurrence **:** CONTINGENCY **2 :** a number of persons representing or drawn from an area or group ⟨a *contingent* of troops from each regiment⟩
con·tin·u·al \kən-'tin-yə(-wə)l\ *adj* **1 :** continuing indefinitely in time without interruption ⟨*continual* fear⟩ **2 :** recurring in rapid succession ⟨*continual* interruptions⟩ **3 :** forming a continuous series — **con·tin·u·al·ly** \-ē\ *adv*
 syn CONTINUOUS, INCESSANT: CONTINUAL implies prolonged succession or recurrence ⟨*continual* showers⟩ CONTINUOUS implies uninterrupted flow ⟨*continuous* roar of the falls⟩ INCESSANT implies ceaseless activity of varying intensity ⟨*incessant* quarreling⟩
con·tin·u·ance \kən-'tin-yə-wən(t)s\ *n* **1 :** the act of continuing in a state, condition, or course of action ⟨during the *continuance* of the illness⟩ **2 :** unbroken succession **:** CONTINUATION **3 :** postponement of proceedings in a court of law to a specified day
con·tin·u·a·tion \kən-,tin-yə-'wā-shən\ *n* **1 :** continuance in or prolongation of a state or activity **2 :** resumption after an interruption **3 :** something that continues, increases, or adds ⟨a *continuation* of last week's story⟩
con·tin·ue \kən-'tin-yü\ *vb* [L *continuare*, fr. *continuus* continuous, fr. *continēre* to hold together, contain] **1 :** to remain in a place or a condition **:** STAY ⟨*continue* in one's present position⟩ **2 :** ENDURE, LAST ⟨cold weather *continued*⟩ **3 :** to go on or carry forward in a course ⟨*continue* to study hard⟩ ⟨*continue* the study of French⟩ **4 :** to go on or carry on after an interruption **:** RESUME ⟨the play *continued* after the intermission⟩ **5 :** to postpone a legal proceeding to a later date **6 :** to allow or cause to remain esp. in a position ⟨the town officials were *continued* in office⟩ — **con·tin·u·er** *n*
con·ti·nu·i·ty \,känt-ᵊn-'(y)ü-ət-ē\ *n, pl* **-ties 1 a :** uninterrupted connection, succession, or union **b :** persistence without change **c :** uninterrupted duration in time **2 a :** a script or scenario in the performing arts **b :** transitional spoken or musical matter for a radio or television program **c :** the story and dialogue of a comic strip
con·tin·u·ous \kən-'tin-yə-wəs\ *adj* **:** being without break or interruption **:** CONTINUED, UNBROKEN ⟨*continuous* line⟩ ⟨*continuous* showing of a moving picture⟩ **syn** see CONTINUAL — **con·tin·u·ous·ly** *adv* — **con·tin·u·ous·ness** *n*
con·tin·u·um \-yə-wəm\ *n, pl* **-ua** \-wə\ *also* **-uums** [L, neut. of *continuus* continuous] **1 :** something that is continuous and the same throughout **2 :** something that consists of a series of definite or indefinite variations or of a sequence of things in regular order
con·tort \kən-'tȯrt\ *vb* [L *contort-, contorquēre*, fr. *com-* + *torquēre* to twist] **:** to twist into an unusual appearance or unnatural shape **:** DEFORM, DISTORT
con·tor·tion \kən-'tȯr-shən\ *n* **1 :** a contorting or a being contorted **2 :** a contorted shape or thing
con·tor·tion·ist \-sh(ə-)nəst\ *n* **:** a person who contorts; *esp* **:** an acrobat who puts himself into unusual postures — **con·tor·tion·is·tic** \-,tȯr-shə-'nis-tik\ *adj*
¹con·tour \'kän-,tü(ə)r\ *n* [F, fr. It *contornare* to round off, outline, fr. L *com-* + *tornare* to turn in a lathe, fr. *tornus* lathe] **1 :** the outline of a figure or body; *also* **:** a line or a drawing representing such an outline ⟨the *contours* of a coast or of a mountain⟩ **2 :** SHAPE, FORM ⟨*contour* of the land⟩
²contour *vt* **1 :** to shape the contour of **2 :** to shape to fit contours
³contour *adj* **:** following or fitted to the contour of something ⟨*contour* plowing⟩
contour feather *n* **:** one of the medium-sized feathers that form the general covering of a bird and determine the external contour

contour line *n* **:** a line (as on a map) connecting the points on a land surface that have the same elevation
contour map *n* **:** a map having contour lines
contra- *prefix* [L, against, opposite]
1 : against **:** contrary **:** contrasting ⟨*contra*distinction⟩ **2 :** pitched below normal bass ⟨*contra*octave⟩

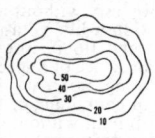
contour map

con·tra·band \'kän-trə-,band\ *n* [It *contrabbando*, fr. ML *contrabannum*, fr. *contra-* + *bannum* decree, ban] **:** goods or merchandise whose importation, exportation, or possession is forbidden; *also* **:** smuggled goods — **contraband** *adj*
contraband of war : something that under international law cannot be supplied to a country at war except at the risk of seizure by the country warring against that country
¹con·tra·bass \'kän-trə-,bās\ *n* **:** DOUBLE BASS
²contrabass *adj* **:** having a pitch range an octave lower than the normal bass ⟨a *contrabass* clarinet⟩
con·tra·bas·soon \,kän-trə-bə-'sün, -ba-\ *n* **:** the largest member of the oboe family an octave lower in pitch than the bassoon
con·tra·cep·tion \,kän-trə-'sep-shən\ *n* [*contra-* + *conception*] **:** voluntary prevention of conception
¹con·tra·cep·tive \-'sep-tiv\ *adj* **:** relating to or used for contraception
²contraceptive *n* **:** a contraceptive agent or device
¹con·tract \'kän-,trakt\ *n* [L *contractus*, fr. *contract-, contrahere* to make a contract, reduce in size, fr. *com-* + *trahere* to draw] **1 a :** a legally binding agreement between two or more persons or parties **:** COVENANT **b :** BETROTHAL **2 :** a writing made by the parties to evidence the terms and conditions of a contract **3 :** an undertaking to win a specified number of tricks or points in bridge
²con·tract \kən-'trakt, *oftenest for 2* 'kän-,\ *vb* **1 :** to enter into by contract ⟨*contract* a marriage⟩ **2 :** to undertake by contract ⟨*contract* to build a bridge⟩ **3 a :** LIMIT, RESTRICT **b :** to draw together or draw up so as to make or to become shorter and broader ⟨brows *contracting* in puzzlement⟩⟨*contract* a muscle⟩⟨muscles *contract*⟩ **4 a :** to diminish in size **:** SHORTEN, SHRINK ⟨metal *contracts* in cold weather⟩ **b :** to shorten (as a word) by omitting one or more sounds or letters ⟨*contract secretary* into *secy*⟩ **5 a :** GET, CATCH ⟨*contract* a cold⟩ **b :** FORM ⟨it is easier to *contract* a habit than to break one⟩ — **con·tract·i·bil·i·ty** \kən-,trak-tə-'bil-ət-ē, ,kän-\ — **con·tract·i·ble** \kən-'trak-tə-bəl, 'kän-,\ *adj*
contract bridge \,kän-,trak(t)-\ *n* **:** a card game identical with auction bridge except that odd tricks do not count toward game or slam bonuses unless undertaken in the contract
con·trac·tile \kən-'trak-tᵊl\ *adj* **:** having the power or property of contracting — **con·trac·til·i·ty** \,kän-,trak-'til-ət-ē\ *n*
contractile vacuole *n* **:** a vacuole in a unicellular organism that contracts regularly to discharge fluid from the body and is held to have an excretory or hydrostatic function
con·trac·tion \kən-'trak-shən\ *n* **1 a :** the act or process of contracting **:** the state of being contracted **b :** the shortening and thickening of a functioning muscle or muscle fiber **2 :** a shortening of a word, syllable, or word group by omission of a sound or letter; *also* **:** a form produced by such shortening ⟨*aren't* is a *contraction* of *are not*⟩ — **con·trac·tion·al** \-'trak-shnəl, -shən-ᵊl\ *adj* — **con·trac·tive** \-'trak-tiv\ *adj*
con·trac·tor \'kän-,trak-tər, kən-'\ *n* **:** one that contracts or is party to a contract; *esp* **:** one who agrees to perform work or provide supplies at a given price or within a given time ⟨building *contractor*⟩
con·trac·tu·al \kən-'trak-chə(-wə)l, kän-\ *adj* **:** of, relating to, or constituting a contract ⟨*contractual* agreements⟩ — **con·trac·tu·al·ly** \-ē\ *adv*
con·tra·dict \,kän-trə-'dikt\ *vt* [L *contradict-, contradicere*, fr. *contra-* + *dicere* to say] **1 :** to deny the truth of (as a statement or a speaker) **:** state the contrary of **2 :** to be contrary or opposed to **:** go counter to ⟨two reports that *contradict* each other⟩⟨his actions *contradict* his words⟩ — **con·tra·dict·a·ble** \-'dik-tə-bəl\ *adj* — **con·tra·dic·tor** \-tər\ *n*

con·tra·dic·tion \-'dik-shən\ *n* **1 a :** a statement that contradicts another **b :** the act of contradicting **:** denial of the truth of something said **2 :** opposition existing between things ⟨a *contradiction* between desire and reality⟩

con·tra·dic·tious \-shəs\ *adj* **1 :** CONTRADICTORY, OPPOSITE **2 :** given to or marked by contradiction **:** CONTRARY

¹con·tra·dic·to·ry \,kän-trə-'dik-t(ə-)rē\ *n, pl* **-ries** **1 a :** something that contradicts **b :** OPPOSITE, CONTRARY **2 :** either of two propositions of which if one is true the other must be false

²contradictory *adj* **1 :** tending to contradict **2 :** involving contradiction **:** OPPOSED ⟨*contradictory* statements⟩ **syn** see CONTRARY — **con·tra·dic·to·ri·ly** \-t(ə-)rə-lē\ *adv* — **con·tra·dic·to·ri·ness** \-t(ə-)rē-nəs\ *n*

con·tra·dis·tinc·tion \,kän-trə-dis-'tiŋ(k)-shən\ *n* **:** distinction by contrast ⟨painting in *contradistinction* to sculpture⟩ — **con·tra·dis·tinc·tive** \-'tiŋ(k)-tiv\ *adj* — **con·tra·dis·tinc·tive·ly** *adv*

con·tra·dis·tin·guish \-'tiŋ-gwish\ *vt* **:** to distinguish by contrast of qualities

con·trail \'kän-,trāl\ *n* [*con*densation *trail*] **:** streaks of condensed water vapor created in the air by an airplane or rocket at high altitudes

con·tra·in·di·cate \,kän-trə-'in-də-,kāt\ *vt* **:** to make (as a treatment or procedure) inadvisable — **con·tra·in·di·ca·tion** \-,in-də-'kā-shən\ *n* — **con·tra·in·dic·a·tive** \-in-'dik-ət-iv\ *adj*

con·tral·to \kən-'tral-tō\ *n, pl* **-tos** [It, fr. *contra-* + *alto* high] **1 a :** the lowest female singing voice **b :** a singer with such a voice **2 :** the part sung by a contralto

con·tra·pos·i·tive \,kän-trə-'päz-ət-iv, -'päz-tiv\ *n* **:** the statement obtained by interchanging the hypothesis and conclusion of a conditional statement and denying both clauses ⟨the *contrapositive* of "if A, then B" is "if not B, then not A"⟩

con·trap·tion \kən-'trap-shən\ *n* **:** CONTRIVANCE, DEVICE, GADGET

con·tra·pun·tal \,kän-trə-'pənt-ᵊl\ *adj* [It *contrappunto* counterpoint, fr. ML *contrapunctus*] **1 :** of or relating to counterpoint **2 :** POLYPHONIC — **con·tra·pun·tal·ly** \-ᵊl-ē\ *adv*

con·tra·pun·tist \-'pənt-əst\ *n* **:** one who writes counterpoint

con·tra·ri·e·ty \,kän-trə-'rī-ət-ē\ *n, pl* **-ties** **1 :** the quality or state of being contrary **2 :** something contrary

con·trari·wise \'kän-,trer-ē-,wīz, kən-'\ *adv* **1 :** on the contrary **2 :** vice versa **:** CONVERSELY **3 :** PERVERSELY, CONTRARILY

¹con·trary \'kän-,trer-ē\ *n, pl* **-trar·ies** **1 :** a fact or condition incompatible with another **:** OPPOSITE **2 :** one of a pair of opposites **3 :** one of two statements in logic of which both may be false but both may not be true — **by contraries :** in a manner opposite to what is logical or expected — **on the contrary :** just the opposite **:** NO — **to the contrary :** NOTWITHSTANDING

²con·trary \'kän-,trer-ē, 4 *is often* kən-'tre(ə)r-ē\ *adj* [L *contrarius*, fr. *contra* against, opposite] **1 :** exactly opposite **:** wholly different ⟨*contrary* opinions⟩ **2 :** OPPOSED ⟨an act *contrary* to law⟩ **3 :** UNFAVORABLE ⟨a *contrary* wind⟩ **4 :** inclined to oppose or resist **:** WAYWARD ⟨a *contrary* child⟩ — **con·trar·i·ly** \-,trer-ə-lē, -'trer-\ *adv* — **con·trar·i·ness** \-,trer-ē-nəs, -'trer-\ *n*

syn OPPOSITE, CONTRADICTORY: CONTRARY implies extreme divergence and often antagonism; OPPOSITE applies to things in sharp contrast or reversed positions; CONTRADICTORY implies the impossibility of two things being true or valid at the same time

³con·trary *like* ²CONTRARY\ *adv* **:** CONTRARILY, CONTRARIWISE

¹con·trast \'kän-,trast\ *n* **1 :** the act or process of contrasting **:** the state of being contrasted **2 :** a person or thing that exhibits differences when contrasted **3 :** difference esp. when sharp or striking between associated things; *esp* **:** diversity of adjacent parts in color, emotion, tone, or brightness ⟨a photograph having good *contrast*⟩

²con·trast \kən-'trast, 'kän-,\ *vb* [F *contraster*, fr. It *contrastare*, fr. *contra-* + *stare* to stand, fr. L] **1 :** to show noticeable differences ⟨black and gold *contrast* sharply⟩ **2 :** to compare two persons or things so as to show the differences between them ⟨*contrast* winter and summer⟩ **syn** see COMPARE — **con·trast·a·ble** \-ə-bəl\ *adj*

con·trasty \'kän-,tras-tē, kən-'\ *adj* **:** having or producing in photography great contrast between highlights and shadows

con·tra·vene \,kän-trə-'vēn\ *vt* [LL *contravent-, contravenire*, fr. L *contra-* + *venire* to come] **1 :** to go or act contrary to ⟨*contravene* a law⟩ **2 :** to oppose in argument **:** CONTRADICT ⟨a proposition that is not likely to be *contravened*⟩ — **con·tra·ven·er** *n*

con·tra·ven·tion \,kän-trə-'ven-chən\ *n* **:** the act of contravening **:** VIOLATION

con·tre·danse *or* **con·tra dance** \'kän-trə-,dan(t)s\ *n* [F *contredanse*, fr. E *country-dance*] **1 :** a folk dance in which couples face each other in two lines or in a square **2 :** a piece of music for a contredanse

con·tre·temps \'kän-trə-,tän\ *n, pl* **con·tre·temps** \-,tän(z)\ [F, fr. *contre-* counter- + *temps* time] **:** an inopportune embarrassing occurrence **:** MISHAP

con·trib·ute \kən-'trib-yət\ *vb* [L *contribuere*, fr. *com-* + *tribuere* to grant] **1 :** to give along with others ⟨*contribute* to charities⟩ ⟨members were asked to *contribute* $5 each⟩ **2 :** to have a share in something ⟨factors *contributing* to an accident⟩ ⟨every member of the class *contributed* to the success of the exhibit⟩ **3 :** to supply (as an article) for publication esp. in a periodical

con·tri·bu·tion \,kän-trə-'byü-shən\ *n* **1 :** LEVY, TAX **2 :** the act of contributing; *also* **:** the sum or thing contributed **3 :** a writing for publication esp. in a periodical

con·trib·u·tive \kən-'trib-yət-iv\ *adj* **:** contributing or tending to contribute — **con·trib·u·tive·ly** *adv*

con·trib·u·tor \-yət-ər\ *n* **:** one that contributes; *esp* **:** one who contributes writings for publication esp. in a periodical

con·trib·u·to·ry \kən-'trib-yə-,tōr-ē, -,tȯr-ē\ *adj* **1 :** that contributes or serves to contribute; *esp* **:** helping to accomplish a result ⟨carelessness *contributory* to an accident⟩ **2 a :** of, relating to, or forming a contribution **b :** supported by contributions ⟨a *contributory* pension plan⟩

con·trite \'kän-,trīt, kən-'\ *adj* [ML *contritus*, lit., bruised, fr. L, pp. of *conterere* to bruise, fr. *com-* + *terere* to rub] **1 :** sorrowful for some wrong that one has done **:** deeply repentant **2 :** caused by repentance ⟨*contrite* tears⟩ — **con·trite·ly** *adv* — **con·trite·ness** *n*

con·tri·tion \kən-'trish-ən\ *n* **:** the state of being contrite **syn** see PENITENCE

con·triv·ance \kən-'trī-vən(t)s\ *n* **1 :** the act or faculty of contriving **:** the state of being contrived **2 :** a thing contrived; *esp* **:** a mechanical device

con·trive \kən-'trīv\ *vb* [ME *controven, contreven*, fr. MF *controver*] **1 :** PLAN, PLOT, SCHEME ⟨*contrive* a means of escape⟩ **2 :** to form or make in some skillful or ingenious way **:** INVENT, DESIGN **3 :** to bring about **:** MANAGE ⟨had a hard time *contriving* to make ends meet⟩ — **con·triv·er** *n*

con·trived *adj* **:** ARTIFICIAL, UNNATURAL

¹con·trol \kən-'trōl\ *vt* **con·trolled; con·trol·ling** [MF *controller*, fr. *controlle* audit, fr. *contre-* counter- + *rolle* roll, account] **1 :** to check, test, or verify by evidence or experiments **2 a :** to exercise restraining or directing influence over **:** REGULATE **b :** to have power over **:** RULE ⟨*control* a territory⟩ **syn** see CONDUCT — **con·trol·la·ble** \-'trō-lə-bəl\ *adj*

²control *n* **1 :** the power or authority to control or command ⟨a child under his parents' *control*⟩ **2 a :** ability to control ⟨anger that is out of *control*⟩ ⟨lose *control* of an automobile⟩ **b :** RESTRAINT, RESERVE **3 :** a means or method of controlling **:** one that controls: as **a :** a mechanism used to regulate or guide the operation of a machine, apparatus, or system ⟨the *controls* of an airplane⟩ ⟨price *controls*⟩ ⟨traffic *control*⟩ **b :** a personality or spirit believed to actuate the utterances or performances of a spiritualist medium **c :** something used in an experiment or a study to provide a basis for comparing results or for checking their accuracy

control experiment *n* **:** an experiment to check the results of other experiments

con·trol·ler \kən-'trō-lər, 'kän-\ *n* **1 a :** COMPTROLLER **b :** the chief accounting officer of a business or institution **2 :** one that controls — **con·trol·ler·ship** \-,ship\ *n*

con·tro·ver·sial \,kän-trə-'vər-shəl, -'vər-sē-əl\ *adj* **1 :** of or relating to controversy **2 :** open to or likely to cause controversy ⟨a *controversial* question⟩ **3 :** fond of con-

---

j joke; **ŋ** sing; **ō** flow; **ȯ** flaw; **ȯi** coin; **th** thin; **t̲h** this; **ü** loot; **u̇** foot; **y** yet; **yü** few; **yu̇** furious; **zh** vision

troversy : ARGUMENTATIVE — **con·tro·ver·sial·ist** \-əst\
n — **con·tro·ver·sial·ly** \-ē\ *adv*
con·tro·ver·sy \'kän-trə-ˌvər-sē\ *n, pl* **-sies** [L *controversia*, fr. *controversus* disputable, lit., turned opposite]
1 : a discussion marked esp. by expression of opposing
views : DISPUTE **2** : QUARREL, STRIFE
con·tro·vert \'kän-trə-ˌvərt, ˌkän-trə-'\ *vt* : to oppose by
argument : DENY, CONTRADICT ⟨a theory *controverted* by
facts⟩ — **con·tro·vert·er** *n* — **con·tro·vert·i·ble** \-ə-bəl\
adj
con·tu·ma·cious \ˌkän-t(y)ə-'mā-shəs, ˌkän-chə-\ *adj*
: stubbornly disobedient : REBELLIOUS — **con·tu·ma·**
cious·ly *adv*
con·tu·ma·cy \kən-'t(y)ü-mə-sē; 'kän-t(y)ə-, 'kän-chə-\ *n*,
pl **-cies** [L *contumacia*, fr. *contumac-, contumax* insubordinate, fr. *com-* + *tumēre* to swell, be proud] : stubborn
opposition to authority : DEFIANCE
con·tu·me·li·ous \ˌkän-t(y)ə-'mē-lē-əs, ˌkän-chə-\ *adj* : insolently abusive and humiliating — **con·tu·me·li·ous·ly**
adv
con·tu·me·ly \kən-'t(y)ü-mə-lē; 'kän-t(y)ə-ˌmē-lē, 'kän-
chə-\ *n, pl* **-lies** [L *contumelia*] : rude language or treatment arising from haughtiness and contempt; *also* : an
instance of such language or treatment
con·tuse \kən-'t(y)üz\ *vt* [L *contus-, contundere* to crush,
bruise, fr. *com-* + *tundere* to beat] : to injure (tissue) usu.
without breaking the skin : BRUISE — **con·tu·sion**
\-'t(y)ü-zhən\ *n*
co·nun·drum \kə-'nən-drəm\ *n* **1** : a riddle whose
answer is or involves a pun **2** : an intricate and difficult
problem
con·ur·ba·tion \ˌkän-(ˌ)ər-'bā-shən\ *n* [*com-* + L *urbs*
city] : a continuous network of urban communities
con·va·lesce \ˌkän-və-'les\ *vi* [L *convalescere*, fr. *com-*
+ *valescere* to grow strong, fr. *valēre* to be strong] : to
recover health and strength gradually after illness or
weakness
con·va·les·cence \ˌkän-və-'les-ᵊn(t)s\ *n* : the process or
period of convalescing — **con·va·les·cent** \-ᵊnt\ *adj or n*
con·vec·tion \kən-'vek-shən\ *n* [L *convect-, convehere* to
bring together, fr. *com-* + *vehere* to carry] : the circulatory
motion that occurs in a gas or liquid at a nonuniform
temperature owing to currents caused by differences in
density with the warmer portions rising and the colder
denser portions sinking; *also* : the transfer of heat by this
automatic circulation of a fluid — **con·vec·tion·al** \-shnəl,
-shən-ᵊl\ *adj* — **con·vec·tive** \-'vek-tiv\ *adj*
con·vec·tor \-'vek-tər\ *n* : a heating unit in which air
heated by contact with a heating device in a casing circulates by convection
con·vene \kən-'vēn\ *vb* [L *convenire*, fr. *com-* + *venire* to
come] **1** : to come together in a group or body : MEET
⟨the legislature *convened* Tuesday⟩ **2** : to cause to assemble : call together ⟨the chairman *convened* the meeting⟩
— **con·ven·er** *n*
con·ve·nience \kən-'vē-nyən(t)s\ *n* **1** : fitness or suitability for meeting a requirement ⟨took the house because
of the *convenience* of its location⟩ **2** : personal comfort
: freedom from trouble ⟨thought only of his own *convenience*⟩ **3** : a suitable time : OPPORTUNITY ⟨come at your
earliest *convenience*⟩ **4** : something⟨as a device or a
service⟩ that gives comfort or advantage ⟨a house with all
modern *conveniences*⟩
con·ve·nient \-nyənt\ *adj* [L *convenient-, conveniens*, fr. prp. of *convenire* to come together, agree, be
suitable] **1 a** : suited to personal comfort or to easy use
⟨*convenient* tools⟩ ⟨*convenient* location⟩ ⟨*convenient* time⟩
b : suited to a particular situation ⟨found it *convenient* not
to be at home⟩ **2** : near at hand : HANDY ⟨schools,
churches, and stores are all *convenient*⟩ — **con·ve·nient·ly**
adv
con·vent \'kän-vənt, -ˌvent\ *n* [ML *conventus*, fr. L,
assembly, fr. *convent-, convenire* to convene] : a local
community or house of a religious order or congregation;
esp : an establishment of nuns — **con·ven·tu·al** \kən-
'vench-(ə-)wəl, kän-\ *adj*
con·ven·ti·cle \kən-'vent-i-kəl\ *n* : ASSEMBLY, MEETING;
esp : a religious meeting not permitted by law
con·ven·tion \kən-'ven-chən\ *n* [L *convent-, convenire* to
convene, be suitable] **1** : AGREEMENT, COVENANT ⟨an
international *convention* for treatment of prisoners of war⟩

2 : generally accepted custom, practice, or belief; *also*
: something accepted by convention as true, useful, or
convenient : RULE ⟨the *convention* of driving on the right⟩
3 : an assembly of persons met for a common purpose
⟨a constitutional *convention*⟩ ⟨teachers' *convention*⟩ **4** : a
practice in bidding or playing that conveys information
between partners in a card game (as bridge)
con·ven·tion·al \kən-'vench-nəl, -'ven-chən-ᵊl\ *adj* **1** : behaving according to convention ⟨a very *conventional* man⟩
2 : settled or prescribed by convention : CUSTOMARY
⟨*conventional* signs and symbols⟩ **3 a** : COMMONPLACE,
ORDINARY ⟨*conventional* remarks⟩ **b** : according to
established rules or traditions : not showing originality
⟨*conventional* musical figures⟩ **4** : of or relating to a convention — **con·ven·tion·al·ly** \-ē\ *adv*
con·ven·tion·al·i·ty \kən-ˌven-chə-'nal-ət-ē\ *n, pl* **-ties**
1 : the quality or state of being conventional; *esp* : formality in social customs and practices **2** : a conventional
practice, custom, or rule : CONVENTION
con·ven·tion·al·ize \kən-'vench-nə-ˌlīz, -'ven-chən-ᵊl-ˌīz\
vt : to make conventional — **con·ven·tion·al·i·za·tion**
\-ˌvench-nə-lə-'zā-shən, -ˌvench-nə-\ *n*
con·verge \kən-'vərj\ *vb* [ML *convergere*, fr. L *com-* +
vergere to incline] **1** : to tend or move toward one point
or one another : MEET **2** : to come together and unite in a
common interest **3** : to approach a limit as the number of
terms increases without limit **4** : to cause to come
together
con·ver·gence \kən-'vər-jən(t)s\ *n* : the act or condition
of converging esp. toward union or uniformity: as **a** : coordinated movement of the eyes that allows an image to
impinge on corresponding parts of the retinas **b** : independent development of similar bodily or cultural characters by individuals in similar environmental relations
— **con·ver·gent** \-jənt\ *adj*
con·ver·sant \kən-'vərs-ᵊnt\ *adj* : having knowledge or
experience : well acquainted : FAMILIAR ⟨*conversant* with
the facts of the case⟩ — **con·ver·sant·ly** *adv*
con·ver·sa·tion \ˌkän-vər-'sā-shən\ *n* : oral exchange of
sentiments, observations, opinions, or ideas; *also* : an instance of such exchange : TALK
con·ver·sa·tion·al \ˌkän-vər-'sā-shnəl, -shən-ᵊl\ *adj*
1 : of, relating to, or suitable for informal friendly talk
⟨written in *conversational* style⟩ **2** : fond of or given to
conversation — **con·ver·sa·tion·al·ly** \-ē\ *adv*
con·ver·sa·tion·al·ist \-shnə-ləst, -shən-ᵊl-əst\ *n* : a
person who is fond of or good at conversation
¹con·verse \kən-'vərs\ *vi* [L *conversari* to live with, keep
company with, freq. of *converter* to turn around, convert]
: to exchange thoughts and opinions in speech : TALK —
con·vers·er *n*
²con·verse \'kän-ˌvərs\ *n* : CONVERSATION
³con·verse \kən-'vərs, 'kän-\ *adj* [L *conversus*, pp. of
convertere to turn around] : reversed in order, relation, or
action — **con·verse·ly** *adv*
⁴con·verse \'kän-ˌvərs\ *n* : something that is the opposite
of something else; *esp* : the statement obtained by interchanging the *if* and *then* clauses of a hypothetical statement
con·ver·sion \kən-'vər-zhən\ *n* **1** : the act of converting
: the state of being converted **2** : a change in the nature or
form of a thing ⟨the *conversion* of water into steam by
boiling⟩ **3** : a spiritual change in a person associated with
a change of religious belief or with the definite adoption
of religion **4** : the taking and using of another's property
without right as one's own **5** : the making of a score on
a try for point after touchdown in football or a free throw
in basketball — **con·ver·sion·al** \-'vərzh-nəl, -ən-ᵊl\ *adj*
¹con·vert \kən-'vərt\ *vb* [L *convertere* to turn around,
convert, fr. *com-* + *vertere* to turn] **1 a** : to bring over
from one belief, view, or party to another **b** : to bring
about a religious conversion in **2 a** : to alter the physical
or chemical nature of **b** : to change from one form or
function to another ⟨*convert* water into ice⟩ ⟨*convert* starch
into sugar⟩ ⟨*convert* iron into steel⟩ **c** : to exchange for an
equivalent **3** : to appropriate without right **4** : to
undergo conversion **5** : to make good on a try for point
after touchdown or on a free throw
²con·vert \'kän-ˌvərt\ *n* : one that is converted; *esp* : one
who has experienced religious conversion
syn CONVERT, PROSELYTE mean one who has changed
from one creed to another. CONVERT implies a change

toward the belief or opinion of the speaker and tends to suggest sincere and voluntary change or acceptance; PROSELYTE implies a change away from the speaker's belief and suggests the effect of persuasion or special inducement

con·vert·er \kən-'vərt-ər\ *n* : one that converts: as **a** : the furnace used in the Bessemer process **b** *or* **con·ver·tor** \-'vərt-ər\ : a device employing mechanical rotation for changing alternating current to direct current **c** : a device for adapting a television receiver to receive channels for which it was not orig. designed

1con·vert·i·ble \kən-'vərt-ə-bəl\ *adj* **1** : capable of being converted ⟨a *convertible* currency⟩ **2** : having a top that may be lowered or removed ⟨*convertible* coupe⟩ — **con·vert·i·bil·i·ty** \-,vərt-ə-'bil-ət-ē\ *n* — **con·vert·i·bly** \-'vərt-ə-blē\ *adv*

2convertible *n* : something convertible; *esp* : a convertible automobile

con·verti·plane *or* **con·verta·plane** \kən-'vərt-ə-,plān\ *n* : an aircraft that takes off and lands like a helicopter and is convertible to a fixed-wing form for forward flight

con·vex \kän-'veks, 'kän-,, kən-'\ *adj* [L *convexus*] : curved or rounded like the exterior of a sphere or circle — **con·vex·ly** *adv* — **con·vex·ness** *n*

con·vex·i·ty \kän-'vek-sət-ē, kän-\ *n, pl* **-ties 1** : the quality or state of being convex **2** : a convex surface or part

con·vexo–con·cave \kən-,vek-sō-'\ *adj* **1** : CONCAVO– CONVEX **2** : having the convex side of greater curvature than the concave

con·vey \kən-'vā\ *vt* [OF *conveier* to escort, fr. L *com-* + *via* way] **1** : to carry from one place to another : TRANS-PORT ⟨*convey* passengers to an airfield by bus⟩ **2** : to serve as a means of transferring or transmitting ⟨pipes *convey* water⟩ **3** : to impart or communicate or serve as a means of imparting or communicating ⟨spoke in words that clearly *conveyed* his meaning⟩⟨a flashing red light *conveys* a warning⟩ **4** : to transfer or deliver to another; *esp* : to transfer real estate or title to real estate by a sealed instrument

con·vey·ance \kən-'vā-ən(t)s\ *n* **1** : the act of conveying **2** : a means or way of conveying: as **a** : an instrument by which title to property is conveyed **b** : a means of transport : VEHICLE

con·vey·anc·ing \-ən(t)-siŋ\ *n* : the procedure or the business of drawing up legal papers for transferring title to property from one person to another — **con·vey·anc·er** \-ən(t)-sər\ *n*

con·vey·er *or* **con·vey·or** \kən-'vā-ər\ *n* **1** : one that conveys **2** *usu* **conveyor** : a mechanical apparatus for carrying (as by an endless moving belt or a chain of receptacles) packages or bulk material from place to place

1con·vict \kən-'vikt\ *vt* [L *convict-, convincere*, fr. *com-* + *vincere* to conquer] : to find or prove to be guilty

2con·vict \'kän-,vikt\ *n* **1** : a person convicted of a crime **2** : a person serving a prison sentence usu. for a long term

con·vic·tion \kən-'vik-shən\ *n* **1** : the act of convicting : the state of being convicted : decision that a person is guilty of a crime or offense **2** : the state of mind of a person who is convinced that what he believes or says is true : CERTITUDE ⟨speaks with *conviction*⟩ **3** : a strong belief or opinion ⟨a man with firm *convictions*⟩ **syn** see CERTAINTY, OPINION

con·vince \kən-'vin(t)s\ *vt* [L *convincere* to refute, convict] : to bring by argument or evidence to assent or belief : overcome the disbelief or objections of ⟨was *convinced* of the man's innocence⟩⟨*convinced* me that he was qualified⟩ — **con·vinc·er** *n*

con·vinc·ing \-'vin(t)-siŋ\ *adj* : having the power or the effect of overcoming objection or disbelief : strongly persuasive ⟨a *convincing* argument⟩⟨a very *convincing* speaker⟩ — **con·vinc·ing·ly** \-siŋ-lē\ *adv* — **con·vinc·ing·ness** *n*

con·viv·i·al \kən-'viv-ē-əl, -'viv-yəl\ *adj* [L *convivium* feast, fr. *com-* + *vivere* to live] : relating to, occupied with, or fond of feasting, drinking, and good company → **con·viv·i·al·ly** \-ē\ *adv*

con·viv·i·al·i·ty \-,viv-ē-'al-ət-ē\ *n, pl* **-ties** : convivial spirit : FESTIVITY

con·vo·ca·tion \,kän-və-'kā-shən\ *n* **1** : the act of convoking : a summons to a meeting **2** : ASSEMBLY, MEETING — **con·vo·ca·tion·al** \-shnəl, -shən-³l\ *adj*

con·voke \kən-'vōk\ *vt* [L *convocare*, fr. *com-* + *vocare* to call] : to call together to a meeting

1con·vo·lute \'kän-və-,lüt\ *vb* [L *convolut-, convolvere*] : TWIST, COIL

2convolute *adj* : rolled or wound together one part upon another ⟨a *convolute* shell⟩ — **con·vo·lute·ly** *adv*

con·vo·lut·ed *adj* **1** : folded in curved or tortuous windings; *esp* : having convolutions **2** : INVOLVED, INTRICATE

con·vo·lu·tion \,kän-və-'lü-shən\ *n* **1** : one of the irregular ridges on the surface of the brain and esp. of the cerebrum of higher mammals **2** : a convoluted form or structure — **con·vo·lu·tion·al** \-shnəl, -shən-³l\ *adj*

con·vol·vu·lus \kən-'väl-vyə-ləs, -'vól-\ *n, pl* **-lus·es** *or* **-li** \-,lī, -,lē\ : any of a genus of erect, trailing, or twining herbs and shrubs of the morning-glory family

1con·voy \'kän-,vói, kən-'\ *vt* [MF *conveier, convoier*, fr. L *com-* + *via* way] : to accompany for protection either by land or by sea : ESCORT ⟨served on a destroyer engaging in *convoying* merchant shipping⟩

2con·voy \'kän-,vói\ *n* **1** : one that convoys; *esp* : a protective escort for ships, persons, or goods **2** : the act of convoying : the state of being convoyed ⟨ships traveling in *convoy*⟩ **3** : a group convoyed or organized for convenience or protection in moving

con·vulse \kən-'vəls\ *vt* [L *convuls-, convellere*, fr. *com-* + *vellere* to pluck] : to shake or agitate violently; *esp* : to shake with or as if with irregular spasms ⟨was *convulsed* with laughter⟩⟨land *convulsed* by an earthquake⟩

con·vul·sion \-'vəl-shən\ *n* **1** : an abnormal violent and involuntary contraction or series of contractions of the muscles **2 a** : a violent disturbance **b** : an uncontrolled fit : PAROXYSM — **con·vul·sion·ary** \-shə-,ner-ē\ *adj*

con·vul·sive \-'vəl-siv\ *adj* : constituting or producing a convulsion; *also* : attended or affected with convulsions — **con·vul·sive·ly** *adv* — **con·vul·sive·ness** *n*

co·ny *var of* CONEY

coo \'kü\ *vi* **1** : to make the low soft cry of a dove or pigeon or a similar sound **2** : to talk fondly or amorously — **coo** *n*

1cook \'kúk\ *n* [OE *cōc*, fr. L *coquus*] **1** : one who prepares food for eating **2** : a technical or industrial process comparable to cooking food; *also* : a substance so processed

2cook *vb* **1** : to prepare food for eating by a heating process **2** : to undergo the action of being cooked **3** : OCCUR, HAPPEN ⟨what's *cooking*⟩ **b** : CONCOCT, IMPROVISE ⟨*cook* up a scheme⟩ **4** : to subject to the action of heat or fire — **cook·er** *n* — **cook one's goose** : to ruin (one) irretrievably

cook·book \'kúk-,búk\ *n* : a book of cooking directions and recipes

cook·ery \'kúk-(ə-)rē\ *n* : the art or practice of cooking

cook·ie *or* **cooky** \'kúk-ē\ *n, pl* **cook·ies** [D *koekje*, dim. of *koek* cake] : any of various small sweet flat or slightly raised cakes

cook·out \'kúk-,aút\ *n* : an outing at which a meal is cooked and served in the open; *also* : the meal cooked

cook·stove \'kúk-,stōv\ *n* : a stove for cooking; *esp* : a cast-iron stove for wood or coal

1cool \'kül\ *adj* [OE *cōl*] **1** : moderately cold : lacking in warmth **2 a** : marked by steady calmness and self-control **b** : lacking ardor, excitement, or friendliness : restrained in emotion **3** : WHOLE, FULL ⟨a *cool* million⟩ **4** : producing an impression of coolness; *esp* : of a hue in the range violet through blue to green — **cool·ish** \'kü-lish\ *adj* — **cool·ly** \'kül-(l)ē\ *adv* — **cool·ness** \'kül-nəs\ *n*

2cool *vb* **1** : to make or become cool **2** : to moderate or calm esp. in emotional intensity ⟨allow tempers to *cool*⟩

3cool *n* : a cool time or place ⟨the *cool* of the night⟩

cool·ant \'kü-lənt\ *n* : a usu. fluid cooling agent

cool·er \'kü-lər\ *n* **1** : one that cools: as **a** : a container for cooling liquids **b** : REFRIGERATOR **2** : LOCKUP, JAIL

coo·lie \'kü-lē\ *n* [Hindi *kulī*] : an unskilled laborer or porter usu. in or from the Far East

coon \'kün\ *n* : RACCOON

coon·skin \-,skin\ *n* : the fur or pelt of the raccoon

1coop \'küp, 'kúp\ *n* [ME *cupe*] **1** : a cage or small enclosure (as for poultry); *also* : a small building for housing poultry **2** : a confined place

2coop *vt* : to place or keep in or as if in a coop : PEN

co-op \'kō-,äp, kō-'äp, 'küp\ *n* : COOPERATIVE

¹coo·per \'kü-pər, 'kup-ər\ *n* [L *cupa* cask] **:** one that makes or repairs wooden casks or tubs

²cooper *vb* **:** to work or work on as a cooper

coo·per·age \'kü-p(ə-)rij, 'kup-(ə-)rij\ *n* **1 :** a cooper's place of business **2 :** a cooper's work or products

co·op·er·ate \kō-'äp-(ə-),rāt\ *vi* [LL *cooperari,* fr. L *co-* + *operari* to work] **:** to act, work, or associate with others esp. for mutual benefit

co·op·er·a·tion \kō-,äp-ə-'rā-shən\ *n* **1 :** the act or process of cooperating **2 :** association of individuals or groups for the purpose of mutual benefit; *also* **:** such association that results in mutual benefit

¹co·op·er·a·tive \kō-'äp-(ə-)rət-iv, -'äp-ə-,rāt-\ *adj* **1 :** marked by cooperation or a willingness to cooperate ⟨*cooperative* neighbors⟩ **2 :** of, relating to, or organized as a cooperative ⟨a *cooperative* store⟩ — **co·op·er·a·tive·ly** *adv* — **co·op·er·a·tive·ness** *n*

²cooperative *n* **:** an association formed to enable its members to buy, sell, or perform other economic functions to better advantage

Coo·per's hawk \,kü-pərz-, ,kup-ərz-\ *n* **:** a common American chicken hawk

co–opt \kō-'äpt\ *vt* [L *cooptare,* fr. *co-* + *optare* to choose] **:** to choose or elect as a fellow member or colleague — **co·op·tion** \-'äp-shən\ *n*

¹co·or·di·nate \kō-'órd-nət, -ᵊn-ət\ *adj* **1 :** equal in rank or order **2 a :** being of equal rank in a compound sentence ⟨*coordinate* clauses⟩ **b :** joining words or word groups of the same grammatical rank ⟨the word *and* is a *coordinate* conjunction⟩ — **co·or·di·nate·ly** *adv* — **co·or·di·nate·ness** *n*

²coordinate *n* **1 :** one who is of equal rank, authority, or importance with another **2 :** any of a set of numbers used in specifying the location of a point on a line or surface or in space

³co·or·di·nate \kō-'órd-ᵊn-,āt\ *vb* **1 :** to make or become coordinate **:** put in the same order or rank **2 :** to bring into a common action, movement, or condition **:** HARMONIZE ⟨*coordinated* the efforts of all the investigating agencies⟩ — **co·or·di·na·tor** \-,āt-ər\ *n*

coordinate system *n* **:** any of various systems for locating points by means of lines; *esp* **:** CARTESIAN COORDINATE SYSTEM

co·or·di·nat·ing *adj* **:** ¹COORDINATE 2b

co·or·di·na·tion \kō-,órd-ᵊn-'ā-shən\ *n* **1 :** the act of coordinating **2 :** the state of being coordinate **:** harmonious working together ⟨muscular *coordination*⟩

coot \'küt\ *n* [ME *coote*] **1 :** any of various sluggish slow≠ flying slaty-black birds of the rail family that somewhat resemble ducks **2 :** a No. American scoter **3 :** a harmless simple person

coo·tie \'küt-ē\ *n* **:** BODY LOUSE

cop \'käp\ *n* [short for ³*copper*] **:** POLICEMAN

co·pal \'kō-pəl, -,pal\ *n* [Sp, fr. Nahuatl *copalli* resin] **:** a recent or fossil resin from various tropical trees used in making varnishes

co·part·ner \(')kō-'pärt-nər\ *n* **:** PARTNER — **co·part·ner·ship** \-,ship\ *n*

¹cope \'kōp\ *n* [OE -*cāp,* fr. LL *cappa* head covering, cloak] **1 :** a long enveloping ecclesiastical vestment **2 :** VAULT, CANOPY; *esp* **:** the vault of heaven **:** SKY

²cope *vt* **:** to cover or furnish with a cope or coping

³cope *vi* [ME *copen* to strike, fight with, fr. MF *couper* to strike, fr. *coup* blow, coup] **:** to struggle or contend esp. with some success ⟨a situation too difficult to *cope* with⟩

co·pe·pod \'kō-pə-,päd\ *n* [Gk *kōpē* oar + *pod-, pous* foot] **:** any of a large group (Copepoda) of usu. tiny freshwater and marine crustaceans — **copepod** *adj*

16th century abbot in cope and miter

Co·per·ni·can \kō-'pər-ni-kən\ *adj* **:** of or relating to Copernicus or his theory that the earth rotates daily on its axis and the planets revolve in orbits round the sun

cope·stone \'kōp-,stōn\ *n* **1 :** a stone forming a coping **2 :** a finishing touch **:** CROWN

cop·i·er \'käp-ē-ər\ *n* **:** one that copies

co·pi·lot \'kō-,pī-lət\ *n* **:** an assistant airplane pilot

cop·ing \'kō-piŋ\ *n* [¹*cope*] **:** the covering course of a wall usu. with a sloping top

coping saw *n* [fr. prp. of *cope* to notch] **:** a ribbon-shaped saw in a U-shaped frame for cutting intricate patterns in wood

co·pi·ous \'kō-pē-əs\ *adj* [L *copia* abundance, fr. *co-* + *ops* wealth] **1 a :** full of thought, information, or matter **b :** profuse or exuberant in words, expression, or style **2 :** very plentiful **:** LAVISH, ABUNDANT **syn** see PLENTIFUL — **co·pi·ous·ly** *adv* — **co·pi·ous·ness** *n*

co·pla·nar \(')kō-'plā-nər\ *adj* **:** lying in the same plane

co·pol·y·mer \(')kō-'päl-ə-mər\ *n* **:** a product of copolymerization

co·po·ly·mer·ize \,kō-pə-'lim-ə-,rīz, (')kō-'päl-ə-mə-\ *vb* **:** to polymerize together — **co·po·ly·mer·i·za·tion** \,kō-pə-,lim-ə-'zā-shən, ,kō-,päl-ə-mə-rə-\ *n*

cop out \(')käp-'aut\ *vi* **:** to withdraw from unwanted responsibility — **cop-out** \'käp-,aut\ *n*

¹cop·per \'käp-ər\ *n* [OE *coper,* fr. LL *cuprum,* fr. Gk *Kypros* Cyprus, island where it was produced] **1 :** a reddish chiefly univalent and bivalent metallic element that is ductile and malleable and one of the best conductors of heat and electricity — see ELEMENT table **2 :** a copper or bronze coin **3 :** any of various small butterflies with copper-colored wings — **cop·pery** \'käp-(ə-)rē\ *adj*

²copper *vt* **:** to cover with copper

³copper *n* [E slang *cop* to catch] **:** POLICEMAN

cop·per·as \'käp-(ə-)rəs\ *n* [ME *coperose,* fr. MF, fr. LL *cuprum* copper + L *rosa* rose] **:** a green sulfate of iron FeSO₄.7H₂O used in making inks and in dyeing

cop·per·head \'käp-ər-,hed\ *n* **1 :** a common largely coppery brown pit viper of upland eastern U.S. **2 :** a person in the northern states who sympathized with the South during the Civil War

cop·per·plate \,käp-ər-'plāt\ *n* **:** an intaglio printing process using engraved or etched copper plates; *also* **:** a print made by this process

cop·per·smith \'käp-ər-,smith\ *n* **:** a worker in copper

copper sulfate *n* **:** a crystalline compound CuSO₄ that is white when anhydrous but that is usu. encountered in the blue hydrated form CuSO₄.5H₂O and that is used in solutions to destroy algae and fungi, in dyeing and printing, and in electric batteries

cop·pice \'käp-əs\ *n* [MF *copeiz,* fr. *couper* to cut] **1 :** a thicket, grove, or growth of small trees **2 :** forest originating mainly from sprouts or root suckers

co·pra \'kō-prə\ *n* [Pg, fr. Malayalam *koppara*] **:** dried coconut meat yielding coconut oil

co·proph·a·gous \kä-'präf-ə-gəs\ *adj* **:** feeding on dung — **co·proph·a·gy** \-ə-jē\ *n*

copse \'käps\ *n* [by alter.] **:** COPPICE 1

Copt \'käpt\ *n* **1 :** a member of a people descended from the ancient Egyptians **2 :** a member of the ancient Christian church of Egypt — **Cop·tic** \'käp-tik\ *adj*

cop·u·la \'käp-yə-lə\ *n* [L, bond] **:** a word or expression (as a form of the verb *to be*) that links a subject with its predicate

cop·u·late \'käp-yə-,lāt\ *vi* **1 :** to engage in sexual intercourse **2** *of gametes* **:** to fuse permanently — **cop·u·la·tion** \,käp-yə-'lā-shən\ *n* — **cop·u·la·to·ry** \'käp-yə-lə-,tōr-ē, -,tor-\ *adj*

¹cop·u·la·tive \'käp-yə-,lāt-iv\ *adj* **1 :** joining together coordinate words or word groups and expressing addition of their meanings ⟨*copulative* conjunction⟩ **2 :** being a copula ⟨*copulative* verb⟩ — **cop·u·la·tive·ly** *adv*

²copulative *n* **:** a copulative word or expression

¹copy \'käp-ē\ *n, pl* **cop·ies** [ML *copia,* fr. L, abundance] **1 :** an imitation, transcript, or reproduction of an original work **2 :** one of the printed reproductions of an original text, engraving, or photograph **3 :** matter to be set up for printing or photoengraving **syn** see DUPLICATE

²copy *vb* **cop·ied; copy·ing** **1 :** to make a copy **:** DUPLICATE **2 :** to model oneself on **:** IMITATE

copy·book \-,buk\ *n* **:** a book containing copies esp. of penmanship for learners to imitate

copy·boy \-,bói\ *n* **:** one that carries copy and runs errands (as in a newspaper office)

copy·cat \-,kat\ *n* **:** a sedulous imitator

copy·desk \-,desk\ *n* **:** the desk at which newspaper copy is edited

copy·hold \-,hōld\ *n* **1 :** a former tenure of land in

England and Ireland by right of being recorded in the court of the manor **2 :** an estate held by copyhold
copy·ist \'käp-ē-əst\ *n* **1 :** one who makes copies **2 :** IMITATOR
copy·read·er \'käp-ē-,rēd-ər\ *n* **:** one who edits and writes headlines for newspaper copy; *also* **:** one who reads and corrects manuscript copy in a publishing house
¹copy·right \-,rīt\ *n* **:** the sole legal right to reproduce, publish, and sell the matter and form of a literary, musical, or artistic work — **copyright** *adj*
²copyright *vt* **:** to secure a copyright on
co·quet *or* **co·quette** \kō-'ket\ *vi* **co·quet·ted; co·quet·ting :** FLIRT
co·quet·ry \'kō-kə-trē, kō-'ke-trē\ *n, pl* **-ries :** the conduct or art of a coquette **:** FLIRTATION
co·quette \kō-'ket\ *n* [F, fem. of *coquet*, fr. dim. of *coq* cock] **:** FLIRT — **co·quett·ish** \-'ket-ish\ *adj* — **co·quett·ish·ly** *adv* — **co·quett·ish·ness** *n*
co·qui·na \kō-'kē-nə\ *n* **1 :** a small marine clam used for broth or chowder **2 :** a soft whitish limestone formed of broken shells and corals cemented together and used for building
cor·a·cle \'kor-ə-kəl, 'kär-\ *n* [W *corwgl*] **:** a boat made of hoops covered with horsehide or tarpaulin
cor·a·coid \'kor-ə-,koid, 'kär-\ *adj* [Gk *korak-, korax* raven] **:** of, relating to, or being a process or bone that in many vertebrates extends from the scapula to or toward the sternum — **coracoid** *n*
cor·al \'kor-əl, 'kär-\ *n* [Gk *korallion*] **1 a :** the calcareous or horny skeletal deposit produced by various polyps; *esp* **:** a richly red material used in jewelry **b :** a polyp or polyp colony together with its membranes and skeleton **2 :** a variable color averaging a deep pink — **coral** *adj*
¹cor·al·line \'kor-ə-,līn, 'kär-\ *adj* **:** of, relating to, or resembling coral or a coralline
²coralline *n* **:** any of various plants or animals (as some red algae and bryozoans) that resemble corals
coral reef *n* **:** a reef made up chiefly of coral
coral snake *n* **:** any of several venomous chiefly tropical New World snakes brilliantly banded in red, black, and yellow or white; *also* **:** any of several harmless snakes resembling the coral snakes
¹cor·bel \'kor-bel\ *n* [MF, fr. dim. of *corp* raven, fr. L *corvus*] **:** a bracket-shaped architectural member that projects from a wall and supports a weight
²corbel *vt* **-beled** *or* **-belled; -bel·ing** *or* **-bel·ling :** to furnish or make into a corbel
¹cord \'kord\ *n* [OF *corde*, fr. L *chorda* string, fr. Gk *chordē*] **1 :** a string or small rope consisting of several strands woven or twisted together **2 :** a moral, spiritual, or emotional bond **3 a :** an anatomical structure (as a tendon or nerve) resembling a cord **b :** a small flexible insulated electrical cable with fittings for connecting an appliance (as a lamp) with a receptacle **4 :** a unit of wood cut for fuel equal to a stack 4x4x8 feet or 128 cubic feet **5 a :** a rib like a cord on a textile **b** (1) **:** a fabric with such ribs ⟨a summer suit of blue cotton *cord*⟩ (2) *pl* **:** trousers made of this fabric
²cord *vt* **1 :** to furnish, bind, or connect with a cord **2 :** to pile up (wood) in cords — **cord·er** *n*
cord·age \'kord-ij\ *n* **1 :** ropes or cords; *esp* **:** the ropes in the rigging of a ship **2 :** the number of cords (as of wood) on a given area
cor·date \'kor-,dāt\ *adj* [L *cord-, cor* heart] **:** shaped like a heart — **cor·date·ly** *adv*
cord·ed \'kord-əd\ *adj* **1 :** having or drawn into ridges or cords ⟨a *corded* seam⟩ ⟨*corded* muscles⟩ **2 :** bound or wound about with cords
¹cor·dial \'kor-jəl\ *adj* [ML *cordialis* of the heart, hearty, fr. L *cord-, cor* heart; akin to E *heart*] **1 :** tending to revive, cheer, or invigorate **2 :** HEARTFELT, HEARTY ⟨a *cordial* greeting⟩ — **cor·di·al·i·ty** \,kor-jē-'al-ət-ē\ *n* — **cor·dial·ly** \'korj-(ə-)lē\ *adv* — **cor·dial·ness** \'kor-jəl-nəs\ *n*
²cordial *n* **1 :** a stimulating medicine or drink **2 :** LIQUEUR
cor·dil·le·ra \,kord-ᵊl-'(y)er-ə, kor-'dil-ə-rə\ *n* [Sp] **:** a system of mountain ranges often consisting of a number of more or less parallel chains — **cor·dil·le·ran** \-'(y)er-ən, -ə-rən\ *adj*
cord·ite \'kor-,dīt\ *n* **:** a smokeless gunpowder composed of nitroglycerin, guncotton, and a stabilizing jelly

cor·do·ba \'kord-ə-bə, -ə-və\ *n* **1 :** the basic monetary unit of Nicaragua **2 :** a currency note representing one cordoba
cor·don \'kord-ᵊn, 'kor-,dän\ *n* **1 :** an ornamental cord used esp. on costumes **2 :** a line of persons or things around a person or place ⟨a *cordon* of police⟩ ⟨a *cordon* of forts⟩ **3 :** a cord or ribbon worn as a badge or decoration
cor·do·van \'kord-ə-vən\ *n* **:** a soft fine-grained colored leather — **cordovan** *adj*
cor·du·roy \'kord-ə-,roi\ *n* **1 a :** a durable ribbed usu. cotton fabric **b** *pl* **:** trousers of corduroy **2 :** a road built of logs laid side by side transversely — **corduroy** *adj*
cord·wain·er \'kord-,wā-nər\ *n* **:** SHOEMAKER
cord·wood \-,wud\ *n* **:** wood cut for fuel and sold by the cord
¹core \'kō(ə)r, 'ko(ə)r\ *n* [ME] **1 :** a central or inmost part: as **a :** the usu. inedible central part of some fruits (as a pineapple or apple) **b :** a bar of iron or a bundle of wires used to intensify an induced magnetic field (as in a transformer or an armature) **2 :** a basic, essential, or enduring part
²core *vt* **:** to remove the core from — **cor·er** *n*
co·re·op·sis \,kor-ē-'äp-səs, ,kor-\ *n* **:** any of a genus of herbs related to the daisies and widely grown for their showy flower heads
co·re·spond·ent \,kō-ri-'spän-dənt\ *n* **:** a person named as guilty of adultery with the defendant in a divorce suit
co·ri·a·ceous \,kor-ē-'ā-shəs, ,kor-\ *adj* **:** resembling leather
co·ri·an·der \'kor-ē-,an-dər, 'kor-\ *n* [Gk *koriandron*] **:** an Old World herb of the carrot family with aromatic fruits
co·rin·thi·an \kə-'rin(t)-thē-ən\ *adj* **:** of or relating to the lightest and most ornate of the three Greek types of architecture characterized esp. by its bell-shaped capital enveloped with acanthuses — see CAPITAL illustration
Cor·in·thi·ans \-ənz\ *n* — see BIBLE table
co·ri·um \'kōr-ē-əm, 'kor-\ *n, pl* **-ria** \-ē-ə\ [L, leather] **:** DERMIS
¹cork \'kork\ *n* [ME, prob. fr. Ar *qurq*, fr. L *cortic-, cortex* bark, cork] **1 a :** the elastic tough outer tissue of a European oak used esp. for stoppers and insulation **b :** the tissue of a woody plant making up most of the bark and arising from an inner cambium **2 :** a usu. cork stopper for a bottle or jug **3 :** an angling float
²cork *vt* **1 :** to furnish, fit, or seal with a cork **2 :** to blacken with burnt cork
cork·er \'kor-kər\ *n* **1 :** one that corks containers **2** *slang* **:** an outstanding person or thing
cork·ing \'kor-kiŋ\ *adj, slang* **:** extremely fine
¹cork·screw \'kork-,skrü\ *n* **:** a pointed spiral piece of metal with a handle that is used to draw corks from bottles
²corkscrew *adj* **:** resembling a corkscrew **:** SPIRAL
cork·wood \'kork-,wud\ *n* **:** any of several trees having light or corky wood
corky \'kor-kē\ *adj* **cork·i·er; -est :** resembling cork esp. in dry porous quality
corm \'korm\ *n* [Gk *kormos* tree trunk] **:** a plant underground resting stage consisting of a rounded thick modified stem base bearing membranous or scaly leaves and buds — compare BULB, TUBER
corm·el \'kor-məl\ *n* **:** a small or secondary corm produced by a larger corm
cor·mo·rant \'korm-(ə-)rənt\ *n* [MF, fr. OF *cormareng*, fr. *corp* raven + *marenc* of the sea] **1 :** any of various dark-colored web-footed seabirds with a long neck, a wedge-shaped tail, a hooked bill, and a patch of bare often brightly colored skin under the mouth **2 :** a greedy or gluttonous person
¹corn \'korn\ *n* [OE] **1 a :** the seeds of a cereal grass and esp. of the important cereal crop of a particular region (as in Britain wheat, in Scotland and Ireland oats, and in the New World and Australia Indian corn) **b :** sweet corn served as a vegetable while the kernels are still soft and milky **2 :** a plant that produces corn **3 :** corny actions or speech
²corn *vb* **:** to preserve by packing with salt or by soaking in brine ⟨*corned* beef⟩
³corn *n* [MF *corne*, fr. L *cornu* horn; akin to E *horn*] **:** a local hardening and thickening of skin (as on a toe)
corn borer *n* **:** any of several insects that bore in corn; *esp*

: a moth larva that is a major pest esp. in the stems and crowns of Indian corn, dahlias, and potatoes

corn bread *n* : bread made with cornmeal

corn·cob \'kȯrn-ˌkäb\ *n* **1** : the woody axis on which the kernels of Indian corn are arranged **2** : a tobacco pipe with a bowl made by hollowing out a piece of corncob

corn cockle *n* : an annual hairy weed with purplish red flowers found in grainfields

corn·crib \'kȯrn-ˌkrib\ *n* : a crib for storing ears of Indian corn

cor·nea \'kȯr-nē-ə\ *n* [ML, fr. L, fem. of *corneus* horny, fr. *cornu* horn] : the transparent part of the coat of the eyeball that covers the iris and pupil and admits light to the interior — **cor·ne·al** \-nē-əl\ *adj*

corn earworm *n* : a large striped yellow-headed moth larva esp. destructive to the ear of Indian corn

cor·nel \'kȯrn-ᵊl\ *n* : any of several shrubs or trees of the dogwood family; *esp* : DOGWOOD

cor·ne·lian \kȯr-'nēl-yən\ *n* : CARNELIAN

cor·ne·ous \'kȯr-nē-əs\ *adj* : HORNY

¹cor·ner \'kȯr-nər\ *n* [OF *corniere*, fr. L *cornu* horn] **1 a** : the point or place where converging lines, edges, or sides meet : ANGLE **b** : the place of intersection of two streets or roads **c** : a piece designed to form, mark, or protect a corner **2** : a position from which escape or retreat is difficult or impossible **3** : control or ownership of enough of the available supply of a commodity or security to permit manipulation of the price — **cor·nered** \-nərd\ *adj*

²corner *vb* **1** : to drive into a corner **2** : to get a corner on ⟨*corner* wheat⟩ **3** : to turn a corner ⟨a car that *corners* well⟩

³corner *adj* **1** : situated at a corner **2** : used or fitted for use in or on a corner

cor·ner·back \-ˌbak\ *n* : a defensive halfback in football who defends the flank

cor·ner·stone \-ˌstōn\ *n* **1** : a stone forming part of a corner in a wall; *esp* : such a stone laid at the formal beginning of the erection of a building **2** : something of basic importance ⟨a *cornerstone* of foreign policy⟩

cor·ner·wise \-ˌwīz\ *or* **cor·ner·ways** \-ˌwāz\ *adv* : DIAGONALLY

cor·net \kȯr-'net\ *n* [MF, dim. of *corn* horn, fr. L *cornu*] **1** : a brass instrument resembling the trumpet but having greater agility and a less brilliant tone **2** : something (as a piece of paper twisted for use as a container) shaped like a cone

cornet

cor·net·ist *or* **cor·net·tist** \kȯr-'net-əst\ *n* : a performer on the cornet

corn·flow·er \'kȯrn-ˌflaú-(ə)r\ *n* : a European plant related to the daisies and often grown for its showy blue, pink, or white flower heads

cor·nice \'kȯr-nəs\ *n* [MF, fr. It] **1** : the ornamental projecting piece that forms the top edge of the front of a building or of a pillar — see ORDER illustration **2** : an ornamental molding placed where the walls meet the ceiling of a room **3** : a decorative band of metal or wood to conceal curtain fixtures

¹Cor·nish \'kȯr-nish\ *adj* : of, relating to, or characteristic of Cornwall, Cornishmen, or Cornish

²Cornish *n* **1** : a Celtic language of Cornwall extinct since the late 18th century **2** : any of an English breed of domestic fowls much used in crossbreeding for meat production

Cor·nish·man \-mən\ *n* : a native or inhabitant of Cornwall, England

corn·meal \'kȯrn-'mēl\ *n* : meal ground from corn

corn pone *n*, *South & Midland* : corn bread often made without milk or eggs and baked or fried

corn snow *n* : granular snow formed by alternate thawing and freezing

corn·stalk \'kȯrn-ˌstȯk\ *n* : a stalk of Indian corn

corn·starch \-ˌstärch\ *n* : a fine starch made from corn and used in cooking as a thickening agent

corn sugar *n* : sugar made by hydrolysis of cornstarch

corn syrup *n* : a syrup obtained by partial hydrolysis of cornstarch and used in baked goods and candy

cor·nu \'kȯr-n(y)ü\ *n*, *pl* **cor·nua** \-n(y)ə-wə\ : HORN;

esp : a horn-shaped anatomical structure — **cor·nu·al** \-nyə-wəl\ *adj*

cor·nu·co·pia \ˌkȯr-n(y)ə-'kō-pē-ə\ *n* [LL, fr. L *cornu copiae* horn of plenty] **1** : a horn-shaped container overflowing with fruits and flowers used as a symbol of abundance **2** : a container shaped like a horn or a cone

corn whiskey *n* : whiskey distilled from a mash made up of not less than 80 percent corn

corny \'kȯr-nē\ *adj* **corn·i·er; -est** : mawkishly old-fashioned or countrified : tiresomely simple or sentimental

co·rol·la \kə-'räl-ə\ *n* [NL, fr. L, dim. of *corona* crown] : the inner floral envelope of a flower consisting of petals and enclosing the stamens and pistil — **co·rol·late** \-'räl-ət\ *adj*

cor·ol·lary \'kȯr-ə-ˌler-ē, 'kär-\ *n*, *pl* **-lar·ies** [LL *corollarium*, fr. L, money paid for a garland, gratuity, fr. *corolla* crown, garland] **1** : an immediate inference from a proved proposition **2** : something that naturally follows : RESULT — **corollary** *adj*

co·ro·na \kə-'rō-nə\ *n* [L, crown] **1** : a usu. colored circle often seen around and close to a luminous body (as the sun or moon) **2** : the outermost part of the atmosphere of the sun appearing as a gray halo around the moon's black disk during a total eclipse of the sun **3** : the upper portion of a body part (as a tooth or the skull) **4** : an appendage on the inner side of the corolla in some flowers (as the daffodil) **5** : a discharge of electricity seen as a faint glow adjacent to the surface of an electrical conductor at high voltage

Corona Bo·re·al·is \-ˌbōr-ē-'al-əs, -ˌbȯr-\ *n* [L, lit., northern crown] : a northern constellation between Hercules and Boötes

cor·o·nach \'kȯr-ə-nək, 'kär-\ *n* : DIRGE

¹cor·o·nal \'kȯr-ən-ᵊl, 'kär-\ *n* : a circlet for the head

²cor·o·nal \'kȯr-ən-ᵊl, 'kär-; *with reference to a corona, also* kə-'rōn-\ *adj* : of or relating to a corona or crown

¹cor·o·nary \'kȯr-ə-ˌner-ē, 'kär-\ *adj* : of, relating to, or being the arteries or veins that supply blood to the heart; *also* : of or relating to the heart

²coronary *n*, *pl* **-nar·ies** **1** : a coronary artery or vein **2** : CORONARY THROMBOSIS

coronary thrombosis *n* : the blocking of an artery of the heart by a thrombus — called also *coronary occlusion*

cor·o·na·tion \ˌkȯr-ə-'nā-shən, ˌkär-\ *n* : the act or ceremony of investing a sovereign or his consort with the royal crown

cor·o·ner \'kȯr-ə-nər, 'kär-\ *n* [ME, officer of the crown, fr. OF *corone* crown, fr. L *corona*] : a public officer whose chief duty is to discover the causes of any death possibly not due to natural causes

cor·o·net \ˌkȯr-ə-'net, ˌkär-\ *n* **1** : a small crown worn by a person of noble but not of royal rank **2** : an ornamental wreath or band worn around the head

¹cor·po·ral \'kȯr-p(ə-)rəl\ *n* : a linen cloth on which the eucharistic elements are placed at mass

²corporal *adj* [L *corporalis*, fr. *corpor-*, *corpus* body] : of or relating to the body ⟨whipping and other *corporal* punishments⟩ — **cor·po·ral·ly** \-p(ə-)rə-lē\ *adv*

³corporal *n* [MF, alteration of *caporal*, fr. It *caporale*, fr. *capo* head, fr. L *caput*] : an enlisted man (as in the army) of the lowest noncommissioned rank

corporal's guard *n* **1** : the small detachment commanded by a corporal **2** : a small group

cor·po·rate \'kȯr-p(ə-)rət\ *adj* [L *corporatus*, pp. of *corporare* to form into a body, fr. *corpor-*, *corpus* body] **1 a** : formed into an association and endowed by law with the rights and liabilities of an individual : INCORPORATED **b** : of, relating to, or being a corporation **2** : of or relating to a whole composed of individuals — **cor·po·rate·ly** *adv*

cor·po·ra·tion \ˌkȯr-pə-'rā-shən\ *n* **1** : the municipal authorities of a town or city **2** : a body authorized by law to carry on an activity (as a business enterprise) with the rights and duties of a single person although constituted by one or more persons and having an identity that survives its incorporators

cor·po·re·al \kȯr-'pōr-ē-əl, -'pȯr-\ *adj* : having, consisting of, or relating to a physical material body : as **a** : not spiritual **b** : not immaterial or intangible : SUBSTANTIAL **c** : of or relating to a human body : BODILY **syn** see MATERIAL — **cor·po·re·al·i·ty** \-ˌpōr-ē-'al-ət-ē, -ˌpȯr-\ *n*

— **cor·po·re·al·ly** \-'pōr-ē-ə-lē, -'pȯr-\ adv — **cor·po·re·al·ness** n

corps \'kō(ə)r, 'kȯ(ə)r\ n, pl **corps** \'kōrz, 'kȯrz\ [F, lit., body, fr. L corpus] **1 a :** an organized branch of a military establishment 〈Marine Corps〉 〈Corps of Engineers〉 **b :** a tactical unit consisting of two or more divisions and supporting forces **2 :** a group of persons associated together or acting under common direction 〈diplomatic corps〉

corps de bal·let \,kōrd-ə-ba-'lā, ,kȯrd-\ n, pl **corps de ballet** \same\ [F] **:** the ensemble or chorus of a ballet company

corpse \'kȯrps\ n [MF corps body, fr. L corpus] **:** a dead body

corps·man \'kōr(z)-mən, 'kȯr(z)-\ n **:** a navy enlisted man trained to give first aid

cor·pu·lent \'kȯr-pyə-lənt\ adj **:** having a large bulky body **:** OBESE — **cor·pu·lence** \-lən(t)s\ or **cor·pu·lency** \-lən-sē\ n — **cor·pu·lent·ly** adv

cor·pus \'kȯr-pəs\ n, pl **cor·po·ra** \-p(ə-)rə\ [L corpor-, corpus body] **1 :** the main or central part of a bodily structure 〈the corpus of the jaw〉 **2 :** the main body or principal substance (as of a field of study)

Cor·pus Chris·ti \,kȯr-pəs-'kris-tē\ n [ML, lit., body of Christ] **:** the Thursday after Trinity Sunday observed as a Roman Catholic festival in honor of the Eucharist

cor·pus·cle \'kȯr-(,)pəs-əl\ n [L corpusculum, dim. of corpus body] **1 :** a minute particle **2 :** a living cell; esp **:** one (as a blood or cartilage cell) not aggregated into continuous tissues — **cor·pus·cu·lar** \kȯr-'pəs-kyə-lər\ adj

cor·pus de·lic·ti \,kȯr-pəs-di-'lik-,tī, -(,)tē\ n, pl **cor·po·ra delicti** \,kȯr-p(ə-)rə-\ [NL, lit., body of the crime] **1 :** the substantial fact necessary to prove the commission of a crime **2 :** the body of a murder victim

cor·pus lu·te·um \,kȯr-pəs-'lüt-ē-əm\ n, pl **cor·po·ra lu·tea** \,kȯr-p(ə-)rə-'lüt-ē-ə\ [NL, lit., yellowish body] **:** a yellowish mass of endocrine tissue formed in an ovarian follicle after the egg is shed

1cor·ral \kə-'ral\ n [Sp, fr. (assumed) VL currale enclosure for vehicles, fr. L currus chariot, fr. currere to run] **1 :** a pen or enclosure for confining or capturing livestock **2 :** an enclosure made with wagons for defense of an encampment

2corral vt **cor·ralled; cor·ral·ling 1 :** to confine in or as if in a corral **:** coop or pen up **2 :** SURROUND, CAPTURE **3 :** to arrange (as wagons) so as to form a corral

1cor·rect \kə-'rekt\ vt [L correct-, corrigere, fr. com- + regere to lead straight] **1 a :** to make or set right **:** AMEND **b :** COUNTERACT, NEUTRALIZE **c :** to alter or adjust so as to bring to some standard or required condition **2 a :** REBUKE, PUNISH **b :** to point out for amendment the errors or faults of 〈correct a student's composition〉 — **cor·rect·a·ble** \-'rek-tə-bəl\ adj — **cor·rec·tor** \-'rek-tər\ n

syn CORRECT, RECTIFY, AMEND mean to make right what is wrong. CORRECT implies taking action to remove errors, faults, or deviations; RECTIFY suggests bringing into a straight line or one direction; AMEND implies improving or restoring by making slight changes

2correct adj **1 :** conforming to an approved or conventional standard **2 :** agreeing with fact, logic, or known truth **:** ACCURATE — **cor·rect·ly** adv — **cor·rect·ness** \-'rek(t)-nəs\ n

syn CORRECT, ACCURATE, EXACT, PRECISE mean conforming to fact, truth, or standard. CORRECT implies little more than freedom from fault or error 〈correct dress for the occasion〉 ACCURATE implies greater fidelity to truth or fact attained by exercise of care 〈accurate description of a situation〉 EXACT stresses a very strict agreement with fact or truth 〈a suit tailored to exact measurements〉 PRECISE adds to EXACT an emphasis on sharpness of definition or delimitation 〈precise terms of a contract〉

cor·rec·tion \kə-'rek-shən\ n **1 :** the action or an instance of correcting **:** making or setting right **2 a :** something substituted in place of what is wrong **b :** a quantity applied by way of correcting (as for adjustment or inaccuracy of an instrument) **3 :** punishment intended to correct faults of character or behavior **4 :** the treatment of offenders through a program involving penal custody, parole, and probation — **cor·rec·tion·al** \-shnəl, -shən-ᵊl\ adj

cor·rec·tive \kə-'rek-tiv\ adj **:** serving to correct **:** having the power of making right, normal, or regular 〈corrective exercises〉 — **corrective** n — **cor·rec·tive·ly** adv — **cor·rec·tive·ness** n

cor·re·late \'kȯr-ə-,lāt, 'kär-\ vb **1 :** to have reciprocal or mutual relations **2 :** to establish a mutual or reciprocal relation of **3 :** to relate so as to each member of one set or series a corresponding member of another is assigned

cor·re·la·tion \,kȯr-ə-'lā-shən, ,kär-\ n **1 :** the act or process of correlating **2 :** the state of being correlated; esp **:** a mutual relation discovered to exist between things 〈the apparent correlation between the degree of poverty in a society and the crime rate〉 — **cor·re·la·tion·al** \-shnəl, -shən-ᵊl\ adj

1cor·rel·a·tive \kə-'rel-ət-iv\ adj **1 :** mutually related **2 :** having a mutual grammatical relation and regularly used together but typically not adjacent 〈either and or are correlative conjunctions〉 — **cor·rel·a·tive·ly** adv

2correlative n **:** either of two correlative things

cor·re·spond \,kȯr-ə-'spänd, ,kär-\ vi [L com- + respondēre to respond] **1 a :** to be in conformity or agreement **:** SUIT **b :** to compare closely **:** MATCH **c :** to be equivalent or parallel **2 :** to communicate with a person by exchange of letters

cor·re·spond·ence \-'spän-dən(t)s\ n **1 a :** the agreement of things with one another **b :** a particular similarity **c :** association of members of one set with each member of a second and of members of the second with each member of the first **2 :** communication by letters; also **:** the letters exchanged

correspondence school n **:** a school that teaches nonresident students by mailing them lessons and exercises which upon completion are returned to the school for grading

1cor·re·spond·ent \,kȯr-ə-'spän-dənt, ,kär-\ adj **1 :** SIMILAR **2 :** CONFORMING, FITTING

2correspondent n **1 :** something that corresponds or conforms to something else **2 a :** one who communicates with another by letter **b :** one who has regular commercial relations with another **c :** one who contributes news or comment to a newspaper often from a distant place

cor·re·spond·ing·ly \-'spän-diŋ-lē\ adv **:** in a corresponding manner **:** in such a way as to correspond

cor·ri·da \kȯ-'rē-thə\ n [Sp corrida, lit., act of running] **:** BULLFIGHT

cor·ri·dor \'kȯr-əd-ər, 'kär-, -ə-,dȯr\ n [It corridore, fr. correre to run, fr. L currere] **1 :** a passageway into which compartments or rooms open (as in a hotel or school) **2 :** a narrow strip of land esp. through foreign-held territory

cor·ri·gen·dum \,kȯr-ə-'jen-dəm, ,kär-\ n, pl **-da** \-də\ [L, thing to be corrected, fr. corrigere to correct] **:** an error in a printed work discovered after printing and shown with its correction on a separate sheet

cor·ri·gi·ble \'kȯr-ə-jə-bəl, 'kär-\ adj [L corrigere to correct] **:** capable of being set right — **cor·ri·gi·bil·i·ty** \,kȯr-ə-jə-'bil-ət-ē, ,kär-\ n — **cor·ri·gi·bly** \'kȯr-ə-jə-blē, 'kär-\ adv

cor·rob·o·rate \kə-'räb-ə-,rāt\ vt [L corroborare to strengthen, fr. com- + robor-, robur strength] **:** to support with evidence or authority **:** make more certain **syn** see CONFIRM — **cor·rob·o·ra·tor** \-,rāt-ər\ n

cor·rob·o·ra·tion \kə-,räb-ə-'rā-shən\ n **1 :** the act of corroborating **2 :** something that corroborates

cor·rob·o·ra·tive \kə-'räb-ə-,rāt-iv, -'räb-(ə-)rət-\ adj **:** serving or tending to corroborate **:** CONFIRMING 〈corroborative evidence〉 — **cor·rob·o·ra·tive·ly** adv

cor·rob·o·ra·to·ry \kə-'räb-(ə-)rə-,tōr-ē, -,tȯr-\ adj **:** CORROBORATIVE

cor·rode \kə-'rōd\ vb [L corros-, corrodere, fr. com- + rodere to gnaw] **:** to eat or be eaten away by degrees as if by gnawing; esp **:** to wear away gradually usu. by chemical action — **cor·rod·i·ble** \-'rōd-ə-bəl\ adj

cor·ro·sion \kə-'rō-zhən\ n **:** the action, process, or effect of corroding

1cor·ro·sive \-'rō-siv, -ziv\ adj **:** tending or having the power to corrode **:** eating away 〈corrosive acids〉 〈corrosive action〉 — **cor·ro·sive·ly** adv — **cor·ro·sive·ness** n

2corrosive n **:** something corrosive

corrosive sublimate n **:** MERCURIC CHLORIDE

cor·ru·gate \'kȯr-ə-ˌgāt, 'kär-\ *vb* [L *corrugare,* fr. *com-* + *ruga* wrinkle] **:** to form or shape into wrinkles or folds or ridges and grooves **:** FURROW ⟨*corrugated* paper⟩ ⟨*corrugated* iron⟩

cor·ru·ga·tion \ˌkȯr-ə-'gā-shən, ˌkär-\ *n* **1 :** the act of corrugating **:** the state of being corrugated **2 :** a ridge or groove of a corrugated surface

¹cor·rupt \kə-'rəpt\ *vb* [L *corrupt-, corrumpere,* fr. *com-* + *rumpere* to break] **1 :** to change from good to bad in morals, manners, or actions; *esp* **:** to influence a public official improperly **2 :** TAINT, ROT **3 :** to alter from the original or correct form ȯr version ⟨*corrupted* text⟩ **4 :** to become debased **syn** see DEBASE — **cor·rupt·er** *or* **cor·rup·tor** \-'rəp-tər\ *n*

²corrupt *adj* **1 :** morally perverted **:** DEPRAVED **2 :** characterized by improper conduct (as bribery or the selling of political favors) ⟨a *corrupt* administration⟩ — **cor·rupt·ly** *adv* — **cor·rupt·ness** \-'rəp(t)-nəs\ *n*

cor·rupt·i·ble \kə-'rəp-tə-bəl\ *adj* **:** capable of being corrupted — **cor·rupt·i·bil·i·ty** \-ˌrəp-tə-'bil-ət-ē\ *n*

cor·rup·tion \kə-'rəp-shən\ *n* **1 a :** physical decay or rotting **b :** impairment of integrity, virtue, or moral principle **:** DEPRAVITY **c :** inducement to do wrong by unlawful or improper means (as bribery) **d :** a departure from what is pure or correct **2** *archaic* **:** an agency or influence that corrupts

cor·rup·tive \kə-'rəp-tiv\ *adj* **:** producing corruption

cor·sage \kȯr-'säzh, -'säj, 'kȯr-,\ *n* [F, fr. OF, bust, fr. *cors* body, fr. L *corpus*] **1 :** the waist or bodice of a woman's dress **2 :** an arrangement of flowers to be worn by a woman

cor·sair \'kȯr-ˌsa(ə)r, -ˌse(ə)r\ *n* [MF *corsaire,* fr. ML *cursarius,* fr. L *cursus* course] **:** PIRATE; *esp* **:** a privateer of the Barbary coast

corse \'kȯrs\ *n* [OF *cors* body] *archaic* **:** CORPSE

corse·let *n* **1** *or* **cors·let** \'kȯr-slət\ **:** the body armor worn by a knight esp. on the upper part of the body **2** \ˌkȯr-sə-'let\ **:** a woman's undergarment somewhat like a corset

¹cor·set \'kȯr-sət\ *n* [OF, a medieval jacket, fr. dim. of *cors* body] **:** a tight-fitting stiffened undergarment worn by women to support or give shape to waist and hips

²corset *vt* **:** to dress in or fit with a corset

cor·tege *also* **cor·tège** \'kȯr-ˌtezh, kȯr-'\ *n* [F *cortège,* fr. It *corteggio,* fr. *corte* court] **1 :** a train of attendants **:** RETINUE **2 :** PROCESSION; *esp* **:** a funeral procession

cor·tes \'kȯr-ˌtez, -ˌtes\ *n, pl* **cor·tes** \-ˌtez\ [Sp, pl. of *corte* court] **:** a Spanish parliament

cor·tex \'kȯr-ˌteks\ *n, pl* **cor·ti·ces** \'kȯrt-ə-ˌsēz\ *or* **cor·tex·es** [L *cortic-, cortex* bark] **:** an outer or investing layer of an organism or one of its parts ⟨the *cortex* of the kidney⟩: as **a :** the outer layer of gray matter of the brain **b :** the layer of tissue outside the vascular tissue and inside the corky or epidermal tissues of a vascular plant; *also* **:** all tissues external to the xylem — **cor·ti·cal** \'kȯrt-i-kəl\ *adj* — **cor·ti·cal·ly** \-i-k(ə-)lē\ *adv*

cor·ti·co·tro·pin \ˌkȯrt-i-kō-'trō-pən\ *n* **:** a preparation of a hormone from the pituitary of various domesticated animals used esp. in the treatment of rheumatic fever and rheumatoid arthritis

cor·tin \'kȯrt-ⁿn\ *n* **:** a hormone mixture from the adrenal cortex

cor·ti·sone \'kȯrt-ə-ˌsōn, -ˌzōn\ *n* **:** a steroid hormone of the adrenal cortex used esp. in the treatment of rheumatoid arthritis

co·run·dum \kə-'rən-dəm\ *n* [Tamil *kuruntam*] **:** a very hard mineral Al_2O_3 that consists of aluminum oxide occurring massive and as variously colored crystals including the ruby and sapphire and that is used as an abrasive

cor·us·cate \'kȯr-ə-ˌskāt, 'kär-\ *vi* [L *coruscare*] **:** FLASH, SPARKLE — **cor·us·ca·tion** \ˌkȯr-ə-'skā-shən, ˌkär-\ *n*

cor·vée \'kȯr-ˌvā\ *n* **:** unpaid labor on public works (as roads) exacted usu. in lieu of taxes

cor·vette \kȯr-'vet\ *n* **1 :** a warship of the old sailing navies smaller than a frigate **2 :** a highly maneuverable armed escort ship smaller than a destroyer

cor·vine \'kȯr-ˌvīn\ *adj* **:** of or relating to the crows **:** resembling a crow

Cor·vus \'kȯr-vəs\ *n* [L, lit., raven] **:** a small constellation adjoining Virgo on the south

Cor·y·bant \'kȯr-ə-ˌbant, 'kär-\ *n, pl* **Cor·y·bants** *or*

Cor·y·ban·tes \ˌkȯr-ə-'ban-ˌtēz, ˌkär-\ **:** one of the attendants or priests of Cybele noted for their orgiastic processions and rites — **cor·y·ban·tic** \ˌkȯr-ə-'bant-ik, ˌkär-\ *adj*

cor·ymb \'kȯr-ˌim, 'kär-\ *n* [Gk *korymbos* cluster of fruit or flowers] **:** a flat-topped indeterminate inflorescence in which the flower stalks arise at different levels on the main axis and reach about the same height — **cor·ym·bose** \-əm-ˌbōs\ *adj*

co·ry·za \kə-'rī-zə\ *n* **:** an acute inflammatory contagious disease involving the upper respiratory tract; *esp* **:** COMMON COLD — **co·ry·zal** \-zəl\ *adj*

co·se·cant \(')kō-'sē-ˌkant, -kənt\ *n* **:** the trigonometric function that for an acute angle in a right triangle is the ratio between the hypotenuse and the side opposite the angle

corymb of a cherry: *1* peduncle; *2, 2* pedicels; *3, 3* bracts

co·sig·na·to·ry \(')kō-'sig-nə-ˌtōr-ē, -ˌtȯr-\ *n, pl* **-ries :** a joint signer

cosily, cosiness *var of* COZILY, COZINESS

co·sine \'kō-ˌsīn\ *n* [NL *cosinus,* fr. *co-* + ML *sinus* sine] **:** the trigonometric function that for an acute angle in a right triangle is the ratio between the side adjacent to the angle and the hypotenuse

¹cos·met·ic \käz-'met-ik\ *n* **:** a cosmetic preparation for external use

²cosmetic *adj* [Gk *kosmein* to adorn, fr. *kosmos* order, adornment] **:** relating to or making for beauty esp. of the complexion **:** BEAUTIFYING ⟨*cosmetic* salves⟩

cos·me·tol·o·gist \ˌkäz-mə-'täl-ə-jəst\ *n* **:** one who gives beauty treatments (as to skin and hair) — **cos·me·tol·o·gy** \-jē\ *n*

cos·mic \'käz-mik\ *adj* **1 :** of or relating to the cosmos ⟨*cosmic* theories⟩ **2 :** extremely vast **:** GRAND ⟨a topic of *cosmic* proportions⟩ — **cos·mi·cal·ly** \-mi-k(ə-)lē\ *adv*

cosmic dust *n* **:** very fine particles of solid matter in any part of the universe and esp. in interstellar space

cosmic radiation *n* **:** radiation consisting of cosmic rays

cosmic ray *n* **:** a stream of atomic nuclei of extremely penetrating character that enter the earth's atmosphere from outer space at speeds approaching that of light

cos·mog·o·ny \käz-'mäg-ə-nē\ *n, pl* **-nies** [Gk *kosmogonia,* fr. *kosmos* universe + *gonos* offspring] **1 :** the creation or origination of the world or universe **2 :** a theory of the origin of the universe — **cos·mog·o·nist** \-nəst\ *n*

cos·mog·ra·phy \käz-'mäg-rə-fē\ *n, pl* **-phies 1 :** a general description of the world or of the universe **2 :** the science that deals with the constitution of the whole order of nature — **cos·mog·ra·pher** \-fər\ *n* — **cos·mo·graph·ic** \ˌkäz-mə-'graf-ik\ *adj*

cos·mol·o·gy \käz-'mäl-ə-jē\ *n, pl* **-gies :** a study that deals with the origin, structure, and space-time relationships of the universe — **cos·mo·log·i·cal** \ˌkäz-mə-'läj-i-kəl\ *adj* — **cos·mol·o·gist** \käz-'mäl-ə-jəst\ *n*

cos·mo·naut \'käz-mə-ˌnȯt, -ˌnät\ *n* [Russ *kosmonavt,* fr. Gk *kosmos* + Russ *-navt* (as in *aeronavt* aeronaut)] **:** a traveler beyond the earth's atmosphere **:** ASTRONAUT

cos·mo·pol·i·tan \ˌkäz-mə-'päl-ət-ⁿn\ *adj* **1 :** having worldwide rather than limited or provincial scope or bearing **2 :** having a broadly sophisticated and international outlook ⟨*cosmopolitan* world travelers⟩ **3 :** composed of persons, constituents, or elements from many parts of the world ⟨a *cosmopolitan* city⟩ **4 :** found in most parts of the world and under varied ecological conditions ⟨a *cosmopolitan* herb⟩— **cosmopolitan** *n* — **cos·mo·pol·i·tan·ism** \-ⁿn-ˌiz-əm\ *n*

cos·mop·o·lite \käz-'mäp-ə-ˌlīt\ *n* [Gk *kosmopolitēs,* fr. *kosmos* cosmos + *politēs* citizen] **:** a cosmopolitan person or organism

cos·mos \'käz-məs, *1 & 2 also* -ˌmōs, -ˌmäs\ *n* [Gk *kosmos* order, adornment, universe] **1 :** the orderly systematic universe **2 :** a complex self-inclusive system having order and harmony among its parts **3 :** a tall garden plant that is related to the daisies and has showy white, pink, or rose-colored flower heads with usu. yellow centers

cos·sack \'käs-ˌak, -ək\ *n* [Russ *kazak* & Ukrainian *kozak,* fr. Turk *kazak* free person] **:** a member of a group of frontiersmen of southern Russia organized as cavalry in the czarist army

¹**cos·set** *n* \'käs-ət\ : a pet lamb; *also* : PET
²**cosset** *vt* : to treat as a pet : FONDLE
¹**cost** \'kȯst\ *n* **1 a** : the amount paid or charged for
something : PRICE **b** : the outlay or expenditure made to
achieve an object ⟨won the battle at the *cost* of many
lives⟩ **2** : loss or penalty incurred in gaining something
3 *pl* : expenses charged to a party before a court of law
⟨fined $50 and *costs*⟩
²**cost** *vb* **cost**; **cost·ing** [MF *coster*, fr. L *costare* to stand
firm, cost, fr. *com-* + *stare* to stand] **1** : to have a price
of : require expenditure or payment ⟨each ticket *costs* one
dollar⟩ **2** : to cause one to pay, spend, or lose ⟨selfishness
cost him many friends⟩
cos·ta \'käs-tə\ *n, pl* **cos·tae** \-(,)tē, -,tī\ [L, rib, side]
: a rib or a body part (as the midrib of a leaf) resembling a
rib — **cos·tal** \'käst-ᵊl\ *adj* — **cos·tate** \'käs-,tāt\ *adj*
cos·tard \'käs-tərd\ **1** : any of several large English
cooking apples **2** *archaic* : HEAD, NODDLE
cos·ter \'käs-tər\ *n, Brit* : COSTERMONGER
cos·ter·mon·ger \'käs-tər-,məŋ-gər, -,mäŋ-\ *n* [*costard*]
Brit : a person who sells fruit or vegetables in the street
from a stand or cart
cos·tive \'käs-tiv\ *adj* [MF *costiver* to constipate, fr. L
constipare] **1** : CONSTIPATED **2** : causing constipation
⟨a *costive* diet⟩ — **cos·tive·ly** *adv* — **cos·tive·ness** *n*
cost·ly \'kȯst-lē\ *adj* **cost·li·er; -est 1** : of great cost
or value ⟨*costly* furs⟩ **2** : made at heavy expense or
sacrifice ⟨*costly* victory⟩ — **cost·li·ness** *n*
syn EXPENSIVE, VALUABLE: COSTLY implies high price and
may suggest luxury or rarity; EXPENSIVE may imply a price
beyond the thing's value or the buyer's means; VALUABLE
suggests worth measured in usefulness as well as price
cost·mary \'kȯst-,mer-ē\ *n, pl* **-mar·ies** : an aromatic
herb related to the daisies and used as a potherb and in
flavoring
¹**cos·tume** \'käs-,t(y)üm\ *n* [F, fr. It, custom, fr. L
consuetudin-, consuetudo] **1** : the prevailing fashion of a
period, country, or class in dress, personal ornaments, and
style of wearing the hair **2** : a suit or dress characteristic
of a period, country, class, or occupation esp. as worn on
the stage or at a masquerade party **3** : a person's ensemble of outer garments; *esp* : a woman's ensemble of
dress with coat or jacket — **costume** *adj*
²**costume** *vt* : to provide with a costume : design costumes for
cos·tum·er \'käs-,t(y)ü-mər\ *or* **cos·tu·mi·er** \käs-'t(y)ü-
mē-ər\ *n* : one that makes, sells, or rents costumes
co·sy \'kō-zē\ *var of* COZY
¹**cot** \'kät\ *n* [OE] **1** : a small house : COTTAGE
2 : SHEATH; *esp* : STALL 4
²**cot** *n* [Hindi *khāṭ* bedstead] : a small often collapsible bed
usu. of fabric stretched on a frame
co·tan·gent \(')kō-'tan-jənt\ *n* : the trigonometric func-
tion that for an acute angle in a right triangle is the ratio
between the side adjacent to the angle and the side
opposite
cote \'kōt, 'kät\ *n* [OE *cot, cote* ¹cot] : a shed or coop for
small domestic animals (as sheep or pigeons)
co·te·rie \'kōt-ə-(,)rē, ,kōt-ə-'\ *n* [F, fr. MF, group of
tenants, fr. ME ¹*cot*] : an often exclusive group
of persons with a common interest or purpose
co·ter·mi·nal \(')kō-'tər-mən-ᵊl\ *adj* : having the same
or coincident boundaries
co·ter·mi·nous \(')kō-'tər-mə-nəs\ *adj* : coextensive in
scope or duration — **co·ter·mi·nous·ly** *adv*
co·til·lion *also* **co·til·lon** \kō-'til-yən\ *n* [F *cotillon*, lit.,
petticoat, fr. OF, fr. *cote* coat] **1** : a ballroom dance for
couples that resembles the quadrille **2** : an elaborate
dance with frequent changing of partners executed under
the leadership of one couple at formal balls **3** : a formal
ball
co·to·ne·as·ter \kə-'tō-nē-,as-tər, 'kät-ᵊn-,ēs-\ *n* : any of a
genus of Old World flowering shrubs of the rose family
often used in hedges
cot·ta \'kät-ə\ *n* : a waist-length surplice
cot·tage \'kät-ij\ *n* **1** : a small usu. frame one-family
house **2** : a small house for vacation use
cottage cheese *n* : a soft uncured cheese made from
soured skim milk
cottage pudding *n* : plain cake covered with a hot sweet
sauce

cot·tag·er \'kät-ij-ər\ *n* : one who lives in a cottage; *esp*
: one occupying a private house at a vacation resort
¹**cot·ter** *or* **cot·tar** \'kät-ər\ *n* [ME *cottar*, fr. ¹*cot*] : a
peasant or rural laborer occupying a small holding usu.
in return for services
²**cot·ter** \'kät-ər\ *n* : a wedge-shaped or tapered piece
used to fasten together parts of a structure
cotter pin *n* : a half-round metal strip bent into a pin whose
ends can be flared after insertion through a slot or hole
¹**cot·ton** \'kät-ᵊn\ *n* [MF, fr. Ar *quṭn*] **1 a** : a soft usu.
white fibrous substance composed of the hairs surrounding
the seeds of various erect freely branching tropical plants
of the mallow family **b** : a plant producing cotton **c** : a
crop of cotton **2 a** : fabric made of cotton **b** : yarn spun
from cotton — **cotton** *adj*
²**cotton** *vi* **cot·toned; cot·ton·ing** \'kät-niŋ, -ᵊn-iŋ\ : to
take a liking ⟨*cottoned* to him at their first meeting⟩
cotton candy *n* : a candy made by spinning sugar that has
been boiled to a high temperature
cotton gin *n* : a machine that separates the seeds, hulls,
and foreign material from cotton
cot·ton·mouth \'kät-ᵊn-,mau̇th\ *n* : WATER MOCCASIN
cot·ton·seed \-,sēd\ *n* : the seed of the cotton plant yielding a protein-rich meal and a fixed oil used esp. in cooking
cot·ton·tail \-,tāl\ *n* : any of several small brownish gray
rabbits with white-tufted tail
cot·ton·wood \-,wu̇d\ *n* : a poplar with a tuft of cottony
hairs on the seed; *esp* : one of the eastern and central U.S.
noted for its rapid growth and luxuriant foliage
cotton wool *n* : raw cotton; *esp* : cotton batting
cot·tony \'kät-nē, -ᵊn-ē\ *adj* : resembling cotton in appearance or character: as **a** : covered with soft hairs
: DOWNY **b** : SOFT
-cot·yl \,kät-ᵊl\ *n comb form* [*cotyledon*] : cotyledon
⟨dicotyl⟩
cot·y·le·don \,kät-ᵊl-'ēd-ᵊn\ *n* [Gk *kotylēdōn* cup-shaped
hollow, fr. *kotylē* cup] **1** : a placental lobule **2** : the first
leaf or one of the first pair or whorl of leaves developed
by the embryo of a seed plant — **cot·y·le·don·ary** \-'ēd-
ᵊn-,er-ē\ *or* **cot·y·le·don·ous** \-'ēd-nəs, -ᵊn-əs\ *adj*
cot·y·lo·saur \'kät-ᵊl-ō-,sȯr\ *n* : any of an order (Coty-
losauria) of ancient extinct primitive reptiles that were
prob. the earliest truly terrestrial vertebrate animals
¹**couch** \'kau̇ch\ *vb* [MF *coucher*, fr. L *collocare* to set
in place, fr. *com-* + *locus* place] **1** : to recline for rest or
sleep **2** : to bring down : LOWER ⟨a knight charging with
couched lance⟩ **3** : to phrase in a specified manner ⟨a
letter *couched* in polite terms⟩ **4** : to lie in ambush
²**couch** *n* : an article of furniture for sitting or reclining;
esp : SOFA
couch·ant \'kau̇-chənt\ *adj* : lying down esp. with the
head up ⟨a heraldic lion *couchant*⟩
couch grass \'kau̇ch-, 'küch-\ *n* : a European creeping
grass naturalized in No. America as a weed
cou·gar \'kü-gər, -,gär\ *n, pl* **cougars** *also* **cougar** [F
couguar, fr. Pg *cuguardo*, fr. Tupi *suasuarana*] : a large
powerful tawny brown cat formerly widespread in the
Americas but now extinct in many areas — called also
mountain lion, panther, puma
¹**cough** \'kȯf\ *vb* [ME *coughen*] **1** : to force air from the
lungs with a sharp short noise or series of noises **2** : to
get rid of by coughing ⟨*cough* up phlegm⟩
²**cough** *n* **1** : a condition marked by repeated or frequent
coughing **2** : an act or sound of coughing
cough up *vt* : DELIVER, PAY ⟨*cough up* the money⟩
could \kəd, 'kud\ [OE *cūthe*] *past of* CAN — used as an
auxiliary verb in the past ⟨he found he *could* go⟩ ⟨he said
he would go if he *could*⟩ and as an alternative to *can* suggesting less force or certainty or as a polite form in the
present ⟨*could* you do this for me⟩ ⟨if you *could* come we
would be pleased⟩
could·est \'kud-əst\ *archaic past 2d sing of* CAN
couldn't \'kud-ᵊnt\ : could not
couldst \kədst, (')kudst\ *archaic past 2d sing of* CAN
cou·lee \'kü-lē\ *n* [CanF *coulée*, lit., flowing] **1** *chiefly
West* **a** : a dry creek bed **b** : a steep-walled valley **2** : a
thick sheet or stream of lava
cou·lomb \'kü-,läm, -,lōm\ *n* [after Charles A. de
*Coulomb d*1806 French physicist] : the practical mks unit
of electric charge equal to the quantity of electricity
transferred by a current of one ampere in one second

---

j joke; ŋ sing; ō flow; ȯ flaw; ȯi coin; th thin; th̲ this; ü loot; u̇ foot; y yet; yü few; yu̇ furious; zh vision

coulter *var of* COLTER

coun·cil \'kaůn(t)-səl\ *n* [OF *concile,* fr. L *concilium,* fr. *com-* + *calare* to call] **1 :** a meeting for consultation, advice, or discussion **2 :** an elected or appointed advisory or legislative body ⟨governor's *council*⟩ **3 :** an administrative body (as of a town) **4 :** deliberation in a council **5 a :** a federation of or a central body uniting a group of organizations or other bodies **b :** a local chapter of an organization **c :** CLUB, SOCIETY

coun·cil·lor *or* **coun·cil·or** \'kaůn(t)-s(ə-)lər\ *n* **:** a member of a council — **coun·cil·lor·ship** \-ˌship\ *n*

coun·cil·man \'kaůn(t)-səl-mən\ *n* **:** a member of a council esp. in a city government

¹coun·sel \'kaůn(t)-səl\ *n* [OF *conseil,* fr. L *consilium,* fr. *consulere* to consult] **1 a :** advice given esp. as a result of consultation **b :** a policy or plan of action or behavior **2 :** DELIBERATION, CONSULTATION **3** *pl* **counsel a :** a lawyer engaged in the trial or management of a case in court **b :** a lawyer appointed to advise and represent a client in legal matters **syn** see ADVICE

²counsel *vb* **-seled** *or* **-selled; -sel·ing** *or* **-sel·ling** \-s(ə-)liŋ\ **1 :** to give counsel to : ADVISE ⟨*counsel* a student on a choice of studies⟩ **2 :** to seek counsel : CONSULT ⟨*counsel* with friends⟩

coun·sel·or *or* **coun·sel·lor** \'kaůn(t)-s(ə-)lər\ *n* **1 :** ADVISER **2 :** LAWYER; *esp* **:** one that manages cases for clients in court **3 :** a supervisor of campers or activities at a summer camp — **coun·sel·or·ship** \-ˌship\ *n*

¹count \'kaůnt\ *vb* [MF *compter,* fr. L *computare,* fr. *com-* + *putare* to consider] **1 a :** to name by units or groups so as to find the total number ⟨*count* the apples in a box⟩ **b :** to name the consecutive numbers up to and including ⟨*count* ten⟩ **c :** to recite the numbers in order by units or groups ⟨*count* to one hundred by fives⟩ **d :** to include in a tally ⟨forty present, *counting* children⟩ **2 a :** CONSIDER ⟨*counts* himself lucky⟩ **b :** to include or exclude by or as if by counting ⟨*count* me as uncommitted⟩ ⟨*counted* himself out⟩ **3 a :** RELY, DEPEND ⟨a man you can *count* on⟩ **b :** RECKON, PLAN ⟨*counted* on going⟩ ⟨didn't *count* on his being there⟩ **4 :** to have value, significance, or importance ⟨every vote *counts*⟩ ⟨a near miss doesn't *count*⟩ — **count·a·ble** \-ə-bəl\ *adj*

²count *n* **1 :** the act or process of counting; *also* **:** a total obtained by counting **:** TALLY **2 :** ALLEGATION, CHARGE; *esp* **:** one stating a separate cause of action in a legal declaration or indictment ⟨guilty on all *counts*⟩ **3 :** the calling off of the seconds from one to ten when a boxer has been knocked down

³count *n* [MF *comte,* fr. LL *comit-, comes,* fr. L, companion, fr. *com-* + *ire* to go] **:** a European nobleman whose rank corresponds to that of a British earl

count·down \'kaůnt-ˌdaůn\ *n* **:** an audible backward counting off in fixed units (as seconds) from an arbitrary starting number to mark the time remaining before an event (as the launching of a rocket)

¹coun·te·nance \'kaůnt-ᵊn-ən(t)s, 'kaůnt-nən(t)s\ *n* [MF *contenance* demeanor, bearing, fr. ML *continentia,* fr. L, restraint, fr. *continent-, continens* content] **1 a :** calm expression **b :** mental composure **c :** LOOK, EXPRESSION **2 :** FACE, VISAGE; *esp* **:** facial indication of mood, emotion, or character **3 :** appearance or expression seeming to approve or encourage ⟨gave no *countenance* to the plan⟩

²countenance *vt* **:** to extend approval or toleration to **:** SANCTION ⟨refused to *countenance* his habitual lateness⟩ — **coun·te·nanc·er** *n*

¹count·er \'kaůnt-ər\ *n* **1 :** a piece (as of metal or ivory) used in counting or in games **2 :** a level surface (as a table) over which transactions are conducted or food is served or on which goods are displayed or work is conducted

²count·er *n* **:** one that counts; *esp* **:** a device for indicating a number or amount

³coun·ter \'kaůnt-ər\ *vb* **coun·tered; coun·ter·ing** \'kaůnt-ə-riŋ, 'kaůn-triŋ\ **1 :** to act in opposition to **:** OPPOSE ⟨*countering* the claim for damages⟩ **2 :** RETALIATE ⟨*countered* with a left hook⟩ ⟨*countered* with a sharp remark of his own⟩

⁴coun·ter *adv* [MF *contre,* fr. L *contra* against, opposite] **:** in a contrary manner or direction ⟨acting *counter* to his wishes⟩ ⟨sailed *counter* to the prevailing winds⟩

⁵coun·ter *n* **1 :** the after portion of a boat from the water-line to the extreme outward swell or overhang **2** [⁴*counter*] **:** the act of giving a retaliatory blow; *also* **:** the blow given **3** [F *contrefort* buttress, counter] **:** a stiffener giving shape to the upper of a shoe around the heel

⁶coun·ter *adj* **1 :** moving in an opposite direction ⟨ship slowed by *counter* tides⟩ **2 :** designed to oppose ⟨a *counter* offer⟩

counter- *prefix* [MF *contre-*] **1 a :** contrary **:** opposite ⟨*counter*clockwise⟩ ⟨*counter*march⟩ **b :** opposing **:** retaliatory ⟨*counter*irritant⟩ ⟨*counter*offensive⟩ **2 :** complementary **:** corresponding ⟨*counter*weight⟩ ⟨*counter*part⟩ **3 :** duplicate **:** substitute ⟨*counter*foil⟩

coun·ter·act \ˌkaůnt-ər-'akt\ *vt* **:** to lessen the force of **:** OFFSET ⟨a drug that *counteracts* the effect of a poison⟩ ⟨*counteracting* an evil influence⟩ — **coun·ter·ac·tion** \-'ak-shən\ *n* — **coun·ter·ac·tive** \-'ak-tiv\ *adj*

coun·ter·at·tack \'kaůnt-ər-ə-ˌtak\ *n* **:** an attack made to counter an enemy's attack — **counterattack** *vb*

¹coun·ter·bal·ance \'kaůnt-ər-ˌbal-ən(t)s, ˌkaůnt-ər-'-\ *n* **1 :** a weight that balances another **2 :** a force or influence that offsets or checks an opposing force ⟨his good sense served as a *counterbalance* to her enthusiasm⟩

²coun·ter·bal·ance \ˌkaůnt-ər-', 'kaůnt-ər-ˌ\ *vt* **1 :** to oppose with an equal weight or force **2 :** to equip with counterbalances

coun·ter·bore \'kaůnt-ər-ˌbōr, -ˌbȯr\ *n* **:** a flat-bottomed enlargement of the mouth of a cylindrical hole — **counterbore** *vt*

¹coun·ter·check \'kaůnt-ər-ˌchek\ *n* **:** a check or restraint often operating against something that is itself a check

²countercheck *vt* **1 :** CHECK, COUNTERACT **2 :** to check a second time for verification

counter check *n* **:** a blank check obtainable at a bank; *esp* **:** one to be cashed at the bank by the drawer

coun·ter·claim \'kaůnt-ər-ˌklām\ *n* **:** an opposing claim esp. in law — **counterclaim** *vb* — **coun·ter·claim·ant** \-ˌklā-mənt\ *n*

coun·ter·clock·wise \ˌkaůnt-ər-'kläk-ˌwīz\ *adv* **:** in a direction opposite to that in which the hands of a clock rotate — **counterclockwise** *adj*

coun·ter·cur·rent \'kaůnt-ər-ˌkər-ənt, -ˌkə-rənt\ *n* **:** a current flowing in a direction opposite to that of another one

coun·ter·es·pi·o·nage \ˌkaůnt-ər-'es-pē-ə-ˌnäzh, -nij, -ˌnäj\ *n* **:** the attempt to discover and defeat enemy espionage

¹coun·ter·feit \'kaůnt-ər-ˌfit\ *vb* **1 :** to imitate or copy esp. with intent to deceive ⟨*counterfeiting* money⟩ **2 :** PRETEND, FEIGN ⟨*counterfeit* an air of indifference⟩ — **coun·ter·feit·er** *n*

²counterfeit *adj* [MF *contrefait,* fr. pp. of *contrefaire* to imitate, fr. *contre-* counter- + *faire* to make, fr. L *facere*] **1 :** made in imitation of something else with intent to deceive **:** FORGED ⟨*counterfeit* money⟩ **2 :** FEIGNED, SHAM ⟨*counterfeit* joy at the news of her friend's engagement⟩

³counterfeit *n* **1 :** something counterfeit **:** FORGERY **2 :** something that is likely to be confused with the genuine thing

coun·ter·foil \ˌkaůnt-ər-ˌfȯil\ *n* [*counter-* + *foil* leaf] **:** a detachable stub usu. serving as a record or receipt (as on a check or ticket)

coun·ter·in·tel·li·gence \ˌkaůnt-ər-ən-'tel-ə-jən(t)s\ *n* **:** organized activities of an intelligence service designed to counter the activities of an enemy's intelligence service by blocking its sources of information and to deceive the enemy through ruses and misinformation

coun·ter·ir·ri·tant \ˌkaůnt-ər-'ir-ə-tənt\ *n* **:** something (as a mustard plaster) used to produce superficial inflammation with the object of reducing inflammation in deeper adjacent structures — **counterirritant** *adj*

coun·ter·man \'kaůnt-ər-ˌman, -mən\ *n* **:** one who tends a counter (as in a lunchroom)

coun·ter·mand \'kaůnt-ər-ˌmand\ *vt* [MF *contremander,* fr. *contre-* counter- + *mander* to command, fr. L *mandare*] **1 :** to revoke (a former command) by a contrary order **2 :** to recall or order back by a superseding contrary order — **countermand** *n*

coun·ter·march \'kaůnt-ər-ˌmärch\ *n* **:** a marching back; *esp* **:** a maneuver by which a unit of troops reverses direction while marching but keeps the same order — **countermarch** *vi*

ə abut; ᵊ kitten; ər further; a back; ā bake; ä cot, cart; aů out; ch chin; e less; ē easy; g gift; i trip; ī life

coun·ter·mea·sure \-,mezh-ər, -,māzh-\ *n* : an action undertaken to counter another

coun·ter·of·fen·sive \'kaủnt-ər-ə-,fen(t)-siv\ *n* : a large-scale military offensive undertaken by a force previously on the defensive

coun·ter·pane \'kaủnt-ər-,pān\ *n* [alter. of ME *countre-pointe*, modif. of MF *coute pointe*, lit., embroidered quilt] : BEDSPREAD

coun·ter·part \'kaủnt-ər-,pärt\ *n* 1 : a part or thing corresponding to another (as in appearance, position, or use) (the left arm is the *counterpart* of the right arm) 2 : something that serves to complete something else : COMPLEMENT 3 : a person closely resembling another person (the twins were *counterparts* of each other)

¹**coun·ter·plot** \-,plät\ *vb* : to plot against or foil with a plot : INTRIGUE

²**counterplot** *n* : a plot opposed to another

coun·ter·point \'kaủnt-ər-,point\ *n* [MF *contrepoint*, fr. ML *contrapunctus*, fr. L *contra-* counter- + ML *punctus* musical note, melody] 1 : one or more independent melodies added above or below a given melody 2 : combination of two or more related independent melodies into a single harmonic texture in which each retains its linear character : POLYPHONY

¹**coun·ter·poise** \-,poiz\ *vt* : COUNTERBALANCE

²**counterpoise** *n* 1 : COUNTERBALANCE 2 : a state of balance

Coun·ter-Ref·or·ma·tion \,kaủnt-ə(r)-,ref-ər-'mā-shən\ *n* : the reform movement in the Roman Catholic Church following the Reformation

coun·ter·rev·o·lu·tion \-,rev-ə-'lü-shən\ *n* : a revolution in opposition to a current or earlier one — **coun·ter·rev·o·lu·tion·ary** \-shə-,ner-ē\ *adj or n* — **coun·ter·rev·o·lu·tion·ist** \-sh(ə-)nəst\ *n*

coun·ter·shaft \'kaủnt-ər-,shaft\ *n* : a shaft that receives motion from a main shaft and transmits it to a working part

¹**coun·ter·sign** \-,sīn\ *n* 1 : a signature attesting the authenticity of a document already signed by another 2 : a sign used in reply to another; *esp* : a secret signal that must be given by one wishing to pass a guard

²**countersign** *vt* : to add one's signature to after another's in order to attest authenticity — **coun·ter·sig·na·ture** \,kaủnt-ər-'sig-nə-,chủ(ə)r, -chər\ *n*

¹**coun·ter·sink** \'kaủnt-ər-,siŋk\ *vt* -**sunk** \-,səŋk\; -**sink·ing** 1 : to form a hollowed-out place around the top of (a hole in wood or metal) into which a screw or bolt is to be placed 2 : to sink the head of (as a screw, bolt, or nail) even with or below the surface

²**countersink** *n* 1 : a funnel-shaped enlargement at the outer end of a drilled hole 2 : a bit or drill for making a countersink

coun·ter·spy \-,spī\ *n* : a spy employed against enemy espionage

coun·ter·ten·or \-,ten-ər\ *n* : a tenor with an unusually high range

coun·ter·weight \-,wāt\ *n* : COUNTERBALANCE — **counterweight** *vt*

count·ess \'kaủnt-əs\ *n* 1 : the wife or widow of a count or an earl 2 : a woman who holds the rank of a count or an earl in her own right

count·ing·house \'kaủnt-iŋ-,haủs\ *n* : a building, room, or office that is used for keeping books and transacting business

counting room *n* : COUNTINGHOUSE

count·less \'kaủnt-ləs\ *adj* : too numerous to be counted : INNUMERABLE **syn** see MANY

coun·tri·fied *or* **coun·try·fied** \'kən-trē-,fīd\ *adj* : looking or acting like a person from the country : RUSTIC

¹**coun·try** \'kən-trē\ *n, pl* **countries** [OF *contree*, fr. ML *contrata*, fr. L *contra* against, on the opposite side] 1 : an indefinite usu. extended expanse of land : REGION (hill *country*) 2 a : the land of a person's birth, residence, or citizenship b : a political state or nation or its territory 3 a : the people of a state or district : POPULACE b : JURY c : ELECTORATE 4 : rural as distinguished from urban areas (lives out in the *country*)

²**country** *adj* : of, relating to, or characteristic of the country

country club *n* : a suburban club for social life and recreation

coun·try–dance \'kən-trē-,dan(t)s\ *n* : an English dance in which partners face each other esp. in rows

coun·try·man \'kən-trē-mən, *3 is often* -,man\ *n* 1 : an inhabitant or native of a specified country (a north *countryman*) 2 : COMPATRIOT (hated by his *countrymen*) 3 : one living in the country or marked by country ways : RUSTIC — **coun·try·wom·an** \-,wùm-ən\ *n*

coun·try·seat \,kən-trē-'sēt\ *n* : a dwelling or estate in the country

coun·try·side \'kən-trē-,sīd\ *n* : a rural area or its people

coun·ty \'kaủnt-ē\ *n, pl* **counties** [OF *conté*, fr. ML *comitatus*, fr. LL, office of a count, fr. *comit-*, *comes* count] 1 : the domain of a count 2 a : one of the chief territorial divisions of Great Britain and Ireland for administrative, judicial, and political purposes b : the largest territorial division for local government within a state of the U.S.

county agent *n* : a government agent employed to promote agricultural improvement in a county

county seat *n* : a town that is the seat of county administration

coup \'kü\ *n, pl* **coups** \'küz\ [F, blow, stroke, fr. LL *colpus*, fr. Gk *kolaphos*] 1 : a brilliant, sudden, and usu. highly successful stroke 2 : COUP D'ETAT

coup de grace \,küd-ə-'gräs\ *n, pl* **coups de grace** \,küd-ə-\ [F *coup de grâce*, lit., stroke of mercy] 1 : a death blow or shot administered to end the suffering of one mortally wounded 2 : a decisive finishing blow or event

coup d'e·tat \,küd-ə-'tä, ,küd-ā-\ *n, pl* **coups d'e·tat** \,küd-ə-'tä(z), ,küd-ā-\ [F *coup d'état*, lit., stroke of state] : a sudden political move by a small group overthrowing an existing government

cou·pé *or* **coupe** \kü-'pā, *2 is often* 'küp\ *n* [F *coupé*, fr. pp. of *couper* to cut, strike, fr. *coup* blow, coup] 1 : a four-wheeled closed horse-drawn carriage for two persons inside with an outside seat for the driver in front 2 *usu* **coupe** : a closed 2-door automobile with one seat compartment and a separate luggage compartment

coupé 1

¹**cou·ple** \'kəp-əl\ *vb* **cou·pled**; **cou·pling** \'kəp-(ə-)liŋ\ 1 : to join together : CONNECT (*coupled* his first request with one for more money) (the freight cars *coupled* end to end) 2 : COPULATE 3 : to bring (two electric circuits) into such close proximity as to permit mutual influence

²**couple** *n* [OF *cople*, fr. L *copula* bond] 1 a : a man and woman married, engaged, or otherwise paired b : any two persons paired together 2 : PAIR, BRACE 3 : two equal and opposite forces that act along parallel lines 4 : an indefinite small number (a *couple* of days ago)

³**couple** *adj* : TWO

cou·pler \'kəp-(ə-)lər\ *n* 1 : one that couples 2 : a contrivance on a keyboard instrument by which keyboards or keys are connected to play together

cou·plet \'kəp-lət\ *n* : two successive lines of verse forming a unit; *esp* : two rhyming lines of the same length — compare HEROIC COUPLET

cou·pling \'kəp-liŋ (*usual for 2*), -ə-liŋ\ *n* 1 : the act of bringing or coming together 2 : PAIRING 2 : something that joins or connects two parts or things (a car *coupling*) (a pipe *coupling*) 3 : the joining of or the part of the body that joins the hindquarters to the forequarters of a quadruped 4 : means of electric connection of two electric circuits by having a part common to both

cou·pon \'k(y)ü-,pän\ *n* [F, fr. *couper* to cut] 1 : a statement of due interest to be cut from a bond and presented for payment on a stated date 2 a : one of a series of attached tickets to be detached and presented as needed b : a ticket or form authorizing purchases of rationed commodities c : a certificate or similar evidence of a purchase redeemable in premiums d : a part of a printed advertisement to be cut off for use as an order blank or inquiry form

cour·age \'kər-ij, 'kə-rij\ *n* [OF *corage*, fr. *cuer* heart, fr. L *cor*] : mental or moral strength to venture, persevere, and withstand danger, fear, or difficulty

syn BRAVERY, VALOR, HEROISM: COURAGE implies strength in overcoming fear and in persisting against odds or difficulties; BRAVERY stresses bold and daring defiance of danger; VALOR applies esp. to bravery in fighting a dangerous enemy; HEROISM suggests bravery and boldness in accepting risk or sacrifice for a noble or generous purpose

cou·ra·geous \kə-'rā-jəs\ *adj* : having or characterized by courage : BRAVE ⟨a *courageous* boy⟩ ⟨a *courageous* act⟩ — **cou·ra·geous·ly** *adv* — **cou·ra·geous·ness** *n*

cou·ri·er \'kùr-ē-ər, 'kər-ē-, 'kə-rē-\ *n* [MF *courrier*, fr. It *corriere*, fr. *correre* to run, fr. L *currere*] : MESSENGER: as **a** : a member of a diplomatic service entrusted with bearing messages **b** : a member of the armed services who carries mail, information, or supplies

¹**course** \'kōrs, 'kórs\ *n* [OF, fr. L *cursus*, fr. *curs-, currere* to run] **1 a** : the act or action of moving in a path from point to point **b** : LIFE HISTORY, CAREER **2** : the path over which something moves: as **a** : RACECOURSE **b** : the direction of flight of an airplane **c** : WATERCOURSE **d** : land laid out for golf **3 a** : accustomed procedure or action ⟨the law taking its *course*⟩ **b** : a manner of conducting oneself : BEHAVIOR ⟨the wisest *course* is to retreat⟩ **c** : progression through a series of acts or events or a development or period ⟨rose quickly in the *course* of his service⟩ **4** : an ordered process or succession; *esp* : a series of lectures or discussions dealing with a subject or a series of such courses constituting a curriculum **5 a** : a part of a meal served at one time **b** : a continuous level range of brick or masonry throughout a wall — **of course 1** : following the ordinary way or procedure ⟨did it as a matter *of course*⟩ **2** : NATURALLY

²**course** *vb* **1 a** : to hunt or pursue (game) with hounds **b** : to cause (dogs) to run (as after game) **2** : to run through or over ⟨when buffalo *coursed* the plains⟩ **3** : to move rapidly : RACE ⟨blood *coursing* through the veins⟩

cours·er \'kōr-sər, 'kór-\ *n* : a swift or spirited horse

¹**court** \'kōrt, 'kórt\ *n* [OF, fr. L *cohort-, cohors* enclosure, throng, cohort; akin to E *yard*] **1 a** : the residence of a sovereign or similar dignitary **b** : a sovereign's formal assembly of his councillors and officers **c** : the sovereign and his officials who constitute the governing power **d** : the family and retinue of a sovereign **e** : a reception held by a sovereign **2 a** : an open space wholly or partly surrounded by buildings **b** : a short street or lane **c** : a space arranged for playing one of various games with a ball ⟨a tennis *court*⟩ **3 a** : an assembly for the transaction of judicial business **b** : a session of a judicial assembly ⟨*court* is now adjourned⟩ **c** : a building or room for the administration of justice **d** : a judge in session **e** : a faculty or agency of judgment or evaluation **4 a** : an assembly or board with legislative or administrative powers **b** : PARLIAMENT, LEGISLATURE **5** : attention designed to win favor or dispel hostility ⟨pay *court* to the king⟩ ⟨paying *court* to a rich widow⟩

²**court** *vb* **1 a** : to try to gain ⟨*courting* favor with the higher-ups⟩ **b** : to act so as to provoke ⟨was *courting* disaster⟩ **2 a** : to seek the affections of ⟨*courted* the neighbor's daughter⟩ **b** : to try to get the support of ⟨both candidates *courted* the independent voters⟩ **3 a** : to engage in the personal relationship and activities usu. leading to marriage ⟨gave her a ring when they were *courting*⟩ **b** : to engage in activity leading to mating ⟨a pair of robins *courting*⟩

cour·te·ous \'kərt-ē-əs\ *adj* **1** : marked by polished manners, gallantry, or ceremonial usage suitable to a court **2** : marked by respect for and consideration of others **syn** see CIVIL — **cour·te·ous·ly** *adv* — **cour·te·ous·ness** *n*

cour·te·san \'kōrt-ə-zən, 'kórt-, 'kərt-\ *n* [MF *courtisane*, fr. It *cortigiana* female courtier, fr. *corte* court, fr. L *cohort-, cohors* cohort] : a prostitute with a courtly, wealthy, or upper-class clientele

cour·te·sy \'kərt-ə-sē\ *n, pl* **-sies 1** : courtly politeness ⟨old-world *courtesy*⟩ **2** : a favor courteously performed **3** : a favor as distinguished from a right ⟨a title by *courtesy* only⟩

court·house \'kōrt-,haùs, 'kórt-\ *n* **1 a** : a building in which courts of law are held **b** : a building in which county offices are housed **2** : COUNTY SEAT ⟨Appomattox *Courthouse*⟩

court·ier \'kōrt-ē-ər, 'kórt-\ *n* **1** : a person in attendance at a royal court **2** : a person who practices flattery

court·ly \'kōrt-lē, 'kórt-\ *adj* **1 a** : of a quality befitting a royal court : ELEGANT ⟨*courtly* manners⟩ **b** : insincerely

flattering **2** : favoring the policy or party of the court — **court·li·ness** *n*

¹**court–mar·tial** \'kōrt-,mär-shəl, 'kórt-\ *n, pl* **courts-martial** *also* **court-martials 1** : a military court for the trial of members of the armed forces or others within its jurisdiction **2** : a trial by court-martial

²**court-martial** *vt* **-mar·tialed** *also* **-mar·tialled**; **-mar·tial·ing** *also* **-mar·tial·ling** \-,märsh-(ə-)liŋ\ : to subject to trial by court-martial

Court of St. James \-sānt-'jāmz\ [fr. *St. James's* Palace, London, former seat of the British court] : the British court ⟨ambassador to the *Court of St. James*⟩

court plaster *n* : an adhesive plaster esp. of silk coated with isinglass and glycerin

court·room \'kōrt-,rüm, 'kórt-, -,rùm\ *n* : a room in which a court of law is held

court·ship \-,ship\ *n* : the act or process of courting

court tennis *n* : a game played with a ball and racket in an enclosed court

court·yard \'kōrt-,yärd, 'kórt-\ *n* : a court or enclosure attached to a building (as a palace)

cous·in \'kəz-°n\ *n* [OF, fr. L *consobrinus*, fr. *com-* + *sobrinus* cousin on the mother's side; akin to E *sister*] **1 a** : a child of one's uncle or aunt **b** : a relative descended from a common ancestor in a different line **2** : a person belonging to an ethnically or culturally related group ⟨our English *cousins*⟩

cous·in-ger·man \,kəz-°n-'jər-mən\ *n, pl* **cousins-german** [MF *cosin germain*, fr. OF, fr. *cosin* cousin + *germain* german] : COUSIN 1a

co·va·lence \(')kō-'vā-lən(t)s\ *or* **co·va·len·cy** \-lən-sē\ *n* : valence characterized by the sharing of electrons in pairs by two atoms in a chemical compound; *also* : the number of pairs of electrons an atom can share with its neighbors — **co·va·lent** \-lənt\ *adj* — **co·va·lent·ly** *adv*

cove \'kōv\ *n* [ME, den, cave, fr. OE *cofa*] **1 a** : an architectural member with a concave cross section **b** : a trough for concealed lighting at the upper part of a wall **2** : a small sheltered inlet or bay **3** : a level area sheltered by hills or mountains

cov·en \'kəv-ən\ *n* [MF *covin*, fr. L *convenire* to come together] : an assembly or band of witches

¹**cov·e·nant** \'kəv-(ə-)nənt\ *n* [OF, fr. prp. of *covenir* to agree, fr. L *convenire*, fr. *com-* + *venire* to come] **1** : a solemn and binding agreement : COMPACT **2 a** : a written agreement or promise between parties usu. under seal **b** : a promise incidental to and contained in an agreement (as a deed) — **cov·e·nan·tal** \,kəv-ə-'nant-°l\ *adj*

²**cov·e·nant** \'kəv-(ə-)nənt, -ə-,nant\ *vb* **1** : to promise by a covenant : PLEDGE **2** : to enter into a covenant : CONTRACT — **cov·e·nant·er** *or* **cov·e·nan·tor** \-ə-,nant-ər\ *n*

Cov·en·try \'kəv-ən-trē, 'käv-\ *n* [fr. *Coventry*, England] : a state of ostracism or exclusion ⟨sent to *Coventry*⟩

¹**cov·er** \'kəv-ər\ *vb* **cov·ered**; **cov·er·ing** \'kəv-(ə-)riŋ\ [OF *covrir*, fr. L *cooperire*, fr. *co-* + *operire* to close, cover] **1 a** : to guard from attack ⟨*covered* the landing with shellfire⟩ **b** : to have within gunshot range **c** (1) : to provide protection or security to : INSURE ⟨this insurance *covers* the traveler in any accident⟩ (2) : to provide protection against or compensation for ⟨the policy *covered* all water damage⟩ **d** : to maintain a check on esp. by patrolling ⟨state police *covering* the highways⟩ **2 a** : to hide from sight or knowledge ⟨*cover* up a scandal⟩ **b** : to conceal something illicit, blameworthy, or embarrassing from notice ⟨*covered* for his friend in the investigation⟩ **c** : to act as a substitute or replacement during an absence ⟨*covered* for me during my vacation⟩ **3** : to overlay so as to protect or shelter ⟨*covered* him with a blanket⟩ **4 a** : to spread or lie over or on ⟨water *covered* the floor⟩ ⟨snow *covering* the hills⟩ **b** : DOT, DAPPLE ⟨resort area *covered* with lakes⟩ **5** : to put something protective or concealing over ⟨*cover* your head⟩ ⟨*cover* the mouth while coughing⟩ **6** : to sit on and incubate (eggs) **7** : to have width or scope enough to include, take in, or make provisions for ⟨an exam *covering* a semester's work⟩ ⟨plans *covering* an enemy attack⟩ **8** : to have as one's territory or field of activity ⟨one salesman *covers* the whole state⟩ ⟨a reporter *covering* the courthouse⟩ **9** : to pass over or through ⟨*covering* 500 miles a day⟩ ⟨*covered* three countries in a week⟩ **10** : to accept an offered bet **11** : to buy securities

or commodities for delivery so as to fulfill (an earlier short sale) — **cov·er·er** \-ər-ər\ *n*

²**cover** *n* **1** : something that protects, shelters, or conceals: as **a** : natural shelter for an animal or the factors that provide such shelter **b** : a position or situation affording protection from enemy fire **2** : something that is placed over or about another thing: **a** : LID, TOP **b** : a binding or case for a book; *also* : the front or back of such a binding **c** : an overlay or outer layer esp. for protection ⟨a mattress *cover*⟩ **d** : a tablecloth and tableware for one person **e** : ROOF **f** : a cloth used on a bed **g** : something (as vegetation or snow) that covers the ground **3** : an envelope or wrapper for mail

cov·er·age \'kəv-(ə-)rij\ *n* **1** : the act or fact of covering or something that covers: as **a** : inclusion within the scope of protection (as of an insurance policy) **b** : inclusion within the scope of discussion or reporting ⟨*coverage* of a political convention⟩ **2 a** : the number or amount covered : SCOPE **b** : all the risks covered by the terms of an insurance contract ⟨a policy with an extensive *coverage*⟩

cov·er·all \'kəv-ər-,ol\ *n* : a one-piece outer garment worn to protect one's clothes — usu. used in pl.

cover charge *n* : a charge made by a restaurant or night-club in addition to the charge for food and drink

cover crop *n* : a crop planted to prevent soil erosion and to provide humus

covered wagon *n* : a wagon with a canvas top supported by bows

cover glass *n* : a piece of very thin glass used to cover material mounted on a glass microscope slide

cov·er·ing \'kəv-(ə-)riŋ\ *n* : something that covers or conceals

cov·er·let \'kəv-ər-lət\ *n* [ME, alter. of *coverlite*, fr. OF *covrir* to cover + *lit* bed] : BEDSPREAD

cov·er·slip \'kəv-ər-,slip\ *n* : COVER GLASS

¹**cov·ert** \'kəv-ərt, 'kō-(,)vərt\ *adj* [OF, pp. of *covrir* to cover] **1** : partly hidden ⟨*covert* smile⟩ **2** : covered over : SHELTERED ⟨a *covert* nook⟩ **syn** see SECRET — **cov·ert·ly** *adv* — **cov·ert·ness** *n*

²**cov·ert** \'kəv-ərt, 'kō-vərt\ *n* **1 a** : hiding place : SHELTER **b** : a thicket affording cover for game **2** : a feather covering the bases of the quills of the wings and tail of a bird — see BIRD illustration **3** : a firm durable twilled sometimes waterproofed cloth usu. of mixed-color yarns

cov·et \'kəv-ət\ *vb* [OF *coveitier*, fr. *coveitié* desire, fr. L *cupiditat-, cupiditas* desire, cupidity] **1** : to wish for enviously **2** : to feel inordinate desire for what belongs to another — **cov·et·a·ble** \-ə-bəl\ *adj* — **cov·et·er** \-ər\ *n* — **cov·et·ing·ly** \-iŋ-lē\ *adv*

cov·et·ous \'kəv-ət-əs\ *adj* : marked by a too eager desire for wealth or possessions or for another's possessions — **cov·et·ous·ly** *adv* — **cov·et·ous·ness** *n*

syn AVARICIOUS, GREEDY: COVETOUS implies excessive desire esp. for what belongs to another; AVARICIOUS implies a strong desire to gain and keep money; GREEDY stresses lack of restraint and often of discrimination in desire

cov·ey \'kəv-ē\ *n, pl* **coveys** [MF *covee*, fr. *cover* to brood, fr. L *cubare* to lie] **1** : a mature bird or pair of birds with a brood of young; *also* : a small flock **2** : COMPANY, GROUP

¹**cow** \'kaù\ *n* [OE *cū*] **1** : the mature female of cattle or of any animal (as the moose) the male of which is called *bull* **2** : a domestic bovine animal regardless of sex or age — **cowy** \-ē\ *adj*

²**cow** *vt* : to subdue the spirits or courage of : make afraid ⟨*cowed* by threats⟩

cow·ard \'kaù-(ə)rd\ *n* [OF *coart*, fr. *coue, coe* tail, fr. L *cauda*] : one who shows ignoble fear or timidity — **coward** *adj*

cow·ard·ice \'kaù-(ə)rd-əs\ *n* : lack of courage to face danger : shameful fear

¹**cow·ard·ly** \'kaù-(ə)rd-lē\ *adv* : in a cowardly manner

²**cowardly** *adj* **1** : lacking courage : disgracefully timid : not brave ⟨a *cowardly* rascal⟩ **2** : characteristic of a coward ⟨a *cowardly* attack from behind cover⟩ ⟨a *cowardly* retreat⟩ — **cow·ard·li·ness** *n*

cow·bane \'kaù-,bān\ *n* : any of several poisonous plants (as a water hemlock) of the carrot family

cow·bell \-,bel\ *n* : a bell hung about the neck of a cow to indicate its whereabouts

cow·bird \-,bərd\ *n* : a small No. American blackbird that lays its eggs in the nests of other birds

cow·boy \-,boi\ *n* : one who tends or drives cattle; *esp* : a usu. mounted cattle ranch hand — **cow·girl** \-,gərl\ *n*

cow·catch·er \-,kach-ər, -,kech-\ *n* : PILOT 3

cow·er \'kaù-(ə)r\ *vi* [ME *couren*, of Scand origin] : to crouch down (as from fear or cold) ⟨*cowered* at the sight of a whip⟩

cow·hand \'kaù-,hand\ *n* : COWBOY

cow·herd \-,hərd\ *n* : one who tends cows

¹**cow·hide** \-,hīd\ *n* **1** : the hide of a cow or leather made from it **2** : a coarse whip of rawhide or braided leather

²**cowhide** *vt* : to whip with a cowhide

cowl \'kaùl\ *n* [OE *cugele*, fr. LL *cuculla*, fr. L *cucullus*] **1** : a hood or long hooded cloak esp. of a monk **2 a** : a chimney covering for improving the draft **b** : the top portion of the front part of an automobile body forward of the two front doors to which are attached the windshield and instrument panel **c** : COWL-ING — **cowled** \'kaùld\ *adj*

cow·lick \'kaù-,lik\ *n* [*cow* + *lick*] : a turned-up tuft of hair that cannot be controlled by brushing

cowl·ing \'kaù-liŋ\ *n* : a removable metal covering for the engine and sometimes a por-tion of the fuselage or nacelle of an airplane; *also* : a metallic cover for any engine

cow·man \'kaù-mən, -,man\ *n* **1** : COW-HERD, COWBOY **2** : a cattle owner or rancher

co·work·er \'kō-,wər-kər\ *n* : a fellow worker

cow·pea \'kaù-,pē\ *n* : a sprawling herb related to the bean and grown in the southern U.S. esp. for forage and green manure; *also* : its edible seed

Cow·per's gland \,kaù-pərz-, ,kü-pərz-, ,kùp-ərz-\ *n* : either of two small glands discharging into the male urethra

cow·poke \'kaù-,pōk\ *n* : COWBOY

cow pony *n* : a light saddle horse trained for herding cattle

cow·pox \'kaù-,päks\ *n* : a mild eruptive disease of the cow that when communicated to man protects against smallpox

cow·punch·er \-,pən-chər\ *n* : COWBOY

cow·rie *or* **cow·ry** \'kaù(ə)r-ē\ *n, pl* **cowries** [Hindi *kaurī*] : any of numerous small snails of warm seas with glossy often brightly colored shells

cow·slip \'kaù-,slip\ *n* [OE *cūslyppe*, lit., cow dung] **1** : a common Old World primrose with fragrant yellow or purplish flowers **2** : MARSH MARIGOLD

cox \'käks\ *n* : COXSWAIN — **cox** *vb*

coxa \'käk-sə *n, pl* **cox·ae** \-,sē, -,sī\ [L, hip] : the basal segment of an arthropod limb — **cox·al** \-səl\ *adj*

cox·comb \'käks-,kōm\ *n* [ME *cokkes comb*, lit., cock's comb] : a conceited foolish person : FOP — **cox·comb·ical** \käks-'kō-mi-kəl, -'käm-i-\ *adj*

cox·swain \'käk-sən, -,swān\ *n* [ME *cokswayne*, fr. *cok* small boat + *swain* servant] **1** : a sailor who has charge of a ship's boat and its crew **2** : a steersman of a racing shell

coy \'koi\ *adj* [MF *coi* quiet, calm, fr. L *quietus*] **1 a** : sen-sitively diffident : BASHFUL **b** : affecting shy or demure reserve **2** : showing reluctance to make a definite com-mitment ⟨a politician *coy* about his intentions⟩ **syn** see SHY — **coy·ly** *adv* — **coy·ness** *n*

coy·ote \'kī-,ōt, kī-'ōt-ē\ *n, pl* **coyotes** *or* **coyote** [MexSp, fr. Nahuatl *coyotl*] : a small wolf native to western No. America

coy·pu \'koi-,pü\ *n* **1** : a So. American aquatic rodent with webbed feet and dorsal mammary glands **2** : NU-TRIA 2

coz·en \'kəz-ᵊn\ *vb* [obs. It *cozzonare*, fr. It *cozzone* horse trader, fr. L *cocion-, cocio* trader] : CHEAT, DEFRAUD, DECEIVE — **coz·en·age** \-ᵊn-ij\ *n* — **coz·en·er** *n*

¹**co·zy** \'kō-zē\ *adj* **co·zi·er; -est** **1** : SNUG, COMFORTABLE **2** : CAREFUL, CAUTIOUS — **co·zi·ly** \-zə-lē\ *adv* — **co·zi·ness** \-zē-nəs\ *n*

²**cozy** *adv* : in a cautious manner ⟨play it *cozy* and wait for your opponent to move⟩

³**cozy** *n, pl* **cozies** : a padded covering for a vessel (as a teapot) to keep the contents hot

C
C cowl 1

¹crab \'krab\ *n* [ME *crabbe*, fr. OE *crabba*] **1** : a crustacean with a short broad usu. flattened carapace, a small abdomen curled forward beneath the body, and a front pair of limbs with strong pincers; *also* : any of various other crustaceans resembling true crabs in having a reduced abdomen **2** : any of various machines for raising or hauling heavy weights **3** : failure to raise an oar clear of the water on recovery of a stroke or missing the water altogether when attempting a stroke ⟨catch a *crab*⟩

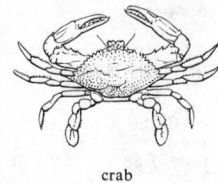

crab

²crab *vi* **crabbed**; **crab·bing** : to fish for crabs — **crab·ber** *n*
³crab *vb* **crabbed**; **crab·bing** : to find fault : COMPLAIN
⁴crab *n* [ME *crabbe*, perh. fr. *crabbe* ¹crab] **1** : CRAB APPLE **2** : a sour ill-tempered person
crab apple *n* **1** : a small wild sour apple **2** : a cultivated apple with small usu. highly colored acid fruit
crab·bed \'krab-əd\ *adj* **1** : MOROSE, PEEVISH **2** : difficult to read or understand — **crab·bed·ly** *adv* — **crab·bed·ness** *n*
crab·by \'krab-ē\ *adj* **crab·bi·er**; **-est** : CROSS, ILL-NATURED
crab·grass \'krab-,gras\ *n* : a weedy grass with creeping or sprawling stems that root freely at the nodes
crab louse *n* : a louse infesting the human pubic region
¹crack \'krak\ *vb* [OE *cracian*] **1 a** : to break or cause to break with a sudden sharp sound : SNAP **b** : to make or cause to make such a sound ⟨*crack* a whip⟩ **2** : to break with or without total separation of parts ⟨the ice *cracked* in several places⟩ **3** : to tell esp. in a clever or witty way ⟨*crack* jokes⟩ **4** : PRAISE, EXTOL ⟨not all he is *cracked* up to be⟩ **5 a** : to lose control **b** : to fail in tone ⟨voice *cracked*⟩ **c** : to smash up a vehicle esp. by losing control ⟨*cracked* up on a curve⟩ **d** : to give or receive a sharp blow ⟨*cracked* his head⟩ **6 a** : to puzzle out and solve or discover the secret of ⟨*crack* a code⟩ **b** : to break into ⟨*crack* a safe⟩ **c** : to break through (as a barrier) **7 a** : to subject (hydrocarbons) to cracking ⟨*crack* petroleum⟩ **b** : to produce by cracking ⟨*cracked* gasoline⟩
²crack *n* **1** : a sudden sharp noise **2** : a sharp witty remark : QUIP **3** : a narrow break : FISSURE **b** : a narrow opening **4 a** : WEAKNESS, FLAW **b** : a broken tone of the voice **5** : MOMENT, INSTANT ⟨the *crack* of dawn⟩ **6** : a sharp resounding blow **7** : ATTEMPT, TRY
³crack *adj* : of superior excellence ⟨*crack* troops⟩
crack·brain \'krak-,brān\ *n* : an erratic person : CRACK-POT — **crack·brained** \-'brānd\ *adj*
crack down \(')krak-'daùn\ *vi* : to take positive disciplinary action
crack·down \'krak-,daùn\ *n* : an act or instance of cracking down ⟨a *crackdown* on gambling⟩
crack·er \'krak-ər\ *n* **1** : something (as a firecracker) that makes a cracking noise **2** : a dry thin crisp bakery product made of flour and water **3** : the equipment in which cracking is carried out
crack·er·jack \'krak-ər(r)-,jak\ *n* : something very excellent — **crackerjack** *adj*
Crack·er Jack \'krak-ə(r)-,jak\ *trademark* — used for a candied popcorn confection
crack·ing *n* : a process in which relatively heavy hydrocarbons (as oils from petroleum) are broken up by heat into lighter products (as gasoline)
¹crack·le \'krak-əl\ *vi* **crack·led**; **crack·ling** \'krak-(ə-)liŋ\ [freq. of ¹crack] **1 a** : to make small sharp sudden repeated noises **b** : to show animation : SPARKLE **2** : to develop a surface network of fine cracks
²crackle *n* **1** : the noise of repeated small cracks or reports **2** : a network of fine cracks on an otherwise smooth surface
crack·ling *n* **1** \'krak-(ə-)liŋ\ : a series of small sharp cracks or reports **2** \'krak-lən, -liŋ\ : the crisp residue left after the fat has been separated from the fibrous tissue (as in frying the skin of pork) — usu. used in pl.
crack·pot \'krak-,pät\ *n* : an eccentric person — **crack·pot** *adj*
crack-up \'krak-,əp\ *n* : CRASH, WRECK
-c·ra·cy \k-rə-sē\ *n comb form*, *pl* **-cracies** [MF *-cratie*,

fr. Gk *-kratia*, fr. *kratos* strength, power; akin to E *hard*] **1** : rule or government of; *also* : state ruled by such a government ⟨mono*cracy*⟩ **2** : dominant social or political class (as of powerful persons) ⟨pluto*cracy*⟩
¹cra·dle \'krād-°l\ *n* [OE *cradol*] **1 a** : a bed or cot for a baby usu. on rockers **b** : place of origin **2** : something serving as a framework or support: as **a** : the support for a telephone receiver or handset **b** : an implement with rods like fingers attached to a scythe and used formerly for harvesting grain **c** : a low frame on casters on which mechanics lie while working under an automobile **3** : a rocking device used in panning for gold
²cradle *vt* **cra·dled**; **cra·dling** \'krād-°l-iŋ, -°l-iŋ\ **1 a** : to place or keep in or as if in a cradle **b** : to shelter in childhood : REAR **c** : to protect and cherish lovingly **2** : to cut (grain) with a cradle scythe **3** : to raise, raise, support, or transport on a cradle **4** : to wash in a miner's cradle
cra·dle·land \'krād-°l-,(l)and\ *n* : region of origin : BIRTHPLACE
cra·dle·song \'krād-°l-,sòŋ\ *n* : LULLABY
craft \'kraft\ *n* [OE *cræft* strength, skill] **1** : DEXTERITY, SKILL **2** : an occupation or trade requiring manual dexterity or artistic skill **3** : skill in deceiving to gain an end **4** : the members of a trade or trade association **5** *pl usu* **craft** : a boat esp. of small size **b** : AIRCRAFT **syn** see ART
crafts·man \'kraf(t)s-mən\ *n* **1** : a workman who practices a trade or handicraft : ARTISAN **2** : a highly skilled worker in any field — **crafts·man·ship** \-,ship\ *n*
craft union *n* : a labor union with membership limited to workmen of the same craft — compare INDUSTRIAL UNION
crafty \'kraf-tē\ *adj* **craft·i·er**; **-est** : skillful at deceiving others : CUNNING **syn** see SLY — **craft·i·ly** \-tə-lē\ *adv* — **craft·i·ness** \-tē-nəs\ *n*
crag \'krag\ *n* [ME, of Celt origin] : a steep rugged rock or cliff — **crag·gy** \-ē\ *adj*
crake \'krāk\ *n* [ME, prob. fr. Scand origin] : any of various mostly short-billed rails
cram \'kram\ *vb* **crammed**; **cram·ming** [OE *crammian*] **1** : to stuff or crowd in ⟨*cram* clothes into a bag⟩ **2** : to fill full ⟨barns *crammed* with hay⟩ **3** : to study hastily in preparation for an examination **4** : to eat greedily : STUFF — **cram·mer** *n*
¹cramp \'kramp\ *n* [MF *crampe*, of Gmc origin] **1** : a sudden painful involuntary contraction of muscle **2** : a temporary paralysis of muscles from overuse **3** : sharp abdominal pain — usu. used in pl.
²cramp *n* [LG or obs. D *krampe* hook] **1** : a usu. iron device bent at the ends and used to hold timbers or blocks of stone together **2** : ¹CLAMP — **cramp** *adj*
³cramp *vt* **1** : to affect with or as if with cramp **2** : CONFINE, RESTRAIN; *also* : HAMPER **3** : to turn (the front wheels of a vehicle) to right or left **4** : to fasten or hold with a cramp
cram·pon \'kram-,pän\ *also* **cram·poon** \kram-'pün\ *n* [MF *crampon*, of Gmc origin] **1** : a hooked clutch or dog for raising heavy objects — usu. used in pl. **2** : CLIMBING IRON — usu. used in pl.
cran·ber·ry \'kran-,ber-ē, -b(ə-)rē\ *n* [LG *kraanbere*, fr. *kraan* crane + *bere* berry] : the bright red sour berry of several trailing plants of the heath family; *also* : a plant producing these
cranberry bush *n* : a shrub or tree with prominently 3-lobed leaves and red fruit — compare SNOWBALL
¹crane \'krān\ *n* [OE *cran*] **1** : any of a family of tall wading birds superficially resembling herons but structurally related to the rails **2** : any of several herons **3 a** : a machine for raising, shifting, and lowering heavy weights by means of a projecting swinging arm or with the hoisting apparatus supported on an overhead track **b** : an iron arm in a fireplace for supporting kettles **c** : a long movable support for a motion-picture or television camera
²crane *vb* **1** : to raise or lift by a crane **2** : to stretch one's neck forward to see better
crane fly *n* : any of numerous long-legged slender two-winged flies that resemble large mosquitoes but do not bite
cranes·bill \'krānz-,bil\ *n* : GERANIUM 1

---

cra·ni·al \'krā-nē-əl\ *adj* **1 :** of or relating to the skull or cranium **2 :** CEPHALIC — **cra·ni·al·ly** \-ə-lē\ *adv*

cranial index *n* **:** the ratio of the maximum breadth of the skull to its maximum height multiplied by 100

cranial nerve *n* **:** any of the paired nerves that arise from the lower surface of the brain and pass through openings in the skull

cra·ni·ate \'krā-nē-ət, -ˌāt\ *adj* **:** having a cranium — **craniate** *n*

cra·ni·ol·o·gy \ˌkrā-nē-'äl-ə-jē\ *n* **:** a science dealing with variations in size, shape, and proportions of skulls among the races of men

cra·ni·om·e·try \-'äm-ə-trē\ *n* **:** a science dealing with cranial measurement

cra·ni·um \'krā-nē-əm\ *n, pl* **-ni·ums** *or* **-nia** \-nē-ə\ [ML, fr. Gk *kranion*] **:** SKULL; *esp* **:** the part that encloses the brain

¹crank \'kraŋk\ *n* [OE *cranc-*] **1 :** a bent part of an axle or shaft or an arm at right angles to the end of a shaft by which circular motion is imparted to or received from it **2 a :** CAPRICE, WHIM, CROTCHET **b :** an eccentric person **c :** a bad-tempered person **:** GROUCH

²crank *vb* **1 :** to move with a winding course **:** ZIGZAG **2 :** to bend into the shape of a crank **3 :** to start or operate by turning a crank

crank·case \'kraŋk-ˌkās\ *n* **:** the housing of a crankshaft

crank·shaft \-ˌshaft\ *n* **:** a shaft turning or driven by a crank

cranky \'kraŋ-kē\ *adj* **crank·i·er; -est 1 :** being out of order **2 :** CROTCHETY, IRRITABLE — **crank·i·ness** *n*

cran·ny \'kran-ē\ *n, pl* **crannies :** a small break or slit **:** CREVICE

crape \'krāp\ *n* **1 :** CREPE **2 :** a band of crepe worn on a hat or sleeve as a sign of mourning

crape myrtle *n* **:** an East Indian shrub of the loosestrife family widely grown in warm regions for its showy flowers

crap·pie \'kräp-ē\ *n* **1 :** BLACK CRAPPIE **2 :** WHITE CRAPPIE

craps \'kraps\ *n pl* [F *craps*, fr. E *crabs* lowest throw at hazard, fr. pl. of **¹crab**] **:** a gambling game played with two dice

crap·shoot·er \'krap-ˌshüt-ər\ *n* **:** a person who plays craps — **crap·shoot·ing** \-ˌshüt-iŋ\ *n*

¹crash \'krash\ *vb* [ME *crasschen*] **1 a :** to break violently and noisily **:** SMASH **b :** to damage an airplane in landing **2 a :** to make or cause to make a loud noise **b :** to move or force through with loud crashing noises **3 :** to enter or attend without invitation or without paying ⟨*crash* a party⟩ **4 :** to decline or break suddenly — **crash·er** *n*

²crash *n* **1 :** a loud sound (as of things smashing) **2 :** a breaking to pieces by or as if by collision; *also* **:** an instance of crashing **3 :** a sudden decline or failure (as of a business or prices) ⟨stock-market *crash*⟩

³crash *adj* **:** effected hastily on an emergency basis with all available means ⟨a *crash* program⟩

⁴crash *n* **:** a coarse fabric used for draperies, toweling, and clothing

crash dive *n* **:** a dive made by a submarine in the least possible time — **crash-dive** \'krash-ˈdīv\ *vi*

crash-land \'krash-ˈland\ *vb* **:** to land an airplane under emergency conditions usu. with damage to the craft — **crash landing** *n*

crass \'kras\ *adj* [L *crassus* thick, gross] **:** GROSS, INSENSITIVE — **crass·ly** *adv* — **crass·ness** *n*

-crat \ˌkrat\ *n comb form* [F *-crate*, back-formation fr. *-cratie* *-cracy*] **:** one that rules or advocates rule of ⟨autocrat⟩ ⟨plutocrat⟩ ⟨theocrat⟩ — **-crat·ic** \'krat-ik\ *adj comb form*

¹crate \'krāt\ *n* [L *cratis* wickerwork, hurdle; akin to E *hurdle*] **1 :** a box usu. ventilated and made of thin wooden slats for packing fruit or vegetables **2 :** an enclosing framework for protecting something (as in shipment)

²crate *vt* **:** to pack in a crate

cra·ter \'krāt-ər\ *n* [Gk *krātēr*, lit., mixing bowl, fr. *kra-*, *kerannynai* to mix] **:** a bowl-shaped depression: as **a :** one around the opening of a volcano **b :** one formed by the impact of a meteorite **c :** a hole in the ground made by the explosion of a bomb or shell

cra·vat \krə-'vat\ *n* [F *cravate*, scarf once worn by

Croatian mercenaries, necktie, fr. obs. *Cravate* Croatian] **:** NECKTIE

crave \'krāv\ *vb* [OE *crafian*] **1 :** to ask earnestly **:** BEG **2 :** to have a strong desire for **3 :** REQUIRE, NEED

¹cra·ven \'krā-vən\ *adj* [ME *cravant*] **:** COWARDLY — **cra·ven·ly** *adv* — **cra·ven·ness** \-vən-nəs\ *n*

²craven *n* **:** COWARD

crav·ing \'krā-viŋ\ *n* **:** a great desire or longing; *esp* **:** an abnormal desire (as for a habit-forming drug)

craw \'krȯ\ *n* [ME *crawe*] **1 :** the crop of a bird or insect **2 :** the stomach esp. of a lower animal

craw·fish \'krȯ-ˌfish\ *n* **1 :** CRAYFISH **2 :** SPINY LOBSTER

¹crawl \'krȯl\ *vb* [ON *krafla*; akin to E *crab*] **1 :** to move slowly with the body close to the ground **:** CREEP **2 :** to drag along slowly or feebly **3 :** to advance by guile or servility **4 :** to be swarming with or have the sensation of swarming with creeping things *syn* see CREEP — **crawl·er** *n*

²crawl *n* **1 :** the act or motion of crawling **2 :** a racing stroke in which a swimmer lying flat in the water propels himself by overarm strokes and a flutter kick

³crawl *n* [Afrik *kraal* pen] **:** an enclosure in shallow waters

cray·fish \'krā-ˌfish\ *n* [MF *crevice*, of Gmc origin; akin to E *crab*] **1 :** any of numerous freshwater crustaceans resembling but usu. much smaller than the lobster **2 :** SPINY LOBSTER

¹cray·on \'krā-ˌän, -ən; 'kran\ *n* [F, crayon, pencil, *craie* chalk, fr. L *creta*] **1 :** a stick of white or colored chalk or of colored wax used for writing or drawing **2 :** a crayon drawing

²crayon *vt* **:** to draw with a crayon — **cray·on·ist** \'krā-ə-nəst\ *n*

¹craze \'krāz\ *vb* [ME *crasen* to crush, craze, of Scand origin] **1 a :** to make insane or as if insane **b :** to become insane **2 :** to develop a mesh of fine cracks

²craze \'krāz\ *n* **1 :** a strong but temporary interest in something or the object of such an interest **:** FAD, MANIA ⟨the latest *craze* among schoolgirls⟩ **2 :** a tiny crack in glaze or enamel or on a painted surface

cra·zy \'krā-zē\ *adj* **cra·zi·er; -est 1 :** full of cracks or flaws **:** UNSOUND; *also* **:** CROOKED, ASKEW **2 a :** mentally disordered **:** INSANE **b** (1) **:** wildly impractical (2) **:** ERRATIC **3 :** distracted with desire or excitement *syn* see INSANE — **cra·zi·ly** \-zə-lē\ *adv* — **cra·zi·ness** \-zē-nəs\ *n*

crazy bone *n* **:** FUNNY BONE

crazy quilt *n* **:** a patchwork quilt without a unified design

¹creak \'krēk\ *vi* [ME *creken*] **:** to make a prolonged grating or squeaking sound

²creak *n* **:** a rasping or grating noise — **creak·i·ly** \'krē-kə-lē\ *adv* — **creaky** \-kē\ *adj*

¹cream \'krēm\ *n* [MF *craime*, fr. LL *cramum*, of Celt origin] **1 :** the yellowish part of milk containing butterfat **2 a :** a food prepared with cream **b :** something having the consistency of cream (as a usu. emulsified medicinal or cosmetic preparation) **3 :** the choicest part **4 :** a pale yellow — **creamy** \'krē-mē\ *adj*

²cream *vb* **1 :** to form cream **2 a :** SKIM 1b **b :** to take the choicest part of something **3 :** to furnish, prepare, or treat with cream **4 a :** to beat into a creamy froth **b :** to work or blend to the consistency of cream

cream cheese *n* **:** an unripened soft white cheese made from whole milk enriched with cream

cream·er \'krē-mər\ *n* **1 :** a device for separating cream from milk **2 :** a small vessel for serving cream

cream·ery \'krēm-(ə-)rē\ *n, pl* **-er·ies :** an establishment where butter and cheese are made or where milk and cream are sold or prepared

cream of tartar *n* **:** a white crystalline salt $C_4H_5KO_6$ used esp. in baking powder **:** potassium acid tartrate

cream puff *n* **:** a round shell of light pastry filled with whipped cream or a cream filling

¹crease \'krēs\ *n* **1 :** a line or mark made by or as if by folding a pliable substance **2 :** a specially marked area in any of various sports (as hockey)

²crease *vb* **1 :** to make a crease in or on **2 :** to wound slightly esp. by grazing **3 :** to become creased — **creas·er** *n*

cre·ate \krē-'āt, 'krē-ˌ\ *vt* [L *creare*] **1 :** to bring into existence **2 :** to invest with a new office or rank ⟨the king *created* him a peer⟩ **3 a :** to bring about **:** CAUSE, MAKE, PRODUCE **b :** DESIGN

cre·a·tine \'krē-ə-ˌtēn\ *n* [Gk *kreat-*, *kreas* flesh] **:** a white crystalline nitrogenous substance $C_4H_9N_3O_2$ found esp. in the muscles of vertebrates

cre·a·tion \krē-'ā-shən\ n 1 : the act of creating or fact of being created; esp : the bringing of the world into existence out of nothing 2 : something created 3 : all created things : WORLD

cre·a·tive \krē-'āt-iv\ adj : able to create; esp : having or showing the power to produce original work (as in literature) — **cre·a·tive·ly** adv — **cre·a·tive·ness** n

cre·a·tiv·i·ty \krē-ā-'tiv-ət-ē, ,krē-ə-\ n : ability to create

cre·a·tor \krē-'āt-ər\ n 1 : one that creates or produces : MAKER 2 cap : ²GOD

crea·ture \'krē-chər\ n 1 : a created being 2 a : a lower animal; esp : a farm animal b : a human being : PERSON c : a being of anomalous or uncertain aspect or nature 3 : one who is the servile dependent or tool of another — **crea·tur·al** \'krēch-(ə-)rəl\ adj

crèche \'kresh\ n [F, fr. OF creche manger, crib, of Gmc origin] 1 : a day nursery or foundling home 2 : a representation of the Nativity scene in the stable at Bethlehem

cre·dence \'krēd-ᵊn(t)s\ n 1 : mental acceptance : BELIEF 2 : a small table where the eucharistic bread and wine rest before consecration

cre·den·tial \kri-'den-chəl\ n 1 : something that gives a title to credit or confidence 2 pl : documents showing that a person is entitled to confidence or has a right to exercise official power

cred·i·ble \'kred-ə-bəl\ adj [L credere to believe] : capable of being believed : deserving to be believed ⟨a credible story⟩ syn see PLAUSIBLE — **cred·i·bil·i·ty** \,kred-ə-'bil-ət-ē\ n — **cred·i·bly** \'kred-ə-blē\ adv

¹cred·it \'kred-ət\ n [L creditum something entrusted to another, fr. neut. of pp. of credere to believe, trust] 1 a : a favorable balance in a bank account b : an entry in an account representing an addition of revenue or net worth ⟨debits and credits⟩ c : an amount or sum put at the disposal of a person or firm by a bank d (1) : the right or privilege of taking present possession of money, goods, or services in exchange for a promise to pay for them at a future date ⟨extended him credit⟩ (2) : faith in the willingness of one to whom credit is extended to perform his promise ⟨buy on credit⟩ (3) : reputation for fulfilling financial obligations ⟨his credit is good⟩ 2 a : reliance on the truth or reality of something : TRUST, BELIEF ⟨a story that deserves little credit⟩ b : reputation for honesty or integrity : good name : ESTEEM 3 : something that adds to a person's reputation or honor ⟨give a person credit for a discovery⟩ 4 : a source of honor ⟨a credit to her school⟩ 5 a : official certification of the completion of a course of study b : a unit of academic work for which such acknowledgment is made

²credit vt 1 : to trust in the truth or truthfulness of : BELIEVE 2 : to enter a sum upon the credit side of ⟨credit his account with $10⟩ 3 a : to give credit to b : to attribute to some person

cred·it·a·ble \'kred-ət-ə-bəl\ adj 1 : worthy of belief 2 : worthy of esteem or praise — **cred·it·a·bil·i·ty** \,kred-ət-ə-'bil-ət-ē\ n — **cred·it·a·bly** \'kred-ət-ə-blē\ adv

credit card n : a card authorizing purchases on credit

cred·i·tor \'kred-ət-ər\ n : a person to whom a debt is owed; esp : a person to whom money or goods are due

credit union n : a cooperative association that makes small loans to its members at low interest rates

cre·do \'krēd-ō, 'krād-\ n, pl credos [L, I believe] : CREED

cre·du·li·ty \kri-'d(y)ü-lət-ē\ n : a willingness to believe statements esp. on little or no evidence

cred·u·lous \'krej-ə-ləs\ adj : ready to believe esp. on slight or uncertain evidence — **cred·u·lous·ly** adv — **cred·u·lous·ness** n

Cree \'krē\ n : a member of an Indian people ranging from Ontario to Saskatchewan and south into Montana

creed \'krēd\ n [OE crēda, fr. L credo I believe (first word of the Apostles' & Nicene creeds), fr. L credere to believe] 1 : a statement of the essential beliefs of a religious faith 2 : a set of guiding principles or beliefs — **creed·al** or **cre·dal** \'krēd-ᵊl\ adj

creek \'krēk, 'krik\ n [ME crike, creke, fr. ON -kriki bend] 1 chiefly Brit : a small narrow inlet extending farther inland than a cove 2 : a natural stream of water usu. smaller than a river

Creek \'krēk\ n : a member of a confederacy of Indian peoples formerly occupying most of Alabama and Georgia and parts of Florida

creel \'krēl\ n [ME creille] : a wicker-work container (as for fish)

creel

¹creep \'krēp\ vi crept \'krept\; creep·ing [OE crēopan] 1 : to move along with the body prone and close to the ground; also : to move slowly on hands and knees 2 : to move or advance slowly, timidly, or stealthily 3 : to spread or grow over a surface usu. rooting at intervals ⟨creeping vine⟩ 4 : to slip or gradually shift position ⟨soil creeping down a slope⟩ 5 : to feel as though insects were crawling on the body ⟨the sudden shriek made my flesh creep⟩

syn CREEP, CRAWL mean to move slowly in a prone or crouching posture. CREEP often suggests the furtive, noiseless movement of one capable of rapid movement ⟨the cat crept closer to the bird⟩ CRAWL suggests the laborious progress of legless insects or reptiles or of maimed animals. CREEP connotes stealth or insinuation ⟨crept into favor⟩ CRAWL often connotes abjectness or submission

²creep n 1 : a creeping movement 2 a : a distressing sensation like that of insects creeping over one's flesh b : a feeling of horror — usu. used in pl. 3 : an enclosure that young animals (as calves) can enter while adults are excluded

creep·er \'krē-pər\ n 1 : one that creeps: as a : a creeping plant b : a bird that creeps about on trees or bushes searching for insects 2 a : a fixture with iron points worn on the shoe to prevent slipping b : a strip (as of sealskin) attachable to the bottom of a ski to prevent sliding backward in uphill climbing 3 : an infant's garment like a romper

creepy \'krē-pē\ adj creep·i·er; -est : having or producing a sensation as of insects creeping on the skin; esp : EERIE — **creep·i·ness** n

cre·mate \'krē-,māt, kri-'\ vt [L cremare] : to reduce (a dead body) to ashes by the action of fire — **cre·ma·tion** \kri-'mā-shən\ n

cre·ma·to·ri·um \,krē-mə-'tōr-ē-əm, ,krem-ə-, -'tòr-\ n, pl -ri·ums or -ria \-ē-ə\ : CREMATORY

¹cre·ma·to·ry \'krē-mə-,tōr-ē, 'krem-ə-, -,tòr-\ n, pl -ries : a furnace for cremating or a structure containing such a furnace

²crematory adj : of, relating to, or used in cremation

crème \'krem, 'krēm\ n, pl crèmes \'krem(z), 'krēmz\ [F] : CREAM

crème de ca·cao \,krēm-də-'kō-kō\ n [F, lit., cream of cacao] : a sweet liqueur flavored with cacao beans and vanilla

crème de menthe \,krēm-də-'mint\ n [F, lit., cream of mint] : a sweet green or white mint-flavored liqueur

cre·nate \'krē-,nāt, 'kren-,āt\ or **cre·nat·ed** \-əd\ adj [ML crena notch] : having the margin cut into rounded scallops ⟨a bicrenate leaf⟩ — **cre·nate·ly** adv — **cre·na·tion** \kri-'nā-shən\ n

cren·el·ate or **cren·el·ate** \'kren-ᵊl-,āt\ vt : to furnish with battlements — **cren·el·la·tion** \,kren-ᵊl-'ā-shən\ n

cren·u·late \'kren-yə-lət, -,lāt\ also **cren·u·lat·ed** \-,lāt-əd\ adj : minutely crenate — **cren·u·la·tion** \,kren-yə-'lā-shən\ n

cre·o·dont \'krē-ə-,dänt\ n : any of a group (Creodonta) of extinct primitive carnivorous mammals that form a link between modern carnivores and the ungulates — **creodont** adj

Cre·ole \'krē-,ōl\ n [F créole, fr. Sp criollo, fr. Pg crioulo] 1 : a white person descended from early French or Spanish settlers in the U.S. Gulf states or Latin America and preserving their speech and culture 2 : a person of mixed French or Spanish and Negro descent speaking a dialect of French or Spanish — **Creole** adj

cre·o·sol \'krē-ə-,sól, -,sōl\ n : a colorless liquid $C_8H_{10}O_2$ obtained from the tar made from beech and a resin

cre·o·sote \'krē-ə-,sōt\ n [Gk kreas flesh + sōtēr preserver, fr. sōzein to preserve, fr. sōs safe] 1 : a clear or yellowish oily liquid mixture of compounds obtained by the distillation of wood tar esp. from beechwood 2 : a brownish oily liquid obtained by distillation of coal tar and used esp. as a wood preservative

crepe or **crêpe** \'krāp\ n [F crêpe, fr. MF crespe curly, fr.

L *crispus*] **:** a thin crinkled fabric (as of silk, wool, or cotton) — **crepe** *adj*

crepe de chine \ˌkrāp-də-'shēn\ *n, often cap 2d C* [F *crêpe de Chine*, lit., China crepe] **:** a soft fine clothing crepe

crepe paper *n* **:** paper with a crinkled or puckered texture

crepe rubber *n* **:** crude rubber in the form of nearly white to brown crinkled sheets used esp. for shoe soles

crepe su·zette \ˌkrāp-sù-'zet\ *n, pl* **crepes suzette** \ˌkrāp(s)-sù-\ *or* **crepe suzettes** \ˌkrāp-sù-'zets\ [F *crêpe Suzette*, fr. *crêpe* pancake + *Suzette* Susy] **:** a thin pancake folded or rolled and heated in a sauce and a liqueur usu. set ablaze for serving

crep·i·tate \'krep-ə-ˌtāt\ *vi* [L *crepitare*, freq. of *crepare* to rattle, crack] **:** CRACKLE — **crep·i·ta·tion** \ˌkrep-ə-'tā-shən\ *n*

cre·pus·cu·lar \kri-'pəs-kyə-lər\ *adj* [L *crepusculum* twilight] **1 :** of, relating to, or resembling twilight **:** DIM **2 :** active in the twilight ⟨*crepuscular* insects⟩

cre·scen·do \kri-'shen-dō\ *n, pl* **-dos** *or* **-does** [It, fr. *crescendo* increasing, fr. *crescere* to increase, fr. L] **:** a swelling in volume of sound in music or a passage so performed — **crescendo** *adv (or adj)*

¹cres·cent \'kres-ᵊnt\ *n* [L *crescent-, crescens*, prp. of *crescere* to increase] **1 a :** the moon at any stage between new moon and first quarter and between last quarter and the succeeding new moon **b :** the figure of the moon defined by a convex and a concave edge **2 :** something shaped like a crescent — **cres·cen·tic** \kre-'sent-ik\ *adj*

crescent 1b: *a* concave side, *b* convex side

²crescent *adj* **:** INCREASING

cre·sol \'krē-ˌsȯl, -ˌsōl\ *n* **:** any of three poisonous colorless crystalline or liquid substances C_7H_8O obtained from coal tar and used as disinfectants or in making resins

cress \'kres\ *n* [OE *cressa*] **:** any of numerous plants of the mustard family whose leaves are used in salads

cres·set \'kres-ət\ *n* **:** an iron vessel or basket holding an illuminant (as burning oil) and serving as a torch or lantern

Cres·si·da \'kres-əd-ə\ *n* **:** a Trojan woman who in medieval legend is unfaithful to her lover Troilus

¹crest \'krest\ *n* [MF *creste*, fr. L *crista*] **1 a :** a showy tuft or process on the head of an animal (as a bird) — see BIRD illustration **b :** the plume worn on a knight's helmet **c :** a heraldic design placed above the escutcheon and also used (as to mark table silver) separately **2 :** something suggesting a crest esp. in being an upper prominence, edge, or limit ⟨the *crest* of a hill⟩ ⟨the *crest* of a wave⟩ ⟨the *crest* of a roof⟩ **3 :** a high point **:** CLIMAX, CULMINATION — **crest·less** \-ləs\ *adj*

²crest *vb* **1 :** to furnish with a crest **:** CROWN **2 :** to reach the crest of ⟨*crest* the hill⟩ **3 :** to rise to a crest ⟨the river *crested* at eight feet⟩

crest·ed \'kres-təd\ *adj* **:** having a crest ⟨fan-*crested*⟩

crest·fall·en \'kres(t)-ˌfȯ-lən\ *adj* **:** having a drooping crest or hanging head **:** DEJECTED; *also* **:** SHAMEFACED, HUMILIATED — **crest·fall·en·ness** *n*

cre·ta·ceous \kri-'tā-shəs\ *adj* [L *cretaceus*, fr. *creta* chalk] **1 :** having the characteristics of or abounding in chalk **2** *cap* **:** of, relating to, or being the 3d and latest period of the Mesozoic era or the corresponding system of rocks with the deposits including chalk and most of the coal of the U.S. west of the Great Plains — **Cretaceous** *n*

cre·tin \'krēt-ᵊn\ *n* [F *crétin*, fr. F dial. *cretin* Christian, human being, kind of idiot found in the Alps, fr. L *christianus* Christian] **:** one afflicted with cretinism; *also* **:** one having a marked mental deficiency — **cre·tin·ous** \-əs\ *adj*

cre·tin·ism \-ˌiz-əm\ *n* **:** a usu. congenital abnormal condition marked by physical and mental stunting and caused by severe thyroid deficiency

cre·tonne \'krē-ˌtän, kri-'\ *n* [F, fr. *Creton*, Normandy] **:** a strong printed cotton or linen cloth used esp. for furniture coverings and curtains

cre·vasse \kri-'vas\ *n* **1 :** a deep crevice or fissure (as in a glacier) **2 :** a breach in a levee

crev·ice \'krev-əs\ *n* [MF *crevace*, fr. *crever* to split, fr. L *crepare* to crack] **:** a narrow opening that results from a split or crack **:** FISSURE, CLEFT ⟨a *crevice* in a rock⟩

¹crew \'krü\ *chiefly Brit past of* CROW

²crew \'krü\ *n* [ME *crue*, lit., reinforcement, fr. MF *creue* increase, fr. *creistre* to increase, fr. L *crescere*] **1 :** a group or gathering of persons ⟨a happy *crew* on a picnic⟩ **2 :** a group of persons associated in joint work ⟨a train *crew*⟩ ⟨a gun *crew*⟩ **3 :** the group of seamen who man a ship **4 :** the oarsmen and steersman of a rowboat or racing shell ⟨rowed on the college *crew*⟩ **5 :** the persons who man an airplane in flight — **crew·man** \-mən\ *n*

crew cut *n* [so called fr. its being the style typically worn by oarsmen] **:** a style of short haircut in which the hair resembles the bristle surface of a brush

crew·el \'krü-əl\ *n* [ME *crule*] **:** slackly twisted worsted yarn used for embroidery — **crew·el·work** \-ˌwərk\ *n*

¹crib \'krib\ *n* [OE *cribb*] **1 :** a manger for feeding animals **2 :** an enclosure esp. of framework: as **a :** a small child's bedstead with high enclosing usu. slatted sides **b :** a building for storage **:** BIN **3 :** the cards discarded in cribbage for the dealer to use in scoring **4 a :** a literal translation; *esp* **:** PONY 3 **b :** a device used for cheating in an examination **5 :** CRÈCHE 2

²crib *vb* **cribbed; crib·bing 1 :** to copy (as an idea or passage) and use as one's own **:** PLAGIARIZE **2 :** to make use of a translation or notes in a forbidden or dishonest way — **crib·ber** *n*

crib·bage \'krib-ij\ *n* [¹*crib*] **:** a card game in which the object is to form various counting combinations and in which each player is dealt six cards and discards one or two to make up the crib

crib·ri·form \'krib-rə-ˌfȯrm\ *adj* **:** pierced with small holes

crick \'krik\ *n* [ME *cryk*] **:** a painful spasm of muscles (as of the neck or back) — **crick** *vt*

¹crick·et \'krik-ət\ *n* [MF *criquet*] **:** a small leaping insect with leathery fore wings and thin hind wings noted for the chirping notes of the males

²cricket *n* **1 :** a game played with a ball and bat by two sides of usu. 11 players each on a large field centering upon two wickets **2 :** fair and honorable behavior — **crick·et·er** *n*

cri·er \'krī(-ə)r\ *n* **:** one that cries; *esp* **:** one who proclaims orders or announcements — compare TOWN CRIER

crime \'krīm\ *n* [MF, fr. L *crimin-, crimen* accusation, fault, crime] **1 a :** the doing of an act forbidden by law **b :** the failure to do an act required by law making the offender liable to punishment **c :** a serious offense against the law **2 :** a grave offense esp. against morality **3 :** criminal activity

¹crim·i·nal \'krim-ən-ᵊl\ *adj* **1 :** involving or being a crime ⟨a *criminal* act⟩ **2 :** relating to crime or its punishment ⟨*criminal* court⟩ **3 :** guilty of crime — **crim·i·nal·i·ty** \ˌkrim-ə-'nal-ət-ē\ *n* — **crim·i·nal·ly** \'krim-ən-ᵊl-ē\ *adv*

²criminal *n* **:** one that has committed a crime **:** MALEFACTOR

crim·i·nol·o·gy \ˌkrim-ə-'näl-ə-jē\ *n* **:** a scientific study of crime as a social phenomenon, of criminals, and of their punishment or correction — **crim·i·no·log·i·cal** \ˌkrim-ən-ᵊl-'äj-i-kəl\ *adj* — **crim·i·nol·o·gist** \ˌkrim-ə-'näl-ə-jəst\ *n*

¹crimp \'krimp\ *vt* [D or LG *krimpen* to shrivel] **1 :** to cause to become wavy, bent, or warped: as **a :** to draw or pinch in or together **b :** to roll the edge of **2 :** INHIBIT, HINDER — **crimp·er** *n*

²crimp *n* **1 :** something produced by or as if by crimping **2 :** something that cramps or inhibits

³crimp *n* **:** a person who traps men into shipping as sailors

⁴crimp *vt* **:** to trap into shipping as a sailor

crimpy \'krim-pē\ *adj* **crimp·i·er; -est :** having a crimped appearance **:** FRIZZY

¹crim·son \'krim-zən\ *n* [OSp *cremesín*, fr. Ar *qirmizī*, fr. *qirmiz* kermes] **:** any of several deep purplish reds — **crimson** *adj*

²crimson *vb* **:** to make or become crimson

¹cringe \'krinj\ *vi* **cringed; cring·ing** [ME *crengen*] **1 :** to draw in or contract one's muscles involuntarily **2 :** to shrink in fear or servility **3 :** to approach someone with fawning and self-abasement — **cring·er** *n*

²cringe *n* **:** an act of cringing

¹crin·kle \'kriŋ-kəl\ *vb* **crin·kled; crin·kling** \-k(ə-)liŋ\ **1 :** to form little waves or wrinkles on the surface **:** WRINKLE, RIPPLE **2 :** RUSTLE ⟨*crinkling* silk⟩

²crinkle *n* **1 :** WINDING, WRINKLE **2 :** any of several

---

j joke; ŋ sing; ō flow; ȯ flaw; ȯi coin; th thin; t̲h̲ this; ü loot; u̇ foot; y yet; yü few; yu̇ furious; zh vision

plant diseases marked by crinkling of leaves — **crin·kly** \-k(ə-)lē\ *adj*

cri·noid \'krī-ˌnȯid\ *n* [Gk *krinon* lily] : any of a large class (Crinoidea) of echinoderms having usu. a cup-shaped body with five or more feathery arms — **crinoid** *or* **cri·noi·dal** \krī-'nȯid-ᵊl\ *adj*

crin·o·line \'krin-ᵊl-ən\ *n* [It *crinolino*, fr. *crino* horsehair + *lino* linen] **1** : a cloth orig. of horsehair and linen thread used for stiffening and lining **2** : a very full stiff skirt; *esp* : one lined with crinoline material **3** : HOOP-SKIRT — **crinoline** *adj*

¹crip·ple \'krip-əl\ *n* [OE *crypel;* akin to E *creep*] : a lame or partly disabled individual

²cripple *vt* **crip·pled; crip·pling** \'krip-(ə-)liŋ\ **1** : to deprive of the use of a limb and esp. a leg **2** : to deprive of strength, efficiency, wholeness, or capability for service — **crip·pler** \-(ə-)lər\ *n*

cri·sis \'krī-səs\ *n, pl* **cri·ses** \'krī-ˌsēz\ [Gk *krisis*, lit., decision, fr. *krinein* to judge, decide] **1** : the turning point for better or worse in an acute disease or fever **2** : a decisive moment or turning point (as in the course of a life or the plot of a story) **3** : an unstable or crucial time or state of affairs ⟨a business *crisis*⟩ **syn** see JUNCTURE

¹crisp \'krisp\ *adj* [OE, fr. L *crispus*] **1** : CURLY, WAVY ⟨*crisp* hair⟩ **2** : easily crumbled : FLAKY ⟨*crisp* pastry⟩ **3** : being firm and fresh ⟨*crisp* lettuce⟩ **4 a** : being sharp, clean-cut, and clear ⟨a *crisp* illustration⟩ **b** : noticeably neat **c** : SPRIGHTLY, LIVELY ⟨*crisp* retort⟩ **d** : FROSTY, SNAPPY ⟨*crisp* weather⟩ **syn** see BRITTLE — **crisp·ly** *adv* — **crisp·ness** *n*

²crisp *vb* : to make or become crisp — **crisp·er** *n*

³crisp *n* **1** : something crisp or brittle **2** *chiefly Brit* : POTATO CHIP

crispy \'kris-pē\ *adj* **crisp·i·er; -est** : CRISP — **crisp·i·ness** *n*

¹criss·cross \'kris-ˌkrȯs\ *n* [earlier *christcross* mark of a cross, fr. *Christ* + *cross*] : a pattern formed by crossed lines — **crisscross** *adj (or adv)*

²crisscross *vb* **1** : to mark with intersecting lines **2** : to go or pass back and forth

cris·tate \'kris-ˌtāt\ *also* **cris·tat·ed** \-ˌtāt-əd\ *adj* : CRESTED

cri·te·ri·on \krī-'tir-ē-ən\ *n, pl* **-ria** \-ē-ə\ *also* **-ri·ons** [Gk *kritērion*, fr. *krinein* to judge, decide] : a standard on which a judgment or decision may be based **syn** see STANDARD

crit·ic \'krit-ik\ *n* [Gk *kritikos*, fr. *krinein* to judge] **1** : a person who gives his judgment of the value, worth, beauty, or excellence of something; *esp* : one whose profession is to write articles expressing trained judgment on work in art, music, drama, or literature **2** : FAULTFINDER

crit·i·cal \'krit-i-kəl\ *adj* **1 a** : inclined to criticize severely and unfavorably **b** : consisting of or involving criticism ⟨*critical* writings⟩ **c** : using or involving careful judgment **2 a** : of, relating to, or being a turning point or specially important juncture ⟨*critical* phase⟩ **b** : relating to or being a state in which or a measurement or point at which some quality, property, or phenomenon suffers a definite change ⟨*critical* temperature⟩ **c** : CRUCIAL, DECISIVE ⟨*critical* test⟩ **d** : indispensable for overcoming a crisis **3** : of sufficient size to sustain a chain reaction — used of a mass of fissionable material — **crit·i·cal·ly** \-i-k(ə-)lē\ *adv* — **crit·i·cal·ness** \-kəl-nəs\ *n*

critical angle *n* : the least angle of incidence at which total reflection takes place

crit·i·cism \'krit-ə-ˌsiz-əm\ *n* **1** : the act of criticizing; *esp* : FAULTFINDING **2** : a critical remark or observation **3** : a careful judgment or review esp. by a critic **4** : the art of judging expertly the merits and faults of works of art or literature

crit·i·cize \'krit-ə-ˌsīz\ *vb* **1** : to examine and judge as a critic : EVALUATE **2** : to express criticism esp. of an unfavorable kind **3** : to find fault with ⟨some people are quick to *criticize* others⟩ — **crit·i·ciz·er** *n*

cri·tique \krə-'tēk\ *n* : an act or instance of criticizing; *esp* : a critical estimate or discussion

crit·ter \'krit-ər\ *n* [by alter.] *dial* : CREATURE

¹croak \'krōk\ *vb* [ME *croken*] **1 a** : to make a deep harsh sound **b** : to speak in a hoarse throaty voice **2 a** : to predict evil **b** : GRUMBLE **3** *slang* **a** : DIE **b** : KILL

²croak *n* : a hoarse harsh cry (as of a frog)

croak·er \'krō-kər\ *n* **1** : an animal that croaks **2** : any of various fishes that produce croaking or grunting noises **3** : one that habitually grumbles or prophesies evil

Croat \'krōt, 'krō-ˌat\ *n* : CROATIAN

Cro·a·tian \krō-'ā-shən\ *n* **1** : a native or inhabitant of Croatia **2** : a south Slavic language spoken by the Croatian people and distinct from Serbian chiefly in its use of the Latin alphabet — **Croatian** *adj*

¹cro·chet \krō-'shā\ *n* [F, fr. dim. of *croche* hook] : needlework consisting of interlocked looped stitches formed with a single thread and a hooked needle

²crochet *vb* : to form a fabric of crochet — **cro·chet·er** \-'shā-ər\ *n*

crock \'kräk\ *n* [OE *crocc*] : a thick earthenware pot or jar

crock·ery \'kräk-(ə-)rē\ *n* : EARTHENWARE

croc·o·dile \'kräk-ə-ˌdīl\ *n* [Gk *krokodilos* lizard, croco-dile] **1 a** : any of several large greedy thick-skinned long-bodied aquatic reptiles of tropical and subtropical waters — compare ALLIGATOR **b** : CROCODILIAN **2** : the skin or hide of a crocodile

crocodile tears *n pl* [fr. the ancient belief that crocodiles weep in sympathy for their victims] : false or pretended tears : insincere sorrow

croc·o·dil·i·an \ˌkräk-ə-'dil-ē-ən\ *n* : any of an order (Loricata) of reptiles including the crocodiles, alligators, and related extinct forms — **crocodilian** *adj*

cro·cus \'krō-kəs\ *n, pl* **cro·cus·es** [Gk *krokos* saffron, of Sem origin] **1** *pl also* **cro·ci** \-ˌkē, -ˌkī, -ˌsī\ : any of a large genus of small herbs of the iris family with showy solitary long-tubed flowers and slender linear leaves **2** : SAFFRON 1b

croft \'krȯft\ *n* [OE] **1** *chiefly Brit* : a small enclosed field **2** *chiefly Brit* : a small farm worked by a tenant — **croft·er** *n*

crois·sant \krə-ˌwä-'säⁿ\ *n, pl* **croissants** \-'säⁿ(z)\ [F, lit., crescent] : a rich crescent-shaped roll

Cro-Mag·non \krō-'mag-nən, -'man-yən\ *n* [*Cro-Magnon*, a cave near Les Eyzies, France] : any of a tall erect race of men known from skeletal remains chiefly from southern France and held to be of the same species as recent man — **Cro-Magnon** *adj*

crom·lech \'kräm-ˌlek\ *n* [W, lit., bent stone] **1** : DOLMEN **2** : a circle of monoliths enclosing a dolmen

crone \'krōn\ *n* [ONF *carogne*, lit., carrion] : a withered old woman

Cro·nus \'krō-nəs\ *n* : a Titan dethroned by his son Zeus

cro·ny \'krō-nē\ *n, pl* **cronies** : an intimate companion

¹crook \'kru̇k\ *n* [ON *krōkr*] **1** : an implement having a bent or hooked form: as **a** : a shepherd's staff **b** : CROSIER **2** : a dishonest person; *esp* : CRIMINAL **3** : BEND, CURVE **4** : a hook-shaped, curved, or bent part

²crook *vb* **1** : BEND **2** : CURVE, WIND

crook·ed \'kru̇k-əd\ *adj* **1** : having a crook or curve : BENT **2** : DISHONEST; *esp* : CRIMINAL — **crook·ed·ly** *adv* — **crook·ed·ness** *n*

syn CROOKED, AWRY, ASKEW mean not straight. CROOKED applies to what is itself not straight but curving, bent, or twisted; AWRY applies to what is out of a straight line in relation to something else; ASKEW implies having a decided slant away from a straight course

crook·neck \'kru̇k-ˌnek\ *n* : a squash with a long curved neck

croon \'krün\ *vb* [MD *cronen* to bellow] **1** : to hum or sing in a low voice ⟨*croon* a lullaby⟩ **2** : to sing popular songs in an exaggerated sentimental style — **croon·er** *n*

¹crop \'kräp\ *n* [OE *cropp* craw, cluster, head of a plant] **1** : the stock or handle of a whip; *also* : a riding whip with a short straight stock and a loop **2** : a pouched enlargement of the gullet of a bird or insect that receives food and prepares it for digestion **3** [²*crop*] **a** : an ear-mark on an animal; *esp* : one made by removing the upper part of the ear **b** : a close cut of the hair **4 a** : a plant or animal or plant or animal product that can be grown and harvested **b** : the product or yield esp. of a harvested crop **c** : BATCH, LOT

²crop *vb* **cropped; crop·ping** **1 a** : to remove the upper or outer parts of ⟨*crop* a hedge⟩ **b** : to cut off short : CLIP **2 a** : to cause (land) to bear produce; *also* : to grow as a crop **b** : HARVEST **3** : to feed by cropping something

4 : to yield or make a crop **5 :** to appear unexpectedly or casually 〈problems *crop* up daily〉

crop·land \'kräp-,land\ *n* **:** land devoted to the production of plant crops

¹crop·per \'kräp-ər\ *n* **1 :** one that crops **2 :** one that raises crops; *esp* **:** SHARECROPPER

²cropper *n* **1 :** a severe fall **2 :** a sudden or violent failure or collapse

crop rotation *n* **:** the practice of growing different crops in succession on the same land chiefly to preserve the productive capacity of the soil

cro·quet \krō-'kā\ *n* [F dial., hockey stick, fr. ONF, crook] **:** a game in which the players use mallets to drive wooden balls through a series of hoops set in the ground

cro·quette \krō-'ket\ *n* [F, fr. *croquer* to crunch] **:** a roll or ball of hashed meat, fish, or vegetables fried in deep fat

cro·sier \'krō-zhər\ *n* [MF *crossier* crosier bearer, fr. *crosse* crosier, of Gmc origin; akin to E *crutch*] **:** a staff carried by bishops and abbots as a symbol of office

¹cross \'krȯs\ *n* [OE, fr. ON *kross*, fr. (assumed) OIr *cross*, fr. L *crux*] **1 a :** a structure consisting of an upright with a transverse beam **b** *often cap* **:** the cross on which Jesus Christ was crucified **2 :** a trying affliction **3 :** a cruciform sign made to invoke the blessing of Christ esp. by touch-

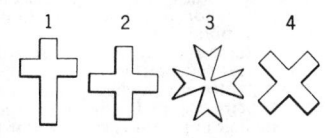

1   2   3   4

crosses 4a: *1* Latin, *2* Greek, *3* Maltese, *4* Saint Andrews

ing the forehead, breast, and shoulders **4 a :** a device or structure composed of an upright bar crossed by a horizontal one; *esp* **:** one used as a Christian emblem **b** *cap* **:** the Christian religion **5 :** a figure or mark formed by two intersecting lines; *esp* **:** one used as a signature **6 :** the intersection of two ways or lines **:** CROSSING **7 a :** an act of crossing unlike individuals **b :** a crossbred individual or kind **8 :** a hook crossed over an opponent's lead in boxing

²cross *vb* **1 a :** to lie or be situated across **b :** INTERSECT **c :** to move, pass, or extend across **2 :** to make the sign of the cross upon or over **3 :** to cancel by marking a cross on or drawing a line through **:** strike out 〈*cross* names off a list〉 **4 :** to place or fold crosswise one over the other 〈*cross* the arms〉 **5 a :** to run counter to **:** OPPOSE, THWART, OBSTRUCT **b :** BETRAY **6 a :** to extend across **:** TRAVERSE **b :** to go from one to the other side of 〈*cross* a street〉〈*cross* a bridge〉 **7 :** to draw a line across 〈*cross* a t〉 **8 :** INTERBREED, HYBRIDIZE **9 :** to meet and pass on the way

³cross *adj* **1 a :** lying across or athwart **b :** moving across 〈*cross* traffic〉 **2 :** running counter **:** OPPOSING, OPPOSED **3 :** marked by bad temper **:** GRUMPY **4 :** CROSSBRED, HYBRID — **cross·ly** *adv* — **cross·ness** *n*

cross·bar \'krȯs-,bär\ *n* **:** a bar, piece, or stripe placed crosswise or across

cross·bill \-,bil\ *n* **:** any of a genus of finches with mandibles strongly curved and crossing each other

cross·bones \-,bōnz\ *n pl* **:** two leg or arm bones placed or depicted crosswise

cross·bow \-,bō\ *n* **:** a short bow mounted crosswise near the end of a wooden stock that discharges stones and square-headed arrows — **cross·bow·man** \-mən\ *n*

cross·bred \'krȯs-'bred\ *adj* **:** HYBRID; *esp* **:** produced by interbreeding two pure but different breeds, strains, or varieties — **cross·breed** \-,brēd\ *n*

¹cross·breed \-,brēd, -'brēd\ *vt* **:** HYBRIDIZE; *esp* **:** to interbreed two varieties or breeds of the same species

²cross·breed \-,brēd\ *n* **:** HYBRID

cross·coun·try \-'kən-trē\ *adj* **1 :** proceeding over the countryside (as fields and woods) rather than by roads **2 :** of or relating to cross-country sports — **cross·country** *adv*

cross·cur·rent \-'kər-ənt, -'kə-rənt\ *n* **1 :** a current running counter to another **2 :** a conflicting tendency

¹cross·cut \-,kət, -'kət\ *vt* **-cut**; **-cut·ting :** to cut or saw crosswise esp. of the grain of wood

²crosscut *adj* **1 :** made or used for cutting transversely 〈a *crosscut* saw〉 **2 :** cut across or transversely 〈a *crosscut* incision〉

³cross·cut \-,kət\ *n* **:** something that cuts across or through

crosse \'krȯs\ *n* **:** the stick used in lacrosse

cross·ex·am·i·na·tion \,krȯs-ig-,zam-ə-'nā-shən\ *n* **:** the questioning of a witness called by the opposing party to a legal action in order to check, alter, expand, or discredit his testimony — **cross·ex·am·ine** \-'zam-ən\ *vt* — **cross·ex·am·in·er** *n*

cross·eye \'krȯs-,ī\ *n* **1 :** an abnormality in which the eye turns inward toward the nose **2** *pl* **:** eyes affected with cross-eye — **cross·eyed** \-'īd\ *adj*

cross·fer·til·i·za·tion \'krȯs-,fərt-ᵊl-ə-'zā-shən\ *n* **1 :** fertilization between gametes produced by separate individuals or sometimes by individuals of different kinds **2 :** CROSS-POLLINATION — **cross·fer·tile** \-'fərt-ᵊl\ *adj* — **cross·fer·til·ize** \-'fərt-ᵊl-,īz\ *vb*

cross fire *n* **1 :** firing (as in combat) from two or more points so that the lines of fire cross; *also* **:** a situation wherein the forces of opposing factions meet or cross **2 :** rapid or heated interchange

cross·grained \'krȯs-'grānd\ *adj* **1 :** having the grain or fibers running diagonally, transversely, or irregularly **2 :** difficult to deal with **:** CONTRARY, PERVERSE

cross hair *n* **:** one of the fine wires or threads in the focus of the eyepiece of an optical instrument used as a reference line

cross·hatch \'krȯs-,hach\ *vb* **:** to mark with a series of parallel lines that cross esp. obliquely — **crosshatch** *n* — **cross·hatch·ing** *n*

cross·ing \'krȯ-siŋ\ *n* **1 a :** the act or action of one that crosses **b :** a voyage across water **c :** INTERBREEDING, HYBRIDIZING **2 :** a point of intersection (as of a street and a railroad track) **3 :** a place where a street or stream is crossed

cross·ing-over \,krȯ-siŋ-'ō-vər\ *n* **:** an interchange of genes or segments between associated parts of homologous chromosomes during synapsis

cross·legged \'krȯs-'leg-(ə)d\ *adv* **:** with the legs crossed and the knees spread wide

cross·over \'krȯs-,ō-vər\ *n* **1 :** a crossing from one side, level, or track to another or a place or passage where such crossing is made **2 :** an instance or product of genetic crossing-over

cross·piece \'krȯs-,pēs\ *n* **:** a horizontal member (as of a figure or a structure)

cross·pol·li·nate \-'päl-ə-,nāt\ *or* **cross·pol·li·nize** \-'päl-ə-,nīz\ *vt* **:** to subject to cross-pollination

cross·pol·li·na·tion \,krȯs-,päl-ə-'nā-shən\ *n* **:** the transfer of pollen from one flower to the stigma of another

cross·pur·pose \'krȯs-'pər-pəs\ *n* **:** an opposing purpose — **at cross·pur·pos·es :** acting contrary to another without meaning to do so

cross·ques·tion \-'kwes-chən\ *vt* **:** to subject to close questioning; *esp* **:** CROSS-EXAMINE — **cross·question** *n*

cross·re·fer \,krȯs-ri-'fər\ *vb* **:** to refer by a notation or direction from one place to another (as in a book, list, or catalog) — **cross·ref·er·ence** \'krȯs-'ref-ərn(t)s, -'ref-(ə-)rən(t)s\ *n*

cross·road \'krȯs-,rōd, -'rōd\ *n* **1 :** a road that crosses a main road or runs cross-country between main roads **2 a :** the place of intersection of two or more roads — usu. used in pl. **b :** a small community located at such a crossroads

cross·ruff \'krȯs-,rəf, -'rəf\ *n* **:** a series of plays in a card game in which partners alternately trump different suits and lead to each other for that purpose — **crossruff** *vb*

cross section *n* **1 a :** a cutting made across something (as a log or apple) **b :** a representation of a cutting made across something 〈a *cross section* of a wire〉 **c :** a piece cut off at right angles to an axis **2 :** a number of persons or things selected from a group to represent or show the general nature of the whole 〈the novel shows a *cross section* of society〉 — **cross·sec·tion·al** \'krȯs-'sek-shnəl, -shən-ᵊl\ *adj*

cross·ster·ile \'krȯs-'ster-əl\ *adj* **:** mutually sterile — **cross·ste·ril·i·ty** \,krȯs-stə-'ril-ət-ē\ *n*

cross·stitch \'krȯs-,stich\ *n* **1 :** a needlework stitch that forms an X **2 :** work having cross-stitch — **cross·stitch** *vb*

cross·town \'krȯs-,taùn, -'taùn\ *adj* **1 :** situated at opposite points of a town 〈*crosstown* neighbors〉 **2 :** extending

---

j joke;   ŋ sing;   ō flow;   ȯ flaw;   ȯi coin;   th thin;   th̲ this;   ü loot;   ù foot;   y yet;   yü few;   yù furious;   zh vision

or running across a town ⟨a *crosstown* bus⟩ ⟨a *crosstown* route⟩ — **crosstown** *adv*

cross-tree \'krȯs-(,)trē\ *n* : two horizontal crosspieces near the top of a ship's mast to spread apart the upper ropes that support the mast — usu. used in pl.

cross-walk \'krȯs-,wȯk\ *n* : a specially paved or marked path for pedestrians crossing a street or road

cross-way \-,wā\ *n* : CROSSROAD — often used in pl.

¹cross-wise \-,wīz\ *also* **cross-ways** \-,wāz\ *adv* **1** *archaic* : in the form of a cross **2** : so as to cross something : ACROSS

²crosswise *adj* : extended or lying across

cross-word puzzle \,krȯs-,wərd-\ *n* : a puzzle in which words are filled into a pattern of numbered squares in answer to similarly numbered clues and in such a way that they read across and down

crotch \'kräch\ *n* [prob. alter. of *crutch*] : an angle formed by the parting of two legs, branches, or members

crotch-et \'kräch-ət\ *n* [MF *crochet*, dim. of *croche* hook] **1** : a small hook or hooked instrument **2** : a peculiar opinion or habit : WHIM **3** : QUARTER NOTE

crotch-ety \'kräch-ət-ē\ *adj* : marked by or given to whims or ill temper ⟨a *crotchety* old man⟩ — **crotch-et-i-ness** *n*

cro-ton \'krōt-°n\ *n* [Gk *krotōn* castor-oil plant] : any of several herbs and shrubs of the spurge family; *esp* : an East Indian plant yielding an oil used as a drastic purgative

Cro-ton bug \'krōt-°n-\ *n* : a small active winged cockroach common where food and moisture are found

crouch \'krauch\ *vb* [ME *crouchen*] **1** : to stoop with the limbs close to the body **2** : to bend or bow servilely : CRINGE — **crouch** *n*

¹croup \'krüp\ *n* [OF *croupe*, of Gmc origin] : the rump of a quadruped

²croup *n* [E dial., to cry hoarsely, cough] : a laryngitis esp. of infants marked by episodes of difficult breathing and a hoarse metallic cough — **croup-ous** \'krü-pəs\ *adj* — **croupy** \-pē\ *adj*

crou-pi-er \'krü-pē-ər, -pē-,ā\ *n* [F, lit., rider on the croup of a horse] : an employee of a gambling casino who collects and pays bets at a gaming table

crou-ton \'krü-,tän, krü-'\ *n* [F *croûton*, dim. of *croûte* crust] : a small cube of bread toasted or fried crisp

¹crow \'krō\ *n* [OE *crāwe*] **1** : any of various large usu. entirely glossy black perching birds related to the jays **2** : CROWBAR — **as the crow flies** : in a straight line

²crow *vi* **crowed** \'krōd\ *also in sense 1 chiefly Brit* **crew** \'krü\; **crow-ing 1** : to make the loud shrill sound characteristic of a cock **2** : to utter a sound expressive of pleasure **3 a** : EXULT, GLOAT **b** : BRAG

³crow *n* **1** : the cry of the cock **2** : a triumphant cry

crow-bar \'krō-,bär\ *n* : an iron or steel bar usu. wedge-shaped at the working end for use as a pry or lever

crow-ber-ry \'krō-,ber-ē\ *n* : any of several heaths or related plants with fruit held to be eaten by crows; *also* : this fruit

¹crowd \'kraud\ *vb* [OE *crūdan*] **1** : to press forward : HURRY **2** : to press close to something ⟨*crowding* the car in front⟩ ⟨*crowd* around the speaker⟩ **3** : to collect in numbers : THRONG, JOSTLE **4** : to fill or pack by pressing or thronging together ⟨*crowd* a room⟩ ⟨*crowd* children into a bus⟩

²crowd *n* **1** : a large number of persons collected into a body without order **2** : the great body of the people : POPULACE ⟨his books appeal to the *crowd*⟩ **3** : a large number of things close together **4** : a group of people having a common interest **syn** *see* MULTITUDE

³crowd \'kraud, 'krüd\ *n* [ME *crowde*] : an ancient Celtic stringed instrument played by plucking or with a short bow — called also *crwth*

crow-foot \'krō-,füt\ *n, pl* **crow-feet** \-,fēt\ **1** *pl usu* **crowfoots** : any of numerous plants having leaves pedately lobed; *esp* : BUTTERCUP **2** : CROW'S-FOOT a — usu. used in pl.

¹crown \'kraun\ *n* [OF *corone*, fr. L *corona* wreath, crown, fr. Gk *korōnē* anything curved or hooked] **1 a** : a wreath or band for the head; *esp* : one worn as a mark of victory or honor **b** : REWARD **2** : a royal or imperial headdress : DIADEM **3** : the highest part: as **a** : the topmost part of the

crown 2

skull or head **b** : the summit of a mountain **c** : the head of foliage of a tree or shrub **d** : the part of a hat covering the crown of the head **e** : the part of a tooth external to the gum or an artificial substitute for this **4** : something resembling a crown **5 a** (1) : *often cap* : imperial or regal power : SOVEREIGNTY (2) *cap* : the executive part of the British government including the monarch and the ministers **b** : SOVEREIGN **6** : the highest point of development : CULMINATION **7 a** : any of several coins; *esp* : an English silver coin worth five shillings **b** : a size of paper usu. 15 x 20 inches **8 a** : the region of a seed plant in which stem and root merge **b** : the thick arching end of the shank of an anchor where the arms join it — see ANCHOR illustration — **crown** *adj, often cap* — **crowned** \'kraund\ *adj*

²crown *vt* **1 a** : to place a crown on; *esp* : to invest with regal dignity and power **b** : to recognize officially as ⟨was *crowned* champion⟩ **2** : BESTOW, ENDOW, ADORN ⟨*crowned* with wisdom⟩ **3** : SURMOUNT, TOP; *esp* : to top (a checker) with a checker to make a king **4** : to bring to a successful conclusion : CLIMAX **5 a** : to fill so that the surface forms a crown **b** : to put an artificial crown upon (a tooth)

crown glass *n* : a very clear alkali-lime glass that is used for optical instruments

crown prince *n* : the heir apparent to a crown or throne

crown princess *n* **1** : the wife of a crown prince **2** : a female heir apparent to a crown or throne

crow's-foot \'krōz-,füt\ *n, pl* **crow's-feet** \-,fēt\ : something resembling a crow's foot: as **a** : any of the wrinkles around the outer corners of the eyes — usu. used in pl. **b** : CROWFOOT 1

crow's nest *n* : a partly enclosed platform high on a ship's mast for a lookout; *also* : any similar lookout

cro-zier *var of* CROSIER

cruces *pl of* CRUX

cru-cial \'krü-shəl\ *adj* [NL *cruc-, crux* crux] **1** : marked by final determination of a doubtful issue : DECISIVE **2** : SEVERE, TRYING — **cru-cial-ly** \'krüsh-(ə-)lē\ *adv*

cru-ci-ate \'krü-shē-,āt\ *adj* : having the shape of a cross — **cru-ci-ate-ly** *adv*

cru-ci-ble \'krü-sə-bəl\ *n* [ML *crucibulum*] **1** : a pot of a very refractory material used for holding a substance for treatment in a process that requires a high degree of heat **2** : a severe test

cru-ci-fer \'krü-sə-fər\ *n* **1** : one who carries a cross esp. at the head of an ecclesiastical procession **2** : any plant of the mustard family — **cru-cif-er-ous** \krü-'sif-(ə-)rəs\ *adj*

cru-ci-fix \'krü-sə-,fiks\ *n* [LL *crucifixus* the crucified Christ, fr. pp. of *crucifigere* to crucify, fr. L *cruc-, crux* cross + *figere* to fasten, fix] : a representation of Christ on the cross

cru-ci-fix-ion \,krü-sə-'fik-shən\ *n* : an act of crucifying; *esp, cap* : the crucifying of Christ

cru-ci-form \'krü-sə-,fȯrm\ *adj* : forming or arranged in a cross — **cru-ci-form-ly** *adv*

cru-ci-fy \'krü-sə-,fī\ *vt* **-fied; -fy-ing 1** : to put to death by nailing or binding the hands and feet to a cross **2** : to treat cruelly : TORTURE, PERSECUTE

¹crude \'krüd\ *adj* [L *crudus* raw; akin to E *raw*] **1** : existing in a natural state and unaltered by processing : not refined : RAW ⟨*crude* oil⟩ ⟨*crude* statistics⟩ **2** : lacking refinement, grace, or tact; *esp* : marked by grossness or vulgarity **3** : rough or inexpert in plan or execution : RUDE **4** : not concealed or glossed over : BARE ⟨the *crude* facts⟩ — **crude-ly** *adv* — **crude-ness** *n* — **cru-di-ty** \'krüd-ət-ē\ *n*

²crude *n* : a substance in its natural unprocessed state; *esp* : unrefined petroleum

cru-el \'krü-(ə)l\ *adj* **cru-el-er** *or* **cru-el-ler; cru-el-est** *or* **cru-el-lest** [OF, fr. L *crudelis*; akin to E *raw*] **1** : disposed to inflict pain **2 a** : causing or helping to cause injury, grief, or pain **b** : devoid of kindness : MERCILESS — **cru-el-ly** \'krü-ə-lē, 'krül-lē\ *adv* — **cru-el-ness** *n*

cru-el-ty \'krü-(ə)l-tē\ *n, pl* **-ties 1** : the quality or state of being cruel **2 a** : a cruel action **b** : inhuman treatment

cru-et \'krü-ət\ *n* [AF, dim. of OF *crue*, of Gmc origin] : a small glass bottle for holding vinegar, oil, or sauce for table use

¹cruise \'krüz\ *vb* [D *kruisen* to make a cross, cruise, fr.

MD *crūce* cross, fr. L *cruc-, crux*\] **1 :** to sail about touching at a series of ports **2 :** to travel for enjoyment **3 :** to go about the streets at random **4 :** to travel at the most efficient operating speed ⟨the *cruising* speed of an airplane⟩ **5 :** to travel over or about **6 :** to inspect (as land) with reference to possible lumber yield

²cruise *n* **:** an act or an instance of cruising

cruis·er \'krü-zər\ *n* **1 :** a boat or vehicle that cruises; *esp* **:** SQUAD CAR **2 :** a large fast moderately armored and gunned warship **3 :** a motorboat with arrangements necessary for living aboard — called also *cabin cruiser*

crul·ler \'krəl-ər\ *n* [D *krulle*, a twisted cake] **1 :** a small sweet cake in the form of a twisted sweet fried in deep fat **2** *North & Midland* **:** an unraised doughnut

¹crumb \'krəm\ *n* [OE *cruma*] **1 :** a small fragment esp. of bread **2 :** BIT

²crumb *vt* **1 :** to break into crumbs **:** CRUMBLE **2 :** to cover or thicken with crumbs **3 :** to remove crumbs from ⟨*crumb* a table⟩

crum·ble \'krəm-bəl\ *vb* **crum·bled; crum·bling** \-b(ə-)liŋ\ **:** to break into small pieces **:** DISINTEGRATE ⟨*crumble* bread in one's hand⟩ ⟨the wall *crumbled*⟩

crum·bly \-b(ə-)lē\ *adj* **crum·bli·er; -est :** easily crumbled — **crum·bli·ness** *n*

crum·pet \'krəm-pət\ *n* **:** a small round cake made of unsweetened batter cooked on a griddle

¹crum·ple \'krəm-pəl\ *vb* **crum·pled; crum·pling** \-p(ə-)liŋ\ [freq. of ME *crumpen* to curve, fr. *crump* crooked, fr. OE] **1 :** to press, bend, or crush out of shape **:** RUMPLE **2 :** to become crumpled **3 :** COLLAPSE

²crumple *n* **:** a wrinkle or crease made by crumpling

¹crunch \'krənch\ *vb* **:** to chew, grind, or press with a crushing noise

²crunch *n* **:** an act or sound of crunching — **crunchy** \'krən-chē\ *adj*

crup·per \'krəp-ər, 'krüp-\ *n* [OF *crupiere*] **1 :** a leather loop passing under a horse's tail and buckled to the saddle of the harness **2 :** the rump of a horse **:** CROUP

¹cru·sade \krü-'sād\ *n* [MF *croisade* & Sp *cruzada*, fr. L *cruc-, crux* cross] **1** *cap* **:** any of the military expeditions undertaken by Christian powers in the 11th, 12th, and 13th centuries to recover the Holy Land from the Muslims **2 :** a campaign to improve conditions that is undertaken with zeal and enthusiasm ⟨a *crusade* against gambling⟩

²crusade *vi* **:** to engage in a crusade — **cru·sad·er** *n*

cruse \'krüz, 'krüs\ *n* **:** a jar, pot, or cup for holding a liquid (as water or oil)

¹crush \'krəsh\ *vb* [fr. MF *cruisir*] **1 a :** to squeeze or force by pressure so as to alter or destroy structure **b :** to squeeze together into a mass **2 :** HUG, EMBRACE **3 :** to reduce to particles by pounding or grinding **4 a :** SUPPRESS, OVERWHELM **b :** OPPRESS **c :** SUBDUE, DEFEAT **5 :** CROWD, PUSH **6 :** to become crushed — **crush·er** *n*

²crush *n* **1 :** an act of crushing **2 :** a tightly packed crowd **3 :** INFATUATION; *also* **:** the object of infatuation

crust \'krəst\ *n* [L *crusta*] **1 a :** the hardened exterior surface of bread **b :** a piece of dry hard bread **2 :** the pastry portion of a pie **3 a :** a hard external covering or surface layer ⟨*crust* of snow⟩ **b :** the outer part of the earth composed essentially of crystalline rocks **c :** SCAB **4** *slang* **:** IMPUDENCE, BRASS — **crust** *vb*

crus·ta·cea \,krəs-'tā-sh(ē-)ə\ *n pl* **:** CRUSTACEANS

crus·ta·cean \,krəs-'tā-shən\ *n* [L *crusta* crust, shell] **:** any of a large class (Crustacea) of mostly aquatic arthropods having a chitinous or calcareous and chitinous exoskeleton and including the lobsters, shrimps, crabs, wood lice, water fleas, and barnacles — **crustacean** *adj*

crus·ta·ceous \-shəs\ *adj* **1 :** of, relating to, having, or forming a crust or shell ⟨a *crustaceous* lichen⟩ **2 :** CRUSTACEAN

crust·al \'krəst-ᵊl\ *adj* **:** relating to a crust esp. of the earth or the moon

crust·ose \'krəs-,tōs\ *adj* **:** forming a firm thin crust ⟨*crustose* lichens⟩

crusty \'krəs-tē\ *adj* **crust·i·er; -est** **1 :** having or being a crust **2 :** SURLY, IRASCIBLE — **crust·i·ly** \-tə-lē\ *adv* — **crust·i·ness** \-tē-nəs\ *n*

crutch \'krəch\ *n* [OE *crycc*] **1 :** a support typically fitting under the armpit for use by the disabled in walking **2 :** a usu. forked support or prop

crux \'krəks, 'krüks\ *n, pl* **crux·es** *also* **cru·ces** \'krü-**

,sēz\ [NL *cruc-, crux*, fr. L, cross, torture] **1 a :** a puzzling or difficult problem **:** an unsolved question **b :** a crucial or critical point ⟨the *crux* of the matter⟩ **2 :** a main or central feature

cru·zei·ro \krü-'zā-rō, -rü\ *n, pl* **-ros** [Pg] **1 :** the basic monetary unit of Brazil **2 :** a coin representing one cruzeiro

crwth \'krüth\ *n* [W] **:** ³CROWD

¹cry \'krī\ *vb* **cried; cry·ing** [OF *crier*, fr. L *quiritare*, lit., to cry for help from a citizen, fr. *Quirit-, Quiris* Roman citizen] **1 :** to call loudly **:** SHOUT **2 :** WEEP, LAMENT **3 :** to utter a characteristic sound or call **4 :** BEG, BESEECH **5 :** to proclaim publicly **:** call out — **cry havoc :** to sound an alarm — **cry wolf :** to give alarm without occasion

²cry *n, pl* **cries** **1 :** a loud call or shout (as of pain, fear, or joy) **2 :** APPEAL ⟨the *cries* of the poor⟩ **3 :** a fit of weeping **4 :** the characteristic sound uttered by an animal (as a bird) **5 :** SLOGAN, WATCHWORD **6 :** a pack of hounds — **a far cry :** a great distance **:** a great change — **in full cry :** in full pursuit

cry·ba·by \'krī-,bā-bē\ *n* **:** one who cries easily or often

cry down *vt* **:** DISPARAGE, BELITTLE

cry·ing \'krī-iŋ\ *adj* **1 :** calling for attention and correction ⟨a *crying* need⟩ **2 :** NOTORIOUS ⟨a *crying* evil⟩

cry·o·gen·ics \,krī-ə-'jen-iks\ *n* [Gk *kryos* icy cold] **:** a branch of physics that relates to the production and effects of very low temperatures

cry·o·lite \'krī-ə-,līt\ *n* **:** a mineral Na_3AlF_6 consisting of sodium, aluminum, and fluorine found in Greenland and used in making soda and aluminum

cry·o·phil·ic \,krī-ə-'fil-ik\ *adj* **:** thriving at low temperatures

crypt \'kript\ *n* [L *crypta*, fr. Gk *kryptē*, fr. *kryptos* hidden, fr. *kryptein* to hide] **1 :** an underground vault or room; *esp* **:** one under the floor of a church used as a burial place **2 :** a simple gland, glandular cavity, or tube **:** FOLLICLE

cryp·tic \'krip-tik\ *adj* **1 :** HIDDEN, SECRET **2 :** having or seeming to have a hidden meaning ⟨a *cryptic* remark⟩ **3 :** serving to conceal **4 :** employing cipher or code — **cryp·ti·cal·ly** \-ti-k(ə-)lē\ *adv*

cryp·to·gam \'krip-tə-,gam\ *n* [Gk *kryptos* hidden + *gamos* marriage] **:** a plant (as a fern, moss, alga, or fungus) reproducing by spores and not producing flowers or seed — **cryp·to·gam·ic** \,krip-tə-'gam-ik\ *or* **cryp·tog·a·mous** \krip-'täg-ə-məs\ *adj*

cryp·to·gen·ic \,krip-tə-'jen-ik\ *adj* **:** of obscure or unknown origin ⟨a *cryptogenic* disease⟩

cryp·to·gram \'krip-tə-,gram\ *n* [Gk *kryptos* hidden] **:** a writing in cipher or code

cryp·to·graph \-,graf\ *n* **:** CRYPTOGRAM — **cryp·to·graph·ic** \,krip-tə-'graf-ik\ *adj* — **cryp·to·graph·i·cal·ly** \-'graf-i-k(ə-)lē\ *adv*

cryp·tog·ra·phy \krip-'täg-rə-fē\ *n* **:** the enciphering and deciphering of messages in secret code — **cryp·tog·ra·pher** \-fər\ *n*

¹crys·tal \'krist-ᵊl\ *n* [Gk *krystallos* ice, crystal] **1 :** quartz that is transparent or nearly so and that is either colorless or only slightly tinged — called also *rock crystal* **2 :** something resembling crystal in transparency and colorlessness

snow crystals greatly magnified

3 : a body that is formed by the solidification of a substance or mixture and has a regularly repeating internal arrangement of its atoms and often external plane faces ⟨a *crystal* of quartz⟩ ⟨a snow *crystal*⟩ ⟨a salt *crystal*⟩ **4 :** a clear colorless glass of superior quality **5 :** the transparent cover over a watch or clock dial

²crystal *adj* **1 :** consisting of or resembling crystal **:** CLEAR, LUCID **2 :** relating to or using a crystal ⟨a *crystal* radio receiver⟩

crys·tal·line \'kris-tə-lən\ *adj* **1 :** made of crystal or composed of crystals **2 :** resembling crystal **:** TRANSPARENT **3 :** of or relating to a crystal — **crys·tal·lin·i·ty** \,kris-tə-'lin-ət-ē\ *n*

crystalline lens *n* **:** the lens of the vertebrate eye

crys·tal·lize \'kris-tə-,līz\ *vb* **1 :** to cause to form crystals or assume crystalline form **2 :** to give a definite form to ⟨tried to *crystallize* his thoughts⟩ **3 :** to become crystallized — **crys·tal·liz·a·ble** \-,lī-zə-bəl\ *adj* — **crys·tal·li·za·tion** \,kris-tə-lə-'zā-shən\ *n*

crys·tal·log·ra·phy \,kris-tə-'läg-rə-fē\ *n* : a science that deals with the form and structure of crystals — **crys·tal·log·ra·pher** \-fər\ *n* — **crys·tal·lo·graph·ic** \-tə-lō-'graf-ik\ *adj*

crys·tal·loid \'kris-tə-,lóid\ *n* : a substance that forms a true solution and is capable of being crystallized

crystal set *n* : a radio receiver having a crystal for a detector and no vacuum tubes

cten·oid \'ten-,óid, 'tē-,nóid\ *adj* [Gk *kten-, kteis* comb] : having the margin toothed ⟨*ctenoid* scale⟩; *also* : having or consisting of ctenoid scales ⟨*ctenoid* fishes⟩

cteno·phore \'ten-ə-,fōr, -,fór\ *n* : any of a phylum (Ctenophora) of marine animals superficially resembling jellyfishes but having decided biradial symmetry and swimming by means of eight bands of transverse ciliated plates — **cte·noph·o·ran** \ti-'näf-ə-rən\ *adj or n*

cub \'kəb\ *n* **1 a** : a young fox or other carnivorous mammal ⟨bear *cubs*⟩ ⟨lion *cubs*⟩ **b** : a young shark **2** : a young person **3** : APPRENTICE; *esp* : an inexperienced newspaper reporter

cub·by·hole \'kəb-ē-,hōl\ *n* [obs. E *cub* pen] **1** : a snug or confined place (as for hiding) **2** : a small closet, cupboard, or compartment for storing things

¹cube \'kyüb\ *n* [L *cubus,* fr. Gk *kybos*] **1** : the regular solid of six equal square sides **2** : the product obtained by taking a number three times as a factor

²cube *vt* **1** : to raise to the third power **2 a** : to form into a cube **b** : to cut into cubes

cu·beb \'kyü-,beb\ *n* [Ar *kubābah*] : the dried unripe berry of a tropical shrub of the pepper family that is crushed and smoked in cigarettes for catarrh

cube

cube root *n* : a number whose cube is a given number ⟨the *cube root* of 27 is 3⟩

cu·bic \'kyü-bik\ *adj* **1** : having the form of a cube : CUBICAL **2** : being the volume of a cube whose edge is a specified unit — **cu·bic·ly** *adv*

cu·bi·cal \'kyü-bi-kəl\ *adj* **1** : CUBIC; *esp* : shaped like a cube **2** : relating to volume — **cu·bi·cal·ly** \-k(ə-)lē\ *adv*

cubic centimeter *n* : a unit of volume equal to the volume of a cube one centimeter long on each side

cubic foot *n* : a unit of volume equal to the volume of a cube one foot long on each side

cubic inch *n* : a unit of volume equal to the volume of a cube one inch long on each side

cu·bi·cle \'kyü-bi-kəl\ *n* [L *cubiculum,* fr. *cubare* to lie, recline] **1** : a sleeping compartment partitioned off from a large room **2** : a small partitioned space

cubic measure *n* : a unit (as a cubic inch or cubic centimeter) for measuring volume — see MEASURE table, METRIC SYSTEM table

cubic meter *n* : a unit of volume equal to the volume of a cube one meter long on each side

cubic yard *n* : a unit of volume equal to the volume of a cube one yard long on each side

cub·ism \'kyü-,biz-əm\ *n* : a phase of Postimpressionism that stresses abstract form largely by use of intersecting often transparent cubes and cones — **cub·ist** \-bəst\ *adj or n*

cu·bit \'kyü-bət\ *n* [L *cubitus* elbow, cubit; akin to E *hip*] : a unit of length based on the length of the forearm from the elbow to the tip of the middle finger and usu. equal to about 18 inches

cu·boi·dal \kyü-'bóid-³l\ *adj* : somewhat cubical : made up of nearly cubical elements ⟨*cuboidal* epithelium⟩

cub scout *n* : a member of the Boy Scouts of America program for boys of the age range 8–10

cuck·ing stool \'kək-in-\ *n* : a chair formerly used for punishing offenders (as dishonest tradesmen) by public exposure or ducking in water

¹cuck·old \'kək-əld, 'kúk-\ *n* [ME *cokewold*] : a man whose wife is unfaithful — **cuck·old·ry** \-əl-drē\ *n*

²cuckold *vt* : to make a cuckold of

¹cuck·oo \'kük-ü, 'kúk-\ *n, pl* **cuckoos** **1** : a largely grayish brown European bird that lays its eggs in the nests of other birds for them to hatch; *also* : any of various related birds **2** : the call of a cuckoo

²cuckoo *adj* **1** : of or resembling the cuckoo **2** : SILLY, CRAZY

cuckoo spit *n* **1** : a frothy secretion exuded upon plants by the nymphs of spittlebugs **2** : SPITTLEBUG

cu·cul·late \'kyü-kə-,lāt, kyü-'kəl-ət\ *also* **cu·cul·lat·ed** \'kyü-kə-,lāt-əd\ *adj* [L *cucullus* hood] : having the shape of a hood ⟨a *cucullate* leaf⟩ : HOODED

cu·cum·ber \'kyü-(,)kəm-bər\ *n* [MF *cocombre,* fr. L *cucumer-, cucumis*] : the long fleshy many-seeded fruit of a vine of the gourd family grown as a garden vegetable; *also* : this vine

cu·cur·bit \kyü-'kər-bət\ *n* : a plant of the gourd family

cud \'kəd, 'kúd\ *n* [OE *cwudu*] : food brought up into the mouth by a ruminating animal (as a cow) from its rumen to be chewed again

¹cud·dle \'kəd-³l\ *vb* **cud·dled; cud·dling** \'kəd-liŋ, -³l-iŋ\ **1** : to hold close for warmth or comfort or in affection **2** : to lie close : NESTLE, SNUGGLE — **cud·dly** \'kəd-lē, -³l-ē\ *adj*

²cuddle *n* : a close embrace : the act of nestling

¹cud·gel \'kəj-əl\ *n* [OE *cycgel*] : a short heavy club

²cudgel *vt* **-geled** *or* **-gelled; -gel·ing** *or* **-gel·ling** : to beat with or as if with a cudgel — **cudgel one s brains** : to think hard (as for a solution to a problem)

¹cue \'kyü\ *n* [prob. fr. *qu,* abbr. (used as a direction in actors' copies of plays) of L *quando* when] **1** : a word, phrase, or action in a play serving as a signal for the next actor to speak or act **2** : something serving as a signal or suggestion : HINT

²cue *n* [F *queue,* lit., tail, fr. L *cauda*] **1** : QUEUE 2 **2** : a tapering rod for striking a ball in games (as billiards or pool)

cue ball *n* : the ball a player strikes with his cue in billiards and pool

¹cuff \'kəf\ *n* **1** : a part of a sleeve or glove encircling the wrist **2** : the turned-back hem of a trouser leg

²cuff *vt* : to strike esp. with or as if with the palm of the hand : BUFFET

³cuff *n* : a blow with the hand esp. when open : SLAP

cui·rass \kwi-'ras\ *n* [MF *curasse,* fr. LL *coreaceus* leathern, fr. L *corium* skin, leather] **1** : a piece of armor covering the body from neck to girdle; *also* : the breastplate of such a piece **2** : something (as bony plates covering an animal) resembling a cuirass

cuir·as·sier \,kwir-ə-'si(ə)r\ *n* : a mounted soldier wearing a cuirass

cui·sine \kwi-'zēn\ *n* [F, lit., kitchen, fr. LL *coquina,* fr. L *coquere* to cook] : manner of preparing food

cuisse \'kwis\ *n* : a piece of plate armor for the thigh esp. in front

cul·de·sac \,kəl-di-'sak, ,kúl-\ *n, pl* **culs·de·sac** \,kəl(z)-, ,kúl(z)-\ *also* **cul·de·sacs** \,kəl-də-'saks, ,kúl-\ [F, lit., bottom of the bag] **1** : a blind diverticulum or pouch **2** : a street or passage closed at one end

cu·lex \'kyü-,leks\ *n* [L, gnat] : any of a large cosmopolitan genus of mosquitoes that includes the common house mosquito of Europe and No. America — **cu·li·cine** \'kyü-lə-,sīn\ *adj or n*

cul·i·nary \'kəl-ə-,ner-ē, 'kyü-lə-\ *adj* [L *culina* kitchen, fr. *coquere* to cook] : of or relating to the kitchen or cookery

¹cull \'kəl\ *vt* **1** : to select from a group : CHOOSE **2** : to identify and remove the culls from — **cull·er** *n*

²cull *n* : something rejected as inferior or worthless

¹culm \'kəlm\ *n* : refuse coal screenings : SLACK

²culm *n* : a monocotyledonous stem

cul·mi·nate \'kəl-mə-,nāt\ *vi* [ML *culminare,* fr. L *culmin-, culmen* top, summit] : to reach the highest or a climactic or decisive point

cul·mi·na·tion \,kəl-mə-'nā-shən\ *n* **1** : the action of culminating **2** : the culminating position : SUMMIT, CLIMAX

cu·lotte \k(y)ù-'lät\ *n* : a divided skirt or a garment with a divided skirt — often used in pl.

cul·pa·ble \'kəl-pə-bəl\ *adj* [L *culpare* to blame, fr. *culpa* fault, guilt] : deserving condemnation or blame ⟨*culpable* negligence⟩ — **cul·pa·bil·i·ty** \,kəl-pə-'bil-ət-ē\ *n* — **cul·pa·ble·ness** \'kəl-pə-bəl-nəs\ *n* — **cul·pa·bly** \-pə-blē\ *adv*

cul·prit \'kəl-prət, -,prit\ *n* [AF *cul.* (abbr. of *culpable* guilty) + *prest, prit* ready (i.e. to prove it), fr. L *praestus*]

ə abut; ᵊ kitten; ər further; a back; ā bake; ä cot, cart; aú out; ch chin; e less; ē easy; g gift; i trip; ī life

1 : one accused of or charged with a crime **·2 :** one who has committed an offense

cult \'kəlt\ *n* [L *cultus*, fr. *cult-*, *colere* to cultivate, worship] **1 :** formal religious veneration **:** WORSHIP **2 :** a system of religious beliefs and ritual; *also* **:** its body of adherents **3 a :** enthusiastic and usu. temporary devotion to a person, idea, or thing **b :** a group of persons showing such devotion — **cult·ist** \'kəl-təst\ *n*

cul·ti·gen \'kəl-tə-jən\ *n* **:** a cultivated organism (as Indian corn) of a variety or species for which a wild ancestor is unknown

cul·ti·va·ble \'kəl-tə-və-bəl\ *adj* **:** capable of being cultivated — **cul·ti·va·bil·i·ty** \,kəl-tə-və-'bil-ət-ē\ *n*

cul·ti·vat·a·ble \'kəl-tə-,vāt-ə-bəl\ *adj* **:** CULTIVABLE

cul·ti·vate \'kəl-tə-,vāt\ *vt* [ML *cultivare*, fr. *cultivus* cultivated, fr. L *cult-*, *colere* to cultivate] **1 :** to prepare or prepare and use for the raising of crops **:** TILL; *also* **:** to loosen or break up the soil about (growing plants) **2 a :** to foster the growth of (*cultivate* vegetables) **b :** CULTURE 2 **c :** REFINE, IMPROVE (*cultivate* the mind) **3 :** FURTHER, ENCOURAGE (*cultivate* the arts) **4 :** to seek the society of

cul·ti·vat·ed *adj* **1 :** subjected to or produced under cultivation (*cultivated* farms) (*cultivated* fruits) **2 :** REFINED, EDUCATED (*cultivated* speech)

cul·ti·va·tion \,kəl-tə-'vā-shən\ *n* **1 :** the act or art of cultivating; *esp* **:** TILLAGE **2 :** CULTURE, REFINEMENT

cul·ti·va·tor \'kəl-tə-,vāt-ər\ *n* **:** one that cultivates; *esp* **:** an implement to loosen the soil while crops are growing

cul·tur·al \'kəlch-(ə-)rəl\ *adj* **1 :** of or relating to culture **2 :** concerned with the fostering of plant or animal growth — **cul·tur·al·ly** \-ē\ *adv*

¹cul·ture \'kəl-chər\ *n* [L *cultura*, fr. *cult-*, *colere* to cultivate] **1 :** CULTIVATION, TILLAGE **2 a :** the rearing or development of a particular product, stock, or crop (bee *culture*) (the *culture* of grapes) **b :** professional or expert care and training (voice *culture*) **3 :** the improvement of the mind, tastes, and manners through careful training or the refinement so acquired **4 a :** a particular stage of advancement in civilization **b :** the characteristic features of a civilization including its beliefs, its artistic and material products, and its social institutions (ancient Greek *culture*) **5 :** cultivation of living material in prepared nutrient media; *also* **:** a product of such cultivation

²culture *vt* **cul·tured; cul·tur·ing** \'kəlch-(ə-)riŋ\ **1 :** CULTIVATE **2 :** to grow in a prepared medium

cul·tured \'kəl-chərd\ *adj* **1 :** CULTIVATED **2 :** produced under artificial conditions (*cultured* viruses) (*cultured* pearls)

cul·tus \'kəl-təs\ *n* **:** CULT

cul·vert \'kəl-vərt\ *n* **1 :** a drain crossing under a road or railroad **2 :** a conduit for a culvert **3 :** a bridge over a culvert

cum·ber \'kəm-bər\ *vt* **cum·bered; cum·ber·ing** \-b(ə-)riŋ\ [ME *cumbren*] **1 :** to hinder or hamper by being in the way **2 :** to weigh down **:** BURDEN (*cumbered* with cares and responsibilities)

cum·ber·some \'kəm-bər-səm\ *adj* **1 :** CLUMSY, UNWIELDY **2 :** slow-moving **:** LUMBERING — **cum·ber·some·ly** *adv* — **cum·ber·some·ness** *n*

cum·brous \'kəm-brəs\ *adj* **:** CUMBERSOME — **cum·brous·ly** *adv* — **cum·brous·ness** *n*

cum·in \'kəm-ən\ *n* **:** a low plant of the carrot family grown for its aromatic seeds

cum lau·de \kùm-'laùd-ə, -ē; ,kəm-'lòd-ē\ *adv (or adj)* [NL, with praise] **:** with academic distinction (graduated *cum laude*)

cum·mer·bund \'kəm-ər-,bənd\ *n* [Hindi *kamarband*] **:** a broad sash worn as a waistband

cu·mu·late \'kyü-myə-,lāt\ *vb* [L *cumulare*, fr. *cumulus* heap] **:** ACCUMULATE — **cu·mu·la·tion** \,kyü-myə-'lā-shən\ *n*

cu·mu·la·tive \'kyü-myə-lət-iv, -,lāt-\ *adj* **1 a :** increasing (as in force, strength, or amount) by successive additions **b :** composed of a series of increases (*cumulative* evidence) **2 :** increasing in severity with repetition of the offense (*cumulative* penalty) **3 :** bearing interest that must be added to a future payment if not paid when due (*cumulative* stock) **4 :** formed by addition of new material of the same kind (*cumulative* book index) **5 :** allotting to each voter as many votes as there are candidates and allowing him to cast all such votes for one candidate (*cumulative* voting) — **cu·mu·la·tive·ly** *adv* — **cu·mu·la·tive·ness** *n*

cu·mu·lo·nim·bus \,kyü-myə-lō-'nim-bəs\ *n* **:** a cumulus often spread out in the shape of an anvil extending to great heights

cu·mu·lo·stra·tus \-'strāt-əs, -'strat-\ *n* **:** a cumulus whose base extends horizontally as a stratus cloud

cu·mu·lous \'kyü-myə-ləs\ *adj* **:** resembling a cumulus

cu·mu·lus \-ləs\ *n, pl* **cu·mu·li** \-,lī, -,lē\ **1** [L] **:** HEAP, ACCUMULATION **2** [NL, fr. L] **:** a massy cloud form having a flat base and rounded outlines often piled up like a mountain

cu·ne·ate \'kyü-nē-,āt, -nē-ət\ *adj* **:** narrowly triangular with the acute angle toward the base (a *cuneate* leaf) — **cu·ne·ate·ly** *adv*

¹cu·ne·i·form \kyù-'nē-ə-,fòrm, 'kyü-n(ē-)ə-\ *adj* [L *cuneus* wedge] **1 :** having the shape of a wedge **2 :** composed of or written in wedge-shaped characters (*cuneiform* alphabet)

²cuneiform *n* **:** cuneiform writing (as of ancient Assyria and Babylonia)

cun·ner \'kən-ər\ *n* **:** either of two small edible wrasses of the Atlantic

¹cun·ning \'kən-iŋ\ *adj* [ME, fr. prp. of *can* know, can] **1 :** exhibiting skill **2 :** CRAFTY, ARTFUL **3 :** prettily appealing **:** CUTE — **cun·ning·ly** \-iŋ-lē\ *adv*

cuneiform writing

²cunning *n* **1 :** SKILL, DEXTERITY **2 :** SLYNESS, CRAFTINESS (the *cunning* of a fox)

¹cup \'kəp\ *n* [OE *cuppe*, fr. LL *cuppa*, fr. L *cupa* tub] **1 :** an open bowl-shaped drinking vessel usu. with a handle **2 a :** the contents of a cup **b :** the consecrated wine of the Communion **3 :** a large ornamental cup offered as a prize **4 :** something (as the corolla of a flower) resembling a cup **5 :** CUPFUL **6 :** a food served in a cup-shaped vessel (fruit *cup*) — **cup·like** \'kəp-,līk\ *adj* — **in one's cups :** DRUNK

²cup *vt* **cupped; cup·ping 1 :** to treat by cupping **2 a :** to curve into the shape of a cup (*cupped* his hands) **b :** to place in or as if in a cup — **cup·per** *n*

cup·bear·er \'kəp-,bar-ər, -,ber-\ *n* **:** one who has the duty of filling and handing cups of wine

cup·board \'kəb-ərd\ *n* **:** a closet with shelves for cups, dishes, or food; *also* **:** a small closet

cup·cake \'kəp-,kāk\ *n* **:** a small cake baked in a cuplike mold

cu·pel \kyü-'pel, 'kyü-pəl\ *n* **:** a small shallow porous cup esp. of bone ash used in assaying to separate precious metals from lead

cup·ful \'kəp-,fùl\ *n, pl* **cup·fuls** \-,fùlz\ *or* **cups·ful** \'kəps-,fùl\ **1 :** the amount held by a cup **2 :** a half pint **:** eight ounces

cu·pid \'kyü-pəd\ *n* **1** *cap* **:** the Roman god of love **2 :** a winged naked figure of an infant often with a bow and arrow that represents the god Cupid

cu·pid·i·ty \kyü-'pid-ət-ē\ *n* [L *cupiditas*, fr. *cupidus* eager, greedy, fr. *cupere* to desire] **:** excessive desire or longing esp. for wealth **:** GREED

cu·po·la \'kyü-pə-lə, -,lō\ *n* [It, fr. LL *cupula*, dim. of L *cupa* tub] **1 :** a rounded roof or ceiling **2 :** a small structure built on top of a roof

cup·ping *n* **:** an operation of drawing blood to or from the surface of the body by use of a glass vessel evacuated by heat

cu·pric \'k(y)ü-prik\ *adj* [LL *cuprum* copper] **:** of, relating to, or containing bivalent copper

cupric sulfate *n* **:** COPPER SULFATE

cu·prite \'k(y)ü-,prīt\ *n* **:** a mineral Cu_2O that consists of oxide of copper and is an ore of copper

cu·prous \-prəs\ *adj* **:** of, relating to, or containing univalent copper

cu·pule \'kyü-,pyül\ *n* **:** a cup-shaped involucre characteristic of the oak — **cu·pu·late** \'kyü-pyə-,lāt\ *adj*

cur \'kər\ *n* **1 :** a mongrel or inferior dog **2 :** an objectionable often surly or cowardly fellow

cur·a·ble \'kyùr-ə-bəl\ *adj* **:** capable of being cured — **cur·a·bil·i·ty** \,kyùr-ə-'bil-ət-ē\ *n* — **cur·a·ble·ness** \'kyùr-ə-bəl-nəs\ *n* — **cur·a·bly** \-nlē\ *adv*

cu·ra·cy \'kyùr-ə-sē\ *n, pl* **-cies** : the office or term of office of a curate

cu·ra·re *or* **cu·ra·ri** \k(y)ù-'rär-ē\ *n* [Pg & Sp *curare*, fr. Carib *kurari*] : a dried aqueous extract esp. of a tropical American vine used in native arrow poisons and in medicine to produce muscular relaxation

cu·rate \'kyùr-ət\ *n* [ML *curatus*, fr. *cura* cure of souls, fr. L, care] **1** : a clergyman in charge of a parish **2** : a clergyman serving as assistant (as to a rector) in a parish

cu·ra·tive \'kyùr-ət-iv\ *adj* : relating to or used in the cure of diseases — **cu·ra·tive·ly** *adv*

cu·ra·tor \kyù-'rāt-ər, 'kyùr-,āt-\ *n* [L, fr. *curare* to care for, fr. *cura* care] : one that has the care and superintendence of something; *esp* : one in charge esp. of a museum or zoo — **cu·ra·to·ri·al** \,kyùr-ə-'tōr-ē-əl, -'tòr-\ *adj* — **cu·ra·tor·ship** *n*

¹curb \'kərb\ *n* [MF *courbe* curved piece of wood or iron, fr. L *curvus* curved] **1** : a chain or strap on a bit used to restrain a horse **2** : CHECK, RESTRAINT 〈price *curbs*〉 **3** : a frame or a raised edge or margin to strengthen or confine 〈the *curb* of a well〉 **4** : an edging built along a street to form part of a gutter **5** [fr. the fact that it orig. transacted its business on the street] : a market for trading in securities not listed on a stock exchange

²curb *vt* : to control by or furnish with a curb

curb·ing \'kər-biŋ\ *n* **1** : the material for a curb **2** : CURB

curb·stone \'kərb-,stōn\ *n* : a stone forming a curb

cur·cu·lio \(,)kər-'kyü-lē-,ō\ *n* : any of various weevils; *esp* : one that injures fruit

¹curd \'kərd\ *n* [ME] **1** : the thick casein-rich part of coagulated milk **2** : something resembling the curd of milk — **curdy** \-ē\ *adj*

²curd *vb* : COAGULATE, CURDLE

cur·dle \'kərd-°l\ *vb* **cur·dled; cur·dling** \'kərd-liŋ, -°l-iŋ\ **1** : to cause curds to form in **2** : to form curds : COAGULATE **3** : SPOIL, SOUR

¹cure \'kyù(ə)r\ *n* [ML *cura* cure of souls, fr. L, care] **1 a** : spiritual charge : CARE **b** : pastoral charge of a parish **2 a** : recovery or relief from a disease **b** : an agency that cures a disease **c** : a course or period of treatment **d** : SPA **3** : a process or method of curing 〈a brine *cure* for meat〉 — **cure·less** \-ləs\ *adj*

²cure *vb* **1 a** : to restore to health, soundness, or normality **b** : to bring about recovery from **2** : RECTIFY, REMEDY **3** : to prepare by chemical or physical processing for keeping or use 〈*cure* bacon〉 **4** : to undergo a curing process 〈hay *curing* in the sun〉 — **cur·er** \'kyùr-ər\ *n*

syn HEAL : CURE applies to restoring to health after disease; HEAL may also apply to this but more commonly suggests restoring a wounded or sore part to soundness

³cu·ré \kyù-'rā\ *n* [F] : a parish priest

cure–all \'kyù(ə)r-,òl\ *n* : a remedy for all ills : PANACEA

cur·few \'kər-,fyü\ *n* [MF *covrefeu* signal given to bank the hearth fire, curfew, fr. *covrir* to cover + *feu* fire] **1** : an order or regulation requiring persons of a usu. specified class to be off the streets at a stated time **2** : a signal (as the ringing of a bell) to announce the beginning of a curfew **3** : the time when a curfew is sounded

cu·ria \'k(y)ùr-ē-ə\ *n, pl* **cu·ri·ae** \'kyùr-ē-,ē, 'kùr-ē-,ī\ **1** : a division of an ancient Roman tribe **2** : a medieval royal court or court of justice **3** *often cap* : the body of congregations, tribunals, and offices through which the pope governs the Roman Catholic Church — **cu·ri·al** \'kyùr-ē-əl\ *adj*

cu·rie \'kyù(ə)r-(,)ē, kyù-'rē\ *n* [Mme. Marie *Curie* †1934 Polish-French chemist] : a unit quantity of any radioactive element in which 37 billion disintegrations occur per second

cu·rio \'kyùr-ē-,ō\ *n, pl* **-ri·os** : a rare or unusual article : CURIOSITY

cu·ri·os·i·ty \,kyùr-ē-'äs-ət-ē\ *n, pl* **-ties** **1** : an eager desire to learn and often to learn what does not concern one : INQUISITIVENESS **2** : something strange or unusual; *esp* : an object or article valued because of its strangeness or rarity

cu·ri·ous \'kyùr-ē-əs\ *adj* [L *curiosus* careful, inquisitive, fr. *cura* care] **1** : eager to learn 〈a *curious* scholar〉 **2** : marked by inquisitiveness about others' concerns : NOSY **3** : STRANGE, RARE, UNUSUAL 〈*curious* insect〉 **4** : ODD, ECCENTRIC 〈the old man had many *curious* ideas〉 — **cu·ri·ous·ly** *adv* — **cu·ri·ous·ness** *n*

syn INQUISITIVE, PRYING : CURIOUS implies an eager desire to learn or observe that may be either justifiable or objectionable; INQUISITIVE implies habitual curiosity esp. about the personal affairs of others; PRYING implies officious, active inquisitiveness

cu·ri·um \'kyùr-ē-əm\ *n* : a metallic radioactive element artificially produced — see ELEMENT table

¹curl \'kərl\ *vb* [ME *curlen*, fr. *crul* curly] **1** : to form into coils or ringlets **2** : to form into a curved shape : TWIST **3 a** : to grow in coils or spirals **b** : to move in curves or spirals

²curl *n* **1** : a lock of hair that coils : RINGLET **2** : something having a spiral or winding form : COIL **3** : the action of curling : the state of being curled **4** : an abnormal rolling or curling of leaves

curl·er \'kər-lər\ *n* **1** : one that curls; *esp* : a device for putting a curl into hair **2** : a player in the game of curling

cur·lew \'kərl-(y)ü\ *n, pl* **curlews** *or* **curlew** [MF *corlieu*] : any of various largely brownish mostly migratory birds related to the woodcocks and distinguished by long legs and a long slender down-curved bill

curli·cue *also* **curly·cue** \'kər-li-,kyü\ *n* : a fancifully curved or spiral figure

curl·ing \'kər-liŋ\ *n* : a game in which two teams of four men each slide special stones over ice toward a target circle

curly \'kər-lē\ *adj* **curl·i·er; -est** **1** : tending to curl; *also* : having curls **2** : having fibers that undulate without crossing 〈*curly* maple〉 — **curl·i·ness** *n*

cur·mudg·eon \(,)kər-'məj-ən\ *n* **1** *archaic* : an avaricious man : MISER **2** : an irascible old man — **cur·mudg·eon·ly** *adj*

cur·rant \'kər-ənt, 'kə-rənt\ *n* [ME *raison of Coraunte*, lit., raisin of Corinth] **1** : a small seedless raisin grown chiefly in the Levant **2** : the acid edible fruit of several shrubs related to the gooseberries; *also* : a plant bearing currants

cur·ren·cy \'kər-ən-sē, 'kə-rən-\ *n, pl* **-cies** **1 a** : circulation as a medium of exchange **b** : general use or acceptance **2** : coin, government notes, and bank notes circulating as a medium of exchange : money in circulation

¹cur·rent \'kər-ənt, 'kə-rənt\ *adj* [L *currere* to run] **1 a** : presently elapsing **b** : occurring in or belonging to the present time **2** : used as a medium of exchange **3** : generally accepted, used, or practiced **syn** see PREVAILING — **cur·rent·ly** *adv* — **cur·rent·ness** *n*

²current *n* **1 a** : the part of a fluid body moving continuously in a certain direction **b** : the swiftest part of a stream **c** : a strong or forceful flow **2** : general course or movement : TREND **3** : a movement of electricity analogous to the flow of a stream of water; *also* : the rate of such movement

current events *n pl* : contemporary developments in local, national, or world affairs; *also* : the organized study of such developments

cur·ri·cle \'kər-i-kəl, 'kə-ri-\ *n* : a 2-wheeled chaise usu. drawn by 2 horses

cur·ric·u·lum \kə-'rik-yə-ləm\ *n, pl* **-la** \-lə\ *or* **-lums** [L, racecourse, course, fr. *currere* to run] : a course of study; *esp* : the body of courses offered in a school or college or in one of its departments — **cur·ric·u·lar** \-lər\ *adj*

¹cur·ry \'kər-ē, 'kə-rē\ *vt* **cur·ried; cur·ry·ing** [OF *correer* to prepare, curry] **1** : to dress the coat of with a currycomb **2** : to treat (tanned leather) esp. by incorporating oil or grease — **cur·ri·er** *n* — **curry fa·vor** \-'fā-vər\ : to seek to gain favor by flattery or attentions

²cur·ry *also* **cur·rie** \'kər-ē, 'kə-rē\ *n, pl* **curries** [Tamil *kari*] **1** : CURRY POWDER **2** : a food seasoned with curry powder

³curry *vt* **cur·ried; cur·ry·ing** : to flavor or cook with curry

cur·ry·comb \-,kōm\ *n* : a comb with rows of metallic teeth or serrated ridges used esp. to curry horses — **currycomb** *vt*

curry powder *n* : a condiment consisting of ground spices

¹curse \'kərs\ *n* [OE *curs*] **1** : a prayer that harm or injury may come upon someone **2** : a word or an expression used in cursing or swearing **3** : evil or misfortune that comes as if in answer to a curse : a cause of great harm or evil 〈floods are the *curse* of this region〉

²curse *vb* **1 a** : to call upon divine or supernatural power to send injury upon **b** : EXECRATE **2 a** : to use profanely insolent language against : BLASPHEME **b** : to utter imprecations : SWEAR **3** : to bring great evil upon : AFFLICT

cursed \'kər-səd, 'kərst\ *also* **curst** \'kərst\ *adj* : being under or deserving a curse — **cursed·ly** *adv* — **cursedness** *n*

¹cur·sive \'kər-siv\ *adj* [L *curs-, currere* to run] : written or formed with the strokes of the letters joined together and the angles rounded ⟨*cursive* handwriting⟩ — **cursive·ly** *adv* — **cur·sive·ness** *n*

²cursive *n* : a style of printed letter imitating handwriting

cur·sor \'kər-sər\ *n* : a part of a mathematical instrument that moves back and forth on another part

cur·so·ri·al \,kər-'sōr-ē-əl, -'sor-\ *adj* : adapted to running

cur·so·ry \'kərs-(ə-)rē\ *adj* [L *curs-, currere* to run] : rapidly and often superficially performed : HASTY **syn** see SUPERFICIAL — **cur·so·ri·ly** \-(ə-)rə-lē\ *adv* — **cur·so·ri·ness** \-(ə-)rē-nəs\ *n*

curt \'kərt\ *adj* [L *curtus* shortened] : short in language : rudely abrupt or brief ⟨a *curt* reply⟩ — **curt·ly** *adv* — **curt·ness** *n*

cur·tail \(,)kər-'tāl\ *vt* : to shorten or reduce by cutting off the end or a part of **syn** see SHORTEN — **cur·tail·er** *n* — **cur·tail·ment** \-'tāl-mənt\ *n*

¹cur·tain \'kərt-ᵊn\ *n* [OF *curtine*, fr. LL *cortina*, fr. L *cohort-, cohors* enclosure, cohort] **1** : a hanging screen that usu. can be drawn up or back; *esp* : a piece of cloth or other material intended to darken, conceal, or divide or to decorate ⟨window *curtains*⟩ ⟨the *curtain* of a theater stage⟩ **2** : the ascent or descent of a theater curtain **3** : something that covers, conceals, or separates like a curtain — compare IRON CURTAIN

²curtain *vt* **cur·tained; cur·tain·ing** \'kərt-niŋ, -ᵊn-iŋ\ **1** : to furnish with curtains **2** : to veil or shut off with a curtain

curtain call *n* : an appearance by a performer at a final curtain (as of a play) in response to the applause of the audience

curtain raiser *n* : a short play usu. of one scene with few characters used to open a performance

¹curt·sy *or* **curt·sey** \'kərt-sē\ *n, pl* **curtsies** *or* **curtseys** [alter. of *courtesy*] : a bow made esp. by women as a sign of respect that consists of a slight lowering of the body and bending of the knees

²curtsy *or* **curtsey** *vi* **curt·sied** *or* **curt·seyed; curt·sy·ing** *or* **curt·sey·ing** : to make a curtsy

cur·va·ceous \,kər-'vā-shəs\ *adj* : having a well-proportioned feminine figure marked by pronounced curves

cur·va·ture \'kər-və-,chù(ə)r, -chər\ *n* **1** : the act of curving : the state of being curved **2** : a measure or amount of curving **3 a** : an abnormal curving **b** : a curved surface

¹curve \'kərv\ *vb* [L *curvare*, fr. *curvus* curved] **1** : to turn, change, or deviate from a straight line without sharp breaks or angularity **2** : to cause to curve : BEND

²curve *n* **1** : a curving line or surface : BEND **2** : something curved **3** : a ball thrown so that it swerves from its normal course — called also *curve ball* **4** : a line representing information graphically — **curved** \'kərvd\ *adj*

¹cur·vet \(,)kər-'vet\ *n* : a prancing leap of a horse in which first the forelegs and then the hind are raised so that for an instant all the legs are in the air

²curvet *vi* **cur·vet·ted** *or* **cur·vet·ed; cur·vet·ting** *or* **cur·vet·ing** : to make a curvet; *also* : CAPER, PRANCE

cur·vi·lin·e·ar \,kər-və-'lin-ē-ər\ *adj* : consisting of or bounded by curved lines

¹cush·ion \'kùsh-ən\ *n* [MF *coissin*, fr. (assumed) VL *coxinus*, fr. L *coxa* hip] **1** : a soft pillow or pad to rest on or against **2** : something resembling a cushion in use, shape, or softness **3** : a pad of springy rubber along the inside of the rim of a billiard table **4** : something serving to mitigate the effects of disturbances or disorders

²cushion *vt* **cush·ioned; cush·ion·ing** \-(ə-)niŋ\ **1** : to seat or place on a cushion **2** : to furnish with a cushion ⟨*cushion* the bench⟩ **3 a** : to mitigate the effects of ⟨*cushion* the blow⟩ **b** : to shield from harm or injury : PROTECT ⟨*cushioned* the children from harsh realities⟩

Cush·it·ic \,kəsh-'it-ik, kùsh-\ *n* [*Cush* (Kush), ancient country in the Nile valley] : a subfamily of the Afro-Asiatic language family comprising various languages spoken in East Africa and esp. in Ethiopia and Somaliland — **Cushitic** *adj*

cushy \'kùsh-ē\ *adj* **cush·i·er; -est** [Hindi *khush* pleasant, fr. Per *khūsh*] : EASY — **cush·i·ly** \'kùsh-ə-lē\ *adv*

cusk \'kəsk\ *n, pl* **cusk** *or* **cusks** : a large edible marine fish related to the cod

cusp \'kəsp\ *n* [L *cuspis*] : POINT, APEX: as **a** : either of the pointed ends of a crescent moon **b** : a pointed projection formed by or arising from the intersection of two arcs **c** : a point on the grinding surface of a tooth **d** : a fold or flap of a cardiac valve

cus·pid \'kəs-pəd\ *n* : a canine tooth

cus·pi·date \'kəs-pə-,dāt\ *or* **cus·pi·dat·ed** \-,dāt-əd\ *adj* : having a cusp : terminating in a point ⟨a *cuspidate* leaf⟩

cus·pi·dor \'kəs-pə-,dor\ *n* [Pg *cuspidouro*] : SPITTOON

¹cuss \'kəs\ *n* **1** : CURSE **2** : FELLOW ⟨an obstinate *cuss*⟩

²cuss *vb* : CURSE — **cuss·er** *n*

cuss·ed \'kəs-əd\ *adj* **1** : CURSED **2** : PERVERSE, OBSTINATE — **cuss·ed·ly** *adv*

cuss·ed·ness \-əd-nəs\ *n* : disposition to perversity : OBSTINACY

cus·tard \'kəs-tərd\ *n* [ME, a kind of pie] : a sweetened mixture of milk and eggs baked, boiled, or frozen

custard apple *n* **1** : any of several chiefly tropical American soft-fleshed edible fruits; *also* : a tree or shrub bearing this fruit **2** : PAPAW 2

cus·to·di·al \,kə-'stōd-ē-əl\ *adj* : of or relating to custodians or custodianship

cus·to·di·an \,kə-'stōd-ē-ən\ *n* : one that guards and protects or maintains: as **a** : one entrusted with guarding prisoners or inmates **b** : one entrusted with guarding and keeping property or records; *esp* : JANITOR — **cus·to·di·an·ship** \-,ship\ *n*

cus·to·dy \'kəs-təd-ē\ *n* [L *custodia* act of guarding, fr. *custod-, custos* guard] **1** : immediate charge and control exercised by a person or an authority **2** : legal confinement; *esp* : IMPRISONMENT ⟨taken into *custody*⟩

¹cus·tom \'kəs-təm\ *n* [OF *costume, custume*, fr. L *consuetudin-, consuetudo*, fr. *consuetus*, pp. of *consuescere* to accustom, fr. *com-* + *suescere* to accustom] **1 a** : a usage or practice common to many or habitual with an individual **b** : long-established practice considered as unwritten law **c** : the whole body of usages, practices, or conventions that regulate social life **2** *pl* : duties, tolls, or imposts imposed by the law of a country on imports or exports **3 a** : business patronage **b** : CUSTOMERS **syn** see HABIT

²custom *adj* **1** : made or performed according to personal order ⟨*custom* clothes⟩ **2** : specializing in custom work or operation ⟨a *custom* tailor⟩

cus·tom·ary \'kəs-tə-,mer-ē\ *adj* **1** : based on or established by custom ⟨*customary* rent⟩ **2** : commonly practiced or observed : HABITUAL ⟨*customary* courtesy⟩ **syn** see USUAL — **cus·tom·ar·i·ly** \,kəs-tə-'mer-ə-lē\ *adv* — **cus·tom·ar·i·ness** \'kəs-tə-,mer-ē-nəs\ *n*

cus·tom-built \,kəs-təm-'bilt\ *adj* : built to individual order

cus·tom·er \'kəs-tə-mər\ *n* **1** : one that buys from or patronizes esp. regularly the same firm **2** : PERSON, FELLOW ⟨a queer *customer*⟩

cus·tom·house \'kəs-təm-,haùs\ *also* **cus·toms·house** \-təmz-\ *n* : a building where customs and duties are paid or collected and where ships are entered and cleared at a port

cus·tom-made \,kəs-təm-'mād\ *adj* : made to individual order

¹cut \'kət\ *vb* **cut; cut·ting** [ME *cutten*] **1 a** : to penetrate with or as if with an edged instrument : GASH ⟨*cut* his hand with a knife⟩ **b** : to function as or like an edged tool ⟨the knife *cuts* well⟩ **c** : to admit of being shaped or penetrated with an edged tool ⟨cheese *cuts* easily⟩ **d** : to work with or as if with an edged tool ⟨a tailor busy *cutting*⟩ **e** : to experience the growth of (a tooth) through the gum **2 a** : to hurt emotionally **b** : to strike sharply or at an angle ⟨*cut* him across the legs with a whip⟩ ⟨*cut* at the ball but missed⟩ **c** : to have validity or effect ⟨that argument *cuts* both ways⟩ **d** : to cause constriction : CHAFE **3 a** : to make less in amount ⟨*cut* costs⟩ **b** : to shorten by omissions ⟨*cut* a manuscript⟩ **c** : DILUTE ⟨*cut* whiskey with water⟩ **4 a** : MOW, REAP **b** : to divide into parts with an edged tool ⟨*cut* bread⟩ **c** : FELL, HEW

5 : to remove as if with an edged tool ⟨*cut* two players from the squad⟩ **6 a :** to turn sharply ⟨*cut* right to avoid a collision⟩⟨*cut* the wheels⟩ **b :** to move fast ⟨*cut* along the road⟩ **c :** to go straight rather than around ⟨*cut* across the campus⟩ **d :** INTERSECT, CROSS ⟨lines *cutting* other lines⟩ **e :** BREAK, INTERRUPT ⟨*cut* our supply line⟩ **f :** to draw a card from or divide a deck of cards **g :** to divide (as money) into shares : SPLIT **7 a :** STOP ⟨*cut* the nonsense⟩ **b :** to refuse to recognize (an acquaintance) **c :** to fail to attend (as a meeting or class) **d :** to stop (a motor) by opening a switch **e :** to cease photographing a motion picture **8 a :** to make or give shape to with or as if with an edged tool ⟨*cut* a hole in the wall⟩⟨the floodwaters *cut* new channels⟩⟨*cut* a diamond⟩ **b :** to record sounds on (a phonograph record) **9 a :** to engage in : PERFORM ⟨*cut* a caper⟩ **b :** to give the appearance of ⟨*cuts* a fine figure⟩
²cut *n* **1 :** something cut or cut off: as **a :** an agricultural yield (as of one harvest) **b :** a part of a meat carcass ⟨a rib *cut*⟩ **c :** an allotted part : SHARE ⟨took his *cut* and left⟩ **2 :** an effect produced by or as if by cutting: as **a :** a wound made by something sharp : GASH **b :** a surface or outline made by cutting ⟨a smooth *cut* in a board⟩ **c :** a passage made by cutting ⟨a railroad *cut*⟩ **d :** a grade or step esp. in a social scale ⟨a *cut* above his neighbors⟩ **e :** a pictorial illustration **3 :** the act or an instance of cutting: as **a :** a gesture or expression that wounds the feelings ⟨an unkind *cut*⟩ **b :** a straight path or course **c :** a cutting stroke or blow ⟨took a *cut* at the ball⟩ **d :** RE-DUCTION ⟨a *cut* in pay⟩ **e :** the act of or a turn at cutting cards ⟨it's your *cut*⟩ **4 :** a voluntary absence from a class **5 :** an abrupt transition from one sound or image to another in motion pictures, radio, or television **6 :** the shape and style in which a thing is cut, formed, or made ⟨clothes of the latest *cut*⟩
cut-and-dried \ˌkət-ᵊn-ˈdrīd\ *adj* **:** according to a plan, set procedure, or formula **:** ROUTINE
cu·ta·ne·ous \kyu̇-ˈtā-nē-əs\ *adj* [L *cutis* skin] **:** of, relating to, or affecting the skin ⟨*cutaneous* infection⟩ — **cu·ta·ne·ous·ly** *adv*
¹cut·away \ˈkət-ə-ˌwā\ *adj* **:** having or showing parts cut away ⟨*cutaway* model⟩
²cutaway *n* **1 :** a coat with skirts tapering from the front waistline to form tails at the back **2 :** a cutaway picture or representation
cut back \ˈkət-ˈbak, ˌkət-\ *vb* **1 :** PRUNE **2 :** REDUCE, DECREASE ⟨*cut back* production⟩ **3 :** to interrupt the sequence of a plot by introducing events prior to those last presented
cut·back \ˈkət-ˌbak\ *n* **1 :** something cut back **2 :** RE-DUCTION
cut down *vb* **1 :** to remake in a smaller size ⟨*cut down* the child's coat⟩ **2 :** to strike down by or as if by cutting **3 a :** REDUCE ⟨*cut down* the accident rate⟩ **b :** to reduce or curtail volume or activity ⟨*cut down* on his smoking⟩
cute \ˈkyüt\ *adj* [short for *acute*] **1 :** CLEVER, SHREWD **2 :** attractive or pretty esp. by reason of daintiness or delicacy **3 :** obviously straining for effect — **cute·ly** *adv* — **cute·ness** *n*
cut glass *n* **:** glass ornamented by cutting and polishing
cu·ti·cle \ˈkyüt-i-kəl\ *n* [L *cuticula*, dim. of *cutis* skin; akin to E ³*hide*] **1 :** SKIN, PELLICLE: as **a :** an external sheathing layer secreted usu. by epidermal cells **b :** the epidermis when it is the outermost layer **c :** a thin continuous fatty film on the external surface of many higher plants **2 :** dead or horny epidermis — **cu·tic·u·lar** \kyu̇-ˈtik-yə-lər\ *adj*
cut in *vb* **1 :** to thrust oneself into a position between others or belonging to another **2 :** to join in something suddenly ⟨*cut in* on the conversation⟩ **3 :** to interrupt a dancing couple and take one of them as a partner **4 :** IN-CLUDE ⟨*cut* me *in* on the profits⟩
cu·tin \ˈkyüt-ᵊn\ *n* **:** an insoluble material containing waxes, fatty acids, soaps, and resinous matter that forms a continuous layer on the outer epidermal wall of a plant — **cu·tin·ized** \-ᵊn-ˌīzd\ *adj*
cu·tis \ˈkyüt-əs\ *n, pl* **cu·tes** \ˈkyü-ˌtēz\ *or* **cu·tis·es** [L] **:** DERMIS
cut·lass \ˈkət-ləs\ *n* [MF *coutelas*, aug. of *coutel* knife, fr. L *cultellus*, dim. of *culter* plowshare, knife] **:** a short curved sword formerly used by sailors on warships
cut·ler \ˈkət-lər\ *n* [MF *coutelier*, fr. LL *cultellarius*, fr. L

cultellus knife] **:** one who makes, deals in, or repairs cutlery
cut·lery \ˈkət-lə-rē\ *n, pl* **-ler·ies** **1 :** edged or cutting tools; *esp* **:** implements for cutting and eating food **2 :** the business of a cutler
cut·let \ˈkət-lət\ *n* [F *côtelette*, dim. of *côte* rib, side, fr. L *costa*] **1 :** a small slice of meat broiled or fried **2 :** a piece of food shaped like a cutlet
cut off \ˌkət-ˈȯf, ˈkət-\ *vt* **1 :** to strike off : SEVER **2 :** to kill usu. suddenly or prematurely **3 :** to stop the passage of ⟨*cut off* our supplies⟩ **4 :** SEPARATE, ISOLATE ⟨*cut off* by the sudden attack⟩ **5 :** DISINHERIT **6 a :** to stop the operation of ⟨*cut off* a motor⟩ **b :** to stop or interrupt while in communication ⟨operator *cut* me *off*⟩
cut·off \ˈkət-ˌȯf\ *n* **1 :** the action or act of cutting off **2 a :** the channel formed when a stream cuts through the neck of an oxbow **b :** SHORTCUT **3 :** a device for cutting off — **cutoff** *adj*
¹cut out \ˌkət-ˈau̇t, ˈkət-\ *vb* **1 :** to form or shape by or as if cutting ⟨*cut out* a pattern⟩ **2 :** to determine or assign through necessity ⟨his work is *cut out* for him⟩ **3 :** to take the place of : SUPPLANT ⟨*cut* her other boyfriends *out*⟩ **4 :** to remove from a series or circuit : DIS-CONNECT **5 :** to cease operating ⟨the engine *cut out*⟩ **6 :** to swerve out of a traffic lane
²cut out *adj* **:** naturally fitted ⟨was just not *cut out* to be a lawyer⟩
cut-out \ˈkət-ˌau̇t\ *n* **1 :** something cut out or prepared for cutting out from something else ⟨a page of animal *cut-outs*⟩ **2 :** one that cuts out — **cutout** *adj*
cut·over \ˌkət-ˌō-vər\ *adj* **:** having most of its salable timber cut ⟨*cutover* land⟩
cut·purse \ˈkət-ˌpərs\ *n* **:** PICKPOCKET
cut-rate \ˈkət-ˈrāt\ *adj* **1 :** marked by, offering, or making use of a reduced rate or price ⟨a *cut-rate* store⟩ **2 :** SECOND-RATE, CHEAP
cut·ter \ˈkət-ər\ *n* **1 :** one that cuts ⟨a diamond *cutter*⟩ ⟨a cookie *cutter*⟩ **2 a :** a boat used by warships for carrying passengers and stores to and from the shore **b :** a small one-masted sailing boat **c :** a small armed boat in the coast guard **3 :** a small sleigh
¹cut·throat \ˈkət-ˌthrōt\ *n* **:** MURDERER
²cutthroat *adj* **1 :** MURDEROUS, CRUEL ⟨a *cutthroat* rogue⟩ **2 :** MERCILESS, RUTHLESS ⟨*cutthroat* competition⟩
cut time *n* **:** ALLA BREVE
¹cut·ting *n* **1 :** something cut or cut off or out: as **a :** a section of a plant capable of developing into a new plant **b :** HARVEST **2 :** something made by cutting; *esp* **:** RE-CORDING
²cutting *adj* **:** given to or designed for cutting: as **a :** EDGED, SHARP **b :** marked by sharp piercing cold ⟨*cutting* wind⟩ **c :** wounding the feelings of others : SAR-CASTIC ⟨could make the most *cutting* remarks in a sweet voice⟩ **d :** INTENSE ⟨*cutting* pain⟩ **syn** see INCISIVE — **cut·ting·ly** \-iŋ-lē\ *adv*
cut·tle·bone \ˈkət-ᵊl-ˌbōn\ *n* [ME *cotul* cuttlefish, fr. OE *cudele*] **:** the shell of cuttlefishes used for making polishing powder or for supplying cage birds with lime and salts
cut·tle·fish \-ˌfish\ *n* [ME *cotul* cuttlefish] **:** a 10-armed marine mollusk differing from the related squid in having a calcified internal shell
cut·ty sark \ˌkət-ē-ˌsärk\ *n* **1** *chiefly Scot* **:** a short garment **2** *chiefly Scot* **:** WOMAN, HUSSY
cut up \ˌkət-ˈəp, ˈkət-\ *vb* **1 a :** to cut or be cut into parts or pieces **b :** to distress deeply ⟨*cut up* by her criticism⟩ **2 :** to damage by or as if by cutting ⟨the truck *cut up* his lawn⟩ **3 :** to clown or act boisterously
cut-up \ˈkət-ˌəp\ *n* **:** one who clowns or acts boisterously
cut·wa·ter \ˈkət-ˌwȯt-ər, -ˌwät-\ *n* **:** the forepart of a ship's stem
cut·worm \-ˌwərm\ *n* **:** any of various smooth-bodied moth larvae that hide by day and feed on plants at night

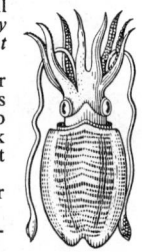

cuttlefish

-cy \sē\ *n suffix, pl* **-cies** [OF *-cie*, fr. L *-tia*, partly fr. *-t-* (final stem consonant) + *-ia* -y, partly fr. Gk *-tia*, *-teia*, fr. *-t-* (final stem consonant) + *-ia*, *-eia* -y] **:** action **:** practice ⟨mendican*cy*⟩ **:** rank **:** office ⟨baronet*cy*⟩

ə abut; ᵊ kitten; ər further; a back; ā bake; ä cot, cart; au̇ out; ch chin; e less; ē easy; g gift; i trip; ī life

⟨chaplain*cy*⟩ : body : class ⟨magistra*cy*⟩ : state : quality ⟨accura*cy*⟩ ⟨bankrupt*cy*⟩ — often replacing a final *-t* or *-te* of the base word

cyan- *or* **cyano-** *comb form* [Gk *kyanos* dark blue enamel] **1** : dark blue : blue ⟨*cyan*ic⟩ **2** : cyanogen ⟨*cyan*ide⟩ **3** : cyanide

cy·an·a·mide *also* **cy·an·a·mid** \sī-'an-ə-məd\ *n* **1** : an acidic compound CH_2N_2 that consists of carbon, hydrogen, and nitrogen and is obtained in various ways **2** : a grayish black lumpy or powdered substance $CaCN_2$ that consists of calcium, carbon, and nitrogen, is made from nitrogen and calcium carbide, and is used as a fertilizer and weed killer — called also *calcium cyanamide*

cy·an·ic \sī-'an-ik\ *adj* : of a blue or bluish color

1cy·a·nide \'sī-ə-,nīd, -nəd\ *n* : a compound of cyanogen with an element or another radical: as **a** : POTASSIUM CYANIDE **b** : SODIUM CYANIDE

2cy·a·nide \-,nīd\ *vt* : to treat with a cyanide

cy·an·o·gen \sī-'an-ə-jən\ *n* **1** : a univalent radical −CN that consists of carbon and nitrogen and is present in simple and complex cyanides **2** : a colorless flammable poisonous gas $(CN)_2$ having an odor of crushed peach leaves

cy·a·no·sis \,sī-ə-'nō-səs\ *n* : a bluish or purplish discoloration (as of skin) due to deficient oxygenation of the blood — **cy·a·nosed** \'sī-ə-,nōzd, -,nōst\ *adj* — **cy·a·not·ic** \,sī-ə-'nät-ik\ *adj*

Cyb·e·le \'sib-ə-lē\ *n* : a nature goddess of the ancient peoples of Asia Minor

cy·ber·net·ics \,sī-bər-'net-iks\ *n* : comparative study of the automatic control system formed by the nervous system and brain and by mechanical-electrical communication systems — **cy·ber·net·ic** *adj*

cy·cad \'sī-kəd\ *n* : any of a family of tropical gymnospermous plants resembling palms — **cy·ca·de·an** \,sī-kə-'dē-ən\ *adj* — **cy·cadi·form** \sī-'kad-ə-,fȯrm\ *adj*

cycl- *or* **cyclo-** *comb form* [Gk *kyklos*] : circle ⟨*cyclo*meter⟩

cy·cla·men \'sī-klə-mən, 'sik-lə-\ *n* : any of a genus of plants of the primrose family grown as pot plants for their showy nodding flowers

1cy·cle \'sī-kəl, 6 *also* 'sik-əl\ *n* [Gk *kyklos*, lit., wheel, circle; akin to E *wheel*] **1** : a period of time taken up by a series of events or actions that repeat themselves regularly and in the same order ⟨the *cycle* of the seasons⟩ **2 a** : a course or series of events or operations that recur regularly and usu. lead back to the starting point ⟨the *cycle* of the blood from the heart, through the blood vessels, and back again⟩ **b** : one complete performance of a series of recurring events; *esp* : one complete series of changes of value of an alternating electric current **3** : a circular or spiral arrangement; *esp* : WHORL **4** : a long period of time : AGE **5 a** : a group of poems, plays, novels, or songs treating the same theme **b** : a series of narratives dealing typically with the exploits of a legendary hero **6 a** : BICYCLE **b** : TRICYCLE **c** : MOTORCYCLE — **cy·clic** \'sī-klik, 'sik-lik\ *or* **cy·cli·cal** \'sī-kli-kəl, 'sik-li-\ *adj* — **cy·cli·cal·ly** \-k(ə-)lē\ *adv*

2cy·cle \'sī-kəl, 2 *also* 'sik-əl\ *vb* **cy·cled**; **cy·cling** \'sī-k(ə-)liŋ, 'sik-(ə)-\ **1 a** : to pass or cause to go through a cycle **b** : to recur in cycles **2** : to ride a cycle — **cy·cler** \'sī-k(ə-)lər, 'sik-(ə)-\ *n*

cy·clist \'sī-k(ə-)ləst, 'sik-(ə)-\ *n* : one who rides a cycle and esp. a bicycle

1cy·cloid \'sī-,klȯid\ *n* : a curve generated by a point on the circumference of a circle that is rolling along a straight line — **cy·cloi·dal** \sī-'klȯid-ə¹l\ *adj*

2cycloid *adj* **1** : CIRCULAR; *esp* : arranged or progressing in circles **2** : smooth with concentric lines of growth ⟨*cycloid* scales⟩; *also* : having or consisting of cycloid scales **3** : CYCLOTHYMIC

cy·clom·e·ter \sī-'kläm-ət-ər\ *n* : a device designed to record revolutions of a wheel and often used to register distance traversed by a wheeled vehicle

cy·clone \'sī-,klōn\ *n* [Gk *kykloun* to go around, fr. *kyklos* circle] **1** : a storm or system of winds that rotates about a center of low atmospheric pressure counterclockwise in the northern hemisphere, advances at a speed of 20 to 30 miles an hour, and often brings abundant rain **2** : TORNADO — **cy·clon·ic** \sī-'klän-ik\ *adj* — **cy·clon·i·cal·ly** \-'klän-i-k(ə-)lē\ *adv*

cy·clo·pe·an \,sī-klə-'pē-ən, sī-'klō-pē-\ *adj* **1** *often cap*

: of, relating to, or characteristic of a Cyclops **2** : HUGE, MASSIVE

cy·clo·pe·dia *or* **cy·clo·pae·dia** \,sī-klə-'pēd-ē-ə\ *n* : ENCYCLOPEDIA — **cy·clo·pe·dic** \-'pēd-ik\ *adj*

cy·clops \'sī-,kläps\ *n* [Gk *Kyklōps*, fr. *kyklos* circle + *ōps* eye] **1** *pl* **cy·clo·pes** \sī-'klō-(,)pēz\ *cap* : one of a race of giants in Greek mythology with a single eye in the middle of the forehead **2** *pl* **cyclops** : WATER FLEA

cy·clo·ra·ma \,sī-klə-'ram-ə, -'räm-\ *n* [*cycl-* + *-orama* (as in *panorama*)] : a large pictorial representation encircling the spectator and often having real objects as a foreground — **cy·clo·ram·ic** \-'ram-ik\ *adj*

cy·clo·sis \sī-'klō-səs\ *n* : the streaming of protoplasm within a cell

cy·clo·stome \'sī-klə-,stōm\ *n* : any of a class (Cyclostomi or Cyclostomata) of lowly craniate vertebrates with a large sucking mouth and no jaws — **cyclostome** *adj*

cy·clo·thy·mia \,sī-klə-'thī-mē-ə\ *n* : a temperament marked by alternate lively and depressed moods — **cy·clo·thy·mic** \-'thī-mik\ *adj*

cy·clo·tron \'sī-klə-,trän\ *n* : a device for giving high speeds to charged particles by means of the combined action of a large magnetic force and a rapidly oscillating electric force

cyg·net \'sig-nət\ *n* [L *cycnus*, *cygnus* swan, fr. Gk *kyknos*] : a young swan

Cyg·nus \'sig-nəs\ *n* [L, lit., swan] : a northern constellation between Lyra and Pegasus in the Milky Way

cyl·in·der \'sil-ən-dər\ *n* [Gk *kylindros*, fr. *kylindein* to roll] **1** : the surface traced by a straight line moving parallel to a fixed straight line and intersecting a fixed curve; *also* : the space bounded by any such surface and two parallel planes cutting all the elements **2** : a long round solid or hollow body (as the piston chamber of an engine, the barrel of a pump, or the part of a revolver which turns and holds the cartridges) — **cyl·in·dered** \-dərd\ *adj*

cy·lin·dri·cal \sə-'lin-dri-kəl\ *or* **cy·lin·dric** \-drik\ *adj* : of, relating to, or having the form or properties of a cylinder — **cy·lin·dri·cal·ly** \-dri-k(ə-)lē\ *adv*

cylinder 1

cym·bal \'sim-bəl\ *n* [OE, fr. L *cymbalum*, fr. Gk *kymbalon*, fr. *kymbē* bowl] : a concave brass plate that produces a brilliant clashing tone and that is struck with a drumstick or is used in pairs struck glancingly together — **cym·bal·ist** \-bə-ləst\ *n*

cym·bid·i·um \sim-'bid-ē-əm\ *n* : any of a genus of tropical Old World orchids with showy boat-shaped flowers

cyme \'sīm\ *n* [L *cyma* cabbage sprout, fr. Gk *kyma* swell, cabbage sprout, fr. *kyein* to be pregnant] : a broad branching often flat-topped determinate inflorescence with a single flower at the end of each branch and with the individual flowers opening in sequence from the center toward the margin of the cluster — see INFLORESCENCE illustration — **cy·mose** \'sī-,mōs\ *adj*

1Cym·ric \'kəm-rik, 'kim-\ *adj* **1** : of, relating to, or characteristic of the non-Gaelic Celtic people of Britain or their language **2** : WELSH

2Cymric *n* **1** : the non-Gaelic Celtic languages **2** : WELSH **2**

cyn·ic \'sin-ik\ *n* [Gk *kynikos*, fr. *kynikos* like a dog, fr. *kyn-, kyōn* dog; akin to E *hound*] **1** *cap* : an adherent or advocate of the view held by some ancient Greek philosophers that virtue is the only good and that its essence lies in self-control and independence **2** : one who believes that human conduct is motivated wholly by self-interest — **cynic** *adj*

cyn·i·cal \'sin-i-kəl\ *adj* : having the attitude or temper of a cynic; *esp* : contemptuously distrustful of human nature and motives ⟨made *cynical* remarks about politicians⟩ — **cyn·i·cal·ly** \-k(ə-)lē\ *adv*

syn MISANTHROPIC, PESSIMISTIC: CYNICAL implies having a sneering disbelief in sincerity or nobility esp. in human motives; MISANTHROPIC suggests a rooted distrust and dislike of people in general and habitual discomfort in their society; PESSIMISTIC implies having a gloomy, distrustful view of things in general and esp. of the future

cyn·i·cism \'sin-ə-,siz-əm\ *n* **1** *cap* : the doctrine of the

---

j joke;　ŋ sing;　ō flow;　ȯ flaw;　ȯi coin;　th thin;　t̲h̲ this;　ü loot;　u̇ foot;　y yet;　yü few;　yu̇ furious;　zh vision

Cynics **2 a :** cynical character or quality **b :** an expression of such quality ⟨pungent *cynicisms*⟩

cy·no·sure \'sī-nə-,shùr, 'sin-ə-\ *n* [Gk *Kynosoura* Ursa Minor, fr. *kynos oura* dog's tail] **1** *cap* **:** the northern constellation Ursa Minor; *also* **:** NORTH STAR **2 :** a center of attraction or attention ⟨the *cynosure* of all eyes⟩

cy·pher *chiefly Brit var of* CIPHER

cy·press \'sī-prəs\ *n* [OF *ciprès*, fr. L *cyparissus*, fr. Gk *kyparissos*] **1 a :** any of a genus of symmetrical mostly evergreen trees of the pine family with overlapping scale-like leaves **b :** any of several related trees; *esp* **:** either of two large swamp trees of the southern U.S. with hard red wood used for shingles **c :** the wood of a cypress tree **2 :** branches of cypress used as a symbol of mourning

cyp·ri·pe·di·um \,sip-rə-'pēd-ē-əm\ *n* **:** any of a genus of leafy-stemmed terrestrial orchids having large usu. showy drooping flowers with the lip inflated or pouched

Cy·ril·lic \sə-'ril-ik\ *adj* [St. *Cyril* d869, apostle of the Slavs and reputed inventor of the Cyrillic alphabet] **:** of, relating to, or constituting an alphabet used for writing Old Church Slavonic and for Russian and various other Slavic languages

cyst \'sist\ *n* [Gk *kystis* bladder, pouch] **1 :** a closed sac developing abnormally in a cavity or structure of the body **2 :** a covering resembling a cyst or a body (as a spore) with such a covering

cys·tic \'sis-tik\ *adj* **1 :** of, relating to, or containing cysts **2 :** of or relating to the urinary bladder or the gallbladder

cys·ti·cer·coid \,sis-tə-'sər-,kòid\ *n* **:** a larval tapeworm having an invaginated scolex and solid tailpiece

cys·ti·cer·cus \-'sər-kəs\ *n, pl* **-ci** \-'sər-,sī\ [Gk *kystis* pouch + *kerkos* tail] **:** a tapeworm larva consisting of a scolex invaginated in a fluid-filled sac

cystic fibrosis *n* **:** an hereditary glandular disease that appears usu. in early childhood and is marked esp. by deficiency of pancreatic enzymes, respiratory symptoms, and excessive loss of salt in the sweat

cys·tine \'sis-,tēn\ *n* **:** an amino acid $C_6H_{12}N_2O_4S_2$ widespread in proteins (as keratins)

cys·ti·tis \sis-'tīt-əs\ *n* **:** inflammation of the urinary bladder

cys·to·scope \'sis-tə-,skōp\ *n* **:** an instrument for the visual examination of and passage of instruments into the bladder — **cys·to·scop·ic** \,sis-tə-'skäp-ik\ *adj*

cyt- *or* **cyto-** *comb form* [Gk *kytos* hollow vessel] **:** cell ⟨*cyto*logy⟩

-cyte \,sīt\ *n comb form* [Gk *kytos* hollow vessel] **:** cell ⟨leuco*cyte*⟩

cy·to·chem·is·try \,sīt-ō-'kem-ə-strē\ *n* **:** the chemistry of cells

cy·to·chrome \'sīt-ə-,krōm\ *n* **:** any of several iron-containing pigments prominent in intracellular oxidations

cy·to·ge·net·ics \,sīt-ə-jə-'net-iks\ *n* **:** a branch of biology that deals with the study of heredity and variation by the methods of both cytology and genetics — **cy·to·ge·net·ic** \-ik\ *or* **cy·to·ge·net·i·cal** \-'net-i-kəl\ *adj* — **cy·to·ge·net·i·cal·ly** \-i-k(ə-)lē\ *adv* — **cy·to·ge·net·i·cist** \-'net-ə-səst\ *n*

cy·tol·o·gy \sī-'täl-ə-jē\ *n* **1 :** a branch of biology dealing with the structure, function, pathology, and life history of cells **2 :** the cytological aspects of a process or structure — **cy·to·log·i·cal** \,sīt-ᵊl-'äj-i-kəl\ *or* **cy·to·log·ic** \-'äj-ik\ *adj* — **cy·to·log·i·cal·ly** \-'äj-i-k(ə-)lē\ *adv* — **cy·tol·o·gist** \sī-'täl-ə-jəst\ *n*

cy·to·plasm \'sīt-ə-,plaz-əm\ *n* **:** the protoplasm of a protoplast external to the nuclear membrane — **cy·to·plas·mic** \,sīt-ə-'plaz-mik\ *adj* — **cy·to·plas·mi·cal·ly** \-mi-k(ə-)lē\ *adv*

cy·to·sine \'sīt-ə-,sēn\ *n* **:** a pyrimidine base regularly present in the polynucleotide chain of deoxyribonucleic acid and ribonucleic acid

czar \'zär\ *n* [obs. Pol, fr. Russ *tsar'*, fr. Goth *kaisar*, fr. L *Caesar*, title of Roman emperors] **1 :** the ruler of Russia until the 1917 revolution **2 :** one having great power or authority ⟨baseball *czar*⟩ — **czar·dom** \'zärd-əm\ *n* — **czar·ism** \'zär-,iz-əm\ *n* — **czar·ist** \'zär-əst\ *adj or n*

cza·ri·na \zä-'rē-nə\ *n* **1 :** the wife of a czar **2 :** a woman who has the rank of czar in her own right

Czech \'chek\ *n* **1 :** a native or inhabitant of Czechoslovakia; *esp* **:** a native or inhabitant of Bohemia, Moravia,

or Silesia provinces **2 :** the Slavic language of the Czechs — **Czech** *adj* — **Czech·ish** \-ish\ *adj*

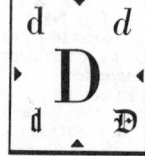

d \'dē\ *n, often cap* **1 :** the 4th letter of the English alphabet **2 :** the roman numeral 500 **3 :** the musical tone D **4 :** a grade rating a student's work as poor

'd \d, əd\ *vb* **1 :** HAD ⟨he'd gone⟩ **2 a :** WOULD ⟨he'd go⟩ **b :** SHOULD ⟨I'd go⟩

¹dab \'dab\ *n* [ME *dabbe*] **1 :** a sudden blow or thrust **:** POKE **2 :** a gentle touch or stroke **:** PAT

²dab *vb* **dabbed; dab·bing 1 :** to strike or touch lightly ⟨*dabs* at her eyes with a handkerchief⟩ **2 :** to apply lightly or irregularly **:** DAUB — **dab·ber** *n*

³dab *n* **1 :** DAUB **2 :** a small amount

⁴dab *n* [AF *dabbe*] **:** FLATFISH; *esp* **:** any of several flounders

dab·ble \'dab-əl\ *vb* **dab·bled; dab·bling** \'dab-(ə-)liŋ\ **1 :** to wet by splashing **:** SPATTER **2 a :** to paddle or play in or as if in water **b :** to reach with the bill to the bottom of shallow water to obtain food **3 :** to work or concern oneself lightly or superficially — **dab·bler** \-(ə-)lər\ *n*

dab·chick \'dab-,chik\ *n* [prob. irreg. fr. obs. E *dop* to dive + E *chick*] **:** any of several small grebes

da ca·po \dä-'käp-ō\ *adv (or adj)* [It] **:** from the beginning — used as a direction in music to repeat

dace \'dās\ *n, pl* **dace** [MF *dars*] **:** a small freshwater European fish related to the carp; *also* **:** any of various similar No. American fishes

da·cha \'däch-ə\ *n* **:** a Russian country house

dachs·hund \'däks-,hùnt\ *n, pl* **dachs·hunds** *or* **dachs·hun·de** \-,hùn-də\ [G, lit., badger dog] **:** a small dog of a breed of German origin with a long body, short legs, and long drooping ears

Da·cron \'dā-,krän, 'dak-,rän\ *trademark* **1 :** — used for a synthetic textile fiber consisting of a complex ester and having great resilience **2 :** a yarn or fabric made of Dacron fiber

dac·tyl \'dak-tᵊl\ *n* [L *dactylus* foot of one long syllable followed by two short syllables, fr. Gk *daktylos*, lit., finger; fr. the fact that the three syllables have the first one longest like the joints of the finger] **:** a metrical foot consisting of one accented syllable followed by two unaccented syllables (as in *tenderly*) — **dac·tyl·ic** \dak-'til-ik\ *adj*

dad \'dad\ *n* **:** FATHER

dad·dy \'dad-ē\ *n, pl* **daddies :** FATHER

dad·dy long·legs \,dad-ē-'lòn,-legz\ *n* **:** any of various animals with long slender legs: as **a :** CRANE FLY **b :** HARVESTMAN

da·do \'dād-ō\ *n, pl* **dadoes** [It, die, plinth] **1 :** the part of a pedestal of a column between the base and the top moldings **2 :** the lower part of an interior wall when specially decorated or faced

Dae·da·lus \'ded-ᵊl-əs\ *n* **:** the builder of the Cretan labyrinth according to Greek legend and inventor of wings whereby he and his son Icarus escaped imprisonment

daemon *var of* DEMON

daf·fo·dil \'daf-ə-,dil\ *n* [prob. fr. D *de affodil* the asphodel] **:** any of a genus of bulbous herbs with long slender leaves and yellow, white, or pinkish flowers borne in spring; *esp* **:** one with flowers whose corolla bears a trumpet-shaped corona — compare JONQUIL

daf·fy \'daf-ē\ *adj* **daf·fi·er; -est** *slang* **:** CRAZY, FOOLISH

daft \'daft\ *adj* [ME *dafte* gentle, stupid] **1 :** SILLY, FOOLISH **2 :** MAD, INSANE — **daft·ly** *adv* — **daft·ness** \'daf(t)-nəs\ *n*

dag·ger \'dag-ər\ *n* [ME] **1 :** a short weapon for stabbing **2 a :** something that resembles a dagger **b :** a character † used as a reference mark or to indicate a death date

da·guerre·o·type \də-'ger-(ē-)ə-,tīp\ *n* [after L. J. M. *Daguerre* d1851 French

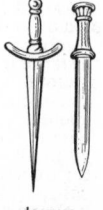

daggers

painter who invented it] **:** an early photograph produced on a silver or a silver-covered copper plate; *also* **:** the process of producing such pictures

dahl·ia \'dal-yə, 'däl-\ *n* [NL, fr. Anders *Dahl* d1789 Swedish botanist] **:** any of a genus of American tuberous-rooted herbs related to the daisies that have opposite pinnate leaves and bright-rayed flower heads

¹dai·ly \'dā-lē\ *adj* **1 a :** occurring, done, produced, or used every day or every weekday ⟨*daily* newspaper⟩ **b :** of or relating to every day ⟨*daily* visitor⟩ **2 :** computed in terms of one day ⟨*daily* wages⟩ — **daily** *adv*

²daily *n, pl* **dailies :** a newspaper published every weekday

daily double *n* **:** a system of betting on races in which the bettor must pick the winners of two stipulated races in order to win

dai·mon \'dī-,mōn\ *n, pl* **dai·mo·nes** \'dī-mə-,nēz\ *or* **dai·mons :** DEMON 1, 3 — **dai·mon·ic** \dī-'män-ik\ *adj*

dai·myo *or* **dai·mio** \'dī-mē-,ō\ *n, pl* **daimyos** *or* **daimios** [Jap *daimyō*] **:** a Japanese feudal baron

¹dain·ty \'dānt-ē\ *n, pl* **dainties** [OF *deintié*, fr. L *dignitat-, dignitas* dignity, worth] **:** something delicious to the taste **:** DELICACY

²dainty *adj* **dain·ti·er; -est 1 :** pleasing to the taste **:** DELICIOUS **2 :** delicately pretty ⟨a *dainty* flower⟩ **3 a :** having or showing delicate or finical taste **b :** FASTIDIOUS ⟨a *dainty* eater⟩ — **dain·ti·ly** \'dānt-ʰl-ē\ *adv* — **dain·ti·ness** \'dānt-ē-nəs\ *n*

dai·qui·ri \'dī-kə-rē\ *n* [*Daiquiri*, Cuba] **:** a cocktail made of rum, lime juice, and sugar

dairy \'de(ə)r-ē\ *n, pl* **dair·ies** [ME *deye* dairymaid, fr. OE *dæge* kneader of dough; akin to E *dough*] **1 :** a room, building, or establishment where milk is kept and butter or cheese is made **2 a :** the department of farming or of a farm concerned with the production of milk, butter, and cheese **b :** a farm devoted to the production of milk — called also *dairy farm* **3 :** an establishment for the sale or distribution chiefly of milk and milk products

dairy breed *n* **:** a cattle breed developed chiefly for milk production

dairy·ing \'der-ē-iŋ\ *n* **:** the business of operating a dairy

dairy·maid \-ē-,mād\ *n* **:** a woman employed in a dairy

dairy·man \-ē-mən, -,man\ *n* **:** one who operates a dairy farm or works in a dairy

da·is \'dā-əs\ *n* [OF *deis*, fr. L *discus* dish, quoit] **:** a raised platform in a hall or large room giving prominence to those who occupy it

dai·sy \'dā-zē\ *n, pl* **daisies** [OE *dægesēage*, lit., day's eye] **1 :** any of numerous plants of the composite family having flower heads with well-developed ray flowers usu. in one or a few whorls: as **a :** a low-growing European herb with white or pink ray flowers — called also *English daisy* **b :** a tall leafy-stemmed American wild flower with yellow disk and long white ray flowers — called also *oxeye daisy* **2 :** the flower head of a daisy

Da·ko·ta \də-'kōt-ə\ *n* **:** a member of a Siouan people of the northern Mississippi valley

Da·lai La·ma \,däl-,ī-'läm-ə\ *n* **:** the spiritual head of Lamaism

dale \'dāl\ *n* [OE *dæl*] **:** VALLEY

dal·li·ance \'dal-ē-ən(t)s\ *n* **1 :** PLAY; *esp* **:** amorous play (as flirting or caressing) **2 :** frivolous action **:** TRIFLING ⟨a short *dalliance* with radical ideas⟩

dal·ly \'dal-ē\ *vi* **dal·lied; dal·ly·ing** [AF *dalier*] **1 :** to act playfully; *esp* **:** to play amorously **2 a :** to waste time ⟨*dally* at one's work⟩ **b :** LINGER, DAWDLE ⟨*dally* on the way home⟩ — **dal·li·er** *n*

dal·ma·tian \dal-'mā-shən\ *n, often cap* **:** a large dog of a breed characterized by a white short-haired coat with black or brown spots

dal·mat·ic \dal-'mat-ik\ *n* **:** a short-sleeved vestment with slit sides worn by a deacon or bishop; *also* **:** a similar robe worn by a British sovereign at his coronation

dal se·gno \däl-'sān-yō\ *adv* [It, from the sign] — used as a direction in music to return to the sign that marks the beginning of a repeat

¹dam \'dam\ *n* [ME *dam, dame* lady, dam] **:** a female parent — used esp. of a domestic animal

²dam *n* **1 :** a barrier preventing the flow of a fluid (as water); *esp* **:** a barrier built across a watercourse **2 :** a body of water confined by a dam

³dam *vt* **dammed; dam·ming 1 :** to provide or restrain with a dam ⟨*dam* a stream⟩ **2 :** to stop up **:** BLOCK ⟨*dammed*-up feelings⟩

¹dam·age \'dam-ij\ *n* [OF, fr. *dam* damage, fr. L *damnum* damage, penalty] **1 :** a loss or harm resulting from injury to person, property, or reputation **2** *pl* **:** compensation in money imposed by law for loss or injury **syn** see INJURY

²damage *vt* **:** to cause damage to

dam·a·scene \'dam-ə-,sēn\ *vt* **:** to ornament (as iron or steel) with wavy patterns or with inlaid work of precious metals

dam·ask \'dam-əsk\ *n* **1 :** a firm lustrous reversible figured fabric used esp. for household linen **2 :** a tough steel having decorative wavy lines — called also *damask steel* **3 :** a grayish red — **damask** *adj*

damask rose *n* **:** a large hardy fragrant pink rose grown in Asia Minor as a source of attar of roses

dame \'dām\ *n* [OF, fr. L *domina*, fem. of *dominus* master] **1 :** a woman of rank, station, or authority: as **a** *archaic* **:** the mistress of a household **b :** the wife or daughter of a lord **c :** a female member of an order of knighthood — used as a title prefixed to the given name **2 a :** an elderly woman **b** *slang* **:** WOMAN

dam·mar *or* **dam·ar** *also* **dam·mer** \'dam-ər\ *n* [Malay *damar*] **:** a clear to yellow resin obtained from Malayan trees and used in varnishes and inks

¹damn \'dam\ *vb* [L *damnare*, fr. *damnum* damage, penalty] **1 :** to condemn to a punishment or fate; *esp* **:** to condemn to hell **2 :** to condemn as bad or as a failure **3 :** to swear at **:** CURSE — **damn·ing·ly** \'dam-iŋ-lē\ *adv*

²damn *n* **1 :** the utterance of the word *damn* as a curse **2 :** something of little value ⟨didn't care a *damn*⟩

³damn *adj* (*or adv*) **:** DAMNED

dam·na·ble \'dam-nə-bəl\ *adj* **1 :** liable to or deserving condemnation ⟨*damnable* conduct⟩ **2 :** very bad **:** EXECRABLE ⟨*damnable* weather⟩ — **dam·na·bly** \-blē\ *adv*

dam·na·tion \dam-'nā-shən\ *n* **1 :** the act of damning **2 :** the state of being damned

¹damned \'damd\ *adj* **damned·er** \'dam-dər\; **damnedest** *or* **damnd·est** \'dam-dəst\ **1 :** DAMNABLE ⟨a *damned* fool⟩ **2 :** UTTER ⟨*damned* nonsense⟩ **3 :** EXTRAORDINARY ⟨the *damnedest* sight⟩

²damned *adv* **:** EXTREMELY, VERY ⟨*damned* fine job⟩

Dam·o·cles \'dam-ə-,klēz\ *n* **:** a courtier of ancient Syracuse held to have been seated at a banquet beneath a sword hung by a single hair

Da·mon \'dā-mən\ *n* **:** a Sicilian held to have pledged his life for his friend Pythias

¹damp \'damp\ *n* [MD or MLG, vapor] **1 :** a noxious gas esp. in a coal mine **2 :** MOISTURE, HUMIDITY **3 :** DISCOURAGEMENT, CHECK

²damp *vt* **1 a :** DEPRESS, DEJECT ⟨failure *damped* his spirits⟩ **b :** RESTRAIN, CHECK ⟨*damp* down a furnace⟩ ⟨*damp* his enthusiasm⟩ **c :** to check the vibration or oscillation of **2 :** DAMPEN

³damp *adj* **1 :** DEPRESSED, DULL ⟨*damp* entertainment⟩ **2 :** slightly or moderately wet **:** MOIST ⟨*damp* cellar⟩ — **damp·ly** *adv* — **damp·ness** *n*

damp·en \'dam-pən\ *vb* **damp·ened; damp·en·ing** \'damp-(ə-)niŋ\ **1 :** to check or diminish in activity or vigor **:** DEADEN **2 :** to make or become damp — **damp·en·er** \'damp-(ə-)nər\ *n*

damp·er \'dam-pər\ *n* **:** one that damps ⟨put a *damper* on the celebration⟩: as **a :** a valve or plate (as in the flue of a furnace) for regulating the draft **b :** a small felted block to stop the vibration of a piano string **c :** a device for checking oscillation

dam·sel \'dam-zəl\ *or* **dam·o·sel** *or* **dam·o·zel** \'dam-ə-,zel\ *n* [OF *dameisele*] **:** GIRL, MAIDEN

dam·sel·fly \'dam-zəl-,flī\ *n* **:** any of numerous insects distinguished from the related dragonflies by laterally projecting eyes and wings folded above the body when at rest

dam·son \'dam-zən\ *n* [L *prunum damascenum*, lit., plum of Damascus] **:** an Asiatic plum grown for its small acid purple fruit; *also* **:** this fruit

Dan·a·ë \'dan-ə-,ē\ *n* **:** the mother of Perseus visited by Zeus as a shower of gold during her imprisonment

¹dance \'dan(t)s\ *vb* [OF *dancier*] **1 :** to perform a rhythmic and patterned succession of bodily movements

---

j joke; **ŋ** sing; **ō** flow; **ȯ** flaw; **ȯi** coin; **th** thin; **th̲** this; **ü** loot; **u̇** foot; **y** yet; **yü** few; **yu̇** furious; **zh** vision

usu. to music **2 :** to move quickly up and down or about **3 :** to perform or take part in as a dancer **4 :** to cause to dance — **danc·er** n
²**dance** n **1 :** an act or instance of dancing **2 :** a social gathering for dancing **3 :** a piece of music by which dancing may be guided **4 :** the art of dancing
dan·de·li·on \'dan-d²l-,ī-ən\ n [MF *dent de lion*, lit., lion's tooth] **:** any of a genus of yellow-flowered herbs related to chicory; *esp* **:** one with long deeply toothed stemless leaves sometimes grown as a potherb
dan·der \'dan-dər\ n [alter. of *dandruff*] **1 :** minute scales from hair, feathers, or skin that may cause allergy **2 :** ANGER, TEMPER ⟨got his *dander* up⟩
dan·di·fy \'dan-di-,fī\ vt **-fied; -fy·ing :** to make characteristic of a dandy
dan·dle \'dan-d²l\ vt **dan·dled; dan·dling** \-dliŋ, -d²l-iŋ\ **1 :** to move up and down in one's arms or on one's knee in affectionate play **2 :** PAMPER, PET
dan·druff \'dan-drəf\ n **:** a scurf that forms on the scalp and comes off in small white or grayish scales — **dan·druffy** \-ē\ adj
¹**dan·dy** \'dan-dē\ n, pl **dandies 1 :** a man unduly attentive to dress **2 :** something excellent in its class — **dan·dy·ish** \-dē-ish\ adj
²**dandy** adj **dan·di·er; -est :** very good **:** FIRST-RATE
Dane \'dān\ n **1 :** a native or inhabitant of Denmark **2 :** a person of Danish descent
dane·geld \'dān-,geld\ n, often cap **:** an annual tax held to have been orig. imposed to buy off Danish invaders in England or to maintain forces to oppose them
Dane·law \'dān-,lo\ n **1 :** the law in force in the part of England held by the Danes before the Norman Conquest **2 :** the part of England under the Danelaw
dan·ger \'dān-jər\ n [ME *daunger* jurisdiction, liability, fr. OF *dongier, dangier* jurisdiction, fr. (assumed) VL *dominiarium*, fr. L *dominium* dominion, ownership] **1 :** exposure or liability to injury, harm, or evil **2 :** something that may cause injury or harm ⟨storms and other *dangers* of the sea⟩
syn DANGER, PERIL, HAZARD mean a threat of loss or injury to life, property, health, or morals. DANGER implies possible but not necessarily inescapable harm; PERIL suggests imminent danger and cause for fear; HAZARD implies danger from chance or something beyond one's control
dan·ger·ous \'dānj-(ə-)rəs\ adj **1 :** exposing to or involving danger ⟨a *dangerous* mission⟩ **2 :** able or likely to inflict injury ⟨*dangerous* weapons⟩ — **dan·ger·ous·ly** adv — **dan·ger·ous·ness** n
dan·gle \'daŋ-gəl\ vb **dan·gled; dan·gling** \-g(ə-)liŋ\ **1 :** to hang loosely esp. with a swinging motion **2 :** to be a hanger-on or dependent **3 :** to be left without proper grammatical connection in a sentence ⟨*dangling* participle⟩ **4 :** to cause to dangle **:** SWING **5 :** to keep hanging uncertainly — **dan·gler** \-g(ə-)lər\ n — **dan·gling·ly** \-g(ə-)liŋ-lē\ adv
Dan·iel \'dan-yəl\ n **1 :** a Hebrew prophet captive in Babylon **2 —** see BIBLE table
¹**Dan·ish** \'dā-nish\ adj **:** of, relating to, or characteristic of Denmark, the Danes, or Danish
²**Danish** n **:** the Germanic language of the Danes
Danish pastry n **:** a rich pastry made of dough raised with yeast with the shortening rolled in
dank \'daŋk\ adj [ME *danke*] **:** unpleasantly moist or wet — **dank·ly** adv — **dank·ness** n
dan·seuse \däⁿ-'sə(r)z, -'süz\ n **:** a female ballet dancer
Daph·ne \'daf-nē\ n **:** a nymph transformed into a laurel tree to escape the pursuing Apollo
daph·nia \'daf-nē-ə\ n **:** any of a genus of tiny freshwater crustaceans **:** WATER FLEA
dap·per \'dap-ər\ adj [MD, quick, strong] **1 :** being neat and trim in dress or appearance **:** SPRUCE **2 :** being alert and lively in movement and manners — **dap·per·ly** adv — **dap·per·ness** n
¹**dap·ple** \'dap-əl\ n **1 :** any of numerous usu. cloudy and rounded spots of a color or shade different from their background **2 :** a dappled state **3 :** a dappled animal
²**dapple** vb **dap·pled; dap·pling** \'dap-(ə-)liŋ\ **:** to mark or become marked with dapples ⟨a *dappled* horse⟩
Dar·by and Joan \,där-bē-ən-'jō(-ə)n, -jō-'an\ n **:** a happily married usu. elderly couple

¹**dare** \'da(ə)r, 'de(ə)r\ vb [OE *dear*, 1st & 3d sing. pres. indic.] **1 a :** to have sufficient courage **:** be bold enough to ⟨try it if you *dare*⟩ **b —** used as an auxiliary verb ⟨no one *dared* say a word⟩ **2 :** to challenge to perform an action esp. as a proof of courage ⟨I *dare* you⟩ **3 :** to confront boldly ⟨*dared* the dangerous crossing⟩
²**dare** n **:** an act or instance of daring **:** CHALLENGE ⟨dived from the bridge on a *dare*⟩
dare·dev·il \'da(ə)r-,dev-əl, 'de(ə)r-\ n **:** a recklessly bold person — **daredevil** adj
¹**dar·ing** adj **:** venturesomely bold — **dar·ing·ly** \-iŋ-lē\ adv — **dar·ing·ness** n
syn DARING, RASH, RECKLESS, FOOLHARDY mean exposing oneself to danger more than is sensible or courageous. DARING stresses fearlessness; RASH implies imprudent hastiness; RECKLESS implies complete heedlessness of consequences; FOOLHARDY suggests recklessness and foolish daring **syn** see in addition ADVENTUROUS
²**daring** n **:** venturesome boldness
¹**dark** \'därk\ adj [OE *deorc*] **1 a :** being without light or without much light ⟨in winter it gets *dark* early⟩ **b :** not giving off light **2 :** not light in color ⟨a *dark* suit⟩ *esp* **:** of low lightness and medium saturation ⟨*dark* blue⟩ **3 :** not bright and cheerful **:** GLOOMY ⟨look on the *dark* side of things⟩ **4 :** being without knowledge and culture **:** IGNORANT **5 :** SILENT, SECRETIVE **6 :** not clear to the understanding ⟨*dark* sayings⟩ **syn** see OBSCURE — **dark·ish** \'där-kish\ adj — **dark·ly** \-klē\ adv — **dark·ness** \'därk-nəs\ n
²**dark** n **1 a :** absence of light **:** DARKNESS **b :** a place or time of little or no light **:** NIGHT, NIGHTFALL ⟨get home before *dark*⟩ **2 :** a dark or deep color
dark adaptation n **:** the whole process by which the eye adapts to seeing in weak light — **dark–adapt·ed** \,därk-ə-'dap-təd\ adj
Dark Ages n pl **:** the period from about A.D. 476 to about 1000; also **:** MIDDLE AGES
dark·en \'där-kən\ vb **dark·ened; dark·en·ing** \'där-(ə-)niŋ\ **1 :** to make or grow dark or darker ⟨*darken* a room⟩ ⟨the sky is *darkening*⟩ **2 :** to make less clear **:** DIM ⟨ignorance *darkens* the understanding⟩ **3 :** BESMIRCH, TARNISH ⟨*darken* a reputation⟩ **4 :** to make or become gloomy or forbidding ⟨his face *darkened* in anger⟩ — **dark·en·er** \'där-(ə-)nər\ n
dark horse n **:** a contestant or a political figure whose abilities and chances as a contender are not known ⟨the deadlocked convention nominated a *dark horse*⟩
dark lantern n **:** a lantern that can be closed to conceal the light
¹**dark·ling** \'där-kliŋ\ adv **:** in the dark
²**darkling** adj **1 :** DARK ⟨a *darkling* plain⟩ **2 :** done or taking place in the dark
dark·room \'därk-,rüm, -,rùm\ n **:** a room protected from rays of light harmful in the process of developing sensitive photographic plates and film
dark·some \'därk-səm\ adj **:** gloomily somber **:** DARK
¹**dar·ling** \'där-liŋ\ n [OE *dēorling*, fr. *dēore* dear] **1 :** a dearly loved person **2 :** FAVORITE
²**darling** adj **1 :** dearly loved **:** FAVORITE **2 :** very pleasing **:** CHARMING — **dar·ling·ly** \-liŋ-lē\ adv
¹**darn** \'därn\ vb **:** to mend with interlacing stitches ⟨*darn* socks⟩
²**darn** n **:** a place that has been darned
³**darn** vb [euphemism] **:** DAMN — **darn** \'därn\ or **darned** \'därn(d)\ adj (or adv)
⁴**darn** n **:** ²DAMN
dar·nel \'därn-²l\ n **:** any of several usu. weedy grasses with bristly flower clusters
darning needle n **1 :** a long needle with a large eye for use in darning **2 :** DRAGONFLY, DAMSELFLY
¹**dart** \'därt\ n [MF, of Gmc origin] **1 a :** a small missile usu. with a shaft pointed at one end and feathered on the other **b** pl **:** a game in which darts are thrown at a target **2 a :** something projected with sudden speed; *esp* **:** a sharp glance **b :** something causing a sudden pain **3 :** a stitched tapering fold in a garment **4 :** a quick movement

dart 1a

²**dart** vb **1 :** to throw with a sudden movement ⟨*dart* a javelin⟩ **2 :** to thrust or move suddenly or rapidly

dart·er \'därt-ər\ *n* : any of numerous small American freshwater fishes closely related to the perches

Dar·win·ian \där-'win-ē-ən\ *adj* : of or relating to Charles Darwin, his theories, or his followers — **Darwinian** *n*

Dar·win·ism \'där-wə-,niz-əm\ *n* : a theory of the origin and perpetuation of new kinds of animals and plants by means of natural selection perpetuating adaptive variations — **Dar·win·ist** \-wə-nəst\ *n* — **darwinist** *or* **dar·win·is·tic** \,där-wə-'nis-tik\ *adj, often cap* — **dar·win·is·ti·cal·ly** \-ti-k(ə-)lē\ *adv, often cap*

¹dash \'dash\ *vb* [ME *dasshen*] **1** : to knock, hurl, or thrust violently ⟨the storm *dashed* the boat against a reef⟩ **2** : to break by striking or knocking ⟨*dashed* a plate against the wall⟩ **3** : SPLASH, SPATTER **4 a** : DESTROY, RUIN ⟨*dash* one's hopes⟩ **b** : DEPRESS, SADDEN **5** : to affect by mixing in something different ⟨*dashed* with vinegar⟩ **6** : to perform or finish hastily ⟨*dash* off a letter⟩ **7** : to move with sudden speed — **dash·er** *n*

²dash *n* **1 a** : BLOW **b** : a sudden burst or splash ⟨a *dash* of cold water⟩ **2 a** : a stroke of a pen **b** : a punctuation mark — used chiefly to indicate a break in the thought or structure of a sentence **3** : a small usu. distinctive addition ⟨add a *dash* of salt⟩ **4** : conspicuous display **5** : animation in style and action ⟨a man of *dash* and vigor⟩ **6 a** : a sudden rush or attempt ⟨made a *dash* for the exit⟩ **b** : a short fast race **7** : a long click or buzz forming a letter or part of a letter (as in the Morse code) **8** : DASHBOARD 2

dash·board \'dash-,bōrd, -,bȯrd\ *n* **1** : a screen on the front of a vehicle (as a carriage) to keep out water, mud, or snow **2** : a panel extending across an automobile or airplane below the windshield and usu. containing dials and controls

da·shi·ki \də-'shē-kē\ *or* **dai·shi·ki** \dī-\ *n* [alter. of Yoruba (a language of western Africa) *danshiki*] : a usu. brightly colored loose-fitting pullover garment

dash·ing *adj* **1** : marked by vigorous action ⟨a *dashing* attack⟩ **2** : marked by smartness esp. in dress and manners ⟨made a *dashing* appearance⟩ — **dash·ing·ly** \-iŋ-lē\ *adv*

das·sie \'däs-ē\ *n* : a hyrax of southern Africa

das·tard \'das-tərd\ *n* [ME] : COWARD; *esp* : one who sneakily commits malicious acts

das·tard·ly \-lē\ *adj* : treacherously cowardly — **das·tard·li·ness** *n*

da·ta \'dāt-ə, 'dat-, 'dät-\ *n sing or pl* [L, pl. of *datum*] **1** : factual information (as measurements or statistics) used as a basis for reasoning, discussion, or calculation **2** : DATUM

¹date \'dāt\ *n* [OF, fr. L *dactylus*, fr. Gk *daktylos*, lit., finger] : the oblong edible fruit of a tall Old World palm; *also* : this palm

²date *n* [MF, fr. LL *data*, fr. *data* (as in *data Romae* given at Rome), fem. of L *datus*, pp. of *dare* to give] **1 a** : the time at which an event occurs **b** : a statement giving the time of execution or making (as of a coin or check) **2** : DURATION **3** : the period of time to which something belongs **4 a** : APPOINTMENT; *esp* : a social engagement between two persons of opposite sex **b** : a person of the opposite sex with whom one has a social engagement — **to date** : up to the present moment

³date *vb* **1** : to determine the date of ⟨*date* the composition of a symphony⟩ **2** : to record the date of or on ⟨*date* a letter⟩ **3** : to mark or reveal the date, age, or period of ⟨the architecture *dates* the house⟩ **4** : to make or have a date with ⟨*dated* only older men⟩ **5 a** : ORIGINATE ⟨*dates* from the sixth century⟩ **b** : EXTEND ⟨*dating* back to childhood⟩ **6** : to show qualities typical of a past period ⟨such formality is *dated*⟩ — **dat·a·ble** *or* **date·a·ble** \'dāt-ə-bəl\ *adj* — **dat·er** *n*

date·less \'dāt-ləs\ *adj* **1** : ENDLESS **2** : having no date **3** : too ancient to be dated **4** : TIMELESS

date·line \'dāt-,līn\ *n* **1** : a line in a publication giving the date and place of composition or issue **2** *usu* **date line** : a hypothetical line approximately along the 180th meridian designated as the place where each calendar day begins — **dateline** *vt*

da·tive \'dāt-iv\ *adj* [L *dativus*, fr. *dare* to give] : of, relating to, or being the grammatical case that marks typically the indirect object of a verb or the object of some prepositions — **dative** *n*

da·tum \'dāt-əm, 'dat-, 'dät-\ *n, pl* **da·ta** \-ə\ *or* **datums**

[L, neut. of *datus*, pp. of *dare* to give] : a single piece of data : FACT

¹daub \'dȯb, 'däb\ *vb* [OF *dauber*] **1** : to cover with soft adhesive matter : PLASTER **2** : SMEAR, SMUDGE **3** : to apply coloring material crudely on **4** *archaic* : to put on a false exterior — **daub·er** *n*

²daub *n* **1** : something daubed on : SMEAR **2** : a crude picture

¹daugh·ter \'dȯt-ər\ *n* [OE *dohtor*] **1 a** : a female offspring esp. of human beings **b** : a human female having a specified ancestor or belonging to a group of common ancestry **2** : something derived from its origin as if feminine — **daugh·ter·ly** \-lē\ *adj*

²daughter *adj* **1** : having the characteristics or relationship of a daughter ⟨*daughter* cities⟩ **2** : being offspring of the first generation ⟨*daughter* cell⟩

daugh·ter-in-law \'dȯt-ə-rən-,lȯ, -ərn-,lȯ\ *n, pl* **daughters-in-law** \-ər-zən-\ : the wife of one's son

daunt \'dȯnt, 'dänt\ *vt* [OF *donter, danter*, fr. L *domitare* to tame, freq. of *domare* to tame] : to lessen the courage of : make afraid

daunt·less \-ləs\ *adj* : FEARLESS, UNDAUNTED — **daunt·less·ly** *adv* — **daunt·less·ness** *n*

dau·phin \'dȯ-fən\ *n, often cap* [MF *dalfin*, fr. OF, title of lords of the Dauphiné, fr. *Dalfin*, a surname] : the eldest son of a king of France

dav·en·port \'dav-ən-,pōrt, -,pȯrt\ *n* : a large upholstered sofa

Da·vid \'dā-vəd\ *n* : the second king of Israel who in his youth killed Goliath and charmed Saul with his music and who is held to be the author of some of the Psalms

da·vit \'dā-vət, 'dav-ət\ *n* : one of a pair of posts with curved arms fitted with ropes and pulleys used for raising and lowering small boats; *also* : a similar hoist (as over a hatchway)

Da·vy Jones \,dā-vē-'jōnz\ *n* : the spirit of the sea

Da·vy Jones's locker \,dā-vē-,jōnz(-əz)-\ *n* : the bottom of the sea

daw \'dȯ\ *n* [ME *dawe*] : JACKDAW

daw·dle \'dȯd-°l\ *vb* **daw·dled; daw·dling** \'dȯd-liŋ, -°l-iŋ\ **1** : to spend time wastefully or idly : LINGER ⟨*dawdled* over her homework⟩ **2** : LOITER ⟨*dawdles* on the way home⟩ **3** : IDLE ⟨*dawdle* the time away⟩ — **daw·dler** \'dȯd-lər, -°l-ər\ *n*

¹dawn \'dȯn, 'dän\ *vi* [ME *dawnen;* akin to E *day*] **1** : to begin to grow light as the sun rises ⟨waited for the day to *dawn*⟩ **2** : to begin to appear or develop ⟨the space age *dawned* with the first sputnik⟩ **3** : to begin to be perceived or understood ⟨the solution *dawned* on him⟩

²dawn *n* **1** : the first appearance of light in the morning **2** : a first appearance : BEGINNING ⟨the *dawn* of a new era⟩

day \'dā\ *n* [OE *dæg*] **1 a** : the time of light between one night and the next **b** : DAYLIGHT **2** : the period of the earth's rotation on its axis **3** : a period of 24 hours beginning at midnight **4** : a specified day or date ⟨the *day* of the picnic⟩ ⟨their wedding *day*⟩ **5** : a specified time or period : AGE ⟨in grandfather's *day*⟩ **6** : the conflict or contention of the day ⟨played hard and carried the *day*⟩ **7** : the time set apart by usage or law for work ⟨the 8-hour *day*⟩

Day·ak \'dī-,ak\ *n* : a member of any of several Indonesian peoples of the interior of Borneo

day·bed \'dā-,bed\ *n* : a couch with low head and foot pieces

day·book \-,buk\ *n* : DIARY, JOURNAL

day·break \-,brāk\ *n* : DAWN

day coach *n* : COACH 1b

¹day·dream \'dā-,drēm\ *n* : a dream experienced while awake; *esp* : a pleasant reverie usu. of wish fulfillment

²daydream *vi* : to have a daydream — **day·dream·er** *n*

day laborer *n* : one who works by the day or for daily wages esp. as an unskilled laborer

day letter *n* : a telegram sent during the day that has a lower priority than a regular telegram

day·light \'dā-,līt\ *n* **1** : the light of day **2** : DAWN **3** : understanding of something that has been obscure ⟨began to see *daylight* on the problem⟩ **4** *pl* **a** : CONSCIOUSNESS **b** : WITS

daylight saving time *n* : time usu. one hour ahead of standard time — called also *daylight time*

day lily *n* **1** : any of various Eurasian plants of the lily family with short-lived flowers resembling lilies that are widespread in cultivation and as escapes **2** : PLANTAIN LILY

day nursery n : a public center for the care and training of young children esp. of working mothers; *also* : NURSERY SCHOOL

Day of Atonement : YOM KIPPUR

days \'dāz\ adv : in the daytime repeatedly

day school n : an elementary or secondary school held on weekdays; *esp* : a private school without boarding facilities

day·star \'dā-,stär\ n **1** : MORNING STAR **2** : SUN 1a

day·time \'dā-,tīm\ n : the period of daylight

¹**daze** \'dāz\ vt [ON *dasask* to exhaust oneself] **1** : to stupefy esp. by a blow : STUN **2** : to dazzle with light

²**daze** n : the state of being dazed

daz·zle \'daz-əl\ vt **daz·zled; daz·zling** \'daz-(ə-)liŋ\ [freq. of ¹*daze*] **1** : to overpower with light ⟨the desert sunlight *dazzled* him⟩ **2** : to impress greatly or confound with brilliance ⟨*dazzled* the crowds with his oratory⟩ — **dazzle** n — **daz·zler** \-(ə-)lər\ n — **daz·zling·ly** \-(ə-)liŋ-lē\ adv

D day n : a day set for launching an operation (as an invasion)

DDT \,dēd-(,)ē-'tē\ n [fr. the initial letters of its chemical components] : a colorless odorless water-insoluble crystalline insecticide

de- prefix [OF de-, des-, partly fr. L de- down, from, away, and partly from L dis- dis-; L de- akin to E to] **1 a** : do the opposite of ⟨devitalize⟩ **b** : reverse of ⟨de-emphasis⟩ **2** : remove (a specified thing) from ⟨delouse⟩ : remove from (a specified thing) ⟨dethrone⟩ **3** : reduce ⟨devalue⟩ **4** : something derived from (a specified thing) ⟨decompound⟩ : derived from something (of a specified nature) ⟨denominative⟩ **5** : get off of (a specified thing) ⟨detrain⟩

dea·con \'dē-kən\ n [OE *dēacon*, fr. LL *diaconus*, fr. Gk *diakonos*, lit., servant] **1 a** : a man in holy orders next below a priest **b** : the cleric (as a priest) serving as first assistant to the celebrant at solemn services (as high mass) **2** : one of several officers in Christian churches; *esp* : a member of a lay board serving in the worship and administration of a Congregational or Baptist church

dea·con·ess \'dē-kə-nəs\ n : a woman assisting in church work; *esp* : one in a Protestant order devoted to community service

de·ac·ti·vate \(')dē-'ak-tə-,vāt\ vt : to make inactive or ineffective — **de·ac·ti·va·tion** \(,)dē-,ak-tə-'vā-shən\ n

¹**dead** \'ded\ adj [OE *dēad*] **1** : deprived of life : having died : LIFELESS **2 a** : having the appearance of death : DEATHLY ⟨in a *dead* faint⟩ **b** : NUMB **c** : very tired **d** : UNRESPONSIVE ⟨*dead* to pity⟩ **e** : EXTINGUISHED ⟨*dead* coals⟩ **3 a** : INANIMATE, INERT ⟨*dead* matter⟩ **b** : no longer producing or functioning : EXHAUSTED ⟨a *dead* battery⟩ **4 a** : lacking power, significance, or effect ⟨a *dead* custom⟩ **b** : no longer in use : OBSOLETE ⟨*dead* language⟩ **c** : no longer active : EXTINCT ⟨*dead* volcano⟩ **d** : lacking in gaiety or animation ⟨*dead* party⟩ **e** : lacking in activity : QUIET **f** : IDLE, UNPRODUCTIVE **g** : lacking elasticity ⟨*dead* tennis ball⟩ **h** : being out of action or out of use; *esp* : free from any connection to a source of voltage and free from electric charges ⟨a *dead* telephone line⟩ **i** : being out of play ⟨*dead* ball⟩ ⟨*dead* cards⟩ **5 a** : not running or circulating : STAGNANT ⟨*dead* air⟩ **b** : lacking warmth, vigor, or taste ⟨a *dead* wine⟩ **6 a** : absolutely uniform ⟨*dead* level⟩ **b** : UNERRING, EXACT ⟨a *dead* shot⟩ ⟨*dead* center of the target⟩ **c** : ABRUPT ⟨a *dead* stop⟩ **d** : COMPLETE, ABSOLUTE ⟨a *dead* loss⟩

²**dead** n, pl **dead 1** : one that is dead — usu. used collectively ⟨the living and the *dead*⟩ **2** : the time of greatest quiet ⟨the *dead* of night⟩

³**dead** adv **1** : UTTERLY ⟨*dead* right⟩ **2** : suddenly and completely ⟨stopped *dead*⟩ **3** : DIRECTLY ⟨*dead* ahead⟩

dead·beat \'ded-,bēt\ n : one who persistently fails to pay his debts or his way

dead·en \'ded-ⁿn\ vt **dead·ened; dead·en·ing** \'ded-niŋ, -ⁿn-iŋ\ **1** : to impair in vigor or sensation : BLUNT ⟨*deaden* pain with drugs⟩ **2 a** : to deprive of luster or spirit **b** : to make (as a wall) soundproof

dead end n : an end (as of a street) without an exit

dead-end \,ded-'end\ adj **1** : leading nowhere ⟨a *dead-end* job⟩ **2** : TOUGH ⟨*dead-end* kids⟩

dead·eye \'ded-,ī\ n **1** : a rounded wood block pierced with holes to receive a lanyard that is used esp. to set up shrouds and stays **2** : a dead shot

dead heat n : a contest in which two or more contestants tie (as by crossing the finish line simultaneously)

dead letter n **1** : something that has lost its force or authority without being formally abolished **2** : a letter that is undeliverable and unreturnable by the post office

dead·line \'ded-,līn\ n : a date or time before which something must be done; *esp* : the time after which copy is not accepted for a particular issue of a publication

dead·lock \'ded-,läk\ n : a stoppage of action because neither of two equally powerful factions in a struggle will give in — **deadlock** vt

¹**dead·ly** \'ded-lē\ adj **dead·li·er; -est 1** : likely to cause or capable of causing death ⟨a *deadly* weapon⟩ **2 a** : aiming to kill or destroy : IMPLACABLE ⟨a *deadly* enemy⟩ **b** : very accurate : UNERRING ⟨a *deadly* marksman⟩ **3** : fatal to spiritual progress **4 a** : tending to deprive of force or vitality ⟨a *deadly* habit⟩ **b** : suggestive of death ⟨*deadly* chill⟩ **5** : very great : EXTREME — **dead·li·ness** n
syn DEADLY, MORTAL, FATAL, LETHAL mean causing or capable of causing death. DEADLY applies to an established or very likely cause of death ⟨a *deadly* disease⟩ MORTAL implies that death has occurred or is inevitable ⟨a *mortal* wound⟩ FATAL stresses the inevitability of what has in fact resulted in death or destruction ⟨*fatal* consequences⟩ LETHAL applies only to something that is bound to cause death or exists for the destruction of life ⟨*lethal* gas⟩ ⟨a *lethal* chamber⟩

²**deadly** adv **1** : suggesting death ⟨*deadly* pale⟩ **2** : EXTREMELY ⟨*deadly* dull⟩

deadly nightshade n : the belladonna plant

deadly sin n : one of seven sins of pride, covetousness, lust, anger, gluttony, envy, and sloth held to be fatal to spiritual progress

dead march n : a solemn march for a funeral

dead pan n : an expressionless immobile face — **dead·pan** \'ded-,pan\ adj or adv

dead reckoning n : the determination without the aid of celestial observations of the position of a ship or airplane from the record of the courses sailed or flown, the distance made, and the known or estimated drift

dead·weight \'ded-'wāt\ n : the unrelieved weight of an inert mass

dead·wood \'ded-,wùd\ n **1** : wood dead on the tree **2** : useless personnel or material

deaf \'def\ adj [OE *dēaf*] **1** : wholly or partly unable to hear **2** : unwilling to hear or listen ⟨*deaf* to all suggestions⟩ — **deaf·ness** n

deaf·en \'def-ən\ vb **deaf·ened; deaf·en·ing** \'def-(ə-)niŋ\ **1** : to make deaf **2** : to cause deafness or stun with noise — **deaf·en·ing·ly** \-(ə-)niŋ-lē\ adv

deaf-mute \'def-'myüt\ n : a deaf person who cannot speak — **deaf-mute** adj — **deaf-mut·ism** \-,myüt-,iz-əm\ n

¹**deal** \'dēl\ n [OE *dǣl* part, quantity] **1 a** : an indefinite quantity or degree ⟨means a great *deal*⟩ **b** : a large quantity ⟨a *deal* of money⟩ **2 a** : the act or right of distributing cards to players in a card game **b** : HAND 11b

²**deal** vb **dealt** \'delt\; **deal·ing** \'dē-liŋ\ **1** : to give as one's portion : DISTRIBUTE ⟨*deal* out sandwiches⟩ ⟨*deal* the cards⟩ **2** : ADMINISTER, BESTOW ⟨*dealt* him a blow⟩ **3** : to have to do : TREAT ⟨the book *deals* with education⟩ **4** : to take action in regard to something ⟨*deal* with offenders⟩ **5 a** : to engage in bargaining : TRADE **b** : to sell or distribute something as a business ⟨*deals* in insurance⟩ — **deal·er** n

³**deal** n **1 a** : BARGAINING, NEGOTIATION **b** : the result of bargaining : a mutual agreement to do business (as to buy or sell) : TRANSACTION ⟨make a *deal* for a used car⟩ **2** : treatment received ⟨a dirty *deal*⟩ **3** : a secret or underhand agreement usu. to mutual advantage or to the disadvantage of other parties **4** : a purchase at a fair or very low price to the purchaser : BARGAIN ⟨a good *deal* in a new suit⟩

⁴**deal** n [MD or MLG *dele* plank] : wood or a board of fir or pine — **deal** adj

deal·ing *n* **1** *pl* : INTERCOURSE, TRAFFIC; *esp* : business transactions ⟨*dealings* with an automobile agency⟩ **2** : a way of acting or of doing business ⟨fair in his *dealing*⟩

de·am·i·nase \(')dē-'am-ə-ˌnās\ *n* : an enzyme that promotes removal of amino groups

de·am·i·nate \-ˌnāt\ *vt* : to remove the amino group from (a compound) — **de·am·i·na·tion** \(ˌ)dē-ˌam-ə-'nā-shən\ *n*

dean \'dēn\ *n* [MF *deien*, fr. LL *decanus*, lit., chief of ten, fr. L *decem* ten] **1 a** : the head of the chapter of a collegiate or cathedral church **b** : a priest who supervises one district of a diocese **2 a** : the head of a division, faculty, college, or school of a university **b** : a college or secondary school administrator in charge of counseling and disciplining students **3** : the senior member of a group ⟨the *dean* of the diplomatic corps⟩ — **dean·ship** \-ˌship\ *n*

dean·ery \'dēn-(ə-)rē\ *n, pl* **-er·ies** : the office, jurisdiction, or official residence of a clerical dean

¹dear \'di(ə)r\ *adj* [OE *dēor*] : SEVERE, SORE

²dear *adj* [ME *dere*, fr. OE *dēore*] **1** *obs* : NOBLE **2** : highly valued : PRECIOUS **3** : AFFECTIONATE, FOND **4** : high‑priced : EXPENSIVE **5** : HEARTFELT — **dear** *adv* — **dear·ly** *adv* — **dear·ness** *n*

³dear *n* : a loved one : DARLING

dearth \'dərth\ *n* **1** : scarcity that makes dear : FAMINE **2** : inadequate supply

death \'deth\ *n* [OE *dēath*] **1** : a permanent cessation of all vital functions : the end of life **2** : the cause of loss of life **3** *cap* : the destroyer of life represented usu. as a skeleton with a scythe **4** : the state of being dead **5** : DESTRUCTION, EXTINCTION **6** : SLAUGHTER — **death·like** \-ˌlīk\ *adj*

death·bed \'deth-'bed\ *n* **1** : the bed in which a person dies **2** : the last hours of life

death·blow \-'blō\ *n* : a destructive or killing stroke or event

death camas *n* : any of several plants of the lily family that cause poisoning of livestock in the western U.S.

death·less \'deth-ləs\ *adj* : IMMORTAL, IMPERISHABLE ⟨*deathless* fame⟩ — **death·less·ly** *adv* — **death·less·ness** *n*

death·ly \'deth-lē\ *adj* **1** : FATAL **2** : of, relating to, or suggestive of death ⟨a *deathly* pallor⟩ — **deathly** *adv*

death's-head \'deths-ˌhed\ *n* : a human skull emblematic of death

¹death·watch \'deth-ˌwäch\ *n* [fr. the superstition that its ticking presages death] : any of several small insects that make a ticking sound

²deathwatch *n* : a vigil kept with the dead or dying

deb \'deb\ *n* : DEBUTANTE

de·ba·cle \di-'bäk-əl, -'bak-\ *n* [F *débâcle*] **1 a** : a breaking up of ice in a river **b** : a tumultuous rush of water and ice following such a breaking up **2** : a violent disruption (as of an army) : ROUT **3** : BREAKDOWN, COLLAPSE ⟨stock market *debacle*⟩

de·bar \di-'bär\ *vt* : to bar from having or doing something : PRECLUDE — **de·bar·ment** \-mənt\ *n*

de·bark \di-'bärk\ *vb* [MF *debarquer*, fr. *de-* + *barque* bark] : DISEMBARK — **de·bar·ka·tion** \ˌdē-ˌbär-'kā-shən\ *n*

de·base \di-'bās\ *vt* : to lower in character, dignity, quality, or value — **de·base·ment** \-mənt\ *n* — **de·bas·er** *n*

syn DEBASE, DEGRADE, CORRUPT, DEPRAVE mean to cause deterioration or lowering in quality or character. DEBASE implies loss of worth, value, or dignity ⟨*debase* morals⟩ ⟨*debase* currency⟩ DEGRADE adds shamefulness or degeneracy to debasement; CORRUPT refers to persons or things characterized by loss of soundness, purity, or integrity through forces that break down, pollute, or destroy; DEPRAVE implies moral deterioration or perversion

de·bat·a·ble \di-'bāt-ə-bəl\ *adj* : able to be debated or disputed : open to question or dispute ⟨a *debatable* question⟩⟨a *decision* of *debatable* wisdom⟩

¹de·bate \di-'bāt\ *n* : a contention by words or arguments: as **a** : the formal discussion of a motion before a deliberative body according to the rules of parliamentary procedure **b** : a regulated discussion of a proposition between two matched sides

²debate *vb* [MF *debatre* to fight, contend, fr. *de-* + *batre* to beat] **1** : to discuss or examine a question by present-

ing and considering arguments on both sides **2** : to take part in a debate **3** : to present or consider the reasons for and against : CONSIDER **syn** see DISCUSS — **de·bat·er** *n*

¹de·bauch \di-'bóch, -'bäch\ *vt* [MF *debaucher* to make disloyal] : to lead away from virtue or morality : SEDUCE, CORRUPT — **de·bauch·ee** \-ˌbóch-'ē, -ˌbäch-\ *n* — **de·bauch·er** \-'bóch-ər, -'bäch-\ *n*

²debauch *n* **1** : an act, occasion, or period of debauchery **2** : ORGY

de·bauch·ery \di-'bóch-(ə-)rē, -'bäch-\ *n, pl* **-er·ies** : excessive indulgence of one's sensual desires : INTEMPERANCE, SENSUALITY

de·ben·ture \di-'ben-chər\ *n* [L *debentur* they are due, fr. *debēre* to owe] : a certificate of indebtedness; *esp* : a bond secured only by the general assets of the issuing government or corporation

de·bil·i·tate \di-'bil-ə-ˌtāt\ *vt* : to impair the strength of : WEAKEN — **de·bil·i·ta·tion** \di-ˌbil-ə-'tā-shən\ *n*

de·bil·i·ty \di-'bil-ət-ē\ *n, pl* **-ties** [L *debilitas*, fr. *debilis* weak] : an infirm or weakened state

¹deb·it \'deb-ət\ *n* [L *debitum* debt] **1** : an entry in an account representing an amount paid out or owed **2** : a disadvantageous or unfavorable quality or character

²debit *vt* : to enter as a debit : charge with or as a debt

deb·o·nair \ˌdeb-ə-'na(ə)r, -'ne(ə)r\ *adj* [OF *debonaire*, *de bonne aire* of good family or nature] : gaily and gracefully charming ⟨a *debonair* manner⟩ — **deb·o·nair·ly** *adv* — **deb·o·nair·ness** *n*

de·bouch \di-'büsh\ *vi* : to march or issue out (as from a defile) into an open area ⟨crowds *debouched* from side streets into the square⟩ — **de·bouch·ment** \-mənt\ *n*

de·bride·ment \də-'brēd-ˌmäⁿ\ *n* : surgical removal of damaged tissue

de·brief \di-'brēf, 'dē-\ *vt* : to interrogate (as a pilot back from a mission) in order to obtain useful information

de·bris \də-'brē, 'dā-ˌbrē\ *n, pl* **de·bris** \-'brēz, -ˌbrēz\ [F *débris*, fr. MF, fr. *debriser* to break to pieces, fr. *de-* + *brisier* to break] **1** : the remains of something broken down or destroyed : RUINS **2** : an accumulation of fragments of rock

debt \'det\ *n* [L *debitum*, fr. neut. of *debitus*, pp. of *debēre* to owe, fr. *de-* + *habēre* to have] **1** : SIN, TRESPASS **2** : something owed to another : a thing or amount due : OBLIGATION ⟨pay a *debt* of $10⟩ **3** : a condition of owing; *esp* : the state of owing money in amounts greater than one can pay ⟨hopelessly in *debt*⟩

debt·or \'det-ər\ *n* **1** : SINNER **2** : one that owes a debt

de·bunk \(')dē-'bəŋk\ *vt* : to expose the sham or falseness in ⟨*debunk* a hero legend⟩ — **de·bunk·er** *n*

de·but \'dā-ˌbyü, dā-'\ *n* [F *début*] **1** : a first public appearance ⟨his *debut* as a novelist⟩ **2** : a formal entrance into society ⟨made her *debut* at eighteen⟩

deb·u·tante \'deb-yu̇-ˌtänt\ *n* : a young woman making her formal entrance into society

deca- *or* **dec-** *or* **deka-** *or* **dek-** *comb form* [Gk *deka*; akin to E ten] : ten ⟨*decahedron*⟩

dec·ade \'dek-ˌād, -əd; de-'kād\ *n* **1** : a group or set of 10 **2** : a period of 10 years **3** : a part of the rosary devoted to one sacred mystery and made up of ten Hail Marys preceded by the Lord's Prayer and followed by the Gloria Patri

dec·a·dence \'dek-əd-ən(t)s, di-'kād-ᵊn(ˌ)s\ *n* [LL *decadere* to fall, sink, fr. L *de-* + *cadere* to fall] **1** : the process of becoming or the quality or state of being decadent **2** : a period of decline

dec·a·dent \'dek-əd-ənt, di-'kād-ᵊnt\ *adj* : marked by decay or decline — **decadent** *n* — **dec·a·dent·ly** *adv*

dec·a·gon \'dek-ə-ˌgän\ *n* : a polygon of 10 angles and 10 sides

decagram *var of* DEKAGRAM

de·cal \'dē-ˌkal, di-'kal, 'dek-əl\ *n* : DECALCOMANIA

de·cal·ci·fy \(')dē-'kal-sə-ˌfī\ *vt* : to remove calcium or calcium compounds from — **de·cal·ci·fi·ca·tion** \(ˌ)dē-ˌkal-sə-fə-'kā-shən\ *n*

de·cal·co·ma·nia \di-ˌkal-kə-'mā-nē-ə\ *n* [F *décalcomanie*, fr. *décalquer* to copy by tracing + *manie* mania] **1** : the art or process of transferring (as to glass) pictures and designs from specially prepared paper **2** : a picture or design prepared for transfer by decalcomania

decaliter *var of* DEKALITER

dec·a·logue \'dek-ə-ˌlóg\ *n* [Gk *dekalogos*, fr. *deka-* deca-

+ *logos* speech, word] **1** *cap* : TEN COMMANDMENTS **2** : a basic set of rules carrying binding authority

decameter *var of* DEKAMETER

de·camp \di-'kamp\ *vi* **1** : to break up a camp **2** : to depart suddenly : ABSCOND ⟨*decamped* with the funds⟩ — **de·camp·ment** \-mənt\ *n*

de·cant \di-'kant\ *vt* [NL *decantare*, fr. L *de-* + (assumed) ML *cantus* edge, fr. L *canthus* iron tire] **1** : to pour from one vessel into another **2** : to draw off gently without disturbing any sediment ⟨*decant* wine⟩ — **de·can·ta·tion** \,dē-,kan-'tā-shən\ *n*

de·cant·er \di-'kant-ər\ *n* : a vessel for decanting liquids or receiving decanted liquids ; *esp* : an ornamental glass bottle used for serving wine

de·cap·i·tate \di-'kap-ə-,tāt\ *vt* [LL *decapitare*, fr. L *de-* + *capit-, caput* head] : to cut off the head of : BEHEAD — **de·cap·i·ta·tion** \di-,kap-ə-'tā-shən\ *n*

dec·a·pod \'dek-ə-,päd\ *n* **1** : any of an order (Decapoda) of crustaceans (as shrimps, lobsters, crabs) with five pairs of thoracic appendages one or more of which are modified into pincers **2** : any of an order (Decapoda) of cephalopod mollusks including the cuttlefishes, squids, and related forms with 10 arms — **decapod** *adj* — **de·cap·o·dan** \di-'kap-əd-ən\ *adj or n*

decanter

de·car·box·yl·ate \,dē-,kär-'bäk-sə-,lāt\ *vt* : to remove carboxyl from — **de·car·box·yl·a·tion** \,dē-,kär-,bäk-sə-'lā-shən\ *n*

decastere *var of* DEKASTERE

deca·syl·lab·ic \,dek-ə-sə-'lab-ik\ *adj* : having 10 syllables : composed of verses having 10 syllables — **deca·syllabic** *n*

de·cath·lon \di-'kath-lən\ *n* [F *décathlon*, fr. Gk *deka-* deca- + *athlon* contest] : an athletic contest in which each competitor participates in each of a series of 10 track-and-field events

¹de·cay \di-'kā\ *vb* [ONF *decaïr*, fr. LL *decadere* to fall, fr. L *de-* + *cadere* to fall] **1** : to decline from a sound or prosperous condition **2** : to decrease gradually in quantity, activity, or force **3** : to fall into ruin **4** : to decline in health, strength, or vigor **5** : to undergo or cause to undergo decomposition ⟨a radioactive element *decays*⟩ **syn** DECAY, DECOMPOSE, ROT mean to undergo disintegration or dissolution. DECAY implies a deterioration, often gradual, from soundness or perfection; DECOMPOSE stresses a breaking down into components or dissolution through corruption ⟨to *decompose* water into oxygen and hydrogen⟩⟨bacteria *decompose* organic products⟩ ROT implies decay with corruption and often suggests offensiveness

²decay *n* **1** : gradual decline in strength, soundness, prosperity, excellence, or value **2** : ROT; *esp* : aerobic decomposition of proteins chiefly by bacteria **3** : a decline in health or vigor **4 a** : spontaneous decrease in the number of radioactive atoms in radioactive material **b** : spontaneous disintegration (as of an atom or a meson)

de·cease \di-'sēs\ *n* [L *decessus* death, fr. *decess-, decedere* to depart, die, fr. *de-* + *cedere* to go] : passing from physical life : DEATH — **decease** *vi*

de·ceased \-'sēst\ *n, pl* **deceased** : a dead person ⟨the will of the *deceased*⟩

de·ce·dent \di-'sēd-ᵊnt\ *n* : a deceased person

de·ceit \di-'sēt\ *n* [fr. OF *deceite, deceivre* to deceive] **1** : the act or practice of deceiving : DECEPTION **2** : an attempt or device to deceive : TRICK **3** : DECEITFULNESS

de·ceit·ful \-fəl\ *adj* **1** : practicing or tending to practice deceit **2** : showing or containing deceit or fraud : MISLEADING, DECEPTIVE ⟨a *deceitful* answer⟩ — **de·ceit·ful·ly** \-fə-lē\ *adv* — **de·ceit·ful·ness** *n*

de·ceive \di-'sēv\ *vb* [OF *deceivre*, fr. L *decipere*, fr. *de-* + *capere* to take] **1** : to cause to believe what is untrue : MISLEAD ⟨*deceived* his father about his real intentions⟩ **2** : to impose upon : deal with dishonestly : CHEAT **3** : to use or practice deceit — **de·ceiv·er** *n* — **de·ceiv·ing·ly** \-'sē-viŋ-lē\ *adv*

syn DECEIVE, MISLEAD mean to lead astray or frustrate usu. by underhandedness. DECEIVE implies imposing a false idea or belief that causes ignorance, bewilderment, or helplessness, and often suggests deliberate entrapping

for the agent's own ends; MISLEAD implies a leading astray that may or may not be intentional

de·cel·er·ate \(')dē-'sel-ə-,rāt\ *vb* **1** : to cause to slow down **2** : to move at decreasing speed — **de·cel·er·a·tion** \(,)dē-,sel-ə-'rā-shən\ *n* — **de·cel·er·a·tor** \(')dē-'sel-ə-,rāt-ər\ *n*

De·cem·ber \di-'sem-bər\ *n* [L, fr. *decem* ten; fr. its having been orig. the tenth month of the Roman calendar] : the 12th month of the year

de·cem·vir \di-'sem-vər\ *n* : one of a body of 10 magistrates in ancient Rome — **de·cem·vi·rate** \-və-rət\ *n*

de·cen·cy \'dēs-ᵊn-sē\ *n, pl* **-cies** **1 a** : the quality or state of being decent : PROPRIETY **b** : conformity to standards of taste, propriety, or quality **2** : standard of propriety — usu. used in pl.

de·cen·ni·al \di-'sen-ē-əl\ *adj* **1** : consisting of 10 years **2** : happening every 10 years ⟨*decennial* census⟩ — **decennial** *n* — **de·cen·ni·al·ly** \-ē-ə-lē\ *adv*

de·cent \'dēs-ᵊnt\ *adj* [L *decent-, decens*, fr. prp. of *decēre* to be fitting] **1 a** : conforming to standards of propriety, good taste, or morality **b** : modestly clothed **2** : free from immodesty or obscenity **3** : fairly good : ADEQUATE ⟨*decent* housing⟩ — **de·cent·ly** *adv*

de·cen·tral·ize \(')dē-'sen-trə-,līz\ *vt* **1** : to disperse or distribute among various regional or local authorities ⟨*decentralize* the administration of flood relief⟩ **2** : to cause to withdraw from urban centers to outlying areas ⟨*decentralize* industries⟩ — **de·cen·tral·i·za·tion** \(,)dē-,sen-trə-lə-'zā-shən\ *n*

de·cep·tion \di-'sep-shən\ *n* [L *decept-, decipere* to deceive] **1 a** : the act of deceiving **b** : the fact or condition of being deceived **2** : something that deceives : TRICK **syn** FRAUD, TRICKERY : DECEPTION applies to any act that misleads whether intentionally or not and includes both deliberate cheating and legitimate tactical resource; FRAUD always implies guilt and often criminality; TRICKERY implies ingenious ways of fooling or cheating

de·cep·tive \di-'sep-tiv\ *adj* : tending or having power to deceive — **de·cep·tive·ly** *adv* — **de·cep·tive·ness** *n*

deci- *comb form* [L *decimus* tenth, fr. *decem* ten] : tenth part ⟨*decigram*⟩

dec·i·bel \'des-ə-,bel, -bəl\ *n* **1** : a unit for expressing the ratio of two amounts of electric or acoustic signal power equal to 10 times the common logarithm of this ratio **2** : a unit for measuring the relative loudness of sounds equal approximately to the smallest degree of difference of loudness ordinarily detectable by the human ear whose range includes about 130 decibels — abbr. *db*

de·cide \di-'sīd\ *vb* [L *decidere*, lit., to cut off, fr. *de-* + *caedere* to cut] **1** : to arrive at a solution that ends uncertainty or dispute about ⟨*decided* the case in favor of the defendant⟩ **2** : to bring to a definitive end ⟨one blow *decided* the fight⟩ **3** : to induce to come to a choice ⟨attractions that *decided* his mind⟩ **4** : to make a choice or judgment ⟨*decided* to go⟩ — **de·cid·a·ble** \-'sīd-ə-bəl\ *adj* — **de·cid·er** *n*

de·cid·ed \-'sīd-əd\ *adj* **1** : CLEAR, UNMISTAKABLE ⟨a *decided* smell of gas⟩ **2** : FIRM, DETERMINED ⟨a *decided* tone of voice⟩ — **de·cid·ed·ly** *adv* — **de·cid·ed·ness** *n*

de·cid·u·ous \di-'sij-ə-wəs\ *adj* [L *deciduus*, fr. *decidere* to fall off, fr. *de-* + *cadere* to fall] **1** : falling off (as at the end of a growing period or stage of development) ⟨antlers are *deciduous*⟩ **2** : having deciduous parts ⟨*deciduous* trees⟩ — opposite EVERGREEN — **de·cid·u·ous·ly** *adv* — **de·cid·u·ous·ness** *n*

deciduous tooth *n* : MILK TOOTH

deci·gram \'des-ə-,gram\ *n* — see METRIC SYSTEM table

deci·li·ter \'des-ə-,lēt-ər\ *n* — see METRIC SYSTEM table

de·cil·lion \di-'sil-yən\ *n* — see NUMBER table

¹dec·i·mal \'des-ə-məl\ *adj* [L *decimus* tenth, fr. *decem* ten; akin to E *ten*] **1** : numbered or proceeding by tens **2** : based on the number 10 ⟨a *decimal* system of currency⟩ **3** : expressed in a decimal fraction — **dec·i·mal·ly** \-mə-lē\ *adv*

²decimal *n* : a proper fraction in which the denominator is a power of 10 usu. not expressed but signified by a point placed at the left of the numerator (as $.2 = \frac{2}{10}$, $.25 = \frac{25}{100}$, $.025 = \frac{25}{1000}$)

decimal point *n* : the dot at the left of a decimal fraction

dec·i·mate \'des-ə-,māt\ *vt* [L *decimare*, fr. *decimus* tenth] **1** : to take or destroy the tenth part of **2** : to destroy a

large part of ⟨a population *decimated* by an epidemic⟩ —
dec·i·ma·tion \‚des-ə-'mā-shən\ *n*
deci·me·ter \'des-ə-‚mēt-ər\ *n* — see METRIC SYSTEM table
de·ci·pher \(')dē-'sī-fər\ *vt* **1 :** to convert into intelligible form; *esp* **:** to translate from secret writing (as code) ⟨*decipher* a message⟩ **2 :** to make out the meaning of despite indistinctness or obscurity ⟨*decipher* partly erased writing⟩ — **de·ci·pher·a·ble** \-f(ə-)rə-bəl\ *adj* — **de·ci·pher·ment** \-fər-mənt\ *n*
de·ci·sion \di-'sizh-ən\ *n* [L *decis-, decidere* to decide] **1 :** the act or result of deciding esp. by giving judgment ⟨the *decision* of the court⟩ **2 :** promptness and firmness in deciding **:** DETERMINATION ⟨a man of courage and *decision*⟩
de·ci·sive \di-'sī-siv\ *adj* **1 :** having the power to decide ⟨the *decisive* vote⟩ **2 :** of such nature as to settle a question or dispute ⟨a *decisive* victory⟩ **3 :** marked by or showing decision ⟨a *decisive* manner⟩ — **de·ci·sive·ly** *adv* — **de·ci·sive·ness** *n*
deci·stere \'des-ə-‚sti(ə)r, -‚ste(ə)r\ *n* **:** a metric unit of capacity equal to ¹⁄₁₀ cubic meter
¹deck \'dek\ *n* **1 :** a platform in a ship serving usu. as a structural element and forming the floor for its compartments **2 :** something resembling the deck of a ship: as **a :** the roadway of a bridge **b :** a flat floored roofless area adjoining a house **3 :** a pack of playing cards — **on deck :** next in line
²deck *vt* [D *dekken* to cover] **1 a :** to clothe elegantly **:** ARRAY ⟨*decked* out in a new suit⟩ **b :** DECORATE **2 :** to furnish with a deck
deck chair *n* **:** a folding chair often having an adjustable leg rest
deck·hand \'dek-‚hand\ *n* **:** a seaman who performs manual duties
deck·le edge \‚dek-əl-\ *n* **:** the rough untrimmed edge of paper — **deck·le–edged** \-'ejd\ *adj*
de·claim \di-'klām\ *vb* [L *declamare*, fr. *de-* + *clamare* to cry out] **:** to speak or deliver in the manner of a formal oration — **de·claim·er** *n* — **dec·la·ma·tion** \‚dek-lə-'mā-shən\ *n*
de·clam·a·to·ry \di-'klam-ə-‚tōr-ē, -‚tor-\ *adj* **:** of, relating to, or marked by declamation or rhetorical display
dec·la·ra·tion \‚dek-lə-'rā-shən\ *n* **1 :** the act of declaring **:** ANNOUNCEMENT **2 :** something declared or a document containing such a declaration ⟨the *Declaration* of Independence⟩ **3 a :** the final bid in auction bridge **b :** the contract in contract bridge
de·clar·a·tive \di-'klar-ət-iv\ *adj* **:** making a declaration or statement ⟨*declarative* sentence⟩
de·clar·a·to·ry \di-'klar-ə-‚tōr-ē, -‚tor-\ *adj* **:** serving to declare
de·clare \di-'kla(ə)r, -'kle(ə)r\ *vb* [L *declarare* to make clear, fr. *de-* + *clarus* clear] **1 :** to make known formally or explicitly ⟨*declare* war⟩ **2 :** to state emphatically **:** AFFIRM ⟨*declares* his innocence⟩ **3 :** to make a full statement of (taxable or dutiable property)
  syn DECLARE, ANNOUNCE, PUBLISH mean to make known publicly or openly. DECLARE suggests a plainness and formality of statement; ANNOUNCE implies a declaration for the first time of something of interest or intended to satisfy curiosity ⟨*announce* an engagement⟩ ⟨*announce* the winner⟩ PUBLISH denotes a making public through print **syn** see in addition ASSERT
de·clar·er \-'klar-ər, -'kler-\ *n* **:** one that declares; *esp* **:** the bridge player who plays both his own hand and that of dummy
de·clas·si·fy \(')dē-'klas-ə-‚fī\ *vt* **:** to remove or reduce the security classification of ⟨*declassify* a secret document⟩
de·clen·sion \di-'klen-chən\ *n* **1 a :** noun, adjective, or pronoun inflection esp. in some prescribed order of the forms **b :** a class of nouns or adjectives having the same type of inflectional forms **2 :** DECLINE, DETERIORATION **3 :** DESCENT, SLOPE — **de·clen·sion·al** \-'klench-nəl, -ən-ʾl\ *adj*
dec·li·nate \'dek-lə-‚nāt\ *adj* **:** bent or curved down or aside
dec·li·na·tion \‚dek-lə-'nā-shən\ *n* **1 :** angular distance north or south from the celestial equator measured along a great circle passing through the celestial poles ⟨the *declination* of a star⟩ **2 :** a decline esp. from vigor **3 :** a bending downward **:** INCLINATION **4 :** a formal refusal **5 :** the angle that the magnetic needle makes with a true north

and south line — **dec·li·na·tion·al** \-'nā-shnəl, -shən-ʾl\ *adj*
¹de·cline \di-'klīn\ *vb* [L *declinare* to turn aside, inflect, fr. *de-* + *clinare* to incline] **1 a :** to slope downward **:** DESCEND **b :** to bend down **:** DROOP ⟨*declined* his head⟩ **2 :** to reach or pass toward a lower level **:** RECEDE **3 :** to draw toward a close **:** WANE **4 a :** to withhold consent **b :** to refuse to undertake, engage in, or comply with **c :** to refuse to accept **5 :** to give in a prescribed order the inflectional forms of a noun, pronoun, or adjective — **de·clin·a·ble** \-'klī-nə-bəl\ *adj*
²decline *n* **1 :** the process of declining: **a :** a gradual sinking and wasting away **b :** a change to a lower state or level **2 :** the time when something is approaching its end **3 :** a downward slope **:** DECLIVITY **4 :** a wasting disease; *esp* **:** pulmonary tuberculosis
de·cliv·i·ty \di-'kliv-ət-ē\ *n*, *pl* **-ties** [L *declivitas*, fr. *declivis* sloping down, fr. *de-* + *clivus* slope] **1 :** downward inclination **2 :** a descending slope
de·coc·tion \di-'käk-shən\ *n* [L *decoct-, decoquere* to cook down, fr. *de-* + *coquere* to cook] **:** an extracting (as of a flavor or active principle) by boiling in water; *also* **:** a product of this process
de·code \(')dē-'kōd\ *vt* **:** to convert (a coded message) into ordinary language — **de·cod·er** *n*
dé·col·le·tage \(‚)dā-‚käl-ə-'täzh, ‚dek-lə-\ *n* [F] **1 :** the low-cut neckline of a dress **2 :** a décolleté dress
dé·col·le·té \(‚)dā-‚käl-ə-'tā, ‚dek-lə-\ *adj* [F] **1 :** wearing a strapless or low-necked dress **2 :** having a low-cut neckline
de·col·or·ize \(')dē-'kəl-ə-‚rīz\ *vt* **:** to remove color from — **de·col·or·iz·er** *n*
de·com·mis·sion \‚dē-kə-'mish-ən\ *vt* **:** to take out of commission ⟨a *decommissioned* battleship⟩
de·com·pen·sa·tion \(‚)dē-‚käm-pən-'sā-shən, -‚pen-\ *n* **:** loss of compensation; *esp* **:** inability of the heart to maintain adequate circulation — **de·com·pen·sate** \(')dē-'käm-pən-‚sāt, -‚pen-\ *vi*
de·com·pose \‚dē-kəm-'pōz\ *vb* **1 :** to separate a thing into its parts or into simpler compounds **2 :** to break down through chemical change **:** ROT **syn** see DECAY — **de·com·pos·a·ble** \-'pō-zə-bəl\ *adj* — **de·com·po·si·tion** \(‚)dē-‚käm-pə-'zish-ən\ *n*
de·com·pos·er \‚dē-kəm-'pō-zər\ *n* **:** an organism (as a bacterium or a fungus) that feeds on and breaks down dead protoplasm
de·com·pound \'dē-'käm-‚paund, ‚dē-‚käm-'\ *adj* **:** having divisions that are themselves compound ⟨a *decompound* leaf⟩
de·com·press \‚dē-kəm-'pres\ *vt* **:** to release (as a diver) from pressure or compression — **de·com·pres·sion** \-'presh-ən\ *n*
de·con·tam·i·nate \‚dē-kən-'tam-ə-‚nāt\ *vt* **:** to rid of contamination — **de·con·tam·i·na·tion** \-‚tam-ə-'nā-shən\ *n*
de·cor *or* **dé·cor** \dā-'kó(ə)r, 'dā-‚\ *n* [F *décor*, fr. *décorer* to decorate, fr. L *decorare*] **:** DECORATION; *esp* **:** the arrangement of accessories in interior decoration
dec·o·rate \'dek-ə-‚rāt\ *vt* [L *decorare*, fr. *decor-, decus* ornament] **1 :** to make more attractive by adding something beautiful or becoming ⟨*decorate* a room⟩ **2 :** to award a decoration of honor to **syn** see ADORN
dec·o·ra·tion \‚dek-ə-'rā-shən\ *n* **1 :** the act or process of decorating **2 :** something that adorns or beautifies **:** ORNAMENT **3 :** a badge of honor (as a medal)
Decoration Day *n* **:** MEMORIAL DAY
dec·o·ra·tive \'dek-ə-‚rāt-iv, 'dek-ə-‚rāt-\ *adj* **:** serving to decorate **:** ORNAMENTAL — **dec·o·ra·tive·ly** *adv* — **dec·o·ra·tive·ness** *n*
dec·o·ra·tor \'dek-ə-‚rāt-ər\ *n* **:** one that decorates; *esp* **:** a person who designs or executes the interiors of buildings and their furnishings
dec·o·rous \'dek-ə-rəs; di-'kōr-əs, -'kor-\ *adj* [L *decorus*, fr. *decor* beauty, grace] **:** marked by propriety and good taste **:** CORRECT ⟨*decorous* conduct⟩ — **dec·o·rous·ly** *adv* — **dec·o·rous·ness** *n*
de·co·rum \di-'kōr-əm, -'kor-\ *n* [L, fr. neut. of *decorus* decorous] **1 :** conformity to accepted standards of conduct **:** proper behavior ⟨social *decorum*⟩ **2 :** ORDERLINESS **syn** PROPRIETY, DIGNITY; DECORUM suggests conduct according with good taste often formally prescribed;

j joke; **ŋ** sing; **ō** flow; **ȯ** flaw; **ȯi** coin; **th** thin; **th** this; **ü** loot; **u̇** foot; **y** yet; **yü** few; **yu̇** furious; **zh** vision

PROPRIETY suggests an artificial standard of what is correct in conduct or speech; DIGNITY implies reserve or restraint in conduct prompted by a sense of personal integrity or social importance

¹de·coy \di-'kȯi, 'dē-,\ n 1 : something intended to lure into a trap; esp : an artificial bird used to attract live birds within shot 2 : a person used to lead another into a trap

²decoy vt : to lure by or as if by a decoy : ENTICE

¹de·crease \di-'krēs, 'dē-,\ vb [L decrescere, fr. de- + crescere to grow] : to grow or cause to grow less

decoy

syn DECREASE, DIMINISH, DWINDLE mean to grow less. DECREASE suggests progressive reduction or lessening; DIMINISH stresses loss, as in numbers or amount, and implies subtraction from the whole; DWINDLE implies progressive lessening, esp. of things growing visibly smaller

²de·crease \'dē-,krēs, di-'\ n 1 : a process of decreasing : DIMINISHING, LESSENING ⟨a decrease in automobile accidents⟩ 2 : the amount by which a thing decreases : REDUCTION ⟨a decrease of three dollars in wages⟩

¹decree \di-'krē\ n [MF decré, fr. L decretum, fr. neut. of pp. of decernere to decide, fr. de- + cernere to sift, decide] 1 : an order usu. having the force of law : EDICT 2 a : a religious ordinance enacted by an ecclesiastical assembly or titular head b : the will of the Deity c : something allotted by fate 3 : a judicial decision esp. in an equity or probate court

²decree vb de·creed; de·cree·ing 1 : to command or enjoin by decree ⟨decree an amnesty⟩ 2 : to determine or order judicially ⟨decree a punishment⟩ — **de·cre·er** \-'krē-ər\ n

dec·re·ment \'dek-rə-mənt\ n [L decrementum, fr. decrescere to decrease] 1 : gradual decrease 2 : the quantity lost by diminution or waste

de·crep·it \di-'krep-ət\ adj [L decrepitus] : broken down with age : worn out — **de·crep·it·ly** adv — **de·crep·it·ness** n

de·crep·i·tate \di-'krep-ə-,tāt\ vi [L de- + crepitare to crackle] : to crackle or fly apart when heated ⟨a crystal that decrepitates⟩ — **de·crep·i·ta·tion** \di-,krep-ə-'tā-shən\ n

de·crep·i·tude \di-'krep-ə-,t(y)üd\ n : the quality or state of being decrepit : infirmity esp. from old age

¹de·cre·scen·do \dā-krə-'shen-dō\ adv (or adj) [It] : with diminishing volume — used as a direction in music

²decrescendo n, pl -dos 1 : a lessening in volume of sound 2 : a decrescendo musical passage

de·cry \di-'krī\ vt [F décrier, fr. OF descrier, fr. des- de- + crier to cry] 1 : to speak slightingly of : belittle publicly ⟨decry a hero's deeds⟩ 2 : to find fault with : CONDEMN ⟨decried the waste of natural resources⟩ — **de·cri·er** \-'krī(-ə)r\ n

de·cum·bent \di-'kəm-bənt\ adj [L decumbere to lie down, fr. de- + -cumbere to lie down] 1 : lying down 2 : resting on the ground but having an ascending tip ⟨decumbent plant stems⟩ — **de·cum·ben·cy** \-bən-sē\ n

de·curved \(')dē-'kərvd\ adj : curved downward : bent down

¹dec·us·sate \'dek-ə-,sāt, di-'kəs-,āt\ vb : INTERSECT

²dec·us·sate \'dek-ə-,sāt, di-'kəs-ət\ adj : arranged in pairs each at right angles to the next pair above or below ⟨decussate leaves⟩

dec·us·sa·tion \,dek-ə-'sā-shən, ,dē-,kəs-'ā-\ n 1 : an intersection in the form of an X 2 : a band of nerve fibers that connects unlike centers of opposite sides of the central nervous system

ded·i·cate \'ded-i-,kāt\ vt [L dedicare, fr. de- + dicare to proclaim, dedicate] 1 : to set apart for some purpose and esp. a sacred or serious purpose : DEVOTE ⟨dedicate a church⟩⟨dedicated his life to helping others⟩ 2 : to address or inscribe as a compliment ⟨dedicated his book to his mother⟩ — **ded·i·ca·tor** \-,kāt-ər\ n

ded·i·ca·tion \,ded-i-'kā-shən\ n 1 a : an act or rite of dedicating to a divine being or to a sacred use b : a setting aside for a particular purpose 2 : a name and often a message prefixed to a literary work in tribute to a person

or cause 3 : self-sacrificing devotion — **ded·i·ca·tive** \'ded-i-,kāt-iv\ adj — **ded·i·ca·to·ry** \'ded-i-kə-,tōr-ē, -,tȯr-\ adj

de·dif·fer·en·ti·a·tion \(')dē-,dif-ə-,ren-chē-'ā-shən\ n : reversion of specialized structures (as cells) to a more generalized state

de·duce \di-'d(y)üs\ vt [L deduct-, deducere, lit., to lead away, fr. de- + ducere to lead] 1 : to trace the course or derivation of 2 a : to draw (a conclusion) necessarily from given premises b : to infer from a general principle — **de·duc·i·ble** \-'d(y)ü-sə-bəl\ adj

de·duct \di-'dəkt\ vt : to take away (an amount) from a total : SUBTRACT

de·duct·i·ble \di-'dək-tə-bəl\ adj : capable of being deducted : allowable as a deduction — **de·duct·i·bil·i·ty** \di-,dək-tə-'bil-ət-ē\ n

de·duc·tion \di-'dək-shən\ n 1 a : an act of taking away b : the deriving of a conclusion by reasoning; esp : inference in which the conclusion follows necessarily from the premises 2 a : a conclusion reached by mental deduction b : something that is or may be subtracted ⟨deductions from taxable income⟩ : ABATEMENT — **de·duc·tive** \-'dək-tiv\ adj — **de·duc·tive·ly** adv

¹deed \'dēd\ n [OE dǣd; akin to E do] 1 : something that is done : ACT ⟨judge a person by his deeds⟩ 2 : a legal document by which one person transfers real property to another **syn** see ACTION — **deed·less** \-ləs\ adj

²deed vt : to convey or transfer by deed

deem \'dēm\ vb [OE dēman] : to come to think or judge : have an opinion : HOLD, JUDGE, SUPPOSE

¹deep \'dēp\ adj [ME dep, fr. OE dēop] 1 a : extending far downward ⟨a deep well⟩ : having a great distance between the top and bottom surfaces ⟨deep water⟩ : not shallow ⟨a deep gash⟩ b : extending well inward from an outer surface ⟨a deep closet⟩ d : extending far outward from a center ⟨deep space⟩ e : occurring or located near the outer limits ⟨deep right field⟩ 3 a : having a specified extension downward or backward ⟨a shelf 20 inches deep⟩ 3 a : difficult to understand ⟨a deep book⟩ b : MYSTERIOUS, OBSCURE ⟨a deep dark secret⟩ c : WISE ⟨a deep thinker⟩ d : ENGROSSED, INVOLVED ⟨deep in thought⟩ e : of great intensity : PROFOUND ⟨deep sleep⟩ 4 a : high in saturation and low in lightness ⟨a deep red⟩ b : having a low musical pitch or range ⟨a deep voice⟩ 5 a : coming from or situated well within ⟨a deep sigh⟩⟨a house deep in the forest⟩ b : covered, enclosed, or filled often to a specified degree ⟨knee-deep in water⟩⟨a road deep with snow⟩ — **deep·ly** adv

²deep adv 1 : to a great depth : DEEPLY 2 : far on : LATE

³deep n 1 : any of the fathom points on a sounding line that is not a mark — see SOUNDING LINE illustration 2 : an extremely deep place or part; esp : OCEAN 3 : the middle or most intense part ⟨the deep of winter⟩

deep·en \'dē-pən\ vb deep·ened; deep·en·ing \'dēp-(ə-)niŋ\ : to make or become deep or deeper

deep–root·ed \'dēp-'rüt-əd, -'rùt-\ adj : deeply implanted or established ⟨a deep-rooted loyalty⟩

deep–sea \'dēp-'sē\ adj : of, relating to, or occurring in the deeper parts of the sea ⟨deep-sea fishing⟩

deep–seat·ed \'dēp-'sēt-əd\ adj 1 : situated far below the surface 2 : firmly established ⟨a deep-seated tradition⟩

deep–set \'dēp-'set\ adj : set far in ⟨deep-set eyes⟩

deer \'di(ə)r\ n, pl deer [OE dēor wild beast] : any of a family of cloven-hoofed ruminant mammals with antlers borne by the males of nearly all and by the females of a few forms

deer·hound \-,haùnd\ n : a large tall slender dog of a breed developed in Scotland and formerly used in hunting deer

deer mouse n : any of numerous No. American field and woodland mice related to the hamsters

deer·skin \'di(ə)r-,skin\ n : leather made from the skin of a deer; also : a garment of such leather

deer·yard \-,yärd\ n : a place where deer herd in winter

de·es·ca·late \(')dē-'es-kə-,lāt\ vb : to decrease in extent, volume, or scope — **de·es·ca·la·tion** \(,)dē-,es-kə-'lā-shən\ n

de·face \di-'fās\ vt [MF desfacier, fr. des- de- + face] : to destroy or mar the face or surface of — **de·face·ment** \-'fās-mənt\ n — **de·fac·er** n

syn DEFACE, DISFIGURE mean to mar the appearance of.

DEFACE suggests superficial injuries or the removal of some part or detail; DISFIGURE implies deeper or more permanent injury that impairs beauty or attractiveness

de fac·to \di-'fak-,tō\ *adj (or adv)* [NL, adv., in fact] **1** : actually exercising power ⟨*de facto* government⟩ — compare DE JURE **2** : actually existing ⟨*de facto* state of war⟩

de·fal·cate \di-'fal-,kāt, -'fòl-; 'def-əl-\ *vi* [ML *defalcare* to deduct, default, fr. L *de-* + *falc-, falx* sickle] : to engage in embezzlement — **de·fal·ca·tor** \-,kāt-ər\ *n*

de·fal·ca·tion \,dē-,fal-'kā-shən, -,fòl-; ,def-əl-\ *n* : a misuse or theft of money by a person who holds it in trust for someone else

def·a·ma·tion \,def-ə-'mā-shən\ *n* : the act of defaming : injury to the good name of another : SLANDER, LIBEL — **de·fam·a·to·ry** \di-'fam-ə-,tōr-ē, -,tòr-\ *adj*

de·fame \di-'fām\ *vt* : to injure or destroy the good name of : speak evil of : LIBEL **syn** see SLANDER — **de·fam·er** *n*

¹de·fault \di-'fòlt\ *n* : failure to do something required by law or duty ⟨the defendant has failed to appear and is held in *default*⟩

²default *vb* : to fail to carry out a contract, obligation, or duty; *also* : to forfeit something by such failure — **de·fault·er** *n*

¹de·feat \di-'fēt\ *vt* [MF *deffait*, pp. of *deffaire* to destroy, fr. ML *disfacere*, fr. L *dis-* + *facere* to do] **1** : NULLIFY, FRUSTRATE ⟨*defeat* a hope⟩ **2** : to win victory over : BEAT

²defeat *n* **1** : frustration by prevention of success **2 a** : an overthrow of an army in battle **b** : loss of a contest (as by a team)

de·feat·ism \-,iz-əm\ *n* : an attitude of expecting the defeat of one's own cause or of accepting such defeat on the ground that further effort would be useless or unwise — **de·feat·ist** \-əst\ *n or adj*

def·e·cate \'def-i-,kāt\ *vb* [L *defaecare*, fr. *de-* + *faec-, faex* dregs, lees] **1** : to free from impurity or corruption : REFINE **2** : to discharge feces from the bowels — **def·e·ca·tion** \,def-i-'kā-shən\ *n*

¹de·fect \'dē-,fekt, di-'\ *n* [L *defectus* lack, fr. *defect-, deficere* to be wanting, fail, fr. *de-* + *facere* to do] : a lack of something necessary for completeness or perfection : FAULT, IMPERFECTION **syn** see BLEMISH

²de·fect \di-'fekt\ *vi* : to desert a cause or party often in order to espouse another — **de·fec·tion** \-'fek-shən\ *n* — **de·fec·tor** \-'fek-tər\ *n*

¹de·fec·tive \di-'fek-tiv\ *adj* **1** : wanting in something essential : FAULTY **2** : lacking one or more of the usual forms of grammatical inflection ⟨the *defective* verb *may*⟩ — **de·fec·tive·ly** *adv* — **de·fec·tive·ness** *n*

²defective *n* : a person who is subnormal physically or mentally

de·fend \di-'fend\ *vb* [L *defendere*, fr. *de-* + *-fendere* to strike] **1** : to repel danger or attack **2** : to act as attorney for **3** : to oppose the claim of another in a lawsuit : CONTEST **4** : to maintain against opposition ⟨*defend* an idea⟩ — **de·fend·er** *n*

syn DEFEND, PROTECT, SHIELD mean to keep secure from danger or against attack. DEFEND denotes warding off actual or threatened attack; PROTECT implies something, as a covering, that serves as a bar to the admission or impact of that which may attack or injure ⟨*protect* one's eyes with dark glasses⟩ ⟨a bird sanctuary *protected* by state law⟩; SHIELD suggests protective intervention in imminent danger or actual attack

de·fend·ant \di-'fen-dənt\ *n* : a person required to make answer in a legal action or suit — compare PLAINTIFF

de·fense *or* **de·fence** \di-'fen(t)s\ *n* [L *defens-, defendere* to defend] **1** : the act of defending : resistance against attack **2** : capability of resisting attack **3 a** : means or method of defending **b** : an argument in support or justification **4** : a defending party or group (as in a court of law or on a playing field) **5** : the answer made by the defendant in a legal action or suit — **de·fense·less** \-ləs\ *adj* — **de·fense·less·ly** *adv* — **de·fense·less·ness** *n*

defense mechanism *n* : a defensive reaction by an organism

de·fen·si·ble \di-'fen(t)-sə-bəl\ *adj* : capable of being defended — **de·fen·si·bil·i·ty** \-,fen(t)-sə-'bil-ət-ē\ *n* — **de·fen·si·bly** \-'fen(t)-sə-blē\ *adv*

¹de·fen·sive \di-'fen(t)-siv\ *adj* : of or relating to defense

: serving or intended to defend or protect ⟨a *defensive* move⟩ — **de·fen·sive·ly** *adv* — **de·fen·sive·ness** *n*

²defensive *n* : a defensive position ⟨put on the *defensive* by an attack⟩

¹de·fer \di-'fər\ *vt* **de·ferred**; **de·fer·ring** [modif. of L *differre* to postpone, fr. *dis-* + *ferre* to carry] : to put off : DELAY ⟨*defer* payment for goods⟩ — **de·fer·ra·ble** \-'fər-ə-bəl\ *adj* — **de·fer·rer** *n*

syn DEFER, POSTPONE, SUSPEND mean to delay an action or proceeding. DEFER may imply a deliberate putting off until a later time. indefinite time or may imply a delay in fulfillment ⟨hopes long *deferred*⟩ POSTPONE implies an intentional deferring usu. to a definite time; SUSPEND implies temporary stopping often until some condition is satisfied

²defer *vi* **de·ferred**; **de·fer·ring** [LL *deferre*, fr. L, to bring down, fr. *de-* + *ferre* to carry] : to submit or yield to another's wish or opinion

def·er·ence \'def-(ə-)rən(t)s\ *n* : courteous, respectful, or ingratiating regard for another's wishes

syn RESPECT, REVERENCE: DEFERENCE implies a courteous yielding of one's own opinion or preference to that of another; RESPECT implies regard for a person or quality or achievement as worthy of honor or confidence; REVERENCE implies profound respect mingled with awe or devotion

def·er·en·tial \,def-ə-'ren-chəl\ *adj* : showing or expressing deference ⟨*deferential* attention⟩ — **def·er·en·tial·ly** \-'rench-(ə-)lē\ *adv*

de·fer·ment \di-'fər-mənt\ *n* : the act of delaying; *esp* : official postponement of military service

de·fi·ance \di-'fī-ən(t)s\ *n* **1** : the act or an instance of defying : CHALLENGE **2** : disposition to resist : contempt of opposition

de·fi·ant \-ənt\ *adj* : full of defiance : BOLD, INSOLENT — **de·fi·ant·ly** *adv*

de·fi·cien·cy \di-'fish-ən-sē\ *n, pl* **-cies** **1** : the quality or state of being deficient **2** : INADEQUACY: as **a** : a shortage of substances necessary to health **b** : absence of one or more genes from a chromosome

deficiency disease *n* : a disease (as scurvy) caused by a lack of essential dietary elements and esp. a vitamin or mineral

¹de·fi·cient \di-'fish-ənt\ *adj* [L *deficient-, deficiens*, prp. of *deficere* to be wanting, fail, fr. *de-* + *facere* to do] : lacking something necessary for completeness : not up to a given or normal standard : DEFECTIVE ⟨a diet *deficient* in proteins⟩ ⟨*deficient* in arithmetic on his first report card⟩ — **de·fi·cient·ly** *adv*

²deficient *n* : one that is deficient ⟨a mental *deficient*⟩

def·i·cit \'def-ə-sət\ *n* [L, it is wanting, fr. *deficere* to be wanting] : a deficiency in amount; *esp* : an excess of expenditures over revenue

¹de·file \di-'fīl\ *vt* [modif. of OF *defouler* to trample, fr. *de-* + *fouler* to trample, lit., to foul] **1** : to make filthy : DIRTY **2** : to corrupt the purity or perfection of **3** : RAVISH, VIOLATE **4** : to make ceremonially unclean : DESECRATE **5** : SULLY, DISHONOR — **de·file·ment** \-mənt\ *n* — **de·fil·er** *n*

²de·file \di-'fīl, 'dē-,\ *vi* [F *défiler*, fr. *dé-* de- + *filer* to move in a column] : to march off in a single line one file after another

³de·file \di-'fīl, 'dē-,\ *n* : a narrow passage or gorge

de·fine \di-'fīn\ *vb* [L *definire*, fr. *de-* + *finis* boundary, end] **1 a** : to fix or mark the limits of **b** : to make distinct in outline **2 a** : to determine the essential qualities or precise meaning of ⟨*define* the concept of loyalty⟩ **b** : to discover and set forth the meaning ⟨*define* a word⟩ — **de·fin·a·ble** \-'fī-nə-bəl\ *adj* — **de·fin·er** *n*

def·i·nite \'def-(ə-)nət\ *adj* **1 a** : having certain or distinct limits : FIXED ⟨a *definite* period of time⟩ **b** : CYMOSE **2** : clear in meaning : EXACT, EXPLICIT ⟨a *definite* answer⟩ **3** : typically designating an identified or immediately identifiable person or thing ⟨the *definite* article *the*⟩ — **def·i·nite·ly** *adv* — **def·i·nite·ness** *n*

syn DEFINITE, DEFINITIVE: DEFINITE denotes that which has limits so clearly fixed, defined, or stated there can be no doubt about the range or meaning ⟨a *definite* sum of money⟩ DEFINITIVE denotes supplying an answer as final and serving to end dispute and doubt ⟨a *definitive* statement of religious belief⟩ **syn** see in addition EXPLICIT

definite integral *n* : a number whose value is the difference between the values of the indefinite integral of a given function at the ends of a specific interval

def·i·ni·tion \,def-ə-'nish-ən\ *n* **1** : an act of determining or settling the limits **2 a** : a statement of the meaning of a word or word group or a sign or symbol **b** : the action or process of stating such a meaning **3 a** : the action or the power of making definite and clear **b** : CLARITY, DISTINCTNESS — **def·i·ni·tion·al** \-'nish-nəl, -'nish-ən-°l\ *adj*

de·fin·i·tive \di-'fin-ət-iv\ *adj* **1** : serving to provide a final solution : CONCLUSIVE ⟨a *definitive* victory⟩ **2** : being authoritative and apparently exhaustive ⟨the *definitive* book on the subject⟩ **3** : serving to define or specify precisely **4** : fully differentiated or developed syn see DEFINITE — **de·fin·i·tive·ly** *adv* — **de·fin·i·tive·ness** *n*

de·flate \di-'flāt, 'dē-\ *vb* [*de-* + *-flate* (as in *inflate*)] **1** : to release air or gas from **2** : to cause to contract from an abnormally high level : reduce from a state of inflation ⟨*deflate* the currency⟩ **3** : to become deflated : COLLAPSE — **de·fla·tor** \-'flāt-ər\ *n*

de·fla·tion \di-'flā-shən, 'dē-\ *n* **1** : an act or instance of deflating : the state of being deflated **2** : a contraction in the volume of available money or credit resulting in a decline of the general price level — **de·fla·tion·ary** \-shə-,ner-ē\ *adj*

de·flect \di-'flekt\ *vb* [L *deflex-, deflectere*, fr. *de-* + *flectere* to bend] : to turn or cause to turn aside (as from a course, direction, or position) ⟨a stream *deflected* from its course⟩ ⟨a bullet *deflected* by striking a wall⟩ — **de·flec·tion** \-'flek-shən\ *n*

de·flexed \di-'flekst, 'dē-\ *adj* : turned abruptly downward ⟨a *deflexed* leaf⟩

de·fo·li·ant \(')dē-'fō-lē-ənt\ *n* : a chemical applied to crop plants to cause the leaves to drop off prematurely

de·fo·li·ate \(')dē-'fō-lē-,āt\ *vt* [L *de-* + *folium* leaf] : to deprive of leaves esp. prematurely — **de·fo·li·ate** \-lē-ət\ *adj* — **de·fo·li·a·tion** \(,)dē-,fō-lē-'ā-shən\ *n* — **de·fo·li·a·tor** \(')dē-'fō-lē-,āt-ər\ *n*

de·for·est \(')dē-'fȯr-əst, -'fär-\ *vt* : to clear of forests — **de·for·es·ta·tion** \(,)dē-,fȯr-ə-'stā-shən, -,fär-\ *n* — **de·for·est·er** \(')dē-'fȯr-ə-stər, -'fär-\ *n*

de·form \di-'fȯrm, 'dē-\ *vb* **1** : to spoil the form or natural appearance of : DISFIGURE ⟨a leg *deformed* by an injury⟩ ⟨a face *deformed* by grief⟩ **2** : to become misshapen or changed in shape — **de·for·ma·tion** \,dē-,fȯr-'mā-shən, ,def-ər-\ *n*

de·formed *adj* : distorted or unshapely in form : MISSHAPEN

de·for·mi·ty \di-'fȯr-mət-ē\ *n, pl* **-ties 1** : the state of being deformed **2** : a physical blemish or distortion : DISFIGUREMENT **3** : a moral or aesthetic flaw

de·fraud \di-'frȯd\ *vt* : to deprive of something by trickery, deception, or fraud ⟨were *defrauded* of their bequests⟩ syn see CHEAT — **de·frau·da·tion** \,dē-,frȯ-'dā-shən\ *n* — **de·fraud·er** \di-'frȯd-ər\ *n*

de·fray \di-'frā\ *vt* [MF *defrayer*, fr. *des-* de- + *frais* expenses] **1** : to pay or provide for the payment of ⟨needs more money to *defray* expenses⟩ **2** *archaic* : to bear the expenses of — **de·fray·a·ble** \-'frā-ə-bəl\ *adj* — **de·fray·al** \-'frā-(ə)l\ *n*

de·frost \di-'frȯst, 'dē-\ *vb* **1** : to release from a frozen state : thaw out ⟨*defrost* meat⟩ **2** : to free from ice ⟨*defrost* a refrigerator⟩ — **de·frost·er** *n*

deft \'deft\ *adj* [ME *defte*] : quick and neat in action : SKILLFUL ⟨dressing the wound with *deft* fingers⟩ syn see DEXTEROUS — **deft·ly** *adv* — **deft·ness** *n*

de·funct \di-'fəŋ(k)t\ *adj* [L *defunctus*, fr. pp. of *defungi* to finish, die, fr. *de-* + *fungi* to perform] : having finished the course of life or existence : DEAD, EXTINCT ⟨a *defunct* organization⟩

de·fy \di-'fī\ *vt* **de·fied; de·fy·ing** [OF *defier* to renounce faith in, challenge, fr. *de-* + *fier* to trust, fr. L *fidere*] **1** : to challenge to do something considered impossible : DARE ⟨the magician *defied* his audience to explain the trick⟩ **2** : to refuse boldly to obey or to yield to : DISREGARD ⟨*defy* public opinion⟩ ⟨*defy* the law⟩ **3** : to resist attempts at : WITHSTAND, BAFFLE ⟨a scene that *defies* description⟩ — **de·fi·er** \-'fī(-ə)r\ *n*

de·gas \(')dē-'gas\ *vt* : to free from gas

de·gauss \(')dē-'gaus\ *vt* : to make (a steel ship) nonmagnetic by electrical means

de·gen·er·a·cy \di-'jen-(ə-)rə-sē\ *n, pl* **-cies 1** : the state

of being or process of becoming degenerate : DEGRADATION, DEBASEMENT **2** : sexual perversion

¹de·gen·er·ate \di-'jen-(ə-)rət\ *adj* [L *degeneratus*, pp. of *degenerare* to degenerate, fr. *de-* + *gener-, genus* race, kind] : having sunk to a condition below that which is normal to a type : having declined (as in nature or character) from an ancestral or former state : DEBASED, DEGRADED — **de·gen·er·ate·ly** *adv* — **de·gen·er·ate·ness** *n*

²degenerate *n* : a degenerate person; *esp* : a sexual pervert

³de·gen·er·ate \di-'jen-ə-,rāt\ *vi* **1** : to pass from a higher to a lower type or condition : DETERIORATE ⟨*degenerate* from the ancestral stock⟩ **2** : to undergo progressive deterioration esp. toward an earlier or less highly organized biological type

de·gen·er·a·tion \di-,jen-ə-'rā-shən\ *n* **1** : a lowering of power, vitality, or essential quality to a feebler and poorer kind or state **2** : a change in a tissue or an organ resulting in diminished activity or usefulness ⟨fatty *degeneration* of the heart⟩; *also* : a condition marked by such changes and esp. by loss of organs present in related forms ⟨tapeworms exhibit extreme degeneration⟩

de·gen·er·a·tive \di-'jen-ə-,rāt-iv\ *adj* : of, relating to, or tending to cause degeneration ⟨a *degenerative* disease⟩

de·glu·ti·tion \,dē-glü-'tish-ən, ,deg-lü-\ *n* [L *deglutire* to swallow down, fr. *de-* + *glutire, gluttire* to swallow] : the act or process of swallowing

deg·ra·da·tion \,deg-rə-'dā-shən\ *n* **1 a** : a reduction in rank, dignity, or standing **b** : removal from office **2** : DISGRACE, HUMILIATION **3** : DETERIORATION, DEGENERATION

de·grade \di-'grād\ *vb* **1** : to reduce from a higher to a lower rank or degree : deprive of an office or position ⟨*degrade* an officer for disobedience⟩ **2** : to lower the character of : DEBASE ⟨a man *degraded* by crime⟩ **3** : to reduce the complexity of : DECOMPOSE syn see DEBASE — **de·grad·er** *n*

de·gree \di-'grē\ *n* [OF *degré* step, stair, fr. L *de-* + *gradus* step, grade] **1** : a step or stage in a process, course, or classificatory order ⟨advance by *degrees*⟩ **2 a** : the extent, intensity, or scope of something esp. as measured by a graded series ⟨murder in the first *degree*⟩ **b** : one of the forms or sets of forms used in the comparison of an adjective or adverb **3 a** : a rank or grade of official, ecclesiastical, or social position **b** : the civil condition or status of a person **4 a** : a grade of membership attained in a ritualistic order or society **b** : the formal ceremonies observed in the conferral of a ritualistic distinction **c** : a title conferred upon students by a college, university, or professional school upon completion of a unified program of study **d** : an academic title conferred honorarily **5** *archaic* : a position or space on the earth or in the heavens as measured by degrees of latitude **6** : one of the divisions or intervals marked on a scale of a measuring instrument — symbol ° **7** : a 360th part of the circumference of a circle **8** : the rank of an algebraic expression that for a monomial term is the sum of the exponents of the variable factors and for a polynomial is the sum of the exponents of the term of highest degree **9 a** : a line or space of the musical staff **b** : a step, note, or tone of a musical scale — **to a degree 1** : to a remarkable extent **2** : in a small way

degrees 7

degree–day *n* : a unit that represents one degree of declination from a given point (as 65°) in the mean daily outdoor temperature and is used to measure heat requirements

de·hisce \di-'his\ *vi* [L *dehiscere* to split open, fr. *de-* + *hiscere* to gape] : to split along a natural line (as a suture) or discharge contents by so splitting ⟨seedpods *dehiscing* at maturity⟩ — **de·his·cence** \-'his-°n(t)s\ *n* — **de·his·cent** \-°nt\ *adj*

de·horn \(')dē-'hȯrn\ *vt* : to deprive of horns — **de·horn·er** *n*

de·hu·man·ize \(')dē-'hyü-mə-,nīz, (')dē-'yü-\ *vt* : to divest of human qualities or personality — **de·hu·man·i·za·tion** \(,)dē-,hyü-mə-nə-'zā-shən, (,)dē-,yü-\ *n*

de·hu·mid·i·fy \,dē-hyü-'mid-ə-,fī, ,dē-yü-\ *vt* : to remove moisture from (as the air) — **de·hu·mid·i·fi·ca·tion** \-,mid-ə-fə-'kā-shən\ *n*

de·hy·drate \(')dē-'hī-,drāt\ *vb* **1** : to remove water

ə abut; ᵊ kitten; ər further; a back; ā bake; ä cot, cart; au̇ out; ch chin; e less; ē easy; g gift; i trip; ī life

from (as foods) **2 :** to lose water or body fluids — **de·hy·dra·tion** \,dē-,hī-'drā-shən\ n

de·hy·drog·e·nase \,dē-,hī-'dräj-ə-,nās, (')dē-'hī-drə-jə-\ n : an enzyme that accelerates the removal and transfer of hydrogen

de·hy·drog·e·nate \,dē-,hī-'dräj-ə-,nāt, (')dē-'hī-drə-jə-\ vt : to remove hydrogen from — **de·hy·drog·e·na·tion** \,dē-,hī-,dräj-ə-'nā-shən, (,)dē-,hī-drə-jə-\ n

de·ice \(')dē-'īs\ vt : to keep free or rid of ice — **de·ic·er** n

de·i·fy \'dē-ə-,fī\ vt **-fied; -fy·ing** [L deus god] **1 a :** to make a god of **b :** to take as an object of worship **2 :** to glorify as of supreme worth ⟨deify money⟩ — **de·i·fi·ca·tion** \,dē-ə-fə-'kā-shən\ n

deign \'dān\ vb [OF deignier, fr. L dignare, fr. dignus worthy] : to think fit or in keeping with one's dignity : CONDESCEND ⟨did not deign to reply to the rude remark⟩ ⟨had not dreamed that the prince would deign to notice her⟩ **syn** see STOOP

de·ion·ize \(')dē-'ī-ə-,nīz\ vt : to remove ions from : DESALT — **de·ion·i·za·tion** \(,)dē-,ī-ə-nə-'zā-shən\ n

de·ism \'dē-,izəm\ n : a movement or system of thought esp. of the 17th and 18th centuries advocating natural religion based on human reason rather than revelation, emphasizing morality, and denying the interference of the Creator with the laws of the universe — **de·ist** \'dē-əst\ n

de·i·ty \'dē-ət-ē\ n, pl **-ties 1 a :** DIVINITY 1 **b** cap : ²GOD ⟨the Deity⟩ **2 a :** GOD **b :** GODDESS

de·jec·ta \di-'jek-tə\ n pl : EXCREMENTS

de·ject·ed \di-'jek-təd\ adj [L deject-, deicere to cast down, fr. de- + jacere to throw] : cast down in spirits : LOW-SPIRITED, SAD, DEPRESSED ⟨dejected over a failure⟩ — **de·ject·ed·ly** adv — **de·ject·ed·ness** n

de·jec·tion \di-'jek-shən\ n : lowness of spirits : SADNESS **syn** see MELANCHOLY

de ju·re \(')dē-'jù(ə)r-ē\ adj (or adv) [NL, by right] : existing or exercising power by legal right ⟨de jure government⟩ — compare DE FACTO

deka- or **dek-** — see DECA-

deka·gram \'dek-ə-,gram\ n : a metric unit of mass and weight equal to 10 grams — see METRIC SYSTEM table

deka·li·ter \'dek-ə-,lēt-ər\ n : a metric unit of capacity equal to 10 liters — see METRIC SYSTEM table

deka·me·ter \'dek-ə-,mēt-ər\ n : a metric unit of length equal to 10 meters — see METRIC SYSTEM table

deka·stere \'dek-ə-,sti(ə)r, -,ste(ə)r\ n : a metric unit of volume equal to 10 cubic meters — see METRIC SYSTEM table

de·lam·i·na·tion \(,)dē-,lam-ə-'nā-shən\ n : separation or splitting into distinct layers — **de·lam·i·nate** \(')dē-'lam-ə-,nāt\ vi

Del·a·ware \'del-ə-,wa(ə)r, -,we(ə)r, -wər\ n : a member of an Indian people of the Delaware valley

1de·lay \di-'lā\ n **1 :** the act of delaying : the state of being delayed **2 :** the time during which something is delayed

2delay vb [OF delaier, fr. de- + laier to leave, alter. of laissier, fr. L laxare to slacken] **1 :** to put off : POSTPONE **2 :** to stop, detain, or hinder for a time ⟨delayed by a storm⟩ **3 :** to move or act slowly — **de·lay·er** n

de·le \'dē-(,)lē\ vt **de·led; de·le·ing** [L, imper. sing. of delēre to delete] : to remove (as a word) from typeset matter : ERASE, DELETE

de·lec·ta·ble \di-'lek-tə-bəl\ adj [L delectare to delight] **1 :** highly pleasing : DELIGHTFUL **2 :** DELICIOUS — **de·lec·ta·bly** \-blē\ adv

de·lec·ta·tion \,dē-,lek-'tā-shən\ n **1 :** DELIGHT **2 :** PLEASURE, ENJOYMENT, DIVERSION

del·e·ga·cy \'del-i-gə-sē\ n, pl **-cies 1 a :** the act of delegating **b :** appointment as delegate **2 :** a body of delegates : BOARD

1del·e·gate \'del-i-gət, -,gāt\ n [L delegatus, pp. of delegare to delegate, fr. de- + legare to send as envoy] : a person sent with power to act for another: as **a :** a representative to a convention, conference, or assembly **b :** a representative of a U.S. territory in the House of Representatives **c :** a member of the lower house of the legislature of Maryland, Virginia, or West Virginia

2del·e·gate \-,gāt\ vt **1 :** to entrust to another ⟨delegate one's authority to an assistant⟩ **2 :** to appoint as one's delegate

del·e·ga·tion \,del-i-'gā-shən\ n **1 :** the act of delegating

power or authority to another **2 :** one or more persons chosen to represent others

de·lete \di-'lēt\ vt [L delet-, delēre] : to eliminate esp. by blotting out, cutting out, or erasing

del·e·te·ri·ous \,del-ə-'tir-ē-əs\ adj [Gk dēlētērios, fr. dēleisthai to hurt] : HARMFUL, NOXIOUS — **del·e·te·ri·ous·ly** adv — **del·e·te·ri·ous·ness** n

de·le·tion \di-'lē-shən\ n **1 :** an act of deleting **2 :** something deleted

delft \'delft\ or **delft·ware** \-,wa(ə)r, -,we(ə)r\ n **1 :** a Dutch brown pottery covered with an opaque white glaze upon which the predominantly blue decoration is painted **2 :** glazed pottery esp. when blue and white

deli \'del-ē\ n, pl **del·is :** DELICATESSEN

1de·lib·er·ate \di-'lib-(ə-)rət\ adj [L deliberatus, pp. of deliberare to weigh in mind, fr. de- + libra scale] **1 :** decided upon as a result of careful thought : carefully considered ⟨a deliberate judgment⟩ **2 :** weighing facts and arguments : careful and slow in deciding ⟨a deliberate man⟩ **3 :** slow in action : not hurried ⟨deliberate movements⟩ **syn** see VOLUNTARY — **de·lib·er·ate·ly** adv — **de·lib·er·ate·ness** n

2de·lib·er·ate \di-'lib-ə-,rāt\ vb : to think about deliberately : ponder issues and decisions carefully : CONSIDER

de·lib·er·a·tion \di-,lib-ə-'rā-shən\ n **1 :** the act of deliberating **2 :** a discussion and consideration of the reasons for and against a measure or question **3 :** the quality of being deliberate : DELIBERATENESS

de·lib·er·a·tive \di-'lib-ə-,rāt-iv, -'lib-(ə-)rət-\ adj : of or relating to deliberation : engaged in or devoted to deliberation ⟨a deliberative assembly⟩ — **de·lib·er·a·tive·ly** adv — **de·lib·er·a·tive·ness** n

del·i·ca·cy \'del-i-kə-sē\ n, pl **-cies 1 :** something pleasing to eat because it is rare or luxurious **2 a :** FINENESS, DAINTINESS ⟨lace of great delicacy⟩ **b :** FRAILTY **3 :** nicety or subtle expressiveness of touch (as in painting or music) **4 a :** precise and refined perception and discrimination **b :** extreme sensitivity : PRECISION **5 a :** nice sensibility in feeling or conduct **b :** SQUEAMISHNESS **6 :** the quality or state of requiring delicate treatment ⟨the delicacy of a situation⟩

del·i·cate \'del-i-kət\ adj [L delicatus] **1 a :** pleasing to the sense of taste or smell esp. in a mild or subtle way ⟨a delicate aroma⟩ **b :** marked by daintiness or charm of color, lines, or proportions **2 :** marked by keen sensitivity or fine discrimination : FASTIDIOUS, SQUEAMISH, SCRUPULOUS **3 a :** marked by minute precision **b :** exhibiting extreme sensitivity **4 :** precariously balanced **5 a :** marked by meticulous technique or operation or by execution with adroit finesse **b :** marked by fineness of structure, workmanship, or texture **c :** easily torn or hurt ⟨a delicate butterfly wing⟩; also : WEAK, SICKLY **d :** marked by fine subtlety ⟨delicate irony⟩ **e :** marked by tact; also : requiring tact — **del·i·cate·ly** adv — **del·i·cate·ness** n

del·i·ca·tes·sen \,del-i-kə-'tes-ᵊn\ n pl **1 :** ready-to-eat food products (as cooked meats and prepared salads) **2** sing, pl **delicatessens :** a store where delicatessen are sold

de·li·cious \di-'lish-əs\ adj : affording great pleasure : DELIGHTFUL; esp : very pleasing to the taste or smell — **de·li·cious·ly** adv — **de·li·cious·ness** n

1de·light \di-'līt\ n **1 :** extreme pleasure or satisfaction : JOY **2 :** something that gives great pleasure ⟨the new car is a delight⟩

2delight vb [OF delitier, fr. L delectare, intens. of delicere to allure, fr. de- + lacere to allure] **1 :** to take great pleasure **2 :** to give keen enjoyment **3 :** to give joy or satisfaction to : please greatly

de·light·ed adj : highly pleased : GRATIFIED, JOYOUS — **de·light·ed·ly** adv — **de·light·ed·ness** n

de·light·ful \di-'līt-fəl\ adj : highly pleasing : giving delight ⟨a delightful vacation⟩ — **de·light·ful·ly** \-fə-lē\ adv — **de·light·ful·ness** n

de·light·some \-'līt-səm\ adj : very pleasing : DELIGHTFUL

De·li·lah \di-'lī-lə\ n : the mistress and betrayer of Samson

de·lim·it \di-'lim-ət\ vt : to fix the limits of : BOUND — **de·lim·i·ta·tion** \-,lim-ə-'tā-shən\ n — **de·lim·i·ta·tive** \-'lim-ə-,tāt-iv\ adj

de·lin·e·ate \di-'lin-ē-,āt\ vt [L delineare, fr. de- + linea line] **1 a :** to indicate by lines drawn in the form or figure of : PORTRAY, SKETCH **b** : to represent accurately **2** : to describe in usu. sharp or vivid detail ⟨*delineate* the characters in a story⟩ — **de·lin·e·a·tor** \-ē-,āt-ər\ *n*

de·lin·e·a·tion \di-,lin-ē-'ā-shən\ *n* **1** : the act of representing, portraying, or describing graphically or verbally **2** : something made by delineating — **de·lin·e·a·tive** \-'lin-ē-,āt-iv\ *adj*

de·lin·quen·cy \di-'liŋ-kwən-sē\ *n, pl* **-cies** : the quality or state of being delinquent

¹de·lin·quent \-kwənt\ *n* : a delinquent person

²delinquent *adj* [L *delinquere* to fail, offend, fr. *de-* + *linquere* to leave] **1** : offending by neglect or violation of duty or of law **2** : being in arrears in payment — **de·lin·quent·ly** *adv*

del·i·quesce \,del-ə-'kwes\ *vi* [L *deliquescere*, fr. *de-* + *liquescere*, incho. of *liquēre* to be fluid] : to melt away: **a** : to dissolve gradually by absorbing moisture from the air ⟨a *deliquescing* substance⟩ **b** : to become soft or liquid ⟨*deliquescing* mushrooms⟩ — **del·i·ques·cence** \-'kwes-°n(t)s\ *n*

del·i·ques·cent \-'kwes-°nt\ *adj* **1** : marked by or undergoing deliquescence **2** : having repeated division into branches ⟨elms are *deliquescent* trees⟩ — compare EXCURRENT

de·lir·i·ous \di-'lir-ē-əs\ *adj* **1** : of or relating to delirium **2** : marked by delirium; *also* : wildly excited — **de·lir·i·ous·ly** *adv* — **de·lir·i·ous·ness** *n*

de·lir·i·um \-'lir-ē-əm\ *n* [L, fr. *delirare* to deviate, be crazy, fr. *de-* + *lira* furrow] **1** : a mental disturbance characterized by confusion, disordered speech, and hallucinations **2** : frenzied excitement

delirium tre·mens \-'trē-mənz\ *n* [NL, lit., trembling delirium] : a violent delirium with tremors that is induced by excessive and prolonged use of alcoholic liquors

de·liv·er \di-'liv-ər\ *vt* **de·liv·ered**; **de·liv·er·ing** \-'liv-(ə-)riŋ\ [OF *delivrer*, fr. LL *deliberare*, fr. L *de-* + *liberare* to liberate] **1** : to set free : SAVE **2** : to hand over : CONVEY, SURRENDER **3** : to assist in giving birth; *also* : to aid in the birth of **4** : UTTER, RELATE, COMMUNICATE **5** : to send to an intended target or destination **syn** see RESCUE — **de·liv·er·a·ble** \-'liv-(ə-)rə-bəl\ *adj* — **de·liv·er·er** \-'liv-ər-ər\ *n*

de·liv·er·ance \di-'liv-(ə-)rən(t)s\ *n* **1** : a delivering or a being delivered : LIBERATION, RESCUE ⟨*deliverance* from the hands of the enemy⟩ **2** : something delivered or communicated; *esp* : a publicly expressed opinion

de·liv·ery \di-'liv-(ə-)rē\ *n, pl* **-er·ies** **1** : a delivering from restraint ⟨jail *delivery*⟩ **2 a** : the act of handing over **b** : a legal conveyance of right or title **c** : something delivered at one time or in one unit **3** : the act of giving birth **4** : a delivering esp. of a speech; *also* : manner or style of uttering in speech or song **5** : the act or manner of sending forth or throwing

dell \'del\ *n* [ME *delle*] : a secluded small valley usu. covered with trees or turf

de·louse \(')dē-'laus, -'lauz\ *vt* : to remove lice from

Del·phi·an \'del-fē-ən\ *or* **Del·phic** \-fik\ *adj* **1** : of or relating to ancient Delphi or its oracle **2** : AMBIGUOUS, OBSCURE

del·phin·i·um \del-'fin-ē-əm\ *n* [Gk *delphinion* larkspur, dim. of *delphin-, delphis* dolphin] : any of a large genus of chiefly perennial erect branching herbs related to the buttercups and widely grown for their irregular flowers in showy spikes — compare LARKSPUR

Del·phi·nus \del-'fī-nəs\ *n* [L, lit., dolphin] : a northern constellation nearly west of Pegasus

del·ta \'del-tə\ *n* **1** : the 4th letter of the Greek alphabet — Δ or δ **2** : something shaped like a capital Δ; *esp* : the triangular or fan-shaped piece of land made by deposits of mud and sand at the mouth of a river **3** : an increment of a variable — **del·ta·ic** \del-'tā-ik\ *adj*

delta ray *n* : an electron ejected by an ionizing particle in its passage through matter

¹del·toid \'del-,toid\ *or* **del·toi·de·us** \del-'toid-ē-əs\ *n, pl* **del·toids** *or* **del·toi·dei** \-'toid-ē-,ī\ : a large triangular muscle that covers the shoulder joint and serves to raise the arm laterally

²deltoid *adj* : shaped like a capital delta : TRIANGULAR ⟨a *deltoid* leaf⟩

de·lude \di-'lüd\ *vt* [L *delus-, deludere*, fr. *de-* + *ludere* to play] : to lead from truth or into error : mislead the mind

or judgment of : DECEIVE, TRICK ⟨*deluded* by false promises⟩ — **de·lud·er** *n* — **de·lud·ing·ly** \-'lüd-iŋ-lē\ *adv*

¹del·uge \'del-(,)yüj\ *n* [MF, fr. L *diluvium*, fr. *diluere* to wash away, fr. *dis-* + *lavere* to wash] **1 a** : an overflowing of the land by water : FLOOD **b** : a drenching rain **2** : an irresistible rush ⟨a *deluge* of Christmas mail⟩

²deluge *vt* **1** : to overflow with water : INUNDATE, FLOOD **2** : to overwhelm as if with a deluge ⟨was *deluged* with inquiries⟩

de·lu·sion \di-'lü-zhən\ *n* **1** : the act of deluding : the state of being deluded **2 a** : something that is falsely or delusively believed or propagated **b** : a false belief regarding the self or persons or objects outside the self that persists despite the facts and is common in some psychotic states — **de·lu·sion·al** \-'lüzh-nəl, -'lü-zhən-°l\ *adj*

syn DELUSION, ILLUSION mean something accepted as true or real that is actually false or unreal. DELUSION implies persistent self-deception concerning facts or situations and usu. suggests a disordered state of mind; ILLUSION implies an attributing of truth or reality to something that seems to normal perception to be true and real but in fact is not

de·lu·sive \-'lü-siv, -'lü-ziv\ *adj* : deluding or apt to delude — **de·lu·sive·ly** *adv* — **de·lu·sive·ness** *n*

de·lu·so·ry \-sə-rē, -zə-rē\ *adj* : DECEPTIVE, DELUSIVE

de·luxe \di-'lüks, -'ləks, -'lüks\ *adj* [F *de luxe*, lit., of luxury] : notably luxurious or elegant ⟨a *deluxe* edition⟩

delve \'delv\ *vi* [OE *delfan*] **1** : to dig or labor with a spade **2** : to seek laboriously for information in written records (as books) ⟨*delve* into the past⟩ — **delv·er** *n*

de·mag·ne·tize \(')dē-'mag-nə-,tīz\ *vt* : to deprive of magnetic properties — **de·mag·ne·ti·za·tion** \(,)dē-,mag-nət-ə-'zā-shən\ *n* — **de·mag·ne·tiz·er** \(')dē-'mag-nə-,tī-zər\ *n*

dem·a·gogue *or* **dem·a·gog** \'dem-ə-,gäg\ *n* [Gk *dēma-gōgos*, fr. *dēmos* people + *agein* to lead] : a person who appeals to the emotions and prejudices of people in order to arouse discontent and advance his own political ends — **dem·a·gog·ic** \,dem-ə-'gäj-ik, -'gäg-\ *or* **dem·a·gog·i·cal** \-i-kəl\ *adj* — **dem·a·gogu·ery** \'dem-ə-,gäg-(ə-)rē\ *n* — **dem·a·gogy** \-,gäj-ē, -,gäg-ē\ *n*

¹de·mand \di-'mand\ *n* **1 a** : an act of demanding or asking esp. with authority **b** : something claimed as due **2 a** : an expressed desire to own or use something ⟨the *demand* for new cars⟩ **b** : the ability and desire to purchase goods or services at a specified time and price **c** : the quantity of an article or service that is wanted at a stated price **3 a** : a seeking or state of being sought after ⟨tickets are in great *demand*⟩ **b** : urgent need **4** : a pressing need or requirement ⟨*demands* that taxed his energy⟩ — **on demand** : upon request for payment

²demand *vb* [ML *demandare*, fr. L *de-* + *mandare* to enjoin] **1** : to ask or call for with authority : claim as one's right ⟨*demand* payment of a debt⟩ ⟨*demand* an apology⟩ **2** : to ask earnestly or in the manner of a command ⟨the sentry *demanded* the password⟩ **3** : to call for : REQUIRE, NEED ⟨an illness that *demands* constant care⟩ — **de·mand·a·ble** \-'man-də-bəl\ *adj* — **de·mand·er** *n*

syn DEMAND, REQUIRE, EXACT mean to ask or call for something as due or as necessary. DEMAND carries a suggestion of authoritativeness, insistence, and a right to make a request that is to be regarded as a command; REQUIRE strictly implies imperativeness arising from inner necessity or the compulsion of law or the urgency of the case; EXACT implies not only demanding but getting what one demands ⟨*exacted* payment of an overdue debt⟩

de·mand·ing *adj* : EXACTING — **de·mand·ing·ly** \-'man-diŋ-lē\ *adv*

de·mar·cate \di-'mär-,kāt, 'dē-,mär-\ *vt* [Sp & Pg *demarcar* to delimit, fr. *de-* + *marcar* to mark] **1** : to mark the limits of **2** : to set apart : SEPARATE — **de·mar·ca·tion** \,dē-,mär-'kā-shən\ *n*

de·marche \dā-'märsh\ *n* : a course of action : MANEUVER

deme \'dēm\ *n* **1** : a unit of local government in ancient Attica **2** : a local population of closely related organisms — usu. used in combination ⟨gamo*deme*⟩

¹de·mean \di-'mēn\ *vt* [OF *demener* to conduct, fr. *de-* + *mener* to lead] : to conduct or behave (oneself) usu. in a proper manner ⟨he *demeans* himself like a true American⟩

²demean *vt* [*de-* + *mean*] : DEGRADE, DEBASE ⟨refused to *demean* himself by dishonesty⟩

de·mean·or \di-'mē-nər\ *n* : outward manner or behavior : CONDUCT, BEARING

de·ment·ed \di-'ment-əd\ *adj* : MAD, INSANE — **de·ment·ed·ly** *adv* — **de·ment·ed·ness** *n*

de·men·tia \di-'men-chə\ *n* [L, fr. dement-, demens mad, fr. de- + mens mind] : a condition of deteriorated mentality : INSANITY

de·mer·it \(')dē-'mer-ət\ *n* **1 :** a quality that deserves blame : FAULT **2 :** a mark placed against a person's record for some fault or offense

de·mesne \di-'mān, -'mēn\ *n* **1 :** manorial land actually possessed by the lord and not held by free tenants **2 a :** the land attached to a mansion **b :** landed property : ESTATE **c :** REGION, TERRITORY **3 :** REALM, DOMAIN

De·me·ter \di-'mēt-ər\ *n* : the Greek goddess of agriculture

demi- *prefix* [MF demi, fr. L dimidius, fr. dis- + medius middle] **1 :** half ⟨demibastion⟩ **2 :** one that partly belongs to (a specified type or class) ⟨demigod⟩

demi·god \'dem-ē-,gäd\ *n* : a mythological being with more power than a mortal but less than a god

demi·john \-,jän\ *n* [by folk etymology fr. F dame-jeanne, lit., Lady Jane] : a large bottle of glass or stoneware enclosed in wicker-work

de·mil·i·ta·rize \(')dē-'mil-ə-tə-,rīz\ *vt* : to strip of military forces, weapons, or fortification ⟨a demilitarized zone⟩ — **de·mil·i·ta·ri·za·tion** \(,)dē-,mil-ə-tə-rə-'zā-shən\ *n*

demi·mon·daine \,dem-ē-,män-'dān\ *n* : a woman of the demimonde

demi·monde \'dem-ē-,mänd\ *n* [F demi-monde, lit., half-world] **1 :** a class of women on the fringes of respectable society supported by wealthy lovers **2 :** a group engaged in activity of doubtful legality or propriety

¹de·mise \di-'mīz\ *vt* : to convey (property) for a period of time : LEASE

²demise *n* [MF, fr. demettre to dismiss, fr. L demittere to send down, fr. de- + mittere to send] **1 :** a letting of property : LEASE **2 :** transfer of sovereignty to a successor ⟨demise of the crown⟩ **3 a :** DEATH **b :** a cessation of existence or activity

demi·tasse \'dem-ē-,tas, -,täs\ *n* [F demi-tasse, lit., half-cup] : a small cup of black coffee; *also* : the cup used to serve it

de·mo·bi·lize \di-'mō-bə-,līz\ *vt* **1 :** to dismiss from military service ⟨demobilize an army⟩ **2 :** to change from a state of war to a state of peace — **de·mo·bi·li·za·tion** \-,mō-bə-lə-'zā-shən\ *n*

de·moc·ra·cy \di-'mäk-rə-sē\ *n, pl* -cies [Gk dēmokratia, fr. dēmos people + -kratia -cracy] **1 a :** government by the people; *esp* : rule of the majority **b :** government in which the supreme power is vested in the people and exercised by them directly or indirectly through representation **2 :** a political unit that has a democratic government **3 a :** the absence of hereditary or arbitrary class distinctions or privileges **b :** belief in or practice of social or economic equality for all people

   syn DEMOCRACY, REPUBLIC: DEMOCRACY is a distribution of political power, not a form of government; REPUBLIC in its general sense is a form of government characterized by any number of ways of distributing political power and may or may not be a democracy ⟨France under the Directory was an oligarchical republic⟩ ⟨some medieval Italian republics were dictatorships⟩ REPUBLIC is widely used in a sense equivalent to representative democracy

dem·o·crat \'dem-ə-,krat\ *n* **1 a :** an adherent of democracy **b :** one who practices social equality **2** *cap* : a member of the Democratic party of the U.S.

dem·o·crat·ic \,dem-ə-'krat-ik\ *adj* **1 :** of, relating to, or favoring political, social, or economic democracy **2** *often cap* : of or relating to a major U.S. political party evolving from the anti-federalists and the Democratic-Republican party and associated with policies of broad social reform and internationalism **3 :** of, relating to, or appealing to the broad masses of the people ⟨democratic art⟩ **4 :** favoring social equality : not snobbish — **dem·o·crat·i·cal·ly** \-i-k(ə-)lē\ *adv*

democratic centralism *n* : participation of Communist party members in discussion of policy and election of higher party organizations and strict obedience of members and lower party bodies to decisions of the higher units

Democratic–Republican *adj* : of or relating to an early 19th century American political party favoring strict interpretation of the constitution to restrict the powers of the federal government and emphasizing states' rights

de·moc·ra·tize \di-'mäk-rə-,tīz\ *vt* : to make democratic — **de·moc·ra·ti·za·tion** \-,mäk-rət-ə-'zā-shən\ *n*

de·mod·u·late \(')dē-'mäj-ə-,lāt\ *vt* : to extract from (a transmitted radio signal) the wave by which the sound or picture is reproduced — **de·mod·u·la·tion** \(,)dē-,mäj-ə-'lā-shən\ *n*

de·mog·ra·phy \di-'mäg-rə-fē\ *n* : the statistical study of human populations and esp. their size and distribution and the number of births and deaths — **de·mog·ra·pher** \-fər\ *n* — **de·mo·graph·ic** \,dē-mə-'graf-ik, ,dem-ə-\ *adj* — **de·mo·graph·i·cal·ly** \-'graf-i-k(ə-)lē\ *adv*

dem·oi·selle \,dem-(w)ə-'zel\ *n* [F] : a young lady

de·mol·ish \di-'mäl-ish\ *vt* [MF demoliss-, demolir, fr. L demoliri, fr. de- + moliri to construct, fr. moles mass] **1 a :** to tear down : RAZE **b :** to break to pieces : SMASH **2 :** to do away with : put an end to **syn** see DESTROY — **de·mol·ish·er** *n* — **de·mol·ish·ment** \-ish-mənt\ *n*

dem·o·li·tion \,dem-ə-'lish-ən, ,dē-mə-\ *n* : the act of demolishing; *esp* : destruction in war by means of explosives — **dem·o·li·tion·ist** \-'lish-(ə-)nəst\ *n*

de·mon *or* **dae·mon** \'dē-mən\ *n* [L daemon divinity, spirit, fr. Gk daimōn] **1** *usu* daemon **:** an attendant power or spirit : GENIUS **2 a :** an evil spirit **b :** an evil or undesirable emotion, trait, or state **3** *usu* daemon : a supernatural being of Greek mythology intermediate between gods and men **4 :** one that has unusual drive or effectiveness ⟨he is a demon for work⟩ — **de·mon·ic** \di-'män-ik\ *adj*

de·mon·e·tize \(')dē-'män-ə-,tīz, -'mən-\ *vt* : to stop using as money or as a monetary standard ⟨demonetize silver⟩— **de·mon·e·ti·za·tion** \(,)dē-,män-ət-ə-'zā-shən, -,mən-\ *n*

¹de·mo·ni·ac \di-'mō-nē-,ak\ *also* **de·mo·ni·a·cal** \,dē-mə-'nī-ə-kəl\ *adj* **1 :** possessed or influenced by a demon **2 :** of, relating to, or suggestive of a demon : DEVILISH, FIENDISH ⟨demoniac cruelty⟩ — **de·mo·ni·a·cal·ly** \,dē-mə-'nī-ə-k(ə-)lē\ *adv*

²demoniac *n* : one possessed by a demon

de·mon·ol·o·gy \,dē-mə-'näl-ə-jē\ *n* **1 :** the study of demons **2 :** belief in demons

de·mon·stra·ble \di-'män(t)-strə-bəl, 'dem-ən-strə-\ *adj* **1 :** capable of being demonstrated or proved **2 :** APPARENT, EVIDENT — **de·mon·stra·bil·i·ty** \di-,män(t)-strə-'bil-ət-ē, ,dem-ən-strə-\ *n* — **de·mon·stra·ble·ness** \di-'män(t)-strə-bəl-nəs, 'dem-ən-strə-\ *n* — **de·mon·stra·bly** \-blē\ *adv*

dem·on·strate \'dem-ən-,strāt\ *vb* [L demonstrare, fr. de- + monstrare to show, fr. monstrum portent, monster] **1 :** to show clearly **2 a :** to prove or make clear by reasoning or evidence **b :** to illustrate and explain esp. with many examples **3 :** to show publicly the good qualities of a product ⟨demonstrate a new car⟩ **4 :** to make a public display ⟨as of feelings or military force⟩ ⟨citizens demonstrated in protest before the capitol⟩

dem·on·stra·tion \,dem-ən-'strā-shən\ *n* **1 :** an outward expression or display ⟨a demonstration of joy⟩ **2 :** an act, process, or means of demonstrating to the intelligence: **a :** conclusive evidence : PROOF **b :** a course of reasoning intended to prove that a certain result or conclusion must follow when certain conditions are accepted as a starting point **c :** a showing to a prospective buyer of the merits of a product ⟨a demonstration of a new vacuum cleaner⟩ **3 :** a show of armed force **4 :** a public display of group feelings toward a person or cause — **dem·on·stra·tion·al** \-shnəl, -shən-ᵊl\ *adj*

¹de·mon·stra·tive \di-'män(t)-strət-iv\ *adj* **1 a :** demonstrating as real or true **b :** characterized or established by demonstration ⟨demonstrative reasoning⟩ **2 :** pointing out the one referred to and distinguishing it from others of the same class ⟨the demonstrative pronoun this in "this is my hat"⟩ ⟨the demonstrative adjective that in "that boy"⟩ **3 :** marked by display of feeling ⟨a demonstrative greeting⟩ — **de·mon·stra·tive·ly** *adv* — **de·mon·stra·tive·ness** *n*

²demonstrative *n* : a demonstrative word; *esp* : a demonstrative pronoun

dem·on·stra·tor \'dem-ən-,strāt-ər\ *n* **1 :** a person who

makes or takes part in a demonstration **2** : a manufactured article (as an automobile) used for purposes of
demonstration

de·mor·al·ize \di-'mȯr-ə-,līz, -'mär-\ *vb* **1** : to corrupt
in morals : make bad **2** : to destroy the morale of
: weaken in discipline or spirit : DISORGANIZE ⟨the
unexpected attack *demoralized* the army⟩ — **de·mor·al-
i·za·tion** \di-,mȯr-ə-lə-'zā-shən, -,mär-\ *n* — **de·mor-
al·iz·er** \-'mȯr-ə-,lī-zər, -'mär-\ *n*

de·mote \di-'mōt, 'dē-\ *vt* [*de-* + *-mote* (as in *promote*)]
: to reduce to a lower grade or rank — **de·mo·tion**
\-'mō-shən\ *n*

de·mot·ic \di-'mät-ik\ *adj* [Gk *dēmos* people] **1** : POPU-
LAR, COMMON **2** : of, relating to, or written in a simplified
form of the ancient Egyptian writing **3** : of or relating
to the form of Modern Greek that is based on colloquial
use

de·mount \('·)dē-'maùnt\ *vt* **1** : to remove from a
mounted position **2** : DISASSEMBLE — **de·mount·a·ble**
\-ə-bəl\ *adj*

¹de·mul·cent \di-'məl-sənt\ *adj* [L *demulcēre* to soothe,
fr. *de-* + *mulcēre* to soothe] : SOOTHING

²demulcent *n* : a usu. oily or somewhat thick and gelatinous preparation used to soothe or protect an abraded
mucous membrane

¹de·mur \di-'mər\ *vi* **de·murred**; **de·mur·ring** [L *de-
morari* to delay, fr. *de-* + *morari* to linger, fr. *mora* delay]
1 : to enter a demurrer **2** : to take exception : OBJECT
3 *archaic* : DELAY, HESITATE

²demur *n* **1** : HESITATION **2** : the act of objecting : PRO-
TEST ⟨accepted without *demur*⟩

de·mure \di-'myù(ə)r\ *adj* [ME] **1** : SOBER, SERIOUS
2 : affectedly modest, reserved, or serious : PRIM — **de-
mure·ly** *adv* — **de·mure·ness** *n*

de·mur·rage \di-'mər-ij, -'mə-rij\ *n* **1** : detention of a
ship by the shipper or receiver beyond the time allowed
for loading or unloading **2** : a charge on a shipper or
receiver of goods for detaining a ship, freight car, or
truck beyond the time necessary for loading or unloading

¹de·mur·rer \di-'mər-ər, -'mə-rər\ *n* **1** : a claim by the
defendant in a legal action that the pleadings of the
plaintiff are insufficient or otherwise defective **2** : OB-
JECTION

²de·mur·rer \-'mər-ər\ *n* : one that demurs

de·my \di-'mī\ *n* [ME *demi* half, fr. MF] : a size of
paper typically 16 × 21 inches

¹den \'den\ *n* [OE *denn*] **1** : the shelter or resting place
of a wild animal **2** : a hiding place (as for thieves)
3 : a dirty wretched place in which people live or gather
⟨*dens* of misery⟩ **4** : a quiet snug room; *esp* : one set apart
for reading and relaxation

²den *vb* **denned**; **den·ning** **1** : to live in or retire to a den
2 : to drive into a den

de·nar·i·us \di-'nar-ē-əs, -'ner-\ *n, pl* **de·nar·ii** \-ē-,ī,
-ē-,ē\ [L, coin worth ten asses, fr. *deni* ten each, fr. *decem*
ten] : a small silver coin of ancient Rome; *also* : a gold
coin equal to 25 silver denarii

de·na·tur·ant \('·)dē-'nāch-(ə-)rənt\ *n* : a denaturing agent

de·na·ture \('·)dē-'nā-chər\ *vt* **de·na·tured**; **de·na·tur·ing**
\-'nāch-(ə-)riŋ\ : to deprive of natural qualities: as
a : to make (alcohol) unfit for drinking without impairing
usefulness for other purposes **b** : to modify (as a native
protein) so that all original properties are removed or
diminished — **de·na·tur·a·tion** \(,)dē-,nā-chə-'rā-shən\ *n*

den·dri·form \'den-drə-,fȯrm\ *adj* : resembling a tree in
structure

den·drite \'den-,drīt\ *n* [Gk *dendron* tree] **1** : a branching
figure (as in a mineral or stone) resembling a tree **2** : any
of the usu. branching protoplasmic processes that conduct impulses toward the body of a nerve cell — **den-
drit·ic** \den-'drit-ik\ *adj*

den·dro·chro·nol·o·gy \,den-drō-krə-'näl-ə-jē\ *n* : the
science of dating events by comparative study of growth
rings in trees and aged wood — **den·dro·chron·o·log·i·cal**
\-,krän-ᵊl-'äj-i-kəl, -,krōn-\ *adj* — **den·dro·chron·o-
log·i·cal·ly** \-k(ə-)lē\ *adv*

den·droid \'den-,drȯid\ *adj* : resembling a tree in form
: ARBORESCENT

den·drol·o·gy \den-'dräl-ə-jē\ *n* : the study of trees —
den·dro·log·ic \,den-drə-'läj-ik\ *adj* — **den·drol·o·gist**
\den-'dräl-ə-jist\ *n*

Den·eb \'den-,eb, -əb\ *n* [Ar *dhanab al-dajāj*, lit., the tail
of the hen] : a star of the first magnitude in Cygnus

den·gue \'deŋ-gē, -,gā\ *n* [Sp] : an acute infectious disease
characterized by headache, severe joint pain, and rash

de·ni·al \di-'nī(-ə)l\ *n* **1** : a refusal to grant something
asked for **2** : a refusal to admit the truth of a statement
: CONTRADICTION ⟨a flat *denial* of the charges⟩ **3** : a refusal to acknowledge something; *esp* : a statement of
disbelief or rejection : DISAVOWAL ⟨make a public *denial*
of political beliefs once held⟩ **4** : a cutting down or
limiting : RESTRICTION ⟨*denial* of her appetite⟩

¹de·ni·er \di-'nī(-ə)r\ *n* : one that denies

²de·nier *n* [MF, fr. L *denarius* denarius] **1** \də-'ni(ə)r,
dən-'yā\ : a small orig. silver coin of France and western
Europe from the 8th to the 19th century **2** \'den-yər\
: a unit of fineness for silk, rayon, or nylon yarn equal
to the fineness of a yarn weighing one gram for each
9000 meters

den·i·grate \'den-i-,grāt\ *vt* [LL *denigrare*, fr. L *de-* +
niger black] : to cast aspersions on : DEFAME — **deni-
gra·tion** \,den-i-'grā-shən\ *n* — **den·i·gra·tor** \'den-i-
,grāt-ər\ *n* — **den·i·gra·to·ry** \-grə-,tōr-ē, -,tȯr-\ *adj*

den·im \'den-əm\ *n* [F *serge de Nîmes* serge of Nîmes,
France] **1** : a firm durable twilled usu. cotton fabric
woven with colored warp and white filling threads **2**
pl : overalls or trousers of usu. blue denim

de·ni·tri·fy \('·)dē-'nī-trə-,fī\ *vt* **1** : to remove nitrogen
or its compound from **2** : to convert (a nitrate or a
nitrite) into a compound of a lower state of oxidation esp.
as a step in the nitrogen cycle — **de·ni·tri·fi·ca·tion**
\(,)dē-,nī-trə-fə-'kā-shən\ *n* — **de·ni·tri·fi·er** \('·)dē-
'nī-trə-,fī(-ə)r\ *n*

den·i·zen \'den-ə-zən\ *n* [MF *denzein*, fr. *denz* within, fr.
LL *deintus*, fr. L *de-* + *intus* within] : INHABITANT; *esp*
: a person, animal, or plant found or naturalized in a
particular region or environment ⟨*denizens* of the forest⟩

de·nom·i·nate \di-'näm-ə-,nāt\ *vt* : to give a name to
: DESIGNATE

de·nom·i·nate number \di-,näm-ə-nət-\ *n* : a number
(as 7 in 7 *feet*) that specifies a quantity in terms of a unit
of measurement

de·nom·i·na·tion \di-,näm-ə-'nā-shən\ *n* **1** : an act of
denominating **2** : NAME, DESIGNATION; *esp* : a general
name for a class of things **3** : a religious body comprising
a number of congregations with similar beliefs **4** : one of
a series of related values each having a special name ⟨a
one-dollar bill and a ten-dollar bill represent two *denominations* of U.S. money⟩ — **de·nom·i·na·tion·al** \-shnəl,
-shən-ᵊl\ *adj* — **de·nom·i·na·tion·al·ly** \-ē\ *adv*

de·nom·i·na·tion·al·ism \-shnəl-,iz-əm, -shən-ᵊl-,iz-\ *n*
1 : devotion to denominational principles or interests
2 : SECTARIANISM

de·nom·i·na·tive \di-'näm-(ə-)nət-iv\ *adj* : derived from
a noun or adjective ⟨*denominative* verb⟩

de·nom·i·na·tor \di-'näm-ə-,nāt-ər\ *n* : the part of a
fraction that is below the line signifying division and that
in fractions with 1 as the numerator indicates into how
many parts the unit is divided : DIVISOR

de·no·ta·tion \,dē-nō-'tā-shən\ *n* **1** : an act or process
of denoting **2** : MEANING; *esp* : a direct specific meaning
as distinct from connotations **3** : a denoting term or
label : NAME, SIGN

de·no·ta·tive \'dē-nō-,tāt-iv, di-'nōt-ət-iv\ *adj* **1** : denoting or tending to denote **2** : relating to denotation

de·note \di-'nōt\ *vt* **1** : to mark out plainly : point out
: INDICATE ⟨the hands of a clock *denote* the time⟩ **2** : to
make known : SHOW ⟨smiled to *denote* pleasure⟩ **3** : to
have the meaning of : MEAN, NAME ⟨in the U.S. the word
corn denotes Indian corn⟩

syn DENOTE and CONNOTE, when used of words, together
equal *mean*. DENOTE implies all that strictly belongs to the
definition of the word; CONNOTE implies all the ideas or
emotions suggested by the word ⟨*home denotes* the place
where one lives, but it *connotes* the comforts, the privacy,
and a whole range of experience one enjoys there⟩

de·noue·ment \,dā-,nü-'mäⁿ, -'nü-,\ *n* [F *dénouement*,
lit., untying] **1** : the final solution or untangling of the
conflicts or difficulties that make up the plot of a literary
work **2** : a solution or working out esp. of a complex or
difficult situation

de·nounce \di-'naùn(t)s\ *vt* [L *denuntiare* to proclaim, fr.

ə abut; ᵊ kitten; ər further; a back; ā bake; ä cot, cart; aù out; ch chin; e less; ē easy; g gift; i trip; ī life

de- + nuntiare to report] **1 :** to point out as deserving blame or punishment **2 :** to inform against **:** ACCUSE **3 :** to announce formally the termination of (as a treaty) — **de·nounce·ment** \-mənt\ *n* — **de·nounc·er** *n*

de no·vo \di-'nō-vō\ *adv* [L] **:** ANEW, AGAIN

dense \'den(t)s\ *adj* [L *densus*] **1 :** marked by compactness or crowding together of parts ⟨a *dense* forest⟩ **2 :** mentally dull **3 :** having high opacity ⟨*dense* fog⟩ ⟨a *dense* photographic negative⟩ **syn** see STUPID — **dense·ly** *adv* — **dense·ness** *n*

den·si·ty \'den(t)-sət-ē\ *n, pl* **-ties 1 :** the quality or state of being dense **2 :** the quantity of something per unit volume, unit area, or unit length: as **a :** the mass of a substance per unit volume ⟨*density* expressed in grams per cubic centimeter⟩ **b :** the average number of individuals or units in a unit of area or volume ⟨population *density*⟩ **3 :** STUPIDITY **4 :** the degree of opacity of a translucent medium

1dent \'dent\ *n* [ME, blow, alter. of *dint*] **1 :** a depression or hollow made by a blow or by pressure **2 a :** an impression or effect made usu. against resistance **b :** initial progress

2dent *vb* **1 :** to make a dent in or on **2 :** to become marked by a dent

1den·tal \'dent-ᵊl\ *adj* [L *dent-, dens* tooth] **1 :** of or relating to the teeth or dentistry **2 :** pronounced with the tip or blade of the tongue against or near the upper front teeth — **den·tal·ly** \-ᵊl-ē\ *adv*

2dental *n* **:** a dental consonant

dental floss *n* **:** a flat waxed thread used to clean between the teeth

dental hygienist *n* **:** one who assists a dentist esp. in cleaning teeth

den·ta·li·um \den-'tā-lē-əm\ *n, pl* **-lia** \-lē-ə\ **:** TOOTH SHELL

den·tate \'den-,tāt\ *or* **den·tat·ed** \-,tāt-əd\ *adj* **:** having pointed conical projections ⟨multi*dentate*⟩ — **den·tate·ly** *adv* — **den·ta·tion** \den-'tā-shən\ *n*

dent corn *n* **:** an Indian corn having kernels that contain both hard and soft starch and that become indented at maturity

den·ti·cle \'dent-i-kəl\ *n* **:** a small conical pointed projection (as a tooth)

den·tic·u·late \den-'tik-yə-lət\ *or* **den·tic·u·lat·ed** \-,lāt-əd\ *adj* **1 :** covered with small pointed projections **2 :** finely dentate

den·ti·frice \'dent-ə-frəs\ *n* [L *dentifricium*, fr. *dent-, dens* tooth + *fricare* to rub] **:** a powder, paste, or liquid for cleaning the teeth

den·til \'dent-ᵊl\ *n* **:** one of a series of small projecting rectangular blocks esp. under a cornice

den·tin \'dent-ᵊn\ *or* **den·tine** \'den-,tēn, den-'\ *n* **:** a calcareous material like bone but harder and denser that composes the principal mass of a tooth — **den·tin·al** \den-'tēn-ᵊl, 'dent-ᵊn-əl\ *adj*

den·tist \'dent-əst\ *n* **:** one whose profession is the care, treatment, and repair of the teeth and the fitting of artificial teeth

den·tist·ry \'dent-ə-strē\ *n* **:** the profession or practice of a dentist

den·ti·tion \den-'tish-ən\ *n* **1 :** the development and cutting of teeth **2 :** the number, kind, and arrangement of teeth (as of a person)

den·tu·lous \'den-chə-ləs\ *adj* [back-formation fr. *edentulous*] **:** having teeth

den·ture \'den-chər\ *n* **1 :** a set of teeth **2 :** an artificial replacement for one or more teeth; *esp* **:** a set of false teeth

dentition (adult human): upper, *A*; lower, *B*; *1* incisors, *2* canines, *3* bicuspids, *4* molars

de·nude \di-'n(y)üd\ *vt* **:** to strip of covering **:** lay bare ⟨forest land *denuded* by fire⟩⟨erosion that *denudes* the rocks of soil⟩ — **de·nu·da·tion** \,dē-(,)n(y)ü-'dā-shən, ,den-yü-'dā-\ *n* — **de·nu·da·tion·al** \-shnəl, -shən-ᵊl\ *adj* — **de·nud·er** \di-'n(y)üd-ər\ *n*

de·nun·ci·a·tion \di-,nən(t)-sē-'ā-shən\ *n* **:** the act of denouncing; *esp* **:** a public accusation ⟨publish a *denuncia*-

---

tion of an official⟩ — **de·nun·ci·a·to·ry** \-'nən(t)-sē-ə-,tōr-ē, -,tor-\ *adj*

de·ny \di-'nī\ *vt* **de·nied; de·ny·ing** [OF *denier*, fr. L *denegare*, fr. *de-* + *negare* to deny] **1 :** to declare not to be true **:** CONTRADICT ⟨*deny* a report⟩ **2 :** to refuse to grant ⟨*deny* a request⟩ **3 :** to refuse to acknowledge **:** DISOWN ⟨*denied* his faith⟩ **4 :** to reject as false ⟨*deny* the theory of evolution⟩ — **de·ny·ing·ly** \-'nī-iŋ-lē\ *adv*

de·o·dar \'dē-ə-,där\ *or* **de·o·da·ra** \,dē-ə-'där-ə\ *n* [Hindi *deodar*, fr. Skt *devadāru*, lit., timber of the gods] **:** an East Indian cedar valued as an ornamental and timber tree

de·odor·ant \dē-'ōd-ə-rənt\ *n* **:** a preparation that destroys or masks unpleasant odors — **deodorant** *adj*

de·odor·ize \dē-'ōd-ə-,rīz\ *vt* **:** to eliminate or prevent the offensive odor of — **de·odor·i·za·tion** \(,)dē-,ōd-ə-rə-'zā-shən\ *n* — **de·odor·iz·er** \(')dē-'ōd-ə-,rī-zər\ *n*

Deo vo·len·te \,dā-ō-və-'lent-ē, ,dē-\ [L] **:** God being willing

de·ox·i·dize \(')dē-'äk-sə-,dīz\ *vt* **:** to remove oxygen from — **de·ox·i·diz·er** *n*

de·ox·y·gen·at·ed \(')dē-'äk-si-jə-,nāt-əd\ *adj* **:** having the hemoglobin in the reduced state

de·oxy·ri·bo·nu·cle·ic acid \(,)dē-,äk-sē-'rī-bō-n(y)ü-,klē-ik-, -,klā-\ *n* **:** any of various nucleic acids that are found esp. in cell nuclei and are the molecular basis of heredity in many organisms

de·oxy·ri·bose \dē-,äk-sē-'rī-,bōs\ *n* **:** a sugar that has five carbon atoms in the molecule and is a constituent of nucleic acids

de·part \di-'pärt\ *vb* **1 a :** to go away or go away from **:** LEAVE **b :** DIE **2 :** to turn aside **:** DEVIATE

de·part·ed *adj* **1 :** BYGONE **2 :** no longer living

de·part·ment \di-'pärt-mənt\ *n* **1 :** a distinct sphere **:** PROVINCE **2 a :** a major administrative division of a government or business **b :** a major territorial administrative division **c :** a division of a college or school giving instruction in a particular subject **d :** a section of a department store — **de·part·men·tal** \di-,pärt-'ment-ᵊl, ,dē-\ *adj* — **de·part·men·tal·ly** *adv*

department store *n* **:** a store having separate departments for a wide variety of goods

de·par·ture \di-'pär-chər\ *n* **1 a :** the act of going away **b** *archaic* **:** DEATH **2 :** a setting out (as on a new course) **3 :** DIVERGENCE

de·pend \di-'pend\ *vi* [L *dependēre*, fr. *de-* + *pendēre* to hang] **1 :** to hang down ⟨a vine *depending* from a tree⟩ **2 :** to rely for support ⟨children *depend* on their parents⟩ **3 :** to be determined by or based on some action or condition ⟨success of the picnic will *depend* on the weather⟩ **4 :** TRUST, RELY ⟨a man you can *depend* on⟩ ⟨you can *depend* on its raining⟩

de·pend·a·ble \di-'pen-də-bəl\ *adj* **:** capable of being depended on **:** TRUSTWORTHY, RELIABLE — **de·pend·a·bil·i·ty** \-,pen-də-'bil-ət-ē\ *n* — **de·pend·a·bly** \-'pen-də-blē\ *adv*

de·pend·ence \di-'pen-dən(t)s\ *n* **1 :** the quality or state of being dependent; *esp* **:** the quality or state of being influenced by or subject to another **2 :** RELIANCE, TRUST **3 :** something on which one relies

de·pend·en·cy \-dən-sē\ *n, pl* **-cies 1 :** DEPENDENCE 1 **2 :** something that is dependent on something else; *esp* **:** a territory under the jurisdiction of a nation but not formally annexed by it

1de·pend·ent \di-'pen-dənt\ *adj* **1 :** hanging down **2 a :** determined or conditioned by another **b :** relying on another for support ⟨*dependent* children⟩ **c :** subject to another's jurisdiction ⟨a *dependent* territory⟩ **3 :** SUBORDINATE 3a — **de·pend·ent·ly** *adv*

2dependent *also* **de·pend·ant** *n* **:** one that is dependent; *esp* **:** a person who relies on another for support

de·pict \di-'pikt\ *vt* [L *depict-, depingere*, fr. *de-* + *pingere* to paint] **1 :** to represent by a picture **2 :** to describe in words — **de·pic·tion** \-'pik-shən\ *n*

dep·i·late \'dep-ə-,lāt\ *vt* [L *depilare*, fr. *de-* + *pilus* hair] **:** to remove hair from — **dep·i·la·tion** \,dep-ə-'lā-shən\ *n*

de·pil·a·to·ry \di-'pil-ə-,tōr-ē, -,tor-\ *n, pl* **-ries :** an agent for removing hair, wool, or bristles — **depilatory** *adj*

de·plane \(')dē-'plān\ *vi* **:** to get off an airplane

de·plete \di-'plēt\ *vt* [L *deplet-, deplēre*, fr. *de-* + *plēre* to fill] **:** to reduce in amount by using up **:** exhaust esp. of strength or resources ⟨soil *depleted* of minerals⟩ ⟨a *depleted*

---

j joke; **ŋ** sing; **ō** flow; **ȯ** flaw; **ȯi** coin; **th** thin; **t̲h̲** this; **ü** loot; **u̇** foot; **y** yet; **yü** few; **yu̇** furious; **zh** vision

treasury) — **de·ple·tion** \-'plē-shən\ *n* — **de·ple·tive** \-'plēt-iv\ *adj*

de·plor·a·ble \di-'plȯr-ə-bəl, -'plȯr-\ *adj* **1 :** deserving to be deplored **:** LAMENTABLE ⟨a *deplorable* accident⟩ **2 :** very bad **:** WRETCHED ⟨*deplorable* conditions⟩ — **de·plor·a·ble·ness** *n* — **de·plor·a·bly** \-blē\ *adv*

de·plore \di-'plō(ə)r, -'plȯ(ə)r\ *vt* [L *deplorare*, fr. *de-* + *plorare* to wail] **1 a :** to feel or express grief for **b :** to regret strongly **2 :** to consider unfortunate or deserving of disapproval — **de·plor·er** *n* — **de·plor·ing·ly** \-iŋ-lē\ *adv*

de·ploy \di-'plȯi\ *vb* [F *déployer*, fr. L *displicare* to scatter, fr. *dis-* + *plicare* to fold] **1 :** to spread out (as troops or ships) in order for battle **2 :** to undergo deployment **de·ploy·ment** \-mənt\ *n* **:** an act of deploying

de·po·lar·ize \(')dē-'pō-lə-,rīz\ *vt* **:** to prevent, reduce, or remove polarization of — **de·po·lar·i·za·tion** \(,)dē-,pō-lə-rə-'zā-shən\ *n* — **de·po·lar·iz·er** \(')dē-'pō-lə-,rī-zər\ *n*

1de·po·nent \di-'pō-nənt\ *adj* [LL *deponent-, deponens*, fr. L, prp. of *deponere* to put down, fr. *de-* + *ponere* to put] **:** occurring with passive or middle voice forms but with active voice meaning ⟨*deponent* verbs in Latin and Greek⟩

2deponent *n* **1 :** a deponent verb **2 :** one who gives evidence

de·pop·u·late \(')dē-'päp-yə-,lāt\ *vt* **:** to reduce greatly the population of (as a city or region) by destroying or driving away the inhabitants ⟨*depopulated* by an epidemic of plague⟩ — **de·pop·u·la·tion** \(,)dē-,päp-yə-'lā-shən\ *n* — **de·pop·u·la·tor** \(')dē-'päp-yə-,lāt-ər\ *n*

de·port \di-'pōrt, -'pȯrt\ *vt* [MF *deporter*, fr. L *deportare* to carry away, fr. *de-* + *portare* to carry] **1 :** CONDUCT, BEHAVE ⟨*deported* himself disgracefully⟩ **2 :** to force (an alien whose presence is unlawful or harmful) to leave a country — **de·por·ta·tion** \,dē-,pōr-'tā-shən, -,pȯr-\ *n* — **de·por·tee** \,dē-,pōr-'tē, -,pȯr-\ *n*

de·port·ment \di-'pōrt-mənt, -'pȯrt-\ *n* **:** manner of conducting oneself **:** BEHAVIOR

de·pose \di-'pōz\ *vb* [OF *deposer*, irreg. fr. LL *deponere*, fr. L, to put down, fr. *de-* + *ponere* to put] **1 :** to remove from a throne or other high position **2** [ME *deposen*, irreg. fr. ML *deponere*, fr. L, to put down] **:** to testify under oath or by affidavit

1de·pos·it \di-'päz-ət\ *vb* **1 :** to place for safekeeping; *esp* **:** to put money in a bank **2 :** to give as a pledge that a purchase will be made or a service used ⟨*deposit* $10 on a new bicycle⟩ **3 :** to lay down **:** PLACE, PUT ⟨*deposit* a parcel on a table⟩ **4 :** to let fall or sink ⟨sand and silt *deposited* by a flood⟩ **5 :** to become deposited **:** SETTLE — **de·pos·i·tor** \-ət-ər\ *n*

2deposit *n* **1 :** the state of being deposited ⟨money on *deposit*⟩ **2 a :** something placed for safekeeping; *esp* **:** money deposited in a bank **b :** money given as a pledge **3 :** an act of depositing **4 :** something laid or thrown down ⟨a *deposit* of silt left by the flood⟩ **5 :** an accumulation of mineral matter (as iron ore, oil, or gas) in nature — **de·pos·i·tary** \di-'päz-ə-,ter-ē\ *n, pl* **-tar·ies 1 :** a person to whom something is entrusted **2 :** DEPOSITORY 2

dep·o·si·tion \,dep-ə-'zish-ən, ,dē-pə-\ *n* **1 :** the act of deposing a person from high office ⟨the *deposition* of the king⟩ **2 :** a statement esp. in writing made under oath **3 :** the action or process of depositing ⟨the *deposition* of silt by a stream⟩ **4 :** something deposited **:** DEPOSIT — **dep·o·si·tion·al** \-'zish-nəl, -ən-ᵊl\ *adj*

de·pos·i·to·ry \di-'päz-ə-,tōr-ē, -,tȯr-\ *n, pl* **-ries 1 :** DEPOSITARY 1 **2 :** a place where something is deposited esp. for safekeeping

de·pot \1 *& 3 are* 'dep-,ō *also* 'dē-,pō, 2 *is* 'dē-,pō *also* 'dep-,ō\ *n* [F *dépôt*] **1 :** a place of deposit for goods **:** STOREHOUSE **2 :** a building for railroad or bus passengers or freight **:** STATION **3 :** a place where military supplies are kept or where troops are assembled and trained

de·prave \di-'prāv\ *vt* [L *depravare* to pervert, fr. *de-* + *pravus* crooked, bad] **:** to make bad **:** corrupt the morals of **:** PERVERT **syn** see DEBASE

de·praved \-'prāvd\ *adj* **:** marked by corruption or evil; *esp* **:** PERVERTED — **de·praved·ly** \-'prā-vəd-lē, -'prāv-dlē\ *adv* — **de·praved·ness** \-'prā-vəd-nəs, -'prāv(d)-nəs\ *n*

de·prav·i·ty \di-'prav-ət-ē\ *n, pl* **-ties 1 :** the quality or state of being depraved **2 :** a corrupt act or practice

dep·re·cate \'dep-ri-,kāt\ *vt* [L *deprecari* to avert by

prayer, fr. *de-* + *precari* to pray] **1 :** to express disapproval of **2 :** DEPRECIATE — **dep·re·cat·ing·ly** \-,kāt-iŋ-lē\ *adv* — **dep·re·ca·tion** \,dep-ri-'kā-shən\ *n*

dep·re·ca·to·ry \'dep-ri-kə-,tōr-ē, -,tȯr-\ *adj* **1 :** serving to deprecate **2 :** expressing deprecation **:** APOLOGETIC

de·pre·ci·ate \di-'prē-shē-,āt\ *vb* [LL *depretiare*, fr. L *de-* + *pretium* price] **1 :** to lower the price or value of ⟨*depreciate* the currency⟩ **2 :** to represent as of little value **:** DISPARAGE **3 :** to fall in value ⟨perishable goods *depreciate* rapidly⟩ — **de·pre·cia·tive** \-shē-,āt-iv, -shē-)ət-\ *adj* — **de·pre·cia·to·ry** \-sh(ē-)ə-,tōr-ē, -,tȯr-\ *adj*

de·pre·ci·a·tion \di-,prē-shē-'ā-shən\ *n* **1 :** a decline in the purchasing power or exchange value of money **2 :** the act of belittling **:** DISPARAGEMENT **3 :** a decline (as from age or wear and tear) in the value of something

dep·re·da·tion \,dep-rə-'dā-shən\ *n* [L *depraedari* to plunder, fr. *de-* + *praedari* to plunder] **:** the action or an act of plundering or laying waste **:** RAVAGING, PILLAGING

de·press \di-'pres\ *vt* [L *depress-, deprimere* to press down, fr. *de-* + *premere* to press] **1** *obs* **:** REPRESS, SUBJUGATE **2 a :** to press down **b :** to cause to sink to a lower position **3 :** to lessen the activity or strength of **4 :** SADDEN, DISCOURAGE **5 :** to lessen in price or value **:** DEPRECIATE — **de·press·i·ble** \-ə-bəl\ *adj* — **de·press·ing·ly** \-iŋ-lē\ *n*

syn DEPRESS, OPPRESS mean to press or weigh down heavily. DEPRESS stresses the resulting state of inactivity or dullness or dejection ⟨*depressed* by failure⟩ OPPRESS emphasizes the burden imposed that may or may not be successfully borne or withstood ⟨*oppressed* by the hot weather⟩

de·pres·sant \di-'pres-ᵊnt\ *n* **:** one that depresses; *esp* **:** an agent that reduces bodily functional activity — **depressant** *adj*

de·pressed *adj* **1 :** low in spirits **:** SAD **2 :** FLATTENED; *esp* **:** lying flat or prostrate ⟨a *depressed* shrub⟩ **3 :** suffering from economic depression; *esp* **:** UNDERPRIVILEGED

de·pres·sion \di-'presh-ən\ *n* **1 :** an act of depressing **:** a state of being depressed: as **a :** a pressing down **:** LOWERING **b :** DEJECTION; *also* **:** a mental disorder marked by sadness, inactivity, and self-depreciation **c** (1) **:** a reduction in activity, amount, quality, or force (2) **:** a lowering of vitality or functional activity **2 a :** a depressed place or part **:** HOLLOW **3 :** a period of low general economic activity with widespread unemployment

de·pres·sive \-'pres-iv\ *adj* **:** of or relating to psychological depression

de·pres·sor \-'pres-ər\ *n* **:** one that depresses: as **a :** a muscle that draws down a part — compare LEVATOR **b :** a device for pressing a part down or aside

de·pres·sur·ize \(')dē-'presh-ə-,rīz\ *vt* **:** to release (as a pressurized aircraft) from pressure

dep·ri·va·tion \,dep-rə-'vā-shən\ *n* **1 :** an act or instance of depriving **:** LOSS **2 :** the state of being deprived

de·prive \di-'prīv\ *vt* [ML *deprivare*, fr. L *de-* + *privare* to deprive] **1 :** to take something away from ⟨*deprive* a king of his power⟩ **2 :** to stop from having something ⟨*deprived* of sleep by street noises⟩

depth \'depth\ *n, pl* **depths** \'dep(th)s\ [ME, prob. fr. *dep* deep] **1 a** (1) **:** a deep place in a body of water (2) **:** a part that is far from the outside or surface ⟨the *depths* of the woods⟩ (3) **:** ABYSS **b** (1) **:** the middle of a time ⟨the *depth* of winter⟩ (2) **:** an extreme state (as of misery) (3) **:** the worst part **2 a :** the perpendicular distance downward from a surface **b :** the distance from front to back **3 :** the quality of being deep **4 :** degree of intensity ⟨the *depth* of a color⟩ — **depth·less** \'depth-ləs\ *adj*

depth charge *n* **:** an explosive projectile for use under water esp. against submarines — called also *depth bomb*

dep·u·ta·tion \,dep-yə-'tā-shən\ *n* **1 :** the act of appointing a deputy **2 :** a group of people appointed to represent others

de·pute \di-'pyüt\ *vt* [LL *deputare* to assign, fr. L *de-* + *putare* to consider] **:** DELEGATE

dep·u·tize \'dep-yə-,tīz\ *vb* **1 :** to appoint as deputy **2 :** to act as deputy

dep·u·ty \'dep-yət-ē\ *n, pl* **-ties 1 :** a person appointed to act for or in place of another **2 :** an assistant empowered to act as a substitute in the absence of his superior **3** : a member of a lower house of a legislative assembly — **deputy** *adj*

de·rail \di-'rāl\ *vt* : to cause to run off the rails ⟨a train *derailed* by heavy snow⟩ — **de·rail·ment** \-mənt\ *n*

de·rail·leur \di-'rā-lər\ *n* [F *dérailleur*, fr. *dérailler* to throw off the track, fr. *dé-* de- + *rail* rail, fr. E] : a mechanism for shifting gears on a bicycle that operates by moving the chain from one set of exposed gears to another; *also* : a bicycle having such a mechanism

de·range \di-'rānj\ *vt* **1** : to put out of order : DIS-ARRANGE, UPSET **2** : to disturb the operation or functions of **3** : to make insane — **de·range·ment** \-mənt\ *n*

der·by \'dər-bē, *esp Brit* 'där-\ *n, pl* **derbies** [after 12th earl of *Derby* d1834] **1** *cap* **a** : a race for three-year-old horses run annually at Epsom Downs, England **b** : a horse race usu. for three-year-olds held annually **2** : a race or contest open to all comers **3** : a man's stiff felt hat with dome-shaped crown and narrow brim

derby

¹**der·e·lict** \'der-ə-‚likt\ *adj* [L *derelictus*, pp. of *derelinquere* to abandon, fr. *de-* + *relinquere* to leave, relinquish] **1** : abandoned by the owner or occupant ⟨a *derelict* ship⟩ **2** : NEGLECTFUL, NEGLIGENT

²**derelict** *n* **1** : something voluntarily abandoned; *esp* : a ship abandoned on the high seas **2** : a person no longer able to support himself : BUM

der·e·lic·tion \‚der-ə-'lik-shən\ *n* **1** : the act of abandoning : the state of being abandoned ⟨the *dereliction* of a cause by its leaders⟩ **2** : a failure in duty : DELINQUENCY

de·ride \di-'rīd\ *vt* [L *deris-, deridēre*, fr. *de-* + *ridēre* to laugh] : to laugh at scornfully : make fun of **syn** see RIDICULE — **de·rid·er** *n* — **de·rid·ing·ly** \-'rīd-iŋ-lē\ *adv*

de ri·gueur \də-(‚)rē-'gər\ *adj* [F] : prescribed or required by fashion, etiquette, or custom : PROPER

de·ri·sion \di-'rizh-ən\ *n* **1** : scornful or contemptuous ridicule **2** : an object of ridicule

de·ri·sive \di-'rī-siv\ *adj* : expressing or causing derision — **de·ri·sive·ly** *adv* — **de·ri·sive·ness** *n*

de·ri·so·ry \di-'rī-sə-rē\ *adj* : DERISIVE

de·riv·a·ble \di-'rī-və-bəl\ *adj* : capable of being derived

der·i·va·tion \‚der-ə-'vā-shən\ *n* **1 a** : the formation (as by the addition of an affix) of a word from an earlier word or root **b** : an act of ascertaining or stating the derivation of a word **c** : ETYMOLOGY 1 **2 a** : SOURCE, ORIGIN **b** : ORIGINATION, DESCENT **c** : an act or process of deriving — **der·i·va·tion·al** \-shnəl, -shən-ᵊl\ *adj*

¹**de·riv·a·tive** \di-'riv-ət-iv\ *adj* **1** : formed by derivation **2** : derived from something else : not original or fundamental ⟨*derivative* poetry⟩ — **de·riv·a·tive·ly** *adv*

²**derivative** *n* **1** : a word formed by derivation **2** : something derived **3** : the limit of the ratio of the change in a function to the corresponding change in its independent variable as the latter change approaches zero **4** : a substance that can be made from another substance in one or more steps ⟨a *derivative* of coal tar⟩

de·rive \di-'rīv\ *vb* **de·rived**; **de·riv·ing** [L *derivare*, fr. *de* from + *rivus* stream] **1 a** : to receive or obtain from a source **b** : to obtain (as a chemical substance) from a parent substance **2** : to trace the origin, descent, or derivation of **3** : to come from a certain source **4** : IN-FER, DEDUCE

derm \'dərm\ *n* **1** : DERMIS **2** : SKIN 2a **3** : CUTICLE 1a

-derm \‚dərm\ *n comb form* [Gk *dermat-, derma*, fr. *derein* to skin; akin to E ³*tear*] : skin : covering : layer ⟨*ectoderm*⟩

der·ma \'dər-mə\ *n* : DERMIS

der·mal \'dər-məl\ *adj* **1** : of or relating to skin and esp. to the dermis : CUTANEOUS **2** : EPIDERMAL

der·map·ter·an \‚dər-'map-tə-rən\ *n* [Gk *derma* skin + *pteron* wing] : any of an order (Dermaptera) of insects including the earwigs — **dermapteran** *adj* — **der·map·ter·ous** \-rəs\ *adj*

dermat- *or* **dermato-** *comb form* [Gk *dermat-, derma*] : skin ⟨*dermatitis*⟩ ⟨*dermatology*⟩

der·ma·ti·tis \‚dər-mə-'tīt-əs\ *n* : inflammation of the skin

der·ma·tol·o·gy \‚dər-mə-'täl-ə-jē\ *n* : a branch of science dealing with the skin — **der·mat·o·log·ic** \‚(‚)dər-‚mat-ᵊl-'äj-ik\ *or* **der·mat·o·log·i·cal** \-'äj-i-kəl\ *adj* — **der·ma·tol·o·gist** \‚dər-mə-'täl-ə-jəst\ *n*

der·mis \'dər-məs\ *n* : the sensitive vascular inner layer of the skin — called also *corium, cutis*

der·mo·trop·ic \‚dər-mə-'träp-ik\ *adj* : attracted to the skin ⟨*dermotropic* viruses⟩

der·o·gate \'der-ə-‚gāt\ *vb* [L *derogare*, to annul (a law), detract, fr. *de-* + *rogare* to ask, propose (a law)] **1** : to cause to seem inferior : DISPARAGE **2** : to take away a part so as to impair : DETRACT — **der·o·ga·tion** \‚der-ə-'gā-shən\ *n* — **de·rog·a·tive** \di-'räg-ət-iv, 'der-ə-‚gāt-\ *adj*

de·rog·a·to·ry \di-'räg-ə-‚tōr-ē, -‚tôr-\ *adj* : intended to lower the reputation of a person or thing : DISPARAGING — **de·rog·a·to·ri·ly** \-‚räg-ə-'tōr-ə-lē, -‚tôr-\ *adv*

der·rick \'der-ik\ *n* [obs. *derrick* hangman, gallows, fr. *Derick*, name of a 17th cent. English hangman] **1** : any of various machines for moving or hoisting heavy weights by means of a long beam fitted with pulleys and ropes or cables **2** : a framework or tower built over an oil well for supporting machinery

der·ri·ere *or* **der·ri·ère** \‚der-ē-'e(ə)r\ *n* [F *derrière*] : BUTTOCKS

der·ring-do \‚der-iŋ-'dü\ *n* [ME *dorring don* daring to do] : daring action : DARING

der·rin·ger \'der-ən-jər\ *n* : a short-barreled pocket pistol

der·ris \'der-əs\ *n* [Gk, skin] : any of a large genus of leguminous tropical Old World shrubs and woody vines including commercial sources of rotenone; *also* : a derris insecticide

der·vish \'dər-vish\ *n* [Turk *derviş*, lit., beggar, fr. Per *darvēsh*] : a member of a Muslim religious order noted for devotional exercises (as bodily movements leading to a trance)

de·salt \(‚)dē-'sólt\ *vt* : to remove salt from — **de·salt·er** *n*

¹**des·cant** \'des-‚kant\ *n* [ML *discantus*, fr. L *dis-* + *cantus* song] **1** : a melody sung above a principal melody **2** : the art of composing or singing part music; *also* : a piece of music so composed **3** : a strain of melody : SONG **4** : a discourse or comment on a subject

²**des·cant** \des-'kant, des-'\ *vi* **1 a** : to sing or play a descant **b** : SING, WARBLE **2** : to talk or write at length

de·scend \di-'send\ *vb* [L *descendere*, fr. *de-* + *scandere* to climb] **1 a** : to pass from a higher to a lower place or level **b** : to pass, move, or climb down or down along **2 a** : to come down from a stock or source : DERIVE ⟨*descended* from an ancient family⟩ **b** : to pass by inheritance **c** : to pass by transmission **3** : to incline, lead, or extend downward ⟨the road *descends* to the river⟩ **4** : to swoop down in a sudden attack **5** : to sink in status or condition — **de·scend·i·ble** \-'sen-də-bəl\ *adj*

¹**de·scend·ant** *or* **de·scend·ent** \di-'sen-dənt\ *adj* **1** : DE-SCENDING **2** : proceeding from an ancestor or source

²**descendant** *or* **descendent** *n* **1** : one descended from another or from a common stock **2** : one deriving directly from a precursor or prototype

de·scent \di-'sent\ *n* **1** : the act or process of descending **2** : a downward step (as in station or value) : DECLINE **3** : derivation from an ancestor : BIRTH, LINEAGE **4 a** : an inclination downward : SLOPE **b** : a descending way (as a downgrade or stairway) **5** : a sudden hostile raid or assault

de·scribe \di-'skrīb\ *vt* [L *descript-, describere*, fr. *de-* + *scribere* to write] **1** : to represent or give an account of in words **2** : to trace or traverse the outline of ⟨*describe* a circle⟩ — **de·scrib·a·ble** \-'skrī-bə-bəl\ *adj* — **de·scrib·er** *n*

de·scrip·tion \di-'skrip-shən\ *n* **1** : an account of something; *esp* : an account that presents a picture to a person who reads or hears it **2** : KIND, SORT ⟨people of every *description*⟩

de·scrip·tive \-'skrip-tiv\ *adj* : serving to describe — **de·scrip·tive·ly** *adv* — **de·scrip·tive·ness** *n*

de·scry \di-'skrī\ *vt* **de·scried**; **de·scry·ing** [OF *descrier* to proclaim, decry] **1** : to catch sight of : spy out or discover by the eye **2** : to discover or detect by observation or investigation

des·e·crate \'des-i-‚krāt\ *vt* [*de-* + *-secrate* (as in *consecrate*)] : to violate the sanctity of : PROFANE — **des·e·crat·er** *or* **des·e·cra·tor** \-‚krāt-ər\ *n* — **des·e·cra·tion** \‚des-i-'krā-shən\ *n*

de·seg·re·gate \(‚)dē-'seg-ri-‚gāt\ *vb* : to eliminate segregation in; *esp* : to end by law the isolation of members of a particular race in separate units ⟨*desegregate* the armed services⟩ — **de·seg·re·ga·tion** \(,)dē-,seg-ri-'gā-shən\ *n*

de·sen·si·tize \('dē-'sen(t)-sə-,tīz\ *vt* : to make (a sensitized or hypersensitive individual) insensitive or nonreactive to a sensitizing agent — **de·sen·si·ti·za·tion** \(,)dē-,sen(t)-sət-ə-'zā-shən\ *n* — **de·sen·si·tiz·er** *n*

¹des·ert \'dez-ərt\ *n* [LL *desertum*, fr. L, neut. of pp. of *deserere* to desert] **1** *archaic* : a wild uninhabited tract : WILDERNESS **2** : an arid barren tract incapable of supporting a considerable population without an artificial water supply

²des·ert \'dez-ərt\ *adj* : of, relating to, or resembling a desert; *esp* : being barren and without life ⟨a *desert* island⟩

³de·sert \di-'zərt\ *n* [OF, fr. *deservir* to deserve] **1** : worthiness of reward or punishment ⟨rewarded according to his *deserts*⟩ **2** : a just reward or punishment

⁴de·sert \di-'zərt\ *vb* [L *desert-, deserere*, fr. *de-* + *serere* to join together] **1** : to withdraw from : LEAVE **2** : to leave in the lurch : FORSAKE **3** : to fail one in time of need **4** : to quit one's post without permission esp. with the intent to remain away permanently **syn** see ABANDON — **de·sert·er** *n*

de·ser·tion \di-'zər-shən\ *n* **1** : an act of deserting; *esp* : the abandonment of a person (as a wife or child) to whom one has legal and moral duties and obligations **2** : a state of being deserted or forsaken : DESOLATION

de·serve \di-'zərv\ *vb* [OF *deservir*, fr. L *deservire* to serve zealously, fr. *de-* + *servire* to serve] : to be worthy of : MERIT ⟨*deserves* another chance⟩ — **de·serv·er** *n*

de·serv·ed·ly \di-'zər-vəd-lē\ *adv* : according to merit ⟨JUSTLY ⟨a prize *deservedly* awarded⟩

¹de·serv·ing *n* : DESERT, MERIT

²deserving *adj* : MERITORIOUS, WORTHY

des·ha·bille \,des-ə-'bēl\ *var of* DISHABILLE

des·ic·cant \'des-i-kənt\ *n* : a drying agent

des·ic·cate \-,kāt\ *vb* [L *desiccare*, fr. *de-* + *siccare* to dry] **1** : to dry up or become dried up **2** : to preserve (a food) by drying : DEHYDRATE — **des·ic·ca·tion** \,des-i-'kā-shən\ *n* — **des·ic·ca·tor** \'des-i-,kāt-ər\ *n*

de·sid·er·a·tum \di-,sid-ə-'rät-əm, -,zid-, -'rāt-\ *n, pl* **-ta** \-ə\ [L] : something desired as essential or needed

¹de·sign \di-'zīn\ *vt* [L *designare*, fr. *de-* + *signare* to mark, mark out] **1 a** : to conceive and plan out in the mind **b** : DEVOTE, CONSIGN **c** : to have as a purpose : INTEND **d** : to devise for a specific function or end **2 a** : to make a pattern or sketch of **b** : to conceive and draw the plans for ⟨*design* an airplane⟩ — **de·sign·er** *n*

²design *n* **1** : a project or scheme in which means to an end are laid down **2** : deliberate purposive planning **3 a** : a secret project or scheme : PLOT **b** *pl* : aggressive or evil intent — used with *on* or *against* **4** : a sketch or plan showing the main features of something to be executed **5** : the arrangement of elements that make up a structure or a work of art **6** : a decorative pattern **syn** see INTENTION, PLAN

¹des·ig·nate \'dez-ig-,nāt, -nət\ *adj* : chosen for an office but not yet installed ⟨ambassador *designate*⟩

²des·ig·nate \-,nāt\ *vt* [L *designare* to design, designate] **1** : to mark or point out : INDICATE **2** : to appoint or choose by name for a special purpose ⟨*designate* someone as chairman⟩ **3** : to call by a name or title — **des·ig·na·tive** \-,nāt-iv\ *adj* — **des·ig·na·tor** \-,nāt-ər\ *n* — **des·ig·na·to·ry** \-nə-,tŏr-ē, -,tór-\ *adj*

des·ig·na·tion \,dez-ig-'nā-shən\ *n* **1** : the act of indicating or identifying **2** : a distinguishing name, sign, or title **3** : appointment to or selection for an office, post, or service

de·sign·ed·ly \di-'zī-nəd-lē\ *adv* : PURPOSELY ⟨came late *designedly*⟩

de·sign·ing *adj* : CRAFTY, SCHEMING ⟨a *designing* woman⟩

de·sir·a·ble \di-'zī-rə-bəl\ *adj* **1** : having pleasing qualities or properties : ATTRACTIVE ⟨a *desirable* location⟩ **2** : worth seeking or doing as advantageous, beneficial, or wise : ADVISABLE ⟨*desirable* legislation⟩ — **de·sir·a·bil·i·ty** \-,zī-rə-'bil-ət-ē\ *n* — **de·sir·a·ble·ness** \-'zī-rə-bəl-nəs\ *n* — **de·sir·a·bly** \-blē\ *adv*

¹de·sire \di-'zī(ə)r\ *vb* [OF *desirer*, fr. L *desiderare*, fr. *de-* + *sider-, sidus* star] **1** : to long for : wish earnestly ⟨*desire* wealth⟩ ⟨*desire* peace⟩ **2** : to express a wish for : REQUEST ⟨the librarian *desires* us to return all overdue books⟩

syn WISH, WANT: DESIRE usu. emphasizes ardor and sometimes striving; WISH, less formal than DESIRE, often connotes longing for the unattainable; WANT may stress need or lack but is often used instead of WISH ⟨they *want* (or *wish*) to leave early⟩ ⟨do you *want* (or *wish*) tea or coffee?⟩

²desire *n* **1** : a strong wish : LONGING; *also* : the mental power or capacity to experience desires **2** : an expressed wish : REQUEST **3** : something desired

de·sir·ous \di-'zī(ə)r-əs\ *adj* : eagerly wishing : DESIRING ⟨*desirous* of an invitation⟩ — **de·sir·ous·ly** *adv*

de·sist \di-'zist, -'sist\ *vi* [L *desistere*, fr. *de-* + *sistere* to stand, stop] : to cease to proceed or act **syn** see STOP — **de·sist·ance** \-'zis-tən(t)s, -'sis-\ *n*

desk \'desk\ *n* [ML *desca*, fr. It *desco* table, fr. L *discus* disk] **1 a** : a table, frame, or case with a flat or sloping surface esp. for writing and reading **b** : a counter at which a person performs his duties **c** : a music stand **2 a** : a specialized division of an organization (as a newspaper) ⟨city *desk*⟩

des·mid \'dez-məd\ *n* [Gk *desmos* bond, ligature] : any of numerous unicellular or colonial green algae (order Zygnematales)

¹des·o·late \'des-ə-lət, 'dez-\ *adj* [L *desolare* to abandon, fr. *de-* + *solus* alone] **1** : lacking inhabitants and visitors : DESERTED **2** : FORSAKEN, LONELY **3 a** : showing the effects of abandonment and neglect : DILAPIDATED **b** : BARREN, LIFELESS **c** : CHEERLESS, GLOOMY **syn** see SOLITARY — **des·o·late·ly** *adv* — **des·o·late·ness** *n*

²des·o·late \-,lāt\ *vt* : to make desolate : **a** : to lay waste **b** : to make wretched

des·o·la·tion \,des-ə-'lā-shən, ,dez-\ *n* **1** : the action of desolating **2** : the condition of being desolated : DEVASTATION, RUIN **3** : a barren wasteland **4 a** : GRIEF, SADNESS **b** : LONELINESS

des·oxy·ri·bo·nu·cle·ic acid \dē-,zäk-sē-'rī-bō-n(y)ü-,klē-ik-, -,klā-\ *n* : DEOXYRIBONUCLEIC ACID

¹de·spair \di-'spa(ə)r, -'spe(ə)r\ *vi* [L *desperare*, fr. *de-* + *sperare* to hope] : to lose all hope or confidence

²despair *n* **1** : utter loss of hope : feeling of complete hopelessness **2** : a cause of hopelessness **syn** see DESPONDENCY

de·spair·ing *adj* : given to, arising from, or marked by despair — **de·spair·ing·ly** \-iŋ-lē\ *adv*

des·patch \dis-'patch\ *var of* DISPATCH

des·per·a·do \,des-pə-'räd-ō, -'rād-\ *n, pl* **-does** or **-dos** : a bold or reckless criminal

des·per·ate \'des-p(ə-)rət\ *adj* [L *desperare* to despair] **1** : being beyond or almost beyond hope : causing despair ⟨a *desperate* illness⟩ **2** : reckless because of despair : RASH ⟨a *desperate* attempt⟩ **3** : extremely intense : OVERPOWERING — **des·per·ate·ly** *adv* — **des·per·ate·ness** *n*

des·per·a·tion \,des-pə-'rā-shən\ *n* **1** : a loss of hope and surrender to misery or dread **2** : a state of hopelessness leading to extreme recklessness **syn** see DESPONDENCY

de·spic·a·ble \di-'spik-ə-bəl, 'des-(,)pik-\ *adj* [L *despicari* to despise] : deserving to be despised ⟨*despicable* traitor⟩ **syn** see CONTEMPTIBLE — **de·spic·a·ble·ness** *n* — **de·spic·a·bly** \-blē\ *adv*

de·spise \di-'spīz\ *vt* [OF *despis-, despire*, fr. L *despicere*, fr. *de-* + *specere* to look] **1** : to look down on with contempt or aversion ⟨*despised* liars⟩ **2** : to regard as negligible, worthless, or distasteful — **de·spis·er** *n*

syn SCORN, DISDAIN: DESPISE may cover a range of feeling from indifferent disdain to active loathing; SCORN suggests either a lively and indignant or a profound and passionate contempt; DISDAIN implies an arrogant or haughty aversion to what is regarded as unworthy

¹de·spite \di-'spīt\ *n* [OF *despit*, fr. L *despectus*, fr. *despect-, despicere* to despise] **1** : the feeling or attitude of despising : CONTEMPT **2** : MALICE, SPITE **3 a** : an act of contempt or defiance **b** : HARM, INJURY — **in despite of** : in spite of

²despite *prep* : in spite of ⟨ran *despite* his injury⟩

de·spite·ful \di-'spīt-fəl\ *adj* : expressing malice or hate — **de·spite·ful·ly** \-fə-lē\ *adv* — **de·spite·ful·ness** *n*

de·spoil \di-'spóil\ *vt* : to strip of belongings, possessions, or value : PLUNDER, PILLAGE — **de·spoil·er** *n* — **de·spoil·ment** \-'spóil-mənt\ *n*

de·spo·li·a·tion \di-,spō-lē-'ā-shən\ *n* : the act of plundering : the state of being despoiled

¹de·spond \di-'spänd\ *vi* [L *despondēre* to give up, despond, fr. *de-* + *spondēre* to promise solemnly] : to become discouraged or disheartened

²despond *n* : DESPONDENCY

de·spond·en·cy \di-'spän-dən-sē\ *n* : the state of being despondent : DEJECTION, DISCOURAGEMENT
syn DESPAIR, DESPERATION : DESPONDENCY may imply a temporary mood of depression and apathy; DESPAIR implies utter loss of hope and suggests a final ceasing of effort or resistance; DESPERATION implies an urgency that drives one to any action offering immediate success regardless of consequences

de·spond·ent \-dənt\ *adj* : feeling extreme discouragement, dejection, or depression ⟨*despondent* about his health⟩ — **de·spond·ent·ly** *adv*

des·pot \'des-pət, -,pät\ *n* [Gk *despotēs* master, lord] 1 : a ruler with absolute power and authority 2 : a person exercising power abusively, oppressively, or tyrannously — **des·pot·ic** \des-'pät-ik\ *adj* — **des·pot·i·cal·ly** \-i-k(ə-)lē\ *adv*

des·po·tism \'des-pə-,tiz-əm\ *n* 1 a : rule by a despot : TYRANNY b : despotic exercise of power 2 : a state or a system of government in which the ruler has unlimited power

des·qua·mate \'des-kwə-,māt\ *vi* [L *desquamare*, fr. *de-* + *squama* scale] : to peel off in scales — **des·qua·ma·tion** \,des-kwə-'mā-shən\ *n*

des·sert \di-'zərt\ *n* [MF, fr. *desservir* to clear the table] : a course of sweet food, fruit, or cheese served at the close of a meal

des·ti·na·tion \,des-tə-'nā-shən\ *n* 1 : an act of appointing, setting aside for a purpose, or predetermining 2 : purpose for which something is destined 3 : a place which is set for the end of a journey or to which something is sent

des·tine \'des-tən\ *vt* [L *destinare*] 1 : to settle in advance ⟨a plan *destined* to fail⟩ 2 : to designate, assign, or dedicate in advance ⟨*destined* his son for the study of law⟩ 3 : to be bound or directed ⟨a ship *destined* for New York⟩

des·ti·ny \'des-tə-nē\ *n, pl* **-nies** 1 : something to which a person or thing is destined : FORTUNE 2 : a predetermined course of events often held to be a resistless power or agency **syn** see FATE

des·ti·tute \'des-tə-,t(y)üt\ *adj* [L *destitutus*, pp. of *destituere* to abandon, deprive, fr. *de-* + *statuere* to set up] 1 : lacking something needed or desirable ⟨*destitute* of the necessities of life⟩ 2 : extremely poor : suffering great want ⟨a *destitute* family⟩ — **des·ti·tute·ness** *n*

des·ti·tu·tion \,des-tə-'t(y)ü-shən\ *n* : the state of being destitute; *esp* : extreme poverty

de·stroy \di-'stroi\ *vb* [OF *destruire*, fr. L *destruct-*, *destruere*, fr. *de-* + *struere* to build] 1 : to put an end to : do away with : RUIN ⟨*destroy* trash by burning⟩ ⟨*destroy* a city with bombs⟩ 2 : KILL ⟨have a sick animal *destroyed*⟩ **syn** DEMOLISH, ANNIHILATE : DESTROY implies any force that wrecks, kills, annihilates, or tears down or apart ⟨*destroy* a friendship by deceit⟩ DEMOLISH implies a pulling or smashing to pieces or a tearing down to the point of ruin; ANNIHILATE suggests destruction so complete as to make any restoration impossible

de·stroy·er \-'stroi-(ə)r\ *n* 1 : a destroying agent or agency 2 : a small fast warship armed with guns, depth charges, torpedoes, and sometimes guided missiles

destroyer escort *n* : a warship similar to but smaller than a destroyer

de·struct \di-'strəkt\ *n* : the deliberate destruction of a rocket after launching

de·struc·ti·ble \di-'strək-tə-bəl\ *adj* : capable of being destroyed — **de·struc·ti·bil·i·ty** \-,strək-tə-'bil-ət-ē\ *n*

de·struc·tion \di-'strək-shən\ *n* [L *destruct-*, *destruere* to destroy] 1 : the action or process of destroying something 2 : the state or fact of being destroyed : RUIN 3 : a destroying agency

de·struc·tive \di-'strək-tiv\ *adj* 1 : causing destruction : RUINOUS ⟨*destructive* storm⟩ 2 : designed or tending to destroy ⟨*destructive* criticism⟩ — **de·struc·tive·ly** *adv* — **de·struc·tive·ness** *n*

destructive distillation *n* : decomposition of a substance (as coal or oil) by heat in a closed container and collection of the volatile products produced

de·struc·tor \di-'strək-tər\ *n* 1 : a furnace for burning

refuse : INCINERATOR 2 : a device for destroying a missile in flight

des·ue·tude \'des-wi-,t(y)üd\ *n* : discontinuance from use or exercise : DISUSE

des·ul·to·ry \'des-əl-,tōr-ē, -,tŏr-\ *adj* [L *desult-*, *desilire* to leap down, fr. *de-* + *salire* to leap] : passing aimlessly from one thing or subject to another : DISCONNECTED ⟨*desultory* reading⟩ — **des·ul·to·ri·ly** \,des-əl-'tōr-ə-lē, -'tŏr-\ *adv* — **des·ul·to·ri·ness** \'des-əl-,tōr-ē-nəs, -,tŏr-\ *n*

de·tach \di-'tach\ *vt* [F *détacher*] 1 : to separate esp. from a larger mass and usu. without violence or damage 2 : DISENGAGE, WITHDRAW — **de·tach·a·ble** \-ə-bəl\ *adj* — **de·tach·a·bly** \-blē\ *adv*

de·tached \-'tacht\ *adj* 1 : not joined or connected : SEPARATE ⟨a *detached* house⟩ 2 : ALOOF, UNCONCERNED, IMPARTIAL ⟨a *detached* attitude⟩ — **de·tached·ly** \-'tach-əd-lē, -'tach-tlē\ *adv* — **de·tached·ness** \-'tach-əd-nəs, -'tach(t)-nəs\ *n*

de·tach·ment \di-'tach-mənt\ *n* 1 : the action or process of detaching : SEPARATION 2 a : the dispatching of a body of troops or part of a fleet from the main body b : a portion dispatched for special service c : a small permanent military unit different in composition from normal units 3 a : indifference to worldly concerns : UNWORLDLINESS b : freedom from bias or prejudice : IMPARTIALITY

¹de·tail \di-'tāl, 'dē-,\ *n* [F *détail*, fr. OF, slice, fr. *detaillier* to cut in pieces] 1 a : a dealing with something item by item ⟨go into *detail* about an adventure⟩ b : a small part : ITEM ⟨the *details* of a story⟩ 2 a : selection (as of a group of soldiers) for some special service b : a soldier or group of soldiers appointed for special duty — **in detail** : item by item omitting nothing : THOROUGHLY ⟨explain *in detail*⟩

²detail *vt* 1 : to report in detail 2 : ENUMERATE, SPECIFY 3 : to assign to a task — **de·tail·er** *n*

de·tailed \di-'tāld, 'dē-,\ *adj* 1 : including many details 2 : furnished with finely finished details ⟨beautifully *detailed* hats⟩ — **de·tailed·ly** \di-'tāl(-ə)d-lē, 'dē-,\ *adv* — **de·tailed·ness** \di-'tā-ləd-nəs, -'tāl(d)-nəs, 'dē-,\ *n*

de·tain \di-'tān\ *vt* [MF *detenir*, fr. L *detinēre*, fr. *de-* + *tenēre* to hold] 1 : to hold or keep in or as if in custody 2 : to keep back (as something due) : WITHHOLD 3 : to restrain esp. from proceeding : STOP — **de·tain·ment** \-mənt\ *n*

de·tect \di-'tekt\ *vt* [L *detect-*, *detegere*, lit., to uncover, fr. *de-* + *tegere* to cover; akin to E *thatch*] 1 : to discover the nature, existence, presence, or fact of ⟨*detect* smoke⟩ ⟨*detect* the approach of an airplane⟩ 2 : DEMODULATE — **de·tect·a·ble** \-'tek-tə-bəl\ *adj*

de·tec·tion \di-'tek-shən\ *n* 1 : the act of detecting : the state or fact of being detected : DISCOVERY 2 : DEMODULATION

¹de·tec·tive \di-'tek-tiv\ *adj* 1 : fitted for or used in detecting something ⟨a *detective* device for coal gas⟩ 2 : of or relating to detectives or their work ⟨a *detective* story⟩

²detective *n* : an individual (as a policeman) whose business is solving crimes and catching criminals or gathering information that is not readily accessible

de·tec·tor \di-'tek-tər\ *n* 1 : one that detects 2 : a device for demodulating a radio signal

de·tent \'dē-,tent, di-'\ *n* : a mechanism that locks or unlocks a movement : PAWL

dé·tente \dā-'tänt\ *n* [F, fr. OF *destendre* to slacken, fr. *des-* dis- + *tendre* to stretch, fr. L *tendere*] : a relaxation of strained relations or tensions (as between nations)

de·ten·tion \di-'ten-chən\ *n* [L *detent-*, *detinēre* to detain] : the act of detaining : the state of being detained: as a : CONFINEMENT; *esp* : temporary custody awaiting trial b : a forced delay

de·ter \di-'tər\ *vt* **de·terred**; **de·ter·ring** [L *deterrēre*, fr. *de-* + *terrēre* to frighten] 1 : to turn aside, discourage, or prevent from acting (as by fear) 2 : INHIBIT — **de·ter·ment** \-'tər-mənt\ *n*

de·ter·gen·cy \di-'tər-jən-sē\ *n* : cleansing quality or power

¹de·ter·gent \-jənt\ *adj* [L *detergēre* to wash off, fr. *de-* + *tergēre* to wipe] : CLEANSING

²detergent *n* : a cleansing agent; *esp* : any of numerous synthetic organic preparations that are chemically dif-

---

j joke; **ŋ** sing; **ō** flow; **ȯ** flaw; **ȯi** coin; **th** thin; **th** this; **ü** loot; **u̇** foot; **y** yet; **yü** few; **yu̇** furious; **zh** vision

ferent from soaps but resemble them in the ability to emulsify oils and hold dirt in suspension

de·te·ri·o·rate \di-'tir-ē-ə-,rāt\ *vb* [L *deterior* worse] : to make or become worse or of less value : DEGENERATE — **de·te·ri·o·ra·tion** \-,tir-ē-ə-'rā-shən\ *n* — **de·te·ri·o·ra·tive** \-'tir-ē-ə-,rāt-iv\ *adj*

de·ter·min·a·ble \di-'tər-mə-nə-bəl\ *adj* : capable of being determined; *esp* : ASCERTAINABLE — **de·ter·min·a·ble·ness** *n* — **de·ter·min·a·bly** \-blē\ *adv*

de·ter·mi·nant \-mə-nənt\ *n* 1 : something that determines or conditions : FACTOR 2 : a square array of numbers bordered on either side by a straight line whose value is the algebraic sum of all the products that can be formed by taking as factors one element from each row and column and giving the products a sign by rule 3 : a gene or a comparable subordinate agent

de·ter·mi·nate \-mə-nət\ *adj* 1 : having fixed limits : DEFINITE: as a : having a limited capacity for elongation 〈*determinate* growth〉; *esp* : CYMOSE b : involving cell division that separates constituents with distinctive and specific potentialities 〈*determinate* cleavage of an embryo〉 2 : definitely settled 〈arranged in a *determinate* order〉 — **de·ter·mi·nate·ly** *adv* — **de·ter·mi·nate·ness** *n*

de·ter·mi·na·tion \di-,tər-mə-'nā-shən\ *n* 1 : the act of coming to a decision; *also* : the decision or conclusion reached 2 : the act of fixing the extent, position, or character of something 〈*determination* of the position of a ship〉 3 : accurate measurement (as of length or volume) 4 : firm or fixed purpose : FIRMNESS 5 : an identification of the taxonomic position of a plant or animal

¹de·ter·mi·na·tive \-'tər-mə-,nāt-iv\ *adj* : having power or tendency to determine — **de·ter·mi·na·tive·ly** *adv* — **de·ter·mi·na·tive·ness** *n*

²determinative *n* : one that serves to determine

de·ter·mine \di-'tər-mən\ *vb* [L *determinare*, fr. *de-* + *terminare* to limit, terminate] 1 a : to fix conclusively or authoritatively 〈two points *determine* a straight line〉 〈*determine* fiscal policy〉 b : REGULATE 2 : to come to a decision : SETTLE, RESOLVE 〈*determine* whom to invite〉 〈*determine* to learn to spell〉 3 : to find out the limits, nature, dimensions, or scope of : gain definite knowledge about 〈*determine* the size of a room〉 〈*determine* the direction of the wind〉 4 : to be the cause of or reason for : DECIDE 〈the quality of a pupil's work *determines* his mark〉 5 : to discover the taxonomic position or the generic and specific names of

de·ter·mined \-mənd\ *adj* 1 : DECIDED, RESOLVED 〈*determined* to succeed〉 2 : FIRM, RESOLUTE 〈a *determined* stance〉 — **de·ter·mined·ly** \-mən-dlē, -mə-nəd-lē\ *adv* — **de·ter·mined·ness** \-mən(d)-nəs\ *n*

de·ter·min·er \-mə-nər\ *n* : one that determines: as a : GENE, DETERMINANT b : a word belonging to a group of noun modifiers characterized by occurrence before descriptive adjectives modifying the same noun 〈*his* in "his new car" is a *determiner*〉

de·ter·min·ism \-mə-,niz-əm\ *n* : a doctrine that acts of the will, natural events, or social changes are determined by preceding causes — **de·ter·min·ist** \-mə-nəst\ *n* or *adj* — **de·ter·min·is·tic** \-,tər-mə-'nis-tik\ *adj*

de·ter·rence \di-'tər-ən(t)s, -'ter-\ *n* : the act, process, or capacity of deterring

de·ter·rent \-ənt\ *adj* 1 : serving to deter 2 : relating to deterrence — **deterrent** *n* — **de·ter·rent·ly** *adv*

de·test \di-'test\ *vt* [L *detestari*, to curse while calling a deity to witness, detest, fr. *de-* + *testari* to call to witness] : to dislike intensely : LOATHE, ABHOR **syn** see HATE — **de·test·er** *n*

de·test·a·ble \di-'tes-tə-bəl\ *adj* : arousing or meriting intense dislike : ABOMINABLE — **de·test·a·ble·ness** *n* — **de·test·a·bly** \-blē\ *adv*

de·tes·ta·tion \,dē-,tes-'tā-shən\ *n* 1 : extreme hatred or dislike : LOATHING 2 : an object of hatred or contempt

de·throne \di-'thrōn\ *vt* : to remove from a throne : DE-POSE — **de·throne·ment** \-mənt\ *n* — **de·thron·er** *n*

det·o·nate \'det-ə-,nāt\ *vb* [L *detonare* to thunder down, fr. *de-* + *tonare* to thunder] : to explode or cause to explode with sudden violence — **det·o·na·tion** \,det-ə-'nā-shən\ *n*

det·o·na·tor \'det-ə-,nāt-ər\ *n* : a device or small quantity of explosive used for detonating a high explosive

¹de·tour \'dē-,tu̇(ə)r, di-'\ *n* [F *détour*] : a deviation from

a direct course or the usual procedure; *esp* : a roundabout way temporarily replacing part of a regular route

²detour *vb* 1 : to send or proceed by a detour 〈*detour* around a pit〉 2 : to avoid by going around 〈*detour* a difficult spot〉

de·tox·i·fy \(')dē-'täk-sə-,fī\ *vt* **-fied; -fy·ing** : to remove poison or the effect of poison from — **de·tox·i·fi·ca·tion** \(,)dē-,täk-sə-fə-'kā-shən\ *n*

de·tract \di-'trakt\ *vb* [L *detract-, detrahere* to withdraw, disparage, fr. *de-* + *trahere* to draw] 1 : to take away : WITHDRAW, SUBTRACT 〈*detract* from a person's reputation〉 2 : DISTRACT 〈*detract* attention〉 — **de·trac·tor** \-'trak-tər\ *n*

de·trac·tion \di-'trak-shən\ *n* : a taking away of a part of the reputation or good name of a person esp. by slander — **de·trac·tive** \-'trak-tiv\ *adj* — **de·trac·tive·ly** *adv*

de·train \(')dē-'trān\ *vb* : to leave or cause to leave a railroad train — **de·train·ment** \-mənt\ *n*

det·ri·ment \'de-trə-mənt\ *n* [L *detrimentum*, fr. *deterere* to wear away, impair, fr. *de-* + *terere* to rub] : injury or damage or its cause : HURT

det·ri·men·tal \,de-trə-'ment-ᵊl\ *adj* : causing detriment : HARMFUL, DAMAGING — **det·ri·men·tal·ly** \-ᵊl-ē\ *adv*

de·tri·tus \di-'trīt-əs\ *n* 1 : loose material that results directly from the natural breaking up of rocks (as by the action of frost) 2 : fragments resulting from disintegration 〈*detritus* from dead animals〉 — **de·tri·tal** \-'trīt-ᵊl\ *adj*

de trop \də-'trō\ *adj* [F] : too much or too many : SUPER-FLUOUS

¹deuce \'d(y)üs\ *n* [MF *deus* two, fr. L *duos*, acc. of *duo* two] 1 a (1) : the face of a dice that bears two spots (2) : a playing card bearing the number two b : a cast of dice yielding a point of two 2 : a tie in tennis with each side having a score of 40 3 [obs. E *deuce* bad luck] : DEVIL, DICKENS — used chiefly as a mild oath

deuces

²deuce *vt* : to bring the score of (a tennis game or set) to deuce

deuc·ed \'d(y)ü-səd\ *adj* : DARNED, CONFOUNDED 〈in a *deuced* fix〉 — **deuced** *or* **deuc·ed·ly** *adv*

deu·te·ri·um \d(y)ü-'tir-ē-əm\ *n* [Gk *deuteros* second] : the hydrogen isotope that is of twice the mass of ordinary hydrogen and that occurs in water — called also *heavy hydrogen;* symbol D

deu·ter·on \'d(y)üt-ə-,rän\ *n* : the nucleus of the deuterium atom that consists of one proton and one neutron

Deu·ter·on·o·my \,d(y)üt-ə-'rän-ə-mē\ *n* — see BIBLE table

deut·sche mark \,dȯi-chə-'märk\ *n* [G] 1 : the German mark as established in 1948 2 : a coin representing one deutsche mark

deut·zia \'d(y)üt-sē-ə\ *n* : any of a genus of ornamental shrubs of the saxifrage family with white or pink flowers

de·val·ue \(')dē-'val-yü\ *vb* : to reduce the international exchange value of a currency — **de·val·u·a·tion** \(,)dē-,val-yə-'wā-shən\ *n*

dev·as·tate \'dev-ə-,stāt\ *vt* [L *devastare*, fr. *de-* + *vastare* to lay waste] 1 : to reduce to ruin : lay waste 2 : to shatter completely : DEMOLISH **syn** see RAVAGE — **dev·as·tat·ing·ly** \-,stāt-iŋ-lē\ *adv* — **dev·as·ta·tor** \-,stāt-ər\ *n*

dev·as·ta·tion \,dev-ə-'stā-shən\ *n* : the action of devastating : the state of being devastated : DESOLATION, RUIN

de·vel·op \di-'vel-əp\ *vb* [F *développer*, fr. OF *desvoloper*, fr. *des-* de- + *voloper* to wrap] 1 a : to unfold gradually or in detail b : to subject (exposed photographic material) to a chemical treatment to produce a visible image c : to elaborate (a musical theme) by working out rhythmic and harmonic changes 2 : to bring out the possibilities of 3 : to make more available or usable 〈*develop* resources〉 4 : to acquire gradually 〈*develop* a taste for olives〉 5 a : to go through a process of natural growth, differentiation, or evolution 〈a blossom *develops* from a bud〉 b : to acquire secondary sex characters c : GROW 6 : to become apparent — **de·vel·op·a·ble** \-'vel-ə-pə-bəl\ *adj*

de·vel·op·er \-'vel-ə-pər\ *n* : one that develops; *esp* : a chemical used to develop exposed photographic materials

de·vel·op·ment \di-'vel-əp-mənt\ *n* 1 : the act, process, or result of developing 2 : the state of being developed

— **de·vel·op·men·tal** \-,vel-əp-'ment-°l\ *adj* — **de·vel·op·men·tal·ly** \-°l-ē\ *adv*

de·vi·ant \'dē-vē-ənt\ *adj* **1** : deviating esp. from some accepted norm **2** : characterized by deviation — **de·vi·ance** \-ən(t)s\ *n* — **deviant** *n*

¹de·vi·ate \'dē-vē-,āt\ *vb* [LL *deviare*, fr. L *de* from + *via* way] **:** to turn aside esp. from an established way

²de·vi·ate \-vē-ət, -vē-,āt\ *adj* : DEVIANT — **deviate** *n*

de·vi·a·tion \,dē-vē-'ā-shən\ *n* : an act or instance of deviating: as **a** : the difference between a value in a frequency distribution and a fixed number **b** : evolutionary differentiation in which new stages are introduced into the ancestral pattern of development **c** : departure from an established ideology or party line **d** : noticeable departure from accepted norms (as of behavior) — **de·vi·a·tion·ism** \-shə-,niz-əm\ *n* — **de·vi·a·tion·ist** \-sh(ə-)nəst\ *n*

de·vice \di-'vīs\ *n* [OF *devis* division, intention, fr. *deviser* to divide, regulate] **1 a** : a scheme to deceive : STRATAGEM **b** : a piece of equipment or a mechanism to serve a special purpose **2** : DESIRE, INCLINATION (left to his own *devices*) **3** : an emblematic design used esp. as a heraldic bearing

¹dev·il \'dev-əl\ *n* [OE *dēofol*, fr. LL *diabolus*, fr. Gk *diabolos*, lit., slanderer, fr. *diaballein* to throw across, slander, fr. *dia-* + *ballein* to throw] **1** *often cap* : the personal supreme spirit of evil often represented in Jewish and Christian belief as the ruler of hell — often used with *the* as a mild imprecation or expression of surprise, vexation, or emphasis **2** : DEMON **3 a** : a wicked person **b** : a reckless or dashing person **c** : a pitiable person — usu. used with *poor*

²devil *vt* **dev·iled** *or* **dev·illed**; **dev·il·ing** *or* **dev·il·ling** \'dev-(ə-)liŋ\ **1** : TEASE, ANNOY **2** : to chop fine and season highly (*deviled* eggs)

dev·il·fish \'dev-əl-,fish\ *n* **1** : any of several extremely large rays widely distributed in warm seas **2** : OCTOPUS

dev·il·ish \'dev-(ə-)lish\ *adj* **1** : characteristic of or resembling the devil (*devilish* tricks) **2** : EXTREME, EXCESSIVE (in a *devilish* hurry) — **devilish** *adv* — **dev·il·ish·ly** *adv* — **dev·il·ish·ness** *n*

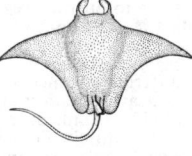
devilfish

dev·il·ment \'dev-əl-mənt, -,ment\ *n* : reckless mischief

dev·il·ry \'dev-əl-rē\ *or* **dev·il·try** \-əl-trē\ *n*, *pl* **-ries** *or* **-tries** **1** : action performed with the help of the devil : WITCHCRAFT **2** : reckless unrestrained conduct : MISCHIEF

devil's advocate *n* **1** : a Roman Catholic official whose duty is to point out defects in the evidence on which a demand for beatification or canonization rests **2** : a person who champions the worse cause for the sake of argument

devil's darning needle *n* **1** : DRAGONFLY **2** : DAMSELFLY

dev·il's food cake \'dev-əlz-,füd-,kāk\ *n* : a rich chocolate cake

devil's paintbrush *n* : any of various hawkweeds found in the eastern U.S.

de·vi·ous \'dē-vē-əs\ *adj* **1** : deviating from a straight line : ROUNDABOUT **2 a** : ERRING **b** : not straightforward : TRICKY — **de·vi·ous·ly** *adv* — **de·vi·ous·ness** *n*

¹de·vise \di-'vīz\ *vt* [OF *deviser* to divide, regulate, fr. L *divis-*, *dividere* to divide] **1 a** : to form in the mind by new combinations or applications of ideas or principles : INVENT **b** : to plan to obtain or bring about : PLOT **2** : to give (real estate) by will — **de·vis·er** *n*

²devise *n* : the act of devising real property; *also* : a will or clause of a will so devising or the property devised

de·vi·tal·ize \(')dē-'vīt-°l-,īz\ *vt* : to deprive of life or vitality

de·void \di-'void\ *adj* : entirely lacking : DESTITUTE (a book *devoid* of interest)

de·voir \dəv-'wär, 'dev-,\ *n* **1** : DUTY **2** : a formal act of civility or respect — usu. used in pl.

dev·o·lu·tion \,dev-ə-'lü-shən, ,dē-və-\ *n* **1** : transference from one individual to another **2** : retrograde evolution : DEGENERATION — **dev·o·lu·tion·ary** \-shə-,ner-ē\ *adj* — **dev·o·lu·tion·ist** \-sh(ə-)nəst\ *n*

de·volve \di-'välv, -'vȯlv\ *vb* [L *devolut-*, *devolvere*, fr.

de- + *volvere* to roll] **:** to pass by transmission or succession from one person to another

dev·on \'dev-ən\ *n*, *often cap* : any of a breed of vigorous red dual-purpose cattle of English origin

De·vo·ni·an \di-'vō-nē-ən\ *n* [*Devon*, England] **:** the period of the Paleozoic era between the Silurian and Mississippian; *also* : the corresponding system of rocks — **Devonian** *adj*

de·vote \di-'vōt\ *vt* [L *devot-*, *devovēre*, fr. *de-* + *vovēre* to vow] **1** : to set apart for a special purpose (as by a vow) : DEDICATE (*devote* an hour to worship) **2** : to give up to wholly (*devoted* herself to her family) (*devote* too much time to sports)

de·vot·ed *adj* **1** : ZEALOUS, ARDENT, DEVOUT (*devoted* admirers) **2** : AFFECTIONATE, LOVING (a *devoted* mother) — **de·vot·ed·ly** *adv* — **de·vot·ed·ness** *n*

dev·o·tee \,dev-ə-'tē, -'tā\ *n* **1** : an esp. ardent adherent of a religion or deity **2** : a zealous follower, supporter, or enthusiast (a *devotee* of sports)

de·vo·tion \di-'vō-shən\ *n* **1 a** : religious fervor : PIETY **b** : a religious exercise or practice other than the regular worship of a church **2 a** (1) : the act of devoting (2) : the quality of being devoted **b** : ardent love, affection, or dedication — **de·vo·tion·al** \-shnəl, -shən-°l\ *adj* — **de·vo·tion·al·ly** \-ē\ *adv*

de·vo·tion·al \-shnəl, -shən-°l\ *n* : a short worship service

de·vour \di-'vaù(ə)r\ *vt* [MF *devourer*, fr. L *devorare*, fr. *de-* + *vorare* to devour] **1** : to eat up greedily **2 a** : to lay waste : CONSUME (fire *devoured* the building) **b** : to use up wastefully (*devoured* his wife's fortune) **3** : to take in eagerly by the senses or mind (*devour* a book)

de·vout \di-'vaùt\ *adj* [LL *devotus*, fr. L, pp. of *devovēre* to devote] **1** : devoted to religion or to religious duties or exercises **2** : expressing devotion or piety **3** : warmly devoted : SINCERE (gave him *devout* thanks) — **de·vout·ly** *adv* — **de·vout·ness** *n*

syn DEVOUT, PIOUS, RELIGIOUS mean showing fervor and reverence in religious practice. DEVOUT stresses an attitude that leads to frequent but not necessarily outward prayer and reverent worship; PIOUS emphasizes the faithful performance of one's religious duties; RELIGIOUS implies devoutness and piety but stresses faith in God or gods and adherence to a way of life conforming to that faith

dew \'d(y)ü\ *n* [OE *dēaw*] **1** : moisture condensed upon the surfaces of cool bodies at night **2** : something resembling dew in purity, freshness, or power to refresh **3** : moisture esp. when appearing in minute droplets — **dew** *vt*

dew·ber·ry \'d(y)ü-,ber-ē\ *n* : any of several sweet edible berries related to and resembling blackberries; *also* : a trailing bramble that bears these

dew·claw \'d(y)ü-,klȯ\ *n* : a vestigial digit on the foot of a mammal or a claw or hoof on such a digit — **dew·clawed** \-,klȯd\ *adj*

dew·drop \'d(y)ü-,dräp\ *n* : a drop of dew

Dew·ey decimal classification \,d(y)ü-ē-\ *n* [after Melvil *Dewey* d1931 American librarian who devised it] **:** a system of classifying publications whereby main classes are designated by a 3-digit number and subdivisions are shown by numbers after a decimal point

dew·fall \'d(y)ü-,fȯl\ *n* : formation of dew; *also* : the time when dew begins to deposit

dew·lap \'d(y)ü-,lap\ *n* : a hanging fold of skin under the neck of bovine animals; *also* : a similar fold on other animals including man — **dew·lapped** \-,lapt\ *adj*

dew point *n* : the temperature at which the moisture in the air begins to condense

dewy \'d(y)ü-ē\ *adj* **dew·i·er**; **-est** : moist with, affected by, or suggestive of dew (eyes as fresh as morning or purity) (eyes *dewy* with tears) — **dew·i·ly** \'d(y)ü-ə-lē\ *adv* — **dew·i·ness** \'d(y)ü-ē-nəs\ *n*

dex·ter \'dek-stər\ *adj* [L, dextral, skillful] **:** being, relating to, or situated on the right esp. of a heraldic shield or escutcheon — **dexter** *adv*

dex·ter·i·ty \dek-'ster-ət-ē\ *n*, *pl* **-ties** **1** : readiness and grace in physical activity; *esp* : skill and ease in using the hands **2** : mental skill or quickness **3** : RIGHT-HANDEDNESS

dex·ter·ous *or* **dex·trous** \'dek-st(ə-)rəs\ *adj* [L *dextr-*, *dexter* dextral, skillful] **1** : skillful and competent with the hands **2** : mentally adroit and skillful : EXPERT

3 : done with skillfulness — **dex·ter·ous·ly** *adv* — **dex·ter·ous·ness** *n*
syn DEXTEROUS, ADROIT, DEFT mean ready and skilled in physical or mental movement. DEXTEROUS implies expertness with facility and agility in manipulation or movement 〈a *dexterous* pianist〉〈*dexterous* diplomacy〉 ADROIT adds artfulness and resourcefulness to dexterity 〈an *adroit* magician〉〈an *adroit* politician〉 DEFT stresses lightness, neatness, and sureness of touch 〈*deft* handling of suspense in a mystery novel〉

dextr- *or* **dextro-** *comb form* [L *dextr-, dexter*] **1** : right : on or toward the right 〈*dextro*rotatory〉 **2** : turning light to the right 〈*dextrose*〉

dex·tral \'dek-strəl\ *adj* : of, relating to, or inclined to the right; *esp* : RIGHT-HANDED — **dex·tral·i·ty** \dek-'stral-ət-ē\ *n* — **dex·tral·ly** \'dek-strə-lē\ *adv*

dex·trin \'dek-strən\ *also* **dex·trine** \-,strēn, -strən\ *n* : any of various soluble gummy substances obtained from starch by the action of heat, acids, or enzymes

dex·trorse \'dek-,strȯrs\ *adj* [L *dextrorsus* toward the right, fr. *dextr-, dexter* dextral + *vers-, vertere* to turn] : twining spirally upward around an axis from left to right — used of a plant or its parts; compare SINISTRORSE — **dex·trorse·ly** *adv*

dex·trose \'dek-,strōs\ *n* : a sugar $C_6H_{12}O_6$ that is a kind of glucose, occurs in plants, fruits, and blood, is a source of energy for living things, may be obtained by acid hydrolysis of starch, and is used in making candy

dey \'dā\ *n* [F, fr. Turk *dayı*, lit., maternal uncle] : a ruling official of the Ottoman Empire in northern Africa

dhar·ma \'dər-mə\ *n* [Skt, fr. *dhārayati* he holds] **1** Hinduism : custom or law regarded as duty **2** *Hinduism & Buddhism* **a** : the basic principles of cosmic or individual existence **b** : conformity to one's duty and nature

dhow \'daů\ *n* [Ar *dāwa*] : an Arab lateen-rigged boat usu. having a long overhang forward and a high poop

di- *comb form* [Gk; akin to E *two*] **1** : twice : twofold **:** double 〈*dichromatic*〉 **2** : containing two atoms, radicals, or groups 〈*dichloride*〉

dia- *also* **di-** *prefix* [Gk, through, apart; akin to E *two*] **:** through 〈*diapositive*〉 **:** across 〈*diactinic*〉

di·a·be·tes \,dī-ə-'bēt-ēz, -'bēt-əs\ *n* [Gk *diabētēs*, fr. *diabainein* to cross over, fr. *dia-* + *bainein* to go] : an abnormal condition marked by discharge of excessive amounts of urine; *esp* : an endocrine disorder in which insulin is deficient and the urine and blood contain excess sugar — called also *diabetes mel·li·tus* \-mə-'līt-əs, -'lēt-\ — **di·a·bet·ic** \,dī-ə-'bet-ik\ *adj or n*

di·a·bol·ic \,dī-ə-'bäl-ik\ *adj* [LL *diabolus* devil] : of, relating to, or characteristic of the devil : FIENDISH — **di·a·bol·i·cal** \-'bäl-i-kəl\ *adj* — **di·a·bol·i·cal·ly** \-i-k(ə-)lē\ *adv* — **di·a·bol·i·cal·ness** \-i-kəl-nəs\ *n*

di·ac·o·nate \dī-'ak-ə-nət\ *n* **1** : the office or period of office of a deacon **2** : an official body of deacons

¹di·a·crit·ic \,dī-ə-'krit-ik\ *or* **di·a·crit·i·cal** \-'krit-i-kəl\ *adj* [Gk *diakrinein* to distinguish, fr. *dia-* + *krinein* to separate] : serving as a diacritic

²diacritic *n* : a mark accompanying a letter or combination of letters and indicating a sound value different from that given the unmarked or otherwise marked letter or combination of letters

di·a·dem \'dī-ə-,dem, -əd-əm\ *n* [Gk *diadēma*, fr. *diadein* to bind around, fr. *dia-* + *dein* to bind] **1** : CROWN; *esp* : a headband worn as a badge of royalty **2** : regal power or dignity

di·aer·e·sis \dī-'er-ə-səs\ *n, pl* **di·aer·e·ses** \-'er-ə-,sēz\ [Gk *diairein* to divide, fr. *dia-* + *hairein* to take] : a mark ¨ placed over a vowel to show that it is pronounced in a separate syllable (as in *naïve* or *Brontë*)

di·ag·nose \'dī-əg-,nōs, -,nōz\ *vb* **:** to recognize (as a disease) by signs and symptoms **:** make a diagnosis 〈*diagnose* a play in football〉

di·ag·no·sis \,dī-əg-'nō-səs\ *n, pl* **-no·ses** \-'nō-,sēz\ [Gk *diagnōsis*, fr. *diagignōskein* to distinguish, fr. *dia-* + *gignōskein* to know] **1** : the art or act of identifying a disease from its signs and symptoms **2** : a concise technical description of a taxon **3 a** : a careful critical study of something esp. to determine its nature or importance **b** : the conclusion reached after a critical study — **di·ag·nos·tic** \-'näs-tik\ *adj* — **di·ag·nos·ti·cal·ly** \-'näs-ti-k(ə-)lē\ *adv* — **di·ag·nos·ti·cian** \-,näs-'tish-ən\ *n*

¹di·ag·o·nal \dī-'ag-ən-⁹l\ *adj* [L *diagonalis*, fr. Gk *diagōnios* from angle to angle, fr. *dia-* + *gōnia* angle] **1** : joining two vertices of a rectilinear or polyhedral figure that are not adjacent **2 a** : running in a slanting direction **b** : having diagonal markings or parts — **di·ag·o·nal·ly** \-'ag-ən-⁹l-ē, -'ag-nə-lē\ *adv*

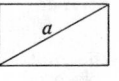
a diagonal

²diagonal *n* **1** : a diagonal line or plane **2 a** : a diagonal direction **b** : a diagonal row, arrangement, or pattern **3** : a mark / used chiefly to denote *or* (as in *and/or*), *and/or* (as in *straggler/deserter*), or *per* (as in *feet/second*) — called also *slant, solidus, virgule*

¹di·a·gram \'dī-ə-,gram\ *n* [Gk *diagramma*, fr. *diagraphein* to mark out by lines, fr. *dia-* + *graphein* to write] : a drawing, sketch, plan, or chart that makes something clearer or easier to understand — **di·a·gram·mat·ic** \,dī-ə-grə-'mat-ik\ *or* **di·a·gram·mat·i·cal** \-'mat-i-kəl\ *adj* — **di·a·gram·mat·i·cal·ly** \-'mat-i-k(ə-)lē\ *adv*

²diagram *vt* **-gramed** *or* **-grammed** \-,gramd\; **-gram·ing** *or* **-gram·ming** \-,gram-iŋ\ : to represent by or put into the form of a diagram 〈*diagram* a sentence〉〈*diagramed* the route for us〉

¹di·al \'dī(-ə)l\ *n* [L *dies* day] **1 a** : the face of a watch or clock **b** : SUNDIAL **2 a** : a face or scale upon which some measurement or other number is registered or indicated usu. by means of numbers and a pointer 〈the *dial* of a pressure gauge〉 **b** : a disk usu. with a knob or slots that may be turned to make electrical connections (as on a telephone) or to regulate the operation of a device (as a radio) and that usu. has guiding marks around its border

²dial *vb* **di·aled** *or* **di·alled**; **di·al·ing** *or* **di·al·ling** **1 a** : to manipulate a telephone dial so as to call **b** : to make a call on a dial telephone **2** : to manipulate a dial so as to operate, regulate, or select

di·a·lect \'dī-ə-,lekt\ *n* [Gk *dialektos* conversation, dialect, fr. *dialegesthai* to converse, fr. *dia-* + *legein* to speak] **1** : a regional variety of a language usu. transmitted orally and differing distinctively from the standard language 〈the Lancashire *dialect* of English〉 **2** : a variety of a language used by the members of an occupational group 〈the *dialect* of the atomic physicist〉 **3** : the customary language of a social class 〈peasant *dialect*〉 — **dialect** *or* **di·a·lec·tal** \,dī-ə-'lek-t⁹l\ *adj* — **di·a·lec·tal·ly** \,dī-ə-'lek-t⁹l-ē\ *adv*
syn DIALECT, LINGO, JARGON, SLANG mean language not recognized as standard. DIALECT applies to a form of language persisting regionally or among the uneducated; LINGO is mildly contemptuous for any language not readily understood; JARGON applies to a special or technical language used by a trade, profession, or cult, and may also be a stronger term than LINGO for language that sounds outlandish; SLANG designates a class of mostly recently coined and often short-lived terms or usages informally preferred to standard usage as being forceful, novel, or fashionable

di·a·lec·tic \,dī-ə-'lek-tik\ *n* [Gk *dialektikē*, fr. *dialektos* conversation] **1** : a process or the art of reasoning through the confrontation of opposing arguments or ideas and their fusion in a truer or more comprehensive concept **2** *or* **dialectics** *pl* : change or development in nature or society in accordance with dialectic — compare DIALECTICAL MATERIALISM

di·a·lec·ti·cal \,dī-ə-'lek-ti-kəl\ *also* **di·a·lec·tic** \-'tik\ *adj* **1** : of, relating to, or in agreement with dialectic **2** : DIALECTAL — **di·a·lec·ti·cal·ly** \-ti-k(ə-)lē\ *adv*

dialectical materialism *n* : a Marxian theory that maintains the material basis of a reality constantly undergoing dialectical change and the priority of matter over mind — compare HISTORICAL MATERIALISM

di·a·lec·tol·o·gy \,dī-ə-,lek-'täl-ə-jē\ *n* : the systematic study of dialect — **di·a·lec·tol·o·gist** \-jəst\ *n*

di·a·logue *or* **di·a·log** \'dī-ə-,lȯg\ *n* [Gk *dialogos*, fr. *dialegesthai* to converse, fr. *dia-* + *legein* to speak] **1 a** : a conversation between two or more persons **b** : an exchange of ideas and opinions **2** : the parts of a literary or dramatic composition that represent conversation

di·al·y·sis \dī-'al-ə-səs\ *n, pl* **-y·ses** \-ə-,sēz\ : the separation of substances in solution by means of their unequal diffusion through semipermeable membranes; *esp* : such a separation of colloids from soluble substances

di·a·lyze \'dī-ə-,līz\ *vt* : to subject to dialysis

ə abut; ⁹ kitten; ər further; a back; ā bake; ä cot, cart; aů out; ch chin; e less; ē easy; g gift; i trip; ī life

dia·mag·net·ic \,dī-ə-,mag-'net-ik\ *adj* : slightly repelled by a magnet — **dia·mag·ne·tism** \-'mag-nə-,tiz-əm\ *n*

di·am·e·ter \dī-'am-ət-ər\ *n* [Gk *diametros*, fr. *dia-* + *metron* measure] **1** : a chord passing through the center of a figure or body — see CIRCLE illustration **2** : the length of a straight line through the center of an object — **di·am·e·tral** \-'am-ə-trəl\ *adj*

di·a·met·ric \,dī-ə-'me-trik\ *adj* **1** : DIAMETRAL **2** : completely opposed or opposite — **di·a·met·ri·cal** \-'me-tri-kəl\ *adj* — **di·a·met·ri·cal·ly** \-tri-k(ə-)lē\ *adv*

di·a·mond \'dī-(ə-)mənd\ *n* [LL *diamant-, diamas*, alter. of L *adamant-, adamas*, hardest metal, diamond, fr. Gk] **1 a** : native crystalline carbon that is usu. nearly colorless, that when transparent and free from flaws is highly valued as a precious stone, and that is used industrially as an abrasive powder and in rock drills; *also* : a piece of this substance esp. when cut and polished **b** : crystallized carbon produced artificially **2** : a square or rhombus-shaped configuration usu. upright or otherwise clearly oriented **3** : a red lozenge used to distinguish a suit of playing cards; *also* : a card of the suit bearing diamonds **4 a** : INFIELD **b** : the entire playing field in baseball or softball

¹di·a·mond·back \'dī-(ə-)mənd(d)-,bak\ *also* **di·a·mond·backed** \,dī-(ə-)mənd(d)-'bakt\ *adj* : having marks like diamonds or lozenges on the back

²diamondback *n* : a large and deadly rattlesnake of the southern U.S.

diamondback terrapin *n* : any of several edible terrapins of coastal salt marshes of the southeastern U.S.

Di·ana \dī-'an-ə\ *n* : the Roman goddess of the moon, wild animals, and hunting

di·a·pa·son \,dī-ə-'pāz-ᵊn, -'pās-\ *n* [Gk (*hē*) *dia pasōn* (*chordōn symphōnia*) the concord through all the notes] **1** : a full deep burst of harmonious sound **2** : one of two principal stops in an organ extending through the complete scale of the instrument **3** : the full range of musical tones

dia·pause \'dī-ə-,póz\ *n* : a period (as in an insect) of spontaneous dormancy between periods of activity

¹di·a·per \'dī-(ə-)pər\ *n* **1** : a usu. white linen or cotton fabric woven in a pattern formed by the repetition of a simple usu. geometric design; *also* : the design on such cloth **2** : a basic garment for infants consisting of a piece of absorbent material drawn up between the legs and fastened about the waist

²diaper *vt* **1** : to ornament with diaper designs **2** : to put a diaper on ⟨*diaper* a baby⟩

di·aph·a·nous \dī-'af-ə-nəs\ *adj* : so fine of texture as to be seen through — **di·aph·a·nous·ly** *adv* — **di·aph·a·nous·ness** *n*

di·a·pho·ret·ic \,dī-ə-fə-'ret-ik\ *adj* : having the power to increase perspiration — **diaphoretic** *n*

di·a·phragm \'dī-ə-,fram\ *n* [Gk *diaphragma*, fr. *dia-phrassein* to barricade, fr. *dia-* + *phrassein* to enclose] **1** : a body partition of muscle and connective tissue; *esp* : the partition separating the chest and abdominal cavities in mammals **2** : a dividing membrane or thin partition (as in a tube) **3** : a device that limits (as in a camera) the aperture of a lens or optical system **4** : a thin flexible disk that vibrates (as in a microphone) — **di·a·phrag·mat·ic** \,dī-ə-,frag-'mat-ik\ *adj* — **di·a·phrag·mat·i·cal·ly** \-'mat-i-k(ə-)lē\ *adv*

di·aph·y·sis \dī-'af-ə-səs\ *n, pl* **di·aph·y·ses** \-'af-ə-,sēz\ : the shaft of a long bone — compare EPIPHYSIS — **di·aph·y·se·al** \,(,)dī-,af-ə-'sē-əl\ *adj*

di·a·rist \'dī-ə-rəst\ *n* : one who keeps a diary

di·ar·rhea *or* **di·ar·rhoea** \,dī-ə-'rē-ə\ *n* [Gk *diarrhoia*, fr. *diarrhein*, to flow through, fr. *dia-* + *rhein* to flow] : an abnormal frequency of intestinal discharge — **di·ar·rhe·al** \-'rē-əl\ *or* **di·ar·rhe·ic** \-'rē-ik\ *adj*

di·a·ry \'dī-(ə-)rē\ *n, pl* **-ries** [L *diarium*, fr. *dies* day] : a daily record esp. of personal experiences, observations, and thoughts; *also* : a book for keeping such private notes and records

Di·as·po·ra \dī-'as-p(ə-)rə\ *n* **1** : the settling of scattered colonies of Jews outside Palestine after the Babylonian exile **2 a** : the area outside Palestine settled by Jews **b** : the Jews living outside Palestine or modern Israel

di·a·stase \'dī-ə-,stās\ *n* [F, fr. Gk *diastasis* separation, fr. *diistanai* to separate, fr. *dia-* + *histanai* to cause to stand]

: AMYLASE; *esp* : a mixture of amylases from malt — **di·a·stat·ic** \,dī-ə-'stat-ik\ *adj*

di·as·ter \'dī-,as-tər\ *n* : a stage in mitosis in which the split and separated chromosomes group themselves near the poles of the spindle — **di·as·tral** \dī-'as-trəl\ *adj*

di·as·to·le \dī-'as-tə-(,)lē\ *n* [Gk *diastolē* dilatation, fr. *diastellein* to expand, fr. *dia-* + *stellein* to send] : a rhythmically recurrent expansion; *esp* : the dilatation of the cavities of the heart during which they fill with blood — **di·a·stol·ic** \,di-ə-'stäl-ik\ *adj*

di·as·tro·phism \dī-'as-trə-,fiz-əm\ *n* : the process of deformation that produces in the earth's crust its continents and ocean basins, plateaus and mountains, folds of strata, and faults — **di·a·stroph·ic** \,dī-ə-'sträf-ik\ *adj*

dia·ther·my \'dī-ə-,thər-mē\ *n* : the generation of heat in tissue for medical or surgical purposes by electric currents — **dia·ther·mic** \,dī-ə-'thər-mik\ *adj*

di·ath·e·sis \dī-'ath-ə-səs\ *n, pl* **di·ath·e·ses** \-'ath-ə-,sēz\ : a constitutional predisposition toward an abnormality or disease — **di·a·thet·ic** \,dī-ə-'thet-ik\ *adj*

di·a·tom \'dī-ə-,täm\ *n* : any of a class (Bacillariophyceae) of minute floating unicellular or colonial algae with silicified skeletons that form diatomite — **di·a·to·ma·ceous** \,dī-ə-tə-'mā-shəs\ *adj*

diatomaceous earth *n* : DIATOMITE

di·atom·ic \,dī-ə-'täm-ik\ *adj* : having two atoms in the molecule

di·at·o·mite \dī-'at-ə-,mīt\ *n* : a light crumbly silica-containing material derived chiefly from diatom remains and used esp. as a filter and as an adsorbent and for heat insulation

dia·ton·ic \,dī-ə-'tän-ik\ *adj* : relating to or being a standard major or minor scale of eight tones to the octave without chromatic deviation — **dia·ton·i·cal·ly** \-'tän-i-k(ə-)lē\ *adv*

di·a·tribe \'dī-ə-,trīb\ *n* [Gk *diatribē* pastime, discourse, fr. *diatribein* to spend (time), wear away, fr. *dia-* + *tribein* to rub] : a bitter or violent attack in speech or writing : an angry criticism or denunciation

di·ba·sic \(')dī-'bā-sik\ *adj* **1** : having two hydrogen atoms replaceable by basic atoms or radicals — used of acids **2** : having two basic hydroxyl groups — used of bases and basic salts

¹dib·ble \'dib-əl\ *n* [ME *debylle*] : a small hand tool that is used to make holes in the ground for plants, seeds, or bulbs

²dibble *vt* **dib·bled; dib·bling** \'dib-(ə-)liŋ\ **1** : to plant with a dibble **2** : to make holes in (soil) with or as if with a dibble

¹dice \'dīs\ *n, pl* **dice** [ME, fr. pl. of *dee* die] **1** : a small cube marked on each face with one to six spots and used usu. in pairs in various games **2** : a gambling game played with dice — **no dice** : nothing doing : no use

dice

²dice *vb* **1** : to cut into small cubes ⟨*diced* carrots⟩ **2** : to play games with dice — **dic·er** *n*

di·chlo·ride \(')dī-'klō(ə)r-,īd, -'klō(ə)r-\ *n* : a binary compound containing two atoms of chlorine combined with an element or radical

di·chog·a·mous \dī-'käg-ə-məs\ *or* **di·cho·gam·ic** \,dī-kə-'gam-ik\ *adj* : producing male and female reproductive elements at different times that ensure cross-fertilization — **di·chog·a·my** \dī-'käg-ə-mē\ *n*

di·chot·o·mous \dī-'kät-ə-məs\ *adj* **1** : dividing into two parts **2** : relating to, involving, or proceeding from dichotomy — **di·chot·o·mous·ly** *adv*

di·chot·o·my \-mē\ *n, pl* **-mies** [Gk *dichotomia*, fr. *dicha* in two + *tom-, temnein* to cut] **1** : a division or the process of dividing into two esp. mutually exclusive or contradictory groups **2 a** : FORKING; *esp* : repeated bifurcation **b** : a system of branching in which the main axis forks repeatedly into two branches

di·chro·ic \dī-'krō-ik\ *adj* : having the property of dichroism

di·chro·ism \'dī-krə-,wiz-əm\ *n* **1** : the property according to which the colors are unlike when a crystal is viewed in the direction of two different axes **2** : the property of a surface of reflecting light of one color and transmitting light of other colors

di·chro·mate \(')dī-'krō-,māt\ *n* : a salt having two

---

j joke; ŋ sing; ō flow; ó flaw; ói coin; th thin; th̲ this; ü loot; ú foot; y yet; yü few; yú̇ furious; zh vision

atoms of chromium in the molecule — called also *bichromate;* compare POTASSIUM DICHROMATE

di·chro·mat·ic \,dī-krō-'mat-ik\ *adj* : having or exhibiting two colors

di·chro·ma·tism \dī-'krō-mə-,tiz-əm\ *n* : the state or condition of being dichromatic

dick·cis·sel \dik-'sis-əl\ *n* [imit.] : a common migratory black-throated finch of the central U.S.

dick·ens \'dik-ənz\ *n* : DEVIL, DEUCE — used chiefly as a mild oath

Dic·ken·si·an \dik-'en-zē-ən\ *adj* : of, relating to, or characteristic of Dickens or his writings

dick·er \'dik-ər\ *vi* **dick·ered; dick·er·ing** \'dik-(ə-)riŋ\ : BARGAIN, HAGGLE — **dicker** *n*

dick·ey *or* **dicky** \'dik-ē\ *n, pl* **dick·eys** *or* **dick·ies** **1** : any of various articles of clothing: as **a** : a man's separate or detachable shirtfront **b** : a small fabric insert worn to fill in the neckline **2** : a small bird **3** *chiefly Brit* **a** : the driver's seat in a carriage **b** : a seat at the back of a carriage or automobile

Dick test \'dik-\ *n* : a test to determine susceptibility or immunity to scarlet fever made by an injection of scarlet fever toxin

di·cli·nous \(')dī-'klī-nəs\ *adj* : having the stamens and pistils in separate flowers — compare MONOCLINOUS — **di·cli·ny** \'dī-,klī-nē\ *n*

di·cot \'dī-,kät\ *also* **di·cot·yl** \-,kät-ᵊl\ *n* : DICOTYLEDON — **dicot** *adj*

di·cot·y·le·don \,dī-,kät-ᵊl-'ēd-ᵊn\ *n* : any of a group (Dicotyledones) of flowering plants having an embryo with two cotyledons and usu. net-veined leaves and flower parts not in threes — **di·cot·y·le·don·ous** \-ᵊn-əs\ *adj*

Dic·ta·phone \'dik-tə-,fōn\ *trademark* — used for a machine for the recording of dictated matter and the reproduction of the words spoken

¹dic·tate \'dik-,tāt\ *vb* [L *dictare,* freq. of *dicere* to say] **1** : to speak or read for a person to transcribe or for a machine to record ⟨*dictate* a letter to a secretary⟩⟨*dictate* a list of words to be spelled⟩ **2** : to say or state with authority : give orders to do a certain thing ⟨*dictate* terms of surrender⟩⟨few people enjoy being *dictated* to⟩

²dictate *n* : an authoritative rule, prescription, or injunction : COMMAND ⟨the *dictates* of conscience⟩⟨the *dictates* of good taste⟩

dic·ta·tion \dik-'tā-shən\ *n* **1** : the act or process of giving arbitrary commands **2 a** : the dictating of words ⟨write from *dictation*⟩⟨an exercise in *dictation*⟩ **b** : something that is dictated or is taken down as dictated ⟨take *dictation*⟩⟨make no mistakes in your *dictation*⟩

dic·ta·tor \'dik-,tāt-ər, dik-'\ *n* **1 a** : a person given absolute emergency power by the ancient Roman senate **b** : a person ruling absolutely and often brutally and oppressively **2** : one that dictates — **dic·ta·tress** \-trəs\ *n*

dic·ta·to·ri·al \,dik-tə-'tōr-ē-əl, -'tòr-\ *adj* : of, relating to, or characteristic of a dictator or a dictatorship : AUTOCRATIC, ARBITRARY ⟨a *dictatorial* regime⟩ ⟨a *dictatorial* manner⟩ — **dic·ta·to·ri·al·ly** \-ē-ə-lē\ *adv* — **dic·ta·to·ri·al·ness** *n*

syn DICTATORIAL, DOGMATIC mean imposing one's will or opinions on others. DICTATORIAL stresses autocratic, high-handed methods and a domineering manner; DOGMATIC implies being unduly and offensively positive in laying down principles and expressing opinions

dic·ta·tor·ship \dik-'tāt-ər-,ship\ *n* **1** : the office or term of office of a dictator **2** : autocratic rule, control, or leadership **3** : a government, form of government, or country in which absolute power is held by a dictator or a small clique

dictatorship of the proletariat : the assumption of political power by the proletariat held in Marxism to be an essential part of the transition from capitalism to communism

dic·tion \'dik-shən\ *n* [L *dict-, dicere* to say] **1** : choice of words esp. with regard to correctness, clearness, or effectiveness : WORDING ⟨careless *diction* in his essay⟩ **2** : quality of vocal expression : ENUNCIATION ⟨a good singer with excellent *diction*⟩

syn STYLE: DICTION applies to choice of words in reference to their effectiveness in expressing ideas or emotions ⟨poetic *diction*⟩ and also to the vocal quality evident in delivering words in acting, singing, or speaking;

STYLE refers to a manner of expression characteristic of its author and having artistic distinction ⟨Hemingway's terse *style*⟩

dic·tio·nary \'dik-shə-,ner-ē\ *n, pl* **-nar·ies** **1** : a reference book containing words usu. alphabetically arranged along with information about their forms, pronunciations, functions, etymologies, meanings, and syntactical and idiomatic uses **2** : a reference book listing alphabetically terms or names important to a particular subject or activity along with discussion of their meanings and applications ⟨a law *dictionary*⟩ **3** : a reference book giving for words of one language equivalents in another ⟨an English-French *dictionary*⟩

Dic·to·graph \'dik-tə-,graf\ *trademark* — used for a telephonic device for picking up sounds in one room and transmitting them to another or recording them

dic·tum \'dik-təm\ *n, pl* **dic·ta** \-tə\ *also* **dic·tums** [L, fr. neut. of pp. of *dicere* to say] **1** : an authoritative statement on some topic : PRONOUNCEMENT **2** : a formal statement of an opinion

did *past of* DO

di·dac·tic \dī-'dak-tik\ *adj* [Gk *didak-, didaskein* to teach] **1** : intended primarily to instruct rather than to entertain; *esp* : intended to teach a moral lesson ⟨*didactic* literature⟩ **2** : having or showing a tendency to instruct or lecture others ⟨a *didactic* manner⟩ — **di·dac·ti·cal** \-ti-kəl\ *adj* — **di·dac·ti·cal·ly** \-ti-k(ə-)lē\ *adv* — **di·dac·ti·cism** \-tə-,siz-əm\ *n*

di·dac·tics \-tiks\ *n sing or pl* : systematic instruction : PEDAGOGY, TEACHINGS

di·dap·per \'dī-,dap-ər\ *n* : a small grebe (as a dabchick)

didn't \'did-ᵊnt\ : did not

di·do \'dīd-ō\ *n, pl* **didoes** *or* **didos** **1** : a foolish or mischievous act ⟨cutting *didoes*⟩ **2** : something frivolous or showy

Di·do \'dīd-ō\ *n* : a queen of Carthage who according to the *Aeneid* entertains Aeneas, falls in love with him, and on his departure stabs herself

didst \(')didst\ *archaic past 2d sing of* DO

¹die \'dī\ *vi* **died; dy·ing** \'dī-iŋ\ [ME *dien;* akin to E *dead*] **1** : to stop living : EXPIRE ⟨*died* of old age⟩ **2 a** : to pass out of existence ⟨a *dying* race⟩ **b** : to disappear or subside gradually ⟨the wind *died* down⟩ **3** : to long keenly or desperately ⟨*dying* to go⟩ **4** : STOP ⟨the motor *died*⟩

²die \'dī\ *n, pl* **dice** \'dīs\ *or* **dies** \'dīz\ [ME *dee,* fr. MF *dé*] **1** *pl* **dice** : DICE **1** **2** *pl usu* **dice** : something determined by or as if by a cast of dice : CHANCE ⟨the *die* is cast; there's no turning back⟩ **3** *pl* **dies** : any of various tools or devices for imparting a desired shape, form, or finish to a material or for impressing an object or material: as **a** : the larger of a pair of cutting or shaping tools that when moved toward each other produce a certain desired form in or impress a desired device on an object **b** : a hollow screw-cutting tool for forming screw threads **c** : a perforated block through which metal or plastic is drawn or extruded

di·ecious *var of* DIOECIOUS

die·hard \'dī-,härd\ *n* : one who resists against hopeless odds; *esp* : an irreconcilable opponent — **die–hard** *adj*

diel·drin \'dēl-drən\ *n* : a white crystalline chlorine-containing insecticide

di·elec·tric \,dī-ə-'lek-trik\ *n* : a nonconductor of electric current

di·en·ceph·a·lon \,dī-,en-'sef-ə-,län\ *n* [*dia-* + *encephalon*] : the posterior subdivision of the forebrain — **di·en·ce·phal·ic** \(,)dī-,en(t)-sə-'fal-ik\ *adj*

di·er·e·sis *var of* DIAERESIS

die·sel \'dē-zəl, -səl\ *n* [Rudolph *Diesel* d1913 German inventor] **1** : DIESEL ENGINE **2** : a vehicle driven by a diesel engine

diesel engine *n* : an internal-combustion engine in which air is compressed to a temperature sufficiently high to ignite fuel injected into the cylinder

Di·es Irae \,dē-,ās-'ē-,rā\ *n* [ML, day of wrath; fr. the first words of the hymn] : a medieval Latin hymn about the Day of Judgment sung in requiem masses

¹di·et \'dī-ət\ *n* [OF *diete,* fr. L *diaeta* prescribed diet, fr. Gk *diaita,* lit., manner of living] **1** : the food and drink that a person, animal, or group usu. takes : customary nourishment **2** : the kind and amount of food selected

for a person or animal for a special reason (as ill health or overweight) ⟨a high-protein *diet*⟩
²diet *vb* **:** to eat or cause to eat less or according to prescribed rules ⟨said she *dieted* but didn't lose a pound⟩ — **di·et·er** *n*
³diet *n* [ML *dieta* day's journey, assembly, fr. L *dies* day] **:** a formal deliberative assembly; *esp* **:** any of various national or provincial legislatures
¹di·e·tary \'dī-ə-,ter-ē\ *n, pl* **-tar·ies :** ¹DIET
²dietary *adj* **:** of or relating to a diet or to the rules of diet
di·e·tar·y \,dī-ə-'tet-ik\ *adj* **:** of or relating to diet or dietetics — **di·e·tet·i·cal·ly** \-'tet-i-k(ə-)lē\ *adv*
di·e·tet·ics \-'tet-iks\ *n* **:** the science or art of applying the principles of nutrition to feeding
di·e·ti·tian *or* **di·e·ti·cian** \,dī-ə-'tish-ən\ *n* **:** a person qualified in or practicing dietetics ⟨a hospital *dietitian*⟩
dif·fer \'dif-ər\ *vi* **dif·fered; dif·fer·ing** \'dif-(ə-)riŋ\ [L *differre* to postpone, be different, fr. *dis-* + *ferre* to carry] **1 :** to be not the same **:** be unlike ⟨brothers who *differ* in looks⟩ **2 :** DISAGREE ⟨they *differ* about what should be done⟩
dif·fer·ence \'dif-ərn(t)s, 'dif-(ə-)rən(t)s\ *n* **1 :** unlikeness between two or more persons or things ⟨the striking *difference* in the sisters' looks⟩ **2 :** the degree or amount by which things differ in quantity or measure; *esp* **:** the number that is obtained by subtracting one number from another ⟨the *difference* between 4 and 6 is 2⟩ **3 :** a disagreement in opinion **:** DISPUTE ⟨persons unable to settle their *differences*⟩
dif·fer·ent \'dif-ərnt, 'dif-(ə-)rənt\ *adj* **1 :** not of the same kind **:** partly or totally unlike another person or thing ⟨this apple is *different* from the others in size and color⟩ **2 :** not the same **:** OTHER, SEPARATE ⟨see the same person at *different* times and places⟩
syn DIFFERENT, DIVERSE, DISPARATE mean unlike in kind or character. DIFFERENT often implies little more than separateness but may also suggest contrast or contrariness; DIVERSE implies both distinctness and marked contrast ⟨a man of *diverse* interests⟩ DISPARATE stresses incongruity or incompatibility
dif·fer·en·tia \,dif-ə-'ren-ch(ē-)ə\ *n, pl* **-ti·ae** \-chē-,ē, -chē-,ī\ **:** the element, feature, or factor that distinguishes two things of the same general class
¹dif·fer·en·tial \,dif-ə-'ren-chəl\ *adj* **1 a :** of, relating to, or constituting a distinction **:** DISTINGUISHING ⟨the *differential* character of voice timbre⟩ **b :** making a distinction between individuals or classes ⟨*differential* legislation⟩ **c :** based upon or resulting from a differential ⟨*differential* freight charges⟩ **d :** functioning or proceeding differently or at a different rate ⟨*differential* melting in a glacier⟩ **2 :** relating to or involving a differential or differentiation ⟨a *differential* equation⟩ **3 :** relating to quantitative differences ⟨*differential* readings on a scale⟩ — **dif·fer·en·tial·ly** \-'rench-(ə-)lē\ *adv*
²differential *n* **1 :** the product of the derivative of a function of one variable by the increment of the independent variable **2 :** an amount or degree of difference between comparable individuals or classes ⟨price *differential* between gasoline grades⟩ ⟨a wage *differential* for night work⟩ **3 :** DIFFERENTIAL GEAR
differential calculus *n* **:** a branch of mathematics dealing chiefly with the rate of change of functions with respect to their variables
differential gear *n* **:** an arrangement of gears in an automobile that allows one of the wheels imparting motion to turn (as in going around a curve) faster than the other
dif·fer·en·ti·ate \,dif-ə-'ren-chē-,āt\ *vb* **1 :** to obtain the mathematical derivative of **2 :** to make a person or a thing different in some way ⟨the color of their eyes *differentiates* the twins⟩ **3 :** to undergo or cause to undergo differentiation in the course of development **4 :** to recognize or state the difference or differences ⟨*differentiate* between two plants⟩
dif·fer·en·ti·a·tion \-,ren-chē-'ā-shən\ *n* **1 :** the act or process of differentiating **2 :** development from the one to the many, the simple to the complex, or the homogeneous to the heterogeneous ⟨the *differentiation* of Latin into the modern Romance languages⟩ **3 :** the sum of the processes whereby apparently indifferent cells, tissues, and structures attain their adult form and function; *also* **:** the result of this

dif·fer·ent·ly \'dif-ərnt-lē, 'dif-(ə-)rənt-\ *adv* **1 :** in a different manner ⟨they talk *differently* from us⟩ **2 :** OTHERWISE ⟨he soon learned *differently*⟩
dif·fi·cult \'dif-i-(,)kəlt\ *adj* **1 :** hard to do, make, or carry out **:** ARDUOUS ⟨a *difficult* climb⟩ **2 a :** hard to deal with, manage, or overcome ⟨a *difficult* child⟩ **b :** hard to understand **:** PUZZLING ⟨*difficult* reading⟩ — **dif·fi·cult·ly** *adv*
dif·fi·cul·ty \-(,)kəl-tē\ *n, pl* **-ties** [L *difficultas*, irreg. fr. *difficilis* difficult, fr. *dis-* + *facilis* easy] **1 :** difficult nature ⟨slowed up by the *difficulty* of a task⟩ **2 :** great effort ⟨accomplish a task only with *difficulty*⟩ **3 :** something that is hard to do **:** OBSTACLE ⟨overcome *difficulties*⟩ **4 :** a difficult or trying situation **:** TROUBLE ⟨in financial *difficulties*⟩ **5 :** DISAGREEMENT ⟨the two partners finally ironed out their *difficulties*⟩
dif·fi·dence \'dif-əd-ən(t)s, -ə-,den(t)s\ *n* **:** the quality or state of being diffident
dif·fi·dent \-əd-ənt, -ə-,dent\ *adj* [L *diffidere* to distrust, fr. *dis-* + *fidere* to trust] **1 :** lacking confidence **:** TIMID **2 :** RESERVED, UNASSERTIVE — **dif·fi·dent·ly** *adv*
dif·flu·gia \dif-'lü-jē-ə\ *n* **:** any of a genus of freshwater amoebas with flask-shaped shells usu. of cemented sand grains
dif·fract \dif-'rakt\ *vb* **:** to undergo or cause to undergo diffraction ⟨*diffract* light⟩
dif·frac·tion \dif-'rak-shən\ *n* [L *diffract-, diffringere* to break apart, fr. *dis-* + *frangere* to break] **:** a modification which light undergoes in passing by the edges of opaque bodies or through narrow slits or in being reflected from ruled surfaces and in which the rays appear to be deflected and produce a series of parallel light and dark or colored bands; *also* **:** a similar modification of other waves
diffraction grating *n* **:** a series of closely and equally spaced parallel lines or bars used for producing spectra by diffraction of light
¹dif·fuse \dif-'yüs\ *adj* [L *diffusus*, pp. of *diffundere* to spread out, fr. *dis-* + *fundere* to pour] **1 :** poured or spread out **:** not concentrated ⟨*diffuse* daylight⟩ **2 :** marked by wordiness **:** VERBOSE ⟨a *diffuse* writer⟩ **3 :** spreading widely or loosely **:** SCATTERED ⟨*diffuse* branches⟩ — **dif·fuse·ly** *adv* — **dif·fuse·ness** *n*
²dif·fuse \dif-'yüz\ *vb* **1 :** to pour out and spread freely **2 :** to subject to or undergo diffusion ⟨gases *diffuse* at different rates⟩ — **dif·fus·er** *also* **dif·fu·sor** \-'yü-zər\ *n*
dif·fus·i·ble \dif-'yü-zə-bəl\ *adj* **:** capable of diffusing or of being diffused — **dif·fus·i·bil·i·ty** \-,yü-zə-'bil-ət-ē\ *n*
dif·fu·sion \dif-'yü-zhən\ *n* **1 :** a diffusing or a being diffused; *also* **:** the state of being diffused **2 :** the intermingling of the particles of liquids, gases, or solids as a result of their spontaneous movement so that in dissolved substances they move from a region of higher to one of lower concentration **3 :** the reflection of light from a rough surface or the transmission of light through a translucent material (as frosted glass) — **dif·fu·sion·al** \-'yüzh-nəl, -'yüzh-ən-ᵊl\ *adj*
dif·fu·sive \dif-'yü-siv, -ziv\ *adj* **:** tending to diffuse **:** characterized by diffusion — **dif·fu·sive·ly** *adv* — **dif·fu·sive·ness** *n*
¹dig \'dig\ *vb* **dug** \'dəg\; **dig·ging** [ME *diggen*] **1 a :** to turn up the soil (as with a spade or hoe) **b :** to hollow out or form by removing earth ⟨*dig* a hole⟩ ⟨*dig* a cellar⟩ **2 :** to uncover or seek by turning up earth ⟨*dig* potatoes⟩ ⟨*dig* for gold⟩ **3 :** to bring to light **:** DISCOVER ⟨*dig* up information⟩ **4 :** POKE, THRUST ⟨*dig* a person in the ribs⟩ **5 :** to work hard **6** *slang* **a :** to pay attention to **b :** UNDERSTAND, APPRECIATE — **dig·ger** *n*
²dig *n* **1 :** THRUST, POKE **2 :** a cutting remark **:** GIBE
di·ge·net·ic \,dī-jə-'net-ik\ *adj* **:** of or relating to a group (Digenea) of trematode worms in which sexual reproduction as an internal parasite of a vertebrate alternates with asexual reproduction in a mollusk
¹di·gest \'dī-,jest\ *n* [L *digestus*, pp. of *digerere* to arrange, digest, fr. *dis-* + *gerere* to carry] **:** a summation or condensation of a body of information or of a literary work ⟨a *digest* of the laws⟩
²di·gest \dī-'jest, də-\ *vb* **1 :** to think over and arrange in the mind **:** assimilate mentally **2 :** to convert food into simpler forms that can be taken in and used by the body **3 :** to soften or decompose or to extract soluble ingredients from by heat and moisture **4 :** to compress

into a short summary **5 :** to become digested — **di-gest-er** *n*

di-gest-i-ble \dī-'jes-tə-bəl, də-\ *adj* **:** capable of being digested — **di-gest-i-bil-i-ty** \(,)dī-,jes-tə-'bil-ət-ē, də-\ *n*

di-ges-tion \dī-'jes-chən, də-\ *n* **:** the process or power of digesting something and esp. food

¹di-ges-tive \-'jes-tiv\ *n* **:** something that aids digestion

²digestive *adj* **1 :** of or relating to digestion **2 :** having the power to cause or promote digestion ⟨*digestive* enzymes⟩ — **di-ges-tive-ly** *adv* — **di-ges-tive-ness** *n*

digger wasp *n* **:** a burrowing wasp; *esp* **:** one that digs nest burrows in the soil and provisions them with insects or spiders paralyzed by stinging

dig-gings \'dig-iŋz\ *n pl* **1 :** a place where ore, metals, or precious stones are dug **2 :** LODGINGS

dight \'dīt\ *vt* **dight-ed** *or* **dight**; **dight-ing** [OE *dihtan* to arrange, compose, fr. L *dictare* to dictate, compose] *archaic* **:** DRESS, ADORN

dig in *vi* **1 :** to dig and take position in defensive trenches **2 :** to go to work

dig-it \'dij-ət\ *n* [L *digitus* finger, toe; akin to E *toe*] **1 a :** any of the arabic numerals 1 to 9 and usu. the symbol 0   **b :** one of the elements that combine to form numbers in a system other than the decimal system **2 :** FINGER, TOE

¹dig-i-tal \'dij-ət-°l\ *adj* **1 :** of or relating to the fingers or toes **:** DIGITATE **2 :** of or relating to calculation directly with digits rather than through measurable physical quantities — **dig-i-tal-ly** \-°l-ē\ *adv*

²digital *n* **:** a key (as of an organ) to be played by the finger

digital computer *n* **:** a computer that operates directly with digits — compare ANALOGUE COMPUTER

dig-i-tal-is \,dij-ə-'tal-əs\ *n* [L *digitus* finger, toe; fr. its finger-shaped corolla] **1 :** FOXGLOVE **2 :** the dried leaf of the common foxglove serving as a powerful heart stimulant and a diuretic

dig-i-tate \'dij-ə-,tāt\ *adj* **:** having or resembling digits; *esp* **:** having divisions arranged like fingers on a hand ⟨*digitate* leaf⟩ — **dig-i-tate-ly** *adv* — **dig-i-ta-tion** \,dij-ə-'tā-shən\ *n*

dig-ni-fied \'dig-nə-,fīd\ *adj* **:** showing or expressing dignity

dig-ni-fy \-,fī\ *vt* **-fied; -fy-ing :** to give dignity or distinction to **:** HONOR

dig-ni-tary \'dig-nə-,ter-ē\ *n, pl* **-tar-ies :** a person of high position or honor ⟨*dignitaries* of the church⟩

dig-ni-ty \'dig-nət-ē\ *n, pl* **-ties** [L *dignitas*, fr. *dignus* worthy] **1 :** the quality or state of being worthy, honored, or esteemed **2 :** high rank, office, or position **3 :** formal reserve of manner or language **syn** see DECORUM

di-graph \'dī-,graf\ *n* **:** a group of two successive letters representing a single sound or a complex sound which is not a combination of the sounds ordinarily represented by each in other occurrences ⟨*ea* in *bread* and *ch* in *chin* are *digraphs*⟩ — **di-graph-ic** \dī-'graf-ik\ *adj*

di-gress \dī-'gres, də-\ *vi* [L *digress-, digredi*, fr. *dis-* + *gradi* to step] **:** to turn aside esp. from the main subject in writing or speaking — **di-gres-sion** \-'gresh-ən\ *n*

di-gres-sive \-'gres-iv\ *adj* **:** characterized by digressions ⟨a *digressive* book⟩ — **di-gres-sive-ly** *adv* — **di-gres-sive-ness** *n*

di-he-dral \dī-'hē-drəl\ *adj* **:** having or formed by two plane faces ⟨*dihedral* angle⟩ — **dihedral** *n*

di-hy-brid \(')dī-'hī-brəd\ *adj* **:** heterozygous in respect to two gene pairs — **dihybrid** *n*

¹dike \'dīk\ *n* [OE *dīc* ditch, dike] **1 :** an artificial watercourse **:** DITCH **2 :** a bank of earth constructed to control or confine water **:** LEVEE **3 a :** a raised causeway **b :** a tabular body of igneous rock that has been injected while molten into a fissure

²dike *vt* **:** to surround or protect with a dike; *also* **:** to drain by a dike — **dik-er** *n*

di-lap-i-dat-ed \də-'lap-ə-,dāt-əd\ *adj* [L *dilapidare* to destroy, fr. *dis-* + *lapidare* to throw stones, fr. *lapid-, lapis* stone] **:** partly ruined or decayed ⟨a *dilapidated* old house⟩

di-lap-i-da-tion \də-,lap-ə-'dā-shən\ *n* **:** a dilapidated condition **:** partial ruin (as from neglect)

dil-a-ta-tion \,dil-ə-'tā-shən, ,dī-lə-\ *n* **1 :** the condition of being stretched beyond normal dimensions esp. as a result of overwork or disease ⟨*dilatation* of the heart⟩ **2 :** DILATION **3 :** a dilated part or formation — **dil-a-ta-tion-al** \-shnəl, -shən-°l\ *adj*

di-late \dī-'lāt, 'dī-,\ *vb* [L *dilatare*, lit., to spread wide, fr. *dis-* + *latus* wide] **:** to make or grow larger or wider **:** SWELL, DISTEND ⟨eyes *dilated* with fear⟩⟨lungs *dilated* with air⟩ **syn** see EXPAND — **di-lat-a-ble** \dī-'lāt-ə-bəl\ *adj* — **di-la-tor** \dī-'lāt-ər, 'dī-,\ *n*

di-la-tion \dī-'lā-shən\ *n* **:** the act of dilating **:** the state of being dilated **:** EXPANSION ⟨*dilation* of the bladder⟩

dil-a-to-ry \'dil-ə-,tōr-ē, -,tòr-\ *adj* [L *dilat-*, used as stem of *differre* to postpone, differ, fr. *dis-* + *ferre* to carry] **1 :** tending or intended to cause delay ⟨*dilatory* tactics⟩ **2 :** characterized by procrastination **:** TARDY — **dil-a-to-ri-ly** \,dil-ə-'tōr-ə-lē, -'tòr-\ *adv* — **dil-a-to-ri-ness** \'dil-ə-,tōr-ē-nəs, -,tòr-\ *n*

di-lem-ma \də-'lem-ə\ *n* [LGk *dilēmmat-, dilēmma*, fr. Gk *di-* + *lēmma* assumption] **:** a choice or a situation in which one has to choose between two or more things, ways, or plans that are equally unsatisfactory **:** a difficult choice **syn** see PREDICAMENT

dil-et-tante \,dil-ə-'tänt(-ē), -'tant(-ē)\ *n, pl* **-tantes** *or* **-tan-ti** \-'tänt-ē, -'tant-ē\ [It, fr. prp. of *dilettare* to delight, fr. L *dilectare*] **1 :** an admirer or lover of the arts **2 :** a person who cultivates esp. superficially an art or branch of knowledge as a pastime — **dilettante** *adj* — **dil-et-tan-tism** \-'tän-,tiz-əm, -'tan-\ *n*

¹dil-i-gence \'dil-ə-jən(t)s\ *n* **:** careful and continued work **:** conscientious effort **:** INDUSTRY

²dil-i-gence \'dil-ə-zhäⁿs, 'dil-ə-jən(t)s\ *n* **:** STAGECOACH

dil-i-gent \'dil-ə-jənt\ *adj* [L *diligent-, diligens*, fr. prp. of *diligere* to love, fr. *di-* + *legere* to select] **:** characterized by steady, earnest, and energetic application and effort **:** PAINSTAKING — **dil-i-gent-ly** *adv*

dill \'dil\ *n* [OE *dile*] **:** any of several plants of the carrot family; *esp* **:** a European herb with aromatic foliage and seeds used in flavoring pickles

dil-ly-dal-ly \'dil-ē-,dal-ē\ *vi* **:** to waste time by loitering or delay **:** DAWDLE

dil-u-ent \'dil-yə-wənt\ *n* **:** a diluting agent

¹di-lute \dī-'lüt, də-\ *vt* [L *dilut-, diluere* to wash away, dilute, fr. *dis-* + *lavere* to wash] **1 :** to make thinner or more liquid by admixture (as with water) **2 :** to diminish the strength, flavor, or brilliance of by admixture ⟨*dilute* wine with water⟩ **3 :** ATTENUATE — **di-lut-er** *or* **di-lu-tor** *n*

²dilute *adj* **:** DILUTED, WEAK ⟨a *dilute* acid⟩ — **di-lute-ness** *n*

di-lu-tion \dī-'lü-shən, də-\ *n* **1 :** the act of diluting **:** the state of being diluted **2 :** something (as a solution) that is diluted

di-lu-vi-al \də-'lü-vē-əl, dī-\ *or* **di-lu-vi-an** \-vē-ən\ *adj* [L *diluvium* deluge] **:** of, relating to, or effected by a flood

¹dim \'dim\ *adj* **dim-mer; dim-mest** [OE] **1 :** not bright or distinct **:** OBSCURE, FAINT ⟨a *dim* light⟩ **2 :** being without luster **:** DULL **3 a :** not seeing or understanding clearly **b :** not seen or understood clearly — **dim-ly** *adv* — **dim-ness** *n*

²dim *vb* **dimmed; dim-ming 1 :** to make or become dim or lusterless **2 :** to reduce the light from (headlights) by switching to the low beam

dime \'dīm\ *n* [MF, tenth part, fr. L *decima*, fr. fem. of *decimus* tenth, fr. *decem* ten] **:** a U.S. coin worth ¹⁄₁₀ dollar

¹di-men-sion \də-'men-chən, dī-\ *n* [L *dimension-, dimensio*, fr. *dimens-, dimetiri* to measure out, fr. *dis-* + *metiri* to measure] **1 a :** extension in one direction **b :** magnitude of extension in one direction or in all directions **:** SIZE **2 :** the range over which something extends **:** SCOPE — **di-men-sion-al** \-'mench-nəl, -'mench-ən-°l\ *adj* — **di-men-sion-al-i-ty** \-,men-chə-'nal-ət-ē\ *n* — **di-men-sion-al-ly** \-'mench-nə-lē, -'men-chən-°l-ē\ *adv* — **di-men-sion-less** \-'men-chən-ləs\ *adj*

²dimension *vt* **1 :** to form to the required dimensions **2 :** to indicate the dimensions on

di-mer-ic \dī-'mer-ik\ *adj* **1 :** consisting of two parts ⟨a *dimeric* chromosome⟩ **2 :** involving or mediated by two factors

dim-er-ous \'dim-ə-rəs\ *adj* **:** consisting of or having two parts — **dim-er-ism** \-,riz-əm\ *n*

dim-e-ter \'dim-ət-ər\ *n* [Gk *dimetros*, adj., being a dimeter, fr. *di-* + *metron* measure] **:** a line consisting of two metrical feet

di-met-ro-don \dī-'me-trə-,dän\ *n* **:** an ancient fossil reptile with a high bony fin on the back

---

di·min·ish \də-'min-ish\ *vb* [ME *diminuen, diminishen,* fr. L *deminuere,* fr. *de-* + *minuere* to lessen] **1 :** to make less or cause to appear less **2 :** to lessen the authority, dignity, or reputation of **:** BELITTLE **3 :** DWINDLE **4 :** TAPER **syn** see DECREASE, MINIMIZE — **di·min·ish·a·ble** \-ish-ə-bəl\ *adj* — **di·min·ish·ment** \-ish-mənt\ *n*

di·min·ished *adj* **:** made one half step less than perfect or minor ⟨the musical interval of a *diminished* fifth⟩

di·min·u·en·do \də-,min-(y)ə-'wen-dō\ *adv (or adj)* [It] **:** DECRESCENDO — **diminuendo** *n*

dim·i·nu·tion \,dim-ə-'n(y)ü-shən\ *n* **:** the act, process, or an instance of diminishing **:** DECREASE

¹di·min·u·tive \də-'min-yət-iv\ *n* **1 :** a diminutive word or affix **2 :** a diminutive object or individual

²diminutive *adj* **1 :** indicating small size and sometimes the state or quality of being lovable, pitiable, or contemptible ⟨the *diminutive* suffixes *-ette* and *-ling*⟩ ⟨the *diminutive* nouns *duckling* and *princeling*⟩ — compare AUGMENTATIVE **2 :** extremely small **:** TINY — **di·min·u·tive·ly** *adv* — **di·min·u·tive·ness** *n*

dim·i·ty \'dim-ət-ē\ *n, pl* **-ties** [alter. of ME *demyt*] **:** a sheer usu. corded cotton fabric of plain weave in checks or stripes

dim·mer \'dim-ər\ *n* **1 :** one that dims **2** *pl* **a :** small lights on an automobile for use in parking **b :** headlights that have been dimmed

di·mor·phic \dī-'mȯr-fik\ *adj* **1 :** DIMORPHOUS **2 :** combining qualities of two kinds of individuals in one

di·mor·phism \-,fiz-əm\ *n* **:** the condition or property of being dimorphous; *esp* **:** occurrence of individuals that might be expected to be similar or identical in two distinguishable forms ⟨sexual *dimorphism* in birds⟩ — compare

di·mor·phous \-fəs\ *adj* **:** occurring or crystallizing in two different forms

¹dim·ple \'dim-pəl\ *n* [ME *dympull;* akin to E *dip*] **1 :** a slight natural indentation in the surface of some part of the human body **2 :** a slight hollow

²dimple *vb* **dim·pled; dim·pling** \-p(ə-)liŋ\ **:** to mark with or form dimples

¹din \'din\ *n* [OE *dyne*] **:** a loud noise; *esp* **:** a welter of confused or discordant sounds

²din *vb* **dinned; din·ning 1 a :** to make a loud noise **b :** to deafen with loud noise **2 :** to impress by insistent repetition

di·nar \di-'när, 'dē-,\ *n* [Ar *dīnār,* fr. L *denarius*] **1 :** a gold coin first struck in the late 7th century A.D. and used as the basic monetary unit in Muslim territories **2 a :** any one of several monetary units; *esp* **:** the basic unit of Yugoslavia **b :** a coin or note representing one dinar

dine \'dīn\ *vb* [OF *diner,* fr. (assumed) VL *disjejunare* to break one's fast, fr. L *dis-* + *jejunus* fasting] **1 :** to eat dinner **2 :** to give a dinner to **:** FEED

din·er \'dī-nər\ *n* **1 :** one that dines **2 a :** DINING CAR **b :** a restaurant in the shape of a railroad car

di·nette \dī-'net\ *n* **:** an alcove or small room used for dining

ding \'diŋ\ *vi* **:** to make a ringing sound **:** CLANG

¹ding-dong \'diŋ-,dȯŋ, -,däŋ\ *n* **:** the sound of repeated strokes on a bell or a similar sound

²dingdong *adj* **:** vigorously contested ⟨a *dingdong* battle⟩

din·ghy \'diŋ-(k)ē\ *n, pl* **dinghies** [Bengali *diṅgi* & Hindi *diṅgī*] **1 :** an East Indian rowboat or sailboat **2 :** a ship's small boat **3 :** a rowboat used as a tender **4 :** a rubber life raft

din·gle \'diŋ-gəl\ *n* **:** a small narrow wooded valley

din·go \'diŋ-,gō\ *n, pl* **dingoes :** a reddish brown bushy-tailed wild dog of Australia

din·gus \'diŋ-(g)əs\ *n* **:** something whose common name is unknown or forgotten

din·gy \'din-jē\ *adj* **din·gi·er; -est 1 :** DARK, DULL ⟨a *dingy* unlighted room⟩ **2 :** not fresh or clean **:** GRIMY ⟨*dingy* wallpaper⟩ — **din·gi·ly** \-jə-lē\ *adv* — **din·gi·ness** \-jē-nəs\ *n*

dining car *n* **:** a railroad car in which meals are served

din·key *or* **din·ky** \'diŋ-kē\ *n, pl* **dinkeys** *or* **dinkies :** a small locomotive used esp. for hauling freight, logging, and shunting

din·ky \'diŋ-kē\ *adj* **din·ki·er; -est** [Sc *dink* neat] **:** SMALL, INSIGNIFICANT

din·ner \'din-ər\ *n* **1 :** the main meal of the day **2 :** a formal banquet

dinner jacket *n* **:** TUXEDO

di·no·flag·el·late \,dī-nō-'flaj-ə-lət\ *n* [Gk *dinos* rotation, eddy] **:** any of an order (Dinoflagellata) of chiefly marine floating plantlike flagellates important in marine food chains

restored skeleton of dinosaur

di·no·saur \'dī-nə-,sȯr\ *n* [Gk *deinos* terrible + *sauros* lizard] **:** any of a group (Dinosauria) of extinct chiefly terrestrial long-tailed reptiles with limbs adapted for walking — **di·no·sau·ri·an** \,dī-nə-'sȯr-ē-ən\ *adj or n*

¹dint \'dint\ *n* [OE *dynt*] **1** *archaic* **:** BLOW **2 :** FORCE, POWER — used chiefly in the phrase *by dint of* **3 :** DENT

²dint *vt* **:** DENT

¹di·oc·e·san \dī-'äs-ə-sən\ *adj* **:** of or relating to a diocese

²diocesan *n* **:** a bishop having jurisdiction over a diocese

di·o·cese \'dī-ə-səs, -,sēz, -,sēs\ *n* [Gk *dioikēsis* administration, administrative division, fr. *dia-* + *oikein* to dwell, manage, fr. *oikos* house] **:** the district over which a bishop has authority

di·ode \'dī-,ōd\ *n* **1 :** a 2-electrode electron tube having a cathode and an anode **2 :** a rectifier consisting of a semiconducting crystal with two terminals

di·oe·cious \dī-'ē-shəs\ *adj* [Gk *di-* + *oikos* house] **1 :** having male reproductive organs in one individual and female in another **2 :** having staminate and pistillate flowers borne on different individuals — **di·oe·cious·ly** *adv* — **di·oe·cism** \-'ē-,siz-əm\ *n*

Di·o·me·des \,dī-ə-'mēd-ēz\ *n* **:** a Greek warrior in the Trojan War

Di·o·ny·sia \,dī-ə-'nizh-ē-ə, -'nis(h)-\ *n pl* **:** any of the ancient Greek festivals in honor of Dionysus; *esp* **:** an autumn festival from which the Greek drama is held to have developed

Di·o·ny·sus \-'nī-səs\ *n* **:** the Greek god of wine

Di·o·phan·tine equation \,dī-ə-,fant-ⁿn-, -,fan-,tīn-\ *n* **:** a polynomial equation for which the unknowns are to be rational numbers

di·o·ra·ma \,dī-ə-'ram-ə, -'räm-\ *n* **:** a scenic representation in which a partly transparent painting is viewed from a distance through an opening or in which lifelike sculptured figures and surrounding details are realistically illuminated against a painted background

di·o·rite \'dī-ə-,rīt\ *n* **:** a granular crystalline igneous rock

Di·os·cu·ri \dī-'äs-kyə-,rī\ *n pl* [Gk *Dioskouroi,* lit., sons of Zeus] **:** the twins Castor and Pollux reunited after Castor's death by Zeus's decree that they live in the upper and lower worlds on alternate days

di·ox·ide \(')dī-'äk-,sīd\ *n* **:** an oxide containing two atoms of oxygen in the molecule

¹dip \'dip\ *vb* **dipped; dip·ping** [OE *dyppan*] **1 a :** to plunge momentarily or partially under the surface (as of a liquid) so as to moisten, cool, or coat **b :** to thrust in a way to suggest immersion ⟨*dips* a hand into his pocket⟩ **2 :** to lift a portion of by reaching below the surface with something shaped to hold liquid **:** LADLE ⟨*dip* water from a pail⟩ **3 :** to lower and then raise again ⟨*dip* a flag in salute⟩ **4 a :** to plunge into a liquid and quickly emerge ⟨oars *dipping* rhythmically⟩ **b :** to immerse something into a processing liquid or finishing material **5 a :** to drop down or out of sight esp. suddenly ⟨the road *dipped* below the crest⟩ **b :** to decrease moderately and usu. temporarily ⟨prices *dipped*⟩ **6 :** to reach down inside or as if inside or below a surface esp. to withdraw a part of the contents ⟨*dipped* into their savings⟩ **7 :** to delve casually or tentatively into something; *esp* **:** to read superficially ⟨*dip* into a book⟩

²dip *n* **1 :** an act of dipping; *esp* **:** a brief plunge into the water for sport or exercise **2 a :** inclination downward **b :** a sharp or slight downward course **:** DROP **3 :** something obtained by or used in dipping **4 :** a liquid preparation into which something may be dipped

---

j *joke;* ŋ *sing;* ō *flow;* ȯ *flaw;* ȯi *coin;* th *thin;* t͟h *this;* ü *loot;* u̇ *foot;* y *yet;* yü *few;* yu̇ *furious;* zh *vision*

di·pep·tide \(')dī-'pep-,tīd\ *n* **:** a peptide that yields two molecules of amino acid on hydrolysis

di·phase \'dī-,fāz\ *or* **di·pha·sic** \(')dī-'fā-zik\ *adj* **:** having two phases

di·phos·pho·pyr·i·dine nucleotide \,dī-,fäs-fō-'pir-ə-,dēn-\ *n* **:** a coenzyme that occurs in most cells and is important in metabolism as an oxidizing agent or in another form as a reducing agent

diph·the·ria \dif-'thir-ē-ə, dip-\ *n* [NL, fr. Gk *diphthera* leather; so called fr. the toughness of the membranous layer] **:** an acute febrile contagious bacterial disease in which the air passages become coated with a membranous layer that often obstructs breathing — **diph·the·ri·al** \-ē-əl\ *or* **diph·the·rit·ic** \,dif-thə-'rit-ik\ *adj*

diph·thong \'dif-,thŏŋ, 'dip-\ *n* [Gk *diphthongos*, fr. *di-* + *phthongos* voice, sound] **1 :** a 2-element speech sound that begins with the tongue position for one vowel and ends with the tongue position for another all within one syllable ⟨the sounds of *ou* in *out* and of *oy* in *boy* are *diphthongs*⟩ **2 :** DIGRAPH **3 :** the letters *a* and *e* or *o* and *e* when they represent a one-syllable sound and are written æ, œ — **diph·thon·gal** \dif-'thŏŋ-(g)əl, dip-\ *adj*

diph·thong·ize \-,thŏŋ-,īz\ *vb* **:** to change into or pronounce as a diphthong — **diph·thong·i·za·tion** \,dif-,thŏŋ-ə-'zā-shən, ,dip-\ *n*

di·phy·let·ic \,dī-fī-'let-ik\ *adj* **:** derived from two lines of descent ⟨*diphyletic* dinosaurs⟩

dipl- *or* **diplo-** *comb form* [Gk *diploos*, fr. *di-* + *-ploos* -fold] **:** double ⟨*diplopia*⟩ **:** twofold ⟨*diploid*⟩

dip·lo·blas·tic \,dip-lō-'blas-tik\ *adj* **:** having two germ layers — used of an embryo or lower invertebrate that lacks a true mesoderm

dip·lo·coc·cus \,dip-lō-'käk-əs\ *n, pl* **-coc·ci** \-'käk-,(s)ī, 'käk-,(,)(s)ē\ **:** any of a genus of parasitic bacteria that occur usu. in pairs in a capsule and include serious pathogens — **dip·lo·coc·cal** \-'käk-əl\ *adj*

di·plod·o·cus \də-'pläd-ə-kəs, dī-\ *n* **:** any of a genus of very large herbivorous dinosaurs from Colorado and Wyoming

dip·loid \'dip-,lȯid\ *adj* **:** double or twofold in appearance or arrangement; *esp* **:** having the basic chromosome number doubled — **diploid** *n* — **dip·loi·dy** \-,lȯid-ē\ *n*

di·plo·ma \də-'plō-mə\ *n* [L, fr. Gk *diplōma* folded paper, passport, fr. *diploun* to double, fr. *diploos* double, fr. *di-* + *-ploos* -fold; akin to E *fold*] **:** a document conferring a privilege, honor, or power; *esp* **:** an official paper bearing record of graduation from or of a degree conferred by an educational institution

di·plo·ma·cy \də-'plō-mə-sē\ *n* **1 :** the art and practice of conducting negotiations between nations **2 :** skill in handling affairs without arousing hostility **:** TACT

dip·lo·mat \'dip-lə-,mat\ *n* **:** a person employed or skilled in diplomacy

dip·lo·mat·ic \,dip-lə-'mat-ik\ *adj* [L *diplomat-, diploma* document, fr. Gk *diplōma*] **1 :** of, relating to, or concerned with diplomacy or diplomats ⟨*diplomatic* immunity⟩ **2 :** TACTFUL ⟨found a *diplomatic* way to say it⟩ — **dip·lo·mat·i·cal·ly** \-'mat-i-k(ə-)lē\ *adv*

di·plo·ma·tist \də-'plō-mət-əst\ *n* **:** DIPLOMAT

dip·lo·pia \dip-'lō-pē-ə\ *n* **:** double vision of an object owing to unequal action of the eye muscles — **dip·lo·pic** \-'lō-pik, -'läp-ik\ *adj*

dip·lo·pod \'dip-lə-,päd\ *n* **:** MILLIPEDE

dip needle *n* **:** a magnetized needle pivoted so that it moves vertically and points in the direction of the earth's greatest magnetic intensity at any place — called also *dipping needle*

dip·no·an \'dip-nə-wən\ *adj* **:** of or relating to a group (Dipnoi) of fishes with pulmonary circulation, gills, and lungs — **dipnoan** *n*

di·pole \'dī-,pōl\ *n* **1 a :** a pair of equal and opposite electric charges or magnetic poles of opposite sign separated by a small distance **b :** a body (as a molecule) having such charges or poles **2 :** a radio antenna consisting of two horizontal rods in line with each other with their ends slightly separated — **di·po·lar** \(')dī-'pō-lər\ *adj*

dip·per \'dip-ər\ *n* **1 :** one that dips; *esp* **:** something (as a long-handled cup) used for dipping **2** *cap* **a :** the seven principal

stars in the constellation of Ursa Major arranged in a form resembling a dipper **b :** the seven principal stars in Ursa Minor similarly arranged with the North Star forming the outer end of the handle **3 :** any of several birds (as a bufflehead) skilled in diving

dip·stick \'dip-,stik\ *n* **:** a graduated rod for indicating depth

dip·ter·an \'dip-tə-rən\ *adj* **:** of, relating to, or being a two-winged fly — **dipteran** *n*

dip·ter·on \'dip-tə-,rän\ *n, pl* **-tera** \-rə\ **:** TWO-WINGED FLY

dip·ter·ous \-rəs\ *adj* [Gk *dipteros*, fr. *di-* + *pteron* wing] **1 :** having two wings or appendages like wings **2 :** DIPTERAN

dip·tych \'dip-(,)tik\ *n* [Gk *di-* + *ptychē* fold] **1 :** a picture or series of pictures (as an altarpiece) painted on two hinged tablets **2 :** a work made up of two matching parts

dire \'dī(ə)r\ *adj* [L *dirus*] **1 :** exciting horror **:** DREADFUL ⟨*dire* suffering⟩ **2 :** warning of disaster ⟨a *dire* forecast⟩ **3 :** EXTREME ⟨*dire* poverty⟩ ⟨*dire* need⟩ — **dire·ly** *adv* — **dire·ness** *n*

¹di·rect \də-'rekt, dī-\ *vt* [L *direct-, dirigere* to set straight, direct, fr. *dis-* + *regere* to lead straight] **1 :** to mark with a name and address ⟨*direct* a letter⟩ **2 :** to cause to turn, move, or point or to follow a straight course **3 :** to point, extend, or project in a specified line, course, or direction **4 :** to show or point out the way for **5 a :** to regulate the activities or course of ⟨*directed* the project⟩ **b :** to guide the organizing, supervising, or performance of ⟨*direct* a play⟩ ⟨*direct* an orchestra⟩ **6 :** to request or instruct with authority ⟨the court *directed* the jury to acquit him⟩ **syn** see CONDUCT

²direct *adj* **1 :** proceeding from one point to another in time or space without deviation or interruption **:** STRAIGHT **2 a :** stemming immediately from a source, cause, or reason ⟨*direct* result⟩ **b :** operating without an intervening agency or step ⟨*direct* action⟩ **c :** being or passing in a straight line of descent from parent to offspring **:** LINEAL ⟨*direct* ancestor⟩ **3 :** NATURAL, STRAIGHTFORWARD ⟨*direct* manner⟩ **4 a :** effected by the action of the people or the electorate and not by representatives **b :** consisting of or reproducing the exact words of a speaker ⟨*direct* discourse⟩ ⟨*direct* question⟩ — **direct** *adv* — **di·rect·ness** \-'rek(t)-nəs\ *n*

direct current *n* **:** an electric current flowing in one direction only — abbr. DC

di·rect·ed *adj* **:** proceeding in a direction designated as positive or negative ⟨*directed* line segment⟩

di·rec·tion \də-'rek-shən, dī-\ *n* **1 a :** guidance or supervision of action or conduct **b :** the art and technique of directing an orchestra or theatrical production **2** *archaic* **:** SUPERSCRIPTION **3 :** an authoritative instruction, indication, or order **4 :** the line or course along which something moves, lies, or points **5 :** TENDENCY, TREND

di·rec·tion·al \-shnəl, -shən-ᵊl\ *adj* **1 :** relating to or indicating direction in space ⟨the *directional* signal lights on an automobile⟩: **a :** suitable for sending out or receiving radio signals in one direction only ⟨a *directional* antenna⟩ **b :** operating most effectively in a particular direction ⟨a *directional* microphone⟩ **2 :** relating to direction or guidance esp. of thought or effort

¹di·rec·tive \də-'rek-tiv, dī-\ *adj* **:** serving to direct, guide, or influence ⟨*directive* language⟩

²directive *n* **:** something that serves to direct, guide, and usu. impel toward an action or goal; *esp* **:** a general instruction as to procedure from a high-level body or official

di·rec·tiv·i·ty \də-,rek-'tiv-ət-ē, (,)dī-\ *n* **:** the property of being directional

di·rect·ly \də-'rek-(t)lē, dī-, *in sense 2 also* 'drek-lē\ *adv* **1 :** in a direct manner ⟨spoke *directly*⟩ **2 :** without delay **:** IMMEDIATELY ⟨go *directly* home⟩

direct object *n* **:** a grammatical object representing the primary goal or the result of the action of its verb ⟨*me* in "he hit me" and *house* in "we built a house" are *direct objects*⟩

di·rec·tor \də-'rek-tər, dī-\ *n* **:** one that directs: as **a :** one of a group of persons who direct the affairs of an organized body (as a nation or corporation) **b :** one that supervises the production of a show (as for stage or screen) **c :** CONDUCTOR b — **di·rec·to·ri·al** \də-,rek-'tōr-ē-əl,

(,)dī-, -'tör-\ *adj* — **di·rec·tor·ship** \də-'rek-tər-,ship, dī-\ *n*

di·rec·tor·ate \də-'rek-t(ə-)rət, dī-\ *n* **1** : the office of director **2** : a board of directors (as of a corporation)

di·rec·to·ry \-t(ə-)rē\ *n, pl* **-ries** **1** : an alphabetical or classified list containing names and addresses **2** : a body of directors (as of a government)

direct primary *n* : a primary at which direct nominations of candidates for office are made

di·rec·trix \də-'rek-triks, dī-\ *n* : a fixed line by relation to which a conic section is described; *also* : a line or curve with which a generatrix of a surface remains in contact

dire·ful \'dī(ə)r-fəl\ *adj* : producing dire effects — **dire·ful·ly** \-fə-lē\ *adv*

dirge \'dərj\ *n* [L *dirige*, imper. of *dirigere* to direct] : a song or hymn of lamentation; *esp* : one intended for funeral or memorial rites

¹dir·i·gi·ble \'dir-ə-jə-bəl, də-'rij-ə-\ *adj* [L *dirigere* to direct] : STEERABLE

²dirigible *n* : AIRSHIP

dirk \'dərk\ *n* [Sc *durk*] : a long straight-bladed dagger — **dirk** *vt*

dirndl \'dərn-dªl\ *n* [short for G *dirndlkleid*, fr. G dial. *dirndl* girl + G *kleid* dress] : a full skirt with a tight waistband

dirt \'dərt\ *n* [ON *drit*] **1** : a filthy or soiling substance (as mud, dust, or grime) **2** : loose or packed earth : SOIL **3** : moral uncleanness: as **a** : OBSCENITY **b** : CORRUPTION **4** : scandalous gossip

¹dirty \'dərt-ē\ *adj* **dirt·i·er**; **-est** **1** : not clean : FILTHY, SOILED ⟨*dirty* clothes⟩ **2** : BASE, UNFAIR ⟨a *dirty* trick⟩ **3** : INDECENT, SMUTTY ⟨*dirty* talk⟩ **4** : FOGGY, STORMY ⟨*dirty* weather⟩ **5** : not clear in color : DULL ⟨a *dirty* red⟩ — **dirt·i·ly** \'dərt-ªl-ē\ *adv* — **dirt·i·ness** \'dərt-ē-nəs\ *n*

syn DIRTY, FILTHY, FOUL, NASTY mean conspicuously unclean or impure and may also imply obscenity. DIRTY applies generally to whatever is soiled by dirt of any kind ⟨*dirty* hands⟩ or is capable of soiling ⟨*dirty* jokes⟩; FILTHY suggests offensiveness and a besmeared, cluttered state ⟨*filthy* rags⟩ FOUL adds to the offensiveness an implication of rottenness or loathsomeness ⟨*foul* sewers⟩ NASTY applies to something that is unpleasant or repugnant to one who is fastidious about cleanliness, sweetness, or freshness ⟨*nasty* smell⟩ and it may also imply mere disagreeableness ⟨received a *nasty* shock⟩

²dirty *vb* **dirt·ied**; **dirty·ing** **1** : to make or become dirty **2** : to stain with dishonor : SULLY

dis- *prefix* [L, lit., apart; akin to E *two*] **1 a** : do the opposite of ⟨*disestablish*⟩ **b** : deprive of (a specified quality, rank, or object) ⟨*disable*⟩ ⟨*disfrock*⟩ **c** : exclude or expel from ⟨*disbar*⟩ **2** : opposite or absence of ⟨*disunion*⟩ ⟨*disaffection*⟩ **3** : not ⟨*disagreeable*⟩ **4** : completely ⟨*disannul*⟩ **5** [by alter.] : DYS- ⟨*disfunction*⟩

Dis \'dis\ *n* : the Roman god of the underworld

dis·abil·i·ty \,dis-ə-'bil-ət-ē\ *n, pl* **-ties** **1** : the condition of being disabled : lack of ability, power, or fitness to do something **2** : a source of disability (as a physical injury); *also* : a legal disqualification that prevents a person from serving or acting in a particular capacity **syn** see INABILITY

dis·able \dis-'ā-bəl\ *vt* **dis·abled**; **dis·abling** \-b(ə-)liŋ\ **1** : to make unable or incapable : deprive of force, strength, or power of action : CRIPPLE ⟨a *disabling* illness⟩ ⟨*disabled* workmen⟩ **2** : to disqualify legally — **dis·able·ment** \-bəl-mənt\ *n*

dis·abuse \,dis-ə-'byüz\ *vt* [F *désabuser*, fr. *dés-* dis- + *abuser* to abuse] : to free from error or fallacy ⟨if that is his notion, we'll have to *disabuse* him⟩

di·sac·cha·ride \(')dī-'sak-ə-,rīd\ *n* : any of a class of sugars (as sucrose) that yield on hydrolysis two monosaccharide molecules

dis·ac·cus·tom \,dis-ə-'kəs-təm\ *vt* : to make no longer accustomed ⟨*disaccustoms* his children to luxury⟩

¹dis·ad·van·tage \,dis-əd-'vant-ij\ *n* **1** : loss or damage esp. to reputation or finances ⟨the deal worked to his *disadvantage*⟩ **2 a** : an unfavorable, inferior, or prejudicial condition ⟨was at a *disadvantage* in educated company⟩ **b** : HANDICAP

²disadvantage *vt* : to place at a disadvantage : HARM

dis·ad·van·ta·geous \(,)dis-,ad-,van-'tā-jəs, -vən-\ *adj* : constituting a disadvantage — **dis·ad·van·ta·geous·ly** *adv* — **dis·ad·van·ta·geous·ness** *n*

dis·af·fect \,dis-ə-'fekt\ *vt* : to alienate the affection or loyalty of : cause discontent in ⟨the troops were *disaffected*⟩ — **dis·af·fec·tion** \,dis-ə-'fek-shən\ *n*

dis·af·firm \,dis-ə-'fərm\ *vt* : DENY, REPUDIATE, ANNUL

dis·agree \,dis-ə-'grē\ *vi* **1** : to fail to agree ⟨the two accounts *disagree*⟩ **2** : to differ in opinion ⟨*disagree* over the price⟩ **3** : to be unsuitable ⟨fried foods *disagree* with me⟩

dis·agree·a·ble \-'grē-ə-bəl\ *adj* **1** : causing discomfort : UNPLEASANT, OFFENSIVE ⟨a *disagreeable* taste⟩ **2** : marked by ill temper : PEEVISH ⟨a *disagreeable* man⟩ — **dis·agree·a·ble·ness** *n* — **dis·agree·a·bly** \-blē\ *adv*

dis·agree·ment \,dis-ə-'grē-mənt\ *n* **1** : the act of disagreeing **2 a** : the state of being different or at variance **b** : QUARREL

dis·al·low \,dis-ə-'laù\ *vt* : to refuse to admit or recognize : REJECT ⟨*disallow* a claim⟩ — **dis·al·low·ance** \-'laù-ən(t)s\ *n*

dis·ap·pear \,dis-ə-'pi(ə)r\ *vi* **1** : to pass from view suddenly or gradually ⟨a ship *disappears* over the horizon⟩ **2** : to cease to be : become lost ⟨the dinosaur *disappeared* ages ago⟩ ⟨the book has *disappeared* from my desk⟩ — **dis·ap·pear·ance** \-'pir-ən(t)s\ *n*

dis·ap·point \,dis-ə-'pòint\ *vt* : to fail to come up to the expectation or hope of : FRUSTRATE

dis·ap·point·ed *adj* : defeated in expectation or hope : THWARTED

dis·ap·point·ment \,dis-ə-'pòint-mənt\ *n* **1** : the act or an instance of disappointing : the state or emotion of being disappointed **2** : one that disappoints ⟨the play proved a *disappointment*⟩

dis·ap·pro·ba·tion \(,)dis-,ap-rə-'bā-shən\ *n* : the act or state of disapproving : the state of being disapproved

dis·ap·prov·al \,dis-ə-'prü-vəl\ *n* **1** : the act of disapproving ⟨frown in *disapproval*⟩ **2** : unfavorable opinion or judgment : CENSURE ⟨the plan met with *disapproval*⟩

dis·ap·prove \-'prüv\ *vb* **1** : to pass unfavorable judgment on : CONDEMN ⟨*disapproved* the boy's conduct⟩ **2** : to refuse approval to : REJECT ⟨*disapproved* the architect's plans⟩ **3** : to feel or express disapproval ⟨*disapproves* of smoking⟩ — **dis·ap·prov·ing·ly** \-'prü-viŋ-lē\ *adv*

dis·arm \(')dis-'ärm\ *vb* **1** : to deprive of arms : take arms or weapons from **2** : to disband or esp. to reduce the size and strength of the armed forces of a country **3** : to make harmless, peaceable, or friendly : remove dislike or suspicion ⟨a *disarming* smile⟩ — **dis·ar·ma·ment** \-'är-mə-mənt\ *n*

dis·ar·range \,dis-ə-'rānj\ *vt* : to disturb the arrangement or order of — **dis·ar·range·ment** \-mənt\ *n*

¹dis·ar·ray \,dis-ə-'rā\ *n* **1** : a lack of order or sequence : CONFUSION **2** : disorderly dress : DISHABILLE

²disarray *vt* **1** : to throw into disorder **2** : UNDRESS

dis·as·sem·ble \,dis-ə-'sem-bəl\ *vt* : to take apart ⟨*disassemble* an engine⟩

dis·as·so·ci·ate \,dis-ə-'sō-s(h)ē-,āt\ *vt* : to detach from association : DISSOCIATE — **dis·as·so·ci·a·tion** \-,sō-sē-'ā-shən, -,sō-shē-\ *n*

di·sas·ter \diz-'as-tər, dis-\ *n* [MF *desastre* unfavorable aspect of a star, fr. L *dis-* + *astrum* star] : a sudden great misfortune; *esp* : one bringing with it destruction of life or property or causing complete ruin

syn DISASTER, CATASTROPHE, CALAMITY, CATACLYSM mean an event or situation that is a terrible misfortune. DISASTER is an unforeseen, ruinous, and often sudden misfortune that happens either through lack of foresight or through some hostile external agency; CATASTROPHE implies a disastrous conclusion, emphasizing finality; CALAMITY heightens the personal reaction to a great public loss; CATACLYSM, originally a deluge or geological convulsion, applies to an event or situation that produces an upheaval or complete reversal

di·sas·trous \-'as-trəs\ *adj* : accompanied by or producing suffering or disaster : CALAMITOUS — **di·sas·trous·ly** *adv*

dis·avow \,dis-ə-'vaù\ *vt* : to refuse to acknowledge : deny responsibility for : REPUDIATE — **dis·avow·al** \-'vaù-(ə)l\ *n*

dis·band \dis-'band\ *vb* : to break up the organization of

: DISPERSE ⟨*disband* an army⟩ — **dis·band·ment** \-'ban(d)-mənt\ *n*
dis·bar \dis-'bär\ *vt* **dis·barred**; **dis·bar·ring** : to deprive (a lawyer) of the rights and privileges of membership in the legal profession — **dis·bar·ment** \-'bär-mənt\ *n*
dis·be·lief \,dis-bə-'lēf\ *n* : the act of disbelieving : mental rejection of a statement as untrue **syn** see UNBELIEF
dis·be·lieve \-'lēv\ *vb* **1** : to hold not to be true or real ⟨*disbelieved* the man's testimony⟩ **2** : to withhold or reject belief ⟨came to *disbelieve* in his sincerity⟩ — **dis·be·liev·er** *n*
dis·bud \(')dis-'bəd\ *vt* : to remove some flower buds to improve the remaining bloom of
dis·bur·den \(')dis-'bərd-ⁿn\ *vt* : to rid of a burden — **dis·bur·den·ment** \-mənt\ *n*
dis·burse \dis-'bərs\ *vt* [MF *desbourser*, fr. *des-* dis- + *bourse* purse, fr. ML *bursa*] : to pay out : EXPEND — **dis·burs·er** *n*
dis·burse·ment \-'bərs-mənt\ *n* : the act of disbursing; *also* : funds paid out
disc *var of* DISK
¹dis·card \dis-'kärd, 'dis-,\ *vb* **1 a** : to let go a playing card from one's hand **b** : to play (a card) from a suit other than trump but different from the one led **2** : to get rid of as useless or unwanted
syn REJECT: DISCARD implies getting rid of something useless, outworn, or burdensome; REJECT implies a refusal to receive or use something offered ⟨*reject* an offer of help⟩
²dis·card \'dis-,kärd\ *n* **1** : the act of discarding **2** : a person or thing cast off or rejected
disc brake *n* : a brake that operates by the friction of two plates pressing against the sides of a rotating disc
dis·cern \dis-'ərn, diz-\ *vt* [L *discernere* to distinguish between, fr. *dis-* + *cernere* to sift] **1** : to detect with the eyes : make out : DISTINGUISH ⟨*discern* an airplane in the clouds⟩ **2** : to come to know, recognize, or discriminate mentally ⟨*discern* the basic issue⟩ — **dis·cern·i·ble** \-'ər-nə-bəl\ *adj* — **dis·cern·i·bly** \-blē\ *adv*
dis·cern·ing *adj* : revealing insight and understanding : DISCRIMINATING ⟨a *discerning* critic⟩ — **dis·cern·ing·ly** \-'ər-niŋ-lē\ *adv*
dis·cern·ment \dis-'ərn-mənt, diz-\ *n* : skill in discerning or discriminating : keenness of insight
¹dis·charge \dis-'chärj, 'dis-,\ *vb* **1 a** : to relieve of a charge, load, or burden : UNLOAD **b** : to throw off or deliver a charge **2** : SHOOT ⟨*discharge* a gun⟩ **3** : to set free ⟨*discharge* a prisoner⟩ **4** : to dismiss from service or employment ⟨*discharge* a soldier⟩ **5** : to let go or let off ⟨*discharge* passengers⟩ **6** : to give forth fluid or other contents ⟨this river *discharges* into the ocean⟩ **7** : to get rid of by paying or doing ⟨*discharge* a debt⟩ ⟨*discharge* a function⟩ **syn** see FREE — **dis·charg·er** *n*
²dis·charge \'dis-,chärj, dis-'\ *n* **1 a** : the act of discharging, unloading, or releasing **b** : something that discharges or releases; *esp* : a certification of release or payment **2** : a firing off **3 a** : a flowing or issuing out; *also* : a rate of flow **b** : something that is emitted **4 a** : release or dismissal esp. from an office or employment **b** : complete separation from military service **5 a** : the equalization of the degree of electrification between two points by a flow of electricity **b** : a flow of electricity through a gas **c** : the converting of the chemical energy of a battery into electrical energy
discharge lamp *n* : an electric lamp in which discharge of electricity between electrodes causes luminosity of the enclosed vapor or gas
discharge tube *n* : an electron tube which contains gas or vapor at low pressure and through which electrical conduction takes place when a high voltage is applied
dis·ci·ple \dis-'ī-pəl\ *n* [L *discipulus* pupil] **1 a** : a pupil or follower who accepts and helps to spread his master's teachings **b** : a convinced adherent **2** *cap* : a member of the Disciples of Christ founded in the U.S. in 1809 — **dis·ci·ple·ship** \-,ship\ *n*
dis·ci·pli·nar·i·an \,dis-ə-plə-'ner-ē-ən\ *n* : one who disciplines or enforces order — **disciplinarian** *adj*
dis·ci·plin·ary \'dis-ə-plə-,ner-ē\ *adj* : of or relating to discipline : CORRECTIVE ⟨*disciplinary* problems⟩ ⟨take *disciplinary* action⟩
¹dis·ci·pline \'dis-ə-plən\ *n* [L *disciplina* teaching, learn-

ing, fr. *discipulus* pupil] **1** : a field of study : SUBJECT **2** : training that corrects, molds, or perfects **3** : PUNISHMENT **4** : control gained by obedience or training : orderly conduct **5** : a system of rules governing conduct or practice
²discipline *vt* **1** : to punish or penalize for the sake of discipline **2** : to train or develop by instruction and exercise esp. in self-control **3 a** : to bring (a group) under control ⟨*discipline* troops⟩ **b** : to impose order upon **syn** see PUNISH — **dis·ci·plin·er** *n*
disc jockey *n* : a person who conducts and announces a radio or television program of musical recordings often with interspersed comments not relating to music
dis·claim \dis-'klām\ *vt* : to deny having a connection with or responsibility for : DISOWN ⟨the prisoner *disclaimed* any part in the crime⟩
dis·claim·er \-'klā-mər\ *n* **1** : an act of disclaiming : a statement that disclaims : DENIAL **2** : REPUDIATION
disclike *var of* DISLIKE
dis·close \dis-'klōz\ *vt* : to expose to view : make known : REVEAL ⟨*disclose* secrets⟩ ⟨the curtain rose *disclosing* a large room⟩ — **dis·clos·er** *n*
dis·clo·sure \-'klō-zhər\ *n* **1** : the act or an instance of disclosing : EXPOSURE **2** : something that is disclosed : REVELATION
dis·cog·ra·phy \dis-'käg-rə-fē\ *n, pl* **-phies** : a descriptive list of phonograph recordings
dis·coid \'dis-,kȯid\ *adj* [Gk *diskos* disk] **1** : resembling a disk esp. in being flat and circular **2** : relating to or forming a disk — **dis·coi·dal** \dis-'kȯid-ⁿl\ *adj*
dis·col·or \(')dis-'kəl-ər\ *vb* : to alter or change in hue or color : STAIN, FADE — **dis·col·or·a·tion** \(,)dis-,kəl-ə-'rā-shən\ *n*
dis·com·bob·u·late \,dis-kəm-'bäb-(y)ə-,lāt\ *vt* : UPSET, CONFUSE
dis·com·fit \dis-'kəm(p)-fət, *esp South* ,dis-kəm-'fit\ *vt* [OF *desconfit*, pp. of *desconfire*, fr. *des-* dis- + *confire* to prepare] : to throw into confusion : UPSET, FRUSTRATE ⟨*discomfit* one's enemies⟩ — **dis·com·fi·ture** \dis-'kəm(p)-fə-,chúr, -fə-chər\ *n*
¹dis·com·fort \dis-'kəm(p)-fərt\ *vt* : to make uncomfortable or uneasy
²discomfort *n* : lack of comfort : physical or mental uneasiness : DISTRESS
dis·com·mode \,dis-kə-'mōd\ *vt* [MF *discommoder*, fr. *dis-* + *commode* convenient] : to cause inconvenience to
dis·com·pose \,dis-kəm-'pōz\ *vt* **1** : to disturb the calmness or peace of : AGITATE ⟨*discomposed* by the bad news⟩ **2** : DISARRANGE ⟨hair *discomposed* by the wind⟩ — **dis·com·po·sure** \-'pō-zhər\ *n*
dis·con·cert \,dis-kən-'sərt\ *vt* **1** : to throw into mental confusion ⟨the unexpected event *disconcerted* their plans⟩ **2** : to disturb the composure of ⟨her frank stare *disconcerted* him⟩ **syn** see EMBARRASS — **dis·con·cert·ing·ly** *adv*
dis·con·nect \,dis-kə-'nekt\ *vt* : to undo or break the connection of ⟨*disconnect* two pipes⟩ ⟨*disconnect* a telephone⟩ — **dis·con·nec·tion** \-'nek-shən\ *n*
dis·con·nect·ed *adj* : not connected : RAMBLING, INCOHERENT — **dis·con·nect·ed·ly** *adv* — **dis·con·nect·ed·ness** *n*
dis·con·so·late \dis-'kän(t)-sə-lət\ *adj* [ML *disconsolatus*, fr. L *dis-* + *consolari* to console] **1** : lacking consolation : hopelessly sad ⟨*disconsolate* in her grief⟩ **2** : causing or suggestive of dejection : CHEERLESS ⟨a bleak *disconsolate* scene⟩ — **dis·con·so·late·ly** *adv* — **dis·con·so·late·ness** *n*
¹dis·con·tent \,dis-kən-'tent\ *adj* : DISCONTENTED
²discontent *vt* : to make discontented — **dis·con·tent·ment** \-mənt\ *n*
³discontent *n* **1** : lack of contentment : UNEASINESS **2** : a yearning for improvement or perfection **syn** see DISSATISFACTION
dis·con·tent·ed *adj* : DISSATISFIED, MALCONTENT — **dis·con·tent·ed·ly** *adv* — **dis·con·tent·ed·ness** *n*
dis·con·tin·u·ance \,dis-kən-'tin-yə-wən(t)s\ *n* : the act or an instance of discontinuing
dis·con·tin·ue \,dis-kən-'tin-yü\ *vb* **1** : to break the continuity of : cease to operate, use, or take **2** : END; *esp* : to cease publication — **dis·con·tin·u·a·tion** \-,tin-yə-'wā-shən\ *n*
dis·con·tin·u·ous \,dis-kən-'tin-yə-wəs\ *adj* : not continuous : having interruptions or gaps : BROKEN ⟨a *discontinuous* flight⟩ — **dis·con·ti·nu·i·ty** \(,)dis-,känt-ⁿn-

¹'(y)ü-ət-ē\ *n* — **dis·con·tin·u·ous·ly** \‚dis-kən-'tin-yə-wəs-lē\ *adv*

dis·cord \'dis-‚kȯrd\ *n* [L *discordia*, fr. *discord-*, *discors* discordant, fr. *dis-* + *cor* heart] **:** lack of agreement or harmony: **a :** DISUNITY, DISSENSION **b :** CONFLICT **c :** OP-POSITION, CONTRAST **d** (1) **:** a harsh combination of musical sounds (2) **:** DISSONANCE **e :** a harsh or unpleasant sound

dis·cord·ance \dis-'kȯrd-ᵊn(t)s\ *n* **1 :** the state or an instance of being discordant **2 :** DISSONANCE

dis·cord·an·cy \-ᵊn-sē\ *n, pl* **-cies :** DISSONANCE, DISPARITY

dis·cord·ant \-ᵊnt\ *adj* **1 a :** being at variance **:** DIS-AGREEING **b :** QUARRELSOME **2 :** relating to or producing a discord **:** JARRING **syn** see DISSONANT — **dis·cord·ant·ly** *adv*

¹dis·count \'dis-‚kaunt\ *n* **1 :** a reduction made from a regular or list price ⟨two percent *discount* for cash⟩ **2 :** a deduction of interest in advance when lending money

²dis·count \'dis-‚kaunt, dis-'\ *vt* **1 a :** to reduce or deduct from the amount of a bill, debt, or charge **b :** to sell or offer for sale at a discount **2 :** to lend money on (a note) after deducting the discount **3 a :** MINIMIZE ⟨*discounted* the value of experience⟩ **b :** to make allowance for bias or exaggeration in ⟨*discount* a romantic tale⟩ **c :** to take into account (as a future event) in present calculations ⟨the stock market has already *discounted* the company's better prospects for next year⟩ — **dis·count·a·ble** \-ə-bəl\ *adj*

dis·coun·te·nance \dis-'kaunt-ᵊn-ən(t)s, -'kaunt-nən(t)s\ *vt* **1 :** to put out of countenance **:** EMBARRASS, DISCONCERT **2 :** to look with disfavor on

dis·cour·age \dis-'kər-ij, -'kə-rij\ *vt* **1 :** to lessen the courage or confidence of **:** DISHEARTEN ⟨*discouraged* by a single failure⟩ **2 a :** to hinder by inspiring fear of consequences **:** DETER ⟨laws that *discourage* speeding⟩ **b :** to attempt to dissuade ⟨*discouraged* his son from becoming a musician⟩ — **dis·cour·ag·ing·ly** \-'kər-i-jiŋ-lē, -'kə-ri-\ *adv*

dis·cour·age·ment \-'kər-ij-mənt, -'kə-rij-\ *n* **1 :** an act of discouraging **:** the state of being discouraged **2 :** something that discourages

¹dis·course \'dis-‚kōrs, -‚kȯrs, dis-'\ *n* [LL *discursus* conversation, fr. L *discurs-*, *discurrere* to run about, fr. *dis-* + *currere* to run] **1** *archaic* **:** the capacity of orderly thought **2 :** verbal interchange of ideas **:** CONVERSATION **3 :** formal and orderly and usu. extended expression of thought on a subject **4** *obs* **:** social familiarity

²dis·course \dis-'kōrs, -'kȯrs, 'dis-‚\ *vi* **1 :** to express oneself in esp. oral discourse **:** hold forth **2 :** TALK, CONVERSE

dis·cour·te·ous \(')dis-'kərt-ē-əs\ *adj* **:** lacking courtesy **:** UNCIVIL, RUDE — **dis·cour·te·ous·ly** *adv* — **dis·cour·te·ous·ness** *n*

dis·cour·te·sy \-'kərt-ə-sē\ *n* **:** RUDENESS; *also* **:** a rude act

dis·cov·er \dis-'kəv-ər\ *vt* **dis·cov·ered; dis·cov·er·ing** \-'kəv-(ə-)riŋ\ [OF *descovrir*, fr. LL *discooperire*, fr. L *dis-* + *cooperire* to cover] **1 :** to make known or visible **2 :** to obtain sight or knowledge of for the first time **:** FIND — **dis·cov·er·a·ble** \-'kəv-(ə-)rə-bəl\ *adj* — **dis·cov·er·er** \-'kəv-ər-ər\ *n*

syn DISCOVER, INVENT mean to bring something new into being. DISCOVER implies the finding of something that preexisted but had been unknown ⟨Newton *discovered* the law of gravity⟩ INVENT suggests fabrication as a result of experiment, study, or ingenuity ⟨the cotton gin was *invented* by Eli Whitney⟩

dis·cov·ery \dis-'kəv-(ə-)rē\ *n, pl* **-er·ies 1 :** the act or process of discovering ⟨hoped for the *discovery* of a cure⟩ **2 :** something discovered ⟨the antique was one of her *discoveries*⟩

¹dis·cred·it \(')dis-'kred-ət\ *vt* **1 :** to refuse to accept as true or accurate **:** DISBELIEVE ⟨*discredit* a rumor⟩ **2 :** to cause disbelief in the accuracy or authority of ⟨*discredit* a witness⟩ **3 :** to destroy the reputation of **:** DISGRACE ⟨involvement in graft *discredited* him⟩

²discredit *n* **1 :** loss of credit or reputation ⟨knew something to the man's *discredit*⟩ **2 :** lack or loss of belief or confidence ⟨bring a story into *discredit*⟩

dis·cred·it·a·ble \-ə-bəl\ *adj* **:** injurious to reputation — **dis·cred·it·a·bly** \-blē\ *adv*

dis·creet \dis-'krēt\ *adj* [MF *discret*, fr. LL *discretus*, fr. L, pp. of *discernere* to distinguish, discern] **:** having or

showing good judgment in conduct and esp. in speech **:** PRUDENT; *esp* **:** capable of observing prudent silence — **dis·creet·ly** *adv* — **dis·creet·ness** *n*

dis·crep·an·cy \dis-'krep-ən-sē\ *n, pl* **-cies 1 :** the quality or state of being discrepant **:** DIFFERENCE ⟨the extent of *discrepancy* between two reports⟩ **2 :** an instance of being discrepant ⟨found *discrepancies* in the firm's financial statements⟩

dis·crep·ant \-ənt\ *adj* [L *discrepare* to sound discordantly, fr. *dis-* + *crepare* to rattle, creak] **:** being at variance **:** DISAGREEING — **dis·crep·ant·ly** *adv*

dis·crete \dis-'krēt, 'dis-‚\ *adj* [L *discretus*, pp. of *discernere* to separate, distinguish between, fr. *dis-* + *cernere* to sift] **1 :** individually distinct **:** SEPARATE ⟨radiation composed of *discrete* particles⟩ **2 :** consisting of unconnected elements **:** DISCONTINUOUS ⟨a *discrete* series⟩ — **dis·crete·ly** *adv* — **dis·crete·ness** *n*

dis·cre·tion \dis-'kresh-ən\ *n* **1 :** the quality of being discreet **:** PRUDENCE; *esp* **:** cautious reserve in speech **2 a :** individual choice or judgment ⟨left the decision to your *discretion*⟩ **b :** power of free decision or latitude of choice ⟨reached the age of *discretion*⟩ — **dis·cre·tion·ary** \-'kresh-ə-‚ner-ē\ *adj*

dis·crim·i·na·ble \dis-'krim-ə-nə-bəl\ *adj* **:** capable of being discriminated — **dis·crim·i·na·bly** \-blē\ *adv*

dis·crim·i·nant \-nənt\ *n* **:** a mathematical expression providing a criterion for the behavior of another more complicated expression, relation, or set of relations

dis·crim·i·nate \dis-'krim-ə-‚nāt\ *vb* [L *discrimin-*, *discrimen* distinction, fr. *discernere* to distinguish, discern] **1 a :** to perceive the distinguishing features of ⟨*discriminate* the geological features of a terrain⟩ **b :** DISTINGUISH, DIFFERENTIATE ⟨*discriminate* hundreds of colors⟩ **2 :** to see and note the differences ⟨*discriminate* among values⟩; *esp* **:** to distinguish one like object from another ⟨*discriminate* between a tree and a bush⟩ **3 :** to make a distinction in favor of or against one person or thing as compared with others ⟨*discriminated* against because of his race⟩

dis·crim·i·nat·ing *adj* **:** marked by discrimination; *esp* **:** DISCERNING, JUDICIOUS ⟨a *discriminating* taste⟩ — **dis·crim·i·nat·ing·ly** \-‚nāt-iŋ-lē\ *adv*

dis·crim·i·na·tion \dis-‚krim-ə-'nā-shən\ *n* **1 :** the act of discriminating **:** DIFFERENTIATION **2 :** the quality or power of finely distinguishing **3 :** distinction and esp. unjust distinction made against one person or group in favor of another ⟨laws to end racial *discrimination*⟩ — **dis·crim·i·na·tion·al** \-shnəl, -shən-ᵊl\ *adj*

dis·crim·i·na·tive \dis-'krim-ə-‚nāt-iv\ *adj* **1 :** making distinctions **2 :** DISCRIMINATORY — **dis·crim·i·na·tive·ly** *adv*

dis·crim·i·na·to·ry \dis-'krim-(ə-)nə-‚tōr-ē, -‚tȯr-\ *adj* **:** marked by esp. unjust discrimination ⟨*discriminatory* treatment⟩

dis·cur·sive \dis-'kər-siv\ *adj* [L *discurs-*, *discurrere* to run about, fr. *dis-* + *currere* to run] **:** passing from one topic to another **:** RAMBLING — **dis·cur·sive·ly** *adv* — **dis·cur·sive·ness** *n*

dis·cus \'dis-kəs\ *n, pl* **dis·cus·es** [L, disk, dish] **:** a disk (as of wood or rubber) thicker in the center than at the perimeter that is hurled for distance

discus (in right hand)

dis·cuss \dis-'kəs\ *vt* [L *discuss-*, *discutere* to shake apart, fr. *dis-* apart + *quatere* to shake] **1 :** to investigate or consider carefully by presenting the various sides **:** debate fully and openly ⟨*discuss* a proposal⟩ **2 :** to talk about ⟨*discuss* the weather⟩

syn DISCUSS, ARGUE, DEBATE mean to talk about in order to reach conclusions or to convince others. DISCUSS implies a presentation of considerations pro and con and suggests an interchange of opinion for the sake of clarifying issues; ARGUE implies the marshaling of evidence and reasons to support a proposition or proposal; DEBATE stresses formal and public argument between opposing parties

dis·cus·sant \dis-'kəs-ᵊnt\ *n* **:** one who takes part in a formal discussion or symposium

dis·cus·sion \dis-'kəsh-ən\ *n* **1 :** consideration of a question in open usu. informal debate **2 :** a formal treatment of a topic ⟨the lecture is billed as a *discussion* of recent research⟩

¹dis·dain \dis-'dān\ *n* : a feeling of contempt for something regarded as beneath one : SCORN

²disdain *vt* [MF *desdeignier*, fr. L *dis-* + *dignare* to deign] **1** : to look with scorn on **2** : to reject or refrain from because of disdain **syn** see DESPISE

dis·dain·ful \-fəl\ *adj* : full of or expressing disdain : SCORNFUL — **dis·dain·ful·ly** \-fə-lē\ *adv* — **dis·dain·ful·ness** *n*

dis·ease \diz-'ēz\ *n* [MF *desaise* trouble, fr. *des-* dis- + *aise* ease] : an alteration of the normal state of the living animal or plant body that impairs the performance of the vital functions : ILLNESS; *also* : a particular instance or kind of such alteration — **dis·eased** \-'ēzd\ *adj*

dis·em·bark \,dis-əm-'bärk\ *vb* : to go or put ashore from a ship — **dis·em·bar·ka·tion** \(,)dis-,em-,bär-'kā-shən, -bər-\ *n*

dis·em·bar·rass \,dis-əm-'bar-əs\ *vt* : to free from something troublesome or superfluous

dis·em·body \,dis-əm-'bäd-ē\ *vt* : to deprive of bodily existence ⟨*disembodied* spirits⟩

dis·em·bow·el \,dis-əm-'bau̇(-ə)l\ *vt* **-eled** *or* **-elled**; **-el·ing** *or* **-el·ling** : to take out the bowels of : EVISCERATE — **dis·em·bow·el·ment** \-mənt\ *n*

dis·en·chant \,dis-ᵊn-'chant\ *vt* : to free from enchantment : DISILLUSION — **dis·en·chant·ment** \-mənt\ *n*

dis·en·cum·ber \,dis-ᵊn-'kəm-bər\ *vt* : to free from something that burdens or obstructs

dis·en·fran·chise \,dis-ᵊn-'fran-,chīz\ *vt* : DISFRANCHISE — **dis·en·fran·chise·ment** \-,chīz-mənt, -chəz-\ *n*

dis·en·gage \,dis-ᵊn-'gāj\ *vb* : to free or release from an engagement, entanglement, or encumbrance : EXTRICATE, DISENTANGLE ⟨*disengage* an automobile clutch⟩; *esp* : to remove oneself from military commitments, alliances, or positions — **dis·en·gage·ment** \-'gāj-mənt\ *n*

dis·en·tan·gle \,dis-ᵊn-'taŋ-gəl\ *vt* : to free from entanglement : straighten out **syn** see EXTRICATE — **dis·en·tan·gle·ment** \-mənt\ *n*

dis·equi·lib·ri·um \(,)dis-,ē-kwə-'lib-rē-əm, -,ek-wə-\ *n* : loss or lack of equilibrium

dis·es·tab·lish \,dis-ə-'stab-lish\ *vt* : to end the establishment of; *esp* : to deprive of the status and privileges of an established church — **dis·es·tab·lish·ment** \-mənt\ *n*

¹dis·es·teem \,dis-ə-'stēm\ *vt* : to regard with disfavor

²disesteem *n* : lack of esteem : DISFAVOR, DISREPUTE

di·seuse \dē-'zə(r)z, -'züz\ *n, pl* **di·seuses** *same or* -'zə(r)z-əz, -'züz-əz\ [F, fem. of *diseur* reciter, fr. *dis-*, *dire* to say, fr. L *dicere*] : a skilled and usu. professional woman reciter

¹dis·fa·vor \(')dis-'fā-vər\ *n* **1** : DISAPPROVAL, DISLIKE **2** : the state or fact of being deprived of favor ⟨in *disfavor* at school⟩

²disfavor *vt* : to regard with disfavor

dis·fig·ure \dis-'fig-yər, *esp Brit* -'fig-ər\ *vt* : to spoil the appearance of ⟨*disfigured* by a scar⟩ **syn** see DEFACE — **dis·fig·ure·ment** \-mənt\ *n*

dis·fran·chise \(')dis-'fran-,chīz\ *vt* : to deprive of a franchise, a legal right, or a privilege or immunity; *esp* : to deprive of the right to vote — **dis·fran·chise·ment** \-,chīz-mənt, -chəz-\ *n*

dis·gorge \(')dis-'górj\ *vb* **1** : VOMIT **2** : to discharge violently, confusedly, or as a result of force **3** : to discharge contents

¹dis·grace \dis-'grās\ *vt* : to bring reproach or shame to — **dis·grac·er** *n*

²disgrace *n* **1** : the condition of being out of favor : loss of respect ⟨in *disgrace* with his schoolmates⟩ **2** : SHAME, DISHONOR ⟨the *disgrace* of being a coward⟩ **3** : a cause of shame ⟨that child's manners are a *disgrace*⟩

dis·grace·ful \-fəl\ *adj* : bringing or involving shame or disgrace — **dis·grace·ful·ly** \-fə-lē\ *adv* — **dis·grace·ful·ness** *n*

dis·grun·tle \dis-'grənt-ᵊl\ *vt* **dis·grun·tled**; **dis·grun·tling** \-'grənt-liŋ, -ᵊl-iŋ\ [*dis-* + ME *gruntlen* grumble, freq. of *grunten* to grunt] : to put in bad humor — **dis·grun·tle·ment** \-ᵊl-mənt\ *n*

¹dis·guise \dis-'gīz\ *vt* **1** : to change the dress or looks of so as to conceal the identity or so as to resemble another ⟨*disguised* himself with a wig⟩ **2 a** : HIDE, CONCEAL ⟨*disguised* their true feelings⟩ **b** : ALTER ⟨tried to

disguise her voice⟩ — **dis·guised·ly** \-'gīz(-ə)d-lē\ *adv* — **dis·guis·er** \-'gī-zər\ *n*

²disguise *n* **1** : clothing put on to conceal one's identity or counterfeit another's **2 a** : an outward form hiding or misrepresenting the true nature or identity of a person or thing **b** : PRETENSE **3** : the act of disguising

syn DISGUISE, CLOAK, MASK mean an appearance that hides one's true identity or nature. DISGUISE implies a change in appearance or behavior that misleads by presenting a different apparent identity; CLOAK suggests a means of hiding a movement or an intention completely; MASK suggests some usu. obvious means of preventing recognition and does not always imply deception or pretense

¹dis·gust \dis-'gəst\ *n* : marked aversion to something distasteful or loathsome : REPUGNANCE

²disgust *vt* [MF *desgouster*, fr. *des-* dis- + *goust* taste, fr. L *gustus*] : to provoke to loathing, repugnance, or aversion : be offensive to — **dis·gust·ed** *adj* — **dis·gust·ed·ly** *adv*

dis·gust·ing *adj* : REVOLTING — **dis·gust·ing·ly** \-'gəs-tiŋ-lē\ *adv*

¹dish \'dish\ *n* [OE *disc*, fr. L *discus* quoit, disk, dish, fr. Gk *diskos*] **1** : a more or less concave vessel from which food is served **2 a** : the food served in a dish ⟨a *dish* of strawberries⟩ **b** : food prepared in a particular way **3** : something resembling a dish esp. in being shallow and concave

²dish *vt* **1** : to put into a dish or set of dishes **2** : to make concave like a dish ⟨a *dished* metal disk⟩

dis·ha·bille \,dis-ə-'bēl\ *n* [F *déshabillé*, fr. pp. of *déshabiller* to undress, fr. *dés-* dis- + *habiller* to dress] **1** : the state of being dressed in a loose or careless style **2** : UNTIDINESS, DISORDER

dis·har·mo·ny \(')dis-'här-mə-nē\ *n* : lack of harmony : DISCORD

dish·cloth \'dish-,klȯth\ *n* : a cloth for washing dishes

dis·heart·en \(')dis-'härt-ᵊn\ *vt* : to deprive of courage and hope : DISCOURAGE — **dis·heart·en·ing** \-'härt-niŋ, -ᵊn-iŋ\ *adj* — **dis·heart·en·ing·ly** \-niŋ-lē, -ᵊn-iŋ-lē\ *adv* — **dis·heart·en·ment** \-'härt-ᵊn-mənt\ *n*

dished \'disht\ *adj* **1** : CONCAVE **2** : nearer together at the bottom than at the top ⟨a *dished* pair of automobile wheels⟩

di·shev·el \dish-'ev-əl\ *vt* **di·shev·eled** *or* **di·shev·elled**; **di·shev·el·ing** *or* **di·shev·el·ling** \-'ev-(ə-)liŋ\ [MF *descheveler* to disarrange the hair, fr. *des-* dis- + *chevel* hair, fr. L *capillus*] : to let hang or fall loosely in disorder : DISARRAY

di·shev·eled *or* **di·shev·elled** *adj* : marked by loose disorder or disarray

dis·hon·est \(')dis-'än-əst\ *adj* **1** : not honest : UNTRUSTWORTHY **2** : marked by fraud : DECEITFUL, CORRUPT ⟨*dishonest* dealings⟩ — **dis·hon·est·ly** *adv*

dis·hon·es·ty \-ə-stē\ *n* : lack of honesty or integrity : disposition to defraud or deceive

¹dis·hon·or \(')dis-'än-ər\ *n* **1 a** : loss of honor or reputation **b** : the state of one who has lost honor or prestige **c** : something dishonorable : a cause of disgrace **2** : the act of dishonoring a piece of commercial paper

²dishonor *vt* **1** : to bring shame on : DISGRACE **2** : to refuse to accept or pay (as a bill or check) — **dis·hon·or·er** *n*

dis·hon·or·a·ble \(')dis-'än-(ə-)rə-bəl, -'än-ər-bəl\ *adj* : not honorable : DISGRACEFUL, SHAMEFUL — **dis·hon·or·a·bly** \-blē\ *adv*

dish·rag \'dish-,rag\ *n* : DISHCLOTH

dish towel *n* : a cloth for drying dishes

dish·wash·er \'dish-,wȯsh-ər, -,wȧsh-\ *n* : a person or a machine that washes dishes

dish·wa·ter \-,wȯt-ər, -,wȧt-\ *n* : water in which dishes have been or are to be washed

¹dis·il·lu·sion \,dis-ə-'lü-zhən\ *n* : DISENCHANTMENT

²disillusion *vt* **dis·il·lu·sioned**; **dis·il·lu·sion·ing** \-'lüzh-(ə-)niŋ\ : to free from or deprive of illusion — **dis·il·lu·sion·ment** \-'lü-zhən-mənt\ *n*

dis·in·cli·na·tion \(,)dis-,in-klə-'nā-shən\ *n* : an unwillingness to do something : a slight dislike or distaste

dis·in·cline \,dis-ᵊn-'klīn\ *vb* : to make or be unwilling ⟨*disinclined* to accept⟩

dis·in·fect \,dis-ᵊn-'fekt\ *vt* : to free from infection esp.

by destroying harmful germs; *also* : CLEANSE — **dis·in·fec·tion** \-'fek-shən\ *n*

dis·in·fect·ant \-'fek-tənt\ *n* : an agent that frees from infection; *esp* : a chemical that destroys vegetative forms of harmful germs but not ordinarily bacterial spores — **disinfectant** *adj*

dis·in·gen·u·ous \ˌdis-°n-'jen-yə-wəs\ *adj* : lacking in candor : not frank or naive — **dis·in·gen·u·ous·ly** *adv* — **dis·in·gen·u·ous·ness** *n*

dis·in·her·it \ˌdis-°n-'her-ət\ *vt* : to prevent from inheriting property that would naturally be passed on

dis·in·te·grate \(')dis-'int-ə-ˌgrāt\ *vb* **1** : to break or decompose into constituent elements, parts, or small particles **2 a** : to destroy the unity or integrity of **b** : to lose unity or integrity by or as if by breaking into parts **3** : to undergo a change in composition ⟨an atomic nucleus that *disintegrates* because of radioactivity⟩ — **dis·in·te·gra·tion** \(ˌ)dis-ˌint-ə-'grā-shən\ *n* — **dis·in·te·gra·tor** \(')dis-'int-ə-ˌgrāt-ər\ *n*

dis·in·ter \ˌdis-°n-'tər\ *vt* **1** : to take out of the grave or tomb **2** : to bring to light : UNEARTH — **dis·in·ter·ment** \-mənt\ *n*

dis·in·ter·est·ed \(')dis-'in-trəs-təd, -'int-ə-rəs-\ *adj* **1** : not interested **2** : free from selfish motive or interest : UNBIASED ⟨a *disinterested* decision⟩ **syn** see UNINTERESTED — **dis·in·ter·est·ed·ly** *adv* — **dis·in·ter·est·ed·ness** *n*

dis·join \(')dis-'join\ *vb* : to end the union of or become separated ⟨chromosome pairs *disjoin* in meiosis⟩

¹dis·joint \(')dis-'joint\ *vb* **1** : to separate the parts of **2** : to take apart or become parted at the joints

²disjoint *adj* : completely separate; *esp* : having no members in common ⟨*disjoint* mathematical sets⟩

dis·joint·ed *adj* **1** : separated at or as if at the joint **2** : DISCONNECTED, DISORDERED; *esp* : INCOHERENT ⟨*disjointed* conversation⟩ — **dis·joint·ed·ly** *adv* — **dis·joint·ed·ness** *n*

dis·junc·tion \dis-'jən(k)-shən\ *n* **1** : DISUNION, SEPARATION **2 a** : a complex proposition that asserts one or more of its terms **b** : a proposition that asserts one and only one of its terms

¹dis·junc·tive \-'jən(k)-tiv\ *n* : a disjunctive conjunction

²disjunctive *adj* **1** : tending to disjoin **2** : expressing an alternative between the meanings of the words connected ⟨the *disjunctive* conjunction *or*⟩

¹disk *or* **disc** \'disk\ *n* [L *discus* dish, disk] **1 a** : the central part of the flower head of a typical composite plant made up of closely packed tubular flowers **b** : any of various rounded and flattened animal anatomical structures **2 a** : a thin circular object : an object that appears to be thin and circular **b** *usu* disc : a phonograph record **3** *usu* disc : a tilling implement (as a harrow or plow) with sharp-edged circular concave cutting blades; *also* : one of these blades

²disk *or* **disc** *vt* : to cultivate (land) with a disc

disk flower *n* : one of the tubular flowers in the disk of a composite plant — called also *disk floret*

disk·like *or* **disc·like** \'disk-ˌlīk\ *adj* : being circular and nearly flat

¹dis·like \(')dis-'līk\ *vt* : to regard with dislike : DISAPPROVE

²dislike *n* : a feeling of distaste or disapproval

dis·lo·cate \'dis-lō-ˌkāt, (')dis-'lō-\ *vt* **1** : to put out of place; *esp* : to displace (a bone) from normal connections with another bone **2** : DISRUPT — **dis·lo·ca·tion** \ˌdis-(ˌ)lō-'kā-shən\ *n*

dis·lodge \(')dis-'läj\ *vt* **1** : to force out of a resting place **2** : to drive from a place of hiding or defense

dis·loy·al \(')dis-'loi-(ə)l\ *adj* : lacking in loyalty **syn** see FAITHLESS — **dis·loy·al·ly** \-'loi-ə-lē\ *adv*

dis·loy·al·ty \-'loi-(ə)l-tē\ *n* : lack of loyalty : UNFAITHFULNESS

dis·mal \'diz-məl\ *adj* [ML *dies mali* evil days] **1** : gloomy to the eye or ear : DREARY, DEPRESSING ⟨a *dismal* sight⟩ **2** : feeling gloom : DEPRESSED ⟨she was *dismal* about her low grades⟩ — **dis·mal·ly** \-mə-lē\ *adv*

dis·man·tle \(')dis-'mant-°l\ *vt* **dis·man·tled; dis·man·tling** \-'mant-liŋ, -°l-iŋ\ [MF *desmanteler* to strip of dress, fr. *des*- dis- + *mantel* mantle] **1** : to strip of furniture and equipment **2** : to take to pieces : take apart ⟨*dismantled* the engine to repair it⟩ — **dis·man·tle·ment** \-'mant-°l-mənt\ *n*

dis·mast \(')dis-'mast\ *vt* : to remove or break off the mast of ⟨a ship *dismasted* in a storm⟩

¹dis·may \dis-'mā, diz-\ *vt* [ME *dismayen*, fr. (assumed) OF *desmaiier*, fr. OF *des*- dis- + *-maiier* (as in *esmaiier* to dismay)] : to cause to lose courage or resolution through alarm or fear : DAUNT — **dis·may·ing·ly** \-iŋ-lē\ *adv*

²dismay *n* **1** : sudden loss of courage or resolution from alarm or fear **2** : a feeling of alarm or disappointment

dis·mem·ber \(')dis-'mem-bər\ *vt* **dis·mem·bered; dis·mem·ber·ing** \-b(ə-)riŋ\ **1** : to cut off or separate the limbs, members, or parts of **2** : to break up or tear into pieces — **dis·mem·ber·ment** \-bər-mənt\ *n*

dis·miss \dis-'mis\ *vt* [modif. of L *dimiss*-, *dimittere*, fr. *dis*- apart + *mittere* to send] **1** : to send away : cause or allow to go ⟨*dismiss* a messenger⟩ **2** : to discharge from office, service, or employment **3** : to put aside or out of mind ⟨*dismiss* the thought⟩ **4** : to refuse further judicial hearing or consideration to ⟨the judge *dismissed* the charge⟩

dis·miss·al \-'mis-əl\ *n* : the act of dismissing : the fact or state of being dismissed

dis·mount \(')dis-'maunt\ *vb* **1** : to get down from something (as a horse or bicycle) **2** : to throw down from a horse : UNHORSE **3** : to take (as a cannon) from the carriage or mountings **4** : to take apart (as a machine) : DISASSEMBLE

dis·obe·di·ence \ˌdis-ə-'bēd-ē-ən(t)s\ *n* : lack of obedience : neglect or refusal to obey — **dis·obe·di·ent** \-ənt\ *adj* — **dis·obe·di·ent·ly** *adv*

dis·obey \ˌdis-ə-'bā\ *vb* : to fail to obey : be disobedient

dis·oblige \ˌdis-ə-'blīj\ *vt* **1** : to go counter to the wishes of **2** : to cause inconvenience to

¹dis·or·der \(')dis-'ord-ər\ *vt* **1** : to disturb the order of **2** : to disturb the regular or normal functions of

²disorder *n* **1 a** : lack of order **b** : a disturbing, neglecting, or breaking away from a due order **2** : an abnormal physical or mental condition : AILMENT — **dis·or·dered** \-'ord-ərd\ *adj*

dis·or·der·ly \-ər-lē\ *adj* **1 a** : UNRULY, TURBULENT **b** (1) : offensive to public order or decency ⟨*disorderly* behavior⟩ (2) : guilty of disorderly conduct ⟨*disorderly* persons⟩ **2** : not in an orderly condition : DISARRANGED ⟨a *disorderly* mass of papers⟩ — **dis·or·der·li·ness** *n*

dis·or·ga·nize \(')dis-'or-gə-ˌnīz\ *vt* : to break up the regular arrangement or system of : throw into disorder : CONFUSE — **dis·or·ga·ni·za·tion** \(ˌ)dis-ˌorg-(ə-)nə-'zā-shən\ *n*

dis·ori·ent \(')dis-'or-ē-ˌent, -'or-\ *vt* : to cause to lose bearings : deprive of the normal sense of position or relationship — **dis·ori·en·ta·tion** \(ˌ)dis-ˌor-ē-ən-'tā-shən, -ˌor-\ *n*

dis·own \(')dis-'ōn\ *vt* : to refuse to acknowledge as one's own : REPUDIATE, RENOUNCE, DISCLAIM

dis·par·age \dis-'par-ij\ *vt* [MF *desparagier* to marry to one of lower class, fr. *des*- dis- + *parage* lineage, fr. *per* peer] **1** : to lower in rank or reputation : DEGRADE **2** : to speak slightingly of : BELITTLE ⟨*disparaged* his acts⟩ — **dis·par·age·ment** \-mənt\ *n* — **dis·par·ag·ing·ly** \-ij-iŋ-lē\ *adv*

dis·par·ate \dis-'par-ət, 'dis-p(ə-)rət\ *adj* [L *disparatus*, pp. of *disparare* to separate, fr. *dis*- + *parare* to prepare] : distinct in quality or character : DISSIMILAR **syn** see DIFFERENT — **dis·par·ate·ly** *adv* — **dis·par·ate·ness** *n* — **dis·par·i·ty** \dis-'par-ət-ē\ *n*

dis·pas·sion·ate \(')dis-'pash-(ə-)nət\ *adj* : not influenced by strong feeling : CALM, IMPARTIAL — **dis·pas·sion·ate·ly** *adv*

¹dis·patch \dis-'pach\ *vt* [Sp *despachar* or It *dispacciare*, fr. Prov *despachar*, fr. OF *despeechier*] **1** : to send away promptly or rapidly to a particular place or for a particular purpose ⟨*dispatch* a messenger⟩ ⟨*dispatch* a train⟩ **2** : to attend to or dispose of speedily ⟨*dispatch* business⟩ **3** : to put to death — **dis·patch·er** *n*

²dispatch *n* **1 a** : the sending of a message or messenger **b** : the shipment of goods **2** : MESSAGE; *esp* : an important official message **3** : the act of putting to death **4** : a news item sent in by a correspondent to a newspaper **5** : promptness and efficiency in performing a task

dis·pel \dis-'pel\ *vt* **dis·pelled; dis·pel·ling** [L *dispellere*, fr. *dis*- + *pellere* to drive] : to drive away by scattering : DISSIPATE **syn** see SCATTER

dis·pens·a·ble \dis-'pen(t)-sə-bəl\ *adj* : capable of being dispensed with : NONESSENTIAL — **dis·pens·a·bil·i·ty** \-,pen(t)-sə-'bil-ət-ē\ n

dis·pen·sa·ry \dis-'pen(t)s-(ə-)rē\ n, pl **-ries** : a place where medical or dental aid is dispensed

dis·pen·sa·tion \,dis-pən-'sā-shən, -,pen-\ n **1 a** : a system of rules for ordering affairs **b** : a particular arrangement or provision esp. of nature **2** : an exemption from a rule or from a vow or oath **3 a** : the act of dispensing **b** : something dispensed or distributed — **dis·pen·sa·tion·al** \-shnəl, -shən-°l\ adj

dis·pen·sa·to·ry \dis-'pen(t)-sə-,tōr-ē, -,tȯr-\ n, pl **-ries** : a book containing descriptions of medicines

dis·pense \dis-'pen(t)s\ vb [L dispens-, dispendere to weigh out, fr. dis- + pendere to weigh] **1 a** : to deal out in portions **b** : ADMINISTER ⟨dispense justice⟩ **2** : to prepare and distribute (medicines) to the sick — **dispense with 1** : to suspend the operation of **2** : to do or get along without

dis·pens·er \dis-'pen(t)-sər\ n : one that dispenses; esp : a container (as a bottle or package) so made as to release part of its contents without being fully opened ⟨a squeeze bottle dispenser for nose drops⟩

dis·pers·al \dis-'pər-səl\ n : the act or result of dispersing

dis·perse \dis-'pərs\ vb [L dispers-, dispergere, fr. dis- + spargere to scatter] **1 a** : to cause to break up and go in different ways **b** : to cause to become spread widely **c** : to drive or clear away **2 a** : DISSEMINATE **b** : to subject (as light) to dispersion **c** : to distribute more or less evenly throughout a medium ⟨disperse particles in water⟩ **3** : to move in different directions : SCATTER **syn** see SCATTER — **dis·pers·i·ble** \-'pər-sə-bəl\ adj

dis·per·sion \dis-'pər-zhən\ n **1** : the act or process of dispersing : the state of being dispersed **2** : the scattering of the values of a frequency distribution from an average **3** : the separation of light into colors by refraction or diffraction with formation of a spectrum **4 a** : a result or product of dispersing : something dispersed **b** : a system consisting of a dispersed substance and the medium in which it is dispersed ⟨a dispersion of fine particles in water⟩ — **dis·per·sive** \-'pər-siv, -ziv\ adj — **dis·per·sive·ly** adv — **dis·per·sive·ness** n

dis·pir·it \(')dis-'pir-ət\ vt [dis- + spirit] : to deprive of cheerful spirit : DISHEARTEN — **dispir·it·ed·ly** adv — **dispir·it·ed·ness** n

dis·place \(')dis-'plās\ vt **1** : to remove from a usual or proper place; esp : to expel or force to flee from home or homeland ⟨displaced persons⟩ **2** : to take the place of : REPLACE — **dis·place·a·ble** \-ə-bəl\ adj

dis·place·ment \-'plās-mənt\ n **1** : the act of displacing : the state of being displaced **2 a** : the volume or weight of a fluid (as water) displaced by a floating body (as a ship) with the weight of the displaced fluid being equal to that of the displacing body ⟨a ship of 3000 tons displacement⟩ **b** : the difference between the initial position of an object and any later position

¹dis·play \dis-'plā\ vt [OF despleier, fr. L displicare to scatter, fr. dis- + plicare to fold] **1** : to show outwardly ⟨display anger⟩ **2 a** : to spread before the view **b** : to set in display **syn** see SHOW

²display n **1 a** : a displaying of something; esp : a device that gives information in visual form in communications ⟨a radar display⟩ **b** : ostentatious show **c** : an eye-catching exhibition **2** : a pattern of behavior exhibited esp. by male birds in the breeding season

dis·please \(')dis-'plēz\ vb **1** : to arouse the disapproval and dislike of **2** : to be offensive to : give displeasure

dis·plea·sure \(')dis-'plezh-ər, -'plāzh-\ n : a feeling of annoyance and dislike accompanying disapproval : DISSATISFACTION

dis·port \dis-'pōrt, -'pȯrt\ vb [MF desporter, fr. des- dis- + porter to carry] **1 a** : DIVERT, AMUSE ⟨disporting themselves on the beach⟩ **b** : FROLIC **2** : DISPLAY

dis·pos·al \dis-'pō-zəl\ n **1** : an orderly distribution : ARRANGEMENT ⟨the disposal of troops for battle⟩ **2 a** : a getting rid of or putting out of the way ⟨trash disposal⟩ **3** : MANAGEMENT, ADMINISTRATION **4** : the transfer of something into new hands ⟨a disposal of property⟩ **5** : the power to dispose of something : CONTROL, COMMAND ⟨funds at his disposal⟩

dis·pose \dis-'pōz\ vb [MF disposer, irreg. fr. L disponere to arrange, fr. dis- apart + ponere to put] **1** : to distribute

and put in place : ARRANGE **2** : to give a tendency to : incline in mind ⟨disposed to refuse⟩ — **dis·pos·a·ble** \-'pō-zə-bəl\ adj — **dispose of 1** : to settle or determine the fate, condition, or use of : deal with conclusively ⟨has the right to dispose of his personal property⟩ **2** : to get rid of : put out of the way : finish with ⟨dispose of rubbish⟩ ⟨dispose of the morning's mail⟩ **3** : to transfer to the control of another

dis·po·si·tion \,dis-pə-'zish-ən\ n **1** : the act or power of disposing : DISPOSAL ⟨money at their disposition⟩ **2** : the giving up or transferring of something ⟨disposition of real estate⟩ **3** : ARRANGEMENT ⟨the disposition of furniture in a room⟩ **4 a** : TENDENCY, INCLINATION ⟨a natural disposition to avoid pain⟩ **b** : natural attitude toward things ⟨a cheerful disposition⟩

dis·pos·sess \,dis-pə-'zes\ vt : to deprive of the possession or occupancy of land or houses : put out : OUST ⟨the landlord dispossessed the tenants for not paying their rent⟩ — **dis·pos·ses·sion** \-'zesh-ən\ n

¹dis·praise \(')dis-'prāz\ vt : to comment on with disapproval or censure — **dis·prais·er** n — **dis·prais·ing·ly** \-'prā-ziŋ-lē\ adv

²dispraise n : the act of dispraising : DISPARAGEMENT

dis·proof \(')dis-'prüf\ n **1** : a proving that something is not as believed or stated **2** : evidence that disproves

¹dis·pro·por·tion \,dis-prə-'pōr-shən, -'pȯr-\ n : lack of proportion, symmetry, or proper relation : DISPARITY; also : an instance of such disparity — **dis·pro·por·tion·al** \-shnəl, -shən-°l\ adj — **dis·pro·por·tion·ate** \-sh(ə-)nət\ adj — **dis·pro·por·tion·ate·ly** adv

²disproportion vt : to make out of proportion : MISMATCH

dis·prove \(')dis-'prüv\ vt : to prove to be false : REFUTE

dis·put·a·ble \dis-'pyüt-ə-bəl, 'dis-pyət-\ adj : open to dispute, debate, or contest : DEBATABLE — **dis·put·a·bly** \-blē\ adv

dis·pu·tant \dis-'pyüt-°nt, 'dis-pyət-ənt\ n : DISPUTER

dis·pu·ta·tion \,dis-pyü-'tā-shən\ n **1** : the act of disputing : DEBATE **2** : an oral defense of an academic thesis

dis·pu·ta·tious \,dis-pyü-'tā-shəs\ adj : inclined to dispute : ARGUMENTATIVE — **dis·pu·ta·tious·ly** adv — **dis·pu·ta·tious·ness** n

¹dis·pute \dis-'pyüt\ vb [L disputare, fr. dis- + putare to think] **1** : to engage in argument : DEBATE **2** : WRANGLE **3 a** : to engage in controversy over : argue about **b** : to call into question : deny the truth or rightness of **4 a** : to struggle against **b** : to struggle over : CONTEST — **dis·put·er** n

²dispute n **1** : verbal controversy : DEBATE **2** : QUARREL

dis·qual·i·fy \(')dis-'kwäl-ə-,fī\ vt **1** : to make or declare unfit or ineligible ⟨disqualify all voters who cannot read and write⟩ **2** : to deprive of necessary qualifications ⟨disqualified for military service by poor vision⟩ — **dis·qual·i·fi·ca·tion** \(,)dis-,kwäl-ə-fə-'kā-shən\ n

¹dis·qui·et \(')dis-'kwī-ət\ vt : to make uneasy or restless : DISTURB — **dis·qui·et·ing·ly** \-iŋ-lē\ adv

²disquiet n : lack of peace or tranquility : ANXIETY

dis·qui·etude \(')dis-'kwī-ə-,t(y)üd\ n : AGITATION, ANXIETY

dis·qui·si·tion \,dis-kwə-'zish-ən\ n [L disquisit-, disquirere to inquire diligently, fr. dis- + quaerere to seek] : a formal inquiry or discussion : DISCOURSE

¹dis·re·gard \,dis-ri-'gärd\ vt : to pay no attention to : treat as unworthy of regard or notice

²disregard n : the act of disregarding : the state of being disregarded : NEGLECT — **dis·re·gard·ful** \-fəl\ adj

¹dis·rel·ish \(')dis-'rel-ish\ vt : to find unpalatable or distasteful

²disrelish n : lack of relish : DISTASTE, DISLIKE

dis·re·pair \,dis-ri-'pa(ə)r, -'pe(ə)r\ n : the state of being in need of repair

dis·rep·u·ta·ble \(')dis-'rep-yət-ə-bəl\ adj : not reputable : DISCREDITABLE, DISGRACEFUL; esp : having a bad reputation — **dis·rep·u·ta·ble·ness** n — **dis·rep·u·ta·bly** \-blē\ adv

dis·re·pute \,dis-ri-'pyüt\ n : loss or lack of reputation : low esteem : DISCREDIT

dis·re·spect \,dis-ri-'spekt\ n : lack of respect : DISCOURTESY — **dis·re·spect·ful** \-fəl\ adj — **dis·re·spect·ful·ly** \-fə-lē\ adv

dis·robe \(')dis-'rōb\ vb : UNDRESS

dis·rupt \dis-'rəpt\ vt [L disrupt-, disrumpere, fr. dis- +

rumpere to break] **1 :** to break apart **:** RUPTURE **2 :** to throw into disorder **:** break up — **dis·rupt·er** *n* — **dis·rup·tion** \-'rəp-shən\ *n* — **dis·rup·tive** \-'rəp-tiv\ *adj* — **dis·rup·tive·ly** *adv* — **dis·rup·tive·ness** *n*

dis·sat·is·fac·tion \(,)dis-,(s)at-əs-'fak-shən\ *n* **:** the quality or state of being dissatisfied

syn DISCONTENT: DISSATISFACTION has usu. a definite cause and is often temporary ⟨*dissatisfaction* with the trend of business⟩ DISCONTENT is more general, personal, and deep-rooted ⟨the *discontent* of colonial peoples⟩

dis·sat·is·fac·to·ry \-'fak-t(ə-)rē\ *adj* **:** causing dissatisfaction

dis·sat·is·fy \(')dis-'(s)at-əs-,fī\ *vt* **:** to fail to satisfy **:** DISPLEASE

dis·sect \dis-'ekt\ *vb* [L *dissect-, dissecare* to cut apart, fr. *dis-* + *secare* to cut] **1 :** to divide (as a plant or animal) into separate parts for examination and study **2 :** to make a searching analysis **:** analyze minutely ⟨*dissect* a proposed plan⟩ — **dis·sec·tion** \-'ek-shən\ *n* — **dis·sec·tor** \-'ek-tər\ *n*

dis·sect·ed *adj* **:** cut deeply into fine lobes ⟨a *dissected* leaf⟩

dis·sem·ble \dis-'em-bəl\ *vb* **-bled; -bling** \-b(ə-)liŋ\ [alter. of ME *dissimulen*, fr. L *dissimulare* to dissimulate, fr. *dis-* + *simulare* to simulate] **1 :** to hide under or put on a false appearance **:** conceal facts, intentions, or feelings under some pretense **2 :** to put on the appearance of **:** SIMULATE — **dis·sem·bler** \-b(ə-)lər\ *n*

dis·sem·i·nate \dis-'em-ə-,nāt\ *vt* [L *disseminare*, fr. *dis-* + *semin-, semen* seed] **:** to spread abroad as though sowing seed ⟨*disseminate* ideas⟩ — **dis·sem·i·na·tion** \-,em-ə-'nā-shən\ *n* — **dis·sem·i·na·tor** \-'em-ə-,nāt-ər\ *n*

dis·sen·sion \dis-'en-chən\ *n* **:** disagreement in opinion **:** DISCORD, QUARRELING

¹dis·sent \dis-'ent\ *vi* [L *dissens-, dissentire*, fr. *dis-* + *sentire* to feel] **1 :** to withhold assent **2 :** to differ in opinion

²dissent *n* **1 :** difference of opinion; *esp* **:** religious nonconformity **2 :** a written statement in which a justice disagrees with the opinion of the majority — called also *dissenting opinion*

dis·sent·er \dis-'ent-ər\ *n* **1 :** one that dissents **2** *cap* **:** an English Nonconformist

dis·sen·tient \dis-'en-chənt\ *adj* **:** expressing dissent — **dissentient** *n*

dis·sep·i·ment \dis-'ep-ə-mənt\ *n* **:** a dividing tissue **:** SEPTUM; *esp* **:** a partition between cells of a compound plant ovary

dis·ser·ta·tion \,dis-ər-'tā-shən\ *n* [L *dissert-, disserere* to discourse, fr. *dis-* + *serere* to join, arrange] **:** an extended usu. written treatment of a subject; *esp* **:** one submitted for a doctorate

dis·ser·vice \(')dis-'(s)ər-vəs\ *n* **:** ill service **:** INJURY

dis·sev·er \dis-'ev-ər\ *vb* **:** to sever thoroughly **:** SEPARATE, DISUNITE — **dis·sev·er·ance** \-'ev-(ə-)rən(t)s\ *n* — **dis·sev·er·ment** \-'ev-ər-mənt\ *n*

dis·si·dence \'dis-əd-ən(t)s\ *n* **:** DISSENT, DISAGREEMENT

dis·si·dent \-ənt\ *adj* [L *dissidēre* to sit apart, disagree, fr. *dis-* + *sedēre* to sit] **:** openly and often violently differing with an opinion or a group **:** DISAFFECTED — **dissident** *n*

dis·sim·i·lar \(')dis-'(s)im-ə-lər\ *adj* **:** UNLIKE — **dis·sim·i·lar·i·ty** \(,)dis-,(s)im-ə-'lar-ət-ē\ *n* — **dis·sim·i·lar·ly** \(')dis-'(s)im-ə-lər-lē\ *adv*

dis·sim·i·la·tion \(,)dis-,im-ə-'lā-shən\ *n* **1 :** CATABOLISM **2 :** the development of dissimilarity between two identical or closely related sounds in a word — **dis·sim·i·la·tive** \dis-'im-ə-,lāt-iv\ *adj*

dis·sim·u·late \(')dis-'im-yə-,lāt\ *vb* **:** to hide under a false appearance **:** DISSEMBLE — **dis·sim·u·la·tion** \(,)dis-,im-yə-'lā-shən\ *n* — **dis·sim·u·la·tor** \(')dis-'im-yə-,lāt-ər\ *n*

dis·si·pate \'dis-ə-,pāt\ *vb* [L *dissipare*, fr. *dis-* + *supare* to throw] **1 a :** to break up and drive off (as a crowd) **b :** to cause to spread out to the point of vanishing **:** DISSOLVE ⟨the breeze *dissipated* the fog⟩ **2 a :** to expend aimlessly or foolishly **b :** SQUANDER **3 :** to separate into parts and scatter or vanish **4 :** to be extravagant or uncontrolled in the pursuit of pleasure; *esp* **:** to drink to excess **syn** see SCATTER

dis·si·pat·ed *adj* **:** given to or marked by dissipation **:** DISSOLUTE — **dis·si·pat·ed·ly** *adv* — **dis·si·pat·ed·ness** *n*

dis·si·pa·tion \,dis-ə-'pā-shən\ *n* **:** the act of dissipating **:** the state of being dissipated: **a :** DISPERSION, DIFFUSION **b :** wasteful expenditure **c :** intemperate living; *esp* **:** excessive drinking

dis·so·ci·ate \(')dis-'ō-s(h)ē-,āt\ *vb* [L *dissociare*, fr. *dis-* + *sociare* to join, fr. *socius* companion] **1 :** to separate from association or union with another **:** DISCONNECT **2 :** DISUNITE; *esp* **:** to subject to chemical dissociation **3 :** to undergo dissociation ⟨salts and acids *dissociate* in water⟩ **4 :** to mutate esp. reversibly

dis·so·ci·a·tion \(,)dis-,ō-sē-'ā-shən, -,ō-shē-\ *n* **:** the act or process of dissociating **:** the state of being dissociated: as **a :** the process by which a chemical combination breaks up into simpler constituents ⟨*dissociation* of hydrochloric acid in water into hydrogen and chlorine ions⟩ **b :** the separation of a biological stock into two or more distinct and relatively permanent strains — **dis·so·cia·tive** \(')dis-'ō-s(h)ē-,āt-iv, -shət-iv\ *adj*

dis·sol·u·ble \dis-'äl-yə-bəl\ *adj* **:** capable of being dissolved — **dis·sol·u·bil·i·ty** \-,äl-yə-'bil-ət-ē\ *n*

dis·so·lute \'dis-ə-,lüt\ *adj* [L *dissolutus*, fr. pp. of *dissolvere* to loosen, dissolve] **:** lacking restraint; *esp* **:** loose in morals or conduct — **dis·so·lute·ly** *adv* — **dis·so·lute·ness** *n*

dis·so·lu·tion \,dis-ə-'lü-shən\ *n* **1 :** the action or process of dissolving: as **a :** separation into component parts **b :** DECAY **2 :** the termination or breaking up of an assembly or a partnership or corporation ⟨*dissolution* of parliament⟩

¹dis·solve \diz-'älv, -'ölv\ *vb* [L *dissolvere*, fr. *dis-* + *solvere* to loosen] **1 :** to break up into component parts **2 :** to pass or cause to pass into solution **:** MELT, LIQUEFY ⟨sugar *dissolves* in water⟩ **3 :** to bring to an end **:** TERMINATE ⟨*dissolve* parliament⟩ **4 :** to waste or fade away as if by breaking up or melting ⟨his courage *dissolved* in the face of danger⟩ **5 :** to fade out (a motion-picture shot) in a dissolve **6 :** to be overcome emotionally **7 :** to resolve itself as if by dissolution — **dis·solv·a·ble** \-ə-bəl\ *adj* — **dis·solv·er** *n*

²dissolve *n* **:** a gradual superimposing of one motion-picture or television shot upon another on a screen

dis·so·nance \'dis-ə-nən(t)s\ *n* **1 :** a mingling of discordant sounds **2 :** lack of agreement **:** DISCORD **3 :** an unresolved musical note or chord

dis·so·nant \'dis-ə-nənt\ *adj* [L *dissonare* to be discordant, fr. *dis-* + *sonare* to sound] **1 :** marked by dissonance in sound **:** DISCORDANT **2 :** not being in harmony or agreement ⟨*dissonant* views of the best course of action⟩ — **dis·so·nant·ly** *adv*

syn DISCORDANT: DISSONANT may apply to lack of harmony intended as a contrast to consonant sounds; DISCORDANT commonly suggests an unpleasant or disagreeable effect on the listener

dis·suade \dis-'wād\ *vt* [L *dissuadēre*, fr. *dis-* + *suadēre* to urge] **:** to advise against a course of action **:** persuade or try to persuade not to do something — **dis·sua·sion** \-'wā-zhən\ *n* — **dis·sua·sive** \-'wā-siv, -ziv\ *adj* — **dis·sua·sive·ly** *adv* — **dis·sua·sive·ness** *n*

dis·syl·lab·ic \,dis-ə-'lab-ik, ,dī-sə-\ *var of* DISYLLABIC

dis·sym·me·try \(')dis-'(s)im-ə-trē\ *n* **:** ASYMMETRY

¹dis·taff \'dis-,taf\ *n* [OE *distæf*] **1 a :** a staff for holding the flax, tow, or wool in spinning **b :** woman's work **2 :** the female branch or side of a family

²distaff *adj* **:** FEMALE

dis·tal \'dist-ᵊl\ *adj* [*distant* + *-al*] **:** far from the point of attachment or origin — compare PROXIMAL — **dis·tal·ly** \-ᵊl-ē\ *adv*

¹dis·tance \'dis-tən(t)s\ *n* **1 a :** separation in time **b :** the shortest space or amount of space between two points, lines, surfaces, or objects **c :** EXPANSE **d :** a full course ⟨go the *distance*⟩ **2 :** the quality or state of being distant: as **a :** spatial remoteness **b :** COLDNESS, RESERVE **c :** DIFFERENCE, DISPARITY **3 :** a distant point or region

²distance *vt* **:** to leave far behind **:** OUTSTRIP

dis·tant \'dis-tənt\ *adj* [L *distare* to stand apart, be distant, fr. *dis-* + *stare* to stand] **1 a :** separated in space

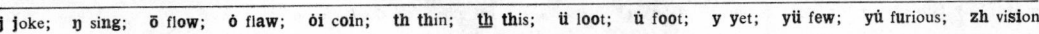

D distaff, *S* spindle

: AWAY **b :** situated at a great distance **:** FAR-OFF **2 :** not close in relationship ⟨*distant* cousin⟩ **3 :** different in kind **4 :** reserved or aloof in personal relationship **:** COLD ⟨*distant* politeness⟩ **5 :** coming from or going to a distance ⟨*distant* voyages⟩ — **dis·tant·ly** *adv* — **dis·tant·ness** *n*

syn DISTANT, FAR, REMOTE mean not close or near in space, time, or relationship. DISTANT is the opposite of *close* and implies separation in space or time; FAR is the opposite of *near* and implies a relatively long distance away; REMOTE applies to what is far removed esp. from what is regarded as a center of interest ⟨spacecraft flying by *remote* control⟩

dis·taste \(')dis-'tāst\ *n* **1 :** dislike of food or drink **2 :** DISINCLINATION, AVERSION ⟨a *distaste* for work⟩

dis·taste·ful \-fəl\ *adj* **1 :** unpleasant to the taste **:** LOATHSOME **2 :** OFFENSIVE, DISAGREEABLE — **dis·taste·ful·ly** \-fə-lē\ *adv* — **dis·taste·ful·ness** *n*

¹dis·tem·per \dis-'tem-pər\ *vt* [ME *distempren,* fr. LL *distemperare* to mix badly, fr. L *dis-* + *temperare* to temper] **:** to throw out of order

²distemper *n* **1 :** bad humor or temper **2 :** a disordered or abnormal bodily state usu. of a lower animal: as **a :** a highly contagious virus disease esp. of dogs marked by fever and by respiratory and sometimes nervous symptoms **b :** PANLEUCOPENIA

³distemper *n* [MF *distemprer* to dilute, fr. L *dis-* + *temperare* to temper] **:** a process of painting in which the pigments are mixed with an emulsion of egg yolk, with size, or with white of egg and which is used esp. for mural decoration; *also* **:** the paint used in this process or a painting done by it

dis·tend \dis-'tend\ *vb* [L *distendere,* fr. *dis-* + *tendere* to stretch] **:** to stretch out or bulge out in all directions **:** SWELL ⟨*distended* cheeks of a horn player⟩ **syn** see EXPAND

dis·ten·si·ble \dis-'ten(t)-sə-bəl\ *adj* [LL *distensus,* pp. of L *distendere* to distend] **:** capable of being distended

dis·ten·sion *or* **dis·ten·tion** \dis-'ten-chən\ *n* **:** the act of distending **:** the state of being distended esp. unduly or abnormally

dis·tich \'dis-(,)tik\ *n* [Gk *distichos* having two rows, fr. *di-* + *stichos* row, verse] **:** a strophic unit of two lines

dis·ti·chous \'dis-ti-kəs\ *adj* **:** divided into or arranged in two groups or segments — **dis·ti·chous·ly** *adv*

dis·till *also* **dis·til** \dis-'til\ *vb* **dis·tilled; dis·till·ing** [LL *distillare,* alter. of L *destillare,* fr. *de-* + *stilla* drop] **1 :** to fall or let fall in drops **2 a :** to subject to or transform by distillation ⟨*distill* water⟩ **b :** to obtain by distillation ⟨*distill* brandy from wine⟩ **3 :** to extract the essence of **:** CONCENTRATE **4 :** to condense from a still after distillation

dis·til·late \'dis-tə-,lāt, dis-'til-ət\ *n* **:** a liquid product condensed from vapor during distillation

dis·til·la·tion \,dis-tə-'lā-shən\ *n* **1 :** a process that consists of driving gas or vapor from liquids or solids by heating and condensing to liquid products and that is used esp. for purification, fractionation, or the formation of new substances **2 :** something obtained by or as if by a process of distilling **:** ESSENCE

dis·till·er \dis-'til-ər\ *n* **:** one that distills; *esp* **:** a person whose business is distilling alcoholic liquors

dis·till·ery \dis-'til-(ə-)rē\ *n, pl* **-er·ies :** a place where distilling esp. of alcoholic liquors is carried on

dis·tinct \dis-'tin(k)t\ *adj* [L *distinctus,* fr. pp. of *distinguere* to distinguish] **1 :** distinguished from others **:** SEPARATE, DIFFERENT ⟨guilty of three *distinct* crimes⟩ **2 :** clearly seen, heard, or understood **:** PLAIN, UNMISTAKABLE — **dis·tinct·ly** *adv* — **dis·tinct·ness** *n*

dis·tinc·tion \dis-'tin(k)-shən\ *n* **1 a :** the act of distinguishing a difference **b :** something that makes a difference **2 :** a distinguishing quality or mark **3 a :** a special recognition **b :** a mark or sign of such recognition **4 :** HONOR

dis·tinc·tive \dis-'tin(k)-tiv\ *adj* **:** clearly marking a person or a thing as different from others **:** CHARACTERISTIC ⟨a *distinctive* way of speaking⟩ **syn** see CHARACTERISTIC — **dis·tinc·tive·ly** *adv* — **dis·tinc·tive·ness** *n*

dis·tin·gué \,dēs-,taŋ-'gā\ *adj* **:** distinguished esp. in manner or bearing

dis·tin·guish \dis-'tiŋ-gwish\ *vb* [L *distinguere,* lit., to separate by pricking, fr. *dis-* + *-stinguere* to prick] **1 :** to

recognize one thing from others by some mark or characteristic ⟨*distinguish* the sound of a piano in an orchestra⟩ **2 :** to hear or see clearly **:** make out **:** DISCERN ⟨*distinguish* a light in the distance⟩ **3 :** to make distinctions ⟨*distinguish* between right and wrong⟩ **4 :** to set apart **:** mark as different **5 :** to separate from others by a mark of honor **:** make outstanding ⟨*distinguished* himself in athletics⟩ — **dis·tin·guish·a·ble** \-ə-bəl\ *adj* — **dis·tin·guish·a·bly** \-blē\ *adv*

dis·tin·guished *adj* **1 :** marked by eminence, distinction, or excellence **2 :** befitting an eminent person

dis·tort \dis-'tȯrt\ *vt* [L *distort-, distorquēre,* fr. *dis-* + *torquēre* to twist] **1 :** to twist out of the true meaning **:** MISREPRESENT **2 :** to twist out of a natural, normal, or original shape or condition — **dis·tort·er** *n*

dis·tor·tion \dis-'tȯr-shən\ *n* **1 :** the act of distorting **2 :** the condition of being distorted or a product of distortion: as **a :** a misshapen condition of an image caused by defects in a lens **b :** falsified reproduction of a sound in radio or of an image in television — **dis·tor·tion·al** \-shnəl, -shən-ᵊl\ *adj*

dis·tract \dis-'trakt\ *vt* [L *distract-, distrahere,* lit., to draw apart, fr. *dis-* + *trahere* to draw] **1 :** to turn aside **:** DIVERT; *esp* **:** to draw (the attention or mind) to a different object **2 :** to stir up or confuse with conflicting emotions or motives **:** HARASS

dis·trac·tion \dis-'trak-shən\ *n* **1 :** the act of distracting or the state of being distracted; *esp* **:** mental confusion **2 :** something that distracts; *esp* **:** AMUSEMENT — **dis·trac·tive** \-'trak-tiv\ *adj*

dis·trait \di-'strā\ *adj* [F, fr. L *distractus,* pp. of *distrahere* to distract] **:** ABSENTMINDED; *esp* **:** inattentive or distracted because of anxiety or apprehension

dis·traught \dis-'trȯt\ *adj* **1 :** agitated with doubt or mental conflict **2 :** CRAZED — **dis·traught·ly** *adv*

¹dis·tress \dis-'tres\ *n* [OF *destresse,* fr. (assumed) VL *districtia,* fr. L *district-, distringere* to draw apart, detain] **1 :** great suffering of body or mind **:** PAIN, ANGUISH ⟨suffer *distress* from loss of a friend⟩ **2 :** MISFORTUNE, TROUBLE, SORROW ⟨the shipwrecked passengers were brothers in *distress*⟩ **3 :** a condition of danger or desperate need ⟨a ship in *distress*⟩

syn SUFFERING, MISERY: DISTRESS implies conditions or circumstances that cause physical or mental stress or strain and suggests the need of assistance ⟨the *distress* of war orphans⟩ SUFFERING applies to human beings and connotes conscious awareness and endurance of pain; MISERY stresses the unhappy or wretched conditions attending distress or suffering

²distress *vt* **1 :** to subject to great strain or difficulties **2 :** to cause to worry or be troubled **:** UPSET — **dis·tress·ing·ly** \-iŋ-lē\ *adv*

dis·tress·ful \-fəl\ *adj* **:** causing distress **:** full of distress — **dis·tress·ful·ly** \-fə-lē\ *adv* — **dis·tress·ful·ness** *n*

dis·trib·u·tary \dis-'trib-yə-,ter-ē\ *n* **:** a river branch flowing away from the main stream

dis·trib·ute \dis-'trib-yət\ *vt* [L *distribut-, distribuere,* fr. *dis-* + *tribuere* to allot] **1 :** to divide among several or many **:** APPORTION **2 :** to spread out so as to cover something **:** SCATTER ⟨*distribute* grass seed over a lawn⟩ **3 :** to divide or separate esp. into kinds **4 :** to market (a line of goods) in a particular area usu. as a wholesaler — **dis·trib·ut·a·ble** \-yət-ə-bəl\ *adj*

dis·tri·bu·tion \,dis-trə-'byü-shən\ *n* **1 :** the act or process of distributing **2 a :** the position, arrangement, or frequency of occurrence (as of the members of a group) over an area or throughout a space or unit of time **b :** the natural geographic range of an organism **3 a :** something distributed **b :** FREQUENCY DISTRIBUTION **4 :** the marketing or merchandising of commodities — **dis·tri·bu·tion·al** \-shnəl, -shən-ᵊl\ *adj*

dis·trib·u·tive \dis-'trib-yət-iv\ *adj* **1 :** of or relating to distribution: as **a :** dealing a proper share to each of a group **b :** diffusing more or less evenly **2 :** referring singly and without exception to the members of a group ⟨the *distributive* adjectives *each* and *every*⟩ **3 :** producing the same element when operating on a whole as when operating on each part and collecting the results ⟨multiplication is *distributive* relative to addition⟩ — **dis·trib·u·tive·ly** *adv* — **dis·trib·u·tive·ness** *n*

dis·trib·u·tor \dis-'trib-yət-ər\ *n* **1 :** one that distributes

2 : an agent or agency for marketing goods **3** : a device for distributing electric current to the spark plugs (as of an automobile engine)

¹dis·trict \'dis-(,)trikt\ *n* [ML *districtus* jurisdiction, district, fr. L *district-, distringere* to draw apart] **1** : a territorial division marked off or defined (as for administrative or electoral purposes) ⟨school *district*⟩ ⟨judicial *district*⟩ **2** : a distinctive area or region

²district *vt* : to divide or organize into districts

district attorney *n* : a public official who prosecutes cases for a state or federal government

district court *n* : one of a group of federal courts that have original jurisdiction in most cases capable of being heard and determined by a federal court and that with certain specialized courts form the lowest system of federal courts

¹dis·trust \(')dis-'trəst\ *vt* : to have no confidence in : SUSPECT

²distrust *n* : a lack of trust or confidence : SUSPICION, WARINESS **syn** see DOUBT — **dis·trust·ful** \-fəl\ *adj* — **dis·trust·ful·ly** \-fə-lē\ *adv* — **dis·trust·ful·ness** *n*

dis·turb \dis-'tərb\ *vt* [L *disturbare*, fr. *dis-* + *turbare* to throw into disorder] **1 a** : to interfere with : INTERRUPT **b** : to alter the position or arrangement of **2 a** : to destroy the tranquillity or composure of : make uneasy **b** : to throw into disorder **c** : to put to inconvenience — **dis·turb·er** *n*

syn PERTURB: DISTURB implies the distracting or distorting effect of worry, conflict, or strain on mental processes; PERTURB applies to the deeper unsettling of the mind by uncertainty, disappointment, or danger

dis·turb·ance \dis-'tər-bən(t)s\ *n* **1** : the act of disturbing **2** : mental confusion : UPSET **3** : public turmoil : DISORDER

dis·turbed *adj* : showing symptoms of mental or emotional illness

di·sul·fide \(')dī-'səl-,fīd\ *n* : a compound containing two atoms of sulfur combined with an element or radical

dis·union \dish-'ü-nyən, (')dis-'yü-\ *n* : lack of union or agreement : SEPARATION

dis·unite \,dish-ü-'nīt, ,dis-yü-\ *vt* : DIVIDE, SEPARATE

dis·uni·ty \dish-'ü-nət-ē, (')dis-'yü-\ *n* : lack of unity; *esp* : DISSENSION

¹dis·use \dish-'üz, (')dis-'yüz\ *vt* : to discontinue the use or practice of

²dis·use \-'üs, -'yüs\ *n* : cessation of use or practice

di·syl·lab·ic \,dī-sə-'lab-ik\ *adj* : having two syllables — **di·syl·la·ble** \'dī-,sil-ə-bəl, (')dī-'-\ *n*

¹ditch \'dich\ *n* [OE *dīc* dike, ditch] : a long narrow excavation dug in the earth for defense, drainage, or irrigation

²ditch *vt* **1 a** : to enclose with a ditch **b** : to dig a ditch in **2** : to drive (a car) into a ditch **3** : to get rid of : DISCARD **4** : to make a forced landing of (an airplane) on water

dith·er \'dith-ər\ *n* [ME *didderen* to shiver] : a highly nervous, excited, or agitated state — **dith·ery** \-ə-rē\ *adj*

dith·y·ramb \'dith-i-,ram\ *n* [Gk *dithyrambos*] **1** : a short poem in a wild inspired strain **2** : an exalted or enthusiastic statement or writing — **dith·y·ram·bic** \,dith-i-'ram-bik\ *adj*

dit·to \'dit-ō\ *n, pl* **dittos** [It dial., pp. of It *dire* to say, fr. L *dicere*] **1** : SAME : more of the same : ANOTHER — used to avoid repeating a word ⟨lost: one shirt (white); *ditto* (blue)⟩ **2** : a mark composed of a pair of inverted commas or apostrophes used as a symbol for the word *ditto*

dit·ty \'dit-ē\ *n, pl* **ditties** [OE] : SONG; *esp* : a short simple song

dit·ty bag \'dit-ē-\ *n* : a small bag used esp. by sailors to hold small articles of gear (as thread, needles, or tape)

di·uret·ic \,dī-yù-'ret-ik\ *adj* [Gk *diourētikos*, fr. *diourein* to urinate, fr. *dia-* + *ourein* to urinate] : tending to increase the flow of urine — **diuretic** *n* — **di·uret·i·cal·ly** \-'ret-i-k(ə-)lē\ *adv*

di·ur·nal \dī-'ərn-ᵊl\ *adj* [L *diurnus* of the day, fr. *dies* day] **1 a** : recurring every day ⟨*diurnal* task⟩ **b** : having a daily cycle ⟨*diurnal* rotation of the heavens⟩ **2 a** : of, relating to, or occurring in the daytime ⟨the city's *diurnal* noises⟩ **b** : opening during the day and closing at night — **di·ur·nal·ly** \-ᵊl-ē\ *adv*

di·va \'dē-və\ *n, pl* **di·vas** or **di·ve** \-(,)vā\ [It, lit., goddess] : PRIMA DONNA I

di·va·gate \'dī-və-,gāt\ *vi* [LL *divagari*, fr. L *dis-* + *vagari* to wander] **1** : to wander about **2** : DIVERGE — **di·va·ga·tion** \,dī-və-'gā-shən\ *n*

di·va·lent \(')dī-'vā-lənt\ *adj* : BIVALENT

di·van \'dī-,van\ *n* [Turk, fr. Per *dīwān* account book] : a large couch or sofa usu. without back or arms often designed for use as a bed

¹dive \'dīv\ *vi* **dived** \'dīvd\ *or* **dove** \'dōv\; **div·ing** [OE *dӯfan* to dip & *dūfan* to dive] **1 a** : to plunge into water headfirst; *esp* : to execute a dive **b** : SUBMERGE **2 a** : to descend or fall precipitously **b** : to descend in a dive ⟨the airplane *dived*⟩ **3 a** : to plunge into some matter or activity **b** : DART, LUNGE ⟨*dived* for his legs⟩

²dive *n* **1** : the act or an instance of diving: as **a** (1) : a plunge into water executed in a prescribed manner (2) : a submerging of a submarine (3) : a steep descent of an airplane with or without power **b** : a sharp decline **2** : a disreputable bar

dive-bomb \'dīv-,bäm\ *vt* : to bomb from an airplane by making a steep dive toward the target before releasing the bomb — **dive-bomb·er** *n*

div·er \'dī-vər\ *n* **1** : one that dives **2 a** : a person who stays under water for long periods by having air supplied from the surface or by carrying a supply of compressed air **b** : any of various diving birds; *esp* : LOON

di·verge \də-'vərj, dī-\ *vb* [ML *divergere*, fr. L *dis-* + *vergere* to incline] **1 a** : to move or extend in different directions from a common point : draw apart ⟨*diverging* rays of light⟩ **b** : to differ in character, form, or opinion **2** : to turn aside from a path or course : DEVIATE **3** : to cause to diverge : DEFLECT

di·ver·gence \-'vər-jən(t)s\ *n* **1** : a drawing apart (as of lines extending from a common center) **2** : DIFFERENCE, DISAGREEMENT **3** : the acquisition of dissimilar characters by related organisms in unlike environments **4** : a deviation from a course or standard

di·ver·gent \-jənt\ *adj* **1** : diverging from each other : SPREADING **2** : differing from each other or from a standard : DEVIANT — **di·ver·gent·ly** *adv*

di·vers \'dī-vərz\ *adj* [ME *divers, diverse*] : VARIOUS

di·verse \dī-'vərs, də-, 'dī-\ *adj* [L *diversus*, fr. pp. of *divertere* to divert] **1** : differing from one another : UNLIKE **2** : having various forms or qualities ⟨*diverse* personality⟩ **syn** see DIFFERENT — **di·verse·ly** *adv* — **di·verse·ness** *n*

di·ver·si·fy \də-'vər-sə-,fī, dī-\ *vb* **-fied; -fy·ing** **1** : to make diverse : give variety to **2** : to distribute one's investments among different kinds of securities **3** : to increase the variety of the products manufactured or distributed **4** : to produce variety **5** : to engage in varied operations — **di·ver·si·fi·ca·tion** \də-,vər-sə-fə-'kā-shən, (,)dī-\ *n*

di·ver·sion \də-'vər-zhən, dī-\ *n* **1** : the act or an instance of diverting from a course, activity, or use : DEVIATION **2** : something that diverts or amuses : PASTIME **3** : an attack made to draw the attention of an enemy from the point of a principal operation — **di·ver·sion·ary** \-zhə-,ner-ē\ *adj*

di·ver·si·ty \də-'vər-sət-ē, dī-\ *n, pl* **-ties** **1** : the condition of being different or having differences **2** : an instance or a point of difference **3** : VARIETY ⟨a great *diversity* of opinion⟩

di·vert \də-'vərt, dī-\ *vb* [L *divertere* to turn in opposite directions, fr. *dis-* + *vertere* to turn] **1 a** : to turn from one course or use to another : DEFLECT **b** : DISTRACT ⟨the scenery *diverted* his attention from the road⟩ **2** : to give pleasure to : turn to **syn** see AMUSE

di·ver·tic·u·lum \,dī-vər-'tik-yə-ləm\ *n, pl* **-la** \-lə\ : a pocket or closed branch opening off a main passage ⟨intestinal *diverticula*⟩

di·ver·ti·men·to \di-,vərt-ə-'ment-ō, -,vert-\ *n, pl* **-men·ti** \-'ment-(,)ē\ *or* **-men·tos** [It, lit., diversion] : an instrumental chamber work in several movements

Di·ves \'dī-,vēz\ *n* : the rich man in the parable recorded in Luke 16:19–31

di·vest \dī-'vest, də-\ *vt* [alter. of *devest*] **1** : to strip esp. of clothing, ornament, or equipment **2** : to deprive esp. of a right

¹di·vide \də-'vīd\ *vb* [L *dividere*, fr. *dis-* + *-videre* to separate] **1 a** : to separate into two or more parts, areas, or groups **b** : to separate into classes, categories,

---

or divisions **c :** CLEAVE, PART **2 a :** to give out in shares **:** DISTRIBUTE **b :** to possess or make use of in common **3 :** to cause to be separate, distinct, or apart from one another **4 a :** to mark divisions on **:** GRADUATE ⟨*divide* a sextant⟩ **b :** to subject to mathematical division **5 a :** to become separated into parts **b :** to branch out *syn* see SEPARATE

²**divide** *n* **:** a dividing ridge between drainage areas **:** WATERSHED

di·vid·ed *adj* **1 a :** separated into parts or pieces ⟨finely *divided* particles of iron⟩ **b :** cut into distinct parts by incisions extending to the base or to the midrib ⟨a *divided* leaf⟩ **c :** having the opposing streams of traffic separated ⟨a *divided* highway⟩ **2 a :** disagreeing with each other **:** DISUNITED **b :** directed or moved toward conflicting goals

div·i·dend \'div-ə-,dend, -əd-ənd\ *n* **1 :** a sum or amount to be distributed or an individual share of such a sum: as **a :** a share of profits distributed to stockholders or of surplus to an insurance policyholder **b :** interest paid on a bank account **2 :** BONUS **3 :** a number to be divided by another

di·vid·er \də-'vīd-ər\ *n* **1 :** one that divides **2** *pl* **:** an instrument for measuring or marking (as in dividing lines and transferring dimensions) **3 :** something that separates

div·i·na·tion \,div-ə-'nā-shən\ *n* **1 :** the art or practice that seeks to foresee or foretell future events or discover hidden knowledge usu. by means of augury or by the aid of supernatural powers **2 :** unusual insight or intuitive perception

¹**di·vine** \də-'vīn\ *adj* [L *divus* god] **1 a :** of, relating to, or proceeding directly from deity **b :** being deity ⟨the *divine* Savior⟩ **c :** directed to deity ⟨*divine* worship⟩ **2 a :** supremely good **:** SUPERB **b :** GODLIKE, HEAVENLY — **di·vine·ly** *adv*

²**divine** *n* **1 :** CLERGYMAN **2 :** THEOLOGIAN

³**divine** *vb* [L *divinare*, fr. *divinus* soothsayer, fr. *divinus*, adj., divine] **1 :** to discover or perceive intuitively **:** INFER, CONJECTURE **2 :** to practice divination **:** PROPHESY — **di·vin·er** *n*

dividers

Divine Liturgy *n* **:** the Eastern Orthodox eucharistic rite

Divine Office *n* **:** the daily devotional office of the breviary

divine right *n* **:** a theory that a monarch receives his right to rule from God and not from the people

diving bell *n* **:** a diving apparatus consisting of a container open only at the bottom and supplied with compressed air by a hose

diving duck *n* **:** any of various ducks that frequent deep waters and obtain their food by diving

divining rod *n* **:** a forked rod believed to indicate the presence of water or minerals by dipping downward when held over a vein

di·vin·i·ty \də-'vin-ət-ē\ *n, pl* **-ties 1 :** the quality or state of being divine **:** GODHEAD **2 a** *often cap* **:** ²GOD **b** (1) **:** GOD (2) **:** GODDESS **c :** DEMIGOD **3 :** THEOLOGY

di·vis·i·ble \də-'viz-ə-bəl\ *adj* **:** capable of being divided or separated — **di·vis·i·bil·i·ty** \-,viz-ə-'bil-ət-ē\ *n*

di·vi·sion \də-'vizh-ən\ *n* [L *divis-, dividere* to divide] **1 a :** the act or process of dividing **:** the state of being divided **b :** DISTRIBUTION **2 :** one of the parts, sections, or groupings into which a whole is divided **3 a :** a large self-contained military unit capable of independent action and usu. made up of five battle groups **b** (1) **:** the basic naval administrative unit (2) **:** a tactical subdivision of a squadron of ships **4 :** an administrative or operating unit of a governmental, business, or educational organization **5 :** a group of organisms forming part of a larger group; *esp* **:** a primary category of the plant kingdom **6 :** something that divides, separates, or marks off **7 a :** difference in opinion or interest **:** DISAGREEMENT **b :** the physical separation of the members of a deliberative body voting for and against a question **8 :** the operation of finding how many times one number or quantity is contained in another — **di·vi·sion·al** \-'vizh-nəl, -ən-ʰl\ *adj*

division of labor *n* **:** the distribution of tasks among members of a group or to different areas to increase efficiency

di·vi·sive \də-'vī-siv, -'viz-iv\ *adj* **:** creating disunity or dissension — **di·vi·sive·ly** *adv* — **di·vi·sive·ness** *n*

di·vi·sor \də-'vī-zər\ *n* **:** the number by which a dividend is divided

¹**di·vorce** \də-'vōrs, -'vȯrs\ *n* [L *divortium*, fr. *divertere, divortere* to turn aside, leave one's husband] **1 :** a complete legal dissolution of a marriage **2 :** complete separation **:** SEVERANCE ⟨the *divorce* of religion and politics⟩

²**divorce** *vt* **1 a :** to get rid of (one's spouse) by divorce **b :** to dissolve the marriage between (two spouses) **2 :** SEPARATE, DISUNITE — **di·vorce·ment** \-mənt\ *n*

di·vor·cée \də-,vōr-'sā, -,vȯr-, -'sē\ *n* [F] **:** a divorced woman

div·ot \'div-ət\ *n* **:** a piece of turf dug from a golf fairway in making a stroke

di·vulge \də-'vəlj, dī-\ *vt* [L *divulgare*, fr. *dis-* + *vulgare* to spread abroad, fr. *vulgus* mob, common people] **:** to make public **:** DISCLOSE, REVEAL ⟨*divulge* a secret⟩ — **di·vul·gence** \-'vəl-jən(t)s\ *n*

Dix·ie \'dik-sē\ *n* [name for the southern states in the song *Dixie* (1859) by Daniel D. Emmett] **:** the southern states of the U.S.

Dix·ie·crat \-,krat\ *n* **:** a dissident southern Democrat; *esp* **:** a supporter of a 1948 presidential ticket opposing the civil rights stand of the regular Democrats — **Dix·ie·crat·ic** \,dik-sē-'krat-ik\ *adj*

diz·zi·ness \'diz-ē-nəs\ *n* **:** the condition of being dizzy

¹**diz·zy** \'diz-ē\ *adj* **diz·zi·er; -est** [OE *dysig* stupid] **1 a :** having a whirling sensation in the head **:** GIDDY **b :** mentally confused **2 a :** causing or caused by giddiness ⟨a *dizzy* height⟩ **b :** extremely rapid — **diz·zi·ly** \'diz-ə-lē\ *adv*

²**dizzy** *vt* **diz·zied; diz·zy·ing :** to make dizzy **:** cause dizziness in

DNA \,dē-,en-'ā\ *n* **:** DEOXYRIBONUCLEIC ACID

¹**do** \(')dü\ *vb* **did** \(')did\; **done** \'dən\; **do·ing** \'dü-iŋ\; **does** \(')dəz\ [OE *dōn*] **1 a :** to accomplish as a purposeful or willful act ⟨do some work⟩⟨crime *done* deliberately⟩ **b :** ACT, BEHAVE ⟨*do* as I say⟩ **c :** to be active or busy ⟨up and *doing* before dawn⟩ **d :** HAPPEN ⟨what's *doing* tonight?⟩ **2 a :** to work at esp. as a vocation ⟨what to *do* after college⟩ **b :** to take appropriate action on **:** PREPARE ⟨*do* your homework⟩ **c :** to put in order (as by cleaning or arranging) ⟨*do* the dishes⟩ **d :** DECORATE ⟨*did* the bedroom in blue⟩ **3 a :** to get along ⟨*does* quite well in school⟩ **b :** to carry on ⟨can *do* without your help⟩ **c :** to feel or function better ⟨could *do* with some coffee⟩ **4 :** to act so as to bring **:** RENDER ⟨sleep will *do* you good⟩ ⟨*do* honor to his memory⟩ **5 :** to bring or come to an end **:** FINISH ⟨it was late when she had *done* washing⟩⟨the result, when he had *done*, was a beautiful picture⟩ **6 :** to put forth **:** EXERT ⟨*did* his best to win⟩ **7 :** PRODUCE ⟨*did* a biography on the president⟩ **8 :** to play the part of ⟨usually *does* old ladies⟩ **9 :** CHEAT ⟨*did* him out of his share⟩ **10 a :** TRAVERSE ⟨*did* 500 miles that day⟩ **b :** TOUR ⟨*did* 12 countries in 3 months⟩ **c :** to travel at a speed of ⟨*doing* 80 on the turnpike⟩ **11 :** to serve in prison ⟨was *doing* five years for forgery⟩ **12 a :** to serve the needs of **:** SUIT ⟨worms will *do* us for bait⟩ **b :** to answer the purpose ⟨half of that will *do*⟩ **c :** to be fitting or proper ⟨it won't *do* to be late⟩ **13** — used with *so* or a pronoun object to stand for part of a preceding predicate ⟨he wants to make the varsity, but to *do* so he'll have to work hard⟩⟨if you must sing, *do* it somewhere else⟩ **14** — used as an auxiliary verb (1) before the subject in an interrogative sentence ⟨*does* he work⟩ and after some adverbs ⟨never *did* he work so hard⟩⟨he works and so *do* I⟩, (2) in a negative statement ⟨he *doesn't* work⟩, (3) for emphasis ⟨he *does* work⟩, and (4) as a substitute for a preceding predicate ⟨he works harder than I *do*⟩⟨he doesn't work, *does* he⟩⟨he likes lobster and she *does* too⟩ — **do away with 1 :** to get rid of ⟨the new program doesn't *do away with* all the red tape⟩ **2 :** DESTROY, KILL ⟨he was *done away with* in the latest purge⟩ — **do by :** to act toward in a specified manner ⟨*did* right *by* her⟩⟨*did* wrong *by* an old friend⟩ — **do for :** to bring about the death or ruin of ⟨he'll be *done for* if they don't help him⟩

²**do** \'dō\ *n* [It] **:** the 1st note of the diatonic scale

do·a·ble \'dü-ə-bəl\ *adj* **:** capable of being done

dob·bin \'däb-ən\ *n* **1 :** a farm horse **2 :** a quiet plodding horse

Do·ber·man pin·scher \,dō-bər-mən-'pin-chər\ *n* **:** a short-haired medium-sized working dog of a breed of German origin

dob·son \'däb-sən\ *n* **:** HELLGRAMMITE

ə abut; ə kitten; ər further; a back; ā bake; ä cot, cart; au̇ out; ch chin; e less; ē easy; g gift; i trip; ī life

dob·son·fly \-ˌflī\ *n* : a large-eyed winged insect with a large carnivorous aquatic larva — compare HELLGRAMMITE

do·cent \'dōs-ᵊnt, dō(t)-'sent\ *n* [L docent-, docens, prp. of docēre to teach] : TEACHER, LECTURER

doc·ile \'däs-əl\ *adj* [L docilis, fr. docēre to teach] : easily taught, led, or managed : TRACTABLE ⟨a docile child⟩ — **doc·ile·ly** \'däs-ə(l)-lē\ *adv* — **do·cil·i·ty** \dä-'sil-ət-ē, dō-\ *n*

¹dock \'däk\ *n* [OE docce] : any of a genus of coarse weedy plants related to buckwheat that are used as potherbs and in folk medicine

²dock *n* [OE -docca (as in fingirdocca finger muscle)] : the solid part of an animal's tail as distinguished from the hair

³dock *vt* **1** : to cut off the end of : cut short ⟨a docked tail⟩ **2** : to take away a part of : make a deduction from ⟨dock a man's wages⟩

⁴dock *n* [prob. fr. MD docke] **1** : an artificial basin to receive ships that has gates to keep the water in or out **2** : a slip or waterway usu. between two piers to receive ships **3** : a wharf or platform for the loading or unloading of materials ⟨a ship moored to the dock⟩⟨a loading dock for trucks⟩ **4** : a place or scaffolding for the inspection and repair of aircraft

⁵dock *vb* **1** : to haul or guide into a dock **2** : to come or go into dock

⁶dock *n* [Flem docke cage] : the place in a criminal court where a prisoner stands or sits during trial

dock·age \'däk-ij\ *n* **1** : a charge for the use of a dock **2** : docking facilities **3** : the docking of ships

¹dock·et \'däk-ət\ *n* [ME doggette, n., brief, abstract] **1 a** : a formal abridged record of the proceedings in a legal action **b** : a register of such records **2 a** : a list of legal causes to be tried **b** : a calendar of matters to be acted on : AGENDA **3** : a label attached to a parcel containing identification or directions (as for handling)

²docket *vt* **1** : to mark with an identifying statement : LABEL **2** : to make a brief abstract of (as a legal matter) and inscribe it in a list **3** : to place on the docket for legal action

dock·hand \'däk-ˌhand\ *n* : LONGSHOREMAN

dock·yard \'däk-ˌyärd\ *n* : a place where ships are built or repaired or where naval supplies or shipbuilding materials are stored

¹doc·tor \'däk-tər\ *n* [L, teacher, fr. doct-, docēre to teach] **1 a** : an eminent theologian declared a sound expounder of doctrine by the Roman Catholic Church — called also doctor of the church **b** : a learned or authoritative teacher **c** : a person holding one of the highest academic degrees (as a PhD) conferred by a university **2 a** : one skilled or specializing in healing arts; *esp* : a physician, surgeon, dentist, or veterinarian licensed to practice his profession **b** : MEDICINE MAN — **doc·tor·al** \-t(ə-)rəl\ *adj* — **doc·tor·ship** \-tər-ˌship\ *n*

²doctor *vb* **doc·tored; doc·tor·ing** \-t(ə-)riŋ\ **1 a** : to give medical treatment to **b** : to practice medicine **c** : to restore to good condition : REPAIR ⟨doctor an old clock⟩ **2 a** : to adapt or modify for a desired end ⟨doctored the play by abridging the last act⟩ **b** : to alter deceptively ⟨doctored the election returns⟩

doc·tor·ate \'däk-t(ə-)rət\ *n* : the degree, title, or rank of a doctor

doc·tri·naire \ˌdäk-trə-'na(ə)r, -'ne(ə)r\ *n* : one who attempts to put an abstract theory into effect without regard to practical difficulties — **doctrinaire** *adj*

doc·trine \'däk-trən\ *n* **1** : something that is taught **2** : a principle or position or the body of principles in a branch of knowledge or system of belief : DOGMA **3** : a principle of law established through past decisions — **doc·tri·nal** \-tran-ᵊl\ *adj* — **doc·tri·nal·ly** \-ᵊl-ē\ *adv*
syn DOCTRINE, DOGMA, TENET mean a principle accepted as authoritative. DOCTRINE strictly implies authoritative teaching accepted by a body of believers or adherents of a philosophy or school ⟨Christian doctrine⟩⟨a mathematical doctrine⟩ but also denotes a theory supported by evidence and proposed for acceptance ⟨the doctrine of evolution⟩ DOGMA implies a doctrine laid down as true and beyond dispute; TENET stresses acceptance and belief of a principle and implies a body of adherents ⟨the tenets of socialism are not identical with the doctrines of Marx⟩

¹doc·u·ment \'däk-yə-mənt\ *n* [L documentum lesson,

proof, fr. docēre to teach] : a usu. original or official written or printed paper furnishing information or used as proof of something else — **doc·u·men·tal** \ˌdäk-yə-'ment-ᵊl\ *adj*

²doc·u·ment \'däk-yə-ˌment\ *vt* : to furnish documentary evidence of ⟨documents his case with his adversary's own statements⟩ — **doc·u·ment·a·ble** \-ə-bəl\ *adj*

¹doc·u·men·ta·ry \ˌdäk-yə-'ment-ə-rē, -'men-trē\ *adj* **1** : consisting of documents : of the nature of documents; *also* : contained or certified in writing ⟨documentary proof⟩ **2** : giving a factual presentation in artistic form ⟨a documentary film⟩ — **doc·u·men·tar·i·ly** \-mən-'ter-ə-lē, -ˌmen-\ *adv*

²documentary *n*, *pl* **-ries** : a documentary presentation (as a film)

doc·u·men·ta·tion \ˌdäk-yə-mən-'tā-shən, -ˌmen-\ *n* **1** : the providing or the using of documents in proof of something **2** : evidence in the form of documents or references (as in footnotes) to documents

¹dod·der \'däd-ər\ *n* [ME doder] : any of a genus of leafless herbs deficient in chlorophyll and parasitic on other plants

²dodder *vi* **dod·dered; dod·der·ing** \'däd-(ə-)riŋ\ **1** : to tremble or shake from weakness or age **2** : to progress feebly

dod·der·ing \'däd-(ə-)riŋ\ *adj* : FOOLISH, SENILE ⟨a doddering old man⟩

do·deca·gon \dō-'dek-ə-ˌgän\ *n* [Gk dōdeka twelve] : a polygon of 12 angles and 12 sides

do·deca·he·dron \(ˌ)dō-ˌdek-ə-'hē-drən\ *n*, *pl* **-drons** *or* **-dra** \-drə\ [Gk dōdeka twelve + hedra seat, base] : a solid having 12 plane faces

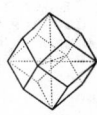
dodecahedron

¹dodge \'däj\ *vb* **1 a** : to move suddenly aside **b** : to avoid by moving quickly aside ⟨dodge a batted ball⟩ **2** : to avoid by trickery or evasion ⟨dodge work⟩ ⟨dodge the truant officer⟩

²dodge *n* **1** : an act of evading by sudden bodily movement **2 a** : an artful device to evade, deceive, or trick ⟨crafty legal dodges⟩ **b** : TECHNIQUE, METHOD ⟨a new market dodge to increase sales⟩

dodg·er \'däj-ər\ *n* **1** : one that dodges; *esp* : one who uses tricky devices **2** : a small handbill **3** : a cake made of cornmeal

do·do \'dōd-ō\ *n*, *pl* **dodoes** *or* **dodos** [Pg doudo] **1** : a heavy flightless extinct bird related to the pigeons but larger than a turkey and formerly found on some of the islands of the Indian ocean **2** : one hopelessly behind the times

doe \'dō\ *n*, *pl* **does** *or* **doe** [OE dā] : an adult female deer; *also* : the female esp. when adult of any mammal (as an antelope or hare) of which the male is called buck

do·er \'dü-ər\ *n* : one that does ⟨a thinker or a doer⟩

doe·skin \'dō-ˌskin\ *n* **1** : the skin of does or leather made of it; *also* : soft leather from sheepskins or lambskins **2** : a soft firm woolen cloth

doesn't \'dəz-ᵊnt\ : does not

do·est \'dü-əst\ *archaic pres 2d sing of* DO

do·eth \'dü-əth\ *archaic pres 3d sing of* DO

doff \'däf, 'dóf\ *vt* [ME doffen, fr. don to do + of off] **1** : to take off (one's clothes); *esp* : to take off or lift up (the hat) **2** : to rid oneself of

¹dog \'dóg\ *n* [OE docga] **1 a** : a variable carnivorous domesticated mammal prob. descended from the common wolf; *also* : an animal of the family to which this mammal belongs **b** : a male dog **2 a** : a worthless fellow **b** : FELLOW, CHAP ⟨a gay dog⟩ **3 a** : any of various devices for holding, gripping, or fastening that consist of a spike, rod, or bar **b** : ANDIRON **4** : affected stylishness or dignity ⟨put on the dog⟩ **5** *cap* **a** : CANIS MAJOR **b** : CANIS MINOR **6** *pl*, *slang* : FEET **7** *pl* : RUIN ⟨go to the dogs⟩ — **dog·like** \-ˌlīk\ *adj*

²dog *vt* **dogged; dog·ging** **1** : to hunt or track like a hound **2** : to worry as if by dogs : HOUND ⟨dogged by bad luck⟩

dog·bane \'dóg-ˌbān\ *n* : any of a genus of chiefly tropical and often poisonous plants with milky juice and usu. showy flowers

dog·cart \-ˌkärt\ *n* **1** : a cart drawn by a dog **2** : a light one-horse carriage with two seats back to back

dog·catch·er \-,kach-ər, -,kech-\ *n* : a community official assigned to catch and dispose of stray dogs

dog days *n pl* [fr. their beginning at the date when the Dog Star (Sirius) rises just before the sun] : the hot sultry period of summer between early July and early September

doge \'dōj\ *n* [It dial., fr. L *duc-, dux* leader] : the chief magistrate in the republics of Venice and Genoa

dog–ear \'dȯg-,i(ə)r\ *n* : the turned-down corner of a leaf of a book — **dog–ear** *vt*

dog–eared \-,i(ə)rd\ *adj* **1** : having dog-ears ⟨a *dog-eared* book⟩ **2** : SHABBY, WORN

dog–eat–dog \,dȯg-,ēt-'dȯg\ *adj* : marked by ruthless self-interest ⟨a *dog-eat-dog* business⟩

dog·face \'dȯg-,fās\ *n, slang* : SOLDIER ; *esp* : INFANTRYMAN

dog·fight \-,fīt\ *n* : a fight between two or more fighter planes usu. at close quarters

dog·fish \-,fish\ *n* : any of various small sharks that often appear in schools near shore

dog·ged \'dȯg-əd\ *adj* : stubbornly determined : TENACIOUS ⟨*dogged* persistence⟩ **syn** see OBSTINATE — **dog·ged·ly** *adv* — **dog·ged·ness** *n*

¹dog·ger·el \'dȯg-(ə-)rəl, 'däg-\ *adj* [ME *dogerel*] : loosely styled and irregular in measure esp. for burlesque or comic effect

²doggerel *n* : doggerel verse

¹dog·gone \'däg-'gän, 'dȯg-'gȯn\ *vb* [euphemism for *God damn*] : DAMN

²doggone *or* **dog·goned** \-'gänd, -'gȯnd\ *adj* (*or adv*) : DAMNED

³doggone *n* : DAMN

¹dog·gy \'dȯg-ē\ *adj* **dog·gi·er; -est 1** : resembling a dog **2** : STYLISH, SHOWY

²dog·gy *or* **dog·gie** \'dȯg-ē\ *n, pl* **doggies** : a small dog

dog·house \'dȯg-,haůs\ *n* : a shelter for a dog — **in the doghouse** : in a state of disfavor

do·gie \'dō-gē\ *n, chiefly West* : a motherless calf in a range herd

dog in the manger [fr. the fable of the dog who prevented an ox from eating hay which he did not want himself] : a person who selfishly withholds from others something useless to himself

dog·ma \'dȯg-mə, 'däg-\ *n, pl* **dog·mas** *also* **dog·ma·ta** \-mət-ə\ [Gk *dogmat-, dogma*, fr. *dokein* to seem, seem good] **1 a** : something held as an established opinion; *esp* : a definite authoritative tenet **b** : a point of view or opinion put forth as authoritative without adequate grounds **2** : a doctrine or body of doctrines concerning faith or morals laid down by a church **syn** see DOCTRINE

dog·mat·ic \dȯg-'mat-ik, däg-\ *adj* **1** : characterized by or given to the use of dogmatism ⟨a *dogmatic* critic⟩ **2** : of or relating to dogma **syn** see DICTATORIAL — **dog·mat·i·cal·ly** \-'mat-i-k(ə-)lē\ *adv*

dog·ma·tism \'dȯg-mə-,tiz-əm, 'däg-\ *n* **1** : positiveness in assertion of opinion esp. when unwarranted or arrogant **2** : a viewpoint or system of ideas based on insufficiently examined premises

dog·ma·tist \-mət-əst\ *n* : one who dogmatizes

dog·ma·tize \-mə-,tīz\ *vb* : to speak or write dogmatically — **dog·ma·tiz·er** *n*

do–good·er \'dü-,gůd-ər\ *n* : an earnest usu. impractical and often naive and ineffectual humanitarian or reformer

Dog Star *n* **1** : SIRIUS **2** : PROCYON

dog tag *n* **1** : a tag worn on a dog's neck bearing a license registration number **2** : a military identification tag

dog·tooth spar \,dȯg-,tüth-\ *n* : the mineral calcite occurring in elongated and pointed crystals

dogtooth violet *n* : any of a genus of small spring-flowering bulbous herbs of the lily family

¹dog·trot \'dȯg-,trät\ *n* : a gentle trot

²dogtrot *vi* : to move or progress at a dogtrot

dog watch *n* : a shipboard watch from 4 to 6 or from 6 to 8 p.m.

dog·wood \'dȯg-,wůd\ *n* : any of a genus of trees and shrubs with heads of small flowers and often showy involucres

doi·ly \'dȯi-lē\ *n, pl* **doilies 1** : a small napkin **2** : a small often decorative mat

do in *vt* **1** : to bring about the defeat or destruction of : RUIN ⟨*done in* by the stock-market crash⟩ **2** : KILL ⟨tried to *do* him *in* with a club⟩ **3** : to wear out : EXHAUST ⟨*done in* at the end of the day⟩

do·ing \'dü-iŋ\ *n* **1** : the act of performing or executing : ACTION ⟨will take some *doing* to beat him⟩ **2** *pl* **a** : things that are done or that occur ⟨everyday *doings*⟩ **b** *dial* : social activities ⟨big *doings* tonight⟩

doit \'dȯit\ *n* [D *duit*] **1** : an old Dutch coin equal to about ¼ cent **2** : TRIFLE

do–it–your·self \,dü-ə-chər-'self\ *adj* : of, relating to, or designed for use in construction, repair, or artistic work done by an amateur or hobbyist ⟨*do-it-yourself* tools⟩ ⟨*do-it-yourself* car model kit⟩

dol·ce \'dōl-(,)chā\ *adv* (*or adj*) [It, lit., sweet, fr. L *dulcis*] : SOFT, SMOOTH — used as a direction in music — **dol·ce·men·te** \,dōl-chä-'ment-ē, -'men-(,)tā\ *adv*

dol·ce far nien·te \'dōl-chē-,fär-nē-'ent-ē\ *n* [It, lit., a sweet doing nothing] : delightful relaxation in carefree idleness

dol·drums \'dōl-drəmz, 'däl-\ *n pl* **1** : a spell of listlessness or despondency **2** : a part of the ocean near the equator abounding in calms and light shifting winds **3** : a state of inactivity, stagnation, or slump

¹dole \'dōl\ *n* [OE *dāl* portion] **1 a** (1) : a giving out of food, money, or clothing to the needy (2) : money, food, or clothing so given **b** : a grant of government funds to the unemployed **2** : something portioned out and distributed

²dole *vt* **1** : to give or distribute as a charity ⟨*doled* out blankets and clothing to the flood victims⟩ **2** : to give or deliver in small portions : PARCEL

³dole *n* [L *dolor*] *archaic* : GRIEF, SORROW

dole·ful \'dōl-fəl\ *adj* : full of grief : SAD — **dole·ful·ly** \-fə-lē\ *adv* — **dole·ful·ness** *n*

dole·some \'dōl-səm\ *adj* : DOLEFUL

dol·i·cho·ce·phal·ic \,däl-i-kō-sə-'fal-ik\ *adj* [Gk *dolichos* long + *kephalē* head] : having a relatively long head with a cephalic index of less than 75 — **dol·i·cho·ceph·a·ly** \-'sef-ə-lē\ *n*

doll \'däl, 'dȯl\ *n* **1** : a small-scale figure of a human being used esp. as a child's plaything **2 a** : a pretty scatter-brained young woman **b** *slang* : WOMAN **c** *slang* : DARLING, SWEETHEART

dol·lar \'däl-ər\ *n* [D or LG *daler*, fr. G *taler*] **1** : TALER **2** : a coin (as a Spanish piece of eight) patterned after the taler **3 a** : a basic monetary unit (as of the U.S. and Canada) **b** : a coin, note, or token representing one dollar

dollar diplomacy *n* : diplomacy held to be designed primarily to further private financial and commercial interests

dol·lop \'däl-əp\ *n* : LUMP, BLOB

doll up *vb* : to dress or adorn formally or elegantly

¹dolly \'däl-ē, 'dȯl-ē\ *n, pl* **doll·ies 1** : DOLL **2** : a platform on a roller or on wheels for transporting heavy objects; *esp* : a wheeled platform for a television or motion-picture camera

²dolly *vi* **doll·ied; doll·y·ing** : to move a motion-picture or television dolly about while shooting a scene

dol·man sleeve \,dōl-mən, ,dȯl-, ,däl-\ *n* [Turk *dolama*, a kind of robe] : a sleeve that is very wide at the armhole and tight at the wrist and that is either set into a deep armhole or cut in one piece with the bodice

dol·men \'dōl-mən, 'dȯl-, 'däl-\ *n* [F, fr. Bret *tolmen*, fr. *tol* table + *men* stone] : a prehistoric monument consisting of two or more upright stones supporting a horizontal stone slab

do·lo·mite \'dō-lə-,mīt, 'däl-ə-\ *n* [fr. Déodat de *Dolomieu* d1801 French geologist] : a mineral CaMg(CO₃)₂ consisting of a calcium magnesium carbonate found in crystals and in extensive beds as a compact limestone — **do·lo·mit·ic** \,dō-lə-'mit-ik, ,däl-ə-\ *adj*

do·lor \'dō-lər, 'däl-ər\ *n* [L *dolor* pain, grief, fr. *dolēre* to feel pain] : mental suffering or anguish : SORROW

do·lor·ous \'dō-lə-rəs, 'däl-ə-\ *adj* : causing, marked by, or expressive of misery or grief — **do·lor·ous·ly** *adv* — **do·lor·ous·ness** *n*

dol·phin \'däl-fən, 'dȯl-\ *n* [MF *dophin*] **1 a** : any of various small long-nosed toothed whales **b** : PORPOISE 1 **2** : either of two active spiny-finned marine food fishes **3** *cap* : DELPHINUS

dolphin 1

dolt \'dōlt\ *n* : a stupid fellow — **dolt·ish** \'dōl-tish\ *adj* — **dolt·ish·ly** *adv* — **dolt·ish·ness** *n*

Dom [L *dominus* master] **1** \(ˌ)däm\ — used as a title prefixed to the name of some monks and canons regular **2** \(ˌ)dōⁿ\ — used as a title prefixed to the Christian name of a Portuguese or Brazilian man of rank

-dom \dəm\ *n suffix* [OE *-dōm*] **1 a :** dignity : office (duke*dom*) **b :** realm : jurisdiction (king*dom*) **c :** geographical area (Anglo-Saxon*dom*) **2 :** state or fact of being (free*dom*) **3 :** those having a (specified) office, occupation, interest, or character (official*dom*)

do·main \dō-'mān, də-\ *n* [MF *domaine*, fr. L *dominium*, fr. *dominus* master] **1 a :** complete and absolute ownership of land — compare EMINENT DOMAIN **b :** land completely owned **2 :** a territory over which dominion is exercised **3 :** a sphere of influence or activity (the widening *domain* of science) **4 :** the set of values to which a variable is limited; *esp* : the set of values that the independent variable of a function may take on **5 :** a small region of a magnetic substance that contains a group of atoms all aligned in the same direction so that each group has the effect of a tiny magnet pointing in a certain direction

¹dome \'dōm\ *n* [ML *domus* church, fr. L, house] **1** *archaic* : a stately building : MANSION **2 :** a large hemispherical roof or ceiling **3 :** a natural formation that resembles the dome or cupola of a building (elevated rock *domes*)

²dome *vb* **1 :** to cover with or as if with a dome **2 :** to form into or swell upward or outward like a dome

Domes·day Book \'dümz-ˌdā-, 'dōmz-\ *n* [ME, fr. *domesday* doomsday] : a record of a survey of English lands made by order of William the Conqueror about 1086

¹do·mes·tic \də-'mes-tik\ *adj* [L *domesticus*, fr. *domus* house, home; akin to E *timber*] **1 :** of or relating to the household or the family (*domestic* life) (*domestic* duties) **2 :** of, relating to, or produced or carried on within one country (*domestic* politics) (*domestic* trade) (*domestic* wines) **3 a :** living near or about the habitations of man (*domestic* vermin) **b :** DOMESTICATED, TAME **4 :** devoted to home duties and pleasures (a man *domestic* in his habits) — **do·mes·ti·cal·ly** \-ti-k(ə-)lē\ *adv*

²domestic *n* : a household servant

domestic animal *n* : any of various animals (as the horse or sheep) domesticated by man so as to live and breed in a tame condition

do·mes·ti·cate \də-'mes-ti-ˌkāt\ *vt* **1 :** to bring into domestic use : ADOPT (European customs *domesticated* in America) **2 :** to fit for domestic life (tried to *domesticate* her explorer husband) **3 :** to adapt to life in intimate association with and to the advantage of man (man *domesticated* the dog) — **do·mes·ti·ca·tion** \də-ˌmes-ti-'kā-shən\ *n*

do·mes·tic·i·ty \ˌdō-ˌmes-'tis-ət-ē, də-\ *n, pl* **-ties 1 :** the quality or state of being domestic or domesticated **2 :** domestic activities or life **3** *pl* : domestic affairs

domestic prelate *n* : a priest having permanent honorary membership in the papal household and ranking above a papal chamberlain

domestic science *n* : instruction and training in domestic management and the household arts (as cooking and sewing)

domestic system *n* : a system of manufacturing by workers in their homes from raw materials supplied by the employer

dom·i·cal \'dō-mi-kəl, 'däm-i-\ *adj* : relating to, shaped like, or having a dome

¹dom·i·cile \'däm-ə-ˌsīl, 'dō-mə-; 'däm-ə-səl\ *n* [L *domicilium*, fr. *domus* house] **1 :** a dwelling place : place of residence : HOME **2 :** a person's fixed, permanent, and principal home for legal purposes — **dom·i·cil·i·ary** \ˌdäm-ə-'sil-ē-ˌer-ē, ˌdō-mə-\ *adj*

²domicile *vt* : to establish in or provide with a domicile

dom·i·nance \'däm-ə-nən(t)s\ *n* : the fact or state of being dominant; *esp* : AUTHORITY

¹dom·i·nant \-nənt\ *adj* **1 :** commanding, controlling, or prevailing over all others (a *dominant* political figure) **2 :** overlooking and commanding from a superior elevation (a *dominant* hill) **3 :** being the more effective or predominant in action of a pair of bodily structures (*dominant* eye) **4 :** predominating over a contrasting allele in manifestation — compare RECESSIVE — **dom·i·nant·ly** *adv*

²dominant *n* **1 a :** a dominant genetic character or factor

b : a kind of organism (as a species) in an ecological association that exerts a controlling influence on the environment **2 :** the 5th note of the diatonic scale

dom·i·nate \'däm-ə-ˌnāt\ *vb* [L *dominari*, fr. *dominus* master; akin to E *tame*] **1 :** RULE, CONTROL (refuse to be *dominated* by his friends) (in primitive societies the strong *dominate* over the weak) **2 :** to have a commanding position or controlling power over (the rock of Gibraltar *dominates* the straits below) **3 :** to rise high above in a position suggesting power to dominate (the mountain range was *dominated* by a single snow-capped peak) — **dom·i·na·tive** \-ˌnāt-iv\ *adj* — **dom·i·na·tor** \-ˌnāt-ər\ *n*

dom·i·na·tion \ˌdäm-ə-'nā-shən\ *n* **1 :** supremacy or preeminence over another **2 :** exercise of mastery or preponderant influence

dom·i·neer \ˌdäm-ə-'ni(ə)r\ *vb* **1 :** to rule in an arrogant manner **2 :** to be overbearing

dom·i·neer·ing *adj* : inclined to domineer **syn** see MASTERFUL — **dom·i·neer·ing·ly** \-iŋ-lē\ *adv* — **dom·i·neer·ing·ness** *n*

Do·min·i·can \də-'min-i-kən\ *n* : a member of the Roman Catholic mendicant Order of Preachers founded in 1215 — **Dominican** *adj*

do·mi·nie *1 oftenest* 'däm-ə-nē, *2 oftenest* 'dō-mə-\ *n* [L *domine*, voc. of *dominus*] **1** *chiefly Scot* : SCHOOLMASTER **2 :** CLERGYMAN

do·min·ion \də-'min-yən\ *n* [MF, modif. of L *dominium*, fr. *dominus* master] **1 :** supreme authority : SOVEREIGNTY **2 :** DOMAIN **3** *often cap* : a self-governing nation of the British Commonwealth other than the United Kingdom that acknowledges the British monarch as chief of state

Dominion Day *n* : July 1 observed in Canada as a legal holiday in commemoration of the proclamation of dominion status in 1867

dom·i·no \'däm-ə-ˌnō\ *n, pl* **-noes** *or* **-nos** [F] **1 :** a long loose hooded cloak usu. worn with a half mask as a masquerade costume **2** [F, fr. It] **a :** a flat rectangular block (as of wood or plastic) whose face is divided into two equal parts that are blank or bear from one to usu. six dots arranged as on dice faces **b** *pl* : any of several games played with a set of usu. 28 dominoes

¹don \'dän\ *n* [Sp, fr. L *dominus* master] **1 :** a Spanish nobleman or gentleman — used as a title prefixed to the Christian name **2 :** a head, tutor, or fellow in a college of Oxford or Cambridge University

²don *vt* **donned; don·ning** [*do* + *on*] : to put on : dress oneself in (don an apron for washing dishes)

do·ña \ˌdō-nyə\ *n* : a Spanish woman of rank — used as a title prefixed to the Christian name

do·nate \'dō-ˌnāt, dō-'\ *vb* [L *donare*, fr. *donum* gift] **1 :** to make a gift of : CONTRIBUTE (*donate* blood) **2 :** to make a donation (*donates* to the community chest every year) **syn** see GIVE — **do·na·tor** \-ˌnāt-ər, -'nāt-\ *n*

do·na·tion \dō-'nā-shən\ *n* **1 :** the action of making a gift esp. to a charity **2 :** a free contribution : GIFT

¹done \'dən\ *past part of* DO

²done *adj* **1 :** conformable to social convention **2 :** physically exhausted : SPENT **3 :** gone by : OVER (when day is *done*) **4 :** doomed to failure, defeat, or death (industry is *done* in this area) **5 :** cooked sufficiently (the meat is *done*)

do·nee \dō-'nē\ *n* : a recipient of a gift

don·jon \'dän-jən, 'dən-\ *n* : a massive inner tower in a medieval castle

Don Juan \(')dän-'(h)wän, dän-'jü-ən\ *n* **1 :** a profligate nobleman of Spanish legend **2 :** LIBERTINE, RAKE

don·key \'däŋ-kē, 'dəŋ-, 'dȯŋ-\ *n, pl* **donkeys 1 :** the domestic ass **2 :** a stupid or obstinate person

donkey engine *n* **1 :** a small usu. portable auxiliary engine **2 :** a small locomotive used in switching

don·na \ˌdän-ə\ *n, pl* **don·ne** \-(ˌ)ā\ [It, fr. L *domina* mistress] : an Italian woman usu. of rank — used as a title prefixed to the Christian name

don·nish \'dän-ish\ *adj* : of, relating to, or characteristic of a university don : PEDANTIC — **don·nish·ly** *adv* — **don·nish·ness** *n*

don·ny·brook \'dän-ē-ˌbrük\ *n* [fr. *Donnybrook* Fair, annual Irish event known for its brawls] : an uproarious brawl

do·nor \'dō-nər, -ˌnȯr\ *n* **1 :** one that gives, donates, or presents **2 :** one used as a source of biological material (a blood *donor*) — **do·nor·ship** \-ˌship\ *n*

do-noth-ing \'dü-,nǝth-iŋ\ *adj* : marked by inactivity; *esp* : marked by lack of initiative, disinclination to disturb the status quo, or failure to make positive progress ⟨a *do-nothing* government⟩ — **do-noth-ing-ism** \-,iŋ-,iz-ǝm\ *n*

Don Qui-xote \,dän-kē-'(h)ōt-ē, dän-'kwik-sǝt\ *n* : the idealistic and impractical hero of Cervantes' *Don Quixote*

don't \(')dōnt\ : do not

doo-dad \'dü-,dad\ *n* : a small article whose common name is unknown or forgotten

¹doo-dle \'düd-ᵊl\ *vb* **doo-dled; doo-dling** \'düd-liŋ, -ᵊl-iŋ\ : to draw or scribble aimlessly and without conscious effort while occupied with something else — **doo-dler** \'düd-lǝr, -ᵊl-ǝr\ *n*

²doodle *n* : something produced by doodling

doo-dle-bug \'düd-ᵊl-,bǝg\ *n* : the larva of an ant lion

doo-hick-ey \'dü-,hik-ē\ *n* : DOODAD

¹doom \'düm\ *n* [OE *dōm* law, judgment] **1 a** : JUDGMENT, DECISION; *esp* : a judicial condemnation or sentence **b** (1) : a final determining of what is just (2) : JUDGMENT DAY **2 a** : DESTINY; *esp* : unhappy destiny **b** : DEATH, RUIN **syn** see FATE

²doom *vt* **1** : to give judgment against : CONDEMN **2 a** : to fix the fate of : DESTINE **b** : to ensure the failure or destruction of

dooms-day \'dümz-,dā\ *n* : JUDGMENT DAY

door \'dō(ǝ)r, 'dȯ(ǝ)r\ *n* [OE *duru* door & *dor* gate] **1** : a usu. swinging or sliding barrier by which an entry is closed and opened; *also* : a similar part of a piece of furniture **2** : DOORWAY **3** : a means of access ⟨the *door* to success⟩

door-jamb \-,jam\ *n* : an upright piece forming the side of a door opening

door-keep-er \-,kē-pǝr\ *n* : one that tends a door

door-knob \-,näb\ *n* : a knob that when turned releases a door latch

door-man \-,man, -mǝn\ *n* **1** : DOORKEEPER **2** : one who tends a door (as of a hotel) and assists people by calling taxis and helping them in and out of cars

door-mat \-,mat\ *n* : a mat placed before or inside a door for wiping dirt from the shoes

door-nail \-,nāl\ *n* : a large-headed nail — used chiefly in the phrase *dead as a doornail*

door-plate \-,plāt\ *n* : a plate or plaque bearing a name (as of a resident) on a door

door-post \-,pōst\ *n* : DOORJAMB

door-step \-,step\ *n* : a step or series of steps before an outer door

door-way \-,wā\ *n* **1** : the opening that a door closes **2** : a means of gaining access

door-yard \-,yärd\ *n* : a yard outside the door of a house

¹dope \'dōp\ *n* [D *doop* sauce; akin to E *dip*] **1 a** : a thick liquid or pasty preparation **b** : a preparation for giving a desired quality to a substance or surface; *esp* : an anti-knock added to gasoline **2 a** : a narcotic preparation **b** : a stupid person **3** : information esp. from a reliable source

²dope *vt* **1** : to treat or affect with dope; *esp* : to give a narcotic to **2** *slang* : to guess the result of : predict (an outcome) esp. by means of special information or skill ⟨*dope* out which team will win⟩ — **dop-er** *n*

dope-ster \'dōp-stǝr\ *n* : a forecaster of the outcome of uncertain public events

dop-ey \'dō-pē\ *adj* **dop-i-er; -est 1** : dulled by or as if by alcohol or a narcotic **2** : DULL, STUPID — **dop-i-ness** *n*

dor-bee-tle \'dȯr-,bēt-ᵊl\ *n* [*dor* buzzing insect] : any of various beetles that fly with a buzzing sound

Do-ri-an \'dōr-ē-ǝn, 'dȯr-\ *n* : one of an ancient Hellenic race that completed the overthrow of Mycenaean civilization and settled esp. in the Peloponnesus and Crete — **Dorian** *adj*

Dor-ic \'dōr-ik, 'där-\ *adj* **1** : of, relating to, or characteristic of the Dorians **2** : belonging to the oldest and simplest Greek architectural order — see CAPITAL illustration

dorm \'dȯrm\ *n* : DORMITORY

dor-mant \'dȯr-mǝnt\ *adj* [MF, stationary, fr. prp. of *dormir* to sleep, fr. L *dormire*] **1** : not active but capable of resuming activity ⟨*dormant* volcano⟩ ⟨*dormant* talent⟩ **2 a** : sleeping or appearing to be asleep : SLUGGISH **b** : biologically inactive; *esp* : not actively growing ⟨a *dormant* bud⟩ **3** : of, relating to, or used during dormancy

⟨a *dormant* condition⟩ ⟨*dormant* sprays⟩ **syn** see LATENT — **dor-man-cy** \-mǝn-sē\ *n*

dor-mer \'dȯr-mǝr\ *n* : a window placed vertically in a roof; *also* : a roofed structure containing such a window

dor-mi-to-ry \'dȯr-mǝ-,tōr-ē, -,tȯr-\ *n, pl* **-ries** [L *dormire* to sleep] **1** : a room for sleeping; *esp* : a large room containing a number of beds **2** : a residence hall providing sleeping rooms

dor-mouse \'dȯ(ǝ)r-,maús\ *n, pl* **dor-mice** \-,mīs\ : any of numerous Old World rodents that resemble small squirrels

dors- *or* **dorsi-** *or* **dorso-** *comb form* [LL *dors-*, fr. L *dorsum*] **1** : back ⟨*dorsad*⟩ **2** : dorsal and ⟨*dorso*lateral⟩

dor-sad \'dȯ(ǝ)r-,sad\ *adv* : toward the back : DORSALLY

¹dor-sal \'dȯr-sǝl\ *adj* **1** : relating to or situated near or on the back (as of an animal) **2** : ABAXIAL — **dor-sal-ly** \-sǝ-lē\ *adv*

²dorsal *n* : a dorsally located part; *esp* : a thoracic vertebra

dorsal fin *n* : a fin on the median ridge of the back of a fish

dor-si-ven-tral \,dȯr-si-'ven-trǝl\ *adj* **1** : having distinct dorsal and ventral surfaces **2** : DORSOVENTRAL 1 — **dor-si-ven-tral-ly** \-trǝ-lē\ *adv*

dor-so-ven-tral \,dȯr-sō-'ven-trǝl\ *adj* **1** : extending from the dorsal toward the ventral side **2** : DORSIVENTRAL 1 — **dor-so-ven-tral-ly** \-trǝ-lē\ *adv*

dor-sum \'dȯr-sǝm\ *n, pl* **dor-sa** \-sǝ\ [L, back] : the dorsal surface (as of an animal or one of its parts)

do-ry \'dōr-ē, 'dȯr-\ *n, pl* **dories** [Miskito *dóri* dugout] : a flat-bottomed boat with a sharp bow and high sides that curve upward and outward

dos-age \'dō-sij\ *n* **1 a** : the giving of medicine in doses **b** : the amount of a single dose **2 a** : the addition of an ingredient or the application of an agent in a measured dose **b** : the presence and relative representation or strength of a factor or agent

¹dose \'dōs\ *n* [Gk *dosis*, lit., act of giving, fr. *didonai* to give] **1 a** : the measured amount of a medicine to be taken at one time **b** : the quantity of radiation administered or absorbed **2** : a portion of a substance added during a process **3** : an experience to which one is exposed ⟨a *dose* of defeat⟩

²dose *vt* **1** : to give medicine to **2** : to divide (as a medicine) into doses **3** : to treat with an application or agent

do-sim-e-ter \dō-'sim-ǝt-ǝr\ *n* : an instrument for measuring doses of X rays or of radioactivity

dos-sier \'dȯs-,yā, 'däs-ē-,ā\ *n* [F, bundle of documents labeled on the back, dossier, fr. *dos* back, fr. L *dorsum*] : a file of papers containing a detailed report or detailed information

dost \(')dǝst\ *archaic pres 2d sing of* DO

¹dot \'dät\ *n* [OE *dott* head of a boil] **1** : a small spot : SPECK **2 a** : a small point made with or as if with a pen **b** (1) : a point after a note or rest in music indicating increase of the time value by one half (2) : a point over or under a note indicating staccato **3** : a precise point in time or space **4** : a short click or buzz forming a letter or part of a letter (as in the Morse code)

²dot *vt* **dot-ted; dot-ting 1** : to mark with a dot ⟨*dot* an *i*⟩ **2** : to cover with or as if with dots ⟨a lake *dotted* with boats⟩ — **dot-ter** *n*

³dot *n* [F, fr. L *dot-, dos* dowry] : DOWRY — **do-tal** \'dōt-ᵊl\ *adj*

dot-age \'dōt-ij\ *n* : a state of feebleness or childishness of mind caused by or accompanying old age : SENILITY

dot-ard \'dōt-ǝrd\ *n* : a person in his dotage

dote \'dōt\ *vi* [ME *doten*] **1** : to be feebleminded esp. from old age **2** : to show excessive or foolish affection or fondness ⟨*doted* on her only nephew⟩ — **dot-er** *n* — **dot-ing-ly** \'dōt-iŋ-lē\ *adv*

doth \(')dǝth\ *archaic pres 3d sing of* DO

dot-ter-el \'dät-ǝ-rǝl, 'dä-trǝl\ *n* [ME *dotrelle*, irreg. fr. *doten* to dote] : a Eurasian plover formerly common in England; *also* : any of several related birds

dot-tle \'dät-ᵊl\ *n* : unburned and partially burned tobacco caked in the bowl of a pipe

dot-ty \'dät-ē\ *adj* **dot-ti-er; -est** : mentally unbalanced : CRAZY

dotterel

Dou·ay Version \dü-'ā-\ *n* [*Douay*, France, where it was published] **:** an English translation of the Vulgate used by Roman Catholics — see BIBLE table

¹**dou·ble** \'dəb-əl\ *adj* [OF, fr. L *duplus*, fr. *duo* two + -*plus* -fold; akin to E *fold*] **1 :** TWOFOLD, DUAL ⟨a *double* function⟩ **2 :** consisting of two members or parts **3 :** being twice as great or as many **4 :** marked by duplicity **:** DECEITFUL **5 :** folded in two **6 :** having more than the usual number of floral leaves ⟨*double* roses⟩ — **dou·ble·ness** *n*

²**double** *n* **1 a :** something twice another in size, strength, speed, quantity, or value ⟨12 is the *double* of 6⟩ **b :** TWO▪ BASE HIT **2 :** COUNTERPART, DUPLICATE ; *esp* **:** a person who closely resembles another **3 :** a sharp turn **:** REVERSAL **4 a :** FOLD **b :** a combined bet placed on two different contests **5** *pl* **:** a game between two pairs of players **6 :** an act of doubling in a card game

³**double** *adv* **1 :** to twice the extent or amount **:** DOUBLY **2 :** two together ⟨sleep *double*⟩

⁴**double** *vb* **dou·bled; dou·bling** \'dəb-(ə-)liŋ\ **1 a :** to make or be twice as great or as many **b :** to make a call in bridge that increases the value of odd tricks or under-tricks at (an opponent's bid) **2 a :** to make of two thicknesses **:** FOLD **b :** CLENCH **c :** to cause to stoop **d :** to become bent or folded usu. in the middle **3 :** to sail around (as a cape) by reversing direction **4 :** to take the place of another **5 a :** to become twice as much or as many ⟨prices *doubled* overnight⟩ **b :** to make a two-base hit **6 :** to turn sharply and suddenly; *esp* **:** to turn back on one's course — **dou·bler** \'dəb-(ə-)lər\ *n*

double bar *n* **:** two vertical lines or a heavy single line separating principal sections of a musical composition

double bass *n* **:** the largest instrument of the viol family

double bassoon *n* **:** CONTRABASSOON

double boiler *n* **:** a cooking utensil consisting of two saucepans fitting into each other so that the contents of the upper can be cooked or heated by boiling water in the lower

dou·ble-breast·ed \,dəb-əl-'bres-təd\ *adj* **:** having one half of the front lapped over the other and usu. two rows of buttons

double cross *n* **1 :** an act of betraying or cheating esp. an associate **2 :** a cross between first-generation hybrids of four separate inbred lines — **dou·ble-cross** \,dəb-əl-'krȯs\ *vt* — **dou·ble-cross·er** *n*

double dagger *n* **:** a character ‡ used as a reference mark

dou·ble-deal·ing \,dəb-əl-'dē-liŋ\ *n* **:** action contradictory to a professed attitude **:** DUPLICITY — **dou·ble-deal·er** *n* — **double-dealing** *adj*

dou·ble-deck·er \'dek-ər\ *n* **1 :** something (as a ship, bus, or bed) having two decks **2 :** a 2-layered sandwich

dou·ble en·ten·dre \,düb-(ə-),läⁿ-'täⁿdr°, ,dəb-\ *n, pl* **double entendres** *same*\ [obs. F, lit., double meaning] **:** a word or expression capable of two interpretations one of which is usu. indelicate

double entry *n* **:** a method of bookkeeping that debits the amount of a business transaction to one account and credits it to another so that the total debits equal the total credits

double fertilization *n* **:** fertilization characteristic of seed plants in which one sperm nucleus fuses with the egg to form an embryo and another fuses with polar nuclei to form endosperm

dou·ble-head·er \,dəb-əl-'hed-ər\ *n* **:** two games, contests, or events held consecutively on the same program

double hyphen *n* **:** a punctuation mark ⸗ used in place of a hyphen at the end of a line to indicate that the word so divided is normally hyphenated

dou·ble-joint·ed \,dəb-əl-'jȯint-əd\ *adj* **:** having a joint that permits exceptional degree of freedom of motion of the parts joined

double-knit *adj* **:** knitted with a double set of needles to produce a double thickness of fabric with each thickness joined by interlocking stitches — **double knit** *n*

double negative *n* **:** a syntactic construction containing two negatives and having a negative meaning (as in *I didn't hear nothing* meaning "I didn't hear anything")

dou·ble-park \,dəb-əl-'pärk\ *vb* **:** to park beside a row of automobiles already parked parallel to the curb

double play *n* **:** a play in baseball by which two players are put out

dou·ble-quick \'dəb-əl-,kwik\ *n* **:** DOUBLE TIME — **double-quick** *vi*

dou·ble-space \,dəb-əl-'spās\ *vb* **:** to type copy leaving every other line blank

double star *n* **1 :** BINARY STAR **2 :** two stars in very nearly the same line of sight but seen as physically separate by means of a telescope

double sugar *n* **:** DISACCHARIDE

dou·blet \'dəb-lət\ *n* **1 :** a close-fitting jacket worn by men of western Europe chiefly in the 16th century **2 :** one of two similar or identical things **3 :** one of two or more words in the same language derived by different routes of transmission from the same source ⟨*dish* and *disk* are *doublets*⟩

dou·ble-talk \'dəb-əl-,tȯk\ *n* **:** language that appears to be meaningful but in fact is a mixture of sense and nonsense

double time *n* **1 :** a marching cadence of 180 36-inch steps per minute **2 :** payment of a worker at twice his regular wage rate

dou·ble-time \'dəb-əl-,tīm\ *vi* **:** to move at double time

double twill *n* **:** a twill weave with intersecting diagonal lines going in opposite directions

dou·bloon \,də-'blün\ *n* [Sp *doblón*] **:** an old gold coin of Spain and Spanish America worth 16 pieces of eight

dou·bly \'dəb-lē\ *adv* **1 :** to twice the degree **2 :** in a twofold manner

¹**doubt** \'daút\ *vb* [OF *douter*, fr. L *dubitare*] **1 :** to be uncertain about **2 :** to lack confidence in **:** DISTRUST, FEAR **3 :** to consider unlikely — **doubt·a·ble** \-ə-bəl\ *adj* — **doubt·er** *n* — **doubt·ing·ly** \-iŋ-lē\ *adv*

²**doubt** *n* **1 :** uncertainty of belief or opinion **2 :** the condition of being objectively uncertain ⟨the outcome of the battle was still in *doubt*⟩ **3 a :** a lack of confidence **:** DISTRUST **b :** an inclination not to believe or accept

syn DISTRUST, SUSPICION: DOUBT implies uncertainty about the truth or reality of something and an inability to make a decision; DISTRUST implies lack of trust or confidence on vague or general grounds; SUSPICION stresses lack of faith in the truth or reality of someone or something and implies an often unfounded charge of wrongdoing **syn** see in addition UNCERTAINTY

doubt·ful \'daút-fəl\ *adj* **1 :** not clear or certain as to fact ⟨a *doubtful* claim⟩ **2 :** questionable in character ⟨*doubtful* intentions⟩ **3 :** not settled in opinion **:** UNDECIDED ⟨*doubtful* about what to do⟩ **4 :** not certain in outcome ⟨a *doubtful* battle⟩ — **doubt·ful·ly** \-fə-lē\ *adv* — **doubt·ful·ness** *n*

doubting Thom·as \-'täm-əs\ *n* [*Thomas*, apostle of Jesus who doubted Jesus' resurrection until he had proof of it (John 20:24–29)] **:** a habitually doubtful person

¹**doubt·less** \'daút-ləs\ *adv* **1 :** without doubt **2 :** PROBABLY

²**doubtless** *adj* **:** free from doubt **:** CERTAIN

douche \'düsh\ *n* [F] **1 a :** a jet of fluid (as water) directed against a part or into a cavity of the body **b :** a cleansing with a douche **2 :** a device for giving douches — **douche** *vb*

dough \'dō\ *n* [OE *dāg*] **:** a soft mass of moistened flour or meal thick enough to knead or roll; *also* **:** any similar soft pasty mass — **doughy** \'dō-ē\ *adj*

dough·boy \'dō-,bȯi\ *n* **:** an American infantryman esp. in World War I

dough·nut \-(,)nət\ *n* **:** a small usu. ring-shaped cake fried in fat

dough·ty \'daút-ē\ *adj* **dough·ti·er; -est** [OE *dohtig*] **:** being strong and valiant **:** BOLD — **dough·ti·ly** \'daút-°l-ē\ *adv* — **dough·ti·ness** \'daút-ē-nəs\ *n*

Doug·las fir \,dəg-ləs-\ *n* **:** a tall evergreen coniferous timber tree of the western U.S.

dour \'daú(ə)r, 'dú(ə)r\ *adj* [L *durus* hard] **1 :** STERN, HARSH **2 :** GLOOMY, SULLEN — **dour·ly** *adv* — **dour·ness** *n*

¹**douse** \'daús\ *vt* **:** to take in ⟨*douse* a sail⟩

²**douse** \'daús, 'daúz\ *vt* **1 a :** to plunge into water **b :** to throw a liquid on **:** DRENCH **2 :** to put out **:** EXTINGUISH

¹**dove** \'dəv\ *n* [ME] **1 :** any of numerous pigeons; *esp* **:** a small wild pigeon **2 :** an individual who takes a conciliatory attitude (as in a dispute) and advocates negotiations and compromise; *esp* **:** an opponent of war — compare HAWK — **dov·ish** \'dəv-ish\ *adj*

²**dove** \'dōv\ *past of* DIVE

dove·cote \'dəv-,kōt, -,kät\ *or* **dove·cot** \-,kät\ *n* **:** a small raised house or box with compartments for domestic pigeons

dove·kie \'dəv-kē\ n : a small short-billed auk breeding on arctic coasts and ranging south in winter

¹**dove·tail** \'dəv-ˌtāl\ n : something resembling a dove's tail; esp : a flaring tenon and a mortise into which it fits tightly making an interlocking joint between two pieces

²**dovetail** vb **1 a** : to join by means of dovetails **b** : to cut to a dovetail **2** : to fit skillfully together to form a whole

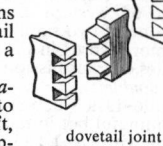

dovetail joint

dow·a·ger \'daù-i-jər\ n [MF douagiere, fr. douage dower, fr. douer to endow, fr. L dotare, fr. dot-, dos gift, dower] **1** : a widow holding property or a title received from her deceased husband **2** : a dignified elderly woman

¹**dowdy** \'daùd-ē\ n, pl **dowd·ies** [dim. of ME doude] : a dowdy woman

²**dowdy** adj **dowd·i·er; -est** : not neatly or becomingly dressed or cared for : SHABBY, UNTIDY — **dowd·i·ly** \'daùd-ᵊl-ē\ adv — **dowd·i·ness** \'daùd-ē-nəs\ n

¹**dow·el** \'daù-(ə)l\ n [ME dowle] : a pin or peg projecting from one of two parts or surfaces (as of wood) to be fastened together and fitting into a hole prepared in the other part

²**dowel** vt **-eled** or **-elled; -el·ing** or **-el·ling** : to fasten by or furnish with dowels

¹**dow·er** \'daù-(ə)r\ n **1** : the part of or interest in the real estate of a deceased husband given by law to his widow during her life **2** : DOWRY

²**dower** vt : to supply with a dower or dowry : ENDOW

¹**down** \'daùn\ n [OE dūn hill] : an undulating usu. treeless upland with sparse soil — usu. used in pl.

²**down** adv [OE dūne, short for adūne, fr. a- off, from (fr. of) + dūne, dat. of dūn hill] **1 a** (1) : toward or in a lower physical position (2) : to a lying or sitting position (3) : toward or to the ground, floor, or bottom **b** : in cash ⟨paid $10 down⟩ **2** : in a direction that is the opposite of up : as **a** : SOUTH **b** : away from a center **3** : to or in a lower or worse condition, level, or status **4** : from a past time ⟨heirlooms handed down⟩ **5** : to or in a state of less activity ⟨excitement died down⟩ **6** : from a thinner to a thicker consistency

³**down** adj **1 a** : occupying a low position; esp : lying on the ground **b** : directed or going downward ⟨a down car⟩ **c** : being at a lower level ⟨sales were down because of bad weather⟩ **2 a** : being in a state of reduced or low activity **b** (1) : DEPRESSED, DEJECTED (2) : SICK ⟨down with flu⟩ (3) : having a low opinion or dislike ⟨down on him⟩ **3** : FINISHED, DONE ⟨eight down and two to go⟩ **4** : being the part of a price paid at the time of purchase or delivery ⟨a down payment⟩

⁴**down** prep : down along : down through : down toward : down in : down into : down on ⟨down the road⟩⟨down the well⟩

⁵**down** n **1** : a low or falling period (as in activity, emotional life, or fortunes) ⟨have their ups and downs⟩ **2** : the ending of an attempt to advance a football by the referee's signal or the attempt itself

⁶**down** vb : to go or cause to go or come down

⁷**down** n [ON dūnn] **1** : a covering of soft fluffy feathers **2** : something soft and fluffy like down

down·beat \'daùn-ˌbēt\ n : the downward stroke of a conductor indicating the principally accented note of a measure of music

down·cast \-ˌkast\ adj **1** : DISCOURAGED, DEJECTED ⟨a downcast manner⟩ **2** : directed down ⟨a downcast glance⟩

down·er \'daù-nər\ n : a depressant drug; esp : BARBITURATE

down·fall \'daùn-ˌfȯl\ n **1** : FALL; esp : a sudden or heavy fall (as of rain) **2** : a sudden descent (as from a high position) : RUIN ⟨the downfall of the beaten champion⟩ — **down·fall·en** \-ˌfȯ-lən\ adj

¹**down·grade** \-ˌgrād\ n **1** : a downward grade or slope **2** : a decline toward a worse condition ⟨a neighborhood on the downgrade⟩ — **down·grade** \-'grād\ adv

²**down·grade** \-ˌgrād\ vt : to lower in grade, rank, position, or status

down·heart·ed \'daùn-'härt-əd\ adj : DEJECTED — **down·heart·ed·ly** adv — **down·heart·ed·ness** n

¹**down·hill** \'daùn-'hil\ adv : toward the bottom of a hill : DOWNWARD

²**downhill** \-ˌhil\ adj : sloping downhill

down·pour \'daùn-ˌpōr, -ˌpȯr\ n : a heavy rain

down·range \-'rānj\ adv (or adj) : toward the target area of a firing range ⟨a missile landing 5000 miles downrange⟩

¹**down·right** \-ˌrīt\ adv : THOROUGHLY ⟨downright mean⟩

²**downright** adj **1** : ABSOLUTE, THOROUGH ⟨a downright lie⟩ **2** : PLAIN, BLUNT ⟨a downright man⟩ — **down·right·ly** adv — **down·right·ness** n

down·stage \-'stāj\ adv (or adj) : toward or at the front of a theatrical stage

¹**down·stairs** \-'sta(ə)rz, -'ste(ə)rz\ adv : down the stairs : on or to a lower floor

²**downstairs** \-ˌsta(ə)rz, -ˌste(ə)rz\ adj : situated on a lower floor or on the main or ground floor

³**downstairs** \'daùn-', ˌdaùn-,\ n : the lower floor of a building

down·stream \'daùn-'strēm\ adv (or adj) : in the direction of flow of a stream

down·stroke \-ˌstrōk\ n : a stroke made in a downward direction

down·swing \-ˌswiŋ\ n **1** : a swing downward **2** : DOWNTURN

down–to–earth \ˌdaùn-tə-'(w)ərth\ adj : PRACTICAL, REALISTIC

¹**down·town** \'daùn-'taùn\ adv : to, toward, or in the lower part or business center of a town or city

²**downtown** \-ˌtaùn\ adj **1** : situated downtown **2** : of or relating to the business center of a town or city

³**downtown** \-ˌtaùn\ n : an urban business center

down·trod·den \'daùn-'träd-ᵊn\ adj : crushed by superior power : OPPRESSED

down·turn \-ˌtərn\ n **1** : a turning downward **2** : a decline esp. in business activity

¹**down·ward** \'daùn-wərd\ also **down·wards** \-wərdz\ adv **1** : in a direction from higher to lower **2** : from a higher to a lower condition **3 a** : from an earlier time **b** : from an ancestor or predecessor

²**downward** adj **1** : directed toward or situated in a lower place or condition : DESCENDING **2** : descending from a head, origin, or source

down·wind \'daùn-'wind\ adv (or adj) : in the direction that the wind is blowing : LEEWARD

downy \'daù-nē\ adj **down·i·er; -est** **1 a** : resembling a bird's down **b** : covered with or made of down **2** : SOFT, SOOTHING

downy mildew n : a parasitic mold that produces whitish masses of sporangia or conidia on the undersurface of the leaves of the host; also : a plant disease caused by a downy mildew

dow·ry \'daù(ə)r-ē\ n, pl **dowries** [AF dowarie, fr. ML dotarium, fr. L dot-, dos gift, dower] : the property that a woman brings to her husband in marriage

dowse \'daùz\ vb : to use a divining rod esp. to find water — **dows·er** n

dox·ol·o·gy \däk-'säl-ə-jē\ n, pl **-gies** [Gk doxa opinion, glory + -logia -logy] : an expression of praise to God; esp, cap : a hymn beginning "Praise God from whom all blessings flow" — compare GLORIA

doze \'dōz\ vi : to sleep lightly — **doze** n — **doz·er** n

doz·en \'dəz-ᵊn\ n, pl **dozens** or **dozen** [OF dozaine, fr. doze twelve, fr. L duodecim, fr. duo two + decem ten] : a group of twelve — **dozen** adj — **doz·enth** \-ᵊn(t)th\ adj

DP \(')dē-'pē\ n : a displaced person

¹**drab** \'drab\ n **1** : SLATTERN **2** : PROSTITUTE

²**drab** n [MF drap cloth, fr. LL drappus] : a light olive brown

³**drab** adj **drab·ber; drab·best** **1** : of the color drab **2** : characterized by dullness and monotony : CHEERLESS ⟨she leads a drab life⟩ — **drab·ly** adv — **drab·ness** n

drachm \'dram\ n **1** : DRACHMA **2** : DRAM

drach·ma \'drak-mə\ n, pl **drach·mas** or **drach·mae** \-(ˌ)mē, -ˌmī\ or **drach·mai** \-ˌmī\ [L, drachma, dram, fr. Gk drachmē] **1 a** : any of various ancient Greek units of weight **b** : any of various modern units of weight; esp : DRAM 1 **2 a** : an ancient Greek silver coin equivalent to 6 obols **b** : the basic monetary unit of modern Greece; also : a coin representing this unit

Dra·co \'drā-kō\ n [L, lit., dragon] : a northern circumpolar constellation between the Big Dipper and Little Dipper

¹draft \'draft, 'dráft\ *n* [ME *draght;* akin to E *draw*] **1** : the act of drawing a net; *also* : the quantity of fish taken at one drawing **2** : the act of moving loads by drawing or pulling : PULL **3 a** : the force required to pull an implement **b** : load or load-pulling capacity **4 a** : the act or an instance of drinking or inhaling; *also* : the portion drunk or inhaled in one such act **b** : a potion prepared for drinking : DOSE **5 a** : DELINEATION, REPRESENTATION; *esp* : a construction plan **b** : SCHEME, DESIGN **c** : a preliminary sketch, outline, or version ⟨submit a rough *draft* of a thesis⟩ **6** : the act, result, or plan of drawing out or stretching **7 a** : the act of drawing (as from a cask) **b** : a portion of liquid so drawn **8** : an allowance granted a buyer for loss in weight **9** : the depth of water a ship draws esp. when loaded **10 a** : the selection of a person esp. for compulsory military service **b** : a group of persons selected **11 a** : an order (as a check) issued by one party to another (as a bank) to pay money to a third party **b** : a heavy demand : STRAIN ⟨a *draft* on national resources⟩ **12 a** : a current of air in a closed-in space **b** : a device for regulating the flow of air (as in a fireplace) **13** : ANGLE, TAPER; *esp* : the taper given to a pattern or die so that the work can be easily withdrawn **14** : a narrow border along the edge of a stone or across its face serving as a stonecutter's guide **15** : a system whereby exclusive rights to selected new players are apportioned among professional teams — **on draft** : ready to be drawn from a receptacle ⟨beer *on draft*⟩

²draft *adj* **1** : used for drawing loads ⟨*draft* animals⟩ **2** : constituting a preliminary or tentative version, sketch, or outline ⟨a *draft* treaty⟩ **3** : being on draft; *also* : DRAWN

³draft *vt* **1** : to select usu. on a compulsory basis; *esp* : to conscript for military service **2 a** : to draw up a preliminary sketch, version, or plan of **b** : to draw up : COMPOSE, PREPARE ⟨*draft* a constitution⟩ **3** : to draw off or away — **draft·er** *n*

draft·ee \draf-'tē, dráf-\ *n* : a person who is drafted esp. into the armed forces

drafts·man \'draf(t)s-mən, 'dráf(t)s-\ *n* : one who draws plans and sketches — **drafts·man·ship** \-,ship\ *n*

drafty \'draf-tē, 'dráf-\ *adj* **draf·ti·er; -est** : relating to or exposed to a draft ⟨a *drafty* hall⟩ — **draft·i·ly** \-tə-lē\ *adv* — **draft·i·ness** \-tē-nəs\ *n*

¹drag \'drag\ *n* **1** : something that is dragged, pulled, or drawn along or over a surface: as **a** : HARROW **b** : a sledge for carrying heavy loads **c** : CONVEYANCE **2** : something used to drag with; *esp* : a device for dragging under water or along the bottom to detect or obtain objects **3 a** : something that retards motion **b** : the retarding force acting on a body (as an airplane) moving through a fluid (as air) parallel and opposite to the direction of motion **c** : friction between engine parts **d** : something that hinders or obstructs progress **4 a** : the act or an instance of dragging or drawing **b** : a drawing along or over a surface with effort or pressure **c** : motion effected with slowness or difficulty; *also* : the condition of having or seeming to have such motion **d** : a draw on a pipe, cigarette, or cigar : PUFF; *also* : a draft of liquid **5** : a movement, inclination, or retardation caused by or as if by dragging **6** *slang* : influence securing special favor or partiality **7** : something characterized by slow retarded motion **8** *slang* : STREET, ROAD ⟨the main *drag*⟩

²drag *vb* **dragged; drag·ging** [ON *draga* or OE *dragan*] **1 a** : to draw slowly or heavily : HAUL **b** : to move or cause to move with painful slowness or difficulty ⟨he *drags* one leg⟩ ⟨the story *drags*⟩ **c** : to force into or out of some situation, condition, or course of action **d** : to pass (a period of time) in lingering pain, tedium, or unhappiness **e** : PROTRACT ⟨*drag* a story out⟩ **2** : to hang or lag behind **3** : to trail along on the ground **4** : to explore, search, or fish with a drag **5** : DRAW, PUFF ⟨*drag* on a cigarette⟩

drag·ger \'drag-ər\ *n* : one that drags; *esp* : a fishing boat operating a trawl or dragnet

drag·gle \'drag-əl\ *vb* **drag·gled; drag·gling** \'drag-(ə-)liŋ\ [freq. of *drag*] **1** : to make or become wet and dirty by dragging **2** : to follow slowly : STRAGGLE

drag·gy \'drag-ē\ *adj* **drag·gi·er; -est** : SLUGGISH, DULL

drag·net \'drag-,net\ *n* **1 a** : a net drawn along the bottom of a body of water : TRAWL **b** : a net used (as for

capturing small game) on the ground **2** : a network of planned actions for pursuing and catching a criminal

drag·o·man \'drag-ə-mən\ *n, pl* **-mans** *or* **-men** \-mən\ [MGk *dragomanos,* fr. Ar *tarjumān,* fr. Aram *tūrgĕmānā*] : an interpreter chiefly of Arabic, Turkish, or Persian employed esp. in the Near East

drag·on \'drag-ən\ *n* [OF, fr. L *dracon-, draco,* lit., serpent, fr. Gk *drakōn*] **1** : a fabulous animal usu. represented as a monstrous winged and scaly serpent or saurian with a crested head and enormous claws **2** : a violent or very strict person **3** *cap* : DRACO

drag·on·fly \-,flī\ *n* : any of an order (Odonata) of large harmless insects that have four long wings and feed esp. on flies, gnats, and mosquitoes — compare DAMSELFLY

¹dra·goon \drə-'gün, dra-\ *n* [F *dragon* dragon, dragoon] : a cavalry soldier

²dragoon *vt* : to force or attempt to force into submission by violent measures

dragonfly

drag race *n* : an acceleration contest between vehicles

¹drain \'drān\ *vb* [OE *drēahnian*] **1 a** : to draw off or flow off gradually or completely ⟨*drain* water from a tank⟩ **b** : to cause the gradual disappearance of : DWINDLE **c** : to exhaust physically or emotionally **2 a** : to make or become gradually dry or empty ⟨let the dishes *drain*⟩ **b** : to carry away the surface water of : discharge surface or surplus water **c** : EMPTY, EXHAUST — **drain·er** *n*

²drain *n* **1** : a means by which liquid or other matter is drained **2 a** : the act of draining **b** : a gradual outflow or withdrawal : DEPLETION **3** : something that causes depletion : BURDEN ⟨a *drain* on one's resources⟩

drain·age \'drā-nij\ *n* **1** : the act, process, or mode of draining; *also* : something drained off **2** : a means for draining; *also* : a system of drains **3** : an area drained

drain·pipe \'drān-,pīp\ *n* : a pipe for drainage

¹drake \'drāk\ *n* [OE *draca* dragon] : MAYFLY

²drake *n* [ME] : a male duck

dram \'dram\ *n* [MF *dragme* dram, drachma, fr. L *drachma,* fr. Gk *drachmē,* lit., handful, fr. *drassesthai* to grasp] **1 a** — see MEASURE table **b** : FLUIDRAM **2 a** : a small portion of something to drink **b** : a small amount

dra·ma \'dräm-ə, 'dram-\ *n* [Gk *dramat-, drama* deed, drama, fr. *dran* to do] **1** : a composition in verse or prose intended to portray life or character or to tell a story through action and dialogue and designed for theatrical performance : PLAY **2** : dramatic art, literature, or affairs **3 a** : a state, situation, or series of events involving interesting or intense conflict of forces ⟨the *drama* of a hockey game⟩ **b** : dramatic state, effect, or quality

Dram·a·mine \'dram-ə-,mēn\ *trademark* — used for a crystalline compound used in the prevention or treatment of motion sickness

dra·mat·ic \drə-'mat-ik\ *adj* **1** : of or relating to the drama **2 a** : suitable to or characteristic of the drama : VIVID **b** : striking in appearance or effect — **dra·mat·i·cal·ly** \-'mat-i-k(ə-)lē\ *adv*

syn DRAMATIC, THEATRICAL, HISTRIONIC, applied to life, mean having a character or an effect like that of acted plays. DRAMATIC applies to situations in life and literature when they give evidence of power to stir deeply the imagination and emotions; THEATRICAL implies a crude appeal through artificiality or exaggeration in gesture or vocal expression ⟨a *theatrical* oration⟩ HISTRIONIC applies to tones, gestures, and motions and suggests a deliberate affectation or staginess ⟨a *histrionic* show of grief⟩

dra·mat·ics \-iks\ *n sing or pl* **1 a** : theatricals esp. as an extracurricular activity in school or college **b** : theatrical technique **2** : dramatic behavior or expression

dra·ma·tis per·so·nae \,dram-ət-əs-pər-'sō-(,)nē, -,nī\ *pl* [NL] : the characters or actors in a drama

dram·a·tist \'dram-ət-əst, 'dräm-\ *n* : PLAYWRIGHT

dram·a·tize \'dram-ə-,tīz, 'dräm-\ *vb* **1** : to adapt for or be suitable for theatrical presentation **2** : to present or represent in a dramatic manner — **dram·a·ti·za·tion** \,dram-ət-ə-'zā-shən, ,dräm-\ *n*

dram·a·tur·gy \'dram-ə-,tər-jē, 'dräm-\ *n* [Gk *dramatourgia* dramatic composition, fr. *dramat-, drama* drama + *ergon* work] : the art or technique of dramatic composi-

---

j joke; ŋ sing; ō flow; ȯ flaw; ȯi coin; th thin; t͟h this; ü loot; u̇ foot; y yet; yü few; yu̇ furious; zh vision

tion and theatrical representation — **dram·a·tur·gic** \,dram-ə-'tər-jik, ,dräm-\ *adj*

drank *past of* DRINK

¹drape \'drāp\ *vb* [MF *drap* cloth, fr. L *drappus*] **1** : to cover or adorn with or as if with folds of cloth ⟨the speaker's platform was *draped* with bunting⟩ **2** : to cause to hang or stretch out loosely or carelessly ⟨he *draped* himself over the counter⟩ **3** : to arrange or become arranged in flowing lines or folds ⟨*drape* a gown⟩

²drape *n* **1** : a drapery esp. for a window : CURTAIN **2** : arrangement in or of folds **3** : the cut or hang of clothing ⟨the *drape* of his jacket⟩

drap·er \'drā-pər\ *n* **1** *Brit* : a dealer in cloth and sometimes also in clothing and dry goods **2** : one that drapes

drap·ery \'drā-p(ə-)rē\ *n, pl* **-er·ies 1** *Brit* : DRY GOODS **2** *Brit* : the occupation of a draper **3 a** : a decorative fabric usu. hung in loose folds and arranged in a graceful design **b** : hangings of heavy fabric for use as a curtain **c** : loose coverings for furniture **4** : the draping or arranging of materials

dras·tic \'dras-tik\ *adj* [Gk *drastikos*, fr. *dran* to do] **1** : acting rapidly or violently ⟨a *drastic* purgative⟩ **2** : extreme in effect : SEVERE ⟨*drastic* changes in the law⟩ — **dras·ti·cal·ly** \-ti-k(ə-)lē\ *adv*

draught \'draft, 'dràft\ *chiefly Brit var of* DRAFT

draughts \'draf(t)s, 'dràf(t)s\ *n, Brit* : CHECKERS

Dra·vid·i·an \drə-'vid-ē-ən\ *n* **1** : a member of an ancient Australoid race of southern India **2** : any of several languages of India, Ceylon, and West Pakistan constituting a language family — **Dravidian** *adj*

¹draw \'drò\ *vb* **drew** \'drü\; **drawn** \'dròn\; **draw·ing** [OE *dragan*] **1** : to cause to move continuously toward or after a force applied in advance : HAUL, DRAG **2 a** : to cause to go in a certain direction (as by leading) ⟨*drew* him aside⟩ **b** : to move or go steadily or gradually ⟨night *draws* near⟩ **3 a** : ATTRACT, ENTICE ⟨honey *draws* flies⟩ **b** : PROVOKE, ROUSE ⟨*drew* enemy fire⟩ **4** : INHALE ⟨*drew* a deep breath⟩ **5 a** : to bring or pull out ⟨*draw* a sword⟩ ⟨*drew*, aimed, and fired⟩ **b** : to force out from cover or possession ⟨*drew* trumps⟩ **c** : to extract the essence from : STEEP ⟨*draw* tea⟩ **d** : EVISCERATE **6** : to require (a specified depth) to float in **7 a** : ACCUMULATE, GAIN ⟨*drawing* interest⟩ **b** : to take money from a place of deposit **c** : WITHDRAW **d** : to receive regularly from a source ⟨*draw* a salary⟩ **8 a** : to take (cards) from a stack or the dealer **b** : to receive or take at random ⟨*drew* a winning number⟩ **9** : to bend (a bow) by pulling back the string **10 a** : to cause to shrink or pucker : WRINKLE **b** : to change shape by or as if by pulling or stretching ⟨a face *drawn* with sorrow⟩ **11** : to strike (a ball) so as to impart a backward spin **12** : to leave (a contest) undecided : TIE **13 a** : to produce a likeness of by making lines on a surface : DELINEATE, SKETCH **b** : to write out in due form : DRAFT ⟨*draw* up a will⟩ **c** : to design or describe in detail : FORMULATE ⟨*draw* comparisons⟩ **14** : DEDUCE ⟨*draw* a conclusion⟩ **15** : to spread or elongate (metal) by hammering or by pulling through dies **16 a** : to produce or allow a draft or current of air ⟨the furnace *draws* well⟩ **b** : to swell out in a wind ⟨all sails *drawing*⟩

²draw *n* **1** : the act, process, or result of drawing **2** : a lot or chance drawn at random ⟨a win at the first *draw*⟩ **3** : the movable part of a drawbridge **4** : a contest left undecided or deadlocked : TIE **5** : something that draws attention or patronage **6** : a gully shallower than a ravine

draw away *vi* : to move ahead (as of an opponent in a race) ⟨the brown horse soon *drew away* from the others⟩

draw·back \'dro-,bak\ *n* : an objectionable feature : HINDRANCE

draw·bar \-,bär\ *n* **1** : a railroad coupler **2** : a beam across the rear of a tractor to which implements are hitched

draw·bridge \-,brij\ *n* : a bridge made to be wholly or partly raised up, let down, or drawn aside so as to permit or hinder passage

draw·ee \dro-'ē\ *n* : the party (as a bank) ordered to pay a draft

draw·er \'dro(-ə)r\ *n* **1** : one that draws: as **a** : a person who draws liquor **b** : DRAFTSMAN **c** : one who

drawbridge of a medieval castle

executes a draft or makes a promissory note **2** : a sliding box or receptacle (as in a table or desk) opened by pulling out and closed by pushing in **3** *pl* : an undergarment for the lower part of the body

draw·ing \'dro-iŋ\ *n* **1** : an act or instance of drawing; *esp* : an occasion when something (as the winner of a raffle) is decided by drawing lots **2** : the act, art, or technique of representing an object or outlining a figure, plan, or sketch by means of lines **3** : something drawn or subject to drawing; *esp* : a representation formed by drawing : SKETCH

drawing board *n* : a board on which paper to be drawn on is fastened

drawing card *n* : something that attracts attention or patronage

drawing room *n* [short for *withdrawing room*] **1 a** : a formal reception room **b** : a private room on a railroad passenger car with three berths and an enclosed toilet **2** : a formal reception ⟨at the queen's *drawing room*⟩

draw·knife \'dro-,nīf\ *n* : a woodworker's tool having a blade with a handle at each end used to shave off surfaces — called also *draw·shave* \-,shāv\

¹drawl \'dròl\ *vb* [prob. freq. of *draw*] : to speak slowly with vowels greatly prolonged : utter in a slow lengthened tone — **drawl·er** *n* — **drawl·ing·ly** \'dro-liŋ-lē\ *adv*

²drawl *n* : a drawling manner of speaking

drawn butter *n* : melted butter often with seasoning

drawn·work \'dron-,wərk\ *n* : decoration on cloth made by drawing out threads according to a pattern

draw on *vb* **1 a** : APPROACH ⟨night *draws on*⟩ **b** : to bring on : CAUSE **2** : to take funds from ⟨*draw on* a bank account⟩

draw out *vt* **1** : REMOVE, EXTRACT **2** : to cause to speak out freely ⟨tried to *draw* him *out* on the subject⟩

draw·string \'dro-,striŋ\ *n* : a string, cord, or tape inserted into hems or casings or laced through eyelets for use in closing a bag or controlling fullness in garments or curtains

draw·tube \-,t(y)üb\ *n* : a telescoping tube (as for the eyepiece of a microscope)

draw up *vb* **1** : to arrange (as a body of troops) in order **2** : to straighten (oneself) to an erect posture **3** : to bring to a halt : STOP

¹dray \'drā\ *n* [ME *draye*, a wheelless vehicle, fr. OE *dræge* dragnet] : a vehicle used to haul goods; *esp* : a strong low cart or wagon without sides

²dray *vb* : to carry or transport on a dray

dray·age \'drā-ij\ *n* : the work or cost of draying

dray·man \'drā-mən\ *n* : one whose work is draying

¹dread \'dred\ *vb* [OE *drǣdan*] **1 a** : to fear greatly : be apprehensive or fearful **b** *archaic* : REVERENCE **2** : to feel extreme reluctance to meet or face

²dread *n* **1 a** : great fear esp. in the face of impending evil or harm **b** *archaic* : AWE **2** : one causing fear or awe **syn** *see* FEAR

³dread *adj* **1** : causing great fear or anxiety **2** : inspiring awe

¹dread·ful \'dred-fəl\ *adj* **1** : inspiring dread or awe : FRIGHTENING **2** : extremely distasteful, unpleasant, or shocking — **dread·ful·ly** \-f(ə-)lē\ *adv* — **dread·ful·ness** \-fəl-nəs\ *n*

²dreadful *n* : a cheap and sensational story or periodical

dread·nought \'dred-,nòt, -,nät\ *n* [fr. *Dreadnought*, a British battleship] : a battleship whose main armament consists entirely of big guns all of the same caliber

¹dream \'drēm\ *n* [OE *drēam* noise, joy] **1** : a series of thoughts, images, or emotions occurring during sleep **2 a** : a visionary creation of the imagination : DAYDREAM **b** : a state of mind in which a person is lost in fancies or reveries **c** : an object seen in a dreamlike state : VISION **3** : something notable for its beauty, excellence, or enjoyable quality **4** : a goal or purpose ardently desired : IDEAL — **dream·like** \-,līk\ *adj*

²dream \'drēm\ *vb* **dreamed** \'drem(p)t, 'drēmd\ *or* **dreamt** \'drem(p)t\; **dream·ing** \'drē-miŋ\ **1** : to have a dream of **2** : to indulge in daydreams or fantasies **:** pass (time) in reverie or inaction **3** : to conceive as possible, fitting, or proper : IMAGINE ⟨*dreamed* of success⟩ **4** : to appear tranquil or dreamy

dream·er \'drē-mər\ *n* **1** : one who dreams **2 a** : one who lives in a world of fancy and imagination **b** : one who has ideas or conceives projects regarded as impractical : VISIONARY

dream·land \'drēm-,land\ *n* : an unreal delightful country existing only in imagination or in dreams

dream·world \'drēm-,wərld\ *n* : DREAMLAND; *also* : a world of illusion or fantasy

dreamy \'drē-mē\ *adj* **dream·i·er; -est 1 a** : full of dreams **b** : VAGUE **2** : given to dreaming or fantasy **3 a** : having the quality or characteristics of a dream **b** : quiet and soothing ⟨*dreamy* music⟩ **c** : DELIGHTFUL, PLEASING — **dream·i·ly** \-mə-lē\ *adv* — **dream·i·ness** \-mē-nəs\ *n*

drear \'dri(ə)r\ *adj* : DREARY

drea·ry \'dri(ə)r-ē\ *adj* **drea·ri·er** \'drir-ē-ər\; **-est** [OE *drēorig* sad, bloody, fr. *drēor* gore] **1** : DOLEFUL, SAD **2** : causing feelings of cheerlessness : GLOOMY ⟨a *dreary* landscape⟩ — **drea·ri·ly** \'drir-ə-lē\ *adv* — **drea·ri·ness** \'drir-ē-nəs\ *n*

¹dredge \'drej\ *n* **1** : an oblong iron frame with an attached bag net used esp. for gathering fish and shellfish **2** : a machine for removing earth usu. by buckets on an endless chain or a suction tube **3** : a barge used in dredging

²dredge *vb* **1** : to dig, gather, or pull out with or as if with a dredge ⟨*dredge* a channel⟩ ⟨*dredge* up something from his memory⟩ **2** : to search with or as if with a dredge ⟨*dredging* for oysters⟩ — **dredg·er** *n*

³dredge *vt* [ME *drage, drege* sweetmeat, fr. MF *dragie,* modif. of L *tragemata* sweetmeats, fr. Gk *tragēmata,* pl. of *tragēma* sweetmeat, fr. *trōgein* to gnaw] : to coat (food) by sprinkling (as with flour) — **dredg·er** *n*

dreg \'dreg\ *n* [ON *dregg*] **1** : sediment contained in a liquid or precipitated from it : LEES — usu. used in pl. **2** : the most undesirable part — usu. used in pl. ⟨the *dregs* of humanity⟩ **3** : the last remaining part : VESTIGE

¹drench \'drench\ *n* **1** : a medicinal potion for a domestic animal **2 a** : something that drenches **b** : a quantity sufficient to drench or saturate

²drench *vt* [OE *drencan;* akin to E *drink*] **1 a** *archaic* : to force to drink **b** : to administer a drench to (an animal) **2** : to wet thoroughly : SATURATE

¹dress \'dres\ *vb* [MF *dresser,* fr. (assumed) VL *directiare,* fr. L *directus* straight, direct] **1 a** : to make or set straight **b** : to arrange (as troops) in a straight line and at proper intervals **2** *archaic* : to dress down **3 a** : to put clothes on **b** : to provide with clothing **c** : to put on or wear formal or fancy clothes **4** : to add decorative details or accessories to : EMBELLISH ⟨*dress* a store window⟩ **5** : to put in order for use or service **6 a** : to apply dressings or medicaments to **b** : to arrange (the hair) by combing, brushing, or curling **c** : to prepare (an animal) by grooming and currying **d** : to kill and prepare for market ⟨*dress* a chicken⟩ **e** : CULTIVATE, TEND; *esp* : to apply manure or fertilizer to **7** : SMOOTH, FINISH ⟨*dress* timber⟩

²dress *n* **1** : APPAREL, CLOTHING **2** : an outer garment for a woman or child : FROCK, GOWN **3** : covering, adornment, or appearance appropriate or peculiar to a particular time **4** : the particular style in which something is presented : GUISE

³dress *adj* **1** : relating to or used for a dress ⟨*dress* goods⟩ **2** : suitable for a formal occasion ⟨*dress* clothes⟩ **3** : requiring or permitting formal dress ⟨a *dress* affair⟩

dres·sage \drə-'säzh\ *n* : the execution by a horse of complex maneuvers in response to barely perceptible movements of a rider's hands, legs, and weight

dress circle *n* : the first or lowest curved tier of seats in a theater

dress down *vt* : to reprove severely — **dressing down** *n*

¹dress·er \'dres-ər\ *n* **1** *obs* : a table or sideboard for preparing and serving food **2** : a cupboard to hold dishes and cooking utensils **3** : a chest of drawers or bureau with a mirror

²dresser *n* : one that dresses ⟨a window *dresser*⟩

dress·ing *n* **1 a** : the act or process of one who dresses **b** : an instance of this act or process **2 a** : a sauce for adding to a dish **b** : a seasoned mixture usu. used as a stuffing (as for poultry) **3 a** : material used to cover an injury **b** : fertilizing material **4** : DRESSING DOWN

dressing gown *n* : a loose robe worn esp. while dressing or resting

dressing room *n* : a room used chiefly for dressing; *esp*

: a room in a theater for changing costumes and makeup

dressing station *n* : a station for giving first aid to the wounded

dressing table *n* : a low table often fitted with drawers and a mirror in front of which one sits while dressing

dress·mak·er \'dres-,mā-kər\ *n* : one that does dressmaking

dress·mak·ing \-kiŋ\ *n* : the process or occupation of making dresses

dress parade *n* : a formal ceremonial parade (as of soldiers) in dress uniform

dress rehearsal *n* : a full rehearsal of a play in costume and with stage properties shortly before the first performance

dress shirt *n* : a man's white shirt esp. for wear with evening dress

dress suit *n* : a suit worn for full dress

dress uniform *n* : a uniform for formal wear

dressy \'dres-ē\ *adj* **dress·i·er; -est 1** : showy in dress **2** : STYLISH, SMART

drew *past of* DRAW

¹drib·ble \'drib-əl\ *vb* **drib·bled; drib·bling** \'drib-(ə-)liŋ\ [freq. of *drib* to dribble] **1** : to fall or flow or let fall or flow in drops or in a thin intermittent stream : TRICKLE **2** : DROOL, SLOBBER **3 a** : to come or issue little by little ⟨replies came *dribbling* in⟩ **b** : FRITTER **4** : to propel by tapping, bouncing, or kicking ⟨*dribble* a basketball⟩ — **drib·bler** \-(ə-)lər\ *n*

²dribble *n* **1 a** : a small trickling stream or flow **b** : a drizzling shower **2** : a tiny or insignificant bit or quantity **3** : an act or instance of dribbling a ball or puck

drib·let \'drib-lət\ *n* **1** : a trifling sum or part : a small amount **2** : a falling drop

dri·er *also* **dry·er** \'drī-(ə)r\ *n* **1** : something that extracts or absorbs moisture **2** : a substance that accelerates drying (as of oils, paints, and printing inks) **3** *usu* dryer : a device for drying

¹drift \'drift\ *n* [ME; akin to E *drive*] **1 a** : the act of driving something along **b** : the flow of a river or ocean stream **2 a** : wind-driven snow, rain, or smoke usu. near the ground surface **b** : a mass of matter (as sand) deposited together by or as if by wind or water **c** : a deposit of clay, sand, gravel, and boulders transported by a glacier or by running water from a glacier **3 a** : a general underlying design or tendency **b** : the meaning, import, or purport of what is spoken or written **4** : a tool for ramming down or driving something **5 a** : a ship's deviation from its course caused by currents **b** : the lateral motion of an airplane due to air currents **6 a** : a gradual shift in attitude, opinion, or position **b** : an aimless course **7** : random change in genotypes of small populations **syn** see TENDENCY

²drift *vb* **1 a** : to become or cause to be driven or carried along by a current of water, wind, or air **b** : to move or float smoothly and effortlessly **2 a** : to move along the line of least resistance **b** : to travel about in a random way esp. in search of work **c** : to become carried along subject to no guidance or control **3 a** : to accumulate or cause to accumulate in a mass : be piled up in heaps by wind or water **b** : to cover or become covered with a drift **4 a** : to vary or deviate from a set adjustment **b** : to vary sluggishly — **drift·er** *n* — **drift·ing·ly** \'drif-tiŋ-lē\ *adv*

drift·age \'drif-tij\ *n* **1** : a drifting of some object esp. through action of wind or water **2** : deviation from a set course due to drifting **3** : something that drifts

drift·wood \'drift-,wùd\ *n* **1** : wood drifted or floated by water **2** : something that drifts aimlessly : FLOTSAM, WRECKAGE

¹drill \'dril\ *vb* [D *drillen*] **1** : to pierce or bore with or as if with a drill ⟨*drill* a tooth⟩ ⟨*drill* a hole⟩ **2 a** : to instruct thoroughly ⟨*drill* a class⟩ **b** : to impart or communicate by repetition ⟨*drill* some sense into a child⟩ **c** : to train or exercise in military evolutions and the use of weapons ⟨*drill* soldiers⟩ — **drill·er** *n*

²drill *n* **1** : an instrument for making holes in hard substances by revolving or by a succession of blows; *also* : such an instrument

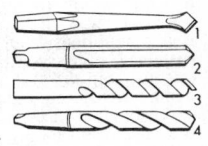

drills 1: *1* flat, *2* straight-flute, *3* single-twist, *4* two-groove

with the machine for operating it **2** : the training of soldiers in military skill and discipline **3** : a physical or mental exercise regularly and repeatedly practiced **4** : a marine snail that destroys oysters by boring through their shells and feeding on the soft parts

³drill *n* : a West African baboon closely related to the typical mandrills

⁴drill *n* **1** : a shallow furrow or trench into which seed is sown **2** : a planting implement that opens a drill, drops in seed, and covers it with earth

⁵drill *vt* : to sow with or as if with a drill

⁶drill *n* [short for *drilling*] : a durable cotton fabric in twill weave

drill·ing \'dril-iŋ\ *n* [modif. of G *drillich*] : ⁶DRILL

drill·mas·ter \'dril-,mas-tər\ *n* : one who drills; *esp* : an instructor in military drill

drill press *n* : an upright drilling machine in which the drill is pressed to the work by a hand lever or by power

drily *var of* DRYLY

¹drink \'driŋk\ *vb* **drank** \'draŋk\; **drunk** \'drəŋk\ *or* **drank**; **drink·ing** [OE *drincan*] **1 a** : to swallow liquid : IMBIBE **b** : to take in or suck up : ABSORB **c** : to take in or receive in a way suggestive of liquid being swallowed ⟨*drink* in the beautiful scenery⟩ **2** : to give or join in a toast ⟨*drink* to the bride⟩ **3 a** : to drink alcoholic beverages **b** : to spend in or on consumption of alcoholic beverages **c** : to bring to a specified state by taking drink

²drink *n* **1 a** : liquid suitable for swallowing : BEVERAGE **b** : alcoholic liquor **2** : a draft or portion of liquid **3** : excessive consumption of alcoholic beverages

¹drink·a·ble \'driŋ-kə-bəl\ *adj* : suitable or safe for drinking

²drinkable *n* : a liquid suitable for drinking : BEVERAGE

drink·er \'driŋ-kər\ *n* **1** : one that drinks **2** : one that drinks alcoholic beverages esp. to excess

¹drip \'drip\ *vb* **dripped** *or* **dript**; **drip·ping** [OE *dryppan*] **1** : to fall or let fall in drops **2 a** : to let fall drops of moisture or liquid ⟨a *dripping* faucet⟩ **b** : to overflow with or as if with moisture — **drip·per** *n*

²drip *n* **1 a** : a falling in drops **b** : liquid that falls, overflows, or is extruded in drops **2** : the sound made by or as if by falling drops **3** : a part of a cornice or other member that projects to throw off rainwater; *also* : an overlapping metal strip serving the same purpose **4** *slang* : a tiresomely dull person

drip–dry \'drip-'drī\ *vi* : to dry with few or no wrinkles when hung dripping wet — **drip–dry** \-,drī\ *adj*

drip pan *n* : a pan for catching drippings — called also *dripping pan*

¹drip·ping \'drip-iŋ\ *n* : fat and juices from meat during cooking — often used in pl.

²dripping *adv* : EXTREMELY ⟨*dripping* wet⟩

¹drive \'drīv\ *vb* **drove** \'drōv\; **driv·en** \'driv-ən\; **driv·ing** \'drī-viŋ\ [OE *drīfan*] **1** : to urge, push, or force onward **2 a** : to direct the movement or course of (as a vehicle or animals drawing a vehicle) ⟨*drive* an automobile⟩ ⟨*drive* into town⟩ **b** : to convey or transport in a vehicle ⟨*drove* him to the airport⟩ **3** : to carry along or keep in motion ⟨*drive* machinery by electricity⟩ **4** : to carry through strongly ⟨*drive* a bargain⟩ **5 a** : to force or compel to work or to act ⟨*driven* by hunger to steal⟩ **b** : to project, inject, or impress forcefully ⟨*drove* the lesson home⟩ **6** : to bring into a specified condition ⟨noise enough to *drive* a person crazy⟩ **7** : to produce by opening a way (as by drilling) ⟨*drive* a well⟩ **8** : to rush and press with violence ⟨the police *drove* into the mob⟩ **9** : to hit a golf ball from the tee **syn** see MOVE, RIDE

²drive *n* **1** : an act of driving: as **a** : a trip in a carriage or automobile **b** : a collecting and driving together of animals **c** : the guiding of logs downstream to a mill **d** : the act of driving a ball **e** : the flight of a ball **2 a** : DRIVEWAY **b** : a public road for driving (as in a park) **3 a** : an offensive or aggressive move; *esp* : a strong sustained military attack **b** : an intensive campaign ⟨membership *drive*⟩ ⟨a *drive* for charity⟩ **4** : the state of being hurried and under pressure **5 a** : an urgent, basic, or instinctual need or longing **b** : dynamic quality **6 a** : the means for giving motion to a machine or machine part ⟨a chain *drive*⟩ **b** : the means by which the movement of an automotive vehicle is controlled and directed

drive-in \'drīv-,in\ *adj* : arranged and equipped so as to

accommodate patrons while they remain in their automobiles ⟨*drive-in* theater⟩ ⟨*drive-in* bank⟩ — **drive–in** *n*

¹driv·el \'driv-əl\ *vb* **driv·eled** *or* **driv·elled**; **driv·el·ing** *or* **driv·el·ling** \'driv-(ə-)liŋ\ [OE *dreflian*] **1** : to let saliva dribble from the mouth : SLAVER **2** : to talk or utter stupidly, carelessly, or in an infantile way — **driv·el·er** *or* **driv·el·ler** \-(ə-)lər\ *n*

²drivel *n* **1** *archaic* : saliva trickling from the mouth **2** : NONSENSE

driv·er \'drī-vər\ *n* : one that drives: as **a** : the operator of a motor vehicle **b** : a golf club having a wooden head with a nearly straight face used in driving — called also *number one wood*

driv·er's seat *n* : the position of top authority or dominance

drive·way \'drīv-,wā\ *n* **1** : a road or way along which animals are driven **2** : a short private road leading from the street to a house, garage, or parking lot

driving iron *n* : a golf iron with a nearly vertical head for distance and little loft — called also *number one iron*

¹driz·zle \'driz-əl\ *vb* **driz·zled**; **driz·zling** \'driz-(ə-)liŋ\ **1** : to rain in very small drops or lightly : SPRINKLE **2** : to shed in minute drops or particles

²drizzle *n* : a fine mistlike rain — **driz·zly** \'driz-(ə-)lē\ *adj*

drogue \'drōg\ *n* [prob. alter. of ¹*drag*] : a small attached parachute for slowing down or stabilizing something (as an astronaut's capsule in landing)

droll \'drōl\ *adj* [F *drôle*] : having a humorous, whimsical, or odd quality ⟨a *droll* expression⟩ — **droll·ness** \'drōl-nəs\ *n* — **drol·ly** \'drōl-lē\ *adv*

droll·ery \'drōl-(ə-)rē\ *n, pl* **-er·ies** **1** : something droll; *esp* : an amusing story or gesture **2** : droll behavior **3** : whimsical humor

-drome \,drōm\ *n comb form* [*hippodrome*] **1** : racecourse ⟨motor*drome*⟩ **2** : large specially prepared place ⟨aero*drome*⟩

drom·e·dary \'dräm-ə-,der-ē\ *n, pl* **-dar·ies** [LL *dromedarius*, fr. L *dromad-, dromas*, fr. Gk, running] **1** : a camel of unusual speed bred and trained esp. for riding **2** : the one-humped camel of western Asia and northern Africa

¹drone \'drōn\ *n* [OE *drān*] **1** : the stingless male bee (as of the honeybee) that gathers no honey **2** : one that lives on the labors of others : PARASITE **3** : a pilotless airplane or ship controlled by radio signals

²drone *vb* : to make or speak with a low dull monotonous humming sound

³drone *n* **1** : one of the pipes on a bagpipe that sound fixed continuous tones **2** : a deep monotonous sound : HUM

drone fly *n* : a large two-winged fly resembling a honeybee

drool \'drül\ *vb* **1 a** : to water at the mouth **b** : to let saliva or some other substance flow from the mouth : SLAVER **2** : to talk foolishly : express in a sentimental or effusive manner

¹droop \'drüp\ *vb* [ON *drūpa*] **1** : to hang or incline downward **2** : to sink gradually **3** : to become depressed or weakened : LANGUISH **4** : to let droop — **droop·ing·ly** \'drü-piŋ-lē\ *adv*

²droop *n* : the condition or appearance of drooping

droopy \'drü-pē\ *adj* **droop·i·er; -est** **1** : drooping or tending to droop **2** : GLOOMY, DEJECTED

¹drop \'dräp\ *n* [OE *dropa*] **1 a (1)** : the quantity of fluid that falls in one spherical mass **(2)** *pl* : a dose of medicine measured by drops **b** : a small quantity of drink **c** : the smallest practical unit of liquid measure **2 a** : a pendent ornament attached to a piece of jewelry; *also* : an earring with such a pendant **b** : a small round candy **3 a** : the act or an instance of dropping : FALL **b** : a decline in quantity or quality **c** : a descent by parachute; *also* : the men or equipment dropped by parachute **4 a** : the distance through which something drops **b** : a fall of electric potential **5** : a slot into which something is to be dropped **6** : an unframed piece of cloth scenery in a theater

²drop *vb* **dropped; drop·ping** **1** : to fall or let fall in drops **2 a** : to let fall ⟨*drop* a book⟩ ⟨*drop* anchor⟩ **b** : to let fall gradually ⟨*dropped* his voice⟩ **3** : SEND ⟨*drop* me a letter⟩ **4** : to let go : DISMISS ⟨*drop* the subject⟩ ⟨*drop* several workmen⟩ **5** : to knock down : cause to fall ⟨*drop* an opponent in a fight⟩ **6** : to go lower ⟨prices *dropped*⟩ **7** : to come or go unexpectedly or informally ⟨*drop* in to call⟩ **8** : to pass from one state into a less active one ⟨*drop* off to sleep⟩ **9** : to move downward or with a current **10** : to withdraw from participation or membership : QUIT — usu. used with *out* **11** : to leave (a letter) unsounded ⟨*drop* the *r* in *farm*⟩ **12** : to give birth to ⟨the cow *dropped* her calf early⟩

drop-forge \'dräp-'förj, -'förj\ *vt* : to forge between dies by a drop hammer or punch press — **drop forger** *n*

drop hammer *n* : a power hammer raised and then released to drop on metal resting on an anvil or die

drop-kick \'dräp-'kik\ *n* : a kick made by dropping a football to the ground and kicking it at the moment it starts to rebound — **drop-kick** *vb* — **drop-kick-er** *n*

drop leaf *n* : a hinged leaf on a table that can be folded down

drop-let \'dräp-lət\ *n* : a very small drop

droplet infection *n* : infection transmitted by airborne droplets of sputum containing infectious organisms

drop-out \'dräp-,aút\ *n* : one who drops out (as from school) before achieving his goal

dropped egg *n* : a poached egg

drop-per \'dräp-ər\ *n* **1** : one that drops **2** : a short glass tube with a rubber bulb used to measure out liquids by drops

drop-pings \'dräp-iηz\ *n pl* : animal dung

drop-sy \'dräp-sē\ *n* [modif. of OF *ydropesie*, fr. L *hydropisis*, modif. of Gk *hydrōps*, fr. *hydōr* water] : EDEMA — **drop-si-cal** \-si-kəl\ *adj*

dros-era \'dräs-ə-rə\ *n* : SUNDEW

drosh-ky \'dräsh-kē\ *n, pl* **droshkies** [Russ *drozhki*, fr. *droga* pole of a wagon; akin to E *draw*] : any of various 2-wheeled or 4-wheeled carriages used esp. in Russia

dro-soph-i-la \drō-'säf-ə-lə\ *n* [Gk *drosos* dew + *-philos* -phil] : any of a genus of small two-winged flies used esp. in the study of inheritance

dross \'dräs, 'drós\ *n* [OE *drōs* dregs] **1** : the scum that forms on the surface of molten metal **2** : waste or foreign matter : IMPURITY

drought *or* **drouth** \'draúth, 'draút\ *n* [OE *drūgath*, fr. *drūgian* to dry up; akin to E *dry*] **1** : lack of rain or water **2** : a long period of dry weather — **droughty** \-ē\ *adj*

drove \'drōv\ *n* [OE *drāf*, fr. *drīfan* to drive] **1** : a group of animals driven or moving in a body **2** : a crowd of people moving or acting together

drov-er \'drō-vər\ *n* [*drove*] : one that drives cattle or sheep

drown \'draún\ *vb* [ME *drounen*] **1 a** : to suffocate by submersion esp. in water **b** : to become drowned **2** : to cover with water : INUNDATE **3** : OVERCOME, OVERPOWER

drowse \'draúz\ *vi* : DOZE — **drowse** *n*

drowsy \'draú-zē\ *adj* **drows-i-er; -est** **1** : ready to fall asleep **2** : making one sleepy — **drows-i-ly** \-zə-lē\ *adv* — **drows-i-ness** \-zē-nəs\ *n*

drub \'drəb\ *vt* **drubbed; drub-bing** **1** : to beat severely with or as if with a stick **2** : to defeat decisively

¹drudge \'drəj\ *vi* [ME *druggen*] : to do hard, menial, or monotonous work — **drudg-er** *n*

²drudge *n* : a person who drudges

drudg-ery \'drəj-(ə-)rē\ *n, pl* **-er-ies** : tiresome or menial work

¹drug \'drəg\ *n* [ME *drogge*] **1** : a substance used as a medicine or in making medicines **2** : something little sought after ⟨a *drug* on the market⟩ **3** : a narcotic substance or preparation

²drug *vb* **drugged; drug-ging** **1** : to affect or treat with a drug; *esp* : to stupefy by a narcotic drug **2** : to lull or stupefy as if with a drug

drug-gist \'drəg-əst\ *n* : one who sells drugs and medicines; *also* : PHARMACIST

drug-store \'drəg-,stōr, -,stór\ *n* : a retail shop where medicines and miscellaneous articles are sold : PHARMACY

dru-id \'drü-əd\ *n, often cap* [L *druides*, pl., fr. Gaulish] : one of an ancient Celtic priesthood of Gaul, Britain, and Ireland appearing in legends as magicians and wizards — **dru-id-ic** \drü-'id-ik\ *or* **dru-id-i-cal** \-'id-i-kəl\ *adj, often cap* — **dru-id-ism** \'drü-ə-,diz-əm\ *n, often cap*

¹drum \'drəm\ *n* [prob. fr. D *trom*] **1** : a musical percussion instrument usu. consisting of a hollow cylinder with a skin head stretched over

drums 1: *1* bass, *2* snare
(for orchestra); *3* snare
(for parades)

each end that is beaten with a stick or pair of sticks in playing **2** : EARDRUM **3** : the sound of a drum; *also* : a similar sound **4** : a drum-shaped object: as **a** : a cylindrical machine or mechanical device or part **b** : a cylindrical container; *esp* : a metal barrel with a capacity of 12 to 110 gallons **c** : a disk-shaped magazine for an automatic weapon **5** : any of various spiny-finned fishes that make a drumming noise

²drum *vb* **drummed; drum-ming** **1** : to beat a drum **2** : to sound rhythmically : THROB, BEAT **3** : to summon or enlist by or as if by beating a drum ⟨*drum* up customers⟩ ⟨*drum* up recruits⟩ **4** : to dismiss ignominiously : EXPEL — usu. used with *out* **5** : to drive or force by steady effort or reiteration ⟨*drum* a lesson into his head⟩ **6** : to strike or tap repeatedly so as to produce rhythmic sounds

drum-beat \'drəm-,bēt\ *n* : a stroke on a drum or its sound

drum-lin \'drəm-lən\ *n* : a long or oval hill of glacial drift

drum major *n* : the marching leader of a band or drum corps

drum ma-jor-ette \,drəm-,mā-jə-'ret\ *n* : a female drum major

drum-mer \'drəm-ər\ *n* **1** : one that plays a drum **2** : TRAVELING SALESMAN

drum-stick \'drəm-,stik\ *n* **1** : a stick for beating a drum **2** : the lower segment of a fowl's leg

¹drunk \'drəηk\ *adj* [ME *drunke*, alter. of *drunken*] **1** : having the faculties impaired by alcohol **2** : controlled by some feeling as if under the influence of alcohol ⟨*drunk* with power⟩ **3** : of, relating to, or caused by intoxication

²drunk *n* **1 a** : a person who is drunk **b** : DRUNKARD **2** : a period of excessive drinking : SPREE

drunk-ard \'drəη-kərd\ *n* : one who is habitually drunk

drunk-en \'drəη-kən\ *adj* [OE *druncen*, fr. pp. of *drincan* to drink] **1 a** : DRUNK **1** **b** : given to habitual excessive use of alcohol **2** : of, relating to, or resulting from intoxication ⟨a *drunken* brawl⟩ **3** : unsteady or lurching as if from intoxication — **drunk-en-ly** *adv* — **drunk-en-ness** \-kən-nəs\ *n*

drunk-om-e-ter \,drəηk-'äm-ət-ər, 'drəηk-ə-,mēt-\ *n* : a device for measuring blood alcohol content by chemical analysis of the breath

drupe \'drüp\ *n* [NL *drupa*, fr. L, overripe olive, fr. Gk *dryppa* olive] : an indehiscent fruit (as the plum, cherry, or peach) having one seed enclosed in a hard bony stone that is usu. covered by a layer of pulpy flesh surrounded in turn by a firm skin — **dru-pa-ceous** \drü-'pā-shəs\ *adj*

drupe-let \'drüp-lət\ *n* : a small drupe; *esp* : one of the individual parts of an aggregate fruit (as the raspberry)

¹dry \'drī\ *adj* **dri-er** \'drī-(ə)r\; **dri-est** \'drī-əst\ [OE *drȳge*] **1** : free or freed from water or liquid **2** : characterized by loss or lack of water: as **a** : lacking precipitation and humidity ⟨a *dry* climate⟩ **b** : lacking freshness : STALE **c** : low in or deprived of succulence ⟨*dry* hay⟩ ⟨achenes and other *dry* fruits⟩ **3** : not being in or under water ⟨*dry* land⟩ **4 a** : THIRSTY **b** : marked by the absence of alcoholic beverages **c** : no longer liquid or sticky ⟨the ink is *dry*⟩ **5** : containing or employing no liquid (as water) ⟨a *dry* creek⟩ ⟨a *dry* fountain pen⟩ ⟨*dry* heat⟩ **6** : not giving milk ⟨a *dry* cow⟩ **7** : lacking natural lubrication : not productive ⟨*dry* cough⟩ **8** : solid as opposed to liquid ⟨*dry* groceries⟩ **9** : not warm or tender in feeling : SEVERE **10** : not yielding : BARREN **11** : marked by a matter-of-fact, ironic, or terse manner of expression ⟨*dry* humor⟩ **12** : UNINTERESTING, WEARISOME ⟨*dry* passages of description⟩ **13** : not sweet **14** : relating to, favoring, or practicing prohibition of alcoholic beverages ⟨a *dry* state⟩— **dry-ly** *adv* — **dry-ness** *n*

²dry *vb* **dried; dry-ing** : to make or become dry

³dry *n, pl* **drys** : PROHIBITIONIST

dry-ad \'drī-əd, -,ad\ *n* [Gk *dryad-, dryas*, fr. *drys* tree; akin to E *tree*] : WOOD NYMPH

dry cell *n* : a small cell producing electricity by the reaction of chemicals that are not spillable ⟨a *dry cell* for a flashlight⟩

dry-clean \'drī-,klēn\ *vt* : to subject to dry cleaning — **dry clean-er** \-,klē-nər\ *n*

dry clean-ing \-,klē-niη\ *n* : the cleansing of fabrics with organic solvents (as naphtha)

dry dock \'drī-,däk\ *n* : a dock that can be kept dry for use during the construction or repairing of ships

---

dry·er *var of* DRIER

dry farm \'drī-'färm\ *n* **:** a farm on dry land operated without irrigation on the basis of moisture-conserving tillage and drought-resistant crops — **dry–farm** *vt* — **dry farmer** *n* — **dry farming** *n*

dry fly *n* **:** an artificial angling fly designed to float upon the surface of the water

dry goods \'drī-,gudz\ *n pl* **:** textiles, ready-to-wear clothing, and notions as distinguished from other goods

Dry Ice *trademark* — used for solidified carbon dioxide usu. in the form of blocks that at −78.5° C changes directly to a gas and that is used chiefly as a refrigerant

drying oil *n* **:** an oil (as linseed oil) that changes readily to a hard tough elastic substance when exposed in a thin film to air

dry measure *n* **:** a series of units of capacity for dry commodities — see MEASURE table, METRIC SYSTEM table

dry·point \'drī-,point\ *n* **:** an engraving made with a pointed instrument (as a needle) instead of a burin directly into the metal plate without the use of acid as in etching

dry rot *n* **:** a fungous decay of seasoned timber in which the cellulose of wood is consumed leaving a soft skeleton readily reduced to powder — **dry–rot** *vb*

dry run *n* **1 :** a practice firing without ammunition **2 :** a practice exercise **:** TRIAL, REHEARSAL ⟨a *dry run* of a television show⟩

dry–shod \'drī-'shäd\ *adj* **:** having dry shoes or feet

d.t.'s \('ꞏ)dē-'tēz\ *n pl, often cap D&T* **:** DELIRIUM TREMENS

du·al \'d(y)ü-əl\ *adj* [L *duo* two] **1 :** consisting of two parts or elements **:** having two like parts **:** DOUBLE **2 :** having a double character or nature — **du·al·i·ty** \d(y)ü-'al-ət-ē\ *n* — **du·al·ly** \'d(y)ü-ə-lē\ *adv*

du·al·ism \'d(y)ü-ə-,liz-əm\ *n* **:** a doctrine that the universe is made up of or governed by two opposing principles (as good and evil) — **du·al·ist** \-ləst\ *n*

du·al–pur·pose \,d(y)ü-əl-'pər-pəs\ *adj* **:** intended for or serving two purposes ⟨*dual-purpose* cattle⟩

¹dub \'dəb\ *vt* **dubbed; dub·bing** [OE *dubbian*] **1 a :** to confer knighthood upon **b :** NAME **2 :** to trim or remove the comb and wattles of **3 :** to execute poorly

²dub *vt* **dubbed; dub·bing** [by shortening & alter. fr. *double*] **1 :** to add (sound effects) to a film or broadcast **2 :** to transpose (recorded sound) to a new record

dub·bin \'dəb-ən\ *n* **:** a dressing of oil and tallow for leather

du·bi·e·ty \d(y)ü-'bī-ət-ē\ *n, pl* **-ties 1 :** DUBIOUSNESS, UNCERTAINTY **2 :** a matter of doubt

du·bi·ous \'d(y)ü-bē-əs\ *adj* [L *dubius*] **1 :** occasioning doubt **:** UNCERTAIN **2 :** feeling doubt **:** UNDECIDED **3 :** of doubtful promise or uncertain outcome ⟨a *dubious* battle⟩ **4 :** questionable in value, quality, or origin ⟨won by *dubious* means⟩ — **du·bi·ous·ly** *adv* — **du·bi·ous·ness** *n*

du·bi·ta·ble \'d(y)ü-bət-ə-bəl\ *adj* **:** open to doubt or question

du·cal \'d(y)ü-kəl\ *adj* **:** of or relating to a duke or dukedom

duc·at \'dək-ət\ *n* [MF, fr. It *ducato* coin with the doge's portrait on it, fr. *duca* doge, fr. L *duc-, dux* leader] **:** a former gold coin of various European countries

du·ce \'dü-(,)chā\ *n* **:** LEADER 2c

duch·ess \'dəch-əs\ *n* **1 :** the wife or widow of a duke **2 :** a woman who holds a ducal title in her own right

duchy \'dəch-ē\ *n, pl* **duch·ies :** the territory of a duke or duchess **:** DUKEDOM

¹duck \'dək\ *n, pl* **duck** *or* **ducks** [OE *dūce*] **1 :** any of various swimming birds with the neck and legs short, the body more or less depressed, the bill often broad and flat, and the sexes almost always different from each other in plumage; *also* **:** a female duck — compare DRAKE **2 a** *chiefly Brit* **:** DARLING **b** *slang* **:** PERSON, CREATURE ⟨a queer *duck*⟩

²duck *vb* [ME *douken*; akin to E **¹***duck*] **1 :** to thrust or plunge under water **2 :** to lower the head or body suddenly **3 :** BOW, BOB **4 a :** to move quickly **:** DODGE **b :** to evade a duty, question, or responsibility ⟨*duck* the issue⟩ — **duck·er** *n*

³duck *n* [D *doek* cloth] **1 :** a durable closely woven usu. cotton fabric **2** *pl* **:** clothes made of duck

⁴duck *n* [*DUKW*, its code designation] **:** an amphibious truck

duck·bill \'dək-,bil\ *n* **1 :** PLATYPUS — called also

duck·billed *platypus* \,dək-,bild-\ **2 :** a common paddlefish

duck·board \'dək-,bōrd, -,bord\ *n* **:** a boardwalk or slatted flooring laid on a wet, muddy, or cold surface — usu. used in pl.

duck·ling \'dək-liŋ\ *n* **:** a young duck

duck·pin \'dək-,pin\ *n* **1 :** a small bowling pin shorter and wider in the middle than a tenpin **2** *pl* **:** a bowling game using duckpins

duck·weed \-,wēd\ *n* **:** a tiny free-floating stemless plant found on a body of still water (as a pond)

duct \'dəkt\ *n* [L *ductus* act of leading, fr. *duct-, ducere* to lead; akin to E *tow*] **1 :** a tube or vessel carrying a bodily fluid (as the secretion of a gland) **2 a :** a pipe, tube, or channel that conveys a fluid (as air or water) **b :** a pipe or tubular passage for conductors (as an electric power line or telephone cables) — **duct·less** \'dək-tləs\ *adj*

duc·tile \'dək-t°l\ *adj* **1 :** capable of being drawn out (as into a wire) or hammered thin ⟨*ductile* metal⟩ **2 :** easily led or influenced **:** DOCILE — **duc·til·i·ty** \,dək-'til-ət-ē\ *n*

ductless gland *n* **:** an endocrine gland

dud \'dəd\ *n* [ME *dudde*] **1** *pl* **a :** CLOTHES **b :** personal belongings **2 :** one that fails completely **3 :** a missile that fails to explode

dude \'d(y)üd\ *n* **1 :** an extremely fastidious man **:** DANDY **2 :** a city man; *esp* **:** an Easterner in the West — **dud·ish** \'d(y)üd-ish\ *adj* — **dud·ish·ly** *adv*

dude ranch *n* **:** a vacation resort offering horseback riding and other activities typical of western ranches

dud·geon \'dəj-ən\ *n* **:** ill humor **:** RESENTMENT

¹due \'d(y)ü\ *adj* [MF *deu*, pp. of *devoir* to owe, fr. L *debēre*] **1 :** owed or owing as a debt **2 a :** owed or owing as a right **b :** according to accepted notions or procedures **:** APPROPRIATE, FITTING **3 a :** SUFFICIENT, ADEQUATE ⟨arrived in *due* time⟩ **b :** REGULAR, LAWFUL ⟨*due* process of law⟩ **4 :** ATTRIBUTABLE, ASCRIBABLE — used with *to* ⟨an accident *due* to negligence⟩ **5 :** having reached the date at which payment is required **:** PAYABLE **6 :** required or expected to happen **:** SCHEDULED ⟨*due* to arrive any time⟩

²due *n* **1 :** something owed **:** DEBT ⟨pay a man his *due*⟩ **2** *pl* **:** a regular or legal charge or fee ⟨membership *dues*⟩

³due *adv* **:** DIRECTLY, EXACTLY ⟨*due* north⟩

¹du·el \'d(y)ü-(-ə)l\ *n* [ML *duellum*, fr. L *duellum, bellum* war] **1 :** a combat between two persons; *esp* **:** one fought with weapons in the presence of witnesses **2 :** a conflict between antagonistic persons, ideas, or forces

²duel *vb* **du·eled** *or* **du·elled; du·el·ing** *or* **du·el·ling :** to fight in a duel — **du·el·er** *n* — **du·el·ist** \'d(y)ü-ə-ləst\ *n*

du·en·na \d(y)ü-'en-ə\ *n* [Sp *dueña*] **1 :** an elderly woman in charge of the younger ladies in a Spanish or Portuguese family **2 :** GOVERNESS, CHAPERON

du·et \d(y)ü-'et\ *n* [It *duetto*, dim. of *duo*] **:** a composition for two performers

due to *prep* **:** because of

duff \'dəf\ *n* [E dial., alter. of *dough*] **1 :** a steamed pudding usu. containing raisins and currants **2 :** partly decayed organic matter on the forest floor

duf·fel \'dəf-əl\ *n* **:** an outfit of supplies (as for camping) **:** KIT

duffel bag *n* **:** a large cylindrical fabric bag for personal belongings

duf·fer \'dəf-ər\ *n* **:** an incompetent or clumsy person

¹dug *past of* DIG

²dug \'dəg\ *n* **:** UDDER, BREAST; *also* **:** TEAT, NIPPLE

du·gong \'dü-,gäŋ, -,goŋ\ *n* [Malay & Tag *duyong* sea cow] **:** an aquatic herbivorous mammal related to the manatees but having a 2-lobed tail and tusks in the male — called also *sea cow*

dug·out \'dəg-,aut\ *n* **1 :** a boat made by hollowing out a large log **2 :** a shelter dug in a hillside or in the ground or in the side of a trench **3 :** a low shelter facing a baseball diamond and containing the players' bench

dui·ker \'dī-kər\ *n* [Afrik., lit., diver] **:** any of several small African antelopes

duke \'d(y)ük\ *n* [OF *duc*, fr. L *duc-, dux* leader, fr. *ducere* to lead] **1 :** a sovereign ruler of a continental European duchy **2 :** a nobleman of the highest rank; *esp* **:** a member of the highest grade of the British peerage **3** *slang* **:** FIST, HAND — usu. used in pl. — **duke·dom** \-dəm\ *n*

dul·cet \'dəl-sət\ *adj* **1** : sweet to the ear : MELODIOUS **2** : AGREEABLE, SOOTHING

dul·ci·mer \'dəl-sə-mər\ *n* [MF *doulcemer*, fr. It *dolcimelo*] : a wire-stringed instrument played with light hammers held in the hands

¹dull \'dəl\ *adj* [ME *dul*] **1** : mentally slow : STUPID **2 a** : slow in perception or sensibility **b** : lacking zest or vivacity **:** LISTLESS **3** : slow in action : SLUGGISH ⟨a *dull* market⟩ **4** : lacking sharpness of edge or point **5** : lacking brilliance or luster **6** : not resonant or ringing **7** : CLOUDY, OVERCAST **8** : TEDIOUS, UNINTERESTING ⟨*dull* sermon⟩ **9** *of a color* : low in saturation and lightness **syn** see BLUNT, STUPID — **dull·ness** *or* **dul·ness** \'dəl-nəs\ *n* — **dul·ly** \'dəl-(l)ē\ *adv*

²dull *vb* : to make or become dull

dull·ard \'dəl-ərd\ *n* : a stupid person

dulse \'dəls\ *n* [ScGael & IrGael *duileasg*] : any of several coarse red seaweeds esp. of northern seas that are used as food

du·ly \'d(y)ü-lē\ *adv* : in a due manner, time, or degree ⟨*duly* authorized⟩ ⟨will be *duly* considered⟩

du·ma \'dü-mə\ *n* [Russ, of Gmc origin; akin to E *doom*] : a representative council in Russia; *esp* : the principal legislative assembly in czarist Russia

dumb \'dəm\ *adj* [OE; akin to E *deaf*] **1 a** : lacking the normal power of speech **b** : naturally incapable of speech ⟨*dumb* animals⟩ **2** : not willing to speak **3 a** : not expressed in uttered words ⟨*dumb* grief⟩ **b** : not having the usual accompaniment of speech or sound **4** : STUPID, FOOLISH — **dumb·ly** \'dəm-lē\ *adv* — **dumb·ness** *n*
syn MUTE, SPEECHLESS: DUMB stresses lack of power to speak that may be natural and permanent ⟨*dumb* animals⟩ or temporary ⟨struck *dumb* with wonder⟩ MUTE stresses the fact of not speaking from whatever cause ⟨stood *mute* and ashamed before his accusers⟩ SPEECHLESS implies esp. inability to find words because of shock or confusion of mind

dumb·bell \'dəm-,bel\ *n* **1** : a weight consisting of two spheres connected by a short bar and used usu. in pairs for calisthenic exercise **2** : a dull or stupid person

dumb·found *or* **dum·found** \,dəm-'faůnd\ *vt* [*dumb* + *-found* (as in *confound*)] : to strike dumb with astonishment

dumbbell

dumb show *n* : signs and gestures without words : PANTOMIME

dumb·wait·er \'dəm-'wāt-ər\ *n* **1** : a portable serving table **2** : a small elevator for conveying food and dishes or small goods from one story of a building to another

dum·dum \'dəm-,dəm\ *n* [fr. *Dum-Dum*, India] : a soft-nosed bullet that expands upon hitting an object

¹dum·my \'dəm-ē\ *n, pl* **dum·mies 1** : a person who lacks or seems to lack the power of speech **2** : one who seems to be acting for himself but is really acting for another **3** : a stupid person **4** : an imitation of something to be used as a substitute ⟨the *dummies* in a store window⟩ **5 a** : an exposed hand in bridge played by one of the players in addition to his own hand **b** : a bridge player whose hand is a dummy **6** : a pattern arrangement of matter to be reproduced esp. by printing

²dummy *adj* : resembling a dummy; *esp* : having the appearance of being real but lacking ability to function ⟨a *dummy* corporation⟩ ⟨*dummy* wooden guns⟩

¹dump \'dəmp\ *vb* **1 a** : to let fall in a heap or mass : UNLOAD ⟨*dump* coal⟩ **b** : to get rid of unceremoniously **c** : to dump refuse ⟨no *dumping* allowed⟩ **2** : to sell in quantity at a very low price; *esp* : to sell abroad at less than the market price at home — **dump·er** *n*

²dump *n* **1 a** : an accumulation of discarded materials (as refuse) **b** : a place where discarded materials are dumped **2 a** : a quantity of reserve and esp. military supplies stored at one place **b** : a place where reserve materials are stored **3** : a disorderly, slovenly, or dilapidated place

dump·ling \'dəm-plin\ *n* **1** : a small mass of dough cooked by boiling or steaming **2** : a dessert of fruit baked in biscuit dough

dumps \'dəm(p)s\ *n pl* : a dull gloomy state of mind : low spirits ⟨in the *dumps*⟩

dump truck *n* : a truck for transporting and dumping loose materials

dumpy \'dəm-pē\ *adj* [E dial. *dump* lump] : short and thick in build : SQUAT — **dump·i·ness** *n*

¹dun \'dən\ *adj* [OE *dunn*] **1** : having a dun color **2** : marked by dullness and drabness — **dun·ness** \'dən-nəs\ *n*

²dun *n* **1** : a pale horse usu. with dark points and dorsal stripe **2** : a variable color averaging a nearly neutral slightly brownish dark gray **3 a** : an immature winged mayfly **b** : CADDIS FLY

³dun *vt* **dunned**; **dun·ning 1** : to make persistent demands upon for payment **2** : to plague or pester constantly

⁴dun *n* **1** : a person who duns another **2** : an urgent request; *esp* : a demand for payment

Dun·can Phyfe \,dən-kən-'fīf\ *adj* : of, relating to, or constituting furniture designed and built by or in the style of Duncan Phyfe

dunce \'dən(t)s\ *n* [fr. John *Duns* Scotus *d ab*1308 Scottish scholastic theologian, whose once accepted writings were ridiculed in the 16th cent.] : a dull-witted and stupid person

dun·der·head \'dən-dər-,hed\ *n* : DUNCE, BLOCKHEAD — **dun·der·head·ed** \,dən-dər-'hed-əd\ *adj*

dune \'d(y)ün\ *n* [F, fr. MD] : a hill or ridge of sand piled up by the wind

¹dung \'dəŋ\ *n* [OE] : the excrement of an animal : MANURE — **dungy** \'dəŋ-ē\ *adj*

²dung *vt* : to fertilize or dress with manure

dun·ga·ree \,dəŋ-gə-'rē\ *n* [Hindi *dūgrī*] **1** : a heavy coarse durable cotton twill woven from colored yarns; *esp* : blue denim **2** *pl* : trousers or work clothes made of dungaree

dung beetle *n* : a beetle (as a dorbeetle or tumblebug) that rolls balls of dung in which to lay eggs and on which the larvae feed

dun·geon \'dən-jən\ *n* [MF *donjon*, fr. (assumed) ML *dominion-, dominio*, fr. L *dominus* lord] **1** : DONJON **2** : a close dark prison commonly underground

dung·hill \'dəŋ-,hil\ *n* **1** : a manure pile **2** : a vile or degraded situation, condition, or thing

dunk \'dəŋk\ *vb* [PaG *dunke*, fr. OHG *dunkōn*] **1** : to dip (as bread or cake) into liquid while eating **2** : to dip or submerge temporarily in liquid **3** : to submerge oneself in water

dun·lin \'dən-lən\ *n, pl* **dunlins** *or* **dunlin** [¹*dun* + *-ling*] (alter. of *-ling*)] : a small sandpiper largely brown above and white below with a black patch on the belly

dun·nage \'dən-ij\ *n* **1** : loose materials used around a cargo to prevent damage; *also* : padding in a shipping container **2** : baggage or personal effects esp. of a sailor

duo \'d(y)ü-ō\ *n, pl* **du·os** [It, fr. L, two] **1** : DUET; *esp* : a composition for two performers at two pianos **2** : PAIR

duo·dec·i·mal \,d(y)ü-ə-'des-ə-məl\ *adj* : of, relating to, or proceeding by twelve or the scale of twelves — **duo·decimal** *n*

du·o·de·num \,d(y)ü-ə-'dē-nəm, d(y)ù-'äd-°n-əm\ *n, pl* **-de·na** \-'dē-nə, -°n-ə\ *or* **-denums** [ML, fr. L *duodeni* twelve each, fr. *duodecim* twelve; fr. its length, about 12 fingers' breadth] : the first part of the small intestine extending from the pylorus to the jejunum — **du·o·de·nal** \-'dēn-°l, -°n-əl\ *adj*

duo·logue \'d(y)ü-ə-,lòg\ *n* : a dialogue between two persons

¹dupe \'d(y)üp\ *n* [F] : one who is easily deceived or cheated

²dupe *vt* : to make a dupe of : DECEIVE — **dup·er** *n*

du·ple \'d(y)ü-pəl\ *adj* **1** : taken by twos : TWOFOLD **2** : having two beats or a multiple of two beats to the measure ⟨*duple* time⟩

¹du·plex \'d(y)ü-,pleks\ *adj* [L *duplic-, duplex*, fr. *duo* two + *-plex* -fold] : DOUBLE, TWOFOLD; *esp* : having two parts that operate at the same time or in the same way ⟨a *duplex* lathe⟩

²duplex *n* : something duplex; *esp* : a 2-family house

duplex apartment *n* : an apartment having rooms on two floors

¹du·pli·cate \'d(y)ü-pli-kət\ *adj* **1** : consisting of or existing in two corresponding or identical parts or examples **2** : being the same as another **3** : of or relating to a card game in which players play identical hands in order to compare scores

²duplicate *n* : a thing that exactly resembles another in appearance, pattern, or content : COPY

---

syn DUPLICATE, COPY, FACSIMILE, REPRODUCTION mean a thing made closely resembling another or an original. DUPLICATE suggests exact sameness of pattern and usu. of material; COPY applies to anything reproduced mechanically or without intentional changes; FACSIMILE implies exact and detailed reproduction of pattern that may differ in scale or material; REPRODUCTION implies an exact or very close imitation of an original in all respects

³**du·pli·cate** \'d(y)ü-pli-‚kāt\ vt **1** : to make double or twofold **2** : to make a duplicate of — **du·pli·ca·tive** \'d(y)ü-pli-‚kāt-iv\ adj

du·pli·ca·tion \‚d(y)ü-pli-'kā-shən\ n **1 a** : an act or process of duplicating **b** : the quality or state of being duplicated **2** : DUPLICATE, COUNTERPART

du·pli·ca·tor \'d(y)ü-pli-‚kāt-ər\ n : one that duplicates; esp : a machine for making copies of typed, drawn, or printed matter

du·plic·i·ty \d(y)ü-'plis-ət-ē\ n, pl **-ties** : deception by pretending to feel and act one way while acting another : DOUBLE-DEALING

du·ra·bil·i·ty \‚d(y)ur-ə-'bil-ət-ē\ n : the quality or state of being durable : ability to last or to stand hard or continued use or wear

du·ra·ble \'d(y)ur-ə-bəl\ adj [L durare to last] : able to last a long time ⟨durable clothing⟩ — **du·ra·ble·ness** n — **du·ra·bly** \-blē\ adv

Du·ral·u·min \d(y)ù-'ral-yə-mən, ‚d(y)ùr-ə-'lü-mən\ trademark — used for a strong light alloy of aluminum, copper, manganese, and magnesium

du·ra ma·ter \'d(y)ur-ə-‚māt-ər, -‚mät-\ n [ML, lit., hard mother] : the outermost and tough fibrous membrane that envelops the brain and spinal cord

du·rance \'d(y)ùr-ən(t)s\ n [MF, fr. durer to last, endure] : IMPRISONMENT

du·ra·tion \d(y)ù-'rā-shən\ n **1** : continuance in time ⟨a storm of short duration⟩ **2** : the time during which something exists or lasts ⟨the duration of the war⟩

dur·bar \'dər-‚bär\ n [Hindi darbār] : a formal reception given by a native Indian prince or by a governor-general

du·ress \d(y)ù-'res\ n **1** : forcible restraint or restriction **2** : compulsion by threat ⟨a confession obtained under duress⟩

Dur·ham \'dər-əm, 'də-rəm\ n : SHORTHORN

du·ri·an \'d(y)ùr-ē-ən\ n [Malay] : a large oval tasty but foul-smelling fruit with a prickly rind and soft pulp; also : the East Indian tree that bears it

dur·ing \d(y)ùr-iŋ\ prep [ME, fr. prp. of duren to last, fr. L durare, fr. durus hard] **1** : throughout the duration of ⟨during his whole lifetime⟩ **2** : at some time or times in the course of ⟨occasional showers during the day⟩

dur·ra \'dúr-ə\ n : any of several grain sorghums grown in warm dry regions

du·rum wheat \‚d(y)ùr-əm-\ n [L durum, neut. of durus hard] : a hard red wheat that yields a glutenous flour used esp. in macaroni and spaghetti

¹**dusk** \'dəsk\ vb [ME dosk, adj., dusky, alter. of OE dox] : to make or become dark or gloomy

²**dusk** n **1** : the darker part of twilight esp. at night **2** : GLOOM

dusky \'dəs-kē\ adj **dusk·i·er; -est** **1** : somewhat dark in color; esp : having dark skin **2** : marked by slight or deficient light : SHADOWY — **dusk·i·ly** \-kə-lē\ adv — **dusk·i·ness** \-kē-nəs\ n

¹**dust** \'dəst\ n [OE dūst] **1** : fine dry powdery particles of earth; also : a fine powder **2** : the earthy remains of bodies once alive; esp : the human corpse **3 a** : a place (as in the earth) of burial **b** : the surface of the ground **4 a** : something worthless **b** : a low or mean condition : state of humiliation **5** Brit : refuse (as sweepings) for disposal — **dust·less** \'dəst-ləs\ adj

²**dust** vb **1** : to make free of dust : brush or wipe away dust **2 a** : to sprinkle with fine particles ⟨dust a pan with flour⟩ **b** : to sprinkle in the form of dust ⟨dust an insecticide on plants⟩ **3** : to sprinkle with dust

dust·bin \'dəs(t)-‚bin\ n, Brit : a trash or garbage can

dust bowl n : a region that suffers from prolonged droughts and dust storms

dust devil n : a small whirlwind containing sand or dust

dust·er \'dəs-tər\ n **1** : one that removes dust **2 a** : a lightweight garment to protect clothing from dust **b** : a dress-length housecoat **3** : one that scatters fine particles;

esp : a device for applying insecticidal or fungicidal dusts to crops

dust jacket n : a removable usu. decorative paper cover folded around the binding of a book

dust·man \'dəs(t)-mən\ n, Brit : a trash or garbage collector

dust·pan \'dəs(t)-‚pan\ n : a shovel-shaped pan for sweepings

dust storm n **1** : a dust-laden whirlwind moving across a dry region and usu. attended by high electrical tension **2** : strong winds bearing clouds of dust

dust-up \'dəs-‚təp\ n : QUARREL, ROW

dusty \'dəs-tē\ adj **dust·i·er; -est** **1** : filled or covered with dust **2** : consisting of dust : POWDERY **3** : resembling dust — **dust·i·ly** \-tə-lē\ adv — **dust·i·ness** \-tē-nəs\ n

dutch \'dəch\ adv, often cap : with each person paying his own way

¹**Dutch** \'dəch\ adj **1 a** archaic : of or relating to the Germanic peoples of Germany, Austria, Switzerland, and the Low Countries **b** slang : GERMAN **2** : of or relating to the Netherlands, its inhabitants, or their language

²**Dutch** n **1 a** archaic : any of the Germanic languages of Germany, Austria, Switzerland, and the Low Countries **b** : the Germanic language of the Netherlands **2 Dutch** pl **a** archaic : the Germanic peoples of Germany, Austria, Switzerland, and the Low Countries **b** : the people of the Netherlands **3** : DISFAVOR, TROUBLE ⟨was in Dutch with the teacher⟩

Dutch clover n : WHITE DUTCH CLOVER

Dutch courage n : courage due to intoxicants

Dutch door n : a door divided horizontally so that the lower part can be shut while the upper part remains open

Dutch elm disease n : a fungous disease of elms characterized by yellowing of the foliage, defoliation, and death

dutch·man \'dəch-mən\ n **1** cap **a** archaic : a member of any of the Germanic peoples of Germany, Austria, Switzerland, and the Low countries **b** : a native or inhabitant of the Netherlands **c** : a person of Dutch descent **d** slang : GERMAN **2** : a device for hiding or counteracting structural defects

Dutch·man's-breech·es \‚dəch-mənz-'brich-əz\ n pl : a delicate spring-flowering herb of the eastern U.S. resembling the related bleeding heart but having cream-white double-spurred flowers

Dutch oven n **1** : a metal shield for roasting before an open fire **2** : a brick oven in which cooking is done by the preheated walls **3 a** : a cast-iron kettle with a tight cover used for baking in an open fire **b** : a heavy pot with a tight-fitting domed cover

Dutch treat n : a treat for which each person pays his own way

Dutch uncle n : one who admonishes sternly and bluntly

du·te·ous \'d(y)üt-ē-əs\ adj : DUTIFUL, OBEDIENT — **du·te·ous·ly** adv — **du·te·ous·ness** n

du·ti·a·ble \'d(y)üt-ē-ə-bəl\ adj : subject to a duty ⟨dutiable imports⟩

du·ti·ful \'d(y)üt-i-fəl\ adj **1** : filled with or motivated by a sense of duty ⟨a dutiful son⟩ **2** : proceeding from or expressive of a sense of duty ⟨dutiful affection⟩ — **du·ti·ful·ly** \-fə-lē\ adv — **du·ti·ful·ness** n

du·ty \'d(y)üt-ē\ n, pl **duties** [AF dueté, fr. OF deu due] **1** : conduct due to parents and superiors : RESPECT **2 a** : the action required by one's position or occupation **b** : assigned service or business; esp : active military service **3 a** : a moral or legal obligation **b** : the force of moral obligation ⟨obey the call of duty⟩ **4** : TAX; esp : a tax on imports **5** : the service required (as of a machine) : USE ⟨this drill has been designed to withstand heavy duty⟩ syn see TASK

du·um·vir \d(y)ù-'əm-vər\ n [L, fr. duum (gen. of duo two) + vir man] : one of two Roman officers or magistrates constituting a board or court

du·um·vi·rate \-və-rət\ n **1** : two people associated in high office **2** : government or control by two people

¹**dwarf** \'dwórf\ n, pl **dwarfs** \'dwórfs\ also **dwarves** \'dwórvz\ [OE dweorg] **1** : a person, lower animal, or plant much below normal size **2** : a small legendary manlike being usu. misshapen and ugly and skilled as an artificer **3** : a star of ordinary or low luminosity and

relatively small mass and size — **dwarf** *adj* — **dwarf·ish** \'dwȯr-fish\ *adj* — **dwarf·ness** *n*

²dwarf *vb* **1** : to restrict the growth of : STUNT ⟨*dwarf* a tree⟩ **2** : to stunt the intellectual or moral development of **3** : to cause to appear smaller **4** : to become smaller

dwarf·ism \'dwȯr-ˌfiz-əm\ *n* : a stunted condition : dwarfish state

dwell \'dwel\ *vi* **dwelt** \'dwelt\ *or* **dwelled** \'dweld, 'dwelt\; **dwell·ing** [OE *dwellan* to delay] **1** : to remain for a time **2** : to live as a resident : RESIDE **3 a** : to linger over something (as with the eyes or mind) : keep the attention directed ⟨*dwelt* on the scene before him⟩ **b** : to write or speak at length or insistently — **dwell·er** *n*

dwell·ing \'dwel-iŋ\ *n* : a building or other shelter in which people live : HOUSE

dwelling place *n* : a place of residence

dwin·dle \'dwin-d°l\ *vb* **dwin·dled; dwin·dling** \'dwin-dliŋ, -d°l-iŋ\ [prob. freq. of *dwine* to waste away] : to make or become less : waste away ⟨*dwindling* supply of coal⟩ **syn** see DECREASE

dy·ad \'dī-ˌad, -əd\ *n* **1** : PAIR **2** : a meiotic chromosome after separation of the two homologous members of a tetrad — **dy·ad·ic** \dī-'ad-ik\ *adj*

dyb·buk \'dib-ək\ *n* [LHeb *dibbūq*] : a wandering soul believed in Jewish folklore to enter and possess a person

¹dye \'dī\ *n* [OE *dēah*] **1** : color from dyeing **2** : a soluble or insoluble coloring matter

²dye *vb* **dyed; dye·ing 1** : to impart a new and often permanent color to esp. by impregnating with a dye **2** : to impart (a color) by dyeing **3** : to take up or impart color in dyeing — **dy·er** \'dī(-ə)r\ *n*

dyed-in-the-wool \ˌdīd-°n-thə-'wu̇l\ *adj* : THOROUGH-GOING, UNCOMPROMISING ⟨a *dyed-in-the-wool* conservative⟩

dye·ing \'dī-iŋ\ *n* : the process or art of fixing coloring matters in fibers (as of wool or cotton)

dye·stuff \'dī-ˌstəf\ *n* : DYE 2

dye·wood \-ˌwu̇d\ *n* : a wood (as logwood) from which coloring matter is extracted for dyeing

dy·ing \'dī-iŋ\ *adj* [fr. prp. of *die*] **1** : being about to die : being in the act of dying or dying out : EXPIRING ⟨a *dying* man⟩ ⟨a *dying* fire⟩ ⟨the *dying* day⟩ **2** : of or relating to dying or death ⟨his *dying* wish⟩ ⟨would remember until his *dying* day⟩

dyke *var of* DIKE

dy·nam·ic \dī-'nam-ik\ *adj* [Gk *dynamis* power, fr. *dynasthai* to be able] **1 a** : of or relating to physical force or energy **b** : of or relating to dynamics : ACTIVE **2 a** : marked by continuous activity or change **b** : marked by energy : FORCEFUL — **dy·nam·i·cal** \-'nam-i-kəl\ *adj* — **dy·nam·i·cal·ly** \-i-k(ə-)lē\ *adv*

dy·nam·ics \dī-'nam-iks\ *n sing or pl* **1** : a branch of mechanics that deals with forces and their relation to the motion and sometimes the equilibrium of bodies of matter **2** : the driving physical, moral, or intellectual forces of any area or the laws relating to them **3** : the pattern of change or growth of an object or phenomenon **4** : variation and contrast in force or intensity (as in music)

dy·na·mism \'dī-nə-ˌmiz-əm\ *n* **1 a** : a theory that explains the universe in terms of forces **b** : DYNAMICS 3 **2** : a dynamic quality

¹dy·na·mite \'dī-nə-ˌmīt\ *n* : a blasting explosive that is made of nitroglycerin absorbed in a porous material and that sometimes contains other chemicals; *also* : any of various blasting explosives that contain no nitroglycerin

²dynamite *vt* : to blow up with dynamite — **dy·na·mit·er** *n*

dy·na·mo \'dī-nə-ˌmō\ *n, pl* **-mos** [short for *dynamo-electric machine*] **1** : GENERATOR 3 **2** : a forceful energetic individual

dy·na·mo·elec·tric \ˌdī-nə-mō-ə-'lek-trik\ *adj* : relating to the conversion by induction of mechanical energy into electrical energy or vice versa

dy·na·mom·e·ter \ˌdī-nə-'mäm-ət-ər\ *n* : an apparatus for measuring mechanical power — **dy·na·mo·met·ric** \ˌdī-nə-mō-'me-trik\ *adj* — **dy·na·mom·e·try** \ˌdī-nə-'mäm-ə-trē\ *n*

dy·na·mo·tor \'dī-nə-ˌmōt-ər\ *n* : a motor generator combining the electric motor and generator

dy·nas·ty \'dī-nə-stē, -ˌnas-tē\ *n, pl* **-ties** [Gk *dynasteia* power, lordship, fr. *dynastēs* ruler, fr. *dynasthai* to be able] **1** : a succession of rulers of the same line of descent **2** : a powerful group or family that maintains its position for a

considerable time — **dy·nas·tic** \dī-'nas-tik\ *adj* — **dy·nas·ti·cal·ly** \-ti-k(ə-)lē\ *adv*

dyne \'dīn\ *n* [F, fr. Gk *dynamis*] : the unit of force in the cgs system equal to the force that would give a free mass of one gram an acceleration of one centimeter per second per second

dys- *prefix* [Gk, bad, difficult] **1** : abnormal ⟨*dys*plasia⟩ **2** : difficult ⟨*dys*phagia⟩ — compare EU- **3** : impaired ⟨*dys*function⟩

dys·en·tery \'dis-°n-ˌter-ē\ *n* [Gk *dys-* bad + *enteron* intestine] **1** : a disease characterized by severe diarrhea with passage of mucus and blood and usu. caused by infection **2** : DIARRHEA — **dys·en·ter·ic** \ˌdis-°n-'ter-ik\ *adj*

dys·func·tion \(')dis-'fəŋ(k)-shən\ *n* : impaired or abnormal functioning — **dys·func·tion·al** \-shnəl, -shən-°l\ *adj*

dys·gen·ic \(')dis-'jen-ik\ *adj* **1** : detrimental to the hereditary qualities of a stock **2** : biologically defective or deficient

dys·men·or·rhea \ˌ(ˌ)dis-ˌmen-ə-'rē-ə\ *n* : painful menstruation — **dys·men·or·rhe·al** \-'rē-əl\ *or* **dys·men·or·rhe·ic** \-'rē-ik\ *adj*

dys·pep·sia \dis-'pep-shə, -sē-ə\ *n* [Gk, fr. *dys-* bad + *pepsis* digestion, fr. *peptein, pessein* to cook, digest] : IN-DIGESTION

¹dys·pep·tic \-'pep-tik\ *adj* **1** : relating to or having dyspepsia **2** : GLOOMY, CROSS — **dys·pep·ti·cal·ly** \-ti-k(ə-)lē\ *adv*

²dyspeptic *n* : a person having dyspepsia

dys·pla·sia \dis-'plā-zh(ē-)ə\ *n* : abnormal growth or development (as of organs or cells); *also* : a resulting abnormal structure — **dys·plas·tic** \-'plas-tik\ *adj*

dys·pnea \'dis(p)-nē-ə, dis(p)-'\ *n* [Gk *dys-* difficult + *pnein*, to breathe] : difficult or labored breathing — **dys·pne·ic** \dis(p)-'nē-ik\ *adj*

dys·pro·si·um \dis-'prō-zē-əm\ *n* : a chemical element that forms highly magnetic compounds — see ELEMENT table

dys·tro·phy \'dis-trə-fē\ *n, pl* **-phies** [Gk *dys-* bad + *-trophia* -trophy] : imperfect nutrition; *esp* : any of several neuromuscular disorders — compare MUSCULAR DYSTROPHY — **dys·tro·phic** \dis-'träf-ik, -'trō-fik\ *adj*

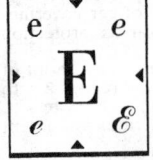

e \'ē\ *n, often cap* **1** : the 5th letter of the English alphabet **2** : the musical tone E **3** : a grade rating a student's work as poor and usu. constituting a conditional pass

e- *prefix* [OF, out, forth, away, fr. L, fr. *ex-*] **1** : not ⟨*e*carinate⟩ **2** : thoroughly ⟨*e*vaporize⟩ **3** : out : forth ⟨*e*radiate⟩

¹each \'ēch\ *adj* [OE *ǣlc*] : being one of two or more distinct individuals

²each *pron* : each one ⟨*each* of us had a twin⟩

³each *adv* : to or for each : APIECE

each other *pron* : each of two or more in reciprocal action or relation ⟨looked at *each other*⟩

ea·ger \'ē-gər\ *adj* [OF *aigre* keen, sharp, fr. L *acer*] : marked by keen, enthusiastic, or sharply expectant desire or interest — **ea·ger·ly** *adv* — **ea·ger·ness** *n*
syn ANXIOUS: EAGER implies ardor and enthusiasm and suggests impatience at delay or restraint; ANXIOUS stresses fear of frustration or failure or disappointment

eager beaver *n* : one who is unduly zealous in performing his assigned duties and in volunteering for more

ea·gle \'ē-gəl\ *n* [OF *aigle*, fr. L *aquila*] **1** : any of various large diurnal birds of prey related to the hawks and noted for their keenness of vision and powers of flight **2** : a seal or standard or an insignia shaped like or bearing an eagle

bald eagle

---

j joke;   ŋ sing;   ō flow;   ȯ flaw;   ȯi coin;   th thin;   t͟h this;   ü loot;   u̇ foot;   y yet;   yü few;   yu̇ furious;   zh vision

3 : a ten-dollar gold coin of the U.S. bearing an eagle on the reverse **4 :** a golf score of two strokes less than par on a hole **5** *cap* **:** AQUILA

ea·glet \'ē-glət\ *n* **:** a young eagle

-ean — see -AN

¹ear \'i(ə)r\ *n* [OE *ēare*] **1 a :** the vertebrate organ of hearing and equilibrium consisting in the typical mammal of a sound-collecting outer ear separated by a membranous drum from a sound-transmitting middle ear that in turn is separated from a sensory inner ear by membranous fenestrae; *also* **:** the outer ear **b :** any of various organs capable of detecting vibratory motion **2 a :** the sense or act of hearing **b :** sensitivity to musical tone and pitch **3 :** ATTENTION; *esp* **:** sympathetic attention **4 :** something resembling an ear in shape or position — **eared** \'i(ə)rd\ *adj* — **ear·less** \'i(ə)r-ləs\ *adj*

²ear *n* [OE *ēar*] **:** the fruiting spike of a cereal (as Indian corn) including both the seeds and protective structures — **ear** *vi*

ear·ache \'i(ə)r-,āk\ *n* **:** an ache or pain in the ear

ear·drum \'i(ə)r-,drəm\ *n* **:** the thin membrane that separates the outer and middle ear and transmits sound waves as vibrations to the chain of tiny bones in the middle ear

eared seal *n* **:** any of a family of seals including the sea lions and fur seals and having small well-developed external ears

ear·ful \-,fúl\ *n* **:** an outpouring of news or gossip

earl \'ərl\ *n* [OE *eorl* warrior, nobleman] **1 :** a great nobleman in Anglo-Saxon or medieval England **2 :** a member of the British peerage ranking below a marquess and above a viscount — **earl·dom** \-dəm\ *n*

earless seal *n* **:** any of a family of seals with hairy coats and no external ears

ear·lobe \'i(ə)r-,lōb\ *n* **:** the pendent part of the ear of man or some fowls

¹ear·ly \'ər-lē\ *adv* **ear·li·er**; **-est** [OE *ǣrlīce*, fr. *ǣr* early, soon] **1 :** near the beginning of a period of time or of a process or series **2 :** before the usual time

²early *adj* **ear·li·er**; **-est 1 a :** of, relating to, or occurring near the beginning of a period of time or of a development or series **b :** PRIMITIVE **2 a :** occurring before the usual time (peaches are *early* this year) **b :** occurring in the near future **c :** maturing or producing sooner than related forms (an *early* peach) — **ear·li·ness** *n*

¹ear·mark \'i(ə)r-,märk\ *n* **1 :** a mark of identification on the ear of an animal **2 :** a distinguishing or identifying mark

²earmark *vt* **1 :** to mark with or as if with an earmark **2 :** to set aside for a specific purpose

ear·muff \'i(ə)r-,məf\ *n* **:** one of a pair of ear coverings connected by a flexible band and worn as protection against cold

earn \'ərn\ *vt* [OE *earnian*] **1 :** to deserve as a result of labor or service (*earned* every cent he was paid) **2 :** to get for services given (*earn* a good salary) — **earn·er** *n*

¹ear·nest \'ər-nəst\ *n* [OE *eornost*] **:** a serious and intent mental state (in *earnest*)

²earnest *adj* **1 :** characterized by or proceeding from an intense and serious state of mind **:** not light or playful **2 :** not trivial **:** IMPORTANT **syn** see SERIOUS — **ear·nest·ly** *adv* — **ear·nest·ness** \-nəs(t)-nəs\ *n*

³earnest *n* [modif. of OF *erres*, pl. of *erre* ³earnest, fr. L *arrabo*, *arra*, fr. Gk *arrhabōn*, fr. Heb '*ērābhōn*] **1 :** something of value given by a buyer to a seller to bind a bargain **2 :** a token of what is to come **:** PLEDGE

earn·ings \'ər-ningz\ *n pl* **1 :** something earned; *esp* **:** WAGES **2 :** revenue after expenses

ear·phone \'i(ə)r-,fōn\ *n* **:** a device that converts electrical energy into sound waves and is worn over or inserted into the ear (a radio *earphone*)

ear·ring \'i(ə)r-,ring\ *n* **:** an ornament for the earlobe

ear shell *n* **:** ABALONE

ear·shot \'i(ə)r-,shät\ *n* **:** the range within which the unaided voice may be heard

ear·split·ting \-,split-ing\ *adj* **:** intolerably loud or shrill

¹earth \'ərth\ *n* [OE *eorthe*] **1 :** the soft or granular material composing part of the surface of the globe; *esp* **:** cultivable soil **2 :** the sphere of mortal life as distinguished from heaven and hell **3 :** areas of land as distinguished from sea and air **:** GROUND **4** *often cap* **:** the

planet which we live on and which is 3d in order of distance from the sun — see PLANET table **5 :** the lair of a burrowing animal **6 :** any of several metallic oxides (as alumina)

syn EARTH, WORLD, UNIVERSE mean the entire area in which man thinks of himself as living. EARTH denotes the material global body, the planet of the sun, but often means the immediate sphere of human action in contrast to the religious concepts of heaven and hell; WORLD often equals EARTH, but may apply to space, earth, and all visible celestial bodies within man's present range of knowledge; UNIVERSE denotes the entire system of created things and physical phenomena regarded as a unit in its arrangement and operation

²earth *vt* **:** to draw soil about (plants)

earth·en \'ər-thən, -thən\ *adj* **:** made of earth or of baked clay (an *earthen* floor) (*earthen* dishes)

earth·en·ware \-,wa(ə)r, -,we(ə)r\ *n* **:** articles (as utensils or ornaments) made of baked clay esp. of the coarser kinds

earth·ling \'ərth-ling\ *n* **:** an inhabitant of the earth

earth·ly \'ərth-lē\ *adj* **1 :** of, relating to, or characteristic of the earth **:** not heavenly or spiritual (*earthly* joys) **2 :** POSSIBLE, IMAGINABLE (that tool is of no *earthly* use) — **earth·li·ness** *n*

syn WORLDLY, MUNDANE: EARTHLY implies chiefly contrast with *heavenly* (*earthly* love) WORLDLY and MUNDANE both imply a relation to the immediate concerns and activities of men, WORLDLY suggesting tangible personal gain or gratification and MUNDANE suggesting reference to the immediate and practical (*mundane* discussion of finances)

earth·quake \'ərth-,kwāk\ *n* **:** a shaking or trembling of a portion of the earth caused by movement of rock masses or by volcanic shocks

earth science *n* **:** any of the sciences (as geology or geography) that deal with the earth or one of its parts

earth·shine \-,shīn\ *n* **:** sunlight reflected by the earth that illuminates the dark part of the moon

earth·work \-,wərk\ *n* **:** an embankment or other construction of earth; *esp* **:** one made as a fortification

earth·worm \-,wərm\ *n* **:** a long slender worm with segmented body that lives in damp earth and moves by means of setae

earthy \'ər-thē, -thē\ *adj* **earth·i·er**; **-est 1 :** consisting of or resembling earth (an *earthy* flavor) **2 a :** DOWN-TO-EARTH, PRACTICAL **b :** CRUDE, GROSS (*earthy* humor) — **earth·i·ness** *n*

ear·wax \'i(ə)r-,waks\ *n* **:** CERUMEN

ear·wig \-,wig\ *n* [OE *ēare* ear + *wicga* insect] **:** any of numerous insects (order Dermaptera) with slender many-jointed antennae and a large forcepslike organ at the end of the body

¹ease \'ēz\ *n* [OF *aise* convenience, comfort, fr. L *adjacens* neighborhood, fr. neut. of prp. of *adjacēre* to lie near, fr. *ad-* + *jacēre* to lie] **1 :** freedom from pain or trouble **:** comfort of body or mind **2 :** freedom from any sense or feeling of difficulty or embarrassment **:** NATURALNESS (speak with *ease*)

²ease *vb* **1 :** to free from something that disquiets or burdens **2 :** to make less painful **:** ALLEVIATE (*ease* his suffering) **3 :** to make less tight or difficult **:** LOOSEN, SLACKEN (*ease* credit) (*ease* up on a rope)

ea·sel \'ē-zəl\ *n* [D *ezel*, lit., ass, fr. L *asinus*] **:** a frame for supporting something (as an artist's canvas)

eas·i·ly \'ēz-(ə-)lē\ *adv* **1 :** in an easy manner (won the game *easily*) **2 :** by far (*easily* the best man)

¹east \'ēst\ *adv* [OE *ēast*] **:** to or toward the east

²east *adj* **1 :** situated toward or at the east **2 :** coming from the east

³east *n* **1 a :** the general direction of sunrise **b :** the compass point directly opposite to west — see COMPASS CARD **2** *cap* **:** regions or countries east of a specified or implied point **3 :** the altar end of a church

east·bound \'ēs(t)-,baùnd\ *adj* **:** headed east

east by north : one point north of due east **:** N78°45'E

east by south : one point south of due east **:** S78°45'E

Eas·ter \'ē-stər\ *n* [OE *ēastre*; akin to E *east*] **:** a feast observed on the first Sunday after the ecclesiastical full moon on or next after March 21 in commemoration of Christ's resurrection

Easter lily *n* **:** any of several white cultivated lilies that bloom in early spring

east·er·ly \'ē-stər-lē\ *adv (or adj)* **1** : from the east **2** : toward the east

east·ern \'ē-stərn\ *adj* [OE *ēasterne*] **1** *often cap* : of, relating to, or characteristic of a region conventionally designated East **2** *cap* **a** : of, relating to, or being the Christian churches originating in the church of the Eastern Roman Empire **b** : Eastern Orthodox **3** : lying toward or coming from the east — **east·ern·most** \-,mōst\ *adj*

East·ern·er \'ē-stə(r)-nər\ *n* : a native or inhabitant of the East (as of the U.S.)

eastern hemisphere *n* : the half of the earth to the east of the Atlantic ocean including Europe, Asia, and Africa

Eastern Orthodox *adj* : of or consisting of the Eastern churches that form a loose federation according primacy of honor to the patriarch of Constantinople and adhering to the decisions of the first seven ecumenical councils and to one rite

Eastern standard time *n* : the time of the 5th time zone west of Greenwich that includes the eastern U.S.

east·ing \'ē-stiŋ\ *n* **1** : difference in longitude to the east from the last preceding point of reckoning **2** : easterly progress

east–northeast *n* — see COMPASS CARD

east–southeast *n* — see COMPASS CARD

¹east·ward \'ēs-twərd\ *adv (or adj)* : toward the east — **east·ward·ly** \-lē\ *adv (or adj)* — **east·wards** \-twərdz\ *adv*

²eastward *n* : eastward direction or part ⟨sail to the *eastward*⟩

easy \'ē-zē\ *adj* **eas·i·er; -est** **1** : not hard to do or get : not difficult ⟨an *easy* lesson⟩ **2** : not severe : LENIENT ⟨an *easy* teacher⟩ **3** : COMFORTABLE ⟨*easy* slippers⟩ **4** : showing ease : NATURAL, UNAFFECTED ⟨an *easy* manner⟩ **5** : free from pain, trouble, or worry ⟨feels *easy* in his mind⟩ **6** : UNHURRIED, LEISURELY ⟨go along at an *easy* pace⟩ **7** : not steep or abrupt ⟨*easy* slope⟩ **syn** see SIMPLE — **eas·i·ness** *n*

easy·go·ing \,ē-zē-'gō-iŋ\ *adj* : taking life easily : CAREFREE — **easy·go·ing·ness** *n*

eat \'ēt\ *vb* **ate** \'āt\; **eat·en** \'ēt-ᵊn\; **eat·ing** [OE *etan*] **1** : to take into the mouth and swallow food : chew and swallow in turn **2** : to take a meal **3** : to destroy, use up, or waste as if by eating : wear away ⟨rocks *eaten* away by waves⟩ ⟨rust *eats* away metal⟩ **4** : to affect something by gradual destruction or consumption — used with *into* ⟨acid *ate* into the metal⟩ — **eat·er** *n*

¹eat·a·ble \'ēt-ə-bəl\ *adj* : fit to be eaten

²eatable *n* **1** : something to eat **2** *pl* : FOOD

eau de co·logne \,ōd-ə-kə-'lōn\ *n, pl* **eaux de cologne** \,ō(z)d-ə-\ [F, lit., water from Cologne] : COLOGNE

eau-de-vie \,ōd-ə-'vē\ *n, pl* **eaux-de-vie** \,ō(z)d-ə-\ [F, lit., water of life] : BRANDY

eaves \'ēvz\ *n sing or pl* [OE *efes*, sing.] : the overhanging lower edge of a roof projecting beyond the wall of a building ⟨icicles hanging from the *eaves*⟩

eaves·drop \'ēvz-,dräp\ *vi* [prob. backᵉformation fr. *eavesdropper*, lit., one standing under the drip from the eaves] : to listen secretly to what is said in private — **eaves·drop·per** *n*

e eaves

eaves trough *n* : GUTTER 1a

¹ebb \'eb\ *n* [OE *ebba*] **1** : the flowing back from the shore of water brought in by the tide ⟨the *ebb* and flow of the sea⟩ **2** : a passing from a high to a low point : a time of decline

²ebb *vi* **1** : to recede from the flood state **2** : DECLINE, WEAKEN

eb·bet \'eb-ət\ *n* : a common green newt of the eastern U.S.

ebb tide *n* **1** : the tide while ebbing **2** : a period or state of decline

eb·on \'eb-ən\ *adj* : EBONY

eb·o·nite \'eb-ə-,nīt\ *n* : hard rubber esp. when black

¹eb·o·ny \'eb-ə-nē\ *n, pl* **-nies** [Gk *ebenos* ebony, fr. Egypt *hbnj*] : a hard heavy wood yielded by various Old World tropical trees related to the persimmon; *also* : a tree yielding ebony

²ebony *adj* **1** : made of or resembling ebony **2** : BLACK, DARK

ebul·lient \i-'bùl-yənt\ *adj* [L *ebullire* to bubble out, fr. *e-* + *bullire* to bubble, boil] **1** : BOILING, AGITATED **2** : characterized by lively or enthusiastic expression of thoughts or feelings : EXUBERANT — **ebul·lience** \-yən(t)s\ *n* — **ebul·lient·ly** *adv*

eb·ul·li·tion \,eb-ə-'lish-ən\ *n* : the process or state of boiling or bubbling up

ecar·i·nate \(')ē-'kar-ə-,nāt\ *adj* : lacking a keel ⟨an *ecarinate* flower⟩

¹ec·cen·tric \ik-'sen-trik, ek-\ *adj* [Gk *ex, ek* out of + *kentron* center] **1** : not having the same center ⟨*eccentric* spheres⟩ **2** : deviating from some established pattern or from conventional or accepted usage or conduct **3 a** : deviating from a circular path ⟨an *eccentric* orbit⟩ **b** : located elsewhere than at the geometrical center — **ec·cen·tri·cal·ly** \-tri-k(ə-)lē\ *adv*

²eccentric *n* **1** : a disklike device that turns around a shaft not at its center and is used in machinery for changing circular motion into back-and-forth motion **2** : an eccentric person

ec·cen·tric·i·ty \,ek-,sen-'tris-ət-ē\ *n, pl* **-ties** **1 a** : the quality or state of being eccentric **b** : deviation from an established pattern, rule, or norm; *esp* : odd or whimsical behavior **2** : the degree of deviation from a circular path ⟨a planet's *eccentricity*⟩

syn ECCENTRICITY, IDIOSYNCRASY mean a peculiar trait, trick, or habit. ECCENTRICITY stresses divergence from the usual or customary and suggests whimsicality or mild mental aberration; IDIOSYNCRASY stresses the following of one's particular bent or temperament and connotes strong individuality and independence of action

Ec·cle·si·as·tes \ik-,lē-zē-'as-(,)tēz\ *n* — see BIBLE table

ec·cle·si·as·tic \-'as-tik\ *n* [Gk *ekklēsia* assembly of citizens, church, fr. *ekkalein* to summon, fr. *ex-* + *kalein* to call] : CLERGYMAN

ec·cle·si·as·ti·cal \-ti-kəl\ *or* **ec·cle·si·as·tic** \-tik\ *adj* : of or relating to the church or its organization or government ⟨*ecclesiastical* history⟩ — **ec·cle·si·as·ti·cal·ly** \-ti-k(ə-)lē\ *adv*

ec·crine \'ek-rən, -,rīn, -,rēn\ *adj* [Gk *ekkrinein* to secrete, fr. *ex-* out + *krinein* to separate] : producing a fluid secretion without removing cytoplasm of the secreting cells ⟨*eccrine* glands⟩

ec·dy·sis \'ek-də-səs\ *n, pl* **-dy·ses** \-də-,sēz\ : the act of molting or of shedding (as by insects and crustaceans) an outer cuticular layer

ech·e·lon \'esh-ə-,län\ *n* [F *échelon*, lit., rung of a ladder] **1 a** : a formation of units (as troops or airplanes) resembling a series of steps **b** : any of several military units **2** : one of a series of levels or grades esp. of authority or the individuals at such a level ⟨policies determined by the higher *echelons*⟩

echid·na \i-'kid-nə\ *n* [Gk, viper] : a spiny-coated toothless burrowing egg-laying mammal of Australia with a tapering snout and long tongue for eating ants

echi·nate \i-'kī-nət\ *adj* : SPINY

echi·no·derm \i-'kī-nə-,dərm\ *n* [Gk *echinos* sea urchin + *derma* skin] : any of a phylum (Echinodermata) of radially symmetrical marine animals that have true coeloms and include the starfishes, sea urchins, and related forms — **echi·no·der·ma·tous** \i,kī-nə-'dər-mət-əs\ *adj*

echi·noid \i-'kī-,noid\ *n* : SEA URCHIN

echin·u·late \i-'kin-yə-lət\ *adj* : set with small spines or prickles — **echin·u·la·tion** \i,kin-yə-'lā-shən\ *n*

echi·nus \i-'kī-nəs\ *n, pl* **-ni** \-,nī\ : SEA URCHIN

¹echo \'ek-ō\ *n, pl* **ech·oes** [Gk *ēchō*] **1** : the repetition of a sound caused by reflection of sound waves **2 a** : a repetition or imitation of another **b** : REPERCUSSION, RESULT **3** : one who closely imitates or repeats another **4 a** : the repetition of a received radio signal due esp. to reflection **b** (1) : the reflection of transmitted radar signals by an object (2) : the visual indication of this reflection on a radarscope — **echo·ic** \i-'kō-ik, e-\ *adj*

²echo *vb* **1** : to resound with echoes **2** : to produce an echo : send back or repeat a sound **3** : REPEAT, IMITATE

echo·lo·ca·tion \,ek-ō-lō-'kā-shən\ *n* : a process for locating distant or invisible objects by means of sound waves reflected back to the sender by the objects

éclair \ā-'kla(ə)r, -'kle(ə)r, 'ā-,\ *n* [F, lit., lightning] : an oblong cream puff with whipped cream or custard filling

eclamp·sia \e-'klam(p)-sē-ə\ *n* : a convulsive state; *esp*

: an attack of convulsions during pregnancy or parturition — **eclamp·tic** \-'klam(p)-tik\ *adj*

éclat \ā-'klä\ *n* [F] **1** : brilliance esp. in performance or achievement **2** : demonstration of approval : ACCLAIM

eclec·tic \e-'klek-tik, i-\ *adj* [Gk *eklektikos*, fr. *eklegein* to select, fr. *ex-* out + *legein* to gather] **1** : selecting elements from various doctrines, methods, or styles **2** : composed of elements drawn from various sources — **eclectic** *n* — **eclec·ti·cal·ly** \-ti-k(ə-)lē\ *adv* — **eclec·ti·cism** \-tə-,siz-əm\ *n*

¹**eclipse** \i-'klips\ *n* [Gk *ekleipsis*, fr. *ekleipein* to omit, suffer eclipse, fr. *ex-* out + *leipein* to leave] **1** : a complete or partial hiding or darkening of the sun or the moon caused when the sun is obscured by the moon's passing between the sun and the earth or when the moon is obscured by its entering the shadow of the earth; *also* : the obscuring of any celestial body by another **2** : a falling into obscurity, decline, or disgrace

²**eclipse** *vt* **1** : to cause an eclipse of **2** : to reduce in fame **3** : to surpass greatly : OUTSHINE

¹**eclip·tic** \i-'klip-tik\ *n* : the great circle of the celestial sphere that is the apparent path of the sun among the stars

²**ecliptic** *adj* : of or relating to the ecliptic or an eclipse

ec·logue \'ek-,lòg\ *n* [L *Eclogae*, title of Vergil's pastorals, lit., selections] : a poem in which shepherds engage in dialogue

ecol·o·gy \i-'käl-ə-jē\ *n* [Gk *oikos* house] **1** : a branch of science concerned with the interrelationship of organisms and their environments **2** : the totality or pattern of relations between organisms and their environment — **ec·o·log·ic** \,ek-ə-'läj-ik, ,ē-kə-\ *or* **ec·o·log·i·cal** \-'läj-i-kəl\ *adj* — **ec·o·log·i·cal·ly** \-'läj-i-k(ə-)lē\ *adv* — **ecol·o·gist** \i-'käl-ə-jəst\ *n*

ec·o·nom·ic \,ek-ə-'näm-ik, ,ē-kə-\ *adj* **1 a** : of or relating to the science of economics **b** : of, relating to, or based on the production, distribution, and consumption of goods and services **c** : of or relating to an economy **2** : having practical or industrial significance or uses : affecting material resources ⟨*economic* pests⟩

ec·o·nom·i·cal \-'näm-i-kəl\ *adj* **1** : given to thrift : FRUGAL **2** : operating with little waste or at a saving ⟨an *economical* car⟩ — **ec·o·nom·i·cal·ly** \-'näm-i-k(ə-)lē\ *adv*

ec·o·nom·ics \,ek-ə-'näm-iks, ,ē-kə-\ *n* **1** : a social science concerned chiefly with description and analysis of the production, distribution, and consumption of goods and services **2** : economic aspect or significance — **econ·o·mist** \i-'kän-ə-məst\ *n*

econ·o·mize \i-'kän-ə-,mīz\ *vb* **1** : to practice economy : be frugal ⟨*economize* on fuel⟩ **2** : to use more economically : SAVE — **econ·o·miz·er** *n*

econ·o·my \i-'kän-ə-mē\ *n, pl* **-mies** [Gk *oikonomia*, fr. *oikos* house + *nom-, nemein* to manage] **1 a** : thrifty use of material resources : frugality in expenditures **b** : the efficient and sparing use of the means available for the end proposed **c** : an act of economizing **2** : systematic arrangement : ORGANIZATION **3** : the structure of economic life in a country, area, or period; *esp* : an economic system

eco·spe·cies \'ek-ō-,spē-(,)shēz, 'ē-kō-, -(,)sēz\ *n* : an ecologic unit comparable to the taxonomic species and made up of ecotypes able to interbreed freely — **eco·spe·cif·ic** \,ek-ō-spi-'sif-ik, ,ē-kō-\ *adj*

eco·sys·tem \'ek-ō-,sis-təm, 'ē-kō-\ *n* : a complex of ecological community and environment forming a functioning whole in nature

eco·tone \-,tōn\ *n* : a transition area between two ecological communities

eco·type \'ek-ō-,tīp, 'ē-kō-\ *n* : an ecological unit comparable to a taxonomic subspecies that is preserved by environmental barriers even though its members form fertile crosses with members of related ecotypes — **eco·typ·ic** \,ek-ō-'tip-ik, ,ē-kō-\ *adj* — **eco·typ·i·cal·ly** \-'tip-i-k(ə-)lē\ *adv*

écru \'ek-rü, 'ā-krü\ *adj* [F *écru* unbleached] : BEIGE

ec·sta·sy \'ek-stə-sē\ *n, pl* **-sies** [Gk *ekstasis*, fr. *existanai* to derange, fr. *ex-* out of + *histanai* to cause to stand] **1** : a state of being beyond reason and self-control **2** : a state of overwhelming emotion; *esp* : rapturous delight

ec·stat·ic \ek-'stat-ik\ *adj* **1** : marked by ecstasy : full of joy and rapture **2** : causing ecstasy — **ec·stat·i·cal·ly** \-i-k(ə-)lē\ *adv*

ect- *or* **ecto-** *comb form* [Gk *ektos*, fr. *ex* out, out of] : outside : external ⟨*ectomere*⟩ — compare END-, EXO-

ec·to·derm \'ek-tə-,dərm\ *n* **1** : the outer cellular layer of a 2-layered animal (as a jellyfish) **2 a** : the outermost of the three primary germ layers of an embryo **b** : a tissue (as skin or nerve) derived from the outermost germ layer — **ec·to·der·mal** \,ek-tə-'dər-məl\ *or* **ec·to·der·mic** \-mik\ *adj*

ec·to·mor·phic \,ek-tə-'mòr-fik\ *adj* : predominating in structures (as nerves) developed from the ectodermal layer of the embryo : light and slender in body build — **ec·to·morph** \'ek-tə-,mòrf\ *n* — **ec·to·mor·phi·cal·ly** \,ek-tə-'mòr-fi-k(ə-)lē\ *adv* — **ec·to·mor·phy** \'ek-tə-,mòr-fē\ *n*

-ec·to·my \'ek-tə-mē\ *n comb form, pl* **-mies** [Gk *ektemnein* to cut out, fr. *ex-* out + *temnein* to cut] : surgical removal ⟨mastoid*ectomy*⟩

ec·to·par·a·site \,ek-tō-'par-ə-,sīt\ *n* : a parasite that lives on the exterior of its host — **ec·to·par·a·sit·ic** \-,par-ə-'sit-ik\ *adj*

ec·to·plasm \'ek-tə-,plaz-əm\ *n* : the outer relatively rigid layer of the cytoplasm usu. held to be a reversible gel — **ec·to·plas·mic** \,ek-tə-'plaz-mik\ *adj*

ec·u·men·i·cal \,ek-yə-'men-i-kəl\ *adj* [Gk *oikoumenē* the inhabited world, fr. fem. of pres. pass. part. of *oikein* to inhabit, fr. *oikos* house] **1** : worldwide or general in extent, influence, or application **2** : of, relating to, or representing the whole of a body of churches **3** : promoting or tending toward worldwide Christian unity or cooperation — **ec·u·men·i·cal·ly** \-i-k(ə-)lē\ *adv* — **ec·u·me·nic·i·ty** \-mə-'nis-ət-ē\ *n*

ecumenical patriarch *n* : the patriarch of Constantinople as the dignitary given first honor in the Eastern Orthodox Church

ec·ze·ma \ig-'zē-mə, 'ek-sə-mə, 'eg-zə-\ *n* [Gk *ekzema*, fr. *ekzein* to erupt, fr. *ex-* out + *zein* to boil] : a skin inflammation marked by redness, itching, and scaly or crusted lesions — **ec·zem·a·tous** \ig-'zem-ət-əs, -'zē-mət-\ *adj*

¹**-ed** \d *after a vowel or* b, g, j, l, m, n, ŋ, r, th, v, z, zh; əd, id *after* d, t; t *after other sounds; exceptions are pronounced at their subentries or entries*\ *vb suffix or adj suffix* [OE *-ed, -od, -d*] **1** — used to form the past participle of regular weak verbs ⟨end*ed*⟩ ⟨fad*ed*⟩ ⟨tri*ed*⟩ ⟨patt*ed*⟩ **2** — used to form adjectives of identical meaning from Latin-derived adjectives ending in *-ate* ⟨crenulat*ed*⟩ **3 a** : having : characterized by ⟨cultur*ed*⟩ ⟨two-legg*ed*⟩ **b** : having the characteristics of ⟨bigot*ed*⟩

²**-ed** *vb suffix* [OE *-ede, -ode, -de*] — used to form the past tense of regular weak verbs ⟨judg*ed*⟩ ⟨deni*ed*⟩ ⟨dropp*ed*⟩

Edam \'ēd-əm, 'ē-,dam\ *n* : a Dutch pressed cheese of yellow color and mild flavor made in balls

edaph·ic \i-'daf-ik\ *adj* [Gk *edaphos* bottom, ground] : of, relating to, or resulting from the soil — **edaph·i·cal·ly** \-'daf-i-k(ə-)lē\ *adv*

Ed·dic \'ed-ik\ *adj* : of, relating to, or resembling the Old Norse *Edda* which is a 13th century collection of chiefly mythological poems in alliterative verse

¹**ed·dy** \'ed-ē\ *n, pl* **eddies** [ME (Sc) *ydy*] **1** : a current of air or water running contrary to the main current; *esp* : a current moving in a circle like a whirlpool **2** : a substance moving like an eddy ⟨*eddies* of dust⟩

²**eddy** *vb* **ed·died; ed·dy·ing** : to move in an eddy or so as to form an eddy ⟨the stream *eddied* about a large rock⟩

edel·weiss \'ād-ºl-,wīs\ *n* [G, fr. *edel* noble + *weiss* white] : a small perennial woolly herb that is related to the thistles and grows high in the Alps

ede·ma \i-'dē-mə\ *n* [Gk *oidēma* swelling, fr. *oidein* to swell] : abnormal accumulation of watery fluid in connective tissue or in a serous cavity; *also* : a condition marked by such accumulation — **edem·a·tous** \i-'dem-ət-əs, -'dē-mət-\ *adj*

Eden \'ēd-ºn\ *n* **1** : the garden where Adam and Eve are held to have first lived **2** : PARADISE **3** — **Eden·ic** \i-'den-ik\ *adj*

eden·tate \(')ē-'den-,tāt\ *n* : any of an order (Edentata) of mammals having few or no teeth and including the sloths, armadillos, and New World anteaters and formerly also the pangolins and the aardvark — **edentate** *adj*

ə abut; ⁰ kitten; ər further; a back; ā bake; ä cot, cart; aú out; ch chin; e less; ē easy; g gift; i trip; ī life

eden·tu·lous \(')ē-'den-chə-ləs\ *adj* : TOOTHLESS

¹edge \'ej\ *n* [OE *ecg*] **1 a** : the cutting side of a blade **b** : the sharpness of a blade **c** : penetrating power : KEENNESS ⟨his voice had a sarcastic *edge*⟩ **2 a** : the line where an object or surface begins or ends : VERGE, BRINK; *also* : the narrow adjacent part : BORDER **b** : the intersection of two plane faces of a solid **3** : a favorable margin : ADVANTAGE **syn** see BORDER — **edged** \'ejd\ *adj* — **on edge** : ANXIOUS, NERVOUS

²edge *vb* **1** : to give an edge to ⟨*edge* a sleeve with lace⟩ **2 a** : to move along gradually ⟨*edged* his chair closer⟩ **b** : to advance very slowly or by short moves ⟨the crowd *edged* closer⟩ **3** : to incline (a ski) sideways

edge tool *n* **1** : a tool (as a chisel, knife, plane, or gouge) with a sharp cutting edge **2** : a tool for forming or dressing an edge

edge·ways \'ej-,wāz\ *or* **edge·wise** \-,wīz\ *adv* : with the edge foremost : SIDEWAYS

edg·ing \'ej-iŋ\ *n* : something that forms an edge or border ⟨a lace *edging*⟩

edgy \'ej-ē\ *adj* **edg·i·er**; **-est 1** : having an edge : SHARP ⟨an *edgy* tone⟩ **2** : being on edge : TENSE, NERVOUS, IRRITABLE — **edg·i·ly** \'ej-ə-lē\ *adv* — **edg·i·ness** \'ej-ē-nəs\ *n*

ed·i·ble \'ed-ə-bəl\ *adj* [L *edere* to eat] : fit or safe to be eaten — **edible** *n* — **ed·i·ble·ness** *n*

edict \'ē-,dikt\ *n* [L *edictum*, fr. neut. of pp. of *edicere* to decree, fr. *e-* + *dicere* to say] : an official public proclamation made by an authority (as a sovereign) having the force of law — **edic·tal** \i-'dik-t⁹l\ *adj*

ed·i·fice \'ed-ə-fəs\ *n* : BUILDING; *esp* : a large or impressive building (as a church)

ed·i·fy \'ed-ə-,fī\ *vt* **-fied**; **-fy·ing** [LL *aedificare*, fr. L, to erect a house, fr. *aedes* temple, house] : to instruct and improve esp. by good example : benefit morally or spiritually ⟨plays that *edify* the audience⟩ — **ed·i·fi·ca·tion** \,ed-ə-fə-'kā-shən\ *n*

ed·it \'ed-ət\ *vt* [L *edit-*, *edere* to bring forth, publish, fr. *e-* + *dare* to give] **1 a** : to correct, revise, and prepare esp. for publication ⟨*edited* Poe's works⟩ **b** : to assemble (as a moving-picture film or tape recording) for use or publication by cutting and rearranging **2** : to direct the publication of

edi·tion \i-'dish-ən\ *n* **1 a** : the form in which a text (as a printed book) is published **b** : the whole number of copies printed or published at one time ⟨a third *edition*⟩ **c** : one of the several issues of a newspaper for a single day **2** : COPY, VERSION ⟨the boy is a smaller *edition* of his father⟩

ed·i·tor \'ed-ət-ər\ *n* **1** : one that edits esp. as an occupation **2** : a person who writes editorials — **ed·i·tor·ship** \-,ship\ *n*

¹ed·i·to·ri·al \,ed-ə-'tōr-ē-əl, -'tor-\ *adj* **1** : of or relating to an editor ⟨an *editorial* staff⟩ **2** : being or resembling an editorial ⟨an *editorial* statement⟩ — **ed·i·to·ri·al·ly** \-ē-ə-lē\ *adv*

²editorial *n* : a newspaper or magazine article that gives the opinions of its editors or publishers

ed·i·to·ri·al·ist \-ē-ə-ləst\ *n* : a writer of editorials

ed·i·to·ri·al·ize \,ed-ə-'tōr-ē-ə-,līz, -'tor-\ *vi* **1** : to express an opinion in the form of an editorial **2** : to introduce opinion into the reporting of facts — **ed·i·to·ri·al·i·za·tion** \-,tōr-ē-ə-lə-'zā-shən, -,tor-\ *n* — **ed·i·to·ri·al·iz·er** \-'tōr-ē-ə-,lī-zər, -'tor-\ *n*

ed·u·ca·ble \'ej-ə-kə-bəl\ *also* **ed·u·cat·a·ble** \-,kāt-ə-bəl\ *adj* : capable of being educated

ed·u·cate \'ej-ə-,kāt\ *vt* [L *educare* to rear, educate] **1** : to provide schooling for **2 a** : to develop mentally and morally esp. by formal instruction **b** : TRAIN **syn** see TEACH — **ed·u·ca·tor** \-,kāt-ər\ *n*

ed·u·cat·ed *adj* **1** : having an education; *esp* : having an education beyond the average **2** : giving evidence of education **3** : based on some knowledge of fact ⟨an *educated* guess⟩

ed·u·ca·tion \,ej-ə-'kā-shən\ *n* **1 a** : the action or process of educating or of being educated **b** : the knowledge and development resulting from an educational process ⟨a man of little *education*⟩ **2** : the field of study that deals mainly with methods and problems of teaching — **ed·u·ca·tion·al** \-shnəl, -shən-⁹l\ *adj* — **ed·u·ca·tion·al·ly** \-ē\ *adv*

syn TRAINING: EDUCATION is the general term for institutional learning and implies the guidance and training intended to develop a person's full capacities and intelligence; TRAINING suggests exercise or practice to gain skill, endurance, or facility in a specific field

ed·u·ca·tive \'ej-ə-,kāt-iv\ *adj* **1** : tending to educate : INSTRUCTIVE **2** : of or relating to education ⟨improvements in *educative* procedures⟩

educe \i-'d(y)üs\ *vt* [L *educere* to draw out, fr. *e-* + *ducere* to lead] **1** : to bring out : draw forth : ELICIT ⟨the questioning *educed* surprising answers⟩ **2** : DEDUCE — **educ·i·ble** \-'d(y)ü-sə-bəl\ *adj* — **educ·tion** \-'dək-shən\ *n* — **educ·tor** \-'dək-tər\ *n*

Ed·war·di·an \ed-'wärd-ē-ən\ *adj* : of, relating to, or characteristic of Edward VII of England or his age — **Edwardian** *n*

¹-ee \'ē, (,)ē\ *n suffix* [MF *-é*, fr. *-é*, pp. ending of some verbs, fr. L *-atus*] **1** : recipient or beneficiary of (a specified action or thing) ⟨appoint*ee*⟩ ⟨grant*ee*⟩ ⟨patent*ee*⟩ **2** : person that performs (a specified action) ⟨escap*ee*⟩

²-ee *n suffix* [prob. alter. of *-y*] **1** : a particular esp. small kind of ⟨boot*ee*⟩ **2** : one resembling or suggestive of ⟨goat*ee*⟩

eel \'ēl\ *n, pl* **eels** *or* **eel** [OE *æl*] **1** : any of numerous long snakelike fishes with smooth slimy skin and no pelvic fins **2** : EELWORM — **eel·like** \'ēl-,līk\ *adj* — **eely** \'ē-lē\ *adj*

eel·grass \'ēl-,gras\ *n* : a monocotyledonous plant that grows underwater and has long narrow leaves

eel·pout \-,paut\ *n* **1** : any of various marine fishes resembling blennies **2** : BURBOT

eel·worm \-,wərm\ *n* : a nematode worm; *esp* : one free-living in soil or parasitic on plants

e'en \(')ēn\ *adv* : EVEN

-eer \'i(ə)r\ *n suffix* [MF *-ier*, fr. L *-arius*] : one that is concerned with or conducts or produces professionally ⟨auction*eer*⟩ ⟨pamphlet*eer*⟩ — often in words with derogatory meaning ⟨profit*eer*⟩

e'er \(')e(ə)r, (')a(ə)r\ *adv* : EVER

ee·rie *also* **ee·ry** \'i(ə)r-ē\ *adj* **ee·ri·er**; **-est** [OE *earg* cowardly, wretched] **1 a** : frightening because of strangeness or gloominess **b** : arousing fear of the supernatural **2** : STRANGE, MYSTERIOUS **syn** see WEIRD — **ee·ri·ly** \'ir-ə-lē\ *adv* — **ee·ri·ness** \'ir-ē-nəs\ *n*

ef·face \i-'fās, e-\ *vt* [MF *effacer*, fr. *ex-* + *face*] **1** : to wipe out : OBLITERATE **2** : to make indistinct by or as if by rubbing out : ERASE ⟨*efface* an inscription⟩ ⟨*efface* unpleasant memories⟩ **3** : to make (oneself) inconspicuous or modestly unnoticeable — **ef·face·a·ble** \-'fā-sə-bəl\ *adj* — **ef·face·ment** \-'fās-mənt\ *n* — **ef·fac·er** *n*

¹ef·fect \i-'fekt\ *n* [L *effectus*, fr. *effect-*, *efficere* to bring about, fr. *ex-* + *facere* to make, do] **1** : an event, condition, or state of affairs that is produced by a cause : the result of something that has been done or has happened : OUTCOME **2** : FULFILLMENT, EXECUTION, OPERATION ⟨the law went into *effect* today⟩ **3** : REALITY, FACT ⟨an excuse that was in *effect* a plain refusal⟩ **4** : the act of making a particular impression ⟨talked merely for *effect*⟩ **5** : INFLUENCE ⟨the *effect* of climate on growth⟩ **6** *pl* : GOODS, POSSESSIONS ⟨household *effects*⟩

syn EFFECT, CONSEQUENCE, RESULT mean a condition or occurrence traceable to a cause. EFFECT designates something that necessarily and directly follows or occurs by reason of a cause ⟨the *effect* of the medicine was a drowsiness⟩ CONSEQUENCE implies a looser or remoter connection with a cause that may no longer be operating ⟨the loss of prestige was a *consequence* of his ill-advised action⟩ RESULT often applies to the last in a series of effects

²effect *vt* : to bring about : ACCOMPLISH **syn** see AFFECT — **ef·fect·er** *n*

¹ef·fec·tive \i-'fek-tiv\ *adj* **1 a** : producing a decided, decisive, or desired effect **b** : IMPRESSIVE, STRIKING **2** : ready for service or action **3** : ACTUAL **4** : being in effect : OPERATIVE — **ef·fec·tive·ly** *adv* — **ef·fec·tive·ness** *n*

syn EFFICIENT, EFFICACIOUS: EFFECTIVE stresses the actual production of an effect when in use or force ⟨the law becomes *effective* immediately⟩ EFFICIENT suggests having given proof of power to produce maximum results with minimum effort ⟨an *efficient* worker⟩ ⟨an *efficient* machine⟩ EFFICACIOUS implies possession of special qualities giving effective power 〈this fluid is *efficacious* in removing ink spots〉

²effective *n* : one that is effective; *esp* : a soldier equipped for duty

ef·fec·tor \i-'fek-tər\ *n* : a bodily organ (as a gland or muscle) that becomes active in response to stimulation

ef·fec·tu·al \i-'fek-chə-wəl, -'fek-chəl\ *adj* : producing or able to produce a desired effect : ADEQUATE, EFFECTIVE 〈an *effectual* remedy〉 — **ef·fec·tu·al·ness** *n*

ef·fec·tu·al·ly \i-'fek-chə-(wə-)lē\ *adv* 1 : in an effectual manner 2 : with great effect : COMPLETELY

ef·fec·tu·ate \i-'fek-chə-ˌwāt\ *vt* : to bring about : EFFECT

ef·fem·i·na·cy \ə-'fem-ə-nə-sē\ *n* : the quality of being effeminate

ef·fem·i·nate \-nət\ *adj* 1 : marked by qualities more characteristic of and suited to women than to men : UNMANLY 2 : marked by weakness and love of ease 〈an *effeminate* civilization〉 **syn** see FEMALE — **ef·fem·i·nate·ly** *adv* — **ef·fem·i·nate·ness** *n*

ef·fen·di \e-'fen-dē, ə-\ *n* [Turk *efendi* master] : a man of property, authority, or education in an eastern Mediterranean country

ef·fer·ent \'ef-ə-rənt, -,er-ənt\ *adj* [L *efferre* to carry outward, fr. *ex-* + *ferre* to carry] : conducting outward from a part or organ; *esp* : conveying nervous impulses to an effector — compare AFFERENT — **efferent** *n* — **ef·fer·ent·ly** *adv*

ef·fer·vesce \ˌef-ər-'ves\ *vi* [L *effervescere*, fr. *ex-* + *fervescere* to begin to boil, fr. *fervēre* to boil] 1 : to bubble, hiss, and foam as gas escapes 〈ginger ale *effervesces*〉 2 : to show liveliness or exhilaration 〈*effervesced* with excitement〉 — **ef·fer·ves·cence** \-'ves-ᵊn(t)s\ *n* — **ef·fer·ves·cent** \-ᵊnt\ *adj* — **ef·fer·ves·cent·ly** *adv*

ef·fete \e-'fēt, i-\ *adj* [L *effetus*, fr. *ex-* + *fetus* fruitful] 1 : no longer productive 2 : worn out : EXHAUSTED; *also* : marked by weakness or decadence 〈an *effete* civilization〉 〈a once mighty empire now become *effete*〉 — **ef·fete·ly** *adv* — **ef·fete·ness** *n*

ef·fi·ca·cious \ˌef-ə-'kā-shəs\ *adj* : having the power to produce a desired effect 〈*efficacious* remedy〉 **syn** see EFFECTIVE — **ef·fi·ca·cious·ly** *adv* — **ef·fi·ca·cious·ness** *n*

ef·fi·ca·cy \'ef-i-kə-sē\ *n, pl* **-cies** : power to produce effects : EFFECTIVENESS 〈a medicine of tested *efficacy*〉

ef·fi·cien·cy \i-'fish-ən-sē\ *n, pl* **-cies** 1 : the quality or degree of being efficient 2 a : efficient operation b : effective operation as measured by a comparison of production with cost (as in energy, time, and money) 3 : the ratio of the useful energy delivered by a dynamic system (as a machine) to the energy supplied to it

efficiency engineer *n* : one who analyzes methods, procedures, and jobs in order to secure maximum efficiency

ef·fi·cient \i-'fish-ənt\ *adj* [L *efficient-, efficiens*, fr. prp. of *efficere* to bring about] : capable of producing desired effects 〈*efficient* worker〉; *esp* : productive without waste 〈*efficient* machine〉 **syn** see EFFECTIVE — **ef·fi·cient·ly** *adv*

ef·fi·gy \'ef-ə-jē\ *n, pl* **-gies** [L *effigies*, fr. *effingere* to form, fr. *ex-* + *fingere* to shape] : an image or likeness esp. of a person: as a : a sculptured image on a tomb b : a crude figure representing a hated person 〈hung him in *effigy*〉

ef·flo·resce \ˌef-lə-'res\ *vi* 1 : to burst forth or become manifest as if flowering 2 a : to change to a powder from loss of water of crystallization on exposure to air 〈a salt that *effloresces*〉 b : to form or become covered with a powdery crust 〈a brick that *effloresces*〉

effigy a

ef·flo·res·cence \-'res-ᵊn(t)s\ *n* 1 : the act, process, period, or result of developing or unfolding 2 : fullness of manifestation : CULMINATION 3 : the process or product of efflorescing chemically 4 : a redness of the skin : ERUPTION — **ef·flo·res·cent** \-ᵊnt\ *adj*

ef·flu·ence \'ef-ˌlü-ən(t)s\ *n* [L *effluere* to flow out, fr. *ex-* + *fluere* to flow] 1 : something that flows out 2 : an action or process of flowing out — **ef·flu·ent** \-ənt\ *adj or n*

ef·flu·vi·um \e-'flü-vē-əm\ *n, pl* **-via** \-vē-ə\ *or* **-vi·ums** : an invisible emanation; *esp* : an offensive exhalation or smell

ef·flux \'ef-ˌləks\ *n* : EFFLUENCE

ef·fort \'ef-ərt, -ˌȯrt\ *n* [OF *esfort*, fr. *esforcier* to force, fr. *ex-* + *forcier* to force] 1 : conscious exertion of power 2 : a serious attempt : TRY 3 : something produced esp. by creative or artistic exertion 4 : the force applied to a simple machine (as a lever) as distinguished from the force exerted by it against the load

syn EFFORT, EXERTION mean the active use of energy in producing a result. EFFORT stresses the calling up or directing of energy by the conscious will and suggests a single action or attempt; EXERTION suggests sustained, laborious, or exhausting effort

ef·fort·less \'ef-ərt-ləs\ *adj* : showing or requiring little or no effort : EASY, SMOOTH — **ef·fort·less·ly** *adv* — **ef·fort·less·ness** *n*

ef·fron·tery \i-'frənt-ə-rē, e-\ *n, pl* **-ter·ies** [F *effronterie*, fr. LL *effront-, effrons* shameless, fr. L *ex-* + *front-, frons* forehead] : shameless boldness : INSOLENCE 〈had the *effrontery* to deny his guilt〉

ef·ful·gence \i-'ful-jən(t)s, e-, -'fəl-\ *n* : radiant splendor : BRILLIANCE 〈the *effulgence* of the sun〉 — **ef·ful·gent** \-jənt\ *adj*

¹ef·fuse \i-'fyüz, e-\ *vb* [L *effus-, effundere*, fr. *ex-* + *fundere* to pour] 1 : to pour out (a liquid) 2 : to give off : RADIATE 3 : to flow out : EMANATE

²ef·fuse \i-'fyüs\ *adj* 1 : poured out freely : OVERFLOWING 2 : DIFFUSE; *esp* : of flat irregular form

ef·fu·sion \i-'fyü-zhən, e-\ *n* 1 : an act of effusing 2 : unrestrained expression of words or feelings 3 a : escape of a fluid from containing vessels b : the fluid that escapes

ef·fu·sive \i-'fyü-siv, e-, -ziv\ *adj* 1 *archaic* : pouring freely 2 : excessively demonstrative or emotional : GUSHING 〈*effusive* thanks for his birthday present〉 3 : characterized or formed by a nonexplosive outpouring of lava — **ef·fu·sive·ly** *adv* — **ef·fu·sive·ness** *n*

eft \'eft\ *n* [OE *efete*] : NEWT

eft·soons \eft-'sünz\ *or* **eft·soon** \-'sün\ *adv* [ME *eftsones*, fr. *eft* after (fr. OE) + *sone* soon + *-s*, adv. suffix] *archaic* : soon afterward; *also* : AGAIN, OFTEN

egad \i-'gad\ *interj* — used as a mild oath

egal·i·tar·i·an \i-ˌgal-ə-'ter-ē-ən\ *adj* [F *égalité* equality, fr. L *aequalitat-, aequalitas*, fr. *aequalis* equal] : asserting, promoting, or marked by egalitarianism — **egalitarian** *n*

egal·i·tar·i·an·ism \-ē-ə-ˌniz-əm\ *n* 1 : a belief in human equality esp. in social, political, and economic affairs 2 : a social philosophy advocating the removal of inequalities among men

egest \i-'jest\ *vt* [L *egest-, egerere* to carry outside, discharge, fr. *e-* + *gerere* to carry] : to rid the body of (waste); *esp* : DEFECATE — **eges·tion** \-'jes-chən\ *n* — **eges·tive** \-'jes-tiv\ *adj*

¹egg \'eg\ *vt* [ON *eggja*] : to incite to action : URGE, ENCOURAGE — usu. used with *on* 〈his comrades *egged* him on to fight〉

²egg *n* [ON] 1 a : the hard-shelled reproductive body produced by a bird and esp. by domestic poultry b : an animal reproductive body consisting of an ovum with its nutritive and protective envelopes and being capable of development into a new individual c : OVUM 2 : something resembling an egg 3 *slang* : FELLOW, GUY

egg and dart *n* : a carved ornamental design consisting of an egg-shaped figure alternating with a figure like the head of an arrow

egg·beat·er \'eg-ˌbēt-ər\ *n* : a rotary beater operated by hand for beating eggs or liquids (as cream)

egg cell *n* : OVUM

egg·head \'eg-ˌhed\ *n* : INTELLECTUAL, HIGHBROW

egg·nog \-ˌnäg\ *n* : a drink consisting of eggs beaten up with sugar, milk or cream, and often alcoholic liquor

egg·plant \-ˌplant\ *n* : a widely cultivated perennial herb that is related to the potato and yields edible fruit; *also* : its usu. smooth and purple ovoid fruit

¹egg·shell \-ˌshel\ *n* : the hard exterior covering of an egg

²eggshell *adj* 1 : being thin and fragile 〈*eggshell* china〉 2 : slightly glossy

egis \'ē-jəs\ *var of* AEGIS

eg·lan·tine \'eg-lən-ˌtīn, -ˌtēn\ *n* [MF *aiglent*] : SWEETBRIER

ego \'ē-gō\ *n, pl* **egos** [L, I; akin to E *I*] 1 : the self as contrasted with another self or the world 2 a : EGOTISM b : SELF-ESTEEM **3** : the conscious part of the personality that is derived from the id through contacts with reality

ego·cen·tric \‚ē-gō-'sen-trik\ *adj* : concerned or overly concerned with the self; *esp* : SELF-CENTERED, SELFISH — **egocentric** *n*

ego·ism \'ē-gə-‚wiz-əm\ *n* **1** : excessive interest in oneself : a self-centered attitude **2** : EGOTISM

ego·ist \'ē-gə-wəst\ *n* : a person whose chief interest is himself : a self-centered person — **ego·is·tic** \‚ē-gə-'wis-tik\ *adj* — **ego·is·ti·cal·ly** \-'wis-ti-k(ə-)lē\ *adv*

syn EGOTIST: EGOIST implies a person whose self-centered concentration on his own desires and aspirations excludes interest in others; EGOTIST may indicate a tendency to attract attention and center interest on oneself and one's achievements

ego·tism \'ē-gə-‚tiz-əm\ *n* [L *ego* + E *-tism* (as in *idiotism*)] **1** : too frequent reference (as by use of the word *I*) to oneself **2** : an exaggerated sense of self≈ importance : CONCEIT **3** : EGOISM

ego·tist \'ē-gə-təst\ *n* : a conceited person syn see EGOIST — **ego·tis·tic** \‚ē-gə-'tis-tik\ *or* **ego·tis·ti·cal** \-'tis-ti-kəl\ *adj* — **ego·tis·ti·cal·ly** \-'tis-ti-k(ə-)lē\ *adv*

ego trip *n* : an act that satisfies one's ego

egre·gious \i-'grē-jəs\ *adj* [L *egregius*, fr. *e-* + *greg-*, *grex* herd] **1** *archaic* : DISTINGUISHED **2** : conspicuously bad : SHOCKING, FLAGRANT ⟨*egregious* errors⟩ — **egre·gious·ly** *adv* — **egre·gious·ness** *n*

egress \'ē-‚gres\ *n* [L *egressus*, fr. *egress-*, *egredi* to go out, fr. *e-* + *gradi* to go] **1** : the act or right of going or coming out ⟨a narrow door was the only means of *egress*⟩ **2** : a place or means of going out : EXIT, OUTLET

egret \'ē-grət, i-'gret, 'ē-‚gret, 'eg-rət\ *n* [MF *aigrette*, of Gmc origin] : any of various herons that bear long plumes during the breeding season

Egyp·tian \i-'jip-shən\ *n* **1** : a native or inhabitant of Egypt **2** : the language spoken by the ancient Egyptians from earliest times to about the 3d century A.D. — **Egyptian** *adj*

Egyptian cotton *n* : a fine long-staple often somewhat brownish cotton grown chiefly in Egypt

Egyp·tol·o·gy \‚ē-gə-(‚)jip-'täl-ə-jē\ *n* : the study of Egyptian antiquities — **Egyp·tol·o·gist** \-jəst\ *n*

eh \'ā, 'e, 'a(i), also with h preceding and/or with nasalization\ *interj* — used to ask for confirmation or to express inquiry

ei·der \'īd-ər\ *n* [ON *æthr*] **1** : a large northern sea duck that is mostly white above and black below and has very soft down — called also *eider duck* **2** : EIDERDOWN 1

ei·der·down \-‚daun\ *n* **1** : the down of the eider **2** : a comforter filled with eiderdown

ei·det·ic \ī-'det-ik\ *adj* [Gk *eidos* form] : marked by or involving peculiarly vivid recall esp. of visual images ⟨an *eidetic* memory⟩ — **ei·det·i·cal·ly** \-'det-i-k(ə-)lē\ *adv*

ei·do·lon \ī-'dō-lən\ *n, pl* **eidolons** *or* **ei·do·la** \-lə\ [Gk *eidōlon*] **1** : an unsubstantial image : PHANTOM **2** : IDEAL

eight \'āt\ *n* [OE *eahta*] **1** — see NUMBER table **2** : the eighth in a set or series **3** : something having eight units or members: as **a** : an 8-oared racing boat or crew **b** : an 8-cylinder engine or automobile — **eight** *adj or pron* — **eighth** \'ātth\ *n, pl* **eighths** \'āts, 'ātths\ — **eighth** *adj or adv*

eight ball *n* : a black pool ball numbered 8 — **behind the eight ball** : in a highly disadvantageous position or baffling situation

eigh·teen \(')ā(t)-'tēn\ *n* — see NUMBER table — **eighteen** *adj or pron* — **eigh·teenth** \-'tēn(t)th\ *adj or n*

eigh·teen·mo \‚ā(t)-'tēn-‚mō\ *n* : the size of a piece of paper cut 18 from a sheet; *also* : a book, a page, or paper of this size

eighth note *n* : a musical note with the time value of one eighth of a whole note

eighty \'āt-ē\ *n, pl* **eight·ies** — see NUMBER table — **eight·i·eth** \-ē-əth\ *adj or n* — **eighty** *adj or pron*

ei·kon \'ī-‚kän\ *var of* ICON

Ein·stein equation \‚īn-‚stīn-\ *n* : MASS-ENERGY EQUATION

ein·stei·ni·um \īn-'stī-nē-əm\ *n* : a radioactive element produced artificially — see ELEMENT table

ei·stedd·fod \ī-'steth-‚vôd\ *n* [W, lit., session, fr. *eistedd* to sit + *bod* being] : a Welsh competitive festival of the arts esp. in singing

¹ei·ther \'ē-thər, 'ī-\ *adj* [OE *æghwæther* both, each]

1 : the one and the other of two : EACH ⟨flowers blooming on *either* side of the walk⟩ **2** : the one or the other of two ⟨take *either* road⟩

²either *pron* : the one or the other

³either *conj* — used as a function word before the first of two or more words or word groups of which the last is preceded by *or* to indicate that they represent alternatives ⟨a statement is *either* true or false⟩

⁴either *adv* **1** : LIKEWISE, MOREOVER — used for emphasis after a negative ⟨not wise or handsome *either*⟩ **2** : for that matter — used for emphasis after an alternative following a question or conditional clause esp. where negation is implied ⟨if his father had come or his mother *either* all would have gone well⟩

ejac·u·late \i-'jak-yə-‚lāt\ *vb* **1** : to utter or eject suddenly and vigorously **2** : to eject a fluid and esp. semen — **ejac·u·la·to·ry** \-yə-lə-‚tōr-ē, -‚tôr-\ *adj*

ejac·u·la·tion \i-‚jak-yə-'lā-shən\ *n* **1** : an act of ejaculating; *esp* : a sudden discharging of a fluid from a duct **2** : something ejaculated; *esp* : a short sudden emotional utterance (as an exclamation)

eject \i-'jekt\ *vt* [L *eject-*, *eicere*, fr. *e-* + *jacere* to throw] **1 a** : to drive out esp. by physical force **b** : to evict from property **2** : to throw out or off from within — **ejec·tor** \-'jek-tər\ *n*

syn EJECT, EXPEL, EVICT mean to drive or force out. EJECT carries a strong implication of throwing or thrusting out from within as a physical action ⟨hot lava *ejected* from a volcano⟩ EXPEL implies usu. a voluntary compulsion to get rid of ⟨slowly *expelled* smoke through his nose⟩ ⟨*expelled* from school⟩ EVICT chiefly applies to turning out of house and home

ejec·tion \i-'jek-shən\ *n* **1** : the act of ejecting : the state of being ejected **2** : ejected matter (as from a volcano)

ejection seat *n* : an emergency escape seat for propelling an occupant out and away from an airplane by means of an explosive charge

¹eke \'ēk\ *adv* [OE *ēac*] *archaic* : ALSO

²eke *vt* [OE *īecan*, *ēcan*] *archaic* : INCREASE, LENGTHEN

eke out *vt* **1 a** : SUPPLEMENT ⟨she *eked* out her small income by sewing for neighbors⟩ **b** : to make (a supply) last by economy **2** : to make (a living) by laborious or precarious means

el \'el\ *n* : ELEVATED RAILROAD

¹elab·o·rate \i-'lab-(ə-)rət\ *adj* [L *elaboratus*, fr. pp. of *elaborare* to work out, fr. *e-* + *laborare* to work] **1** : planned or carried out with great care : DETAILED ⟨*elaborate* preparations⟩ **2** : marked by complexity, fullness of detail, or ornateness ⟨an *elaborate* design⟩ — **elab·o·rate·ly** *adv* — **elab·o·rate·ness** *n*

²elab·o·rate \i-'lab-ə-‚rāt\ *vb* **1** : to produce by labor **2** : to build up (complex organic compounds) from simple ingredients ⟨a substance *elaborated* by a gland⟩ **3** : to work out in detail : DEVELOP ⟨*elaborate* an idea⟩ **4** : to give esp. additional details ⟨*elaborate* on a story⟩ — **elab·o·ra·tion** \-‚lab-ə-'rā-shən\ *n* — **elab·o·ra·tive** \i-'lab-ə-‚rāt-iv\ *adj* — **elab·o·ra·tor** \-‚rāt-ər\ *n*

Elaine \i-'lān\ *n* : a woman in Arthurian legend who dies for unrequited love of Lancelot

élan \ā-'läⁿ\ *n* [F] : SPIRIT, ARDOR, DASH

eland \'ē-lənd\ *n* [Afrik, elk, fr. D] : either of two large African antelopes resembling oxen and having short spirally twisted horns in both sexes

elapse \i-'laps\ *vi* [L *elaps-*, *elabi*, fr. *e-* + *labi* to slip] : to slip or glide away : PASS

elas·mo·branch \i-'laz-mə-‚braŋk\ *n, pl* **-branchs** [Gk *elasmos* metal plate + L *branchia* gill] : any of a class (Chondrichthyes) of fishes with cartilage skeletons and platelike gills that include the sharks, rays, chimeras, and extinct related fishes — **elasmobranch** *adj*

¹elas·tic \i-'las-tik\ *adj* [LGk *elastos* beaten, ductile, fr. Gk *elaunein* to beat out] **1 a** : capable of recovering shape or size after being stretched, pressed, or squeezed together : SPRINGY ⟨sponges are *elastic*⟩ **b** : capable of indefinite expansion ⟨gases are *elastic* substances⟩ **2** : able to recover quickly esp. from depression or fatigue ⟨youthful, *elastic* spirit⟩ **3** : FLEXIBLE, ADAPTABLE ⟨a plan *elastic* enough to be changed at any time⟩ — **elas·ti·cal·ly** \-ti-k(ə-)lē\ *adv*

syn RESILIENT, BUOYANT: ELASTIC may indicate an ability to recover quickly from discouragement or dejection ⟨an

---

j joke;   ŋ sing;   ō flow;   ô flaw;   ȯi coin;   th thin;   th̲ this;   ü loot;   u̇ foot;   y yet;   yü few;   yu̇ furious;   zh vision

elastic power of throwing off painful memories) RE-SILIENT may stress speed of return to usual good or high spirits after strain, depression, or setback ⟨the *resilient* energy of the storm-wracked villagers⟩ BUOYANT may indicate a lightness of spirit incapable of lasting dejection

²**elastic** *n* **1 a :** an elastic fabric usu. made of yarns containing rubber   **b :** something made from elastic fabric   **2 :** easily stretched rubber; *esp* **:** a rubber band

elas·tic·i·ty \i-ˌlas-ˈtis-ət-ē, ˌē-ˌlas-\ *n, pl* **-ties :** the quality or state of being elastic : RESILIENCE, ADAPTABILITY

elas·ti·cized \i-ˈlas-tə-ˌsīzd\ *adj* **:** made with elastic thread or inserts

elas·to·mer \i-ˈlas-tə-mər\ *n* **:** any of various elastic substances resembling rubber — **elas·to·mer·ic** \i-ˌlas-tə-ˈmer-ik\ *adj*

elate \i-ˈlāt\ *vt* [L *elat-*, used as stem of *efferre* to carry out, elevate, fr. *e-* + *ferre* to carry] **:** to fill with joy or pride

elat·ed \i-ˈlāt-əd\ *adj* **:** marked by high spirits : EXULTANT ⟨*elated* over the team's victory⟩ — **elat·ed·ly** *adv* — **elat·ed·ness** *n*

el·a·ter \ˈel-ət-ər\ *n* [Gk *elatēr* driver, fr. *elaunein* to beat out] **1 :** CLICK BEETLE   **2 :** an elastic or expansible filament that aids in the distribution of a plant's spores

elat·er·ite \i-ˈlat-ə-ˌrīt\ *n* **:** a dark brown elastic mineral resin occurring in soft flexible masses

ela·tion \i-ˈlā-shən\ *n* **:** the quality or state of being elated ⟨alternating moods of *elation* and despair⟩

E layer *n* **:** a layer of the ionosphere that occurs at about 60 miles above the earth's surface and is capable of reflecting radio waves

¹**el·bow** \ˈel-ˌbō\ *n* [OE *elboga*] **1 a :** the joint of the arm; *also* **:** the outer curve of a bent arm   **b :** a corresponding joint in the front limb of an animal   **2 :** something resembling an elbow; *esp* **:** an angular pipe fitting

²**elbow** *vb* **1 :** to push or shove aside by pushing with the elbow : JOSTLE   **2 :** to force or advance by or as if by pushing with the elbow ⟨*elbowed* their way through the crowd⟩

elbows: *1* water pipe, *2* stovepipe

elbow grease *n* **:** energy vigorously exerted esp. in physical labor

el·bow·room \-ˌrüm, -ˌru̇m\ *n* **1 :** room for moving the elbows freely   **2 :** enough space for work or operation

eld \ˈeld\ *n* **1** *archaic* **:** old age   **2** *archaic* **:** ancient times : ANTIQUITY

¹**el·der** \ˈel-dər\ *n* [OE *ellærn*] **:** any of a genus of shrubs or trees of the honeysuckle family with flat clusters of small white or pink flowers and black or red drupes resembling berries

²**elder** *adj* [ME, fr. OE *ieldra*, compar. of *eald* old] **1 :** of earlier birth or greater age : OLDER ⟨the *elder* brother⟩   **2 :** of or relating to earlier times : FORMER ⟨in *elder* days⟩   **3** *obs* **:** of or relating to a more advanced time of life   **4 :** prior or superior in rank, office, or validity

³**elder** *n* **1 :** one living in an earlier period   **2 a :** one who is older : SENIOR   **b** *archaic* **:** an aged person   **3 :** a person having authority by virtue of age and experience ⟨the village elders⟩   **4 :** any of various church officers: as   **a :** PRESBYTER 1   **b :** a permanent officer elected by a Presbyterian congregation and ordained to serve on the session and assist the pastor at communion   **c :** MINISTER 2a, 2b   **d :** a Mormon ordained to the higher priesthood — **el·der·ship** \-ˌship\ *n*

el·der·ber·ry \ˈel-də(r)-ˌber-ē\ *n* **1 :** the edible fruit of an elder   **2 :** ¹ELDER

el·der·ly \ˈel-dər-lē\ *adj* **1 :** rather old; *esp* **:** past middle age   **2 :** of, relating to, or characteristic of later life ⟨*elderly* pursuits⟩ — **el·der·li·ness** *n*

elder statesman *n* **:** an eminent senior member of a group or organization; *esp* **:** a retired statesman who unofficially advises current leaders

el·dest \ˈel-dəst\ *adj* **:** OLDEST

El Do·ra·do \ˌel-də-ˈräd-ō, -ˈrād-\ *n* **1 :** a city or country of fabulous riches held by 16th century explorers to exist in So. America   **2 :** a place of great wealth, abundance, or opportunity

¹**elect** \i-ˈlekt\ *adj* [L *electus* choice, fr. pp. of *eligere* to select, fr. *e-* + *legere* to choose] **1 :** carefully selected : CHOSEN   **2 :** chosen for eternal life through divine mercy   **3 :** chosen for office or position but not yet installed ⟨president-*elect*⟩

²**elect** *n pl* **:** a carefully chosen group — used with *the*

³**elect** *vb* **1 :** to select usu. by vote for an office, position, or membership   **2 :** CHOOSE, SELECT

elec·tion \i-ˈlek-shən\ *n* **1 a :** an act or process of electing; *esp* **:** the process of voting to choose a person to hold an office   **b :** the fact of being elected   **2 :** predestination to eternal life   **3 :** the power or privilege of making a choice

elec·tion·eer \i-ˌlek-shə-ˈni(ə)r\ *vi* **:** to work in the interest of a candidate or party in an election

¹**elec·tive** \i-ˈlek-tiv\ *adj* **1 :** chosen by election ⟨an *elective* official⟩   **2 :** filled by a person who is elected and not appointed ⟨the presidency is an *elective* office⟩   **3 :** of, relating to, or based on elections ⟨*elective* functions⟩ ⟨an *elective* government⟩   **4 :** followed or taken by choice : not required ⟨an *elective* subject in school⟩ — **elec·tive·ly** *adv* — **elec·tive·ness** *n*

²**elective** *n* **:** an elective course or subject in school

elec·tor \i-ˈlek-tər\ *n* **1 :** one qualified to vote in an election   **2 :** one entitled by his office to participate in an election: as   **a :** one of the German princes entitled to take part in choosing the Holy Roman emperor   **b :** a member of the electoral college in the U.S.

elec·tor·al \i-ˈlek-t(ə-)rəl\ *adj* **:** of or relating to an election or electors

electoral college *n* **:** a body of electors; *esp* **:** one that elects the president and vice-president of the U.S.

elec·tor·ate \i-ˈlek-t(ə-)rət\ *n* **1 :** the territory, jurisdiction, or dignity of a German elector   **2 :** a body of people entitled to vote

electr- *or* **electro-** *comb form* [NL *electricus* electric] **1 a :** electricity ⟨*electrometer*⟩   **b :** electric ⟨*electrode*⟩ : electric and ⟨*electrochemical*⟩ : electrically ⟨*electropositive*⟩   **2 :** electron ⟨*electrovalence*⟩

Elec·tra \i-ˈlek-trə\ *n* **:** a sister of Orestes who urges her brother to avenge their father's murder

¹**elec·tric** \i-ˈlek-trik\ *or* **elec·tri·cal** \-tri-kəl\ *adj* [NL *electricus* produced from amber by friction, electric, fr. L *electrum* amber, fr. Gk *ēlektron*] **1 :** of, relating to, operated by, or produced by electricity   **2 :** ELECTRIFYING, THRILLING ⟨an *electric* performance⟩ — **elec·tri·cal·ly** \-tri-k(ə-)lē\ *adv* — **elec·tri·cal·ness** \-kəl-nəs\ *n*

²**electric** *n* **:** something operated by electricity; *esp* **:** an electric automobile

electrical engineering *n* **:** engineering that deals with the practical applications of electricity — **electrical engineer** *n*

electrical transcription *n* **1 :** a phonograph record esp. designed for use in radiobroadcasting   **2 :** a radio program broadcast from an electrical transcription

electric chair *n* **1 :** a chair used in legal electrocution   **2 :** the penalty of death by electrocution

electric charge *n* **:** a definite quantity of electricity

electric eel *n* **:** a large So. American eel-shaped fish able to give a severe electric shock

electric eye *n* **:** PHOTOELECTRIC CELL

elec·tri·cian \i-ˌlek-ˈtrish-ən\ *n* **1 :** a specialist in electricity   **2 :** one who installs, operates, or repairs electrical equipment

elec·tric·i·ty \i-ˌlek-ˈtris-ət-ē, -ˈtris-tē\ *n* **1 a :** a fundamental phenomenon of nature consisting of negative and positive kinds composed respectively of electrons and protons, observable in the attractions and repulsions of bodies electrified by friction and in natural phenomena (as lightning), and usu. utilized as a source of energy in the form of electric currents   **b :** electric current   **2 :** a science that deals with the phenomena and laws of electricity

electric ray *n* **:** any of various round-bodied short-tailed rays of warm seas able to give a severe electric shock

elec·tri·fy \i-ˈlek-trə-ˌfī\ *vt* **-fied; -fy·ing 1 a :** to charge with electricity   **b (1) :** to equip for use of electric power   **(2) :** to supply with electric power   **2 :** to excite intensely or suddenly : THRILL ⟨an acrobat who has *electrified* audiences with his daring⟩ — **elec·tri·fi·ca·tion** \i-ˌlek-trə-fə-ˈkā-shən\ *n*

ə abut; ᵊ kitten; ər further; a back; ā bake; ä cot, cart; au̇ out; ch chin; e less; ē easy; g gift; i trip; ī life

elec·tro·anal·y·sis \i-ˌlek-trō-ə-'nal-ə-səs\ n : chemical analysis by electrolytic methods — **elec·tro·an·a·lyt·ic** \-ˌan-ᵊl-'it-ik\ adj

elec·tro·car·dio·gram \i-ˌlek-trō-'kärd-ē-ə-ˌgram\ n : the tracing made by an electrocardiograph

elec·tro·car·dio·graph \-ˌgraf\ n : an instrument for recording the changes of electrical potential occurring during the heartbeat — **elec·tro·car·dio·graph·ic** \-ˌkärd-ē-ə-'graf-ik\ adj — **elec·tro·car·dio·graph·i·cal·ly** \-'graf-i-k(ə-)lē\ adv — **elec·tro·car·di·og·ra·phy** \-ē-'äg-rə-fē\ n

elec·tro·chem·is·try \i-ˌlek-trō-'kem-ə-strē\ n : a science that deals with the relation of electricity to chemical changes and with the mutual conversion of chemical and electrical energy — **elec·tro·chem·i·cal** \-'kem-i-kəl\ adj — **elec·tro·chem·i·cal·ly** \-i-k(ə-)lē\ adv

elec·tro·cute \i-'lek-trə-ˌkyüt\ vt [electr- + -cute (as in execute)] : to kill by electric shock; esp : to execute (a criminal) in this way — **elec·tro·cu·tion** \i-ˌlek-trə-'kyü-shən\ n

elec·trode \i-'lek-ˌtrōd\ n : a conductor (as a metal or carbon) used to establish electrical contact with a nonmetallic part of a circuit (as in a storage battery, electron tube, or arc lamp)

elec·tro·de·pos·it \i-ˌlek-trō-di-'päz-ət\ vt : to deposit (as a metal or rubber) by electrolysis — **elec·tro·dep·o·si·tion** \-ˌdep-ə-'zish-ən, -ˌdē-pə-\ n

elec·tro·dy·nam·ics \-ˌdī-'nam-iks\ n : physics that deals with the effects arising from the interactions of electric currents with magnets, with other currents, or with themselves — **elec·tro·dy·nam·ic** \-ik\ adj

elec·tro·dy·na·mom·e·ter \-ˌdī-nə-'mäm-ət-ər\ n : an instrument that measures electric current by indicating the strength of the forces between a current flowing in fixed coils and one flowing in movable coils

elec·tro·en·ceph·a·lo·gram \-en-'sef-ə-lō-ˌgram\ n : the tracing of brain waves that is made by an electroencephalograph

elec·tro·en·ceph·a·lo·graph \-ˌgraf\ n : an apparatus for detecting and recording brain waves — **elec·tro·en·ceph·a·lo·graph·ic** \-en-ˌsef-ə-lō-'graf-ik\ adj — **elec·tro·en·ceph·a·log·ra·phy** \-ˌsef-ə-'läg-rə-fē\ n

elec·tro·form \i-'lek-trə-ˌfȯrm\ vb : to form (shaped articles) by electrodeposition on a mold

elec·tro·jet \-ˌjet\ n : an overhead concentration of electric current found in the regions of strong auroral displays and along the magnetic equator

elec·tro·ki·net·ic \-trō-kə-'net-ik, -kī-\ adj : of or relating to the motion of particles or liquids that results from or produces a difference of electric potential

elec·trol·y·sis \i-ˌlek-'träl-ə-səs\ n 1 a : the producing of chemical changes by passage of an electric current through an electrolyte with the ions carrying the current by migrating to the electrodes where they may form new substances that are given off as gases or deposited as solids b : subjection to this action 2 : the destruction of hair roots with an electric current

elec·tro·lyte \i-'lek-trə-ˌlīt\ n 1 : a nonmetallic electric conductor in which current is carried by the movement of ions with the liberation of matter at the electrodes 2 : a substance that when dissolved in a suitable solvent or when fused becomes an ionic conductor

elec·tro·lyt·ic \i-ˌlek-trə-'lit-ik\ adj : of or relating to electrolysis or an electrolyte — **elec·tro·lyt·i·cal·ly** \-i-k(ə-)lē\ adv

elec·tro·lyze \i-'lek-trə-ˌlīz\ vt : to subject to electrolysis

elec·tro·mag·net \i-ˌlek-trō-'mag-nət\ n : a core of magnetic material (as soft iron) surrounded by a coil of wire through which an electric current is passed to magnetize the core

electromagnetic spectrum n : the entire range of wavelengths or frequencies of electromagnetic waves extending from gamma rays to the longest radio waves and including visible light

electromagnetic wave n : a wave (as a radio wave, infrared wave, wave of visible light, or X ray) that is propagated at the speed of light by regular variations of the intensity of associated electric and magnetic fields at right angles to each other

elec·tro·mag·ne·tism \i-ˌlek-trō-'mag-nə-ˌtiz-əm\ n 1 : magnetism developed by a current of electricity

2 : physical science that deals with the physical relations between electricity and magnetism — **elec·tro·mag·net·ic** \-mag-'net-ik\ adj — **elec·tro·mag·net·i·cal·ly** \-'net-i-k(ə-)lē\ adv

elec·tro·met·al·lur·gy \-'met-ᵊl-ˌər-jē\ n : metallurgy that deals with the applications of electric current either for electrolytic deposition or as a source of heat

elec·trom·e·ter \i-ˌlek-'träm-ət-ər\ n : an instrument for detecting or measuring electric-potential differences or ionizing radiations — **elec·tro·met·ric** \i-ˌlek-trə-'me-trik\ adj

elec·tro·mo·tive force \i-ˌlek-trə-ˌmōt-iv-\ n : an influence that tends to change the motion of electricity or maintain its motion against opposing forces ⟨a battery is a source of electromotive force⟩ — abbr. EMF or emf

elec·tron \i-'lek-ˌträn\ n [electr- + ²-on] : a negatively charged elementary particle that forms the part of an atom outside the nucleus and that is of the kind of particles whose flow along a conductor is an electric current

elec·tro·neg·a·tive \i-ˌlek-trō-'neg-ət-iv\ adj 1 : charged with negative electricity 2 : capable of acting as the negative electrode of a voltaic cell 3 : having a tendency to attract valence electrons ⟨a fluorine atom is electronegative⟩ — **elec·tro·neg·a·tiv·i·ty** \-ˌneg-ə-'tiv-ət-ē\ n

electron gun n : the electron-emitting cathode and its surrounding assembly in a cathode-ray tube for directing, controlling, and focusing the stream of electrons to a spot of desired size

elec·tron·ic \i-ˌlek-'trän-ik\ adj 1 : of or relating to electrons 2 : of, relating to, or utilizing devices constructed or working by principles of electronics — **elec·tron·i·cal·ly** \-'trän-i-k(ə-)lē\ adv

elec·tron·ics \-'trän-iks\ n : a branch of physics that deals with the emission, behavior, and effects of electrons in vacuums and gases and with the use of electronic devices (as electron tubes, radar, radio, and television)

electron lens n : a device for causing an electron beam to converge or diverge by means of either an electric or magnetic field

electron microscope n : an instrument in which a beam of electrons is used to produce an enlarged image of a minute object in a way similar to that in which light is used to form the image in an ordinary microscope

elec·tro·nog·ra·phy \i-ˌlek-trə-'näg-rə-fē\ n : a printing process in which the ink is transferred by electrostatic action across a gap between printing plate and impression cylinder

electron optics n : electronics that deals with those properties of beams of electrons that are analogous to the properties of rays of light

electron tube n : a device in which conduction by electrons takes place through a vacuum or a gas within a sealed glass or metal container and which has various common uses (as in radio and television) based on the controlled flow of electrons

electron volt n : a unit of energy equal to the energy gained by an electron in passing from a point of low potential to a point one volt higher in potential

elec·tro·pho·re·sis \i-ˌlek-trə-fə-'rē-səs\ n [Gk phorein, freq. of pherein to carry] : the movement of suspended particles through a fluid under the action of an electromotive force applied to electrodes in contact with the suspension — **elec·tro·pho·ret·ic** \-'ret-ik\ adj

elec·troph·o·rus \i-ˌlek-'träf-ə-rəs\ n, pl -ri \-ˌrī, -ˌrē\ [Gk phor-, pherein to carry] : an instrument for the production of electric charges by induction

elec·tro·plate \i-'lek-trə-ˌplāt\ vt : to cover with a coating (as of metal or rubber) by means of electrolysis

elec·tro·pos·i·tive \i-ˌlek-trō-'päz-ət-iv, -'päz-tiv\ adj 1 a : charged with positive electricity b : capable of acting as the positive electrode of a voltaic cell 2 : having a tendency to release electrons ⟨an electropositive atom⟩

elec·tro·scope \i-'lek-trə-ˌskōp\ n : any of various instruments for detecting the presence of an electric charge on a body, for determining whether the charge is positive or negative, or for indicating and measuring intensity of radiation

elec·tro·shock therapy \-ˌshäk-\ n : the treatment of mental disorder by the induction of coma with an electric current

---

elec·tro·stat·ic \i-,lek-trə-'stat-ik\ *adj* **:** of or relating to static electricity or electrostatics — **elec·tro·stat·i·cal·ly** \-'stat-i-k(ə-)lē\ *adv*

electrostatic generator *n* **:** an apparatus for the production of electrical discharges at high voltage commonly consisting of an insulated hollow conducting sphere that accumulates in its interior the charge continuously conveyed from a source of direct current by an endless belt

elec·tro·stat·ics \i-,lek-trə-'stat-iks\ *n* **:** physics that deals with phenomena due to attractions or repulsions of electric charges but not dependent upon their motion

elec·tro·sur·gery \i-,lek-trō-'sərj-(ə-)rē\ *n* **:** surgery by means of diathermy — **elec·tro·sur·gi·cal** \-'sər-ji-kəl\ *adj*

elec·tro·ther·a·py \-'ther-ə-pē\ *n* **:** treatment of disease by means of diathermy or electrically generated heat

elec·tro·ther·mal \-'thər-məl\ *or* **elec·tro·ther·mic** \-mik\ *adj* **:** relating to the generation of heat by electricity

elec·trot·o·nus \i-,lek-'trät-ᵊn-əs\ *n* **:** altered sensitivity of a nerve when a constant current of electricity passes through — **elec·tro·ton·ic** \i-,lek-trə-'tän-ik\ *adj*

elec·tro·type \i-'lek-trə-,tīp\ *n* **1 :** a plate for use in printing made by making a mold of the matter to be printed, covering this mold with a thin shell of metal by electrolysis, and putting on a backing (as of heavy metal or plastic) **2 :** a print made from an electrotype — **elec·tro·typ·er** \-,tī-pər\ *n*

elec·tro·va·lence \i-,lek-trō-'vā-lən(t)s\ *or* **elec·tro·va·len·cy** \-lən-sē\ *n* **:** valence characterized by the transfer of electrons from one atom to another with the formation of ions; *also* **:** the number of charges acquired by an atom by the loss or gain of electrons — **elec·tro·va·lent** \-lənt\ *adj*

elec·trum \i-'lek-trəm\ *n* **:** a natural pale yellow alloy of gold and silver

elec·tu·ary \i-'lek-chə-,wer-ē\ *n, pl* **-ar·ies** [L *electuarium*] **:** a medicinal preparation made as a paste with honey or syrup

el·ee·mos·y·nary \,el-i-'mäs-ᵊn-,er-ē\ *adj* [ML *eleemosynarius,* fr. LL *eleemosyna* alms, fr. Gk *eleēmosynē* mercy, alms, fr. *eleein* to have mercy] **:** of, relating to, or supported by charity

el·e·gance \'el-i-gən(t)s\ *n* **1 :** refined gracefulness **2 :** tasteful richness of design or ornamentation

el·e·gan·cy \-gən-sē\ *n, pl* **-cies :** ELEGANCE

el·e·gant \'el-i-gənt\ *adj* [L *elegant-, elegans*] **1 :** marked by elegance **2 :** EXCELLENT, SPLENDID — **el·e·gant·ly** *adv*

el·e·gy \'el-ə-jē\ *n, pl* **-gies** [Gk *elegeia* poem in elegiac couplets, fr. *elegos* song of mourning] **1 :** a poem expressing sorrow for one who is dead **2 :** a poem that is sad or mournful in spirit — **el·e·gi·ac** \,el-ə-'jī-ək, i-'lē-jē-,ak\ *adj* — **el·e·gize** \'el-ə-,jīz\ *vb*

el·e·ment \'el-ə-mənt\ *n* [L *elementum*] **1 a :** one of the four substances air, water, fire, or earth formerly believed to compose the physical universe **b** *pl* **:** forces of nature; *esp* **:** stormy or cold weather **c :** the state or sphere natural or suited to a person or an organism **2 :** a constituent part: as **a** *pl* **:** the simplest principles of a subject of study **:** RUDIMENTS **b** (1) **:** a part of a geometric magnitude (2) **:** a generator of a geometric figure (3) **:** a basic member of a mathematical class or set **c :** any of more than 100 fundamental substances that consist of atoms of only one kind ⟨gold and carbon are *elements*⟩ **d :** a distinct part of a composite device **e :** a subdivision of a military unit **3** *pl* **:** the bread and wine used in the sacrament of Communion

syn COMPONENT, CONSTITUENT, INGREDIENT: ELEMENT applies to anything that is a part of a compound or complex whole and often connotes irreducible simplicity; COMPONENT and CONSTITUENT are often interchangeable in designating any of the substances or qualities that enter into a compound or complex product; COMPONENT applies to one of the parts that make up a compounded or complex thing ⟨the *components* of a carburetor⟩ CONSTITUENT implies the essential or formative character of the parts ⟨atoms are the *constituents* of molecules⟩ INGREDIENT is applicable to any substance that combines with others to form something else and may imply intangible matters ⟨*ingredients* of a chocolate cake⟩ ⟨*ingredients* of successful comedy⟩

CHEMICAL ELEMENTS

ELEMENT & SYMBOL	ATOMIC NUMBER	ATOMIC WEIGHT (O = 16) formerly	(C = 12)
actinium (Ac)	89		
aluminum (Al)	13	26.98	26.9815
americium (Am)	95		
antimony (Sb)	51	121.76	121.75
argon (Ar)	18	39.944	39.948
arsenic (As)	33	74.91	74.9216
astatine (At)	85		
barium (Ba)	56	137.36	137.34
berkelium (Bk)	97		
beryllium (Be)	4	9.013	9.01218
bismuth (Bi)	83	209.00	208.9806
boron (B)	5	10.82	10.81
bromine (Br)	35	79.916	79.904
cadmium (Cd)	48	112.41	112.40
calcium (Ca)	20	40.08	40.08
californium (Cf)	98		
carbon (C)	6	12.011	12.011
cerium (Ce)	58	140.13	140.12
cesium (Cs)	55	132.91	132.9055
chlorine (Cl)	17	35.457	35.453
chromium (Cr)	24	52.01	51.996
cobalt (Co)	27	58.94	58.9332
columbium (Cb)	(see niobium)		
copper (Cu)	29	63.54	63.546
curium (Cm)	96		
dysprosium (Dy)	66	162.51	162.50
einsteinium (Es)	99		
erbium (Er)	68	167.27	167.26
europium (Eu)	63	152.0	151.96
fermium (Fm)	100		
fluorine (F)	9	19.00	18.9984
francium (Fr)	87		
gadolinium (Gd)	64	157.26	157.25
gallium (Ga)	31	69.72	69.72
germanium (Ge)	32	72.60	72.59
gold (Au)	79	197.0	196.9665
hafnium (Hf)	72	178.50	178.49
helium (He)	2	4.003	4.00260
holmium (Ho)	67	164.94	164.9303
hydrogen (H)	1	1.008	1.0080
indium (In)	49	114.82	114.82
iodine (I)	53	126.91	126.9045
iridium (Ir)	77	192.2	192.22
iron (Fe)	26	55.85	55.847
krypton (Kr)	36	83.80	83.80
lanthanum (La)	57	138.92	138.9055
lawrencium (Lr)	103		
lead (Pb)	82	207.21	207.2
lithium (Li)	3	6.940	6.941
lutetium (Lu)	71	174.99	174.97
magnesium (Mg)	12	24.32	24.305
manganese (Mn)	25	54.94	54.9380
mendelevium (Md)	101		
mercury (Hg)	80	200.61	200.59
molybdenum (Mo)	42	95.95	95.94
neodymium (Nd)	60	144.27	144.24
neon (Ne)	10	20.183	20.179
neptunium (Np)	93		237.0482
nickel (Ni)	28	58.71	58.71
niobium (Nb)	41	92.91	92.9064
nitrogen (N)	7	14.008	14.0067
nobelium (No)	102		
osmium (Os)	76	190.2	190.2
oxygen (O)	8	16.000	15.9994
palladium (Pd)	46	106.4	106.4
phosphorus (P)	15	30.975	30.9738
platinum (Pt)	78	195.09	195.09
plutonium (Pu)	94		
polonium (Po)	84		
potassium (K)	19	39.100	39.102
praseodymium (Pr)	59	140.92	140.9077
promethium (Pm)	61		
protactinium (Pa)	91		231.0359
radium (Ra)	88		226.0254
radon (Rn)	86		
rhenium (Re)	75	186.22	186.2

ELEMENT & SYMBOL	ATOMIC NUMBER	ATOMIC WEIGHT	
		(O=16)	(C=12)
rhodium (Rh)	45	102.91	102.9055
rubidium (Rb)	37	85.48	85.4678
ruthenium (Ru)	44	101.1	101.07
samarium (Sm)	62	150.35	150.4
scandium (Sc)	21	44.96	44.9559
selenium (Se)	34	78.96	78.96
silicon (Si)	14	28.09	28.086
silver (Ag)	47	107.880	107.868
sodium (Na)	11	22.991	22.9898
strontium (Sr)	38	87.63	87.62
sulfur (S)	16	32.066	32.06
tantalum (Ta)	73	180.95	180.9479
technetium (Tc)	43		98.9062
tellurium (Te)	52	127.61	127.60
terbium (Tb)	65	158.93	158.9254
thallium (Tl)	81	204.39	204.37
thorium (Th)	90	232.05	232.0381
thulium (Tm)	69	168.94	168.9342
tin (Sn)	50	118.70	118.69
titanium (Ti)	22	47.90	47.90
tungsten (W)	74	183.86	183.85
uranium (U)	92	238.07	238.029
vanadium (V)	23	50.95	50.9414
wolfram (W)	(see tungsten)		
xenon (Xe)	54	131.30	131.30
ytterbium (Yb)	70	173.04	173.04
yttrium (Y)	39	88.92	88.9059
zinc (Zn)	30	65.38	65.37
zirconium (Zr)	40	91.22	91.22

el·e·men·tal \,el-ə-'ment-ᵊl\ *adj* **1 a :** of, relating to, or being an element; *esp :* existing as an uncombined chemical element **b :** of, relating to, or being an ultimate constituent **c :** ELEMENTARY **d :** ESSENTIAL **2 :** of, relating to, or resembling a great force of nature — **el·e·men·tal·ly** \-ᵊl-ē\ *adv*

el·e·men·ta·ry \,el-ə-'ment-ə-rē, -'men-trē\ *adj* **1 a :** of or relating to the simplest principles of a subject **b :** of, relating to, or teaching the basic subjects of education ⟨*elementary* school⟩ **2 :** ELEMENTAL 1a ⟨an *elementary* substance⟩

elementary particle *n :* any of the ultimate constituents (as the electron, proton, or neutron) of matter that are extremely small charged or uncharged bodies

el·e·phant \'el-ə-fənt\ *n* [Gk *elephant-, elephas*\ : a huge thickset nearly hairless mammal having the snout prolonged as a trunk and two upper incisors developed into long outward=curving pointed tusks which furnish ivory

elephant bird *n :* a gigantic extinct flightless bird of Madagascar whose eggs are held to have a volume of two gallons

el·e·phan·ti·a·sis \,el-ə-fən-'tī-ə-səs, -,fan-\ *n*, *pl* **-ti·a·ses** \-'tī-ə-,sēz\ [Gk, a kind of leprosy, fr. *elephant-, elephas* elephant] : enlargement and thickening of tissues caused by obstruction of lymphatics (as by filarial worms)

elephants: *1* Indian, *2* African

el·e·phan·tine \,el-ə-'fan-,tēn, -,tīn\ *adj* **1 a :** HUGE, MASSIVE **b :** CLUMSY, PONDEROUS, UNGAINLY **2 :** of or relating to an elephant

el·e·vate \'el-ə-,vāt\ *vb* [L *elevare,* fr. *e- + levare* to raise] **1 :** to lift up : RAISE **2 :** to raise in rank or status : EXALT **3 :** to improve morally, intellectually, or culturally **4 :** to raise the spirits of : ELATE

¹el·e·vat·ed \-,vāt-əd\ *adj* **1 :** raised esp. above the ground ⟨*elevated* highway⟩ **2 a :** morally or intellectually on a high plane ⟨*elevated* mind⟩ **b :** FORMAL, DIGNIFIED ⟨*elevated* diction⟩

²elevated *n :* ELEVATED RAILROAD

elevated railroad *n :* a railroad supported by a structure of trestles and girders high enough to permit movement of traffic underneath — called also *elevated railway*

el·e·va·tion \,el-ə-'vā-shən\ *n* **1 :** the height to which something is elevated: as **a :** the angular distance of a celestial object above the horizon **b :** the degree to which a gun is aimed above the horizon **c :** the height above sea level : ALTITUDE **2 :** an act or instance of elevating **3 a :** something that is elevated **b :** an elevated place or station **4 :** the quality or state of being elevated **5 :** a scale drawing showing a vertical structural section (as of a building) as viewed horizontally **syn** see HEIGHT

el·e·va·tor \'el-ə-,vāt-ər\ *n* **1 a :** an endless belt or chain conveyor with cleats, scoops, or buckets for raising material **b :** a cage or platform and its hoisting machinery for conveying something to different levels **c :** a building for elevating, storing, discharging, and sometimes processing grain **2 :** a movable airfoil usu. attached to the tail plane of an airplane for producing motion up or down

elev·en \i-'lev-ən\ *n* [OE *endleofan,* adj.] **1 —** see NUMBER table **2 :** the eleventh in a set or series **3 :** something having 11 units or members — **eleven** *adj or pron* — **elev·enth** \-ən(t)th\ *n* — **eleventh** *adj or adv*

el·e·von \'el-ə-,vän\ *n :* an airplane control surface that combines the functions of elevator and aileron

elf \'elf\ *n, pl* **elves** \'elvz\ [OE *ælf*] : a small often mischievous fairy — **elf·ish** \'el-fish\ *adj* — **elf·ish·ly** *adv*

elf·in \'el-fən\ *adj* **1 :** of or relating to elves **2 :** resembling an elf; *esp :* having a strange beauty or charm

Eli \'ē-,lī\ *n :* an early Hebrew judge and priest

Eli·as \i-'lī-əs\ *var of* ELIJAH

elic·it \i-'lis-ət\ *vt* [L *elicit-, elicere,* fr. *e- + lacere* to allure] : to draw forth or bring out often by skillful questioning or discussion ⟨*elicit* the truth from an unwilling witness⟩ — **elic·i·ta·tion** \i-,lis-ə-'tā-shən\ *n* — **elic·i·tor** \i-'lis-ət-ər\ *n*

elide \i-'līd\ *vt* [L *elis-, elidere* to strike out, fr. *e- + laedere* to injure by striking] **1 :** to suppress or alter by elision **2 :** OMIT, IGNORE

el·i·gi·ble \'el-ə-jə-bəl\ *adj* [L *eligere* to choose] : qualified to be chosen ⟨*eligible* to be president⟩ : ENTITLED ⟨*eligible* to retire⟩ — **el·i·gi·bil·i·ty** \,el-i-jə-'bil-ət-ē\ *n* — **eligible** *n* — **el·i·gi·bly** \'el-i-jə-blē\ *adv*

Eli·jah \i-'lī-jə\ *n :* a Hebrew prophet of the 9th century B.C.

elim·i·nate \i-'lim-ə-,nāt\ *vt* [L *eliminare,* fr. *e- + limin-, limen* threshold] **1 a :** to get rid of : EXPEL **b :** to set aside as unimportant : IGNORE **2 :** to expel from the living body **3 :** to cause (a symbol) to disappear by combining two or more equations — **elim·i·na·tion** \i-,lim-ə-'nā-shən\ *n* — **elim·i·na·tive** \i-'lim-ə-,nāt-iv\ *adj* — **elim·i·na·tor** \-,nāt-ər\ *n*

Elis·a·beth \i-'liz-ə-bəth\ *n :* the mother of John the Baptist

Eli·sha \i-'lī-shə\ *n :* a Hebrew prophet who was a disciple and successor of Elijah

eli·sion \i-'lizh-ən\ *n* [L *elis-, elidere* to strike out] : the omission of a final or initial sound of a word ⟨*is* has become *'s* in *there's* by *elision*⟩; *esp :* the omission of an unstressed vowel or syllable in a verse to achieve a uniform rhythm

elite \ā-'lēt\ *n* [F *élite,* fr. OF *eslite,* fr. fem. of pp. of *eslire* to choose, fr. L *eligere*] **1 a :** the choice part; *esp* : a socially superior group **b :** a small group exercising power by virtue of real or claimed superiority in ability or technical competence **2 :** a typewriter type providing 12 characters to the inch — **elite** *adj*

elix·ir \i-'lik-sər\ *n* [ML, fr. Ar *al-iksīr* the elixir] **1 a :** a substance held to be capable of changing metals into gold **b :** a substance held to be capable of prolonging life indefinitely **c :** CURE-ALL **2 :** a sweetened usu. alcoholic liquid used as a vehicle for medicinal agents **3 :** the essential principle

Eliz·a·be·than \i-,liz-ə-'bē-thən\ *adj* : of, relating to, or characteristic of Elizabeth I of England or her age — **Eliza·bethan** *n*

elk \'elk\ *n, pl* **elk** *or* **elks** [ME] **1 :** the largest existing deer of Europe and Asia resembling but not so large as the moose of No. America **2 :** WAPITI **3 :** any of various large Asiatic deer

elk

¹ell \'el\ *n* [OE *eln*] : a former English unit of length for cloth equal to 45 inches

²ell *n* [fr. the resulting shape like the letter *L*] : an extension at right angles to a building

el·lipse \i-'lips, e-\ *n* **1** : OVAL **2** : a closed plane curve generated by a point moving in such a way that the sums of its distances from two fixed points is a constant : a conic section that is a closed curve

el·lip·sis \i-'lip-səs, e-\ *n, pl* **-lip·ses** \-'lip-ˌsēz\ [Gk *elleipsis* ellipsis, ellipse, fr. *elleipein* to leave out, fall short, fr. *en-* in- + *leipein* to leave] **1** : the omission of one or more words that can be obviously understood and supplied to make a construction seem more complete ⟨"fire when ready" for "fire when you are ready" is an example of *ellipsis*⟩ **2** : marks or a mark (as . . . or * * * or —) used to show the omission esp. of letters or words

el·lip·soid \i-'lip-ˌsȯid, e-\ *n* : a surface all plane sections of which are ellipses or circles; *esp* : SPHEROID — **ellipsoid** *or* **el·lip·soi·dal** \i-ˌlip-'sȯid-ᵊl, (ˌ)e-\ *adj*

el·lip·tic \i-'lip-tik, e-\ *or* **el·lip·ti·cal** \-ti-kəl\ *adj* **1 a** : of, relating to, or shaped like an ellipse **b** : OVAL **2** : of, relating to, or marked by ellipsis — **el·lip·ti·cal·ly** \-ti-k(ə-)lē\ *adv*

elm \'elm\ *n* [OE] **1** : any of a genus of large graceful trees with alternate toothed leaves and small flowers without petals often grown as shade trees **2** : the wood of an elm

el·o·cu·tion \ˌel-ə-'kyü-shən\ *n* [L *elocut-, eloqui* to speak out] **1** : the art of effective public speaking **2** : a style of speaking esp. in public — **el·o·cu·tion·ary** \-shə-ˌner-ē\ *adj* — **el·o·cu·tion·ist** \-sh(ə-)nəst\ *n*

elo·dea \i-'lōd-ē-ə\ *n* [Gk *helōdēs* marshy, fr. *helos* marsh] : any of a small genus of American aquatic monocotyledonous herbs

¹elon·gate \i-'lȯŋ-ˌgāt\ *vb* **1** : to extend the length of **2** : to grow in length — **elon·ga·tion** \i-ˌlȯŋ-'gā-shən, ˌē-\ *n*

²elongate *adj* **1** : stretched out : LENGTHENED **2** : long in proportion to width

elon·gat·ed \i-'lȯŋ-ˌgāt-əd\ *adj* : ELONGATE

elope \i-'lōp\ *vi* [AF *aloper*] **1 a** : to run away from one's husband with a lover **b** : to run away secretly with the intention of getting married usu. without parental consent **2** : to depart secretly : slip away — **elope·ment** \-mənt\ *n* — **elop·er** *n*

el·o·quence \'el-ə-kwən(t)s\ *n* : discourse marked by force and persuasiveness; *also* : the art or power of using such discourse

el·o·quent \-kwənt\ *adj* [L *eloquent-, eloquens,* fr. prp. of *eloqui* to speak out, fr. *e-* + *loqui* to speak] **1** : marked by forceful and fluent expression **2** : vividly or movingly expressive or revealing — **el·o·quent·ly** *adv*

¹else \'els\ *adv* [OE *elles*] **1 a** : in a different manner or place or at a different time **b** : in an additional manner or place or at an additional time **2** : if the facts are or were different : if not : OTHERWISE

²else *adj* : OTHER : **a** : being different in identity ⟨somebody *else*⟩ **b** : being in addition ⟨what *else*⟩

else·where \-ˌhwe(ə)r, -ˌhwa(ə)r\ *adv* : in or to another place

elu·ci·date \i-'lü-sə-ˌdāt\ *vt* [L *e-* + *lucidus* lucid] : to make clear or plain : EXPLAIN — **elu·ci·da·tion** \i-ˌlü-sə-'dā-shən\ *n* — **elu·ci·da·tive** \i-'lü-sə-ˌdāt-iv\ *adj* — **elu·ci·da·tor** \-ˌdāt-ər\ *n*

elude \i-'lüd\ *vt* [L *elus-, eludere,* fr. *e-* + *ludere* to play] : to avoid or escape by being quick, skillful, or tricky ⟨*elude* a blow⟩ ⟨*elude* the police⟩ **syn** see EVADE

elu·sion \i-'lü-zhən\ *n* : an act of eluding : ESCAPE, EVASION

elu·sive \i-'lü-siv, -ziv\ *adj* **1** : tending to elude : EVASIVE **2** : hard to comprehend or define ⟨an *elusive* idea⟩ — **elu·sive·ly** *adv* — **elu·sive·ness** *n*

elu·so·ry \i-'lüs-(ə-)rē, -'lüz-\ *adj* : ELUSIVE

elute \i-'lüt\ *vt* [Gk *eluere* to wash out, fr. *ex-, e-* out + *lavere* to wash] : to extract esp. by means of a solvent — **elu·tion** \i-'lü-\ *n*

elu·vi·al \ē-'lü-vē-əl\ *adj* : of or relating to eluvium

elu·vi·um \-vē-əm\ *n* [NL, fr. L *eluere* to wash out] **1** : fine material produced where found by weathering of rock **2** : fine soil material deposited by wind

el·ver \'el-vər\ *n* [alter. of *eelfare* migration of eels] : a young eel

elves *pl of* ELF

elv·ish \'el-vish\ *adj* : ELFISH, MISCHIEVOUS

Ely·si·um \i-'liz(h)-ē-əm\ *n* **1** : the abode of the good after death in classical mythology **2** : a place or condition of ideal happiness : PARADISE — **Ely·sian** \i-'lizh-ən\ *adj*

el·y·tron \'el-ə-ˌträn\ *also* **el·y·trum** \-trəm\ *n, pl* **-tra** \-trə\ [Gk *elytron* sheath, wing case, fr. *eilyein* to roll, wrap] : one of the thick modified anterior wings in beetles and some other insects that protect the posterior pair of functional wings

em \'em\ *n* **1** : the width of the body of a piece of type bearing the letter *M* used as a unit of measure of printed matter **2** : PICA 2

em- — see EN-

ema·ci·ate \i-'mā-shē-ˌāt\ *vt* [L *emaciare,* fr. *e-* + *macies* leanness, fr. *macer* lean] **1** : to cause to lose flesh so as to become very thin **2** : to make feeble — **ema·ci·a·tion** \i-ˌmā-s(h)ē-'ā-shən\ *n*

em·a·nate \'em-ə-ˌnāt\ *vb* [L *emanare,* fr. *e-* + *manare* to flow] **1** : to come out from a source **2** : to give out : EMIT

em·a·na·tion \ˌem-ə-'nā-shən\ *n* **1** : the action of emanating **2** : something that emanates or is produced by emanation — **em·a·na·tion·al** \-shnəl, -shən-ᵊl\ *adj* — **em·a·na·tive** \'em-ə-ˌnāt-iv\ *adj*

eman·ci·pate \i-'man(t)-sə-ˌpāt\ *vt* [L *emancipare,* fr. *e-* + *mancipare* to transfer ownership of, fr. *mancip-, manceps* purchaser, fr. *manus* hand + *capere* to take] : to free from restraint, control, or the power of another; *esp* : to free from bondage ⟨*emancipated* the slaves⟩ — **eman·ci·pa·tion** \i-ˌman(t)-sə-'pā-shən\ *n* — **eman·ci·pa·tor** \i-'man(t)-sə-ˌpāt-ər\ *n*

emar·gin·ate \(ˌ)ē-'mär-jə-nət, -ˌnāt\ *adj* : having a notched margin

emas·cu·late \i-'mas-kyə-ˌlāt\ *vt* **1** : CASTRATE **2** : to deprive of masculine vigor or spirit : WEAKEN — **emas·cu·la·tion** \i-ˌmas-kyə-'lā-shən\ *n* — **emas·cu·la·tor** \i-'mas-kyə-ˌlāt-ər\ *n*

em·balm \im-'bäm, -'bälm\ *vb* [MF *embaumer,* fr. *en-* + *basme* balm] **1** : to treat a dead body with special preparations to preserve it from decay **2** : PERFUME **3** : to preserve in one's memory — **em·balm·er** *n* — **em·balm·ment** \-'bäm-mənt, -'bälm-\ *n*

em·bank \im-'baŋk\ *vt* : to enclose or confine by an embankment

em·bank·ment \-mənt\ *n* **1** : the action of embanking **2** : a raised bank or wall to carry a roadway, prevent floods, or hold back water

em·bar·go \im-'bär-gō\ *n, pl* **-goes** [Sp., fr. *embargar* to bar, fr. L *in-* + (assumed) VL *barra* bar] **1** : an order of a government prohibiting the departure of commercial ships from its ports **2** : legal prohibition or restriction of commerce **3** : STOPPAGE, IMPEDIMENT; *esp* : PROHIBITION — **embargo** *vt*

em·bark \im-'bärk\ *vb* [MF *embarquer,* fr. OProv *embarcar,* fr. *em-* + *barca* bark] **1** : to go or put on board a ship or airplane **2** : to enter into some enterprise or undertaking : begin activities ⟨*embark* on a career⟩ — **em·bar·ka·tion** \ˌem-ˌbär-'kā-shən\ *n* — **em·bark·ment** \im-'bärk-mənt\ *n*

em·bar·rass \im-'bar-əs\ *vt* [F *embarrasser,* fr. Sp *embarazar,* fr. Pg *embaraçar*] **1** : to hamper the freedom of movement of : IMPEDE ⟨soldiers *embarrassed* by heavy packs⟩ **2** : to make confused or upset in mind : cause a feeling of uneasiness in : DISCONCERT ⟨unexpected laughter *embarrassed* the speaker⟩ **3** : to involve in financial difficulties **4** : to impair the activity or functioning of ⟨lungs *embarrassed* by asthma⟩ — **em·bar·rass·ing·ly** \-'bar-ə-siŋ-lē\ *adv*

syn ABASH, DISCONCERT: EMBARRASS implies an influence or circumstance that checks or constrains one's freedom of action, speech, or choice and causes uneasiness or confusion of mind; ABASH suggests producing feelings of shame, shyness, or unworthiness by suddenly destroying self-confidence; DISCONCERT implies producing uncertainty, hesitancy, or confusion esp. through an unexpected discovery or turn of events

em·bar·rass·ment \-mənt\ *n* **1** : the state of being embarrassed: as **a** : confusion or discomposure of mind **b** : difficulty arising from the want of money to pay debts **2 a** : something that embarrasses : IMPEDIMENT

b : an excessive quantity from which to select — used esp. in the phrase *embarrassment of riches*

em·bas·sa·dor \im-\ *var of* AMBASSADOR

em·bas·sy \'em-bə-sē\ *n, pl* **-sies** [MF *embassee*, of Gmc origin] **1** : the function or position of an ambassador **2** : the business entrusted to an ambassador **3** : the person or group of persons sent as ambassadors **4** : the residence or office of an ambassador

em·bat·tle \im-'bat-ᵊl\ *vt* **1** : to arrange in order of battle : prepare for battle **2** : FORTIFY

em·bed \im-'bed\ *vb* **1** : to enclose closely in or as if in a surrounding mass : set solidly in or as if in a bed ⟨*embed* a post in concrete⟩ **2** : to become embedded

em·bel·lish \im-'bel-ish\ *vt* [MF *embeliss-, embelir*, fr. *en-* + *bel* beautiful] **1** : to make beautiful with ornamentation : DECORATE **2** : to heighten the attractiveness of by adding ornamental details **syn** see ADORN — **em·bel·lish·ment** \-mənt\ *n*

em·ber \'em-bər\ *n* [ME *eymere*, fr. ON *eimyrja*] **1** : a glowing piece of coal or wood from a fire; *esp* : such a piece smoldering in ashes **2** *pl* : smoldering remains of a fire

em·ber day \'em-bər-\ *n* [OE *ymbrendæg*, fr. *ymbrene* anniversary + *dæg* day] : a Wednesday, Friday, or Saturday following the first Sunday in Lent, Whitsunday, September 14, or December 13 and set apart for fasting and prayer

em·bez·zle \im-'bez-əl\ *vt* **em·bez·zled**; **em·bez·zling** \-'bez-(ə-)liŋ\ [AF *embeseiller*, fr. MF *en-* + *bessiller* to destroy] : to take (property entrusted to one's care) dishonestly for one's own use — **em·bez·zle·ment** \-'bez-əl-mənt\ *n* — **em·bez·zler** \-'bez-(ə-)lər\ *n*

em·bit·ter \im-'bit-ər\ *vt* : to make bitter or more bitter; *esp* : to arouse bitter feeling in — **em·bit·ter·ment** \-mənt\ *n*

em·bla·zon \im-'blāz-ᵊn\ *vt* **1** : to inscribe or ornament with markings or emblems used in heraldry **2 a** : to deck in bright colors **b** : CELEBRATE, EXTOL

em·blem \'em-bləm\ *n* [Gk *emblēmat-, emblēma* inlaid work, fr. *emballein* to insert, fr. *en-* + *ballein* to throw] **1** : an object or a likeness of an object used to suggest a thing that cannot be pictured : SYMBOL ⟨the flag is the *emblem* of one's country⟩ **2** : a device, symbol, design, or figure used as an identifying mark

em·blem·at·ic \,em-blə-'mat-ik\ *also* **em·blem·at·i·cal** \-'mat-i-kəl\ *adj* : of, relating to, or constituting an emblem : SYMBOLIC

em·bod·i·ment \im-'bäd-i-mənt\ *n* **1** : the act of embodying : the state of being embodied **2** : a thing that embodies something

em·body \im-'bäd-ē\ *vt* **-bod·ied**; **-body·ing** **1** : to bring together so as to form a body or system ⟨the Constitution *embodies* the fundamental laws of the United States⟩ **2** : to make a part of a body or system **3** : to express in a concrete or definite form ⟨*embodied* his ideas in suitable words⟩ **4** : to represent in visible form ⟨a man who *embodies* courage⟩ — **em·bod·i·er** *n*

em·bold·en \im-'bōl-dən\ *vt* : to make bold

em·bo·lism \'em-bə-,liz-əm\ *n* **1** : the sudden obstruction of a blood vessel by an embolus **2** : EMBOLUS — **em·bol·ic** \em-'bäl-ik\ *adj*

em·bo·lus \'em-bə-ləs\ *n, pl* **-li** \-,lī, -,lē\ [Gk *embolos* wedge-shaped object, stopper, fr. *emballein* to insert, intercalate] : an abnormal particle (as an air bubble) circulating in the blood — compare THROMBUS

em·bon·point \ä"-bō"-'pwa"\ *n* [F] : plumpness of person : STOUTNESS

em·bo·som \im-'bůz-əm\ *vt* **1** : to take to one's heart : EMBRACE **2** : ENCLOSE, SHELTER

em·boss \im-'bäs, -'bós\ *vt* : to ornament with a pattern or design having a raised surface — **em·boss·er** *n* — **em·boss·ment** \-mənt\ *n*

em·bou·chure \,äm-bù-'shù(ə)r\ *n* [F, fr. (s')*emboucher* to flow into, fr. *en-* + *bouche* mouth] **1** : the position and use of the lips in producing a musical tone on a wind instrument **2** : the mouthpiece of a musical instrument

em·bow·er \im-'baů-(ə)r\ *vt* : to shelter or enclose in or as if in a bower

¹em·brace \im-'brās\ *vb* [OF *embracier*, fr. *en-* + *brace* two arms, fr. L *bracchia*, pl. of *bracchium* arm] **1 a** : to clasp in the arms : HUG **b** : CHERISH, LOVE **2** : ENCIRCLE,

ENCLOSE **3 a** : to take up esp. readily or gladly ⟨*embrace* a cause⟩ **b** : to avail oneself of : WELCOME **4** : to take in : INCLUDE — **em·brace·a·ble** \-'brā-sə-bəl\ *adj* — **em·brace·ment** \-'brās-mənt\ *n* — **em·brac·er** *n*

²embrace *n* : a close encircling with the arms and pressure to the bosom

em·bra·sure \im-'brā-zhər\ *n* **1** : a recess of a door or window **2** : an opening with sides flaring outward in a wall or parapet usu. for allowing the firing of cannon

em·bro·cate \'em-brə-,kāt\ *vt* : to moisten and rub (a part of the body) with a medicinal lotion or liniment — **em·bro·ca·tion** \,em-brə-'kā-shən\ *n*

em·broi·der \im-'bróid-ər\ *vb* **em·broi·dered**; **em·broi·der·ing** \-'bróid-(ə-)riŋ\ [MF *embroder*] **1** : to make or fill in a design with needlework **2** : to ornament with needlework **3** : to add to the interest of with details far beyond the truth : elaborate on : EXAGGERATE — **em·broi·der·er** \-'bróid-ər-ər\ *n*

em·broi·dery \im-'bróid-(ə-)rē\ *n, pl* **-der·ies** **1 a** : the process or art of embroidering **b** : needlework done to decorate cloth **c** : embroidered work **2** : elaboration in details esp. to add interest

em·broil \im-'bróil\ *vt* [F *embrouiller*, fr. *en-* + *brouiller* to broil] **1** : to throw into disorder or confusion **2** : to involve in conflict or difficulties — **em·broil·ment** \-mənt\ *n*

em·brown \im-'braůn\ *vt* **1** : DARKEN **2** : to make brown

em·bryo \'em-brē-,ō\ *n, pl* **em·bry·os** [ML *embryon-, embryo*, fr. Gk *embryon*, fr. *en-* + *bryein* to swell] **1** : an animal in the early stages of growth and differentiation that are characterized by cleavage, the laying down of fundamental tissues, and the formation of primitive organs and organ systems — compare FETUS **2** : the young sporophyte within a seed usu. having the form of a rudimentary plant with plumule, radicle, and cotyledons **3** : a beginning or undeveloped stage — used esp. in the phrase *in embryo*

em·bry·og·e·ny \,em-brē-'äj-ə-nē\ *or* **em·bry·o·gen·e·sis** \,em-brē-ō-'jen-ə-səs\ *n* : the formation and development of the embryo — **em·bry·o·gen·ic** \,em-brē-ə-'jen-ik\ *adj* — **em·bry·o·ge·net·ic** \,em-brē-(,)ō-jə-'net-ik\ *adj*

em·bry·ol·o·gy \,em-brē-'äl-ə-jē\ *n* **1** : a branch of biology dealing with embryos and their development **2** : the features and phenomena exhibited in the formation and development of an embryo — **em·bry·o·log·ic** \,em-brē-ə-'läj-ik\ *or* **em·bry·o·log·i·cal** \-'läj-i-kəl\ *adj* — **em·bry·o·log·i·cal·ly** \-i-k(ə-)lē\ *adv* — **em·bry·ol·o·gist** \,em-brē-'äl-ə-jəst\ *n*

em·bry·o·nal \'em-brē-ən-ᵊl\ *adj* : EMBRYONIC 1 — **em·bry·o·nal·ly** \-brē-ə-nə-lē\ *adv*

em·bry·on·ic \,em-brē-'än-ik\ *adj* **1** : of or relating to an embryo **2** : being in an early or undeveloped stage : being in embryo ⟨an *embryonic* idea⟩ — **em·bry·on·i·cal·ly** \-i-k(ə-)lē\ *adv*

em·bry·o·phyte \'em-brē-ə-,fīt\ *n* : a plant (as a fern or seed plant) producing an embryo and developing vascular tissues

embryo sac *n* : the female gametophyte of a seed plant consisting of a thin-walled sac containing the egg nucleus and others which give rise to endosperm

¹em·cee \'em-'sē\ *n* [*M.C.*] : MASTER OF CEREMONIES

²emcee *vb* **em·ceed**; **em·cee·ing** : to act as master of ceremonies

emend \ē-'mend\ *vt* [L *emendare* to emend, amend] : to correct usu. by textual alterations — **emend·a·ble** \-'men-də-bəl\ *adj*

emen·da·tion \(,)ē-,men-'dā-shən, ,em-ən-\ *n* **1** : the act of emending **2** : an alteration designed to correct or improve

¹em·er·ald \'em-(ə-)rəld\ *n* [MF *esmeralde*, fr. (assumed) VL *smaralda*, fr. L *smaragdus*, fr. Gk *smaragdos*] **1** : a rich green beryl prized as a gemstone **2** : a green gemstone (as synthetic corundum)

²emerald *adj* : brightly or richly green

emerald green *n* **1** : a clear bright green resembling that of the emerald **2** : a strong green

emerge \i-'mərj\ *vi* [L *emergere*, fr. *e-* + *mergere* to plunge] **1** : to rise from or as if from an enveloping fluid : come out into view **2** : to become known or apparent **3** : to rise from an obscure or inferior condition

---

j joke; **ŋ** sing; **ō** flow; **ó** flaw; **ói** coin; **th** thin; **th̲** this; **ü** loot; **ů** foot; **y** yet; **yü** few; **yů** furious; **zh** vision

emer·gence \i-'mər-jən(t)s\ *n* **1** : the act or an instance of emerging **2** : a superficial outgrowth of plant tissue usu. containing both epidermis and underlying tissues

emer·gen·cy \i-'mər-jən-sē\ *n, pl* **-cies** **1** : an unforeseen combination of circumstances or the resulting state that calls for immediate action **2** : a pressing need : EXIGENCY **syn** see JUNCTURE

¹emer·gent \i-'mər-jənt\ *adj* : rising out of or as if out of a fluid

²emergent *n* : a plant rooted in shallow water and having most of its growth above water

emer·i·tus \i-'mer-ət-əs\ *adj* [L, pp. of *emereri* to serve out one's term, fr. *e-* + *mereri, merēre* to earn, deserve, serve] **1** : holding after retirement an honorary title corresponding to that held last during active service ⟨professor *emeritus*⟩ **2** : retired from an office or position — *emeritus n*

emer·sion \ē-'mər-zhən\ *n* [L *emers-, emergere* to emerge] : an act of emerging : EMERGENCE

em·ery \'em-(ə-)rē\ *n* [MF *emeri*, fr. It *smeriglio*, fr. ML *smiriglum*, fr. Gk *smyrid-, smyris* powdered emery; akin to E *smear*] : a dark granular corundum used esp. in the form of powder or grains for grinding and polishing

emet·ic \i-'met-ik\ *n* : an agent that induces vomiting — **emetic** *adj* — **emet·i·cal·ly** \-'met-i-k(ə-)lē\ *adv*

-emia *or* **-ae·mia** \'ē-mē-ə\ *n comb form* [Gk *haima* blood] : condition of having (such) blood ⟨leuk*emia*⟩

em·i·grant \'em-i-grənt\ *n* **1** : one that emigrates **2** : a migrant plant or animal — **emigrant** *adj*
syn EMIGRANT, IMMIGRANT mean one who leaves his country to settle in another. EMIGRANT applies to the person leaving his country; IMMIGRANT applies to the same person entering and settling in another country

em·i·grate \'em-ə-ˌgrāt\ *vi* [L *emigrare*, fr. *e-* + *migrare* to migrate] : to leave a place of abode or a country for life or residence elsewhere — **em·i·gra·tion** \ˌem-ə-'grā-shən\ *n*

émi·gré *or* **emi·gré** \ˌem-ə-'grā, ˌā-mə-\ *n* : EMIGRANT; *esp* : a person who emigrates because of political conditions

em·i·nence \'em-ə-nən(t)s\ *n* **1** : a condition or station of prominence or superiority **2** — used as a title for a cardinal **3 a** : a person of high rank or attainments **b** : a natural elevation : HEIGHT

em·i·nent \-nənt\ *adj* [L *eminent- eminens*, fr. prp. of *eminēre* to stand out] **1** : standing above all others esp. in rank, merit, or virtue : NOTABLE **2** : LOFTY, TOWERING — **em·i·nent·ly** *adv*

eminent domain *n* : a right of a government to take private property for public use by virtue of the superior dominion of the sovereign power over all lands within its jurisdiction

emir \i-'mi(ə)r, ā-\ *n* [Ar *amīr* commander] : a Muslim prince — **emir·ate** \-'mi(ə)r-ət, -ˌāt\ *n*

em·is·sary \'em-ə-ˌser-ē\ *n, pl* **-sar·ies** : one sent as the agent of another often in secret to gather information

emis·sion \ē-'mish-ən\ *n* **1** : an act or instance of emitting **2** : something emitted : DISCHARGE — **emis·sive** \ē-'mis-iv\ *adj*

em·is·siv·i·ty \ˌem-ə-'siv-ət-ē, ˌē-, -mi-\ *n* : the relative power of a surface to emit heat by radiation

emit \ē-'mit\ *vt* **emit·ted**; **emit·ting** [L *emiss-, emittere* to send out, fr. *e-* + *mittere* to send] **1 a** : to throw or give off or out (as light) **b** : to send out : EJECT **2** : to issue with authority **3** : to give utterance to : EXPRESS — **emit·ter** *n*

em·mer \'em-ər\ *n* : a hard red wheat having spikelets with two kernels that remain in the glumes after threshing

em·met \'em-ət\ *n* [ME *emete*] *chiefly dial* : ANT

¹emol·lient \i-'mäl-yənt\ *adj* [L *emollire* to soften, fr. *e-* + *mollis* soft] : making soft or supple; *also* : soothing esp. to the skin or mucous membrane

²emollient *n* : something that softens or soothes

emol·u·ment \i-'mäl-yə-mənt\ *n* [L *emolumentum*, lit., miller's fee, fr. *emolere* to grind up] : profit from one's employment or from an office held : SALARY, WAGES

emote \i-'mōt\ *vi* : to give expression to emotion in or as if in a play

emo·tion \i-'mō-shən\ *n* [MF, fr. *emouvoir* to stir up, fr. L *exmovēre*, lit., to move away, fr. *ex-* + *movēre* to move] **1** : strong feeling : EXCITEMENT ⟨speak with *emotion*⟩

2 : a mental and bodily reaction (as anger, joy, hate, or fear) marked by strong feeling and physiological responses that prepare the body for action **syn** see FEELING

emo·tion·al \i-'mō-shnəl, -shən-ᵊl\ *adj* **1** : of or relating to the emotions ⟨an *emotional* upset⟩ **2** : inclined to show or express emotion : easily moved ⟨an *emotional* person⟩ **3** : appealing to or arousing emotion ⟨an *emotional* speech⟩ — **emo·tion·al·ly** \-ē\ *adv*

emo·tive \i-'mōt-iv\ *adj* **1** : of or relating to the emotions **2** : appealing to or expressing emotion — **emo·tive·ly** *adv*

em·pa·thy \'em-pə-thē\ *n* : the capacity for experiencing as one's own the feelings of another — **em·path·ic** \em-'path-ik\ *adj*

em·pen·nage \ˌäm-pə-'näzh, ˌem-\ *n* : the tail assembly of an airplane

em·per·or \'em-pər-ər, -prər\ *n* [OF *empereor*, fr. L *imperator*, lit., commander, fr. *imperare* to command, fr. *in-* + *parare* to prepare, arrange] : the sovereign ruler of an empire — compare MONARCH

em·pery \'em-pə-rē\ *n* : wide dominion : EMPIRE

em·pha·sis \'em(p)-fə-səs\ *n, pl* **-pha·ses** \-fə-ˌsēz\ [Gk, exposition, emphasis, fr. *emphainein* to indicate, fr. *en-* in- + *phainein* to show] **1 a** : a forcefulness of expression that gives special impressiveness or importance **b** : a particular prominence given in reading or speaking to a word or syllable **2** : special stress or insistence upon something

em·pha·size \'em(p)-fə-ˌsīz\ *vt* : to give emphasis to or place emphasis upon : STRESS

em·phat·ic \im-'fat-ik, em-\ *adj* **1** : uttered with or marked by emphasis **2** : tending to express oneself in forceful speech or to take decisive action **3** : attracting special attention ⟨an *emphatic* contrast⟩ **4** : constituting or belonging to a set of verb forms in English that have the auxiliary *do* and are used rarely for emphasis and regularly to take the place of a simple verb form in questions or negative statements ⟨the *emphatic* form "do know" or "do . . . know" in "but I tell you I do know him", "do you know him?", and "I do not know him"⟩ — **em·phat·i·cal·ly** \-'fat-i-k(ə-)lē\ *adv*

em·phy·se·ma \ˌem(p)-fə-'sē-mə, -'zē-\ *n* : a disorder marked by air-filled expansions of tissues esp. of the lung — **em·phy·se·ma·tous** \-mət-əs\ *adj*

em·pire \'em-ˌpī(ə)r\ *n* [OF, fr. L *imperium*, fr. *imperare* to command] **1 a** (1) : a major political unit with a great extent of territory or a number of territories or peoples under one sovereign authority; *esp* : one having an emperor as chief of state (2) : the territory of such a unit **b** : something held to resemble a political empire; *esp* : an extensive territory or enterprise under one control **2** : imperial sovereignty, rule, or dominion

Em·pire \'äm-ˌpī(ə)r, 'em-ˌpī(ə)r\ *adj* [F, fr. *le premier Empire* the first Empire of France] : of or relating to an early 19th century French style (as of clothing or furniture) characterized by elaborateness and refinement

em·pir·ic \im-'pir-ik, em-\ *n* [Gk *empeirikos* doctor relying on experience alone, fr. *empeiria* experience, fr. *en-* + *peiran* to attempt] : one who relies upon practical experience

em·pir·i·cal \-'pir-i-kəl\ *or* **em·pir·ic** \-'pir-ik\ *adj* **1** : relying on experience or observation usu. without due regard for system and theory ⟨*empirical* medicine⟩ **2** : originating in or based on observation or experience **3** : capable of being verified or disproved by observation or experiment ⟨*empirical* laws⟩ — **em·pir·i·cal·ly** \-'pir-i-k(ə-)lē\ *adv*

empirical formula *n* : a chemical formula showing the simplest ratio of elements in a compound

em·pir·i·cism \im-'pir-ə-ˌsiz-əm, em-\ *n* **1** : QUACKERY, CHARLATANRY **2** : the practice of relying upon observation and experiment esp. in the natural sciences **3** : a theory that knowledge originates in experience — **em·pir·i·cist** \-səst\ *adj or n*

em·place \im-'plās\ *vt* : to put into place

em·place·ment \im-'plās-mənt\ *n* **1** : a prepared position for weapons or military equipment **2** : a putting into position : PLACEMENT

¹em·ploy \im-'plói\ *vt* [MF *emploier*, fr. L *implicare* to involve, implicate] **1 a** : to make use of **b** : to occupy (as time) advantageously **c** : to use or engage the services of : provide with a job that pays wages or a salary **2** : to devote (as time or energy) to or direct toward a particular activity or person **syn** see HIRE, USE — **em·ploy·a·ble** \-ə-bəl\ *adj*

²**employ** *n* : the state of being employed esp. for wages or a salary ⟨generous to men in his *employ*⟩

em·ploy·ee or **em·ploye** \im-ˌplȯi-ˈē, (ˌ)em-; im-ˈplȯi-ˌē\ *n* : one employed by another usu. for wages or salary

em·ploy·er \im-ˈplȯi(-ə)r\ *n* : one that employs others

em·ploy·ment \im-ˈplȯi-mənt\ *n* **1** : USE, PURPOSE; *also* : the act of using **2 a** : the act of engaging a person for work : HIRING **b** : the work at which one is employed : OCCUPATION **c** : the state of being employed ⟨*employment* in the machine trade⟩ **d** : the extent or degree to which a labor force is employed ⟨*employment* is high⟩

em·po·ri·um \im-ˈpōr-ē-əm, em-, -ˈpȯr-\ *n, pl* **-ri·ums** or **-ria** \-ē-ə\ [Gk *emporion*, fr. *emporos* traveler, trader, fr. *en* in + *poros* passage] **1** : a place of trade : MARKETPLACE; *esp* : a commercial center **2** : a store carrying a wide variety of merchandise

em·pow·er \im-ˈpau̇(-ə)r\ *vt* : to give official authority or legal power to **syn** see ENABLE

em·press \ˈem-prəs\ *n* **1** : the wife or widow of an emperor **2** : a woman who holds an imperial title in her own right

em·prise \em-ˈprīz\ *n* : UNDERTAKING, ENTERPRISE; *esp* : a chivalric enterprise

¹**emp·ty** \ˈem(p)-tē\ *adj* **emp·ti·er; -est** [OE *ǣmettig* unoccupied, fr. *ǣmetta* leisure] **1** : containing nothing ⟨*empty* box⟩ **2** : UNOCCUPIED, VACANT ⟨*empty* house⟩ **3** : being without reality or substance ⟨*empty* dreams⟩ **4** : lacking in value, sense, effect, or sincerity ⟨*empty* pleasures⟩ ⟨*empty* threats⟩ **5** : HUNGRY ⟨feel *empty* before dinner⟩ **6** : NULL 4 — **emp·ti·ly** \-tə-lē\ *adv* — **emp·ti·ness** \-tē-nəs\ *n*

syn VACANT, VOID, BLANK: EMPTY implies a complete lack or absence of usual content or significance ⟨*empty* words⟩ VACANT implies lack of what is considered as or intended to be the usual occupant, tenant, or attribute ⟨a *vacant* lot⟩ ⟨a *vacant* store⟩ VOID intensifies emptiness ⟨the *void* expanse of sea⟩ ⟨*void* of compassion⟩ BLANK stresses what is free from writing or marking and implies lack of signs of expression, comprehension, or meaning ⟨a *blank* page⟩ ⟨*blank* surprise⟩

²**empty** *vb* **1** : to make empty : remove the contents of ⟨*empty* a barrel⟩ **2** : to transfer by emptying **3** : to become empty **4** : to give forth its contents (as fluid) : DISCHARGE ⟨the river *empties* into the ocean⟩

³**empty** *n, pl* **empties** : an empty container

emp·ty-hand·ed \ˌem(p)-tē-ˈhan-dəd\ *adj* **1** : having nothing in the hands **2** : having acquired or gained nothing

em·pur·ple \im-ˈpər-pəl\ *vb* **em·pur·pled; em·pur·pling** \-ˈpər-p(ə-)liŋ\ : to tinge or color purple

em·py·ema \ˌem-ˌpī-ˈē-mə, -pē-\ *n* : the presence of pus in a bodily cavity — **em·py·emic** \-ˈē-mik, -ˈem-ik\ *adj*

em·py·re·al \ˌem-ˌpī-ˈrē-əl, -pə-\ *adj* [Gk *en* in + *pyr* fire] **1** : of or relating to the empyrean : CELESTIAL **2** : SUBLIME

¹**em·py·re·an** \-ˈrē-ən\ *adj* : EMPYREAL

²**empyrean** *n* **1** : the highest heaven or heavenly sphere **2** : FIRMAMENT, HEAVENS

emu \ˈē-ˌmyü\ *n* [modif. of Pg *ema* rhea] : a swift-running Australian bird with undeveloped wings that is related to but smaller than the ostrich

em·u·late \ˈem-yə-ˌlāt\ *vt* [L *aemulari*, fr. *aemulus* emulous] **1 a** : to strive to equal or excel **b** : IMITATE **2** : to equal or approach equality with — **em·u·la·tor** \-ˌlāt-ər\ *n*

em·u·la·tion \ˌem-yə-ˈlā-shən\ *n* : ambition or endeavor to equal or excel; *also* : IMITATION — **em·u·la·tive** \ˈem-yə-ˌlāt-iv\ *adj*

emu

em·u·lous \ˈem-yə-ləs\ *adj* : eager or ambitious to equal or excel another ⟨*emulous* competitors⟩ — **em·u·lous·ly** *adv* — **em·u·lous·ness** *n*

emul·si·fi·er \i-ˈməl-sə-ˌfī(-ə)r\ *n* : an agent (as a soap) promoting the formation and stabilization of an emulsion

emul·si·fy \-ˌfī\ *vt* **-fied; -fy·ing** : to convert (as an oil) into an emulsion — **emul·si·fi·a·ble** \-ˌfī-ə-bəl\ *adj* — **emul·si·fi·ca·tion** \i-ˌməl-sə-fə-ˈkā-shən\ *n*

emul·sion \i-ˈməl-shən\ *n* [L *emuls-, emulgēre* to milk out, fr. *e-* + *mulgēre* to milk] **1** : a material consisting of a mixture of liquids that do not dissolve in each other and having droplets of one liquid dispersed throughout the other ⟨an *emulsion* of oil in water⟩ **2** : a light-sensitive coating on photographic plates, film, or paper consisting of particles of a silver salt suspended in a thick substance (as a gelatin solution) — **emul·sive** \-siv\ *adj*

emul·soid \-ˌsȯid\ *n* : a colloid consisting of one liquid dispersed in another

en \ˈen\ *n* : the width of the body of a piece of type bearing the letter *n* used as a unit of measure of printed matter : one half of an em

¹**en-** *also* **em-** \e\ *also occurs in these prefixes although only i may be shown as in "engage"* \ *prefix* [OF, fr. L *in-*] **1** : put into or on to ⟨*encradle*⟩ ⟨*enthrone*⟩ : cover with ⟨*enverdure*⟩ : go into or on to ⟨*embus*⟩ **2** : cause to be ⟨*enslave*⟩ **3** : provide with ⟨*empower*⟩ **4** : so as to cover ⟨*enwrap*⟩ : thoroughly ⟨*entangle*⟩ — in all senses usu. *em-* before *b, m,* or *p*

²**en-** *also* **em-** *prefix* [Gk] : in : within ⟨*enzootic*⟩ — usu. *em-* before *b, m,* or *p* ⟨*empathy*⟩

¹**-en** \ən, ᵊn\ *also* **-n** \n\ *adj suffix* [OE] : made of : consisting of ⟨earthe*n*⟩ ⟨woole*n*⟩ ⟨silver*n*⟩

²**-en** *vb suffix* [OE *-nian*] **1** : become or cause to be ⟨sharpe*n*⟩ **2** : cause or come to have ⟨lengthe*n*⟩

en·able \in-ˈā-bəl\ *vt* **en·abled; en·abling** \-b(ə-)liŋ\ **1 a** : to make able ⟨glasses *enable* him to read⟩ **b** : to make possible, practical, or easy **2** : to give legal power, capacity, or sanction to

syn ENABLE, EMPOWER mean to make one able to do something. ENABLE implies provision of the means or opportunity for doing; EMPOWER implies the granting of power or delegation of authority to do

en·act \in-ˈakt\ *vt* **1** : to establish by legal and authoritative act; *esp* : to make (as a bill) into law **2** : to act out : REPRESENT — **en·ac·tor** \-ˈak-tər\ *n*

en·act·ment \-ˈak(t)-mənt\ *n* **1** : the act of enacting : the state of being enacted **2** : LAW, STATUTE

¹**enam·el** \in-ˈam-əl\ *vt* **enam·eled** or **enam·elled; enam·el·ing** or **enam·el·ling** \-ˈam-(ə-)liŋ\ [MF *enamailler,* fr. *en-* + *esmail* enamel] **1** : to cover or inlay with enamel **2** : to form a glossy surface on

²**enamel** *n* **1** : a usu. opaque vitreous composition applied by fusion to the surface of metal, glass, or pottery **2** : a surface that resembles enamel **3** : a usu. glossy paint that flows out to a smooth hard coat when applied **4** : a very hard outer layer covering the crown of a tooth

enam·el·ware \-ˌwa(ə)r, -ˌwe(ə)r\ *n* : metal utensils (as pots and pans) coated with enamel

en·am·or \in-ˈam-ər\ *vt* [OF *enamourer,* fr. *en-* + *amour* love] : to inflame with love

en bloc \ä⁼-ˈbläk\ *adv (or adj)* [F] : as a whole : in a mass

en·camp \in-ˈkamp\ *vb* **1** : to set up and occupy a camp : CAMP **2** : to place or establish in a camp ⟨*encamp* troops⟩

en·camp·ment \-mənt\ *n* **1** : the act of encamping : the state of being encamped **2** : CAMP

en·cap·su·late \in-ˈkap-sə-ˌlāt\ *vb* : to encase or become encased in a capsule — **en·cap·su·la·tion** \-ˌkap-sə-ˈlā-shən\ *n*

en·case \in-ˈkās\ *vt* : to enclose in or as if in a case — **en·case·ment** \-mənt\ *n*

en·caus·tic \in-ˈkȯ-stik\ *n* : a paint mixed with melted beeswax and after application fixed by heat

-ence \ən(t)s, ᵊn(t)s\ *n suffix* [OF, fr. L *-entia,* fr. *-ent-, -ens,* prp. ending of some verbs + *-ia -y*] **1** : action or process ⟨emerg*ence*⟩ : instance of an action or process ⟨refer*ence*⟩ **2** : quality or state ⟨despond*ence*⟩

en·ceinte \ä⁼-ˈsant, än-\ *adj* [MF, modif. of L *incient-, inciens*] : PREGNANT

encephal- or **encephalo-** *comb form* [Gk *enkephalos,* fr. *en* in + *kephalē* head] : brain ⟨encephalitis⟩ ⟨encephalogram⟩

en·ceph·a·li·tis \(ˌ)en-ˌsef-ə-ˈlīt-əs\ *n* : inflammation of the brain — **en·ceph·a·lit·ic** \-ˈlit-ik\ *adj*

en·ceph·a·lo·my·e·li·tis \en-ˌsef-ə-lō-ˌmī-ə-ˈlīt-əs\ *n* : concurrent inflammation of the brain and spinal cord

en·ceph·a·lon \en-ˈsef-ə-ˌlän, -lən\ *n, pl* **-la** \-lə\ : the vertebrate brain — **en·ce·phal·ic** \ˌen(t)-sə-ˈfal-ik\ *adj*

---

j joke; **ŋ** sing; **ō** flow; **ȯ** flaw; **ȯi** coin; **th** thin; **th** this; **ü** loot; **u̇** foot; **y** yet; **yü** few; **yu̇** furious; **zh** vision

en·chain \in-'chān\ vt **1** : to bind with or as if with chains **2** : to attract and hold (as the attention) — **en·chain·ment** \-mənt\ n

en·chant \in-'chant\ vt [MF *enchanter*, fr. L *incantare*, fr. *in-* + *cantare* to sing] **1** : to influence by charms and incantation : BEWITCH **2** : THRILL, ENRAPTURE

en·chant·er \-ər\ n : one that enchants; *esp* : SORCERER

en·chant·ing adj : CHARMING, ATTRACTIVE — **en·chant·ing·ly** \-iŋ-lē\ adv

en·chant·ment \in-'chant-mənt\ n **1** : the act or art of enchanting : the state of being enchanted **2** : something that enchants : SPELL, CHARM

en·chant·ress \in-'chan-trəs\ n **1** : a woman who practices magic : SORCERESS **2** : a fascinating woman

en·chi·la·da \,en-chə-'läd-ə\ n [AmerSp] : a tortilla rolled with meat filling and served with tomato sauce seasoned with chili

en·ci·pher \in-'sī-fər, en-\ vt : to convert (a message) into cipher

en·cir·cle \in-'sər-kəl\ vt **1** : to form a circle around : SURROUND **2** : to pass completely around — **en·cir·cle·ment** \-kəl-mənt\ n

en·clave \'en-,klāv, 'än-\ n [MF, fr. *enclaver* to enclose, fr. L *in-* + *clavis* key] : a territorial or culturally distinct unit enclosed within foreign territory

en·clit·ic \en-'klit-ik\ adj [Gk *enklitikos*, fr. *enklinesthai* to lean on, fr. *en-* + *klinein* to lean] : being without independent accent and treated in pronunciation as forming a part of the preceding word ⟨*thee* in *prithee* and *not* in *cannot* are *enclitic*⟩ — **enclitic** n

en·close \in-'klōz\ vt **1 a** : to close in : SURROUND; *esp* : to mark off (land) by or as if by a fence for one's own use **b** : to hold in : CONFINE **2** : to place in a parcel or envelope

en·clo·sure \in-'klō-zhər\ n **1** : the act of enclosing : the state of being enclosed **2** : an enclosed space **3** : something (as a fence) that encloses **4** : something enclosed (a letter with two *enclosures*)

en·code \in-'kōd\ vt : to transfer from one system of communication into another; *esp* : to convert (a message) into code

en·co·mi·ast \en-'kō-mē-,ast, -mē-əst\ n : EULOGIST — **en·co·mi·as·tic** \-,kō-mē-'as-tik\ adj

en·co·mi·um \en-'kō-mē-əm\ n, pl **-mi·ums** or **-mia** \-mē-ə\ [Gk *enkōmion*, fr. *en* in + *kōmos* celebration] : warm or high praise esp. when formally expressed : EULOGY

en·com·pass \in-'kəm-pəs, -'käm-\ vt **1** : to form a circle about : ENCLOSE **2 a** : ENVELOP **b** : INCLUDE — **en·com·pass·ment** \-mənt\ n

¹en·core \'än-,kō(ə)r, -,kȯ(ə)r\ n [F, again] : a demand for repetition or reappearance made by an audience; *also* : a further performance in response to such a demand

²encore vt : to call for a further performance or appearance of or by

¹en·coun·ter \in-'kaunt-ər\ vt **en·coun·tered**; **en·coun·ter·ing** \-'kaunt-ə-riŋ, -'kaun-triŋ\ [OF *encontrer*, fr. L *in-* + *contra* against] **1** : to meet as an adversary or enemy : engage in conflict with **2** : to come upon face to face : MEET **3** : to come upon unexpectedly

²encounter n **1 a** : a meeting between hostile factions or persons **b** : a sudden often violent clash : COMBAT **2 a** : a chance meeting **b** : a meeting face to face

en·cour·age \in-'kər-ij, -'kə-rij\ vt **1** : to inspire with courage, spirit, or hope : HEARTEN **2** : to spur on : STIMULATE **3** : to give help to : FOSTER — **en·cour·ag·ing·ly** \-iŋ-lē\ adv

en·cour·age·ment \-mənt\ n **1** : the act of encouraging : the state of being encouraged **2** : something that encourages

en·croach \in-'krōch\ vi [MF *encrochier*, fr. *en-* + *croche* hook] **1** : to enter or force oneself gradually upon another's property or rights : TRESPASS, INTRUDE (*encroach* upon a neighbor's land) **2** : to advance beyond the usual or proper limits (the gradually *encroaching* sea) — **en·croach·ment** \-mənt\ n

en·crust \in-'krəst\ vb **1** : to cover, line, or overlay with a crust **2** : to form a crust

en·crus·ta·tion \(,)in-,krəs-'tā-shən, ,en-\ var of INCRUSTATION

en·cum·ber \in-'kəm-bər\ vt **en·cum·bered**; **en·cum·**

ber·ing \-b(ə-)riŋ\ [MF *encombrer*] **1** : to weigh down : BURDEN **2** : to impede or hamper the function or activity of : HINDER **3** : to burden with a legal charge (as a mortgage) (*encumber* an estate)

en·cum·brance \in-'kəm-brən(t)s\ n **1** : something that encumbers : LOAD, BURDEN **2** : a legal claim (as a mortgage) against property

-en·cy \ən-sē, °n-\ n suffix, pl **-encies** [L *-entia* -ency, -ence] : quality or state (despond*ency*)

¹en·cyc·li·cal \in-'sik-li-kəl, en-\ adj [Gk *enkyklios* circular, general, fr. *en* in + *kyklos* circle] : addressed to all the individuals of a group : GENERAL

²encyclical n : an encyclical letter; *esp* : a papal letter to the bishops of the church as a whole or to those in one country

en·cy·clo·pe·dia also **en·cy·clo·pae·dia** \in-,sī-klə-'pēd-ē-ə\ n [Gk *enkyklios paideia* general education] : a work that contains information on all branches of knowledge or treats comprehensively a particular branch of knowledge usu. in articles arranged alphabetically by subject

en·cy·clo·pe·dic also **en·cy·clo·pae·dic** \-'pēd-ik\ adj **1** : of or relating to an encyclopedia **2** : covering a wide range of subjects (*encyclopedic* knowledge) — **en·cy·clo·pe·di·cal·ly** \-'pēd-i-k(ə-)lē\ adv

en·cyst \in-'sist, en-\ vi : to form or become enclosed in a cyst — **en·cyst·ment** \-'sis(t)-mənt\ n

¹end \'end\ n [OE *ende*] **1 a** : the part of an area that lies at the boundary **b** : a point that marks the extent or limit of something **c** : the point where something ceases to exist (world without *end*) **d** : the extreme or last part lengthwise : TIP **e** : a football lineman whose position is at the extremity of the line **2 a** : cessation of a course of action, pursuit, or activity **b** : DEATH, DESTRUCTION **c** (1) : the ultimate state (2) : RESULT, ISSUE **d** : the complex of events, parts, or sections that forms an extremity, termination, or finish **3** : something left over : REMNANT **4** : the goal toward which an agent acts or should act **5 a** : a share in an undertaking **b** : a particular phase of an undertaking or organization — **end·ed** \'en-dəd\ adj

syn END, TERMINATION, ENDING mean the point or line beyond which a thing does not or cannot go. END implies the final limit in time, space, extent, influence, or range of possibility; TERMINATION applies to the end of something complete or finished or having a set limit (the *termination* of the treaty) ENDING also includes a portion prior to the termination (the *ending* of a play) (a long *ending* to a symphony)

²end vb **1 a** : to bring or come to an end : STOP **b** : DESTROY **2** : to make up the end of **syn** see CLOSE

end- or **endo-** comb form [Gk *endon*] **1** : within : inside (*endo*skeleton) — compare ECT-, EXO- **2** : taking in (*endo*thermal)

end·amoe·ba \,en-də-'mē-bə\ n : any of a genus of parasitic amoebas that in some classifications include those causing amebic dysentery in man — **end·amoe·bic** \-bik\ adj

en·dan·ger \in-'dān-jər\ vt **en·dan·gered**; **en·dan·ger·ing** \-'dānj-(ə-)riŋ\ : to bring into danger or peril

end·brain \'en(d)-,brān\ n : the anterior subdivision of the forebrain

end brush n : the end plate of a nerve fiber

end bulb n : a bulbous termination of a sensory nerve fiber (as in the skin)

en·dear \in-'di(ə)r\ vt : to cause to become dear or beloved

en·dear·ment \-mənt\ n : a word or an act (as a caress) showing love or affection

¹en·deav·or \in-'dev-ər\ vb **en·deav·ored**; **en·deav·or·ing** \-'dev-(ə-)riŋ\ [ME *en-* + *dever* duty, fr. OF *devoir* to owe, fr. L *debēre*] : to make an effort : work for a particular end : TRY (*endeavor* to do better)

²endeavor n : a serious determined effort

¹en·dem·ic \en-'dem-ik\ adj [Gk *en* in + *dēmos* people, populace] : restricted or peculiar to a locality or region (*endemic* diseases) (an *endemic* plant) — **en·dem·i·cal·ly** \-'dem-i-k(ə-)lē\ adv — **en·de·mic·i·ty** \,en-,dem-'is-ət-ē, -də-'mis-\ n

²endemic n : NATIVE 2b

end·er·gon·ic \,en-(,)dər-'gän-ik\ adj : requiring expenditure of energy (an *endergonic* biochemical reaction)

end·ing \'en-diŋ\ *n* **1** : CONCLUSION, END ⟨a novel with a happy *ending*⟩ **2** : one or more sounds or letters added at the end of a word esp. in inflection **syn** see END

en·dive \'en-,dīv\ *n* [LL *endivia*, fr. LGk *entubion*, fr. L *intubus*] **1** : an annual or biennial herb closely related to chicory and widely grown as a salad plant — called also *escarole* **2** : the developing crown of chicory when blanched for use as salad

end·less \'en-(d)ləs\ *adj* **1** : being or seeming to be without end ⟨waited *endless* hours⟩ ⟨the *endless* prairie⟩ **2** : joined at the ends : CONTINUOUS ⟨an *endless* ·belt⟩ **syn** see ETERNAL — **end·less·ly** *adv* — **end·less·ness** *n*

end man *n* : a man at each end of the line of performers in a minstrel show who engages in comic repartee with the interlocutor

end·most \'en(d)-,mōst\ *adj* : situated at the very end

en·do·car·di·tis \,en-dō-kär-'dīt-əs\ *n* : inflammation of the lining of the heart and its valves

en·do·car·di·um \,en-dō-'kärd-ē-əm\ *n* [Gk *kardia* heart] : a thin serous membrane lining the cavities of the heart — **en·do·car·di·al** \-ē-əl\ *adj*

en·do·carp \'en-də-,kärp\ *n* : the inner layer of the pericarp of a fruit (as the stony wall enclosing the seed of a peach) — compare EPICARP, MESOCARP — **en·do·car·pal** \,en-də-'kär-pəl\ *or* **en·do·car·pic** \-pik\ *adj*

¹en·do·crine \'en-də-krən, -,krīn, -,krēn\ *adj* [Gk *krinein* to separate] **1 a** : producing secretions that are distributed in the body by way of the bloodstream ⟨*endocrine* glands⟩ **b** : of, relating to, or resembling that of an endocrine gland **2** : HORMONAL

²endocrine *n* **1** : HORMONE **2** : an endocrine gland

en·do·cri·nol·o·gy \,en-də-kri-'näl-ə-jē, -krī-\ *n* : a branch of knowledge dealing with the endocrine glands — **en·do·cri·no·log·i·cal** \-,krin-ᵊl-'äj-i-kəl, -,krīn-\ *adj* — **en·do·cri·nol·o·gist** \-kri-'näl-ə-jəst, -krī-\ *n*

en·do·derm \'en-də-,dərm\ *n* : the innermost of the three primary germ layers of an embryo giving rise to the epithelium of the digestive tract and its derivatives; *also* : a tissue derived from this layer — **en·do·der·mal** \,en-də-'dər-məl\ *or* **en·do·der·mic** \-mik\ *adj*

en·do·der·mis \,en-də-'dər-məs\ *n* : the innermost tissue of the cortex in many roots and stems

en·do·en·zyme \,en-dō-'en-,zīm\ *n* : an enzyme that functions inside the cell

en·dog·a·my \en-'däg-ə-mē\ *n* : sexual reproduction between near relatives; *esp* : pollination of a flower by pollen from another flower of the same plant — compare AUTOGAMY — **en·dog·a·mous** \-məs\ *adj*

en·dog·e·nous \en-'däj-ə-nəs\ *adj* : developing or originating within the cell or body — **en·dog·e·nous·ly** *adv*

en·do·lymph \'en-də-,lim(p)f\ *n* : the watery fluid in the inner ear

en·do·mor·phic \,en-də-'mor-fik\ *adj* [*endoderm* + *-morphic*] : predominating in structures (as the internal organs) developed from the endodermal layer of the embryo : broad and heavy in build — **en·do·morph** \'en-də-,mórf\ *n* — **en·do·mor·phy** \-,mór-fē\ *n*

en·do·par·a·site \,en-dō-'par-ə-,sīt\ *n* : a parasite that lives in the internal organs or tissues of its host — **en·do·par·a·sit·ic** \-,par-ə-'sit-ik\ *adj* — **en·do·par·a·sit·ism** \-'par-ə-,sīt-,iz-əm\ *n*

en·do·plasm \'en-də-,plaz-əm\ *n* : the inner relatively fluid part of the cytoplasm — **en·do·plas·mic** \,en-də-'plaz-mik\ *adj*

end organ *n* : a structure forming the end of a neural path and consisting of an effector or a receptor with its associated nerve terminations

en·dorse \in-'dórs\ *vt* [alter. of ME *endosen*, fr. MF *endosser*, fr. *en-* + *dos* back, fr. L *dorsum*] **1** : to write one's signature and often other matter esp. on the back of (a commercial document) for some special purpose ⟨*endorse* a check⟩ **2** : to give one's support to ⟨*endorse* a candidate⟩ **syn** see APPROVE — **en·dors·er** *n*

en·dorse·ment \in-'dórs-mənt\ *n* **1** : the act or process of endorsing **2** : something written in the process of endorsing **3** : SANCTION, APPROVAL

en·do·scope \'en-də-,skōp\ *n* : an instrument with which the interior of a hollow organ (as the rectum) may be visualized — **en·do·scop·ic** \,en-də-'skäp-ik\ *adj* — **en·dos·co·py** \en-'däs-kə-pē\ *n*

en·do·skel·e·ton \,en-dō-'skel-ət-ᵊn\ *n* : an internal

skeleton or supporting framework in an animal — **en·do·skel·e·tal** \-ət-ᵊl\ *adj*

end·os·mo·sis \,en-,däs-'mō-səs, -,däz-\ *n* : passage of material through a membrane from a region of lower to a region of higher concentration — **end·os·mot·ic** \-'mät-ik\ *adj*

en·do·sperm \'en-də-,spərm\ *n* : a nutritive tissue in seed plants formed within the embryo sac — **en·do·sper·mic** \,en-də-'spər-mik\ *adj* — **en·do·sper·mous** \-məs\ *adj*

en·do·spore \'en-də-,spōr, -,spór\ *n* : an asexual spore developed within the cell esp. in bacteria — **en·do·spor·ic** \,en-də-'spōr-ik, -'spór-\ *adj* — **en·do·spo·rous** \,en-də-'spōr-əs, -'spór-; en-'däs-pə-rəs\ *adj*

end·os·te·um \en-'däs-tē-əm\ *n, pl* **-tea** \-tē-ə\ [NL, fr. Gk *osteon* bone] : a vascular connective tissue lining the cavity of a bone — **end·os·te·al** \-tē-əl\ *adj*

end·os·tra·cum \en-'däs-tri-kəm\ *n, pl* **-ca** \-kə\ [NL, fr. Gk *ostrakon* shell] : the inner layer of a shell (as of a crab or mussel)

en·do·the·li·um \,en-də-'thē-lē-əm\ *n, pl* **-lia** \-lē-ə\ [*end-* + epi*thelium*] : an inner layer (as of epithelium or of a seed coat) — **en·do·the·li·al** \-lē-əl\ *adj*

en·do·ther·mic \,en-də-'thər-mik\ *or* **en·do·ther·mal** \-məl\ *adj* : characterized by or formed with absorption of heat ⟨*endothermic* chemical reactions⟩

en·do·tox·in \,en-dō-'täk-sən\ *n* : a poisonous substance of a bacterium (as of typhoid fever) separable from the cell only on its disintegration

en·dow \in-'daù\ *vt* [MF *en-* + *douer* to endow, fr. L *dotare*, fr. *dot-*, *dos* gift] **1** : to furnish with money for support or maintenance ⟨*endow* a hospital⟩ **2** : to provide or equip gratuitously ⟨man is *endowed* with reason⟩

en·dow·ment \-mənt\ *n* **1** : the providing of a permanent fund for support or the fund provided ⟨a college with a large *endowment*⟩ **2** : a person's natural ability or talent

endowment policy *n* : a life-insurance policy that provides for payment of a sum to the policyholder at the end of a stated period or to the beneficiary if the policyholder dies during that period

end plate *n* : a flat plate or structure at the end of something

end·point \'en(d)-,póint\ *n* : either of two points that mark the ends of a line segment or a point that marks the end of a ray

end run *n* : a football play in which the ballcarrier attempts to run wide around the end

end table *n* : a small table used beside a larger piece of furniture

en·due \in-'d(y)ü\ *vt* [MF *enduire* to bring in, fr. L *inducere*, fr. *in-* + *ducere* to lead] : to provide with a quality or power ⟨*endued* with grace⟩

en·dur·ance \in-'d(y)ùr-ən(t)s\ *n* **1** : PERMANENCE, DURATION **2** : the ability to withstand hardship, adversity, or stress **3** : SUFFERING, TRIAL

en·dure \in-'d(y)ü(ə)r\ *vb* [MF *endurer*, fr. L *in-* + *durare* to harden, endure] **1** : to continue in the same state : LAST **2 a** : to remain firm under suffering or misfortune without yielding **b** : to bear patiently : SUFFER **3** : TOLERATE, PERMIT — **en·dur·a·ble** \-'d(y)ùr-ə-bəl\ *adj* — **en·dur·a·bly** \-blē\ *adv*

en·dur·ing *adj* : LASTING, DURABLE — **en·dur·ing·ly** \-iŋ-lē\ *adv* — **en·dur·ing·ness** *n*

end·ways \'en-,dwāz\ *or* **end·wise** \-,dwīz\ *adv* (*or adj*) **1** : with the end forward **2** : LENGTHWISE **3** : on end : UPRIGHT

En·dym·i·on \en-'dim-ē-ən\ *n* : a beautiful youth loved by Selene

end zone *n* : the area at each end of a football field bounded by the end line, the goal line, and the sidelines

-ene \,ēn\ *n suffix* [Gk *-ēnē*, fem. of *-ēnos*, adj. suffix] : unsaturated carbon compound ⟨benz*ene*⟩; *esp* : carbon compound with one double bond ⟨ethyl*ene*⟩

en·e·ma \'en-ə-mə\ *n* [Gk, fr. *enienai* to inject, fr. *en-* + *hienai* to send] : the injection of liquid into the intestine by way of the anus; *also* : the material injected

en·e·my \'en-ə-mē\ *n, pl* **-mies** [OF *enemi*, fr. L *inimicus*, fr. *in-* ¹*in-* + *amicus* friend] **1** : one that hates another : one that attacks or tries to harm another **2** : something that harms **3 a** : a nation with which one's own country

is at war **b :** a military force, a ship, or a person belonging to such a nation
syn ENEMY, FOE mean one who shows hostility or ill will. ENEMY stresses antagonism showing itself in hatred or destructive attitude or action; FOE stresses active fighting or struggle and is used poetically for an enemy in war **syn** see in addition OPPONENT

en·er·get·ic \,en-ər-'jet-ik\ *adj* **:** having or showing energy **:** ACTIVE, FORCEFUL ⟨an *energetic* salesman⟩ **syn** see VIGOROUS — **en·er·get·i·cal·ly** \-'jet-i-k(ə-)lē\ *adv*

en·er·gid \'en-ər-jəd\ *n* **:** a nucleus together with the mass of cytoplasm with which it interacts

en·er·gize \'en-ər-,jīz\ *vb* **1 :** to put forth energy **:** ACT **2 a :** to impart energy to **b :** to make energetic or vigorous **3 :** to apply voltage to — **en·er·giz·er** *n*

en·er·gy \'en-ər-jē\ *n, pl* **-gies** [Gk *energeia* activity, fr. *en* in + *ergon* work] **1 :** power or capacity to be active **:** strength of body or mind to do things or to work ⟨a man of great intellectual *energy*⟩ **2 :** natural power vigorously exerted **:** vigorous action ⟨work with *energy*⟩ **3 :** the capacity for performing work — compare KINETIC ENERGY, POTENTIAL ENERGY **syn** see POWER

energy level *n* **:** one of the stable states of constant energy that may be assumed by a physical system — used esp. of electrons in atoms

en·er·vate \'en-ər-,vāt\ *vt* **:** to cause to grow less in strength or vigor **:** WEAKEN — **en·er·va·tion** \,en-ər-'vā-shən\ *n*

en·fant ter·ri·ble \ä"-fä"-te-rēblᵉ\ *n* [F, lit., terrible child] **:** one whose remarks or unconventional actions cause embarrassment

en·fee·ble \in-'fē-bəl\ *vt* **en·fee·bled**; **en·fee·bling** \-b(ə-)liŋ\ **:** to make feeble — **en·fee·ble·ment** \-bəl-mənt\ *n*

¹en·fi·lade \'en-fə-,lād, -,läd\ *n* [F, fr. *enfiler* to thread, enfilade, fr. *en-* + *fil* thread] **:** gunfire directed along the length of an enemy battle line

²enfilade *vt* **:** to rake or be in a position to rake with gunfire in a lengthwise direction

en·fold \in-'fōld\ *vt* **1 a :** to cover with folds **:** ENVELOP **b :** CONTAIN **2 :** to clasp within the arms **:** EMBRACE

en·force \in-'fōrs, -'fors\ *vt* **1 :** FORCE, COMPEL ⟨*enforce* obedience⟩ **2 :** to carry out effectively ⟨*enforce* the law⟩ — **en·force·a·ble** \-ə-bəl\ *adj* — **en·force·ment** \-mənt\ *n* — **en·forc·er** *n*

en·fran·chise \in-'fran-,chīz\ *vt* [MF *enfranchiss-*, *enfranchir*, fr. *en-* + *franc* free] **1 :** to set free (as from slavery) **2 :** to admit to the privileges of a citizen; *esp* **:** to admit to the right of suffrage — **en·fran·chise·ment** \-,chīz-mənt, -chəz-\ *n*

en·gage \in-'gāj\ *vb* [MF *engagier*, fr. *en-* + *gage* ¹gage] **1 :** to interlock with **:** MESH; *also* **:** to cause to mesh **2 :** to bind oneself to do something; *esp* **:** to bind by a pledge to marry **3 a :** to arrange to obtain the use or services of **:** HIRE **b :** ENGROSS, OCCUPY ⟨the task *engaged* his attention⟩ **4 :** to enter into contest with ⟨*engage* the enemy⟩ **5 a :** to begin and carry on an enterprise ⟨*engaged* in sales⟩ **b :** PARTICIPATE

en·gaged \in-'gājd\ *adj* **1 :** OCCUPIED, EMPLOYED, BUSY ⟨*engaged* in conversation⟩ **2 :** pledged to be married **:** BETROTHED ⟨an *engaged* couple⟩

en·gage·ment \in-'gāj-mənt\ *n* **1 a :** the act of engaging **:** the state of being engaged **b :** BETROTHAL **2 :** PLEDGE, OBLIGATION ⟨financial *engagements* to fulfill⟩ **3 a :** a promise to be present at a specified time and place **b :** employment esp. for a stated time **4 :** the state of being in gear **5 :** a hostile encounter between military forces

en·gag·ing \in-'gā-jiŋ\ *adj* **:** ATTRACTIVE, PLEASING — **en·gag·ing·ly** \-jiŋ-lē\ *adv*

en·gen·der \in-'jen-dər\ *vt* **en·gen·dered**; **en·gen·der·ing** \-d(ə-)riŋ\ [MF *engendrer*, fr. L *ingenerare*, fr. *in-* + *generare* to generate] **1 :** BEGET, PROCREATE **2 :** to cause to exist **:** PRODUCE, CREATE ⟨angry words *engender* strife⟩

en·gine \'en-jən\ *n* [OF *engin* ingenuity, fr. L *ingenium* talent, fr. *in-* + *gen-*, *gignere* to beget] **1 a :** a mechanical tool (as an instrument of war or torture) **b :** a mechanical appliance — compare FIRE ENGINE **2 :** a machine for converting energy into mechanical force and motion **3 :** a railroad locomotive

¹en·gi·neer \,en-jə-'ni(ə)r\ *n* **1 :** a member of a military

group devoted to engineering work **2 a :** a designer or builder of engines **b :** a person who is trained in or follows as a profession a branch of engineering **c :** a person who skillfully carries out an enterprise **3 :** a person who runs or supervises an engine or an apparatus

²engineer *vt* **1 :** to plan, build, or manage as an engineer **2 :** to guide the course of ⟨*engineer* a fund-raising campaign⟩

en·gi·neer·ing *n* **1 :** the art of managing engines **2 :** a science by which the properties of matter and the sources of energy in nature are made useful to man

en·gine·ry \'en-jən-rē\ *n* **1 :** instruments of war **2 :** machines, tools, and mechanical devices

en·gla·cial \en-'glā-shəl\ *adj* **:** embedded in a glacier

¹English \'iŋ-glish\ *adj* **:** of, relating to, or characteristic of England, the English people, or the English language

²English *n* **1 a :** the language of the people of England and the U.S. and many areas now or formerly under British control **b :** English language, literature, or composition that is a subject of study **2 English** *pl* **:** the people of England **3 :** a sideways spin given to a ball by striking it to right or left of center (as in pool) or by the manner of releasing it (as in bowling)

³English *vt* **:** to translate into English

English horn *n* **:** a double-reed woodwind instrument similar to the oboe but a fifth lower in pitch

English horn

En·glish·man \'iŋ-glish-mən\ *n* **:** a native or inhabitant of England — **En·glish·wom·an** \-,wum-ən\ *n*

English setter *n* **:** any of a breed of bird dogs with a flat silky coat of white or white with color

English shepherd *n* **:** any of a breed of medium-sized working dogs with a long and glossy black coat and usu. tan to brown markings

English sonnet *n* **:** a sonnet consisting of three quatrains and a couplet with a rhyme scheme of *abab cdcd efef gg*

English sparrow *n* **:** HOUSE SPARROW

English walnut *n* **:** a Eurasian walnut valued for its large edible nut and its hard richly figured wood; *also* **:** its nut

en·gorge \in-'gorj\ *vb* **1 :** GORGE, GLUT **2 :** to fill with blood **:** CONGEST — **en·gorge·ment** \-mənt\ *n*

en·graft \in-'graft\ *vt* **:** GRAFT 1

en·gram *also* **en·gramme** \'en-,gram\ *n* **:** a physical alteration in nervous tissue postulated to explain the persistence of memory

en·grave \in-'grāv\ *vt* **1 a :** to form by incisions (as upon wood or metal) **b :** to impress deeply ⟨the incident was *engraved* in his memory⟩ **2 a :** to cut figures, letters, or devices upon for printing; *also* **:** to print from an engraved plate **b :** PHOTOENGRAVE — **en·grav·er** *n*

en·grav·ing \in-'grā-viŋ\ *n* **1 :** the art of cutting letters, pictures, or patterns in wood, stone, or metal **2 :** a print made from an engraved surface

en·gross \in-'grōs\ *vt* [AF *engrosser*] **1 a :** to copy or write in a large hand **b :** to prepare the usu. final handwritten or printed text of (an official document) **2** [ME *engrossen*, fr. MF *en gros* in large quantities] **:** to take up the whole interest of **:** occupy fully **:** ABSORB — **en·gross·er** *n* — **en·gross·ment** \-'grōs-mənt\ *n*

en·gulf \in-'gəlf\ *vt* **:** to flow over and enclose; *also* **:** to take in (food) by such means — **en·gulf·ment** \-mənt\ *n*

en·hance \in-'han(t)s\ *vt* [AF *enhauncer*, alter of OF *enhaucier*, fr. L *in* + *altus* high] **:** to make greater (as in value, desirability, or attractiveness) **:** HEIGHTEN **syn** see INTENSIFY — **en·hance·ment** \-mənt\ *n*

en·har·mon·ic \,en-,här-'män-ik\ *adj* **:** relating to a change of letter names of notes that does not change the pitch ⟨*enharmonic* change from A flat to G sharp⟩ — **en·har·mon·i·cal·ly** \-i-k(ə-)lē\ *adv*

enig·ma \i-'nig-mə\ *n* [Gk *ainigmat-*, *ainigma*, fr. *ainissesthai* to speak in riddles, fr. *ainos* fable, riddle] **:** something hard to understand or explain **:** PUZZLE ⟨his behavior was an *enigma* to his family⟩ **syn** see MYSTERY — **en·ig·mat·ic** \,en-ig-'mat-ik, ,ē-nig-\ *or* **en·ig·mat·i·cal** \-'mat-i-kəl\ *adj* — **en·ig·mat·i·cal·ly** \-i-k(ə-)lē\ *adv*

en·isle \in-'īl\ *vt* **1 :** ISOLATE **2 :** to make an island of

en·jamb·ment *or* **en·jambe·ment** \in-'jam-mənt, -'jam-bmənt\ *n* [F *enjambement*, fr. *enjamber* to straddle, fr. *en-* + *jambe* leg\ : the running over of a sentence from one verse or couplet into another so that closely related words fall in different lines

en·join \in-'join\ vt **1** : to direct or impose by authoritative order **2** : FORBID, PROHIBIT

en·joy \in-'joi\ vt **1** : to take pleasure or satisfaction in **2** : to have for one's use, benefit, or lot — **en·joy·a·ble** \-ə-bəl\ adj — **en·joy·a·ble·ness** n — **en·joy·a·bly** \-blē\ adv

en·joy·ment \in-'joi-mənt\ n **1** : the condition of enjoying something : possession and use of something with satisfaction ⟨the enjoyment of good health⟩ **2** : PLEASURE, SATISFACTION ⟨find enjoyment in skating⟩ **3** : something that gives pleasure

en·kin·dle \in-'kin-dᵊl\ vb : KINDLE

en·lace \in-'lās\ vt **1** : ENCIRCLE, ENFOLD **2** : ENTWINE, INTERLACE

en·large \in-'lärj\ vb **1** : to make or grow larger : INCREASE, EXPAND **2** : ELABORATE ⟨enlarge on a story⟩ — **en·larg·er** n

en·large·ment \in-'lärj-mənt\ n **1** : an act or instance of enlarging : the state of being enlarged **2** : a photographic print that is larger than the negative and is made by projecting an image of the negative upon a photographic printing surface

en·light·en \in-'līt-ᵊn\ vt **en·light·ened**; **en·light·en·ing** \-'līt-niŋ, -ᵊn-iŋ\ **1** : to furnish knowledge to : INSTRUCT **2** : to give spiritual insight to — **en·light·en·ment** \-'līt-ᵊn-mənt\ n

en·list \in-'list\ vb **1** : to enroll oneself or another for military or naval service; esp : to join one of the armed services voluntarily **2** : to obtain the help or support of ⟨enlisted her friends in the campaign⟩; also : to participate heartily (as in a cause or drive) — **en·list·ment** \-'lis(t)-mənt\ n

en·list·ed adj : of, relating to, or constituting the part of a military or naval force below commissioned or warrant officers

en·liv·en \in-'lī-vən\ vt : to give life, action, or spirit to : ANIMATE

en masse \än-'mas, äⁿ-\ adv [F] : in a body : as a whole

en·mesh \in-'mesh\ vt : to catch or entangle in or as if in meshes

en·mi·ty \'en-mət-ē\ n, pl **-ties** [MF enemité, fr. enemi enemy] : ILL WILL, HATRED; esp : mutual hatred or ill will **syn** HOSTILITY, ANIMOSITY: ENMITY suggests positive hatred which may be open or concealed; HOSTILITY suggests enmity showing itself in attacks or aggression; ANIMOSITY implies intense ill will and vindictiveness that threaten to kindle hostility

en·no·ble \in-'ō-bəl\ vt **-bled**; **-bling** \-b(ə-)liŋ\ **1** : to make noble : ELEVATE **2** : to raise to the rank of nobility — **en·no·ble·ment** \-bəl-mənt\ n

en·nui \'än-'wē\ n [F, fr. OF enui annoyance, fr. enuier to annoy] : a feeling of weariness and dissatisfaction : BOREDOM

enor·mi·ty \i-'nor-mət-ē\ n, pl **-ties** **1** : huge size **2** : great wickedness : OUTRAGEOUSNESS ⟨the enormity of the offense⟩ **3** : an outrageous act or offense

enor·mous \i-'nor-məs\ adj [L enormis, fr. e, ex out of + norma norm] **1** archaic **a** : ABNORMAL, INORDINATE **b** : exceedingly wicked : OUTRAGEOUS **2** : extraordinarily great in size, number, or degree — **enor·mous·ly** adv — **enor·mous·ness** n
  syn IMMENSE, HUGE, VAST: ENORMOUS implies exceeding ordinary bounds in size, amount, or degree ⟨the enormous expenditures for war⟩ IMMENSE suggests size far in excess of ordinary measurements or concepts ⟨an immense waste of natural resources⟩ HUGE suggests immensity of bulk, size, or capacity ⟨huge wine vats⟩ VAST usu. suggests immensity of extent ⟨vast stretches of desert⟩

¹enough \i-'nəf; after t, d, s, z often ⁿ-'əf\ adj [ME ynough, fr. OE genōg] : occurring in such quantity, quality, or scope as to fully satisfy demands or needs **syn** see SUFFICIENT

²enough adv **1** : in sufficient amount or degree : SUFFICIENTLY ⟨did not run fast enough⟩ **2** : FULLY, QUITE ⟨ready enough to admit the truth⟩ **3** : TOLERABLY ⟨sang well enough⟩

³enough n : a sufficient quantity ⟨we have enough to meet our needs⟩

enow \i-'naù\ adv (or adj) [ME inow, fr. OE genōg] archaic : ENOUGH

en·plane \in-'plān\ vi : to board an airplane

en·quire \in-'kwī(ə)r\, **en·qui·ry** \'in-,kwī(ə)r-ē, in-; 'in-kwə-rē, 'in-\ var of INQUIRE, INQUIRY

en·rage \in-'rāj\ vt : to fill with rage : ANGER, MADDEN

en·rapt \in-'rapt\ adj : RAPT, ENRAPTURED

en·rap·ture \in-'rap-chər\ vt **-rap·tured**; **-rap·tur·ing** \-'rap-chə-riŋ, -'rap-shriŋ\ : to fill with delight

en·rich \in-'rich\ vt **1** : to make rich or richer ⟨enrich the mind⟩ **2** : ADORN, ORNAMENT **3 a** : to make (soil) more fertile **b** : to improve (a food) in nutritive value by adding vitamins and minerals in processing — **en·rich·ment** \-mənt\ n

en·robe \in-'rōb\ vt : to invest or adorn with a robe

en·roll or **en·rol** \in-'rōl\ vb **en·rolled**; **en·roll·ing** **1** : to insert, register, or enter in a list, catalog, or roll **2** : to enroll oneself or cause oneself to be enrolled — **en·roll·ment** \-'rōl-mənt\ n

en route \än-'rüt, en-, in-\ adv [F] : on or along the way

en·sconce \in-'skän(t)s\ vt **1** : to place or hide securely : CONCEAL ⟨ensconced himself behind a tree⟩ **2** : to establish comfortably : settle snugly

en·sem·ble \än-'säm-bəl\ n [F, fr. L insimul at the same time, fr. in- + simul at the same time] : a group constituting a whole or producing a single effect: as **a** : SET **b** : concerted music of two or more parts or the musicians that perform it **c** : a complete set of harmonizing clothes **d** : a group of supporting performers

en·sheathe \in-'shēth\ vt : to cover with or as if with a sheath

en·shrine \in-'shrīn\ vt **1** : to enclose in or as if in a shrine **2** : to preserve or cherish as sacred

en·shroud \in-'shraùd\ vt : SHROUD

en·si·form \'en(t)-sə-,form\ adj [L ensis sword] : having sharp edges and tapering to a slender point

en·sign \'en(t)-sən, in senses 1 & 2 also 'en-,sīn\ n [MF enseigne, fr. L insignia insignia, flags] **1** : a flag flown as the symbol of nationality **2** : a badge of office, rank, or power **3** : a commissioned officer of the lowest rank in the navy

en·si·lage \'en(t)-sə-lij\ n : SILAGE

en·sile \en-'sīl\ vt : to prepare and store (fodder) for silage

en·slave \in-'slāv\ vt : to reduce to slavery : SUBJUGATE — **en·slave·ment** \-mənt\ n — **en·slav·er** n

en·snare \in-'sna(ə)r, -'sne(ə)r\ vt : SNARE, ENTRAP

en·sue \in-'sü\ vi [MF ensuivre, fr. en- + suivre to follow] : to come after in time or as a result : FOLLOW ⟨ensuing effects⟩

en·sure \in-'shù(ə)r\ vt [AF enseurer, prob. alter. of OF aseürer] : to make sure, certain, or safe : GUARANTEE

ent- or **ento-** comb form [Gk entos within] : inner : within ⟨entoblast⟩

en·tab·la·ture \in-'tab-lə-,chùr, -chər\ n : the upper section of a wall or story usu. supported on columns or pilasters and in classical orders consisting of architrave, frieze, and cornice — see ORDER illustration

en·ta·ble·ment \in-'tā-bəl-mənt\ n : a platform supporting a statue and above the dado

¹en·tail \in-'tāl\ vt **1** : to limit the inheritance of (property) to the owner's lineal descendants or to a class thereof **2** : to impose, involve, or imply as a necessary accompaniment or result — **en·tail·ment** \-mənt\ n

²entail n **1 a** : an entailing esp. of lands **b** : an entailed estate **2** : the rule fixing descent by entailment

en·tan·gle \in-'taŋ-gəl\ vt **1** : to make tangled, complicated, or confused **2** : to involve in or as if in a tangle — **en·tan·gle·ment** \-gəl-mənt\ n

en·tente \än-'tänt\ n [F, lit., intent] **1** : an international understanding providing for a common course of action **2** : a coalition of parties to an entente

en·ter \'ent-ər\ vb **en·tered**; **en·ter·ing** \'ent-ə-riŋ, 'en-triŋ\ [OF entrer, fr. L intrare, fr. intra within] **1** : to go or come into : go or come in ⟨enter a room⟩ ⟨enter and leave by the same door⟩ **2** : to pass into or through usu. by overcoming resistance : PIERCE **3** : to cause to go into or be admitted to ⟨enter a child in kindergarten⟩ **4** : to become a member of : JOIN ⟨enter the hikers' club⟩ **5** : to make a beginning ⟨enter into business⟩ **6** : to take part or play a part ⟨enter into a discussion⟩ ⟨tin enters into the com-

---

j joke; ŋ sing; ō flow; ȯ flaw; ȯi coin; th thin; th̲ this; ü loot; u̇ foot; y yet; yü few; yu̇ furious; zh vision

position of pewter⟩ **7 :** to take possession ⟨*entered* upon their inheritance⟩ **8 :** to set down in a book or list ⟨*enter* words in a dictionary⟩ ⟨pupils' names are *entered* in the class register⟩ **9 :** to place formally before a legal authority as a court ⟨*enter* a complaint⟩ — **en·ter·a·ble** \'ent-ə-rə-bəl\ *adj*

syn ENTER, PENETRATE, PIERCE mean to make way into something. ENTER is the general term and may imply going in or forcing a way in; PENETRATE carries a strong implication of an impelling force or compelling power that achieves entrance; PIERCE adds an implication of running through with a sharp-pointed instrument

enter- *or* **entero-** *comb form* [Gk *enteron*] **:** intestine ⟨*enter*itis⟩

en·ter·ic \en-'ter-ik\ *adj* **:** of or relating to the alimentary canal **:** INTESTINAL

en·ter·i·tis \,ent-ə-'rīt-əs\ *n* **:** inflammation of the intestines or a disease marked by this

en·tero·coc·cus \,ent-ə-rō-'käk-əs\ *n* **:** STREPTOCOCCUS; *esp* **:** one normally present in the intestine — **en·tero·coc·cal** \-'käk-əl\ *adj*

en·tero·coele *or* **en·tero·coel** \'ent-ə-rō-,sēl\ *n* **:** a coelom originating by outgrowth from the archenteron — **en·tero·coe·lic** \,ent-ə-rō-'sē-lik\ *adj* — **en·tero·coe·lous** \-ləs\ *adj*

en·tero·ki·nase \,ent-ə-rō-'kīn-,ās, -'kin-\ *n* **:** an intestinal enzyme that converts trypsinogen to trypsin

en·ter·on \'ent-ə-,rän, -rən\ *n* **:** the alimentary canal or system — used esp. of the embryo

en·ter·prise \'ent-ə(r)-,prīz\ *n* [MF *entreprise*, fr. *entreprendre* to undertake, fr. *entre-* inter- + *prendre* to take, fr. L *prehendere* to seize] **1 :** a difficult, complicated, or risky project or undertaking **:** VENTURE **2 a :** a business organization **b :** a systematic purposeful activity **3 :** readiness to engage in daring action **:** INITIATIVE — **en·ter·pris·er** \-,prī-zər\ *n*

en·ter·pris·ing \-,prī-ziŋ\ *adj* **:** marked by an independent energetic spirit and by readiness to undertake or experiment

en·ter·tain \,ent-ər-'tān\ *vb* [MF *entretenir*, fr. *entre-* inter- + *tenir* to hold, fr. L *tenēre*] **1 :** to receive and provide for as host **:** have as a guest ⟨*entertain* friends over the weekend⟩ **2 :** to provide entertainment esp. for guests **3 :** to have in mind **:** CONSIDER ⟨*entertained* thoughts of quitting his job⟩ **4 :** AMUSE, DIVERT ⟨his jokes never ceased to *entertain* the spectators⟩ **syn** see AMUSE

en·ter·tain·er \-'tā-nər\ *n* **:** one that entertains; *esp* **:** one who gives or takes part in public entertainments

en·ter·tain·ment \-'tān-mənt\ *n* **1 :** provision for guests esp. in public places (as hotels and inns) **2 :** AMUSEMENT, RECREATION, DIVERSION **3 :** something that entertains **:** a means of amusement or recreation; *esp* **:** a public performance

en·thrall *or* **en·thral** \in-'thról\ *vt* **en·thralled; en·thrall·ing 1 :** to hold in or reduce to slavery **2 :** to hold spellbound **:** CHARM — **en·thrall·ment** \-'thról-mənt\ *n*

en·throne \in-'thrōn\ *vt* **1 :** to seat ceremonially on a throne **2 :** to place on high **:** EXALT — **en·throne·ment** \-mənt\ *n*

en·thuse \in-'th(y)üz\ *vb* [back-formation fr. *enthusiasm*] **1 :** to make enthusiastic **2 :** to show enthusiasm

en·thu·si·asm \in-'th(y)ü-zē-,az-əm\ *n* [Gk *enthousiasmos*, fr. *enthousiazein* to be inspired, fr. *entheos* inspired, fr. *en-* in- + *theos* god] **1 :** strong excitement of feeling **:** FERVOR **2 :** something inspiring zeal or fervor **syn** see ZEAL

en·thu·si·ast \-zē-,ast, -əst\ *n* **:** a person filled with enthusiasm

en·thu·si·as·tic \in-,th(y)ü-zē-'as-tik\ *adj* **:** filled with or marked by enthusiasm ⟨*enthusiastic* about foreign movies⟩ ⟨an *enthusiastic* welcome⟩ — **en·thu·si·as·ti·cal·ly** \-ti-k(ə-)lē\ *adv*

en·tice \in-'tīs\ *vt* [OF *enticier*] **:** to attract by arousing hope or desire **:** TEMPT — **en·tice·ment** \-mənt\ *n*

en·tire \in-'tī(ə)r, 'en-,\ *adj* [MF *entir*, fr. L *integer*, lit., untouched, fr. *in-* + *tangere* to touch] **1 :** having no element or part left out **2 :** COMPLETE, TOTAL, FULL ⟨an *entire* regiment was lost⟩ **3 a :** consisting of one piece **:** HOMOGENOUS **b :** INTACT **4 :** having the margin continuous and free from indentations ⟨an *entire* leaf⟩ **syn** see WHOLE — **entire** *adv* — **en·tire·ly** *adv* — **en·tire·ness** *n*

en·tire·ty \in-'tī-rət-ē, -'tī(ə)rt-ē\ *n* **1 :** the state of being entire or complete **2 :** sum total **:** WHOLE

en·ti·tle \in-'tīt-ºl\ *vt* **en·ti·tled; en·ti·tling** \-'tīt-liŋ, -ºl-iŋ\ **1 :** to give a title to **:** DESIGNATE **2 a :** to give a legal right to **b :** to qualify for something — **en·ti·tle·ment** \-'tīt-ºl-mənt\ *n*

en·ti·ty \'ent-ət-ē\ *n, pl* **-ti·ties** [ME *entitas*, fr. L *ent-, ens* existing thing, fr. coined prp. of *esse* to be] **:** something that has a real existence either as a thing (as a chair or a building) knowable through the senses or as a thing (as a nation or a religion) conceivable by the mind

ento- — see ENT-

en·tomb \in-'tüm\ *vt* **:** to place in a tomb **:** BURY — **en·tomb·ment** \-'tüm-mənt\ *n*

en·to·mol·o·gy \,ent-ə-'mäl-ə-jē\ *n* [Gk *entomon* insect, fr. neut. of *entomos* cut up, fr. *en-* + *temnein* to cut] **:** a branch of zoology that deals with insects — **en·to·mo·log·ic** \,ent-ə-mə-'läj-ik\ *or* **en·to·mo·log·i·cal** \-'läj-i-kəl\ *adj* — **en·to·mo·log·i·cal·ly** \-i-k(ə-)lē\ *adv* — **en·to·mol·o·gist** \,ent-ə-'mäl-ə-jəst\ *n*

en·to·moph·a·gous \,ent-ə-'mäf-ə-gəs\ *adj* **:** feeding on insects

en·to·moph·i·lous \,ent-ə-'mäf-ə-ləs\ *adj* **:** normally pollinated by insects — **en·to·moph·i·ly** \-lē\ *n*

en·to·mos·tra·can \,ent-ə-'mäs-tri-kən\ *n* **:** any of a large group of small simple crustaceans (as copepods or barnacles)

en·tou·rage \,änt-ə-'räzh, än-tü-\ *n* [F] **:** one's attendants or associates **:** RETINUE

en·tr'acte \'än-,trakt, än-'\ *n* [F, fr. *entre-* inter- + *acte* act] **1 :** the interval between two acts of a play **2 :** a dance, piece of music, or interlude performed between two acts of a play

en·trails \'en-trəlz, -,trālz\ *n pl* [MF *entrailles*, fr. ML *intralia*, alter. of L *interanea*, fr. neut. pl. of *interaneus* interior] **:** internal parts **:** VISCERA; *esp* **:** INTESTINES

en·train \in-'trān\ *vb* **:** to put or go aboard a railroad train

¹en·trance \'en-trən(t)s\ *n* **1 :** the act of entering **2 :** the means or place of entry **3 :** power or permission to enter **:** ADMISSION

²en·trance \in-'tran(t)s\ *vt* **1 :** to put into a trance **2 :** to fill with delight, wonder, or rapture — **en·trance·ment** \-mənt\ *n*

en·trant \'en-trənt\ *n* **:** one that enters; *esp* **:** one that enters a contest

en·trap \in-'trap\ *vt* **1 :** to catch in or as if in a trap **2 :** to lure into a compromising statement or act — **en·trap·ment** \-mənt\ *n*

en·treat \in-'trēt\ *vb* [MF *entraitier* to treat, fr. *en-* + *traitier* to treat] **:** to ask earnestly or urgently **:** PLEAD, BEG — **en·treat·ing·ly** \-iŋ-lē\ *adv*

en·treaty \in-'trēt-ē\ *n, pl* **-treat·ies :** earnest request **:** APPEAL, PLEA

en·tre·chat \,än-trə-'shä\ *n* [F] **:** a leap in which a ballet dancer repeatedly crosses the legs and sometimes beats them together

en·trée *or* **en·tree** \'än-(,)trā\ *n* [F *entrée*] **1 a :** the act or manner of entering **:** ENTRANCE **b :** freedom of entry or access **2 a :** a dish served between the main courses **b :** the principal dish of the meal

en·trench \in-'trench\ *vb* **1 a :** to dig, place within, surround with, or occupy a trench esp. for defense **b :** to establish solidly **2 :** to cut into **:** FURROW; *esp* **:** to erode downward so as to form a trench **3 :** ENCROACH — used with *on* or *upon*

en·trench·ment \in-'trench-mənt\ *n* **1 :** the act of entrenching **:** the state of being entrenched **2 :** DEFENSE; *esp* **:** a defensive work consisting of a trench and a wall of earth

en·tre·pre·neur \,än-trə-p(r)ə-'nər\ *n* [F] **:** one who organizes, manages, and assumes the risks of a business or enterprise

en·tro·py \'en-trə-pē\ *n* [Gk *en-* + *trop-*, *trepein* to turn, change] **1 :** a measure of the unavailable energy in a closed thermodynamic system **2 :** the degradation of the matter and energy in the universe to an ultimate state of inert uniformity

en·trust \in-'trəst\ *vt* **1 :** to give into the care of another (as for safekeeping) ⟨*entrust* your savings to a bank⟩ **2 :** to give custody, care, or charge of something to as a

---

ə abut; ᵊ kitten; ər further; a back; ā bake; ä cot, cart; au̇ out; ch chin; e less; ē easy; g gift; i trip; ī life

trust ⟨*entrusted* a bank with his savings⟩ — **en·trust·ment** \-'trəs(t)-mənt\ *n*

en·try \'en-trē\ *n, pl* **entries** **1** **:** the act of entering **:** ENTRANCE **2** **:** a place through which entrance is made **:** HALL, VESTIBULE **3 a :** the act of making (as in a book or list) a written record of something **b :** the thing thus recorded: as (1) **:** HEADWORD (2) **:** a headword with its definition or identification (3) **:** VOCABULARY ENTRY **4 :** a person, thing, or group entered in a contest or race

en·twine \in-'twīn\ *vb* **:** to twine together or around

enu·cle·ate \(')ē-'n(y)ü-klē-ˌāt\ *vt* [L *enucleare*, lit., to remove the kernel from, fr. *e-* + *nucleus* kernel] **:** to remove without cutting into — **enu·cle·ation** \(ˌ)ē-ˌn(y)ü-klē-'ā-shən\ *n*

enu·mer·ate \i-'n(y)ü-mə-ˌrāt\ *vt* **1 :** to ascertain the number of **:** COUNT **2 :** to specify one after another **:** LIST — **enu·mer·a·ble** \-'n(y)üm-(ə-)rə-bəl\ *adj* — **enu·mer·a·tion** \-ˌn(y)ü-mə-'rā-shən\ *n* — **enu·mer·a·tor** \-'n(y)ü-mə-ˌrāt-ər\ *n*

enun·ci·ate \ē-'nən(t)-sē-ˌāt\ *vb* [L *enuntiare*, fr. *e-* + *nuntiare* to report, fr. *nuntius* messenger] **1 :** ANNOUNCE, PROCLAIM **2 :** ARTICULATE, PRONOUNCE **3 :** to utter articulate sounds — **enun·ci·a·tion** \-ˌnən(t)-sē-'ā-shən\ *n*

en·ure·sis \ˌen-yu̇-'rē-səs\ *n* [Gk *en-* in- + *ourein* to urinate] **:** involuntary discharge of urine **:** bed wetting — **en·uret·ic** \-'ret-ik\ *adj or n*

en·vel·op \in-'vel-əp\ *vt* [MF *enveloper*, fr. *en-* + *voloper* to wrap] **1 :** to enclose or enfold completely with or as if with a covering **2 :** to mount an attack on (an enemy's flank) — **en·vel·op·ment** \-mənt\ *n*

en·ve·lope \'en-və-ˌlōp, 'än-\ *n* **1 :** something that envelops **2 :** a flat usu. paper container (as for a letter) **3 :** the bag containing the gas in a balloon or airship **4 :** a natural enclosing covering (as a membrane)

en·ven·om \in-'ven-əm\ *vt* **1 :** to taint or fill with poison **2 :** EMBITTER

en·vi·a·ble \'en-vē-ə-bəl\ *adj* **:** worthy of envy **:** highly desirable — **en·vi·a·ble·ness** *n* — **en·vi·a·bly** \-blē\ *adv*

en·vi·ous \'en-vē-əs\ *adj* **:** feeling or showing envy **:** caused by or proceeding from envy ⟨*envious* of a neighbor's wealth⟩ — **en·vi·ous·ly** *adv* — **en·vi·ous·ness** *n*

syn JEALOUS: ENVIOUS suggests a spiteful or malicious grudging of another's possessions and accomplishments; JEALOUS implies a grudging of something regarded as properly belonging to oneself; it may also indicate a vigilant guarding ⟨*jealous* of his good name and honor⟩

en·vi·ron \in-'vī-rən\ *vt* [MF *environner*, fr. *environ* around, fr. *en* in + *viron* circle] **:** ENCIRCLE, SURROUND

en·vi·ron·ment \in-'vī-rən-mənt\ *n* **:** something that environs **:** SURROUNDINGS: as **a :** the climatic, edaphic, and biotic factors that determine the form and survival of an organism or ecological community **b :** the social and cultural conditions that influence the life of a person or human community — **en·vi·ron·men·tal** \in-ˌvī-rən-'ment-°l\ *adj* — **en·vi·ron·men·tal·ly** \-°l-ē\ *adv*

en·vi·ron·men·tal·ist \-ˌvī-rən-'ment-°l-əst\ *n* **:** one concerned about the quality of the human environment

en·vi·rons \in-'vī-rənz\ *n pl* **1 :** the districts around a city **2 :** SURROUNDINGS

en·vis·age \in-'viz-ij\ *vt* **:** to have a mental picture of esp. in advance of realization **:** VISUALIZE

en·vi·sion \in-'vizh-ən\ *vt* **:** to picture to oneself

en·voi *or* **en·voy** \'en-ˌvȯi, 'än-\ *n* [F *envoi*, lit., message, fr. OF *envoier* to send on one's way, fr. L *in* on + *via* way] **:** the usu. explanatory or commendatory concluding remarks to a poem, essay, or book

en·voy \'en-ˌvȯi, 'än-\ *n* [F *envoyé*, fr. pp. of *envoyer* to send, fr. L *in-* + *via* way] **1 a :** a minister plenipotentiary accredited to a foreign government who ranks between an ambassador and a minister resident — called also *envoy extraordinary* **b :** a representative sent by one government to another **2 :** MESSENGER, REPRESENTATIVE

¹**en·vy** \'en-vē\ *n, pl* **envies** [OF *envie*, fr. L *invidia*, fr. *invidus* envious, fr. *invidēre* to look askance at, envy, fr. *in-* + *vidēre* to see] **1 :** painful or resentful awareness of an advantage enjoyed by another joined with a desire to possess the same advantage **2 :** an object of envy

²**envy** *vt* **en·vied; en·vy·ing :** to feel envy toward or on account of — **en·vi·er** *n* — **en·vy·ing·ly** \-iŋ-lē\ *adv*

en·wrap \in-'rap\ *vt* **1 :** ENFOLD **2 :** ENVELOP **3 :** ENGROSS

en·wreathe \in-'rēth\ *vt* **:** WREATHE, ENVELOP

en·zyme \'en-ˌzīm\ *n* [Gk *en-* in- + *zymē* leaven] **:** a complex organic and predominantly protein substance produced by living cells that brings about or accelerates reaction (as in the digestion of food) at body temperatures without itself being permanently altered — **en·zy·mat·ic** \ˌen-zə-'mat-ik\ *adj* — **en·zy·mat·i·cal·ly** \-'mat-i-k(ə-)lē\ *adv*

eo- *comb form* [Gk *ēos* dawn] **:** earliest **:** oldest ⟨*eolithic*⟩

Eo·cene \'ē-ə-ˌsēn\ *n* **:** the epoch of the Tertiary between the Paleocene and the Oligocene; *also* **:** the corresponding system of rocks — **Eocene** *adj*

eo·hip·pus \ˌē-ō-'hip-əs\ *n* [Gk *hippos* horse] **:** any of a genus of small primitive 4-toed horses from the Lower Eocene of the western U.S.

eo·li·an \ē-'ō-lē-ən\ *adj* [L *Aeolus*, god of the winds] **:** borne, deposited, produced, or eroded by the wind ⟨*eolian* sand⟩

eo·lith \'ē-ə-ˌlith\ *n* **:** a very crudely chipped flint from the earliest phase of human culture

Eo·lith·ic \ˌē-ə-'lith-ik\ *adj* **:** of or relating to the early period of the Stone Age marked by the use of eoliths

eon \'ē-ən, 'ē-ˌän\ *var of* AEON

Eos \'ē-ˌäs\ *n* **:** the Greek goddess of dawn

eo·sin \'ē-ə-sən\ *or* **eo·sine** \-sən, -ˌsēn\ *n* [Gk *ēos* dawn] **:** a red synthetic fluorescent dye used esp. in cosmetics and as a toner; *also* **:** a salt of this dye used esp. in red pigments and as a stain for biological tissue

eo·sin·o·phil \ˌē-ə-'sin-ə-ˌfil\ *or* **eo·sin·o·phile** \-ˌfīl\ *n* **:** a white blood cell with cytoplasmic inclusions readily stained by eosin — **eo·sin·o·phil·ic** \-ˌsin-ə-'fil-ik\ *adj*

-eous *adj suffix* [L *-eus*] **:** like **:** resembling ⟨aqueous⟩

ep·au·let *also* **ep·au·lette** \ˌep-ə-'let\ *n* [F *épaulette*] **:** a shoulder ornament on a uniform esp. of a military or naval officer

épée \'ep-ˌā, ā-'pā\ *n* [F, fr. L *spatha* spoon, sword] **:** a fencing or dueling sword having a bowl-shaped guard and a tapering rigid blade with no cutting edge

epergne \i-'pərn\ *n* **:** an often ornate tiered centerpiece consisting typically of a frame of wrought metal (as silver or gold) bearing dishes, vases, or candle holders or a combination of these

epaulet

ephah \'ē-fə, 'ef-ə\ *n* **:** an ancient Hebrew unit of dry measure equal to a little more than a bushel

ephed·rine \i-'fed-rən\ *n* **:** a crystalline alkaloid extracted from Chinese woody gymnospermous plants or synthesized and used as a salt in relieving hay fever, asthma, and nasal congestion

ephem·era \i-'fem-(ə-)rə\ *n pl* **:** ephemeral things

ephem·er·al \i-'fem-(ə-)rəl\ *adj* [Gk *ephēmeros* lasting a day, daily, fr. *epi-* + *hēmera* day] **1 :** lasting one day only **2 :** lasting a very short time — **ephem·er·al·ly** \i-'fem-(ə-)rə-lē\ *adv*

ephem·er·id \i-'fem-ə-rəd\ *n* [Gk *ephēmeron*, fr. neut. of *ephēmeros* ephemeral] **:** MAYFLY — **ephemerid** *adj*

ephem·er·is \-rəs\ *n, pl* **eph·e·mer·i·des** \ˌef-ə-'mer-ə-ˌdēz\ [Gk *ephēmerid-, ephēmeris* diary, journal, fr. *ephēmeros* daily] **:** any tabular statement of the assigned places of a celestial body for regular intervals

Ephe·sians \i-'fē-zhənz\ *n* — see BIBLE table

eph·od \'ef-ˌäd\ *n* **1 :** a linen apron worn in ancient Hebrew rites; *esp* **:** a vestment for the high priest **2 :** an ancient Hebrew instrument of priestly divination

eph·or \'ef-ər, -ˌȯr\ *n* [Gk *ephoros*, fr. *epi-* + *horan* to see] **:** one of five ancient Spartan magistrates having power over the king

epi- *or* **ep-** *prefix* [Gk] **:** upon ⟨*epiphyte*⟩ **:** besides ⟨*epiphenomenon*⟩ **:** near to ⟨*epencephalon*⟩ **:** over ⟨*epicenter*⟩ **:** outer ⟨*epiblast*⟩ **:** anterior ⟨*episternum*⟩ **:** after ⟨*epigenesis*⟩

¹**ep·ic** \'ep-ik\ *adj* [Gk *epos* word, speech, poem] **1 :** of, relating to, or having the characteristics of an epic **2 a :** unusually long esp. in size or scope **b :** HEROIC

²**epic** *n* **1 :** a long narrative poem in elevated style relating the deeds of a legendary or historical hero **2 :** a work of art that resembles or suggests an epic **3 :** a series of events or body of tradition held to form the proper subject of an epic

epi·ca·lyx \ˌep-ə-'kā-liks, -'kal-iks\ *n* **:** a whorl of bracts resembling but below the calyx

epi·car·di·um \,ep-ə-'kärd-ē-əm\ *n* : the part of the pericardium that closely invests the heart — **epi·car·di·al** \-ē-əl\ *adj*

epi·carp \'ep-ə-,kärp\ *n* : the usu. thin membranous outermost layer of the pericarp of a fruit (as the skin of a peach) — compare ENDOCARP, MESOCARP

epi·cen·ter \'ep-ə-,sent-er\ *n* **1** : the part of the earth's surface directly above the focus of an earthquake **2** : CENTER 2

ep·i·cot·yl \'ep-ə-,kät-ˀl\ *n* : the part of a plant embryo or seedling above the cotyledons — **ep·i·cot·y·le·don·ary** \-ˀl-'ēd-ˀn-,er-ē\ *adj*

ep·i·cure \'ep-i-,kyur\ *n* [after *Epicurus d270* B.C. Gk philosopher] : a person with sensitive and discriminating tastes in food or wine

¹ep·i·cu·re·an \,ep-i-kyu̇-'rē-ən, -'kyur-ē-\ *adj* **1** *cap* : of or relating to Epicurus or Epicureanism **2** : of, relating to, or suited to an epicure

²epicurean *n* **1** *cap* : a follower of Epicurus **2** : EPICURE

Ep·i·cu·re·an·ism \-ə-,niz-əm\ *n* : the philosophy of Epicurus that pleasure is the only good and the pleasures of wise, just, and moderate living are the best

¹ep·i·dem·ic \,ep-ə-'dem-ik\ *adj* [Gk *epidēmia* visit, epidemic, fr. *epi-* + *dēmos* people] **1** : affecting many individuals and esp. persons at one time **2** : excessively prevalent — **ep·i·dem·i·cal·ly** \-'dem-i-k(ə-)lē\ *adv* — **ep·i·de·mic·i·ty** \-,dem-'is-ət-ē\ *n*

²epidemic *n* **1** : an outbreak of epidemic disease **2** : an outbreak or product of sudden rapid spread or development

ep·i·de·mi·ol·o·gy \,ep-ə-,dē-mē-'äl-ə-jē\ *n* **1** : a branch of medical science that deals with the incidence, distribution, and control of disease in a population **2** : the sum of the factors controlling the presence or absence of a particular disease — **ep·i·de·mi·o·log·ic** \-mē-ə-'läj-ik\ *or* **ep·i·de·mi·o·log·i·cal** \-'läj-i-kəl\ *adj* — **ep·i·de·mi·o·log·i·cal·ly** \-i-k(ə-)lē\ *adv* — **ep·i·de·mi·ol·o·gist** \-mē-'äl-ə-jəst\ *n*

ep·i·den·drum \,ep-ə-'den-drəm\ *n* : any of a large genus of often showy tropical American epiphytic orchids

epi·der·mis \,ep-ə-'dər-məs\ *n* **1** : the thin outer epithelial layer of the animal body that is derived from ectoderm and in vertebrates forms an insensitive covering over the dermis **2** : a thin surface layer of primary tissue in higher plants **3** : any of various covering layers resembling the epidermis of the skin — **epi·der·mal** \-məl\ *adj*

ep·i·did·y·mis \,ep-ə-'did-ə-məs\ *n, pl* **-mi·des** \-mə-,dēz\ [Gk *epi-* + *didymos* testicle, fr. *dyo* two] : a mass at the back of the testis composed of coiled tubes in which sperms are stored — **epi·did·y·mal** \-'did-ə-məl\ *adj*

epi·gen·e·sis \,ep-ə-'jen-ə-səs\ *n, pl* **-gen·e·ses** \-ə-,sēz\ : development in which an initially undifferentiated entity (as a spore) gradually develops new characters (as of a whole plant) — **epi·ge·net·ic** \-jə-'net-ik\ *adj*

epi·glot·tis \,ep-ə-'glät-əs\ *n* : a thin plate of flexible cartilage in front of the glottis that folds back over and protects the glottis during swallowing — **epi·glot·tal** \-'glät-ˀl\ *adj*

ep·i·gram \'ep-ə-,gram\ *n* **1** : a short often satirical poem ending with an ingenious turn of thought **2** : a brief witty saying — **ep·i·gram·ma·tist** \,ep-ə-'gram-ət-əst\ *n*

ep·i·gram·mat·ic \,ep-i-grə-'mat-ik\ *adj* **1** : of, relating to, or resembling an epigram **2** : marked by or given to the use of epigrams — **ep·i·gram·mat·i·cal** \-'mat-i-kəl\ *adj* — **ep·i·gram·mat·i·cal·ly** \-i-k(ə-)lē\ *adv*

epig·ra·phy \i-'pig-rə-fē\ *n* [Gk *epigraphein* to inscribe, fr. *epi-* + *graphein* to write] : the study of inscriptions and esp. of ancient inscriptions

epig·y·nous \i-'pij-ə-nəs, e-\ *adj* **1** : grown to and appearing to arise from the top of a plant ovary ⟨*epigynous* stamens⟩ **2** : having epigynous floral organs — **epig·y·ny** \-nē\ *n*

ep·i·lep·sy \'ep-ə-,lep-sē\ *n* [Gk *epilēpsia*, fr. *epilambanein* to seize, fr. *epi-* + *lambanein* to take, seize] : a disorder marked by disturbed electrical rhythms of the central nervous system and typically manifested by convulsive attacks usu. with clouding of consciousness — **ep·i·lep·tic** \,ep-ə-'lep-tik\ *adj or n*

ep·i·logue \'ep-ə-,lȯg\ *n* **1** : a concluding section that rounds out the design of a literary work **2 a** : a speech often in verse addressed to the audience by an actor at the end of a play **b** : the actor speaking such an epilogue **3** : a concluding event or development

ep·i·my·si·um \,ep-ə-'miz(h)-ē-əm\ *n* [NL, fr. Gk *mys* mouse, muscle] : the outer connective tissue sheath of a muscle

ep·i·neph·rine *or* **ep·i·neph·rin** \,ep-ə-'nef-,rēn, -rən\ *n* : ADRENALINE

epiph·a·ny \i-'pif-ə-nē\ *n, pl* **-nies** [LL *epiphania*, fr. LGk, pl., prob. alter. of Gk *epiphaneia* appearance, manifestation, fr. *epi-* + *phainein* to show] : an appearance or manifestation esp. of a divine being

Epiphany *n* : January 6 observed as a church festival in commemoration of the coming of the three wise men to Jesus at Bethlehem

ep·i·phragm \'ep-ə-,fram\ *n* : a closing membrane or septum

epiph·y·sis \i-'pif-ə-səs\ *n, pl* **-y·ses** \-ə-,sēz\ : the end of a long bone — compare DIAPHYSIS — **epiph·y·se·al** \i-,pif-ə-'sē-əl\ *adj*

ep·i·phyte \'ep-ə-,fīt\ *n* : a plant that derives its moisture and nutrients from the air and rain and grows usu. on another plant

ep·i·phyt·ic \,ep-ə-'fit-ik\ *adj* **1** : of, relating to, or being an epiphyte **2** : living on the surface of plants — **ep·i·phyt·i·cal·ly** \-'fit-i-k(ə-)lē\ *adv*

¹ep·i·phy·tot·ic \-,fī-'tät-ik\ *adj* : of, relating to, or being a disease that affects many plants of one kind at the same time — **ep·i·phy·tot·i·cal·ly** \-'tät-i-k(ə-)lē\ *adv*

²epiphytotic *n* : an epiphytotic disease

epi·scia \i-'pish-(ē-)ə\ *n* : any of a genus of tropical American herbs often grown for their showy hairy foliage and reddish flowers

epis·co·pa·cy \i-'pis-kə-pə-sē\ *n, pl* **-cies** **1** : government of the church by bishops or by a hierarchy **2** : EPISCOPATE

epis·co·pal \i-'pis-kə-pəl\ *adj* [Gk *episkopos* overseer, bishop, fr. *epi-* + *skop-, skeptesthai* to look at] **1** : of or relating to a bishop **2** : having or constituting government by bishops **3** *cap* : of or relating to the Protestant Episcopal Church representing the Anglican communion in the U.S. — **epis·co·pal·ly** \-p(ə-)lē\ *adv*

Epis·co·pa·lian \i-,pis-kə-'pāl-yən\ *n* **1** : an adherent of the episcopal form of church government **2** : a member of the Protestant Episcopal Church — **Episcopalian** *adj* — **Epis·co·pa·lian·ism** \-yə-,niz-əm\ *n*

epis·co·pate \i-'pis-kə-pət\ *n* **1** : the rank, office, or term of office of a bishop **2** : the whole body of bishops

ep·i·sode \'ep-ə-,sōd\ *n* [Gk *epeisodion*, fr. neut. of *epeisodios* coming in besides, fr. *epi-* + *eis* into + *hodos* road] **1 a** : a developed situation integral to but separable from a continuous narrative : INCIDENT **b** : one of a series of loosely connected stories or scenes **2** : an event that is distinctive and separate esp. in history or in a life **3** : a digressive subdivision in a musical composition *syn* see OCCURRENCE — **ep·i·sod·ic** \,ep-ə-'säd-ik\ *also* **ep·i·sod·i·cal** \-'säd-i-kəl\ *adj* — **ep·i·sod·i·cal·ly** \-i-k(ə-)lē\ *adv*

ep·i·stax·is \,ep-ə-'stak-səs\ *n* [Gk, fr. *epistazein* to drip on, to bleed from the nose again] : NOSEBLEED

epis·tle \i-'pis-əl\ *n* [OF, lit., letter, fr. L *epistula, epistola*, fr. Gk *epistolē*, fr. *epi-* + *stellein* to send] **1** *cap* **a** : one of the letters of the New Testament **b** : a liturgical reading usu. from one of the New Testament Epistles **2** : LETTER; *esp* : a formal or elegant letter

epis·to·lary \i-'pis-tə-,ler-ē\ *adj* **1** : of, relating to, or suitable to a letter **2** : contained in or carried on by letters **3** : written in the form of a series of letters ⟨*epistolary* novel⟩

ep·i·taph \'ep-ə-,taf\ *n* [Gk *epitaphion* funeral oration, fr. *epi-* + *taphos* tomb, funeral] : an inscription (as on a tombstone) in memory of a dead person

ep·i·tha·la·mi·um \,ep-ə-thə-'lā-mē-əm\ *n, pl* **-mi·ums** *or* **ep·i·tha·la·mi·on** \-mē-ən\, *n, pl* **epi·tha·la·mi·ums** *or* **ep·i·tha·la·mia** \-mē-ə\ [L, fr. Gk *epithalamion*, fr. *epi-* + *thalamos* room, bridal chamber] : a song or poem in honor of a bride and bridegroom

ep·i·the·li·o·ma \,ep-ə-,thē-lē-'ō-mə\ *n* : a tumor derived from epithelial cells

epi·the·li·um \,ep-ə-'thē-lē-əm\ *n, pl* **-lia** \-lē-ə\ [Gk *epi-* + *thēlē* nipple] **1** : a membranous cellular tissue that covers a free surface or lines a tube or cavity of an animal body and usu. encloses parts of the body, produces secretions and excretions, or functions in assimilation **2** : a usu. thin layer of parenchyma that lines a cavity or tube of a plant — **ep·i·the·li·al** \-lē-əl\ *adj* — **ep·i·the·li·oid** \-lē-,ȯid\ *adj*

ep·i·thet \'ep-ə-,thet\ *n* [Gk *epitheton*, fr. *epitithenai* to add, fr. *epi-* + *tithenai* to put] **1** : a characterizing word or phrase accompanying or occurring in place of the name of a person or thing **2** : a disparaging or abusive word or phrase **3** : the part of a taxonomic name identifying a subordinate unit within a genus — **ep·i·thet·ic** \,ep-ə-'thet-ik\ *or* **ep·i·thet·i·cal** \-'thet-i-kəl\ *adj*

epit·o·me \i-'pit-ə-mē\ *n* [Gk *epitomē*, fr. *epitemnein* to cut short, fr. *epi-* + *temnein* to cut] **1** : a brief condensed statement of the contents of a work : SUMMARY, ABSTRACT **2** : a part that is typical of a whole : something considered to represent or embody the characteristics of something else

epit·o·mize \i-'pit-ə-,mīz\ *vt* : to make or serve as an epitome of : SUMMARIZE

ep·i·zo·ic \,ep-ə-'zō-ik\ *adj* : living on the body of an animal ⟨an *epizoic* plant⟩ — **ep·i·zo·ism** \-'zō-,iz-əm\ *n* — **ep·i·zo·ite** \-'zō-,īt\ *n*

¹ep·i·zo·ot·ic \,ep-ə-zə-'wät-ik\ *adj* : of, relating to, or being a disease that affects many animals of one kind at the same time — **ep·i·zo·ot·i·cal·ly** \-'wät-i-k(ə-)lē\ *adv*

²epizootic *n* : an epizootic disease

e plu·ri·bus unum \,ē-,plu̇r-ə-bəs-'yü-nəm\ [L, one out of many] : one composed of many — used on the seal of the U.S. and on several U.S. coins

ep·och \'ep-ək, -,äk\ *n* [Gk *epochē* cessation, fixed point, fr. *epechein* to hold back, fr. *epi-* + *echein* to hold] **1** : an instant of time selected as a point of reference in astronomy **2 a** : an event or a time that begins a new period or development **b** : a memorable event or date **3 a** : an extended period of time characterized by a distinctive development or by a memorable series of events **b** : a division of geologic time less than a period and greater than an age **syn** see PERIOD — **ep·och·al** \-əl\ *adj* — **ep·och·al·ly** \-ə-lē\ *adv*

epon·y·mous \i-'pän-ə-məs, e-'pän-\ *adj* [Gk *epōnymos*, fr. *epi-* + *onyma* name] : of, relating to, or being the person for whom something is named or is believed to be named

ep·oxy resin \(,)e-,päk-sē-\ *n* : a flexible usu. thermosetting resin made by polymerization of an oxygen-containing compound and used chiefly in coatings and adhesives

ep·si·lon \'ep-sə-,län, -lən\ *n* : the 5th letter of the Greek alphabet — E or ε

Ep·som salt \,ep-səm-\ : a bitter colorless or white crystalline salt $MgSO_4.7H_2O$ that is a hydrated sulfate of magnesium with cathartic properties — usu. used in pl.

eq·ua·ble \'ek-wə-bəl, 'ē-kwə-\ *adj* : EVEN, UNIFORM; *esp* : free from extremes or sudden or harsh changes ⟨an *equable* temper⟩ ⟨an *equable* climate⟩ — **eq·ua·bly** \-blē\ *adv*

¹equal \'ē-kwəl\ *adj* [L *aequus* level, equal] **1 a** (1) : of the same measure, quantity, amount, or number as another : LIKE (2) : identical in value : EQUIVALENT **b** : like in quality, nature, or status **c** : not varying : UNIFORM **2 a** : evenly balanced **b** : IMPARTIAL **3 a** : free from extremes **b** : tranquil of mind or mood **4** : capable of meeting requirements

²equal *n* **1** : one that is equal ⟨has no *equal* at shooting marbles⟩ **2** : an equal quantity

³equal *vt* **equaled** *or* **equalled; equal·ing** *or* **equal·ling** **1** : to be equal to; *esp* : to be identical in value to **2** : to produce something equal to : MATCH

equal–area *adj* : preserving the true extent of area of the forms represented although with distortion of shape ⟨*equal-area* maps⟩

equal·i·tar·i·an \i-,kwäl-ə-'ter-ē-ən\ *adj or n* : EGALITARIAN

equal·i·ty \i-'kwäl-ət-ē\ *n, pl* **-ties** **1** : the quality or state of being equal **2** : EQUATION 2a

equal·ize \'ē-kwə-,līz\ *vt* **1** : to make equal **2** : to make uniform; *esp* : to distribute evenly or uniformly : BALANCE — **equal·i·za·tion** \,ē-kwə-lə-'zā-shən\ *n* — **equal·iz·er** \'ē-kwə-,lī-zər\ *n*

equal·ly \'ē-kwə-lē\ *adv* **1** : in an equal manner : EVENLY **2** : to an equal degree : ALIKE

equa·nim·i·ty \,ē-kwə-'nim-ət-ē, ,ek-wə-\ *n* [L *aequo animo* with even mind] : evenness of mind : calm temper : COMPOSURE ⟨accept misfortunes with *equanimity*⟩

equate \i-'kwāt\ *vt* : to make or treat as equal : represent or express as equal or equivalent

equa·tion \i-'kwā-zhən, -shən\ *n* **1 a** : the act or process of equating **b** : a state of being equated; *esp* : the regarding of two or more things as identical or similar **2 a** : a statement of the equality of two mathematical expressions **b** : an expression representing a chemical reaction in which chemical symbols for reacting substances are placed on the left and those for products on the right of the sign → or = or of the sign ⇆ or ⇌ if the reaction is reversible

equa·tion·al \i-'kwāzh-nəl, -'kwāsh-, -ən-°l\ *adj* : of, using, or involving equations or the equating of elements

equa·tor \i-'kwāt-ər, 'ē-,kwāt-\ *n* [ME, fr. ML *aequator*, lit., equalizer, fr. L *aequare* to make equal; fr. its containing the equinoxes] **1** : the great circle of the celestial sphere whose plane is perpendicular to the axis of the earth **2** : a great circle of the earth that is everywhere equally distant from the two poles and divides the earth's surface into the northern and southern hemispheres — see ZONE illustration **3** : a circle dividing a body into two usu. equal and symmetrical parts

equa·to·ri·al \,ē-kwə-'tōr-ē-əl, ,ek-wə-, -'tȯr-\ *adj* **1** : of, relating to, or located at the equator or an equator **2** : of, originating in, or suggesting the region around the geographic equator ⟨*equatorial* heat⟩

eq·uer·ry \'ek-wə-rē, i-'kwer-ē\ *n, pl* **-ries** [MF *escuirie* office of a squire, stable, fr. *escuier* squire] **1** : an officer in charge of the horses of a prince or nobleman **2** : a personal attendant of a member of the British royal family

¹eques·tri·an \i-'kwes-trē-ən\ *adj* [L *equestr-, equester*, fr. *eques* horseman, fr. *equus* horse] **1** : of or relating to horses, horsemen, or horsemanship **2** : mounted on horseback ⟨*equestrian* troops⟩ **3** : representing a person on horseback ⟨an *equestrian* statue⟩ **4** : of, relating to, or composed of knights

²equestrian *n* : one who rides on horseback

eques·tri·enne \i-,kwes-trē-'en\ *n* : a female equestrian

equi- *comb form* [L *aequus*] : equal ⟨*equipoise*⟩ : equally ⟨*equiprobable*⟩

equi·an·gu·lar \,ē-kwi-'aŋ-gyə-lər\ *adj* : having all or corresponding angles equal

equi·dis·tant \,ē-kwə-'dis-tənt\ *adj* : equally distant

equi·lat·er·al \,ē-kwə-'lat-ə-rəl, -'la-trəl\ *adj* **1** : having all sides equal — see TRIANGLE illustration **2** : having all the faces equal ⟨*equilateral* polyhedron⟩

equil·i·brant \i-'kwil-ə-brənt\ *n* : a counterbalancing force or system of forces

equil·i·brate \-,brāt\ *vb* **1** : to bring into or keep in equilibrium : BALANCE **2** : to bring about, come to, or be in equilibrium — **equil·i·bra·tion** \i-,kwil-ə-'brā-shən\ *n*

equil·i·brist \,ē-kwə-'lib-rəst, i-'kwil-ə-brəst\ *n* : one who balances himself in unnatural positions and hazardous movements

equi·lib·ri·um \,ē-kwə-'lib-rē-əm, ,ek-wə-\ *n, pl* **-ri·ums** *or* **-ria** \-rē-ə\ [L *aequilibrium*, fr. *aequi-* equi- + *libra* weight] **1** : a static or dynamic state of balance between opposing forces or actions **2** : a state of adjustment between opposing or divergent influences or elements **3** : the normal oriented state of the animal body in respect to its environment

equi·mo·lal \,ē-kwə-'mō-ləl\ *adj* **1** : having equal molal concentration **2** : EQUIMOLAR 1

equi·mo·lar \-lər\ *adj* **1** : of or relating to an equal number of moles ⟨an *equimolar* mixture⟩ **2** : having equal molar concentration

equine \'ē-,kwīn\ *adj* [L *equinus*, fr. *equus* horse] : of, relating to, or resembling a horse or the horse family — **equine** *n* — **equine·ly** *adv*

¹equi·noc·tial \,ē-kwə-'näk-shəl, ,ek-wə-\ *adj* **1** : of, relating to, or occurring at or near an equinox ⟨*equinoctial* storms⟩ **2** : of or relating to the regions or climate of the equator ⟨*equinoctial* lands⟩ ⟨*equinoctial* heat⟩

²equinoctial *n* **1** : EQUATOR 1 **2** : an equinoctial storm

---

equinoctial circle *n* : EQUATOR 1 — called also *equinoctial line*

equi·nox \'ē-kwə-ˌnäks, 'ek-wə-\ *n* [MF *equinoxe*, fr. L *aequinoctium*, fr. *aequi-* equi- + *noct-*, *nox* night] **1** : either of the two times each year when the sun crosses the equator and day and night are everywhere of equal length that occur about March 21 and September 23 **2** : either of the two points on the celestial sphere where the celestial equator intersects the ecliptic

equip \i-'kwip\ *vt* **equipped; equip·ping** [MF *equiper*, fr. OF *eschiper* to equip a ship, of Gmc origin; akin to E *ship*] **1** : to furnish for service or action : PREPARE **2** : DRESS, ARRAY

eq·ui·page \'ek-wə-pij\ *n* **1 a** : material or articles used in equipment : OUTFIT **b** : TRAPPINGS **2** : a horse-drawn carriage with its retinue of servants or such a carriage alone

equip·ment \i-'kwip-mənt\ *n* **1 a** : the equipping of a person or thing **b** : the state of being equipped **2 a** : the set of articles or resources serving to equip a person or thing: as (1) : the implements used in an operation or activity : APPARATUS (2) : the rolling stock of a railway **b** : a piece of such equipment

eq·ui·poise \'ek-wə-ˌpȯiz, 'ē-kwə-\ *n* **1** : a state of balance : EQUILIBRIUM **2** : a weight used to balance another weight

equi·pol·lent \ˌē-kwə-'päl-ənt\ *adj* [L *pollēre* to be able, have power] **1** : equal in force, power, or validity **2** : EQUIVALENT — **equi·pol·lence** \-ən(t)s\ *n*

equi·pon·der·ant \-'pän-də-rənt\ *adj* : equally balanced

equi·pon·der·ate \-də-ˌrāt\ *vb* : to be or make equal in weight or force

equi·po·tent \ˌē-kwə-'pōt-ᵊnt\ *adj* : having equal effects or capacities ⟨*equipotent* genes⟩

equi·po·ten·tial \-pə-'ten-chəl\ *adj* : having the same electrical potential ⟨*equipotential* points⟩ : of uniform potential throughout

eq·ui·se·tum \ˌek-wə-'sēt-əm\ *n* [L *equisaetum* horsetail (plant), fr. *equus* horse + *saeta* bristle] : any of a genus of primitive perennial vascular plants with creeping rhizomes and leaves reduced to nodal sheaths on the hollow jointed grooved shoots — called also *horsetail*, *scouring rush*

eq·ui·ta·ble \'ek-wət-ə-bəl\ *adj* **1** : having or exhibiting equity : JUST **2** : existing or valid in equity as distinguished from law **syn** see FAIR — **eq·ui·ta·ble·ness** *n* — **eq·ui·ta·bly** \-blē\ *adv*

eq·ui·ta·tion \ˌek-wə-'tā-shən\ *n* : the act or art of riding on horseback

eq·ui·ty \'ek-wət-ē\ *n, pl* **-ties 1** : fairness or justice in dealings between persons **2** : a system of law originating in the English chancery supplementary to common and statute law and designed to protect rights and enforce duties fixed by substantive law **3** : the value of an owner's interest in a property in excess of claims or liens against it

equiv·a·lent \i-'kwiv(-ə)-lənt\ *adj* [LL *aequivalēre* to have equal power, fr. L *aequi-* equi- + *valēre* to be strong] **1** : equal in force, amount, or value; *also* : equal in area or volume but not admitting of superposition ⟨a square *equivalent* to a triangle⟩ **2** : like in meaning **3** : corresponding or virtually identical in effect or function **4** : having the same chemical combining capacity — **equiv·a·lence** \-lən(t)s\ *n* — **equivalent** *n* — **equiv·a·lent·ly** *adv*

equiv·o·cal \i-'kwiv-ə-kəl\ *adj* [LL *aequivocus*, fr. L *aequi-* equi- + *voc-*, *vox* voice] **1** : having two or more possible meanings : AMBIGUOUS ⟨an *equivocal* answer⟩ **2** : UNCERTAIN, DOUBTFUL ⟨an *equivocal* result⟩ **3** : SUSPICIOUS, QUESTIONABLE ⟨*equivocal* behavior⟩ — **equiv·o·cal·ly** \-k(ə-)lē\ *adv* — **equiv·o·cal·ness** \-kəl-nəs\ *n*

equiv·o·cate \i-'kwiv-ə-ˌkāt\ *vi* **1** : to use equivocal language esp. with intent to deceive : LIE **2** : to avoid committing oneself in what one says — **equiv·o·ca·tion** \-ˌkwiv-ə-'kā-shən\ *n* — **equiv·o·ca·tor** \i-'kwiv-ə-ˌkāt-ər\ *n*

¹-er \ər; *after some vowels, often* r; *after* ŋ, *usu* gər\ *adj suffix or adv suffix* [OE *-ra*, in adjectives, *-or*, in adverbs] — used to form the comparative degree of adjectives and adverbs of one syllable ⟨hott*er*⟩ ⟨dri*er*⟩ and of some adjectives and adverbs of two syllables ⟨complet*er*⟩ and sometimes of longer ones

²-er \ər; *after some vowels, often* r\ *also* **-ier** \ē-ər, yər\ *or* **-yer** \yər\ *n suffix* [ME , partly fr. OE *-ere*, partly fr. OF *-ier*, both fr. L *-arius* -ary] **1 a** : a person occupationally connected with ⟨hatt*er*⟩ ⟨furri*er*⟩ ⟨law*yer*⟩ **b** : person or thing belonging to or associated with ⟨head*er*⟩ ⟨old-tim*er*⟩ **c** : native of : resident of ⟨cottag*er*⟩ ⟨New York*er*⟩ **d** : one that has ⟨three-deck*er*⟩ **e** : one that produces or yields ⟨pork*er*⟩ **2 a** : one that does or performs (a specified action) ⟨report*er*⟩ — sometimes added to both elements of a compound ⟨build*er*-upp*er*⟩ **b** : one that is a suitable object of (a specified action) ⟨broil*er*⟩ **3** : one that is ⟨foreign*er*⟩

era \'ir-ə, 'er-ə, 'ē-rə\ *n* [LL *aera*, fr. L, counters, pl. of *aer-*, *aes* copper, money; akin to E *ore*] **1** : a period of time reckoned from some special date or event ⟨the Christian *era* is computed from the birth of Christ⟩ **2** : an important or distinctive period of history ⟨the Revolutionary *era*⟩ **3** : one of the major divisions of geologic time **syn** see PERIOD

erad·i·cate \i-'rad-ə-ˌkāt\ *vt* [L *eradicare*, fr. *e-* + *radic-*, *radix* root] : to remove by or as if by uprooting : ELIMINATE, EXTIRPATE ⟨*eradicate* weeds⟩ ⟨*eradicating* an endemic disease⟩ — **erad·i·ca·ble** \-'rad-i-kə-bəl\ *adj* — **erad·i·ca·tion** \-ˌrad-ə-'kā-shən\ *n* — **erad·i·ca·tive** \-'rad-ə-ˌkāt-iv\ *adj* — **erad·i·ca·tor** \-ˌkāt-ər\ *n*

eras·a·ble \i-'rā-sə-bəl\ *adj* : capable of being erased — **eras·a·bil·i·ty** \i-ˌrā-sə-'bil-ət-ē\ *n*

erase \i-'rās\ *vb* [L *eras-*, *eradere*, fr. *e-* + *radere* to scratch] **1** : to rub or scrape out (as something written) **2** : to remove as if by erasing ⟨*erased* the event from their memories⟩ ⟨*erase* a recording from a tape⟩ **3** : to yield to being erased

syn CANCEL, OBLITERATE: ERASE implies rubbing or wiping out symbols or impressions often for correction or insertion of new matter; CANCEL implies an action (as marking, revoking, or neutralizing) that makes a thing no longer effective or usable; OBLITERATE implies a covering up or defacing that removes all distinct traces of a thing's existence

eras·er \i-'rā-sər\ *n* : one that erases; *esp* : a sharp instrument or a piece of rubber or cloth used to erase marks

era·sure \i-'rā-shər, -zhər\ *n* : an act or instance of erasing

Er·a·to \'er-ə-ˌtō\ *n* : the Greek Muse of lyric and esp. love poetry

er·bi·um \'ər-bē-əm\ *n* : a rare metallic element that occurs with yttrium — see ELEMENT table

¹ere \(ˌ)e(ə)r, (ˌ)a(ə)r\ *prep* [OE *ǣr*, adv., early, soon] : ²BEFORE 2

²ere *conj* : ³BEFORE

¹erect \i-'rekt\ *adj* [L *erectus*, fr. pp. of *erigere* to erect fr. *e-* + *regere* to lead straight] **1 a** : vertical in position : UPRIGHT ⟨an *erect* pole⟩ ⟨*erect* poplars⟩ **b** : marked by straightness of bodily posture ⟨a man of *erect* bearing⟩ **c** : standing up or out from the body ⟨a porcupine with quills *erect*⟩ **2** : directed upward ⟨a tree with *erect* branches⟩ — **erect·ly** *adv* — **erect·ness** \-'rek(t)-nəs\ *n*

²erect *vt* **1 a** : to put up by the fitting together of materials : BUILD ⟨*erect* a building⟩ **b** : to fix in an upright position ⟨*erect* a flagpole⟩ **c** : to cause to stand up or out **2** : to elevate in status ⟨*erects* a few odd notions into a philosophy⟩ **3** : ESTABLISH ⟨*erect* a civilization⟩ **4** : to construct (as a perpendicular) upon a given base — **erec·tor** \-'rek-tər\ *n*

erec·tile \i-'rek-tᵊl, -ˌtīl\ *adj* : capable of being raised to an erect position

erec·tion \i-'rek-shən\ *n* **1** : an erecting or a being erected : RAISING, BUILDING, CONSTRUCTING **2** : something erected

E region *n* : the part of the ionosphere that occurs between 40 and 90 miles above the surface of the earth

ere·long \e(ə)r-'lȯŋ, a(ə)r-\ *adv* : before long : SOON

er·e·mite \'er-ə-ˌmīt\ *n* [ME] : HERMIT; *esp* : a religious recluse

erep·sin \i-'rep-sən\ *n* : a mixture of peptidases from the intestinal juice

erg \'ərg\ *n* [Gk *ergon* work; akin to E *work*] : a cgs unit of work equal to the work done by a force of one dyne acting through a distance of one centimeter

er·go \'e(ə)r-ˌgō, 'ər-\ *adv* [L] : THEREFORE, HENCE

er·go·graph \'ər-gə-ˌgraf\ *n* : an apparatus for measuring the work capacity of a muscle

---

ə abut; ᵊ kitten; ər further; a back; ā bake; ä cot, cart; aù out; ch chin; e less; ē easy; g gift; i trip; ī life

er·gos·ter·ol \,ər-'gäs-tə-,ról, -,rōl\ *n* [*ergot* + *sterol*] : a crystalline steroid alcohol that occurs esp. in yeast, molds, and ergot and is converted by ultraviolet irradiation into vitamin D

er·got \'ər-gət, -,gät\ *n* [F, lit., cock's spur] **1 a** : the dark club-shaped fruiting body of several fungi that replaces the seed of a grass (as rye) **b** : a disease of cereals (as rye) caused by ergot-producing fungi **2** : dried ergots that contain several alkaloids and are used medicinally for their contractile effect on smooth muscle — **er·got·ic** \,ər-'gät-ik\ *adj*

er·got·a·mine \,ər-'gät-ə-,mēn\ *n* : an alkaloid from ergot that has the pharmacological action of ergot and is used esp. in treating migraine

er·got·ism \'ər-gət-,iz-əm\ *n* : a toxic condition caused by consumption of ergot (as in grain or bread)

er·i·ca·ceous \,er-ə-'kā-shəs\ *adj* [NL *Erica*, genus name, fr. Gk *ereikē* heather] : of, relating to, or being heath plants

Erie \'i(ə)r-ē\ *n* : a member of an Iroquoian people of the Lake Erie region

Er·in \'er-ən\ *n* : Ireland

Erin·ys \i-'rin-əs, -'rī-nəs\ *n, pl* **Eriny·es** \-'rin-ē-,ēz\ : one of the Furies in Greek mythology

Eris \'ir-əs, 'er-\ *n* : the Greek goddess of discord

Er·len·mey·er flask \,ər-lən-,mī(-ə)r-, ,er-lən-\ *n* : a flat-bottomed conical laboratory flask

er·mine \'ər-mən\ *n, pl* **ermine** or **ermines** [OF, of Gmc origin] **1 a** : any of several weasels that assume a white winter coat usu. with more or less black on the tail **b** : the white fur of an ermine **2** : a rank or office whose robe is ornamented with ermine — **er·mined** \-mənd\ *adj*

erne or **ern** \'ərn, 'e(ə)rn\ *n* [OE *earn*] : EAGLE; *esp* : a white-tailed sea eagle

erode \i-'rōd\ *vb* [L *eros-, erodere* to eat away, fr. *e-* + *rodere* to gnaw] **1** : to diminish or destroy by degrees: **a** : to eat into or away by slow destruction of substance : CORRODE **b** : to wear away by or as if by the action of water, wind, or glacial ice (*eroded* the soil) **2** : to undergo erosion — **erod·i·ble** \-'rōd-ə-bəl\ *adj*

Eros \'e(ə)r-,äs, 'i(ə)r-\ *n* : the Greek god of love

erose \i-'rōs\ *adj* : IRREGULAR, UNEVEN; *esp* : having the margin irregularly notched as if gnawed (an *erose* leaf) — **erose·ly** *adv*

ero·sion \i-'rō-zhən\ *n* : the process of eroding : the state of being eroded — **ero·sion·al** \-'rōzh-nəl, -'rō-zhən-ºl\ *adj*

ero·sive \i-'rō-siv, -ziv\ *adj* : eating or wearing away (the *erosive* effect of water upon rock) (an *erosive* ulcer) — **ero·sive·ness** *n* — **ero·siv·i·ty** \i-,rō-'siv-ət-ē\ *n*

erot·ic \i-'rät-ik\ *adj* [Gk *erōt-, erōs* love] : of, relating to, or marked by sexual love or desire — **erot·i·cal·ly** \-i-k(ə-)lē\ *adv* — **erot·i·cism** \-'rät-ə-,siz-əm\ *n*

err \'e(ə)r, 'ər\ *vi* [L *errare* to stray] **1** : to make a mistake (*erred* in his calculations) **2** : to violate an accepted standard of conduct : do wrong : SIN

er·ran·cy \'er-ən-sē\ *n, pl* **-cies** : the state or an instance of erring

er·rand \'er-ənd\ *n* [OE *ærend*] : a short trip taken to attend to some business esp. for another; *also* : the object or purpose of such a trip

er·rant \'er-ənt\ *adj* **1** : wandering esp. in search of adventure (an *errant* knight) **2 a** : straying outside the proper bounds (an *errant* calf) **b** : deviating from what is true or right (an *errant* child) — **er·rant·ry** \-ən-trē\ *n*

er·ra·ta \e-'rät-ə, -'rāt-, -'rat-\ *n* [fr. pl. of *erratum*] : a list of corrigenda

er·rat·ic \ir-'at-ik\ *adj* [L *erraticus*, fr. *errare* to stray] **1** : having no fixed course : WANDERING (an *erratic* comet) **2** : marked by lack of consistency or regularity : ECCENTRIC (*erratic* behavior) — **er·rat·i·cal·ly** \-'at-i-k(ə-)lē\ *adv*

er·ra·tum \e-'rät-əm, -'rāt-, -'rat-\ *n, pl* **-ta** \-ə\ [L, fr. neut. of pp. of *errare* to stray] : CORRIGENDUM

er·ro·ne·ous \ir-'ō-nē-əs, e-'rō-\ *adj* : containing or characterized by error : MISTAKEN, INCORRECT — **er·ro·ne·ous·ly** *adv* — **er·ro·ne·ous·ness** *n*

er·ror \'er-ər\ *n* **1 a** : deviation from a code of behavior (saw the *error* of his ways) **b** : an act involving an unintentional deviation from truth or accuracy (an arithmetic *error*) **c** : an act that through ignorance, deficiency, or accident fails to achieve what should be done (an *error* of judgment) **d** : a defensive misplay made by a baseball player when normal play would have resulted in an out or prevented an advance by a base runner **2 a** : the quality or state of erring **b** : an instance of false belief **3** : something produced by mistake **4** : the difference between an observed or estimated value and the actual value — **er·ror·less** \-ləs\ *adj*

syn ERROR, MISTAKE, BLUNDER mean a departure from what is true, right, or proper. ERROR is a deviation from what is right, correct, or sanctioned (an *error* in reasoning) (an *error* in addition) MISTAKE implies misunderstanding or an oversight or unintentional wrongdoing and connotes less severe judgment than ERROR; BLUNDER suggests ignorance, stupidity, carelessness, or lack of foresight and sometimes implies blame

er·satz \'er-,zäts, er-'\ *adj* [G, n., substitute] : SUBSTITUTE, SYNTHETIC (*ersatz* flour)

Erse \'ərs\ *n* **1** : SCOTTISH GAELIC **2** : IRISH GAELIC — **Erse** *adj*

erst \'ərst\ *adv* [OE *ærest*, superl. of *ær* early] *archaic* : FORMERLY

erst·while \'ərst-,hwīl\ *adv* : in the past : FORMERLY — **erstwhile** *adj*

eruct \i-'rəkt\ *vb* : BELCH — **eruc·tate** \i-'rək-,tāt\ *vb* — **eruc·ta·tion** \i-,rək-'tā-shən, ,ē-,rək-\ *n*

er·u·dite \'er-(y)ə-,dīt\ *adj* [L *e-* + *rudis* rude, ignorant] : characterized by erudition — **er·u·dite·ly** *adv*

er·u·di·tion \,er-(y)ə-'dish-ən\ *n* : extensive knowledge acquired chiefly from books : LEARNING

erum·pent \i-'rəm-pənt\ *adj* : bursting forth (*erumpent* fungi)

erupt \i-'rəpt\ *vb* [L *erupt-, erumpere* to burst forth, fr. *e-* + *rumpere* to break] **1 a** : to force out or release suddenly and often violently something pent up **b** : to burst forth; *also* : to break through a surface (teeth *erupting* from the gum) **c** : EXPLODE **2** : to break out (as with a skin eruption) — **erupt·i·ble** \i-'rep-tə-bəl\ *adj*

erup·tion \i-'rəp-shən\ *n* **1 a** : an act, process, or instance of erupting **b** : the breaking out of a rash on the skin **2** : a product (as a skin rash) of erupting — **erup·tive** \-'rəp-tiv\ *adj*

-ery \(ə-)rē\ *n suffix, pl* **-er·ies** [OF *-erie*, fr. *-ier* -er + *-ie* -y] **1** : qualities collectively : character : -NESS (snobb*ery*) **2** : art : practice (cook*ery*) **3** : place of doing, keeping, producing, or selling (the thing specified) (fish*ery*) (bak*ery*) **4** : collection : aggregate (fin*ery*) **5** : state or condition (slav*ery*)

er·y·sip·e·las \,er-ə-'sip-(ə-)ləs, ,ir-\ *n* : an acute disease marked by fever and intense local inflammation of the skin and subcutaneous tissues and caused by a hemolytic streptococcus

eryth·ro·cyte \i-'rith-rə-,sīt\ *n* [Gk *erythros* red] : RED BLOOD CELL — **eryth·ro·cyt·ic** \-,rith-rə-'sit-ik\ *adj*

eryth·ro·my·cin \i-,rith-rə-'mīs-ºn\ *n* : an antibiotic produced by an actinomycete and active against amebiasis

eryth·ro·sin \i-'rith-rə-sən\ *n* : any of several dyes made from fluorescein that yields reddish shades

1-es \əz, iz *after* s, z, sh, ch; z *after* v *or a vowel*\ *n pl suffix* [OE *-as*, nom. & acc. pl. ending of some masc. nouns] **1** — used to form the plural of most nouns that end in *s* (glass*es*), *z* (fuzz*es*), *sh* (bush*es*), *ch* (peach*es*), or a final *y* that changes to *i* (lad*ies*) and of some nouns ending in *f* that changes to *v* (loav*es*) — compare **1-s** 1 **2** : **1-s** 2

2-es *vb suffix* [OE *-es, -as*] — used to form the third person singular present of most verbs that end in *s* (bless*es*), *z* (fizz*es*), *sh* (hush*es*), *ch* (catch*es*), or a final *y* that changes to *i* (def*ies*) — compare **2-s**

Esau \'ē-,só\ *n* : the elder son of Isaac and Rebekah and brother of Jacob

es·ca·drille \'es-kə-,dril, -,drē\ *n* : a unit of a European air command containing usu. six airplanes

es·ca·late \'es-kə-,lāt\ *vb* [back-formation fr. *escalator*] : to increase in extent or intensity — **es·ca·la·tion** \,es-kə-'lā-shən\ *n*

1es·ca·la·tor \'es-kə-,lāt-ər\ *n* [fr. *Escalator*, a trademark] : a power-driven set of stairs arranged like an endless belt that ascend or descend continuously

2escalator *adj* : providing for a periodic proportional upward or downward adjustment (as of prices or wages)

es·cal·lop \is-'käl-əp, -'kal-\ *var of* SCALLOP

---

j joke; ŋ sing; ō flow; ó flaw; ói coin; th thin; t͟h this; ü loot;   u̇ foot; y yet; yü few; yu̇ furious; zh vision

es·ca·pade \'es-kə-ˌpād\ *n* : a mischievous adventure : PRANK

¹**es·cape** \is-'kāp\ *vb* [ONF *escaper,* fr. L *ex-* + LL *cappa* head covering] **1 a** : to get away (as by flight) ⟨*escape* from a burning building⟩ **b** : to issue from confinement ⟨gas is *escaping*⟩ **c** : to run wild from cultivation **2** : to get out of the way of : AVOID ⟨*escaped* the plague by moving to the country⟩ **3** : to fail to be noticed or recallable by ⟨his name *escapes* me⟩ **4** : to come out from or be uttered by involuntarily ⟨a sigh *escaped* him⟩ — **es·cap·er** *n*

²**escape** *n* **1** : an act or instance of escaping **2** : a means of escaping **3** : a cultivated plant run wild

³**escape** *adj* **1** : relating to escape from reality ⟨*escape* literature⟩ **2** : providing a means of escape ⟨an *escape* clause⟩

es·cap·ee \(ˌ)es-ˌkā-'pē, is-ˌkā-, ˌes-kə-\ *n* : one that has escaped; *esp* : an escaped prisoner

escape mechanism *n* : a mode of behavior or thinking adopted to evade unpleasant facts or responsibilities

es·cape·ment \is-'kāp-mənt\ *n* **1** : a device in a timepiece through which the energy of the weight or spring is transmitted to the pendulum or balance by means of impulses that permit one tooth on a wheel to escape from a projecting part at regular intervals **2** : a device (as the spacing mechanism of a typewriter) that permits motion in one direction only in equal steps

escapement

escape velocity *n* : the minimum velocity that a moving body (as a rocket) must have to escape from the gravitational field of the earth or of a celestial body and move outward into space

es·cap·ism \is-'kā-ˌpiz-əm\ *n* : habitual diversion of the mind to purely imaginative activity or entertainment in order to escape from reality or routine — **es·cap·ist** \-pəst\ *adj or n*

es·ca·role \'es-kə-ˌrōl\ *n* [F, fr. LL *escariola*] : ENDIVE 1

es·carp·ment \is-'kärp-mənt\ *n* **1** : a steep slope in front of a fortification **2** : a long cliff

-es·cence \'es-ᵊn(t)s\ *n suffix* : process of becoming ⟨obsol*escence*⟩

-es·cent \'es-ᵊnt\ *adj suffix* [L *-escent-, -escens,* prp. ending of incho. verbs in *-escere*] **1** : beginning : beginning to be : slightly ⟨alkal*escent*⟩ **2** : reflecting or emitting light (in a specified way) ⟨fluor*escent*⟩

es·char \'es-ˌkär, -kər\ *n* [LL *eschara,* fr. Gk, hearth, scab] : SCAB; *esp* : a crust formed over a burn — **es·cha·rot·ic** \ˌes-kə-'rät-ik\ *adj*

¹**es·cheat** \is-'chēt\ *n* [ME *eschete,* fr. OF, fr. *escheoir* to fall, devolve, irreg. fr. L *ex-* + *cadere* to fall] : the reversion of property to the state when there are no persons (as heirs) legally entitled to hold it; *also* : the property that reverts

²**escheat** *vb* : to revert or cause to revert by escheat — **es·cheat·a·ble** \-ə-bəl\ *adj*

es·chew \is-'chü\ *vt* [MF *eschiuver*] : SHUN, AVOID

¹**es·cort** \'es-ˌkȯrt\ *n* [F *escorte,* fr. It *scorta,* fr. *scorgere* to guide, fr. L *ex-* + *corrigere* to make straight, correct] **1 a** : a person or group of persons accompanying another to give protection or show courtesy **b** : the man who goes on a date with a woman **c** : a protective screen of warships or fighter planes used to fend off enemy attack from one or more vulnerable craft **2** : accompaniment by a person or an armed protector (as a ship)

²**es·cort** \is-'kȯrt, es-', 'es-,\ *vt* : to accompany as an escort **syn** see ACCOMPANY

escort carrier *n* : a small aircraft carrier

escort fighter *n* : a fighter airplane for escorting heavy bombers

es·cri·toire \'es-krə-ˌtwär\ *n* : a writing table or desk; *esp* : SECRETARY 4

es·crow \'es-ˌkrō, es-'\ *n* [MF *escroue* scroll] : something (as a deed or a sum of money) delivered by one person to another to be delivered by him to a third party only upon the fulfillment of a condition — **in escrow** : in trust as an escrow

es·cu·do \is-'küd-ō\ *n, pl* **-dos** **1** : any of various former gold or silver coins of Hispanic countries **2 a** : the basic monetary unit of Portugal and Chile **b** : a coin representing this unit

es·cu·lent \'es-kyə-lənt\ *adj* : EDIBLE — **esculent** *n*

es·cutch·eon \is-'kəch-ən\ *n* : the usu. shield-shaped surface on which a coat of arms is shown

¹**-ese** \'ēz, 'ēs\ *adj suffix* [Pg *-ês* & It *-ese,* fr. L *-ensis*] : of, relating to, or originating in (a certain place or country) ⟨Japan*ese*⟩

²**-ese** *n suffix, pl* **-ese** **1** : native or resident of (a specified place or country) ⟨Chin*ese*⟩ **2 a** : language of (a particular place, country, or nationality) ⟨Siam*ese*⟩ **b** : speech, literary style, or diction peculiar to (a specified place, person, or group) — usu. in words applied in depreciation ⟨journal*ese*⟩

escutcheon

es·ker \'es-kər\ *n* [IrGael *eiscir* ridge] : a long narrow mound of material deposited by a stream flowing on, within, or beneath a stagnant glacier

Es·ki·mo \'es-kə-ˌmō\ *n* **1** : a member of a group of peoples of northern Canada, Greenland, Alaska, and eastern Siberia **2** : the language of the Eskimo people — **Es·ki·mo·an** \ˌes-kə-'mō-ən\ *adj*

Eskimo dog *n* **1** : a broad-chested powerful dog native to Greenland and Labrador that has a heavy double coat **2** : a sled dog of American origin

esoph·a·gus \i-'säf-ə-gəs\ *n, pl* **-gi** \-ˌgī, -ˌjī, -ˌgē\ [Gk *oisophagos,* fr. *ois-* (used as stem of *pherein* to bear) + *phagein* to eat] : a muscular tube that leads from the pharynx to the stomach — **esoph·a·ge·al** \i-ˌsäf-ə-'jē-əl\ *adj*

es·o·ter·ic \ˌes-ə-'ter-ik\ *adj* [Gk *esōterikos,* fr. *esōterō,* compar. of *eisō, esō* within] **1** : designed for, limited to, or understood by the specially initiated alone ⟨an *esoteric* ritual⟩ ⟨*esoteric* pursuits⟩ **2** : of or relating to knowledge that is restricted to a small group : RECONDITE ⟨*esoteric* writings⟩ — **es·o·ter·i·cal·ly** \-'ter-i-k(ə-)lē\ *adv*

es·pa·drille \ˌes-pə-'dril\ *n* : a flat sandal usu. having a fabric upper and a flexible sole

es·pal·ier \is-'pal-yər\ *n* : a plant (as a fruit tree) trained to grow flat against a support (as a wall or trellis) — **espalier** *vt*

es·pe·cial \is-'pesh-əl\ *adj* : SPECIAL, PARTICULAR — **es·pe·cial·ly** \-'pesh-(ə-)lē\ *adv*

Es·pe·ran·to \ˌes-pə-'rant-ō, -'ränt-\ *n* [Dr. *Esperanto,* pseudonym of L.L. Zamenhof *d*1917 Polish oculist, its inventor] : an artificial international language based as far as possible on words common to the chief European languages

es·pi·al \is-'pī(-ə)l\ *n* **1** : OBSERVATION **2** : an act of noticing : DISCOVERY

es·pi·o·nage \'es-pē-ə-ˌnäzh, -nij, -ˌnäj\ *n* [F *espionnage,* fr. MF *espionner* to spy, fr. *espion* spy, fr. OIt *spione,* aug. of *spia* spy, of Gmc origin] : the practice of spying or the use of spies esp. to obtain information about the plans and activities of a foreign government

es·pla·nade \'es-plə-ˌnäd, -ˌnād\ *n* [F] : a level open stretch or area; *esp* : one designed for walking or driving along a shore

es·pous·al \is-'pau̇-zəl, -səl\ *n* **1 a** : BETROTHAL **b** : WEDDING **2** : MARRIAGE **3** : a taking up of a cause or belief as a supporter

es·pouse \is-'pau̇z, -'pau̇s\ *vt* **1** : MARRY **2** : to take up the cause of : SUPPORT — **es·pous·er** *n*

espres·so \e-'spres-ō\ *n* [It *caffè espresso,* lit., pressed out coffee] : coffee brewed by forcing steam through finely ground darkly roasted coffee beans

es·prit \is-'prē\ *n* [F] : vivacious cleverness or wit

es·prit de corps \is-ˌprēd-ə-'kō(ə)r, -'kȯ(ə)r\ *n* [F] : the common spirit existing in the members of a group and inspiring enthusiasm, devotion, and strong regard for the honor of the group

es·py \is-'pī\ *vt* **es·pied** \-'pīd\; **es·py·ing** : to catch sight of

-esque \'esk\ *adj suffix* [F, fr. It *-esco,* of Gmc origin; akin to E *-ish*] : in the manner or style of : like ⟨statu*esque*⟩ ⟨Roman*esque*⟩

es·quire \'es-ˌkwī(ə)r, is-'\ *n* [MF *esquier* squire] **1** : a member of the English gentry ranking immediately below a knight **2** : a candidate for knighthood serving as attendant to a knight **3** — used as a title of courtesy usu. placed in its abbreviated form after the surname ⟨John Smith, *Esq.*⟩

-ess \əs, is *also* ˌes\ *n suffix* [OF *-esse*, fr. LL *-issa*, fr. Gk] : female ⟨author*ess*⟩

¹es·say \'es-ˌā, *in sense 1 also* e-'sā\ *n* [MF *essai*, fr. LL *exagium* act of weighing, fr. L *exigere* to drive out, weigh, fr. *ex-* + *agere* to drive] **1** : ATTEMPT; *esp* : an initial tentative effort **2** : an analytic or interpretative literary composition usu. dealing with its subject from a limited or personal point of view

²es·say \e-'sā, 'es-ˌā\ *vt* : to make an effort to perform ⟨*essayed* the role of mediator⟩

es·say·ist \'es-ˌā-əst\ *n* : a writer of essays

es·sence \'es-ᵊn(t)s\ *n* [L *essentia*, fr. *esse* to be; akin to E *is*] **1** : the basic nature of a thing : the quality or sum of qualities that make a thing what it is ⟨the *essence* of love is unselfishness⟩ **2** : a substance distilled or otherwise extracted from another substance (as a plant or drug) and having the special qualities of the original substance ⟨*essence* of peppermint⟩ **3** : PERFUME, SCENT

Es·sene \is-'ēn, 'es-ˌ\ *n* : a member of a monastic brotherhood of Jews in Palestine from the 2d century B.C. to the 2d century A.D.

¹es·sen·tial \i-'sen-chəl\ *adj* **1** : forming or belonging to the fundamental nature of a thing ⟨free speech is an *essential* right of citizenship⟩ **2** : containing or having the character of a volatile essence ⟨*essential* oils⟩ **3** : important in the highest degree : NECESSARY ⟨food is *essential* to life⟩ **4** : IDIOPATHIC ⟨*essential* hypertension⟩ — **es·sen·ti·al·i·ty** \-ˌsen-chē-'al-ət-ē\ *n* — **es·sen·tial·ly** \-'sench-(ə-)lē\ *adv* — **es·sen·tial·ness** \-əl-nəs\ *n*
syn ESSENTIAL, FUNDAMENTAL, VITAL mean so important as to be indispensable. ESSENTIAL implies belonging to the very nature of a thing and therefore being incapable of removal without destroying the thing itself or its character; FUNDAMENTAL suggests something that is of the nature of a foundation without which an entire system or complex whole would collapse ⟨the *fundamental* principles of a democracy⟩ VITAL suggests that which is as necessary to continuance as air, food, and water are to living things ⟨resources *vital* to security⟩ **syn** see in addition NECESSARY

²essential *n* : something basic, necessary, or indispensable ⟨the *essentials* for success⟩

es·so·nite \'es-ᵊn-ˌīt\ *n* : a yellow to brown garnet

¹-est \əst, ist\ *adj suffix or adv suffix* [OE] — used to form the superlative degree of adjectives and adverbs of one syllable ⟨fatt*est*⟩ ⟨lat*est*⟩, of some adjectives and adverbs of two syllables ⟨lucki*est*⟩ ⟨often*est*⟩, and less often of longer ones ⟨beggarli*est*⟩

²-est \əst, ist\ *or* **-st** \st\ *suffix* [OE] — used to form the archaic second person singular of English verbs (with *thou*) ⟨gett*est*⟩ ⟨did*st*⟩

es·tab·lish \is-'tab-lish\ *vb* [MF *establiss-*, *establir*, fr. L *stabilire*, fr. *stabilis* stable] **1** : to make firm or stable ⟨*establish* a gun on its base⟩ **2** : to enact permanently ⟨*establish* a constitution⟩ **3 a** : to bring into existence : FOUND ⟨*establish* a republic⟩ **b** : to bring about : EFFECT ⟨*establish* a good relationship⟩ **4 a** : to set on a firm basis ⟨*establish* his son in business⟩ **b** : to put into a favorable position ⟨the *established* order⟩ **c** : to gain full recognition or acceptance of ⟨*establish* a claim⟩ **5** : to put beyond doubt : PROVE ⟨*established* his innocence⟩ **6** : to become naturalized ⟨a grass that *establishes* on poor soil⟩ — **es·tab·lish·er** *n*

established church *n* : a church recognized by law as the official church of a nation and supported by civil authority

es·tab·lish·ment \is-'tab-lish-mənt\ *n* **1 a** : the act of establishing : the state or fact of being established **b** : the granting of a favorable or privileged position ⟨*establishment* of a church⟩ **2** : something (as an organized force for carrying on public or private affairs) that is established ⟨the military *establishment* of a country⟩ **3** : a settled place for residence or business; *also* : such a place with its grounds, buildings, furnishings, and employees ⟨a dry-cleaning *establishment*⟩ **4** : an established order of society; *also* : the social, economic, and political leaders of such an order ⟨was generally hostile to the *establishment*⟩

es·ta·mi·net \e-stá-mē-nā\ *n, pl* **estaminets** \-nā(z)\ [F] : a small café

es·tate \is-'tāt\ *n* [MF *estat*, fr. L *status* state] **1** : STATE, CONDITION **2** : social standing or rank esp. of a high order **3** : a social or political class; *esp* : one of the great classes (as the nobility, clergy, and commons) formerly vested with distinct political powers **4 a** : the nature and extent of one's interest in property (as land) **b** : POSSESSIONS, PROPERTY; *esp* : a person's property in land and tenements **c** : the assets and liabilities left by a person at death **5** : a landed property usu. with a large house on it

Es·tates Gen·er·al \is-ˌtāts-'jen-(ə-)rəl\ *n* : a legislative assembly of nobility, clergy, and commons in France prior to the revolution of 1789

¹es·teem \is-'tēm\ *n* : high regard

²esteem *vt* [L *aestimare* to estimate] **1 a** : REGARD, CONSIDER ⟨*esteem* it a privilege⟩ **b** : THINK, BELIEVE **2** : to set a high value on : PRIZE *see* REGARD
syn VALUE, APPRECIATE: ESTEEM implies a high evaluation and adds to it warmth of feeling or close attachment; VALUE suggests a judgment that combines analytical and subjective evaluation ⟨*valued* their services⟩ ⟨*valued* his contribution to literature⟩ APPRECIATE implies recognition of worth or merit through wise judgment, perception, and insight ⟨*appreciates* freedom⟩

es·ter \'es-tər\ *n* [G, fr. *essigäther* ethyl acetate, fr. *essig* vinegar + *äther* ether] : an organic compound formed by the reaction between an acid and an alcohol

es·ter·ase \'es-tə-ˌrās\ *n* : an enzyme that accelerates the hydrolysis or synthesis of esters

es·ter·i·fy \e-'ster-ə-ˌfī\ *vt* **-fied; -fy·ing** : to convert into an ester — **es·ter·i·fi·ca·tion** \-ˌster-ə-fə-'kā-shən\ *n*

Es·ther \'es-tər\ *n* **1** : a Hebrew woman who became Xerxes' queen during the Babylonian captivity and delivered her people from destruction **2** — *see* BIBLE table

es·the·sia \es-'thē-zh(ē-)ə\ *n* [back-formation fr. *anesthesia*] : capacity for sensation and feeling : SENSIBILITY

esthete, esthetic, esthetics *var of* AESTHETE, AESTHETIC, AESTHETICS

es·ti·ma·ble \'es-tə-mə-bəl\ *adj* : worthy of esteem — **es·ti·ma·ble·ness** *n*

¹es·ti·mate \'es-tə-ˌmāt\ *vt* [L *aestimare*] **1** : to judge or determine tentatively or approximately the value, size, or cost of ⟨*estimate* a distance⟩ ⟨*estimate* a painting job⟩ **2** : to form an opinion of : JUDGE, CONCLUDE — **es·ti·ma·tor** \-ˌmāt-ər\ *n*
syn ESTIMATE, APPRAISE, EVALUATE, ASSESS mean to judge a thing with respect to its worth. ESTIMATE implies a judgment, considered or casual, that precedes or takes the place of actual measuring, counting, or testing; APPRAISE implies the fixing of the monetary worth of a thing by an expert; EVALUATE suggests an attempt to determine the relation or intrinsic worth of something in terms other than of money ⟨*evaluate* a new novel⟩ ASSESS implies a critical weighing or appraising often of a particular element or aspect for the purpose of understanding or interpreting a larger whole or as a guide in taking action ⟨*assess* the deterrent effect of punishment⟩

²es·ti·mate \'es-tə-mət\ *n* **1** : the act of appraising or valuing : CALCULATION **2** : an opinion or judgment of the nature, character, or quality of a thing **3** : a rough or approximate calculation **4** : a statement of the cost of a job

es·ti·ma·tion \ˌes-tə-'mā-shən\ *n* **1** : JUDGMENT, OPINION **2 a** : the act of estimating **b** : ESTIMATE **3** : ESTEEM, HONOR

Es·to·nian \e-'stō-nē-ən, -nyən\ *n* **1** : a member of a Finno-Ugric-speaking people chiefly of Estonia **2** : the Finno-Ugric language of the Estonians — **Estonian** *adj*

estr- *or* **estro-** *or* **oestr-** *or* **oestro-** *comb form* : estrus ⟨*estrogen*⟩

es·tra·di·ol \ˌes-trə-'dī-ˌol, -ˌōl\ *n* : a powerful steroid estrogenic hormone usu. made synthetically for medicinal use

es·trange \is-'trānj\ *vt* **1** : to remove from customary environment or associations **2** : to destroy the affection of : ALIENATE ⟨*estranged* from his wife⟩ — **es·trange·ment** \-mənt\ *n*

es·trin \'es-trən\ *n* : an estrogenic hormone

es·tri·ol \'es-ˌtrī-ˌol, e-'strī-, -ˌōl\ *n* : a crystalline estrogenic hormone usu. obtained from the urine of pregnant women

es·tro·gen \'es-trə-jən\ *n* : a substance (as a sex hormone) tending to promote estrus and stimulate the development of secondary sex characteristics in the female — **es·tro-**

---

j joke; ŋ sing; ō flow; ȯ flaw; ȯi coin; th thin; th̲ this; ü loot; u̇ foot; y yet; yü few; yu̇ furious; zh vision

gen·ic \‚es-trə-'jen-ik\ *adj* — **es·tro·gen·i·cal·ly** \-'jen-i-k(ə-)lē\ *adv*

es·trone \'es-‚trōn\ *n* : a ketonic estrogenic hormone from the urine of pregnant females

estrous cycle *n* : the correlated phenomena of the endocrine and generative systems of a female mammal from the beginning of one period of estrus to the beginning of the next

es·trus \'es-trəs\ *or* **es·trum** \-trəm\ *n* [L *oestrus* gadfly, frenzy, fr. Gk *oistros*] **1** : a regularly recurrent state of sexual excitability during which the female of most mammals will accept the male and is capable of conceiving : HEAT **2** : ESTROUS CYCLE — **es·trous** \-trəs\ *adj*

es·tu·a·rine \'es-chə-wə-‚rīn\ *adj* : of, relating to, or formed in an estuary

es·tu·ary \'es-chə-‚wer-ē\ *n, pl* **-ar·ies** [L *aestuarium*, fr. *aestus* boiling, tide] : a water passage where the tide meets a river current; *esp* : an arm of the sea at the lower end of a river

-et \'et, ‚et, ət, it\ *n suffix* [OF, fr. LL *-itus*] **1** : small one : lesser one ⟨islet⟩ **2** : group ⟨octet⟩

eta \'āt-ə\ *n* : the 7th letter of the Greek alphabet — H or η

et cet·era \et-'set-ə-rə, -'se-trə\ [L] : and others esp. of the same kind : and so forth

etch \'ech\ *vt* [D *etsen*, fr. G *ätzen*, lit., to feed] **1** : to produce esp. on metal or glass by the corrosive action of an acid; *also* : to subject to such etching **2** : to impress sharply or clearly — **etch·er** *n*

etch·ing *n* **1** : the art of producing pictures or designs by printing from an etched metal plate **2** : an impression from an etched plate

eter·nal \i-'tərn-ºl\ *adj* [L *aeternus*] **1** : having no beginning and no end : lasting forever **2** : continuing without interruption : UNCEASING ⟨that dog's *eternal* barking⟩ — **eter·nal·ly** \-ºl-ē\ *adv* — **eter·nal·ness** *n*

syn EVERLASTING, ENDLESS: ETERNAL implies being without either beginning or end and so unaffected by time or change ⟨*eternal* truths⟩ EVERLASTING and ENDLESS apply to what exists and endures in time without end or limit, EVERLASTING stressing the quality of permanence or the fact of duration and ENDLESS frequently suggesting a wearisome stretching out without conclusion or final rest ⟨*endless* arguments⟩ ⟨*endless* punishment⟩

Eternal *n* : ²GOD — used with *the*

eter·ni·ty \i-'tər-nət-ē\ *n, pl* **-ties 1** : the quality or state of being eternal **2** : infinite time **3** *pl* : AGES **4** : the state after death : IMMORTALITY **5** : a seemingly endless time

¹-eth \əth, ith\ *or* **-th** \th\ *vb suffix* [OE *-eth, -ath, -th*] — used to form the archaic third person singular present of verbs ⟨goeth⟩ ⟨doth⟩

²-eth — see -TH

eth·ane \'eth-‚ān\ *n* [*ethyl* + *-ane*] : a colorless odorless gas C_2H_6 that consists of carbon and hydrogen, is found in natural gas, and is used esp. as a fuel

eth·a·nol \'eth-ə-‚nȯl, -‚nōl\ *n* : ALCOHOL 1

eth·ene \'eth-‚ēn\ *n* : ETHYLENE

ether \'ē-thər\ *n* [Gk *aithēr*, fr. *aithein* to ignite] **1** : the upper regions of space : HEAVENS **2 a** : a medium formerly held to permeate all space and transmit transverse waves (as light) **b** : the medium that transmits radio waves **3 a** : a light volatile flammable liquid $(C_2H_5)_2O$ obtained by the distillation of alcohol with sulfuric acid and used chiefly as a solvent esp. of fats and as an anesthetic **b** : any of various organic compounds characterized by an oxygen atom attached to two carbon atoms

ethe·re·al \i-'thir-ē-əl\ *adj* **1** : HEAVENLY ⟨*ethereal* spirits⟩ **2** : being light and airy : DELICATE ⟨*ethereal* music⟩ — **ethe·re·al·i·ty** \i-‚thir-ē-'al-ət-ē\ *n* — **ethe·re·al·ly** \-'thir-ē-ə-lē\ *adv* — **ethe·re·al·ness** *n*

ether·ize \'ē-thə-‚rīz\ *vt* : to treat or anesthetize with ether — **ether·i·za·tion** \‚ē-thə-rə-'zā-shən\ *n*

eth·i·cal \'eth-i-kəl\ *or* **eth·ic** \-ik\ *adj* [Gk *ēthikos*, fr. *ēthos* character] **1** : of or relating to ethics **2** : conforming to accepted and esp. professional standards of conduct ⟨*ethical* practices⟩ **3** : sold only on a doctor's prescription ⟨*ethical* drugs⟩ **syn** see MORAL — **eth·i·cal·ly** \'eth-i-k(ə-)lē\ *adv*

eth·ics \'eth-iks\ *n sing or pl* [ME *ethik*, fr. MF *ethique*, fr. L *ethice*, fr. Gk *ēthikē*, fr. *ēthikos*] **1** : a branch of

philosophy dealing with what is good and bad and with moral duty and obligation **2** : the principles of moral conduct governing an individual or a group

Ethi·o·pi·an \‚ē-thē-'ō-pē-ən\ *n* **1** : a member of any of the mythical or actual peoples usu. described by the ancient Greeks as dark-skinned and living far to the south **2** : a native or inhabitant of Ethiopia — **Ethiopian** *adj*

Ethi·op·ic \-'äp-ik, -'ō-pik\ *n* : a Semitic language formerly spoken in Ethiopia and still used as the liturgical language of the Christian church in Ethiopia

eth·moid \'eth-‚mȯid\ *or* **eth·moi·dal** \eth-'mȯid-ºl\ *adj* : of, relating to, adjoining, or being one or more bones of the walls and septum of the nasal cavity — **ethmoid** *n*

eth·nic \'eth-nik\ *adj* [Gk *ethnikos* national, fr. *ethnos* nation] : of or relating to races or large groups of people classed according to common traits and customs ⟨*ethnic* minorities⟩ — **eth·ni·cal·ly** \-ni-k(ə-)lē\ *adv*

eth·no·cen·tric \‚eth-nō-'sen-trik\ *adj* : favoring esp. unduly one's own ethnic group ⟨*ethnocentric* views⟩

eth·nog·ra·phy \eth-'näg-rə-fē\ *n* : ETHNOLOGY; *esp* : descriptive anthropology — **eth·nog·ra·pher** \-fər\ *n* — **eth·no·graph·ic** \‚eth-nə-'graf-ik\ *or* **eth·no·graph·i·cal** \-'graf-i-kəl\ *adj* — **eth·no·graph·i·cal·ly** \-i-k(ə-)lē\ *adv*

eth·nol·o·gy \eth-'näl-ə-jē\ *n* [Gk *ethnos* nation, people] : a science that deals with the division of mankind into races and their origin, distribution, relations, and characteristics — **eth·no·log·ic** \‚eth-nə-'läj-ik\ *or* **eth·no·log·i·cal** \-'läj-i-kəl\ *adj* — **eth·no·log·i·cal·ly** \-i-k(ə-)lē\ *adv* — **eth·nol·o·gist** \eth-'näl-ə-jəst\ *n*

eth·yl \'eth-əl\ *n* [*ether* + *-yl*] : a chemical radical C_2H_5 or CH_3CH_2 consisting of carbon and hydrogen

ethyl alcohol *n* : ALCOHOL 1a

eth·yl·ate \'eth-ə-‚lāt\ *vt* : to introduce the ethyl radical into (a compound) — **eth·yl·a·tion** \‚eth-ə-'lā-shən\ *n*

ethyl cellulose *n* : any of various plastics made by ethylating cellulose

ethyl chloride *n* : a colorless pungent flammable compound C_2H_5Cl used esp. as a surface anesthetic

eth·yl·ene \'eth-ə-‚lēn\ *n* **1** : a colorless flammable gas C_2H_4 found in coal gas or obtained from petroleum hydrocarbons and used to ripen fruits or as an anesthetic **2** : a bivalent hydrocarbon radical $-CH_2CH_2-$ derived from ethane — **eth·yl·en·ic** \‚eth-ə-'lē-nik\ *adj*

ethylene gly·col \-'glī-‚kȯl, -‚kōl\ *n* : a thick liquid alcohol $(CH_2OH)_2$ used as an antifreeze and in making resins

-et·ic \'et-ik\ *adj suffix* [Gk *-etikos, -ētikos*, fr. *-etos, -ētos*, ending of certain verbals] : -IC ⟨limnetic⟩ — often in adjectives corresponding to nouns ending in *-esis* ⟨genetic⟩

eti·o·late \'ēt-ē-ə-‚lāt\ *vt* **1** : to make (a green plant) pale and spindling by lack of light **2** : to make pale and sickly — **eti·o·la·tion** \‚ēt-ē-ə-'lā-shən\ *n*

eti·ol·o·gy \‚ēt-ē-'äl-ə-jē\ *n* [Gk *aitia* cause] : the cause or origin esp. of a disease — **eti·o·log·ic** \‚ēt-ē-ə-'läj-ik\ *or* **eti·o·log·i·cal** \-'läj-i-kəl\ *adj* — **eti·o·log·i·cal·ly** \-i-k(ə-)lē\ *adv*

et·i·quette \'et-i-kət, -‚ket\ *n* [F *étiquette*, lit., ticket] : the body of rules governing the way in which people behave in social or official life or the way in which a ceremony is conducted

Eton collar \‚ēt-ºn-\ *n* [*Eton* College, English public school] : a large stiff turnover collar

Eton jacket *n* : a short black jacket with long sleeves, wide lapels, and an open front

Etrus·can \i-'trəs-kən\ *n* **1** : a native or inhabitant of ancient Etruria **2** : the language of the Etruscans — **Etruscan** *adj*

-ette \'et, ‚et, ət, it\ *n suffix* [MF, fem. of *-et*] **1** : little one ⟨kitchenette⟩ **2** : female ⟨farmerette⟩ **3** : imitation ⟨beaverette⟩

étude \'ā-‚t(y)üd\ *n* **1** : a piece of music for the practice of a point of technique **2** : a composition built on a technical motive but played for its artistic value

et·y·mol·o·gy \‚et-ə-'mäl-ə-jē\ *n, pl* **-gies** [Gk *etymologia*, fr. *etymon* the literal meaning of a word according to its origin, fr. *etymos* true; akin to E *sooth*] **1** : the history of a word as shown esp. by tracing its transmission from one language to another, by analyzing it into its component parts, by identifying its cognates in other languages, or by tracing it and its cognates to a common ancestral form in an ancestral language **2** : a branch of language study concerned with etymologies — **et·y·mo·log·i·cal** \-mə-'läj-i-kəl\ *adj* — **et·y·mo·log·i·cal·ly** \-'läj-i-k(ə-)lē\ *adv* — **et·y·mol·o·gist** \,et-ə-'mäl-ə-jəst\ *n*

eu- *comb form* [Gk] **1 a** : well : easily ⟨euplastic⟩ — compare DYS- **b** : good ⟨eudaemon⟩ — compare DYS- **2 a** : true ⟨euchromosome⟩ **b** : truly ⟨eucoelomate⟩

eu·ca·lypt \'yü-kə-,lipt\ *n* : EUCALYPTUS

eu·ca·lyp·tus \,yü-kə-'lip-təs\ *n, pl* **-ti** \-,tī, -,tē\ *or* **-tus·es** [Gk *eu-* + *kalyptein* to conceal; fr. the conical covering of the buds] : any of a genus of mostly Australian evergreen trees of the myrtle family including many that are widely cultivated for their gums, resins, oils, and useful woods

Eu·cha·rist \'yü-k(ə-)rəst\ *n* [LL *eucharistia*, ·fr. Gk, gratitude, Eucharist, fr. *eu-* + *charis* favor, grace, gratitude] : COMMUNION 2a; *esp* : a Roman Catholic sacrament renewing Christ's propitiatory sacrifice of his body and blood — **eu·cha·ris·tic** \,yü-kə-'ris-tik\ *adj, often cap*

eu·chre \'yü-kər\ *n* : a card game in which each player is dealt five cards and the player making trump must take three tricks to win a hand

eu·clid·e·an \yü-'klid-ē-ən\ *adj, often cap* : of or relating to the geometry of Euclid

eu·gen·ic \yü-'jen-ik\ *adj* **1** : relating to or fitted for the production of good offspring **2** : of or relating to eugenics — **eu·gen·i·cal·ly** \-'jen-i-k(ə)lē\ *adv*

eu·gen·ics \yü-'jen-iks\ *n* : a science that deals with the improvement (as by control of human mating) of hereditary qualities of a race or breed — compare EUTHENICS — **eu·gen·ist** \yü-'jen-əst, 'yü-jə-nəst\ *also* **eu·gen·i·cist** \yü-'jen-ə-səst\ *n*

eu·gle·na \yü-'glē-nə\ *n* : any of a large genus of green freshwater flagellates often classed as algae — **eu·gle·noid** \-,nóid\ *adj or n*

euglenoid movement *n* : writhing protoplasmic movement typical of some euglenoid flagellates

eu·lo·gize \'yü-lə-,jīz\ *vt* : to speak or write in high praise of : EXTOL — **eu·lo·gist** \-jəst\ *n* — **eu·lo·gis·tic** \,yü-lə-'jis-tik\ *adj* — **eu·lo·gis·ti·cal·ly** \-ti-k(ə-)lē\ *adv*

eu·lo·gy \'yü-lə-jē\ *n, pl* **-gies** **1** : a speech or a writing in praise of a person or thing; *esp* : a formal speech in praise of a dead person **2** : high praise

Eu·men·i·des \yü-'men-ə-,dēz\ *n pl* : ERINYES

eu·nuch \'yü-nək\ *n* [Gk *eunouchos*, fr. *eunē* bed + *echein* to have, have charge of] : a castrated man; *esp* : one placed in charge of a harem or employed as a chamberlain in a palace

eu·on·y·mus \yü-'än-ə-məs\ *n* : any of a genus of mostly shrubs and small trees often grown as ornamentals

eu·phe·mism \'yü-fə-,miz-əm\ *n* [Gk *euphēmismos*, fr. *eu-* + *phēmē* speech, fr. *phanai* to speak] : the substitution of an agreeable or inoffensive expression for one that may offend or suggest something unpleasant; *also* : the expression so substituted ⟨*pass away* is a widely used *euphemism for die*⟩ — **eu·phe·mis·tic** \,yü-fə-'mis-tik\ *adj* — **eu·phe·mis·ti·cal·ly** \-ti-k(ə-)lē\ *adv*

eu·pho·ni·ous \yü-'fō-nē-əs\ *adj* : pleasing to the ear : smooth-sounding — **eu·pho·ni·ous·ly** *adv* — **eu·pho·ni·ous·ness** *n*

eu·pho·ni·um \-nē-əm\ *n* : a tenor tuba like a baritone but mellower in tone

eu·pho·ny \'yü-fə-nē\ *n, pl* **-nies** [Gk *euphōnia*, fr. *eu-* + *phōnē* voice] : pleasing or sweet sound; *esp* : the effect of words so combined as to please the ear — **eu·phon·ic** \yü-'fän-ik\ *adj* — **eu·phon·i·cal·ly** \-'fän-i-k(ə-)lē\ *adv*

eu·phor·bia \yü-'fór-bē-ə\ *n* : a typical milky-juiced spurge

eu·pho·ria \yü-'fōr-ē-ə, -'fór-\ *n* [Gk, fr. *eu-* + *pherein* to bear] : an often unaccountable feeling of well-being or elation — **eu·phor·ic** \-'fór-ik, -'fär-\ *adj*

Eu·phros·y·ne \yü-'fräs-°n-(,)ē\ *n* : one of the three Graces

eu·ploid \'yü-,plóid\ *adj* : having a chromosome number that is an exact multiple of the monoploid number — **euploid** *n* — **eu·ploi·dy** \-,plóid-ē\ *n*

Eur·asian \yü-'rā-zhən, -shən\ *adj* **1** : of or relating to Eurasia **2** : of mixed European and Asiatic origin — **Eurasian** *n*

eu·re·ka \yü-'rē-kə\ *interj* [Gk *heurēka* I have found, fr. *heuriskein* to find; fr. the exclamation attributed to

Archimedes on discovering a method for determining the purity of gold] — used to express triumph on a discovery

Eu·ro·pa \yü-'rō-pə\ *n* : a Phoenician princess carried off by Zeus in the form of a white bull

Eu·ro·pe·an \,yür-ə-'pē-ən\ *n* **1** : a native or inhabitant of Europe **2** : a person of European descent — **European** *adj*

European plan *n* : a hotel rate whereby guests are charged a fixed sum for room without meals — compare AMERICAN PLAN

eu·ro·pi·um \yü-'rō-pē-əm\ *n* : a metallic chemical element found in a sand — see ELEMENT table

eury- *comb form* [Gk *eurys*] : broad : wide ⟨*eury*pterid⟩

Eu·ryd·i·ce \yü-'rid-ə-(,)sē\ *n* : the wife of Orpheus

eu·ry·ha·line \,yür-i-'hā-,līn\ *adj* : able to live in waters of a wide range of salinity

eu·ryp·ter·id \yü-'rip-tə-rəd\ *n* [Gk *pteron* wing] : any of an order (Eurypterida) of usu. large aquatic Paleozoic arthropods related to the king crabs — **eurypterid** *adj*

eu·ry·therm \'yür-i-,thərm\ *n* : an organism that tolerates a wide range of temperature — **eu·ry·ther·mal** \,yür-i-'thər-məl\ *or* **eu·ry·ther·mic** \-mik\ *or* **eu·ry·ther·mous** \-məs\ *adj*

eu·ry·top·ic \,yür-i-'täp-ik\ *adj* : tolerant of wide variation in environmental factors

eu·sta·chian tube \yü-,stā-shən-, -,stā-kē-ən-\ *n, often cap E* [fr. Bartolommeo *Eustachio* d1574 Italian anatomist] : a tube connecting the middle ear with the throat and equalizing air pressure on both sides of the eardrum

eu·stat·ic \yü-'stat-ik\ *adj* : relating to or characterized by worldwide change of sea level

Eu·ter·pe \yü-'tər-pē\ *n* : the Greek Muse of music

eu·tha·na·sia \,yü-thə-'nā-zh(ē-)ə\ *n* [Gk, easy death, fr. *eu-* + *thanatos* death] : the act or practice of killing (as an incurable invalid) for reasons of mercy — **eu·tha·na·sic** \-zik, -sik\ *adj*

eu·then·ics \yü-'then-iks\ *n* : a science that deals with human improvement by control and improvement of environment — compare EUGENICS — **eu·then·ic** \-ik\ *adj* — **eu·then·ist** \yü-'then-əst, 'yü-thə-nəst\ *n*

eu·the·ri·an \yü-'thir-ē-ən\ *adj* : of or relating to the placental mammals — **eutherian** *n*

evac·u·ate \i-'vak-yə-,wāt\ *vb* [L *evacuare*, fr. *e-* + *vacuus* empty] **1** : to make empty **2** : to discharge waste matter from the body : VOID **3** : to remove something esp. by pumping **4 a** : to remove or withdraw from a military or occupation zone or from a dangerous area **b** : VACATE — **evac·u·a·tion** \i-,vak-yə-'wā-shən\ *n* — **evac·u·a·tive** \i-'vak-yə-,wāt-iv\ *adj*

evac·u·ee \i-,vak-yə-'wē\ *n* : an evacuated person

evade \i-'vād\ *vb* [L *evas-, evadere*, fr. *e-* + *vadere* to go, walk] **1** : to get away or avoid by skill or trickery ⟨*evade* a question⟩ ⟨*evade* punishment⟩ **2** : to avoid facing up to ⟨*evade* responsibility⟩ **3** : BAFFLE, FOIL ⟨the problem *evades* all efforts at solution⟩ — **evad·a·ble** \i-'vād-ə-bəl\ *adj* — **evad·er** *n*

syn ELUDE: EVADE implies adroitness, ingenuity, or lack of scruple in escaping or avoiding a pursuer or attacker; ELUDE implies a slippery or elusive quality that baffles attempts to seize or keep or identify the person or thing that escapes

evag·i·nate \i-'vaj-ə-,nāt\ *vt* : to turn inside out — **evag·i·na·tion** \i-,vaj-ə-'nā-shən\ *n*

eval·u·ate \i-'val-yə-,wāt\ *vt* **1** : to determine or fix the value of **2** : to examine and judge the quality or degree of **syn** see ESTIMATE — **eval·u·a·tion** \-,val-yə-'wā-shən\ *n* — **eval·u·a·tive** \-'val-yə-,wāt-iv\ *adj*

ev·a·nesce \,ev-ə-'nes\ *vi* [L *evanescere*, fr. *e-* + *vanus* empty] : to dissipate like vapor

ev·a·nes·cence \,ev-ə-'nes-°n(t)s\ *n* **1** : the process or fact of evanescing **2** : evanescent quality

ev·a·nes·cent \-°nt\ *adj* : tending to vanish like vapor : not lasting : quickly passing ⟨*evanescent* pleasures⟩

¹**evan·gel** \i-'van-jəl\ *n* [LL *evangelium*, fr. Gk *euangelion*, lit., good news, fr. *eu-* + *angelos* messenger] : GOSPEL

²**evangel** *n* : EVANGELIST

evan·gel·i·cal \,ē-,van-'jel-i-kəl, ,ev-ən-\ *also* **evan·gel·ic** \-'jel-ik\ *adj* **1** : of, relating to, or in agreement with the Christian gospel esp. as it is presented in the four Gospels **2** : PROTESTANT **3** : emphasizing salvation by faith in the atoning death of Jesus Christ through personal conversion, the authority of Scripture, and the importance of preaching as contrasted with ritual **4** *often cap* **a** : FUNDAMENTALIST **b** : Low Church **5** : EVANGELISTIC, ZEALOUS — **Evan·gel·i·cal·ism** \-i-kə-,liz-əm\ *n* — **evan·gel·i·cal·ly** \-i-k(ə-)lē\ *adv*

Evangelical *n* : one holding evangelical principles or belonging to an evangelical party or church

evan·ge·lism \i-'van-jə-,liz-əm\ *n* **1** : the winning or revival of personal commitments to Christ **2** : militant or crusading zeal — **evan·ge·lis·tic** \i-,van-jə-'lis-tik\ *adj* — **evan·ge·lis·ti·cal·ly** \-ti-kə-lē\ *adv*

evan·ge·list \i-'van-jə-ləst\ *n* **1** *often cap* : a writer of any of the four Gospels **2** : one who evangelizes; *esp* : a Protestant minister or layman who preaches at services of evangelism

evan·ge·lize \i-'van-jə-,līz\ *vb* **1** : to preach the gospel **2** : to convert to Christianity — **evan·ge·li·za·tion** \-,van-jə-lə-'zā-shən\ *n* — **evan·ge·liz·er** \-'van-jə-,lī-zər\ *n*

evap·o·rate \i-'vap-ə-,rāt\ *vb* **1** : to change into vapor ⟨ether *evaporates* rapidly in air⟩; *also* : to pass off or cause to pass off in usu. invisible minute particles **2 a** : to pass off or away : DISAPPEAR **b** : to diminish quickly **3** : to expel moisture from (as by heat) ⟨*evaporate* apples⟩ — **evap·o·ra·tion** \-,vap-ə-'rā-shən\ *n* — **evap·o·ra·tive** \-'vap-ə-,rāt-iv\ *adj* — **evap·o·ra·tor** \-,rāt-ər\ *n*

evaporated milk *n* : milk concentrated by evaporation without the addition of sugar to one half or less of its bulk

evapo·trans·pi·ra·tion \i-,vap-ō-,tran(t)-spə-'rā-shən\ *n* : soil water loss through evaporation and through transpiration by plants

eva·sion \i-'vā-zhən\ *n* **1** : the act or an instance of evading : ESCAPE ⟨tax *evasion*⟩ **2** : a means of evading

eva·sive \i-'vā-siv, -ziv\ *adj* : marked by a tendency or purpose to evade : EQUIVOCAL — **eva·sive·ly** *adv* — **eva·sive·ness** *n*

eve \'ēv\ *n* [ME *even, eve*] **1** : EVENING **2** : the evening or the day before a special day ⟨Christmas *Eve*⟩ **3** : the period immediately preceding an event

Eve \'ēv\ *n* : the first woman and wife of Adam

¹even \'ē-vən\ *n* [ME, fr. OE *æfen*] *archaic* : EVENING

²even *adj* [OE *efen*] **1 a** : having a horizontal surface : FLAT ⟨*even* ground⟩ **b** : being without break or irregularity : SMOOTH **c** : being in the same plane or line **2** : being without variation : UNIFORM **3 a** : EQUAL, FAIR **b** : SQUARE, QUITS **c** : BALANCED; *esp* : showing neither profit nor loss **4** : being exactly divisible by two ⟨*even* number⟩ **5** : EXACT, PRECISE ⟨an *even* dozen⟩ **syn** see STEADY — **even·ly** *adv* — **even·ness** *n*

³even *adv* **1 a** : PRECISELY, EXACTLY ⟨*even* as you and I⟩ **b** : at the very same time ⟨*even* as the clock struck⟩ **2 a** — used as an intensive to indicate something unexpected ⟨honored *even* by his enemies⟩ **b** — used as an intensive to stress the comparative degree ⟨are *even* more at home⟩

⁴even *vb* **evened**; **even·ing** \'ēv-(ə-)niŋ\ : to make or become even — **even·er** \'ēv-(ə-)nər\ *n*

even·hand·ed \,ē-vən-'han-dəd\ *adj* : FAIR, IMPARTIAL

eve·ning \'ēv-niŋ\ *n* **1** : the latter part and close of the day and early part of the night **2** : the latter part ⟨the *evening* of life⟩

evening dress *n* : conventional dress for formal or semiformal evening social occasions

evening prayer *n, often cap E&P* : an evening service of the Anglican communion

evening primrose *n* : a coarse biennial herb with yellow flowers that open in the evening; *also* : any of several related plants

eve·nings \'ēv-niŋz\ *adv* : in the evening repeatedly

evening star *n* : a bright planet (as Venus) seen in the western sky at or after sunset

even·song \'ē-vən-,sȯŋ\ *n, often cap* **1** : VESPERS **2** : evening prayer esp. when sung

event \i-'vent\ *n* [L *eventus*, fr. *event-, evenire* to turn out, happen, fr. *e-* + *venire* to come] **1 a** : something that happens : OCCURRENCE **b** : a noteworthy happening **c** : a social occasion or activity **2 a** : OUTCOME, RESULT **b** : CONTINGENCY, EVENTUALITY ⟨in the *event* of rain the ceremony will be held indoors⟩ **3** : any of the contests in a program of sports **syn** see OCCURRENCE — **at all events** : in any case — **in any event** : in any case

event·ful \-fəl\ *adj* **1** : full of or rich in events ⟨an *eventful* day⟩ **2** : MOMENTOUS — **event·ful·ly** \-fə-lē\ *adv* — **event·ful·ness** *n*

even·tide \'ē-vən-,tīd\ *n* : EVENING

even·tu·al \i-'vench-(ə-)wəl, -'ven-chəl\ *adj* : taking place at an unspecified later time : ULTIMATE ⟨*eventual* success⟩ — **even·tu·al·ly** \-ē\ *adv*

even·tu·al·i·ty \i-,ven-chə-'wal-ət-ē\ *n, pl* **-ties** : a possible outcome : POSSIBILITY

even·tu·ate \i-'ven-chə-,wāt\ *vi* : to come out finally

ev·er \'ev-ər\ *adv* [OE *æfre*] **1** : ALWAYS ⟨*ever* faithful⟩ **2 a** : at any time ⟨seldom if *ever* home⟩ **b** : in any way **3** — used as an intensive esp. with *so*

ev·er·bloom·ing \,ev-ər-'blü-miŋ\ *adj* : blooming more or less continuously throughout the growing season

ev·er·glade \'ev-ər-,glād\ *n* : a low-lying tract of swampy or marshy land

¹ev·er·green \'ev-ər-,grēn\ *adj* : having foliage that remains green and functional through more than one growing season ⟨most conifers are *evergreen* trees⟩ — compare DECIDUOUS

²evergreen *n* **1** : an evergreen plant; *also* : CONIFER **2** *pl* : twigs and branches of evergreen plants used for decoration

¹ev·er·last·ing \,ev-ər-'las-tiŋ\ *adj* **1** : lasting or enduring through all time : ETERNAL **2 a** (1) : continuing long or indefinitely : PERPETUAL (2) : retaining form or color when dried ⟨*everlasting* flowers⟩ **b** : TEDIOUS **3** : wearing indefinitely : DURABLE **syn** see ETERNAL — **ev·er·last·ing·ly** \-tiŋ-lē\ *adv* — **ev·er·last·ing·ness** *n*

²everlasting *n* **1** *cap* : ²GOD — used with *the* **2** : ETERNITY ⟨from *everlasting*⟩ **3** : a plant esp. of the daisy family with everlasting flowers; *also* : its flower

ev·er·more \,ev-ər-'mō(ə)r, -'mȯ(ə)r\ *adv* : ALWAYS, FOREVER

evert \i-'vərt\ *vt* [L *evers-, evertere* to overturn, fr. *e-* + *vertere* to turn] : to turn outward or inside out — **ever·si·ble** \-'vər-sə-bəl\ *adj* — **ever·sion** \-'vər-zhən\ *n*

ever·tor \i-'vərt-ər\ *n* : a muscle that rotates a part outward

ev·ery \'ev-rē\ *adj* [ME *everich*, fr. OE *æfre ælc*, fr. *æfre* ever + *ælc* each] **1** : being each individual or part of a group without exception **2** : COMPLETE, ENTIRE ⟨have *every* confidence in him⟩

ev·ery·body \'ev-ri-,bäd-ē\ *pron* : every person

ev·ery·day \'ev-rē-,dā\ *adj* : encountered or used routinely or typically : ORDINARY ⟨*everyday* clothes⟩

ev·ery·one \-(,)wən\ *pron* : EVERYBODY

ev·ery·thing \'ev-rē-,thiŋ\ *pron* **1 a** : all that exists **b** : all that relates to the subject ⟨tell *everything*⟩ **2** : a most important or excellent thing ⟨to some people money is *everything*⟩

ev·ery·where \-,hwe(ə)r, -,hwa(ə)r\ *adv* : in every place or part

evict \i-'vikt\ *vt* [LL *evict-, evincere*, fr. L, to vanquish, fr. *e-* + *vincere* to conquer] : to put (a person) out from property by legal process **syn** see EJECT — **evic·tion** \-'vik-shən\ *n* — **evic·tor** \-'vik-tər\ *n*

¹ev·i·dence \'ev-əd-ən(t)s, -ə-,den(t)s\ *n* **1 a** : an outward sign : INDICATION **b** : something that furnishes proof : TESTIMONY; *esp* : material legally submitted to a tribunal to ascertain the truth of a matter **2** : one who bears witness; *esp* : one who voluntarily confesses a crime and testifies for the prosecution against his accomplices — **ev·i·den·tial** \,ev-ə-'den-chəl\ *adj* — **in evidence** : to be seen : CONSPICUOUS

²evidence *vt* : to serve as or offer evidence of

ev·i·dent \'ev-əd-ənt, -ə-,dent\ *adj* [L *evident-, evidens*, fr. *e-* + *videns*, prp. of *videre* to see] : clear to the sight and to the mind : PLAIN ⟨was *evident* that the boy and girl were twins⟩ **syn** see APPARENT — **ev·i·dent·ly** *adv*

¹evil \'ē-vəl\ *adj* **evil·er** *or* **evil·ler**; **evil·est** *or* **evil·lest** [OE *yfel*] **1 a** : not good morally : WICKED **b** : arising from bad character or conduct **2 a** : causing discomfort or repulsion : OFFENSIVE **b** : DISAGREEABLE **3 a** : causing harm : PERNICIOUS **b** : marked by misfortune : UNLUCKY — **evil·ly** \-və(l)-lē\ *adv*

²evil *n* **1** : something that brings sorrow, distress, or calamity **2** : the fact of suffering, misfortune, and wrongdoing — **evil·do·er** \,ē-vəl-'dü-ər\ *n* — **evil·do·ing** \-'dü-iŋ\ *n*

ə abut; ᵊ kitten; ər further; a back; ā bake; ä cot, cart; aú out; ch chin; e less; ē easy; g gift; i trip; ī life

evil eye *n* : an eye or glance held to be capable of inflicting harm

evil-mind·ed \ˌē-vəl-'mīn-dəd\ *adj* : having an evil disposition or evil thoughts

Evil One *n* : DEVIL, SATAN — used with *the*

evince \i-'vin(t)s\ *vt* **1** : to constitute evidence of : SHOW **2** : to display clearly : REVEAL ⟨his musical talent *evinced* itself early in his life⟩ — **evinc·i·ble** \i-'vin(t)-sə-bəl\ *adj*

evis·cer·ate \i-'vis-ə-ˌrāt\ *vt* **1** : to take out the entrails of **2** : to deprive of vital content or force — **evis·cer·a·tion** \i-ˌvis-ə-'rā-shən\ *n*

evo·ca·tion \ˌē-vō-'kā-shən, ˌev-ə-\ *n* **1** : the act or fact of evoking : SUMMONING **2** : INDUCTION 3c

evoke \i-'vōk\ *vt* [L *evocare*, fr. *e-* + *vocare* to call] **1 a** : to call forth or up : SUMMON **b** : INVOKE **2** : ELICIT **3** : to re-create imaginatively — **evo·ca·ble** \'ev-ə-kə-bəl, i-'vō-kə-\ *adj* — **evoc·a·tive** \i-'väk-ət-iv\ *adj* — **evoc·a·tive·ly** *adv* — **evo·ca·tor** \'e-vō-ˌkāt-ər, 'ev-ə-\ *n*

evo·lu·tion \ˌev-ə-'lü-shən, ˌē-və-\ *n* **1 a** : a process of change esp. from a lower to a higher state : GROWTH **b** : something evolved **2** : one of a set of prescribed movements **3** : the process of working out or developing **4** : the extraction of a mathematical root **5 a** : PHYLOGENY **b** : the process by which through a series of changes or steps a living organism has acquired its distinguishing characters **c** : a theory that the various types of animals and plants have their origin in other preexisting types and that the distinguishable differences are due to modifications in successive generations **6** : a process in which the whole universe is a progression of interrelated phenomena — **ev·o·lu·tion·ary** \-shə-ˌner-ē\ *adj* — **ev·o·lu·tion·ism** \-shə-ˌniz-əm\ *n* — **ev·o·lu·tion·ist** \-sh(ə-)nəst\ *n or adj*

evolve \i-'välv, -'vólv\ *vb* [L *evolut-*, *evolvere* to unroll, fr. *e-* + *volvere* to roll] **1** : to give off : EMIT **2 a** : DERIVE, EDUCE **b** : to work out : DEVELOP **c** : to produce by natural evolutionary processes **3** : to undergo evolutionary change — **evolve·ment** \-mənt\ *n*

ev·zone \'ev-ˌzōn\ *n* [NGk *euzōnos*, fr. Gk, active, lit., well girt, fr. *eu-* + *zōne* girdle] : a member of a select Greek infantry unit

ewe \'yü\ *n* [OE *ēowu*] : the female of the sheep or a related animal esp. when mature

ew·er \'yü-ər, 'yu̇(-ə)r\ *n* [AF, fr. OF *evier*, fr. L *aquarium*, neut. of *aquarius* of water, fr. *aqua* water] : a vase-shaped pitcher or jug

ex \ˌ(ˌ)eks\ *prep* [L] **1 a** : out of : FROM ⟨goods supplied *ex* stock or *ex* factory⟩ **b** : from a specified dam ⟨a promising colt by Ranger *ex* Margot⟩ **2** : without an indicated value or right — used esp. of securities ⟨*ex* dividend⟩

ewer

¹ex- \e *also occurs in this prefix where only i is shown below (as in* "express") *and ks sometimes occurs where only gz is shown (as in* "exact"); *3 is* \ˌ(ˌ)eks, 'eks\ *prefix* [L, out, out of, thoroughly] **1** : out of : outside ⟨exterritorial⟩ **2** : not ⟨*ex*stipulate⟩ **3** : former ⟨*ex*-president⟩ ⟨*ex*-child actor⟩

²ex- *see* EXO-

ex·ac·er·bate \ig-'zas-ər-ˌbāt, ek-'sas-\ *vt* [L *exacerbare*, fr. *ex-* + *acerbus* harsh, bitter, fr. *acer* sharp] : to make more violent, bitter, or severe — **ex·ac·er·ba·tion** \ig-ˌzas-ər-'bā-shən, ˌ(ˌ)ek-ˌsas-\ *n*

¹ex·act \ig-'zakt\ *vt* [L *exact-*, *exigere* to drive out, demand, fr. *ex-* + *agere* to drive] **1** : to demand and compel peremptorily : EXTORT **2** : to call for as necessary, appropriate, or desirable *syn see* DEMAND — **ex·act·a·ble** \-'zak-tə-bəl\ *adj*

²exact *adj* **1** : showing strict, particular, and complete accordance with fact ⟨*exact* knowledge⟩ **2** : marked by thorough consideration or minute measurement of small factual details ⟨build an *exact* replica⟩ : not incomplete or approximate *syn see* CORRECT — **exact·ness** \-'zak(t)-nəs\ *n*

ex·act·ing \ig-'zak-tiŋ\ *adj* : making many or difficult demands upon a person : TRYING ⟨an *exacting* task⟩ ⟨an *exacting* teacher⟩ — **ex·act·ing·ly** \-tiŋ-lē\ *adv* — **ex·act·ing·ness** *n*

ex·ac·tion \ig-'zak-shən\ *n* **1 a** : the act or process of

exacting **b** : EXTORTION **2** : something exacted; *esp* : something demanded with compelling force

ex·ac·ti·tude \ig-'zak-tə-ˌt(y)üd\ *n* : EXACTNESS

ex·act·ly \ig-'zak-(t)lē\ *adv* **1** : in an exact manner : PRECISELY ⟨copy *exactly*⟩ ⟨at *exactly* three⟩ **2** : quite so : just as you say — used to express agreement

ex·ag·ger·ate \ig-'zaj-ə-ˌrāt\ *vb* [L *exaggerare*, lit., to heap up, fr. *ex-* + *agger* heap] **1** : to enlarge a fact or statement beyond what is actual or true : OVERSTATE **2** : to enlarge or increase esp. beyond the normal — **ex·ag·ger·at·ed·ly** \-ˌrāt-əd-lē\ *adv* — **ex·ag·ger·a·tion** \-ˌzaj-ə-'rā-shən\ *n* — **ex·ag·ger·a·tor** \-'zaj-ə-ˌrāt-ər\ *n*

ex·alt \ig-'zólt\ *vb* [L *exaltare*, fr. *ex-* + *altus* high] **1** : to raise high : ELEVATE **2** : to raise in rank, power, or character **3** : to elevate by praise or in estimation : GLORIFY — **ex·alt·er** *n*

ex·al·ta·tion \ˌeg-ˌzól-'tā-shən\ *n* **1** : the act of exalting : the state of being exalted **2** : a greatly heightened sense of personal well-being, power, or importance

ex·am \ig-'zam\ *n* : EXAMINATION

ex·am·i·na·tion \ig-ˌzam-ə-'nā-shən\ *n* **1** : the act or process of examining : the state of being examined **2** : an exercise designed to examine progress or test qualification or knowledge **3** : a formal interrogation — **ex·am·i·na·tion·al** \-shnəl, -shən-°l\ *adj*

ex·am·ine \ig-'zam-ən\ *vb* [L *examinare*, fr. *examin-*, *examen* tongue of a balance, examination, fr. *exigere* to drive out, weigh] **1 a** : to look at or inspect closely ⟨*examine* rock specimens⟩ **b** : to inquire into carefully : INVESTIGATE **2** : to test the condition of ⟨had his eyes *examined*⟩ **3** : to question closely in order to determine progress, fitness, or knowledge ⟨*examine* a class in arithmetic⟩ *syn see* SCRUTINIZE — **ex·am·in·er** *n*

ex·am·ple \ig-'zam-pəl\ *n* [MF, fr. L *exemplum*, fr. *eximere* to take out, fr. *ex-* + *emere* to take] **1** : a sample of something taken to show what the whole is like ⟨a striking *example* of scientific method⟩ **2** : a problem to be solved in order to show how a rule works ⟨an *example* in arithmetic⟩ **3** : something to be imitated : MODEL ⟨set a good *example* for others⟩ **4** : punishment inflicted as a warning to others *syn see* INSTANCE

ex·an·them \ig-'zan(t)-thəm\ *also* **ex·an·the·ma** \ˌeg-zan-'thē-mə\ *n, pl* **exanthems** *also* **ex·an·them·a·ta** \ˌeg-ˌzan-'them-ət-ə, -'thē-mət-\ *or* **exanthemas** [Gk *exanthēma*, fr. *exanthein* to bloom, break out, fr. *ex-* + *anthos* flower] : an eruptive disease (as measles) or its symptomatic eruption — **ex·an·them·a·tous** \ˌeg-ˌzan-'them-ət-əs\ *adj*

ex·arch \'ek-ˌsärk\ *n* : an Eastern bishop ranking below a patriarch and above a metropolitan; *esp* : the head of an independent church — **ex·ar·chal** \ek-'sär-kəl\ *adj* — **ex·arch·ate** \'ek-ˌsär-kət\ *n* — **ex·ar·chy** \'ek-ˌsär-kē\ *n*

ex·as·per·ate \ig-'zas-pə-ˌrāt\ *vt* [L *exasperare*, fr. *ex-* + *asper* rough] **1** : to make angry : ENRAGE **2** : to cause irritation or annoyance to *syn see* IRRITATE

ex·as·per·a·tion \ig-ˌzas-pə-'rā-shən\ *n* **1** : the act of exasperating : PROVOCATION **2** : the state of being exasperated : extreme irritation or annoyance : ANGER

Ex·cal·i·bur \ek-'skal-ə-bər\ *n* : the sword of King Arthur

ex ca·the·dra \ˌeks-kə-'thē-drə\ *adv* (*or adj*) [NL, lit., from the chair] : by virtue of or in the exercise of one's office

ex·ca·vate \'ek-skə-ˌvāt\ *vt* **1** : to hollow out : form a hole in **2** : to make by hollowing out ⟨*excavate* a tunnel⟩ **3** : to dig out and remove ⟨*excavate* sand⟩ **4** : to uncover by digging away covering earth — **ex·ca·va·tor** \-ˌvāt-ər\ *n*

ex·ca·va·tion \ˌek-skə-'vā-shən\ *n* : the act or process of excavating **2** : a hollowed-out place formed by excavating

ex·ceed \ik-'sēd\ *vb* [L *excedere*, fr. *ex-* + *cedere* to go] **1** : to extend outside of ⟨the river will *exceed* its banks⟩ **2** : to be greater than or superior to : SURPASS, PREDOMINATE **3** : to go beyond a limit set by ⟨*exceeded* his authority⟩

syn EXCEL, SURPASS, TRANSCEND: EXCEED implies going beyond a limit or standard set by authority, custom, or previous achievement ⟨*exceed* last year's production⟩ EXCEL implies preeminence in achievement or quality

⟨*excelling* in athletics⟩ ⟨*excels* in writing dialogue⟩ SURPASS suggests superiority in quality, merit, or skill; TRANSCEND implies a rising or extending notably above or beyond ordinary limits ⟨writing that *transcends* prosaic statement⟩

ex·ceed·ing *adj* : exceptional in amount, quality, or degree : EXTRAORDINARY

ex·ceed·ing·ly \ik-'sēd-iŋ-lē\ *or* **ex·ceed·ing** *adv* : EXTREMELY

ex·cel \ik-'sel\ *vb* **ex·celled**; **ex·cel·ling** [L *excellere*, fr. *ex-* + *-cellere* to rise, project; akin to E *hill*] : to outdo others (as in good qualities or ability) : be better than others : SURPASS ⟨a pupil that *excels* in arithmetic⟩ ⟨a jump *excelling* the previous record⟩ **syn** see EXCEED

ex·cel·lence \'ek-s(ə-)lən(t)s\ *n* **1** : the quality of being excellent **2** : an excellent or valuable quality : VIRTUE **3** : EXCELLENCY **2**

ex·cel·len·cy \'ek-s(ə-)lən-sē\ *n, pl* **-cies** **1** : EXCELLENCE **2** — used as a title for high dignitaries of state (as a governor or an ambassador) and church (as a Roman Catholic archbishop or bishop)

ex·cel·lent \'ek-s(ə-)lənt\ *adj* : very good of its kind : eminently good : FIRST-CLASS — **ex·cel·lent·ly** *adv*

ex·cel·si·or \ik-'sel-sē-ər\ *n* [trade name, fr. L, higher, compar. of *excelsus* high, fr. pp. of *excellere* to excel] : fine curled wood shavings used esp. for packing fragile items

¹ex·cept \ik-'sept\ *vt* [L *exceptare*, freq. of *excipere* to take out, except, fr. *ex-* + *capere* to take] : to take or leave out from a number or a whole : EXCLUDE

²except *also* **ex·cept·ing** *prep* **1** : with the exclusion or exception of ⟨everybody *except* him⟩ **2** : otherwise than : other than ⟨take no orders *except* from me⟩

³except *also* **excepting** *conj* : UNLESS ⟨*except* you repent⟩

ex·cep·tion \ik-'sep-shən\ *n* **1** : the act of excepting : EXCLUSION **2** : one that is excepted **3** : something offered as objection or taken as objectionable

ex·cep·tion·a·ble \ik-'sep-sh(ə-)nə-bəl\ *adj* : likely to cause objection : OBJECTIONABLE — **ex·cep·tion·a·bly** \-blē\ *adv*

ex·cep·tion·al \ik-'sep-shnəl, -shən-ⁿl\ *adj* **1** : forming an exception : RARE **2** : better than average : SUPERIOR — **ex·cep·tion·al·ly** \-ē\ *adv* — **ex·cep·tion·al·ness** *n*

¹ex·cerpt \ek-'sərpt, eg-'zərpt, 'ek-ˌ, 'eg-ˌ\ *vt* [L *excerpere*, fr. *ex-* + *carpere* to gather, pluck] : to select for quoting : EXTRACT

²ex·cerpt \'ek-ˌsərpt, 'eg-ˌzərpt\ *n* : a passage selected or copied : EXTRACT

¹ex·cess \ik-'ses, 'ek-ˌ\ *n* [LL *excessus*, fr. L *excess-*, *excedere* to exceed] **1 a** : a state of surpassing limits : SUPERFLUITY **b** : something that exceeds what is usual, proper, or specified **c** : the amount or degree by which one thing or quantity exceeds another **2** : INTEMPERANCE

²excess *adj* : more than the usual, proper, or specified amount

ex·ces·sive \ik-'ses-iv\ *adj* : exceeding the usual, proper, or normal — **ex·ces·sive·ly** *adv* — **ex·ces·sive·ness** *n* **syn** EXCESSIVE, EXORBITANT, INORDINATE mean going beyond a normal limit. EXCESSIVE implies an amount or degree too great to be reasonable or acceptable ⟨*excessive* bail was required⟩ EXORBITANT applies to what is grossly excessive ⟨*exorbitant* demands⟩ INORDINATE implies an exceeding of the limits dictated by reason or good judgment ⟨*inordinate* appetite⟩ ⟨*inordinate* desire for power⟩

¹ex·change \iks-'chānj, 'eks-ˌ\ *n* **1** : a giving or taking one thing in return for another : TRADE **2** : the act of substituting one thing for another **3** : something offered, given, or received in an exchange **4 a** : funds payable at a distant point in foreign or domestic currency **b** (1) : interchange of two kinds of money (as money of two different countries) with allowance for difference in value (2) : the amount of one currency that will buy a given amount of another **5** : a place where things or services are exchanged: as **a** : an organized market or center for trading in securities or commodities **b** : a central office in which telephone lines are connected to permit communication

²exchange *vt* **1** : to give in exchange : TRADE, SWAP ⟨*exchange* a knife for a book⟩ **2** : to part with for a substitute ⟨unwilling to *exchange* his home for a palace⟩ — **ex·change·a·ble** \-ə-bəl\ *adj* — **ex·chang·er** *n*

exchange student *n* : a student from a usu. foreign country

received into an institution in exchange for one sent to that country

ex·che·quer \'eks-ˌchek-ər, iks-'\ *n* **1** : the department or office of state in Great Britain and Northern Ireland charged with the receipt and care of the national revenue **2** : TREASURY; *esp* : a national or royal treasury **3** : pecuniary resources : FUNDS

ex·cip·i·ent \ik-'sip-ē-ənt\ *n* [L *excipient-, excipiens*, prp. of *excipere* to take out, take up, fr. *ex-* + *capere* to take] : an inert substance that forms a vehicle (as for a drug)

¹ex·cise \'ek-ˌsīz, -ˌsīs\ *n* [obs. D *excijs*] : an internal tax levied on the manufacture, sale, or consumption of a commodity within a country

²ex·cise \ek-'sīz\ *vt* [L *excis-, excidere*, fr. *ex-* + *caedere* to cut] : to remove by cutting out — **ex·ci·sion** \-'sizh-ən\ *n*

ex·cit·a·ble \ik-'sīt-ə-bəl\ *adj* : readily roused into action or an active state; *esp* : capable of activation by and reaction to stimuli — **ex·cit·a·bil·i·ty** \-ˌsīt-ə-'bil-ət-ē\ *n*

ex·ci·ta·tion \ˌek-ˌsī-'tā-shən, ˌek-sə-\ *n* : EXCITEMENT; *esp* : the irritability induced in protoplasm by a stimulus

ex·cit·a·to·ry \ik-'sīt-ə-ˌtōr-ē, -ˌtòr-\ *adj* : exhibiting or marked by excitement or excitation

ex·cite \ik-'sīt\ *vt* [L *excitare*, fr. *ex-* + *citare* to rouse] **1 a** : to call to activity **b** : to rouse to feeling **2 a** : ENERGIZE **b** : to produce a magnetic field in **3** : to increase the activity of (as nervous tissue) : STIMULATE **4** : to raise (as an atom) to a higher energy level **syn** see PROVOKE

ex·cit·ed \-'sīt-əd\ *adj* : having or showing strong feeling : worked up : STIRRED — **ex·cit·ed·ly** *adv*

ex·cite·ment \ik-'sīt-mənt\ *n* **1** : the act of exciting : the state of being excited **2** : something that excites or rouses

ex·cit·er \-'sīt-ər\ *n* : one that excites

ex·cit·ing \-'sīt-iŋ\ *adj* : causing excitement : STIRRING — **ex·cit·ing·ly** \-iŋ-lē\ *adv*

ex·claim \iks-'klām\ *vb* [L *exclamare*, fr. *ex-* + *clamare* to cry out] **1** : to cry out or speak in strong or sudden emotion **2** : to speak loudly or vehemently

ex·cla·ma·tion \ˌeks-klə-'mā-shən\ *n* **1** : a sharp or sudden utterance : OUTCRY **2** : vehement expression of protest or complaint

exclamation point *n* : a punctuation mark ! used chiefly after an interjection or exclamation to show forceful utterance or strong feeling

ex·clam·a·to·ry \iks-'klam-ə-ˌtōr-ē, -ˌtòr-\ *adj* : containing, expressing, using, or relating to exclamation ⟨an *exclamatory* phrase⟩

ex·clude \iks-'klüd\ *vt* [L *exclus-, excludere*, fr. *ex-* + *claudere* to close] **1 a** : to shut out **b** : to bar from participation, consideration, or inclusion **2** : to put out : EXPEL — **ex·clud·a·ble** \-'klüd-ə-bəl\ *adj* — **ex·clud·er** *n* — **ex·clu·sion** \-'klü-zhən\ *n*

ex·clu·sive \iks-'klü-siv, -ziv\ *adj* **1** : excluding or inclined to exclude certain persons or classes (as from ownership, membership, or privileges) : catering to a special esp. fashionable class ⟨an *exclusive* neighborhood⟩ ⟨an *exclusive* school⟩ **2** : SOLE, SINGLE ⟨*exclusive* use of a beach⟩ **3** : COMPLETE, UNDIVIDED ⟨gave their *exclusive* attention⟩ **4** : not taking account : not inclusive ⟨for five days *exclusive* of today⟩ — **ex·clu·sive·ly** *adv* — **ex·clu·sive·ness** *n*

ex·cog·i·tate \eks-'käj-ə-ˌtāt\ *vt* : to think out : DEVISE — **ex·cog·i·ta·tion** \eks-ˌkäj-ə-'tā-shən\ *n* — **ex·cog·i·ta·tive** \eks-'käj-ə-ˌtāt-iv\ *adj*

ex·com·mu·ni·cate \ˌeks-kə-'myü-nə-ˌkāt\ *vt* : to bar officially from the rights of church membership — **ex·com·mu·ni·ca·tion** \-ˌmyü-nə-kā-shən\ *n* — **ex·com·mu·ni·ca·tor** \-'myü-nə-ˌkāt-ər\ *n*

ex·co·ri·ate \ek-'skōr-ē-ˌāt, -'skòr-\ *vt* [LL *excoriare*, fr. L *ex-* + *corium* skin, hide] **1** : to wear off the skin of : ABRADE **2** : to censure scathingly — **ex·co·ri·a·tion** \(ˌ)ek-ˌskōr-ē-'ā-shən, -ˌskòr-\ *n*

ex·cre·ment \'ek-skrə-mənt\ *n* : waste matter discharged from the body and esp. from the alimentary canal — **ex·cre·men·tal** \ˌek-skrə-'ment-ⁿl\ *or* **ex·cre·men·ti·tious** \-ˌmen-'tish-əs\ *adj*

ex·cres·cence \ek-'skres-ⁿn(t)s\ *n* : OUTGROWTH; *esp* : an abnormal outgrowth (as a wart) on the body

ex·cres·cent \-ⁿnt\ *adj* [L *excrescere* to grow out, fr. *ex-*

+ *crescere* to grow] **:** being or forming an excrescence — **ex·cres·cent·ly** *adv*

ex·cre·ta \ek-'skrēt-ə\ *n pl* **:** waste matter eliminated or separated from an organism

ex·crete \ek-'skrēt\ *vt* [L *excret-, excernere* to sift out, discharge, fr. *ex-* + *cernere* to sift] **:** to separate and eliminate (waste) from the blood or tissues or from the active protoplasm usu. in the form of sweat or urine — **ex·cret·er** *n*

ex·cre·tion \ek-'skrē-shən\ *n* **1 :** the act or process of excreting **2 :** excreted matter

ex·cre·to·ry \'ek-skrə-,tōr-ē, -,tòr-\ *adj* **:** of, relating to, or functioning in excretion

ex·cru·ci·ate \ik-'skrü-shē-,āt\ *vt* [L *excruciare,* fr. *ex-* + *cruciare* to crucify, fr. *cruc-, crux* cross] **:** to subject to intense pain or mental distress — **ex·cru·ci·a·tion** \-,skrü-s(h)ē-'ā-shən\ *n*

ex·cru·ci·at·ing \-'skrü-shē-,āt-iŋ\ *adj* **1 :** causing great pain or anguish **:** AGONIZING **2 :** very intense **:** EXTREME — **ex·cru·ci·at·ing·ly** \-iŋ-lē\ *adv*

ex·cul·pate \'ek-(,)skəl-,pāt, ek-'\ *vt* [L *ex* + *culpa* blame] **:** to clear from alleged fault or guilt — **ex·cul·pa·tion** \,ek-(,)skəl-'pā-shən\ *n* — **ex·cul·pa·to·ry** \ek-'skəl-pə-,tōr-ē, -,tòr-\ *adj*

ex·cur·rent \ek-'skər-ənt, -'skə-rənt\ *adj* **1 :** having a main stem continuous to the apex (the spruce is an *excurrent* tree)—compare DELIQUESCENT **2 :** characterized by a current that flows outward (*excurrent* canals of a sponge)

ex·cur·sion \ik-'skər-zhən\ *n* [L *excurs-, excurrere* to run out, fr. *ex-* + *currere* to run] **1 a :** a going out or forth **:** EXPEDITION **b :** a usu. brief pleasure trip; *esp* **:** such a trip at special reduced rates **2 :** deviation from a direct or proper course; *esp* **:** DIGRESSION **3 :** a movement outward or from a mean position or axis; *also* **:** the distance traversed **:** AMPLITUDE

ex·cur·sion·ist \ik-'skərzh-(ə-)nəst\ *n* **:** a person who goes on an excursion

ex·cur·sive \ik-'skər-siv\ *adj* **:** constituting a digression **:** characterized by digression — **ex·cur·sive·ly** *adv* — **ex·cur·sive·ness** *n*

ex·cur·sus \ik-'skər-səs\ *n, pl* **ex·cur·sus·es** *also* **ex·cur·sus** \-səs, -,süs\ **:** an appendix or a digression containing further exposition of some point or topic

¹ex·cuse \ik-'skyüz\ *vt* [L *excusare,* fr. *ex-* + *causa* cause, explanation] **1 :** to make apology for **:** try to remove blame from (*excused* himself for being late) **2 :** to accept an excuse for **:** PARDON **3 :** to free or let off from doing something (*excuse* a person from a debt) **4 :** to serve as an acceptable reason or explanation for (something said or done) **:** JUSTIFY (nothing can *excuse* dishonesty) — **ex·cus·a·ble** \-'skyü-zə-bəl\ *adj* — **ex·cus·a·bly** \-blē\ *adv* — **ex·cus·er** *n*

syn CONDONE, PARDON, FORGIVE: EXCUSE implies an overlooking of a fault, omission, or failure without censure or due punishment; CONDONE suggests accepting without protest or censure a reprehensible act or condition (condemning murder while *condoning* war) PARDON implies freeing from penalty due for admitted or proved offense; FORGIVE implies a sincere change of feeling that makes no claim to retaliation and gives up resentment or desire for revenge

²ex·cuse \ik-'skyüs\ *n* **1 :** the act of excusing **2 a :** something offered as grounds for being excused **b :** a note of explanation of an absence **3 :** JUSTIFICATION, REASON **syn** see APOLOGY

ex·ec \ig-'zek\ *n* **:** EXECUTIVE OFFICER

ex·e·cra·ble \'ek-si-krə-bəl\ *adj* **:** DETESTABLE, ABOMINABLE — **ex·e·cra·ble·ness** *n* — **ex·e·cra·bly** \-blē\ *adv*

ex·e·crate \'ek-sə-,krāt\ *vt* [L *exsecrari* to put under a curse, fr. *ex* + *sacr-, sacer* sacred] **1 :** to declare to be evil or detestable **:** DENOUNCE **2 :** to detest utterly **:** ABHOR — **ex·e·cra·tion** \,ek-sə-'krā-shən\ *n* — **ex·e·cra·tor** \'ek-sə-,krāt-ər\ *n*

ex·e·cute \'ek-sə-,kyüt\ *vt* [L *exsecut-, exsequi,* fr. *ex-* + *sequi* to follow] **1 :** to put into effect **:** carry out **:** PERFORM **2 :** to do what is provided or required by (*execute* a decree) **3 :** to put to death in compliance with a legal sentence **4 :** to make or produce esp. by carrying out a design **5 :** to perform what is required to give validity to (*execute* a deed) — **ex·e·cut·er** *n*

ex·e·cu·tion \,ek-sə-'kyü-shən\ *n* **1 :** the act or process of executing **:** PERFORMANCE (put a plan into *execution*) **2 :** a putting to death as a legal penalty **3 :** a judicial writ empowering an officer to carry out a judgment **4 :** the act or mode or result of performance in something requiring special skill or technique (a statue perfect in its *execution*) **5 :** effective and esp. destructive action (did terrible *execution* among the enemy's ships)

ex·e·cu·tion·er \-'kyü-sh(ə-)nər\ *n* **:** one that executes; *esp* **:** one who puts into effect a sentence of death

¹ex·ec·u·tive \ig-'zek-(y)ət-iv\ *adj* **1 :** designed for or relating to the execution of affairs (*executive* ability) **2 :** of or relating to the execution of the laws and the conduct of public affairs **3 :** of or relating to an executive

²executive *n* **1 :** the executive branch of a government **2 :** an individual or group constituting the agency that directs an organization **3 :** one who holds a position of administrative or managerial responsibility

executive agreement *n* **:** an agreement between the U.S. and a foreign government made by the executive

executive officer *n* **:** the officer second in command of a military or naval organization

executive session *n* **:** a usu. closed session esp. of a legislative body

ex·ec·u·tor \ig-'zek-(y)ət-ər, *in sense 1 also* 'ek-sə-,kyüt-\ *n* **1 :** one who executes something **2 :** the person designated in a will as the one to carry out its provisions

ex·ec·u·trix \ig-'zek-(y)ə-(,)triks\ *n, pl* **ex·ec·u·trix·es** *or* **ex·ec·u·tri·ces** \-,zek-(y)ə-'trī-,sēz\ **:** a female executor

ex·e·ge·sis \,ek-sə-'jē-səs\ *n, pl* **-ge·ses** \-'jē-,sēz\ [Gk *exēgēsis,* fr. *exēgeisthai* to explain, fr. *ex-* + *hēgeisthai* to lead] **:** explanation or critical interpretation of a text — **ex·e·get·ic** \-'jet-ik\ *or* **ex·e·get·i·cal** \-'jet-i-kəl\ *adj* — **ex·e·get·i·cal·ly** \-i-k(ə-)lē\ *adv*

ex·e·gete \'ek-sə-,jēt\ *n* **:** one who practices exegesis

ex·em·plar \ig-'zem-,plär, -plər\ *n* [L, fr. *exemplum* example] **1 a :** one that serves as a model or pattern; *esp* **:** an ideal model **b :** ARCHETYPE **2 :** a typical instance **:** EXAMPLE; *esp* **:** a typical or standard specimen

ex·em·pla·ry \ig-'zem-plə-rē\ *adj* **1 a :** serving as a pattern **b :** deserving imitation **:** COMMENDABLE **2 :** serving as a warning **3 :** serving as an example, instance, or illustration — **ex·em·plar·i·ly** \,eg-zəm-'pler-ə-lē\ *adv* — **ex·em·pla·ri·ness** \ig-'zem-plə-rē-nəs\ *n*

ex·em·pli·fy \ig-'zem-plə-,fī\ *vt* **-fied; -fy·ing 1 :** to show or illustrate by example **2 :** to serve as an example of — **ex·em·pli·fi·ca·tion** \-,zem-plə-fə-'kā-shən\ *n*

¹ex·empt \ig-'zem(p)t\ *adj* [L *exemptus,* pp. of *eximere* to take out, fr. *ex-* + *emere* to take] **:** free or released from an obligation or requirement to which others are subject

²exempt *vt* **:** to make exempt **:** free from a requirement to which others are subject **:** EXCUSE

ex·emp·tion \ig-'zem(p)-shən\ *n* **1 :** the act of exempting **:** the state of being exempt **:** IMMUNITY **2 :** one that exempts or is exempted; *esp* **:** a source of income exempted from taxation

ex·e·quy \'ek-sə-kwē\ *n, pl* **-quies** [L *exsequiae,* pl., fr. *exsequi* to follow out] **:** a funeral rite — usu. used in pl.

¹ex·er·cise \'ek-sər-,sīz\ *n* [MF *exercice,* fr. L *exercitium,* fr. *exercit-, exercēre* to drive on, fr. *ex-* + *arcēre* to hold off] **1 :** the act of bringing into play or realizing in action **:** USE (by the *exercise* of his authority as governor) **2 a :** regular or repeated use of a faculty or bodily organ **b :** bodily exertion for the sake of physical fitness **3 :** something performed or practiced in order to develop, improve, or display a specific power or skill **4 a :** a maneuver or drill carried out for training and discipline **b** *pl* **:** a program including speeches, announcements of awards and honors, and various traditional practices

²exercise *vb* **1 :** to bring to bear **:** EXERT (*exercise* patience) (*exercise* influence) **2 a :** to use repeatedly in order to strengthen or develop (*exercise* a muscle) **b :** to train (as troops) by drills and maneuvers **c :** to put through exercises **:** give exercise to (*exercise* a dog) **3 :** to engage the attention of; *esp* **:** to cause anxiety, alarm, or indignation in (came home to find his family greatly *exercised* about his absence) **4 :** to take exercise — **ex·er·cis·a·ble** \-'sī-zə-bəl\ *adj* — **ex·er·cis·er** *n*

ex·er·gon·ic \,ek-sər-(,)sər-'gän-ik\ *adj* **:** liberating energy (an *exergonic* biochemical reaction)

---

j joke; ŋ sing; ō flow; ò flaw; òi coin; th thin; th̲ this; ü loot; u̇ foot; y yet; yü few; yu̇ furious; zh vision

ex·ert \ig-'zərt\ *vt* [L *exsert-, exserere* to thrust out, fr. *ex-* + *serere* to join] **1** : to put forth (as strength, force, power, or influence) : bring into play **2** : to put (oneself) into action or to tiring effort

ex·er·tion \ig-'zər-shən\ *n* : the act or an instance of exerting; *esp* : laborious or perceptible effort **syn** see EFFORT

ex·e·unt \'ek-sē-(,)ənt\ [L, they go out, fr. *exire* to go out, fr. *ex-* + *ire* to go] — used as a stage direction to specify that all or certain named characters leave the stage

ex·fo·li·ate \(')eks-'fō-lē-,āt\ *vb* : to shed or remove in thin layers or scales — **ex·fo·li·a·tion** \(,)eks-,fō-lē-'ā-shən\ *n* — **ex·fo·li·a·tive** \eks-'fō-lē-,āt-iv\ *adj*

ex·hal·ant \eks-'hā-lənt\ *adj* : bearing out or outward ⟨an *exhalant* siphon of a clam⟩

ex·ha·la·tion \,eks-(h)ə-'lā-shən\ *n* : an act or product of exhaling

ex·hale \eks-'hāl\ *vb* [L *exhalare*, fr. *ex-* + *halare* to breathe] **1** : to breathe out **2** : to send forth (as gas or odor) : EMIT ⟨the fragrance that flowers *exhale*⟩ **3** : to rise or be given off as vapor

1ex·haust \ig-'zȯst\ *vb* [L *exhaust-, exhaurire*, fr. *ex-* + *haurire* to draw] **1 a** : to draw off or let out completely ⟨*exhaust* the air from the jar⟩ **b** : to empty by drawing something from; *esp* : to create a vacuum in **2 a** : to use up the whole supply of **b** : to deprive wholly of (as strength, patience, or resources) **3 a** : to develop (a subject) completely **b** : to try out the whole number of ⟨had *exhausted* all possibilities⟩ **4** : to destroy the fertility of (soil) **5** : to pass or flow out : DISCHARGE, EMPTY — **ex·haust·er** *n* — **ex·haust·i·bil·i·ty** \-,zȯ-stə-'bil-ət-ē\ *n* — **ex·haust·i·ble** \-'zȯ-stə-bəl\ *adj*

2exhaust *n* **1 a** : the escape of used steam or gas from an engine **b** : the gas thus escaping **2 a** : a conduit through which used gases escape **b** : an arrangement for withdrawing fumes, dusts, or odors from an enclosure

ex·haus·tion \ig-'zȯs-chən\ *n* **1** : the act or process of exhausting **2** : the state of being exhausted; *esp* : extreme weariness or fatigue

ex·haus·tive \ig-'zȯ-stiv\ *adj* **1** : serving or tending to exhaust **2** : testing all possibilities or considering all elements : THOROUGH, COMPLETE — **ex·haus·tive·ly** *adv* — **ex·haus·tive·ness** *n*

ex·haust·less \ig-'zȯst-ləs\ *adj* : INEXHAUSTIBLE

1ex·hib·it \ig-'zib-ət\ *vt* [L *exhibit-, exhibēre*, fr. *ex-* + *habēre* to have, hold] **1** : to show outwardly : REVEAL ⟨*exhibit* an interest in music at an early age⟩ **2** : to put on display ⟨*exhibit* a collection of paintings⟩ **3** : to present in legal form (as to a court) **syn** see SHOW — **ex·hib·i·tor** *also* **ex·hib·it·er** \-ət-ər\ *n*

2exhibit *n* **1** : an act or instance of exhibiting **2** : something exhibited; *esp* : a document or material object produced and identified (as in a court) for use as evidence

ex·hi·bi·tion \,ek-sə-'bish-ən\ *n* **1** : an act or instance of exhibiting **2** *Brit* : a grant drawn from the funds of a school or university to help maintain a student **3** : a public showing (as of works of art, objects of manufacture, or athletic skill)

ex·hi·bi·tion·er \-'bish-(ə-)nər\ *n, Brit* : one who holds an exhibition (sense 2)

ex·hi·bi·tion·ism \-'bish-ə-,niz-əm\ *n* **1 a** : a perversion marked by a tendency to indecent exposure **b** : an act of such exposure **2** : the act or practice of behaving so as to attract attention to oneself — **ex·hi·bi·tion·ist** \-'bish-(ə-)nəst\ *n* — **exhibitionist** *or* **ex·hi·bi·tion·is·tic** \-,bish-ə-'nis-tik\ *adj*

ex·hil·a·rate \ig-'zil-ə-,rāt\ *vt* [L *exhilarare*, fr. *ex-* + *hilarus* cheerful] **1** : to make cheerful or jolly ⟨were *exhilarated* by the unexpected victory⟩ **2** : to fill with a lively sense of well-being : INVIGORATE ⟨an *exhilarating* autumn day⟩ — **ex·hil·a·ra·tive** \-,rāt-iv\ *adj*

ex·hil·a·ra·tion \ig-,zil-ə-'rā-shən\ *n* **1** : the action of exhilarating **2** : the state or the feeling of being exhilarated : high spirits : LIVELINESS

ex·hort \ig-'zȯrt\ *vb* [L *exhortari*, fr. *ex-* + *hortari* to incite] : to arouse by words (as of advice, encouragement, or warning) : urge or appeal strongly — **ex·hort·er** *n*

ex·hor·ta·tion \,eks-,ȯr-'tā-shən, ,egz-\ *n* **1** : an act or instance of exhorting **2** : a speech intended to exhort others : earnestly spoken words of urgent advice or warning

ex·hort·a·tive \ig-'zȯrt-ət-iv\ *adj* : serving to exhort

ex·hort·a·to·ry \-ə-,tȯr-ē, -,tȯr-\ *adj* : HORTATORY

ex·hume \igz-'(y)üm, iks-'(h)yüm\ *vt* [L *ex* out of + *humus* earth] **1** : to dig out of the ground; *esp* : to uncover and take out of a place of burial : DISINTER **2** : to bring back from neglect or obscurity — **ex·hu·ma·tion** \,eks-(h)yü-'mā-shən, ,egz-(y)ü-\ *n* — **ex·hum·er** *n*

ex·i·gence \'ek-sə-jən(t)s\ *n* : EXIGENCY

ex·i·gen·cy \'ek-sə-jən-sē, ig-'zij-ən-\ *n, pl* **-cies** : a case or a state of affairs demanding immediate action or remedy : an urgent need ⟨capable of dealing with the *exigencies* of any situation likely to arise⟩ **syn** see NEED

ex·i·gent \'ek-sə-jənt\ *adj* [L *exigere* to demand, fr. *ex-* + *agere* to drive] **1** : requiring immediate aid or action : URGENT **2** : requiring or calling for much : DEMANDING, EXACTING — **ex·i·gent·ly** *adv*

ex·ig·u·ous \eg-'zig-yə-wəs\ *adj* : scanty in amount — **ex·i·gu·i·ty** \,ek-sə-'gyü-ət-ē\ *n* — **ex·ig·u·ous·ly** \eg-'zig-yə-wəs-lē\ *adv* — **ex·ig·u·ous·ness** *n*

1ex·ile \'eg-,zīl, 'ek-,sīl\ *n* [L *exilium*] **1** : forced removal or voluntary absence from one's native country; *also* : the state of one so absent **2** : a person expelled from his country by authority

2exile *vt* : to banish or expel from one's own country or home

ex·ine \'ek-,sēn, -,sīn\ *n* : an outer layer (as of a spore)

ex·ist \ig-'zist\ *vi* [L *exsistere* to come into being, exist, fr. *ex-* + *sistere* to stand] **1** : to have actual being : be real : BE ⟨do unicorns *exist*⟩ **2** : to continue to be : LIVE ⟨earn hardly enough to *exist* on⟩ **3** : to be found : OCCUR ⟨a disease that once *existed* but has been wiped out⟩

ex·ist·ence \ig-'zis-tən(t)s\ *n* **1** : the fact or the state of having being or of being real ⟨believed in the *existence* of dragons⟩ ⟨the largest animal in *existence*⟩ **2** : continuance in living or way of living : LIFE ⟨owed his *existence* to a doctor's skill⟩ ⟨a happy *existence*⟩ **3** : actual occurrence ⟨recognized the *existence* of a state of war⟩ **4 a** : the sum total of existing things **b** : a specific being

ex·ist·ent \-tənt\ *adj* **1** : having being : EXISTING **2** : existing now : EXTANT

1ex·it \'eg-zət, 'ek-sət\ [L, he goes out, fr. *exire* to go out, fr. *ex-* + *ire* to go] — used as a stage direction to specify who goes off stage

2exit *n* [L *exitus*, fr. *exit-, exire* to go out] **1** [*1exit*] : a departure from a stage **2** : the act of going out or going away **3** : a way out of an enclosed place or space — **exit** *vi*

ex libris \eks-'lē-brəs\ *n, pl* **ex libris** [NL, from the books; used before the owner's name on bookplates] : BOOKPLATE

exo- *or* **ex-** *comb form* [Gk *exō* out, outside] : outside ⟨*exogamy*⟩ ⟨outer ⟨*exoskeleton*⟩ — compare ECT-, END-

exo·carp \'ek-sō-,kärp\ *n* : EPICARP

exo·crine \'ek-sə-krən, -,krīn, -,krēn\ *adj* [Gk *krinein* to separate] : secreting or secreted externally ⟨*exocrine* glands⟩

ex·o·don·tist \,ek-sə-'dänt-əst\ *n* [Gk *odont-, odous* tooth] : a dentist that specializes in the extraction of teeth

ex·o·dus \'ek-səd-əs\ *n* **1** *cap* — see BIBLE table **2** : a mass departure

exo·en·zyme \,ek-sō-'en-,zīm\ *n* : an enzyme that functions (as in the stomach) outside the cell

ex of·fi·cio \,eks-ə-'fish-ē-,ō\ *adv* (*or adj*) [LL] : by virtue or because of an office ⟨*ex officio* chairman⟩

ex·og·a·my \ek-'säg-ə-mē\ *n* **1** : marriage outside a specific group esp. as required by custom or law **2** : sexual reproduction between organisms not closely related — **ex·og·a·mous** \-məs\ *adj*

ex·og·e·nous \ek-'säj-ə-nəs\ *adj* : developing or originating outside the cell or body — **ex·og·e·nous·ly** *adv*

ex·on·er·ate \ig-'zän-ə-,rāt\ *vt* [L *exonerare*, fr. *ex-* + *oner-, onus* burden] : to clear from an accusation or from blame : declare innocent — **ex·on·er·a·tion** \ig-,zän-ə-'rā-shən\ *n* — **ex·on·er·a·tive** \ig-'zän-ə-,rāt-iv\ *adj*

ex·oph·thal·mos \,ek-,säf-'thal-məs, -,säp-'thal-\ *also* **ex·oph·thal·mus** \-məs\ *n* [Gk *ex* out + *ophthalmos* eye] : abnormal protrusion of the eyeball — **ex·oph·thal·mic** \-mik\ *adj*

ex·or·bi·tant \ig-'zȯr-bət-ənt\ *adj* : going beyond the limits of what is fair, reasonable, or expected : EXCESSIVE ⟨*exorbitant* prices⟩ ⟨a task that requires an *exorbitant* amount of time) **syn** see EXCESSIVE — **ex·or·bi·tance** \-bət-ən(t)s\ *n* — **ex·or·bi·tant·ly** *adv*

ex·or·cise \'ek-ˌsȯr-ˌsīz, -sər-\ *vt* [Gk *exorkizein,* fr. *ex-* + *horkizein* to bind by oath, fr. *horkos* oath] **1 :** to drive (as an evil spirit) off by calling upon some holy name or by spells **2 :** to free (as a person or place) from an evil spirit — **ex·or·cis·er** *n*

ex·or·cism \-ˌsiz-əm\ *n* **1 :** the act or practice of exorcising **2 :** a spell or formula used in exorcising — **ex·or·cist** \-ˌsist, -səst\ *n*

ex·or·di·um \eg-'zȯrd-ē-əm\ *n, pl* **-di·ums** *or* **-dia** \-ē-ə\ **:** a beginning or introduction esp. to a discourse or composition — **ex·or·di·al** \-ē-əl\ *adj*

exo·skel·e·ton \ˌek-sō-'skel-ət-ᵊn\ *n* **:** a hard supporting or protective structure (as of a crustacean) developed on the outside of the body — **exo·skel·e·tal** \-ət-ᵊl\ *adj*

ex·os·mo·sis \ˌek-ˌsäs-'mō-səs, -ˌsäz-\ *n* **:** passage of material through a membrane from a region of higher to a region of lower concentration — **ex·os·mot·ic** \-'mät-ik\ *adj*

exo·sphere \'ek-sō-ˌsfi(ə)r\ *n* **:** the outer fringe region of the atmosphere

ex·os·to·sis \ˌek-ˌsäs-'tō-səs\ *n, pl* **-to·ses** \-'tō-ˌsēz\ [Gk *ex* out of + *osteon* bone] **:** a bony or cartilaginous spur (as on a bone)

ex·o·ter·ic \ˌek-sə-'ter-ik\ *adj* **1 a :** suitable to be imparted to the public (the *exoteric* doctrine) **b :** belonging to the outer or less initiate circle **2 :** relating to the outside — **ex·o·ter·i·cal·ly** \-'ter-i-k(ə-)lē\ *adv*

exo·ther·mic \ˌek-sō-'thər-mik\ *or* **exo·ther·mal** \-məl\ *adj* **:** characterized by evolution of heat (an *exothermic* chemical reaction)

¹ex·ot·ic \ig-'zät-ik\ *adj* [Gk *exōtikos,* fr. *exō* outside, fr. *ex* out of] **1 :** introduced from another country **2** *archaic* **:** OUTLANDISH, ALIEN **3 :** strikingly or excitingly different or unusual (as in color or design) — **ex·ot·i·cal·ly** \-'zät-i-k(ə-)lē\ *adv* — **ex·ot·ic·ness** \-ik-nəs\ *n*

²exotic *n* **:** something (as a plant) that is exotic

ex·ot·i·cism \ig-'zät-ə-ˌsiz-əm\ *n* **1 :** the quality or state of being exotic **2 :** EXOTIC

exo·tox·in \ˌek-sō-'täk-sən\ *n* **:** a soluble poisonous substance given off by a microorganism

ex·pand \ik-'spand\ *vb* [L *expans-, expandere,* fr. *ex-* + *pandere* to spread] **1 :** to open wide : UNFOLD (a bird with wings *expanded*) **2 :** to take up or to cause to take up more space : ENLARGE, SWELL (metals *expand* under heat) **3 :** to develop more fully : work out in greater detail (*expand* an argument) (*expand* a sentence into a paragraph) **4 :** to state in enlarged form : write out in full (*expand* an equation) **5 :** to increase in quantity or scope (*expand* the currency) (*expand* a business) — **ex·pand·a·ble** \-'span-də-bəl\ *adj* — **ex·pand·er** *n*

syn EXPAND, DILATE, DISTEND, INFLATE mean to increase in size or volume. EXPAND applies to any enlarging that comes from within or outside or in any way, as in growth, unfolding, or addition of parts; DILATE suggests expansion of diameter or circumference (the drops *dilated* the pupils of his eyes) DISTEND implies swelling or stretching caused by pressure from within forcing extension outward (*distended* nostrils) INFLATE implies distension by the introduction of air or something insubstantial and suggests a liability to sudden collapse (*inflated* balloon) (*inflated* currency)

ex·panse \ik-'span(t)s\ *n* **:** the extent to which something spreads out : a wide space, area, or stretch (the vast *expanse* of the ocean)

ex·pan·si·ble \ik-'span(t)-sə-bəl\ *adj* **:** capable of being expanded

ex·pan·sile \ik-'span(t)-səl\ *adj* **:** of, relating to, or capable of expansion

ex·pan·sion \ik-'span-chən\ *n* **1 :** the act or process of expanding **2 :** the quality or state of being expanded **3 :** EXPANSE **4 a :** an expanded part **b :** something that results from an act of expanding **5 :** the result of an indicated operation : the expression of a function in the form of a series (the *expansion* of $(a + b)^2$ is $a^2 + 2ab + b^2$)

ex·pan·sive \ik-'span(t)-siv\ *adj* **1 :** having a capacity or a tendency to expand (gases are *expansive*) **2 :** causing or tending to cause expansion (an *expansive* force) **3 :** characterized by high spirits or benevolent inclina-

tions (in an *expansive* mood) **4 :** having considerable extent (*expansive* grounds) (too *expansive* a subject for brief treatment) — **ex·pan·sive·ly** *adv* — **ex·pan·sive·ness** *n*

ex par·te \(')eks-'pärt-ē\ *adj* (*or adv*) [ML, on behalf] **:** from a one-sided or partisan point of view

ex·pa·ti·ate \ek-'spā-shē-ˌāt\ *vi* **:** to speak or write at length or in detail — **ex·pa·ti·a·tion** \(ˌ)ek-ˌspā-shē-'ā-shən\ *n*

¹ex·pa·tri·ate \ek-'spā-trē-ˌāt\ *vb* **1 :** to drive into exile : BANISH **2 :** to withdraw (oneself) from residence in or allegiance to one's native country **3 :** to leave one's native country; *esp* **:** to renounce allegiance to one's native country — **ex·pa·tri·a·tion** \(ˌ)ek-ˌspā-trē-'ā-shən\ *n*

²ex·pa·tri·ate \ek-'spā-trē-ˌāt, -trē-ət\ *adj* **:** living in a foreign country : EXPATRIATED — **expatriate** *n*

ex·pect \ik-'spekt\ *vb* [L *exspectare* to look forward to, fr. *ex-* + *spectare,* freq. of *specere* to look] **1 :** to look forward **2 :** to anticipate the birth of a child (she is *expecting*) **3 :** SUPPOSE, THINK **4 :** to anticipate or look forward to the coming or occurrence of (was *expecting* a telephone call) **5 a :** to consider probable or certain (*expect* to be forgiven) **b :** to consider reasonable, due, or necessary (*expect* an honest day's work) **c :** to consider obligated or in duty bound (told him they *expected* him to pay his dues) — **ex·pect·a·ble** \-'spek-tə-bəl\ *adj* — **ex·pect·a·bly** \-blē\ *adv*

ex·pect·ance \ik-'spek-tən(t)s\ *n* **:** EXPECTATION

ex·pect·an·cy \ik-'spek-tən-sē\ *n, pl* **-cies 1 a :** the act or state of expecting **b :** the state of being expected **2 a :** something expected **b :** the expected amount (as of the number of years of life) based on statistical probability

ex·pect·ant \-tənt\ *adj* **:** characterized by or being in a state of expectation — **expectant** *n* — **ex·pect·ant·ly** *adv*

ex·pec·ta·tion \ˌek-ˌspek-'tā-shən, ik-\ *n* **1 :** the act or state of expecting **:** a looking forward to or waiting for something **2 :** prospect of the future **:** grounds for expecting something; *esp* **:** prospects of inheritance — usu. used in pl. **3 :** something expected **4 :** the product of the probability that an event will occur and the amount to be received if it does occur — called also *mathematical expectation*

ex·pec·to·rant \ik-'spek-tə-rənt\ *adj* **:** tending to promote discharge of mucus from the respiratory tract — **expectorant** *n*

ex·pec·to·rate \ik-'spek-tə-ˌrāt\ *vb* [L *expectorare* to cast out of mind, fr. *ex* out of + *pector-, pectus* breast, soul] **:** to discharge (as phlegm) from the throat or lungs by coughing and spitting; *also* **:** SPIT — **ex·pec·to·ra·tion** \-ˌspek-tə-'rā-shən\ *n*

ex·pe·di·ence \ik-'spēd-ē-ən(t)s\ *n* **:** EXPEDIENCY

ex·pe·di·en·cy \ik-'spēd-ē-ən-sē\ *n, pl* **-cies 1 :** the quality or state of being suited to the end in view **:** suitability or convenience in a particular situation **2 :** the use of means and methods advantageous to oneself without regard to principles of fairness and rightness (was guided in his life solely by *expediency*)

¹ex·pe·di·ent \ik-'spēd-ē-ənt\ *adj* [L *expedient-, expediens,* prp. of *expedire* to extricate, be advantageous, fr. *ex-* + *ped-, pes* foot] **:** suitable for bringing about a desired result often without regard to fairness or rightness (the cheaper and more *expedient* of two methods) — **ex·pe·di·ent·ly** *adv*

syn POLITIC, ADVISABLE: EXPEDIENT usu. applies to what is immediately advantageous often without regard for ethics; POLITIC may apply to what is judicious and of tactical value and sometimes suggests an artful ulterior motive (found it *politic* to have the children on her side) ADVISABLE applies to what is practical, prudent, or advantageous without derogatory implication (*advisable* to drive carefully)

²expedient *n* **1 :** something expedient **2 :** a means to accomplish an end; *esp* **:** one used in place of a better means that is not available

ex·pe·dite \'ek-spə-ˌdīt\ *vt* **1 :** to carry out rapidly : execute promptly **2 :** to accelerate the process or progress of : FACILITATE **3 :** to send out : DISPATCH

ex·pe·dit·er *also* **ex·pe·di·tor** \-ˌdīt-ər\ *n* **:** one that expedites; *esp* **:** one employed to ensure adequate supplies of raw materials and equipment or to coordinate the flow of materials, tools, parts, and processed goods within a plant

ex·pe·di·tion \,ek-spə-'dish-ən\ *n* **1 :** efficient promptness **:** SPEED, EXPEDITIOUSNESS **2 a :** a sending or setting forth for some object or purpose **b :** a journey or trip undertaken for a specific purpose (as for war or exploring) **c :** a group (as a military force) making such a journey

ex·pe·di·tion·ary \-'dish-ə-,ner-ē\ *adj* **:** of, relating to, or constituting an expedition; *esp* **:** sent on military service abroad (an *expeditionary* force)

ex·pe·di·tious \,ek-spə-'dish-əs\ *adj* **:** characterized by or acting with promptness and efficiency **:** SPEEDY — **ex·pe·di·tious·ly** *adv* — **ex·pe·di·tious·ness** *n*

ex·pel \ik-'spel\ *vt* **ex·pelled; ex·pel·ling** [L *expuls-, expellere,* fr. *ex-* + *pellere* to drive] **1 :** to drive or force out (*expel* air from the lungs) **2 :** to drive away; *esp* **:** DEPORT **3 :** to cut off from membership (*expelled* from college) **syn** see EJECT — **ex·pel·la·ble** \-'spel-ə-bəl\ *adj*

ex·pel·lant *or* **ex·pel·lent** \ik-'spel-ənt\ *adj* [L *expellent-, expellens,* prp. of *expellere*] **:** tending or serving to expel (an *expellant* medicine) — **expellant** *n*

ex·pend \ik-'spend\ *vt* [L *expens-, expendere,* fr. *ex-* + *pendere* to weigh, pay] **1 :** to pay out **:** SPEND (social services for which public funds are *expended*) **2 :** to consume by use **:** use up

¹ex·pend·a·ble \ik-'spen-də-bəl\ *adj* **:** that may be used up in an ordinary way or sacrificed to accomplish a mission (*expendable* ammunition) (*expendable* troops) — **ex·pend·a·bil·i·ty** \-,pen-də-'bil-ət-ē\ *n* — **ex·pend·a·bly** \-'pen-də-blē\ *adv*

²expendable *n* **:** an item of equipment or a member or unit of an armed force that is regarded as expendable

ex·pen·di·ture \ik-'spen-di-chər, -də-,chur\ *n* **1 :** the act or process of expending **2 :** an amount (as of money or time) expended **:** DISBURSEMENT, EXPENSE

ex·pense \ik-'spen(t)s\ *n* **1 a :** something expended to secure a benefit or bring about a result **b :** financial burden or outlay **:** COST **2 :** a cause of expenditure **3 :** SACRIFICE — usu. used in the phrase *at the expense of*

expense account *n* **:** an account of expenses reimbursable to an employee

ex·pen·sive \ik-'spen(t)-siv\ *adj* **1 :** occasioning expense (*expensive* journey) **2 :** high-priced **:** DEAR **syn** see COSTLY — **ex·pen·sive·ly** *adv* — **ex·pen·sive·ness** *n*

¹ex·pe·ri·ence \ik-'spir-ē-ən(t)s\ *n* [L *experientia* act of trying, fr. *experiri* to try] **1 a :** the usu. conscious perception or apprehension of reality or of an event **b :** the sum total of the conscious events that make up an individual life or the past of a community, nation, or mankind generally **2 a :** the actual living through an event or series of events (learn by *experience*) **b :** something that one has actually done or lived through (a soldier's *experiences* in war) **3 a :** the skill or knowledge gained by actually doing or feeling a thing (a job that requires men with *experience*) **b :** the amount or kind of work a person or animal has done or the time during which work has been done (a man with five years' *experience*) — **ex·pe·ri·en·tial** \-,spir-ē-'en-chəl\ *adj*

²experience *vt* **1 :** to have experience of **:** UNDERGO **2 :** to learn by experience

ex·pe·ri·enced \ik-'spir-ē-ən(t)st\ *adj* **:** having experience **:** made skillful or wise through experience (an *experienced* pilot)

¹ex·per·i·ment \ik-'sper-ə-mənt\ *n* **1 a :** TEST, TRIAL **b :** a tentative procedure or policy **c :** an operation carried out under controlled conditions in order to discover an unknown effect or law, to test or establish a hypothesis, or to illustrate a known law **2 :** the process of testing **:** EXPERIMENTATION

²ex·per·i·ment \-,ment\ *vi* **:** to make experiments — **ex·per·i·men·ta·tion** \ik-,sper-ə-mən-'tā-shən, -,men-\ *n* — **ex·per·i·ment·er** \-'sper-ə-,ment-ər\ *n*

ex·per·i·men·tal \ik-,sper-ə-'ment-ᵊl\ *adj* **1 :** of, relating to, or based on experience **:** EMPIRICAL **2 :** founded on or derived from experiment **3 :** serving the ends of or used for experimentation **4 :** relating to or having the characteristics of experiment **:** TENTATIVE — **ex·per·i·men·tal·ly** \-ᵊl-ē\ *adv*

experiment station *n* **:** an establishment for scientific

research (as in agriculture) esp. of practical application and for the dissemination of information

¹ex·pert \'ek-,spərt, ik-'\ *adj* [L *expertus,* fr. pp. of *experiri* to try] **:** having, involving, or displaying special skill or knowledge derived from training or experience **syn** see PROFICIENT — **ex·pert·ly** *adv* — **ex·pert·ness** *n*

²ex·pert \'ek-,spərt\ *n* **:** one who has acquired special skill in or knowledge of a subject

ex·per·tise \,ek-(,)spər-'tēz, -,sper-\ *n* **:** EXPERTNESS

ex·pi·ate \'ek-spē-,āt\ *vt* [L *expiare* to atone for, fr. *ex-* + *piare* to appease] **1 :** to atone for **:** to pay the penalty for **2 :** to make amends for — **ex·pi·a·ble** \-spē-ə-bəl\ *adj* — **ex·pi·a·tor** \-,āt-ər\ *n*

ex·pi·a·tion \,ek-spē-'ā-shən\ *n* **1 :** the act of making atonement **2 :** the means by which atonement is made

ex·pi·a·to·ry \'ek-spē-ə-,tōr-ē, -,tȯr-\ *adj* **:** serving to expiate

ex·pi·ra·tion \,ek-spə-'rā-shən\ *n* **1 a :** the expelling of air from the lungs in breathing; *also* **:** air or vapor so expelled **b** *archaic* **:** the last emission of breath **:** DEATH **2 :** the fact of coming to an end **:** TERMINATION

ex·pi·ra·to·ry \(')ek-'spī-rə-,tōr-ē, -,tȯr-\ *adj* **:** of, relating to, or used in respiratory expiration

ex·pire \ik-'spī(ə)r, oftenest for 3 ek-\ *vb* [L *exspirare,* fr. *ex-* + *spirare* to breathe] **1 :** DIE **2 :** to come to an end **:** STOP **3 a :** to emit the breath **b :** to breathe out from or as if from the lungs

ex·pi·ry \ik-'spī(ə)r-ē, 'ek-spə-rē\ *n, pl* **-ries 1 a :** exhalation of breath **b :** DEATH **2 :** TERMINATION; *esp* **:** the termination of a time or period fixed by law, contract, or agreement

ex·plain \ik-'splān\ *vb* [L *explanare,* lit., to make level, fr. *ex-* + *planus* level] **1 :** to make plain or understandable **2 :** to give the reason for or cause of **3 :** to show the logical development or relationships of — **ex·plain·a·ble** \-'splā-nə-bəl\ *adj* — **ex·plain·er** *n*

syn EXPOUND, INTERPRET: EXPLAIN implies making plain or intelligible; EXPOUND implies a careful, often elaborate explanation (*expounding* his philosophy of life) INTERPRET adds the use of the imagination, sympathy, or special knowledge to clarify something of more than obvious difficulty (*interpret* a poem) (*interpret* the law)

ex·pla·na·tion \,ek-splə-'nā-shən\ *n* **1 :** the act or process of explaining **2 :** something that explains **:** a statement that makes clear

ex·plan·a·to·ry \ik-'splan-ə-,tōr-ē, -,tȯr-\ *adj* **:** serving to explain (*explanatory* notes) — **ex·plan·a·to·ri·ly** \-,splan-ə-'tȯr-ə-lē, -'tȯr-\ *adv*

ex·plant \(')eks-'plant\ *vt* **:** to remove (living tissue) esp. to a tissue culture medium

ex·ple·tive \'ek-splət-iv\ *n* **1 :** a syllable, word, or phrase inserted to fill a vacancy (as in a sentence or a line of verse) without adding to the sense; *esp* **:** a word that occupies the position of the subject or object of a verb in normal English word order and anticipates a subsequent word or phrase that supplies the needed meaningful content (*it* in "it is easy to say so" and in "make it clear which you prefer" is an *expletive*) **2 :** an exclamatory word or phrase; *esp* **:** one that is obscene or profane — **expletive** *adj*

ex·pli·cate \'ek-splə-,kāt\ *vt* [L *explicare,* lit., to unfold, fr. *ex-* + *plicare* to fold] **:** to give a detailed explanation of — **ex·plic·a·ble** \ek-'splik-ə-bəl, 'ek-(,)splik-\ *adj* — **ex·pli·ca·tion** \,ek-splə-'kā-shən\ *n* — **ex·pli·ca·tive** \ek-'splik-ət-iv, 'ek-splə-,kāt-\ *adj* — **ex·pli·ca·tor** \'ek-splə-,kāt-ər\ *n* — **ex·plic·a·to·ry** \ek-'splik-ə-,tōr-ē, -,tȯr-\ *adj*

ex·plic·it \ik-'splis-ət\ *adj* [L *explicitus,* fr. pp. of *explicare* to explicate] **:** so clear in statement that there is no doubt about the meaning **:** fully stated (*explicit* instructions) — compare IMPLICIT — **ex·plic·it·ly** *adv* — **ex·plic·it·ness** *n*

syn EXPLICIT, DEFINITE, EXPRESS, SPECIFIC mean perfectly clear in meaning. EXPLICIT implies such verbal plainness and distinctness that there is no room for doubt or difficulty in understanding; DEFINITE stresses precise, clear statement or arrangement that leaves no doubt or indecision; EXPRESS implies explicitness and utterance with directness and positiveness (*express* denial of the charges) SPECIFIC applies to what is precisely and fully treated in detail or particular

ə abut; ᵊ kitten; ər further; a back; ā bake; ä cot, cart; au̇ out; ch chin; e less; ē easy; g gift; i trip; ī life

ex·plode \ik-'splōd\ vb [L explos-, explodere to drive off the stage by clapping or hissing, fr. ex- + plaudere to clap] **1 :** to cause to be given up or rejected **:** DISCREDIT ⟨science has exploded many old ideas⟩ **2 a :** to burst or cause to burst violently and noisily **b :** to burn suddenly so that there is a violent expansion of hot gases with great disruptive force and a loud noise; also **:** to undergo an atomic nuclear reaction with similar but more violent effects **3 :** to burst forth (as with anger or laughter)

ex·plod·ed adj **:** showing the parts separated but in correct relationship to each other ⟨an exploded view of a carburetor⟩

¹ex·ploit \'ek-,sploit, ik-'\ n [OF, outcome, success, fr. L explicitum, neut. of pp. of explicare to explicate] **:** DEED, ACT; esp **:** a notable or heroic act **syn** see FEAT

²ex·ploit \ik-'sploit, 'ek-,\ vt **1 :** to extract value or use from **:** UTILIZE ⟨exploit a mine⟩ **2 :** to make use of unfairly for one's own advantage — **ex·ploit·a·ble** \-ə-bəl\ adj — **ex·ploi·ta·tion** \,ek-,sploi-'tā-shən\ n — **ex·ploit·er** \ik-'sploit-ər, 'ek-,\ n

ex·plo·ra·tion \,ek-splə-'rā-shən\ n **:** the act or an instance of exploring — **ex·plor·ative** \ik-'splōr-ət-iv, -'splor-\ adj — **ex·plor·a·to·ry** \-ə-,tōr-ē, -,tor-\ adj

ex·plore \ik-'splō(ə)r, -'splo(ə)r\ vb [L explorare to seek for, fr. ex- + plorare to cry out] **1 a :** to search through or into **b :** to examine carefully and in detail esp. for diagnostic purposes ⟨explore a wound⟩ **c :** to penetrate into or range over for purposes of discovery ⟨explore an uncharted sea⟩ **2 :** to make or conduct a systematic search

ex·plor·er \ik-'splōr-ər, -'splor-\ n **:** one that explores; esp **:** a person who travels in search of geographical or scientific information

ex·plo·sion \ik-'splō-zhən\ n **1 :** the act or an instance of exploding **2 :** a large-scale, rapid, and spectacular expansion, outbreak, or upheaval **3 :** a violent outburst of feeling

¹ex·plo·sive \ik-'splō-siv, -ziv\ adj **1 :** relating to, characterized by, or operated by explosion **2 :** tending to explode — **ex·plo·sive·ly** adv — **ex·plo·sive·ness** n

²explosive n **1 :** an explosive substance **2 :** ²STOP 8

ex·po·nent \ik-'spō-nənt, 'ek-,\ n [L exponere to set forth, explain, fr. ex- + ponere to put] **1 :** a symbol written above and to the right of a mathematical expression to indicate the operation of raising to a power ⟨in the expression a^3, the exponent 3 indicates that a is to be taken as a factor three times⟩ **2 a :** one that expounds or interprets **b :** one that champions or advocates

ex·po·nen·tial \,ek-spə-'nen-chəl\ adj **1 :** of or relating to an exponent **2 :** involving a variable exponent ⟨10^x is an exponential function⟩ **3 :** capable of being expressed or approximated by an exponential equation ⟨exponential growth⟩ — **ex·po·nen·tial·ly** \-'nench-(ə-)lē\ adv

¹ex·port \ek-'spōrt, -'sport, 'ek-,\ vt [L exportare, fr. ex- + portare to carry] **1 :** to carry away **:** REMOVE **2 :** to carry or send (as a commodity) to another country or place esp. for sale — **ex·port·a·ble** \-ə-bəl\ adj — **ex·por·ta·tion** \,ek-,spōr-'tā-shən, -,spor-, -spər-\ n — **ex·port·er** \ek-'spōrt-ər, -'sport-, 'ek-,\ n

²ex·port \'ek-,spōrt, -,sport\ n **1 :** something exported; esp **:** a commodity conveyed from one country or region to another for purposes of trade **2 :** an act of exporting **:** EXPORTATION

³export \'ek-,\ adj **1 :** of or relating to exportation or exports ⟨export duties⟩ **2 :** intended for export ⟨export goods⟩

ex·pose \ik-'spōz\ vt [MF exposer, irreg. fr. L exponere to set forth, explain, fr. ex- + ponere to put, place] **¹1 a :** to deprive of shelter, protection, or care ⟨expose troops needlessly⟩ **b :** to submit or subject to an action or influence; esp **:** to subject (a sensitive photographic film, plate, or paper) to the action of radiant energy (as light) **c :** to abandon (an infant) esp. in the open **:** DESERT **2 :** to lay open to view: as **a :** to offer publicly for sale **b :** to exhibit for public veneration **c :** to reveal the face of (a playing card) **3 :** to bring to light **:** UNMASK ⟨expose a murderer⟩ — **ex·pos·er** n

²ex·po·sé \,ek-(,)spō-'zā\ n [F] **:** an exposure of something discreditable

ex·po·si·tion \,ek-spə-'zish-ən\ n **1 :** an explaining of the meaning or purpose of something (as a piece of writing)

2 : a composition that explains something **3 :** a public exhibition or show **4 :** the first part of a musical composition in sonata form in which the thematic material of the movement is presented — **ex·pos·i·to·ry** \ik-'späz-ə-,tōr-ē, -,tor-\ adj

ex·pos·i·tor \ik-'späz-ət-ər\ n **:** one that expounds or explains

ex post fac·to law \,eks-,pōst-'fak-(,)tō-\ n [LL ex post facto from a thing done afterward] **:** a law that declares to be criminal an act that was not punishable when committed or that subjects a prior crime to a penalty heavier than that applicable when committed

ex·pos·tu·late \ik-'späs-chə-,lāt\ vi **:** to reason earnestly with a person against something he has done or intends to do **:** REMONSTRATE — **ex·pos·tu·la·tion** \-,späs-chə-'lā-shən\ n — **ex·pos·tu·la·to·ry** \-'späs-chə-lə-,tōr-ē, -,tor-\ adj

ex·po·sure \ik-'spō-zhər\ n **1 :** the act or an instance of exposing: as **a :** disclosure to view **b :** UNMASKING **c :** an act of abandoning esp. in the open **d** (1) **:** a section of a film for a single picture (2) **:** the time during which a sensitive photographic film is exposed **2 a :** a condition or an instance of being exposed; esp **:** the condition of being exposed to danger (as from the elements) **b :** a position with respect to direction or to general weather conditions ⟨a southern exposure⟩

ex·pound \ik-'spaùnd\ vt [MF expondre, fr. L exponere to explain] **1 a :** to set forth **:** STATE **b :** to defend (as a theory) with argument **2 :** to make clear the meaning of **:** INTERPRET **syn** see EXPLAIN — **ex·pound·er** n

¹ex·press \ik-'spres\ adj [L expressus, fr. pp. of exprimere to press out, fr. ex- + premere to press] **1 a :** directly and distinctly stated **:** EXPLICIT **b :** EXACT, PRECISE **2 :** of a particular sort **:** SPECIAL **3 a :** traveling at high speed; esp **:** traveling with few or no stops ⟨express train⟩ **b :** adapted or suitable for travel at high speed **syn** see EXPLICIT

²express adv **:** by express ⟨send a package express⟩

³express n **1 a :** a system for special transportation of goods at premium rates **b :** a company operating such a service or the goods or shipments so transported **2 :** an express vehicle

⁴express vt **1 a :** to represent esp. in words **:** STATE **b :** to give expression to the opinions, feelings, or abilities of (oneself) **c :** to represent by a sign or symbol **:** SYMBOLIZE **2 :** to press or squeeze out of an object **3 :** to send by express — **ex·press·er** n — **ex·press·i·ble** \-ə-bəl\ adj

ex·pres·sion \ik-'spresh-ən\ n **1 :** the act or process of expressing esp. in words **2 a :** a word, phrase, or sign that expresses a thought, feeling, or quality; esp **:** a significant word or phrase **b :** a mathematical symbol or a combination of symbols and signs representing a quantity or operation **3 :** a way of speaking or of singing or of playing an instrument so as to show mood or feeling **4 :** LOOK, APPEARANCE ⟨a pleased expression⟩ **5 :** the detectable effect of a gene; also **:** EXPRESSIVITY **6 :** an act or product of pressing out — **ex·pres·sion·less** \-ləs\ adj

ex·pres·sion·ism \ik-'spresh-ə-,niz-əm\ n **:** a theory or practice in art of seeking to depict the artist's subjective responses to objects and events — **ex·pres·sion·ist** \-'spresh-(ə-)nəst\ n or adj — **ex·pres·sion·is·tic** \-,spresh-ə-'nis-tik\ adj

ex·pres·sive \ik-'spres-iv\ adj **1 :** of or relating to expression **2 :** serving to express, utter, or represent **3 :** full of expression **:** SIGNIFICANT — **ex·pres·sive·ly** adv — **ex·pres·sive·ness** n

ex·pres·siv·i·ty \,ek-,spres-'iv-ət-ē\ n, pl -ties **:** the relative capacity of a gene to modify the organism of which it is a part

ex·press·ly \ik-'spres-lē\ adv **1 :** in an express manner **:** EXPLICITLY **2 :** for the express purpose **:** PARTICULARLY

ex·press·man \ik-'spres-,man, -mən\ n **:** a person employed in the express business

ex·press·way \ik-'spres-,wā\ n **:** a high-speed divided highway for through traffic with controlled access and grade separations at intersections

ex·pro·pri·ate \ek-'sprō-prē-,āt\ vt [ML expropriare, fr. L ex- + proprius own] **:** to take away from a person the possession of or right to (property) — **ex·pro·pri·a·tion**

\(,)ek-,sprō-prē-'ā-shən\ *n* — **ex·pro·pri·a·tor** \ek-'sprō-prē-,āt-ər\ *n*

ex·pul·sion \ik-'spəl-shən\ *n* [L expuls-, expellere to expel] **:** the act of expelling **:** the state of being expelled — **ex·pul·sive** \-'pəl-siv\ *adj*

ex·punge \ik-'spənj\ *vt* [L expungere to mark for deletion by dots, fr. ex- + pungere to prick] **1 :** to blot out **:** rub out **:** ERASE **2 :** CANCEL — **ex·pung·er** *n*

ex·pur·gate \'ek-spər-,gāt\ *vt* [L expurgare, fr. ex- + purgare to purge] **:** to clear of something wrong or objectionable; *esp* **:** to clear (as a book) of objectionable words or passages — **ex·pur·ga·tion** \,ek-spər-'gā-shən\ *n* — **ex·pur·ga·tor** \'ek-spər-,gāt-ər\ *n*

¹ex·quis·ite \ek-'skwiz-ət, 'ek-(,)skwiz-\ *adj* [L exquisitus, fr. pp. of exquirere to search out, fr. ex- + quaerere to seek] **1 :** marked by flawless craftsmanship or delicate execution **2 :** keenly appreciative **:** DISCRIMINATING **3 :** pleasing through beauty, fitness, or perfection **4 :** ACUTE, INTENSE — **ex·quis·ite·ly** *adv* — **ex·quis·ite·ness** *n*

²exquisite *n* **:** one who is overly fastidious in dress or ornament — FOP

ex·san·gui·nate \ek(s)-'san-gwə-,nāt\ *vt* **:** to drain of blood

ex·sert·ed \ek-'sərt-əd\ *adj* **:** projecting beyond an enclosing organ or part

ex·sic·cate \'ek-si-,kāt\ *vt* [L exsiccare, fr. ex- + siccus dry] **:** to remove moisture from **:** DRY — **ex·sic·ca·tion** \,ek-si-'kā-shən\ *n*

ex·stip·u·late \(')ek(s)-'stip-yə-lət\ *adj* **:** having no stipules

ex·tant \'ek-stənt, ek-'stant\ *adj* [L exstare to stand out, be in existence, fr. ex- + stare to stand] **:** currently existing **:** not destroyed or lost

ex·tem·po·ra·ne·ous \(,)ek-,stem-pə-'rā-nē-əs\ *adj* [LL extemporaneus, fr. L ex tempore on the spur of the moment] **1 :** composed, performed, or uttered on the spur of the moment **:** IMPROMPTU **2 :** carefully prepared but delivered without notes or text **3 :** provided, made, or put to use as an expedient — **ex·tem·po·ra·ne·ous·ly** *adv* — **ex·tem·po·ra·ne·ous·ness** *n*

ex·tem·po·rary \ik-'stem-pə-,rer-ē\ *adj* **:** EXTEMPORANEOUS — **ex·tem·po·rar·i·ly** \-,stem-pə-'rer-ə-lē\ *adv*

ex·tem·po·re \ik-'stem-pə-(,)rē\ *adv* **:** EXTEMPORANEOUSLY — **extempore** *adj*

ex·tem·po·rize \ik-'stem-pə-,rīz\ *vb* **:** to do, make, or utter extempore **:** IMPROVISE — **ex·tem·po·ri·za·tion** \ik-,stem-pə-rə-'zā-shən\ *n* — **ex·tem·po·riz·er** \-'stem-pə-,rī-zər\ *n*

ex·tend \ik-'stend\ *vb* [L extens-, extendere, fr. ex- + tendere to stretch] **1 :** to straighten out or stretch forth ⟨*extended* his arm⟩ **2 :** to make active at full capacity ⟨*extended* himself to win the race⟩ **3 :** to increase the bulk of (a product) by the addition of a cheaper substance **4 a :** to make the offer of **:** PROFFER **b :** to make available **5 a :** to cause to reach **b :** to cause to be longer; *esp* **:** to prolong the time of payment of **6 a :** to cause to be of greater area or volume **:** ENLARGE **b :** to increase the scope, meaning, or application of **:** BROADEN **7 :** to stretch out in distance, space, or time **:** REACH **8 :** to span an interval of distance, space, or time — **ex·tend·i·ble** \-'sten-də-bəl\ *or* **ex·ten·si·ble** \-'sten(t)-sə-bəl\ *adj* — **ex·ten·si·bil·i·ty** \-,sten(t)-sə-'bil-ət-ē\ *n*

syn EXTEND, LENGTHEN, PROLONG, PROTRACT mean to draw out or add to so as to increase in length. EXTEND and LENGTHEN imply a drawing out in space or time; EXTEND may also imply increase in width, scope, area, or range ⟨*extend* a vacation⟩ ⟨*extend* welfare services⟩ ⟨*lengthen* a skirt⟩ ⟨*lengthened* her life⟩ PROLONG suggests chiefly increase in duration esp. beyond usual limits ⟨*prolonged* illness⟩ PROTRACT adds to PROLONG implications of needlessness, vexation, or indefiniteness ⟨*protracted* litigation⟩

ex·tend·er \ik-'sten-dər\ *n* **:** something added to another thing usu. as a diluent, adulterant, or modifier

ex·ten·sion \ik-'sten-chən\ *n* **1 a :** the act of extending **:** the state of being extended **b :** something extended **2 :** the total range over which something extends **:** COMPASS **3 :** the property of occupying space **4 :** an increase in length of time; *esp* **:** a granting of extra time to fulfill an obligation **5 :** the making available of educational resources by special programs (as correspondence courses)

to persons otherwise unable to take advantage of them **6 a :** a part constituting an addition **b :** a section forming an additional length **c :** an extra telephone connected to the principal line — **ex·ten·sion·al** \-'stench-nəl, -'sten-chən-°l\ *adj* — **ex·ten·sion·al·ly** \-ē\ *adv*

ex·ten·sive \ik-'sten(t)-siv\ *adj* **1 :** EXTENSIONAL **2 :** having wide or considerable extent — **ex·ten·sive·ly** *adv* — **ex·ten·sive·ness** *n*

ex·ten·sor \ik-'sten(t)-sər\ *n* **:** a muscle serving to extend a limb or other bodily part — compare ABDUCTOR, ADDUCTOR

ex·tent \ik-'stent\ *n* **1 a :** the range, distance, or space over or through which something extends **b :** the point, degree, or limit to which something extends **2 :** an extended tract or region

ex·ten·u·ate \ik-'sten-yə-,wāt\ *vt* [L extenuare, fr. ex- + tenuis thin] **:** DIMINISH, UNDERESTIMATE; *esp* **:** to represent (as a crime, fault, or mistake) as of less importance than is real or apparent **:** make excuses for ⟨an offense that could not be *extenuated* by the offender's youth⟩ — **ex·ten·u·a·tion** \-,sten-yə-'wā-shən\ *n* — **ex·ten·u·a·tor** \-'sten-yə-,wāt-ər\ *n* — **ex·ten·u·a·to·ry** \-wə-,tōr-ē, -,tȯr-\ *adj*

¹ex·te·ri·or \ek-'stir-ē-ər\ *adj* [L, compar. of exter, exterus being on the outside, fr. ex] **1 :** EXTERNAL, OUTER **2 a :** happening or coming from outside **b :** suitable for use on outside surfaces ⟨*exterior* paint⟩ — **ex·te·ri·or·ly** *adv*

²exterior *n* **1 a :** an exterior part or surface **:** OUTSIDE **b :** outward manner or appearance **2 :** a representation of an outdoor scene

exterior angle *n* **1 :** the angle between a side of a polygon and an adjacent side prolonged **2 :** an angle between a transversal and either of two parallel lines on the exterior of the latter

ex·ter·mi·nate \ik-'stər-mə-,nāt\ *vt* [L exterminare, fr. ex- + terminus boundary] **:** to get rid of completely **:** ANNIHILATE — **ex·ter·mi·na·tion** \-,stər-mə-'nā-shən\ *n* — **ex·ter·mi·na·tor** \-'stər-mə-,nāt-ər\ *n*

ex·tern *also* **ex·terne** \'ek-,stərn\ *n* **:** a person (as a doctor) professionally connected with an institution but not living in it

¹ex·ter·nal \ek-'stərn-°l\ *adj* [L externus external] **1 a :** outwardly visible ⟨external signs⟩ **b :** not intrinsic or essential **:** SUPERFICIAL **2 a :** of, relating to, or connected with the outside or an outer part **b :** applied or applicable to the outside **3 a (1) :** situated outside, apart, or beyond **(2) :** arising or acting from outside ⟨external force⟩ **b :** of or relating to relationships with foreign countries **c :** having existence independent of the mind **:** PHYSICAL ⟨external reality⟩ — **ex·ter·nal·ly** \-°l-ē\ *adv*

²ex·ter·nal *n* **:** something external **:** an external feature or aspect — usu. used in pl.

external–combustion engine *n* **:** a heat engine (as a steam engine) that derives its heat from fuel consumed outside the engine cylinder

external ear *n* **:** the outer part of the ear consisting of the sound-collecting pinna and the canal leading from this to the eardrum

external respiration *n* **:** exchange of gases between the external environment and a distributing system of the animal body (as gills or lungs) or between the alveoli of the lungs and the blood — compare INTERNAL RESPIRATION

ex·tero·cep·tive \,ek-stə-rō-'sep-tiv\ *adj* **:** activated by, relating to, or being stimuli impinging on the organism from outside — **ex·tero·cep·tor** \-'sep-tər\ *n*

ex·tinct \ik-'stin(k)t, 'ek-,\ *adj* [L exstinctus, pp. of exstinguere to extinguish] **1 :** no longer burning **:** EXTINGUISHED **2 :** no longer active ⟨an *extinct* volcano⟩ **3 :** no longer existing ⟨an *extinct* animal⟩ — **ex·tinc·tion** \ik-'stin(k)-shən\ *n*

ex·tin·guish \ik-'stin-gwish\ *vt* [L exstinguere, fr. ex- + stinguere to extinguish] **1 a :** to cause to cease burning **:** QUENCH **b :** to cause to die out **:** DESTROY **c :** to dim the brightness of **:** ECLIPSE **2 :** to end the force or existence of ⟨*extinguish* a claim⟩ ⟨*extinguish* a debt⟩ — **ex·tin·guish·a·ble** \-ə-bəl\ *adj* — **ex·tin·guish·er** \-ər\ *n* — **ex·tin·guish·ment** \-mənt\ *n*

ex·tir·pate \'ek-stər-,pāt, ek-'\ *vt* [L exstirpare, fr. ex- + stirp-, stirps trunk, root] **1 :** to pull up by the roots

---

ə abut; ə kitten; ər further; a back; ā bake; ä cot, cart; aú out; ch chin; e less; ē easy; g gift; i trip; ī life

2 : to eradicate (as by surgery) or destroy wholly — **ex·tir·pa·tion** \,ek-(,)stər-'pā-shən\ *n* — **ex·tir·pa·tive** \'ek-stər-,pāt-iv, ek-'stər-pət-\ *adj* — **ex·tir·pa·tor** \-,pāt-ər, -pət-\ *n*

ex·tol *also* **ex·toll** \ik-'stōl\ *vt* **ex·tolled; ex·tol·ling** [L *extollere,* fr. *ex-* + *tollere* to lift up] : to praise highly : GLORIFY ⟨*extolled* the virtues of his country⟩ — **ex·tol·ler** *n* — **ex·tol·ment** \-'stōl-mənt\ *n*

ex·tort \ik-'stòrt\ *vt* [L *extort-, extorquēre* to wrench out, fr. *ex-* + *torquēre* to twist] : to wring (as money or a confession) from a person by the use of force or threats — **ex·tort·er** *n* — **ex·tor·tive** \-'stòrt-iv\ *adj*

ex·tor·tion \ik-'stòr-shən\ *n* **1** : the act or practice of extorting; *esp* : the offense committed by an official engaging in this practice **2 a** : something extorted **b** : a gross overcharge — **ex·tor·tion·er** \-'stòr-sh(ə-)nər\ *n* — **ex·tor·tion·ist** \-sh(ə-)nəst\ *n*

ex·tor·tion·ate \ik-'stòr-sh(ə-)nət\ *adj* **1** : characterized by extortion **2** : EXCESSIVE, EXORBITANT ⟨*extortionate* prices⟩ ⟨*extortionate* fees⟩ — **ex·tor·tion·ate·ly** *adv*

¹**ex·tra** \'ek-strə\ *adj* **1 a** : more than is due, usual, or necessary : ADDITIONAL ⟨*extra* work⟩ **b** : subject to an additional charge **2** : SUPERIOR ⟨*extra* quality⟩

²**extra** *n* : something extra or additional: as **a** : an added charge **b** : a special edition of a newspaper **c** : an additional worker; *esp* : one hired to act in a group scene in a motion picture or stage production

³**extra** *adv* : beyond the usual size, extent, or degree ⟨*extra* long⟩

extra- *prefix* [L, fr. *extra,* adv. & prep., outside, except, beyond] : outside : beyond ⟨*extra*judicial⟩

ex·tra·cel·lu·lar \,ek-strə-'sel-yə-lər\ *adj* : situated or occurring outside a cell or the cells of the body — **ex·tra·cel·lu·lar·ly** *adv*

¹**ex·tract** \ik-'strakt, *oftenest in sense 5* 'ek-,\ *vt* [L *extract-, extrahere,* fr. *ex-* + *trahere* to draw] **1 a** : to draw forth; *esp* : to pull out forcibly **b** : to obtain by much effort from someone unwilling **2** : to separate or otherwise obtain (as a juice or a constituent element) by physical or chemical process **3** : to separate (a metal) from an ore **4** : to determine (a mathematical root) by calculation **5** : to select (excerpts) and copy out or cite — **ex·tract·a·ble** *or* **ex·tract·i·ble** \-ə-bəl\ *adj* — **ex·trac·tor** \-ər\ *n*

²**ex·tract** \'ek-,strakt\ *n* **1** : a selection from a writing or discourse : EXCERPT **2** : a product (as an essence or concentrate) prepared by extracting; *esp* : a solution of essential constituents of a complex material (as meat or an aromatic plant)

ex·trac·tion \ik-'strak-shən\ *n* **1** : the act or process of extracting ⟨*extraction* of a tooth⟩ **2** : ORIGIN, LINEAGE **3** : something extracted

¹**ex·trac·tive** \ik-'strak-tiv\ *adj* **1 a** : of, relating to, or involving extraction ⟨*extractive* processes⟩ **b** : capable of being extracted ⟨*extractive* by-products of coal tar⟩ **2** : drawing on natural and esp. irreplaceable resources ⟨*extractive* industries such as mining and lumbering⟩

²**extractive** *n* : an extractive substance

ex·tra·cur·ric·u·lar \,ek-strə-kə-'rik-yə-lər\ *adj* **1** : not falling within the curriculum; *esp* : of or relating to those activities (as debating and athletics) that form part of the life of students but are not part of the courses of study **2** : lying outside one's regular duties or routine

ex·tra·dite \'ek-strə-,dīt\ *vt* [back-formation fr. *extradition*] : to cause to be delivered or given up to a different legal authority as an alleged criminal for trial ⟨the prisoner was *extradited* from New York to New Jersey⟩ — **ex·tra·dit·a·ble** \-,dīt-ə-bəl\ *adj*

ex·tra·di·tion \,ek-strə-'dish-ən\ *n* [L *ex-* + *tradition-, traditio* act of handing over] : the surrender or delivery of an alleged criminal by one authority (as a state) to another having jurisdiction to try the charge

ex·tra·dos \'ek-strə-,däs, -,dō; ek-'strā-,däs\ *n, pl* **extrados** \-,dōz, -,däs\ *or* **ex·tra·dos·es** \-,däs-əz\ : the exterior curve of an arch

ex·tra·ga·lac·tic \,ek-strə-gə-'lak-tik\ *adj* : lying or coming from outside the Milky Way

ex·tra·mu·ral \-'myùr-əl\ *adj* : relating to or taking part in informal con-

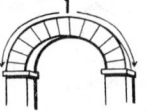

l extrados

tests between teams of different schools other than varsity teams

ex·tra·ne·ous \ek-'strā-nē-əs\ *adj* [L *extraneus* external, strange, fr. *extra* outside] **1** : existing or coming from the outside **2 a** : not forming an essential or vital part : ACCIDENTAL **b** : IRRELEVANT — **ex·tra·ne·ous·ly** *adv* — **ex·tra·ne·ous·ness** *n*

ex·tra·nu·cle·ar \,ek-strə-'n(y)ü-klē-ər\ *adj* : CYTO-PLASMIC

ex·traor·di·nary \ik-'stròrd-°n-,er-ē, ,ek-strə-'òrd-\ *adj* **1 a** : going beyond what is usual, regular, or customary ⟨*extraordinary* powers⟩ **b** : exceptional to a very marked extent : REMARKABLE ⟨*extraordinary* beauty⟩ **2** : employed for or sent on a special function or service ⟨an ambassador *extraordinary*⟩ — **ex·traor·di·nar·i·ly** \ik-,stròrd-°n-'er-ə-lē, ,ek-strə-,òrd-\ *adv* — **ex·traor·di·nar·i·ness** \ik-'stròrd-°n-,er-ē-nəs, ,ek-strə-'òrd-\ *n*

extra point *n* **1** : a point scored in football after a touchdown by drop-kicking or place-kicking **2** *pl* : a score of two points scored after a touchdown by advancing the ball across the goal line in one play

ex·trap·o·late \ik-'strap-ə-,lāt\ *vt* [L *extra* outside + E *-polate* (as in *interpolate*)] : to infer (data in an unknown area or interval) from data in a known area or interval — **ex·trap·o·la·tion** \-,strap-ə-'lā-shən\ *n* — **ex·trap·o·la·tive** \-'strap-ə-,lāt-iv\ *adj* — **ex·trap·o·la·tor** \-,lāt-ər\ *n*

ex·tra·sen·so·ry \,ek-strə-'sen(t)s-(ə-)rē\ *adj* : extending or occurring beyond the known senses

ex·tra·ter·ri·to·ri·al \-,ter-ə-'tōr-ē-əl, -'tòr-\ *adj* **1** : located outside the territorial limits of a jurisdiction **2** : of or relating to extraterritoriality ⟨*extraterritorial* rights⟩ — **ex·tra·ter·ri·to·ri·al·ly** \-ē-ə-lē\ *adv*

ex·tra·ter·ri·to·ri·al·i·ty \-,tōr-ē-'al-ət-ē, -,tòr-\ *n* : exemption from the application or jurisdiction of local law or tribunals ⟨diplomats enjoy *extraterritoriality*⟩

ex·trav·a·gance \ik-'strav-i-gən(t)s\ *n* **1 a** : an extravagant act; *esp* : an excessive outlay of money **b** : something extravagant **2** : the quality or fact of being extravagant

ex·trav·a·gant \-gənt\ *adj* [ML *extravagant-, extravagans,* fr. L *extra-* + *vagans,* prp. of *vagari* to wander about] **1** : going beyond what is reasonable or suitable ⟨*extravagant* praise⟩ **2** : wasteful esp. of money **3** : too high in price — **ex·trav·a·gant·ly** *adv*

ex·trav·a·gan·za \ik-,strav-ə-'gan-zə\ *n* **1** : a literary or musical work marked by extreme freedom of style and structure and usu. by elements of burlesque or parody **2** : a lavish or spectacular show or event

ex·trav·a·sate \ik-'strav-ə-,sāt\ *vb* : to escape or cause to escape from a proper vessel or channel — **ex·trav·a·sa·tion** \-,strav-ə-'sā-shən\ *n*

ex·tra·ve·hic·u·lar \,ek-strə-vē-'hik-yə-lər\ *adj* : taking place outside a vehicle (as a spacecraft)

¹**ex·treme** \ik-'strēm\ *adj* [L *extremus,* superl. of *exter, exterus* being on the outside] **1 a** : existing in the highest or the greatest possible degree ⟨*extreme* poverty⟩ **b** : going to great or exaggerated lengths **c** : exceeding the ordinary, usual, or expected ⟨*extreme* measures⟩ **2** : situated at the farthest possible point from a center **3 a** : most advanced : UTMOST **b** : MAXIMUM ⟨the *extreme* penalty⟩ — **ex·treme·ly** *adv* — **ex·treme·ness** *n*

²**extreme** *n* **1** : an extreme state or condition **2 a** : something situated at or marking one end or the other of a range ⟨*extremes* of heat and cold⟩ **b** : the first term or the last term of a mathematical proportion **3 a** : a very pronounced or excessive degree **b** : MAXIMUM **4** : an extreme measure or expedient ⟨go to *extremes*⟩

extremely high frequency *n* : a radio frequency in the range between 30,000 and 300,000 megacycles — abbr. *ehf*

extreme unction *n* : a Roman Catholic sacrament in which a priest anoints a critically ill or injured person and prays for his recovery and salvation

ex·trem·ism \ik-'strē-,miz-əm\ *n* : advocacy or practice of extreme measures esp. in politics; *esp* : RADICALISM — **ex·trem·ist** \-məst\ *n or adj*

ex·trem·i·ty \ik-'strem-ət-ē\ *n, pl* **-ties 1 a** : the farthest or most remote part, section, or point **b** : a limb of the body; *esp* : a human hand or foot **2 a** : extreme danger or critical need **b** : a moment of such danger or need **3** : the utmost degree (as of emotion or pain) **4** : a drastic or desperate act or measure

ex·tri·cate \'ek-strə-ˌkāt\ *vt* [L *extricare,* fr. *ex-* + *tricae* trifles, perplexities] **:** to free or remove from an entanglement or difficulty — **ex·tri·ca·ble** \ek-'strik-ə-bəl, 'ek-(ˌ)strik-\ *adj* — **ex·tri·ca·tion** \ˌek-strə-'kā-shən\ *n*
syn EXTRICATE, DISENTANGLE, UNTANGLE mean to free from what binds or holds back. EXTRICATE implies the use of care or ingenuity in freeing from a difficult position or situation; DISENTANGLE implies a painstaking separating of two or more things that are confused together or closely interrelated; UNTANGLE suggests straightening out something whose parts are confusingly tangled or disordered
ex·trin·sic \ek-'strin-zik, -'strin(t)-sik\ *adj* **1 a :** not forming part of or belonging to a thing **:** EXTRANEOUS **b :** originating from or on the outside; *esp* **:** originating outside of but acting upon a part ⟨*extrinsic* muscles of the eye⟩ **2 :** EXTERNAL — **ex·trin·si·cal·ly** \-zi-k(ə-)lē, -si-\ *adv*
ex·trorse \'ek-ˌstrȯrs\ *adj* [LL *extrorsus,* adv., outward, fr. L *extra-* + *-orsus* (as in *introrsus* introrse)] **:** turned away from the axis of growth ⟨an *extrorse* anther⟩ — **ex·trorse·ly** *adv*
ex·tro·ver·sion *also* **ex·tra·ver·sion** \ˌek-strə-'vər-zhən\ *n* **:** the state of an extrovert — **ex·tro·ver·sive** \-siv, -ziv\ *adj* — **ex·tro·ver·sive·ly** *adv*
ex·tro·vert \'ek-strə-ˌvərt\ *n* [*extro-* (fr. L *extra-*) + L *vers-, vertere* to turn] **:** a person more interested in what he does and what goes on about him than in what he thinks or imagines **:** one who finds most of his interests and satisfactions in external things — **ex·tro·vert·ed** \'ek-strə-ˌvərt-əd\ *or* **ex·tro·vert** \-ˌvərt\ *adj*
ex·trude \ik-'strüd\ *vb* [L *extrus-, extrudere,* fr. *ex-* + *trudere* to thrust] **1 :** to force, press, or push out **2 :** to shape (as metal) by forcing through a die **3 :** to become extruded — **ex·trud·er** *n*
ex·tru·sion \ik-'strü-zhən\ *n* **:** the act or process of extruding; *also* **:** a form produced by this process
ex·u·ber·ant \ig-'zü-b(ə-)rənt\ *adj* [L *exuberare* to be abundant, fr. *ex-* + *uber* fruitful] **1 :** characterized by great abundance **:** PLENTEOUS, LUXURIANT **2 :** filled with life, vigor, and high spirits **3 :** carried to or experienced in an extreme degree — **ex·u·ber·ance** \-b(ə-)rən(t)s\ *n* — **ex·u·ber·ant·ly** *adv*
ex·u·date \'eks-ə-ˌdāt, 'egz-\ *n* **:** exuded matter
ex·ude \ig-'züd\ *vb* [L *exsudare,* fr. *ex-* + *sudare* to sweat; akin to E *sweat*] **1 :** to discharge slowly through pores or cuts **:** OOZE ⟨*exude* sweat⟩ ⟨sap *exuding* from a cut stem⟩ **2 :** to cause to spread out in all directions ⟨*exuded* charm⟩ — **ex·u·da·tion** \ˌeks-ə-'dā-shən, ˌegz-\ *n* — **ex·u·da·tive** \ig-'züd-ət-iv\ *adj*
ex·ult \ig-'zəlt\ *vi* [L *exsultare,* lit., to leap up, fr. *ex-* + *saltare* to leap] **:** to be extremely joyful **:** REJOICE — **ex·ult·ing·ly** \-'zəl-tiŋ-lē\ *adv*
ex·ult·ant \ig-'zəlt-°nt\ *adj* **:** filled with or expressing extreme joy **:** JUBILANT — **ex·ult·ant·ly** *adv*
ex·ul·ta·tion \ˌeks-(ˌ)əl-'tā-shən, ˌegz-\ *n* **:** the act of exulting **:** the state of being exultant
ex·urb \'ek-ˌsərb, 'eg-ˌzərb\ *n* **:** a region or district outside a city and usu. beyond its suburbs inhabited chiefly by well-to-do families — **ex·ur·bia** \ek-'sər-bē-ə, eg-'zər-\ *n*
ex·ur·ban·ite \ek-'sər-bə-ˌnīt, eg-'zər-\ *n* **:** one who lives in an exurb
ex·u·vi·ate \ig-'zü-vē-ˌāt\ *vb* **:** MOLT — **ex·u·vi·a·tion** \-ˌzü-vē-'ā-shən\ *n*
-ey — see -Y
¹eye \'ī\ *n* [OE *ēage*] **1 a :** an organ of sight; *esp* **:** a rounded hollow organ lined with a sensitive retina and lodged in a bony orbit in the vertebrate skull **b :** the faculty of seeing with eyes **c :** the faculty of intellectual perception or appreciation **d :** LOOK, GLANCE **e :** POINT OF VIEW, JUDGMENT **2 :** something suggestive of an eye: as **a :** the hole through the head of a needle **b :** a loop to receive a hook **c :** an undeveloped bud (as on a potato) **3 :** something central **:** CENTER ⟨the *eye* of a hurricane⟩ — **eyed** \'īd\ *adj* — **eye·less** \'ī-ləs\ *adj*
²eye *vt* **eyed; eye·ing** *or* **ey·ing** **:** to fix the eyes on **:** watch closely
eye·ball \'ī-ˌbȯl\ *n* **:** the vertebrate eye
eye·brow \'ī-ˌbrau̇\ *n* **:** the ridge over the eye or hair growing on it

eye–catch·er \'ī-ˌkach-ər, -ˌkech-\ *n* **:** something strongly attracting the eye — **eye–catch·ing** \-iŋ\ *adj*
eye–cup \'ī-ˌkəp\ *n* **:** a small oval cup with a rim curved to fit the orbit of the eye used for applying liquid remedies to the eyes
eye doctor *n* **:** OPTOMETRIST
eye–drop·per \'ī-ˌdräp-ər\ *n* **:** DROPPER 2
eye·ful \'ī-ˌful\ *n* **1 :** a satisfying view **2 :** one that is visually attractive; *esp* **:** a strikingly beautiful woman
eye·glass \'ī-ˌglas\ *n* **1 a :** a glass lens used to improve faulty eyesight **b :** GLASSES **2 :** an eyepiece esp. of a telescope or microscope
eye·hole \'ī-ˌhōl\ *n* **1 :** ORBIT 1 **2 :** PEEPHOLE
eye·lash \'ī-ˌlash\ *n* **:** the fringe of hair edging the eyelid; *also* **:** a single hair of this fringe
eye·let \'ī-lət\ *n* **1 a :** a small hole designed to receive a cord or used for decoration (as in embroidery) **b :** a small usu. metal ring to reinforce an eyelet **:** GROMMET **2 :** PEEPHOLE
eye·lid \'ī-ˌlid\ *n* **:** one of the movable lids of skin and muscle that can be closed over the eyeball
eye·piece \'ī-ˌpēs\ *n* **:** the lens or combination of lenses at the eye end of an optical instrument

eyelets 1a

eye·sight \'ī-ˌsīt\ *n* **:** SIGHT, VISION ⟨keen *eyesight*⟩ ⟨stay within *eyesight*⟩
eye·sore \'ī-ˌsōr, -ˌsȯr\ *n* **:** something displeasing to the sight ⟨that old building is an *eyesore*⟩
eye·spot \'ī-ˌspät\ *n* **:** a simple or primitive visual organ
eye·stalk \'ī-ˌstȯk\ *n* **:** a movable stalk bearing an eye at the tip in a crustacean
eye·strain \'ī-ˌstrān\ *n* **:** weariness or a strained state of the eye
eye·tooth \'ī-ˌtüth\ *n* **:** a canine tooth of the upper jaw
eye·wash \'ī-ˌwȯsh, -ˌwäsh\ *n* **1 :** an eye lotion **2 :** misleading or deceptive statements, actions, or procedures
eye·wit·ness \'ī-ˌwit-nəs\ *n* **:** a person who sees an occurrence with his own eyes and is able to give a firsthand account of it ⟨an *eyewitness* to an accident⟩
ey·rie \'ī(ə)r-ē, *or like* AERIE\ *var of* AERIE
Eze·kiel \i-'zē-kyəl\ *n* **1 :** a Hebrew prophet of the 6th century B.C. **2** — see BIBLE table
Ez·ra \'ez-rə\ *n* **1 :** a Hebrew priest of the 5th century B.C. **2** — see BIBLE table

F

f \'ef\ *n, often cap* **1 :** the 6th letter of the English alphabet **2 :** the musical tone F **3 :** a grade rating a student's work as failing
fa \'fä\ *n* [ML] **:** the 4th note of the diatonic scale
Fa·bi·an \'fā-bē-ən\ *adj* **1 a :** of, relating to, or being in the manner of the Roman general Quintus Fabius Maximus known for his defeat of Hannibal in the Second Punic War by the avoidance of decisive contests **b :** CAUTIOUS, DELAYING **2** [the *Fabian* Society; fr. the members' belief in slow rather than revolutionary change in government] **:** of, relating to, or being a society of socialists organized in England in 1884 to spread socialist principles gradually — **Fabian** *n* — **Fa·bi·an·ism** \-ə-ˌniz-əm\ *n*
¹fa·ble \'fā-bəl\ *n* [MF, fr. L *fabula* conversation, story, fr. *fari* to speak] **:** a fictitious narrative or statement: as **a :** a legendary story of supernatural happenings **b :** a narration intended to teach a lesson; *esp* **:** one in which animals speak and act like human beings **c :** FALSEHOOD, LIE **syn** see MYTH
²fable *vt* **fa·bled; fa·bling** \-b(ə-)liŋ\ **:** to talk or write about as if true — **fa·bler** \-b(ə-)lər\ *n*
fa·bled \'fā-bəld\ *adj* **1 :** FICTITIOUS **2 :** told of or celebrated in fable ⟨*fabled* mountain of glass⟩
fab·ric \'fab-rik\ *n* [L *fabrica* workshop, structure, fr. *faber* artisan, smith] **1 a :** STRUCTURE **b :** underlying

structure : FRAMEWORK ⟨the *fabric* of society⟩ **2 a** : a cloth woven or knitted from natural or synthetic fibers ⟨cotton *fabrics*⟩ **b** : a material that resembles cloth

fab·ri·cate \'fab-ri-ˌkāt\ *vt* **1** : CONSTRUCT, MANUFACTURE; *esp* : to construct from standardized parts **2** : INVENT, CREATE **3** : to make up for the purpose of deception — **fab·ri·ca·tion** \ˌfab-ri-'kā-shən\ *n* syn see FICTION — **fab·ri·ca·tor** \'fab-ri-ˌkāt-ər\ *n*

Fab·ri·koid \'fab-ri-ˌkȯid\ *trademark* — used for a plastic-treated cloth used for bookbinding, luggage, and upholstery

fab·u·list \'fab-yə-ləst\ *n* : a creator or writer of fables

fab·u·lous \'fab-yə-ləs\ *adj* **1** : told in or based on fable ⟨*fabulous* animals⟩ **2** : resembling a fable esp. in exaggeration : being beyond belief : EXTRAORDINARY, WONDERFUL ⟨*fabulous* adventures of an explorer⟩ — **fab·u·lous·ly** *adv* — **fab·u·lous·ness** *n*

syn FABULOUS, LEGENDARY, MYTHICAL mean having the character of what is invented or imagined. FABULOUS stresses marvelousness or incredibility often without implying actual nonexistence or impossibility ⟨the company made *fabulous* profits⟩ LEGENDARY suggests having a fabulous character created by the distortions or exaggerations of historical fact by popular tradition ⟨*legendary* deeds of Robin Hood⟩ MYTHICAL applies to what is or has been popularly believed but does not in fact exist ⟨*mythical* wood nymphs⟩

fa·cade *also* **fa·çade** \fə-'säd\ *n* **1** : the front of a building usu. given special architectural treatment **2** : a false, superficial, or artificial appearance ⟨a *facade* of wealth⟩

facade

¹face \'fās\ *n* [OF, fr. ML *facia*, fr. L *facies* make, form, face, fr. *facere* to make] **1** : the front part of the human head including the chin, mouth, nose, cheeks, eyes, and usu. the forehead **2** : PRESENCE ⟨brave in the *face* of danger⟩ **3 a** : facial expression ⟨put a sad *face* on⟩ **b** : GRIMACE **4 a** : outward appearance ⟨suspicious on the *face* of it⟩ **b** : BOLDNESS **c** : DIGNITY, PRESTIGE ⟨afraid to lose *face*⟩ **5** : SURFACE: **a** : a front, upper, or outer surface; *esp* : an exposed surface of rock **b** : any of the plane surfaces that bound a geometric solid **c** : a surface or side that is marked or specially prepared ⟨the *face* of a clock⟩⟨the *face* of a document⟩ **6** : the end or wall (as of a mine tunnel) at which work is progressing — **faced** \'fāst\ *adj*

²face *vb* **1** : to confront brazenly ⟨*face* out a compromising situation⟩ **2 a** : to line near the edge esp. with a different material **b** : to cover the front or surface of ⟨*faced* the building with marble⟩ **3** : to bring face to face ⟨*faced* him with the evidence⟩ **4 a** : to stand or sit with the face toward ⟨*face* the class⟩ **b** : to front on ⟨a house *facing* the park⟩ **5 a** : to oppose firmly ⟨*faces* danger bravely⟩⟨*faced* up to his foe⟩ **b** : to master by confronting with determination ⟨*faced* down the critics of his policy⟩ **6** : to turn or cause to turn the face or body in a specified direction

face card *n* : a king, queen, or jack in a deck of cards

face·down \'fās-'daủn\ *adv* : with the face downward

face·lift·ing \'fās-ˌlif-tiŋ\ *n* **1** : a plastic operation for removal of facial defects (as wrinkles or sagging) usu. associated with aging **2** : MODERNIZATION

face·plate \'fās-ˌplāt\ *n* : a disk fixed with its face at right angles to the live spindle of a lathe for the attachment of the work

fac·et \'fas-ət\ *n* **1** : a small plane surface (as on a cut gem) **2** : ASPECT, PHASE **3** : the external corneal surface of a functional unit of a compound eye — **fac·et·ed** \'fas-ət-əd\ *adj*

fa·ce·tious \fə-'sē-shəs\ *adj* [L *facetia* jest, fr. *facetus* witty] **1 a** : COMICAL **b** : JOCULAR **2** : marked by unseemly jesting or ironic levity : FLIPPANT ⟨welcomes serious and relevant but not *facetious* questions⟩ — **fa·ce·tious·ly** *adv* — **fa·ce·tious·ness** *n*

face-to-face \ˌfās-tə-'fās\ *adv* (*or adj*) **1** : within each other's sight or presence : involving close contacts : in person ⟨a *face-to-face* meeting of the two leaders⟩⟨we met *face-to-face* for the first time⟩ **2** : under the necessity of

having to make a decision or to take action ⟨surgeon *face-to-face* with an emergency case⟩

face value *n* **1** : the value indicated on the face of a bill, security, or instrument **2** : the apparent value or significance ⟨can't take a braggart's statements at *face value*⟩

¹fa·cial \'fā-shəl\ *adj* : of or relating to the face — **fa·cial·ly** \-shə-lē\ *adv*

²facial *n* : a facial treatment or massage

facial nerve *n* : either of a pair of mixed nerves that are the seventh cranial nerves, control facial and ear movements, and transmit sensations of taste

fa·cies \'fā-shēz, -shē-ˌēz\ *n, pl* facies [NL, fr. L, face] : a particular form or appearance; *esp* : a rock or group of rocks that differs (as in composition) from comparable rocks

fac·ile \'fas-əl\ *adj* [L *facilis* easy, fr. *facere* to do, make] **1 a** : easily accomplished, handled, or attained ⟨a *facile* material to work with⟩⟨a *facile* success⟩ **b** : SPECIOUS, SUPERFICIAL ⟨too *facile* a solution to a complex problem⟩ **c** : readily manifested and often insincere ⟨*facile* tears⟩ **2** : mild or yielding in disposition : PLIANT **3** : READY, FLUENT ⟨a *facile* writer⟩ — **fac·ile·ly** \-ə(l)-lē\ *adv*

fa·cil·i·tate \fə-'sil-ə-ˌtāt\ *vt* : to make easier — **fa·cil·i·ta·tion** \-ˌsil-ə-'tā-shən\ *n*

fa·cil·i·ty \fə-'sil-ət-ē\ *n, pl* -ties **1** : the quality of being easily performed **2** : ease in performance : APTITUDE **3** : readiness to be influenced : PLIANCY **4 a** : something that facilitates an action, operation, or course of conduct — usu. used in pl. ⟨library *facilities*⟩⟨*facilities* for graduate study⟩ **b** : something (as a hospital) that is built, installed, or established to serve a particular purpose

fac·ing \'fā-siŋ\ *n* **1 a** : a lining at the edge esp. of a garment **b** *pl* : the collar, cuffs, and trimmings of a uniform coat **2** : an ornamental or protective layer ⟨a frame house with brick *facing*⟩ **3** : material for facing

fac·sim·i·le \fak-'sim-ə-lē\ *n* [L *fac* make + *simile* similar] **1** : an exact copy **2** : the process of transmitting printed matter or still pictures by wire or radio for reproduction syn see DUPLICATE

fact \'fakt\ *n* [L *factum*, fr. neut. of pp. of *facere* to make, do; akin to E *do*] **1** : a thing done : DEED; *esp* : CRIME ⟨accessory after the *fact*⟩ **2** : the quality of being actual **3 a** : something that exists or occurs : EVENT, ACTUALITY **b** : a piece of information about such a fact ⟨it is a *fact* that he was there⟩

fac·tion \'fak-shən\ *n* [L *faction-, factio* party, side, fr. *facere* to make, do, take sides] **1** : a group or combination acting together within and usu. against a larger body (as in a state, political party, or church) : CLIQUE **2** : party spirit esp. when marked by dissension — **fac·tion·al** \-shnəl, -shən-ᵊl\ *adj* — **fac·tion·al·ism** \-ˌiz-əm\ *n* — **fac·tion·al·ist** \-shnəl-əst, -shən-ᵊl-\ *n*

fac·tious \'fak-shəs\ *adj* **1** : of, relating to, or caused by faction ⟨*factious* disputes⟩ **2 a** : inclined to faction or the formation of factions ⟨*factious* politicians⟩ **b** : SEDITIOUS — **fac·tious·ly** *adv* — **fac·tious·ness** *n*

fac·ti·tious \fak-'tish-əs\ *adj* : not natural or genuine : ARTIFICIAL ⟨a *factitious* display of grief⟩ syn see FICTITIOUS — **fac·ti·tious·ly** *adv* — **fac·ti·tious·ness** *n*

¹fac·tor \'fak-tər\ *n* [L, doer, maker, fr. *facere* to do, make] **1 a** : one that buys or sells property for another **b** : an agent in charge of a trading post **2** : something that actively contributes to the production of a result : INGREDIENT **3** : GENE **4** : any of the numbers or symbols in mathematics that when multiplied together form a product — **fac·tor·ship** \-ˌship\ *n*

²factor *vb* fac·tored; fac·tor·ing \-t(ə-)riŋ\ **1** : to resolve into factors **2** : to work as a factor — **fac·tor·a·ble** \-t(ə-)rə-bəl\ *adj*

¹fac·to·ri·al \fak-'tōr-ē-əl, -'tȯr-\ *n* : the product of all the positive integers from one to a given number

²factorial *adj* : of or relating to factors, factoring, or factorials

fac·to·ry \'fak-t(ə-)rē\ *n, pl* -ries **1** : a trading station where resident factors trade **2** : a building or set of buildings with facilities for manufacturing

factory system *n* : a system of manufacturing based on concentration of industry into large establishments that began with the Industrial Revolution

fac·to·tum \fak-'tōt-əm\ *n* [L *fac* do + *totum* everything] : an employee with numerous varied duties

---

j joke; ŋ sing; ō flow; ȯ flaw; ȯi coin; th thin; th̲ this; ü loot; u̇ foot; y yet; yü few; yu̇ furious; zh vision

fac·tu·al \'fak-chǝ(-wǝ)l\ *adj* **1** : of or relating to facts **2** : restricted to or based on fact — **fac·tu·al·i·ty** \,fak-chǝ-'wal-ǝt-ē\ *n* — **fac·tu·al·ly** \'fak-chǝ(-wǝ)-lē\ *adv* — **fac·tu·al·ness** *n*

fac·u·la \'fak-yǝ-lǝ\ *n, pl* **-lae** \-,lē, -,lī\ [NL, fr. L, dim. of *fac-, fax* torch] : any of the bright regions of the sun's photosphere

fac·ul·ta·tive \'fak-ǝl-,tāt-iv\ *adj* : OPTIONAL; *also* : capable of more than one relationship or response ⟨*facultative* parasites⟩ — **fac·ul·ta·tive·ly** *adv*

fac·ul·ty \'fak-ǝl-tē\ *n, pl* **-ties** [L *facultas,* fr. *facilis* easy, fr. *facere* to do] **1** : ability to do something : TALENT ⟨a *faculty* for making friends⟩ **2** : one of the powers of the mind or body ⟨the *faculty* of hearing⟩ **3 a** : the teachers in a school or college **b** : a department of instruction in a university **4** : the members of a profession

fad \'fad\ *n* : a practice or interest followed for a time with exaggerated zeal : CRAZE — **fad·dist** \'fad-ǝst\ *n*

¹fade \'fād\ *vb* [MF *fader,* fr. *fade* feeble, insipid] **1** : to lose freshness or vitality : WITHER **2** : to lose or cause to lose freshness or brilliance of color **3** : to grow dim or faint : disappear gradually **4** : to change gradually in loudness or visibility — used of a motion-picture image or of an electronics signal and usu. with *in* or *out*

²fade *n* : a gradual changing of one picture to another in a motion-picture or television sequence

fade·less \'fād-lǝs\ *adj* : not susceptible to fading

fae·cal, fae·ces *var of* FECAL, FECES

fa·er·ie *also* **fa·ery** \'fā-(ǝ-)rē, 'fa(ǝ)r-ē, 'fe(ǝ)r-ē\ *n, pl* **fa·er·ies** [MF *faerie*] **1** : FAIRYLAND **2** : FAIRY — **faery** *adj*

¹fag \'fag\ *vb* **fagged; fag·ging 1** : DRUDGE **2** : to act as a fag **3** : to tire by strenuous activity : EXHAUST

²fag *n* **1** : an English public-school boy who acts as servant to another **2** : MENIAL, DRUDGE

³fag *n* [*fag end*] : CIGARETTE

fag end *n* [ME *fagge* flap] **1 a** : the last part or coarser end of a web of cloth **b** : the untwisted end of a rope **2 a** : a poor or worn-out end **b** : the extreme end

fag·ot *or* **fag·got** \'fag-ǝt\ *n* [MF] : a bundle of sticks or twigs esp. as used for fuel

fag·ot·ing *or* **fag·got·ing** \'fag-ǝt-iŋ\ *n* : an embroidery produced by tying threads in hourglass-shaped clusters

Fahr·en·heit \'far-ǝn-,hīt\ *adj* [after Gabriel D. *Fahrenheit* d1736 German physicist] : relating or conforming to a thermometric scale on which under standard atmospheric pressure the boiling point of water is at 212 degrees above the zero of the scale and the freezing point is at 32 degrees above zero — abbr. F

fa·ience *or* **fa·ïence** \fā-'än(t)s\ *n* [F, fr. *Faenza,* Italy] : earthenware decorated with opaque colored glazes

¹fail \'fāl\ *vb* [OF *faillir,* fr. L *fallere* to deceive, disappoint] **1 a** : to lose strength : WEAKEN **b** : to die away **c** : to stop functioning **2 a** : to fall short ⟨*failed* in his duty⟩⟨*failed* of reelection⟩ **b** : to be or become absent or inadequate ⟨the water supply *failed*⟩ **c** : to be unsuccessful ⟨as in passing an examination⟩ **d** : to become bankrupt **3** : DISAPPOINT, DESERT ⟨*fail* a friend in his need⟩ **4** : NEGLECT ⟨*fail* to answer the telephone⟩

²fail *n* : FAILURE — usu. used in the phrase *without fail*

¹fail·ing \'fā-liŋ\ *n* : WEAKNESS, SHORTCOMING **syn** see FAULT

²failing *prep* : in the absence or lack of ⟨*failing* a purchaser, he rented the house⟩

faille \'fīl\ *n* [F] : a somewhat shiny closely woven ribbed silk, rayon, or cotton fabric

fail-safe \'fāl-,sāf\ *adj* : incorporating some feature for automatically counteracting the effect of an anticipated possible source of failure

fail·ure \'fāl-yǝr\ *n* **1 a** : a failing to do or perform : neglect of an assigned, expected, or appropriate action **b** : a state of inability to perform a normal function adequately ⟨heart *failure*⟩ **2 a** : a lack of success **b** : BANKRUPTCY **3 a** : a falling short : DEFICIENCY ⟨crop *failure*⟩ **b** : DETERIORATION, BREAKDOWN ⟨a *failure* of memory⟩ **4** : one that has failed

¹fain \'fān\ *adj* [OE *fægen*] **1** *archaic* : GLAD **2** *archaic* : INCLINED **3** *archaic* : OBLIGED

²fain *adv* **1** *archaic* : WILLINGLY **2** *archaic* : RATHER

fai·né·ant \'fā-nē-ǝnt, fā-nā-ä"\ *n* : an irresponsible idler

¹faint \'fānt\ *adj* [OF *feint, faint,* fr. pp. of *feindre,*

faindre to feign, shirk] **1** : lacking courage and spirit : COWARDLY ⟨*faint* heart⟩ **2** : being weak, dizzy, and likely to faint ⟨feels *faint* at the sight of blood⟩ **3** : lacking strength : FEEBLE ⟨a *faint* attempt⟩⟨*faint* praise⟩ **4** : lacking distinctness : barely perceptible ⟨a *faint* sound⟩ ⟨a *faint* impression⟩ — **faint·ly** *adv* — **faint·ness** *n*

²faint *vi* **1** *archaic* : to lose courage or spirit **2** : to lose consciousness because of a temporary decrease in the blood supply to the brain

³faint *n* : an act or condition of fainting

faint·heart·ed \'fānt-'härt-ǝd\ *adj* : lacking courage or resolution : TIMID — **faint·heart·ed·ly** *adv* — **faint·heart·ed·ness** *n*

¹fair \'fa(ǝ)r, 'fe(ǝ)r\ *adj* [OE *fæger*] **1** : attractive in appearance : BEAUTIFUL ⟨*fair* lady⟩⟨our *fair* city⟩ **2** : SPECIOUS ⟨don't trust his *fair* words⟩ **3 a** : CLEAN, PURE ⟨sullied her *fair* name⟩ **b** : CLEAR, LEGIBLE ⟨make a *fair* copy⟩ **4** : not stormy or cloudy ⟨*fair* weather⟩ **5 a** : marked by impartiality and honesty : JUST **b** : conforming with the rules : ALLOWED ⟨*fair* play⟩ **c** : open to legitimate pursuit or attack ⟨*fair* game⟩ **6 a** : PROMISING, LIKELY ⟨a *fair* chance of winning⟩ **b** : favorable to a ship's course ⟨a *fair* wind⟩ **7** : not dark : BLOND **8** : ADEQUATE ⟨made a *fair* grade⟩— **fair·ness** *n*

syn FAIR, EQUITABLE, IMPARTIAL, UNBIASED mean free from favor toward either or any side. FAIR implies eliminating one's own feelings, prejudices, or desires so as to achieve a proper balance of conflicting interests ⟨a *fair* settlement of property claims⟩ EQUITABLE stresses equal treatment of all concerned ⟨*equitable* sharing in the profits of a venture⟩ IMPARTIAL implies absence or suppression of favor or prejudice in making a judgment ⟨an *impartial* referee⟩ UNBIASED stresses more definitely complete absence of prejudice or predisposition ⟨*unbiased* history⟩ **syn** see in addition BEAUTIFUL

²fair *adv* : FAIRLY

³fair *n* [OF *feire,* fr. ML *feria,* fr. L *feriae* (pl.) holidays] **1** : a gathering of buyers and sellers at a particular place and time for trade **2** : a competitive exhibition ⟨as of farm products⟩ usu. with accompanying entertainment and amusements **3** : a sale of a collection of articles usu. for a charitable purpose

fair ball *n* : a batted baseball that settles within the foul lines in the infield, that first touches the ground within the foul lines in the outfield, or that is within the foul lines when bounding to the outfield past first or third base or when going beyond the outfield for a home run

fair catch *n* : a catch of a kicked football by a player who having given a prescribed signal forfeits his right to advance the ball and may not be tackled

Fair Deal *n* : the political, economic, and social program of the administration of President Truman

fair·ground \'fa(ǝ)r-,graund, 'fe(ǝ)r-\ *n* : an area set aside for the holding of fairs and similar gatherings

¹fair·ing \'fa(ǝ)r-iŋ, 'fe(ǝ)r-\ *n, Brit* : GIFT; *esp* : a present bought or given at a fair

²fairing *n* : a structure whose function is to produce a smooth outline and reduce resistance to motion through the air

fair·ish \'fa(ǝ)r-ish, 'fe(ǝ)r-\ *adj* : fairly good or large

fair·ly \'fa(ǝ)r-lē, 'fe(ǝ)r-\ *adv* **1** : HANDSOMELY, FAVORABLY ⟨*fairly* situated⟩ **2** : QUITE, COMPLETELY ⟨*fairly* bursting with pride⟩ **3** : in a fair manner : JUSTLY ⟨treat each person *fairly*⟩ **4** : MODERATELY ⟨a *fairly* easy job⟩

fair-spo·ken \'fa(ǝ)r-'spō-kǝn, 'fe(ǝ)r-\ *adj* : using fair speech : COURTEOUS

fair-trade \-'trād\ *adj* : of, relating to, or being an agreement between a producer and a seller that branded merchandise will be sold at or above a specified price ⟨*fair-trade* items⟩ — **fair-trade** *vt*

fair·way \-,wā\ *n* **1** : a navigable part of a river, bay, or harbor **2** : an open path or space **3** : the mowed part of a golf course between a tee and a green

fairy \'fa(ǝ)r-ē, 'fe(ǝ)r-\ *n, pl* **fair·ies** [ME *fairie* fairyland, fairy people, fr. OF *faerie,* fr. *fee* fairy, fr. L *Fata,* goddess of fate, fr. *fatum* fate] : a mythical being of folklore and romance usu. having diminutive human form and magic powers — **fairy** *adj* — **fairy·like** \-,līk\ *adj*

fairy·land \-,land\ *n* **1** : the land of fairies **2** : a place of delicate beauty or magical charm

fairy ring *n* : a ring of mushrooms produced at the outer margin of a body of mycelium; *also* **:** a mushroom that commonly grows in fairy rings

fairy shrimp *n* **:** any of several delicate transparent fresh-water crustaceans (order Anostraca)

fairy tale *n* **1 :** a simple children's story about super-natural beings — called also *fairy story* **2 :** a made-up story usu. designed to mislead

fait ac·com·pli \fā-tà-kōⁿ-plē\ *n, pl* **faits accomplis** \fā-tà-kōⁿ-plē(z)\ [F, accomplished fact] **:** a thing ac-complished and presumably irreversible

faith \'fāth\ *n* [ME *feith*, fr. OF *feid*, fr. L *fides*] **1 a :** al-legiance to duty or a person **:** LOYALTY   **b :** fidelity to one's promises **2 a (1) :** belief and trust in and loyalty to God **(2) :** belief in the traditional doctrines of a religion **b (1) :** firm belief in something for which there is no proof **(2) :** complete confidence **3 :** something that is believed esp. with strong conviction; *esp* **:** a system of religious beliefs **syn** see BELIEF — **in faith :** by my faith **:** TRULY

¹faith·ful \'fāth-fəl\ *adj* **1 :** full of faith esp. in God **2 :** steadfast in keeping promises or in fulfilling duties ⟨a *faithful* worker⟩ **3 :** steady, firm, and dependable in allegiance or devotion **:** LOYAL ⟨a *faithful* friend⟩ **4 :** true to the facts **:** ACCURATE ⟨*faithful* copy⟩ — **faith·ful·ly** \-fə-lē\ *adv* — **faith·ful·ness** *n*

syn LOYAL, CONSTANT: FAITHFUL implies unswerving ad-herence to a person or to an oath or promise; LOYAL im-plies a firm resistance to any temptation to desert or betray; CONSTANT implies continuing firmness of emo-tional attachment ⟨a *constant* friend⟩ ⟨*constant* lovers⟩

²faithful *n, pl* **faith·ful** *or* **faith·fuls :** one that is faithful: as **a :** a member of a religious body ⟨the *faithful* observe the holy days⟩ **b :** a loyal follower or member ⟨party *faithfuls* gather on election night⟩

faith·less \'fāth-ləs\ *adj* **1 :** not having faith **2 :** not worthy of trust or reliance **:** false to promises — **faith·less·ly** *adv* — **faith·less·ness** *n*

syn FALSE, DISLOYAL: FAITHLESS may apply to any failure to keep a promise or pledge or to any breach of allegiance or loyalty; FALSE often implies a degree of premeditation and deception in betrayal or treachery ⟨*false* friends⟩ DISLOYAL implies a lack of complete faithfulness to a friend, cause, leader, or country ⟨*disloyal* officers⟩

¹fake \'fāk\ *vt* **1 :** to treat so as to falsify **:** DOCTOR ⟨*faked* the statistics to make them support his argument⟩ **2 :** COUNTERFEIT ⟨*fake* a rare first edition⟩ **3 :** PRETEND, SIMULATE ⟨*fake* surprise⟩ — **fak·er** \'fā-kər\ *n* — **fak·ery** \-k(ə-)rē\ *n*

²fake *n* **1 :** an imitation or fabrication that is passed off as genuine **:** FRAUD, COUNTERFEIT ⟨the supposed antique was a *fake*⟩ **2 :** IMPOSTOR, CHARLATAN

³fake *adj* **:** COUNTERFEIT, SHAM

fa·kir \fə-'ki(ə)r\ *n* [Ar *faqīr*, lit., poor man] **1 :** a Muslim mendicant **:** DERVISH **2 :** an itinerant Hindu ascetic or wonder-worker

Fa·lange \fə-'län-hā, 'fā-,lanj\ *n* **:** a fascist political party governing Spain after the civil war of 1936–39 — **Fa·lan·gist** \fə-'lan-jəst, 'fā-,\ *n*

fal·cate \'fal-,kāt, 'fól-\ *also* **fal·cat·ed** \-,kāt-əd\ *adj* **:** hooked or curved like a sickle

fal·chion \'fól-chən\ *n* [OF *fauchon*, fr. L *falc-, falx* sickle, scythe] **:** a broad-bladed slightly curved medieval sword

fal·ci·form \'fal-sə-,fórm, 'fól-\ *adj* **:** having the shape of a scythe or sickle

fal·con \'fal-kən, 'fól-; 'fó-kən\ *n* [LL *falcon-, falco*] **1 :** a hawk trained for use in falconry; *esp* **:** a female peregrine — compare TIERCEL **2 :** any of various hawks with long wings and a notch and tooth on the upper mandible

fal·con·er \-kə-nər\ *n* **:** one that hunts with hawks or breeds or trains hawks for hunting

fal·con·ry \'fal-kən-rē, 'fól-; 'fó-kən-\ *n* **1 :** the art of training falcons to pursue game **2 :** the sport of hunting with falcons

fal·de·ral \'fäl-də-,räl\ *var of* FOLDEROL

¹fall \'fól\ *vi* **fell** \'fel\; **fall·en** \'fó-lən\; **fall·ing** [OE *feallan*] **1 a :** to descend freely by the force of gravity **b :** to hang freely **c :** to drop oneself to a lower position ⟨*fell* to his knees⟩ **d :** to come as if by descending ⟨darkness *falls* early in winter⟩ **2 a :** to be-come of lower degree or level ⟨the tempera-

falcon: *h* hood, *j* jess

ture *fell* 10°⟩ **b :** to drop in pitch or volume **c :** to become uttered **d :** to become lowered ⟨her eyes *fell*⟩ **3 a :** to leave an erect position suddenly and involuntarily **b :** STUMBLE, STRAY **c :** to drop down wounded or dead; *esp* **:** to die in battle **d :** to become captured or defeated ⟨the fortress *fell*⟩ **e :** to suffer ruin or failure **4 :** to com-mit an immoral act; *esp* **:** to lose one's chastity **5 a :** to move or extend in a downward direction ⟨the ground *falls* away to the east⟩ **b :** SUBSIDE, ABATE **c :** to decline in quality, activity, quantity, or value **d :** to lose weight — used with *off* or *away* **e :** to assume a look of shame or dejection ⟨his face *fell* when he lost⟩ **6 a :** to occur at a certain time **b :** to come by chance **:** DEVOLVE **d :** to have the proper place or station ⟨the accent *falls* on the second syllable⟩ **7 :** to come within the scope of some-thing **8 :** to pass from one condition of body or mind to another ⟨*fall* ill⟩ ⟨*fall* asleep⟩ **9 :** to set about heartily or actively ⟨*fell* to work⟩ — **fall flat :** to produce no response or result — **fall for 1 :** to fall in love with **2 :** to become a victim of — **fall foul 1 :** to have a collision — used chiefly of ships **2 :** to have a quarrel **:** CLASH — often used with *of* — **fall from grace 1 :** to lapse morally **:** SIN **2 :** BACKSLIDE — **fall into line :** to comply with a certain course of action — **fall over oneself :** to display excessive eagerness — **fall short 1 :** to be deficient **2 :** to fail to attain

²fall *n* **1 :** the act of falling by the force of gravity ⟨a *fall* from a horse⟩ **2 a :** a falling out, off, or away **:** DROPPING ⟨the *fall* of the leaves⟩ **b :** AUTUMN **c :** a thing or quantity that falls ⟨a heavy *fall* of snow⟩ **3 :** one of the three outer and often drooping segments of the flower of an iris **4 a :** loss of greatness **:** COLLAPSE **b :** the surrender or capture of a besieged place **c :** lapse or departure from innocence or goodness; *esp, often cap* **:** the act of Adam and Eve in eating the forbidden fruit **d :** loss of a woman's chastity **5 a :** the descent of land or a hill **:** SLOPE **b :** WATERFALL — usu. used in pl. **6 :** a decrease in size, quantity, degree, activity, or value **7 :** the distance which something falls **8 a :** an act of forcing a wrestler's shoul-ders to the mat **b :** a bout of wrestling

fal·la·cious \fə-'lā-shəs\ *adj* **1 :** embodying a fallacy ⟨a *fallacious* argument⟩ **2 :** MISLEADING, DELUSIVE ⟨cherish a *fallacious* hope⟩ — **fal·la·cious·ly** *adv* — **fal·la·cious·ness** *n*

fal·la·cy \'fal-ə-sē\ *n, pl* **-cies** [L *fallacia*, fr. *fallac-, fallax* deceptive, fr. *fallere* to deceive] **1 :** a false or mis-taken idea ⟨the popular *fallacy* that poets are impractical⟩ **2 :** false or illogical reasoning or an instance of such rea-soning

fall back *vi* **:** RETREAT, RECEDE

fall·er \'fó-lər\ *n* **:** a logger who fells trees

fall·fish \'fól-,fish\ *n* **:** any of several common No. American minnows

fall guy *n* **1 :** one that is easily duped **2 :** SCAPEGOAT

fal·li·ble \'fal-ə-bəl\ *adj* [ML *fallibilis*, fr. L *fallere* to de-ceive] **1 :** liable to be erroneous ⟨a *fallible* generalization⟩ **2 :** capable of making a mistake ⟨even experts are *fallible*⟩ — **fal·li·bil·i·ty** \,fal-ə-'bil-ət-ē\ *n* — **fal·li·bly** \'fal-ə-blē\ *adv*

fall in *vi* **:** to take one's proper place in a military formation

fall·ing-out \,fó-liŋ-'aút\ *n, pl* **fallings-out** *or* **falling-outs :** QUARREL

falling star *n* **:** METEOR

fal·lo·pi·an tube \fə-,lō-pē-ən-\ *n, often cap F* [after Gabriel *Fallopius d*1562 Italian anatomist] **:** either of the pair of tubes conducting the egg from the ovary to the uterus

fall out \(')fól-'aút\ *vi* **1 :** HAPPEN **2 :** to have a quarrel **3 a :** to leave one's place in the ranks **b :** to leave a building to meet a military formation

fall·out \'fól-,aút\ *n* **:** the often radioactive particles stirred up by or resulting from a nuclear explosion and descending through the atmosphere

¹fal·low \'fal-ō\ *adj* [OE *fealu*] **:** of a light yellowish brown

²fallow *n* [OE *fealga*, pl., plowed land] **1 a :** usu. culti-vated land allowed to lie idle during the growing season **b :** the tilling of land without sowing it for a season **2 :** the state or period of being fallow

³fallow *vt* **:** to till (land) without seeding

⁴fallow *adj* **1 :** left untilled or unsown **2 :** DORMANT, INACTIVE — **fal·low·ness** *n*

---

j joke; ŋ sing; ō flow; ó flaw; ói coin; th thin; th̲ this; ü loot; ú foot; y yet; yü few; yú furious; zh vision

fallow deer *n* : a small European deer with broad antlers and a pale yellow coat spotted white in the summer

¹false \'fóls\ *adj* [L *falsus*, fr. pp. of *fallere* to deceive] **1** : not genuine ⟨*false* documents⟩⟨*false* teeth⟩ **2 a** : intentionally untrue ⟨*false* testimony⟩ **b** : adjusted or made so as to deceive ⟨*false* scales⟩ **c** : tending to mislead ⟨*false* promise⟩ **3** : not true ⟨*false* concepts⟩ **4** : not faithful or loyal : TREACHEROUS **5** : not essential to structure ⟨*false* ceiling⟩⟨*false* front⟩ **6** : inaccurate in pitch ⟨a *false* note⟩ **7 a** : based on mistaken ideas ⟨*false* pride⟩ **b** : inconsistent with the true facts ⟨a *false* claim⟩ **syn** see FAITHLESS — **false·ly** *adv* — **false·ness** *n*

²false *adv* : FAITHLESSLY, TREACHEROUSLY

false fruit *n* : a fruit formed from tissues other than those of the plant ovary

false·hood \'fóls-,húd\ *n* **1** : an untrue statement : LIE **2** : absence of truth or accuracy **3** : the practice of lying

false rib *n* : a rib whose cartilages unite indirectly or not at all with the sternum — compare FLOATING RIB

¹fal·set·to \fól-'set-ō\ *n, pl* **-tos** [It] **1** : an artificially high voice; *esp* : an artificial singing voice that overlaps and extends above the range of the full voice esp. of a tenor **2** : a singer who uses falsetto

²falsetto *adv* : in falsetto

fal·si·fy \'fól-sə-,fī\ *vb* **-fied; -fy·ing** **1** : to make false : change so as to deceive ⟨*falsify* financial accounts⟩ **2 a** : to tell lies : LIE **b** : MISREPRESENT **3** : to prove to be false ⟨promises *falsified* by events⟩ — **fal·si·fi·ca·tion** \,fól-sə-fə-'kā-shən\ *n* — **fal·si·fi·er** \'fól-sə-,fī(-ə)r\ *n*

fal·si·ty \'fól-sət-ē, -stē\ *n, pl* **-ties** **1** : something false : LIE **2** : the quality or state of being false

falt·boat \'fält-,bōt\ *n* [part trans. of G *faltboot*, fr. *falten* to fold + *boot* boat] : a small collapsible canoe made of rubberized cloth stretched over a framework

¹fal·ter \'fól-tər\ *vb* **fal·tered; fal·ter·ing** \'fól-t(ə-)riŋ\ [ME *falteren*] **1** : to move unsteadily : WAVER **2** : to stumble or hesitate in speech : STAMMER ⟨*falter* out thanks⟩ **3** : to hesitate in purpose or action ⟨courage that never *falters*⟩ **syn** see HESITATE — **fal·ter·er** \-tər-ər\ *n* — **fal·ter·ing·ly** \-t(ə-)riŋ-lē\ *adv*

²falter *n* : an act or instance of faltering

fame \'fām\ *n* [L *fama* talk, report, fame, fr. *fari* to speak] : the fact or condition of being known to the public : REPUTATION, RENOWN

famed \'fāmd\ *adj* : FAMOUS, WELL-KNOWN, RENOWNED

fa·mil·ial \fə-'mil-yəl\ *adj* : of, relating to, or characteristic of a family

¹fa·mil·iar \fə-'mil-yər\ *n* **1** : an intimate associate : COMPANION **2** : a spirit held to attend and serve or guard a person — called also *familiar spirit* **3** : one that frequents a place

²familiar *adj* [L *familiaris*, fr. *familia* family] **1** : closely acquainted : INTIMATE **2** : of or relating to a family **3 a** : marked by casualness, informality, and lack of constraint : INFORMAL ⟨*familiar* essay⟩ **b** : overly intimate : FORWARD, PRESUMPTUOUS **4 a** : frequently seen or experienced **b** : of everyday occurrence **5** : having a good knowledge ⟨*familiar* with the rules of soccer⟩ — **fa·mil·iar·ly** *adv*

fa·mil·iar·i·ty \fə-,mil-'yar-ət-ē, -,mil-ē-'ar-\ *n, pl* **-ties** **1** : close friendship : INTIMACY **2** : close acquaintance with or knowledge of something ⟨acquire a *familiarity* with French⟩ **3** : lack of formality : freedom and ease in personal relations **4** : an unduly bold or forward act or expression

fa·mil·iar·ize \fə-'mil-yə-,rīz\ *vt* **1** : to make thoroughly acquainted : ACCUSTOM ⟨*familiarized* himself with his new job⟩ **2** : to make well known ⟨advertising *familiarizes* the name of a product⟩ — **fa·mil·iar·i·za·tion** \-,mil-yə-rə-'zā-shən\ *n*

fam·i·ly \'fam-(ə-)lē\ *n, pl* **-lies** [L *familia* household (including servants and free persons), fr. *famulus* servant] **1** : a group of persons of common ancestry : CLAN **2** : a group of individuals living under one roof and under one head : HOUSEHOLD **3** : a group of things having common characteristics or properties **4** : a social group composed of parents and their children **5** : a group of related plants or animals forming a category ranking above a genus and below an order and usu. comprising several to many genera **6** : a set of curves or surfaces whose equations differ only in certain constant terms

family name *n* : SURNAME 2

family tree *n* **1** : GENEALOGY **2** : a diagram showing genealogical relationships

fam·ine \'fam-ən\ *n* [MF, fr. L *fames* hunger] **1** : an extreme general scarcity of food **2** : a great shortage

fam·ish \'fam-ish\ *vb* **1** : STARVE **2** : to suffer or cause to suffer from extreme hunger — **fam·ish·ment** \-mənt\ *n*

fa·mous \'fā-məs\ *adj* **1** : much talked about : very well known ⟨*famous* explorer⟩ **2** : deserving to be remembered : SPLENDID, FIRST-CLASS

syn RENOWNED, CELEBRATED: FAMOUS may imply no more than being widely and popularly known for any reason and any length of time; RENOWNED implies glory and acclamation ⟨heroes *renowned* in song and story⟩ CELEBRATED stresses frequent public notice and mention esp. in print ⟨a *celebrated* murder trial⟩

fa·mous·ly \'fā-məs-lē\ *adv* : SPLENDIDLY, EXCELLENTLY ⟨got along *famously* together⟩

¹fan \'fan\ *n* [OE *fann*, fr. L *vannus*] **1** : any of various devices for winnowing grain **2** : an instrument for producing a current of air: as **a** : a device that consists of material (as paper or silk) often in the shape of a segment of a circle and is waved to and fro by hand **b** : a device that consists of a series of vanes radiating from a hub rotated on its axle by a motor **3** : something shaped like or suggesting a hand fan

²fan *vb* **fanned; fan·ning** **1** : to drive away the chaff from grain by winnowing **2** : to move or impel air with a fan **3 a** : to direct a current of air upon with a fan **b** : to stir up to activity as if by fanning : STIMULATE **4** : to spread out or move like a fan **5** : to strike out in baseball **6** : to fire a gun by squeezing the trigger and striking the hammer to the rear with the free hand — **fan·ner** *n*

³fan *n* [prob. short for *fanatic*] **1** : an enthusiastic follower of a sport or entertainment **2** : an enthusiastic admirer (as of an athlete or movie star)

fa·nat·ic \fə-'nat-ik\ *adj* [L *fanaticus* inspired by a deity, frenzied, fr. *fanum* temple] : marked or moved by excessive enthusiasm and intense uncritical devotion — **fanatic** *n* — **fa·nat·i·cal** \-i-kəl\ *adj* — **fa·nat·i·cal·ly** \-i-k(ə-)lē\ *adv* — **fa·nat·i·cism** \-ə-,siz-əm\ *n*

fan·ci·er \'fan(t)-sē-ər\ *n* : one with a special liking or interest; *esp* : a person who breeds or grows a particular animal or plant for points of excellence

fan·ci·ful \'fan(t)-si-fəl\ *adj* **1 a** : full of fancy ⟨a *fanciful* tale of an imaginary kingdom⟩ **b** : guided by fancy ⟨a *fanciful* impractical person⟩ **2** : coming from the fancy rather than from the reason ⟨a *fanciful* scheme for getting rich⟩ **3** : curiously made or shaped ⟨*fanciful* forms of ice on a windowpane⟩ — **fan·ci·ful·ly** \-f(ə-)lē\ *adv* — **fan·ci·ful·ness** \-fəl-nəs\ *n*

¹fan·cy \'fan(t)-sē\ *n, pl* **fancies** [ME *fantasie, fantsy* fantasy, fancy, fr. MF *fantasie* fantasy] **1** : the power of the mind to think of things not present : IMAGINATION **2** : LIKING ⟨take a *fancy* to a person⟩ **3** : THOUGHT, IDEA, WHIM ⟨a passing *fancy*⟩ **4** : taste or judgment esp. in art, literature, or decoration **5 a** : devotees of an art, practice, or amusement : FANCIERS **b** : the object of such interest

²fancy *vt* **fan·cied; fan·cy·ing** **1** : to have a fancy for : LIKE **2** : to form a conception of : IMAGINE **3** : to believe without evidence

³fancy *adj* **fan·ci·er; -est** **1** : based on fancy : WHIMSICAL **2 a** : not plain : ORNAMENTAL **b** : of particular excellence **c** : bred primarily for showiness **3** : executed with technical skill and superior grace ⟨*fancy* diving⟩ — **fan·ci·ly** \'fan(t)-sə-lē\ *adv* — **fan·ci·ness** \-sē-nəs\ *n*

fancy dress *n* : a costume (as for a masquerade) chosen to suit the wearer's fancy — **fancy–dress** *adj*

fan·cy–free \'fan(t)-sē-,frē\ *adj* : not centering the attention on any one person or thing; *esp* : not in love

fan·cy·work \-,wərk\ *n* : ornamental needlework (as embroidery)

fan·dan·go \fan-'daŋ-gō\ *n, pl* **-gos** [Sp] : a lively Spanish or Spanish-American dance

fane \'fān\ *n* [L *fanum*] : TEMPLE

fan·fare \'fan-,fa(ə)r, -,fe(ə)r\ *n* [F] **1** : a flourish of trumpets **2** : a showy outward display

fang \'faŋ\ *n* [OE] **1** : a long sharp tooth: as **a** : one by which an animal's prey is seized and held or torn **b** : one of the long hollow or grooved teeth of a venomous snake

ə abut; ᵊ kitten; ər further; a back; ā bake; ä cot, cart; aú out; ch chin; e less; ē easy; g gift; i trip; ī life

2 : the root of a tooth or one of the prongs into which a root divides — **fanged** \'faŋd\ *adj*

fan·jet \'fan-ˌjet\ *n* **1 :** a jet engine having a fan that operates in a duct and draws in extra air whose compression and expulsion provide extra thrust **2 :** an airplane powered by a fan-jet engine

fan·light \'fan-ˌlīt\ *n* **:** a semicircular window with radiating sash bars like the ribs of a fan placed over a door or window

fan·tail \'fan-ˌtāl\ *n* **1 :** a fan-shaped tail or end **2 a :** a domestic pigeon having a broad rounded tail **b :** a fancy goldfish with the tail fins double **3 :** an architectural part resembling a fan; *esp* **:** a centering (as of an arch) of radiating struts **4 :** an overhang at the stern of a ship

fan·tan \'fan-ˌtan\ *n* [Chin (Pek) *fan¹-t'an¹*] **:** a Chinese gambling game; *also* **:** a card game

fan·ta·sia \fan-'tā-zhə, ˌfan-ə-'zē-ə\ *also* **fan·ta·sie** \ˌfant-ə-'zē\ *n* [It *fantasia*, lit., fancy] **:** a free instrumental composition not in strict form

fan·tas·tic \fan-'tas-tik, fən-\ *also* **fan·tas·ti·cal** \-ti-kəl\ *adj* **1 :** produced by the fancy or resembling something produced by the fancy **:** IMAGINARY, UNREAL ⟨*fantastic* dreams⟩⟨a *fantastic* scheme⟩ **2 :** going beyond belief **:** incredible or hardly credible ⟨airplanes now travel at *fantastic* speeds⟩ **3 :** extremely individual or eccentric ⟨*fantastic* behavior⟩ — **fan·tas·ti·cal·ly** \-ti-k(ə-)lē\ *adv*
   syn BIZARRE, GROTESQUE: FANTASTIC may connote unrestrained extravagance in conception ⟨*fantastic* theory⟩ ⟨*fantastic* prices⟩ or merely elaborateness of decorative invention; BIZARRE implies strangeness produced by violence of contrast or incongruity of combination ⟨*bizarre* architecture of an amusement park⟩ GROTESQUE implies violent distortion of the natural with a comic, startling, or pathetic result ⟨*grotesque* masks⟩⟨her *grotesque* attempts at operatic roles⟩

fan·ta·sy \'fant-ə-sē, -ə-zē\ *n, pl* **-sies** [MF *fantasie* fancy, fr. L *phantasia*, fr. Gk, imagination, fr. *phantazesthai* to imagine, fr. *phan-, phainein* to show] **1 :** IMAGINATION, FANCY **2 :** something produced by a person's imagination; *esp* **:** ILLUSION **3 :** FANTASIA

¹far \'fär\ *adv* **far·ther** \-thər\ *or* **fur·ther** \'fər-\; **farthest** *or* **fur·thest** \-thəst\ [ME *fer*, fr. OE *feorr*] **1 :** at or to a considerable distance in space or time ⟨*far* from home⟩ **2 :** by a broad interval **:** WIDELY, MUCH ⟨*far* better⟩ **3 :** to or at a definite distance, point, or degree ⟨as *far* as I know⟩ **4 :** to an advanced point or extent **:** a long way ⟨go *far* in his field⟩ — **by far :** GREATLY — **far and away :** DECIDEDLY

²far *adj* **farther** *or* **further**; **farthest** *or* **furthest** **1 a :** very distant in space **b :** remote in time **2 :** LONG ⟨a *far* journey⟩ **3 :** the more distant of two ⟨on the *far* side of the lake⟩ **syn** see DISTANT

far·ad \'far-ˌad, -əd\ *n* [after Michael *Faraday* d1867 English physicist] **:** the unit of capacitance equal to the capacitance of a capacitor between whose plates there appears a potential of one volt when it is charged by one coulomb of electricity

far·a·day \'far-ə-ˌdā\ *n* **:** the quantity of electricity transferred in electrolysis per equivalent weight of an element or ion equal to about 96,500 coulombs

fa·rad·ic \fə-'rad-ik\ *adj* **:** of or relating to an alternating current of electricity produced by an induction coil

far·away \ˌfär-ə-'wā\ *adj* **1 :** DISTANT ⟨*faraway* lands⟩ **2 :** DREAMY, ABSTRACTED ⟨a *faraway* look⟩

farce \'färs\ *n* [MF, stuffing, farce, fr. L *fars*, *farcire* to stuff] **1 :** a play made up of ridiculous and absurd situations and happenings and intended to make people laugh **2 :** humor of the kind characteristic of a farce **3 :** a ridiculous action, display, or pretense

far·ceur \fär-'sər\ *n* **:** a writer or actor of farce

far·ci·cal \'fär-si-kəl\ *adj* **:** of, relating to, or resembling farce **:** LUDICROUS, ABSURD

¹fare \'fa(ə)r, 'fe(ə)r\ *vi* [OE *faran*] **1 :** GO, TRAVEL ⟨*fare* forth on a journey⟩ **2 :** to get along **:** SUCCEED **3 :** EAT, DINE

²fare *n* **1 :** the money a person pays to travel on a public conveyance **2 :** a person paying a fare **3 :** FOOD

¹fare·well \fa(ə)r-'wel, fe(ə)r-\ *imperative verb* **:** get along well — used interjectionally or to or by one departing

²farewell *n* **1 :** a wish of welfare at parting **:** GOOD-BYE **2 :** an act of departure **:** LEAVE-TAKING

³fare·well \ˌfa(ə)r-ˌwel, ˌfe(ə)r-\ *adj* **:** PARTING, FINAL

far-fetched \'fär-'fecht\ *adj* **:** not easily or naturally deduced or introduced **:** IMPROBABLE

far-flung \'fär-'fləŋ\ *adj* **:** covering great areas **:** having wide range ⟨a *far-flung* empire⟩

fa·ri·na \fə-'rē-nə\ *n* [L, meal, flour, fr. *far* spelt] **:** a fine meal of vegetable matter (as nuts or a cereal grain) used chiefly for puddings or as a breakfast cereal

far·i·na·ceous \ˌfar-ə-'nā-shəs\ *adj* **1 :** containing or rich in starch **2 :** having a mealy texture or surface

far·i·nose \'far-ə-ˌnōs\ *adj* **1 :** yielding or resembling farina **2 :** covered with a whitish mealy powder — **far·i·nose·ly** *adv*

¹farm \'färm\ *n* [ME *ferme* rent, lease, fr. OF, lease, fr. *fermer* to make a contract, fr. L *firmare* to make firm, fr. *firmus* firm] **1 a :** a tract of land devoted to the raising of crops or livestock **b :** a tract of water used for the cultivation of an aquatic life form ⟨oyster *farms*⟩ **2 :** a minor-league subsidiary of a major-league baseball club to which recruits are assigned for training

²farm *vb* **1 :** to turn over for performance or use usu. on contract or for an agreed payment — usu. used with *out* **2 a :** to devote to agriculture ⟨*farm* land⟩ **b :** to engage in raising crops or livestock — **farm·er** *n*

farm·hand \'färm-ˌhand\ *n* **:** a farm laborer

farm·house \-ˌhaüs\ *n* **:** a dwelling on a farm

farm·ing \'fär-miŋ\ *n* **:** the occupation or business of a person who farms **:** AGRICULTURE

farm·land \'färm-ˌland\ *n* **:** land used or suitable for farming

farm·stead \-ˌsted\ *n* **:** the buildings and adjacent service areas of a farm

farm·yard \-ˌyärd\ *n* **:** space around or enclosed by farm buildings

faro \'fa(ə)r-ō, 'fe(ə)r-\ *n, pl* **far·os :** a banking game in which players bet on cards drawn from a dealing box

far-off \'fär-'öf\ *adj* **:** remote in time or space

fa·rouche \fə-'rüsh\ *adj* [F, wild, shy, fr. LL *forasticus* belonging outside] **:** marked by shyness and lack of polish; *also* **:** WILD

far-out \'fär-'aüt\ *adj* **:** marked by a considerable departure from the conventional or traditional **:** EXTREME

far point *n* **:** the point farthest from the eye at which an object can be accurately focused on the retina — compare NEAR POINT

far·ra·go \fə-'räg-ō, -'rā-gō\ *n, pl* **-goes** [L] **:** a confused collection **:** MIXTURE

far-reach·ing \'fär-'rē-chiŋ\ *adj* **:** having a wide range, influence, or effect ⟨a *far-reaching* decision⟩

far·ri·er \'far-ē-ər\ *n* **:** a blacksmith who shoes horses; *also* **:** VETERINARIAN

¹far·row \'far-ō\ *vb* [ME *farwen*, fr. (assumed) OE *feargian*, fr. OE *fearh* young pig] **:** to give birth to pigs

²farrow *n* **:** a litter of pigs

far-see·ing \'fär-'sē-iŋ\ *adj* **:** FARSIGHTED

far·sight·ed \-'sīt-əd\ *adj* **1 :** able to see distant things more clearly than near ones **2 :** able to judge how something will work out in the future **:** SHREWD — **far·sight·ed·ly** *adv* — **far·sight·ed·ness** *n*

¹far·ther \'fär-thər\ *adv* [ME *ferther*, alter. of *further*] **1 :** at or to a greater distance or more advanced point **2 :** more completely

²farther *adj* **1 :** more distant **:** REMOTER **2 :** ²FURTHER

far·ther·most \-ˌmōst\ *adj* **:** most distant **:** FARTHEST

¹far·thest \'fär-thəst\ *adj* **:** most distant in space or time

²farthest *adv* **1 :** to or at the greatest distance in space or time **:** REMOTEST **2 :** to the most advanced point **3 :** by the greatest degree or extent **:** MOST

far·thing \'fär-thiŋ\ *n* [OE *fēorthung*, fr. *fēortha* fourth] **:** a British monetary unit equal to ¼ of a penny; *also* **:** a coin representing this unit

far·thin·gale \'fär-thən-ˌgāl, -thiŋ-\ *n* [modif. of MF *verdugale*, fr. Sp *verdugado*, fr. *verdugo* young shoot of a tree, fr. *verde* green, fr. L *viridis*] **:** a support (as of hoops) worn esp. in the 16th century to swell out a skirt

fas·ces \'fas-ˌēz\ *n sing or pl* [L, fr. pl. of *fascis* bundle] **:** a bundle of rods surrounding an ax with projecting blade borne before ancient Roman magistrates as a badge of authority

fas·cia \'fash-(ē-)ə, 'fāsh-\ *n, pl* **fas·ci·ae** \-ē,ē\   fasces *or* **fas·cias** [It, fr. L, band, bandage] **1 :** one of the three bands making up the architrave in the Ionic order **2 :** a sheet of connective tissue covering or binding together body structures — **fas·cial** \'fash-(ē-)əl, 'fāsh-\ *adj*

fas·ci·ate \'fash-ē-ˌāt\ *or* **fas·ci·at·ed** \-ˌāt-əd\ *adj* **1 :** being banded or striped; *esp* **:** broadly banded with color **2 :** exhibiting fasciation

fas·ci·a·tion \ˌfas(h)-ē-'ā-shən\ *n* **:** a malformation in which a plant stem is enlarged and flattened as if several stems were fused into one

fas·ci·cle \'fas-i-kəl\ *n* [L *fasciculus,* dim. of *fascis* bundle] **1 :** a small bundle or cluster (as of flowers or roots) **2 :** one of the divisions of a book published in parts — **fas·ci·cled** \-kəld\ *adj* — **fas·cic·u·lar** \fə-'sik-yə-lər, fa-\ *adj* — **fas·cic·u·late** \-lət\ *adj*

fas·cic·u·lus \fə-'sik-yə-ləs, fa-\ *n, pl* **-li** \-ˌlī\ **:** a slender bundle of fibers and esp. nerve fibers

fas·ci·nate \'fas-°n-ˌāt\ *vb* [L *fascinare,* fr. *fascinum* witchcraft] **1 :** to grip the attention of esp. so as to take away the power to move, act, or think for oneself **2 :** to allure and hold by charming qualities **:** be attractive — **fas·ci·na·tion** \ˌfas-°n-'ā-shən\ *n*

fas·ci·na·tor \'fas-°n-ˌāt-ər\ *n* **1 :** one that fascinates **2 :** a crocheted head covering for women

fas·cine \fa-'sēn, fə-\ *n* **:** a long bundle of sticks of wood bound together and used for such purposes as filling ditches and making parapets

fas·cism \'fash-ˌiz-əm\ *n* [It *fascismo,* fr. *fascio* bundle, fasces, group, fr. L *fascis* bundle & *fasces* fasces] **1** *cap* **:** the principles of an Italian political organization headed by Mussolini that governed Italy 1922–1943 and that advocated nationalism and racial superiority, a centralized dictatorial regime, severe economic and social regimentation, and forcible suppression of opposition; *also* **:** the movement advocating or the regime following these principles **2 :** a political philosophy, movement, or regime (as Nazism) similar to Fascism — **fas·cist** \'fash-əst\ *n or adj, often cap* — **fas·cis·tic** \fa-'shis-tik\ *adj, often cap*

Fa·sci·sta \fä-'shē-stä\ *n, pl* **Fa·sci·sti** \-(ˌ)stē\ **:** a member of the Italian Fascist movement

¹fash·ion \'fash-ən\ *n* [OF *façon,* fr. L *faction-, factio* act of making, faction, fr. *facere* to make] **1 :** the make or form of something **2 :** MANNER, WAY **3 a :** a prevailing custom, usage, or style **b :** the prevailing style (as in dress) during a particular time

syn STYLE, MODE, VOGUE: FASHION may apply to any way of dressing, behaving, writing, or performing that is favored at any one time or place; STYLE often implies the fashion approved by the wealthy or socially prominent, or it may suggest a distinctive way of conforming to fashion; MODE suggests the fashion among those anxious to appear elegant and sophisticated; VOGUE applies to a temporary widespread style

²fashion *vt* **fash·ioned; fash·ion·ing** \'fash-(ə-)niŋ\ **1 :** to give shape or form to **:** MOLD, CONSTRUCT **2 :** FIT, ADAPT — **fash·ion·er** \'fash-(ə-)nər\ *n*

fash·ion·a·ble \'fash-(ə-)nə-bəl\ *adj* **1 a :** following the fashion or established style **:** STYLISH ⟨*fashionable* clothes⟩ **b :** dressing or behaving according to fashion ⟨*fashionable* people⟩ **2 :** of or relating to the world of fashion **:** popular among those who conform to fashion ⟨*fashionable* stores⟩ — **fash·ion·a·ble·ness** *n* — **fash·ion·a·bly** \-blē\ *adv*

¹fast \'fast\ *adj* [OE *fæst*] **1 a :** firmly fixed or bound **b :** tightly shut **c :** adhering firmly **d :** UNCHANGEABLE **2 :** firmly loyal **3 a :** characterized by quick motion, operation, or effect: **(1) :** moving or able to move rapidly **:** SWIFT **(2) :** taking a comparatively short time ⟨a *fast* trip⟩ **(3) :** imparting quickness of motion ⟨a *fast* bowler⟩ **b :** conducive to rapidity of play or action ⟨a *fast* track⟩ **c (1) :** indicating ahead of the correct time **(2) :** according to daylight saving time **d :** contributing to a shortening of photographic exposure time ⟨*fast* lens⟩ **4 :** not easily disturbed **5 a :** permanently dyed **b :** proof against fading by a particular agency **6 a :** DISSIPATED, WILD **b :** daringly unconventional esp. in sexual matters

syn RAPID, SWIFT, FLEET: FAST and RAPID are very close in meaning but FAST applies esp. to the thing that moves ⟨a *fast* horse⟩ and RAPID to the movement ⟨a *rapid* series of blows⟩ SWIFT suggests great rapidity together with ease of movement ⟨*swift* play of his imagination⟩ FLEET adds

an implication of lightness and nimbleness ⟨*fleet* little ponies⟩

²fast *adv* **1 :** in a fast or fixed manner ⟨stuck *fast* in the mud⟩ **2 :** SOUNDLY, DEEPLY ⟨*fast* asleep⟩ **3 :** SWIFTLY **4 :** in a dissipated manner **:** RECKLESSLY

³fast *vi* [OE *fæstan*] **1 :** to abstain from food **2 :** to eat sparingly or abstain from some foods

⁴fast *n* **1 :** the act or practice of fasting **2 :** a time of fasting

fast·back \'fas(t)-ˌbak\ *n* **:** an automobile roof with a long curving downward slope to the rear; *also* **:** an automobile with such a roof

fas·ten \'fas-°n\ *vb* **fas·tened; fas·ten·ing** \'fas-niŋ, -°n-iŋ\ **1 :** to attach or join by or as if by pinning, tying, or nailing ⟨*fasten* clothes on a line⟩⟨*fasten* blame on someone⟩ **2 :** to make fast **:** fix securely ⟨*fasten* a door⟩ **3 :** to fix or set steadily ⟨*fastened* his eyes on the distant ship⟩ **4 :** to become fixed or joined ⟨a shoe that *fastens* with a buckle⟩ — **fas·ten·er** \'fas-nər, -°n-ər\ *n*

fas·ten·ing \'fas-niŋ, -°n-iŋ\ *n* **:** something that fastens **:** FASTENER

fas·tid·i·ous \fa-'stid-ē-əs\ *adj* [L *fastidiosus* disgusted, fastidious, fr. *fastidium* disgust] **1 a :** overly difficult to please **b :** showing or demanding excessive delicacy or care **2 :** having complex nutritional requirements ⟨*fastidious* microorganisms⟩ — **fas·tid·i·ous·ly** *adv* — **fas·tid·i·ous·ness** *n*

fas·tig·i·ate \fa-'stij-ē-ət\ *or* **fas·tig·i·at·ed** \-ē-ˌāt-əd\ *adj* [L *fastigium* gable end, top] **:** narrowing toward the top — **fas·tig·i·ate·ly** *adv*

fast·ness \'fas(t)-nəs\ *n* **1 :** the quality or state of being fast **2 :** a fortified or secure place **:** STRONGHOLD

¹fat \'fat\ *adj* **fat·ter; fat·test** [OE *fǣtt,* fr. pp. of *fǣtan* to cram] **1 a :** PLUMP, FLESHY **b :** OILY, GREASY **2 :** well stocked **:** ABUNDANT ⟨a *fat* purse⟩ **3 :** richly rewarding **:** PROFITABLE — **fat·ness** *n*

²fat *n* **1 :** animal tissue consisting chiefly of cells distended with greasy or oily matter **2 a :** any of numerous compounds of carbon, hydrogen, and oxygen that are esters of glycerol and fatty acids, the chief constituents of plant and animal fat, and a major class of energy-rich food, and that are soluble in organic solvents (as ether) but not in water **b :** a solid or semisolid fat as distinguished from an oil **3 :** the best or richest part ⟨lived on the *fat* of the land⟩ **4 :** excess matter

³fat *vt* **fat·ted; fat·ting :** to make fat **:** FATTEN

fa·tal \'fāt-°l\ *adj* **1 :** causing death or ruin **:** MORTAL ⟨a *fatal* accident⟩ **2 :** determining one's fate ⟨a *fatal* day in his life⟩ **syn** see DEADLY — **fa·tal·ly** \-°l-ē\ *adv*

fa·tal·ism \'fāt-°l-ˌiz-əm\ *n* **:** the belief that events are determined in advance by powers beyond man's control; *also* **:** the attitude of mind of a person holding this belief — **fa·tal·ist** \-°l-əst\ *n* — **fa·tal·is·tic** \ˌfāt-°l-'is-tik\ *adj* — **fa·tal·is·ti·cal·ly** \-'is-ti-k(ə-)lē\ *adv*

fa·tal·i·ty \fā-'tal-ət-ē, fə-\ *n, pl* **-ties** **1 a :** the quality or state of causing death **:** DEADLINESS **b :** the quality or condition of being destined for disaster **:** FATE 1 **3 :** a death resulting from a disaster or accident

fat·back \'fat-ˌbak\ *n* **:** a fatty strip from the back of the hog usu. cured by salting and drying

¹fate \'fāt\ *n* [L *fatum,* lit., what has been spoken, fr. neut. of *fatus,* pp. of *fari* to speak] **1 :** a power beyond men's control that is held to determine what happens **:** DESTINY ⟨blamed his failure on *fate*⟩ **2 :** something that happens as though determined by fate **:** FORTUNE ⟨it was his *fate* to outlive his children⟩ **3 :** END, OUTCOME ⟨awaited news of the *fate* of the polar expedition⟩ **4 :** DISASTER; *esp* **:** DEATH

syn FATE, DESTINY, LOT, DOOM mean a predetermined state or end. FATE implies an inevitable and usu. adverse outcome or end; DESTINY implies something foreordained and usu. suggests a great or notable course or end; LOT implies a distribution of success or happiness by fate or destiny according to blind chance; DOOM implies a grim or calamitous fate

²fate *vt* **:** DESTINE; *also* **:** DOOM

fate·ful \'fāt-fəl\ *adj* **1 :** having serious consequences **:** IMPORTANT ⟨a *fateful* decision⟩ **2 :** OMINOUS, PROPHETIC ⟨the *fateful* circling of the vultures overhead⟩ **3 :** determined by fate **4 :** DEADLY, DESTRUCTIVE — **fate·ful·ly** \-fə-lē\ *adv* — **fate·ful·ness** *n*

ə abut; ə kitten; ər further; a back; ā bake; ä cot, cart; au̇ out; ch chin; e less; ē easy; g gift; i trip; ī life

Fates \'fāts\ *n pl* : the three goddesses in classical mythology who determine the course of human life — compare ATROPOS, CLOTHO, LACHESIS

¹**fa·ther** \'fäth-ər\ *n* [OE *fæder*] **1 a** : a male parent **b** *cap* (1) : ²GOD (2) : the first person of the Trinity **2** : FOREFATHER **3 a** : one who cares for another as a father might **b** : one deserving the respect and love given to a father ⟨the *father* of his country⟩ **4** *often cap* : a pre‑Scholastic Christian writer accepted by the church as an authoritative witness to its teaching and practice **5** : ORIGINATOR, AUTHOR **6** : PRIEST — used esp. as a title **7** : one of the leading men (as of a city) — usu. used in pl.

²**father** *vt* **fa·thered; fa·ther·ing** \'fäth-(ə-)riŋ\ **1 a** : BEGET **b** : to be the founder, producer, or author of **2** : to treat or care for as a father

fa·ther·hood \'fäth-ər-,hùd\ *n* : the condition of being a father

fa·ther-in-law \'fäth-(ə-)rən-,lȯ, -ərn-,lȯ\ *n, pl* **fathers-in-law** \'fäth-ər-zən-\ : the father of one's spouse

fa·ther·land \'fäth-ər-,land\ *n* **1** : one's native land or country **2** : the native land or country of one's ancestors

fa·ther·less \-ləs\ *adj* : having no father : ORPHANED

fa·ther·ly \-lē\ *adj* **1** : of or resembling a father ⟨a *fatherly* old man⟩ **2** : showing the affection or concern of a father ⟨*fatherly* advice⟩ — **fa·ther·li·ness** *n*

Father's Day *n* : the 3d Sunday in June appointed for the honoring of fathers

¹**fath·om** \'fath-əm\ *n* [OE *fæthm* outstretched arms, length of the outstretched arms] : a unit of length equal to 6 feet that is used esp. for measuring the depth of water

²**fathom** *vb* **1** : to measure by a sounding line : take soundings; *also* : PROBE **2** : to penetrate and come to understand — **fath·om·a·ble** \'fath-ə-mə-bəl\ *adj*

Fa·thom·e·ter \fa-'tham-ət-ər, 'fath-ə(m)-,mēt-\ *trademark* — used for a sonic depth finder

fath·om·less \'fath-əm-ləs\ *adj* : incapable of being fathomed

¹**fa·tigue** \fə-'tēg\ *n* [F, fr. L *fatigare*] **1 a** : weariness from labor or exertion **b** : temporary loss of power to respond (as of a sense organ) after prolonged stimulation **2 a** : manual or menial work performed by military personnel **b** *pl* : the uniform or work clothing worn on fatigue and in the field **3** : the tendency of a material (as metal) to break under repeated stress (as bending)

²**fatigue** *vb* **1** : to weary or become weary with labor or exertion **2** : to induce a condition of fatigue in

fat·ling \'fat-liŋ\ *n* : a young animal fattened for slaughter

fats·hed·era \fats-'(h)ed-ə-rə\ *n* : a hybrid plant grown as a houseplant for its glossy deeply lobed leaves

fat-soluble *adj* : soluble in fats or fat solvents

fat·ten \'fat-ᵊn\ *vb* **fat·tened; fat·ten·ing** \'fat-niŋ, -ᵊn-iŋ\ **1** : to make or become fat ⟨*fatten* pigs for market⟩ ⟨cattle *fattening* on the range⟩ **2** : to make (as land) fertile — **fat·ten·er** \'fat-nər, -ᵊn-ər\ *n*

fat·ty \'fat-ē\ *adj* **fat·ti·er; -est** **1** : containing fat esp. in unusual amounts; *also* : unduly stout : CORPULENT **2** : GREASY — **fat·ti·ly** \'fat-ᵊl-ē\ *adv* — **fat·ti·ness** \'fat-ē-nəs\ *n*

fatty acid *n* : any of numerous saturated or unsaturated acids that contain only carbon, hydrogen, and oxygen and that occur naturally in the form of glycerides in fats and various oils

fa·tu·ity \fə-'t(y)ü-ət-ē, fa-\ *n, pl* **-ities** : FOOLISHNESS, STUPIDITY

fat·u·ous \'fach-(ə-)wəs\ *adj* [L *fatuus*] : complacently or inanely foolish : SILLY — **fat·u·ous·ly** *adv* — **fat·u·ous·ness** *n*

fau·bourg \fō-'bù(ə)r\ *n* [MF *fauxbourg*, alter. of OF *forsborc*, fr. *fors* outside + *borc* town] **1** : SUBURB; *esp* : a suburb of a French city **2** : a city quarter

fau·ces \'fȯ-,sēz\ *n pl* : the narrow passage between the soft palate and the base of the tongue that joins the mouth to the pharynx — **fau·cial** \'fȯ-shəl\ *adj*

fau·cet \'fȯ-sət, 'fäs-ət\ *n* [MF *fausset* bung, fr. *fausser* to breach, fr. LL *falsare* to falsify, fr. L *falsus* false] : a fixture for drawing a liquid from a pipe, cask, or other vessel

¹**fault** \'fȯlt\ *n* [OF *faute*, fr. (assumed) VL *fallitus*, pp. of L *fallere* to deceive, disappoint] **1 a** : a weakness in character : FAILING; *esp* : a moral weakness less serious than a vice **b** : a physical or intellectual imperfection or impairment **c** : an error in a service in tennis **2 a** : MISDEMEANOR **b** : MISTAKE **3** : responsibility for wrongdoing or failure **4** : a fracture in the earth's crust accompanied by a displacement of rock masses in a direction parallel to the fracture

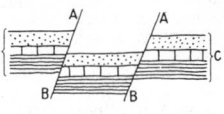

fault 4: *AB* fault; *C* strata originally continuous

syn FAULT, FAILING, FOIBLE mean a weakness or imperfection of character. FAULT applies to any failure, serious or trivial, to attain a standard of perfection in action, disposition, or habit; FAILING suggests a minor shortcoming in character; FOIBLE implies a harmless or even endearing weakness

— **at fault** : open to blame : RESPONSIBLE — **to a fault** : EXCESSIVELY ⟨generous *to a fault*⟩

²**fault** *vb* **1** : to commit a fault : ERR **2** : to fracture so as to produce a geologic fault **3** : to find a fault in ⟨could not *fault* his argument⟩

fault·find·er \'fȯlt-,fīn-dər\ *n* : a person who is inclined to find fault or complain — **fault·find·ing** \-diŋ\ *n or adj*

fault·less \'fȯlt-ləs\ *adj* : free from fault : being without error or imperfection : PERFECT — **fault·less·ly** *adv* — **fault·less·ness** *n*

faulty \'fȯl-tē\ *adj* : marked by fault, blemish, or defect : IMPERFECT — **fault·i·ly** \-tə-lē\ *adv* — **fault·i·ness** \-tē-nəs\ *n*

faun \'fȯn, 'fän\ *n* [L *faunus*, fr. *Faunus*, god of animals] : an ancient Italian deity of fields and herds represented as part goat and part man

fau·na \'fȯn-ə, 'fän-\ *n, pl* **faunas** *also* **fau·nae** \-,ē, -,ī\ : animals or animal life esp. of a region, period, or environment — compare FLORA — **fau·nal** \'fȯn-ᵊl\ *adj* — **fau·nal·ly** \-ᵊl-ē\ *adv*

fau·nis·tic \fȯ-'nis-tik, fä-\ *adj* : dealing with faunas and esp. their distribution : ZOOGEOGRAPHIC — **fau·nis·ti·cal·ly** \-ti-k(ə-)lē\ *adv*

Faust \'faùst\ *n* : a German magician and astrologer held to have sold his soul to the devil in exchange for worldly experience and power

fau·vism \'fō-,viz-əm\ *n, often cap* [F *fauvisme*, fr. *fauve* wild animal] : a movement in painting typified by the work of Matisse and characterized by vivid colors, free treatment of form, and a resulting vibrant and decorative effect — **fau·vist** \-vəst\ *n, often cap*

faux pas \(')fō-'pä\ *n, pl* **faux pas** \-'pä(z)\ [F, lit., false step] : BLUNDER; *esp* : a social blunder

fa·va bean \,fäv-ə-\ *n* [It *fava* bean] : BROAD BEAN

¹**fa·vor** \'fā-vər\ *n* **1** : friendly regard, fr. *favēre* to show favor] **1** *archaic* **a** : APPEARANCE **b** : COUNTENANCE **2 a** : friendly regard shown toward another esp. by a superior ⟨enjoyed the *favor* of the king⟩ **b** : APPROVAL, APPROBATION ⟨look with *favor* on a project⟩ **c** : PARTIALITY ⟨the judge showed *favor* to the defendant⟩ **d** : POPULARITY ⟨a fad loses *favor* quickly⟩ **3 a** : gracious kindness; *also* : an act of such kindness **b** *pl* : effort in one's behalf or interest : ATTENTION **4 a** : a token of love (as a ribbon) usu. worn conspicuously **b** : a small gift or decorative item given out at a party **5** : a special privilege or right granted or conceded **6** *archaic* : LETTER **7** : BEHALF, INTEREST — **in favor of** **1** : in accord or sympathy with **2** : in support of

²**favor** *vt* **fa·vored; fa·vor·ing** \'fāv-(ə-)riŋ\ **1 a** : to regard or treat with favor **b** (1) : to do a kindness for : OBLIGE (2) : ENDOW ⟨*favored* by nature⟩ **c** : to treat gently or carefully : SPARE ⟨*favor* a lame leg⟩ **2** : PREFER **3 a** : to give support to : SUSTAIN **b** : to afford advantages for success to : FACILITATE ⟨darkness *favors* attack⟩ **4** : to bear a resemblance to ⟨*favors* his father⟩ — **fa·vor·er** \'fā-vər-ər\ *n*

fa·vor·a·ble \'fāv-(ə-)rə-bəl, 'fā-vər-bəl\ *adj* **1** : showing favor : APPROVING ⟨a *favorable* opinion⟩ **2** : HELPFUL, PROMISING, ADVANTAGEOUS ⟨*favorable* weather⟩ — **fa·vor·a·ble·ness** *n* — **fa·vor·a·bly** \-blē\ *adv*

¹**fa·vor·ite** \'fāv-(ə-)rət\ *n* [It *favorito*, pp. of *favorire* to favor, fr. *favore* favor, fr. L *favor*] **1** : a person or a thing that is favored above others **2** : the contestant regarded as having the best chance to win

²**favorite** *adj* : constituting a favorite; *esp* : best-liked ⟨playing his *favorite* tune⟩

favorite son *n* : a candidate supported by the delegates of his state at a presidential nominating convention

fa·vor·it·ism \'fāv-(ə-)rət-,iz-əm\ *n* : unfairly favorable treatment of some to the neglect of others : PARTIALITY

fa·vus \'fā-vəs\ *n* [NL, fr. L, honeycomb] : a contagious skin disease caused by a fungus that may occur in man, domestic animals, and birds

¹**fawn** \'fȯn, 'fän\ *vi* [OE *fagnian* to rejoice, fr. *fægen* glad, fain] **1** : to show affection — used esp. of a dog **2** : to court favor by a cringing or flattering manner : GROVEL — **fawn·er** *n* — **fawn·ing·ly** \-iŋ-lē\ *adv*

²**fawn** *n* [MF *feon, faon* young of an animal, fr. L *fetus* offspring] **1** : a young deer; *esp* : one still unweaned or retaining a distinctive baby coat **2** : a variable color averaging a light grayish brown

fay \'fā\ *n* [MF *feie*] : FAIRY, ELF — **fay** *adj*

faze \'fāz\ *vt* [OE *fēsian* to drive away] : to disturb the composure or courage of : DAUNT

F clef *n* : BASS CLEF

fe·al·ty \'fē-(ə)l-tē\ *n* [OF *feelté, fealté*, fr. L *fidelitat-, fidelitas* fidelity] **1** : the loyalty of a feudal vassal to his lord **2** : LOYALTY, ALLEGIANCE

¹**fear** \'fi(ə)r\ *n* [OE *fær* sudden danger] **1 a** : an unpleasant often strong emotion caused by expectation or awareness of danger **b** : an instance of this emotion; *esp* : a state marked by this emotion **2** : anxious concern : SOLICITUDE **3** : reverential awe esp. toward God

syn FEAR, DREAD, FRIGHT, PANIC mean a painful emotion in the presence or expectation of danger. FEAR is the general term and implies great anxiety and usu. loss of courage; DREAD adds the idea of intense aversion and reluctance to face something; FRIGHT suggests the shock of sudden, startling appearance of danger or threat; PANIC implies completely dominating fear that causes hysterical activity

²**fear** *vb* **1** : to have a reverential awe of ⟨*fear* God⟩ **2** : to be afraid of : have fear **3** : to be apprehensive ⟨*feared* he would miss the train⟩ — **fear·er** *n*

fear·ful \'fi(ə)r-fəl\ *adj* **1** : causing fear ⟨the *fearful* roar of a lion⟩ **2** : filled with fear ⟨*fearful* of danger⟩ **3** : showing or caused by fear ⟨a *fearful* glance⟩ **4** : extremely bad, large, or intense ⟨*fearful* cold⟩ — **fear·ful·ly** \-fə-lē\ *adv* — **fear·ful·ness** *n*

fear·less \'fi(ə)r-ləs\ *adj* : free from fear : BRAVE — **fear·less·ly** *adv* — **fear·less·ness** *n*

fear·some \'fi(ə)r-səm\ *adj* **1** : causing fear **2** : TIMID, TIMOROUS — **fear·some·ly** *adv* — **fear·some·ness** *n*

fea·si·ble \'fē-zə-bəl\ *adj* [MF *faisible*, fr. *fais-, faire* to do, fr. L *facere*] **1** : capable of being done or carried out ⟨a *feasible* plan⟩ **2** : capable of being used or dealt with successfully : SUITABLE **3** : REASONABLE, LIKELY **syn** see POSSIBLE — **fea·si·bil·i·ty** \,fē-zə-'bil-ət-ē\ *n* — **fea·si·ble·ness** \'fē-zə-bəl-nəs\ *n* — **fea·si·bly** \-blē\ *adv*

¹**feast** \'fēst\ *n* [ME *feste*, fr. OF, festival, fr. L *festa*, pl. of *festum* festival, fr. *festus* solemn, festal] **1 a** : an elaborate meal : BANQUET **b** : something that gives great pleasure ⟨a *feast* of wit⟩ **2** : a religious festival : HOLY DAY

²**feast** *vb* **1** : to eat plentifully : participate in a feast **2** : to entertain with rich and plentiful food **3** : DELIGHT ⟨*feasted* his eyes on a beautiful scene⟩ — **feast·er** *n*

¹**feat** \'fēt\ *adj* **1** *archaic* : BECOMING, NEAT **2** *archaic* : SKILLFUL, DEXTEROUS

²**feat** *n* [MF *fait*, fr. L *factum*, fr. neut. of pp. of *facere* to do] **1** : ACT, DEED **2 a** : a deed notable esp. for courage **b** : an act or product of skill, endurance, or ingenuity **syn** FEAT, EXPLOIT, ACHIEVEMENT mean a remarkable deed. FEAT implies strength or dexterity or daring in achieving; EXPLOIT applies to an adventurous or heroic act that brings fame; ACHIEVEMENT implies hard-won success in the face of difficulty or opposition

¹**feath·er** \'feth-ər\ *n* [OE *fether*] **1 a** : one of the light horny outgrowths that form the external covering of the body of a bird **b** : the vane of an arrow **2 a** : KIND, NATURE **b** : ATTIRE, DRESS **c** : CONDITION, MOOD **3** : a feathery tuft or fringe of hair **4** : a projecting strip, rib, fin, or flange **5** : the act of feathering an oar — **feath·ered** \-ərd\ *adj* — **feath·er·less** \'feth-ər-ləs\ *adj* — **a feather in one's cap** : a mark of distinction : HONOR

²**feather** *vb* **feath·ered; feath·er·ing** \'feth-(ə-)riŋ\ **1 a** : to furnish (as an arrow) with a feather **b** : to cover, clothe, or adorn with feathers **2 a** : to turn (an oar blade) almost horizontal when lifting from the water at the end of a stroke in order to reduce air resistance **b** : to change the angle of (airplane propeller blades) so that the chords become approximately parallel to the line of flight **3** : to grow or form feathers **4** : to move, spread, or grow like feathers — **feather one's nest** : to provide for oneself esp. reprehensibly while in a position of trust

feath·er bed \'feth-ər-,bed\ *n* : a mattress filled with feathers; *also* : a bed with such a mattress

feath·er·bed·ding \-,bed-iŋ\ *n* : the requiring of an employer usu. under a union rule or safety statute to employ more workers than are needed or to limit production

feath·er·brain \'feth-ər-,brān\ *n* : a foolish scatterbrained person — **feath·er·brained** \,feth-ər-'brānd\ *adj*

feath·er·edge \'feth-ər-,ej\ *n* : a very thin sharp edge; *esp* : one that is easily broken or bent over — **featheredge** *vt*

feath·er·weight \-ər-,wāt\ *n* **1** : a very light weight; *esp* : the lightest weight a racehorse may carry in a handicap **2** : one that is very light in weight; *esp* : a boxer weighing more than 118 but not over 126 pounds

feath·ery \'feth-(ə-)rē\ *adj* : resembling, suggesting, or covered with feathers

¹**fea·ture** \'fē-chər\ *n* [MF *feture*, fr. L *factura* act of making, fr. *facere* to do, make] **1 a** : the shape or appearance of the face ⟨a man stern of *feature*⟩ **b** : a single part of the face (as the nose or the mouth) **2** : something esp. noticeable : a prominent part or detail : CHARACTERISTIC ⟨such earth *features* as mountains and rivers⟩ **3** : a main or outstanding attraction: as **a** : the principal motion picture on a program **b** : a special column or section in a newspaper or magazine

²**feature** *vb* **fea·tured; fea·tur·ing** \'fēch-(ə-)riŋ\ **1** : to outline or mark the features of **2** : to give special prominence to ⟨*feature* a story in a newspaper⟩ **3** : to play an important part

fea·ture·less \'fē-chər-ləs\ *adj* : having no distinctive features

feaze \'fēz, 'fāz\ *var of* FAZE

feb·ri·fuge \'feb-rə-,fyüj\ *n* [F *fébrifuge*, fr. L *febris* fever + *fugare* to put to flight] : a medicine for relieving fever — **febrifuge** *or* **fe·brif·u·gal** \fi-'brif-(y)i-gəl\ *adj*

fe·brile \'feb-rəl, 'fēb-, -,rīl\ *adj* : of or relating to fever : FEVERISH

Feb·ru·ary \'feb-(y)ə-,wer-ē, 'feb-rə-\ *n* [L *Februarius*, fr. *Februa*, pl., a festival held during the month] : the 2d month of the year

fe·ces \'fē-(,)sēz\ *n pl* [ME, sediment, dregs, fr. L *faeces*, pl. of *faec-, faex*] : bodily waste discharged through the anus : EXCREMENT — **fe·cal** \'fē-kəl\ *adj*

feck·less \'fek-ləs\ *adj* [Sc *feck* value] **1** : INEFFECTUAL, WEAK **2** : WORTHLESS — **feck·less·ly** *adv* — **feck·less·ness** *n*

fe·cund \'fē-kənd, 'fek-ənd\ *adj* [L *fecundus*] **1** : fruitful in offspring or vegetation : PROLIFIC **2** : intellectually productive or inventive to a marked degree — **fe·cun·di·ty** \fi-'kən-dət-ē\ *n*

fe·cun·date \'fek-ən-,dāt, 'fē-kən-\ *vt* : FERTILIZE — **fe·cun·da·tion** \,fek-ən-'dā-shən, ,fē-kən-\ *n*

fed·er·al \'fed-(ə-)rəl\ *adj* [L *foeder-, foedus* compact, league] **1 a** : formed by a compact between political units that surrender individual sovereignty to a central authority but retain certain limited powers **b** : of or constituting a form of government in which power is distributed between a central authority and constituent territorial units **c** : of or relating to the central government of a federation **2** *often cap* : FEDERALIST **3** *often cap* : of, relating to, or loyal to the federal government or the Union armies of the U.S. in the American Civil War — **fed·er·al·ly** \-ē\ *adv*

Federal *n* **1** : a supporter of the government of the U.S. in the Civil War; *esp* : a soldier in the federal armies **2** : a federal agent or officer

federal district *n* : a district (as the District of Columbia) set apart as the seat of the central government of a federation

fed·er·al·ism \'fed-(ə-)rə-,liz-əm\ *n* **1 a** *often cap* : the federal principle of organization **b** : support or advocacy of this principle **2** *cap* : the principles of the Federalists

fed·er·al·ist \-ləst\ *n* **1** : an advocate of federalism; *esp*, *often cap* : an advocate of a federal union between the American colonies after the Revolution and of the adoption of the U.S. Constitution **2** *cap* : a member of a major political party in the early years of the U.S. favoring a strong centralized national government — **federalist** adj, often cap

fed·er·al·ize \'fed-(ə-)rə-,līz\ vt **1** : to unite in or under a federal system **2** : to bring under the jurisdiction of a federal government — **fed·er·al·i·za·tion** \,fed-(ə-)rə-lə-'zā-shən\ n

Federal Reserve system n : a system of 12 central banks in the U.S. that serve as a depository for reserves of affiliated banks, engage in rediscounting, and serve as a clearinghouse for checks

fed·er·ate \'fed-ə-,rāt\ vb : to join in a federation

fed·er·a·tion \,fed-ə-'rā-shən\ n **1** : the act of federating; esp : the formation of a federal union **2** : something formed by federation: as **a** : a federal government **b** : a union of organizations

fed·er·a·tive \'fed-ə-,rāt-iv, 'fed-(ə-)rət-\ adj : FEDERAL

fe·do·ra \fi-'dōr-ə, -'dȯr-\ n [Fédora (1882), drama by V. Sardou in which a type of fedora was introduced] : a low soft felt hat with the crown creased lengthwise

fedora

fed up adj : tired, sated, or disgusted beyond endurance ⟨fed up with his mistakes⟩

fee \'fē\ n [OF fief, fé, of Gmc origin] **1 a** : an estate in land held from a feudal lord in return for homage and service paid him **b** : an inherited or heritable estate in land **2 a** : a fixed charge ⟨admission fee to a museum⟩ ⟨license fee⟩ **b** : a charge for a professional service ⟨a doctor's fees⟩ **c** : GRATUITY, TIP syn see WAGE — **in fee** : as a fee ⟨land held in fee⟩

fee·ble \'fē-bəl\ adj fee·bler \-b(ə-)lər\; -blest \-b(ə-)ləst\ [OF feble, fr. L flebilis lamentable, wretched, fr. flēre to weep] **1** : lacking in strength or endurance : WEAK **2** : not vigorous or loud : INEFFECTIVE, INADEQUATE ⟨a feeble cry⟩ ⟨a feeble protest⟩ — **fee·ble·ness** \-bəl-nəs\ n — **fee·bly** \-blē\ adv

fee·ble·mind·ed \,fē-bəl-'mīn-dəd\ adj : lacking normal intelligence : mentally deficient — **fee·ble·mind·ed·ness** n

¹feed \'fēd\ vb fed \'fed\; feed·ing [OE fēdan] **1 a** : to give food to **b** : to give as food **c** : to consume food : EAT **d** : PREY — used with on, upon, or off **2 a** : to furnish with something essential to growth, sustenance, or operation **b** : to become nourished or satisfied as if by food **3** : to give satisfaction to : GRATIFY **4 a** : to supply (as material) for use or consumption **b** : to supply (a signal) to an electronic circuit **5** : to supply with cues and situations that make a role more effective

²feed n **1 a** : an act of eating **b** : MEAL; esp : a large meal **2 a** : food for livestock **b** : the amount given at each feeding **3 a** : material supplied (as to a furnace) **b** : a mechanism by which the action of feeding is effected

feed·back \'fēd-,bak\ n : the return to the input of a part of the output of a machine, system, or process

feed·er \'fēd-ər\ n : one that feeds: as **a** : a device or apparatus for supplying food : TRIBUTARY **c** : a source of supply **d** : an animal being fattened or suitable for fattening **e** : an actor or role that serves as a foil for another

feed·stuff \'fēd-,stəf\ n : FEED 2a; also : any of the nutrients in an animal ration

¹feel \'fēl\ vb felt \'felt\; feel·ing [OE fēlan] **1 a** : to perceive as a result of physical contact ⟨feel a blow⟩ ⟨feel cold⟩ **b** : to examine or test by touching : HANDLE ⟨felt the silk between her fingers⟩ **2 a** : EXPERIENCE **b** : to suffer from **3** : to ascertain by cautious trial — often used with out **4 a** : to be aware of : BELIEVE, THINK **5** : to search for something with the fingers **6** : to seem esp. to the sense of touch ⟨feels like wool⟩ **7** : to have sympathy or pity ⟨I feel for you⟩

²feel n **1** : the sense of touch **2** : SENSATION, FEELING **3** : the quality of a thing as imparted through touch

feel·er \'fē-lər\ n **1** : one that feels; esp : a tactile process (as a tentacle) of an animal **2** : a proposal or remark made to find out the views of other people

¹feel·ing \'fē-liŋ\ n **1 a** : a sense which is mediated chiefly through receptors in the skin and of which the sensations of touch and temperature are characteristic; esp : TOUCH 3 **b** : a sensation experienced through this sense **2 a** : an often indefinite state of mind ⟨a feeling of loneliness⟩; also : such a state with regard to something ⟨feeling of dislike⟩ **b** pl : general emotional

condition : SENSIBILITIES **3 a** : the overall quality of one's awareness **b** : conscious recognition : SENSE **4 a** : OPINION, BELIEF **b** : unreasoned attitude : SENTIMENT **c** : PRESENTIMENT **5** : capacity to respond emotionally esp. with the higher emotions : SYMPATHY **6** : the quality of a work of art that embodies and conveys the emotion of the artist

syn EMOTION, SENTIMENT: FEELING applies to any response or awareness marked by pleasure, pain, attraction, or repulsion; it may suggest the existence of a response without implying anything definite about its nature or intensity; EMOTION implies a clearly defined feeling and usu. greater excitement or agitation; SENTIMENT may imply emotion inspired by an idea or belief ⟨he argued more from grounds of moral sentiment than cold logic⟩

²feeling adj **1** : SENSITIVE; esp : easily moved emotionally — **feel·ing·ly** \'fē-liŋ-lē\ adv — **feel·ing·ness** n

feet pl of FOOT

feet-first \'fēt-'fərst\ adv : with both feet or all four feet foremost ⟨jumped into the water feetfirst⟩

feign \'fān\ vb [OF feign-, feindre, fr. L fingere to shape, feign] **1** : to represent by a false appearance of : SHAM ⟨feign an excuse⟩ **2** : to assert as if true : PRETEND ⟨feign illness⟩ — **feign·er** n

feint \'fānt\ n [F feinte, fr. feindre to feign] : something feigned; esp : a mock blow or attack at one point in order to distract attention from the point one really intends to attack — **feint** vi

feist \'fīst\ n [obs. fisting hound, fr. obs. fist to break wind] chiefly dial : a small dog

feld·spar \'fel(d)-,spär\ n [modif. of G feldspat, lit., field spar] : any of a group of crystalline minerals that consist of silicates of aluminum with either potassium, sodium, calcium, or barium and that are an essential constituent of nearly all crystalline rocks

fe·lic·i·tate \fi-'lis-ə-,tāt\ vt : to wish joy to : CONGRATULATE — **fe·lic·i·ta·tion** \-,lis-ə-'tā-shən\ n — **fe·lic·i·ta·tor** \-'lis-ə-,tāt-ər\ n

fe·lic·i·tous \fi-'lis-ət-əs\ adj **1** : suitably expressed : APT ⟨felicitous wording⟩ **2** : possessing a talent for apt expression ⟨a felicitous speaker⟩ — **fe·lic·i·tous·ly** adv — **fe·lic·i·tous·ness** n

fe·lic·i·ty \fi-'lis-ət-ē\ n, pl -ties [L felicitas, fr. felic-, felix happy] **1** : the quality or state of being happy; esp : great happiness **2** : something that causes happiness **3** : a pleasing faculty esp. in art or language : APTNESS **4** : an apt expression

fe·lid \'fē-ləd\ n : CAT 1b — **felid** adj

fe·line \'fē-,līn\ adj [L felinus, fr. felis cat] **1 a** : of or relating to cats or the cat family **b** : resembling a cat **2 a** : SLY, TREACHEROUS **b** : STEALTHY — **feline** n — **fe·line·ly** adv — **fe·lin·i·ty** \fē-'lin-ət-ē\ n

¹fell \'fel\ n [OE] : SKIN, HIDE, PELT

²fell vt [OE fellan; akin to E fall] **1 a** : to cut, beat, or knock down ⟨fell trees for lumber⟩ **b** : KILL **2** : to sew (a seam) by folding one raw edge under the other — **fell·a·ble** \-ə-bəl\ adj

³fell past of FALL

⁴fell adj [OF fel, fr. ML fello villain, felon] : FIERCE, CRUEL; also : DEADLY

fel·lah \'fel-ə, fə-'lä\ n, pl fel·la·hin \,fel-ə-'hēn, fə-,lä-'hēn\ [Ar fallāḥ] : a peasant or agricultural laborer in Arab countries (as Egypt or Syria)

¹fel·low \'fel-ō\ n [OE fēolaga, fr. ON fēlagi, fr. fē cattle, money + lag act of laying] **1** : COMRADE, ASSOCIATE **2 a** : an equal in rank, power, or character : PEER **b** : one of a pair : MATE **3** : a member of an incorporated literary or scientific society **4 a** : a worthless man or boy : MAN, BOY **c** : BOYFRIEND **5** : a person granted a stipend for advanced study

²fellow adj : being a companion, mate, or associate ⟨a fellow lodge member⟩

fel·low·man \,fel-ō-'man\ n : a kindred human being

fel·low·ship \'fel-ō-,ship\ n **1** : the condition of friendly relationship existing among persons **2** : a community of interest or feeling **3** : a group with similar interests **4 a** : the position of a fellow (as of a university) **b** : the stipend granted a fellow or a foundation providing such a stipend

fellow traveler n [trans. of Russ poputchik] : a person who sympathizes with and often furthers the ideals and program of an organized group (as the Communist party) without joining it or regularly participating in its activities

fel·ly \'fel-ē\ *or* **fel·loe** \-ō\ *n, pl* **fellies** *or* **felloes** [OE *felg*] : the outside rim or a part of the rim of a wheel supported by the spokes

¹**fel·on** \'fel-ən\ *n* [OF, villain, fr. ML *fellon-, fello*] : CRIMINAL; *esp* : one who has committed a felony

²**felon** *n* [OF, lit., villain] : a deep inflammation of the finger or toe esp. near the end or around the nail and usu. with pus

fel·o·ny \'fel-ə-nē\ *n, pl* **-nies** : a serious crime usu. punishable by a sentence heavier than that for a misdemeanor — **fe·lo·ni·ous** \fə-'lō-nē-əs\ *adj* — **fe·lo·ni·ous·ly** *adv* — **fe·lo·ni·ous·ness** *n*

fel·spar \'fel-,spär\ *var of* FELDSPAR

¹**felt** \'felt\ *n* [OE] **1** : a cloth made of wool and fur often mixed with natural or synthetic fibers through the action of heat, moisture, chemicals, and pressure **2** : an article (as a hat) made of felt **3** : a material resembling felt

²**felt** *vt* **1** : to make into felt **2** : to cause to adhere and mat together **3** : to cover with felt

³**felt** *past of* FEEL

felt·ing \'fel-tiŋ\ *n* **1** : the process by which felt is made **2** : FELT

fe·luc·ca \fə-'lü-kə, -'lək-ə\ *n* [It *feluca*] : a narrow fast lateen-rigged sailing ship of the Mediterranean

¹**fe·male** \'fē-,māl\ *n* [ME *femelle*, fr. MF & ML; MF, fr. ML *femella*, fr. L, girl, dim. of *femina* woman] : a female plant or animal

²**female** *adj* **1 a** : of, relating to, or being the sex that bears young **b** : PISTILLATE; *esp* : having only pistillate flowers ⟨a *female* holly⟩ **2 a** : of, relating to, or characteristic of the female sex ⟨a high *female* voice⟩ **b** : made up of females ⟨a large *female* population⟩ **3** : designed with a hollow into which a corresponding male part fits ⟨a *female* hose coupling⟩ — **fe·male·ness** *n*

syn FEMININE, WOMANLY, EFFEMINATE: FEMALE applies to animals and plants in distinguishing sex; FEMININE applies to qualities or attitudes characteristic of women and not shared by men ⟨*feminine* grace and softness⟩; WOMANLY suggests qualities esp. associated with the ideal wife or mother; EFFEMINATE applies to qualities in men that imply a lack of virility or masculinity or strength ⟨a drooping *effeminate* pose⟩

¹**fem·i·nine** \'fem-ə-nən\ *adj* [L *femininus*, fr. *femina* woman] **1** : of the female sex **2** : characteristic of or belonging to women : WOMANLY ⟨a *feminine* concern with clothes⟩ **3** : of, relating to, or constituting the class of words that ordinarily includes most of those referring to females ⟨a *feminine* noun⟩⟨*feminine* gender⟩ **4** : having or occurring in an unstressed extra final syllable ⟨*feminine* rhyme⟩ **syn** see FEMALE — **fem·i·nine·ly** *adv* — **fem·i·nine·ness** \-nən-nəs\ *n*

²**feminine** *n* **1** : the female principle ⟨eternal *feminine*⟩ **2 a** : a word or form of the feminine gender **b** : the feminine gender

fem·i·nin·i·ty \,fem-ə-'nin-ət-ē\ *n* **1** : the quality or nature of the female sex **2** : EFFEMINACY **3** : WOMEN, WOMANKIND

fem·i·nism \'fem-ə-,niz-əm\ *n* **1** : the theory of the political, economic, and social equality of the sexes **2** : organized activity on behalf of women's rights and interests — **fem·i·nist** \-nəst\ *n or adj* — **fem·i·nis·tic** \,fem-ə-'nis-tik\ *adj*

fe·mur \'fē-mər\ *n, pl* **fe·murs** *or* **fem·o·ra** \'fem-(ə-)rə\ [NL *femor-, femur*, fr. L, thigh] **1** : the long bone of the hind or lower limb extending from the hip to the knee and supporting the thigh — called also *thighbone* **2** : the segment of an insect's leg that is third from the body — **fem·o·ral** \'fem-(ə-)rəl\ *adj*

fen \'fen\ *n* [OE *fenn*] : low land covered naturally in whole or in part with water

¹**fence** \'fen(t)s\ *n* [ME, defense, short for *defense*] **1** : a barrier intended to prevent escape or intrusion or to mark a boundary; *esp* : such a barrier made of posts and wire or boards **2** : a person who receives stolen goods or a shop where stolen goods are disposed of — **fence·less** \-ləs\ *adj* — **on the fence** : in a state of indecision (as between two plans or policies)

²**fence** *vb* **1 a** : to enclose with a fence **b** : to keep in or out with a fence **2 a** : to practice fencing **b** : to use tactics

of attack and defense esp. in debate resembling those of fencing — **fenc·er** *n*

fenc·ing *n* **1** : the art or practice of attack and defense with a sword or foil **2 a** : the fences of a property or region **b** : material used for building fences

fend \'fend\ *vb* [ME *fenden*, short for *defenden*] **1** : to keep or ward off : REPEL **2** : to try to get along without help : SHIFT ⟨*fend* for himself⟩

fend·er \'fen-dər\ *n* : a device that protects: as **a** : a cushion to lessen shock **b** : RAILING **c** : a device in front of a locomotive or streetcar to lessen injury to animals or pedestrians in case of collision **d** : a guard over the wheel of a motor vehicle **e** : a screen or a low metal frame before an open fireplace

fe·nes·tra \fi-'nes-trə\ *n, pl* **-trae** \-,trē, -,trī\ [L, window] : a small opening; *esp* : either of two apertures in the bone between the middle and inner ear — **fe·nes·tral** \-trəl\ *adj*

fe·nes·trat·ed \fi-'nes-,trāt-əd, 'fen-əs-\ *adj* : having openings or transparent spots

fen·es·tra·tion \,fen-əs-'trā-shən\ *n* : the arrangement, proportioning, and design of windows and doors in a building

Fe·ni·an \'fē-nē-ən\ *n* **1** : one of a legendary band of Irish warriors of the 2d and 3d centuries A.D. **2** : a member of a secret 19th century Irish and Irish-American organization dedicated to the overthrow of British rule in Ireland — **Fenian** *adj*

fen·nec \'fen-ik\ *n* [Ar *fanak*] : a small large-eared African fox

fen·nel \'fen-ᵊl\ *n* [OE *finugl*, fr. L *feniculum*, dim. of *fenum* hay] : a perennial European herb of the carrot family grown for its aromatic seeds

fen·ny \'fen-ē\ *adj* **1** : BOGGY **2** : peculiar to or found in a fen

fen·u·greek \'fen-yə-,grēk\ *n* [MF *fenugrec*, fr. L *fenum graecum*, lit., Greek hay] : a white-flowered Old World legume with aromatic seeds once used in medicine

fe·ral \'fir-əl, 'fer-\ *adj* [L *ferus* wild] : having escaped from domestication and become wild

fer·bam \'fər-,bam\ *n* : an agricultural fungicide used esp. on fruit trees

fer-de-lance \,ferd-ᵊl-'an(t)s, -'än(t)s\ *n, pl* **fer-de-lance** [F, lit., lance iron] : a large extremely poisonous pit viper of Central and So. America

fe·ria \'fir-ē-ə\ *n* : a weekday of the Roman Catholic or Anglican church calendar on which no feast is celebrated — **fe·ri·al** \-ē-əl\ *adj*

¹**fer·ment** \(,)fər-'ment\ *vb* **1** : to undergo or cause to undergo fermentation **2** : to be or cause to be in a state of agitation or intense activity : EXCITE — **fer·ment·a·ble** \-ə-bəl\ *adj* — **fer·ment·er** *n*

²**fer·ment** \'fər-,ment\ *n* [L *fermentum* yeast] **1** : an agent capable of bringing about fermentation **2 a** : FERMENTATION **1 b** : a state of unrest : AGITATION

fer·men·ta·tion \,fər-mən-'tā-shən, -,men-\ *n* **1** : chemical decomposition of an organic substance (as in the souring of milk or the formation of alcohol from sugar) produced by an enzyme and often accompanied by the evolution of a gas; *esp* : such an energy-yielding decomposition proceeding without the aid of free oxygen **2** : FERMENT **2b** — **fer·men·ta·tive** \(,)fər-'ment-ət-iv\ *adj*

fer·mi·um \'fer-mē-əm, 'fər-\ *n* [after Enrico *Fermi* d1954 Italian physicist] : a radioactive metallic element artificially produced (as by bombardment of plutonium with neutrons) — see ELEMENT table

fern \'fərn\ *n* [OE *fearn*] : any of a class (Filicineae) of flowerless seedless vascular plants; *esp* : any of an order (Filicales) resembling seed plants in being differentiated into root, stem, and leaflike fronds but reproducing by spores — **fern·like** \-,līk\ *adj* — **ferny** \'fər-nē\ *adj*

fern·ery \'fərn-(ə-)rē\ *n, pl* **-er·ies** **1** : a place for growing ferns **2** : a collection of growing ferns

fe·ro·cious \fə-'rō-shəs\ *adj* [L *feroc-, ferox*] **1** : CRUEL, SAVAGE **2** : unbearably intense ⟨*ferocious* heat⟩ **syn** see FIERCE — **fe·ro·cious·ly** *adv* — **fe·ro·cious·ness** *n*

fe·roc·i·ty \fə-'räs-ət-ē\ *n, pl* **-ties** : the quality or state of being ferocious

-fer·ous \f-(ə-)rəs\ *adj comb form* [L *-fer*, fr. *ferre* to bear; akin to E *bear*] : bearing : producing ⟨coniferous⟩

¹**fer·ret** \'fer-ət\ *n* [MF *furet*, fr. L *fur* thief] : a partially

domesticated usu. albino European polecat used esp. for hunting rodents
²ferret *vb* **1 :** to hunt game with ferrets **2 a :** to drive out of a hiding place **b :** to find and bring to light by searching — usu. used with *out* — **fer·ret·er** *n*
fer·ric \'fer-ik\ *adj* **1 :** of, relating to, or containing iron **2 :** being or containing iron with a higher valence (as three) than in ferrous compounds
ferric oxide *n* **:** the red or black oxide of iron Fe_2O_3 that is found in nature as hematite and as rust and is obtained synthetically and that is used as a pigment and for polishing
Fer·ris wheel \'fer-əs-\ *n* **:** an amusement device consisting of a large upright power-driven wheel carrying seats that remain horizontal around its rim
ferro- *comb form* [L *ferrum*] **1 :** iron ⟨*ferro*concrete⟩ **2 :** iron and ⟨*ferro*nickel⟩
fer·ro·con·crete \,fer-ō-'kän-,krēt, -,kän-'\ *n* **:** REINFORCED CONCRETE
fer·ro·mag·net·ic \-mag-'net-ik\ *adj* **:** of or relating to substances having magnetic properties similar to but weaker than those of iron and steel
¹fer·ro·type \'fer-ə-,tīp\ *n* **:** a photograph on a thin iron plate having a darkened surface
²ferrotype *vt* **:** to give a gloss to (a photographic print) by pressing with the face down while wet on a metal plate and allowing to dry
fer·rous \'fer-əs\ *adj* **1 :** of, relating to, or containing iron **2 :** being or containing bivalent iron
ferrous oxide *n* **:** the monoxide of iron FeO
ferrous sulfate *n* **:** a salt FeSO₄ that consists of iron, sulfur, and oxygen and is used in making pigments and ink, in treating industrial wastes, and in medicine
fer·ru·gi·nous \fə-'rü-jə-nəs, fe-\ *or* **fer·ru·gin·e·ous** \,fer-(y)ü-'jin-ē-əs\ *adj* [L *ferrugin-, ferrugo* iron rust, fr. *ferrum* iron] **1 :** of, relating to, or containing iron **2 :** resembling iron rust in color
fer·rule \'fer-əl\ *n* [alter. of ME *virole*, fr. MF, fr. L *viriola* little bracelet] **:** a metal ring or cap placed around the end of a slender shaft of wood (as a cane) or around a tool handle to prevent splitting or to provide a strong well-fitting joint
¹fer·ry \'fer-ē\ *vb* **fer·ried; fer·ry·ing** [OE *ferian* to carry, convey; akin to L *fare*] **1 a :** to carry by boat over a body of water **b :** to cross by a ferry **2 a :** to fly (an airplane) from the shipping point to a delivery point or from one base to another **b :** to transport in an airplane
²ferry *n*, *pl* **ferries 1 :** a place where persons or things are carried across a body of water (as a river) in a boat **2 :** FERRYBOAT **3 :** an organized service and route for flying airplanes — **fer·ry·man** \-mən\ *n*
fer·ry·boat \-,bōt\ *n* **:** a boat used to ferry passengers, vehicles, or goods
fer·tile \'fərt-əl\ *adj* [L *fertilis*, fr. *ferre* to bear] **1 :** producing or bearing fruit in great quantities **:** PRODUCTIVE **2 a (1) :** capable of sustaining abundant plant growth **(2) :** affording abundant possibilities for development **b :** capable of growing or developing ⟨*fertile* egg⟩ **c :** capable of reproducing or of producing reproductive cells ⟨a *fertile* bull⟩ ⟨*fertile* fungous hyphae⟩ — **fer·tile·ly** \-əl-(l)ē\ *adv* — **fer·tile·ness** \-əl-nəs\ *n* — **fer·til·i·ty** \(,)fər-'til-ət-ē\ *n*
syn FRUITFUL, PROLIFIC: FERTILE implies having the inherent power to reproduce in kind or to assist in reproduction and growth ⟨*fertile* soil⟩ FRUITFUL adds the implication of actually producing desirable and useful results ⟨*fruitful* methods⟩ PROLIFIC stresses the power of multiplying and spreading rapidly ⟨*prolific* rabbits⟩ or of creating freely ⟨*prolific* writer⟩
fer·til·i·za·tion \,fərt-əl-ə-'zā-shən\ *n* **:** an act or process of making fertile: as **a :** the application of fertilizer **b :** the process of union of male and female germ cells whereby a zygote is formed — **fer·til·i·za·tion·al** \-shnəl, -shən-əl\ *adj*
fer·til·ize \'fərt-əl-,īz\ *vt* **:** to make fertile: as **a :** to cause the fertilization of **b :** to apply a fertilizer to ⟨*fertilize* land⟩ — **fer·til·iz·a·ble** \-,ī-zə-bəl\ *adj*
fer·til·iz·er \-,ī-zər\ *n* **:** one that fertilizes; *esp* **:** a substance (as manure or a chemical mixture) used to make soil more fertile
fer·ule \'fer-əl\ *n* [L *ferula*] **:** a rod or ruler used in punishing children

fer·ven·cy \'fər-vən-sē\ *n* **:** FERVOR
fer·vent \'fər-vənt\ *adj* [L *fervent-, fervens*, prp. of *fervēre* to boil, glow] **1 :** very hot **:** GLOWING **2 :** marked by great warmth of feeling **:** ARDENT — **fer·vent·ly** *adv*
fer·vid \'fər-vəd\ *adj* [L *fervidus*, fr. *fervēre* to boil] **1 :** very hot **:** BURNING **2 :** ARDENT, ZEALOUS — **fer·vid·ly** *adv* — **fer·vid·ness** *n*
fer·vor \'fər-vər\ *n* **1 :** intense heat **2 :** intensity of feeling **:** fervid emotion or words **:** ENTHUSIASM **syn** see PASSION
fes·cue \'fes-kyü\ *n* [MF *festu* stalk, straw, fr. L *festuca*] **:** a tufted perennial grass with panicled spikelets
fess \'fes\ *n* [MF *faisse*, fr. L *fascia* band] **:** a broad horizontal bar across the middle of a heraldic field
-fest \,fest\ *n comb form* [G *fest* celebration, fr. L *festum*] **:** meeting or occasion marked by (such) activity ⟨talk*fest*⟩
fes·tal \'fest-əl\ *adj* [L *festum* feast, festival] **:** of or relating to a feast or festival **:** FESTIVE — **fes·tal·ly** \-əl-ē\ *adv*
¹fes·ter \'fes-tər\ *n* [MF *festre*, fr. L *fistula* pipe, fistula] **:** a pus-filled sore **:** PUSTULE
²fester *vb* **fes·tered; fes·ter·ing** \-t(ə-)riŋ\ **1 a :** to form pus **b :** to become painful and inflamed **2 :** PUTREFY, ROT **3 :** to grow or cause to grow increasingly more acute and harder to bear **:** RANKLE ⟨resentment *festered* in his mind⟩
¹fes·ti·val \'fes-tə-vəl\ *adj* **:** of, relating to, appropriate to, or set apart as a festival
²festival *n* **1 :** a time of celebration marked by special observances **2 :** a periodic season or program of cultural events or entertainment ⟨a music *festival*⟩
Festival of Lights *n* **:** HANUKKAH
fes·tive \'fes-tiv\ *adj* **1 :** of, relating to, or suitable for a feast or festival **2 :** JOYOUS, GAY — **fes·tive·ly** *adv* — **fes·tive·ness** *n*
fes·tiv·i·ty \fe-'stiv-ət-ē\ *n*, *pl* **-ties 1 :** FESTIVAL 1 **2 :** the quality or state of being festive **:** GAIETY **3 :** festive activity
¹fes·toon \fe-'stün\ *n* [F *feston*, fr. It *festone*, fr. L *festa* festival] **1 :** a decorative chain or strip hanging between two points **2 :** a carved, molded, or painted ornament representing a decorative chain
²festoon *vt* **1 :** to hang or form festoons on **2 :** to shape into festoons
¹fetch \'fech\ *vb* [OE *feccan*] **1 :** to go after and bring back ⟨teach a dog to *fetch* a stick⟩ **2 :** to cause to come **:** bring out ⟨*fetched* tears from the eyes⟩ **3 a :** to take in ⟨*fetching* her breath⟩ **b :** HEAVE ⟨*fetch* a sigh⟩ **4 :** to bring as a price **:** sell for **5 :** to give by striking ⟨*fetch* him a blow in the face⟩ **6 :** ARRIVE ⟨*fetched* up at the wharf on time⟩ — **fetch·er** *n*
²fetch *n* **1 :** an act or instance of fetching **2 :** TRICK, STRATAGEM
fetch·ing *adj* **:** ATTRACTIVE, PLEASING — **fetch·ing·ly** \-iŋ-lē\ *adv*
¹fete *or* **fête** \'fāt\ *n* [F *fête*, fr. OF *feste*] **1 :** FESTIVAL **2 a :** a lavish often outdoor entertainment **b :** an elaborate usu. large party
²fete *or* **fête** *vt* **1 :** to honor or commemorate with a fete **2 :** to pay high honor to
fet·er·i·ta \,fet-ə-'rēt-ə\ *n* **:** a grain sorghum with compact heads of soft white seeds
fet·id \'fet-əd\ *adj* [L *foetidus*, fr. *foetēre* to stink] **:** having an offensive smell **:** STINKING — **fet·id·ly** *adv* — **fet·id·ness** *n*
fet·ish *or* **fet·ich** \'fet-ish, 'fēt-\ *n* [F *fétiche*, fr. Pg *feitiço*, fr. *feitiço* artificial, fr. L *facticius*, fr. *fact-, facere* to make] **1 :** an object (as an idol or image) believed to have supernatural or magical powers **2 :** something that is made an object of unreasoning devotion or concern ⟨make a *fetish* of social position⟩ — **fet·ish·ism** \-,iz-əm\ *n*
fet·lock \'fet-,läk\ *n* [ME *fitlok;* akin to E *foot*] **1 :** a projection with a tuft of hair on the back of a horse's leg above the hoof **2 :** the tuft of hair growing out of the fetlock
¹fet·ter \'fet-ər\ *n* [OE *feter;* akin to E *foot*] **1 :** a chain or shackle for the feet **2 :** something that confines **:** RESTRAINT
²fetter *vt* **1 :** to put fetters on **:** SHACKLE **2 :** to restrain from motion or action **:** CONFINE **syn** see HAMPER

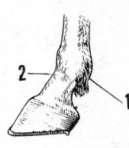

1 fetlock;
2 pastern

fet·tle \'fet-ᵊl\ *n* [ME *fetlen* to prepare] : a state of fitness or order : CONDITION ⟨in fine *fettle*⟩

fe·tus \'fēt-əs\ *n* [L, act of bearing young, offspring] : an unborn or unhatched vertebrate esp. after attaining the basic structural plan of its kind — compare EMBRYO — **fe·tal** \'fēt-ᵊl\ *adj*

¹feud \'fyüd\ *n* [alter. of ME *feide*, fr. MF, of Gmc origin; akin to E *foe*] : a prolonged quarrel; *esp* : a lasting conflict between families or clans marked by violent attacks undertaken for revenge — **feud** *vi*

²feud *n* [ML *feodum*, *feudum*, of Gmc origin] : FEE 1a

feu·dal \'fyüd-ᵊl\ *adj* 1 : of, relating to, or having the characteristics of a medieval fee 2 : of, relating to, or characteristic of feudalism — **feu·dal·ly** \-ᵊl-ē\ *adv*

feu·dal·ism \-,iz-əm\ *n* : a system of political organization prevailing in medieval Europe in which a vassal rendered service (as military) to a lord and received protection and a holding of land in return; *also* : any of various similar political or social systems — **feu·dal·is·tic** \,fyüd-ᵊl-'is-tik\ *adj*

¹feu·da·to·ry \'fyüd-ə-,tōr-ē, -,tor-\ *adj* : owing feudal allegiance : being in the relation of a vassal to his lord

²feudatory *n, pl* **-ries** 1 : a person who holds lands by feudal law or usage 2 : FIEF

fe·ver \'fē-vər\ *n* [OE *fēfer*, fr. L *febris*] 1 a : a rise of body temperature above the normal b : a disease of which fever is a prominent symptom 2 a : a state of heightened or intense emotion or activity b : a contagious transient enthusiasm : CRAZE

fever blister *n* : COLD SORE

fe·ver·few \'fē-vər-,fyü\ *n* : a perennial European herb related to the daisies

fe·ver·ish \'fēv-(ə-)rish\ *adj* 1 a : marked by fever b : of, relating to, or being fever c : tending to cause fever 2 : marked by intense emotion, activity, or instability — **fe·ver·ish·ly** *adv* — **fe·ver·ish·ness** *n*

¹few \'fyü\ *pron* [OE *fēawa*] : not many persons or things ⟨*few* were present⟩ ⟨*few* of his stories are true⟩

²few *adj* 1 : consisting of or amounting to a small number ⟨one of his *few* pleasures⟩ 2 : not many but some ⟨caught a *few* fish⟩ — **few·ness** *n*

³few *n* 1 : a small number of units or individuals ⟨a *few* of them⟩ 2 : a special limited number ⟨the discriminating *few*⟩

¹few·er \'fyü-ər\ *adj* : not so many : a smaller number of
syn LESS: FEWER is applied to countable things ⟨*fewer* dollars⟩ ⟨*fewer* hours⟩ LESS may refer to amount, degree, or value ⟨*less* pay⟩ ⟨*less* heat⟩ ⟨*less* beauty⟩

²fewer *pron* : a smaller number of persons or things ⟨*fewer* came than were expected⟩

fey \'fā\ *adj* 1 *chiefly Scot* : fated to die; *also* : marked by a foreboding of death or calamity 2 : ELFIN

fez \'fez\ *n, pl* **fez·zes** [F, fr. *Fez*, Morocco] : a round flat-crowned hat that usu. has a tassel, is made of red felt, and is worn by men in eastern Mediterranean countries

fia·cre \fē-'äkrᵊ\ *n, pl* **fi·acres** \-'äkrᵊ, -'äk-rəz\ [F, fr. the Hotel St. *Fiacre*, Paris] : a small hackney coach

fi·an·cé \,fē-,än-'sā, fē-'än-,sā\ *n* [F] : a man engaged to be married

fi·an·cée \,fē-,än-'sā, fē-'än-,sā\ *n* : a woman engaged to be married

fi·as·co \fē-'as-kō\ *n, pl* **-coes** [It] : a complete or ridiculous failure

fi·at \'fī-,at, 'fē-,ät\ *n* [L, let it be done, fr. *fieri* to be done, become; akin to E *be*] : an authoritative and often arbitrary order or decree

fiat money *n* : paper currency backed only by the authority of the government and not by metal

¹fib \'fib\ *n* : a lie about some trivial matter

²fib *vi* **fibbed**; **fib·bing** : to tell a fib — **fib·ber** *n*

fi·ber *or* **fi·bre** \'fī-bər\ *n* [F *fibre*, fr. L *fibra*] 1 : a thread or a structure or object resembling a thread: as a : a slender root (as of a grass) b : a long tapering thick-walled plant cell esp. of vascular tissue c : a muscle cell d : a slender and greatly elongated natural or synthetic unit of material (as wool, cotton, asbestos, gold, glass, or rayon) typically capable of being spun into yarn 2 : material made of fibers; *esp* : a tough hard or flexible material made from cellulose fibers and used for luggage 3 a : an element that gives texture or substance : basic toughness : STRENGTH

fi·ber·board \'fī-bər-,bōrd, -,bord\ *n* : a material made by compressing fibers (as of wood) into stiff sheets

fiber glass *n* : glass in fibrous form used in making various products (as yarn and insulation)

fi·bril \'fīb-rəl, 'fib-\ *n* : a small filament or fiber (as a root hair) — **fi·bril·lar** \-rə-lər\ *adj* — **fi·bril·lose** \-rə-,lōs\ *adj*

fi·bril·la·tion \,fib-rə-'lā-shən, ,fīb-\ *n* : rapid irregular contractions of muscle fibers (as of the heart)

fi·brin \'fī-brən\ *n* : a white insoluble fibrous protein formed from fibrinogen by the action of thrombin esp. in the clotting of blood — **fi·brin·ous** \-brə-nəs\ *adj*

fi·brin·o·gen \fī-'brin-ə-jən\ *n* : a globulin produced in the liver, present esp. in blood plasma, and converted into fibrin during clotting of blood

fi·bro·blast \'fī-brə-,blast\ *n* : a cell giving rise to connective tissue — **fi·bro·blas·tic** \,fī-brə-'blas-tik\ *adj*

fi·broid \'fī-,broid\ *adj* : resembling, forming, or consisting of fibrous tissue ⟨*fibroid* tumors⟩

fi·bro·sis \fī-'brō-səs\ *n* : a condition in which fibrous tissue infiltrates other tissues — **fi·brot·ic** \-'brät-ik\ *adj*

fi·brous \'fī-brəs\ *adj* 1 : containing, consisting of, or resembling fibers 2 : TOUGH, STRINGY

fibrous root *n* : a root that is one of many similar slender roots branching directly from the base of the stem of a plant — compare TAPROOT

fibrous tissue *n* : a connective tissue rich in fibers that infiltrates and supports body structures and is prominent in healing wounds

fi·bro·vas·cu·lar bundle \,fī-brō-,vas-kyə-lər-\ *n* : VASCULAR BUNDLE

fib·u·la \'fib-yə-lə\ *n, pl* **-lae** \-,lē, -,lī\ *or* **-las** [L, clasp, brace] : the outer and usu. the smaller of the two bones of the hind limb below the knee — **fib·u·lar** \-lər\ *adj*

-f·ic \f-ik\ *adj suffix* [L *-ficus*, fr. *facere* to make] : making : causing ⟨sudori*fic*⟩

-fi·ca·tion \fə-'kā-shən\ *n comb form* [L *-fication-*, *-ficatio*, fr. *-ficatus*, pp. ending of verbs in *-ficare* to make, fr. *-ficus* *-fic*] : the act or process of or the result of ⟨ampli*fication*⟩ ⟨forti*fication*⟩

fichu \'fish-ü\ *n* : a woman's light triangular scarf draped over the shoulders and fastened in front

fick·le \'fik-əl\ *adj* [OE *ficol* deceitful] : not firm or steadfast in disposition or character : INCONSTANT ⟨*fickle* friends⟩ — **fick·le·ness** *n*

fic·tion \'fik-shən\ *n* [L *fict-*, *fingere* to shape, invent, feign; akin to E *dough*] 1 : something told or written that is not fact : something made up ⟨both fact and *fiction* in that story⟩ 2 : a made-up story about real or imaginary persons or events; *also* : such stories as a class ⟨a writer of *fiction*⟩ ⟨science *fiction*⟩ — **fic·tion·al** \'fik-shnəl, -shən-ᵊl\ *adj* — **fic·tion·al·ly** \-ē\ *adv*
syn FIGMENT, FABRICATION: FICTION implies imaginative creation of events, characters, or circumstances with or more often without intent to deceive ⟨King Arthur belongs to *fiction* rather than to history⟩ FIGMENT suggests a creation of the imagination that deceives its own creator ⟨a *figment* of his fevered brain⟩ FABRICATION implies something deliberately made up to deceive or mislead ⟨his story of being robbed was pure *fabrication*⟩

fic·tion·al·ize \'fik-shnəl-,īz, -shən-ᵊl-\ *or* **fic·tion·ize** \-shə-,nīz\ *vt* : to make into fiction ⟨the novel is a *fictionalized* version of the author's youth⟩ — **fic·tion·al·i·za·tion** \,fik-shnəl-ə-'zā-shən, -shən-ᵊl-\ *or* **fic·tion·i·za·tion** *n*

fic·ti·tious \fik-'tish-əs\ *adj* : not real : MADE-UP, IMAGINARY ⟨a *fictitious* alibi⟩ — **fic·ti·tious·ly** *adv* — **fic·ti·tious·ness** *n*
syn FICTITIOUS, FACTITIOUS are easily confused. FICTITIOUS applies to what is invented by the imagination ⟨a child's *fictitious* playmate⟩ ⟨*fictitious* characters in a novel⟩ FACTITIOUS applies to what has actual existence but an artificial rather than natural origin or cause ⟨*factitious* enthusiasm⟩ ⟨*factitious* scarcity of goods in a controlled market⟩

fid \'fid\ *n* 1 : a square bar of wood or iron used to support a topmast 2 : a pin usu. of hard wood that tapers to a point and is used in opening the strands of a rope

¹fid·dle \'fid-ᵊl\ *n* [OE *fithele*] : VIOLIN

²fiddle *vb* **fid·dled**; **fid·dling** \'fid-liŋ, -ᵊl-iŋ\ 1 : to play on a fiddle 2 a : to move the hands or fingers restlessly

b : to spend time in aimless activity **: PUTTER c :** MEDDLE, TAMPER — **fid·dler** \'fid-lər, -ᵊl-ər\ *n*

fiddler crab *n* **:** a burrowing crab with one claw much enlarged in the male

fid·dle·stick \'fid-ᵊl-ˌstik\ *n* **1 :** a violin bow **2** *pl* **:** NONSENSE — used as an interjection

fi·del·i·ty \fə-'del-ət-ē, fī-\ *n, pl* **-ties** [L *fidelitas*, fr. *fidelis* faithful, fr. *fides* faith] **1 a :** the quality or state of being faithful **b :** accuracy in details **:** EXACTNESS **2 :** the degree to which an electronic device (as a radio or phonograph) accurately reproduces its effect (as sound)

syn ALLEGIANCE, LOYALTY: FIDELITY implies strict and continuous faithfulness to an obligation, trust, or duty; ALLEGIANCE implies the formal obedient adherence of a subject to his sovereign or a citizen to his state; LOYALTY implies personal steadfast adherence in the face of any temptation to desert or betray

¹fid·get \'fij-ət\ *n* [irreg. fr. Sc *fidge* to fidget] **1** *pl* **:** uneasiness or restlessness as shown by nervous movements **2 :** one that fidgets — **fid·gety** \-ət-ē\ *adj*

²fidget *vb* **:** to move or cause to move or act nervously or restlessly

¹fi·du·cia·ry \fə-'d(y)ü-shē-ˌer-ē, fī-, -shə-rē\ *n, pl* **-cia·ries** **1 :** one that acts as a trustee for another **2 :** one that acts in a confidential capacity

²fiduciary *adj* [L *fiducia* confidence, trust, fr. *fidere* to trust] **1 :** involving a confidence or trust ⟨employed in a *fiduciary* capacity⟩ **2 :** held or holding in trust for another ⟨*fiduciary* accounts⟩

fie \'fī\ *interj* — used to express disgust or shock

fief \'fēf\ *n* [F, fr. OF *fief, fé,* of Gmc origin] **:** a feudal estate **:** FEE

¹field \'fēld\ *n* [OE *feld*] **1 a :** open country — usu. used in pl. **b :** a piece of open cleared or cultivated land **c :** a piece of land put to some special use or yielding some special product ⟨athletic *field*⟩⟨oil *field*⟩ **d :** a place where a battle is fought **:** the region in which military operations are carried on **e :** an open space or expanse ⟨a *field* of ice⟩ **2 :** a sphere or range of activity or influence ⟨the *field* of science⟩ **3 :** a background on which something is drawn, painted, or mounted ⟨the American flag has white stars on a blue *field*⟩ **4 :** the individuals that make up all or part of a sports activity: as **a :** all the participants in a contest or sporting event (as a golf tournament) **b :** the baseball team not at bat **5 :** a set of mathematical elements subject to two operations for both of which the commutative and associative laws hold and both of which have the property of closure providing the identity element of the second operation is excluded and the second of which is distributive relative to the first **6 :** a region or space in which a given effect (as gravity, electricity, or magnetism) exists **7 :** the area visible through the lens of an optical instrument

²field *vb* **1 :** to put into the field ⟨*field* an army⟩ **2 :** to catch, stop, or throw a ball as a fielder ⟨can hit but can't *field*⟩⟨*field* a grounder⟩

³field *adj* **:** of or relating to a field: as **a :** growing in or inhabiting open country **b :** made, conducted, used, or operating in the field

field artillery *n* **:** artillery other than antiaircraft artillery used with armies in the field

field corn *n* **:** an Indian corn with starchy kernels grown for feeding livestock or for market grain

field day *n* **1 :** a day devoted to outdoor sports and athletic competition **2 :** a time of unusual pleasure or unexpected success

field·er \'fēl-dər\ *n* **:** one that fields; *esp* **:** a baseball player stationed in the outfield

field event *n* **:** an event in a track meet other than a race

field glass *n* **:** a hand-held optical instrument for use outdoors usu. consisting of two telescopes on a single frame with a focusing device — usu. used in pl.

field goal *n* **1 :** a score in football made by drop-kicking or place-kicking the ball over the crossbar from ordinary play **2 :** a basket in basketball made while the ball is in play

field magnet *n* **:** a magnet for producing and maintaining a magnetic field esp. in a generator or electric motor

field glasses

field marshal *n* **:** an officer (as in the British army) of the highest rank

field pea *n* **:** a small-seeded pea widely grown chiefly for forage

field·piece \'fēld-ˌpēs\ *n* **:** a gun or howitzer for use in the field

field trial *n* **:** a trial of sporting dogs in actual performance

fiend \'fēnd\ *n* [OE *fēond, fiend,* lit., enemy] **1 :** DEMON, DEVIL **2 :** an extremely wicked or cruel person **3 a :** a person excessively devoted to a pursuit **:** FANATIC ⟨golf *fiend*⟩ **b :** a person who uses immoderate quantities of something **:** ADDICT ⟨dope *fiend*⟩

fiend·ish \'fēn-dish\ *adj* **:** extremely cruel or wicked **:** DIABOLICAL — **fiend·ish·ly** *adv* — **fiend·ish·ness** *n*

fierce \'fi(ə)rs\ *adj* [OF *fiers,* fr. L *ferus* wild, savage] **1 a :** violently hostile or aggressive in temperament **b :** given to fighting or killing **:** PUGNACIOUS **2 :** marked by unrestrained zeal or vehemence **:** INTENSE **3 :** furiously active or determined **4 :** wild or menacing in aspect — **fierce·ly** *adv* — **fierce·ness** *n*

syn FEROCIOUS: FIERCE implies inspiring fear because of a wild and menacing aspect or display of fury in attack ⟨*fierce* mountain tribes⟩ FEROCIOUS implies extreme fierceness and unrestrained violence and brutality

fi·ery \'fī-(ə-)rē\ *adj* **fi·eri·er; -est** **1 a :** consisting of fire **b :** BURNING, BLAZING **c :** FLAMMABLE **2 a :** hot like a fire **b** (1) **:** INFLAMED (2) **:** feverish and flushed **3 a :** of the color of fire **:** RED **b :** intensely or unnaturally red **4 a :** full of emotion or spirit **b :** easily provoked **:** IRRITABLE — **fi·eri·ness** *n*

fi·es·ta \fē-'es-tə\ *n* [Sp, fr. L *festa,* pl. of *festum*] **:** FESTIVAL; *esp* **:** a saint's day celebrated in Spain and Latin America with processions and dances

fife \'fīf\ *n* [G *pfeife* pipe, fife] **:** a small shrill musical instrument resembling a flute

fif·teen \(')fif-'tēn\ *n* **1** — see NUMBER table **2 :** the 1st point scored by a side in a game of tennis — called also *five* — **fifteen** *adj or pron* — **fif·teenth** \-'tēn(t)th\ *adj or n*

fifth \'fif(t)th, 'fift\ *n, pl* **fifths** \'fif(t)s, 'fifths\ **1** — see NUMBER table **2 a :** the musical interval embracing five diatonic degrees **b :** the harmonic combination of two tones at this interval **3 :** a unit of measure for liquor equal to one fifth of a U.S. gallon — **fifth** *adj or adv* — **fifth·ly** *adv*

fifth column *n* [name applied to rebel sympathizers in Madrid in 1936 when four rebel columns were advancing on the city] **:** a group of secret sympathizers or supporters of a nation's enemy that engage in espionage or sabotage within the country — **fifth columnist** *n*

fif·ty \'fif-tē\ *n, pl* **fifties** — see NUMBER table — **fif·ti·eth** \-tē-əth\ *adj or n* — **fifty** *adj or pron*

fif·ty–fif·ty \ˌfif-tē-'fif-tē\ *adj* **1 :** shared equally ⟨a *fifty-fifty* proposition⟩ **2 :** half favorable and half unfavorable ⟨a *fifty-fifty* chance to live⟩ — **fifty–fifty** *adv*

fig \'fig\ *n* [OF *figue,* fr. OProv *figa,* fr. L *ficus* fig tree, fig] **:** the usu. edible oblong or pear-shaped fruit of a tree of the mulberry family; *also* **:** a tree bearing figs

¹fight \'fīt\ *vb* **fought** \'fot\; **fight·ing** [OE *feohtan*] **1 a :** to contend against another in battle or physical combat; *esp* **:** to strive to overcome a person by blows **b :** to engage in prizefighting **:** BOX **2 :** to put forth a determined effort **3 a :** to act in opposition **:** STRUGGLE, CONTEND ⟨*fight* for the right⟩ **b :** to attempt to prevent the success or effectiveness of **4 :** to carry on **:** WAGE **5 :** to gain by struggle ⟨*fights* his way through⟩

²fight *n* **1 a :** a combat or hostile encounter **:** BATTLE **b :** a boxing match **c :** a verbal disagreement **2 :** a struggle for a goal or an objective **3 :** strength or disposition for fighting ⟨full of *fight*⟩

fight·er \'fīt-ər\ *n* **:** one that fights: **a :** WARRIOR, SOLDIER **b :** BOXER **c :** an airplane of high speed and maneuverability with armament for destroying enemy aircraft

fig·ment \'fig-mənt\ *n* [L *figmentum,* fr. *fingere* to shape, feign] **:** something imagined or made up ⟨a *figment* of a child's imagination⟩ **syn** see FICTION

fig·u·ra·tion \ˌfig-(y)ə-'rā-shən\ *n* **1 :** FORM, OUTLINE **2 :** an act or instance of representation in figures and shapes

fig·u·ra·tive \'fig-(y)ə-rət-iv, 'fig-(y)ərt-iv\ *adj* **1 :** repre-

---

ǰ joke; ŋ sing; ō flow; ȯ flaw; ȯi coin; th thin; th this; ü loot;   u̇ foot; y yet; yü few; yu̇ furious; zh vision

senting by a figure or resemblance : EMBLEMATIC **2 a :** expressing one thing in terms normally denoting something analogous : METAPHORICAL **b :** characterized by figures of speech — **fig·u·ra·tive·ly** *adv* — **fig·u·ra·tive·ness** *n*

¹fig·ure \'fig-yər, *esp Brit* 'fig-ər\ *n* [L *figura*, fr. *fingere* to shape] **1 a :** a number symbol : NUMERAL **b** *pl* **:** arithmetical calculations **c :** a written or printed character **d :** value. esp. as expressed in numbers : PRICE **2 a :** the external shape or outline of something **b :** bodily shape or form esp. of a person **c :** an object noticeable only as a shape or form **3 a :** the graphic representation of a form esp. of a person **b :** a diagram or pictorial illustration of textual matter **c :** a combination of points, lines, or surfaces in geometry **4 :** an expression (as in metonymy, metaphor, irony, or hyperbole) that uses words in other than a plain or literal way **5 :** PATTERN, DESIGN **6 :** appearance made or impression produced ⟨the couple cut quite a *figure*⟩ **7 a :** a series of movements in a dance **b :** an outline representation of a form traced by a series of evolutions **8 :** a prominent personality : PERSONAGE **syn** see FORM

²figure *vb* **1 :** to represent by or as if by a figure or outline : PORTRAY **2 :** to decorate with a pattern **3 a :** to indicate or represent by numerals **b :** REGARD, CONSIDER **4 :** to be or appear important or conspicuous **5 :** COMPUTE, CALCULATE — **fig·ur·er** \-(y)ər-ər\ *n* — **figure on 1 :** to take into consideration **2 :** to rely on **3 :** PLAN

fig·ured *adj* **1 :** REPRESENTED, PORTRAYED **2 :** adorned with, formed into, or marked with a figure **3 :** indicated by figures esp. in music

figure eight *n* **:** something (as a skating figure) resembling the arabic numeral 8 in form or shape

fig·ure·head \'fig-(y)ər-,hed\ *n* **1 :** a figure, statue, or bust on the bow of a ship **2 :** a person who has the title but not the powers of the head of something

figure of speech : a form of expression (as a simile or metaphor) used to convey meaning or heighten effect often by comparing or identifying one thing with another that has a meaning or connotation familiar to the reader or listener

figure out : to work out mentally

fig·u·rine \,fig-(y)ə-'rēn\ *n* **:** a small carved or molded figure

fig·wort \'fig-,wərt, -,wòrt\ *n* **:** any of a genus of chiefly coarse erect herbs with toothed leaves having no stipules and clustered flowers with irregular 2-lipped corollas

fil·a·ment \'fil-ə-mənt\ *n* [ML *filamentum*, fr. LL *filare* to spin, fr. L *filum* thread] **:** a single thread or a thin flexible threadlike object, process, or appendage: as **a :** a wire in an electric lamp made incandescent by the passage of an electric current; *esp* **:** a cathode in the form of a metal wire in an electron tube **b :** the anther-bearing stalk of a stamen — see FLOWER illustration — **fil·a·men·tous** \,fil-ə-'ment-əs\ *adj*

fi·lar \'fī-lər\ *adj* [L *filum* thread] **:** of or relating to a thread or line

fi·lar·ia \fə-'lar-ē-ə, -'ler-\ *n, pl* **-i·ae** \-ē-,ē, -ē-,ī\ **:** any of numerous slender filamentous nematodes that as adults are parasites in the blood or tissues of mammals and as larvae usu. develop in biting insects — **fi·lar·i·al** \-ē-əl\ *adj* — **fil·a·ri·a·sis** \,fil-ə-'rī-ə-səs\ *n*

fil·bert \'fil-bərt\ *n* [fr. St. *Philibert* d684 Frankish abbot whose feast day falls in the nutting season] **1 :** either of two European hazels; *also* **:** the sweet thick-shelled nut of a filbert **2 :** HAZELNUT

filch \'filch\ *vt* [ME *filchen*] **:** to steal furtively : PILFER

¹file \'fīl\ *n* [OE *fēol*] **:** a usu. steel tool with sharp ridges or teeth on its surface for smoothing or rubbing down a hard substance (as metal)

²file *vt* **:** to rub, smooth, or cut away with a file

³file *vb* [MF *filer* to string documents on a string or wire, fr. *fil* thread, fr. L *filum*] **1 :** to arrange in order for preservation or reference **2 a :** to enter or record officially or as prescribed by law ⟨*file* a mortgage⟩⟨*file* a lawsuit⟩ **b :** to send (copy) to a newspaper **3 :** to register as a candidate esp. in a primary election

file: 1 tang, 2 heel, 3 face, 4 tip, 5 edge

⁴file *n* **1 :** a device (as a folder, case, or cabinet) by means of which papers or records may be kept in order **2 :** a collection of papers or records kept in a file

⁵file *n* [L *filum* thread] **:** a row of persons, animals, or things arranged one behind the other

⁶file *vi* **:** to march or proceed in file

fi·let \fi-'lā\ *n* **:** a lace with a square mesh and geometric designs

fi·let mi·gnon \,fil-(,)ā-mēn-'yōⁿ, fi-,lā-\ *n, pl* **filets mignons** *same or* -'yōⁿz\ [F, lit., dainty fillet] **:** a fillet of beef cut from the thick end of a beef tenderloin

fil·i·al \'fil-ē-əl, 'fil-yəl\ *adj* [L *filius* son] **1 :** of, relating to, or befitting a son or daughter **2 :** having or assuming the relation of a child or offspring — **fil·i·al·ly** \-ē\ *adv*

filial generation *n* **:** a generation in a cross successive to a parental generation

¹fil·i·bus·ter \'fil-ə-,bəs-tər\ *n* [Sp *filibustero*, fr. E *freebooter*] **1 :** an irregular military adventurer; *esp* **:** an American engaged in fomenting insurrections in Latin America in the mid-19th century **2 a :** the use of delaying tactics (as extremely long speeches) in an attempt to delay or prevent action esp. in a legislative assembly **b :** an instance of this practice

²filibuster *vb* **fil·i·bus·tered; fil·i·bus·ter·ing** \-t(ə-)riŋ\ **1 :** to carry out insurrectionist or revolutionary activities in a foreign country **2 :** to engage in a legislative filibuster **3 :** to subject to a filibuster — **fil·i·bus·ter·er** \-tər-ər\ *n*

fil·i·form \'fil-ə-,fòrm, 'fī-lə-\ *adj* **:** shaped like a filament

fil·i·gree \'fil-ə-,grē\ *n* [F *filigrane*, fr. It *filigrana*, fr. L *filum* thread + *granum* grain] **1 :** ornamental work esp. of fine wire applied chiefly to gold and silver surfaces **2 a :** ornamental openwork of delicate or intricate design **b :** a pattern or design resembling this openwork

fil·ing \'fī-liŋ\ *n* **1 :** the act of one who files **2 :** a small piece scraped off by a file ⟨iron *filings*⟩

Fil·i·pi·no \,fil-ə-'pē-nō\ *n, pl* **-nos 1 :** a native or inhabitant of the Philippines **2 :** a person of Filipino descent — **Filipino** *adj*

¹fill \'fil\ *vb* [OE *fyllan*] **1 :** to put into as much as can be held or conveniently contained **2 :** to become full **3 :** SATISFY ⟨*fill* all requirements⟩ **4 :** to occupy fully : take up whatever space there is **5 :** to spread through ⟨laughter *filled* the room⟩ **6 :** to stop up (as crevices or holes) : PLUG ⟨*fill* a crack with putty⟩⟨*fill* a tooth⟩ **7 a :** to have and perform the duties of : OCCUPY ⟨*fill* the office of president⟩ **b :** to put a person in ⟨*filled* several vacancies⟩ **8 :** to supply according to directions ⟨*fill* a prescription⟩ — **fill one's shoes :** to take one's place or position — **fill the bill :** to serve the purpose satisfactorily

²fill *n* **1 :** a full supply; *esp* **:** a quantity that satisfies or satiates **2 :** material used esp. for filling a ditch or hollow in the ground

fill·er \'fil-ər\ *n* **:** one that fills: as **a :** a substance added to another substance to increase bulk or weight **b :** a material used for filling cracks and pores in wood before painting **c :** a pack of paper for insertion in a binder

¹fil·let \'fil-ət\ *also* **fi·let** \fi-'lā, 'fil-(,)ā\ *n* [MF *filet*, dim. of *fil* thread, fr. L *filum*] **1 :** a narrow strip of material (as a ribbon) used as a headband **2 :** a thin narrow strip of material: as **a :** a band of anatomical fibers **b :** a piece or slice of boneless meat or fish; *esp* **:** the tenderloin of beef **3 a :** a flat molding separating other moldings **b :** the space between two flutings in a shaft

²fillet *vt* **1 :** to bind or adorn with or as if with a fillet **2 :** to cut into fillets

fill in *vb* **1 :** to furnish with specified information ⟨*fill in* an application⟩ **2 :** to fill a vacancy usu. temporarily : SUBSTITUTE ⟨*filled in* during the emergency⟩

fill·ing \'fil-iŋ\ *n* **1 :** material that is used to fill something ⟨a *filling* for a tooth⟩ **2 :** something that completes: as **a :** the yarn interlacing the warp in a fabric **b :** a food mixture used to fill pastry or sandwiches

filling station *n* **:** a retail station for servicing motor vehicles esp. with gasoline and oil

¹fil·lip \'fil-əp\ *n* **1 :** a blow or gesture made by the sudden forcible straightening of a finger curled up against the thumb **2 :** something tending to arouse or excite

²fillip *vt* **1 :** to tap with the finger by flicking the fingernail outward across the end of the thumb **2 :** STIMULATE

fill out *vi* **:** to put on flesh

fil·ly \'fil-ē\ *n, pl* **fillies** [ON *fylja*] : a young female horse usu. of less than four years

¹film \'film\ *n* [OE *filmen*] **1** : a thin skin or membrane **2** : a thin coating or layer ⟨a *film* of ice on a windshield⟩ **3** : a roll or strip of thin flexible transparent material coated with a chemical substance sensitive to light and used in taking pictures **4** : MOTION PICTURE ⟨a *film* about Mexico⟩

²film *vb* **1** : to cover or become covered with film ⟨eyes *filmed* with tears⟩ **2** : to photograph on a film; *esp* : to make a motion picture of ⟨a picture *filmed* in Europe⟩ ⟨*film* a battle scene⟩

film·dom \-dəm\ *n* **1** : the motion-picture industry **2** : the personnel of the motion-picture industry

film·ic \'fil-mik\ *adj* : of, relating to, or resembling motion pictures

film·strip \'film-,strip\ *n* : a strip of usu. 35 mm. film bearing photographs, diagrams, or graphic matter for still projection upon a screen

filmy \'fil-mē\ *adj* **film·i·er; -est 1** : of, resembling, or composed of film **2** : covered with a haze or film — **film·i·ness** *n*

filo·plume \'fil-ə-,plüm, 'fī-lə-\ *n* : a filamentous feather

¹fil·ter \'fil-tər\ *n* [ML *filtrum*, piece of felt used as a filter, of Gmc origin; akin to E *felt*] **1** : a porous article or mass through which a gas or liquid is passed to separate out matter in suspension **2** : an apparatus containing a filter medium **3** : a device or material for suppressing or minimizing waves or oscillations of certain frequencies (as of electricity, light, or sound); *esp* : COLOR FILTER

²filter *vb* **fil·tered; fil·ter·ing** \-t(ə-)riŋ\ **1** : to subject to the action of a filter **2** : to remove by means of a filter **3** : to pass through or as if through a filter

fil·ter·a·ble *also* **fil·tra·ble** \'fil-t(ə-)rə-bəl\ *adj* : capable of being separated by or of passing through a filter ⟨*filterable* microorganisms⟩⟨a *filterable* liquid⟩ — **fil·ter·a·bil·i·ty** \,fil-t(ə-)rə-'bil-ət-ē\ *n*

filterable virus *n* : VIRUS 1a

filter bed *n* : a bed of sand or gravel through which liquid (as from sewage) is passed to purify it

filter paper *n* : porous paper used for filtering

filter tip *n* : a cigar or cigarette with a tip designed to filter the smoke

filth \'filth\ *n* [OE *fȳlth*, fr. *fūl* foul] **1** : foul or putrid matter; *esp* : loathsome dirt or refuse **2 a** : moral corruption or defilement **b** : something that tends to corrupt or defile : OBSCENITY

filthy \'fil-thē\ *adj* **filth·i·er; -est 1** : covered with or containing filth : disgustingly dirty **2 a** : UNDERHANDED, VILE **b** : OBSCENE **syn** see DIRTY — **filth·i·ly** \-thə-lē\ *adv* — **filth·i·ness** \-thē-nəs\ *n*

fil·trate \'fil-,trāt\ *n* : the fluid that has passed through a filter

fil·tra·tion \fil-'trā-shən\ *n* : the act or process of filtering

fim·bria \'fim-brē-ə\ *n, pl* **-bri·ae** \-brē-,ē, -brē-,ī\ [L, fringe] : a bordering fringe esp. at the entrance of a fallopian tube — **fim·bri·al** \-brē-əl\ *adj* — **fim·bri·ate** \-brē-,āt\ *or* **fim·bri·at·ed** \-,āt-əd\ *adj* — **fim·bri·a·tion** \,fim-brē-'ā-shən\ *n*

fin \'fin\ *n* [OE *finn*] **1** : a thin external process of an aquatic animal (as a fish) used in propelling or guiding the body **2 a** : a fin-shaped part (as on an airplane, boat, or automobile) **b** : FLIPPER 2 **c** : a projecting rib on a radiator or an engine cylinder — **fin·like** \-,līk\ *adj* — **finned** \'find\ *adj*

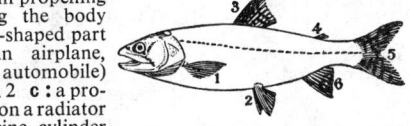

fins 1: *1* pectoral, *2* pelvic, *3* first dorsal, *4* second dorsal, *5* caudal, *6* anal

fi·na·gle \fə-'nā-gəl\ *vb* **fi·na·gled; fi·na·gling** \-'nā-g(ə-)liŋ\ **1** : to arrange for : WANGLE **2** : to obtain by trickery **3** : to use devious dishonest methods to achieve one's ends — **fi·na·gler** \-g(ə-)lər\ *n*

¹fi·nal \'fīn-°l\ *adj* [L *finalis* of the end, fr. *finis* end, boundary] **1** : not to be altered or undone : CONCLUSIVE **2** : constituting the ultimate in degree or development ⟨the *final* climax⟩ **3** : of or relating to the ultimate purpose or result of a process ⟨the *final* goal of life⟩

4 : relating to or occurring at the end or conclusion **syn** see LAST — **fi·nal·ly** \'fīn-°l-ē, 'fīn-lē\ *adv*

²final *n* : something final: as **a** : a deciding match, game, or trial **b** : the last examination in a course

fi·na·le \fə-'nal-ē, fi-'näl-\ *n* [It] : the close or termination of something; *esp* : the last section of an instrumental musical composition

fi·nal·ist \'fīn-°l-əst\ *n* : a contestant in the finals of a competition

fi·nal·i·ty \fī-'nal-ət-ē, fə-\ *n, pl* **-ties 1** : the character or condition of being final, settled, or complete **2** : something final

fi·nal·ize \'fīn-°l-,īz\ *vt* : to put in final or finished form

¹fi·nance \fə-'nan(t)s, 'fī-, fī-'\ *n* [ME, payment, fr. MF, fr. *finer* to pay, fr. *fin* payment, fine] **1** *pl* : liquid resources (as money) available esp. to a government or business **2** : the obtaining of funds or capital : FINANCING **3** : the system that includes the circulation of money, the granting of credit, the making of investments, and the provision of banking facilities

²finance *vt* **1 a** : to raise or provide funds or capital for **b** : to furnish with necessary funds **2** : to sell or supply on credit

finance company *n* **1** : a company that pays to the seller the cost of an article (as an automobile) purchased on the installment plan and is reimbursed with interest in installments by the purchaser **2** : a company that makes small loans to individuals usu. at high rates of interest

fi·nan·cial \fə-'nan-chəl, fī-\ *adj* : having to do with finance or with finances — **fi·nan·cial·ly** \-'nanch-(ə-)lē\ *adv*

syn MONETARY, PECUNIARY: FINANCIAL implies money matters involving a large scale or some degree of complexity ⟨*financial* aspects of a business⟩ MONETARY refers to money as coined, distributed, or circulating ⟨*monetary* reform⟩ PECUNIARY implies reference to money matters affecting the individual ⟨*pecuniary* rewards of an office⟩

fin·an·cier \,fin-ən-'si(ə)r, fə-,nan-, ,fī-,nan-\ *n* **1** : a person skilled in managing large funds **2** : a person who carries on financial operations; *esp* : a person who invests large sums of money

fin·back \'fin-,bak\ *n* : RORQUAL; *esp* : a large whale of the Atlantic

finch \'finch\ *n* [OE *finc*] : any of numerous songbirds including the sparrows, grosbeaks, crossbills, goldfinches, linnets, buntings, and related birds and having a short stout conical bill adapted for crushing seeds

¹find \'fīnd\ *vb* **found** \'faůnd\; **find·ing** [OE *findan*] **1** : to come upon : meet with someone or something by chance ⟨*find* a kitten on the porch⟩ **2** : to come upon by searching or study : DISCOVER **3** : to obtain by effort or management ⟨*find* time to do it⟩ **4** : to arrive at : REACH ⟨*find* his place in the world⟩ **5** : to make a decision and declare it ⟨*find* a verdict⟩⟨*find* for the defendant⟩ **6** : to know by experience ⟨people *found* the boy honest⟩ **7** : to gain or regain the use of ⟨*found* her voice again⟩ **8** : PROVIDE, SUPPLY ⟨*find* room for a guest⟩ — **find fault** : to criticize unfavorably

²find *n* **1** : an act or instance of finding **2** : something found; *esp* : a valuable item of discovery

find·er \'fīn-dər\ *n* : one that finds: as **a** : a small telescope attached to a larger one for finding an object **b** : a lens on a camera that shows the view being photographed by the camera

fin de siè·cle \,faⁿ-dəs-'yekl°\ *adj* [F, end of the century] : of, relating to, or characteristic of the close of the 19th century

find·ing *n* **1 a** : the act of one that finds **b** : FIND 2 **2** : the result of a judicial proceeding or investigation

find out *vt* **1** : to learn by study or observation **2** : DETECT, DISCOVER

¹fine \'fīn\ *n* [OF *fin*, fr. ML *finis* end, settlement, fine, fr. L, end, boundary] : a sum of money imposed as punishment for an offense — **in fine** : in short

²fine *vt* : to impose a fine on : punish by a fine

³fine *adj* [OF *fin* extreme, excellent, fr. L *finis* end, limit] **1 a** : free from impurity **b** : having a stated proportion of pure metal in the composition ⟨silver 800/1000 *fine*⟩ **2 a** : very thin in gauge or texture **b** : not coarse ⟨*fine* sand⟩ **3** : subtle or sensitive in perception or discrimination ⟨a *fine* distinction⟩ **4** : superior in quality, conception, or appearance **5** : marked by or affecting elegance or refinement — **fine·ly** adv — **fine·ness** \'fīn-nəs\ n

⁴fine adv : FINELY

⁵fi·ne \'fē-(ˌ)nā\ n [It, fr. L finis end] : END — used as a direction in music to mark the closing point after a repeat

fine art n : art (as painting, sculpture, or music) concerned primarily with the creation of beautiful objects — usu. used in pl.

fin·ery \'fīn-(ə-)rē\ n, pl **-er·ies** : ORNAMENT, DECORATION; esp : showy clothing and jewels

fines \'fīnz\ n pl : finely crushed or powdered material (as ore or coal)

¹fi·nesse \fə-'nes\ n [MF, fr. fin fine] **1** : refinement or delicacy of workmanship, structure, or texture ⟨a painting executed with finesse⟩ **2** : skillful handling of a situation : CUNNING, SUBTLETY ⟨accomplish by finesse what could not have been done by force⟩ **3** : the withholding of one's highest card or trump on the assumption that a lower card will take the trick because the taking card is in the hand of an opponent who has already played

²finesse vb **1 a** : to make a finesse in playing cards **b** : to play (a card) as a finesse **2 a** : to bring about by adroit maneuvering **b** : EVADE, TRICK

¹fin·ger \'fiŋ-gər\ n [OE] **1** : one of the five terminating members of the hand; esp : one other than the thumb **2 a** : something that resembles or does the work of a finger **b** : a part of a glove into which a finger is inserted **3** : the breadth of a finger — **fin·ger·like** \-ˌlīk\ adj

²finger vb **fin·gered; fin·ger·ing** \'fiŋ-g(ə-)riŋ\ **1** : to touch with the fingers : HANDLE **2** : to perform with the fingers or with a certain fingering **3** : to mark the notes of a piece of music to show what fingers are to be used **4** : to point out : IDENTIFY

fin·ger·board \'fiŋ-gər-ˌbōrd, -ˌbȯrd\ n : the part of a stringed instrument against which the fingers press the strings to vary the pitch

finger bowl n : a basin to hold water for rinsing the fingers at table

finger hole n : a hole in a wind instrument by means of which the pitch of the tone is changed when it is left open or closed by the finger

fin·ger·ing n **1** : the act or process of handling or touching with the fingers **2 a** : the act or method of using the fingers in playing an instrument **b** : the marking of the method of fingering

fin·ger·ling \'fiŋ-gər-liŋ\ n : a young fish esp. up to one year of age

fin·ger·nail \'fiŋ-gər-ˌnāl, ˌfiŋ-gər-'\ n : the nail of a finger

finger painting n **1** : a technique of spreading pigment on wet paper chiefly with the fingers **2** : a picture produced by finger painting

fin·ger·post \'fiŋ-gər-ˌpōst\ n : a post bearing one or more signs often terminating in a pointing finger

fin·ger·print \'fiŋ-gər-ˌprint\ n : the pattern of marks made by pressing the tip of a finger or thumb on a surface; esp : an ink impression of the lines on the tip of a finger or thumb taken for the purpose of identification — **finger·print** vb

fin·i·al \'fin-ē-əl\ n : an ornamental projection or end (as on a spire or gable end)

fin·i·cal \'fin-i-kəl\ adj [prob. fr. ³fine] : FINICKY — **fin·i·cal·ly** \-k(ə-)lē\ adv — **fin·i·cal·ness** \-kəl-nəs\ n

fin·ick·ing \'fin-i-kiŋ, -kən\ adj [alter. of finical] : FINICKY

fin·icky \'fin-i-kē\ adj [alter. of finicking] : excessively nice, exacting, or meticulous in taste or standards — **fin·ick·i·ness** n

fin·is \'fin-əs, 'fī-nəs\ n [L] : END, CONCLUSION

¹fin·ish \'fin-ish\ vb [MF finiss-, finir, fr. L finire, fr. finis end] **1 a** : to bring or come to an end : TERMINATE **b** : to use or dispose of entirely **2 a** : to bring to completion or issue : PERFECT **b** : to put a final coat or surface on **3** : to bring about the death of **4** : to come to the end of a course, task, or undertaking — **fin·ish·er** n

syn COMPLETE: FINISH implies accomplishing the final act or stage in producing, performing, or perfecting something ⟨needed more paint to finish the job⟩ COMPLETE stresses a bringing of something to a state of wholeness, fullness, or soundness ⟨still another link was needed to complete the circle⟩

²finish n **1** : END, CONCLUSION ⟨a close finish in a race⟩ **2** : the treatment given a surface or the appearance given

by finishing ⟨shiny finish on a new car⟩ **3** : cultivation in manners and speech : social polish

finishing school n : a private school for girls that emphasizes cultural studies and prepares students esp. for social activities

fi·nite \'fī-ˌnīt\ adj [L finitus, pp. of finire to limit, fr. finis end, limit] **1 a** : having definite or definable limits **b** : having a limited nature or existence **2 a** : completely determinable in theory or in fact by counting, measurement, or thought **b** : neither infinite nor infinitesimal **3** : showing distinction of grammatical person and number ⟨a finite verb⟩ — **fi·nite·ly** adv — **fi·nite·ness** n

fin·i·tude \'fin-ə-ˌt(y)üd, 'fī-nə-\ n : finite quality or state

Finn \'fin\ n **1** : a member of a people speaking Finnish or a related language **2 a** : a native or inhabitant of Finland **b** : a person of Finnish descent

fin·nan had·die \ˌfin-ən-'had-ē\ n [alter. of Findon haddock, fr. Findon, village in Scotland] : smoked haddock — called also finnan haddock

¹Finn·ish \'fin-ish\ adj : of, relating to, or characteristic of Finland, the Finns, or Finnish

²Finnish n : a Finno-Ugric language spoken in Finland, Karelia, and small areas of Sweden and Norway

Fin·no-Ugric \ˌfin-ō-'(y)ü-grik\ adj **1** : of or relating to any of various peoples including the Finnish, Hungarian, and Bulgarian peoples and the Lapps and Estonians **2** : of, relating to, or constituting a subfamily of the Uralic family of languages comprising various languages spoken in Hungary, Finland, Estonia, and northwestern Russia — **Finno-Ugric** n

fin·ny \'fin-ē\ adj **1** : resembling or having fins **2** : of, relating to, or full of fish

fiord var of FJORD

fip·ple flute \ˌfip-əl-\ n : a wind instrument (as the recorder) in which air is blown through a flue in the mouthpiece

fir \'fər\ n [OE fyrh] **1** : any of various usu. large symmetrical evergreen trees of the pine family some of which yield useful lumber or resins **2** : the wood of a fir

¹fire \'fī(ə)r\ n [OE fȳr] **1** : the light and heat and esp. the flame produced by burning **2** : fuel that is burning (as in a fireplace or stove) **3** : the destructive burning of something (as a building or a forest) **4** : ardent liveliness : ENTHUSIASM **5** : the discharge of firearms : SHOOTING ⟨the sound of rifle fire⟩ — **on fire 1** : BURNING **2** : ARDENT, EAGER — **under fire 1** : exposed to the firing of an enemy's guns **2** : under attack

²fire vb **1 a** : to set on fire : KINDLE, IGNITE **b** : STIR, ENLIVEN ⟨fires the imagination⟩ **2** : to dismiss from employment : DISCHARGE **3** : to cause to explode ⟨fire dynamite⟩ **4** : to propel from or as if from a gun ⟨fire an arrow⟩ **a** : DISCHARGE ⟨fire a gun⟩ **b** : LAUNCH ⟨fire a rocket⟩ **c** : to throw with speed : HURL ⟨fired the ball to first base⟩ **5 a** : to subject to intense heat ⟨fire pottery⟩ **b** : to feed or serve the fire of ⟨fire a furnace⟩ **6 a** : to take fire : KINDLE **b** : to have the explosive charge ignite at the proper time ⟨cylinder that does not fire right⟩ **7 a** : to discharge a firearm **b** : to emit or let fly an object — **fir·er** n

fire·arm \'fī(ə)r-ˌärm\ n : a weapon from which a shot is discharged by gunpowder — usu. used only of a small arm (as a rifle or pistol)

fire·ball \-ˌbȯl\ n **1** : a ball of fire **2** : a brilliant meteor that may trail bright sparks **3** : the highly luminous cloud of vapor and dust created by a nuclear explosion (as of an atom bomb)

fire·boat \-ˌbōt\ n : a ship equipped with apparatus (as pumps) for fighting fire

fire·box \-ˌbäks\ n **1** : a chamber (as of a furnace or steam boiler) that contains a fire **2** : a box containing an apparatus for transmitting an alarm to a fire station

fire·brand \-ˌbrand\ n **1** : a piece of burning wood **2** : a person who creates unrest or strife : AGITATOR

fire·break \-ˌbrāk\ n : a barrier of cleared or plowed land intended to check a forest or grass fire

fire·brick \-ˌbrik\ n : a brick capable of withstanding great heat and used for lining furnaces or fireplaces

fire·bug \-ˌbəg\ n : a person who deliberately sets destructive fires : INCENDIARY

fir (balsam): leaves and fruit

ə abut; ᵊ kitten; ər further; a back; ā bake; ä cot, cart; aù out; ch chin; e less; ē easy; g gift; i trip; ī life

fire·clay \-,klā\ *n* : clay capable of withstanding high temperatures and used esp. for firebrick and crucibles

fire·crack·er \-,krak-ər\ *n* : a paper cylinder containing an explosive and a fuse and usu. discharged for amusement to make a noise

fire–cured \-'kyu̇(ə)rd\ *adj* : cured over open fires in direct contact with the smoke

fire·damp \-,damp\ *n* : a combustible mine gas that consists chiefly of methane; *also* : the explosive mixture of this gas with air

fire·dog \-,do̍g\ *n* : ANDIRON

fire drill *n* : a practice drill in extinguishing fires or in the conduct and manner of exit in case of fire

fire engine *n* : a usu. mobile apparatus for directing water or an extinguishing chemical on fires; *esp* : a motortruck equipped with an apparatus for this purpose

fire escape *n* : a stairway or ladder that provides a means of escape from a building in case of fire

fire extinguisher *n* : something used to put out a fire; *esp* : a portable hand-operated metal contrivance for ejecting a stream or spray of fire-extinguishing chemicals

fire·fly \'fī(ə)r-,flī\ *n* : a winged nocturnal insect producing a bright soft intermittent light; *esp* : the male of various long flat beetles

fire·house \-,hau̇s\ *n* : FIRE STATION

fire irons *n pl* : implements for tending a fire esp. in a fireplace

fire·light \'fī(ə)r-,līt\ *n* : the light of a fire and esp. of one burning in a fireplace

fire·man \-mən\ *n* 1 : a member of a company organized to fight fires   2 : one who tends or feeds fires : STOKER

fire·place \-,plās\ *n* 1 : a framed rectangular opening made in a chimney to hold an open fire : HEARTH   2 : an outdoor structure of brick or stone made for an open fire

fire·plug \-,pləg\ *n* : a hydrant to which a large hose can be attached for drawing water from the main water pipes to extinguish fires

fire·pow·er \-,pau̇(-ə)r\ *n* : the relative ability to deliver gunfire or warheads on a target

¹**fire·proof** \-'prüf\ *adj* : proof against or resistant to fire

²**fireproof** *vt* : to make fireproof

fire sale *n* : a sale of merchandise damaged by fire

fire screen *n* : a protecting wire screen before a fireplace

fire·side \'fī(ə)r-,sīd\ *n* 1 : a place near the fire or hearth   2 : HOME

fire station *n* : a building housing fire apparatus and usu. firemen

fire tower *n* 1 : a tower from which a watch for fires is kept (as in a forest)   2 : a fireproof compartment extending from top to bottom of a building and containing a stairway

fire·trap \'fī(ə)r-,trap\ *n* : a building or place apt to catch on fire or difficult to escape from in case of fire

fire wall *n* : a wall for preventing the spread of fire

fire·wa·ter \-,wȯt-ər, -,wät-\ *n* : intoxicating liquor

fire·weed \-,wēd\ *n* : any of several weeds that spring up in clearings or burned areas

fire·wood \-,wu̇d\ *n* : wood cut for fuel

fire·work \-,wərk\ *n* 1 : a device for producing a striking display (as of light, noise, or smoke) by the combustion of explosive or flammable compositions   2 *pl* : a display of fireworks   3 *pl* : a display of temper

firing line *n* 1 : a line from which fire is delivered against a target   2 : the forefront of an activity

firing squad *n* 1 : a detachment detailed to fire volleys over the grave of one buried with military honors   2 : a detachment detailed to carry out a death sentence by shooting

fir·kin \'fər-kən\ *n* [ME *firdekyn, fyrkyn*, fr. (assumed) MD *vierdelkijn*, dim. of MD *vierdel* quarter] 1 : a small wooden vessel or cask   2 : any of various British units of capacity usu. equal to ¼ barrel

¹**firm** \'fərm\ *adj* [L *firmus*] 1 a : securely or solidly fixed in place   b : SOLID, VIGOROUS   c : having a solid or compact texture   2 a : not subject to change or fluctuation : STEADY   b : not easily moved or disturbed : STEADFAST   c : WELL-FOUNDED   3 : indicating firmness or resolution ⟨*firm* mouth⟩ — **firm·ly** *adv* — **firm·ness** *n*

²**firm** *vb* 1 : to make solid or compact   2 : to become firm

³**firm** *n* [G *firma*, fr. It, signature, fr. *firmare* to sign, fr. L, to confirm, fr. *firmus*, adj., firm] 1 : the name under

which a company does business   2 : a business partnership of two or more persons   3 : a business enterprise

fir·ma·ment \'fər-mə-mənt\ *n* : the arch of the sky : HEAVENS

¹**first** \'fərst\ *adj* [OE *fyrst*] 1 — see NUMBER table   2 : preceding all others in time, order, or importance: as   a : EARLIEST   b : being the lowest forward gear or speed in an automotive shift   c : highest or most prominent in carrying the melody ⟨*first* violin⟩

²**first** *adv* 1 a : before any other in time, space, or importance   b : for the first time   2 : in preference to something else : SOONER

³**first** *n* 1 — see NUMBER table   2 : something that is first: as   a : the 1st gear or speed in an automotive vehicle   b : the winning place in a competition or contest

first aid *n* : emergency care or treatment given to an ill or injured person

first base *n* 1 : the base that must be touched first by a base runner in baseball   2 : the position of the player defending the area around first base   3 : the first step or stage in a course ⟨his plan never got to *first base*⟩ — **first base·man** \-'bās-mən\ *n*

first·born \'fərs(t)-'bȯrn\ *adj* : born first : ELDEST — **firstborn** *n*

first class *n* : the best or highest group in a classification: as   a : the highest class of accommodations in a passenger ship   b : a class of mail that comprises letters, postcards, or matter sealed against inspection — **first–class** *adj or adv*

first·hand \'fərst-'hand\ *adj* : coming directly from the original source — **firsthand** *adv*

first lady *n, often cap F&L* : the wife or hostess of the chief executive of a political unit (as a country)

first lieutenant *n* : a commissioned officer (as in the army) ranking above a second lieutenant and below a captain

first·ling \'fərst-liŋ\ *n* 1 : the first of a class or kind   2 : the first produce or result of something

first·ly \-lē\ *adv* : in the first place

first person *n* : a set of words or forms (as pronouns or verb forms) referring to the speaker or writer of the utterance in which they occur; *also* : a word or form belonging to such a set

first–rate \'fərst-'rāt\ *adj* : of the first order of size, importance, or quality — **first–rate** *adv* — **first–rat·er** \-'rāt-ər\ *n*

First Reader *n* : a Christian Scientist chosen to conduct meetings for a specified time and specifically to read aloud from the writings of Mary Baker Eddy

first sergeant *n* 1 : a noncommissioned officer serving as chief enlisted assistant to the commander (as of a company)   2 : a master sergeant in the army

first–string \'fərs(t)-'striŋ\ *adj* : being a regular as distinguished from a substitute

first water *n* 1 : the purest luster   2 : the highest grade, degree, or quality

firth \'fərth\ *n* [ON *fjörthr*] : a narrow arm of the sea; *also* : the opening of a river into the sea

fis·cal \'fis-kəl\ *adj* [L *fiscus* treasury, lit., basket] 1 : of or relating to taxation, public revenues, or public debt   2 : of or relating to financial matters — **fis·cal·ly** \-kə-lē\ *adv*

¹**fish** \'fish\ *n, pl* **fish** *or* **fish·es** [OE *fisc*] 1 a : an aquatic animal — usu. used in combination ⟨star*fish*⟩ ⟨cuttle*fish*⟩   b : any of numerous cold-blooded aquatic water-breathing vertebrates with a usu. long somewhat spindle-shaped body terminating in a broad caudal fin and limbs in the form of fins when present at all   2 : the flesh of fish used as food   3 : FELLOW, CHAP ⟨a queer *fish*⟩   4 : a piece of wood or iron fastened alongside another member to strengthen it — **fish·like** \'fish-,līk\ *adj*

²**fish** *vb* 1 : to catch fish   2 : to catch or try to catch fish in ⟨*fish* the stream⟩   3 : to search (as with a hook) for something underwater   4 : to seek something by or as if by groping or feeling

fish–and–chips *n pl* : fried fish and french fried potatoes

fish cake *n* : a round fried cake made of shredded fish and mashed potato — called also *fish ball*

fish·er \'fish-ər\ *n* 1 : one that fishes   2 : a large dark brown No. American arboreal carnivorous mammal related to the weasels; *also* : its valuable fur or pelt

fish·er·man \-mən\ *n* 1 : one who engages in fishing as an occupation or for pleasure **2** : a ship used in commercial fishing

fish·ery \'fish-(ə-)rē\ *n, pl* **-er·ies 1** : the activity or business of taking aquatic products (as fish) **2** : a place or establishment for catching fish often together with its personnel

fish hawk *n* : OSPREY

fish·hook \'fish-,hůk\ *n* : a usu. barbed hook for catching fish

fish·ing *n* : the sport or business of catching fish

fish ladder *n* : an arrangement of pools by which fish can pass around a dam

fish·mon·ger \'fish-,məŋ-gər, -,mäŋ-\ *n, chiefly Brit* : a fish dealer

fish·plate \-,plāt\ *n* : a steel plate used to lap a butt joint

fish stick *n* : a small elongated fillet of fish breaded and fried

fish story *n* : an extravagant or incredible story

fish·wife \'fish-,wīf\ *n* **1** : a woman who sells fish **2** : a scurrilously abusive woman

fishy \'fish-ē\ *adj* **fish·i·er; -est 1** : of, relating to, or resembling fish ⟨a *fishy* odor⟩ **2** : inspiring doubt or suspicion : QUESTIONABLE ⟨that story sounds *fishy* to me⟩

fis·sile \'fis-əl\ *adj* **1** : capable of being split or divided along the grain or along planes ⟨a *fissile* rock⟩ **2** : FISSIONABLE

¹fis·sion \'fish-ən, 'fizh-\ *n* [L *fiss-, findere* to split; akin to E *bite*] **1** : a splitting or breaking up into parts **2** : reproduction by spontaneous division of a body or a cell into two or more parts each of which grows into a complete individual **3** : the splitting of an atomic nucleus resulting in the release of large amounts of energy

²fission *vb* : to undergo or cause to undergo fission

fis·sion·a·ble \'fish-(ə-)nə-bəl, 'fizh-\ *adj* : capable of undergoing fission ⟨*fissionable* material⟩

fission bomb *n* : ATOM BOMB 1

fis·sip·a·rous \fis-'ip-ə-rəs\ *adj* **1** : reproducing by fission **2** : tending to disrupt or divide

fis·si·ped \'fis-ə-,ped\ *adj* [L *fiss-, findere* to split + *ped-, pes* foot] : having the toes separated to the base — **fissiped** *n*

¹fis·sure \'fish-ər\ *n* : a narrow opening or crack of some length and depth ⟨a *fissure* of the skull⟩ ⟨a *fissure* in rock⟩

²fissure *vb* **1** : to break into fissures : CLEAVE **2** : CRACK, DIVIDE

fist \'fist\ *n* [OE *fȳst*] **1** : the hand clenched with fingers doubled into the palm **2** : CLUTCH, GRASP **3** : INDEX 6

fist·ic \'fis-tik\ *adj* : of or relating to boxing or to fist fighting

fist·i·cuffs \'fis-ti-,kəfs\ *n pl* [alter. of *fisty cuff*, fr. *fisty fistic + cuff*] : a fight with usu. bare fists

fis·tu·la \'fis-chə-lə\ *n, pl* **-las** *or* **-lae** \-,lē, -,lī\ [L, reed, pipe, fistula] : an abnormal passage leading from an abscess or hollow organ — **fis·tu·lous** \-ləs\ *adj*

¹fit \'fit\ *n* [OE *fitt* strife] **1** : a sudden violent attack of a disorder (as epilepsy) esp. when marked by convulsions or loss of consciousness **2** : a sudden outburst (as of laughter) —**by fits** *or* **by fits and starts** : in an impulsive or irregular manner

²fit *adj* **fit·ter; fit·test** [ME] **1** : adapted to an end or design : APPROPRIATE ⟨water *fit* for drinking⟩ **2** : BECOMING, PROPER **3** : READY, PREPARED **4** : QUALIFIED, COMPETENT **5** : sound physically and mentally : HEALTHY — **fit·ly** *adv* — **fit·ness** *n*
syn FIT, SUITABLE, PROPER, APPROPRIATE mean right with respect to the nature, condition, or use of the thing qualified. FIT stresses adaptability to the end in view or special readiness for a particular activity ⟨*fit* to teach young children⟩ SUITABLE implies answering the demands or requirements of an occasion ⟨*suitable* clothes for the reception⟩ PROPER suggests a suitability through essential nature ⟨a *proper* diet⟩ or in accordance with custom ⟨a request made in *proper* form⟩ APPROPRIATE implies a marked or distinctive fitness or suitability ⟨*appropriate* words of congratulation⟩

³fit *vb* **fit·ted; fit·ting 1** : to be suitable for or to : BEFIT **2 a** : to be correctly adjusted to or shaped for **b** : to insert or adjust until correctly in place **c** : to make a place or room for **3** : to be in agreement or accord with ⟨the theory *fits* the facts⟩ **4 a** : to make ready : PREPARE **b** : to bring to a required form and size : ADJUST **c** : to cause to conform to or suit something else **5** : SUPPLY, EQUIP **6** : to be in harmony or accord : BELONG

⁴fit *n* **1 a** : the state or manner of being fitted **b** : the degree of closeness with which surfaces are brought together in an assembly of parts **2** : a piece of clothing that fits

fitch \'fich\ *or* **fitch·ew** \'fich-ü\ *n* [ME *fiche, ficheux,* fr. MF or MD; MF *fichau,* fr. MD *vitsau*] : POLECAT 1; *also* : its fur or pelt

fitch·et \'fich-ət\ *n* : POLECAT 1

fit·ful \'fit-fəl\ *adj* : not regular : RESTLESS ⟨*fitful* sleep⟩ — **fit·ful·ly** \-fə-lē\ *adv* — **fit·ful·ness** *n*

fit·ter \'fit-ər\ *n* : one that fits: as **a** : a person who tries on and adjusts articles of dress **b** : a person who fits, adjusts, or assembles parts (as of machinery)

¹fit·ting *adj* : APPROPRIATE, SUITABLE — **fit·ting·ly** \-iŋ-lē\ *adv* — **fit·ting·ness** *n*

²fitting *n* **1** : the action or act of one that fits; *esp* : a trying on of clothes being made or altered **2** : a small often standardized accessory part ⟨a plumbing *fitting*⟩ ⟨an electrical *fitting*⟩ ⟨an airplane *fitting*⟩

five \'fīv\ *n* [OE *fīf*] **1** — see NUMBER table **2** : the fifth in a set or series **3** : something having five units or members; *esp* : a male basketball team **4** : FIFTEEN 2 — **five** *adj or pron*

five-and-ten \,fī-vən-'ten\ *also* **five-and-dime** \-vən-'dīm\ *n* : a store selling articles priced at 5 or 10 cents and other inexpensive articles

five-year plan *n* : one of a series of detailed plans for development (as economic) each of which covers a 5-year period

¹fix \'fiks\ *vb* [L *fix-, figere* to fasten, fix] **1 a** : to make firm, stable, or fast **b** : to give a permanent or final form to: as (1) : to change into a stable or available form ⟨bacteria that *fix* nitrogen⟩ (2) : to kill, harden, and preserve for microscopic study (3) : to make the image of (a photographic film or print) permanent by chemical treatment **c** : AFFIX, ATTACH **2** : to hold or direct steadily ⟨*fixes* his eyes on the horizon⟩ **3 a** : to set or place definitely : ESTABLISH ⟨*fix* the date of a meeting⟩ **b** : ASSIGN ⟨*fix* blame⟩ **4** : to set in order : ADJUST **5** : to get ready : PREPARE **6** : to make sound or whole again: **a** : REPAIR, MEND **b** : RESTORE, CURE **7** : to influence the actions, outcome, or effect of by improper or illegal methods ⟨*fix* a horse race⟩ — **fix·a·ble** \'fik-sə-bəl\ *adj* — **fix·er** *n*
syn FIX, REPAIR mean to restore to sound condition or working order. FIX tends to stress the arranging, straightening out, or adjusting of parts ⟨*fix* a clock⟩ ⟨getting his teeth *fixed*⟩ REPAIR usu. stresses the replacing or remaking of damaged or lost parts ⟨*repair* a broken toy⟩ ⟨*repair* a collapsed bridge⟩

²fix *n* **1** : a position of difficulty or embarrassment : PREDICAMENT **2** : the position (as of a ship) determined by bearings, observations, or radio; *also* : a determination of one's position **3** : a shot of a narcotic

fix·ate \'fik-,sāt\ *vb* **1** : to make fixed or unchanging : FIX **2 a** : to focus one's eyes upon **b** : to focus or concentrate one's attention

fix·a·tion \fik-'sā-shən\ *n* **1** : the act, process, or result of fixing or fixating ⟨*fixation* of nitrogen⟩ **2** : an obsessive or unhealthy preoccupation or attachment

fix·a·tive \'fik-sət-iv\ *n* : something that stabilizes or sets: as **a** : a substance added to a perfume esp. to prevent too rapid evaporation **b** : a varnish used esp. for the protection of crayon drawings — **fixative** *adj*

fixed \'fikst\ *adj* **1 a** : securely placed or fastened : STATIONARY **b** (1) : NONVOLATILE ⟨*fixed* oil⟩ (2) : COMBINED ⟨*fixed* nitrogen⟩ **c** : not subject to change or fluctuation : SETTLED, FINAL **d** : recurring on the same date from year to year **e** : INTENT ⟨a *fixed* stare⟩ **2** : supplied with a definite amount of something needed (as money) — **fix·ed·ly** \'fik-səd-lē\ *adv* — **fix·ed·ness** \'fik-səd-nəs\ *n*

fixed star *n* : a star so distant that its motion can be measured only by very precise observations over long periods

fix·ing \'fik-siŋ, 2 is often -sənz\ *n* **1** : a putting in permanent form **2** *pl* : ARRANGEMENTS, TRIMMINGS ⟨a birthday party with all the *fixings*⟩

fix·i·ty \'fik-sət-ē\ *n* : the quality or state of being fixed or stable

fix·ture \'fiks-chər\ *n* **1** : the act of fixing : the state of being fixed **2 :** one firmly established in a place **3 :** something attached to another thing as a permanent part ⟨bathroom *fixtures*⟩

¹fizz \'fiz\ *vi* : to make a hissing or sputtering sound

²fizz *n* **1 :** a hissing sound **2 :** an effervescent beverage — **fizzy** \'fiz-ē\ *adj*

¹fiz·zle \'fiz-əl\ *vi* **fiz·zled**; **fiz·zling** \'fiz-(ə-)liŋ\ **1 :** FIZZ **2 :** to fail or end feebly esp. after a promising start

²fizzle *n* : an abortive effort : FAILURE

fjord \fē-'ȯrd, 'fyȯrd\ *n* [Norw] : a narrow inlet of the sea between cliffs or steep slopes

flab·ber·gast \'flab-ər-,gast\ *vt* : to overwhelm with shock, surprise, or wonder : ASTOUND

flab·by \'flab-ē\ *adj* **flab·bi·er**; **-est** [alter. of *flappy*, fr. ²*flap*] **1 :** lacking resilience or firmness : FLACCID **2 :** being weak and ineffective : FEEBLE **syn** see LIMP — **flab·bi·ly** \'flab-ə-lē\ *adv* — **flab·bi·ness** \'flab-ē-nəs\ *n*

fla·bel·late \flə-'bel-ət, 'flab-ə-,lāt\ *or* **fla·bel·li·form** \flə-'bel-ə-,fȯrm\ *adj* [L *flabellum* fan] : shaped like a fan

flac·cid \'flak-səd\ *adj* [L *flaccidus*] : FLABBY; *also* : deficient in turgor ⟨*flaccid* stems⟩ **syn** see LIMP — **flac·cid·i·ty** \flak-'sid-ət-ē\ *n* — **flac·cid·ly** \'flak-səd-lē\ *adv*

flac·on \'flak-ən\ *n* [F] : a small usu. ornamental bottle with a tight cap

¹flag \'flag\ *n* [ME *flagge* reed, rush] : any of various monocotyledonous plants with long narrow leaves: as **a :** IRIS; *esp* : a wild iris **b :** SWEET FLAG **c :** CATTAIL

²flag *n* [ON *flaga* slab; akin to E *flay*] **1 :** a hard stone that is composed of even layers and splits into flat pieces suitable for paving **2 :** a thin piece of flag used for paving

³flag *vt* **flagged**; **flag·ging** : to pave (as a walk) with flags

⁴flag *n* [perh. fr. ¹*flag*] **1 :** a usu. rectangular piece of fabric of distinctive design that is used as a symbol (as of nationality) or as a signaling device and is usu. displayed hanging free from a staff or halyard to which it is attached by one edge **2 :** one of the cross strokes of a musical note less than a quarter note in value

⁵flag *vt* **flagged**; **flag·ging 1 :** to put a flag on **2 :** to signal with or as if with a flag; *esp* : to signal to stop ⟨*flag* a taxi⟩

⁶flag *vi* **flagged**; **flag·ging 1 :** to be loose, yielding, or limp; *also* : to droop from lack of water ⟨plants *flagging* under the summer sun⟩ **2 a :** to become feeble ⟨his interest *flagged*⟩ **b :** to decline in interest or attraction ⟨the topic *flagged*⟩

Flag Day *n* : June 14 observed in various states in commemoration of the adoption in 1777 of the official U.S. flag

flag·el·lant \'flaj-ə-lənt, flə-'jel-ənt\ *n* : one that whips; *esp* : a person who scourges himself as a public penance

¹flag·el·late \'flaj-ə-,lāt\ *vt* : to punish by whipping : WHIP — **flag·el·la·tion** \,flaj-ə-'lā-shən\ *n*

²flag·el·late \'flaj-ə-lət, flə-'jel-ət\ *adj* **1 a** *or* **flag·el·lat·ed** \'flaj-ə-,lāt-əd\ : having flagella **b :** resembling a flagellum **2 :** of, relating to, or caused by flagellates

³flagellate *like* ²\ *n* : a flagellate protozoan or alga

fla·gel·lum \flə-'jel-əm\ *n, pl* **-gel·la** \-'jel-ə\ *also* **-gellums** [L, whip] : a long slender appendage: as **a :** the distal part of an antenna **b :** a tapering process that projects singly or in groups from a cell and is the primary organ of motion of many microorganisms — **fla·gel·lar** \-'jel-ər\ *adj*

fla·geo·let \,flaj-ə-'let\ *n* [F] : a small woodwind instrument belonging to the flute class

flag·ging \'flag-iŋ\ *n* : a pavement of flagstones

fla·gi·tious \flə-'jish-əs\ *adj* [L *flagitium* shameful thing] : marked by outrageous or scandalous crime or vice : VILLAINOUS — **fla·gi·tious·ly** *adv* — **fla·gi·tious·ness** *n*

flag·man \'flag-mən\ *n* : one who signals with or as if with a flag esp. to warn of danger

flag of truce : a white flag carried or displayed to an enemy to signal a desire to negotiate or surrender

flag·on \'flag-ən\ *n* [MF *flascon*, *flacon* bottle, fr. LL *flascon-*, *flasco*] : a container for liquids usu. having a handle, spout, and lid

flag·pole \'flag-,pōl\ *n* : a pole to raise a flag on

flag rank *n* : any of the ranks in the navy above a captain

fla·grant \'flā-grənt\ *adj* [L *flagrant-*, *flagrans*, prp. of *flagrare* to blaze, burn; akin to E *black*] : conspicuously bad : OUTRAGEOUS, NOTORIOUS ⟨*flagrant* disobedience⟩ ⟨a *flagrant* criminal⟩ — **fla·gran·cy** \-grən-sē\ *n* — **fla·grant·ly** *adv*

syn FLAGRANT, GLARING, GROSS mean conspicuously bad or objectionable. FLAGRANT applies to behavior, errors, or offenses so bad that they cannot escape notice or be excused ⟨*flagrant* disobedience⟩ GLARING suggests painful or damaging obtrusiveness ⟨*glaring* imperfection⟩ GROSS applies to utterly inexcusable faults or offenses ⟨*gross* dishonesty⟩ ⟨*gross* carelessness⟩

fla·gran·te de·lic·to \flə-,grant-ē-di-'lik-,tō\ *adv* [ML, lit., while the crime is blazing] : in the very act of committing a misdeed

flag·ship \'flag-,ship\ *n* : the ship that carries the commander of a fleet or subdivision thereof and flies his flag

flag·staff \-,staf\ *n* : FLAGPOLE

flag·stone \-,stōn\ *n* : ²FLAG 2

flag stop *n* : a point at which a vehicle in public transportation stops only on prearrangement or signal

flag-wav·ing \'flag-,wā-viŋ\ *n* : passionate appeal to patriotic or partisan sentiment : CHAUVINISM

¹flail \'flāl\ *n* [MF *flaiel*, fr. LL *flagellum*, fr. L, whip] : a hand threshing tool consisting of a wooden handle with a stout short stick at the end so hung as to swing freely

²flail *vb* : to strike with or as if with a flail

flair \'fla(ə)r, 'fle(ə)r\ *n* [F, lit., sense of smell, fr. OF, odor, fr. *flairier* to give off an odor, fr. LL *flagrare*, alter. of L *fragrare*] **1 :** discriminating sense ⟨a *flair* for logical analysis⟩ **2 :** natural aptitude : BENT **syn** see PENCHANT

flak \'flak\ *n* [G] : antiaircraft guns or the bursting shells fired from them

¹flake \'flāk\ *n* [ME, of Scand origin] : a thin flattened usu. loose piece : CHIP ⟨a *flake* of snow⟩ ⟨a *flake* of dandruff⟩ ⟨soap *flakes*⟩

²flake *vb* : to form or separate into flakes : make or become flaky ⟨this paint *flakes* off⟩

flaky \'flā-kē\ *adj* **flak·i·er**; **-est 1 :** consisting of flakes **2 :** tending to flake ⟨pie with a crisp *flaky* crust⟩ — **flak·i·ness** *n*

flam·beau \'flam-,bō\ *n, pl* **flam·beaux** \-,bōz\ *or* **flambeaus** [F] : a flaming torch

flam·boy·ant \flam-'bȯi-ənt\ *adj* [F, fr. prp. of *flamboyer* to flame, fr. OF, fr. *flambe* flame] **1** *often cap* : characterized by waving curves suggesting flames ⟨*flamboyant* window tracery⟩ **2 :** FLORID, ORNATE; *also* : RESPLENDENT **3 :** given to dashing display : SHOWY — **flam·boy·ance** \-ən(t)s\ *also* **flam·boy·an·cy** \-ən-sē\ *n* — **flam·boy·ant·ly** *adv*

¹flame \'flām\ *n* [ME *flaume*, fr. MF *flamme*, fr. L *flamma*] **1 :** the glowing gaseous part of a fire **2 a :** a state of blazing combustion **b :** a condition or appearance suggesting a flame **c :** BRILLIANCE, BRIGHTNESS **3 :** burning zeal or passion **4 :** SWEETHEART

²flame *vb* **1 :** to burn with a flame : BLAZE **2 :** to burst or break out violently or passionately **3 :** to shine brightly : GLOW **4 :** to treat or affect with flame — **flam·er** *n*

flame cell *n* : a hollow excretory cell of various lower invertebrates that has a tuft of vibratile cilia

fla·men·co \flə-'meŋ-kō\ *n, pl* **-cos** [Sp, Flemish, like a gypsy, fr. MD *Vlaminc* Fleming] : a vigorous rhythmic dance style of the Andalusian gypsies

flame-out \'flām-,aut\ *n* : the cessation of operation of a jet airplane engine

flame·proof \-'prüf\ *adj* **1 :** resistant to the action of flame **2 :** rendered so on contact with flame

flame·throw·er \-,thrō-(ə)r\ *n* : a device that expels from a nozzle a burning stream of liquid or semiliquid fuel under pressure

flam·ing \'flā-miŋ\ *adj* **1 :** BLAZING **2 :** suggesting a flame in brilliance or wavy outline **3 :** ARDENT, PASSIONATE — **flam·ing·ly** \-miŋ-lē\ *adv*

fla·min·go \flə-'miŋ-gō\ *n, pl* **-gos** *also* **-goes** [obs. Sp *flamengo* Fleming, flamingo, fr. MD *Vlaminc* Fleming; so called fr. the ruddy complexion of Flemings] : any of several aquatic long-legged and long-necked birds with a broad bill bent downward at the end and usu. rosy-white plumage with scarlet wing coverts

flam·ma·ble \'flam-ə-bəl\ *adj* : capable of being easily ignited and of burning with extreme rapidity ⟨a *flammable*

fla-geo-let

liquid⟩ — **flam·ma·bil·i·ty** \,flam-ə-'bil-ət-ē\ *n* — **flammable** *n*

fla·neur \flä-'nər\ *n* [F *flâneur* idler] **:** MAN-ABOUT-TOWN; *also* **:** an intellectual trifler

¹flange \'flanj\ *n* **:** a rib or rim used for strength, for guiding, or for attachment to another object ⟨the *flange* on a locomotive wheel⟩

²flange *vt* **:** to furnish with a flange

¹flank \'flaŋk\ *n* [OF *flanc*] **1 a :** the fleshy part of the side between the ribs and the hip; *also* **:** the side of a quadruped **b :** a cut of meat from this part of an animal **2 a :** SIDE **b :** the right or left of a formation

²flank *vt* **1 a :** to attack or threaten the flank of **b :** to turn the flank of **2 :** to be situated at the side of **:** BORDER

flank·er \'flaŋ-kər\ *n* **1 :** one that flanks **2 :** a football player stationed wide of the formation; *esp* **:** an offensive halfback who lines up on the flank and serves chiefly as a pass receiver — called also *flanker back*

flan·nel \'flan-ᵊl\ *n* [ME *flaunneol* woolen cloth or garment] **1 a :** a soft twilled wool or worsted fabric with a napped surface **b :** a stout cotton fabric napped on one side **2** *pl* **:** flannel underwear or trousers

flan·nel·ette \,flan-ᵊl-'et\ *n* **:** a cotton flannel napped on one or both sides

¹flap \'flap\ *n* [ME *flappe*] **1 :** a stroke with something broad **:** SLAP **2 :** something broad, limber, or flat and usu. thin that hangs loose: as **a :** a piece on a garment that hangs free **b :** an extended part forming the closure (as of an envelope) **3 :** the motion of something broad and limber **4 :** a movable auxiliary airfoil attached to the trailing edge of an airplane wing permitting a steeper gliding angle in landing

²flap *vb* **flapped; flap·ping 1 :** to beat with something broad and flat **2 :** to move or cause to move with a beating motion ⟨birds *flapping* their wings⟩ **3 :** to sway loosely usu. with a noise of striking ⟨the tent *flapped* in the rising breeze⟩

flap·jack \'flap-,jak\ *n* **:** GRIDDLE CAKE

flap·per \'flap-ər\ *n* **1 :** one that flaps **2 :** a young woman esp. of the 1920s who shows bold freedom from conventions in conduct and dress

¹flare \'fla(ə)r, 'fle(ə)r\ *vb* **1 :** to burn with an unsteady flame **2 a :** to shine with a sudden light **b :** to become suddenly excited or angry ⟨*flare* up⟩ **3 :** to open or spread outward

²flare *n* **1 :** an unsteady glaring light **2 a :** a fire or blaze of light used to signal, illuminate, or attract attention; *also* **:** a device or composition used to produce such a flare **b :** a temporary outburst of energy from a small area of the sun's surface **3 :** a sudden outburst (as of sound, excitement, or anger) **4 :** a spreading outward; *also* **:** a place or part that spreads ⟨the *flare* of a vase⟩⟨the *flare* of a trumpet⟩

flare-up \-,əp\ *n* **:** a sudden burst (as of flame or anger)

¹flash \'flash\ *vb* [ME *flaschen*] **1 :** to break forth in or like a sudden flame ⟨lightning *flashed*⟩ **2 :** to send out in or as if in flashes ⟨*flash* a message⟩ **3 :** to appear or pass very suddenly ⟨a car *flashed* by⟩ **4 :** to make a sudden display (as of brilliance or feeling) ⟨the girl's eyes *flashed* with excitement⟩ **5 :** to gleam or glow intermittently **6 :** to fill by a sudden rush of water **7 :** to expose to view very briefly ⟨*flash* a badge⟩

syn FLASH, GLANCE, GLINT, SPARKLE mean to send forth light. FLASH implies a sudden brief outburst of bright light; GLANCE suggests a darting light reflected from a quickly moving surface ⟨sunlight *glancing* from the ripples⟩ GLINT suggests a cold glancing light; SPARKLE implies innumerable moving points of bright light

²flash *n* **1 a :** a sudden burst of light **b :** a movement of a flag or light in signaling **2 :** a sudden and brilliant burst (as of wit) **3 :** a brief time **4 a :** SHOW, DISPLAY; *esp* **:** ostentatious display **b :** one that attracts notice; *esp* **:** an outstanding athlete **5 :** something flashed: as **a :** GLIMPSE, LOOK **b :** a first brief news report **c :** FLASHLIGHT 2 **d :** a quick-spreading flame or momentary intense outburst of radiant heat

³flash *adj* **1 :** FLASHY, SPORTY **2 :** of sudden origin and short duration ⟨a *flash* fire⟩

flash·back \'flash-,bak\ *n* **:** injection into the chronological sequence of events in a literary or theatrical work of an event of earlier occurrence

flash·bulb \-,bəlb\ *n* **:** an electric flash lamp in which metal foil or wire is burned

flash card *n* **:** a card bearing words, numbers, or pictures briefly displayed by a teacher to a class during drills (as in reading, spelling, or arithmetic)

flash color *n* **:** a patch of bright color on an otherwise dull-colored animal that is visible only during motion and is thought to distract a predator

flash·cube \'flash-,kyüb\ *n* **:** a cubical device incorporating four flashbulbs for taking four pictures in succession

flash flood *n* **:** a local flood of great volume and short duration generally resulting from heavy rainfall in the immediate vicinity

flash·gun \'flash-,gən\ *n* **:** a device for holding and operating a flashbulb

flash·ing \'flash-in\ *n* **:** sheet metal used in waterproofing roof valleys or the angle between a chimney and a roof

flash lamp *n* **:** a usu. electric lamp for producing a brief but intense flash of light for taking photographs

flash·light \'flash-,līt\ *n* **1 :** a flash of light or a light that flashes **2 a :** a sudden bright artificial light used in taking photographic pictures **b :** a photograph taken by such a light **3 :** a small battery-operated portable electric light

flash·over \-,ō-vər\ *n* **:** an abnormal electrical discharge (as through the air to the ground from a high potential source)

flash point *n* **:** the lowest temperature at which vapors above a volatile combustible substance ignite in air when exposed to flame

flashy \'flash-ē\ *adj* **flash·i·er; -est 1 :** momentarily dazzling **2 a :** superficially attractive **:** BRIGHT **b :** SHOWY **syn** see GAUDY — **flash·i·ly** \'flash-ə-lē\ *adv* — **flash·i·ness** \'flash-ē-nəs\ *n*

flask \'flask\ *n* [MF *flasque* powder flask, fr. LL *flasco* bottle] **1 :** a bottle-shaped container often somewhat narrowed toward the outlet and often fitted with a closure **2 :** a frame that holds molding sand used in a foundry

¹flat \'flat\ *adj* **flat·ter; flat·test** [ON *flatr*] **1 :** having a smooth level horizontal surface ⟨*flat* ground⟩ **2 :** having a smooth even surface ⟨*flat* pavement⟩ **3 :** spread out on or along a surface ⟨was *flat* on the ground⟩ **4 :** having a broad smooth surface and little thickness ⟨a phonograph record is *flat*⟩ **5 :** DOWNRIGHT, POSITIVE ⟨a *flat* refusal⟩ **6 :** FIXED, UNCHANGING ⟨charge a *flat* rate⟩ **7 :** EXACT ⟨*flat* four minutes⟩ **8 :** DULL, UNINTERESTING, INSIPID ⟨a *flat* story⟩⟨water that tastes *flat*⟩ **9 :** DEFLATED — used of tires **10 a :** lower than the true pitch **b :** lower by a half step ⟨tone of A *flat*⟩ **c :** having a flat in the signature ⟨key of B *flat*⟩ **11 :** pronounced like the vowel of *hat* ⟨a *flat* a⟩ **12 :** being an adverb with no distinctive ending **13 a :** having little or no illusion of depth ⟨a *flat* painting⟩ **b :** lacking contrast ⟨a *flat* photographic negative⟩ **c :** free from gloss ⟨*flat* paint⟩ — **flat·ly** *adv* — **flat·ness** *n*

²flat *n* **1 :** a level surface of land with little or no relief **:** PLAIN **2 :** a flat part or surface **3 a :** a musical note or tone one half step lower than a specified note or tone **b :** a character ♭ on a line or space of the staff indicating such a note or tone **4 :** something flat: as **a :** a flat piece of theatrical scenery **b :** a shoe or slipper having a flat heel or no heel **5 :** a deflated tire

³flat *adv* **1 :** FLATLY: as **a :** on or against a flat surface ⟨lie *flat*⟩ **b :** EXACTLY **c :** below the true musical pitch

⁴flat *vb* **flat·ted; flat·ting 1 :** FLATTEN **2 a :** to lower in pitch esp. by a half step **b :** to sing or play below the true pitch

⁵flat *n* **1 :** a floor or story in a building **2 :** an apartment on one floor

flat·bed \'flat-,bed\ *n* **:** a motortruck or trailer with a body in the form of a platform or shallow box

flat·boat \'flat-,bōt\ *n* **:** a large flat-bottomed boat with square ends used for transporting heavy freight on rivers

flat·car \-,kär\ *n* **:** a railroad freight car without permanent raised sides, ends, or covering

flat·fish \-,fish\ *n* **:** any of an order (Heterosomata) of marine teleost fishes (as halibuts, flounders, or soles) that as adults swim on one side of the laterally compressed body and have both eyes on the upper side

flat·foot \-,füt (*always so in sense 3*), -'füt\ *n*, *pl* **flat·feet 1 :** a condition in which the main arch of the foot is so flattened that the entire sole rests upon the ground **2 :** a foot affected with flatfoot **3** *or pl* **flatfoots** *slang*

: POLICEMAN; *esp* : PATROLMAN — **flat·foot·ed** \-'fut-əd\ *adj*

flat·iron \'flat-,ī(-ə)rn\ *n* : an iron for pressing clothes

flat·ten \'flat-°n\ *vb* **flat·tened**; **flat·ten·ing** \'flat-niŋ, -°n-iŋ\ : to make or become flat esp. in surface or position

flat·ter \'flat-ər\ *vt* [ME *flateren*, irreg. fr. OF *flater* to lick, flatter] **1** : to praise too much or without sincerity in order to gain some advantage or benefit for oneself or to gratify another's vanity **2** : to represent too favorably ⟨a picture that *flatters* her⟩ **3** : to judge (oneself) favorably or too favorably esp. in respect to an accomplishment or ability ⟨*flattered* himself on his skill as a swimmer⟩ — **flat·ter·er** \'flat-ər-ər\ *n* — **flat·ter·ing·ly** \'flat-ə-riŋ-lē\ *adv*

flat·tery \'flat-ə-rē\ *n, pl* **-ter·ies** **1** : the act of flattering **2** : flattering speech or attentions : insincere or excessive praise

flat·top \'flat-,täp\ *n* : AIRCRAFT CARRIER

flat·u·lent \'flach-ə-lənt\ *adj* [MF, fr. L *flatus* act of blowing, wind, fr. *flat-*, *flare* to blow; akin to E *blow*] **1 a** : marked by or affected with gases formed in the intestine or stomach **b** : likely to cause alimentary flatulence **2** : pretentious without real worth or substance : POMPOUS — **flat·u·lence** \-lən(t)s\ *n* — **flat·u·lent·ly** *adv*

fla·tus \'flāt-əs\ *n* : gas formed in the intestine or stomach

flat·ware \'flat-,wa(ə)r, -,we(ə)r\ *n* : tableware more or less flat and usu. formed or cast in a single piece

flat·wise \-,wīz\ *or* **flat·ways** \-,wāz\ *adv* : with the flat side downward or next to another object

flat·work \-,wərk\ *n* : articles that in laundering can be finished mechanically as distinguished from those requiring hand ironing

flat·worm \-,wərm\ *n* : any of a phylum (Platyhelminthes) of flat bilaterally symmetrical unsegmented worms that lack a body cavity and include the turbellarians, flukes, and tapeworms

flaunt \'flont, 'flänt\ *vb* **1** : to wave or flutter showily **2** : to display or obtrude oneself to public notice **3** : to display ostentatiously or impudently : PARADE — **flaunt** *n* **syn** FLAUNT, FLOUT are often confused. FLAUNT implies displaying something shamelessly, boastfully, or offensively ⟨*flaunting* their criminal exploits in the tabloids⟩ FLOUT implies scoffing or jeering at in contempt or defiance ⟨openly *flouting* the nation's laws⟩ — **flaunt·ing·ly** \-iŋ-lē\ *adv*

flau·tist \'flot-əst, 'flaut-\ *n* [It *flauto* flute] : FLUTIST

fla·vo·pro·tein \,flā-vō-'prō-,tēn, -'prōt-ē-ən\ *n* : an enzyme that serves in the removal and transport of hydrogen and plays a major role in biological oxidations

¹fla·vor \'flā-vər\ *n* [ME, fr. MF *flaor*] **1 a** : the quality of something that affects the sense of taste : SAVOR **b** : the blend of taste and smell sensations evoked by a substance in the mouth **2** : a substance that flavors **3** : characteristic or predominant quality — **fla·vored** \-vərd\ *adj* — **fla·vor·ful** \-fəl\ *adj* — **fla·vor·less** \-ləs\ *adj*

²flavor *vt* **fla·vored**; **fla·vor·ing** \'flāv-(ə-)riŋ\ : to give or add flavor to

fla·vor·ing *n* : FLAVOR 2

fla·vour \'flā-vər\ *chiefly Brit var of* FLAVOR

¹flaw \'flo\ *n* [ME] : an imperfect part : CRACK, FAULT ⟨a *flaw* in a plan⟩ ⟨a *flaw* in a diamond⟩ **syn** see BLEMISH — **flaw·less** \-ləs\ *adj* — **flaw·less·ly** *adv* — **flaw·less·ness** *n*

²flaw *vb* **1** : to make flaws in : CRACK **2** : to become defective

³flaw *n* : a sudden brief burst of wind; *also* : a spell of stormy weather

flax \'flaks\ *n* [OE *fleax*] : a slender erect blue-flowered plant grown for its fiber and seeds; *also* : its fiber esp. prepared for spinning — compare LINEN

flax·en \'flak-sən\ *adj* **1** : made of flax **2** : resembling flax esp. in pale soft straw color

flax·seed \'flak-,sēd\ *n* : the seed of flax used as a source of linseed oil and medicinally

flay \'flā\ *vt* [OE *flēan*] **1** : to strip off the skin or surface of : SKIN **2** : to criticize harshly : SCOLD

F layer *n* : the highest and most densely ionized regular layer of the ionosphere

flea \'flē\ *n* [OE *flēa*] : any of an order (Siphonaptera) of wingless bloodsucking insects with a hard laterally compressed body and legs adapted to leaping

flea·bane \-,bān\ *n* : any of various of the daisy family believed to drive away fleas

flea beetle *n* : any of various small beetles that leap like fleas, feed on foliage, and sometimes transmit virus diseases of plants

flea-bit·ten \'flē-,bit-°n\ *adj* : bitten by or infested with fleas

flea market *n* : a street market for cheap or secondhand articles

¹fleck \'flek\ *vt* [back-formation fr. *flecked* spotted, fr. ME, prob. fr. ON *flekkōttr*] : STREAK, SPOT ⟨yellow bananas *flecked* with brown⟩

²fleck *n* **1** : SPOT, MARK **2** : FLAKE, PARTICLE

flec·tion \'flek-shən\ *n* [L *flectere* to bend] **1** : the act of flexing or bending **2** : a part bent : BEND **3** : FLEXION — **flec·tion·al** \-shnəl, -shən-°l\ *adj*

fledge \'flej\ *vb* [OE *-flycge* capable of flying] **1** : to develop the feathers necessary for flying **2** : to furnish with feathers ⟨*fledge* an arrow⟩

fledg·ling \'flej-liŋ\ *n* **1** : a young bird just fledged **2** : an immature or inexperienced person

flee \'flē\ *vb* **fled** \'fled\; **flee·ing** [OE *flēon*] **1 a** : to run away from danger or evil : FLY **b** : to run away from : SHUN **2** : to pass away swiftly : VANISH

¹fleece \'flēs\ *n* [OE *flēos*] **1** : the coat of wool covering an animal (as a sheep) **2** : a soft or woolly covering

²fleece *vt* **1** : to remove the fleece from : SHEAR **2** : to strip of money or property by fraud or extortion

fleecy \'flē-sē\ *adj* **fleec·i·er**; **-est** : covered with, made of, or resembling fleece — **fleec·i·ness** *n*

fleer \'fli(ə)r\ *vi* [ME *fleryen*, of Scand origin] : to laugh or grimace in a coarse manner : SNEER — **fleer** *n*

¹fleet \'flēt\ *vi* [OE *flēotan* to float, flow] : to fly swiftly : pass rapidly ⟨time is *fleeting*⟩

²fleet *n* [OE *flēot* ship, fr. *flēotan* to float] **1 a** : a group of warships under one command **b** : a country's navy **2** : a group of ships or vehicles that move together or are operated under one management ⟨a *fleet* of trucks⟩ ⟨a *fleet* of airplanes⟩

³fleet *adj* [prob. fr. **¹fleet**] **1** : swift in motion : NIMBLE **2** : not enduring : FLEETING **syn** see FAST — **fleet·ly** *adv* — **fleet·ness** *n*

fleet admiral *n* : an admiral of the highest rank whose insignia is five stars

Flem·ing \'flem-iŋ\ *n* : a member of the Germanic people inhabiting northern Belgium and a small section of northern France bordering on Belgium

Flem·ish \'flem-ish\ *n* **1** : the Germanic language of the Flemings **2 Flemish** *pl* : FLEMINGS — **Flemish** *adj*

¹flesh \'flesh\ *n* [OE *flæsc*] **1** : the soft parts of the body of an animal and esp. of a vertebrate; *esp* : skeletal muscle as distinguished from visceral structures, bone, and integuments **b** : sleek well-fatted condition of body **2** : parts of an animal used as food **3** : the physical being of man as distinguished from the soul **4 a** : human beings **b** : living beings **c** : STOCK, KINDRED **5** : a fleshy plant part used as food; *esp* : the fleshy part of a fruit — **fleshed** \'flesht\ *adj*

²flesh *vb* **1** : to initiate into warfare by a first experience of battle ⟨*flesh* green troops⟩ **2** : to give substance to ⟨*flesh* out a story with details⟩ **3** : to remove flesh from **4** : to become fleshy — often used with *up* or *out*

flesh fly *n* : a two-winged fly whose maggots feed on flesh

flesh·ing \'flesh-iŋ\ *n* : the distribution of the lean and fat on an animal

flesh·ly \'flesh-lē\ *adj* **1** : CORPOREAL, BODILY **2 a** : CARNAL, SENSUAL **b** : not spiritual : WORLDLY

flesh·pot \'flesh-,pät\ *n* **1** *pl* : bodily comfort : LUXURY **2** : a place of luxurious entertainment

fleshy \'flesh-ē\ *adj* **flesh·i·er**; **-est** **1 a** : resembling or consisting of flesh **b** : having abundant flesh; *esp* : CORPULENT **2** : SUCCULENT, PULPY ⟨*fleshy* fruits⟩ — **flesh·i·ness** *n*

fleur-de-lis *or* **fleur-de-lys** \,flərd-°l-'ē, ,flùrd-\ *n, pl* **fleurs-de-lis** *or* **fleur-de-lis** *or* **fleurs-de-lys** *or* **fleur-de-lys** \,flərd-°l-'ē(z), ,flùrd-\ [MF *flor de lis*, lit., lily flower] **1** : IRIS 3 **2** : a conventionalized iris in art and heraldry

flew *past of* FLY

flews \'flüz\ *n pl* : the pendulous lateral parts of a dog's upper lip

fleur-de-lis 2

j joke; ŋ sing; ō flow; ȯ flaw; ȯi coin; th thin; ṯh this; ü loot; ù foot; y yet; yü few; yù furious; zh vision

flex \'fleks\ *vb* [L *flex-, flectere*] **:** to bend esp. repeatedly **:** cause flexion of

flex·i·ble \'flek-sə-bəl\ *adj* **1 :** capable of being flexed **:** PLIANT **2 :** readily changed or changing **:** ADAPTABLE ⟨a *flexible* mind⟩ — **flex·i·bil·i·ty** \,flek-sə-'bil-ət-ē\ *n* — **flex·i·bly** \'flek-sə-blē\ *adv*

flex·ion \'flek-shən\ *n* **:** muscular movement that lessens the angle between bones or parts; *also* **:** the resulting state or relation of parts

flex·or \'flek-sər\ *n* **:** a muscle that produces flexion — **flexor** *adj*

flex·u·ous \'fleksh-(ə-)wəs\ *adj* **1 :** having turns or windings **2 :** FLEXIBLE — **flex·u·os·i·ty** \,flek-shə-'wäs-ət-ē\ *n* — **flex·u·ous·ly** *adv*

flex·ure \'flek-shər\ *n* **1 :** the quality or state of being flexed **2 :** TURN, FOLD, BEND — **flex·ur·al** \-sh(ə-)rəl\ *adj*

flib·ber·ti·gib·bet \,flib-ərt-ē-'jib-ət\ *n* **:** a silly restless person

¹flick \'flik\ *n* [imit.] **1 :** a light sharp jerky stroke or movement **2 :** a sound produced by a flick **3 :** DAUB

²flick *vb* **1 :** to strike lightly with a quick sharp motion ⟨*flicked* a speck off her coat⟩ **2 :** FLUTTER, DART, FLIT

¹flick·er \'flik-ər\ *vb* **flick·ered; flick·er·ing** \'flik-(ə-)riŋ\ [OE *flicorian*] **1 a :** to waver unsteadily **:** FLUTTER **b :** FLIT, DART **2 :** to burn fitfully or with a fluctuating light ⟨a *flickering* candle⟩ **3 :** to produce by flickering

²flicker *n* **1 :** a brief interval of brightness ⟨a *flicker* of light⟩ **2 :** a flickering light **3 :** a brief stirring ⟨a *flicker* of interest⟩ — **flick·ery** \'flik-(ə-)rē\ *adj*

³flicker *n* **:** a common large brightly marked woodpecker of eastern No. America

flied *past of* FLY

fli·er \'flī(-ə)r\ *n* **1 :** one that flies; *esp* **:** AVIATOR **2 :** something (as an express train) that travels very fast **3 :** a speculative undertaking; *esp* **:** an attempt to gain large profits in a business venture by one who is inexperienced or uninformed **4 :** a printed notice or message (as an advertising leaflet) distributed in large numbers

¹flight \'flīt\ *n* [OE *flyht*; akin to E *fly*] **1 :** an act or instance of passing through the air by the use of wings ⟨a *flight* in a plane⟩ ⟨the *flight* of birds⟩ **2 a :** a passing through the air or through space outside the earth's atmosphere ⟨a balloon *flight*⟩ ⟨the *flight* of a bullet⟩ ⟨the *flight* of a rocket to the moon⟩ **b :** the distance covered in a flight **c :** swift movement **3 :** an airplane making a scheduled flight **4 :** a group of similar things flying through the air together ⟨a *flight* of ducks⟩ ⟨a *flight* of bombers⟩ **5 :** a brilliant, imaginative, or unrestrained exercise or display ⟨a *flight* of fancy⟩ **6 :** a continuous series of stairs from one landing or floor to another

²flight *n* [ME *fliht*; akin to E *flee*] **:** an act or instance of running away

flight control *n* **:** the control from a ground station of an airplane esp. by radio

flight engineer *n* **:** a flight crewman responsible for mechanical operation

flight feather *n* **:** one of the quills of a bird's wing or tail that support it in flight

flight·less \'flīt-ləs\ *adj* **:** unable to fly ⟨*flightless* birds⟩

flight line *n* **:** a parking and servicing area for airplanes

flight path *n* **:** the path of the center of gravity of an airplane in flight

flighty \'flīt-ē\ *adj* **flight·i·er; -est :** lacking stability or steadiness: **a :** easily upset **:** VOLATILE ⟨a *flighty* temper⟩ **b :** easily excited **:** SKITTISH ⟨*flighty* horses⟩ **c :** SCATTER-BRAINED, SILLY, FRIVOLOUS ⟨a *flighty* young girl⟩ — **flight·i·ly** \'flīt-ᵊl-ē\ *adv* — **flight·i·ness** \'flīt-ē-nəs\ *n*

flim·flam \'flim-,flam\ *n* **1 :** DECEPTION, FRAUD **2 :** HANKY-PANKY — **flimflam** *vb*

flim·sy \'flim-zē\ *adj* **flim·si·er; -est 1 a :** lacking strength or substance **b :** of inferior materials and workmanship **2 :** having little worth or plausibility ⟨a *flimsy* excuse⟩ — **flim·si·ly** \-zə-lē\ *adv* — **flim·si·ness** \-zē-nəs\ *n*

flinch \'flinch\ *vi* [MF *flenchir* to bend] **:** to shrink from or as if from physical pain **:** WINCE — **flinch** *n* — **flinch·er** *n*

flin·ders \'flin-dərz\ *n pl* [ME *flendris*] **:** SPLINTERS, FRAGMENTS

¹fling \'fliŋ\ *vb* **flung** \'fləŋ\; **fling·ing** \'fliŋ-iŋ\ [ME *flingen*, of Scand origin] **1 :** to move in a brusque or headlong manner ⟨*flung* out of the room⟩ **2 :** to kick or plunge vigorously **3 a :** to throw or swing with force or recklessness **b :** to cast aside **:** DISCARD **4 :** to place or put suddenly and unexpectedly into a state or condition ⟨*flung* the enemy troops into confusion⟩ **syn** *see* THROW — **fling·er** \-ər\ *n*

²fling *n* **1 :** an act or instance of flinging **2 :** a casual try **:** ATTEMPT **3 :** a period of self-indulgence

flint \'flint\ *n* **1 :** a grayish or dark hard quartz that strikes fire with steel **2 :** an alloy (as of iron and cerium) used for striking fire in cigarette lighters

flint glass *n* **:** heavy glass that contains lead oxide and is used for optical structures (as lenses)

flint·lock \'flint-,läk\ *n* **1 :** a lock for a 17th and 18th century firearm using a flint to ignite the charge **2 :** a firearm fitted with a flintlock

flinty \'flint-ē\ *adj* **flint·i·er; -est 1 :** composed of or covered with flint **2 a :** notably hard ⟨*flinty* seeds⟩ **b :** UNYIELDING, STERN — **flint·i·ly** \'flint-ᵊl-ē\ *adv* — **flint·i·ness** \'flint-ē-nəs\ *n*

¹flip \'flip\ *vb* **flipped; flip·ping 1 :** to turn by tossing ⟨*flip* a coin⟩ **2 :** to turn quickly ⟨*flip* the pages of a book⟩ **3 :** FLICK, JERK ⟨*flip* a light switch⟩ **4 :** to lose self-control

²flip *n* **1 :** an act or instance of flipping **:** TOSS, FLICK **2 :** any of several mixed drinks

³flip *adj* **:** FLIPPANT, IMPERTINENT

flip·pant \'flip-ənt\ *adj* **:** treating lightly something serious or worthy of respect **:** lacking earnestness **:** SAUCY — **flip·pan·cy** \-ən-sē\ *n* — **flip·pant·ly** *adv*

flip·per \'flip-ər\ *n* **1 :** a broad flat limb (as of a seal) adapted for swimming **2 :** a flat rubber shoe with the front expanded into a paddle used in skin diving

¹flirt \'flərt\ *vi* **1 :** to move erratically **:** FLIT **2 a :** to behave amorously without serious intent **b :** TOY — **flir·ta·tion** \,flər-'tā-shən\ *n* — **flir·ta·tious** \-shəs\ *adj* — **flir·ta·tious·ness** *n* — **flirt·er** \'flərt-ər\ *n*

²flirt *n* **1 :** an act or instance of flirting **2 :** a person who flirts

flit \'flit\ *vi* **flit·ted; flit·ting** [ME *flitten*, of Scand origin] **:** to move or progress in quick erratic darts — **flit** *n*

flitch \'flich\ *n* **:** a side of pork cured and smoked as bacon

flit·ter \'flit-ər\ *vi* **:** FLUTTER, FLICKER

fliv·ver \'fliv-ər\ *n* **:** a small cheap usu. old automobile

¹float \'flōt\ *n* [ME *flote* boat, float, fr. OE *flota* ship; akin to E *fleet*] **1 :** an act or instance of floating **2 :** something that floats in or on the surface of a fluid: as **a :** a cork or bob buoying up the baited end of a fishing line **b :** a floating platform anchored near a shoreline for use by swimmers or boats **c :** a hollow ball that controls the flow or level of the liquid it floats on (as in a tank or cistern) **d :** a watertight structure giving an airplane buoyancy on water **3 a :** a vehicle with a platform used to carry an exhibit in a parade **b :** the vehicle and exhibit together **4 :** a drink consisting of ice cream floating in a beverage

²float *vb* **1 :** to rest or cause to rest in or on the surface of a fluid **2 a :** to drift or cause to drift on or through or as if on or through a fluid ⟨dust *floating* through the air⟩ ⟨*float* logs down a river⟩ **b :** WANDER **3 :** FLOOD **4 a :** to offer (an issue of stocks or bonds) in order to finance an enterprise **b :** to finance (an enterprise) by floating an issue of stocks or bonds **c :** to arrange for ⟨*float* a loan⟩

float·er \'flōt-ər\ *n* **1 a :** one that floats **b :** a person who floats something **2 :** a person without a permanent home or job **:** VAGRANT

float·ing *adj* **1 :** buoyed on or in a fluid **2 a :** not settled or committed **:** not established ⟨*floating* capital⟩ ⟨*floating* population⟩ **b :** not funded ⟨*floating* debt⟩ **3 :** connected or constructed so as to operate and adjust smoothly ⟨*floating* axle⟩

floating island *n* **:** a dessert consisting of custard with floating masses of whipped white of egg

floating rib *n* **:** a rib (as one of the last two pairs in man) that has no attachment to the sternum — compare FALSE RIB

¹floc·cu·late \'fläk-yə-lət\ *adj* **:** bearing small tufts of hairs

²floc·cu·late \-,lāt\ *vb* **:** to aggregate or cause to aggregate into a flocculent mass ⟨certain clays *flocculate* readily⟩ — **floc·cu·la·tion** \,fläk-yə-'lā-shən\ *n*

floc·cu·lent \\'fläk-yə-lənt\\ *adj* [L *floccus* flock of wool] **1** : resembling wool esp. in loose fluffy texture **2** : covered with woolly material — **floc·cu·lence** \\-lən(t)s\\ *n*

¹flock \\'fläk\\ *n* [OE *flocc* crowd, band] **1** : a group of birds or mammals assembled or herded together **2** : a group under the guidance of a leader **3** : a large number

²flock *vi* : to gather or move in a crowd 〈they *flocked* to the beach〉

³flock *n* [ME] **1** : a tuft of wool or cotton fiber **2** : woolen or cotton refuse used for stuffing furniture and mattresses **3** : very short or pulverized fiber used to form a pattern on cloth or paper or a protective covering on metal

⁴flock *vt* **1** : to fill with flock **2** : to decorate with flock

flock·ing \\'fläk-iŋ\\ *n* : a design in flock

floe \\'flō\\ *n* [prob. fr. Norw *flo* flat layer] : a sheet or mass of floating ice

flog \\'fläg\\ *vt* **flogged; flog·ging** : to beat severely with a rod or whip — **flog·ger** *n*

¹flood \\'fləd\\ *n* [OE *flōd*] **1 a** : a great flow of water that rises and spreads over the land **b** *cap* : a flood described in the Bible as covering the earth in the time of Noah **2** : the flowing in of the tide **3** : an overwhelming quantity or volume 〈a *flood* of mail〉

²flood *vb* **1** : to cover or become filled with a flood : IN-UNDATE 〈the river *flooded* the lowlands〉〈the cellar *flooded* after a rain〉 **2** : to fill abundantly or excessively 〈a room *flooded* with light〉〈*flood* a carburetor〉 **3** : to pour forth in a flood

flood·gate \\'fləd-,gāt\\ *n* **1** : a gate (as in a canal) for shutting out, admitting, or releasing a body of water : SLUICE **2** : something serving to restrain an outburst

¹flood·light \\-,līt\\ *n* **1** : artificial illumination in a broad beam **2** : a lighting unit for projecting a beam of light

²floodlight *vt* : to illuminate by means of one or more floodlights

flood·plain \\-,plān\\ *n* **1** : low flat land along a stream that may be submerged by floodwaters **2** : a plain built up by deposits of earth from floodwaters

flood tide *n* **1** : the tide while rising at or its greatest height **2 a** : an overwhelming quantity **b** : a high point : PEAK 〈his success was at *flood tide*〉

flood·wa·ter \\'fləd-,wot-ər, -,wät-\\ *n* : the water of a flood

flood·way \\-,wā\\ *n* : a channel for diverting floodwaters

¹floor \\'flō(ə)r, 'flo(ə)r\\ *n* [OE *flōr*] **1** : the part of a room on which one stands **2 a** : the lower inside surface of a hollow structure **b** : a ground surface 〈the ocean *floor*〉 〈the *floor* of a forest〉 **3 a** : a structure dividing a building into stories **b** : STORY 〈he lives on the first *floor*〉 **c** : the occupants of a story **4** : the surface of a structure on which one travels 〈the *floor* of a bridge〉 **5 a** : a main level space (as in a legislative chamber) distinguished from a platform or gallery **b** : the right to speak from one's place in an assembly 〈the senator has the *floor*〉 **6** : a lower limit (as of prices)

²floor *vt* **1** : to cover with a floor or flooring **2 a** : to knock to the floor **b** : SHOCK, OVERWHELM 〈the news *floored* us〉 **c** : DEFEAT

floor·age \\'flōr-ij, 'flor-\\ *n* : floor space

floor·board \\'flō(ə)r-,bōrd, 'flo(ə)r-,bord\\ *n* **1** : a board in a floor **2** : the floor of an automobile

floor·ing \\'flōr-iŋ, 'flor-\\ *n* **1** : FLOOR **2** : material for floors

floor lamp *n* : a tall lamp that stands on the floor

floor leader *n* : a member of a legislative body chosen by his party to have charge of its organization and strategy on the floor

floor show *n* : a series of acts presented in a nightclub

floor·walk·er \\'flō(ə)r-,wo-kər, 'flo(ə)r-\\ *n* : a man employed in a retail store to oversee the sales force and aid customers

floo·zy \\'flü-zē\\ *n, pl* **floozies** : a tawdry or immoral woman

¹flop \\'fläp\\ *vb* **flopped; flop·ping** [alter. of ²*flap*] **1** : to swing or bounce loosely : flap about 〈the brim of her hat *flopping* in the wind〉 **2 a** : to throw oneself down heavily, clumsily, or in a completely relaxed manner 〈he *flopped* into the chair with a sigh〉 **b** : to throw or drop suddenly and usu. heavily or noisily 〈she *flopped* her bundles on the table〉 **3** : to fail completely 〈in spite of some good reviews the play *flopped*〉

²flop *n* **1** : an act or sound of flopping **2** : a complete failure : DUD 〈he was a *flop* as a teacher〉

³flop *adv* : RIGHT, SQUARELY 〈fell *flop* on his face〉

flop·house \\-,haus\\ *n* : a cheap rooming house or hotel

flop·py \\'fläp-ē\\ *adj* **flop·pi·er; -est** : tending to flop; *esp* : being soft and flexible 〈a hat with a *floppy* brim〉

flo·ra \\'flōr-ə, 'flor-\\ *n, pl* **floras** *also* **flo·rae** \\'flō(ə)r-,ē, 'flo(ə)r-, -,ī\\ **1** *cap* : the Roman goddess of flowers **2 a** : a treatise on or list of the plants of an area or period **b** : plants or plant life esp. of a region, period, or environment — compare FAUNA

flo·ral \\'flōr-əl, 'flor-\\ *adj* [L *flor-, flos* flower] : of or relating to flowers or a flora — **flo·ral·ly** \\-ə-lē\\ *adv*

Flor·ence flask \\,flor-ən(t)s-, ,flär-\\ *n* : a round usu. flat-bottomed glass laboratory vessel with a long neck

flo·res·cence \\flō-'res-ⁿn(t)s, flə-\\ *n* [L *florescere*, incho. of *florēre* to blossom, flourish] : a state or period of being in bloom or flourishing 〈the highest *florescence* of a civilization〉 — **flo·res·cent** \\-ⁿnt\\ *adj*

flo·ret \\'flōr-ət, 'flor-\\ *n* : a small flower; *esp* : one of the small flowers forming the head of a composite plant (as a daisy)

flori- *comb form* [L *flor-, flos* flower] : flower or flowers 〈*flori*culture〉 : something resembling a flower or flowers 〈*flori*ated〉

flo·ri·cul·ture \\'flōr-ə-,kəl-chər, 'flor-\\ *n* : the cultivation and management of ornamental and flowering plants — **flo·ri·cul·tur·al** \\,flōr-ə-'kəlch-(ə-)rəl, ,flor-\\ *adj* — **flo·ri·cul·tur·al·ly** \\-ē\\ *adv* — **flo·ri·cul·tur·ist** \\-'kəlch-(ə-)rəst\\ *n*

flor·id \\'flōr-əd, 'flär-\\ *adj* **1** : excessively flowery in style : ORNATE 〈*florid* writing〉〈a *florid* musical composition〉 **2** : tinged with red : RUDDY 〈a *florid* complexion〉 — **flo·rid·i·ty** \\flə-'rid-ət-ē, flō-\\ *n* — **flor·id·ly** \\'flōr-əd-lē, 'flär-\\ *adv* — **flor·id·ness** *n*

flo·rif·er·ous \\flō-'rif-(ə-)rəs\\ *adj* : bearing flowers; *esp* : blooming freely — **flo·rif·er·ous·ly** *adv* — **flo·rif·er·ous·ness** *n*

flo·ri·gen \\'flōr-ə-jən, 'flor-, 'flär-\\ *n* : a hormone that promotes flowering — **flo·ri·gen·ic** \\,flōr-ə-'jen-ik, ,flor-, ,flär-\\ *adj*

flor·in \\'flōr-ən, 'flär-, 'flor-\\ *n* [MF, fr. It *fiorino*, fr. *fiore* flower, fr. L *flor-, flos*; fr. the lily on the first florins] **1 a** : an old gold coin first struck at Florence in 1252 **b** : any of various gold coins of European countries patterned after the Florentine florin **2 a** : a British silver coin worth two shillings **b** : any of several similar coins issued in British Commonwealth countries **3** : GULDEN

flo·rist \\'flōr-əst, 'flor-, 'flär-\\ *n* : one who sells flowers and ornamental plants

flo·ris·tic \\flō-'ris-tik\\ *adj* : of or relating to flowers, a flora, or floristics — **flo·ris·ti·cal·ly** \\-ti-k(ə-)lē\\ *adv*

flo·ris·tics \\-tiks\\ *n* : a branch of botany dealing numerically with plants and plant groups

-flo·rous \\'flōr-əs, 'flor-\\ *adj comb form* [L *flor-, flos* flower] : having or bearing (such or so many) flowers 〈uni*florous*〉

floss \\'fläs, 'flos\\ *n* [D *vlos*] **1** : waste or short silk fibers that cannot be reeled **2 a** : soft thread of silk or mercerized cotton used for embroidery **b** : a lightweight wool knitting yarn **3** : fluffy fibrous material; *esp* : SILK COTTON

flossy \\'fläs-ē, 'flos-\\ *adj* **floss·i·er; -est 1 a** : of, relating to, or having the characteristics of floss **b** : DOWNY **2** : STYLISH, GLAMOROUS

flo·ta·tion \\flō-'tā-shən\\ *n* **1** : the act, process, or state of floating **2** : the separation of the particles of a mass of pulverized ore according to their relative capacity for floating on a given liquid

flo·til·la \\flō-'til-ə\\ *n* [Sp, dim. of *flota* fleet, fr. OF *flote*, fr. ON *floti*; akin to E *float*] : a fleet of ships; *esp* : a fleet of small ships

flot·sam \\'flät-səm\\ *n* [AF *floteson*, fr. OF *floter* to float] : floating wreckage of a ship or its cargo

¹flounce \\'flaun(t)s\\ *vi* **1 a** : to move with exaggerated jerky motions **b** : to go with sudden determination 〈she *flounced* out of the room in anger〉 **2** : FLOUNDER, STRUGGLE

²flounce *n* : an act or instance of flouncing

³flounce *n* [alter. of ME *frounce* to curl] : a strip of fabric attached by the upper edge 〈a wide *flounce* at the bottom of her skirt〉

---

j joke; ŋ sing; ō flow; o̊ flaw; o̊i coin; th thin; th this; ü loot; u̇ foot; y yet; yü few; yu̇ furious; zh vision

⁴flounce *vt* : to trim with flounces

¹floun·der \'flaùn-dər\ *n, pl* **flounder** *or* **flounders** [ME, of Scand origin] : FLATFISH; *esp* : any of various important marine food fishes

²flounder *vi* **floun·dered; floun·der·ing** \-d(ə-)riŋ\ [prob. alter. of *founder*] **1** : to struggle to move or obtain footing ⟨horses *floundering* in a swamp⟩ **2** : to proceed clumsily ⟨*floundered* through a recitation⟩

¹flour \'flaù(ə)r\ *n* [ME, flower, best of anything, flour] **1 a** : finely ground powdery meal of wheat usu. largely freed from bran **b** : a similar meal of any cereal grain or edible seed **2** : a fine soft powder
syn FLOUR, MEAL mean the product of grinding cereal grain or other seeds. FLOUR used alone denotes wheat kernels finely ground and sifted to remove the bran; MEAL applies to any grain or seed coarsely ground and unsifted

²flour *vt* : to coat with flour

¹flour·ish \'flər-ish, 'flə-rish\ *vb* [MF *floriss-, florir,* fr. L *florēre,* fr. *flor-, flos* flower] **1** : to grow luxuriantly : THRIVE **2 a** : to achieve success : PROSPER **b** : to be in a state of activity or production ⟨*flourished* around 1850⟩ **c** : to reach a height of development or influence **3** : to make bold and sweeping gestures **4** : to wield with dramatic gestures : BRANDISH ⟨*flourish* a sword⟩

²flourish *n* **1** : a period of thriving **2 a** : a florid embellishment or passage ⟨handwriting with *flourishes*⟩ ⟨a *flourish* of drums⟩ **b** : an act or instance of brandishing : WAVE ⟨with a *flourish* of his cane⟩ **c** : a dramatic action ⟨introduces her with a *flourish*⟩

floury \'flaù(ə)r-ē\ *adj* **1** : of, relating to, or resembling flour **2** : covered with flour

¹flout \'flaùt\ *vb* **1** : to treat with contemptuous disregard : SCORN ⟨*flouting* her mother's advice⟩ **2** : to indulge in scornful behavior **syn** see FLAUNT — **flout·er** *n*

²flout *n* **1** : INSULT **2** : MOCKERY

¹flow \'flō\ *vi* [OE *flōwan*] **1 a** : to issue or move in a stream **b** : to move with a continual change of place among the constituent particles ⟨the molasses *flowed* slowly⟩ **2** : RISE ⟨the tide ebbs and *flows*⟩ **3** : ABOUND ⟨a land that *flows* with milk and honey⟩ **4 a** : to proceed smoothly and readily ⟨the words *flowed* from his mouth⟩ **b** : to have a smooth uninterrupted continuity **5** : to hang loose and billowing ⟨a flag *flowing* in the breeze⟩ **6** : COME, ARISE **7** : MENSTRUATE — **flow·ing·ly** \-iŋ-lē\ *adv*

²flow *n* **1** : an act of flowing **2** : FLOOD 1a, 2 **3 a** : a smooth uninterrupted movement **b** : a stream of fluid; *also* : a mass of matter that has flowed ⟨a lava *flow*⟩ **4** : the quantity that flows in a certain time ⟨the *flow* of water over a dam⟩ **5 a** : MENSTRUATION **b** : YIELD, PRODUCTION **6** : a continuous transfer of energy ⟨a *flow* of electricity⟩

flow chart *n* : a diagram showing progress of material through a process (as of manufacturing)

¹flow·er \'flaù(-ə)r\ *n* [ME *flour,* fr. OF, fr. L *flor-, flos;* akin to E ³*blow*] **1 a** : BLOSSOM, INFLORESCENCE **b** : a shoot of the sporophyte of a higher plant that is modified for reproduction and consists of a shortened axis bearing modified leaves (as petals and sporophylls) **c** : a plant cultivated or esteemed for its blossoms **2 a** : the best part or example ⟨the *flower* of the family⟩ **b** : the finest most vigorous period **c** : a state of blooming or flourishing ⟨when knighthood was in *flower*⟩ **3** *pl* : a chemical element in the form of a finely divided powder produced esp. by condensation or sublimation ⟨*flowers* of sulfur⟩ — **flow·er·less** \-ləs\ *adj* — **flow·er·like** \-,līk\ *adj*

flower in section: *1* filament, *2* anther, *3* stigma, *4* style, *5* petal, *6* ovary, *7* sepal, *8* pedicel, *9* stamen, *10* pistil, *11* perianth

²flower *vb* **1** : to produce flowers : BLOOM **2 a** : DEVELOP ⟨*flowered* into young womanhood⟩ **b** : FLOURISH **3** : to decorate with floral designs

flow·ered \'flaù(-ə)rd\ *adj* **1** : having or bearing flowers **2** : decorated with flowers or flowerlike figures ⟨*flowered* silk⟩

flow·er·et \'flaù(ə)r-ət\ *n* : FLORET

flower girl *n* : a little girl who carries flowers at a wedding

flower head *n* : a tight cluster of small sessile flowers so

arranged that the whole inflorescence looks like a single flower

flowering plant *n* : any of a major group (Angiospermae) of higher plants that comprises those which produce flowers, fruits, and seeds — compare SEED PLANT

flow·er·pot \'flaù(-ə)r-,pät\ *n* : a pot in which to grow plants

flow·ery \'flaù(-ə)r-ē\ *adj* **flow·er·i·er; -est** **1** : full of or covered with flowers **2** : full of fine words or phrases : FLORID ⟨*flowery* language⟩ — **flow·er·i·ness** *n*

flown *past part of* FLY

flu \'flü\ *n* **1** : INFLUENZA **2** : any of several virus diseases marked esp. by respiratory symptoms

flub \'fləb\ *vb* **flubbed; flub·bing** **1** : to make a mess of : BOTCH ⟨the actor *flubbed* his lines⟩ ⟨*flubbed* his chance⟩ **2** : BLUNDER — **flub** *n*

fluc·tu·ate \'flək-chə-,wāt\ *vi* [L *fluctuare,* fr. *fluctus* flow, wave, fr. *fluct-, fluere* to flow] **1** : to move up and down or back and forth like a wave **2** : to be constantly changing (as between two points, levels, or conditions) : rise and fall usu. with regularity : WAVER ⟨*fluctuating* temperatures⟩ ⟨*fluctuated* in his mind between hope and fear⟩ — **fluc·tu·a·tion** \,flək-chə-'wā-shən\ *n*

flue \'flü\ *n* : an enclosed passageway for directing a current: as **a** : a channel in a chimney for conveying flame and smoke to the outer air **b** : a pipe for conveying flame and hot gases around or through water in a steam boiler **c** : an air channel to the lip of a wind instrument **d** : FLUE PIPE

flu·en·cy \'flü-ən-sē\ *n* : the quality or state of being fluent esp. in speech

flu·ent \'flü-ənt\ *adj* [L *fluere* to flow] **1** : capable of flowing : FLUID **2 a** : ready or facile in speech ⟨*fluent* in Spanish⟩ **b** : effortlessly smooth and rapid : POLISHED ⟨*fluent* speech⟩ — **flu·ent·ly** *adv*

flue pipe *n* : an organ pipe whose tone is produced by an air current striking the lip and causing the air within to vibrate

flue stop *n* : an organ stop made up of flue pipes

¹fluff \'fləf\ *n* **1** : NAP, DOWN ⟨soft *fluff* from a pillow⟩ **2** : something fluffy **3** : something inconsequential **4** : BLUNDER; *esp* : an actor's lapse of memory

²fluff *vb* **1** : to make or become fluffy ⟨*fluff* up a pillow⟩ **2** : to make or spoil by a mistake : BOTCH **3** : to deliver badly or forget (one's lines) in a play

fluffy \'fləf-ē\ *adj* **fluff·i·er; -est** **1 a** : having, covered with, or resembling fluff or down ⟨the *fluffy* fur of a kitten⟩ **b** : being light and soft or airy ⟨a *fluffy* omelet⟩ **2** : FATUOUS, SILLY — **fluff·i·ness** *n*

¹flu·id \'flü-əd\ *adj* [L *fluidus,* fr. *fluere* to flow] **1 a** : capable of flowing like a liquid or gas : being liquid or gaseous ⟨a substance in a *fluid* state⟩ **b** : likely or tending to change or move **2** : characterized by or employing a smooth easy style **3 a** : available for various uses **b** : easily converted into cash ⟨*fluid* assets⟩ — **flu·id·i·ty** \flü-'id-ət-ē\ — **flu·id·ly** \'flü-əd-lē\ *adv* — **flu·id·ness** *n*

²fluid *n* : a substance tending to flow or conform to the outline of its container ⟨liquids and gases are *fluids*⟩

flu·id·ounce \,flü-əd-'aùn(t)s\ *n* : a unit of liquid capacity equal to ¹⁄₁₆ pint — see MEASURE table

flu·idram \,flü-ə(d)-'dram\ *n* [blend of ¹*fluid* and *dram*] : a unit of liquid capacity equal to ⅛ fluidounce — see MEASURE table

¹fluke \'flük\ *n* [OE *flōc*] **1** : FLATFISH **2** : TREMATODE

²fluke *n* **1** : the part of an anchor that fastens in the ground — see ANCHOR illustration **2** : a barbed head (as of a harpoon) **3** : one of the lobes of a whale's tail

³fluke *n* **1** : an accidentally successful stroke at billiards or pool **2** : a stroke of luck ⟨he won by a *fluke*⟩

fluky \'flü-kē\ *adj* **fluk·i·er; -est** **1** : happening by or depending on chance **2** : UNCERTAIN, CHANGEABLE ⟨*fluky* wind⟩

flume \'flüm\ *n* **1** : a ravine or gorge with a stream running through it **2** : an inclined channel for conveying water (as for power)

flum·mery \'fləm-(ə-)rē\ *n, pl* **-mer·ies** [W *llymru*] **1 a** : a soft jelly or porridge made with flour or meal **b** : any of several sweet desserts **2 a** : something trashy **b** : empty compliment : HUMBUG

flum·mox \'fləm-əks, -iks\ *vt* : CONFUSE

flung *past of* FLING

flunk \'fləŋk\ vb **1** : to fail an examination or course ⟨*flunked* English⟩ **2** : to give a failing grade to ⟨the math teacher *flunked* four boys⟩ — **flunk** n

flunk out vb : to dismiss or be dismissed from a school or college for failure

flun·ky or **flun·key** \'fləŋ-kē\ n, pl **flunkies** or **flunkeys** [Sc] **1** : a servant in livery : esp : FOOTMAN **2** : a person who fawns upon or does menial duties for another : TOADY

fluor- or **fluoro-** comb form **1** : fluorine ⟨*fluoride*⟩ **2** also **fluori-** : fluorescence ⟨*fluoroscope*⟩

flu·o·resce \(ˌ)flü-(ə)r-'es\ vi [back-formation fr. *fluorescence*] : to produce, undergo, or exhibit fluorescence

flu·o·res·ce·in \-'es-ē-ən\ n : a yellow or red crystalline dye with a bright yellow-green fluorescence in alkaline solution

flu·o·res·cence \-'es-°n(t)s\ n : emission of or the property of emitting electromagnetic radiation usu. as visible light resulting from and only during the absorption of radiation from some other source; also : the radiation emitted — **flu·o·res·cent** \-°nt\ adj

fluorescent lamp n : a tubular electric lamp in which light is produced on the inside fluorescent coating by the action of ultraviolet light

flu·o·ri·date \'flur-ə-ˌdāt\ vt : to add a fluoride to — **flu·o·ri·da·tion** \ˌflur-ə-'dā-shən\ n

flu·o·ride \'flu̇(-ə)r-ˌīd\ n : a compound of fluorine with another chemical element or a radical

flu·o·rin·ate \'flur-ə-ˌnāt\ vt : to treat or cause to combine with fluorine or a compound of fluorine — **flu·o·rin·a·tion** \ˌflur-ə-'nā-shən\ n

flu·o·rine \'flu̇(-ə)r-ˌēn, -ən\ n [NL *fluor*, mineral belonging to a group including fluorite (in which fluorine is found) and used as fluxes, fr. L, flow, fr. *fluere* to flow] : a nonmetallic univalent chemical element that is normally a pale yellowish flammable irritating toxic gas — see ELEMENT table

flu·o·rite \'flu̇(-ə)r-ˌīt\ n : a transparent or translucent mineral CaF_2 of different colors that consists of a fluoride of calcium and is used as a flux and in making glass

¹flu·o·ro·scope \'flur-ə-ˌskōp\ n : an instrument that is used for studying an object by observing light and shadows produced on a screen by the action of X rays passing through the object and that is useful in examining inner parts of the body (as the lungs) — **flu·o·ro·scop·ic** \ˌflur-ə-'skäp-ik\ adj — **flu·o·ros·co·py** \(ˌ)flu̇(-ə)r-'äs-kə-pē\ n

²fluoroscope vt : to examine by fluoroscopy

flu·or·spar \'flu̇(-ə)r-ˌspär\ n : FLUORITE

¹flur·ry \'flər-ē, 'flə-rē\ n, pl **flurries** **1 a** : a gust of wind **b** : a brief light snowfall **2** : nervous commotion : BUSTLE ⟨the news caused a *flurry*⟩ **3** : a brief outburst of activity ⟨a *flurry* of trading in the stock exchange⟩

²flurry vb **flur·ried**; **flur·ry·ing** : to become or cause to become agitated and confused : EXCITE, FLUSTER

¹flush \'fləsh\ vb [ME *flusshen*] : to begin flight or cause to begin flight suddenly ⟨*flushed* a covey of quail⟩

²flush n **1** : a sudden flow **2** : a sudden increase or expansion; esp : a surge of emotion ⟨a *flush* of triumph⟩ **3 a** : a tinge of red : BLUSH **b** : a fresh and vigorous state ⟨in the *flush* of youth⟩ **4** : a transitory sensation of extreme heat

³flush vb **1** : to flow and spread suddenly and freely : RUSH **2 a** : to glow brightly **b** : BLUSH **3** : to pour liquid over or through; esp : to wash out with a rush of liquid **4** : INFLAME, EXCITE ⟨troops *flushed* with victory⟩ **5** : to make red or hot ⟨face *flushed* with fever⟩

⁴flush adj **1 a** : filled to overflowing **b** : fully supplied esp. with money **2 a** : full of life and vigor : LUSTY **b** : of a ruddy healthy color **3** : readily available : ABUNDANT **4 a** : having an unbroken or even surface ⟨*flush* paneling⟩ **b** : being on a level with an adjacent surface ⟨a river *flush* with the top of its bank⟩ **c** : directly abutting or immediately adjacent **d** : set even with an edge of a type page or column — **flush·ness** n

⁵flush adv **1** : in a flush manner **2** : SQUARELY ⟨dealt him a blow *flush* on the chin⟩

⁶flush vt : to make flush

⁷flush n [MF *flus*, fr. L *fluxus* flow] : a hand of playing cards all of the same suit

¹flus·ter \'fləs-tər\ vt **flus·tered**; **flus·ter·ing** \-t(ə-)riŋ\ **1** : to make tipsy **2** : to put into a state of agitated confusion : UPSET ⟨*flustered* by his stares⟩

²fluster n : a state of agitated confusion

¹flute \'flüt\ n [MF *flahute*, fr. OProv *flaut*] **1 a** : RECORDER **3 b** : a keyed woodwind instrument played by blowing across a hole near the closed end and producing a soft clear tone **c** : an organ flue pipe with a flutelike tone or a stop composed of such pipes **2 a** : a grooved pleat **b** : a rounded groove; esp : one of the vertical parallel grooves on a classical architectural column — **flute-like** \-ˌlīk\ adj

²flute vb **1** : to play a flute **2** : to utter with or produce a flutelike sound ⟨*fluted* notes⟩ **3** : to form flutes in ⟨*fluted* columns⟩

flut·ing \'flüt-iŋ\ n : fluted material or decoration

flut·ist \'flüt-əst\ n : a flute player

¹flut·ter \'flət-ər\ vb [OE *floterian*, freq. of *flotian* to float] **1** : to move or cause the wings to move rapidly without flying or in short flights ⟨butterflies *flutter*⟩ **2 a** : to move with quick wavering or flapping motions ⟨flags *fluttered* in the breeze⟩ **b** : to vibrate in irregular spasms ⟨a *fluttering* pulse⟩ **3** : to move about or behave in an agitated aimless manner ⟨she *fluttered* about the house⟩ — **flut·tery** \'flət-ə-rē\ adj

²flutter n **1** : an act of fluttering **2 a** : a state of nervous confusion or excitement **b** : FLURRY, COMMOTION **3** : a distortion in reproduced sound similar to but of a higher pitch than wow

flutter kick n : an alternating whipping motion of the legs used in various swimming styles

flu·vi·al \'flü-vē-əl\ adj [L *fluvius* river, fr. *fluere* to flow] : produced by stream action ⟨a *fluvial* plain⟩

¹flux \'fləks\ n [L *fluxus* flow, fr. *flux-*, *fluere* to flow] **1** : an excessive fluid discharge from the body and esp. the bowels **2 a** : a flowing in ⟨*flux* of the tide⟩ **b** : a series of changes : a state of continuous change **3** : a substance used to promote fusion esp. of metals or minerals **4** : the rate of flow of fluid, particles, or energy across a given surface

²flux vb **1** : to become or cause to become fluid : FUSE **2** : to treat with a flux

¹fly \'flī\ vb **flew** \'flü\; **flown** \'flōn\; **fly·ing** [OE *flēogan*] **1 a** : to move in or pass through the air with wings **b** : to move through the air or before the wind **c** : to float or cause to float, wave, or soar in the air **2 a** : to take flight : escape from : FLEE; also : AVOID, SHUN **b** : to fade and disappear : VANISH **3** : to move or pass swiftly ⟨*fly* to the rescue⟩ ⟨time *flies*⟩ **4** : to become expended or dissipated rapidly **5** : to pursue or attack in flight **6** past or past part **flied** \'flīd\ : to hit a fly in baseball **7 a** : to operate or travel in an airplane **b** : to journey over by flying ⟨to *fly* the Atlantic⟩ **c** : to transport by airplane ⟨to *fly* passengers⟩ — **fly at** : to assail suddenly and violently — **fly blind** : to fly an airplane solely by instruments — **fly contact** : to fly an airplane with the aid of visible landmarks or reference points — **fly high** : to be elated — **fly in the face of** or **fly in the teeth of** : to act forthrightly or brazenly in defiance or disobedience of

²fly n, pl **flies** **1** : the action or process of flying : FLIGHT **2 a** : a horse-drawn public coach or delivery wagon **b** chiefly Brit : a light covered carriage or cab **3** pl : the space over a theater stage **4** : something attached by one edge: as **a** : a garment closing concealed by a fold of cloth extending over the fastener **b** : the outer canvas of a tent with double top **c** : the length of an extended flag from its staff or support; also : the outer or loose end of a flag **5** : a baseball hit high into the air — **on the fly** : in motion : as **a** : continuously active : very busy **b** : while still in the air

³fly n, pl **flies** [OE *flēoge*; akin to E ¹*fly*] **1** : a winged insect **2** : a winged or rarely wingless insect (order Diptera); esp : a large stout-bodied two-winged fly — compare GNAT **3** : a fishhook dressed to suggest an insect — **fly in the ointment** : a detracting factor or element

fly·a·ble \'flī-ə-bəl\ adj : suitable for flying or being flown

fly 3

fly agaric n : a poisonous mushroom with a usu. bright red cap

fly ash *n* : fine solid particles of noncombustible ash carried out of a bed of burning solid fuel by the draft

fly·blow \'flī-,blō\ *n* [³*fly* + *blow* deposit of insect eggs] : an egg or young larva deposited by a flesh fly or blowfly — **flyblow** *vt*

fly·blown \-,blōn\ *adj* : TAINTED, SPOILED ⟨a *flyblown* reputation⟩

fly·by \-,bī\ *n* : a usu. low-altitude flight past an appointed place by an airplane

fly casting *n* : the act or practice of throwing the lure in angling with artificial flies — **fly·cast·er** *n*

fly·catch·er \'flī-,kach-ər, -,kech-\ *n* : a small bird that feeds on insects that it captures in the air

fly·er *var of* FLIER

¹fly·ing \'flī-iŋ\ *adj* **1 a** : rapidly moving **b** : HASTY ⟨a *flying* visit⟩ **2** : ready to move or act : MOBILE

²flying *n* **1** : travel by air **2** : the operation of an airplane

flying boat *n* : a seaplane with a hull adapted for floating

flying buttress *n* : a projecting arched structure to support a wall or building

flying colors *n pl* : complete success ⟨passed his exams with *flying colors*⟩

Flying Dutchman *n* **1** : a legendary Dutch mariner condemned to sail the seas until Judgment Day **2** : a spectral ship held by sailors to haunt the seas near the Cape of Good Hope in stormy weather

flying field *n* : a field with a graded area for airplane landings and takeoffs

flying fish *n* : any of numerous sea fishes that have long pectoral fins suggesting wings and are able to move some distance through the air

flying jib *n* : a sail outside the jib on an extension of the jibboom

flying machine *n* : AIRCRAFT

flying saucer *n* : any of various unidentified moving objects repeatedly reported as seen in the air and usu. alleged to be saucer-shaped or disk-shaped — called also *flying disk*

flying squirrel *n* : a squirrel with folds of skin connecting the forelegs and hind legs and enabling it to make long gliding leaps

fly·leaf \'flī-,lēf\ *n* : a blank leaf at the beginning or end of a book

fly·pa·per \-,pā-pər\ *n* : paper poisoned or coated with a sticky substance for killing or catching flies

fly·speck \-,spek\ *n* **1** : a speck of fly dung **2** : something small and insignificant — **flyspeck** *vt*

fly·strike \-,strīk\ *n* : infestation with fly maggots

fly·way \-,wā\ *n* : an established air route of migratory birds

fly·weight \-,wāt\ *n* : a boxer weighing 112 pounds or less

fly·wheel \-,hwēl\ *n* : a heavy wheel for opposing by its inertia a fluctuation of speed in the machinery with which it revolves

f-num·ber \'ef-,nəm-bər\ *n* [*focal* length] : a number following the symbol f/ that expresses the effectiveness of the aperture of a camera lens in relation to brightness of image so that the smaller the number the brighter the image and therefore the shorter the exposure required

¹foal \'fōl\ *n* [OE *fola*] : the young of an animal of the horse family; *esp* : one under one year

²foal *vb* : to give birth to a foal

¹foam \'fōm\ *n* [OE *fām*] **1** : a light frothy mass of fine bubbles formed in or on the surface of a liquid **2** : a froth formed (as by a horse) in salivating or sweating **3** : SEA **4** : a stabilized froth produced chemically and used esp. in fighting oil fires **5** : a material (as rubber) in a lightweight cellular form resulting from introduction of gas bubbles during manufacture

syn FOAM, FROTH mean masses of small bubbles. FOAM is likely to stress whiteness and delicacy, and to imply a distinct separation from the liquid forming the bubbly mass; FROTH may stress insubstantiality or worthlessness ⟨all *froth* and no beer⟩ or madness or feverishness

²foam *vb* **1 a** : to produce or form foam **b** : to froth at the mouth esp. in anger; *also* : to be angry **2** : to gush out in foam **3** : to cause to form foam; *esp* : to cause air bubbles to form in **4** : to convert (as a plastic) into a foam

foam rubber *n* : spongy rubber of fine texture made from latex by foaming before vulcanization

foamy \'fō-mē\ *adj* **foam·i·er**; **-est** **1** : covered with

foam : FROTHY **2** : full of, consisting of, or resembling foam — **foam·i·ly** \-mə-lē\ *adv* — **foam·i·ness** \-mē-nəs\ *n*

fob \'fäb\ *n* **1** : a watch chain or ribbon; *esp* : one hanging from a small watch pocket near the waistband in trousers **2** : a small ornament worn on a watch chain

fob off *vt* **1** : to put off with a trick or excuse **2** : to pass or offer as genuine **3** : to put aside

fo·cal \'fō-kəl\ *adj* : of, relating to, or having a focus — **fo·cal·ly** \-kə-lē\ *adv*

focal infection *n* : a persistent localized infection esp. when causing symptoms elsewhere in the body

focal length *n* : the distance of the focus from the surface of a lens or concave mirror

fo'·c'sle *var of* FORECASTLE

¹fo·cus \'fō-kəs\ *n, pl* **fo·cus·es** *or* **fo·ci** \-,sī\ [L, hearth] **1** : a point at which rays (as of light, heat, or sound) converge or from which they diverge or appear to diverge; *esp* : the point at which an image is formed by a mirror, lens, or optical system — see LENS illustration **2 a** : FOCAL LENGTH **b** : adjustment (as of the eye or field glasses) for distinct vision; *also* : the area that may be seen distinctly or resolved into a clear image **3** : one of the points that with the corresponding directrix defines a conic section **4** : a center of activity, attraction, or attention

²focus *vb* **fo·cused** *also* **fo·cussed**; **fo·cus·ing** *also* **fo·cus·sing** **1** : to bring to a focus ⟨*focus* rays of light⟩ **2** : to cause to be concentrated ⟨*focus* public attention on a problem⟩ **3** : to adjust the focus of ⟨*focus* the eyes⟩ ⟨*focus* a telescope⟩ **4** : to come to a focus **5** : to adjust one's eye or a camera to a particular range ⟨*focus* at 8 feet⟩

fod·der \'fäd-ər\ *n* [OE *fōdor*] : coarse dry food (as cornstalks) for livestock — **fodder** *vt*

foe \'fō\ *n* [OE *fāh*] **1** : one who has personal enmity for another : ENEMY **2** : an enemy in war : ADVERSARY **3** : something prejudicial or injurious **syn** see ENEMY

foe·man \'fō-mən\ *n* : an enemy in war : FOE

foe·tal, foe·tus *var of* FETAL, FETUS

¹fog \'fög, 'fäg\ *n* **1 a** : fine particles of water suspended in the lower atmosphere that differ from cloud only in being near the ground **b** : a fine spray or a foam for fire fighting **2** : a murky condition of the atmosphere or a substance causing it **3** : a state of mental confusion **4** : a density in a developed photographic image caused by chemical action or stray radiation

²fog *vb* **fogged**; **fog·ging** **1** : to cover or become covered with or as if with fog **2** : to make obscure or confusing **3** : to make confused

fog·bound \'fög-,baùnd, 'fäg-\ *adj* **1** : covered with or surrounded by fog ⟨*fogbound* coast⟩ **2** : unable to move because of fog ⟨*fogbound* ship⟩

fog·bow \-,bō\ *n* : a nebulous arc or circle of white or yellowish light seen in fog

fog·gy \'fög-ē, 'fäg-\ *adj* **fog·gi·er**; **-est** **1 a** : filled or abounding with fog **b** : covered or made opaque by moisture or grime **2** : MUDDLED — **fog·gi·ly** \-ə-lē\ *adv* — **fog·gi·ness** \-ē-nəs\ *n*

fog·horn \'fög-,hörn, 'fäg-\ *n* : a horn sounded in foggy weather to warn ships

fo·gy *also* **fo·gey** \'fō-gē\ *n, pl* **fogies** *also* **fogeys** : a person with old-fashioned ideas — usu. used with *old* — **fo·gy·ish** \-gē-ish\ *adj* — **fo·gy·ism** \-gē-,iz-əm\ *n*

foi·ble \'föi-bəl\ *n* [obs. F, fr. OF *feble* feeble] : a minor flaw or shortcoming in personal character or behavior : WEAKNESS **syn** see FAULT

¹foil \'föil\ *vt* [ME *foilen* to full cloth, trample, modif. of MF *fouler*] **1** : to prevent from attaining an end : DEFEAT **2** : to bring to naught

²foil *n* **1** : a fencing weapon with a flat guard and a light flexible blade tapering to a blunt point **2** *pl* : the art or practice of fencing with foils

³foil *n* [MF, fr. L *folium*] **1** : a plant leaf — used in compounds **2** : a leaf-shaped architectural ornamentation or one of the arcs or rounded spaces between its projections **3** : a very thin sheet of metal ⟨tin or aluminum *foil*⟩ **4** : a thin leaf of polished and colored metal used in jewelry to give color and brilliance to paste and inferior stones **5** : one that serves as a contrast to another

foils·man \'föilz-mən\ *n* : FENCER

foist \'föist\ *vt* : to pass off (something false or worthless) as genuine

---

ə abut; ⁹ kitten; ər further; a back; ā bake; ä cot, cart; aù out; ch chin; e less; ē easy; g gift; i trip; ī life

¹fold \'fōld\ *n* [OE *falod, fald*] **1** : an enclosure for or a flock of sheep **2** : a group of people with a common faith, belief, or interest

²fold *vt* : to pen up or confine (as sheep) in a fold

³fold *vb* [OE *fealdan*] **1** : to double or become doubled over itself ⟨*fold* a blanket⟩ **2** : to clasp together ⟨*folded* his hands⟩ **3** : to lay one part over or against another part of something ⟨birds *folding* their wings⟩⟨*fold* the leaves of the table⟩ **4** : to enclose in or as if in a fold ⟨a letter with a circular *folded* in it⟩ **5** : EMBRACE ⟨*folding* her doll in her arms⟩ **6** : to incorporate (a food ingredient) into a mixture by repeated overturnings without stirring or beating **7** : FAIL, COLLAPSE ⟨the new enterprise *folded* rapidly⟩

⁴fold *n* **1** : a doubling or folding over **2** : a part doubled or laid over another part

-fold \‚fōld, 'fōld\ *suffix* [OE *-feald*] **1** : multiplied by (a specified number) : times — in adjectives ⟨a twelve*fold* increase⟩ and adverbs ⟨repay you ten*fold*⟩ **2** : having (so many) parts ⟨three*fold* aspect of the problem⟩

fold·boat \'fōl(d)-‚bōt\ *n* : FALTBOAT

fold·er \'fōl-dər\ *n* **1** : one that folds **2** : a printed circular of folded sheets **3** : a folded cover or large envelope for holding or filing loose papers

fol·de·rol \'fäl-də-‚räl\ *n* [fr. *fol-de-rol*, a refrain in some old songs] **1** : a useless trifle **2** : NONSENSE

fo·li·a·ceous \‚fō-lē-'ā-shəs\ *adj* **1** : of, relating to, or resembling a plant leaf **2** : consisting of thin layers

fo·li·age \'fō-l(ē-)ij, -lyij\ *n* [MF *fuellage*, fr. *foille* leaf, fr. L *folium*] **1** : the mass of leaves of a plant **2** : a representation of leaves, flowers, and branches for architectural ornamentation — **fo·li·aged** \-l(ē-)ijd, -lyijd\ *adj*

foliage plant *n* : a plant grown for its decorative foliage

fo·li·ar \'fō-lē-ər\ *adj* : of or relating to leaves

¹fo·li·ate \'fō-lē-ət\ *adj* **1** : having or made up of leaves ⟨3-*foliate*⟩ **2** : FOLIOLATE

²fo·li·ate \-lē-‚āt\ *vb* **1** : to number the leaves of (as a manuscript) **2** : to ornament with foils **3** : to divide into layers or leaves — **fo·li·at·ed** \-‚āt-əd\ *adj*

fo·li·a·tion \‚fō-lē-'ā-shən\ *n* **1** : the leafing out of a plant : the state of being in leaf **2** : the act of numbering the leaves of a book; *also* : the total count of leaves numbered **3** : a decoration resembling a leaf **4** : foliated texture

fo·lic acid \‚fō-lik-\ *n* [L *folium* leaf] : a crystalline vitamin of the B complex used esp. in the treatment of nutritional anemias

fo·lio \'fō-lē-‚ō\ *n, pl* **fo·li·os** [L, abl. of *folium* leaf] **1** : a leaf of a manuscript or book **2** : a sheet of paper folded once **3 a** : the size of a piece of paper cut two from a sheet **b** : a book printed on folio pages **c** : a very large book

fo·li·o·late \'fō-lē-ə-‚lāt\ *adj* : having or made up of leaflets — usu. used in combination

fo·li·ose \'fō-lē-‚ōs\ *adj* : suggesting a leaf or an arrangement of leaves ⟨*foliose* lichens⟩

¹folk \'fōk\ *n, pl* **folk** *or* **folks** [OE *folc*] **1** : a group of people forming a tribe or nation; *also* : the largest number or most characteristic part of such a group **2** : people in general : persons as a group ⟨country *folk*⟩ ⟨old *folks*⟩ **3** : the persons of one's own family ⟨visit her *folks* during the holidays⟩

²folk *adj* : of, relating to, or originating among the common people ⟨*folk* dances⟩

folk etymology *n* : the transformation of words so as to give them an apparent relationship to other better-known or better-understood words (as the change of *chaise longue* to *chaise lounge*)

folk·lore \'fōk-‚lō(ə)r, -‚lò(ə)r\ *n* : customs, beliefs, stories, and sayings of a people handed down from generation to generation — **folk·lor·ist** \-‚lōr-əst, -‚lòr-\ *n*

folk medicine *n* : traditional medicine involving esp. the empirical use of vegetable remedies

folk·moot \-‚müt\ *or* **folk·mote** \-‚mōt\ *n* : a general assembly of the people (as of a shire) in early England

folk song *n* : a song originated or traditional among the common people of a country or region — **folk singer** *n*

folksy \'fōk-sē\ *adj* **folks·i·er; -est** **1** : SOCIABLE, FRIENDLY **2** : informal, casual, or familiar in manner or style — **folks·i·ly** \-sə-lē\ *adv* — **folks·i·ness** \-sē-nəs\ *n*

folk·tale \'fōk-‚tāl\ *n* : a characteristically anonymous, timeless, and placeless tale circulated orally among a people

folk·way \'fōk-‚wā\ *n* : a way of thinking, feeling, or acting common to a people or to a social group

fol·li·cle \'fäl-i-kəl\ *n* [L *folliculus* small bag, pod, dim. of *follis* bellows, inflated ball, bag] **1 a** : a small anatomical cavity or deep narrow-mouthed depression (as from which a hair grows) **b** : a small lymph node **2** : a dry one-celled fruit that develops (as in the peony, larkspur, or milkweed) from a single carpel and splits open by one seam only when ripe — **fol·lic·u·lar** \fə-'lik-yə-lər, fä-\ *adj* — **fol·lic·u·late** \-lət\ *also* **fol·lic·u·lat·ed** \-‚lāt-əd\ *adj*

follicle–stimulating hormone *n* : a hormone from the anterior lobe of the pituitary body that stimulates the growth of ovarian follicles

¹fol·low \'fäl-ō\ *vb* [OE *folgian*] **1** : to go or come after ⟨night *follows* day⟩ **2** : to take as a leader : OBEY ⟨*followed* her conscience⟩⟨*follow* instructions⟩ **3** : PURSUE ⟨*follow* a clue⟩ **4** : to proceed along ⟨*follow* a path⟩ **5** : to attend upon (as a business or profession) steadily ⟨*follow* the sea⟩ **6** : to come after in order of rank or natural sequence ⟨two *follows* one⟩ **7** : to keep one's eyes or attention fixed on ⟨*follow* a speech⟩⟨*follow* a lesson⟩ **8** : to result from something ⟨disaster *followed* the captain's blunder⟩⟨it does not necessarily *follow* that the accused is guilty⟩

syn FOLLOW, SUCCEED mean to come after or later than something or someone. FOLLOW may apply to a coming after in time, position, or logical sequence ⟨continue the sentence on the *following* page⟩ ⟨the punishment that *follows* crime⟩ SUCCEED may add a stronger implication of displacing or replacing ⟨*succeeded* his father as president⟩ **syn** see in addition CHASE

— follow suit 1 : to play a card of the same suit as the card led **2** : to follow an example set

²follow *n* : the act or process of following

fol·low·er \'fäl-ə-wər\ *n* **1 a** : ATTENDANT, RETAINER **b** : SUPPORTER, ADHERENT **c** : DISCIPLE **d** : one that imitates another **2** : a machine part that receives motion from another part

¹fol·low·ing \'fäl-ə-wiŋ\ *adj* **1** : next after : SUCCEEDING ⟨the *following* day⟩ **2** : that immediately follows ⟨trains will leave at the *following* times⟩

²following *n* : a group of followers, adherents, or partisans

³following *prep* : subsequent to ⟨*following* the lecture tea was served⟩

follow out *vt* **1** : to follow to the end or to a conclusion **2** : to carry out : EXECUTE

follow through *vi* **1** : to complete a stroke or swing **2** : to press on in an activity to a conclusion ⟨*follow through* with an investigation⟩

follow up \‚fäl-ə-'wəp\ *vt* : to pursue closely or show continued interest in often with subsequent supplementary action ⟨*follow up* his initial effort⟩⟨*follow up* a news story⟩ ⟨*follow up* a patient⟩

fol·low-up \'fäl-ə-‚wəp\ *n* : a system or instance of pursuing an initial effort by supplementary action — **follow-up** *adj*

fol·ly \'fäl-ē\ *n, pl* **follies** [OF *folie*, fr. *fol* fool] **1** : lack of good sense or normal prudence and foresight **2 a** : a foolish act or idea **b** : foolish actions or conduct **3** : an excessively costly or unprofitable undertaking

Fol·som \'fōl-səm\ *adj* : of or relating to a prehistoric culture of No. America on the east side of the Rocky mountains characterized esp. by a leaf-shaped flint projectile point

fo·ment \fō-'ment\ *vt* [LL *fomentare*, fr. L *fomentum* fomentation, fr. *fovēre* to warm, fondle, foment] **1** : to treat with moist heat (as for easing pain) **2** : to stir up : ROUSE, INSTIGATE ⟨*foment* rebellion⟩ — **fo·men·ta·tion** \‚fō-mən-'tā-shən, -‚men-\ *n* — **fo·ment·er** \fō-'ment-ər\ *n*

fond \'fänd\ *adj* [ME *fonned, fond*, fr. *fonne* fool] **1** : FOOLISH, SILLY ⟨*fond* pride⟩ **2 a** : prizing highly : DESIROUS ⟨*fond* of praise⟩ **b** : strongly attracted or predisposed ⟨*fond* of music⟩ **3** : TENDER, LOVING, AFFECTIONATE **4** : doted on : DEAR ⟨his *fondest* hopes⟩ — **fond·ly** *adv* — **fond·ness** \'fän(d)-nəs\ *n*

fon·dant \'fän-dənt\ *n* [F, fr. *fondre* to melt] **1** : a creamy preparation of sugar used as a basis for candies or icings **2** : a candy consisting chiefly of fondant

fon·dle \'fän-d'l\ *vt* **fon·dled; fon·dling** \-dliŋ, -d'l-iŋ\ : to touch or handle in a tender or loving manner : CARESS, PET — **fon·dler** \-dlər, -d'l-ər\ *n*

j joke;   ŋ sing;   ō flow;   ò flaw;   òi coin;   th thin;   th this;   ü loot;   u̇ foot;   y yet;   yü few;   yu̇ furious;   zh vision

fon·due \fän-'d(y)ü\ *n* [F] : a preparation of melted cheese usu. flavored with wine or brandy

¹font \'fänt\ *n* [OE, fr. L *font-, jons* fountain] **1** : a receptacle for baptismal or holy water **2** : FOUNTAIN, SOURCE

²font *n* [MF *jonte* act of founding, fr. *jondre* to found] : an assortment of type all of one size and style

fon·ta·nel *also* **fon·ta·nelle** \,fänt-ᵊn-'el\ *n* [ME *jontinelle*, a bodily hollow or pit, fr. MF *jontenele*, dim. of *jontaine* fountain] : a membrane-covered opening in bone or between bones; *esp* : one between the bones of a fetal or young skull

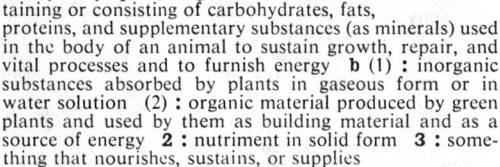

font 1

food \'füd\ *n* [OE *jōda*] **1 a** : material containing or consisting of carbohydrates, fats, proteins, and supplementary substances (as minerals) used in the body of an animal to sustain growth, repair, and vital processes and to furnish energy **b** (1) : inorganic substances absorbed by plants in gaseous form or in water solution (2) : organic material produced by green plants and used by them as building material and as a source of energy **2** : nutriment in solid form **3** : something that nourishes, sustains, or supplies

food chain *n* : a sequence of organisms in which each uses the next usu. lower member of the sequence for food

food·less \-ləs\ *adj* : lacking food — **food·less·ness** *n*

food poisoning *n* : an acute digestive disorder caused by bacteria or their toxic products or by chemical residues in food

food pyramid *n* : an ecological hierarchy of food relationships esp. when expressed quantitatively (as in mass, numbers, or energy) in which a chief predator is at the top, each level preys on the next lower level, and usu. green plants are at the bottom

food·stuff \'füd-,stəf\ *n* : a substance with food value; *esp* : a specific nutrient (as protein or fat)

food vacuole *n* : a vacuole (as in an amoeba) in which ingested food is digested

food web *n* : the totality of interacting food chains in an ecological community

¹fool \'fül\ *n* [MF *jol*, fr. LL *jollis*, fr. L, bellows, bag] **1** : a person who lacks sense or judgment **2** : a person formerly kept in a noble or royal household for casual entertainment — called also *jester* **3** : a person lacking in common powers of understanding : IDIOT **4** : DUPE

²fool *vb* **1 a** : to spend time idly or aimlessly **b** : to meddle or tamper thoughtlessly or ignorantly ⟨don't *fool* with that gun⟩ **2** : to speak or act in jest : JOKE ⟨I was only *fooling*⟩ **3** : to make a fool of : DECEIVE **4** : to spend on trifles or without advantage : FRITTER — used with *away*

fool·ery \'fül-(ə-)rē\ *n, pl* **-er·ies 1** : the habit of fooling : the behavior of a fool **2** : a foolish act : HORSEPLAY

fool·har·dy \'fül-,härd-ē\ *adj* : foolishly adventurous and bold : RASH **syn** see DARING — **fool·har·di·ly** \-,härd-ᵊl-ē\ *adv* — **fool·har·di·ness** \-,härd-ē-nəs\ *n*

fool·ish \'fü-lish\ *adj* : showing or arising from folly or lack of judgment — **fool·ish·ly** *adv* — **fool·ish·ness** *n*

fool·proof \'fül-'prüf\ *adj* : so simple, plain, or reliable as to leave no opportunity for error, misuse, or failure

fools·cap *or* **fool's cap** \'fül-,skap\ *n* **1** : a cap or hood usu. with bells worn by jesters **2** [fr. the watermark of a fool's cap formerly applied to such paper] *usu foolscap* : a size of paper typically 16x13 inches

fool's errand *n* : a needless or profitless errand

fool's gold *n* : PYRITE

fool's paradise *n* : a state of delusory happiness

¹foot \'füt\ *n, pl* **feet** \'fēt\ *also* **foot** [OE *jōt*] **1 a** : the terminal part of the vertebrate leg upon which an individual stands **b** : an invertebrate organ of locomotion or attachment; *esp* : a ventral muscular part of a mollusk **2** : any of various units of length based on the length of the human foot; *esp* : a unit equal to ⅓ yard and comprising 12 inches ⟨a 10-*foot* pole⟩ ⟨6 *feet* tall⟩ — see MEASURE table **3** : the basic unit of verse meter consisting of any of various fixed combinations or groups of accented and unaccented syllables **4** : something (as the lower end of the leg of a chair) resembling an animal's foot in position or use **5** *foot pl, chiefly Brit* : INFANTRY **6** : the lower edge (as of a sail) **7** : the lowest part : BOTTOM **8** : the end that is lower or opposite the head ⟨the *foot* of the bed⟩

9 foots *pl* : material deposited esp. on aging or refining : DREGS — **foot·like** \'füt-,līk\ *adj* — **on foot 1** : by walking ⟨toured the campus *on foot*⟩ **2** : under way : in progress ⟨plans for a new building are *on foot*⟩

²foot *vb* **1** : DANCE **2 a** : to go on foot **b** : to walk, run, or dance on, over, or through **3** : to make speed : MOVE **4 a** : to add up **b** : to pay or provide for paying

foot·age \'füt-ij\ *n* : length expressed in feet

foot-and-mouth disease *n* : an acute virus disease esp. of cattle marked by fever and by ulcers in the mouth, about the hooves, and on the udder

foot·ball \'füt-,bol\ *n* **1** : any of several games that are played with an inflated ball on a rectangular field having two goalposts at each end by two teams whose object is to get the ball over a goal line between goalposts: as **a** *Brit* : SOCCER **b** *Brit* : RUGBY **c** : a game played between two teams of 11 players each in which the ball is advanced by running or passing **2** : the ball used in football **3** : something shifted rapidly from one party to another esp. because no one wants to be held liable for it ⟨a political *football*⟩

foot·board \'füt-,bōrd, -,bord\ *n* **1** : a narrow platform on which to stand or brace the feet **2** : a board forming the foot of a bed

foot·boy \-,boi\ *n* : a serving boy : PAGE

foot brake *n* : a brake operated by foot pressure

foot·bridge \-,brij\ *n* : a bridge for pedestrians

foot·can·dle \'füt-'kan-dᵊl\ *n* : a unit for measuring illumination equal to the illumination on a surface all parts of which are one foot from a light of one candle

foot·ed \'füt-əd\ *adj* **1** : having a foot or feet ⟨a *footed* stand⟩⟨*footed* creatures⟩ **2** : having such or so many feet ⟨flat-*footed*⟩⟨four-*footed*⟩

foot·fall \'füt-,fol\ *n* : FOOTSTEP; *also* : the sound of a footstep

foot·gear \-,gi(ə)r\ *n* : covering (as shoes) for the feet

foot·hill \-,hil\ *n* : a hill at the foot of higher hills

foot·hold \-,hōld\ *n* **-1** : a hold for the feet : FOOTING **2** : a position usable as a base for further advance

foot·ing \'füt-iŋ\ *n* **1 a** : the placing of one's feet in a position to secure a firm or safe stand **b** : a place for the foot to rest on : FOOTHOLD **2** : a moving on foot : WALK, TREAD, DANCE **3 a** : position with respect to one another : STATUS ⟨nations on a friendly *footing*⟩ **b** : BASIS **4 a** : the action of adding up a column of figures **b** : the total amount of such a column

foot·lights \'füt-,līts\ *n pl* **1** : a row of lights set across the front of a stage floor **2** : the stage as a profession

foot·ling \-liŋ\ *adj* **1** : INEPT **2** : TRIVIAL

foot·lock·er \-,läk-ər\ *n* : a small flat trunk designed to be placed at the foot of a bed (as in barracks)

foot·loose \-,lüs\ *adj* : having no ties : FREE, UNTRAMMELED

foot·man \'füt-mən\ *n* : a male servant who attends a carriage, waits on table, admits visitors, and runs errands

foot·mark \-,märk\ *n* : FOOTPRINT

foot·note \-,nōt\ *n* : a note of reference, explanation, or comment placed below the text on a printed page — **footnote** *vt*

foot·pad \-,pad\ *n* : a highwayman or robber on foot

foot·path \-,path, -,påth\ *n* : a narrow path for pedestrians

foot–pound \-'paund\ *n, pl* **foot–pounds** : a unit of work equal to the work done by a force of one pound acting through a distance of one foot

foot–pound–second *adj* : being or relating to a system of units based upon the foot as the unit of length, the pound as the unit of weight or mass, and the second as the unit of time — *abbr. fps*

foot·print \'füt-,print\ *n* : an impression left by the foot

foot·race \-,rās\ *n* : a race run on foot

foot·rest \-,rest\ *n* : a support for the feet

foot soldier *n* : INFANTRYMAN

foot·sore \'füt-,sō(ə)r, -,sò(ə)r\ *adj* : having sore or tender feet (as from much walking)

foot·step \-,step\ *n* **1 a** : a step or tread of the foot **b** : distance covered by a step : PACE **2** : the mark of the foot : TRACK **3** : a step on which to ascend or descend

foot·stone \-,stōn\ *n* : a stone placed at the foot of a grave

foot·stool \-,stül\ *n* : a low stool to support the feet

foot·way \-,wā\ *n* : a narrow way or path for pedestrians

foot·wear \-,wa(ə)r, -,we(ə)r\ *n* : FOOTGEAR; *esp* : SHOES, BOOTS

foot·work \-,wərk\ *n* : the management of the feet (as in boxing)

foo·zle \'fü-zəl\ *vt* **foo·zled; foo·zling** \'füz-(ə-)liŋ\ : to manage or play awkwardly : BUNGLE — **foozle** *n*

fop \'fäp\ *n* [ME] : a man who is vain about his dress or appearance : DANDY — **fop·pish** \'fäp-ish\ *adj* — **fop·pish·ly** *adv* — **fop·pish·ness** *n*

fop·pery \'fäp-(ə-)rē\ *n, pl* **fop·per·ies** **1** : foolish character or action : FOLLY **2** : the distinguishing marks (as behavior or dress) of a fop

¹for \fər, (')fȯ(ə)r\ *prep* [OE; akin to E *fore*] **1** — used as a function word to indicate purpose ⟨money *for* studying⟩, intended destination ⟨left *for* home⟩, or object toward which one's desire or activity is directed ⟨now *for* a good rest⟩ **2** : as being ⟨take him *for* a fool⟩ **3** : because of ⟨cried *for* joy⟩ **4 a** : in support of ⟨fighting *for* their country⟩ **b** — used as a function word to indicate appropriateness or belonging ⟨medicine *for* a cold⟩ **c** — used as a function word with a following noun or pronoun to introduce an infinitive construction equivalent to a noun clause (as *that someone should* or *that he might*) ⟨shouted the news *for* all to hear⟩ **5 a** : in place of ⟨Doe batting *for* Roe⟩ **b** : in exchange as the equivalent of ⟨paid $10 *for* a hat⟩ **6** : in spite of ⟨unconvinced *for* all his clever arguments⟩ **7** : CONCERNING ⟨a stickler *for* detail⟩ **8** — used as a function word to indicate equality or proportion ⟨point *for* point⟩⟨tall *for* his age⟩ **9** — used as a function word to indicate duration of time or extent of space ⟨waited *for* several hours⟩ **10** : ²AFTER 3b ⟨named *for* his grandfather⟩

²for *conj* : for this reason or on this ground, namely : in view of the fact that ⟨he was certainly there, *for* I heard him⟩ **syn** see BECAUSE

for- *prefix* [OE] **1** : so as to involve prohibition, exclusion, omission, failure, neglect, or refusal ⟨*for*say⟩ **2** : destructively or detrimentally ⟨*for*storm⟩ **3** : completely : excessively : to exhaustion : to pieces ⟨*for*spent⟩

fora *pl of* FORUM

¹for·age \'fȯr-ij, 'fär-\ *n* [MF, fr. *forre* fodder, of Gmc origin; akin to E *fodder*] **1** : food for animals esp. when taken by browsing or grazing **2** : an act of foraging : a search for provisions

²forage *vb* **1** : to collect forage from **2** : to wander in search of provisions **3** : to get by foraging — **for·ag·er** *n*

fo·ram \'fȯr-əm, 'fȯr-\ *n* : FORAMINIFER

fo·ra·men \fə-'rā-mən\ *n, pl* **-ram·i·na** \-'ram-ə-nə\ *or* **-ra·mens** \-'rā-mənz\ [L *foramin-, foramen,* fr. *forare* to bore] : a small opening, perforation, or orifice : FENESTRA — **fo·ram·i·nal** \-'ram-ən-ºl\ *or* **fo·ram·i·nous** \-ə-nəs\ *adj*

fo·ra·men mag·num \fə-,rā-mən-'mag-nəm\ *n* [NL, lit., great opening] : the opening in the skull through which the spinal cord joins the brain

for·a·min·i·fer \,fȯr-ə-'min-ə-fər, ,fär-\ *n* : any of an order (Foraminifera) of large chiefly marine amoeboid protozoans usu. having perforated calcareous shells that are important sources of chalk and limestone — **fo·ra·mi·nif·er·al** \-rə,ram-ə-'nif-(ə-)rəl; fȯr-ə-mə-'nif-, ,fär-\ *or* **fo·ra·mi·nif·er·ous** \-(ə-)rəs\ *adj* — **fo·ra·mi·nif·er·an** \-(ə-)rən\ *adj or n*

for·as·much as \'fȯr-əz-,məch-əz\ *conj* : in consideration that : in view of the fact that : SINCE

¹for·ay \'fȯr-,ā\ *vb* [MF *forrer,* fr. *forre* fodder] : to raid esp. in search of plunder : PILLAGE

²foray *n* : a sudden invasion or attack for war or spoils : RAID

forb \'fȯrb\ *n* [Gk *phorbē* fodder, food, fr. *pherbein* to graze] : an herb other than grass

¹for·bear \fȯr-'ba(ə)r, fər-, -'be(ə)r\ *vb* **-bore** \-'bō(ə)r, -'bȯ(ə)r\; **-borne** \-'bōrn, -'bȯrn\; **-bear·ing** [OE *forberan* to endure, do without, fr. *for-* + *beran* to bear] **1** : to refrain or desist from : ABSTAIN **2** : to control oneself when provoked : be patient — **for·bear·er** *n*

²forbear *var of* FOREBEAR

for·bear·ance \fȯr-'bar-ən(t)s, fər-, -'ber-\ *n* **1** : the act of forbearing **2** : the quality of being forbearing : LENIENCY, PATIENCE

for·bid \fər-'bid, fȯr-\ *vt* **-bade** \-'bad, -'bād\ *or* **-bad** \-'bad\; **-bid·den** \-'bid-ºn\; **-bid·ding** [OE *forbēodan,* fr. *for-* + *bēodan* to bid] **1** : to command against : PROHIBIT **2 a** : to exclude or warn off by express command **b** : to bar from use ⟨cameras are *forbidden*⟩ **3** : to hinder

or prevent as if by an effectual command ⟨space *forbids* quoting in full⟩ — **for·bid·der** *n*

syn PROHIBIT, INHIBIT: FORBID implies absolute proscription with expectation of obedience; PROHIBIT implies more generality and suggests the effect of statutes or ordinances; INHIBIT implies hampering or restricting by authority or more often by circumstances or involuntary self-restraint

for·bid·ding *adj* : discouraging approach : frightening away : REPELLENT, DISAGREEABLE — **for·bid·ding·ly** \-iŋ-lē\ *adv* — **for·bid·ding·ness** *n*

forbode *var of* FOREBODE

¹force \'fōrs, 'fȯrs\ *n* [MF, fr. (assumed) VL *fortia,* fr. L *fortis* strong] **1 a** : strength or energy exerted or brought to bear : cause of motion or change : active power ⟨*forces* of nature⟩ **b** : moral or mental strength **c** (1) : capacity to persuade or convince (2) : legal efficacy ⟨that law is still in *force*⟩ **2 a** : military strength **b** (1) : a body (as of troops or ships) assigned to a military purpose (2) *pl* : the whole military strength (as of a nation) **c** : a body of persons available for a particular end ⟨labor *force*⟩ **3** : violence, compulsion, or constraint exerted upon or against a person or thing **4** : an influence (as a push or pull) that if applied to a material free body results chiefly in an acceleration of the body and sometimes in other effects (as deformation) **syn** see POWER — **force·less** \-ləs\ *adj*

²force *vt* **1** : to compel by physical, moral, or intellectual means : COERCE **2** : to make or cause through natural or logical necessity ⟨*forced* to admit he was right⟩ **3** : to attain to or effect against resistance or inertia ⟨*force* your way through⟩ **4** : to achieve or win by strength in struggle or violence: **a** : to win one's way into ⟨*forced* the mountain passes⟩ **b** : to break open or through ⟨*force* a lock⟩ **5 a** : to raise or accelerate to the utmost ⟨*forcing* the pace⟩ **b** : to produce with unnatural or unwilling effort ⟨*forced* laughter⟩ **6 a** : to hasten the rate of progress or growth of **b** : to bring (as plants) to maturity out of the normal season ⟨*forcing* lilies for the Easter trade⟩ — **forc·er** *n*

syn COMPEL, COERCE: FORCE implies the use of physical power to overcome resistance of persons or things ⟨*forced* him to his knees⟩⟨*forced* the door with a crowbar⟩ COMPEL and COERCE take only personal objects, COMPEL implying the working of an irresistible force ⟨hunger *compelled* them to surrender⟩ and COERCE suggesting the use of threatened violence or other injury

forced \'fōrst, 'fȯrst\ *adj* **1** : compelled or extracted by force : INVOLUNTARY ⟨*forced* labor⟩ **2** : done or produced with effort, exertion, or pressure ⟨a *forced* march⟩ — **forc·ed·ly** \'fōr-səd-lē, 'fȯr-\ *adv*

force·ful \'fōrs-fəl, 'fȯrs-\ *adj* : possessing or filled with force : VIGOROUS — **force·ful·ly** \-fə-lē\ *adv* — **force·ful·ness** *n*

force·meat \'fōrs-,mēt, 'fȯrs-\ *n* [*force* (alter. of *farce* stuffing) + *meat*] : chopped and seasoned meat or fish served alone or used as a stuffing

for·ceps \'fȯr-səps\ *n, pl* **forceps** [L, fr. *formus* warm + *capere* to take] : an instrument for grasping, holding, or exerting traction on objects esp. for delicate operations (as by jewelers or surgeons) — **for·ceps·like** \-,līk\ *adj*

force pump *n* : a pump with a solid piston for drawing and forcing through valves a liquid (as water) under a considerable pressure

forc·i·ble \'fōr-sə-bəl, 'fȯr-\ *adj* **1** : got, made, or done by force or violence ⟨a *forcible* entrance⟩ **2** : showing force or energy ⟨a *forcible* speech⟩⟨a *forcible* effort⟩ — **forc·i·bly** \-blē\ *adv*

¹ford \'fōrd, 'fȯrd\ *n* [OE] : a shallow part of a body of water that may be crossed by wading

²ford *vt* : to cross (a body of water) by wading — **ford·a·ble** \-ə-bəl\ *adj*

for·do *or* **fore·do** \fȯr-'dü, fōr-\ *vt* **-did** \-'did\; **-done** \-'dən\; **-do·ing** [OE *fordōn* to destroy, fr. *for-* + *dōn* to do] **1** *archaic* : DESTROY **2** : to overcome with fatigue : EXHAUST

¹fore \'fō(ə)r, 'fȯ(ə)r\ *adv* [OE] : in, toward, or adjacent to the front : FORWARD ⟨the shell lifts *fore* of the mast⟩

²fore *adj* : being or coming before in time, order, or space

³fore *n* : a prominent place or position : FRONT ⟨crowded schools bring new educational problems to the *fore*⟩

⁴fore *interj* [prob. short for *before*] — used by a golfer to warn anyone within range of the probable line of flight of his ball

fore- *comb form* [OE, fr. *fore*, adv.] **1 a** : earlier : beforehand ⟨*fore*see⟩ **b** : occurring earlier : occurring beforehand ⟨*fore*payment⟩ **2 a** : situated at the front : in front ⟨*fore*leg⟩ **b** : front part of (something specified) ⟨*fore*arm⟩

fore and aft *adv* : lengthwise of a ship : from stem to stern

fore-and-aft \,fōr-ən-'aft, ,fȯr-\ *adj* **1** : lying, running, or acting in the general line of the length of a ship or other construction⟨*fore-and-aft* sails⟩ **2** : having no square sails

fore-and-aft·er \-'af-tər\ *n* : a ship with a fore-and-aft rig; *esp* : SCHOONER

fore-and-aft rig *n* : a sailing-ship rig in which most or all of the sails are not attached to yards but are bent to gaffs or set on the masts or on stays in a fore-and-aft line — **fore-and-aft rigged** *adj*

¹fore·arm \(')fōr-'ärm, (')fȯr-\ *vt* : to arm in advance : PREPARE

²fore·arm \'fōr-,ärm, 'fȯr-\ *n* : the part of the arm between the elbow and the wrist

fore·bear *or* **for·bear** \'fōr-,ba(ə)r, 'fȯr-, -,be(ə)r\ *n* [ME (Sc) *forebear*, fr. *fore-* + *-bear* one that is, fr. *been* to be] : ANCESTOR, FOREFATHER

fore·bode *also* **for·bode** \fōr-'bōd, fȯr-\ *vb* **1** : FORETELL, PORTEND ⟨such heavy air *forebodes* storm⟩ **2** : to have an inward and anticipatory conviction of (as misfortune) **3** : to have a feeling of something about to happen — **fore·bod·er** *n*

¹fore·bod·ing *n* : an omen, prediction, or presentiment esp. of coming evil : PORTENT

²foreboding *adj* : indicative of or marked by foreboding ⟨*foreboding* glance⟩ — **fore·bod·ing·ly** \-iŋ-lē\ *adv* — **fore·bod·ing·ness** *n*

fore·brain \'fōr-,brān, 'fȯr-\ *n* : the anterior division of the embryonic vertebrate brain or the parts developed from it

¹fore·cast \'fōr-,kast, 'fȯr-\ *vb* **forecast** *or* **fore·cast·ed**; **fore·cast·ing 1** : to calculate or predict (a future event or condition) usu. as a result of rational study and analysis of data; *esp* : to predict (weather conditions) on the basis of meteorological observations **2** : to indicate as likely to occur ⟨*forecast* an easy victory at the polls⟩ **syn** see FORETELL — **fore·cast·er** *n*

²forecast *n* : a prophecy, estimate, or prediction of a future happening or condition ⟨weather *forecasts*⟩ ⟨business *forecasts*⟩

fore·cas·tle \'fōk-səl; 'fōr-,kas-əl, 'fȯr-\ *n* **1** : the part of the upper deck of a ship forward of the foremast **2** : the part of a merchantman having crew quarters forward

fore·close \fōr-'klōz, fȯr-\ *vb* **1** : to shut out ⟨didn't *foreclose* the possibility of a second term⟩ **2** : to take legal measures to terminate a mortgage and take possession of the mortgaged property because the conditions of the mortgage have not been met by the mortgagor

fore·clo·sure \-'klō-zhər\ *n* : the act of foreclosing; *esp* : the legal procedure of foreclosing a mortgage

fore·deck \'fōr-,dek, 'fȯr-\ *n* : the forepart of a ship's main deck

foredo *var of* FORDO

fore·doom \fōr-'düm, fȯr-\ *vt* : to doom beforehand ⟨efforts *foredoomed* to failure⟩

fore·fa·ther \'fōr-,fäth-ər, 'fȯr-\ *n* **1** : ANCESTOR 1 **2** : a person of an earlier period and common heritage

fore·fin·ger \'fōr-,fiŋ-gər, 'fȯr-\ *n* : the finger next to the thumb

fore·foot \-,fút\ *n* **1** : one of the front feet of a quadruped **2** : the forward part of a ship where the stem and keel meet

fore·front \-,frənt\ *n* : the foremost part or place : the place of greatest activity or interest ⟨an event in the *forefront* of the news⟩

foregather *var of* FORGATHER

¹fore·go \fōr-'gō, fȯr-\ *vb* **-went** \-'went\; **-gone** \-'gȯn, -'gän\; **-go·ing** \-'gō-iŋ\ : to go before : PRECEDE — **fore·go·er** \-'gō(-ə)r\ *n*

²forego *var of* FORGO

fore·go·ing \fōr-'gō-iŋ, fȯr-\ *adj* : going before; *esp* : said, written, or listed before or above ⟨the *foregoing* paragraphs⟩ **syn** see PRECEDING

fore·gone \,fōr-'gȯn, ,fȯr-, -,gän\ *adj* : determined or settled in advance ⟨his success seemed a *foregone* conclusion⟩

fore·ground \'fōr-,graúnd, 'fȯr-\ *n* **1** : the part of a scene or representation that is nearest to and in front of the spectator **2** : a position of prominence : FOREFRONT

fore·gut \-,gət\ *n* : the part of the alimentary canal of a vertebrate embryo that develops into the pharynx, esophagus, stomach, and first part of the intestine

¹fore·hand \'fōr-,hand, 'fȯr-\ *n* : a stroke made with the palm of the hand turned in the direction of movement

²forehand *adv* : with a forehand

³forehand *adj* : using or made with a forehand

fore·hand·ed \'fōr-'han-dəd, 'fȯr-\ *adj* **1** : mindful of the future : THRIFTY, PRUDENT **2** : FOREHAND — **fore·hand·ed·ly** *adv* — **fore·hand·ed·ness** *n*

fore·head \'fȯr-əd, 'fär-; 'fōr-,hed, 'fȯr-\ *n* **1** : the part of the face above the eyes **2** : the front or forepart of something

forehand

for·eign \'fȯr-ən, 'fär-\ *adj* [OF *forein*, fr. LL *foranus* being outside, fr. L *foris* outside; akin to E *door*] **1** : situated outside a place or country; *esp* : situated outside one's own country ⟨*foreign* nations⟩ **2** : born in, belonging to, or characteristic of some place or country other than the one under consideration ⟨*foreign* language⟩ ⟨*foreign* customs⟩ **3** : alien in character : not connected or pertinent ⟨material *foreign* to the topic under discussion⟩ **4** : related to or dealing with other nations⟨*foreign* affairs⟩ ⟨*foreign* office⟩ **5** : occurring in an abnormal situation in the living body and commonly introduced from without ⟨a *foreign* body in the eye⟩ — **for·eign·ness** \-ən-nəs\ *n*

for·eign·er \'fȯr-ə-nər, 'fär-\ *n* : a person belonging to or owing allegiance to a foreign country : ALIEN

for·eign·ism \'fȯr-ə-,niz-əm, 'fär-\ *n* : something peculiar to a foreign language or people; *esp* : a foreign idiom or custom

foreign minister *n* : a governmental minister for foreign affairs

fore·know \(')fōr-'nō, (')fȯr-\ *vt* **-knew** \-'n(y)ü\; **-known** \-'nōn\; **-know·ing** : to have previous knowledge of : know beforehand — **fore·knowl·edge** \-'näl-ij\ *n*

fore·la·dy \'fōr-,lād-ē, 'fȯr-\ *n* : a woman who acts as a foreman

fore·land \-lənd\ *n* : PROMONTORY, HEADLAND

fore·leg \-,leg\ *n* : a front leg

fore·limb \-,lim\ *n* : an arm, fin, wing, or leg that is a foreleg or homologous to it

fore·lock \-,läk\ *n* : a lock of hair growing from the front of the head

fore·man \'fōr-mən, 'fȯr-\ *n* : a first or chief man: as **a** : a member of a jury who acts as chairman and spokesman **b** : a workman in charge of a group of workers

fore·mast \-,mast, -məst\ *n* : the mast nearest the bow of a ship

¹fore·most \'fōr-,mōst, 'fȯr-\ *adj* [OE *formest*, superl. of *forma* first] : first in time, place, or order : most important : PREEMINENT

²foremost *adv* : in the first place

fore·name \-,nām\ *n* : a first name

fore·named \-,nāmd\ *adj* : previously named : AFORESAID

fore·noon \-,nün, 'fȯr-\ *n* : the early part of the day ending with noon : MORNING

¹fo·ren·sic \fə-'ren(t)-sik, -'ren-zik\ *adj* [L *forensis*, fr. *forum*] : belonging to, used in, or suitable to courts of law or to public discussion and debate — **fo·ren·si·cal·ly** \-si-k(ə-)lē, -zi-\ *adv*

²forensic *n* **1** : an argumentative exercise **2** *pl* : the art or study of argumentative discourse

fore·or·dain \,fōr-ȯr-'dān, ,fȯr-\ *vt* : to ordain or decree in advance : PREDESTINE ⟨a *foreordained* course of events⟩ — **fore·or·di·na·tion** \-,ȯrd-ᵊn-'ā-shən\ *n*

fore·part \'fōr-,pärt, 'fȯr-\ *n* : the part most advanced or first in place or time

fore·paw \-,pȯ\ *n* : the paw of a foreleg

fore·quar·ter \-,kwȯrt-ər\ *n* : the front half of a lateral half of the body or carcass of a quadruped ⟨a *forequarter* of beef⟩

fore·reach \fōr-'rēch, fȯr-\ *vb* **1** : to gain ground in tacking **2** : to gain on or overhaul and go ahead of (a ship) when close-hauled

fore·run·ner \'fōr-,rən-ər, 'fȯr-\ *n* **1** : one that goes or is sent before to give notice of the approach of others : HARBINGER ⟨the dark clouds were *forerunners* of a storm⟩ **2** : PREDECESSOR, ANCESTOR

fore·sail \'fōr-,sāl, 'fōr-, -səl\ *n* **1** : the lowest sail on the foremast of a square-rigged ship **2** : the lower sail set toward the stern on the foremast of a schooner

fore·see \fōr-'sē, fȯr-\ *vt* **-saw** \-'sȯ\; **-seen** \-'sēn\; **-see·ing** : to see or realize (as a development) beforehand : EXPECT — **fore·see·a·ble** \-ə-bəl\ *adj* — **fore·se·er** \-'sē-ər\ *n*

syn FORESEE, ANTICIPATE mean to know beforehand. FORESEE may apply to ordinary reasoning and of itself implies nothing concerning either action or feeling; ANTICIPATE implies responding emotionally to or taking action about something before it happens

fore·shad·ow \-'shad-ō\ *vt* : to give a hint or suggestion of beforehand : represent beforehand ⟨events *foreshadowed* a victory⟩ — **fore·shad·ow·er** *n*

fore·shank \'fōr-,shaŋk, 'fȯr-\ *n* : a beef shin

fore·sheet \-,shēt\ *n* **1** : one of the sheets of a foresail **2** *pl* : the forward part of an open boat

fore·shore \-,shōr, -,shȯr\ *n* : the part of a seashore between high-water and low-water marks

fore·short·en \fōr-'shȯrt-ᵊn, fȯr-\ *vt* : to shorten (a detail) in a drawing or painting so that the composition appears to have depth

fore·show \-'shō\ *vt* **1** : FORETELL **2** : to show beforehand

fore·side \'fōr-,sīd, 'fȯr-\ *n* : the front side or part : FRONT

fore·sight \'fōr-,sīt, 'fȯr-\ *n* **1** : the act or power of foreseeing : knowledge of something before it happens **2** : the act of looking forward; *also* : a view forward **3** : care or provision for the future : PRUDENCE — **fore·sight·ed** \-,sīt-əd\ *adj* — **fore·sight·ed·ly** *adv* — **fore·sight·ed·ness** *n*

fore·skin \-,skin\ *n* : a fold of skin that covers the end of the penis — called also *prepuce*

for·est \'fȯr-əst, 'fär-\ *n* [ML *forestis* unfenced wood, fr. L *foris* outside] **1** : a dense growth of trees and underbrush covering a large tract; *also* : the area covered by a forest **2** : something resembling a forest esp. in profusion ⟨a *forest* of masts⟩

fore·stage \'fōr-,stāj, 'fȯr-\ *n* : APRON 2a

fore·stall \fōr-'stȯl, fȯr-\ *vt* : to keep out, hinder, or prevent by measures taken in advance ⟨*forestall* unnecessary questions by giving careful directions⟩ **syn** see PREVENT — **fore·stall·er** *n* — **fore·stall·ment** \-'stȯl-mənt\ *n*

for·es·ta·tion \,fȯr-ə-'stā-shən, ,fär-\ *n* : the planting and care of a forest

fore·stay \'fōr-,stā, 'fȯr-\ *n* : a stay from the top of a ship's foremast to the deck

for·est·ed \'fȯr-ə-stəd, 'fär-\ *adj* : covered with trees or forests : WOODED ⟨*forested* slopes⟩

for·est·er \'fȯr-ə-stər, 'fär-\ *n* **1** : a person trained in forestry **2** : an inhabitant of a forest

forest floor *n* : the upper layer of mixed soil and organic debris typical of forested land

forest green *n* : a dark yellowish or moderate olive green

forest ranger *n* : an officer who patrols and guards a forest

for·est·ry \'fȯr-ə-strē, 'fär-\ *n* **1** : the science of developing and caring for forests **2** : the management of growing timber

foreswear *var of* FORSWEAR

¹fore·taste \'fōr-,tāst, 'fȯr-\ *n* : a preliminary or partial experience of something that will not be fully experienced until later : an advance notion ⟨through field maneuvers a soldier gets a *foretaste* of real campaigning⟩

²fore·taste \fōr-'tāst, fȯr-', 'fōr-,, 'fȯr-,\ *vt* : to taste beforehand : ANTICIPATE

fore·tell \fōr-'tel, fȯr-\ *vt* **-told** \-'tōld\; **-tell·ing** : to tell of or describe beforehand : PROPHESY

syn FORETELL, PREDICT, FORECAST mean to tell or announce beforehand. FORETELL often implies seeing the future through occult or unexplained powers ⟨sorcerers *foretold* his death by drowning⟩ PREDICT implies often exact foretelling through scientific methods ⟨*predict* an eclipse⟩ FORECAST commonly deals in probabilities and eventualities rather than certainties ⟨*forecasting* the week's weather⟩ — **fore·tell·er** *n*

fore·thought \'fōr-,thȯt, 'fȯr-\ *n* **1** : a thinking or plan-

ning out in advance : PREMEDITATION **2** : consideration for the future — **fore·thought·ful** \-fəl\ *adj* — **fore·thought·ful·ly** \-fə-lē\ *adv* — **fore·thought·ful·ness** *n*

¹fore·to·ken \'fōr-,tō-kən, 'fȯr-\ *n* : a premonitory sign

²fore·to·ken \fōr-'tō-kən, fȯr-\ *vt* **fore·to·kened; fore·to·ken·ing** \-'tōk-(ə-)niŋ\ : to indicate in advance ⟨the bright sunset *foretokened* good weather⟩

fore·top \'fōr-,täp, 'fȯr-; 'fōrt-əp, 'fȯrt-\ *n* : the platform at the head of a ship's foremast

fore·top·gal·lant \'fōr-,täp-,gal-ənt\ *adj* : being the part next above the fore-topmast

fore·top·mast \'fōr-,täp-məst\ *n* : a mast next above the foremast

fore·top·sail \'fōr-,täp-səl\ *n* : the sail above the foresail

for·ev·er \fə-'rev-ər\ *adv* **1** : for a limitless time : EVERLASTINGLY **2** : at all times : ALWAYS, CONSTANTLY ⟨a dog that was *forever* chasing cars⟩

for·ev·er·more \-,rev-ə(r)-'mō(ə)r, -'mȯ(ə)r\ *adv* : FOREVER

fore·warn \fōr-'wȯrn, fȯr-\ *vt* : to warn in advance ⟨*forewarned* of danger⟩

fore wing *n* : either of the front wings of a 4-winged insect

fore·wom·an \'fōr-,wùm-ən, 'fȯr-\ *n* : FORELADY

fore·word \'fōr-(,)wərd, 'fȯr-\ *n* : PREFACE

¹for·feit \'fōr-fət\ *n* [MF *forfait*, fr. pp. of *forfaire* to commit a crime, forfeit] **1** : something lost by or taken away from a person because of an offense or error committed by him : PENALTY, FINE ⟨pay for the crime of murder with the *forfeit* of his own life⟩ **2** *pl* : a game in which the players redeem personal articles by paying amusing or embarrassing penalties

²forfeit *vt* : to lose or lose the right to by some error, offense, or crime — **for·feit·er** *n*

³forfeit *adj* : forfeited or subject to forfeiture ⟨if they caught the spy his life would be *forfeit*⟩

for·fei·ture \'fōr-fə-,chùr, -chər\ *n* **1** : the act of forfeiting **2** : something forfeited : PENALTY

for·fend \fōr-'fend\ *vt* **1 a** *archaic* : FORBID **b** : to ward off **2** : PROTECT, PRESERVE

for·gath·er *or* **fore·gath·er** \fōr-'gath-ər, fȯr-\ *vi* **1** : to come together : ASSEMBLE **2** : to meet someone usu. by chance

¹forge \'fōrj, 'fȯrj\ *n* [OF, fr. L *fabrica* workshop, fr. *fabr-*, *faber* artisan, smith] **1** : a furnace or a shop with its furnace where metal is heated and wrought **2** : a workshop where wrought iron is produced or where iron is made malleable

²forge *vt* **1 a** : to form (as metal) by heating and hammering **b** : to form (metal) by a mechanical or hydraulic press **2** : to form or shape out in any way : FASHION ⟨*forged* an agreement⟩ **3** : to make or imitate falsely esp. with intent to defraud : COUNTERFEIT ⟨*forge* a check⟩ ⟨*forge* a signature⟩

³forge *vi* : to move forward steadily but gradually ⟨*forge* ahead in the voting for class president⟩

forg·er \'fōr-jər, 'fȯr-\ *n* : one that forges; *esp* : a person guilty of forgery

forg·ery \'fōrj-(ə-)rē, 'fȯrj-\ *n, pl* **-er·ies** **1** : the crime of falsely making or changing a written paper or signing someone else's name **2** : something (as a signature) that has been forged

for·get \fər-'get, fȯr-\ *vb* **-got** \-'gät\; **-got·ten** \-'gät-ᵊn\ *or* **-got**; **-get·ting** [OE *forgietan*] **1** : to be unable to think of or recall ⟨*forgot* his address⟩ ⟨he *forgets* easily⟩ **2 a** : to fail to become mindful at the proper time ⟨*forgot* about paying the bill⟩ **b** : NEGLECT ⟨*forgot* his old friends⟩ — **for·get·ter** *n* — **forget oneself** : to lose one's dignity, temper, or self-control

for·get·ful \-'get-fəl\ *adj* **1** : having a poor memory **2** : CARELESS, NEGLECTFUL ⟨*forgetful* of responsibilities⟩ — **for·get·ful·ly** \-fə-lē\ *adv* — **for·get·ful·ness** *n*

for·get-me-not \fər-'get-mē-,nät, fȯr-\ *n* : any of a genus of small herbs with bright blue or white flowers usu. in a curving spike

for·get·ta·ble \-'get-ə-bəl\ *adj* : likely to be forgotten

forg·ing \'fōr-jiŋ, 'fȯr-\ *n* : a piece of forged work

for·give \fər-'giv, fȯr-\ *vb* **-gave** \-'gāv\; **-giv·en** \-'giv-ən\; **-giv·ing** [OE *forgifan*, fr. *for-* + *gifan* to give] **1** : to cease to feel resentment against (an offender) : PARDON ⟨*forgive* your enemies⟩ **2 a** : to give up resentment of or claim to requital for ⟨*forgive* an insult⟩ **b** : to grant relief from payment of ⟨*forgive* a debt⟩ **syn** see EXCUSE — **for·giv·a·ble** \-'giv-ə-bəl\ *adj* — **for·giv·er** *n*

for·give·ness \-'giv-nəs\ *n* : the act of forgiving : PARDON
for·giv·ing \-'giv-iŋ\ *adj* : showing forgiveness : inclined or ready to forgive ⟨a person with a *forgiving* nature⟩ — **for·giv·ing·ly** \-iŋ-lē\ *adv* — **for·giv·ing·ness** *n*
for·go *or* **fore·go** \fȯr-'gō, fōr-\ *vt* **-went** \-'went\; **-gone** \-'gȯn, -'gän\; **-go·ing** \-'gō-iŋ\ [OE *forgān* to pass by, forgo, fr. *for-* + *gān* to go] : to give up : let pass : go without ⟨*forgo* lunch⟩⟨*forgo* an opportunity⟩
¹fork \'fȯrk\ *n* [ME *forke*, fr. OE *forca* & ONF *forque*; both fr. L *furca*] **1** : an implement with two or more prongs used esp. for taking up (as in eating), pitching, or digging **2** : a forked part, tool, or piece of equipment **3 a** : a dividing into branches or the place where something divides into branches ⟨a *fork* in the road⟩ **b** : a branch of a fork ⟨take the left *fork* at the crossroads⟩
²fork *vb* **1** : to divide into two or more branches ⟨the road *forks*⟩ **2** : to give the form of a fork to ⟨*forking* her fingers⟩ **3** : to raise or pitch with a fork ⟨*fork* hay⟩ — **fork·er** *n*

forks 1

forked \'fȯrkt, 'fȯr-kəd\ *adj* : having a fork : shaped like a fork ⟨*forked* lightning⟩ ⟨a *forked* tongue⟩
fork·ful \'fȯrk-,fu̇l\ *n, pl* **forkfuls** \'fȯrk-,fu̇lz\ *or* **forks·ful** \'fȯrks-,fu̇l\ : as much as a fork will hold
fork·lift \'fȯrk-,lift\ *n* : a machine for hoisting heavy objects by means of steel fingers inserted under the load
for·lorn \fər-'lȯrn\ *adj* [OE *forloren*, pp. of *forlēosan* to abandon, fr. *for-* + *lēosan* to lose] **1** : DESERTED, FORSAKEN **2** : feeling deserted or neglected : WRETCHED **3** : nearly hopeless ⟨a *forlorn* cause⟩ **syn** see SOLITARY — **for·lorn·ly** *adv* — **for·lorn·ness** \-'lȯrn-nəs\ *n*
forlorn hope *n* [by folk etymology fr. D *verloren hoop*, lit., lost band] **1** : a body of men selected to perform a perilous service **2** : a desperate or extremely difficult enterprise
¹form \'fȯrm\ *n* [L *forma*] **1 a** : the shape and structure of something as distinguished from its material **b** : a body (as of a person) esp. in its external appearance or as distinguished from the face **2** : the essential nature of a thing as distinguished from its matter **3 a** : established manner of doing or saying something **b** : a prescribed and set order of words : FORMULA ⟨the *form* of the marriage service⟩ **4** : a printed or typed document with blank spaces for insertion of required information ⟨tax *form*⟩ **5 a** : conduct regulated by custom or etiquette : CEREMONY, CONVENTIONALITY; *also* : show without substance ⟨outward *forms* of mourning⟩ **b** : manner or style of performing or accomplishing according to recognized standards of technique ⟨such behavior is bad *form*⟩ **6** : a long seat : BENCH **7 a** : a supporting frame model of the human figure used for displaying clothes **b** : a mold in which concrete is placed to set **8** : the printing type or matter arranged and secured in a chase ready for printing **9** : one of the different modes of existence, action, or manifestation of a particular thing or substance ⟨coal is a *form* of carbon⟩ **10 a** : orderly method of arrangement (as in the presentation of ideas) : manner of coordinating elements (as of an artistic production); *also* : a particular kind or instance of such arrangement ⟨the sonnet is a poetical *form*⟩ **b** : the structural element, plan, or design of a work of art **c** : a visible and measurable unit defined by a contour : a bounded surface or volume **11** : a grade in a British secondary school or in some American private schools **12 a** : a table with information on the past performances of racehorses **b** (1) : known ability to perform (2) : condition suitable for performing (as in athletic competition) **13 a** : a meaningful unit of speech (as a morpheme, word, or sentence) **b** : any of the different pronunciations or spellings a word may take in inflection or compounding
syn FIGURE, SHAPE: FORM may refer both to internal structure and external outline and often suggests the principle giving unity to the whole ⟨early *forms* of animal life⟩; FIGURE applies chiefly to the bounding or enclosing lines of a form ⟨cutting doll *figures* out of paper⟩ SHAPE may also suggest an outline, but carries a stronger implication of a three-dimensional body ⟨the *shape* of the monument was pyramidal⟩
²form *vb* **1** : to give form or shape to : FASHION, MAKE

⟨*form* a letter of the alphabet⟩ **2** : TRAIN, INSTRUCT ⟨education *forms* the mind⟩ **3** : DEVELOP, GET, CONTRACT ⟨*form* a habit⟩ **4** : to make up : CONSTITUTE ⟨bonds *formed* the bulk of the estate⟩ **5** : to arrange in order ⟨*form* a battle line⟩ **6** : to take form : ARISE ⟨fog *forms* in the valleys⟩ **7** : to take a definite form, shape, or arrangement ⟨each column of soldiers marched away as soon as it *formed*⟩ — **form·er** *n*
-form \,fȯrm\ *adj comb form* [L *-formis*, fr. *forma* form] : in the form or shape of : resembling ⟨*oviform*⟩
¹for·mal \'fȯr-məl\ *adj* **1 a** : belonging to or being the essential constitution or structure ⟨*formal* cause⟩ **b** : relating to, concerned with, or constituting the outward form of something as distinguished from its content ⟨the *formal* features of a thing can be misleading⟩ **2 a** : following or according with established form, custom, or rule : CONVENTIONAL ⟨paying *formal* attention to his hostess⟩ **b** : done in due or lawful form ⟨a *formal* contract⟩ **3 a** : based on conventional forms and rules ⟨a *formal* reception⟩ **b** : characterized by punctilious respect for form ⟨very *formal* in all his dealings⟩ **4** : NOMINAL ⟨a purely *formal* requirement⟩ — **for·mal·ly** \-mə-lē\ *adv*
²formal *n* : something (as a social event) formal in character
form·al·de·hyde \fȯr-'mal-də-,hīd, fər-\ *n* [*form*ic acid + *aldehyde*] : a colorless gas HCHO that consists of carbon, hydrogen, and oxygen, has a sharp irritating odor, and in solution in water is used as a disinfectant and preservative
For·ma·lin \'fȯr-mə-lən\ *trademark* — used for a clear water solution of formaldehyde containing a small amount of methanol
for·mal·ism \'fȯr-mə-,liz-əm\ *n* : the strict observance of forms or conventions (as in religion or art) — **for·mal·ist** \-ləst\ *n* — **for·mal·is·tic** \,fȯr-mə-'lis-tik\ *adj* — **for·mal·is·ti·cal·ly** \-ti-k(ə-)lē\ *adv*
for·mal·i·ty \fȯr-'mal-ət-ē\ *n, pl* **-ties** **1** : the quality or state of being formal **2** : compliance with formal or conventional rules : CEREMONY **3** : an established form that is required or conventional
for·mal·ize \'fȯr-mə-,līz\ *vt* **1** : to give a certain or definite form to : SHAPE **2 a** : to make formal **b** : to give formal status or approval to — **for·mal·iz·er** *n*
for·mat \'fȯr-,mat\ *n* [G, fr. L *formatus*, pp. of *formare* to form, fr. *forma* form] **1** : the shape, size, and general makeup of a publication **2** : the general plan of organization or arrangement of something
for·ma·tion \fȯr-'mā-shən\ *n* **1** : a forming of something ⟨the *formation* of good habits during childhood⟩ **2** : something that is formed ⟨new word *formations*⟩ **3** : the manner in which a thing is formed : STRUCTURE, SHAPE ⟨an abnormal *formation* of the jaw⟩ **4** : the primary subdivision in an ecological community **5** : an arrangement or grouping of persons, ships, or airplanes ⟨battle *formation*⟩ ⟨planes flying in *formation*⟩ **6** : a bed of rocks or series of beds recognizable as a unit — **for·ma·tion·al** \-shnəl, -shən-ᵊl\ *adj*
for·ma·tive \'fȯr-mət-iv\ *adj* **1** : giving or capable of giving form : CONSTRUCTIVE ⟨a *formative* influence⟩ **2** : capable of alteration by growth and development ⟨*formative* tissue⟩ **3** : of, relating to, or characterized by important growth or formation ⟨*formative* years⟩ — **for·ma·tive·ly** *adv* — **for·ma·tive·ness** *n*
form class *n* : a class of linguistic forms that can be used in the same position in a construction and that have one or more morphological or syntactical features in common
for·mer \'fȯr-mər\ *adj* [ME, compar. of *forme* first, fr. OE *forma*] **1** : coming before in time; *esp* : of, relating to, or occurring in the past ⟨*former* correspondence⟩ **2** : preceding in place or arrangement : FOREGOING ⟨*former* part of the chapter⟩ **3** : first mentioned or in order of two things mentioned or understood ⟨of these two evils the *former* is the lesser⟩
for·mer·ly \-mə(r)-lē\ *adv* : at an earlier time : PREVIOUSLY
form·fit·ting \'fȯrm-,fit-iŋ\ *adj* : conforming to the outline of the body : close-fitting ⟨a *formfitting* sweater⟩
For·mi·ca \fȯr-'mī-kə, fər-\ *trademark* — used for any of various laminated plastic products used esp. for surface finish
for·mic acid \,fȯr-mik-\ *n* [L *formica* ant] : a colorless strong-smelling liquid acid CH_2O_2 that irritates the skin, is

found in insects (as ants) and in many plants, and is used chiefly in dyeing and finishing textiles

for·mi·cary \'for-mə-‚ker-ē\ *n, pl* **-car·ies** [ML *formicarium,* fr. L *formica* ant] **:** an ant nest

for·mi·da·ble \'for-məd-ə-bəl, for-'mid-\ *adj* [L *formidare* to fear, fr. *formido* fear] **1 :** arousing fear ⟨a *formidable* foe⟩ **2 :** imposing serious difficulties or hardships ⟨the mountains were a *formidable* barrier⟩ **3 :** tending to inspire awe or wonder ⟨his *formidable* accomplishments as a scientist⟩ — **for·mi·da·bil·i·ty** \‚for-məd-ə-'bil-ət-ē, for-‚mid-\ *n* — **for·mi·da·ble·ness** *n* — **for·mi·da·bly** \-blē\ *adv*

form·less \'form-ləs\ *adj* **:** having no regular form or shape — **form·less·ly** *adv* — **form·less·ness** *n*

for·mu·la \'for-myə-lə\ *n, pl* **-las** *also* **-lae** \-‚lē, -‚lī\ [L, dim. of *forma* form] **1 :** a set form of words for use in a ceremony or ritual **2 a :** RECIPE, PRESCRIPTION **b :** a milk mixture or substitute for a baby **3 a :** a symbolic expression of the composition or constitution of a substance ⟨the *formula* for water is H₂O⟩ **b :** a group of numerical symbols associated to express briefly a single concept **4 :** a prescribed or set form or method — **for·mu·la·ic** \‚for-myə-'lā-ik\ *adj* — **for·mu·la·ical·ly** \-'lā-ə-k(ə-)lē\ *adv*

for·mu·la·rize \'for-myə-lə-‚rīz\ *vt* **:** to state in or reduce to a formula : FORMULATE — **for·mu·la·riz·er** *n*

for·mu·lary \'for-myə-‚ler-ē\ *n, pl* **-lar·ies** **1 :** a book or collection of stated and prescribed forms **2 :** a prescribed form or model : FORMULA **3 :** a book containing a list of medicinal substances and formulas — **formulary** *adj*

for·mu·late \'for-myə-‚lāt\ *vt* **1 :** to express in a formula **2 :** to put in systematic form : state definitely and clearly ⟨*formulate* a plan⟩ — **for·mu·la·tion** \‚for-myə-'lā-shən\ *n* — **for·mu·la·tor** \'for-myə-‚lāt-ər\ *n*

¹for·ni·cate \'for-nə-‚kāt\ *vi* [LL *fornicare,* fr. L *fornic-, fornix* arch, vaulted basement, brothel] **:** to commit fornication — **for·ni·ca·tor** \-‚kāt-ər\ *n*

²for·ni·cate \'for-ni-kət, -nə-‚kāt\ *adj* [L *fornicatus,* fr. *fornic-, fornix* arch] **:** ARCHED, VAULTED ⟨*fornicate* leaves⟩; *also* **:** having fornices

for·ni·ca·tion \‚for-nə-'kā-shən\ *n* **:** human sexual intercourse other than between a man and his wife : sexual intercourse between a spouse and an unmarried person **:** sexual intercourse between unmarried people — used in some translations (as AV, DV) of the Bible (as in Matthew 5:32) for *unchastity* (as in RSV) or *immorality* (as in NCE) to cover all sexual intercourse except between husband and wife or concubine

for·nix \'for-niks\ *n, pl* **for·ni·ces** \-nə-‚sēz\ **:** an anatomical arch or fold

for·sake \fər-'sāk, for-\ *vt* **for·sook** \-'suk\; **for·sak·en** \-'sā-kən\; **for·sak·ing** [OE *forsacan,* fr. *for-* + *sacan* to dispute] **1 :** to give up : RENOUNCE **2 :** to quit or leave entirely ⟨*forsook* the theater for other work⟩; *also* **:** DESERT ⟨*forsaken* by false friends⟩ **syn** see ABANDON

for·sooth \fər-'süth\ *adv* **:** in truth : INDEED

for·swear *or* **fore·swear** \for-'swa(ə)r, for-, -'swe(ə)r\ *vb* **-swore** \-'swō(ə)r, -'swo(ə)r\; **-sworn** \-'sworn, -'sworn\; **-swear·ing** **1 :** to swear falsely : commit perjury **2 :** to pledge oneself to give up ⟨*forswear* gambling⟩

for·syth·ia \fər-'sith-ē-ə\ *n* [after William *Forsyth* d1804 British botanist] **:** any of a genus of shrubs of the olive family widely grown for their yellow bell-shaped flowers appearing before the leaves in early spring

fort \'fort, 'fort\ *n* [MF, fr. *fort* strong, fr. L *fortis*] **1 :** a strong or fortified place; *esp* **:** a place surrounded with defenses and occupied by soldiers **2 :** a permanent army post

¹forte \'fort, 'fort, 'for-‚tā\ *n* **:** something in which a person excels or shows special ability : a strong point ⟨baseball and not books was that boy's *forte*⟩

²for·te \'for-‚tā, 'fort-ē\ *adv (or adj)* [It, fr. *forte* strong, fr. L *fortis*] **:** LOUDLY, POWERFULLY — used as a direction in music

forth \'forth, 'forth\ *adv* [OE; akin to E *fore*] **1 :** FORWARD, ONWARD ⟨from that time *forth*⟩ ⟨and so *forth*⟩ ⟨back and *forth*⟩ **2 :** out into view : OUT ⟨plants putting *forth* leaves⟩

¹forth·com·ing \(')forth-'kəm-iŋ, (')forth-\ *adj* **1 :** being about to appear : APPROACHING ⟨the *forthcoming* holidays⟩

2 : readily available or approachable ⟨confident that the needed supplies will be *forthcoming*⟩

²forthcoming *n* **:** a coming forth : APPROACH

forth·right \'forth-‚rīt, 'forth-\ *adj* **:** STRAIGHTFORWARD, DIRECT ⟨a *forthright* answer⟩ — **forth·right·ly** *adv* — **forth·right·ness** *n*

forth·with \(')forth-'with, (')forth-, -'with\ *adv* **:** IMMEDIATELY ⟨expect an answer *forthwith*⟩

for·ti·fi·ca·tion \‚fort-ə-fə-'kā-shən\ *n* **1 :** the act of fortifying; *esp* **:** the building of military defenses **2 a :** a construction built for the defense of a place : FORT **b** *pl* **:** defensive works

for·ti·fy \'fort-ə-‚fī\ *vt* **-fied; -fy·ing** [MF *fortifier,* fr. LL *fortificare,* fr. L *fortis* strong] **:** to make strong: **a :** to strengthen and secure by military defenses ⟨*fortify* a town⟩ **b :** to give physical strength, courage, or endurance to ⟨temperate habits *fortify* the body against illness⟩ **c :** to add mental or moral strength to : ENCOURAGE **d :** to add material to for strengthening or improving : ENRICH ⟨*fortify* a soil with fertilizer⟩ — **for·ti·fi·er** \-‚fī(-ə)r\ *n*

for·tis·si·mo \for-'tis-ə-‚mō\ *adv (or adj)* [It] **:** very loudly — used as a direction in music

for·ti·tude \'fort-ə-‚t(y)üd\ *n* [L *fortitudo* strength, fr. *fortis* strong, brave] **:** strength of mind that enables a person to encounter danger or bear pain or adversity with courage

fort·night \'fort-‚nīt, 'fort-\ *n* [ME *fourtene night* fourteen nights] **:** the space of 14 days : two weeks

¹fort·night·ly \-lē\ *adj* **:** occurring or appearing once in a fortnight

²fortnightly *adv* **:** once in a fortnight

³fortnightly *n, pl* **-lies** **:** a publication issued fortnightly

for·tress \'for-trəs\ *n* [MF *forteresce,* fr. L *fortis* strong] **:** a fortified place; *esp* **:** a large and permanent fortification sometimes including a town

for·tu·i·tous \for-'t(y)ü-ət-əs, fər-\ *adj* [L *fortuitus*] **:** occurring by chance **syn** see ACCIDENTAL — **for·tu·i·tous·ly** *adv* — **for·tu·i·tous·ness** *n*

for·tu·i·ty \-'t(y)ü-ət-ē\ *n, pl* **-ties** **1 :** the quality or state of being fortuitous **2 :** a chance event or occurrence

for·tu·nate \'forch-(ə-)nət\ *adj* **1 :** coming or happening by good luck : bringing a benefit or good that was not expected or was not foreseen as certain ⟨a storm-tossed sailing ship saved by a *fortunate* change in the wind⟩ **2 :** receiving some unexpected good : LUCKY ⟨a *fortunate* man⟩ ⟨considered herself *fortunate* in having good health⟩ **syn** see LUCKY — **for·tu·nate·ly** *adv* — **for·tu·nate·ness** *n*

for·tune \'for-chən\ *n* [L *fortuna*] **1 :** an apparent cause of something that happens to one suddenly and unexpectedly : CHANCE, LUCK **2 :** what happens to a person : good or bad luck ⟨the *fortunes* of war⟩ ⟨have the good *fortune* to be elected class president⟩ **3 :** a person's destiny or fate ⟨tell his *fortune* with cards⟩ **4 a :** possession of material goods : WEALTH ⟨a man of *fortune*⟩ **b :** a store of material possessions : RICHES ⟨was left a *fortune* by his father⟩

fortune hunter *n* **:** a person who seeks wealth esp. by marriage

for·tune–tell·er \-‚tel-ər\ *n* **:** a person who professes to foretell future events — **for·tune–tell·ing** \-‚tel-iŋ\ *n or adj*

for·ty \'fort-ē\ *n, pl* **forties** **1** — see NUMBER table **2 :** the 3d point scored by a side in a game of tennis — **for·ti·eth** \-ē-əth\ *adj or n* — **forty** *adj or pron*

for·ty–five \‚fort-ē-'fīv\ *n* **1 :** a 45 caliber pistol — usu. written .45 **2 :** a phonograph record for play at 45 revolutions per minute

Forty Hours *n sing or pl* **:** a Roman Catholic devotion in which the churches of a diocese in two-day turns maintain continuous daytime prayer before the exposed Blessed Sacrament

for·ty–nin·er \‚fort-ē-'nī-nər\ *n* **:** a person in California in the gold rush of 1849

forty winks *n sing or pl* **:** a short sleep : NAP

fo·rum \'for-əm, 'for-\ *n, pl* **forums** *also* **fo·ra** \-ə\ [L] **1 a :** the marketplace or public place of an ancient Roman city serving as the center of judicial and public business **b :** a medium of open discussion ⟨the publication serves as a *forum* for the examination of controversial issues⟩ **2 :** a judicial body or assembly : COURT **3 a :** a public meeting or lecture involving audience discussion **b :** a program (as on radio or television) involving discussion of a problem usu. by several authorities

¹for·ward \'fȯr-wərd\ *adj* **1** : near, being at, or belonging to the front ⟨a ship's *forward* gun⟩ **2 a** : strongly inclined : READY **b** : tending to push oneself : BRASH ⟨a flashy *forward* young woman⟩ **3** : notably advanced or developed : PRECOCIOUS **4** : moving, tending, or leading toward a position in front ⟨*forward* movement⟩ **5** : of, relating to, or getting ready for the future ⟨*forward* buying of produce⟩ — **for·ward·ly** *adv* — **for·ward·ness** *n*

²forward *adv* **:** to or toward what is before or in front

³forward *n* **:** a mainly offensive player in any of several games (as basketball) stationed at or near the front of his side or team

⁴forward *vt* **1** : to help onward : ADVANCE ⟨*forwarded* his friend's career⟩ **2 a** : to send forward : TRANSMIT **b** : to send or ship onward from an intermediate post or station in transit ⟨*forward* a letter⟩

for·ward·er \'fȯr-wərd-ər\ *n* : one that forwards; *esp* : an agent who forwards goods ⟨a freight *forwarder*⟩

for·ward·ing \-wərd-iŋ\ *n* : the act of one that forwards; *esp* : the business of a forwarder of goods

forward pass *n* : a pass in football thrown in the direction of the opponents' goal

for·wards \'fȯr-wərdz\ *adv* : FORWARD

fos·sa \'fäs-ə\ *n, pl* **fos·sae** \'fäs-ē, -ī\ [L, ditch] : an anatomical pit or depression — **fos·sate** \-ˌāt\ *adj*

fosse *or* **foss** \'fäs\ *n* [OF *fosse*, fr. L *fossa*, fr. fem. of pp. of *fodere* to dig] : DITCH, MOAT

¹fos·sil \'fäs-əl\ *n* [L *fossilis* dug up, fr. *foss-, fodere* to dig] **1** : a trace or impression or the remains of a plant or animal of a past age preserved in the earth's crust **2 a** : a person whose ideas are out-of-date **b** : something that has become rigidly fixed

²fossil *adj* **1** : extracted from the earth ⟨*fossil* fuels such as coal⟩ **2** : being or resembling a fossil ⟨*fossil* plants⟩

fos·sil·if·er·ous \ˌfäs-ə-'lif-(ə-)rəs\ *adj* : containing fossils

fos·sil·ize \'fäs-ə-ˌlīz\ *vb* **1** : to convert or become converted into a fossil **2** : to make outmoded, rigid, or fixed — **fos·sil·i·za·tion** \ˌfäs-ə-lə-'zā-shən\ *n*

fos·so·ri·al \fä-'sōr-ē-əl, -'sȯr-\ *adj* : adapted to or occupied in digging ⟨a *fossorial* foot⟩⟨*fossorial* animals⟩

¹fos·ter \'fȯs-tər, 'fäs-\ *adj* [OE *fōstor-*, fr. *fōstor* food, feeding] : affording, receiving, or sharing nurture or parental care though not related by blood or legal ties ⟨*foster* parent⟩⟨*foster* child⟩⟨*foster* brother⟩

²foster *vt* **fos·tered; fos·ter·ing** \-t(ə-)riŋ\ **1** : to give parental care to : NURTURE **2** : to promote the growth or development of : ENCOURAGE ⟨*foster* the spread of higher education⟩ — **fos·ter·er** \-tər-ər\ *n*

fos·ter·ling \-tər-liŋ\ *n* : a foster child

fought *past of* FIGHT

¹foul \'faul\ *adj* [OE *fūl*] **1 a** : offensive to the senses : LOATHSOME ⟨a *foul* sewer⟩ **b** : clogged or covered with dirt **2** : morally or spiritually odious : DETESTABLE ⟨*foul* crimes⟩ **3** : OBSCENE, ABUSIVE ⟨*foul* language⟩ **4** : being wet and stormy ⟨*foul* weather⟩ **5 a** : TREACHEROUS, DISHONORABLE ⟨fair means or *foul*⟩ **b** : violating a rule in a game or sport ⟨a *foul* blow in boxing⟩ **6** : marked up or defaced by changes ⟨*foul* manuscript⟩ **7** : ENTANGLED **8** : being outside the foul lines in baseball ⟨*foul* grounder⟩ **syn** see DIRTY — **foul·ly** \'faul(l)-lē\ *adv*

²foul *n* **1** : an entanglement or collision esp. in angling or sailing **2 a** : an infringement of the rules in a game or sport **b** : FREE THROW **3** : FOUL BALL

³foul *adv* : FOULLY

⁴foul *vb* **1** : to make or become foul or filthy ⟨*foul* the air⟩ ⟨*foul* a stream⟩ **2** : DISGRACE, DISHONOR ⟨*fouled* his good name⟩ **3 a** : to commit a violation of the rules in a sport or game **b** : to hit a foul ball **4** : to entangle or become entangled ⟨*foul* a rope⟩⟨the anchor *fouled*⟩ **5** : to collide with ⟨*foul* a launch in moving away from the dock⟩

fou·lard \fu̇-'lärd\ *n* [F] **1** : a lightweight silk of plain or twill weave usu. decorated with a printed pattern **2** : an article of clothing (as a scarf) made of foulard

foul ball *n* : a baseball batted into foul territory

foul·brood \'faul-ˌbrüd\ *n* : a destructive bacterial disease of honeybee larvae

foul line *n* **1** : either of two straight lines extending from the rear corner of home plate through the outer corners of first and third base and continued to the boundary of a

baseball field **2** : a line across a bowling alley that a player must not step over when delivering the ball

foul-mouthed \'faul-ˌmauthd, -'mautht\ *adj* : given to the use of obscene, profane, or abusive language

foul·ness \'faul-nəs\ *n* **1** : the quality or state of being foul **2** : something that is foul

foul play *n* : unfair play or dealing : dishonest conduct; *esp* : VIOLENCE ⟨the dead man was clearly a victim of *foul play*⟩

foul tip *n* : a pitched baseball that is slightly deflected by the bat

¹found \'faund\ *past of* FIND

²found *vt* [OF *fonder*, fr. L *fundare*, fr. *fundus* bottom] **1** : to take the first steps in building ⟨*found* a colony⟩ **2** : to set or ground on something solid : BASE ⟨a house *founded* on rock⟩ **3** : to establish and often to provide for the future maintenance of ⟨*found* a college⟩

³found *vt* [MF *fondre* to pour, melt, found, fr. L *fundere*] : to melt (metal) and pour into a mold

foun·da·tion \faun-'dā-shən\ *n* **1** : the act of founding **2** : the base or basis upon which something stands or is supported ⟨suspicions with no *foundation* in fact⟩ **3** : funds given for the permanent support of an institution : ENDOWMENT; *also* : an organization or institution so endowed **4** : an underlying natural or prepared base or support; *esp* : the whole masonry substructure of a building **5 a** : a body or ground upon which something is built up or overlaid **b** : a woman's supporting undergarment : CORSET — **foun·da·tion·al** \-shnəl, -shən-³l\ *adj*

¹found·er \'faun-dər\ *n* : one that founds or establishes ⟨the *founders* of the town⟩

²foun·der \'faun-dər\ *vb* **foun·dered; foun·der·ing** \-d(ə-)riŋ\ [MF *fondrer* to send to the bottom, collapse, fr. L *fundus* bottom] **1** : to become or make disabled; *esp* : to go lame ⟨his horse *foundered*⟩ **2** : to give way : COLLAPSE ⟨the building *foundered* in the fire⟩ **3** : to sink below the surface of the water ⟨a *foundering* ship⟩ **4** : to come to grief : FAIL ⟨their efforts all *foundered*⟩

³found·er *n* : one that founds metal; *esp* : TYPEFOUNDER

found·ling \'faun-dliŋ\ *n* : an infant found after its unknown parents have abandoned it

found·ry \'faun-drē\ *n, pl* **foundries** **1** : the act, process, or art of casting metals; *also* : CASTINGS **2** : an establishment where founding is carried on

¹fount \'faunt\ *n* : FOUNTAIN, SOURCE

²fount \'fänt, 'faunt\ *n* [F *fonte*] *Brit* : a type font

foun·tain \'faunt-³n\ *n* [MF *fontaine*, fr. LL *fontana*, fr. L *font-, fons*] **1** : a spring of water issuing from the earth **2** : SOURCE **3** : an artificially produced jet of water; *also* : the structure from which it rises **4** : a reservoir containing a liquid that can be drawn off as needed

foun·tain·head \-ˌhed\ *n* **1** : a fountain or spring that is the source of a stream **2** : a primary source : ORIGIN ⟨the *fountainhead* of our liberties⟩ ⟨a *fountainhead* of wisdom⟩

fountain pen *n* : a pen with a reservoir that automatically feeds the writing point with ink

four \'fō(ə)r, 'fȯ(ə)r\ *n* [OE *fēower*] **1** — see NUMBER table **2** : the fourth in a set or series **3** : something having four units or members — **four** *adj or pron*

four-flush \'fȯr-ˌfləsh, 'fȯr-\ *vi* : to make a false claim : BLUFF — **four-flush·er** *n*

four·fold \-ˌfōld, -'fōld\ *adj* **1** : having four units or members **2** : of or amounting to 400 percent — **fourfold** *adv*

four-foot·ed \-'fut-əd\ *adj* : QUADRUPED

4-H \-'āch\ *adj* : of or relating to a program set up by the U.S. Department of Agriculture to instruct rural young people in modern farm practices and in good citizenship ⟨4-H club⟩ — **4-H'er** \-'āch-ər\ *n*

four-hand \'fȯr-ˌhand, 'fȯr-\ *adj* : FOUR-HANDED

four-hand·ed \-'han-dəd\ *adj* **1** : designed for four hands **2** : engaged in by four persons ⟨a *four-handed* card game⟩

Four Horsemen *n pl* [fr. the apocalyptic vision in Revelation 6:2–8] : war, famine, pestilence, and death personified as the four major plagues of mankind

Four Hundred *or* **400** *n* : the exclusive social set of a community — used with *the*

four-in-hand \'fȯr-ən-ˌhand, 'fȯr-\ *n* **1 a** : a team of four horses driven by one person **b** : a vehicle drawn by such a team   **2 :** a necktie tied in a slipknot with long ends overlapping vertically in front

four-o'clock \-ə-,kläk\ *n* **:** an American garden plant with fragrant yellow, red, or white flowers opening late in the afternoon

four-post-er \-'pō-stər\ *n* **:** a bed with tall corner posts orig. designed to support curtains or a canopy

four-ra-gère \,fur-ə-'zhe(ə)r\ *n* [F] **:** a braided cord worn (as by a soldier in uniform) usu. around the left shoulder

four-score \'fōr-,skōr, 'fȯr-,skȯr\ *adj* **:** being four times twenty **:** EIGHTY

four-some \'fōr-səm, 'fȯr-\ *n* **1 :** a group of four persons or things **2 :** a golf match between two pairs of partners

four-square \-'skwa(ə)r, -'skwe(ə)r\ *adj* **1 :** SQUARE **2 :** marked by boldness and conviction **:** FORTHRIGHT — **foursquare** *adv*

four-teen \(')fōr(t)-'tēn, (')fȯr(t)-\ *n* — see NUMBER table — **fourteen** *adj or pron* — **four-teenth** \-'tēn(t)th\ *adj or n*

four-teen-er \-'tē-nər\ *n* **:** a verse consisting of 14 syllables or esp. of 7 iambic feet

fourth \'fōrth, 'fȯrth\ *n* **1** — see NUMBER table **2 a :** the musical interval embracing four diatonic degrees **b :** the harmonic combination of two tones a fourth apart **3 :** the 4th forward gear or speed of a motor vehicle — **fourth** *adj or adv* — **fourth-ly** *adv*

fourth estate *n, often cap F&E* **:** the public press

Fourth of July : INDEPENDENCE DAY

four-wheel \'fōr-,hwēl, 'fȯr-\ *or* **four-wheeled** \-'hwēld\ *adj* **1 :** having four wheels **2 :** acting on or by means of four wheels of an automotive vehicle ⟨four-wheel drive⟩

four-wheel-er \-'hwē-lər\ *n* **:** a four-wheel vehicle

fo-vea \'fō-vē-ə\ *n, pl* **-ve-ae** \-vē-,ē, -vē-,ī\ [L, pit] **:** an area of the retina containing only cones and affording acute vision — **fo-ve-al** \-vē-əl\ *adj* — **fo-ve-ate** \-vē-,āt\ *adj*

¹**fowl** \'faul\ *n, pl* **fowl** *or* **fowls** [ME *foul,* fr. OE *fugel*] **1 :** BIRD 1 **: a :** a domestic cock or hen; *esp* **:** an adult hen **b :** any of several domesticated or wild birds related to the common domestic cock and hen **2 :** the flesh of fowls used as food

²**fowl** *vi* **:** to seek, catch, or kill wildfowl — **fowl-er** *n*

fowling piece *n* **:** a light gun for shooting birds or small quadrupeds

¹**fox** \'fäks\ *n, pl* **fox-es** *or* **fox** [OE] **1 a :** any of various alert carnivorous mammals of the dog family related to the wolves but smaller and with shorter legs and more pointed muzzle **b :** the fur of a fox **2 :** a clever crafty person

²**fox** *vt* **:** to trick by ingenuity or cunning **:** OUTWIT

foxed \'fäkst\ *adj* **:** discolored with yellowish brown stains ⟨an old book with some pages *foxed*⟩

fox fire *n* **:** an eerie phosphorescent light (as of decaying wood); *also* **:** a luminous fungus that causes decaying wood to glow

red fox

fox-glove \'fäks-,gləv\ *n* **:** any of a genus of erect herbs of the figwort family; *esp* **:** a common European biennial or perennial cultivated for its showy racemes of closed white or purple tubular flowers and as a source of digitalis

fox grape *n* **:** any of several native grapes of eastern No. America with sour or musky fruit

fox-hole \'fäks-,hōl\ *n* **:** a pit dug hastily during combat for individual cover against enemy fire

fox-hound \-,haund\ *n* **:** any of various large swift powerful hounds used in hunting foxes

fox-i-ly \'fäk-sə-lē\ *adv* **:** in a foxy manner

fox-i-ness \-sē-nəs\ *n* **:** the quality or state of being foxy

fox-tail millet \,fäks-,tāl-\ *n* **:** a coarse drought-resistant but frost-sensitive annual grass grown for grain, hay, and forage

fox terrier *n* **:** a small lively terrier formerly used to dig out foxes and known in smooth-haired and wirehaired varieties — see TERRIER illustration

fox-trot \'fäks-,trät\ *n* **1 :** a short broken slow trotting gait in which the hind foot of the horse hits the ground a trifle before the diagonally opposite forefoot **2 :** a ball-

room dance in duple time that includes slow walking steps, quick running steps, and two-steps — **fox-trot** *vi*

foxy \'fäk-sē\ *adj* **fox-i-er; -est 1 :** resembling a fox in appearance or disposition **:** WILY **b :** being alert and knowing **:** CLEVER **2 :** having the color of a fox **3 :** FOXED

foy-er \'fȯi-(ə)r, 'fȯi-,(y)ā\ *n* [F, lit., fireplace, fr. ML *focarius,* fr. L *focus* hearth] **:** an anteroom or lobby esp. of a theater; *also* **:** an entrance hallway **:** VESTIBULE

fra-cas \'frā-kəs, 'frak-əs\ *n* [F] **:** a noisy quarrel **:** BRAWL

frac-tion \'frak-shən\ *n* [LL *fraction-, fractio* act of breaking, fr. L *fract-, frangere* to break] **1 :** a numerical representation (as ¾, ⅝, 3.234) of two numbers whose quotient is to be determined **2 a :** FRAGMENT **b :** PORTION, SECTION

frac-tion-al \-shnəl, -shən-°l\ *adj* **1 :** of, relating to, or being a fraction **2 :** relatively small **:** INCONSIDERABLE **3 :** of, relating to, or involving a separating of components from a mixture through differences in physical or chemical properties ⟨*fractional* distillation⟩ — **frac-tion-al-ly** \-ē\ *adv*

frac-tion-ate \'frak-shə-,nāt\ *vt* **:** to separate into different portions, *esp* **:** to subject to fractional distillation — **frac-tion-ation** \,frak-shə-'nā-shən\ *n*

frac-tious \'frak-shəs\ *adj* [*fraction* + -*ous*] **1 :** tending to be troublesome **:** hard to handle or control **2 :** QUARRELSOME, IRRITABLE — **frac-tious-ly** *adv* — **frac-tious-ness** *n*

¹**frac-ture** \'frak-chər\ *n* [L *fract-, frangere* to break; akin to E *break*] **1 :** the act or process of breaking or the state of being broken; *esp* **:** the breaking of bone — compare SIMPLE FRACTURE, COMPOUND FRACTURE **2 :** the result of fracturing; *esp* **:** an injury resulting from fracture of a bone **syn** FRACTURE, RUPTURE mean a break in tissue. FRACTURE applies to the cracking of hard substances ⟨*fractured* bones⟩ RUPTURE applies to the tearing or bursting of soft tissues ⟨*ruptured* blood vessel⟩

²**fracture** *vb* **frac-tured; frac-tur-ing** \-chə-riŋ, -shriŋ\ **1 :** to cause a fracture in **:** BREAK **2 :** to break up **:** DESTROY **3 :** to undergo fracture

frae \(')frā\ *prep* [ON *frā*] *Scot* **:** FROM

frag-ile \'fraj-əl, -,īl\ *adj* [L *fragilis,* fr. *frangere* to break] **1 :** easily broken or destroyed **:** DELICATE **2 :** TENUOUS, SLIGHT ⟨*fragile* evidence⟩ **syn** see BRITTLE — **fra-gil-i-ty** \frə-'jil-ət-ē\ *n*

frag-ment \'frag-mənt\ *n* [L *fragmentum,* fr. *frangere* to break] **1 :** a part broken off, detached, or incomplete **2 :** SENTENCE FRAGMENT — **frag-ment** \-,ment\ *vb*

frag-men-tary \'frag-mən-,ter-ē\ *adj* **:** consisting of fragments **:** INCOMPLETE ⟨*fragmentary* evidence⟩⟨a *fragmentary* report⟩ — **frag-men-tar-i-ness** *n*

frag-men-tate \'frag-mən-,tāt\ *vb* **:** to break or fall into pieces — **frag-men-ta-tion** \,frag-mən-'tā-shən, -,men-\ *n*

frag-men-tize \'frag-mən-,tīz\ *vb* **:** to break into fragments

fra-grance \'frā-grən(t)s\ *n* **1 :** a sweet, pleasing, and often flowery or fruity odor ⟨the *fragrance* of new-mown hay⟩ — compare AROMA **2 :** a particular odor (as of a perfume or toilet water)

fra-grant \-grənt\ *adj* [L *fragrant-, fragrans,* fr. prp. of *fragrare* to be fragrant] **:** having fragrance — **fra-grant-ly** *adv*

frail \'frāl\ *adj* [MF *fraile,* fr. L *fragilis* fragile] **1 :** morally weak ⟨*frail* humanity⟩ **2 :** FRAGILE **3 a :** physically weak **b :** SLIGHT, UNSUBSTANTIAL — **frail-ly** \'frāl-lē\ *adv* — **frail-ness** *n*

frail-ty \'frā-(ə)l-tē\ *n, pl* **frailties 1 :** the quality or state of being frail **2 :** a fault due to weakness esp. of moral character

¹**frame** \'frām\ *vt* [OE *framian* to make progress, be profitable] **1 a :** PLAN, CONTRIVE **b :** to give expression to **:** FORMULATE **c :** SHAPE, CONSTRUCT **d :** to draw up ⟨*frame* a constitution⟩ **2 :** to fit or adjust for a purpose **3 :** to construct by fitting and uniting the parts of the skeleton of (a structure) **4 :** to enclose in a frame ⟨*frame* a picture⟩ **5 :** to make (an innocent person) appear guilty — **fram-er** *n*

²**frame** *n* **1 a :** something composed of parts fitted together and united **b :** the physical makeup of an animal and esp. a human body **:** PHYSIQUE, FIGURE **2 a :** an arrangement of structural parts that gives form or support to something ⟨*frame* of a cart⟩⟨the bony *frame* of the

body); *esp* **:** one (as of girders, beams, and joists) that forms the main support of a structure (as a building) **b :** a skeletal structure on or in which something rests ⟨the *frame* of a bucksaw⟩⟨the *frame* that rests on the axles and supports the remainder of the chassis of an auto⟩; *also* **:** a machine built on or in a frame ⟨a spinning *frame*⟩ **c :** a supporting or enclosing border or open case (as for a window or a picture) **d :** matter or an area enclosed by a border: as **(1) :** one of the squares in which scores for each round are recorded (as in bowling); *also* **:** a round in bowling **(2) :** one picture of the series on a length of film **(3) :** a complete image being transmitted by television **3 :** a particular state or disposition (as of the mind) **:** MOOD

³frame *adj* **:** having a wood frame ⟨*frame* houses⟩

frame of reference : a set or system (as of facts or ideas) serving to orient or give particular meaning

frame-up \'frām-,əp\ *n* **:** a scheme to cause an innocent person to be accused of a crime; *also* **:** the action resulting from such a scheme

frame-work \'frām-,wərk\ *n* **1 :** a skeletal, openwork, or structural frame **2 :** a basic structure (as of ideas)

fram-ing \'frā-miŋ\ *n* **:** FRAME, FRAMEWORK

franc \'fraŋk\ *n* [F, fr. ML *Francorum Rex*, king of the French, device on 14th cent. francs] **1 :** the basic monetary unit of any of several countries (as France, Belgium, or Switzerland) **2 :** a coin representing one franc

fran-chise \'fran-,chīz\ *n* [OF, freedom from a restriction, fr. *franchir* to free, fr. *franc* free, frank] **1 :** a special privilege granted to an individual or group: as **a :** the right to be and exercise the powers of a corporation **b :** the right to market a company's goods or services in a particular territory; *also* **:** the territory covered by grant of such a right **2 :** a constitutional or statutory right or privilege, *esp* **:** the right to vote

¹Fran-cis-can \fran-'sis-kən\ *adj* **:** of or relating to St. Francis of Assisi or one of the orders under his monastic rule

²Franciscan *n* **:** a member of the Order of Friars Minor observing the unmodified rule of the first order of St. Francis of Assisi and engaging chiefly in preaching and in missionary and charitable work

fran-ci-um \'fran(t)-sē-əm\ *n* [after *France*, the country] **:** a radioactive chemical element obtained artificially by the bombardment of thorium with protons — see ELEMENT table

Franco- *comb form* [ML *Francus* Frenchman, fr. LL, Frank] **:** French and ⟨*Franco*-German⟩ **:** French ⟨*Franco*-phile⟩

fran-co-lin \'fraŋ-kə-lən\ *n* [F, fr. It *francolino*] **:** any of various African or Asiatic partridges

Fran-co-phile \'fraŋ-kə-,fīl\ *adj* **:** markedly friendly to France or French culture — **Francophile** *n*

fran-gi-ble \'fran-jə-bəl\ *adj* [ML *frangibilis*, fr. L *frangere* to break] **:** BREAKABLE — **fran-gi-bil-i-ty** \,fran-jə-'bil-ət-ē\ *n*

fran-gi-pani \,fran-jə-'pan-ē\ *n, pl* **frangipani** *or* **fran-gi-pan-is** [modif. of It *frangipane*] **:** a perfume derived from or imitating the odor of the flower of the red jasmine; *also* **:** red jasmine or a related tropical American shrub or small tree

¹frank \'fraŋk\ *adj* [OF *franc* free, frank, fr. ML *francus*, fr. LL *Francus* Frank] **1 :** free and forthright in expressing one's feelings and opinions **:** OUTSPOKEN **2 :** unmistakably evident **:** MANIFEST, CLEAR ⟨*frank* treason⟩ ⟨*frank* pus in a wound⟩ — **frank-ly** *adv* — **frank-ness** *n*
syn FRANK, CANDID, OPEN mean showing willingness to tell one's thoughts or feelings. FRANK implies absence of the evasiveness that springs from considerations of tact or of expedience ⟨*frank* declaration of selfish motives⟩ CANDID stresses sincerity and honesty of expression esp. in offering unwelcome criticism or opinion ⟨a *candid* appraisal of her friend's behavior⟩ OPEN implies frankness but suggests more indiscretion than FRANK and less earnestness than CANDID ⟨*open* betrayal of his friend⟩

²frank *vt* **:** to mark (a piece of mail) with an official signature or sign indicating the right of the sender to free mailing; *also* **:** to mail in this manner

³frank *n* **1 :** a signature, mark, or stamp on a piece of mail indicating that it can be mailed free **2 :** the privilege of sending mail free of charge

Frank \'fraŋk\ *n* **:** a member of a West Germanic people entering the Roman provinces in A.D. 253 and establishing themselves in the Netherlands, in Gaul, and along the Rhine — **Frank-ish** \'fraŋ-kish\ *adj*

Fran-ken-stein \'fraŋ-kən-,stīn, -,stēn\ *n* **1 :** a student of physiology in Mary W. Shelley's novel *Frankenstein* whose life is ruined by a monster he creates **2 :** a work or agency that ruins its originator **3 :** a monster in the shape of a man

frank-furt-er *or* **frank-fort-er** \'fraŋk-fə(r)t-ər\ *or* **frank-furt** *or* **frank-fort** \-fərt\ *n* [G *frankfurter* of Frankfurt, fr. *Frankfurt*, Germany] **:** a seasoned beef or beef and pork sausage

frank-in-cense \'fraŋ-kən-,sen(t)s\ *n* [ME *frank* frank, pure + *incense*] **:** a fragrant gum resin from African or Arabian trees that is an important incense resin

frank-lin \'fraŋ-klən\ *n* [AF *fraunclein*, fr. OF *franc* free] **:** a free medieval English landowner not of noble birth

Frank-lin stove \,fraŋ-klən-\ *n* [Benjamin *Franklin*, its inventor] **:** a metal heating stove resembling an open fireplace but designed to conserve and radiate heat

fran-tic \'frant-ik\ *adj* [ME *frenetik*, *frantik* mentally deranged, fr. L *phreneticus*, fr. Gk *phrenitis* inflammation of the brain, fr. *phrēn* mind] **:** wildly or uncontrollably excited **:** FRENZIED ⟨*frantic* with pain⟩⟨*frantic* cries for help⟩ — **fran-ti-cal-ly** \-i-k(ə-)lē\ *adv* — **fran-tic-ly** \-i-klē\ *adv* — **fran-tic-ness** *n*

frap-pé \fra-'pā\ *or* **frappe** \'frap, fra-'pā\ *n* [F *frappé*, iced, lit., struck] **1 :** an iced or frozen mixture or drink **2 :** a thick milk shake — **frappé** *adj*

fra-ter-nal \frə-'tərn-ᵊl\ *adj* [L *fraternus*, fr. *frater* brother; akin to E *brother*] **1 a :** of, relating to, or involving brothers **b :** of, relating to, or being a fraternity or society **2 :** derived from two ova ⟨*fraternal* twins⟩ **3 :** FRIENDLY, BROTHERLY — **fra-ter-nal-ism** \-ᵊl-,iz-əm\ *n* — **fra-ter-nal-ly** \-ᵊl-ē\ *adv*

fra-ter-ni-ty \frə-'tər-nət-ē\ *n, pl* **-ties** **1 :** a social, honorary, or professional organization; *esp* **:** a social club of male college students **2 :** BROTHERLINESS, BROTHERHOOD **3 :** men of the same class, profession, character or tastes ⟨the legal *fraternity*⟩ **4 a :** the entire progeny of a single mating **b :** a group of siblings

frat-er-nize \'frat-ər-,nīz\ *vi* **1 :** to associate or mingle as brothers or friends **2 :** to associate on intimate terms with citizens or troops of a hostile nation — **frat-er-ni-za-tion** \,frat-ər-nə-'zā-shən\ *n* — **frat-er-niz-er** \'frat-ər-,nī-zər\ *n*

frat-ri-cide \'fra-trə-,sīd\ *n* [L *fratr-*, *frater* brother] **1 :** one that murders or kills his own brother or sister **2 :** the act of a fratricide — **frat-ri-cid-al** \,fra-trə-'sīd-ᵊl\ *adj*

Frau \'frau̇\ *n, pl* **Frau-en** \'frau̇-ən\ [G] **:** a German married woman **:** WIFE — used as a title equivalent to *Mrs.*

fraud \'frȯd\ *n* [L *fraud-*, *fraus*] **1 a :** DECEIT; *esp* **:** intentional perversion of truth in order to induce another to part with something of value or to surrender a legal right **b :** an act of deceiving or misrepresenting **:** TRICK **2 a :** one who is not what he pretends to be **:** IMPOSTOR **b :** one who defrauds **:** CHEAT **syn** see DECEPTION

fraud-u-lent \'frȯj-ə-lənt\ *adj* **:** characterized by, based on, or done by fraud **:** DECEITFUL ⟨*fraudulent* claims of injury from an automobile accident⟩ — **fraud-u-lence** \-lən(t)s\ *n* — **fraud-u-lent-ly** *adv* — **fraud-u-lent-ness** *n*

fraught \'frȯt\ *adj* [ME, freighted, fr. pp. of *fraughten* to load, fr. *fraught* freight, fr. MD or MLG *vracht*, *vrecht*] **:** bearing promise or menace **:** PREGNANT ⟨a situation *fraught* with danger⟩⟨words *fraught* with meaning⟩

Fräu-lein \'frȯi-,līn\ *n* [G] **:** an unmarried German girl or woman — used as a title equivalent to *Miss*

¹fray \'frā\ *n* [ME, short for *affray*] **:** BRAWL, FIGHT; *also* **:** DISPUTE

²fray *vb* [MF *frayer* to rub, fr. L *fricare*] **1 a :** to wear (as an edge of cloth) by rubbing **:** FRET **b :** to separate the threads at the edge of **c :** to wear out or into shreds **2 :** STRAIN, IRRITATE

fraz-zle \'fraz-əl\ *vb* **fraz-zled**; **fraz-zling** \'fraz-(ə-)liŋ\ **1 :** FRAY **2 :** to put in a state of extreme physical or nervous fatigue — **frazzle** *n*

¹freak \'frēk\ *n* **1 a :** WHIM **b :** a seemingly capricious action or event **2 :** something markedly unusual or abnormal; *esp* **:** one with a physical oddity who appears in a

ə abut; ə kitten; ər further; a back; ā bake; ä cot, cart; au̇ out; ch chin; e less; ē easy; g gift; i trip; ī life

circus sideshow **3** *slang* **:** a person who uses an illicit drug **4** *slang* **:** an ardent enthusiast — **freak·ish** \'frē-kish\ *adj* — **freak·ish·ly** *adv* — **freak·ish·ness** *n*

²freak *adj* **:** having the character of a freak ⟨involved in a *freak* accident⟩

freak–out \'frēk-,aut\ *n* **1 :** a withdrawal from reality esp. by means of drugs **2 :** a drug-induced state of mind characterized by nightmarish hallucinations **:** a bad trip — **freak out** \-'aut\ *vb*

¹freck·le \'frek-əl\ *n* [ME *freken, frekel,* of Scand origin] **:** a small brownish spot in the skin usu. due to precipitation of pigment on exposure to sunlight — **freck·ly** \'frek-(ə-)lē\ *adv*

²freckle *vb* **freck·led; freck·ling** \'frek-(ə-)liŋ\ **:** to mark or become marked with freckles or small spots

¹free \'frē\ *adj* **fre·er** \'frē-ər\; **fre·est** \'frē-əst\ [OE *frēo*] **1 a :** having liberty **:** not being a slave **b** (1) **:** not controlled by others **:** INDEPENDENT ⟨a *free* country⟩ (2) **:** not controlled or influenced by any power outside itself ⟨a *free* press⟩ **c :** not allowing slavery ⟨*free* state⟩ **2 :** not subject to a duty, tax, or other charge **3 :** released or not suffering from something unpleasant or painful ⟨*free* from worry⟩ **4 :** given without charge ⟨*free* ticket⟩ **5 :** made or done voluntarily ⟨a *free* offer⟩ **6 :** LAVISH ⟨a *free* spender⟩ **7 :** PLENTIFUL, COPIOUS ⟨a *free* supply⟩ **8 :** not held back by fear or distrust **:** OPEN, FRANK ⟨*free* expression of opinion⟩ **9 :** not restricted by or made in accordance with conventional forms **10 :** not literal or exact ⟨a *free* translation⟩ **11 a :** not obstructed **:** CLEAR ⟨a road *free* of ice⟩ **b :** not being used or occupied ⟨*free* time⟩ **c :** not fastened or bound **:** able to act, move, or turn ⟨*free* energy⟩ **12 :** performed under the rules without interference from the opponents ⟨a *free* kick⟩ **13 :** UNCOMBINED ⟨*free* oxygen⟩ **14 :** capable of being used meaningfully apart from another linguistic form ⟨the word *hats* is a *free* form⟩ — compare BOUND — **free·ly** *adv*
syn FREE, INDEPENDENT, SOVEREIGN mean not subject to the rule or control of another. FREE stresses the complete absence of external rule and the full right to make decisions ⟨*free* society of equals⟩ INDEPENDENT implies standing alone; applied to a state it implies that no other state has power to interfere with its citizens, laws, or policies; SOVEREIGN stresses supremacy within one's own domain or sphere and implies the absence of any superior power

²free *adv* **1 :** FREELY **2 :** without charge ⟨admitted *free*⟩

³free *vt* **freed; free·ing 1 :** to cause to be free **:** set free ⟨*free* a prisoner⟩ **2 :** RELIEVE, RID **3 :** DISENTANGLE, CLEAR
syn FREE, RELEASE, LIBERATE, DISCHARGE mean to set loose from restraint or constraint. FREE implies usu. permanent removal from whatever binds, entangles, or oppresses; RELEASE suggests a setting loose from confinement or from a state of pressure or tension; LIBERATE stresses the state resulting from freeing or releasing; DISCHARGE may imply removing from a lighter degree of restraint or constraint

free·board \'frē-,bōrd, -,bȯrd\ *n* **:** the vertical distance between the waterline and the deck of a ship

free·boo·ter \'frē-,büt-ər\ *n* [D *vrijbuiter,* fr. *vrijbuit* plunder, fr. *vrij* free + *buit* booty] **:** PLUNDERER, PIRATE

free·born \'frē-'bȯrn\ *adj* **1 :** not born in vassalage or slavery **2 :** relating to or befitting one that is freeborn

free city *n* **:** a self-governing city

freed·man \'frēd-mən\ *n* **1 :** a man freed from slavery

free·dom \'frēd-əm\ *n* **1 :** the quality or state of being free: as **a :** the absence of necessity, coercion, or constraint in choice or action **b :** liberation from slavery or restraint or from the power of another **:** INDEPENDENCE **c :** EXEMPTION, RELEASE **d :** EASE, FACILITY **e :** FRANKNESS, OUTSPOKENNESS **f :** unrestricted use **2 a :** a political right **b :** FRANCHISE, PRIVILEGE
syn LIBERTY, LICENSE: FREEDOM has a broad range of application from total absence of restraint to merely a sense of not being unduly hampered or frustrated; LIBERTY suggests release from former restraint or compulsion; LICENSE implies freedom specially granted or conceded and may connote an abuse of freedom

free enterprise *n* **:** freedom of private business to organize and operate for profit in competition with other businesses with a minimum of interference by the government; *also* **:** an economic system providing this freedom to business and freedom of choice of goods, services, and occupations to individuals

free–for–all \'frē-fər-,ȯl\ *n* **:** a competition, dispute, or fight open to all comers and usu. with no rules **:** BRAWL

free·hand \'frē-,hand\ *adj* **:** done without mechanical aids or devices **:** FREE ⟨*freehand* drawing⟩ — **freehand** *adv*

free·hand·ed \-'han-dəd\ *adj* **:** OPENHANDED, GENEROUS

free·hold \'frē-,hōld\ *n* **:** ownership of real estate for life usu. with the right of leaving it to one's heirs; *also* **:** an estate so owned — **free·hold·er** \-,hōl-dər\ *n*

free lance *n* **1 :** a knight whose services could be bought by any ruler or state **2 :** one who pursues a profession (as writing, art, or acting) on his own without being committed to work for one employer for a long period — **free–lance** *adj* — **free–lance** *vb* — **free–lanc·er** *n*

free–liv·ing \'frē-'liv-iŋ\ *adj* **1 :** marked by more than usual freedom in the gratification of appetites **2 :** being neither parasitic nor symbiotic

free·man \'frē-mən\ *n* **1 :** a person enjoying civil or political liberty **2 :** one having the full rights of a citizen

free·mar·tin \-,märt-°n\ *n* **:** a sexually imperfect usu. sterile female calf twinborn with a male

Free·ma·son \-'mās-°n\ *n* **:** a member of a secret fraternal society called Free and Accepted Masons

free·ma·son·ry \-rē\ *n* **1** *cap* **:** the principles, institutions, or practices of Freemasons — called also *Masonry* **2 :** natural or instinctive fellowship or sympathy

free on board *adv* (*or adj*) **:** without charge for delivery to and placing on board a means of transportation at a specified point

free·sia \'frē-zh(ē-)ə\ *n* [after F. H. T. *Freese* d1876 German physician] **:** any of a genus of sweet-scented African herbs with showy red, white, or yellow flowers

free silver *n* **:** the free coinage of silver often at a fixed ratio with gold

free soil *n* **:** U.S. territory where prior to the Civil War slavery was prohibited

free–soil *adj* **1 :** characterized by free soil **2** *cap F&S* **:** of, relating to, or constituting a minor U.S. political party prior to the Civil War opposing the extension of slavery into U.S. territories and the admission of slave states into the Union — **Free–Soil·er** \-,sȯi-lər\ *n*

free–spo·ken \'frē-'spō-kən\ *adj* **:** OUTSPOKEN

free·stand·ing \-'stan-diŋ\ *adj* **:** standing alone or on its own foundation free of architectural or supporting frame or attachment

free·stone \'frē-,stōn\ *n* **1 :** a stone that may be cut freely without splitting **2 a :** a fruit stone to which the flesh does not cling **b :** a fruit (as a peach or cherry) having such a stone

free·think·er \-'thiŋ-kər\ *n* **:** one who forms opinions on the basis of reason independently of authority; *esp* **:** one who doubts or denies religious dogma **syn** see ATHEIST — **free·think·ing** \-kiŋ\ *n or adj*

free throw *n* **:** an unhindered shot in basketball made from behind a set line and usu. awarded because of a foul by an opponent

free trade *n* **:** trade based upon the unrestricted international exchange of goods with tariffs used only as a source of revenue

free verse *n* **:** verse whose meter is irregular or whose rhythm is not metrical

free·way \'frē-,wā\ *n* **1 :** an expressway with fully controlled access **2 :** a toll-free highway

free·wheel \'frē-'hwēl\ *vi* **:** to move, live, or drift along freely or irresponsibly

free will *n* **:** the power asserted of moral beings of willing or choosing within limitations or with respect to some matters without restraint of physical or divine necessity or causal law

free·will \,frē-'wil\ *adj* **:** VOLUNTARY ⟨a *freewill* offering⟩

free world *n* **:** the part of the world where political democracy and capitalism or moderate socialism rather than totalitarian or Communist political and economic systems prevail

¹freeze \'frēz\ *vb* **froze** \'frōz\; **fro·zen** \'frōz-°n\; **freez·ing** [OE *frēosan*] **1 :** to harden into or be hardened into ice or a like solid by loss of heat ⟨the river *froze* over⟩ ⟨*freeze* cream⟩ ⟨*freeze* the molten metal⟩ **2 a :** to chill or become chilled with cold ⟨almost *froze* to death⟩ **b :** to become coldly formal in manner ⟨*froze* when introduced to him⟩ **c :** to act toward in a stiff and formal way **3 a :** to act on usu. destructively by frost ⟨*froze* the tomato plants⟩ **b** : to anesthetize by cold **4 a** : to adhere solidly by freezing **b** : to cause to grip tightly or remain in immovable contact ⟨fear *froze* the driver to the wheel⟩ **5** : to clog or become clogged with ice ⟨the water pipes *froze*⟩ **6** : to become fixed or motionless; *esp* : to become incapable of acting or speaking ⟨*froze* in his tracks⟩ **7 a** : to fix at a certain stage or level ⟨*freeze* rents to avoid inflation⟩ **b** : to halt by governmental regulation the expenditure, withdrawal, or exchange of foreign-owned assets

²freeze *n* **1** : a state of weather marked by low temperature **2 a** : an act or instance of freezing **b** : the state of being frozen

freeze–dry \'frēz-ˌdrī\ *vt* : to dry in a frozen state under high vacuum esp. for preservation

freez·er \'frē-zər\ *n* : one that freezes or keeps cool; *esp* : an insulated compartment or room for keeping food at a subfreezing temperature or for freezing perishable food rapidly

freezing point *n* : the temperature at which a liquid solidifies ⟨the *freezing point* of water is 0° C or 32° F⟩

F region *n* : the highest region of the atmosphere occurring from 90 to more than 250 miles above the earth

¹freight \'frāt\ *n* [MD or MLG *vracht, vrecht*] **1** : the amount paid (as to a railroad or a steamship company) for carrying goods **2** : goods or cargo carried by a ship, train, truck, or airplane; *also* : the carrying of goods from one place to another by such a vehicle ⟨ship the order by *freight*⟩ **3** : a train that carries freight

²freight *vt* **1 a** : to load with goods for transportation **b** : BURDEN, CHARGE **2** : to transport or ship by freight

freight·age \'frāt-ij\ *n* : FREIGHT

freight·er \'frāt-ər\ *n* **1** : one that loads or charters and loads a ship **2** : SHIPPER **3** : a ship or airplane used chiefly to carry freight

¹French \'french\ *adj* : of, relating to, or characteristic of France, its people, or their language — **French·man** \-mən\ *n* — **French·wom·an** \-ˌwùm-ən\ *n*

²French *n* **1** : a Romance language developing out of the Vulgar Latin of Transalpine Gaul and becoming the literary and official language of France **2 French** *pl* : the French people

French Canadian *n* : one of the descendants of French settlers in lower Canada — **French–Canadian** *adj*

French door *n* : a light door with glazed rectangular panels extending the full length; *also* : one of a pair of such doors in a single frame

¹french fry *vt, often cap 1st F* : to fry (as strips of potato) in deep fat until brown

²french fry *n, often cap 1st F* : a strip of potato fried in deep fat — usu. used in pl.

French horn *n* : a brass wind instrument consisting of a long curved conical tube with a narrow funnel-shaped mouthpiece at one end and a flaring bell at the other

French leave *n* : an informal, hasty, or secret departure

French telephone *n* : HANDSET

French window *n* **1** : a French door paired in an exterior wall **2** : a casement window

French horn

fre·net·ic \fri-'net-ik\ *adj* [MF *frenetique* insane, fr. L *phreneticus*, fr. Gk *phrenitis* inflammation of the brain, fr. *phrēn* mind] : FRENZIED, FRANTIC — **fre·net·i·cal·ly** \-'net-i-k(ə-)lē\ *adv*

fre·num \'frē-nəm\ *n, pl* **frenums** *or* **fre·na** \-nə\ [L, lit., bridle] : a fold of membrane (as beneath the tongue) that supports or restrains

fren·zied \'fren-zēd\ *adj* : marked by frenzy : wildly excited — **fren·zied·ly** *adv*

fren·zy \'fren-zē\ *n, pl* **frenzies** [MF *frenesie*, fr. L *phrensis*, fr. *phreneticus* insane, frantic] **1** : a temporary madness or violent agitation **2** : intense and usu. wild and often disorderly activity — **frenzy** *vt*

Fre·on \'frē-ˌän\ *trademark* — used for any of various nonflammable gaseous and liquid hydrocarbons used as refrigerants and as propellants for aerosols

fre·quence \'frē-kwən(t)s\ *n* : FREQUENCY

fre·quen·cy \'frē-kwən-sē\ *n, pl* **-cies** **1** : the fact or condition of occurring frequently **2** : rate of occurrence: as

a : the number of times that a periodic function repeats the same sequence of values during a unit variation of the independent variable **b** : the number of individuals in a single class when objects are classified according to variations in one or more specified qualities **3** : the number of repetitions of a periodic process in a unit of time: as **a** : the number of complete alternations per second of an alternating current ⟨a current having a *frequency* of 60 cycles per second⟩ **b** : the number of sound waves per second produced by a sounding body ⟨a sound having a *frequency* of 1500 cycles per second⟩ **c** : the number of complete oscillations per second of an electromagnetic wave ⟨the *frequency* of a radio wave⟩ ⟨the *frequency* of yellow light⟩

frequency distribution *n* : an arrangement of statistical data that exhibits the frequency of the occurrence of the values of a variable

frequency modulation *n* : modulation of the frequency of the carrier wave in accordance with the audio or video signal; *esp* : the system of broadcasting using this method of modulation — abbr. *FM*

¹fre·quent \'frē-kwənt\ *adj* [L *frequent-, frequens* crowded, frequent] **1** : happening often or at short intervals ⟨made *frequent* trips to town⟩ **2** : HABITUAL, CONSTANT ⟨a *frequent* visitor⟩ — **fre·quent·ly** *adv* — **fre·quent·ness** *n*

²fre·quent \frē-'kwent, 'frē-kwənt\ *vt* : to visit often : associate with, be in, or resort to habitually ⟨*frequented* a café in the neighborhood⟩ — **fre·quent·er** *n*

¹fre·quen·ta·tive \frē-'kwent-ət-iv\ *adj* : denoting repeated or recurrent action ⟨*frequentative* verb⟩

²frequentative *n* : a frequentative verb or verb form

fres·co \'fres-ˌkō\ *n, pl* **frescoes** *or* **frescos** [It, fr. *fresco* fresh, of Gmc origin] **1** : the art of painting on freshly spread moist lime plaster with pigments suspended in a water vehicle **2** : a painting executed in fresco — **fresco** *vt*

¹fresh \'fresh\ *adj* [OF *freis*, of Gmc origin] **1 a** : not salt ⟨*fresh* water⟩ **b** : PURE, INVIGORATING ⟨*fresh* air⟩ **c** : fairly strong : BRISK ⟨*fresh* breeze⟩ **2 a** : not altered by processing (as freezing, canning, or pickling) ⟨*fresh* vegetables⟩ **b** : having its original qualities unimpaired: as (1) : full of or renewed in vigor : REFRESHED (2) : not stale, sour, or decayed ⟨*fresh* bread⟩ (3) : not faded (4) : not worn or rumpled **3 a** (1) : experienced, made, or received newly or anew (2) : ADDITIONAL, ANOTHER ⟨make a *fresh* start⟩ **b** : ORIGINAL, VIVID **c** : INEXPERIENCED, RAW **d** : newly or just come or arrived ⟨*fresh* from school⟩ **4** : disposed to take liberties : IMPUDENT **syn** see NEW — **fresh·ly** *adv* — **fresh·ness** *n*

²fresh *adv* : just recently : FRESHLY ⟨a *fresh* laid egg⟩

fresh·en \'fresh-ən\ *vb* **fresh·ened; fresh·en·ing** \'fresh-(ə-)niŋ\ **1** : to make or become fresh: as **a** : to become brisk or strong ⟨the wind *freshened*⟩ **b** : to make or become fresh in appearance or vitality ⟨*freshen* up with a shower⟩ **c** : to lose saltiness **2** : to come into milk ⟨when the cow *freshens*⟩ — **fresh·en·er** \-(ə-)nər\ *n*

fresh·et \'fresh-ət\ *n* [fr. *fresh* increased flow, freshet] : a great rise or overflowing of a stream caused by heavy rains or melted snow

fresh·man \'fresh-mən\ *n* **1** : NOVICE, NEWCOMER **2** : a student in his first year or having chiefly first-year standing (as in a college)

fresh·wa·ter \ˌfresh-ˌwòt-ər, -ˌwät-\ *adj* **1** : of, relating to, or living in fresh water **2** : accustomed to navigating only in fresh waters; *also* : UNSKILLED

¹fret \'fret\ *vb* **fret·ted; fret·ting** [OE *fretan* to devour] **1** : to suffer or cause to suffer emotional strain : become irritated : WORRY, VEX ⟨*fretted* over petty problems⟩ **2 a** : to eat into or wear away : CORRODE ⟨rock *fretted* by rainwater⟩ **b** : FRAY **c** : to cause by wearing away ⟨the stream *fretted* a channel⟩ **3** : to affect something as if by gnawing or biting : GRATE ⟨the voice *frets* at his nerves⟩ **4** : AGITATE, RIPPLE

²fret *n* : an irritated or worried state ⟨be in a *fret*⟩

³fret *vt* **fret·ted; fret·ting** : to decorate with interlaced designs

⁴fret *n* [MF *frete* interlaced design] : ornamental work often in relief consisting of small straight bars intersecting one another in right or oblique angles

⁵fret *n* : one of a series of ridges fixed across the fingerboard of a stringed musical instrument — **fret·ted** \'fret-əd\ *adj*

frets

fret·ful \'fret-fəl\ *adj* **1** : disposed to fret : IRRITABLE **2 a** : TROUBLED ⟨*fretful* waters⟩ **b** : GUSTY ⟨a *fretful* wind⟩ — **fret·ful·ly** \-fə-lē\ *adv* — **fret·ful·ness** *n*

fret·saw \'fret-,sò\ *n* : a narrow-bladed fine-toothed saw for cutting curved outlines

fret·work \-,wərk\ *n* **1** : decoration consisting of work adorned with frets **2** : ornamental openwork or work in relief

Freud·ian \'fróid-ē-ən\ *adj* : of, relating to, or according with the psychoanalytic theories or practices of Freud — **Freudian** *n* — **Freud·ian·ism** \-ē-ə,niz-əm\ *n*

fri·a·ble \'frī-ə-bəl\ *adj* [L *friabilis,* fr. *friare* to crumble] : easily crumbled or pulverized **syn** see BRITTLE — **fri·a·bil·i·ty** \,frī-ə-'bil-ət-ē\ *n* — **fri·a·ble·ness** \'frī-ə-bəl-nəs\ *n*

fri·ar \'frī(-ə)r\ *n* [ME *frere,* fr. OF, lit., brother, fr. L *frater*] : a member of one of several Roman Catholic religious orders for men in which monastic life is combined with preaching and other priestly duties — compare MONK

fri·ary \'frī-(ə-)rē\ *n, pl* **-ar·ies** : a monastery of friars

¹fric·as·see \'frik-ə-,sē\ *n* [MF] : a dish of meat (as chicken or veal) cut into pieces and stewed in a gravy

²fricassee *vt* **-seed; -see·ing** : to cook as a fricassee

¹fric·a·tive \'frik-ət-iv\ *adj* [L *fricare* to rub] : characterized by frictional passage of the expired breath against a narrowing at some point in the mouth or throat ⟨\f v th th s z sh zh h\ are *fricative*⟩

²fricative *n* : a fricative consonant

fric·tion \'frik-shən\ *n* [L *frict-, fricare* to rub] **1 a** : the rubbing of one body against another **b** : resistance to motion between two bodies in contact ⟨the *friction* of a box sliding along the floor⟩⟨the *friction* between a moving rocket and the air⟩ ⟨lubrication reduces the *friction* of an axle in its support⟩ **2** : the clashing between two persons or parties of opposed views : DISAGREEMENT — **fric·tion·less** \-ləs\ *adj*

fric·tion·al \'frik-shnəl, -shən-°l\ *adj* **1** : of or relating to friction **2** : moved or produced by friction — **fric·tion·al·ly** \-ē\ *adv*

friction tape *n* : a usu. cloth tape impregnated with insulating material and an adhesive and used esp. to protect and insulate electrical conductors

Fri·day \'frīd-ē\ *n* [OE *frīgedæg,* trans. of L *Veneris dies* day of Venus] : the 6th day of the week

fried-cake \'frīd-,kāk\ *n* : DOUGHNUT, CRULLER

friend \'frend\ *n* [OE *frēond*] **1 a** : one attached to another by affection or esteem **b** : ACQUAINTANCE **2** : one who is not hostile ⟨are you *friend* or foe⟩ **3** : one who supports or favors something ⟨a *friend* of liberal education⟩ **4** *cap* : a member of a Christian group that stresses Inner Light, rejects ostentation, outward rites, and an ordained ministry, and opposes war — called also *Quaker* — **friend·less** \'fren-dləs\ *adj* — **friend·less·ness** *n*

friend·ly \'fren-(d)lē\ *adj* **friend·li·er; -est** : of, relating to, or befitting a friend: as **a** : showing kindly interest and goodwill ⟨a *friendly* gesture⟩ **b** : not hostile ⟨*friendly* Indians⟩ **c** : serving a beneficial or helpful purpose : FAVORABLE ⟨a *friendly* breeze⟩ **d** : COMFORTING, CHEERFUL ⟨the *friendly* glow of the fire⟩ — **friend·li·ness** *n*

friend·ship \'fren(d)-,ship\ *n* **1** : the state of being friends **2** : FRIENDLINESS

fri·er *var of* FRYER

¹frieze \'frēz, frē-'zā\ *n* [MF *frise,* fr. MD *vriese*] : a woolen cloth with a shaggy surface

²frieze \'frēz\ *n* [MF *frise*] **1** : the part of an entablature between the architrave and the cornice — see ORDER illustration **2** : a sculptured or richly ornamented band (as around a building)

frig·ate \'frig-ət\ *n* [MF, fr. It *fregata*] **1** : a square-rigged warship intermediate between a corvette and a ship of the line **2** : a British or Canadian escort ship between a corvette and a destroyer in size **3** : a U.S. warship smaller than a cruiser and larger than a destroyer

frigate bird *n* : any of several strong-winged seabirds noted for their greedy ways

¹fright \'frīt\ *n* [OE *fyrhto, fryhto*] **1** : fear caused by sudden danger : sudden terror : ALARM ⟨cry out in *fright*⟩ **2** : something that frightens **3** : something that is ugly or shocking ⟨his beard was a *fright*⟩ **syn** see FEAR

²fright *vt* : to alarm suddenly : FRIGHTEN

fright·en \'frīt-°n\ *vb* **fright·ened; fright·en·ing** \'frīt-niŋ, -°n-iŋ\ **1** : to make afraid : TERRIFY **2** : to drive away or out by frightening **3** : to become frightened — **fright·en·ing·ly** \-niŋ-lē, -°n-iŋ-lē\ *adv*

fright·ful \'frīt-fəl\ *adj* **1** : causing fear or alarm : TERRIFYING **2** : causing shock or horror : STARTLING **3** : EXTREME ⟨*frightful* thirst⟩ — **fright·ful·ly** \-fə-lē\ *adv* — **fright·ful·ness** *n*

frig·id \'frij-əd\ *adj* [L *frigidus,* fr. *frigēre* to be cold] **1** : intensely cold **2** : lacking warmth or ardor : INDIFFERENT — **fri·gid·i·ty** \frij-'id-ət-ē\ *n* — **frig·id·ly** \'frij-əd-lē\ *adv* — **frig·id·ness** *n*

Frig·i·daire \,frij-ə-'da(ə)r, -'de(ə)r\ *trademark* — used for a mechanical refrigerator

frigid zone *n* : the area or region between the arctic circle and the north pole or between the antarctic circle and the south pole — see ZONE illustration

fri·jol \frē-'hōl\ *also* **fri·jo·le** \-'hō-lē\ *n, pl* **fri·jo·les** \-'hō-lēz\ [Sp *frijol*] *chiefly Southwest* : BEAN 1b

¹frill \'fril\ *vt* : to provide or decorate with a frill

²frill *n* **1** : a gathered, pleated, or ruffled edging (as of lace) **2** : an addition that is merely ornamental : something unessential **3** : a ruff of hair or feathers about the neck of an animal — **frilly** \'fril-ē\ *adj*

¹fringe \'frinj\ *n* [MF *frenge,* fr. L *fimbriae* (pl.) fibers, fringe] **1** : an ornamental border consisting of short straight or twisted threads or strips hanging from cut or raveled edges or from a separate band **2** : something resembling a fringe : BORDER **3 a** : something on the margin of an activity, process, or subject matter **b** : a group with marginal or extremist views

²fringe *vt* **1** : to furnish or adorn with a fringe **2** : to serve as a fringe for : BORDER

fringe area *n* : a region in which reception from a broadcasting station is weak or subject to serious distortion

fringe benefit *n* : an employment benefit paid for by an employer without affecting basic wage rates

frip·pery \'frip-(ə-)rē\ *n, pl* **-per·ies** [MF *friperie* cast-off clothes] **1** : cheap showy finery **2** : affected elegance : pretentious display — **frippery** *adj*

Fri·sian \'frizh-ən, 'frē-zhən\ *n* **1** : a member of a people that inhabit principally the Netherlands province of Friesland and the Frisian islands in the North sea **2** : the Germanic language of the Frisian people — **Frisian** *adj*

frisk \'frisk\ *vb* [obs. *frisk* lively, fr. MF *frisque*] **1** : to leap, skip, or dance in a lively or playful way : GAMBOL **2** : to search (a person) rapidly esp. for concealed weapons by running the hand over the clothing — **frisk·er** *n*

frisky \'fris-kē\ *adj* **frisk·i·er; -est** : inclined to frisk : FROLICSOME — **frisk·i·ly** \-kə-lē\ *adv* — **frisk·i·ness** \-kē-nəs\ *n*

frit·il·lar·ia \,frit-°l-'er-ē-ə, -'ar-\ *n* [NL, fr. L *fritillus* dice cup; so called fr. its spotted markings] : any of a genus of bulbous herbs of the lily family with mottled or checkered flowers

frit·il·lary \'frit-°l-,er-ē\ *n, pl* **-laries 1** : FRITILLARIA **2** : any of numerous spotted butterflies

¹frit·ter \'frit-ər\ *n* [MF *friture,* fr. L *frict-, frigere* to fry] : a small quantity of fried or sautéed batter often containing fruit or meat

²fritter *vb* [*fritter,* n., fragment] **1** : to reduce or waste piecemeal ⟨*frittering* away his time on trifles⟩ **2** : to break into small fragments **3** : DISSIPATE, DWINDLE — **frit·ter·er** \-ər-ər\ *n*

fri·vol·i·ty \friv-'äl-ət-ē\ *n, pl* **-ties 1** : the quality or state of being frivolous **2** : a frivolous act or thing

friv·o·lous \'friv-(ə-)ləs\ *adj* [L *frivolus*] **1** : of little importance : TRIVIAL **2** : lacking in seriousness : PLAYFUL ⟨a *frivolous* attitude⟩ — **friv·o·lous·ly** *adv* — **friv·o·lous·ness** *n*

¹frizz \'friz\ *vb* : to curl in small tight curls

²frizz *n* **1** : a tight curl or hair that is tightly curled — **frizzy** \'friz-ē\ *adj*

¹friz·zle \'friz-əl\ *vb* **friz·zled; friz·zling** \'friz-(ə-)liŋ\ : FRIZZ, CURL — **frizzle** *n* — **friz·zly** \-(ə-)lē\ *adj*

²frizzle *vb* **1** : to fry until crisp and curled **2** : to cook with a sizzling noise

fro \'frō\ *adv* [ME, fr. *fra, fro* from, fr. ON *frā;* akin to E *from*] : BACK, AWAY — used in the phrase *to and fro*

frock \'fräk\ *n* [MF *froc,* a monk's garment, of Gmc origin] **1** : a friar's habit **2 a** : an outer garment worn by men; *esp* : a loose shirt of coarse linen or cotton formerly worn by workmen **b** : a woolen jersey worn esp. by sailors **3** : a woman's or child's dress

frock coat *n* : a man's usu. double-breasted coat with knee-length skirts

frog \'frȯg, 'fräg\ *n* [OE *frogga*]
1 a : any of various smooth-skinned web-footed largely aquatic tailless agile leaping amphibians — compare TOAD **b** : a condition in the throat that produces hoarseness ⟨had a *frog* in his throat⟩ **2** : the triangular elastic horny pad on the sole of the hoof of a horse **3** : an ornamental braiding for fastening the front of a garment by a loop through which a button passes **4** : a device permitting the wheels on one rail of a track to cross an intersecting rail

frog

frog·man \-,man, -mən\ *n* : a swimmer having equipment (as oxygen helmet and flippers) that permits an extended stay under water usu. for observation or demolition; *esp* : a member of a military unit so equipped

frog spit *n* : CUCKOO SPIT 1 — called also *frog spittle*

¹frol·ic \'fräl-ik\ *vi* **frol·icked; frol·ick·ing** [*frolic*, adj., merry, fr. D *vroolijk*, fr. MD *vro* happy] **1** : to make merry **2** : to play about happily : ROMP ⟨children *frolicking* on the beach⟩

²frolic *n* **1** : a playful mischievous action **2** : FUN, MERRIMENT

frol·ic·some \'fräl-ik-səm\ *adj* : full of gaiety : SPORTIVE

from \(')frəm, 'främ\ *prep* [OE *fram, from*; akin to E *fore*]
1 — used as a function word to indicate a starting point: as (1) a place where a physical movement begins ⟨came here *from* the city⟩ (2) a starting point in a statement of limits ⟨cost *from* $5 to $10⟩ ⟨an avid reader *from* childhood⟩ **2** — used as a function word to indicate separation: as (1) physical separation ⟨a child taken *from* its mother⟩ (2) an act or condition of removal, abstention, exclusion, release, or differentiation ⟨refrain *from* interrupting⟩ ⟨far *from* safe⟩ **3** — used as a function word to indicate the source, cause, agent, or basis ⟨reading aloud *from* a book⟩ ⟨suffering *from* a cold⟩

frond \'fränd\ *n* [L *frond-, frons* foliage] : a leaf or leaflike part: as **a** : a palm leaf **b** : a fern leaf **c** : a leaflike thallus or shoot (as of a lichen) — **frond·ed** \'frän-dəd\ *adj* — **fron·dose** \-,dōs\ *adj*

¹front \'frənt\ *n* [L *front-, frons*] **1 a** : FOREHEAD; *also* : the whole face **b** : DEMEANOR, BEARING **c** : external often feigned appearance ⟨put up a good *front*⟩ **2 a** (1) : a region in which active warfare is taking place (2) : a sphere of active struggle or striving **b** : the lateral space occupied by a military unit ⟨advanced on a 4-mile *front*⟩ **3** : the side of a building containing the principal entrance **4 a** : the forward part or surface ⟨the *front* of a shirt⟩ **b** : FRONTAGE **c** : the boundary between two dissimilar air masses **5 a** : a position directly before or ahead of something else ⟨stood in the *front* of the room⟩ **b** — used as a call by a hotel desk clerk in summoning a bellboy **c** : a position of leadership or superiority ⟨at the *front* of his profession⟩ **6** : a person, group, or thing used to mask the identity or true character or activity of the actual controlling agent ⟨the candy store was a *front* for a bookie joint⟩ **7** : a political coalition of diverse parties or movements to achieve certain common objectives

²front *vb* **1** : FACE ⟨the cottage *fronts* on the lake⟩ ⟨the house *fronts* the street⟩ **2** : to serve as a front **3** : CONFRONT

³front *adj* **1** : of, relating to, or situated at the front **2** : pronounced with closure or narrowing at or toward the front of the oral passage ⟨the *front* vowels \i\ and \e\⟩ — **front** *adv*

front·age \'frənt-ij\ *n* **1 a** : the front face (as of a building) **b** : the direction in which something faces **2 a** : the front boundary line of a lot abutting on a street **b** : the length of such a line

front·al \'frənt-°l\ *adj* **1** : of, relating to, or adjacent to the forehead or the frontal bone **2 a** : of, relating to, or situated at the front **b** : directed against the front or at the main point or issue : DIRECT ⟨*frontal* assault⟩ — **fron·tal·ly** \-°l-ē\ *adv*

frontal bone *n* : either of a pair of bones forming the forehead

frontal lobe *n* : the anterior division of each cerebral hemisphere

fron·tier \,frən-'ti(ə)r, frän-\ *n* [MF *frontiere*, fr. *front* front] **1** : a border between two countries **2 a** : a region that forms the margin of settled territory in a country being populated **b** : the outer limits of knowledge or achievement ⟨the *frontiers* of science⟩ — **frontier** *adj*

fron·tiers·man \-'ti(ə)rz-mən\ *n* : a man living on the frontier

fron·tis·piece \'frənt-ə-,spēs\ *n* [LL *frontispicium* front of a building, fr. *front-, frons* front + *specere* to look] : an illustration preceding and usu. facing the title page of a book

front·let \'frənt-lət\ *n* **1** : a band worn on the forehead **2** : the forehead esp. of a bird when distinctively marked

front man *n* : a person serving as a front or figurehead

¹frost \'frȯst\ *n* [OE; akin to E *freeze*] **1 a** : the process of freezing **b** : the temperature that causes freezing **c** : a covering of minute ice crystals on a cold surface **2** : coldness of deportment or temperament : INDIFFERENCE

²frost *vb* **1 a** : to cover with or as if with frost; *esp* : to put icing on (as cake) **b** : to produce a fine-grained slightly roughened surface on (as glass) **2** : to injure or kill by frost : FREEZE

¹frost·bite \'frȯs(t)-,bīt\ *vt* : to blight or nip with frost

²frostbite *n* : the freezing or the local effect of a partial freezing of some part of the body

frost·ed \'frȯ-stəd\ *adj* **1** : covered with frost or with something resembling frost ⟨*frosted* glass⟩ **2** : ornamented with frosting ⟨a *frosted* cake⟩ **3** : QUICK-FROZEN ⟨*frosted* foods⟩

frost heave *n* : an upthrust of ground or pavement caused by freezing of moist soil — called also *frost heaving*

frost·ing \'frȯ-stiŋ\ *n* **1** : ICING **2** : dull finish on metal or glass

frosty \'frȯ-stē\ *adj* **frost·i·er; -est** **1** : attended with or producing frost : FREEZING **2** : covered or appearing as if covered with frost : HOARY **3** : marked by coolness or extreme reserve in manner — **frost·i·ly** \-stə-lē\ *adv* — **frost·i·ness** \-stē-nəs\ *n*

¹froth \'frȯth\ *n* [ON *frotha*] **1 a** : bubbles formed in or on a liquid by fermentation or agitation **b** : a foamy slaver sometimes accompanying disease or exhaustion **2** : something light or frivolous and of little value *syn* see FOAM

²froth \'frȯth, 'frȯth\ *vb* **1** : to cause to foam **2** : to cover with froth **3** : to produce or throw up froth

frothy \'frȯ-thē, -_the_\ *adj* **froth·i·er; -est** **1** : full of or consisting of froth **2** : gaily frivolous or light ⟨*frothy* music⟩ — **froth·i·ly** \-thə-lē, -thə-\ *adv* — **froth·i·ness** \-thē-nəs, -_the_-\ *n*

frou-frou \'frü-,frü\ *n* [F] **1** : a rustling esp. of a woman's skirts **2** : frilly ornamentation esp. in women's clothing

fro·ward \'frō-(w)ərd\ *adj* [ME, turned away, froward, fr. *fro* + *-ward*] : habitually disposed to disobedience and opposition — **fro·ward·ly** *adv* — **fro·ward·ness** *n*

frown \'fraun\ *vb* [MF *froigner* to snort, frown] **1** : to wrinkle the forehead (as in anger, displeasure, or thought) : put on a stern look **2** : to look with disapproval ⟨*frowns* on rudeness⟩ **3** : to express with a frown ⟨*frowned* her disapproval⟩ — **frown** *n* — **frown·er** *n* — **frown·ing·ly** \'frau-niŋ-lē\ *adv*

frow·zy *or* **frow·sy** \'frau-zē\ *adj* **frow·zi·er** *or* **frow·si·er; -est** : having a slovenly or uncared-for appearance

froze *past of* FREEZE

fro·zen \'frōz-°n\ *adj* **1 a** : affected or crusted over by freezing **b** : subject to long and severe cold ⟨the *frozen* north⟩ **c** : CHILLED, REFRIGERATED ⟨*frozen* pies⟩ **2 a** : expressing or characterized by cold unfriendliness ⟨a *frozen* stare⟩ **b** : incapable of being changed, moved, or undone : FIXED ⟨wages were *frozen*⟩ **c** : not available for present use ⟨*frozen* capital⟩ — **fro·zen·ly** *adv* — **fro·zen·ness** \-°n-(n)əs\ *n*

frozen food *n* : food that has been subjected to rapid freezing and is kept frozen until used

fruc·ti·fi·ca·tion \,frək-tə-fə-'kā-shən, ,frük-\ *n* **1** : the forming or producing of fruit **2** : FRUIT 1c

fruc·ti·fy \'frək-tə-,fī, 'frük-\ *vb* **-fied; -fy·ing** [L *fructus* fruit] **1** : to bear fruit **2** : to make fruitful or productive

fruc·tose \-,tōs\ *n* [L *fructus* fruit] : a very sweet soluble sugar $C_6H_{12}O_6$ that occurs esp. in fruit juices and honey

fru·gal \'frü-gəl\ adj [L frugi virtuous, frugal, fr. dat. of frug-, frux value, fruit] : characterized by or reflecting economy in the expenditure of resources — **fru·gal·i·ty** \frü-'gal-ət-ē\ n — **fru·gal·ly** \'frü-gə-lē\ adv

¹**fruit** \'früt\ n [OF, fr. L fructus use, benefit, fruit, fr. fruct-, frui to enjoy] **1 a** : a usu. useful product of plant growth ⟨fruits of the earth⟩ **b** : the usu. edible reproductive body of a seed plant; esp : one (as a strawberry) having a sweet pulp **c** : a product of fertilization in a plant with its envelopes or appendages; esp : the ripened ovary of a seed plant and its contents **2** : CONSEQUENCE, RESULT — **fruit·ed** \-əd\ adj

²**fruit** vb : to bear or cause to bear fruit

fruit·age \'früt-ij\ n **1** : the condition or process of bearing fruit **2** : FRUIT

fruit bat n : any of numerous large Old World fruit-eating bats of warm regions

fruit·cake \'früt-ˌkāk\ n : a rich cake containing nuts, dried or candied fruits, and spices

fruit·er·er \'früt-ər-ər\ n : one that deals in fruit

fruit fly n : any of various small two-winged flies whose larvae feed on fruit or decaying vegetable matter

fruit·ful \'früt-fəl\ adj **1** : yielding or producing fruit **2** : abundantly productive : bringing results **syn** see FERTILE — **fruit·ful·ly** \-fə-lē\ adv — **fruit·ful·ness** n

fruiting body n : a plant organ specialized for producing spores

fru·i·tion \frü-'ish-ən\ n [LL fruit-, frui, alter. of L fruct-, frui to enjoy] **1** : pleasurable use or possession : ENJOYMENT **2 a** : the state of bearing fruit **b** : REALIZATION, ACCOMPLISHMENT

fruit·less \'früt-ləs\ adj **1** : lacking or not bearing fruit **2** : productive of no good effect : UNSUCCESSFUL ⟨a fruitless attempt⟩ — **fruit·less·ly** adv — **fruit·less·ness** n

fruit sugar n : FRUCTOSE

fruity \'früt-ē\ adj **fruit·i·er**; -**est** : relating to or suggesting fruit ⟨a fruity odor⟩

frus·trate \'frəs-ˌtrāt\ vt [L frustrare, fr. frustra in vain] **1** : to prevent from carrying out a purpose : DEFEAT, BLOCK **2** : to bring to nothing : NULLIFY — **frus·tra·tion** \(ˌ)frəs-'trā-shən\ n

syn THWART, BAFFLE: FRUSTRATE implies making even the best or most persistent efforts vain and ineffectual; THWART implies frustrating or checking esp. by deliberately crossing or opposing; BAFFLE implies frustrating by confusing or puzzling

frus·tum \'frəs-təm\ n, pl **frustums** or **frus·ta** \-tə\ [L, piece, bit] : the part of a cone or pyramid formed by cutting off the top by a plane parallel to the base

fru·tes·cence \frü-'tes-°n(t)s\ n : shrubby habit of growth — **fru·tes·cent** \-°nt\ adj

fru·ti·cose \'früt-i-ˌkōs\ adj [L fruticosus, fr. frutic-, frutex shrub] : occurring in the form of or resembling a shrub : SHRUBBY

¹**fry** \'frī\ vb **fried**; **fry·ing** [OF frire, fr. L frigere] **1** : to cook in a pan or on a griddle over a fire esp. with the use of fat **2** : to undergo frying

²**fry** n, pl **fries 1** : a dish of something fried **2** : a social gathering where fried food is eaten

³**fry** n, pl **fry** [ME] **1 a** : recently hatched fishes **b** : the young of other animals **2** : very small adult fishes **3** : members of a group or class : PERSONS ⟨small fry⟩

fry·er \'frī(-ə)r\ n : something intended for or used in frying: as **a** : a young chicken **b** : a deep utensil for frying foods

f-stop \'ef-ˌstäp\ n : a camera lens aperture setting indicated by an f= number

fuch·sia \'fyü-shə\ n [after Leonhard Fuchs d1566 German botanist] **1** : any of a genus of shrubs of the evening-primrose family widely grown for their showy nodding flowers usu. in deep pinks, reds, and purples **2** : a vivid reddish purple

fuch·sine or **fuch·sin** \'fyük-sən, -ˌsēn\ n : a synthetic dye that yields a brilliant bluish red

fu·cus \'fyü-kəs\ n [L, a lichen, fr. Gk phykos seaweed, a lichen] : any of various brown algae common along rocky shores — called also rockweed — **fu·coid** \-ˌkȯid\ adj or n

fuchsia

fud·dle \'fəd-°l\ vt **fud·dled**; **fud·dling** \'fəd-liŋ, -°l-iŋ\ : to make confused : MUDDLE

fud·dy-dud·dy \'fəd-ē-ˌdəd-ē\ n, pl -**dies** : one who is old-fashioned, pompous, unimaginative, or concerned about trifles

¹**fudge** \'fəj\ vb **1** : to act dishonestly **2** : to avoid commitment : HEDGE **3 a** : to devise as a substitute : FAKE **b** : FALSIFY

²**fudge** n **1** : foolish nonsense **2** : a soft creamy candy of sugar, milk, butter, and flavoring

¹**fu·el** \'fyü-əl\ n [OF fouaille, fr. feu fire, fr. LL focus, fr. L, hearth] **1 a** : a material used to produce heat or power by burning **b** : a material from which atomic energy can be liberated esp. in a reactor **2** : a source of sustenance or incentive

²**fuel** vb -**eled** or -**elled**; -**el·ing** or -**el·ling 1** : to provide with or take in fuel **2** : SUPPORT, STIMULATE

fuel cell n : a cell that continuously changes the chemical energy of a fuel and oxidant to electrical energy

fuel oil n : an oil that is used for fuel and that usu. ignites at a higher temperature than kerosene

fu·ga·cious \fyü-'gā-shəs\ adj [L fugac-, fugax, fr. fugere to flee] : lasting but a short time

¹**fu·gi·tive** \'fyü-jət-iv\ adj [L fugitivus, fr. fugere to flee] **1** : running away or trying to escape ⟨a fugitive slave⟩ **2** : likely to vanish suddenly : not fixed or lasting ⟨fugitive thoughts⟩ — **fu·gi·tive·ly** adv — **fu·gi·tive·ness** n

²**fugitive** n **1** : one who flees or tries to escape **2** : something elusive or hard to find

fugue \'fyüg\ n [L fuga flight, fr. fugere to flee] : a musical composition in which one or two themes are imitated by successively entering voices and contrapuntally developed — **fu·gal** \'fyü-gəl\ adj

füh·rer or **fueh·rer** \'fyur-ər, 'fir-\ n [G] : LEADER 2c — used chiefly of the leader of the German Nazis

¹-**ful** \fəl\ adj suffix, sometimes -**ful·er**; sometimes -**fullest 1** : full of ⟨eventful⟩ **2** : characterized by ⟨peaceful⟩ **3** : having the qualities of ⟨masterful⟩ **4** : -ABLE ⟨mournful⟩

²-**ful** \ˌful\ n suffix : number or quantity that fills or would fill ⟨roomful⟩

ful·crum \'ful-krəm, 'fəl-\ n, pl **fulcrums** or **ful·cra** \-krə\ [LL, support, fr. L, bedpost, fr. fulcire to prop] : the support about which a lever turns

F fulcrum, L lever

ful·fill or **ful·fil** \ful-'fil\ vt **ful·filled**; **ful·fill·ing** [OE fullfyllan, fr. full + fyllan to fill] **1** : to put into effect ⟨fulfill a promise⟩ **2** : to bring to an end **3** : to measure up to : SATISFY ⟨fulfill requirements⟩ — **ful·fill·er** n — **ful·fill·ment** \-mənt\ n

ful·gent \'ful-jənt, 'fəl-\ adj [L fulgēre to shine] : dazzingly bright — **ful·gent·ly** adv

fu·lig·i·nous \fyü-'lij-ə-nəs\ adj [LL fuliginosus, fr. L fuligin-, fuligo soot] : having a dark or dusky color — **fu·lig·i·nous·ly** adv

¹**full** \'ful\ adj [OE] **1** : containing as much or as many as is possible or normal ⟨a bin full of corn⟩ **2 a** : complete as to number, amount, or duration ⟨his full share⟩ **b** : having all the distinguishing characteristics ⟨a full member⟩ **c** : being at the highest degree : MAXIMUM ⟨full strength⟩ **3 a** : plump and rounded in outline ⟨a full figure⟩ **b** : having an abundance of material ⟨a full skirt⟩ **4 a** : possessing or containing an abundance ⟨a full life⟩ **b** : rich in detail ⟨a full report⟩ **5** : satisfied esp. with food or drink **6** : having both parents in common ⟨full sisters⟩ **7** : having volume or depth of sound ⟨full tones⟩ **8** : completely occupied esp. with a thought or plan ⟨full of his own concerns⟩ — **full·ness** also **ful·ness** n

²**full** adv **1 a** : VERY, EXTREMELY **b** : ENTIRELY **2 a** : EXACTLY **b** : STRAIGHT, SQUARELY ⟨the blow hit him full in the face⟩

³**full** n **1 a** : the utmost extent ⟨enjoy to the full⟩ **b** : the highest or fullest state or degree **2** : the requisite or complete amount

⁴**full** vt [MF fouler, fr. L fullo fuller] : to shrink and thicken ⟨woolen cloth⟩ by moistening, heating, and pressing

full·back \'ful-ˌbak\ n : an offensive football back who usu. lines up between the halfbacks

full-blood·ed \'ful-'bləd-əd\ adj : of unmixed ancestry : PUREBRED — **full-blood·ed·ness** n

full-blown \-'blōn\ *adj* **1** : being at the height of bloom **2** : fully mature or developed

full-bod·ied \-'bäd-ēd\ *adj* : marked by richness and fullness

full dress *n* : the style of dress prescribed for ceremonial or formal social occasions — **full–dress** *adj*

full·er \'fül-ər\ *n* : a person whose occupation is fulling cloth

fuller's earth *n* : a clayish earthy substance used in fulling cloth, as a filter medium, and as a catalyst

full-fledged \'fül-'flejd\ *adj* **1** : fully developed : MATURE **2** : having full plumage

full house *n* : a poker hand containing three of a kind and a pair

full moon *n* : the moon with its whole apparent disk illuminated

full-scale \'fül-'skāl\ *adj* **1** : identical to an original in proportion and size ⟨*full-scale* drawing⟩ **2** : involving full use of available resources ⟨a *full-scale* biography⟩

full tilt *adv* : at high speed

full time *n* : the standard working time for a given job or period — **full–time** *adj*

ful·ly \'fül-(l)ē\ *adv* **1** : in a full manner or degree : COMPLETELY **2** : at least ⟨*fully* nine tenths of us⟩

ful·mar \'fül-mər, -,mär\ *n* [of Scand origin] : an Arctic seabird closely related to the petrels

ful·mi·nate \'fül-mə-,nāt, 'fəl-\ *vb* [ML *fulminare*, fr. L, to flash with lightning, strike with lightning, fr. *fulmin-, fulmen* lightning, fr. *fulgēre* to shine] **1** : to utter or send out censure or invective : condemn scathingly **2** : to make a sudden loud noise : EXPLODE — **ful·mi·na·tion** \,fül-mə-'nā-shən, ,fəl-\ *n* — **ful·mi·na·tor** \-,nāt-ər\ *n*

ful·mi·nate of mercury \,fül-mə-,nāt-, ,fəl-\ : MERCURY FULMINATE

ful·some \'fül-səm\ *adj* [ME, copious, cloying, fr. *full*] : offensive esp. from insincerity or baseness of motive ⟨*fulsome* praise⟩ — **ful·some·ly** *adv* — **ful·some·ness** *n*

ful·vous \'fül-vəs, 'fəl-\ *adj* [L *fulvus*] : of a dull brownish yellow : TAWNY

fu·ma·role \'fyü-mə-,rōl\ *n* : a hole in a volcanic region from which hot gases and vapors issue

¹fum·ble \'fəm-bəl\ *vb* **fum·bled; fum·bling** \-b(ə-)liŋ\ **1** : to feel or grope about clumsily ⟨*fumbled* in his pocket for a key⟩ **2** : to handle or manage something clumsily : to fail to grasp firmly; *esp* : to fail to hold, catch, or handle the ball properly in a game (as baseball or football) — **fum·bler** \-b(ə-)lər\ *n*

²fumble *n* **1** : an act or instance of fumbling **2** : a fumbled ball

¹fume \'fyüm\ *n* [L *fumus* smoke] **1** : a usu. irritating or offensive smoke, vapor, or gas — usu. used in pl. ⟨motorcar *fumes*⟩ ⟨acid *fumes*⟩ ⟨*fumes* of burning sulfur⟩ **2** : a state of excited irritation or anger — **fumy** \'fyü-mē\ *adj*

²fume *vb* **1** : to expose to or treat with fumes **2** : to give off fumes **3** : to show bad temper : express annoyance or irritation

fu·mi·gant \'fyü-mi-gənt\ *n* : a substance used for fumigation

fu·mi·gate \'fyü-mə-,gāt\ *vt* : to apply smoke, vapor, or gas to esp. for the purpose of disinfecting or of destroying pests — **fu·mi·ga·tion** \,fyü-mə-'gā-shən\ *n* — **fu·mi·ga·tor** \'fyü-mə-,gāt-ər\ *n*

fu·mi·to·ry \'fyü-mə-,tōr-ē, -,tȯr-\ *n, pl* **-ries** : any of a genus of erect or climbing herbs with showy irregular flowers

¹fun \'fən\ *n* [E dial. *fun* to hoax] **1** : something that provides amusement or enjoyment; *esp* : playful boisterous action or speech **2** : AMUSEMENT, ENJOYMENT

²fun *vi* **funned; fun·ning** : to indulge in banter or play : JOKE

¹func·tion \'fəŋ(k)-shən\ *n* [L *function-, functio* performance, fr. *funct-, fungi* to perform] **1** : professional position or duties : OCCUPATION **2** : the action for which a person or thing is specially fitted or used or for which a thing exists **3** : an impressive, elaborate, or formal ceremony or social gathering **4** : one of a group of related actions contributing to a larger action; *esp* : the normal and specific contribution of a bodily part to the economy of a living organism **5 a** : a mathematical relationship between each element of one set and at least one element of the same or another set **b** : a quality, trait, or fact dependent on and varying with another — **func·tion·less** \-ləs\ *adj*

²function *vi* **func·tioned; func·tion·ing** \-sh(ə-)niŋ\ **1** : to have a function : SERVE ⟨an attributive noun *functions* as an adjective⟩ **2** : to be in action : OPERATE ⟨a government *functions* through numerous divisions⟩

func·tion·al \'fəŋ(k)-shnəl, -shən-°l\ *adj* **1 a** : of, connected with, or being a function **b** : affecting functions but not structure ⟨*functional* heart disease⟩ **2** : serving in a larger whole; *also* : designed or developed chiefly from the point of view of use ⟨*functional* architecture⟩ **3** : performing or able to perform a regular function **4** : organized by functions — **func·tion·al·ly** \-ē\ *adv*

func·tion·ary \'fəŋ(k)-shə-,ner-ē\ *n, pl* **-ar·ies** : a person charged with the performance of a certain function; *esp* : OFFICIAL

function word *n* : a word expressing primarily grammatical relationship

¹fund \'fənd\ *n* [L *fundus* bottom, piece of landed property] **1** : an available quantity of material or intangible resources : SUPPLY **2 a** : a sum of money or other resources the principal or interest of which is set apart for a specific objective **b** : available money — usu. used in pl. **3** : an organization administering a special fund

²fund *vt* : to convert (a short-term obligation) into a debt payable at a distant date or at no definite date and bearing a fixed interest ⟨*fund* a debt⟩

fun·da·ment \'fən-də-mənt\ *n* [L *fundamentum*, fr. *fundare* to found, fr. *fundus* bottom] **1** : FOUNDATION, BASE **2 a** : BUTTOCKS **b** : ANUS

¹fun·da·men·tal \,fən-də-'ment-°l\ *adj* **1 a** : serving as an original or generating source : PRIMARY **b** : serving as a basis supporting existence or determining essential structure or function : BASIC **2** : of or relating to essential structure, function, or facts : RADICAL ⟨*fundamental* change⟩; *esp* : of or dealing with general principles rather than practical application ⟨*fundamental* science⟩ **3 a** : having the root in the bass ⟨*fundamental* chord⟩ **b** : of, relating to, or produced by the lowest component of a complex vibration **4** : of central importance : PRINCIPAL ⟨*fundamental* purpose⟩ **syn** see ESSENTIAL — **fun·da·men·tal·ly** \-°l-ē\ *adv*

²fundamental *n* **1** : something fundamental; *esp* : one of the basic constituents essential to a thing or system **2 a** : the prime tone of a harmonic series **b** : the root of a chord **3** : the harmonic component of a wave that has the lowest frequency and commonly the greatest amplitude

fun·da·men·tal·ism \-°l-,iz-əm\ *n* **1** *often cap* : a movement in 20th century Protestantism emphasizing as fundamental the literal interpretation of and absence of error in the Scriptures, the second coming of Jesus Christ, the virgin birth, physical resurrection, and substitutionary atonement **2 a** : the beliefs associated with fundamentalism **b** : adherence to such beliefs — **fun·da·men·tal·ist** \-°l-əst\ *adj or n*

fundamental particle *n* : ELEMENTARY PARTICLE

fundamental tissue *n* : plant tissue other than dermal and vascular tissues that consists typically of relatively undifferentiated parenchymatous and supportive cells

fun·dus \'fən-dəs\ *n, pl* **fun·di** \-,dī, -,dē\ [NL, fr. L, bottom] : the bottom of or part opposite the aperture of a hollow organ: as **a** : the great curvature of the stomach **b** : the large upper end of the uterus — **fun·dic** \-dik\ *adj*

¹fu·ner·al \'fyün-(ə-)rəl\ *adj* [LL *funeralis*, fr. L *funer-, funus*, n., funeral] **1** : of, relating to, or constituting a funeral **2** : FUNEREAL 2

²funeral *n* **1** : the ceremonies held for a dead person usu. before burial or cremation **2** : a funeral party in transit

funeral director *n* : one who manages funerals and is usu. an embalmer

funeral home *n* : a set of rooms with facilities for the preparation of the dead for burial or cremation, for the viewing of the body, and for funerals — called also *funeral parlor*

fu·ner·ary \'fyü-nə-,rer-ē\ *adj* : of, used for, or associated with burial ⟨a pharaoh's *funerary* chamber⟩

fu·ne·re·al \fyü-'nir-ē-əl\ *adj* **1** : of or relating to a funeral **2** : suggesting a funeral ⟨*funereal* gloom⟩ — **fu·ne·re·al·ly** \-ē-ə-lē\ *adv*

fungi- *comb form* : fungus ⟨*fungi*form⟩

fun·gi·cid·al \,fən-jə-'sīd-°l, ,fəŋ-gə-\ *adj* : destroying or inhibiting the growth of fungi — **fun·gi·cid·al·ly** \-ºl-ē\ *adv* — **fun·gi·cide** \'fən-jə-ˌsīd, 'fəŋ-gə-\ *n*

fun·go \'fəŋ-gō\ *n, pl* **fungoes** : a fly ball hit by a player who tosses a ball in the air and hits it as it comes down

fun·goid \'fəŋ-ˌgóid\ *adj* : resembling, characteristic of, or being a fungus — **fungoid** *n*

fun·gous \'fəŋ-gəs\ *or* **fun·gal** \-gəl\ *adj* **1** : of, relating to, or resembling fungi **2** : caused by a fungus

fun·gus \'fəŋ-gəs\ *n, pl* **fun·gi** \'fən-ˌjī, 'fəŋ-ˌgī\ *also* **fun·gus·es** [L] **1** : any of a major group (Fungi) of saprophytic and parasitic lower plants that lack chlorophyll and include molds, rusts, mildews, smuts, mushrooms, and usu. bacteria **2** : infection with a fungus — **fungus** *adj*

¹**fu·nic·u·lar** \fyü-'nik-yə-lər, fə-\ *adj* : of, relating to, or being a funiculus

²**funicular** *n* : a cable railway ascending a mountain; *esp* : one in which an ascending car counterbalances a descending car

fu·nic·u·lus \-ləs\ *n, pl* **-li** \-ˌlī, -ˌlē\ [NL, fr. L, dim. of *funis* rope] : an anatomical stalk, band, or cord (as the umbilical cord or the stalk of a plant ovule)

¹**funk** \'fəŋk\ *n* : a state of paralyzed fear : PANIC

²**funk** *vb* **1** : to become frightened and shrink back **2** : to be afraid of : DREAD

¹**fun·nel** \'fən-ºl\ *n* [OProv *fonilh*, fr. ML *fundibulum*, short for L *infundibulum*, fr. *infundere* to pour in, fr. *in-* + *fundere* to pour] **1** : a utensil usu. shaped like a hollow cone with a tube extending from the point and designed to catch and direct a downward flow (as of liquid) **2** : a stack or flue for the escape of smoke or for ventilation

funnel 1

²**funnel** *vb* **-neled** *also* **-nelled**; **-nel·ing** *also* **-nel·ling** **1** : to pass through or as if through a funnel **2** : to move or cause to move to a focal point or into a central channel

fun·ny \'fən-ē\ *adj* **fun·ni·er**; **-est** **1 a** : affording light mirth and laughter : AMUSING **b** : seeking or intended to amuse : FACETIOUS **2** : differing from the ordinary in a suspicious way : QUEER **3** : involving trickery or deception — **fun·ni·ly** \'fən-ºl-ē\ *adv* — **fun·ni·ness** \'fən-ē-nəs\ *n*

funny bone *n* : a place at the back of the elbow where a blow compresses a nerve and causes a painful tingling sensation

¹**fur** \'fər\ *vb* **furred**; **fur·ring** [MF *fourrer*, fr. OF *fuerre* sheath] : to cover, line, trim, or clothe with fur

²**fur** *n* **1** : a piece of the dressed pelt of an animal used to make, trim, or line wearing apparel **2** : an article of clothing made of or with fur **3** : the hairy coat of a mammal esp. when fine, soft, and thick **4** : a coating (as on the tongue) resembling fur — **fur·less** \'fər-ləs\ *adj* — **furred** \'fərd\ *adj*

fur·bear·er \'fər-ˌbar-ər, -ˌber-\ *n* : an animal that bears fur esp. of a commercially desired quality

fur·be·low \'fər-bə-ˌlō\ *n* **1** : FLOUNCE, RUFFLE **2** : showy trimming

fur·bish \'fər-bish\ *vt* [MF *fourbiss-, fourbir*] **1** : to make lustrous : POLISH **2** : RENOVATE, REVIVE

fur·cate \'fər-ˌkāt\ *vi* [L *furca* fork] : to branch like a fork — **furcate** *adj* — **furcate·ly** *adv* — **fur·ca·tion** \ˌfər-'kā-shən\ *n*

fu·ri·ous \'fyür-ē-əs\ *adj* **1** : being in a fury : FIERCE, ANGRY **2** : RUSHING, VIOLENT ⟨a *furious* assault⟩ — **fu·ri·ous·ly** *adv*

¹**furl** \'fərl\ *vb* [MF *ferler*, fr. ONF *ferlier* to tie tightly, fr. OF *ferm, fer* tight (fr. L *firmus* firm) + *lier* to tie, fr. L *ligare*] **1** : to wrap or roll (as a sail or a flag) close to or around something **2** : to curl or fold in furls

²**furl** *n* **1** : the act of furling **2** : a furled coil

fur·long \'fər-ˌlóŋ\ *n* [ME, fr. OE *furlang*, fr. *furh* furrow + *lang* long] : a unit of distance equal to 220 yards

¹**fur·lough** \'fər-lō\ *n* [D *verlof*, lit., permission; akin to E *leave*] : a leave of absence from duty granted esp. to a soldier

²**furlough** *vt* **1** : to grant a furlough to **2** : to lay off from work

fur·nace \'fər-nəs\ *n* [OF *fornaise*, fr. L *fornac-, fornax*] : an enclosed structure in which heat is produced (as for heating a house or melting metals)

fur·nish \'fər-nish\ *vt* [MF *fourniss-, fournir*, of Gmc

origin] **1** : to provide with what is needed; *esp* : to equip with furniture **2** : SUPPLY, GIVE — **fur·nish·er** *n*

fur·nish·ings \-nish-iŋz\ *n pl* **1** : articles or accessories of dress **2** : objects that tend to increase comfort or utility; *esp* : articles of furniture for a room

fur·ni·ture \'fər-ni-chər\ *n* : equipment that is necessary, useful, or desirable; *esp* : movable articles (as chairs, tables, or beds) used in making a room ready for occupancy or use

fu·ror \'fyü(ə)r-ˌór, -ˌor\ *n* [L, fr. *furere* to rage] **1** : ANGER, RAGE **2** : FURORE

fu·rore \-ˌór, -ˌor\ *n* **1** : a contagious excitement; *esp* : a fashionable craze **2** : a public disturbance : UPROAR

fur·ri·er \'fər-ē-ər\ *n* : a person who prepares or deals in furs — **fur·ri·ery** \-ē-ə-rē\ *n*

fur·ring \'fər-iŋ\ *n* **1** : a fur trimming or lining **2** : the application of thin wood, brick, or metal to joists, studs, or walls to form a level surface or an air space; *also* : the material used in this process

¹**fur·row** \'fər-ō, 'fə-rō\ *n* [OE *furh*] **1** : a trench in the earth made by or as if by a plow **2** : something (as a groove or wrinkle) that resembles the track of a plow

²**furrow** *vb* **1** : to make furrows in **2** : to form furrows

fur·ry \'fər-ē\ *adj* **fur·ri·er**; **-est** **1** : consisting of or resembling fur **2** : covered with fur **3** : clogged as if with fur

fur seal *n* : a seal with a dense soft undercoat valued for fur — compare HAIR SEAL

¹**fur·ther** \'fər-thər\ *adv* [OE *furthor*, compar. of *forth*] **1** : ¹FARTHER 1 **2** : in addition : MOREOVER **3** : to a greater degree or extent

²**further** *adj* **1** : ²FARTHER 1 **2** : going or extending beyond : ADDITIONAL ⟨*further* education⟩

³**further** *vt* **fur·thered**; **fur·ther·ing** \'fərth-(ə-)riŋ\ : to help forward : PROMOTE — **fur·ther·er** \'fər-thər-ər\ *n*

fur·ther·ance \'fərth-(ə-)rən(t)s\ *n* : the act of furthering : ADVANCEMENT

fur·ther·more \'fər-thə(r)-ˌmōr, -ˌmór\ *adv* : in addition to what precedes : BESIDES

fur·ther·most \-ˌmōst\ *adj* : most distant : FARTHEST

fur·thest \'fər-thəst\ *adv (or adj)* : FARTHEST

fur·tive \'fərt-iv\ *adj* [L *furtivus*, fr. *furtum* theft, fr. *fur* thief] : done by stealth : SLY, SECRET ⟨a *furtive* look⟩ — **fur·tive·ly** *adv* — **fur·tive·ness** *n*

fu·run·cle \'fyü(ə)r-ˌəŋ-kəl\ *n* : a localized inflammatory swelling of the skin and underlying tissues : BOIL — **fu·run·cu·lar** \fyü-'rəŋ-kyə-lər\ *adj* — **fu·run·cu·lous** \-ləs\ *adj*

fu·ry \'fyü(ə)r-ē\ *n, pl* **furies** [L *furia*, fr. *furere* to rage] **1** : violent anger : RAGE **2 a cap** : one of the avenging spirits in classical mythology **b** : a violently angry or spiteful person **3** : extreme fierceness or violence ⟨the *fury* of the storm⟩ **syn** see ANGER

furze \'fərz\ *n* [OE *fyrs*] : a prickly evergreen shrub of the pea family with yellow flowers

¹**fuse** \'fyüz\ *n* [It *fuso* spindle, fr. L *fusus*] **1** : a continuous train of a combustible substance enclosed in a cord or cable for setting off an explosive charge by transmitting fire to it **2** *usu* **fuze** : a mechanical or electrical detonating device for setting off the bursting charge of a projectile, bomb, or torpedo

²**fuse** *or* **fuze** *vt* : to equip with a fuse

³**fuse** *vb* [L *fus-, fundere* to pour, melt] **1** : to reduce to a liquid or plastic state by heat **2** : to become fluid with heat **3** : to unite by or as if by melting together : BLEND, INTEGRATE

⁴**fuse** *n* : an electrical safety device consisting of or including a wire or strip of fusible metal that melts and interrupts the circuit when the current becomes too strong

fu·see \fyü-'zē\ *n* **1** : a friction match with a bulbous head not easily blown out **2** : a red signal flare used esp. for protecting stalled trains and trucks

fu·se·lage \'fyü-sə-ˌläzh, 'fyü-zə-\ *n* [F, fr. *fuselé* spindle-shaped, fr. L *fusus* spindle] : the central body portion of an airplane which holds the crew, passengers, and cargo

fu·sel oil \'fyü-zəl-\ *n* : an acrid oily liquid occurring in insufficiently distilled alcoholic liquors and consisting chiefly of amyl alcohol

fus·i·ble \'fyü-zə-bəl\ *adj* : capable of being fused and esp. liquefied by heat — **fus·i·bil·i·ty** \ˌfyü-zə-'bil-ət-ē\ *n*

fu·si·form \'fyü-zə-ˌfórm\ *adj* : tapering toward each end

j joke; **ŋ** sing; **ō** flow; **ó** flaw; **ói** coin; **th** thin; **th̲** this; **ü** loot; **ù** foot; **y** yet; **yü** few; **yù** furious; **zh** vision

fu·sil \'fyü-zəl\ *n* [F, steel for striking fire, fusil, fr. LL *focus* fire, fr. L, hearth] : a light flintlock musket

fu·sil·ier *or* **fu·sil·eer** \,fyü-zə-'li(ə)r\ *n* 1 : a soldier armed with a fusil 2 : a member of a British regiment formerly armed with fusils

fu·sil·lade \'fyü-sə-,läd, -zə-, -,läd\ *n* 1 : a number of shots fired simultaneously or in rapid succession 2 : a spirited outburst esp. of criticism

fu·sion \'fyü-zhən\ *n* 1 : the act or process of melting or making fluid by heat 2 : union by or as if by melting; *esp* : a merging of diverse elements into a unified whole 3 : the union of atomic nuclei to form heavier nuclei resulting in the release of enormous quantities of energy when certain light elements unite

fusion bomb *n* : a bomb in which nuclei of a light chemical element unite to form nuclei of heavier elements with a release of energy; *esp* HYDROGEN BOMB

¹**fuss** \'fəs\ *n* 1 a : needless bustle or excitement : COMMOTION b : effusive praise 2 : a state of agitation esp. over a trivial matter

²**fuss** *vi* 1 a : to create or be in a state of restless activity; *esp* : to shower flattering attentions b : to pay undue attention to small details 2 : to become upset : WORRY — **fuss·er** *n*

fuss·budg·et \'fəs-,bəj-ət\ *n* : one who fusses about trifles

fussy \'fəs-ē\ *adj* **fuss·i·er; -est** 1 : easily upset : IRRITABLE 2 a : requiring or giving close attention to details b : revealing a concern for niceties : FASTIDIOUS — **fuss·i·ly** \'fəs-ə-lē\ *adv* — **fuss·i·ness** \'fəs-ē-nəs\ *n*

fus·tian \'fəs-chən\ *n* 1 : a strong cotton and linen fabric 2 : pretentious writing or speech — **fustian** *adj*

fus·tic \'fəs-tik\ *n* : the wood of a tropical American tree related to the mulberry that yields a yellow dye; *also* : a tree yielding fustic

fus·ty \'fəs-tē\ *adj* **fus·ti·er; -est** 1 : MOLDY, MUSTY 2 : rigidly conservative : OLD-FASHIONED — **fus·ti·ly** \-tə-lē\ *adv* — **fus·ti·ness** \-tē-nəs\ *n*

fu·tile \'fyüt-ºl, 'fyü-,tīl\ *adj* [L *futilis*, lit., that pours out easily] 1 : having no result or effect : USELESS ⟨a *futile* struggle against overwhelming forces⟩ ⟨waste time in *futile* talk⟩ 2 : UNIMPORTANT, TRIVIAL ⟨*futile* pleasures⟩ **syn** see VAIN — **fu·tile·ly** \-ºl-(l)ē, -,tīl-lē\ *adv* — **fu·til·i·ty** \fyü-'til-ət-ē\ *n*

fut·tock \'fət-ək\ *n* : one of the curved timbers scarfed together to form the lower part of the compound rib of a ship

¹**fu·ture** \'fyü-chər\ *adj* [L *futurus*, used as future participle of *esse* to be; akin to E *be*] 1 a : that is to be b : existing after death 2 : of, relating to, or constituting a verb tense formed in English with *will* and *shall* and expressive of time yet to come

²**future** *n* 1 a : time that is to come b : what is going to happen 2 : expectation of advancement or development ⟨a promising *future*⟩ 3 : a stock or commodity sold for delivery at a future time — usu. used in pl. 4 a : the future tense b : a verb form in the future tense

fu·ture·less \-ləs\ *adj* : having no prospect of future success

future perfect *adj* : of, relating to, or constituting a verb tense formed in English with *will have* and *shall have* and expressing completion of an action by a specified time that is yet to come — **future perfect** *n*

fu·tur·ism \'fyü-chə-,riz-əm\ *n* : a movement in art, music, and literature begun in Italy about 1910 and marked esp. by an effort to give formal expression to the dynamic energy and movement of mechanical processes — **fu·tur·ist** \'fyüch-(ə-)rəst\ *n*

fu·tur·is·tic \,fyü-chə-'ris-tik\ *adj* : of or relating to the future or to futurism — **fu·tur·is·ti·cal·ly** \-ti-k(ə-)lē\ *adv*

fu·tu·ri·ty \fyü-'t(y)ùr-ət-ē, -'chùr-\ *n, pl* **-ties** 1 : FUTURE 2 : the quality or state of being future 3 *pl* : future events or prospects

fuze, fuzee *var of* FUSE, FUSEE

fuzz \'fəz\ *n* : fine light particles or fibers (as of down or fluff)

fuzzy \'fəz-ē\ *adj* **fuzz·i·er; -est** 1 : covered with or resembling fuzz 2 : not clear : INDISTINCT — **fuzz·i·ly** \'fəz-ə-lē\ *adv* — **fuzz·i·ness** \'fəz-ē-nəs\ *n*

-fy \,fī\ *vb suffix* **-fied; -fy·ing** [OF *-fier*, fr. L *-ficare*, fr. *-ficus* -fic] 1 : make : form into ⟨dandi*fy*⟩ 2 : invest with the attributes of : make similar to ⟨citi*fy*⟩

---

g \'jē\ *n, often cap* 1 : the 7th letter of the English alphabet 2 : the musical tone G 3 : a unit of force equal to a person's weight and used to express forces he experiences (as when he is in an airplane that is pulling out of a dive or that is making a sharp turn) ⟨the pilot of the plane experienced a force of three *G's*⟩

gab \'gab\ *vi* **gabbed; gab·bing** : to talk idly : CHATTER — **gab** *n*

gab·ar·dine \'gab-ər-,dēn\ *n* [MF *gaverdine*] 1 : GABERDINE 2 a : a firm durable twilled fabric having diagonal ribs and made of various fibers b : a garment of gabardine

gab·ble \'gab-əl\ *vb* **gab·bled; gab·bling** \'gab-(ə-)liŋ\ : to talk fast or foolishly : JABBER, BABBLE — **gabble** *n* — **gab·bler** \'gab-(ə-)lər\ *n*

gab·bro \'gab-rō\ *n, pl* **gabbros** [It] : a granular igneous rock rich in magnesium and low in quartz — **gab·bro·ic** \ga-'brō-ik\ *adj*

gab·by \'gab-ē\ *adj* **gab·bi·er; -est** : TALKATIVE, GARRULOUS

gab·er·dine \'gab-ər-,dēn\ *n* [MF *gaverdine*] 1 a : a long smock worn chiefly by Jews in medieval times b : an English laborer's smock 2 : GABARDINE

gab·fest \'gab-,fest\ *n* 1 : an informal gathering for general talk 2 : an extended conversation

ga·ble \'gā-bəl\ *n* [MF, of Gmc origin] : the triangular part of an outside wall of a building that is formed by the sides of the roof sloping down from the ridgepole to the eaves; *also* : a similar triangular structure (as over a door or window) — **ga·bled** \-bəld\ *adj*

gable roof *n* : a double-sloping roof that forms a gable at each end

Ga·bri·el \'gā-brē-əl\ *n* : one of the archangels

¹**gad** \'gad\ *vi* **gad·ded; gad·ding** [ME *gadden*] : to roam about : wander restlessly and without purpose — **gad·der** *n*

²**gad** *interj* [euphemism for *God*] — used as a mild oath

gad·about \'gad-ə-,baùt\ *n* : a person who flits about in social activity — **gadabout** *adj*

gad·fly \'gad-,flī\ *n* 1 : any of various flies (as a horsefly or botfly) that bite or harass livestock 2 : an intentionally annoying person who stimulates or provokes others esp. by persistent criticism

gad·get \'gaj-ət\ *n* : CONTRIVANCE, DEVICE ⟨a *gadget* for peeling potatoes⟩ ⟨a house filled with all the latest *gadgets*⟩ — **gad·ge·teer** \,gaj-ə-'ti(ə)r\ *n* — **gad·get·ry** \'gaj-ə-trē\ *n*

gad·o·lin·i·um \,gad-ºl-'in-ē-əm\ *n* : a magnetic metallic chemical element occurring in several minerals — see ELEMENT table

gad·wall \'gad-,wòl\ *n, pl* **gadwalls** *or* **gadwall** : a grayish brown duck about the size of the mallard

Gael \'gāl\ *n* 1 : a Scottish Highlander 2 : a Celtic esp. Gaelic-speaking inhabitant of Ireland, Scotland, or the Isle of Man

Gael·ic \'gā-lik\ *adj* 1 : of or relating to the Gaels and esp. the Celtic Highlanders of Scotland 2 : of, relating to, or constituting the Goidelic speech of the Celts in Ireland, the Isle of Man, and the Scottish Highlands — **Gaelic** *n*

¹**gaff** \'gaf\ *n* [F *gaffe*] 1 a : a spear or spearhead for taking fish or turtles b : a handled hook for holding or lifting heavy fish c : a metal spur for a gamecock 2 : the spar upon which the head of a fore-and-aft sail is extended 3 : rough treatment : ABUSE

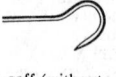

gaff (without handle) 1b

²**gaff** *vt* : to strike, take, or handle with a gaff

gaffe \'gaf\ *n* [F] : a social blunder

gaf·fer \'gaf-ər\ *n* [prob. alter. of *godfather*] : an old man

¹**gag** \'gag\ *vb* **gagged; gag·ging** [ME *gaggen* to strangle] 1 a : to prevent from speaking or crying out by stopping up the mouth b : to prevent from speaking freely 2 a : to retch or cause to retch b : OBSTRUCT, CHOKE 3 : BALK 4 : to make quips

²**gag** *n* 1 a : something thrust into the mouth esp. to prevent speech or outcry b : CLOTURE c : a check to free speech 2 : a laugh-provoking remark or act 3 : HOAX, TRICK

---

ga·ga \'gä-,gä\ *adj* **1** : CRAZY, FOOLISH **2** : INFATUATED

¹gage \'gāj\ *n* [MF] **1** : a token of defiance; *esp* : a glove or cap cast on the ground as a pledge of combat **2** : something deposited as a pledge : SECURITY

²gage *var of* GAUGE

gag·man \'gag-,man\ *n* **1** : a gag writer **2** : a comedian who uses gags

gag rule *n* : a rule restricting freedom of debate or expression esp. in a legislative body

gag·ster \'gag-stər\ *n* : GAGMAN

gai·e·ty \'gā-ət-ē\ *n, pl* **gai·e·ties** **1** : MERRYMAKING **2** : gay spirits or manner **3** : FINERY

gai·ly \'gā-lē\ *adv* : in a gay manner

¹gain \'gān\ *n* [MF *gaigne*] **1** : an increase in or addition to what is of profit **2** : the obtaining of profit or possessions **3** : an increase in amount, magnitude, or degree

²gain *vb* **1 a** : to get possession of : EARN **b** : to win in competition or conflict ⟨*gain* a victory⟩ **c** : to get by a natural development or process : ACHIEVE ⟨*gain* strength⟩ **d** : to arrive at ⟨*gained* the river that night⟩ **2** : to win to one's side : PERSUADE **3** : to increase in ⟨*gain* momentum⟩ **4** : to run fast ⟨my watch *gains* a minute a day⟩ **5** : to get advantage : PROFIT **6 a** : INCREASE **b** : to improve in health — **gain ground** : to make progress

gain·er \'gā-nər\ *n* **1** : one that gains **2** : a fancy dive in which the diver from a forward position rotates backward and enters the water feetfirst and facing away from the board

gain·ful \'gān-fəl\ *adj* : producing gain : PROFITABLE, PAID ⟨*gainful* employment⟩ — **gain·ful·ly** \-fə-lē\ *adv* — **gain·ful·ness** *n*

gain·ly \'gān-lē\ *adj* : GRACEFUL, SHAPELY

gain·say \gān-'sā\ *vt* **gain·said** \-'sād, -'sed\; **gain·say·ing** \-'sā-iŋ\ [ME *gainsayen*, fr. *gain-* against + *sayen* to say] **1** : DENY, DISPUTE **2** : to speak against : CONTRADICT — **gain·say·er** *n*

gait \'gāt\ *n* [ME *gate* way, path, fr. ON *gata*] : manner of moving on foot ⟨his *gait* was deliberate⟩; *also* : a particular pattern or style of such movement ⟨the walk, trot, and canter are *gaits* of the horse⟩ — **gait·ed** \-əd\ *adj*

gai·ter \'gāt-ər\ *n* [F *guêtre*] **1** : a cloth or leather leg covering reaching from the instep to ankle, mid calf, or knee **2 a** : an ankle-high shoe with elastic gores in the sides **b** : an overshoe with fabric upper

gal \'gal\ *n* [*Galileo* d1642 Italian astronomer and physicist] : a unit of acceleration equivalent to one centimeter per second per second

ga·la \'gā-lə, 'gal-ə\ *n* [It] : a gay celebration : FESTIVITY — **gala** *adj*

ga·lac·tic \gə-'lak-tik\ *adj* : of or relating to a galaxy

galactic noise *n* : radio-frequency radiation from the Milky Way

ga·lac·tose \gə-'lak-,tōs\ *n* : a sugar $C_6H_{12}O_6$ less soluble and less sweet than glucose

ga·lah \gə-'lä\ *n* : a showy Australian cockatoo

Gal·a·had \'gal-ə-,had\ *n* : a knight of the Round Table who finds the Holy Grail

Gal·a·tea \,gal-ə-'tē-ə\ *n* : an ivory statue of a maiden carved by Pygmalion according to Greek legend and given life by Aphrodite in response to the sculptor's prayer

Ga·la·tians \gə-'lā-shənz\ *n* — see BIBLE table

ga·lax \'gā-,laks\ *n* : an evergreen herb related to the heaths that has shiny leaves used in decorations

gal·axy \'gal-ək-sē\ *n, pl* **gal·ax·ies** [Gk *galaxias*, fr. *galakt-, gala* milk] **1 a** *often cap* : MILKY WAY GALAXY **b** : one of billions of systems each including stars, nebulae, clusters of stars, gas, and dust that make up the universe **2** : an assemblage of brilliant or notable persons or things

gale \'gāl\ *n* **1** : a strong current of air; *esp* : a wind of from 32 to 63 miles per hour **2** : an emotional outburst

ga·lea \'gā-lē-ə\ *n* [L, helmet] : an anatomical part suggesting a helmet — **ga·le·ate** \-lē-,āt\ *adj*

ga·le·na \gə-'lē-nə\ *n* [L, lead ore] : a bluish gray mineral PbS with metallic luster consisting of sulfide of lead and constituting the principal ore of lead

¹gall \'gol\ *n* [OE *gealla*; akin to E *yellow*] **1 a** : BILE **b** : something bitter to endure **c** : bitterness of spirit : RANCOR **2** : EFFRONTERY, IMPUDENCE

²gall *n* [OE *gealla*, fr. L *galla* gall on a plant] **1** : a skin sore caused by chronic irritation **2** : a cause or state of exasperation

³gall *vb* **1 a** : to fret and wear away by friction : CHAFE **b** : to become sore or worn by rubbing **2** : IRRITATE, VEX **3** : HARASS

⁴gall *n* [MF *galle*, fr. L *galla*] : a swelling or overgrowth of plant tissue usu. due to fungi or insect parasites

¹gal·lant \gə-'lant, gə-'länt, 'gal-ənt\ *n* **1** : a young man of fashion **2 a** : a man who shows a marked fondness for the company of women and who is esp. attentive to them **b** : SUITOR

²gal·lant \'gal-ənt (*usu in sense 2b*); gə-'lant, gə-'länt (*usu in sense 3*)\ *adj* [MF *galant*, fr. prp. of *galer* to have a good time, fr. *gale* pleasure, fr. Gmc origin; akin to E *weal*] **1** : showy in dress or bearing : SMART **2 a** : SPLENDID, STATELY **b** : SPIRITED, BRAVE **c** : CHIVALROUS, NOBLE **3** : polite and attentive to women — **gal·lant·ly** *adv*

gal·lant·ry \'gal-ən-trē\ *n, pl* **-ries** **1** *archaic* : gallant appearance **2 a** : an act of marked courtesy **b** : courteous attention to a woman **3** : conspicuous bravery

gall·blad·der \'gol-,blad-ər\ *n* : a membranous muscular sac in which bile from the liver is stored

gal·le·on \'gal-ē-ən\ *n* [Sp *galeón*, fr. MF *galion*] : a heavy square-rigged sailing ship of the 15th to early 18th centuries used for war or commerce esp. by the Spanish

gal·lery \'gal-(ə)-rē\ *n, pl* **gal·ler·ies** [ML *galeria*] **1 a** : a roofed promenade : COLONNADE **b** : an outdoor balcony **c** *South & Midland* : PORCH, VERANDA **d** : a balcony in a theater, auditorium, or church; *esp* : the highest balcony in a theater or the people who sit in this balcony ⟨play to the *gallery*⟩ **e** : a body of spectators at a tennis or golf match **2 a** : a long narrow room, hall, or passage; *esp* : one having windows along one side **b** : a subterranean passageway (as in a cave or mine) **c** : a passage (as in earth or wood) made by an animal and esp. an insect **3 a** : a room or building devoted to the exhibition of works of art **b** : an institution or business exhibiting or dealing in works of art **4** : a photographer's studio — **gal·ler·ied** \-rēd\ *adj*

gal·ley \'gal-ē\ *n, pl* **galleys** [OF *galie*, fr. MGk *galea*] **1** : a large low usu. single-decked ship propelled by oars and sails and used in ancient times and in the Middle Ages chiefly in the Mediterranean sea **2** : the kitchen of a ship **3 a** : an oblong tray with upright sides to hold printer's type that has been set **b** : GALLEY PROOF

galley proof *n* : a proof from type on a galley before it is made up in pages; *also* : such proofs

galley slave *n* **1** : a slave or criminal acting as a rower on a galley **2** : one who engages in hard, menial, or monotonous work

gall·fly \'gol-,flī\ *n* : an insect that deposits its eggs in plants and causes galls in which the larvae feed

Gal·lic \'gal-ik\ *adj* : of or relating to Gaul or France

gal·lic acid \,gal-ik-, ,gò-lik-\ *n* : a crystalline acid $C_7H_6O_5 \cdot H_2O$ found in plants and used esp. in dyes and writing ink

Gal·li·can·ism \'gal-i-kə-,niz-əm\ *n* : a movement originating in France and advocating administrative independence from papal control for the Roman Catholic Church in each nation — **Gal·li·can** \-kən\ *adj or n*

gal·li·cism \'gal-ə-,siz-əm\ *n, often cap* : a characteristic French idiom, expression, or trait

gal·li·gas·kins \,gal-i-'gas-kənz\ *n pl* **1** : loose wide breeches worn in the 16th and 17th centuries **2** *chiefly dial* : LEGGINGS

gal·li·mau·fry \,gal-ə-'mò-frē\ *n, pl* **-fries** [MF *galimafree* hash] : MEDLEY, JUMBLE

gal·li·na·ceous \,gal-ə-'nā-shəs\ *adj* [L *gallinaceus* of domestic fowl, fr. *gallina* hen, fr. *gallus* cock] : of or relating to an order (Galliformes) of heavy-bodied largely terrestrial birds including the pheasants, turkeys, grouse, and the common domestic fowl

gall·ing \'gò-liŋ\ *adj* : CHAFING, VEXING

gal·li·nip·per \'gal-ə-,nip-ər\ *n* : a large American mosquito

gal·li·nule \'gal-ə-,n(y)ül\ *n* [L *gallina* hen] : any of several aquatic birds related to the rails but having unlobed feet and a frontal shield on the head

gal·li·um \'gal-ē-əm\ *n* : a rare bluish white metallic chemical element that is hard and brittle at low temperatures but melts just above room temperature — see ELEMENT table

gal·li·vant \'gal-ə-,vant\ *vi* **1** : to go about ostentatiously with the opposite sex **2** : to travel or roam about for pleasure

gall mite *n* : any of various minute 4-legged mites that form galls on plants

gal·lon \'gal-ən\ *n* [ME *galon*, a liquid measure, fr. ONF, fr. ML *galeta*] — see MEASURE table

gal·lon·age \'gal-ə-nij\ *n* : amount in gallons

¹gal·lop \'gal-əp\ *n* [MF *galop*] **1** : a springing gait of a quadruped; *esp* : a fast natural 3-beat gait of the horse — compare CANTER **2** : a ride or run at a gallop

²gallop *vb* **1** : to move or ride at a gallop **2** : to run fast **3** : to cause to gallop — **gal·lop·er** *n*

gal·lows \'gal-ōz\ *n, pl* **gallows** *or* **gal·lows·es** [ME *galwes*, pl. of *galwe*, fr. OE *gealga*] **1** : a frame usu. of two upright posts and a traverse beam from which criminals are hanged — called also *gallows tree* **2** : a structure consisting of an upright frame with a crosspiece

gall·stone \'gól-,stōn\ *n* : a concretion formed in the gallbladder or bile passages

gall wasp *n* : a wasp that is a gallfly

ga·loot \gə-'lüt\ *n, slang* : a disreputable-looking man : FELLOW

ga·lop \'gal-əp, ga-'lō\ *n* : a lively dance in duple measure

ga·lore \gə-'lō(ə)r, -'ló(ə)r\ *adj* [IrGael *go leor* enough] : ABUNDANT, PLENTIFUL — used after the word it modifies ⟨presents *galore*⟩

ga·losh \gə-'läsh\ *n* [MF *galoche*, a heavy-soled shoe] : a high overshoe worn esp. in snow and slush — **ga·loshed** \-'läsht\ *adj*

gal·van·ic \gal-'van-ik\ *adj* **1** : of, relating to, or producing a direct current of electricity by chemical action ⟨a *galvanic* cell⟩ **2** : having an electric effect : STIMULATING ⟨a *galvanic* personality⟩ — **gal·van·i·cal·ly** \-i-k(ə-)lē\ *adv*

gal·va·nism \'gal-və-,niz-əm\ *n* [after Luigi *Galvani* d1798 Italian physician and physicist] : a direct current of electricity produced by chemical action

gal·va·nize \'gal-və-,nīz\ *vt* **1 a** : to subject to the action of an electric current **b** : to stimulate or excite by or as if by an electric shock ⟨*galvanize* a muscle⟩ **2** : to coat (as iron) with zinc for protection — **gal·va·ni·za·tion** \,gal-və-nə-'zā-shən\ *n*

gal·va·nom·e·ter \,gal-və-'näm-ət-ər\ *n* : an instrument for detecting or measuring a small electric current by movements of a magnetic needle or of a coil in a magnetic field — **gal·va·no·met·ric** \,gal-və-nō-'me-trik\ *adj*

gal·vano·scope \gal-'van-ə-,skōp\ *n* : an instrument for detecting the presence and direction of an electric current by the deflection of a magnetic needle

gal·yak \'gal-,yak\ *n* : a short sleek fur from the pelt of a stillborn lamb or kid

gam- *or* **gamo-** *comb form* [Gk *gamos* marriage] **1** : united : joined ⟨*gamo*phyllous⟩ **2** : sexual : sexuality ⟨*gamic*⟩ ⟨*gamo*genesis⟩

gam·bit \'gam-bət\ *n* [It *gambetto*, lit., act of tripping someone, fr. *gamba* leg, fr. LL *gamba*] **1** : a chess opening in which a player risks one or more minor pieces to gain an advantage in position **2** : a calculated move : STRATAGEM

¹gam·ble \'gam-bəl\ *vb* **gam·bled; gam·bling** \-b(ə-)liŋ\ **1 a** : to play a game for money or other stakes **b** : to bet on an uncertain outcome **2** : to stake something on a doubtful event : BET, WAGER **3** : VENTURE, HAZARD — **gam·bler** \-blər\ *n*

²gamble *n* : a risky undertaking

gam·boge \gam-'bōj, -'büzh\ *n* : an orange to brown gum resin from southeast Asian trees that is used as a yellow pigment and cathartic

gam·bol \'gam-bəl\ *vi* **gam·boled** *or* **gam·bolled; gam·bol·ing** *or* **gam·bol·ling** \-b(ə-)liŋ\ [MF *gambade* spring of a horse, gambol] : to skip about in play : FRISK — **gambol** *n*

gam·brel roof \,gam-brəl-\ *n* : a roof having a double slope on each side with a lower steeper slope and an upper flatter one — see ROOF illustration

gam·bu·sia \gam-'byü-zh(ē-)ə\ *n* : any of several top-minnows used as exterminators of mosquito larvae in warm fresh waters

¹game \'gām\ *n* [OE *gamen*] **1 a** : AMUSEMENT, DIVERSION **b** : FUN, SPORT **2 a** : a procedure for gaining an end **b** : a line of work : PROFESSION **3 a** (1) : a physical

or mental contest (2) : a division of a larger contest (3) : the number of points necessary to win (4) : the manner of playing in a contest **b** : a situation involving opposing interests given specific information and allowed a choice of moves with the object of maximizing their wins and minimizing their losses **4 a** (1) : animals pursued or taken in hunting esp. for sport or food (2) : the flesh of game animals **b** : an object of ridicule or attack — often used in the phrase *fair game*

²game *vb* : to play for a stake : GAMBLE

³game *adj* : having a resolute unyielding spirit ⟨*game* to the end⟩ — **game·ly** *adv* — **game·ness** *n*

⁴game *adj* : LAME ⟨a *game* leg⟩

game·cock \'gām-,käk\ *n* : a male game fowl

game fish *n* : a fish of the trout family; *also* : a fish regularly sought by anglers for sport

game fowl *n* : a domestic fowl of a strain developed for the production of fighting cocks

game·keep·er \'gām-,kē-pər\ *n* : one that has charge of the breeding and protection of game animals or birds on a private preserve

game·some \'gām-səm\ *adj* : GAY, FROLICSOME — **game·some·ly** *adv* — **game·some·ness** *n*

game·ster \'gām-stər\ *n* : one who plays games; *esp* : GAMBLER

gam·etan·gi·um \,gam-ə-'tan-jē-əm\ *n, pl* **-gia** \-jē-ə\ [*gamete* + Gk *angeion* vessel] : a cell or organ in which gametes are developed — **gam·etan·gial** \-'tan-j(ē-)əl\ *adj*

ga·mete \gə-'mēt, 'gam-,ēt\ *n* [Gk *gametēs* husband, fr. *gamos* marriage] : a matured germ cell capable of uniting with another such cell to form a new plant or animal individual — **ga·met·ic** \gə-'met-ik\ *adj* — **ga·met·i·cal·ly** \-'met-i-k(ə-)lē\ *adv*

ga·me·to·cyte \gə-'mēt-ə-,sīt\ *n* : a cell that divides to produce gametes

ga·me·to·gen·e·sis \gə-,mēt-ə-'jen-ə-səs\ *n* : the production of gametes — **ga·me·to·gen·ic** \-'jen-ik\ *or* **gam·e·tog·e·nous** \,gam-ə-'täj-ə-nəs\ *adj* — **gam·e·tog·e·ny** \-nē\ *n*

ga·me·to·phyte \gə-'mēt-ə-,fīt\ *n* : the individual or generation of a plant exhibiting alternation of generations that bears sex organs — compare SPOROPHYTE — **ga·me·to·phyt·ic** \-,mēt-ə-'fit-ik\ *adj*

game warden *n* : an official whose duties are to enforce the laws regulating the taking of game

gam·in \'gam-ən\ *n* [F] **1** : a boy who runs the streets : URCHIN **2** : GAMINE 2

ga·mine \ga-'mēn\ *n* **1** : a girl who runs the streets : TOMBOY **2** : a girl of elfin appeal

gam·ing \'gā-miŋ\ *n* : the practice of gambling

gam·ma \'gam-ə\ *n* : the 3d letter of the Greek alphabet — Γ or γ

gamma globulin *n* : a protein fraction of blood plasma rich in antibodies

gamma rays *n pl* : very penetrating radiation of the same nature as X rays but of shorter wavelength emitted by various radioactive atomic nuclei — called also *gamma radiation*

gam·mer \'gam-ər\ *n* [prob. alter. of *godmother*] : an old woman

Gam·mex·ane \ga-'mek-,sān\ *trademark* — used for lindane

¹gam·mon \'gam-ən\ *n* : a ham or flitch of cured bacon

²gammon *n* : deceptive talk : HUMBUG — **gammon** *vb*

gamo- — see GAM-

gamo·gen·e·sis \,gam-ə-'jen-ə-səs\ *n* : sexual reproduction

gam·ut \'gam-ət\ *n* [ML *gamma*, lowest note of Guido's scale (fr. Gk, third letter of the alphabet) + *ut*, first note of the diatonic scale] **1** : the whole series of recognized musical notes **2** : an entire range or series

gamy \'gā-mē\ *adj* **gam·i·er; -est** **1** : GAME, PLUCKY **2** : having the flavor of game esp. when slightly tainted ⟨*gamy* meat⟩ — **gam·i·ly** \'gā-mə-lē\ *adv* — **gam·i·ness** \'gā-mē-nəs\ *n*

gamecock

-g·a·my \g-ə-mē\ *n comb form, pl* **-gamies** [Gk *-gamia*, fr. *gamos* marriage] **1** : marriage ⟨exogamy⟩ **2** : union for propagation or reproduction ⟨allogamy⟩

Gan·da \'gän-də\ *n, pl* **Ganda** *or* **Gandas** **1** : a member of a Bantu-speaking people of Uganda **2** : the Bantu language of the Ganda people

1gan·der \'gan-dər\ *n* [OE *gandra*] : a male goose

2gander *n, slang* : LOOK, GLANCE

gan·dy dancer \'gan-dē-\ *n* **1** : a laborer in a railroad section gang **2** : an itinerant or seasonal laborer

1gang \'gaŋ\ *n* [ME, set of things or persons, fr. OE, journey, act of going] **1** : a group of persons working or going about together ⟨a *gang* of laborers⟩ ⟨a *gang* of boys in swimming⟩ **2** : a group of persons associated or acting together for unlawful or antisocial purposes ⟨a *gang* of thieves⟩ **3** : two or more similar implements or devices arranged to work together in order to save time and labor or to produce a unified effect ⟨a *gang* of saws⟩

2gang *vb* **1** : to attack in a gang — usu. used with *up* ⟨the crowd *ganged* up on the referee⟩ **2** : to form into or move or act as a gang

gang·land \'gaŋ-,land\ *n* : the world of organized crime

gan·gling \'gaŋ-gliŋ, -glən\ *adj* : LANKY, SPINDLING

gan·gli·on \'gaŋ-glē-ən\ *n, pl* **-glia** \-glē-ə\ *also* **-gli·ons** [Gk] : a mass of neural tissue lying external to the brain or spinal cord and containing nerve cells; *also* : NUCLEUS c — **gan·gli·on·at·ed** \'gaŋ-glē-ə-,nāt-əd\ *adj* — **gan·gli·on·ic** \,gaŋ-glē-'än-ik\ *adj*

gan·gly \'gaŋ-glē\ *adj* : GANGLING, LANKY

gang·plank \'gaŋ-,plaŋk\ *n* [E dial. *gang* passage] : a movable bridge used in boarding or leaving a ship at a pier

gang·plow \-,plaù\ *n* : a plow designed to turn two or more furrows at one time

1gan·grene \'gaŋ-,grēn, gaŋ-', 'gan-,, gan-'\ *n* [Gk *gangraina*] : local death of soft tissues due to loss of blood supply — **gan·gre·nous** \'gaŋ-grə-nəs\ *adj*

2gangrene *vb* : to make or become gangrenous

gang·ster \'gaŋ-stər\ *n* : a member of a gang of criminals : RACKETEER — **gang·ster·ism** \-stə-,riz-əm\ *n*

gangue \'gaŋ\ *n* [F, fr. G *gang* vein of metal] : the worthless rock or vein matter in which valuable metals or minerals occur

gang·way \'gaŋ-,wā\ *n* **1** : a passage into, through, or out of an enclosed place **2** : GANGPLANK **3** : a clear passage through a crowd — often used as an interjection

gan·net \'gan-ət\ *n, pl* **gannets** *also* **gannet** [OE *ganot*] : any of several large fish-eating seabirds that remain at sea for long periods and breed chiefly on offshore islands

gan·oid \'gan-,òid\ *adj* : of or relating to a group (Ganoidei) of teleost fishes with usu. hard rhombic enameled scales — **ganoid** *n* — **ga·noi·de·an** \ga-'nòid-ē-ən\ *adj or n*

gant·let \'gónt-lət, 'gänt-\ *var of* GAUNTLET

gan·try \'gan-trē\ *n, pl* **gantries** **1** : a platform made to carry a traveling crane and supported by towers or side frames running on parallel tracks; *also* : a movable structure with platforms at different levels used for erecting and servicing rockets before launching **2** : a structure spanning several railroad tracks and displaying signals for each

Gan·y·mede \'gan-ə-,mēd\ *n* : the cupbearer of the gods in classical mythology

gaol \'jāl\, **gaol·er** *chiefly Brit var of* JAIL, JAILER

gap \'gap\ *n* [ON, chasm, hole] **1** : an opening made by a break or a parting : BREACH, CLEFT **2** : a mountain pass **3** : a break or separation in continuity : a blank space ⟨a *gap* where the tooth had been⟩

1gape \'gāp\ *vi* [ON *gapa*; akin to E *yawn*] **1 a** : to open the mouth wide **b** : to open or part widely **2** : to stare openmouthed **3** : YAWN — **gap·er** *n* — **gap·ing·ly** *adv*

2gape *n* **1** : an act or instance of gaping: **a** : YAWN **b** : an openmouthed stare **2** : the line along which the mandibles of a bird close **3** *pl* : a disease of young birds in which gapeworms invade and irritate the trachea

gape·worm \'gāp-,wərm\ *n* : a nematode worm that causes gapes of birds

gar \'gär\ *n* : any of various fishes with a long body like that of a pike and long narrow jaws; *esp* : any of several predaceous No. American freshwater ganoid fishes with rank tough flesh

1ga·rage \gə-'räzh, -'räj\ *n* [F] **1** : a building where automobiles are housed **2** : a repair shop for automobiles — **ga·rage·man** \-,man\ *n*

2garage *vt* : to keep or put in a garage

1garb \'gärb\ *n* [MF *garbe* grace, fr. It *garbo*] **1** : style of dress **2** : CLOTHING, DRESS

2garb *vt* : CLOTHE, ARRAY

gar·bage \'gär-bij\ *n* [ME, animal entrails] : food waste : REFUSE

gar·ble \'gär-bəl\ *vt* **gar·bled**; **gar·bling** \-b(ə-)liŋ\ [ME *garbelen* to cull, fr. It *garbellare* to sift, fr. Ar *ghirbāl* sieve, fr. LL *cribellum*] : to distort the meaning or sound of ⟨*garble* a story⟩ ⟨*garble* words⟩ — **gar·bler** \-b(ə-)lər\ *n*

gar·çon \gär-'sōⁿ\ *n, pl* **garçons** \-'sōⁿ(z)\ [F, boy, servant] : WAITER

1gar·den \'gärd-ⁿn\ *n* [ONF *gardin*, of Gmc origin; akin to E *yard*] **1** : a plot of ground where herbs, fruits, flowers, or vegetables are grown **2 a** : a public recreation area or park; *esp* : one for the exhibition of plants or animals ⟨a botanical *garden*⟩ **b** : an open-air eating or drinking place

2garden *vb* **gar·dened**; **gar·den·ing** \'gärd-niŋ, -ⁿn-iŋ\ **1** : to lay out or work in a garden **2** : to make into a garden — **gar·den·er** \'gärd-nər, -ⁿn-ər\ *n*

3garden *adj* **1** : of, relating to, or frequenting gardens **2** : of a kind grown under cultivation esp. in the open **3** : ORDINARY, COMMONPLACE

garden heliotrope *n* : a tall Old World valerian widely grown for its fragrant tiny flowers and roots which yield the drug valerian

gar·de·nia \gär-'dē-nyə\ *n* [after Alexander *Garden* d1791 Scottish naturalist] : any of various Old World tropical trees and shrubs of the madder family with leathery leaves and fragrant white or yellow flowers; *also* : one of the flowers

Gar·gan·tua \gär-'ganch-(ə-)wə\ *n* : a gigantic king in Rabelais's *Gargantua* having a great capacity for food and drink — **gar·gan·tu·an** \-wən\ *adj, often cap*

1gar·gle \'gär-gəl\ *vb* **gar·gled**; **gar·gling** \-g(ə-)liŋ\ : to rinse the throat with a liquid kept in motion by air forced through it from the lungs

2gargle *n* **1** : a liquid used in gargling **2** : a gargling sound

gar·goyle \'gär-,gòil\ *n* [MF *gargouille*] : a spout in the form of a grotesque human or animal figure projecting from a roof gutter to throw rainwater away from a building — **gar·goyled** \-,gòild\ *adj*

gargoyle

gar·ish \'ga(ə)r-ish, 'ge(ə)r-\ *adj* **1 a** : excessively vivid : FLASHY **b** : offensively bright : GLARING **2** : tastelessly showy **syn** see GAUDY — **gar·ish·ly** *adv* — **gar·ish·ness** *n*

1gar·land \'gär-lənd\ *n* [MF *garlande*] : a wreath or rope of leaves or flowers

2garland *vt* : to form into or deck with a garland

gar·lic \'gär-lik\ *n* [OE *gārlēac*, fr. *gār* spear + *lēac* leek] : a European bulbous herb of the lily family widely grown for its pungent compound bulbs much used in cookery; *also* : one of the bulbs — **gar·licky** \-li-kē\ *adj*

1gar·ment \'gär-mənt\ *n* [MF *garnement*, fr. OF *garnir* to equip] : an article of clothing

2garment *vt* : to clothe with or as if with a garment

1gar·ner \'gär-nər\ *n* : a bin or building for storing grain

2garner *vt* **1** : to gather into or as if into a granary **2 a** : to acquire by effort : EARN **b** : ACCUMULATE, COLLECT

gar·net \'gär-nət\ *n* [MF *grenat*, fr. *grenat*, adj., red like a pomegranate, fr. *pome grenate* pomegranate] **1** : a brittle and more or less transparent usu. red silicate mineral that occurs mainly in crystals and is used as a semiprecious stone and as an abrasive **2** : a variable color averaging a dark red

gar·net·if·er·ous \,gär-nət-'if-(ə-)rəs\ *adj* : containing garnets

garnet paper *n* : an abrasive paper with crushed garnet as the abrasive

1gar·nish \'gär-nish\ *vt* [MF *garniss-*, *garnir* to warn, equip, garnish, of Gmc origin; akin to E *warn*] **1** : DECO-

RATE, EMBELLISH **2** : to add decorative or savory touches to (food) **3** : GARNISHEE
²garnish *n* **1** : EMBELLISHMENT, ORNAMENT **2** : a savory and usu. decorative condiment
gar·nish·ee \‚gär-nə-'shē\ *vt* **gar·nish·eed**; **gar·nish·ee·ing** **1** : to serve with a garnishment **2** : to take (as a debtor's wages) by legal authority
gar·nish·ment \'gär-nish-mənt\ *n* **1** : GARNISH **2** : a legal warning to a party holding property of a debtor to give it to a creditor; *also* : the attachment of such property (as a bank account or pending wages) to satisfy a creditor
gar·ni·ture \'gär-ni-chər, -nə-‚chúr\ *n* : EMBELLISHMENT, TRIMMING
gar·ret \'gar-ət\ *n* [MF *garite* watchtower] : a room or unfinished part of a house just under the roof
¹gar·ri·son \'gar-ə-sən\ *n* [OF *garison* protection, fr. *garir* to protect, of Gmc origin] **1** : a military post; *esp* : a permanent military installation **2** : the troops stationed at a garrison
²garrison *vt* **1** : to furnish (as a fort or a town) with troops for defense **2** : to protect with forts and soldiers ⟨*garrison* a frontier⟩
garrison house *n* **1** : a house fortified against Indian attack **2** : a colonial house having the second story overhanging the first in the front elevation
garrison state *n* : a state organized on a primarily military basis
¹gar·rote *or* **ga·rotte** \gə-'rät, -'rōt\ *n* [Sp *garrote*] **1 a** : a method of execution by strangling with an iron collar **b** : the iron collar used **2 a** : strangulation esp. for the purpose of robbery **b** : an implement for this purpose
²garrote *or* **garotte** *vt* **1** : to execute with or as if with a garrote **2** : to strangle and rob — **gar·rot·er** *n*
gar·ru·lous \'gar-ə-ləs\ *adj* [L *garrulus*, fr. *garrire* to chatter] : very talkative esp. about trifles : WORDY **syn** see TALKATIVE — **gar·ru·li·ty** \gə-'rü-lət-ē\ *n* — **gar·ru·lous·ly** \'gar-ə-ləs-lē\ *adv* — **gar·ru·lous·ness** *n*
¹gar·ter \'gär-tər\ *n* [ONF *gartier*, fr. *garet* bend of the knee, of Celt origin] **1** : a band or strap worn to hold up a stocking or sock **2 cap a** : the British Order of the Garter **b** : the blue velvet garter that is its badge **c** : membership in the order
²garter *vt* : to support with or as if with a garter
garter snake *n* : any of numerous harmless viviparous American snakes with stripes along the back
¹gas \'gas\ *n, pl* **gas·es** *also* **gas·ses** [NL, alter. of L *chaos* space, chaos] **1** : a fluid (as hydrogen or air) that has neither independent shape nor volume but tends to expand indefinitely **2 a** : a gas or gaseous mixture used as a fuel or as an anesthetic **b** : a gaseous, liquid, or solid substance (as tear gas or mustard gas) that can be used to produce a poisonous, asphyxiating, or irritant atmosphere **3** *slang* : empty talk : BOMBAST **4** : GASOLINE
²gas *vb* **gassed**; **gas·sing** **1 a** : to treat chemically with gas **b** : to poison with gas **2** : to supply with gas or esp. gasoline ⟨*gas* up the automobile⟩ **3** *slang* : to talk idly
gas chamber *n* : a chamber in which people are executed by poison gas
gas·con \'gas-kən\ *n* **1** *cap* : a native of Gascony **2** : a boastful swaggering person — **Gascon** *adj*
gas·con·ade \‚gas-kə-'nād\ *n* **1** : BOASTING, BRAVADO — **gas·conade** *vi*
gas·e·ous \'gas-ē-əs, 'gash-əs\ *adj* **1 a** : having the form of or being gas; *also* : of or relating to gas **b** : SUPERHEATED **2** : lacking substance or solidity
gas fitter *n* : a workman who installs or repairs gas pipes or fittings
gash \'gash\ *vb* [ONF *garser*] : to make a long deep cut in : CUT — **gash** *n*
gas·hold·er \'gas-‚hōl-dər\ *n* : a large cylindrical tank for storing fuel gas under pressure
gas·house \-‚haús\ *n* : GASWORKS
gas·i·fy \'gas-ə-‚fī\ *vb* **-fied**; **-fy·ing** **1** : to convert into gas **2** : to become gaseous — **gas·i·fi·ca·tion** \‚gas-ə-fə-'kā-shən\ *n*
gas·ket \'gas-kət\ *n* **1** : a line or band used to lash a furled sail **2** : material (as asbestos, rubber, or metal) used as packing (as for pistons or pipe joints)

gas·light \'gas-‚līt\ *n* **1** : light made by burning illuminating gas **2 a** : a gas flame **b** : a gas lighting fixture — **gas·light·ing** \-iŋ\ *n*
gas·lit \-‚lit\ *adj* : illuminated by gaslight
gas log *n* : a hollow perforated imitation log used as a gas burner in a fireplace
gas mask *n* : a mask connected to a chemical air filter and used to protect the face and lungs against poison gases
gas·o·gene \'gas-ə-‚jēn\ *n* **1** : an apparatus carried by a vehicle to produce gas for fuel by partial burning of charcoal or wood **2** : a portable apparatus for carbonating liquids
gas·o·line *or* **gas·o·lene** \‚gas-ə-'lēn, 'gas-ə-‚\ *n* : a flammable liquid that evaporates easily, that consists of a mixture of hydrocarbons produced by blending products from natural gas and petroleum or from coal gas or water gas, and that is used esp. as a fuel for automobiles and as a cleaning fluid
gasoline engine *n* : an internal-combustion engine using gasoline as fuel
gas·om·e·ter \ga-'säm-ət-ər\ *n* **1** : a laboratory apparatus for holding and measuring gases **2** : GASHOLDER
gasp \'gasp\ *vb* [ME *gaspen*] **1** : to catch the breath with shock or other emotion **2** : to breathe laboriously : PANT **3** : to utter in a gasping manner — **gasp** *n*
gas·ser \'gas-ər\ *n* : an oil well that yields gas
gas station *n* : FILLING STATION
gas·sy \'gas-ē\ *adj* **gas·si·er**; **-est** **1** : full of or containing gas **2** : having the characteristics of gas **3** : FLATULENT — **gas·si·ness** *n*
gas·tight \'gas-'tīt\ *adj* : impervious to gas
gastr- *or* **gastro-** *also* **gastri-** *comb form* [Gk *gastr-*, *gastēr*] **1** : belly ⟨*gastro*pod⟩ : stomach ⟨*gastri*tis⟩ **2** : gastric and ⟨*gastro*intestinal⟩
gas·tral \'gas-trəl\ *adj* : of or relating to the stomach or digestive tract
gas·tric \'gas-trik\ *adj* : of, relating to, or located near the stomach
gastric juice *n* : a watery acid digestive fluid secreted by glands in the mucous membrane of the stomach
gas·trin \'gas-trən\ *n* : a hormone that induces secretion of gastric juice
gas·tri·tis \gas-'strīt-əs\ *n* : inflammation of the stomach and esp. of its mucous membrane
gas·tro·cne·mi·us \‚gas-trō-'nē-mē-əs, -‚träk-'nē-\ *n* [Gk *gastroknēmē* calf of the leg, fr. *gastēr* belly + *knēmē* leg] : the largest muscle of the calf of the leg
gas·tro·en·ter·ol·o·gy \‚gas-trō-‚ent-ə-'räl-ə-jē\ *n* [Gk *enteron* intestine] : a branch of medicine dealing with the alimentary canal — **gas·tro·en·ter·ol·o·gist** \-jəst\ *n*
gas·tro·in·tes·ti·nal \‚gas-trō-in-'tes-tən-ᵊl\ *adj* : of, relating to, or including both stomach and intestine
gas·tron·o·my \ga-'strän-ə-mē\ *n* [Gk *gastronomia*, fr. *gastēr* belly + *-nomia* (as in *astronomia* astronomy)] : the art of good eating — **gas·tro·nom·ic** \‚gas-trə-'näm-ik\ *adj* — **gas·tro·nom·i·cal** \-'näm-i-kəl\ *adj*
gas·tro·pod \'gas-trə-‚päd\ *n* [Gk *pod-*, *pous* foot] : any of a large class (Gastropoda) of mollusks (as snails) having a muscular ventral foot and usu. a distinct head bearing sensory organs — **gastropod** *also* **gas·trop·o·dan** \ga-'sträp-əd-ən\ *or* **gas·trop·o·dous** \-əd-əs\ *adj*
gas·tro·trich \'gas-trə-‚trik\ *n* : any of a small group (Gastrotricha) of minute freshwater multicellular animals superficially resembling infusorians — **gas·trot·ri·chan** \ga-'strä-tri-kən\ *adj or n*
gas·tro·vas·cu·lar \‚gas-trō-'vas-kyə-lər\ *adj* : functioning in both digestion and circulation
gas·tru·la \'gas-trə-lə\ *n, pl* **-las** *or* **-lae** \-‚lē, -‚lī\ : an early metazoan embryo typically consisting of a double cup-shaped layer of cells produced by a folding in of the wall of the blastula — **gas·tru·lar** \-lər\ *adj*
gas·tru·late \-‚lāt\ *vi* : to become or form a gastrula — **gas·tru·la·tion** \‚gas-trə-'lā-shən\ *n*
gas turbine *n* : an engine in which turbine blades are driven by hot compressed gases produced during combustion
gas·works \'gas-‚wərks\ *n pl* : a plant for manufacturing gas
¹gat \(')gat\ *archaic past of* GET
²gat \'gat\ *n* [short for *Gatling gun*] *slang* : PISTOL
¹gate \'gāt\ *n* [OE *geat*] **1** : an opening in a wall or

fence **2 :** a city or castle entrance often with towers or other defensive structures **3 :** the frame or door that closes a gate **4 :** a means of entrance or exit **5 :** a door, valve, or other device for controlling the passage esp. of fluid **6 :** the total admission receipts or the number of spectators at a sports event

²gate *vt* **:** to control by means of a gate

gate-crash·er \'gāt-,krash-ər\ *n* **:** one who enters without paying admission or attends without invitation — **gate-crash·ing** \-iŋ\

gate·leg table \,gāt-,leg-\ *n* **:** a table with drop leaves supported by movable paired legs

gate·post \'gāt-,pōst\ *n* **:** the post to which a gate is hung or the one against which it closes

gate·way \-,wā\ *n* **1 :** an opening for a gate in a wall or fence **2 :** a passage into or out of a place or state ⟨Gibraltar is the *gateway* to the Mediterranean⟩ ⟨knowledge is the *gateway* to wisdom⟩

¹gath·er \'gath-ər\ *vb* **gath·ered; gath·er·ing** \'gath-(ə-)riŋ\ [OE *gaderian*] **1 :** to bring together ⟨*COLLECT* **2 a :** PICK, HARVEST **b :** to pick up little by little **c :** to gain by gradual increase ⟨*gather* speed⟩ **d :** to accumulate and place in order or readiness ⟨*gathered* up his tools⟩ **3 a :** to summon up ⟨*gather* courage to dive⟩ **b :** to prepare (as oneself) by mustering strength **4 a :** to bring together the parts of **b :** to draw about or close to something ⟨*gathering* his cloak about him⟩ **c :** to pull (fabric) along a line of stitching into puckers **5 :** GUESS, DEDUCE **6 a :** to come together in a body **b :** to cluster around a focus of attraction **7 a :** to swell and fill with pus **b :** GROW, INCREASE ⟨the storm *gathered* in intensity as it advanced⟩ — **gath·er·er** \'gath-ər-ər\ *n*

syn COLLECT, ASSEMBLE: GATHER is the general term for bringing or coming together from a spread-out or scattered state ⟨a crowd *gathered* at the scene of the accident⟩ ⟨*gathered* all the leaves into one pile⟩ COLLECT often implies careful selection or orderly arrangement ⟨*collect* rare coins⟩ ASSEMBLE implies an ordered gathering for a definite purpose often into a unified whole ⟨*assembled* a team of experts for an antarctic expedition⟩

²gather *n* **:** a drawing together; *esp* **:** a puckering in cloth made by gathering

gath·er·ing *n* **1 a :** ASSEMBLY, MEETING **b :** a pus-filled swelling (as an abscess) **2 :** the collecting of food and raw materials from the wild **3 :** COLLECTION, COMPILATION **4 :** a gather in cloth

Gat·ling gun \'gat-liŋ-\ *n* **:** an early machine gun with a revolving cluster of barrels fired once each per revolution

gauche \'gōsh\ *adj* [F, lit., left] **:** lacking social experience or grace **:** CRUDE **syn** see AWKWARD — **gauche·ness** *n*

gau·che·rie \,gō-shə-'rē\ *n* **:** a tactless or awkward action **:** CRUDITY

gau·cho \'gaü-chō\ *n, pl* **gauchos** [AmerSp] **:** a cowboy of the So. American pampas

gaud \'gȯd, 'gäd\ *n* [ME *gaude*, prob. fr. L *gaudēre* to rejoice] **:** ORNAMENT, TRINKET

gaudy \-ē\ *adj* **gaud·i·er; -est :** ostentatiously or tastelessly ornamented — **gaud·i·ly** \-ᵊl-ē\ *adv* — **gaud·i·ness** \-ē-nəs\ *n*

syn GARISH, FLASHY: GAUDY implies a tasteless use of overly bright colors or lavish ornamentation; GARISH stresses an unpleasant brightness; FLASHY applies to what is momentarily dazzling but soon revealed to be shallow and vulgar

¹gauge \'gāj\ *n* [ONF] **1 a :** measurement according to some standard or system **b :** DIMENSIONS, SIZE **2 :** an instrument for measuring, testing, or registering ⟨steam *gauge*⟩ **3 :** the distance between the rails of a railroad **4 :** the size of a shotgun expressed as the number of lead balls each just fitting the interior diameter of the barrel required to make a pound ⟨a 12-*gauge* shotgun⟩ **5 :** the thickness of sheet metal or the diameter of wire or a screw **6 :** the fineness of a knitted fabric in loops per 1½ inch **syn** see STANDARD

²gauge *vt* **1 a :** to measure exactly the size, dimensions, or other measurable quantity of **b :** to determine the capacity or contents of **2 :** ESTIMATE, JUDGE — **gauge·a·ble** \'gā-jə-bəl\ *adj* — **gaug·er** *n*

Gaul \'gȯl\ *n* **:** a Celt of ancient Gaul

¹Gaul·ish \'gȯ-lish\ *adj* **:** of or relating to the Gauls or their language or land

²Gaulish *n* **:** the Celtic language of the ancient Gauls

gaunt \'gȯnt, 'gänt\ *adj* [ME] **1 :** being thin and angular **2 :** attenuated by suffering or weariness **3 :** BARREN, DESOLATE **syn** see LANK — **gaunt·ly** *adv* — **gaunt·ness** *n*

¹gaunt·let \'gȯnt-lət, 'gänt-\ *n* [MF *gantelet*, dim. of *gant* glove, of Gmc origin] **1 :** a protective glove worn with medieval armor **2 :** a protective glove used in industry **3 :** a challenge to combat **4 :** a dress glove extending above the wrist — **gaunt·let·ed** \-lət-əd\ *adj*

²gauntlet *n* **1 :** a double file of men armed with weapons (as clubs) with which to strike at an individual who is made to run between them **2 :** CROSS FIRE; *also* **:** ORDEAL

gauntlet 1

gaur \'gaü(ə)r\ *n* [Hindi, fr. Skt *gaura;* akin to E *cow*] **:** an East Indian wild ox

gauss \'gaüs\ *n, pl* **gauss** *also* **gauss·es** [after Karl F. *Gauss d*1855 German mathematician] **:** the cgs unit of magnetic induction

gauze \'gȯz\ *n* [MF *gaze*] **1 :** a thin often transparent fabric used chiefly for clothing or draperies **2 :** a loosely woven cotton surgical dressing **3 :** a woven fabric of metal or plastic filaments — **gauzy** \'gȯ-zē\ *adj*

gave *past of* GIVE

gav·el \'gav-əl\ *n* **:** the mallet of a presiding officer or auctioneer

ga·votte \gə-'vät\ *n* [F] **:** a dance of French peasant origin in moderately quick 4/4 time marked by the raising rather than sliding of the feet — **gavotte** *vi*

Ga·wain \gə-'wān, 'gä-,wān\ *n* **:** a nephew of King Arthur and knight of the Round Table

¹gawk \'gȯk\ *vi* **:** to gape or stare stupidly

²gawk *n* **:** a clumsy stupid person **:** LOUT

gawky \'gȯ-kē\ *adj* **gawk·i·er; -est :** AWKWARD, CLUMSY ⟨a tall *gawky* youth⟩ — **gawk·i·ly** \-kə-lē\ *adv* — **gawk·i·ness** \-kē-nəs\ *n*

gay \'gā\ *adj* [MF *gai*] **1 :** happily excited **:** MERRY **2 a :** BRIGHT, LIVELY **b :** brilliant in color **3 :** given to social pleasures; *also* **:** LICENTIOUS **4 :** HOMOSEXUAL — **gay** *adv* — **gay·ness** *n*

gay·e·ty *var of* GAIETY

gay·ly *var of* GAILY

gaze \'gāz\ *vi* [ME *gazen*] **:** to fix the eyes in a steady intent look — **gaze** *n* — **gaz·er** *n*

ga·ze·bo \gə-'zā-bō, -'zē-\ *n, pl* **-bos :** BELVEDERE

gaze·hound \'gāz-,haùnd\ *n* **:** a dog that hunts chiefly by sight; *esp* **:** GREYHOUND

ga·zelle \gə-'zel\ *n, pl* **gazelles** *also* **gazelle** [F, fr. Ar *ghazāl*] **:** any of numerous small graceful swift antelopes with soft lustrous eyes

¹ga·zette \gə-'zet\ *n* [F, fr. It *gazzetta*] **1 :** NEWSPAPER **2 :** an official journal

²gazette *vt, chiefly Brit* **:** to announce or publish in a gazette

gaz·et·teer \,gaz-ə-'ti(ə)r\ *n* **1** *archaic* **:** JOURNALIST, PUBLICIST **2** [*The Gazetteer's: or, Newsman's Interpreter*, a geographical index edited by Laurence Echard] **:** a geographical dictionary

G clef *n* **:** TREBLE CLEF

ge- *or* **geo-** *comb form* [Gk *gē-, geo-*, fr. *gē*] **1 :** earth **:** ground **:** soil ⟨*geanticline*⟩ ⟨*geophyte*⟩ **2 :** geographical **:** geography and ⟨*geopolitics*⟩

¹gear \'gi(ə)r\ *n* [OE *gearwe*] **1 :** CLOTHING, GARMENTS **2 :** EQUIPMENT, PARAPHERNALIA ⟨fishing *gear*⟩ ⟨camping *gear*⟩ ⟨electronic *gear*⟩ **3 :** the rigging of a ship or boat **4 a** (1) **:** a mechanism that performs a specific function in a complete machine ⟨steering *gear*⟩ (2) **:** a toothed wheel **:** COGWHEEL (3) **:** working relation or adjustment ⟨in *gear*⟩ **b :** one of two or more adjustments of a motor-vehicle transmission that determine the direction of travel and the relative speed between the engine and the motion of the vehicle ⟨reverse *gear*⟩ ⟨a car goes slower in first *gear* than in third *gear*⟩ — **gear·less** \-ləs\ *adj*

²gear *vb* **1 a :** to provide with gearing **b :** to connect by gearing **c :** to put into gear **2 a :** to make ready for effective operation **b :** to adjust or become adjusted so as to match or blend with something **3 :** to be in or come into gear

gear·box \'gi(ə)r-,bäks\ *n* **:** TRANSMISSION

gear·ing *n* **1 :** the act or process of providing or fitting with gears **2** : the parts by which motion is transmitted from one portion of machinery to another

gear·shift \'gi(ə)r-,shift\ *n* : a mechanism by which the transmission gears in a power-transmission system are engaged and disengaged

gear wheel *n* : a toothed wheel that gears with another piece of a mechanism; *esp* : COGWHEEL

Geat \'gēt, 'yaot\ *n* : a member of a Scandinavian people of southern Sweden subjugated by the Swedes in the 6th century — **Geat·ish** \-ish\ *adj*

gecko \'gek-ō\ *n, pl* **geck·os** *or* **geck·oes** [Malay *ge'kok*] : any of numerous small harmless chiefly tropical and nocturnal insect-eating lizards

¹gee \'jē\ *imperative verb* — used as a direction to turn to the right or move ahead; compare **⁴HAW**

²gee *interj* [euphemism for *Jesus*] — used to express surprise or enthusiasm

geese *pl of* GOOSE

gee·zer \'gē-zər\ *n, slang* : a queer, odd, or eccentric man

ge·gen·schein \'gā-gən-,shīn\ *n, often cap* [G, fr. *gegen* against, counter- + *schein* shine] : a faint light on the celestial sphere opposite the sun

Ge·hen·na \gi-'hen-ə\ *n* **1** : HELL **2** : a place or state of misery

Gei·ger counter \,gī-gər-'\ *or* **Geiger–Mül·ler counter** \-'myül-ər-, -'mil-, -'məl-\ *n* : an electronic instrument for detecting the presence of cosmic rays or radioactive substances by means of the ionizing particles that come from them, enter the instrument, and cause pulses of electricity that are indicated visibly or audibly (as by clicks)

gei·sha \'gā-shə, 'gē-\ *n, pl* **geisha** *or* **geishas** [Jap, fr. *gei* art + *-sha* person] : a Japanese girl who is trained to provide entertaining company for men

¹gel \'jel\ *n* [*gelatin*] : a colloid in a more solid form than a sol (fruit jelly and gelatin dessert are *gels*)

²gel *vi* **gelled; gel·ling** : to change into or take on the form of a gel — **gel·a·ble** \'jel-ə-bəl\ *adj*

gel·ate \'jel-,āt\ *vi* : GEL — **gel·a·tion** \je-'lā-shən\ *n*

gel·a·tin *also* **gel·a·tine** \'jel-ət-ᵊn\ *n* [F *gélatine*, fr. It *gelatina*, fr. *gelare* to freeze, fr. L; akin to E *cold*] **1** : gummy or sticky material obtained from animal tissues by boiling; *esp* : a colloidal protein used as a food, in ᵗ hotography, and in medicine **2 a** : any of various substances resembling gelatin **b** : an edible jelly formed with gelatin **c** : a thin colored transparent sheet used to color a stage light

ge·lat·i·nous \jə-'lat-nəs, -ᵊn-əs\ *adj* **1** : resembling gelatin or jelly (a *gelatinous* precipitate) **2** : relating to, or containing gelatin — **ge·lat·i·nous·ly** *adv* — **ge·lat·i·nous·ness** *n*

geld \'geld\ *vt* [ON *gelda*] : CASTRATE; *also* : SPAY

geld·ing \'gel-diŋ\ *n* : a castrated animal; *esp* : a castrated male horse

gel·id \'jel-əd\ *adj* [L *gelidus*, fr. *gelu* frost, cold; akin to E *cold*] : extremely cold : ICY — **ge·lid·i·ty** \jə-'lid-ət-ē, je-\ *n* — **gel·id·ly** \'jel-əd-lē\ *adv*

¹gem \'jem\ *n* [L *gemma* bud, gem] **1 a** : JEWEL **b** : a precious or sometimes semiprecious stone cut and polished for ornament **2** : something usu. small or brief that is prized for great beauty or perfection

²gem *vt* **gemmed; gem·ming** : to adorn with or as if with gems

Ge·ma·ra \gə-'mär-ə\ *n* [Aram *gĕmārā* completion] : a commentary on the Mishnah forming the second part of the Talmud

gem·i·nate \'jem-ə-,nāt\ *vb* [L *geminus* twin] : DOUBLE — **gem·i·na·tion** \,jem-ə-'nā-shən\ *n*

Gem·i·ni \'jem-ə-(,)nē, -,nī\ *n* [L, lit., the twins (Castor and Pollux)] **1** : the 3d zodiacal constellation pictorially represented as the twins Castor and Pollux sitting together and located on the opposite side of the Milky Way from Taurus and Orion **2** : the 3d sign of the zodiac — see ZODIAC table

gem·ma \'jem-ə\ *n, pl* **gem·mae** \'jem-,ē\ [L] : BUD; *also* : a many-celled asexual reproductive body that becomes detached from a parent plant — **gem·ma·ceous** \jə-'mā-shəs\ *adj* — **gem·mate** \'jem-,āt\ *adj* — **gem·ma·tion** \je-'mā-shən\ *n*

gem·mo·log·i·cal *or* **gem·o·log·i·cal** \,jem-ə-'läj-i-kəl\ *adj* : of or relating to a gem or gemmology

gem·mol·o·gy *or* **gem·ol·o·gy** \je-'mäl-ə-jē\ *n* : the science of gems

gem·mule \'jem-yül\ *n* : a small bud; *esp* : an internal resistant reproductive bud (as of a sponge) — **gem·mu·la·tion** \,jem-yə-'lā-shən\ *n*

gem·stone \'jem-,stōn\ *n* : a mineral or petrified material that when cut and polished can be used in jewelry

gen- *or* **geno-** *comb form* [Gk *genos* birth, race, kind] **1** : race (*geno*cide) **2** : genus : kind (*geno*type)

-gen \jən, ,jen\ *also* **-gene** \,jēn\ *n comb form* [Gk *-genēs* born, fr. *gignesthai* to be born; akin to E *kin*] **1** : producer (andro*gen*) **2** : one that is (so) produced (culti*gen*) (phos*gene*)

gen·darme \'zhän-,därm, 'jän-\ *n* [F] : one of a body of soldiers esp. in France serving as an armed police force for the maintenance of public order

gen·dar·mer·ie *or* **gen·dar·mery** \jän-'dä(r)m-ə-rē, zhän-\ *n, pl* **-mer·ies** : a body of gendarmes

gen·der \'jen-dər\ *n* [MF *genre, gendre*, fr. L *gener-, genus* kind, gender] **1** : SEX **2** : any of two or more classes of words (as nouns or pronouns) or of forms of words (as adjectives) in a language that are partly arbitrary but also partly based on distinguishable characteristics (as sex) and that determine agreement with and selection of other words or grammatical forms; *also* : membership of a word or a grammatical form in such a class — compare COMMON, FEMININE, MASCULINE, NEUTER

gene \'jēn\ *n* [G *gen*, short for *pangen*, fr. *pan-* + *-gen*] : an element of the germ plasm that transmits a hereditary character and forms a specific part of a self-perpetuating deoxyribonucleic acid in the cell nucleus

ge·ne·al·o·gy \,jē-nē-'äl-ə-jē, ,jen-ē-, -'al-\ *n, pl* **-gies** [Gk *genealogia*, fr. *genea* race, family + *-logia* -logy] **1** : a history of the descent of a person or family from an ancestor **2** : the descent of a person or family from an ancestor : PEDIGREE, LINEAGE **3** : the study of family pedigrees — **ge·ne·a·log·i·cal** \,jē-nē-ə-'läj-i-kəl, ,jen-ē-\ *adj* — **ge·ne·a·log·i·cal·ly** \-'läj-i-k(ə-)lē\ *adv* — **ge·ne·al·o·gist** \-'äl-ə-jəst, -'al-\ *n*

gene mutation *n* : mutation due to fundamental change in a gene

genera *pl of* GENUS

¹gen·er·al \'jen-(ə-)rəl\ *adj* [L *generalis*, fr. *gener-, genus* kind, class] **1** : of or relating to the whole : not local (a *general* election) **2** : taken as a whole (the *general* body of citizens) **3** : relating to or covering all instances or individuals of a class or group (a *general* conclusion) **4** : not limited in meaning : not specific or in detail (a *general* outline) **5** : common to many (a *general* custom) **6** : not special : not specialized (a *general* store) **7** : not precise or definite (*general* comments) **8** : superior in rank : concerned with administration or counseling (*general* manager) (inspector *general*) syn see UNIVERSAL

²general *n* **1** : something that involves or is applicable to the whole **2** *archaic* : the general public : PEOPLE **3 a** : a military officer ranking above a colonel **b** (1) : a commissioned officer in the army or air force ranking above a lieutenant general and below a general of the army or a general of the air force (2) : a commissioned officer of the highest rank in the marine corps — **in general** : for the most part : GENERALLY

general assembly *n* **1** : a legislative assembly; *esp* : a U.S. state legislature **2** *cap G&A* : the supreme deliberative body of the United Nations

General Court *n* : the state legislature in Massachusetts and New Hampshire

general delivery *n* : a department of a post office that handles the delivery of mail at a post office window to persons who call for it

gen·er·a·lis·si·mo \,jen-(ə-)rə-'lis-ə-,mō\ *n, pl* **-mos** [It] : the chief commander of an army : COMMANDER IN CHIEF

gen·er·al·i·ty \,jen-ə-'ral-ət-ē\ *n, pl* **-ties** **1** : the quality or state of being general **2 a** : GENERALIZATION **2 b** : a vague or inadequate statement **3** : the greatest part : BULK

gen·er·al·i·za·tion \,jen-(ə-)rə-lə-'zā-shən\ *n* **1** : the act or process of generalizing **2** : a general statement, law, principle, or proposition

gen·er·al·ize \'jen-(ə-)rə-,līz\ *vb* **1** : to make general **2** : to draw general conclusions from (*generalized* their experiences) **3** : to reach a general conclusion esp. on

---

ə abut; ᵊ kitten; ər further; a back; ā bake; ä cot, cart; aú out; ch chin; e less; ē easy; g gift; i trip; ī life

the basis of particular instances **4** : to extend throughout the body — **gen·er·al·iz·er** n

gen·er·al·ized adj : made general; esp : not highly specialized biologically nor strictly adapted (as to a particular environment)

gen·er·al·ly \'jen-(ə-)rə-lē, 'jen-ər-lē\ adv : in a general manner: as **a** : in disregard of specific instances and with regard to an overall picture ⟨generally speaking⟩ **b** : as a rule : USUALLY

general of the air force : a general of the highest rank in the air force whose insignia is five stars

general of the army : a general of the highest rank in the army whose insignia is five stars

general practitioner n : a physician or veterinarian who does not limit his practice to a specialty

gen·er·al·ship \'jen-(ə-)rəl-,ship\ n **1** : office or tenure of office of a general **2** : military skill as a high commander **3** : LEADERSHIP

general staff n : a group of officers who assist a high-level commander in planning, coordinating, and supervising operations

general store n : a retail store that carries a wide variety of goods but is not divided into departments

general strike n : a strike involving all union workers in all the trades and industries of an area

gen·er·ate \'jen-ə-,rāt\ vt [L generare, fr. gener-, genus birth, kind] : to bring into existence: as **a** : to originate esp. by a vital or chemical process : PRODUCE ⟨generate an electric current⟩ ⟨heat generated by friction⟩ **b** : to trace out mathematically by a moving point, line, or surface — **gen·er·a·tive** \-ə-,rāt-iv, -rət-\ adj

gen·er·a·tion \,jen-ə-'rā-shən\ n **1 a** : a body of living beings constituting a single step in the line of descent from an ancestor **b** : a group of individuals born and living at the same time **c** : a type or class of objects developed from an earlier type **2** : the average span of time between the birth of parents and that of their offspring **3** : the action or process of generating ⟨generation of an electric current⟩

generative cell n : GAMETE

generative nucleus n : the nucleus of a developing pollen grain that produces sperm nuclei — compare TUBE NUCLEUS

gen·er·a·tor \'jen-ə-,rāt-ər\ n **1** : one that generates **2** : an apparatus in which vapor or gas is formed **3** : a machine by which mechanical energy is changed into electrical energy

gen·er·a·trix \,jen-ə-'rā-triks\ n, pl **-tri·ces** \-trə-,sēz\ : a point, line, or surface whose motion generates a line, surface, or solid

ge·ner·ic \jə-'ner-ik\ adj **1** : of, relating to, or characteristic of a whole group or class : not specific : GENERAL **2** : of, relating to, or ranking as a biological genus — **ge·ner·i·cal·ly** \-'ner-i-k(ə-)lē\ adv

gen·er·os·i·ty \,jen-ə-'räs-ət-ē\ n, pl **-ties 1 a** : liberality in spirit or act; esp : liberality in giving **b** : a generous act **2** : ABUNDANCE, LARGENESS

gen·er·ous \'jen-(ə-)rəs\ adj [L generosus highborn, magnanimous, fr. gener-, genus birth, family] **1** : free in giving or sharing : not mean or stingy : UNSELFISH ⟨a generous giver⟩ **2** : HIGH-MINDED, NOBLE ⟨generous in dealing with a defeated enemy⟩ **3** : ABUNDANT, PLENTIFUL, AMPLE ⟨a generous supply⟩ — **gen·er·ous·ly** adv — **gen·er·ous·ness** n

syn GENEROUS, BOUNTIFUL, MUNIFICENT mean giving freely and unstintingly. GENEROUS stresses warmheartedness in giving rather than the size or importance of the gift; BOUNTIFUL implies giving lavishly from ample means or an inexhaustible source of supply; MUNIFICENT suggests a scale of giving appropriate to lords and princes

gen·e·sis \'jen-ə-səs\ n, pl **-e·ses** \-ə-,sēz\ [Gk, fr. gignesthai to be born] : the origin or coming into being of something

Genesis — see BIBLE table

gen·et \'jen-ət\ n [MF genete, fr. Ar jarnayt] : an Old World carnivorous mammal related to the civets

ge·net·ic \jə-'net-ik\ adj **1** : of or relating to the origin, development, or causes of something **2 a** : of, relating to, or involving genetics **b** : GENIC — **ge·net·i·cal** \-i-kəl\ adj — **ge·net·i·cal·ly** \-i-k(ə-)lē\ adv

genetic code n : the biochemical basis of heredity consist-

ing of triplets of nucleotides that determine the specific amino acid sequence in proteins and that are uniform for the forms of life studied so far

ge·net·ics \jə-'net-iks\ n **1** : a branch of biology that deals with the heredity and variation of organisms **2** : the genetic makeup and phenomena of an organism, type, group, or condition — **ge·net·i·cist** \-'net-ə-səst\ n

Ge·ne·va bands \jə-,nē-və-\ n pl [fr. their use by the Calvinist clergy of Geneva, Switzerland] : two strips of white cloth suspended from the front of a clerical collar and sometimes used by Protestant clergymen

Geneva gown n : a loose large-sleeved black academic gown widely used as a vestment by Protestant clergymen

¹**ge·nial** \'jē-nyəl, -nē-əl\ adj [L genialis, fr. genius] **1** : favorable to growth or comfort ⟨a genial climate⟩ **2** : being cheerful and cheering : KINDLY — **ge·ni·al·i·ty** \,jē-nē-'al-ət-ē, jēn-'yal-\ n — **ge·nial·ly** \'jē-nyə-lē, -nē-ə-lē\ adv

²**ge·ni·al** \jə-'nī(-ə)l\ adj [Gk geneion chin, fr. genys jaw; akin to E chin] : of or relating to the chin

gen·ic \'jē-nik\ adj : of, relating to, or being a gene — **gen·i·cal·ly** \-ni-k(ə-)lē\ adv

-gen·ic \'jen-ik\ adj comb form [-gen & -geny + -ic] **1** : producing : forming ⟨carcinogenic⟩ **2** : produced by : formed from ⟨phytogenic⟩ **3** [photogenic] : suitable for production or reproduction by (such) a medium ⟨telegenic⟩

ge·nic·u·late \jə-'nik-yə-lət\ or **ge·nic·u·lat·ed** \-,lāt-əd\ adj : bent abruptly at an angle like a bent knee — **ge·nic·u·late·ly** adv

ge·nie \'jē-nē\ n, pl **ge·nies** \-nēz\ also **ge·nii** \-nē-,ī\ [F génie, fr. Ar jinnīy] : JINN

¹**gen·i·tal** \'jen-ə-t²l\ adj [L genitalis, fr. genit-, gignere to beget] : of or relating to reproduction or the sexual organs

²**genital** n : one of the genitalia

gen·i·ta·lia \,jen-ə-'tāl-ē-ə, -'tāl-yə\ n pl : reproductive organs; esp : the external genital organs — **gen·i·tal·ic** \-'tal-ik\ adj

gen·i·tive \'jen-ət-iv\ adj : of, relating to, or constituting a grammatical case marking typically a relationship esp. of possessor or source — compare POSSESSIVE — **gen·i·ti·val** \,jen-ə-'tī-vəl\ adj — **genitive** n

gen·i·to·uri·nary \,jen-ə-tō-'yùr-ə-,ner-ē\ adj : of or relating to the genital and urinary organs or functions

ge·nius \'jē-nyəs\ n, pl **ge·nius·es** or **ge·nii** \-nē-,ī\ [L, tutelary spirit, fondness for social enjoyment, fr. gignere to beget] **1** pl genii : an attendant spirit of a person or place **2** : a strong leaning or inclination : PENCHANT **3 a** : a peculiar, distinctive, or identifying character or spirit **b** : the associations and traditions of a place **4** pl genii **a** : an elemental spirit : JINN **b** : a person who influences another for good or bad ⟨his brother was his evil genius⟩ **5** pl geniuses **a** : a single strongly marked capacity or aptitude **b** : extraordinary intellectual power esp. as manifested in creative activity **c** : a person endowed with transcendent mental superiority; esp : a person with a very high intelligence quotient **syn** see TALENT

geno- — see GEN-

gen·o·cide \'jen-ə-,sīd\ n : the deliberate and systematic destruction of a racial, political, or cultural group — **gen·o·cid·al** \,jen-ə-'sīd-²l\ adj

ge·nome \'jē-,nōm\ or **ge·nom** \-,näm\ n : one haploid set of chromosomes with the genes they contain — **ge·no·mic** \ji-'nō-mik, -'näm-ik\ adj

ge·no·type \'jē-nə-,tīp, 'jen-ə-\ n : the genetic constitution of an individual or group; also : a class or group of individuals with a particular genetic makeup — **ge·no·typ·ic** \,jē-nə-'tip-ik, ,jen-ə-\ also **ge·no·typ·i·cal** \-'tip-i-kəl\ adj — **ge·no·typ·i·cal·ly** \-i-k(ə-)lē\ adv

-ge·nous \jə-nəs\ adj comb form [-gen + -ous] **1** : producing : yielding ⟨alkaligenous⟩ **2** : having (such) an origin ⟨endogenous⟩

genre \'zhä(ⁿ)n-rə, 'zhäⁿ'(-ə)r\ n [F] **1** : KIND, SORT **2 a** : paintings that depict scenes or events from everyday life usu. realistically; also : the style of painting featuring such subject matter **b** : a distinctive type or category of literary composition

gens \'jenz, 'gen(t)s\ n, pl **gen·tes** \'jen-,tēz, 'gen-,tās\ [L gent-, gens] : a Roman clan embracing the families of the same stock in the male line

---

j joke; **ŋ** sing; **ō** flow; **ȯ** flaw; **ȯi** coin; **th** thin; **th** this; **ü** loot; **ù** foot; **y** yet; **yü** few; **yù** furious; **zh** vision

gent \'jent\ *n* [short for *gentleman*] : MAN, FELLOW
gen·teel \jen-'tēl\ *adj* [MF *gentil* gentle] **1 a** : ARISTO-
CRATIC **b** : ELEGANT, GRACEFUL **c** : STYLISH **d** : POLITE,
REFINED **2 a** : maintaining the appearance of superior
or middle-class social status or respectability **b** : marked
by false delicacy, prudery, or affectation — **gen·teel·ly**
\-'tēl-lē\ *adv* — **gen·teel·ness** *n*
gen·tian \'jen-chən\ *n* [L *gentiana*]
: any of various herbs with opposite
smooth leaves and showy usu. blue
flowers

gentian violet *n*, *often cap G&V* : a
violet dye in the form of a green powder
produced chemically and used as a biological stain and as a bactericide and
fungicide
gen·tile \'jen-ˌtīl\ *n* [LL *gentilis*
heathen, fr. L *gent-*, *gens* clan, nation;
akin to E *kin*] **1** *often cap* : a person
who is not Jewish **2** : HEATHEN,
PAGAN **3** *often cap* : a person who is
not a Mormon — **gentile** *adj*, *often cap*

fringed gentian

gen·til·i·ty \jen-'til-ət-ē\ *n*, *pl* **-ties**
1 : good birth and family **2** : the qualities characteristic
of a well-bred person **3** : good manners **4** : maintenance
of the appearance of superior or middle-class social status
¹gen·tle \'jent-ᵊl\ *adj* [OF *gentil*, fr. L *gentilis* of a clan,
fr. *gent-*, *gens* clan, nation] **1 a** : belonging or suitable
to a family of high social station **b** : of, relating to, or
characteristic of a gentleman **c** : KIND, AMIABLE ⟨*gentle*
reader⟩ **2 a** : TRACTABLE, DOCILE **b** : not harsh or stern
: MILD **3** : SOFT, DELICATE **4** : MODERATE ⟨*gentle* slopes⟩
— **gen·tle·ness** \'jent-ᵊl-nəs\ *n* — **gen·tly** \'jent-lē\ *adv*
²gentle *vt* **gen·tled**; **gen·tling** \'jent-liŋ, -ᵊl-iŋ\ **1** : to
make mild, docile, soft, or moderate **2** : MOLLIFY,
PLACATE
gen·tle·folk \'jent-ᵊl-ˌfōk\ *also* **gen·tle·folks** \-ˌfōks\
n pl : persons of good family and breeding
gen·tle·man \'jent-ᵊl-mən\ *n* **1** : a man of good family
2 : a well-bred man of good education and good social
position **3** : MAN — used in the plural as a form of address
in speaking to a group of men
gen·tle·man·ly \-lē\ *adj* : characteristic of or having the
character of a gentleman — **gen·tle·man·li·ness** *n*
gentleman's agreement *n* : an agreement secured only by
the honor of the participants — called also *gentlemen's
agreement*
gen·tle·wom·an \'jent-ᵊl-ˌwùm-ən\ *n* **1** : a woman of
good family or breeding **2** : a woman attending a lady
of rank
gen·try \'jen-trē\ *n* **1** : people of good birth, breeding,
and education : ARISTOCRACY **2** : the class of English
people between the nobility and the yeomanry **3** : PEOPLE;
esp : persons of a designated class
gen·u·flect \'jen-yə-ˌflekt\ *vt* [L *genu* knee (akin to E
knee) + *flectere* to bend] **1** : to bend the knee **2** : to
touch the knee to the floor or ground esp. in worship —
gen·u·flec·tion \ˌjen-yə-'flek-shən\ *n*
gen·u·ine \'jen-yə-wən\ *adj* [L *genuinus*] **1** : being
actually what it seems to be : REAL ⟨*genuine* gold⟩ ⟨a
genuine antique⟩ **2** : SINCERE, HONEST ⟨a *genuine* interest
in classical music⟩ **syn** see AUTHENTIC — **gen·u·ine·ly** *adv*
— **gen·u·ine·ness** *n*
ge·nus \'jē-nəs\ *n*, *pl* **gen·era** \'jen-ə-rə\ [L *gener-*,
genus birth, race, kind; akin to E *kin*] **1** : a category of
biological classification ranking between the family and
the species, comprising structurally or genetically related
species and being designated by a Latin or latinized
capitalized singular noun **2** : a class of objects divided
into several subordinate groups
-ge·ny \j-ə-nē\ *n comb form*, *pl* **-genies** [Gk *-genēs* born]
: generation : production ⟨bio*geny*⟩
geo- — see GE-
geo·cen·tric \ˌjē-ō-'sen-trik\ *adj* **1** : relating to or measured from the earth's center **2** : having or relating to
the earth as a center — compare HELIOCENTRIC
geo·chem·is·try \-'kem-ə-strē\ *n* : a science that deals
with the chemical composition of and chemical changes
in the crust of the earth — **geo·chem·i·cal** \-'kem-i-
kəl\ *adj*
geo·chro·nol·o·gy \ˌjē-ō-krə-'näl-ə-jē\ *n* : the chronology

of the past as indicated by geologic data — **geo·chron·o-
log·i·cal** \-ˌkrän-ᵊl-'äj-i-kəl, -ˌkrōn-\ *adj*
ge·ode \'jē-ˌōd\ *n* [Gk *geōdēs* earthlike, fr. *gē* earth] : a
nodule of stone having a cavity lined with crystals or
mineral matter; *also* : the cavity in a geode
¹ge·o·des·ic \ˌjē-ə-'des-ik, -'dē-sik\ *adj* : made of a framework of light straight-sided polygons in tension ⟨a *geo-
desic* dome⟩
²geodesic *n* : the shortest line between two points on a
surface
ge·od·e·sy \jē-'äd-ə-sē\ *n* [Gk *geōdaisia*, fr. *geō-* ge- +
daiesthai to divide] : a branch of applied mathematics
that determines the exact positions of points and the figures
and areas of large portions of the earth's surface, the shape
and size of the earth, and the variations of terrestrial
gravity and magnetism — **ge·od·e·sist** \-səst\ *n* —
ge·o·det·ic \ˌjē-ə-'det-ik\ *adj* — **ge·o·det·i·cal·ly** \-'det-
i-k(ə-)lē\ *adv*
ge·og·ra·pher \jē-'äg-rə-fər\ *n* : a specialist in geography
ge·o·graph·ic \ˌjē-ə-'graf-ik\ *adj* **1** : of or relating to
geography ⟨the *geographic* center of the U.S.⟩ **2** : belonging to or characteristic of a particular region ⟨a
geographic industry⟩ — **ge·o·graph·i·cal** \-i-kəl\ *adj* —
ge·o·graph·i·cal·ly \-i-k(ə-)lē\ *adv*
geographical mile *n* : MILE 2
ge·og·ra·phy \jē-'äg-rə-fē\ *n*, *pl* **-phies** **1** : a science
that deals with the natural features of the earth and its
climate, products, and inhabitants **2** : the natural features of an area
ge·o·log·ic \ˌjē-ə-'läj-ik\ *adj* : of, relating to, or based on
geology — **ge·o·log·i·cal** \-i-kəl\ *adj* — **ge·o·log·i·cal·ly**
\-i-k(ə-)lē\ *adv*
geologic time *n* : the long period of time that deals with
the sequence of events in the earth's geological history
ge·ol·o·gist \jē-'äl-ə-jəst\ *n* : a specialist in geology
ge·ol·o·gize \-ˌjīz\ *vi* : to study geology or make geologic
investigations
ge·ol·o·gy \jē-'äl-ə-jē\ *n*, *pl* **-gies** **1 a** : a science that
deals with the history of the earth and its life esp. as
recorded in rocks **b** : a study of the features of a celestial
body (as the moon) **2** : the geologic features of an area
geo·mag·net·ic \ˌjē-ō-mag-'net-ik\ *adj* : of or relating
to the magnetism of the earth — **geo·mag·ne·tism**
\-'mag-nə-ˌtiz-əm\ *n*
ge·om·e·ter \jē-'äm-ət-ər\ *n* : a specialist in geometry
ge·o·met·ric \ˌjē-ə-'me-trik\ *adj* **1** : of, relating to, or
based on the methods or principles of geometry **2** : utilizing rectilinear or simple curvilinear motifs or outlines in
design — **ge·o·met·ri·cal** \-'me-tri-kəl\ *adj* — **ge·o·
met·ri·cal·ly** \-tri-k(ə-)lē\ *adv*
ge·om·e·tri·cian \(ˌ)jē-ˌäm-ə-'trish-ən\ *n* : GEOMETER
geometric mean *n* **1** : the square root of the product of
two terms : a term between any two terms of a geometric
progression **2** : the *n*th root of the product of *n* numbers
geometric progression *n* : a progression (as 1, ½, ¼) in
which the ratio of a term to its predecessor is always the
same
ge·o·met·rid \ˌjē-ə-'me-trəd, jē-'äm-ə-\ *n* : any of a family
of medium-sized moths with large wings and larvae that
are loopers — **geometrid** *adj*
ge·om·e·trize \jē-'äm-ə-ˌtrīz\ *vb* **1** : to work by or as
if by geometric methods or laws **2** : to represent geo-
metrically
ge·om·e·try \jē-'äm-ə-trē\ *n* [Gk *geōmetria*, lit., measurement of the earth] **1 a** : a branch of mathematics that
deals with the measurement, properties, and relationships of points, lines, angles, surfaces, and solids **b** : a
particular type or system of geometry **2 a** : the arrangement of the parts of a device ⟨the *geometry* of an electron
tube⟩ **b** : SHAPE ⟨the *geometry* of a crystal⟩
geo·mor·phol·o·gy \ˌjē-ō-mór-'fäl-ə-jē\ *n* : a science that
deals with the land and submarine relief features of the
earth's surface — **geo·mor·pho·log·i·cal** \-ˌmór-fə-
'läj-i-kəl\ *adj*
geo·phys·ics \ˌjē-ō-'fiz-iks\ *n* : the physics of the earth
including the fields of meteorology, hydrology, oceanog-
raphy, seismology, volcanology, magnetism, radioactivity, and geodesy — **geo·phys·i·cal** \-'fiz-i-kəl\ *adj*
— **geo·phys·i·cist** \-'fiz-ə-səst\ *n*
geo·pol·i·tics \ˌjē-ō-'päl-ə-tiks\ *n* : a science based on
the theory that domestic and foreign politics of a country

GEOLOGIC TIME AND FORMATIONS

ERAS	PERIODS AND SYSTEMS	EPOCHS AND SERIES	APPROXIMATE NO. OF YEARS AGO	EARLIEST RECORD OF	
				ANIMALS	PLANTS
Cenozoic	Quaternary	Holocene (Recent) Pleistocene (Glacial)		mankind	
	Tertiary	Pliocene Miocene Oligocene Eocene Paleocene	70,000,000	placental mammals	
Mesozoic	Cretaceous	Upper			
		Lower			grasses and cereals
	Jurassic		160,000,000	birds mammals	flowering plants
	Triassic				
	Permian		230,000,000		ginkgoes cycads and conifers
Paleozoic	Pennsylvanian			insects	primitive gymnosperms
	Mississippian			reptiles	
	Devonian		390,000,000	amphibians	seed ferns vascular plants: lycopods, equisetums, ferns, etc.
	Silurian				
	Ordovician			fishes	
	Cambrian		500,000,000		mosses
Protero-zoic	not divided into periods		620,000,000	invertebrates	spores of uncertain relationship marine algae
			1,420,000,000		
Archeo-zoic			2,300,000,000		

j joke; ŋ sing; ō flow; ȯ flaw; ȯi coin; th thin; <u>th</u> this; ü loot; u̇ foot; y yet; yü few; yu̇ furious; zh vision

are dependent on physical geography; *also* : the physical geography of a region as affecting politics — **geo·po·lit·i·cal** \,jē-ō-pǝ-'lit-i-kǝl\ *adj*

Geor·gette \jȯr-'jet\ *trademark* — used for a thin strong clothing crepe

¹**Geor·gian** \'jȯr-jǝn\ *adj* **1** : of, relating to, or characteristic of the reigns of the first four Georges of Great Britain ⟨*Georgian* architecture⟩ **2** : of, relating to, or characteristic of the reign of George V of Great Britain

²**Georgian** *n* : one belonging to either of the Georgian periods

Geor·gia pine \,jȯr-jǝ-\ *n* : LONGLEAF PINE

geo·sci·ence \,jē-ō-'sī-ǝn(t)s\ *n* : any of the sciences dealing with the earth

geo·tax·is \-'tak-sǝs\ *n* : a taxis in which the force of gravity is the directive factor — **geo·tac·tic** \-'tak-tik\ *adj* — **geo·tac·ti·cal·ly** \-ti-k(ǝ-)lē\ *adv*

geo·ther·mal -\'thǝr-mǝl\ *or* **geo·ther·mic** \-mik\ *adj* : of or relating to the heat of the earth's interior

geo·trop·ic \,jē-ō-'träp-ik\ *adj* : of or relating to geotropism — **geo·trop·i·cal·ly** \-i-k(ǝ-)lē\ *adv*

ge·ot·ro·pism \jē-'ä-trǝ-,piz-ǝm\ *n* : a tropism involving turning or movement toward the earth

ge·ra·ni·um \jǝ-'rā-nē-ǝm\ *n* [Gk *geranion*, fr. dim. of *geranos* crane; akin to E *crane*] **1** : any of a widely distributed genus of herbs with usu. deeply cut leaves, regular flowers in which glands alternate with the petals, and long slender dry fruits **2** : PELARGONIUM

ger·bera \'gǝr-bǝ-rǝ\ *n* [Traugott *Gerber* d1743 German naturalist] : any of a genus of Old World composite herbs often grown for their showy yellow, pink, or orange flower heads

gerfalcon *var of* GYRFALCON

ger·i·at·ric \,jer-ē-'a-trik\ *adj* [Gk *gēras* old age + *iatros* physician] : of or relating to geriatrics, the aged, or the process of aging

ger·i·at·rics \,jer-ē-'a-triks\ *n* : a branch of medicine that deals with the problems and diseases of old age and aging people — compare GERONTOLOGY — **ger·i·a·tri·cian** \,jer-ē-ǝ-'trish-ǝn\ *n*

germ \'jǝrm\ *n* [F *germe*, fr. L *germin-*, *germen*, fr. *gignere* to beget] **1** : a small mass of living substance capable of developing into an organism or one of its parts **2** : something that serves or may serve as an origin : RUDIMENT ⟨the *germ* of an idea⟩ **3** : MICROBE

ger·man \'jǝr-mǝn\ *adj* [ME *germain*, fr. MF, fr. L *germanus*] : having the same parents ⟨brother-*german*⟩ or the same grandparents on either the maternal or paternal side ⟨cousin-*german*⟩

Ger·man \'jǝr-mǝn\ *n* **1 a** : a native or inhabitant of Germany **b** : a person of German descent **c** : one who speaks German **2** : the Germanic language of Germany, Austria, and parts of Switzerland **3** *often not cap* **a** : a dance consisting of capriciously involved figures intermingled with waltzes **b** *chiefly Midland* : a dancing party; *esp* : one at which the german is danced — **German** *adj*

ger·man·der \(,)jǝr-'man-dǝr\ *n* **1** : a plant of the mint family with dense spikes of purple flowers **2** : any of several speedwells

ger·mane \(,)jǝr-'mān\ *adj* [ME *germain* german, closely akin] : having a significant connection : PERTINENT — **ger·mane·ly** *adv*

¹**Ger·man·ic** \(,)jǝr-'man-ik\ *adj* **1** : GERMAN **2** : of, relating to, or characteristic of the Germanic-speaking peoples **3** : of, relating to, or constituting Germanic

²**Germanic** *n* : a branch of the Indo-European language family containing English, German, Dutch, Afrikaans, Flemish, Frisian, the Scandinavian languages, and Gothic

ger·ma·ni·um \(,)jǝr-'mā-nē-ǝm\ *n* : a grayish white hard brittle chemical element that resembles silicon and is used as a semiconductor — see ELEMENT table

ger·man·ize \'jǝr-mǝ-,nīz\ *vt*, *often cap* **1** *archaic* : to translate into German **2** : to cause to acquire German characteristics — **ger·man·i·za·tion** \,jǝr-mǝ-nǝ-'zā-shǝn\ *n*, *often cap*

German measles *n sing or pl* : an acute contagious virus disease like but usu. milder than typical measles though damaging to the fetus when occurring early in pregnancy

Ger·mano- \(,)jǝr-'man-ō\ *comb form* : German ⟨*Germanophile*⟩ : German and ⟨*Germano*-Russian⟩

German shepherd *n* : a large erect-eared intelligent dog of a breed originating in northern Europe that is often used in police work and as a guide dog for the blind

German silver *n* : NICKEL SILVER

germ cell *n* : an egg or sperm or one of their antecedent cells

ger·mi·cid·al \,jǝr-mǝ-'sīd-ᵊl\ *adj* : of or relating to a germicide; *also* : destroying germs

ger·mi·cide \'jǝr-mǝ-,sīd\ *n* : an agent that destroys germs

ger·mi·nal \'jǝr-mǝn-ᵊl\ *adj* : of or relating to a germ or germ cell; *also* : EMBRYONIC — **ger·mi·nal·ly** \-ᵊl-ē\ *adv*

ger·mi·nate \'jǝr-mǝ-,nāt\ *vb* [L *germinare* to sprout, fr. *germin-*, *germen* bud, germ] **1** : to cause to sprout or develop **2** : to begin to grow : SPROUT **3** : to come into being : EVOLVE — **ger·mi·na·tion** \,jǝr-mǝ-'nā-shǝn\ *n*

ger·mi·na·tive \'jǝr-mǝ-,nāt-iv\ *adj* : having the power to germinate or to develop

germ layer *n* : any of the three primary layers of cells differentiated in most embryos during and immediately following gastrulation — called also *primary germ layer;* compare ECTODERM, ENDODERM, MESODERM

germ plasm *n* **1** : germ cells and their precursors serving as the bearers of heredity — compare SOMA **2** : GENES

germ theory *n* : a theory that infectious and contagious disorders result from the action of living organisms

germ warfare *n* : the use of harmful bacteria as weapons in war

ger·on·tol·o·gy \,jer-ǝn-'täl-ǝ-jē\ *n* [Gk *geront-*, *gerōn* old man] : a branch of knowledge dealing with aging and the problems of the aged — compare GERIATRICS — **ger·on·to·log·i·cal** \,jer-,änt-ᵊl-'äj-i-kǝl\ *adj* — **ger·on·tol·o·gist** \,jer-ǝn-'täl-ǝ-jǝst\ *n*

¹**ger·ry·man·der** \,jer-ē-'man-dǝr, ,ger-\ *n* [Elbridge *Gerry* d1814 American statesman + *-mander* (as in sala*mander*); so called fr. the shape of an election district formed during Gerry's governorship] **1** : the act or method of gerrymandering **2** : a district or pattern of districts varying greatly in size or population as a result of gerrymandering

²**gerrymander** *vt* **ger·ry·man·dered;** **ger·ry·man·der·ing** \-d(ǝ-)riŋ\ : to divide (as a state or county) into election districts so as to give one political party an advantage over its opponents

gerrymander of Essex County, Massachusetts, 1812

ger·und \'jer-ǝnd\ *n* [LL *gerundium*, fr. L *gerere* to carry, carry on] **1** : a verbal noun in Latin that expresses the action of the verb as generalized or in continuance **2** : an English verbal noun in *-ing* used as a substantive and at the same time capable of taking adverbial modifiers and having an object

ge·run·dive \jǝ-'rǝn-div\ *n* : a Latin verbal adjective that expresses necessity or fitness and has the same suffix as the gerund

ges·so \'jes-ō\ *n* [It, lit., gypsum, fr. L *gypsum*] **1** : plaster of paris or gypsum prepared with glue for use in painting or making bas-reliefs **2** : a paste prepared by mixing whiting with size or glue and spread upon a surface to fit it for painting or gilding

gest *or* **geste** \'jest\ *n* [OF, fr. L *gesta* exploits, fr. neut. pl. of pp. of *gerere* to carry, perform] **1** : ADVENTURE, EXPLOIT **2** : a tale of adventures; *esp* : a romance in verse

Ge·sta·po \gǝ-'stäp-ō\ *n* [G, fr. *Ge*heime *Staatspoli*zei, lit., secret state police] : the Nazi secret-police organization operating esp. against suspected political criminals by means of terror

ges·tate \'jes-,tāt\ *vt* **1** : to carry in the uterus during pregnancy **2** : to conceive and gradually develop in the mind

ges·ta·tion \je-'stā-shǝn\ *n* [L *gestare*, freq. of *gerere* to carry] **1** : the carrying of young in the uterus : PREGNANCY **2** : conception and development esp. in the mind — **ges·ta·tion·al** \-shnǝl, -shǝn-ᵊl\ *adj*

ges·tic·u·late \je-'stik-yə-,lāt\ *vi* : to make gestures esp. when speaking — **ges·tic·u·la·tor** \-,lāt-ər\ *n*

ges·tic·u·la·tion \(,)jes-,tik-yə-'lā-shən\ *n* **1** : the action of making gestures **2** : GESTURE; *esp* : an expressive gesture made in showing strong feeling or in enforcing an argument

ges·tic·u·la·tive \je-'stik-yə-,lāt-iv\ *adj* : inclined to or marked by gesticulation

¹**ges·ture** \'jes-chər\ *n* [ML *gestura* mode of action, fr. L *gest-, gerere* to carry on] **1** : the use of motions of the limbs or body as a means of expression **2** : a movement usu. of the body or limbs that expresses or emphasizes an idea, sentiment, or attitude **3** : something said or done by way of formality or courtesy, as a symbol or token, or for its effect on the attitudes of others

²**gesture** *vb* **1** : to make a gesture **2** : to express or direct by a gesture

ge·sund·heit \gə-'zùnt-,hīt\ *interj* [G, lit., health] — used to wish good health esp. to one who has just sneezed

¹**get** \(')get, *esp when unemphatic also* git\ *vb* **got** \(')gät\; **got** *or* **got·ten** \'gät-³n\; **get·ting** [ON *geta*] **1 a** : to gain possession of (as by receiving, acquiring, earning, buying, or winning) ⟨*get* a present⟩ ⟨*got* first prize⟩ ⟨*get* a dog⟩ **b** : to seek out and obtain as planned ⟨planned to *get* dinner at the inn⟩ **c** : FETCH ⟨*get* your father his slippers⟩ **d** : to acquire wealth ⟨*getting* and spending⟩ ⟨those that have, *get*⟩ **2 a** : to succeed in coming or going ⟨*got* to the city on time⟩⟨*got* home early⟩ **b** : to cause to come or go ⟨*got* the dog out in a hurry⟩ **3** : BEGET **4 a** : to cause to be in a certain condition ⟨*got* his hair cut⟩ ⟨*got* his feet wet⟩ **b** : BECOME ⟨*get* sick⟩⟨*get* better⟩⟨it's *getting* warmer⟩ **c** : PREPARE ⟨started *getting* dinner⟩ **5 a** : SEIZE ⟨*got* the thief by the leg⟩ **b** : to move emotionally ⟨a song that always *got* him⟩ **c** : BAFFLE, PUZZLE ⟨the third question *got* everybody⟩ **d** : IRRITATE ⟨don't let it *get* you⟩ **e** : HIT ⟨*got* him in the leg⟩ **f** : KILL ⟨swore to *get* him⟩ **6 a** : to be subjected to ⟨*get* a broken nose⟩⟨*got* the measles⟩ **b** : to receive as punishment ⟨*got* six months for larceny⟩ **7 a** : to find out by calculation ⟨*got* the right answer⟩ **b** : to hear correctly ⟨I didn't *get* your name⟩ **c** : UNDERSTAND **8** : PERSUADE, INDUCE ⟨couldn't *get* him to agree⟩ **9 a** : HAVE — used in the present perfect form with present meaning ⟨I've *got* no money⟩ **b** : to have as an obligation or necessity — used in the present perfect form with present meaning ⟨he has *got* to come⟩ **10** : to establish communication with ⟨*got* him on the telephone⟩ **11** : to be able : CONTRIVE, MANAGE ⟨never *got* to go to college⟩ **12** : to leave at once : clear out ⟨told him to *get*⟩ **13** : to put out in baseball — **get ahead** : to achieve success — **get around 1** : to get the better of **2** : EVADE — **get at 1** : to reach effectively **2** : to influence corruptly **3** : to turn one's attention to **4** : to try to prove or make clear ⟨what is he *getting* at⟩ — **get away with** : to perform without suffering unpleasant consequences — **get back at** : to get even with — **get even** : to get revenge — **get even with** : to repay in kind — **get it** : to receive a scolding or punishment — **get one's goat** : to make one angry or annoyed — **get over 1** : OVERCOME **2** : to recover from — **get through 1** : to reach the end of : COMPLETE **2** : to while away — **get to 1** : BEGIN **2** : to have an effect on : INFLUENCE — **get together 1** : to bring together : ACCUMULATE **2** : to come together : ASSEMBLE **3** : to reach agreement — **get wind of** : to become aware of

²**get** \'get\ *n* **1** : something begotten : OFFSPRING, PROGENY **2** : a difficult return of a shot in a game

get along *vi* **1 a** : PROGRESS **b** : to approach old age **2** : to meet one's needs : MANAGE **3** : to be or remain on congenial terms

get·at·a·ble \get-'at-ə-bəl\ *adj* : ACCESSIBLE

get·away \'get-ə-,wā\ *n* **1** : the action or fact of getting away : ESCAPE **2** : the action of starting or getting under way (as by horses in a race or an automobile starting from a dead stop)

get by *vi* **1** : to avoid failure or catastrophe : barely succeed **2** : to proceed without being discovered, criticized, or punished

Geth·sem·a·ne \geth-'sem-ə-nē\ *n* **1** : the garden outside Jerusalem mentioned in the New Testament as the scene of the agony and arrest of Jesus **2** : a place or occasion of great suffering esp. in mind or spirit

get in *vt* : to allow for : INCLUDE

get off *vb* **1** : UTTER ⟨*get off* a joke⟩ **2** : START, LEAVE **3** : to escape or help to escape **4** : to leave work with permission

get on *vi* **1** : to get along **2** : to gain knowledge or understanding ⟨*got on* to the racket⟩

get out *vb* **1** : to bring before the public; *esp* : PUBLISH **2** : to escape or help to escape **3** : to become known : leak out ⟨their secret *got out*⟩

get·ter \'get-ər\ *n* : one that gets; *esp* : a substance introduced into a vacuum tube or incandescent electric lamp to remove traces of gas

get-to·geth·er \'get-tə-,geth-ər\ *n* : MEETING; *esp* : an informal social gathering

get up \get-'əp, git-\ *vb* **1 a** : to arise from bed **b** : to rise to one's feet **2** : to go ahead or faster — used as a command to a horse **3** : to make preparations for : ORGANIZE ⟨*get up* a party⟩ ⟨*get up* a petition⟩ **4** : to arrange as to external appearance : DRESS ⟨was *got up* as a pirate⟩

get·up \'get-,əp\ *n* **1** : general composition or structure **2** : OUTFIT, COSTUME

gew·gaw \'g(y)ü-,gò\ *n* : a showy trifle : BAUBLE, TRINKET

gey·ser \'gī-zər, *Brit usu* 'gē- *for 2*\ *n* [Icel *geysir* gusher] **1** : a spring that throws forth intermittent jets of heated water and steam **2** *Brit* : an apparatus for heating water rapidly esp. by injected steam

gey·ser·ite \'gī-zə-,rīt\ *n* : a hydrous silica that constitutes one variety of opal and is deposited around some hot springs and geysers

¹**ghast·ly** \'gast-lē\ *adj* **ghast·li·er; -est** [OE *gāstlīc* ghostly, fr. *gāst* ghost] **1** : HORRIBLE, SHOCKING ⟨a *ghastly* crime⟩ **2** : resembling a ghost : DEATHLIKE, PALE ⟨a *ghastly* face⟩ — **ghast·li·ness** *n*

syn GRUESOME, GRIM, LURID: GHASTLY suggests the horrifying aspects of corpses or skeletons; GRUESOME suggests additionally the effects of cruelty or extreme violence; GRIM implies a fierce and forbidding aspect; LURID adds to GRUESOME the suggestion of shuddering fascination with violent death and esp. with murder

²**ghastly** *adv* : in a ghastly manner ⟨turned *ghastly* pale⟩

ghat \'gòt, 'gät\ *n* [Hindi *ghāṭ*] : a landing place with stairs descending to a river in India

gher·kin \'gər-kən\ *n* [D *gurken*, pl. of *gurk* cucumber] **1** : a small prickly cucumber used for pickling; *also* : the vine that bears it **2** : the immature fruit of the common cucumber

ghet·to \'get-ō\ *n, pl* **ghettos** *or* **ghettoes** [It] : a quarter of a city in which Jews are required to live; *also* : a quarter of a city in which members of a minority group live because of social, legal, or economic pressure

Ghib·el·line \'gib-ə-,lēn, -,līn, -lən\ *n* : a member of an aristocratic political party in medieval Italy supporting the authority of the German emperors — compare GUELF

ghillie *var of* GILLIE

¹**ghost** \'gōst\ *n* [OE *gāst*] **1** : the seat of life : SOUL ⟨give up the *ghost*⟩ **2** : a disembodied soul; *esp* : the soul of a dead person believed to be an inhabitant of the unseen world or to appear to the living in bodily likeness **3** : SPIRIT, DEMON **4** : a faint shadowy trace or suggestion ⟨a *ghost* of a smile⟩ **5** : a false image in a photographic negative or on a television screen caused esp. by reflection **6** : one who ghostwrites — **ghost·like** \-,līk\ *adj* — **ghosty** \'gō-stē\ *adj*

²**ghost** *vb* **1** : to haunt like a ghost **2** : to move silently like a ghost **3** : GHOSTWRITE

ghost·ly \'gōst-lē\ *adj* **ghost·li·er; -est** **1** : of or relating to the soul : SPIRITUAL **2** : of, relating to, or having the characteristics of a ghost : SPECTRAL — **ghost·li·ness** *n*

ghost town *n* : a once flourishing town deserted or nearly so often after exhaustion of some natural resource (as gold)

ghost·write \'gōst-,rīt\ *vb* : to write for and in the name of another — **ghost-writ·er** *n*

ghoul \'gül\ *n* [Ar *ghūl*] **1** : a legendary evil being that robs graves and feeds on corpses **2** : a person (as a grave robber) whose activities suggest those of a ghoul — **ghoul·ish** \'gü-lish\ *adj* — **ghoul·ish·ly** *adv* — **ghoul·ish·ness** *n*

¹**GI** \(')jē-'ī\ *adj* [galvanized iron; fr. abbr. used in listing

such articles as garbage cans, but taken as abbr. for *government issue*] **1 :** provided by an official U.S. military supply department ⟨*GI* shoes⟩ **2 :** of, relating to, or characteristic of U.S. military personnel **3 :** conforming to military regulations or customs ⟨a *GI* haircut⟩

²GI *n* **:** a member or former member of the U.S. armed forces; *esp* **:** an enlisted man

³GI *vt* **GI'd; GI'ing :** to prepare for military inspection by cleaning

¹gi·ant \'jī-ənt\ *n* [MF *geant*, L *gigant-*, *gigas*, fr. Gk] **1 :** a legendary being of great stature and strength and of more than mortal but less than godlike power **2 a :** a living being of great size **b :** a person of extraordinary powers **3 :** something unusually large or powerful

²giant *adj* **:** characterized by extremely large size, proportion, or power

gi·ant·ess \'jī-ənt-əs\ *n* **:** a female giant; *esp* **:** an unusually large woman

gi·ant·ism \'jī-ənt-,iz-əm\ *n* **1 :** the quality or state of being a giant **2 :** GIGANTISM 2

giant star *n* **:** a star of great luminosity and of large mass

giaour \'jaú(ə)r\ *n* [Turk *gâvur*] **:** one outside the Muslim faith **:** INFIDEL

¹gib \'gib\ *n* **:** a male cat

²gib *n* **:** a plate (as of metal) machined to hold other parts in place, to afford a bearing surface, or to take up wear

gib·ber \'jib-ər\ *vi* **gib·bered; gib·ber·ing** \'jib-(ə-)riŋ\ **:** to speak rapidly, inarticulately, and often foolishly **:** CHATTER — **gibber** *n*

gib·ber·el·lic acid \,jib-ə-,rel-ik-\ *n* **:** a crystalline organic acid associated with and similar in effect to the gibberellins

gib·ber·el·lin \-'rel-ən\ *n* [NL *Gibberella*, genus of fungi] **:** any of several plant-growth regulators produced by a fungus that in low concentrations promote shoot growth

gib·ber·ish \'jib-(ə-)rish, 'gib-\ *n* **:** unintelligible, confused, or meaningless speech or language

¹gib·bet \'jib-ət\ *n* [OF *gibet*] **:** GALLOWS; *esp* **:** an upright post with a projecting arm for hanging the bodies of executed criminals as a warning

²gibbet *vt* **1 a :** to hang on a gibbet **b :** to expose to public scorn **2 :** to execute by hanging

gib·bon \'gib-ən\ *n* **:** any of several tailless apes of southeastern Asia and the East Indies that are the smallest and most arboreal anthropoid apes

gib·bos·i·ty \jib-'äs-ət-ē, gib-\ *n*, *pl* **-ties :** PROTUBERANCE, SWELLING

gib·bous \'jib-əs, 'gib-\ *adj* [LL *gibbosus* humpbacked, fr. L *gibbus* hump] **1 a :** convexly rounded in form **:** PROTUBERANT **b :** seen with more than half but not all of the apparent disk illuminated ⟨*gibbous* moon⟩ **c :** swollen on one side **2 :** having a hump **:** HUMPBACKED — **gib·bous·ly** *adv* — **gib·bous·ness** *n*

¹gibe \'jīb\ *vb* **:** to utter or reproach with taunting or sarcastic words — **gib·er** *n*

²gibe *n* **:** JEER, TAUNT

gib·let \'jib-lət\ *n* [ME *gibelet* entrails, fr. MF, stew of wildfowl] **:** the edible viscera of a bird (as a fowl) — usu. used in pl.

gid \'gid\ *n* [back-formation fr. *giddy*] **:** a disease usu. of sheep caused by a tapeworm larva in the brain

gid·dap \gid-'ap\ *imperative verb* — a command to a horse to go ahead or go faster

gid·dy \'gid-ē\ *adj* **gid·di·er; -est** [OE *gydig* possessed, mad; akin to E *god*] **1 :** having a feeling of whirling or reeling about **2 :** causing dizziness ⟨a *giddy* height⟩ **3 :** not serious **:** lightheartedly silly **:** FRIVOLOUS, FICKLE — **gid·di·ly** \'gid-°l-ē\ *adv* — **gid·di·ness** \'gid-ē-nəs\ *n*

Gid·e·on \'gid-ē-ən\ *n* **:** a biblical hero noted for his defeat of the Midianites

gie \'gē\ *chiefly Scot var of* GIVE

gift \'gift\ *n* [ON, something given; akin to E *give*] **1 :** the act or power of giving ⟨the appointment was not in his *gift*⟩ **2 :** something given **:** PRESENT **3 :** a special ability **:** TALENT ⟨a *gift* for music⟩

gift·ed \'gif-təd\ *adj* **:** having great natural ability **:** TALENTED ⟨a class for *gifted* children⟩⟨*gifted* musician⟩

gift wrap *vt* **:** to wrap (merchandise intended as a gift) in specially attractive or fancy wrappings usu. with ribbons

¹gig \'gig\ *n* **1 a :** a long light ship's boat propelled by

oars, sail, or motor **b :** a rowboat designed for speed rather than for work **2 :** a light 2-wheeled one-horse carriage

²gig *n* **:** a pronged spear for catching fish

³gig *vb* **gigged; gig·ging :** to spear or fish with a gig

⁴gig *n* **:** a military demerit

⁵gig *vt* **gigged; gig·ging :** to give a military gig to ⟨*gigged* for dirty shoes⟩

giga- \'jig-ə\ *comb form* [Gk *gigas* giant] **:** billion ⟨*giga*volt⟩

gi·gan·tesque \,jī-,gan-'tesk\ *adj* **:** of enormous proportions

gi·gan·tic \jī-'gant-ik\ *adj* [Gk *gigant-*, *gigas* giant] **1 a :** resembling a giant ⟨*gigantic* stature⟩ **b :** greater in size than the usual or expected ⟨*gigantic* wave⟩ **2 :** extremely large or great ⟨*gigantic* industry⟩ — **gi·gan·ti·cal·ly** \-'gant-i-k(ə-)lē\ *adv*

gi·gan·tism \jī-'gan-,tiz-əm\ *n* **1 :** GIGANTISM 1 **2 :** development to abnormally large size; *esp* **:** excessive somatic growth with delayed or inhibited reproduction

¹gig·gle \'gig-əl\ *vi* **gig·gled; gig·gling** \'gig-(ə-)liŋ\ **:** to laugh with repeated short catches of the breath **:** laugh in a silly manner — **gig·gler** \-(-ə-)lər\ *n*

²giggle *n* **:** the act of giggling **:** a light silly laugh

gig·gly \'gig-(ə-)lē\ *adj* **:** given to giggling

gig·o·lo \'jig-ə-,lō\ *n*, *pl* **-los** [F] **1 :** a man living on the earnings of a woman **2 :** a professional dancing partner or male escort

gi·got \'jig-ət, zhē-'gō\ *n*, *pl* **gigots** \-əts, -'gō(z)\ [MF, dim. of *gigue* fiddle; fr. its shape] **1 :** a leg (as of lamb) esp. when cooked **2 :** a leg-of-mutton sleeve

Gi·la monster \,hē-lə-\ *n* [*Gila* river, Arizona] **:** a large orange and black venomous lizard of the southwestern U.S.; *also* **:** a related Mexican lizard

¹gild \'gild\ *vt* **gild·ed** *or* **gilt** \'gilt\; **gild·ing** [OE *gyldan;* akin to E *gold*] **1 :** to cover with or as if with a thin coating of gold **2 :** to give an attractive but often deceptive appearance to — **gild·er** *n* — **gild the lily :** to add unnecessary ornamentation to something beautiful in its own right

²gild *var of* GUILD

gild·ing *n* **1 a :** the art or practice of coating with gold **b :** the material used **2 :** a superficial coating or appearance

¹gill \'jil\ *n* [ME *gille*] — see MEASURE table

²gill \'gil\ *n* [ME *gile*, *gille*] **1 :** an organ (as of a fish) for obtaining oxygen from water **2 :** the flesh under or about the chin or jaws — usu. used in pl. **3 :** one of the radiating plates forming the undersurface of the cap of a mushroom — **gilled** \'gild\ *adj*

gill arch *n* **:** one of the several bony or cartilaginous bars that are paired on either side of the throat and support the gills of water-breathing vertebrates

gil·lie *or* **gil·ly** *or* **ghil·lie** \'gil-ē\ *n*, *pl* **gillies** *or* **ghillies** [ScGael *gille* boy] **1 :** a male attendant on a Scottish Highland chief **2** *Scot & Irish* **:** a fishing and hunting guide **3** *usu* **ghillie :** a lowcut shoe with decorative lacing

gill net *n* **:** a net that allows the head of a fish to pass but entangles it as it seeks to withdraw — **gill·net** \'gil-,net\ *vt*

gill raker *n* **:** one of the bony processes on a gill arch that divert debris from the gills

gill slit *n* **:** any of the openings between gill clefts through which water passes from the gills; *also* **:** an embryonic rudiment of one of these characteristic of vertebrate development

gil·ly·flow·er \'jil-ē-,flaú(-ə)r\ *n* [by folk etymology fr. ME *gilofre* clove, fr. MF *girofle*, *gilofre*, fr. L *caryophyllum*, fr. Gk *karyophyllon*, fr. *karyon* nut + *phyllon* leaf] **:** an Old World pink that is grown for its clove-scented flowers and is the source of garden carnations — called also *clove pink*

¹gilt \'gilt\ *adj* [fr. pp. of **¹gild**] **:** of the color of gold

²gilt *n* **1 :** gold or something that resembles gold laid on a surface **2 :** superficial brilliance

³gilt *n* [ON *gyltr*] **:** a young female swine

gilt-edged \'gilt-'ejd\ *or* **gilt-edge** \-'ej\ *adj* **1 :** having a gilt edge **2 :** of the best quality; *esp* **:** extremely safe for investment ⟨*gilt-edged* securities⟩

gim·bal \'gim-bəl, 'jim-\ *n* **:** a device that permits a body to incline freely in any direction or suspends something (as a ship's compass) so that it will remain level when its support is tipped — usu. used in pl.; called also *gimbal ring*

gim·crack \'jim-ˌkrak\ *n* : a showy object of little use or value — GEWGAW — **gimcrack** *adj* — **gim·crack·ery** \-ˌkrak-(ə-)rē\ *n*

¹**gim·let** \'gim-lət\ *n* [MF *guimbelet*] : a small tool with a screw point, grooved shank, and cross handle for boring holes

²**gimlet** *adj* : having a piercing or penetrating quality

gim·mick \'gim-ik\ *n* 1 : CONTRIVANCE, GADGET; *esp* : one used in secret or for an illicit purpose 2 a : an important feature that is not immediately apparent : CATCH b : a new and ingenious scheme

¹**gimp** \'gimp\ *n* : an ornamental flat braid or round cord used as a trimming

²**gimp** *n* : SPIRIT, VIM

³**gimp** *n* : CRIPPLE; *also* : LIMP — **gimpy** \'gim-pē\ *adj*

¹**gin** \'jin\ *n* [modif. of OF *engin* engine] : a mechanical tool or device: as a : a snare or trap for game b : COTTON GIN

²**gin** *vt* **ginned**; **gin·ning** 1 : SNARE 2 : to separate (cotton fiber) from seeds and waste material — **gin·ner** *n*

³**gin** *n* [by shortening & alter. fr. *geneva*, modif. of obs. D *genever*, lit., juniper, fr. L *juniperus*] : a strong alcoholic liquor made by distilling a mash of grain with juniper berries

gin·ger \'jin-jər\ *n* [OE *gingifer*, fr. ML *gingiber*, alter. of L *zingiber*, fr. Gk *zingiberi*] 1 : any of a genus of tropical Old World herbs with pungent aromatic rhizomes used as a condiment and in medicine; *also* : this rhizome 2 : high spirit : PEP — **gin·gery** \'jinj-(ə-)rē\ *adj*

ginger ale *n* : a nonalcoholic drink flavored with ginger extract

ginger beer *n* : a nonalcoholic drink heavily flavored with ginger or capsicum or both

gin·ger·bread \'jin-jər-ˌbred\ *n* 1 : a cake made with molasses and flavored with ginger 2 : tawdry, gaudy, or superfluous ornament — **gingerbread** *adj*

gin·ger·ly \'jin-jər-lē\ *adj* : very cautious or careful — **gingerly** *adv*

gin·ger·snap \-ˌsnap\ *n* : a thin brittle cookie flavored with ginger

ging·ham \'giŋ-əm\ *n* [Malay *genggang* checkered cloth] : a clothing fabric usu. of yarn-dyed cotton in plain weave

gin·gi·vi·tis \ˌjin-jə-'vīt-əs\ *n* [L *gingiva* gum] : inflammation of the gums

gink·go *also* **ging·ko** \'giŋ-kō\ *n*, *pl* **ginkgoes** [Jap *ginkyo*] : a large gymnospermous tree of eastern China with fan-shaped leaves often grown as a shade tree — called also *maidenhair tree*

gin rummy *n* [³*gin*] : a rummy game for 2 players in which each player is dealt 10 cards and in which a player may win a hand by matching all his cards or may end play when his unmatched cards count up to less than 10

gin·seng \'jin-ˌsaŋ, -ˌseŋ\ *n* [Chin (Pek) *jen²-shen¹*] 1 : a perennial Chinese herb with small greenish flowers in a rounded cluster and scarlet berries; *also* : a closely related No. American herb 2 : the forked aromatic root of the ginseng used in oriental medicine

Gipsy *var of* GYPSY

gi·raffe \jə-'raf\ *n*, *pl* **giraffe** *or* **giraffes** [It *giraffa*, fr. Ar *zirāfah*] : a large fleet African ruminant mammal that is the tallest of living quadrupeds and has a very long neck and a black-blotched coat — **gi·raff·ish** \-'raf-ish\ *adj*

gird \'gərd\ *vb* **gird·ed** *or* **girt** \'gərt\; **gird·ing** [OE *gyrdan*; akin to E *yard*] 1 : to encircle or fasten with or as if with a belt or cord : GIRDLE ⟨*gird* on a sword⟩ 2 : to clothe or invest esp. with power or authority 3 : to make or get ready : BRACE ⟨*girded* themselves for a struggle⟩

gird·er \'gərd-ər\ *n* : a horizontal main supporting beam (as of wood or steel) ⟨the *girders* of a bridge⟩ ⟨a *girder* supporting floor joists⟩

¹**gir·dle** \'gərd-ᵊl\ *n* [OE *gyrdel*] : something that encircles or confines: as a : a belt or sash encircling the waist b : a

woman's supporting undergarment that extends from the waist to below the hips c : a bony arch for the support of a limb d : a ring made by the removal of the bark and cambium around a plant stem

²**girdle** *vt* **gir·dled**; **gir·dling** \'gərd-liŋ, -ᵊl-iŋ\ 1 : to bind or encircle with a girdle 2 : to move around : CIRCLE 3 : to cut a girdle around (a plant)

girl \'gərl\ *n* [ME *girle* young person of either sex] 1 : a female child : young woman 2 : a female servant or employee 3 : SWEETHEART — **girl·hood** \-ˌhud\ *n*

girl friend *n* 1 : a female friend 2 : a frequent or regular female companion of a boy or man 3 : a female paramour

girl guide *n* : a member of the British Girl Guides

girl·ish \'gər-lish\ *adj* : of, relating to, or having the characteristics of a girl or girlhood ⟨*girlish* laughter⟩ — **girl·ish·ly** *adv* — **girl·ish·ness** *n*

girl scout *n* : a member of the Girl Scouts of the United States of America

Gi·rond·ist \jə-'rän-dəst\ *n* [F *Gironde*, a political party, fr. *Gironde*, department of France] : a member of the moderate republican party in the French legislative assembly in 1791

girt \'gərt\ *vt* [ME *girten*, alter. of *girden*] 1 : GIRD 2 : to fasten by means of a girth

¹**girth** \'gərth\ *n* [ON *gjörth*] 1 : a band or strap that encircles the body of an animal to fasten something (as a saddle) upon its back 2 : a measure around a body

²**girth** *vt* 1 : ENCIRCLE 2 : to bind or fasten with a girth

gist \'jist\ *n* [AF, it lies, (in *cest action gist* this action lies, statement laying the foundation of a legal action)] : the main point of a matter : ESSENCE

git·tern \'git-ərn\ *n* : a medieval stringed instrument of the guitar family

¹**give** \'giv\ *vb* **gave** \'gāv\; **giv·en** \'giv-ən\; **giv·ing** [ME *given*, of Scand origin] 1 : to make a present of 2 a : GRANT, BESTOW b : to accord or yield to another ⟨*gave* her confidence to him⟩ 3 a : to put into the possession or keeping of another : HAND b : to offer to another : PROFFER ⟨*gave* his hand to the visitor⟩ c : DELIVER; *esp* : to deliver in exchange d : PAY ⟨*give* a fair price⟩ 4 a : to present in public performance ⟨*give* a concert⟩ b : to present to view or observation ⟨*gave* the signal to start⟩ 5 : to provide by way of entertainment ⟨*give* a party⟩ 6 : to designate as a share or portion : ALLOT 7 : to ATTRIBUTE, ASCRIBE ⟨*gave* all the glory to God⟩ 8 : to yield as a product or result : PRODUCE ⟨cows *give* milk⟩ ⟨24 divided by 12 *gives* 7⟩ 9 a : to deliver by some bodily action ⟨*gave* him a push⟩ b : to carry out (a movement of or as if of the body) : EXECUTE : UTTER, PRONOUNCE ⟨*give* judgment⟩ 10 : to offer for consideration or acceptance ⟨*gives* no reason for his absence⟩ 11 : to apply freely or fully : DEVOTE ⟨*gave* himself to the cause⟩ 12 : to cause to have or receive : OCCASION ⟨*gave* pleasure to the reader⟩ 13 : to make gifts or presents : CONTRIBUTE, DONATE 14 a : to yield to physical force or strain b : to collapse from the application of force or pressure — **giv·er** *n*

syn PRESENT, DONATE: GIVE is the general term applying to delivering, passing over, or transmitting in any manner; PRESENT implies more ceremony or formality and suggests a degree of complexity or value in what is given; DONATE implies a free but usu. publicized giving, as to charity — **give ground** : to withdraw before superior force : RETREAT — **give it to** : to attack vigorously ⟨*gave it to* him right between the eyes⟩ — **give tongue** : to begin barking on the scent ⟨the hounds *gave tongue*⟩ — **give way** 1 : RETREAT 2 : to yield oneself without restraint or control 3 a : COLLAPSE, FAIL b : CONCEDE 4 : to yield place

²**give** *n* 1 : capacity or tendency to yield to force or strain 2 : the quality or state of being springy

give–and–take \ˌgiv-ən-'tāk\ *n* : an exchange (as of remarks or ideas) esp. on fair or equal terms

give away \ˌgiv-ə-'wā\ *vt* 1 : to deliver (a bride) to the bridegroom at a wedding 2 a : BETRAY b : DISCLOSE, REVEAL

give·away \'giv-ə-ˌwā\ *n* 1 : an unintentional revelation or betrayal 2 : something given away free; *esp* : PREMIUM 3 : a radio or television program on which prizes are given away

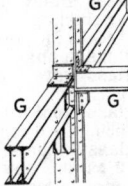

gimlet

G, G, G, girders

give back *vi* : RETIRE, RETREAT

give in *vi* : YIELD, SURRENDER

giv·en \'giv-ən\ *adj* **1** : DISPOSED, INCLINED ⟨*given* to swearing⟩ **2** : SPECIFIED, FIXED ⟨at a *given* time⟩ **3** : granted as true : ASSUMED **4** : EXECUTED, DATED ⟨*given* under my hand and seal⟩

given name *n* : CHRISTIAN NAME

give off *vt* : EMIT

give out *vb* **1** : EMIT **2** : to become exhausted : COLLAPSE **3** : to break down

give up *vb* **1** : to hand over to another : SURRENDER **2** : to abandon (oneself) to a feeling, influence, or activity **3** : to withdraw from an activity or course of action

giz·mo *or* **gis·mo** \'giz-mō\ *n, pl* **gizmos** *or* **gismos** : GADGET

giz·zard \'giz-ərd\ *n* [alter. of ME *giser*, fr. ONF *guisier*, fr. L *gigeria*, pl., giblets] **1** : a muscular enlargement of the digestive canal (as of a bird) that follows the crop and has usu. a horny lining for grinding the food **2** : INNARDS

gla·bres·cent \glā-'bres-ʔnt\ *adj* : somewhat glabrous

gla·brous \'glā-brəs\ *adj* [L *glabr-, glaber* smooth, bald] : SMOOTH; *esp* : having a surface without hairs or projections — **gla·brous·ness** *n*

gla·cé \gla-'sā\ *adj* **1** : made or finished so as to have a smooth glossy surface **2** : coated with a glaze : CANDIED

gla·cial \'glā-shəl\ *adj* **1 a** : extremely cold : FRIGID **b** : lacking warmth and cordiality **2 a** : of, relating to, or produced by glaciers **b** (1) : of, relating to, or being any of those parts of geologic time when a large portion of the earth was covered by glaciers (2) *cap* : PLEISTOCENE — **gla·cial·ly** \-shə-lē\ *adv*

glacial acetic acid *n* : acetic acid containing less than one percent of water obtained as a caustic liquid that crystallizes easily

gla·ci·ate \'glā-shē-ˌāt\ *vt* **1** : to subject to glacial action **2** : to produce glacial effects in or on — **gla·ci·a·tion** \ˌglā-s(h)ē-'ā-shən\ *n*

gla·cier \'glā-shər\ *n* [F dial., fr. MF *glace* ice, fr. L *glacies*] : a large body of ice moving slowly down a slope or valley or spreading outward on a land surface

gla·ci·ol·o·gy \ˌglā-s(h)ē-'äl-ə-jē\ *n* : a branch of geology dealing with snow or ice accumulation, glaciation, or glacial epochs — **gla·ci·ol·o·gist** \-jəst\ *n*

gla·cis \gla-'sē, 'glā-səs\ *n, pl* **gla·cis** \gla-'sēz\ *also* **glac·is·es** \'glas-ə-səz\ : a slope that runs downward from the outside of a fortification

¹glad \'glad\ *adj* **glad·der; glad·dest** [OE *glæd*] **1 a** : experiencing pleasure, joy, or delight : made happy **b** : GRATIFIED, PLEASED **c** : very willing ⟨*glad* to do it⟩ **2** : causing happiness and joy : PLEASANT ⟨*glad* tidings⟩ **3** : full of brightness and cheerfulness — **glad·ly** *adv* — **glad·ness** *n*

²glad *n* : GLADIOLUS

glad·den \'glad-ʔn\ *vt* **glad·dened; glad·den·ing** \'glad-niŋ, -ʔn-iŋ\ : to make glad

glade \'glād\ *n* : a grassy open space in a forest

glad·i·a·tor \'glad-ē-ˌāt-ər\ *n* [L, fr. *gladius* sword] **1** : a person engaged in a fight to the death for public entertainment in ancient Rome **2** : a person engaging in a fierce fight or controversy — **glad·i·a·to·ri·al** \ˌglad-ē-ə-'tōr-ē-əl, -'tȯr-\ *adj*

glad·i·o·lus \ˌglad-ē-'ō-ləs, glə-'dī-ə-ləs\ *n, pl* **-o·li** \-'ō-(ˌ)lē, -'ō-ˌlī; -ə-ˌlī\ *or* **-o·lus** *or* **-o·lus·es** [L, fr. dim. of *gladius* sword] : any of a genus of chiefly African plants of the iris family with erect sword-shaped leaves and spikes of brilliantly colored irregular flowers arising from flattened corms

glad·some \'glad-səm\ *adj* : giving or showing joy : CHEERFUL — **glad·some·ly** *adv* — **glad·some·ness** *n*

glad·stone \'glad-ˌstōn\ *n, often cap* [after W. E. *Gladstone* d1898 British statesman] : a traveling bag with flexible sides on a rigid frame that opens flat into two compartments

glam·or·ize \'glam-ə-ˌrīz\ *vt* **1** : to make glamorous **2** : ROMANTICIZE, GLORIFY — **glam·or·i·za·tion** \ˌglam-ə-rə-'zā-shən\ *n* — **glam·or·iz·er** *n*

glam·or·ous \'glam-(ə-)rəs\ *adj* : full of glamour — **glam·or·ous·ly** *adv* — **glam·or·ous·ness** *n*

gladiolus

glam·our *or* **glam·or** \'glam-ər\ *n* [Sc *glamour* magic spell, alter. of E *grammar;* fr. the popular association of erudition with occult practices] : a romantic, exciting, and often illusory attractiveness; *esp* : alluring or fascinating personal attraction

¹glance \'glan(t)s\ *vb* [ME *glencen*] **1** : to strike and fly off at an angle ⟨the arrow *glanced* off the shield⟩ **2 a** : to give a quick or hasty look ⟨*glanced* at his watch⟩ ⟨*glanced* up from a book⟩ **b** : to refer briefly to something by way of indirect criticism or satire **3** : GLINT ⟨polished metal *glancing* in the sun⟩ **syn** see FLASH — **glanc·ing·ly** \'glan(t)-siŋ-lē\ *adv*

²glance *n* **1** : a quick intermittent flash or gleam **2** : a deflected impact or blow **3 a** : a swift movement of the eyes **b** : a quick or cursory look **4** *archaic* : a brief or slight allusion

syn GLANCE, GLIMPSE are not synonymous even though both mean a brief view or viewing. GLANCE implies that one looks at something only briefly when he could have looked longer ⟨gave the paper hardly a *glance*⟩ GLIMPSE implies that only a brief look is possible ⟨got a *glimpse* of the deer before it vanished into the woods⟩

gland \'gland\ *n* [F *glande*, fr. L *gland-, glans* acorn] **1** : a cell or group of cells that prepares and secretes a product for further use in the body or for elimination from the body **2** : any of various animal structures suggestive of glands ⟨lymph *gland*⟩ — **gland** *adj*

glan·ders \'glan-dərz\ *n sing or pl* : a destructive bacterial disease esp. of horses characterized by nodules that tend to ulcerate — **glan·dered** \-dərd\ *adj*

glan·du·lar \'glan-jə-lər\ *adj* **1** : of, relating to, or involving glands, gland cells, or their products **2** : having the characteristics or function of a gland — **glan·du·lar·ly** *adv*

glans \'glanz\ *n, pl* **glan·des** \'glan-ˌdēz\ : a conical vascular body forming the extremity of the penis or clitoris

¹glare \'gla(ə)r, 'gle(ə)r\ *vb* [ME *glaren*] **1 a** : to shine with a harsh uncomfortably brilliant light **b** : to stand out offensively : OBTRUDE **2 a** : to stare angrily or fiercely **b** : to express (as hostility) by staring angrily

²glare *n* **1** : a harsh uncomfortably bright light; *esp* : painfully bright sunlight **2** : an angry or fierce stare

³glare *n* : a surface or sheet of ice with a smooth slippery surface

glar·ing *adj* **1** : having a fixed look of hostility, fierceness, or anger **2 a** : shining with or reflecting a harsh uncomfortably bright light **b** (1) : GARISH (2) : vulgarly ostentatious **3** : painfully obvious ⟨a *glaring* mistake⟩ **syn** see FLAGRANT — **glar·ing·ly** \-iŋ-lē\ *adv* — **glar·ing·ness** *n*

glary \'gla(ə)r-ē, 'gle(ə)r-\ *adj* **glar·i·er; -est** : having a dazzling brightness : GLARING

¹glass \'glas\ *n* [OE *glæs*] **1 a** : a hard brittle usu. transparent or translucent noncrystalline inorganic substance commonly formed by melting a mixture (as of silica sand and metallic oxides) and cooling to a rigid condition **b** : a substance (as a rock formed by the rapid cooling of molten minerals) resembling glass **2 a** : something (as a water tumbler, lens, mirror, barometer, or telescope) that is made of glass or has a glass lens **b** *pl* : a pair of glass lenses used to correct defects of vision — called also *eyeglasses, spectacles* **3** : GLASSFUL

²glass *vt* : to fit or protect with glass

glass·blow·ing \-ˌblō-iŋ\ *n* : the art of shaping a mass of glass that has been softened by heat by blowing air into it through a tube — **glass·blow·er** \-ˌblō(-ə)r\ *n*

glass·ful \'glas-ˌful\ *n* : the quantity held by a glass

glass·mak·ing \-ˌmā-kiŋ\ *n* : the art or process of manufacturing glass

glass·man \-ˌman\ *n* : a dealer in or maker of glass

glass snake *n* : a limbless lizard of the southern U.S. resembling a snake and having a fragile tail that readily breaks into pieces

glass sponge *n* : a sponge with a glassy skeleton of silica

glass·ware \'glas-ˌwa(ə)r, -ˌwe(ə)r\ *n* : articles made of glass

glass wool *n* : glass fibers in a mass resembling wool and being used esp. for thermal insulation and air filters

glassy \'glas-ē\ *adj* **glass·i·er; -est** **1** : resembling glass **2** : DULL, LIFELESS ⟨*glassy* eyes⟩ — **glass·i·ly** \'glas-ə-lē\ *adv* — **glass·i·ness** \'glas-ē-nəs\ *n*

Glau·ber's salt \ˌglau̇-bər(z)-'sȯlt\ *n* : a colorless crystalline sulfate of sodium $Na_2SO_4.10H_2O$ used esp. as a cathartic

glau·co·ma \glȯ-'kō-mə, glau̇-\ *n* [Gk *glaukōma* cataract, fr. *glaukos* gray] : a state of increased pressure within the eyeball resulting in retinal damage and gradual loss of vision

glau·cous \'glȯ-kəs\ *adj* [Gk *glaukos* gleaming, gray] **1 a** : of a pale yellow green color **b** : of a light bluish gray or bluish white color **2** : having a powdery or waxy coating ⟨*glaucous* fruits like plums or grapes⟩ — **glau·cous·ness** *n*

¹glaze \'glāz\ *vb* **1** : to furnish or fit with glass **2 a** : to coat with or as if with glass **b** : to apply a glaze to **3** : to give a smooth glossy surface to **4** : to become glazed — **glaz·er** *n*

²glaze *n* **1** : a smooth slippery coating of thin ice **2 a** : a transparent or translucent substance used as a coating (as on food or pottery) to produce a gloss **b** : a smooth glossy or lustrous surface or finish

gla·zier \'glā-zhər\ *n* : a person who sets glass in window frames

glaz·ing \'glā-zin\ *n* : GLAZE

¹gleam \'glēm\ *n* [OE *glǣm*] **1 a** : a transient subdued or partly obscured light **b** : a small bright light : GLINT **2** : a brief or faint appearance : TRACE ⟨*gleam* of hope⟩

²gleam *vi* **1** : to shine with subdued light or moderate brightness **2** : to appear briefly or faintly

glean \'glēn\ *vb* [MF *glener*, fr. LL *glennare*] **1** : to gather from a field or vineyard what has been left (as by reapers) **2** : to gather little by little : collect with patient effort ⟨*glean* knowledge from books⟩ — **glean·er** *n*

glean·ings \'glē-ninz\ *n pl* : things acquired by gleaning

glebe \'glēb\ *n* [L *gleba* clod, land] : land belonging or yielding revenue to a parish church or ecclesiastical benefice

glee \'glē\ *n* [OE *glēo* entertainment, music] **1** : exultant high-spirited joy : HILARITY **2** : an unaccompanied song for three or more solo usu. male voices **syn** see MIRTH

glee club *n* : a chorus organized for singing usu. short choral pieces

glee·ful \'glē-fəl\ *adj* : full of glee : MERRY — **glee·ful·ly** \-fə-lē\ *adv* — **glee·ful·ness** *n*

glee·man \'glē-mən\ *n* : MINSTREL

gleet \'glēt\ *n* [MF *glete* mucous matter, fr. L *glittus* viscous] : chronic inflammation about a bodily opening accompanied by an abnormal discharge; *also* : this discharge

glen \'glen\ *n* : a small secluded narrow valley

glen·gar·ry \glen-'gar-ē\ *n, often cap* [Glengarry, valley in Scotland] : a woolen cap of Scottish origin

glib \'glib\ *adj* **glib·ber; glib·best** [prob. modif. of LG *glibberig* slippery] : speaking or spoken with careless ease and often with little regard for truth ⟨a *glib* talker⟩ ⟨a *glib* excuse⟩ — **glib·ly** *adv* — **glib·ness** *n*

¹glide \'glīd\ *vi* [OE *glīdan*] **1** : to move smoothly, continuously, and effortlessly **2** : to pass gradually and imperceptibly **3** : to descend at a normal angle without engine power sufficient for level flight ⟨*glide* in an airplane⟩

²glide *n* **1** : the act or action of gliding **2 a** : PORTAMENTO **b** : a transitional sound produced by the passing of the vocal organs to or from the position for the articulation of a speech sound

glid·er \'glīd-ər\ *n* : one that glides: as **a** : an aircraft without an engine **b** : a porch seat suspended from an upright framework by short chains or straps

¹glim·mer \'glim-ər\ *vi* **glim·mered; glim·mer·ing** \'glim-(ə-)rin\ : to shine faintly or unsteadily

²glimmer *n* **1 a** : a feeble or intermittent light **b** : a soft shimmer **2 a** : a dim perception or faint idea : INKLING **b** : a small amount : BIT

glim·mer·ing *n* : GLIMMER

¹glimpse \'glim(p)s\ *vb* [ME *glimsen*] : to take a brief look : see momentarily or incompletely — **glimps·er** *n*

²glimpse *n* **1** : a short hurried view ⟨catch a *glimpse* of something rushing by⟩ **2** : a faint idea : GLIMMER **syn** see GLANCE

¹glint \'glint\ *vi* **1** : GLANCE **2** : to shine by reflection: **a** : to shine with small bright flashes **b** : GLITTER **c** : GLEAM **3** : to appear briefly or faintly ⟨fear *glinted* in his eyes⟩ **syn** see FLASH

²glint *n* **1** : a small bright flash of light : SPARKLE **2** : a brief or faint manifestation

glis·san·do \gli-'sän-dō\ *n, pl* **-di** \-(,)dē\ *or* **-dos** : a rapid sliding up or down the musical scale

¹glis·ten \'glis-ᵊn\ *vi* **glis·tened; glis·ten·ing** \'glis-nin, -ᵊn-in\ [OE *glisnian*] : to shine by reflection with a soft luster or sparkle

syn GLISTEN, GLITTER, SCINTILLATE mean to give out bright flashes of light. GLISTEN implies a subdued shining as from a wet or oily surface; GLITTER implies a dancing brightness often with a suggestion of coldness or evil ⟨eyes *glittering* with greed⟩ SCINTILLATE stresses brilliance and showiness ⟨clear sky with *scintillating* stars⟩ ⟨a *scintillating* infielder⟩

²glisten *n* : GLITTER, SPARKLE

glis·ter \'glis-tər\ *vi* **glis·tered; glis·ter·ing** \-t(ə-)rin\ : GLISTEN — **glister** *n*

¹glit·ter \'glit-ər\ *vi* [ON *glitra*] **1 a** : to shine with brilliant or metallic luster ⟨*glittering* sequins⟩ **b** : SPARKLE **c** : to shine with a cold glassy brilliance ⟨little eyes *glittered* cruelly⟩ **2** : to be brilliantly attractive esp. in a superficial way **syn** see GLISTEN

²glitter *n* **1** : sparkling brilliancy, showiness, or attractiveness **2** : small glittering objects used for ornamentation — **glit·tery** \'glit-ə-rē\ *adj*

gloam·ing \'glō-min\ *n* [ME (Sc) *gloming*, fr. OE *glōming*, fr. *glōm* twilight; akin to E *glow*] : TWILIGHT, DUSK

gloat \'glōt\ *vi* **1** : to gaze at or think about something with great self-satisfaction, gratification, or joy ⟨*gloating* over his gold⟩ **2** : to linger over or dwell upon something with malicious pleasure — **gloat·er** *n*

glob \'gläb\ *n* : a small drop : BLOB

glob·al \'glō-bəl\ *adj* **1** : SPHERICAL **2** : WORLDWIDE ⟨*global* war⟩ — **glob·al·ly** \-bə-lē\ *adv*

glo·bate \'glō-,bāt\ *adj* : GLOBULAR

globe \'glōb\ *n* [MF, fr. L *globus*] : something spherical or rounded: as **a** : a spherical representation of the earth or heavens **b** : EARTH — usu. used with *the* or *this*

globe·fish \-,fish\ *n* : any of numerous marine spiny-finned fishes that can distend themselves to a globular form

globe·trot·ter \-,trät-ər\ *n* : one that travels widely — **globe·trot·ting** \-,trät-in\ *n or adj*

glo·bose \'glō-,bōs\ *adj* : GLOBULAR — **glo·bose·ly** *adv* — **glo·bos·i·ty** \glō-'bäs-ət-ē\ *n*

glob·u·lar \'gläb-yə-lər\ *adj* : having the shape of a globe or globule

glob·ule \'gläb-yül\ *n* : a tiny globe or ball ⟨*globules* of fat⟩

glob·u·lin \'gläb-yə-lən\ *n* : any of a class of simple proteins insoluble in pure water but soluble in dilute salt solutions that occur widely in plant and animal tissues

glo·chid·i·um \glō-'kid-ē-əm\ *n, pl* **-ia** \-ē-ə\ : a larval freshwater mussel that develops as an external parasite on fish

glock·en·spiel \'gläk-ən-,s(h)pēl\ *n* [G, fr. *glocke* bell + *spiel* play] : a percussion musical instrument consisting of a series of graduated metal bars tuned to the chromatic scale and played with two hammers

glom·er·ate \'gläm-ə-rət\ *adj* [L *glomeratus*, pp. of *glomerare* to wind into a ball, fr. *glomer-, glomus* ball] : collected into a ball, heap, or mass : CONGLOMERATE — **glom·er·a·tion** \,gläm-ə-'rā-shən\ *n*

glom·er·ule \'gläm-ər-,(y)ül\ *n* : a compacted cyme like the flower head of a composite

glo·mer·u·lus \glä-'mer-(y)ə-ləs\ *n, pl* **-li** \-,lī, -,lē\ : a tuft of capillaries at the point of origin of each functional tubule of the vertebrate kidney — **glo·mer·u·lar** \-lər\ *adj*

¹gloom \'glüm\ *vi* [ME *gloumen*] **1** : to look sullen or despondent **2** : to be or become overcast

²gloom *n* **1** : partial or total darkness **2 a** : lowness of spirits : DEJECTION **b** : an atmosphere of despondency

gloomy \'glü-mē\ *adj* **gloom·i·er, -est 1** : DUSKY, DIM ⟨a *gloomy* cave⟩ **2** : MELANCHOLY, LOW-SPIRITED ⟨feel *gloomy*⟩ **3** : causing gloom : DISMAL ⟨*gloomy* weather⟩ ⟨*gloomy* news⟩ — **gloom·i·ly** \-mə-lē\ *adv* — **gloom·i·ness** \-mē-nəs\ *n*

Glo·ria \'glōr-ē-ə, 'glȯr-\ *n* : one of two Christian doxologies: **a** *or* **Gloria in Ex·cel·sis** \-,in-ik-'skel-səs, -,sēs, -,in-ek-'chel-\ : one beginning "Glory be to God on high" **b** *or* **Gloria Pa·tri** \-'pä-(,)trē\ **:** one beginning "Glory be to the Father"

glo·ri·fy \'glȯr-ə-,fī, 'glȯr-\ *vt* **-fied; -fy·ing** **1 :** to make glorious by bestowing glory upon; *esp* **:** to elevate to celestial glory **2 :** to shed radiance or splendor on **3 :** to make glorious by presentation in a favorable aspect **4 :** to give glory to — **glo·ri·fi·ca·tion** \,glȯr-ə-fə-'kā-shən, ,glȯr-\ *n* — **glo·ri·fi·er** \'glȯr-ə-,fī(-ə)r, 'glȯr-\ *n*

glo·ri·ous \'glȯr-ē-əs, 'glȯr-\ *adj* **1 a :** possessing or deserving glory **:** ILLUSTRIOUS **b :** conferring glory ⟨*glorious* victory⟩ **2 :** RESPLENDENT, MAGNIFICENT ⟨*glorious* heavens⟩ **3 :** DELIGHTFUL, WONDERFUL **syn** see SPLENDID — **glo·ri·ous·ly** *adv* — **glo·ri·ous·ness** *n*

¹glo·ry \'glȯr-ē, 'glȯr-\ *n, pl* **glories** [L *gloria*] **1 a :** praise, honor, or distinction extended by common consent **:** RENOWN **b :** worshipful praise, honor, and thanksgiving **2 a :** something that secures praise or renown **b :** a brilliant asset **3 a :** RESPLENDENCE, MAGNIFICENCE **b :** the splendor and beatific happiness of heaven **4 :** a height of prosperity or achievement **5 :** a ring or spot of light: as **a :** AUREOLE **b :** CORONA 1, 2

²glory *vi* **:** to rejoice proudly **:** EXULT

¹gloss \'gläs, 'glȯs\ *n* [prob. of Scand origin] **1 :** brightness from a smooth surface **:** LUSTER, SHEEN **2 :** a deceptively attractive appearance **:** outward show ⟨a thin *gloss* of good manners⟩

²gloss *vt* **1 :** to give a deceptive appearance to **2 :** to pass over quickly in an attempt to ignore ⟨*gloss* over inadequacies⟩

³gloss *n* [OF *glose*, fr. L *glossa* unusual word requiring explanation, fr. Gk *glōssa, glōtta*, lit., tongue, language] **1 :** a brief explanation (as in the margin of a text) of a difficult or obscure word or expression **2 a :** GLOSSARY **b :** an interlinear translation **c :** a continuous commentary accompanying a text

⁴gloss *vt* **:** to furnish glosses for

glos·sa·ry \'gläs-(ə-)rē, 'glȯs-\ *n, pl* **-ries :** a list in the back of a book of the hard or unusual words found in the text; *also* **:** a dictionary of the special terms found in a particular field of study — **glos·sar·i·al** \glä-'sar-ē-əl, -'ser-\ *adj*

glos·so·pha·ryn·geal \,gläs-ō-fə-'rin-j(ē-)əl, ,glȯs-, -,farən-'jē-əl\ *adj* [Gk *glōssa* tongue] **:** of or relating to both tongue and pharynx ⟨the *glossopharyngeal* nerve⟩

glossy \'gläs-ē, 'glȯs-\ *adj* **gloss·i·er; -est :** having a superficial luster or brightness — **gloss·i·ness** *n*

glot·tis \'glät-əs\ *n, pl* **glot·tis·es** *or* **glot·ti·des** \'glät-ə-,dēz\ [Gk *glōttis*, fr. *glōtta* tongue] **:** the elongated opening between the pharynx and trachea — compare EPIGLOTTIS — **glot·tal** \'glät-ᵊl\ *adj*

glove \'gləv\ *n* [OE *glōf*] **1 a :** a covering for the hand having separate sections for each finger **b :** GAUNTLET **2 a :** a padded leather covering for the hand used in baseball — compare MITT **b :** BOXING GLOVE — **gloved** \'gləvd\ *adj*

¹glow \'glō\ *vi* [OE *glōwan*] **1 a :** to shine with or as if with an intense heat **b** (1) **:** to have a rich warm usu. ruddy color (2) **:** FLUSH, BLUSH **2 a :** to experience a sensation of heat **b :** to show exuberance or elation ⟨*glow* with pride⟩

²glow *n* **1 :** brightness or warmth of color; *esp* **:** REDNESS **2 a :** warmth of feeling or emotion **b :** a sensation of warmth **3 :** light such as is emitted by something that is intensely hot but not flaming ⟨the *glow* of coals in the fireplace⟩

glow·er \'glau̇(-ə)r\ *vi* [ME (Sc) *glowren*] **:** to look or stare with sullen annoyance or anger — **glower** *n*

glow·worm \'glō-,wərm\ *n* **:** an insect or insect larva that gives off light

glox·in·ia \gläk-'sin-ē-ə\ *n* [after B. P. *Gloxin*, 18th cent. German botanist] **:** any of a genus of Brazilian tuberous herbs related to the African violets; *esp* **:** one often grown for its showy bell-shaped flowers

gloze \'glōz\ *vt* **:** to make appear right or acceptable **:** GLOSS ⟨*gloze* over a person's faults⟩

glu·cose \'glü-,kōs\ *n* [F, modif. of Gk *gleukos* must, sweet wine] **1 :** a sugar $C_6H_{12}O_6$ known in three different forms; *esp* **:** DEXTROSE **2 :** CORN SYRUP

glu·co·side \'glü-kə-,sīd\ *n* **:** GLYCOSIDE

¹glue \'glü\ *n* [MF *glu*, fr. LL *glut-, glus;* akin to E *clay*] **1 :** any of various strong adhesive substances; *esp* **:** a

hard protein substance that absorbs water to form a viscous solution with strong adhesive properties and is obtained by cooking down animal materials (as hides or bones) **2 :** a solution of glue used to stick things together

²glue *vt* **glued; glu·ing** *also* **glue·ing :** to make fast with or as if with glue

glu·ey \'glü-ē\ *adj* **glu·i·er; -est** **1 :** covered with glue **2 :** sticky like glue — **glu·i·ly** \'glü-ə-lē\ *adv*

glum \'gləm\ *adj* **glum·mer; glum·mest** **1 :** MOROSE, SULLEN **2 :** DREARY, GLOOMY — **glum·ly** *adv* — **glum·ness** *n*

glume \'glüm\ *n* [L *gluma* hull, husk] **:** a chaffy bract; *esp* **:** either of two empty bracts at the base of the spikelet in a grass — **glu·ma·ceous** \glü-'mā-shəs\ *adj* — **glu·mif·er·ous** \glü-'mif-(ə-)rəs\ *adj*

¹glut \'glət\ *vt* **glut·ted; glut·ting** **1 :** to fill esp. with food to satiety **:** SATIATE **2 :** to flood with goods so that supply exceeds demand ⟨the market was *glutted* with fruit⟩

²glut *n* **:** an excessive quantity **:** OVERSUPPLY

glu·ta·mate \'glüt-ə-,māt\ *n* **:** a salt or ester of glutamic acid

glu·tam·ic acid \(,)glü-,tam-ik-\ *n* [*gluten* + *amino* + *-ic*] **:** a crystalline amino acid $C_5H_9NO_4$ widely distributed in plant and animal proteins and used in the form of a sodium salt as a seasoning

glu·ten \'glüt-ᵊn\ *n* [L *glutin-, gluten* glue] **:** a tough elastic protein substance in flour esp. from wheat that holds together dough and makes it sticky — **glu·ten·ous** \'glüt-nəs, -ᵊn-əs\ *adj*

glu·te·us \'glüt-ē-əs\ *n, pl* **-tei** \-ē-,ī\ **:** any of the large muscles of the buttocks — **glu·te·al** \-ē-əl\ *adj*

glu·ti·nous \'glüt-nəs, -ᵊn-əs\ *adj* **:** resembling glue **:** STICKY — **glu·ti·nous·ly** *adv*

glut·ton \'glət-ᵊn\ *n* [OF *gloton*, fr. L *glutton-, glutto*] **1 :** one that eats too much **2 a :** a shaggy thickset carnivorous mammal of northern Europe and Asia related to the marten and the sable **b :** WOLVERINE — **glut·ton·ous** \'glət-nəs, -ᵊn-əs\ *adj* — **glut·ton·ous·ly** *adv*

glut·tony \'glət-nē, -ᵊn-ē\ *n, pl* **-ton·ies :** excess in eating or drinking

glyc·er·ide \'glis-ə-,rīd\ *n* **:** an ester of glycerol esp. with fatty acids — **glyc·er·id·ic** \,glis-ə-'rid-ik\ *adj*

glyc·er·in *or* **glyc·er·ine** \'glis-(ə-)rən\ *n* [F *glycérine*, fr. Gk *glykeros* sweet] **:** GLYCEROL

glyc·er·ol \'glis-ə-,rȯl, -,rōl\ *n* **:** a sweet colorless syrupy alcohol $C_3H_5(OH)_3$ usu. obtained by the hydrolysis of fats and oils and used esp. as a solvent and plasticizer

gly·cine \'glī-,sēn, 'glīs-ᵊn\ *n* **:** a sweet crystalline amino acid $C_2H_5NO_2$ formed esp. by hydrolysis of proteins

gly·co·gen \'glī-kə-jən\ *n* [Gk *glykys* sweet] **:** a white tasteless substance that is the chief storage carbohydrate of animals

gly·col·y·sis \glī-'käl-ə-səs\ *n* **:** enzymatic breakdown of carbohydrate (as glucose) by way of phosphate derivatives — **gly·co·lyt·ic** \,glī-kə-'lit-ik\ *adj*

gly·co·side \'glī-kə-,sīd\ *n* **:** any of numerous derivatives of sugars that on hydrolysis yield a sugar (as glucose) — **gly·co·sid·ic** \,glī-kə-'sid-ik\ *adj*

gly·cos·uria \,glī-kō-'s(h)u̇r-ē-ə\ *n* **:** the presence of abnormal amounts of sugar in the urine

G-man \'jē-,man\ *n* [prob. fr. *government man*] **:** a special agent of the Federal Bureau of Investigation

gnarl \'närl\ *n* **:** a hard protuberance with twisted grain on a tree — **gnarled** \'närld\ *adj* — **gnarly** \'när-lē\ *adj*

gnash \'nash\ *vt* **:** to strike or grind (the teeth) together

gnat \'nat\ *n* [OE *gnætt*] **:** any of various small usu. biting two-winged flies — compare FLY

gnath·ic \'nath-ik\ *adj* [Gk *gnathos* jaw] **:** of or relating to the jaw

gnaw \'nȯ\ *vb* [OE *gnagan*] **1 a :** to bite or chew with the teeth; *esp* **:** to wear away by persistent biting or nibbling ⟨dog *gnawing* a bone⟩ **b :** to make by gnawing ⟨rats *gnawed* a hole⟩ **2 a :** to be a source of vexation to **:** PLAGUE **b :** to affect like gnawing ⟨*gnawing* hunger⟩ **3 :** ERODE, CORRODE — **gnaw·er** \'nȯ(-ə)r\ *n*

gneiss \'nīs\ *n* [G *gneis*] **:** a metamorphic rock in layers that is similar in composition to granite or feldspar

gnome \'nōm\ *n* [NL *gnomus*] **:** a dwarf of folklore living inside the earth and guarding precious ore or treasure — **gnom·ish** \'nō-mish\ *adj*

ə abut; ᵊ kitten; ər further; a back; ā bake; ä cot, cart; au̇ out; ch chin; e less; ē easy; g gift; i trip; ī life

gno·mon \'nō-,män, -mən\ *n* : an object that by the position or length of its shadow serves as an indicator of the hour of the day; *esp* : the style of an ordinary sundial

gno·sis \'nō-səs\ *n* : immediate knowledge of spiritual truth held by the ancient Gnostics to be attainable through faith alone

Gnos·tic \'näs-tik\ *n* [Gk *gnōstikos* of knowledge, fr. *gignōskein* to know; akin to E *know*] : an adherent of one of various cults of late pre-Christian and early Christian centuries distinguished by the conviction that matter is evil and that emancipation comes through gnosis — **Gnostic** *adj* — **gnos·ti·cism** \-tə-,siz-əm\ *n, often cap*

gnu \'n(y)ü\ *n, pl* **gnu** *or* **gnus** [Bushman *nqu*] : any of several large African antelopes with a head like that of an ox, short mane, long tail, and horns in both sexes that curve downward and outward

gnu

¹**go** \'gō\ *vb* **went** \'went\; **gone** \'gȯn, 'gän\; **go·ing** \'gō-iŋ\; **goes** \'gōz\ [OE *gān*] **1** : to move on a course : PROCEED ⟨*go* slow⟩ **2** : to move away from one point to or toward another : LEAVE, DEPART **3 a** : to take a certain course or follow a certain procedure **b** : to pass by a process like journeying ⟨the message *went* by wire⟩ **c** (1) : EXTEND, RUN ⟨his land *goes* to the river⟩ (2) : to give access : LEAD ⟨that door *goes* to the cellar⟩ **4** : to be habitually in a certain state ⟨*goes* bareheaded⟩ ⟨*goes* armed after dark⟩ **5 a** : to become lost, consumed, or spent **b** : to slip away : ELAPSE, PASS **c** : to pass by sale ⟨*went* for a good price⟩ **d** : to become impaired or weakened ⟨his hearing started to *go*⟩ **e** : to give way under force or pressure : BREAK **6 a** : to take place : HAPPEN ⟨what's *going* on⟩ **b** : to be in general or on an average ⟨cheap, as yachts *go*⟩ **c** : to become esp. as the result of a contest ⟨decision *went* against him⟩ **7 a** : to apply oneself **b** : to put or subject oneself ⟨*went* to great expense⟩ **8** : to have recourse : RESORT ⟨*go* to court to recover damages⟩ **9 a** : to begin or maintain an action or motion ⟨drums had been *going* strong⟩ **b** : to function properly ⟨get the motor to *go*⟩ **10** : to have currency : CIRCULATE ⟨the report *goes*⟩ **11 a** : to be or act in accordance ⟨a good rule to *go* by⟩ **b** : to come to be applied **c** : to pass by award, assignment, or lot ⟨the prize *went* to a sophomore⟩ **d** : to contribute to a result ⟨qualities that *go* to make a hero⟩ **12 a** : to be about, intending, or expecting something ⟨is *going* to leave town⟩ **b** : to come or arrive at a certain state or condition ⟨*go* to sleep⟩ **c** : to come to be ⟨the tire *went* flat⟩ **13 a** : to be capable of passing, extending, or being contained or inserted ⟨these clothes will *go* in your suitcase⟩ **b** : to have a usual or proper place or position : BELONG ⟨these books *go* on the top shelf⟩ **c** : to be capable of being divided ⟨5 *goes* into 60 12 times⟩ **14** : to have a tendency : CONDUCE ⟨the incident *goes* to show that he can be trusted⟩ **15** : to be acceptable, satisfactory, or adequate ⟨any kind of dress *goes*⟩ **16 a** : to proceed along or according to : FOLLOW ⟨if I was *going* his way⟩ **b** : TRAVERSE **17** : to make a wager or offer of : BET, BID ⟨willing to *go* $50⟩ **18 a** : to assume the function or obligation of ⟨*go* bail for his friend⟩ **b** : to participate to the extent of ⟨*go* halves⟩ **19** : YIELD, WEIGH — **go at 1** : ATTACK, ATTEMPT **2** : UNDERTAKE — **go back on 1** : ABANDON **2** : BETRAY **3** : FAIL — **go by the board** : to be discarded — **go down the line** : to give wholehearted support — **go for 1** : to pass for or serve as **2** : to have an interest in or liking for : FAVOR — **go one better** : OUTDO, SURPASS — **go over 1** : EXAMINE **2 a** : REPEAT **b** : STUDY, REVIEW — **go places** : to be on the way to success — **go steady** : to date one person exclusively and frequently — **go through 1** : to subject to thorough examination, consideration, or study **2** : EXPERIENCE, UNDERGO **3** : to carry out : PERFORM ⟨*went through* his act perfectly⟩ — **to go** : REMAINING, LEFT ⟨five minutes *to go* before the train leaves⟩

²**go** *n, pl* **goes** **1** : the act or manner of going **2** : the height of fashion **3** : a turn of affairs : OCCURRENCE **4** : ENERGY, VIGOR **5** : ATTEMPT, TRY **6** : a spell of activity — **no go** : to no avail : USELESS — **on the go** : constantly or restlessly active

goad \'gōd\ *n* [OE *gād*] **1** : a pointed rod used to urge an animal on **2** : something that urges : SPUR — **goad** *vt*

goal \'gōl\ *n* [ME *gol* boundary, limit] **1** : the terminal point of a race **2** : the end toward which effort is directed : AIM **3 a** : an area or object toward which players in various games attempt to advance a ball or puck to score points **b** : the score resulting from such an act

goal·keep·er \-,kē-pər\ *n* : a player who defends the goal in various games — called also *goal·ie* \'gō-lē\, *goaltend·er* \'gōl-,ten-dər\

goal·post \'gōl-,pōst\ *n* : one of two vertical posts that with a crossbar constitute the goal in various games

goat \'gōt\ *n, pl* **goat** *or* **goats** [OE *gāt*] **1** : any of various hollow-horned ruminant mammals related to the sheep but of lighter build and with backwardly arching horns, a short tail, and usu. straight hair **2** : SCAPEGOAT — **goat·like** \-,līk\ *adj*

goa·tee \gō-'tē\ *n* : a small trim pointed or tufted beard on a man's chin

goat·fish \'gōt-,fish\ *n* : MULLET 2

goat·suck·er \-,sək-ər\ *n* : any of various medium-sized long-winged nocturnal birds (as the whippoorwills and nighthawks) having a short wide bill, short legs, and soft mottled plumage and feeding on insects which they catch on the wing

¹**gob** \'gäb\ *n* **1** : LUMP, MASS **2** : a large amount — usu. used in pl. ⟨*gobs* of money⟩

²**gob** *n* : SAILOR

gob·bet \'gäb-ət\ *n* [MF *gobet* mouthful, piece] : LUMP, MASS

¹**gob·ble** \'gäb-əl\ *vt* **gob·bled**; **gob·bling** \'gäb-(ə-)liŋ\ **1** : to swallow or eat greedily **2** : to take eagerly : GRAB — usu. used with *up*

²**gobble** *vi* : to make the natural guttural noise of a male turkey — **gobble** *n*

gob·ble·dy·gook *or* **gob·ble·de·gook** \,gäb-əl-dē-'gúk\ *n* : wordy and generally unintelligible jargon

gob·bler \'gäb-lər\ *n* : a male turkey

Go·be·lin \'gō-bə-lən, 'gäb-ə-\ *adj* : of, relating to, or characteristic of tapestry produced at the Gobelin works in Paris — **Gobelin** *n*

go-be·tween \'gō-bə-,twēn\ *n* : a person who acts as a messenger or an intermediary between two parties

gob·let \'gäb-lət\ *n* [MF *gobelet*] : a drinking glass with a foot and stem — compare TUMBLER

goblet cell *n* : a mucus-secreting cell distended at the free end by secretion

gob·lin \'gäb-lən\ *n* [MF *gobelin*, fr. ML *gobelinus*, fr. Gk *kobalos* rogue, goblin] : an ugly grotesque sprite with evil or mischievous ways

go·by \'gō-bē\ *n, pl* **gobies** *also* **goby** [L *gobius* gudgeon, fr. Gk *kōbios*] : any of numerous spiny-finned fishes with the pelvic fins often united to form a sucking disk

go-cart \'gō-,kärt\ *n* **1 a** : WALKER **b** : STROLLER **2** : a light open carriage

¹**god** \'gäd, 'gȯd\ *n* [OE] **1** : a being possessing more than human powers ⟨ancient peoples worshiped many *gods*⟩ **2** : a natural or man-made physical object (as an image or idol) worshiped as divine **3** : something held to be the most important thing in existence ⟨make a *god* of money⟩

²**God** *n* : the supreme or ultimate reality; *esp* : the Being perfect in power, wisdom, and goodness whom men worship as creator and ruler of the universe

god·child \-,chīld\ *n* : a person for whom another person stands as sponsor at baptism and promises to see that the baptized person receives a Christian training : GODSON, GODDAUGHTER

god·daugh·ter \-,dȯt-ər\ *n* : a female godchild

god·dess \'gäd-əs\ *n* **1** : a female god **2** : a woman whose great charm or beauty arouses adoration

god·fa·ther \'gäd-,fäth-ər, 'gȯd-\ *n* : a man who stands as sponsor for a child at its baptism

god·head \-,hed\ *n* [ME *godhed*, fr. *god* + *-hed* -hood] **1** : divine nature or essence : DIVINITY **2** *cap* **a** : ²GOD, DEITY **b** : the nature of God esp. as existing in three persons — used with *the*

god·hood \-,húd\ *n* : DIVINITY

Go·di·va \gə-'dī-və\ *n* : a Saxon lady noted in legend for

j joke; **ŋ** sing; **ō** flow; **ȯ** flaw; **ȯi** coin; **th** thin; **th** this; **ü** loot; **ú** foot; **y** yet; **yü** few; **yú** furious; **zh** vision

riding naked through the streets of Coventry to relieve the town of a burdensome tax levied by her husband

god·less \'gäd-ləs, 'gód-\ *adj* : not acknowledging a deity or divine law — **god·less·ness** *n*

god·like \-,līk\ *adj* : resembling or having the qualities of God or a god : DIVINE — **god·like·ness** *n*

god·ling \-liŋ\ *n* : an inferior or local god

god·ly \-lē\ *adj* **god·li·er; -est** : PIOUS, DEVOUT ⟨a *godly* man⟩ — **god·li·ness** *n*

god·moth·er \-,məth-ər\ *n* : a woman who stands as sponsor for a child at its baptism

go·down \'gō-,daún\ *n* [Malay *gudang*] : a warehouse in an oriental country

god·par·ent \'gäd-,par-ənt, 'gód-, -,per-\ *n* : a sponsor at baptism

God's acre *n* : a churchyard burial ground

god·send \'gäd-,send, 'gód-\ *n* : a desirable or needed thing or event that comes unexpectedly as if sent by God

god·son \-,sən\ *n* : a male godchild

God·speed \-'spēd\ *n* : a wish for success given to a person on parting

god·wit \'gäd-,wit\ *n* : any of a genus of long-billed wading birds related to the snipes but similar to curlews

go·er \'gō-(ə)r\ *n* : one that goes

go·get·ter \'gō-,get-ər\ *n* : an aggressively enterprising person : HUSTLER — **go·get·ting** \-,get-iŋ\ *adj or n*

¹**gog·gle** \'gäg-əl\ *vi* **gog·gled; gog·gling** \'gäg-(ə-)liŋ\ [ME *gogelen* to squint] : to stare with wide or protuberant eyes — **gog·gler** \-(ə-)lər\ *n*

²**goggle** *adj* : PROTUBERANT, STARING ⟨*goggle* eyes⟩ — **gog·gly** \-(ə-)lē\ *adj*

gog·gle-eyed \,gäg-əl-'īd\ *adj* : having bulging or rolling eyes

gog·gles \'gäg-əlz\ *n pl* : protective eyeglasses typically with shields at the side

Goi·del·ic \gói-'del-ik\ *n* : a branch of the Celtic languages that includes Irish Gaelic, Scottish Gaelic, and Manx — **Goidelic** *adj*

go in *vi* : ENTER — **go in for** **1** : to make one's particular interest or specialty **2** : to take part in out of interest or liking ⟨*go in for* track⟩

¹**go·ing** \'gō-iŋ\ *n* **1** : DEPARTURE **2** : the condition of the ground esp. for walking or driving **3** : advance toward an objective : PROGRESS

²**going** *adj* **1** : EXISTING, LIVING ⟨best novelist *going*⟩ **2** : CURRENT, PREVAILING ⟨*going* price⟩ **3** : being successful and likely to continue successful ⟨a *going* concern⟩

go·ings-on \,gō-iŋz-'ón, -'än\ *n pl* : ACTIONS, EVENTS

goi·ter *also* **goi·tre** \'góit-ər\ *n* [F *goitre*, fr. MF *goitron* throat, fr. (assumed) VL *guttrion-, guttrio*, fr. L *guttur*] : an enlargement of the thyroid gland visible as a swelling of the front of the neck — compare HYPERTHYROIDISM, HYPOTHYROIDISM — **goi·trous** \'gói-trəs, 'góit-ə-rəs\ *adj*

gold \'gōld\ *n* [OE; akin to E *yellow*] **1** : a malleable ductile yellow trivalent and univalent metallic element that occurs chiefly free but also in a few minerals and is used esp. in coins and jewelry — see ELEMENT table **2 a** : gold coins **b** : MONEY **3** : a variable color averaging deep yellow — **gold** *adj*

gold·beat·er \'gōl(d)-,bēt-ər\ *n* : one that beats gold into gold leaf

gold·brick \'gōl(d)-,brik\ *n* : a person (as a soldier) who shirks assigned work — **goldbrick** *vi*

gold·en \'gōl-dən\ *adj* **1** : consisting of, relating to, or containing gold **2 a** : having the color of gold **b** : BLOND **1a** **3** : SHINING, LUSTROUS **4** : of a high degree of excellence : SUPERB **5** : FLOURISHING, PROSPEROUS ⟨a *golden* age⟩ **6** : radiantly youthful and vigorous **7** : FAVORABLE, ADVANTAGEOUS ⟨*golden* opportunity⟩ **8** : MELLOW, RESONANT ⟨smooth *golden* tenor⟩ — **gold·en·ly** *adv* — **gold·en·ness** \-dən-nəs\ *n*

golden alga *n* : any of a major group (Chrysophyta) of algae with golden brown pigments usu. hiding the chlorophyll — called also *golden-brown alga*

gold·en·eye \'gōl-dən-,ī\ *n* **1** : a northern diving duck having the male strikingly marked in black and white **2** : LACEWING

Golden Fleece *n* : a fleece of gold recovered from a dragon= guarded grove by the Argonauts

golden glow *n* : a tall branching herb related to the daisies that has showy yellow very double flower heads

golden mean *n* : the medium between extremes : MODERATION

gold·en·rod \'gōl-dən-,räd\ *n* : any of numerous chiefly No. American biennial or perennial plants that are related to the daisies and have stems resembling wands and heads of small yellow or sometimes white flowers usu. in panicles

golden rule *n* : a rule that one should do to others as he would have others do to him

gol·den·seal \'gōl-dən-,sēl\ *n* : a perennial American herb of the crowfoot family with a thick knotted yellow rootstock and large rounded leaves

golden section *n* : division of a line segment in which the ratio of the smaller division to the larger is equal to the ratio of the larger to the whole segment

gold·field \'gōl(d)-,fēld\ *n* : a gold-mining district

gold-filled \'gōl(d)-'fild\ *adj* : covered with a layer of gold ⟨a *gold-filled* bracelet⟩

gold·finch \-,finch\ *n* **1** : a small largely red, black, and yellow European finch often kept as a cage bird **2** : any of several small American finches usu. having the male in summer plumage yellow with black wings, tail, and crown

gold·fish \-,fish\ *n* : a small usu. golden yellow or orange carp much used as an aquarium and pond fish

gold leaf *n* : a thin sheet of gold used esp. for gilding

gold·smith \'gōl(d)-,smith\ *n* : one who makes or deals in articles of gold

gold standard *n* : a monetary standard under which the basic unit of currency is defined by a stated quantity of gold and which is usu. characterized by the coinage and circulation of gold

golf \'gälf, 'gólf\ *n* [ME (Sc)] : a game whose object is to sink a ball into each of the 9 or 18 holes on a course by using as few strokes with a club as possible and avoiding various obstacles — **golf** *vi* — **golf·er** *n*

Gol·gi apparatus \'gól-(,)jē-\ *n* [Camillo *Golgi* d1926 Italian physician] : a cytoplasmic component that prob. plays a part in elaboration and secretion of cell products

Golgi body *n* : a single particle of the Golgi apparatus

Gol·go·tha \'gäl-gə-thə\ *n* : CALVARY

Go·li·ath \gə-'lī-əth\ *n* : a Philistine giant held in the Old Testament to have been killed by David with a sling

Go·mor·rah \gə-'mór-ə, -'mär-\ *n* : a wicked city whose destruction by God is described in the book of Genesis

gon- *or* **gono-** *comb form* [Gk *gonos* procreation, seed, fr. *gen-, gon-, gignesthai* to be born] : sexual : generative : semen : seed ⟨*gono*duct⟩

-gon \,gän\ *n comb form* [Gk *-gōnon*, fr. *gōnia* angle] : figure having (so many) angles ⟨deca*gon*⟩

go·nad \'gō-,nad\ *n* [NL *gonad-, gonas*] : a primary sex gland : OVARY, TESTIS — **go·nad·al** \gō-'nad-ºl\ *adj*

go·nad·o·trop·ic \gō-,nad-ə-'träp-ik\ *also* **go·nad·o·troph·ic** \-'träf-ik\ *adj* : acting on or stimulating the gonads ⟨*gonadotropic* hormone⟩ — **go·nad·o·tro·pin** \-'trō-pən\ *n*

gon·do·la \'gän-də-lə (*usual for sense 1*), gän-'dō-\ *n* [It] **1** : a long narrow flat-bottomed boat with a high prow and stern used on the canals of Venice **2** : a railroad car with flat bottom, fixed sides, and no top used chiefly for hauling heavy bulk commodities **3 a** : an elongated car attached to the underside of an airship **b** : an often spherical airtight enclosure suspended from a balloon for carrying passengers or instruments **4** : a motortruck or trailer having a large hopper-shaped container for transporting mixed concrete

gondola 1

gon·do·lier \,gän-də-'li(ə)r\ *n* : one who propels a gondola

gone \'gón, 'gän\ *adj* [fr. pp. of *go*] **1** : PAST **2 a** : ADVANCED, ABSORBED ⟨far *gone* in hysteria⟩ **b** : INFATUATED **c** : PREGNANT **3 a** : DEAD **b** : LOST, RUINED **c** : SINKING, WEAK ⟨a *gone* feeling from hunger⟩

gon·er \'gón-ər, 'gän-\ *n* : one whose case is hopeless

gon·fa·lon \'gän-fə-,län\ *n* [It *gonfalone*] **1** : the ensign of certain princes or states (as the medieval republics of Italy) **2** : a flag that hangs from a crosspiece or frame

gong \'gäŋ, 'góŋ\ *n* **1** : a metallic disk that produces a resounding tone when struck **2** : a flat saucer-shaped bell

---

ə abut; ᵊ kitten; ər further; a back; ā bake; ä cot, cart; aú out; ch chin; e less; ē easy; g gift; i trip; ī life

go·ni·a·tite \'gō-nē-ə-,tīt\ *n* : any of various discoidal Paleozoic ammonoids with angular-lobed sutures — **go·ni·a·tit·ic** \,gō-nē-ə-'tit-ik\ *adj*

go·nid·i·um \gō-'nid-ē-əm\ *n, pl* **-ia** \-ē-ə\ : an asexual reproductive cell or group of cells of a gametophyte — **go·nid·i·al** \-ē-əl\ *adj*

gono·coc·cus \,gän-ə-'käk-əs\ *n, pl* **-coc·ci** \-'käk-,(s)ī, -'käk-(,)(s)ē\ : a pus-producing bacterium that causes gonorrhea — **gono·coc·cal** \-'käk-əl\ *or* **gono·coc·cic** \-'käk-(s)ik\ *adj*

gon·or·rhea \,gän-ə-'rē-ə\ *n* : a contagious inflammatory disease of the genitourinary tract caused by the gonococcus — **gon·or·rhe·al** \-'rē-əl\ *adj*

-g·o·ny \g-ə-nē\ *n comb form, pl* **-gonies** [Gk *-gonia*, fr. *gen-, gon-, gignesthai* to be born] : reproduction ⟨sporog*ony*⟩

goo \'gü\ *n* : a viscid or sticky substance — **goo·ey** \'gü-ē\ *adj*

goo·ber \'gü-bər, 'gùb-ər\ *n* [of African origin] *dial* : PEANUT

¹good \'gùd\ *adj* **bet·ter** \'bet-ər\; **best** \'best\ [OE *gōd*] **1 a** (1) : of a favorable character or tendency ⟨*good* news⟩ (2) : BOUNTIFUL, FERTILE ⟨*good* land⟩ (3) : COMELY, ATTRACTIVE ⟨*good* looks⟩ **b** (1) : SUITABLE, FIT ⟨*good* to eat⟩ (2) : SOUND, WHOLE ⟨one *good* arm⟩ (3) : not depreciated ⟨bad money drives out *good*⟩ (4) : commercially reliable ⟨a *good* risk⟩ (5) : certain to last or live ⟨*good* for another year⟩ (6) : certain to pay or contribute ⟨*good* for a hundred dollars⟩ (7) : certain to elicit a specified result ⟨always *good* for a laugh⟩ **c** (1) : AGREEABLE, PLEASANT (2) : SALUTARY, WHOLESOME ⟨*good* for a cold⟩ **d** (1) : CONSIDERABLE, AMPLE ⟨a *good* margin⟩ (2) : FULL ⟨*good* measure⟩ **e** (1) : WELL-FOUNDED, COGENT ⟨*good* reasons⟩ (2) : TRUE ⟨holds *good* for society at large⟩ (3) : ACTUALIZED, REAL ⟨made *good* his promises⟩ (4) : recognized or valid esp. in law ⟨member in *good* standing⟩ ⟨has a *good* title⟩ **f** (1) : ADEQUATE, SATISFACTORY ⟨*good* care⟩ (2) : conforming to a standard ⟨*good* English⟩ (3) : DISCRIMINATING, CHOICE ⟨*good* taste⟩ **2 a** (1) : COMMENDABLE, VIRTUOUS, JUST ⟨a *good* man⟩ (2) : RIGHT ⟨*good* conduct⟩ **b** : UPPER-CLASS ⟨*good* family⟩ **c** : COMPETENT, SKILLFUL ⟨a *good* doctor⟩ **d** : LOYAL ⟨a *good* member of his political party⟩ ⟨a *good* Catholic⟩ **3** : containing less fat and being less tender than higher grades — used of meat and esp. beef — **as good as** : in effect : VIRTUALLY ⟨as good as dead⟩ — **good and** : VERY, ENTIRELY ⟨was *good* and mad⟩

²good *n* **1 a** : something good **b** : praiseworthy character : GOODNESS **2** : PROSPERITY, BENEFIT, WELFARE ⟨*good* of the community⟩ **3 a** : something that has economic utility or satisfies an economic need or desire **b** *pl* : personal property (as one's clothing, furniture, automobile, or collection of rare coins) **c** *pl* : CLOTH **d** *pl* : WARES, COMMODITIES **4** : good persons — used with *the* **5** *pl* : proof of wrongdoing ⟨got the *goods* on him⟩

³good *adv* : WELL

good book *n, often cap G&B* : BIBLE

good-bye *or* **good-by** \gùd-'bī\ *n* [alter. of *God be with you*] : a concluding remark at parting — often used interjectionally

good fellow *n* : a hearty companionable person — **good·fel·low·ship** *n*

Good Friday *n* : the Friday before Easter observed as the anniversary of the crucifixion of Christ

good-heart·ed \'gùd-'härt-əd\ *adj* : having a kindly generous disposition — **good-heart·ed·ly** *adv* — **good-heart·ed·ness** *n*

good-hu·mored \-'hyü-mərd, -'yü-\ *adj* : GOOD-NATURED, CHEERFUL — **good-hu·mored·ly** *adv* — **good-hu·mored·ness** *n*

good·ish \'gùd-ish\ *adj* : fairly good

good·ly \'gùd-lē\ *adj* **good·li·er; -est 1** : of pleasing appearance **2** : LARGE, CONSIDERABLE ⟨a *goodly* number⟩

good·man \'gùd-mən\ *n* **1** *archaic* : the head of a household : HUSBAND **2** *archaic* : MISTER

good-na·tured \'gùd-'nā-chərd\ *adj* : of a pleasant cheerful disposition — **good-na·tured·ly** *adv* — **good-na·tured·ness** *n*

good-neighbor policy *n* : a policy of friendship, cooperation, and noninterference in the internal affairs of another country

good·ness \'gùd-nəs\ *n* : the quality or state of being good; *esp* : excellence of character

Good Shepherd *n* : JESUS

good-sized \'gùd-'sīzd\ *adj* : large enough : fairly large

good-tem·pered \-'tem-pərd\ *adj* : having an even temper — **good-tem·pered·ly** *adv* — **good-tem·pered·ness** *n*

good·wife \'gùd-,wīf\ *n* **1** *archaic* : the mistress of a household **2** *archaic* — used as a title equivalent to *Mrs.*

good·will \'gùd-'wil\ *n* **1** : kindly feeling : BENEVOLENCE **2** : the value of the trade a business has built up over a considerable time **3 a** : cheerful consent **b** : willing effort

goody \'gùd-ē\ *n, pl* **good·ies** : something that is particularly good to eat or otherwise attractive

goody-goody \,gùd-ē-'gùd-ē\ *adj* : affectedly good — **goody-goody** *n*

goof \'güf\ *vb* : BLUNDER — **goof** *n*

go off *vi* **1** : EXPLODE **2** : to undergo decline or deterioration **3** : to follow the expected or desired course : PROCEED

goofy \'gü-fē\ *adj* **goof·i·er; -est** : CRAZY, SILLY — **goof·i·ness** *n*

goose \'güs\ *n, pl* **geese** \'gēs\ [OE *gōs*] **1 a** : any of numerous long-necked birds intermediate in size between the related swans and ducks **b** : a female goose as distinguished from a gander **2** : SIMPLETON, DOLT **3** *pl* **goos·es** : a tailor's smoothing iron with a goose-neck handle

goose·ber·ry \'güs-,ber-ē, 'güz-\ *n* : the acid usu. prickly fruit of any of several shrubs related to the currant

goose

goose egg *n* : ZERO, NOTHING

goose·flesh \'güs-,flesh\ *n* : a roughening of the skin caused usu. by cold or fear

goose·foot \-,fùt\ *n, pl* **goosefoots** : any of numerous mostly weedy glabrous herbs with branched clusters of small petalless greenish or whitish flowers — compare BEET, SPINACH

goose·neck \-,nek\ *n* : something (as a flexible jointed metal pipe) curved like the neck of a goose or U-shaped — **goose·necked** \-,nekt\ *adj*

goose pimples *n pl* : GOOSEFLESH

goose step *n* : a straight-legged stiff-kneed step used by troops of some armies when passing in review — **goose-step** \'güs-,step\ *vi*

go out *vi* **1** : to go forth; *esp* : to leave one's house **2** : to become extinguished ⟨the hall light *went out*⟩ **3** : to go on strike **4** : to become a candidate ⟨*went out* for the football team⟩

go·pher \'gō-fər\ *n* **1** : a burrowing American land tortoise **2 a** : any of several burrowing American rodents with large cheek pouches **b** : a small striped ground squirrel of the prairie region of the U.S.

Gor·di·an knot \,górd-ē-ən-\ *n* : a knot tied by Gordius, king of Phrygia, held to be capable of being untied only by the future ruler of Asia and cut by Alexander the Great with his sword

¹gore \'gō(ə)r, 'gó(ə)r\ *n* [OE *gor* filth] : BLOOD; *esp* : clotted blood

²gore *n* [OE *gāra* triangular piece of land] : a tapering or triangular piece (as of cloth in a skirt)

³gore *vt* **1** : to cut into a tapering triangular form **2** : to provide with a gore

⁴gore *vt* [ME *goren*] : to pierce or wound with a horn or tusk

¹gorge \'górj\ *n* [MF, fr. LL *gurga*, alter. of L *gurges* throat, whirlpool] **1** : THROAT **2** : a narrow passage (as between two mountains) **3** : a mass of matter that chokes up a passage ⟨an ice *gorge* in the river⟩

²gorge *vb* : to eat greedily : stuff to capacity : GLUT — **gorg·er** *n*

gor·geous \'gór-jəs\ *adj* [MF *gorgias* elegant, fr. *gorgias* neckerchief, fr. *gorge*] : resplendently beautiful ⟨*gorgeous* sunset⟩ — **syn** see SPLENDID — **gor·geous·ly** *adv* — **gor·geous·ness** *n*

gor·get \'gór-jət\ *n* : a piece of armor defending the throat and shoulders

gor·gon \'gȯr-gən\ *n* [Gk *Gorgōn*] **1** *cap* : any of three snaky-haired sisters in Greek mythology having glaring eyes capable of turning the beholder to stone **2** : an ugly or repulsive woman

go·ril·la \gə-'ril-ə\ *n* [Gk *Gorillai*, African creatures believed to be hairy women] : an anthropoid ape of west equatorial Africa related to but less erect and much larger than the chimpanzee

gor·man·dize \'gȯr-mən-,dīz\ *vb* [*gormand*, alter. of *gourmand*] : to eat greedily or ravenously — **gor·man·diz·er** *n*

gorse \'gȯrs\ *n* [OE *gorst*] **1** : FURZE **2** : JUNIPER — **gorsy** \'gȯr-sē\ *adj*

gory \'gō(ə)r-ē, 'gȯ(ə)r-\ *adj* **gor·i·er; -est 1** : covered with gore : BLOODSTAINED **2** : BLOODCURDLING, SENSATIONAL

gos·hawk \'gäs-,hȯk\ *n* [OE *gōshafoc*, fr. *gōs* goose + *hafoc* hawk] : any of several long-tailed short-winged hawks noted for their powerful flight, activity, and vigor

gos·ling \'gäz-liŋ, 'gȯz-, -lən\ *n* : a young goose

¹gos·pel \'gäs-pəl\ *n* [ME, fr. OE *gōdspel*, fr. *gōd* good + *spell* tale, news] **1 a** *often cap* : the Christian message concerning Christ, the kingdom of God, and salvation **b** *cap* : one of the first four New Testament books telling of the life, death, and resurrection of Jesus Christ; *also* : a similar apocryphal book **2** *cap* : a liturgical reading from one of the New Testament Gospels **3** : the message or teachings of a religious teacher **4** : something accepted as infallible truth or as a guiding principle

²gospel *adj* **1** : relating to or in accordance with the gospel : EVANGELICAL **2** : EVANGELISTIC ⟨a *gospel* team⟩ **3** : of or relating to religious songs associated with evangelism and popular devotion ⟨a *gospel* singer⟩

Gos·plan \'gäs-,plan\ *n* : a Soviet Russian agency that makes long-term economic and social plans and generally supervises their execution

gos·sa·mer \'gäs-ə-mər, 'gäz-\ *n* [ME *gossomer*, fr. *gos* goose + *somer* summer] **1** : a film of cobwebs floating in air **2** : something light, delicate, or tenuous — **gossamer** *adj* — **gos·sa·mery** \-mə-rē\ *adj*

¹gos·sip \'gäs-əp\ *n* [ME, crony, fr. OE *godsibb* godparent, fr. *god* + *sibb* kinsman] **1** : a person who habitually reveals personal or sensational facts **2 a** : rumor or report of an intimate nature **b** : chatty talk –- **gossipy** \-ə-pē\ *adj*

²gossip *vi* : to relate gossip — **gos·sip·er** *n*

got *past of* GET

Goth \'gäth\ *n* : a member of a Germanic people that in the early centuries of the Christian era overran the Roman Empire

¹Goth·ic \'gäth-ik\ *adj* **1** : of, relating to, or resembling the Goths, their civilization, or their language **2** : of or relating to a style of architecture prevalent in western Europe from the middle 12th to the early 16th century and characterized by weights and strains converging at isolated points on slender vertical piers and counterbalancing buttresses and by pointed arches and vaulting — **goth·i·cal·ly** \-i-k(ə-)lē\ *adv* — **Goth·ic·ness** *n*

²Gothic *n* **1** : the Germanic language of the Goths **2** : the Gothic architectural style or decoration

gotten *past part of* GET

gouache \'gwäsh\ *n* [F] **1** : painting with opaque colors that have been ground in water and mingled with a preparation of gum **2** : a picture painted by gouache

¹gouge \'gauj\ *n* [MF, fr. LL *gulbia*] **1** : a chisel with a curved blade for scooping or cutting holes **2** : a hole or groove made with or as if with a gouge

²gouge *vt* **1** : to cut holes or grooves in with or as if with a gouge **2** : to force out (an eye) with the thumb **3** : to charge excessively : DEFRAUD, CHEAT — **goug·er** *n*

gou·lash \'gü-,läsh, -,lash\ *n* [Hung *gulyás*] : a beef stew with onion, paprika, and caraway

gourd \'gōrd, 'gȯrd, 'gurd\ *n* [MF *gourde*, fr. L *cucurbita*] **1** : any of a family of chiefly herbaceous tendril-bearing vines including the cucumber, melon, squash, and pumpkin **2** : the fruit of a gourd; *esp* : any of various hard-rinded inedible fruits often used for ornament or for vessels and utensils

gourde \'gurd\ *n* [AmerF] **1** : the basic monetary unit of Haiti **2** : a coin representing one gourde

gour·mand \'gu(ə)r-,mänd\ *n* [MF *gourmant*] **1** : one who is excessively fond of eating and drinking **2** : a luxurious eater : GOURMET — **gour·mand·ism** \'gu(ə)r-,män-,diz-əm, -mən-, -mən-\ *n*

gour·met \-,mā\ *n* [F, alter. of MF *gromet* groom, wine merchant's assistant, fr. ME *grom* groom] : a connoisseur in eating and drinking

gout \'gaut\ *n* [OF *goute* drop, gout, fr. L *gutta* drop] **1** : a metabolic disease marked by a painful inflammation and swelling of the joints **2** : a drop or clot usu. of blood — **gouty** \-ē\ *adj*

gov·ern \'gəv-ərn\ *vb* [OF *governer*, fr. L *gubernare* to steer, govern, fr. Gk *kybernan*] **1** : to exercise continuous sovereign or delegated authority over; *esp* : to control and direct the making and administration of policy in **2** : to control the speed of by automatic means **3 a** : to control, direct, or strongly influence the actions and conduct of **b** : to hold in check : RESTRAIN **4 a** : to require a word to be in a certain case or mood ⟨in German a transitive verb *governs* a noun in the accusative case⟩ **b** : to require a certain case or mood ⟨in Latin the preposition *cum governs* the ablative case⟩ **5** : to constitute a rule or law for **6** : to exercise authority : RULE — **gov·ern·a·ble** \-ər-nə-bəl\ *adj*

syn GOVERN, RULE mean to exercise power or authority over others. GOVERN implies the aim of keeping in a straight course or smooth operation for the common good; RULE more often suggests the exercise of arbitrary or despotic power

gov·ern·ance \'gəv-ər-nən(t)s\ *n* : the exercise of control : GOVERNMENT

gov·ern·ess \'gəv-ər-nəs\ *n* : a woman who teaches and trains a child esp. in a private home

gov·ern·ment \'gəv-ər(n)-mənt\ *n* **1** : the act or process of governing; *esp* : authoritative direction or control **2 a** : the continuous exercise of authority over a political unit : RULE **b** : the making of policy as distinguished from the administration of policy decisions **3 a** : the organization, machinery, or agency through which a political unit exercises authority and performs functions and which is usu. classified according to the distribution of power within it ⟨republican *government*⟩ **b** : the institutions, laws, and customs through which a political unit is governed **4** : the body of persons that constitutes the governing authority of a political unit: as **a** : the officials comprising the governing body of a political unit **b** *cap* : the executive branch of the U.S. federal government **c** *cap* : a small group of persons holding simultaneously the principal political executive offices of a political unit and responsible for the direction and supervision of public affairs: (1) : such a group in a parliamentary system constituted by the cabinet or by the ministry (2) : ADMINISTRATION 4b **5** : POLITICAL SCIENCE — **government** *adj* — **gov·ern·men·tal** \,gəv-ər(n)-'ment-ºl\ *adj* — **gov·ern·men·tal·ly** \-ºl-ē\ *adv*

gov·er·nor \'gəv-ə(r)-nər\ *n* **1** : one that governs: as **a** : one that exercises authority esp. over an area or group **b** : an official elected or appointed to act as ruler, chief executive, or nominal head of a political unit (as a colony, state, or province) **c** : COMMANDANT ⟨*governor* of a fortress⟩ **d** : the managing director and usu. the principal officer of an institution or organization ⟨*governor* of a bank⟩ **e** : a member of a group that directs or controls an institution or society ⟨board of *governors*⟩ **2** : TUTOR **3** : an attachment to a machine for automatic control of speed

gov·er·nor-gen·er·al \,gəv-ə(r)-nər-'jen-(ə-)rəl\ *n, pl* **governors–general** *or* **governor–generals** : a governor of high rank; *esp* : one who governs a large territory or has lieutenant governors under him ⟨the *Governor=General* of Canada⟩

governor's council *n* : an executive or legislative council chosen to advise or assist a governor

gov·er·nor·ship \'gəv-ə(r)-nər-,ship\ *n* **1** : the office or position of governor **2** : the term of office of a governor

gown \'gaun\ *n* [MF *goune*, fr. LL *gunna*, a fur garment] **1 a** : a loose flowing outer garment formerly worn by men **b** : an official robe worn esp. by a judge, clergyman, or teacher **c** : a woman's dress; *esp* : one suitable for afternoon or evening wear **d** : a loose robe (as a dressing gown or a nightgown) **e** : a coverall worn in an operating room **2 a** : an office or profession symbolized by a distinctive robe **b :** a body of college students and faculty — **gown** *vt*

Graaf·ian follicle \ˌgräf-ē-ən-, ˌgraf-\ *n* **:** a vesicle in a mammal ovary enclosing a developing egg

¹grab \'grab\ *vb* **grabbed; grab·bing** [obs. D or LG *grabben*] **:** to take hastily **:** CLUTCH, SNATCH — **grab·ber** *n*

²grab *n* **1 a :** a sudden snatch **b :** an unlawful seizure **c :** something grabbed **2 a :** a device for clutching an object **b :** CLAMSHELL

¹grace \'grās\ *n* [OF, fr. L *gratia* favor, thanks, fr. *gratus* pleasing, grateful] **1 a :** help given man by God esp. in overcoming temptation or in leading a good life **b :** a state of freedom from sin and of love for God enjoyed through divine grace **c :** a virtue coming from God **2 :** a short prayer at a meal asking a blessing or giving thanks **3 a :** KINDNESS, FAVOR **b :** a temporary respite granted from the performance of an obligation (as the payment of a debt) **c :** APPROVAL, ACCEPTANCE ⟨stayed in his good *graces*⟩ **4 a :** a charming trait or accomplishment **b** (1) **:** ATTRACTIVENESS, BEAUTY (2) **:** fitness or proportion of line or expression (3) **:** ease of movement **:** charm of bearing **5 :** a musical trill, turn, or appoggiatura **6** — used as a title for a duke, a duchess, or an archbishop — **grace·ful** \-fəl\ *adj* — **grace·ful·ly** \-fə-lē\ *adv* — **grace·ful·ness** *n*

²grace *vt* **1 :** HONOR **2 :** ADORN, EMBELLISH

grace·less \'grās-ləs\ *adj* **:** having no grace, charm, or elegance; *esp* **:** showing lack of feeling for what is fitting ⟨*graceless* behavior⟩ — **grace·less·ly** *adv* — **grace·less·ness** *n*

grace note *n* **:** a musical note added as an ornament; *esp* **:** APPOGGIATURA

Grac·es \'grā-səz\ *n pl* **:** three sister goddesses in Greek mythology who are the givers of charm and beauty

gra·cious \'grā-shəs\ *adj* **1 a :** marked by kindness and courtesy **b :** GRACEFUL **c :** characterized by charm, good taste, and urbanity ⟨*gracious* living⟩ **2 :** MERCIFUL, COMPASSIONATE — used conventionally of royalty and high nobility — **gra·cious·ly** *adv* — **gra·cious·ness** *n*

grack·le \'grak-əl\ *n* [L *graculus* jackdaw] **1 :** any of various Old World starlings **2 :** any of several rather large American blackbirds with glossy iridescent black plumage

gra·da·tion \grā-'dā-shən, grə-\ *n* **1 a :** a series forming successive stages **b :** a step, degree, or stage in a series **2 :** an advance by regular degrees **3 :** the act or process of grading — **gra·da·tion·al** \-shnəl, -shən-ᵊl\ *adj* — **gra·da·tion·al·ly** \-ē-\ *adv*

purple grackle

¹grade \'grād\ *n* [L *gradus* step, degree] **1 :** a stage, step, or degree in a series, order, or ranking **2 :** position in a scale of rank, quality, or order ⟨the *grade* of sergeant⟩ ⟨leather of the highest *grade*⟩ **3 :** a class of things that are of the same rank, quality, or order **4 a :** a division of the school course representing a year's work ⟨finish the fourth *grade*⟩ **b :** the pupils in a school division **c** *pl* **:** the elementary school system ⟨teach in the *grades*⟩ **5 :** a mark or rating esp. of accomplishment in school ⟨a *grade* of 90 in a test⟩ **6 :** a standard of quality ⟨government *grades* for meat⟩ **7 a :** the degree of slope (as of a road, railroad track, or embankment) **:** SLOPE **b :** ground level **8 :** a domestic animal with only one parent purebred

²grade *vb* **1 :** to arrange in grades **:** SORT ⟨*grade* apples⟩ **2 :** to make level or evenly sloping ⟨*grade* a highway⟩ **3 :** to give a grade to ⟨*grade* a pupil in arithmetic⟩ **4 :** to assign to a grade **5 :** to form a series having only slight differences ⟨colors that *grade* into one another⟩

grade crossing *n* **:** a crossing of highways, railroad tracks, or pedestrian walks or combinations of these on the same level

grad·er \'grād-ər\ *n* **1 :** one that grades **2 :** a machine for leveling earth **3 :** a pupil in a school grade ⟨a 5th *grader*⟩

grade school *n* **:** a public school including the first six or the first eight grades

gra·di·ent \'grād-ē-ənt\ *n* [L *gradient-, gradiens*, prp. of *gradi* to step, go] **1 a :** the rate of ascent or descent **:** INCLINATION ⟨the *gradient* of a rock layer⟩ **b :** a part (as of a road) sloping upward or downward **:** GRADE **2 :** change in the value of a quantity per unit distance in a specified direction ⟨vertical temperature *gradient*⟩ **3 :** a graded difference in physiological activity along an axis

¹grad·u·al \'graj-(ə-)wəl\ *n*, *often cap* **1 :** a response following the Epistle at Mass **2** *or* **gra·du·a·le** \ˌgräd-ə-'wäl-,ā\ **:** a book containing the choral parts of the Mass

²gradual *adj* **1 :** proceeding by steps or degrees **2 :** moving or changing by slight degrees — **grad·u·al·ly** \'graj-ə-(wə-)lē\ *adv* — **grad·u·al·ness** \'graj-(ə-w)əl-nəs\ *n*

grad·u·al·ism \'graj-ə(-wə)-ˌliz-əm\ *n* **:** the policy of approaching a desired end by gradual stages — **grad·u·al·ist** \-ləst\ *n or adj*

¹grad·u·ate \'graj-ə-wət, -ˌwāt\ *n* **1 :** a holder of an academic degree or diploma **2 :** a graduated cup, cylinder, or flask for measuring contents

²graduate *adj* **1 :** holding an academic degree or diploma **2 :** of or relating to studies beyond the first or bachelor's degree ⟨*graduate* school⟩

³grad·u·ate \'graj-ə-ˌwāt\ *vb* **1 :** to grant or receive an academic degree or diploma **2 :** to admit to a particular standing or grade **3 a :** to mark with degrees of measurement ⟨*graduate* a thermometer⟩ **b :** to divide into grades, classes, or intervals ⟨*graduated* income tax⟩ **4 :** to change gradually — **grad·u·a·tor** \-ˌwāt-ər\ *n*

grad·u·a·tion \ˌgraj-ə-'wā-shən\ *n* **1 :** a mark on an instrument or vessel indicating degrees or quantity; *also* **:** these marks **2 a :** an act or process of graduating **b :** the ceremony or exercises marking the completion by a student of a course of study at a school or college **:** COMMENCEMENT **3 :** arrangement in degrees or ranks

Graeco- — see GRECO-

graf·fi·to \grə-'fēt-ō\ *n*, *pl* **-ti** \-(ˌ)ē\ [It] **:** a rude inscription or drawing found on rocks or walls

¹graft \'graft\ *vb* [ME *graffen, graften*, fr. *graffe* graft, fr. ML *graphium*, fr. L, stylus, fr. Gk *grapheion*, fr. *graphein* to write] **1 a :** to insert a shoot from one plant into another plant so that they are joined and grow together **b :** to join one thing to another as if by grafting ⟨*graft* skin over a scar⟩ **2 :** to gain money or advantage by dishonest means — **graft·er** *n*

²graft *n* **1 a :** a grafted plant **b :** the point of insertion of a scion upon a stock **2 a :** the act of grafting **b :** something used in grafting: as (1) **:** SCION (2) **:** living tissue used in surgical grafting **3 a :** the getting of money or advantage by dishonest means through misuse of an official position **b :** the money or advantage gained dishonestly

gra·ham flour \ˌgrā-əm-\ *n* [after Sylvester *Graham d*1851 American dietary reformer] **:** whole wheat flour

Grail \'grāl\ *n* [MF *graal*] **:** the cup or platter used according to medieval legend by Christ at the Last Supper and thereafter the object of knightly quests — called also *Holy Grail*

¹grain \'grān\ *n* [MF, fr. L *granum*; akin to E *corn*] **1 a :** a seed or fruit of a cereal grass **b :** the seeds or fruits of various food plants and esp. the cereal grasses **c :** plants producing grain **2 :** a small hard particle or crystal **3 a :** a granulated surface or appearance **b :** the outer or hair side of a skin or hide **4 :** a unit of weight based on the weight of a grain of wheat — see MEASURE table **5 a :** the arrangement of fibers in wood **b :** appearance or texture due to constituent particles or fibers ⟨the *grain* of a rock⟩ **6 :** natural disposition **:** TEMPER — **grained** \'grānd\ *adj* — **with a grain of salt :** SKEPTICALLY ⟨take his predictions *with a grain of salt*⟩

²grain *vt* **1 :** to form into grains **:** GRANULATE **2 :** to paint in imitation of the grain of wood or stone — **grain·er** *n*

grain alcohol *n* **:** ALCOHOL 1

grain·field \'grān-ˌfēld\ *n* **:** a field where grain is grown

grain rust *n* **:** a rust that attacks a cereal grass

grain sorghum *n* **:** any of several sorghums cultivated primarily for grain — compare SORGO

grainy \'grā-nē\ *adj* **grain·i·er; -est** **1 :** consisting of or resembling grains **:** GRANULAR **2 :** resembling the grain of wood — **grain·i·ness** *n*

gram *or* **gramme** \'gram\ *n* [Gk *gramma* writing, a small weight, fr. *graphein* to write] **:** a metric unit of mass and weight equal to ¹⁄₁₀₀₀ kilogram and nearly equal to one cubic centimeter of water at its maximum density — see METRIC SYSTEM table

-gram \,gram\ *n comb form* [Gk *gramma* writing, fr. *graphein* to write] : drawing : writing : record ⟨chrono-gram⟩ ⟨telegram⟩

grama \'gram-ə\ *n* [Sp] : a pasture grass of the western U.S.

gram atom *n* : the weight in grams of a chemical element that is equal numerically to its atomic weight ⟨a *gram atom* of oxygen is 16 grams⟩ — called also *gram-atomic weight*

gra·mer·cy \grə-'mər-sē\ *interj* [MF *grand merci* great thanks] *archaic* — used to express gratitude or astonishment

gram·i·ci·din \,gram-ə-'sīd-ᵊn\ *n* : a toxic crystalline antibiotic produced by a soil bacterium and used against bacteria in local infections

gra·min·e·ous \grə-'min-ē-əs\ *adj* [L *gramin-, gramen* grass] : of or relating to grasses

gram·mar \'gram-ər\ *n* [MF *gramaire*, modif. of L *grammatica*, fr. Gk *grammatikē*, fr. *grammat-, gramma* letter, writing, fr. *graphein* to write] **1** : the study of the classes of words, their inflections, and their functions and relations in the sentence **2** : the facts of language with which grammar deals **3 a** : a grammar textbook **b** : speech or writing evaluated according to its conformity to grammatical rules — **gram·mar·i·an** \grə-'mer-ē-ən\ *n*

grammar school *n* **1 a** : a secondary school emphasizing Latin and Greek in preparation for college **b** : a British college preparatory school **2** : an elementary school

gram·mat·i·cal \grə-'mat-i-kəl\ *adj* **1** : of or relating to grammar **2** : conforming to the rules of grammar — **gram·mat·i·cal·ly** \-k(ə-)lē\ *adv*

gram–mo·lec·u·lar \,gram-mə-'lek-yə-lər\ *or* **gram–mo·lar** \'gram-'mō-lər\ *adj* : of, relating to, or containing a gram molecule

gram molecule *n* : the quantity of a chemical compound or element that has a weight in grams numerically equal to the molecular weight — called also *gram-molecular weight*

Gram·o·phone \'gram-ə-,fōn\ *trademark* — used for a phonograph

gram·pus \'gram-pəs\ *n* [modif. of MF *graspeis*, fr. *gras* fat + *peis* fish] : a small whale (as the killer) related to the blackfish; *also* : BLACKFISH

grana *pl of* GRANUM

gran·a·dil·la \,gran-ə-'dil-ə\ *n* [Sp, fr. dim. of *granada* pomegranate] : the edible fruit of a tropical American passionflower

gra·na·ry \'grän-(ə-)rē, 'gran-\ *n, pl* **-ries** [L *granum* grain] **1** : a storehouse for threshed grain **2** : a region producing grain in abundance

¹grand \'grand\ *adj* [MF, large, grand, fr L *grandis*] **1** : higher in rank than others of the same class : FORE-MOST, PRINCIPAL ⟨*grand* champion⟩ ⟨*grand* prize⟩ **2** : great in size **3** : INCLUSIVE, COMPLETE ⟨a *grand* total⟩ **4 a** : marked by magnificence or splendor **b** : showing wealth or high social standing ⟨the airs of a *grand* lady⟩ **5** : IMPRESSIVE, STATELY ⟨a *grand* old man⟩ **6** : very good : FINE ⟨*grand* weather⟩ ⟨have a *grand* time⟩ — **grand·ly** *adv* — **grand·ness** \'gran(d)-nəs\ *n*

syn MAGNIFICENT, MAJESTIC, GRANDIOSE: GRAND often adds to greatness of size implications of handsomeness and dignity; MAGNIFICENT implies an impressive largeness achieved without sacrifice of dignity or taste ⟨*magnificent* palace⟩ MAJESTIC adds to MAGNIFICENT connotations of awe-inspiring grandeur or loftiness ⟨*majestic* waterfall⟩ GRANDIOSE commonly implies inflated pretension or pomposity ⟨*grandiose* schemes of world conquest⟩

²grand *n* **1** : GRAND PIANO **2** *slang* : a thousand dollars

gran·dam \'gran-,dam, -dəm\ *or* **gran·dame** \-,dām, -dəm\ *n* [AF *graund dame*, lit., great lady] **1** : GRAND-MOTHER **2** : an old woman

grand·aunt \'gran-'dant, -'dànt\ *n* : an aunt of one's father or mother

grand·child \'gran(d)-,chīld\ *n* : a child of one's son or daughter

grand·daugh·ter \'gran-,dȯt-ər\ *n* : a daughter of one's son or daughter

grand duchess *n* **1** : the wife or widow of a grand duke **2** : a woman who rules a grand duchy in her own right

grand duchy *n* : the territory or dominion of a grand duke or grand duchess

grand duke *n* **1** : the sovereign duke of any of various European states **2** : a son or male descendant of a Russian czar

grande dame \grän(d)-dȧm\ *n* [F] : a usu. elderly woman of great prestige

gran·dee \gran-'dē\ *n* [Sp *grande*] : a man of elevated rank or station; *esp* : a high-ranking Spanish or Portuguese nobleman

gran·deur \'gran-jər\ *n* **1** : the quality or state of being grand : awe-inspiring magnificence **2** : something grand or conducive to grandness

grand·fa·ther \'gran(d)-,fȧth-ər\ *n* : the father of one's father or mother; *also* : ANCESTOR 1

grandfather clause *n* : a provision in several southern state constitutions that waives voting requirements for descendants of men voting before 1867

grandfather clock *n* : a tall pendulum clock standing directly on the floor — called also *grandfather's clock*

gran·dil·o·quence \gran-'dil-ə-kwən(t)s\ *n* [L *grandiloquus* using lofty language, fr. *grandis* grand + *loqui* to speak] : lofty or pompous eloquence : BOMBAST — **gran·dil·o·quent** \-kwənt\ *adj* — **gran·dil·o·quent·ly** *adv*

gran·di·ose \'gran-dē-,ōs\ *adj* [F, fr. It *grandioso*, fr. L *grandis* grand] **1** : impressive because of uncommon largeness, scope, effect, or grandeur **2** : characterized by affectation of grandeur or splendor or by absurd exaggeration **syn** see GRAND — **gran·di·ose·ly** *adv* — **gran·di·os·i·ty** \,gran-dē-'äs-ət-ē\ *n*

grand jury *n* : a jury that chiefly examines accusations of crime made against persons and if the evidence warrants makes formal charges on which the accused persons are later tried

grand mal \'gran(d)-'mäl\ *n* [F, lit., great illness] : severe epilepsy

grand march *n* : a march at the opening of a ball in which all the guests participate

grand·moth·er \'gran(d)-,məth-ər\ *n* : the mother of one's father or mother; *also* : a female ancestor

grand·neph·ew \-'nef-yü\ *n* : a grandson of one's brother or sister

grand·niece \-'nēs\ *n* : a granddaughter of one's brother or sister

grand opera *n* : opera in which the plot is elaborated as in serious drama and the entire text set to music

grand·par·ent \'gran(d)-,par-ənt, -,per-\ *n* : a parent of one's father or mother

grand piano *n* : a piano with horizontal frame and strings

grand·sire \'gran(d)-,sī(ə)r\ *or* **grand·sir** \'gran(t)-sər\ *n* **1** *dial* : GRANDFATHER **2** *archaic* : an aged man

grand slam *n* : the winning of all the tricks of one hand in a card game (as bridge)

grand·son \'gran(d)-,sən\ *n* : a son of one's son or daughter

grand·stand \'gran(d)-,stand\ *n* : a usu. roofed stand for spectators at a racecourse or stadium

grand tour *n* : an extended European tour formerly a usual part of the education of youth of the British aristocracy

grand·un·cle \'gran-'dəŋ-kəl\ *n* : an uncle of one's father or mother

grange \'grānj\ *n* [MF, granary, fr. ML *granica*, fr. L *granum* grain] **1** : FARM; *esp* : a farmhouse with outbuildings **2** *cap* : one of the lodges of a national fraternal association of farmers; *also* : the association itself

grang·er \'grān-jər\ *n* : a member of a Grange

gran·ite \'gran-ət\ *n* [It *granito*, fr. pp. of *granire* to granulate, fr. *grano* grain, fr. L *granum*] : a very hard igneous rock of visibly crystalline texture formed essentially of quartz and orthoclase or microcline and used for building and for monuments — **gra·nit·ic** \gra-'nit-ik\ *adj*

gran·ite·ware \'gran-ət-,wa(ə)r, -,we(ə)r\ *n* : enameled ironware

gra·niv·o·rous \grə-'niv-ə-rəs, grā-\ *adj* : feeding on seeds or grain

gran·ny *or* **gran·nie** \'gran-ē\ *n, pl* **grannies** **1** : GRAND-MOTHER **2** : a fussy person

granny knot *n* : an insecure knot often made instead of a square knot

---

ə abut; ᵊ kitten; ər further; a back; ā bake; ä cot, cart; aů out; ch chin; e less; ē easy; g gift; i trip; ī life

¹grant \'grant\ *vt* [OF *creanter, graanter*, fr. L *credent-, credens*, prp. of *credere* to believe, trust] **1 a :** to consent to **:** ALLOW **b :** to permit as a right, privilege, or favor **2 :** to give the possession or benefit of formally or legally **3 :** to concede (something not yet proved) to be true — **grant·er** \ər\ *n* — **grant·or** \'grant-ər, grant-'òr\ *n*
syn GRANT, CONCEDE mean to give as a favor or a right. GRANT implies giving voluntarily something that could be as well withheld ·or denied ⟨*granted* his assistant a week's leave⟩ CONCEDE implies yielding with reluctance to a rightful or compelling claim ⟨*conceded* the justice of their demands⟩

²grant *n* **1 :** the act of granting ⟨land ceded by *grant*⟩ **2 :** something granted; *esp* **:** a gift for a particular purpose ⟨a *grant* for a summer's study in Europe⟩ **3 a :** a transfer of property by deed or writing **b :** the instrument by which such a transfer is made; *also* **:** the property so transferred

grant·ee \grant-'ē\ *n* **:** one to whom a grant is made
gran·tia \'grant-ē-ə\ *n* [after Robert E. *Grant d*1874 Scottish anatomist] **:** a small cylindrical calcareous sponge
grant–in–aid \,grant-ⁿ-'ād\ *n*, *pl* **grants–in–aid** \,gran(t)-sⁿ-'nād\ **1 :** a grant from public funds paid by a central to a local government in aid of a public undertaking **2 :** a grant to a school or individual for an educational or artistic project
gran·u·lar \'gran-yə-lər\ *adj* **:** consisting of or appearing to consist of granules **:** having a grainy texture — **gran·u·lar·i·ty** \,gran-yə-'lar-ət-ē\ *n*
gran·u·late \'gran-yə-,lāt\ *vb* **1 :** to form or crystallize into grains or granules **2 :** to collect into grains or granules — **gran·u·lat·ed** *adj*
gran·u·la·tion \,gran-yə-'lā-shən\ *n* **1 :** the act or process of granulating or the condition of being granulated **2 :** a product of granulating (as a tiny knot of vascular tissue in a healing wound)
granulation tissue *n* **:** tissue made up of granulations that temporarily replaces lost tissue in a wound
gran·ule \'gran-yül\ *n* [LL *granulum*, fr. dim. of *granum* grain] **:** a small grain or particle ⟨*granules* of sugar⟩
gran·u·lose \'gran-yə-,lōs\ *adj* **:** GRANULAR; *esp* **:** having the surface roughened with granules
gra·num \'grā-nəm\ *n* [L, grain, seed] **:** one of the small laminated disks bearing the chlorophyll of a chloroplast
grape \'grāp\ *n* [OF] **1 :** a smooth-skinned juicy greenish white to deep red or purple berry eaten dried or fresh as a fruit or fermented to produce wine **2 :** a woody vine widely grown for its clustered grapes **3 :** GRAPESHOT — **grapy** \'grā-pē\ *adj*
grape·fruit \'grāp-,früt\ *n* **:** a large citrus fruit with a bitter yellow rind and a highly flavored somewhat acid juicy pulp; *also* **:** a small roundheaded tree that bears this fruit
grape hyacinth *n* **:** any of several small bulbous spring‐flowering herbs of the lily family with racemes of usu. blue flowers
grape·shot \'grāp-,shät\ *n* **:** a cluster of small iron balls used as a cannon charge
grape sugar *n* **:** DEXTROSE
grape·vine \'grāp-,vīn\ *n* **1 :** GRAPE 2 **2 a :** RUMOR, REPORT; *esp* **:** a baseless rumor **b** (1) **:** an informal means of circulating information or gossip (2) **:** a secret source of information
¹graph \'graf\ *n* [short for *graphic formula*] **1 :** a diagram that represents change in one variable factor in comparison with that of one or more other factors **2 :** the collection of all points whose coordinates satisfy a given functional relation
²graph *vt* **1 :** to represent by a graph **2 :** to plot upon a graph
-graph \,graf\ *n comb form* [Gk *graphein* to write; akin to E *carve*] **1 :** something written ⟨auto*graph*⟩ **2 :** instrument for making or transmitting records ⟨chrono*graph*⟩
-g·ra·pher \g-rə-fər\ *n comb form* **:** one that writes about (specified) material or in a (specified) way ⟨bio*grapher*⟩
¹graph·ic \'graf-ik\ *or* **graph·i·cal** \-i-kəl\ *adj* [Gk *graphein* to write] **1 :** being written, drawn, or engraved **2 a :** described or related with vivid clarity or striking imaginative power **b :** sharply outlined or delineated **3 a :** of or relating to the pictorial arts **b :** of, relating to, or involving methods of reproduction (as painting,

engraving, etching, lithography, or photography) **4 :** of, relating to, or represented by a graph **5 :** of or relating to writing — **graph·i·cal·ly** \-i-k(ə-)lē\ *adv* — **graph·ic·ness** *n*
syn GRAPHIC, VIVID, PICTURESQUE mean giving a clear visual impression through words. GRAPHIC stresses the evoking of a lifelike picture esp. of an action; VIVID suggests conveying a strong or lasting impression of reality; PICTURESQUE implies the presenting of a striking or effective picture often without regard to reality ⟨*picturesque* metaphors⟩

²graphic *n* **1 a :** a product of graphic art **b** *pl* **:** the graphic media **2 :** a picture, map, or graph used for illustration or demonstration
graphic arts *n pl* **:** the fine and applied arts of representation, decoration, and writing or printing on flat surfaces together with the techniques and crafts associated with each
graph·ite \'graf-,īt\ *n* [G *graphit*, fr. Gk *graphein* to write] **:** a soft black carbon with a metallic luster that conducts electricity and is used in making lead pencils, as a dry lubricant, and for electrodes — **gra·phit·ic** \gra-'fit-ik\ *adj*
graph·i·tize \'graf-ə-,tīz\ *vb* **1 :** to convert into graphite **2 :** to impregnate or coat with graphite — **graph·it·i·za·tion** \,graf-,īt-ə-'zā-shən\ *n*
gra·phol·o·gy \gra-'fäl-ə-jē\ *n* **:** the study of handwriting esp. for the purpose of character analysis — **gra·phol·o·gist** \-jəst\ *n*
graph paper *n* **:** paper ruled (as into small squares) for drawing graphs or making diagrams
-g·ra·phy \g-rə-fē\ *n comb form, pl* **-graphies 1 :** writing or representation in a (specified) manner or by a (specified) means of or of a (specified) object ⟨phono*graphy*⟩ ⟨photo*graphy*⟩ ⟨steno*graphy*⟩ **2 :** writing on a (specified) subject or in a (specified) field ⟨organo*graphy*⟩
grap·nel \'grap-nºl\ *n* **:** a small anchor with two or more claws used in dragging or grappling operations and for anchoring a small boat
¹grap·ple \'grap-əl\ *n* [MF *grappelle*, dim. of *grape* hook, grape] **1 :** the act of grappling or seizing **:** GRIP, HOLD **2 :** an implement used or designed for grappling; *esp* **:** GRAPNEL

grapnel

²grapple *vb* **grap·pled; grap·pling** \'grap-(ə-)liŋ\ **1 :** to seize or hold with or as if with a hooked implement **2 :** to seize one another **:** struggle in or as if in a close fight **3 :** to attempt to deal **:** COPE ⟨*grapple* with a problem⟩ — **grap·pler** \-(ə-)lər\ *n*
grappling iron *n* **:** a hooked iron for anchoring a boat, grappling ships to each other, or recovering sunken objects
grap·to·lite \'grap-tə-,līt\ *n* [Gk *graptos* painted, written, fr. *graphein* to write] **:** any of numerous Paleozoic fossil colonial animals with zooids in cups along a chitinous axis
¹grasp \'grasp\ *vb* [ME *graspen*] **1 :** to make the motion of seizing **:** CLUTCH ⟨*grasp* at straws⟩ **2 :** to take or seize firmly ⟨*grasp* a bat⟩ **3 :** to clasp or embrace with or as if with the fingers or arms **4 :** to lay hold of with the mind **:** COMPREHEND **syn** see TAKE — **grasp·a·ble** \'gras-pə-bəl\ *adj* — **grasp·er** *n*
²grasp *n* **1 a :** HANDLE **b :** EMBRACE **2 :** HOLD, CONTROL **3 a :** the reach of the arms **b :** the power of seizing and holding **4 :** COMPREHENSION
grasp·ing *adj* **:** AVARICIOUS — **grasp·ing·ly** \'gras-piŋ-lē\ *adv* — **grasp·ing·ness** *n*
¹grass \'gras\ *n* [OE *græs*] **1 :** herbage suitable or used for grazing animals **2 :** any of a large family of mostly herbaceous monocotyledonous plants with jointed stems, slender sheathing leaves, and flowers borne in spikelets of bracts **3 :** grass-covered land **4 :** MARIJUANA — **grass·like** \-,līk\ *adj*
²grass *vt* **:** to seed to grass
grass·hop·per \'gras-,häp-ər\ *n* **:** any of numerous plant‐eating insects (order Orthoptera) having the hind legs adapted for leaping
grass·land \-,land\ *n* **:** land covered naturally or under cultivation with grasses and other low-growing herbs
grass roots *n pl* **:** society at the local and popular level

esp. in rural areas as distinguished from the centers of political leadership

grass widow *n* **1 :** a woman divorced or separated from her husband **2 :** a woman whose husband is temporarily away

grass widower *n* **1 :** a man divorced or separated from his wife **2 :** a man whose wife is temporarily away

grassy \'gras-ē\ *adj* **grass·i·er; -est 1 :** containing or covered or abounding with grass **2 :** resembling grass ⟨a *grassy* odor⟩ ⟨*grassy*-leaved⟩

¹grate \'grāt\ *n* [ML *crata, grata* hurdle, fr. L *cratis;* akin to E *hurdle*] **1 :** a frame containing parallel or crossed bars (as in a prison window) **2 :** a frame or basket of iron bars for holding burning fuel (as in a furnace or a fireplace)

²grate *vt* **:** to furnish with a grate

³grate *vb* [MF *grater* to scratch, of Gmc origin] **1 :** to make into small particles by rubbing against something rough ⟨*grate* cheese⟩ **2 :** to grind or rub against something with a rasping noise ⟨a door that *grates* on its hinges⟩ **3 :** to have a harsh or rasping effect ⟨a noise that *grates* on one's nerves⟩ — **grat·er** *n*

grate·ful \'grāt-fəl\ *adj* [obs. *grate* pleasing, thankful, fr. L *gratus*] **1 a :** appreciative of benefits received **b :** expressing gratitude **2 a :** affording pleasure or contentment **:** PLEASING **b :** pleasing by reason of comfort supplied or discomfort alleviated ⟨*grateful* warmth of a fire on a frosty day⟩ — **grate·ful·ly** \-fə-lē\ *adv* — **grate·ful·ness** *n*

   syn GRATEFUL, THANKFUL mean feeling or expressing gratitude. GRATEFUL applies to an appropriate sense of having received favors from other persons ⟨very *grateful* for his help⟩ THANKFUL suggests a more generalized acknowledgment of what is felt to be providential ⟨*thankful* for a good harvest⟩

grat·i·fi·ca·tion \ˌgrat-ə-fə-'kā-shən\ *n* **1 :** the act of gratifying **:** the state of being gratified **2 :** a source of satisfaction or pleasure

grat·i·fy \'grat-ə-ˌfī\ *vt* **-fied; -fy·ing** [L *gratificari,* lit., to make oneself pleasing, fr. *gratus* pleasing + *-ificari,* pass. of *-ificare* -ify] **1 :** to give or be a source of pleasure or satisfaction to **2 :** to confer a favor on **:** INDULGE

grat·ing \'grāt-iŋ\ *n* **:** a partition, covering, or frame of parallel bars or crossbars **:** GRATE

gra·tis \'grāt-əs, 'grat-\ *adv (or adj)* [L *gratiis, gratis,* fr. abl. pl. of *gratia* favor] **:** without charge or recompense **:** FREE

grat·i·tude \'grat-ə-ˌt(y)üd\ *n* **:** the state of being grateful **:** THANKFULNESS

gra·tu·i·tous \grə-'t(y)ü-ət-əs\ *adj* **1 :** done or provided without return or expectation of return or payment; *also* **:** acting without compensation **2 :** not called for by the circumstances **:** UNWARRANTED ⟨a *gratuitous* insult⟩ — **gra·tu·i·tous·ly** *adv* — **gra·tu·i·tous·ness** *n*

gra·tu·i·ty \grə-'t(y)ü-ət-ē\ *n, pl* **-ties :** something given freely, *esp* **:** something given in return for a favor or service

gra·va·men \grə-'vām-ən, -'väm-\ *n, pl* **-vamens** *or* **-va·mi·na** \-'vam-ə-nə, -'vām-, -'väm-\ [LL, burden, fr. L *gravare* to burden, fr. *gravis* heavy] **:** the basic or significant part of a grievance or complaint

¹grave \'grāv\ *vt* **graved; grav·en** \'grā-vən\ *or* **graved; grav·ing** [OE *grafan* to dig, engrave] **1 a :** to carve or shape with a chisel **:** SCULPTURE **b :** to carve or cut (as letters or figures) into a hard surface **:** ENGRAVE **c :** to impress or fix (as a thought) deeply

²grave *n* **:** an excavation for burial of a body; *also* **:** TOMB

³grave \'grāv, *in sense 4 also* 'gräv\ *adj* [L *gravis* heavy, grave] **1 a** *obs* **:** AUTHORITATIVE, WEIGHTY **b :** meriting serious consideration **:** IMPORTANT **c :** threatening great harm or danger **:** MORTAL **2 :** dignified in appearance or demeanor **:** SOLEMN, SERIOUS **3 :** drab in color **:** SOMBER **4 :** of, marked by, or being an accent mark having the form ` — **grave·ly** *adv* — **grave·ness** *n*

⁴gra·ve \'gräv-(ˌ)ā\ *adv (or adj)* [It, fr. L *gravis* grave] **:** in a slow and solemn manner — used as a direction in music

grave·clothes \'grāv-ˌklō(th̲)z\ *n pl* **:** the clothes in which a dead person is buried

¹grav·el \'grav-əl\ *n* [MF *gravele,* dim. of *grave, greve* pebbly ground] **1 :** loose rounded fragments of rock

coarser than sand **2 :** a deposit of small concretions in the kidneys and urinary bladder

²gravel *adj* **:** GRAVELLY 2

³gravel *vt* **grav·eled** *or* **grav·elled; grav·el·ing** *or* **grav·el·ling** \'grav-(ə-)liŋ\ **:** to cover or spread with gravel

grave·less \'grāv-ləs\ *adj* **1 :** UNBURIED ⟨these *graveless* bones⟩ **2 :** not requiring graves **:** DEATHLESS ⟨the *graveless* home of the blessed⟩

grav·el·ly \'grav-(ə-)lē\ *adj* **1 :** of, containing, or covered with gravel **2 :** having a harsh grating sound ⟨a *gravelly* voice⟩

grav·er \'grā-vər\ *n* **1 :** ENGRAVER, SCULPTOR **2 :** any of various cutting or shaving tools

grave·stone \'grāv-ˌstōn\ *n* **:** a burial monument

grave·yard \-ˌyärd\ *n* **:** CEMETERY

grav·id \'grav-əd\ *adj* [L *gravidus,* fr. *gravis* heavy] **:** PREGNANT — **gra·vid·i·ty** \gra-'vid-ət-ē\ *n* — **grav·id·ly** \'grav-əd-lē\ *adv* — **grav·id·ness** *n*

grav·i·da \'grav-əd-ə\ *n* [L, fr. *gravis* heavy] **:** a pregnant woman

gra·vim·e·ter \gra-'vim-ət-ər, 'grav-ə-ˌmēt-\ *n* **1 :** a device similar to a hydrometer for determining specific gravity **2 :** an instrument for measuring differences in the force of gravity at different places — **gravi·met·ric** \ˌgrav-ə-'me-trik\ *adj*

grav·i·tate \'grav-ə-ˌtāt\ *vi* **1 :** to move or tend to move under the influence of gravitation **2 :** to move toward something

grav·i·ta·tion \ˌgrav-ə-'tā-shən\ *n* **1 a :** a force of attraction between two material particles or bodies that is proportional to the product of their masses and inversely proportional to the square of the distance between them **b :** the action or process of gravitating **2 :** an attraction or tendency toward something — **grav·i·ta·tion·al** \-shnəl, -shən-°l\ *adj* — **grav·i·ta·tion·al·ly** \-ē\ *adv* — **grav·i·ta·tive** \'grav-ə-ˌtāt-iv\ *adj*

grav·i·ty \'grav-ət-ē\ *n, pl* **-ties** [L *gravis* heavy] **1 a :** dignity or sobriety of bearing **b :** IMPORTANCE, SIGNIFICANCE; *esp* **:** SERIOUSNESS **2 :** WEIGHT — used chiefly in the phrase *center of gravity* **3 a :** the gravitational attraction of the earth's mass for bodies at or near its surface **b :** GRAVITATION **c :** ACCELERATION OF GRAVITY — **gravity** *adj*

gra·vure \grə-'vyu̇(ə)r, grā-\ *n* [F, fr. *graver* to grave, of Gmc origin] **1 a :** a process for producing an intaglio printing plate on wood or copper **b :** a gravure plate or print **2 :** PHOTOGRAVURE

gra·vy \'grā-vē\ *n, pl* **gravies** [MF *gravé*] **1 :** a sauce made from the thickened and seasoned juices of cooked meat **2 :** unearned or illicit gain **:** GRAFT

¹gray \'grā\ *adj* [OE *grǣg*] **1 :** of the color gray; *also* **:** dull in color **2 :** having gray hair **3 :** dull in mood or outlook **:** DISMAL ⟨a *gray* day⟩ — **gray·ness** *n*

²gray *n* **1 :** something of a gray color **2 :** one of the series of neutral colors ranging between black and white

³gray *vb* **:** to make or become gray

gray·beard \'grā-ˌbi(ə)rd\ *n* **:** an old man

gray·ish \'grā-ish\ *adj* **1 :** somewhat gray **2 :** low in saturation

gray·ling \'grā-liŋ\ *n, pl* **grayling** *also* **graylings :** any of several freshwater fishes related to the trouts and valued for food and sport

gray matter *n* **1 :** neural tissue esp. of the brain and spinal cord that contains nerve-cell bodies as well as nerve fibers and has a brownish gray color **2 :** BRAINS, INTELLECT

gray mullet *n* **:** MULLET 1

gray trout *n* **:** a common weakfish of the U.S. Atlantic coast

¹graze \'grāz\ *vb* [OE *grasian,* fr. *græs* grass] **1 :** to feed on growing herbage **2 :** to feed on or put cattle to feed on the herbage of **3 :** to put to graze

   syn GRAZE, BROWSE means to feed on growing vegetation. GRAZE applies esp. to animals wandering freely on open grassland; BROWSE implies specifically feeding on leaves and shoots of trees or shrubs

²graze *n* **1 :** an act of grazing **2 :** herbage for grazing

³graze *vt* **1 :** to rub or touch lightly in passing **:** touch against and glance off ⟨*graze* the curb with the wheel of a car⟩ **2 :** to scratch or scrape by rubbing against something

---

ə **abut;** ᵊ **kitten;** ər **further;** a **back;** ā **bake;** ä **cot, cart;** au̇ **out;** ch **chin;** e **less;** ē **easy;** g **gift;** i **trip;** ī **life**

⁴graze n : a scraping along a surface or an abrasion made by it; esp : a superficial skin injury

gra·zier \'grā-zhər\ n : a person who grazes cattle; also : RANCHER

¹grease \'grēs\ n [OF craisse, graisse, fr. L crassus, adj., fat] **1** : rendered animal fat **2** : oily matter **3** : a thick lubricant ⟨a grease made from petroleum⟩ ⟨a silicone grease⟩

²grease \'grēs, 'grēz\ vt **1** : to smear or daub with grease **2** : to lubricate with grease — **greas·er** n

grease·paint \'grēs-ˌpānt\ n : theater makeup

grease·wood \-ˌwu̇d\ n : a low stiff shrub of the goose-foot family common in alkaline soils in the western U.S.

greasy \'grē-sē, -zē\ adj **greas·i·er; -est 1** : smeared with grease **2** : containing grease ⟨greasy food⟩ **3** : resembling grease or oil : SLIPPERY, SLICK — **greas·i·ly** \-sə-lē, -zə-\ adv — **greas·i·ness** \-sē-nəs, -zē-\ n

great \'grāt, in South also 'gre(ə)t\ adj [OE grēat] **1** : large in size : not small or little **2** : large in number : NUMEROUS ⟨a great crowd⟩ **3** : long continued ⟨a great while⟩ **4** : much beyond the average or ordinary : MIGHTY, HEAVY, INTENSE ⟨a great weight⟩ ⟨in great pain⟩ **5** : EMINENT, DISTINGUISHED ⟨a great artist⟩ ⟨great men⟩ **6** : remarkable in knowledge of or skill in something ⟨the boy is great at dividing⟩ **7** : much favored or much used ⟨a great joke of my father's⟩ **8** : EXCELLENT, FINE ⟨a great time at the beach⟩ **9** : more distant in relationship by one generation ⟨great-grandchildren⟩ **syn** see LARGE — **great·ly** adv — **great·ness** n

great ape n : any of the recent anthropoid apes

great auk n : an extinct large flightless auk formerly abundant along No. Atlantic coasts

great-aunt n : GRANDAUNT

Great Bear n : URSA MAJOR

great circle n : a circle formed on the surface of a sphere by the intersection of a plane that passes through the center of the sphere; esp : such a circle on the surface of the earth an arc of which constitutes the shortest distance between any two terrestrial points — compare SMALL CIRCLE

great·coat \'grāt-ˌkōt\ n : a heavy overcoat

Great Dane n : any of a breed of tall massive powerful smooth-coated dogs

great divide n **1** : a watershed between major drainage systems **2** : a significant point of division; esp : DEATH ⟨he crossed the great divide bravely⟩

great·heart·ed \'grāt-'härt-əd\ adj **1** : COURAGEOUS **2** : MAGNANIMOUS — **great·heart·ed·ly** adv — **great·heart·ed·ness** n

great-nephew n : GRANDNEPHEW

great-niece n : GRANDNIECE

great power n : one of the nations that figure most decisively in international affairs

Great Russian n : a member of the Russian-speaking people of central and northeastern Soviet Russia

great-uncle n : GRANDUNCLE

greave \'grēv\ n [MF greve] : armor for the leg below the knee — usu. used in pl.

grebe \'grēb\ n [F grèbe] : any of a family of swimming and diving birds closely related to the loons

Gre·cian \'grē-shən\ adj : GREEK — **Grecian** n

Greco- or **Graeco-** comb form [L Graecus] **1** : Greece : Greeks ⟨Grecophile⟩ ⟨Grecomania⟩ **2** : Greek and ⟨GraecoRoman⟩

grebe

greed \'grēd\ n [back-formation fr. greedy] : excessive or blameworthy acquisitiveness : AVARICE

greedy \'grēd-ē\ adj **greed·i·er; -est** [OE grǣdig] **1** : having a driving appetite for food or drink : very hungry ⟨a lion greedy for its prey⟩ **2** : having an eager and often selfish desire or longing ⟨greedy for praise⟩ **3** : wanting more than one needs or more than one's fair share (as of food or wealth) **syn** see COVETOUS — **greed·i·ly** \'grēd-ºl-ē\ adv — **greed·i·ness** \'grēd-ē-nəs\ n

¹Greek \'grēk\ n [OE Grēca, fr. L Graecus, fr. Gk Graikos] **1 a** : a native or inhabitant of ancient or modern Greece **b** : a person of Greek descent **2 a** : the Indo-European language used by the Greeks from prehistoric times to the present **b** : ancient Greek as used from the time of the earliest records to the end of the 2d century A.D.

²Greek adj **1** : of, relating to, or characteristic of Greece, the Greeks, or Greek ⟨Greek architecture⟩ **2 a** : EASTERN ORTHODOX **b** : of or relating to an Eastern rite of the Roman Catholic Church **c** : of or relating to the established Orthodox church of Greece

Greek cross n : a cross having an upright and a transverse shaft equal in length and intersecting at their middles — see CROSS illustration

Greek fire n [so called fr. the Byzantine Greeks who used it in warfare] : an incendiary composition of uncertain ingredients that burn in water

Greek Orthodox adj : EASTERN ORTHODOX; esp : GREEK 2c

¹green \'grēn\ adj [OE grēne; akin to E grow] **1** : of the color green **2 a** : covered by green foliage or herbage ⟨green hills⟩ **b** : consisting of green plants or of the leafy part of a plant ⟨a green salad⟩ ⟨green food for rabbits⟩ **3 a** : YOUTHFUL, VIGOROUS **b** : FRESH, NEW **4** : not fully grown or ripe ⟨green apples⟩ ⟨tender green grasses⟩ **5** : marked by a sickly appearance ⟨green with envy⟩ **6 a** : not fully processed or treated **b** : not being in condition for a particular use or activity ⟨green troops⟩ **7 a** : lacking training, knowledge, or experience ⟨green troops⟩ **b** : GULLIBLE, NAÏVE ⟨too green to suspect a trick⟩ — **green·ly** adv — **green·ness** \'grēn-nəs\ n

²green vb : to make or become green

³green n **1** : a color whose hue is somewhat less yellow than that of growing fresh grass or of the emerald or is that of the part of the spectrum lying between blue and yellow **2** : something of a green color **3 a** : green vegetation **b** pl : leafy parts of plants used for some purpose (as ornament or food) **4** : a grassy plain or plot; esp : PUTTING GREEN — **greeny** \'grē-nē\ adj

green alga n : an alga (esp. group Chlorophyta) in which the chlorophyll is not masked by other pigments

green·back \'grēn-ˌbak\ n : a legal-tender note issued by the U.S. government; esp : one without gold or silver backing issued during the Civil War

Green·back·er \-ər\ n : a member of a post-Civil War American political party opposing reduction in the amount of greenbacks in circulation

green bean n : a kidney bean with the pods green when suitably matured for use as snap beans

green·belt \'grēn-ˌbelt\ n : a belt of parkways or farmlands that encircles a community and is designed to prevent undesirable encroachments

green·bri·er \'grēn-ˌbrī(-ə)r\ n : a prickly vine of the lily family of the eastern U.S. with thick leaves and umbels of small greenish flowers

green·ery \'grēn-(ə-)rē\ n, pl **-er·ies** : green foliage or plants : VERDURE

green·gland n : a greenish excretory organ in the head of some crustaceans (as a lobster)

green·gro·cer \'grēn-ˌgrō-sər\ n, chiefly Brit : a retailer of fresh vegetables and fruit — **green·gro·cery** \-ˌgrōs-(ə-)rē\ n

green·horn \'grēn-ˌhȯrn\ n : an inexperienced person; esp : one easily tricked or cheated

green·house \-ˌhau̇s\ n : a glassed enclosure used for the cultivation or protection of tender plants

green·ish \'grē-nish\ adj : somewhat green — **green·ishness** n

green light n [fr. the green traffic light which signals permission to proceed] : authority or permission to undertake a project

green·ling \'grēn-liŋ\ n : any of several spiny-finned food fishes of the rocky coasts of the northern Pacific

green manure n : an herbaceous crop (as clover) plowed under while green to enrich the soil

green mold n : a green or green-spored mold (as a penicillium)

green onion n : a young onion pulled before the bulb has enlarged esp. for use in salad

green·room \'grēn-ˌrüm, -ˌru̇m\ n : a room in a theater or concert hall where actors or musicians relax before, between, or after appearances

green·sick \-ˌsik\ adj : affected by chlorosis

---

j joke; **ŋ** sing; **ō** flow; **ȯ** flaw; **ȯi** coin; **th** thin; **th̲** this; **ü** loot; **u̇** foot; **y** yet; **yü** few; **yu̇** furious; **zh** vision

green snake *n* : either of two bright green harmless largely insectivorous No. American snakes

green soap *n* : a soft soap made from vegetable oils and used esp. in skin diseases

green·stick fracture \('\)grēn-'stik-\ *n* : a bone fracture in which the bone is partly broken and partly bent and which occurs in young individuals

green·sward \'grēn-,swórd\ *n* : turf green with growing grass

green thumb *n* : an unusual ability to make plants grow — **green–thumbed** \'grēn-'thəmd\ *adj*

green turtle *n* : a large edible sea turtle with a smooth greenish shell

Green·wich time \'grin-ij-, 'gren-, -ich-\ *n* [*Greenwich*, England] : the time of the meridian of Greenwich used as the basis of standard time throughout the world

green·wood \'grēn-,wùd\ *n* : a forest green with foliage

greet \'grēt\ *vt* [OE *grētan*] **1** : to address with expressions of kind wishes : HAIL **2** : to meet or react to in a specified manner ⟨candidate was *greeted* with cheers and catcalls⟩ **3** : to be perceived by ⟨a sight *greeted* her eyes⟩ — **greet·er** *n*

greet·ing *n* **1** : a salutation at meeting **2** : an expression of good wishes : REGARDS — usu. used in pl.

gre·gar·i·ous \gri-'gar-ē-əs, -'ger-\ *adj* [L *gregarius* of a herd, fr. *greg-, grex* herd] **1** : tending to associate with others of one's kind : SOCIAL **2** : habitually living or moving with others of one's own kind : tending to flock together ⟨*gregarious* insects⟩ — **gre·gar·i·ous·ly** *adv* — **gre·gar·i·ous·ness** *n*

Gre·go·ri·an calendar \gri-,gōr-ē-ən-, -,gòr-\ *n* : a calendar introduced by Pope Gregory XIII in 1582 and adopted in Great Britain and the American colonies in 1752 — compare JULIAN CALENDAR

Gregorian chant *n* : a rhythmically free unaccompanied melody sung in unison in services of the Roman Catholic Church

grem·lin \'grem-lən\ *n* [perh. modif. of IrGael *gruaimín* ill-humored little fellow] : a small gnome held to be responsible for malfunction of equipment esp. in an airplane

gre·nade \grə-'nād\ *n* [MF, pomegranate, fr. LL *granata*, fr. L *granum* grain] **1** : a small bomb filled with a destructive agent (as gas, high explosive, or incendiary chemicals) and made to be hurled often by hand **2** : a container (as of glass) of volatile chemicals that can be burst by throwing (as in extinguishing a fire)

gren·a·dier \,gren-ə-'di(ə)r\ *n* : a member of a European regiment formerly armed with grenades

gren·a·dine \,gren-ə-'dēn\ *n* : a syrup flavored with pomegranates and used in mixed drinks

Gret·na Green \,gret-nə-'grēn\ *n* [fr. *Gretna Green*, village in Scotland near the English border] : a place where many eloping couples are married

grew *past of* GROW

grew·some *var of* GRUESOME

grey *var of* GRAY

grey friar *n*, *often cap G&F* : a Franciscan friar

grey·hound \'grā-,haùnd\ *n* [OE *grīghund*] : a tall slender graceful smooth-coated dog noted for swiftness and keen sight and used for coursing game and racing

grey·lag \-,lag\ *n* : the common gray wild goose of Europe

grib·ble \'grib-əl\ *n* : a small marine crustacean that destroys submerged timbers

grid \'grid\ *n* [back-formation fr. *gridiron*] **1** : GRATING **2** : a perforated or ridged metal plate used as a conductor in a storage battery **3** : an electrode consisting of a mesh or a spiral of fine wire placed between two other elements of an electron tube so as to control the amount of current that flows between them **4 a** : a network of horizontal and perpendicular lines for locating points by means of coordinates ⟨a *grid* of longitude and latitude lines on a map⟩ **b** : GRIDIRON 2

grid·dle \'grid-ᵊl\ *n* [ONF *gredil* gridiron, fr. L *craticulum*, dim. of *cratis* wickerwork, hurdle] : a flat surface or pan on which food is cooked by dry heat

griddle cake *n* : a flat cake made of thin batter and cooked on both sides on a griddle

grid·iron \'grid-,ī(-ə)rn\ *n* [ME *gredire*] **1** : a grate for broiling food **2** : something consisting of or covered with a network; *esp* : a football field

grief \'grēf\ *n* [OF, heavy, grave, fr. L *gravis*] **1** : deep sorrow : SADNESS, DISTRESS **2** : a cause of sorrow **3** : MISHAP, DISASTER ⟨the boat came to *grief* on the rocks⟩ *syn* see SORROW

griev·ance \'grē-vən(t)s\ *n* **1** : a cause of distress (as an unsatisfactory working condition) affording reason for complaint or resistance **2** : the formal expression of a grievance : COMPLAINT

grieve \'grēv\ *vb* [OF *grever*, fr. L *gravare* to burden, fr. *gravis* heavy, grave] **1** : to cause grief or sorrow to : cause to suffer : DISTRESS **2** : to feel grief : SORROW — **griev·er** *n*

griev·ous \'grē-vəs\ *adj* **1** : OPPRESSIVE, ONEROUS ⟨the *grievous* cost of war⟩ **2** : causing or characterized by esp. severe pain, suffering, or sorrow ⟨a *grievous* wound⟩ ⟨*grievous* news⟩ **3** : SERIOUS, GRAVE ⟨*grievous* fault⟩ — **griev·ous·ly** *adv* — **griev·ous·ness** *n*

grif·fin *or* **grif·fon** \'grif-ən\ *n* [MF *grifon*, fr. L *gryphus*, fr. Gk *gryp-, gryps*] : a fabulous animal typically half eagle and half lion

grig \'grig\ *n* : a gay lively person

¹**grill** \'gril\ *vt* **1** : to broil on a grill **2 a** : to torment as if by broiling **b** : to question intensely

²**grill** *n* [F *gril*, fr. L *craticulum*, dim. of *cratis* wickerwork, hurdle] **1** : a cooking utensil of parallel bars on which food is exposed to heat **2** : food that is broiled usu. on a grill **3** : a restaurant featuring broiled foods

grille *or* **grill** \'gril\ *n* **1** : a grating forming a barrier or screen **2** : an opening covered with a grille

grill·work \'gril-,wərk\ *n* : work constituting or resembling a grille

grilse \'grils\ *n, pl* **grilse** : a young mature salmon returning from the sea to spawn for the first time

grim \'grim\ *adj* **grim·mer**; **grim·mest** [OE *grimm*] **1** : CRUEL, SAVAGE, FIERCE **2 a** : harsh and forbidding in appearance **b** : ghastly, repellent, or sinister in character **3** : UNFLINCHING, UNYIELDING ⟨*grim* determination⟩ *syn* see GHASTLY — **grim·ly** *adv* — **grim·ness** *n*

grim·ace \'grim-əs, grim-'ās\ *n* [F] : a twisting or distortion of the face or features expressive usu. of disgust or disapproval — **grimace** *vi*

gri·mal·kin \grim-'al-kən, -'ò(l)-kən\ *n* : CAT 1a; *esp* : an old female cat

grime \'grīm\ *n* [Flem *grijm*] : soot, smut, or dirt adhering to or embedded in a surface; *also* : accumulated dirtiness and disorder — **grime** *vt*

grimy \'grī-mē\ *adj* **grim·i·er**; **-est** : full of or covered with grime : DIRTY — **grim·i·ness** *n*

grin \'grin\ *vi* **grinned**; **grin·ning** [OE *grennian*] : to draw back the lips so as to show the teeth esp. in amusement or laughter — **grin** *n*

¹**grind** \'grīnd\ *vb* **ground** \'graùnd\; **grind·ing** [OE *grindan*] **1** : to reduce to powder or small fragments by friction (as in a mill or with the teeth) **2** : to wear down, polish, or sharpen by friction : WHET **3** : to press with a grating noise : GRIT ⟨*grind* the teeth⟩ **4** : OPPRESS, HARASS **5 a** : to operate or produce by turning a crank **b** : to produce in a laborious and mechanical way ⟨*grind* out a composition⟩ **6** : to move with difficulty or friction esp. so as to make a grating noise ⟨gears *grinding* when an automobile is shifted into high⟩ **7** : DRUDGE; *esp* : to study hard

²**grind** *n* **1** : an act of grinding **2 a** : monotonous labor or routine; *esp* : intensive study **b** : a student who studies excessively **3** : the result of grinding; *esp* : the size of particle obtained by grinding

grind·er \'grīn-dər\ *n* **1 a** : MOLAR **b** *pl* : TEETH **2** : one that grinds **3** *chiefly NewEng* : a large sandwich usu. consisting of a long roll split lengthwise with various fillings (as meatballs or meat, cheese, tomato, and lettuce)

grind·stone \'grīn-,stōn\ *n* : a flat circular stone of natural sandstone that revolves on an axle and is used for grinding, shaping, or smoothing

grin·go \'grin-gō\ *n, pl* **gringos** [Sp, alter. of *griego* Greek, stranger, fr. L *Graecus* Greek] : a foreigner in Spain or Latin America esp. when of English or American origin — often used disparagingly

¹**grip** \'grip\ *vt* **gripped**; **grip·ping** [OE *grippan*] **1** : to seize firmly **2** : to hold strongly the interest of ⟨the story *grips* the reader⟩

²**grip** *n* **1 a** : a strong or tenacious grasp **b** : strength in

gripping **c** : a mode of clasping the hand by which members of a secret order recognize or greet one another **d** : arrangement of the hands in grasping **2 a** : CONTROL, MASTERY **b** : mental grasp : UNDERSTANDING **3** : a part or device for gripping **4** : a part by which something is grasped; *esp* : HANDLE **5** : SUITCASE

¹**gripe** \'grīp\ *vb* [OE *grīpan*] **1** : SEIZE, GRIP **2 a** : AFFLICT, DISTRESS **b** : IRRITATE, VEX **3** : to cause or experience spasms of pain in the bowels **4** : COMPLAIN — **grip·er** *n*

²**gripe** *n* **1** : CLUTCH, GRASP; *also* : CONTROL, MASTERY **2 a** : AFFLICTION **b** : COMPLAINT **3** : a spasm of intestinal pain **4** : HANDLE, GRIP **5** : a device (as a brake) for grasping or holding

grippe \'grip\ *n* [F, lit., seizure] : an acute febrile virus disease identical with or resembling influenza — **grippy** \'grip-ē\ *adj*

grip·sack \'grip-,sak\ *n* : TRAVELING BAG

Gri·sel·da \griz-'el-də\ *n* : a woman noted in medieval literature for her meekness and patience

gris-gris \'grē-,grē\ *n, pl* **gris-gris** \-,grēz\ : an amulet or incantation used chiefly by people of African Negro ancestry

gris·ly \'griz-lē\ *adj* **gris·li·er; -est** [OE *grislic*] : HORRIBLE, GRUESOME — **gris·li·ness** *n*

grist \'grist\ *n* [OE *grīst;* akin to E *grind*] : grain to be ground or already ground

gris·tle \'gris-əl\ *n* [OE] : CARTILAGE — **gris·tli·ness** \'gris-(ə-)lē-nəs\ *n* — **gris·tly** \'gris-(ə-)lē\ *adj*

grist·mill \'grist-,mil\ *n* : a mill for grinding grain

¹**grit** \'grit\ *n* [OE *grēot*] **1** : a hard sharp granule (as of sand); *also* : material (as many abrasives) composed of such granules **2** : firmness of mind or spirit : unyielding courage

²**grit** *vb* **grit·ted; grit·ting** : to grind or cause to grind : GRATE

grits \'grits\ *n pl* : coarsely ground hulled grain — compare HOMINY

grit·ty \'grit-ē\ *adj* **grit·ti·er; -est 1** : containing or resembling grit **2** : courageously persistent : PLUCKY — **grit·ti·ness** *n*

griz·zled \'griz-əld\ *adj* : sprinkled, streaked, or mixed with gray

¹**griz·zly** \'griz-lē\ *adj* **griz·zli·er; -est** [*grizzle* gray, fr. MF *grisel,* fr. OF *gris*] : GRIZZLED

²**grizzly** *n, pl* **grizzlies** : GRIZZLY BEAR

grizzly bear *n* : a large powerful usu. brownish yellow bear of the uplands of western No. America

groan \'grōn\ *vb* [OE *grānian*] **1** : to utter a deep moan of pain, grief, or annoyance **2** : to make a harsh sound under sudden or prolonged strain ⟨the chair *groaned* under his weight⟩ — **groan** *n* — **groan·er** *n*

¹**groat** \'grōt\ *n* [OE *grot*] **1** : hulled grain broken into fragments larger than grits **2** : a grain (as of oats) exclusive of the hull

²**groat** *n* [ME *groot*] : a former British coin worth four pennies

gro·cer \'grō-sər\ *n* [ME, fr. MF *grossier* wholesaler, fr. *gros* gross, wholesale] : a dealer in staple foodstuffs and household supplies

gro·cery \'grōs-(ə-)rē\ *n, pl* **-cer·ies 1** *pl* : foodstuffs sold by a grocer ⟨went out to buy the *groceries*⟩ **2** : a grocer's store

grog \'gräg\ *n* [fr. Old *Grog,* nickname of Edward Vernon *d*1757 English admiral responsible for diluting the sailors' rum] : alcoholic liquor; *esp* : liquor (as rum) cut with water — **grog·gery** \'gräg-ə-rē\ *n* — **grog·shop** \'gräg-,shäp\ *n*

grog·gy \'gräg-ē\ *adj* **grog·gi·er; -est** [*grog*] : being weak and dazed and unsteady on the feet or in action — **grog·gi·ly** \'gräg-ə-lē\ *adv* — **grog·gi·ness** \'gräg-ē-nəs\ *n*

¹**groin** \'groin\ *n* [alter. of ME *grynde,* fr. OE, abyss; akin to E *ground*] **1** : the fold marking the juncture of the lower abdomen and thigh; *also* : the region of this line **2** : the projecting curved line along which two intersecting structural vaults meet

²**groin** *vt* : to build or equip with groins

grom·met \'gräm-ət, 'grəm-\ *n* **1** : a ring of rope **2** : an eyelet of firm material to strengthen or protect an opening

¹**groom** \'grüm, 'grùm\ *n* [ME *grom*] **1** : a male servant; *esp* : one in charge of horses **2** [by shortening] : BRIDEGROOM

²**groom** *vb* **1** : to clean and care for (an animal) **2** : to make neat, attractive, or acceptable : POLISH

grooms·man \'grümz-mən, 'grùmz-\ *n* : a male friend who attends a bridegroom at his wedding

groove \'grüv\ *n* [ME *groof;* akin to E *grave*] **1** : a long narrow channel or depression **2** : a fixed routine : RUT — **groove** *vt* — **in the groove** : in top form

grope \'grōp\ *vb* [OE *grāpian*] **1** : to feel about or cast about blindly or uncertainly in search ⟨*groped* for his arm⟩⟨*grope* for the right word⟩ **2** : to feel one's way by groping ⟨*grope* along a wall⟩

gros·beak \'grōs-,bēk\ *n* [F *grosbec,* fr. *gros* gross, thick + *bec* beak] : any of several finches of Europe or America having large stout conical bills

gro·schen \'grō-shən, 'grò-\ *n, pl* **groschen** [G] **1** : a unit of value equal to 1/100 schilling **2** : a coin representing one groschen

gros·grain \'grō-,grān\ *n* : a silk or rayon fabric with crosswise cotton ribs

¹**gross** \'grōs\ *adj* [MF *gros* thick, coarse, fr. L *grossus*] **1 a** : glaringly noticeable ⟨*gross* error⟩ **b** : OUT-AND-OUT, UTTER ⟨*gross* fool⟩ **c** : SHAMEFUL ⟨*gross* injustice⟩ **2 a** : BIG, BULKY; *esp* : excessively fat **b** : excessively luxuriant : RANK **3 a** : GENERAL, BROAD **b** : consisting of an overall total exclusive of deductions ⟨*gross* earnings⟩ **4** : EARTHY, CARNAL ⟨*gross* pleasures⟩ **5** : not fastidious in taste : UNDISCRIMINATING **6** : lacking knowledge or culture : UNREFINED **7** : COARSE, VULGAR ⟨*gross* epithets⟩ **syn** see FLAGRANT — **gross·ly** *adv* — **gross·ness** *n*

²**gross** *n* **1** : an overall total exclusive of deductions (as for taxes or expenses) **2** *archaic* : main body : MASS

³**gross** *vt* : to earn (an overall total) exclusive of deductions

⁴**gross** *n, pl* **gross** [MF *grosse,* fr. fem. of *gros* thick, coarse] : a total of 12 dozen things ⟨a *gross* of pencils⟩

gross national product *n* : the total value of the goods and services produced in a nation during a year

grot \'grät\ *n* : GROTTO

¹**gro·tesque** \grō-'tesk\ *adj* [grotesque, n., work of decorative art combining fanciful animal forms with foliage, fr. MF, fr. It *pittura grottesca,* lit., cave painting] **1** : combining (as in a painting or poem) details never found together in nature and rarely in art : using distortion and incongruity for artistic effect **2** : absurdly awkward or incongruous ⟨*grotesque* appearance of a clown⟩ **syn** see FANTASTIC — **gro·tesque·ly** *adv* — **gro·tesque·ness** *n*

²**grotesque** *n* : something that is grotesque

grot·to \'grät-ō\ *n, pl* **grottoes** *also* **grottos** [It, fr. L *crypta* cavern, crypt] **1** : CAVE **2** : an artificial recess or structure made to resemble a natural cave

grouch \'grauch\ *n* **1** : a fit of bad temper **2** : an habitually irritable or complaining person — **grouch** *vi* — **grouch·i·ly** \'grau-chə-lē\ *adv* — **grouch·i·ness** \-chē-nəs\ *n* — **grouchy** \-chē\ *adj*

¹**ground** \'graund\ *n* [OE *grund*] **1 a** : the bottom of a body of water ⟨the boat struck *ground*⟩ **b** *pl* : sediment at the bottom of a liquid : LEES **2** : a basis for belief, action, or argument ⟨*grounds* for divorce⟩ **3 a** : a surrounding area : BACKGROUND ⟨a picture on a gray *ground*⟩ **b** : material that serves as a substratum : FOUNDATION **4 a** : the surface of the earth **b** : an area used for a particular purpose ⟨parade *ground*⟩ **c** *pl* : the area around and belonging to a building ⟨the capitol *grounds*⟩ **5** : SOIL, EARTH **6 a** : an object that makes an electrical connection with the earth **b** : a large conducting body (as the earth) used as a common return for an electric circuit

²**ground** *vb* **1** : to bring to or place on the ground ⟨*ground* a rifle⟩ **2** : to provide a reason or justification for **b** : to instruct in fundamentals ⟨well *grounded* in mathematics⟩ **3** : to connect electrically with a ground **4** : to restrict to the ground ⟨*ground* a pilot⟩ **5** : to run aground ⟨the ship *grounded* on a reef⟩ **6** : to hit a grounder ⟨*grounded* to the shortstop⟩

³**ground** *past of* GRIND

ground–cher·ry \'graun(d)-'cher-ē\ *n* : a plant related to the nightshades that is sometimes grown for its edible but insipid yellow fruits enclosed in papery husks

ground cloth *n* : GROUNDSHEET

ground cover *n* : low plants that cover the ground (as

in a forest or as a substitute for turf); *also* : a plant used as ground cover

ground crew *n* : the mechanics and technicians who maintain and service an airplane

ground·er \'graùn-dər\ *n* : a batted ball that strikes the ground almost immediately — called also *ground ball*

ground floor *n* : the floor of a house most nearly on a level with the ground

ground glass *n* : glass with a roughened light-diffusing nontransparent surface

ground·hog \'graùnd-,hòg, -,häg\ *n* : WOODCHUCK

Groundhog Day *n* [fr. the legend that the groundhog comes out of hibernation on this date, but is frightened back for six more weeks if the day is sunny and he sees his shadow, thus betokening six more weeks of winter] : February 2

ground·less \'graùn-dləs\ *adj* : being without foundation or reason ⟨*groundless* fears⟩ — **ground·less·ly** *adv* — **ground·less·ness** *n*

ground·ling \'graùn-dliŋ\ *n* **1 a** : a spectator in the pit or cheaper part of a theater **b** : a person of inferior taste **2** : one that lives or works on or near the ground

ground loop *n* : a sharp uncontrollable turn made by an airplane in landing, taking off, or taxiing

ground·mass \'graùn(d)-,mas\ *n* : the fine-grained base of a rock in which larger crystals are embedded

ground pine *n* : any of several club mosses with long creeping stems and erect branches

ground plan *n* **1** : a plan of a floor of a building **2** : a first or basic plan

ground rule *n* : a rule of procedure

ground·sel \'graùn(d)-səl\ *n* [OE *grundeswelge,* fr. *grund* ground + *swelgan* to swallow] : any of a large genus of plants related to the daisies that have mostly yellow flower heads

ground·sheet \'graùn(d)-,shēt\ *n* : a waterproof sheet placed on the ground for protection from moisture

ground squirrel *n* : any of numerous burrowing rodents (as the gophers and chipmunks) differing from true squirrels in having cheek pouches and shorter fur

ground state *n* : the energy level of a system of interacting elementary particles having the least energy of all its possible states

ground swell *n* : a broad deep ocean swell caused by a distant storm or earthquake

ground·wa·ter \'graùn-,dwòt-ər, -,dwät-\ *n* : water within the earth that supplies wells and springs

ground wave *n* : a radio wave that is propagated along the surface of the earth

ground·work \'graùn-,dwərk\ *n* : FOUNDATION, BASIS

¹group \'grüp\ *n* [F *groupe,* fr. It *gruppo,* of Gmc origin] **1** : two or more figures forming a complete unit in a composition **2 a** : a number of individuals assembled together or having common interests **b** : a number of objects regarded as a unit **3 a** : an assemblage of related organisms **b** : an assemblage of atoms forming part of a molecule ⟨a methyl *group* (CH₃)⟩ **4** : a mathematical system consisting of a set of elements (as integers) and an operation (as multiplication or addition) such that two elements under the operation yield a third member of the set, the elements behave associatively, there exists an identity element, and for each element there is an inverse such that the product of the two equals the identity element

²group *vb* **1** : to combine in a group **2** : to assign to a group : CLASSIFY **3** : to form a group

grou·per \'grü-pər\ *n, pl* **groupers** *also* **grouper** [Pg *garoupa*] **1** : any of numerous mostly large solitary bottom fishes of warm seas related to the sea basses **2** : any of several rockfishes

group·ing *n* **1** : the act, process, or manner of combining in groups **2** : GROUP

¹grouse \'graùs\ *n, pl* **grouse** : any of numerous plump-bodied game birds usu. protectively colored and less brilliant in plumage than the related pheasants

²grouse *vi* : COMPLAIN, GRUMBLE — **grous·er** *n*

ruffed grouse

grout \'graùt\ *n* [OE *grūt* coarse meal] **1** : thin mortar **2** : PLASTER — **grout** *vt*

grove \'grōv\ *n* [OE *grāf*] : a small wood; *esp* : a group of trees without underbrush ⟨a picnic *grove*⟩ ⟨an orange *grove*⟩

grov·el \'gräv-əl, 'grəv-\ *vi* **-eled** *or* **-elled; -el·ing** *or* **-el·ling** \-(ə-)liŋ\ **1** : to lie or creep with the body prostrate in token of subservience or abasement **2** : to abase oneself : CRINGE — **grov·el·er** *or* **grov·el·ler** \-(ə-)lər\ *n*

grow \'grō\ *vb* **grew** \'grü\; **grown** \'grōn\; **grow·ing** [OE *grōwan*] **1 a** : to spring up and develop to maturity **b** : to be able to grow in some place or situation ⟨rice *grows* in water⟩ ⟨fruits that *grow* only in the tropics⟩ **c** : to assume some relation through or as if through a process of natural growth ⟨a tree with limbs *grown* together⟩ ⟨ferns *growing* from the rocks⟩ **2 a** : to become larger and often more complex by addition of material either by assimilation into the living organism or by accretion in a natural inorganic process (as crystallization) **b** : INCREASE, EXPAND ⟨the city is *growing* rapidly⟩ ⟨*grows* in wisdom⟩ **3 a** : RESULT, ORIGINATE ⟨the project *grew* out of a mere suggestion⟩ **b** : to come into existence : ARISE **4 a** : to pass into a condition : BECOME ⟨*grew* pale⟩ **b** : to obtain influence ⟨habit *grows* on a man⟩ **5** : to cause to grow : CULTIVATE, RAISE ⟨*grow* wheat⟩ — **grow·er** \'grō-(ə)r\ *n*

growing pains *n pl* : pains in the legs of growing children having no demonstrable relation to growth

growing point *n* : the tip of a plant shoot from which additional shoot tissues differentiate

growl \'graùl\ *vb* **1 a** : RUMBLE **b** : to utter a deep guttural threatening sound ⟨the dog *growled* at the stranger⟩ ⟨*growled* a stern warning⟩ **2** : to complain angrily : GRUMBLE — **growl** *n* — **growl·er** *n*

grown \'grōn\ *adj* : fully grown : MATURE ⟨*grown* man⟩

grown-up \'grōn-,əp\ *adj* : ADULT ⟨*grown-up* books⟩ — **grown-up** *n*

growth \'grōth\ *n* [ON *grōthr,* fr. *grōa* to grow] **1 a** : stage or condition attained in growing : SIZE ⟨hasn't reached his full *growth*⟩ **b** : a process of growing ⟨*growth* of a crystal⟩ **c** : progressive development ⟨the *growth* of civilization⟩; *also* : INCREASE ⟨*growth* of wealth⟩ **2** : a result or product of growing: as **a** : vegetation or a cover of vegetation ⟨covered with a *growth* of mold⟩ ⟨a *growth* of new rye⟩ **b** : an abnormal mass of tissue (as a tumor) **3** : a producing esp. by growing ⟨fruits of his own *growth*⟩

growth factor *n* : a substance (as a vitamin) that promotes the growth of an organism

growth hormone *n* : an anterior pituitary hormone that regulates growth

growth ring *n* : a layer of wood (as an annual ring) produced during a single period of growth

¹grub \'grəb\ *vb* **grubbed; grub·bing** [ME *grubben;* akin to E *grave*] **1** : to clear or root out by digging ⟨*grub* up roots⟩ ⟨*grub* land for planting⟩ **2** : to work hard : DRUDGE **3 a** : to dig in the ground usu. for a hidden object ⟨*grub* for potatoes⟩ **b** : to search about : RUMMAGE ⟨*grubbing* about in the cupboard⟩ — **grub·ber** *n*

²grub *n* **1** : a soft thick wormlike larva of an insect **2 a** : DRUDGE **b** : a slovenly person **3** : FOOD

grub·by \'grəb-ē\ *adj* **grub·bi·er; -est 1** : DIRTY, SLOVENLY **2** : BASE, CONTEMPTIBLE — **grub·bi·ly** \'grəb-ə-lē\ *adv* — **grub·bi·ness** \'grəb-ē-nəs\ *n*

grub·stake \'grəb-,stāk\ *n* : supplies or funds furnished a mining prospector in return for a promise of a share in his finds — **grubstake** *vt* — **grub·stak·er** *n*

¹grudge \'grəj\ *vt* [ME *grucchen, grudgen* to grumble, complain, fr. OF *groucier*] : to be unwilling to give or admit : BEGRUDGE — **grudg·er** *n* — **grudg·ing·ly** \'grəj-iŋ-lē\ *adv*

²grudge *n* : a feeling of deep-seated resentment or ill will

gru·el \'grü-əl\ *n* [MF, of Gmc origin] : a thin porridge

gru·el·ing *or* **gru·el·ling** \'grü-(ə-)liŋ\ *adj* [fr. prp. of obs. *gruel* to exhaust] : requiring extreme effort : EXHAUSTING, PUNISHING ⟨a *grueling* race⟩

grue·some \'grü-səm\ *adj* [ME *gruen* to shiver] : inspiring horror or repulsion : GRISLY syn see GHASTLY — **grue·some·ly** *adv* — **grue·some·ness** *n*

gruff \'grəf\ *adj* [D *grof*] **1** : rough or stern in manner, speech, or look ⟨a *gruff* reply⟩ **2** : being deep and harsh : HOARSE ⟨a *gruff* voice⟩ — **gruff·ly** *adv* — **gruff·ness** *n*

grum·ble \'grəm-bəl\ *vb* **grum·bled**; **grum·bling** \-b(ə-)liŋ\ **1** : to mutter in discontent **2 a** : GROWL **b** : RUMBLE — **grumble** *n* — **grum·bler** \-b(ə-)lər\ *n*

grump \'grəmp\ *n* **1** *pl* : a fit of ill humor **2** : a person given to complaining — **grump** *vi* — **grump·i·ly** \'grəm-pə-lē\ *adv* — **grump·i·ness** \-pē-nəs\ *n* — **grumpy** \-pē\ *adj*

grun·ion \'grən-yən\ *n* : a silversides of the California coast notable for the regularity with which it comes inshore to spawn at nearly full moon

¹grunt \'grənt\ *vb* **1** : to make the characteristic throat sound of a hog **2** : to utter with a grunt — **grunt·er** *n*

²grunt *n* **1 a** : the deep short sound characteristic of a hog **b** : a similar sound **2** : any of numerous marine fishes related to the snappers

gryph·on *var of* GRIFFIN

G suit *n* : an aviator's or astronaut's suit designed to counteract the physiological effects of acceleration

gua·nine \'gwän-,ēn\ *n* : a purine base regularly present in the polynucleotide chain of deoxyribonucleic acid and ribonucleic acid

gua·no \'gwän-ō\ *n, pl* **guanos** [Sp, fr. Quechua *huanu* dung] : a substance composed chiefly of the excrement of seabirds and used as a fertilizer

gua·ra·ni \,gwär-ə-'nē\ *n, pl* **-nis** *or* **-nies** : the basic monetary unit of Paraguay; *also* : a note representing this unit

¹guar·an·tee \,gar-ən-'tē\ *n* **1** : GUARANTOR **2** : GUAR-ANTY 1 **3 a** : an agreement by which one party undertakes to secure another in the possession or enjoyment of something **b** : an assurance of the quality of or of the length of use to be expected from a product offered for sale often with a promise of reimbursement in case of defect or failure **4** : GUARANTY 3

²guarantee *vt* **-teed**; **-tee·ing 1** : to undertake to answer for the debt, failure to perform, or faulty performance of (another) **2** : to undertake an obligation to establish, perform, or continue ⟨*guaranteed* annual wage⟩ **3** : to give security to : SECURE

guar·an·tor \,gar-ən-'tó(ə)r, 'gar-ən-tər\ *n* : a person who gives a guarantee

¹guar·an·ty \'gar-ən-tē\ *n, pl* **-ties** [MF *garantie*, fr. *garantir* to guarantee, fr. *garant* warrant, of Gmc origin] **1** : an undertaking to answer for another's failure to pay a debt or perform a duty **2** : GUARANTEE 3 **3** : something given as security : PLEDGE **4** : GUARANTOR

²guaranty *vt* **-tied**; **-ty·ing** : GUARANTEE

¹guard \'gärd\ *n* [MF *garde*, fr. *garder* to guard, of Gmc origin; akin to E *ward*] **1** : a posture of defense **2 a** : the act or duty of protecting or defending **b** : PROTECTION **3 a** : a man or a body of men on sentinel duty **b** *pl* : troops attached to the person of the sovereign **c** (1) : BRAKEMAN (2) *Brit* : CONDUCTOR **4 a** : a football player who lines up inside the tackle and next to the center **b** : either of two primarily defensive players stationed to the rear of the court in basketball **5** : a protective or safety device (as on a machine)

²guard *vb* **1** : to protect from danger : DEFEND **2 a** : to watch over so as to prevent escape, disclosure, or indiscretion ⟨*guard* a prisoner⟩ ⟨a closely *guarded* secret⟩ ⟨*guard* his tongue⟩ **b** : to attempt to prevent (an opponent) from scoring **3** : to be on guard : take precautions ⟨*guard* against infection⟩

guard cell *n* : one of the two crescent-shaped epidermal cells that border and open and close a plant stoma

guard·ed \'gärd-əd\ *adj* **1** : PROTECTED **2** : CAUTIOUS, NONCOMMITTAL ⟨a *guarded* answer⟩ — **guard·ed·ly** *adv*

guard hair *n* : one of the long coarse hairs forming a protective coating over the underfur of a mammal

guard·house \'gärd-,haús\ *n* **1** : a building occupied by a guard or used as a headquarters by soldiers on guard duty **2** : a military jail

guard·i·an \'gärd-ē-ən\ *n* **1** : one that guards : CUSTODIAN **2** : one who has the care of the person or property of another — **guard·i·an·ship** \-,ship\ *n*

guard of honor : a guard turned out to greet or accompany a distinguished person or to accompany the casket at a military funeral

guard·room \'gärd-,rüm, -,rúm\ *n* **1** : a room used by

a military guard while on duty **2** : a room where military prisoners are confined

guards·man \'gärdz-mən\ *n* : a member of a military body organized as guards

gua·va \'gwäv-ə\ *n* [Sp *guayaba*, of AmerInd origin] **1** : any of several tropical American shrubs or small trees of the myrtle family; *esp* : one widely grown for its sweet-to-acid yellow fruit **2** : the fruit of a guava

gua·yu·le \(g)wī-'ü-lē\ *n* : a low shrubby plant related to the daisies and found in Mexico and the southwestern U.S. that has been grown as a source of rubber

gu·ber·na·to·ri·al \,gü-bə(r)-nə-'tōr-ē-əl, ,gyü-, -'tòr-\ *adj* [L *gubernator* governor, fr. *gubernare* to govern] : of or relating to a governor

gud·geon \'gəj-ən\ *n* [MF *goujon*, fr. L *gobion-*, *gobio*, alter. of *gobius* goby] : a small European freshwater fish related to the carps; *also* : any of several fishes (as a goby or killifish)

Guelf *or* **Guelph** \'gwelf\ *n* : a member of a papal and popular political party in medieval Italy opposing the authority of the German emperors — compare GHIBELLINE

gue·non \gə-'nōⁿ\ *n* : any of various long-tailed chiefly arboreal African monkeys

guer·don \'gərd-°n\ *n* [MF, modif. of OHG *widarlōn*, fr. *widar* back + *lōn* reward] : REWARD, RECOMPENSE

guern·sey \'gərn-zē\ *n, pl* **guernseys** [*Guernsey*, Channel islands] : any of a breed of fawn and white dairy cattle that are larger than jerseys and produce rich yellowish milk

guer·ril·la *or* **gue·ril·la** \gə-'ril-ə\ *n* [Sp *guerrilla*, fr. dim. of *guerra* war, of Gmc origin] : a person who engages in irregular warfare esp. as a member of an independent unit carrying out harassment and sabotage — **guerrilla** *adj*

guess \'ges\ *vb* [ME *gessen*] **1** : to form an opinion from little or no evidence **2** : to conjecture correctly about : DISCOVER **3** : BELIEVE, SUPPOSE ⟨I *guess* you're right⟩ *syn* see CONJECTURE — **guess** *n* — **guess·er** *n* — **guess-work** \'ges-,wərk\ *n*

guest \'gest\ *n* [ON *gestr*] **1 a** : a person entertained in one's house **b** : a person to whom hospitality is extended **c** : a patron of a commercial establishment (as a hotel or restaurant) **2** : an organism that lives in close association with another kind of organism

guf·faw \(,)gə-'fó\ *n* : a loud burst of laughter — **guf-faw** *vi*

guid·ance \'gīd-°n(t)s\ *n* **1** : the act or process of guiding **2** : advice on vocational or educational problems given to students

¹guide \'gīd\ *n* [MF, fr. OProv *guida*, of Gmc origin] **1 a** : one who leads or directs another in his way **b** : one who exhibits and explains points of interest **c** : something that provides a person with guiding information **d** : SIGNPOST **e** : one who directs a person in his conduct or course of life **2 a** : a contrivance for steadying or directing the motion of something **b** : a sheet or a card with projecting tab for labeling inserted in a card index to facilitate reference

²guide *vb* **1** : to act as a guide : CONDUCT ⟨*guide* a group on a tour⟩ **2 a** : MANAGE, DIRECT ⟨*guide* a car through traffic⟩ **b** : to superintend the training of — **guid·a·ble** \'gīd-ə-bəl\ *adj*

guide·book \'gīd-,búk\ *n* : a book of information for travelers

guid·ed missile \,gīd-əd-\ *n* : a missile whose course toward a target may be changed (as by radio signals or a built-in target-seeking device) during flight

guide word *n* : CATCHWORD 1

gui·don \'gīd-,än, -°n\ *n* **1** : a small flag; *esp* : one borne by a military unit as a unit marker **2** : one who carries a guidon

guild \'gild\ *n* [ON *gildi*] : an association of men with kindred pursuits or common interests or aims; *esp* : a medieval association of merchants or craftsmen — **guild-ship** \-,ship\ *n*

guil·der \'gil-dər\ *n* : GULDEN

guild·hall \'gild-,hól\ *n* : a hall where a guild or corporation usu. assembles : TOWN HALL

guile \'gīl\ *n* [OF] : deceitful cunning : DUPLICITY — **guile·ful** \-fəl\ *adj* — **guile·ful·ly** \-fə-lē\ *adv* — **guile-ful·ness** *n*

guile·less \'gīl-ləs\ *adj* : free from deceit or cunning

: INNOCENT, NAÏVE ⟨a *guileless* person⟩ ⟨a *guileless* smile⟩
— **guile·less·ly** *adv* — **guile·less·ness** *n*

guil·le·mot \'gil-ə-,mät\ *n* [F, fr. MF, dim. of *Guillaume*
William] : any of several narrow-billed auks of northern
seas

guil·lo·tine \'gil-ə-,tēn, 'gē-(y)ə-\ *n* [F,
after Joseph *Guillotin* d1814 French physician who proposed its use] : a machine for
cutting off a person's head by means of a
heavy blade sliding in two upright grooved
posts — **guillotine** *vb*

guilt \'gilt\ *n* [OE *gylt*] 1 : the fact of
having committed an offense and esp. one
that is punishable by law 2 : BLAME-
WORTHINESS 3 : a feeling of responsibility
for offenses — **guilt·less** \-ləs\ *adj*

guilty \'gil-tē\ *adj* **guilt·i·er; -est** 1
: having committed a breach of conduct
2 a : suggesting or involving guilt ⟨a *guilty*
manner⟩ b : aware of or suffering from guilt — **guilt·i·ly**
\-tə-lē\ *adv* — **guilt·i·ness** \-tē-nəs\ *n*

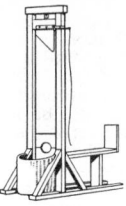

guillotine

guin·ea \'gin-ē\ *n* [*Guinea*, West Africa, supposed source
of the gold from which it was made] 1 : a British gold
coin no longer issued worth 21 shillings 2 : a unit of
value equal to 21 shillings

guinea fowl *n* : an African bird related to the pheasants,
widely raised for food, and marked by a bare neck and
head and white-speckled usu. slaty plumage

guinea hen *n* : a female guinea fowl; *also* : GUINEA FOWL

guinea pig *n* 1 : a small stout-bodied short-eared nearly
tailless rodent often kept as a pet and widely used in
biological research — called also *cavy* 2 : a subject of
scientific research, experimentation, or testing

Guin·e·vere \'gwin-ə-,vi(ə)r\ *n* : the wife of King
Arthur and mistress of Lancelot in Arthurian legend

guise \'gīz\ *n* [ME, fr. OF, of Gmc origin; akin to E
1*wise*] 1 : a form or style of dress : COSTUME ⟨appeared in
the *guise* of a shepherd⟩ 2 *obs* : MANNER 3 : external
appearance : SEMBLANCE ⟨swindled people under the *guise*
of friendship⟩

gui·tar \gə-'tär\ *n* [F *guitare*, fr. Sp *guitarra*, fr.
Ar *qītār*, fr. Gk *kithara* cithara] : a flat-bodied
stringed instrument with a long fretted neck
and usu. six strings plucked with a plectrum or
with the fingers

gu·lar \'g(y)ü-lər\ *adj* [L *gula* throat] : of, relating to, or situated on the throat

gulch \'gəlch\ *n* : a deep steep-sided ravine;
esp : one that is the bed of a stream

gul·den \'gül-dən\ *n, pl* **guldens** or **gulden**
[MD *gulden florijn* golden florin] 1 : the basic
monetary unit of the Netherlands 2 : a coin
or note representing one gulden

gules \'gyülz\ *n, pl* **gules** [MF *goules*] : the
heraldic color red

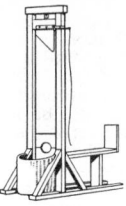

guitar

gulf \'gəlf\ *n* [MF *golfe*, fr. It *golfo*, fr. LL *colpus*, fr. Gk
kolpos bosom, gulf] 1 : a part of an ocean or sea extending into the land 2 : a deep hollow in the earth : CHASM,
ABYSS 3 : WHIRLPOOL 4 : a wide separation : an un-
bridgeable gap

syn BAY : GULF implies a body of water of considerable
size and importance and usu. suggests deep penetration
of the land and a relatively narrow entrance; BAY commonly implies a shallow penetration and wide entrance
but may apply to a body of water of almost any size or
shape that is connected with or is part of a larger one

Gulf Stream *n* : a warm ocean current in the north
Atlantic flowing from the Gulf of Mexico along the eastern
coast of the U.S. to Nantucket Island and thence eastward

gulf·weed \'gəlf-,wēd\ *n* : any of several marine brown
algae; *esp* : a branching olive-brown
seaweed of tropical American seas
with numerous air vesicles suggesting
berries

1**gull** \'gəl\ *n* [ME, of Celt origin] : any
of numerous mostly white or gray long⸗
winged web-footed aquatic birds

2**gull** *vt* : to make a dupe of : DECEIVE

3**gull** *n* : a person easily deceived or
cheated : DUPE

gull

gul·let \'gəl-ət\ *n* [MF *goulet*, dim. of *goule* throat, fr.

L *gula*] 1 : ESOPHAGUS; *also* : THROAT 2 : the space
between adjacent saw teeth

gull·i·ble \'gəl-ə-bəl\ *adj* : easily deceived, cheated, or
duped — **gull·i·bil·i·ty** \,gəl-ə-'bil-ət-ē\ *n* — **gull·i·bly**
\'gəl-ə-blē\ *adv*

gul·ly \'gəl-ē\ *n, pl* **gullies** [obs. E *gully* gullet] : a trench
worn in the earth by running water after rains — **gully** *vb*

gully erosion *n* : soil erosion produced by running water

gulp \'gəlp\ *vb* [ME *gulpen*] 1 : to swallow hurriedly
or greedily or in one swallow 2 : to keep back as if by
swallowing ⟨*gulp* down a sob⟩ 3 : to catch the breath as
if in taking a long drink — **gulp** *n* — **gulp·er** *n*

1**gum** \'gəm\ *n* [OE *gōma* palate] : the tissue along the
jaws of animals that surrounds the necks of the teeth

2**gum** *vt* **gummed; gum·ming** 1 : to enlarge gullets of
(a saw) 2 : to chew with the gums

3**gum** *n* [OF *gomme*, fr. L *cummi, gummi*, fr. Gk *kommi*,
fr. Egypt *qmyt*] 1 : any of numerous complex colloidal
substances (as gum arabic) that are exuded by plants or
are extracted from them by solvents, that are thick or
sticky when moist but harden on drying and are either
soluble in water or swell up in contact with water, and
that are used in pharmacy (as for emulsifiers), for adhesives, as food thickeners, and in inks; *also* : any of
various gummy plant exudates including natural resins,
oleoresins, rubber, and rubberlike substances 2 : a
substance or deposit resembling a plant gum (as in sticky
quality) 3 a : a tree that yields a gum b *Austral*
: EUCALYPTUS 4 : the wood of a gum — called also
gumwood \-,wùd\ 5 : CHEWING GUM

4**gum** *vt* **gummed; gum·ming** : to smear, seal, or clog
with or as if with gum ⟨*gum* up the works⟩

gum arabic *n* : a water-soluble gum obtained from several
acacias and used esp. in adhesives, in confectionery, and
in pharmacy

gum·bo \'gəm-,bō\ *n, pl* **gumbos** [AmerF *gombo*, of
Bantu origin] 1 : OKRA 2 : a soup thickened with okra
pods 3 : any of various fine-grained silty soils that when
wet become very sticky

gum·boil \'gəm-,bòil\ *n* : an abscess in the gum

gum·drop \-,dräp\ *n* : a candy made usu. from corn
syrup with gelatin or gum arabic and coated with sugar
crystals

gum·ma \'gəm-ə\ *n, pl* **gummas** *also* **gum·ma·ta** \'gəm-
ət-ə\ [LL *gummat-, gumma* gum, alter. of L *gummi*] : a
gummy or rubbery tumor associated esp. with late stages
of syphilis — **gum·ma·tous** \-ət-əs\ *adj*

gum·my \'gəm-ē\ *adj* **gum·mi·er; -est** 1 : consisting of,
containing, or covered with gum 2 : VISCOUS, STICKY
— **gum·mi·ness** *n*

gump·tion \'gəm(p)-shən\ *n* 1 : shrewd common sense
2 : courageous or vigorous initiative : SPUNK

gum resin *n* : a plant product consisting essentially of a
mixture of gum and resin

gum·shoe \'gəm-,shü\ *n* : DETECTIVE — **gumshoe** *vi*

gum tragacanth *n* : TRAGACANTH

1**gun** \'gən\ *n* [ME *gunne*] 1 a : a piece of ordnance usu.
with high muzzle velocity and comparatively flat trajec-
tory : CANNON b : a portable firearm (as a rifle or pistol)
c : a device that throws a projectile 2 a : a discharge of
a gun b : a signal marking a beginning or ending ⟨the
opening *gun* of his campaign⟩ 3 : one who is skilled with
a gun 4 : something suggesting a gun in shape or function 5 : THROTTLE — **gunned** \'gənd\ *adj*

2**gun** *vb* **gunned; gun·ning** 1 : to hunt with a gun
2 : SHOOT 3 : to open up the throttle of so as to increase
speed ⟨*gun* the engine⟩

gun·boat \'gən-,bōt\ *n* : a small lightly armed ship for
use in shallow waters

gun·cot·ton \-,kät-°n\ *n* : an explosive that consists of
cellulose nitrate with a high nitrogen content and is used
chiefly in smokeless powder

gun·fight \-,fīt\ *n* : a duel with guns — **gun·fight·er** *n*

gun·fire \-,fī(ə)r\ *n* : the firing of guns

gun·lock \-,läk\ *n* : a device on a firearm by which the
charge is ignited

gun·man \-mən\ *n* : a man armed with a gun; *esp* : an
armed bandit or gangster

gun·met·al \'gən-,met-°l\ *n* 1 : a bronze formerly much
used for making cannon; *also* : a metal treated to look
like gunmetal 2 : a slightly purplish dark gray

gun·ner \'gən-ər\ *n* **1 :** a soldier or airman who operates or aims a gun **2 :** one that hunts with a gun

gun·nery \'gən-(ə-)rē\ *n* **:** the use of guns; *esp* **:** the science of the flight of projectiles and of the effective use of guns

gun·ny \'gən-ē\ *n, pl* **gunnies** [Hindi *ganī*] **1 :** coarse jute sacking **2 :** BURLAP

gun·ny·sack \-,sak\ *n* **:** a sack made of gunny or burlap

gun·point \'gən-,point\ *n* **:** the point of a gun — **at gunpoint :** under a threat of death by being shot

gun·pow·der \-,paùd-ər\ *n* **:** an explosive mixture of potassium nitrate, charcoal, and sulfur used in gunnery and blasting; *also* **:** any of various explosive powders used in guns

gun·shot \-,shät\ *n* **1 :** shot or a projectile fired from a gun **2 :** the range of a gun ⟨within *gunshot*⟩

gun·shy \-,shī\ *adj* **1 :** afraid of a loud noise (as of a gun) **2 :** markedly distrustful

gun·smith \-,smith\ *n* **:** one whose business is the making and repair of firearms

gun·wale *or* **gun·nel** \'gən-ᵊl\ *n* [so called fr. its former use as a support for guns] **:** the upper edge of a ship's side

gup·py \'gəp-ē\ *n, pl* **guppies** [R.J.L. *Guppy* of Trinidad, donor of specimens to the British Museum] **:** a small tropical topminnow frequently kept as an aquarium fish

gur·gle \'gər-gəl\ *vi* **gur·gled; gur·gling** \'gər-g(ə-)liŋ\ **1 :** to flow in a broken irregular current **2 :** to make a sound like that of a gurgling liquid — **gurgle** *n*

Gur·kha \'gù(ə)r-kə, 'gər-\ *n* **:** a soldier from Nepal in the British or Indian army

gur·nard \'gər-nərd\ *n, pl* **gurnard** *or* **gurnards** [MF *gornart*] **:** any of various marine spiny-finned fishes with a spiny armored head and three pairs of modified fin rays used esp. in crawling

gu·ru \gə-'rü\ *n* [Hindi *gurū*, fr. Skt *guru*, fr. *guru* heavy, venerable] **:** a personal religious teacher and spiritual guide in Hinduism

gush \'gəsh\ *vb* [ME *guschen*] **1 :** to issue or pour forth copiously or violently **:** SPOUT ⟨oil *gushed* from the new well⟩ **2 :** to make an effusive display of affection or enthusiasm ⟨girls *gushed* over the latest movie star⟩ — **gush** *n*

gush·er \'gəsh-ər\ *n* **:** one that gushes; *esp* **:** an oil well with a copious natural flow

gushy \'gəsh-ē\ *adj* **gush·i·er; -est :** marked by effusive sentimentality — **gush·i·ness** *n*

gus·set \'gəs-ət\ *n* [ME, piece of armor covering the joints in a suit of armor, fr. MF *gouchet*] **:** a usu. triangular or diamond-shaped insert (as in a seam of a sleeve or glove) to give width or strength

gust \'gəst\ *n* **1 :** a sudden brief rush of wind **2 :** a sudden outburst **:** SURGE ⟨a *gust* of anger⟩ — **gusty** \'gəs-tē\ *adj*

gus·ta·tion \,gəs-'tā-shən\ *n* **:** the act or sensation of tasting

gus·ta·to·ry \'gəs-tə-,tōr-ē, -,tòr-\ *adj* **:** relating to, associated with, or being the sense or sensation of taste

gus·to \'gəs-,tō\ *n* [Sp, fr. L *gustus* taste; akin to E *choose*] **1 :** keen and usu. vigorous enjoyment or appreciation **:** high relish ⟨eat with *gusto*⟩ **2 :** capacity for taking delight in experience **:** strength of appetite ⟨a man of gigantic *gusto*⟩ **syn** see TASTE

¹gut \'gət\ *n* [OE *guttas*, pl.] **1 a :** VISCERA, ENTRAILS — usu. used in pl. **b :** the alimentary canal or part of it **c :** BELLY, ABDOMEN **2** *pl* **:** the inner essential parts **3** *pl* **:** COURAGE

²gut *vt* **gut·ted; gut·ting 1 :** EVISCERATE **2 :** to destroy the inside of ⟨fire *gutted* the building⟩

gut·ta-per·cha \,gət-ə-'pər-chə\ *n* [Malay *gĕtah-pĕrcha*] **:** a tough plastic substance from the latex of several Malaysian trees that resembles but contains more resin than rubber and that is used esp. as insulation and in dentistry

gut·tate \'gə-,tāt\ *adj* [L *gutta* drop] **:** having small usu. colored spots or drops

gut·ta·tion \,gə-'tā-shən\ *n* **:** physiological exudation of liquid water from a plant

¹gut·ter \'gət-ər\ *n* [OF *goutiere*, fr. *goute* drop, fr. L *gutta*] **1 a :** a trough along the eaves to catch and carry off water from a roof **b :** a low area (as at a roadside) to carry off surface water **2 :** a narrow channel or groove

²gutter *vb* **1 :** to form gutters in **2 a :** to flow in small streams **b :** to melt away rapidly by becoming channeled down the sides ⟨a *guttering* candle⟩ **3 :** to flicker in a draft

gut·ter·snipe \-,snīp\ *n* **:** a person of the lowest moral or economic station; *esp* **:** a street urchin

gut·tur·al \'gət-ə-rəl\ *adj* [L *guttur* throat] **1 :** of or relating to the throat **2 a :** formed or pronounced in the throat ⟨*guttural* sounds⟩ **b :** being or marked by an utterance that is strange, unpleasant, or disagreeable **c :** VELAR, PALATAL — **guttural** *n* — **gut·tur·al·ly** \-rə-lē\ *adv* — **gut·tur·al·ness** *n*

gut·ty \'gət-ē\ *adj* **gut·ti·er; -est :** being vital, bold, and challenging ⟨*gutty* realism⟩

¹guy \'gī\ *n* [prob. fr. D *gei* brail] **:** a rope, chain, or rod attached to something as a brace or guide

²guy *vt* **guyed; guy·ing :** to steady or reinforce with a guy

³guy *n* [*guy* grotesque effigy of Guy Fawkes paraded and burned in England on November 5, fr. *Guy* Fawkes *d*1606 English conspirator who plotted to blow up the Houses of Parliament] **:** MAN, FELLOW

⁴guy *vt* **guyed; guy·ing :** to make fun of **:** RIDICULE

guz·zle \'gəz-əl\ *vb* **guz·zled; guz·zling** \'gəz-(ə-)liŋ\ **:** to drink greedily — **guz·zler** \-(ə-)lər\ *n*

gybe \'jīb\ *var of* JIBE

gym \'jim\ *n* **:** GYMNASIUM

gym·kha·na \jim-'kan-ə, -'kän-\ *n* **:** a meet featuring sports contests (as horseback-riding events)

gymn- *or* **gymno-** *comb form* [Gk *gymnos*] **:** naked **:** bare ⟨*gymno*gynous⟩

gym·na·si·um *in sense 1* jim-'nā-zē-əm, *in sense 2* gim-'nä-zē-əm\ *n, pl* **-si·ums** *or* **-sia** \-zē-ə\ [Gk *gymnasion* exercise ground, school, fr. *gymnazein* to exercise naked, fr. *gymnos* naked] **1 :** a room or building for sports activities **2 :** a German secondary school preparing students for the university

gym·nast \'jim-,nast\ *n* **:** an expert in gymnastics

gym·nas·tics \jim-'nas-tiks\ *n sing or pl* **:** physical exercises developing or exhibiting skill, strength, and control in the use of the body — **gym·nas·tic** \-tik\ *adj*

gym·no·din·i·um \,jim-nō-'din-ē-əm\ *n* **:** any of a genus of naked marine dinoflagellates some of which cause red tides

gym·no·sperm \'jim-nə-,spərm\ *n* [*gymn-* + Gk *sperma* seed] **:** any of a group (Gymnospermae) of woody vascular seed plants that produce naked seeds not enclosed in a true fruit — **gym·no·sper·mous** \,jim-nə-'spər-məs\ *adj* — **gym·no·sper·my** \'jim-nə-,spər-mē\ *n*

gyn- *or* **gyno-** *comb form* [Gk *gynaik-, gynē* woman; akin to E *queen*] **1 :** woman ⟨*gyn*archy⟩ **2 :** female reproductive organ ⟨*gyno*phore⟩

gyn·an·dro·morph \jin-'an-drə-,mòrf, gīn-\ *n* **:** an abnormal individual exhibiting characters of both sexes in various parts of the body — **gyn·an·dro·mor·phic** \-,an-drə-'mòr-fik\ *adj* — **gyn·an·dro·mor·phism** \-,fiz-əm\ *n* — **gyn·an·dro·mor·phous** \-fəs\ *adj* — **gyn·an·dro·mor·phy** \-'an-drə-,mòr-fē\ *n*

gy·ne·col·o·gy \,jin-i-'käl-ə-jē, ,gīn-\ *n* [Gk *gynaik-, gynē* woman] **:** a branch of medicine that deals with women, their diseases, and their hygiene — **gy·ne·co·log·ic** \-kə-'läj-ik\ *or* **gy·ne·co·log·i·cal** \-'läj-i-kəl\ *adj* — **gy·ne·col·o·gist** \-'käl-ə-jəst\ *n*

gy·noe·ci·um \jin-'ē-s(h)ē-əm, gīn-\ *n, pl* **-cia** \-s(h)ē-ə\ [NL, alter. of L *gynaeceum* women's apartments, fr. Gk *gynaikeion*, fr. *gynaik-, gynē* woman] **:** the carpels in a flower

-g·y·nous \j-ə-nəs\ *adj comb form* [Gk *gynē* woman] **1 :** of, relating to, or having (such or so many) females ⟨hetero*gynous*⟩ **2 :** having (such or so many) styles or pistils ⟨tetra*gynous*⟩

¹gyp \'jip\ *n* **1 :** CHEAT, SWINDLER **2 :** an act or instance of cheating **:** FRAUD, SWINDLE

²gyp *vb* **gypped; gyp·ping :** CHEAT, SWINDLE

gyp·soph·i·la \jip-'säf-ə-lə\ *n* **:** any of a large genus of Old World herbs of the pink family having open panicles of tiny flowers

gyp·sum \'jip-səm\ *n* [L, fr. Gk *gypsos*] **:** a colorless mineral $CaSO_4.2H_2O$ that consists of hydrous calcium sulfate occurring in crystals or masses and that is used esp. as a soil improver and in making plaster of paris

Gyp·sy \'jip-sē\ *n, pl* **Gypsies** [by shortening & alter. fr. *Egyptian*] **1 :** one of a dark Caucasoid people coming orig. from India to Europe in the 14th or 15th century and living and maintaining a migratory way of life chiefly in Europe and the U.S. **2 :** ROMANY 2

gypsy moth *n* **:** an Old World tussock moth introduced about 1869 into the U.S. that has a grayish mottled hairy caterpillar which is a destructive defoliator of many trees

gyr- *or* **gyro-** *comb form* [Gk *gyros*] **1 :** ring **:** circle **:** spiral ⟨*gyro*magnetic⟩ **2 :** gyroscope ⟨*gyro*compass⟩

gy·rate \'jī-‚rāt\ *vi* **1 :** to revolve around a point or axis **2 :** to oscillate with or as if with a circular or spiral motion — **gy·ra·tion** \jī-'rā-shən\ *n* — **gy·ra·tion·al** \-shnəl, -shən-ᵊl\ *adj*

gyr·fal·con \'jər-‚fal-kən, -‚fȯl-; -‚fȯ-kən\ *n* **:** any of various large arctic falcons more powerful though less active than the peregrine falcon

gy·ro \'jī-rō\ *n, pl* **gyros 1 :** GYROSCOPE **2 :** GYRO-COMPASS

gy·ro·com·pass \'jī-rō-‚kəm-pəs, -‚käm-\ *n* **:** a compass in which the horizontal axis of a constantly spinning gyroscope points to the north and which is often used instead of a magnetic compass where metal in the vicinity (as on a ship) would interfere with the working of a magnetic compass

gy·ro·scope \'jī-rə-‚skōp\ *n* [so called fr. its original use to illustrate the rotation of the earth] **:** a wheel or disk mounted to spin rapidly about an axis that is free to turn in various directions — **gy·ro·scop·ic** \‚jī-rə-'skäp-ik\ *adj*

gy·rus \'jī-rəs\ *n, pl* **gy·ri** \-‚rī\ [NL, fr. L, circle, fr. Gk *gyros*] **:** a convoluted ridge between anatomical grooves

gyve \'jīv\ *n* [ME] **:** FETTER — usu. used in pl. — **gyve** *vt*

h \'āch\ *n, often cap* **:** the 8th letter of the English alphabet

ha \'hä\ *interj* — used to express surprise, joy, or grief or sometimes doubt or hesitation

Hab·ak·kuk \'hab-ə-‚kək, hə-'bak-ək\ *n* **1 :** a Hebrew prophet of Old Testament times **2** — see BIBLE table

ha·ba·ne·ra \‚(h)äb-ə-'ner-ə\ *n* [Sp *danza habanera*, lit., dance of Havana] **1 :** a Cuban dance in slow duple time **2 :** the music for the habanera

hab·da·lah \‚häv-də-'lä, häv-'dȯ-lə\ *n, often cap* **:** a Jewish ceremony that marks the close of a Sabbath or of a holy day

ha·be·as cor·pus \‚hā-bē-əs-'kȯr-pəs\ *n* [ML, you should have the body] **1 :** any of several writs obtained for the purpose of bringing a person before a court; *esp* **:** one ordering an inquiry to determine whether or not a person has been lawfully imprisoned **2 :** the right of a citizen to obtain a writ of habeas corpus as a protection against illegal imprisonment

hab·er·dash·er \'hab-ə(r)-‚dash-ər\ *n* [ME, fr. AF *hapertas* petty merchandise] **:** a dealer in men's wear (as gloves, neckties, socks, and shirts)

hab·er·dash·ery \-‚dash-(ə)rē\ *n, pl* **-er·ies 1 :** goods sold by a haberdasher **2 :** a haberdasher's shop

hab·er·geon \'hab-ər-jən\ *n* [MF *haubergeon*, dim. of *hauberc* hauberk] **1 :** a medieval jacket of mail shorter than a hauberk **2 :** HAUBERK

ha·bil·i·ment \hə-'bil-ə-mənt\ *n* [MF *habillement*, fr. *habiller* to dress a log, dress, fr. *bille* log] **1 :** the dress characteristic of an occupation or occasion — usu. used in pl. ⟨the *habiliments* of a priest⟩ **2 :** CLOTHES — usu. used in pl.

¹hab·it \'hab-ət\ *n* [L *habitus* condition, custom, dress, fr. *habēre* to have, hold] **1 :** a costume characteristic of a calling, rank, or function ⟨riding *habit*⟩ **2 :** bodily appearance or makeup **:** PHYSIQUE **3 :** the prevailing disposition or character of a person's thoughts and feelings **:** mental makeup **4 :** a usual manner of behavior **:** CUSTOM **5 a :** a behavior pattern acquired and fixed by frequent repetition — compare REFLEX **b** (1) **:** an acquired mode of behavior that has become nearly or completely involuntary (2)

: ADDICTION **6 :** characteristic mode of growth or occurrence ⟨elms have a spreading *habit*⟩

syn HABIT, PRACTICE, USAGE, CUSTOM mean a way of acting that has become fixed through repetition. HABIT implies doing something unconsciously, often involuntarily or without forethought, and as a result of much repetition ⟨*habits* of speech⟩ ⟨pocketed his car keys by force of *habit*⟩ PRACTICE suggests an act performed with regularity and usu. by choice; USAGE suggests a customary action or practice followed so generally that it has become a social norm; CUSTOM applies to practice or usage so long and continuously associated with an individual or group as to have the force of unwritten law ⟨the *custom* of senatorial courtesy in the U.S. senate⟩

²habit *vt* **:** CLOTHE, DRESS

hab·it·a·ble \'hab-ət-ə-bəl\ *adj* **:** suitable or fit to live in ⟨the *habitable* parts of the earth⟩ — **hab·it·a·bil·i·ty** \‚hab-ət-ə-'bil-ət-ē\ *n* — **hab·it·a·ble·ness** \'hab-ət-ə-bəl-nəs\ *n* — **hab·it·a·bly** \-blē\ *adv*

hab·i·tant *n* **1** \'hab-ət-ənt\ **:** INHABITANT, RESIDENT **2** \‚(h)ab-i-'tän\ **:** a French settler or a farmer of French origin in Canada

hab·i·tat \'hab-ə-‚tat\ *n* [L, it dwells, fr. *habitare* to dwell] **1 :** the place or type of site where a plant or animal naturally or usu. lives or grows **2 :** the place where something is commonly found

hab·i·ta·tion \‚hab-ə-'tā-shən\ *n* [L *habitare* to dwell, freq. of *habēre* to have, hold] **1 :** the act of inhabiting **:** OCCUPANCY **2 :** a dwelling place **:** RESIDENCE

hab·it-form·ing *adj* **:** inducing the formation of an addiction

ha·bit·u·al \hə-'bich-(ə-w)əl\ *adj* **1 :** according to or constituting a habit ⟨*habitual* tardiness⟩ **2 :** doing or acting by force of habit ⟨*habitual* smoker⟩ **3 :** REGULAR ⟨*habitual* evening walk⟩ **syn** see USUAL — **ha·bit·u·al·ly** \-ē\ *adv* — **ha·bit·u·al·ness** *n*

ha·bit·u·ate \hə-'bich-ə-‚wāt\ *vt* **:** to make used to **:** ACCUSTOM — **ha·bit·u·a·tion** \hə-‚bich-ə-'wā-shən\ *n*

hab·i·tude \'hab-ə-‚t(y)üd\ *n* **1 :** habitual disposition or mode of behavior or procedure **2 :** CUSTOM

ha·bi·tué \hə-'bich-ə-‚wā\ *n* [F] **:** one who frequents a place or type of place

hab·i·tus \'hab-ət-əs\ *n, pl* **hab·i·tus** \-ət-əs, -ə-‚tüs\ [NL, fr. L] **:** HABIT; *esp* **:** body build and constitution

Habs·burg \'haps-, 'häps-\ *var of* HAPSBURG

ha·chure \ha-'shu̇(ə)r\ *n* [F] **:** a short line used in drawing and engraving esp. in shading and in representing different surfaces (as slopes of the ground on a map)

ha·ci·en·da \‚(h)äs-ē-'en-də\ *n* [Sp, business, wealth, estate, fr. L *facienda* things to be done, fr. *facere* to do] **1 :** a large estate in present or formerly Spanish-speaking countries **:** PLANTATION **2 :** the main building of a farm or ranch

¹hack \'hak\ *vb* [OE *-haccian*] **1 a :** to cut with repeated irregular or unskillful blows **b :** to sever with repeated blows **:** CHOP **2 :** to cough in a short dry manner — **hack·er** *n*

²hack *n* **1 :** an implement for hacking **2 :** NICK, NOTCH **3 :** a short dry cough **4 :** a hacking blow

³hack *n* [short for *hackney*] **1 a** (1) **:** a horse let out for common hire (2) **:** a horse used in all kinds of work **b :** a horse worn out in service **c :** a light easy saddle horse; *esp* **:** a three-gaited saddle horse **2 a :** HACKNEY **b** (1) **:** TAXICAB (2) **:** a driver of a cab **3 a :** a writer who works mainly for hire or for commercial success rather than literary achievement **b :** one who serves a cause not out of enthusiasm or devotion but merely for reward ⟨party *hacks* in a political campaign⟩

⁴hack *adj* **1 :** working for hire **2 :** done by or characteristic of a hack ⟨*hack* writing⟩ **3 :** HACKNEYED, TRITE

⁵hack *vi* **1 :** to ride or drive at an ordinary pace or over the roads as distinguished from racing or riding across country **2 :** to operate a taxicab

hack·a·more \'hak-ə-‚mōr, -‚mȯr\ *n* [by folk etymology fr. Sp *jaquima*] **:** a bridle with the bit replaced by a loop capable of being tightened about the nose or by a slip noose passed over the lower jaw

hack·ber·ry \'hak-‚ber-ē\ *n* **:** any of a genus of trees and shrubs of the elm family with small often edible berries; *also* **:** its wood

hack·ie \'hak-ē\ *n* **:** a driver of a cab

¹**hack·le** \'hak-əl\ *n* [ME *hakell*] **1** : a comb for dressing fibers (as flax or hemp) **2** : one of the long narrow feathers on the neck or lower back of a bird **3** *pl* **a** : erectile hairs along the neck and back esp. of a dog **b** : TEMPER, DANDER

²**hackle** *vt* **hack·led**; **hack·ling** \'hak-(ə-)liŋ\ [freq. of ¹*hack*] : to chop up or chop off roughly : HACK

hack·ly \'hak-lē\ *adj* : looking as if hacked : JAGGED

hack·man \'hak-mən\ *n* : a driver of a cab

hack·ma·tack \'hak-mə-,tak\ *n* [of Algonquian origin] : TAMARACK; *also* : any of several coniferous trees (as a juniper or poplar)

¹**hack·ney** \'hak-nē\ *n, pl* **hack·neys** [ME *hakeney*] **1 a** : a horse suitable for ordinary riding or driving **b** : any of a breed of rather compact English horses with a conspicuously high knee and hock flexion **2** : a carriage or automobile kept for hire

²**hackney** *adj* : kept for public hire **2** : HACKNEYED

³**hackney** *vt* **1** : to make common or frequent use of **2** : to make trite, vulgar, or commonplace

hack·neyed \'hak-nēd\ *adj* : worn out from too long or too much use : COMMONPLACE ⟨a *hackneyed* expression⟩ **syn** see TRITE

hack·saw \'hak-,sò\ *n* : a fine-tooth saw with blade under tension in a bow-shaped frame for cutting hard materials (as metal)

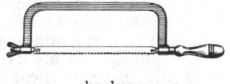

hacksaw

hack·work \-,wərk\ *n* : literary, artistic, or professional work done on order usu. according to formula and in conformity with commercial standards

had *past of* HAVE

had·dock \'had-ək\ *n, pl* **haddock** *also* **haddocks** [ME *haddok*] : an important Atlantic food fish usu. smaller than the related common cod

Ha·des \'hād-(,)ēz\ *n* **1** : the abode of the dead in Greek mythology **2** *often not cap* : HELL

hadn't \'had-ᵊnt\ : had not

hadst \(')hadst, (h)ədst\ *archaic past 2d sing of* HAVE

hae \(')hā\ *chiefly Scot var of* HAVE

haem- or haemo- — see HEM-

haemat- or haemato- — see HEMAT-

haf·ni·um \'haf-nē-əm\ *n* [NL, fr. *Hafnia* (Copenhagen), Denmark] : a metallic chemical element that resembles zirconium chemically and is useful because of its ready emission of electrons — see ELEMENT table

¹**haft** \'haft\ *n* [OE *hæft*] : the handle of a weapon or tool (as a sword or knife)

²**haft** *vt* : to set in or furnish with a haft

haf·ta·rah \,häf-tə-'rä, häf-'tò-rə\ *n, pl* **haf·ta·rot** \,häf-tə-'rōt\ *or* **haftarahs** : one of the biblical selections from the Books of the Prophets read at the conclusion of the Jewish synagogue service

hag \'hag\ *n* [ME *hagge*] **1** : WITCH **2** : an ugly, slatternly, or evil-looking old woman

Ha·gar \'hā-,gär, -gər\ *n* : a concubine of Abraham driven into the desert with her son Ishmael because of Sarah's jealousy

hag·fish \'hag-,fish\ *n* : any of several marine cyclostomes that are related to the lampreys and in general resemble eels

Hag·ga·dah \hə-'gäd-ə, -'gód-\ *n, pl* **Hag·ga·doth** \-'gäd-,ōt(h), -'gód-\ **1** : ancient Jewish lore forming esp. the nonlegal part of the Talmud **2** : the Jewish ritual for the Seder — **hag·gad·ic** \-'gad-ik, -'gäd-, -'gód-\ *adj, often cap*

Hag·gai \'hag-ē-,ī, 'hag-,ī\ *n* **1** : a Hebrew prophet of the 6th century B.C. **2** — see BIBLE table

hag·gard \'hag-ərd\ *adj* [MF *hagard*] : having the expression of a person who is suffering esp. from great hunger, worry, or pain or who is wasted with age : GAUNT

hag·gis \'hag-əs\ *n* [ME *hagese*] : a pudding esp. popular in Scotland made of the heart, liver, and lungs of a sheep or a calf minced with suet, onions, oatmeal, and seasonings and boiled in the stomach of the animal

¹**hag·gle** \'hag-əl\ *vb* **hag·gled**; **hag·gling** \'hag-(ə-)liŋ\ **1** : to cut roughly or clumsily : HACK **2** : to dispute or argue esp. over a bargain or a price — **hag·gler** \-(ə-)lər\ *n*

²**haggle** *n* : an act or instance of haggling

Hag·i·og·ra·pha \,hag-ē-'äg-rə-fə, ,hä-jē-\ *n sing or pl*

[LGk, lit., holy writings] : the third part of the Jewish scriptures — compare LAW, PROPHETS

hag·i·og·ra·phy \-fē\ *n* [Gk *hagios* saint, fr. *hagios* holy] **1** : biography of saints or venerated persons **2** : idealizing or idolizing biography — **hag·i·og·ra·pher** \-fər\ *n*

hah *var of* HA

ha-ha \(')hä-'hä\ *interj* — used to express amusement or derision

¹**hail** \'hāl\ *n* [OE *hægl*] **1** : precipitation in the form of small balls or lumps usu. consisting of concentric layers of clear ice and compact snow **2** : something that gives the effect of falling hail ⟨a *hail* of bullets⟩

²**hail** *vb* **1** : to precipitate hail **2** : to pour down like hail **3** : to hurl forcibly ⟨*hailed* curses on him⟩

³**hail** *interj* [ON *heill*, fr. *heill* healthy, hale] **1** — used to express acclamation **2** *archaic* — used as a greeting or welcome

⁴**hail** *vb* **1 a** : SALUTE, GREET **b** : to greet with enthusiastic approval : ACCLAIM ⟨they *hailed* him as a hero⟩ **2** : to greet or summon by calling ⟨*hail* a taxi⟩ **3** : to call out; *esp* : to call a greeting to a passing ship — **hail from** : to come from ⟨he *hails from* New York⟩

⁵**hail** *n* **1** : an exclamation of greeting or acclamation **2** : a calling to attract attention **3** : hailing distance ⟨within *hail*⟩

hail-fel·low \'hāl-,fel-ō\ *or* **hail-fellow-well-met** \-,wel-'met\ *adj* : heartily informal

Hail Mary *n* : AVE MARIA

hail·stone \'hāl-,stōn\ *n* : a pellet of hail

hail·storm \-,stórm\ *n* : a storm accompanied by hail

hair \'ha(ə)r, 'he(ə)r\ *n* [OE *hær*] **1 a** : a slender thread-like outgrowth of the epidermis of an animal; *esp* : one of the usu. pigmented filaments that form the characteristic coat of a mammal **b** : the hairy covering of an animal or a body part **2** : HAIRCLOTH **3 a** : a minute distance or amount : TRIFLE ⟨won by a *hair*⟩ **b** : a precise degree : NICETY ⟨aligned to a *hair*⟩ **4** : a filamentous structure that resembles hair ⟨leaf *hair*⟩ — **haired** \'ha(ə)rd, 'he(ə)rd\ *adj* — **hair·less** \'ha(ə)r-ləs, 'he(ə)r-\ *adj* — **hair·like** \-,līk\ *adj*

¹**hair·breadth** \'ha(ə)r-,bredth, 'he(ə)r-\ *or* **hairs·breadth** \'ha(ə)rz-, 'he(ə)r-\ *n* : a very small distance or margin

²**hairbreadth** *adj* : very narrow : CLOSE ⟨a *hairbreadth* escape⟩

hair·brush \'ha(ə)r-,brəsh, 'he(ə)r-\ *n* : a brush for the hair

hair cell *n* : a sensory cell (as of the organ of hearing) bearing hairlike processes

hair·cloth \-,klòth\ *n* : any of various stiff wiry fabrics esp. of horsehair or camel's hair used for upholstery or stiffening in garments

hair·cut \-,kət\ *n* : the act, process, or style of cutting and shaping the hair — **hair·cut·ter** \-,kət-ər\ *n* — **hair·cut·ting** \-,kət-iŋ\ *n*

hair·do \-,dü\ *n, pl* **hairdos** : a way of dressing a woman's hair : COIFFURE ⟨the very latest in *hairdos*⟩

hair·dress·er \-,dres-ər\ *n* : one who dresses or cuts women's hair — **hair·dress·ing** \-,dres-iŋ\ *n*

hair·line \-,līn\ *n* **1** : a very slender line **2** : the outline of the scalp or of the hair on the head — **hairline** *adj*

hair·pin \-,pin\ *n* **1** : a 2-pronged U-shaped pin to hold the hair in place **2** : something shaped like a hairpin; *esp* : a sharp turn in a road — **hairpin** *adj*

hair-rais·er \'ha(ə)r-,rā-zər, 'he(ə)r-\ *n* : THRILLER

hair-rais·ing \-,rā-ziŋ\ *adj* : causing terror, excitement, or astonishment ⟨a *hair-raising* climax⟩ — **hair-rais·ing·ly** \-,ziŋ-lē\ *adv*

hair seal *n* : any of a family of seals with a coarse hairy coat and no external ears — compare FUR SEAL

hair shirt *n* : a shirt made of rough animal hair worn next to the skin as a penance

hair-split·ter \'ha(ə)r-,split-ər, 'he(ə)r-\ *n* : a person who makes unnecessarily fine distinctions in reasoning or argument — **hair-split·ting** \-,split-iŋ\ *adj or n*

hair·spring \-,spriŋ\ *n* : a slender spiraled spring that regulates the motion of the balance wheel of a timepiece

hair·streak \-,strēk\ *n* : any of various small usu. dark butterflies with filamentous projections from the hind wings

hair trigger *n* : a trigger so adjusted as to permit a firearm to be fired by a very slight pressure

---

hair·worm \'ha(ə)r-ˌwərm, 'he(ə)r-\ *n* : any of various very slender worms; *esp* : HORSEHAIR WORM

hairy \'ha(ə)r-ē, 'he(ə)r-\ *adj* **hair·i·er; -est** **1** : bearing or covered with or as if with hair **2** : made of or resembling hair — **hair·i·ness** *n*

hake \'hāk\ *n* : any of several marine food fishes related to the cod

hal- *or* **halo-** *comb form* [Gk *hals* salt, sea; akin to E *salt*] : salt ⟨*halophyte*⟩

ha·la·kah \hä-'läk-ə, ˌhä-lə-'kä\ *n, pl* **ha·la·koth** \hə-'läk̲-ˌōt(h), ˌhä-lə-'kōt(h)\ *or* **halakahs** *often cap* : the body of Jewish law supplementing the scriptural law and forming esp. the legal part of the Talmud — **ha·lak·ic** \hə-'lak-ik, -'läk-\ *adj, often cap*

ha·la·tion \hā-'lā-shən\ *n* [*halo*] : the spreading (as in a developed photographic image) of light beyond its proper boundaries

hal·berd \'hal-bərd, 'hȯl-\ *or* **hal·bert** \-bərt\ *n* [MF *hallebarde*] : a long-handled weapon used both as a spear and as a battle-ax esp. in the 15th and 16th centuries — **hal·berd·ier** \ˌhal-bər-'di(ə)r, ˌhȯl-\ *n*

¹hal·cy·on \'hal-sē-ən\ *n* [Gk *halkyōn*] **1** : a bird identified with the kingfisher and held in ancient legend to nest at sea about the time of the winter solstice and to calm the waves during incubation **2** : KINGFISHER

²halcyon *adj* **1** : of or relating to the halcyon or its nesting period **2 a** : CALM, PEACEFUL **b** : HAPPY, GOLDEN ⟨the *halcyon* days of youth⟩

¹hale \'hāl\ *adj* [partly fr. northern ME *hale*, fr. OE *hāl* whole; partly fr. ME *hail*, fr. ON *heill*; akin to E *whole*] : free from defect, disease, or infirmity : SOUND, HEALTHY ⟨a *hale* and hearty old man⟩

²hale *vt* [MF *haler*] **1** : HAUL, PULL **2** : to compel to go ⟨*haled* him into court⟩

¹half \'haf, 'håf\ *n, pl* **halves** \'havz, 'håvz\ [OE *healf*] **1 a** : one of two equal parts into which a thing is divisible; *also* : a part of a thing approximately equal to the remainder **b** : half an hour **2** : one of a pair: as **a** : PARTNER **b** : SEMESTER, TERM **c** (1) : one of the two playing periods usu. separated by an interval that together make up the playing time of various games (2) : the turn of one team to bat in baseball — **by half** : by a great deal — **by halves** : in part : HALF-HEARTEDLY — **in half** : into two equal or nearly equal parts

²half *adj* **1 a** : being one of two equal parts **b** (1) : amounting to nearly half (2) : PARTIAL, IMPERFECT **2** : of half the usual size or extent — **half·ness** *n*

³half *adv* **1 a** : to the extent of half ⟨*half* full⟩ **b** : PARTIALLY ⟨*half* persuaded⟩ **2** : at all : by any means ⟨the song wasn't *half* bad⟩

half-and-half \ˌhaf-ən-'haf, ˌhåf-ən-'håf\ *n* : something that is half one thing and half another; *esp* : a mixture of two malt beverages — **half-and-half** *adj or adv*

half·back \'haf-ˌbak, 'håf-\ *n* : a football back who lines up on or near either flank; *also* : one of the players stationed behind the forward line in other games (as soccer or field hockey)

half-baked \-'bākt\ *adj* **1** : imperfectly baked : UNDERDONE **2 a** : not well planned **b** : lacking judgment, intelligence, or common sense

half blood *n* **1** : the relation between individuals having but one parent or parent strain in common **2** : one related to another in the half blood — **half-blood·ed** \-'bləd-əd\ *adj*

half boot *n* : a boot with a top reaching above the ankle

half-breed \'haf-ˌbrēd, 'håf-\ *n* : the offspring of parents of different races; *esp* : the offspring of an American Indian and a white person — **half-breed** *adj*

half brother *n* : a brother by one parent only

half-caste \'haf-ˌkast, 'håf-\ *n* : one of mixed racial descent : HALF-BREED — **half-caste** *adj*

half cock *n* **1** : the position of the hammer of a firearm when it is partly drawn back and locked in position so that it cannot be operated by a pull on the trigger **2** : a state of inadequate preparation or mental confusion — **half-cocked** \'haf-'käkt, 'håf-\ *adj*

half crown *n* : a British coin worth 2s 6d

half-dollar \'haf-'däl-ər, 'håf-\ *n* **1** : a coin representing one half of a dollar **2** : the sum of fifty cents

half eagle *n* : a five-dollar gold piece issued by the U.S. 1795–1916 and in 1929

half-ev·er·green \'haf-'ev-ər-ˌgrēn, 'håf-\ *adj* : tending to be evergreen in a mild climate but deciduous in a rigorous climate

half gainer *n* : a gainer in which the diver executes a half backward somersault and enters the water headfirst and facing the board

half-heart·ed \'haf-'härt-əd, 'håf-\ *adj* : lacking spirit or interest — **half-heart·ed·ly** *adv* — **half-heart·ed·ness** *n*

half hitch *n* : a simple knot so made as to be easily unfastened — see KNOT illustration

half hour *n* **1** : thirty minutes **2** : the middle point of an hour — **half-hour·ly** \'haf-'au̇(ə)r-lē, 'håf-\ *adv (or adj)*

half-knot \'haf-ˌnät, 'håf-\ *n* : a knot joining the ends of two cords and used in tying other knots

half-life \-ˌlīf\ *n* : the time required for half of the atoms of a radioactive substance to become disintegrated

half line *n* : a straight line extending from a point in one direction only

half-mast \'haf-'mast, 'håf-\ *n* : a point some distance but not necessarily halfway down below the top of a mast or staff or the peak of a gaff ⟨flags hanging at *half-mast*⟩

half-moon \-ˌmün\ *n* **1** : the moon when half its disk appears illuminated **2** : something shaped like a crescent **3** : the lunule of a fingernail

half nelson *n* : a wrestling hold in which one arm is thrust under the corresponding arm of the opponent generally from behind and the hand placed on the back of his neck

half note *n* : a musical note of half the value of a whole note

half·pen·ny \'hāp-(ə-)nē, *US also* 'haf-ˌpen-ē, 'håf-\ *n, pl* **half·pence** \'hā-pən(t)s, *US also* 'haf-ˌpen(t)s, 'håf-\ *or* **halfpennies** **1** : a British coin representing one half of a penny **2** : the sum of half a penny **3** : a small amount — **halfpenny** *adj*

half plane *n* : a part of a plane on one side of a straight line

half sister *n* : a sister by one parent only

half-slip \'haf-ˌslip, 'håf-\ *n* : PETTICOAT 1b

half sole *n* : a shoe sole extending from the shank forward — **half-sole** \'haf-'sōl, 'håf-\ *vt*

half sovereign *n* : a British gold coin worth ten shillings

half-staff \'haf-'staf, 'håf-\ *n* : HALF-MAST

half step *n* : the pitch interval between any two adjacent tones on a keyboard instrument — called also *semitone*

half tide *n* : the time or state halfway between flood and ebb

half tim·ber \'haf-'tim-bər, 'håf-\ *or* **half-tim·bered** \-bərd\ *adj* : constructed of wood framing with spaces filled with masonry ⟨a *half-timbered* house⟩

half time *n* : an intermission marking the completion of half of a game

half·tone \'haf-ˌtōn, 'håf-\ *n* **1** : HALF STEP **2 a** : any of the shades of gray between the darkest and the lightest parts of a photographic image **b** : a photoengraving made from an image photographed through a screen having a lattice of horizontal and vertical lines and then etched so that the details of the image are reproduced in dots

half-track \-ˌtrak\ *n* **1** : one of the endless-chain tracks used in place of rear wheels on a heavy-duty vehicle **2** : a motor vehicle propelled by half-tracks; *esp* : such a vehicle lightly armored for military use — **half-track** *or* **half-tracked** \-ˌtrakt\ *adj*

half-truth \-ˌtrüth\ *n* : a statement that is only partially true; *esp* : one that mingles truth and falsehood and is deliberately intended to deceive

half·way \-'wā\ *adj* **1** : midway between two points ⟨stop at the *halfway* mark⟩ **2** : PARTIAL ⟨*halfway* measures⟩ — **halfway** *adv*

half-wit \-ˌwit\ *n* : a foolish or imbecilic person — **half-wit·ted** \-'wit-əd\ *adj*

hal·i·but \'hal-ə-bət, 'häl-\ *n, pl* **halibut** *also* **halibuts** [ME *halybutte*, fr. *haly, holy* + *butte* flatfish; so called fr. its being eaten on holy days] : a marine food fish that is the largest flatfish of both the Atlantic and Pacific oceans

hal·ide \'hal-ˌīd, 'hā-ˌlīd\ *n* : a compound of a halogen with another element or a radical

hal·i·dom \'hal-əd-əm\ *or* **hal·i·dome** \-ə-ˌdōm\ *n* [OE *hāligdōm*, lit., holiness] *archaic* : a holy place or relic

hal·ite \'hal-ˌīt, 'hā-ˌlīt\ *n* : native sodium chloride

hal·i·to·sis \ˌhal-ə-'tō-səs\ *n* [L *halitus* breath, fr. *halare* to breathe] : a condition of having offensive breath

---

hall \hȯl\ *n* [OE *heall*] **1 a** : a large or imposing residence; *esp* : MANOR HOUSE **b** : a large building used for public purposes ⟨city *hall*⟩ **c** : one of the buildings of a college or university set apart for a special purpose ⟨Science *Hall*⟩⟨residence *halls*⟩ **d** : a college or a division of a college at some universities **e** : the common dining room of an English college **2** : the chief living room in a medieval castle **3 a** : the entrance room of a building : LOBBY **b** : a corridor or passage in a building **4** : a large room for assembly : AUDITORIUM **5** : a place used for public entertainment

Hal·lel \hä-'lāl\ *n* : a selection comprising Psalms 113–118 chanted during a Jewish feast (as the Passover)

¹hal·le·lu·jah \,hal-ə-'lü-yə\ *interj* [Hebrew *halălūyāh* praise ye Jehovah] — used to express praise, joy, or thanks

²hallelujah *n* : a shout or song of praise or thanksgiving

¹hall·mark \'hȯl-,märk\ *n* [Goldsmiths' *Hall*, London, England, where gold and silver articles were assayed and stamped] **1 a** : an official mark stamped on gold and silver articles in England to attest their purity **b** : a mark or device placed on an article to indicate origin, purity, or genuineness **2** : a distinguishing characteristic, trait, or feature

²hallmark *vt* : to stamp with a hallmark

hal·lo \hə-'lō, ha-\ *or* **hal·loo** \-'lü\ *var of* HOLLO

hal·low \'hal-ō\ *vt* [OE *hālgian*, fr. *hālig* holy] **1** : to make holy or set apart for holy use : CONSECRATE **2** : to respect greatly : VENERATE

hal·lowed \'hal-ōd, *in the Lord's Prayer also* 'hal-ə-wəd\ *adj* : CONSECRATED, SACRED

Hal·low·een \,hal-ə-'wēn, ,häl-\ *n* [short for *All Hallow even* the eve of All Saints' Day] : October 31 observed with merrymaking and the playing of pranks by children during the evening

Hal·low·mas \'hal-ō-,mas, -məs\ *n* : ALL SAINTS' DAY

hal·lu·ci·na·tion \hə-,lüs-ᵊn-'ā-shən\ *n* [L *hallucinari* to wander in mind] : the perceiving of objects or the experiencing of feelings that have no cause outside one's mind esp. as the result of a mental disorder or as the effect of a drug; *also* : something so perceived or experienced — **hal·lu·ci·nate** \-'lüs-ᵊn-,āt\ *vb* — **hal·lu·ci·na·tion·al** \-,lüs-ᵊn-'ā-shnəl, -shən-ᵊl\ *adj* — **hal·lu·ci·na·to·ry** \-'lüs-ᵊn-ə-,tōr-ē, -,tȯr-\ *adj*

hal·lu·ci·no·gen \hə-'lüs-ᵊn-ə-jən\ *n* : a substance that induces hallucinations — **hal·lu·ci·no·gen·ic** \-,lüs-ᵊn-ə-'jen-ik\ *adj*

hal·lux \'hal-əks\ *n, pl* **hal·lu·ces** \'hal-(y)ə-,sēz\ [L] : BIG TOE

hall·way \'hȯl-,wā\ *n* **1** : an entrance hall **2** : CORRIDOR

¹ha·lo \'hā-lō\ *n, pl* **halos** *or* **haloes** [Gk *halōs* threshing floor, disk, halo] **1** : a circle of light around the sun or moon caused by the presence of tiny ice crystals in the air **2** : something resembling a halo: as **a** : NIMBUS **b** : a differentiated zone surrounding a central object **3** : the aura of glory, veneration, or sentiment surrounding an idealized person or thing

²halo *vt* : to form into or surround with a halo

halo- — see HAL-

hal·o·bi·ont \,hal-ō-'bī-,änt\ *n* [Gk *biount-, biōn*, prp. of *bioun* to live, fr. *bios* life] : HALOPHILE

hal·o·gen \'hal-ə-jən\ *n* : any of the five elements fluorine, chlorine, bromine, iodine, and astatine existing in the free state normally as diatomic molecules

hal·o·ge·ton \,hal-ə-'jēt-ᵊn\ *n* [Gk *geitōn* neighbor] : a coarse annual herb related to the goosefoots that is a noxious weed in western No. America

hal·o·phile \'hal-ə-,fīl\ *n* : an organism that flourishes in a salty environment — **hal·o·phil·ic** \,hal-ə-'fil-ik\ *adj*

hal·o·phyte \'hal-ə-,fīt\ *n* : a plant that grows in salty soil. wet soil and physiologically resembles a true xerophyte — **hal·o·phyt·ic** \,hal-ə-'fit-ik\ *adj* — **hal·o·phyt·ism** \'hal-ə-,fīt,-iz-əm\ *n*

¹halt \'hȯlt\ *adj* [OE *healt*] : LAME

²halt *vi* **1** : to walk or proceed lamely : LIMP **2** : to stand in perplexity or doubt between alternate courses : WAVER **3** : to display weakness or imperfection : FALTER

³halt *n* : STOP ⟨call a *halt*⟩

⁴halt *vb* [G, fr. *halten* to hold, stop; akin to E *hold*] **1** : to cease marching or journeying **2** : DISCONTINUE, TERMINATE **3** : to bring to a stop : END

¹hal·ter \'hȯl-tər\ *n* [OE *hælftre*] **1 a** : a rope or strap for leading or tying an animal **b** : a headstall to which a lead may be attached **2** : a rope for hanging criminals : NOOSE; *also* : death by hanging **3** : a woman's blouse that is typically held in place by straps around the neck and across the back and leaves the back, arms, and midriff bare

²halter *vt* **hal·tered; hal·ter·ing** \-t(ə-)riŋ\ **1 a** : to catch with or as if with a halter; *also* : to put a halter on **b** : HANG **2** : to put restraint upon : HAMPER

³hal·ter \'hȯl-tər\ *or* **hal·tere** \-,ti(ə)r\ *n, pl* **hal·teres** \hȯl-'ti(ə)r-(,)ēz, 'hȯl-,ti(ə)rz\ [NL *halter*, fr. Gk *halter* weight held in the hand to assist jumping, fr. *hallesthai* to jump] : one of a pair of club-shaped organs that are the modified second pair of wings of a 2-winged insect and serve to maintain balance in flight

halt·ing \'hȯl-tiŋ\ *adj* **1** : LAME, LIMPING **2** : UNCERTAIN, FALTERING — **halt·ing·ly** \-tiŋ-lē\ *adv*

halve \'hav, 'håv\ *vt* **1** : to divide into two equal parts **b** : to reduce to one half ⟨*halving* the cost⟩ **c** : to share equally **2** : to play (as a hole) in the same number of strokes as one's opponent at golf

halv·ers \'hav-ərz, 'håv-\ *n pl* : half shares : HALVES

halves *pl of* HALF

hal·yard *or* **hal·liard** \'hal-yərd\ *n* [ME *halier*, fr. *halen* to pull, haul] : a rope or tackle for hoisting and lowering

¹ham \'ham\ *n* [OE *hamm* hollow of the knee] **1** : a buttock with its associated thigh — usu. used in pl. **2** : a cut of meat consisting of a thigh; *esp* : one from a hog **3 a** : an unskillful but showy performer **b** : an operator of an amateur radio station — **ham** *adj*

²ham *vb* **hammed; ham·ming** : to execute with exaggerated speech or gestures : OVERACT

hama·dry·ad \,ham-ə-'drī-əd, -,ad\ *n* [Gk *hamadryad-, hamadryas*] : WOOD NYMPH

Ha·man \'hā-mən\ *n* : an enemy of the Jews hanged according to the book of Esther for plotting their destruction

ha·mate \'hā-,māt\ *also* **ha·mat·ed** \-,māt-əd\ *adj* : shaped like a hook

ham·burg·er \'ham-,bər-gər\ *or* **ham·burg** \-,bərg\ *n* [G, of Hamburg, fr. *Hamburg*, Germany] **1 a** : ground beef **b** : a cooked patty of ground beef **2** : a sandwich consisting of a patty of hamburger in a split round bun

hame \'hām\ *n* : one of two curved projections which are attached to the collar of a draft horse and to which the traces are fastened

Ham·ite \'ham-,īt\ *n* [fr. *Ham*, son of Noah, their supposed ancestor] : a member of a mainly Caucasoid group of chiefly northern African peoples

Ham·it·ic \ha-'mit-ik, hə-\ *adj* : of, relating to, or characteristic of the Hamites or one of the Hamitic languages

Hamitic languages *n pl* : the Berber, Cushitic, and sometimes Egyptian branches of the Afro-Asiatic languages

ham·let \'ham-lət\ *n* [MF *hamelet*, dim. of *ham* dwelling, village, of Gmc origin; akin to E *home*] : a small group of houses in the country

¹ham·mer \'ham-ər\ *n* [OE *hamor*] **1 a** : a hand tool that consists of a solid head set crosswise on a handle and is used for pounding (as in driving nails) **b** : a power tool that substitutes a metal block or a drill for the head for pounding (as in driving posts or breaking rock) **2** : something that resembles a hammer in shape or action (as the part of a gun whose striking action causes explosion of the charge) **3** : MALLEUS **4** : a metal sphere usu. weighing about 16 pounds that is hurled in an athletic event

heads of hammers

²hammer *vb* **ham·mered; ham·mer·ing** \'ham-(ə-)riŋ\ **1** : to strike blows esp. repeatedly with or as if with a hammer : POUND **2 a** : to make repeated efforts **b** : to reiterate an opinion or attitude **3 a** : to beat, drive, or shape with repeated blows of a hammer **b** : to fasten or build with a hammer **4** : to produce or bring about as if by repeated blows ⟨*hammer* out a policy⟩

hammer and sickle *n* : an emblem consisting of a crossed hammer and sickle used chiefly as a symbol of Russian Communism

hammer and tongs *adv* : with great force and violence

ham·mered *adj* : having surface indentations produced or appearing to have been produced by hammering ⟨*hammered* copper⟩

ham·mer·head \'ham-ər-,hed\ *n* **1** : the striking part of a hammer **2** : BLOCKHEAD **3** : any of various active voracious medium-sized sharks that have the eyes at the ends of lateral extensions of the flattened head

ham·mer·less \-ləs\ *adj* : having the hammer concealed ⟨*hammerless* gun⟩

ham·mer·lock \-,läk\ *n* : a wrestling hold in which an opponent's arm is held bent behind his back

ham·mer·toe \-,tō\ *n* : a toe (as the second) deformed by permanent angular flexion

¹ham·mock \'ham-ək\ *n* [Sp *hamaca*, of AmerInd origin] : a swinging couch or bed usu. made of netting or canvas and slung by cords from supports at each end

²hammock *n* : HUMMOCK

ham·my \'ham-ē\ *adj* **ham·mi·er**; **-est** : characteristic of a ham actor

¹ham·per \'ham-pər\ *vt* **ham·pered**; **ham·per·ing** \-p(ə-)riŋ\ [ME *hamperen*] **1** : to restrict or interfere with the movement or operation of : IMPEDE, DISRUPT ⟨fog *hampered* the traffic⟩ **2** : ENCUMBER

syn FETTER, SHACKLE: HAMPER may imply the effect of any hindering or restraining influence; FETTER suggests a restraining so severe that freedom to move or progress is almost lost; SHACKLE is still stronger and suggests total loss of freedom to act or to move from one position

²hamper *n* [ME *hanaper*, fr. MF *hanapier* case to hold goblets] : a large basket usu. with a cover ⟨a clothes *hamper*⟩ ⟨a picnic *hamper*⟩

ham·ster \'ham(p)-stər\ *n* [G, of Slavic origin] : any of various stocky short-tailed Old World rodents with large cheek pouches

¹ham·string \'ham-,striŋ\ *n* **1** : either of two groups of tendons at the back of the human knee **2** : a large tendon above and behind the hock of a quadruped

²hamstring *vt* **-strung** \-,strəŋ\; **-string·ing** \-,striŋ-iŋ\ **1** : to cripple by cutting the leg tendons **2** : to make ineffective or powerless : CRIPPLE

ham·u·lus \'ham-yə-ləs\ *n, pl* **-li** \-,lī, -,lē\ [L, dim. of *hamus* hook] : a hooked process : HOOK

Han \'hän\ *n* : a Chinese dynasty dated 207 B.C.–A.D. 220 and marked by centralized bureaucratic control, a revival of learning, and the penetration of Buddhism

¹hand \'hand\ *n* [OE] **1 a** : the free end part of the fore-limb when modified (as in man) for handling, grasping, and holding **b** : any of various anatomical parts that are homologous or analogous to the hand (as the hind foot of an ape or the chela of a crab) **2** : something resembling a hand: as **a** : an indicator or pointer on a dial **b** : a figure of a hand with forefinger extended to point a direction or call attention to something **c** : a cluster of bananas developed from a single flower group **3** : personal possession : CONTROL, DIRECTION ⟨in the *hands* of the enemy⟩ **4 a** : SIDE, DIRECTION ⟨fighting on either *hand*⟩ **b** : a side or aspect of an issue or argument ⟨on the one *hand* . . . on the other *hand*⟩ **5** : a pledge esp. of betrothal or bestowal in marriage **6 a** : style of penmanship : HANDWRITING **b** : SIGNATURE **7 a** : SKILL, ABILITY **b** : a part or share in doing something ⟨take a *hand* in the work⟩ **8** : SOURCE ⟨learn at first *hand*⟩ **9** : a unit of measure equal to 4 inches used esp. for the height of horses **10** : a round of applause ⟨give him a *hand*⟩ **11 a** (1) : a player in a card game or board game (2) : the cards or pieces held by a player **b** : a single round in a game **12 a** : one who performs or executes a particular work ⟨two portraits by the same *hand*⟩ **b** : a hired worker : LABORER **c** : a member of a ship's crew ⟨all *hands* on deck⟩ **d** : one skilled in a particular activity or field **13 a** : HANDIWORK **b** : style of execution : WORKMANSHIP ⟨the *hand* of a master⟩ **c** : TOUCH, FEEL — **at hand 1** : near in time or place — **by hand** : with the hands — **in hand 1** : in one's possession or control **2** : in preparation — **off one's hands** : out of one's care or charge — **on all hands** *or* **on every hand** : EVERYWHERE — **on hand 1** : in present possession ⟨goods *on hand*⟩ **2** : about to appear : PENDING **3** : in attendance : PRESENT — **out of hand 1** : without delay : FORTHWITH **2** : done with **3** : out of control — **to hand 1** : into possession **2** : within reach **3** : into control or subjection

²hand *vt* **1** : to lead, guide, or assist with the hand

: CONDUCT ⟨*hand* a lady into a bus⟩ **2 a** : to give, pass, or transmit with the hand ⟨*hand* a person a letter⟩ **b** : PRESENT, PROVIDE ⟨*handed* him a surprise⟩

hand and foot *adv* : TOTALLY, COMPLETELY ⟨she waited on her husband *hand and foot*⟩

hand·bag \'han(d)-,bag\ *n* **1** : TRAVELING BAG **2** : a woman's bag used for carrying small personal articles and money

hand·ball \-,bȯl\ *n* **1** : a small rubber ball used in the game of handball **2** : a game played in a walled court or against a single wall or board by two or four players who use their hands to strike the ball

hand·bar·row \-,bar-ō\ *n* : a flat rectangular frame with handles at both ends that is carried by two persons

hand·bill \-,bil\ *n* : a small printed sheet to be distributed by hand

hand·book \-,buk\ *n* : a small book of facts or useful information usu. about a particular subject : MANUAL

hand·breadth \-,bredth\ *n* : any of various units of length based on the breadth of a hand varying from about 2½ to 4 inches

hand·car \'han(d)-,kär\ *n* : a small four-wheeled railroad car propelled by a hand-operated mechanism or by a small motor

hand·cart \-,kärt\ *n* : a cart drawn or pushed by hand

hand·clasp \-,klasp\ *n* : HANDSHAKE

¹hand·craft \-,kraft\ *n* : HANDICRAFT

²handcraft *vt* : to fashion by handicraft ⟨*handcrafted* materials⟩

¹hand·cuff \-,kəf\ *vt* : to apply handcuffs to : MANACLE

²handcuff *n* : a metal fastening that can be locked around a wrist and that is usu. connected by a chain or bar with another handcuff — usu. used in pl.

handcuffs

hand down *vt* **1** : to transmit in succession ⟨*handed down* from generation to generation⟩ **2** : to make official formulation of and express ⟨the opinion of a court⟩

hand·ed \'han-dəd\ *adj* : having or using such or so many hands ⟨a right-*handed* person⟩ — **hand·ed·ness** *n*

hand·ful \'han(d)-,ful\ *n, pl* **handfuls** \-,fulz\ *or* **hands·ful** \'han(d)z-,ful\ **1** : as much or as many as the hand will grasp **2** : a small quantity or number **3** : as much as one can control or manage

hand glass *n* : a small mirror with a handle

hand·grip \'han(d)-,grip\ *n* **1** : a grasping with the hand **2** : HANDLE

hand·gun \'han(d)-,gən\ *n* : a firearm held and fired with one hand

¹hand·i·cap \'han-di-,kap\ *n* [obs. E *handicap*, a game in which forfeits were held in a cap, fr. *hand in cap*] **1** : a race or contest in which an artificial advantage is given to or disadvantage imposed on a contestant to equalize chances of winning; *also* : the advantage given or disadvantage imposed **2 a** : a disadvantage that makes progress or success more difficult ⟨his overweight was a *handicap*⟩

²handicap *vt* **-capped**; **-cap·ping 1 a** : to give a handicap to **b** : to assign handicaps to **2** : to put at a disadvantage ⟨*handicapped* by poor health⟩

hand·i·craft \'han-di-,kraft\ *n* [alter. of *handcraft*] **1** : an occupation (as weaving or pottery making) requiring skill with the hands **2** : the articles fashioned by those engaged in handicraft — **hand·i·craft·er** \-,kraf-tər\ *n* — **hand·i·crafts·man** \-,kraf(t)s-mən\ *n*

Hand·ie-Talk·ie \,han-dē-'tȯ-kē\ *trademark* — used for a small portable radio transmitter-receiver

hand·i·ly \'han-də-lē\ *adv* : in a handy manner : EASILY, CONVENIENTLY

hand·i·ness \-dē-nəs\ *n* : the quality or state of being handy

hand in glove *or* **hand and glove** *adv* : in extremely close relationship or agreement

hand in hand *adv* : in union : CONJOINTLY

hand·i·work \'han-di-,wərk\ *n* [OE *handgeweorc*, fr. *hand* + *geweorc* work, fr. *ge-*, collective prefix, + *weorc* work] **1** : work done by the hands **2** : work one has done himself ⟨a writer's pride in his *handiwork*⟩

hand·ker·chief \'haŋ-kər-chəf, -,(,)chif, -,chēf\ *n, pl* **-chiefs** *also* **-chieves** \-chəfs, -,(,)chifs, -,chēvz⟩ ⟨used by many who

---

ə abut; ᵊ kitten; ər further; a back; ā bake; ä cot, cart; au̇ out; ch chin; e less; ē easy; g gift; i trip; ī life

have sing. -chəf *or* -(,)chif\, -,chēfs, -chəvz, -(,)chivz\ **1** : a small usu. square piece of cloth used for various personal purposes or as a costume accessory **2** : KERCHIEF 1

hand language *n* : communication by means of a manual alphabet

¹han·dle \'han-dᵊl\ *n* [OE] **1** : a part that is designed esp. to be grasped by the hand **2** : something that resembles a handle **3** *slang* : NAME — **han·dled** \-dᵊld\ *adj* — **off the handle** : into a state of sudden and violent anger

²handle *vb* **han·dled; han·dling** \-dliŋ, -dᵊl-iŋ\ [OE *handlian*] **1 a** : to touch, feel, hold, or otherwise affect with the hand **b** : to manage with the hands 〈*handle* a horse〉 **2 a** : to deal with in writing or speaking or in the plastic arts **b** : CONTROL, DIRECT **c** : to train and act as second for (a prizefighter) **3** : to deal with or act on 〈*handle* a problem〉 **4** : to deal or trade in 〈a store that *handles* rugs〉 **5** : to act, behave, or feel in a certain way when managed or directed 〈a car that *handles* well〉

han·dle·a·ble \'han-dᵊl-ə-bəl\ *adj* : capable of being handled

han·dle·bar \'han-dᵊl-,bär\ *n* : a straight or bent bar with a handle (as for steering a bicycle) at each end

hand lens *n* : a magnifying glass to be held in the hands

han·dler \'han-dlər, -dᵊl-ər\ *n* **1** : one that handles **2** : one that helps to train a prizefighter or acts as his second during a match

hand·made \'han(d)-'mād\ *adj* : made by hand and not by machine

hand·maid \-,mād\ *or* **hand·maid·en** \-,mād-ᵊn\ *n* : a female servant or attendant

hand-me-down \'han(d)-mē-,daún\ *adj* : worn or put in use by one person or group after being discarded by another — **hand-me-down** *n*

hand·off \'han-,dóf\ *n* : a football play in which the ball is handed by one player to another nearby

hand on *vt* : to hand down (sense 1)

hand organ *n* : a barrel organ operated by a hand crank

hand·out \'han-,daút\ *n* **1** : a portion of food, clothing, or money given to or as if to a beggar **2** : an information sheet for free distribution **3** : a prepared statement released to the press

hand over *vt* : to yield control of

hand·pick \'han(d)-'pik\ *vt* : to select personally 〈a *hand-picked* successor〉

hand·rail \'han-,drāl\ *n* : a narrow rail for grasping with the hand as a support (as on a staircase)

hand·saw \'han(d)-,só\ *n* : a saw used with one hand; *esp* : a woodworker's ripsaw or crosscut saw

hands·breadth \'han(d)z-,bredth\ *var of* HANDBREADTH

hands down *adv* : without question : EASILY

hand·sel \'han(t)-səl\ *n* [ME *hansell*] **1** : a gift made as a token of good wishes or luck esp. at the beginning of a new year **2** : EARNEST, FORETASTE

hand·set \'han(d)-,set\ *n* : a combined telephone transmitter and receiver mounted on a handle

hand·shake \-,shāk\ *n* : a clasping (as in greeting or farewell) of right hands by two people

hand·some \'han(t)-səm\ *adj* [ME *handsom* easy to manipulate] **1** : moderately large : SIZABLE 〈a *handsome* fortune〉 **2** : marked by graciousness or generosity : LIBERAL (paid him a *handsome* tribute) 〈a *handsome* tip〉 **3** : having a pleasing and usu. impressive or dignified appearance — **hand·some·ly** *adv* — **hand·some·ness** *n*

hand·spike \'han(d)-,spīk\ *n* : a bar used as a lever (as in working a windlass on a boat)

hand·spring \-,spriŋ\ *n* : a feat of tumbling in which the body turns forward or backward in a full circle from a standing position and lands first on the hands and then on the feet

hand-to-hand \,han-tə-'hand\ *adj* : being at very close quarters 〈*hand-to-hand* combat〉

hand-to-mouth \-tə-'maúth\ *adj* : having or providing nothing to spare : PRECARIOUS 〈a *hand-to-mouth* existence〉

hand·wheel \'han(d)-,hwēl\ *n* : a wheel worked by hand

hand·work \'han-,dwərk\ *n* : work done with the hands and not by machine

hand·wo·ven \'han-'dwō-vən\ *adj* : produced on a hand-operated loom

hand·writ·ing \'han-,drīt-iŋ\ *n* **1** : writing done by

hand; *esp* : the cast or form of writing peculiar to a particular person **2** : something written by hand : MANUSCRIPT — **hand·writ·ten** \-,drit-ᵊn\ *adj*

handy \'han-dē\ *adj* **hand·i·er; -est** **1 a** : conveniently near **b** : convenient for use 〈a *handy* reference book〉 **c** : easily handled 〈a *handy* sloop〉 **2** : clever in using the hands : DEXTEROUS 〈*handy* with a needle〉

handy·man \-dē-,man\ *n* : a man who does odd jobs

¹hang \'haŋ\ *vb* **hung** \'həŋ\ *also* **hanged** \'haŋd\; **hang·ing** \'haŋ-iŋ\ [OE *hōn* (v.t.) & OE *hangian* (v.i. & v.t.)] **1 a** : to fasten or be fastened to some elevated point without support from below : SUSPEND, DANGLE **b** : to put to death or be put to death by hanging from a rope tied round the neck 〈sentenced to be *hanged*〉 **c** : to fasten so as to allow free motion upon a point of suspension 〈*hang* a door〉 **d** : to fit or fix in position or at a proper angle 〈*hang* an ax to its helve〉 **e** : to adjust the hem of (a skirt) so as to hang evenly and at a proper height when worn **2** : to cover, decorate, or furnish by hanging pictures, trophies, or drapery **3** : to hold or bear in a suspended or inclined manner : DROOP 〈*hung* his head in shame〉 **4** : to fasten to a wall 〈*hang* wallpaper〉 **5** : to display (pictures) in a gallery **6** : to remain poised or stationary in the air 〈clouds *hanging* low overhead〉 **7** : to stay with persistence **8** : IMPEND 〈evils *hang* over the nation〉 **9** : DEPEND 〈election *hangs* on one vote〉 **10 a** (1) : to take hold for support : CLING 〈she *hung* on his arm〉 (2) : to keep persistent contact 〈dogs *hung* to the trail〉 **b** : to be burdensome or oppressive 〈time *hangs* on his hands〉 **c** : LEAN **11 a** : to be in suspense : suffer delay 〈the decision is still *hanging*〉 **b** : to occupy an uncertain mid-position **12** : to lean, incline, or jut over or downward **13** : to be in a state of rapt attention 〈*hung* on his every word〉 **14** : LINGER, LOITER **15** : to fit or fall from the figure in easy lines 〈the coat *hangs* loosely〉 — **hang·able** \'haŋ-ə-bəl\ *adj* — **hang fire 1** : to be slow in the explosion of a charge after its primer has been discharged **2** : DELAY, HESITATE

²hang *n* **1** : the manner in which a thing hangs 〈the *hang* of a skirt〉 **2 a** : peculiar and significant meaning 〈the *hang* of an argument〉 **b** : the special method of doing, using, or dealing with something : KNACK 〈get the *hang* of driving a car〉 — **give a hang** *or* **care a hang** : to be concerned or worried

¹hang·ar \'haŋ-ər, 'haŋ-,gər\ *n* [F] : SHELTER, SHED; *esp* : a covered and usu. enclosed area for housing and repairing airplanes

²hangar *vt* : to place in a hangar

hang around *vi* **1** : to pass time or stay aimlessly : loiter idly 〈*hang around* in drugstores〉 **2** : to spend one's time in company

hang back *vi* **1** : to drag behind others **2** : to be reluctant : HESITATE, FALTER

hang·dog \'haŋ-,dóg\ *adj* **1** : ASHAMED, GUILTY 〈had a *hangdog* look about him when caught〉 **2** : ABJECT, COWED

hang·er \'haŋ-ər\ *n* **1** : one that hangs or causes to be hung or hanged **2** : something that hangs, overhangs, or is suspended; *esp* : a small sword formerly used by seamen **3** : a device by which or to which something is hung or hangs: as **a** : a strap on a sword belt by which a sword or dagger can be suspended **b** : a loop (as on a collar) by which a garment is hung up **c** : a device that fits inside or around a garment (as a suit or a pair of trousers) for hanging from a hook or rod

hang·er-on \'haŋ-ər-,ón, -,än\ *n*, *pl* **hangers-on** : one that hangs around a person, place, or institution in hope of personal gain

¹hang·ing \'haŋ-iŋ\ *n* **1** : an execution by strangling or breaking the neck by a suspended noose **2** : something hung: as **a** : CURTAIN — usu. used in pl. **b** : a covering (as a tapestry) for a wall — usu. used in pl. **3** : a downward slope : DECLIVITY

²hanging *adj* **1** : situated or lying on steeply sloping ground 〈*hanging* gardens〉 **2 a** : OVERHANGING **b** : supported only by the wall on one side 〈a *hanging* staircase〉 **3** : adapted for sustaining a hanging object **4** : punishable by death by hanging 〈a *hanging* offense〉

hanging indention *n* : indention of all the lines of a paragraph except the first

hang·man \'haŋ-mən\ *n* : a person who hangs condemned criminals

hang·nail \-,nāl\ *n* : a bit of skin hanging loose at the side or base of a fingernail

hang on *vi* **1** : to keep hold : hold onto something **2** : to persist tenaciously ⟨a cold that *hung on* all spring⟩ — **hang on to** : to hold, grip, or keep tenaciously ⟨learned to *hang on to* his money⟩

hang out \(')han-'aùt\ *vb* **1** : to protrude in a downward direction **2** : to habitually spend one's time idly ⟨*hangs out* in poolrooms⟩ **3** : to display outside as an announcement to the public

hang-out \'han-,aùt\ *n* : a place in which a person spends a great deal of time or which he visits repeatedly

hang·over \'han-,ō-vər\ *n* **1** : something (as a surviving custom) that remains from what is past **2** : disagreeable aftereffects following great excitement or excess (as in consumption of alcohol)

hang together *vi* **1** : to remain united : stand by one another **2** : to form a consistent or coherent whole

hang up \(')han-'əp\ *vb* **1 a** : to place on a hook or hanger designed for the purpose ⟨*hung up* his coat⟩ **b** : to replace (a telephone receiver) on the cradle so that the connection is broken; *also* : to terminate a telephone conversation **2** : to stick or snag or cause to stick or snag so as to be immovable ⟨the ship *hung up* on a sandbar⟩

hang-up \'han-,əp\ *n* : a source of mental or emotional difficulty

hank \'hank\ *n* [of Scand origin] : COIL, LOOP, SKEIN; *esp* : a coiled or looped bundle (as of yarn)

han·ker \'han-kər\ *vi* **han·kered; han·ker·ing** \-k(ə-)rin\ : to have an eager or persistent desire ⟨*hanker* after fame and fortune⟩ **syn** see LONG — **han·ker·er** \-kər-ər\ *n*

han·ky-pan·ky \,han-kē-'pan-kē\ *n* : questionable or underhand activity : TRICKERY

Han·o·ve·ri·an \,han-ə-'vir-ē-ən, -'ver-\ *adj* : of, relating to, or supporting the German ducal house of Hanover or the descendant British royal house furnishing sovereigns from 1714 to 1901 — **Hanoverian** *n*

Han·sa \'han(t)-sə\ *or* **Hanse** \'han(t)s\ *n* : a league of merchants of various free German cities in the medieval period and later of the cities themselves organized to secure greater safety and privileges in trading — **Han·se·at·ic** \,han(t)-sē-'at-ik\ *n or adj*

han·sel *var of* HANDSEL

Han·sen's disease \'han(t)-sənz-\ *n* [after Armauer *Hansen* d1912 Norwegian physician] : LEPROSY

han·som \'han(t)-səm\ *n* [after Joseph A. *Hansom* d1882 English architect who designed it] : a light 2-wheeled covered carriage with the driver's seat elevated behind

hansom

Ha·nuk·kah \'kän-ə-kə, 'hän-\ *n* [Heb *hănukkāh* dedication] : an 8-day Jewish festival of lights celebrated in November or December in commemoration of the rededication of the Temple of Jerusalem after its defilement by Antiochus of Syria

hao·le \'haù-(,)lā\ *n* [Hawaiian] : one who is not a member of the native race of Hawaii; *esp* : WHITE

¹hap \'hap\ *n* [ON *happ* good luck] **1** : HAPPENING **2** : CHANCE, FORTUNE

²hap *vi* **happed; hap·ping** : HAPPEN

¹hap·haz·ard \hap-'haz-ərd\ *n* : CHANCE

²haphazard *adj* : marked by lack of plan, order, or direction : AIMLESS **syn** see RANDOM — **haphazard** *adv* — **hap·haz·ard·ly** *adv* — **hap·haz·ard·ness** *n*

hapl- *or* **haplo-** *comb form* [Gk *haploos*] **1** : single : simple **2** : of or relating to the haploid generation or condition ⟨*haplosis*⟩

hap·less \'hap-ləs\ *adj* : having no luck : UNFORTUNATE ⟨a *hapless* child⟩ — **hap·less·ly** *adv* — **hap·less·ness** *n*

hap·loid \'hap-,lòid\ *adj* : having the gametic number of chromosomes or half the number characteristic of somatic cells — **haploid** *n* — **hap·loi·dy** \-,lòid-ē\ *n*

hap·ly \'hap-lē\ *adv* : by chance, luck, or accident

hap·pen \'hap-ən, -ᵊm\ *vi* **hap·pened; hap·pen·ing** \'hap-(ə-)nin\ [ME *happenen*, fr. ¹*hap*] **1** : to occur or come about by chance **2** : to take place **3** : to have occasion or opportunity without intention : CHANCE ⟨*happened* to overhear⟩ **4 a** : to meet or find something by chance

⟨*happened* on the right answer⟩ **b** : to appear casually or by chance **5** : to come esp. by way of injury or harm ⟨I promise nothing will *happen* to you⟩

syn HAPPEN, CHANCE, OCCUR, TRANSPIRE mean to come about. HAPPEN applies to whatever comes about without cause or intention; CHANCE stresses lack of plan or apparent cause; OCCUR, often interchangeable with HAPPEN, stresses a being brought to sight or to mind or attention ⟨theoretically possible, but not *occurring* in reality⟩ ⟨it never *occurred* to him she would not like it⟩ TRANSPIRE implies a coming out or becoming known but is often equal to OCCUR ⟨what *happened* that day only *transpired* much later⟩

hap·pen·ing \'hap-(ə-)nin\ *n* **1** : OCCURRENCE **2** : an event or series of events designed to evoke a spontaneous reaction to sensory, emotional, or spiritual stimuli

hap·pen·stance \'hap-ən-,stan(t)s, 'hap-ᵊm-\ *n* : a circumstance regarded as due to chance

hap·pi·ly \'hap-ə-lē\ *adv* **1** : FORTUNATELY, LUCKILY ⟨*happily*, no one was injured⟩ **2** : in a happy manner or state ⟨lived *happily* ever after⟩ **3** : APTLY, SUCCESSFULLY ⟨his remarks were *happily* worded⟩

hap·pi·ness \'hap-i-nəs\ *n* **1** *archaic* : good fortune : PROSPERITY **2 a** : a state of well-being and contentment : JOY **b** : a pleasurable satisfaction **3** : APTNESS, FELICITY

hap·py \'hap-ē\ *adj* **hap·pi·er; -est** [ME, fr. *hap*] **1** : FORTUNATE, LUCKY **2** : notably well adapted or fitting : FELICITOUS ⟨a *happy* choice for governor⟩ **3 a** : enjoying well-being and contentment : JOYOUS ⟨*happy* in his work⟩ **b** : expressing or suggestive of happiness : PLEASANT ⟨*happy* laughter⟩ **c** : PLEASED, GRATIFIED ⟨*happy* to accept an invitation⟩

hap·py-go-lucky \,hap-ē-(,)gō-'lək-ē\ *adj* : blithely unconcerned : CAREFREE

Haps·burg \'haps-,bərg, 'häps-,bùrg\ *adj* : of or relating to a princely German family furnishing the rulers of Austria from 1278 to 1918 and of Spain from 1516 to 1700 and many of the Holy Roman emperors — **Hapsburg** *n*

hap·ten \'hap-,ten\ *n* [G, fr. Gk *haptesthai* to touch] : a substance that is not an antigen but has some antigenic properties

hara-kiri \,har-i-'ki(ə)r-ē, -'kar-ē\ *n* [Jap *harakiri*] : suicide by disembowelment formerly practiced by the Japanese samurai

ha·rangue \hə-'ran\ *n* [MF, fr. It *aringa*] **1** : a speech addressed to a public assembly **2** : a bombastic ranting speech or writing **3** : LECTURE — **harangue** *vb* — **ha·rangu·er** \-'ran-ər\ *n*

ha·rass \hə-'ras, 'har-əs\ *vt* [F *harasser*, fr. MF *harer* to set dogs on, fr. OF *hare*, interj. used to incite dogs] **1** : to tire out by persistent efforts : worry or annoy with repeated attacks **2** : to lay waste : HARRY **syn** see ANNOY — **ha·rass·ment** \-mənt\ *n*

¹har·bin·ger \'här-bən-jər\ *n* [ME *herbergere* lodging keeper, one sent ahead to provide lodgings, fr. OF, lodging keeper, fr. *herberge* inn, of Gmc origin] : a messenger sent on ahead : one that announces or shows what is coming : FORERUNNER ⟨robins are *harbingers* of spring⟩

²harbinger *vt* : to be a harbinger of : PRESAGE

¹har·bor \'här-bər\ *n* [ME *herberge*, *herborowe*] **1** : place of security : REFUGE **2** : a part of a body of water protected and deep enough to furnish anchorage; *esp* : one with port facilities — **har·bor·less** \-ləs\ *adj*

²harbor *vb* **har·bored; har·bor·ing** \-b(ə-)rin\ **1 a** : to give shelter or refuge to **b** : to be the home or habitat of : CONTAIN **2** : to hold a thought or feeling of **3** : to take shelter in or as if in a harbor — **har·bor·er** *n*

har·bor·age \'här-bə-rij\ *n* : SHELTER, HARBOR

har·bour \'här-bər\ *chiefly Brit var of* HARBOR

¹hard \'härd\ *adj* [OE *heard*] **1** : not easily penetrated, cut, or divided into parts : not soft **2 a** : strong in alcoholic content ⟨*hard* distilled liquors⟩ **b** : characterized by the presence of salts that prevent lathering with soap ⟨*hard* water⟩ **3 a** : having high penetrating power ⟨*hard* X rays⟩ **b** : having or producing relatively great photographic contrast ⟨*hard* negative⟩ **4 a** : metallic as distinct from paper ⟨*hard* money⟩ **b** : convertible into gold : stable in value ⟨*hard* currency⟩ **5** : NAPLESS ⟨*hard* woolens⟩ **6 a** : physically fit (in good *hard* condition) **b** : free of weakness or flaw **7 a** (1) : FIRM, DEFINITE ⟨*hard* agreement⟩ (2) : FACTUAL, ACTUAL ⟨*hard* evidence⟩

b : CLOSE, SEARCHING ⟨*hard* look⟩ **c :** free from sentimentality or illusion **:** REALISTIC ⟨good *hard* sense⟩ **d :** OBDURATE, UNFEELING ⟨*hard* heart⟩ **8 a** (1) **:** difficult to bear or endure ⟨*hard* luck⟩ ⟨*hard* times⟩ (2) **:** OPPRESSIVE, UNJUST ⟨*hard* greedy landlord⟩ **b :** INCORRIGIBLE, TOUGH ⟨*hard* gang⟩ **c** (1) **:** harsh, severe, or offensive in tendency or effect ⟨said some *hard* things⟩ (2) **:** RESENTFUL ⟨*hard* feelings⟩ (3) **:** STRICT, UNRELENTING ⟨drives a *hard* bargain⟩ **d :** INCLEMENT ⟨*hard* winter⟩ **e** (1) **:** intense in force, manner, or degree ⟨*hard* blow⟩ (2) **:** ARDUOUS, STRENUOUS ⟨*hard* work⟩ (3) **:** performing or carrying on with great energy, intensity, or persistence ⟨*hard* worker⟩ **9 a :** characterized by sharp or harsh outline, rigid execution, and stiff drawing **b :** sharply defined **:** STARK ⟨*hard* shadows⟩ **c :** lacking in shading, delicacy, or resonance ⟨*hard* singing tone⟩ **d :** sounding as in *arcing* and *geese* respectively — used of *c* and *g* **10 a :** difficult to accomplish or resolve **:** TROUBLESOME ⟨*hard* problem⟩ **b :** difficult to comprehend or explain ⟨*hard* words⟩ — **hard up** **1 :** short of money **:** POOR ⟨family was *hard up* for years⟩ **2 :** poorly provided ⟨he's *hard up* for friends⟩

²**hard** *adv* **1 a :** with great or utmost effort or energy **:** STRENUOUSLY **b :** VIOLENTLY, FIERCELY **c :** to the full extent — used in nautical directions **d :** INTENTLY **2 a :** HARSHLY, SEVERELY **b :** with rancor, bitterness, or grief ⟨took his defeat *hard*⟩ **3 :** TIGHTLY, FIRMLY ⟨hold *hard* to something⟩ **4 :** to the point of hardness **5 :** close in time or space ⟨the school stood *hard* by a church⟩

hard–and–fast \ˌhärd-ᵊn-ˈfast\ *adj* **:** rigidly binding **:** STRICT ⟨a *hard-and-fast* rule⟩

hard·back \ˈhärd-ˌbak\ *n* **:** a book bound in hard covers

hard·ball \-ˌból\ *n* **:** BASEBALL

hard–bit·ten \-ˈbit-ᵊn\ *adj* **:** SEASONED, TOUGH, DOGGED ⟨*hard-bitten* campaigners⟩

hard·board \-ˌbōrd, -ˌbórd\ *n* **:** composition board made by compressing shredded wood chips often with a binder at high temperatures

hard–boiled \-ˈbóild\ *adj* **1 :** boiled until both white and yolk have solidified ⟨*hard-boiled* eggs⟩ **2 a :** lacking sentiment **:** CALLOUS ⟨a *hard-boiled* drill sergeant⟩ **b :** PRACTICAL, REALISTIC ⟨*hard-boiled* business dealings⟩

hard candy *n* **:** a candy made of sugar and corn syrup boiled without crystallizing and usu. fruit-flavored

hard clam *n* **:** a hard-shelled clam; *esp* **:** QUAHOG

hard coal *n* **:** ANTHRACITE

hard core *n* **:** a usu. resistant and enduring central part; *esp* **:** a militant nucleus of a group — **hard-core** *adj*

hard·en \ˈhärd-ᵊn\ *vb* **hard·ened; hard·en·ing** \ˈhärd-niŋ, -ᵊn-iŋ\ **1 :** to make or become hard or harder **2 :** to make or become hardy or strong ⟨muscles *hardened* by exercise⟩ **3 a :** to make or become stubborn, unfeeling, or unsympathetic ⟨*harden* his heart⟩ **b :** to become confirmed ⟨a *hardened* criminal⟩ — **hard·en·er** \ˈhärd-nər, -ᵊn-ər\ *n*

hard·hack \ˈhärd-ˌhak\ *n* **:** a shrubby American spirea with rusty hairy leaves and dense terminal panicles of pink or occas. white flowers

hard·hand·ed \-ˈhan-dəd\ *adj* **1 :** having hands made hard by labor **2 :** STRICT, OPPRESSIVE

hard·head·ed \-ˈhed-əd\ *adj* **1 :** STUBBORN **2 :** marked by sound judgment **:** REALISTIC ⟨a *hardheaded* reappraisal⟩ — **hard·head·ed·ly** *adv* — **hard·head·ed·ness** *n*

hard·heart·ed \-ˈhärt-əd\ *adj* **:** UNFEELING, PITILESS — **hard·heart·ed·ly** *adv* — **hard·heart·ed·ness** *n*

har·di·hood \ˈhärd-ē-ˌhúd\ *n* **1 a :** resolute courage and fortitude **b :** disdainful insolence **2 :** VIGOR, ROBUSTNESS

hard labor *n* **:** compulsory labor of imprisoned criminals that is a part of the prison discipline

hard·ly \ˈhärd-lē\ *adv* **1 :** with force **:** VIGOROUSLY **2 :** SEVERELY, HARSHLY **3 :** with difficulty **:** PAINFULLY **4 :** not quite **:** BARELY, SCARCELY ⟨it *hardly* ever rains there⟩

hard·ness *n* **1 :** the quality or state of being hard **2 :** the cohesion of the particles on the surface of a mineral as determined by its capacity to scratch another or be itself scratched

hard–of–hearing \ˌhärd-ə(v)-ˈhi(ə)r-iŋ\ *adj* **:** of or relating to a defective but functional sense of hearing

hard palate *n* **:** the bony front part of the palate forming the roof of the mouth

hard·pan \ˈhärd-ˌpan\ *n* **1 :** a cemented or compacted and often clayey layer in soil that roots cannot readily penetrate **2 :** a fundamental part **:** BEDROCK, BASIS

hard put *adj* **:** barely able ⟨*hard put* to find an explanation⟩

hard rubber *n* **:** a firm rubber or rubber product that is relatively incapable of being stretched

hard sauce *n* **:** a creamed mixture of butter and powdered sugar often with added cream and flavoring

hard sell *n* **:** aggressive high-pressure salesmanship

hard–shell \ˈhärd-ˌshel\ *adj* **:** CONFIRMED, UNCOMPROMISING ⟨a *hard-shell* conservative⟩

hard–shell crab \-ˌshel-\ *n* **:** a crab that has not recently shed its shell — called also *hard-shelled crab* \-ˌshel(d)-\

hard·ship \ˈhärd-ˌship\ *n* **1 :** SUFFERING, PRIVATION **2 :** something that causes or entails suffering or privation

hard·stand \-ˌstand\ *n* **:** a hard-surfaced area for parking an airplane

hard–sur·face \-ˈsər-fəs\ *vt* **:** to provide (as a road) with a paved surface

hard·tack \ˈhärd-ˌtak\ *n* **:** a hard biscuit or bread made of flour and water without salt

hard·top \-ˌtäp\ *n* **:** an automobile styled to resemble a convertible but having a rigid top of metal or plastic

hard·ware \-ˌwa(ə)r, -ˌwe(ə)r\ *n* **1 :** articles (as fittings, cutlery, tools, utensils, or parts of machines) made of metal **2 :** the physical components (as electronic and electrical devices) of a vehicle (as a spacecraft) or an apparatus (as a computer)

hard wheat *n* **:** a wheat with hard flinty kernels high in gluten that yield a flour esp. suitable for bread and macaroni

¹**hard·wood** \ˈhärd-ˌwùd\ *n* **1 :** the wood of an angiospermous tree as distinguished from that of a coniferous tree **2 :** a tree that yields hardwood

²**hardwood** *adj* **1 :** having or made of hardwood ⟨*hardwood* floors⟩ **2 :** consisting of mature woody tissue ⟨a *hardwood* cutting⟩

hard–wood·ed \-ˈwùd-əd\ *adj* **1 :** having wood that is hard ⟨a *hard-wooded* pine⟩ **2 :** HARDWOOD 1 •

hard·work·ing \-ˈwər-kiŋ\ *adj* **:** INDUSTRIOUS

har·dy \ˈhärd-ē\ *adj* **har·di·er; -est** [OF *hardi*, fr. pp. of (assumed) OF *hardir* to make hard, of Gmc origin; akin to E *hard*] **1 :** BOLD, BRAVE **2 :** AUDACIOUS, BRAZEN **3 a :** inured to fatigue or hardships **:** ROBUST **b :** able to withstand adverse conditions (as of weather) ⟨a *hardy* rose⟩ — **har·di·ly** \ˈhärd-ᵊl-ē\ *adv* — **har·di·ness** \ˈhärd-ē-nəs\ *n*

hare \ˈha(ə)r, ˈhe(ə)r\ *n, pl* **hare** *or* **hares** [OE *hara*] **:** any of various swift timid long-eared mammals (order Lagomorpha) with a divided upper lip, long hind legs, a short cocked tail, and the young open-eyed and furred at birth — compare RABBIT

hare and hounds *n* **:** a game in which some of the players scatter bits of paper for a trail and others try to find and catch them

hare·bell \ˈha(ə)r-ˌbel, ˈhe(ə)r-\ *n* **1 :** a slender herb with bright blue bell-shaped flowers **2 :** WOOD HYACINTH

hare·brained \-ˈbränd\ *adj* **:** FLIGHTY, GIDDY

hare·lip \-ˈlip\ *n* **:** a deformity in which the upper lip is split like that of a hare — **hare·lipped** \-ˈlipt\ *adj*

har·em \ˈhar-əm, ˈher-\ *n* [Ar *harīm*] **1 a :** the rooms assigned to the women in a Muslim household **b :** the women of a Muslim household **2 :** a group of females associated with one male — used of polygamous animals

hark \ˈhärk\ *vi* [ME *herken*] **:** to pay close attention

hark back *vi* **:** to go back to something earlier

harken *var of* HEARKEN

har·le·quin \ˈhär-li-k(w)ən\ *n* [It *arlecchino*] **1 a** *cap* **:** a character in comedy and pantomime with a shaved head, masked face, variegated tights, and wooden sword **b :** BUFFOON, CLOWN **2 :** a variegated pattern (as of a textile)

har·le·quin·ade \ˌhär-li-k(w)ə-ˈnād\ *n* **:** a play or pantomime in which Harlequin has a leading role

har·lot \ˈhär-lət\ *n* [OF *herlot* rogue] **:** PROSTITUTE

har·lot·ry \-lə-trē\ *n, pl* **-ries :** PROSTITUTION

¹**harm** \ˈhärm\ *n* [OE *hearm*] **1 :** physical or mental damage **:** INJURY **2 :** MISCHIEF, HURT **syn** see INJURY

²**harm** *vt* **:** to cause harm to

harm·ful \ˈhärm-fəl\ *adj* **:** DAMAGING, INJURIOUS — **harm·ful·ly** \-fə-lē\ *adv* — **harm·ful·ness** *n*

harm·less \ˈhärm-ləs\ *adj* **1 :** free from harm, liability, or loss **2** : lacking capacity or intent to injure : INNOCU-OUS ⟨a *harmless* joke⟩ — **harm·less·ly** *adv* — **harm·less·ness** *n*

¹**har·mon·ic** \härˈmän-ik\ *adj* **1** : of or relating to musical harmony as opposed to melody or rhythm **2** : of an integrated nature : CONGRUOUS — **har·mon·i·cal·ly** \-ˈmän-i-k(ə-)lē\ *adv*

²**harmonic** *n* **1 a** : OVERTONE; *esp* : one whose frequency is a multiple of the fundamental **b** : a flutelike tone produced (as on a violin) by lightly touching a vibrating string with a finger **2** : a component frequency of a harmonic motion (as of an electromagnetic wave) that is an integral multiple of the fundamental frequency

har·mon·i·ca \härˈmän-i-kə\ *n* : a small rectangular wind instrument with free metallic reeds recessed in air slots from which tones are sounded by exhaling and inhaling — called also *mouth organ*

harmonic motion *n* : a periodic motion that has a single frequency or amplitude (as of a sounding violin string or swinging pendulum) or a vibratory motion that is composed of two or more such simple periodic motions

har·mon·ics \härˈmän-iks\ *n* : the study of the physical characteristics of musical sounds

har·mo·ni·ous \härˈmō-nē-əs\ *adj* **1** : musically concordant ⟨a *harmonious* song⟩ **2** : having the parts agreeably related : CONGRUOUS ⟨*harmonious* colors⟩ **3** : marked by accord in sentiment or action ⟨a *harmonious* family⟩ — **har·mo·ni·ous·ly** *adv* — **har·mo·ni·ous·ness** *n*

har·mo·ni·um \-nē-əm\ *n* : REED ORGAN

har·mo·nize \ˈhär-mə-ˌnīz\ *vb* **1** : to play or sing in harmony **2** : to be in harmony **3** : to bring into harmony or agreement **4** : to provide or accompany with harmony ⟨*harmonize* a melody⟩ — **har·mo·ni·za·tion** \ˌhär-mə-nə-ˈzā-shən\ *n* — **har·mo·niz·er** \ˈhär-mə-ˌnī-zər\ *n*

har·mo·ny \ˈhär-mə-nē\ *n, pl* **-nies** [Gk *harmonia* fastening, music] **1** *archaic* : tuneful sound **2 a** : the combination of simultaneous musical notes in a chord **b** : the structure of music with respect to the composition and progression of chords **c** : the science of the structure, relation, and progression of chords **3 a** : pleasing or congruent arrangement of parts ⟨a picture showing *harmony* of color and design⟩ **b** : CORRESPONDENCE, ACCORD ⟨lives in *harmony* with her neighbors⟩ **c** : internal calm : TRANQUILLITY **4 a** : an interweaving of different accounts into a single narrative **b** : an arrangement of different accounts in parallel columns with corresponding passages side by side ⟨a *harmony* of the Gospels⟩

¹**har·ness** \ˈhär-nəs\ *n* [OF *herneis* baggage, gear] **1 a** (1) : the gear other than a yoke of a draft animal (2) : GEAR, EQUIPMENT **b** (1) : occupational surroundings or routine ⟨back in *harness* after a vacation⟩ (2) : close association **2** : military equipment for horse or man **3** : a part of a loom that holds and controls the heddles

²**harness** *vt* **1 a** : to put a harness on **b** : to attach by means of a harness **2** : to tie together : YOKE **3** : to put to work : UTILIZE ⟨*harness* a waterfall⟩

harness horse *n* : a horse for racing or working in harness

¹**harp** \ˈhärp\ *n* [OE *hearpe*] : an instrument having strings of graded length stretched across an open triangular frame with a curving top and played by plucking with the fingers — **harp·ist** \ˈhär-pəst\ *n*

²**harp** *vi* **1** : to play on a harp **2** : to dwell on or recur to a subject tiresomely or monotonously ⟨always *harping* on his shortcomings⟩

harp·er \ˈhär-pər\ *n* **1** : HARPIST **2** : one that harps

har·poon \härˈpün\ *n* [prob. fr. D *harpoen*, fr. MF *harpon* clamp] : a barbed spear used esp. in hunting large fish or whales — **harpoon** *vt* — **har·poon·er** *n*

harp·si·chord \ˈhärp-si-ˌkórd\ *n* [modif. of It *arpicordo*, fr. *arpa* harp + *corda* string] : a keyboard instrument resembling the grand piano and producing tones by the plucking of wire strings with quills or leather points

har·py \ˈhär-pē\ *n, pl* **harpies** [Gk *harpyia*] **1** *cap* : a foul malign creature of classical mythology that is part woman and part bird **2 a** : a greedy or grasping person : LEECH **b** : a shrewish woman

har·que·bus \ˈhär-kwi-(ˌ)bəs\ *n* [MF *harquebuse, arquebuse*] : a portable firearm of the 15th and 16th centuries later replaced by the musket

har·ri·dan \ˈhar-əd-³n\ *n* : a scolding old woman

¹**har·ri·er** \ˈhar-ē-ər\ *n* [irreg. fr. *hare*] **1** : a hunting dog

like a small foxhound used esp. for hunting rabbits **2** : a runner on a cross-country team

²**harrier** *n* **1** : one that harries **2** : any of various slender long-legged hawks

¹**har·row** \ˈhar-ō\ *vt* [ME *harwen*, fr. OE *hergian*] *archaic* : PILLAGE, PLUNDER

²**harrow** *n* [ME *harwe*] : a cultivating implement set with spikes, spring teeth, or disks and used primarily for pulverizing and smoothing the soil

³**harrow** *vt* **1** : to cultivate with a harrow **2** : TORMENT, VEX ⟨*harrowed* by grief⟩ — **har·row·er** \ˈhar-ə-wər\ *n*

har·ry \ˈhar-ē\ *vt* **har·ried**; **har·ry·ing** [ME *harien*, fr. OE *hergian*] **1** : RAID, RAVAGE, PILLAGE **2** : to torment by or as if by constant attack ⟨*harried* by cares⟩

harsh \ˈhärsh\ *adj* [ME *harsk*, of Scand origin] **1** : disagreeable to the touch **2** : causing discomfort or pain **3** : unduly exacting : SEVERE ⟨*harsh* discipline⟩ **4** : aesthetically jarring ⟨*harsh* combination of colors⟩ **syn** see ROUGH — **harsh·en** \ˈhär-shən\ *vb* — **harsh·ly** *adv* — **harsh·ness** *n*

hart \ˈhärt\ *n* [OE *heort*] *chiefly Brit* : a male red deer esp. over five years old : STAG — compare HIND

harte·beest \ˈhärt-(ə-)ˌbēst\ *n* [Afrik] : a large nearly extinct African antelope with ringed horns

harts·horn \ˈhärts-ˌhórn\ *n* : a preparation of ammonia used as smelling salts

har·um–scar·um \ˌhar-əm-ˈskar-əm, ˌher-əm-ˈsker-\ *adj* : RECKLESS, IRRESPONSIBLE — **harum–scarum** *n* — **harum–scarum** *adv*

ha·rus·pex \hə-ˈrəs-ˌpeks, ˈhar-əs-\ *n, pl* **ha·rus·pi·ces** \hə-ˈrəs-pə-ˌsēz\ [L] : a diviner in ancient Rome basing his predictions on inspection of the entrails of sacrificial animals

¹**har·vest** \ˈhär-vəst\ *n* [OE *hærfest*] **1** : the season when grains and fruits are gathered **2** : the gathering of a crop **3** : a ripe crop (as of grain or fruit); *also* : the quantity of a crop gathered in a single season **4** : the product or reward of effort

²**harvest** *vb* **1 a** : to gather in a crop : REAP **b** : to gather as if by harvesting **2** : to win by achievement — **har·vest·a·ble** \-və-stə-bəl\ *adj* — **har·vest·er** *n*

harvest fly *n* : CICADA

har·vest·man \ˈhär-vəs(t)-mən\ *n* : an arachnid (order Phalangida) that superficially resembles a true spider but has a small rounded body and very long slender legs — called also *daddy longlegs*

harvest moon *n* : the full moon nearest the time of the September equinox

has *pres 3d sing of* HAVE

has–been \ˈhaz-ˌbin\ *n* : one that has passed the peak of ability, power, effectiveness, or popularity

ha·sen·pfef·fer \ˈhäz-ˀn-ˌ(p)fef-ər\ *n* [G, fr. *hase* hare + *pfeffer* pepper] : a stew made of marinated rabbit meat

¹**hash** \ˈhash\ *vt* [F *hacher*, fr. *hache* ax] **1 a** : to chop into small pieces **b** : CONFUSE, MUDDLE **2** : to talk about : REVIEW, CONSIDER

²**hash** *n* **1** : chopped food; *esp* : chopped meat mixed with potatoes and browned **2** : a restatement of something that is already known **3** : HODGEPODGE, JUMBLE

³**hash** *n* : HASHISH

Hash·im·ite or **Hash·em·ite** \ˈhash-ə-ˌmīt\ *n* : a member of an Arab family having common ancestry with Muhammad and founding dynasties in countries of the eastern Mediterranean

hash·ish \ˈhash-ˌēsh, -(ˌ)ish\ *n* [Ar *hashīsh*] : a narcotic preparation from hemp that is smoked, chewed, or drunk for its intoxicating effect

Ha·sid or **Has·sid** \ˈhas-əd, ˈkäs-\ *n, pl* **Ha·si·dim** or **Has·si·dim** \ˈhas-əd-əm, kə-ˈsēd-\ : a member of a Jewish mystical sect founded in Poland about 1750 in opposition to rationalism and ritual laxity — **Ha·sid·ic** \hə-ˈsid-ik, ha-\ *adj* — **Has·i·dism** \ˈhas-ə-ˌdiz-əm\ *n*

Has·mo·nae·an or **Has·mo·ne·an** \ˌhaz-mə-ˈnē-ən\ *n* : a member of the Maccabees — **Hasmonaean** or **Hasmonean** *adj*

hasn't \ˈhaz-ˀnt\ : has not

hasp \ˈhasp\ *n* [OE *hæsp*] : any of several devices for fastening; *esp*

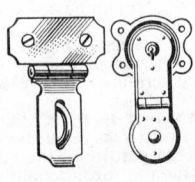

hasps

: a fastener esp. for a door or lid consisting of a hinged metal strap that fits over a staple and is secured by a pin or padlock

has·sle \'has-əl\ *n* **1** : a heated argument : WRANGLE **2** : a violent skirmish : FIGHT — **hassle** *vi*

has·sock \'has-ək\ *n* [OE *hassuc*] **1** : TUSSOCK **2 a** : a cushion to kneel on in prayer **b** : a cushion that serves as a seat or as a leg rest

hast \(')hast, (h)əst\ *archaic pres 2d sing of* HAVE

has·tate \'has-,tāt\ *adj* [L *hasta* spear] : shaped like an arrow with flaring barbs ⟨*hastate* leaf⟩ — **has·tate·ly** *adv*

¹haste \'hāst\ *n* [OF] **1** : rapidity of motion or action : SWIFTNESS **2** : rash or headlong action : PRECIPITATE-NESS **3** : undue eagerness to act : URGENCY

syn HURRY, SPEED: HASTE implies quickness impelled by urgency, eagerness, or rashness; HURRY suggests agitation, bustle, or confusion; SPEED stresses swiftness without confusion and often with success ⟨increase the *speed* of social progress⟩

²haste *vb* : to move or act swiftly : HASTEN, HURRY

has·ten \'hās-ºn\ *vb* **has·tened; has·ten·ing** \'hās-niŋ, -ºn-iŋ\ **1** : to urge on **2** : to speed up : ACCELERATE ⟨*hastened* his steps⟩ **3** : to move or act quickly : HURRY ⟨*hasten* home⟩ ⟨*hastened* to the aid of our allies⟩ — **has·ten·er** \-nər, -ºn-ər\ *n*

hasty \'hā-stē\ *adj* **hast·i·er; -est** **1 a** : rapid in action or movement : SPEEDY **b** : done or made in a hurry : HURRIED ⟨a *hasty* trip⟩ **2** : EAGER, IMPATIENT **3** : PRE-CIPITATE, RASH **4** : prone to anger : IRRITABLE ⟨a *hasty* temper⟩ — **hast·i·ly** \-stə-lē\ *adv* — **hast·i·ness** \-stē-nəs\ *n*

hasty pudding *n* **1** *Brit* : a porridge of oatmeal or flour boiled in water **2** *New Eng* : cornmeal mush

hat \'hat\ *n* [OE *hæt*] : a covering for the head usu. having a shaped crown and brim — **hat in the ring** : an announcement of entry into a usu. political contest

hat·box \'hat-,bäks\ *n* : a round piece of luggage esp. for carrying hats

¹hatch \'hach\ *n* [OE *hæc* lower half of a divided door] **1** : an opening in the deck of a ship or in the floor or roof of a building; *also* : a small door or opening (as in an airplane) ⟨an escape *hatch*⟩ ⟨a cargo *hatch*⟩ **2** : the covering for a hatch

²hatch *vb* [ME *hacchen*] **1** : to produce young by incubation : INCUBATE **2** : to bring into being : ORIGINATE; *esp* : to concoct in secret ⟨*hatch* a plot⟩ **3** : to emerge from an egg or chrysalis — **hatch·a·bil·i·ty** \,hach-ə-'bil-ət-ē\ *n* — **hatch·a·ble** \'hach-ə-bal\ *adj*

³hatch *n* **1** : an act or instance of hatching **2** : a brood of hatched young

⁴hatch *vt* [ME *hachen*, fr. MF *hachier* to chop up, hatch, fr. *hache* ax] **1** : to inlay in fine lines **2** : to mark (as the shading in a picture) with fine closely spaced lines

⁵hatch *n* : STROKE, LINE; *esp* : one used to give the effect of shading

hatch·ery \'hach-(ə-)rē\ *n, pl* **-er·ies** : a place for hatching eggs

hatch·et \'hach-ət\ *n* [MF *ha-chette*, dim. of *hache* ax] **1** : a short-handled ax for use with one hand that has a part opposite the blade for hammering **2** : TOMA-HAWK

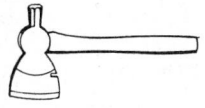

hatchet

hatchet face *n* : a thin sharp face — **hatch·et-faced** \,hach-ət-'fāst\ *adj*

hatchet man *n* : one hired for murder, coercion, or unscrupulous attack

hatch·ing \'hach-iŋ\ *n* : the engraving or drawing of fine lines in close proximity chiefly to give an effect of shading; *also* : the pattern so created

hatch·ment \'hach-mənt\ *n* : a panel on which a coat of arms of a deceased person is temporarily displayed

hatch·way \'hach-,wā\ *n* : a hatch giving access to an enclosed space (as a compartment or cellar) and usu. having a ladder or stairs

¹hate \'hāt\ *n* **1 a** : intense hostility and aversion **b** : distaste coupled with sustained ill will **c** : a very strong dislike : ANTIPATHY **2** : an object of hatred

²hate *vt* [OE *hatian*] **1** : to feel extreme enmity toward ⟨*hates* his country's enemies⟩ **2 a** : to have a strong aver-

sion to : DETEST ⟨*hate* hypocrisy⟩ **b** : to find distasteful : DISLIKE ⟨*hates* cold weather⟩ — **hat·er** *n*

syn DETEST, ABHOR, LOATHE: HATE implies strong dislike coupled with enmity or malice; DETEST suggests violent or intense dislike but may lack the hostility implied in HATE; ABHOR suggests a deep often shuddering repugnance; LOATHE implies utter disgust and intolerance

hate·ful \'hāt-fəl\ *adj* **1** : full of hate : MALICIOUS ⟨*hateful* enemies⟩ **2** : exciting or deserving hate ⟨a *hateful* crime⟩ — **hate·ful·ly** \-fə-lē\ *adv* — **hate·ful·ness** *n*

hath \(')hath, (h)əth\ *archaic pres 3d sing of* HAVE

ha·tred \'hā-trəd\ *n* **1** : HATE **2** : prejudiced hostility or animosity

hat·ter \'hat-ər\ *n* : one that makes, sells, or cleans and repairs hats

hau·berk \'hò-(,)bərk\ *n* [OF *hauberc*, of Gmc origin] : a tunic of chain mail worn as defensive armor from the 12th to the 14th century — see MAIL illustration

haugh·ty \'hòt-ē, 'hät-\ *adj* **haugh·ti·er; -est** [ME *haute*, fr. MF *haut*, lit., high, fr. L *altus*] : disdainfully proud : ARROGANT — **haugh·ti·ly** \-ºl-ē\ *adv* — **haugh·ti·ness** \-ē-nəs\ *n*

¹haul \'hòl\ *vb* [ME *halen* to pull, draw, fr. OF *haler*, of Gmc origin] **1** : to change the course of (a ship) esp. so as to sail closer to the wind **2 a** : to exert traction : DRAW, PULL ⟨the horse *hauled* a cart⟩ **b** : to obtain or move by hauling **c** : to transport in a vehicle : HALE **4** : SHIFT ⟨the wind *hauled* around to the south⟩ — **haul·er** *n*

²haul *n* **1 a** : the act or process of hauling : PULL **b** : a device for hauling **2 a** : an amount collected : TAKE ⟨a burglar's *haul*⟩ **b** : the fish taken in a single draft of a net **3** : transportation by hauling **b** : the distance or route over which a load is transported ⟨a long *haul*⟩ **c** : a quantity transported : LOAD

haul·age \'hò-lij\ *n* : the act or process of hauling

haulm \'hòm\ *n* [OE *healm*] : the stems or tops of a plant (as peas or potatoes) esp. after the crop is gathered; *also* : a plant stem

haunch \'hònch, 'hänch\ *n* [OF *hanche*] **1 a** : HIP 1 **b** : HINDQUARTER 2 — usu. used in pl. **2** : HINDQUARTER 1

¹haunt \'hònt, 'hänt\ *vb* [OF *hanter*] **1 a** : to visit often : FREQUENT ⟨she *haunted* the antique shops⟩ **b** : to continually seek the company of **c** : to stay around or persist : LINGER **2 a** : to recur constantly and spontaneously to ⟨the tune *haunted* her all day⟩ **b** : to reappear continually in **3** : to visit or inhabit as a ghost ⟨the murdered man *haunted* the house⟩ — **haunt·ing·ly** \-iŋ-lē\ *adv*

²haunt \'hònt, 'hänt, *2 is usu* 'hant\ *n* **1** : a place habitually frequented or repeatedly visited ⟨the favorite *haunts* of birds⟩ **2** *chiefly dial* : GHOST

haus·to·ri·um \hò-'stōr-ē-əm, -'stòr-\ *n, pl* **-ria** \-ē-ə\ [NL, fr. L *haust-*, *haurire* to drink, drain] : a food-absorbing outgrowth of a plant — **haus·to·ri·al** \-ē-əl\ *adj*

haut·bois *or* **haut·boy** \'(h)ō-,bói\ *n, pl* **hautbois** \-,bóiz\ *or* **hautboys** [MF *hautbois*, fr. *haut* high + *bois* wood] : OBOE

haute cou·ture \,ōt-kù-'tù(ə)r\ *n* : the establishments or designers that create fashions for women; *also* : the fashions created

hau·teur \hò-'tər\ *n* [F, fr. *haut* high, fr. L *altus*] : HAUGH-TINESS, ARROGANCE

Ha·vana \hə-'van-ə\ *n* : a cigar made from Cuban tobacco

¹have \(')hav, (h)əv, v; *before* "to" *usu* 'haf\ *vb, past & past part* **had** \(')had, (h)əd, d\; *pres part* **hav·ing** \'hav-iŋ\; *pres 3d sing* **has** \(')haz, (h)əz, z, s; *before* "to" *usu* 'has\ [OE *habban*] **1 a** : POSSESS, OWN ⟨*have* a car⟩ **b** : to hold in one's use, service, or affection or at one's disposal ⟨can't *have* your cake and eat it too⟩ **c** : to consist of : CONTAIN ⟨April *has* 30 days⟩ **2** : to feel obligation or necessity in regard to ⟨*have* to go⟩ ⟨*have* a letter to write⟩ **3** : to stand in relationship to ⟨*have* enemies⟩ **4 a** : to acquire or get possession of : OBTAIN ⟨best to be *had*⟩ **b** : RECEIVE ⟨*had* bad news from her mother⟩ **c** : ACCEPT; *esp* : to accept in marriage ⟨she wouldn't *have* him⟩ **5 a** : to be marked or characterized by ⟨*have* red hair⟩ **b** : SHOW ⟨*had* the gall to refuse⟩ **c** : USE, EXERCISE ⟨*have* mercy on us⟩ **6 a** : to experience esp. by submitting to, undergoing, or suffering ⟨*have* a cold⟩ **b** : to carry on : PERFORM, TAKE ⟨*have* a look at that cut⟩ ⟨*have* a fight⟩ **c** : to entertain in the mind : CHERISH

⟨*have* an opinion⟩ **7 a :** to cause to by persuasive or forceful means ⟨please *have* the children stay⟩ **b :** to cause to be **8 :** ALLOW ⟨we'll *have* no more of that⟩ **9 :** to be competent in ⟨*has* only a little French⟩ **10 a :** to hold an advantage over ⟨we *have* him now⟩ **b :** TRICK, FOOL ⟨been *had* by a partner⟩ **11 :** to be able to exercise ⟨I *have* my rights⟩ **12 :** BEGET, BEAR ⟨*have* a baby⟩ **13 :** to partake of ⟨*have* dinner⟩ **14 :** BRIBE ⟨can be *had* for a price⟩ **15** — used as an auxiliary verb with the past participle to form the present perfect, past perfect, or future perfect ⟨*has* gone home⟩ ⟨*had* already eaten⟩ ⟨will *have* finished dinner by then⟩ — **have at** \ha-'vat\ **:** to go at or deal with **:** ATTACK — **have done :** FINISH, STOP — **have it in for** \,hav-ət-'in-fər, -,fór\ **:** to intend to do harm to — **have it out :** to settle a matter of contention by discussion or a fight — **have to do with 1 :** to deal with **2 :** to have in the way of connection or relation with or effect on
²**have** \'hav\ *n* **:** one that has material wealth as distinguished from one that is poor
ha·ven \'hā-vən\ *n* [OE *hæfen*] **1 :** HARBOR, PORT **2 :** a place of safety **:** ASYLUM
have-not \'hav-,nät, -'nät\ *n* **:** one that is poor in material wealth as distinguished from one that is rich
haven't \'hav-ənt\ **:** have not
hav·er·sack \'hav-ər-,sak\ *n* [F *havresac*, fr. G *habersack* bag for oats, fr. *haber* oats + *sack* bag] **:** a bag similar to a knapsack but worn over one shoulder
Ha·ver·sian canal \hə-,vər-zhən-\ *n* [Clopton *Havers* d1702 English physician] **:** one of the small canals by which blood vessels traverse bone
hav·oc \'hav-ək\ *n* [AF *havok*, modif. of OF *havot* plunder] **1 :** wide and general destruction **:** DEVASTATION **2 :** great confusion and disorder
¹**haw** \'hó\ *n* **1 :** a hawthorn berry **2 :** HAWTHORN
²**haw** *vi* **:** to utter the sound represented by *haw* ⟨hemmed and *hawed* before answering⟩
³**haw** *n* **:** a vocalized pause in speaking or an instance of uttering this sound
⁴**haw** *imperative verb* — used as a direction to turn to the left; compare GEE
Ha·wai·ian \hə-'wä-yən, -'wī-(y)ən, -'wó-yən\ *n* **1 :** a native or resident of Hawaii; *esp* **:** one of Polynesian ancestry **2 :** the Polynesian language of the Hawaiians — **Hawaiian** *adj*
Ha·wai·ian guitar *n* **:** a flat-bodied stringed musical instrument with a long fretted neck and usu. 6 to 8 strings that are plucked
Hawaii standard time *n* **:** the time of the 10th time zone west of Greenwich that includes the Hawaiian islands and central Alaska — compare ALASKA STANDARD TIME
haw·finch \'hó-,finch\ *n* [¹*haw*] **:** a heavy-billed Old World finch with the male marked in black, white, and brown
¹**hawk** \'hók\ *n* [OE *hafoc*] **1 :** any of numerous birds of prey including all the smaller members of this group active mostly by day — compare OWL **2 :** an individual who takes a militant attitude (as in a dispute) and advocates immediate vigorous action; *esp* **:** a supporter of a war or warlike policy — compare DOVE — **hawk·ish** \'hó-kish\ *adj*
²**hawk** *vb* **1 :** to hunt birds by means of a trained hawk **2 :** to hunt on the wing like a hawk
³**hawk** *vt* [back-formation fr. ²*hawker*] **:** to offer for sale by calling out in the street ⟨*hawk* vegetables⟩
⁴**hawk** *vb* **1 :** to utter a harsh guttural sound in or as if in clearing the throat **2 :** to raise by hawking ⟨*hawk* up phlegm⟩
⁵**hawk** *n* **:** an act or sound of hawking
¹**hawk·er** \'hó-kər\ *n* **:** FALCONER
²**hawker** *n* [LG *höker*] **:** one that hawks wares
hawk-moth \'hók-,móth\ *n* **:** any of numerous stout-bodied moths with long strong narrow pointed fore wings and small hind wings
hawks·bill \'hóks-,bil\ *n* **:** a carnivorous sea turtle whose shell yields the best tortoiseshell of commerce
hawk·weed \'hók-,wēd\ *n* **:** any of several plants that are related to the daisies and usu. have flower heads with red or orange rays
hawse \'hóz\ *n* [ON *hals* neck, hawse] **1 a :** HAWSEHOLE **b :** the part of a ship's bow that contains the hawseholes **2 :** the distance between a ship's bow and her anchor

hawse·hole \-,hōl\ *n* **:** a hole in the bow of a ship through which a cable passes
haw·ser \'hó-zər\ *n* [AF *hauceour*, fr. MF *haucier* to hoist, fr. (assumed) VL *altiare*, fr. L *altus* high] **:** a large rope for towing, mooring, or securing a ship
haw·thorn \'hó-,thórn\ *n* [OE *hagathorn*, fr. *haga* hedge + *thorn*] **:** any of a genus of spring-flowering spiny shrubs or small trees of the rose family with glossy and often lobed leaves, white or pink fragrant flowers, and small red fruits
¹**hay** \'hā\ *n* [ME *hey*, fr. OE *hīeg*] **:** herbage (as grass) mowed and cured for fodder
²**hay** *vb* **1 :** to cut, cure, and store herbage for hay **2 :** to feed with hay — **hay·er** *n*
hay·cock \'hā-,käk\ *n* **:** a conical pile of hay
hay fever *n* **:** an acute allergic catarrh of the mucous membranes of the eyes, nose, and throat
hay·fork \'hā-,fórk\ *n* **:** a hand or mechanically operated fork for loading or unloading hay
hay·loft \-,lóft\ *n* **:** a loft for hay
hay·mak·er \-,mā-kər\ *n* **1 :** HAYER **2 :** a powerful blow (as in boxing)
hay·mow \-,mau\ *n* **:** a mow of or for hay
hay·rack \-,rak\ *n* **1 :** a frame mounted on the running gear of a wagon and used esp. in hauling hay or straw **2 :** a feeding rack that holds hay for livestock
hay·rick \-,rik\ *n* **:** a large sometimes thatched outdoor stack of hay
hay·seed \-,sēd\ *n* **1 a :** seed shattered from hay **b :** clinging bits of straw or chaff from hay **2 :** BUMPKIN
hay·wire \-,wī(ə)r\ *adj* [fr. the frequent use of baling wire for makeshift repairs] **1 :** hastily or shoddily made **2 :** being out of order **:** MALFUNCTIONING ⟨something went *haywire* with the radio⟩ **3 :** emotionally or mentally upset
ha·zan \kə-'zän, 'käz-ⁿn\ *n, pl* **ha·za·nim** \kə-'zän-əm\ **:** CANTOR 2
¹**haz·ard** \'haz-ərd\ *n* [MF *hasard*, fr. Ar *az-zahr* the die] **1 :** a game of chance played with two dice **2 :** CHANCE, ACCIDENT **3 :** RISK, PERIL ⟨the *hazards* of war⟩ **4 :** a source of danger ⟨a fire *hazard*⟩ **5 :** an obstruction on a golf course **syn** see DANGER — **at hazard :** at stake
²**hazard** *vt* **:** VENTURE, RISK ⟨*hazard* a guess⟩
haz·ard·ous \'haz-ərd-əs\ *adj* **:** DANGEROUS, RISKY — **haz·ard·ous·ly** *adv* — **haz·ard·ous·ness** *n*
¹**haze** \'hāz\ *vb* **:** to make or become hazy or cloudy
²**haze** *n* **1 :** fine dust, smoke, or light vapor causing lack of transparency in the air **2 :** vagueness of mind or mental perception
³**haze** *vt* **1 :** to harass by exacting unnecessary, disagreeable, or difficult work **2 a :** to harass by banter, ridicule, or criticism **b :** to play abusive and humiliating tricks on by way of initiation — **haz·er** *n*
ha·zel \'hā-zəl\ *n* [OE *hæsel*] **1 :** any of a genus of shrubs or small trees of the birch family bearing edible nuts enclosed in a leafy case **2 :** a light brown to a strong yellowish brown — **hazel** *adj* — **ha·zel·ly** \'hāz-(ə)lē\ *adj*
hazel hen *n* **:** a European grouse
ha·zel·nut \'hā-zəl-,nət\ *n* **:** the nut of a hazel
hazy \'hā-zē\ *adj* **haz·i·er; -est 1 :** obscured or darkened by or as if by haze ⟨*hazy* weather⟩ **2 :** VAGUE, INDEFINITE ⟨a *hazy* idea⟩ **3 :** CLOUDED — **haz·i·ly** \-zə-lē\ *adv* — **haz·i·ness** \-zē-nəs\ *n*
H-bomb \'āch-,bäm\ *n* **:** HYDROGEN BOMB
¹**he** \(')hē, ē\ *pron* [OE *hē*] **1 :** that male one ⟨*he* is my father⟩ — compare HIM, HIS, IT, SHE, THEY **2 :** that one whose sex is unknown or immaterial ⟨*he* that runs may read⟩
²**he** \'hē\ *n* **:** a male person or animal
¹**head** \'hed\ *n* [OE *hēafod*] **1 :** the upper or front division of the body (as of a man or an insect) that contains the brain, the chief sense organs, and the mouth **2 a :** MIND, UNDERSTANDING ⟨a good *head* for figures⟩ **b :** mental or emotional control **:** POISE ⟨a level *head*⟩ **3 :** the obverse of a coin **4 a :** each one among a number **:** INDIVIDUAL **b** *pl* **head :** a unit of number (as of livestock) **5 a :** the end that is upper or higher or opposite the foot ⟨the *head* of the bed⟩ **b :** the source of a stream **c :** either end of something (as a drum) whose two ends need not be distinguished **d :** a horizontal passage in a coal mine **6 a :** HEADMASTER **b :** a person responsible for directing the actions and duties of others **:** CHIEF, LEADER ⟨the *head* of a company⟩ **7 a :** CAPITULUM 2 **b :** a compact mass

of plant parts (as leaves or flowers) ⟨a *head* of cabbage⟩
8 a : the leading element of a military column or a procession **b** : HEADWAY **9 a** : the uppermost extremity or projecting part of an object : TOP **b** : the striking part of a weapon **10** : a body of water kept in reserve at a height **11 a** : the difference in elevation between two points in a body of fluid **b** : the resulting pressure of the fluid at the lower point expressible as this height; *also* : pressure of a fluid ⟨a *head* of steam⟩ **12 a** : the bow and adjacent parts of a ship **b** : a ship's toilet **13** : the place of leadership or command ⟨the man at the *head* of the group⟩ **14 a** (1) : a word often in larger letters placed above a passage in order to introduce or categorize (2) : a separate part or topic **b** : a portion of a page or sheet that is above the first line of printing **15** : the foam that rises on an effervescing liquid **16 a** : the part of a boil, pimple, or abscess at which it is likely to break **b** : CRISIS ⟨events came to a *head*⟩ **17** : a part of a machine or machine tool containing a device (as a cutter, drill) ⟨a machine with a grinding *head*⟩; *also* : the part of an apparatus that performs the chief function or a particular function ⟨a shower *head*⟩ — **off one's head** : CRAZY, DISTRACTED — **out of one's head** : DELIRIOUS — **over one's head** **1** : beyond one's comprehension **2** : so as to bypass or ignore one's superior standing or authority
²head *adj* **1** : of, relating to, or used for the head **2** : PRINCIPAL, CHIEF ⟨*head* cook⟩ **3** : situated at the head **4** : coming from in front ⟨*head* sea⟩
³head *vb* **1** : to cut back or off the upper or terminal growth of (a plant or plant part) **2 a** : to provide with or form a head ⟨*head* an arrow⟩ ⟨this cabbage *heads* early⟩ **b** : to form the head or top of ⟨tower *headed* by a spire⟩ **3** : to put oneself at the head of : act as leader to ⟨*head* a revolt⟩ **4 a** : to get in front of so as to hinder, stop, or turn back ⟨*head* him off at the pass⟩ **b** : to take a lead over (as in a race) : SURPASS **c** : to pass (a stream) by going round above the source **5 a** : to put something at the head of (as a list) **b** : to stand as the first or leading member of ⟨*heads* the list of heroes⟩ **6** : to take or cause to take a specified course ⟨we *headed* for home⟩ ⟨*head* the ship north⟩
head·ache \'hed-ˌāk\ *n* **1** : pain in the head **2** : an annoying or baffling situation or problem — **head·achy** \-ˌā-kē\ *adj*
head·band \-ˌband\ *n* : a band worn on or around the head
head·board \-ˌbōrd, -ˌbórd\ *n* : a board forming the head (as of a bed)
head·cheese \-ˌchēz\ *n* : a product made from the edible parts of the head, feet, and sometimes the tongue and heart esp. of a pig cut up fine, seasoned, boiled, and pressed
head cold *n* : a common cold centered in the nasal passages and adjacent mucous tissues
head·dress \'he(d)-ˌdres\ *n* : a covering or ornament for the head
head·ed \'hed-əd\ *adj* **1** : having a head or a heading ⟨a *headed* bolt⟩ **2** : having such a head or so many heads ⟨curly-*headed*⟩ ⟨three-*headed* monster⟩
head·er \'hed-ər\ *n* **1** : one that removes heads; *esp* : a grain-harvesting machine that cuts off the grain heads and lifts them into a wagon **2 a** : a brick or stone laid in a wall with its end toward the face of the wall **b** : a beam fitted between trimmers and across the ends of tailpieces in a building frame **3** : a fall or dive head foremost ⟨took a *header* downstairs⟩

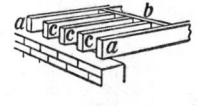

timbers with header: *a, a* trimmers; *b* header; *c, c, c* tailpieces

head·first \'hed-ˈfərst\ *also* **head·fore·most** \-ˈfór-ˌmōst, -ˈfór-\ *adv* : with the head foremost : HEADLONG — **headfirst** *adj*
head gate *n* **1** : a gate at the upper end of a canal lock **2** : a gate for controlling the water flowing into a race, sluice, or irrigation ditch
head·gear \'hed-ˌgi(ə)r\ *n* **1** : a covering or protective device for the head **2** : harness for a horse's head
head·hunt·ing \-ˌhənt-iŋ\ *n* : the practice of cutting off and preserving as trophies the heads of enemies — **head·hunt·er** *n*

head·i·ly \'hed-ºl-ē\ *adv* : in a heady manner
head·i·ness \'hed-ē-nəs\ *n* : the quality or state of being heady
head·ing \'hed-iŋ\ *n* **1** : the compass direction in which the longitudinal axis of a ship or aircraft points **2** : something that forms or serves as a head; *esp* : an inscription, headline, or title standing at the top or beginning (as of a letter or chapter)
head·land \'hed-lənd, -ˌland\ *n* : a point of usu. high land jutting out into the sea : PROMONTORY
head·less \-ləs\ *adj* **1** : having no head **2** : having no chief **3** : lacking good sense or prudence : FOOLISH — **head·less·ness** *n*
head·light \-ˌlīt\ *n* : a light on the front of a vehicle
¹head·line \-ˌlīn\ *n* **1** : a line at the top of a page (as in a book) giving a title or heading **2** : the title over an item or article in a newspaper
²headline *vt* **1** : to provide with a headline **2** : to publicize highly
head·lin·er \-ˌlī-nər\ *n* : a performer whose name is given prominent billing : STAR
head·lock \'hed-ˌläk\ *n* : a wrestling hold in which one encircles his opponent's head with one arm
¹head·long \-ˈlóŋ\ *adv* [ME *hedlong*, alter. of *hedling*, fr. *hed head*] **1** : HEADFIRST **2** : without deliberation : RECKLESSLY ⟨dash *headlong* into traffic⟩ **3** : without pause or delay
²head·long \-ˌlóŋ\ *adj* **1** : PRECIPITATE, RASH ⟨*headlong* flight⟩ **2** : plunging headfirst ⟨a *headlong* dive into the pool⟩
head louse *n* : a louse that lives on the scalp of man
head·man \'hed-ˈman, -ˌman\ *n* : one who is a leader (as of a tribe, clan, or village) : CHIEF
head·mas·ter \'hed-ˌmas-tər\ *n* : a male head of a private school : PRINCIPAL — **head·mis·tress** \-ˌmis-trəs\ *n*
head·most \-ˌmōst\ *adj* : most advanced : LEADING
head-on \'hed-ˈón, -ˈän\ *adj* : having the head or front facing forward : front to front ⟨a *head-on* collision⟩
head over heels *adv* **1** : in or as if in a somersault ⟨fell *head over heels* down the hill⟩ **2** : HOPELESSLY, DEEPLY ⟨*head over heels* in love⟩
head·phone \'hed-ˌfōn\ *n* : an earphone held over the ear by a band worn on the head
head·piece \-ˌpēs\ *n* **1** : a protective or defensive covering for the head **2** : BRAINS, INTELLIGENCE **3** : an ornament esp. at the beginning of a chapter
head·pin \-ˌpin\ *n* : a pin that stands at the apex in a triangular arrangement of bowling pins
head·quar·ters \'hed-ˌkwórt-ərz\ *n sing or pl* **1** : a place from which a commander exercises command **2** : the administrative center of an enterprise
head·race \-ˌrās\ *n* : a race for conveying water to a place of industrial application
head·rest \-ˌrest\ *n* : a support for the head
head·set \-ˌset\ *n* : a pair of headphones
head·ship \-ˌship\ *n* : the position, office, or dignity of a head
heads·man \'hedz-mən\ *n* : one that beheads : EXECUTIONER
head·stall \'hed-ˌstól\ *n* : a part of a bridle or halter that encircles the head
head·stand \-ˌstand\ *n* : the gymnastic feat of standing on one's head usu. with support from the hands
head·stock \-ˌstäk\ *n* : a part of a lathe that holds the revolving spindle and its attachments
head·stone \-ˌstōn\ *n* : a memorial stone placed at the head of a grave
head·strong \-ˌstróŋ\ *adj* **1** : not easily restrained : WILLFUL ⟨a *headstrong* child⟩ **2** : directed by ungovernable will ⟨violent *headstrong* actions⟩
head·wait·er \'hed-ˈwāt-ər\ *n* : the head of the dining-room staff of a restaurant or hotel
head·wa·ters \-ˌwót-ərz, -ˌwät-\ *n pl* : the source and upper part of a stream
head·way \-ˌwā\ *n* **1 a** : motion or rate of motion (as of a ship) in a forward direction **b** : ADVANCE, PROGRESS **2** : clear space (as under an arch) **3** : the time interval between two vehicles traveling in the same direction on the same route
head wind *n* : a wind blowing in a direction opposite to a course esp. of a ship or aircraft

head·word \'hed-,wərd\ *n* **1** : a word or term placed at the beginning (as of a chapter or entry) **2** : a word qualified by a modifier

head·work \-,wərk\ *n* : mental work or effort : THINKING

heady \'hed-ē\ *adj* **head·i·er; -est 1** : WILLFUL, RASH **2** : likely to make one dizzy ⟨*heady* wine⟩⟨a *heady* height⟩

heal \'hēl\ *vb* [OE *hǣlan;* akin to E *whole*] **1** : to make healthy or whole **2** : to return to a sound or healthy condition **syn** see CURE

heal·er \'hē-lər\ *n* **1** : one that heals **2** : a Christian Science practitioner

health \'helth\ *n* [ME *helthe,* fr. OE *hǣlth,* fr. *hāl* whole, hale] **1 a** : the condition of being sound in body, mind, or spirit; *esp* : freedom from physical disease or pain **b** : general functional condition of an individual ⟨in poor *health*⟩ **2** : flourishing condition : WELL-BEING ⟨the *health* of the economy⟩ **3** : a toast to someone's health or prosperity ⟨drink a *health*⟩

health·ful \-fəl\ *adj* **1** : beneficial to health of body or mind ⟨*healthful* exercise⟩ **2** : HEALTHY — **health·ful·ly** \-fə-lē\ *adv* — **health·ful·ness** *n*

syn WHOLESOME, SALUTARY: HEALTHFUL means being both conducive to and indicative of health or soundness ⟨a *healthful* climate⟩ WHOLESOME applies to what benefits, builds up, or sustains physically, mentally, or spiritually ⟨*wholesome* meals⟩ ⟨*wholesome* literature⟩ SALUTARY describes something corrective or beneficially effective, even though it may in itself be unpleasant ⟨the *salutary* nature of satire⟩ ⟨the *salutary* influence of constructive criticism⟩

healthy \'hel-thē\ *adj* **health·i·er; -est 1** : enjoying or typical of good health : WELL **2** : conducive to health **3 a** : PROSPEROUS, FLOURISHING **b** : not small or feeble : CONSIDERABLE — **health·i·ly** \-thə-lē\ *adv* — **health·i·ness** \-thē-nəs\ *n*

syn WELL, SOUND: HEALTHY implies full strength and vigor as well as freedom from disease; WELL implies merely freedom from disease or illness; SOUND stresses perfect health, absence of all defects, disease, or morbidity ⟨a *sound* mind in a *sound* body⟩

¹heap \'hēp\ *n* [OE *hēap*] **1** : a collection of things thrown one on another : PILE ⟨a rubbish *heap*⟩ **2** : a great number or large quantity : LOT ⟨*heaps* of people⟩⟨a *heap* of fun⟩

²heap *vt* **1** : to throw or lay in a heap : AMASS, PILE ⟨*heap* up leaves⟩ **2** : to cast or bestow in large quantities ⟨*heaped* scorn upon him⟩ **3** : to fill (a measure or container) more than even full

hear \'hi(ə)r\ *vb* **heard** \'hərd\; **hear·ing** \'hi(ə)r-iŋ\ [OE *hīeran*] **1** : to perceive or apprehend by the ear ⟨*hear* music⟩; *also* : to have the power of apprehending sound ⟨doesn't *hear* well⟩ **2** : to gain knowledge of by hearing : LEARN ⟨*heard* you're leaving⟩ **3** : to listen to with attention : HEED ⟨*hear* me out⟩ **4 a** : to give a legal hearing to ⟨*hear* a case⟩ **b** : to take testimony from ⟨*hear* witnesses⟩ **5 a** : to get news ⟨*heard* from him yesterday⟩ **b** : to have knowledge or information ⟨never *heard* of such a thing⟩ **6** : to entertain the idea ⟨wouldn't *hear* of it⟩ — **hear·er** \'hir-ər\ *n*

syn LISTEN: HEAR implies the actual sensation and response of the auditory nerves to a stimulus; LISTEN implies the conscious or voluntary effort to hear

hear·ing *n* **1 a** : the process, function, or power of perceiving sound; *esp* : the special sense by which noises and tones are received as stimuli **b** : EARSHOT ⟨stay within *hearing*⟩ **2 a** : opportunity to present one's case **b** : a listening to arguments **c** : a session (as of a legislative committee) in which the testimony of witnesses is heard

hearing aid *n* : an electronic device usu. worn by a person for amplifying sound before it reaches the receptor organs

hear·ken \'här-kən\ *vi* **hear·kened; hear·ken·ing** \'härk-(ə-)niŋ\ [OE *heorcnian*] **1** : to give ear : LISTEN **2** : to give respectful attention

hear·say \'hi(ə)r-,sā\ *n* **1** : something heard from another : RUMOR **2** : evidence based not on a witness's personal knowledge but on matters told him by another

hearse \'hərs\ *n* [ME *herse* framework holding candles placed over a bier, fr. MF *herce* harrow, frame for holding candles, fr. L *hirpic-, hirpex* harrow] **1 a** *archaic* : COFFIN **b** *obs* : BIER **2** : a vehicle for conveying the dead to the grave

heart \'härt\ *n* [OE *heorte*] **1 a** : a hollow muscular

organ of vertebrate animals that by its rhythmic contraction acts as a force pump maintaining the circulation of the blood **b** : a structure in an invertebrate animal functionally analogous to the vertebrate heart **2** : the part nearest the center ⟨the *heart* of a forest⟩⟨the *heart* of a flower⟩ **3** : the most essential part of something **4** : something resembling a heart in shape **5 a** : the whole personality including intellectual as well as emotional functions or traits **b** : human feelings : AFFECTION, KINDNESS ⟨a man seemingly without *heart*⟩ **c** : COURAGE, SPIRIT ⟨take *heart*⟩ **6** : MOOD ⟨with a merry *heart*⟩ **7** : the real meaning : hidden meaning ⟨get to the *heart* of a subject⟩ **8** : MEMORY ⟨learn by *heart*⟩ **9** : PERSON ⟨dear *heart*⟩ ⟨a sailing ship manned by a crew of stout *hearts*⟩ **10 a** : a red stylized heart used to distinguish a suit of playing cards; *also* : a card of the suit bearing hearts **b** *pl* : a card game in which the object is to avoid taking tricks containing hearts — **to heart** : with deep concern

heart·ache \'härt-,āk\ *n* : anguish of mind : SORROW

heart attack *n* : an acute episode of heart disease or disorder; *esp* : CORONARY THROMBOSIS

heart·beat \'härt-,bēt\ *n* : one complete pulsation of the heart

heart block *n* : defective coordination of the events of the heartbeat

heart·break \'härt-,brāk\ *n* : crushing grief

heart·break·ing \-,brā-kiŋ\ *adj* : causing intense sorrow or distress — **heart·break·ing·ly** \-kiŋ-lē\ *adv*

heart·bro·ken \-,brō-kən\ *adj* : overcome by sorrow

heart·burn \-,bərn\ *n* : a burning discomfort behind the lower part of the sternum usu. related to spasm of the lower esophagus or the upper stomach

heart·burn·ing \-,bər-niŋ\ *n* : intense or rancorous jealousy or resentment

heart·ed \'härt-əd\ *adj* : having a specified kind of heart ⟨stout*hearted*⟩

heart·en \'härt-ⁿn\ *vt* **heart·ened; heart·en·ing** \'härt-niŋ, -ⁿn-iŋ\ : to cheer up : ENCOURAGE ⟨*heartened* by the confidence of a friend⟩

heart·felt \'härt-,felt\ *adj* : deeply felt : EARNEST ⟨*heartfelt* thanks⟩

heart-free \-,frē\ *adj* : not in love

hearth \'härth\ *n* [OE *heorth*] **1 a** : a brick, stone, or cement area in front of a fireplace **b** : the floor of a fireplace **c** : the lowest section of a blast furnace **b** : the floor of a metal-processing furnace **2** : HOME, FIRESIDE

hearth·side \-,sīd\ *n* : FIRESIDE

hearth·stone \-,stōn\ *n* **1** : stone forming a hearth **2** : FIRESIDE

heart·i·ly \'härt-ⁿl-ē\ *adv* **1** : with sincerity, goodwill, or enthusiasm ⟨set to work *heartily*⟩⟨eat *heartily*⟩ **2** : CORDIALLY ⟨make a guest feel *heartily* welcome⟩ **3** : COMPLETELY, THOROUGHLY ⟨*heartily* sick of his complaints⟩

heart·i·ness \'härt-ē-nəs\ *n* : the quality or state of being hearty

heart·land \'härt-,land\ *n* : a central land area; *esp* : one thought of as economically and militarily self-sufficient and able to control the landmass around it

heart·less \-ləs\ *adj* **1** *archaic* : SPIRITLESS **2** : lacking feeling : CRUEL — **heart·less·ly** *adv* — **heart·less·ness** *n*

heart·rend·ing \-,ren-diŋ\ *adj* : causing intense grief, anguish, or distress ⟨a *heartrending* experience⟩

hearts·ease \'härts-,ēz\ *n* **1** : peace of mind : TRANQUILLITY **2** : any of various violas; *esp* : WILD PANSY

heart·sick \'härt-,sik\ *adj* : very despondent : DEPRESSED — **heart·sick·ness** *n*

heart·sore \-,sōr, -,sȯr\ *adj* : HEARTSICK

heart-strick·en \-,strik-ən\ *or* **heart-struck** \-,strək\ *adj* : stricken to the heart (as with grief or dismay)

heart·string \-,striŋ\ *n* **1** *obs* : a nerve once believed to sustain the heart **2** : the deepest emotions or affections ⟨pulled at his *heartstrings*⟩

heart·throb \-,thräb\ *n* **1** : the throb of a heart **2 a** : sentimental emotion : PASSION **b** : SWEETHEART

heart-to-heart \'härt-tə-,härt\ *adj* : SINCERE, FRANK ⟨a *heart-to-heart* talk⟩

heart-whole \'härt-,hōl\ *adj* **1** : HEART-FREE **2** : SINCERE, GENUINE

heart·wood \-,wu̇d\ *n* : the older harder nonliving and usu. darker wood of the central portion of a stem that is surrounded by sapwood

---

ə abut; ⁰ kitten; ər further; a back; ā bake; ä cot, cart; au̇ out; ch chin; e less; ē easy; g gift; i trip; ī life

¹hearty \'härt-ē\ *adj* **heart·i·er; -est** **1 a** : giving unqualified support : THOROUGHGOING ⟨*hearty* agreement⟩ **b** : enthusiastically or exuberantly cordial : JOVIAL ⟨a *hearty* welcome⟩ **c** : expressed unrestrainedly ⟨*hearty* laughter⟩ **2 a** : exhibiting vigorous good health ⟨a hale and *hearty* old man⟩ **b** (1) : having a good appetite ⟨a *hearty* eater⟩ (2) : abundant and satisfying ⟨a *hearty* meal⟩ **c** : NOURISHING ⟨*hearty* beef stock⟩ **3** : ENERGETIC, VIGOROUS ⟨gave a *hearty* pull⟩

²hearty *n, pl* **heart·ies** : a bold brave fellow : COMRADE; *also* : SAILOR

¹heat \'hēt\ *vb* [OE *hǣtan;* akin to E *hot*] **1** : to make or become warm or hot **2** : to make or become excited or angry

²heat *n* [OE *hǣtu;* akin to E *hot*] **1 a** : a condition of being hot : WARMTH **b** : a marked or notable degree of hotness **c** : a hot place or situation **d** : a period of heat **e** : a form of energy that causes substances to rise in temperature, fuse, evaporate, expand, or undergo any of various other changes and that flows to a body by contact with or radiation from bodies at higher temperatures **2 a** : intensity of feeling or reaction ⟨answered with some *heat*⟩ **b** : the height of an action or condition ⟨the *heat* of battle⟩ **c** : sexual excitement esp. in a female mammal; *esp* : ESTRUS **3** : pungency of flavor **4** : a single continuous effort: as **a** : a single course in a race **b** : one of several preliminary races held to eliminate less competent contenders **c** : PRESSURE, COERCION — **heatless** \'hēt-ləs\ *adj*

heat·ed \'hēt-əd\ *adj* **1** : HOT ⟨a *heated* engine⟩ **2** : marked by emotional heat : ANGRY ⟨*heated* words⟩

heat·ed·ly \-əd-lē\ *adv* : ANGRILY

heat engine *n* : a mechanism for converting heat energy into mechanical energy

heat·er \'hēt-ər\ *n* : a device that imparts heat or holds something to be heated

heat exchanger *n* : a device (as an automobile radiator) for transferring heat from one fluid to another without allowing them to mix

heat exhaustion *n* : a condition marked by weakness, nausea, dizziness, and profuse sweating that results from physical exertion in a hot environment — called also *heat prostration;* compare HEATSTROKE

heath \'hēth\ *n* [OE *hǣth*] **1** : any of a family of shrubby dicotyledonous and often evergreen plants that thrive on open barren soil usu. acid and ill-drained soil; *esp* : a low evergreen shrub with whorls of needlelike leaves and clusters of small flowers **2** : a tract of usu. level and poorly drained wasteland commonly overgrown with low shrubs — **heath·like** \-,līk\ *adj* — **heathy** \'hē-thē\ *adj*

¹hea·then \'hē-thən\ *adj* [OE *hǣthen*] **1** : of or relating to the heathen, their religions, or their customs **2** : FOREIGN, UNCIVILIZED

²heathen *n, pl* **heathens** *or* **heathen** **1** : an unconverted member of a people or nation that does not acknowledge the God of the Bible : PAGAN **2** : an uncivilized or irreligious person — **hea·then·dom** \-dəm\ *n* — **hea·then·ism** \-thə-,niz-əm\ *n*

hea·then·ish \'hē-thə-nish\ *adj* : resembling or characteristic of heathens : BARBAROUS — **hea·then·ish·ly** *adv*

¹heath·er \'heth-ər\ *n* [ME (northern) *hather*] : HEATH 1; *esp* : a common evergreen heath of northern and alpine regions with small crowded stemless leaves and tiny usu. purplish pink flowers in one-sided spikes — **heath·ery** \'heth-(ə-)rē\ *adj*

²heather *adj* **1** : of, relating to, or resembling heather **2** : having flecks of various colors ⟨a soft *heather* tweed⟩

heath hen *n* : an extinct grouse of the northeastern U.S. related to the prairie chicken

heating element *n* : the part of an electrical heating appliance that changes electrical energy into heat by offering great resistance to the passage of an electrical current

heat lightning *n* : flashes of light without thunder seen near the horizon and ascribed to far-off lightning reflected by high clouds

heat rash *n* : PRICKLY HEAT

heat-stroke \'hēt-,strōk\ *n* : a condition marked esp. by cessation of sweating, high body temperature, and collapse that results from prolonged exposure to high temperature — compare HEAT EXHAUSTION

¹heave \'hēv\ *vb* **heaved** *or* **hove** \'hōv\; **heav·ing** [OE

hebban] **1** : to raise with an effort : LIFT ⟨*heave* a trunk onto a truck⟩ **2** : THROW, CAST, HURL ⟨*heave* a rock⟩ **3** : to utter with an effort ⟨*heave* a sigh⟩ **4** : to rise and fall repeatedly ⟨the runner's chest was *heaving*⟩ **5** : to be thrown up or raised ⟨the ground *heaved* during the earthquake⟩ **6** : RETCH **syn** see LIFT — **heav·er** *n* — **heave in sight** : to seem to rise above the horizon and come into view — **heave to** : to bring a ship to a stop

²heave *n* **1 a** : an effort to heave or raise **b** : a forceful throw : CAST **2** : an upward motion; *esp* : a rhythmical rising (as of the chest in breathing)

heav·en \'hev-ən\ *n* [OE *heofon*] **1** : the expanse of space that seems to be over the earth like a dome : FIRMAMENT — usu. used in pl. **2** *often cap* : the dwelling place of God and the joyful abode of the blessed dead **b** : a spiritual state of everlasting communion with God **3** *cap* : ²GOD **4** : a place or condition of utmost happiness

heav·en·ly \'hev-ən-lē\ *adj* **1** : of or relating to heaven or the heavens ⟨*heavenly* bodies such as the sun, moon, and stars⟩ **2** : DIVINE, SACRED, BLESSED ⟨*heavenly* grace⟩ **3** : supremely delightful ⟨a *heavenly* day⟩ — **heav·en·li·ness** *n*

heav·en·ward \'hev-ən-wərd\ *adv* (*or adj*) : toward heaven

heav·en·wards \-wərdz\ *adv* : HEAVENWARD

heav·i·ly \'hev-ə-lē\ *adv* **1** : with or as if with weight ⟨bear down *heavily*⟩⟨*heavily* burdened with cares⟩ **2** : in a slow laborious manner ⟨breathe *heavily*⟩ **3** : SEVERELY ⟨*heavily* punished⟩ **4** : THICKLY ⟨a *heavily* populated district⟩

heav·i·ness \'hev-ē-nəs\ *n* : the quality or state of being heavy

¹heavy \'hev-ē\ *adj* **heav·i·er; -est** [OE *hefig*] **1 a** : having great weight or weight greater than the usual or normal **b** : weighty in proportion to bulk : having a high specific gravity ⟨gold is a *heavy* metal⟩ **2** : hard to bear; *esp* : GRIEVOUS ⟨a *heavy* sorrow⟩ **3** : of weighty import : SERIOUS ⟨words *heavy* with meaning⟩ **4 a** : OPPRESSED, BURDENED **b** : PREGNANT; *esp* : approaching parturition **5 a** : slow or dull from loss of vitality or resiliency ⟨a *heavy* step⟩ **b** : lacking sparkle or vivacity ⟨a *heavy* writing style⟩ **c** : lacking mirth or gaiety : DOLEFUL **6** : dulled with weariness : DROWSY **7** : greater in volume or force than the average of its kind or class ⟨*heavy* traffic⟩⟨*heavy* seas⟩ **8 a** : OVERCAST **b** : full of clay and inclined to hold water ⟨*heavy* soils⟩ **c** : LOUD **d** : THICK ⟨a *heavy* growth of timber⟩ **e** : OPPRESSIVE ⟨a *heavy* odor⟩ **f** : STEEP, ACUTE ⟨a *heavy* grade⟩ **g** : LABORIOUS, DIFFICULT ⟨a *heavy* task⟩ **h** : of large capacity or output ⟨a *heavy* drinker⟩ **9 a** : digested with difficulty because of excessive richness or seasoning ⟨*heavy* fruitcake⟩ **b** : not properly raised or leavened ⟨*heavy* bread⟩ **10** : producing goods (as coal or steel) used in the production of other goods ⟨*heavy* industry⟩ **11** : heavily armed or armored ⟨*heavy* tank⟩ **12** : ACCENTED ⟨*heavy* syllables⟩

²heavy *adv* : in a heavy manner : HEAVILY ⟨time hung *heavy* on their hands⟩

³heavy *n, pl* **heav·ies** **1** : HEAVYWEIGHT 2 **2 a** : a theatrical role or an actor representing a dignified or imposing person **b** : VILLAIN

heavy–du·ty \,hev-ē-'d(y)üt-ē\ *adj* : able or designed to withstand unusual strain

heavy–foot·ed \-'füt-əd\ *adj* : heavy and slow in movement : DULL

heavy–hand·ed \-'han-dəd\ *adj* **1** : CLUMSY, UNGRACEFUL **2** : OPPRESSIVE, HARSH — **heavy–hand·ed·ly** *adv* — **heavy–hand·ed·ness** *n*

heavy–heart·ed \-'härt-əd\ *adj* : SADDENED, DESPONDENT — **heavy·heart·ed·ly** *adv* — **heavy·heart·ed·ness** *n*

heavy hydrogen *n* : DEUTERIUM

heavy·set \,hev-ē-'set\ *adj* : being stocky and compact and sometimes tending to stoutness in build

heavy water *n* : water containing more than the usual proportion of heavy isotopes; *esp* : water enriched in deuterium

heavy·weight \'hev-ē-,wāt\ *n* **1** : one above average in weight **2** : one in the heaviest class of contestants; *esp* : a boxer weighing over 175 pounds

heb·dom·a·dal \heb-'däm-əd-ᵊl\ *adj* [Gk *hebdomad-, hebdomas* group of seven, week; akin to E *seven*] : WEEKLY — **heb·dom·a·dal·ly** \-ᵊl-ē\ *adv*

j joke; ŋ sing; ō flow; ȯ flaw; ȯi coin; th thin; t͟h this; ü loot; u̇ foot; y yet; yü few; yu̇ furious; zh vision

He·be \'hē-bē\ *n* : the Greek goddess of youth
He·bra·ic \hi-'brā-ik\ *adj* : of, relating to, or character-istic of the Hebrews or their language or culture
He·bra·ism \'hē-brā-,iz-əm\ *n* 1 : a Hebrew idiom oc-curring in another language 2 : the thought, spirit, or practice characteristic of the Hebrews
He·bra·ist \-,brā-əst\ *n* : a specialist in Hebrew and Hebraic studies
He·bra·is·tic \,hē-brā-'is-tik\ *adj* 1 : HEBRAIC 2 : marked by Hebraisms
He·brew \'hē-,brü\ *n* 1 : a member of or descendant from one of a group of northern Semitic peoples including the Israelites; *esp* : ISRAELITE 2 a : the Semitic language of the ancient Hebrews b : any of various later forms of this language — **Hebrew** *adj*
He·brews \'hē-,brüz\ *n* — see BIBLE table
Hec·a·te \'hek-ət-ē\ *n* : the Greek goddess of the under-world
hec·a·tomb \'hek-ə-,tōm\ *n* [Gk *hekatombē,* fr. *hekaton* hundred + *bous* cow] 1 : an ancient Greek and Roman sacrifice of 100 oxen or cattle 2 : a great slaughter
heck·le \'hek-əl\ *vt* **heck·led; heck·ling** \'hek-(ə-)liŋ\ [ME *hekelen,* fr. *hakell, hekele* hackle] : to interrupt with questions or comments usu. with the intention of annoy-ing or hindering : BADGER 〈*heckle* a public speaker〉 — **heck·ler** \-(ə-)lər\ *n*
hect- or **hecto-** *comb form* [F, irreg. fr. Gk *hekaton;* akin to E *hundred*] : hundred 〈*hectograph*〉
hect·are \'hek-,ta(ə)r, -,te(ə)r, -,tär\ *n* — see METRIC SYSTEM table
hec·tic \'hek-tik\ *adj* [LL *hecticus,* fr. Gk *hektikos* habit-ual, consumptive, fr. *hek-, echein* to have, hold] 1 a : char-acteristic of a wasting disease; *esp* : being a fluctuating but persistent fever (as in tuberculosis) b : affected by or appearing as if affected by a hectic fever; *esp* : FLUSHED 2 : filled with excitement or confusion 〈bought all the gifts in three *hectic* days of Christmas shopping〉 — **hec-ti·cal·ly** \-ti-k(ə-)lē\ *adv*
hec·to·gram \'hek-tə-,gram\ *n* — see METRIC SYSTEM table
hec·to·graph \-,graf\ *n* : a machine for making copies of a writing or drawing — **hectograph** *vt* — **hec·to·graph·ic** \,hek-tə-'graf-ik\ *adj*
hec·to·li·ter \'hek-tə-,lēt-ər\ *n* — see METRIC SYSTEM table
hec·to·me·ter \'hek-tə-,mēt-ər\ *n* — see METRIC SYSTEM table
hec·tor \'hek-tər\ *vb* **hec·tored; hec·tor·ing** \-t(ə-)riŋ\ [*Hector*] 1 : to play the bully : SWAGGER 2 : to intimi-date by bluster or personal pressure
Hec·tor \'hek-tər\ *n* : a son of Priam and bravest of the Trojans in Homer's *Iliad*
Hec·u·ba \'hek-yə-bə\ *n* : the wife of Priam and mother of Hector in Homer's *Iliad*
he'd \(,)hēd, ēd\ : he had : he would
hed·dle \'hed-ᵊl\ *n* : one of the sets of parallel cords or wires that with their mounting compose the harness used to guide warp threads in a loom
¹hedge \'hej\ *n* [OE *hecg*] 1 a : a fence or boundary formed by a dense row of shrubs or low trees b : BAR-RIER, LIMIT 2 : a protection against financial loss 3 : a statement that avoids a direct answer or promise
²hedge *vb* 1 : to enclose or protect with or as if with a hedge 2 : to hem in or obstruct with or as if with a barrier : HINDER 〈*hedged* in by restrictions〉 3 : to protect oneself from losing by making a second balancing transac-tion 〈*hedge* on a bet〉 4 : to avoid giving a direct or definite answer or promise 〈*hedged* when asked to support a candidate for office〉 — **hed·ger** *n*
³hedge *adj* : of, relating to, or designed for a hedge
hedge·hog \'hej-,hóg, -,häg\ *n* 1 : an Old World insectiv-orous mammal having sharp spines mixed with the hair on its back and able to roll itself up into a spiny ball 2 : PORCUPINE
hedge·hop \-,häp\ *vi* : to fly an airplane so low that it is sometimes necessary to climb to avoid obstacles (as trees) — **hedge·hop·per** *n*
hedge·row \-,rō\ *n* : a row of shrubs or trees bounding or separating fields
he·do·nism \'hēd-ᵊn-,iz-əm\ *n* [Gk *hēdonē* pleasure; akin to E *sweet*] 1 : a doctrine that pleasure or happiness is the sole or chief good in life 2 : a way of life based on

hedonism — **he·do·nist** \-ᵊn-əst\ *n* — **he·do·nis·tic** \,hēd-ᵊn-'is-tik\ *adj*
-he·dral \'hē-drəl\ *adj comb form* : having (such) a surface or (such or so many) surfaces 〈di*hedral*〉
-he·dron \'hē-drən\ *n comb form, pl* **-hedrons** or **-he·dra** \-drə\ [Gk *hedra* seat] : crystal or geometrical figure having a (specified) form or number of surfaces 〈penta-*hedron*〉〈deca*hedron*〉
¹heed \'hēd\ *vb* [OE *hēdan*] 1 : to pay attention 2 : to concern oneself with : MIND
²heed *n* : ATTENTION, NOTICE 〈gave no *heed* to the warning〉
heed·ful \'hēd-fəl\ *adj* : taking heed : CAREFUL 〈*heedful* of the rights of others〉 — **heed·ful·ly** \-fə-lē\ *adv* — **heed-ful·ness** *n*
heed·less \-ləs\ *adj* : not taking heed : CARELESS 〈*heedless* of danger〉 — **heed·less·ly** *adv* — **heed·less·ness** *n*
hee-haw \'hē-,hò\ *n* 1 : the bray of a donkey 2 : a loud rude laugh : GUFFAW — **hee-haw** *vi*
¹heel \'hēl\ *n* [OE *hēla*] 1 : the back part of the human foot behind the arch and below the ankle; *also* : the cor-responding part of a lower vertebrate 2 a : a part (as of a shoe) that covers the human heel b : a solid attachment of a shoe or boot forming the back of the sole under the heel of the foot 3 : something resembling a heel in form, function, or position: as a (1) : one of the crusty ends of a loaf of bread (2) : one of the rind ends of a cheese b (1) : the after end of a ship's keel (2) : the lower end of a mast c : the base of a tuber or cutting of a plant used for propagation d : the base of a ladder 4 : a contempt-ible person — **heel·less** \'hēl-ləs\ *adj*
²heel *vt* : to furnish with a heel
³heel *vb* [ME *heelden,* fr. OE *hieldan*] : to tilt or cause to tilt to one side : TIP, LIST 〈a boat *heeling* badly〉
⁴heel *n* : a tilt to one side
heel–and–toe \,hē-lən-'tō\ *adj* : marked by a stride in which the heel of one foot touches the ground before the toe of the other foot leaves it 〈a *heel-and-toe* walking race〉
heel·er \'hē-lər\ *n* : one that heels
heel·tap \'hēl-,tap\ *n* : a small quantity of liquor remain-ing (as in a glass after drinking)
¹heft \'heft\ *n* [irreg. fr. *heave*] : WEIGHT, HEAVINESS
²heft *vt* 1 : to heave up : HOIST, LIFT, RAISE 2 : to test the weight of by lifting
hefty \'hef-tē\ *adj* **heft·i·er; -est** 1 : quite heavy 2 : marked by bigness, bulk, and usu. strength — **heft·i·ly** \-tə-lē\ *adv* — **heft·i·ness** \-tē-nəs\ *n*
he·gari \hi-'gar-ē\ *n* [Sudanese Ar *hegiri*] : a grain sor-ghum with chalky white seeds
he·gem·o·ny \hi-'jem-ə-nē, 'hej-ə-,mō-nē\ *n* [Gk *hēge-monia,* fr. *hēgemōn* leader, fr. *hēgeisthai* to lead] : prepon-derant influence or authority esp. of one nation over others
he·gi·ra or **he·ji·ra** \hi-'jī-rə, 'hej-ə-rə\ *n* [ML *hegira,* fr. Ar *hijrah,* lit., flight] 1 *cap* : the flight of Muhammad from Mecca in A.D. 622 2 : a journey esp. when under-taken to seek refuge away from a dangerous or undesir-able environment
Hei·del·berg man \,hīd-ᵊl-,bərg\ *n* [*Heidelberg,* Ger-many] : an early Pleistocene man known only from a massive fossilized jaw with distinctly human dentition
heif·er \'hef-ər\ *n* [OE *hēahfore*] : a young cow; *esp* : one that has not had a calf
heigh \'hī, 'hā\ *interj* : HEY
heigh–ho \-'hō\ *interj* — used typically to express bore-dom, weariness, or sadness or sometimes as a cry of en-couragement
height \'hīt, 'hītth\ *n* [OE *hiehthu;* akin to E *high*] 1 a : the highest part : SUMMIT b : the highest or most advanced point : CLIMAX 〈the *height* of stupidity〉 2 a : the distance from the bottom to the top of something stand-ing upright b : the extent of elevation above a level : ALTITUDE 3 : the condition of being tall or high 4 a : an extent of land rising to a considerable degree above the surrounding country b : a high point or position
syn ELEVATION, ALTITUDE: HEIGHT refers to something measured vertically whether high or low 〈a wall six feet in *height*〉 〈lettering not more than one inch in *height*〉 ELEVATION and ALTITUDE suggest reckoning of height by angular measurement or atmospheric pressure 〈fly at an *elevation* of 30,000 feet〉 〈Mexico City has a high *altitude*〉 ELEVATION is also applicable to things that are

raised or thought of as raised ⟨aimed the gun at an *elevation* of 40 degrees⟩

height·en \'hīt-ᵊn\ *vb* **height·ened; height·en·ing** \'hīt-niŋ, -ᵊn-iŋ\ **1 a :** to increase the amount or degree of **:** AUGMENT ⟨*heightened* the citizens' awareness⟩ **b :** to make or become brighter or more intense **:** DEEPEN ⟨excitement *heightened* the pinkness of her cheeks⟩ **c :** to bring out more strongly **:** point up ⟨*heighten* a contrast⟩ **2 a :** to raise high or higher **:** ELEVATE **b :** to raise above the ordinary or trite **syn** see INTENSIFY

hei·nous \'hā-nəs\ *adj* [ME, fr. MF *haineus* hateful, fr. *haine* hate, fr. *hair* to hate, of Gmc origin; akin to E *hate*] **:** hatefully or shockingly evil **:** ABOMINABLE — **hei·nous·ly** *adv* — **hei·nous·ness** *n*

heir \'a(ə)r, 'e(ə)r\ *n* [OF, fr. L *hered-, heres*] **1 :** a person who inherits or is entitled to inherit property **2 :** a person who has legal claim to a title or a throne when the person holding it dies — **heir·ship** \-,ship\ *n*

heir apparent *n, pl* **heirs apparent :** an heir who cannot legally be deprived of his right to succeed (as to a throne or a title) if he survives the present holder

heir·ess \'ar-əs, 'er-\ *n* **:** a female heir; *esp* **:** a female heir to great wealth

heir·loom \'a(ə)r-,lüm, 'e(ə)r-\ *n* [ME *heirlome*, fr. *heir* + *lome* implement] **:** a piece of personal property handed down by inheritance; *esp* **:** a piece of intrinsic or sentimental value owned by a family for several generations

heir presumptive *n, pl* **heirs presumptive :** an heir whose present right to inherit could be lost through the birth of a nearer relative

¹heist \'hīst\ *vt* **1** *chiefly dial* **:** HOIST **2** *slang* **a :** to commit armed robbery on **b :** STEAL

²heist *n, slang* **:** armed robbery **:** HOLDUP; *also* **:** THEFT

held *past of* HOLD

Hel·en of Troy \,hel-ən-əv-'troi\ **:** the beautiful wife of Menelaus whose abduction by Paris caused the Trojan War

heli- *or* **helio-** *comb form* [Gk *hēlios*] **:** sun ⟨*heliocentric*⟩ ⟨*heliograph*⟩

hel·i·cal \'hel-i-kəl, 'hē-li-\ *adj* **:** of, relating to, or having the form of a helix; *also* **:** SPIRAL 1a — **hel·i·cal·ly** \-k(ə-)lē\ *adv*

hel·i·coid \'hel-ə-,koid, 'hē-lə-\ *or* **hel·i·coi·dal** \,hel-ə-'koid-ᵊl, ,hē-lə-\ *adj* **1 :** forming or arranged in a spiral **2 :** having the form of a flat coil or flattened spiral ⟨*helicoid* snail shell⟩

hel·i·con \'hel-ə-,kän, -i-kən\ *n* **:** a large circular bass tuba used in military bands

¹hel·i·cop·ter \'hel-ə-,käp-tər, 'hē-lə-\ *n* [Gk *helik-, helix* helix + *pteron* wing] **:** an aircraft that is supported in the air by propellers revolving on a vertical axis

²helicopter *or* **hel·i·copt** \-,käpt\ *vb* **:** to travel or transport by helicopter

he·lio·cen·tric \,hē-lē-ō-'sen-trik\ *adj* **1 :** referred to or measured from the sun's center or appearing as if seen from it ⟨a *heliocentric* position⟩ **2 :** having or relating to the sun as a center ⟨a *heliocentric* theory of the solar system⟩ — compare GEOCENTRIC

¹he·lio·graph \'hē-lē-ə-,graf\ *n* **:** an apparatus for telegraphing by means of the sun's rays reflected from a mirror

²heliograph *vb* **:** to signal by means of a heliograph

He·li·os \'hē-lē-,äs\ *n* **:** the sun god in Greek mythology represented as driving a 4-horse chariot through the heavens

he·lio·tax·is \,hē-lē-ō-'tak-səs\ *n* **:** phototaxis for which sunlight is the stimulus

he·lio·trope \'hēl-yə-,trōp, 'hē-lē-ə-\ *n* [Gk *hēliotropion* plant that turns its flowers towards the sun, fr. *hēlios* sun + *trop-, trepein* to turn] **1 :** any of a genus of herbs or shrubs of the borage family — compare GARDEN HELIOTROPE **2 :** BLOODSTONE **3 a :** a variable color averaging a moderate purple **b :** a moderate reddish purple

he·li·ot·ro·pism \,hē-lē-'ä-trə-,piz-əm\ *n* **:** phototropism in which sunlight is the orienting stimulus — **he·lio·tro·pic** \,hē-lē-ə-'trōp-ik, -'träp-\ *adj* — **he·lio·tro·pi·cal·ly** \-i-k(ə-)lē\ *adv*

heli·port \'hel-ə-,pōrt, 'hē-lə-, -,port\ *n* **:** a landing and takeoff place for a helicopter

he·li·um \'hē-lē-əm\ *n* [NL, fr. Gk *hēlios* sun; so called because first observed in the sun's atmosphere] **:** a light

colorless nonflammable gaseous chemical element in various natural gases — see ELEMENT table

he·lix \'hē-liks\ *n, pl* **he·li·ces** \'hel-ə-,sēz, 'hē-lə-\ *also* **he·lix·es** \'hē-lik-səz\ [L *helic-, helix*, fr. Gk *helik-, helix*] **1 :** something (as a wire coiled around a cylinder, a cone-shaped wire spring, or a corkscrew) spiral in form **2 :** the incurved rim of the external ear **3 a :** a curve in space traced by a point rotating around an axis and progressing in a direction parallel to the axis (as the curve formed by a screw thread) **b :** SPIRAL 1 b

hell \'hel\ *n* [OE] **1 :** the abode of souls after death **2 :** the place or state of punishment for the wicked after death **:** the home of evil spirits **3 :** a place or condition of misery or wickedness **4 :** something that causes torment; *esp* **:** a severe scolding

he'll \(,)hēl, hil, ēl, il\ **:** he shall **:** he will

hell·ben·der \'hel-,ben-dər\ *n* **:** a large aquatic salamander of the Ohio valley

hell·bent \-,bent\ *adj* **1 :** stubbornly and often recklessly determined **2 :** going full tilt

hell·cat \-,kat\ *n* **1 :** WITCH 2 **2 :** TORMENTOR; *esp* **:** SHREW

hel·le·bore \'hel-ə-,bōr, -,bȯr\ *n* [Gk *helleboros*] **1 :** any of a genus of herbs of the buttercup family; *also* **:** its dried root formerly used in medicine **2 :** a poisonous herb of the lily family; *also* **:** its dried root or a product of this containing alkaloids used in medicine and insecticides

Hel·lene \'hel-,ēn\ *n* [Gk *Hellēn*] **:** GREEK — **Hel·len·ic** \he-'len-ik, hə-\ *adj*

Hel·le·nism \'hel-ə-,niz-əm\ *n* **1 :** devotion to or imitation of esp. ancient Greek thought, customs, or styles **2 :** Greek civilization **3 :** a body of humanistic and classical ideals associated with ancient Greece

Hel·le·nist \-nəst\ *n* **1 :** a person living in Hellenistic times not Greek in ancestry but Greek in language, outlook, and way of life; *esp* **:** a hellenized Jew **2 :** a specialist in the language or culture of ancient Greece

Hel·le·nis·tic \,hel-ə-'nis-tik\ *adj* [fr. the hellenization of non-Greek lands resulting from their conquest by Alexander] **1 :** of or relating to Greek history, culture, or art after Alexander the Great **2 :** of or relating to the Hellenists — **Hel·le·nis·ti·cal·ly** \-ti-k(ə-)lē\ *adv*

hel·le·nize \'hel-ə-,nīz\ *vb, often cap* **:** to make or become Greek or Hellenistic in form or culture — **hel·le·ni·za·tion** \,hel-ə-nə-'zā-shən\ *n, often cap*

hell·er \'hel-ər\ *n, chiefly dial* **:** HELLION

hel·leri \'hel-ə-,rī, -,rē\ *n* [NL (specific epithet of *Xiphophorus helleri*), fr. C. *Heller*, 20th cent. tropical fish collector] **1 :** SWORDTAIL **2 :** any of various brightly colored topminnows that are hybrids of swordtails and platys

hell·gram·mite \'hel-grə-,mīt\ *n* **:** the carnivorous aquatic larva of a dobsonfly much used as a fish bait

hel·lion \'hel-yən\ *n* **:** a troublesome or mischievous person

hell·ish \'hel-ish\ *adj* **:** of, resembling, or befitting hell **:** DEVILISH — **hell·ish·ly** *adv* — **hell·ish·ness** *n*

hel·lo \hə-'lō, he-\ *n, pl* **hellos :** an expression or gesture of greeting — used interjectionally in greeting, in answering the telephone, or to express surprise

¹helm \'helm\ *n* [OE] **:** HELMET 1

²helm *vt* **:** to cover or furnish with a helmet

³helm *n* [OE *helma*] **1 :** a lever or wheel controlling the rudder of a ship for steering; *also* **:** the entire apparatus for steering a ship **2 :** a position of control **:** HEAD ⟨at the *helm* of a growing business⟩

⁴helm *vt* **:** to direct with or as if with a helm **:** STEER

hel·met \'hel-mət\ *n* [MF, dim. of *helme* helmet, of Gmc origin; akin to E *helm*] **1 :** a covering or enclosing head-piece of ancient or medieval armor **2 :** any of various protective head coverings usu. made of a hard material to resist impact **3 :** something resembling a helmet — **hel·met·like** \-,līk\ *adj*

hel·minth \'hel-,min(t)th\ *n* [Gk *helminth-, helmis*] **:** WORM; *esp* **:** an intestinal worm (as a tapeworm) — **hel·min·thic** \hel-'min(t)-thik\ *adj*

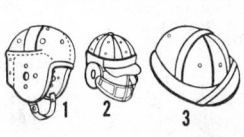
helmets 2: *1* football, *2* lacrosse, *3* polo

hel·min·thi·a·sis \,hel-,min-'thī-ə-səs\ *n* : infestation with or disease caused by parasitic worms

hel·min·thol·o·gy \-'thäl-ə-jē\ *n* : a branch of zoology concerned with helminths; *esp* : the study of parasitic worms

helms·man \'helmz-mən\ *n* : the man at the helm : STEERSMAN

hel·ot \'hel-ət\ *n* [Gk *heilōt-, heilōs*] **1** *cap* : a member of a class of serfs of ancient Sparta **2** : SERF, SLAVE — **hel·ot·ry** \-ə-trē\ *n*

hel·ot·ism \'hel-ət-,iz-əm\ *n* **1** : SERFDOM **2** : a symbiotic relation in which one member functions as the slave of the other

¹help \'help\ *vb* [OE *helpan*] **1 a** : to give aid or assistance ⟨we *helped* him⟩ ⟨tries to *help* but gets in the way⟩ **b** : to aid in doing a certain act ⟨*helped* him study⟩ ⟨*helped* me to get a job⟩ **c** : to be of aid in putting or bringing into a certain place, position, or condition ⟨*helped* him home⟩ ⟨*help* her up⟩ **2 a** : REMEDY, RELIEVE ⟨rest *helps* a cold⟩ **b** : to get (oneself) out of a difficulty **3** : to further the advancement of : PROMOTE ⟨*helping* industrial development with loans⟩ **4 a** : to change for the better ⟨people get used to what they can't *help*⟩ **b** : to refrain from ⟨couldn't *help* laughing⟩ **c** : to keep from occurring : PREVENT ⟨blamed him for something he couldn't *help*⟩ **5** : to serve with food or drink esp. at a meal **6** : to appropriate for the use of (oneself) — **cannot help but** : cannot but — **so help me** : I swear it

²help *n* **1** : an act or instance of helping ⟨give *help*⟩ ⟨thank someone for his *help*⟩ **2** : the state of being helped : RELIEF ⟨a situation that is beyond *help*⟩ **3** : a person or a thing that helps ⟨a *help* in time of trouble⟩ **4** : a hired helper or a body of hired helpers ⟨hire additional *help* in a business⟩

help·er \'hel-pər\ *n* : one that helps; *esp* : a relatively unskilled worker who assists a skilled worker usu. by manual labor

help·ful \'help-fəl\ *adj* : furnishing help : ASSISTING, USEFUL ⟨a *helpful* neighbor⟩ ⟨a *helpful* reference book⟩ — **help·ful·ly** \-fə-lē\ *adv* — **help·ful·ness** *n*

help·ing \'hel-piŋ\ *n* : a portion of food : SERVING ⟨asked for a second *helping* of potatoes⟩

helping verb *n* : an auxiliary verb

help·less \'hel-pləs\ *adj* **1** : lacking protection or support : DEFENSELESS **2** : lacking strength or effectiveness : POWERLESS ⟨was *helpless* to prevent him from going⟩ — **help·less·ly** *adv* — **help·less·ness** *n*

help·mate \'help-,māt\ *n* : one who is a companion and helper; *esp* : WIFE

help·meet \-,mēt\ *n* : HELPMATE

¹hel·ter-skel·ter \,hel-tər-'skel-tər\ *adv* **1** : in headlong disorder : PELL-MELL ⟨ran *helter-skelter* down the hill⟩ **2** : in random order : HAPHAZARDLY ⟨clothes strewn *helter-skelter* about the room⟩

²helter-skelter *n* : a disorderly confusion : TURMOIL

³helter-skelter *adj* **1** : confusedly hurried : PRECIPITATE ⟨*helter-skelter* rush-hour traffic⟩ **2** : HIT-OR-MISS, HAPHAZARD ⟨does things in a *helter-skelter* manner⟩

helve \'helv\ *n* [OE *hielfe*] : a handle of a tool or weapon : HAFT

Hel·ve·tian \hel-'vē-shən\ *adj* : of or relating to the Helvetii or Helvetia : SWISS — **Helvetian** *n*

Hel·ve·tii \-shē-,ī\ *n pl* : an early Celtic people of western Switzerland in the time of Julius Caesar

¹hem \'hem\ *n* [OE] : a border of a garment or cloth; *esp* : one made by folding back an edge and sewing it down

²hem *vb* **hemmed; hem·ming** **1** : to finish with or make a hem in sewing **2** : to surround in a restrictive manner : CONFINE ⟨a town *hemmed* in by mountains⟩ — **hem·mer** *n*

³hem \a *throat-clearing sound; often read as* 'hem\ *n* : a vocalized pause in speaking — often used interjectionally to call attention or to express hesitation or doubt

⁴hem \'hem\ *vi* **hemmed; hem·ming** **1** : to utter the sound represented by *hem* **2** : EQUIVOCATE ⟨*hemmed* and hawed and refused to act⟩

hem- *or* **hemo-** *or* **haem-** *or* **haemo-** *comb form* [Gk *haima*] : blood ⟨*hem*al⟩ ⟨*hemo*flagellate⟩

he·ma·cy·tom·e·ter \,hē-mə-sī-'täm-ət-ər\ *n* : an instrument for counting blood cells

hem·ag·glu·ti·na·tion \,hē-mə-,glüt-ᵊn-'ā-shən\ *n* : ag-

glutination of red blood cells — **hem·ag·glu·ti·nate** \-'glüt-ᵊn-,āt\ *vt*

he·mal \'hē-məl\ *adj* : of or relating to the blood or blood vessels; *also* : situated on the side of the spinal cord adjacent to the heart and chief blood vessels

he-man \'hē-'man\ *n* : an obviously strong virile man

hemat- *or* **hemato-** *or* **haemat-** *or* **haemato-** *comb form* [Gk *haimat-, haima* blood] : HEM- ⟨*hemat*oid⟩ ⟨*hemato*genous⟩

he·ma·tin·ic \,hē-mə-'tin-ik\ *n* : an agent that tends to stimulate blood cell formation or to increase the hemoglobin in the blood — **hematinic** *adj*

he·ma·tite \'hē-mə-,tīt\ *n* : a mineral Fe_2O_3 consisting of ferric oxide, constituting an important iron ore, and occurring in crystals or in a red earthy form

he·ma·tog·e·nous \,hē-mə-'täj-ə-nəs\ *adj* **1** : producing blood **2** : spread by or arising in the blood

he·ma·tol·o·gy \-'täl-ə-jē\ *n* : a branch of biology that deals with the blood and blood-forming organs — **he·ma·to·log·ic** \,hē-mət-ə-'läj-ik\ *or* **he·ma·to·log·i·cal** \-'läj-i-kəl\ *adj* — **he·ma·tol·o·gist** \,hē-mə-'täl-ə-jəst\ *n*

he·ma·to·ma \,hē-mə-'tō-mə\ *n* : a blood-containing tumor or swelling

he·mato·poi·e·sis \hi-,mat-ə-pói-'ē-səs\ *n* [Gk *poiēsis* production, fr. *poiein* to make] : the formation of blood or of blood cells in the living body — **he·mato·poi·et·ic** \-pói-'et-ik\ *adj*

he·ma·tox·y·lon \,hē-mə-'täk-sə-,län, ,hem-ə-\ *n* [Gk *xylon* wood] : the wood or dye of logwood

heme \'hēm\ *n* : a deep red iron-containing pigment obtained from hemoglobin

hem·ero·cal·lis \,hem-ə-rō-'kal-əs\ *n* : DAY LILY 1

hemi- *prefix* [Gk *hēmi-*] : half ⟨*hemi*hedral⟩ — compare SEMI-

hemi·chor·date \,hem-i-'kórd-ət, -'kór-,dāt\ *n* : any of a small group (Hemichordata) of lowly marine animals resembling worms but having a proboscis that contains a structure held to be a degenerate notochord — compare CHORDATE

he·mip·ter·an \hi-'mip-tə-rən\ *n* [Gk *pteron* wing] : any of a large order (Hemiptera) of insects comprising the true bugs (as the bedbug and chinch bug) and related forms (as plant lice) and having flattened bodies, two pairs of wings, and heads with piercing and sucking organs — **he·mip·ter·on** \-tə-,rän\ *n* — **he·mip·ter·ous** \-tə-rəs\ *adj*

hemi·sphere \'hem-ə-,sfi(ə)r\ *n* **1** : the northern or southern half of the earth divided by the equator or the eastern or western half divided by a meridian **2** : one of two half spheres formed by a plane through the sphere's center **3** : CEREBRAL HEMISPHERE — **hemi·spher·ic** \,hem-ə-'sfi(ə)r-ik, -'sfer-\ *or* **hemi·spher·i·cal** \-'sfir-i-kəl, -'sfer-\ *adj*

hemi·stich \'hem-i-,stik\ *n* [Gk *stichos* line, verse] : half a poetic line usu. divided by a caesura

hem·line \'hem-,līn\ *n* : the line formed by the lower edge of a dress, skirt, or coat

hem·lock \'hem-,läk\ *n* [OE *hemlic*] **1** : any of several poisonous herbs of the carrot family having finely cut leaves and small white flowers **2** : any of a genus of evergreen trees of the pine family; *also* : the soft light splintery wood of a hemlock

he·mo·cy·a·nin \,hē-mō-'sī-ə-nən\ *n* : a copper-containing respiratory pigment in the blood of some mollusks and arthropods

he·mo·glo·bin \'hē-mə-,glō-bən\ *n* : an iron-containing protein respiratory pigment that is the chief means of oxygen transport in the vertebrate body where it occurs in the red blood cells and is able to combine loosely with oxygen in regions (as the lungs) of high concentration and release it in regions (as the visceral tissues) of low concentration; *also* : any of various chemically or functionally similar iron-containing compounds

he·mo·ly·sin \,hē-mə-'līs-ᵊn\ *n* : a substance that causes the dissolution of red blood cells

he·mol·y·sis \hi-'mäl-ə-səs\ *n* : a breaking down of red blood cells resulting in release of hemoglobin — **he·mo·lyt·ic** \,hē-mə-'lit-ik\ *adj* — **he·mo·lyze** \'hē-mə-,līz\ *vb*

he·mo·phil·ia \,hē-mə-'fil-ē-ə\ *n* : a usu. hereditary

tendency to uncontrollable bleeding — **he·mo·phil·i·ac** \-ē-,ak\ *adj or n*

he·mo·phil·ic \-'fil-ik\ *adj* **1** : blood-loving ⟨*hemophilic* bacteria⟩ **2** : HEMOPHILIAC

hem·or·rhage \'hem-(ə-)rij\ *n* [Gk *haimorrhagia*, fr. *haima* blood + *rhag-*, *rhēgnynai* to break] : a copious discharge of blood from the blood vessels — **hemorrhage** *vi* — **hem·or·rhag·ic** \,hem-ə-'raj-ik\ *adj*

hem·or·rhoid \'hem-(ə-),ròid\ *n* [Gk *haimorrhoides*, pl., fr. *haima* blood + *rho-*, *rhein* to flow] : a swollen mass of dilated veins situated at or just within the anus — usu. used in pl.; called also *piles* — **hem·or·rhoid·al** \,hem-ə-'ròid-ᵊl\ *adj* — **hem·or·rhoid·ec·to·my** \,hem-(ə-),ròi-'dek-tə-mē\ *n*

he·mo·sta·sis \,hē-mə-'stā-səs\ *n* [Gk *stasis* act of stopping, fr. *histanai* to cause to stand] : an arrest of bleeding; *also* : sluggishness of blood flow — **he·mo·stat·ic** \-'stat-ik\ *adj*

hemp \'hemp\ *n* [OE *hænep*] : a tall Asiatic herb of the mulberry family widely grown for its tough bast fiber that is used esp. in cordage or for its flowers that yield hashish — **hemp·en** \'hem-pən\ *adj*

¹hem·stitch \'hem-,stich\ *vt* : to embroider (fabric) by drawing out parallel threads and stitching the exposed threads in groups to form various designs — **hem·stitch·er** *n*

²hemstitch *n* **1** : decorative needlework **2** : a stitch used in hemstitching

hen \'hen\ *n* [OE *henn*] **1 a** : a female domestic fowl esp. over a year old; *also* : a female bird **b** : the female of various mostly aquatic animals (as lobsters or fish) **2** : WOMAN; *esp* : a fussy middle-aged woman

hen·bane \'hen-,bān\ *n* : a poisonous fetid Old World herb of the nightshade family having sticky hairy toothed leaves and yellowish brown flowers

hence \'hen(t)s\ *adv* [ME *hennes*, *henne*, fr. OE *heonan*] **1** : from this place : AWAY **2** : from this time ⟨a week *hence*⟩ **3** : CONSEQUENTLY, THEREFORE ⟨was a newcomer and *hence* had no close friends in the city⟩

hence·forth \-,fòrth, -,fòrth\ *adv* : from this point on

hence·for·ward \hen(t)s-'fòr-wərd\ *adv* : HENCEFORTH

hench·man \'hench-mən\ *n* [ME *hengestman* groom, fr. *hengest* stallion + *man*] **1** : a trusted follower or supporter **2** : a political follower serving for his own advantage

hen·e·quen \'hen-i-kən, ,hen-i-'ken\ *n* [Sp *henequén*] : a strong hard cordage fiber from the leaves of a tropical American agave; *also* : this plant

hen harrier *n* : a widely distributed hawk with the bluish gray adult male differing so much from the brown and buff female and immature forms as to be often mistaken for a different species

¹hen·na \'hen-ə\ *n* [Ar *hinnā'*] **1** : an Old World tropical shrub with panicles of fragrant white flowers **2** : a reddish brown dye obtained from leaves of the henna and used esp. on hair

²henna *vt* **hen·naed** \'hen-əd\; **hen·na·ing** : to dye or tint with henna

hen·nery \'hen-ə-rē\ *n, pl* **-ner·ies** : a poultry farm; *also* : an enclosure for poultry

hen party *n* : a party for women only

hen·peck \'hen-,pek\ *vt* : to subject (one's husband) to persistent nagging and domination

hen·ry \'hen-rē\ *n, pl* **henries** *also* **henrys** [after Joseph Henry d1878 American physicist] : the mks unit of inductance equal to the self-inductance of a circuit or the mutual inductance of two circuits in which the variation of one ampere per second results in an induced electromotive force of one volt

hep \'hep\ *adj* **1** : characterized by a keen informed awareness of or interest in the newest developments **2** : WISE, ALERT

hep·a·rin \'hep-ə-rən\ *n* : a compound found esp. in liver that slows the clotting of blood and is used medically

¹he·pat·ic \hi-'pat-ik\ *adj* [Gk *hēpat-*, *hēpar* liver] : of, relating to, or resembling the liver

²hepatic *n* : LIVERWORT

he·pat·i·ca \hi-'pat-i-kə\ *n* : any of a genus of herbs of the buttercup family with lobed leaves and delicate white, pink, or bluish flowers; *also* : this flower

hep·a·ti·tis \,hep-ə-'tīt-əs\ *n* : inflammation of the liver;

also : an acute virus disease marked by hepatitis, jaundice, fever, and gastrointestinal symptoms

He·phaes·tus \hi-'fes-təs\ *n* : the Greek god of fire and of metalworking

hepped up \'hep-'təp\ *adj* : ENTHUSIASTIC ⟨was all *hepped up* about his summer job⟩

Hep·ple·white \'hep-əl-,hwīt\ *adj* [after George *Hepplewhite* d1786 English cabinetmaker] : of or relating to a late 18th century English furniture style characterized by light and elegant construction and the use of curves

hepta- *or* **hept-** *comb form* [Gk *hepta*; akin to E *seven*] : seven ⟨*hepta*meter⟩

hep·ta·gon \'hep-tə-,gän\ *n* : a polygon of seven angles and seven sides — **hep·tag·o·nal** \hep-'tag-ən-ᵊl\ *adj*

hep·tam·e·ter \hep-'tam-ət-ər\ *n* : a line consisting of seven metrical feet

¹her \(h)ər, ,hər\ *adj* [OE *hiere*, gen. of *hēo* she; akin to E *he*] : of or relating to her or herself esp. as possessor, agent, or object of an action ⟨*her* house⟩ ⟨*her* research⟩ ⟨*her* rescue⟩ — compare ¹SHE

²her \ər, (')hər\ *pron, objective case of* SHE

He·ra \'hir-ə\ *n* : the queen of heaven in Greek mythology, sister and wife of Zeus, and goddess of women and marriage

Her·a·kles *or* **Her·a·cles** \'her-ə-,klēz\ *n* : HERCULES

¹her·ald \'her-əld\ *n* [MF *hiraut*, of Gmc origin] **1 a** : an official at a medieval tournament **b** : an officer acting as messenger between leaders of warring parties **c** : an officer responsible for granting and registering coats of arms **2** : an official crier or messenger **3 a** : HARBINGER **b** : ANNOUNCER

²herald *vt* **1** : to give notice of : ANNOUNCE **2 a** : PUBLICIZE **b** : HAIL, GREET

he·ral·dic \he-'ral-dik\ *adj* : of or relating to heralds or heraldry — **he·ral·di·cal·ly** \-di-k(ə-)lē\ *adv*

her·ald·ry \'her-əl-drē\ *n, pl* **-ries** **1** : the art or science of a herald : the science of tracing a person's family and determining what coat of arms he is entitled to have **2** : COAT OF ARMS **3** : heraldic pomp or ceremony

herb \'(h)ərb\ *n* [L *herba* grass, herb] **1** : an annual, biennial, or perennial seed plant that does not develop persistent woody tissue but dies down at the end of a growing season — compare SHRUB **2** : a plant or plant part valued for its medicinal, savory, or aromatic qualities — **her·ba·ceous** \,(h)ər-'bā-shəs\ *adj* — **herb·like** \'(h)ərb-,līk\ *adj* — **herby** \'(h)ər-bē\ *adj*

herb·age \'(h)ər-bij\ *n* **1** : herbaceous vegetation (as grass) esp. when used for grazing **2** : the succulent parts of herbaceous plants

¹herb·al \'(h)ər-bəl\ *n* : a book about plants esp. with reference to their medical properties

²herbal *adj* : of, relating to, or made of herbs

herb·al·ist \'(h)ər-bə-ləst\ *n* : one that collects, grows, or deals in herbs

her·bar·i·um \,(h)ər-'bar-ē-əm, -'ber-\ *n, pl* **-ia** \-ē-ə\ **1** : a collection of dried plant specimens **2** : a place that houses an herbarium

her·bi·cide \'(h)ər-bə-,sīd\ *n* : an agent used to destroy or inhibit plant growth — **her·bi·cid·al** \,(h)ər-bə-'sīd-ᵊl\ *adj*

her·biv·o·ra \,(h)ər-'biv-ə-rə\ *n pl* [NL] : HERBIVORES

her·bi·vore \'(h)ər-bə-,vōr, -,vòr\ *n* [NL *herbivorus* plant-eating, fr. L *herba* grass + *vorare* to devour] : a plant-eating animal; *esp* : UNGULATE — **her·biv·o·rous** \,(h)ər-'biv-ə-rəs\ *adj*

Her·cu·le·an \,hər-kyə-'lē-ən, ,hər-'kyü-lē-\ *adj* **1** : of, relating to, or characteristic of Hercules **2** *often not cap* : of extraordinary power, size, or difficulty ⟨a *herculean* task⟩

Her·cu·les \'hər-kyə-,lēz\ *n* **1** : a hero of classical mythology noted for great strength and esp. for achieving twelve labors imposed on him by Hera **2** [L] : a northern constellation between Corona Borealis and Lyra

Her·cu·les'–club \,hər-kyə-,lēz-'kläb\ *n* : a small prickly eastern U.S. tree of the ginseng family; *also* : a prickly shrub or tree of the rue family

¹herd \'hərd\ *n* [OE *heord*] **1** : a number of animals of one kind kept or living together **2** : the common people : MASSES

²herd *vb* **1** : to assemble or move in a herd **2 a** : to keep or move (animals) as a herd ⟨*herd* cattle⟩ **b** : to gather, lead, or drive as if in a herd ⟨*herded* her guests into the music room⟩ **3 :** to place or place oneself in a group **:** ASSOCIATE ⟨*herded* with other jazz fans⟩ — **herd·er** *n*

herds·man \'hərdz-mən\ *n* **:** a manager, breeder, or tender of livestock

1here \'hi(ə)r\ *adv* [OE *hēr*] **1 a :** in or at this place ⟨turn *here*⟩ **b :** NOW ⟨*here* it's morning already⟩ **2 :** at or in this point or particular ⟨*here* we agree⟩ **3 :** in the present life or state **4 :** to this place ⟨come *here*⟩ **5** — used interjectionally in rebuke or encouragement ⟨*here*, that's enough⟩

2here *n* **:** this place ⟨get away from *here*⟩

here·abouts \'hir-ə-ˌbaüts\ *or* **here·about** \-ˌbaüt\ *adv* **:** near or around this place **:** in this vicinity

1here·af·ter \hir-'af-tər\ *adv* **1 :** after this **2 :** in some future time or state

2hereafter *n*, *often cap* **1 :** FUTURE **2 :** an existence beyond earthly life ⟨belief in the *hereafter*⟩

here·by \hir-'bī\ *adv* **:** by means of this

her·e·dit·a·ment \ˌher-ə-'dit-ə-mənt\ *n* **:** heritable property

he·red·i·tary \hə-'red-ə-ˌter-ē\ *adj* **1 :** genetically transmitted or transmittable from parent to offspring ⟨*hereditary* traits⟩ **2 a :** received or passing by inheritance ⟨*hereditary* rank⟩ **b :** having title or possession through inheritance ⟨*hereditary* ruler⟩ **3 :** TRADITIONAL **4 :** of or relating to inheritance or heredity

he·red·i·ty \hə-'red-ət-ē\ *n*, *pl* **-ties** [L *hereditas* inheritance, fr. *hered-, heres* heir] **1 :** the sum of the qualities and potentialities genetically derived from one's ancestors **2 :** the transmission of qualities from ancestor to descendant through genes

Her·e·ford \'hər-fərd, 'her-ə-\ *n* **:** any of an English breed of hardy red white-faced beef cattle widely raised in the western U.S.

here·in \hir-'in\ *adv* **:** in this

here·of \hir-'əv, -'äv\ *adv* **:** of this

here·on \-'ón, -'än\ *adv* **:** on this

her·e·sy \'her-ə-sē\ *n*, *pl* **-sies** [LGk *hairesis*, fr. Gk, choice, sect, fr. *haireisthai* to choose, middle voice of *hairein* to take] **1 :** religious opinion contrary to church dogma **2 :** opinion or doctrine contrary to a dominant or generally accepted belief

her·e·tic \'her-ə-ˌtik\ *n* **1 :** a person who believes or teaches something contrary to church dogma **2 :** one that dissents from an accepted belief or doctrine

he·ret·i·cal \hə-'ret-i-kəl\ *also* **her·e·tic** \'her-ə-ˌtik, hə-'ret-ik\ *adj* **:** of, relating to, or characterized by heresy **:** UNORTHODOX **syn** see HETERODOX — **he·ret·i·cal·ly** \hə-'ret-i-k(ə-)lē\ *adv* — **he·ret·i·cal·ness** \-kəl-nəs\ *n*

here·to \hir-'tü\ *adv* **:** to this document

here·to·fore \'hirt-ə-ˌfōr, -ˌfór\ *adv* **:** up to this time **:** HITHERTO

here·un·der \hir-'ən-dər\ *adv* **:** under or in accordance with this

here·un·to \hir-'ən-tü\ *adv* **:** to this; *esp* **:** to this writing or document

here·up·on \'hir-ə-ˌpón, -ˌpän\ *adv* **:** on this **:** immediately after this

here·with \hir-'wiṯẖ, -'wiẖ\ *adv* **:** with this **:** enclosed in this

her·i·ot \'her-ē-ət\ *n* **:** a feudal duty or tribute due under English law to a lord upon the death of a tenant

her·i·ta·ble \'her-ət-ə-bəl\ *adj* **1 :** capable of being inherited or of passing by inheritance **2 :** HEREDITARY — **her·i·ta·bil·i·ty** \ˌher-ət-ə-'bil-ət-ē\ *n*

her·i·tage \'her-ət-ij\ *n* [MF, fr. *heriter* to inherit, fr. LL *hereditare*, fr. L *hereditas* heredity] **1 :** property that descends to an heir **2 :** something transmitted by or acquired from a predecessor **:** LEGACY **3 :** BIRTHRIGHT

syn INHERITANCE: HERITAGE may imply anything passed on to heirs or succeeding generations, but applies usu. to something other than actual property or material things ⟨our *heritage* of freedom⟩ INHERITANCE applies to anything acquired by an heir ⟨received a large *inheritance* from his aunt⟩ ⟨his optimistic nature was considered a maternal *inheritance*⟩

her·maph·ro·dite \(ˌ)hər-'maf-rə-ˌdīt\ *n* [Gk *hermaphroditos*, fr. *Hermaphroditos*] **1 :** an animal or plant having both male and female reproductive organs **2 :** HOMOSEXUAL — **hermaphrodite** *adj* — **her·maph·ro·dit·ic** \(ˌ)hər-ˌmaf-rə-'dit-ik\ *adj* — **her·maph·ro·dit·i·cal·ly**

\-'dit-i-k(ə-)lē\ *adv* — **her·maph·ro·dit·ism** \(ˌ)hər-'maf-rə-ˌdīt-ˌiz-əm\ *n*

Her·maph·ro·di·tus \(ˌ)hər-ˌmaf-rə-'dīt-əs\ *n* **:** a son of Hermes and Aphrodite who according to Greek mythology became joined in one body with a nymph while bathing

Her·mes \'hər-(ˌ)mēz\ *n* **:** a Greek god who serves as herald and messenger of the other gods and conducts the dead to Hades

her·met·ic \(ˌ)hər-'met-ik\ *adj* [NL *hermeticus*, fr. *Hermes Trismegistus*, legendary inventor of a magic seal to keep vessels airtight] **:** AIRTIGHT; *also* **:** impervious to external influence — **her·met·i·cal** \-'met-i-kəl\ *adj* — **her·met·i·cal·ly** \-i-k(ə-)lē\ *adv*

her·mit \'hər-mət\ *n* [ME *eremite*, fr. LL *eremita*, fr. LGk *erēmitēs*, fr. Gk *erēmia* solitude, desert, fr. *erēmos* solitary] **1 :** one that lives in solitude esp. for religious reasons **:** RECLUSE **2** *obs* **:** BEADSMAN **3 :** a spiced molasses cookie

her·mit·age \'hər-mət-ij\ *n* **:** the habitation of a hermit; *also* **:** a secluded residence **:** RETREAT

hermit crab *n* **:** any of various marine decapod crustaceans having soft asymmetrical abdomens and occupying the empty shells of gastropods

her·nia \'hər-nē-ə\ *n*, *pl* **her·ni·as** *or* **her·ni·ae** \-nē-ˌē, -nē-ˌī\ [L] **:** a protrusion of an organ or part through connective tissue or through a wall of the cavity in which it is normally enclosed — called also *rupture* — **her·ni·al** \-nē-əl\ *adj* — **her·ni·ate** \-nē-ˌāt\ *vi* — **her·ni·a·tion** \ˌhər-nē-'ā-shən\ *n*

hermit crab

he·ro \'hē-rō, 'hi(ə)r-ō\ *n*, *pl* **heroes** [Gk *hērōs*] **1 a :** a mythological or legendary figure often of divine descent endowed with great strength or ability **b :** an illustrious warrior **c :** a man admired for his achievements and qualities ⟨he was a *hero* to his secretary⟩ **d :** one that shows great courage ⟨the *hero* of a rescue⟩ **2 a :** the principal male character in a literary work **b :** the central figure in an event or period

Hero *n* **:** a priestess of Aphrodite loved by Leander

he·ro·ic \hi-'rō-ik\ *adj* **1 :** of, relating to, or resembling heroes esp. of antiquity ⟨the *heroic* age⟩ ⟨*heroic* legends⟩ **2 :** exhibiting or marked by courage, daring, or desperate enterprise ⟨a *heroic* rescue⟩ ⟨the surgeon's last *heroic* efforts to save him⟩ **3 a :** GRAND, NOBLE ⟨a *heroic* plan for civic improvement⟩ **b :** larger than life-size ⟨a *heroic* statue⟩ — **he·ro·i·cal** \-'rō-i-kəl\ *adj* — **he·ro·i·cal·ly** \-i-k(ə-)lē\ *adv*

heroic couplet *n* **:** a rhyming couplet in iambic pentameter

he·ro·ics \hi-'rō-iks\ *n pl* **:** extravagant display of heroic attitudes in action or expression

heroic verse *n* **:** the iambic pentameter used in English poetry (as epic) during the 17th and 18th centuries

her·o·in \'her-ə-wən\ *n* [fr. *Heroin*, a trademark] **:** a strongly addictive narcotic made from but more potent than morphine — **her·o·in·ism** \-wə-ˌniz-əm\ *n*

her·o·ine \'her-ə-wən\ *n* **1 :** a woman of courage and daring **2 :** a woman admired for her achievements and qualities **3 :** the chief female figure in a literary work or in an event or period

her·o·ism \'her-ə-ˌwiz-əm\ *n* **1 :** heroic conduct **2 :** the qualities of a hero **syn** see COURAGE

her·on \'her-ən\ *n*, *pl* **herons** *also* **heron** [MF *hairon*, of Gmc origin] **:** any of various long-necked wading birds with a long tapering bill, large wings, and soft plumage

hero worship *n* **1 :** veneration of a hero **2 :** foolish or excessive adulation for an individual

her·pes \'hər-(ˌ)pēz\ *n* [Gk *herpēs* shingles, fr. *herpein* to creep] **:** any of several virus diseases characterized by the formation of blisters on the skin or mucous membranes — **her·pet·ic** \(ˌ)hər-'pet-ik\ *adj* — **her·pet·i·form** \(ˌ)hər-'pet-ə-ˌfórm\ *adj*

her·pe·tol·o·gy \ˌhər-pə-'täl-ə-jē\ *n* [Gk *herpeton* reptile, lit., creeping thing, fr. *herpein* to creep] **:** a branch of zoology dealing with reptiles and amphibians — **her·pe·to·log·ic** \ˌhər-pət-ə-'läj-ik\ *or* **her·pe·to·log·i·cal** \-'läj-i-kəl\ *adj* — **her·pe·to·log·i·cal·ly** \-i-k(ə-)lē\ *adv* — **her·pe·tol·o·gist** \ˌhər-pə-'täl-ə-jəst\ *n*

Herr \(ˌ)he(ə)r\ *n*, *pl* **Her·ren** \ˌher-ən, (ˌ)he(ə)rn\ [G] used among German-speaking people as a title equivalent to *mister*

her·ring \'her-iŋ\ *n, pl* **herring** *or* **herrings** [OE *hæring*] : a valuable soft-rayed food fish abundant in the temperate and colder parts of the north Atlantic; *also* : any of various similar and related fishes

¹her·ring·bone \'her-iŋ-,bōn\ *n* **1** : a pattern made up of rows of parallel lines with adjacent rows slanting in reverse directions **2** : a twilled fabric with a herringbone pattern

²herringbone *vb* **1** : to produce a herringbone pattern on a surface **2** : to arrange in a herringbone pattern

hers \'hərz\ *pron* : her one : her ones — used without a following noun as a pronoun equivalent in meaning to the adjective *her*

her·self \(h)ər-'self\ *pron* **1** : that identical female one — compare ¹SHE; used reflexively, for emphasis, or in absolute constructions ⟨she considers *herself* lucky⟩ ⟨she *herself* did it⟩ ⟨*herself* an orphan, she understood the situation⟩ **2** : her normal, healthy, or sane condition or self ⟨was *herself* again after a good night's sleep⟩

hertz \'hərts, 'he(ə)rts \n [after Heinrich R. *Hertz d*1894 German physicist] : a unit of frequency equal to one cycle per second — *abbr. Hz*

hertz·ian wave \,hərt-sē-ən-, ,hert-\ *n* [after Heinrich R. *Hertz d*1894 German physicist] : an electromagnetic wave produced by the oscillation of electricity in a conductor (as a radio antenna)

he's \(,)hēz, ēz\ : he is : he has

hes·i·tance \'hez-ə-tən(t)s\ *n* : HESITANCY

hes·i·tan·cy \-tən-sē\ *n, pl* **-cies** **1** : the quality or state of being hesitant **2** : an act or instance of hesitating

hes·i·tant \'hez-ə-tənt\ *adj* : tending to hesitate — **hes·i·tant·ly** *adv*

hes·i·tate \'hez-ə-,tāt\ *vi* [L *haesitare*, freq. of *haerēre* to stick] **1** : to stop or pause because of forgetfulness, uncertainty, or indecision ⟨*hesitate* before answering⟩ **2** : to hold back because of scruples : be reluctant ⟨*hesitate* to ask a favor⟩ **3** : to falter in speaking : STAMMER — **hes·i·tat·er** *n* — **hes·i·tat·ing·ly** \-,tāt-iŋ-lē\ *adv*

syn HESITATE, WAVER, VACILLATE, FALTER mean to show irresolution or uncertainty. HESITATE implies a pause before deciding, acting, or choosing; WAVER implies hesitation after a decision and connotes weakness or a retreat; VACILLATE implies prolonged hesitation from inability to reach a decision; FALTER suggests a wavering or stumbling due to emotional stress, lack of courage, or fear

hes·i·ta·tion \,hez-ə-'tā-shən\ *n* **1** : an act or instance of hesitating **2** : STAMMERING

Hes·pe·ri·an \he-'spir-ē-ən\ *adj* [Gk *Hesperia*, the west, fr. *hesperos* evening] : WESTERN, OCCIDENTAL

Hes·per·i·des \he-'sper-ə-,dēz\ *n pl* : a legendary garden at the western extremity of the world producing golden apples

hes·per·or·nis \,hes-pə-'ror-nəs\ *n* [Gk *hesperos* western + *ornis* bird] : any of a genus of Cretaceous toothed swimming birds resembling loons

Hes·per·us \'hes-p(ə)rəs\ *n* : Venus when appearing as an evening star

Hes·sian \'hesh-ən\ *n* **1** : a native or inhabitant of Hesse **2** : a German mercenary serving in the British forces during the American Revolution

Hessian fly *n* : a small two-winged fly destructive to wheat in America

hest \'hest\ *n* [ME *hest, hes,* fr. OE *hǣs*] *archaic* : COMMAND, PRECEPT

Hes·tia \'hes-tē-ə, 'hes-chə\ *n* : the Greek goddess of the hearth

heter- *or* **hetero-** *comb form* [Gk *heteros* other] : other than usual : other : different ⟨*hetero*phyllous⟩

het·ero·chro·mat·ic \,het-ə-rō-krə-'mat-ik\ *adj* **1** : of, relating to, or having different colors esp. in a complex pattern **2** : of or relating to heterochromatin — **het·ero·chro·ma·tism** \-'krō-mə-,tiz-əm\ *n*

het·ero·chro·ma·tin \-'krō-mət-ən\ *n* : densely staining chromatin appearing as nodules in or along chromosomes

het·ero·chro·mo·some \,het-ə-rō-'krō-mə-,sōm\ *n* : SEX CHROMOSOME

het·er·o·crine \'het-ə-rə-,krin, -,krīn, -,krēn\ *adj* : having both an endocrine and an exocrine secretion

het·er·o·dox \'het-ə-rə-,däks\ *adj* [Gk *heterodoxos* holding

a different opinion, fr. *heteros* other + *doxa* opinion] **1** : contrary to prevailing opinions, beliefs, or standards; *esp* : not orthodox in religion **2** : holding or expressing unorthodox beliefs or opinions

syn HERETICAL: HETERODOX implies only not being in conformity with orthodox teachings; HERETICAL implies divergence regarded as destructive of truth

het·er·o·doxy \-,däk-sē\ *n, pl* **-dox·ies** **1** : the quality or state of being heterodox **2** : a heterodox opinion or doctrine

het·ero·dyne \'het-ə-rə-,dīn\ *vt* : to combine (a radio frequency) with a different frequency so that a beat is produced — **heterodyne** *adj*

het·er·oe·cious *or* **het·er·e·cious** \,het-ə-'rē-shəs\ *adj* [*heter-* + Gk *oikia* house] : passing through different stages in the life cycle on different hosts — **het·er·oe·cism** \-'rē-,siz-əm\ *n*

het·ero·ga·mete \,het-ə-rō-gə-'mēt, -'gam-,ēt\ *n* : either of a pair of gametes that differ in form, size, or behavior and occur typically as large immobile eggs and small motile sperms — **het·ero·ga·met·ic** \-gə-'met-ik\ *adj*

het·er·og·a·mous \,het-ə-'räg-ə-məs\ *adj* : having diversity of reproductive elements or processes: as **a** : HETEROGAMETIC **b** : exhibiting alternation of generations in which two kinds of sexual generation alternate **c** : bearing flowers of two kinds — **het·er·og·a·my** \-mē\ *n*

het·er·o·ge·ne·ity \,het-ə-rō-jə-'nē-ət-ē\ *n* : the quality or state of being heterogeneous

het·er·o·ge·ne·ous \,het-ə-rə-'jē-nē-əs\ *adj* [ML *heterogeneus,* fr. Gk *heterogenēs,* fr. *heteros* other + *genos* kind] : differing in kind : consisting of dissimilar ingredients or constituents : MIXED ⟨a *heterogeneous* population⟩ — **het·er·o·ge·ne·ous·ly** *adv* — **het·er·o·ge·ne·ous·ness** *n*

het·er·o·gen·e·sis \,het-ə-rō-'jen-ə-səs\ *n* : ALTERNATION OF GENERATIONS

het·er·ol·o·gous \,het-ə-'räl-ə-gəs\ *adj* **1** : characterized by heterology **2** : derived from a different species — **het·er·ol·o·gous·ly** *adv*

het·er·ol·o·gy \-'räl-ə-jē\ *n* [*heter-* + *-logy* (as in *analogy*)] : a lack of correspondence of apparently similar bodily parts due to differences in fundamental makeup or origin

het·ero·mor·phous \,het-ə-rō-'mor-fəs\ *or* **het·ero·mor·phic** \-fik\ *adj* : exhibiting diversity of form

het·ero·ploid \'het-ə-rə-,ploid\ *adj* : having a chromosome number that is not a simple multiple of the haploid chromosome number — **heteroploid** *n* — **het·ero·ploi·dy** \-,ploid-ē\ *n*

het·er·op·ter·ous \,het-ə-'räp-tə-rəs\ *adj* [Gk *pteron* wing] : of or relating to a group (Heteroptera) of insects comprising the true bugs — **het·er·op·ter·an** \-tə-rən\ *adj or n*

het·ero·sex·u·al \,het-ə-rō-'sek-sh(ə-w)əl\ *adj* : of, relating to, or marked by sexual orientation toward members of the opposite sex — **heterosexual** *n* — **het·ero·sex·u·al·i·ty** \-,sek-shə-'wal-ət-ē\ *n*

het·er·o·sis \,het-ə-'rō-səs\ *n* : exceptional vigor or capacity for growth on the part of a hybrid — **het·er·ot·ic** \-'rät-ik\ *adj*

het·ero·spo·rous \,het-ə-rə-'spor-əs, -'spor-; ,het-ə-'räs-pə-rəs\ *adj* : producing spores of more than one kind — **het·ero·spo·ry** \'het-ə-rə-,spor-ē, -,spor-; ,het-ə-'räs-pə-rē\ *n*

het·ero·thal·lic \,het-ə-rō-'thal-ik\ *adj* [Gk *thallein* to sprout, grow] : having two or more morphologically similar but functionally different phases that behave as opposite sexes — compare HOMOTHALLIC — **het·ero·thal·lism** \-'thal-,iz-əm\ *n*

het·ero·troph·ic \,het-ə-rə-'träf-ik, -'trō-fik\ *adj* : unable to live and grow without complex organic compounds of nitrogen and carbon — **het·ero·troph** \'het-ə-rə-,träf\ *n* — **het·ero·troph·i·cal·ly** \,het-ə-rə-'träf-i-k(ə)lē, -'trō-fi-\ *adv* — **het·er·ot·ro·phism** \,het-ə-'rä-trə-,fiz-əm\ *or* **het·er·ot·ro·phy** \-trə-fē\ *n*

het·ero·zy·gote \-'zī-,gōt\ *n* : a heterozygous individual — **het·ero·zy·gos·i·ty** \-,zī-'gäs-ət-ē\ *n*

het·ero·zy·gous \-'zī-gəs\ *adj* : containing both members of at least one pair of alleles ⟨a plant *heterozygous* for yellow seed⟩ — **het·ero·zy·gous·ly** *adv*

het·man \'het-mən\ *n, pl* **hetmans** [Pol] : a cossack leader

het up \('')het-'əp\ *adj* : highly excited : UPSET

hew \'hyü\ *vb* **hewed**; **hewed** *or* **hewn** \'hyün\; **hew·ing**

[OE *hēawan*] **1** : to chop down : CHOP ⟨*hew* logs⟩ ⟨*hew* trees⟩ **2** : to make or shape by or as if by cutting with an ax ⟨*hew* a beam⟩⟨a cabin built of rough-*hewn* logs⟩ **3** : to conform strictly : ADHERE ⟨*hew* to the line⟩ — **hew·er** *n*

¹**hex** \'heks\ *vt* [PaG *hexe*, fr. G *hexen*, fr. *hexe* witch] **1** : to put a hex on **2** : to affect as if by an evil spell : JINX — **hex·er** *n*

²**hex** *n* **1** : SPELL, JINX **2** : a person who practices witchcraft : WITCH

³**hex** *adj* : HEXAGONAL

hexa- *or* **hex-** *comb form* [Gk, fr. *hex;* akin to E *six*] : six ⟨*hexa*merous⟩

hex·a·gon \'hek-sə-ˌgän\ *n* : a polygon of six angles and six sides

hex·ag·o·nal \hek-'sag-ən-ᵊl\ *adj* **1** : having six angles and six sides **2** : relating to or being a crystal system characterized by three equal lateral axes intersecting at angles of 60 degrees and a vertical axis of variable length at right angles ⟨quartz occurs in *hexagonal* crystals⟩ — **hex·ag·o·nal·ly** \-ᵊl-ē\ *adv* — hexagon

hex·a·he·dron \ˌhek-sə-'hē-drən\ *n, pl* **-drons** *also* **-dra** \-drə\ : a polyhedron of six faces

hex·am·e·ter \hek-'sam-ət-ər\ *n* : a line consisting of six metrical feet

hex·ane \'hek-ˌsān\ *n* : any of five isomeric volatile liquid hydrocarbons C_6H_{14} found in petroleum

hex·a·ploid \'hek-sə-ˌplȯid\ *adj* : having or being six times the monoploid chromosome number — **hexaploid** *n* — **hex·a·ploidy** \-ˌplȯid-ē\ *n*

¹**hex·a·pod** \'hek-sə-ˌpäd\ *n* : INSECT 2

²**hexapod** *adj* : six-footed **2** : of or relating to insects

Hex·a·teuch \'hek-sə-ˌt(y)ük\ *n* [Gk *teuchos* tool, vessel, book] : the first six books of the Old Testament

hex·ose \'hek-ˌsōs\ *n* : a saccharide $C_6H_{12}O_6$ containing six carbon atoms in the molecule

hey \'hā\ *interj* — used esp. to call attention or to express interrogation, surprise, or exultation

hey·day \'hā-ˌdā\ *n* : the time of greatest strength or vigor ⟨a nation in the *heyday* of its power⟩

hi \'hī-(ē)\ *interj* — used esp. as a greeting

hi·a·tus \hī-'āt-əs\ *n* [L, fr. *hiare* to gape, yawn] **1** : a gap in space or in time; *esp* : a break occurring where a part is missing ⟨a *hiatus* in an old manuscript⟩ **2** : the occurrence of two vowel sounds without pause or intervening consonantal sound

hi·ba·chi \hē-'bäch-ē\ *n* [Jap] : a charcoal brazier

hi·ber·nal \hī-'bərn-ᵊl\ *adj* : of or relating to winter : WINTRY

hi·ber·nate \'hī-bər-ˌnāt\ *vi* [L *hibernare* to pass the winter, fr. *hibernus* of winter] : to pass the winter in a torpid or resting state — **hi·ber·na·tion** \ˌhī-bər-'nā-shən\ *n* — **hi·ber·na·tor** \'hī-bər-ˌnāt-ər\ *n*

hi·bis·cus \hī-'bis-kəs, hə-\ *n* [L, marshmallow] : any of a large genus of herbs, shrubs, or small trees of the mallow family with toothed leaves and large showy flowers

¹**hic·cup** *also* **hic·cough** \'hik-(ˌ)əp\ *n* : a spasmodic breathing movement checked by sudden closure of the glottis accompanied by a peculiar sound

²**hiccup** *also* **hiccough** *vi* **hic·cuped** *also* **hic·cupped; hic·cup·ing** *also* **hic·cup·ping** : to make a hiccup or be affected with hiccups

hic ja·cet \(ˈ)hik-'jā-sət\ *n* [L, here lies] : EPITAPH

hick \'hik\ *n* [*Hick*, nickname for *Richard*] : an awkward provincial person

hick·ey \'hik-ē\ *n* : DEVICE, GADGET

hick·o·ry \'hik-(ə-)rē\ *n, pl* **-ries** [of AmerInd origin] **1 a** : any of a genus of No. American hardwood trees of the walnut family often with sweet edible nuts **b** : the usu. tough pale wood of a hickory **2** : a switch or cane (as of hickory wood) used esp. for punishing a child

hi·dal·go \hid-'al-gō, ē-'thäl-\ *n, pl* **-gos** [Sp] : a member of the lower nobility of Spain

hidden hunger *n* : a bodily disorder caused by a badly balanced diet

hidden tax *n* : a tax on commodities which is passed on to the consumer in higher prices and of whose presence the consumer is not generally aware

¹**hide** \'hīd\ *n* [OE *higid*] : any of various old English units of land area; *esp* : a unit of 120 acres

²**hide** *vb* **hid** \'hid\; **hid·den** \'hid-ᵊn\ *or* **hid; hid·ing** \'hīd-iŋ\ [OE *hȳdan*] **1** : to put or get out of sight : SECRETE ⟨*hide* a treasure⟩ ⟨*hid* in a closet⟩ **2** : to keep secret ⟨*hid* her grief⟩ **3** : to screen from view ⟨a house *hidden* by trees⟩ **4** : to seek protection or evade responsibility ⟨*hides* behind dark glasses⟩ — **hid·er** \'hīd-ər\ *n*

³**hide** *n* [OE *hȳd*] : the skin of an animal whether raw or dressed

⁴**hide** *vt* **hid·ed; hid·ing** : to give a beating to : FLOG

hide-and-seek \ˌhīd-ᵊn-'sēk\ *n* : a children's game in which one player covers his eyes and after giving the others time to hide goes looking for and tries to catch them — called also *hide-and-go-seek* \-ᵊn-ˌgō-'sēk\

hide·away \'hīd-ə-ˌwā\ *n* : RETREAT, HIDEOUT

hide·bound \'hīd-ˌbau̇nd\ *adj* **1** : having a dry skin lacking in pliancy and adhering closely to the underlying flesh ⟨a *hidebound* horse⟩ **2** : obstinately conservative : NARROW

hid·e·ous \'hid-ē-əs\ *adj* [alter. of ME *hidous*, fr. OF, fr. *hide* terror] : horribly ugly or disgusting : FRIGHTFUL, SHOCKING — **hid·e·ous·ly** *adv* — **hid·e·ous·ness** *n*

hide·out \'hīd-ˌau̇t\ *n* : a place of refuge or concealment

¹**hid·ing** \'hīd-iŋ\ *n* : a state or place of concealment ⟨go into *hiding*⟩

²**hiding** *n* : FLOGGING, WHIPPING ⟨got a severe *hiding*⟩

hie \'hī\ *vb* **hied; hy·ing** *or* **hie·ing** [OE *hīgian*] : HURRY, HASTEN

hi·er·arch \'hī-(ə-)ˌrärk\ *n* [Gk *hieros* holy + *archein* to rule] **1** : a religious leader in a position of authority **2** : a person high in a hierarchy — **hi·er·ar·chal** \ˌhī-(ə-)-'rär-kəl\ *adj*

hi·er·ar·chy \'hī-(ə-)ˌrär-kē\ *n, pl* **-chies** **1** : a ruling body of clergy organized into ranks each subordinate to the one above it; *esp* : the bishops of a province or nation **2** : a governing body whose members are arranged in ordered ranks; *also* : any body of persons in authority **3 a** : arrangement into a graded series **b** : persons or things arranged in ranks or classes — **hi·er·ar·chi·cal** \ˌhī-(ə-)'rär-ki-kəl\ *or* **hi·er·ar·chic** \-'rär-kik\ *adj* — **hi·er·ar·chi·cal·ly** \-'rär-ki-k(ə-)lē\ *adv*

hi·er·at·ic \ˌhī-(ə-)'rat-ik\ *adj* [Gk *hieratikos* sacerdotal, fr. *hieros* holy] **1** : constituting or belonging to a form of ancient Egyptian writing simpler than the hieroglyphic **2** : SACERDOTAL — **hi·er·at·i·cal·ly** \-'rat-i-k(ə-)lē\ *adv*

hi·er·o·glyph \'hī-(ə-)rə-ˌglif\ *n* : a character used in a system of hieroglyphic writing

¹**hi·er·o·glyph·ic** \ˌhī-(ə-)rə-'glif-ik\ *adj* [Gk *hieroglyphikos*, fr. *hieros* holy + *glyphein* to carve] **1** : written in, constituting, or belonging to a system of writing mainly in pictorial characters **2** : inscribed with hieroglyphic characters **3** : resembling hieroglyphic in difficulty of decipherment

²**hieroglyphic** *n* **1** : HIERO-GLYPH **2** : a system of hieroglyphic writing; *esp* : the picture script of the ancient Egyptian p r i e s t h o o d **3** : characters that resemble a hieroglyphic esp. in difficulty of decipherment

Egyptian hieroglyphics

hi-fi \'hī-'fī\ *n* **1** : HIGH FIDELITY **2** : equipment for reproduction of sound with high fidelity

hig·gle \'hig-əl\ *vi* **hig·gled; hig·gling** \'hig-(ə-)liŋ\ : HAGGLE — **hig·gler** \-(ə-)lər\ *n*

hig·gle·dy–pig·gle·dy \ˌhig-əl-dē-'pig-əl-dē\ *adv* : in confusion : TOPSY-TURVY — **higgledy–piggledy** *adj*

¹**high** \'hī\ *adj* [OE *hēah*] **1 a** : extending or raised up : ELEVATED ⟨a *high* building⟩ **b** : having a specified elevation : TALL ⟨six feet *high*⟩ **2** : advanced toward fullness or culmination ⟨*high* summer⟩ **3** : SHRILL, SHARP ⟨*high* note⟩ **4** : relatively far from the equator ⟨*high* latitude⟩ **5** : exalted in character : NOBLE ⟨a man of *high* purpose⟩ **6** : of greater degree, size, amount, or content than average or ordinary ⟨*high* pressure⟩ **7** : of relatively great importance: as **a** : foremost in rank, dignity, or standing ⟨*high* society⟩ **b** : SERIOUS, GRAVE ⟨*high* crimes⟩ **8** : FORCIBLE, STRONG ⟨*high* winds⟩ **9** : showing elation or excitement ⟨*high* spirits⟩ **10** : COSTLY, DEAR ⟨everything's *high* nowadays⟩ **11** : advanced in complexity, development, or elaboration ⟨*higher* mathematics⟩⟨*higher* algae⟩ **12** : pronounced with some part of the tongue close to the palate ⟨\ē\ is a *high* vowel⟩

²**high** *adv* **1** : at or to a high place, altitude, or degree

⟨knocked the ball *high* into the bleachers⟩ **2** : RICHLY, LUXURIOUSLY ⟨lived *high* after getting his inheritance⟩

³high *n* **1** : an elevated place or region: as **a** : HILL, KNOLL **b** : SKY, HEAVEN ⟨birds wheeling on *high*⟩ **2** : a region of high barometric pressure **3 a** : a high point or level : HEIGHT ⟨prices reached a new *high* this year⟩ **b** : the transmission gear of an automotive vehicle giving the highest ratio of propeller-shaft to engine-shaft speed and consequently the highest speed of travel

high·ball \'hī-ˌbȯl\ *n* : a drink of alcoholic liquor with water or a carbonated beverage served in a tall glass

high·bind·er \-ˌbīn-dər\ *n* **1** : a professional killer operating in the Chinese quarter of an American city **2** : a corrupt or scheming politician

high blood pressure *n* : HYPERTENSION

high·born \'hī-'bȯrn\ *adj* : of noble birth

high·boy \'hī-ˌbȯi\ *n* : a high chest of drawers mounted on a base with long legs

high·bred \-'bred\ *adj* : coming from superior stock

high·brow \-ˌbraú\ *n* : a person of superior learning or culture : INTELLECTUAL — **high·brow** *adj*

high chair *n* : a child's chair with long legs, a feeding tray, and a footrest

High Church *adj* : tending toward or stressing sacerdotal, liturgical, ceremonial, traditional, and Catholic elements as appropriate to the life of the Christian church — **High Churchman** *n*

highboy

high command *n* **1** : the supreme headquarters of a military force **2** : the highest leaders in an organization

high commissioner *n* : a principal or high-ranking commissioner; *esp* : an ambassadorial representative of the government of one country stationed in another

higher education *n* : education provided by a college or university

higher fungus *n* : a fungus with hyphae well-developed and septate

high·er-up \ˌhī-ər-'əp\ *n* : a superior officer or official

high explosive *n* : an explosive (as TNT) that generates gas with extreme rapidity and has a shattering effect

high·fa·lu·tin \ˌhī-fə-'lüt-ᵊn\ *adj* : PRETENTIOUS, POMPOUS ⟨*highfalutin* talk⟩⟨*highfalutin* people⟩

high fidelity *n* : the reproduction of sound with a high degree of faithfulness to the original

high·fli·er *or* **high·fly·er** \'hī-'flī-(-ə)r\ *n* **1** : an extravagant, pretentious, or excessively ambitious person **2** : an extremely orthodox or doctrinaire person

high-flown \-'flōn\ *adj* **1** : ELEVATED, PROUD **2** : not plain or simple : EXTRAVAGANT ⟨*high-flown* language⟩

high frequency *n* : a radio frequency in the range between 3 and 30 megacycles — abbr. *hf*

High German *n* : German as natively used in southern and central Germany

high-grade \'hī-'grād\ *adj* : of a grade rated as superior

high-hand·ed \-'han-dəd\ *adj* : OVERBEARING, ARBITRARY ⟨*high-handed* actions⟩ — **high-hand·ed·ly** *adv* — **high-hand·ed·ness** *n*

¹high-hat \'hī-'hat\ *adj* : SUPERCILIOUS, SNOBBISH

²high-hat *vt* : to treat in a high-hat manner

High Holiday *n* : either of two important Jewish holidays: **a** : ROSH HASHANAH **b** : YOM KIPPUR

high horse *n* : an arrogant mood or attitude

high jinks \-'jiŋ(k)s\ *n pl* : wild or boisterous behavior

high jump *n* : a jump for height in a track-and-field contest — **high jumper** *n*

¹high·land \'hī-lənd\ *n* : elevated or mountainous land

²highland *adj* **1** : of or relating to a highland **2** *cap* : of or relating to the Highlands of Scotland

high·land·er \-lən-dər\ *n* **1** : an inhabitant of a highland **2** *cap* : an inhabitant of the Highlands of Scotland

Highland fling *n* : a lively Scottish folk dance

¹high·light \'hī-ˌlīt\ *n* **1 a** : one of the spots or areas on an object that reflect the most light **b** : the brightest spot (as in a painting or drawing) **2** : an event or scene of major interest ⟨the *highlights* of a trip⟩

²highlight *vt* **1** : to throw a strong light on ⟨the match flared, *highlighting* his face⟩ **2 a** : to center attention on : EMPHASIZE ⟨his television speech *highlighted* the presi-

dent's concern⟩ **b** : to constitute a highlight of ⟨a bullfight *highlighted* their trip to Mexico⟩

high·ly \'hī-lē\ *adv* **1** : to a high degree : very much : EXTREMELY ⟨*highly* pleased⟩ **2** : with much approval ⟨*highly* recommended⟩⟨speak *highly* of a person⟩

high mass *n, often cap H&M* : a sung mass with full ceremonials and incense and with the celebrant assisted by a deacon and subdeacon

high-mind·ed \'hī-'mīn-dəd\ *adj* : having or marked by elevated principles and feelings — **high-mind·ed·ly** *adv* — **high-mind·ed·ness** *n*

high-muck-a-muck \ˌhī-ˌmək-i-'mək\ *or* **high-muck·ety-muck** \ˌhī-mək-ət-ē-'mək\ *n* : a person of importance; *esp* : one who is arrogant

high·ness \'hī-nəs\ *n* **1** : the quality or state of being high **2** — used as a title for persons (as a king or prince) of exalted rank ⟨His Royal *Highness*⟩

high-octane *adj* : having a high octane number and hence good antiknock properties ⟨*high-octane* gasoline⟩

¹high-pressure *adj* **1 a** : having or involving a high or comparatively high pressure esp. greatly exceeding that of the atmosphere **b** : having a high atmospheric pressure **2** : using or involving aggressive and insistent sales techniques

²high-pressure *vt* : to sell or influence by high-pressure tactics

high relief *n* : sculptural relief in which at least half of the circumference of the modeled form projects

high·road \'hī-ˌrōd\ *n* **1** *chiefly Brit* : HIGHWAY **2** : the easiest course

high school *n* : a secondary school usu. comprising the 9th to 12th or 10th to 12th years of study

high seas *n pl* : the open part of a sea or ocean esp. outside territorial waters

high-sound·ing \'hī-'saún-diŋ\ *adj* : POMPOUS, IMPOSING

high-spir·it·ed \'hī-'spir-ət-əd\ *adj* : characterized by a bold or lofty spirit : METTLESOME — **high-spir·it·ed·ly** *adv* — **high-spir·it·ed·ness** *n*

high-strung \-'strəŋ\ *adj* : having or marked by an extremely nervous or sensitive temperament

hight \'hīt\ *adj* [ME, pp. of *hoten* to command, call, be called, fr. OE *hātan*] *archaic* : CALLED, NAMED

high-tail \'hī-ˌtāl\ *vi* : to retreat at full speed

high-tension *adj* : having a high voltage; *also* : relating to apparatus to be used at high voltage

high-test *adj* : passing a difficult test; *esp* : having a high volatility ⟨*high-test* gasoline⟩

high tide *n* **1** : the tide when the water is at its greatest height **2** : culminating point : CLIMAX

high-toned \'hī-'tōnd\ *adj* **1** : high in social, moral, or intellectual quality **2** : PRETENTIOUS, POMPOUS

high treason *n* : TREASON 2

high·way \'hī-ˌwā\ *n* : a public road or way; *esp* : a main direct road

high·way·man \-mən\ *n* : a person who robs travelers on a highway

hi·jack *or* **high-jack** \'hī-ˌjak\ *vt* **1** : to steal by stopping a vehicle on the highway ⟨*hijack* a load of furs⟩; *also* : to stop and steal from (a vehicle in transit) **2** : to commandeer a flying airplane (as by coercing the pilot at gunpoint)

¹hike \'hīk\ *vb* **1 a** : to move or raise up **b** : to raise in amount sharply or suddenly ⟨*hike* rents⟩ **2** : to go on a long walk — **hik·er** *n*

²hike *n* **1** : a long walk esp. for pleasure or exercise **2** : an upward movement : RISE ⟨a price *hike*⟩

hi·lar·i·ous \hil-'ar-ē-əs, -'er-; hī-'lar-, -'ler-\ *adj* [L *hilarus, hilaris* cheerful, fr. Gk *hilaros*] : marked by or affording hilarity — **hi·lar·i·ous·ly** *adv* — **hi·lar·i·ous·ness** *n*

hi·lar·i·ty \-ət-ē\ *n* : boisterous merriment **syn** see MIRTH

¹hill \'hil\ *n* [OE *hyll*] **1** : a usu. rounded natural elevation of land lower than a mountain **2** : an artificial heap or mound (as of earth) **3** : several seeds or plants planted in a group rather than a row ⟨a *hill* of beans⟩

²hill *vt* **1** : to form into a heap **2** : to draw earth around the roots or base of — **hill·er** *n*

hill·bil·ly \'hil-ˌbil-ē\ *n, pl* **-lies** : a person from a mountainous backwoods area

hillbilly music *n* : music deriving from or imitating the folk style of the southern U.S. or of the Western cowboy

hill myna *n* : a largely black Asiatic starling often tamed and taught to pronounce words

hill·ock \'hil-ək\ *n* : a small hill — **hill·ocky** \-ə-kē\ *adj*

hill·side \'hil-‚sīd\ *n* : the side of a hill

hill·top \'hil-‚täp\ *n* : the highest part of a hill

hilly \'hil-ē\ *adj* **hill·i·er; -est** **1** : abounding in hills ⟨a *hilly* city⟩ **2** : STEEP ⟨a *hilly* climb⟩

hilt \'hilt\ *n* [OE] : a handle esp. of a sword or dagger — **to the hilt** : COMPLETELY

hi·lum \'hī-ləm\ *n, pl* **hi·la** \-lə\ [NL, fr. L, trifle] **1** : a scar on a seed at the point of attachment of the ovule **2** : a notch in or opening from a bodily part suggesting the hilum of a bean — **hi·lar** \-lər\ *adj*

him \im, (')him\ *pron, objective case of* HE

him·self \(h)im-'self\ *pron* **1** : that identical male one : that identical one whose sex is unknown or immaterial — compare **¹HE**; used reflexively, for emphasis, or in absolute constructions ⟨everyone must look out for *himself*⟩ ⟨he *himself* did it⟩ ⟨*himself* unhappy, he understood the situation⟩ **2** : his normal, healthy, or sane condition or self ⟨he's *himself* again⟩

Hi·na·ya·na \‚hē-nə-'yän-ə\ *n* [Skt *hīnayāna*, lit., lesser vehicle] : a southern conservative branch of Buddhism adhering to the Pali scriptures and the nontheistic ideal of purification of the self to nirvana — compare MAHAYANA

¹hind \'hīnd\ *n, pl* **hinds** *also* **hind** [OE] **1** : a female red deer — compare HART **2** : any of various usu. spotted groupers

²hind *adj* : located behind : REAR ⟨*hind* legs⟩

hind·brain \'hīn(d)-‚brān\ *n* : the posterior division of the embryonic vertebrate brain or the parts developed from it

¹hin·der \'hin-dər\ *vb* **hin·dered; hin·der·ing** \-d(ə-)riŋ\ [OE *hindrian*, fr. *hinder* behind] **1** : to make slow or difficult : HAMPER **2** : to hold back : CHECK

²hind·er \'hīn-dər\ *adj* [ME, fr. OE, behind] : HIND

hind·gut \'hīn(d)-‚gət\ *n* : the posterior part of the alimentary canal

Hin·di \'hin-(‚)dē\ *n* **1** : a literary and official language of northern India **2** : a complex of Indic dialects of northern India for which Hindi is the usual literary language — **Hindi** *adj*

hind·most \'hīn(d)-‚mōst\ *adj* : farthest to the rear

hind·quar·ter \-‚kwòrt-ər\ *n* **1** : the back half of a lateral half of the body or carcass of a quadruped ⟨a *hindquarter* of beef⟩ **2** *pl* : the part of a quadruped lying behind the attachment of the hind legs to the trunk

hin·drance \'hin-drən(t)s\ *n* **1** : the state of being hindered **2** : the action of hindering **3** : something that hinders : IMPEDIMENT

hind·sight \'hīn(d)-‚sīt\ *n* **1** : a rear sight of a firearm **2** : perception of the significance of an event only after it has happened ⟨*hindsight* is easier than foresight⟩

¹Hin·du *also* **Hin·doo** \'hin-‚dü\ *n* [Per *Hindū* inhabitant of India, fr. *Hind* India] **1** : an adherent of Hinduism **2** : a native or inhabitant of India

²Hindu *also* **Hindoo** *adj* : of, relating to, or characteristic of the Hindus or Hinduism

Hin·du·ism \-‚iz-əm\ *n* **1** : a body of social, cultural, and religious beliefs and practices native to the Indian subcontinent; *esp* : devotion to the cult of one of the chief gods and goddesses **2** : a religious philosophy based on Hinduism — compare KARMA

Hin·du·stani *also* **Hin·do·stani** \‚hin-dù-'stan-ē, -'stän-ē\ *n* **1** : a group of Indic dialects of northern India of which literary Hindi and Urdu are considered diverse written forms **2** : a form of speech allied to Urdu but less divergent from Hindi — **Hindustani** *adj*

¹hinge \'hinj\ *n* [ME *heng*; akin to E *hang*] **1** : a jointed piece on which one surface (as a door, gate, or lid) turns or swings on another **2** : the ligamentous joint between valves of a bivalve's shell — compare HINGE JOINT

hinges: *1* hook-andeye, *2* strap, *3* T hinge

²hinge *vb* **1** : to attach by or furnish with hinges **2** : to hang or turn as if on a hinge : DEPEND ⟨success *hinges* on the decision⟩

hinge joint *n* : a joint between bones (as at the elbow) that permits motion in but one plane

hin·ny \'hin-ē\ *n, pl* **hinnies** [L *hinnus*] : a hybrid between a stallion and a she ass — compare MULE

¹hint \'hint\ *n* **1** : a slight mention : an indirect suggestion or reminder ⟨a *hint* of winter in the air⟩ **2** : a very small amount : TRACE ⟨a *hint* of garlic⟩ **syn** see SUGGESTION

²hint *vb* : to bring to mind by or give a hint ⟨*hinting* at what she wanted for Christmas⟩ ⟨*hinted* that something was up⟩ — **hint·er** *n*

hin·ter·land \'hint-ər-‚land\ *n* [G, fr. *hinter* hinder + *land*] **1** : a region behind a coast **2** : a region that provides supplies **3** : a region remote from cities and towns

¹hip \'hip\ *n* [OE *hēope*] : the fruit of a rose consisting of a fleshy receptacle filled with achenes

²hip *n* [OE *hype*] **1** : the part of the body that curves outward below the waist on either side formed by the side part of the pelvis and the upper part of the thigh **2** : HIP JOINT

³hip *var of* HEP

hip and thigh *adv* : OVERWHELMINGLY, UNSPARINGLY

hip·bone \'hip-‚bōn, -‚bōn\ *n* : INNOMINATE BONE

hip joint *n* : the articulation between the femur and the innominate bone

hip·par·i·on \hip-'ar-ē-‚än, -'er-\ *n* : any of a genus of extinct Miocene and Pliocene 3-toed horses

¹hipped \'hipt\ *adj* : having hips ⟨broad-*hipped*⟩

²hipped *adj* **1** : DEPRESSED **2** : extremely interested

hip·pie *or* **hip·py** \'hip-ē\ *n, pl* **hippies** [³hip + -ie] : a usu. young person who rejects the mores of established society (as by dressing unconventionally or favoring communal living), advocates a nonviolent ethic, and often uses psychedelic drugs or marijuana; *also* : a long-haired unconventionally dressed young person

hip·po \'hip-ō\ *n, pl* **hippos** : HIPPOPOTAMUS

Hip·po·crat·ic oath \‚hip-ə-‚krat-ik-\ *n* [after *Hippocrates* d ab377 B.C. Greek physician believed to have formulated it] : an oath embodying a code of medical ethics usu. taken by those about to begin medical practice

Hip·po·crene \'hip-ə-‚krēn, ‚hip-ə-'krē-nē\ *n* : a fountain on Mount Helicon sacred to the Muses and believed to be a source of poetic inspiration

hip·po·drome \'hip-ə-‚drōm\ *n* [Gk *hippodromos*, fr. *hippos* horse + *dromos* racecourse] **1** : an oval stadium for horse and chariot races in ancient Greece **2** : an arena for equestrian performances

hip·po·pot·a·mus \‚hip-ə-'pät-ə-məs\ *n, pl* **-mus·es** *or* **-mi** \-‚mī, -(‚)mē\ [Gk *hippopotamos*, fr. *hippos* horse + *potamos* river] : any of several large herbivorous 4-toed chiefly aquatic African mammals related to the swine and characterized by an extremely large head and mouth, very thick hairless skin, and short legs

hip roof *n* : a roof having sloping ends and sloping sides — see ROOF illustration

hip·ster \'hip-stər\ *n* : a person who is unusually aware of and interested in new and unconventional patterns esp. in jazz, in the use of stimulants (as narcotics), and in exotic religion

¹hire \'hī(ə)r\ *n* [OE *hȳr*] **1 a** : payment for temporary use **b** : payment for services : WAGES ⟨not worth his *hire*⟩ **2 a** : the act of hiring **b** : the state of being hired : EMPLOYMENT

²hire *vb* **1 a** : to engage the personal services of for a set sum ⟨*hire* a new crew⟩ **b** : to engage the temporary use of for a fixed sum ⟨*hire* a hall⟩ **2** : to grant the personal services of for a fixed sum ⟨*hire* themselves out⟩ **3** : to take employment ⟨*hire* out as a cook⟩ — **hir·er** *n*

syn HIRE, LET, LEASE, RENT mean to engage or grant for use at a price. HIRE and LET are complementary terms, HIRE implying the act of engaging or taking for use and LET the granting of use ⟨we *hired* a car for the summer⟩ ⟨we had difficulty finding a cottage to *let*⟩ LEASE strictly implies a letting but is often applied to hiring on a lease ⟨the diplomat *leased* an apartment for a year⟩⟨the landlord refused to *lease* to tenants with pets⟩ RENT stresses the payment of money for the full use of property and may imply either hiring or letting

syn HIRE, EMPLOY mean to engage for work. HIRE stresses the act of engaging a person's services for pay; EMPLOY stresses the continued or regular use of a person's services — **for hire** : available for use or service at a price

hire·ling \'hī(ə)r-liŋ\ *n* : a person who serves for wages; *esp* : one whose only interest in his work is the money he receives

hire purchase *n, chiefly Brit* : purchase on the installment plan

hiring hall *n* : a union-operated placement office where registered applicants are referred in rotation to jobs

hir·sute \'hər-ˌsüt, 'hi(ə)r-\ *adj* [L *hirsutus*] : roughly hairy; *esp* : pubescent with coarse stiff hairs — **hir·sute·ness** *n*

hir·su·tu·lous \ˌhər-'sü-chə-ləs, hir-\ *adj* : minutely or slightly hirsute

¹**his** \(h)iz, hiz\ *adj* [OE, gen. of *hē* he] : of or relating to him or himself esp. as possessor, agent, or object of an action ⟨*his* house⟩ ⟨*his* writings⟩ ⟨*his* confirmation⟩ — compare ¹HE

²**his** \'hiz\ *pron* : his one : his ones — used without a following noun as a pronoun equivalent in meaning to the adjective *his*

His·pan·ic \his-'pan-ik\ *adj* [L *Hispania* Iberian peninsula, Spain] : of or relating to the people, speech, or culture of Spain or Latin America

his·pid \'his-pəd\ *adj* [L *hispidus*] : rough or covered with bristles, stiff hairs, or minute spines ⟨*hispid* leaf⟩ — **his·pid·i·ty** \his-'pid-ət-ē\ *n*

hiss \'his\ *vb* : to condemn with or make a sharp sibilant sound like that of the speech sound \s\ or that emitted by an alarmed goose or snake — **hiss** *n* — **hiss·er** *n*

hist \s *often prolonged and usu with* p *preceding and* t *following; often read as* 'hist\ *interj* — used to attract attention

hist- *or* **histo-** *comb form* [Gk *histos* mast, loom beam, web] : tissue ⟨*histo*physiology⟩

his·tam·i·nase \his-'tam-ə-ˌnās, 'his-tə-mə-\ *n* : an enzyme that breaks down histamine

his·ta·mine \'his-tə-ˌmēn, -mən\ *n* : a compound occurring in many animal tissues that is believed to play an important part in allergic reactions (as hives and asthma) and in certain respiratory diseases

his·to·gen·e·sis \ˌhis-tə-'jen-ə-səs\ *n, pl* **-gen·e·ses** \-ə-ˌsēz\ : the formation and differentiation of tissues — **his·to·ge·net·ic** \-jə-'net-ik\ *adj* — **his·to·ge·net·i·cal·ly** \-i-k(ə-)lē\ *adv*

his·to·gram \'his-tə-ˌgram\ *n* : a representation of a frequency distribution by means of rectangles whose widths represent class intervals and whose heights represent the number of items found within each class interval

his·tol·o·gy \his-'täl-ə-jē\ *n, pl* **-gies** 1 : a branch of anatomy that deals with the structure of animal and plant tissues as revealed by the microscope 2 : tissue structure or organization — **his·to·log·i·cal** \ˌhis-tə-'läj-i-kəl\ *or* **his·to·log·ic** \-'läj-ik\ *adj* — **his·to·log·i·cal·ly** \-i-k(ə-)lē\ *adv* — **his·tol·o·gist** \his-'täl-ə-jəst\ *n*

his·tol·y·sis \his-'täl-ə-səs\ *n* : the breakdown of bodily tissues — **his·to·lyt·ic** \ˌhis-tə-'lit-ik\ *adj*

his·to·ri·an \his-'tōr-ē-ən, -'tór-\ *n* 1 : a student or writer of history; *esp* : one that produces a scholarly historical study 2 : CHRONICLER

his·tor·ic \his-'tór-ik, -'tär-\ *adj* : HISTORICAL; *esp* : famous in history ⟨*historic* events⟩

his·tor·i·cal \-i-kəl\ *adj* 1 a : of, relating to, or having the character of history; *esp* : known to be true ⟨*historical* fact⟩ b : based on history ⟨*historical* novels⟩ 2 : famous in history ⟨*historical* personages⟩ — **his·tor·i·cal·ly** \-i-k(ə-)lē\ *adv* — **his·tor·i·cal·ness** \-kəl-nəs\ *n*

historical materialism *n* : a Marxist theory of history and society that holds that ideas and social institutions develop only as the superstructure of a material economic base — compare DIALECTICAL MATERIALISM

historical present *n* : the present tense used to relate past events

his·to·ric·i·ty \ˌhis-tə-'ris-ət-ē\ *n* : historical actuality : FACT

his·to·ri·og·ra·pher \his-ˌtōr-ē-'äg-rə-fər, -ˌtór-\ *n* : a usu. official writer of history : HISTORIAN — **his·to·rio·graph·ic** \-ē-ə-'graf-ik\ *or* **his·to·ri·o·graph·i·cal** \-'graf-i-kəl\ *adj* — **his·to·ri·o·graph·i·cal·ly** \-i-k(ə-)lē\ *adv* — **his·to·ri·og·ra·phy** \-ē-'äg-rə-fē\ *n*

his·to·ry \'his-t(ə-)rē\ *n, pl* **-ries** [Gk *historia*, lit., research, fr. *istōr, histōr* knowing, learned; akin to E *wit*] 1 : TALE, STORY 2 a : a chronological record of significant events with an explanation of their causes b : an account of a sick person's medical background 3 : a branch of knowledge that records and explains past events 4 a : events that form the subject matter of a history b : past events

his·tri·on·ic \ˌhis-trē-'än-ik\ *adj* [L *histrion-, histrio* actor] 1 : of or relating to actors, acting, or the theater 2 : deliberately affected : THEATRICAL *syn* see DRAMATIC — **his·tri·on·i·cal·ly** \-'än-i-k(ə-)lē\ *adv*

his·tri·on·ics \-'än-iks\ *n pl* 1 : theatrical performances 2 : deliberate display of emotion for effect

¹**hit** \'hit\ *vb* **hit; hit·ting** [ON *hitta*] 1 a : to strike usu. with force ⟨*hit* a ball⟩ ⟨the ball *hit* the house⟩ ⟨*hit* the stick against the railing⟩ ⟨the stone *hit* against the window⟩ b : to make usu. forceful contact with something ⟨tipped over and *hit* hard⟩ 2 a : ATTACK ⟨tried to guess when and where the enemy would *hit*⟩ b : to affect detrimentally ⟨her death *hit* him pretty hard⟩ 3 : OCCUR, HAPPEN ⟨the storm *hit* just at sundown⟩ 4 a : COME, STUMBLE ⟨*hit* upon the answer accidentally⟩ b : to experience or find esp. by chance ⟨finally *hit* pay dirt⟩ c : to get to : REACH ⟨*hit* town that night⟩ ⟨prices *hit* a new high⟩ d : to reflect accurately ⟨*hits* the right note⟩ 5 : to fire the charge in the cylinders ⟨an automobile engine not *hitting*⟩ — **hit·ter** *n*

²**hit** *n* 1 a : a blow striking an object aimed at b : COLLISION 2 a : a stroke of luck b : something that is conspicuously successful ⟨the show was a *hit*⟩ 3 : a telling remark *x* : BASE HIT

hit-and-miss \ˌhit-ən-'mis\ *adj* : sometimes successful and sometimes not : HAPHAZARD

hit-and-run \-'rən\ *adj* 1 : being or relating to a baseball play in which a base runner starts for the next base as the pitcher starts to pitch and the batter attempts to hit the ball 2 : being or involving a motor-vehicle driver who does not stop after being involved in an accident 3 : involving or intended for quick specific action or results ⟨small *hit-and-run* troop units⟩

¹**hitch** \'hich\ *vb* [ME *hytchen*] 1 : to move by jerks ⟨*hitched* his pants up⟩ 2 a : to catch or fasten by or as if by a hook or knot ⟨*hitch* a horse to a rail⟩ b : to connect to or with a hitch 3 : HITCHHIKE — **hitch·er** *n*

²**hitch** *n* 1 : a jerky movement or pull ⟨gave his trousers a *hitch*⟩ 2 : a sudden stop : an unforeseen obstacle : HALT ⟨a plan that went off without a *hitch*⟩ 3 : the connection between something towed (as a plow or trailer) and its mover (as a tractor, automobile, or animal) 4 : a knot used for a temporary fastening ⟨barrel *hitch*⟩ 5 *slang* : a period of time in a specified state or activity ⟨a *hitch* in the infantry⟩

hitch·hike \'hich-ˌhīk\ *vb* : to travel by or secure free rides — **hitch·hik·er** *n*

hitch up *vi* : to harness and hitch a draft animal or team

¹**hith·er** \'hith-ər\ *adv* [OE *hider*] : to this place ⟨come *hither*⟩

²**hither** *adj* : being on the near or adjacent side ⟨the *hither* side of the hill⟩

hith·er·most \-ˌmōst\ *adj* : nearest on this side

hith·er·to \-ˌtü\ *adv* : up to this time ⟨*hitherto* unknown facts⟩

hith·er·ward \'hith-ə(r)-wərd\ *adv* : HITHER

hit off *vb* 1 : to characterize precisely and usu. satirically 2 : HARMONIZE, AGREE

hit or miss *adv* : HAPHAZARDLY — **hit-or-miss** \ˌhit-ər-'mis\ *adj*

Hit·tite \'hi-ˌtīt\ *n* 1 : a member of a conquering people in Asia Minor and Syria ruling an empire in the 2d millennium B.C. 2 : an Indo-European language of the Hittite people known from cuneiform texts — **Hittite** *adj*

¹**hive** \'hīv\ *n* [OE *hȳf*] 1 a : a container for housing honeybees b : a colony of bees 2 : a place swarming with busy occupants — **hive·less** \-ləs\ *adj*

²**hive** *vb* 1 a : to collect (as bees) into a hive b : to enter and take over a hive 2 : to store up in or as if in a hive ⟨*hive* honey⟩ 3 : to reside in close association

³**hive** *n* : an urticarial wheal

hives *n sing or pl* : an allergic disorder in which the skin or mucous membrane is affected by itching wheals

ho \'hō\ *interj* — used esp. to attract attention

¹**hoar** \'hō(ə)r, 'ho(ə)r\ *adj* [OE *hār*] *archaic* : HOARY

²**hoar** *n* : FROST 1c

hoard \'hōrd, 'hórd\ *n* [OE *hord*] : a hidden supply or fund stored up — **hoard** *vt* — **hoard·er** *n*

hoard·ing \'hȯrd-iŋ, 'hȯrd-\ n [obs. *hourd, hoard* hoarding] **1** : a temporary board fence put about a building being erected or repaired — called also *hoard* **2** *Brit* : BILLBOARD

hoar·frost \'hō(ə)r-,frȯst, 'hȯ(ə)r-\ n : FROST 1c

hoar·i·ness \'hōr-ē-nəs, 'hȯr-\ n : the quality or state of being hoary

hoarse \'hōrs, 'hȯrs\ adj [ME *hos, hors,* fr. OE *hās*] **1** : harsh in sound ⟨a crow's *hoarse* caw⟩ **2** : having a rough grating voice ⟨a cold made him *hoarse*⟩ — **hoarse·ly** adv — **hoarse·ness** n

hoary \'hōr-ē, 'hȯr-\ adj **hoar·i·er; -est 1** : grayish or whitish esp. from age ⟨bowed his *hoary* head⟩ **2** : very old : ANCIENT ⟨*hoary* legends⟩

hoa·tzin \wä(t)-'sēn\ n [AmerSp, fr. Nahuatl *uatzin*] : a crested So. American bird with claws on the first and second fingers of the wing

¹hoax \'hōks\ vt : to trick into believing or accepting as genuine something false and often preposterous — **hoax·er** n

²hoax n **1** : an act intended to trick or dupe **2** : something false passed off or accepted as genuine

¹hob \'häb\ n **1** dial Eng : HOBGOBLIN, ELF **2** : MISCHIEF, TROUBLE ⟨raise *hob*⟩

²hob n **1** : a projection at the back or side of a fireplace on which something may be kept warm **2** : a cutting tool used for cutting the teeth of worm wheels or gear wheels

³hob vt **hobbed; hob·bing 1** : to furnish with hobnails **2** : to cut with a hob

¹hob·ble \'häb-əl\ vb **hob·bled; hob·bling** \'häb-(ə-)liŋ\ [ME *hoblen*] **1 a** : to move along unsteadily or with difficulty; *esp* : to limp along ⟨*hobble* along on crutches⟩ **b** : to cause to limp : make lame : CRIPPLE ⟨*hobbled* by an ankle injury⟩ **2 a** : to keep (as a horse) from straying by joining two legs with a short length (as of rope) **b** : HAMPER, IMPEDE — **hob·bler** \-(ə-)lər\ n

²hobble n **1** : a hobbling movement **2** : something used to hobble an animal

hob·ble·de·hoy \'häb-əl-di-,hȯi\ n : an awkward gawky youth

hobble skirt n : a skirt very narrow at the ankles

hob·by \'häb-ē\ n, pl **hobbies** [short for *hobbyhorse*] : an interest or activity which is outside a person's main occupation but to which he devotes much time for pleasure ⟨the *hobby* of stamp collecting⟩ — **hob·by·ist** \-ē-əst\ n

hob·by·horse \-ē-,hȯrs\ n [ME *hoby* small light horse] **1** : a stick sometimes with a horse's head on which children pretend to ride **2 a** : a toy horse **b** : ROCKING HORSE **3** : something (as a pet idea or scheme or favorite topic) to which one constantly reverts

hob·gob·lin \'häb-,gäb-lən\ n **1** : a mischievous elf or goblin **2** : BOGEY 2, BUGABOO

hob·nail \'häb-,nāl\ n : a short large-headed nail used to stud the soles of heavy shoes as a protection against wear — **hob·nailed** \-,nāld\ adj

hob·nob \-,näb\ vi **hob·nobbed; hob·nob·bing** : to associate familiarly ⟨*hobnobbing* with royalty⟩ — **hob·nob·ber** n

ho·bo \'hō-bō\ n, pl **hoboes** also **hobos 1** : a migratory worker **2** : TRAMP — **hobo** vi

Hob·son's choice \,häb-sənz-\ n [Thomas *Hobson* d1631 English liveryman, who required every customer to take the horse nearest the door] : apparently free choice with no real alternative

¹hock \'häk\ n [OE *hōh* heel] : the tarsal joint or region in the hind limb of a quadruped (as the horse) corresponding to the ankle of man

²hock n, often cap [G *hochheimer,* fr. *Hochheim,* Germany] chiefly Brit : RHINE WINE

³hock n [D *hok* pen, prison] : ¹PAWN 2 ⟨got his watch out of *hock*⟩

⁴hock vt : PAWN ⟨*hocked* his watch⟩

hock·ey \'häk-ē\ n : a game played on a field or on ice in which two sides try to drive a ball or puck through opposite goals by hitting it with a curved or hooked stick

ho·cus \'hō-kəs\ vt **ho·cused** or **ho·cussed; ho·cus·ing** or **ho·cus·sing 1** : DECEIVE, CHEAT **2 a** : ADULTERATE **b** : DRUG

ho·cus-po·cus \,hō-kəs-'pō-kəs\ n **1** : a set form of words used by those skilled in tricks of illusion **2** : nonsense that serves as a means of deception

hod \'häd\ n **1** : a long-handled wooden tray or trough used for carrying mortar or bricks on the shoulder **2** : a bucket for holding or carrying coal

hod carrier n : a laborer employed in carrying supplies to bricklayers, stonemasons, cement finishers, or plasterers on the job

hodge·podge \'häj-,päj\ n : MIXTURE, MESS, JUMBLE

hoe \'hō\ n [MF *houe,* of Gmc origin; akin to E *hew*] : a farm or garden tool with a thin flat blade at nearly a right angle to a long handle that is used for weeding, loosening the earth about plants, and hilling — **hoe** vb — **ho·er** \'hō(-ə)r\ n

hod 1

hoe·cake \'hō-,kāk\ n : a cornmeal cake often baked on a griddle

hoe·down \-,daȯn\ n **1** : SQUARE DANCE **2** : a gathering featuring hoedowns

¹hog \'hȯg, 'häg\ n, pl **hogs** also **hog** [OE *hogg*] **1** : a domestic swine esp. when weighing more than 120 pounds; also : any of various animals related to the domestic swine **2** : a selfish, gluttonous, or filthy person

²hog vt **hogged; hog·ging** : to take in excess of one's share ⟨*hogged* all the good seats⟩

ho·gan \'hō-,gän\ n [Navaho] : an earth-covered dwelling of the Navaho Indians

hog·back \'hȯg-,bak, 'häg-\ n **1** : a ridge of land formed by the outcropping edges of tilted strata **2** : a ridge with a sharp summit and steeply sloping sides

hog cholera n : a highly infectious often fatal virus disease of swine

hog·gish \'hȯg-ish, 'häg-\ adj : very selfish, gluttonous, or filthy — **hog·gish·ly** adv — **hog·gish·ness** n

hog·nose snake \,hȯg-,nōz-, ,häg-\ n : any of several rather small harmless stout-bodied No. American snakes that hiss belligerently when disturbed — called also **hog-nosed snake** \-,nōz(d)-\

hogs·head \'hȯgz-,hed, 'hägz-\ n **1** : a large cask or barrel; esp : one containing from 63 to 140 gallons **2** : a U.S. measure for liquids equal to 63 gallons

hog-tie \'hȯg-,tī, 'häg-\ vt **1** : to tie together the feet of ⟨*hog-tie* a calf⟩ **2** : to make helpless ⟨operations *hog-tied* by red tape⟩

hog·wash \-,wȯsh, -,wäsh\ n **1** : SWILL 1, SLOP 4a **2** : worthless or nonsensical language

Ho·hen·stau·fen \'hō-ən-,s(h)taȯ-fən\ n : a member of a princely German family furnishing monarchs of the Holy Roman Empire from 1138–1254 and of Sicily from 1194–1266 — **Hohenstaufen** adj

Ho·hen·zol·lern \'hō-ən-,zäl-ərn\ adj : of or relating to a princely German family furnishing kings of Prussia from 1701 to 1918 and German emperors from 1871 to 1918 — **Hohenzollern** n

hoi pol·loi \,hȯi-pə-'lȯi\ n pl [Gk, the many] : the common people : MASSES

hoise \'hȯiz\ vt **hoised** \'hȯizd\ or **hoist** \'hȯist\; **hois·ing** \'hȯi-ziŋ\ : HOIST — **hoist with one's own petard** : affected or hurt by one's own scheme

¹hoist \'hȯist, chiefly dial 'hīst\ vb [alter. of *hoise*] : to raise or become raised into position by or as if by means of tackle syn see LIFT — **hoist·er** n

²hoist n **1** : an act of hoisting : LIFT **2** : an apparatus for hoisting heavy loads

hoi·ty-toi·ty \,hȯit-ē-'tȯit-ē, ,hīt-ē-'tīt-ē\ adj **1** : GIDDY, FLIGHTY **2** : HAUGHTY, PATRONIZING

ho·key-po·key \,hō-kē-'pō-kē\ n : HOCUS-POCUS

ho·kum \'hō-kəm\ n **1** : a device used (as by showmen) to evoke a desired response esp. of mirth or sentiment **2** : HOCUS-POCUS, BUNKUM

hol- or **holo-** comb form [Gk *holos* whole] **1** : complete : total ⟨*holo*hedral⟩ **2** : completely : totally ⟨*Holo*cene⟩

¹hold \'hōld\ vb **held** \'held\; **hold·ing** [OE *healdan*] **1 a** : to maintain possession of : POSSESS, HAVE ⟨*hold* title to property⟩ **b** : to retain by force ⟨the soldiers *held* the bridge⟩ **2 a** : to impose restraint upon esp. by keeping back ⟨*hold* the dogs⟩ **b** : STAY, ARREST ⟨*held* his hand as he was about to strike⟩ **c** : DELAY ⟨*held* the plane⟩ **3** : to keep from advancing or succeeding in attack **e** : to bind legally or morally : CONSTRAIN ⟨*held* him to his word⟩

3 a : to have or keep in the grasp **b :** to cause to be or remain in a particular situation, position, or relation ⟨*hold* a ladder steady⟩ **c :** SUPPORT, SUSTAIN ⟨the floor will *hold* 10 tons⟩ **d :** to keep in custody **e :** to have in one's keeping : RESERVE ⟨*hold* a room⟩ **4 :** BEAR, CARRY, COMPORT ⟨the soldierly way he *holds* himself⟩ **5 a :** to maintain in being or action : keep up without interruption or flagging ⟨*hold* silence⟩ **b :** to keep the uninterrupted interest, attention, or devotion of **6 a :** to receive and retain : CONTAIN, ACCOMMODATE ⟨the can *holds* 20 gallons⟩ **b :** to have in reserve ⟨what the future *holds*⟩ **7 a :** HARBOR, ENTERTAIN ⟨*hold* a theory⟩ **b :** CONSIDER, REGARD, JUDGE ⟨truths *held* to be self-evident⟩ **c :** ESTEEM, VALUE **8 :** CONVOKE, CONVENE ⟨*hold* a meeting of the council⟩ **9 a :** to have (as an office) by election or appointment ⟨*holds* a captaincy in the navy⟩ **b :** to have earned or been awarded ⟨*holds* a Ph.D.⟩ **10 :** to handle (as reins or a gun) so as to guide or manage **11 a :** to maintain position : not retreat **b** (1) : to continue in the same way or state : LAST ⟨hopes the weather will *hold*⟩ (2) : to endure a test or trial ⟨if his interest *holds* up⟩ **c :** to remain steadfast or faithful ⟨*held* to his beliefs⟩ **12 :** to maintain a grasp on something : remain fastened to something ⟨the anchor *held* in the rough sea⟩ **13 :** to bear or carry oneself ⟨asked him to *hold* still⟩ **14 :** to be or remain valid : APPLY ⟨the rule *holds* in most cases⟩ **15 :** to forbear an intended or threatened action : HALT, PAUSE **syn** see CONTAIN — **hold forth :** to preach or harangue at length — **hold one's own :** to prove at least equal to opposition — **hold the bag 1 :** to be left empty-handed **2 :** to bear alone a responsibility that should have been shared by others — **hold water :** to stand up under criticism or analysis — **hold with :** to agree with or approve of

²hold *n* **1 :** STRONGHOLD **2 :** something that holds, secures, or fastens **3 :** the act or manner of holding : SEIZURE, GRASP ⟨lost his *hold* on the rope⟩ **4 :** a manner of grasping the opponent in wrestling **5 :** the authority to take or keep : POWER ⟨the law has no *hold* over this man⟩ **6 :** something that may be grasped or held **7 :** a prolonged note or rest in music; *also* : a sign ⁀ or ‿ denoting a hold **8 :** an order or indication that something is to be reserved or delayed

³hold *n* [alter. of *hole*] **1 :** the interior of a ship below decks; *esp* : the cargo deck of a ship **2 :** the cargo compartment of an airplane

hold·all \'hōl-ˌdȯl\ *n* : a container for miscellaneous articles; *esp* : an often cloth traveling case or bag

hold·back \'hōl(d)-ˌbak\ *n* **1 :** a device that retains or restrains **2 a :** the act of holding back **b :** something held back

hold·er \'hōl-dər\ *n* **1 :** a person that holds: **a** (1) : OWNER (2) : TENANT **b :** a person in possession of and legally entitled to receive payment of a bill, note, or check **2 :** a device that holds ⟨cigarette *holder*⟩

hold·fast \'hōl(d)-ˌfast\ *n* **1 :** a part by which a plant or animal clings (as to a flat surface or the body of a host) **2 :** something to which something else (as a guy line) may be secured firmly

hold·ing \'hōl-diŋ\ *n* **1 a :** land held (as for farming or residence) **b :** property (as bonds or stocks) owned **2 :** a ruling of a court esp. on an issue of law raised in a case

holding company *n* : a company that owns part or all of other companies for purposes of control

hold out \(')hōl-'daʉt\ *vb* **1 :** OFFER, PROFFER ⟨*held out* no chance for advancement⟩ **2 :** REPRESENT, DESCRIBE ⟨*holds* himself *out* as a singer⟩ **3 :** to remain unsubdued or operative : continue to cope **4 :** to refuse to come to an agreement — **hold·out** \'hōl-ˌdaʉt\ *n*

hold over \(')hōl-'dō-vər\ *vb* **1 :** to continue (as in office) beyond the normal term **2 :** to prolong the engagement or tenure of — **hold·over** \'hōl-ˌdō-vər\ *n*

hold up \(')hōl-'dəp\ *vt* **1 :** DELAY, IMPEDE ⟨only *holding* things *up*⟩ **2 :** to rob at gunpoint

hold·up \'hōl-ˌdəp\ *n* **1 :** a robbery at the point of a gun **2 :** DELAY

hole \'hōl\ *n* [OE *hol* hole, hollow & *holh* hole, hollow] **1 :** an opening into or through a thing ⟨a *hole* in a wall⟩ **2 a :** a hollow place; *esp* : PIT, CAVE **b :** a deep place in a body of water ⟨trout *holes*⟩ **3 :** an underground habitation : BURROW ⟨a fox in its *hole*⟩ **4 :** FLAW, FAULT ⟨a big *hole* in his argument⟩ **5 :** the unit of play from the tee to the cup in golf **6 :** a mean or dingy place ⟨lives in a real *hole*⟩ **7 :** an awkward position : FIX — **hole** *vb* — **hol·ey** \'hō-lē\ *adj* — **in the hole :** in debt : ¹BEHIND 2b

hol·i·day \'hal-ə-ˌdā\ *n* [OE *hāligdæg* holy day] **1 :** HOLY DAY **2 :** a day on which one is exempt from work; *esp* : a day marked by a general suspension of work in commemoration of an event **3 :** a period of relaxation : VACATION ⟨home for the Christmas *holiday*⟩ — **holiday** *vi* — **hol·i·day·er** *n*

hol·i·days \-ˌdāz\ *adv* : on holidays repeatedly : on any holiday ⟨the ferry runs *holidays*⟩

ho·li·ness \'hō-lē-nəs\ *n* **1 :** the quality or state of being holy **2 —** used as a title for various high religious dignitaries ⟨His *Holiness* Pope Paul VI⟩

hol·land \'hal-ənd\ *n* : a cotton or linen fabric in plain weave usu. heavily sized or glazed and used for window shades, bookbinding, and clothing

hol·lan·daise \ˌhal-ən-'dāz\ *n* [F *sauce hollandaise*, lit., Dutch sauce] : a sauce made of butter, yolks of eggs, and lemon juice or vinegar

Hol·lands \'hal-ən(d)z\ *n* : gin made in the Netherlands — called also *Holland gin*

¹hol·ler \'hal-ər\ *vb* **hol·lered**; **hol·ler·ing** \'hal-(ə-)riŋ\ **1 :** to cry or call out : SHOUT **2 :** GRIPE, COMPLAIN

²holler *n* **1 :** SHOUT, CRY **2 :** COMPLAINT

hol·lo \hä-'lō, hə-; 'hal-ō\ *or* **hol·la** \hə-'lä, hal-ä\ *interj* **1 —** used to attract attention **2 —** used as a call of encouragement or jubilation

¹hol·low \'hal-ō\ *adj* [ME *holh, holw*, fr. *holh* hole, hollow, fr. OE] **1 :** CONCAVE, SUNKEN ⟨*hollow* cheeks⟩ **2 :** having a hole inside : not solid throughout ⟨*hollow* tree⟩ **3 :** devoid of value or significance ⟨*hollow* victory⟩ **4 :** reverberating like a sound made in or by beating on a large empty enclosure : MUFFLED **5 :** FALSE, DECEITFUL — **hol·low·ly** *adv* — **hol·low·ness** *n*

²hollow *vb* : to make or become hollow

³hollow *n* **1 :** a low spot in a surface; *esp* : VALLEY **2 :** an empty space within something : HOLE ⟨the *hollow* of a tree⟩

hollow ware *n* : vessels usu. of pottery, glass, or metal (as bowls, cups, or vases) with a significant depth and volume — compare FLATWARE

hol·ly \'hal-ē\ *n, pl* **hollies** [OE *holegn*] : any of a genus of trees and shrubs with thick glossy spiny-margined leaves and usu. bright red berries; *also* : the foliage or branches of a holly

hol·ly·hock \'hal-ē-ˌhäk, -ˌhȯk\ *n* [ME *holihoc*, fr. *holi* holy + *hoc* mallow, fr. OE] : a tall widely grown perennial Chinese herb of the mallow family with large coarse rounded leaves and tall spikes of showy flowers

Hol·ly·wood bed \ˌhal-ē-ˌwȯd-\ *n* : a mattress on a box spring supported by low legs sometimes with an upholstered headboard

hol·mi·um \'hōl-mē-əm\ *n* [NL, fr. *Holmia* (Stockholm), Sweden] : a metallic element that occurs with yttrium and forms highly magnetic compounds — see ELEMENT table

holo- — see HOL-

hol·o·caust \'hal-ə-ˌkȯst, 'hō-lə-\ *n* [Gk *holokaustos* burnt whole, fr. *holos* whole + *kaustos* burnt, fr. *kaiein* to burn] **1 :** a sacrifice consumed by fire **2 :** a thorough destruction esp. by fire

Ho·lo·cene \'hō-lə-ˌsēn, 'hal-ə-\ *adj* : RECENT 2 — **Holocene** *n*

ho·lo·gram \'hō-lə-ˌgram, 'hal-ə-\ *n* : a three-dimensional picture that is made on a photographic film or plate without the use of a camera, that consists of a pattern of interference produced by a split coherent beam of light, and that for viewing is illuminated with coherent light from behind

ho·lo·graph \'hō-lə-ˌgraf, 'hal-ə-\ *n* : a document wholly in the handwriting of the purported author — **holograph** *adj* — **ho·lo·graph·ic** \ˌhō-lə-'graf-ik, ˌhal-ə-\ *adj*

ho·lo·phyt·ic \ˌhō-lə-'fit-ik\ *adj* : obtaining food after the manner of a green plant by photosynthetic activity — compare HOLOZOIC

ho·lo·thu·ri·an \ˌhō-lə-'th(y)ur-ē-ən\ *n* : any of a class (Holothurioidea) of echinoderms having a long flexible tough muscular body — **holothurian** *adj*

ho·lo·zo·ic \ˌhō-lə-'zō-ik\ *adj* : obtaining food after the manner of most animals by ingesting complex organic matter — compare HOLOPHYTIC

---

j joke; **ŋ** sing; **ō** flow; **ȯ** flaw; **ȯi** coin; **th** thin; **t͟h** this; **ü** loot; ** u̇** foot; **y** yet; **yü** few; **yu̇** furious; **zh** vision

hol·stein-frie·sian \ˌhōl-ˌstēn-'frē-zhən, -ˌstīn-\ n [*Holstein*, Germany, its later locality + *Friesian* Frisian] : any of a breed of large black-and-white dairy cattle that produce large quantities of comparatively low-fat milk — called also *holstein*

hol·ster \'hōl(t)-stər\ n [D] : a usu. leather case for a pistol

ho·lus-bo·lus \ˌhō-ləs-'bō-ləs\ adv : all at once : ALTOGETHER

ho·ly \'hō-lē\ adj **ho·li·er; -est** [OE *hālig*] **1** : set apart to the service of God or a god : SACRED **2 a** : characterized by perfection and transcendence : commanding absolute adoration and reverence **b** : spiritually pure : SAINTLY **3 a** : evoking or meriting veneration or awe **b** : being awesome, frightening, or beyond belief ⟨a *holy* terror⟩

Holy Communion n : COMMUNION 2

holy day n : a day observed as a religious feast or fast

holy day of obligation : a feast on which Roman Catholics are obliged to hear mass

Holy Father n : POPE

Holy Ghost n : the third person of the Trinity : HOLY SPIRIT

Holy Grail n : GRAIL

Holy Hour n : an hour of prayer and meditation before the Blessed Sacrament esp. in memory of the Passion

Holy Office n : a congregation and tribunal of the curia charged with protecting faith and morals

holy of holies : the innermost chamber of the Jewish tabernacle and temple

holy oil n : olive oil blessed by a bishop for use in a sacrament or sacramental

holy order n, *often cap H&O* **1** : MAJOR ORDER **2** pl : the rite or sacrament of ordination

Holy Roman Empire n : a loose confederation of German and Italian territories under an emperor existing from the 9th or 10th century to 1806

Holy Saturday n : the Saturday before Easter

Holy See n : the see of the pope

Holy Spirit n : the active presence of God in human life constituting the third person of the Trinity

ho·ly·stone \'hō-lē-ˌstōn\ n : a soft sandstone used to scrub a ship's decks — **holystone** vb

Holy Synod n : the governing body of a self-governing Eastern church

Holy Thursday n : MAUNDY THURSDAY

holy water n : water blessed by a priest and used as a purifying sacramental

Holy Week n : the week before Easter

Holy Writ n : BIBLE 1, 2

Holy Year n : a jubilee year

hom- or **homo-** comb form [Gk *homos*] : one and the same : similar : alike ⟨*homo*graph⟩ ⟨*homo*sporous⟩

hom·age \'(h)äm-ij\ n [OF *hommage*, fr. *homme* man, vassal, fr. L *homin-, homo* man] **1** : a ceremony in which a person pledged allegiance to a lord and became his vassal **2** : something done or given as an acknowledgment of a vassal's duty to his lord **3** : RESPECT, HONOR

hom·bre \'äm-brē, -brā\ n [Sp, man, fr. L *homin-, homo*] : GUY, FELLOW

hom·burg \'häm-bərg\ n [*Homburg*, Germany] : a man's felt hat with a stiff curled brim and a high crown creased lengthwise

¹home \'hōm\ n [OE *hām* village, home] **1** : the house in which one lives or in which one's family lives **2** : the country or place where one lives or where one's ancestors lived **3** : the place where something is usu. or naturally found : HABITAT ⟨the *home* of the elephant⟩ **4** : a place for the care of persons unable to care for themselves ⟨a *home* for old people⟩ **5** : the social unit formed by a family living together in one dwelling ⟨a city of 20,000 *homes*⟩ **6** : a dwelling house ⟨new modern *homes* for sale⟩ **7** : the goal or point to be reached in some games

²home adv **1** : to or at home ⟨he went *home*⟩ ⟨she's not *home*⟩ **2** : to a final, closed, or standard position ⟨drive a nail *home*⟩ **3** : to a vital core ⟨the truth struck *home*⟩

³home vb **1 a** : to go or return home **b** : to return home accurately from a distance ⟨a pigeon *homes* to its loft⟩ **c** : to proceed to or toward a source of radiated energy used as a guide ⟨missiles *home* in on radar⟩ **2** : to have a home **3** : to send to or provide with a home

home- or **homeo-** also **homoi-** or **homoio-** comb form

[Gk *homoios*, fr. *homos* same] : like : similar ⟨*homeo*stasis⟩ ⟨*homoio*thermic⟩

home·body \'hōm-ˌbäd-ē\ n : one whose life centers around the home

home·bred \-'bred\ adj : produced at home : INDIGENOUS

home brew n : an alcoholic beverage made at home

home·com·ing \'hōm-ˌkəm-iŋ\ n **1** : a return home **2** : the return of a group of people esp. on a special occasion to a place formerly frequented

home economics n : the study of the various arts and skills involved in the care and management of a household — **home economist** n

home front n : the sphere of civilian activity in war

home·grown \'hōm-'grōn\ adj **1** : NATIVE, LOCAL ⟨*homegrown* corn⟩ **2** : DOMESTIC, INDIGENOUS

home·land \'hōm-ˌland\ n : native land : FATHERLAND

home·less \'hōm-ləs\ adj : having no home ⟨a *homeless* kitten⟩ ⟨a family left *homeless* by a fire⟩

home·like \-ˌlīk\ adj : characteristic of a home: **a** : CHEERFUL, COZY **b** : SIMPLE, WHOLESOME

home·ly \'hōm-lē\ adj **home·li·er; -est** **1** : characteristic of home : PLAIN, SIMPLE ⟨*homely* meals⟩ **2** : lacking polish or refinement : RUDE ⟨*homely* manners⟩ **3** : not handsome ⟨a *homely* person⟩ — **home·li·ness** n

home·made \'hōm-'mād\ adj : made in the home or on the premises ⟨*homemade* bread⟩

home·mak·er \'hōm-ˌmā-kər\ n : one who manages a household esp. as a wife and mother — **home·mak·ing** \-kiŋ\ n or adj

ho·me·op·a·thy \ˌhō-mē-'äp-ə-thē\ n : a system of medical practice that treats disease esp. with minute doses of dilute drugs — **home·o·path** \'hō-mē-ə-ˌpath\ n — **home·o·path·ic** \-mē-ə-'path-ik\ adj

ho·me·o·sta·sis \ˌhō-mē-ō-'stā-səs, -mē-'äs-tə-səs\ n : a relatively stable state of equilibrium or a tendency toward such a state between the different but interdependent elements or groups of elements of an organism or group — **ho·meo·stat·ic** \-mē-ō-'stat-ik\ adj

home plate n : a rubber slab at the apex of a baseball diamond that a base runner must touch in order to score

hom·er \'hō-mər\ n **1** : HOMING PIGEON **2** : HOME RUN

home range n : the area to which an animal confines his activities — compare TERRITORY

Ho·mer·ic \hō-'mer-ik\ adj : of, relating to, or characteristic of the Greek poet Homer, his age, or his writings — **Ho·mer·i·cal·ly** \-i-k(ə-)lē\ adv

home·room \'hōm-ˌrüm, -ˌrúm\ n : a schoolroom where pupils of the same class report at the opening of school

home rule n : self-government in internal affairs by the people of a dependent political unit **2** : limited autonomy in local affairs granted by a state to a county or municipality

home run n : a hit in baseball that enables the batter to make a complete circuit of the bases and score a run — called also *homer*

home·sick \'hōm-ˌsik\ adj : longing for home and family while absent from them — **home·sick·ness** n

¹home·spun \-ˌspən\ adj **1 a** : spun or made at home **b** : made of homespun **2** : SIMPLE, HOMELY ⟨*homespun* humor⟩

²homespun n : a loosely woven usu. woolen or linen fabric orig. made from homespun yarn

¹home·stead \'hōm-ˌsted\ n **1 a** : the home and adjoining land occupied by a family **b** : an ancestral home **2** : a tract of land acquired from U.S. public lands by filing a record and living on and cultivating it

²homestead vb : to acquire or settle on land for use as a homestead ⟨*homesteaded* in Alaska⟩

home·stead·er \-ˌsted-ər\ n : one who holds a homestead; *esp* : one who has acquired a homestead under laws authorizing the sale of public lands in parcels of 160 acres to settlers

home·stretch \'hōm-'strech\ n **1** : the part of a racecourse between the last curve and the winning post **2** : a final stage

home·ward \'hōm-wərd\ or **home·wards** \-wərdz\ adv : toward or in the direction of home — **homeward** adj

home·work \-ˌwərk\ n : work and esp. school lessons to be done at home

hom·ey \'hō-mē\ adj **hom·i·er; -est** : HOMELIKE, INTIMATE — **hom·ey·ness** or **hom·i·ness** n

hom·i·cid·al \ˌhäm-ə-'sīd-ᵊl, ˌhō-mə-\ *adj* : having or showing tendencies toward homicide : MURDEROUS — **hom·i·cid·al·ly** \-ᵊl-ē\ *adv*

hom·i·cide \'häm-ə-ˌsīd, 'hō-mə-\ *n* **1** [L *homicida*, fr. *homo* man + *-cida* -cide] : a person who kills another **2** [L *homicidium*, fr. *homo* man + *-cidium* -cide] : a killing of one human being by another

hom·i·let·ic \ˌhäm-ə-'let-ik\ *adj* **1** : of the nature of a homily **2** : of or relating to homiletics — **hom·i·let·i·cal** \-i-kəl\ *adj* — **hom·i·let·i·cal·ly** \-i-k(ə-)lē\ *adv*

hom·i·let·ics \-'let-iks\ *n* : the art of preaching

hom·i·ly \'häm-ə-lē\ *n, pl* **-lies** [LL *homilia*, fr. LGk, fr. Gk, conversation, discourse, fr. *homilein* to consort with, address, fr. *homilos* crowd, assembly] **1** : SERMON; *esp* : an informal exposition of Scripture **2** : a moral lecture

homing pigeon *n* : a racing pigeon trained to return home

hom·i·nid \'häm-ə-nəd\ *n* [L *homin-*, *homo* man] : any of a family (Hominidae) of 2-footed primate mammals comprising recent man, his immediate ancestors, and related extinct forms — **hominid** *adj*

hom·i·noid \'häm-ə-ˌnȯid\ *adj* : resembling or related to man — **hominoid** *n*

hom·i·ny \'häm-ə-nē\ *n* [of AmerInd origin] : hulled corn with the germ removed — compare GRITS

ho·mo \'hō-mō\ *n* [NL *Homo*, genus name, fr. L, man] : any of a genus (*Homo*) of primate mammals that consists of mankind and is usu. held to include a single recent species (*H. sapiens*) comprising all surviving and various extinct men

homo- — see HOM-

ho·mog·e·nate \hō-'mäj-ə-ˌnāt\ *n* : a product of homogenizing

ho·mo·ge·ne·i·ty \ˌhō-mə-jə-'nē-ət-ē\ *n* : the quality or state of being homogeneous

ho·mo·ge·ne·ous \ˌhō-mə-'jē-nē-əs\ *adj* [ML *homogeneus*, fr. Gk *homogenēs*, fr. *homos* same + *genos* kind] **1** : of the same or a similar kind or nature **2** : of uniform structure or composition throughout **3** : HOMOGENOUS 1 — **ho·mo·ge·ne·ous·ly** *adv* — **ho·mo·ge·ne·ous·ness** *n*

ho·mog·e·nize \hō-'mäj-ə-ˌnīz\ *vt* **1** : to make homogeneous **2 a** : to reduce to small particles of uniform size and distribute evenly 〈*homogenize* peanut butter〉 〈*homogenize* paint〉 **b** : to break up the fat globules of (milk) into very fine particles esp. by forcing through minute openings — **ho·mog·e·ni·za·tion** \-ˌmäj-ə-nə-'zā-shən\ *n* — **ho·mog·e·niz·er** \-'mäj-ə-ˌnī-zər\ *n*

ho·mog·e·nous \-'mäj-ə-nəs\ *adj* **1** : of, relating to, or exhibiting homogeny **2** : HOMOGENEOUS

ho·mog·e·ny \-nē\ *n* : correspondence between parts or organs due to descent from the same ancestral type

hom·o·graph \'häm-ə-ˌgraf, 'hō-mə-\ *n* : one of two or more words alike in spelling but different in origin or meaning 〈*fair* meaning "market" and *fair* meaning "beautiful" are *homographs*〉 — **hom·o·graph·ic** \ˌhäm-ə-'graf-ik, ˌhō-mə-\ *adj*

homoi- *or* **homoio-** — see HOME-

ho·moio·ther·mic \hō-ˌmȯi-ə-'thər-mik\ *or* **ho·moio·ther·mal** \-məl\ *or* **ho·moio·ther·mous** \-məs\ *adj* : WARM-BLOODED — **ho·moio·therm** \-'mȯi-ə-ˌthərm\ *n* — **ho·moio·ther·my** \-ˌthər-mē\ *n*

ho·mol·o·gize \hō-'mäl-ə-ˌjīz\ *vt* **1** : to make homologous **2** : to demonstrate the homology of

ho·mol·o·gous \hō-'mäl-ə-gəs\ *adj* [Gk *homologos* agreeing, fr. *homos* same + *legein* to say] **1 a** : having the same relative position, value, or structure 〈*homologous* chromosomes〉 **b** : corresponding in structure because of community of origin 〈arms and wings are *homologous* structures〉 **c** : belonging to or consisting of a chemical series whose members exhibit homology **2** : derived from or developed in response to organisms of the same species 〈*homologous* tissue graft〉

ho·mo·logue *or* **ho·mo·log** \'hō-mə-ˌlȯg, 'häm-ə-\ *n* : something that exhibits homology

ho·mol·o·gy \hō-'mäl-ə-jē\ *n, pl* **-gies** **1** : a similarity often attributable to common origin **2 a** : structural likeness between corresponding parts of different organisms due to differentiation from a remote common ancestor — compare ANALOGY **b** : structural likeness between different parts of the same individual **3** : the relation existing between chemical compounds in a series whose successive members have in composition a regular difference

hom·o·nym \'häm-ə-ˌnim, 'hō-mə-\ *n* [Gk *homōnymon*, fr. *homōnymos* having the same name, fr. *homos* same + *onoma*, *onyma* name] **1** : HOMOPHONE **2** : one of two or more words spelled and pronounced alike but different in meaning 〈*pool* of water and *pool* (the game) are *homonyms*〉 — **hom·o·nym·ic** \ˌhäm-ə-'nim-ik, ˌhō-mə-\ *adj*

hom·o·phone \'häm-ə-ˌfōn, 'hō-mə-\ *n* [hom- + Gk *phōnē* voice, sound] : one of two or more words pronounced alike but different in meaning or derivation or spelling 〈*to*, *too*, and *two* are *homophones*〉 — **ho·moph·o·nous** \hō-'mäf-ə-nəs\ *adj*

hom·o·phon·ic \ˌhäm-ə-'fän-ik, ˌhō-mə-\ *adj* [Gk *homophōnos* being in unison, fr. *homos* same + *phōnē* sound] : of, relating to, or being music consisting of a single accompanied melodic line — **ho·moph·o·ny** \hō-'mäf-ə-nē\ *n*

ho·mop·ter·ous \hō-'mäp-tə-rəs\ *adj* [Gk *pteron* wing] : of or relating to a group (Homoptera) of insects having sucking mouthparts and comprising the cicadas, aphids, scale insects, and related forms — **ho·mop·ter·an** \-rən\ *adj or n*

ho·mo sa·pi·ens \ˌhō-mō-'sap-ē-ənz, -'sā-pē-\ *n* [NL, species name, fr. *Homo*, genus name + *sapiens*, specific epithet, fr. L, wise, intelligent] : MANKIND 1

ho·mo·sex·u·al \ˌhō-mə-'sek-sh(ə-w)əl\ *adj* : of, relating to, or exhibiting sexual desire toward a member of one's own sex — **homosexual** *n* — **ho·mo·sex·u·al·i·ty** \-ˌsek-shə-'wal-ət-ē\ *n*

ho·mo·thal·lic \ˌhō-mō-'thal-ik\ *adj* [Gk *thallein* to sprout, grow] : having a single phase that produces two kinds of gametes capable of fusing to form a zygote — compare HETEROTHALLIC — **ho·mo·thal·lism** \-'thal-ˌiz-əm\ *n*

ho·mo·zy·gote \-'zī-ˌgōt\ *n* : a homozygous individual — **ho·mo·zy·gos·i·ty** \-ˌzī-'gäs-ət-ē\ *n*

ho·mo·zy·gous \-'zī-gəs\ *adj* [Gk *zygon* yoke] : containing either but not both members of at least one pair of alleles 〈a plant *homozygous* for yellow seed〉〈*homozygous* gametes〉 — **ho·mo·zy·gous·ly** *adv*

ho·mun·cu·lus \hō-'məŋ-kyə-ləs\ *n, pl* **-li** \-ˌlī, -lē\ [L, dim. of *homin-*, *homo* man] : a little man : MANIKIN

homy \'hō-mē\ *var of* HOMEY

¹hone \'hōn\ *n* [OE *hān* stone] **1** : a fine-grit whetstone; *esp* : one for sharpening razors **2** : a tool for enlarging holes to precise measurements by means of a rotated abrasive

²hone *vt* : to sharpen, enlarge, or smooth with a hone — **hon·er** *n*

hon·est \'än-əst\ *adj* [L *honestus* honorable, fr. *honos*, *honor* honor] **1 a** : free from fraud or deception : TRUTHFUL 〈an *honest* plea〉 **b** : GENUINE, REAL 〈made an *honest* error〉 **c** : HUMBLE, PLAIN **2 a** : REPUTABLE, RESPECTABLE 〈poor but *honest* people〉 **b** *chiefly Brit* : GOOD, WORTHY **3** : CREDITABLE **4 a** : marked by integrity : UPRIGHT **b** : marked by frankness or sincerity : STRAIGHTFORWARD **c** : INNOCENT, SIMPLE — **hon·est·ly** *adv*

hon·es·ty \'än-ə-stē\ *n* **1** : fairness and straightforwardness of conduct : INTEGRITY **2** : TRUTHFULNESS, SINCERITY 〈*honesty* is the best policy〉

¹hon·ey \'hən-ē\ *n, pl* **honeys** [OE *hunig*] **1** : a thick sugary material prepared by bees from floral nectar and stored by them in a honeycomb for food **2 a** : SWEETHEART, DEAR — often used as a term of endearment **b** : something superlative 〈a *honey* of a play〉 **3** : SWEETNESS 〈coaxed him with *honey* in her voice〉 — **honey** *adj*

²honey *vb* **hon·eyed** *also* **hon·ied; hon·ey·ing** **1** : to sweeten with or as if with honey **2** : to speak ingratiatingly : FLATTER

hon·ey·bee \'hən-ē-ˌbē\ *n* : a social honey-producing bee; *esp* : a European bee widely kept for its honey and wax

honeybee

¹hon·ey·comb \-ˌkōm\ *n* **1** : a mass of 6-sided wax cells built by honeybees in their nest to contain brood and stores of honey **2** : something that resembles a honeycomb in structure or appearance

²honeycomb *vb* **1** : to make or become full of holes like a honeycomb **2** : SUBVERT, WEAKEN

hon·ey·dew \'hən-ē-ˌd(y)ü\ *n* : a sugary deposit secreted on the leaves of plants usu. by aphids or scale insects but sometimes by a fungus

j joke; **ŋ** sing; **ō** flow; **ȯ** flaw; **ȯi** coin; **th** thin; **th** this; **ü** loot; **ù** foot; **y** yet; **yü** few; **yù** furious; **zh** vision

honeydew melon *n* : a pale smooth-skinned muskmelon with greenish sweet flesh

hon·ey·moon \'hən-ē-ˌmün\ *n* **1** : the time immediately after marriage **2** : the holiday spent by a couple after marriage — **honeymoon** *vi* — **hon·ey·moon·er** *n*

hon·ey·suck·le \-ˌsək-əl\ *n* : any of a genus of shrubs with opposite leaves and often showy flowers rich in nectar; *also* : any of various plants (as a columbine or azalea) with tubular flowers rich in nectar

honk \'häŋk, 'hóŋk\ *n* : the cry of a goose; *also* : a similar sound (as of a horn) — **honk** *vb*

hon·ky-tonk \'häŋ-kē-ˌtäŋk\ *n* : a cheap nightclub or dance hall : DIVE

¹hon·or \'än-ər\ *n* [L *honos, honor*] **1 a** : good name : public esteem : REPUTATION **b** : outward respect : RECOGNITION ⟨a dinner in *honor* of a new coach⟩ **2** : PRIVILEGE **3** : a person of superior standing ⟨if your *Honor* please⟩ — used esp. as a title for a holder of high office **4** : one whose worth brings respect or fame : CREDIT ⟨was an *honor* to his profession⟩ **5** : an evidence or symbol of distinction: as **a** : an exalted title or rank **b** : BADGE, DECORATION **c** : a ceremonial rite or observance **d** *pl* : an academic distinction conferred on a superior student **e** : an award in a contest or field of competition **6** : CHASTITY, PURITY **7 a** : a keen sense of ethical conduct : INTEGRITY ⟨a man of *honor*⟩ **b** : one's word given as a guarantee of performance **8** *pl* : social courtesies or civilities extended by a host ⟨did the *honors* at the table⟩ **9 a** (1) : the ace, king, queen, jack, or ten of the trump suit in bridge or any ace when the contract is no-trump (2) : the scoring value of honors held in bridge — usu. used in pl. **b** : the privilege of playing first from the tee in golf

²honor *vt* **hon·ored; hon·or·ing** \'än-(ə-)riŋ\ **1 a** : to regard or treat with honor : RESPECT ⟨*honor* your parents⟩ **b** : to confer honor on **2** : to live up to or fulfill the terms of; *esp* : to accept and pay when due ⟨*honor* a check⟩ **3** : to salute with a bow in square dancing

hon·or·a·ble \'än-(ə-)rə-bəl, 'än-ər-bəl\ *adj* **1** : deserving of honor **2** : performed or accompanied with marks of honor or respect ⟨an *honorable* burial⟩ **3 a** : of great renown : ILLUSTRIOUS **b** — used as a title for children of some British noblemen and for various government officials **4 a** : doing credit to the possessor **b** : consistent with an untarnished reputation **5** : characterized by integrity : ETHICAL — **hon·or·a·bly** \-blē\ *adv*

hon·o·rar·i·um \ˌän-ə-ˈrer-ē-əm\ *n, pl* **-ia** \-ē-ə\ *also* **-i·ums** : a reward usu. for services on which custom or propriety forbids a price to be set

hon·or·ary \'än-ə-ˌrer-ē\ *adj* **1 a** : having or conferring distinction **b** : COMMEMORATIVE ⟨*honorary* plaque⟩ **2 a** : conferred in recognition of achievement or service without the usual prerequisites or obligations ⟨received an *honorary* degree⟩ **b** : UNPAID, VOLUNTARY ⟨*honorary* chairman⟩ — **hon·or·ar·i·ly** \ˌän-ə-ˈrer-ə-lē\ *adv*

¹hon·or·if·ic \ˌän-ə-ˈrif-ik\ *adj* **1** : conferring or conveying honor **2** : belonging to or constituting a class of grammatical forms used in speaking to or about a social superior

²honorific *n* : an honorific word, phrase, or form

hon·our \'än-ər\ *chiefly Brit var of* HONOR

hooch \'hüch\ *n, slang* : alcoholic liquor esp. when inferior or illicitly made or obtained

¹hood \'hud\ *n* [OE *hōd*] **1 a** : a flexible covering for the head and neck **b** : a protective covering for the head and face **2 a** : an ornamental fold at the back of an academic gown or ecclesiastical vestment **b** : a color marking, crest, or expansive fold on the head of an animal **3 a** : something resembling a hood in form or use **b** : a cover for parts of mechanisms; *esp* : the movable metal covering over the engine of an automobile — **hood** *vt* — **hood·like** \-ˌlīk\ *adj*

²hood \'hud, 'hüd\ *n, slang* : HOODLUM

-hood \ˌhud\ *n suffix* [OE *-hād*] **1** : state : condition : quality : character ⟨boy*hood*⟩ ⟨hardi*hood*⟩ **2** : instance of a (specified) state or quality ⟨false*hood*⟩ **3** : individuals sharing a (specified) state or character ⟨brother*hood*⟩

hood·ed \'hud-əd\ *adj* : having or shaped like a hood — **hood·ed·ness** *n*

hood·lum \'hüd-ləm\ *n* **1** : THUG, MOBSTER **2** : a young ruffian

hoo·doo \'hüd-ü\ *n, pl* **hoodoos** [of African origin] **1** : VOODOO **2** : something that brings bad luck — **hoodoo** *vt* — **hoo·doo·ism** \-ˌiz-əm\ *n*

hood·wink \'hud-ˌwiŋk\ *vt* **1** *archaic* : BLINDFOLD **2** : to deceive by false appearance : impose upon

hoo·ey \'hü-ē\ *n* : NONSENSE

¹hoof \'huf, 'hüf\ *n, pl* **hooves** \'huvz, 'hüvz\ *or* **hoofs** [OE *hōf*] **1** : a curved covering of horn that protects the front of or encloses the ends of the toes of some mammals and that corresponds to a nail or claw **2** : a hoofed foot esp. of a horse — **hoofed** \'huft, 'hüft, 'huvd, 'hüvd\ *adj* — **on the hoof** : LIVING ⟨meat animals bought *on the hoof*⟩

²hoof *vb* **1** : WALK **2** : KICK, TRAMPLE **3** : to move on the feet; *esp* : DANCE

hoof·er \'huf-ər, 'hü-fər\ *n* : a professional dancer

¹hook \'huk\ *n* [OE *hōc*] **1** : a curved or bent implement for catching, holding, or pulling **2** : something (as a sharp bend in a road) curved or bent like a hook **3** : a flight of a ball that deviates from a straight course in a direction opposite to the dominant hand of the player propelling it **4** : a short blow delivered with a circular motion by a boxer while the elbow remains bent and rigid — **by hook or by crook** : by any means — **off the hook** : out of trouble — **on one's own hook** : by oneself : INDEPENDENTLY

²hook *vb* **1** : to form into a hook : CROOK, CURVE **2 a** : to seize, make fast, or connect by or as if by a hook **b** : to become secured or connected by or as if by a hook **3** : STEAL, PILFER **4** : to strike or pierce as if with a hook **5** : to make (as a rug) by drawing loops of thread, yarn, or cloth through a coarse fabric with a hook **6** : to hit or throw (a ball) so that a hook results

hook·ah \'huk-ə, 'hü-kə\ *n* [Ar *huqqah* bottle of a hookah] : a pipe for smoking that has a long flexible tube whereby the smoke is cooled by passing through water

hook and eye *n* : a 2-part fastening device (as on a garment or a door) consisting of a wire hook that catches over a bar or into a loop of wire

hooked \'hukt\ *adj* **1** : shaped like or furnished with a hook **2** : made by hooking ⟨a *hooked* rug⟩

hook·er \'huk-ər\ *n* [D *hoeker*, fr. *hoec* fishhook] **1** : a one-masted fishing boat **2** : an outmoded or clumsy boat

hook·let \'huk-lət\ *n* : a small hook

hook·up \'huk-ˌəp\ *n* **1** : an assemblage (as of circuits) used for a specific purpose (as in radio); *also* : the plan of such an assemblage **2** : an arrangement of mechanical parts **3** : connection often between antagonistic elements : ALLIANCE ⟨a *hookup* between two countries⟩

hook·worm \'huk-ˌwərm\ *n* **1** : a parasitic nematode worm having strong hooks or plates about the mouth and including serious bloodsucking pests **2** : a disordered state marked by blood loss, paleness, and weakness due to hookworms in the intestine — called also *hookworm disease*

hooky \'huk-ē\ *n* : TRUANCY ⟨play *hooky*⟩

hoo·li·gan \'hü-li-gən\ *n* : RUFFIAN, HOODLUM — **hoo·li·gan·ism** \-gə-ˌniz-əm\ *n*

¹hoop \'hup, 'hüp\ *n* [OE *hōp*] **1** : a circular strip used esp. for holding together the staves of containers or as a plaything **2** : a circular figure or object : RING **3** : a circle or series of circles of flexible material used to expand a woman's skirt

²hoop *vt* : to bind or fasten with or as if with a hoop — **hoop·er** *n*

hoop·la \'hü-ˌplä\ *n* **1** : TO-DO **2** : utterances designed to bewilder or confuse

hoop·skirt \'hup-ˌskərt, 'hüp-\ *n* : a skirt stiffened with or as if with hoops

hoo·ray \hu-ˈrā\ *var of* HURRAH

hoose·gow \'hüs-ˌgaú\ *n* [Sp *juzgado* panel of judges, courtroom, fr. *juzgar* to judge, fr. L *judicare*] *slang* : JAIL

¹hoot \'hüt\ *vb* **1** : to utter a loud shout usu. in contempt **2** : to make the natural throat noise of an owl or a similar cry **3** : to assail or drive out by hooting — **4** : to express in or by hoots ⟨*hooted* disapproval⟩ — **hoot·er** *n*

²hoot *n* **1** : a sound of hooting; *esp* : the cry of an owl **2** : a very small amount ⟨don't care a *hoot* about the book⟩

hoo·te·nan·ny \'hüt-ᵊn-ˌan-ē\ *n, pl* **-nies** : a gathering

hooks: *1* coat, *2* hammock, *3* screw

at which folk singers entertain often with the audience joining in

¹hop \'häp\ *vb* **hopped; hop·ping** [OE *hoppian*] **1 :** to move by a quick springy leap or in a series of leaps; *esp* **:** to jump on one foot **2 :** to jump over ⟨*hop* a puddle⟩ **3 :** to get aboard by or as if by hopping ⟨*hop* a train⟩ **4 :** to make a quick trip esp. by air

²hop *n* **1 a :** a short brisk leap esp. on one leg **b :** BOUNCE, REBOUND **2 :** DANCE, BALL ⟨the junior *hop*⟩ **3 a :** a flight in an airplane **b :** a short trip **c :** a free ride

³hop *n* [MD *hoppe*] **1 :** a twining vine of the mulberry family with lobed leaves and pistillate flowers in cone≠shaped catkins **2** *pl* **:** the ripe dried pistillate catkins of a hop used esp. to impart a bitter flavor to malt liquors

⁴hop *vt* **hopped; hop·ping 1 :** to flavor with hops **2 :** to increase the power of beyond an original rating ⟨*hop* up an engine⟩

¹hope \'hōp\ *vb* [OE *hopian*] **1 :** to desire with expectation of fulfillment ⟨*hope* to succeed⟩ **2 :** to long for with expectation of obtainment **3 :** to expect with desire **:** TRUST ⟨*hope* he'll accept the invitation⟩

²hope *n* **1 :** TRUST, RELIANCE ⟨our *hope* is in the Lord⟩ **2 a :** desire accompanied by expectation of or belief in fulfillment ⟨in *hope* of an early recovery⟩ **b :** someone or something on which hopes are centered ⟨a healthy quarterback was the team's only *hope* for victory⟩ **c :** something hoped for

hope chest *n* **:** a young woman's accumulation of clothes and domestic furnishings (as silver or linen) kept in or as if in a chest in anticipation of her marriage; *also* **:** a chest for such an accumulation

¹hope·ful \'hōp-fəl\ *adj* **1 :** full of or inclined to hope **2 :** having qualities which inspire hope — **hope·ful·ly** \-fə-lē\ *adv* — **hope·ful·ness** *n*

²hopeful *n* **:** a person who has hopes or is considered promising esp. as a new political candidate

hope·less \'hōp-ləs\ *adj* **1 a :** having no expectation of good or success **:** DESPAIRING **b :** not susceptible of remedy or cure **:** INCURABLE **2 a :** giving no ground for hope **:** DESPERATE ⟨a *hopeless* situation⟩ **b :** incapable of solution, management, or accomplishment **:** IMPOSSIBLE ⟨a *hopeless* task⟩ — **hope·less·ly** *adv* — **hope·less·ness** *n*

Ho·pi \'hō-pē\ *n* **1 :** a member of a Pueblo Indian people of northeastern Arizona **2 :** the language of the Hopi people

hop·lite \'häp-,līt\ *n* [Gk *hoplitēs*, fr. *hopla* arms] **:** a heavily armed infantry soldier of ancient Greece

hop·per \'häp-ər\ *n* **1 a :** one that hops **b :** a leaping insect; *esp* **:** an immature hopping form of an insect **2** [fr. the shaking motion of hoppers used to feed grain into a mill] **a :** a usu. funnel-shaped receptacle for delivering material (as grain or coal) **b :** a box in which a bill to be considered by a legislative body is dropped **c :** a tank holding liquid and having a device for releasing its contents through a pipe

hop·scotch \'häp-,skäch\ *n* **:** a child's game in which a player tosses an object (as a stone) consecutively into areas of a figure outlined on the ground and hops through the figure and back to regain the object

ho·ra *also* **ho·rah** \'hōr-ə, 'hȯr-ə\ *n* [NHeb *hōrāh*, fr. Romanian *horă*] **:** a circle dance of Romania and Israel

Ho·rae \'hō(ə)r-,ē, 'hȯ(ə)r-, -ī\ *n pl* **:** the goddesses of the seasons in Greek mythology

Ho·ra·tian \hə-'rā-shən\ *adj* **:** of, relating to, or characteristic of Horace or his poetry

Ho·ra·tius \hə-'rā-sh(ē-)əs\ *n* **:** a hero in Roman legend noted for his defense of a bridge over the Tiber against the Etruscans

horde \'hōrd, 'hȯrd\ *n* [Pol *horda*, of Mongolic origin] **1 a :** a tribal group of Mongolian nomads **b :** a nomadic people or tribe **2 :** a great multitude **:** THRONG, SWARM ⟨*hordes* of tourists⟩

hore·hound \'hō(ə)r-,haund, 'hȯ(ə)r-\ *n* [OE *hārhūne*, fr. *hār* hoary + *hūne* horehound] **:** an aromatic bitter mint with hoary downy leaves; *also* **:** an extract or confection made from this plant

ho·ri·zon \hə-'rīz-°n\ *n* [Gk *horizont-, horizōn*, fr. prp. of *horizein* to bound, fr. *horos* boundary] **1 :** the apparent junction of earth and sky **2 :** the limit or range of a person's outlook or experience ⟨reading broadens our *horizons*⟩ **3 a :** the geological deposit of a particular time

b : a distinct layer of soil or its underlying material in a vertical section of land — **ho·ri·zon·al** \-(°-)nəl\ *adj*

¹hor·i·zon·tal \,hȯr-ə-'zänt-°l, ,här-\ *adj* **1 a :** of, relating to, or situated near the horizon **b :** parallel to, in the plane of, or operating in a plane parallel to the horizon or to a base line **:** LEVEL ⟨*horizontal* distance⟩ ⟨*horizontal* engine⟩ **2 :** consisting of individuals or groups of similar level in a hierarchy ⟨*horizontal* labor unions⟩ — **hor·i·zon·tal·ly** \-°l-ē\ *adv*

²horizontal *n* **:** something (as a line or plane) that is horizontal — see PERPENDICULAR illustration

hor·mone \'hȯr-,mōn\ *n* [Gk *hormōn*, prp. of *horman* to stir up, set in motion] **:** a product of living cells that circulates in body fluids or sap and produces a specific and usu. stimulatory effect on cells remote from its point of origin — **hor·mon·al** \hȯr-'mōn-°l\ *adj* — **hor·mon·al·ly** \-°l-ē\ *adv*

horn \'hȯrn\ *n* [OE] **1 a** (1) **:** one of the hard bony growths on the head of many hoofed animals including the true permanent horns of cattle, goats, and sheep with a bony core enclosed in a sheath and the deciduous antlers of deer (2) **:** a part like an animal's horn attributed esp. to the devil **b** (1) **:** a tough fibrous material that consists chiefly of keratin and forms the sheath of a true horn and horny parts (as hooves or nails) (2) **:** a manufactured product (as a plastic) resembling horn **c :** a hollow horn used to hold something **2 :** something resembling or suggestive of a horn: as **a :** one of the curved ends of a crescent **b :** a high pommel of a saddle **3 a :** an animal's horn used as a wind instrument **b :** a brass wind instrument; *esp* **:** FRENCH HORN **c :** a usu. electrical device that makes a noise like that of a horn ⟨an automobile *horn*⟩ **4 :** a source of strength — **horned** \'hȯrnd\ *adj* — **horn·less** \'hȯrn-ləs\ *adj* — **horn·less·ness** *n* — **horn·like** \-,līk\ *adj*

horn·beam \'hȯrn-,bēm\ *n* **:** any of a genus of trees of the birch family having smooth gray bark and hard white wood

horn·bill \-,bil\ *n* **:** any of a family of large nonpasserine Old World birds having enormous bills

horn·blende \-,blend\ *n* [G, fr. *horn* horn + *blende* sphalerite] **:** a black, dark green, or brown mineral that occurs as distinct crystals and in columnar, fibrous, and granular form

horn·book \-,bùk\ *n* **1 :** a child's primer consisting of a sheet of parchment or paper protected by a sheet of transparent horn **2 :** a rudimentary treatise

horned owl *n* **:** any of several owls with conspicuous tufts of feathers on the head

horned pout *n* **:** a common bullhead of the eastern U.S.

horned toad *n* **:** any of several small harmless insect-eating lizards of the western U.S. and Mexico having hornlike spines

hor·net \'hȯr-nət\ *n* [OE *hyrnet*] **:** any of the larger social wasps — compare YELLOW JACKET

horn in *vi* **:** to participate without invitation or consent **:** INTRUDE ⟨*horn in* on a conversation⟩

horn of plenty *n* **:** CORNUCOPIA

horn·pipe \'hȯrn-,pīp\ *n* **1 :** a single reed wind instrument consisting of a wooden or bone pipe with holes at intervals and a bell and mouthpiece usu. of horn **2 :** a lively folk dance of the British Isles orig. accompanied by hornpipe playing

horn·tail \-,tāl\ *n* **:** any of various insects related to the sawflies

horn·wort \-,wərt, -,wȯrt\ *n* **:** any of an order (Anthocerotales) of mostly aquatic plants related to the liverworts

horny \'hȯr-nē\ *adj* **horn·i·er; -est 1 a :** made of or as if of horn **b** (1) **:** resembling horn esp. in appearance or texture (2) **:** HARD, CALLOUS ⟨*horny*-handed⟩ **2 :** having horns

hor·o·loge \'hȯr-ə-,lōj, 'här-\ *n* **:** a timekeeping device (as a sundial)

ho·rol·o·ger \hə-'räl-ə-jər\ *n* **:** HOROLOGIST

ho·rol·o·gy \-jē\ *n* [Gk *hōra* time, hour] **1 :** the science of measuring time **2 :** the art of constructing instruments for indicating time — **hor·o·log·ic** \,hȯr-ə-'läj-ik, ,här-, -'lōj-\ *adj* — **hor·o·log·i·cal** \-i-kəl\ *adj* — **ho·rol·o·gist** \hə-'räl-ə-jəst\ *n*

hor·o·scope \'hȯr-ə-,skōp, 'här-\ *n* [L *horoscopus*, fr. Gk *hōroskopos* astrologer, fr. *hōra* time, hour + *skopein* to look at] **:** a diagram of the relative positions of planets and signs of the zodiac used by astrologers to foretell events of a person's life

hor·ren·dous \hȯ-'ren-dəs, hä-\ *adj* [L *horrendus,* fr. *horrēre* to shudder] **:** DREADFUL, HORRIBLE — **hor·ren·dous·ly** *adv*

hor·ri·ble \'hȯr-ə-bəl, 'här-\ *adj* **1 :** marked by or conducive to horror **2 :** extremely unpleasant or disagreeable — **horrible** *n* — **hor·ri·bly** \-blē\ *adv*

hor·rid \'hȯr-əd, 'här-\ *adj* **1 :** HIDEOUS, SHOCKING **2 :** REPULSIVE, OFFENSIVE — **hor·rid·ly** *adv* — **hor·rid·ness** *n*

hor·rif·ic \hȯ-'rif-ik, hä-\ *adj* **:** HORRIFYING, HORRIBLE

hor·ri·fy \'hȯr-ə-,fī, 'här-\ *vt* **-fied; -fy·ing :** to cause to feel horror

hor·ror \'hȯr-ər, 'här-\ *n* [L, fr. *horrēre* to bristle, shudder] **1 a :** painful and intense fear, dread, or dismay **:** CONSTERNATION **b :** intense aversion or repugnance **2 a :** the quality of inspiring horror **b :** something that inspires horror **3** *pl* **:** a state of extreme depression or apprehension

hors de com·bat \,ȯrd-ə-kōⁿ-'bä\ *adv (or adj)* [F] **:** out of combat **:** DISABLED

hors d'oeuvre \ȯr-'dərv\ *n, pl* **hors d'oeuvres** *also* **hors d'oeuvre** \-'dərv(z)\ [F *hors-d'œuvre,* lit., outside of work] **:** any of various savory foods usu. served as appetizers at the beginning of a meal

¹horse \'hȯrs\ *n, pl* **hors·es** *also* **horse** [OE *hors*] **1 a :** a large solid-hoofed herbivorous mammal domesticated by man since a prehistoric period and used as a beast of burden, a draft animal, or for riding — compare PONY **b :** a male horse **:** STALLION **2 a :** a frame that supports something (as wood while being cut or clothes while being dried) **b :** a piece of gymnasium equipment used for vaulting exercises **3** *horse pl* **:** CAVALRY ⟨a regiment of *horse*⟩ — **from the horse's mouth :** from the original source

²horse *vb* **1 :** to provide with a horse **2 :** to lift, pull, or push by brute force **3 :** to engage in horseplay **:** FOOL ⟨*horsed* around instead of studying⟩

³horse *adj* **1 a :** of or relating to the horse **b :** worked by horsepower ⟨a *horse* barge⟩ **2 :** large or coarse of its kind **3 :** mounted on horses ⟨*horse* guards⟩

¹horse·back \'hȯrs-,bak\ *n* **:** the back of a horse

²horseback *adv* **:** on horseback

horse·car \'hȯrs-,kär\ *n* **1 :** a streetcar drawn by horses **2 :** a car for transporting horses

horse chestnut *n* **:** a large Asiatic tree with palmate leaves and erect conical clusters of showy flowers widely grown as an ornamental and shade tree and naturalized as an escape; *also* **:** its large glossy brown seed

horse·flesh \'hȯrs-,flesh\ *n* **:** horses for riding, driving, or racing

horse·fly \-,flī\ *n* **:** any of a family of swift usu. large two-winged flies with bloodsucking females

horse·hair \-,ha(ə)r, -,he(ə)r\ *n* **1 :** the hair of a horse esp. from the mane or tail **2 :** cloth made from horsehair — **horsehair** *adj*

horsehair worm *n* **:** any of various long slender worms whose adults are found in water and whose larvae parasitize insects — called also *horsehair snake*

horse·hide \'hȯrs-,hīd\ *n* **:** a horse's hide or leather made from it

horse latitudes *n pl* **:** either of two belts or regions in the neighborhood of 30° N. and 30° S. latitude characterized by high pressure, calms, and light changeable winds

horse·laugh \'hȯrs-,laf, -,láf\ *n* **:** a loud boisterous laugh **:** GUFFAW

horse·less carriage \,hȯrs-ləs-\ *n* **:** AUTOMOBILE

horse mackerel *n* **:** any of several large fishes (as a tuna)

horse·man \'hȯrs-mən\ *n* **1 a :** a rider on horseback **b :** one skilled in managing horses **2 :** a breeder or raiser of horses — **horse·man·ship** \-,ship\ *n*

horse·mint \-,mint\ *n* **:** any of various coarse mints; *esp* **:** MONARDA

horse nettle *n* **:** a coarse prickly yellow-flowered weed related to the nightshades

horse opera *n* **:** a motion picture or radio or television play usu. about western cowboys

horse pistol *n* **:** a large pistol formerly carried by horsemen

horse·play \'hȯrs-,plā\ *n* **:** rough or boisterous play

horse·pow·er \-,pau̇(-ə)r\ *n* **:** a unit of power equal in the U.S. to 746 watts and nearly equivalent to the English gravitational unit of the same name that equals 550 foot-pounds of work per second

horse·rad·ish \-,rad-ish\ *n* **:** a tall coarse white-flowered herb of the mustard family; *also* **:** its pungent root used as a condiment

horse sense *n* **:** COMMON SENSE

horse·shoe \'hȯrs(h)-,shü\ *n* **1 :** a shoe for horses usu. consisting of a narrow plate of iron shaped to fit the rim of a horse's hoof **2 :** something (as a valley) shaped like a horseshoe **3** *pl* **:** a game like quoits played with horseshoes or with horseshoe-shaped pieces of metal — **horseshoe** *vt* — **horse·sho·er** \-,shü-ər\ *n*

horseshoe crab *n* **:** KING CRAB 1

horseshoe magnet *n* **:** a U-shaped magnet

horse·tail \'hȯrs-,tāl\ *n* **:** EQUISETUM

horse trade *n* **:** negotiation accompanied by shrewd bargaining and reciprocal concessions — **horse–trade** *vi* — **horse trader** *n*

horse·whip \-,hwip\ *vt* **:** to flog with or as if with a whip made to be used on a horse

horse·wom·an \-,wu̇m-ən\ *n* **1 :** a woman horseback rider **2 :** a woman skilled in riding horseback or in caring for or managing horses

hors·ey *or* **horsy** \'hȯr-sē\ *adj* **hors·i·er; -est 1 :** of, relating to, or suggesting a horse **2 :** having to do with horses or horse racing **b :** characteristic of horsemen — **hors·i·ness** *n*

hor·ta·tive \'hȯrt-ət-iv\ *adj* [L *hortari* to urge] **:** giving exhortation **:** ADVISORY — **hor·ta·tive·ly** *adv*

hor·ta·to·ry \'hȯrt-ə-,tōr-ē, -,tȯr-\ *adj* **:** HORTATIVE, EXHORTATORY

hor·ti·cul·ture \'hȯrt-ə-,kəl-chər\ *n* [L *hortus* garden; akin to E *yard*] **:** the science and art of growing fruits, vegetables, flowers, or ornamental plants — **hor·ti·cul·tur·al** \,hȯrt-ə-'kəlch-(ə)-rəl\ *adj* — **hor·ti·cul·tur·al·ly** \-rə-lē\ *adv* — **hor·ti·cul·tur·ist** \-'kəlch-(ə)-rəst\ *n*

ho·san·na \hō-'zan-ə\ *interj* [Gk *hōsanna,* fr. Heb *hōshī'āh-nnā* pray, save (us)!] — used as a cry of acclamation and adoration

¹hose \'hōz\ *n, pl* **hose** *or* **hos·es** [OE *hosa*] **1** *pl* **hose a** (1) **:** a cloth leg covering that sometimes covers the foot (2) **:** STOCKING, SOCK **b** (1) **:** a close-fitting garment covering the legs and waist that is usu. attached to a doublet or points (2) **:** short breeches reaching to the knee **2 :** a flexible tube for conveying (as from a faucet) a fluid

²hose *vt* **:** to spray, water, or wash with a hose

Ho·sea \hō-'zē-ə, -'zā-\ *n* **1 :** a Hebrew prophet of the 8th century B.C. **2** — see BIBLE table

ho·siery \'hōzh-(ə)-rē, 'hōz-(ə)-\ *n* [*hosier* dealer in hose] **1 :** HOSE 1a **2** *chiefly Brit* **:** KNITWEAR

hos·pice \'häs-pəs\ *n* [F, fr. L *hospitium* hospitality, lodging, fr. *hospit-, hospes* host] **:** an inn for travelers; *esp* **:** one kept by a religious order

hos·pit·a·ble \hä-'spit-ə-bəl, 'häs-(,)pit-\ *adj* **1 a :** showing hospitality **:** generous and cordial in receiving guests **b :** promising or suggesting generous and cordial welcome **c :** offering a pleasant or sustaining environment **2 :** readily receptive **:** OPEN ⟨*hospitable* to new ideas⟩ — **hos·pit·a·bly** \-blē\ *adv*

hos·pi·tal \'häs-,pit-ºl\ *n* [ML *hospitale,* fr. LL, hospice, fr. L *hospit-, hospes* host] **1 :** an institution where the sick or injured are given medical or surgical care **2 :** a repair shop for specified small objects ⟨doll *hospital*⟩

Hos·pi·tal·er *or* **Hos·pi·tal·ler** \-ºl-ər\ *n* **:** a member of a religious military order established in Jerusalem in the 12th century

hos·pi·tal·i·ty \,häs-pə-'tal-ət-ē\ *n, pl* **-ties :** hospitable treatment, reception, or disposition (as of visitors and guests)

hos·pi·tal·ize \'häs-,pit-ºl-,īz\ *vt* **:** to place in a hospital for care and treatment — **hos·pi·tal·i·za·tion** \,häs-,pit-ºl-ə-'zā-shən\ *n*

¹host \'hōst\ *n* [LL *hostis,* fr. L, stranger, enemy; akin to E *guest*] **1 :** ARMY **2 :** a great number **:** MULTITUDE

²host *n* [OF *hoste* host, guest, fr. L *hospit-, hospes* fr. *hostis* stranger] **1 :** one who receives or entertains guests socially or as a business **2 :** a living animal or plant affording subsistence or lodgment to a parasite — **host** *vt* — **host·al** \'hōst-ºl\ *adj*

ə abut; ᵊ kitten; ər further; a back; ā bake; ä cot, cart; aù out; ch chin; e less; ē easy; g gift; i trip; ī life

³host *n, often cap* [L *hostia* sacrifice] : the bread or wafer consecrated in the Mass

hos·tage \'häs-tij\ *n* [MF, lodging, condition of a hostage, hostage, fr. *hoste* host, guest] : a person held by one party in a conflict as a pledge that promises will be kept or terms met by the other

hos·tel \'häst-ʔl\ *n* [OF, fr. LL *hospitale* hospice] **1** : INN **2** : a supervised lodging for use by youth esp. on bicycling trips — called also *youth hostel*

hos·tel·er \'häs-tə-lər\ *n* **1** : one that lodges guests or strangers **2** : a young traveler who stops at hostels overnight

hos·tel·ry \'häst-ʔl-rē\ *n, pl* **-ries** : INN, HOTEL

host·ess \'hō-stəs\ *n* : a woman who acts as host; *esp* : one who receives and arranges for the care of patrons in a restaurant

hos·tile \'häst-ʔl, 'häs-,tīl\ *adj* [L *hostilis*, fr. *hostis* enemy] **1** : of or relating to an enemy ⟨*hostile* troops⟩ **2** : marked by open antagonism : UNFRIENDLY **3** : not hospitable : FORBIDDING ⟨a *hostile* environment⟩ — **hos·tile·ly** \-ʔl-ē, -,tīl-lē\ *adv*

hos·til·i·ty \hä-'stil-ət-ē\ *n, pl* **-ties 1 a** : a hostile state **b** (1) : hostile action (2) *pl* : overt acts of warfare : WAR **2** : antagonism, opposition, or resistance in thought or principle **syn** see ENMITY

hos·tler \'(h)äs-lər\ *n* [ME, innkeeper, hostler, fr. *hostel*] **1** : one who takes care of horses or mules **2** : one who services a vehicle (as a locomotive or truck) or machine (as a crane)

¹hot \'hät\ *adj* **hot·ter**; **hot·test** [OE *hāt*] **1 a** : having a relatively high temperature **b** : capable of giving a sensation of heat or of burning, searing, or scalding **2 a** : ARDENT, FIERY ⟨*hot* temper⟩ **b** : VIOLENT, RAGING **c** : LUSTFUL, LECHEROUS **d** : EAGER ⟨*hot* for reform⟩ **e** : ecstatic and emotionally exciting and marked by strong rhythms and free melodic improvisations ⟨*hot* jazz⟩ **3** : having or causing the sensation of an uncomfortable degree of body heat **4** : newly made : FRESH ⟨*hot* scent⟩; *also* : close to something sought **5 a** : suggestive of heat or of burning or glowing objects **b** : PUNGENT, PEPPERY ⟨*hot* relish⟩ **6 a** : unusually lucky or favorable ⟨*hot* dice⟩ **b** : temporarily capable of unusual performance **c** : currently popular **d** (1) — used as a generalized term of approval (2) : ABSURD, UNBELIEVABLE **7 a** : electrically energized **b** : RADIOACTIVE; *also* : dealing with radioactive material **8** : recently and illegally obtained ⟨*hot* jewels⟩ — **hot·ly** *adv* — **hot·ness** *n*

²hot *adv* : HOTLY ⟨took a club and gave it to him *hot* and heavy⟩

hot air *n* : empty talk

hot·bed \'hät-,bed\ *n* **1** : a bed of soil enclosed in glass, heated usu. by fermenting manure, and used for forcing or for raising seedlings **2** : an environment that favors rapid growth or development ⟨a *hotbed* of dissent⟩

hot–blood \-,bləd\ *n* : THOROUGHBRED 1

hot–blood·ed \-'bləd-əd\ *adj* : easily roused or excited : ARDENT — **hot–blood·ed·ness** *n*

hot·box \'hät-,bäks\ *n* : a journal bearing (as of a railroad car) overheated by friction

hotch·potch \'häch-,päch\ *n* [MF *hochepot*, fr. *hochier* to shake + *pot*] : HODGEPODGE

hot dog \'hät-,dȯg\ *n* : a cooked frankfurter usu. served in a long split roll

ho·tel \hō-'tel\ *n* [F *hôtel*, fr. OF *hostel*] : a building that provides lodging and usu. meals, entertainment, and various personal services esp. for transients : INN

¹hot·foot \'hät-,fu̇t\ *adv* : in haste

²hotfoot *vi* : to go hotfoot : HURRY ⟨*hotfooted* it home⟩

³hotfoot *n, pl* **hotfoots** : a practical joke in which a match is surreptitiously inserted into the side of a victim's shoe and lighted

hot·head \'hät-,hed\ *n* : a hotheaded person

hot·head·ed \-'hed-əd\ *adj* : HASTY, RASH, FIERY — **hot·head·ed·ly** *adv* — **hot·head·ed·ness** *n*

¹hot·house \'hät-,haus\ *n* : a heated glass-enclosed house for raising plants

²hothouse *adj* **1** : grown in a hothouse **2** : having the qualities of a plant raised in a hothouse; *esp* : DELICATE

hot pants *n pl* : very short shorts

hot pepper *n* **1** : pungent often thin-walled and small capsicum fruit **2** : a pepper plant bearing hot peppers

hot plate *n* : a simple portable appliance for heating or for cooking

hot rod *n* : an automobile rebuilt or modified for high speed and fast acceleration — **hot–rod·der** \'hät-'räd-ər\ *n*

hot·shot \'hät-,shät\ *n* : a showily skillful person

Hot·ten·tot \'hät-ʔn-,tät\ *n* : a member of a people of southern Africa apparently akin to both the Bushmen and the Bantus

hot war *n* : a conflict involving actual fighting

hot water *n* : a distressing predicament : DIFFICULTY ⟨got into *hot water* over his income tax⟩

¹hound \'haund\ *n* [OE *hund*] **1 a** : DOG **b** : a dog of any of various hunting breeds typically having large drooping ears and a deep voice and following their prey by scent **2** : a despicable person **3** : ADDICT, FAN

²hound *vt* : to pursue with or as if with hounds

hour \'au̇(ə)r\ *n* [OF *heure*, fr. L *hora* hour of the day, fr. Gk *hōra* time, season, hour] **1** : a time or office for daily liturgical devotion; *esp* : CANONICAL HOUR **2** : one of the 24 divisions of a day : 60 minutes **3 a** : the time of day indicated by a timepiece **b** : the time reckoned from midnight to midnight ⟨attack at 0900 *hours*⟩ **4 a** : a customary time **b** : a particular time ⟨lunch *hour*⟩ **5** : the work done or distance traveled at normal rate in an hour **6** : a class session ⟨a 50-minute *hour*⟩

hour·glass \-,glas\ *n* : an instrument for measuring time consisting of a glass vessel with two compartments from the uppermost of which a quantity of sand, water, or mercury runs in an hour into the lower one — **hourglass** *adj*

hourglass

hou·ri \'hu̇(ə)r-ē\ *n* [F, fr. Per. *hūri*, fr. Ar *hūrīyah*] : one of the beautiful maidens among the pleasures of the Muslim paradise

hour·ly \'au̇(ə)r-lē\ *adj* **1 a** : occurring hour by hour **b** : FREQUENT, CONTINUAL **2** : computed in terms of one hour — **hourly** *adv*

¹house \'haus\ *n, pl* **hous·es** \'hau̇-zəz\ [OE *hūs*] **1** : a building that serves as living quarters for one or more families **2 a** : something that serves an animal for shelter or habitation **b** : a building in which something is housed ⟨carriage *house*⟩ **3 a** : one of the 12 equal sectors in which the celestial sphere is divided in astrology : a zodiacal sign that is the seat of a planet's greatest influence **4 a** : HOUSEHOLD **b** : FAMILY 1; *esp* : a royal or noble family ⟨the *house* of Windsor⟩ **5 a** : a residence for a religious community or for students **b** : the community or students in residence **6 a** : a legislative, deliberative, or consultative assembly; *esp* : one constituting a division of a bicameral body **b** : the place where an assembly meets **7 a** : a place of business or entertainment **b** (1) : a business organization (2) : the operator of a gambling establishment **c** : the audience in a theater or concert hall

²house \'hauz\ *vb* **1 a** : to provide with living quarters or shelter **b** : to store in a house **2** : to encase, enclose, or shelter as if by putting in a house **3** : to take shelter : LODGE

house·boat \'haus-,bōt\ *n* : a barge fitted for use as a dwelling or for leisurely cruising

house·boy \-,bȯi\ *n* : a boy or man hired to act as a general household servant

house·break \-,brāk\ *vt* : to make housebroken

house·break·ing \-,brā-kin\ *n* : the act of breaking into and entering a person's dwelling house with the intent of committing a felony — **house·break·er** \-kər\ *n*

house·bro·ken \-,brō-kən\ *adj* : trained to excretory habits acceptable in indoor living

house·clean \'haus-,klēn\ *vb* **1** : to clean a house and its furniture **2** : to clean the surfaces and furnishings of **3** : to get rid of unwanted or undesirable items or people — **house·clean·ing** *n*

house·coat \-,kōt\ *n* : a woman's usu. long-skirted informal garment for wear around the house

house·fly \-,flī\ *n* : a two-winged fly that is common about human habitations and acts as a vector of diseases (as typhoid fever)

¹house·hold \-,hōld\ *n* : those who dwell under the same roof and compose a family; *also* : such a family and its servants or retainers

²household *adj* **1** : of or relating to a household : DOMESTIC **2** : FAMILIAR, COMMON ⟨names that have become *household* words⟩

house·hold·er \-,hōl-dər\ *n* : one who occupies a dwelling alone or as the head of a household
house·keep \'haús-,kēp\ *vi* : to keep house
house·keep·er \-,kē-pər\ *n* : a woman employed to keep house
house·keep·ing \-piŋ\ *n* : the care and management of a house and home affairs
house·less \'haús-ləs\ *adj* 1 : HOMELESS 2 : destitute of houses — **house·less·ness** *n*
house·lights \-,līts\ *n pl* : the lights that illuminate the parts of a theater occupied by the audience
house·maid \-,mād\ *n* : a female servant employed to do housework
housemaid's knee *n* : a swelling over the knee due to an enlargement of the bursa in the front of the kneecap
house·man \'haús-mən\ *n* : a person who performs general work about a house : HOUSEBOY
house·moth·er \-,məth-ər\ *n* : a woman acting as hostess, chaperon, and often housekeeper in a residence for young people
House of Burgesses : the colonial representative assembly of Virginia
House of Commons : the lower house of the British and Canadian parliaments
house of correction : an institution where persons are confined who have committed a minor offense and are considered capable of reformation
House of Lords : the upper house of the British Parliament composed of the peers temporal and spiritual
house of representatives : the lower house of a legislative body (as the U.S. Congress or a state legislature)
house organ *n* : a periodical distributed by a business concern among its employees, sales personnel, and customers
house party *n* : a party lasting over one or more nights at a home, fraternity house, or other residence
house·plant \-,plant\ *n* : a plant grown or kept indoors
house·rais·ing \-,rā-ziŋ\ *n* : the joint erection of a house or its framework by a gathering of neighbors
house sparrow *n* : an Old World sparrow widely naturalized in the New World — called also *English sparrow*
house·top \'haús-,täp\ *n* : ROOF
house·warm·ing \-,wór-miŋ\ *n* : a party to celebrate the taking possession of a house or premises
house·wife \'haús-,wīf, *2 is often* 'həz-əf, 'həs-əf\ *n* 1 : a married woman in charge of a household 2 : a small container for small articles (as thread) — **house·wife·li·ness** \'haús-,wī-flē-nəs\ *n* — **house·wife·ly** \-flē\ *adj* — **house·wif·ery** \-,wī-f(ə-)rē\ *n*
house·work \-,wərk\ *n* : the work of housekeeping
¹**hous·ing** \'haú-ziŋ\ *n* 1 a : SHELTER, LODGING b : dwellings provided for people ⟨*housing* for the aged⟩ 2 a : something that covers or protects b : a support (as a frame) for mechanical parts
²**housing** *n* [ME *howssing*, fr. *howse* housing, fr. MF *housse*] 1 : a usu. ornamental covering for the back and sides of a horse : CAPARISON 2 *pl* : TRAPPINGS
hove *past of* HEAVE
hov·el \'həv-əl, 'häv-\ *n* [ME] 1 : an open shed or shelter 2 : TABERNACLE 3 : a small mean house : HUT
hov·er \'həv-ər, 'häv-\ *vb* **hov·ered; hov·er·ing** \-(ə-)riŋ\ [ME *hoveren*] 1 a : to hang fluttering in the air or on the wing ⟨hawks *hovering* over their prey⟩ b : to remain suspended over a place or object 2 a : to move to and fro near a place ⟨waiters *hovered* about⟩ b : to be in a state of uncertainty, irresolution, or suspense ⟨*hovering* between life and death⟩ 3 : to brood over ⟨hen *hovers* her chicks⟩ — **hover** *n* — **hov·er·er** \-ər-ər\ *n*
¹**how** \(')haú\ *adv* [OE *hū*] 1 a : in what manner or way b : with what meaning : to what effect c : by what name or title d : for what reason : WHY 2 : to what degree or extent 3 : in what state or condition ⟨*how* are you⟩ 4 : at what price ⟨*how* do you sell your eggs⟩ — **how about** : what do you say to or think of ⟨*how about* another game⟩
²**how** *conj* 1 : in what manner or condition ⟨remember *how* they fought⟩⟨asked him *how* he was⟩ 2 : in whatever way or manner : HOWEVER ⟨do it *how* you like⟩
³**how** \'haú\ *n* 1 : MANNER, METHOD ⟨the *hows* and whys of this action⟩ 2 : a question about manner or method
¹**how·be·it** \haú-'bē-ət\ *adv* : NEVERTHELESS

²**howbeit** *conj* : ALTHOUGH
how·dah \'haúd-ə\ *n* [Hindi *hauda*] : a seat or covered pavilion on the back of an elephant or camel
¹**how·ev·er** \haú-'ev-ər\ *conj* : in whatever way or manner ⟨can go *however* he likes⟩ **syn** see BUT
²**however** *adv* 1 a : to whatever degree or extent b : in whatever manner or way 2 : in spite of that : on the other hand : BUT ⟨still seems possible, *however*, that conditions will improve⟩⟨would like to go; *however*, I think I'd better not⟩ 3 : how in the world ⟨*however* did you manage to do it⟩
how·it·zer \'haú-ət-sər\ *n* [D *houwitser*, fr. G *haubitze*, fr. Czech *houfnice* machine for hurling missiles] : a short cannon used to fire projectiles at medium muzzle velocities and with relatively high trajectories
howl \'haú(ə)l\ *vb* [ME *houlen*] 1 : to emit a loud sustained doleful sound ⟨*howling* dogs⟩ 2 : to cry out or exclaim without restraint under strong impulse (as pain, grief, or rage) 3 : to utter with unrestrained outcry 4 : to affect, effect, or drive by adverse outcry ⟨*howl* down all opposition⟩ — **howl** *n*
howl·er \'haú-lər\ *n* 1 : one that howls 2 : a stupid and ridiculous blunder
how·so·ev·er \,haú-sə-'wev-ər\ *adv* 1 : in whatever manner 2 : to whatever degree or extent
hoy·den \'hóid-ⁿn\ *n* : a girl or woman of saucy, boisterous, or carefree behavior — **hoy·den·ish** \-ish\ *adj*
hua·ra·che \wə-'räch-ē\ *n* [MexSp] : a low-heeled sandal having an upper made of interwoven leather thongs
hub \'həb\ *n* [prob. alter. of ²*hob*] 1 : the central part of a wheel, propeller, or fan 2 : a center of activity ⟨the *hub* of the universe⟩
hub·bub \'həb-,əb\ *n* 1 : a noisy confusion of sound : UPROAR 2 : TURMOIL
hu·bris \'hyü-brəs\ *n* [Gk *hybris*] : overweening pride or self-confidence : ARROGANCE
huck·a·back \'hək-ə-,bak\ *n* : an absorbent durable fabric of cotton, linen, or both used chiefly for towels
huck·le·ber·ry \'hək-əl-,ber-ē\ *n* 1 : an American shrub related to the blueberry; *also* : its edible dark blue to black usu. acid berry with 10 bony nutlets 2 : BLUEBERRY
huck·ster \'hək-stər\ *n* [MD *hoekester*, fr. *hoeken* to peddle] 1 : HAWKER, PEDDLER 2 : a writer of advertising esp. for radio or television
¹**hud·dle** \'həd-ⁿl\ *vb* **hud·dled; hud·dling** \'həd-liŋ, -ⁿl-iŋ\ 1 *Brit* : to throw together, arrange, or complete carelessly or hurriedly 2 : to crowd, push, or pile together ⟨*huddled* in a doorway⟩ 3 : to gather in a group for conference : CONFER; *esp* : to gather (as in a circle for receiving signals from the quarterback) behind the line of scrimmage in a football game 4 : to curl up : CROUCH ⟨a child *huddled* in its crib⟩ — **hud·dler** \'həd-lər, -ⁿl-ər\ *n*
²**huddle** *n* 1 : a close-packed group : BUNCH 2 a : CONFERENCE b : a strategy conference of football players behind the line of scrimmage
Hud·son seal \,həd-sən-\ *n* : the fur of the muskrat dressed to simulate seal
hue \'hyü\ *n* [OE *hīw*] 1 : SHAPE, ASPECT 2 a : gradation of color b : a chromatic color as distinct from white, gray, and black ⟨one of the *hues* of the rainbow⟩ c : the attribute of colors that permits them to be classed as red, yellow, green, blue, or an intermediate between any contiguous pair of these colors **syn** see COLOR
hue and cry \,hyü-\ *n* [*hue* outcry] 1 : a loud outcry formerly used in the pursuit of felons 2 : a clamor of pursuit or protest
¹**huff** \'həf\ *vb* 1 : PUFF ⟨tourists *huffing* up the steps behind their guide⟩ 2 a : BLUSTER b : to react indignantly 3 : to make angry : PROVOKE ⟨was *huffed* over his cavalier treatment of her⟩
²**huff** *n* : a fit of anger or pique
huffy \'həf-ē\ *adj* **huff·i·er; -est** 1 : HAUGHTY 2 a : easily offended : TOUCHY b : SULKY — **huff·i·ly** \'həf-ə-lē\ *adv* — **huff·i·ness** *n*
hug \'həg\ *vb* **hugged; hug·ging** 1 : to press tightly esp. in the arms : EMBRACE 2 : to hold fast : CHERISH ⟨*hugged* her fancied grievances⟩ 3 : to stay close to ⟨drives along *hugging* the curb⟩ — **hug** *n*
huge \'hyüj, 'yüj\ *adj* [OF *ahuge*] : very large or extensive: as a : of great size or area b : of sizable scale or degree

c : of limitless scope or character **syn** see ENORMOUS —
huge·ly adv — **huge·ness** n
hug·ger-mug·ger \'həg-ər-,məg-ər\ n 1 : SECRECY
2 : CONFUSION, MUDDLE — **hugger-mugger** adj
Hu·gue·not \'hyü-gə-,nät\ n [MF, fr. MF dial., adherent
of a Swiss political movement, fr. Besançon *Hugues* d1532
Swiss political leader + MF dial. *eidgnot* confederate, fr.
G dial. *eidgnoss*] : a French Protestant of the 16th and
17th centuries
hu·la \'hü-lə\ or **hu·la-hu·la** \,hü-lə-'hü-lə\ n [Hawaiian]
: a sinuous mimetic Polynesian dance usu. accompanied
by chants and rhythmic drumming
¹hulk \'həlk\ n [OE *hulc*, fr. ML *holcas*, fr. Gk *holkas*,
fr. *helkein* to pull, drag] 1 : a heavy clumsy ship 2 : a
bulky, unwieldy, or clumsy person or thing 3 a : the
body of an old ship unfit for service or of an abandoned
wreck b : a ship used as a prison — usu. used in pl.
²hulk vi : to appear impressively large : BULK
hulk·ing \'həl-kiŋ\ adj : MASSIVE, HUSKY
¹hull \'həl\ n [OE *hulu*] 1 a : the outer covering of a
fruit or seed b : the persistent calyx or involucre that
clings to the base of some fruits 2 a : the frame or body
of a ship or flying boat b : the main structure of a rigid
airship 3 : COVERING, CASING
²hull vt : to remove the hulls of — **hull·er** n
hul·la·ba·loo \'həl-ə-bə-,lü\ n, pl **-loos** : a confused
noise : UPROAR
hum \'həm\ vb **hummed**; **hum·ming** [ME *hummen*] 1 a
: to utter a sound like that of the speech sound \m\ prolonged b : to make the natural buzzing noise of an insect
in motion or a similar sound : DRONE c : to give forth
a low continuous blend of sound 2 : to sing with the
lips closed and without articulation 3 : to be busily
active — **hum·mer** n
hu·man \'hyü-mən, 'yü-\ adj [L *humanus*] 1 : of, relating
to, or characteristic of man ⟨the *human* body⟩ ⟨*human*
history⟩ ⟨to err is *human*⟩ 2 a : being a man ⟨a *human*
being⟩ b : consisting of men ⟨the *human* race⟩ 3 : having
human form or attributes ⟨the dog's expression was almost
human⟩ — **human** n — **hu·man·ness** \-mən-nəs\ n
syn HUMANE: HUMAN applies to whatever is characteristic of mankind ⟨*human* love⟩ ⟨*human* achievements⟩
HUMANE stresses an attitude of compassion and implies
moral progress attained through this attitude ⟨the growth
of the *humane* treatment of prisoners in recent history⟩
hu·mane \hyü-'mān, yü-\ adj [L *humanus*, lit., human]
1 : marked by compassion, sympathy, or consideration
for other human beings or for animals 2 : HUMANISTIC
syn see HUMAN — **hu·mane·ly** adv — **hu·mane·ness**
\-'mān-nəs\ n
hu·man·ism \'hyü-mə-,niz-əm, 'yü-\ n 1 : a revival of
classical letters, an individualistic and critical spirit, and
an emphasis on secular concerns characteristic of the
Renaissance 2 : a doctrine or way of life centered on
human interests or values; *esp* : a philosophy that asserts
the dignity and worth of man and his capacity for
self-realization through reason and that often rejects
supernaturalism — **hu·man·ist** \-nəst\ n or adj — **hu·man·-
is·tic** \,hyü-mə-'nis-tik, ,yü-\ adj
hu·man·i·tar·i·an \(,)hyü-,man-ə-'ter-ē-ən, (,)yü-\ n : a
person promoting human welfare and social reform
: PHILANTHROPIST — **humanitarian** adj — **hu·man·i·-
tar·i·an·ism** \-ē-ə-,niz-əm\ n
hu·man·i·ty \hyü-'man-ət-ē, yü-\ n, pl **-ties** 1 : the
quality or state of being humane ⟨treated the beaten foe
with *humanity*⟩ 2 : the quality or state of being human
⟨the common *humanity* of all peoples⟩ 3 pl : the branches
of learning having primarily a cultural character 4
: MANKIND 1
hu·man·ize \'hyü-mə-,nīz, 'yü-\ vt 1 : to adapt to
human nature or use 2 : to make humane : CIVILIZE,
REFINE — **hu·man·i·za·tion** \,hyü-mə-nə-'zā-shən, ,yü-\ n
hu·man·kind \'hyü-mən-,kīnd, 'yü-\ n : MANKIND 1
hu·man·ly \'hyü-mən-lē, 'yü-\ adv 1 a : from the viewpoint of man b : within the range of human capacity
⟨a task not *humanly* possible⟩ 2 : in a human manner
hu·man·oid \-mə-,nȯid\ adj : HOMINID — **humanoid** n
¹hum·ble \'həm-bəl, 'əm-\ adj **hum·bler** \-b(ə-)lər\;
hum·blest \-b(ə-)ləst\ [OF, fr. L *humilis* low, humble, fr.
humus earth] 1 : modest or meek in spirit or manner
: not proud or assertive ⟨a great man is often *humble*⟩

2 : expressing a spirit of deference or submission ⟨*humble*
apology⟩ 3 : low in rank or status : UNPRETENTIOUS
⟨*humble* birth⟩ ⟨a *humble* position⟩ — **hum·bly** \-blē\ adv
²humble vt **hum·bled**; **hum·bling** \-b(ə-)liŋ\ 1 : to make
humble in spirit or manner ⟨*humbled* himself before the
king⟩ 2 : to destroy the power or prestige of ⟨*humbled*
their opponents with a crushing attack⟩ — **hum·bler**
\-b(ə-)lər\ n
hum·ble-bee \'həm-bəl-,bē\ n [ME *humbylbee*] : BUMBLE-
BEE
Hum·boldt current \,həm-,bōlt-\ n : PERU CURRENT
hum·bug \'həm-,bəg\ n 1 a : something designed to
deceive and mislead : FRAUD ⟨took his fervent denials as
humbug⟩ b : CHARLATAN 2 : DRIVEL, NONSENSE ⟨his
speech was full of *humbug*⟩ — **humbug** vb — **hum·bug·-
gery** \-,bəg-(ə-)rē\ n
hum·ding·er \'həm-'diŋ-ər\ n : a person or thing of
striking excellence
hum·drum \'həm-,drəm\ adj : MONOTONOUS, DULL
hu·mec·tant \hyü-'mek-tənt\ n [L *humectus* moist, fr.
humēre to be moist] : a substance that promotes retention
of moisture
hu·mer·al \'hyüm-(ə-)rəl\ adj : of, relating to, or used or
located in the region of the humerus or shoulder — **hu·-
meral** n
humeral veil n : an oblong vestment worn around the
shoulders and over the hands by a priest or subdeacon
holding a sacred vessel
hu·mer·us \'hyüm-(ə-)rəs\ n, pl **hu·meri** \'hyü-mə-,rī,
-,rē\ [NL, fr. L *umerus, humerus* upper arm, shoulder] : the
long bone of the upper arm or forelimb extending from
the shoulder to the elbow
hu·mic \'hyü-mik, 'yü-\ adj : of, relating to, or derived
from humus ⟨a *humic* acid⟩
hu·mid \'hyü-məd, 'yü-\ adj [L *umidus, humidus*, fr.
umēre, humēre to be moist] : containing or characterized
by perceptible moisture : DAMP ⟨a *humid* day⟩ ⟨a *humid*
climate⟩ — **hu·mid·ly** adv
hu·mid·i·fy \hyü-'mid-ə-,fī, yü-\ vt **-fied; -fy·ing** : to
make (as the air of a room) humid : MOISTEN — **hu·mid·i·-
fi·ca·tion** \-,mid-ə-fə-'kā-shən\ n — **hu·mid·i·fi·er**
\-'mid-ə-,fī(-ə)r\ n
hu·mid·i·ty \-'mid-ət-ē\ n, pl **-ties** : DAMPNESS, MOISTURE;
esp : the amount of moisture in the air — compare RELA-
TIVE HUMIDITY
hu·mi·dor \'hyü-mə-,dȯr, 'yü-\ n [*humid* + *-or* (as in
cuspidor)] : a case usu. for storing cigars in which the air
is kept properly humidified
hu·mil·i·ate \hyü-'mil-ē-,āt, yü-\ vt [LL *humiliare*, fr.
L *humilis* low, fr. *humus* earth] : to reduce to a lower position in one's own eyes or others' eyes : HUMBLE ⟨the public
reprimand *humiliated* him⟩ — **hu·mil·i·a·tion** \-,mil-ē-'ā-
shən\ n
hu·mil·i·ty \hyü-'mil-ət-ē, yü-\ n : the quality or state
of being humble
hum·ming·bird \'həm-iŋ-,bərd\ n : any of numerous tiny
brightly colored American birds related to the swifts and
having narrow swiftly beating wings, a slender bill, and a
long tongue for sipping nectar
hum·mock \'həm-ək\ n 1 : a rounded mound of earth
: KNOLL 2 : a ridge or pile of ice — **hum·mocky** \-ə-kē\
adj
¹hu·mor \'hyü-mər, 'yü-\ n [L *umor, humor* moisture,
fluid, fr. *umēre* to be moist] 1 : state of mind or disposition ⟨he is in a good *humor*⟩ 2 : the amusing quality of
things ⟨the *humor* of a situation⟩ 3 : the power to see or
tell about the amusing side of things : a keen perception
of the comic or the ridiculous ⟨a writer famous for his
humor⟩ 4 : WHIM, FANCY 5 : something comical or
amusing **syn** see MOOD, WIT — **hu·mor·less** \-ləs\ adj
— **hu·mor·less·ness** n
²humor vt **hu·mored; hu·mor·ing** \'hyüm-(ə-)riŋ, 'yüm-\
: to comply with the wishes or mood of ⟨*humor* an invalid⟩
hu·mor·al \'hyüm-(ə-)rəl, 'yüm-\ adj : of, relating to,
proceeding from, or involving a bodily fluid (as a secretion)
hu·mor·esque \,hyü-mə-'resk, ,yü-\ n [G *humoreske*] : a
musical composition typically whimsical or fanciful in
character
hu·mor·ist \'hyüm-(ə-)rəst, 'yüm-\ n : a person specializing in or noted for humor

---

j joke; ŋ sing; ō flow; ȯ flaw; ȯi coin; th thin; th͟ this; ü loot; u̇ foot; y yet; yü few; yu̇ furious; zh vision

hu·mor·ous \'hyüm-(ə-)rəs, 'yüm-\ *adj* : full of, characterized by, or expressive of humor : AMUSING, DROLL ⟨a *humorous* story⟩ — **hu·mor·ous·ly** *adv* — **hu·mor·ous·ness** *n*

hu·mour \'hyü-mər, 'yü-\ *chiefly Brit var of* HUMOR

¹hump \'həmp\ *n* **1** : a rounded bulge or lump (as on the back of a camel) **2** : MOUND, HUMMOCK **3** : a difficult phase ⟨help him over the *hump*⟩ **4** : strenuous effort ⟨get a *hump* on and finish the job⟩ — **humped** \'həm(p)t\ *adj* — **humpy** \'həm-pē\ *adj*

²hump *vb* **1** : to exert oneself vigorously : HUSTLE **2** : to make hump-shaped : HUNCH

hump·back \'həmp-,bak\ *n* **1** : a humped or crooked back **2** : HUNCHBACK **3** : a large whalebone whale with very long flippers

hump·backed \-'bakt\ *or* **hump·back** \-,bak\ *adj* : having a humped back

hu·mus \'hyü-məs, 'yü-\ *n* [L, earth] : a brown or black product of partial decomposition of plant or animal matter that forms the organic portion of soil

Hun \'hən\ *n* **1** : a member of a nomadic Mongolian people gaining control of a large part of central and eastern Europe under Attila about A.D. 450 **2** *often not cap* : a person who is wantonly destructive

¹hunch \'hənch\ *vb* **1** : to thrust oneself forward ⟨*hunch* nearer the fire⟩ **2** : to assume a bent or crooked posture ⟨sat *hunched* over the table⟩ **3** : to thrust into a hump ⟨*hunches* his shoulders⟩

²hunch *n* **1** : HUMP **2** : a strong intuitive feeling as to how something (as a course of action) will turn out

hunch·back \'hənch-,bak\ *n* **1** : HUMPBACK 1 **2** : a person with a humpback — **hunch·backed** \-'bakt\ *adj*

hun·dred \'hən-drəd, -dərd\ *n, pl* **hundreds** *or* **hundred** [OE] **1** — see NUMBER table **2** : the number in the third decimal place to the left of the decimal point in arabic numerals **3** : a subdivision of some English and American counties **4** : a very large or indefinitely great number ⟨*hundreds* of times⟩ — **hundred** *adj*

hun·dredth \-drədth\ *n* **1** : one of 100 equal parts of something **2** : the one numbered 100 in a countable series — see NUMBER table — **hundredth** *adj*

hun·dred·weight \'hən-drəd-,wāt, -dərd-\ *n, pl* **-weight** *or* **-weights** **1** : a unit of weight equal to 100 pounds — called also *short hundredweight;* see MEASURE table **2** *Brit* : a unit of weight equal to 112 pounds — called also *long hundredweight*

hung *past of* HANG

Hun·gar·i·an \,hən-'ger-ē-ən, -'gar-\ *n* **1 a** : a native or inhabitant of Hungary : MAGYAR **b** : a person of Hungarian descent **2** : MAGYAR 2 — **Hungarian** *adj*

¹hun·ger \'hən-gər\ *n* [OE *hungor*] **1** : a desire or a need for food; *also* : an uneasy feeling or weakened condition resulting from lack of food **2** : a strong desire : CRAVING ⟨a *hunger* for praise⟩ — **hunger** *adj*

²hunger *vi* **hun·gered; hun·ger·ing** \-g(ə-)riŋ\ **1** : to feel or suffer hunger **2** : to have an eager desire

hunger strike *n* : refusal esp. by a prisoner to eat enough to sustain life

hung jury *n* : a jury that is unable to reach a unanimous verdict

hun·gry \'hən-grē\ *adj* **hun·gri·er; -est 1** : feeling or showing hunger **2** : EAGER, AVID **3** : not rich or fertile : BARREN — **hun·gri·ly** \-grə-lē\ *adv* — **hun·gri·ness** \-grē-nəs\ *n*

hunk \'həŋk\ *n* [Flem *hunke*] : a large lump or piece ⟨*hunks* of iron⟩ ⟨a *hunk* of bread⟩

hun·ker \'həŋ-kər\ *vi* : CROUCH, SQUAT

hun·kers \-kərz\ *n pl* : HAUNCHES

hun·ky-do·ry \,hən-kē-'dōr-ē, -'dor-\ *adj* : quite satisfactory : FINE

¹hunt \'hənt\ *vb* [OE *huntian*] **1 a** : to pursue for food or in sport ⟨*hunt* squirrel⟩ **b** : to use in hunting game ⟨*hunts* a pack of dogs⟩ **2 a** : to pursue with intent to capture **b** : to search out : SEEK **3** : to drive or chase esp. by harrying ⟨*hunt* a criminal out of town⟩ **4** : to search through in quest of prey ⟨*hunts* the woods⟩ **5** : to take part in a hunt

²hunt *n* **1** : the act, the practice, or an instance of hunting **2** : a group of hunters; *esp* : persons with horses and dogs engaged in hunting or riding to hounds

hunt·er \'hənt-ər\ *n* **1 a** : a person who hunts game

b : a dog or horse used or trained for hunting **2** : a person who searches for something

hunt·ing *n* : the act of one that hunts; *esp* : the pursuit of game

hunt·ress \'hən-trəs\ *n* : a female hunter

hunts·man \'hən(t)s-mən\ *n* **1** : HUNTER 1a **2** : a person who manages a hunt and looks after the hounds

¹hur·dle \'hərd-²l\ *n* [OE *hyrdel*] **1** : a movable frame (as of woven twigs) used for enclosing land or livestock **2** : a barrier to be jumped in a race **3** : OBSTACLE

²hurdle *vt* **hur·dled; hur·dling** \'hərd-liŋ, -²l-iŋ\ **1** : to leap over while running **2** : OVERCOME, SURMOUNT — **hur·dler** \'hərd-lər, -²l-ər\ *n*

hur·dy-gur·dy \,hərd-ē-'gərd-ē\ *n, pl* **-dies** : a musical instrument in which the sound is produced by turning a crank; *esp* : BARREL ORGAN

hurl \'hərl\ *vb* [ME *hurlen*] **1** : to throw violently or powerfully ⟨*hurl* a spear⟩ **2** : PITCH **syn** see THROW — **hurl·er** *n*

hurdle 2

hur·ly-bur·ly \,hər-lē-'bər-lē\ *n, pl* **-lies** : UPROAR, TUMULT

Hu·ron \'hyur-ən, 'hyù(ə)r-,än\ *n* : a member of an Iroquoian people orig. of the St. Lawrence valley and Ontario

¹hur·rah \hù-'rô, -'rä\ *also* **hur·ray** \-'rä\ *interj* — used to express joy, approval, or encouragement

²hurrah *n* **1** : EXCITEMENT, FANFARE **2** : FUSS, CONTROVERSY

³hurrah *vb* : to shout hurrah : CHEER

hur·ri·cane \'hər-ə-,kān, -i-kən, 'hə-rə-, 'hə-ri-\ *n* [Sp *huracán*, of AmerInd origin] : a tropical cyclone with winds of 73 miles per hour or greater but rarely exceeding 150 miles per hour usu. accompanied by rain, thunder, and lightning

hurricane deck *n* : PROMENADE DECK

hurricane lamp *n* : a candlestick or an electric lamp with a glass chimney

hur·ried \'hər-ēd, 'hə-rēd\ *adj* **1** : going or working at speed ⟨the *hurried* life of the city⟩ **2** : done in a hurry : HASTY ⟨a *hurried* meal⟩ — **hur·ried·ly** \-ēd-lē, -(r)əd-\ *adv*

¹hur·ry \'hər-ē, 'hə-rē\ *vb* **hur·ried; hur·ry·ing 1 a** : to carry or cause to go with haste ⟨*hurry* him to the hospital⟩ **b** : to move or act with haste ⟨had to *hurry* to arrive in time⟩ **2** : to impel to greater speed : PROD **b** : EXPEDITE ⟨*hurry* a repair job⟩ — **hur·ri·er** *n*

²hurry *n, pl* **hurries 1** : DISTURBANCE, COMMOTION **2** : a recurrent agitation of sound ⟨a *hurry* of voices⟩ **3** : excessive haste : PRECIPITANCY **b** : a state of eagerness or urgency : RUSH ⟨in a *hurry* to get there⟩ **syn** see HASTE

¹hurt \'hərt\ *vb* **hurt; hurt·ing** [ME *hurten*] **1 a** : to inflict with physical pain **b** : to do harm to : DAMAGE **2 a** : to cause anguish to : OFFEND **b** : HAMPER **3** : to feel or cause pain ⟨a *hurting* tooth⟩ — **hurt·er** *n*

²hurt *n* **1** : a wounding blow : a cause of injury or damage **2 a** : a bodily injury or wound **b** : mental distress : SUFFERING **3** : WRONG, HARM

hurt·ful \'hərt-fəl\ *adj* : causing injury or suffering : DAMAGING — **hurt·ful·ly** \-fə-lē\ *adv* — **hurt·ful·ness** *n*

hur·tle \'hərt-²l\ *vb* **hur·tled; hur·tling** \'hərt-liŋ, -²l-iŋ\ [ME *hurtlen* to collide, freq. of *hurten* to cause to strike, hurt] **1** : to move with or as if with a rushing sound ⟨boulders *hurtled* down the hill⟩ **2** : HURL, FLING ⟨*hurtled* himself through the doorway⟩

¹hus·band \'həz-bənd\ *n* [OE *hūsbonda* master of a house, fr. ON *hūsbōndi*, fr. *hūs* house + *bōndi* householder] : a married man

²husband *vt* **1** : to manage prudently and economically : use carefully : CONSERVE ⟨*husbanded* their resources⟩ **2** *archaic* : to be a husband to : MARRY — **hus·band·er** *n*

hus·band·man \'həz-bən(d)-mən\ *n* : FARMER; *also* : a specialist in farm husbandry

hus·band·ry \-bən-drē\ *n* **1** : the management or judicious use of resources : ECONOMY **2** : FARMING, AGRICULTURE; *esp* : the technical and scientific aspects of farming and esp. of the care and production of domestic animals

¹hush \'həsh\ *vb* **1** : to make quiet, calm, or still : SOOTHE

⟨*hush* a baby⟩ **2 :** to become quiet **3 :** to keep from public knowledge **:** SUPPRESS ⟨*hush* up a scandal⟩
²**hush** *n* **:** a silence or calm esp. following noise **:** QUIET
hush-hush \'həsh-,həsh\ *adj* **:** SECRET, CONFIDENTIAL
¹**husk** \'həsk\ *n* [ME] **1 :** a usu. thin dry outer covering of a seed or fruit **2 :** an outer layer **:** SHELL
²**husk** *vt* **:** to strip the husk from — **husk·er** *n*
husk·ing *n* **:** a gathering of farm families to husk corn
¹**husky** \'həs-kē\ *adj* **husk·i·er; -est :** resembling, containing, or full of husks
²**husky** *adj* **husk·i·er; -est :** hoarse with or as if with emotion — **husk·i·ly** \'həs-kə-lē\ *adv* — **husk·i·ness** \-kē-nəs\ *n*
³**husky** *adj* **husk·i·er; -est 1 :** BURLY, ROBUST **2 :** LARGE
⁴**husky** *n, pl* **husk·ies :** one that is husky
⁵**hus·ky** \'həs-kē\ *n, pl* **hus·kies** [prob. by shortening & alter. fr. *Eskimo*] **:** a heavy-coated working dog of the New World arctic region
hus·sar \(,)hə-'zär\ *n* [Hung *huszár* highwayman, hussar, fr. Serb *husar* pirate, fr. ML *cursarius* corsair] **:** a member of any of various European military units orig. of light cavalry
Huss·ite \'həs-,īt, 'hüs-\ *n* **:** a member of the Bohemian religious and nationalist movement originating with John Huss — **Hussite** *adj*
hus·sy \'həz-ē, 'həs-\ *n, pl* **hus·sies** [alter. of *housewife*] **1 :** a lewd or brazen woman **2 :** a pert or mischievous girl
hus·tings \'həs-tiŋz\ *n pl* [OE *hūsting*, fr. ON *hūsthing*, fr. *hūs* house + *thing* assembly] **:** a place where political campaign speeches are made; *also* **:** the proceedings in an election campaign
hus·tle \'həs-əl\ *vb* **hus·tled; hus·tling** \'həs-(ə-)liŋ\ [D *husselen* to shake] **1 :** to push, crowd, or force forward roughly ⟨*hustled* the prisoner to jail⟩ **2 :** to move or work rapidly and tirelessly; *also* **:** to obtain by such work ⟨*hustled* new customers⟩ — **hustle** *n* — **hus·tler** \-(ə-)lər\ *n*
hut \'hət\ *n* [MF *hutte*, fr. of Gmc origin] **:** an often small and temporary dwelling or shelter **:** SHACK — **hut** *vb*
hutch \'həch\ *n* [OF *huche*] **1 a :** a chest or compartment for storage **b :** a low cupboard usu. surmounted by open shelves **2 :** a pen or coop for an animal **3 :** SHACK, SHANTY
hut·ment \'hət-mənt\ *n* **1 :** a collection of huts **:** ENCAMPMENT **2 :** HUT
huz·zah *or* **huz·za** \(,)hə-'zä\ *interj* — used to express joy or approbation
hwan \'hwän\ *n, pl* **hwan** [Korean] **:** the basic monetary unit of So. Korea
hy·a·cinth \'hī-ə-(,)sin(t)th\ *n* [Gk *hyakinthos*, a flowering plant, a precious stone] **1 :** a red or brownish gem zircon or essonite **2 :** any of a genus of bulbous herbs of the lily family; *esp* **:** a common garden plant widely grown for the beauty and fragrance of its bell-shaped 6-lobed flowers **2 :** a light violet to moderate purple — **hy·a·cin·thine** \,hī-ə-'sin(t)-thən\ *adj*
Hy·a·des \'hī-ə-,dēz\ *n pl* [Gk] **:** a V-shaped cluster of stars in the head of the constellation Taurus held by the ancients to indicate rainy weather when they rise with the sun
hy·ae·na *var of* HYENA
¹**hy·a·line** \'hī-ə-lən, -,līn\ *adj* [Gk *hyalos* glass] **1 :** transparent or nearly so and usu. homogeneous **2 :** GLASSY
²**hyaline** *n* **:** something (as the clear atmosphere) that is transparent
hyaline cartilage *n* **:** translucent bluish cartilage with an apparently homogeneous matrix that is present in joints and respiratory passages and the fetal skeleton
hy·a·lite \'hī-ə-,līt\ *n* **:** a colorless opal that is clear as glass, translucent, or whitish
hy·brid \'hī-brəd\ *n* [L *hybrida*] **1 :** an offspring of parents of different genotype or of different races, breeds, varieties, species, or genera **2 a :** something of mixed origin or composition **b :** a word composed of elements from different languages — **hybrid** *adj* — **hy·brid·ism** \'hī-brə-,diz-əm\ *n* — **hy·brid·i·ty** \hī-'brid-ət-ē\ *n*
hy·brid·ize \'hī-brə-,dīz\ *vb* **:** to produce or cause to produce hybrids **:** INTERBREED — **hy·brid·i·za·tion** \,hī-brəd-ə-'zā-shən\ *n* — **hy·brid·iz·er** \'hī-brə-,dī-zər\ *n*

hyacinth 2

hybrid vigor *n* **:** HETEROSIS
hy·da·tid \'hīd-ə-təd\ *n* [Gk *hydatid-, hydatis* watery cyst, fr. *hydat-, hydōr* water] **:** a larval tapeworm that occurs in the host's tissues as a fluid-filled sac containing daughter cysts and scolices
hydr- *or* **hydro-** *comb form* [Gk, fr. *hydōr;* akin to E *water*] **1 :** water ⟨*hydrous*⟩ ⟨*hydroelectricity*⟩ **2 :** containing or combined with hydrogen ⟨*hydrocarbon*⟩ ⟨*hydroxyl*⟩ **3 :** hydroid ⟨*hydromedusa*⟩
Hy·dra \'hī-drə\ *n* **1 :** a 9-headed serpent or monster of Greek mythology slain by Hercules **2** [L, fr. Gk, lit., water serpent] **:** a southern constellation that is represented on old maps by a serpent **3** *not cap* **:** any of numerous small tubular freshwater animals related to the jellyfishes and having a mouth surrounded by tentacles at one end
hy·dran·gea \hī-'drān-jə\ *n* [Gk *hydr-* + *angeion,* dim. of *angos* vessel] **:** any of a genus of mostly shrubs of the saxifrage family with showy clusters of usu. sterile white, pink, or blue flowers
hy·drant \'hī-drənt\ *n* **1 :** a discharge pipe with a valve and spout at which water may be drawn from a main **2 :** FAUCET
hy·dranth \'hī-,dran(t)th\ *n* [Gk *hydr-* + *anthos* flower] **:** a nutritive zooid of a hydroid colony
¹**hy·drate** \'hī-,drāt\ *n* **1 :** a compound or complex ion formed by the union of water with some other substance ⟨a *hydrate* of copper sulfate⟩ **2 :** HYDROXIDE ⟨calcium *hydrate*⟩
²**hydrate** *vt* **:** to cause to take up or combine with water or the elements of water — **hy·dra·tion** \hī-'drā-shən\ *n*
hy·drau·lic \hī-'dro-lik\ *adj* [Gk *hydraulikos,* fr. *hydraulis* hydraulic organ, fr. *hydr-* + *aulos* reed instrument] **1 :** operated, moved, or effected by means of water **2 :** of or relating to hydraulics ⟨*hydraulic* engineer⟩ **3 :** operated by the resistance offered or the pressure transmitted when a quantity of liquid is forced through a comparatively small orifice or through a tube ⟨*hydraulic* brakes⟩ **4 :** hardening or setting under water ⟨*hydraulic* cement⟩ — **hy·drau·li·cal·ly** \-li-k(ə-)lē\ *adv*
hydraulic ram *n* **:** a pump that forces running water to a higher level by utilizing the kinetic energy of flow
hy·drau·lics \-liks\ *n* **:** a science that deals with practical applications of liquid (as water) in motion
hy·dra·zine \'hī-drə-,zēn\ *n* [*hydr-* + *azote* + *-ine*] **:** a colorless fuming corrosive liquid NH_2NH_2 used esp. in fuels for rocket engines
hy·dride \'hī-,drīd\ *n* **:** a compound of hydrogen with another element or radical
hy·dri·od·ic acid \,hī-drē-,äd-ik-\ *n* **:** an aqueous solution of hydrogen iodide HI that is a strong acid
hy·dro \'hī-drō\ *adj* **:** HYDROELECTRIC ⟨*hydro* power⟩
hy·dro·bro·mic acid \,hī-drə-,brō-mik-\ *n* **:** an aqueous solution of hydrogen bromide HBr that is a strong acid
hy·dro·car·bon \,hī-drə-'kär-bən\ *n* **:** an organic compound (as acetylene or benzene) containing only carbon and hydrogen
hy·dro·ceph·a·lus \,hī-drō-'sef-ə-ləs\ *also* **hy·dro·ceph·a·ly** \-lē\ *n* [Gk *hydr-* + *kephalē* head] **:** an abnormal state in which increased cerebrospinal fluid results in expansion of the cerebral ventricles, enlargement of the skull, and atrophy of the brain — **hy·dro·ce·phal·ic** \-sə-'fal-ik\ *adj or n*
hy·dro·chlo·ric acid \,hī-drə-,klōr-ik-, -,klòr-\ *n* **:** an aqueous solution of hydrogen chloride HCl that is a strong corrosive liquid acid, is normally present in dilute form in gastric juice, and is widely used in industry and in the laboratory
hy·dro·chlo·ride \-'klōr-,īd, -'klòr-\ *n* **:** a compound of hydrochloric acid
hy·dro·cor·ti·sone \,hī-drō-'kòrt-ə-,sōn, -,zōn\ *n* **:** a hormone of the adrenal cortex that is derived from cortisone and used similarly
hy·dro·cy·an·ic acid \,hī-drō-(,)sī-,an-ik-\ *n* **:** an aqueous solution of hydrogen cyanide HCN that is a weak poisonous acid and is used in fumigating
hy·dro·dy·nam·ics \,hī-drō-dī-'nam-iks\ *n* **:** a science that deals with the motion of fluids and the forces acting on solid bodies immersed in fluids and in motion relative to them — **hy·dro·dy·nam·ic** \-ik\ *adj*
hy·dro·elec·tric \,hī-drō-i-'lek-trik\ *adj* **:** of or relating to

production of electricity by waterpower ⟨a *hydroelectric power plant*⟩ — **hy·dro·elec·tric·i·ty** \-,lek-'tris-ət-ē, -'tris-tē\ *n*

hy·dro·flu·or·ic acid \,hī-drō-flū-,ȯr-ik, -,är-\ *n* : a weak poisonous acid that consists of a solution of hydrogen fluoride in water and is used esp. in polishing and etching glass

hy·dro·foil \'hī-drə-,fȯil\ *n* : a body similar to an air-foil but designed for action in or on the water

hy·dro·gen \'hī-drə-jən\ *n* [F *hydrogène*, fr. *hydr-* + *-gène* -gen; fr. the fact that water is generated by its combustion] : a univalent chemical element that is the simplest and lightest of the elements and is normally a colorless odorless highly flammable diatomic gas — compare DEUTERIUM, TRITIUM; see ELEMENT table — **hy·drog·e·nous** \hī-'dräj-ə-nəs\ *adj*

hy·dro·ge·nate \'hī-drə-jə-,nāt, hī-'dräj-ə-\ *vt* : to combine or treat with hydrogen; *esp* : to add hydrogen to the molecule of ⟨*hydrogenate* a vegetable oil to form a fat⟩ — **hy·dro·ge·na·tion** \,hī-drə-jə-'nā-shən, (,)hī-,dräj-ə-\ *n*

hydrogen bomb *n* : a bomb whose violent explosive power is due to the sudden release of atomic energy resulting from the union of light nuclei (as of hydrogen atoms)

hydrogen chloride *n* : a colorless pungent poisonous gas HCl that fumes in moist air and yields hydrochloric acid when dissolved in water

hydrogen fluoride *n* : a colorless corrosive fuming poisonous liquid or gas HF that yields hydrofluoric acid when dissolved in water

hydrogen ion *n* **1** : the cation H^+ of acids consisting of a hydrogen atom whose electron has been transferred to the anion of the acid **2** : HYDRONIUM

hydrogen peroxide *n* : an unstable liquid compound H_2O_2 used esp. as an oxidizing and bleaching agent, an antiseptic, and a propellant

hydrogen sulfide *n* : a flammable poisonous gas H_2S of disagreeable odor found esp. in many mineral waters and in putrefying matter

hy·drog·ra·phy \hī-'dräg-rə-fē\ *n* **1** : the study of seas, lakes, rivers, and other waters esp. with reference to their use by man **2** : the mapping of bodies of water **3** : bodies of water — **hy·drog·ra·pher** \-fər\ *n* — **hy·dro·graph·ic** \,hī-drə-'graf-ik\ *adj*

¹hy·droid \'hī-,drȯid\ *adj* : of or relating to the hydrozoans; *esp* : resembling a typical hydra

²hydroid *n* : HYDROZOAN; *esp* : a hydrozoan polyp as distinguished from a hydrozoan jellyfish

hy·drol·o·gy \hī-'dräl-ə-jē\ *n* : a science dealing with the properties, distribution, and circulation of water on and below the surface of the land and in the atmosphere — **hy·dro·log·ic** \,hī-drə-'läj-ik\ *adj* — **hy·drol·o·gist** \hī-'dräl-ə-jəst\ *n*

hy·drol·y·sis \hī-'dräl-ə-səs\ *n* : a chemical process of decomposition involving splitting of a bond and addition of the elements of water — **hy·dro·lyt·ic** \,hī-drə-'lit-ik\ *adj*

hy·dro·lyze \'hī-drə-,līz\ *vb* : to subject to or undergo hydrolysis

hy·drom·e·ter \hī-'dräm-ət-ər\ *n* : a floating instrument for determining specific gravities of liquids and hence the strength (as of alcoholic liquors, saline solutions) — **hy·dro·met·ric** \,hī-drə-'me-trik\ *adj* — **hy·drom·e·try** \hī-'dräm-ə-trē\ *n*

hy·dro·ni·um \hī-'drō-nē-əm\ *n* : a hydrated hydrogen ion H_3O^+

hy·dro·phil·ic \,hī-drə-'fil-ik\ *or* **hy·dro·phile** \'hī-drə-,fil\ *adj* : of, relating to, or having a strong affinity for water

hy·dro·pho·bia \,hī-drə-'fō-bē-ə\ *n* **1** : a morbid dread of water **2** : RABIES

hy·dro·pho·bic \-'fō-bik, -'fäb-ik\ *adj* **1** : of, relating to, or suffering from rabies **2** : lacking affinity for water — **hy·dro·pho·bic·i·ty** \-,fō-'bis-ət-ē\ *n*

hy·dro·phone \'hī-drə-,fōn\ *n* : an instrument for listening to sound transmitted through water

hy·dro·phyte \-,fīt\ *n* : a plant growing in water or in waterlogged soil — **hy·dro·phyt·ic** \,hī-drə-'fit-ik\ *adj*

¹hy·dro·plane \'hī-drə-,plān\ *n* **1** : a speedboat with fins or a stepped bottom so that the hull is raised wholly or partly out of the water **2** : SEAPLANE

²hydroplane *vi* **1** : to skim over the water with the hull

more or less clear of the surface **2** : to drive or ride in a hydroplane

hy·dro·pon·ics \,hī-drə-'pän-iks\ *n* [*-ponics* (as in *geoponics* agriculture, fr. Gk *geōponein*, fr. *geō-* ge- + *ponein* to toil] : the growing of plants in nutrient solutions — **hy·dro·pon·ic** \-ik\ *adj* — **hy·dro·pon·i·cal·ly** \-'pän-i-k(ə-)lē\ *adv*

hy·dro·qui·none \,hī-drō-kwin-'ōn, -'kwin-,ōn\ *n* : a white crystalline compound used as a photographic developer and as an antioxidant and stabilizer

hy·dro·sphere \'hī-drə-,sfi(ə)r\ *n* **1** : the water vapor that surrounds the earth as part of the atmosphere **2** : the surface waters of the earth and the water vapor in the atmosphere

hy·dro·stat·ic \,hī-drə-'stat-ik\ *adj* : of or relating to liquids at rest or to the pressures they exert or transmit

hy·dro·stat·ics \-iks\ *n* : a branch of physics that deals with the characteristics of liquids at rest and esp. with the pressure in a liquid or exerted by a liquid on an immersed body

hy·dro·sul·fu·ric acid \,hī-drō-,səl-,fyür-ik-\ *n* : an acid that consists of a solution of hydrogen sulfide in water

hy·dro·sul·fu·rous acid \,hī-drō-,səl-f(y)ə-rəs-, -,fyür-əs-\ *n* : an unstable acid $H_2S_2O_4$ known only in aqueous solution

hy·dro·tax·is \,hī-drō-'tak-səs\ *n* : a taxis in which moisture is the directive factor — **hy·dro·tac·tic** \-'tak-tik\ *adj*

hy·dro·ther·a·py \-'ther-ə-pē\ *n* : the use of water in the treatment of disease

hy·drot·ro·pism \hī-'drä-trə-,piz-əm\ *n* : a tropism (as in plant roots) in which water or water vapor is the orienting factor — **hy·dro·trop·ic** \,hī-drə-'träp-ik\ *adj* — **hy·dro·trop·i·cal·ly** \-'träp-i-k(ə-)lē\ *adv*

hy·drous \'hī-drəs\ *adj* : containing water usu. chemically combined

hy·drox·ide \hī-'dräk-,sīd\ *n* : a compound of hydroxyl with an element or radical

hydroxide ion *n* : the anion OH^- of basic hydroxides — called also *hydroxyl ion*

hy·drox·yl \hī-'dräk-səl\ *n* : the univalent group OH consisting of one atom of hydrogen and one of oxygen that is characteristic of hydroxides

hy·dro·zo·an \,hī-drə-'zō-ən\ *n* : any of a class (Hydrozoa) of coelenterates including the hydras and various polyps and jellyfishes — **hydrozoan** *adj* — **hy·dro·zo·on** \-'zō-,än, -'zō-ǝn\ *n*

hy·e·na \hī-'ē-nə\ *n* [Gk *hyaina*, fr. *hys* hog; akin to E *¹sow*] : any of several large strong nocturnal carnivorous Old World mammals

Hy·ge·ia \hī-'jē-(y)ə\ *n* : the Greek goddess of health

hy·giene \'hī-,jēn\ *n* [F *hygiène*, fr. Gk *hygieinos* healthful, fr. *hygiēs* healthy] **1** : a science dealing with the establishment and maintenance of health **2** : conditions or practices (as of cleanliness) conducive to health — **hy·gi·en·ic** \,hī-jē-'en-ik, hī-'jen-, hī-'jēn-\ *adj* — **hy·gi·en·i·cal·ly** \-i-k(ə-)lē\ *adv* — **hy·gien·ist** \hī-'jēn-əst, -'jen-, 'hī-,\ *n*

hygr- *also* **hygro-** *comb form* [Gk *hygros* wet] : humidity : moisture ⟨*hygroscope*⟩

hy·gro·graph \'hī-grə-,graf\ *n* : an instrument for automatic recording of variations in atmospheric humidity

hy·grom·e·ter \hī-'gräm-ət-ər\ *n* : any of several instruments for measuring the humidity of the atmosphere — **hy·gro·met·ric** \,hī-grə-'me-trik\ *adj*

hy·gro·scop·ic \,hī-grə-'skäp-ik\ *adj* **1 a** : readily taking up and retaining moisture ⟨salt is somewhat *hygroscopic*⟩ **b** : taken up and being retained ⟨*hygroscopic* moisture⟩ **2** : involving or induced by the taking up of moisture

hying *pres part of* HIE

Hyk·sos \'hik-,sōs\ *n* : a Semitic dynasty ruling Egypt from about 1750 to 1580 B.C.

hy·la \'hī-lə\ *n* [Gk *hylē* wood] : TREE TOAD

hymen \'hī-mən\ *n* [Gk *hymēn* membrane] : a fold of mucous membrane partly closing the opening of the vagina — **hy·men·al** \'hī-mən-°l\ *adj*

Hy·men *n* : the god of marriage in Greek mythology

hy·me·ne·al \,hī-mə-'nē-əl\ *adj* : of or relating to marriage : NUPTIAL

hy·me·nop·ter·on \,hī-mə-'näp-tə-,rän, -rən\ *n*, *pl* **-tera** \-rə\ [NL, fr. Gk *hymēn* membrane + *pteron* wing]

ə abut; ᵊ kitten; ǝr further; a back; ā bake; ä cot, cart; aù out; ch chin; e less; ē easy; g gift; i trip; ī life

: any of an order (Hymenoptera) of highly specialized and often colonial insects that have usu. four membranous wings and the abdomen on a slender stalk and include the bees, wasps, ants, and related forms — **hy·me·nop·ter·an** \-rən\ *adj or n* — **hy·me·nop·ter·ous** \-rəs\ *adj*

¹hymn \'him\ *n* [Gk *hymnos*] **1** : a song of praise esp. to God : PAEAN **2** : a religious song

²hymn *vb* **hymned; hymn·ing** \'him-iŋ\ **1 a** : to praise or worship in hymns ⟨*hymned* their god⟩ **b** : to sing the praises of : EXTOL ⟨*hymned* the joys of rural life⟩ **2 a** : to express in or as if in a hymn ⟨*hymns* his belief in human goodness⟩ **b** : SING; *esp* : to sing hymns

hymn·al \'him-nᵊl\ *n* : a book of hymns

hymn·book \'him-ˌbu̇k\ *n* : HYMNAL

hymn·o·dy \'him-nəd-ē\ *n* **1** : hymn singing **2** : hymn writing **3** : the hymns of a time, place, or church

hym·nol·o·gy \him-'näl-ə-jē\ *n* **1** : HYMNODY **2** : the study of hymns

hy·oid bone \ˌhī-ˌo͝id-\ *n* [Gk *hyoeidēs* shaped like the letter upsilon (υ), fr. *hy* upsilon] : a bone or complex of bones supporting the tongue and its muscles — **hy·oid** \'hī-ˌo͝id\ *adj or n*

hyp- — see HYPO-

hyper- *prefix* [Gk *hyper-*; akin to E *over*] **1** : above : beyond : SUPER- ⟨*hyper*physical⟩ **2 a** : excessively ⟨*hyper*sensitive⟩ **b** : excessive ⟨*hyper*emia⟩

hy·per·ac·id \ˌhī-pər-'as-əd\ *adj* : containing more than the normal amount of acid — **hy·per·acid·i·ty** \-ə-'sid-ət-ē\ *n*

hy·per·ac·tive \-'ak-tiv\ *adj* : excessively or pathologically active

hy·per·bo·la \hī-'pər-bə-lə\ *n, pl* **-las** or **-lae** \-ˌlē\ [NL, fr. Gk *hyperbolē*] : a plane curve generated by a point so moving that the difference of the distances from two fixed points is a constant : a curve formed by the intersection of a double right circular cone with a plane that cuts both halves of the cone — see CONIC SECTION illustration

hy·per·bo·le \hī-'pər-bə-(ˌ)lē\ *n* [Gk *hyperbolē* excess, hyperbole, hyperbola, fr. *hyperballein* to exceed, fr. *hyper-* + *ballein* to throw] : extravagant exaggeration used as a figure of speech

hy·per·bol·ic \ˌhī-pər-'bäl-ik\ *adj* **1** : of, characterized by, or given to hyperbole **2** : of or relating to a hyperbola — **hy·per·bol·i·cal** \-i-kəl\ *adj* — **hy·per·bol·i·cal·ly** \-i-k(ə-)lē\ *adv*

hy·per·bo·re·an \ˌhī-pər-'bōr-ē-ən, -'bȯr-\ *adj* : of, relating to, or inhabiting a remote northern region

Hyperborean *n* [Gk *Hyperboreoi*, pl., fr. *hyper-* + *Boreas*] **1** : a member of a people held by the ancient Greeks to live beyond the north wind in a region of perpetual sunshine **2** : an inhabitant of a remote northern region

hy·per·crit·i·cal \ˌhī-pər-'krit-i-kəl\ *adj* : excessively critical : CAPTIOUS — **hy·per·crit·i·cal·ly** \-k(ə-)lē\ *adv*

hy·per·e·mia \ˌhī-pə-'rē-mē-ə\ *n* : excess of blood in a body part : CONGESTION — **hy·per·e·mic** \-mik\ *adj*

hy·per·es·the·sia \ˌhī-pər-es-'thē-zhə\ *n* : abnormal or unusual sensitivity (as of the skin) — **hy·per·es·thet·ic** \-'thet-ik\ *adj*

hy·per·gly·ce·mia \ˌhī-pər-glī-'sē-mē-ə\ *n* [Gk *glykys* sweet] : excess of sugar in the blood — **hy·per·gly·ce·mic** \-mik\ *adj*

Hy·pe·ri·on \hī-'pir-ē-ən\ *n* : a Titan in Greek mythology and father of Helios

hy·per·me·tro·pia \ˌhī-pər-mi-'trō-pē-ə\ *n* : HYPEROPIA — **hy·per·me·tro·pic** \-'trōp-ik, -'träp-\ *adj* — **hy·per·me·tro·pi·cal** \-i-kəl\ *adj* — **hy·per·met·ro·py** \-'me-trə-pē\ *n*

hy·per·o·pia \ˌhī-pə-'rō-pē-ə\ *n* : a condition in which visual images come to a focus behind the retina and the eye is farsighted — **hy·per·ope** \'hī-pə-ˌrōp\ *n* — **hy·per·o·pic** \ˌhī-pə-'rōp-ik, -'räp-\ *adj*

hy·per·par·a·site \ˌhī-pər-'par-ə-ˌsīt\ *n* : a parasite of a parasite — **hy·per·par·a·sit·ism** \-ˌsīt-iz-əm\ *n*

hy·per·pla·sia \ˌhī-pər-'plā-zh(ē-)ə\ *n* : an abnormal or unusual increase in the elements (as tissue cells) composing a part — **hy·per·plas·tic** \-'plas-tik\ *adj*

hy·per·pnea \ˌhī-pər-'nē-ə, -ˌpərp-'nē-\ *n* : abnormally rapid or deep breathing — **hy·per·pne·ic** \-'nē-ik\ *adj*

hy·per·py·rex·ia \ˌhī-pər-pī-'rek-sē-ə\ *n* : exceptionally high fever — **hy·per·py·ret·ic** \-'ret-ik\ *adj*

hy·per·sen·si·tive \-'sen(t)-sət-iv, -'sen(t)-stiv\ *adj* : ex-

cessively or abnormally sensitive — **hy·per·sen·si·tive·ness** *n* — **hy·per·sen·si·tiv·i·ty** \-ˌsen(t)-sə-'tiv-ət-ē\ *n*

hy·per·son·ic \-'sän-ik\ *adj* [L *sonus* sound] **1** : of or relating to speed five or more times that of sound in air — compare SONIC **2** : moving, capable of moving, or utilizing air currents that move at hypersonic speed ⟨*hypersonic* wind tunnel⟩

hy·per·ten·sion \ˌhī-pər-'ten-chən\ *n* : abnormally high blood pressure and esp. arterial blood pressure — **hy·per·ten·sive** \-'ten(t)-siv\ *adj or n*

hy·per·thy·roid·ism \-'thī-ˌro͝id-,diz-əm\ *n* : excessive activity of the thyroid gland; *also* : the resulting abnormal state of health — compare GOITER — **hy·per·thy·roid** \-ˌro͝id\ *adj*

hy·per·ton·ic \-'tän-ik\ *adj* **1** : having excessive tone or tension **2** : having a higher osmotic pressure than a fluid under comparison — **hy·per·to·nic·i·ty** \-tə-'nis-ət-ē\ *n*

hy·per·tro·phy \hī-'pər-trə-fē\ *n, pl* **-phies** : excessive development of a bodily part; *esp* : increase in bulk without multiplication of constituent units — **hy·per·tro·phic** \ˌhī-'pər-trə-fik, ˌhī-pər-'träf-ik\ *adj* — **hypertrophy** *vb*

hy·pha \'hī-fə\ *n, pl* **hy·phae** \-(ˌ)fē\ [NL, fr. Gk *hyphē* web] : one of the threads that make up the mycelium of a fungus — **hy·phal** \-fəl\ *adj*

¹hy·phen \'hī-fən\ *n* [Gk, fr. *hyph' hen* under one] : a mark - used to divide or to compound words or word elements

²hyphen *vt* : to connect or mark with a hyphen

hy·phen·ate \'hī-fə-ˌnāt\ *vt* : HYPHEN

hyp·no·sis \hip-'nō-səs\ *n, pl* **-no·ses** \-'nō-ˌsēz\ [Gk *hypnoun* to put to sleep, fr. *hypnos* sleep] : an induced state which resembles sleep but in which the subject is very responsive to suggestions of the hypnotizer

hyp·no·ther·a·py \ˌhip-nō-'ther-ə-pē\ *n* : the use of hypnotism in medical or psychiatric practice

¹hyp·not·ic \hip-'nät-ik\ *adj* [Gk *hypnōtikos*, fr. *hypnoun* to put to sleep, fr. *hypnos* sleep] **1** : tending to induce sleep : SOPORIFIC **2** : of or relating to hypnosis or hypnotism — **hyp·not·i·cal·ly** \-i-k(ə-)lē\ *adv*

²hypnotic *n* **1** : a sleep-inducing agent : SOPORIFIC **2** : one that is or can be hypnotized

hyp·no·tism \'hip-nə-ˌtiz-əm\ *n* **1** : the study of or act of inducing hypnosis **2** : HYPNOSIS — **hyp·no·tist** \-təst\ *n*

hyp·no·tize \-ˌtīz\ *vt* **1** : to induce hypnosis in **2** : to deaden (judgment or resistance) by or as if by hypnotic suggestion — **hyp·no·tiz·a·ble** \-ˌtī-zə-bəl\ *adj* — **hyp·no·ti·za·tion** \ˌhip-nət-ə-'zā-shən\ *n* — **hyp·no·tiz·er** \'hip-nə-ˌtī-zər\ *n*

¹hy·po \'hī-pō\ *n* : HYPOCHONDRIA

²hypo *n* [short for *hyposulfite*] : sodium thiosulfate used in photography as a fixing agent

³hypo *n, pl* **hypos** : a hypodermic syringe or injection

hypo- or **hyp-** *prefix* [Gk] **1** : under : beneath : down ⟨*hypo*dermic⟩ **2** : less than normal or normally ⟨*hyp*esthesia⟩ ⟨*hypo*tension⟩ **3** : in a lower state of oxidation : in a low and usu. the lowest position in a series of compounds ⟨*hypo*nitrous acid⟩

hy·po·chlo·rite \ˌhī-pə-'klōr-ˌīt, -'klȯr-\ *n* : a salt or ester of hypochlorous acid

hy·po·chlo·rous acid \ˌhī-pə-ˌklōr-əs-, -ˌklȯr-\ *n* : an unstable weak acid HClO obtained in solution by reaction of chlorine with water and used esp. in the form of salts as an oxidizing agent, bleaching agent, and disinfectant

hy·po·chon·dria \ˌhī-pə-'kän-drē-ə\ *n* [NL, fr. LL, pl., upper abdomen (formerly regarded as the seat of hypochondria), fr. Gk, lit., the parts under the cartilage (of the breastbone), fr. *hypo-* + *chondros* cartilage] : severe depression of mind or spirits often centered on imaginary physical ailments — **hy·po·chon·dri·ac** \-drē-ˌak\ *adj or n* — **hy·po·chon·dri·a·cal** \-kən-'drī-ə-kəl, -ˌkän-\ *adj* — **hy·po·chon·dri·a·cal·ly** \-'drī-ə-k(ə-)lē\ *adv*

hy·po·cot·yl \'hī-pə-ˌkät-ᵊl\ *n* : the part of the axis of a plant embryo or seedling below the cotyledons

hy·poc·ri·sy \hip-'äk-rə-sē\ *n, pl* **-sies** : a pretending to be what one is not or to believe what one does not; *esp* : the false assumption of an appearance of virtue or religion

hyp·o·crite \'hip-ə-ˌkrit\ *n* [Gk *hypokritēs* actor, hypocrite, lit., one who answers, fr. *hypokrinesthai* to answer] : one who affects virtues or qualities he does not have : DISSEMBLER — **hyp·o·crit·i·cal** \ˌhip-ə-'krit-i-kəl\ *adj* — **hyp·o·crit·i·cal·ly** \-i-k(ə-)lē\ *adv*

¹hy·po·der·mic \,hī-pə-'dər-mik\ *adj* [Gk *derma* skin] : of, relating to, or injected into the parts beneath the skin — **hy·po·der·mi·cal·ly** \-mi-k(ə-)lē\ *adv*

²hypodermic *n* **1** : HYPODERMIC INJECTION **2** : HYPODERMIC SYRINGE

hypodermic injection *n* : an injection made into the subcutaneous tissues

hypodermic syringe *n* : a small syringe used with a hollow needle for injection of material into or beneath the skin

hy·po·der·mis \,hī-pə-'dər-məs\ *n* : a layer of tissue immediately beneath an outermost layer; *esp* : a layer just beneath the epidermis of a plant and often modified to serve as a supporting and protecting layer

hy·po·ge·al \,hī-pə-'jē-əl\ *or* **hy·po·ge·ous** \-'jē-əs\ *adj* [Gk *gē* earth] : growing or living below the surface of the ground — **hy·po·ge·al·ly** \-'jē-ə-lē\ *adv*

hy·po·glos·sal \,hī-pə-'gläs-əl\ *adj* [Gk *glossa, glotta* tongue] : of, relating to, or being the 12th and final pair of cranial nerves that are motor nerves arising from the medulla oblongata and supplying muscles of the tongue in higher vertebrates — **hypoglossal** *n*

hy·po·gly·ce·mia \,hī-pə-,glī-'sē-mē-ə\ *n* [Gk *glykys* sweet] : abnormal decrease of sugar in the blood — **hy·po·gly·ce·mic** \-mik\ *adj*

hy·pog·y·nous \hī-'päj-ə-nəs\ *adj* **1** : growing from the receptacle below and free from the ovary ⟨*hypogynous* petals⟩ **2** : having hypogynous floral organs — **hy·pog·y·ny** \-nē\ *n*

hy·po·phar·ynx \,hī-pō-'far-iŋ(k)s\ *n* : an appendage or fold of the mouth of some insects that resembles a tongue

hy·po·phos·phite \,hī-pə-'fäs-,fīt\ *n* : a salt of hypophosphorous acid

hy·po·phos·phor·ic acid \,hī-pə-,fäs-,fór-ik-, -,fär-\ *n* : an unstable acid $H_4P_2O_6$ usu. obtained in the form of its salts

hy·po·phos·pho·rous acid \-,fäs-f(ə-)rəs-\ *n* : a crystalline strong acid H_3PO_2 used as a reducing agent

hy·poph·y·sis \hī-'päf-ə-səs\ *n, pl* **-y·ses** \-ə-,sēz\ [Gk, attachment underneath, fr. *hypophyein* to grow beneath] : PITUITARY BODY — **hy·poph·y·se·al** \(,)hī-,päf-ə-'sē-əl\ *adj*

hy·po·pla·sia \,hī-pə-'plā-zh(ē-)ə\ *n* : arrested development of an organ or part — **hy·po·plas·tic** \-'plas-tik\ *adj*

hy·po·sen·si·tize \,hī-pō-'sen(t)-sə-,tīz\ *vt* : to reduce the sensitivity of esp. to an allergen : DESENSITIZE — **hy·po·sen·si·ti·za·tion** \-,sen-sət-ə-'zā-shən\ *n*

hy·po·style \'hī-pə-,stīl\ *adj* [Gk *stylos* pillar] : having the roof resting on rows of columns

hy·po·sul·fite \,hī-pō-'səl-,fīt\ *n* : THIOSULFATE — used chiefly in photography

hy·po·sul·fu·rous acid \,hī-pō-,səl-f(y)ə-rəs-, -,fyùr-əs-\ *n* : HYDROSULFUROUS ACID

hy·po·ten·sion \,hī-pō-'ten-chən\ *n* : deficiency of tension; *esp* : abnormally low blood pressure — **hy·po·ten·sive** \-'ten(t)-siv\ *adj or n*

hy·pot·e·nuse \hī-'pät-°n-,(y)üs, -,(y)üz\ *n* [Gk *hypoteinousa,* fr. fem. of *hypoteinōn,* prp. of *hypoteinein* to subtend, fr. *hypo-* + *teinein* to stretch] : the side of a right-angled triangle that is opposite the right angle

hy·po·thal·a·mus \,hī-pō-'thal-ə-məs\ *n* : a basal part of the diencephalon that lies beneath the thalamus and is usu. held to contain vital autonomic centers — **hy·po·tha·lam·ic** \-thə-'lam-ik\ *adj*

¹hy·poth·e·cate \hip-'äth-ə-,kāt, hī-'päth-\ *vt* [Gk *hypothēkē,* n., deposit, pledge, fr. *hypotithenai* to put under, pledge] : to pledge as collateral without delivery of title or possession — **hy·poth·e·ca·tion** \hip-,äth-ə-'kā-shən, hī-,päth-\ *n* — **hy·poth·e·ca·tor** \hip-'äth-ə-,kāt-ər, hī-'päth-\ *n*

²hy·poth·e·cate \hī-'päth-ə-,kāt\ *vb* : HYPOTHESIZE

hy·poth·e·sis \hī-'päth-ə-səs\ *n, pl* **-e·ses** \-ə-,sēz\ [Gk, supposition, fr. *hypotithenai* to put under, suppose, fr. *hypo-* + *tithenai* to put] : something not proved but assumed to be true for purposes of argument or further study or investigation

syn HYPOTHESIS, THEORY, LAW mean a formula derived by inference from scientific data that explains a principle operating in nature. HYPOTHESIS implies insufficient evidence to provide more than a tentative explanation; THEORY implies a greater range of evidence and greater likelihood of truth; LAW denotes a statement of order and relation in nature that has been found to be invariable under the same conditions

hy·poth·e·size \hī-'päth-ə-,sīz\ *vb* **1** : to make a hypothesis **2** : to adopt as a hypothesis

hy·po·thet·i·cal \,hī-pə-'thet-i-kəl\ *adj* **1** : involving hypothesis : ASSUMED **2** : of or depending on supposition : CONJECTURAL — **hy·po·thet·i·cal·ly** \-i-k(ə-)lē\ *adv*

hy·po·thy·roid·ism \,hī-pō-'thī-,rói-,diz-əm\ *n* : deficient activity of the thyroid gland; *also* : the resultant condition marked esp. by lowered metabolic rate and loss of vigor — compare GOITER — **hy·po·thy·roid** \-,róid\ *adj*

hy·po·ton·ic \,hī-pə-'tän-ik\ *adj* **1** : having deficient tone or tension **2** : having a lower osmotic pressure than a fluid under comparison — **hy·po·to·nic·i·ty** \-tə-'nis-ət-ē\ *n*

hyp·som·e·ter \hip-'säm-ət-ər\ *n* [Gk *hypsos* height] : any of various instruments for determining the height of trees by triangulation

hy·rax \'hī(ə)r-,aks\ *n, pl* **hy·rax·es** *also* **hy·ra·ces** \'hī-rə-,sēz\ [Gk *hyrak-, hyrax* shrewmouse] : any of several small thickset Old World ungulate mammals (order Hyracoidea) — called also *coney*

hys·sop \'his-əp\ *n* [Gk *hyssōpos,* of Sem origin] **1** : a plant used in purificatory sprinkling rites by the ancient Hebrews **2** : a woody European mint with pungent aromatic leaves sometimes used in folk medicine for bruises

hys·ter·e·sis \,his-tə-'rē-səs\ *n* [NL, fr. Gk *hysterein* to be late, fr. *hysteros* later] : a lagging in the values of resulting magnetization in a magnetic material (as iron) due to a changing magnetizing force

hys·te·ria \his-'ter-ē-ə, -'tir-\ *n* [NL, fr. Gk *hystera* womb; fr. the former notion that hysteric women were suffering from disturbances of the womb] **1** : a psychoneurosis marked by emotional excitability **2** : unmanageable fear or emotional excess — **hys·ter·ic** \-'ter-ik\ *n* — **hysteric** *or* **hys·ter·i·cal** \-'ter-i-kəl\ *adj* — **hys·ter·i·cal·ly** \-i-k(ə-)lē\ *adv*

hys·ter·ics \his-'ter-iks\ *n sing or pl* : a fit of uncontrollable laughter or crying : HYSTERIA

i \'ī\ *n, often cap* **1** : the 9th letter of the English alphabet **2** : the roman numeral 1

I \(')ī, ə\ *pron* [OE *ic*] : the one who is speaking or writing ⟨*I* feel fine⟩⟨it wasn't *I*⟩ — compare ME, MINE, MY, WE

-i- [L, stem vowel of most nouns and adjectives in combination] — used as a connective vowel to join word elements esp. of Latin origin ⟨pesticide⟩

-ia *n suffix* [NL, fr. L & Gk, suffix forming feminine nouns] **1** : pathological condition ⟨hyster*ia*⟩ **2** : genus of plants or animals ⟨Fuchs*ia*⟩

-ial *adj suffix* [L *-ialis,* fr. *-i-* + *-alis* -al] : ¹-AL ⟨gerund*ial*⟩

iamb \'ī-,am\ *n* [L *iambus,* fr. Gk *iambos*] : a metrical foot consisting of one unaccented syllable followed by one accented syllable (as in *away*) — **iam·bic** \ī-'am-bik\ *adj*

iam·bus \ī-'am-bəs\ *n, pl* **-bus·es** *also* **-bi** \-,bī\ : IAMB

-ian — see -AN

-iana — see -ANA

-i·a·sis \'ī-ə-səs\ *n suffix, pl* **-i·a·ses** \'ī-ə-,sēz\ [NL, fr. Gk, suffix of action, fr. denominative verbs in *-ian, -iazein*] : disease having characteristics of or produced by (something specified) ⟨elephant*iasis*⟩ ⟨ameb*iasis*⟩

iat·ro·gen·ic \ī-,a-trə-'jen-ik\ *adj* [Gk *iatros* physician] : caused by the physician ⟨*iatrogenic* illness⟩

-i·a·try \'ī-ə-trē, in a few words ē-,a-trē\ *n comb form* [Gk *iatreia* art of healing, fr. *iatros* physician] **:** medical treatment **:** healing ⟨pod*iatry*⟩

Ibe·ri·an \ī-'bir-ē-ən\ *n* [*Iberia*, peninsula in Europe] **1 :** a member of one or more Caucasoid peoples anciently inhabiting the peninsula comprising Spain and Portugal **2 :** a native or inhabitant of Spain or Portugal — **Iberian** *adj*

ibex \'ī-,beks\ *n, pl* **ibex** *or* **ibex·es** [L] **:** any of several wild goats living chiefly in high mountain areas of the Old World and having large recurved horns transversely ridged in front

ibi·dem \'ib-ə-,dem, ib-'īd-əm\ *adv* [L] **:** in the same place

-ibility — see -ABILITY

ibis \'ī-bəs\ *n, pl* **ibis** *or* **ibis·es** [Gk, fr. Egypt *hby*] **:** any of several wading birds related to the herons but distinguished by a long slender bill that curves downward

-ible — see -ABLE

1-ic \ik\ *adj suffix* [L *-icus* & Gk *-ikos;* akin to E *-y*] **1 :** having the character or form of **:** being ⟨panoram*ic*⟩ **:** consisting of ⟨run*ic*⟩ **2 a :** of or relating to ⟨alderman*ic*⟩ **b :** related to, derived from, or containing ⟨alcohol*ic*⟩ ⟨ole*ic*⟩ **3 :** in the manner of **:** like that of **:** characteristic of ⟨Byron*ic*⟩ **4 :** associated or dealing with ⟨Ved*ic*⟩ **5 :** characterized by **:** exhibiting ⟨nostalg*ic*⟩ **:** affected with ⟨allerg*ic*⟩ **6 :** caused by ⟨amoeb*ic*⟩ **7 :** tending to produce ⟨analges*ic*⟩ **8 :** having a valence relatively higher than in compounds or ions named with an adjective ending in *-ous* ⟨ferr*ic* iron⟩

2-ic *n suffix* **:** one having the character or nature of **:** one belonging to or associated with **:** one exhibiting or affected by **:** one that produces

-i·cal \i-kəl\ *adj suffix* [LL *-icalis,* fr. nouns in *-icus, -ica, -icum* + L *-alis -al*] **:** -IC ⟨symmetr*ical*⟩ ⟨geolog*ical*⟩ — sometimes differing from *-ic* in that adjectives formed with *-ical* have a wider or more transferred semantic range than corresponding adjectives in *-ic*

Ic·a·rus \'ik-ə-rəs\ *n* **:** the son of Daedalus who in escaping from imprisonment fell into the sea when the wax of his wings melted as he flew too near the sun — **Icar·i·an** \ik-'ar-ē-ən, -'er-\ *adj*

1ice \'īs\ *n* [OE *īs*] **1 a :** frozen water **b :** an expanse of frozen water **2 :** a state of coldness (as from formality or reserve) **3 :** a substance resembling ice **4 :** a frozen dessert; *esp* **:** one containing no milk or cream — **on ice 1 :** with every likelihood of being won or accomplished **2 :** in reserve or safekeeping — **on thin ice :** in a situation involving great risk

2ice *vb* **1 a :** to coat or become coated with ice **:** change into ice **b :** to chill with ice **c :** to supply with ice **2 :** to cover with or as if with icing

Ice Age *n* **:** the Pleistocene glacial epoch

ice bag *n* **:** a waterproof bag to hold ice for local application of cold to the body

ice·berg \'īs-,bərg\ *n* [prob. part trans. of Norw *isberg,* fr. *is* ice + *berg* mountain] **:** a large floating mass of ice detached from a glacier

ice·boat \-,bōt\ *n* **:** a skeleton boat or frame on runners propelled on ice usu. by sails

ice·bound \-,baůnd\ *adj* **:** surrounded or obstructed by ice

ice·box \-,bäks\ *n* **:** REFRIGERATOR

ice·break·er \-,brā-kər\ *n* **1 :** a ship equipped to make and maintain a channel through ice **2 :** something that breaks the ice (as at a social occasion)

ice cap *n* **:** a glacier forming on an extensive area of relatively level land and flowing outward from its center — called also *ice sheet*

ice-cold \'īs-'kōld\ *adj* **:** extremely cold

ice cream \(')īs-'krēm, 'īs-,\ *n* **:** a frozen food containing cream or butterfat, flavoring, sweetening, and usu. eggs

ice field *n* **1 :** an extensive sheet of sea ice **2 :** ICE CAP

ice floe *n* **:** a flat free mass of floating sea ice

ice·house \'īs-,haůs\ *n* **:** a building for storing ice

1Ice·lan·dic \'īs-'lan-dik\ *adj* **:** of, relating to, or characteristic of Iceland, the Icelanders, or Icelandic

2Icelandic *n* **:** the Germanic language of the Icelandic people

Ice·land moss \,īs-lən(d)-, -,lan(d)-\ *n* **:** an arctic lichen sometimes used medicinally or as food

Iceland spar *n* **:** a doubly refracting transparent calcite

ice·man \'īs-,man\ *n* **:** one who sells or delivers ice

ice pack *n* **:** an expanse of pack ice

ice pick *n* **:** a hand tool ending in a spike for chipping ice

ice-skate \'ī(s)-,skāt\ *vi* **:** to skate on ice — **ice skater** *n*

ice water *n* **:** chilled or iced water esp. for drinking

ich·neu·mon \ik-'n(y)ü-mən\ *n* [Gk *ichneumōn,* lit., tracker, fr. *ichneuein* to track, fr. *ichnos* track, trail] **:** MONGOOSE

ichneumon fly *n* **:** any of numerous small hymenopterous insects whose larvae are usu. internal parasites of other insect larvae

ichor \'īk-,òr, 'īk-ər, 'ik-\ *n* [Gk *ichōr*] **:** an ethereal fluid taking the place of blood in the veins of the ancient Greek gods — **ichor·ous** \-ə-rəs\ *adj*

ichthy- *or* **ichthyo-** *comb form* [Gk *ichthys*] **:** fish ⟨*ichthy*ic⟩

ich·thy·ol·o·gy \,ik-thē-'äl-ə-jē\ *n* **:** a branch of zoology that deals with fishes — **ich·thy·o·log·i·cal** \,ik-thē-ə-'läj-i-kəl\ *adj* — **ich·thy·o·log·i·cal·ly** \-i-k(ə-)lē\ *adv* — **ich·thy·ol·o·gist** \,ik-thē-'äl-ə-jəst\ *n*

ich·thy·or·nis \,ik-thē-'òr-nəs\ *n* [Gk *ornis* bird] **:** any of a genus of extinct toothed birds

ich·thy·o·saur \'ik-thē-ə-,sòr\ *n* **:** any of an order (Ichthyosauria) of extinct marine reptiles with fish-shaped body and elongated snout — **ich·thy·o·sau·ri·an** \,ik-thē-ə-'sòr-ē-ən\ *adj or n*

ich·thy·o·sis \,ik-thē-'ō-səs\ *n* **:** a congenital disorder in which the skin is rough, thick, and scaly — **ich·thy·ot·ic** \-'ät-ik\ *adj*

-i·cian \'ish-ən\ *n suffix* [OF *-icien,* fr. L *-ica* -ic, -ics + OF *-ien* -ian] **:** specialist **:** practitioner ⟨beaut*ician*⟩

ici·cle \'ī-,sik-əl\ *n* [ME *isikel,* fr. *is* ice + *ikel* icicle, fr. OE *gicel*] **:** a hanging mass of ice formed by the freezing of dripping water

ic·ing \'ī-siŋ\ *n* **:** a coating for baked goods usu. made from sugar and butter combined with water, milk, or egg white and flavoring

icon \'ī-,kän\ *n* [Gk *eikōn,* fr. *eikenai* to resemble] **1 :** IMAGE **2 :** a conventional religious image typically painted on a small wooden panel and venerated by Eastern Christians — **icon·ic** \ī-'kän-ik\ *adj* — **icon·i·cal·ly** \-'kän-i-k(ə-)lē\ *adv*

icon·o·clasm \ī-'kän-ə-,klaz-əm\ *n* **:** the doctrine, practice, or attitude of an iconoclast

icon·o·clast \-,klast\ *n* [MGk *eikonoklastēs,* fr. Gk *eikōn* image + *klan* to break] **1 :** one who destroys religious images or opposes their veneration **2 :** one who attacks established beliefs or institutions — **icon·o·clas·tic** \ī-,kän-ə-'klas-tik\ *adj* — **icon·o·clas·ti·cal·ly** \-ti-k(ə-)lē\ *adv*

icon·o·scope \ī-'kän-ə-,skōp\ *n* **:** a television camera containing an electron gun and a photoemissive screen

ico·sa·he·dron \,ī-,kō-sə-'hē-drən\ *n, pl* **-drons** *or* **-dra** \-drə\ [Gk *eikosaedron,* fr. *eikosi* twenty + *-edron* *-hedron*] **:** a polyhedron having 20 faces

-ics \iks\ *n sing or pl suffix* [*-ic* + *-s;* trans. of Gk *-ika,* fr. neut. pl. of *-ikos* -ic] **1 :** study **:** knowledge **:** skill **:** practice ⟨linguist*ics*⟩ ⟨electron*ics*⟩ **2 :** characteristic actions or activities ⟨acrobat*ics*⟩ **3 :** characteristic qualities, operations, or phenomena ⟨mechan*ics*⟩

ic·ter·us \'ik-tə-rəs\ *n* **:** JAUNDICE — **ic·ter·ic** \ik-'ter-ik\ *adj*

ic·tus \'ik-təs\ *n* [L *ictus,* fr. *icere* to strike] **:** the recurring stress or beat in a rhythmic or metrical series of sounds

icy \'ī-sē\ *adj* **ic·i·er; -est 1 a :** covered with, full of, or consisting of ice ⟨*icy* roads⟩ **b :** intensely cold ⟨*icy* weather⟩ **2 :** characterized by coldness **:** FRIGID ⟨an *icy* stare⟩ — **ic·i·ly** \-sə-lē\ *adv* — **ic·i·ness** \-sē-nəs\ *n*

1id \'id\ *n* [L, it] **:** the primitive undifferentiated part of the psychic apparatus that reacts blindly on a pleasure-pain level, is the seat of psychic energy, and is the ultimate source of higher psychic components (as ego and superego)

2id *n* **:** an allergic skin rash secondary to an infection

I'd \(,)īd\ **:** I had **:** I should **:** I would

-ide \-,īd\ *also* **-id** \əd, (,)id\ *n suffix* [F *-ide* (as in *oxide*)] **1 :** binary chemical compound ⟨hydrogen sulf*ide*⟩ ⟨cyan*ide*⟩ **2 :** chemical compound derived from or related to another (usu. specified) compound ⟨anhydr*ide*⟩ ⟨glucos*ide*⟩

idea \ī-'dē-ə, *esp South* 'īd-ē-\ *n* [Gk, form, notion, fr. *idein* to see] **1 :** a plan of action **:** INTENTION ⟨his *idea* is to study law⟩ **2 :** something imagined or pictured in the mind **:** NOTION ⟨form an *idea* of a foreign country from reading⟩ **3 :** a central meaning or purpose ⟨the *idea* of the game is to keep from getting caught⟩ — **idea·less** \ī-'dē-ə-ləs\ *adj*

syn CONCEPT, CONCEPTION: IDEA may apply to a mental image of something seen, known, or imagined or to an abstraction or to something assumed or vaguely sensed ⟨the *idea* of interplanetary travel⟩⟨a new *idea* for redecorating a room⟩ ⟨*ideas* about the nature of democracy⟩ CONCEPT may apply to the idea formed after knowing many instances of a type or to an idea of what a thing ought to be ⟨the *concepts* of modern architecture⟩⟨the *concept* of the role of a citizen in a democracy⟩ CONCEPTION is often interchangeable with CONCEPT, but it may stress the act of imagining or formulating rather than the result ⟨the primitive *conception* of all nature as animate⟩

¹ide·al \ī-'dē(-ə)l\ *adj* **1** : existing only in the mind : not real **2** : embodying or symbolizing an ideal : PERFECT ⟨an *ideal* place for a picnic⟩⟨*ideal* weather⟩

²ideal *n* **1** : a standard of perfection, beauty, or excellence **2** : a perfect type : a model for imitation **3** : an ultimate object or aim of endeavor : GOAL — **ide·al·less** \ī-'dē(-ə)l-ləs\ *adj*

ideal gas *n* : a theoretical gas in which there is no attraction between the molecules and which conforms exactly to the general laws governing the behavior of real gases

ide·al·ism \ī-'dē-(ə-),liz-əm\ *n* **1 a** : a theory that ultimate reality lies in a realm transcending phenomena **b** : a theory that reality lies essentially in consciousness or reason **2** : the practice of forming ideals or living under their influence **3** : literary or artistic theory or practice that values ideal or subjective types or aspects of beauty more than formal or sensible qualities or the representation of objective reality

ide·al·ist \ī-'dē-(ə-)ləst\ *n* **1 a** : an adherent of a philosophical theory of idealism **b** : an artist or author who advocates or practices idealism in art or writing **2** : one guided by ideals; *esp* : one that places ideals before practical considerations — **ide·al·is·tic** \-,dē-(ə-)'lis-tik\ *adj* — **ide·al·is·ti·cal·ly** \-ti-k(ə-)lē\ *adv*

ide·al·ize \ī-'dē-(ə-),līz\ *vt* : to think of or represent as ideal ⟨*idealize* life on a farm⟩ — **ide·al·i·za·tion** \ī-,dē-(ə-)lə-'zā-shən\ *n* — **ide·al·iz·er** *n*

ide·al·ly \ī-'dē-(ə-)lē\ *adv* **1** : in idea or imagination : MENTALLY ⟨realizable only *ideally*, not in fact⟩ **2** : conformably to an ideal : PERFECTLY ⟨*ideally* suited to the position⟩

ide·a·tion \,īd-ē-'ā-shən\ *n* : the capacity for or process of forming or entertaining ideas — **ide·ate** \'īd-ē-,āt\ *vb* — **ide·a·tion·al** \,īd-ē-'ā-shnəl, -shən-ᵊl\ *adj*

idem \'īd-,em\ *pron* [L, same] : something previously mentioned : SAME

iden·ti·cal \ī-'dent-i-kəl, ə-\ *adj* **1** : being one and the same ⟨the *identical* place we stopped before⟩ **2** : being essentially the same or exactly alike ⟨*identical* hats⟩ — **iden·ti·cal·ly** \-i-k(ə-)lē\ *adv* — **iden·ti·cal·ness** \-kəl-nəs\ *n*

identical equation *n* : an equation that is satisfied for all values of the symbols

identical twin *n* : either member of a pair of twins produced from a single fertilized egg and marked by extreme physical and mental similarity

iden·ti·fi·ca·tion \ī-,dent-ə-fə-'kā-shən, ə-\ *n* **1** : an act of identifying : the state of being identified **2** : evidence of identity ⟨carry *identification* at all times⟩

iden·ti·fy \ī-'dent-ə-,fī, ə-\ *vt* **-fied; -fy·ing 1 a** : to cause to be or become identical ⟨*identifies* democracy with capitalism⟩ **b** : ASSOCIATE ⟨*identified* himself with the movement⟩ **2** : to establish the identity of ⟨*identified* the dog as her lost pet⟩ — **iden·ti·fi·a·ble** \-,fī-ə-bəl\ *adj* — **iden·ti·fi·a·bly** \-blē\ *adv* — **iden·ti·fi·er** \-,fī(-ə)r\ *n*

iden·ti·ty \ī-'dent-ət-ē, ə-\ *n, pl* **-ties** [LL *identitas*, irreg. fr. L *idem* same, fr. *is* that] **1** : the fact or condition of being exactly alike : SAMENESS ⟨an *identity* of interests⟩ **2** : distinctness with regard to character or appearance : INDIVIDUALITY ⟨members of a mob often lose their *identity*⟩ **3** : the fact of being the same person or thing as one described or known to exist ⟨proved his *identity* with the wanted man⟩ **4 a** : IDENTICAL EQUATION **b** : a mathematical element that leaves a quantity unchanged under a specific operation — called also *identity element*

id·e·o·gram \'id-ē-ə-,gram, 'īd-\ *n* **1** : a picture or symbol used in a system of writing to represent a thing or an idea

but not a particular word or phrase for it **2** : a character or symbol used in a system of writing to represent an entire word without providing separate representation of the individual sounds in it

id·e·o·graph \-,graf\ *n* : IDEOGRAM — **id·e·o·graph·ic** \,id-ē-ə-'graf-ik, ,īd-\ *adj* — **id·e·o·graph·i·cal·ly** \-'graf-i-k(ə-)lē\ *adv*

ide·ol·o·gy \,īd-ē-'äl-ə-jē, ,id-\ *n, pl* **-gies 1** : a systematic body of concepts esp. about human life or culture **2** : a manner or the content of thinking characteristic of an individual, group, or culture **3** : the integrated assertions, theories, and aims that constitute a political, social, and economic program — **ide·o·log·i·cal** \-ē-ə-'läj-i-kəl\ — **ide·o·log·i·cal·ly** \-i-k(ə-)lē\ *adv* — **ide·ol·o·gist** \-ē-'äl-ə-jəst\ *n*

ides \'īdz\ *n pl* [L *Idus*] : the 15th day of March, May, July, or October or the 13th day of any other month in the ancient Roman calendar

id·i·o·cy \'id-ē-ə-sē\ *n, pl* **-cies** [*idiot*] **1** : extreme mental deficiency commonly due to incomplete or abnormal development of the brain **2** : something notably stupid or foolish

id·i·o·lect \'id-ē-ə-,lekt\ *n* : the speech pattern of one individual

id·i·om \'id-ē-əm\ *n* [Gk *idiōmat-*, *idiōma* individual peculiarity of language, fr. *idios* one's own] **1** : the language peculiar to a group ⟨doctors speaking in their professional *idiom*⟩ **2** : the characteristic form or structure of a language ⟨know the vocabulary of a foreign language but not its *idiom*⟩ **3** : an expression that cannot be understood from the meanings of its separate words but must be learned as a whole ⟨the expression *give way*, meaning "retreat", is an *idiom*⟩ — **id·i·om·at·ic** \,id-ē-ə-'mat-ik\ *adj* — **id·i·om·at·i·cal·ly** \-'mat-i-k(ə-)lē\ *adv* — **id·i·om·at·ic·ness** \-'mat-ik-nəs\ *n*

id·i·o·path·ic \,id-ē-ə-'path-ik\ *adj* : arising spontaneously or from an obscure or unknown cause — **id·i·o·path·i·cal·ly** \-'path-i-k(ə-)lē\ *adv* — **id·i·op·a·thy** \,id-ē-'äp-ə-thē\ *n*

id·i·o·syn·cra·sy \,id-ē-ə-'siŋ-krə-sē\ *n, pl* **-sies** [Gk *idiosynkrasia*, fr. *idios* one's own + *syn-* + *kerannynai* to mix] **1** : characteristic peculiarity of habitual behavior or of structure **2** : individual hypersensitiveness (as to a drug or food) **syn** see ECCENTRICITY — **id·i·o·syn·crat·ic** \,id-ē-ō-sin-'krat-ik\ *adj* — **id·i·o·syn·crat·i·cal·ly** \-'krat-i-k(ə-)lē\ *adv*

id·i·ot \'id-ē-ət\ *n* [L *idiota* ignorant person, fr. Gk *idiōtēs* one in a private station, layman, ignorant person, fr. *idios* one's own, private] **1** : a person afflicted with idiocy; *esp* : a feebleminded person having a mental age not exceeding three years and requiring complete custodial care **2** : a silly or foolish person — **idiot** *adj*

syn IDIOT, IMBECILE, MORON mean one who is mentally defective and technically designate three grades of mental deficiency. An IDIOT is incapable of coherent speech and of avoiding ordinary hazards and therefore requires constant care; an IMBECILE is incapable of earning a living but can be taught to attend to his simple wants and to avoid ordinary dangers; a MORON can learn a simple trade but requires constant supervision in work and play

id·i·ot·ic \,id-ē-'ät-ik\ *adj* : characterized by idiocy : FOOLISH — **id·i·ot·i·cal·ly** \-'ät-i-k(ə-)lē\ *adv*

¹idle \'īd-ᵊl\ *adj* **idler** \'īd-lər, -ᵊl-ər\; **idlest** \'īd-ləst, -ᵊl-əst** [OE *īdel*] **1** : not based on facts : WORTHLESS ⟨*idle* rumor⟩⟨mere *idle* talk⟩ **2** : USELESS ⟨it is *idle* to want what you cannot have⟩ **3** : not employed : doing nothing ⟨*idle* workmen⟩⟨*idle* machines⟩ **4** : LAZY **syn** see INACTIVE, VAIN — **idle·ness** \'īd-ᵊl-nəs\ *n* — **idly** \'īd-lē\ *adv*

²idle *vb* **idled; idling** \'īd-liŋ, -ᵊl-iŋ\ **1 a** : to spend time in idleness **b** : to move idly **2** : to run disconnected so that power is not used for useful work ⟨the engine is *idling*⟩ **3** : to pass in idleness : WASTE — **idler** \'īd-lər, -ᵊl-ər\ *n*

idol \'īd-ᵊl\ *n* [Gk *eidōlon* image, idol, fr. *eidos* form] **1** : an image of a god made or used as an object of worship **2** : one that is very greatly or excessively loved and admired

idol·a·ter \ī-'däl-ət-ər\ *n* [Gk *eidōlolatrēs*, fr. *eidōlon* idol + *-latrēs* wor-

idol 1

shiper] **1 :** a worshiper of idols **2 :** a person that admires or loves intensely and often blindly — **idol·a·tress** \-'däl-ə-trəs\ n

idol·a·trous \ī-'däl-ə-trəs\ adj **1 :** of, relating to, or having the character of idolatry **2 :** given to idolatry — **idol·a·trous·ly** adv — **idol·a·trous·ness** n

idol·a·try \-trē\ n, pl **-tries** **1 :** the worship of a physical object as a god **2 :** immoderate attachment or devotion to something

idol·ize \'īd-ᵊl-,īz\ vb **1 :** to worship idolatrously **2 :** to love or admire to excess — **idol·i·za·tion** \,īd-ᵊl-ə-'zā-shən\ n — **idol·iz·er** \'īd-ᵊl-,ī-zər\ n

idyll or **idyl** \'īd-ᵊl\ n [Gk eidyllion, fr. dim. of eidos form] **1 a :** a simple poetic or prose work descriptive of peaceful rustic life or pastoral scenes **b :** a romantic narrative poem **2 :** a fit subject for an idyll — **idyl·lic** \ī-'dil-ik\ adj — **idyl·li·cal·ly** \-'dil-i-k(ə-)lē\ adv

-ie also **-y** \ē\ n suffix, pl **-ies** [ME] **1 :** little one : dear little one (birdie) (sonny) — sometimes in names of articles of apparel (pantie) **2 :** one belonging to : one having to do with (towny) **3 :** one of (such) a kind or quality (cutie) (toughie)

-ier — see -ER

¹**if** \(,)if, əf\ conj [OE gif] **1 :** in the event that (come if you can) **2 :** WHETHER (asked if the mail had come) **3 —** used as a function word to introduce an exclamation expressing a wish (if it would only rain) **4 :** even though (an interesting if untenable argument)

²**if** \'if\ n **1 :** CONDITION, STIPULATION **2 :** SUPPOSITION

-if·er·ous \'if-(ə-)rəs\ adj comb form : -FEROUS

if·fy \'if-ē\ adj [if] : abounding in contingencies or unknown qualities or conditions

-i·form \ə-,form\ adj comb form : -FORM (ramiform)

-i·fy \ə-,fī\ vb suffix **-i·fied; -i·fy·ing** [OF -ifier, fr. L -ificare, fr. -i- + -ficare -fy] : -FY

ig·loo \'ig-lü\ n, pl **igloos** [Eskimo iglu house] **1 :** an Eskimo house often made of snow blocks and in the shape of a dome **2 :** a structure shaped like a dome

ig·ne·ous \'ig-nē-əs\ adj [L igneus, fr. ignis fire] **1 :** of, relating to, or resembling fire : FIERY **2 :** formed by solidification of molten magma (igneous rock)

igloo

ig·nes·cent \ig-'nes-ᵊnt\ adj **1 :** capable of emitting sparks **2 :** flaring up

ig·nis fat·u·us \,ig-nəs-'fach-ə-wəs\ n, pl **ig·nes fat·ui** \-,nēz-'fach-ə-,wī\ [ML, lit., foolish fire] **1 :** a light that sometimes appears in the night over marshy ground and is often attributable to the combustion of gas from decomposed organic matter **2 :** WILL-O'-THE-WISP 2

ig·nit·a·ble \ig-'nīt-ə-bəl\ adj : capable of being ignited

ig·nite \ig-'nīt\ vb [L ignire, fr. ignis fire] **1 a :** to set afire (ignite a piece of paper); also : KINDLE (ignite a fire) **b :** to cause (a fuel mixture) to burn **2 :** to catch fire (dry wood ignites quickly) — **ig·nit·er** or **ig·ni·tor** \-'nīt-ər\ n

ig·ni·tion \ig-'nish-ən\ n **1 :** the act or action of igniting : KINDLING **2 :** the process or means (as an electric spark) of igniting a fuel mixture

ig·no·ble \ig-'nō-bəl\ adj [L ignobilis, fr. in- ¹in- + nobilis, gnobilis noble] **1 :** of low birth : PLEBEIAN **2 :** characterized by baseness or meanness (ignoble conduct) — **ig·no·ble·ness** n — **ig·no·bly** \-blē\ adv

ig·no·min·i·ous \,ig-nə-'min-ē-əs\ adj **1 :** marked by disgrace or shame : DISHONORABLE **2 :** DESPICABLE **3 :** HUMILIATING, DEGRADING — **ig·no·min·i·ous·ly** adv — **ig·no·min·i·ous·ness** n

ig·no·mi·ny \'ig-nə-,min-ē, ig-'näm-ə-nē\ n, pl **-nies** [L ignominia, fr. ig- ¹in- (as in ignorare to ignore) + nomin-, nomen name, repute] **1 :** deep personal humiliation and disgrace : DISHONOR **2 :** disgraceful conduct, quality, or action

ig·no·ra·mus \,ig-nə-'rā-məs\ n, pl **-mus·es** [fr. Ignoramus, an ignorant lawyer in Ignoramus (1615), a play by George Ruggle] : an utterly ignorant person : DUNCE

ig·no·rance \'ig-nə-rən(t)s\ n : the state of being ignorant

ig·no·rant \-rənt\ adj [L ignorare to be ignorant of, ignore] **1 :** having no knowledge or very little knowledge : not educated **2 :** not knowing : UNAWARE (ignorant of the true facts) **3 :** resulting from or showing lack of

knowledge (an ignorant mistake) — **ig·no·rant·ly** adv — **ig·no·rant·ness** n

syn ILLITERATE: IGNORANT indicates a lack of knowledge in general or of a particular thing; ILLITERATE implies inability to read or write or complete unfamiliarity with the world of learning (the vast problem of teaching the illiterate millions of this world)

ig·nore \ig-'nō(ə)r, -'nȯ(ə)r\ vt [L ignorare to be ignorant of, ignore, fr. ignarus ignorant, fr. in- ¹in- + gnarus having knowledge; akin to E know] : to refuse to take notice of (ignore an interruption) — **ig·nor·er** n

Igraine \i-'grān\ n : the wife of Uther and mother of Arthur in Arthurian legend

igua·na \i-'gwän-ə\ n [Sp, of AmerInd origin] : any of various large herbivorous tropical American lizards with a serrated dorsal crest that are locally important as human food

IHS \,ī-,āch-'es\ [LL, part transliteration of Gk IHΣ, abbreviation for IHΣOTΣ Iēsous Jesus] — used as a Christian symbol and monogram for Jesus

ikon var of ICON

il- — see IN-

il·e·i·tis \,il-ē-'īt-əs\ n : inflammation of the ileum

il·e·um \'il-ē-əm\ n, pl **il·ea** \-ē-ə\ [L ilium, ileum groin, viscera] : the part of the small intestine between the jejunum and the large intestine — **il·e·al** \-ē-əl\ adj

il·e·us \'il-ē-əs\ n [L, fr. Gk eileos, fr. eilyein to roll] : obstruction of the intestine

ilex \'ī-,leks\ n [L] **1 :** a southern European evergreen oak — called also holm oak **2 :** HOLLY

il·i·um \'il-ē-əm\ n, pl **il·ia** \-ē-ə\ [NL, fr. L, groin] : the dorsal and upper one of the three bones composing either lateral half of the pelvis — **il·i·ac** \-ē-,ak\ adj

ilk \'ilk\ n [ME, pron., same, fr. OE ilca] : SORT, FAMILY — used chiefly in the phrase of that ilk

il·ka \'il-kə\ adj, chiefly Scot : EACH, EVERY

¹**ill** \'il\ adj **worse** \'wərs\; **worst** \'wərst\ [ME, fr. ON illr evil] **1 :** showing or implying evil intention (ill deeds) **2 a :** causing suffering or distress : DISAGREEABLE (ill weather) **b** (1) **:** not normal or sound : FAILING (ill health) (2) **:** not in good health (an ill person); also : NAUSEATED (felt ill) **3 :** UNFORTUNATE, UNLUCKY (ill omen) **4 :** UNKIND, UNFRIENDLY (ill feeling) **5 :** not right or proper (ill use of power) **syn** see SICK

²**ill** adv **worse; worst** **1 a :** with displeasure (the remark was ill received) **b :** HARSHLY (ill treated) **2 :** in a reprehensible manner (ill-gotten gains) **3 :** SCARCELY (can ill afford it) **4 :** BADLY, POORLY (ill equipped)

³**ill** n **1 :** EVIL **2 a :** MISFORTUNE **b :** SICKNESS **c :** TROUBLE, AFFLICTION **3 :** something that reflects unfavorably

I'll \(,)īl\ : I shall : I will

ill–ad·vised \,il-əd-'vīzd\ adj : showing lack of wise and sufficient counsel or deliberation : UNWISE — **ill–ad·vis·ed·ly** \-'vī-zəd-lē\ adv

ill–bred \'il-'bred\ adj : badly brought up : IMPOLITE

il·le·gal \il-'(l)ē-gəl\ adj : not lawful — **il·le·gal·i·ty** \,il-ē-'gal-ət-ē\ n — **il·le·gal·ly** \il-'(l)ē-gə-lē\ adv

il·leg·i·ble \il-'(l)ej-ə-bəl\ adj : not legible : impossible or very hard to read (illegible handwriting) **syn** see UNREADABLE — **il·leg·i·bil·i·ty** \il-,ej-ə-'bil-ət-ē\ n — **il·leg·i·bly** \il-'(l)ej-ə-blē\ adv

il·le·git·i·mate \,il-i-'jit-ə-mət\ adj **1 :** born of a father and mother who are not married **2 :** not correctly deduced or reasoned (an illegitimate conclusion) **3 :** not lawful or proper — **il·le·git·i·ma·cy** \-'jit-ə-mə-sē\ n — **il·le·git·i·mate·ly** adv

ill–fat·ed \'il-'fāt-əd\ adj : having an evil fate : UNFORTUNATE — **ill–fated** adj : ill-fated expedition)

ill–fa·vored \-'fā-vərd\ adj **1 :** unattractive in physical appearance; esp : having an ugly face **2 :** OFFENSIVE

ill–got·ten \-'gät-ᵊn\ adj : acquired by evil means

ill–hu·mored \'il-'hyü-mərd, -'yü-\ adj : SURLY, IRRITABLE — **ill–hu·mored·ly** adv

il·lib·er·al \il-'(l)ib-(ə-)rəl\ adj : not liberal : as **a** archaic : not generous : STINGY **b :** not broad-minded : BIGOTED **c :** opposed to liberalism — **il·lib·er·al·i·ty** \il-,ib-ə-'ral-ət-ē\ n — **il·lib·er·al·ly** \-'(l)ib-(ə-)rə-lē\ adv — **il·lib·er·al·ness** n

il·lic·it \il-'(l)is-ət\ adj : not permitted : UNLAWFUL — **il·lic·it·ly** adv

il·lim·it·a·ble \il-'(l)im-ət-ə-bəl\ adj : incapable of being limited : BOUNDLESS — **il·lim·it·a·bil·i·ty** \-,(l)im-ət-ə-'bil-ət-ē\ *n* — **il·lim·it·a·ble·ness** \-'(l)im-ət-ə-bəl--nəs\ *n* — **il·lim·it·a·bly** \-blē\ *adv*

il·lit·er·a·cy \il-'(l)it-ə-rə-sē, -'(l)i-trə-sē\ *n, pl* **-cies** **1** : the quality or state of being illiterate; *esp* : inability to read or write **2** : a mistake or crudity made by one who is illiterate

il·lit·er·ate \-'(l)it-ə-rət, -'(l)i-trət\ *adj* **1** : having little or no education; *esp* : unable to read or write **2 a** : showing or marked by a lack of familiarity with language and literature **b** : showing ignorance of the fundamentals of a particular field of knowledge **syn** see IGNORANT — **illiterate** *n* — **il·lit·er·ate·ly** *adv* — **il·lit·er·ate·ness** *n*

ill–man·nered \'il-'man-ərd\ *adj* : marked by bad manners : RUDE

ill–na·tured \-'nā-chərd\ *adj* : having a bad disposition : CROSS, SURLY — **ill–na·tured·ly** *adv*

ill·ness \'il-nəs\ *n* : an unhealthy condition of body or mind : SICKNESS

il·log·i·cal \il-'(l)äj-i-kəl\ *adj* : not observing the principles of logic or good reasoning — **il·log·i·cal·ly** \-i-k(ə-)lē\ *adv* — **il·log·i·cal·ness** \-kəl-nəs\ *n*

ill–starred \'il-'stärd\ *adj* : ILL-FATED, UNLUCKY ⟨ill-starred lovers⟩

ill–tem·pered \-'tem-pərd\ *adj* : ILL-NATURED, QUARREL-SOME — **ill–tem·pered·ly** *adv*

ill–treat \-'trēt\ *vt* : to treat cruelly or improperly : MAL-TREAT — **ill–treat·ment** \-mənt\ *n*

il·lume \il-'üm\ *vt* : ILLUMINATE

il·lu·mi·nant \il-'ü-mə-nənt\ *n* : an illuminating device (as an electric lamp) or substance (as natural gas)

il·lu·mi·nate \-,nāt\ *vt* [L *illuminare,* fr. *in-* [2]*in-* + *lumin-, lumen* light] **1 a** : to supply or brighten with light : light up ⟨*illuminate* a building⟩ **b** : ENLIGHTEN **2** : to make clear : ELUCIDATE ⟨*illuminated* the subject with explanatory comments⟩ **3** : to decorate (as a manuscript) with gold or silver or brilliant colors or with elaborate designs or miniature pictures — **il·lu·mi·na·tive** \-,nāt-iv\ *adj* — **il·lu·mi·na·tor** \-,nāt-ər\ *n*

illuminating gas *n* : a gas that is burned for illumination

il·lu·mi·na·tion \il-,ü-mə-'nā-shən\ *n* **1** : the action of illuminating or state of being illuminated: as **a** : spiritual or intellectual enlightenment **b** : decorative lighting or lighting effects **c** : decoration by the art of illuminating **2** : the quantity of light or the luminous flux per unit area on an intercepting surface at any given point

il·lu·mine \il-'ü-mən\ *vt* : ILLUMINATE

ill–us·age \'il-'yü-sij, -'yü-zij\ *n* : harsh or abusive treatment

ill–use \-'yüz\ *vt* : MALTREAT, ABUSE — **ill–use** \-'yüs\ *n*

il·lu·sion \il-'ü-zhən\ *n* [L *illus-, illudere* to mock at, fr. *in-* [2]*in-* + *ludere* to play] **1** : a misleading image presented to the eye **2** : the state or fact of being led to accept as true something unreal or imagined **3** : a mistaken idea ⟨*illusions* of childhood about the world of grown-ups⟩ **syn** see DELUSION — **il·lu·sion·ary** \-zhə-,ner-ē\ *adj*

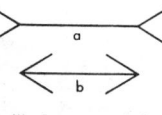

illusion: *a* equals *b*

il·lu·sion·ist \il-'üzh-(ə-)nəst\ *n* : one that produces illusions; *esp* : a ventriloquist or sleight-of-hand performer

il·lu·sive \il-'ü-siv, -'ü-ziv\ *adj* : ILLUSORY — **il·lu·sive·ly** *adv* — **il·lu·sive·ness** *n*

il·lu·so·ry \il-'üs-(ə)-rē, -'üz-(ə)-\ *adj* : based on or producing illusion : DECEPTIVE ⟨inflation gave the nation an *illusory* appearance of prosperity⟩ — **il·lu·so·ri·ly** \-rə-lē\ *adv* — **il·lu·so·ri·ness** \-rē-nəs\ *n*

il·lus·trate \'il-ə-,strāt\ *vb* [L *illustrare,* fr. *in-* [2]*in-* + *lustrare* to make bright] **1** : to make clear esp. by giving or by serving as an example or instance ⟨*illustrated* his point with cases from his own experience⟩ **2 a** : to provide with pictures or figures intended to explain or decorate ⟨*illustrate* a book with color plates⟩ **b** : to serve to explain or decorate ⟨*illustrates* the operation of a computer⟩ **3** : DEMONSTRATE — **il·lus·tra·tor** \-,strāt-ər\ *n*

il·lus·tra·tion \,il-ə-'strā-shən\ *n* **1** : the action of illustrating : the condition of being illustrated **2 a** : an example or instance intended to make something clear **b** : a picture or diagram intended to explain or decorate

il·lus·tra·tive \il-'əs-trət-iv\ *adj* : serving, tending, or de-

signed to illustrate ⟨an *illustrative* diagram⟩ ⟨*illustrative* examples⟩ — **il·lus·tra·tive·ly** *adv*

il·lus·tri·ous \il-'əs-trē-əs\ *adj* : notably outstanding because of rank or achievement : EMINENT — **il·lus·tri·ous·ly** *adv* — **il·lus·tri·ous·ness** *n*

ill will *n* : unfriendly feeling

ill–wish·er \'il-'wish-ər\ *n* : one that wishes ill to another

il·ly \'il-(l)ē\ *adv* : BADLY, ILL ⟨*illy* chosen⟩

il·men·ite \'il-mə-,nīt\ *n* : an iron-black mineral composed of iron, titanium, and oxygen that is an ore of titanium

im– — see IN-

I'm \(,)īm\ : I am

[1]**im·age** \'im-ij\ *n* [OF, fr. L *imago*] **1** : a reproduction or imitation of the form of a person or thing; *esp* : an imitation in solid form : DEVICE **2 a** : a picture of an object produced by a lens, a mirror, or an electronic system **b** : a likeness of an object produced on a photographic material **3** : exact likeness **4 a** : a tangible or visible representation : INCARNATION **b** *archaic* : an illusory form : APPARITION **5 a** : a mental picture of something not actually present : IMPRESSION **b** : IDEA, CONCEPT **6** : a vivid or graphic representation or description **7** : something introduced to represent something else that it strikingly resembles or suggests (as the use of *sleep* for *death*) **8** : a person strikingly like another person ⟨the boy is the *image* of his father⟩

[2]**image** *vt* **1** : to describe or portray in language esp. vividly **2** : to call up a mental picture of : IMAGINE **3 a** : REFLECT, MIRROR **b** : to make appear : PROJECT **4 a** : to create a representation of **b** : to represent symbolically

im·ag·ery \'im-ij-(ə-)rē\ *n, pl* **-er·ies** **1** : the product of image makers : IMAGES; *also* : the art of making images **2** : figurative language ⟨*imagery* of a poem⟩ **3** : mental images; *esp* : the products of imagination

imag·in·a·ble \im-'aj-(ə-)nə-bəl\ *adj* : capable of being imagined : CONCEIVABLE — **imag·in·a·bly** \-blē\ *adv*

imag·i·nary \im-'aj-ə-,ner-ē\ *adj* : existing only in imagination : FANCIED — **imag·i·nar·i·ly** \-,maj-ə-'ner-ə-lē\ *adv* — **imag·i·nar·i·ness** \-'maj-ə-,ner-ē-nəs\ *n*

imaginary number *n* **1** : an even root of a negative number — called also *imaginary* **2** : a complex number in which the part (as $3\sqrt{-1}$ in $2 + 3\sqrt{-1}$) containing the positive square root of minus 1 is not equal to zero

imag·i·na·tion \im-,aj-ə-'nā-shən\ *n* **1** : the act or power of forming a mental image of something not present to the senses or never before wholly perceived in reality **2 a** : creative ability **b** : ability to confront and deal with a problem : RESOURCEFULNESS **3 a** : a creation of the mind; *esp* : an idealized or poetic creation **b** : fanciful or empty assumption **4** : popular or traditional belief or conception

imag·i·na·tive \im-'aj-(ə-)nət-iv, -'aj-ə-,nāt-\ *adj* **1** : of, relating to, or characterized by imagination **2** : given to imagining : having a lively imagination **3** : of or relating to images; *esp* : showing a command of imagery — **imag·i·na·tive·ly** *adv* — **imag·i·na·tive·ness** *n*

imag·ine \im-'aj-ən\ *vb* **imag·ined; imag·in·ing** \-'aj-(ə-)niŋ\ [L *imaginari,* fr *imagin-, imago* image] **1** : to form a mental image of something not present : use the imagination **2** : THINK, SUPPOSE, GUESS ⟨I *imagine* it will rain⟩

im·ag·ism \'im-ij-,iz-əm\ *n* : a movement in poetry advocating free verse and the expression of ideas and emotions through clear precise images — **im·ag·ist** \-ij-əst\ *n* — **imagist** *or* **im·ag·is·tic** \,im-ij-'is-tik\ *adj* — **im·ag·is·ti·cal·ly** \,im-ij-'is-ti-k(ə-)lē\ *adv*

ima·go \im-'ā-gō, -'äg-ō\ *n, pl* **imagoes** *or* **ima·gi·nes** \-'ā-gə-,nēz, -'äg-ə-\ [NL, fr. L, image] : an insect in its final adult, sexually mature, and usu. winged state — **ima·gi·nal** \-'ā-gən-ºl, -'äg-ən-\ *adj*

imam \i-'mäm, -'mam\ *n* [Ar *imām*] **1** : the prayer leader of a mosque **2** *cap* : a Muslim leader held to be a divinely appointed successor of Muhammad **3** : any of various Muslim rulers that claim descent from Muhammad — **imam·ate** \-,āt\ *n, often cap*

im·bal·ance \(')im-'bal-ən(t)s\ *n* : lack of balance : the state of being out of equilibrium or out of proportion

im·be·cile \'im-bə-səl, -,sil\ *n* [L *imbecillus* weak, weak-minded] **1** : a mentally deficient person; *esp* : a feeble-minded person having a mental age of three to seven years

ə abut; ə kitten; ər further; a back; ā bake; ä cot, cart; au̇ out; ch chin; e less; ē easy; g gift; i trip; ī life

and requiring supervision in the performance of routine daily tasks of caring for himself **2** : FOOL, SIMPLETON **syn** see IDIOT — **imbecile** *or* **im·be·cil·ic** \,im-bə-'sil-ik\ *adj* — **im·be·cile·ly** \'im-bə-sə(l)-lē, -,sil-lē\ *adv*

im·be·cil·i·ty \,im-bə-'sil-ət-ē\ *n, pl* **-ties 1** : the quality or state of being imbecile or an imbecile **2 a** : utter foolishness; *also* : FUTILITY **b** : something that is foolish or nonsensical

imbed *var of* EMBED

im·bibe \im-'bīb\ *vb* [L *imbibere* to drink in, fr. *in-* + *bibere* to drink] **1** : to receive into the mind and retain ⟨*imbibe* knowledge⟩ **2 a** : DRINK **b** : to drink in : ABSORB ⟨sponges *imbibe* moisture⟩ — **im·bib·er** *n*

im·bi·bi·tion \,im-bə-'bish-ən\ *n* : the act or action of imbibing; *esp* : the taking up of fluid by a colloidal system resulting in swelling — **im·bi·bi·tion·al** \-'bish-nəl, -ən-°l\ *adj*

imbitter *var of* EMBITTER

imbosom *var of* EMBOSOM

¹im·bri·cate \'im-bri-kət\ *adj* [L *imbric-, imbrex* roofing tile, fr. *imber* rain] : lying lapped over each other in regular order ⟨*imbricate* scales⟩ — **im·bri·cate·ly** *adv*

²im·bri·cate \'im-brə-,kāt\ *vb* : OVERLAP

im·bri·ca·tion \,im-brə-'kā-shən\ *n* **1** : an overlapping of edges (as of tiles) **2** : a decoration or pattern showing imbrication

im·bro·glio \im-'brōl-yō\ *n, pl* **-glios** [It, fr. *imbrogliare* to embroil, fr. F *embrouiller*] **1** : a confused mass ⟨an *imbroglio* of papers and books⟩ **2 a** : an intricate or complicated situation (as in a novel) **b** : an acutely painful or embarrassing misunderstanding : EMBROILMENT ⟨an *imbroglio* between foreign ministers⟩

imbrown *var of* EMBROWN

im·brue \im-'brü\ *vt* [ME *embrewen*] : DRENCH, STAIN ⟨*imbrued* with blood⟩

im·brute \im-'brüt\ *vb* : to sink or degrade to the level of a brute

im·bue \im-'byü\ *vt* [L *imbuere*] **1** : to tinge or dye deeply **2** : to cause to become penetrated : PERMEATE ⟨men *imbued* with a deep sense of loyalty to their country⟩

im·i·ta·ble \'im-ət-ə-bəl\ *adj* : capable or worthy of being imitated or copied

im·i·tate \'im-ə-,tāt\ *vt* [L *imitari*] **1** : to follow as a pattern, model, or example **2** : to be or appear similar to : RESEMBLE **3** : to copy exactly : COUNTERFEIT — **im·i·ta·tor** \-,tāt-ər\ *n*

syn MIMIC, APE, MOCK : IMITATE suggests following a model or a pattern but may allow for some variation; MIMIC implies a close copying as of voice or mannerism often for fun, ridicule, or lifelike imitation ⟨*mimicked* the bird's notes⟩ ⟨children *mimicking* adults⟩ APE may suggest presumptuous, slavish, or inept imitating of a superior original ⟨peasants *aping* their feudal lords⟩ MOCK usu. implies imitation with derision

¹im·i·ta·tion \,im-ə-'tā-shən\ *n* **1** : an act of imitating **2** : something produced as a copy **3** : a literary work designed to reproduce the style of another author **4** : the repetition in a voice part of the melodic theme, phrase, or motive previously found in another part **5** : participation by a sensible object in a transcendent idea — **im·i·ta·tion·al** \-shnəl, -shən-°l\ *adj*

²imitation *adj* : resembling something else esp. of better quality : not real ⟨*imitation* leather⟩

im·i·ta·tive \'im-ə-,tāt-iv\ *adj* **1 a** : marked by imitation **b** : ONOMATOPOEIC **c** : exhibiting mimicry **2** : inclined to imitate **3** : imitating something superior — **im·i·ta·tive·ly** *adv* — **im·i·ta·tive·ness** *n*

im·mac·u·late \im-'ak-yə-lət\ *adj* [L *macula* stain] **1** : having no stain or blemish : PURE ⟨an *immaculate* heart⟩ **2** : containing no flaw or error **3** : spotlessly clean ⟨*immaculate* linen⟩ — **im·mac·u·late·ly** *adv* — **im·mac·u·late·ness** *n*

Immaculate Conception *n* : December 8 observed as a Roman Catholic festival in commemoration of the conception of the Virgin Mary as free from original sin

im·ma·nent \'im-ə-nənt\ *adj* [LL *immanēre* to remain in, fr. L *in-* + *manēre* to remain] **1** : INDWELLING; *esp* : having existence only in the mind **2** : dwelling in nature and the souls of men — compare TRANSCENDENT — **im·ma·nence** \-nən(t)s\ *or* **im·ma·nen·cy** \-nən-sē\ *n* — **im·ma·nent·ly** *adv*

im·ma·te·ri·al \,im-ə-'tir-ē-əl\ *adj* **1** : not consisting of matter : INCORPOREAL **2** : of no consequence : UNIMPORTANT — **im·ma·te·ri·al·i·ty** \-,tir-ē-'al-ət-ē\ *n* — **im·ma·te·ri·al·ly** \-'tir-ē-ə-lē\ *adv* — **im·ma·te·ri·al·ness** *n*

im·ma·ture \,im-ə-'t(y)ú(ə)r\ *adj* **1** : lacking complete development : not yet mature **2** : YOUNG, UNRIPE **2** : CRUDE, UNFINISHED — **immature** *n* — **im·ma·ture·ly** *adv* — **im·ma·ture·ness** *n* — **im·ma·tu·ri·ty** \-'t(y)ùr-ət-ē\ *n*

im·mea·sur·a·ble \('m-'ezh-(ə-)rə-bəl, -'ezh-ər-bəl, -'āzh-\ *adj* : incapable of being measured : indefinitely extensive ⟨the *immeasurable* sea⟩ — **im·mea·sur·a·ble·ness** *n* — **im·mea·sur·a·bly** \-blē\ *adv*

im·me·di·a·cy \im-'ēd-ē-ə-sē\ *n, pl* **-cies 1 a** : the quality or state of being immediate; *esp* : lack of an intervening object, place, time, or agent **b** : URGENCY **2** : something that is of immediate importance ⟨*immediacies* of daily life⟩

im·me·di·ate \im-'ēd-ē-ət\ *adj* [LL *immediatus*, fr. L *in-* ¹*in-* + *medius* middle] **1** : next in line or relationship ⟨the king's *immediate* heir⟩ **2** : closest in importance ⟨his *immediate* interest⟩ **3** : acting directly and alone without anything intervening ⟨an *immediate* cause of disease⟩ **4** : not distant or separated : NEXT ⟨their *immediate* neighbors⟩ **5** : close in time ⟨the *immediate* past⟩ **6** : made or done at once ⟨ask for an *immediate* reply⟩ — **im·me·di·ate·ness** *n*

im·me·di·ate·ly *adv* **1** : with nothing between : DIRECTLY, CLOSELY ⟨the house *immediately* beyond this one⟩ **2** : without delay : STRAIGHTWAY ⟨do it *immediately*⟩

im·med·i·ca·ble \('')im-'ed-i-kə-bəl\ *adj* : INCURABLE — **im·med·i·ca·bly** \-blē\ *adv*

im·me·mo·ri·al \,im-ə-'mōr-ē-əl, -'mòr-\ *adj* : extending beyond the reach of memory, record, or tradition — **im·me·mo·ri·al·ly** \-ē-ə-lē\ *adv*

im·mense \im-'en(t)s\ *adj* [L *immensus* immeasurable, fr. *in-* + *mensus*, pp. of *metiri* to measure] **1** : very great in size or degree : HUGE **2** : supremely good : EXCELLENT **syn** see ENORMOUS — **im·mense·ly** *adv* — **im·mense·ness** *n*

im·men·si·ty \im-'en(t)-sət-ē\ *n, pl* **-ties 1** : the quality or state of being immense **2** : something immense

im·men·su·ra·ble \('')im-'en(t)-sə-rə-bəl, -'en-chə-\ *adj* : IMMEASURABLE

im·merge \im-'ərj\ *vi* : to plunge into or immerse oneself in something ⟨*immerge* into silence⟩

im·merse \im-'ərs\ *vt* [L *immers-, immergere*, fr. *in-* ²*in-* + *mergere* to dip] **1** : to plunge into something that surrounds or covers; *esp* : to plunge or dip into a fluid **2** : to baptize by submerging in water **3** : ENGROSS, ABSORB

im·mersed \im-'ərst\ *adj* : growing wholly under water ⟨*immersed* plants⟩

im·mer·sion \im-'ər-zhən, -shən\ *n* : an act of immersing : a state of being immersed

im·mesh \im-'esh\ *var of* ENMESH

im·mi·grant \'im-i-grənt\ *n* : one that immigrates: **a** : a person who comes to a country to become a permanent resident **b** : a plant or animal that becomes established in an area where it was previously unknown **syn** see EMIGRANT — **immigrant** *adj*

im·mi·grate \'im-ə-,grāt\ *vi* : to enter and usu. become established; *esp* : to come into a country of which one is not a native to take up permanent residence — **im·mi·gra·tion** \,im-ə-'grā-shən\ *n*

im·mi·nence \'im-ə-nən(t)s\ *n* **1** *also* **im·mi·nen·cy** \-nən-sē\ : the quality or state of being imminent **2** : something imminent; *esp* : impending evil or danger

im·mi·nent \-nənt\ *adj* [L *imminēre* to project, threaten] : ready to take place; *esp* : hanging threateningly over one's head **syn** see IMPENDING — **im·mi·nent·ly** *adv* — **im·mi·nent·ness** *n*

im·mis·ci·ble \(')im-'is-ə-bəl\ *adj* : incapable of mixing ⟨ether and water are *immiscible*⟩ — **im·mis·ci·bil·i·ty** \(,)im-,is-ə-'bil-ət-ē\ *n*

im·mit·i·ga·ble \(')im-'it-i-gə-bəl\ *adj* : not capable of being mitigated — **im·mit·i·ga·ble·ness** *n* — **im·mit·i·ga·bly** \-blē\ *adv*

im·mo·bile \(')im-'ō-bəl, -,bēl, -,bīl\ *adj* : incapable of being moved : FIXED — **im·mo·bil·i·ty** \,im-(,)ō-'bil-ət-ē\ *n*

im·mo·bi·lize \im-'ō-bə-,līz\ *vt* : to make immobile; *esp*

: to prevent freedom of movement or effective use of — **im·mo·bi·li·za·tion** \im-ˌō-bə-lə-'zā-shən\ *n* — **im·mo·bi·liz·er** \(')im-ˈō-bə-ˌlī-zər\ *n*

im·mod·er·ate \(')im-ˈäd-(ə-)rət\ *adj* : lacking in moderation : EXCESSIVE — **im·mod·er·a·cy** \-(ə-)rə-sē\ *n* — **im·mod·er·ate·ly** *adv* — **im·mod·er·ate·ness** *n* — **im·mod·er·a·tion** \(ˌ)im-ˌäd-ə-'rā-shən\ *n*

im·mod·est \(')im-ˈäd-əst\ *adj* : not modest; *esp* : INDECENT ⟨*immodest* clothing⟩ — **im·mod·est·ly** *adv* — **im·mod·es·ty** \-ə-stē\ *n*

im·mo·late \'im-ə-ˌlāt\ *vt* [L *immolare*, fr. *in-* ²in- + *mola* meal; fr. the custom of sprinkling victims with sacrificial meal] **1** : to offer in sacrifice; *esp* : to kill as a sacrificial victim **2** : KILL, DESTROY — **im·mo·la·tion** \ˌim-ə-'lā-shən\ *n* — **im·mo·la·tor** \'im-ə-ˌlāt-ər\ *n*

im·mor·al \(')im-ˈȯr-əl, -ˈär-\ *adj* : not moral : WICKED, LEWD, LICENTIOUS — **im·mor·al·ly** \-ə-lē\ *adv*

im·mor·al·ist \-ə-ləst\ *n* : an advocate of immorality

im·mo·ral·i·ty \ˌim-ˌȯ-'ral-ət-ē, ˌim-ə-'ral-\ *n, pl* **-ties** **1** : the quality or state of being immoral; *esp* : UNCHASTITY **2** : an immoral act or practice

¹im·mor·tal \(')im-ˈȯrt-ᵊl\ *adj* **1** : exempt from death ⟨the *immortal* gods⟩ **2** : connected with or relating to immortality ⟨*immortal* longings⟩ **3** : living or lasting forever ⟨*immortal* fame⟩ — **im·mor·tal·ly** \-ᵊl-ē\ *adv*

²immortal *n* **1 a** : one exempt from death **b** *pl, often cap* : the gods of the Greek and Roman pantheon **2** : a person whose fame is lasting ⟨one of the *immortals* of baseball⟩

im·mor·tal·i·ty \ˌim-ˌȯr-'tal-ət-ē\ *n* : the quality or state of being immortal: **a** : unending existence **b** : lasting fame

im·mor·tal·ize \im-ˈȯrt-ᵊl-ˌīz\ *vt* : to make immortal ⟨a man *immortalized* by his writings⟩ — **im·mor·tal·i·za·tion** \-ˌȯrt-ᵊl-ə-'zā-shən\ *n* — **im·mor·tal·iz·er** \-ˈȯrt-ᵊl-ˌī-zər\ *n*

im·mor·telle \ˌim-ˌȯr-'tel\ *n* [F, fr. fem. of *immortel* immortal] : EVERLASTING 3

im·mo·tile \(')im-ˈōt-ᵊl, -ˈō-ˌtīl\ *adj* : lacking motility — **im·mo·til·i·ty** \ˌim-ō-'til-ət-ē\ *n*

im·mov·a·ble \(')im-ˈü-və-bəl\ *adj* **1 a** : incapable of being moved ⟨*immovable* mountains⟩ **b** : STATIONARY **2 a** : STEADFAST, UNYIELDING ⟨an *immovable* purpose⟩ **b** : not capable of being moved in feeling : IMPASSIVE — **im·mov·a·bil·i·ty** \(ˌ)im-ˌü-və-'bil-ət-ē\ *n* — **im·mov·a·ble·ness** \(')im-ˈü-və-bəl-nəs\ *n* — **im·mov·a·bly** \-blē\ *adv*

im·mune \im-ˈyün\ *adj* [L *immunis*, fr. *in-* ¹in- + *munia* services, obligations] **1** : FREE, EXEMPT ⟨*immune* from punishment⟩ **2 a** : not susceptible or responsive ⟨*immune* to fatigue⟩ ⟨*immune* to persuasion⟩ **b** : having a special capacity for resistance ⟨*immune* to diphtheria⟩ **3** : containing or producing antibodies ⟨an *immune* serum⟩ — **im·mune** *n*

im·mu·ni·ty \im-ˈyü-nət-ē\ *n, pl* **-ties** : the quality or state of being immune; *esp* : bodily power to resist an infectious disease usu. by preventing development of its causative microorganism or by neutralizing poisons produced by it

im·mu·nize \'im-yə-ˌnīz\ *vt* : to make immune — **im·mu·ni·za·tion** \ˌim-yə-nə-'zā-shən\ *n*

im·mu·no·ge·net·ic \ˌim-yə-nō-jə-'net-ik\ *adj* **1** : dealing with the interrelation of disease resistance and genetic makeup **2** : of or relating to the study of biological relationships by serological means

im·mu·no·gen·ic \-'jen-ik\ *adj* : producing immunity — **im·mu·no·gen·i·cal·ly** \-i-k(ə-)lē\ *adv* — **im·mu·no·ge·nic·i·ty** \-jə-'nis-ət-ē\ *n*

im·mu·nol·o·gy \ˌim-yə-'näl-ə-jē\ *n* : a science that deals with the phenomena and causes of immunity — **im·mu·no·log·ic** \ˌim-yə-nə-'läj-ik\ *or* **im·mu·no·log·i·cal** \-'läj-i-kəl\ *adj* — **im·mu·no·log·i·cal·ly** \-i-k(ə-)lē\ *adv* — **im·mu·nol·o·gist** \ˌim-yə-'näl-ə-jəst\ *n*

im·mu·no·sup·pres·sion \ˌim-yə-nō-sə-'presh-ən\ *n* : suppression (as by drugs) of natural immune responses — **im·mu·no·sup·pres·sant** \-'pres-ᵊnt\ *n or adj* — **im·mu·no·sup·pres·sive** \-'pres-iv\ *adj*

im·mure \im-ˈyu̇(ə)r\ *vt* [ML *immurare*, fr. L *in-* ²in- + *murus* wall] **1 a** : to enclose within or as if within walls **b** : to shut up : IMPRISON **2** : to build into a wall; *esp* : to entomb in a wall — **im·mure·ment** \-mənt\ *n*

im·mu·ta·ble \(')im-ˈyüt-ə-bəl\ *adj* : not capable or susceptible of change — **im·mu·ta·bil·i·ty** \(ˌ)im-ˌyüt-ə-

'bil-ət-ē\ *n* — **im·mu·ta·ble·ness** \(')im-'yüt-ə-bəl-nəs\ *n* — **im·mu·ta·bly** \-blē\ *adv*

imp \'imp\ *n* [ME *impe* offspring, child, fr. OE *impa* bud, shoot, scion] **1** : a small demon : FIEND **2** : a mischievous child

¹im·pact \'im-ˌpakt\ *vt* [L *impact-, impingere* to impinge] **1 a** : to fix firmly by or as if by packing or wedging **b** : to press together **2** : to impinge upon

²impact \'im-ˌpakt\ *n* **1 a** : an impinging or striking (as of one body against another) **b** : a forceful contact, collision, or onset; *also* : the impetus communicated in or as if in a collision **2** : the force of impression or operation of one thing on another : EFFECT ⟨the full *impact* of war upon the world⟩

im·pact·ed \im-'pak-təd\ *adj* : wedged between the jawbone and another tooth

im·pac·tion \im-'pak-shən\ *n* : the act of becoming or the state of being impacted; *also* : lodgment of something (as feces) in a body passage or cavity

im·pair \im-'pa(ə)r, -'pe(ə)r\ *vt* [MF *empeirer*, fr. (assumed) VL *impejorare*, fr. L *in-* ²in- + L *pejor* worse] : to diminish in quantity, value, excellence, or strength : DAMAGE — **im·pair·er** *n* — **im·pair·ment** \-mənt\ *n*

im·pa·la \im-'pal-ə, -'päl-\ *n* [Zulu] : a large brownish African antelope that in the male has slender lyrate horns

im·pale \im-'pāl\ *vt* : to pierce with or as if with something pointed; *esp* : to torture or kill by fixing on a sharp stake — **im·pale·ment** \-mənt\ *n*

im·pal·pa·ble \(')im-'pal-pə-bəl\ *adj* **1** : incapable of being felt by the touch : INTANGIBLE **2** : not readily discerned or apprehended — **im·pal·pa·bil·i·ty** \(ˌ)im-ˌpal-pə-'bil-ət-ē\ *n* — **im·pal·pa·bly** \(')im-'pal-pə-blē\ *adv*

im·pan·el \im-'pan-ᵊl\ *vt* **-eled** *or* **-elled; -el·ing** *or* **-el·ling** : to enter in or on a panel or list : ENROLL

im·par·a·dise \im-'par-ə-ˌdīs, -ˌdīz\ *vt* : to put in paradise : ENRAPTURE

im·par·i·ty \(')im-'par-ət-ē\ *n, pl* **-ties** : INEQUALITY, DISPARITY

im·part \im-'pärt\ *vt* **1** : to give or grant from one's store or abundance : TRANSMIT ⟨the sun *imparts* warmth⟩ **2** : to communicate the knowledge of : DISCLOSE ⟨*imparted* her plans⟩ — **im·part·a·ble** \-ə-bəl\ *adj* — **im·par·ta·tion** \ˌim-ˌpär-'tā-shən\ *n* — **im·part·ment** \im-'pärt-mənt\ *n*

im·par·tial \(')im-'pär-shəl\ *adj* : not partial : UNBIASED **syn** see FAIR — **im·par·ti·al·i·ty** \(ˌ)im-ˌpär-shē-'al-ət-ē, -ˌpär-'shal-\ *n* — **im·par·tial·ly** \(')im-'pärsh-(ə-)lē\ *adv*

im·pass·a·ble \(')im-'pas-ə-bəl\ *adj* : incapable of being passed, traversed, or circulated — **im·pass·a·bil·i·ty** \(ˌ)im-ˌpas-ə-'bil-ət-ē\ *n* — **im·pass·a·ble·ness** \(')im-'pas-ə-bəl-nəs\ *n* — **im·pass·a·bly** \-blē\ *adv*

im·passe \'im-ˌpas, im-'\ *n* [F, fr. *in-* ¹in- + *passer* to pass] **1** : an impassable road or way **2 a** : a predicament from which there is no obvious escape **b** : DEADLOCK

im·pas·si·ble \(')im-'pas-ə-bəl\ *adj* [LL *impassibilis* incapable of feeling, fr. L *in-* ¹in- + *pass-, pati* to suffer] **1 a** : incapable of suffering or of experiencing pain **b** : inaccessible to injury **2** : incapable of feeling : IMPASSIVE — **im·pas·si·bil·i·ty** \(ˌ)im-ˌpas-ə-'bil-ət-ē\ *n* — **im·pas·si·bly** \(')im-'pas-ə-blē\ *adv*

im·pas·sioned \im-'pash-ənd\ *adj* : filled with passion or zeal : showing great warmth or intensity of feeling ⟨*impassioned* plea for justice⟩

syn IMPASSIONED, PASSIONATE mean showing intense feeling. IMPASSIONED implies warmth and intensity without violence and suggests a fluent verbal expression; PASSIONATE implies great vehemence and often violence and wasteful diffusion of emotion

im·pas·sive \(')im-'pas-iv\ *adj* **1** : not feeling or not showing any emotion : CALM, UNMOVED ⟨an *impassive* expression on his face⟩ **2** : MOTIONLESS — **im·pas·sive·ly** *adv* — **im·pas·sive·ness** \im-'pas-siv-i-ty\ \ˌim-ˌpas-'iv-ət-ē\ *n*

syn IMPASSIVE, APATHETIC, STOLID, PHLEGMATIC mean unresponsive to something that might normally excite interest or emotion. IMPASSIVE stresses the absence of any external sign of emotion in action or facial expression; APATHETIC may imply a puzzling or deplorable indifference or inertness ⟨a public *apathetic* to the evils of gambling⟩ STOLID implies an habitual absence of interest, responsiveness, or curiosity; PHLEGMATIC implies a temperament hard to arouse

im·pas·to \im-'pas-tō, -'päs-\ *n* [It] **:** the thick application of a pigment to a canvas or panel in painting; *also* **:** the body of pigment so applied

im·pa·tience \(')im-'pā-shən(t)s\ *n* **:** the quality or state of being impatient: as **a :** restlessness of spirit (as under irritation, delay, or opposition) **b :** restless or eager desire or longing

im·pa·tiens \im-'pā-shənz, -shən(t)s, -shē-,enz\ *n* [NL, genus name, fr. L, impatient] **:** any of a large genus of watery-juiced annual herbs with often showy irregular flowers

im·pa·tient \(')im-'pā-shənt\ *adj* **1 a :** not patient : restless or short of temper esp. under irritation, delay, or opposition ⟨an *impatient* disposition⟩ **b :** INTOLERANT ⟨*impatient* of poverty⟩ **2 :** prompted or marked by impatience ⟨an *impatient* answer⟩ **3 :** eagerly desirous : ANXIOUS — **im·pa·tient·ly** *adv*

im·peach \im-'pēch\ *vt* [MF *empeechier* to hinder, fr. LL *impedicare* to fetter, fr. L *in-* [2]in- + *pedica* fetter, fr. *ped-, pes* foot] **1 :** to charge (a public official) before a competent tribunal with misconduct in office **2 :** to cast doubt on; *esp* **:** to challenge the credibility or validity of ⟨*impeach* the testimony of a witness⟩ — **im·peach·a·ble** \-'pē-chə-bəl\ *adj* — **im·peach·ment** \-'pēch-mənt\ *n*

im·pearl \im-'pərl\ *vt* **:** to form into pearls; *also* **:** to form of or adorn with pearls

im·pec·ca·ble \(')im-'pek-ə-bəl\ *adj* [L *peccare* to sin] **1 :** not capable of sinning or liable to sin **2 :** free from fault or blame : FLAWLESS ⟨a man of *impeccable* character⟩ — **im·pec·ca·bil·i·ty** \(,)im-,pek-ə-'bil-ət-ē\ *n* — **im·pec·ca·bly** \(')im-'pek-ə-blē\ *adv*

im·pe·cu·ni·ous \,im-pi-'kyü-nē-əs, -nyəs\ *adj* [L *pecunia* money] **:** having very little or no money usu. habitually : PENNILESS — **im·pe·cu·ni·os·i·ty** \-,kyü-nē-'äs-ət-ē\ *n* — **im·pe·cu·ni·ous·ly** \-'kyü-nē-əs-lē, -nyəs-\ *adv* — **im·pe·cu·ni·ous·ness** *n*

im·ped·ance \im-'pēd-ᵊn(t)s\ *n* **:** the apparent opposition in an electrical circuit to the flow of an alternating current as a result of a combination of resistance and reactance

im·pede \im-'pēd\ *vt* [L *impedire*, fr. *in-* [2]in- + *ped-, pes* foot] **:** to interfere with the progress of : BLOCK, HINDER ⟨traffic *impeded* by heavy rain⟩ — **im·ped·er** *n*

im·ped·i·ment \im-'ped-ə-mənt\ *n* [L *impedimentum*, fr. *impedire* to impede] **1 :** something that impedes, hinders, or obstructs **2 :** a defect in speech

im·ped·i·men·ta \im-,ped-ə-'ment-ə\ *n pl* [L, pl. of *impedimentum* impediment] **:** things (as baggage or supplies) that impede

im·pel \im-'pel\ *vt* **im·pelled; im·pel·ling** [L *impellere*, fr. *in-* [2]in- + *pellere* to drive] **1 :** to urge or drive forward or into action ⟨felt *impelled* to speak up in his defense⟩ **2 :** PROPEL ⟨*impel* water through a pipe⟩ **syn** see MOVE — **im·pel·ler** *also* **im·pel·lor** \-'pel-ər\ *n*

im·pend \im-'pend\ *vi* [L *impendēre*, fr. *in-* [2]in- + *pendēre* to hang] **1** *archaic* **:** to hang suspended **2 a :** to hover threateningly : MENACE ⟨warning of a danger that *impends*⟩ **b :** to be about to occur

im·pend·ing *adj* **:** threatening to occur soon : APPROACHING **syn** IMPENDING, IMMINENT mean threatening to occur very soon. IMPENDING implies signs that keep one in suspense ⟨an *impending* thunderstorm kept us from going on a picnic⟩ IMMINENT emphasizes the shortness of time before happening ⟨execution of the death sentence was now *imminent*⟩

im·pen·e·tra·bil·i·ty \(,)im-,pen-ə-trə-'bil-ət-ē\ *n* **1 :** the quality or state of being impenetrable **2 :** the inability of two portions of matter to occupy the same space at the same time

im·pen·e·tra·ble \(')im-'pen-ə-trə-bəl\ *adj* **1 a :** incapable of being penetrated or pierced ⟨*impenetrable* rock⟩ ⟨*impenetrable* jungle⟩ **b :** inaccessible to knowledge, reason, or sympathy : IMPERVIOUS **2 :** incapable of being comprehended : INSCRUTABLE ⟨*impenetrable* mystery⟩ **3 :** having the property of impenetrability — **im·pen·e·tra·ble·ness** *n* — **im·pen·e·tra·bly** \-blē\ *adv*

im·pen·i·tent \(')im-'pen-ə-tənt\ *adj* **:** not penitent : not sorry for having done wrong — **im·pen·i·tence** \-tən(t)s\ *n* — **im·pen·i·tent·ly** *adv*

[1]im·per·a·tive \im-'per-ət-iv\ *adj* [L *imperare* to com-

mand] **1 a :** of, relating to, or constituting the grammatical mood that expresses a command, request, or strong encouragement **b :** expressive of a command, entreaty, or exhortation ⟨an *imperative* gesture⟩ **c :** having power to restrain, control, and direct : AUTHORITATIVE **2 :** not to be avoided or evaded : URGENT ⟨*imperative* business⟩ — **im·per·a·tive·ly** *adv* — **im·per·a·tive·ness** *n*

[2]imperative *n* **1 :** the imperative mood of a verb **:** a verb in this mood **2 :** something that is imperative: **a :** COMMAND, ORDER **b :** an obligatory act or duty

im·pe·ra·tor \,im-pə-'rät-ər\ *n* **:** a supreme leader of the ancient Romans : EMPEROR — **im·per·a·to·ri·al** \(,)im-,per-ə-'tōr-ē-əl, -'tȯr-\ *adj*

im·per·cep·ti·ble \,im-pər-'sep-tə-bəl\ *adj* **1 :** not perceptible by a sense or by the mind **2 :** extremely slight, gradual, or subtle — **im·per·cep·ti·bil·i·ty** \-,sep-tə-'bil-ət-ē\ *n* — **im·per·cep·ti·bly** \-'sep-tə-blē\ *adv*

im·per·cep·tive \,im-pər-'sep-tiv\ *adj* **:** not perceptive — **im·per·cep·tive·ness** *n*

im·per·cip·i·ent \,im-pər-'sip-ē-ənt\ *adj* **:** UNPERCEPTIVE

[1]im·per·fect \(')im-'pər-fikt\ *adj* **1 :** not perfect : DEFECTIVE **2 :** of, relating to, or constituting a verb tense used to designate a continuing state or an incomplete action esp. in the past — **im·per·fect·ly** \-'fik-(t)lē\ *adv* — **im·per·fect·ness** \-'fik(t)-nəs\ *n*

[2]imperfect *n* **:** the imperfect tense of a verb **:** a verb in this tense

imperfect flower *n* **:** a flower with stamens or pistils but not both

imperfect fungus *n* **:** any of an order (Fungi Imperfecti) of fungi of which only the conidial stage is known

im·per·fec·tion \,im-pər-'fek-shən\ *n* **:** the quality or state of being imperfect; *also* : FAULT, BLEMISH

im·per·fo·rate \(')im-'pər-f(ə-)rət, -fə-,rāt\ *adj* **1 :** having no opening or aperture; *esp* : lacking the usual or normal opening **2 :** lacking perforations or rouletting ⟨*imperforate* postage stamps⟩ — **imperforate** *n*

[1]im·pe·ri·al \im-'pir-ē-əl\ *adj* [L *imperium* command, empire] **1 a :** of, relating to, or befitting an empire or an emperor ⟨by *imperial* decree⟩ **b :** of or relating to the British Commonwealth or Empire **2 a :** SOVEREIGN **b :** REGAL, IMPERIOUS **3 :** of superior or unusual size or excellence **4 :** belonging to the official British series of weights and measures ⟨an *imperial* gallon is equal to about 1.2 U.S. gallon⟩ — **im·pe·ri·al·ly** \-ē-ə-lē\ *adv*

[2]imperial *n* **1 :** a size of paper usu. 23 x 31 inches **2** [fr. the beard worn by Napoleon III] **:** a pointed beard growing below the lower lip

im·pe·ri·al·ism \im-'pir-ē-ə,liz-əm\ *n* **1 a :** imperial government or authority **b :** an imperial system **2 :** the policy or practice of extending the power and dominion of one nation by direct territorial acquisitions or by indirect control over the political or economic life of other areas; *also* : advocacy of such policies or practice **3 :** the final stage of capitalism in Leninist theory in which capitalists seek new territories and markets in order to keep their economies from collapsing from internal contradictions — **im·pe·ri·al·ist** \-ləst\ *n* — **imperialist** *or* **im·pe·ri·al·is·tic** \im-,pir-ē-ə-'lis-tik\ *adj* — **im·pe·ri·al·is·ti·cal·ly** \-ti-k(ə-)lē\ *adv*

imperial 2

im·per·il \im-'per-əl\ *vt* **-iled** *or* **-illed; -il·ing** *or* **-il·ling** **:** to bring into peril : ENDANGER ⟨*imperil* the lives of others by reckless driving⟩ — **im·per·il·ment** \-əl-mənt\ *n*

im·pe·ri·ous \im-'pir-ē-əs\ *adj* [L *imperium* command] **1 :** COMMANDING, LORDLY **2 :** ARROGANT, DOMINEERING **3 :** IMPERATIVE, URGENT ⟨*imperious* need⟩ — **im·pe·ri·ous·ly** *adv* — **im·pe·ri·ous·ness** *n*

im·per·ish·a·ble \(')im-'per-ish-ə-bəl\ *adj* **:** not perishable or subject to decay : INDESTRUCTIBLE ⟨*imperishable* fame⟩ — **im·per·ish·a·bil·i·ty** \(,)im-,per-ish-ə-'bil-ət-ē\ *n* — **im·per·ish·a·ble·ness** \(')im-'per-ish-ə-bəl-nəs\ *n* — **im·per·ish·a·bly** \-blē\ *adv*

im·pe·ri·um \im-'pir-ē-əm\ *n* [L] **1 a :** supreme power or dominion **b :** the right to supreme power : SOVEREIGNTY **2 :** EMPIRE

im·per·ma·nent \(')im-'pər-mə-nənt\ *adj* **:** not permanent : TRANSIENT — **im·per·ma·nence** \-nən(t)s\ *n* — **im·per·ma·nent·ly** *adv*

im·per·me·a·ble \(')im-'pər-mē-ə-bəl\ *adj* **:** not permitting passage (as of a fluid) through its substance : IMPERVIOUS

— im·per·me·a·bil·i·ty \(,)im-,pər-mē-ə-'bil-ət-ē\ n — im·per·me·a·ble·ness \(')im-'pər-mē-ə-bəl-nəs\ n — im·per·me·a·bly \-blē\ adv

im·per·mis·si·ble \,im-pər-'mis-ə-bəl\ adj : not permissible

im·per·son·al \(')im-'pərs-nəl, -°n-əl\ adj 1 : of, relating to, or being a verb used with no expressed subject or with a merely formal subject ⟨methinks in "methinks you are wrong" and rained in "it rained" are impersonal verbs⟩ 2 a : having no personal reference or connection ⟨impersonal criticism⟩ b : not engaging the human personality or emotions ⟨impersonal attitude of a doctor⟩ c : not existing as a person ⟨an impersonal deity⟩ — im·per·son·al·i·ty \(,)im-,pərs-°n-'al-ət-ē\ n — im·per·son·al·ize \(')im-'pərs-nə-,līz, -°n-ə-,līz\ vt — im·per·son·al·ly \-nə-lē, -°n-ə-lē\ adv

im·per·son·ate \im-'pərs-°n-,āt\ vt 1 : to act the part of or pretend to be some other person ⟨impersonate a circus barker⟩ 2 : TYPIFY, EXEMPLIFY — im·per·son·a·tion \-,pərs-°n-'ā-shən\ n — im·per·son·a·tor \-'pərs-°n-,āt-ər\ n

im·per·ti·nence \(')im-'pərt-°n-ən(t)s\ also im·per·ti·nen·cy \-ən-sē\ n, pl -nences also -nencies 1 : the quality or state of being impertinent: as a : IRRELEVANCE, UNFITNESS b : INCIVILITY, INSOLENCE 2 : something impertinent

im·per·ti·nent \-ənt\ adj 1 : not pertinent : IRRELEVANT 2 : not restrained within due or proper bounds : RUDE, INSOLENT — im·per·ti·nent·ly adv

im·per·turb·a·ble \,im-pər-'tər-bə-bəl\ adj : marked by extreme calm, impassivity, and steadiness : SERENE — im·per·turb·a·bil·i·ty \-,tər-bə-'bil-ət-ē\ n — im·per·turb·a·bly \-'tər-bə-blē\ adv

im·per·vi·ous \(')im-'pər-vē-əs\ adj 1 : not allowing entrance or passage : IMPENETRABLE ⟨a coat impervious to rain⟩ 2 : not capable of being affected or disturbed ⟨impervious to criticism⟩ — im·per·vi·ous·ly adv — im·per·vi·ous·ness n

im·pe·ti·go \,im-pə-'tē-gō, -'tī-\ n [L, fr. impetere to attack] : an acute contagious skin disease characterized by vesicles, pustules, and yellowish crusts — im·pe·tig·i·nous \-'tij-ə-nəs\ adj

im·pet·u·os·i·ty \im-,pech-ə-'wäs-ət-ē\ n, pl -ties 1 : the quality or state of being impetuous 2 : an impetuous action or impulse

im·pet·u·ous \im-'pech-(ə-)wəs\ adj 1 : marked by force and violence 2 : marked by impulsive vehemence — im·pet·u·ous·ly adv — im·pet·u·ous·ness n

im·pe·tus \'im-pət-əs\ n [L, assault, impetus, fr. impetere to attack, fr. in- ²in- + petere to go to, seek] 1 a : a driving force : IMPULSE b : INCENTIVE, STIMULUS 2 : the property possessed by a moving body in virtue of its mass and its motion : MOMENTUM ⟨the impetus of a bullet⟩

im·pi·e·ty \(')im-'pī-ət-ē\ n, pl -ties 1 a : the quality or state of being impious : UNGODLINESS b : UNDUTIFULNESS 2 : an impious act

im·pinge \im-'pinj\ vi [L impingere, fr. in- ²in- + pangere to fasten, drive in] 1 : to strike or dash esp. with a sharp collision ⟨sound waves impinge upon the eardrums⟩ 2 : to come into close contact 3 : ENCROACH, INFRINGE ⟨impinge on another person's rights⟩ — im·pinge·ment \-mənt\ n

im·pi·ous \'im-pē-əs, (')im-'pī-\ adj : not pious: a : IRREVERENT, PROFANE b : UNDUTIFUL, UNFILIAL — im·pi·ous·ly adv

imp·ish \'im-pish\ adj : of, relating to, or befitting an imp; esp : MISCHIEVOUS — imp·ish·ly adv — imp·ish·ness n

im·plac·a·ble \(')im-'plak-ə-bəl, -'plā-kə-\ adj 1 : not placable : not capable of being appeased, pacified, or mitigated ⟨implacable enemy⟩ 2 : UNALTERABLE — im·plac·a·bil·i·ty \(,)im-,plak-ə-'bil-ət-ē, -,plā-kə-\ n — im·plac·a·ble·ness \(')im-'plak-ə-bəl-nəs, -'plā-kə-\ n — im·plac·a·bly \-blē\ adv

im·plant \im-'plant\ vt 1 a : to fix or set securely or deeply b : to set as permanent in the consciousness or habit patterns : INCULCATE ⟨implant patriotism in children⟩ 2 : to insert in a living site ⟨implant a hormone pellet⟩ — im·plan·ta·tion \,im-,plan-'tā-shən\ n — im·plant·er n

im·plau·si·ble \(')im-'plȯ-zə-bəl\ adj : not plausible — im·plau·si·bil·i·ty \(,)im-,plȯ-zə-'bil-ət-ē\ n — im·plau·si·bly \(')im-'plȯ-zə-blē\ adv

¹im·ple·ment \'im-plə-mənt\ n [LL implementum action of filling up, fr. L implēre to fill up, fr. in- ²in- + plēre to fill] 1 : an article serving to equip ⟨implements of war⟩ 2 : one that serves as an instrument or tool

syn IMPLEMENT, TOOL, UTENSIL, INSTRUMENT apply to any device for performing work. IMPLEMENT may apply to anything necessary to bring about an end or perform a task ⟨propaganda as an implement of peace and war⟩ ⟨agricultural and garden implements⟩ TOOL suggests an implement adapted to a specific task and implies the need of skill in its use ⟨carpenter's tools⟩ UTENSIL suggests a device useful for domestic tasks and often equals vessel ⟨kitchen utensils⟩ ⟨an altar and its sacred utensils⟩ INSTRUMENT suggests a device capable of delicate or precise work ⟨a surgeon's instruments⟩

²im·ple·ment \-,ment\ vt 1 : to carry out : FULFILL; esp : to give practical effect to by concrete measures ⟨implement the provisions of a treaty⟩ 2 : to provide implements for — im·ple·men·ta·tion \,im-plə-mən-'tā-shən, -,men-\ n

im·pli·cate \'im-plə-,kāt\ vt [L implicare, lit., to enfold, fr. in- + plicare to fold] : to bring into connection : INVOLVE ⟨his confession implicated several others in the crime⟩

im·pli·ca·tion \,im-plə-'kā-shən\ n 1 a : the act of implicating : the state of being implicated b : an incriminating involvement 2 a : the act of implying : the state of being implied b : something implied — im·pli·ca·tive \'im-plə-,kāt-iv\ adj — im·pli·ca·tive·ly adv — im·pli·ca·tive·ness n

im·plic·it \im-'plis-ət\ adj [L implicitus, pp. of implicare to enfold, implicate] 1 : understood though not directly stated ⟨an implicit agreement⟩ 2 : being without reserve : COMPLETE, UNQUESTIONING ⟨have implicit confidence in a person⟩ — compare EXPLICIT — im·plic·it·ly adv — im·plic·it·ness n

im·plode \im-'plōd\ vi [in- + -plode (as in explode)] : to burst inward — im·plo·sion \-'plō-zhən\ n — im·plo·sive \-'plō-siv, -ziv\ adj

im·plore \im-'plō(ə)r, -'plȯ(ə)r\ vt [L implorare, fr. in- + plorare to cry out] 1 : to call upon in supplication : BESEECH 2 : to call or pray for earnestly : ENTREAT syn see BEG

im·ply \im-'plī\ vt im·plied; im·ply·ing [MF emplier, fr. L implicare to enfold, implicate] 1 : to include or involve as a natural or necessary though not expressly stated part or effect ⟨military maneuvers implying threats of war⟩ ⟨the rights of citizenship imply certain obligations⟩ 2 : to express indirectly : suggest rather than state plainly ⟨remarks that implied consent⟩ — im·plied·ly \-'plī-(ə)d-lē\ adv

syn INFER : INFER is sometimes used for IMPLY but to most users the two words are complementary rather than synonymous. IMPLY means conveying or drawing attention to a fact or relationship by suggestion or hint rather than by direct statement ⟨his silence implied disapproval⟩ INFER means to arrive at a conclusion by reasoning from evidence and if the evidence is slight, comes close to surmise ⟨I inferred his disapproval from his silence⟩ ⟨a future rise in the number of college students may be inferred from the present population statistics⟩

im·po·lite \,im-pə-'līt\ adj : not polite : RUDE — im·po·lite·ly adv — im·po·lite·ness n

im·pol·i·tic \(')im-'päl-ə-,tik\ adj : not politic : UNWISE — im·pol·i·tic·ly adv

im·pon·der·a·ble \(')im-'pän-d(ə-)rə-bəl\ adj [L ponderare to weigh, ponder] : incapable of being weighed or evaluated with exactness — im·pon·der·a·bil·i·ty \(,)im-,pän-d(ə-)rə-'bil-ət-ē\ n — imponderable n — im·pon·der·a·ble·ness \(')im-'pän-d(ə-)rə-bəl-nəs\ n — im·pon·der·a·bly \-blē\ adv

¹im·port \im-'pōrt, -'pȯrt, 'im-,\ vb [MF importer, fr. It importare, fr. L, to bring in, fr. in- + portare to carry] 1 a : MEAN, SIGNIFY b : to be of importance or consequence : MATTER ⟨events that imported little to the country as a whole⟩ 2 : to bring in or introduce from a foreign country; esp : to bring in goods to be sold ⟨import coffee⟩ ⟨deals in imported sports cars⟩ — im·port·a·ble \-ə-bəl\ adj — im·port·er n

²im·port \'im-,pōrt, -,pȯrt\ n 1 : MEANING, SIGNIFICATION 2 : IMPORTANCE, SIGNIFICANCE 3 a : something imported b : IMPORTATION

im·por·tance \im-'pȯrt-°n(t)s, -ən(t)s\ n 1 : the quality

or state of being important : CONSEQUENCE **2** : an important aspect or bearing : SIGNIFICANCE

im·por·tant \im-'pȯrt-°nt, -ənt\ *adj* **1** : marked by or possessing weight or consequence : SIGNIFICANT ⟨an *important* change in printing methods⟩ **2** : marked by self-complacency, ostentation, or pompousness ⟨has an *important* air about him⟩ — **im·por·tant·ly** *adv*

im·por·ta·tion \,im-,pōr-'tā-shən, -,pȯr-, -pər-\ *n* **1** : the act or practice of importing **2** : something imported : IMPORT

im·por·tu·nate \im-'pȯrch-(ə-)nət\ *adj* **1** : TROUBLESOME **2** : troublesomely urgent : overly persistent in request or demand ⟨*importunate* beggar⟩ — **im·por·tu·nate·ly** *adv* — **im·por·tu·nate·ness** *n*

¹im·por·tune \,im-pər-'t(y)ün, im-'pȯr-chən\ *adj* : IMPORTUNATE — **im·por·tune·ly** *adv*

²importune *vb* [L *importunus* troublesome, fr. ¹*in-* + *-portunus* (as in *opportunus* opportune)] **1** : to press, beg, or urge with troublesome persistence **2** : ANNOY, TROUBLE — **im·por·tun·er** *n*

im·por·tu·ni·ty \,im-pər-'t(y)ü-nət-ē\ *n*, *pl* **-ties** : the quality or state of being importunate : persistence in requests or demands

im·pose \im-'pōz\ *vb* [MF *imposer*, irreg. fr. L *imponere*, lit., to put upon, fr. *in-* + *ponere* to put] **1 a** : to establish or apply as a charge or penalty : LEVY ⟨*impose* a fine⟩ ⟨*impose* a tax⟩ **b** : to make prevail by force ⟨*imposed* himself as their leader⟩ **2** : to use trickery or deception to get what one wants ⟨*impose* on an ignorant person⟩ **3** : to arrange (as typeset or plated pages) in order for printing **4** : to take unwarranted advantage of something : exploit a personal relationship ⟨*impose* upon a friend's good nature⟩ — **im·pos·er** *n*

im·pos·ing \im-'pō-ziŋ\ *adj* : impressive because of size, bearing, dignity, or grandeur ⟨an *imposing* building⟩ — **im·pos·ing·ly** \-ziŋ-lē\ *adv*

im·po·si·tion \,im-pə-'zish-ən\ *n* [L *imposit-*, *imponere* to impose] **1** : the act of imposing **2** : something imposed: as **a** : LEVY, TAX **b** : an excessive or unduly burdensome requirement or demand **3** : DECEPTION, TRICK

im·pos·si·bil·i·ty \(,)im-,päs-ə-'bil-ət-ē\ *n*, *pl* **-ties** **1** : the quality or state of being impossible **2** : something impossible

im·pos·si·ble \(')im-'päs-ə-bəl\ *adj* **1 a** : incapable of being or of occurring **b** : felt to be incapable of being done, attained, or fulfilled : insuperably difficult : HOPELESS ⟨found himself in an *impossible* situation⟩ **2 a** : extremely undesirable : UNACCEPTABLE **b** : markedly difficult to deal with : OBJECTIONABLE — **im·pos·si·bly** \-blē\ *adv*

¹im·post \'im-,pōst\ *n* [MF, fr. L *impositus*, pp. of *imponere* to impose] : TAX; *esp* : a customs duty

²impost *n* : a block, capital, or molding (as of a pillar or pier) from which an arch springs

im·pos·tor \im-'päs-tər\ *n* [LL, fr. L *impositus*, *impostus*, pp. of *imponere* to impose] : a person who practices deceit; *esp* : one who represents himself as being someone else

im·pos·ture \im-'päs-chər\ *n* : the act or conduct of an impostor; *esp* : fraudulent impersonation

im·po·tence \'im-pət-ən(t)s\ *n* : the quality or state of being impotent

im·po·tent \'im-pət-ənt\ *adj* **1** : not potent : lacking in power, strength, or vigor : HELPLESS **2** : unable to copulate; *also* : STERILE — usu. used of males — **impotent** *n* — **im·po·tent·ly** *adv*

im·pound \im-'paünd\ *vt* **1** : to shut up in or as if in a pound : CONFINE **2** : to seize and hold in legal custody ⟨*impound* funds pending decision of a case⟩ **3** : to collect (water) in a reservoir

im·pound·ment \im-'paün(d)-mənt\ *n* **1** : the act of impounding : the state of being impounded **2** : a body of water formed by impounding

im·pov·er·ish \im-'päv-(ə-)rish\ *vt* [MF *empovriss-*, *empovrir*, fr. *en-* + *povre* poor, fr. L *pauper*] **1** : to make poor **2** : to deprive of strength, richness, or fertility ⟨*impoverished* soil⟩ — **im·pov·er·ish·er** *n* — **im·pov·er·ish·ment** \-mənt\ *n*

im·prac·ti·ca·ble \(')im-'prak-ti-kə-bəl\ *adj* **1** : not practicable : incapable of being put into practice or use ⟨an *impracticable* plan⟩ **2** : IMPASSABLE ⟨an *impracticable* road⟩ — **im·prac·ti·ca·bil·i·ty** \(,)im-,prak-ti-kə-'bil-

ət-ē\ *n* — **im·prac·ti·ca·ble·ness** \(')im-'prak-ti-kə-bəl-nəs\ *n* — **im·prac·ti·ca·bly** \-blē\ *adv*

im·prac·ti·cal \(')im-'prak-ti-kəl\ *adj* : not practical: as **a** : not wise to put into or keep in practice or effect **b** : IDEALISTIC, THEORETICAL **c** : incapable of dealing sensibly or prudently with practical matters **d** : IMPRACTICABLE — **im·prac·ti·cal·i·ty** \(,)im-,prak-ti-'kal-ət-ē\ *n* — **im·prac·ti·cal·ness** \(')im-'prak-ti-kəl-nəs\ *n*

im·pre·cate \'im-pri-,kāt\ *vb* [L *imprecari*, fr. *in-* ²*in-* + *precari* to pray] : to invoke evil upon : CURSE — **im·pre·ca·tion** \,im-pri-'kā-shən\ *n* — **im·pre·ca·to·ry** \'im-pri-kə-,tōr-ē, im-'prek-ə-, -,tȯr-\ *adj*

im·pre·cise \,im-pri-'sīs\ *adj* : not precise — **im·pre·cise·ly** *adv* — **im·pre·cise·ness** *n* — **im·pre·ci·sion** \-'sizh-ən\ *n*

im·preg·na·ble \im-'preg-nə-bəl\ *adj* [alter. of ME *imprenable*, fr. MF, fr. *in-* + *prenable* vulnerable to capture, fr. *prendre* to take, fr. L *prehendere*] : incapable of being taken by assault : UNCONQUERABLE; *also* : UNASSAILABLE — **im·preg·na·bil·i·ty** \-,preg-nə-'bil-ət-ē\ *n* — **im·preg·na·ble·ness** \-'preg-nə-bəl-nəs\ *n* — **im·preg·na·bly** \-blē\ *adv*

im·preg·nate \im-'preg-,nāt\ *vt* [LL *impraegnare*, fr. L *in-* ²*in-* + *praegnas* pregnant] **1 a** (1) : to make pregnant (2) : to introduce sperm cells into **b** : to make fertile or fruitful **2** : to cause (a material or substance) to be filled, permeated, or saturated ⟨*impregnate* wood with a preservative⟩ ⟨*impregnate* water with carbon dioxide⟩ — **im·preg·na·tion** \,im-,preg-'nā-shən\ *n* — **im·preg·na·tor** \im-'preg-,nāt-ər\ *n*

im·pre·sa·rio \,im-prə-'sär-ē-,ō, -'sar-, -'ser-\ *n*, *pl* **-rios** [It, fr. *impresa* undertaking] **1** : the projector, manager, or conductor of an opera or concert company **2** : one who puts on or sponsors an entertainment **3** : MANAGER, PRODUCER

im·pre·scrip·ti·ble \,im-pri-'skrip-tə-bəl\ *adj* : INALIENABLE — **im·pre·scrip·ti·bly** \-blē\ *adv*

¹im·press \im-'pres\ *vb* [L *impress-*, *imprimere*, fr. *in-* ²*in-* + *premere* to press] **1 a** : to apply with pressure so as to imprint **b** : to produce (as a mark) by pressure **c** : to mark by or as if by pressure or stamping **2 a** : to produce a vivid impression of **b** : to affect esp. forcibly or deeply : INFLUENCE ⟨*impressed* by his appearance⟩ **3** : to transmit (force or motion) by pressure; *esp* : to apply (as an electromotive force) to a circuit from an outside source

²im·press \'im-,pres\ *n* **1** : the act of impressing **2 a** : a mark made by pressure : IMPRINT **b** : an image of something formed by or as if by pressure; *esp* : SEAL **c** : a product of pressure or influence **3** : a characteristic or distinctive mark : STAMP **4** : IMPRESSION, EFFECT

³im·press \im-'pres\ *vt* [²*in-* + ³*press*] **1** : to seize for public service; *esp* : to force into naval service **2** : to enlist the aid or services of by strong argument or appeal ⟨*impress* helpers into a fund-raising campaign⟩

⁴im·press \'im-,pres\ *n* : IMPRESSMENT

im·press·i·ble \im-'pres-ə-bəl\ *adj* : capable of being impressed : SENSITIVE — **im·press·i·bil·i·ty** \-,pres-ə-'bil-ət-ē\ *n* — **im·press·i·bly** \-'pres-ə-blē\ *adv*

im·pres·sion \im-'presh-ən\ *n* **1** : the act or process of impressing **2** : the effect produced by impressing: as **a** : a stamp, form, or figure resulting from physical contact **b** : an esp. marked influence or effect on feeling, sense, or mind **3 a** : a characteristic trait or feature resulting from influence **b** : an effect of alteration or improvement **c** : a telling image impressed on the senses or the mind **4 a** : one instance of the meeting of a printing surface and the material being printed; *also* : a single print or copy so made **b** : all the copies of a publication (as a book) printed in one continuous operation from a single makeready **5** : a usu. indistinct or imprecise notion or remembrance **6** : an imitation or representation of salient features in an artistic or theatrical medium; *esp* : an imitation in caricature of a noted personality as a form of theatrical entertainment — **im·pres·sion·al** \-'presh-nəl, -ən-°l\ *adj*

im·pres·sion·a·ble \im-'presh-(ə-)nə-bəl\ *adj* : capable of being easily impressed : easily molded or influenced : PLASTIC — **im·pres·sion·a·bil·i·ty** \-,presh-(ə-)nə-'bil-ət-ē\ *n* — **im·pres·sion·a·ble·ness** \-'presh-(ə-)nə-bəl-nəs\ *n* — **im·pres·sion·a·bly** \-blē\ *adv*

im·pres·sion·ism \im-'presh-ə-,niz-əm\ *n* **1** *often cap*

: a theory or practice in painting esp. among French painters of about 1870 of depicting the natural appearances of objects by means of dabs or strokes of primary unmixed colors in order to simulate actual reflected light **2 a** : the depiction of scene, emotion, or character by details evoking impressions rather than by re-creating reality **b** : a style of musical composition designed to create moods through rich and varied harmonies **3** : a practice of presenting and elaborating one's reactions to a work of art — **im·pres·sion·ist** \-'presh-(ə-)nəst\ *n or adj* — **im·pres·sion·is·tic** \-ˌpresh-ə-'nis-tik\ *adj* — **im·pres·sion·is·ti·cal·ly** \-ti-k(ə-)lē\ *adv*

im·pres·sive \im-'pres-iv\ *adj* : making or tending to make a marked impression : stirring deep feeling esp. of awe or admiration ⟨an *impressive* speech⟩ — **im·pres·sive·ly** *adv* — **im·pres·sive·ness** *n*

im·press·ment \im-'pres-mənt\ *n* : the act of seizing for public use or of impressing into public service

im·pri·ma·tur \ˌim-prə-'mät-ər\ *n* [NL, let it be printed, fr. *imprimere* to print, fr. L, to impress, imprint] **1 a** : a license to print or publish **b** : official approval of a publication by a censor **2** : SANCTION, APPROVAL

¹im·print \im-'print, 'im-ˌ\ *vt* **1 a** : to mark by or as if by pressure : STAMP, IMPRESS **b** *archaic* : PRINT **c** : to add an imprint to **2** : to fix indelibly or firmly (as in the memory) ⟨her smile was *imprinted* on his memory⟩

²im·print \'im-ˌprint\ *n* : something imprinted or printed : as **a** : IMPRESS **b** : a publisher's name often with address and date of publication printed at the foot of a title page **c** : an indelible distinguishing effect or influence ⟨the teacher left her *imprint* on several generations of students⟩

im·pris·on \im-'priz-ⁿn\ *vt* **-pris·oned; -pris·on·ing** \-'priz-niŋ, -ⁿn-iŋ\ : to put in or as if in prison : CONFINE — **im·pris·on·ment** \-'priz-ⁿn-mənt\ *n*

im·prob·a·ble \(')im-'präb-ə-bəl\ *adj* : unlikely to be true or to occur — **im·prob·a·bil·i·ty** \(ˌ)im-ˌpräb-ə-'bil-ət-ē\ *n* — **im·prob·a·ble·ness** \(')im-'präb-ə-bəl-nəs\ *n* — **im·prob·a·bly** \-'präb-ə-blē\ *adv*

im·pro·bi·ty \(')im-'prō-bət-ē, -'präb-ət-\ *n* : lack of probity or integrity : DISHONESTY

im·promp·tu \im-'präm(p)-t(y)ü\ *adj* [F, fr. *impromptu* extemporaneously, fr. L *in promptu* in readiness] **1** : made or done on or as if on the spur of the moment : IMPROVISED **2** : composed or uttered without previous study or preparation : EXTEMPORANEOUS ⟨an *impromptu* speech⟩ — **impromptu** *adv or n*

im·prop·er \(')im-'präp-ər\ *adj* **1** : not proper, fit, or suitable ⟨*improper* dress for the occasion⟩ **2** : INCORRECT, INACCURATE ⟨*improper* deduction⟩⟨*improper* address on a letter⟩ **3** : not in accordance with good taste or good manners ⟨*improper* language⟩ **syn** see INDECOROUS — **im·prop·er·ly** *adv* — **im·prop·er·ness** *n*

improper fraction *n* : a fraction whose numerator is equal to or larger than the denominator

im·pro·pri·e·ty \ˌim-prə-'prī-ət-ē\ *n, pl* **-ties** **1** : the quality or state of being improper **2** : an improper or indecorous act or remark; *esp* : an unacceptable use of a word or of language

im·prove \im-'prüv\ *vb* [AF *emprouer* to invest profitably, fr. OF *en-* + *prou* advantage] **1** : to make greater in amount or degree : INCREASE **2 a** : to enhance in value or quality : make or grow better ⟨*improved* his health⟩ **b** : to increase the value of real estate (as by cultivation or the erection of buildings) **c** : to grade and drain (a road) and apply surfacing material other than pavement **3** : to turn to good account ⟨*improved* their time by studying⟩ **4** : to make useful additions or amendments ⟨*improve* on the carburetor⟩ — **im·prov·a·ble** \-'prü-və-bəl\ *adj* — **im·prov·er** *n*

im·prove·ment \im-'prüv-mənt\ *n* **1** : the act or process of improving **2 a** : the state of being improved; *esp* : enhanced value or excellence **b** : an instance or result of such improvement **3** : something that increases the value esp. of real estate ⟨add a number of *improvements* to an old house⟩

im·prov·i·dent \(')im-'präv-əd-ənt, -ə-ˌdent\ *adj* : not provident : not foreseeing or providing for the future : THRIFTLESS — **im·prov·i·dence** \-əd-ən(t)s, -ə-ˌden(t)s\ *n* — **im·prov·i·dent·ly** *adv*

im·prov·i·sa·tion \im-ˌpräv-ə-'zā-shən, ˌim-prə-və-\ *n*

1 : the act or art of improvising **2** : something that is improvised — **im·prov·i·sa·tion·al** \-shnəl, -shən-ⁿl\ *adj*

im·prov·i·sa·tor \im-'präv-ə-ˌzāt-ər\ *n* : IMPROVISER — **im·prov·i·sa·to·ri·al** \-ˌpräv-ə-zə-'tōr-ē-əl, -'tȯr-\ *or* **im·prov·i·sa·to·ry** \-'präv-ə-zə-ˌtōr-ē, -ˌtȯr-\ *adj*

im·pro·vise \'im-prə-ˌvīz\ *vb* [L *improvisus* sudden, fr. *in-* ¹in- + *provisus*, pp. of *providēre* to see ahead, provide] **1** : to compose, recite, or sing on the spur of the moment : EXTEMPORIZE **2** : to make, invent, or arrange offhand — **im·pro·vis·er** *n*

im·pru·dent \(')im-'prüd-ⁿnt\ *adj* : not prudent : lacking discretion — **im·pru·dence** \-ⁿn(t)s\ *n* — **im·pru·dent·ly** *adv*

im·pu·dent \'im-pyəd-ənt\ *adj* [L *impudent-, impudens*, fr. *in-* ¹in- + *pudēre* to feel shame] : marked by contemptuous or cocky boldness or disregard of others : INSOLENT, DISRESPECTFUL, FORWARD — **im·pu·dence** \-ən(t)s\ *n* — **im·pu·dent·ly** *adv*

im·pugn \im-'pyün\ *vt* [L *impugnare*, fr. *in-* ²in- + *pugnare* to fight] : to oppose or attack as false : cast doubt on ⟨*impugn* the motives of an opponent⟩ — **im·pugn·er** *n*

im·puis·sance \(')im-'pwis-ⁿn(t)s, -'pyü-ə-sən(t)s\ *n* : POWERLESSNESS, WEAKNESS

im·pulse \'im-ˌpəls\ *n* [L *impulsus*, fr. *impellere* to impel] **1 a** : a force that starts a body into motion : IMPULSION **b** : the motion produced by such an impulse **2 a** : a sudden spontaneous arousing of the mind and spirit to do something : an inclination to act ⟨have an *impulse* to run away⟩⟨acts on the *impulse* of the moment⟩ **3** : a wave of excitation transmitted esp. through nerves and muscles that results in altered activity of a bodily part **4** : the product of the average value of a force and the time during which it acts **syn** see MOTIVE

im·pul·sion \im-'pəl-shən\ *n* **1 a** : the action of impelling : the state of being impelled **b** : an impelling force **c** : IMPETUS **2** : IMPULSE 2 **3** : COMPULSION 2

im·pul·sive \im-'pəl-siv\ *adj* **1** : having the power of driving or impelling **2** : acting or liable to act on impulse : moved or caused by an impulse : IMPETUOUS **syn** see SPONTANEOUS — **im·pul·sive·ly** *adv* — **im·pul·sive·ness** *n*

im·pu·ni·ty \im-'pyü-nət-ē\ *n* [L *impunitat-, impunitas*, fr. *impune* without punishment, fr. *in-* ¹in- + *poena* pain, penalty] : exemption or freedom from punishment, harm, or loss

im·pure \(')im-'pyü(ə)r\ *adj* : not pure: as **a** : UNCHASTE, OBSCENE ⟨*impure* language⟩ **b** : containing something unclean : FOUL ⟨*impure* water⟩ **c** : ritually unclean **d** : marked by an intermixture of foreign elements or by substandard, incongruous, or objectionable locutions **e** : mixed with some other substance and esp. some inferior substance ⟨an *impure* chemical⟩ **f** : MIXED, BASTARD ⟨an *impure* style of ornamentation⟩ — **im·pure·ly** *adv* — **im·pure·ness** *n*

im·pu·ri·ty \(')im-'pyür-ət-ē\ *n, pl* **-ties** **1** : the quality or state of being impure **2** : something that is impure or that makes something else impure ⟨a filter to remove *impurities* from water⟩

im·pute \im-'pyüt\ *vt* [L *imputare*, fr. *in-* ²in- + *putare* to reckon] **1** : to lay the responsibility or blame for : CHARGE **2** : to credit to a person or a cause : ATTRIBUTE **syn** see ASCRIBE — **im·put·a·ble** \-'pyüt-ə-bəl\ *adj* — **im·put·a·bly** \-blē\ *adv* — **im·pu·ta·tion** \ˌim-pyə-'tā-shən\ *n* — **im·pu·ta·tive** \im-'pyüt-ət-iv\ *adj* — **im·pu·ta·tive·ly** *adv*

¹in \(')in, ən, ⁿn\ *prep* [OE] **1 a** — used as a function word to indicate location or inclusion in space or in something immaterial ⟨swimming *in* the lake⟩ ⟨*in* the summer⟩ **b** : INTO 1a ⟨went *in* the house⟩ **2** — used as a function word to indicate means ⟨written *in* pencil⟩ **3 a** — used as a function word to indicate a qualification ⟨alike *in* some respects⟩ ⟨left *in* a hurry⟩ **b** : INTO 2a ⟨broke *in* pieces⟩ **4** — used as a function word to indicate purpose ⟨said *in* reply⟩

²in \'in\ *adv* **1 a** : to or toward the inside ⟨went *in* and closed the door⟩ **b** : to or toward some particular place ⟨flew *in* on the first plane⟩ **c** : at close quarters : NEAR ⟨play close *in*⟩ **d** : into the midst of something ⟨mix *in* the flour⟩ **e** : to or at its proper place ⟨fit a piece *in*⟩ **f** : into line ⟨fell *in* with our plans⟩ **2 a** : WITHIN **b** : in the position of insider **c** : on good terms **d** : in a position of assured success; *also* : in vogue or season **e** : at hand or on hand ⟨the evidence is all *in*⟩ ⟨harvests are *in*⟩

³in \'in\ *adj* **1 a :** being inside or within ⟨the *in* part⟩ **b :** being in position, operation, or power ⟨the *in* party⟩ **2 :** directed or bound inward **: INCOMING** ⟨the *in* train⟩ **3 :** keenly aware of and responsive to what is new and smart ⟨the *in* crowd⟩ **4 :** extremely fashionable ⟨the *in* thing to do⟩

⁴in \'in\ *n* **1 :** one who is in office or power or on the inside **2 : INFLUENCE, PULL**

¹in- *or* **il-** *or* **im-** *or* **ir-** *prefix* [L] **:** not **: NON-, UN-** — usu. *il-* before *l* ⟨*il*logical⟩ and *im-* before *b*, *m*, or *p* ⟨*im*balance⟩ ⟨*im*moral⟩ ⟨*im*practical⟩ and *ir-* before *r* ⟨*ir*reducible⟩ and *in-* before other sounds ⟨*in*conclusive⟩

²in- *or* **il-** *or* **im-** *or* **ir-** *prefix* [L; akin to E *in*] **1 :** in **:** within **:** into **:** toward **:** on ⟨*im*mingle⟩ ⟨*ir*radiance⟩ — usu. *il-* before *l*, *im-* before *b*, *m*, or *p*, *ir-* before *r*, and *in-* before other sounds **2 : ¹EN-** ⟨*im*peril⟩ ⟨*in*spirit⟩

¹-in \ən, °n\ *n suffix* [F *-ine*, fr. L *-ina*, fem. of *-īnus* **²-ine**] **:** chemical compound ⟨insul*in*⟩ ⟨penicill*in*⟩ ⟨epinephr*in*⟩

²-in \-ˌin\ *comb form* [**²***in* (as in *sit-in*)] **1 :** organized public protest by means of or in favor of **:** demonstration ⟨teach-*in*⟩ **2 :** public group activity ⟨sing-*in*⟩

in·abil·i·ty \ˌin-ə-'bil-ət-ē\ *n* **:** the condition of being unable **:** lack of ability, power, or means

syn INABILITY, DISABILITY both denote lack of ability to perform a given act or to pursue a specific trade or profession. INABILITY implies lack of power to perform and suggests lack of means, health, training, or temperamental fitness ⟨*inability* to see⟩ ⟨*inability* to understand⟩ DISABILITY implies the loss of power to perform due to accident, illness, or disqualification and applies both to the resulting inability and to the cause of it ⟨because of *disabilities* many a veteran failed to return to his former occupation⟩

in ab·sen·tia \ˌin-ab-'sen-ch(ē-)ə\ *adv* [L] **:** in one's absence ⟨was awarded the degree *in absentia*⟩

in·ac·ces·si·ble \ˌin-ik-'ses-ə-bəl, ˌin-ak-\ *adj* **:** not accessible — **in·ac·ces·si·bil·i·ty** \-ˌses-ə-'bil-ət-ē\ *n* — **in·ac·ces·si·bly** \-'ses-ə-blē\ *adv*

in·ac·cu·ra·cy \('\)in-'ak-yə-rə-sē\ *n, pl* **-cies 1 :** the quality or state of being inaccurate **2 : MISTAKE, ERROR**

in·ac·cu·rate \-rət\ *adj* **:** not accurate **:** not exact **: FAULTY** — **in·ac·cu·rate·ly** *adv*

in·ac·tion \('\)in-'ak-shən\ *n* **:** lack of action or activity

in·ac·ti·vate \('\)in-'ak-tə-ˌvāt\ *vt* **:** to make inactive — **in·ac·ti·va·tion** \(ˌ)in-ˌak-tə-'vā-shən\ *n*

in·ac·tive \('\)in-'ak-tiv\ *adj* **:** not active: as **a :** INDOLENT, SLUGGISH **b :** being out of use or activity **c :** relating to members of the armed forces who are not performing or available for military duties **d :** chemically inert — **in·ac·tive·ly** *adv* — **in·ac·tiv·i·ty** \ˌin-ak-'tiv-ət-ē\ *n*

syn INERT, IDLE: INACTIVE applies to anyone or anything not in action or in operation or at work ⟨an *inactive* mine⟩ ⟨an *inactive* reserve officer⟩ INERT as applied to a thing implies being powerless to move itself or to affect other things ⟨*inert* gas⟩ ⟨*inert* stocks⟩ and applied to a person suggests an inherent or habitual indisposition to activity ⟨politically *inert* citizens⟩ IDLE applies to people who are not busy or occupied or to their powers or implements ⟨talents left *idle* because of indifference⟩

in·ad·e·quate \('\)in-'ad-i-kwət\ *adj* **:** not adequate **:** INSUFFICIENT — **in·ad·e·qua·cy** \-kwə-sē\ *n* — **in·ad·e·quate·ly** *adv* — **in·ad·e·quate·ness** *n*

in·ad·mis·si·ble \ˌin-əd-'mis-ə-bəl\ *adj* **:** not admissible — **in·ad·mis·si·bil·i·ty** \-ˌmis-ə-'bil-ət-ē\ *n* — **in·ad·mis·si·bly** \-'mis-ə-blē\ *adv*

in·ad·ver·tence \ˌin-əd-'vərt-°n(t)s\ *n* **:** INATTENTION; *also* **:** a result of inattention **:** OVERSIGHT

in·ad·ver·ten·cy \-°n-sē\ *n, pl* **-cies :** INADVERTENCE

in·ad·ver·tent \-°nt\ *adj* [L *in-* **¹***in-* + *advertent-, advertens*, prp. of *advertere* to notice, short for *advertere animum*, lit., to turn the mind to] **1 :** HEEDLESS, INATTENTIVE **2 :** UNINTENTIONAL — **in·ad·ver·tent·ly** *adv*

in·ad·vis·a·ble \ˌin-əd-'vī-zə-bəl\ *adj* **:** not advisable **:** UNWISE — **in·ad·vis·a·bil·i·ty** \-ˌvī-zə-'bil-ət-ē\ *n*

in·alien·a·ble \('\)in-'āl-yə-nə-bəl, -'ā-lē-ə-nə-\ *adj* **:** not capable of being taken away, given up, or transferred ⟨*inalienable* rights⟩ — **in·alien·a·bil·i·ty** \(ˌ)āl-yə-nə-'bil-ət-ē, -ˌā-lē-ə-nə-\ *n* — **in·alien·a·bly** \('\)in-'āl-yə-nə-blē, -'ā-lē-ə-nə-\ *adv*

in·al·ter·a·ble \('\)in-'ȯl-t(ə-)rə-bəl\ *adj* **:** not alterable **:** UNALTERABLE — **in·al·ter·a·bil·i·ty** \(ˌ)in-ˌȯl-t(ə-)rə-

'bil-ət-ē\ *n* — **in·al·ter·a·ble·ness** \(ˌ)in-'ȯl-t(ə-)rə-bəl-nəs\ *n* — **in·al·ter·a·bly** \-blē\ *adv*

in·amo·ra·ta \(ˌ)in-ˌam-ə-'rät-ə\ *n* [It *innamorata*, fr. *innamorare* to inspire with love, fr. *in-* **²***in-* + *amore* love, fr. L *amor*] **:** a woman with whom one is in love

inane \in-'ān\ *adj* [L *inanis*] **1 :** EMPTY, INSUBSTANTIAL **2 :** lacking significance, meaning, or point **:** SILLY **syn** see INSIPID — **inane·ly** *adv* — **inane·ness** \-'ān-nəs\ *n*

in·an·i·mate \('\)in-'an-ə-mət\ *adj* **1 :** not animate: **a :** not endowed with life or spirit **b :** lacking consciousness or power of motion **2 :** not animated or lively **:** DULL — **in·an·i·mate·ly** *adv* — **in·an·i·mate·ness** *n*

in·a·ni·tion \ˌin-ə-'nish-ən\ *n* [L *inanire* to empty, fr. *inanis* inane] **:** a weak lethargic state resulting from or as if from lack of food and water

inan·i·ty \in-'an-ət-ē\ *n, pl* **-ties 1 :** the quality or state of being inane: as **a :** EMPTINESS **b :** FATUOUSNESS **2 :** something that is inane; *esp* **:** a senseless or foolish remark

in·ap·par·ent \ˌin-ə-'par-ənt, -'per-\ *adj* **:** not apparent

in·ap·peas·a·ble \ˌin-ə-'pē-zə-bəl\ *adj* **:** UNAPPEASABLE

in·ap·pe·tence \('\)in-'ap-ət-ən(t)s\ *n* **:** lack of appetite

in·ap·pli·ca·ble \('\)in-'ap-li-kə-bəl, ˌin-ə-'plik-ə-\ *adj* **:** not applicable **:** UNSUITABLE, IRRELEVANT — **in·ap·pli·ca·bil·i·ty** \(ˌ)in-ˌap-li-kə-'bil-ət-ē, ˌin-ə-ˌplik-ə-\ *n* — **in·ap·pli·ca·bly** \('\)in-'ap-li-kə-blē, ˌin-ə-'plik-ə-\ *adv*

in·ap·po·site \('\)in-'ap-ə-zət\ *adj* **:** not apposite — **in·ap·po·site·ly** *adv* — **in·ap·po·site·ness** *n*

in·ap·pre·cia·ble \ˌin-ə-'prē-shə-bəl\ *adj* **:** too small to be perceived **:** very slight — **in·ap·pre·cia·bly** \-blē\ *adv*

in·ap·pre·cia·tive \ˌin-ə-'prē-shət-iv, -shē-ˌāt-\ *adj* **:** not appreciative — **in·ap·pre·cia·tive·ly** *adv* — **in·ap·pre·cia·tive·ness** *n*

in·ap·proach·a·ble \ˌin-ə-'prō-chə-bəl\ *adj* **:** not approachable **:** INACCESSIBLE

in·ap·pro·pri·ate \ˌin-ə-'prō-prē-ət\ *adj* **:** not appropriate — **in·ap·pro·pri·ate·ly** *adv* — **in·ap·pro·pri·ate·ness** *n*

in·apt \('\)in-'apt\ *adj* **1 :** not suitable **2 :** INEPT — **in·apt·ly** *adv* — **in·apt·ness** \-'ap(t)-nəs\ *n*

in·ap·ti·tude \-'ap-tə-ˌt(y)üd\ *n* **:** lack of aptitude

in·ar·tic·u·late \ˌin-är-'tik-yə-lət\ *adj* **1 a :** not understandable as spoken words ⟨*inarticulate* cries⟩ **b :** incapable of speech esp. under stress of emotion **:** MUTE **c :** incapable of being expressed by speech ⟨*inarticulate* longings⟩ **d :** UNSPOKEN **2 :** incapable of giving coherent, clear, or effective expression to one's ideas or feelings **3 a :** having no distinct body segments **b :** lacking a hinge — used esp. of a brachiopod shell — **in·ar·tic·u·late·ly** *adv* — **in·ar·tic·u·late·ness** *n*

in·ar·tis·tic \ˌin-är-'tis-tik\ *adj* **:** not artistic — **in·ar·tis·ti·cal·ly** \-ti-k(ə-)lē\ *adv*

in·as·much as \ˌin-əz-ˌməch-əz\ *conj* **1 :** to the extent that **2 :** in view of the fact that **:** SINCE

in·at·ten·tion \ˌin-ə-'ten-chən\ *n* **:** failure to pay attention

in·at·ten·tive \-'tent-iv\ *adj* **:** not attentive — **in·at·ten·tive·ly** *adv* — **in·at·ten·tive·ness** *n*

in·au·di·ble \('\)in-'ȯd-ə-bəl\ *adj* **:** not audible — **in·au·di·bil·i·ty** \(ˌ)in-ˌȯd-ə-'bil-ət-ē\ *n* — **in·au·di·bly** \('\)in-'ȯd-ə-blē\ *adv*

¹in·au·gu·ral \in-'ȯ-gyə-rəl, -g(ə-)rəl\ *adj* **1 :** of or relating to an inauguration ⟨*inaugural* address⟩ ⟨*inaugural* ball⟩ **2 :** marking a beginning **:** first in a projected series ⟨*inaugural* run of a new luxury liner⟩

²inaugural *n* **1 :** an inaugural address **2 :** INAUGURATION

in·au·gu·rate \in-'ȯ-g(y)ə-ˌrāt\ *vt* [L *inaugurare* to practice augury, inaugurate, fr. *in-* **²***in-* + *augur*; fr. the consulting of omens at inaugurations] **1 :** to introduce into office with suitable ceremonies **:** INSTALL ⟨*inaugurate* a president⟩ **2 :** to celebrate or mark the opening of ⟨the teams chosen to *inaugurate* the new athletic field⟩ **3 :** to commence or enter upon **:** BEGIN ⟨*inaugurate* a reform⟩ ⟨*inaugurate* a policy⟩ — **in·au·gu·ra·tor** \-ˌrāt-ər\ *n*

in·au·gu·ra·tion \in-ˌȯ-g(y)ə-'rā-shən\ *n* **:** an act of inaugurating; *esp* **:** a ceremonial introduction into office

in·aus·pi·cious \ˌin-ȯ-'spish-əs\ *adj* **:** not auspicious — **in·aus·pi·cious·ly** *adv* — **in·aus·pi·cious·ness** *n*

in·board \'in-ˌbȯrd, -ˌbȯrd\ *adv* **1 :** inside the line of a ship's bulwarks or hull **:** toward the center line of a ship **2 :** in a position closer or closest to the longitudinal axis of an aircraft — **inboard** *adj*

in·born \'in-'bȯrn\ *adj* **1 :** born in or with one **:** not acquired by training or experience : NATURAL **2** : IN-HERITED, HEREDITARY **syn** see INNATE

in·bound \'in-ˌbaůnd\ *adj* : inward bound ⟨*inbound* traffic⟩

in·breathe \'in-ˈbrēth\ *vt* : INHALE

in·bred \'in-ˈbred\ *adj* **1 a** : present from birth **b** : planted in by early teaching or training : INCULCATED **2** : subjected to or produced by inbreeding **syn** see INNATE

in·breed \'in-ˈbrēd\ *vb* : to produce by or subject to inbreeding

in·breed·ing \'in-ˌbrēd-iŋ\ *n* **1** : the interbreeding of closely related individuals esp. to preserve and fix desirable characters of and to eliminate unfavorable characters from a stock **2** : confinement to a narrow range or a local or limited field of choice

In·ca \'iŋ-kə\ *n* **1** : a noble or a member of the ruling family of an Indian empire of Peru, Bolivia, and Ecuador until the Spanish conquest **2** : a member of the leading people of the empire of the Incas — **In·can** \-kən\ *adj*

in·cal·cu·la·ble \(')in-ˈkal-kyə-lə-bəl\ *adj* **1** : not capable of being calculated; *esp* : too large or numerous to be calculated **2** : not capable of being known in advance : UNCERTAIN — **in·cal·cu·la·bil·i·ty** \(ˌ)in-ˌkal-kyə-lə-'bil-ət-ē\ *n* — **in·cal·cu·la·bly** \-blē\ *adv*

in·can·desce \ˌin-kən-'des\ *vb* : to become or cause to become incandescent

in·can·des·cence \ˌin-kən-'des-ᵊn(t)s\ *n* : a glowing condition of a body due to its high temperature

in·can·des·cent \-ᵊnt\ *adj* [L *incandescere* to become white-hot, fr. *in-* ²in- + *candēre* to be white] **1 a** : white or glowing with intense heat **b** : strikingly bright, radiant, or clear **c** : BRILLIANT **2 a** : of, relating to, or being light produced by incandescence **b** : producing light by incandescence — **in·can·des·cent·ly** *adv*

incandescent lamp *n* : a lamp whose light is produced by the glow of a filament heated by an electric current

in·can·ta·tion \ˌin-ˌkan-'tā-shən\ *n* [L *incantare* to enchant, fr. *in-* ²in- + *cantare*, freq. of *canere* to sing] : a use of spells or charms spoken or sung as part of a ritual of magic; *also* : a formula of words so used — **in·can·ta·tion·al** \-shnəl, -shən-ᵊl\ *adj* — **in·can·ta·to·ry** \in-'kant-ə-ˌtōr-ē, -ˌtör-\ *adj*

in·ca·pa·ble \(')in-ˈkā-pə-bəl\ *adj* : not capable : lacking capacity, ability, or qualification for the purpose or end in view: as **a** : not in a state of a kind to admit : INSUSCEPTIBLE ⟨*incapable* of precise measurement⟩ **b** : not able or fit : UNQUALIFIED, INCOMPETENT — **in·ca·pa·bil·i·ty** \(ˌ)in-ˌkā-pə-'bil-ət-ē\ *n* — **in·ca·pa·ble·ness** \(')in-ˈkā-pə-bəl-nəs\ *n* — **in·ca·pa·bly** \-blē\ *adv*

in·ca·pac·i·tate \ˌin-kə-'pas-ə-ˌtāt\ *vt* **1** : to deprive of natural capacity or power : DISABLE **2** : to make legally incapable or ineligible — **in·ca·pac·i·ta·tion** \-ˌpas-ə-'tā-shən\ *n*

in·ca·pac·i·ty \ˌin-kə-'pas-ət-ē, -'pas-tē\ *n, pl* **-ties** : lack of ability or power ⟨a seeming *incapacity* for telling the truth⟩

in·car·cer·ate \in-ˈkär-sə-ˌrāt\ *vt* [L *incarcerare*, fr. *in-* ²in- + *carcer* prison] : IMPRISON, CONFINE — **in·car·cer·a·tion** \(ˌ)in-ˌkär-sə-'rā-shən\ *n*

¹in·car·na·dine \in-ˈkär-nə-ˌdīn, -ˌdēn\ *adj* : RED; *esp* : BLOODRED

²incarnadine *vt* : to make incarnadine : REDDEN

¹in·car·nate \in-ˈkär-nət, -ˌnāt\ *adj* [LL *incarnatus*, pp. of *incarnare* to incarnate, fr. L *in-* ²in- + *carn-, caro* flesh] **1** : invested with bodily esp. human nature and form **2** : EMBODIED, PERSONIFIED ⟨a fiend *incarnate*⟩

²in·car·nate \-ˌnāt\ *vt* : to make incarnate

in·car·na·tion \ˌin-ˌkär-'nā-shən\ *n* **1** : the act of incarnating : the state of being incarnate **2 a** : the embodiment of a deity or spirit in an earthly form; *esp, cap* : the union of divinity with humanity in Jesus Christ **b** : a concrete or actual form of a quality or concept; *esp* : a person showing a trait or typical character to a marked degree

incase *var of* ENCASE

in·cau·tious \(')in-ˈkȯ-shəs\ *adj* : lacking in caution : HEEDLESS, RASH — **in·cau·tious·ly** *adv* — **in·cau·tious·ness** *n*

in·cen·di·a·rism \in-'sen-dē-ə-ˌriz-əm\ *n* : incendiary action or behavior

¹in·cen·di·ary \in-'sen-dē-ˌer-ē\ *n, pl* **-ar·ies** [L *incendiarius*, fr. *incendium* conflagration, fr. *incendere* to set on fire] **1 a** : a person who maliciously sets fire to property **b** : an incendiary agent (as a bomb) **2** : a person who excites quarrels : AGITATOR

²incendiary *adj* **1** : of, relating to, or involving malicious burning of property **2** : tending to excite or inflame quarrels : INFLAMMATORY **3 a** : igniting combustible materials spontaneously **b** : relating to or being a missile containing chemicals that ignite on bursting or on contact

¹in·cense \'in-ˌsen(t)s\ *n* [LL *incensum*, fr. L *incens-, incendere* to set on fire] **1** : material used to produce a fragrant odor when burned **2 a** : the perfume exhaled from some spices and gums when burned **b** : a pleasing scent

²in·cense \in-'sen(t)s\ *vt* [L *incens-, incendere*, lit., to set on fire] : to inflame with anger or indignation ⟨*incensed* by his bad behavior⟩

in·cen·ter \'in-ˌsent-ər\ *n* : the point of intersection of the bisectors of the angles of a triangle

in·cen·tive \in-'sent-iv\ *n* [L *incent-, incinere* to set the tune, fr. *in-* ²in- + *canere* to sing] : something that arouses or spurs one on to action or effort : STIMULUS **syn** see MOTIVE — **incentive** *adj*

in·cept \in-'sept\ *vi* : to enter upon a career — **in·cep·tor** \-'sep-tər\ *n*

in·cep·tion \in-'sep-shən\ *n* [L *incept-, incipere* to begin, fr. *in-* ²in- + *capere* to take] : an act, process, or instance of beginning : COMMENCEMENT ⟨the program has been a success since its *inception*⟩ **syn** see ORIGIN

in·cep·tive \in-'sep-tiv\ *adj* **1** : BEGINNING **2** : INCHOATIVE **2** — **inceptive** *n* — **in·cep·tive·ly** *adv*

in·cer·ti·tude \(')in-'sərt-ə-ˌt(y)üd\ *n* **1** : UNCERTAINTY: **a** : absence of assurance : DOUBT, INDECISION **b** : INSECURITY, INSTABILITY

in·ces·sant \(')in-'ses-ᵊnt\ *adj* [LL *incessant-, incessans*, fr. L *in-* ¹in- + *cessare* to delay, be idle, freq. of *cedere* to withdraw] : continuing without interruption : UNCEASING ⟨*incessant* rains⟩ **syn** see CONTINUAL — **in·ces·sant·ly** *adv*

in·cest \'in-ˌsest\ *n* [L *incestum*, fr. neut. of *incestus* impure, fr. *in-* ¹in- + *castus* pure] : sexual intercourse between persons so closely related that they are forbidden by law to marry; *also* : the statutory crime of such a relationship

in·ces·tu·ous \in-'ses-chə-wəs\ *adj* **1** : constituting or involving incest **2** : guilty of incest — **in·ces·tu·ous·ly** *adv* — **in·ces·tu·ous·ness** *n*

¹inch \'inch\ *n* [OE *ynce*, fr. L *uncia* twelfth part, inch, ounce] **1** : a unit of length equal to ¹⁄₃₆ yard — see MEASURE table **2** : a small amount, distance, or degree ⟨wouldn't move an *inch*⟩ **3** *pl* : STATURE, HEIGHT

²inch *vb* : to move by small degrees

³inch *n* [ScGael *innis*] *chiefly Scot* : ISLAND

inch·meal \'inch-ˌmēl\ *adv* : little by little : GRADUALLY

in·cho·ate \in-'kō-ət, 'in-kə-ˌwāt\ *adj* [L *inchoatus*, pp. of *inchoare* to begin] : being recently begun or only partly in existence or operation : INCIPIENT, INCOMPLETE — **in·cho·ate·ly** *adv* — **in·cho·ate·ness** *n*

in·cho·a·tive \in-'kō-ət-iv\ *adj* **1** : INITIAL, FORMATIVE **2** : denoting a beginning — used of verbs — **inchoative** *n* — **in·cho·a·tive·ly** *adv*

inch·worm \'inch-ˌwərm\ *n* : LOOPER 1

in·ci·dence \'in(t)-səd-ən(t)s, -sə-ˌden(t)s\ *n* **1 a** : an act or fact of affecting : OCCURRENCE **b** : rate of occurrence or influence **2 a** : the arrival of something (as a projectile or a ray of light) at a surface **b** : ANGLE OF INCIDENCE

¹in·ci·dent \'in(t)-səd-ənt, -sə-ˌdent\ *n* [ME, fr. MF, fr. ML *incident-, incidens*, fr. L, prp. of *incidere* to fall on, occur, fr. *in-* + *cadere* to fall] **1 a** : an occurrence that is a separate unit of experience : HAPPENING **b** : an accompanying minor occurrence **2** : an action likely to lead to grave consequences esp. in matters diplomatic **3** : something dependent on or subordinate to something else of greater importance **syn** see OCCURRENCE

²incident *adj* **1** : occurring or likely to occur as an esp. minor consequence or accompaniment ⟨a question *incident* to the main topic⟩ **2** : dependent on or relating to another thing **3** : falling or striking on something ⟨*incident* light rays⟩

¹in·ci·den·tal \ˌin(t)-sə-'dent-ᵊl\ *adj* **1** : occurring merely by chance or without intention **2** : being likely to happen as a chance or minor consequence ⟨*incidental* expenses of a trip⟩ **syn** see ACCIDENTAL — **in·ci·den·tal·ly** \-'dent-lē, -'l-ē\ *adv*

²incidental *n* **1** : something that is incidental **2** *pl* : minor items (as of expense) that are not particularized

in·cin·er·ate \in-'sin-ə-,rāt\ *vt* [L *in-* ²*in-* + *ciner-, cinis* ashes] : to burn to ashes — **in·cin·er·a·tion** \(,)in-,sin-ə-'rā-shən\ *n*

in·cin·er·a·tor \in-'sin-ə-,rāt-ər\ *n* : one that incinerates; *esp* : a furnace or a container for incinerating waste materials

in·cip·i·ent \in-'sip-ē-ənt\ *adj* [L *incipient-, incipiens*, prp. of *incipere* to begin, fr. *in-* + *capere* to take] : beginning to be or become apparent — **in·cip·i·en·cy** \-ən-sē\ *also* **in·cip·i·ence** \-ən(t)s\ *n* — **in·cip·i·ent·ly** *adv*

in·cise \in-'sīz\ *vt* [L *incis-, incidere*, fr. *in-* + *caedere* to cut] **1** : to cut into **2** : ENGRAVE

in·cised \-'sīzd\ *adj* **1** : cut in; *esp* : decorated with incised figures **2** : having a deeply and sharply notched margin ⟨an *incised* leaf⟩

in·ci·sion \in-'sizh-ən\ *n* **1 a** : a marginal notch (as in a leaf) **b** : CUT, GASH; *esp* : an incised wound made surgically into the body **2** : an act of incising **3** : incisive quality

in·ci·sive \in-'sī-siv\ *adj* **1** : CUTTING, PENETRATING **2** : ACUTE, CLEAR-CUT — **in·ci·sive·ly** *adv* — **in·ci·sive·ness** *n*

syn TRENCHANT, CUTTING: INCISIVE implies a power to impress the mind by keen penetration, directness, and decisiveness ⟨no one could ignore that *incisive* command⟩ TRENCHANT implies an energetic cutting or deep probing so as to reveal distinctions or get to the heart of the matter ⟨a *trenchant* critic of political pretensions⟩ CUTTING suggests sarcasm or penetrating accuracy that wounds the feelings ⟨she makes the most *cutting* remarks in that sweet tone of voice⟩

in·ci·sor \in-'sī-zər\ *n* : a tooth adapted for cutting; *esp* : one of the cutting teeth in front of the canines of a mammal — see DENTITION illustration, TOOTH illustration — **incisor** *adj*

in·ci·ta·tion \,in-,sī-'tā-shən, ,in(t)-sə-\ *n* : INCITEMENT

in·cite \in-'sīt\ *vt* [L *incitare*, fr. *in-* ²*in-* + *citare* to rouse, cite] : to move to action : stir up : spur on : urge on — **in·cit·er** *n*

syn INSTIGATE: INCITE stresses a stirring up and urging on and may or may not imply initiative ⟨propaganda *inciting* war⟩ INSTIGATE implies responsibility for initiating another's action and often connotes dubious or evil intention ⟨pamphleteers whose writings *instigated* rebellion⟩ ⟨the theft was *instigated* by desperate hunger⟩

in·cite·ment \in-'sīt-mənt\ *n* **1** : the act of inciting : the state of being incited ⟨charged with *incitement* to riot⟩ **2** : something that incites : INCENTIVE

in·ci·vil·i·ty \,in(t)-sə-'vil-ət-ē\ *n, pl* **-ties** **1** : the quality or state of being uncivil : DISCOURTESY, RUDENESS **2** : a rude or discourteous act

in·clem·ent \(')in-'klem-ənt\ *adj* **1** : harsh or severe in temper or action : UNMERCIFUL **2** : STORMY, ROUGH ⟨*inclement* weather⟩ — **in·clem·en·cy** \-ən-sē\ *n* — **in·clem·ent·ly** *adv*

in·clin·a·ble \in-'klī-nə-bəl\ *adj* : having a tendency or inclination : DISPOSED; *also* : FAVORABLE

in·cli·na·tion \,in-klə-'nā-shən, ,in-\ *n* **1** : an act or the action of bending or inclining: as **a** : BOW, NOD **b** : a tilting of something **2** : PROPENSITY, BENT; *esp* : LIKING **3 a** : a departure from the true vertical or horizontal : SLANT ⟨the *inclination* of the earth's axis⟩; *also* : the degree of such departure **b** : an inclined surface : SLOPE **4** : a tendency to a particular state, character, or action — **in·cli·na·tion·al** \-shnəl, -shən-ᵊl\ *adj*

¹in·cline \in-'klīn\ *vb* [L *inclinare*, fr. *in-* ²*in-* + *clinare* to bend; akin to E ¹*lean*] **1** : to bend the head or body forward : BOW **2** : to lean in one's mind : be favorable (as toward a person, an opinion, or a course of action) : TEND ⟨*inclined* toward the second of two proposals⟩ **3** : to deviate from a line, direction, or course : LEAN, SLOPE, SLANT; *esp* : to deviate from the vertical or horizontal **4** : to cause to bend, bow, slope, or slant **5** : to have influence on (as in direction, course of action, or opinion) — **in·clin·er** *n*

²in·cline \'in-,klīn\ *n* : an inclined plane : GRADE, SLOPE

in·clined \in-'klīnd, 2 also 'in-,\ *adj* **1** : having inclina-

tion, disposition, or tendency **2 a** : having a slant or slope **b** : making an angle with a line or plane

inclined plane *n* : a plane surface that makes an oblique angle with the plane of the horizon

in·cli·nom·e·ter \,in-klə-'näm-ət-ər, ,in-\ *n* **1** : an apparatus for determining the direction of the earth's magnetic field with reference to the plane of the horizon **2** : an instrument for indicating the inclination to the horizontal of the lateral or longitudinal axis of an airplane

inclose, inclosure *var of* ENCLOSE, ENCLOSURE

in·clude \in-'klüd\ *vt* [L *inclus-, includere*, fr. *in-* ²*in-* + *claudere* to close] **1** : to shut up : ENCLOSE **2** : to take in or comprise as a part of a whole **3** : to contain between ⟨two sides and the *included* angle⟩ — **in·clud·a·ble** *or* **in·clud·i·ble** \-'klüd-ə-bəl\ *adj*

syn INCLUDE, COMPREHEND, INVOLVE mean to contain within as a part of the whole. INCLUDE suggests containing something as a constituent or subordinate part of a larger whole ⟨one of several species of oak *included* in the genus *Quercus*⟩ COMPREHEND implies that something comes within the range or scope of a statement or definition ⟨in some cases the term *commerce* does not *comprehend* navigation⟩ INVOLVE suggests an inclusion or entanglement in a whole by virtue of its being its result or a necessary element of its definition ⟨surrender *involves* submission⟩ ⟨freedom *involves* responsibility⟩ **syn** see in addition COMPRISE

in·clu·sion \in-'klü-zhən\ *n* **1** : the act of including : the state of being included **2** : something that is included; *esp* : a passive product of cell activity (as a starch grain) within the protoplasm

in·clu·sive \in-'klü-siv, -ziv\ *adj* **1** : INCLUDING ⟨the cost *inclusive* of materials⟩; *esp* : including one or more limits ⟨pages ten to twenty *inclusive*⟩⟨*inclusive* of today⟩ **2** : broad in orientation, scope, or coverage ⟨an *inclusive* insurance policy⟩ — **in·clu·sive·ly** *adv* — **in·clu·sive·ness** *n*

in·co·erc·i·ble \,in-kō-'ər-sə-bəl\ *adj* : incapable of being controlled, checked, or confined

in·cog·i·tant \in-'käj-ət-ənt\ *adj* : THOUGHTLESS, INCONSIDERATE

¹in·cog·ni·to \,in-,käg-'nēt-ō, in-'käg-nə-,tō\ *adv (or adj)* [It, fr. L *incognitus* unknown, fr. *in-* + *cognitus* known, fr. pp. of *cognoscere* to know] : with one's identity concealed (as by a name or title not arousing special recognition) ⟨traveling *incognito* to avoid publicity⟩

²incognito *n, pl* **-tos** **1** : one appearing or living incognito **2** : the state or disguise of an incognito ⟨his *incognito* was quickly discovered⟩

in·co·her·ence \,in-kō-'hir-ən(t)s, -'her-\ *n* **1** : the quality or state of being incoherent **2** : an incoherent utterance

in·co·her·ent \-ənt\ *adj* : not coherent: as **a** : not sticking closely or compactly together : LOOSE **b** : not clearly or logically connected : RAMBLING ⟨the victim told an *incoherent* story⟩ — **in·co·her·ent·ly** *adv*

in·com·bus·ti·ble \,in-kəm-'bəs-tə-bəl\ *adj* : not combustible : incapable of being burned

in·come \'in-,kəm\ *n* : a gain usu. measured in money that derives from capital or labor; *also* : the amount of such gain received by an individual in a given period of time

income tax \,in-(,)kəm-\ *n* : a tax on the net income of an individual or business concern

¹in·com·ing \'in-,kəm-iŋ\ *n* : the act of coming in

²incoming *adj* : coming in

in·com·men·su·ra·ble \,in-kə-'men(t)s-(ə-)rə-bəl, -'mench-(ə-)rə-\ *adj* : not commensurable — **in·com·men·su·ra·bil·i·ty** \-,men(t)s-(ə-)rə-'bil-ət-ē, -,mench-(ə-)rə-\ *n* — **incommensurable** *n* — **in·com·men·su·ra·bly** \-'men(t)s-(ə-)rə-blē, -'mench-(ə-)rə-\ *adv*

in·com·men·su·rate \-'men(t)s-(ə-)rət, -'mench-(ə-)rət\ *adj* : not commensurate; *esp* : not adequate : not enough to satisfy ⟨funds *incommensurate* with need⟩

in·com·mode \,in-kə-'mōd\ *vt* [L *incommodare*, fr. *incommodus* inconvenient] : to give inconvenience or trouble to : DISCOMMODE

in·com·mo·di·ous \,in-kə-'mōd-ē-əs\ *adj* : not commodious : INCONVENIENT — **in·com·mo·di·ous·ly** *adv* — **in·com·mo·di·ous·ness** *n*

in·com·mod·i·ty \-'mäd-ət-ē\ *n* : INCONVENIENCE, DISADVANTAGE

in·com·mu·ni·ca·ble \,in-kə-'myü-ni-kə-bəl\ *adj* : not capable of being communicated or imparted — **in·com·**

j **joke**; ŋ **sing**; ō **flow**; ȯ **flaw**; ȯi **coin**; th **thin**; t̶h **this**; ü **loot**; u̇ **foot**; y **yet**; yü **few**; yu̇ **furious**; zh **vision**

mu·ni·ca·bil·i·ty \-ˌmyü-ni-kə-'bil-ət-ē\ *n* — **in·com-mu·ni·ca·bly** \-'myü-ni-kə-blē\ *adv*
in·com·mu·ni·ca·do \ˌin-kə-ˌmyü-nə-'käd-ō\ *adv (or adj)* [Sp *incomunicado,* fr. pp. of *incomunicar* to deprive of communication] : without means of communication with others; *also* : in solitary confinement ⟨a prisoner held *incommunicado*⟩
in·com·mu·ni·ca·tive \ˌin-kə-'myü-nə-ˌkāt-iv, -ni-kət-\ *adj* : UNCOMMUNICATIVE
in·com·mut·a·ble \ˌin-kə-'myüt-ə-bəl\ *adj* : not commutable — **in·com·mut·a·bly** \-blē\ *adv*
in·com·pa·ra·ble \('\)in-'käm-p(ə-)rə-bəl\ *adj* **1** : eminent beyond comparison : MATCHLESS **2** : not suitable for comparison — **in·com·pa·ra·bil·i·ty** \(ˌ)in-ˌkäm-p(ə-)rə-'bil-ət-ē\ *n* — **in·com·pa·ra·bly** \('\)in-'käm-p(ə-)rə-blē\ *adv*
in·com·pat·i·bil·i·ty \ˌin-kəm-ˌpat-ə-'bil-ət-ē\ *n, pl* **-ties 1** : the quality or state of being incompatible **2** *pl* : mutually antagonistic things or qualities
¹**in·com·pat·i·ble** \ˌin-kəm-'pat-ə-bəl\ *adj* : incapable of or unsuitable for association ⟨were temperamentally *incompatible*⟩: as **a** : lacking harmony or congruity : DISCORDANT ⟨*incompatible* colors⟩⟨conduct *incompatible* with a sense of honor⟩ **b** : having undesirable chemical or physiological effects when used together ⟨*incompatible* drugs⟩ **c** : infertile in a particular reproductive association ⟨*incompatible* plants⟩ — **in·com·pat·i·bly** \-blē\ *adv*
²**incompatible** *n* : one that is incompatible — usu. used in pl.
in·com·pe·tence \('\)in-'käm-pət-ən(t)s\ *also* **in·com·pe·ten·cy** \-ən-sē\ *n, pl* **-tenc·es** *also* **-tencies** : the quality, state, or fact of being incompetent
¹**in·com·pe·tent** \('\)in-'käm-pət-ənt\ *adj* **1** : lacking the qualities (as knowledge, skill, or ability) necessary to effective independent action **2** : not legally qualified **3** : inadequate to or unsuitable for the purpose ⟨an *incompetent* heart valve⟩⟨an *incompetent* system of government⟩ — **in·com·pe·tent·ly** *adv*
²**incompetent** *n* : an incompetent person
in·com·plete \ˌin-kəm-'plēt\ *adj* : not complete : lacking some part : UNFINISHED, IMPERFECT — **in·com·plete·ly** *adv* — **in·com·plete·ness** *n*
in·com·pli·ant \ˌin-kəm-'plī-ənt\ *adj* : not compliant or pliable : UNYIELDING
in·com·pre·hen·si·ble \(ˌ)in-ˌkäm-pri-'hen(t)-sə-bəl\ *adj* : incapable of being comprehended : impossible to understand — **in·com·pre·hen·si·bil·i·ty** \-ˌhen(t)-sə-'bil-ət-ē\ *n* — **in·com·pre·hen·si·ble·ness** \-'hen(t)-sə-bəl-nəs\ *n* — **in·com·pre·hen·si·bly** \-blē\ *adv*
in·com·pre·hen·sion \(ˌ)in-ˌkäm-pri-'hen-chən\ *n* : lack of comprehension or understanding
in·com·press·i·ble \ˌin-kəm-'pres-ə-bəl\ *adj* : incapable of or resistant to compression — **in·com·press·i·bil·i·ty** \-ˌpres-ə-'bil-ət-ē\ *n* — **in·com·press·i·bly** \-'pres-ə-blē\ *adv*
in·com·put·a·ble \ˌin-kəm-'pyüt-ə-bəl\ *adj* : not computable : very great — **in·com·put·a·bly** \-blē\ *adv*
in·con·ceiv·a·ble \ˌin-kən-'sē-və-bəl\ *adj* : impossible to imagine or conceive : hard to believe : INCREDIBLE, UNTHINKABLE — **in·con·ceiv·a·bil·i·ty** \-ˌsē-və-'bil-ət-ē\ *n* — **in·con·ceiv·a·ble·ness** \-'sē-və-bəl-nəs\ *n* — **in·con·ceiv·a·bly** \-blē\ *adv*
in·con·clu·sive \ˌin-kən-'klü-siv, -ziv\ *adj* : leading to no conclusion or definite result — **in·con·clu·sive·ly** *adv* — **in·con·clu·sive·ness** *n*
in·con·dens·a·ble \ˌin-kən-'den(t)-sə-bəl\ *adj* : incapable of being condensed
in·con·form·i·ty \ˌin-kən-'fȯr-mət-ē\ *n* : NONCONFORMITY
in·con·gru·ence \ˌin-kən-'grü-ən(t)s, ('\)in-'käŋ-grə-wən(t)s\ *n* : INCONGRUITY
in·con·gru·ent \ˌin-kən-'grü-ənt, ('\)in-'käŋ-grə-wənt\ *adj* : not congruent — **in·con·gru·ent·ly** *adv*
in·con·gru·i·ty \ˌin-kən-'grü-ət-ē, -ˌkän-\ *n, pl* **-ties 1** : the quality or state of being incongruous **2** : something that is incongruous
in·con·gru·ous \('\)in-'käŋ-grə-wəs\ *adj* : not consistent with or suitable to the surroundings or associations : not harmonious, appropriate, or proper : out of place ⟨*incongruous* colors⟩⟨had manners *incongruous* with his appearance⟩ — **in·con·gru·ous·ly** *adv* — **in·con·gru·ous·ness** *n*

in·con·sec·u·tive \ˌin-kən-'sek-(y)ət-iv\ *adj* : not consecutive
in·con·se·quence \('\)in-'kän(t)-sə-ˌkwen(t)s, -si-kwən(t)s\ *n* : the quality or state of being inconsequent
in·con·se·quent \-kwənt, -ˌkwent\ *adj* **1 a** : lacking reasonable sequence : ILLOGICAL **b** : not consecutive **2** : IRRELEVANT **3** : INCONSEQUENTIAL 2 — **in·con·se·quent·ly** \-ˌkwent-lē, -kwənt-\ *adv*
in·con·se·quen·tial \(ˌ)in-ˌkän(t)-sə-'kwen-chəl\ *adj* **1 a** : ILLOGICAL **b** : IRRELEVANT **2** : of no significance : UNIMPORTANT — **in·con·se·quen·ti·al·i·ty** \-ˌkwen-chē-'al-ət-ē\ *n* — **in·con·se·quen·tial·ly** \-'kwench-(ə-)lē\ *adv*
in·con·sid·er·a·ble \ˌin-kən-'sid-ər-(ə-)bəl, -'sid-rə-bəl\ *adj* : not worth considering : SLIGHT, TRIVIAL — **in·con·sid·er·a·ble·ness** *n* — **in·con·sid·er·a·bly** \-blē\ *adv*
in·con·sid·er·ate \ˌin-kən-'sid-(ə-)rət\ *adj* **1** : HEEDLESS, THOUGHTLESS **2** : careless of the rights or feelings of others — **in·con·sid·er·ate·ly** *adv* — **in·con·sid·er·ate·ness** *n*
in·con·sis·ten·cy \ˌin-kən-'sis-tən-sē\ *n, pl* **-cies 1** : the quality or state of being inconsistent **2** : an instance of being inconsistent
in·con·sis·tent \ˌin-kən-'sis-tənt\ *adj* **1 a** : not being in agreement or harmony : INCOMPATIBLE ⟨offered an explanation *inconsistent* with the facts⟩ ⟨two *inconsistent* statements⟩ **b** : containing incompatible elements ⟨an *inconsistent* argument⟩ **2** : not logical in thought or actions : CHANGEABLE ⟨a very *inconsistent* man⟩ — **in·con·sis·tent·ly** *adv*
in·con·sol·a·ble \ˌin-kən-'sō-lə-bəl\ *adj* : incapable of being consoled : not to be comforted : DISCONSOLATE — **in·con·sol·a·ble·ness** *n* — **in·con·sol·a·bly** \-blē\ *adv*
in·con·so·nance \('\)in-'kän(t)-s(ə-)nən(t)s\ *n* : lack of consonance or harmony : DISAGREEMENT
in·con·so·nant \-s(ə-)nənt\ *adj* : not consonant : DISCORDANT
in·con·spic·u·ous \ˌin-kən-'spik-yə-wəs\ *adj* : not readily noticeable — **in·con·spic·u·ous·ly** *adv* — **in·con·spic·u·ous·ness** *n*
in·con·stan·cy \('\)in-'kän(t)-stən-sē\ *n, pl* **-cies** : the quality or state of being inconstant : lack of constancy
in·con·stant \-stənt\ *adj* : likely to change frequently without apparent reason : CHANGEABLE — **in·con·stant·ly** *adv*
in·con·sum·a·ble \ˌin-kən-'sü-mə-bəl\ *adj* : not capable of being consumed — **in·con·sum·a·bly** \-blē\ *adv*
in·con·test·a·ble \ˌin-kən-'tes-tə-bəl\ *adj* : not open to doubt or contest : INDISPUTABLE, UNQUESTIONABLE — **in·con·test·a·bil·i·ty** \-ˌtes-tə-'bil-ət-ē\ *n* — **in·con·test·a·bly** \-'tes-tə-blē\ *adv*
in·con·ti·nent \('\)in-'känt-ⁿn-ənt\ *adj* : lacking in self-restraint esp. in the gratification of sensuous desires — **in·con·ti·nence** \-ən(t)s\ *n* — **in·con·ti·nent·ly** *adv*
in·con·trol·la·ble \ˌin-kən-'trō-lə-bəl\ *adj* : UNCONTROLLABLE
in·con·tro·vert·i·ble \(ˌ)in-ˌkän-trə-'vərt-ə-bəl\ *adj* : not open to question : INDISPUTABLE ⟨*incontrovertible* evidence⟩ — **in·con·tro·vert·i·bly** \-blē\ *adv*
¹**in·con·ve·nience** \ˌin-kən-'vē-nyən(t)s\ *n* **1** : the quality or state of being inconvenient : lack of suitability for personal ease or comfort **2** : something inconvenient : something that disturbs or that causes discomfort or annoyance
²**inconvenience** *vt* : to subject to inconvenience : cause discomfort to : put to trouble : INCOMMODE
in·con·ve·nient \-nyənt\ *adj* : not convenient : causing difficulty, discomfort, or annoyance — **in·con·ve·nient·ly** *adv*
in·con·vert·i·ble \ˌin-kən-'vərt-ə-bəl\ *adj* : not convertible into something else; *esp* : not exchangeable for a foreign currency or into specie — **in·con·vert·i·bil·i·ty** \-ˌvərt-ə-'bil-ət-ē\ *n* — **in·con·vert·i·bly** \-'vərt-ə-blē\ *adv*
in·con·vinc·i·ble \ˌin-kən-'vin(t)-sə-bəl\ *adj* : incapable of being convinced
in·co·or·di·nate \ˌin-kō-'ȯrd-nət, -ⁿn-ət\ *adj* : not coordinate
in·co·or·di·na·tion \ˌin-kō-ˌȯrd-ⁿn-'ā-shən\ *n* : lack of coordination esp. of muscular movements
in·cor·po·ra·ble \in-'kȯr-p(ə-)rə-bəl\ *adj* : capable of being incorporated
¹**in·cor·po·rate** \in-'kȯr-pə-ˌrāt\ *vb* [L *in-* ²*in-* + *corpor-,*

corpus body] **1** : to unite with or work into something already existent **2** : to unite or combine to form a single body or a consistent whole **3** : to give material form to : EMBODY **4** : to form, form into, or become a corporation ⟨*incorporate* a firm⟩⟨an *incorporated* town⟩ — **in·cor·po·ra·tion** \(,)in-,kȯr-pə-'rā-shən\ *n* — **in·cor·po·ra·tive** \in-'kȯr-pə-,rāt-iv, -p(ə-)rət-\ *adj* — **in·cor·po·ra·tor** \-pə-,rāt-ər\ *n*

²in·cor·po·rate \in-'kȯr-p(ə-)rət\ *adj* : INCORPORATED

in·cor·po·rat·ed \-pə-,rāt-əd\ *adj* : united in one body; *esp* : formed into a legal corporation

in·cor·po·re·al \,in-kȯr-'pōr-ē-əl, -'pȯr-\ *adj* : not corporeal : having no material body or form : IMMATERIAL — **in·cor·po·re·al·ly** \-ə-lē\ *adv*

in·cor·po·re·i·ty \,in-,kȯr-pə-'rē-ət-ē\ *n* : the quality or state of being incorporeal : IMMATERIALITY

in·cor·rect \,in-kə-'rekt\ *adj* **1 a** : INACCURATE, FAULTY **b** : not true : WRONG **2** : UNBECOMING, IMPROPER — **in·cor·rect·ly** *adv* — **in·cor·rect·ness** \-'rek(t)-nəs\ *n*

¹in·cor·ri·gi·ble \(')in-'kȯr-ə-jə-bəl, -'kär-\ *adj* [L ¹in- + *corrigere* to correct] : not to be corrected or improved: as **a** : incapable of being reformed ⟨an *incorrigible* gambler⟩ **b** : UNRULY, UNMANAGEABLE — **in·cor·ri·gi·bil·i·ty** \(,)in-,kȯr-ə-jə-'bil-ət-ē, -,kär-\ *n* — **in·cor·ri·gi·ble·ness** \(')in-'kȯr-ə-jə-bəl-nəs, -'kär-\ *n* — **in·cor·ri·gi·bly** \-blē\ *adv*

²incorrigible *n* : an incorrigible person

in·cor·rupt·i·ble \,in-kə-'rəp-tə-bəl\ *adj* : not to be corrupted: as **a** : not subject to decay **b** : incapable of being bribed or morally corrupted — **in·cor·rupt·i·bil·i·ty** \-,rəp-tə-'bil-ət-ē\ *n* — **in·cor·rupt·i·bly** \-'rəp-tə-blē\ *adv*

¹in·crease \in-'krēs, 'in-,\ *vb* [MF *encreistre*, fr. L *increscere*, fr. in- ²in- + *crescere* to grow] **1** : to make or become greater (as in size, number, value, or power) ⟨*increase* speed⟩ ⟨skill *increases* with practice⟩ **2** : to multiply by the production of young — **in·creas·a·ble** \-'krē-sə-bəl, -,krē-\ *adj* — **in·creas·er** *n*

²in·crease \'in-,krēs, in-'\ *n* **1** : the act of increasing : addition or enlargement in size, extent, or quantity **2** : something (as offspring, produce, or profit) added to an original stock by enlargement or growth

in·creas·ing·ly \in-'krē-siŋ-lē, 'in-,krē-\ *adv* : to an increasing degree : more and more

in·cre·ate \,in-krē-'āt, in-'krē-ət\ *adj* : not created — **in·cre·ate·ly** *adv*

in·cred·i·ble \(')in-'kred-ə-bəl\ *adj* : too extraordinary or improbable to be believed; *also* : hard to believe — **in·cred·i·bil·i·ty** \(,)in-,kred-ə-'bil-ət-ē\ *n* — **in·cred·i·bly** \(')in-'kred-ə-blē\ *adv*

in·cre·du·li·ty \,in-kri-'d(y)ü-lət-ē\ *n* : the quality or state of not believing or of doubting; *also* : an instance of disbelieving **syn** see UNBELIEF

in·cred·u·lous \(')in-'krej-ə-ləs\ *adj* **1** : not credulous : tending to disbelieve : SKEPTICAL **2** : expressing incredulity ⟨listened with an *incredulous* smile⟩ — **in·cred·u·lous·ly** *adv*

in·cre·ment \'iŋ-krə-mənt, 'in-\ *n* [L *incrementum*, fr. *increscere* to increase] **1** : an increasing or growth esp. in quantity or value : ENLARGEMENT, INCREASE; *also* : QUANTITY **2 a** : something gained or added **b** : one of a series of regular consecutive additions **c** : a minute increase in quantity — **in·cre·men·tal** \,iŋ-krə-'ment-ᵊl, ,in-\ *adj*

in·cres·cent \in-'kres-ᵊnt\ *adj* : INCREASING, WAXING ⟨the *increscent* moon⟩

in·crim·i·nate \in-'krim-ə-,nāt\ *vt* [L *in-* ²in- + *crimin-, crimen* accusation, crime] : to charge with or involve in a crime or fault : ACCUSE — **in·crim·i·na·tion** \(,)in-,krim-ə-'nā-shən\ *n* — **in·crim·i·na·to·ry** \in-'krim-(ə)nə-,tōr-ē, -,tȯr-\ *adj*

in·cross \'in-,krȯs\ *n* : an individual produced by crossing inbred lines of the same breed or strain

in·cross·bred \'in-'krȯs-,bred\ *n* : an individual produced by crossing inbred lines of separate breeds or strains

incrust *var of* ENCRUST

in·crus·ta·tion \,in-,krəs-'tā-shən\ *n* **1** : the act of encrusting : the state of being encrusted **2** : a hard coating : CRUST **3 a** : OVERLAY **b** : INLAY

in·cu·bate \'iŋ-kyə-,bāt, 'in-\ *vb* [L *incubare*, fr. *in-* ²in- + *cubare* to lie] **1** : to sit upon eggs to hatch them by warmth **2** : to maintain (as bacteria or a chemically active system)

under conditions favorable for development or reaction **3** : to undergo incubation — **in·cu·ba·tive** \-,bāt-iv\ *adj*

in·cu·ba·tion \,iŋ-kyə-'bā-shən, ,in-\ *n* **1** : the act or process of incubating **2** : the period between infection and the manifestation of a disease — **in·cu·ba·tion·al** \-shnəl, -shən-ᵊl\ *adj*

in·cu·ba·tor \'iŋ-kyə-,bāt-ər, 'in-\ *n* : one that incubates; *esp* : an apparatus providing suitable conditions (as of warmth and moisture) for incubating something ⟨an *incubator* for premature babies⟩

in·cu·bus \'iŋ-kyə-bəs, 'in-\ *n, pl* **-bi** \-,bī, -,bē\ *also* **-bus·es** [LL, fr. L *incubare* to lie on] **1** : an evil spirit held to lie upon persons in their sleep **2** : NIGHTMARE **3** : a person or thing that oppresses or burdens like a nightmare

in·cul·cate \in-'kəl-,kāt, 'in-(,)kəl-\ *vt* [L *inculcare*, lit., to tread in, fr. *in-* + *calc-, calx* heel] : to teach and impress upon the mind by frequent repetition ⟨childhood training that had *inculcated* a deep sense of responsibility⟩ — **in·cul·ca·tion** \,in-(,)kəl-'kā-shən\ *n* — **in·cul·ca·tor** \in-'kəl-,kāt-ər, 'in-(,)kəl-\ *n*

in·cul·pa·ble \(')in-'kəl-pə-bəl\ *adj* : free from guilt : BLAMELESS

in·cul·pate \in-'kəl-,pāt, 'in-(,)kəl-\ *vt* [L *in-* ²in- + *culpa* blame, fault] : INCRIMINATE — **in·cul·pa·tion** \,in-(,)kəl-'pā-shən\ *n*

in·cum·ben·cy \in-'kəm-bən-sē\ *n, pl* **-cies** **1** : the quality or state of being incumbent **2** : the office or period of office of an incumbent

¹in·cum·bent \-bənt\ *n* [L *incumbere* to lie down on, fr. *in-* + *-cumbere* to lie down] : the holder of an office or position

²incumbent *adj* **1** : lying or resting on something else **2** : imposed as a duty : OBLIGATORY **3** : bent over so as to rest on or touch an underlying surface

incumber, incumbrance *var of* ENCUMBER, ENCUMBRANCE

in·cu·nab·u·lum \,in-kyə-'nab-yə-ləm, ,iŋ-\ *n, pl* **-la** \-lə\ [NL, fr. L *incunabula*, pl., swaddling clothes, cradle, fr. *in-* + *cunae* cradle] : a book printed before 1501; *also* : a work of art or of human industry of an early epoch

in·cur \in-'kər\ *vt in-curred; in·cur·ring* [L *incurrere*, lit., to run into, fr. *in-* + *currere* to run] **1** : to meet with (as an inconvenience) ⟨*incur* expenses⟩ **2** : to become liable or subject to : bring down upon oneself ⟨*incur* punishment⟩

¹in·cur·a·ble \(')in-'kyur-ə-bəl\ *adj* : not capable of being cured — **in·cur·a·bil·i·ty** \(,)in-,kyur-ə-'bil-ət-ē\ *n* — **in·cur·a·ble·ness** \(')in-'kyur-ə-bəl-nəs\ *n* — **in·cur·a·bly** \-blē\ *adv*

²incurable *n* : a person suffering from a disease that is beyond cure

in·cu·ri·ous \(')in-'kyur-ē-əs\ *adj* : not curious or inquisitive : UNINTERESTED — **in·cu·ri·ous·ly** *adv* — **in·cu·ri·ous·ness** *n*

in·cur·rence \in-'kər-ən(t)s, -'kə-rən(t)s\ *n* : the act or process of incurring

in·cur·rent \in-'kər-ənt, -'kə-rənt\ *adj* : characterized by a current that flows inward ⟨*incurrent* canals of a sponge⟩

in·cur·sion \in-'kər-zhən\ *n* [L *incurs-, incurrere* to run into, invade] : a sudden usu. temporary invasion : RAID

in·cur·sive \in-'kər-siv\ *adj* : making incursions

in·cur·vate \'in-,kər-,vāt, in-'\ *vt* : to cause to curve inward : BEND — **in·cur·vate** \in-,kər-,vāt, in-'kər-vət\ *adj* — **in·cur·va·tion** \,in-,kər-'vā-shən\ *n* — **in·cur·va·ture** \(')in-'kər-və-,chur, -chər\ *n*

¹in·curve \'in-,kərv\ *vb* : to bend so as to curve inward

²in·curve \'in-,kərv\ *n* : a curving in

in·cus \'iŋ-kəs\ *n, pl* **in·cu·des** \iŋ-'kyüd-(,)ēz\ [NL *incud-, incus,* fr. L, anvil] : the middle of a chain of three small bones in the ear of a mammal — called also *anvil;* compare STAPES

Ind \'ind, 'īnd\ *n* **1** *archaic* : India **2** *obs* : Indies

Ind- *or* **Indo-** *comb form* **1** : India or the East Indies ⟨*Indo*phile⟩ ⟨*Indo*-Briton⟩ **2** : Indo-European ⟨*Indo*-Hittite⟩

in·debt·ed \in-'det-əd\ *adj* : being in debt : owing something (as money, gratitude, or services)

in·debt·ed·ness *n* **1** : the condition of being indebted **2** : an amount owed

in·de·cen·cy \(')in-'dēs-ᵊn-sē\ *n, pl* **-cies** **1** : lack of decency **2** : an indecent act or word

in·de·cent \-ᵊnt\ *adj* : not decent: **a** : UNBECOMING, UNSEEMLY ⟨remarried in *indecent* haste⟩ **b** : morally offensive — **in·de·cent·ly** *adv*

---

j joke; **ŋ** sing; **ō** flow; **ȯ** flaw; **ȯi** coin; **th** thin; **th** this; **ü** loot; ** u̇** foot; **y** yet; **yü** few; **yu̇** furious; **zh** vision

in·de·ci·pher·a·ble \,in-di-'sī-f(ə-)rə-bəl\ *adj* : that cannot be deciphered

in·de·ci·sion \,in-di-'sizh-ən\ *n* : a wavering between two or more possible courses of action : IRRESOLUTION

in·de·ci·sive \-'sī-siv\ *adj* **1** : not decisive or final ⟨an *indecisive* battle⟩ **2** : characterized by indecision : HESITATING, UNCERTAIN ⟨an *indecisive* person⟩ — **in·de·ci·sive·ly** *adv* — **in·de·ci·sive·ness** *n*

in·de·clin·a·ble \,in-di-'klī-nə-bəl\ *adj* : having no grammatical inflections

in·dec·o·rous \(')in-'dek-ə-rəs; ,in-di-'kōr-əs, -'kòr-\ *adj* : not decorous : UNBECOMING — **in·dec·o·rous·ly** *adv* — **in·dec·o·rous·ness** *n*

syn IMPROPER, UNSEEMLY : INDECOROUS suggests a violation of accepted standards of good manners ⟨*indecorous* talking in church⟩ IMPROPER applies to a broader range of violation of rules not only of social behavior but also of ethical practice or logical procedure ⟨an *improper* conclusion inferred from the premises⟩ ⟨telling *improper* jokes⟩ UNSEEMLY adds a suggestion of an offensiveness to good taste ⟨city outskirts made ugly by *unseemly* junk piles⟩

in·de·co·rum \,in-di-'kōr-əm, -'kòr-\ *n* : lack of decorum : IMPROPRIETY

in·deed \in-'dēd\ *adv* **1** : in fact : in reality : TRULY — often used interjectionally to express disbelief or surprise **2** : ADMITTEDLY, UNDENIABLY

in·de·fat·i·ga·ble \,in-di-'fat-i-gə-bəl\ *adj* [L *indefatigabilis*, fr. *in-* ¹in- + *defatigare* to wear down, fr. *de-* + *fatigare* to fatigue] : capable of working a long time without tiring : not giving in to fatigue : TIRELESS — **in·de·fat·i·ga·bil·i·ty** \-,fat-i-gə-'bil-ət-ē\ *n* — **in·de·fat·i·ga·ble·ness** \-'fat-i-gə-bəl-nəs\ *n* — **in·de·fat·i·ga·bly** \-blē\ *adv*

in·de·fea·si·ble \,in-di-'fē-zə-bəl\ *adj* [¹in- + AF *defaisible* capable of being annulled, fr. OF *deffais-*, *deffaire* to undo, fr. ML *disfacere*, fr. L *dis-* + *facere* to do] : not capable of being abolished or annulled ⟨*indefeasible* rights⟩ — **in·de·fea·si·bil·i·ty** \-,fē-zə-'bil-ət-ē\ *n* — **in·de·fea·si·bly** \-'fē-zə-blē\ *adv*

in·de·fec·ti·ble \,in-di-'fek-tə-bəl\ *adj* **1** : not subject to failure or decay : LASTING **2** : free of faults : FLAWLESS — **in·de·fec·ti·bil·i·ty** \-,fek-tə-'bil-ət-ē\ *n* — **in·de·fec·ti·bly** \-'fek-tə-blē\ *adv*

in·de·fen·si·ble \,in-di-'fen(t)-sə-bəl\ *adj* : not capable of being defended ⟨an *indefensible* position⟩ ⟨*indefensible* conduct⟩ — **in·de·fen·si·bil·i·ty** \-,fen(t)-sə-'bil-ət-ē\ *n* — **in·de·fen·si·bly** \-'fen(t)-sə-blē\ *adv*

in·de·fin·a·ble \,in-di-'fī-nə-bəl\ *adj* : incapable of being precisely described or analyzed — **in·de·fin·a·bil·i·ty** \-,fī-nə-'bil-ət-ē\ *n* — **in·de·fin·a·ble·ness** \-'fī-nə-bəl-nəs\ *n* — **in·de·fin·a·bly** \-blē\ *adv*

in·def·i·nite \(')in-'def-(ə-)nət\ *adj* **1** : not clear or fixed in meaning or details : VAGUE ⟨*indefinite* about their plans⟩ ⟨an *indefinite* answer⟩ **2** : not fixed or limited (as in amount or length) ⟨an *indefinite* period⟩ **3** : being a pronoun or grammatical modifier that typically designates an unidentified or not immediately identifiable person or thing ⟨the *indefinite* article⟩ — **in·def·i·nite·ly** *adv* — **in·def·i·nite·ness** *n*

indefinite integral *n* : a mathematical function which is a function of another function and whose derivative is the other function

in·de·his·cent \,in-di-'his-ᵊnt\ *adj* : remaining closed at maturity ⟨*indehiscent* fruits⟩ — **in·de·his·cence** \-ᵊn(t)s\ *n*

in·del·i·ble \in-'del-ə-bəl\ *adj* [L *indelebilis*, fr. *in-* ¹in- + *delēre* to destroy, delete] **1** : not capable of being erased, removed, or blotted out ⟨*indelible* impression⟩ **2** : making marks not easily erased ⟨an *indelible* pencil⟩ — **in·del·i·bil·i·ty** \(,)in-,del-ə-'bil-ət-ē\ *n* — **in·del·i·bly** \in-'del-ə-blē\ *adv*

in·del·i·ca·cy \(')in-'del-i-kə-sē\ *n, pl* **-cies** **1** : the quality or state of being indelicate : COARSENESS **2** : an indelicate act or utterance

in·del·i·cate \-kət\ *adj* : not delicate : offensive to good manners or refined taste : IMMODEST, COARSE — **in·del·i·cate·ly** *adv* — **in·del·i·cate·ness** *n*

in·dem·ni·fy \in-'dem-nə-,fī\ *vt* **-fied; -fy·ing** [L *indemnis* unharmed, fr. *in-* ¹in- + *damnum* damage] **1** : to insure or protect against loss, damage, or injury **2** : to make compensation to for loss, damage, or injury ⟨*indemnify* victims of a disaster⟩ **3** : to make compensation for : make good ⟨have their losses *indemnified*⟩ — **in·dem·ni·fi·ca·tion** \-,dem-nə-fə-'kā-shən\ *n* — **in·dem·ni·fi·er** \-'dem-nə-,fī(-ə)r\ *n*

in·dem·ni·ty \in-'dem-nət-ē\ *n, pl* **-ties** **1** : protection from loss, damage, or injury : INSURANCE **2** : freedom or exemption from penalty for past offenses **3** : compensation paid for loss, damage, or injury

¹in·dent \in-'dent\ *vt* [OF *endenter*, fr. *en-* + *dent* tooth, fr. L *dent-*, *dens*] **1 a** : to notch the edge of : make jagged **b** : to cut into for the purpose of mortising or dovetailing **2** : to set (as a line of a paragraph) in from the margin **3** : to join together by or as if by mortises or dovetails — **in·dent·er** *n*

²indent *vt* **1** : to force inward so as to form a depression **2** : to form a dent in — **in·dent·er** *n*

³indent *n* : INDENTATION

in·den·ta·tion \,in-,den-'tā-shən\ *n* **1 a** : an angular cut in an edge : NOTCH **b** : a usu. deep recess (as in a coastline) **2 a** : the action of indenting : the state of being indented **b** : a blank or empty space produced by indenting **3** : DENT

in·den·tion \in-'den-chən\ *n* : an indentation esp. in printing ⟨*indention* of a paragraph⟩

¹in·den·ture \in-'den-chər\ *n* [MF *endenture* document carrying two or more copies and divided by an irregular notched cut so that the sections might be proved to belong to the same document by matching the divided edges, fr. *endenter* to indent, notch] **1** : a written agreement : CONTRACT **2** : a contract that binds a person to serve another for a specified period — usu. used in pl.

²indenture *vt* : to bind (as an apprentice) by indentures

in·de·pend·ence \,in-də-'pen-dən(t)s\ *n* **1** : the quality or state of being independent : freedom from outside control **2** *archaic* : COMPETENCE 1

Independence Day *n* : July 4 observed as a legal holiday in commemoration of the adoption of the Declaration of Independence in 1776

in·de·pend·en·cy \,in-də-'pen-dən-sē\ *n* **1** : INDEPENDENCE 1 **2** *cap* : the polity or movement of the Independents

¹in·de·pend·ent \,in-də-'pen-dənt\ *adj* **1** : not subject to control or rule by another : SELF-GOVERNING, FREE ⟨an *independent* nation⟩ **2** : not having connections with another : SEPARATE ⟨the same story told by *independent* witnesses⟩ **3** : not supported by or relying on another : having or providing enough money to live on ⟨a person of *independent* means⟩ **4** : not easily influenced : showing self-reliance ⟨an *independent* mind⟩ **5** : refusing to accept help from or to come under obligation to others **6 a** : having full meaning in itself and capable of standing alone as a simple sentence : MAIN ⟨*independent* clause⟩ **b** : varying without respect to other variables **7** : not tied to a political party **syn** see FREE — **in·de·pend·ent·ly** *adv*

²independent *n* **1** *cap* : a sectarian of an English religious movement for congregational autonomy originating in the late 16th century, giving rise to Congregationalists, Baptists, and Friends, and forming a major political force in the period of Cromwell **2** : one that is independent; *esp* : one not committed to a political party

in·de·scrib·a·ble \,in-di-'skrī-bə-bəl\ *adj* : incapable of being described : surpassing description ⟨*indescribable* beauty⟩ — **in·de·scrib·a·ble·ness** *n* — **in·de·scrib·a·bly** \-bə-blē\ *adv*

in·de·struc·ti·ble \,in-di-'strək-tə-bəl\ *adj* : incapable of being destroyed — **in·de·struc·ti·bil·i·ty** \-,strək-tə-'bil-ət-ē\ *n* — **in·de·struc·ti·ble·ness** \-'strək-tə-bəl-nəs\ *n* — **in·de·struc·ti·bly** \-blē\ *adv*

in·de·ter·min·a·ble \,in-di-'tər-mə-nə-bəl\ *adj* : incapable of being definitely decided or ascertained — **in·de·ter·min·a·ble·ness** *n* — **in·de·ter·min·a·bly** \-blē\ *adv*

in·de·ter·mi·nate \,in-di-'tər-mə-nət\ *adj* **1 a** : not definitely or precisely determined : VAGUE **b** : not known in advance **c** : not leading to a definite end or result **2** : capable of continued growth; *esp* : RACEMOSE ⟨an *indeterminate* inflorescence⟩ — **in·de·ter·mi·na·cy** \-mə-nə-sē\ *n* — **in·de·ter·mi·nate·ly** *adv* — **in·de·ter·mi·nate·ness** *n*

in·de·ter·mi·na·tion \-,tər-mə-'nā-shən\ *n* **1** : INDETERMINATENESS **2** : a state of mental indecision

in·de·vout \,in-di-'vaùt\ *adj* : not devout — **in·de·vout·ly** *adv*

¹in·dex \'in-,deks\ n, pl in·dex·es or in·di·ces \-də-,sēz\ [L indic-, index pointer, forefinger, guide, index, fr. indicare to indicate] 1 : a guide (as a table or file) for facilitating reference; esp : an alphabetical list of items treated in a printed work that gives with each item the page number where it may be found 2 : POINTER, INDICATOR 3 : SIGN, INDICATION, TOKEN ⟨an index of his mood⟩ 4 [NL Index Librorum Prohibitorum, lit., index of prohibited books] : a list of restricted or prohibited material; esp, cap : a list of books prohibited or restricted for Roman Catholics by church authorities 5 pl indices : a mathematical figure, letter, or expression (as the figure 3 in a³) : EXPONENT 6 : a character ☞ used to direct attention — called also fist 7 : a number derived from a series of observations and used as an indicator or measure; esp : INDEX NUMBER— in·dex·i·cal \in-'dek-si-kəl\ adj

²index vt 1 a : to provide with an index   b : to list in an index   2 : to serve as an index of — in·dex·er n

index finger n : the finger next to the thumb

index fossil n : a fossil with a usu. narrow temporal range that can be used in dating formations in which it is found

index number n : a number used to indicate change in magnitude (as of cost or price) as compared with the magnitude at some specified time usu. taken as 100

index of refraction : the ratio of the velocity of light in the first of two media to its velocity in the second as it passes from one into the other

index finger

in·dia ink \,in-dē-ə-\ n, often cap 1st I : a solid black pigment (as lampblack) used in drawing and lettering; also : a fluid consisting of a fine suspension of india ink in a liquid

In·dia·man \'in-dē-ə-mən\ n : a large sailing ship formerly used in trade with India

In·di·an \'in-dē-ən\ n 1 : a native or inhabitant of the Republic of India, the subcontinent of India, or the East Indies   2 a [fr. the belief held by Columbus that the lands he discovered were part of Asia] : a member of any of the aboriginal peoples of No. and So. America except the Eskimos   b : an American Indian language — Indian adj

Indian club n : a wooden club that is swung for gymnastic exercise

Indian corn n 1 : a tall widely cultivated American cereal grass bearing seeds on elongated ears   2 : the ears of Indian corn; also : its edible seeds

Indian file n : SINGLE FILE

Indian giver n : one who gives something to another and then takes it back or expects an equivalent in return — Indian giving n

Indian meal n : CORNMEAL

Indian paintbrush n : any of several plants with orange-red flowers or bracts; esp : a European hawkweed that is a widely naturalized weed in No. America

Indian pipe n : a waxy white leafless saprophytic herb with a solitary nodding bell-shaped flower

Indian club

Indian pudding n : a pudding made chiefly of cornmeal, milk, and molasses

Indian summer n : a period of mild weather in late autumn or early winter

Indian tobacco n : any of several plants resembling or used in place of tobacco; esp : an American wild lobelia with small blue flowers

Indian turnip n : JACK-IN-THE-PULPIT; also : its acrid root

India paper n : a thin tough opaque printing paper

india rubber n, often cap I 1 : RUBBER 2 : something made of rubber

In·dic \'in-dik\ adj 1 : of or relating to the subcontinent of India : INDIAN   2 : of, relating to, or constituting the Indian branch of the Indo-European languages — Indic n

in·di·cate \'in-də-,kāt\ vt [L indicare, fr. in- ²in- + dicare to proclaim] 1 a : to point out or point to   b : to be a sign, symptom, or index of   2 : to state or express briefly : SUGGEST

in·di·ca·tion \,in-də-'kā-shən\ n 1 : the action of indicating   2 : something that indicates : SIGN, SUGGESTION   3 : the degree or amount indicated on a graduated instrument

¹in·dic·a·tive \in-'dik-ət-iv\ adj 1 : of, relating to, or

constituting the grammatical mood that represents the denoted act or state as an objective fact   2 : pointing out : giving a sign or indication of something not visible or obvious : SUGGESTIVE ⟨remarks indicative of resentment⟩ — in·dic·a·tive·ly adv

²indicative n : the indicative mood of a verb or a verb in this mood

in·di·ca·tor \'in-də-,kāt-ər\ n 1 : one that indicates: as a : an index hand (as on a dial) : POINTER   b : a pressure gauge   2 : a substance used to show visually (as by change of color) the condition of a solution with respect to the presence of free acid, alkali, or other substance — in·dic·a·to·ry \in-'dik-ə-,tōr-ē, -,tȯr-\ adj

indices pl of INDEX

in·di·cia \in-'dish-(ē-)ə\ n pl [L, pl. of indicium sign, fr. indicare to indicate] 1 : distinctive marks : INDICATIONS   2 : postal markings often imprinted on mail or on labels to be affixed to mail

in·dict \in-'dīt\ vt [alter. of ME inditen, fr. AF enditer, fr. OF, to write down, indite] 1 : to charge with an offense : ACCUSE   2 : to charge with a crime by the finding of a grand jury — in·dict·a·ble \-ə-bəl\ adj — in·dict·er or in·dict·or \-ər\ n

in·dict·ment \in-'dīt-mənt\ n 1 : the act or the legal process of indicting   2 : a formal written statement drawn up by a prosecuting attorney and reported by a grand jury after an inquiry charging a person with an offense — syn see CHARGE

in·dif·fer·ence \in-'dif-ərn(t)s, -'dif-(ə-)rən(t)s\ n 1 : the condition or the fact of being indifferent : lack of feeling for or against something   2 : lack of importance ⟨a matter of indifference to everyone but himself⟩

syn UNCONCERN: INDIFFERENCE implies neutrality of feeling from lack of inclination, preference, or prejudice; UNCONCERN suggests a lack of sensitivity or regard for others' needs or troubles

in·dif·fer·ent \in-'dif-ərnt, -'dif-(ə-)rənt\ adj 1 : having no choice or preference : not interested in or concerned about something ⟨indifferent to heat or cold⟩ ⟨indifferent to the troubles of others⟩   2 : showing neither interest nor dislike ⟨the audience was indifferent⟩   3 : neither good nor bad : MEDIOCRE ⟨indifferent health⟩   4 : of no special influence or value : not important   5 : capable of development in more than one direction — in·dif·fer·ent·ly adv

in·dif·fer·ent·ism \-ərnt-,iz-əm, -(ə-)rənt-\ n : INDIFFER-ENCE; esp : belief that all religions are equally valid — in·dif·fer·ent·ist \-ərnt-əst, -(ə-)rənt-\ n

in·di·gene \'in-di-,jēn\ n : NEEDINESS, POVERTY

in·dig·e·nous \in-'dij-ə-nəs\ adj [LL indigenus, fr. L indu in + gigni to be born] 1 : produced, growing, or living naturally in a particular region or environment   2 : IN-BORN, INNATE   syn see NATIVE — in·dig·e·nous·ly adv — in·dig·e·nous·ness n

in·di·gent \'in-di-jənt\ adj [L indigent-, indigens, fr. prp. of indigēre to need, fr. indu in + egēre to need] : POOR, NEEDY

in·di·gest·i·ble \,in-dī-'jes-tə-bəl, -də-\ adj : not digestible : not easily digested — in·di·gest·i·bil·i·ty \-,jes-tə-'bil-ət-ē\ n

in·di·ges·tion \-'jes-chən\ n 1 : inability to digest or difficulty in digesting something   2 : a case or attack of indigestion — in·di·ges·tive \-'jes-tiv\ adj

in·dig·nant \in-'dig-nənt\ adj [L indignari to be indignant, fr. indignus unworthy, fr. in- ¹in- + dignus worthy] : filled with or marked by indignation — in·dig·nant·ly adv

in·dig·na·tion \,in-dig-'nā-shən\ n : anger aroused by something unjust, unworthy, or mean

in·dig·ni·ty \in-'dig-nət-ē\ n 1 : an act that offends against a person's dignity or self-respect : INSULT   2 : humiliating treatment

in·di·go \'in-di-,gō\ n, pl -gos or -goes [It dial., fr. L indicum, fr. Gk indikon, fr. neut. of indikos Indian] 1 : a blue dye made artificially and formerly obtained from plants and esp. indigo plants   2 : a variable color averaging a dark grayish blue

indigo plant n : any of various mostly leguminous plants that yield indigo

indigo snake n : a large harmless blue-black snake of the southern U.S.

in·di·rect \,in-də-'rekt, -dī-\ adj 1 : not straight : not

the shortest ⟨an *indirect* route⟩ **2 :** not straightforward **: ROUNDABOUT** ⟨*indirect* methods⟩ **3 :** not having a plainly seen connection ⟨an *indirect* cause⟩ **4 :** not straight to the point ⟨an *indirect* answer⟩ **5 :** stating what a real or supposed original speaker said with changes in wording that conform the statement grammatically to the sentence in which it is included ⟨*indirect* discourse⟩ — **in·di·rect·ly** *adv* — **in·di·rect·ness** \-'rek(t)-nəs\ *n*

in·di·rec·tion \-'rek-shən\ *n* **1 :** lack of straightforwardness and openness **: DECEITFULNESS 2 :** indirect action or procedure **: DECEIT**

indirect lighting *n* **:** lighting in which the light emitted by a source is diffusely reflected (as by the ceiling)

indirect object *n* **:** a grammatical object representing the secondary goal of the action of its verb ⟨*me* in "gave me the book" is an *indirect object*⟩

indirect proof *n* **: REDUCTIO AD ABSURDUM**

indirect tax *n* **:** a tax exacted from a person other than the one on whom the ultimate burden of the tax is expected to fall

in·dis·cern·i·ble \,in-dis-'ər-nə-bəl, -diz-'ər-\ *adj* **1 :** incapable of being discerned **2 :** not recognizable as distinct

in·dis·cov·er·a·ble \,in-dis-'kəv-(ə-)rə-bəl\ *adj* **:** not discoverable

in·dis·creet \,in-dis-'krēt\ *adj* **:** not discreet **: IMPRUDENT** — **in·dis·creet·ly** *adv* — **in·dis·creet·ness** *n*

in·dis·crete \,in-dis-'krēt, (')in-'dis-,\ *adj* **:** not separated into distinct parts ⟨an *indiscrete* mass⟩

in·dis·cre·tion \-'kresh-ən\ *n* **1 :** lack of discretion **: IMPRUDENCE 2 :** an indiscreet act or remark

in·dis·crim·i·nate \,in-dis-'krim-ə-nət\ *adj* **:** showing lack of discrimination **:** not making careful distinction between persons or things ⟨an *indiscriminate* reader⟩ ⟨an *indiscriminate* enthusiasm for everything new⟩ — **in·dis·crim·i·nate·ly** *adv* — **in·dis·crim·i·nate·ness** *n*

syn MISCELLANEOUS, PROMISCUOUS: INDISCRIMINATE implies lack of selectivity or consideration of individual distinctions or merits ⟨*indiscriminate* praise⟩ MISCELLANEOUS implies a mixture showing few if any signs of selectivity and often connoting dependence on chance ⟨a collection of books on *miscellaneous* subjects⟩ PROMISCUOUS suggests lack of good judgment, prudence, or restraint ⟨a *promiscuous* arrangement of paintings⟩

in·dis·crim·i·na·tion \-,krim-ə-'nā-shən\ *n* **:** lack of discrimination

in·dis·pens·a·ble \,in-dis-'pen(t)-sə-bəl\ *adj* **:** absolutely necessary ⟨an *indispensable* employee⟩ — **in·dis·pens·a·bil·i·ty** \-,pen(t)-sə-'bil-ət-ē\ *n* — **indispensable** *n* — **in·dis·pens·a·ble·ness** \-'pen(t)-sə-bəl-nəs\ *n* — **in·dis·pens·a·bly** \-blē\ *adv*

in·dis·pose \,in-dis-'pōz\ *vt* **1 :** to make unfit **: DISQUALIFY 2 :** to make averse **: DISINCLINE**

in·dis·posed \-'pōzd\ *adj* **1 :** slightly ill **2 : AVERSE**

in·dis·po·si·tion \(,)in-,dis-pə-'zish-ən\ *n* **1 :** a slight illness **2 : DISINCLINATION, UNWILLINGNESS**

in·dis·put·a·ble \,in-dis-'pyüt-ə-bəl, (')in-'dis-pyət-\ *adj* **:** not disputable **: UNQUESTIONABLE** ⟨*indisputable* proof⟩ — **in·dis·put·a·ble·ness** *n* — **in·dis·put·a·bly** \-blē\ *adv*

in·dis·sol·u·ble \,in-dis-'äl-yə-bəl\ *adj* **:** not capable of being dissolved, undone, broken up, or decomposed ⟨an *indissoluble* contract⟩ ⟨a substance *indissoluble* in water⟩ — **in·dis·sol·u·bil·i·ty** \-,äl-yə-'bil-ət-ē\ *n* — **in·dis·sol·u·ble·ness** \-'äl-yə-bəl-nəs\ *n* — **in·dis·sol·u·bly** \-blē\ *adv*

in·dis·tinct \,in-dis-'tiŋ(k)t\ *adj* **:** not distinct: as **a : CONFUSED, BLURRED b : FAINT, DIM c : UNCERTAIN** — **in·dis·tinct·ly** *adv* — **in·dis·tinct·ness** *n*

in·dis·tinc·tive \-'tiŋ(k)-tiv\ *adj* **:** lacking distinctive qualities

in·dis·tin·guish·a·ble \,in-dis-'tiŋ-gwish-ə-bəl\ *adj* **:** not capable of being clearly distinguished — **in·dis·tin·guish·a·ble·ness** *n* — **in·dis·tin·guish·a·bly** \-blē\ *adv*

in·dite \in-'dīt\ *vt* **[ME** *enditen,* fr. OF *enditer* to write down, proclaim, fr. L *indict-, indicere* to proclaim, fr. *in-* + *dicere* to say] **1 :** to make up **: COMPOSE** ⟨*indite* an epistle⟩ **2 :** to compose and put down in writing — **in·dit·er** *n*

in·di·um \'in-dē-əm\ *n* **[NL,** fr. *indicum* indigo; fr. the indigo lines in its spectrum] **:** a malleable fusible silvery metallic chemical element — see **ELEMENT table**

in·di·vert·i·ble \,in-də-'vərt-ə-bəl, -dī-\ *adj* **:** not to be diverted or turned aside — **in·di·vert·i·bly** \-blē\ *adv*

¹in·di·vid·u·al \,in-də-'vij-(ə-w)əl\ *adj* **[L** *individuus* indivisible, fr. *in-* **¹in-** + *dividere* to divide] **1 a :** of or relating to an individual ⟨*individual* traits⟩ **b :** intended for one person ⟨*individual* servings⟩ **2 : PARTICULAR, SEPARATE** ⟨*individual* copies⟩ **3 :** having marked individuality ⟨an *individual* style⟩ **syn** see **CHARACTERISTIC** — **in·di·vid·u·al·ly** \-ē\ *adv*

²individual *n* **1 :** a particular being or thing as distinguished from a class, species, or collection: as **a :** one human being esp. contrasted with a social group or institution **b :** one organism distinguished from a group **2 :** a particular person

in·di·vid·u·al·ism \-'vij-ə(-wə-),liz-əm\ *n* **1 :** an ethical doctrine that the interests of the individual are primary **2 a :** a doctrine that the chief end of society is to promote the welfare of its individual members **b :** a doctrine holding that the individual has certain political or economic rights with which the state must not interfere **3 : INDIVIDUALITY**

in·di·vid·u·al·ist \-ləst\ *n* **1 :** a person who shows marked individuality or independence of others in thought or behavior **2 :** a supporter of the doctrines of individualism — **in·di·vid·u·al·is·tic** \-,vij-ə(-wə)-'lis-tik\ *adj* — **in·di·vid·u·al·is·ti·cal·ly** \-ti-k(ə-)lē\ *adv*

in·di·vid·u·al·i·ty \,in-də-,vij-ə-'wal-ət-ē\ *n, pl* **-ties 1 :** the qualities that distinguish one person or thing from all others **2 :** the condition of having separate existence **3 : INDIVIDUAL, PERSON**

in·di·vid·u·al·ize \-'vij-(ə-w)əl-,īz\ *vt* **1 :** to make individual in character **2 :** to treat or notice individually **: PARTICULARIZE 3 :** to adapt to a particular individual — **in·di·vid·u·al·i·za·tion** \-,vij-(ə-w)əl-ə-'zā-shən\ *n*

in·di·vid·u·a·tion \-,vij-ə-'wā-shən\ *n* **1 :** a giving of individuality or definitive form **: DIFFERENTIATION** ⟨*individuation* of an embryo⟩ **2 :** differentiated state **: INDIVIDUALITY**

in·di·vis·i·ble \,in-də-'viz-ə-bəl\ *adj* **:** not capable of being divided or separated — **in·di·vis·i·bil·i·ty** \-,viz-ə-'bil-ət-ē\ *n* — **in·di·vis·i·ble·ness** \-'viz-ə-bəl-nəs\ *n* — **in·di·vis·i·bly** \-blē\ *adv*

Indo- — see IND-

In·do-Ary·an \,in-dō-'ar-ē-ən, -'er-\ *n* **1 :** a member of one of the peoples of India of Aryan speech and physique **2 :** one of the early Indo-European invaders of Persia, Afghanistan, and India — **Indo-Aryan** *adj*

in·doc·ile \(')in-'däs-əl\ *adj* **:** unwilling or indisposed to be taught or disciplined **: INTRACTABLE** — **in·do·cil·i·ty** \,in-dä-'sil-ət-ē, -dō-\ *n*

in·doc·tri·nate \in-'däk-trə-,nāt\ *vt* **[MF** *endoctriner,* fr. *en-* + *doctrine*] **1 :** to instruct esp. in fundamentals **2 :** to imbue with a usu. partisan or sectarian opinion, point of view, or principle — **in·doc·tri·na·tion** \(,)in-,däk-trə-'nā-shən\ *n* — **in·doc·tri·na·tor** \in-'däk-trə-,nāt-ər\ *n*

¹In·do-Eu·ro·pe·an \,in-dō-,yùr-ə-'pē-ən\ *adj* **:** of, relating to, or constituting a family of languages comprising those spoken in most of Europe and in the parts of the world colonized by Europeans since 1500 and also in Iran, the subcontinent of India, and some other parts of Asia

²Indo-European *n* **1 :** the Indo-European languages **2 :** a member of a people whose original tongue is one of the Indo-European languages

in·dole·ace·tic acid \,in-,dōl-ə-,sēt-ik-\ *n* [*indole* C_8H_7N, fr. G *indol,* fr. L *indicum* indigo] **:** a crystalline plant hormone that promotes growth and rooting of plants

in·dole·bu·tyr·ic acid \-byü-,tir-ik-\ *n* **:** a crystalline acid similar to indoleacetic acid in its effects on plants

in·do·lent \'in-də-lənt\ *adj* **[LL** *indolent-, indolens* insensitive to pain, fr. L *in-* **¹in-** + *dolēre* to feel pain] **1 :** slow to develop or heal **2 :** averse to exertion **: LAZY, IDLE** ⟨felt *indolent* every spring⟩ — **in·do·lence** \-lən(t)s\ *n* — **in·do·lent·ly** *adv*

in·dom·i·ta·ble \in-'däm-ət-ə-bəl\ *adj* **[LL** *indomitabilis,* fr. L *in-* **¹in-** + *domitare* to tame, daunt] **:** incapable of being subdued **: UNCONQUERABLE** ⟨*indomitable* courage⟩ — **in·dom·i·ta·bil·i·ty** \-,däm-ət-ə-'bil-ət-ē\ *n* — **in·dom·i·ta·ble·ness** \-'däm-ət-ə-bəl-nəs\ *n* — **in·dom·i·ta·bly** \-blē\ *adv*

syn INVINCIBLE: INDOMITABLE stresses courage or determination that cannot be overcome or subdued; IN-

---

ə abut; ˀ kitten; ər further; a back; ā bake; ä cot, cart; aù out; ch chin; e less; ē easy; g gift; i trip; ī life

VINCIBLE implies having strength and ability superior to all enemies

In·do·ne·sian \ˌin-də-'nē-zhən, -shən\ n **1** : a native or inhabitant of the Malay archipelago **2 a** : a native or inhabitant of the Republic of Indonesia **b** : the language based on Malay that is the national language of the Republic of Indonesia — **Indonesian** adj

in·door \ˈin-ˌdōr, -ˌdȯr\ adj **1** : of or relating to the interior of a building **2** : done, living, or belonging within doors

in·doors \(ˈ)in-'dō(ə)rz, -'dȯ(ə)rz\ adv : in or into a building ⟨games to be played indoors⟩

indorse, indorsement var of ENDORSE, ENDORSEMENT

in·drawn \ˈin-ˌdrȯn\ adj **1** : drawn in **2** : ALOOF, RESERVED

in·du·bi·ta·ble \(ˈ)in-'d(y)ü-bət-ə-bəl\ adj : too evident to be doubted : UNQUESTIONABLE — **in·du·bi·ta·ble·ness** n — **in·du·bi·ta·bly** \-blē\ adv

in·duce \in-'d(y)üs\ vt [L induct-, inducere, fr. in- ²in- + ducere to lead] **1** : to lead on to do something : influence by persuasion **2** : to bring about : CAUSE ⟨an illness induced by overwork⟩ **3** : to conclude or infer by reasoning from particular instances **4** : to produce (as an electric current) by induction — **in·duc·er** n — **in·duc·i·ble** \-'d(y)ü-sə-bəl\ adj

in·duce·ment \in-'d(y)üs-mənt\ n **1** : the act of inducing **2** : something that induces ⟨a money-back guarantee is a good inducement to buy⟩ **syn** see MOTIVE

in·duct \in-'dəkt\ vt **1** : to place formally in office : INSTALL **2** : to enroll into military service in accordance with a draft law — **in·duct·ee** \ˌ(ˌ)in-ˌdək-'tē\ n

in·duc·tance \in-'dək-tən(t)s\ n **1** : a property of an electric circuit by which an electromotive force is induced in it by a variation of current either in the circuit itself or in a neighboring circuit **2** : a circuit or a device possessing inductance

in·duc·tion \in-'dək-shən\ n **1 a** : the act or process of inducting (as into office) **b** : an initial experience : INITIATION **c** : the procedure by which a civilian is inducted into military service **2 a** : reasoning from particular instances to a general conclusion; also : the conclusion so reached **b** : mathematical demonstration of the validity of a law concerning all the positive integers by proving that it holds for the first integer and that if it holds for all the integers preceding a given integer it must hold for the next following integer **3 a** : the act of causing or bringing on or about **b** : the process by which an electrical conductor becomes electrified when near a charged body, by which a body becomes magnetized when in a magnetic field or in the flux set up by a magnetizing force, or by which an electromotive force is produced in a circuit by varying the magnetic field linked with the circuit **c** : the sum of the processes by which the fate of embryonic cells is fixed and morphological differentiation brought about

induction coil n : an apparatus for obtaining intermittent high voltage consisting of a primary coil through which the direct current flows, an interrupter, and a secondary coil of a larger number of turns in which the high voltage is induced

induction heating n : heating material by means of an electric current that is caused to flow through the material or its container by electromagnetic induction

in·duc·tive \in-'dək-tiv\ adj : relating to, employing, or based on induction — **in·duc·tive·ly** adv — **in·duc·tive·ness** n

in·duc·tor \in-'dək-tər\ n **1** : one that inducts **2** : a part of an electrical apparatus that acts upon another or is itself acted upon by induction **3** : something (as a kind of tissue) able to cause embryonic induction

indue var of ENDUE

in·dulge \in-'dəlj\ vb [L indult-, indulgēre] **1** : to be tolerant toward : give way to : HUMOR, GRATIFY ⟨indulges his appetite⟩ **2** : to allow oneself to take pleasure ⟨indulge in a new suit⟩ — **in·dulg·er** n

in·dul·gence \in-'dəl-jən(t)s\ n **1** : a release from purgatorial punishment gained by performing pious acts authorized by the Roman Catholic Church **2 a** : the act of indulging : the state of being indulgent **b** : an indulgent act **c** : something indulged in

in·dul·gent \-jənt\ adj : indulging or characterized by indulgence : LENIENT — **in·dul·gent·ly** adv

in·dult \'in-ˌdəlt, in-'\ n : a temporary or personal privilege granted in the Roman Catholic Church

¹in·du·rate \'in-d(y)ə-rət, in-'d(y)ür-ət\ adj : physically or morally hardened

²in·du·rate \'in-d(y)ə-ˌrāt\ vb [L indurare, fr. in- ²in- + durus hard] **1** : to make unfeeling, stubborn, or obdurate **2** : to make hardy : INURE **3** : to make fibrous or hard ⟨great heat indurates clay⟩ ⟨indurated tissue⟩ **4** : to grow hard : HARDEN — **in·du·ra·tion** \ˌin-d(y)ə-'rā-shən\ n — **in·du·ra·tive** \'in-d(y)ə-ˌrāt-iv, in-'d(y)ür-ət-\ adj

in·dus·tri·al \in-'dəs-trē-əl\ adj **1** : of, relating to, or engaged in industry **2** : characterized by highly developed industries ⟨an industrial nation⟩ **3** : derived from human industry **4** : used in industry ⟨industrial diamonds⟩ — **in·dus·tri·al·ly** \-trē-ə-lē\ adv

industrial arts n sing or pl : a subject taught in elementary and secondary schools that aims at developing manual skill and familiarity with tools and machines

in·dus·tri·al·ism \-trē-ə-ˌliz-əm\ n : social organization in which large-scale industries are dominant

in·dus·tri·al·ist \-ləst\ n : a person owning or engaged in the management of an industry : MANUFACTURER

in·dus·tri·al·ize \in-'dəs-trē-ə-ˌlīz\ vb : to make or become industrial : convert to an industrial economy ⟨industrialize an agricultural region⟩ — **in·dus·tri·al·i·za·tion** \-ˌdəs-trē-ə-lə-'zā-shən\ n

industrial revolution n : a rapid major change in an economy (as in England in the late 18th century) marked by the general introduction of power-driven machinery or by an important change in the prevailing types and methods of use of such machines

industrial school n : a school specializing in the teaching of the industrial arts

industrial union n : a labor union that admits to membership all workers in an industry irrespective of their occupation or craft — compare CRAFT UNION

in·dus·tri·ous \in-'dəs-trē-əs\ adj : constantly, regularly, or habitually occupied : DILIGENT — **in·dus·tri·ous·ly** adv — **in·dus·tri·ous·ness** n

in·dus·try \'in-(ˌ)dəs-trē\ n, pl -tries [L industria] **1** : diligence in an employment or pursuit **2 a** : systematic labor esp. for the creation of value **b** : a department or branch of a craft or art or of business or manufacturing; esp : one that employs a large number of persons and considerable capital esp. in manufacturing **c** : a distinct group of productive or profit-making enterprises ⟨the steel industry⟩ ⟨the tourist industry⟩ **d** : manufacturing activity as a whole ⟨commerce and industry⟩

in·dwell \(ˈ)in-'dwel\ vb : to exist within as an activating spirit, force, or principle — **in·dwell·er** n

¹-ine \ˌīn, ən, (ˌ)in, ˌēn\ adj suffix **1** [L -īnus] : of or relating to ⟨alkaline⟩ **2** [L -īnus, fr. Gk -inos] : made of : like ⟨opaline⟩

²-ine \ˌēn, 'ēn, ən, (ˌ)in\ n suffix [L -īna, fr. fem. of -īnus, adj. suffix] **1** : chemical substance: as **a** : halogen element ⟨chlorine⟩ **b** : basic or base-containing carbon compound ⟨quinine⟩ ⟨cystine⟩ **c** : mixture of chemical compounds (as of hydrocarbons) ⟨gasoline⟩ **d** : hydride ⟨arsine⟩ **2** : -IN

ine·bri·ate \in-'ē-brē-ˌāt\ vt [L inebriare, fr. in- ²in- + ebrius drunk] : to make drunk : INTOXICATE — **ine·bri·ate** \-'brē-ət\ adj or n — **ine·bri·a·tion** \in-ˌē-brē-'ā-shən\ n

ine·bri·at·ed \-ˈē-brē-ˌāt-əd\ adj : exhilarated or confused by or as if by alcohol : INTOXICATED

in·e·bri·e·ty \ˌin-i-'brī-ət-ē\ n : INEBRIATION, DRUNKENNESS

in·ed·i·ble \(ˈ)in-'ed-ə-bəl\ adj : not fit or safe for food ⟨inedible mushrooms⟩

in·ed·it·ed \(ˈ)in-'ed-ət-əd\ adj : UNPUBLISHED

in·ed·u·ca·ble \(ˈ)in-'ej-ə-kə-bəl\ adj : incapable of being educated

in·ef·fa·ble \-'ef-ə-bəl\ adj [L ineffabilis, fr. in- ¹in- + effari to utter, fr. ex- + fari to speak] : being beyond the power of language to describe : UNUTTERABLE ⟨ineffable bliss⟩ — **in·ef·fa·bil·i·ty** \(ˌ)in-ˌef-ə-'bil-ət-ē\ n — **in·ef·fa·ble·ness** \(ˈ)in-'ef-ə-bəl-nəs\ n — **in·ef·fa·bly** \-blē\ adv

in·ef·face·a·ble \ˌin-ə-'fā-sə-bəl\ adj : not effaceable : INERADICABLE — **in·ef·face·a·bil·i·ty** \-ˌfā-sə-'bil-ət-ē\ n — **in·ef·face·a·bly** \-'fā-sə-blē\ adv

in·ef·fec·tive \ˌin-ə-'fek-tiv\ adj **1** : not effective : IN-

EFFECTUAL ⟨an *ineffective* law⟩ **2** : not efficient : INCAPABLE ⟨an *ineffective* leader⟩ — **in·ef·fec·tive·ly** *adv* — **in·ef·fec·tive·ness** *n*

in·ef·fec·tu·al \‚in-ə-'fek-chə(-wə)l\ *adj* : not producing the proper or usual effect : FUTILE — **in·ef·fec·tu·al·ly** \-ē\ *adv* — **in·ef·fec·tu·al·ness** *n*

in·ef·fi·ca·cious \(‚)in-‚ef-ə-'kā-shəs\ *adj* : lacking the power to produce a desired effect : INADEQUATE — **in·ef·fi·ca·cious·ly** *adv* — **in·ef·fi·ca·cious·ness** *n* — **in·ef·fi·ca·cy** \-'ef-ə-kə-sē\ *n*

in·ef·fi·cient \‚in-ə-'fish-ənt\ *adj* **1** : not producing the effect intended or desired : INEFFICACIOUS **2** : INCAPABLE, INCOMPETENT — **in·ef·fi·cien·cy** \-'fish-ən-sē\ *n* — **in·ef·fi·cient·ly** *adv*

in·elas·tic \‚in-ə-'las-tik\ *adj* **1** : not elastic **2** : slow to react or respond to changing conditions — **in·elas·tic·i·ty** \‚in-i-‚las-'tis-ət-ē\ *n*

in·el·e·gance \(')in-'el-i-gən(t)s\ *n* : lack of elegance

in·el·e·gant \(')in-'el-i-gənt\ *adj* : lacking in refinement, grace, or good taste — **in·el·e·gant·ly** *adv*

in·el·i·gi·ble \(')in-'el-ə-jə-bəl\ *adj* : not qualified to be chosen for an office — **in·el·i·gi·bil·i·ty** \(‚)in-‚el-ə-jə-'bil-ət-ē\ *n* — **ineligible** *n*

in·eluc·ta·ble \‚in-i-'lək-tə-bəl\ *adj* [L *ineluctabilis,* fr. *in-* + *eluctari* to struggle out, fr. *ex-* + *luctari* to struggle] : not to be avoided, changed, or resisted : INEVITABLE — **in·eluc·ta·bil·i·ty** \-‚lək-tə-'bil-ət-ē\ *n* — **in·eluc·ta·bly** \-'lək-tə-blē\ *adv*

in·elud·i·ble \‚in-i-'lüd-ə-bəl\ *adj* : INESCAPABLE

in·ept \in-'ept\ *adj* [L *ineptus,* fr. *in-* ²*in-* + *aptus* apt] **1** : lacking in fitness or aptitude : UNFIT **2** : not apt for the occasion : INAPPROPRIATE **3** : lacking sense or reason : FOOLISH **4** : generally incompetent : BUNGLING — **in·ep·ti·tude** \-'ep-tə-‚t(y)üd\ *n* — **in·ept·ly** *adv* — **in·ept·ness** \-'ep(t)-nəs\ *n*

in·equal·i·ty \‚in-i-'kwäl-ət-ē\ *n* **1** : the quality of being unequal or uneven **2** : an instance of being unequal (as an irregularity in a surface) **3** : a formal statement of inequality between two quantities

in·eq·ui·ta·ble \(')in-'ek-wət-ə-bəl\ *adj* : not equitable : UNFAIR — **in·eq·ui·ta·bly** \-blē\ *adv*

in·eq·ui·ty \-wət-ē\ *n, pl* **-ties** **1** : INJUSTICE, UNFAIRNESS **2** : an instance of injustice or unfairness

in·erad·i·ca·ble \‚in-i-'rad-i-kə-bəl\ *adj* : incapable of being eradicated — **in·erad·i·ca·bly** \-blē\ *adv*

in·er·ran·cy \(')in-'er-ən-sē\ *n* : exemption from error : INFALLIBILITY — **in·er·rant** \-ənt\ *adj*

in·ert \in-'ərt\ *adj* [L *inert-, iners* unskilled, idle, fr. *in-* + *art-, ars* skill, art] **1** : not having the power to move itself **2** : deficient in active properties; *esp* : lacking a usual or anticipated chemical or biological action **3** : very slow to move or act : SLUGGISH **syn** see INACTIVE — **in·ert·ly** *adv* — **in·ert·ness** *n*

in·er·tia \in-'ər-shə, -shē-ə\ *n* [NL, fr. L, lack of skill, fr. *inert-, iners* unskilled] **1** : a property of matter by which it remains at rest or in uniform motion in the same straight line unless acted upon by some external force; *also* : an analogous property of other physical quantities (as electricity) **2** : indisposition to motion, exertion, or change : INERTNESS — **in·er·tial** \-shəl\ *adj*

inertial guidance *n* : guidance (as of an aircraft) by means of self-contained automatically controlling devices that respond to changes in velocity or direction

in·es·cap·a·ble \‚in-ə-'skā-pə-bəl\ *adj* : incapable of being escaped : INEVITABLE — **in·es·cap·a·bly** \-blē\ *adv*

in·es·sen·tial \‚in-ə-'sen-chəl\ *adj* : not essential

in·es·ti·ma·ble \(')in-'es-tə-mə-bəl\ *adj* **1** : incapable of being estimated or computed **2** : too valuable or excellent to be measured or appreciated — **in·es·ti·ma·bly** \-blē\ *adv*

in·ev·i·ta·ble \in-'ev-ət-ə-bəl\ *adj* [L *inevitabilis,* fr. *in-* ¹*in-* + *evitare* to avoid, fr. *ex-* + *vitare* to shun] : incapable of being avoided or evaded : bound to happen : CERTAIN — **in·ev·i·ta·bil·i·ty** \(‚)in-‚ev-ət-ə-'bil-ət-ē\ *n* — **in·ev·i·ta·ble·ness** \(')in-'ev-ət-ə-bəl-nəs\ *n* — **in·ev·i·ta·bly** \-blē\ *adv*

in·ex·act \‚in-ig-'zakt\ *adj* : not precisely correct or true : INACCURATE — **in·ex·ac·ti·tude** \-'zak-tə-‚t(y)üd\ *n* — **in·ex·act·ly** \-'zak-(t)lē\ *adv* — **in·ex·act·ness** \-'zak(t)-nəs\ *n*

in·ex·cus·a·ble \‚in-ik-'skyüz-ə-bəl\ *adj* : not to be

excused : not justifiable ⟨*inexcusable* rudeness⟩ — **in·ex·cus·a·ble·ness** *n* — **in·ex·cus·a·bly** \-blē\ *adv*

in·ex·haust·i·ble \‚in-ig-'zo-stə-bəl\ *adj* **1** : plentiful enough not to give out or be used up : UNFAILING ⟨an *inexhaustible* supply⟩ **2** : UNTIRING — **in·ex·haust·i·bil·i·ty** \-‚zo-stə-'bil-ət-ē\ *n* — **in·ex·haust·i·bly** \-'zo-stə-blē\ *adv*

in·ex·ist·ence \‚in-ig-'zis-tən(t)s\ *n* : NONEXISTENCE

in·ex·ist·ent \-tənt\ *adj* : not having being : NONEXISTENT

in·ex·o·ra·ble \(')in-'eks-(ə-)rə-bəl\ *adj* [L *inexorabilis,* fr. *in-* ¹*in-* + *exorare* to beg off, fr. *ex-* + *orare* to pray] : not to be persuaded or moved by entreaty : RELENTLESS — **in·ex·o·ra·bil·i·ty** \(‚)in-‚eks-(ə-)rə-'bil-ət-ē\ *n* — **in·ex·o·ra·ble·ness** \(')in-'eks-(ə-)rə-bəl-nəs\ *n* — **in·ex·o·ra·bly** \-blē\ *adv*

in·ex·pe·di·ent \‚in-ik-'spēd-ē-ənt\ *adj* : not suited to bring about a desired result : UNWISE — **in·ex·pe·di·en·cy** \-ən-sē\ *n* — **in·ex·pe·di·ent·ly** *adv*

in·ex·pen·sive \‚in-ik-'spen(t)-siv\ *adj* : reasonable in price : CHEAP — **in·ex·pen·sive·ly** *adv* — **in·ex·pen·sive·ness** *n*

in·ex·pe·ri·ence \‚in-ik-'spir-ē-ən(t)s\ *n* : lack of experience or of knowledge or proficiency gained by experience — **in·ex·pe·ri·enced** \-ən(t)st\ *adj*

in·ex·pert \(')in-'ek-‚spərt, ‚in-ik-'\ *adj* : not expert : UNSKILLED — **in·ex·pert·ly** *adv* — **in·ex·pert·ness** *n*

in·ex·pi·a·ble \(')in-'ek-spē-ə-bəl\ *adj* : incapable of being atoned for ⟨an *inexpiable* crime⟩ — **in·ex·pi·a·bly** \-blē\ *adv*

in·ex·plain·a·ble \‚in-ik-'splā-nə-bəl\ *adj* : INEXPLICABLE

in·ex·plic·a·ble \‚in-ik-'splik-ə-bəl, (')in-'ek-(‚)splik-\ *adj* : incapable of being explained, interpreted, or accounted for — **in·ex·plic·a·bil·i·ty** \‚in-ik-‚splik-ə-'bil-ət-ē, (‚)in-‚ek-(‚)splik-ə-‚bil-\ *n* — **in·ex·plic·a·ble·ness** \‚in-ik-'splik-ə-bəl-nəs, (')in-'ek-(‚)splik-\ *n* — **in·ex·plic·a·bly** \-blē\ *adv*

in·ex·plic·it \‚in-ik-'splis-ət\ *adj* : not explicit

in·ex·press·i·ble \‚in-ik-'spres-ə-bəl\ *adj* : being beyond one's power to express : INDESCRIBABLE ⟨*inexpressible* joy⟩ — **in·ex·press·i·bil·i·ty** \-‚spres-ə-'bil-ət-ē\ *n* — **in·ex·press·i·ble·ness** \-'spres-ə-bəl-nəs\ *n* — **in·ex·press·i·bly** \-blē\ *adv*

in·ex·pres·sive \-'spres-iv\ *adj* **1** *obs* : INEXPRESSIBLE **2** : lacking expression or meaning — **in·ex·pres·sive·ly** *adv* — **in·ex·pres·sive·ness** *n*

in·ex·ten·si·ble \‚in-ik-'sten(t)-sə-bəl\ *adj* : incapable of being stretched

in ex·ten·so \‚in-ik-'sten(t)-sō\ *adv* [ML] : at full length

in·ex·tin·guish·a·ble \‚in-ik-'stin-gwish-ə-bəl\ *adj* : not extinguishable : UNQUENCHABLE — **in·ex·tin·guish·a·bly** \-blē\ *adv*

in ex·tre·mis \‚in-ik-'strā-məs, -‚mēs\ *adv* [L] : in extreme circumstances; *esp* : at the point of death

in·ex·tri·ca·ble \‚in-ik-'strik-ə-bəl, (')in-'ek-(‚)strik-\ *adj* **1** : forming a tangle from which one cannot free oneself **2** : not capable of being disentangled — **in·ex·tri·ca·bly** \-blē\ *adv*

in·fal·li·ble \(')in-'fal-ə-bəl\ *adj* **1** : not capable of being wrong : UNERRING **2** : not liable to fail, deceive, or disappoint : SURE, CERTAIN ⟨an *infallible* remedy⟩ — **in·fal·li·bil·i·ty** \(‚)in-‚fal-ə-'bil-ət-ē\ *n* — **in·fal·li·bly** \(')in-'fal-ə-blē\ *adv*

in·fa·mous \'in-fə-məs\ *adj* [L *infamis,* fr. *in-* ¹*in* + *fama* fame, reputation] **1** : having an evil reputation ⟨an *infamous* person⟩ **2** : DETESTABLE, DISGRACEFUL ⟨an *infamous* crime⟩ — **in·fa·mous·ly** *adv*

in·fa·my \-mē\ *n, pl* **-mies** **1** : evil reputation brought about by something grossly criminal, shocking, or brutal **2 a** : an infamous act **b** : the state of being infamous

in·fan·cy \'in-fən-sē\ *n, pl* **-cies** **1** : early childhood **2** : a beginning or early period of existence **3** : the legal status of an infant

in·fant \'in-fənt\ *n* [L *infant-, infans,* fr. *infant-, infans,* incapable of speech, young, fr. *in-* ¹*in-* + *fari* to speak] **1** : a child in the first period of life **2** : MINOR; *esp* : a person under the age of 21 — **infant** *adj*

in·fan·ta \in-'fant-ə, -'fänt-\ *n* : a daughter of a Spanish or Portuguese monarch

in·fan·ti·cide \in-'fant-ə-‚sīd\ *n* **1** : the killing of an infant **2** : one who kills an infant

in·fan·tile \'in-fən-‚tīl, -təl, -‚tēl\ *adj* **1** : of, relating to,

---

ə abut; ⁹ kitten; ər further; a back; ā bake; ä cot, cart; aů out; ch chin; e less; ē easy; g gift; i trip; ī life

or resembling infants or infancy : CHILDISH **2** : being in a very early stage of development following an uplift or equivalent change ⟨an *infantile* river⟩ — **in·fan·til·i·ty** \ˌin-fən-ˈtil-ət-ē\ *n*

infantile paralysis *n* : POLIOMYELITIS

in·fan·til·ism \ˈin-fən-ˌtīl-ˌiz-əm, -təl-, -ˌtēl-\ *n* : retention of childish qualities in adult life; *esp* : failure to attain sexual maturity

in·fan·try \ˈin-fən-trē\ *n, pl* **-tries** [MF *infanterie,* fr. It *infanteria,* fr. *infante* boy, foot soldier, fr. L *infant-, infans* infant] **1** : soldiers trained, armed, and equipped to fight on foot **2** : a branch of an army composed of infantry — **in·fan·try·man** \-mən\ *n*

in·farct \ˈin-ˌfärkt\ *n* [L *infarctus,* pp. of *infarcire* to stuff in, fr. *in-* + *farcire* to stuff] : an area of dead tissue (as of the heart wall) caused by blockage of local blood circulation — **in·farc·tion** \in-ˈfärk-shən\ *n*

in·fat·u·ate \in-ˈfach-ə-ˌwāt\ *vt* [L *infatuare,* fr. *in-* ²*in-* + *fatuus* fatuous] : to inspire with a foolish or extravagant love or admiration — **in·fat·u·at·ed** *adj* — **in·fat·u·a·tion** \in-ˌfach-ə-ˈwā-shən\ *n*

in·fea·si·ble \(ˈ)in-ˈfē-zə-bəl\ *adj* : not feasible : IMPRACTICABLE

in·fect \in-ˈfekt\ *vt* [L *infect-, inficere,* fr. *in-* ²*in-* + *facere* to make] **1** : to contaminate with a disease-producing substance or organism ⟨*infected* bedding⟩ **2** : to communicate a germ or disease to ⟨coughing people who *infect* others⟩ **b** : to enter and cause disease in ⟨bacteria that *infect* wounds⟩ **3** a : CONTAMINATE, CORRUPT **b** : to work upon or seize upon so as to induce sympathy, belief, or support — **in·fec·tious** \-ˈfek-shəs\ *adj* — **in·fec·tious·ly** *adv* — **in·fec·tious·ness** *n* — **in·fec·tor** \-ˈfek-tər\ *n*

in·fec·tion \in-ˈfek-shən\ *n* **1** : an act or process of infecting **2** : the state produced by the establishment of a germ in or on a suitable host; *also* : a contagious or infectious disease **3** : an infective agent or material contaminated with an infective agent **4** : the communication of emotions or qualities through example or contact

in·fec·tive \in-ˈfek-tiv\ *adj* : producing or able to produce infection — **in·fec·tiv·i·ty** \(ˌ)in-ˌfek-ˈtiv-ət-ē\ *n*

in·fe·lic·i·tous \ˌin-fi-ˈlis-ət-əs\ *adj* **1** : UNHAPPY, UNFORTUNATE ⟨an *infelicitous* time⟩ **2** : not apt : not suitably chosen for the occasion ⟨an *infelicitous* word⟩ — **in·fe·lic·i·tous·ly** *adv*

in·fe·lic·i·ty \-ət-ē\ *n, pl* **-ties** **1** : UNHAPPINESS, WRETCHEDNESS **2** : a lack of suitability or aptness **3** : an unsuitable or inappropriate act or utterance

in·fer \in-ˈfər\ *vt* **in·ferred; in·fer·ring** [L *inferre,* lit., to carry into, fr. *in-* + *ferre* to carry] **1** : to derive as a conclusion from facts or premises **2** : GUESS, SURMISE **3** a : to involve as a normal outcome of thought **b** : to point out : INDICATE **4** : HINT, SUGGEST **syn** see IMPLY — **in·fer·a·ble** *or* **in·fer·ri·ble** \-ˈfər-ə-bəl\ *adj* — **in·fer·rer** \-ˈfər-ər\ *n*

in·fer·ence \ˈin-f(ə-)rən(t)s\ *n* **1** : the act or process of inferring **2** : something inferred; *esp* : a proposition arrived at by inference

in·fer·en·tial \ˌin-fə-ˈren-chəl\ *adj* : deduced or deducible by inference — **in·fer·en·tial·ly** \-ˈren-chə-lē\ *adv*

in·fe·ri·or \in-ˈfir-ē-ər\ *adj* [L, compar. of *inferus* low, situated beneath; akin to E *under*] **1** : situated lower down : LOWER **2** : of low or lower degree or rank **3** : of little or less importance, value, or merit — **inferior** *n* — **in·fe·ri·or·i·ty** \(ˌ)in-ˌfir-ē-ˈòr-ət-ē, -ˈär-\ *n* — **in·fe·ri·or·ly** \in-ˈfir-ē-ər-lē\ *adv*

inferiority complex *n* : an acute sense of personal inferiority resulting either in timidity or in exaggerated aggressiveness

in·fer·nal \in-ˈfərn-ᵊl\ *adj* [LL *infernus* hell, fr. L, lower; akin to E *under*] **1** : of or relating to a netherworld of the dead **2** a : of or relating to hell **b** : HELLISH, DIABOLICAL **3** : DAMNABLE, DAMNED — **in·fer·nal·ly** \-ᵊl-ē\ *adv*

infernal machine *n* : a machine or apparatus designed to explode and destroy life or property

in·fer·no \in-ˈfər-nō\ *n, pl* **-nos** [It, hell, fr. LL *infernus*] : a place or a state that resembles or suggests hell esp. in intense heat or raging fire

in·fer·tile \(ˈ)in-ˈfərt-ᵊl\ *adj* : not fertile or productive : BARREN — **in·fer·til·i·ty** \in-(ˌ)fər-ˈtil-ət-ē\ *n*

in·fest \in-ˈfest\ *vt* [L *infestus* hostile] **1** : to spread or

swarm in or over in a troublesome manner **2** : to live in or on as a parasite — **in·fes·ta·tion** \ˌin-ˌfes-ˈtā-shən\ *n* — **in·fest·er** \in-ˈfes-tər\ *n*

in·fi·del \ˈin-fəd-ᵊl, -fə-ˌdel\ *n* [LL *infidelis* unbelieving, fr. L, unfaithful, fr. *in-* ¹*in-* + *fidelis* faithful, fr. *fides* faith] : a person who does not believe in a religion and esp. in Christianity — **infidel** *adj*

in·fi·del·i·ty \ˌin-fə-ˈdel-ət-ē, -fī-\ *n, pl* **-ties** **1** : lack of faith in a religion **2** : unfaithfulness esp. to one's husband or wife

in·field \ˈin-ˌfēld\ *n* **1** a : the part of a baseball field enclosed by the three bases and home plate and including the base paths **b** : the defensive positions comprising first base, second base, shortstop, and third base **2** : the area enclosed by a racetrack or running track — **in·field·er** \-ˌfēl-dər\ *n*

in·fight·ing \ˈin-ˌfīt-iŋ\ *n* **1** : fighting or boxing at close quarters **2** : rough-and-tumble fighting — **in·fight·er** *n*

in·fil·trate \in-ˈfil-ˌtrāt, ˈin-(ˌ)fil-\ *vb* **1** : to pass into or through by filtering or permeating **2** : to enter or become established gradually or unobtrusively — **in·fil·tra·tion** \ˌin-(ˌ)fil-ˈtrā-shən\ *n* — **in·fil·tra·tor** \ˈin-(ˌ)fil-ˌtrāt-ər, in-ˈfil-\ *n*

in·fi·nite \ˈin-fə-nət\ *adj* **1** : being without limits of any kind : ENDLESS ⟨*infinite* space⟩ **2** : seeming to be without limits : VAST, INEXHAUSTIBLE ⟨*infinite* patience⟩ ⟨*infinite* wealth⟩ **3** : extending or lying beyond any preassigned value however large — **infinite** *n* — **in·fi·nite·ly** *adv* — **in·fi·nite·ness** *n*

in·fin·i·tes·i·mal \(ˌ)in-ˌfin-ə-ˈtes-ə-məl\ *adj* **1** : arbitrarily small **2** : immeasurably or incalculably small — **in·fin·i·tes·i·mal·ly** \-mə-lē\ *adv*

in·fin·i·tive \in-ˈfin-ət-iv\ *n* : a verb form serving as a noun or as a modifier and at the same time showing certain characteristics of a verb (as association with objects and adverbial modifiers) ⟨*have* in "let him have it" and *to run* in "able to run fast" are *infinitives*⟩ — **infinitive** *adj*

in·fin·i·tude \in-ˈfin-ə-ˌt(y)üd\ *n* **1** : INFINITENESS **2** : something infinite esp. in extent **3** : an infinite number or quantity

in·fin·i·ty \in-ˈfin-ət-ē\ *n, pl* **-ties** **1** a : the quality of being infinite **b** : unlimited extent of time, space, or quantity : BOUNDLESSNESS **2** : an indefinitely great number or amount **3** : a distance so great that the rays of light from a point source at that distance may be regarded as parallel ⟨a camera focused at *infinity*⟩

in·firm \in-ˈfərm\ *adj* **1** : poor or weakened in vitality; *esp* : feeble from age **2** : not solid or stable : INSECURE — **in·firm·ly** *adv*

in·fir·ma·ry \in-ˈfərm-(ə-)rē\ *n, pl* **-ries** : a place where the infirm or sick are lodged for care and treatment

in·fir·mi·ty \in-ˈfər-mət-ē\ *n, pl* **-ties** : the quality or state of being infirm: as **a** : FEEBLENESS, FRAILTY **b** : DISEASE, AILMENT **c** : a personal failing : FOIBLE

in·fix \ˈin-ˌfiks, in-ˈ\ *vt* **1** : to fasten or fix by piercing or thrusting in **2** : INSTILL, INCULCATE

in flagrante delicto \ˌin-\ *adv* : flagrante delicto

in·flame \in-ˈflām\ *vb* [L *inflammare,* fr. *in-* ²*in-* + *flamma* flame] **1** : to set on fire : KINDLE **2** a : to excite to excessive or unnatural action or feeling **b** : to make more heated or violent : INTENSIFY **3** : to cause to redden or grow hot from anger or excitement **4** : to cause inflammation in (bodily tissue) **5** : to become affected with inflammation — **in·flam·er** *n*

in·flam·ma·ble \in-ˈflam-ə-bəl\ *adj* [L *inflammare* to inflame] **1** : FLAMMABLE **2** : easily inflamed : EXCITABLE — **in·flam·ma·bil·i·ty** \-ˌflam-ə-ˈbil-ət-ē\ *n* — **inflammable** *n* — **in·flam·ma·ble·ness** \-ˈflam-ə-bəl-nəs\ *n* — **in·flam·ma·bly** \-blē\ *adv*

in·flam·ma·tion \ˌin-flə-ˈmā-shən\ *n* **1** : the act of inflaming : the state of being inflamed **2** : a local bodily response to injury in which an affected area becomes red, hot, painful, and congested with blood and which is a physiological mechanism for the elimination of noxious agents and of damaged tissue

in·flam·ma·to·ry \in-ˈflam-ə-ˌtōr-ē, -ˌtòr-\ *adj* **1** : tending to excite anger, disorder, or tumult : SEDITIOUS **2** : causing or accompanied by inflammation ⟨*inflammatory* diseases⟩

in·flate \in-ˈflāt\ *vb* [L *inflare,* fr. *in-* ²*in-* + *flare* to blow;

---

j joke; ŋ sing; ō flow; ò flaw; òi coin; th thin; t̲h̲ this; ü loot; ù foot; y yet; yü few; yù furious; zh vision

akin to E *blow*] **1 :** to swell with air or gas ⟨*inflate* a balloon⟩ **2 :** to puff up **:** ELATE ⟨*inflated* with a sense of his own importance⟩ **3 :** to increase abnormally ⟨*inflated* prices⟩ ⟨*inflated* currency⟩ **syn** see EXPAND — **in·flat·a·ble** \in-'flāt-ə-bəl\ *adj* — **in·fla·tor** \-'flāt-ər\ *n*

in·fla·tion \in-'flā-shən\ *n* **1 :** an act of inflating **:** the state of being inflated **2 :** an increase in the volume of money and credit relative to available goods resulting in a substantial and continuing rise in prices

in·fla·tion·ary \-shə-,ner-ē\ *adj* **:** of, relating to, or tending to cause inflation

in·flect \in-'flekt\ *vb* [L *inflex-, inflectere, fr. in-* ²*in-* + *flectere* to bend] **1 :** to turn from a direct line or course **:** CURVE **2 :** to vary a word by inflection **:** DECLINE, CONJUGATE **3 :** to vary the pitch of the voice **:** MODULATE

in·flec·tion \in-'flek-shən\ *n* **1 :** the act or result of curving or bending **2 :** a change in the pitch or tone of a person's voice **3 :** the change in the form of a word showing its case, gender, number, person, tense, mood, voice, or comparison — **in·flec·tion·al** \-shnəl, -shən-ᵊl\ *adj* — **in·flec·tion·al·ly** \-ē\ *adv*

in·flexed \(')in-'flekst\ *adj* **:** bent or turned abruptly inward or downward ⟨flowers with *inflexed* petals⟩

in·flex·i·ble \(')in-'flek-sə-bəl\ *adj* **1 :** not easily bent or twisted **:** RIGID, STIFF **2 :** not easily influenced or persuaded **:** FIRM ⟨an *inflexible* judge⟩ **3 :** incapable of change **:** UNALTERABLE ⟨*inflexible* laws⟩ — **in·flex·i·bil·i·ty** \(,)in-,flek-sə-'bil-ət-ē\ *n* — **in·flex·i·bly** \(')in-'flek-sə-blē\ *adv*

in·flex·ion \in-'flek-shən\ *chiefly Brit var of* INFLECTION

in·flict \in-'flikt\ *vt* [L *inflict-, infligere, fr. in-* ²*in-* + *fligere* to strike] **1 a :** to give by striking **b :** to cause (something damaging or painful) to be endured **:** IMPOSE **2 :** AFFLICT — **in·flic·tive** \-'flik-tiv\ *adj*

in·flic·tion \in-'flik-shən\ *n* **1 :** the act of inflicting **2 :** something inflicted

in·flo·res·cence \,in-flə-'res-ᵊn(t)s\ *n* [LL *inflorescere* to

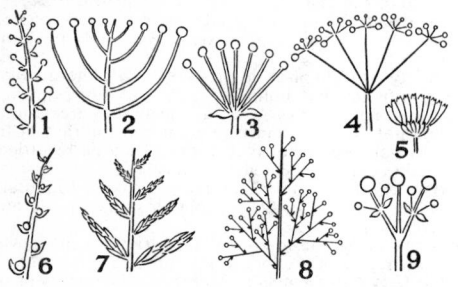

inflorescence (types): *1* raceme, *2* corymb, *3* umbel, *4* compound umbel, *5* capitulum, *6* spike, *7* compound spike, *8* panicle, *9* cyme

begin to bloom, fr. L *in-* ²*in-* + *flor-, flos* flower] **1 a :** the mode of development and arrangement of flowers on an axis **b :** a floral axis with its appendages; *also* **:** a flower cluster or sometimes a solitary flower **2 :** BLOSSOMING, FLOWERING — **in·flo·res·cent** \-ᵊnt\ *adj*

in·flow \'in-,flō\ *n* **1 :** the act of flowing in **2 :** something that flows in

¹**in·flu·ence** \'in-,flü-ən(t)s\ *n* [ML *influentia* ethereal fluid thought to flow from the stars and affect the actions of men, fr. L *influere* to flow in, fr. *in-* + *fluere* to flow] **1 :** the act or power of producing an effect without apparent exertion of force or direct exercise of command **2 :** corrupt interference with authority for personal gain **3 :** the power or capacity of causing an effect in indirect or intangible ways **:** SWAY **4 :** a person or thing that exerts influence

syn INFLUENCE, PRESTIGE, AUTHORITY mean power exerted over the minds or behavior of others. INFLUENCE may apply either to a force exercised and received unknowingly or to a conscious and deliberate affecting ⟨the *influence* of feelings on a worker's productivity⟩ ⟨a leader whose *influence* was creative⟩ PRESTIGE implies a reputation for conspicuous excellence or superiority that

compels deference ⟨the *prestige* and power of the landowners were unshaken in spite of the revolt of the peasants⟩ AUTHORITY implies the power to win devotion and allegiance or to gain acceptance and belief

²**influence** *vt* **1 :** to affect or alter (as behavior) by indirect or intangible means **2 :** to have an effect on the condition or development of **:** MODIFY — **in·flu·enc·er** *n*

syn AFFECT, SWAY: INFLUENCE applies to a force that brings about a change or determines a course of action or behavior ⟨traditions that *influenced* resistance to change⟩ AFFECT applies to a stimulus strong enough to bring about a reaction or modification without a total change ⟨rainfall *affects* the rate of growth in plants⟩ ⟨the child's forlorn little figure *affected* her deeply⟩ ⟨the new law *affects* only some aspects of commerce⟩ SWAY applies to forces that either are not resisted or are irresistible and bring about a change ⟨advertising that *sways* the choices of the public⟩

in·flu·ent \'in-,flü-ənt\ *adj* **:** flowing in

in·flu·en·tial \,in-flü-'en-chəl\ *adj* **:** having or exerting influence — **in·flu·en·tial·ly** \-'ench-(ə-)lē\ *adv*

in·flu·en·za \,in-flü-'en-zə\ *n* [It, lit., influence, fr. ML *influentia;* fr. the belief that epidemics were due to the influence of the stars] **1 :** an acute and very contagious virus disease with sudden onset, fever, prostration, severe aches and pains, and inflammation of the respiratory tract **2 :** any of various feverish usu. virus diseases of man or domestic animals typically with respiratory symptoms and inflammation and often with systemic involvement

in·flux \'in-,fləks\ *n* [LL *influxus, fr. L influx-, influere* to flow in] **:** a flowing in **:** INFLOW

in·fold *vb* **1** \in-'fōld\ **:** ENFOLD **2** \'in-,fōld\ **:** to fold inward or toward one another

in·form \in-'fȯrm\ *vb* [ME *informen* to give form to, direct, inform] **1 :** to let a person know something **:** TELL **2 :** to give information so as to accuse or cast suspicion ⟨*inform* against him to the police⟩

in·for·mal \(')in-'fȯr-məl\ *adj* **1 :** conducted or carried out without formality or ceremony **2 :** appropriate for ordinary or casual use ⟨*informal* clothes⟩ — **in·for·mal·i·ty** \,in-fȯr-'mal-ət-ē, -fər-\ *n* — **in·for·mal·ly** \(')in-'fȯr-mə-lē\ *adv*

in·form·ant \in-'fȯr-mənt\ *n* **:** INFORMER

in·for·ma·tion \,in-fər-'mā-shən\ *n* **1 :** the communication or reception of knowledge or intelligence **2 a :** knowledge obtained from investigation, study, or instruction **b :** INTELLIGENCE, NEWS **c :** FACTS, DATA **d :** a signal or mark put into or put out by a computing machine **3 :** a formal accusation of a crime made by a prosecuting officer as distinguished from an indictment presented by a grand jury — **in·for·ma·tion·al** \-shnəl, -shən-ᵊl\ *adj*

information theory *n* **:** a theory that deals statistically with the efficiency of processes of communication (as in telecommunication or in computing machines) between men and machines

in·form·a·tive \in-'fȯr-mət-iv\ *adj* **:** imparting knowledge **:** INSTRUCTIVE — **in·form·a·tive·ly** *adv* — **in·form·a·tive·ness** *n*

in·form·a·to·ry \-mə-,tōr-ē, -,tȯr-\ *adj* **:** conveying information ⟨an *informatory* double in bridge⟩

in·formed \in-'fȯrmd\ *adj* **:** EDUCATED, INTELLIGENT

in·form·er \in-'fȯr-mər\ *n* **:** one that informs; *esp* **:** a person who informs against someone else

infra- *prefix* [L *infra;* akin to E *under*] **1 :** below ⟨*infra*human⟩ ⟨*infra*sonic⟩ **2 :** within ⟨*infra*specific⟩ **3 :** below in a scale or series ⟨*infra*red⟩

in·fract \in-'frakt\ *vt* **:** INFRINGE, VIOLATE — **in·frac·tor** \-'frak-tər\ *n*

in·frac·tion \in-'frak-shən\ *n* [L *infract-, infringere* to infringe] **:** the act of infringing **:** VIOLATION

in·fra dig \,in-frə-'dig\ *adj* [short for L *infra dignitatem*] **:** being beneath one's dignity **:** UNDIGNIFIED

in·fra·hu·man \,in-frə-'hyü-mən, -'yü-\ *adj* **:** less or lower than human ⟨*infrahuman* primates⟩ — **infrahuman** *n*

in·fran·gi·ble \(')in-'fran-jə-bəl\ *adj* **1 :** not capable of being broken or separated into parts **2 :** not to be violated — **in·fran·gi·bil·i·ty** \(,)in-,fran-jə-'bil-ət-ē\ *n* — **in·fran·gi·ble·ness** \(,)in-'fran-jə-bəl-nəs\ *n* — **in·fran·gi·bly** \-blē\ *adv*

in·fra·red \,in-frə-'red, -(,)frä-\ *adj* **1 :** lying outside the visible spectrum at its red end — used of heat radiation of wavelengths longer than those of visible light **2 :** relating to, producing, or employing infrared radiation ⟨*infrared* photography⟩ — **infrared** *n*

in·fra·son·ic \-'sän-ik\ *adj* [L *sonus* sound] **1** : having a frequency below the audibility range of the human ear **2** : utilizing or produced by infrasonic waves or vibrations

in·fre·quent \(')in-'frē-kwənt\ *adj* **1** : seldom happening or occurring : RARE **2** : placed or occurring at considerable distances or intervals : OCCASIONAL — **in·fre·quen·cy** \-kwən-sē\ *n* — **in·fre·quent·ly** *adv*

syn SPORADIC: INFREQUENT applies to that which occurs at wide intervals in time or space ⟨*infrequent* church attendance⟩⟨*infrequent* stands of pine alongside the highway⟩ SPORADIC applies to that which occurs in scattered instances without continuity or continuous existence ⟨*sporadic* cases of food poisoning⟩⟨*sporadic* fighting on the border⟩

in·fringe \in-'frinj\ *vb* [L *infringere*, fr. *in-* ²in- + *frangere* to break] **1** : VIOLATE, TRANSGRESS ⟨*infringe* a treaty⟩ ⟨*infringe* a patent⟩ **2** : ENCROACH ⟨*infringe* upon a person's rights⟩ — **infringement** *n* — **in·fring·er** *n*

in·fun·dib·u·li·form \,in-(,)fən-'dib-yə-lə-,fórm\ *adj* : shaped like a funnel or cone

in·fun·dib·u·lum \,in-(,)fən-'dib-yə-ləm\ *n, pl* **-la** \-lə\ [NL, fr. L, funnel, fr. *infundere* to pour in, fr. *in-* + *fundere* to pour] : any of various conical or dilated anatomical parts: as **a** : the conical stalk by which the pituitary body is continuous with the brain **b** : the abdominal opening of a fallopian tube — **in·fun·dib·u·lar** \-lər\ *adj*

in·fu·ri·ate \in-'fyur-ē-,āt\ *vt* : to make furious : ENRAGE — **in·fu·ri·at·ing·ly** \-,āt-iŋ-lē\ *adv* — **in·fu·ri·a·tion** \-,fyur-ē-'ā-shən\ *n*

in·fuse \in-'fyüz\ *vt* [L *infus-*, *infundere* to pour in, fr. *in-* ²in- + *fundere* to pour] **1** : to put in as if by pouring ⟨*infused* courage into his followers⟩ **2** : INSPIRE **3** : to steep (as tea) without boiling — **in·fus·er** *n*

in·fus·i·ble \(')in-'fyü-zə-bəl\ *adj* [¹in- + *fusible*] : incapable or very difficult of fusion — **in·fus·i·bil·i·ty** \(,)in-,fyü-zə-'bil-ət-ē\ *n* — **in·fus·i·ble·ness** \(')in-'fyü-zə-bəl-nəs\ *n*

in·fu·sion \in-'fyü-zhən\ *n* **1** : the act or process of infusing **2** : a substance extracted esp. from a plant material by steeping or soaking in water ⟨a strong *infusion* of tea⟩

in·fu·so·ri·an \,in-fyü-'zōr-ē-ən, -'zòr-\ *n* : any of a heterogeneous group of minute organisms found esp. in decomposing infusions of organic matter; *esp* : a ciliated protozoan — **in·fu·so·ri·al** \-ē-əl\ *or* **infusorian** *adj*

¹-ing \iŋ\ *; in some dialects usu., in other dialects informally,* ən, in, *or (in certain phonetic contexts)* °n, °m, °ŋ\ *vb suffix or adj suffix* [ME, alter. of *-ende*, fr. OE] — used to form the present participle ⟨sail*ing*⟩ and sometimes to form an adjective resembling a present participle but not derived from a verb ⟨swashbuckl*ing*⟩

²-ing *n suffix* [OE] : one of a (specified) kind ⟨sweet*ing*⟩

³-ing *n suffix* [OE] **1** : action or process ⟨runn*ing*⟩⟨sleep*ing*⟩ : instance of an action or process ⟨a meet*ing*⟩ **2 a** : product or result of an action or process ⟨an engrav*ing*⟩ — often in pl. ⟨earn*ings*⟩ **b** : something used in an action or process ⟨a bed cover*ing*⟩ **3** : action or process connected with (a specified thing) ⟨iceboat*ing*⟩ **4** : something connected with, consisting of, or used in making (a specified thing) ⟨scaffold*ing*⟩ **5** : something related to (a specified concept) ⟨off*ing*⟩

in·gath·er·ing \'in-,gath-(ə-)riŋ\ *n* **1** : COLLECTION, HARVEST **2** : ASSEMBLY

in·gem·i·nate \in-'jem-ə-,nāt\ *vt* : REDOUBLE, REITERATE — **in·gem·i·na·tion** \-,jem-ə-'nā-shən\ *n*

in·ge·nious \in-'jē-nyəs\ *adj* [L *ingenium* natural capacity, fr. *in-* ²in- + *gen-, gigni* to be born] **1** : marked by especial aptitude at discovering, inventing, or contriving **2** : marked by originality, resourcefulness, and cleverness in conception or execution ⟨*ingenious* device⟩ — **in·ge·nious·ly** *adv* — **in·ge·nious·ness** *n*

syn INGENIOUS, INGENUOUS are not synonymous but they are readily confused. INGENIOUS implies having inborn inventiveness and cleverness; INGENUOUS implies keeping a childlike innocence, frankness, or lack of sophistication

in·ge·nue *or* **in·gé·nue** \'an-jə-,nü, 'aⁿ-zhə-\ *n* [F *ingénue*, fr. fem. of *ingénu* ingenuous, fr. L *ingenuus*] : a naïve girl or young woman; *esp* : an actress representing such a person

in·ge·nu·i·ty \,in-jə-'n(y)ü-ət-ē\ *n, pl* **-ties** [obs. *ingenuity* ingenuousness] **1 a** : skill or cleverness in devising or combining : INVENTIVENESS **b** : cleverness or aptness of design or contrivance **2** : an ingenious device or contrivance

in·gen·u·ous \in-'jen-yə-wəs\ *adj* [L *ingenuus* native, freeborn, ingenuous, fr. *in-* ²in-, *gigni* to be born] **1** : STRAIGHTFORWARD, FRANK **2** : showing innocent or childlike simplicity : NAÏVE **syn** see INGENIOUS — **in·gen·u·ous·ly** *adv* — **in·gen·u·ous·ness** *n*

in·gest \in-'jest\ *vt* : to take in for or as if for digestion — **in·gest·i·ble** \-'jes-tə-bəl\ *adj* — **in·ges·tion** \-'jes-chən\ *n* — **in·ges·tive** \-'jes-tiv\ *adj*

in·ges·ta \in-'jes-tə\ *n pl* [NL] : material taken into the body by way of the mouth

in·gle \'iŋ-(g)əl\ *n* [ScGael *aingeal*] **1** : FLAME, BLAZE **2** : FIREPLACE

in·gle·nook \-,núk\ *n* **1** : a corner by the fire or chimney **2** : a high-backed wooden settle placed close to a fireplace

in·glo·ri·ous \(')in-'glōr-ē-əs, -'glòr-\ *adj* **1** : not glorious : lacking fame or honor **2** : bringing disgrace : SHAMEFUL ⟨*inglorious* defeat⟩ — **in·glo·ri·ous·ly** *adv* — **in·glo·ri·ous·ness** *n*

inglenooks 2

in·got \'iŋ-gət\ *n* [ME] : a mass of metal cast into a convenient shape for storage or transportation

ingraft *var of* ENGRAFT

¹in·grain \(')in-'grān\ *vt* : to work indelibly into the natural texture or mental or moral constitution : IMBUE

²in·grain \'in-,grān\ *adj* **1 a** : made of fiber that is dyed before being spun into yarn **b** : made of yarn that is dyed before being woven or knitted ⟨*ingrain* carpet⟩ **2** : thoroughly worked in : INNATE — **ingrain** *n*

in·grained \'in-,grānd, (')in-'\ *adj* : worked into the grain or fiber : DEEP-SEATED ⟨*ingrained* prejudice⟩ — **in·grain·ed·ly** \-,grā-nəd-lē, -'grā-\ *adv*

in·grate \'in-,grāt\ *n* [L *ingratus* ungrateful, fr. *in-* ¹in- + *gratus* grateful] : an ungrateful person

in·gra·ti·ate \in-'grā-shē-,āt\ *vt* [²in- + L *gratia* grace] : to gain favor or favorable acceptance for by deliberate effort ⟨the new teacher quickly *ingratiated* herself with her pupils⟩ — **in·gra·ti·a·tion** \-,grā-shē-'ā-shən\ *n* — **in·gra·tia·to·ry** \-'grā-sh(ē-)ə-,tōr-ē, -,tòr-\ *adj*

in·gra·ti·at·ing *adj* **1** : capable of winning favor : PLEASING ⟨*ingratiating* smile⟩ **2** : intended or adopted in order to gain favor : FLATTERING ⟨*ingratiating* manner⟩ — **in·gra·ti·at·ing·ly** \-,āt-iŋ-lē\ *adv*

in·grat·i·tude \(')in-'grat-ə-,t(y)üd\ *n* : lack of gratitude or thankfulness : UNGRATEFULNESS

in·gre·di·ent \in-'grēd-ē-ənt\ *n* [L *ingredi* to go into, fr. *in-* + *gradi* to go] : one of the substances that make up a mixture ⟨*ingredients* of a cake⟩ **syn** see ELEMENT — **ingredient** *adj*

in·gress \'in-,gres\ *n* [L *ingressus*, fr. *ingredi* to go into] **1** : the act of entering : ENTRANCE **2** : the power or liberty of entrance or access ⟨free *ingress* to the circus grounds⟩

in·grow·ing \'in-,grō-iŋ\ *adj* : growing or tending inward

in·grown \-,grōn\ *adj* : grown in; *esp* : having the free tip or edge embedded in the flesh ⟨*ingrown* toenail⟩ — **in·grown·ness** \-,grōn-nəs\ *n*

in·growth \'in-,grōth\ *n* **1** : a growing inward (as to fill a void) **2** : something that grows in or into a space

in·gui·nal \'iŋ-gwən-°l\ *adj* [L *inguin-, inguen* groin] : of, relating to, or situated in the region of the groin

in·gur·gi·tate \in-'gər-jə-,tāt\ *vt* [L *ingurgitare*, fr. *in-* + *gurgit-, gurges* whirlpool] : to swallow greedily or in large quantity — **in·gur·gi·ta·tion** \-,gər-jə-'tā-shən\ *n*

in·hab·it \in-'hab-ət\ *vt* [L *inhabitare*, fr. *in-* ²in- + *habitare* to dwell, fr. freq. of *habēre* to have] : to live or dwell in — **in·hab·it·a·ble** \-ə-bəl\ *adj* — **in·hab·i·ta·tion** \-,hab-ə-'tā-shən\ *n* — **in·hab·it·er** \-'hab-ət-ər\ *n*

in·hab·it·an·cy \-ən-sē\ *n* : OCCUPANCY

in·hab·it·ant \in-'hab-ət-ənt\ *n* : one who lives permanently in a place

¹in·hal·ant \in-'hā-lənt\ *n* : something (as an allergen or medicated spray) that is inhaled

²**inhalant** adj 1 : of or relating to an inhalant 2 : bearing in or inward ⟨an *inhalant* siphon of a clam⟩

in·ha·la·tion \,in-(h)ə-'lā-shən\ n : the act or an instance of inhaling — **in·ha·la·tion·al** \-shnəl, -shən-ᵊl\ adj

in·ha·la·tor \'in-(h)ə-,lāt-ər\ n : an apparatus used in inhaling something (as a mixture of oxygen and carbon dioxide)

in·hale \in-'hāl\ vb [²in- + -hale (as in *exhale*)] 1 : to draw in by breathing 2 : to breathe in

in·hal·er \in-'hā-lər\ n 1 : one that inhales 2 : INHALATOR

in·har·mon·ic \,in-(,)här-'män-ik\ adj : not harmonic : DISCORDANT

in·har·mo·ni·ous \-'mō-nē-əs\ adj 1 : not harmonious : DISCORDANT 2 : not fitting or congenial : CONFLICTING ⟨*inharmonious* ideas⟩ — **in·har·mo·ni·ous·ly** adv — **in·har·mo·ni·ous·ness** n

in·har·mo·ny \(')in-'här-mə-nē\ n : DISCORD

in·here \in-'hi(ə)r\ vi [L *inhaerēre*, fr. ²in- + *haerēre* to stick] : to be inherent : BELONG ⟨power to make laws *inheres* in the state⟩

in·her·ent \in-'hir-ənt, -'her-\ adj : belonging to or being a part of the essential character of a person or thing : belonging by nature : INTRINSIC ⟨an *inherent* sense of fair play⟩⟨fluidity is an *inherent* quality of gas⟩ — **in·her·ence** \-ən(t)s\ n — **in·her·ent·ly** adv

in·her·it \in-'her-ət\ vt [MF *inheriter* to make heir, fr. LL *inhereditare*, fr. L in- ²in- + *hereditas* inheritance, fr. *hered-, heres* heir] 1 : to come into possession of : RECEIVE 2 : to receive by legal right from an ancestor at his death 3 a : to receive from ancestors by genetic transmission ⟨*inherit* a strong constitution⟩ b : to have in turn or receive as if from an ancestor ⟨*inherited* the problem of unemployment from his predecessor⟩ — **in·her·i·tor** \-ət-ər\ n — **in·her·i·tress** \-ə-trəs\ or **in·her·i·trix** \-ə-(,)triks\ n

in·her·it·a·ble \in-'her-ət-ə-bəl\ adj : capable of being inherited : TRANSMISSIBLE — **in·her·it·a·ble·ness** n

in·her·it·ance \in-'her-ət-ən(t)s\ n 1 : the act of inheriting 2 : something that is or may be inherited **syn** see HERITAGE

in·hib·it \in-'hib-ət\ vt [L *inhibit-, inhibēre*, fr. in- ²in- + *habēre* to have, hold] 1 : to prohibit from doing something 2 a : to hold in check : RESTRAIN b : to discourage from free or spontaneous activity : REPRESS **syn** see FORBID — **in·hib·i·tive** \-ət-iv\ adj — **in·hib·i·to·ry** \-ə-,tōr-ē, -,tor-\ adj

in·hi·bi·tion \,in-(h)ə-'bish-ən\ n 1 a : the act of inhibiting : the state of being inhibited b : something that forbids or debars 2 : an inner impediment to free activity, expression, or functioning

in·hib·i·tor or **in·hib·it·er** \in-'hib-ət-ər\ n : one that inhibits; esp : an agent that slows or interferes with a chemical action

in·hos·pit·a·ble \,in-,häs-'pit-ə-bəl, (')in-'häs-(,)pit-\ adj 1 : not showing hospitality 2 : providing no shelter or sustenance : BARREN ⟨miles of *inhospitable* desert⟩ — **in·hos·pit·a·ble·ness** n — **in·hos·pit·a·bly** \-blē\ adv

in·hos·pi·tal·i·ty \(,)in-,häs-pə-'tal-ət-ē\ n : the quality or state of being inhospitable

in·hu·man \(')in-'hyü-mən, (')in-'yü-\ adj 1 a : lacking pity or kindness : SAVAGE b : COLD, IMPERSONAL c : not worthy of or conforming to the needs of human beings 2 : of or suggesting a nonhuman class of beings — **in·hu·man·ly** adv

in·hu·mane \,in-hyü-'mān, ,in-yü-\ adj : not humane : INHUMAN 1 — **in·hu·mane·ly** adv

in·hu·man·i·ty \-'man-ət-ē\ n, pl -ties 1 : the quality or state of being cruel or barbarous 2 : a cruel or barbarous act

in·hu·ma·tion \,in-hyü-'mā-shən\ n : BURIAL, INTERMENT

in·hume \in-'hyüm\ vt [L *inhumare*, fr. ²in- + *humus* earth] : BURY, INTER

in·im·i·cal \in-'im-i-kəl\ adj [L *inimicus* enemy, fr. ¹in- + *amicus* friend] 1 a : having the disposition of an enemy : HOSTILE b : reflecting or indicating hostility : UNFRIENDLY ⟨*inimical* stares⟩ 2 : HARMFUL, ADVERSE ⟨habits *inimical* to health⟩— **in·im·i·cal·ly** \-'im-i-k(ə-)lē\ adv

in·im·i·ta·ble \(')in-'im-ət-ə-bəl\ adj : not capable of being imitated : MATCHLESS — **in·im·i·ta·bil·i·ty** \(,)in-

,im-ət-ə-'bil-ət-ē\ n — **in·im·i·ta·ble·ness** \(')in-'im-ət-ə-bəl-nəs\ n — **in·im·i·ta·bly** \-blē\ adv

in·iq·ui·tous \in-'ik-wət-əs\ adj : characterized by iniquity : WICKED — **in·iq·ui·tous·ly** adv — **in·iq·ui·tous·ness** n

in·iq·ui·ty \in-'ik-wət-ē\ n, pl -ties [L *iniquitas*, fr. *iniquus* unfair, fr. in- ¹in- + *aequus* equal, fair] 1 : gross injustice : WICKEDNESS 2 : an iniquitous act or thing : SIN

¹**ini·tial** \in-'ish-əl\ adj [L *initium* beginning, fr. *inire* to go into, fr. in- + *ire* to go] 1 : of, relating to, or existing at the beginning : INCIPIENT ⟨*initial* stages of a disease⟩ 2 : placed or standing at the beginning : FIRST ⟨*initial* letter of a word⟩ — **ini·tial·ly** \-'ish-(ə-)lē\ adv — **ini·tial·ness** \-'ish-əl-nəs\ n

²**initial** n 1 a : the first letter of a name b : a large letter beginning a text or a division or paragraph 2 : PRECURSOR; esp : a meristematic cell

³**initial** vt **ini·tialed** or **ini·tialled**; **ini·tial·ing** or **ini·tial·ling** \-'ish-(ə-)liŋ\ : to affix an initial to : mark with an initial ⟨*initial* a memorandum⟩⟨*initial* a handkerchief⟩

initial side n : a straight line containing a point about which another line rotates to generate an angle

¹**ini·ti·ate** \in-'ish-ē-,āt\ vt 1 : to set going : ORIGINATE, START, BEGIN ⟨*initiate* a new policy⟩ 2 : to instruct in the rudiments or principles of something : INTRODUCE ⟨*initiate* pupils into the mysteries of algebra⟩ 3 : to induct into membership by or as if by special rites — **ini·ti·a·tor** \-,āt-ər\ n

²**ini·tiate** \in-'ish-(ē-)ət\ adj : INITIATED

³**ini·tiate** \in-'ish-(ē-)ət\ n 1 : a person who is undergoing or has passed an initiation 2 : a person who is instructed or adept in a special field

ini·ti·a·tion \in-,ish-ē-'ā-shən\ n 1 : an initiating or a being initiated : INTRODUCTION 2 : the ceremonies with which a person is made a member of a society or club

ini·tia·tive \in-'ish-ət-iv\ n 1 : an introductory step or movement ⟨take the *initiative* in becoming acquainted⟩ 2 : energy or aptitude displayed in initiation of action : ENTERPRISE ⟨he has ability but lacks *initiative*⟩ 3 a : the right to initiate legislative action b : a procedure enabling a specified number of voters to propose a law for approval of the electorate or the legislature — compare REFERENDUM

ini·tia·to·ry \in-'ish-(ē-)ə-,tōr-ē, -,tor-\ adj 1 : constituting a beginning : INTRODUCTORY ⟨*initiatory* remarks⟩ 2 : tending or serving to initiate ⟨*initiatory* rites of a fraternal order⟩

in·ject \in-'jekt\ vt [L *inject-, inicere*, fr. in- + *jacere* to throw] 1 a : to throw, drive, or force into something ⟨*inject* fuel into an engine⟩ b : to force a fluid into esp. for medical purposes 2 : to introduce as an element or factor in or into some situation or subject ⟨*injected* humor into his speech⟩ — **in·ject·a·ble** \-'jek-tə-bəl\ adj — **in·jec·tor** \-tər\ n

in·jec·tion \in-'jek-shən\ n 1 : an act or instance of injecting (as by a syringe or pump) 2 : something (as a medication) that is injected

in·ju·di·cious \,in-jù-'dish-əs\ adj : not judicious : INDISCREET, UNWISE — **in·ju·di·cious·ly** adv — **in·ju·di·cious·ness** n

in·junc·tion \in-'jəŋ(k)-shən\ n [L *injunct-, injungere* to enjoin, fr. in- + *jungere* to join] 1 : the act or an instance of enjoining : ORDER, ADMONITION 2 : a writ granted by a court of equity requiring a party to do or refrain from doing a specified act ⟨sought an *injunction* against the strike⟩ — **in·junc·tive** \-'jəŋ(k)-tiv\ adj

in·jure \'in-jər\ vt **in·jured**; **in·jur·ing** \'inj-(ə-)riŋ\ [back-formation fr. *injury*] 1 a : to do an injustice to : WRONG b : to harm, impair, or tarnish the standing of c : to give pain to ⟨*injure* a man's pride⟩ 2 a : to inflict bodily hurt on b : to impair the soundness of c : to inflict material damage or loss on

in·ju·ri·ous \in-'jùr-ē-əs\ adj : causing injury : HARMFUL — **in·ju·ri·ous·ly** adv — **in·ju·ri·ous·ness** n

in·ju·ry \'inj-(ə-)rē\ n, pl -ries [L *injuria* injustice, wrong, fr. in- ¹in- + *jur-, jus* justice, right] 1 : an act that damages or hurts : WRONG 2 : hurt, damage, or loss sustained **syn** DAMAGE, HARM : INJURY implies an act or result detrimental to one's rights, well-being, freedom, property, or success; DAMAGE applies to injury involving loss ⟨the pest did considerable *damage* to the crop⟩⟨scandal that resulted in *damage* to the company's prestige⟩ HARM applies to any evil that injures and often suggests suffering, pain, or annoyance ⟨assured there would be no bodily *harm*⟩

in·jus·tice \(')in-'jǝs-tǝs\ *n* **1** : absence of justice : violation of the rights of another : UNFAIRNESS **2** : an unjust act or deed

¹ink \'iŋk\ *n* [OF *enke,* fr. LL *encaustum,* fr. Gk *enkaustos* burned in, painted in encaustic, fr. *enkaiein* to burn in, fr. *en-* + *kaiein* to burn] **1** : a usu. liquid and colored material for writing and printing **2** : the black protective secretion of a cephalopod

²ink *vt* : to put ink on — **ink·er** *n*

ink·ber·ry \'iŋk-,ber-ē\ *n* **1** : a black-berried American holly **2** : POKEWEED **3** : the fruit of an inkberry

ink·blot \'iŋk-,blät\ *n* : any of several plates showing blots of ink for use in psychological testing

¹ink·horn \-,hórn\ *n* : a small portable bottle (as of horn) for holding ink

²inkhorn *adj* : ostentatiously learned : PEDANTIC ⟨*inkhorn* terms⟩

in·kling \'iŋ-kliŋ\ *n* [ME *yngkiling*] **1** : HINT, INTIMATION **2** : a slight knowledge or vague notion ⟨he had no *inkling* of what it all meant⟩

ink·stand \'iŋk-,stand\ *n* : INKWELL; *also* : a pen and ink-well

ink·well \-,wel\ *n* : a container for ink

inky \'iŋ-kē\ *adj* **ink·i·er; -est** **1** : consisting of, using, or resembling ink ⟨*inky* blackness of the sea⟩ **2** : soiled with ink **3** : of the color of ink : BLACK — **ink·i·ness** *n*

inky cap *n* : a small mushroom whose cap dissolves into an inky fluid after the spores mature

in·laid \'in-'lād\ *adj* **1** : set into a surface in a decorative design **2** : decorated with a design or material set into a surface ⟨a table with an *inlaid* top⟩

¹in·land \'in-,land, -lǝnd\ *n* : the interior part of a country : the land away from the coast or boundaries

²inland *adj* **1** *chiefly Brit* : not foreign : DOMESTIC, INTERNAL ⟨*inland* revenue⟩ **2** : of or relating to the interior of a country

³inland *adv* : into or toward the interior

in·land·er \'in-,lan-dǝr, -lǝn-\ *n* : one who lives inland

in·law \'in-,ló\ *n* [back-formation fr. *mother-in-law,* etc.] : a relative by marriage

¹in·lay \(')in-'lā\ *vt* **in·laid; in·lay·ing** : to set into a surface or ground material for decoration or reinforcement — **in·lay·er** *n*

²in·lay \'in-,lā\ *n* **1** : inlaid work or material used in inlaying **2** : a tooth filling shaped to fit a cavity and then cemented into place

in·let \'in-,let, -lǝt\ *n* **1** : an act of letting in **2 a** : a bay or recess in a shore; *also* : CREEK **b** : an opening for intake

in·ly \'in-lē\ *adv* **1** : INWARDLY, WITHIN **2** : INTIMATELY, THOROUGHLY

in·mate \'in-,māt\ *n* : one of a group occupying a single residence; *esp* : a person confined in an asylum, prison, or poorhouse

in me·di·as res \in-,mād-ē-,äs-'räs\ *adv* [L, lit., into the midst of things] : in or into the middle of a narrative or plot

in me·mo·ri·am \,in-mǝ-'mōr-ē-ǝm, -'mór-\ *prep* [L] : in memory of — used esp. in epitaphs

in·most \'in-,mōst\ *adj* : deepest within : INNERMOST

inn \'in\ *n* [OE] **1** : a public house that provides lodging and food for travelers : HOTEL **2** : TAVERN

in·nards \'in-ǝrdz\ *n pl* [alter. of *inwards*] **1** : the internal organs of a man or animal; *esp* : VISCERA **2** : the internal parts of a structure or mechanism

in·nate \in-'āt, 'in-,\ *adj* [L *innatus,* fr. pp. of *innasci* to be born in, fr. *in-* + *nasci* to be born] **1** : existing in or belonging to an individual from birth : NATIVE **2** : belonging to the essential nature of something : INHERENT — **in·nate·ly** *adv* — **in·nate·ness** *n*

syn INBORN, INBRED: INNATE applies to qualities or characteristics that are part of the essential nature of a person or thing ⟨an ability to develop the *innate* talent of the young⟩⟨the *innate* defect of the scheme⟩ INBORN suggests a quality or tendency either present at birth or so deep-seated as to seem so ⟨an *inborn* ability to act⟩ INBRED suggests something deeply rooted acquired from parents by heredity or early nurture ⟨a natural *inbred* dignity⟩⟨an *inbred* hatred of injustice⟩

in·ner \'in-ǝr\ *adj* **1 a** : situated farther in ⟨*inner* room⟩

b : near a center esp. of influence ⟨belong to the *inner* circle⟩ **2** : of or relating to the mind or spirit ⟨the *inner* life of man⟩ — **in·ner·ly** *adv*

inner city *n* : the usu. older and more densely populated central section of a city — **inner-city** *adj*

inner ear *n* : a cavity in the temporal bone that contains a complex membranous labyrinth containing sense organs of hearing and of awareness of position in space and that is separated from the middle ear by membranous fenestrae

inner light *n, often cap I & L* : a divine presence held (as in Quaker doctrine) to enlighten and guide the soul

in·ner·most \'in-ǝr-,mōst\ *adj* : farthest inward : INMOST

in·ner·sole \,in-ǝr-'sōl\ *n* : INSOLE

inner tube *n* : an airtight tube of rubber placed inside the casing of a pneumatic tire to hold air under pressure

in·ner·vate \in-'ǝr-,vāt, 'in-(,)ǝr-\ *vt* : to supply with nerves — **in·ner·va·tion** \,in-(,)ǝr-'vā-shǝn\ *n* — **in·ner·va·tion·al** \-shnǝl, -shǝn-²l\ *adj*

in·ning \'in-iŋ\ *n* [²in] **1** : a baseball team's turn at bat ending with the 3d out; *also* : a division of a baseball game consisting of a turn at bat for each team **2** : a chance or turn for action or accomplishment ⟨time for the opposition to have its *innings*⟩

inn·keep·er \'in-,kē-pǝr\ *n* : the landlord of an inn

in·no·cence \'in-ǝ-sǝn(t)s\ *n* **1 a** : freedom from guilt, sin, or blame **b** : GUILELESSNESS, SIMPLICITY **c** : IGNORANCE **2** : BLUET

in·no·cent \-sǝnt\ *adj* [L *innocent-, innocens,* fr. *in-* ¹in- + *nocēre* to harm] **1** : free from sin : knowing nothing of evil **2** : free from guilt or blame : GUILTLESS ⟨*innocent* of the crime⟩ **3** : free from evil influence or effect : HARMLESS ⟨an *innocent* pastime⟩ **4** : ARTLESS, SIMPLE, UNSOPHISTICATED ⟨an *innocent* country boy⟩ — **innocent** *n* — **in·no·cent·ly** *adv*

in·noc·u·ous \in-'äk-yǝ-wǝs\ *adj* [L *innocuus,* fr. *in-* ¹in- + *nocēre* to harm] **1** : working no injury : HARMLESS **2 a** : not likely to give offense : INOFFENSIVE **b** : INSIPID, INSIGNIFICANT ⟨*innocuous* poems⟩ — **in·noc·u·ous·ly** *adv* — **in·noc·u·ous·ness** *n*

in·nom·i·nate \in-'äm-ǝ-nǝt\ *adj* [LL *innominatus,* fr. L *in-* + *nomin-, nomen* name] : having no name : UNNAMED; *also* : ANONYMOUS

innominate artery *n* : a short artery arising from the arched first part of the aorta and dividing into the carotid and subclavian arteries of the right side

innominate bone *n* : the large flaring bone that makes a lateral half of the pelvis in mammals and is composed of the fused ilium, ischium, and pubis

innominate vein *n* : either of a pair of veins that receive blood from the head and upper limbs and fuse to form the superior vena cava

in·no·vate \'in-ǝ-,vāt\ *vb* [L *innovare,* fr. *in-* ²in- + *novus* new] **1** : to introduce as or as if new **2** : to make changes — **in·no·va·tive** \-,vāt-iv\ *adj* — **in·no·va·tor** \-,vāt-ǝr-\ *n*

in·no·va·tion \,in-ǝ-'vā-shǝn\ *n* **1** : the introduction of something new **2** : a new idea, method, or device

in·nu·en·do \,in-yǝ-'wen-dō\ *n, pl* **-dos** or **-does** [L, by hinting, fr. *innuere* to hint, fr. *in-* ²in- + *nuere* to nod] : an oblique allusion : HINT, INSINUATION; *esp* : a veiled or equivocal reflection on character or reputation

in·nu·mer·a·ble \in-'(y)üm-(ǝ-)rǝ-bǝl\ *adj* : too many to be numbered : COUNTLESS — **in·nu·mer·a·ble·ness** *n* — **in·nu·mer·a·bly** \-blē\ *adv*

in·nu·mer·ous \-(ǝ-)rǝs\ *adj* : INNUMERABLE

in·ob·ser·vance \,in-ǝb-'zǝr-vǝn(t)s\ *n* **1** : lack of attention : HEEDLESSNESS **2** : failure to fulfill : NONOBSERVANCE — **in·ob·ser·vant** \-vǝnt\ *adj*

in·oc·u·lant \in-'äk-yǝ-lǝnt\ *n* : INOCULUM

in·oc·u·late \in-'äk-yǝ-,lāt\ *vt* [L *inoculare* to insert a bud in a plant, fr. *in-* + *oculus* eye, bud] **1 a** : to introduce a microorganism into ⟨*inoculate* mice with anthrax⟩ ⟨beans *inoculated* with nitrogen-fixing bacteria⟩ **b** : to introduce (a microorganism) into a suitable situation for growth **c** : to introduce a serum, antibody, or antigen into in order to treat or prevent a disease **2** : to introduce something into the mind of — **in·oc·u·la·tive** \-,lāt-iv\ *adj* — **in·oc·u·la·tor** \-,lāt-ǝr\ *n*

in·oc·u·la·tion \in-,äk-yǝ-'lā-shǝn\ *n* **1** : the act or process or an instance of inoculating **2** : INOCULUM

in·oc·u·lum \in-'äk-yǝ-lǝm\ *n, pl* **-la** \-lǝ\ : material used for inoculation

---

j joke; **ŋ** sing; **ō** flow; **ò** flaw; **òi** coin; **th** thin; **t̲h̲** this; **ü** loot; **u̇** foot; **y** yet; **yü** few; **yu̇** furious; **zh** vision

in·of·fen·sive \‚in-ə-'fen(t)-siv\ *adj* **1** : causing no harm or injury **2 a** : giving no provocation : PEACEABLE **b** : unobjectionable to the senses — **in·of·fen·sive·ly** *adv* — **in·of·fen·sive·ness** *n*

in·op·er·a·ble \(')in-'äp-(ə-)rə-bəl\ *adj* **1** : not suitable for surgery **2** : not operable

in·op·er·a·tive \-'äp-(ə-)rət-iv, -'äp-ə-‚rāt-\ *adj* : not functioning : producing no effect ⟨an *inoperative* law⟩ — **in·op·er·a·tive·ness** *n*

in·op·er·cu·late \‚in-ō-'pər-kyə-lət\ *adj* : lacking an operculum ⟨*inoperculate* snails⟩

in·op·por·tune \(‚)in-‚äp-ər-'t(y)ün\ *adj* : INCONVENIENT, UNSEASONABLE ⟨happened at an *inopportune* time⟩ — **in·op·por·tune·ly** *adv* — **in·op·por·tune·ness** \-'t(y)ün-nəs\ *n*

in order that *conj* : THAT

in·or·di·nate \in-'ord-ᵊn-ət, -'ord-nət\ *adj* [L *inordinatus* disordered, fr. *in-* + *ordin-, ordo* order] : not kept within bounds : IMMODERATE ⟨an *inordinate* curiosity⟩ **syn** see EXCESSIVE — **in·or·di·nate·ly** *adv* — **in·or·di·nate·ness** *n*

in·or·gan·ic \‚in-ór-'gan-ik\ *adj* **1** : being or composed of matter of other than plant or animal origin : MINERAL **2** : of or relating to a branch of chemistry concerned with substances not usu. classed as organic — **in·or·gan·i·cal·ly** \-'gan-i-k(ə-)lē\ *adv*

in·pa·tient \'in-‚pā-shənt\ *n* : a hospital patient who receives lodging and food as well as treatment

in pet·to \in-'pet-ō\ *adv* (*or adj*) [It, lit., in the breast] : in private : SECRETLY

in·put \'in-‚put\ *n* **1** : something that is put in; *esp* : power or energy put into a machine or system **2** : a point at which something (as power, an electronic signal, or data) is put in **3** : the act or process of putting in

in·quest \'in-‚kwest\ *n* [OF *enqueste*, fr. (assumed) VL *inquaestus*, fr. L *inquirere* to inquire] **1** : a judicial or official inquiry or investigation esp. before a jury **2** : a body of men assembled to conduct an inquest **3** : the finding of an inquest

in·qui·e·tude \(')in-'kwī-ə-‚t(y)üd\ *n* : disturbed state : UNEASINESS, RESTLESSNESS

in·qui·line \'in-kwə-‚līn, 'iŋ-, -lən\ *n* [L *inquilinus* tenant, lodger, fr. *in-* + *colere* to cultivate, dwell] : an animal that habitually lives in the nest or den of another kind of animal — **in·qui·lin·ism** \-‚iz-əm\ *n* — **in·qui·li·nous** \‚in-kwə-'lī-nəs, iŋ-\ *adj*

in·quire \in-'kwī(ə)r\ *vb* [L *inquirere*, fr. *in-* ²*in-* + *quaerere* to seek] **1** : to ask about **2** : to make investigation or inquiry : search into : INVESTIGATE **3** : to put a question — **in·quir·er** *n* — **in·quir·ing·ly** \-iŋ-lē\ *adv* — **inquire after** : to ask about the health of

in·qui·ry \'in-‚kwī(ə)r-ē, in-'; 'in-kwə-rē, 'iŋ-\ *n, pl* **-ries** **1 a** : the act of inquiring ⟨learn by *inquiry*⟩ **b** : a request for information ⟨make *inquiries* at the station⟩ **2** : a search for truth or knowledge **3** : a systematic examination : INVESTIGATION

in·qui·si·tion \‚in-kwə-'zish-ən\ *n* [L *inquisit-, inquirere* to inquire] **1** : the act of inquiring **2** : a judicial or official inquiry **3 a** *cap* : a former Roman Catholic tribunal for the discovery and punishment of heresy **b** : an investigation conducted with little regard for individual rights **c** : a severe questioning — **in·qui·si·tion·al** \-'zish-nəl, -ən-ᵊl\ *adj*

in·quis·i·tive \in-'kwiz-ət-iv\ *adj* **1** : given to examination or investigation **2** : QUESTIONING; *esp* : PRYING **syn** see CURIOUS — **in·quis·i·tive·ly** *adv* — **in·quis·i·tive·ness** *n*

in·quis·i·tor \in-'kwiz-ət-ər\ *n* : one who inquires or conducts an inquisition — **in·quis·i·to·ri·al** \-‚kwiz-ə-'tōr-ē-əl, -'tòr-\ *adj* — **in·quis·i·to·ri·al·ly** \-ē-ə-lē\ *adv*

in re \in-'rē, -'rā\ *prep* [L] : in the matter of : CONCERNING, RE

in·road \'in-‚rōd\ *n* **1** : a sudden hostile incursion : RAID **2** : a serious encroachment ⟨an extended illness made *inroads* on his savings⟩

in·rush \'in-‚rəsh\ *n* : a crowding or flooding in : INFLUX

in·sa·lu·bri·ous \‚in(t)-sə-'lü-brē-əs\ *adj* : UNWHOLESOME, NOXIOUS — **in·sa·lu·bri·ty** \-brət-ē\ *n*

in·sane \(')in-'sān\ *adj* **1** : not sane : unsound in mind : MAD, CRAZY **2** : showing evidence of an unsound mind ⟨an *insane* look⟩ **3** : used by or for the insane ⟨an *insane* asylum⟩ **4** : FOOLISH, WILD ⟨an *insane* attempt⟩ — **in·sane·ly** *adv* — **in·sane·ness** \-'sān-nəs\ *n*

syn MAD, CRAZY : INSANE technically means such unsoundness of mind that one is not responsible for one's actions; in general use it implies utter folly or irrationality ⟨*insane* ravings⟩ MAD carries implications of wildness or rashness or lack of restraint ⟨*mad* pursuit of fortunes⟩ CRAZY suggests a distraught state of mind induced by intense emotion ⟨*crazy* with anxiety⟩

in·san·i·tary \in-'san-ə-‚ter-ē\ *adj* : unclean enough to endanger health : CONTAMINATED

in·san·i·ty \in-'san-ət-ē\ *n, pl* **-ties** **1 a** : unsoundness or derangement of the mind **b** : a mental disorder **2** : such unsoundness of mind as excuses one from criminal or civil responsibility **3 a** : extreme folly or unreasonableness **b** : something utterly foolish or unreasonable

syn INSANITY, LUNACY, MANIA denote serious mental disorder. INSANITY implies unfitness to manage one's own affairs or to behave safely in a state of freedom; LUNACY may imply alternating periods of madness and lucidity and commonly stresses wildness of thought and behavior; MANIA is often used specif. of one of the spells of intense excitement characteristic of some mental disorders

in·sa·tia·ble \(')in-'sā-shə-bəl\ *adj* : incapable of being satisfied : QUENCHLESS ⟨*insatiable* thirst⟩ ⟨an *insatiable* desire for knowledge⟩ — **in·sa·tia·bil·i·ty** \(‚)in-‚sā-shə-'bil-ət-ē\ *n* — **in·sa·tia·ble·ness** \(')in-'sā-shə-bəl-nəs\ *n* — **in·sa·tia·bly** \-blē\ *adv*

in·sa·tiate \-'sā-sh(ē-)ət\ *adj* : not satiated or satisfied; *also* : INSATIABLE ⟨*insatiate* cruelty⟩ — **in·sa·tiate·ly** *adv* — **in·sa·tiate·ness** *n*

in·scribe \in-'skrīb\ *vt* [L *inscript-, inscribere*, fr. *in-* ²*in-* + *scribere* to write] **1 a** : to write, engrave, or print as a lasting record **b** : to enter on a list : ENROLL **c** : to write (letters or other characters) in a particular format in cryptography **2 a** : to write, engrave, or print characters on **b** : to autograph or address as a gift **c** : to stamp deeply : IMPRESS ⟨a scene *inscribed* on her memory⟩ **3** : to dedicate (as a poem) to someone **4** : to draw within a figure so as to touch in as many places as possible — **in·scrib·er** *n*

in·scrip·tion \in-'skrip-shən\ *n* **1** : something that is inscribed; *also* : TITLE, SUPERSCRIPTION **2** : the wording on a coin, medal, or seal : LEGEND **3** : the dedication of a book or work of art **4 a** : the act of inscribing **b** : the entering of a name on or as if on a list : ENROLLMENT — **in·scrip·tion·al** \-shnəl, -shən-ᵊl\ *adj*

in·scrip·tive \in-'skrip-tiv\ *adj* : relating to or constituting an inscription — **in·scrip·tive·ly** *adv*

in·scru·ta·ble \in-'skrüt-ə-bəl\ *adj* [L *in-* ¹*in-* + *scrutari* to search] : not readily understood : ENIGMATIC ⟨an *inscrutable* mystery⟩ — **in·scru·ta·bil·i·ty** \-‚skrüt-ə-'bil-ət-ē\ *n* — **in·scru·ta·ble·ness** \-'skrüt-ə-bəl-nəs\ *n* — **in·scru·ta·bly** \-blē\ *adv*

in·seam \'in-‚sēm\ *n* : an inner seam of a garment or shoe

in·sect \'in-‚sekt\ *n* [L *insectum*, fr. *insecare* to cut into, fr. *in-* + *secare* to cut] **1** : any of numerous small animals that are usu. more or less obviously segmented **2** : any of a class (Insecta) of arthropods (as bugs or bees) with well-defined head, thorax, and abdomen, three pairs of jointed legs, and typically one or two pairs of wings

in·sect·a·ry \'in-‚sek-tə-rē\ *or* **in·sec·tar·i·um** \‚in-‚sek-'ter-ē-əm\ *n, pl* **-taries** \-tə-rēz\ *or* **-tar·ia** \-'ter-ē-ə\ : a place for rearing or keeping live insects

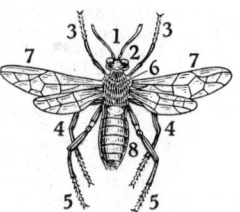

insect: *1* antennae, *2* head, *3* front leg, *4* middle leg, *5* hind leg, *6* thorax, *7* wing, *8* abdomen

in·sec·ti·cide \in-'sek-tə-‚sīd\ *n* : an agent that destroys insects — **in·sec·ti·cid·al** \-‚sek-tə-'sīd-ᵊl\ *adj*

in·sec·ti·vore \in-'sek-tə-‚vōr, -‚vór\ *n* **1** : any of an order (Insectivora) of mammals comprising the moles, shrews, hedgehogs, and related forms that are mostly small, insectivorous, and nocturnal **2** : an insectivorous plant or animal

in·sec·tiv·o·rous \ˌin-ˌsek-ˈtiv-(ə-)rəs\ *adj* : depending on insects as food

in·se·cure \ˌin(t)-si-ˈkyu̇(ə)r\ *adj* **1** : UNCERTAIN, UNSURE **2** : UNPROTECTED, UNSAFE **3** : LOOSE, SHAKY **4** : lacking stability : INFIRM **5** : beset by fear or anxiety — **in·se·cure·ly** *adv* — **in·se·cure·ness** *n* — **in·se·cu·ri·ty** \-ˈkyu̇r-ət-ē\ *n*

in·sem·i·nate \in-ˈsem-ə-ˌnāt\ *vt* : to introduce semen into the genital tract of (a female) — **in·sem·i·na·tion** \-ˌsem-ə-ˈnā-shən\ *n*

in·sen·sate \(ˈ)in-ˈsen-ˌsāt\ *adj* [L in- ¹in + sensus sense] **1** : lacking animate awareness or sensation **2** : lacking sense or understanding; *also* : FOOLISH **3** : UNFEELING, BRUTAL, INHUMAN ⟨insensate hatred⟩ — **in·sen·sate·ly** *adv* — **in·sen·sate·ness** *n*

in·sen·si·ble \(ˈ)in-ˈsen(t)-sə-bəl\ *adj* **1** : incapable or bereft of feeling or sensation: as **a** : INANIMATE, INSENTIENT ⟨insensible earth⟩ **b** : UNCONSCIOUS **c** : lacking or deprived of sensory perception ⟨insensible to pain⟩⟨insensible from cold⟩ **2 a** : IMPERCEPTIBLE **b** : SLIGHT, GRADUAL ⟨insensible motion⟩ **3** : APATHETIC, INDIFFERENT ⟨insensible to fear⟩; *also* : UNAWARE ⟨insensible of their danger⟩ **4** : not intelligible : MEANINGLESS **5** : lacking delicacy or refinement — **in·sen·si·bil·i·ty** \(ˌ)in-ˌsen(t)-sə-ˈbil-ət-ē\ *n* — **in·sen·si·ble·ness** \(ˈ)in-ˈsen(t)-sə-bəl-nəs\ *n* — **in·sen·si·bly** \-blē\ *adv*

in·sen·si·tive \(ˈ)in-ˈsen(t)-sət-iv, -ˈsen(t)-stiv\ *adj* : not sensitive; *esp* : lacking feeling — **in·sen·si·tive·ly** *adv* — **in·sen·si·tive·ness** *n* — **in·sen·si·tiv·i·ty** \(ˌ)in-ˌsen(t)-sə-ˈtiv-ət-ē\ *n*

in·sen·tient \(ˈ)in-ˈsen-ch(ē-)ənt\ *adj* : lacking perception, consciousness, or animation — **in·sen·tience** \-ch(ē-)ən(t)s\ *n*

in·sep·a·ra·ble \(ˈ)in-ˈsep-(ə-)rə-bəl\ *adj* : incapable of being separated or disjoined ⟨inseparable friends⟩ — **in·sep·a·ra·bil·i·ty** \(ˌ)in-ˌsep-(ə-)rə-ˈbil-ət-ē\ *n* — **inseparable** *n* — **in·sep·a·ra·ble·ness** \(ˈ)in-ˈsep-(ə-)rə-bəl-nəs\ *n* — **in·sep·a·ra·bly** \-blē\ *adv*

¹in·sert \in-ˈsərt\ *vb* [L inserere, fr. in- + serere to join] **1** : to put or thrust in ⟨inserted the key in the lock⟩ **2** : to put or introduce into the body of : INTERPOLATE ⟨insert a word in a sentence⟩ **3** : to set in and make fast; *esp* : to insert by sewing between two cut edges **4** : to attach by natural growth to something and esp. a part to be moved **syn** see INTRODUCE — **in·sert·er** *n*

²in·sert \ˈin-ˌsərt\ *n* : something that is inserted or is for insertion; *esp* : written or printed material inserted (as between the leaves of a book)

in·ser·tion \in-ˈsər-shən\ *n* **1** : the act or process of inserting **2** : something that is inserted: as **a** : the part of a muscle that inserts on a part to be moved **b** : the mode or place of attachment of an organ or part **c** : embroidery or needlework inserted as ornament between two pieces of fabric — **in·ser·tion·al** \-shnəl, -shən-ᵊl\ *adj*

in·ses·so·ri·al \ˌin-ˌse-ˈsōr-ē-əl, -ˈsȯr-\ *adj* [L insess-, insidēre to sit on, fr. in- + sedēre to sit] : adapted for perching : PERCHING ⟨insessorial birds⟩

¹in·set \ˈin-ˌset\ *n* : something that is inset: as **a** : a small graphic representation (as a map or picture) set within the compass of a larger one **b** : a piece of cloth set into a garment for decoration

²in·set \ˈin-ˌset, in-ˈ\ *vt* **inset** *or* **in·set·ted**; **in·set·ting** : to set in : insert as an inset

¹in·shore \ˈin-ˈshō(ə)r, -ˈshȯ(ə)r\ *adj* **1** : situated or carried on near shore ⟨inshore fishing⟩ **2** : moving toward shore ⟨an inshore wind⟩

²inshore *adv* : to or toward shore ⟨debris drifting inshore⟩

¹in·side \(ˈ)in-ˈsīd, ˈin-ˌ\ *n* **1** : an inner side or surface **2 a** : an interior or internal part : the part within **b** : inward nature, thoughts, or feeling **c** : VISCERA, ENTRAILS — usu. used in pl. — **inside** *adj*

²inside *prep* **1 a** : in or into the interior of ⟨went inside the house⟩ **b** : on the inner side of ⟨put the dot inside the curve⟩ **2** : before the end of : WITHIN ⟨inside an hour⟩

³inside *adv* **1** : on the inner side ⟨cleaned his car inside and out⟩ **2** : in or into the interior ⟨went inside⟩

inside of *prep* : INSIDE

in·sid·er \(ˈ)in-ˈsīd-ər\ *n* : a person who has access to confidential information

inside track *n* **1** : the inner side of a curved racecourse **2** : an advantageous competitive position

in·sid·i·ous \in-ˈsid-ē-əs\ *adj* [L insidiae ambush, fr. insidēre to sit in, fr. in- + sedēre to sit] **1 a** : awaiting a chance to entrap : TREACHEROUS **b** : harmful but enticing : SEDUCTIVE **2** : having a gradual and cumulative effect ⟨an insidious disease⟩ — **in·sid·i·ous·ly** *adv* — **in·sid·i·ous·ness** *n*

in·sight \ˈin-ˌsīt\ *n* **1** : the power or act of seeing into a situation : PENETRATION **2** : the act of apprehending the inner nature of things or of seeing intuitively

in·sig·nia \in-ˈsig-nē-ə\ *or* **in·sig·ne** \-(ˌ)nē\ *n, pl* **-nia** *or* **-ni·as** [L insignia, pl. of insigne mark, badge, fr. in- ²in + signum mark, sign] : a distinguishing mark esp. of authority, office, or honor : BADGE, EMBLEM

in·sig·nif·i·cance \ˌin(t)-sig-ˈnif-i-kən(t)s\ *n* : the quality or state of being insignificant

in·sig·nif·i·cant \-kənt\ *adj* : not significant: as **a** : lacking meaning or import : INCONSEQUENTIAL ⟨insignificant quarrel⟩ **b** : INCONSIDERABLE, UNIMPORTANT ⟨losses were insignificant⟩ **c** : lacking weight, position, or influence : CONTEMPTIBLE ⟨an insignificant hanger-on⟩ **d** : LITTLE, SMALL ⟨an insignificant amount⟩ — **in·sig·nif·i·cant·ly** *adv*

in·sin·cere \ˌin(t)-sin-ˈsi(ə)r\ *adj* : not sincere : HYPOCRITICAL — **in·sin·cere·ly** *adv* — **in·sin·cer·i·ty** \-ˈser-ət-ē, -ˈsir-\ *n*

in·sin·u·ate \in-ˈsin-yə-ˌwāt\ *vt* [L insinuare, fr. in- ²in- + sinus curve, bosom] **1 a** : to introduce (as an idea) gradually or in a subtle, indirect, or covert way **b** : HINT, IMPLY **2** : to introduce (as oneself) by stealthy, smooth, or artful means — **in·sin·u·a·tive** \-ˌwāt-iv\ *adj* — **in·sin·u·a·tor** \-ˌwāt-ər\ *n*

in·sin·u·at·ing *adj* **1** : tending gradually to cause doubt, distrust, or change of outlook ⟨insinuating remarks⟩ **2** : winning favor and confidence by imperceptible degrees ⟨insinuating voice⟩ — **in·sin·u·at·ing·ly** \-ˌwāt-iŋ-lē\ *adv*

in·sin·u·a·tion \in-ˌsin-yə-ˈwā-shən\ *n* **1** : a subtle suggestion : INNUENDO **2** : the artful pursuit of favor : INGRATIATION

in·sip·id \in-ˈsip-əd\ *adj* [LL insipidus, fr. L in- ¹in + sapidus savory, fr. sapere to taste] **1** : lacking taste or savor : TASTELESS **2** : lacking in qualities that interest, stimulate, or challenge : DULL, FLAT ⟨insipid fiction⟩ — **in·si·pid·i·ty** \ˌin(t)-sə-ˈpid-ət-ē\ *n* — **in·sip·id·ly** \in-ˈsip-əd-lē\ *adv*

syn VAPID, INANE: INSIPID implies a lack of sufficient taste or savor to please or interest ⟨overcooked insipid cabbage⟩ ⟨insipid art and dull prose⟩ VAPID suggests lack of liveliness, force, or spirit ⟨exchange of vapid remarks⟩ INANE implies lacking any significant or convincing quality ⟨a purposeless inane life⟩⟨inane criticism⟩

in·sist \in-ˈsist\ *vb* [L insistere to stand upon, insist, fr. in- ²in- + sistere to stand] **1** : to place special emphasis or great importance ⟨insists on punctuality⟩⟨insisted on his going⟩ **2** : to make a demand : request urgently

in·sist·ence \in-ˈsis-tən(t)s\ *n* **1** : the act of insisting **2** : the quality or state of being insistent : URGENCY ⟨the insistence of a need⟩

in·sist·ent \-tənt\ *adj* : compelling attention : PERSISTENT — **in·sist·ent·ly** *adv*

in si·tu \in-ˈsī-tü\ *adv (or adj)* [L, in position] : in the natural or original position

in·so·cia·ble \(ˈ)in-ˈsō-shə-bəl\ *adj* : not sociable — **in·so·cia·bil·i·ty** \(ˌ)in-ˌsō-shə-ˈbil-ət-ē\ *n* — **in·so·cia·bly** \(ˈ)in-ˈsō-shə-blē\ *adv*

in·so·far as \ˈin(t)-sə-ˌfär-əz\ *conj* : to the extent or degree that

in·so·la·tion \ˌin-ˌsō-ˈlā-shən\ *n* [L insolare to expose to the sun, fr. in- ²in- + sol sun] **1** : solar radiation that has been received **2** : the rate of delivery of all direct solar energy per unit of horizontal surface

in·sole \ˈin-ˌsōl\ *n* **1** : an inside sole of a shoe **2** : a loose thin strip placed inside a shoe for warmth or comfort

in·so·lence \ˈin(t)-sə-lən(t)s\ *n* : a haughty attitude or insulting act

in·so·lent \-lənt\ *adj* [L insolent-, insolens] **1** : arrogant in speech or conduct ⟨an insolent child⟩ **2** : exhibiting boldness or effrontery ⟨an insolent act⟩ — **in·so·lent·ly** *adv*

in·sol·u·bil·i·ty \(ˌ)in-ˌsäl-yə-ˈbil-ət-ē\ *n* : the quality or state of being insoluble: as **a** : INDISSOLUBILITY **b** : INEXPLICABILITY

in·sol·u·ble \(ˈ)in-ˈsäl-yə-bəl\ *adj* : not soluble: as

a : having or admitting of no solution or explanation **b** : incapable of being dissolved in a liquid or soluble only with difficulty or to a slight degree — **insoluble** n — **in·sol·u·ble·ness** n — **in·sol·u·bly** \-blē\ adv

in·solv·a·ble \(')in-'säl-və-bəl, -'sȯl-\ adj : admitting no solution — **in·solv·a·bly** \-blē\ adv

in·sol·vent \(')in-'säl-vənt\ adj **1** : unable or having ceased to pay debts as they fall due **2** : insufficient to pay all debts ⟨an *insolvent* estate⟩ **3** : IMPOVERISHED, DEFICIENT — **in·sol·ven·cy** \-vən-sē\ n — **insolvent** n

in·som·nia \in-'säm-nē-ə\ n [L, fr. in- ¹in- + *somnus* sleep] : prolonged and usu. abnormal inability to get enough sleep — **in·som·ni·ac** \-nē-,ak\ adj or n

in·so·much as \,in(t)-sə-,məch-əz\ conj : inasmuch as

insomuch that \-thət\ conj : to such a degree that : so that

in·sou·ci·ance \in-'sü-sē-ən(t)s\ n [F] : a lighthearted unconcern : NONCHALANCE — **in·sou·ci·ant** \-ənt\ adj — **in·sou·ci·ant·ly** adv

in·spect \in-'spekt\ vb [L inspect-, inspicere, fr. in- ²in- + specere to look] **1** : to examine closely (as for judging quality or condition) ⟨*inspect* foodstuffs⟩ **2** : to view and examine (as troops) officially **3** : to make an examination ⟨they're *inspecting* this afternoon⟩ — **in·spec·tive** \-'spek-tiv\ adj

in·spec·tion \in-'spek-shən\ n **1** : the act of inspecting : EXAMINATION **2** : a checking or testing of an individual against established standards

in·spec·tor \in-'spek-tər\ n **1** : a person employed to make inspections ⟨meat *inspector*⟩ **2** : a police officer ranking next below a superintendent or deputy superintendent — **in·spec·tor·ate** \-t(ə-)rət\ n — **in·spec·tor·ship** \-tər-,ship\ n

in·spi·ra·tion \,in(t)-spə-'rā-shən\ n **1** : the act of inspiring **2 a** : the act of inhaling or drawing in **b** : the drawing of air into the lungs in breathing : INHALATION; *also* : air or vapor so drawn in **3** : the act or power of moving the intellect or emotions ⟨the *inspiration* of music⟩ **4 a** : the quality or state of being inspired ⟨the artist's *inspiration* came from many sources⟩ **b** : something that is inspired ⟨a scheme that was an *inspiration*⟩ **5** : an inspiring agent or influence — **in·spi·ra·tion·al** \-shnəl, -shən-ᵊl\ adj — **in·spi·ra·tion·al·ly** \-ē\ adv

in·spi·ra·to·ry \(')in-'spī-rə-,tōr-ē, -,tȯr-\ adj : relating to, used for, or associated with inspiration

in·spire \in-'spī(ə)r\ vb [L inspirare, lit., to breathe into, fr. in- ²in- + *spirare* to breathe] **1 a** (1) : to move or guide by divine or supernatural influence ⟨prophets *inspired* by God⟩ (2) : to exert an animating, enlivening, or exalting influence on ⟨*inspired* by his mother⟩ **b** : to give inspiration **c** : AFFECT ⟨a childhood that *inspired* him with a desire for education⟩ **2** : INHALE **3 a** : to communicate to an agent supernaturally ⟨words *inspired* by God⟩ **b** : to infuse or introduce into the mind : AROUSE ⟨*inspires* confidence in his followers⟩ **4** : to bring about : OCCASION ⟨studies that *inspired* several inventions⟩ **5** : to spread (rumor) by indirect means or through the agency of another — **in·spir·er** n

in·spir·it \in-'spir-ət\ vt : ANIMATE, HEARTEN

in·spis·sate \in-'spis-,āt\ vb [L spissus dense] : CONDENSE, THICKEN — **in·spis·sa·tion** \,in(t)-spə-'sā-shən\ n — **in·spis·sa·tor** \in-'spis-,āt-ər\ n

in·sta·bil·i·ty \,in(t)-stə-'bil-ət-ē\ n : the quality or state of being unstable

in·sta·ble \(')in-'stā-bəl\ adj : UNSTABLE

in·stall or **in·stal** \in-'stȯl\ vt **in·stalled**; **in·stall·ing** [ML installare, fr. in- + *stallum* stall, of Gmc origin] **1** : to place formally in office : induct into an office, rank, or order **2** : to establish in an indicated place, condition, or status ⟨*installed* himself in the best chair in the room⟩ **3** : to set up for use or service ⟨*install* a TV set⟩ — **in·stall·er** n

in·stal·la·tion \,in(t)-stə-'lā-shən\ n **1** : the act of installing : the state of being installed **2** : something that is installed for use **3** : a military camp, fort, or base

¹in·stall·ment or **in·stal·ment** \in-'stȯl-mənt\ n : INSTALLATION 1

²installment also **instalment** n [alter. of earlier *estallment* payment by installment, fr. OF *estaler* to place, fix, fr. *estal* place, of Gmc origin] **1** : one of the parts into which a debt is divided when payment is made at intervals

2 : one of several parts (as of a publication) presented at intervals — **installment** adj

installment plan n : a system of buying goods by paying for them in installments

¹in·stance \'in(t)-stən(t)s\ n **1** : SUGGESTION, REQUEST ⟨entered a contest at the *instance* of his teacher⟩ **2** : EXAMPLE ⟨an *instance* of rare courage⟩ **3** : OCCASION, CASE ⟨in the first instance⟩

syn CASE, EXAMPLE: INSTANCE applies to any individual person, act, or thing that may be offered to illustrate or explain ⟨a good *instance* of the power of suggestion⟩ CASE is used to direct attention to a real or assumed occurrence or situation that is to be considered, studied, or dealt with ⟨reported isolated *cases* of typhoid⟩ EXAMPLE applies to a typical or illustrative instance or case ⟨a fine *example* of Georgian architecture⟩ — **for instance** : as an example

²instance vt **1** : to illustrate or demonstrate by an instance **2** : to mention as a case or example : CITE

¹in·stant \'in(t)-stənt\ n [ML instant-, instans, fr. L, present, urgent, fr. prp. of *instare* to stand on, impend, urge, fr. in- ²in- + *stare* to stand] : a very small space of time : MOMENT

²instant adj [L instant-, instans, fr. prp. of *instare* to urge] **1** : IMPORTUNATE, URGENT ⟨in *instant* need⟩ **2** : of or occurring in the present month **3** : IMMEDIATE, DIRECT ⟨an *instant* reponse⟩ **4 a** : partially prepared by the manufacturer to make final preparation easy ⟨*instant* cake mix⟩ **b** : immediately soluble in water ⟨*instant* coffee⟩ — **in·stant·ness** n

in·stan·ta·ne·ous \,in(t)-stən-'tā-nē-əs\ adj **1** : done, occurring, or acting without any perceptible duration of time **2** : done without any dclay being introduced purposely **3** : occurring or present at a particular instant ⟨*instantaneous* velocity⟩ — **in·stan·ta·ne·ous·ly** adv — **in·stan·ta·ne·ous·ness** n

in·stan·ter \in-'stant-ər\ adv [ML, fr. instant-, instans present] : at once : INSTANTLY

in·stant·ly \'in(t)-stənt-lē\ adv **1** : IMPORTUNATELY, URGENTLY **2** : without the least delay : IMMEDIATELY

in·star \'in-,stär\ n [NL, fr. L, likeness] : a stage in the life of an insect between two successive molts

in·state \in-'stāt\ vt : to set or establish in a rank or office : INSTALL

in sta·tu quo \in-,stā-tü-'kwō\ [NL, lit., in the state in which] : in the former or same state

in·stead \in-'sted\ adv **1** : as a substitute or equivalent ⟨was going to write but called *instead*⟩ **2** : as an alternative to something expressed or implied : RATHER ⟨cut class and went *instead* to a movie⟩

instead of \in-,sted-ə(v), -,stid-\ prep : as a substitute for or alternative to ⟨called *instead of* writing⟩

in·step \'in-,step\ n **1** : the arched middle part of the human foot in front of the ankle joint **2** : the part of a shoe or stocking over the instep

in·sti·gate \'in(t)-stə-,gāt\ vt [L instigare] : to goad or urge forward : set on **syn** see INCITE — **in·sti·ga·tion** \,in(t)-stə-'gā-shən\ n — **in·sti·ga·tive** \'in(t)-stə-,gāt-iv\ adj — **in·sti·ga·tor** \-,gāt-ər\ n

in·still also **in·stil** \in-'stil\ vt **in·stilled**; **in·still·ing** [L instillare, fr. in- + *stillare* to drip] **1** : to cause to enter drop by drop **2** : to impart gradually ⟨*instill* a love of music⟩ — **in·stil·la·tion** \,in(t)-stə-'lā-shən\ n — **in·still·er** \in-'stil-ər\ n — **in·still·ment** \-'stil-mənt\ n

¹in·stinct \'in(t)-,stiŋ(k)t\ n [L instinctus impulse, fr. instinct-, instinguere to incite] **1** : a natural aptitude, impulse, or capacity **2 a** : complex but unreasoned response by an organism to environmental stimuli that is largely hereditary and unalterable **b** : behavior based on reactions below the conscious level — **in·stinc·tu·al** \in-'stiŋ(k)-chə(-wə)l\ adj

²in·stinct \in-'stiŋ(k)t, 'in-,\ adj : FILLED, INFUSED

in·stinc·tive \in-'stiŋ(k)-tiv\ adj : of, relating to, or prompted by instinct **syn** see SPONTANEOUS — **in·stinc·tive·ly** adv

¹in·sti·tute \'in(t)-stə-,t(y)üt\ vt [L institut-, instituere, fr. in- ²in- + *statuere* to set up, fr. status condition, state] **1** : to set up : ESTABLISH, FOUND ⟨*institute* a society⟩ **2** : INAUGURATE, BEGIN ⟨*institute* an inquiry⟩ — **in·sti·tut·er** or **in·sti·tu·tor** \-,t(y)üt-ər\ n

²institute n **1** : something that is instituted: as **a** : an elementary principle recognized as authoritative **b** *pl* : a collection of such principles and precepts **2 a** : an organization for the promotion of a cause : ASSOCIATION ⟨an *institute* for psychical research⟩ **b** : an educational institution **3** : a meeting for instruction or a brief course of such meetings ⟨teachers' *institute*⟩

in·sti·tu·tion \,in(t)-stə-'t(y)ü-shən\ *n* **1** : the act of instituting : ESTABLISHMENT **2** : an established custom, practice, or law ⟨the turkey dinner is a Thanksgiving *institution*⟩ **3 a** : an established society or corporation; *esp* : a public one ⟨educational and charitable *institutions*⟩ ⟨a financial *institution*⟩ **b** : the building used by such an organization — **in·sti·tu·tion·al** \-shnəl, -shən-ºl\ *adj* — **in·sti·tu·tion·al·ly** \-ē\ *adv*

in·sti·tu·tion·al·ize \-'t(y)ü-shnə-,līz, -shən-ºl-,īz\ *vt* **1** : to make into or treat like an institution ⟨*institutionalized* housing⟩ **2** : to put in the care of an institution ⟨*institutionalized* alcoholics⟩

in·struct \in-'strəkt\ *vt* [L *instruct-, instruere* to construct, instruct, fr. *in-* ²*in-* + *struere* to build] **1** : to impart knowledge to : TEACH **2** : to give information to : INFORM **3** : to give directions or commands to syn see TEACH

in·struct·ed *adj* **1** : TAUGHT, INFORMED **2** : subject to specific instructions ⟨*instructed* delegates⟩

in·struc·tion \in-'strək-shən\ *n* **1 a** : LESSON **b** : COMMAND, ORDER **c** *pl* : an outline or manner of procedure to be followed : DIRECTIONS **2** : the action or practice of an instructor or teacher — **in·struc·tion·al** \-shnəl, -shən-ºl\ *adj*

in·struc·tive \in-'strək-tiv\ *adj* : giving knowledge : serving to instruct or inform ⟨an *instructive* experience⟩ — **in·struc·tive·ly** *adv* — **in·struc·tive·ness** *n*

in·struc·tor \-tər\ *n* : one that instructs : TEACHER; *esp* : a college teacher below professorial rank — **in·struc·tor·ship** \-,ship\ *n* — **in·struc·tress** \-'strək-trəs\ *n*

in·stru·ment \'in(t)-strə-mənt\ *n* [L *instrumentum*, fr. *instruere* to construct, instruct] **1 a** : a means whereby something is achieved, performed, or furthered **b** : DUPE **2 a** : UTENSIL, IMPLEMENT, TOOL ⟨a surgical *instrument*⟩ **b** : a device used to produce music **3** : a formal legal document (as a deed, bond, or agreement) **4 a** : a measuring device for determining the present value of a quantity under observation **b** : an electrical or mechanical device used in navigating an airplane; *esp* : such a device used as the sole means of navigating syn see IMPLEMENT

in·stru·men·tal \,in(t)-strə-'ment-ºl\ *adj* **1** : acting as an instrument or means ⟨*instrumental* in sending a thief to jail⟩ **2** : having to do with an instrument : designed for or performed with or on an instrument and esp. a musical instrument ⟨an unusual *instrumental* arrangement⟩ — **in·stru·men·tal·ly** \-ºl-ē\ *adv*

in·stru·men·tal·ist \-ºl-əst\ *n* : a player on a musical instrument

in·stru·men·tal·i·ty \,in(t)-strə-mən-'tal-ət-ē, -,men-\ *n*, *pl* **-ties** **1** : the quality or state of being instrumental **2** : MEANS, AGENCY ⟨metals purified through the *instrumentality* of heat⟩

in·stru·men·ta·tion \,in(t)-strə-mən-'tā-shən, -,men-\ *n* **1** : the use or application of instruments for observation, measurement, or control **2** : the arrangement or composition of music for the instruments esp. of a band or orchestra **3** : instruments for a particular purpose

instrument flying *n* : navigation of an airplane by instruments only

instrument landing *n* : a landing made with little or no external visibility by means of instruments within an airplane and by ground radio devices

instrument panel *n* : a panel on which instruments are mounted; *esp* : DASHBOARD **2** — called also *instrument board*

in·sub·or·di·nate \,in(t)-sə-'bord-ºn-ət, -'bord-nət\ *adj* : unwilling to submit to authority : DISOBEDIENT, REBELLIOUS — **in·sub·or·di·nate·ly** *adv* — **in·sub·or·di·na·tion** \,in(t)-sə-,bord-ºn-'ā-shən\ *n*

in·sub·stan·tial \,in(t)-səb-'stan-chəl\ *adj* **1** : lacking substance or reality : IMAGINARY **2** : lacking firmness or solidity — **in·sub·stan·ti·al·i·ty** \-,stan-chē-'al-ət-ē\ *n*

in·suf·fer·a·ble \('')in-'səf-(ə-)rə-bəl\ *adj* : incapable of being endured : INTOLERABLE ⟨*insufferable* bore⟩ ⟨*insufferable* wrongs⟩ — **in·suf·fer·a·ble·ness** *n* — **in·suf·fer·a·bly** \-blē\ *adv*

in·suf·fi·cien·cy \,in(t)-sə-'fish-ən-sē\ *n*, *pl* **-cies** **1** : the quality or state of being insufficient: as **a** : lack of mental or moral fitness **b** : lack of adequate supply **c** : lack of physical competence ⟨cardiac *insufficiency*⟩ **2** : something insufficient ⟨aware of his own *insufficiencies*⟩

in·suf·fi·cient \-'fish-ənt\ *adj* : not sufficient : INADEQUATE; *also* : INCOMPETENT — **in·suf·fi·cient·ly** *adv*

in·su·lar \'in(t)-s(y)ə-lər, 'in-shə-lər\ *adj* [L *insula* island] **1** : of, relating to, or forming an island **2** : ISOLATED, DETACHED **3** : of or relating to the inhabitants of islands **4** : being isolated and illiberal : NARROW — **in·su·lar·ism** \-lə-,riz-əm\ *n* — **in·su·lar·i·ty** \,in(t)s-(y)ə-'lar-ət-ē, ,in-shə-'lar-\ *n* — **in·su·lar·ly** *adv*

in·su·late \'in(t)-sə-,lāt\ *vt* : to place in a detached situation : ISOLATE; *esp* : to separate from conducting bodies by means of nonconductors so as to prevent transfer of electricity, heat, or sound

in·su·la·tion \,in(t)-sə-'lā-shən\ *n* **1** : the act of insulating : the state of being insulated **2** : material used in insulating

in·su·la·tor \'in(t)-sə-,lāt-ər\ *n* : one that insulates; *esp* : a material that is a poor conductor of electricity or a device made of such material

in·su·lin \'in(t)-s(ə-)lən\ *n* [NL *insula* islet of Langerhans, fr. L, island] : a protein pancreatic hormone essential esp. for the metabolism of carbohydrates and used in the treatment and control of diabetes

insulin shock *n* : a condition of deficient blood sugar associated with excessive insulin in the system and marked by progressive development of coma

insulator

¹**in·sult** \in-'səlt\ *vt* [L *insultare*, lit., to spring upon, fr. *in-* + *saltare* to leap] **1** : to treat with insolence, indignity, or contempt : AFFRONT **2** : to make little of : BELITTLE syn see OFFEND — **in·sult·er** *n*

²**in·sult** \'in-,səlt\ *n* **1** : an act or speech showing disrespect or contempt **2** : damage to the body or one of its parts; *also* : a cause of this ⟨thermal *insult*⟩ syn see AFFRONT

in·su·per·a·ble \(')in-'sü-p(ə-)rə-bəl\ *adj* [L *insuperabilis*, fr. *in-* ²*in-* + *superare* to surmount, fr. *super* over] : incapable of being surmounted, overcome, or passed over ⟨*insuperable* difficulties⟩ ⟨an *insuperable* barrier⟩ — **in·su·per·a·bly** \-blē\ *adv*

in·sup·port·a·ble \,in(t)-sə-'pōrt-ə-bəl, -'port-\ *adj* : not supportable: **a** : UNENDURABLE ⟨an *insupportable* burden⟩ **b** : UNJUSTIFIABLE ⟨*insupportable* charges⟩ — **in·sup·port·a·ble·ness** *n* — **in·sup·port·a·bly** \-blē\ *adv*

in·sup·press·i·ble \,in(t)-sə-'pres-ə-bəl\ *adj* : IRREPRESSIBLE — **in·sup·press·i·bly** \-blē\ *adv*

in·sur·a·ble \in-'shúr-ə-bəl\ *adj* : capable of being insured against loss, damage, or death — **in·sur·a·bil·i·ty** \in-,shúr-ə-'bil-ət-ē\ *n*

in·sur·ance \in-'shúr-ən(t)s\ *n* **1** : the act of insuring : the state of being insured **2 a** : the business of insuring persons or property **b** : coverage by contract whereby one party undertakes to guarantee another against loss by a specified event or peril **c** : the sum for which something is insured

in·sure \in-'shu̇(ə)r\ *vt* **1** : to give or procure insurance on or for **2** : to make certain : ENSURE

in·sured *n* : a person whose life or property is insured

in·sur·er \in-'shu̇r-ər\ *n* : one that insures; *esp* : a company issuing insurance

in·sur·gence \in-'sər-jən(t)s\ *n* : UPRISING, INSURRECTION

in·sur·gen·cy \-jən-sē\ *n* **1** : the quality or state of being insurgent; *esp* : a state of revolt against a government that is less than an organized revolution **2** : INSURGENCE

¹**in·sur·gent** \in-'sər-jənt\ *n* [L *insurgere* to rise up, fr. *in-* ²*in-* + *surgere* to rise] : a person who revolts; *esp* : a rebel not recognized as a belligerent

²**insurgent** *adj* : rising in opposition to authority : REBELLIOUS — **in·sur·gent·ly** *adv*

in·sur·mount·a·ble \,in(t)-sər-'maúnt-ə-bəl\ *adj* : incapable of being surmounted : INSUPERABLE ⟨*insurmountable* difficulties⟩ — **in·sur·mount·a·bly** \-blē\ *adv*

in·sur·rec·tion \,in(t)-sə-'rek-shən\ *n* [L *insurrect-, insurgere* to rise up] : an act or instance of revolting against civil authority or an established government — **in·sur·rec·tion·ary** \-shə-,ner-ē\ *adj or n* — **in·sur·rec·tion·ist** \-shə-nəst\ *n*

---

j joke;   **ŋ** sing;   **ō** flow;   **ȯ** flaw;   **ȯi** coin;   **th** thin;   **th̲** this;   **ü** loot;   **u̇** foot;   **y** yet;   **yü** few;   **yu̇** furious;   **zh** vision

in·sus·cep·ti·bil·i·ty \,in(t)-sə-,sep-tə-'bil-ət-ē\ *n* : the quality or state of being insusceptible

in·sus·cep·ti·ble \-'sep-tə-bəl\ *adj* : not susceptible — **in·sus·cep·ti·bly** \-blē\ *adv*

in·tact \in-'takt\ *adj* [L *intactus,* fr. *in-* ¹*in-* + *tactus,* pp. of *tangere* to touch] : untouched esp. by anything that harms or diminishes : ENTIRE, UNINJURED — **in·tact·ness** \-'tak(t)-nəs\ *n*

in·ta·glio \in-'tal-yō, -'tag-lē-,ō\ *n, pl* **-glios** [It., fr. *intagliare* to engrave, fr. ML *intaliare,* fr. L *in-* + LL *taliare* to cut] **1 a** : an engraving or incised figure in a hard material (as stone) depressed below the surface of the material **b** : the process of making intaglios **c** : printing (as in die stamping and gravure) done from a plate in which the image is sunk below the surface **2** : something (as a gem) carved in intaglio

in·take \'in-,tāk\ *n* **1** : a place where liquid or air is taken into something (as a pump) **2** : the act of taking in **3** : something taken in ⟨food *intake*⟩

¹in·tan·gi·ble \(')in-'tan-jə-bəl\ *adj* : not tangible: as **a** : incapable of being touched ⟨light is *intangible*⟩ **b** : incapable of being thought of as matter or substance : ABSTRACT ⟨goodwill is an *intangible* asset⟩— **in·tan·gi·bil·i·ty** \(,)in-,tan-jə-'bil-ət-ē\ *n* — **in·tan·gi·ble·ness** \(')in-'tan-jə-bəl-nəs\ *n* — **in·tan·gi·bly** \-blē\ *adv*

²intangible *n* : something intangible

in·te·ger \'int-i-jər\ *n* [L, adj., whole, entire, fr. *in-* ¹*in-* + *tangere* to touch] **1** : a number that is a natural number (as 1, 2, or 3), the negative of a natural number, or 0 — called also *whole number* **2** : a complete entity

in·te·gra·ble \'int-i-grə-bəl\ *adj* : capable of being integrated

¹in·te·gral \'int-i-grəl (*usu so in mathematics*); in-'teg-rəl, -'tēg-\ *adj* **1 a** : essential to completeness : CONSTITUENT ⟨an *integral* part of his plan⟩ **b** : of or relating to a mathematical integer, an integral, or integration **c** : formed as a unit with another part **2** : composed of integral parts : INTEGRATED **3** : lacking nothing essential : ENTIRE — **in·te·gral·i·ty** \,int-ə-'gral-ət-ē\ *n* — **in·te·gral·ly** \'int-i-grə-lē; in-'teg-rə-, -'tēg-\ *adv*

²integral *n* : the result of a mathematical integration — compare DEFINITE INTEGRAL, INDEFINITE INTEGRAL

integral calculus *n* : a branch of mathematics applying integration to the determination of lengths, areas, and volumes and to the solution of differential equations

in·te·grate \'int-ə-,grāt\ *vb* **1** : to form into a whole : UNITE ⟨*integrate* the countries' economies⟩ **2 a** : to unite with something else ⟨free enterprise *integrated* with some government controls⟩ **b** : to incorporate into a larger unit ⟨*integrate* migrant workers into the organized labor movement⟩ **3** : to subject to mathematical integration **4 a** : to end the segregation of and bring into common and equal membership in society or an organization **b** : DESEGREGATE ⟨*integrate* school districts⟩ **5** : to become integrated

integrated circuit *n* : a tiny complex of electronic components and their connections that is produced in or on a small slice of material (as silicon) — **integrated circuitry** *n*

in·te·gra·tion \,int-ə-'grā-shən\ *n* **1** : the act, the process, or an instance of integrating; *esp* : incorporation as equals into society or an organization of persons from different groups (as races) **2** : the operation of finding a function whose differential is known

in·te·gra·tion·ist \-sh(ə-)nəst\ *n* : a person who believes in, advocates, or practices social integration

in·teg·ri·ty \in-'teg-rət-ē\ *n* **1** : an unimpaired condition : SOUNDNESS **2** : adherence to a code of moral, artistic, or other values **3** : the quality or state of being complete or undivided : COMPLETENESS

in·teg·u·ment \in-'teg-yə-mənt\ *n* [L *integumentum,* fr. *integere* to cover over, fr. *in-* ²*in-* + *tegere* to cover] : something that covers or encloses; *esp* : an enveloping layer (as a skin, membrane, or husk) of an organism or one of its parts — **in·teg·u·men·tal** \(,)in-,teg-yə-'ment-ºl\ *adj* — **in·teg·u·men·ta·ry** \-'ment-ə-rē, -'men-trē\ *adj*

in·tel·lect \'int-ºl-,ekt\ *n* [L *intellectus,* fr. *intellect-, intellegere* to understand] **1 a** : the power of knowing **b** : the capacity for thought esp. when highly developed **2** : a person of notable intellect

in·tel·lec·tion \,int-ºl-'ek-shən\ *n* **1** : exercise of the intellect : REASONING **2** : a specific act of the intellect : THOUGHT — **in·tel·lec·tive** \-'ek-tiv\ *adj* — **in·tel·lec·tive·ly** *adv*

¹in·tel·lec·tu·al \,int-ºl-'ek-ch(ə-w)əl\ *adj* **1 a** : having to do with the intellect or understanding **b** : performed by the intellect ⟨*intellectual* processes⟩ **2** : having intellect to a high degree : engaged in or given to learning and thinking ⟨*intellectual* person⟩ **3** : requiring study and thought ⟨*intellectual* work⟩ **syn** see INTELLIGENT, MENTAL — **in·tel·lec·tu·al·i·ty** \-,ek-chə-'wal-ət-ē\ *n* — **in·tel·lec·tu·al·ly** \-'ek-ch(ə-w)ə-lē\ *adv* — **in·tel·lec·tu·al·ness** \-ch(ə-w)əl-nəs\ *n*

²intellectual *n* : an intellectual person

in·tel·lec·tu·al·ism \,int-ºl-'ek-chə(-wə)-,liz-əm\ *n* : devotion to the exercise of intellect or to intellectual pursuits — **in·tel·lec·tu·al·ist** \-ləst\ *n* — **in·tel·lec·tu·al·is·tic** \-,ek-chə(-wə)-'lis-tik\ *adj*

in·tel·lec·tu·al·ize \,int-ºl-'ek-chə(-wə)-,līz\ *vt* : to give rational form or content to

in·tel·li·gence \in-'tel-ə-jən(t)s\ *n* **1 a** : the ability to learn and understand or to deal with new or trying situations : REASON, INTELLECT **b** : mental acuteness : SHREWDNESS **2** : the act of understanding : COMPREHENSION **3 a** : INFORMATION, NEWS **b** : information concerning an enemy or possible enemy or an area; *also* : an agency engaged in obtaining such information

intelligence quotient *n* : a number held to express the relative intelligence of a person and determined by dividing his mental age by his chronological age and multiplying by 100 — abbr. *IQ*

intelligence test *n* : a test designed to measure the relative mental capacity of a person

in·tel·li·gent \in-'tel-ə-jənt\ *adj* [L *intellegere, intelligere* to understand, fr. *inter-* + *legere* to select] : having or showing intelligence or intellect — **in·tel·li·gent·ly** *adv*

syn INTELLECTUAL: INTELLIGENT implies having quickness of perception and understanding of any sort; INTELLECTUAL suggests having greater than average interest in things of the mind or in thinking abstractly and often implies a contrast with practical activity or capacity for simple emotional response to experience **syn** see in addition CLEVER

in·tel·li·gen·tsia \in-,tel-ə-'jen(t)-sē-ə, -'gen(t)-\ *n* [Russ *intelligentsiya,* fr. L *intelligentia* intelligence] : intellectuals who form an artistic, social, or political elite

in·tel·li·gi·ble \in-'tel-ə-jə-bəl\ *adj* : capable of being understood : COMPREHENSIBLE — **in·tel·li·gi·bil·i·ty** \-,tel-ə-jə-'bil-ət-ē\ *n* — **in·tel·li·gi·ble·ness** \-'tel-ə-jə-bəl-nəs\ *n* — **in·tel·li·gi·bly** \-blē\ *adv*

in·tem·per·ance \(')in-'tem-p(ə-)rən(t)s\ *n* : lack of moderation esp. in satisfying an appetite or passion; *esp* : habitual or excessive use of intoxicants

in·tem·per·ate \-p(ə-)rət\ *adj* : not temperate: as **a** : not moderate or mild : EXCESSIVE, EXTREME, SEVERE ⟨*intemperate* weather⟩ **b** : lacking or showing lack of restraint or self-control **c** : given to excessive use of intoxicants — **in·tem·per·ate·ly** *adv* — **in·tem·per·ate·ness** *n*

in·tend \in-'tend\ *vt* [L *intendere* to stretch tight, purpose, fr. *in-* ²*in-* + *tendere* to stretch] : to have in mind as a purpose or aim : PLAN ⟨*intend* to do better work⟩ ⟨*intend* no harm⟩

in·ten·dan·cy \in-'ten-dən-sē\ *n, pl* **-cies** **1** : the office or term of office of an intendant **2** : the territory administered by an intendant

in·ten·dant \-dənt\ *n* [F, fr. L *intendere* to intend, give attention to] : a governor or similar administrative official esp. under the French, Spanish, or Portuguese monarchies

¹in·tend·ed \in-'ten-dəd\ *adj* **1** : INTENTIONAL ⟨an *intended* insult⟩ **2** : PROPOSED; *esp* : BETROTHED

²intended *n* : an affianced person : BETROTHED

in·tense \in-'ten(t)s\ *adj* [L *intensus,* pp. of *intendere* to stretch out, intend] **1 a** : existing in an extreme degree ⟨an *intense* light⟩ **b** : having or showing a characteristic in extreme degree ⟨an *intense* sun shone down⟩ **c** : very large : CONSIDERABLE ⟨*intense* amounts of radiation⟩ **2** : strained or straining to the utmost ⟨*intense* study⟩ **3 a** : feeling deeply esp. by nature or temperament ⟨an *intense* person⟩ **b** : deeply felt ⟨*intense* convictions⟩ — **in·tense·ly** *adv* — **in·tense·ness** *n*

in·ten·si·fy \in-'ten(t)-sə-,fī\ *vb* **-fied; -fy·ing** **1** : to make or become intense or more intensive : STRENGTHEN **2** : to make or become more acute : SHARPEN — **in·ten·si-**

fi·ca·tion \-,ten(t)-sə-fə-'kā-shən\ *n* — **in·ten·si·fi·er** \-'ten(t)-sə-,fī(-ə)r\ *n*

syn INTENSIFY, HEIGHTEN, ENHANCE mean to increase markedly in measure or degree. INTENSIFY implies a deepening or strengthening of a thing or its characteristics ⟨*intensify* efforts for peace⟩ ⟨colors were *intensified* by the clear atmosphere⟩ HEIGHTEN suggests a lifting above the ordinary or accustomed ⟨tried to *heighten* awareness of possible danger⟩ ENHANCE suggests a raising above normal in desirability or attractiveness ⟨shrubbery *enhances* property⟩

in·ten·si·ty \in-'ten(t)-sət-ē\ *n, pl* **-ties** **1** : the quality or state of being intense; *esp* : extreme degree of strength, force, or energy **2 a** : the degree or amount of a quality or condition **b** : the magnitude of force or energy per unit (as of surface, charge, or mass) ⟨the *intensity* of an electric or magnetic field⟩ **3** : SATURATION 3a

¹in·ten·sive \in-'ten(t)-siv\ *adj* **1** : involving or marked by special effort : THOROUGH, EXHAUSTIVE ⟨an *intensive* campaign⟩ ⟨*intensive* agriculture⟩ **2** : serving to give emphasis ⟨the *intensive* pronoun *himself* in the sentence "he himself was present"⟩ — **in·ten·sive·ly** *adv* — **in·ten·sive·ness** *n*

²intensive *n* : an intensive word

¹in·tent \in-'tent\ *n* [LL *intentus*, fr. L *intens-, intent-, intendere* to intend] **1** : the act, fact, or state of mind of intending : PURPOSE, INTENTION ⟨with *intent* to kill⟩ **2** : MEANING, SIGNIFICANCE ⟨understand the *intent* of the message⟩

²intent *adj* **1** : directed with strained or eager attention : CONCENTRATED ⟨an *intent* gaze⟩ **2 a** : closely occupied : ENGROSSED ⟨*intent* upon his own thoughts⟩ **b** : set on some end or purpose ⟨*intent* on going⟩ — **in·tent·ly** *adv* — **in·tent·ness** *n*

in·ten·tion \in-'ten-chən\ *n* **1** : a determination to act in a certain way ⟨done without *intention*⟩ **2** : an intended object : PURPOSE, END ⟨unable to carry out all his *intentions*⟩ **3** : IMPORT, SIGNIFICANCE ⟨understanding the *intention* of a line of poetry⟩

syn PURPOSE, DESIGN, AIM: INTENTION applies to what one has in mind to do or bring about; PURPOSE suggests a more settled determination; DESIGN implies a carefully calculated plan; AIM adds implications of definite purpose and effort to attain or accomplish an end

in·ten·tion·al \in-'tench-nəl, -'ten-chən-°l\ *adj* : done by intention or design : not accidental : INTENDED ⟨*intentional* damage⟩ ⟨the batter was given an *intentional* pass to bring up a weaker hitter⟩ **syn** see VOLUNTARY — **in·ten·tion·al·i·ty** \-,ten-chə-'nal-ət-ē\ *n* — **in·ten·tion·al·ly** \in-'tench-nə-lē, -'ten-chən-°l-ē\ *adv*

in·ter \in-'tər\ *vt* **in·terred; in·ter·ring** [L *in-* ²*in-* + *terra* earth] : to deposit (a dead body) in the earth or in a tomb : BURY

inter- *prefix* [L; akin to E *under, in*] **1** : between : among : in the midst ⟨*inter*crop⟩ ⟨*inter*penetrate⟩ ⟨*inter*stellar⟩ **2** : reciprocal ⟨*inter*relation⟩ : reciprocally ⟨*inter*marry⟩ **3** : located between ⟨*inter*face⟩ **4** : carried on between ⟨*inter*national⟩ **5** : occurring between : intervening ⟨*inter*glacial⟩ **6** : shared by or derived from two or more ⟨*inter*faith⟩ **7** : between the limits of : within ⟨*inter*tropical⟩

in·ter·act \,int-ər-'akt\ *vi* : to act upon one another — **in·ter·ac·tion** \int-ər-'ak-shən\ *n* — **in·ter·ac·tion·al** \-shnəl, -shən-°l\ *n*

in·ter alia \,int-ər-'ā-lē-ə, -'äl-ē-ə\ *adv* [L] : among other things

in·ter·atom·ic \,int-ər-ə-'täm-ik\ *adj* : situated or acting between atoms

in·ter·breed \,int-ər-'brēd\ *vb* **-bred** \-'bred\; **-breed·ing** : to breed or cause to breed together: as **a** : CROSSBREED **b** : to breed within a closed population

in·ter·ca·lary \in-'tər-kə-,ler-ē\ *adj* **1** : INTERCALATED ⟨February 29 is an *intercalary* day⟩ **2** : INTERPOLATED

in·ter·ca·late \in-'tər-kə-,lāt\ *vt* [L *intercalare*, fr. *inter-* + *calare* to call, summon] **1** : to insert (as a day) in a calendar **2** : to insert between or among existing elements or layers — **in·ter·ca·la·tion** \-,tər-kə-'lā-shən\ *n*

in·ter·cede \,int-ər-'sēd\ *vi* [L *intercedere*, fr. *inter-* + *cedere* to go] **1** : to act as a go-between between parties who are unfriendly **2** : to beg or plead in behalf of another ⟨*intercede* for a friend who is to be punished⟩ **syn** see INTERPOSE

in·ter·cel·lu·lar \,int-ər-'sel-yə-lər\ *adj* : lying between cells ⟨*intercellular* spaces⟩

¹in·ter·cept \,int-ər-'sept\ *vt* [L *intercept-, intercipere*, fr. *inter-* + *capere* to take] **1** : to take or seize on the way to or before arrival at a destination : stop the progress of ⟨*intercept* a letter⟩ ⟨*intercept* an enemy bomber⟩ **2** : to cut through : INTERSECT ⟨a line *intercepted* between points A and B⟩

²in·ter·cept \'int-ər-,sept\ *n* : the distance from the origin to a point where a graph crosses a coordinate axis

in·ter·cept·er \,int-ər-'sep-tər\ *n* : INTERCEPTOR

in·ter·cep·tion \,int-ər-'sep-shən\ *n* : the act of intercepting : the state of being intercepted ⟨the *interception* of a message⟩; *also* : an act of intercepting ⟨made four *interceptions* in his last football game⟩

in·ter·cep·tor \,int-ər-'sep-tər\ *n* : one that intercepts; *esp* : a light high-speed fast-climbing fighter plane designed for defense against raiding bombers

in·ter·ces·sion \,int-ər-'sesh-ən\ *n* [L *intercess-, intercedere* to intercede] : the act of interceding : MEDIATION — **in·ter·ces·sion·al** \-'sesh-nəl, -ən-°l\ *adj* — **in·ter·ces·sor** \-'ses-ər\ *n* — **in·ter·ces·so·ry** \-'ses-(ə-)rē\ *adj*

¹in·ter·change \,int-ər-'chānj\ *vb* **1** : to put each in the place of the other ⟨*interchange* the front tires⟩ **2** : EXCHANGE ⟨*interchange* ideas⟩ **3** : to change places mutually ⟨square dancers *interchanging* in complex movements⟩ — **in·ter·chang·er** *n*

²in·ter·change \'int-ər-,chānj\ *n* **1** : the act, the process, or an instance of interchanging : EXCHANGE **2** : a joining of two or more highways by a system of separate levels that permit traffic to pass from one to another without the crossing of traffic streams

in·ter·change·a·ble \,int-ər-'chān-jə-bəl\ *adj* : capable of being interchanged; *esp* : permitting mutual substitution ⟨*interchangeable* parts⟩ — **in·ter·change·a·bil·i·ty** \-,chān-jə-'bil-ət-ē\ *n* — **in·ter·change·a·ble·ness** \-'chān-je-bəl-nəs\ *n* — **in·ter·change·a·bly** \-blē\ *adv*

in·ter·col·le·giate \,int-ər-kə-'lē-j(ē-)ət\ *adj* : existing or carried on between colleges ⟨*intercollegiate* athletics⟩

in·ter·com \'int-ər-,käm\ *n* : INTERCOMMUNICATION SYSTEM

in·ter·com·mu·ni·cate \,int-ər-kə-'myü-nə-,kāt\ *vi* **1** : to exchange communication with one another **2** : to afford passage from one to another ⟨the rooms *intercommunicate*⟩ — **in·ter·com·mu·ni·ca·tion** \-,myü-nə-'kā-shən\ *n*

intercommunication system *n* : a two-way communication system with microphone and loudspeaker at each station for localized use

in·ter·com·mu·nion \,int-ər-kə-'myü-nyən\ *n* : interdenominational participation in communion

in·ter·con·nect \,int-ər-kə-'nekt\ *vb* : to connect with one another ⟨the rooms *interconnect*⟩ ⟨*interconnected* switches⟩ — **in·ter·con·nec·tion** \-'nek-shən\ *n*

in·ter·con·ti·nen·tal \,int-ər-,känt-°n-'ent-°l\ *adj* **1** : extending among or carried on between continents ⟨*intercontinental* trade⟩ **2** : capable of traveling between continents ⟨*intercontinental* missile⟩

in·ter·con·ver·sion \,int-ər-kən-'vər-zhən\ *n* : mutual conversion ⟨*interconversion* of chemical compounds⟩ — **in·ter·con·vert** \-'vərt\ *vt* — **in·ter·con·vert·i·ble** \-'vərt-ə-bəl\ *adj*

in·ter·cool·er \,int-ər-'kü-lər\ *n* : a device for cooling a fluid between successive heat-generating processes

in·ter·cos·tal \,int-ər-'käst-°l\ *adj* [L *costa* rib] : situated between the ribs; *also* : of or relating to an intercostal part — **intercostal** *n* — **in·ter·cos·tal·ly** \-'käs-tə-lē\ *adv*

in·ter·course \'int-ər-,kōrs, -,kȯrs\ *n* [ML *intercursus*, fr. L, act of running between, fr. *intercurrere* to run between, fr. *inter-* + *currere* to run] **1** : connection between persons or groups : COMMUNICATION **2** : COPULATION, COITUS

in·ter·crop \,int-ər-'kräp\ *vb* : to grow two or more crops at one time on the same piece of land ⟨*intercrop* corn and pumpkins⟩

in·ter·cross \'int-ər-,krȯs\ *n* : an instance or a product of crossbreeding — **in·ter·cross** \,int-ər-'krȯs\ *vb*

in·ter·cul·tur·al \,int-ər-'kəlch-(ə-)rəl\ *adj* : occurring between or relating to two or more cultures

in·ter·de·nom·i·na·tion·al \,int-ər-di-,näm-ə-'nā-shnəl, -shən-°l\ *adj* : involving or occurring between different denominations — **in·ter·de·nom·i·na·tion·al·ism** \-,iz-əm\ *n*

---

j joke; ŋ sing; ō flow; ȯ flaw; ȯi coin; th thin; t͟h this; ü loot; u̇ foot; y yet; yü few; yu̇ furious; zh vision

in·ter·de·part·men·tal \,int-ər-di-,pärt-'ment-ᵊl, -,dē-\ *adj* : carried on between or involving different departments (as of a college) 〈*interdepartmental* committee〉 — **in·ter·de·part·men·tal·ly** \-ᵊl-ē\ *adv*

in·ter·de·pend \,int-ər-di-'pend\ *vi* : to depend upon one another — **in·ter·de·pend·ence** \-'pen-dən(t)s\ *n* — **in·ter·de·pend·en·cy** \-dən-sē\ *n* — **in·ter·de·pend·ent** \-dənt\ *adj* — **in·ter·de·pend·ent·ly** *adv*

¹**in·ter·dict** \'int-ər-,dikt\ *n* [L *interdictum* official prohibition, fr. *interdicere* to interpose, forbid, fr. *inter-* + *dicere* to say] **1** : a Roman Catholic ecclesiastical censure withdrawing most sacraments and Christian burial from a person or district **2** : PROHIBITION

²**in·ter·dict** \,int-ər-'dikt\ *vt* : to prohibit or forbid esp. by an interdict — **in·ter·dic·tion** \,int-ər-'dik-shən\ *n* — **in·ter·dic·tor** \-'dik-tər\ *n* — **in·ter·dic·to·ry** \-'dik-t(ə-)rē\ *adj*

in·ter·dig·i·tate \-'dij-ə-,tāt\ *vi* [L *digitus* finger] : to interlock like the fingers of folded hands — **in·ter·dig·i·ta·tion** \-,dij-ə-'tā-shən\ *n*

in·ter·dis·ci·pli·nary \,int-ər-'dis-ə-plə-,ner-ē\ *adj* : involving two or more academic disciplines

¹**in·ter·est** \'in-trəst, 'int-ə-rəst\ *n* [ME, alter. of *interesse*, fr. L, to make a difference, concern, fr. *inter-* + *esse* to be] **1** : a right, title, or legal share in something **2** : WELFARE, BENEFIT; *esp* : SELF-INTEREST **3 a** : a charge for borrowed money that is generally a percentage of the amount borrowed **b** : the return received by capital on its investments **4** *pl* : a group financially interested in an industry or enterprise 〈mining *interests*〉 **5 a** : readiness to be concerned with or moved by an object or class of objects **b** : the quality in a thing that arouses interest 〈her plans are of great *interest* to me〉

²**interest** *vt* **1** : to involve the interest of : AFFECT, CONCERN 〈had *interested* herself in his behalf〉 **2** : to persuade to participate or take part **3** : to arouse the interest of 〈a market that should *interest* any businessman〉

in·ter·est·ed *adj* : having the attention occupied : having or showing interest 〈an *interested* listener〉 — **in·ter·est·ed·ly** *adv*

interest group *n* : a group of persons having a common identifying interest that often provides a basis for action

in·ter·est·ing *adj* : holding the attention : arousing interest — **in·ter·est·ing·ly** \-iŋ-lē\ *adv*

in·ter·face \'int-ər-,fās\ *n* : a surface forming a common boundary of two bodies, spaces, or phases 〈an *interface* between oil and water〉 — **in·ter·fa·cial** \,int-ər-'fā-shəl\ *adj*

in·ter·faith \'int-ər-,fāth\ *adj* : involving persons of different religious faiths 〈*interfaith* conference〉

in·ter·fere \,int-ə(r)-'fi(ə)r\ *vi* [MF *s'entreferir* to strike one another, fr. *entre-* inter- + *ferir* to strike, fr. L *ferire*] **1** : to strike one foot against the opposite foot or ankle in walking or running **2** : to come in collision or be in opposition : CLASH 〈the relatives' arrival *interfered* with his plans〉 **3** : to take a part in the concerns of others 〈she *interferes* continually〉 **4** : to act so as to augment, diminish, or otherwise affect one another 〈*interfering* light waves〉 **5 a** : to run ahead of and provide blocking for the ballcarrier in football **b** : to hinder illegally an attempt of a football player to receive a pass **syn** see INTERPOSE — **in·ter·fer·er** *n*

in·ter·fer·ence \,int-ə(r)-'fir-ən(t)s\ *n* **1 a** : the act or process of interfering **b** : something that interferes : OBSTRUCTION **2** : the mutual effect on meeting of two waves (as of light or sound) whereby the resulting neutralization at some points and reinforcement at others produces in the case of light waves alternate light and dark bands or colored bands **3** : the act of hampering or blocking an opponent in football **4** : confusion of received radio signals due to undesired signals or electrical effects; *also* : an electrical effect that produces such confusion — **in·ter·fer·en·tial** \-fə-'ren-chəl, -,fir-'en-\ *adj*

in·ter·fer·tile \,int-ər-'fərt-ᵊl\ *adj* : capable of interbreeding — **in·ter·fer·til·i·ty** \-(,)fər-'til-ət-ē\ *n*

in·ter·fruit·ful \-'früt-fəl\ *adj* : capable of reciprocal pollination

in·ter·fuse \,int-ər-'fyüz\ *vb* [L *interfus-, interfundere* to pour between, fr. *inter-* + *fundere* to pour] **1** : to combine by or as if by fusing : INTERMINGLE **2** : PERVADE, PERMEATE — **in·ter·fu·sion** \-'fyü-zhən\ *n*

in·ter·ga·lac·tic \,int-ər-gə-'lak-tik\ *adj* : situated or occurring in the spaces between galaxies

in·ter·ge·ner·ic \-jə-'ner-ik\ *adj* : existing or occurring between genera 〈*intergeneric* hybridization〉

in·ter·gla·cial \,int-ər-'glā-shəl\ *adj* : occurring or relating to the time between successive glaciations

in·ter·grade \,int-ər-'grād\ *vi* : to merge gradually one with another through a continuous series of intermediate forms, kinds, or types — **in·ter·gra·da·tion** \,grā-'dā-shən, -grə-\ *n* — **in·ter·gra·da·tion·al** \-shnəl, -shən-ᵊl\ *adj*

in·ter·im \'in-tə-rəm, -,rim\ *n* [L, adv., meanwhile, fr. *inter* between] : a time intervening : INTERVAL — **interim** *adj*

¹**in·te·ri·or** \in-'tir-ē-ər\ *adj* [L, fr. *in* in] **1** : lying, occurring, or functioning within the limits : INNER **2** : remote from the border or shore : INLAND — **in·te·ri·or·ly** *adv*

²**interior** *n* **1** : the internal or inner part of a thing 〈*interior* of a house〉 **2** : the inland part (as of a country or continent) **3** : internal nature : CHARACTER **4** : the internal affairs of a state or nation — **in·te·ri·or·i·ty** \(,)in-,tir-ē-'ór-ət-ē, -'är-\ *n*

interior angle *n* **1** : the inner of the two angles formed where two sides of a polygon come together **2** : any of the four angles formed in the area between a pair of parallel lines when a third line cuts them

interior decoration *n* : the art of planning the layout and furnishings of the interior of a building

in·ter·ject \,int-ər-'jekt\ *vt* [L *interject-, intericere*, fr. *inter-* + *jacere* to throw] : to throw in between or among other things : INSERT 〈*interject* a remark〉 — **in·ter·jec·tor** \-'jek-tər\ *n* — **in·ter·jec·to·ry** \-t(ə-)rē\ *adj*

in·ter·jec·tion \,int-ər-'jek-shən\ *n* **1** : an interjecting of something **2** : something interjected 〈the speaker was interrupted several times by *interjections* from the audience〉 **3** : a word or cry expressing sudden or strong feeling and usu. lacking grammatical connection — **in·ter·jec·tion·al** \-shnəl, -shən-ᵊl\ *adj* — **in·ter·jec·tion·al·ly** \-ē\ *adv*

in·ter·lace \,int-ər-'lās\ *vb* **1** : to unite by or as if by lacing together : INTERWEAVE 〈*interlaced* fibers〉 **2** : to vary by alternation or intermixture : INTERSPERSE **3** : to cross one another as if woven together : INTERTWINE 〈*interlacing* boughs〉 — **in·ter·lace·ment** \-mənt\ *n*

in·ter·lard \,int-ər-'lärd\ *vt* : to insert or introduce at intervals : INTERSPERSE 〈a speech *interlarded* with quotations〉

in·ter·lay·er \,int-ər-'lā-ər, -,le(-ə)r\ *n* : a layer placed between other layers

¹**in·ter·leaf** \,int-ər-'lēf\ *vt* : INTERLEAVE

²**in·ter·leaf** \'int-ər-,lēf\ *n* **1** : a usu. blank leaf inserted between two leaves of a book **2** : SLIP SHEET

in·ter·leave \,int-ər-'lēv\ *vt* : to equip with an interleaf

¹**in·ter·line** \,int-ər-'līn\ *vt* : to insert between lines already written or printed; *also* : to insert something between the lines of 〈*interline* a page〉 — **in·ter·lin·e·a·tion** \-,lin-ē-'ā-shən\ *n*

²**interline** *vt* : to provide (a garment) with an interlining

in·ter·lin·e·ar \,int-ər-'lin-ē-ər\ *adj* [L *linea* line] **1** : inserted between lines already written or printed **2** : written or printed in different languages or texts in alternate lines — **in·ter·lin·e·ar·ly** *adv*

in·ter·lin·ing \'int-ər-,lī-niŋ\ *n* : a lining between the ordinary lining and the outside fabric

in·ter·link \,int-ər-'liŋk\ *vt* : to link together

in·ter·lock \,int-ər-'läk\ *vb* **1** : to lock together : interlace firmly : UNITE 〈*interlocked* fingers〉 〈a series of rings *interlocking* to form a chain〉 — **in·ter·lock** \'int-ər-,läk\ *n* — **in·ter·lock·er** \,int-ər-'läk-ər\ *n*

interlocking directorate *n* : a board of corporate directors linked by common membership to the board of another corporation in such a way that the two businesses are under one control

in·ter·lo·cu·tion \,int-ər-lō-'kyü-shən\ *n* : interchange of speech : CONVERSATION

in·ter·loc·u·tor \,int-ər-'läk-yət-ər\ *n* [L *interlocut-, interloqui* to speak between, interrupt, fr. *inter-* + *loqui* to speak] **1** : one who takes part in dialogue or conversation **2** : a man in a minstrel show who questions the end men

in·ter·lop·er \,int-ər-'lō-pər, 'int-ər-,\ *n* : a person who intrudes or interferes wrongly or officiously : INTRUDER

in·ter·lude \'int-ər-,lüd\ *n* [ML *interludium*, fr. L *inter-* +

ludus play] **1** : a performance or entertainment between the acts of a play **2** : an intervening or interruptive period, space, or event : INTERVAL ⟨an *interlude* of peace between wars⟩ **3** : a musical composition inserted between the parts of a longer composition, a drama, or a religious service

in·ter·mar·riage \ˌint-ər-'mar-ij\ *n* : marriage between members of different racial, social, or religious groups

in·ter·mar·ry \-'mar-ē\ *vi* **1** : to marry each other **2** : to become connected by intermarriage

in·ter·med·dle \ˌint-ər-'med-ºl\ *vi* : MEDDLE, INTERFERE — **in·ter·med·dler** \-'med-lər, -ºl-ər\ *n*

¹in·ter·me·di·ary \ˌint-ər-'mēd-ē-ˌer-ē\ *adj* **1** : INTER-MEDIATE ⟨an *intermediary* stage⟩ **2** : acting as a mediator ⟨*intermediary* agent⟩

²intermediary *n, pl* **-ar·ies** : MEDIATOR, GO-BETWEEN

¹in·ter·me·di·ate \ˌint-ər-'mēd-ē-ət\ *adj* [L *intermedius,* fr. *inter-* + *medius* middle] : being or occurring at the middle place or degree or between extremes — **in·ter·me·di·ate·ly** *adv* — **in·ter·me·di·ate·ness** *n*

²intermediate *n* **1** : an intermediate term, thing, or class **2** : MEDIATOR, GO-BETWEEN

in·ter·me·din \ˌint-ər-'mēd-ºn\ *n* : a pituitary hormone that induces expansion of vertebrate chromatophores

in·ter·ment \in-'tər-mənt\ *n* : the act or ceremony of interring : BURIAL

in·ter·mez·zo \ˌint-ər-'met-sō, -'med-zō\ *n, pl* **-zi** \-(ˌ)sē, -(ˌ)zē\ *or* **-zos** [It, fr. L *intermedius* intermediate] **1** : a short light piece between the acts of a serious drama or opera **2 a** : a short movement connecting major sections of an extended musical work (as a symphony) **b** : a short independent instrumental composition

in·ter·mi·na·ble \(')in-'tərm-(ə-)nə-bəl\ *adj* : ENDLESS; *esp* : wearisomely dragged out ⟨an *interminable* speech⟩ — **in·ter·mi·na·ble·ness** *n* — **in·ter·mi·na·bly** \-blē\ *adv*

in·ter·min·gle \ˌint-ər-'min-gəl\ *vb* : INTERMIX

in·ter·mis·sion \ˌint-ər-'mish-ən\ *n* **1** : INTERRUPTION ⟨continuing without *intermission*⟩ **2** : a pause or interval esp. between the acts of a play

in·ter·mit \-'mit\ *vb* **-mit·ted; -mit·ting** [L *intermiss-, intermittere,* fr. *inter-* + *mittere* to send] : to stop for a time : discontinue at intervals and then continue again — **in·ter·mit·ter** *n*

in·ter·mit·tence \-'mit-ºn(t)s\ *n* : the quality or state of being intermittent

in·ter·mit·tent \-'mit-ºnt\ *adj* : coming and going at intervals : starting, stopping, and starting again ⟨an *intermittent* electric current⟩ ⟨an *intermittent* fever⟩ — **in·ter·mit·tent·ly** *adv*

in·ter·mix \ˌint-ər-'miks\ *vb* : to mix together — **in·ter·mix·ture** \-'miks-chər\ *n*

in·ter·mo·lec·u·lar \ˌint-ər-mə-'lek-yə-lər\ *adj* : existing or acting between molecules — **in·ter·mo·lec·u·lar·ly** *adv*

¹in·tern \'in-ˌtərn, in-'\ *vt* [F *interner,* fr. L *internus* internal] : to confine or impound esp. during a war ⟨*interned* enemy aliens⟩

²in·tern *or* **in·terne** \'in-ˌtərn\ *n* : an advanced student or graduate esp. in medicine gaining supervised practical experience (as in a hospital) — **in·tern·ship** \-ˌship\ *n*

³in·tern \'in-ˌtərn\ *vi* : to act as an intern

in·ter·nal \in-'tərn-ºl\ *adj* [L *internus*] **1 a** : existing or situated within the limits or surface of something ⟨*internal* structure⟩ **b** : having to do with or situated in the inside of the body ⟨*internal* organs⟩⟨*internal* pain⟩ **2** : relating or belonging to or existing within the mind **3** : INTRINSIC, INHERENT ⟨*internal* evidence⟩ ⟨*internal* consistency⟩ **4** : of or relating to the domestic affairs of a state ⟨*internal* revenue⟩ — **in·ter·nal·i·ty** \ˌin-ˌtər-'nal-ət-ē\ *n* — **in·ter·nal·ly** \in-'tərn-ºl-ē\ *adv*

internal–combustion engine *n* : an engine run by a fuel mixture ignited within the engine cylinder

internal respiration *n* : exchange of gases between the cells of the body and the blood — compare EXTERNAL RESPIRA-TION

internal rhyme *n* : rhyme between a word within a line and another at the end of the same line or within another line

internal secretion *n* : HORMONE

¹in·ter·na·tion·al \ˌint-ər-'nash-nəl, -ən-ºl\ *adj* **1** : of, relating to, or affecting two or more nations ⟨*international* trade⟩ **2** : of, relating to, or constituting a group having

members in two or more nations ⟨*international* union⟩ — **in·ter·na·tion·al·i·ty** \-ˌnash-ə-'nal-ət-ē\ *n* — **in·ter·na·tion·al·ly** \-'nash-nə-lē, -ən-ºl-ē\ *adv*

²in·ter·na·tion·al \-'nash-nəl, -ən-ºl, *in sense 1 often* -ˌnash-ə-'nal, -'näl\ *n* **1** : one of several socialist or communist organizations of international scope **2** : a labor union having locals in more than one country

international date line *n* : DATE LINE

in·ter·na·tion·al·ism \ˌint-ər-'nash-nəl-ˌiz-əm, -'nash-ən-ºl-\ *n* **1** : international character or outlook **2 a** : a policy of political and economic cooperation among nations **b** : an attitude favoring such a policy — **in·ter·na·tion·al·ist** \-əst\ *n or adj*

in·ter·na·tion·al·ize \-'nash-nəl-ˌīz, -'nash-ən-ºl-\ *vt* : to make international; *esp* : to place under international control — **in·ter·na·tion·al·i·za·tion** \-ˌnash-nəl-ə-'zā-shən, -ˌnash-ən-ºl-\ *n*

international law *n* : a body of rules that control or affect the rights of nations in their relations with each other

international unit *n* : a quantity (as of a vitamin) that barely produces a particular biological effect agreed upon as an international standard of activity

in·ter·nec·ine \ˌint-ər-'nes-ˌēn, -'nē-ˌsīn; in-'tər-nə-ˌsēn\ *adj* [L *internecinus,* fr. *internecare* to slay, fr. *inter-* + *necare* to kill, fr. *nec-, nex* violent death] **1** : marked by slaughter : DEADLY **2** : of, relating to, or involving conflict within a group ⟨bitter *internecine* feuds⟩

in·tern·ee \ˌin-ˌtər-'nē\ *n* : an interned person

in·ter·neu·ron \ˌint-ər-'n(y)ü-ˌrän, -'n(y)ù(ə)r-ˌän\ *n* : a nerve cell that carries an impulse from one nerve cell to another

in·ter·nist \in-'tər-nəst\ *n* : a specialist in medicine as distinguished from surgery

in·tern·ment \in-'tərn-mənt\ *n* : the act of interning : the state of being interned

in·ter·node \'int-ər-ˌnōd\ *n* : an interval or part between two nodes (as of a stem) : SEGMENT

in·ter·nu·cle·ar \ˌint-ər-'n(y)ü-klē-ər\ *adj* : situated or occurring between nuclei

in·ter·nun·ci·al \ˌint-ər-'nən(t)-sē-əl, -'nùn(t)-\ *adj* **1** : of or relating to an internuncio **2** : serving to link sensory and motor neurons — **in·ter·nun·ci·al·ly** \-sē-ə-lē\ *adv*

in·ter·nun·cio \-sē-ˌō\ *n* [It *internunzio,* lit., messenger between two parties, fr. L *internuntius,* fr. *inter-* + *nuntius* messenger] : a papal legate of lower rank than a nuncio

in·tero·cep·tive \ˌint-ə-rō-'sep-tiv\ *adj* : of, relating to, or being stimuli arising within the body and esp. the viscera — **in·tero·cep·tor** \-'sep-tər\ *n*

in·ter·of·fice \ˌint-ər-'òf-əs, -'äf-\ *adj* : functioning or communicating between the offices of an organization ⟨an *interoffice* memo⟩

in·ter·pen·e·trate \ˌint-ər-'pen-ə-ˌtrāt\ *vb* **1** : to penetrate between, within, or throughout : PERMEATE **2** : to penetrate mutually — **in·ter·pen·e·tra·tion** \-ˌpen-ə-'trā-shən\ *n*

in·ter·phase \'int-ər-ˌfāz\ *n* : the period between the end of one mitotic division and the beginning of the next

In·ter·phone \'int-ər-ˌfōn\ *trademark* — used for a telephone system for intercommunication between points within a short distance of each other

in·ter·plan·e·tary \ˌint-ər-'plan-ə-ˌter-ē\ *adj* : existing, carried on, or operating between planets ⟨designing rockets for *interplanetary* travel⟩

in·ter·plant \ˌint-ər-'plant\ *vt* : to plant (a crop) between plants of another kind

in·ter·play \'int-ər-ˌplā\ *n* : mutual action or influence : INTERACTION ⟨an *interplay* of thought and feeling⟩ — **in·ter·play** \ˌint-ər-'plā\ *vi*

in·ter·po·late \in-'tər-pə-ˌlāt\ *vb* [L *interpolare*] **1 a** : to alter or corrupt (as a text) by inserting new or foreign matter **b** : to insert (words) into a text or into a conversation **2** : to insert between other things or parts **3** : to estimate values of (a function) between two known values **4** : to make insertions *syn* see INTRODUCE — **in·ter·po·la·tion** \-ˌtər-pə-'lā-shən\ *n* — **in·ter·po·la·tive** \-'tər-pə-ˌlāt-iv\ *adj* — **in·ter·po·la·tor** \-ˌlāt-ər\ *n*

in·ter·pose \ˌint-ər-'pōz\ *vb* [MF *interposer,* irreg. fr. L *interponere,* fr. *inter-* + *ponere* to put] **1 a** : to place in an intervening position **b** : to put (oneself) between : IN-TRUDE, INTERRUPT **2** : to introduce or throw in between the parts of a conversation or argument **3** : to be or

come between; *esp* : to step in between opposing parties — **in·ter·pos·er** *n* — **in·ter·po·si·tion** \-pə-'zish-ən\ *n*
syn INTERPOSE, INTERFERE, INTERVENE, INTERCEDE mean to come or go between. INTERPOSE implies no more than this ⟨*interposed* in the argument⟩ INTERFERE implies a getting in the way or otherwise hindering ⟨strikes *interfere* with production plans⟩ INTERVENE may imply an occurring in space or time between two things or a stepping in to halt or settle a dispute ⟨years *intervening* between graduation and marriage⟩ INTERCEDE implies acting in behalf of an offender or between two parties needing reconciliation ⟨the UN *intercedes* in international disputes⟩

in·ter·pret \in-'tər-prət\ *vb* [L *interpretari*, fr. *interpret-*, *interpres* agent, interpreter] **1** : to explain or tell the meaning of : TRANSLATE ⟨*interpret* a dream⟩ **2** : to understand according to one's own belief, judgment, or interest ⟨*interpret* an action as unfriendly⟩ **3** : to bring out the meaning or significance of by performing ⟨*interpret* a symphonic score⟩ ⟨an actor *interprets* a role⟩ **4** : to act as an oral translator for speakers of different languages **syn** see EXPLAIN — **in·ter·pret·a·ble** \-prət-ə-bəl\ *adj* — **in·ter·pret·er** *n* — **in·ter·pre·tive** \-prət-iv\ *adj* — **in·ter·pre·tive·ly** *adv*
in·ter·pre·ta·tion \in-ˌtər-prə-'tā-shən\ *n* **1** : the act or the result of interpreting : EXPLANATION **2** : an instance of artistic interpretation in performance or adaptation — **in·ter·pre·ta·tion·al** \-'shnəl, -shən-ᵊl\ *adj* — **in·ter·pre·ta·tive** \-'tər-prə-ˌtāt-iv\ *adj* — **in·ter·pre·ta·tive·ly** *adv*
in·ter·ra·cial \ˌint-ə(r)-'rā-shəl\ *adj* : of, involving, or designed for members of different races
in·ter·reg·num \ˌint-ə-'reg-nəm\ *n, pl* **-nums** *or* **-na** \-nə\ [L, fr. *inter-* + *regnum* reign] **1** : a period between two successive reigns or regimes **2** : a lapse or pause in a continuous series
in·ter·re·late \ˌint-ə(r)-ri-'lāt\ *vb* : to bring into or have a mutual relationship — **in·ter·re·la·tion** \-'lā-shən\ *n* — **in·ter·re·la·tion·ship** \-ˌship\ *n*
in·ter·ro·gate \in-'ter-ə-ˌgāt\ *vt* [L *interrogare*, fr. *inter-* + *rogare* to ask] : to question formally and systematically ⟨*interrogate* a prisoner of war⟩ — **in·ter·ro·ga·tion** \-ˌter-ə-'gā-shən\ *n* — **in·ter·ro·ga·tion·al** \-'shnəl, -shən-ᵊl\ *adj* — **in·ter·ro·ga·tor** \-'ter-ə-ˌgāt-ər\ *n*
interrogation point *n* : QUESTION MARK
¹in·ter·rog·a·tive \ˌint-ə-'räg-ət-iv\ *adj* **1** : having the form or force of a question ⟨an *interrogative* phrase⟩ **2** : used in a question ⟨an *interrogative* pronoun⟩ — **in·ter·rog·a·tive·ly** *adv*
²interrogative *n* : a word used in asking questions ⟨*who, what,* and *which* are *interrogatives*⟩
in·ter·rog·a·to·ry \-'räg-ə-ˌtōr-ē, -ˌtȯr-\ *adj* : containing, expressing, or implying a question ⟨an *interrogatory* tone of voice⟩
in·ter·rupt \ˌint-ə-'rəpt\ *vb* [L *interrupt-*, *interrumpere*, fr. *inter-* + *rumpere* to break] **1** : to stop or hinder by breaking in ⟨*interrupt* a conversation⟩ **2** : to break the uniformity or continuity of ⟨*interrupt* a sequence⟩ **3** : to break in upon an action; *esp* : to break in with questions or remarks while another is speaking ⟨a bad habit of *interrupting*⟩ — **in·ter·rup·tion** \-'rəp-shən\ *n* — **in·ter·rup·tive** \-'rəp-tiv\ *adj*
in·ter·rupt·er *n* : one that interrupts; *esp* : a device for periodically and automatically interrupting an electric current
in·ter·scho·las·tic \ˌint-ər-skə-'las-tik\ *adj* : existing or carried on between schools ⟨*interscholastic* athletics⟩
in·ter·school \ˌint-ər-'skül\ *adj* : INTERSCHOLASTIC
in·ter se \ˌint-ər-'sā, -'sē\ *adv (or adj)* [L] : among or between themselves
in·ter·sect \ˌint-ər-'sekt\ *vb* [L *intersect-*, *intersecare*, fr. *inter-* + *secare* to cut] **1** : to pierce or divide by passing through or across : CROSS ⟨one line *intersecting* another⟩ **2** : to meet and cross at a point ⟨streets *intersecting* at right angles⟩
in·ter·sec·tion \ˌint-ər-'sek-shən\ *n* **1** : the act or process of intersecting **2** : the place or point where two or more things and esp. streets intersect ⟨a busy *intersection*⟩ **3** : the set of elements common to two sets; *esp* : the set of points common to two geometric configurations
in·ter·sex \'int-ər-ˌseks\ *n* : an intersexual individual
in·ter·sex·u·al \ˌint-ər-'sek-sh(ə-w)əl\ *adj* **1** : existing between sexes ⟨*intersexual* hostility⟩ **2** : intermediate in

sexual characters between a typical male and a typical female — **in·ter·sex·u·al·i·ty** \-ˌsek-shə-'wal-ət-ē\ *n* — **in·ter·sex·u·al·ly** \-'sek-sh(ə-w)ə-lē, -'seksh-lē\ *adv*
¹in·ter·space \'int-ər-ˌspās\ *n* : an intervening space : INTERVAL
²in·ter·space \ˌint-ər-'spās\ *vt* : to separate by spaces
in·ter·spe·cif·ic \ˌint-ər-spi-'sif-ik\ *or* **in·ter·spe·cies** \-'spē-(ˌ)shēz, -(ˌ)sēz\ *adj* : existing or arising between species ⟨*interspecific* hybrid⟩
in·ter·sperse \ˌint-ər-'spərs\ *vt* [L *interspersus* interspersed, fr. *inter-* + *sparsus*, pp. of *spargere* to scatter] **1** : to scatter or set here and there among others ⟨*intersperse* pictures in a book⟩ **2** : to vary with things inserted here and there ⟨a serious talk *interspersed* with a few jokes⟩ — **in·ter·sper·sion** \-'spər-zhən\ *n*
in·ter·state \ˌint-ər-'stāt\ *adj* : of, connecting, or existing between two or more states esp. of the U.S.
in·ter·stel·lar \-'stel-ər\ *adj* : located or taking place among the stars ⟨*interstellar* space⟩
in·ter·ster·ile \-'ster-əl\ *adj* : unable to pollinate one another — **in·ter·ste·ril·i·ty** \-stə-'ril-ət-ē\ *n*
in·ter·stice \in-'tər-stəs\ *n, pl* **in·ter·stic·es** \-stə-ˌsēz, -stə-səz\ [LL *interstitium*, fr. L *interstit-*, *intersistere* to stand in the middle, fr. *inter-* + *sistere* to stand] : a little space between one thing and another : CHINK, CREVICE
in·ter·sti·tial \ˌint-ər-'stish-əl\ *adj* **1** : relating to or situated in the interstices **2** : situated within organs or tissues ⟨*interstitial* connective tissue⟩; *also* : affecting the interstitial tissues of a body part — **in·ter·sti·tial·ly** \-'stish-ə-lē\ *adv*
in·ter·tid·al \-'tīd-ᵊl\ *adj* : of, relating to, or being the area that is above low-tide mark but exposed to tidal flooding
in·ter·twine \-'twīn\ *vb* : to twine or cause to twine about one another : INTERLACE — **in·ter·twine·ment** \-mənt\ *n*
¹in·ter·twist \-'twist\ *vb* : INTERTWINE
²in·ter·twist \'int-ər-ˌtwist\ *n* : an act or instance of intertwisting : the state of being intertwisted
in·ter·ur·ban \ˌint-ər-'ər-bən\ *adj* : connecting cities or towns ⟨an *interurban* bus line⟩
in·ter·val \'int-ər-vəl\ *n* [L *intervallum*, lit., space between ramparts, fr. *inter-* + *vallum* rampart] **1** : a space of time between events or states : PAUSE ⟨the *interval* between elections⟩ ⟨an *interval* of three months⟩ **2 a** : a space between things ⟨the *interval* between two desks⟩ **b** : difference in pitch between tones **3** : a set of numbers between two numbers; *also* : the set of numbers greater or less than some number
in·ter·vene \ˌint-ər-'vēn\ *vi* [L *intervenire*, fr. *inter-* + *venire* to come] **1** : to happen or come in between as an unrelated event ⟨rain *intervened* and we postponed the match⟩ **2** : to happen or come between points of time or between events ⟨a second *intervened* between the flash and the report⟩ **3** : to come in or between in order to stop, settle, or change something : step in ⟨*intervene* in a quarrel⟩ **4** : to lie between ⟨*intervening* mountains⟩ **syn** see INTERPOSE — **in·ter·ve·nor** \-'vē-nər, -ˌnȯr\ *also* **in·ter·ven·er** \-'vē-nər\ *n* — **in·ter·ven·tion** \-'ven-chən\ *n*
in·ter·ven·tion·ism \-'ven-chə-ˌniz-əm\ *n* : the theory or practice of intervening; *esp* : interference by one country in the political affairs of another — **in·ter·ven·tion·ist** \-'vench-(ə-)nəst\ *n or adj*
in·ter·ver·te·bral \-'vərt-ə-brəl\ *adj* : situated between adjacent vertebrae ⟨*intervertebral* disks⟩
in·ter·view \'int-ər-ˌvyü\ *n* **1** : a meeting face to face esp. for the purpose of talking or consulting with someone **2** : a meeting between a representative of a newspaper or magazine and another person in order to get news or an article to be published; *also* : the written account of such a meeting — **interview** *vt* — **in·ter·view·er** *n*
in·ter·vo·cal·ic \ˌint-ər-vō-'kal-ik\ *adj* : immediately preceded and immediately followed by a vowel
in·ter·weave \ˌint-ər-'wēv\ *vb* **1** : to weave together **2** : to blend or cause to blend together : INTERMINGLE — **in·ter·wo·ven** \-'wō-vən\ *adj*
¹in·tes·tate \in-'tes-ˌtāt, -'tes-tət\ *adj* **1** : not having made a will ⟨he died *intestate*⟩ **2** : not disposed of by will — **in·tes·ta·cy** \-'tes-tə-sē\ *n*
²intestate *n* : one who dies intestate
in·tes·ti·nal \in-'tes-tən-ᵊl\ *adj* **1** : of or relating to the

intestine **2** : affecting or occurring in the intestine — **in·tes·ti·nal·ly** \-ᵊl-ē\ *adv*

intestinal fortitude *n* [euphemism for *guts*] : COURAGE, STAMINA

¹in·tes·tine \in-'tes-tən\ *adj* [L *intestinus*, fr. *intus* within] : INTERNAL; *esp* : of or relating to the internal affairs of a state or country

²intestine *n* : the tubular part of the alimentary canal that extends from the stomach to the anus

in·ti·ma·cy \'int-ə-mə-sē\ *n, pl* **-cies** **1** : the state of being intimate : FAMILIARITY **2** : an instance of esp. objectionable intimacy

¹in·ti·mate \'int-ə-ˌmāt\ *vt* [LL *intimare* to put in, announce, fr. L *intimus* innermost] **1** : ANNOUNCE, DECLARE **2** : to communicate indirectly : HINT — **in·ti·mat·er** *n* — **in·ti·ma·tion** \ˌint-ə-'mā-shən\ *n*

²in·ti·mate \'int-ə-mət\ *adj* [alter. of obs. *intime*, fr. L *intimus* inmost] **1** : belonging to or characterizing one's deepest nature ⟨*intimate* reflections⟩ **2** : marked by very close association or contact ⟨the *intimate* relations between economics and politics⟩ **3 a** : marked by a warm friendship developing through long association ⟨on *intimate* terms with a neighbor⟩ **b** : suggesting informal warmth or privacy ⟨*intimate* clubs⟩ **4** : of a very personal or private nature ⟨*intimate* family affairs⟩ — **in·ti·mate·ly** *adv* — **in·ti·mate·ness** *n*

³in·ti·mate \'int-ə-mət\ *n* : an intimate friend : CONFIDANT

in·tim·i·date \in-'tim-ə-ˌdāt\ *vt* : to make timid or fearful; *esp* : to compel or deter by or as if by threats — **in·tim·i·da·tion** \-ˌtim-ə-'dā-shən\ *n* — **in·tim·i·da·tor** \-'tim-ə-ˌdāt-ər\ *n*

in·tinc·tion \in-'tiŋ(k)-shən\ *n* [L *intinct-*, *intingere* to dip in, fr. *in-* + *tingere* to dip, moisten] : the administration of the sacrament of Communion by dipping the bread in the wine and giving both together to the communicant

in·tine \'in-ˌtēn, -ˌtīn\ *n* [L *intus* within] : an inner layer (as of a spore)

in·to \'in-tə, -tü\ *prep* [OE *intō*, fr. ²*in* + *tō* to] **1 a** : to the inside of ⟨came *into* the room⟩ **b** — used as a function word to indicate entry, introduction, insertion, or inclusion ⟨enter *into* an alliance⟩ **2 a** : to the state, condition, or form of ⟨got *into* trouble⟩ **b** : to the occupation, action, or possession of ⟨go *into* farming⟩ **c** : involved with ⟨they were *into* hard drugs⟩ **3** : to a position of contact with : AGAINST ⟨ran *into* a wall⟩

in·tol·er·a·bil·i·ty \(ˌ)in-ˌtäl-(ə-)rə-'bil-ət-ē\ *n* : the quality or state of being intolerable

in·tol·er·a·ble \(')in-'täl-(ə-)rə-bəl, -'täl-ər-bəl\ *adj* **1** : not tolerable : UNBEARABLE **2** : EXCESSIVE — **in·tol·er·a·ble·ness** *n* — **in·tol·er·a·bly** \-blē\ *adv*

in·tol·er·ance \(')in-'täl-ə-rən(t)s\ *n* : the quality or state of being intolerant; *also* : exceptional sensitivity (as to a drug or food)

in·tol·er·ant \-rənt\ *adj* **1** : unable to endure **2 a** : unwilling to endure **b** : unwilling to grant equality or freedom esp. in religious matters or other social rights : BIGOTED — **in·tol·er·ant·ly** *adv*

in·to·nate \'in-tə-ˌnāt\ *vt* : INTONE, UTTER

in·to·na·tion \ˌin-tə-'nā-shən\ *n* **1** : the act of intoning and esp. of chanting; *also* : something intoned **2** : the act of producing tones on a musical instrument esp. with regard to proper pitch **3** : the rise and fall in pitch of the voice in speech — **in·to·na·tion·al** \-shnəl, -shən-ᵊl\ *adj*

in·tone \in-'tōn\ *vb* : to utter in musical or prolonged tones : CHANT — **in·ton·er** *n*

in to·to \in-'tōt-ō\ *adv* [L, on the whole] : TOTALLY, ENTIRELY ⟨accepted the plan *in toto*⟩

in·tox·i·cant \in-'täk-si-kənt\ *n* : something that intoxicates; *esp* : an alcoholic drink — **intoxicant** *adj*

in·tox·i·cate \in-'täk-sə-ˌkāt\ *vt* [ML *intoxicare*, fr. L ²*in-* + *toxicum* poison] **1 a** : POISON **b** : to affect by alcohol or a narcotic esp. to the point where physical and mental control is markedly diminished **2** : to excite or elate to the point of enthusiasm or frenzy ⟨*intoxicated* with joy⟩

in·tox·i·ca·tion \in-ˌtäk-sə-'kā-shən\ *n* **1 a** : an abnormal state that is essentially a poisoning ⟨intestinal *intoxication*⟩ **b** : the condition of being drunk : INEBRIATION **2** : a strong excitement or elation

in·tra- \ˌin-trə\ *also but not shown at individual entries*

\ˌin-ˌträ\ *prefix* [L *intra*, adv. & prep.] **1 a** : within ⟨*intra*mural⟩ ⟨*intra*-English⟩ **b** : during ⟨*intra*natal⟩ **2** : INTRO- ⟨an *intra*muscular injection⟩

in·tra·cel·lu·lar \ˌin-trə-'sel-yə-lər\ *adj* : being or occurring within a protoplasmic cell — **in·tra·cel·lu·lar·ly** *adv*

in·trac·ta·ble \(')in-'trak-tə-bəl\ *adj* **1** : not easily governed, managed, or directed ⟨an *intractable* child⟩ **2** : not easily relieved or cured ⟨*intractable* pain⟩ — **in·trac·ta·bil·i·ty** \(ˌ)in-ˌtrak-tə-'bil-ət-ē\ *n* — **in·trac·ta·ble·ness** \(')in-'trak-tə-bəl-nəs\ *n* — **in·trac·ta·bly** \-blē\ *adv*

in·tra·cu·ta·ne·ous \ˌin-trə-kyü-'tā-nē-əs\ *adj* : INTRADERMAL

in·tra·der·mal \-'dər-məl\ *adj* : situated or done within or between the layers of the skin

in·tra·dos \'in-trə-ˌdäs, -ˌdō; in-'trā-ˌdäs\ *n, pl* **-dos** \-ˌdōz, -ˌdäs\ *or* **-dos·es** \-ˌdäs-əz\ [F, fr. L *intra* within + F *dos* back, fr. L *dorsum*] : the interior curve of an arch

in·tra·mo·lec·u·lar \ˌin-trə-mə-'lek-yə-lər\ *adj* : situated, acting, or occurring within the molecule — **in·tra·mo·lec·u·lar·ly** *adv*

in·tra·mu·ral \-'myur-əl\ *adj* [L *murus* wall] : being, occurring, or undertaken within the limits usu. of a community or institution (as a school) ⟨*intramural* sports⟩ — **in·tra·mu·ral·ly** \-'myur-ə-lē\ *adv*

in·tran·si·geance \in-'tran(t)s-ə-jən(t)s, -'tranz-\ *n* : INTRANSIGENCE — **in·tran·si·geant** \-jənt\ *adj or n* — **in·tran·si·geant·ly** *adv*

in·tran·si·gence \-jən(t)s\ *n* : the quality or state of being intransigent

in·tran·si·gent \-jənt\ *adj* [Sp *intransigente*, fr. *in-* ¹*in-* + *transigir* to compromise, fr. L *transigere* to transact] **1 a** : refusing to compromise or to abandon an extreme position or attitude : UNCOMPROMISING **b** : IRRECONCILABLE **2** : characteristic of an intransigent person — **intransigent** *n* — **in·tran·si·gent·ly** *adv*

in·tran·si·tive \(')in-'tran(t)s-ət-iv, -'tranz-\ *adj* : not transitive; *esp* : characterized by not having or containing a direct object ⟨an *intransitive* verb⟩ — **in·tran·si·tive·ly** *adv* — **in·tran·si·tive·ness** *n*

in·tra·spe·cif·ic \ˌin-trə-spi-'sif-ik\ *also* **in·tra·spe·cies** \-'spē-(ˌ)shēz, -(ˌ)sēz\ *adj* : occurring within a species or involving members of one species ⟨*intraspecific* variation⟩

in·tra·state \ˌin-trə-'stāt\ *adj* : existing or occurring within a state

in·tra·uter·ine \-'yüt-ə-rən, -ˌrīn\ *adj* : being or occurring within the uterus ⟨*intrauterine* growth⟩

intrauterine device *n* : a device inserted and left in the uterus to prevent effective conception

in·tra·ve·nous \ˌin-trə-'vē-nəs\ *adj* : being within or entering by way of the veins ⟨*intravenous* feeding⟩ — **in·tra·ve·nous·ly** *adv*

in·tra·vi·tam \-'vī-ˌtam, -'wē-ˌtäm\ *adj* [NL *intra vitam* during life] : performed or acting upon or found in a living subject

in·tra·zon·al \ˌin-trə-'zōn-ᵊl\ *adj* : of, relating to, or being a soil or a major soil group having relatively well-developed characteristics — compare AZONAL, ZONAL

intrench *var of* ENTRENCH

in·trep·id \in-'trep-əd\ *adj* [L *intrepidus*, fr. *in-* ¹*in-* + *trepidus* alarmed] : characterized by resolute fearlessness, fortitude, and endurance — **in·tre·pid·i·ty** \ˌin-trə-'pid-ət-ē\ *n* — **in·trep·id·ly** \in-'trep-əd-lē\ *adv* — **in·trep·id·ness** *n*

in·tri·ca·cy \'in-tri-kə-sē\ *n, pl* **-cies** **1** : the quality or state of being intricate **2** : something intricate ⟨the *intricacies* of the law⟩

in·tri·cate \'in-tri-kət\ *adj* [L *intricatus*, pp. of *intricare* to entangle, fr. *in-* ²*in-* + *tricae* trifles, impediments] **1** : having many complexly interrelating parts or elements : COMPLICATED ⟨an *intricate* machine⟩ **2** : difficult to resolve or analyze ⟨an *intricate* problem⟩ **syn** see COMPLEX — **in·tri·cate·ly** *adv* — **in·tri·cate·ness** *n*

¹in·trigue \in-'trēg\ *vb* [F *intriguer*, fr. It *intrigare*, fr. L *intricare* to entangle] **1** : to make or accomplish by intrigue ⟨*intrigued* his way into power⟩ **2** : PLOT, SCHEME **3** : to arouse the interest or curiosity of — **in·trigu·er** *n*

²in·trigue \'in-ˌtrēg, in-'\ *n* **1** : a secret and involved

---

1 intrados

---

j **joke**; ŋ **sing**; ō **flow**; ȯ **flaw**; ȯi **coin**; th **thin**; t͟h **this**; ü **loot**; u̇ **foot**; y **yet**; yü **few**; yu̇ **furious**; zh **vision**

stratagem : MACHINATION **2** : a clandestine love affair **syn** see PLOT

in·trin·sic \in-'trin-zik, -'trin(t)-sik\ *adj* [LL *intrinsecus* internal, fr. L, *adv.,* inwardly] **1** : belonging to the essential nature or constitution of a thing : REAL ⟨the lost ring has great sentimental but little *intrinsic* value⟩ **2** : originating or situated within the body or part acted on — **in·trin·si·cal** \-zi-kəl, -si-\ *adj* — **in·trin·si·cal·ly** \-k(ə-)lē\ *adv* — **in·trin·si·cal·ness** \-kəl-nəs\ *n*

intro- *prefix* [L, fr. *intro* inside, to the inside] : inward : within ⟨*introvert*⟩

in·tro·duce \,in-trə-'d(y)üs\ *vt* [L *introducere,* fr. *intro-* + *ducere* to lead] **1** : to bring into practice or use ⟨*introduce* a new fashion⟩ **2** : to lead or bring in ⟨*introduce* birds from other countries into America⟩; *esp* : to present formally ⟨*introduce* a person into society⟩ ⟨*introduce* a legislative bill⟩ **3** : to cause to become acquainted : make known ⟨*introduced* two of his friends⟩ ⟨*introduce* the speaker to an audience⟩ **4** : to present or bring forward for discussion ⟨*introduce* a subject⟩ **5** : to put in : INSERT ⟨*introduce* a probe into a cavity⟩ — **in·tro·duc·er** *n*

syn INSERT, INTERPOLATE : INTRODUCE is the general term for bringing or putting a thing or person into a body or thing already in existence; INSERT implies putting into an open, fixed, or prepared space between or among things; INTERPOLATE applies esp. to the inserting of something extraneous or spurious

in·tro·duc·tion \,in-trə-'dək-shən\ *n* **1 a** : the action of introducing **b** : something introduced; *esp* : a new or exotic plant or animal **2** : the part of a book that leads up to and explains what will be found in the main part : PREFACE ⟨a textbook with an *introduction* and notes⟩ **3** : a book intended for beginners in a subject : GUIDE ⟨an *introduction* to chemistry⟩ **4** : the action of making persons known to each other ⟨gave two of his friends an *introduction*⟩

in·tro·duc·to·ry \,in-trə-'dək-t(ə-)rē\ *adj* : serving to introduce : PRELIMINARY — **in·tro·duc·to·ri·ly** \-t(ə-)rə-lē\ *adv*

in·troit \'in-,trō-ət, -,tróit, in-'\ *n* [ML *introitus,* fr. L, entrance, fr. *introire* to go in, fr. *intro-* + *ire* to go] **1** *often cap* : the first part of the proper of the Mass consisting of an antiphon, verse from a psalm, and the Gloria Patri **2** : a piece of music sung or played at the beginning of a worship service

in·tro·mis·sion \,in-trə-'mish-ən\ *n* : the act or process of intromitting; *esp* : COPULATION

in·tro·mit \-'mit\ *vt* **in·tro·mit·ted; in·tro·mit·ting** [L *intromittere,* fr. *intro-* + *mittere* to send] : to send or put in : INSERT — **in·tro·mit·tent** \-'mit-ᵊnt\ *adj* — **in·tro·mit·ter** \-'mit-ər\ *n*

in·trorse \'in-,trórs\ *adj* [L *introrsus,* adv., inward, fr. *intro-* + *versus* toward, fr. pp. of *vertere* to turn] : facing inward or toward the axis of growth — **in·trorse·ly** *adv*

in·tro·spect \,in-trə-'spekt\ *vi* [L *introspect-, introspicere* to look inside, fr. *intro-* + *specere* to look] : to engage in introspection — **in·tro·spec·tive** \-'spek-tiv\ *adj* — **in·tro·spec·tive·ly** *adv*

in·tro·spec·tion \,in-trə-'spek-shən\ *n* : a reflective looking inward : an examination of one's own thoughts and feelings — **in·tro·spec·tion·al** \-shnəl, -shən-ᵊl\ *adj*

in·tro·ver·sion \,in-trə-'vər-zhən, -shən\ *n* **1** : the act of introverting : the state of being introverted **2** : a tendency toward preoccupation with one's own mental life — **in·tro·ver·sive** \-'vər-siv, -ziv\ *adj* — **in·tro·ver·sive·ly** *adv*

¹in·tro·vert \'in-trə-,vərt\ *vt* [*intro-* + L *vers-, vertere* to turn] : to turn inward or in upon itself: as **a** : to bend or draw inward **b** : to concentrate or direct upon oneself — **in·tro·ver·tive** \-,vərt-iv\ *adj*

²introvert *n* **1** : one that is or can be introverted **2** : a person characterized by introversion

in·trude \in-'trüd\ *vb* [L *intrus-, intrudere* to thrust in, fr. *in-* + *trudere* to thrust] **1** : to bring in or introduce unasked ⟨*intruded* his views into the discussion⟩ **2** : to come or go in without invitation or welcome : TRESPASS ⟨*intrude* on another's property⟩ **3** : to enter or cause to enter as if by force — **in·trud·er** *n*

syn INTRUDE, OBTRUDE mean to thrust oneself or something in without invitation or authorization. INTRUDE implies rudeness, officiousness, or encroachment ⟨no wish to *intrude* on your privacy⟩ OBTRUDE suggests more

strongly the impropriety, boldness, futility, or disagreeableness of an intrusion ⟨intended to write plain prose, but rhyme *obtruded*⟩

in·tru·sion \in-'trü-zhən\ *n* **1** : the act of intruding : the state of being intruded **2** : the forcible entry of molten rock or magma into or between other rock formations; *also* : the intruded magma

in·tru·sive \in-'trü-siv, -ziv\ *adj* **1** : characterized by intrusion; *esp* : intruding where one is not welcome or invited **2** : having been forced while in a plastic state into cavities or between layers ⟨*intrusive* rock⟩ — **in·tru·sive·ly** *adv* — **in·tru·sive·ness** *n*

intrust *var of* ENTRUST

in·tu·it \in-'t(y)ü-ət\ *vt* : to apprehend by intuition — **in·tu·it·a·ble** \-ə-bəl\ *adj*

in·tu·i·tion \,in-t(y)ù-'ish-ən\ *n* [L *intuit-, intueri* to contemplate, fr. *in-* ²in- + *tueri* to look at] **1** : the power of knowing immediately and without conscious reasoning **2** : something known or understood at once and without an effort of the mind ⟨act upon an *intuition*⟩ — **in·tu·i·tion·al** \-'ish-nəl, -ən-ᵊl\ *adj*

in·tu·i·tive \in-'t(y)ü-ət-iv\ *adj* **1** : knowing or understanding by intuition ⟨an *intuitive* person⟩ **2** : having or characterized by intuition ⟨an *intuitive* mind⟩ **3** : known or understood by intuition ⟨*intuitive* knowledge⟩ — **in·tu·i·tive·ly** *adv* — **in·tu·i·tive·ness** *n*

in·tu·mesce \,in-t(y)ù-'mes\ *vi* : ENLARGE, SWELL — **in·tu·mes·cence** \-'mes-ᵊn(t)s\ *n* — **in·tu·mes·cent** \-ᵊnt\ *adj*

in·tus·sus·cep·tion \,int-ə-sə-'sep-shən\ *n* [L *intus* within + *suscept-, suscipere* to take up, fr. *sub-, sus-* up + *capere* to take] : a drawing in of something from without: as **a** : INVAGINATION **b** : the assimilation of new material and its dispersal among preexistent matter (as in the growth of protoplasm) — **in·tus·sus·cep·tive** \-'sep-tiv\ *adj*

in·u·lin \'in-yə-lən\ *n* [NL *Inula,* genus of composite plants] : a white polysaccharide that consists of fructose molecules and occurs as a storage carbohydrate esp. in the roots or tubers of composite plants

in·un·date \'in-ən-,dāt\ *vt* [L *inundare,* fr. *in-* ²in- + *unda* wave] : to cover with a flood : OVERFLOW — **in·un·da·tion** \,in-ən-'dā-shən\ *n* — **in·un·da·tor** \'in-ən-,dāt-ər\ *n* — **in·un·da·to·ry** \in-'ən-də-,tōr-ē, -,tòr-\ *adj*

in·ure \in-'(y)ù(ə)r\ *vb* [ME *enuren,* fr. *en-* + *ure* use, custom, fr. MF *uevre* work, fr. L *opera*] **1** : to make less sensitive : HARDEN ⟨living in Alaska had *inured* him to cold⟩ **2** : to become of advantage ⟨the benefits that *inure* to our descendants⟩ ⟨the profits *inure* to the benefit of the hospital⟩ — **in·ure·ment** \-'(y)ù(ə)r-mənt\ *n*

in·urn \in-'ərn\ *vt* **1** : to enclose in an urn **2** : ENTOMB

in·utile \(')in-'yüt-ᵊl, -'yü-,tīl\ *adj* : USELESS, UNUSABLE — **in·util·i·ty** \,in-yù-'til-ət-ē\ *n*

in vac·uo \in-'vak-yə-,wō\ *adv* [NL] : in a vacuum

in·vade \in-'vād\ *vt* [L *invadere,* fr. *in-* ²in- + *vadere* to go] **1** : to enter for conquest or plunder ⟨*invade* a country⟩ **2** : to encroach upon : INFRINGE **3** : to spread progressively over or into and usu. affect injuriously ⟨bacteria *invading* tissue⟩ ⟨stores *invading* a residential section⟩ — **in·vad·er** *n*

in·vag·i·nate \in-'vaj-ə-,nāt\ *vb* [L *vagina* sheath] : to fold or cause to fold in on itself so that an outer becomes an inner surface — **in·vag·i·na·tion** \-,vaj-ə-'nā-shən\ *n*

¹in·val·id \(')in-'val-əd\ *adj* : having no force or effect : not valid ⟨a license that is *invalid* unless signed by the person to whom it was issued⟩ — **in·va·lid·i·ty** \,in-və-'lid-ət-ē\ *n* — **in·val·id·ly** \(')in-'val-əd-lē\ *adv* — **in·val·id·ness** *n*

²in·va·lid \'in-və-ləd\ *adj* [F *invalide,* fr. L *invalidus* weak, fr. *in-* ¹in- + *valēre* to be well] **1** : suffering from disease or disability : SICKLY **2** : of, relating to, or suited to one that is sick

³invalid \like ²\ *n* : one that is sickly or disabled — **in·va·lid·ism** \-,iz-əm\ *n*

⁴in·va·lid \'in-və-ləd, -,lid\ *vt* **1** : to make sickly or disabled ⟨has been *invalided* since childhood⟩ **2** : to remove from active duty by reason of sickness or disability ⟨*invalided* home after the battle⟩

in·val·i·date \(')in-'val-ə-,dāt\ *vt* : to make invalid ⟨a petition *invalidated* by false signatures⟩; *esp* : to weaken or destroy the cogency of **syn** see NULLIFY — **in·val·i·da-**

tion \(,)in-,val-ə-'dā-shən\ *n* — **in·val·i·da·tor** \in-'val-ə-,dāt-ər\ *n*

in·val·u·able \(')in-'val-yə-(wə-)bəl\ *adj* [¹in- + ²value] : having value too great to be estimated : PRICELESS — **in·val·u·able·ness** *n* — **in·val·u·ably** \-blē\ *adv*

in·var·i·a·bil·i·ty \(,)in-,ver-ē-ə-'bil-ət-ē, -,var-\ *n* : the quality or state of being invariable

in·var·i·a·ble \(')in-'ver-ē-ə-bəl, -'var-\ *adj* : not changing or capable of change : CONSTANT ⟨followed an *invariable* routine each morning⟩ — **invariable** *n* — **in·var·i·a·ble·ness** *n* — **in·var·i·a·bly** \-blē\ *adv*

in·var·i·ant \-ē-ənt\ *adj* : CONSTANT, UNCHANGING — **in·variant** *n*

in·va·sion \in-'vā-zhən\ *n* [L *invas-, invadere* to invade] : an act of invading; *esp* : entrance of an army into a country for conquest or plunder

in·va·sive \-'vā-siv, -ziv\ *adj* : of, relating to, or engaged in invasion — **in·va·sive·ness** *n*

in·vec·tive \in-'vek-tiv\ *n* [L *invect-, invehi* to inveigh] : condemnation written or spoken in a harsh or bitter tone ⟨attack the opposing candidate with *invective*⟩ **syn** see ABUSE

in·veigh \in-'vā\ *vi* [L *invehi* to attack, inveigh, pass. of *invehere* to carry in, fr. *in-* + *vehere* to carry] : to protest or complain bitterly or vehemently : RAIL ⟨*inveighing* against the tax laws⟩ — **in·veigh·er** *n*

in·vei·gle \in-'vā-gəl, -'vē-\ *vt* **in·vei·gled; in·vei·gling** \-g(ə-)liŋ\ [modif. of MF *aveugler* to blind, hoodwink, fr. *avogle* blind, fr. ML *aboculis*, lit., lacking eyes] **1** : to bring or lead by flattery : ENTICE ⟨*inveigled* him into marriage⟩ **2** : to acquire by ingenuity or flattery ⟨*inveigled* a loan⟩ — **in·vei·gle·ment** \-gəl-mənt\ *n* — **in·vei·gler** \-g(ə-)lər\ *n*

in·vent \in-'vent\ *vt* [L *invent-, invenire* to come upon, find, fr. *in-* + *venire* to come] **1 a** : to think up : IMAGINE **b** : to make up : FABRICATE ⟨*invent* an excuse⟩ **2** : to create or produce for the first time : DEVISE **syn** see DISCOVER — **in·ven·tor** \-'vent-ər\ *n*

in·ven·tion \in-'ven-chən\ *n* **1** : INVENTIVENESS **2** : something invented: as **a** : a product of the imagination; *esp* : a false conception **b** : a device or process originated after study and experiment **3** : the act or process of inventing

in·ven·tive \in-'vent-iv\ *adj* : gifted with the skill and imagination to invent ⟨an *inventive* mind⟩ ⟨an *inventive* genius⟩ — **in·ven·tive·ly** *adv* — **in·ven·tive·ness** *n*

¹in·ven·to·ry \'in-vən-,tōr-ē, -,tór-\ *n, pl* **-ries** **1 a** : an itemized list of current assets **b** : a list of goods on hand **2** : the quantity of goods or materials on hand : STOCK **3** : the act or process of making an inventory — **in·ven·to·ri·al** \,in-vən-'tōr-ē-əl, -'tór-\ *adj* — **in·ven·to·ri·al·ly** \-ē-ə-lē\ *adv*

²inventory *vt* **-ried; -ry·ing** : to make an inventory of : CATALOG

in·ver·ness \,in-vər-'nes\ *n* [*Inverness*, Scotland] : a loose belted coat having a cape with a close round collar

¹in·verse \(')in-'vərs, 'in-,\ *adj* [L *inversus* inverted, fr. pp. of *invertere* to invert] : opposite in order, nature, or effect; *esp* : so relating two quantities that their product is a constant ⟨an *inverse* proportion⟩ — **in·verse·ly** *adv*

²inverse *n* : something inverse or resulting in or from inversion: as **a** : an inverse function or operation in mathematics ⟨addition is the *inverse* of subtraction⟩ **b** : an inverse quantity; *esp* : RECIPROCAL 2 **c** : the statement formed by contradicting both the hypothesis and the conclusion of another statement

inverse square law *n* : a statement in physics: a physical quantity (as illumination) varies with the distance from the source inversely as the square of the distance

in·ver·sion \in-'vər-zhən\ *n* **1** : the act or process of inverting **2** : a reversal of position, order, or relationship: as **a** : a change in normal word order; *esp* : the placing of a verb before its subject **b** : the process or result of reversing the relative positions of the elements of an interval, chord, or phrase; *esp* : a chord having its root in a voice other than the bass **3** : HOMOSEXUALITY

in·ver·sive \in-'vər-siv, -ziv\ *adj* : marked by inversion

in·vert \in-'vərt\ *vt* [L *invertere*, fr. *in-* ²in- + *vertere* to turn] **1 a** : to turn inside out or upside down **b** : to turn inward **2** : to reverse the position, order, or relationship of **syn** see REVERSE — **in·vert·i·ble** \-ə-bəl\ *adj*

in·ver·tase \in-'vərt-,ās, 'in-vər-,tās\ *n* : an enzyme that splits sucrose into glucose and fructose

in·ver·te·brate \(')in-'vərt-ə-brət, -,brāt\ *adj* : lacking a spinal column; *also* : of or relating to invertebrate animals — **invertebrate** *n*

in·vert·er \in-'vərt-ər\ *n* : a device for converting direct current into alternating current

invert sugar \,in-,vərt-\ *n* : a mixture of dextrose and levulose found in fruits or produced artificially from sucrose

¹in·vest \in-'vest\ *vt* [L *investire* to clothe, surround, fr. *in-* ²in- + *vestis* garment] **1 a** : to array in the symbols of office or honor **b** : to furnish with power or authority **2** : to cover completely : ENVELOP **3** : CLOTHE, ADORN **4** : to surround with troops or ships : BESIEGE **5** : to endow with a quality or characteristic : INFUSE ⟨*invest* an incident with mystery⟩

²invest *vb* [It *investire* to clothe, invest money, fr. L, to clothe] **1** : to commit money in order to earn a financial return **2** : to expend for future benefits or advantages ⟨had a lot of time and energy *invested* in the project⟩ — **in·vest·a·ble** \-'ves-tə-bəl\ *adj* — **in·ves·tor** \-'tər\ *n*

in·ves·ti·gate \in-'ves-tə-,gāt\ *vb* [L *investigare* to track, investigate, fr. *in-* ²in- + *vestigium* footprint] : to observe or study by close examination and systematic inquiry — **in·ves·ti·ga·tion** \-,ves-tə-'gā-shən\ *n* — **in·ves·ti·ga·tive** \-'ves-tə-,gāt-iv\ *adj* — **in·ves·ti·ga·tor** \-,gāt-ər\ *n* — **in·ves·ti·ga·to·ry** \in-'ves-tə-gə-,tōr-ē, -,tór-\ *adj*

in·ves·ti·ture \in-'ves-tə-,chúr, -chər\ *n* **1** : the action of investing a person esp. with the robes of office **2** : CLOTHING, APPAREL

¹in·vest·ment \in-'ves(t)-mənt\ *n* **1 a** *archaic* : VESTMENT **b** : an outer layer : ENVELOPE **2** : INVESTITURE 1 **3** : BLOCKADE, SIEGE

²investment *n* : the outlay of money for income or profit; *also* : the sum invested or the property purchased

in·vet·er·a·cy \in-'vet-ə-rə-sē, -'ve-trə-\ *n* : the quality or state of being inveterate

in·vet·er·ate \in-'vet-ə-rət, -'ve-trət\ *adj* [L *inveteratus*, fr. pp. of *inveterare* to age, fr. *in-* ²in- + *veter-, vetus* old] **1** : firmly established by age or by being long continued **2** : HABITUAL ⟨an *inveterate* smoker⟩ — **in·vet·er·ate·ly** *adv*

in·vi·a·ble \(')in-'vī-ə-bəl\ *adj* : incapable of surviving — **in·vi·a·bil·i·ty** \(,)in-,vī-ə-'bil-ət-ē\ *n*

in·vid·i·ous \in-'vid-ē-əs\ *adj* [L *invidiosus*, fr. *invidia* envy] : tending to arouse dislike, ill will, or envy; *esp* : discriminating unfairly between two things ⟨an *invidious* comparison⟩ — **in·vid·i·ous·ly** *adv* — **in·vid·i·ous·ness** *n*

in·vig·o·rate \in-'vig-ə-,rāt\ *vt* : to give life and energy to : ANIMATE — **in·vig·o·ra·tion** \-,vig-ə-'rā-shən\ *n* — **in·vig·o·ra·tor** \-'vig-ə-,rāt-ər\ *n*

in·vin·ci·bil·i·ty \(,)in-,vin(t)-sə-'bil-ət-ē\ *n* : the quality or state of being invincible

in·vin·ci·ble \(')in-'vin(t)-sə-bəl\ *adj* [LL *invincibilis*, fr. L *in-* ¹in- + *vincere* to conquer] : incapable of being defeated, overcome, or subdued ⟨*invincible* determination⟩ ⟨an *invincible* army⟩ **syn** see INDOMITABLE — **in·vin·ci·ble·ness** *n* — **in·vin·ci·bly** \-blē\ *adv*

in·vi·o·la·ble \(')in-'vī-ə-lə-bəl\ *adj* **1** : too sacred to be violated ⟨an *inviolable* oath⟩ **2** : incapable of being harmed or destroyed by violence — **in·vi·o·la·bil·i·ty** \(,)in-,vī-ə-lə-'bil-ət-ē\ *n* — **in·vi·o·la·bly** \(')in-'vī-ə-lə-blē\ *adv*

in·vi·o·late \(')in-'vī-ə-lət\ *adj* : not violated; *esp* : PURE, UNPROFANED — **in·vi·o·late·ly** *adv* — **in·vi·o·late·ness** *n*

in·vis·i·bil·i·ty \(,)in-,viz-ə-'bil-ət-ē\ *n* : the quality or state of being invisible

in·vis·i·ble \(')in-'viz-ə-bəl\ *adj* **1 a** : incapable by nature of being seen ⟨sound is *invisible*⟩ **b** : inaccessible to view : HIDDEN ⟨the sun *invisible* on a cloudy day⟩ **2** : not reflected in statistics ⟨*invisible* imports⟩ **3** : IMPERCEPTIBLE, INCONSPICUOUS ⟨an *invisible* plaid⟩ — **invisible** *n* — **in·vis·i·ble·ness** *n* — **in·vis·i·bly** \-blē\ *adv*

in·vi·ta·tion \,in-və-'tā-shən\ *n* **1** : the act of inviting **2** : the written, printed, or spoken expression by which a person is invited — **in·vi·ta·tion·al** \-shnəl, -shən-°l\ *adj*

¹in·vite \in-'vīt\ *vt* [L *invitare*] **1 a** : to offer an incentive or inducement to : ENTICE **b** : to increase the likelihood of ⟨*invite* disaster by speeding⟩ **2 a** : to request the presence or participation of **b** : to request formally **c** : to urge politely : ENCOURAGE — **in·vit·er** *n*

---

j joke; **ŋ** sing; **ō** flow; **ó** flaw; **ói** coin; **th** thin; **th̲** this; **ü** loot; **ú** foot; **y** yet; **yü** few; **yú** furious; **zh** vision

syn SOLICIT: INVITE commonly implies a formal or courteous request for one's presence or participation but may also apply simply to an attracting or tempting ⟨*invited* a few friends for dinner⟩ ⟨the title of the book *invited* interest⟩ SOLICIT suggests urgency in encouraging or asking ⟨they offered to *solicit* contributions for the hospital⟩

²**in·vite** \'in-ˌvīt\ *n, chiefly dial* : INVITATION

in·vit·ing \in-'vīt-iŋ\ *adj* : ATTRACTIVE, TEMPTING ⟨a very *inviting* prospect⟩ — **in·vit·ing·ly** \-iŋ-lē\ *adv*

in vi·tro \in-'vē-,trō\ *adv (or adj)* [NL, lit., in glass] : outside the living body and in an artificial environment

in vi·vo \in-'vē-vō\ *adv (or adj)* [NL, lit., in the living] : in the living body of a plant or animal

in·vo·cate \'in-və-ˌkāt\ *vt, archaic* : INVOKE — **in·voc·a·to·ry** \in-'väk-ə-ˌtōr-ē, -ˌtȯr-\ *adj*

in·vo·ca·tion \ˌin-və-'kā-shən\ *n* **1 a** (1) : the act or process of petitioning for help or support : SUPPLICATION (2) *often cap* : an invocatory prayer **b** : a calling upon for authority or justification ⟨*invocation* of the law⟩ **2** : a formula for conjuring : INCANTATION — **in·vo·ca·tion·al** \-shnəl, -shən-ᵊl\ *adj*

¹**in·voice** \'in-ˌvȯis\ *n* [MF *envois*, pl. of *envoi* message, *envoi*] : an itemized statement furnished to a purchaser by a seller and usu. specifying the price of goods or services and the terms of sale; *also* : a shipment of goods sent with such a statement

²**invoice** *vt* : to submit an invoice for : BILL

in·voke \in-'vōk\ *vt* [L *invocare*, fr. *in-* ²*in-* + *vocare* to call] **1** : to call on for aid or protection (as in prayer) ⟨*invoke* God's blessing⟩ **2** : to call forth by magic : CONJURE ⟨*invoke* spirits⟩ **3** : to appeal to as an authority or for support ⟨*invoke* a little-known law⟩ — **in·vok·er** *n*

in·vo·lu·cre \'in-və-ˌlü-kər\ *n* [L *involucrum* envelope, fr. *involvere* to wrap, involve] : one or more whorls of bracts immediately below a flower, flower cluster, or fruit — **in·vo·lu·cral** \ˌin-və-'lü-krəl\ *adj* — **in·vo·lu·cred** \'in-və-ˌlü-kərd\ *or* **in·vo·lu·crate** \ˌin-və-'lü-krət\ *adj* — **in·vo·lu·cri·form** \-'lü-krə-ˌfȯrm\ *adj*

in·vol·un·tary \(')in-'väl-ən-ˌter-ē\ *adj* **1** : not made or done willingly or from choice : UNWILLING **2** : COMPULSORY **3** : not subject to control by the will : REFLEX, AUTONOMIC ⟨*involuntary* muscles⟩ — **in·vol·un·tar·i·ly** \(ˌ)in-ˌväl-ən-'ter-ə-lē\ *adv* — **in·vol·un·tar·i·ness** \(')in-'väl-ən-ˌter-ē-nəs\ *n*

¹**in·vo·lute** \'in-və-ˌlüt\ *adj* [L *involutus*, pp. of *involvere* to roll in, involve] **1 a** : curled spirally and usu. closely ⟨*involute* shell⟩ **b** : curled or curved inward ⟨an *involute* leaf⟩ **2** : INVOLVED, INTRICATE — **in·vo·lute·ly** *adv*

²**involute** *n* : a spiral curve traced by a point on a taut thread as the thread is unwound from around a geometric figure (as a circle or polygon)

in·vo·lu·tion \ˌin-və-'lü-shən\ *n* **1 a** : the act or an instance of enfolding or entangling : INVOLVEMENT **b** : COMPLEXITY, INTRICACY **2** : the act or process of raising a quantity to any power **3** : an inward curving or penetration ⟨a gastrula formed by *involution*⟩ **4 a** : a shrinking or return to a former size **b** : the regressive alteration characteristic of aging and marked by a decrease of bodily vigor — **in·vo·lu·tion·al** \-shnəl, -shən-ᵊl\ *adj* — **in·vo·lu·tion·ary** \-shə-ˌner-ē\ *adj*

in·volve \in-'välv, -'vȯlv\ *vt* [L *involut-, involvere* to roll in, wrap, fr. *in-* + *volvere* to roll] **1 a** : to draw in as a participant : ENGAGE ⟨many workmen are *involved* in the operation⟩ **b** : to oblige to become associated ⟨was *involved* in a lawsuit⟩ **c** : to occupy absorbingly ⟨*involved* in the hero's fate⟩ **2** : to make difficult : COMPLICATE ⟨an *involved* explanation⟩ **3 a** : to have within or as part of itself : INCLUDE ⟨one problem *involves* others⟩ **b** : to require as a necessary accompaniment ⟨the road job *involved* the building of 10 bridges⟩ **c** : to have an effect on : AFFECT ⟨breathing *involves* the whole organism⟩ **syn** see INCLUDE — **in·volve·ment** \-mənt\ *n* — **in·volv·er** *n*

in·volved \-'välvd, -'vȯlvd\ *adj* **1** : TWISTED **2 a** : COMPLICATED, INTRICATE **b** : CONFUSED, TANGLED **3** : AFFECTED, IMPLICATED **syn** see COMPLEX — **in·volved·ly** \-'välv-(ə-)dlē, -'vȯlv-\ *adv*

in·vul·ner·a·bil·i·ty \(ˌ)in-ˌvəl-nə-rə-'bil-ət-ē\ *n* : the quality or state of being invulnerable

in·vul·ner·a·ble \(')in-'vəl-nə-rə-bəl\ *adj* **1** : incapable of being wounded, injured, or damaged **2** : immune to or

proof against attack : IMPREGNABLE — **in·vul·ner·a·ble·ness** *n* — **in·vul·ner·a·bly** \-blē\ *adv*

¹**in·ward** \'in-wərd\ *adj* **1** : situated on the inside : INNER **2 a** : MENTAL **b** : SPIRITUAL **3** : directed toward the interior ⟨an *inward* flow⟩

²**inward** *or* **in·wards** \-wərdz\ *adv* **1** : toward the inside, center, or interior ⟨slope *inwards*⟩ **2** : toward the inner being ⟨turned his thoughts *inward*⟩

³**inward** *n* **1** : something that is inward **2 in·wards** \'in-ərdz, -wərdz\ *pl* : INNARDS

in·ward·ly \'in-wərd-lē\ *adv* **1** : MENTALLY, SPIRITUALLY **2 a** : INTERNALLY ⟨bled *inwardly*⟩ **b** : to oneself : PRIVATELY ⟨cursed *inwardly*⟩ **3** : towards the inside ⟨curving *inwardly*⟩

in·ward·ness *n* **1** : fundamental nature or meaning **2** : absorption in one's own mental or spiritual life

in·weave \(')in-'wēv\ *vt* : to weave in or together : INTERLACE

in·wrought \(')in-'rȯt\ *adj* **1** : worked in among other things : inwoven in a fabric ⟨an *inwrought* design⟩ **2** : ADORNED, DECORATED ⟨silver *inwrought* with gold⟩

iod- *or* **iodo-** *comb form* [F *iode*] : iodine ⟨*iod*ize⟩ ⟨*iodo*form⟩

¹**io·date** \'ī-ə-ˌdāt, -əd-ət\ *n* : a salt of iodic acid

²**io·date** \'ī-ə-ˌdāt\ *vt* : to impregnate or treat with iodine

iod·ic acid \ˌī-ˌäd-ik-\ *n* : a crystalline oxidizing solid HIO_3 formed by oxidation of iodine

io·dide \'ī-ə-ˌdīd\ *n* : a compound of iodine with another element or radical

io·dine *also* **io·din** \'ī-ə-ˌdīn, -əd-ᵊn, -ə-ˌdēn\ *n* [modif. of F *iode*, fr. Gk *ioeidēs* violet colored, fr. *ion* violet] **1** : a nonmetallic usu. univalent chemical element that occurs in seawater, seaweeds, and underground brines, is obtained usu. as heavy shining blackish gray crystals, and is used esp. in medicine, photography, and analysis — see ELEMENT table **2** : a solution of iodine in alcohol used as an antiseptic

io·dize \'ī-ə-ˌdīz\ *vt* : to treat with iodine or an iodide

io·do·form \ī-'ōd-ə-ˌfȯrm, -'äd-\ *n* [*iod-* + *-form* (as in *chloroform*)] : a yellow crystalline volatile iodine compound that is used as an antiseptic dressing

io·dop·sin \ˌī-ə-'däp-sən\ *n* [Gk *ioeidēs* violet colored + *opsis* vision] : a violet light-sensitive pigment in the retinal cones that is formed from vitamin A and is important in daylight vision — compare RHODOPSIN

io moth \'ī-(ˌ)ō-\ *n* : a large yellowish American moth with a large spot on each hind wing

ion \'ī-ən, 'ī-ˌän\ *n* [Gk, neut. of *iōn*, prp. of *ienai* to go] : an atom or group of atoms that carries a positive or negative electric charge as a result of having lost or gained one or more electrons

-ion *n suffix* [L *-ion-, -io*] **1 a** : act or process ⟨valid*ation*⟩ **b** : result of an act or process ⟨regul*ation*⟩ **2** : state or condition ⟨hydr*ation*⟩

Io·ni·an \ī-'ō-nē-ən\ *n* **1** : one of an ancient Greek people who settled in Attica on the islands of the Aegean sea, and on the shore of Asia Minor **2** : a native or inhabitant of Ionia — **Ionian** *adj*

ion·ic \ī-'än-ik\ *adj* : of, relating to, or existing in the form of ions

Ion·ic \ī-'än-ik\ *adj* **1** : of or relating to Ionia or the Ionians **2** : belonging to or resembling the Ionic order of architecture characterized esp. by the spiral volutes of its capital — see CAPITAL illustration

io·ni·um \ī-'ō-nē-əm\ *n* [*ion;* fr. its ionizing action] : a natural radioactive isotope of thorium having a mass number of 230

ion·ize \'ī-ə-ˌnīz\ *vb* **1** : to convert wholly or partly into ions **2** : to become ionized — **ion·i·za·tion** \ˌī-ə-nə-'zā-shən\ *n* — **ion·iz·er** \'ī-ə-ˌnī-zər\ *n*

iono·sphere \ī-'än-ə-ˌsfi(ə)r\ *n* : the part of the earth's atmosphere beginning at an altitude of about 25 miles and extending outward 250 miles or more and containing free electrically charged particles by means of which radio waves are transmitted to great distances around the earth — **iono·spher·ic** \(ˌ)ī-ˌän-ə-'sfi(ə)r-ik, -'sfer-\ *adj*

io·ta \ī-'ōt-ə\ *n* **1** : the 9th letter of the Greek alphabet — I or ι **2** : an infinitesimal amount : JOT ⟨the story contained not one *iota* of truth⟩

IOU \ˌī-(ˌ)ō-'yü\ *n* [fr. the pronunciation of *I owe you*] : a paper that has on it the letters IOU, a stated sum, and a signature and that is given as an acknowledgment of debt

-ious *adj suffix* [partly fr. L *-iosus*, fr. *-i-* (penultimate vowel of some noun stems) + *-osus* -ous; partly fr. L *-ius*, adj. suffix] : -OUS ⟨capaci*ous*⟩

ip·e·cac \'ip-i-,kak\ *or* **ipe·ca·cu·an·ha** \ē-,pek-ə-kù-'an-yə\ *n* [Pg *ipecacuanha*, of AmerInd origin] : a So. American creeping plant of the madder family; *also* : its dried rhizome and roots or an extract of these used esp. formerly in medicine esp. as an emetic and purgative

Iph·i·ge·nia \,if-ə-jə-'nī-ə\ *n* : a daughter of Agamemnon offered by her father as a sacrifice but saved and made a priestess of Artemis

ip·se dix·it \,ip-sē-'dik-sət\ *n* [L, he himself said it] : an assertion made but not proved : DICTUM

ip·si·lat·er·al \,ip-si-'lat-ə-rəl, -'la-trəl\ *adj* [L *ipse* self + *later-, latus* side] : situated on or affecting the same side of the body — **ip·si·lat·er·al·ly** \-ē\ *adv*

ip·so fac·to \,ip-sō-'fak-tō\ *adv* [NL, lit., by the fact itself] : by the very nature of the case

ir- — *see* IN-

Ira·ni·an \ir-'ā-nē-ən\ *n* **1** : a native or inhabitant of Iran **2** : a branch of the Indo-European family of languages that includes Persian — **Iranian** *adj*

iras·ci·ble \ir-'as-ə-bəl, ī-'ras-\ *adj* [L *irasci* to become angry, fr. *ira* ire] : marked by hot temper and easily provoked anger — **iras·ci·bil·i·ty** \ir-,as-ə-'bil-ət-ē, ī-,ras-\ *n* — **iras·ci·ble·ness** \ir-'as-ə-bəl-nəs, ī-'ras-\ *n* — **iras·ci·bly** \-blē\ *adv*

syn IRASCIBLE, CHOLERIC, TESTY, TOUCHY mean easily angered. IRASCIBLE implies a tendency to be fiery tempered ⟨an *irascible* peppery old codger⟩ CHOLERIC may suggest impatient excitability and unreasonable irritability; TESTY implies a quick temper irritated by trivial annoyances; TOUCHY suggests oversensitive readiness to take offense or flare up at slight or implied criticism

irate \ī-'rāt\ *adj* **1** : roused or given to ire : INCENSED ⟨*irate* over acts of vandalism⟩ **2** : arising from anger ⟨*irate* words⟩ — **irate·ly** *adv* — **irate·ness** *n*

ire \'ī(ə)r\ *n* [L *ira*] : ANGER, WRATH — **ire** *vt* — **ire·ful** \-fəl\ *adj* — **ire·ful·ly** \-fə-lē\ *adv*

iren·ic \ī-'ren-ik\ *adj* [Gk *eirēnē* peace] : conducive to or operating toward peace or conciliation — **iren·i·cal·ly** \-'ren-i-k(ə-)lē\ *adv*

ir·i·des·cence \,ir-ə-'des-ᵊn(t)s\ *n* : a play of colors producing rainbow effects (as in mother-of-pearl) — **ir·i·des·cent** \-ᵊnt\ *adj* — **ir·i·des·cent·ly** *adv*

irid·ic \ir-'id-ik\ *adj* : of or relating to iridium; *esp* : containing tetravalent iridium

irid·i·um \ir-'id-ē-əm\ *n* [NL, fr. Gk *irid-, iris* rainbow] : a silver-white hard brittle very heavy metallic chemical element — *see* ELEMENT table

iris \'ī-rəs\ *n, pl* **iris·es** *or* **iri·des** \'ī-rə-,dēz, 'ir-ə-\ [Gk *irid-, iris*] **1** : RAINBOW **2** : the opaque contractile diaphragm perforated by the pupil and forming the colored portion of the eye **3** : any of a large genus of perennial herbaceous plants with linear usu. basal leaves and large showy flowers

Iris \'ī-rəs\ *n* : the goddess of the rainbow and messenger of the gods in Greek mythology

iris diaphragm *n* : an adjustable diaphragm of thin opaque plates used for changing the diameter of a central opening to control the amount of light passing (as into a microscope or camera)

Irish \'ī(ə)r-ish\ *n* **1** **Irish** *pl* : the natives or inhabitants of Ireland or their descendants **2** : the Celtic language of Ireland — **Irish** *adj*

Irish Gaelic *n* : the Celtic language of Ireland esp. as used since the end of the medieval period

Irish·ism \'ī-rish-,iz-əm\ *n* : a word, phrase, or expression characteristic of the Irish

Irish·man \'ī-rish-mən\ *n* **1** : a native or inhabitant of Ireland **2** : a man of Irish descent — **Irish·wom·an** \-,wùm-ən\ *n*

Irish moss *n* : either of two red algae; *also* : the dried and bleached plants of these used esp. as a thickening or emulsifying agent

Irish potato *n* : POTATO 2b

Irish setter *n* : any of a breed of bird dogs generally comparable to English setters but with a chestnut-brown or mahogany-red coat

irk \'ərk\ *vt* [ME *irken*] : to make weary, irritated, or bored : ANNOY ⟨his lack of interest *irked* her⟩

irk·some \'ərk-səm\ *adj* : TIRESOME, TEDIOUS, ANNOYING ⟨an *irksome* task⟩ — **irk·some·ly** *adv* — **irk·some·ness** *n*

¹iron \'ī(-ə)rn\ *n* [OE *īsern, īren*] **1** : a heavy malleable ductile magnetic chiefly bivalent and trivalent silver-white metallic chemical element that readily rusts in moist air, occurs in meteorites and combined in rocks, and is vital to biological processes — *see* ELEMENT table **2** : something made of iron: as **a** : something (as handcuffs or chains) used to bind or restrain — usu. used in pl. **b** : a heated metal implement used for branding **c** : FLATIRON **d** : one of a set of golf clubs numbered 1 through 9 with heads that are metal blades laid progressively farther back to provide progressively more height and less distance **3** : STRENGTH, HARDNESS ⟨muscles of *iron*⟩

²iron *adj* **1** : of, relating to, or made of iron **2** : resembling iron (as in hardness or strength) **3 a** : being strong and healthy : ROBUST ⟨an *iron* constitution⟩ **b** : INFLEXIBLE, UNRELENTING ⟨*iron* determination⟩ **c** : holding or binding fast ⟨*iron* ties of kinship⟩

³iron *vb* **1** : to furnish or cover with iron **2 a** : to smooth or press with a heated flatiron ⟨*iron* a shirt⟩ **b** : to remove by ironing ⟨*iron* out wrinkles⟩ **3** : to iron clothes ⟨spent all day *ironing*⟩

Iron Age *n* : the period of human culture characterized by the smelting and use of iron and beginning somewhat before 1000 B.C. in western Asia and Egypt

iron·bound \'ī(-ə)rn-'baùnd\ *adj* : bound with or as if with iron: as **a** : HARSH, RUGGED ⟨*ironbound* coast⟩ **b** : STERN, RIGOROUS

¹iron·clad \-'klad\ *adj* **1** : sheathed in iron armor **2** : RIGOROUS, EXACTING ⟨*ironclad* laws⟩

²iron·clad \-,klad\ *n* : an armored naval vessel

iron curtain *n* : a political, military, and ideological barrier that cuts off and isolates an area; *esp* : one between an area under Soviet Russian control and other areas

iron·er \'ī(-ə)r-nər\ *n* : one that irons; *esp* : MANGLE

iron horse *n* : a locomotive engine

iron·ic \ī-'rän-ik\ *adj* **1** : relating to, containing, or constituting irony ⟨an *ironic* turn of events⟩ ⟨an *ironic* laugh⟩ **2** : given to irony — **iron·i·cal** \-i-kəl\ *adj* — **iron·i·cal·ly** \-i-k(ə-)lē\ *adv*

iro·nist \'ī-rə-nəst\ *n* : a person given to irony

iron lung *n* : a device for artificial respiration in which rhythmic alternations in the air pressure in a chamber surrounding a patient's chest force air into and out of the lungs

iron·mon·ger \'ī(-ə)rn-,məŋ-gər, -,mäŋ-\ *n, Brit* : a dealer in iron and hardware — **iron·mon·gery** \-g(ə-)rē\ *n*

iron oxide *n* **1** : FERRIC OXIDE **2** : FERROUS OXIDE **3** : a black magnetic oxide of iron Fe_3O_4 used as a pigment and polishing material

iron pyrites *n* : PYRITE — called also *iron pyrite*

iron·stone \'ī(-ə)rn-,stōn\ *n* **1** : a hard sedimentary rock rich in iron **2** : a hard white pottery first made in England during the 18th century — called also *ironstone china*

iron·ware \-,wa(ə)r, -,we(ə)r\ *n* : articles made of iron

iron·wood \-,wùd\ *n* **1** : any of numerous trees and shrubs with exceptionally tough or hard wood **2** : the wood of an ironwood

iron·work \-,wərk\ *n* **1** : work in iron **2** *sing or pl* : a mill or building where iron or steel is smelted or heavy iron or steel products are made — **iron·work·er** \-,wər-kər\ *n*

iro·ny \'ī-rə-nē\ *n, pl* **-nies** [Gk *eirōnia*, fr. *eirōn* dissembler] **1** : the humorous or sardonic use of words to express the opposite of what one really means (as when words of praise are given but blame is intended); *also* : an ironic expression or utterance **2** : incongruity between the actual result of a sequence of events and the expected result; *also* : an event or result marked by such incongruity

Ir·o·quoi·an \,ir-ə-'kwòi-ən\ *n* **1** : a language family of eastern No. America including the languages spoken by the Cayugas, Cherokees, Eries, Mohawks, Onondagas, Oneidas, Senecas, and Tuscaroras **2** : a member of any of the peoples constituting the Iroquois — **Iroquoian** *adj*

Ir·o·quois \'ir-ə-,kwòi\ *n, pl* **Iroquois** \-,kwòi(z)\ : a member of an Indian confederacy consisting orig. of the Cayugas, Mohawks, Oneidas, Onondagas, and Senecas of New York and later including the Tuscaroras

ir·ra·di·ance \ir-'ād-ē-ən(t)s\ *n* **:** something emitted like rays of light

ir·ra·di·ant \ir-'ād-ē-ənt\ *adj* **:** emitting rays of light — **ir·ra·di·an·cy** \-ən-sē\ *n*

ir·ra·di·ate \ir-'ād-ē-,āt\ *vt* **1 a :** to cast rays of light on **:** ILLUMINATE **b :** to enlighten intellectually or spiritually **c :** to affect or treat by exposure to radiations (as of ultraviolet light, X rays, or gamma rays) **2 :** to emit like rays of light **:** RADIATE — **ir·ra·di·a·tion** \-,ād-ē-'ā-shən\ *n* — **ir·ra·di·a·tive** \-'ād-ē-,āt-iv\ *adj*

ir·rad·i·ca·ble \(')ir-'ad-i-kə-bəl\ *adj* [ML *irradicabilis*, fr. L in- ¹in- + *radic-, radix* root] **:** impossible to eradicate **:** DEEP-ROOTED — **ir·rad·i·ca·bly** \-blē\ *adv*

ir·ra·tio·nal \(')ir-'ash-nəl, -ən-ᵊl\ *adj* **1 a** (1) **:** incapable of reasoning ⟨*irrational* beasts⟩ (2) **:** defective in mental power ⟨*irrational* with fever⟩ **b :** coming from or as if from a mind incapable of reasoning ⟨*irrational* fear⟩ **2 :** of or relating to an irrational number — **ir·ra·tio·nal·i·ty** \(,)ir-,ash-ə-'nal-ət-ē\ *n* — **ir·ra·tio·nal·ly** \(')ir-'ash-nə-lē, -'ash-ən-ᵊl-ē\ *adv* — **ir·ra·tio·nal·ness** \-nal-nəs, -ən-ᵊl-nəs\ *n*

syn IRRATIONAL, UNREASONABLE mean not guided by reason. IRRATIONAL may imply mental derangement but oftener suggests lack of control or guidance by reason ⟨*irrational* fears⟩ UNREASONABLE suggests control by some force other than reason which makes for a deficiency in good sense ⟨*unreasonable* demands⟩

irrational number *n* **:** a real number that is not expressible as the quotient of two integers

ir·re·claim·a·ble \,ir-i-'klā-mə-bəl\ *adj* **:** incapable of being reclaimed — **ir·re·claim·a·bly** \-blē\ *adv*

ir·rec·on·cil·a·ble \(,)ir-,ek-ən-'sī-lə-bəl, (')ir-'ek-ən-,\ *adj* **:** impossible to reconcile, adjust, or harmonize ⟨*irreconcilable* enemies⟩ ⟨*irreconcilable* ideas⟩ — **ir·rec·on·cil·a·bil·i·ty** \(,)ir-,ek-ən-,sī-lə-'bil-ət-ē\ *n* — **ir·rec·on·cil·a·ble·ness** \(,)ir-,ek-ən-'sī-lə-bəl-nəs, (')ir-'ek-ən-,\ *n* — **ir·rec·on·cil·a·bly** \-blē\ *adv*

ir·re·cov·er·a·ble \,ir-i-'kəv-(ə-)rə-bəl\ *adj* **:** not capable of being recovered or rectified **:** IRREPARABLE ⟨an *irrecoverable* debt⟩ — **ir·re·cov·er·a·ble·ness** *n* — **ir·re·cov·er·a·bly** \-blē\ *adv*

ir·re·deem·a·ble \,ir-i-'dē-mə-bəl\ *adj* **1 :** not redeemable; *esp* **:** not convertible into gold or silver at the will of the holder **2 :** being beyond remedy **:** HOPELESS ⟨*irredeemable* mistakes⟩ — **ir·re·deem·a·bly** \-blē\ *adv*

ir·re·den·tism \,ir-i-'den,-tiz-əm\ *n* [It *Italia irredenta* unredeemed Italy, used of Italian-speaking areas not incorporated in Italy] **:** a principle or policy directed toward the incorporation of a territory historically or ethnically part of another into that other — **ir·re·den·tist** \-'dent-əst\ *n or adj*

ir·re·duc·i·ble \,ir-i-'d(y)ü-sə-bəl\ *adj* **:** not reducible — **ir·re·duc·i·bil·i·ty** \-,d(y)ü-sə-'bil-ət-ē\ *n* — **ir·re·duc·i·bly** \-'d(y)ü-sə-blē\ *adv*

ir·ref·ra·ga·ble \(')ir-'ef-rə-gə-bəl\ *adj* [L in- ¹in- + *refragari* to oppose, fr. re- + *-fragari* (as in *suffragari* to vote for)] **:** impossible to deny or refute **:** INVIOLABLE — **ir·ref·ra·ga·bil·i·ty** \(,)ir-,ef-rə-gə-'bil-ət-ē\ *n* — **ir·ref·ra·ga·bly** \(')ir-'ef-rə-gə-blē\ *adv*

ir·re·fut·a·ble \,ir-i-'fyüt-ə-bəl, (')ir-'ef-yət-\ *adj* **:** not capable of being proved wrong **:** INDISPUTABLE — **ir·re·fut·a·bil·i·ty** \,ir-i-,fyüt-ə-'bil-ət-ē, (,)ir-,ef-yət-ə-'bil-\ *n* — **ir·re·fut·a·bly** \,ir-i-'fyüt-ə-blē, (')ir-'ef-yət-\ *adv*

¹**ir·reg·u·lar** \(')ir-'eg-yə-lər\ *adj* **1 a :** not conforming to established laws, customs, or moral principles **b :** not belonging to a recognized or organized body ⟨*irregular* troops⟩ ⟨*irregular* Democrats⟩ **2 :** not conforming to the normal or usual manner of inflection ⟨the *irregular* verbs *sell* and *cast*⟩; *esp* **:** STRONG ⟨the *irregular* verb *write*⟩ **3 :** lacking perfect symmetry or evenness; *esp* **:** not radially symmetrical ⟨*irregular* flowers⟩ **4 :** lacking continuity or regularity esp. of occurrence or activity ⟨*irregular* intervals⟩ ⟨*irregular* payments⟩ — **ir·reg·u·lar·ly** *adv*

²**irregular** *n* **:** an irregular soldier

ir·reg·u·lar·i·ty \(,)ir-,eg-yə-'lar-ət-ē\ *n, pl* **-ties 1 :** the quality or state of being irregular **2 :** something (as dishonest conduct) that is irregular

ir·rel·a·tive \(')ir-'el-ət-iv\ *adj* **:** not relative — **ir·rel·a·tive·ly** *adv*

ir·rel·e·vant \(')ir-'el-ə-vənt\ *adj* **:** not relevant **:** not applicable or pertinent **:** FOREIGN — **ir·rel·e·vance**

\-vən(t)s\ *or* **ir·rel·e·van·cy** \-vən-sē\ *n* — **ir·rel·e·vant·ly** *adv*

ir·re·li·gion \,ir-i-'lij-ən\ *n* **:** the quality or state of being irreligious

ir·re·li·gious \-'lij-əs\ *adj* **1 :** lacking religious emotions, doctrines, or practices **2 :** indicating lack of religion — **ir·re·li·gious·ly** *adv*

ir·re·me·di·a·ble \,ir-i-'mēd-ē-ə-bəl\ *adj* **:** not remediable; *esp* **:** INCURABLE — **ir·re·me·di·a·ble·ness** *n* — **ir·re·me·di·a·bly** \-blē\ *adv*

ir·re·mov·a·ble \,ir-i-'mü-və-bəl\ *adj* **:** not removable — **ir·re·mov·a·bil·i·ty** \-,mü-və-'bil-ət-ē\ *n* — **ir·re·mov·a·bly** \-'mü-və-blē\ *adv*

ir·rep·a·ra·ble \(')ir-'ep-(ə-)rə-bəl\ *adj* **:** not capable of being repaired, recovered, regained, or remedied ⟨an *irreparable* loss⟩ — **ir·rep·a·ra·ble·ness** *n* — **ir·rep·a·ra·bly** \-blē\ *adv*

ir·re·place·a·ble \,ir-i-'plā-sə-bəl\ *adj* **:** not replaceable

ir·re·press·i·ble \,ir-i-'pres-ə-bəl\ *adj* **:** not capable of being checked or held back ⟨*irrepressible* laughter⟩ — **ir·re·press·i·bil·i·ty** \-,pres-ə-'bil-ət-ē\ *n* — **ir·re·press·i·bly** \-'pres-ə-blē\ *adv*

ir·re·proach·a·ble \-'prō-chə-bəl\ *adj* **:** not reproachable **:** BLAMELESS — **ir·re·proach·a·ble·ness** *n* — **ir·re·proach·a·bly** \-blē\ *adv*

ir·re·sist·i·ble \-'zis-tə-bəl\ *adj* **:** impossible to successfully resist or oppose ⟨an *irresistible* attraction⟩ — **ir·re·sist·i·bil·i·ty** \-,zis-tə-'bil-ət-ē\ *adj* — **ir·re·sist·i·ble·ness** \-'zis-tə-bəl-nəs\ *n* — **ir·re·sist·i·bly** \-blē\ *adv*

ir·res·o·lute \(')ir-'ez-ə-,lüt, -lət\ *adj* **:** uncertain how to act or proceed — **ir·res·o·lute·ly** *adv* — **ir·res·o·lute·ness** *n* — **ir·res·o·lu·tion** \(,)ir-,ez-ə-'lü-shən\ *n*

ir·re·solv·a·ble \,ir-i-'zäl-və-bəl, -'zól-\ *adj* **:** incapable of being resolved

ir·re·spec·tive \,ir-i-'spek-tiv\ *adj* **:** having no regard for persons, conditions, or consequences — **ir·re·spec·tive·ly** *adv*

irrespective of *prep* **:** without regard to

ir·re·spon·si·ble \,ir-i-'spän(t)-sə-bəl\ *adj* **:** not responsible: as **a :** not answerable **b :** said or done with no sense of responsibility ⟨*irresponsible* charges⟩ **c :** lacking a sense of responsibility **d :** unable esp. mentally or financially to bear responsibility — **ir·re·spon·si·bil·i·ty** \-,spän(t)-sə-'bil-ət-ē\ *n* — **ir·re·spon·si·bly** \-'spän(t)-sə-blē\ *adv*

ir·re·spon·sive \-'spän(t)-siv\ *adj* **:** not responsive; *esp* **:** not able, ready, or inclined to respond — **ir·re·spon·sive·ness** *n*

ir·re·triev·a·ble \,ir-i-'trē-və-bəl\ *adj* **:** not capable of being recovered, regained, or remedied ⟨an *irretrievable* mistake⟩ — **ir·re·triev·a·bly** \-blē\ *adv*

ir·rev·er·ence \(')ir-'ev-(ə-)rən(t)s, -'ev-ərn(t)s\ *n* **1 :** lack of reverence **2 :** an irreverent act or utterance

ir·rev·er·ent \-'ev-(ə-)rənt, -'ev-ərnt\ *adj* **:** showing lack of reverence **:** DISRESPECTFUL — **ir·rev·er·ent·ly** *adv*

ir·re·vers·i·ble \,ir-i-'vər-sə-bəl\ *adj* **:** incapable of being reversed — **ir·re·vers·i·bil·i·ty** \-,vər-sə-'bil-ət-ē\ *n* — **ir·re·vers·i·bly** \-'vər-sə-blē\ *adv*

ir·rev·o·ca·ble \(')ir-'ev-ə-kə-bəl\ *adj* **:** not capable of being revoked ⟨an *irrevocable* decision⟩ — **ir·rev·o·ca·bil·i·ty** \(,)ir-,ev-ə-kə-'bil-ət-ē\ *n* — **ir·rev·o·ca·bly** \(')ir-'ev-ə-kə-blē\ *adv*

ir·ri·gate \'ir-ə-,gāt\ *vb* [L *irrigare*, fr. in- ²in- + *rigare* to water] **1 :** WET, MOISTEN: as **a :** to supply (as land) with water by artificial means **b :** to flush with a liquid ⟨*irrigate* a wound⟩ **2 :** to refresh as if by watering **3 :** to practice irrigation — **ir·ri·ga·tion** \,ir-ə-'gā-shən\ *n* — **ir·ri·ga·tor** \'ir-ə-,gāt-ər\ *n*

ir·ri·ta·bil·i·ty \,ir-ət-ə-'bil-ət-ē\ *n, pl* **-ties :** the quality or state of being irritable: as **a :** quick or excessive excitability esp. to annoyance, impatience, or anger **:** PETULANCE **b :** the property of protoplasm and of living organisms that permits them to react to stimuli

ir·ri·ta·ble \'ir-ət-ə-bəl\ *adj* **:** capable of being irritated; *esp* **:** readily or easily irritated — **ir·ri·ta·ble·ness** *n* — **ir·ri·ta·bly** \-blē\ *adv*

ir·ri·tant \'ir-ə-tənt\ *adj* **:** IRRITATING; *esp* **:** tending to produce physical irritation — **irritant** *n*

ir·ri·tate \'ir-ə-,tāt\ *vb* [L *irritare*] **1 :** to excite impatience, anger, or displeasure in **:** ANNOY **2 a :** to induce irritability in or of **:** act as a stimulus toward **b :** to make sore or inflamed : act as an irritant toward — **ir·ri·ta·tive** \-ˌtāt-iv\ *adj*

syn AGGRAVATE, EXASPERATE: IRRITATE implies arousing feelings that may range from impatience to rage; AGGRAVATE may apply to repeated action that intensifies anger or irritation; EXASPERATE suggests intense annoyance or patience strained beyond endurance

ir·ri·ta·tion \ˌir-ə-ˈtā-shən\ *n* **1** : the act of irritating **2** : something that irritates **3** : the state of being irritated

ir·rupt \(ˈ)ir-ˈəpt\ *vi* [L *irrupt-, irrumpere,* fr. *in-* ²*in-* + *rumpere* to break] **1** : to rush in forcibly or violently **2** : to increase suddenly in numbers ⟨rabbits *irrupt* in cycles⟩ — **ir·rup·tion** \(ˈ)ir-ˈəp-shən\ *n*

ir·rup·tive \(ˈ)ir-ˈəp-tiv\ *adj* : irrupting or tending to irrupt — **ir·rup·tive·ly** *adv*

is [OE] *pres 3d sing of* BE

is- *or* **iso-** *comb form* [Gk *isos*] **1** : equal : uniform ⟨*isobar*⟩ **2** : isomeric ⟨*isopropyl*⟩

Isaac \ˈī-zik, -zək\ *n* : a Hebrew patriarch who was the son of Abraham and father of Jacob

Isa·iah \ī-ˈzā-ə\ *or* **Isa·ias** \-əs\ *n* **1** : a Hebrew prophet of the 8th century B.C. **2** — see BIBLE table

is·che·mia \is-ˈkē-mē-ə\ *n* [NL, fr. Gk *ischaimos* styptic, fr. *ischein* to restrain + *haima* blood] : local deficiency of blood due to decreased arterial inflow — **is·che·mic** \-mik\ *adj*

is·chi·um \ˈis-kē-əm\ *n, pl* **-chia** \-kē-ə\ [NL, fr. Gk *ischion* hip joint] : the dorsal and posterior of the three principal bones composing either half of the pelvis — **is·chi·al** \-kē-əl\ *adj*

-ise \ˌīz\ *vb suffix, chiefly Brit* : -IZE

Iseult \i-ˈsült, -ˈzült\ *var of* ISOLDE

-ish \ish\ *adj suffix* [OE *-isc*] **1** : of, relating to, or being ⟨Finn*ish*⟩ **2 a** : characteristic of ⟨boy*ish*⟩ : having the undesirable qualities of ⟨mul*ish*⟩ **b** (1) : having a touch or trace of ⟨summer*ish*⟩ : somewhat ⟨purpl*ish*⟩ (2) : having the approximate age of ⟨forty*ish*⟩ (3) : being or occurring at the approximate time of ⟨eight*ish*⟩

Ish·ma·el \ˈish-mē-əl\ *n* **1** : the outcast son of Abraham and Hagar **2** : a social outcast

Ish·ma·el·ite \-mē-ə-ˌlīt\ *n* **1** : a descendant of Ishmael **2** : ISHMAEL 2 — **Ish·ma·el·it·ish** \-ˌlīt-ish\ *adj* — **Ish·ma·el·it·ism** \-ˌlīt-ˌiz-əm\ *n*

Ish·tar \ˈish-ˌtär\ *n* : the chief goddess of the Babylonian and Assyrian pantheons

isin·glass \ˈīz-ᵊn-ˌglas, ˈī-ziŋ-\ *n* **1** : a very pure gelatin prepared from the air bladders of fishes (as sturgeons) **2** : mica in thin sheets

Isis \ˈī-səs\ *n* : the Egyptian goddess of motherhood and fertility and wife of Osiris

Is·lam \is-ˈläm, iz-, -ˈlam, ˈis-, ˈiz-\ *n* [Ar *islām* submission (to the will of God)] **1** : a religion dominant in much of Asia and northern Africa since the 7th century A.D. that is marked by belief in Allah as the sole deity, in Muhammad as his prophet, and in the Koran **2 a** : the civilization erected upon Islamic faith **b** : the group of modern nations in which Islam is the dominant religion — **Is·lam·ic** \is-ˈläm-ik, iz-, -ˈlam-\ *adj* — **Is·lam·ize** \ˈiz-lə-ˌmīz\ *vt*

¹**is·land** \ˈī-lənd\ *n* [alter. of ME *iland,* fr. OE *igland*] **1** : an area of land surrounded by water and smaller than a continent **2** : something (as a safety zone in a street) suggestive of an island **3** : a superstructure on the deck of an aircraft carrier

²**island** *vt* **1 a** : to make into or as if into an island **b** : to dot with or as if with islands **2** : ISOLATE

is·land·er \ˈī-lən-dər\ *n* : a native or inhabitant of an island

island of Langerhans : ISLET OF LANGERHANS

island universe *n* : a galaxy other than the Milky Way

isle \ˈīl\ *n* [OF, fr. L *insula*] : ISLAND; *esp* : a small island

is·let \ˈī-lət\ *n* : a little island

islet of Lang·er·hans \-ˈläŋ-ər-ˌhän(t)s, -ˌhänz\ [Paul *Langerhans* d1888 German physician] : any of the groups of small granular endocrine cells that form interlacing strands in the pancreas and secrete insulin

ism \ˈiz-əm\ *n* [-ism] : a distinctive doctrine, cause, or theory

-ism \ˌiz-əm\ *n suffix* [Gk *-isma* & *-ismos,* fr. verbs in *-izein* -ize] **1 a** : act : practice : process ⟨critic*ism*⟩ ⟨plagiar*ism*⟩ **b** : manner of action or behavior characteristic of a (specified) person or thing ⟨animal*ism*⟩ **2 a** : state : condition : property ⟨barbarian*ism*⟩ **b** : abnormal state or condition resulting from excess of a (specified) thing ⟨alcohol*ism*⟩ or marked by resemblance to (such) a person or thing ⟨mongol*ism*⟩ **3 a** : doctrine : theory : cult ⟨Buddh*ism*⟩ **b** : adherence to a system or a class of principles ⟨stoic*ism*⟩ **4** : characteristic or peculiar feature or trait ⟨colloquial*ism*⟩

isn't \ˈiz-ᵊnt\ : is not

iso·bar \ˈī-sə-ˌbär\ *n* [Gk *baros* weight] : a line drawn on a map to indicate areas having the same atmospheric pressure at a given time or for a given period — **iso·bar·ic** \ˌī-sə-ˈbär-ik, -ˈbar-\ *adj*

iso·di·a·met·ric \ˌī-sō-ˌdī-ə-ˈme-trik\ *adj* : having equal diameters

iso·elec·tric \ˌī-sō-i-ˈlek-trik\ *adj* : having or representing zero difference of electrical potential

iso·ga·mete \ˌī-sō-gə-ˈmēt, -ˈgam-ˌēt\ *n* : a gamete indistinguishable from another gamete with which it can unite to form a zygote — **iso·ga·met·ic** \-gə-ˈmet-ik\ *adj*

isog·a·mous \ī-ˈsäg-ə-məs\ *adj* : having or involving isogametes — **isog·a·mous·ly** *adv* — **isog·a·my** \-mē\ *n*

iso·gon·ic line \ˌī-sə-ˌgän-ik-\ *n* [Gk *gōnia* angle] : an imaginary line or a line on a map joining points on the earth's surface at which the magnetic declination is the same

iso·late \ˈī-sə-ˌlāt, ˈis-ə-\ *vb* [back-formation fr. *isolated* set apart, fr. F *isolé,* fr. It *isolato,* fr. *isola* island, fr. L *insula*] **1** : to set apart from others; *also* : QUARANTINE **2** : to select from among others; *esp* : to separate from other substances so as to obtain pure or in a free state

iso·la·tion \ˌī-sə-ˈlā-shən, ˌis-ə-\ *n* : the act of isolating : the condition of being isolated

iso·la·tion·ism \-shə-ˌniz-əm\ *n* : a policy of national isolation by avoiding international political and economic relations (as alliances) — **iso·la·tion·ist** \-sh(ə-)nəst\ *n or adj*

Isol·de \i-ˈzōl-də\ *n* : an Irish princess married to King Mark of Cornwall and loved by Tristram

iso·leu·cine \ˌī-sō-ˈlü-ˌsēn\ *n* : a crystalline essential amino acid isomeric with leucine

iso·mer \ˈī-sə-mər\ *n* : a compound, radical, ion, or nuclide exhibiting isomerism with one or more others

isom·er·ism \ī-ˈsäm-ə-ˌriz-əm\ *n* **1** : the relation of two or more chemical compounds, radicals, or ions that contain the same numbers of atoms of the same elements but differ in structural arrangement and properties **2** : the relation of two or more nuclides with the same mass numbers and atomic numbers but different energy states and rates of radioactive decay **3** : the condition of being isomerous — **iso·mer·ic** \ˌī-sə-ˈmer-ik\ *adj*

isom·er·ize \ī-ˈsäm-ə-ˌrīz\ *vb* : to change or cause to change into an isomeric form — **isom·er·i·za·tion** \ī-ˌsäm-ə-rə-ˈzā-shən\ *n*

isom·er·ous \ī-ˈsäm-ə-rəs\ *adj* : having an equal number of parts (as ridges or markings); *esp* : having the members of each floral whorl equal in number

iso·met·ric \ˌī-sə-ˈme-trik\ *adj* **1** : of, relating to, or characterized by equality of measure **2** : relating to or being a crystallographic system characterized by three equal axes at right angles — **iso·met·ri·cal·ly** \-tri-k(ə-)lē\ *adv*

iso·mor·phic \ˌī-sə-ˈmòr-fik\ *adj* : having or involving structural similarity or identity — **iso·morph** \ˈī-sə-ˌmòrf\ *n* — **iso·mor·phism** \ˌī-sə-ˈmòr-ˌfiz-əm\ *n*

iso·ni·a·zid \ˌī-sə-ˈnī-ə-zəd\ *n* : a crystalline compound used in the treatment of tuberculosis

iso·pod \ˈī-sə-ˌpäd\ *n* : any of a large order (Isopoda) of small sessile-eyed crustaceans having seven free thoracic segments each bearing a pair of similar legs — **isopod** *adj* — **isop·o·dan** \ī-ˈsäp-əd-ən\ *adj or n*

isos·ce·les trapezoid \ī-ˌsäs-ə-ˌlēz-\ *n* : a trapezoid whose two nonparallel sides are equal

isosceles triangle *n* [Gk *isoskelēs* having two equal sides, fr. *skelos* leg] : a triangle having two equal sides — see TRIANGLE illustration

isos·ta·sy \ī-ˈsäs-tə-sē\ *n* [Gk *-stasia* condition of standing, fr. *histanai* to cause to stand] : general equilibrium in the earth's crust maintained by a yielding flow of rock material beneath the surface under the force of gravity — **iso·stat·ic** \ˌī-sə-ˈstat-ik\ *adj*

---

j joke; ŋ sing; ō flow; ò flaw; òi coin; th thin; th̲ this; ü loot; u̇ foot; y yet; yü few; yu̇ furious; zh vision

iso·therm \\'ī-sə-ˌthərm\\ *n* [Gk *thermē* heat] : a line on a map connecting points having the same temperature at a given time or the same mean temperature for a given period

iso·ther·mal \\ˌī-sə-'thər-məl\\ *adj* : of, relating to, or marked by equality of temperature

iso·ton·ic \\ˌī-sə-'tän-ik\\ *adj* [Gk *tonos* tension, tone] : having the same or equal osmotic pressure ⟨a salt solution *isotonic* with red blood cells⟩ — **iso·ton·i·cal·ly** \\-'tän-i-k(ə-)lē\\ *adv*

iso·tope \\'ī-sə-ˌtōp\\ *n* [Gk *topos* place] : any of two or more species of atoms of a chemical element with the same atomic number and position in the periodic table and nearly identical chemical behavior but with differing atomic mass or mass number and different physical properties — **iso·top·ic** \\ˌī-sə-'täp-ik, -'tō-pik\\ *adj* — **iso·top·i·cal·ly** \\-'täp-i-k(ə-)lē, -'tō-pi-\\ *adv*

Is·ra·el \\'iz-rē-əl\\ *n* 1 : JACOB 2 : the Jewish people 3 : God's chosen people — **Israel** *adj*

Is·ra·el·ite \\'iz-rē-ə-ˌlīt\\ *n* : a descendant of the Hebrew patriarch Jacob; *esp* : a native or inhabitant of the ancient northern kingdom of Israel — **Israelite** *or* **Is·ra·el·it·ish** \\-ˌlīt-ish\\ *adj*

is·su·a·ble \\'ish-ə-ə-bəl\\ *adj* : capable of being issued

is·su·ance \\'ish-ə-ən(t)s\\ *n* : the act of issuing or giving out esp. officially

¹is·sue \\'ish-(ˌ)ü\\ *n* [MF, fr. *issir* to come out, go out, fr. L *exire*, fr. *ex-* + *ire* to go] 1 : the action of going, coming, or flowing out : EGRESS, EMERGENCE 2 : a means or place of going out : EXIT, OUTLET 3 : OFFSPRING, PROGENY 4 : final outcome : RESULT 5 a : a matter in dispute : a point of debate or controversy b : a final result or conclusion : DECISION 6 : a discharge (as of blood) from the body 7 : something coming forth from a specified source ⟨*issues* of a disordered imagination⟩ 8 a : the act of officially giving out (as new currency, supplies, or an order) : PUBLICATION b : the thing or the whole quantity of things given out at one time ⟨new *issue* of stamps⟩ ⟨stock *issue*⟩ — **at issue** 1 : in a state of controversy : in disagreement 2 *also* **in issue** : under discussion or in dispute

²issue *vb* 1 a : to go, come, or flow out b : to come forth or cause to come forth : EMERGE, DISCHARGE, EMIT 2 : ACCRUE 3 : to descend from a specified parent or ancestor 4 : to be a consequence or final outcome : RESULT 5 : to appear through issuance or publication 6 : to have an outcome : result in 7 a : to put forth or distribute officially ⟨government *issued* a new airmail stamp⟩ ⟨*issue* orders to advance⟩ ⟨*issued* rifles and rations⟩ b : to send out for sale or circulation : PUBLISH — **is·su·er** *n*

¹-ist \\əst\\ *n suffix* [Gk *-istēs*, fr. verbs in *-izein* *-ize*] 1 a : one that performs a (specified) action ⟨cyclist⟩ b : one that plays a (specified) musical instrument ⟨harpist⟩ c : one that operates a (specified) mechanical instrument or contrivance ⟨automobilist⟩ 2 : one that specializes in a (specified) art or science or skill ⟨geologist⟩ ⟨ventriloquist⟩ 3 : one that adheres to or advocates a (specified) doctrine or system or code of behavior ⟨socialist⟩ ⟨royalist⟩ ⟨hedonist⟩ or that of a (specified) individual ⟨Calvinist⟩ ⟨Darwinist⟩

²-ist *adj suffix* : of, relating to, or characteristic of ⟨dilettantist⟩

¹isth·mi·an \\'is-mē-ən\\ *n* : a native or inhabitant of an isthmus

²isthmian *adj* : of, relating to, or situated in or near an isthmus: as a *often cap* : of or relating to the Isthmus of Corinth in Greece or the games anciently held there b *often cap* : of or relating to the Isthmus of Panama

isth·mic \\'is-mik\\ *adj* : ISTHMIAN

isth·mus \\'is-məs\\ *n* [Gk *isthmos*] 1 : a narrow strip of land connecting two larger land areas 2 : a narrow anatomical part or passage connecting two larger structures or cavities

-is·tic \\'is-tik\\ *also* **-is·ti·cal** \\-ti-kəl\\ *adj suffix* [Gk *-istikos*, fr. *-istēs* *-ist* + *-ikos* *-ic*] : of, relating to, or characteristic of ⟨altruistic⟩

is·tle \\'ist-lē\\ *n* [AmerSp *ixtle*, fr. Nahuatl *ichtli*] : a strong fiber (as for cordage or basketry) from tropical American plants

¹it \\(')it, ət\\ *pron* [OE *hit*, neut. of *hē* he] 1 : that one —

used usu. in reference to a lifeless thing ⟨caught the ball and threw *it* back⟩, a plant, a person or animal whose sex is unknown or disregarded ⟨don't know who *it* is⟩, a group of individuals or things, or an abstract entity; compare HE, ITS, SHE, THEY 2 — used as subject of a verb that expresses a condition or action without reference to an agent ⟨*it* is raining⟩ 3 a — used as anticipatory subject or object of a verb ⟨*it* is necessary to repeat the whole thing⟩; often used to shift emphasis to a part of a statement other than the subject ⟨*it* was in this city that the treaty was signed⟩ b — used with many verbs as a direct object with little or no meaning ⟨footed *it* back to camp⟩ 4 : the general state of affairs or circumstances ⟨how is *it* going⟩

²it \\'it\\ *n* : the player in a game who performs a function (as trying to catch others in a game of tag) essential to the nature of the game

Ital·ian \\ə-'tal-yən, i-\\ *n* 1 a : a native or inhabitant of Italy b : a person of Italian descent 2 : the Romance language of the Italians — **Italian** *adj*

Italian sonnet *n* : a sonnet consisting of an octave rhyming *abba abba* and a sestet rhyming in any of several patterns (as *cde cde* or *cdc dcd*)

¹ital·ic \\ə-'tal-ik, i-, ī-\\ *adj* 1 *cap* : of or relating to ancient Italy, its peoples, or their Indo-European languages 2 : of or relating to a type style with characters that slant upward to the right (as in "*these words are italic*")

²italic *n* : an italic character or type

ital·i·cize \\ə-'tal-ə-ˌsīz, i-, ī-\\ *vt* : to print in italics : underscore with a single line

¹itch \\'ich\\ *vb* [ME *icchen*, fr. OE *giccan*] 1 : to have or produce an itch 2 : to cause to itch 3 : to have a strong persistent desire for something ⟨just *itching* to get at the new car⟩

²itch *n* 1 a : an uneasy irritating sensation in the skin usu. held to result from mild stimulation of pain receptors b : a skin disorder accompanied by an itch; *esp* : a contagious eruption caused by a mite 2 a : a restless usu. constant often compulsive desire b : LUST, PRURIENCE — **itch·i·ness** \\'ich-ē-nəs\\ *n* — **itchy** \\-ē\\ *adj*

it'd \\ˌit-əd\\ : it had : it would

¹-ite \\ˌīt\\ *n suffix* [Gk *-itēs*] 1 a : native : resident ⟨Brooklynite⟩ b : descendant ⟨Ishmaelite⟩ c : adherent : follower ⟨Jacobite⟩ 2 : product ⟨metabolite⟩ ⟨ebonite⟩ 3 : fossil ⟨ammonite⟩ 4 : mineral ⟨halite⟩ : rock ⟨quartzite⟩ 5 : segment or constituent part ⟨somite⟩

²-ite *n suffix* [F, alter. of *-ate* ¹*-ate*, fr. NL *-atum*] : salt or ester of an acid with a name ending in *-ous* ⟨sulfite⟩ ⟨nitrite⟩

¹item \\'ī-ˌtem, 'īt-əm\\ *adv* [L, fr. *ita* thus] : and in addition : ALSO — used to introduce each article in a list or enumeration

²item \\'īt-əm\\ *n* 1 : a separate particular in an enumeration, account, or series : ARTICLE ⟨one *item* in a bill⟩ 2 : a separate piece of news or information : a short news paragraph ⟨column of local *items*⟩

item·i·za·tion \\ˌīt-ə-mə-'zā-shən\\ *n* : the act of itemizing; *also* : an itemized list

item·ize \\'īt-ə-ˌmīz\\ *vt* : to set down in detail or by particulars : LIST ⟨*itemize* expenditures⟩

it·er·ance \\'it-ə-rən(t)s\\ *n* : REITERATION

it·er·ant \\-rənt\\ *adj* : ITERATING

it·er·ate \\'it-ə-ˌrāt\\ *vt* [L *iterare*, fr. *iterum* again] : REITERATE, REPEAT — **it·er·a·tion** \\ˌit-ə-'rā-shən\\ *n* — **it·er·a·tive** \\'it-ə-ˌrāt-iv, -rət-\\ *adj*

itin·er·ant \\ī-'tin-ə-rənt, ə-'tin-\\ *adj* [LL *itinerari* to journey, fr. L *itiner-, iter* journey, fr. *ire* to go] : traveling from place to place; *esp* : covering a circuit ⟨*itinerant* preacher⟩ — **itin·er·an·cy** \\-rən-sē\\ *or* **itin·er·a·cy** \\-rə-sē\\ *n* — **itinerant** *n* — **itin·er·ant·ly** *adv*

itin·er·ary \\ī-'tin-ə-ˌrer-ē, ə-\\ *n, pl* **-ar·ies** 1 : the route of a journey 2 : a travel diary 3 : a traveler's guidebook — **itinerary** *adj*

itin·er·ate \\ī-'tin-ə-ˌrāt, ə-\\ *vi* : to travel about on a circuit esp. for the purpose of preaching — **itin·er·a·tion** \\(ˌ)ī-ˌtin-ə-'rā-shən, ə-ˌtin-\\ *n*

-i·tious \\'ish-əs\\ *adj suffix* [L *-icius, -itius*] : of, relating to, or having the characteristics of ⟨cementitious⟩

-i·tis \\'īt-əs *also* but not shown at individual entries '−ēt-\\ *n suffix, pl* **-i·tis·es** *also* **-it·i·des** \\'it-ə-ˌdēz\\ *sometimes* **-i·tes** \\'īt-(ˌ)ēz, 'ēt-\\ 1 : inflamed state or inflammatory disorder of ⟨bronchitis⟩ 2 a : heated or excessive response (as of distress or enthusiasm) to ⟨vacationitis⟩

ə abut; ə kitten; ər further; a back; ā bake; ä cot, cart; aú out; ch chin; e less; ē easy; g gift; i trip; ī life

⟨television*itis*⟩ **b** : excess of the qualities of ⟨big-business-*itis*⟩

it'll \,it-ºl\ : it shall : it will

its \(,)its, əts\ *adj* : of or relating to it or itself esp. as possessor ⟨going to *its* kennel⟩, agent ⟨a child proud of *its* first drawings⟩, or object of an action ⟨*its* final enactment into law⟩

it's \(,)its, əts\ **1** : it is **2** : it has

it·self \it-'self, ət-\ *pron* **1** : that identical one — compare ¹IT 1; used reflexively ⟨watched the cat giving *itself* a bath⟩ or for emphasis ⟨the letter *itself* was missing⟩ **2** : its normal, healthy, or sane condition or self

-ity \ət-ē\ *n suffix, pl* **-ities** [OF or L; OF *-ité*, fr. L *-itat-*, *-itas*, fr. *-i-* (stem vowel of adjs.) + *-tat-*, *-tas* -ity] : quality : state : degree ⟨alkalin*ity*⟩

IUD \,ī-,yü-'dē\ *n* : INTRAUTERINE DEVICE

-ium *n suffix* [NL, fr. L, ending of some neut. nouns] **1** : chemical element ⟨sod*ium*⟩ **2** : chemical radical ⟨ammon*ium*⟩

-ive \iv\ *adj suffix* [L *-ivus*] : that performs or tends toward an (indicated) action ⟨regress*ive*⟩ ⟨correct*ive*⟩

I've \(,)īv\ : I have

ivied \'ī-vēd\ *adj* : overgrown with ivy

ivo·ry \'īv-(ə-)rē\ *n, pl* **-ries** [OF *ivoire*, fr. L *eboreus* of ivory, fr. *ebor-, ebur* ivory, fr. Egypt *;b* elephant, ivory] **1** : the hard creamy-white modified dentine that composes the tusks of a tusked mammal (as an elephant) **2** : a variable color averaging a pale yellow **3** *slang* : TOOTH **4** : something (as piano keys) made of ivory or of a similar substance

ivory black *n* : a fine black pigment made by calcining ivory

ivory tower *n* : a secluded place for meditation : RETREAT

ivy \'ī-vē\ *n, pl* **ivies** [OE *īfig*] **1** : a widely cultivated woody Eurasian vine of the ginseng family with glossy evergreen leaves, small yellowish flowers, and black berries **2** : any of several plants resembling ivy

Ivy League *adj* : of, relating to, or characteristic of a group of long-established eastern U.S. colleges widely regarded as high in scholastic and social prestige

iwis \ē-'wis, ī-\ *adv* [ME, fr. OE *gewis* certain] *archaic* : CERTAINLY

Ix·i·on \ik-'sī-ən\ *n* : a Thessalian king punished by Zeus for aspiring to love Hera by being bound in Tartarus to an endlessly revolving wheel

ivy

-iza·tion \ə-'zā-shən *also esp when an unstressed syllable precedes but not shown at individual entries* (,)ī-'zā-\ *n suffix* : action : process : state

-ize \,īz\ *vb suffix* [Gk *-izein*] **1 a** (1) : cause to be or conform to or resemble ⟨system*ize*⟩ ⟨american*ize*⟩ : cause to be formed into ⟨union*ize*⟩ (2) : subject to a (specified) action ⟨satir*ize*⟩ (3) : saturate, treat, or combine with ⟨oxid*ize*⟩ ⟨macadam*ize*⟩ **b** : treat like ⟨idol*ize*⟩ **2 a** : become : become like ⟨crystall*ize*⟩ **b** : be productive in or of ⟨hypothes*ize*⟩ : engage in a (specified) activity ⟨philosoph*ize*⟩ **c** : adopt or spread the manner of activity or the teaching of ⟨calvin*ize*⟩

iz·zard \'iz-ərd\ *n* [alter. of earlier *ezod, ezed*, prob. fr. MF *et zede* and Z] *chiefly dial* : the letter z

---

j \'jā\ *n, often cap* : the 10th letter of the English alphabet

jab \'jab\ *vb* **jabbed**; **jab·bing** : to thrust quickly or abruptly with or as if with something sharp : POKE — **jab** *n*

¹jab·ber \'jab-ər\ *vb* **jab·bered**; **jab·ber·ing** \-(ə-)riŋ\ [ME *jaberen*] : to talk or speak rapidly, indistinctly, or unintelligibly — **jab·ber·er** \'jab-ər-ər\ *n*

²jabber *n* : GIBBERISH, CHATTER

jab·ber·wocky \'jab-ər-,wäk-ē\ *n* [*Jabberwocky*, nonsense poem by Lewis Carroll] : meaningless speech or writing

---

ja·bot \zha-'bō, ja-\ *n* [F] : a ruffle of cloth or lace that falls from the collar down the front of a dress or shirt

jac·a·ran·da \,jak-ə-,ran-'dä, -'ran-də\ *n* [Pg] : a tropical American tree often grown for its showy panicles of blue flowers

ja·cinth \'jās-ºn(t)th\ *n* [OF *jacinthe*, fr. L *hyacinthus*] : HYACINTH

¹jack \'jak\ *n* [*Jack*, nickname for *John*] **1** *often cap* **a** : MAN; *esp* : one of the common people **b** : SAILOR **2 a** : a device for turning a spit (as in roasting meat) **b** : any of various portable mechanisms for exerting pressure or lifting a heavy body a short distance **3** : any of various animals: as **a** : a young male salmon **b** : a male ass **c** : JACKDAW **d** : JACKRABBIT **4 a** : something small of its kind ⟨*jack* rafter⟩ **b** : a small target ball in lawn bowling **c** : a small national flag flown by a ship **d** (1) : a small 6-pointed metal object used in a game (2) *pl* : a game played with jacks **5** : a playing card bearing the stylized figure of a man **6** *slang* : MONEY **7** : a socket in an electric circuit used with a plug to make a connection with another circuit

jack 2b

²jack *vb* **1** : to hunt or fish for game at night with a jacklight **2** : to move or lift by or as if by a jack **3** : INCREASE, RAISE ⟨*jack* up prices⟩ — **jack·er** *n*

jack·al \'jak-əl, -,ȯl\ *n* [Turk *çakal*, fr. Per *shagāl*, fr. Skt *śṛgāla*] **1** : any of several Old World wild dogs smaller than the related wolves **2** : a person who performs routine or menial and often base tasks for another

jack·a·napes \'jak-ə-,nāps\ *n* [ME *Jack Napis*, nickname for William de la Pole *d*1450 duke of Suffolk] **1** : MONKEY, APE **2** : an impudent or conceited person

jack·ass \'jak-,as\ *n* **1** : a male ass; *also* : DONKEY **2** : a stupid person : FOOL

jack·ass·ery \-,as-(ə-)rē\ *n* : a stupid or foolish act

jack·boot \'jak-,büt\ *n* **1** : a heavy military boot of glossy black leather extending above the knee **2** : a laceless military boot reaching to the calf

jack·daw \'jak-,dȯ\ *n* : a common black and gray Eurasian bird related to but smaller than the common crow

jack·et \'jak-ət\ *n* [MF *jaquet*, dim. of *jaque* peasant's coat, fr. *jacques* peasant, fr. *Jaques* James] **1** : a garment for the upper body usu. having a front opening, collar, and sleeves **2** : an outer covering or casing: as **a** : a tough metal covering on a bullet or projectile **b** : a coating or covering of a nonconducting material used to prevent heat radiation **c** : a detachable outer paper wrapper on a bound book — **jack·et·ed** \-ət-əd\ *adj*

Jack Frost *n* : frost or frosty weather personified

jack-in-the-box \'jak-ən-thə-,bäks\ *n, pl* **jack-in-the-boxes** *or* **jacks-in-the-box** : a small box out of which a figure (as of a clown's head) springs when the lid is raised

jack-in-the-pul·pit \,jak-ən-thə-'pul-,pit\ *n, pl* **jack-in-the-pulpits** *or* **jacks-in-the-pulpit** : any of several plants of the arum family; *esp* : an American spring-flowering woodland herb with an upright club-shaped flower cluster arched over by a green and purple spathe

¹jack·knife \'jak-,nīf\ *n* **1** : a large strong clasp knife for the pocket **2** : a dive in which the diver bends from the waist and touches his ankles before straightening out

²jackknife *vi* **1** : to double up like a jackknife **2** : to turn or twist and form an angle of 90 degrees or less with each other — used esp. of a pair of connected vehicles

jack·leg \'jak-,leg\ *adj* **1** : lacking skill or training : AMATEUR ⟨*jackleg* carpenter⟩ **2** : designed as a temporary expedient : MAKESHIFT

jack·light \'jak-,līt\ *n* : a light used esp. in hunting or fishing at night

jack-of-all-trades \,jak-ə-'vȯl-,trādz\ *n, pl* **jacks-of-all-trades** : a person who can do passable work at various trades : HANDYMAN

jack-o'-lan·tern \'jak-ə-,lant-ərn\ *n* **1** : IGNIS FATUUS **2** : a lantern made of a pumpkin cut to look like a human face

jack pine *n* : a No. American pine with paired twisted needles that is used for pulp and box lumber

jack·pot \'jak-,pät\ *n* **1 a** : a large pot (as in poker) formed by the accumulation of stakes from previous play **b** (1) : a combination on a slot machine that wins a top

---

prize or all the coins in the machine (2) **:** the sum so won **2 :** an impressive often unexpected success or reward

jack·rab·bit \-‚rab-ət\ n [jackass + rabbit; fr. its long ears] **:** any of several large hares of western No. America with long ears and long hind legs

jack·screw \-‚skrü\ n **:** a screw-operated jack for lifting or for exerting pressure

Jack·so·ni·an \jak-'sō-nē-ən\ adj **:** of, relating to, or characteristic of Andrew Jackson or his political principles or policies — **Jacksonian** n

jack·stone \'jak-‚stōn\ n **1 :** JACK 4d(1) **2** pl **:** JACK 4d(2)

jack·straw \-‚strȯ\ n **1 :** one of the pieces used in the game jackstraws **2** pl **:** a game in which a set of straws or thin strips are let fall in a heap with each player in turn trying to remove them one at a time without disturbing the rest

jack·tar \-'tär\ n, often cap **:** SAILOR

Ja·cob \'jā-kəb\ n **:** a Hebrew patriarch who was the son of Isaac and Rebekah

Jac·o·be·an \‚jak-ə-'bē-ən\ adj [LL Jacobus James] **:** of, relating to, or characteristic of James I of England or his age — **Jacobean** n

Jac·o·bin \'jak-ə-bən\ n [F, fr. Jacobin Dominican (fr. LL Jacobus James; fr. the location of the first Dominican convent in Paris in the street of St. James — Rue St. Jacques); so called fr. the group's having been founded in a former Dominican convent] **:** a member of a radical political group advocating egalitarian democracy and engaging in terrorist activities during the French Revolution of 1789 — **Jac·o·bin·ism** \-bə-‚niz-əm\ n

Jac·o·bite \'jak-ə-‚bīt\ n **:** a partisan of James II of England or of the Stuarts after the revolution of 1688 — **Jac·o·bit·i·cal** \‚jak-ə-'bit-i-kəl\ adj — **Jac·o·bit·ism** \'jak-ə-‚bīt-‚iz-əm\ n

Jacob's ladder n **1 :** a ladder extending from earth to heaven seen by the patriarch Jacob in a dream **2 :** a ship's ladder of rope or chain with wooden or iron rungs

jac·o·net \'jak-ə-‚net\ n **:** a lightweight cotton cloth used for clothing and bandages

jac·quard \'jak-‚ärd\ n, often cap [after Joseph Jacquard d1834 French inventor of a loom head] **:** a fabric of intricate variegated weave or pattern

¹jade \'jād\ n [ME] **1 :** a broken-down, vicious, or worthless horse **2 :** a disreputable woman

²jade vb **1 a :** to wear out by overwork or abuse **b :** to tire by tedious tasks **2 :** to become weary

³jade n [F, fr. obs. Sp piedra de la ijada, lit., loin stone; fr. the belief that it cured renal colic] **:** a tough compact usu. green gemstone that takes a high polish

jad·ed \'jād-əd\ adj **1 :** EXHAUSTED **2 :** SATIATED — **jad·ed·ly** adv — **jad·ed·ness** n

jade green n **:** a variable color averaging a light bluish green

jae·ger \'yā-gər\ n [G jäger hunter] **:** any of several large dark-colored rapacious birds of northern seas

¹jag \'jag\ vb **jagged** \'jagd\; **jag·ging** [ME jaggen] **:** to make ragged **:** NOTCH

²jag n **:** a sharp projecting part **:** BARB

³jag n **1 :** a small load (as of hay) **2 :** a drunken spree

jag·ged \'jag-əd\ adj **:** sharply notched **:** ROUGH ⟨a jagged edge⟩ — **jag·ged·ly** adv — **jag·ged·ness** n

jag·uar \'jag-‚wär, 'jag-yə-‚wär\ n [Sp yaguar & Pg jaguar, of AmerInd origin] **:** a large cat of tropical America that is larger and stockier than the leopard and is brownish yellow or buff with black spots

jag·ua·run·di \‚jag-wə-'rən-dē\ n [AmerSp & Pg, of AmerInd origin] **:** a slender long-tailed short-legged grayish wildcat of Central and So. America

jai alai \'hī-‚lī, ‚hī-ə-'lī\ n [Sp, fr. Basque, fr. jai festival + alai merry] **:** a court game played by two or four players with a ball and a long curved wicker basket strapped to the right wrist

¹jail \'jāl\ n [OF jaiole, fr. (assumed) VL caveola, dim. of L cavea cage] **:** PRISON; esp **:** a building for the confinement of persons held in temporary custody

²jail vt **:** to confine in or as if in a jail

jail·bird \'jāl-‚bərd\ n **:** a person confined in jail; esp **:** a habitual criminal

jail·break \-‚brāk\ n **:** a forcible escape from jail

jail·er or **jail·or** \'jā-lər\ n **:** the keeper of a jail

Jain \'jīn\ or **Jai·na** \'jī-nə\ n **:** an adherent of Jainism

Jain·ism \'jī-‚niz-əm\ n **:** a religion of India originating in the 6th century B.C. and teaching liberation of the soul by right knowledge, right faith, and right conduct

jal·ap \'jal-əp, 'jäl-\ n [F jalap, fr. Sp jalapa, fr. Jalapa, Mexico] **:** a purgative tuberous root obtained esp. from a Mexican plant related to the morning glory; also **:** a drug prepared from this

ja·lopy \jə-'läp-ē\ n, pl **-lop·ies :** a dilapidated old automobile or airplane

jal·ou·sie \'jal-ə-sē\ n [F, lit., jealousy] **1 :** a blind with adjustable horizontal slats for admitting light and air while excluding sun and rain **2 :** a window made of adjustable glass louvers that control ventilation

¹jam \'jam\ vb **jammed; jam·ming 1 a :** to press into a close or tight position ⟨jam his hat on⟩ **b :** to cause to become wedged so as to be unworkable ⟨jam the typewriter keys⟩ **c :** to block passage of **:** OBSTRUCT **d :** to fill full or to excess **:** PACK **2 :** to push forcibly; esp **:** to apply the brakes suddenly with full force **3 :** CRUSH, BRUISE **4 :** to make unintelligible by sending out interfering signals or messages ⟨jam a radio program⟩ **5 :** to become unworkable through the jamming of a movable part ⟨the burglar was unable to shoot when his gun jammed⟩ **6 :** to force one's way into a restricted space — **jam·mer** n

²jam n **1 a :** an act or instance of jamming **b :** a crowded mass that impedes or blocks ⟨traffic jam⟩ **2 :** a difficult state of affairs

³jam n **:** a food made by boiling fruit and sugar to a thick consistency

jamb \'jam\ n [MF jambe, lit., leg, fr. LL gamba] **:** an upright piece forming the side of an opening (as of a door)

jam·ba·laya \‚jəm-bə-'lī-ə\ n [LaF] **:** rice cooked with ham, sausage, chicken, shrimp, or oysters and seasoned with herbs

jam·bo·ree \‚jam-bə-'rē\ n **1 :** a large festive gathering **2 :** a national or international camping assembly of boy scouts

James \'jāmz\ n **1 :** one of the twelve apostles, a son of Zebedee and brother of the apostle John **2 :** one of the twelve apostles, a son of Alphaeus — called also James the Less **3 a :** a brother of Jesus held to be the author of the New Testament Epistle of James **b** — see BIBLE table

jam session n **:** an impromptu performance by a group of jazz musicians characterized by group improvisation

¹jan·gle \'jaŋ-gəl\ vb **jan·gled; jan·gling** \-g(ə-)liŋ\ [OF jangler] **1 :** to quarrel verbally **2 a :** to make a harsh or discordant sound **b :** to cause to sound harshly or inharmoniously — **jan·gler** \-g(ə-)lər\ n

²jangle n **1 :** noisy quarreling **2 :** discordant sound

jan·is·sary or **jan·i·zary** \'jan-ə-‚ser-ē, -‚zer-\ n, pl **-sar·ies** or **-zar·ies** [It gianizzero, fr. Turk yeniçeri] often cap **:** a soldier of a select corps of Turkish troops organized in the 14th century and abolished in 1826

jan·i·tor \'jan-ət-ər\ n [L, fr. janua door, fr. Janus] **1 :** DOORKEEPER **2 :** a person who has the care of a building (as a school or an apartment house) — **jan·i·to·ri·al** \‚jan-ə-'tōr-ē-əl, -'tȯr-\ adj — **jan·i·tress** \'jan-ə-trəs\ n

Jan·u·ary \'jan-yə-‚wer-ē\ n [L Januarius, fr. Janus] **:** the 1st month of the year

Ja·nus \'jā-nəs\ n **:** an ancient Roman god of gates and doors and of beginnings and endings represented with two opposite faces

¹ja·pan \jə-'pan\ n [Japan, country of Asia] **1 :** a varnish giving a hard brilliant surface coating **2 :** work varnished and figured in the Japanese manner

²japan vt **ja·panned; ja·pan·ning :** to cover with or as if with a coat of japan

Japan current n **:** a warm current of the north Pacific flowing from the east coast of the Philippines north along the east coast of Japan and thence eastward — called also Japanese current

Jap·a·nese \‚jap-ə-'nēz, -'nēs\ n, pl **Japanese 1 a :** a native or inhabitant of Japan **b :** a person of Japanese descent **2 :** the language of the Japanese — **Japanese** adj

Japanese beetle n **:** a small metallic green and brown scarab beetle introduced into America from Japan that as a grub feeds on the roots of grasses and decaying vegetation and as an adult eats foliage and fruits

Japanese iris *n* : any of various beardless garden irises with very large showy flowers

Japanese mink *n* : an Asiatic weasel; *also* : its pale yellowish brown fur

Japanese persimmon *n* : an Asiatic persimmon widely grown for its large edible fruits

Japanese quince *n* : a hardy Chinese ornamental shrub of the rose family with scarlet flowers

¹**jape** \'jāp\ *vb* [ME *japen*] **1** : JOKE, FOOL **2** : MOCK — **jap·er** \'jā-pər\ *n* — **jap·ery** \'jā-p(ə-)rē\ *n*

²**jape** *n* : JEST, GIBE

ja·pon·i·ca \jə-'pän-i-kə\ *n* : JAPANESE QUINCE

¹**jar** \'jär\ *vb* **jarred; jar·ring** **1 a** : to make a harsh or discordant sound **b** : to have a harsh or disagreeable effect **2** : to undergo severe vibration **3** : to make unstable **4** : SHAKE, CLASH, QUARREL

²**jar** *n* **1** : a harsh sound **2** : JOLT **3** : QUARREL, DISPUTE **4** : a painful effect : SHOCK

³**jar** *n* [MF *jarre*, fr. OProv *jarra*, fr. Ar *jarrah*] **1** : a widemouthed container usu. of earthenware or glass **2** : JARFUL

jar·di·niere \,järd-ᵊn-'i(ə)r\ *n* [F *jardinière*, lit., female gardener] : an ornamental stand or pot for plants or flowers

jar·ful \'jär-,fúl\ *n, pl* **jarfuls** \-,fúlz\ *or* **jars·ful** \'järz-,fúl\ : the quantity held by a jar

jar·gon \'jär-gən, -,gän\ *n* [MF] **1 a** : confused unintelligible language **b** : a hybrid language or dialect used for communication between peoples of different speech **2** : the special vocabulary or idiom of a particular activity or group **3** : obscure and often pretentious language marked by circumlocutions and abstract words **syn** see DIALECT

jas·mine \'jaz-mən\ *n* [F *jasmin*, fr. Ar *yāsamīn*, fr. Per] : any of numerous often climbing shrubs of the olive family with extremely fragrant flowers; *also* : any of various plants noted for sweet-scented flowers — compare YELLOW JESSAMINE

Ja·son \'jās-ᵊn\ *n* : a hero noted in Greek legend for his successful quest of the Golden Fleece

jas·per \'jas-pər\ *n* [MF *jaspre*, fr. L *jaspis*, fr. Gk *iaspis*, of Sem origin] : an opaque fine-grained usu. red, yellow, or brown quartz; *esp* : green chalcedony — **jas·pery** \-pə-rē\ *adj*

ja·to unit \'jāt-ō-\ *n* [*jet-assisted takeoff*] : a special rocket engine to help an airplane take off

¹**jaun·dice** \'jón-dəs, 'jän-\ *n* [MF *jaunisse*, fr. *jaune* yellow] **1** : yellowish discoloration of the skin, tissues, and body fluids caused by the deposition of bile pigments; *also* : a disease or abnormal condition marked by jaundice **2** : a state or attitude characterized by satiety, distaste, or hostility

²**jaundice** *vt* **1** : to affect with jaundice **2** : to affect by envy, distaste, or hostility

¹**jaunt** \'jónt, 'jänt\ *vi* : to make a short journey for pleasure

²**jaunt** *n* : a short excursion for pleasure or recreation

jaun·ty \'jónt-ē, 'jänt-\ *adj* **jaun·ti·er; -est** [alter. of earlier *jentee* genteel, fr. F *gentil*] **1** *archaic* : STYLISH **2** : sprightly in manner or appearance : LIVELY — **jaun·ti·ly** \'jónt-ᵊl-ē, 'jänt-\ *adv* — **jaun·ti·ness** \'jónt-ē-nəs, 'jänt-\ *n*

Ja·va man \,jäv-ə-, ,jav-\ *n* : either of two primitive small-brained prehistoric men known chiefly from skulls found in Java : PITHECANTHROPUS

jav·e·lin \'jav-(ə-)lən\ *n* [MF *javeline*] **1** : a light spear **2** : a slender metal-tipped shaft of wood thrown for distance in an athletic field event

¹**jaw** \'jó\ *n* [ME] **1 a** : either of two cartilaginous or bony structures that support the soft parts enclosing the mouth and usu. bear teeth on their oral margin: (1) : MANDIBLE (2) : MAXILLA **b** : the parts constituting the walls of the mouth and serving to open and close it — usu. used in pl. **c** : any of various organs of invertebrates that perform the function of the vertebrate jaws **2** : something resembling the jaw of an animal in form or action ⟨the *jaws* of a mountain pass⟩; *esp* : one of a set of opposing parts that open and close for holding or crushing something between them ⟨the *jaws* of a vise⟩ — **jawed** \'jód\ *adj*

²**jaw** *vi, slang* : to talk in a scolding or boring manner

jaw·bone \'jó-'bōn, -,bōn\ *n* : JAW 1a; *esp* : MANDIBLE

jaw·break·er \-,brā-kər\ *n* **1** : a word difficult to pronounce **2** : a round hard candy

jaw·less fish \,jó-ləs-\ *n* : CYCLOSTOME

jaw·line \'jó-,līn\ *n* : the outline of the lower jaw

jay \'jā\ *n* [MF *jai*, fr. L *gaius*] : any of several noisy birds of the crow family that are smaller and more graceful than a crow and usu. more brightly colored

Jay·cee \'jā-'sē\ *n* [*junior chamber*] : a member of a junior chamber of commerce

jay·vee \'jā-'vē\ *n* [*junior varsity*] **1** : JUNIOR VARSITY **2** : a member of a junior varsity team

jay·walk \'jā-,wók\ *vi* [*jay* greenhorn] : to cross a street carelessly without paying attention to traffic regulations — **jay·walk·er** *n*

¹**jazz** \'jaz\ *vt* **1** : ENLIVEN — usu. used with *up* **2** : to play in the manner of jazz

²**jazz** *n* **1 a** : American music characterized by group and solo improvisation, syncopated rhythms, and contrapuntal ensemble playing **b** : rhythmic popular dance music influenced by jazz **2** : empty talk : STUFF — **jazz·man** \-mən, -,man\ *n*

jazzy \'jaz-ē\ *adj* **jazz·i·er; -est** **1** : having the characteristics of jazz **2** : marked by unrestraint, animation, or flashiness — **jazz·i·ly** \'jaz-ə-lē\ *adv* — **jazz·i·ness** \'jaz-ē-nəs\ *n*

jeal·ous \'jel-əs\ *adj* [OF *jelous*, fr. (assumed) VL *zelosus*, fr. LL *zelus* zeal, fr. Gk *zēlos*] **1** : demanding complete devotion **2** : fearful or suspicious of a rival or competitor : feeling a spiteful envy toward someone more successful than oneself **3** : suspicious that a person one loves is not faithful **4** : WATCHFUL, CAREFUL ⟨*jealous* of her rights⟩ — **jeal·ous·ly** *adv*

jeal·ou·sy \'jel-ə-sē\ *n, pl* **-sies** **1** : a jealous disposition, attitude, or feeling **2** : zealous vigilance

jean \'jēn\ *n* [short for *jean fustian*, fr. ME *Gene, Jene* Genoa] **1** : a durable twilled cotton cloth used esp. for sportswear and work clothes **2** *pl* : pants made of jean or denim

jeep \'jēp\ *n* [alter. of *gee pee*, fr. *general-purpose*] : a small general-purpose motor vehicle with ¼-ton capacity and four-wheel drive used by the U.S. Army in World War II

Jeep *trademark* — used for a civilian automotive vehicle

¹**jeer** \'ji(ə)r\ *vb* **1** : to speak or cry out in derision **2** : DERIDE, RIDICULE — **jeer·er** \'jir-ər\ *n* — **jeer·ing·ly** \-iŋ-lē\ *adv*

²**jeer** *n* : a jeering remark or sound : TAUNT

Jef·fer·so·ni·an \,jef-ər-'sō-nē-ən\ *adj* : of, relating to, or characteristic of Thomas Jefferson or his political principles — **Jeffersonian** *n*

Je·ho·vah \ji-'hō-və\ *n* [NL, false reading (as *Yĕhōwāh*) of Heb *Yahweh*] : ²GOD

Jehovah's Witness *n* : a member of a group that witness by distributing literature and by personal evangelism to beliefs in the theocratic rule of God, the sinfulness of organized religions and governments, and an approaching millennium

je·hu \'jē-h(y)ü\ *n* [Heb *Yēhū*] **1** *cap* : a king of Israel in the 9th century B.C. **2** [fr. the biblical reference to Jehu's driving (2 Kings 9:20)] : a driver of a coach or cab

je·june \ji-'jün\ *adj* [L *jejunus* fasting, dry] **1** : lacking nutritive value ⟨*jejune* diets⟩ **2** : lacking interest or significance : DULL **3** : lacking maturity : CHILDISH ⟨*jejune* remarks on world affairs⟩ — **je·june·ly** *adv* — **je·june·ness** \-'jün-nəs\ *n*

je·ju·num \ji-'jü-nəm\ *n* [L, fr. neut. of *jejunus*] : the section of the small intestine between the duodenum and the ileum — **je·ju·nal** \-'jün-ᵊl\ *adj*

jell \'jel\ *vb* [back-formation fr. *jelly*] **1** : to come to the consistency of jelly **2** : to take shape : CRYSTALLIZE ⟨an idea *jelled* in his mind⟩ **3** : to cause to jell

¹**jel·ly** \'jel-ē\ *n, pl* **jellies** [MF *gelee*, fr. pp. of *geler* to freeze, congeal, fr. L *gelare*] **1** : a food with a soft somewhat elastic consistency due usu. to the presence of gelatin or pectin; *esp* : a fruit product made by boiling sugar and the juice of fruit **2** : a substance resembling jelly in consistency — **jel·ly·like** \-ē-,līk\ *adj*

²**jelly** *vb* **jel·lied; jel·ly·ing** **1** : to make into or become jelly **2** : to set in jelly ⟨*jellied* tongue⟩

jel·ly·fish \'jel-ē-,fish\ *n* : a free-swimming sexually reproducing coelenterate animal with a gelatinous, disk‑shaped, and usu. nearly transparent body; *also* : any of various somewhat similar sea animals (as a ctenophore)

jelly roll *n* : a thin sheet of sponge cake spread with jelly and rolled up while hot

jen·net \'jen-ət\ *n* [MF *genet*, fr. Catalan] **1** : a small Spanish horse **2 a** : a female donkey **b** : HINNY

jen·ny \'jen-ē\ *n, pl* **jennies 1 a** : a female bird ⟨*jenny* wren⟩ **b** : a female donkey **2** : SPINNING JENNY

jeop·ar·dize \'jep-ər-,dīz\ *vt* : to expose to danger : IMPERIL; *also* : RISK

jeop·ar·dy \'jep-ərd-ē\ *n* [ME *jeopardie* even chance, problem, risk, fr. OF *jeu parti*, lit., divided game] **1** : exposure to death, loss, or injury : DANGER **2** : the danger that an accused person is subjected to when on trial for a criminal offense

jer·boa \jər-'bō-ə\ *n* [Ar *yarbū'*] : any of several social nocturnal Old World jumping rodents with long hind legs and long tail

jer·e·mi·ad \,jer-ə-'mī-əd, -'mī-,ad\ *n* [LL *Jeremias* Jeremiah] : a prolonged lamentation or complaint

Jer·e·mi·ah \-'mī-ə\ *n* **1** : a Hebrew prophet of the 6th and 7th centuries B.C. **2** — see BIBLE table

jerboa

¹jerk \'jərk\ *vb* **1** : to give a sharp quick push, pull, or twist to **2 a** : to make a sudden sharp motion **b** : to move in short abrupt motions or with frequent jolts **3** : to mix and dispense (as sodas) behind a soda fountain — **jerk·er** *n*

²jerk *n* **1** : a short quick pull or twist : TWITCH **2 a** : an involuntary spasmodic muscular movement due to reflex action **b** *pl* : involuntary twitchings due to nervous excitement **3** : a stupid, foolish, or eccentric person

³jerk *vt* [back-formation fr. *jerky* jerked meat, fr. Sp *charqui*] : to cut (meat) into long slices or strips and dry in the sun

jer·kin \'jər-kən\ *n* : a close-fitting hip-length sleeveless jacket

jerk·wa·ter \'jərk-,wȯt-ər, -,wät-\ *adj* : of minor importance : INSIGNIFICANT ⟨*jerkwater* towns⟩

jerky \'jər-kē\ *adj* **jerk·i·er; -est** : moving by sudden starts and stops — **jerk·i·ly** \-kə-lē\ *adv* — **jerk·i·ness** \-kē-nəs\ *n*

jer·ry-build \'jer-ē-,bild\ *vt* **–built** \-,bilt\; **–build·ing** : to build cheaply and flimsily — **jer·ry-build·er** *n* — **jer·ry-built** \-,bilt\ *adj*

jer·sey \'jər-zē\ *n, pl* **jerseys** [*Jersey*, Channel islands] **1** : a plain knitted fabric of wool, cotton, nylon, rayon, or silk **2** : any of various close-fitting knitted garments **3** : any of a breed of small usu. fawn-colored dairy cattle noted for their rich milk

Je·ru·sa·lem artichoke \jə-,rü-s(ə-)ləm-, -,rüz-(ə-)ləm-\ *n* : a perennial American sunflower grown for its edible tubers

Jerusalem cherry *n* : a plant of the nightshade family grown as a houseplant for its showy orange or red berries

jess \'jes\ *n* : a leg strap to which the leash of a falconer's hawk is attached — see FALCON illustration — **jessed** \'jest\ *adj*

jes·sa·mine \'jes-(ə-)mən\ *var of* JASMINE

¹jest \'jest\ *n* [ME *geste* exploit, tale, fr. OF, fr. L *gesta* exploits, fr. neut. pl. of pp. of *gerere* to carry, perform] **1 a** : an act intended to provoke laughter : PRANK **b** : a comic incident **2 a** : JEER **b** : a witty remark **3 a** : a frivolous mood or manner ⟨spoken in *jest*⟩ **b** : a state of gaiety and merriment **4** : LAUGHINGSTOCK

syn JEST, JOKE, QUIP, WISECRACK mean something said for the purpose of evoking laughter. JEST applies to an utterance not seriously intended whether sarcastic, ironic, witty, or merely playful; JOKE may apply to an act as well as an utterance and suggests no intent to hurt feelings; QUIP suggests a quick, light, neatly phrased remark; WISECRACK stresses cleverness of phrasing and may suggest unfeeling flippancy

²jest *vi* : JOKE, BANTER

jest·er \'jes-tər\ *n* **1** : FOOL 2 ⟨court *jester*⟩ **2** : one given to jests

Je·su·it \'jezh-(ə-)wət, 'jez-(ə-)\ *n* **1** : a member of the

---

Roman Catholic Society of Jesus founded by St. Ignatius Loyola in 1534 and composed of clerks regular devoted esp. to missions and education **2** : one given to intrigue or equivocation — **je·su·it·ic** \,jez(h)-ə-'wit-ik\ *or* **je·su·it·i·cal** \-i-kəl\ *adj, often cap* — **je·su·it·i·cal·ly** \-i-k(ə-)lē\ *adv, often cap*

Je·sus \'jē-zəs\ *n* : the founder of the Christian religion — called also *Jesus Christ*

¹jet \'jet\ *n* [MF *jaiet*, fr. Gk *gagatēs*, fr *Gagas*, town and river in Asia Minor] **1** : a compact velvet-black mineral similar to coal in composition that takes a good polish and is often used for jewelry **2** : a very dark black

²jet *vb* **jet·ted; jet·ting** [MF *jeter*, lit., to throw, fr. L *jactare*, freq. of *jacere* to throw] : to spout or emit in a stream : SPURT

³jet *n* **1 a** : a forceful rush of liquid, gas, or vapor through a narrow opening or a nozzle **b** : a nozzle for a jet of fluid (as gas or water) **2 a** : JET ENGINE **b** : JET AIRPLANE

⁴jet *vi* **jet·ted; jet·ting** : to travel by jet airplane

jet airplane *n* : an airplane powered by a jet engine that utilizes the surrounding air in the combustion of fuel or by a rocket-type jet engine that carries its fuel and all the oxygen needed for combustion — called also *jet plane*

jet engine *n* : an engine that produces motion as a result of the rearward discharge of a jet of fluid; *esp* : an airplane engine having one or more exhaust nozzles for discharging rearwardly a jet of heated air and exhaust gases

jet–pro·pelled \,jet-prə-'peld\ *adj* : propelled by a jet engine

jet propulsion *n* : propulsion of a body produced by the forwardly directed forces of the reaction resulting from the rearward discharge of a jet of fluid; *esp* : propulsion of an airplane by jet engines

jet·sam \'jet-səm\ *n* [alter. of *jettison*] : goods thrown overboard to lighten a ship in distress; *esp* : such goods when washed ashore

jet stream *n* : a long narrow meandering current of high‑speed winds blowing from a generally westerly direction several miles above the earth's surface

¹jet·ti·son \'jet-ə-sən\ *n* [OF *getaison* act of throwing, fr. L *jactation-*, *jactatio*, fr. *jactare*, freq. of *jacere* to throw] : a voluntary sacrifice of cargo to lighten a ship's load in time of distress

²jettison *vt* **1 a** : to throw (goods) overboard to lighten a ship in distress **b** : to drop from an airplane in flight **2** : to cast away or aside : DISCARD — **jet·ti·son·a·ble** \-sə-nə-bəl\ *adj*

jet·ty \'jet-ē\ *n, pl* **jetties** [MF *jetee*, fr. pp. of *jeter* to throw] **1** : a pier built out into the water to influence the current or to protect a harbor **2** : a landing wharf

jeu d'es·prit \zhœ-des-prē\ *n, pl* **jeux d'esprit** \same\ [F, lit., play of wit] : a witty comment or composition

Jew \'jü\ *n* **1 a** : a member of the tribe of Judah **b** : ISRAELITE **2** : a member of a nation existing in Palestine from the 6th century B.C. to the 1st century A.D. **3** : one whose religion is Judaism

¹jew·el \'jü(-ə)l\ *n* [OF *juel*, fr. dim. of *jeu* game, play, fr. L *jocus* joke, game] **1** : an ornament of precious metal set with stones or finished with enamel and worn as an accessory of dress **2** : one that is highly esteemed **3** : a precious stone : GEM **4** : a bearing for a pivot in a watch made of a crystal or of a precious stone

²jewel *vt* **-eled** *or* **-elled; -el·ing** *or* **-el·ling** : to adorn or equip with jewels

jew·el·er *or* **jew·el·ler** \'jü-(ə-)lər\ *n* : a person who makes or deals in jewelry and related articles

jew·el·ry \'jü(-ə)l-rē\ *n* : JEWELS; *esp* : objects of precious metal set with gems and worn for personal adornment

jew·el·weed \'jü-(ə)l-,wēd\ *n* : IMPATIENS

Jew·ess \'jü-əs\ *n* : a female Jew

jew·fish \'jü-,fish\ *n* : any of various large groupers that are usu. dusky green or blackish, thickheaded, and rough‑scaled

Jew·ish \'jü-ish\ *adj* : of, relating to, or characteristic of the Jews — **Jew·ish·ly** *adv* — **Jew·ish·ness** *n*

Jewish calendar *n* : a calendar in use among Jewish peoples that is reckoned from the year 3761 B.C. and dates in its present form from about A.D. 360

Jew·ry \'jü(ə)r-ē, 'jü-rē\ *n, pl* **Jewries 1** : a district of a city inhabited by Jews : GHETTO **2** : the Jewish people

---

ə abut; ᵊ kitten; ər further; a back; ā bake; ä cot, cart; au̇ out; ch chin; e less; ē easy; g gift; i trip; ī life

Jew's harp *or* **Jews' harp** \'jüz-,härp\ *n* : a small lyre=shaped instrument that when placed between the teeth gives tones from a metal tongue struck by the finger

Jez·e·bel \'jez-ə-,bel\ *n* **1** : a queen of Israel noted for her wickedness **2** *often not cap* : an impudent or wicked woman

¹jib \'jib\ *n* : a triangular sail set on a stay extending from the head of the foremast to the bowsprit or the jibboom

Jew's harp

²jib *vb* **jibbed; jib·bing 1** : to shift or swing from one side of a ship to the other **2** : to cause (a sail) to jib

³jib *n* **1** : the projecting arm of a crane **2** : a derrick boom

⁴jib *vi* **jibbed; jib·bing** : to refuse to go : BALK

jib·boom \'jib-'(b)üm\ *n* : a spar that serves as an extension of the bowsprit

¹jibe \'jīb\ *vb* **1** : to shift suddenly from one side to the other **2** : to change the course of a ship so that the sail jibes **3** : to cause (a sail) to jibe

²jibe *var of* GIBE

³jibe *vi* : to be in accord : AGREE

jif·fy \'jif-ē\ *n, pl* **jiffies** : MOMENT, INSTANT ⟨in a *jiffy*⟩

¹jig \'jig\ *n* **1** : a lively springy dance in triple rhythm **2** : TRICK, GAME ⟨the *jig* is up⟩ **3 a** : any of several fishing devices that are jerked up and down or drawn through the water **b** : a device used to maintain mechanically the correct position of a piece of work and a tool or of parts of work during assembly

²jig *vb* **jigged; jig·ging 1** : to dance a jig **2** : to jerk up and down or to and fro **3** : to fish or catch with a jig **4** : to machine by means of a jig-controlled tool operation

¹jig·ger \'jig-ər\ *n* **1** : one that jigs or operates a jig **2** : JIG 3a **3 a** : a small mast stepped in the stern **b** : the aftermost mast of a 4-masted ship **4 a** : a mechanical device; *esp* : one operating with a jerky reciprocating motion **b** : GADGET **5** : a measure used in mixing drinks that usu. holds 1½ ounces

²jigger *n* [of African origin] : CHIGGER

¹jig·gle \'jig-əl\ *vb* **jig·gled; jig·gling** \'jig-(ə-)liŋ\ [freq. of *²jig*] : to move or cause to move with quick little jerks

²jiggle *n* : a jiggling motion

jig·saw \'jig-,só\ *n* **1** : a machine saw with a narrow blade that moves up and down for cutting curved and irregular lines or openwork patterns **2** : SCROLL SAW

jigsaw puzzle *n* : a puzzle consisting of small irregular pieces fitted together to form a picture

¹jilt \'jilt\ *n* [alter. of *jillet* flirtatious girl] : a woman who jilts a man

²jilt *vt* : to cast (as a lover) aside unfeelingly

jim crow \'jim-'krō\ *n, often cap J & C* [fr. *Jim Crow*, stereotype Negro in a 19th cent. song-and-dance act] : discrimination against the Negro by legal enforcement or traditional sanctions — **jim crow·ism** \-,iz-əm\ *n, often cap J & C*

jim–dan·dy \'jim-'dan-dē\ *n* : something excellent of its kind

¹jim·my \'jim-ē\ *n, pl* **jimmies** : a short crowbar used by burglars

²jimmy *vt* **jim·mied; jim·my·ing** : to force open with or as if with a jimmy

jim·son·weed \'jim(p)-sən-,wēd\ *n, often cap* [alter. of *Jamestown weed*, fr. *Jamestown*, Va.] : a poisonous coarse annual weed of the nightshade family with rank-smelling foliage and large white or violet trumpet-shaped flowers

¹jin·gle \'jiŋ-gəl\ *vb* **jin·gled; jin·gling** \-g(ə-)liŋ\ [ME *ginglen*] **1** : to make a light clinking or tinkling sound **2** : to rhyme or sound in a catchy repetitious manner **3** : to cause to jingle — **jin·gler** \-g(ə-)lər\ *n*

²jingle *n* **1 a** : a light clinking or tinkling sound **b** : a catchy repetition of sounds in a poem **2** : a short verse or song marked by catchy repetition — **jin·gly** \-g(ə-)lē\ *adj*

¹jin·go \'jiŋ-gō\ *interj* — used as a mild oath usu. in the phrase *by jingo*

²jingo *n, pl* **jingoes** [fr. the fact that the phrase *by jingo* appeared in the refrain of a chauvinistic song] : one characterized by jingoism — **jin·go·ish** \-ish\ *adj*

jin·go·ism \'jiŋ-gō-,iz-əm\ *n* : extreme chauvinism or nationalism marked esp. by a belligerent foreign policy

— jin·go·ist \-əst\ *n* **— jin·go·is·tic** \,jiŋ-gō-'is-tik\ *adj* **— jin·go·is·ti·cal·ly** \-'is-ti-k(ə-)lē\ *adv*

jinn \'jin\ *or* **jin·ni** \jə-'nē, 'jin-ē\ *n, pl* **jinns** *or* **jinn** [Ar *jinnīy* demon (pl. *jinn*)] : one of a class of spirits held by the Muslims to inhabit the earth, to assume various forms, and to exercise supernatural power

jin·rik·i·sha \jin-'rik-,shò\ *n* [Jap, fr. *jin* man + *riki* power + *sha* carriage] : a small 2-wheeled covered vehicle pulled by one man and used orig. in Japan

¹jinx \'jiŋ(k)s\ *n* [prob. fr. *jynx* wryneck, fr. Gk *iynx*; fr. the traditional use of the wryneck as a charm] : one that brings bad luck

²jinx *vt* : to foredoom to failure or misfortune

jit·ney \'jit-nē\ *n, pl* **jitneys**   jinrikisha **1** *slang* : NICKEL 2a **2** [fr. the 5 cent fare] : BUS 1a; *esp* : a small bus that carries passengers over a regular route according to a flexible schedule

jit·ter·bug \'jit-ər-,bəg\ *n* **1** : a dance in which couples two-step, balance, and twirl in standardized patterns or with vigorous acrobatics **2** : one who dances the jitterbug — **jitterbug** *vi*

jit·ters \'jit-ərz\ *n pl* : extreme nervousness — **jit·tery** \-ə-rē\ *adj*

jiu·jit·su *or* **jiu·jut·su** *var of* JUJITSU

¹jive \'jīv\ *n* **1** : swing music or dancing performed to it **2 a** : the jargon of hipsters **b** : a special jargon of difficult or slang terms

²jive *vi* : to dance to or play jive

jo \'jō\ *n, pl* **joes** [alter. of *joy*] *chiefly Scot* : SWEETHEART, DEAR

¹job \'jäb\ *n* **1 a** : a piece of work; *esp* : one undertaken on order at a stated rate **b** : the object or material on which work is being done **c** : something produced by or as if by work **2** : something done for private advantage **3 a** : something that has to be done : TASK **b** : a specific duty, role, or function **c** : a regular remunerative position **syn** see TASK — **job·less** \-ləs\ *adj* — **job·less·ness** *n*

²job *vb* **1** : to do occasional pieces of work for hire **2** : to hire or let by the job

Job \'jōb\ *n* **1** : an Old Testament patriarch who endured afflictions with fortitude and faith **2** — see BIBLE table

job·ber \'jäb-ər\ *n* **1** : a person who buys goods and then sells them to other dealers : MIDDLEMAN **2** : a person who does work by the job

job·hold·er \'jäb-,hōl-dər\ *n* : one having a regular job; *esp* : a government employee

job lot *n* **1** : a miscellaneous collection of goods for sale as a lot usu. to a retailer **2** : a miscellaneous and usu. inferior collection or group

Job's tears *n* : an Asiatic grass with large hard pearly white seeds often used as beads

job work *n* : commercial printing of miscellaneous orders

Jo·cas·ta \jō-'kas-tə\ *n* : a queen of Thebes and mother of Oedipus

¹jock·ey \'jäk-ē\ *n, pl* **jockeys** [fr. *Jockey*, Sc nickname for *John*] **1** : one who rides a horse esp. as a professional in a race **2** : OPERATOR

²jockey *vb* **jock·eyed; jock·ey·ing 1** : to ride (a horse) as a jockey **2 a** : to maneuver or manipulate by adroit or devious means ⟨*jockey* a truck into position⟩ **b** : to maneuver for advantage **3** : OUTWIT, TRICK, CHEAT

jockey club *n* : an association for the promotion and regulation of horse racing

jo·cose \jō-'kōs\ *adj* [L *jocosus*, fr. *jocus* joke, sport] **1** : given to joking : MERRY **2** : characterized by joking : HUMOROUS — **jo·cose·ly** *adv* — **jo·cose·ness** *n*

joc·u·lar \'jäk-yə-lər\ *adj* **1** : given to jesting : MIRTHFUL **2** : said or done in jest : PLAYFUL — **joc·u·lar·ly** *adv*

joc·u·lar·i·ty \,jäk-yə-'lar-ət-ē\ *n, pl* **-ties 1** : the quality or state of being jocular **2** : a jocular act or remark

joc·und \'jäk-ənd, 'jō-kənd\ *adj* [LL *jocundus* pleasant, agreeable, alter. of L *jucundus*, fr. *juvare* to help, give pleasure to] : marked by or suggestive of mirth or cheerfulness : GAY — **joc·und·ly** *adv*

jodh·pur \'jäd-pər\ *n* [*Jodhpur*, India] **1** *pl* : riding breeches loose above the knee and tight-fitting below **2** : an ankle-high boot fastened with a strap that is buckled at the side

Jo·el \'jō-əl\ *n* **1** : a Hebrew prophet of Old Testament times **2** — see BIBLE table

¹jog \'jäg\ *vb* **jogged**; **jog·ging 1** : to give a slight shake or push to : NUDGE **2** : to rouse to alertness **3** : to move up and down or about with a short heavy motion **4 a** : to go or cause to go at a jog **b** : to go at a jog or monotonous pace : TRUDGE — **jog·ger** *n*

²jog *n* **1** : a slight shake : PUSH **2 a** : a jogging movement, pace, or trip **b** : a horse's slow gait with marked beats

³jog *n* **1** : a projecting or retreating part of a line or surface **2** : a brief abrupt change in direction

¹jog·gle \'jäg-əl\ *vb* **jog·gled**; **jog·gling** \'jäg-(ə-)liŋ\ [freq. of ¹*jog*] **1** : to shake slightly **2** : to move shakily or jerkily — **jog·gler** \-(ə-)lər\ *n*

²joggle *n* : ²JOG 2a

John \'jän\ *n* **1** : the baptizer of Jesus — called also *John the Baptist* **2 a** : one of the twelve apostles who is held to have written the fourth Gospel, three Epistles, and the Book of Revelation **b** — see BIBLE table

john·boat \'jän-,bōt\ *n* : a narrow flat-bottomed square-ended boat propelled by a pole or paddle and used on inland waterways

John Bull \'jän-'bul\ *n* **1** : the English nation personified : the English people **2** : a typical Englishman

John Doe \-'dō\ *n* : a party to legal proceedings whose true name is unknown

John Do·ry \-'dōr-ē, -'dȯr-\ *n* : a yellow to olive compressed marine food fish with a dark spot on each side

John Han·cock \-'han-,käk\ *n* [fr. the prominence of John Hancock's signature on the Declaration of Independence] : an autograph signature

john·ny \'jän-ē\ *n, pl* **johnnies** : a short gown opening in the back that is used by hospital bed patients

john·ny·cake \'jän-ē-,kāk\ *n* : a bread made with cornmeal, flour, eggs, and milk

John·ny-jump-up \,jän-ē-'jəmp-,əp\ *n* : any of various small-flowered pansies or violets

Johnny Reb \-'reb\ *n* [*reb*, short for *rebel*] : a Confederate soldier

John·so·ni·an \jän-'sō-nē-ən\ *adj* : of, relating to, or characteristic of Samuel Johnson or his writings

joie de vi·vre \,zhwäd-ə-'vēvrᵊ\ *n* [F, lit., joy of living] : keen or buoyant enjoyment of life

¹join \'join\ *vb* [OF *joindre*, fr. L *jungere*; akin to E *yoke*] **1 a** : to bring or fasten together in close physical contact ⟨*join* hands⟩ **b** : to connect (as points) by a line **2** : to put or bring into close association or relationship ⟨*join* in marriage⟩ **3 a** : to come into the company of **b** : to associate oneself with : become a member of ⟨*join* a church⟩ **4 a** : to come together so as to be connected ⟨nouns *join* to form compounds⟩ **b** : ADJOIN **5** : to take part in a collective activity ⟨*join* in singing⟩ — **join·a·ble** \-ə-bəl\ *adj*

syn JOIN, COMBINE, UNITE, CONNECT mean to bring or come together in some kind of union. JOIN suggests a physical contact or conjunction between two or more things ⟨*join* the ends with glue⟩ ⟨*joined* forces in a common purpose to reach victory⟩ COMBINE implies some merging or mingling with corresponding loss of identity of each unit; UNITE implies a greater loss of separate identity; CONNECT suggests a loose or external attachment with little or no loss of separate identity

²join *n* : point of joining : JOINT

join·er \'joi-nər\ *n* : one that joins: as **a** : a person whose occupation is to construct articles by joining pieces of wood **b** : a gregarious person who joins many organizations

join·ery \'join-(ə-)rē\ *n* **1** : the art or trade of a joiner **2** : things made by a joiner

¹joint \'joint\ *n* [OF *jointe*, fr. pp. of *joindre* to join] **1 a** (1) : the point of contact between elements of an animal skeleton with the parts that surround and support it (2) : NODE 4b **b** : a part or space included between two articulations, knots, or nodes **c** : a large piece of meat for roasting **2 a** : a place where two things or parts are joined ⟨a *joint* in a pipe⟩ **b** : a space between the adjacent surfaces of two bodies joined and held together

by an adhesive material (as cement or mortar) ⟨a thin *joint*⟩ **c** : a fracture or crack in rock **3 a** : a shabby or disreputable place of entertainment **b** : PLACE, ESTABLISHMENT — **joint·ed** \-əd\ *adj* — **out of joint** : DISLOCATED

²joint *adj* **1** : UNITED, COMBINED ⟨a *joint* effort⟩ **2** : done by or shared by two or more persons ⟨a *joint* account⟩ **3** : sharing with another ⟨*joint* owner⟩

³joint *vb* **1 a** : to unite by a joint : fit together **b** : to provide with a joint **2** : to separate the joints of — **joint·er** *n*

joint·ly *adv* : in a joint manner : TOGETHER ⟨owned *jointly*⟩

joint stock *n* : capital stock held by a group of persons in common

joint–stock company *n* : an association of individuals organized to conduct a business for gain in which the shares held by a member are transferable without the consent of the other owners

joist \'joist\ *n* [MF *giste*, fr. *gesir* to lie, fr. L *jacēre*] : any of the small timbers or metal beams ranged parallel from wall to wall in a building to support the floor or ceiling

F floor, J joist

¹joke \'jōk\ *n* [L *jocus* joke, sport] **1 a** : something said or done to provoke laughter; *esp* : a brief oral narrative with a climactic humorous twist **b** (1) : the humorous or ridiculous element in something (2) : RAILLERY, KIDDING ⟨can't take a *joke*⟩ **c** : PRACTICAL JOKE **d** : LAUGHINGSTOCK **2 a** : something lacking substance, genuineness, or quality **b** : something presenting no difficulty **syn** see JEST

²joke *vb* **1** : to make jokes : JEST **2** : to make the object of a joke : KID — **jok·ing·ly** \'jō-kiŋ-lē\ *adv*

jok·er \'jō-kər\ *n* **1** : a person who jokes **2** : a part (as of an agreement) meaning something quite different from what it seems to mean and changing the apparent intention of the whole **3** : an extra card used in some card games

jol·li·fi·ca·tion \,jäl-i-fə-'kā-shən\ *n* : a festive celebration : MERRYMAKING

jol·li·ty \'jäl-ət-ē\ *n, pl* **-ties** : GAIETY, MERRIMENT

¹jol·ly \'jäl-ē\ *adj* **jol·li·er**; **-est** [OF *joli*] **1 a** (1) : full of high spirits : JOYOUS (2) : given to conviviality : JOVIAL **b** : expressing, suggesting, or inspiring gaiety : CHEERFUL **2** : extremely pleasant or agreeable : SPLENDID **syn** see MERRY

²jolly *adv* : VERY ⟨had a *jolly* good time⟩

³jolly *vb* **jol·lied**; **jol·ly·ing 1** : to engage in good-natured banter **2** : to put in good humor esp. in order to gain an end

jol·ly boat \'jäl-ē-\ *n* : a medium-sized ship's boat used for general rough or small work

Jol·ly Rog·er \,jäl-ē-'räj-ər\ *n* : a black flag with a white skull and crossbones

¹jolt \'jōlt\ *vb* **1** : to give a quick hard knock or blow to : JAR **2** : to disturb the composure of **3** : to interfere with roughly and abruptly **4** : to move or cause to move with a sudden jerky motion — **jolt·er** *n*

²jolt *n* **1 a** : an abrupt sharp jerky blow or movement **b** : a jarring blow **2** : a sudden shock, surprise, or disappointment

Jo·nah \'jō-nə\ *n* **1** : a Hebrew prophet cast overboard during a storm sent by God because of his disobedience, swallowed by a great fish, and vomited up after three days in its belly **2** — see BIBLE table

Jon·a·than \'jän-ə-thən\ *n* : a son of Saul and friend of David

jon·gleur \zhōⁿ-'glər\ *n* [F, fr. OF *jogleour*, fr. *jogler* to perform as a minstrel, lit., to joke] : an itinerant medieval minstrel

jon·quil \'jän-kwəl, 'jäŋ-\ *n* [F *jonquille*, fr. Sp *junquillo*, dim. of *junco* reed, fr. L *juncus*] : a Mediterranean perennial bulbous herb with long linear leaves that is widely grown for its yellow or white fragrant short-tubed clustered flowers — compare DAFFODIL

Jor·dan almond \,jȯrd-ᵊn-\ *n* [ME *jardin almande*, fr. MF *jardin* garden + ME *almande* almond] **1** : an almond imported from Málaga **2** : an almond coated with sugar

jo·seph \'jō-zəf\ *n* **1** *cap* **a** : a Hebrew patriarch who in his youth was given a coat of many colors by his father Jacob, was sold into slavery because of his brothers' jealousy, and became a ruler in Egypt and saved his father and his brothers in time of famine **b** : the husband of Mary the mother of Jesus **2** : a long cloak worn esp. by women in the 18th century

Joseph's coat *n* [*Joseph;* fr. his coat of many colors] : any of several plants with variegated foliage; *esp* : COLEUS

josh \'jäsh\ *vb* : to make fun of : TEASE, JOKE — **josh·er** *n*

Josh·ua \'jäsh-ə-wə\ *n* **1** : a Hebrew leader and successor of Moses during the settlement of the Israelites in Canaan **2** — see BIBLE table

Joshua tree *n* : a tall branched yucca of the southwestern U.S. with short leaves and clustered greenish white flowers

joss \'jäs, 'jós\ *n* [pidgin E, fr. Pg *deus* god, fr. L] : a Chinese idol or cult image

joss house *n* : a Chinese temple or shrine

¹jos·tle \'jäs-əl\ *vb* **jos·tled**; **jos·tling** \'jäs-(ə-)liŋ\ [alter. of earlier *justle*, freq. of *joust*] **1** : to run or knock against so as to jar : push roughly ⟨*jostled* by a crowd⟩ **2** : to make one's way by pushing and shoving : ELBOW

²jostle *n* **1** : a jostling encounter or experience **2** : the state of being jostled together

¹jot \'jät\ *n* [L *iota, jota* iota] : the least bit : IOTA

²jot *vt* **jot·ted**; **jot·ting** : to write briefly or hurriedly : set down in the form of a note ⟨*jot* this down⟩

jot·ting \'jät-iŋ\ *n* : a brief note : MEMORANDUM

joule \'jül, 'jaúl\ *n* [after James P. *Joule* d1889 English physicist] : the mks unit of work or energy equal to 10^7 ergs or approximately 0.7375 foot-pounds

jounce \'jaún(t)s\ *vb* : JOLT — **jounce** *n*

jour·nal \'jərn-ⁿl\ *n* [MF, service book containing the day hours, fr. *journal* daily, fr. L *diurnalis*, fr. *diurnus* of the day, fr. *dies* day] **1 a** : a brief account of daily events **b** : a record of experiences, ideas, or reflections kept for private use **c** : a record of transactions kept by a deliberative or legislative body **2 a** : a daily newspaper **b** : a periodical dealing esp. with current events **3** : the part of a rotating shaft, axle, roll, or spindle that turns in a bearing

jour·nal·ese \,jərn-ⁿl-'ēz, -'ēs\ *n* : a style of writing held to be characteristic of newspapers

jour·nal·ism \'jərn-ⁿl-,iz-əm\ *n* **1** : the business of writing for, editing, or publishing periodicals (as newspapers) **2** : writing designed for or characteristic of newspapers or popular magazines

jour·nal·ist \-ⁿl-əst\ *n* : an editor of or writer for a periodical

jour·nal·is·tic \,jərn-ⁿl-'is-tik\ *adj* : of, relating to, or characteristic of journalism or journalists — **jour·nal·is·ti·cal·ly** \-ti-k(ə-)lē\ *adv*

jour·nal·ize \'jərn-ⁿl-,īz\ *vt* : to record in a journal — **jour·nal·iz·er** *n*

¹jour·ney \'jər-nē\ *n, pl* **journeys** [OF *journee* day's journey, fr. *jour* day, fr. LL *diurnum*, fr. L *diurnus* of a day, fr. *dies* day] : travel or passage from one place to another

²journey *vb* **jour·neyed**; **jour·ney·ing** **1** : to go on a journey : TRAVEL **2** : to travel over or through : TRAVERSE — **jour·ney·er** *n*

jour·ney·man \'jər-nē-mən\ *n* **1** : a worker who has learned a trade and works for another person usu. by the day **2** : an experienced reliable workman in any field

¹joust \'jaúst, 'jəst\ *vi* [OF *juster*, fr. (assumed) VL *juxtare* to touch, fr. L *juxta* near] : to engage in a joust : TILT — **joust·er** *n*

²joust *n* : a combat on horseback between two knights with lances esp. as part of a tournament

Jove \'jōv\ *n* : JUPITER — **Jo·vi·an** \'jō-vē-ən\ *adj*

jo·vi·al \'jō-vē-əl\ *adj* [L *Jov-, Juppiter* Jupiter; fr. the supposed character conferred by Jupiter as a natal planet] : marked by good humor : full of fun : JOLLY **syn** see MERRY — **jo·vi·al·i·ty** \,jō-vē-'al-ət-ē\ *n* — **jo·vi·al·ly** \'jō-vē-ə-lē\ *adv*

¹jowl \'jaúl, 'jōl\ *n* [alter. of ME *chavel*, fr. OE *ceafl*] **1** : JAW; *esp* : MANDIBLE **2** : CHEEK 1

²jowl *n* [ME *cholle*] : usu. slack flesh (as a wattle) associated with the lower jaw or throat — **jowly** \-ē\ *adj*

¹joy \'jói\ *n* [OF *joie*, fr. L *gaudium*, fr. *gaudēre* to rejoice] **1** : a feeling of great pleasure or happiness that comes

from success, good fortune, or a sense of well-being : GLADNESS **2** : something that gives great pleasure or happiness ⟨a *joy* to behold⟩

²joy *vi* : to experience great pleasure or delight : REJOICE

joy·ance \'jói-ən(t)s\ *n* : DELIGHT, ENJOYMENT

joy·ful \'jói-fəl\ *adj* : experiencing, causing, or showing joy : HAPPY — **joy·ful·ly** \-fə-lē\ *adv* — **joy·ful·ness** *n*

joy·less \'jói-ləs\ *adj* : not feeling or causing joy : CHEERLESS — **joy·less·ly** *adv* — **joy·less·ness** *n*

joy·ous \'jói-əs\ *adj* : JOYFUL — **joy·ous·ly** *adv* — **joy·ous·ness** *n*

joy·ride \'jói-,rīd\ *n* : a ride taken for pleasure and often marked by reckless driving — **joy·rid·er** *n* — **joy·rid·ing** *n*

ju·bi·lant \'jü-bə-lənt\ *adj* [L *jubilare* to rejoice] : expressing great joy : EXULTANT — **ju·bi·lant·ly** *adv*

Ju·bi·la·te \,yü-bə-'lä-,tā, ,jü-\ *n* [L, rejoice!; fr. its first word] : the 100th Psalm in the Authorized Version

ju·bi·la·tion \,jü-bə-'lā-shən\ *n* **1** : an act of rejoicing : the state of being jubilant **2** : an expression of great joy

ju·bi·lee \'jü-bə-,lē\ *n* [LL *jubilaeus*, fr. LGk *iōbēlaios*, fr. Heb *yōbhēl*] **1 a** : a special anniversary; *esp* : a 50th anniversary **b** : a celebration of such an anniversary **2 a** : a period of time proclaimed by the Roman Catholic pope ordinarily every 25 years as a time of special solemnity **b** : a special plenary indulgence granted during a year of jubilee to Roman Catholics who perform specified works of repentance and piety **3** : a Negro folk song about a future happy time

Ju·da·ic \jü-'dā-ik\ *adj* [Gk *ioudaikos*, fr. *Ioudaios* Jew, fr. Heb *Yĕhūdhī*, fr. *Yĕhūdhāh* Kingdom of Judah] : of, relating to, or characteristic of Jews or Judaism — **Ju·da·ical** \-'dā-ə-kəl\ *adj*

Ju·da·ism \'jüd-ə-,iz-əm, 'jüd-ē-\ *n* **1** : a religion developed among the ancient Hebrews and marked by belief in one God who is creator, ruler, and redeemer of the universe and by the moral and ceremonial laws of the Old Testament and the rabbinic tradition **2** : conformity to Jewish rites, ceremonies, and practices **3** : the cultural, social, and religious beliefs and practices of the Jews **4** : the whole body of Jews — **Ju·da·ist** \-ə-əst, -ē-əst\ *n* — **Ju·da·is·tic** \,jüd-ə-'is-tik, ,jüd-ē-\ *adj*

Ju·da·ize \'jüd-ə-,īz, 'jüd-ē-\ *vb* **1** : to adopt the customs, beliefs, or character of a Jew **2** : to make Jewish — **Ju·da·i·za·tion** \,jüd-ə-ə-'zā-shən, ,jüd-ē-ə-\ *n* — **Ju·da·iz·er** *n*

Ju·das \'jüd-əs\ *n* **1** : an apostle and betrayer of Jesus — called also *Judas Is·car·i·ot* \is-'kar-ē-ət\ **2** : TRAITOR

Judas tree *n* : a leguminous tree often grown for its showy usu. rosy flowers borne before the leaves appear

Jude \'jüd\ *n* — see BIBLE table

¹judge \'jəj\ *vb* [OF *jugier*, fr. L *judicare*, fr. *judic-, judex* judge, fr. *jus* right, law + *dicere* to say] **1** : to form an authoritative opinion **2** : to decide as a judge : TRY **3** : to determine or pronounce after inquiry and deliberation : CONSIDER **4** : GOVERN, RULE — used of a Hebrew tribal leader **5** : to form an estimate, conclusion, or evaluation about something : THINK — **judg·er** *n*

²judge *n* : one who judges: as **a** : a public official authorized to decide questions brought before a court **b** *often cap* : a tribal hero exercising authority over the Hebrews after the death of Joshua **c** : one appointed to decide in a contest or competition : UMPIRE **d** : one who gives an authoritative opinion : CRITIC — **judge·ship** \-,ship\ *n*

Judg·es \'jəj-əz\ *n* — see BIBLE table

judg·ment *or* **judge·ment** \'jəj-mənt\ *n* **1 a** : the act of judging **b** : a decision or opinion given after judging **2 a** : a formal decision given by a court **b** : a court decree that a defendant has an obligation to the plaintiff for a specified amount **3** *cap* : the final judging of mankind by God — called also *Last Judgment* **4 a** : the process of forming an opinion by discerning and comparing **b** : an opinion so formed **5** : the capacity for judging : DISCERNMENT — **judg·men·tal** \,jəj-'ment-ⁿl\ *adj*

Judgment Day *n* : the day of the Last Judgment

ju·di·ca·ture \'jüd-i-kə-,chúr\ *n* [L *judicare* to judge] **1** : the administration of justice **2** : JUDICIARY 1

ju·di·cial \jü-'dish-əl\ *adj* [L *judicium* judgment, fr. *judic-, judex* judge] **1** : of or relating to a judgment, the function of judging, the administration of justice, or the

judiciary 2 : pronounced, ordered, or enforced by a court ⟨a *judicial* decision⟩ **3 :** of, characterized by, or expressing judgment **:** CRITICAL 1c — **ju·di·cial·ly** \-'dish-(ə-)lē\ *adv*

ju·di·ci·ary \jù-'dish-ē-,er-ē, -'dish-ə-rē\ *n, pl* **-ries 1 a :** a system of courts of law **b :** the judges of these courts **2 :** a branch of government in which judicial power is vested — **judiciary** *adj*

ju·di·cious \jù-'dish-əs\ *adj* **:** having, exercising, or characterized by sound judgment **:** DISCREET — **ju·di·cious·ly** *adv* — **ju·di·cious·ness** *n*

ju·do \'jüd-ō\ *n, pl* **judos** [Jap *jūdō*] **:** a modern refined form of jujitsu that uses special applications of the principles of movement, balance, and leverage

¹jug \'jəg\ *n* **1 a :** a large deep usu. earthenware or glass container with a narrow mouth and a handle **b :** JUGFUL **2 :** JAIL

²jug *vt* **jugged; jug·ging :** IMPRISON

jug·ful \'jəg-,fúl\ *n, pl* **jugfuls** \-,fúlz\ *or* **jugs·ful** \'jəgz-,fúl\ **:** the quantity held by a jug

jug·ger·naut \'jəg-ər-,nót\ *n* [Hindi *Jagannāth*, title of Vishnu, lit., lord of the world] **:** a massive inexorable force or object that crushes whatever is in its path

¹jug·gle \'jəg-əl\ *vb* **jug·gled; jug·gling** \'jəg-(ə-)liŋ\ [MF *jogler* to entertain as a minstrel, lit., to joke, fr. L *joculari*, fr. *joculus*, dim. of *jocus* joke] **1 :** to keep several objects in motion in the air at the same time **2 :** to manipulate esp. in order to achieve a desired and often fraudulent end ⟨*juggle* an account to hide a loss⟩ **3 :** to hold or balance insecurely — **jug·gler** \-(ə-)lər\ *n*

²juggle *n* **:** an act or instance of juggling **:** a show of manual dexterity

jug·glery \'jəg-lə-rē\ *n, pl* **-gler·ies 1 :** the art or practice of a juggler **2 :** TRICKERY

jug·u·lar \'jəg-yə-lər\ *adj* [L *jugulum* collarbone, throat, fr. dim. of *jugum* yoke; akin to E *yoke*] **1 :** of, relating to, or situated in or on the throat or neck **2 :** of or relating to the jugular vein

jugular vein *n* **:** any of several veins of each side of the neck that return blood from the head

juice \'jüs\ *n* [OF *jus*, broth, juice, fr. L] **1 :** the extractable fluid contents of cells or tissues **2 a :** any of several chiefly digestive secretions **b :** the liquid or moisture contained in something **3 :** a medium (as electricity or gasoline) that supplies power — **juiced** \'jüst\ *adj* — **juice·less** \'jüs-ləs\ *adj*

juic·er \'jü-sər\ *n* **:** an appliance for extracting juice from fruit or vegetables

juice up *vt* **:** to give life, energy, or spirit to

juicy \'jü-sē\ *adj* **juic·i·er; -est 1 :** having much juice **:** SUCCULENT **2 a :** rich in interest **:** COLORFUL **b :** PIQUANT, RACY — **juic·i·ly** \-sə-lē\ *adv* — **juic·i·ness** \-sē-nəs\ *n*

ju·jit·su *or* **ju·jut·su** \jü-'jit-sü\ *n* [Jap *jūjutsu*, fr. *jū* weakness + *jutsu* art] **:** the Japanese art of defending oneself by grasping or striking an opponent so that his own strength and weight are used against him

ju·jube \'jü-,jüb\ *n* [ML *jujuba*] **1 :** the edible fruit of a tree of the buckthorn family; *also* **:** this tree **2 :** a fruit-flavored gumdrop or lozenge

juke·box \'jük-,bäks\ *n* [Gullah *juke* disorderly, of W. African origin] **:** a cabinet containing an automatic player of phonograph records that is started by inserting a coin in a slot

juke joint *n* **:** a small inexpensive establishment for eating, drinking, or dancing to the music of a jukebox

ju·lep \'jü-ləp\ *n* [Ar *julāb*, a drink made from syrup, fr. Per *gulāb*, fr. *gul* rose + *āb* water] **:** a drink consisting of bourbon, sugar, and mint served in a frosted tumbler filled with crushed ice

Ju·lian calendar \,jül-yən-\ *n* [Gaius *Julius* Caesar, who introduced it] **:** a calendar introduced in Rome in 46 B.C. establishing the 12-month year of 365 days with each 4th year having 366 days and the months each having 31 or 30 days except for February which has 28 or in leap years 29 days — compare GREGORIAN CALENDAR

Ju·ly \jù-'lī\ *n* [L *Julius*, after Gaius *Julius* Caesar] **:** the 7th month of the year

¹jum·ble \'jəm-bəl\ *vb* **jum·bled; jum·bling** \-b(ə-)liŋ\ **:** to mix in a confused mass

²jumble *n* **:** a disorderly mass or pile

jum·bo \'jəm-bō\ *n, pl* **jumbos** [after *Jumbo*, a huge elephant exhibited by P. T. Barnum] **:** a very large specimen of its kind

¹jump \'jəmp\ *vb* **1 a :** to spring into the air **:** LEAP **b :** to give a sudden movement **:** START **c :** to move over a position occupied by an opponent's man in a board game **d :** SKIP ⟨his typewriter *jumps*⟩ **e :** to begin a forward movement — usu. used with *off* **2 a :** to rise suddenly in rank or status **b :** to undergo or cause a sudden sharp increase ⟨prices *jumped*⟩ **3 :** to make a sudden attack ⟨*jumped* on him for his criticism⟩ **4 :** to bustle with activity **5 a :** to pass over by a leap ⟨*jump* a hurdle⟩ **b :** BYPASS ⟨*jump* electrical connections⟩ **c :** ANTICIPATE ⟨*jump* the gun in starting the race⟩ **d :** to leap aboard ⟨*jump* a freight⟩ **6 a :** to escape from usu. in a hasty or furtive manner ⟨*jump* town without paying his bills⟩ **b :** to abscond while at liberty under (bail) **c :** to depart from a normal course ⟨*jump* the track⟩ **7 :** to occupy illegally ⟨*jump* a mining claim⟩ **8 a :** to cause to leap **b :** to elevate in rank or status **c :** to make a bridge bid of more tricks than are necessary to overcall the preceding bid

²jump *n* **1 a** (1) **:** an act of jumping **:** LEAP (2) **:** a sports competition featuring a leap, spring, or bound (3) **:** a space covered by a leap **b :** a sudden involuntary movement **:** START **c :** a move made in a board game by jumping **2 a :** a sharp sudden increase **b :** one in a series of moves from one place to another **3 :** an advantage at the start

¹jump·er \'jəm-pər\ *n* **1 :** one that jumps **2 :** any of various devices operating with a jumping motion **3 :** a short wire used to close a break or cut out part of a circuit

²jumper *n* **1 :** a loose blouse or jacket worn by workmen **2 :** a sleeveless one-piece dress worn usu. with a blouse **3** *pl* **:** a child's coverall

jumping bean *n* **:** a seed of any of several Mexican shrubs of the spurge family that tumbles about because of the movements of the larva of a small moth inside it

jumping jack *n* **:** a toy figure of a man jointed and made to jump or dance by means of strings or a sliding stick

jumper 2

jumping mouse *n* **:** any of several small hibernating No. American rodents with long hind legs and tail and no cheek pouches

jump·ing-off place \,jəm-piŋ-'óf-\ *n* **1 :** a remote or isolated place **2 :** a place from which an enterprise is launched

jump pass *n* **:** a pass made by a player (as in football or basketball) while jumping

jump seat *n* **1 :** a movable carriage seat **2 :** a folding seat between the front and rear seats of a passenger automobile

jump shot *n* **:** a shot made by a basketball player at the peak of a jump

jumpy \'jəm-pē\ *adj* **jump·i·er; -est :** NERVOUS, JITTERY — **jump·i·ness** *n*

jun·co \'jəŋ-kō\ *n, pl* **juncos** *or* **juncoes** [obs. Sp *junco* ave, a long-tailed bird, fr. *junco* reed, rush (fr. L *juncus*) + *ave* bird, fr. L *avis*] **:** any of a genus of small American finches usu. with a pink bill, ashy gray head and back, and conspicuous white lateral tail feathers

junc·tion \'jəŋ(k)-shən\ *n* [L *junct-*, *jungere* to join] **1 :** an act of joining **:** the state of being joined **2 :** a place or point of meeting ⟨a railroad *junction*⟩ **3 :** something that joins — **junc·tion·al** \-shnəl, -shən-°l\ *adj*

junc·ture \'jəŋ(k)-chər\ *n* **1 :** an instance of joining **:** UNION **2 a :** JOINT, CONNECTION **b :** the manner of transition between two consecutive sounds in speech **3 :** a point of time; *esp* **:** one made critical by a concurrence of circumstances — **junc·tur·al** \-chə-rəl, -shrəl\ *adj*

syn JUNCTURE, EMERGENCY, CRISIS mean a critical or crucial time or state of affairs. JUNCTURE stresses the significant convergence of events or developments; EMERGENCY emphasizes the sudden unforeseen nature of a situation and the need for quick action; CRISIS applies to a juncture whose outcome will make a decisive difference

June \'jün\ *n* [L *Junius*, fr. *Junius*, a Roman clan name] **:** the 6th month of the year

june beetle *n, often cap J* : any of various large leaf-eating beetles that fly chiefly in late spring and have as larvae white grubs that live in soil and feed on roots — called also *june bug*

June·ber·ry \'jün-ˌber-ē\ *n* : any of various No. American trees and shrubs of the rose family sometimes grown for their white flowers or edible fruits

jun·gle \'jəŋ-gəl\ *n* [Hindi *jaṅgal*] **1 a** : a thick tangled mass of tropical vegetation **b** : a tract overgrown with jungle or other rank vegetation **2** : a hobo camp **3** : a place of ruthless struggle for survival — **jun·gly** \-g(ə-)lē\ *adj*

jungle fowl *n* : any of several Asiatic wild birds related to the pheasants; *esp* : one from which domestic fowls are held to have descended

jungle gym *n* : a structure of vertical and horizontal bars for use of children at play

¹ju·nior \'jü-nyər\ *n* [L, fr. *junior* younger, compar. of *juvenis* young] **1** : a person who is younger or of lower rank than another **2** : a student in his next-to-last year before graduating from an educational institution of secondary or higher level

²junior *adj* **1 a** : YOUNGER — used chiefly to distinguish a son with the same given name as his father **b** : of more recent date **2** : lower in standing or rank ⟨*junior* partner⟩ **3** : of or relating to juniors in an educational institution

ju·nior·ate \'jü-nyə-ˌrāt, -rət\ *n* **1** : a course of high school or college study for candidates for the priesthood, brotherhood, or sisterhood; *esp* : one preparatory to the course in philosophy **2** : a seminary for the juniorate

junior college *n* : an educational institution that offers two years of studies similar to those in the first two years of a four-year college

junior high school *n* : a school usu. including the 7th, 8th, and 9th grades

junior varsity *n* : the members of a varsity squad lacking the experience or class qualification for the first team

ju·ni·per \'jü-nə-pər\ *n* [L *juniperus*] **1** : any of a genus of evergreen shrubs and trees of the pine family; *esp* : one of prostrate or shrubby habit **2** : any of various coniferous trees resembling true junipers

¹junk \'jəŋk\ *n* [ME *jonke* old cable] **1** : hard salted beef for use on shipboard **2 a** : old iron, glass, paper, or waste : discarded articles **b** : a shoddy product : TRASH — **junk·man** \-ˌman\ *n* — **junky** *adj*

²junk *vt* : to get rid of as worthless : SCRAP

³junk *n* [Pg *junco*, of Austronesian origin] : a ship of Chinese waters with bluff lines, a high poop and overhanging stem, little or no keel, high pole masts, and a deep rudder

Jun·ker \'yùŋ-kər\ *n* : a member of the Prussian landed aristocracy

¹jun·ket \'jəŋ-kət\ *n* **1** : a dessert of sweetened flavored milk set in a jelly **2 a** : a festive social affair **b** : a trip made by an official at public expense

junk

²junket *vi* **1** : FEAST, BANQUET **2** : to go on a junket

Ju·no \'jü-nō\ *n* : the queen of heaven in Roman mythology

jun·ta \'hùn-tə, 'jənt-ə\ *n* [Sp, fr. fem. of *junto* joined, fr. L *junctus*, pp. of *jungere* to join] **1** : a council or committee for political or governmental purposes; *esp* : a group of persons controlling a government after a revolutionary seizure of power **2** : JUNTO

jun·to \'jənt-ō\ *n, pl* **juntos** : a group of persons joined for a common purpose

Ju·pi·ter \'jü-pət-ər\ *n* **1** : the chief god in Roman mythology and husband of Juno **2** : the largest of the planets and 5th in order of distance from the sun — see PLANET table

Ju·ras·sic \jù-'ras-ik\ *n* [F *jurassique*, fr. *Jura* mountain range] : the period of the Mesozoic era between the Triassic and Comanchean marked by the presence of dinosaurs and the first appearance of birds; *also* : the corresponding system of rocks — **Jurassic** *adj*

ju·rel \hü-'rel\ *n* [Sp] : any of several food fishes of warm seas

ju·rid·i·cal \jù-'rid-i-kəl\ *adj* **1** : of or relating to the administration of justice or the office of a judge **2** : of or relating to law or jurisprudence : LEGAL — **ju·rid·i·cal·ly** \-k(ə-)lē\ *adv*

ju·ris·dic·tion \ˌjùr-əs-'dik-shən\ *n* [L *jurisdiction-, jurisdictio*, fr. *juris dictio*, lit., pronouncement of justice] **1** : the power, right, or authority to interpret and apply the law **2** : the authority of a sovereign power to govern or legislate **3** : the limits or territory within which authority may be exercised — **ju·ris·dic·tion·al** \-shnəl, -shən-ᵊl\ *adj* — **ju·ris·dic·tion·al·ly** \-ē\ *adv*

ju·ris·pru·dence \ˌjùr-ə-'sprüd-ᵊn(t)s\ *n* **1** : a system of laws **2** : the science or philosophy of law **3** : a department of law ⟨medical *jurisprudence*⟩ — **ju·ris·pru·den·tial** \-sprü-'den-chəl\ *adj* — **ju·ris·pru·den·tial·ly** \-'dench-(ə-)lē\ *adv*

ju·rist \'jù(ə)r-əst\ *n* [L *jur-, jus* law] : one having a thorough knowledge of law

ju·ris·tic \jù-'ris-tik\ *adj* **1** : of or relating to a jurist or jurisprudence **2** : of, relating to, or recognized in law — **ju·ris·ti·cal·ly** \-ti-k(ə-)lē\ *adv*

ju·ror \'jùr-ər\ *n* : a member of or a person summoned to serve on a jury

¹ju·ry \'jù(ə)r-ē\ *n, pl* **juries** [AF *juree*, fr. OF, pp. of *jurer* to swear, fr. L *jurare*, fr. *jur-, jus* law] **1** : a body of persons sworn to inquire into and test a matter submitted to them and to give their verdict according to the evidence presented **2** : a committee that judges and awards prizes at an exhibition or contest — **ju·ry·man** \-mən\ *n*

²jury *adj* : improvised for temporary use esp. in an emergency : MAKESHIFT ⟨a *jury* mast⟩

¹just \'jəst\ *adj* [L *justus* righteous, fr. *jus* right, justice, law] **1 a** : having a basis in or conforming to fact or reason : REASONABLE ⟨a *just* comment⟩ **b** *archaic* : faithful to an original **c** : conforming to a standard of correctness : PROPER ⟨*just* proportions⟩ **2 a** (1) : morally right or good : RIGHTEOUS ⟨a *just* war⟩ (2) : MERITED, DESERVED ⟨*just* punishment⟩ **b** : legally right ⟨a *just* title⟩ — **just·ly** \'jəs(t)-nəs\ *adv* — **just·ness** \'jəs(t)-nəs\ *n*

²just \(ˌ)jəst, (ˌ)jist\ *adv* **1 a** : EXACTLY, PRECISELY ⟨*just* right⟩ **b** : very recently ⟨the bell *just* rang⟩ **2 a** : by a very small margin : BARELY ⟨*just* over the line⟩ **b** : IMMEDIATELY, DIRECTLY ⟨*just* west of here⟩ **3 a** : ONLY, MERELY ⟨*just* a note⟩ **b** : QUITE, VERY ⟨*just* wonderful⟩

jus·tice \'jəs-təs\ *n* **1 a** : the maintenance or administration of what is just **b** : JUDGE **c** : the administration of law **2 a** : the quality of being just, impartial, or fair **b** : RIGHTEOUSNESS **c** : the quality of conforming to law

justice of the peace : a local magistrate empowered chiefly to try minor cases, to administer oaths, and to perform marriages

jus·ti·fi·a·ble \'jəs-tə-ˌfī-ə-bəl\ *adj* : capable of being justified : EXCUSABLE — **jus·ti·fi·a·bly** \-blē\ *adv*

jus·ti·fi·ca·tion \ˌjəs-tə-fə-'kā-shən\ *n* **1** : the act, process, or state of being justified by God **2 a** : the act or an instance of justifying : VINDICATION **b** : something that justifies : DEFENSE

jus·ti·fy \'jəs-tə-ˌfī\ *vb* **-fied; -fy·ing** **1 a** : to prove or show to be just, right, or reasonable : VINDICATE **b** : to show a sufficient lawful reason for an act done **2 a** : to make righteous **b** : to release from the guilt of sin and accept as righteous **3** : to adjust or arrange exactly; *esp* : to set type so as to fill a full line **syn** see MAINTAIN — **jus·ti·fi·er** \-ˌfī(-ə)r\ *n*

¹jut \'jət\ *vb* **jut·ted; jut·ting** : to shoot or cause to shoot out, up, or forward : PROJECT

²jut *n* : something that juts : PROJECTION

jute \'jüt\ *n* [Hindi & Bengali *jūṭ*] : a glossy fiber from either of two East Indian plants that is used chiefly for sacking and twine

Jute \'jüt\ *n* : a member of a Germanic people invading England from the Continent and settling in Kent in the 5th century A.D. — compare ANGLO-SAXON — **Jut·ish** \'jüt-ish\

ju·ve·nal \'jü-vən-ᵊl\ *adj* : JUVENILE

¹ju·ve·nile \'jü-və-ˌnīl, -vən-ᵊl\ *adj* [L, youthful, fr. *juvenis* young person, fr. *juvenis* young; akin to E *young*] **1** : showing incomplete development : IMMATURE, CHILDISH **2** : of, relating to, or characteristic of children or young people — **ju·ve·nil·i·ty** \ˌjü-və-'nil-ət-ē\ *n*

²juvenile *n* **1 a** : a young person : YOUTH **b** : a book for young people **2 a** : a fledged bird not yet in adult plumage **b** : a 2-year-old racehorse **3** : an actor or actress who plays youthful parts

juvenile delinquency *n* : violation of the law or antisocial behavior by a juvenile — **juvenile delinquent** *n*

jux·ta·pose \'jək-stə-,pōz\ *vt* : to place side by side

jux·ta·po·si·tion \,jək-stə-pə-'zish-ən\ *n* [L *juxta* near, next] : a placing or being placed side by side — **jux·ta·po·si·tion·al** \-'zish-nəl, -ən-°l\ *adj*

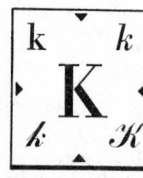

k \'kā\ *n, often cap* : the 11th letter of the English alphabet

Kaa·ba \'käb-ə\ *n* [Ar *ka'bah*, lit., square building] : a small stone building in the court of the Great Mosque at Mecca that contains a sacred black stone and is the goal of Islamic pilgrimage and the point toward which Muslims turn in praying

ka·bob \'kā-,bäb, kə-'\ *n* [Ar *kabāb*, fr. Turk *kebap*] : cubes of meat cooked with vegetables usu. on a skewer

Ka·bu·ki \kə-'bü-kē, 'käb-ù-(,)kē\ *n* : traditional Japanese popular drama with singing and dancing performed in a highly stylized manner

kad·dish \'käd-ish\ *n, often cap* [Aram *qaddīsh* holy] : a Jewish prayer recited in the daily ritual of the synagogue and by mourners at public services after the death of a close relative

kaf·fee·klatsch \'kóf-ē-,klach, 'käf-\ *n, often cap* [G, fr. *kaffee* coffee + *klatsch* gossip] : an informal social gathering for coffee and talk

Kaf·fir or **Kaf·ir** \'kaf-ər\ *n* : a member of a group of southern African Bantu-speaking peoples

kaf·ir \'kaf-ər\ *n* : a stocky grain sorghum with erect heads

kai·ser \'kī-zər\ *n* [ON *keisari* & G *kaiser;* both fr. L *Caesar,* cognomen of the Emperor Augustus] : EMPEROR; *esp* : the ruler of Germany from 1871 to 1918 — **kai·ser·dom** \-zərd-əm\ *n* — **kai·ser·ism** \-,riz-əm\ *n*

ka·ka \'käk-ə\ *n* [Maori] : a brownish New Zealand parrot with gray and red markings that is a good mimic and talker

kal·an·choe \,kal-ən-'kō-ē\ *n* : any of a genus of succulent tropical Old World plants including several grown as ornamentals

kale \'kāl\ *n* [Sc, fr. OE *cāl*] : a hardy cabbage with curled often finely cut leaves that do not form a dense head

ka·lei·do·scope \kə-'līd-ə-,skōp\ *n* [Gk *kalos* beautiful + *eidos* shape, form + E *-scope*] **1** : an instrument containing loose bits of colored glass between two flat plates and two plane mirrors so placed that changes of position of the bits of glass are reflected in an endless variety of patterns **2** : a variegated changing pattern or scene — **ka·lei·do·scop·ic** \-,līd-ə-'skäp-ik\ *adj* — **ka·lei·do·scop·i·cal·ly** \-'skäp-i-k(ə-)lē\ *adv*

kalends *var of* CALENDS

Kal·muck or **Kal·muk** \'kal-,mək, kal-'\ *n* **1** : a member of a Buddhist Mongol people of northern Sinkiang, China **2** : the language of the Kalmucks

kal·so·mine *var of* CALCIMINE

ka·ma·ai·na \,käm-ə-'ī-nə\ *n* : one who has lived in Hawaii for a long time

kam·a·la \'käm-ə-lə\ *n* [Skt] : an East Indian tree; *also* : a reddish powder from its fruit used as a dye and a worm remedy

kame \'kām\ *n* [Sc, lit., comb, fr. OE *camb*] : a short ridge or mound of material deposited by water from a melting glacier

ka·mi·ka·ze \,käm-i-'käz-ē\ *n* [Jap, lit., divine wind] : a member of a corps of Japanese pilots assigned to make a crash on a target; *also* : an airplane flown in such an attack

kan·ga·roo \,kaŋ-gə-'rü\ *n, pl* **-roos** : any of various herbivorous leaping marsupial mammals of Australia, New Guinea, and adjacent islands with a small head,

long powerful hind legs, and a long thick tail used as a support and in balancing

kangaroo rat *n* : a pouched burrowing rodent of dry regions of the western U.S.

kangaroo

Kant·ian \'kant-ē-ən, 'känt-\ *adj* : of, relating to, or characteristic of Kant or his philosophy

ka·o·lin *also* **ka·o·line** \'kā-ə-lən\ *n* [F *kaolin,* fr. *Kao-ling,* hill in China] : a fine usu. white clay that is used in ceramics and refractories and as an adsorbent

ka·pok \'kā-,päk\ *n* [Malay] : a mass of silky fibers that clothe the seeds of the ceiba tree and are used esp. as a filling for mattresses, life preservers, and sleeping bags and as insulation

kap·pa \'kap-ə\ *n* : the 10th letter of the Greek alphabet — K or κ

ka·put \kä-'pùt\ *adj* [G, fr. F *capot* not having made a trick at piquet] **1** : utterly defeated or destroyed **2** : made useless or unable to function **3** : hopelessly outmoded

kar·a·kul \'kar-ə-kəl\ *n* [*Kara Kul,* lake in Soviet Central Asia] **1** : any of a breed of hardy fat-tailed Asiatic sheep with coarse wiry brown fur **2** : the tightly curled glossy black coat of the newborn lamb of a karakul valued as fur

kar·at \'kar-ət\ *n* [alter. of ¹*carat,* fr. ²*carat*] : a unit of fineness for gold equal to ½₄ part of pure gold in an alloy

ka·ra·te \kə-'rät-ē\ *n* [Jap] : a Japanese system of self-defense without a weapon

kar·ma \'kär-mə, 'kər-\ *n, often cap* [Skt *karman* (nom. *karma*), lit., work] : the force generated by a person's actions held in Hinduism and Buddhism to perpetuate transmigration and to determine his destiny in his next existence — **kar·mic** \-mik\ *adj, often cap*

kar·roo or **ka·roo** \kə-'rü\ *n* : a dry tableland of southern Africa

kary- or **karyo-** *comb form* [Gk *karyon* nut] : nucleus of a cell ⟨*karyo*kinesis⟩

karyo·ki·ne·sis \,kar-ē-ō-kə-'nē-səs, -kī-'nē-\ *n* : MITOSIS — **karyo·ki·net·ic** \-'net-ik\ *adj*

karyo·type \'kar-ē-ə-,tīp\ *n* : the distinguishing features (as chromosome number and form) of a particular cell nucleus — **karyo·typ·ic** \,kar-ē-ə-'tip-ik\ *n*

ka·sher \kä-'she(ə)r\ *var of* KOSHER

Kash·mir goat \,kash-,mi(ə)r-, ,kazh-\ *n* : an Indian goat whose soft woolly undercoat forms cashmere wool

kash·ruth or **kash·rut** \kä-'shrüt(h)\ *n* **1** : the state of being kosher **2** : the Jewish dietary laws

Kas·site \'kas-,īt\ *n* : a member of a people from the Iranian plateau ruling Babylon between 1600 and 1200 B.C.

katabolism *var of* CATABOLISM

ka·ty·did \'kāt-ē-,did\ *n* : any of several large green American long-horned grasshoppers having stridulating organs on the fore wings of the males that produce a loud shrill sound

kau·ri \'kaù(ə)r-ē\ *n* [Maori *kawri*] **1** : any of several trees of the pine family; *esp* : a tall New Zealand timber tree **2** : a recent or fossil resin from New Zealand kauris used esp. in varnish and linoleum

Kay \'kā\ : a boastful malicious Knight of the Round Table who is foster brother and seneschal of King Arthur

kay·ak \'kī-,ak\ *n* [Esk *qajaq*] **1** : an Eskimo canoe made of a frame entirely covered with skins except for a small opening in the center where one or two paddlers may sit **2** : a canvas-covered small canoe resembling a kayak

kayak

¹**kayo** \kā-'ō, 'kā-ō\ *n, pl* **kay·os** : KNOCKOUT

²**kayo** *vt* **kay·oed; kayo·ing** : to knock out

ka·zoo \kə-'zü\ *n, pl* **kazoos** : a toy musical instrument consisting of a tube with a membrane sealing one end and a side hole into which one sings or hums

kea \'kē-ə\ *n* [Maori] : a New Zealand parrot that is normally insectivorous but sometimes destroys sheep by slashing the back to feed on the kidney fat

ke·bab or **ke·bob** \'kā-,bäb, kə-'\ *var of* KABOB

ə abut; ᵊ kitten; ər further; a back; ā bake; ä cot, cart; aù out; ch chin; e less; ē easy; g gift; i trip; ī life

¹kedge \'kej\ *vt* : to move (a ship) by hauling on a line attached to a small anchor dropped at the distance and in the direction desired

²kedge *n* : a small anchor used esp. in kedging

¹keel \'kēl\ *n* [ME *kele*, fr. ON *kjölr*] **1** : a timber or plate running lengthwise along the center of the bottom of a ship and usu. projecting from the bottom **2 a** : something (as the breastbone of a bird) like a ship's keel in form or use; *esp* : a ridged part **b** : the lower two petals of a pea flower **3** : SHIP

²keel *vb* **1 a** : to turn over **b** : to fall in or as if in a faint — usu. used with *over* **2** : to provide with a keel

keel·boat \'kēl-,bōt\ *n* : a shallow covered riverboat with a keel that is usu. rowed, poled, or towed and used for freight — **keel·boat·man** \-mən\ *n*

keel·haul \-,hȯl\ *vt* **1** : to haul under the keel of a ship as punishment or torture **2** : to rebuke severely

keel·son \'kel-sən, 'kēl-\ *n* : a structure running above and fastened to the keel of a ship in order to stiffen and strengthen its framework

¹keen \'kēn\ *adj* [OE *cēne* bold, fierce] **1** : having a fine edge or point : SHARP ⟨a *keen* knife⟩ **2** : CUTTING, STINGING, SEVERE ⟨a *keen* wind⟩ **3** : STRONG, ACUTE ⟨a *keen* sense of smell⟩ **4** : EAGER, ENTHUSIASTIC ⟨*keen* eyesight⟩ **5** : having or showing mental sharpness ⟨a *keen* mind⟩ **syn** see SHARP — **keen·ly** *adv* — **keen·ness** \'kēn-nəs\ *n*

²keen *vb* [IrGael *caoinim* I lament] : to lament with a keen — **keen·er** *n*

³keen *n* : a lamentation for the dead uttered in a loud wailing voice or in a wordless cry

¹keep \'kēp\ *vb* **kept** \'kept\; **keep·ing** [OE *cēpan*] **1** : to perform as a duty : FULFILL, OBSERVE ⟨*keep* a promise⟩ ⟨*keep* a holiday⟩ **2 a** : GUARD ⟨*keep* us from harm⟩ **b** : to take care of ⟨*keep* a war orphan⟩ **3** : to continue doing something : MAINTAIN ⟨*keep* silence⟩ ⟨*keep* on working⟩ **4** : STAY, REMAIN ⟨*keep* off the grass⟩ **5** : to have in one's service or at one's disposal ⟨*keep* a maid⟩ ⟨*keep* a car⟩ **6** : to preserve a record in ⟨*keep* a diary⟩ ⟨*keep* books⟩ **7** : to have on hand regularly for sale ⟨*keep* neckties⟩ **8** : to possess permanently ⟨*keep* what one has earned⟩ **9** : HOLD, DETAIN ⟨*keep* a person in jail⟩ **10** : to hold back : WITHHOLD ⟨*keep* a secret⟩ **11 a** : to cause to remain in a given place, situation, or condition ⟨*keep* him waiting⟩ **b** : to continue in an unspoiled condition ⟨milk does not *keep* well in warm weather⟩ **12** : REFRAIN ⟨unable to *keep* from talking⟩

syn KEEP, OBSERVE, CELEBRATE mean to notice or honor a day, occasion, or deed. KEEP stresses the idea of not neglecting or violating ⟨*keep* a fast⟩ OBSERVE implies marking by ceremonial performance ⟨not all holidays are *observed* nationally⟩ CELEBRATE suggests acknowledging an occasion by festivity

²keep *n* **1** : FORTRESS; *esp* : the strongest part of a medieval castle **2** : the means or provisions by which one is kept ⟨earned his *keep*⟩ — **for keeps 1 a** : with the provision that one keep what he has won ⟨play marbles *for keeps*⟩ **b** : with deadly seriousness **2** : PERMANENTLY

keep·er \'kē-pər\ *n* : a person who watches, guards, or takes care of something : a person in charge : WARDEN, CUSTODIAN

keep·ing \'kē-piŋ\ *n* **1** : OBSERVANCE ⟨the *keeping* of a holiday⟩ **2** : CARE, CHARGE, CUSTODY **3** : AGREEMENT, HARMONY ⟨in *keeping* with good taste⟩ **4** : the means by which something is kept : SUPPORT

keep·sake \'kēp-,sāk\ *n* : something kept or given to be kept as a memento

keep up *vb* **1** : MAINTAIN, SUSTAIN ⟨*keep* standards *up*⟩ **2** : to keep adequately informed ⟨*keep up* on international relations⟩ **3** : to continue without interruption ⟨rain *kept up* all night⟩ **4** : to stay even with others (as in a race)

keet \'kēt\ *n* : a young guinea fowl

keg \'keg, 'kag\ *n* [ME *kag*, of Scand origin] **1** : a small cask or barrel holding 30 gallons or less **2** : the contents of a keg

keg·ler \'keg-lər\ *n* [G] : ¹BOWLER

kelp \'kelp\ *n* [ME *culp*] **1** : any of various large brown seaweeds; *also* : a mass of these **2** : the ashes of seaweed used esp. as a source of iodine

kel·pie \'kel-pē\ *n* : an Australian sheep dog of a breed developed by crossing the dingo with British sheep dogs

Kelt \'kelt\, **Kelt·ic** \'kel-tik\ *var of* CELT, CELTIC

Kel·vin \'kel-vən\ *adj* [after William Thomson, Lord *Kelvin* d1907 British physicist] : relating to, conforming to, or having a thermometric scale on which the unit of measurement is the same size as the centigrade degree and according to which absolute zero is 0° or the equivalent of −273.16°C — *abbr.* K

¹ken \'ken\ *vb* **kenned**; **ken·ning** [ON *kenna* to perceive; akin to E *can*] *chiefly Scot* : KNOW

²ken *n* **1 a** : range of vision **b** : SIGHT, VIEW **2** : range of understanding

ke·naf \kə-'naf\ *n* [Per] : an East Indian hibiscus that yields a strong cordage fiber; *also* : its fiber

¹ken·nel \'ken-°l\ *n* [(assumed) ONF *kenil*, fr. (assumed) VL *canile*, fr. L *canis* dog] **1 a** : a shelter for a dog **b** : an establishment for the breeding or boarding of dogs **2** : a pack of dogs

²kennel *vb* **-neled** *or* **-nelled**; **-nel·ing** *or* **-nel·ling** : to put, keep, or take shelter in or as if in a kennel

ken·ning \'ken-iŋ\ *n* [ON, fr. *kenna* to know, name] : a metaphorical compound word or phrase used esp. in Old English and Old Norse poetry

Ken·tucky coffee tree \kən-,tək-ē-\ *n* : a tall No. American leguminous tree with large woody pods whose seeds have been used as a substitute for coffee

ke·pi \'kā-pē, 'kep-ē\ *n* [F *képi*] : a military cap with a round flat top sloping toward the front and a visor

ker·a·tin \'ker-ət-°n\ *n* [Gk *kerat-, keras* horn] : any of various sulfur-containing fibrous proteins that form the chemical basis of hair and horny tissues — **ke·rat·i·nous** \kə-'rat-°n-əs, ,ker-ə-'tī-nəs\ *adj*

kerb \'kərb\ *n, Brit* : CURB 4

ker·chief \'kər-chəf, -,chēf\ *n, pl* **kerchiefs** \-chəfs\ *also* **kerchieves** \-,chēvz\ [ME *courchef*, fr. OF *cuevrechief*, fr. *covrir* to cover + *chief* head, fr. L *caput*] **1** : a square of cloth worn by women as a head covering or around the neck **2** : HANDKERCHIEF 1

kerf \'kərf\ *n* : a slit or notch made by a saw or cutting torch

ker·mes \'kər-mēz\ *n* [Ar *qirmiz*] : the dried bodies of the females of various scale insects used as a red dyestuff

ker·mis *or* **ker·mess** \'kər-məs\ *n* [D *kermis*, fr. MD *kerc* church + *misse* mass, festival] **1** : an outdoor festival of the Low Countries **2** : a fair held usu. for charitable purposes

kern \'kərn\ *n* [F *carne* corner, fr. L *cardin-, cardo* hinge] : a part of the face of a type-cast letter that projects beyond the body

ker·nel \'kərn-°l\ *n* [OE *cyrnel*, dim. of *corn*] **1 a** : the inner softer part of a seed, fruit stone, or nut **b** : a whole seed of a cereal **2** : a central or essential part : CORE

kern·ite \'kər-,nīt\ *n* : a mineral $Na_2B_4O_7.4H_2O$ that consists of sodium, boron, and water and is an important source of borax

ker·o·sene *or* **ker·o·sine** \'ker-ə-,sēn\ *n* [Gk *kēros* wax] : a thin oil consisting of a mixture of hydrocarbons usu. obtained by distillation of petroleum and used for a fuel and as a solvent and thinner (as for paints)

ker·ria \'ker-ē-ə\ *n* [NL, fr. William *Kerr* d1814 English gardener] : any of a genus of yellow-flowered shrubs related to the roses

Ker·ry blue terrier \,ker-ē-\ *n* : any of an Irish breed of medium-sized terriers with a long head, deep chest, and silky bluish coat

ker·sey \'kər-zē\ *n* : a coarse ribbed woolen cloth for hose and work clothes

kes·trel \'kes-trəl\ *n* [MF *crecerelle*] : a small European falcon that hovers in the air against a wind

ketch \'kech\ *n* [ME *cache*] : a fore-and-aft-rigged ship similar to a yawl but with a larger mizzen and with the mizzenmast stepped farther forward

ketch·up *var of* CATSUP

ke·to acid \,kēt-ō-\ *n* : a compound that is both a ketone and an acid

ke·to·gen·e·sis \,kēt-ō-'jen-ə-səs\ *n* : the production of ketone bodies (as in diabetes) — **ke·to·gen·ic** \-'jen-ik\ *adj*

ke·tone \'kē-,tōn\ *n* [G *keton*] : an organic compound with a carbonyl group attached to two carbon atoms or in a bivalent radical — **ke·ton·ic** \kē-'tän-ik\ *adj*

ketone body *n* : a ketone or related compound found in

blood or urine as abnormal by-products of fatty acid
metabolism (as in diabetes)
ke·to·ste·roid \,kēt-ō-'sti(ə)r-,ȯid, -'ste(ə)r-\ *n* : a steroid
containing a ketone group
ket·tle \'ket-ᵊl\ *n* [ME *ketel*, fr. ON *ketill*, fr. L *catillus*,
dim. of *catinus* bowl] : a metallic vessel for boiling
liquids; *esp* : TEAKETTLE
ket·tle·drum \-,drəm\ *n* : a brass or copper kettle-shaped
drum with parchment stretched across the top and
capable of being tuned to definite pitches
¹key \'kē\ *n* [OE *cǣg*] **1 a** : a usu. metal instrument by
which the bolt of a lock is turned
b : a device having the form or
function of a key ⟨a *key* for winding a clock⟩ ⟨a *key* for opening a
coffee can⟩ **2** : a means of gaining
or preventing entrance, possession,
or control **3 a** : something that
gives an explanation or provides a
solution **b** : a list of words or
phrases giving an explanation of
symbols or abbreviations **c** : an

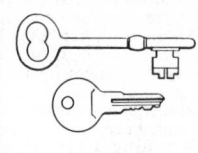

keys 1a

arrangement of usu. opposed characters of a group of
plants or animals used for identification **d** : a map
legend **4** : a small piece of wood or metal used as a
wedge or for preventing motion between parts **5** : one
of the levers with a flat surface that is pressed by a finger
in operating or playing an instrument (as a typewriter,
piano, or clarinet) **6** : SAMARA **7** : a leading individual
or principle ⟨the *key* to the situation⟩ **8** : a system of
seven tones based on their relationship to a tonic; *esp*
: the tonality of a scale **9 a** : characteristic style or tone
b : the tone or pitch of a voice **10** : a small switch for
opening or closing an electric circuit
²key *vb* **1 a** : to lock with a key **b** : to secure (as a pulley
on a shaft) by a key **2** : to regulate the musical pitch of
3 : to make conformable : ATTUNE **4** : to make nervous
or tense — usu. used with *up* ⟨was all *keyed* up about the
examination⟩ **5** : to use a key
³key *adj* : of basic importance : FUNDAMENTAL
⁴key *n* [Sp *cayo*, of AmerInd origin] : a low island or reef;
esp : one of the coral islets off the southern coast of Florida
key·board \'kē-,bȯrd, -,bȯrd\ *n* **1** : a row of keys (as on
a piano) **2** : the whole arrangement of keys (as on a
typewriter)
keyed \'kēd\ *adj* **1** : furnished with keys **2** : reinforced
by a key or keystone **3** : set to a key **4** : ADJUSTED,
ATTUNED
key·hole \'kē-,hōl\ *n* : a hole for receiving a key
¹key·note \-,nōt\ *n* **1** : the first and harmonically
fundamental tone of a scale **2** : the fundamental or central fact, idea, or mood
²keynote *vt* **1** : to set the keynote of **2** : to deliver the
keynote address at — **key·not·er** *n*
keynote address *n* : an address designed to present the
issues of primary interest to an assembly and often to
arouse unity and enthusiasm — called also *keynote speech*
key signature *n* : the sharps or flats placed after a clef
in music to indicate the key
key·stone \'kē-,stōn\ *n* **1** : the wedge-
shaped piece at the crown of an arch
that locks the other pieces in place
2 : something on which associated things
depend for support
key·way \'kē-,wā\ *n* : a groove or
channel for a key
key word *n* : a word that is a key; *esp*
: a word exemplifying the meaning or
value of a letter or symbol
khaki \'kak-ē, 'käk-\ *n* [Hindi *k͟hākī*
dust-colored, fr. *k͟hāk* dust] **1** : a light
yellowish brown **2 a** : a khaki-colored cloth made usu.
of cotton or wool **b** : a military uniform of this cloth
Khal·kha \'kal-kə\ *n* **1** : a member of a Mongol people
of Outer Mongolia **2** : the language of the Khalkha
people used as the official language of the Mongolian
People's Republic
¹khan \'kän, 'kan\ *n* [MF *caan*, of Turkic origin] **1** : a
Mongol leader; *esp* : one of the successors of Genghis
Khan **2** : a local chieftain or man of rank in some
countries of central Asia — **khan·ate** \-,āt\ *n*

K keystone

²khan *n* : a building (as a caravansary) used for shelter
by travelers in some Asian countries
khe·dive \kə-'dēv\ *n* [Turk *hidiv*] : a ruler of Egypt from
1867 to 1914 governing as a viceroy of the sultan of
Turkey
Khmer \kə-'me(ə)r\ *n* : a member of an aboriginal people
of Cambodia — **Khmer·ian** \-'mer-ē-ən\ *adj*
kib·butz \kib-'ùts, -'üts\ *n, pl* **kib·but·zim** \-,ùt-'sēm,
-,üt-\ [NHeb *qibbūṣ*, fr. Heb, gathering] : a collective
farm or settlement in Israel
kibe \'kīb\ *n* : CHILBLAIN
kib·itz·er \'kib-ət-sər\ *n* [Yiddish *kibitsen* to kibitz, fr.
G *kiebitzen*, fr. *kiebitz* pewit, busybody] : one who looks
on and often offers unwanted advice or comment esp.
at a card game — **kib·itz** \-əts\ *vb*
ki·bosh \'kī-,bäsh\ *n* : something that serves as a check
or stop ⟨put the *kibosh* on⟩
¹kick \'kik\ *vb* [ME *kiken*] **1** : to strike out (as in defense
or at a ball in games) with the foot or feet **2** : to strike,
thrust, or hit violently with the foot **3** : to object strongly
: PROTEST ⟨*kick* because prices were raised⟩ **4** : to recoil
when fired **5** : to score by kicking a ball ⟨*kick* the point
after touchdown⟩ — **kick·er** *n*
²kick *n* **1 a** : a blow with the foot; *esp* : a propelling of
a ball with the foot **b** : the power to kick **c** : a rhythmic
motion of the legs in swimming **2** : a forceful jolt or thrust
suggesting a kick; *esp* : the recoil of a gun **3 a** : a feeling
or expression of opposition or objection **b** : the grounds
for objection **4** : a stimulating effect esp. of pleasure
: THRILL
kick around *vt* **1** : to treat in an inconsiderate or high-
handed fashion **2** *slang* : to consider, examine, or discuss
from various angles
kick·back \'kik-,bak\ *n* **1** : a sharp violent reaction
2 : a secret return of a part of a sum received
kick in *vb, slang* : CONTRIBUTE
kick off \('kik-'ȯf\ *vi* **1** : to start or resume play in
football by a place-kick **2** : to begin proceedings
kick·off \'kik-,ȯf\ *n* **1** : a kick that puts the ball into
play in a football or soccer game **2** : COMMENCEMENT
kick out *vt* : to dismiss or eject forcefully or summarily
kick·shaw \'kik-,shȯ\ *n* [modif. of F *quelque chose* some-
thing] **1** : a fancy dish : DELICACY **2** : BAUBLE, GEWGAW
¹kid \'kid\ *n* [ME *kide*, of Scand origin] **1** : the young
of a goat or of a related animal **2 a** : the flesh, fur, or
skin of a kid **b** : something (as leather) made of kid
3 : CHILD, YOUNGSTER — **kid·dish** \'kid-ish\ *adj*
²kid *vb* **kid·ded; kid·ding 1** : to deceive as a joke : FOOL
2 : to make fun of : TEASE — **kid·der** *n*
kid·dush \'kid-,ùsh, kid-'üsh\ *n* : a Jewish blessing
customarily recited before the evening meal at the beginning of a Sabbath or festival
kid glove *n* : a dress glove made of kidskin — **kid–gloved**
\'kid-'gləvd\ *adj* — **with kid gloves** : with special
consideration
kid·nap \'kid-,nap\ *vb* **kid·napped** \-,napt\ *or* **kid-
naped; kid·nap·ping** \-,nap-iŋ\ *or* **kid·nap·ing** [prob.
back-formation fr. *kidnapper*, fr. **¹kid** + obs. *napper*
thief] : to carry away a person by unlawful force or by
fraud against his will — **kid·nap·per** \-,nap-ər\ *or*
kid·nap·er *n*
kid·ney \'kid-nē\ *n, pl* **kidneys** [ME] **1 a** : either of a
pair of oval to bean-shaped organs situated in the body
cavity near the spinal column that excrete waste products
of metabolism in the form of urine **b** : an excretory organ
of an invertebrate animal **2 a** : TEMPERAMENT, DISPOSI-
TION **b** : KIND, SORT
kidney bean *n* : a common garden bean grown esp. for
its nutritious seeds; *also* : a rather large dark red bean seed
kid·skin \'kid-,skin\ *n* : the skin of a young goat or
leather made from or resembling this
kie·sel·guhr *or* **kie·sel·gur** \'kē-zəl-,gùr\ *n* : loose or
porous diatomite
¹kill \'kil\ *vb* [ME *cullen, killen* to strike, kill] **1** : to
deprive of life : put to death : SLAY **2** : DESTROY, RUIN
⟨*kill* all chance of success⟩ **3** : to use up ⟨*kill* time⟩
4 : DEFEAT ⟨*kill* a proposed law⟩ **5** : to mark matter for
omission ⟨*kill* a news story⟩ **6** : to hit a return (as in
tennis) so hard that it cannot be played back
syn KILL, SLAY, MURDER, ASSASSINATE mean to deprive of
life. KILL simply states the fact of death by any agency in

any manner; SLAY implies deliberateness and violence but not necessarily motive; MURDER implies motive and premeditation and usu. secrecy and stresses full moral responsibility; ASSASSINATE applies to open or secret killing often for political motives

²**kill** *n* **1** : an act of killing **2 a** : an animal killed in a hunt, season, or particular period of time **b** : an enemy airplane, submarine, or ship destroyed by military action

kill·deer \'kil-‚di(ə)r\ *n, pl* **killdeers** *or* **killdeer** : a No. American plover with a plaintive penetrating cry

kill·er \'kil-ər\ *n* **1** : one that kills **2** : a fierce carnivorous gregarious largely black whale 20 to 30 feet long — called also *killer whale*

kil·li·fish \'kil-ē-‚fish\ *n* : any of numerous small fishes including some used as bait, in mosquito control, and as aquarium fishes

kill·ing \'kil-iŋ\ *n* : a sudden notable gain or profit

kill·joy \'kil-‚jòi\ *n* : one who spoils the pleasure of others

¹**kiln** \'kil(n)\ *n* [OE *cyln*, fr. L *culina* kitchen] : an oven, furnace, or heated enclosure for processing a substance by burning, firing, or drying

²**kiln** *vt* : to burn, fire, or dry in a kiln

ki·lo \'kē-lō, 'kil-ō\ *n, pl* **kilos 1** : KILOGRAM **2** : KILOMETER

kilo- *comb form* [F, modif. of Gk *chilioi*] : thousand ⟨*kiloton*⟩

kilo·cal·o·rie \'kil-ə-‚kal-(ə-)rē\ *n* : CALORIE 1b

kilo·cy·cle \'kil-ə-‚sī-kəl\ *n* : one thousand cycles; *esp* : one thousand cycles per second

kilo·gram \'kil-ə-‚gram\ *n* : the basic metric unit of mass and weight equal to 1000 grams or approximately 2.2046 pounds avoirdupois — see METRIC SYSTEM table

kilo·li·ter \'kil-ə-‚lēt-ər\ *n* — see METRIC SYSTEM table

ki·lom·e·ter \kil-'äm-ət-ər, 'kil-ə-‚mēt-\ *n* — see METRIC SYSTEM table

kilo·ton \'kil-ə-‚tən\ *n* **1** : one thousand tons **2** : an explosive force equivalent to that of one thousand tons of TNT

kilo·volt \'kil-ə-‚vōlt\ *n* : a unit of electromotive force equal to one thousand volts

kilo·watt \'kil-ə-‚wät\ *n* : a unit of power equal to 1000 watts

kilowatt–hour *n* : a unit of work or energy equal to that expended by one kilowatt in one hour

¹**kilt** \'kilt\ *vt* [of Scand origin] *chiefly dial* : to tuck up (as a skirt)

²**kilt** *n* **1** : a knee-length pleated skirt usu. of tartan worn by men in Scotland and by Scottish regiments in the British army **2** : a garment that resembles a Scottish kilt — **kilt·ed** \'kil-təd\ *adj*

kil·ter \'kil-tər\ *n* : proper condition : ORDER ⟨out of *kilter*⟩

ki·mo·no \kə-'mō-nə\ *n, pl* **-nos** [Jap] **1** : a loose robe with wide sleeves and a broad sash traditionally worn as an outer garment by the Japanese **2** : a loose dressing gown worn chiefly by women

¹**kin** \'kin\ *n* [OE *cyn*] **1 a** : a person's relatives : KINDRED **b** : KINSMAN **2** *archaic* : KINSHIP

²**kin** *adj* : KINDRED, RELATED

-kin \kən\ *also* **-kins** \kənz\ *n suffix* [MD *-kin*] : little ⟨cat*kin*⟩⟨baby*kins*⟩

¹**kind** \'kīnd\ *n* [OE *cynd* birth, nature; akin to E *kin*] **1 a** : a natural group : SPECIES **b** : a group united by common traits or interests : CATEGORY **c** : VARIETY ⟨all *kinds* of people⟩ **d** : a doubtful or barely admissible member of a category ⟨a *kind* of gray⟩ **2** : essential quality or character ⟨punishment different in *kind* rather than degree⟩ **3 a** : goods or commodities as distinguished from money **b** : the equivalent of what has been offered or received

syn SORT, TYPE: KIND and SORT are close synonyms and usu. imply a group with less specific resemblances than TYPE; KIND may suggest natural or logical grouping; SORT sometimes suggests disparagement ⟨the flashier *sort* of holiday resorts⟩ TYPE may suggest clearly marked similarity throughout the items included so that each is typical of the group

— **of a kind 1** : of the same sort, class, or value **2** : of an imperfect or untypical quality or character : of a sort

²**kind** *adj* [OE *gecynde* natural, fr. *cynd* nature] **1** : having the will to do good and to bring happiness to others

: SYMPATHETIC, CONSIDERATE, GENTLE **2** : showing or growing out of gentleness or goodness of heart ⟨a *kind* act⟩

kin·der·gar·ten \'kin-dər-‚gärt-°n, -‚gärd-\ *n* [G, lit., garden cf children] : a school or class for very young children in which teaching is done largely through activities based on the normal aptitudes and desire of the pupils for exercise and play

kin·der·gart·ner \-‚gärt-nər, -‚gärd-\ *n* **1** : a kindergarten pupil **2** : a kindergarten teacher

kind·heart·ed \'kīnd-'härt-əd\ *adj* : having or showing a kind and sympathetic nature — **kind·heart·ed·ly** *adv* — **kind·heart·ed·ness** *n*

kin·dle \'kin-d°l\ *vb* **kin·dled; kin·dling** \-dliŋ, -d°l-iŋ\ [ME *kindlen*, fr. ON *kynda*] **1** : to set on fire or take fire : start burning : LIGHT ⟨*kindle* a fire⟩ **2** : AROUSE, PROVOKE, EXCITE ⟨*kindle* a person's anger⟩ **3** : to begin to be excited : grow warm and animated **4** : to light up as if with flame ⟨with *kindling* eyes⟩ — **kin·dler** \-dlər, -d°l-ər\ *n*

kin·dling \'kin-dliŋ\ *n* : easily combustible material for starting a fire

¹**kind·ly** \'kīn-dlē\ *adj* **kind·li·er; -est** [OE *cyndelīc* natural, fr. *cynd*] **1** : of an agreeable or beneficial nature : PLEASANT ⟨*kindly* climate⟩ **2** : of a sympathetic or generous nature : FRIENDLY ⟨*kindly* men⟩ — **kind·li·ness** *n*

²**kindly** *adv* **1** : READILY ⟨does not take *kindly* to criticism⟩ **2 a** : SYMPATHETICALLY **b** : as a gesture of good will **c** : COURTEOUSLY, OBLIGINGLY

kind·ness \'kīn(d)-nəs\ *n* **1** : a kind deed : FAVOR **2** : the quality or state of being kind

¹**kin·dred** \'kin-drəd\ *n* **1 a** : a group of related individuals **b** : one's relatives **2** *archaic* : family relationship : KINSHIP

²**kindred** *adj* : of like nature or character

kine \'kīn\ *archaic pl of* COW

kin·e·mat·ics \‚kin-ə-'mat-iks, ‚kī-nə-\ *n* [Gk *kinēmat-, kinēma* motion, fr. *kinein* to move] : a science that deals with aspects of motion apart from considerations of mass and force — **kin·e·mat·ic** \-'mat-ik\ *adj*

¹**kin·e·scope** \'kin-ə-‚skōp\ *n* **1** : a cathode-ray tube on which the picture appears in a television receiver **2** : a moving picture made from the image on a kinescope

²**kinescope** *vt* : to make a kinescope of

ki·ne·si·ol·o·gy \kə-‚nē-sē-'äl-ə-jē, kī-, -‚nē-zē-\ *n* : the study of the mechanical and anatomical relations involved in human movement

kin·es·the·sia \‚kin-əs-'thē-zh(ē-)ə\ *or* **kin·es·the·sis** \-'thē-səs\ *n, pl* **-the·sias** *or* **-the·ses** \-'thē-‚sēz\ : a sense based on receptors in muscles, tendons, and joints that are stimulated by bodily movements and tensions; *also* : sensory experience derived from this sense — **kin·es·thet·ic** \-'thet-ik\ *adj* — **kin·es·thet·i·cal·ly** \-'thet-i-k(ə-)lē\ *adv*

ki·net·ic \kə-'net-ik, kī-\ *adj* [Gk *kinein* to move] : of or relating to the motion of material bodies and the forces and energy associated therewith

kinetic energy *n* : energy associated with motion

ki·net·ics \kə-'net-iks, kī-\ *n sing or pl* **1** : a science that deals with the effects of forces upon the motions of material bodies or with changes in a physical or chemical system **2** : the means by which a physical or chemical change is effected

kin·folk \'kin-‚fōk\ *n* : RELATIVES

king \'kiŋ\ *n* [OE *cyning*] **1 a** : a male monarch of a major territorial unit; *esp* : one who inherits his position and rules for life **b** : a paramount chief **2** *cap* : GOD, CHRIST **3** : one that holds a preeminent position; *esp* : a chief among competitors **4** : the piece in a set of chessmen that can move ordinarily one square in any direction and has the power to capture but is obliged never to enter or remain in exposure to capture **5** : a playing card bearing the stylized figure of a king **6** : a checker that has been crowned

king·bird \-‚bərd\ *n* : an American tyrant flycatcher

king crab *n* **1** : a large marine arthropod (order Xiphosura and class Merostomata) with a broad crescentic cephalothorax **2** : any of several very large crabs

king·dom \'kiŋ-dəm\ *n* **1** : a political community or territorial unit having a monarchical form of government headed by a king or queen **2** *often cap* **a** : the eternal kingship of God **b :** the realm in which God's will is fulfilled **3 :** a realm or region in which something or someone is dominant ⟨the cotton *kingdom*⟩ **4 :** one of the three primary divisions of lifeless material, plants, and animals into which natural objects are grouped — called also respectively *mineral kingdom, plant kingdom, animal kingdom*

king·fish \'kiŋ-,fish\ *n* **:** any of various sea fishes; *esp* **:** a large sport and food fish of the warm western Atlantic resembling the related Spanish mackerel

king·fish·er \-,fish-ər\ *n* **:** any of a family of usu. crested and bright-colored nonpasserine birds with a short tail and a long stout sharp bill

King James Version \kiŋ-'jāmz-\ *n* [James I *d*1625 king of England] **:** AUTHORIZED VERSION

king·let \'kiŋ-lət\ *n* **1 :** a weak or petty king **2 :** any of several small birds that resemble warblers but have some of the habits of titmice

king·ly \'kiŋ-lē\ *adj* **1 :** having royal rank **2 :** of, relating to, or befitting a king **3 :** MONARCHICAL — **king·li·ness** *n* — **kingly** *adv*

king·pin \'kiŋ-,pin\ *n* **1 :** any of several bowling pins: as **a :** HEAD-PIN **b :** the number 5 pin **2 :** the chief person in a group or undertaking **3 :** a vertical bolt by which the forward axle and wheels of a vehicle are connected with other parts

kingfisher

king post *n* **1 :** a vertical member connecting the apex of a triangular truss with the base **2 :** a mast that supports a shipboard derrick

Kings \'kiŋz\ *n* — see BIBLE table

King's English *n* **:** standard, pure, or correct English speech or usage

king's evil *n, often cap K&E* [fr. the former belief that it could be healed by a king's touch] **:** SCROFULA

king·ship \'kiŋ-,ship\ *n* **1 :** the position, office, or dignity of a king **2 :** the personality of a king **:** MAJESTY **3 :** government by a king

king-size \'kiŋ-,sīz\ *or* **king-sized** \-,sīzd\ *adj* **1 :** longer than the regular or standard size **2 :** unusually large

king snake *n* **:** any of numerous harmless brightly marked snakes of the southern and central U.S. that feed on rodents

¹kink \'kiŋk\ *n* [D] **1 :** a short tight twist or curl **2 :** QUIRK, WHIM **3 :** a cramp in some part of the body **4 :** an imperfection likely to cause difficulties in operation — **kinky** \'kiŋ-kē\ *adj*

²kink *vb* **:** to form a kink **:** make a kink in

kin·ka·jou \'kiŋ-kə-,jü\ *n* [F, of Algonquian origin] **:** a slender long-tailed mammal of Central and So. America related to the raccoon

-kins — see -KIN

kins·folk \'kinz-,fōk\ *n* **:** RELATIVES

kin·ship \'kin-,ship\ *n* **:** the quality or state of being kin **:** RELATIONSHIP

kins·man \'kinz-mən\ *n* **:** RELATIVE; *esp* **:** a male relative

kins·wom·an \'kinz-,wům-ən\ *n* **:** a female relative

ki·osk \'kē-,äsk, kē-'\ *n* [Turk *köşk*, fr. Per *kūshk* portico] **1 :** an open summerhouse or pavilion **2 :** a small light structure with one or more open sides used esp. as a newsstand or a telephone booth

kip \'kip\ *n* **:** the undressed hide of a young or small animal

¹kip·per \'kip-ər\ *n* [OE *cypera* spawning salmon] **:** a kippered herring or salmon

²kipper *vt* **kip·pered; kip·per·ing** \'kip-(ə-)riŋ\ **:** to cure by splitting, cleaning, salting, and smoking

Kir·ghiz \ki(ə)r-'gēz\ *n* **:** a member of a Mongolian people with some Caucasian intermixture inhabiting chiefly Soviet Central Asia

kirk \'ki(ə)rk, 'kərk\ *n* [ON *kirkja*, fr. OE *cirice*] **1** *chiefly Scot* **:** CHURCH **2** *cap* **:** the national church of Scotland as distinguished from the Church of England or the Anglican Church in Scotland

kir·tle \'kərt-ᵊl\ *n* [OE *cyrtel*] **:** a woman's dress, skirt, or petticoat

kis·met \'kiz-,met, -mət\ *n, often cap* [Turk *kısmet*, fr. Ar *qismah* portion, lot] **:** FATE 1, 2

¹kiss \'kis\ *vb* [OE *cyssan*] **1 :** to touch with the lips as a mark of affection or greeting **2 :** to touch gently or lightly ⟨wind gently *kissing* the trees⟩ — **kiss·a·ble** \-ə-bəl\ *adj*

²kiss *n* **1 :** a caress with the lips **2 :** a gentle touch or contact **3 :** a bite-size candy often wrapped in paper or foil

kiss·er \'kis-ər\ *n* **1 :** one that kisses **2** *slang* **:** MOUTH; *also* **:** FACE

¹kit \'kit\ *n* [ME, wooden tub] **1 a :** a collection of articles for personal use ⟨a travel *kit*⟩ **b :** a set of tools or implements ⟨a carpenter's *kit*⟩ **c :** a set of parts to be assembled ⟨model-airplane *kit*⟩ **d :** a packaged collection of related material ⟨convention *kit*⟩ **2 :** a container (as a bag or case) for a kit

²kit *n* **:** a small violin

³kit *n* **1 :** KITTEN **2 :** a young or undersized fur-bearing animal; *also* **:** its pelt

kitch·en \'kich-ən\ *n* [OE *cycene*, fr. LL *coquina*, fr. L *coquere* to cook] **1 :** a place (as a room) with cooking facilities **2 :** the personnel that prepares, cooks, and serves food

kitchen cabinet *n* **1 :** a cupboard with drawers and shelves for use in a kitchen **2 :** an informal group of advisers to the head of a government

kitch·en·ette \,kich-ə-'net\ *n* **:** a small kitchen or an alcove containing cooking facilities

kitchen garden *n* **:** a plot in which vegetables are grown for domestic use

kitchen midden *n* **:** a refuse heap; *esp* **:** a mound marking the site of a primitive human habitation

kitchen police *n* **1 :** enlisted men detailed to assist the cooks in a military mess **2 :** the work done by kitchen police

kitch·en·ware \'kich-ən-,wa(ə)r, -,we(ə)r\ *n* **:** hardware for use in a kitchen

kite \'kīt\ *n* [OE *cȳta*] **1 :** any of various hawks with long narrow wings, a deeply forked tail, and feet adapted for taking insects and small reptiles as prey **2 :** a light frame covered with paper or cloth, often provided with a balancing tail, and designed to be flown in the air at the end of a long string **3** *pl* **:** the lightest and usu. the loftiest sails carried only in a light breeze

kith \'kith\ *n* [ME, fr. OE *cȳthth*, fr. *cūth* known] **:** familiar friends, neighbors, or relatives ⟨*kith* and kin⟩

kit·ten \'kit-ᵊn\ *n* [ME *kitoun*] **:** the young of a small mammal and esp. of a cat

kit·ten·ish \'kit-nish, -ᵊn-ish\ *adj* **:** resembling a kitten; *esp* **:** PLAYFUL — **kit·ten·ish·ly** *adv* — **kit·ten·ish·ness** *n*

kit·ti·wake \'kit-ē-,wāk\ *n* **:** any of various gulls having the hind toe short and the wing tips black

¹kit·ty \'kit-ē\ *n, pl* **kitties :** CAT 1a; *esp* **:** KITTEN

²kitty *n, pl* **kitties 1 :** a fund in a poker game made up of contributions from each pot **2 :** a sum of money or a collection of goods made up of small contributions **:** POOL

kit·ty-cor·ner *or* **kit·ty-cor·nered** *var of* CATERCORNER

ki·va \'kē-və\ *n* **:** a Pueblo Indian ceremonial structure that is usu. round and partly underground

Ki·wa·ni·an \kə-'wän-ē-ən\ *n* **:** a member of one of the major service clubs

ki·wi \'kē-(,)wē\ *n* [Maori] **:** a flightless New Zealand bird with rudimentary wings, stout legs, a long bill, and grayish brown hairlike plumage

Klan \'klan\ *n* **:** an organization of Ku Kluxers; *also* **:** a subordinate unit of such an organization — **Klansman** \'klanz-mən\ *n*

Klee·nex \'klē-,neks\ *trademark* — used for a cleansing tissue

klep·to·ma·nia \,klep-tə-'mā-nē-ə, -nyə\ *n* [Gk *kleptein* to steal] **:** a persistent neurotic impulse to steal esp. without economic motive — **klep·to·ma·ni·ac** \-nē-,ak\ *adj or n*

klieg light *or* **kleig light** \'klēg-,līt\ *n* [after John H. *Kliegl d*1959 & Anton T. *Kliegl d*1927 American lighting experts] **:** an arc light used in taking motion pictures

knack \'nak\ *n* [ME *knak* trick, artifice] **1 :** a clever way of doing something **:** TRICK **2 :** a special ready capacity that is hard to analyze or teach

knack·er \'nak-ər\ *n, Brit* **:** a buyer or processor of wornout animals or their carcasses esp. for animal feed and fertilizer — **knack·ery** \-ə-rē\ n

knap·sack \'nap-,sak\ n [LG *knappsack*, fr. *knappen* to eat + *sack* bag] : a usu. canvas or leather bag or case strapped on the back and used esp. for carrying supplies while on a march or hike

knap·weed \'nap-,wēd\ n : any of several weedy plants related to the cornflower

knave \'nāv\ n [ME, fr. OE *cnafa*, lit., boy] **1** archaic **a** : a male servant **b** : a man of humble birth or position **2** : a tricky deceitful fellow : ROGUE **3** : JACK 5

knav·ery \'nāv-(ə-)rē\ n, pl **-er·ies 1** : the practices of a knave : RASCALITY **2** : a roguish or mischievous act

knav·ish \'nā-vish\ adj : of, relating to, or characteristic of a knave; esp : DISHONEST — **knav·ish·ly** adv

knead \'nēd\ vt [OE *cnedan*] **1** : to work and press into a mass with or as if with the hands **2 a** : to form or shape as if by kneading **b** : to treat as if by kneading : MASSAGE — **knead·er** n

knee \'nē\ n [OE *cnēow*] **1** : the joint or middle part of the human leg in which the femur, tibia, and patella come together; *also* : a corresponding part of a quadruped **2** : something resembling the human knee **3** : the part of a garment covering the knee — **kneed** \'nēd\ adj

knee·cap \'nē-,kap\ n : PATELLA

knee·hole \-,hōl\ n : a space (as under a desk) for the knees

knee jerk n : an involuntary forward kick produced by a light blow on the tendon below the patella

kneel \'nēl\ vi **knelt** \'nelt\ or **kneeled** \'nēld\; **kneel·ing** [OE *cnēowlian*] : to bend the knee : fall or rest on the knees — **kneel·er** n

¹knell \'nel\ vb [OE *cnyllan*] **1** : to ring esp. for a death, funeral, or disaster : TOLL **2** : to sound in an ominous manner or with an ominous effect **3** : to summon, announce, or proclaim by or as if by a knell

²knell n **1** : a stroke or sound of a bell esp. when rung slowly for a death, funeral, or disaster **2** : a sound or other indication of a death or of the end or failure of something

knew past of KNOW

knick·er·bock·ers \'nik-ə(r)-,bäk-ərz\ n pl [Diedrich *Knickerbocker*, fictitious author of *History of New York* (1809) by Washington Irving] : KNICKERS

knick·ers \'nik-ərz\ n pl : loose-fitting short pants gathered at the knee

knick·knack \'nik-,nak\ n : a small trivial article intended for ornament

¹knife \'nīf\ n, pl **knives** \'nīvz\ [OE *cnīf*] **1 a** : a cutting instrument consisting of a sharp blade fastened to a handle **b** : a weapon resembling a knife **2** : a sharp cutting blade or tool in a machine

²knife vt **1** : to stab, slash, or wound with a knife **2** : to move like a knife in ⟨birds *knifing* the evening sky⟩

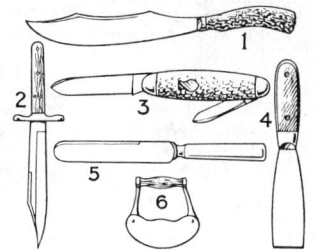

knives: *1* carving, 2 hunting, *3* pocket, 4 putty, *5* table, 6 chopping

knife pleat n : one of a series of narrow sharply pressed pleats all turned in one direction

¹knight \'nīt\ n [ME, fr. OE *cniht* boy, military follower] **1 a** : a mounted warrior of feudal times serving a superior (as a king); *esp* : one who after a period of early service has been awarded a special military rank and has sworn to obey certain rules of conduct **b** : a man honored by a sovereign for merit and in Great Britain ranking below a baronet **c** : a person of another age or area resembling a medieval knight in rank or way of life **d** : a member of any of various orders or societies **e** : a man devoted to the service of a lady as her attendant or champion **2** : a chess piece that can move two squares in any direction to a square of the opposite color regardless of whether the intervening squares are occupied

²knight vt : to make a knight of : confer the rank of knight on

knight bachelor n, pl **knights bachelor** : a knight of the most ancient and lowest order of English knights

knight–er·rant \'nīt-'er-ənt\ n, pl **knights-errant** : a knight traveling in search of adventures in which to exhibit his military skill, prowess, and generosity — **knight-er·rant·ry** \'nīt-'er-ən-trē\ n

knight·hood \'nīt-,húd\ n **1** : the rank, dignity, or profession of a knight **2** : the qualities befitting a knight : CHIVALRY **3** : knights as a class or body

knight·ly \'nīt-lē\ adj **1** : of, relating to, or characteristic of a knight **2** : made up of knights — **knight·li·ness** n — **knightly** adv

Knight of Co·lum·bus \-kə-'ləm-bəs\ n, pl **Knights of Columbus** [after Christopher *Columbus* d1506 Italian explorer] : a member of a fraternal and benevolent society of Roman Catholic men

Knight Templar n, pl **Knights Templars** or **Knights Templar 1** : TEMPLAR 1 **2** : a member of an order of Freemasonry

knit \'nit\ vb **knit** or **knit·ted**; **knit·ting** [OE *cnyttan*; akin to E *knot*] **1** : to form a fabric by interlacing yarn or thread in connected loops with needles ⟨knit a sweater⟩ **2** : to draw or come together closely as if knitted : unite firmly ⟨wait for a broken bone to *knit*⟩ **3** : WRINKLE ⟨knit her brow⟩ **4** : to bind closely by a tie of any kind ⟨knit by common interests⟩ — **knit·ter** n

knit stitch n : a basic knitting stitch usu. made with the yarn at the back of the work by inserting the right needle into the front part of a loop on the left needle from the left side, catching the yarn with the point of the right needle, and bringing it through the first loop to form a new loop — compare PURL STITCH

knit·ting n **1** : the action or method of one that knits **2** : work done or being done by one that knits

knit·wear \'nit-,wa(ə)r, -,we(ə)r\ n : knitted clothing

knob \'näb\ n [ME *knobbe*] **1 a** : a rounded protuberance : LUMP **b** : a small rounded ornament or handle **2** : a rounded usu. isolated hill or mountain — **knobbed** \'näbd\ adj — **knob·by** \'näb-ē\ adj

¹knock \'näk\ vb [OE *cnocian*] **1 a** : to strike something with a sharp blow : to drive, force, or make by so striking **2** : to collide with something **3 a** : BUSTLE ⟨knocked around in the kitchen most of the afternoon⟩ **b** : WANDER ⟨knocked about the mountains during his vacation⟩ **4** : to make a pounding noise esp. as a result of abnormal ignition ⟨an automobile engine that *knocks*⟩ **5** : to find fault with

²knock n **1 a** : a sharp blow **b** : a severe misfortune or hardship **2** : a pounding noise; *esp* : one in an automobile engine caused by abnormal ignition

¹knock·about \'näk-ə-,baút\ adj **1** : suitable for rough use **2** : being noisy and rough : BOISTEROUS

²knockabout n **1** : knockabout comedy **2** : a sloop with a simple rig and no bowsprit and topmast

knock down \(')näk-'daún\ vt **1** : to dispose of to a bidder at an auction sale **2** : to take apart : DISASSEMBLE

¹knock·down \'näk-,daún\ n **1** : a knocking down of something or someone (as a boxer) **2** : something that strikes down or overwhelms **3** : something easily assembled or disassembled

²knockdown adj **1** : having such force as to strike down or overwhelm **2** : that can easily be assembled or disassembled

knock·er \'näk-ər\ n : one that knocks; *esp* : a device hinged to a door for use in knocking

knock–knee \'näk-,nē, -,nē\ n : a condition in which the legs curve inward at the knees — **knock-kneed** \-'nēd\ adj

knock off vb : to discontinue doing something : STOP

knock out \(')näk-'aút\ vt **1** : to fell (a boxing opponent) by hitting with an immobilizing blow **2** : to make inoperative, useless, or unconscious

knock·out \'näk-,aút\ n **1 a** : the act of knocking out : the condition of being knocked out **b** : a blow that knocks out an opponent **2** : something sensationally striking or attractive — **knockout** adj

knoll \'nōl\ n [OE *cnoll*] : a small round hill : MOUND

¹knot \'nät\ n [OE *cnotta*] **1** : an interlacing (as of string or ribbon) that forms a lump or knob **2** : something hard to solve : PROBLEM **3** : a bond of union; *esp* : the marriage bond **4 a** : a protuberant lump or swelling in tissue **b** : the base of a woody branch enclosed in the stem from which it arises; *also* : its section in lumber **5** : a cluster of persons or things : GROUP **6** : an ornamental bow of ribbon : COCKADE **7 a** : one nautical mile per hour **b** : one nautical mile

knots 1 : *1* square, 2 overhand knot, 3 half hitch, 4 slipknot

²knot *vb* **knot·ted; knot·ting 1** : to tie in or with a knot : form knots in **2** : to unite closely or intricately : ENTANGLE

³knot *n* [ME *knott*] : any of several sandpipers that breed in the Arctic and winter in temperate or warm regions

knot·grass \'nät-,gras\ *n* : a weed related to buckwheat with bluish gray grassy leaves and tiny flowers

knot·hole \-,hōl\ *n* : a hole in a board or tree trunk where a knot has come out

knot·ted *adj* **1** : tied in or with a knot **2** : full of knots : GNARLED **3** : ENTANGLED, PUZZLING **4** : ornamented with knots or knobs

knot·ty \'nät-ē\ *adj* **knot·ti·er; -est 1** : marked by or full of knots **2** : puzzling because of intricacy : COMPLEX ⟨a *knotty* problem⟩

knotty pine *n* : pine wood with decorative distribution of knots used esp. for interior finish

knout \'naut, 'nüt\ *n* [Russ *knut*, of Gmc origin; akin to E *knot*] : a whip for flogging criminals

know \'nō\ *vb* **knew** \'n(y)ü\; **known** \'nōn\; **know·ing** [OE *cnāwen*] **1 a** (1) : to perceive directly : have direct cognition (2) : to have understanding of ⟨*know* yourself⟩ (3) : to recognize the nature of : DISCERN ⟨*knew* him to be honest⟩ **b** (1) : to recognize as being the same as something previously known ⟨*knew* him by his walk⟩ (2) : to be acquainted or familiar with ⟨*knows* the city very well⟩ **2 a** : to be aware of the truth or factuality of ⟨*know* that the earth is round⟩ **b** : to have a practical understanding of ⟨*knows* how to write⟩ **3** : to have knowledge **4** : to be or become aware ⟨*knew* about her⟩ — **know·a·ble** \'nō-ə-bəl\ *adj* — **know·er** \'nō-(ə)r\ *n*

know-how \'nō-,hau\ *n* : knowledge of how to do something smoothly and efficiently

¹know·ing \'nō-iŋ\ *n* : ACQUAINTANCE, COGNIZANCE

²knowing *adj* **1** : having or reflecting knowledge, information, or intelligence ⟨a *knowing* glance⟩ **2** : shrewdly and keenly alert : ASTUTE **3** : DELIBERATE, INTENTIONAL — **know·ing·ly** \-iŋ-lē\ *adv*

knowl·edge \'näl-ij\ *n* [ME *knowlege* acknowledgment, cognizance, fr. *knowlechen* to acknowledge, fr. *knowen* to know] **1** : understanding gained by actual experience : practical skill ⟨a *knowledge* of carpentry⟩ **2 a** : the state of being aware of something or of having information **b** : range of information ⟨within my *knowledge*⟩ **3** : the act of understanding : clear perception of truth **4** : something learned and kept in the mind : LEARNING, ENLIGHTENMENT ⟨a man of vast *knowledge* of history⟩

knowl·edge·a·ble \'näl-i-jə-bəl\ *adj* : having or exhibiting knowledge or intelligence : WISE — **knowl·edge·a·ble·ness** *n* — **knowl·edge·a·bly** \-blē\ *adv*

know-noth·ing \'nō-,nəth-iŋ\ *n* **1** : IGNORAMUS **2** *cap K & N* : a member of a 19th century secret American political organization hostile to the political influence of recent immigrants and Roman Catholics

¹knuck·le \'nək-əl\ *n* [ME *knokel*] **1** : the rounded lump formed by the ends of two bones where they come together in a joint; *esp* : such a lump at a finger joint **2** : a cut of meat consisting of a tarsal or carpal joint with the adjoining flesh **3** *pl* : a set of joined metal finger rings worn over the front of the fist for use as a weapon — called also *brass knuckles*

²knuckle *vb* **knuck·led; knuck·ling** \'nək-(ə-)liŋ\ **1** : to place the knuckles on the ground in shooting a marble **2** : to give in : SUBMIT — usu. used with *under* **3** : to apply oneself earnestly — usu. used with *down*

knuck·le·bone \,nək-əl-'bōn, 'nək-əl-,\ *n* : the bone of a knuckle joint; *esp* : a metacarpal or metatarsal bone of a sheep formerly used in gaming or divination

knur \'nər\ *n* : a hard excrescence : GNARL

knurl \'nərl\ *n* **1** : a small protuberance or knob; *also* : a gnarl or twisted knot of wood **2** : one of a series of

small ridges or beads on a metal surface (as of a thumbscrew) to aid in gripping — **knurled** \'nərld\ *adj*

¹KO \kā-'ō, 'kā-ō\ *n* [*knock out*] : a knockout in boxing

²KO *vt* **KO'd; KO'·ing** : to knock out in boxing

ko·a·la \kō-'äl-ə\ *n* : an Australian arboreal marsupial that has large hairy ears, gray fur, and no tail and feeds on eucalyptus leaves

ko·bold \'kō-,bold\ *n* **1** : a gnome that in German folklore inhabits underground places **2** : an often mischievous spirit of German folklore

Koch's postulates \'kōks-\ *n pl* [after Robert *Koch d*1910 German bacteriologist] : a statement of the steps required to identify a microorganism as the cause of a disease

Ko·dak \'kō-,dak\ *trademark* — used for a small hand camera

Koh-i-noor \'kō-ə-,nur\ *n* [Per *Kōh-i-nūr*, lit., mountain of light] : a large diamond discovered in India and made one of the British crown jewels

kohl \'kōl\ *n* [Ar *kuḥl*] : a preparation used by women esp. in Arabia and Egypt to darken the edges of the eyelids

kohl·ra·bi \kōl-'räb-ē, -'rab-\ *n, pl* **-rab·ies** [G, fr. It *cavolo rapa*, fr. *cavolo* cabbage + *rapa* turnip] : a cabbage that forms no head but has a swollen fleshy edible stem

kok-sa·ghyz *or* **kok-sa·gyz** \,kōk-sə-'gēz\ *n* [Russ *kok-sagyz*, fr. Turki *kok-sagīz*, fr. *kok* root + *sagīz* rubber] : a perennial Asiatic dandelion cultivated for its thick rubber-containing roots

ko·la nut \'kō-lə-\ *n* [of African origin] : the bitter seed of an African tree containing much caffeine and used in beverages and medicine for its stimulant effect

ko·lin·sky *or* **ko·lin·ski** \kə-'lin(t)-skē\ *n* [Russ *kolinskiĭ* of Kola, fr. *Kola*, U.S.S.R.] **1** : any of several Asiatic minks **2** : the fur or pelt of a kolinsky

kol·khoz \käl-'kòz\ *n, pl* **kol·kho·zy** \-'kò-zē\ *or* **kol·khoz·es** [Russ] : a collective farm of the U.S.S.R. — compare SOVKHOZ

Kol Ni·dre \kōl-'nid-(,)rā\ *n* [Aram *kol nidhrē* all the vows; fr. its opening phrase] : an Aramaic prayer chanted in the synagogue on the eve of Yom Kippur

Kom·so·mol \,käm(p)-sə-'mòl\ *n* **1** : the Young Communist League of the U.S.S.R. that comprises youth from 15 to 26 **2** : a member of the Komsomol

koo·doo *or* **ku·du** \'küd-ü\ *n* [Afrik *koedoe*] : a large grayish brown African antelope with large ringed spirally twisted horns

kook·a·bur·ra \'kuk-ə-,bər-ə, -,bə-rə\ *n* : an Australian kingfisher that is about the size of a crow and has a call resembling loud laughter

ko·peck *also* **ko·pek** \'kō-,pek\ *n* [Russ *kopeĭka*] **1** : a unit of value equal to ¹⁄₁₀₀ ruble **2** : a coin representing one kopeck

Ko·ran \kə-'ran\ *n* [Ar *qur'ān*] : the book composed of writings accepted by Muslims as revelations made to Muhammad by Allah — **Ko·ran·ic** \kə-'ran-ik\ *adj*

Ko·re·an \kə-'rē-ən\ *n* **1** : a native or inhabitant of Korea **2** : the language of the Korean people — **Korean** *adj*

¹ko·sher \'kō-shər\ *adj* [Yiddish, fr. Heb *kāshēr* fit, proper] **1** : sanctioned by Jewish law; *esp* : ritually fit for use **2** : selling or serving food ritually fit according to Jewish law

²kosher *vt* : to make kosher

kou·miss *or* **ku·miss** \'kü-'mis, 'kü-məs\ *n* [Russ *kumys*] : a fermented milk beverage made orig. by the nomadic peoples of central Asia from mare's milk

¹kow·tow \kau-'tau, 'kau-,\ *n* [Chin (Pek) *k'o¹ t'ou²*, fr. *k'o¹* to bump + *t'ou²* head] : an act of kowtowing

²kowtow *vi* **1** : to kneel and touch the forehead to the ground to show homage, worship, or deep respect **2** : to show obsequious deference

¹kraal \'krol, 'kräl\ *n* [Afrik, fr. Pg *curral* enclosure, corral] **1** : a village of southern African natives **2** : an enclosure for domestic animals in southern Africa

²kraal *vt* : to pen in a kraal

kraft \'kraft\ *n* [G, lit., strength] : a strong paper or board made from wood pulp derived from wood chips boiled in an alkaline solution

krait \'krīt\ *n* : any of several brightly banded extremely venomous mostly Asiatic snakes

kraut \'kraut\ *n* : SAUERKRAUT

Krebs cycle \'krebz-\ *n* [after H. A. *Krebs d*1900 English biochemist] : a sequence of reactions in the living organism in which oxidation of acetic acid or acetyl equivalent provides energy for storage in phosphate bonds

krem·lin \'krem-lən\ n [Russ *kreml'*] **1** : the citadel of a Russian city **2** [the *Kremlin*, citadel of Moscow and governing center of the U.S.S.R.] *cap* : the Russian government

kreu·zer \'kroit-sər\ n [G] : a small coin formerly used in Austria and Germany

krill \'kril\ n [Norw *kril* recently hatched fishes] : small planktonic organisms (as crustaceans and larvae) that form a major food of whales

krim·mer \'krim-ər\ n : a gray fur made from the pelts of young lambs of the Crimean peninsula region

kris \'krēs\ n [Malay *kěris*] : a Malay or Indonesian dagger with a ridged and twisting blade

Kriss Krin·gle \'kris-'krin-gəl\ n [G *Christkindl* Christ child] : SANTA CLAUS

¹kro·na \'krō-nə\ n, pl **kro·nur** \-nər\ [Icel *krōna*, lit., crown] **1** : the basic monetary unit of Iceland **2** : a coin representing one krona

²kro·na \'krō-nə, 'krü-\ n, pl **kro·nor** \-,nȯr\ **1** : the basic monetary unit of Sweden **2** : a coin representing one krona

¹kro·ne \'krō-nə\ n, pl **kro·nen** \-nən\ **1** : the basic monetary unit of Austria from 1892 to 1925 **2** : a coin representing one krone

²kro·ne \'krō-nə, 'krü-\ n, pl **kro·ner** \-nər\ **1** : the basic monetary unit of Denmark and Norway **2** : a coin representing one krone

kris

kryp·ton \'krip-,tän\ n [Gk, neut. of *kryptos* hidden, fr. *kryptein* to hide] : a colorless inert gaseous chemical element found in air and used esp. in electric lamps — see ELEMENT table

ku·dos \'k(y)ü-,däs, -,dōs\ n, pl **ku·dos** \-,dōz\ [Gk *kydos*] : FAME, GLORY

kud·zu \'kud-zü\ n : a trailing Asiatic leguminous vine used widely for hay and forage and for erosion control

Ku Klux·er \'k(y)ü-,klək-sər\ n : a member of the Ku Klux Klan — **Ku Klux·ism** \-,klək-,siz-əm\ n

Ku Klux Klan \-,k(y)ü-,kləks-'klan\ n **1** : a post-Civil War secret society advocating the inherent superiority of the white race over the Negro race **2** : a 20th-century secret fraternal group held to confine its membership to American-born Protestant whites

ku·lak \k(y)ü-'lak\ n [Russ, tightwad, kulak, lit., fist] : a prosperous peasant farmer in Czarist and early Soviet Russia

kul·tur \kul-'tü(ə)r\ n, *often cap* : German culture held esp. by militant Nazi and Hohenzollern expansionists to be superior esp. in its emphasis on practical efficiency and individual subordination to the state

kum·quat \'kəm-,kwät\ n [Chin (Cant) *kam kwat*, fr. *kam* gold + *kwat* orange] **1** : a small citrus fruit with sweet spongy rind and somewhat acid pulp used esp. for preserves **2** : a tree or shrub that bears kumquats

Kuo·min·tang \'gwō-'min-'däŋ\ n [Chin (Pek) *kuo² min² tang³*, lit., national people's party] : a Chinese political party founded by Sun Yat-sen and headed by Chiang Kai-shek that is the dominant party of the Nationalist Republic of China : the Chinese Nationalist party

Kurd \'kurd, 'kərd\ n : a member of a pastoral and agricultural people inhabiting a plateau region in adjoining parts of Turkey, Iran, Iraq, Syria, and Soviet Armenia and Azerbaidzhan — **Kurd·ish** \-ish\ adj

kwa·shi·or·kor \,kwäsh-ē-'ȯr-kər\ n : a disease of young children resulting from deficient intake of protein

ky·mo·gram \'kī-mə-,gram\ n : a record made by a kymograph

ky·mo·graph \'kī-mə-,graf\ n [Gk *kyma* wave] : a recording device on which a graphic record of motion or pressure may be automatically traced

ky·pho·sis \kī-'fō-səs\ n [Gk *kyphōsis*, fr. *kyphos* humpbacked] : abnormal backward curvature of the spine — compare LORDOSIS, SCOLIOSIS — **ky·phot·ic** \-'fät-ik\ adj

ky·rie \'kir-ē-,ā\ n, *often cap* [LL *kyrie eleison*, transliteration of Gk *kyrie eleēson* Lord, have mercy] : a short liturgical prayer that begins with or consists of the words "Lord, have mercy" — called also *kyrie elei·son* \-ə-'lā-(ə-),sän\

l \'el\ n, *often cap* **1** : the 12th letter of the English alphabet **2** : the roman numeral 50

la \'lä\ n [ML] : the 6th note of the diatonic scale

lab \'lab\ n : LABORATORY

lab·da·num \'lab-də-nəm\ n [ML *lapdanum*] : a fragrant resinous plant substance used in perfumes

¹la·bel \'lā-bəl\ n [MF, strip of cloth, ribbon] **1** : a slip (as of paper or cloth) that is attached to something and gives an identification or description of it : TAG, STICKER **2** : a descriptive or identifying word or phrase : EPITHET

²label vt **la·beled** or **la·belled**; **la·bel·ing** or **la·bel·ling** \'lā-b(ə-)liŋ\ **1** : to affix a label to ⟨*label* a medicine bottle⟩ **2** : to describe or designate with a label ⟨*labeled* his opponent a visionary⟩ **3** : to make (a chemical element) traceable (as through the steps of a biochemical process) by substitution of a radioactive or special isotope — **la·bel·er** \-b(ə-)lər\ n

la·bel·lum \lə-'bel-əm\ n, pl **-bel·la** \-'bel-ə\ [NL, fr. L, dim. of *labrum* lip] **1** : the median and often spurred petal of the corolla of an orchid **2** : a terminal part of the labium or labrum of various insects — **la·bel·late** \lə-'bel-ət\ adj

¹la·bi·al \'lā-bē-əl\ adj [L *labium* lip] **1** : of or relating to the lips or labia **2** : uttered with the participation of one or both lips ⟨the *labial* sounds \f\, \p\, and \ü\⟩ — **la·bi·al·ly** \-ə-lē\ adv

²labial n : a labial consonant

¹la·bi·ate \'lā-bē-ət, -bē-,āt\ adj **1** : LIPPED; esp : having a tubular corolla or calyx divided into two unequal parts projecting one over the other like lips **2** : of or relating to the mint family

²labiate n : a plant of the mint family

la·bile \'lā-,bīl, -bəl\ adj [LL *labilis* fleeting, transient, fr. L *labi* to slip] **1** : characterized by a ready capability for change : ADAPTABLE **2** : readily or continually undergoing chemical or physical change : UNSTABLE ⟨a *labile* mineral⟩ — **la·bil·i·ty** \lā-'bil-ət-ē\ n

labio- comb form [L *labium* lip] : labial and ⟨*labio*dental⟩

la·bio·den·tal \,lā-bē-ō-'dent-°l\ adj : uttered with the participation of lip and teeth ⟨the *labiodental* sounds \f\ and \v\⟩ — **labiodental** n

la·bi·um \'lā-bē-əm\ n, pl **-bia** \-bē-ə\ [NL, fr. L, lip] **1** : any of the folds at the margin of the vulva **2** : the lower lip of a labiate corolla **3 a** : the lower lip of an insect **b** : a liplike part of various invertebrates

¹la·bor \'lā-bər\ n [L] **1 a** : expenditure of physical or mental effort esp. when difficult or compulsory **b** (1) : human activity that provides the goods or services in an economy (2) : the services performed by workers for wages as distinguished from those rendered by entrepreneurs for profits **c** (1) : the physical activities involved in parturition (2) : the period of such labor **2** : TASK **3** : a product of labor **4 a** : those who do labor or work for wages **b** : labor unions or their officials **5** *usu* **La·bour** \-bər\ : the Labour party of the United Kingdom or cf another nation of the British Commonwealth

²labor vb **la·bored**; **la·bor·ing** \-b(ə-)riŋ\ **1** : to exert one's body or mind : WORK; esp : to work for wages and in actual production of goods **2** : to move with great effort **3** : to suffer from some disadvantage or distress ⟨*labor* under a delusion⟩ **4** : to pitch or roll heavily ⟨the ship *labored* in a rough sea⟩ **5** : to treat or work out in often laborious detail ⟨*labor* the obvious⟩

³labor adj **1** : of or relating to labor **2** *usu* **Labour** : of, relating to, or constituting a political party held to represent the interests of workingmen or characterized by a membership in which organized labor groups predominate

lab·o·ra·to·ry \'lab-(ə-)rə-,tōr-ē, -,tȯr-\ n, pl **-ries** : a place equipped for experimental study in a science or for testing and analysis; *also* : a place providing opportunity for experimentation, observation, or practice in a field of study — **laboratory** adj

labor camp n **1** : a penal colony where forced labor is performed **2** : a camp for migratory labor

Labor Day n : the 1st Monday in September observed as a legal holiday in recognition of the workingman

la·bored adj **1** : produced or performed with labor; esp

: not freely or easily done ⟨*labored* breathing⟩ **2** : lacking ease or spontaneity of expression ⟨a *labored* essay⟩ ⟨*labored* poetry⟩

la·bor·er \'lā-bər-ər\ *n* : one that works; *esp* : a worker on jobs requiring strength rather than skill

la·bo·ri·ous \lə-'bōr-ē-əs, -'bȯr-\ *adj* **1** : INDUSTRIOUS **2** : requiring or characterized by hard or toilsome effort; *also* : LABORED — **la·bo·ri·ous·ly** *adv* — **la·bo·ri·ous·ness** *n*

La·bor·ite \'lā-bə-,rīt\ *n* **1** : a member of a political party devoted chiefly to the interests of labor **2** *usu* **La·bour·ite** : a member of the British Labour party

la·bor·sav·ing \'lā-bər-,sā-viŋ\ *adj* : adapted to replace or decrease human labor and esp. manual labor

labor union *n* : an organization of workers formed to advance its members' interests in respect to wages and working conditions

la·bour \'lā-bər\ *chiefly Brit var of* LABOR

Lab·ra·dor current \,lab-rə-'dȯr-\ *n* : a cold ocean current flowing south from Baffin Bay through Davis strait to Newfoundland

lab·ra·dor·ite \'lab-rə-,dȯr-,īt\ *n* : a feldspar showing a play of several colors

Labrador retriever *n* : a retriever developed from stock originating in Newfoundland and characterized by a short dense usu. black coat and broad head and chest

la·brum \'lā-brəm\ *n* [NL, fr. L, lip] : the upper lip of an arthropod in front of or above the mandibles

la·bur·num \lə-'bər-nəm\ *n* [L] : any of several poisonous Eurasian leguminous shrubs and trees with pendulous racemes of bright yellow flowers

lab·y·rinth \'lab-ə-,rin(t)th\ *n* [Gk *labyrinthos*] **1** : a place constructed of or full of passageways and blind alleys so arranged as to make it difficult for a person to find his way around : MAZE **2** : something extremely complex or tortuous **3** : a tortuous anatomical structure; *esp* : the internal ear or its bony or membranous part — **lab·y·rin·thine** \,lab-ə-'rin(t)-thən\ *adj*

lac \'lak\ *n* [Per *lak* & Hindi *lākh*, fr. Skt *lākṣā*] : a resinous substance secreted by a scale insect and used in the manufacture of shellac, lacquers, and sealing wax

lac·co·lith \'lak-ə-,lith\ *n* [Gk *lakkos* cistern] : a mass of igneous rock that intrudes between sedimentary beds and produces a dome-shaped bulge

¹lace \'lās\ *n* [OF *laz*, fr. L *laqueus* noose, snare] **1** : a cord or string used for drawing together two edges (as of a garment or a shoe) **2** : an ornamental braid for trimming men's coats or uniforms **3** : a fine openwork usu. figured fabric made of thread and used chiefly for household coverings or for ornament of dress — **laced** \'lāst\ *adj* — **lace·like** \'lās-,līk\ *adj*

²lace *vb* **1** : to draw together the edges of by or as if by a lace passed through eyelet holes **2 a** : to adorn with or as if with lace **b** : INTERTWINE **3** : BEAT, LASH **4 a** : to add a dash esp. of an alcoholic liquor to **b** : to give savor or zest to — **lac·er** *n*

¹lac·er·ate \'las-ə-rət\ *adj* : having the edges deeply and irregularly cut ⟨a flower with *lacerate* petals⟩

²lac·er·ate \'las-ə-,rāt\ *vt* [L *lacerare*] **1** : to tear roughly ⟨flesh *lacerated* by the wolf's fangs⟩ **2** : to cause sharp mental or emotional pain to : DISTRESS — **lac·er·a·tive** \-,rāt-iv\ *adj*

lac·er·a·tion \,las-ə-'rā-shən\ *n* : an act or instance of lacerating; *also* : a torn and ragged wound

lac·er·til·i·an \,las-ər-'til-ē-ən\ *adj* [L *lacerta* lizard] : of or relating to the lizards — **lacertilian** *n*

lace·wing \'lās-,wiŋ\ *n* : any of various neuropterous insects with delicate lacy wings, long antennae, and brilliant eyes

Lach·e·sis \'lak-ə-səs\ *n* : the one of the three Fates in classical mythology who determines the length of the thread of life

lach·ry·mose \'lak-rə-,mōs\ *adj* [L *lacrima* tear] **1** : given to tears or weeping : TEARFUL **2** : tending to cause tears : MOURNFUL ⟨*lachrymose* ballads⟩ — **lach·ry·mose·ly** *adv*

lac·ing \'lā-siŋ\ *n* **1** : the action of one that laces **2** : something that laces : LACE

la·cin·i·ate \lə-'sin-ē-ət, -,āt\ *or* **la·cin·i·at·ed** \-,āt-əd\ *adj* : bordered with a fringe — **la·cin·i·a·tion** \lə-,sin-ē-'ā-shən\ *n*

¹lack \'lak\ *vb* [MD *laken*] **1** : to be wanting or missing

⟨the will to win is *lacking*⟩ **2** : to need, want, or be deficient in ⟨*lacks* financial support⟩

²lack *n* **1** : the fact or state of being wanting or deficient ⟨a *lack* of good manners⟩ **2** : something that is lacking or is needed ⟨money is the club's biggest *lack*⟩

lack·a·dai·si·cal \,lak-ə-'dā-zi-kəl\ *adj* [*lackaday*, interj. used to express regret] : lacking life, spirit, or zest : LANGUID — **lack·a·dai·si·cal·ly** \-k(ə-)lē\ *adv*

lack·ey \'lak-ē\ *n, pl* **lackeys** [MF *laquais*] **1** : a liveried retainer : FOOTMAN **2** : a servile follower : TOADY

lack·lus·ter \'lak-,ləs-tər\ *adj* : lacking in sheen, radiance, or vitality : DULL

la·con·ic \lə-'kän-ik\ *adj* [Gk *lakōnikos* Spartan, Laconian; fr. the Spartan reputation for terseness of speech] : sparing of words : TERSE — **la·con·i·cal·ly** \-'kän-i-k(ə-)lē\ *adv*

¹lac·quer \'lak-ər\ *n* [Pg *lacré* sealing wax, fr. *laca* lac, fr. Ar *lakk*, fr. Per *lak*] **1** : any of numerous preparations that consist of a substance in solution (as shellac in alcohol), dry rapidly usu. by evaporation of the solvent to form a glossy film, and are used to coat objects (as wood or metal); *esp* : a solution of a cellulose derivative (as nitrocellulose) with or without pigments or other ingredients **2** : any of various durable natural varnishes; *esp* : one from an Asiatic sumac

²lacquer *vt* **lac·quered**; **lac·quer·ing** \'lak-(ə-)riŋ\ : to coat with lacquer

¹lac·ri·mal *also* **lach·ry·mal** \'lak-rə-məl\ *adj* [L *lacrima* tear; akin to E *tear*] : of, relating to, or being the glands that produce tears

²lacrimal *n* : a small bone of the median front part of the orbit of the eye

lac·ri·ma·tion \,lak-rə-'mā-shən\ *n* : the secretion of tears esp. when abnormal or excessive

lac·ri·ma·tor *or* **lach·ry·ma·tor** \'lak-rə-,māt-ər\ *n* : TEAR GAS

la·crosse \lə-'krȯs\ *n* [CanF *la crosse*, lit., the crosier] : a game played on a turfed field in which the players use a long-handled racket to catch, carry, or throw the ball toward or into the opponents' goal

lact- *or* **lacti-** *or* **lacto-** *comb form* [L *lact-, lac*] **1** : milk ⟨*lacti*genous⟩ **2 a** : lactic acid ⟨*lactate*⟩ **b** : lactose ⟨*lacto*se⟩

lac·tase \'lak-,tās\ *n* : an enzyme that hydrolyzes lactose and related compounds and occurs esp. in the intestines of young mammals and in yeasts

¹lac·tate \'lak-,tāt\ *n* : a salt or ester of lactic acid

²lactate *vi* : to secrete milk — **lac·ta·tion** \lak-'tā-shən\ *n* — **lac·ta·tion·al** \-shnəl, -shən-ᵊl\ *n* — **lac·ta·tion·al·ly** \-ē\ *adv*

¹lac·te·al \'lak-tē-əl\ *adj* [L *lacteus* of milk, fr. *lact-, lac* milk] **1** : consisting of, producing, or resembling milk **2 a** : conveying or containing a milky fluid **b** : of or relating to the lacteals

²lacteal *n* : one of the lymphatic vessels arising from the villi of the small intestine and conveying chyle to the thoracic duct

lac·tic \'lak-tik\ *adj* **1** : of or relating to milk **2** : obtained from sour milk or whey **3** : involving the production of lactic acid

lactic acid *n* : an organic acid $C_3H_6O_3$ present in cells and esp. muscle, produced from carbohydrate usu. by bacterial fermentation, and used esp. in food and medicine

lac·tif·er·ous \lak-'tif-(ə-)rəs\ *adj* **1** : secreting or conveying milk **2** : yielding or containing a milky juice — **lac·tif·er·ous·ness** *n*

lac·to·ba·cil·lus \,lak-tō-bə-'sil-əs\ *n* : any of a genus of lactic-acid-forming bacteria

lac·to·gen·ic \,lak-tə-'jen-ik\ *adj* : inducing lactation

lac·tose \'lak-,tōs\ *n* : a sugar $C_{12}H_{22}O_{11}$ present in milk that on hydrolysis yields glucose and galactose and on fermentation yields esp. lactic acid

la·cu·na \lə-'k(y)ü-nə\ *n, pl* **-cu·nae** \-'kyü-(,)nē, -'kü-,nī\ *or* **-cu·nas** \-'k(y)ü-nəz\ [L, pool, pit, cavity, lacuna, fr. *lacus* lake] **1** : a blank space or a missing part : GAP **2** : a small cavity, pit, or discontinuity in an anatomical structure — **la·cu·nal** \-'k(y)ün-ᵊl\ *adj* — **la·cu·nar** \-'k(y)ü-nər\ *adj* — **la·cu·nary** \'lak-yə-,ner-ē\ *adj* — **la·cu·nate** \lə-'k(y)ü-nət\ *adj*

la·cus·trine \lə-'kəs-trən\ *adj* [L *lacus* lake] : of, relating to, or growing in lakes

---

ə abut; ᵊ kitten; ər further; a back; ā bake; ä cot, cart; au̇ out; ch chin; e less; ē easy; g gift; i trip; ī life

lacy \'lā-sē\ *adj* **lac·i·er; -est** : resembling or consisting of lace

lad \'lad\ *n* [ME *ladde*] **1** : BOY, YOUTH **2** : FELLOW, CHAP

lad·der \'lad-ər\ *n* [OE *hlæder*] **1** : a structure for climbing up or down that consists of two long parallel sidepieces joined at intervals by crosspieces on which one may step **2** : something that suggests a ladder in form or use **3** : a series of usu. ascending steps or stages : SCALE

ladder

lad·die \'lad-ē\ *n* : a young lad

lade \'lād\ *vb* **lad·ed; lad·ed** *or* **lad·en** \'lād-ᵊn\; **lad·ing** [OE *hladan*] **1 a** : to put a load or burden on or in : LOAD ⟨*lade* a vessel⟩ ⟨a truck *laden* with gravel⟩ **b** : STOW, SHIP ⟨*lading* a rich cargo⟩ **2** : to burden heavily : OPPRESS ⟨*laden* with cares⟩ **3** : LADLE

la-di-da \,läd-ē-'dä\ *adj* : affectedly refined or polished

ladies' man *n* : a man who shows a marked fondness for the company of women or is esp. attentive to women

lad·ing \'lād-iŋ\ *n* **1** : the act of one that lades **2** : CARGO, FREIGHT

la·di·no \lə-'dī-nō, -nə\ *n, pl* **-nos** : a large rapidly growing white clover widely planted for hay or silage

¹la·dle \'lād-ᵊl\ *n* [OE *hlædel*, fr. *hladan* to lade] : a deep-bowled long-handled spoon or dipper used esp. for taking up and conveying liquids

²ladle *vt* **la·dled; la·dling** \'lād-liŋ, -ᵊl-iŋ\ : to take up and convey in or as if in a ladle ⟨*ladle* soup⟩

la·dy \'lād-ē\ *n, pl* **ladies** [OE *hlǣfdīge*, fr. *hlāf* loaf of bread + *-dīge* one that kneads; akin to E *dough*] **1 a** : a woman of property, rank, or authority; *esp* : one having a standing equivalent to that of a lord or the wife of a lord **b** : a woman receiving the homage or devotion of a knight or lover **2** *cap* : VIRGIN MARY — usu. used with *Our* **3 a** : a woman of superior social position **b** : a woman of refinement and gentle manners **c** : WOMAN, FEMALE **4** : WIFE **5 a** — used as a title of a woman of rank in Great Britain **b** : a female member of an order of knighthood — compare DAME

lady beetle *n* : LADYBUG

la·dy·bird \'lād-ē-,bərd\ *n* : LADYBUG

la·dy·bug \-,bəg\ *n* : any of numerous small nearly hemispherical often brightly colored beetles that usu. feed both as larvae and adults on other insects

lady chapel *n, often cap L&C* : a chapel dedicated to the Virgin Mary

Lady Day *n* : the feast of the Annunciation

la·dy·fin·ger \'lād-ē-,fiŋ-gər\ *n* : a small finger-shaped sponge cake

la·dy-in-wait·ing \,lād-ē-in-'wāt-iŋ\ *n, pl* **ladies-in-waiting** : a lady appointed to attend or wait on a queen or princess

la·dy·like \'lād-ē-,līk\ *adj* **1** : resembling a lady in appearance or manners : WELL-BRED **2** : suitable to a lady ⟨*ladylike* behavior⟩

la·dy·love \'lād-ē-,ləv, 'lād-ē-'\ *n* : SWEETHEART, MISTRESS

la·dy's-ear·drop \,lād-ēz-'i(ə)r-,dräp\ *n* : a plant with flowers suggesting earrings; *esp* : FUCHSIA

la·dy·ship \'lād-ē-,ship\ *n* : the condition of being a lady : rank of lady — used as a title for a woman having the rank of lady ⟨her *Ladyship* is not at home⟩ ⟨if your *Ladyship* please⟩

lady's slipper *or* **lady slipper** \'lād-ē(z)-,slip-ər\ *n* : any of several No. American temperate-zone orchids with flowers whose shape suggests a slipper

¹lag \'lag\ *vb* **lagged; lag·ging** **1** : to stay or fall behind: as **a** : to hang back : LINGER, LOITER ⟨*lagged* behind the other hikers⟩ **b** : to move, function, or develop with comparative slowness ⟨*lagged* behind the production schedule⟩ **c** : to become retarded in attaining maximum value or development ⟨the current *lags* behind the voltage⟩ **2** : to slacken little by little : FLAG ⟨interest never *lagged* during the play⟩ **3** : to pitch or shoot something (as a marble) at a mark — **lag·ger** *n*

²lag *n* **1 a** : the action or condition of lagging **b** : comparative slowness or retardation **2 a** : an amount of lagging or time during which lagging continues **b** : INTERVAL

la·ger \'läg-ər\ *n* [G *lagerbier*, fr. *lager* storehouse + *bier* beer] : a beer brewed by slow fermentation and stored in refrigerated cellars for maturing

lag·gard \'lag-ərd\ *adj* : lagging or tending to lag : DILATORY, SLOW — **laggard** *n* — **lag·gard·ly** *adv or adj* — **lag·gard·ness** *n*

la·gniappe \'lan-,yap, lan-'\ *n* : something given gratis or by way of good measure

lago·morph \'lag-ə-,mȯrf\ *n* [Gk *lagōs* hare + *morphē* form] : any of an order (Lagomorpha) of gnawing mammals having two pairs of upper incisors one behind the other and comprising the rabbits, hares, and pikas — compare RODENT — **lago·mor·phic** \,lag-ə-'mȯr-fik\ *adj* — **lago·mor·phous** \-fəs\ *adj*

la·goon \lə-'gün\ *n* [F *lagune*, fr. It *laguna*, fr. L *lacuna* pit, pool, fr. *lacus* lake] : a shallow sound, channel, or pond near or communicating with a larger body of water

la·i·cal \'lā-ə-kəl\ *or* **la·ic** \'lā-ik\ *adj* : of or relating to the laity : SECULAR — **laic** *n* — **la·i·cal·ly** \'lā-ə-k(ə-)lē\ *adv*

la·i·cism \'lā-ə-,siz-əm\ *n* : a political system characterized by the exclusion of ecclesiastical control and influence

la·i·cize \'lā-ə-,sīz\ *vt* **1** : to reduce to lay status **2** : to put under the direction of or throw open to laymen — **la·i·ci·za·tion** \,lā-ə-sə-'zā-shən\ *n*

laid *past of* LAY

lain *past part of* LIE

lair \'la(ə)r, 'le(ə)r\ *n* [OE *leger*; akin to E ¹*lie*] : the resting or living place of a wild animal : DEN; *also* : REFUGE, HIDEAWAY

laird \'la(ə)rd, 'le(ə)rd\ *n* [ME (northern) *lard* lord] *Scot* : a landed proprietor

lais·sez-faire \,les-,ā-'fa(ə)r, -'fe(ə)r\ *n* [F *laissez faire*, let do, leave without interference] : a doctrine opposing governmental interference in economic affairs beyond the minimum necessary for the maintenance of peace and property rights — **laissez-faire** *adj*

la·i·ty \'lā-ət-ē\ *n, pl* **-ties** [⁵*lay*] **1** : the people of a religious faith as distinguished from its clergy **2** : the mass of the people as distinguished from those of a particular profession or skill

¹lake \'lāk\ *n* [OF *lac*, fr. L *lacus*] : a considerable inland body of standing water; *also* : a pool of liquid (as lava, oil, or pitch)

²lake *n* [F *laque* lac, fr. OProv *laca*, fr. Ar *lakk*, fr. Per *lak*] **1** : any of numerous bright pigments composed of a soluble dye adsorbed on or combined with an inorganic substance **2** : a vivid red

lake dwelling *n* : a dwelling built on piles in a lake; *esp* : one built in prehistoric times — **lake dweller** *n*

lake herring *n* : a commercially important whitefish of northern lakes

lake trout *n* : any of several lake fishes; *esp* : a large dark American char that is an important sport and commercial fish in northern lakes — called also *nam·ay·cush* \'nam-i-,kəsh\

la·ma \'läm-ə\ *n* [Tibetan *blama*] : a Lamaist monk

La·ma·ism \'läm-ə-,iz-əm\ *n* : the Mahayana Buddhism of Tibet and Mongolia marked by a dominant hierarchy of monks — **La·ma·ist** \'läm-ə-əst\ *n or adj* — **La·ma·is·tic** \,läm-ə-'is-tik\ *adj*

La·marck·ism \lə-'mär-,kiz-əm\ *n* [J. B. de Monet *Lamarck* d1829 French biologist] : a theory of organic evolution asserting that environmental changes cause structural changes in animals and plants that are transmitted to offspring — **La·marck·ian** \-'mär-kē-ən\ *adj or n*

la·ma·sery \'läm-ə-,ser-ē\ *n, pl* **-ser·ies** [F *lamaserie*, fr. *lama* + Per *sarāī* palace] : a monastery of lamas

¹lamb \'lam\ *n* [OE] **1 a** : a young sheep esp. less than one year old or without permanent teeth **b** : the young of various animals (as the smaller antelopes) **2 a** : an innocent, weak, or gentle person **b** *cap* : JESUS — called also *Lamb of God* **3** : the flesh of a lamb used as food

²lamb *vb* **1** : to bring forth a lamb **2** : to tend (ewes) at lambing time — **lamb·er** \'lam-ər\ *n*

lam·baste *or* **lam·bast** \lam-'bāst, -'bast\ *vt* **1** : to assault violently : BEAT **2** : to thrash verbally : EXCORIATE

lamb·da \'lam-də\ *n* : the 11th letter of the Greek alphabet — Λ or λ

lam·bent \'lam-bənt\ *adj* [L *lambere* to lick; akin to E ³*lap*] **1** : playing lightly over a surface : FLICKERING ⟨a *lambent* flame⟩ **2** : softly radiant ⟨*lambent* eyes⟩ **3** : marked by lightness or brilliance ⟨*lambent* humor⟩ — **lam·ben·cy** \-bən-sē\ *n*

lam·bre·quin \'lam-bər-kən, -bri-kən\ *n* [F] : a short decorative drapery for a shelf edge or for the top of a window casing : VALANCE

lamb·skin \'lam-,skin\ *n* : a lamb's skin or a small fine= grade sheepskin or the leather made from either

lamb's–quar·ters \'lamz-,kwȯrt-ərz\ *n* : a goosefoot with glaucous foliage that is sometimes used as a potherb

¹**lame** \'lām\ *adj* [OE *lama*] **1 a** : physically disabled; *also* : having a part and esp. a limb so disabled as to impair freedom of movement **b** : halting in movement : LIMPING **2** : lacking substance : UNSATISFACTORY, WEAK ⟨a *lame* excuse⟩ — **lame·ly** *adv* — **lame·ness** *n*

²**lame** *vt* **1** : to make lame : CRIPPLE **2** : to make weak or ineffective : DISABLE

³**la·mé** \lä-'mā, la-\ *n* [F] : a brocaded clothing fabric made from any of various fibers combined with tinsel filling threads often of gold or silver

lame duck *n* : an elected officer continuing to hold political office after his defeat and before the inauguration of a successor

la·mel·la \lə-'mel-ə\ *n, pl* **-mel·lae** \-'mel-(,)ē, -,ī\ *also* **-mellas** [NL, fr. L, dim. of *lamina*] : a thin flat scale or part — **la·mel·lar** \lə-'mel-ər\ *adj* — **la·mel·late** \-'mel-ət\ *adj* — **la·mel·late·ly** *adv*

lam·el·la·tion \,lam-ə-'lā-shən\ *n* **1** : formation or division into lamellae **2** : LAMELLA

la·mel·li·branch \lə-'mel-ə-,braŋk\ *n, pl* **-branchs** \-,braŋ(k)s\ [NL *lamella* + L *branchia* gill] : any of a class (Lamellibranchia) of mollusks (as clams, oysters, or mussels) with a shell made up of right and left parts joined by a hinge — **lamellibranch** *adj* — **la·mel·li·bran·chi·ate** \lə-,mel-ə-'braŋ-kē-ət\ *adj or n*

la·mel·li·corn \lə-'mel-ə-,kȯrn\ *adj* [L *cornu* horn] : having or constituting antennae ending in flattened plates — **lamellicorn** *n*

¹**la·ment** \lə-'ment\ *vb* [L *lamentari*, fr. *lamentum*, n., lament] **1** : to mourn aloud : WAIL **2** : to express sorrow for : BEWAIL

²**lament** *n* **1** : a crying out in grief : WAILING **2** : DIRGE, ELEGY

lam·en·ta·ble \'lam-ən-tə-bəl, lə-'ment-ə-\ *adj* **1** : that is to be regretted or lamented : DEPLORABLE ⟨a *lamentable* error in judgment⟩ **2** : expressing grief : MOURNFUL ⟨a *lamentable* cry⟩ — **lam·en·ta·ble·ness** *n* — **lam·en·ta·bly** \-blē\ *adv*

lam·en·ta·tion \,lam-ən-'tā-shən\ *n* : an act or instance of lamenting

Lam·en·ta·tions \,lam-ən-'tā-shənz\ *n* — see BIBLE table

la·mia \'lā-mē-ə\ *n* [L, fr. Gk] : a female demon : VAMPIRE

lam·i·na \'lam-ə-nə\ *n, pl* **-nae** \-,nē, -,nī\ *or* **-nas** [L] **1** : a thin plate or scale **2** : BLADE 1b — **lam·i·nar** \-nər\ *adj*

lam·i·nar·ia \,lam-ə-'ner-ē-ə, -'nar-\ *n* : any of various large kelps with an unbranched cylindrical or flattened stalk and a smooth or convoluted blade — **lam·i·nar·i·an** \-ē-ən\ *adj*

¹**lam·i·nate** \'lam-ə-,nāt\ *vt* **1** : to roll or compress into a thin plate **2** : to make by uniting superposed layers of one or more materials — **lam·i·na·tor** \-,nāt-ər\ *n*

²**lam·i·nate** \-nət, -,nāt\ *adj* **1** : consisting of laminae **2** : bearing or covered with laminae

³**lam·i·nate** \-nət, -,nāt\ *n* : a product made by laminating

lam·i·nat·ed \-,nāt-əd\ *adj* : composed of layers of firmly united material; *esp* : made by bonding or impregnating superposed layers of paper, wood, or fabric with resin and compressing under heat

lam·i·na·tion \,lam-ə-'nā-shən\ *n* **1** : the process of laminating **2** : a laminate structure **3** : LAMINA

Lam·mas \'lam-əs\ *n* [OE *hlāfmæsse*, fr. *hlāf* loaf + *mæsse* mass; so called because formerly loaves made from the first ripe grain were consecrated on this day] : August 1

lam·mer·gei·er *or* **lam·mer·gey·er** \'lam-ər-,gī(-ə)r\ *n* [G *lämmergeier*, fr. *lämmer* (pl. of *lamm* lamb) + *geier* vulture] : the largest Eurasian bird of prey found chiefly in mountainous regions

lamp \'lamp\ *n* [Gk *lampas*, fr. *lampein* to shine] **1** : a vessel with a wick for burning an inflammable liquid (as oil) to produce artificial light **2** : a device for producing light or heat

lamp·black \-,blak\ *n* : a finely powdered deep black soot made by incomplete burning of carbon-containing material and used esp. as a pigment in paints and ink

lamp·light·er \-,līt-ər\ *n* : one that lights a lamp; *esp* : a person employed to go about lighting street lights that burn gas

¹**lam·poon** \lam-'pün\ *n* [F *lampon*] **1** : a harsh satire usu. directed against an individual **2** : a light mocking satire

²**lampoon** *vt* : to make (as a political opponent) the subject of a lampoon : RIDICULE — **lam·poon·er** *n* — **lam·poon·ery** \-'pün-(ə-)rē\ *n*

lam·prey \'lam-prē\ *n, pl* **lampreys** [OF *lampreie*, fr. ML *lampreda*] : any of an order (Hyperoartia) of aquatic vertebrates that resemble eels but have a large sucking mouth with no jaws

lamp·shell \'lamp-,shel\ *n* : BRACHIOPOD

la·nai \lə-'nī, lä-\ *n* [Hawaiian] : a porch furnished for use as a living room

la·nate \'lā-,nāt, 'lan-,āt\ *adj* [L *lana* wool; akin to E *wool*] : covered with fine hair or filaments : WOOLLY

Lan·cas·tri·an \lan-'kas-trē-ən, laŋ-\ *n* : a member or supporter of the English royal house of Lancaster furnishing sovereigns from 1399 to 1461 — compare YORKIST — **Lancastrian** *adj*

¹**lance** \'lan(t)s\ *n* [L *lancea*] **1** : a weapon of war consisting of a long shaft with a sharp steel head and carried by mounted knights or light cavalry **2** : any of various sharp objects suggestive of a lance; *esp* : LANCET **3** : LANCER 1b

²**lance** *vt* **1** : to pierce with a lance or similar weapon **2** : to open with or as if with a lancet ⟨*lance* a boil⟩

lance·let \'lan(t)s-lət\ *n* : any of various small translucent marine animals related to the vertebrates — called also *amphioxus*

Lan·ce·lot \'lan(t)-sə-,lät\ *n* : a knight of the Round Table and lover of Queen Guinevere in Arthurian legend

lan·ce·o·late \'lan(t)-sē-ə-,lāt\ *also* **lan·ce·o·lat·ed** \-,lāt-əd\ *adj* [L *lanceola*, dim. of *lancea* lance] : shaped like a lance head; *esp* : being narrow and tapering to a point at the tip ⟨*lanceolate* leaves⟩

lanc·er \'lan(t)-sər\ *n* **1 a** : one who carries a lance **b** : a light cavalryman armed with a lance **2** *pl* **a** : a set of five quadrilles each in a different meter **b** : the music for such dances

lan·cet \'lan(t)-sət\ *n* : a sharp-pointed and usu. 2-edged surgical instrument

lancet arch *n* : an acutely pointed arch — see ARCH illustration

¹**land** \'land\ *n* [OE] **1 a** : the solid part of the surface of the earth **b** : a portion of the earth's surface in some way distinguishable (as by natural or political boundaries, ownership, or physical quality) ⟨his *land* bordered the river⟩ ⟨drained the marshy *land*⟩ **c** : REALM, DOMAIN ⟨the *land* of Egypt⟩ **d** *pl* : territorial possessions : REAL ESTATE **2** : the people of a country : NATION — **land·less** \'lan-dləs\ *adj*

²**land** *vb* **1 a** : to set or go ashore from a ship : DISEMBARK ⟨*land* troops⟩ ⟨*landed* in the early afternoon⟩ **b** : to stop at or near a place on shore ⟨the ship *landed* at the dock⟩ **2** : to alight or cause to alight on a surface ⟨the plane *landed* on instruments⟩ ⟨*landed* his plane in a field of corn⟩ **3 a** : to bring or get to a destination : ARRIVE ⟨this train will *land* you there before dark⟩ ⟨*landed* back in his home town⟩ **b** : to reach or cause to reach a certain place or position ⟨*landed* in jail⟩ ⟨*landed* a haymaker on his jaw⟩ **c** : to bring to a specified condition ⟨his foolishness *landed* him in trouble⟩ **4 a** : to catch with a hook and bring in ⟨*land* a fish⟩ **b** : GAIN, SECURE ⟨*landed* a good job⟩

lan·dau \'lan-,dau, -dȯ\ *n* [*Landau*, Germany] **1** : a four-wheeled carriage with a top divided into two sections that can be lowered, thrown back, or removed **2** : a closed automobile body with

landau

provision for opening or folding down the rear quarter top

land breeze *n* : a breeze blowing toward the sea

land bridge *n* : a strip of land connecting two landmasses (as continents)

land·ed \'lan-dəd\ *adj* **1** : having an estate in land ⟨*landed* proprietors⟩ **2** : consisting of real estate ⟨*landed* property⟩

land·fall \'lan(d)-,fȯl\ *n* **1** : a sighting or making of land after a voyage or flight **2** : the shore or land first sighted on a voyage or flight

land·form \-,fȯrm\ *n* : a feature of the earth's surface attributable to natural causes

land grant *n* : a grant of land by a government; *esp* : one granted by the federal government to a state for the support of an agricultural and mechanical college

land·grave \'lan(d)-,grāv\ *n* [G *landgraf*, fr. *land* land + *graf* count] : a German count having a certain territorial jurisdiction — used also as a title of some German princes

land·hold·er \'land-,hōl-dər\ *n* : a holder or owner of land — **land·hold·ing** \-diŋ\ *n*

land·ing \'lan-diŋ\ *n* **1** : the action of one that lands **2** : a place for discharging or taking on passengers and cargo **3** : the level part of a staircase at the end of a flight of stairs or connecting one flight with another

landing craft *n* : any of numerous naval craft specially designed for putting ashore troops and equipment

landing field *n* : a field where aircraft may land and take off

landing gear *n* : the undercarriage of an airplane

landing net *n* : a small net with a handle used to take a hooked fish from the water

landing strip *n* : AIRSTRIP

land·la·dy \'lan(d)-,lād-ē\ *n* : a female landlord

land·locked \-,läkt\ *adj* **1** : enclosed or nearly enclosed by land ⟨a *landlocked* harbor⟩ **2** : confined to fresh water by some barrier ⟨*landlocked* salmon⟩

land·lord \-,lȯrd\ *n* **1** : the owner of property (as land) which he leases or rents to another **2** : a man who runs an inn or rooming house : INNKEEPER

land·lub·ber \-,ləb-ər\ *n* **1** : LANDSMAN **2** : one who is unacquainted with the sea or seamanship — **land·lub·ber·ly** *adj*

land·mark \-,märk\ *n* **1** : an object (as a stone or tree) that marks the boundary of land **2 a** : a conspicuous object on land that marks a course, serves as a guide, or characterizes a locality ⟨pick out a good *landmark* when hiking⟩ **b** : an anatomical structure used as a point of orientation in locating other structures **3** : an event or development that marks a turning point or a stage ⟨his symphony was a musical *landmark*⟩

land·mass \-,mas\ *n* : a large area of land

land–office business *n* : extensive and rapid business

land·own·er \'land-,ō-nər\ *n* : an owner of land — **land·own·ing** \-niŋ\ *adj*

land–poor \'lan(d)-,pü(ə)r\ *adj* : owning so much unprofitable or encumbered land as to lack funds to develop the land or pay the charges due thereon

land reform *n* : more equitable distribution of agricultural land esp. by governmental action

¹**land·scape** \'lan(d)-,skāp\ *n* [D *landschap*, fr. *land* + -*schap* -ship] **1** : a picture representing a view of natural inland scenery **2** : a portion of land that the eye can see in one glance

²**landscape** *vb* : to improve the natural beauties of a tract of land by grading, clearing, or gardening

landscape gardener *n* : one skilled in the development and decorative planting of gardens and grounds

land·slide \'lan(d)-,slīd\ *n* **1** : the slipping down of a mass of rocks or earth on a steep slope; *also* : the mass of material that slides **2** : an overwhelming material victory esp. in a political contest

lands·man \'lan(d)z-mən\ *n* : a person who lives or works on land; *esp* : one who knows little or nothing of the sea and ships

¹**land·ward** \'land-wərd\ *adj* : lying or being toward the land or on the side toward the land

²**landward** *also* **land·wards** \-wərdz\ *adv* : to or toward the land

lane \'lān\ *n* [OE *lanu*] **1** : a narrow passageway between fences, hedges, or buildings **2** : a relatively narrow way or track: as **a** : an ocean route for ships; *also* : AIR LANE **b** : a strip of roadway for a single line of vehicles **c** : a bowling alley

Lan·go·bard \'laŋ-gə-,bärd\ *n* : LOMBARD

lan·gouste \lä²-'güst\ *n* [F] : SPINY LOBSTER

lang syne \laŋ-'zīn, -'sīn\ *n* [ME (Sc), fr. *lang* long + *syne* since] : times past : old times — **lang syne** *adv or adj, chiefly Scot*

lan·guage \'laŋ-gwij\ *n* [ME, fr. OF, fr. *langue* tongue, language, fr. L *lingua*] **1 a** : the words, their pronunciation, and the methods of combining them used and understood by a large group of people **b** (1) : audible, articulate, and meaningful sound as produced by the action of the vocal organs (2) : a systematic means of communicating ideas by signs or marks with understood meanings ⟨sign *language*⟩ **2 a** : form or manner of verbal expression; *esp* : STYLE ⟨forceful *language*⟩ **b** : the vocabulary and phraseology belonging to an art or department of knowledge ⟨the *language* of medicine⟩ **3** : the study of language esp. as a school subject

langue d'oc \läⁿg-'dȯk\ *n* [F, fr. OF, lit., language of *oc*; fr. the Provençal use of the word *oc* for "yes"] : PROVENÇAL

langue d'oïl \-dȯ-ēl\ *n* [F, fr. OF, lit., language of *oïl*; fr. the French use of the word *oïl* for "yes"] : FRENCH 1

lan·guid \'laŋ-gwəd\ *adj* [L *languidus*, fr. *languēre* to languish] **1** : drooping or flagging from or as if from exhaustion : WEAK **2** : sluggish in character or disposition : LISTLESS **3** : lacking force or quickness of movement : SLOW ⟨*languid* life in the tropics⟩ — **lan·guid·ly** *adv* — **lan·guid·ness** *n*

lan·guish \'laŋ-gwish\ *vi* [MF *languiss-*, *languir*, fr. L *languēre*] **1** : to become weak or languid **2** : to lose strength or force : waste away with longing : PINE ⟨*languish* in prison⟩ **3** : to appeal for sympathy by putting on a weary or sorrowful look — **lan·guish·er** *n* — **lan·guish·ing** *adj* — **lan·guish·ing·ly** \-iŋ-lē\ *adv* — **lan·guish·ment** \-gwish-mənt\ *n*

lan·guor \'laŋ-(g)ər\ *n* **1** : weakness or weariness of body or mind **2** : a state of dreamy inactivity **syn** see LETHARGY — **lan·guor·ous** \-(g)ə-rəs\ *adj* — **lan·guor·ous·ly** *adv*

lan·gur \läŋ-'gü(ə)r\ *n* [Hindi *lāgūr*] : any of various slender long-tailed Asiatic monkeys

lank \'laŋk\ *adj* [OE *hlanc*] **1** : not well filled out : SLENDER, THIN ⟨*lank* cattle⟩ **2** : hanging straight and limp without spring or curl ⟨*lank* hair⟩ — **lank·ly** *adv* — **lank·ness** *n*

syn LANKY, GAUNT: LANK implies tallness as well as leanness of figure; LANKY suggests awkwardness and loose-jointedness as well as thinness; GAUNT implies marked thinness as from overwork, suffering, or undernourishment

lanky \'laŋ-kē\ *adj* **lank·i·er; -est** : being tall, thin, and usu. loose-jointed ⟨a *lanky* boy⟩ **syn** see LANK — **lank·i·ly** \-kə-lē\ *adv* — **lank·i·ness** \-kē-nəs\ *n*

lan·ner \'lan-ər\ *n* [MF *lanier*, fr. *lanier* coward, fr. L *lanarius* woolworker, fr. *lana* wool] : a widely distributed Old World falcon

lan·o·lin \'lan-ᵊl-ən\ *n* [L *lana* wool + *oleum* oil] : the fatty coating of sheep's wool esp. when refined for use in ointments and cosmetics

lan·ta·na \lan-'tän-ə\ *n* : any of a genus of tropical shrubs related to vervains that have showy heads of small bright flowers

lan·tern \'lant-ərn\ *n* [L *lanterna*, fr. Gk *lamptēr*, fr. *lampein* to shine] **1** : a usu. portable light that has a protective transparent or translucent covering **2 a** : the chamber in a lighthouse containing the light **b** : a structure with glazed or open sides above an opening in a roof for light, ventilation, or decoration **3** : PROJECTOR 2b

lantern jaw *n* **1** : an undershot jaw **2** : a long thin jaw — **lan·tern·jawed** \,lant-ərn-'jȯd\ *adj*

lanterns: *1* barn, *2* bull's-eye

lan·tha·nide series \'lan(t)-thə-,nīd-\ *n* : a group of chemical elements consisting of the rare-earth metals

lan·tha·num \'lan(t)-thə-nəm\ *n* [NL, fr. Gk *lanthanein* to escape notice] **:** a white soft malleable metallic chemical element that occurs in rare-earth minerals — see ELEMENT table

lant·horn \'lant-ərn\ *n, chiefly Brit* **:** LANTERN

la·nu·gi·nous \lə-'n(y)ü-jə-nəs\ *adj* [L *lanugin-, lanugo* down] **:** covered with down or fine soft hair **:** DOWNY

lan·yard \'lan-yərd\ *n* [ME *lanyer* thong, strap, fr. MF *laniere*] **1 :** a piece of rope or line for fastening something in ships **2 a :** a cord worn around the neck to hold a knife or a whistle **b :** a cord worn as a symbol of a military citation **3 :** a strong cord with a hook at one end used in firing cannon

Lao \'laů\ *or* **Lao·tian** \lā-'ō-shən, 'laů-shən\ *n* **1 :** a member of a Buddhist people living in Laos and northeastern Thailand and constituting a branch of the Tai race **2 :** the Thai language of the Lao people — **Lao** *or* **Laotian** *adj*

La·oc·o·ön \lā-'äk-ə-,wän\ *n* **:** a Trojan priest killed with his two sons by sea serpents after warning the Trojans against the wooden horse

¹lap \'lap\ *n* [OE *læppa*] **1 a :** a loose panel or hanging flap esp. of a garment **b** *archaic* **:** the skirt of a coat or dress **2 a** (1) **:** the clothing that lies on the knees, thighs, and lower part of the trunk when one sits (2) **:** the front part of the lower trunk and thighs of a seated person **b :** an environment of nurture ⟨the *lap* of luxury⟩ **3 :** CHARGE, CONTROL ⟨in the *lap* of the gods⟩

²lap *vb* **lapped; lap·ping 1 :** FOLD ⟨*lap* cloth in making a seam⟩ **2 :** WRAP ⟨the mother *lapped* her coat around the child⟩ **3 a :** to lay over or near something else so as to partly cover it ⟨*lap* one shingle over another⟩ **b :** to project or spread beyond a certain point **4 :** to smooth or polish (as a metal surface) to a high degree of refinement — **lap·per** *n*

³lap *n* **1 a :** the amount by which one object overlaps or projects beyond another ⟨shingles with a 2-inch *lap*⟩ **b :** the part of an object that overlaps another **2 :** a smoothing and polishing tool **3 a :** one circuit around a racecourse **b :** one segment of a journey **c :** one complete turn (as of a rope around a drum)

⁴lap *vb* **lapped; lap·ping** [OE *lapian*] **1 :** to scoop up food or drink with the tip of the tongue; *also* **:** DEVOUR — usu. used with *up* **2 :** to wash or splash gently ⟨the sea *lapping* the shore⟩ ⟨waves *lapping* against the dock⟩ — **lap·per** *n*

⁵lap *n* **1 a :** an act or instance of lapping **b :** the amount that can be carried to the mouth by one lick or scoop of the tongue **2 :** a gentle splashing sound

lap·board \'lap-,bȯrd, -,bȯrd\ *n* **:** a board used on the lap as a table or desk

lap·dog \-,dȯg\ *n* **:** a small dog that may be held in the lap

la·pel \lə-'pel\ *n* [dim. of ¹*lap*] **:** the part of a garment that is turned back; *esp* **:** the fold of the front of a coat that is usu. a continuation of the collar

lap·ful \'lap-,fúl\ *n, pl* **lapfuls** \-,fúlz\ *or* **laps·ful** \'laps-,fúl\ **:** as much as the lap can hold or support

¹lap·i·dary \'lap-ə-,der-ē\ *n, pl* **-dar·ies** [L *lapid-, lapis* stone] **:** a person who cuts, polishes, and engraves precious stones

²lapidary *adj* **1 :** of or relating to precious stones or the art of cutting them **2 :** of, relating to, or suitable for engraved inscriptions

lap·in \'lap-ən\ *n* [F, rabbit] **:** rabbit fur usu. sheared and dyed

la·pis la·zu·li \,lap-əs-'laz(h)-ə-lē\ *n* [ML, fr. L *lapis* stone + ML *lazuli,* gen. of *lazulum* lapis lazuli, fr. Ar *lāzaward*] **:** a deep blue semiprecious stone that is essentially a complex silicate often with spangles of iron pyrites

lap joint *n* **:** a joint made by overlapping two ends or edges and fastening them together — **lap-jointed** \'lap-'jȯint-əd\ *adj*

Lapp \'lap\ *n* **:** a member of a people of northern Scandinavia, Finland, and the Kola peninsula of Russia

lap·pet \'lap-ət\ *n* **1 :** a fold or flap on a garment or headdress **2 :** a flat overlapping or hanging piece (as the wattle of a bird)

¹lapse \'laps\ *n* [L *lapsus,* fr. *labi* to slip] **1 a :** a slight error or slip ⟨*lapse* of memory⟩ **b :** a temporary deviation or fall esp. from a higher to a lower state ⟨*lapse* from grace⟩ **2 :** LOWERING, DECLINE **3 a :** the termination of a right or privilege through failure to meet requirements

b : INTERRUPTION, DISCONTINUANCE ⟨*lapse* of a custom⟩ **4 :** APOSTASY **5 :** a passage of time; *also* **:** INTERVAL

²lapse *vi* **1 :** to commit apostasy **2 :** to slip, pass, or fall gradually ⟨*lapse* into silence⟩ **3 :** to fall into disuse ⟨a custom that had *lapsed*⟩ **4 :** to come to end **:** pass to someone else because of failure to meet requirements ⟨his insurance *lapsed* from failure to pay premiums⟩ — **laps·er** *n*

lap·wing \'lap-,wiŋ\ *n* **:** a crested Old World plover noted for its slow irregular flapping flight and its shrill wailing cry

lar·board \'lär-bərd\ *n* [ME *ladeborde*] **:** PORT — **larboard** *adj*

lar·ce·ny \'lärs-nē, -³n-ē\ *n, pl* **-nies** [MF *larcin,* fr. L *latrocinium* robbery, fr. *latro* brigand] **:** the unlawful taking and carrying away of personal property with intent to deprive the owner of it permanently **:** THEFT — **lar·ce·nous** \'lärs-nəs, -³n-əs\ *adj*

larch \'lärch\ *n* **1 :** any of a genus of trees of the pine family with short deciduous needles; *also* **:** any of several related trees **2 :** the wood of a larch

¹lard \'lärd\ *vt* **1 :** to insert strips of usu. pork fat into (meat) before cooking **2 :** to smear with lard, fat, or grease **3 :** to add to; *esp* **:** ENRICH ⟨a book *larded* with illustrations⟩

larch: needles and cones

²lard *n* [OF, hog fat, fr. L *lardum*] **:** a soft white solid or semisolid fat obtained by rendering fatty tissue of the hog — **lardy** \'lärd-ē\ *adj*

lar·der \'lärd-ər\ *n* **:** a place where foods (as meat) are kept

lar·es and pe·na·tes \,lar-ēz-³n-pə-'nāt-ēz, ,ler-\ *n pl* [L *lares,* tutelary gods] **1 :** household gods **2 :** personal or household effects

¹large \'lärj\ *adj* [OF, abundant, generous, broad, fr. L *largus* abundant, generous] **:** greater, bigger, more extended, or more powerful than usual ⟨*large* expenditures⟩ ⟨a *large* house⟩ — **large·ness** *n*

syn BIG, GREAT: LARGE is likely to be chosen when the dimensions, extent, capacity, or quantity are considered as a simple fact ⟨*large* sum of money⟩ BIG suggests emphasis on bulk, weight, or volume ⟨*big* box⟩ GREAT may imply physical magnitude usu. with connotations of emotional effect but more often implies degree of intensity ⟨*great* kindness⟩ ⟨*great* fear⟩ LARGE figuratively implies breadth, comprehensiveness, or generosity; BIG suggests impressiveness often at the expense of solidity; GREAT implies eminence, distinction, or supremacy

²large *n, obs* **:** LIBERALITY, GENEROSITY — **at large 1 :** free; FREE ⟨the escaped prisoner is still *at large*⟩ **2 :** as a whole **:** in general ⟨the opinion of the public *at large*⟩ **3 :** representing a whole state or area rather than one of its subdivisions — used in combination with a preceding noun ⟨congressman-*at-large* from Ohio⟩ ⟨delegate-*at-large*⟩

large-heart·ed \'lärj-'härt-əd\ *adj* **:** GENEROUS, SYMPATHETIC

large intestine *n* **:** the posterior division of the vertebrate intestine consisting of the cecum, colon, and rectum and functioning esp. in the dehydration of digestive residues into feces

large·ly \'lärj-lē\ *adv* **1 :** GENEROUSLY, COMPREHENSIVELY **2 :** for the most part **:** in the main **:** CHIEFLY ⟨the statement is *largely* true⟩

large-mind·ed \'lärj-'mīn-dəd\ *adj* **:** generous or comprehensive in outlook, range, or capacity — **large·mind·ed·ly** *adv* — **large-mind·ed·ness** *n*

large-scale \-'skāl\ *adj* **:** larger than others of its kind

lar·gess *or* **lar·gesse** \lär-'jes, 'lär-,\ *n* [MF *largesse,* fr. *large* generous] **1 :** liberal giving **2 :** a generous gift

¹lar·ghet·to \lär-'get-ō\ *adv* (*or adj*) [It, fr. dim. of *largo*] **:** a little less slowly than largo — used as a direction in music

²larghetto *n, pl* **-tos :** a larghetto movement

larg·ish \'lär-jish\ *adj* **:** rather large

¹lar·go \'lär-gō\ *adv* (*or adj*) [It, lit., broad, fr. L *largus* abundant] **:** in a very slow and broad manner — used as a direction in music

²largo *n, pl* **largos :** a largo movement

lar·i·at \'lar-ē-ət\ *n* [AmerSp *la reata* the lasso] **:** a long light rope to catch livestock or to picket grazing animals **:** LASSO

¹lark \'lärk\ *n* [OE *lāwerce*] **1 :** any of numerous Old World singing birds; *esp* **:** SKYLARK **2 :** any of various usu. dull-colored ground-living birds (as the meadowlark or titlark)

²lark *vi* **:** FROLIC, SPORT

³lark *n* **:** FROLIC, ROMP; *also* **:** PRANK

lark·spur \'lärk-ˌspər\ *n* **:** DELPHINIUM; *esp* **:** a cultivated annual delphinium grown for its flowers

lar·rup \'lar-əp\ *vt, dial* **:** BEAT, WHIP

lar·va \'lär-və\ *n, pl* **lar·vae** \-(ˌ)vē, -ˌvī\ *also* **larvas** [NL, fr. L, specter, mask] **1 :** the immature, wingless, and often wormlike form that hatches from the egg of many insects — see SILKWORM illustration **2 :** the early form of any animal that at birth or hatching is fundamentally unlike its parent ⟨the tadpole is the *larva* of the frog⟩ — **lar·val** \-vəl\ *adj*

lar·vi·cide \'lär-və-ˌsīd\ *n* **:** an agent for killing larval pests — **lar·vi·cid·al** \ˌlär-və-'sīd-ᵊl\ *adj*

¹la·ryn·geal \lə-'rin-j(ē-)əl, ˌlar-ən-'jē-əl\ *adj* [NL *laryngeus*, fr. *laryng-, larynx* larynx] **:** of, relating to, or used on the larynx — **la·ryn·geal·ly** \-ē\ *adv*

²laryngeal *n* **:** a laryngeal part

lar·yn·gi·tis \ˌlar-ən-'jīt-əs\ *n* **:** inflammation of the larynx — **lar·yn·git·ic** \-'jit-ik\ *adj*

lar·ynx \'lar-iŋ(k)s\ *n, pl* **la·ryn·ges** \lə-'rin-(ˌ)jēz\ *or* **lar·ynx·es** [NL *laryng-, larynx*, fr. Gk] **:** the modified upper part of the trachea that in man and most mammals contains the vocal cords

las·car \'las-kər\ *n* [Hindi *lashkar* army] **:** an East Indian sailor, army servant, or native artilleryman

las·civ·i·ous \lə-'siv-ē-əs\ *adj* [L *lascivia* wantonness, fr. *lascivus* wanton] **:** LEWD, LUSTFUL — **las·civ·i·ous·ly** *adv* — **las·civ·i·ous·ness** *n*

la·ser \'lā-zər\ *n* [*light amplification* by *stimulated emission* of *radiation*] **:** a device that utilizes the natural oscillations of atoms for amplifying or generating electromagnetic waves in the visible region of the spectrum

¹lash \'lash\ *vb* [ME *lashen*] **1 :** to move violently or suddenly ⟨a lion *lashing* his tail⟩ **2 :** to strike with or as if with a whip ⟨*lashed* at the dogs with a rope⟩⟨rain *lashing* the window⟩ **3 :** to attack or retort verbally — **lash·er** *n*

²lash *n* **1 a** (1) **:** a stroke with a whip or with anything slender, pliant, and tough (2) **:** the flexible part of a whip; *also* **:** WHIP **b :** a sudden swinging blow **2 :** a verbal blow **3 :** EYELASH

³lash *vt* [ME *lasschen* to lace, fr. MF *lacier*] **:** to bind with a rope, cord, or chain — **lash·er** *n*

lash·ing *n* **:** something used for binding, wrapping, or fastening

lass \'las\ *n* [ME *las*] **1 :** young woman **:** GIRL **2 :** SWEETHEART

lass·ie \'las-ē\ *n* **:** LASS, GIRL

las·si·tude \'las-ə-ˌt(y)üd\ *n* [L *lassitudo*, fr. *lassus* weary] **1 :** WEARINESS, FATIGUE **2 :** LISTLESSNESS, LANGUOR

las·so \'las-ō, la-'sü\ *n, pl* **lassos** *or* **lassoes** [Sp *lazo*, fr. L *laqueus* noose, snare] **:** a rope or long thong of leather with a running noose that is used esp. for catching livestock — **lasso** *vt*

¹last \'last\ *vb* [OE *lǣstan*] **1 :** to continue in existence or operation **:** go on ⟨the meeting *lasted* three hours⟩ **2 a :** to remain valid, valuable, or important **:** ENDURE ⟨a book that will *last*⟩ **b :** to manage to continue (as in a course of action) ⟨he won't *last* on that job⟩ **3 :** to be enough for the needs of ⟨these supplies will *last* you for a week⟩ — **last·er** *n*

²last *adj* [OE *latost*, superl. of *læt* late] **1 a :** following all the rest ⟨*last* one out⟩ **b :** being the only remaining ⟨his *last* dollar⟩ **2 a :** belonging to the final stage ⟨the four *last* things⟩ **b :** administered to the dying ⟨*last* sacraments⟩ **3 :** next before the present **:** LATEST ⟨*last* week⟩ **4 :** least likely ⟨an investigation is the *last* thing he'd want⟩ **5 a :** CONCLUSIVE, ULTIMATE **b :** highest in degree **:** SUPREME

syn FINAL, ULTIMATE: LAST applies to something that comes at the end of a series but does not always imply that the series is completed or stopped ⟨*last* stop on the bus line⟩⟨*last* news bulletin I heard⟩ FINAL stresses a definite closing of a series, process, or stage of progress

⟨*final* exams⟩ ULTIMATE implies the last degree or stage of a long process beyond which further change or change is impossible ⟨*ultimate* collapse of civilization⟩

³last *adv* **1 :** at the end ⟨ran *last* in the race⟩ **2 :** most lately ⟨saw him *last* in New York⟩ **3 :** in conclusion ⟨and, *last*, I'd like to talk about money⟩

⁴last *n* **:** something that is last **:** END

⁵last *n* [OE *lǣste*] **:** a wooden or metal form which is shaped like the human foot and on which a shoe is shaped or repaired

⁶last *vb* **:** to shape with a last — **last·er** *n*

Las·tex \'las-ˌteks\ *trademark* — used for an elastic yarn

last·ing *adj* **:** existing or continuing a long while **:** ENDURING — **last·ing·ly** \'las-tiŋ-lē\ *adv* — **last·ing·ness** *n*

syn LASTING, PERMANENT mean enduring for so long as to seem fixed or established. LASTING implies a capacity to continue indefinitely ⟨*lasting* stain⟩ PERMANENT may add the implication of being designed to stand or continue indefinitely ⟨*permanent* arrangement⟩ ⟨*permanent* buildings⟩

last·ly \'last-lē\ *adv* **:** in conclusion **:** in the last place

Last Supper *n* **:** the supper of Christ and his disciples on the night of his betrayal

last word *n* **1 :** the final remark in a verbal exchange ⟨she always has to have the *last word*⟩ **2 :** the power of final decision **3 :** the most advanced, up-to-date, or fashionable exemplar of its kind ⟨the *last word* in sports cars⟩

lat·a·kia \ˌlat-ə-'kē-ə\ *n* [*Latakia*, Syria] **:** an aromatic Turkish smoking tobacco

¹latch \'lach\ *vi* [OE *læccan*] **1 :** to catch or get hold ⟨*latch* onto a pass⟩ **2 :** to attach oneself

²latch *n* **:** a device that holds something in place by entering a notch or cavity; *esp* **:** a catch (as a spring bolt) that holds a door or gate closed and that sometimes is operated by a key on one side and a knob on the other

³latch *vb* **:** CATCH, FASTEN

latch·et \'lach-ət\ *n* [MF *lachet*, fr. *laz* snare, fr. L *laqueus*] **:** a narrow leather strap, thong, or lace that fastens a shoe or sandal on the foot

latch·key \'lach-ˌkē\ *n* **:** a key by which a door latch may be opened from the outside

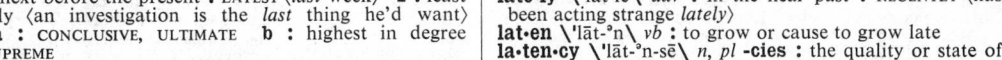

latches: *1* door, *2* gate

latch·string \-ˌstriŋ\ *n* **:** a string on a latch that may be left hanging outside the door for raising the latch

¹late \'lāt\ *adj* [OE *lǣt*] **1 a :** coming or remaining after the due, usual, or proper time ⟨*late* spring⟩ **b :** of or relating to an advanced stage in point of time or development ⟨*late* Middle Ages⟩; *esp* **:** far advanced toward the close of the day or night ⟨*late* hours⟩ **2 a :** living comparatively recently **b :** holding some position or relationship recently but not now ⟨*late* belligerents⟩ **c :** made, appearing, or happening just previous to the present time ⟨*late* quarrel⟩ syn see RECENT — **late·ness** *n*

²late *adv* **1 a :** after the usual or proper time ⟨came in *late*⟩ **b :** at or to an advanced point in time ⟨saw her *later* in the day⟩ **2 :** not long ago **:** RECENTLY ⟨a man *late* of Chicago⟩ — **of late :** LATELY, RECENTLY

late·com·er \'lāt-ˌkəm-ər\ *n* **:** one who arrives late; *also* **:** a recent arrival

¹la·teen \lə-'tēn\ *adj* [F *voile latine* lateen sail] **:** of, relating to, or being a sailing rig used esp. on the north coast of Africa and characterized by a triangular sail extended by a long spar slung to a low mast

²lateen *n* **1** *also* **la·teen·er** \-'tē-nər\ **:** a lateen-rigged ship **2 :** a lateen sail

Late Latin *n* **:** the Latin language used by writers in the 3d to 6th centuries

late·ly \'lāt-lē\ *adv* **:** in the near past **:** RECENTLY ⟨has been acting strange *lately*⟩

lat·en \'lāt-ᵊn\ *vb* **:** to grow or cause to grow late

la·ten·cy \'lāt-ᵊn-sē\ *n, pl* **-cies :** the quality or state of being latent **:** DORMANCY

la·tent \'lāt-ᵊnt\ *adj* [L *latent-, latens*, fr. prp. of *latēre* to lie hidden] **:** present but not visible or active ⟨*latent* abilities⟩⟨*latent* infection⟩ — **la·tent·ly** *adv*

syn LATENT, DORMANT, QUIESCENT mean not now showing its presence or existence. LATENT applies to a power or quality that has not yet come forth but may emerge and develop ⟨talents which were *latent* in childhood⟩ DORMANT suggests inactivity as though sleeping ⟨a *dormant* volcano⟩ QUIESCENT suggests a temporary cessation of activity ⟨*quiescent* lung disease⟩

latent heat *n* : heat energy absorbed or evolved in a process (as fusion or vaporization) other than a change of temperature

latent image *n* : an invisible image produced by the action of light on a photographic film that can be made visible by developing

latent period *n* : the interval between causation and effect (as the incubation period of a disease)

lat·er·ad \'lat-ə-ˌrad\ *adv* : toward the side

¹**lat·er·al** \'lat-ə-rəl, 'la-trəl\ *adj* [L *later-*, *latus* side] : of or relating to the side : situated on, directed toward, or coming from the side ⟨the *lateral* branches of a tree⟩ — **lat·er·al·ly** \-ē\ *adv*

²**lateral** *n* **1** : a lateral part or branch **2** : a lateral pass in football

lateral line *n* : a sense organ of the skin of most fishes that is sensitive to low vibrations and extends along each side of the body

lateral pass *n* : a pass in football thrown parallel to the line of scrimmage or in a direction away from the opponent's goal

lat·er·ite \'lat-ə-ˌrīt\ *n* [L *later* brick] : a residual product of rock decay that is red in color and has a high content in the oxides of iron and hydroxide of aluminum — **lat·er·it·ic** \ˌlat-ə-'rit-ik\ *adj*

la·tex \'lā-ˌteks\ *n*, *pl* **la·ti·ces** \'lat-ə-ˌsēz\ *or* **la·tex·es** [NL *latic-*, *latex*, fr. L, fluid] **1** : a milky juice produced by plants esp. of the milkweed family ⟨rubber, gutta-percha, chicle, and balata are products of various *latexes*⟩ **2** : a water emulsion of a synthetic rubber or plastic used esp. in paints and adhesives — **lat·i·cif·er·ous** \ˌlat-ə-'sif-(ə-)rəs\ *adj*

¹**lath** \'lath\ *n*, *pl* **laths** \'lathz, 'laths\ [OE *lætt*] **1** : a thin narrow strip of wood used esp. as a base for plaster **2** : material (as wire cloth) used in sheets as a substitute for wooden laths **3** : a quantity of laths together

²**lath** *vt* : to cover or line with laths

lathe \'lāth\ *n* : a machine in which a piece of material is held and turned while being shaped by a tool

¹**lath·er** \'lath-ər\ *n* [(assumed) ME, fr. OE *lēathor* washing soda, lather; akin to E *lye*] **1 a** : a foam or froth formed when a detergent (as soap) is agitated in water **b** : foam or froth from profuse sweating (as on a horse) **2** : an agitated or overwrought state : DITHER

²**lather** *vb* **lath·ered; lath·er·ing** \'lath-(ə-)riŋ\ **1 a** : to spread lather over ⟨*lathered* his face⟩ **b** : to form a lather or a froth like lather ⟨this soap *lathers* well⟩ **2** : to beat severely : FLOG — **lath·er·er** \'lath-ər-ər\ *n* — **lath·ery** \'lath-(ə-)rē\ *adj*

³**lath·er** \'lath-ər, 'lath-\ *n* : a workman who makes or applies laths

lath·ing \'lath-iŋ, 'lath-\ *n* **1** : the action or process of placing laths **2** : a quantity or an installation of laths

lath·work \'lath-ˌwərk\ *n* : LATHING

lat·i·me·ria \ˌlat-ə-'mir-ē-ə\ *n* : any of a genus of living coelacanth fishes of deep seas off southern Africa — compare LOBE-FIN

¹**Lat·in** \'lat-ᵊn\ *adj* **1** : of or relating to Latium or the Latins **2 a** : of, relating to, or composed in Latin ⟨*Latin* grammar⟩ **b** : ROMANCE **3** : of or relating to the part of the Catholic Church that uses a Latin rite and forms the patriarchate of the pope **4** : of or relating to the peoples or countries using Romance languages; *esp* : of or relating to the peoples or countries of Latin America

²**Latin** *n* **1** : the Italic language of ancient Latium and of Rome and until modern times the dominant language of school, church, and state in western Europe **2** : a member of the people of ancient Latium **3** : a Catholic of the Latin rite **4** : a member of one of the Latin peoples; *esp* : a native or inhabitant of Latin America

Lat·in·ate \'lat-ᵊn-ˌāt\ *adj* : of, relating to, resembling, or derived from Latin

Latin cross *n* : a cross having a long upright shaft and a shorter crossbar above the middle — see CROSS illustration

Lat·in·ism \'lat-ᵊn-ˌiz-əm\ *n* **1** : a word, idiom, or mode

of speech derived from or imitative of Latin **2** : Latin quality, character, or mode of thought

Lat·in·ist \-ᵊn-əst\ *n* : a specialist in the Latin language or Roman culture

la·tin·i·ty \la-'tin-ət-e, lə-\ *n*, *often cap* **1** : a manner of speaking or writing Latin **2** : LATINISM

lat·in·i·za·tion \ˌlat-ᵊn-ə-'zā-shən\ *n* : the act or result of latinizing

lat·in·ize \'lat-ᵊn-ˌīz\ *vt*, *often cap* **1** *obs* : to translate into Latin **2** : to give Latin characteristics or forms to

lat·ish \'lāt-ish\ *adj* (*or adv*) : somewhat late

lat·i·tude \'lat-ə-ˌt(y)üd\ *n* [ME, fr. L *latitudin-*, *latitudo* width, breadth, fr. *latus* wide] **1 a** : angular distance north or south from the earth's equator measured in degrees **b** : angular distance of a celestial body from the ecliptic **c** : a region or locality as marked by its latitude **2** : the range of exposures within which a film or plate will produce a negative or positive of satisfactory quality **3** : freedom from narrow restrictions ⟨was allowed great *latitude* in his editorials⟩ — **lat·i·tu·di·nal** \ˌlat-ə-'t(y)üd-nəl, -ᵊn-əl\ *adj* — **lat·i·tu·di·nal·ly** \-ē\ *adv*

hemisphere marked with parallels of latitude

lat·i·tu·di·nar·i·an \ˌlat-ə-ˌt(y)üd-ᵊn-'er-ē-ən\ *n* : a person who is broad and liberal in his standards of religious belief and conduct — **latitudinarian** *adj* — **lat·i·tu·di·nar·i·an·ism** \-ē-ə-ˌniz-əm\ *n*

la·trine \lə-'trēn\ *n* [F, fr. L *latrina* bath, toilet, fr. *lavere* to wash] **1** : a receptacle (as a pit in the earth) for use as a toilet **2** : TOILET

lat·ter \'lat-ər\ *adj* [OE *lætra*, compar. of *læt* late] **1 a** : more recent : LATER **b** : of or relating to the end : FINAL **2** : of, relating to, or being the second of two things referred to

lat·ter-day \ˌlat-ər-ˌdā\ *adj* **1** : of a later or subsequent time **2** : of present or recent times

Latter–Day Saint *n* : a member of a religious body founded by Joseph Smith in 1830 and accepting the Book of Mormon as divine revelation : MORMON

lat·ter·ly \'lat-ər-lē\ *adv* : LATELY, RECENTLY

lat·tice \'lat-əs\ *n* [MF *lattis*] **1 a** : a framework or structure of crossed wood or metal strips **b** : a window, door, or gate having a lattice **2** : a regular geometrical arrangement of points or objects over an area or in space ⟨the *lattice* of atoms in a crystal⟩ — **lattice** *vt* — **lat·ticed** \-əst\ *adj*

lat·tice·work \'lat-əs-ˌwərk\ *n* : a lattice or work made of lattices

¹**Lat·vi·an** \'lat-vē-ən\ *adj* : of, relating to, or characteristic of Latvia, the Latvians, or Latvian

²**Latvian** *n* **1** : a native or inhabitant of Latvia **2** : the Baltic language of the Latvian people

¹**laud** \'lod\ *n* [ML *laudes*, pl., fr. L, pl. of *laud-*, *laus* praise] **1** *pl* : an office of solemn praise to God forming with matins the first of the canonical hours **2** : ACCLAIM, PRAISE

²**laud** *vt* [L *laudare*, fr. *laud-*, *laus*, n., praise] : PRAISE, EXTOL

laud·a·bil·i·ty \ˌlod-ə-'bil-ət-ē\ *n* : the quality or state of being laudable

laud·a·ble \'lod-ə-bəl\ *adj* : worthy of praise : COMMENDABLE — **laud·a·ble·ness** *n* — **laud·a·bly** \-blē\ *adv*

lau·da·num \'lod-nəm, -ᵊn-əm\ *n* [NL] **1** : a formerly used preparation of opium **2** : a tincture of opium

lau·da·tion \lo-'dā-shən\ *n* **1** : the act of lauding **2** : PRAISE

lau·da·to·ry \'lod-ə-ˌtor-ē, -ˌtor-\ *adj* : of, relating to, or expressing praise

¹**laugh** \'laf, 'laf\ *vb* [OE *hliehhan*, *hlæhan*] **1 a** : to show mirth, joy, or scorn with a smile and chuckle or explosive sound **b** : to become amused or derisive ⟨*laughed* at his early efforts⟩ **2** : to produce the sound or appearance of laughter **3** : to utter with a laugh ⟨*laughs* her consent⟩ — **laugh·er** *n*

²**laugh** *n* **1** : the act or sound of laughing **2** : a cause for derision or merriment

laugh·a·ble \'laf-ə-bəl, 'laf-\ *adj* : such as to provoke laughter or derision : RIDICULOUS — **laugh·a·ble·ness** n — **laugh·a·bly** \-blē\ adv

syn LUDICROUS, RIDICULOUS: LAUGHABLE may apply to anything that arouses laughter; LUDICROUS suggests obvious absurdity or preposterousness that excites both laughter and scorn or sometimes pity; RIDICULOUS implies extreme absurdity, foolishness, or ineptness

laugh·ing adj : fit to be treated or accompanied with laughter : LAUGHABLE ⟨this is no *laughing* matter⟩

laughing gas n : NITROUS OXIDE

laughing jackass n : KOOKABURRA

laugh·ing·ly \'laf-iŋ-lē, 'laf-\ adv : with laughter

laugh·ing·stock \'laf-iŋ-ˌstäk, 'laf-\ n : an object of ridicule

laugh·ter \'laf-tər, 'laf-\ n : the action or sound of laughing

¹launch \'lonch, 'länch\ vb [ONF lancher, fr. LL lanceare to wield a lance, fr. L lancea lance] **1 a** : to throw forward : HURL ⟨*launch* a spear⟩ **b** : to spring forward : take off **c** : to send off (a self-propelled object) ⟨*launch* a rocket⟩ **d** : to set (a ship) afloat **2 a** : to put in operation : BEGIN ⟨*launch* an attack⟩ **b** : to give (a person) a start ⟨*launched* his son in business⟩ **c** : to make a start ⟨had *launched* on a difficult course of study⟩ **3** : to throw oneself energetically : PLUNGE ⟨*launched* into a dreary monologue⟩

²launch n : an act of launching

³launch n [Pg lancha, fr. Malay lancharan] **1** archaic : a large ship's boat **2** : a small open or half-decked motorboat used for pleasure or short-distance transportation

launch·er \'lon-chər, 'län-\ n : one that launches: as **a** : a device for firing a grenade from a rifle **b** : a device for launching a rocket or rocket shell **c** : CATAPULT

launching pad n : a nonflammable platform from which a rocket can be launched

laun·der \'lon-dər, 'län-\ vb **laun·dered; laun·der·ing** \-d(ə-)riŋ\ [ME launder launderer, fr. MF lavandier, fr. ML lavandarius, fr. L lavandus to be washed, fr. lavare to wash] **1 a** : to wash (as clothes) in water **b** : to iron after washing ⟨a freshly *laundered* shirt⟩ **2** : to wash or wash and iron clothing or household linens **3** : to undergo washing and ironing ⟨fabrics guaranteed to *launder* well⟩ — **laun·der·er** \-dər-ər\ n — **laun·dress** \-drəs\ n

laun·dry \'lon-drē, 'län-\ n, pl **-dries 1** : clothes or linens that have been or are to be laundered **2** : a place where laundering is done

laun·dry·man \-mən\ n : a male laundry worker — **laun·dry·wom·an** \-ˌwùm-ən\ n

lau·re·ate \'lor-ē-ət, 'lär-\ n [L laureatus crowned with laurel, fr. laurea laurel wreath, fr. laurus laurel] : the recipient of honor for achievement in an art or science; esp : POET LAUREATE — **laureate** adj — **lau·re·ate·ship** \-ˌship\ n

lau·rel \'lor-əl, 'lär-\ n [modif. of OF lorier, fr. lor laurel, fr. L laurus] **1** : any of a genus of trees or shrubs related to the sassafras and cinnamon; esp : a small evergreen tree of southern Europe with foliage used by the ancient Greeks to crown victors in various contests **2** : a tree or shrub (as a mountain laurel) like the true laurel **3** : a crown of laurel : HONOR

la·va \'läv-ə, 'lav-\ n [It] : melted rock coming from a volcano; also : such rock that has cooled and hardened

la·va·bo \lə-'väb-ō\ n [L, I shall wash, fr. lavare to wash] often cap : a ceremony at Mass in which the celebrant washes his hands after offering the oblations and says Psalm 25:6–12

la·vage \lə-'väzh\ n : WASHING; esp : the washing out (as of a wound or hollow organ) for medicinal reasons

la·va·liere or **la·val·liere** \ˌläv-ə-'li(ə)r, ˌlav-\ n [F lavallière necktie with a large bow] : a pendant on a fine chain that is worn as a necklace

lav·a·to·ry \'lav-ə-ˌtōr-ē, -ˌtor-\ n, pl **-ries** [ML lavatorium, fr. L lavare to wash] **1** : a vessel for washing; esp : a fixed bowl or basin with running water and drainpipe **2** : a room with conveniences for washing and usu. with one or more toilets **3** : WATER CLOSET

lave \'lāv\ vb [OE lafian, fr. L lavare] **1 a** : WASH **b** archaic : to wash oneself : BATHE **2** : to flow along or against ⟨water *laving* the shore⟩

lav·en·der \'lav-ən-dər\ n [AF lavendre, fr. ML lavandula]

1 : a Mediterranean mint widely cultivated for its narrow aromatic leaves and spikes of lilac-purple flowers which are dried and used in sachets; also : any of several related plants used similarly **2** : a variable color averaging a pale purple

¹la·ver \'lā-vər\ n **1** archaic : a vessel, trough, or cistern for washing **2** : a large basin used for ceremonial ablutions in ancient Judaism

²laver n : any of several mostly edible seaweeds; esp : SEA LETTUCE

¹lav·ish \'lav-ish\ adj [ME lavas abundance, fr. MF lavasse downpour of rain, fr. laver to wash, fr. L lavare] **1** : spending or giving more than is necessary : EXTRAVAGANT ⟨*lavish* with money⟩ ⟨*lavish* of praise⟩ **2** : spent, produced, or given freely ⟨*lavish* gifts⟩ ⟨*lavish* hospitality⟩ — **lav·ish·ly** adv — **lav·ish·ness** n

²lavish vt : to spend or give freely : SQUANDER ⟨*lavish* affection on a person⟩

law \'lo\ n [OE lagu, of Scand. origin] **1 a** : a rule of conduct or action laid down and enforced by the supreme governing authority (as the legislature) of a community, state, or nation or established by custom **b** : the whole collection of customs and rules ⟨the *law* of the land⟩ **c** : the control brought about by enforcing rules ⟨forces of *law* and order⟩ **2** : a rule, principle, or formula of construction or procedure ⟨the *laws* of poetry⟩ **3** : a rule or principle stating something that always works in the same way under the same conditions ⟨the *law* of gravity⟩ **4** : the observed regularity of nature **5 cap a** : the revelation of the divine will set forth in the Old Testament **b** : the first part of the Jewish scriptures — compare HAGIOGRAPHA, PROPHETS **6** : trial in a court to determine what is just and right according to the laws ⟨go to *law*⟩ **7** : the science that deals with laws and their interpretation and application ⟨study *law*⟩ **8** : the profession of a lawyer : lawyers as a group

syn LAW, REGULATION, STATUTE, ORDINANCE mean a principle that governs action or procedure. LAW implies imposition by a sovereign authority and obligation of obedience by all; REGULATION carries an implication of authority exercised in order to control an organization or system; STATUTE implies a law enacted by a legislative body often as distinguished from the common or unwritten law; ORDINANCE applies to an order governing some detail or procedure enforced by a limited authority such as a municipality ⟨city *ordinances* for traffic regulation⟩ syn see in addition HYPOTHESIS

law-abid·ing \'lo-ə-ˌbīd-iŋ\ adj : obedient to the law

law-break·er \'lo-ˌbrā-kər\ n : a person who breaks the law — **law-break·ing** \-kiŋ\ adj or n

law·ful \'lo-fəl\ adj **1** : permitted by law ⟨having *lawful* business to transact⟩ **2** : recognized by law : RIGHTFUL ⟨the *lawful* owner⟩ — **law·ful·ly** \-f(ə-)lē\ adv — **law·ful·ness** \-fəl-nəs\ n

syn LAWFUL, LEGAL, LEGITIMATE mean being in accordance with law. LAWFUL implies conformity to law of any kind; LEGAL implies reference to the law of courts; LEGITIMATE implies a legal right or one supported by tradition, custom, or accepted standards of authenticity ⟨*legitimate* heir to the throne⟩

law·giv·er \'lo-ˌgiv-ər\ n **1** : one who gives a code of laws to a people **2** : LEGISLATOR

law·less \'lo-ləs\ adj **1** : having no laws : not based on or regulated by law ⟨the *lawless* society of the frontier⟩ **2** : not controlled by law : UNRULY, DISORDERLY ⟨a *lawless* mob⟩ — **law·less·ly** adv — **law·less·ness** n

law·mak·er \'lo-ˌmā-kər\ n : a person who has a part in framing laws : LEGISLATOR — **law·mak·ing** adj or n

¹lawn \'lon, 'län\ n [Laon, France] : a fine sheer linen or cotton fabric of plain weave that is thinner than cambric — **lawny** \-ē\ adj

²lawn n [ME launde glade, pasture, fr. MF lande heath] : ground (as around a house or in a park) covered with grass that is kept mowed

lawn bowling n : a bowling game played on a green with wooden balls which are rolled at a jack

lawn mower n : a machine for cutting grass on lawns

lawn tennis n : tennis played on a grass court

law of conservation of energy : CONSERVATION OF ENERGY

law of conservation of mass : CONSERVATION OF MASS

law of definite proportions : a statement in chemistry:

every definite compound always contains the same elements in the same proportions by weight

law of dominance : the 3d of Mendel's laws

law of independent assortment : the 2d of Mendel's laws

law of mass action : a statement in chemistry: the rate of a chemical reaction is directly proportional to the molecular concentrations of the reacting substances

law of Mo·ses \-'mō-zəz, -zəs\ : PENTATEUCH

law of multiple proportions : a statement in chemistry: when two elements combine in more than one proportion to form two or more compounds the weights of one element that combine with a given weight of the other element are in the ratios of small whole numbers

law of segregation : the first of Mendel's laws

law of unit characters : LAW OF INDEPENDENT ASSORTMENT

law·ren·ci·um \lȯ-'ren(t)-sē-əm\ n [NL, fr. Ernest O. *Lawrence* d1958 American physicist] : a short-lived radioactive element produced from californium — see ELEMENT table

law·suit \'lȯ-ˌsüt\ n : a suit in law : a case before a court

law·yer \'lȯ-yər\ n : one whose profession is to conduct lawsuits for clients or to advise as to legal rights and obligations in other matters

lax \'laks\ adj [L *laxus* loose] **1 a :** LOOSE, OPEN ⟨*lax* bowels⟩ **b :** having loose bowels **2 :** not strict or stringent ⟨*lax* discipline⟩ **3 a :** not tense : not firm or rigid : SLACK **b :** having an open or loose texture ⟨a *lax* flower cluster⟩ **4 :** produced with the speech muscles in a relatively relaxed state ⟨the *lax* vowels \i\ and \u̇\⟩ — compare TENSE — **lax·ly** adv — **lax·ness** n

¹lax·a·tive \'lak-sət-iv\ adj : having a tendency to loosen or relax; esp : relieving constipation — **lax·a·tive·ly** adv — **lax·a·tive·ness** n

²laxative n : a usu. mild laxative drug — compare PURGATIVE

lax·i·ty \'lak-sət-ē\ n : the quality or state of being lax ⟨*laxity* in discipline⟩

¹lay \'lā\ vb **laid** \'lād\; **lay·ing** [OE *lecgan* to cause to lie; akin to E ¹*lie*] **1 :** to beat or strike down ⟨*laid* him in the dust who blow⟩ **2 a :** to put or set on or against a surface ⟨*lay* the book on the table⟩ ⟨*laid* his watch to his ear⟩ **b :** to place for rest or sleep; also : BURY **3 :** to produce and deposit eggs **4 :** to cause to settle or be less turbulent ⟨a shower *laid* the dust⟩; also : CALM, ALLAY ⟨*laid* his fears⟩ **5 :** to press down smooth and even ⟨*lay* the nap of a fabric⟩ **6 a :** to spread over a surface ⟨*lay* plaster⟩ **b :** to place down or together in orderly sequence ⟨*lay* track⟩ ⟨*lay* bricks⟩ **7 a :** to put and arrange dishes, linens, and silver on : SET ⟨*lay* a table⟩ **b :** to gather and arrange fuel for ⟨*lay* a fire⟩ **8 :** to deposit as a wager : BET ⟨I'll *lay* you ten dollars on that⟩ **9 a :** SET, IMPOSE ⟨*lay* a tax on liquor⟩ **b :** to put as a burden of reproach ⟨*laid* the blame on him⟩ **10 :** to place or assign in one's scheme of things ⟨*lays* great stress on manners⟩ **11 :** CONTRIVE, DEVISE ⟨a well-*laid* plan⟩ **12 :** to bring to a specified condition ⟨*lay* waste the land⟩ **13 :** to put forward : SUBMIT ⟨*lay* claim to an estate⟩ ⟨*laid* his case before the committee⟩ **14 :** to apply oneself vigorously ⟨*laid* to his oars⟩ **15 :** TAKE, GRAB ⟨*lay* hold of that line⟩ — **lay for :** to wait and look for a chance to attack ⟨was *laying for* him after school⟩ — **lay on :** ATTACK, BEAT ⟨grabbed a club and *laid on* for all he was worth⟩

²lay n **1 :** something (as a layer) that lies or is laid **2 :** the way in which a thing lies or is laid in relation to something else ⟨*lay* of the land⟩ **3 :** an egg-laying condition

³lay past of LIE

⁴lay n [OF *lai*] **1 :** a simple narrative poem : BALLAD **2 :** MELODY, SONG

⁵lay adj [OF *lai*, fr. LL *laicus*, fr. Gk *laikos* of the people, fr. *laos* people] **1 :** of or relating to the laity : not ecclesiastical **2 :** of or relating to members of a religious house occupied with domestic or manual work ⟨*lay* brother⟩ **3 :** not of or from a particular profession : UNPROFESSIONAL ⟨*lay* public⟩

lay away vt : to put aside for future use or delivery

lay by vt : to store for future use : SAVE

lay down vt **1 :** to give up : SURRENDER ⟨*lay down* your arms⟩ **2 a :** ESTABLISH, PRESCRIBE ⟨*lays down* standards⟩ ⟨scale *laid down* for a map⟩ **b :** to assert or command dogmatically ⟨*lay down* the law⟩ **3 :** STORE, PRESERVE

¹lay·er \'lā-ər, 'le(-ə)r\ n **1 :** one that lays ⟨his hens were

poor *layers*⟩ **2 :** one thickness, course, or fold laid or lying over or under another ⟨a *layer* of rock⟩ **3 :** a shoot used in or a plant developed by layering — **lay·ered** \'lā-ərd, 'le(-ə)rd\ adj

²layer vt : to propagate (a plant) by layering

lay·er·age \'lā-ə-rij, 'le-ə-\ n : the practice or art of layering plants

lay·er·ing \'lā-ə-riŋ, 'le(-ə)r-iŋ\ n : the production of new plants by surrounding a stem which is often partly cut through with a rooting medium (as soil) until new roots have formed

lay·ette \lā-'et\ n [F, fr. MF, dim. of *laye* box, drawer, fr. MD *lade* box; akin to OE *hladan* to load] : a complete outfit of clothing and equipment for a newborn infant

lay figure \'lā-\ n [obs. *layman* lay figure, fr. D *ledeman, leeman*, fr. *lede* limb + *man* man] **1 :** a jointed model of the human body used by artists to show the disposition of drapery **2 :** a person of no importance or individuality : DUMMY, PUPPET

lay in vt : to lay by : SAVE

lay·man \'lā-mən\ n **1 :** a person who is not a clergyman **2 :** a person who is not a member of a particular profession

lay off \(')lā-'ȯf\ vb **1 :** to mark or measure off **2 :** to cease to employ (a worker) usu. temporarily **3 a :** to leave undisturbed ⟨*lay off* him — he's had enough⟩ **b :** AVOID, QUIT ⟨*lay off* smoking⟩ **4 :** to stop or rest from work

lay·off \'lā-ˌȯf\ n **1 :** the act of laying off an employee or a work force **2 :** a period of inactivity or idleness

lay out \(')lā-'au̇t\ vt **1 :** to prepare (a corpse) for burial **b :** to knock flat or unconscious **2 :** to plan in detail ⟨*lay out* a campaign⟩ **3 :** to mark (work) for drilling, machining, or filing **4 :** ARRANGE, DESIGN **5 :** SPEND

lay·out \'lā-ˌau̇t\ n **1 :** ARRANGEMENT, PLAN ⟨the *layout* of a house⟩ **2 :** something that is laid out ⟨a model train *layout*⟩ **3 :** the way in which a piece of printed matter is arranged ⟨the *layout* of a page⟩ ⟨the *layout* of a book⟩ **4 :** a set or outfit esp. of tools

lay over \(')lā-'ō-vər\ vi : to make a temporary halt or stop ⟨*laid over* in New York for three days before flying back⟩

lay·over \'lā-ˌō-vər\ n : STOPOVER

lay reader n : an Anglican layman licensed to read sermons and conduct some religious services

lay to \(')lā-'tü\ vb : to bring (a ship) into the wind and hold stationary; also : to lie to

lay up \(')lā-'əp\ vt **1 :** to store up : lay by **2 :** to disable or confine with illness or injury **3 :** to take out of active service

lay·up \'lā-ˌəp\ n : the action of laying up or the condition of being laid up; esp : a jumping one-hand shot in basketball made off the backboard from close under the basket

lay·wom·an \-ˌwu̇m-ən\ n : a woman who is a member of the laity

laz·ar \'laz-ər, 'lā-zər\ n [ML *lazarus*, fr. LL *Lazarus*, beggar in parable in Luke 16:20–31] : a person afflicted with a repulsive disease; esp : LEPER

laz·a·ret·to \ˌlaz-ə-'ret-ō\ or **laz·a·ret** \-'ret\ n, pl **-rettos** or **-rets** [It dial. *lazareto*, alter. of *nazareto*, fr. *Santa Maria di Nazaret*, church in Venice that maintained a hospital] **1** usu *lazaretto* : a hospital for contagious diseases **2 :** a building or a ship used for detention in quarantine **3** usu *lazaret* : a space in a ship between decks used as a storeroom

Laz·a·rus \'laz-(ə-)rəs\ n **1 :** a brother of Mary and Martha raised by Jesus from the dead **2 :** the diseased beggar in the biblical parable of the rich man and the beggar

laze \'lāz\ vb : to pass time in idleness or relaxation : IDLE

lazuli n : LAPIS LAZULI

la·zy \'lā-zē\ adj **la·zi·er; -est 1 :** not willing to act or work : IDLE, INDOLENT **2 :** SLOW, SLUGGISH ⟨a *lazy* stream⟩ — **la·zi·ly** \-zə-lē\ adv — **la·zi·ness** \-zē-nəs\ n

la·zy·bones \'lā-zē-ˌbōnz\ n : a lazy person

la·zy·ish \'lā-zē-ish\ adj : somewhat lazy

lazy Su·san \ˌlā-zē-'süz-ᵊn\ n : a revolving tray placed on a dining table for serving food, condiments, or relishes

lea or **ley** \'lē, 'lā\ n [OE *lēah*] **1 :** GRASSLAND, PASTURE **2** usu *ley* : arable land used temporarily for hay or grazing

leach \'lēch\ vt : to pass a liquid and esp. water through

¹lead \'lēd\ *vb* **led** \'led\; **lead·ing** \'lēd-iŋ\ [OE *lǣdan*] **1 a :** to guide on a way esp. by going in advance **:** CONDUCT **b :** to direct on a course or in a direction **c :** to serve as a channel for ⟨pipes *lead* water into canals⟩ **d :** to lie, run, or open in a specified place or direction ⟨path *leads* uphill⟩ **2 :** to go through **:** LIVE ⟨*lead* a quiet life⟩ **3 a :** to direct the operations, activity, or performance of ⟨*lead* an orchestra⟩ ⟨*lead* a campaign⟩ **b** (1) **:** to go at the head of ⟨*lead* a parade⟩ (2) **:** to be first in or among ⟨*lead* the league⟩; *also* **:** BEGIN, OPEN ⟨*lead* off for the home team⟩ (3) **:** to have a margin over ⟨*led* his opponent⟩ **4 :** to begin play with **:** play the first card ⟨*lead* trumps⟩ **5 :** to direct (a blow) at an opponent in boxing **6 :** to tend toward a definite result **:** EVENTUATE ⟨study *leading* to a degree⟩

²lead *n* **1 a** (1) **:** position at the front **:** VANGUARD (2) **:** INITIATIVE (3) **:** the act or privilege of leading in cards; *also* **:** the card or suit led **b** (1) **:** LEADERSHIP (2) **:** EXAMPLE, PRECEDENT **c :** a margin or measure of advantage or superiority or position in advance **2 :** one that leads: as **a :** INDICATION, CLUE **b :** a principal role in a dramatic production; *also* **:** one who plays such a role **c :** LEASH 1 **d :** an introductory section of a news story; *also* **:** a news story of chief importance **e :** the first in a series or exchange of blows in boxing **3 :** an insulated electrical conductor **4 :** a position taken by a base runner off a base toward the next **5 :** the amount that a screw or spiral advances in one complete turn

³lead *adj* **:** acting or serving as a leader ⟨the *lead* article in this month's issue⟩

⁴lead \'led\ *n* [OE *lēad*] **1 :** a heavy soft malleable bivalent or tetravalent bluish white metallic chemical element that is found mostly in combination and is used in pipes, cable sheaths, solder, and type metal — see ELEMENT table **2 a :** a mass of lead used on a line for finding the depth of water (as in the ocean) **b** *pl* **:** lead framing for panes in windows **c :** a thin strip of metal used to separate lines of type in printing **3 a :** a thin stick of marking substance (as graphite) in or for a pencil **b :** WHITE LEAD **4 :** BULLETS, PROJECTILES **5 :** TETRAETHYL LEAD — **lead·less** \-ləs\ *adj*

⁵lead \'led\ *vt* **1 :** to cover, line, or weight with lead **2 :** to fix (window glass) in position with lead **3 :** to place lead or other spacing material between the lines of (type matter) **4 :** to treat or mix with lead or a lead compound ⟨*leaded* gasoline⟩

lead acetate *n* **:** a poisonous soluble salt of lead $Pb(C_2H_3O_2)_2.3H_2O$ used in dyeing and printing

lead arsenate *n* **:** an acid salt of lead $PbHAsO_4$ used as an insecticide

lead dioxide *n* **:** a poisonous compound PbO_2 that occurs as a mineral and is produced artificially and that is used as an oxidizing agent — called also *lead peroxide*

lead·en \'led-ᵊn\ *adj* **1 :** made of lead **b :** of the color of lead **:** dull gray **2 :** low in quality **:** POOR **3 a :** oppressively heavy **b :** SLUGGISH **c :** lacking spirit or animation **:** DULL ⟨*leaden* spirits⟩ — **lead·en·ly** *adv* — **lead·en·ness** \-ᵊn-(n)əs\ *n*

lead·er \'lēd-ər\ *n* **1 :** something that leads: as **a :** a main shoot of a plant **b :** TENDON, SINEW **c :** dots or hyphens (as in an index) used to lead the eye horizontally **:** ELLIPSIS 2 **d** *chiefly Brit* **:** a newspaper editorial **e :** a short length of material for attaching the end of a fishing line to a lure or hook **f :** a pipe for conducting fluid **g :** an article offered at an attractive special low price to stimulate business **h :** something that ranks first **2 :** a person that leads: as **a :** GUIDE, CONDUCTOR **b :** COMMANDER **c :** the authoritarian head of a totalitarian party or state **d :** CONDUCTOR **b e :** a first or principal performer of a group **3 :** a horse placed in front of the other horses of a team **4 :** STRAW BOSS, FOREMAN — **lead·er·less** \-ləs\ *adj* — **lead·er·ship** \-,ship\ *n*

lead-in \'lēd-,in\ *n* **:** something that leads in; *esp* **:** the part of a radio antenna that runs to the transmitting or receiving set — **lead-in** *adj*

lead·ing \'lēd-iŋ\ *adj* **1 :** coming or ranking first or among the first **:** FOREMOST **2 :** exercising leadership **3 :** GUIDING, DIRECTING ⟨*leading* question⟩ **4 :** given most prominent display ⟨*leading* story⟩

leading lady *n* **:** an actress who plays the leading feminine role in a play or movie

leading man *n* **:** an actor who plays the leading male role in a play or movie

leading tone *n* [so called because it leads harmonically to the tonic] **:** the seventh musical degree of a major or minor scale — called also *subtonic*

lead monoxide *n* **:** a yellow to brownish red poisonous compound PbO used in rubber manufacture and glassmaking

lead-off \'lēd-,óf\ *n* **1 :** a beginning or leading action **2 :** the player who heads the batting order or bats first in any inning in baseball — **lead-off** *adj*

lead on *vt* **:** to entice or induce to proceed in a course esp. when unwise or mistaken ⟨*led* her *on* to believe him⟩

lead oxide *n* **:** a compound of lead and oxygen; *esp* **:** LEAD MONOXIDE

lead pencil \'led-\ *n* **:** a pencil using graphite as the marking material

lead up \(')lēd-'əp\ *vi* **1 :** to prepare the way **2 :** to make a gradual or indirect approach to a topic

¹leaf \'lēf\ *n, pl* **leaves** \'lēvz\ [OE *lēaf*] **1 a :** a usu. flat lateral outgrowth from a stem that is a unit of plant foliage and functions primarily in food manufacture by photosynthesis **b :** FOLIAGE **2 :** something suggestive of a leaf: as **a :** a part of a book or folded sheet containing a page on each side **b :** a part (as of window shutters, folding doors, or gates) that slides or is hinged **c :** the movable part of a table top **d :** a thin sheet (as of metal) **:** LAMINA **e :** one of the plates of a leaf spring — **leaf·less** \'lēf-ləs\ *adj* — **leaf·like** \-,līk\ *adj*

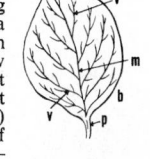

leaf 1a: *a* apex, *b* blade, *p* petiole, *v* vein, *m* midrib

²leaf *vb* **1 :** to produce leaves **2 :** to turn the pages of a book

leaf·age \'lē-fij\ *n* **:** FOLIAGE

leaf bud *n* **:** a bud that develops into a leafy shoot and does not produce flowers

leaf fat *n* **:** the fat that lines the abdominal cavity and encloses the kidneys; *esp* **:** that of a hog used in the manufacture of lard

leaf·hop·per \'lēf-,häp-ər\ *n* **:** any of numerous small leaping insects related to the cicadas that suck the juices of plants

leaf lard *n* **:** high quality lard made from leaf fat

leaf·let \'lēf-lət\ *n* **1 a :** one of the divisions of a compound leaf **b :** a small or young foliage leaf **2 a :** a single printed sheet of paper unfolded or folded but not trimmed at the fold **b :** a sheet of small pages folded but not stitched

leaf miner *n* **:** any of various small insects that as larvae burrow in and eat the tissue of leaves

leaf mold *n* **:** a compost or layer composed chiefly of decayed vegetable matter

leaf spring *n* **:** a spring made of superposed strips, plates, or leaves — see SPRING illustration

leaf·stalk \'lēf-,stók\ *n* **:** PETIOLE

leafy \'lē-fē\ *adj* **leaf·i·er; -est 1 a :** having or abounding in leaves ⟨*leafy* woodlands⟩ **b :** consisting mostly of leaves ⟨*leafy* vegetables⟩ **2 :** resembling a leaf; *esp* **:** LAMINATE

¹league \'lēg\ *n* [LL *leuga*, of Celt origin] **:** any of various units of distance from about 2.4 to 4.6 statute miles

²league *n* [ME (Sc) *ligg*, fr. MF *ligue*, fr. It *liga*, fr. *ligare* to bind, fr. L] **1 a :** an association or alliance of nations for a common purpose **b :** an association of persons or groups united for common interests or goals **2 :** CLASS, CATEGORY — **league** *vb*

leagu·er \'lē-gər\ *n* **:** a member of a league

Le·ah \'lē-ə\ *n* **:** one of the wives of Jacob

¹leak \'lēk\ *vb* [ON *leka*] **1 a :** to enter or escape or permit to enter or escape through an opening usu. by a fault or mistake ⟨fumes *leak* in⟩ **b :** to let a substance or light in or out through an opening **2 :** to become known despite efforts at concealment ⟨the secret *leaked* out⟩ **3 :** to give out (information) surreptitiously ⟨*leaked* the story to the press before the official announcement⟩

²leak *n* **1 a :** a crack or hole that usu. by mistake admits or lets escape **b :** something that permits the admission or escape of something else usu. with prejudicial effect **2** : LEAKAGE 1a

leak·age \'lē-kij\ *n* **1 a** : the act, process, or an instance of leaking **b** : loss of electricity due esp. to faulty insulation **2** : something or the amount that leaks

leaky \'lē-kē\ *adj* **leak·i·er; -est** : permitting fluid to leak in or out — **leak·i·ness** *n*

leal \'lēl\ *adj* [OF *leial, leel,* fr. L *legalis* legal] *chiefly Scot* : LOYAL, TRUE

¹lean \'lēn\ *vb* **leaned** \'lēnd, *chiefly Brit* 'lent\; **lean·ing** \'lē-niŋ\ [OE *hleonian*] **1 a** : to incline, deviate, or bend from a vertical position **b** : to cast one's weight to one side for support 〈*lean* on me〉 **2** : to rely for support or inspiration **3** : to incline in opinion, taste, or desire 〈*lean* toward simplicity〉

²lean *n* : the act or an instance of leaning : INCLINATION

³lean *adj* [OE *hlǣne*] **1 a** : lacking or deficient in flesh 〈*lean* cattle〉 **b** : containing little or no fat 〈*lean* meat〉 **2** : lacking richness, sufficiency, or productiveness **3** : characterized by economy of style or expression — **lean·ness** \'lēn-nəs\ *n*

⁴lean *n* : the part of meat that consists principally of fat-free muscle

Le·an·der \lē-'an-dər\ *n* : a youth noted in Greek legend for swimming the Hellespont nightly to visit Hero

lean·ing \'lē-niŋ\ *n* : TENDENCY, INCLINATION

leant \'lent\ *chiefly Brit past of* LEAN

¹lean-to \'lēn-,tü\ *n, pl* **lean-tos 1** : a wing or extension of a building having a lean-to roof **2** : a rough shed or shelter with a lean-to roof

²lean-to *adj* : having only one slope or pitch 〈*lean-to* roof〉 — see ROOF illustration

¹leap \'lēp\ *vb* **leaped** *or* **leapt** \'lept, 'lept\; **leap·ing** \'lē-piŋ\ [OE *hlēapan*] **1** : to spring or cause to spring free from or as if from the ground : JUMP 〈*leap* over a fence〉〈a fish *leaps* out of the water〉〈*leap* a horse over a ditch〉 **2 a** : to pass abruptly from one state or topic to another **b** : to act precipitately 〈*leaped* at the chance〉 — **leap·er** \'lē-pər\ *n*

²leap *n* **1 a** : an act of leaping : SPRING, BOUND **b** (1) : a place leaped over or from (2) : the distance covered by a leap **2** : a sudden transition — **by leaps and bounds** : with extraordinary rapidity 〈improved *by leaps and bounds*〉

leap·frog \'lēp-,frôg, -,fräg\ *n* : a game in which one player bends down and another leaps over him

leap year *n* **1** : a year in the Gregorian calendar containing 366 days with February 29 as the extra day **2** : an intercalary year in any calendar

learn \'lərn\ *vb* **learned** \'lərnd, 'lərnt\ *also* **learnt** \'lərnt\; **learn·ing** [OE *leornian;* akin to E *lore*] **1 a** (1) : to gain knowledge or understanding of or skill in by study, instruction, or experience (2) : MEMORIZE 〈*learn* the lines of a play〉 **b** : to come to be able to 〈*learn* to swim〉 **c** : to come to realize **2** *substand* : to cause to learn : TEACH **3** : to find out : ASCERTAIN **4** : to acquire knowledge (never too late to *learn*) — **learn·a·ble** \'lər-nə-bəl\ *adj* — **learn·er** *n*

syn LEARN and TEACH are not synonyms; though LEARN has been used for TEACH this is not accepted usage. LEARN implies acquiring knowledge; TEACH implies imparting it

learned *adj* **1** \'lər-nəd\ : characterized by or associated with learning : ERUDITE **2** \'lərnd, 'lərnt\ : acquired by learning — **learn·ed·ly** \'lər-nəd-lē\ *adv* — **learn·ed·ness** \'lər-nəd-nəs\ *n*

learn·ing *n* **1** : the act or experience of one that learns **2** : knowledge or skill acquired by instruction or study

¹lease \'lēs\ *n* [AF *les,* fr. OF *laissier* to let go, leave, fr. L *laxare* to loosen, fr. *laxus* loose] **1** : a contract by which one party conveys real estate to another for a term of years or at will usu. for a specified rent; *also* : the act of such conveyance or the term for which it is made **2** : a piece of land or property that is leased

²lease *vt* **1** : to grant by lease : LET **2** : to hold under a lease **syn** see HIRE

lease·hold \'lēs-,hōld\ *n* **1** : a tenure by lease **2** : land held by lease — **lease·hold·er** \-,hōl-dər\ *n*

leash \'lēsh\ *n* [OF *laisse,* fr. *laissier* to let go, fr. L *laxare* to loosen] **1** : a line for leading or restraining an animal **2** : a set of three animals (as dogs) — **leash** *vt*

¹least \'lēst\ *adj* [OE *lǣst,* superl. of *lǣssa* lesser] **1** : lowest in importance or position **2 a** : smallest in size or degree **b** : smallest possible : SLIGHTEST

²least *n* : one that is least : something of the lowest possible value, importance, or scope 〈not to care in the *least*〉〈the *least* that can be said〉 — **at least 1** : at the minimum **2** : in any case

³least *adv* : in the smallest or lowest degree

least common denominator *n* : the lowest common multiple of the denominators of two or more fractions

least common multiple *n* : LOWEST COMMON MULTIPLE

least·wise \'lēst-,wīz\ *adv* : at least

¹leath·er \'leth-ər\ *n* [OE *lether-*] **1** : animal skin dressed for use **2** : something wholly or partly made of leather — **leather** *adj*

²leather *vt* **leath·ered; leath·er·ing** \'leth-(ə-)riŋ\ **1** : to cover with leather **2** : to beat with a strap : THRASH

leath·er·back \'leth-ər-,bak\ *n* : a very large sea turtle with a flexible carapace

Leath·er·ette \,leth-ə-'ret\ *trademark* — used for a product colored, finished, and embossed in imitation of leather grains

leath·ern \'leth-ərn\ *adj* : made of, consisting of, or resembling leather

leath·er·neck \'leth-ər-,nek\ *n* : MARINE

leath·ery \'leth-(ə-)rē\ *adj* : resembling leather in appearance or texture : TOUGH

¹leave \'lēv\ *vb* **left** \'left\; **leav·ing** [OE *lǣfan*] **1** : to allow or cause to remain behind 〈*leave* your books at home〉 **2** : DELIVER 〈*leave* a book at the library〉〈the postman *left* three letters〉 **3** : to have remaining (as after death or subtraction) 〈*leave* a widow and two children〉 〈taking 7 from 10 *leaves* 3〉 **4** : to give by will : BEQUEATH **5** : to let stay without interference 〈*leave* a kettle to boil〉 〈*leave* someone alone〉 **6** : to go away 〈*leave* at ten o'clock〉 **7** : to depart from 〈*leave* the house〉

syn LEAVE, LET mean to refrain from preventing but they are not interchangeable in construction. LEAVE implies not interfering with, disturbing, or taking action concerning someone or something 〈*leave* him in peace〉〈he was *left* to follow his own choice〉 LET is always followed by an infinitive without *to* and may imply a positive giving of permission 〈*let* the prisoner go〉 or a failure to prevent 〈*let* the plate fall from her hand〉

²leave *n* **1 a** : PERMISSION **b** : authorized absence from duty or employment **2** : an act of leaving : DEPARTURE

³leave *vi* **leaved; leav·ing** : LEAF

leaved \'lēvd\ *adj* : having leaves 〈broad-*leaved*〉

¹leav·en \'lev-ən\ *n* [MF *levain,* fr. (assumed) VL *levamen,* fr. L *levare* to raise] **a** : a substance (as yeast) used to produce a gaseous fermentation (as in dough) **b** : a material (as baking powder) used to produce a gas that lightens dough or batter **2** : something that modifies or lightens a mass or aggregate 〈a *leaven* of common sense〉

²leaven *vt* **leav·ened; leav·en·ing** \'lev-(ə-)niŋ\ **1** : to raise (dough) with a leaven **2** : to mingle or permeate with some modifying, alleviating, or vivifying element

leav·en·ing *n* : a leavening agent : LEAVEN

leave off *vb* : STOP, CEASE

leaves *pl of* LEAF

leave-tak·ing \'lēv-,tā-kiŋ\ *n* : DEPARTURE, FAREWELL

leav·ings \'lē-viŋz\ *n pl* : REMNANT, RESIDUE

lech·ery \'lech-(ə-)rē\ *n, pl* **-er·ies** [OF *lecherie* gluttony, lechery, fr. *lechier* to lick, of Gmc origin; akin to E *lick*] : inordinate indulgence in sexual activity — **lech·er** *n* — **lech·er·ous** \-(ə-)rəs\ *adj* — **lech·er·ous·ly** *adv* — **lech·er·ous·ness** *n*

lec·i·thin \'les-ə-thən\ *n* [Gk *lekithos* egg yolk] : any of several waxy phosphorus-containing substances that are common in animals and plants, form colloidal solutions in water, and have emulsifying, wetting, and antioxidant properties

lec·tern \'lek-tərn\ *n* [MF *letrun,* fr. ML *lectorinum,* fr. L *lector* reader] : READING DESK; *esp* : one from which scripture lessons are read in a church service

lec·tor \'lek-tər\ *n* [L, reader, fr. *lect-, legere* to read] : one whose chief duty is to read the lessons in a church service

¹lec·ture \'lek-chər\ *n* [ME, act of reading,

lectern

fr. LL *lectura*, fr. L *lect-*, *legere* to gather, pick out, read] **1** : a discourse given before an audience or class esp. for instruction **2** : REPRIMAND, SCOLDING

²lecture *vb* **lec·tured**; **lec·tur·ing** \'lek-chə-riŋ, 'lek-shriŋ\ **1** : to deliver a lecture or a course of lectures **2** : to instruct by lectures **3** : REPRIMAND, SCOLD — **lec·tur·er** \-chər-ər, -shrər\ *n*

led *past of* LEAD

Le·da \'lēd-ə\ *n* : the mother of Clytemnestra and Castor by her husband Tyndareus, King of Sparta, and of Helen of Troy and Pollux by Zeus in the guise of a swan

le·der·ho·sen \'lād-ər-,hōz-ᵊn\ *n pl* [G, lit., leather trousers] : knee-length leather trousers worn esp. in Bavaria

ledge \'lej\ *n* [ME *legge* bar of a gate] **1** : a projecting ridge or raised edge along a surface : SHELF **2** : an underwater ridge or reef esp. near the shore **3** : a narrow flat surface or shelf; *esp* : one that projects (as from a wall of rock) **4** : LODE, VEIN

led·ger \'lej-ər\ *n* [ME *legger*] : a book containing accounts to which debits and credits are posted in final form

ledger line *n* : a short line added above or below a musical staff for notes that are too high or too low to be placed on the staff

¹lee \'lē\ *n* [OE *hlēo*] **1** : protecting shelter **2** : the side (as of a ship) that is sheltered from the wind

²lee *adj* : of or relating to the lee — compare WEATHER

¹leech \'lēch\ *n* [OE *lǣce*] **1** *archaic* : PHYSICIAN, SURGEON **2** [fr. its former use by physicians for bleeding patients] : any of numerous carnivorous or bloodsucking segmented usu. flattened freshwater worms (class Hirudinea) having a sucker at each end **3** : a hanger-on who seeks advantage or gain : PARASITE

²leech *vb* **1** : to drain the substance of : EXHAUST **2** : to attach oneself to a person as a leech

³leech *n* [MLG *līk* boltrope] **1** : either vertical edge of a square sail **2** : the after edge of a fore-and-aft sail

leek \'lēk\ *n* [OE *lēac*] : a garden herb closely related to the onion and grown for its mildly pungent leaves and thick stalk

¹leer \'li(ə)r\ *vi* : to cast a sidelong glance; *esp* : to give a suggestive, knowing, or malicious look

²leer *n* : a suggestive, knowing, or malicious look

leery \'li(ə)r-ē\ *adj* : SUSPICIOUS, WARY

lees \'lēz\ *n pl* [ME *lie*, fr. MF, fr. ML *lia*] : the settlings of liquor during fermentation and aging : DREGS, SEDIMENT

lee shore *n* : a shore lying off a ship's leeward side and constituting a severe danger in storm

¹lee·ward \'lē-wərd, 'lü-ərd\ *adj* : situated away from the wind : DOWNWIND — compare WINDWARD — **leeward** *adv*

²leeward *n* : the lee side

lee·way \'lē-,wā\ *n* **1** : off-course lateral movement of a ship when under way **2** : an allowable margin of freedom or variation : TOLERANCE ⟨allow enough *leeway* to arrive on time⟩

¹left \'left\ *adj* [OE, weak] **1** : of, relating to, or being the side of the body in which the heart is mostly located ⟨the *left* leg⟩ **2** : located nearer to the left side of the body than to the right ⟨the *left* arm of his chair⟩; *also* : lying in the direction that an observer's left hand would naturally extend ⟨the *left* fork of the road⟩ **3** *often cap* : of, adhering to, or constituted by the political Left — **left** *adv*

²left *n* **1 a** : the left hand **b** : the location or direction of or part on the left side **2** *often cap* **a** : the part of a legislative chamber located to the left of the presiding officer **b** : the members of a continental European legislative body occupying the left and holding more radical political views than other members **3** *cap* **a** : those professing views usu. characterized by desire to reform or overthrow the established order esp. in politics and usu. advocating greater freedom or well-being of the common man **b** : a liberal as distinguished from a conservative position

³left *past of* LEAVE

left field *n* **1** : the part of the baseball outfield to the left looking out from the plate **2** : the position of the player defending left field — **left fielder** *n*

left-hand \,left-,hand\ *adj* **1** : situated on the left **2** : LEFT-HANDED

left-hand·ed \'left-'han-dəd\ *adj* **1** : using the left hand habitually or more easily than the right **2** : relating to,

designed for, or done with the left hand **3** : CLUMSY, AWKWARD; *also* : INSINCERE, MALICIOUS, DUBIOUS ⟨*left-handed* compliment⟩ **4 a** : COUNTERCLOCKWISE **b** : having a structure involving a counterclockwise direction ⟨*left-handed* screw⟩ — **left-handed** *adv* — **left-hand·ed·ly** *adv* — **left-hand·ed·ness** *n* — **left-hand·er** \-'han-dər\ *n*

left·ist \'lef-təst\ *n* : a person who advocates or adheres to the policies of the left or who belongs to a left political party

left·over \'left-,ō-vər\ *n* : an unused or unconsumed residue; *esp* : food left over from one meal and served at another — **leftover** *adj*

left shoulder arms — used as a command in the manual of arms to bring the rifle to a position in which the butt is held in the left hand, the barrel rests on the left shoulder, and the muzzle is inclined to the rear

left·ward \'left-wərd\ *also* **left·wards** \-wərdz\ *adv* : toward or on the left — **leftward** *adj*

left wing *n* : the leftist division of a group **2** : LEFT 3a — **left-wing** *adj* — **left-wing·er** \'left-,wiŋ-ər\ *n*

¹leg \'leg\ *n* [ON *leggr*] **1** : a limb of an animal used esp. for supporting the body and for walking; *esp* : the part of the vertebrate limb between the knee and foot **2** : something resembling an animal leg in shape or use ⟨*legs* of a table⟩ **3** : the part of an article of clothing that covers the leg **4** : OBEISANCE, BOW ⟨make a *leg*⟩ **5** : either side of a triangle as distinguished from the base or hypotenuse **6** : BOOST — called also *leg up* **7 a** : the course and distance sailed by a boat on a single tack **b** : a portion of a trip : STAGE **c** : one section of a relay race **8** : a branch or part of an object or system ⟨*legs* of a pair of compasses⟩

²leg *vi* **legged**; **leg·ging** : to use the legs in walking or esp. in running

leg·a·cy \'leg-ə-sē\ *n, pl* **-cies** [ML *legatia* office or jurisdiction of a legate, fr. L *legatus* legate] **1** : something left to a person by will : INHERITANCE, BEQUEST **2** : something that has come from an ancestor or predecessor or the past ⟨a *legacy* of ill will⟩

le·gal \'lē-gəl\ *adj* [L *leg-*, *lex* law] **1** : of or relating to law or lawyers **2 a** : deriving authority from or founded on law : de jure **b** : established by law; *esp* : STATUTORY **3** : conforming to or permitted by law or established rules **4** : recognized or made effective at law rather than in equity **syn** see LAWFUL — **le·gal·ly** \-gə-lē\ *adv*

legal age *n* : the age at which a person enters into full adult legal rights and responsibilities (as of voting or making contracts or wills)

legal holiday *n* : a holiday established by legal authority and characterized by legal restrictions on work and transaction of official business

le·gal·ism \'lē-gə-,liz-əm\ *n* : strict, literal, or excessive conformity to the law or to a religious or moral code — **le·gal·ist** \-gə-ləst\ *n* — **le·gal·is·tic** \,lē-gə-'lis-tik\ *adj* — **le·gal·is·ti·cal·ly** \-ti-k(ə-)lē\ *adv*

le·gal·i·ty \li-'gal-ət-ē\ *n, pl* **-ties** : the quality or state of being legal : LAWFULNESS

le·gal·ize \'lē-gə-,līz\ *vt* : to make legal; *esp* : to give legal validity or sanction to — **le·gal·i·za·tion** \,lē-gə-lə-'zā-shən\ *n*

legal tender *n* : currency in the amounts and denominations that the law authorizes a debtor to tender and requires a creditor to receive in payment of money obligations

leg·ate \'leg-ət\ *n* [L *legatus* deputy, emissary, fr. *legare* to depute, bequeath, fr. *leg-*, *lex* law] : an official representative (as an ambassador or envoy)

leg·a·tee \,leg-ə-'tē\ *n* : a person to whom a legacy is bequeathed

le·ga·tion \li-'gā-shən\ *n* **1** : a body of deputies sent on a mission; *esp* : a diplomatic mission headed by a minister **2** : the official residence and office of a diplomatic minister to a foreign government

le·ga·to \li-'gät-ō\ *adv (or adj)* [It, lit., tied, fr. pp. of *legare* to tie, fr. L *ligare*] : in a manner that is smooth and connected between successive tones — used as a direction in music

leg·end \'lej-ənd\ *n* [ML *legenda*, fr. L, fem. of *legendus* to be read, fr. *legere* to read] **1 a** : a story coming down from the past and popularly regarded as historical although not verifiable **b** : a popular myth of recent origin c : a person or thing that inspires legends **2 a** : an inscription or title on an object **b** : CAPTION 2 **c** : an explanatory list of the symbols on a map or chart **syn** see MYTH

leg·end·ary \'lej-ən-,der-ē\ *adj* : of or resembling a legend ⟨*legendary* heroes⟩ : consisting of legends ⟨*legendary* writings⟩ **syn** see FABULOUS

leg·end·ry \-ən-drē\ *n* : LEGENDS

leg·er·de·main \,lej-ərd-ə-'mān\ *n* [MF *leger de main* light of hand] **1** : SLEIGHT OF HAND **2** : an artful deception

legged \'leg(-ə)d\ *adj* : having legs ⟨four-*legged*⟩

leg·ging *or* **leg·gin** \'leg-ən, 'leg-iŋ\ *n* : a covering for the leg usu. of leather or cloth — usu. used in pl.

leg·gy \'leg-ē\ *adj* **leg·gi·er; -est 1 a** : having disproportionately long legs **b** : SPINDLY ⟨a *leggy* plant⟩ **2** : having attractive legs

leg·horn \'leg-,(h)òrn, 'leg-ərn\ *n* [*Leghorn*, Italy] **1 a** : a fine plaited straw made from an Italian wheat **b** : a hat of this straw **2** : any of a Mediterranean breed of small hardy fowls noted for their large production of white eggs

leg·i·ble \'lej-ə-bəl\ *adj* [L *legere* to read] : capable of being read or deciphered : PLAIN — **leg·i·bil·i·ty** \,lej-ə-'bil-ət-ē\ *n* — **leg·i·bly** \'lej-ə-blē\ *adv*

le·gion \'lē-jən\ *n* [L *legion-, legio,* fr. *legere* to gather, pick out, read] **1** : the principal unit of the Roman army comprising 3000 to 6000 foot soldiers with cavalry **2** : ARMY 1a **3** : a very large number : MULTITUDE **4** : a national association of ex-servicemen

¹le·gion·ary \'lē-jə-,ner-ē\ *adj* : of, relating to, or constituting a legion

²legionary *n, pl* **-ar·ies** : LEGIONNAIRE

le·gion·naire \,lē-jə-'na(ə)r, -'ne(ə)r\ *n* [F *légionnaire*] : a member of a legion

leg·is·late \'lej-ə-,slāt\ *vb* [back-formation fr. *legislator*] **1** : to make or enact laws **2** : to cause, create, or bring about by legislation

leg·is·la·tion \,lej-ə-'slā-shən\ *n* **1** : the action of making laws **2** : the laws made by a legislator or legislative body

leg·is·la·tive \'lej-ə-,slāt-iv\ *adj* **1** : having the power or performing the function of legislating ⟨the *legislative* branch⟩ **2** : of or relating to a legislature or legislation — **leg·is·la·tive·ly** *adv*

legislative assembly *n, often cap L&A* **1** : a bicameral legislature in an American state or its lower house **2** : a unicameral legislature esp. in a Canadian province

legislative council *n, often cap L&C* : a permanent committee from both houses of a state legislature that meets between sessions to study state problems and plan a legislative program

leg·is·la·tor \'lej-ə-,slāt-ər\ *n* [L *legis lator* proposer of a law] : a person who makes laws for a state or community; *esp* : a member of a legislature

leg·is·la·ture \'lej-ə-,slā-chər\ *n* : an organized body of persons having the authority to make laws for a political unit

le·git \li-'jit\ *adj, slang* : LEGITIMATE

¹le·git·i·mate \li-'jit-ə-mət\ *adj* **1** : born of parents who are married : lawfully begotten ⟨*legitimate* children⟩ **2** : being in accordance with law or established requirements : LAWFUL ⟨a *legitimate* claim⟩ **3** : being in keeping with what is right or in accordance with standards permitted ⟨a *legitimate* excuse for absence⟩ **4** : relating to acted plays not including burlesque, revues, or musical comedy ⟨*legitimate* theater⟩ **syn** see LAWFUL — **le·git·i·ma·cy** \-mə-sē\ *n* — **le·git·i·mate·ly** *adv*

²le·git·i·mate \-,māt\ *vt* [ML *legitimare,* fr. *legitimus* lawful, fr. *leg-, lex* law] : to make lawful or legal — **le·git·i·ma·tion** \li-,jit-ə-'mā-shən\ *n*

le·git·i·ma·tize \li-'jit-ə-mə,tīz\ *vt* : LEGITIMATE

le·git·i·mize \li-'jit-ə-,mīz\ *vt* : LEGITIMATE

leg·less \'leg-ləs\ *adj* : having no legs ⟨*legless* insect⟩

leg·man \'leg-,man\ *n* **1** : a newspaperman assigned usu. to gather information **2** : an assistant who gathers information and runs errands

leg-of-mut·ton \,leg-ə(v)-'mət-°n\ *adj* : having the approximately triangular shape or outline of a leg of mutton ⟨*leg-of-mutton* sleeve⟩⟨*leg-of-mutton* sail⟩

le·gume \'leg-,yüm, li-'gyüm\ *n* [F *légume,* fr. L *legumin-, legumen* leguminous plant, fr. *legere* to gather] **1 a** : any

of a large family of dicotyledonous herbs, shrubs, and trees having fruits that are dry single-celled pods and split into two valves when ripe, bearing nodules on the roots that contain nitrogen-fixing bacteria, and including important food and forage plants (as peas, beans, or clovers) **b** : the part (as seeds or pods) of a legume used as food; *also* : VEGETABLE 1b **2** : the pod characteristic of a legume — compare LOMENT — **le·gu·mi·nous** \li-'gyü-mə-nəs, le-\ *adj*

leg·work \'leg-,wərk\ *n* : the work of a legman

le·hua \lā-'hü-ə\ *n* [Hawaiian] : a showy tree of the myrtle family with corymbs of bright red flowers and a hard wood; *also* : its flower

lei \'lā, 'lā-,ē\ *n* [Hawaiian] : a wreath or necklace usu. of flowers

lei·sure \'lēzh-ər, 'lezh-, 'lāzh-\ *n* [OF *leisir,* fr. *leisir* to be permitted, fr. L *licēre*] **1** : freedom provided by the cessation of activities; *esp* : time free from work or duties **2 a** : EASE **b** : CONVENIENCE — **leisure** *adj*

lei·sure·ly \-lē\ *adj* : characterized by leisure : UNHURRIED ⟨a *leisurely* pace⟩ — **lei·sure·li·ness** *n* — **leisurely** *adv*

leit·mo·tiv *or* **leit·mo·tif** \'līt-mō-,tēf\ *n* [G *leitmotiv,* lit., leading motif] : a dominant recurring theme (as in a musical or literary work)

lem·an \'lem-ən, 'lē-mən\ *n, archaic* : SWEETHEART, LOVER; *esp* : MISTRESS

lem·ma \'lem-ə\ *n* [Gk, husk] : the lower of the two bracts enclosing the flower in the spikelet of grasses

lem·ming \'lem-iŋ\ *n* [Norw] : any of several small short-tailed northern rodents with furry feet and small ears

¹lem·on \'lem-ən\ *n* [MF *limon,* fr ML *limon-, limo,* fr. Ar *laymūn*] **1 a** : an acid fruit that is botanically a many-seeded pale yellow nearly oval berry **b** : the stout thorny citrus tree that bears this fruit **2** : DUD, FAILURE ⟨the new car proved to be a *lemon*⟩

²lemon *adj* **1 a** : containing lemon **b** : having the flavor or scent of lemon **2** : of the color lemon yellow

lem·on·ade \,lem-ə-'nād\ *n* : a drink made of lemon juice, sugar, and water

lemon balm *n* : a perennial Old World mint often grown for its fragrant lemon-flavored leaves

lemon yellow *n* : a variable color averaging a brilliant greenish yellow

lem·pi·ra \lem-'pir-ə\ *n* **1** : the basic monetary unit of Honduras **2** : a coin or note representing one lempira

le·mur \'lē-mər\ *n* [L *lemures,* pl., ghosts] : any of numerous arboreal and mostly nocturnal mammals that are related to the monkeys and usu. have a muzzle like a fox, large eyes, very soft woolly fur, and a long furry tail

lend \'lend\ *vb* **lent** \'lent\; **lend·ing** [OE *lǣnan,* fr. *lǣn* loan] **1** : to allow the use of something on the condition that it or its equivalent be returned ⟨*lend* a book⟩ ⟨*lend* money⟩ **2** : to give for the time being ⟨*lend* assistance⟩ **3** : to have the quality or nature that makes suitable ⟨a voice that *lends* itself to singing in opera⟩ — **lend·er** *n*

syn LOAN: LEND implies a giving of anything for a temporary use or purpose ⟨offered to *lend* his help to win the campaign⟩ LOAN chiefly applies to lending money at interest ⟨*loaned* him a hundred dollars at six percent⟩

lend–lease \'len-'dlēs\ *n* : the transfer of goods and services to an ally to aid in a common cause with payment being made by a return of the original items or their use in the common cause or by a similar transfer of other goods and services — **lend–lease** *vt*

length \'leŋ(k)th\ *n* [OE *lengthu,* fr. *lang* long] **1 a** : the longer or longest dimension of an object **b** : a measured distance or dimension ⟨10-inch *length*⟩ — see MEASURE table, METRIC SYSTEM table **c** : the quality or state of being long ⟨criticized the *length* of the story⟩ **2 a** : duration or extent in time ⟨the *length* of an interview⟩ **b** : relative duration or stress of a sound **3** : the length of something taken as a unit of measure ⟨horse led by a *length*⟩ **4** : a piece constituting or usable as part of a whole or of a connected series : SECTION ⟨a *length* of pipe⟩ **5** : a vertical dimension of an article of clothing — **at length 1** : COMPREHENSIVELY, FULLY **2** : at last : FINALLY

length·en \'leŋ(k)-thən\ *vb* **length·ened; length·en·ing** \'leŋ(k)th-(ə)-niŋ\ : to make or become longer **syn** see EXTEND — **length·en·er** \-(ə-)nər\ *n*

length·ways \'leŋ(k)th-,wāz\ *adv* : LENGTHWISE

length·wise \-,wīz\ *adv* : in the direction of the length

ə abut; ᵊ kitten; ər further; a back; ā bake; ä cot, cart; aù out; ch chin; e less; ē easy; g gift; i trip; ī life

: LONGITUDINALLY ⟨fold the paper *lengthwise*⟩ — **lengthwise** *adj*

lengthy \'len(k)-thē\ *adj* **length·i·er; -est** **1** : excessively drawn out : OVERLONG ⟨a *lengthy* speech⟩ **2** : EXTENDED, LONG ⟨a *lengthy* stay⟩ — **length·i·ly** \-thə-lē\ *adv* — **length·i·ness** \-thē-nəs\ *n*

le·ni·en·cy \'lē-nē-ən-sē\ *or* **le·ni·ence** \-ən(t)s\ *n* : the quality or state of being lenient **syn** see MERCY

le·ni·ent \'lē-nē-ənt\ *adj* [L *lenire* to soothe, fr. *lenis* mild] : of mild and tolerant disposition or effect; *esp* : INDULGENT ⟨looked on the child's mistakes with a *lenient* eye⟩ — **le·ni·ent·ly** *adv*

Len·in·ism \'len-ə-,niz-əm, 'lān-\ *n* : the political, economic, and social principles and policies advocated by Lenin; *esp* : the theory and practice of communism developed by or associated with Lenin — **Len·in·ist** \-nəst\ *n or adj*

len·i·tive \'len-ət-iv\ *adj* : alleviating pain or acrimony : MITIGATING — **lenitive** *n*

len·i·ty \'len-ət-ē\ *n* : MILDNESS, LENIENCY

lens \'lenz\ *n* [NL *lent-, lens*, fr. L, lentil; so called fr. its shape] **1** : a piece of transparent substance (as glass) that has two opposite regular surfaces either both curved or one curved and the other plane and that is used either singly or combined in an optical instrument for forming an image by focusing rays of light **2** : a device for directing or focusing radiation (as sound waves or electrons) other than light **3** : something shaped like a double-convex optical lens ⟨a mineral occurring in the form of *lenses*⟩ **4** : a transparent biconvex lens-shaped or nearly spherical body in the eye that focuses light rays (as upon the retina)

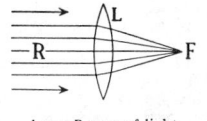

lens: *R* rays of light, *F* focus, *L* lens

Lent \'lent\ *n* [OE *lengten* springtime] : a period of penitence and fasting observed on the 40 weekdays from Ash Wednesday to Easter by many churches

Lent·en \'lent-°n\ *adj* : of, relating to, or suitable to Lent; *esp* : MEAGER, SOMBER

len·ti·cel \'lent-ə-,sel\ *n* : a pore in a stem of a woody plant through which gases are exchanged between the atmosphere and the stem tissues — **len·ti·cel·late** \,lent-ə-'sel-ət\ *adj*

len·tic·u·lar \len-'tik-yə-lər\ *adj* : shaped like a doubleconvex lens

len·til \'lent-°l\ *n* [OF *lentille*, fr. L *lenticula*, dim. of *lent-, lens*] : a Eurasian annual legume widely grown for its flattened edible seeds and leafy stalks used as fodder; *also* : its seed

len·to \'len-,tō\ *adv (or adj)* [It, fr. *lento*, adj., slow, fr. L *lentus* pliant, sluggish] : in a slow manner — used as a direction in music

Leo \'lē-ō\ *n* [L, lit., lion] **1** : a northern constellation east of Cancer **2** : the 5th sign of the zodiac — see ZODIAC table

le·o·nine \'lē-ə-,nīn\ *adj* [L *leon-, leo* lion] : of, relating to, or resembling a lion

leop·ard \'lep-ərd\ *n* [Gk *leopardos*, fr. *leōn* lion + *pardos* leopard] : a large strong cat of southern Asia and Africa that is usu. tawny or buff with black spots arranged in broken rings or rosettes — called also *panther* — **leop·ard·ess** \-əs\ *n*

leopard frog *n* : the common spotted frog of the eastern U.S.

le·o·tard \'lē-ə-,tärd\ *n* [Jules *Léotard*, 19th cent. French aerial gymnast] : a close-fitting garment usu. with long sleeves, a high neck, and ankle-length legs worn for practice or performance by dancers, acrobats, and aerialists

lep·er \'lep-ər\ *n* [OF *lepre* leprosy, fr. LL *lepra*, fr. Gk, fr. *lepein* to peel] **1** : a person affected with leprosy **2** : OUTCAST

lep·i·dop·ter·an \,lep-ə-'däp-tə-rən\ *n* : any of a large order (Lepidoptera) of insects that comprise the butterflies and moths, as adults have four wings usu. covered with minute overlapping often brightly colored scales, and as larvae are caterpillars — **lep·i·dop·ter** \-tər\ *n* — **lepidopteran** *adj* — **lep·i·dop·ter·ous** \-tə-rəs\ *adj*

lep·i·dop·ter·on \-tə-rən, -,rän\ *n, pl* **-tera** \-rə\ [NL, fr. Gk *lepid-, lepis* scale + *pteron* wing] : LEPIDOPTERAN

lep·i·do·sis \,lep-ə-'dō-səs\ *n, pl* **-do·ses** \-'dō-,sēz\ [Gk *lepid-, lepis* scale] : arrangement of scales (as on a snake)

lep·re·chaun \'lep-rə-,kän, -,kón\ *n* [IrGael *leipreachān*] : a mischievous elf of Irish folklore usu. believed to reveal the hiding place of treasure if caught

lep·rose \'lep-,rōs\ *adj* : SCALY, SCURFY

lep·ro·sy \'lep-rə-sē\ *n* : a chronic bacterial disease marked by slow-growing spreading swellings accompanied by loss of sensation, wasting, and deformities — **lep·rot·ic** \le-'prät-ik\ *adj*

lep·rous \'lep-rəs\ *adj* : infected with, relating to, or resembling leprosy — **lep·rous·ly** *adv* — **lep·rous·ness** *n*

lep·to·ceph·a·lus \,lep-tə-'sef-ə-ləs\ *n, pl* **-li** \-,lī\ : the slender transparent first larva of an eel

les·bi·an \'lez-bē-ən\ *adj, often cap* : of or relating to homosexuality between females — **lesbian** *n, often cap* — **les·bi·an·ism** \-bē-ə-,niz-əm\ *n*

lese maj·es·ty *or* **lèse ma·jes·té** \'lēz-'maj-ə-stē\ *n* [MF *lese majesté*, fr. L *laesa majestas*, lit., injured majesty] **1 a** : a crime committed against a sovereign power **b** : an offense violating the dignity of a ruler as the representative of a sovereign power **2** : a detraction from or affront to dignity or importance

le·sion \'lē-zhən\ *n* [L *laes-, laedere* to injure] **1** : INJURY, HARM **2** : an abnormal structural change in an organ or part due to injury or disease

les·pe·de·za \,les-pə-'dē-zə\ *n* : any of a genus of herbaceous or shrubby leguminous plants including some widely used for forage, soil improvement, and esp. hay

¹**less** \'les\ *adj* [partly fr. OE *lǣs*, adv. & n.; partly fr. OE *lǣssa*, adj.] **1** : of a smaller number : FEWER ⟨*less* than three⟩ **2** : of lower rank, degree, or importance ⟨no *less* a person than the principal⟩ **3 a** : SMALLER, SLIGHTER **b** : more limited in quantity ⟨in *less* time⟩ **syn** see FEWER

²**less** *adv* : to a lesser extent or degree ⟨a *less* difficult lesson⟩

³**less** *prep* : diminished by ⟨full price *less* the discount⟩

⁴**less** *n, pl* **less** **1** : a smaller portion or quantity ⟨spent *less* than usual⟩ **2** : something of less importance ⟨could have killed him for *less*⟩

-less \ləs\ *adj suffix* [OE *-lēas*, fr. *lēas* devoid; akin to E *lose*] **1** : destitute of : not having ⟨wit*less*⟩ ⟨child*less*⟩ **2** : unable to be acted on or to act (in a specified way) ⟨daunt*less*⟩ ⟨fade*less*⟩

les·see \le-'sē\ *n* : a tenant under a lease

less·en \'les-°n\ *vb* **less·ened; less·en·ing** \'les-niŋ, -°n-iŋ\ : to make or become less : DECREASE

¹**less·er** \'les-ər\ *adj* **1** : LESS, SMALLER ⟨choose the *lesser* evil⟩ **2** : INFERIOR ⟨the *lesser* nobility⟩

²**lesser** *adv* : LESS ⟨*lesser*-known⟩

¹**les·son** \'les-°n\ *n* [OF *leçon*, fr. L *lection-, lectio* act of reading, fr. *legere* to read] **1** : a passage from sacred writings read in a service of worship **2 a** : a piece of instruction : TEACHING ⟨the story carries a *lesson*⟩; *esp* : a reading or exercise to be studied by a pupil ⟨master each *lesson* before going on to the next⟩ **b** : something learned by study or experience ⟨the *lessons* of history⟩ **3 a** : a period of instruction usu. lasting an hour or less in a single subject ⟨has her music *lesson* at four⟩ **b** : an instructive example; *also* : REPRIMAND

²**lesson** *vt* **les·soned; les·son·ing** \'les-niŋ, -°n-iŋ\ **1** : to give a lesson to **2** : REBUKE

les·sor \'les-,ór, le-'só(ə)r\ *n* : one that conveys property by a lease

lest \(,)lest\ *conj* [ME *les the, leste*, fr. OE *thȳ lǣs the*] **1** : for fear that ⟨bound him *lest* he should escape⟩ **2** : THAT — used after an expression denoting fear or apprehension ⟨worried *lest* he should be late⟩

¹**let** \'let\ *vt* **let·ted; letted** *or* **let; let·ting** [OE *lettan*] *archaic* : HINDER, PREVENT

²**let** *n* **1** : HINDRANCE, OBSTACLE ⟨go ahead without *let* or hindrance⟩ **2** : a served ball (as in tennis) that strikes the top of the net and lands in the service court and that must be served over; *also* : a point that must be played over because of interference with the play

³**let** *vb* **let; let·ting** [OE *lǣtan*] **1** : to cause to : MAKE ⟨*let* it be known⟩ **2 a** : RENT, LEASE ⟨*let* rooms⟩ **b** : to assign esp. after bids ⟨*let* a contract⟩ **3 a** : to give opportunity to ⟨live and *let* live⟩ **b** — used in the imperative to introduce a request or proposal ⟨*let* us pray⟩ **c** — used imperatively as an auxiliary to express a warning ⟨*let* him

---

j joke; **ŋ** sing; **ō** flow; **ȯ** flaw; **ȯi** coin; **th** thin; **th** this; **ü** loot; **u̇** foot; **y** yet; **yü** few; **yu̇** furious; **zh** vision

try〉 **4 :** to free from confinement **:** RELEASE 〈*let* the prisoner go〉 **5 :** to allow to enter, pass, or leave 〈*let* them through〉 **syn** see HIRE, LEAVE

-let \lət\ *n suffix* [MF *-elet*, fr. *-el*, dim. suffix (fr. L *-ellus*) + *-et*] **1 :** small one 〈book*let*〉 **2 :** article worn on 〈wrist*let*〉

let down \(')let-'daùn\ *vb* **1 :** to fail to support **:** DESERT 〈*let down* a friend in a crisis〉 **2 :** DISAPPOINT 〈the end of the story *lets* the reader *down*〉 **3 :** to slacken effort **:** RELAX 〈the team *let down* in the second half〉

let-down \'let-,daùn\ *n* **1 :** DISAPPOINTMENT **2 :** a slackening of effort **:** RELAXATION

¹le·thal \'lē-thəl\ *adj* [L *letalis, lethalis,* fr. *letum* death] **1 :** of, relating to, or causing death **2 :** capable of causing death **syn** see DEADLY — **le·thal·i·ty** \lē-'thal-ət-ē\ *n* — **le·thal·ly** \'lē-thə-lē\ *adv*

²lethal *n* **1 :** an abnormality of genetic origin causing the death of the organism possessing it **2 :** LETHAL GENE

lethal gene *n* **:** a gene capable of preventing development or causing the death of an organism or its germ cells — called also *lethal factor*

le·thar·gic \li-'thär-jik, le-\ *adj* **1 :** of, relating to, or characterized by lethargy **:** SLUGGISH **2 :** LISTLESS — **le·thar·gi·cal·ly** \-ji-k(ə-)lē\ *adv*

leth·ar·gy \'leth-ər-jē\ *n* [Gk *lēthargos* lethargic, fr. *lēthē* forgetfulness + *argos* lazy, fr. *a-* ²*a-* + *ergon* work] **1 :** abnormal drowsiness **2 :** the quality or state of being lazy or indifferent

syn LETHARGY, LANGUOR, STUPOR, TORPOR mean physical or mental inertness. LETHARGY implies drowsiness or apathy induced by disease, injury, or drugs; LANGUOR suggests inertia induced by enervating climate, illness, or amorous emotion; STUPOR implies a deadening of the mind and senses by shock, narcotics, or intoxicants; TORPOR implies a state of suspended animation or extreme sluggishness

Le·the \'lē-thē\ *n* [Gk *Lēthē,* fr. *lēthē* forgetfulness, fr. *lanthanesthai* to forget] **1 :** a river of Hades held in Greek mythology to cause forgetfulness of the past in those who drink its water **2 :** OBLIVION, FORGETFULNESS — **Le·the·an** \'lē-thē-ən\ *adj*

Le·to \'lē-,tō\ *n* **:** the mother of Apollo and Artemis by Zeus

let on *vb* **1 a :** ADMIT 〈didn't *let on* he was the author〉 **b :** REVEAL, DISCLOSE 〈don't *let on* that I told you〉 **2 :** PRETEND 〈not so surprised as he *let on*〉

let's \(,)lets, (,)les\ : let us

Lett \'let\ *n* **:** a member of a people closely related to the Lithuanians and mainly inhabiting Latvia

¹let·ter \'let-ər\ *n* [OF *lettre,* fr. L *littera* letter of the alphabet & *litterae,* pl., epistle, literature] **1 :** a symbol in writing or print that stands for a speech sound and constitutes a unit of an alphabet **2 :** a direct or personal written or printed message addressed to a person or organization **3** *pl* **a :** LITERATURE, BELLES LETTRES **b :** LEARNING 〈a man of *letters*〉 **4 :** the strict or outward meaning 〈the *letter* of the law〉 **5 a :** a single piece of type **b :** a style of type 〈roman *letter*〉

²letter *vt* **1 :** PRINT **2 :** to mark with letters **:** INSCRIBE — **let·ter·er** \-ər-ər\ *n*

letter carrier *n* **:** MAILMAN

let·tered \'let-ərd\ *adj* **1 a :** LEARNED, EDUCATED **b :** of, relating to, or characterized by learning **:** CULTURED 〈a *lettered* environment〉 **2 :** inscribed with or as if with letters 〈a *lettered* sign〉

let·ter·head \'let-ər-,hed\ *n* **:** stationery having a printed or engraved heading; *also* **:** the heading itself

let·ter·ing *n* **:** letters used in an inscription

let·ter–per·fect \,let-ər-'pər-fikt\ *adj* **:** correct to the smallest detail; *esp* **:** VERBATIM

let·ter·press \'let-ər-,pres\ *n* **1 :** printing done directly by impressing the paper on an inked raised surface **2 :** printed reading matter **:** TEXT

letters of marque \-'märk\ **:** written authority granted to a private person by a government to seize the subjects of a foreign state or their goods; *esp* **:** a license granted to a private person to fit out an armed ship to plunder the enemy

letters pat·ent \-'pat-ᵊnt, *Brit also* 'pāt-\ *n pl* **:** a writing (as from a sovereign) that confers on a designated person a grant in a form readily open for inspection by all

Lett·ish \'let-ish\ *adj* **:** of or relating to the Latvians or their language — **Lettish** *n*

let·tre de ca·chet \,le-trə-də-,ka-'shā\ *n, pl* **lettres de cachet** \-trə(z)-də-\ [F] **:** a letter bearing an official seal and usu. authorizing imprisonment without trial of a named person

let·tuce \'let-əs\ *n* [ME *letuse,* fr. OF *laitues,* pl. of *laitue* lettuce, fr. L *lactuca,* fr. *lact-, lac* milk] **:** a common garden vegetable related to the daisies that has succulent leaves used esp. in salads

let up \(')let-'əp\ *vi* **1 :** to slow down **:** DIMINISH **2 :** CEASE, STOP

let·up \'let-,əp\ *n* **:** a lessening of effort **:** CESSATION

leuc- *or* **leuco-** *also* **leuk-** *or* **leuko-** *comb form* [Gk *leukos;* akin to E ¹*light*] **1 :** white **:** colorless **:** weakly colored 〈*leuco*cyte〉 〈*leuko*rrhea〉 **2 :** leucocyte 〈*leuk*emia〉 **3 :** white matter of the brain 〈*leuco*tomy〉

leu·cine \'lü-,sēn\ *n* **:** an essential amino acid obtained by the hydrolysis of most dietary proteins

leu·co·cyte *or* **leu·ko·cyte** \'lü-kə-,sīt\ *n* **:** a white or colorless nucleated blood cell — **leu·co·cyt·ic** \,lü-kə-'sit-ik\ *adj*

leu·co·plast \'lü-kə-,plast\ *n* **:** a colorless plastid of a plant cell usu. concerned with starch formation and storage

leu·co·sin \'lü-kə-sən\ *n* **:** an insoluble carbohydrate reserve of some algae

leu·ke·mia \lü-'kē-mē-ə\ *n* **:** a cancerous disease of warm⸗ blooded animals (as man) in which leucocytes increase abnormally in the tissues and often in the blood — **leu·ke·mic** \-mik\ *adj* — **leu·ke·moid** \-,mòid\ *adj*

leu·ko·cy·to·sis \,lü-kə-,sī-'tō-səs\ *n, pl* **-to·ses** \-'tō-,sēz\ **:** an increase in the number of leucocytes in the circulating blood — **leu·ko·cy·tot·ic** \-'tät-ik\ *adj*

leu·ko·pe·nia \,lü-kə-'pē-nē-ə\ *n* [Gk *penia* poverty, lack] **:** a condition in which the number of leucocytes circulating in the blood is abnormally low — **leu·ko·pe·nic** \-nik\ *adj*

leu·ko·sis \lü-'kō-səs\ *n* **:** LEUKEMIA — **leu·kot·ic** \-'kät-ik\ *adj*

lev- *or* **levo-** *comb form* [L *laevus* left] **:** turning light to the left 〈*levo*lose〉

le·va·tor \li-'vāt-ər\ *n, pl* **lev·a·to·res** \,lev-ə-'tōr-(,)ēz\ *or* **le·va·tors** \li-'vāt-ərz\ [NL, fr. L *levare* to raise] **:** a muscle that serves to raise a body part — compare DEPRESSOR

¹lev·ee \'lev-ē; lə-'vē, -'vā\ *n* [F *lever,* lit., act of arising, fr. *se lever* to raise oneself, rise] **1 :** a reception held by a person of distinction orig. on rising from bed **2 :** a reception usu. in honor of a particular person

²levee \'lev-ē\ *n* [F *levée,* fr. *lever* to raise] **1 :** an embankment or dike to prevent flooding **2 :** a river landing place **:** PIER

¹lev·el \'lev-əl\ *n* [MF *livel,* fr. (assumed) VL *libellum,* dim. of L *libra* pound, balance] **1 :** a device for establishing a horizontal line or plane 〈a carpenter's *level*〉 〈a surveyor's *level*〉 **2 :** horizontal condition; *esp* **:** a condition of liquids marked by a horizontal surface of even altitude 〈water seeks its own *level*〉 **3 :** a horizontal position, line, or surface taken as an index of altitude 〈placed at eye *level*〉; *also* **:** a flat area of ground 〈easier to walk on the *level*〉 **4 :** height, position, rank, or size in or as if in a scale of values 〈the *level* of water in a gauge〉 〈a high blood-sugar *level*〉 〈students at the same *level* of learning〉 — **on the level :** bona fide **:** HONEST

²level *vb* **lev·eled** *or* **lev·elled; lev·el·ing** *or* **lev·el·ling** \'lev-(ə-)liŋ\ **1 :** to make (a line or surface) horizontal **:** make flat or level **2 :** AIM, DIRECT **3 :** to bring to a common level or plane **:** EQUALIZE **4 :** to lay level with the ground **:** RAZE **5 :** to attain or come to a level — **lev·el·er** *or* **lev·el·ler** \-(ə-)lər\ *n*

³level *adj* **1 :** having a flat even surface 〈a *level* lawn〉 **2 :** being on a line with the floor or even ground **:** HORIZONTAL 〈in a *level* position〉 **3 a :** of the same height or rank **:** being on a line **:** EVEN 〈stood in water *level* with his shoulders〉 **b :** UNIFORM **4 :** steady and cool in judgment 〈a *level* head〉 — **lev·el·ly** \'lev-(l)-lē\ *adv* — **lev·el·ness** \-əl-nəs\ *n* — **level best :** very best

level crossing *n, Brit* **:** GRADE CROSSING

lev·el·head·ed \,lev-əl-'hed-əd\ *adj* **:** having sound judgment **:** SENSIBLE — **lev·el·head·ed·ness** *n*

---

level off *vb* : to attain or come to a level

¹**lev·er** \'lev-ər, 'lē-vər\ *n* [OF *levier*, fr. *lever* to raise, fr. L *levare*, fr. *levis* light] **1 a** : a bar used for prying or dislodging something **b** : an instrument or agency used to achieve one's purpose : TOOL ⟨used food distribution as a *lever* to gain votes⟩ **2 a** : a rigid bar used to exert a pressure or sustain a weight at one point of its length by the application of a force at a second and turning at a third on a fulcrum **b** : a projecting piece by which a mechanism is operated or adjusted

²**lever** *vt* **lev·ered; lev·er·ing** \'lev-(ə-)riŋ, 'lēv-\ : to pry, raise, or move with or as if with a lever

levers; *F* fulcrum, *P* power, *W* weight

lev·er·age \'lev-(ə-)rij, 'lēv-\ *n* **1** : the action of a lever or the mechanical advantage gained by it **2** : EFFECTIVENESS, POWER ⟨the strike threat gave the union bargaining *leverage*⟩

lev·er·et \'lev-(ə-)rət\ *n* [ME, fr. MF *levre* hare, fr. L *lepor-, lepus*] : a hare in its first year

le·vi·a·than \li-'vī-ə-thən\ *n* [Heb *liwyāthān*] **1 a** *often cap* : a sea monster often symbolizing evil in the Old Testament and Christian literature **b** : a large sea animal **2** : something very large, powerful, or formidable esp. of its kind — **leviathan** *adj*

lev·in \'lev-ən\ *n, archaic* : LIGHTNING

Le·vi's \'lē-,vīz\ *trademark* — used for close-fitting heavy blue denim pants reinforced at strain points with copper rivets

lev·i·tate \'lev-ə-,tāt\ *vb* : to rise or cause to rise in the air in seeming defiance of gravitation — **lev·i·ta·tion** \,lev-ə-'tā-shən\ *n*

Le·vite \'lē-,vīt\ *n* **1** : a member of the Hebrew tribe of Levi, a son of Jacob **2** : a descendant of Levi assigned to assist the priests in the care of the temple — **Le·vit·i·cal** \li-'vit-i-kəl\ *adj*

Le·vit·i·cus \li-'vit-i-kəs\ *n* — see BIBLE table

lev·i·ty \'lev-ət-ē\ *n, pl* **-ties** [L *levitas*, lit., lightness, fr. *levis* light; akin to E ⁴*light*] : excessive or unseemly lack of earnestness in conduct or character : FRIVOLITY

lev·u·lose \'lev-yə-,lōs\ *n* [irreg. fr. *lev-* + *-ose*] : FRUCTOSE

¹**levy** \'lev-ē\ *n, pl* **lev·ies** [MF *levee*, lit., act of raising, fr. *lever* to raise, fr. L *levare*] **1 a** : the imposition or collection of an assessment **b** : an amount levied **2 a** : the enlistment or conscription of men for military service **b** : troops raised by levy

²**levy** *vb* **lev·ied; lev·y·ing** **1 a** : to impose or collect by legal authority ⟨*levy* a tax⟩ ⟨*levy* a fine⟩ **b** : to require by authority **2** : to enlist or conscript for military service **3** : to carry on (war) : WAGE **4** : to seize property in satisfaction of a legal claim — **lev·i·er** *n*

lewd \'lüd\ *adj* [ME *lewed* vulgar, fr. OE *lǣwede* laical, ignorant] **1** : sexually unchaste : LASCIVIOUS **2** : OBSCENE, SALACIOUS — **lewd·ly** *adv* — **lewd·ness** *n*

lex·i·cog·ra·pher \,lek-sə-'käg-rə-fər\ *n* : an author or compiler of a dictionary

lex·i·cog·ra·phy \-fē\ *n* **1** : the editing or making of a dictionary **2** : the principles and practices of dictionary making — **lex·i·co·graph·ic** \-kō-'graf-ik\ *or* **lex·i·co·graph·i·cal** \-'graf-i-kəl\ *adj* — **lex·i·co·graph·i·cal·ly** \-i-k(ə-)lē\ *adv*

lex·i·con \'lek-sə-,kän, -si-kən\ *n, pl* **lex·i·ca** \-si-kə\ *or* **lexicons** [LGk *lexikon*, fr. neut. of *lexikos* of words, fr. Gk *lexis* speech, word, fr. *legein* to say] : DICTIONARY

ley *var of* LEA

Ley·den jar \,līd-ᵊn-\ *n* [*Leiden, Leyden*, Netherlands] : an electrical condenser consisting of a glass jar coated inside and outside with metal foil and having the inner coating connected to a conducting rod passed through the insulating stopper

li·a·bil·i·ty \,lī-ə-'bil-ət-ē\ *n, pl* **-ties** **1** : the state of being liable ⟨*liability* for his debts⟩ ⟨*liability* to disease⟩ **2** *pl* : that for which a person is liable : DEBTS **3** : something that is a drawback or disadvantage

li·a·ble \'lī-ə-bəl\ *adj* [OF *lier* to bind, fr. L *ligare*]

1 : bound by law : OBLIGATED, RESPONSIBLE ⟨*liable* for damage done to a neighbor's property⟩ ⟨men *liable* for military service⟩ **2** : exposed to or likely to experience something undesirable : LIKELY ⟨*liable* to slip⟩ ⟨*liable* to be hurt⟩ **3** : SUSCEPTIBLE ⟨*liable* to disease⟩ **syn** see APT

li·aise \lē-'āz\ *vi* **1** : to establish liaison **2** : to act as a liaison officer

li·ai·son \'lē-ə-,zän, lē-'ā-\ *n* [F, fr. *lier* to bind, fr. L *ligare*] **1 a** : a connecting link; *esp* : a linking or co-ordinating of activities **b** : AFFAIR 3a **2** : the pronunciation of an otherwise absent consonant sound at the end of the first of two consecutive words when the second begins with a vowel sound and follows without pause **3** : intercommunication esp. between parts of an armed force

li·a·na \lē-'än-ə, -'an-ə\ *or* **li·ane** \-'än, -'an\ *n* [F *liane*] : a climbing plant that roots in the ground

li·ar \'lī-(ə)r\ *n* : one that tells lies

li·ba·tion \lī-'bā-shən\ *n* [L *libare* to pour a libation] **1** : the act of pouring a liquid (as wine) esp. in honor of a god; *also* : the liquid poured out **2** : DRINK — **li·ba·tion·ary** \-shə-,ner-ē\ *adj*

¹**li·bel** \'lī-bəl\ *n* [MF, written declaration, fr. L *libellus*, fr. dim. of *liber* book] **1** : the action or the crime of injuring a person's reputation by means of something printed or written or by some visible representation (as a picture) — compare SLANDER **2** : a spoken or written statement or a representation that gives an unjustly unfavorable impression of a person or thing — **li·bel·ous** *or* **li·bel·lous** \-bə-ləs\ *adj*

²**libel** *vb* **li·beled** *or* **li·belled; li·bel·ing** *or* **li·bel·ling** **1** : to make libelous statements **2** : to make or publish a libel against — **li·bel·er** *or* **li·bel·ler** \-bə-lər\ *n*

¹**lib·er·al** \'lib-(ə-)rəl\ *adj* [L *liberalis* suitable for a freeman, generous, fr. *liber* free] **1** : of, relating to, or based on the liberal arts ⟨*liberal* education⟩ **2 a** : marked by generosity and openhandedness ⟨*liberal* giver⟩ **b** : AMPLE, BOUNTIFUL **3** : not literal : LOOSE ⟨a *liberal* translation⟩ **4** : BROAD-MINDED, TOLERANT; *esp* : not bound by authoritarianism, orthodoxy, or traditional forms **5 a** : of, favoring, or based on the principles of liberalism : not conservative **b** *cap* : of or constituting a political party (as in the United Kingdom) advocating or associated with the principles of political liberalism — **lib·er·al·ly** \-rə-lē\ *adv*

syn RADICAL: LIBERAL suggests an independence of mind, a freedom from conventionality, tradition, or dogma, a practical tolerant recognition of changing conditions and the need to adapt to them, and readiness to experiment; RADICAL usu. suggests extremeness in breaking with established order and in a political desire to uproot and destroy

²**liberal** *n* : one who is liberal: as **a** : one who is open-minded or not strict in the observance of orthodox or traditional forms **b** *cap* : a member or supporter of a Liberal party **c** : an advocate of liberalism esp. in individual rights

liberal arts *n pl* : the studies (as language, philosophy, mathematics, history, literature, or abstract science) in a college or university intended to provide chiefly general knowledge and to develop the general intellectual capacities

lib·er·al·ism \'lib(-ə)-rə-,liz-əm\ *n* **1** : the quality or state of being liberal **2 a** *often cap* : a movement in modern Protestantism emphasizing intellectual liberty and the spiritual and ethical content of Christianity **b** : a theory in economics emphasizing individual freedom from restraint and usu. based on free competition, the self-regulating market, and the gold standard **c** : a political philosophy based on belief in progress, the essential goodness of man, and the autonomy of the individual and standing for the protection of political and civil liberties **d** *cap* : the principles or policies of a Liberal party — **lib·er·al·ist** \-rə-ləst\ *n or adj* — **lib·er·al·is·tic** \,lib(-ə)-rə-'lis-tik\ *adj*

lib·er·al·i·ty \,lib-ə-'ral-ət-ē\ *n, pl* **-ties** **1** : the quality or state of being liberal: **a** : GENEROSITY **b** : BROAD-MINDEDNESS **2** : a liberal gift **3** : AMPLENESS, BROADNESS

lib·er·al·ize \'lib-(ə)-rə-,līz\ *vb* : to make or become liberal — **lib·er·al·i·za·tion** \,lib(-ə)rə-lə-'zā-shən\ *n* — **lib·er·al·iz·er** \'lib-(ə)-rə-,lī-zər\ *n*

lib·er·ate \'lib-ə-ˌrāt\ vt [L liberare, fr. liber free] **1** : to free from bondage or restraint : set at liberty ⟨liberate a prisoner⟩ ⟨liberate the mind from worry⟩ **2** : to free (as a gas) from combination **syn** see FREE — **lib·er·a·tion** \ˌlib-ə-'rā-shən\ n — **lib·er·a·tor** \'lib·er·a·tor \'lib-ə-ˌrāt-ər\ n

lib·er·tar·i·an \ˌlib-ər-'ter-ē-ən\ n **1** : an advocate of the doctrine of free will **2** : one who upholds the principles of liberty esp. of thought and action — **libertarian** adj — **lib·er·tar·i·an·ism** \-ē-ə-ˌniz-əm\ n

lib·er·tine \'lib-ər-ˌtēn\ n [L libertus, libertinus freedman, fr. liber free] : a person who leads a life of unrestrained dissoluteness — **libertine** adj — **lib·er·tin·ism** \-ˌtē-ˌniz-əm\ n

lib·er·ty \'lib-ərt-ē\ n, pl **-ties** [L libertas, fr. liber free] **1** : the condition of those who are free and independent : freedom from slavery, imprisonment, or control by another **2** : power to do what one pleases : freedom from restraint ⟨give a child some liberty to manage his own affairs⟩ **3** : permission for a sailor to go ashore off duty for a certain number of hours **4** : excessive freedom of action : the act of a person who is too free or bold or familiar ⟨took liberties with his health⟩ ⟨take liberties with a stranger⟩ **syn** see FREEDOM — **at liberty 1** : not confined **2** : at leisure : not busy **3** : having the right : FREE ⟨at liberty to go or stay⟩

liberty cap n : a close-fitting conical cap used as a symbol of liberty by the French revolutionists and in the U.S. esp. before 1800

li·bid·i·nous \lə-'bid-°n-əs\ adj [L libidin-, libido desire, lust, fr. libēre to please; akin to E love] **1** : having or marked by lustful desires : LASCIVIOUS **2** : LIBIDINAL — **li·bid·i·nous·ly** adv — **li·bid·i·nous·ness** n

li·bi·do \lə-'bēd-ō, -'bīd-\ n, pl **-dos** [NL libidin-, libido, fr. L, desire, lust] **1** : emotion or psychic energy derived from primitive biological urges **2** : sexual drive — **li·bid·i·nal** \-'bid-°n-əl\ adj — **li·bid·i·nal·ly** \-°n-ə-lē\ adv

Li·bra \'lī-brə, 'lē-\ n [L, lit., scales, pound] **1** : a southern zodiacal constellation between Virgo and Scorpius represented by a pair of scales **2** : the 7th sign of the zodiac — see ZODIAC table

li·brar·i·an \lī-'brer-ē-ən\ n : a specialist in the care or management of a library — **li·brar·i·an·ship** \-ˌship\ n

li·brary \'lī-ˌbrer-ē\ n, pl **-brar·ies** [ML librarium, fr. L libr-, liber book] **1** : a place in which books, manuscripts, musical scores, or other literary and artistic materials are kept for use but not for sale **2** : a collection of literary or artistic materials (as books or prints)

library paste n : a thick white adhesive made from starch

li·bret·tist \lə-'bret-əst\ n : the writer of a libretto

li·bret·to \lə-'bret-ō\ n, pl **-tos** or **-ti** \-(ˌ)ē\ [It, dim. of libro book, fr. L libr-, liber] : the text of a work (as an opera) for the musical theater; also : a book containing such a text

lice pl of LOUSE

¹li·cense or **li·cence** \'līs-°n(t)s\ n [MF licence, fr. L licentia, fr. licent-, licens, prp. of licēre to be permitted] **1 a** : permission to act **b** : freedom of action **2 a** : permission granted by competent authority to engage in a business, occupation, or activity otherwise unlawful **b** : a document, plate, or tag evidencing a license granted **3 a** : freedom that is used with irresponsibility **b** : LICENTIOUSNESS **4** : deviation from fact, form, or rule by an artist or writer for the sake of the effect gained **syn** see FREEDOM

²license also **licence** vt **1** : to issue a license to **2** : to permit or authorize esp. by formal license — **li·cens·a·ble** \-ə-bəl\ adj

li·cens·ee \ˌlīs-°n-'sē\ n : a licensed person

li·cen·ti·ate \lī-'sen-chē-ət\ n [ML licentiatus, fr. pp. of licentiare to license, fr. L licentia license] : one licensed (as by a university) to practice a profession

li·cen·tious \lī-'sen-chəs\ adj : loose and lawless in behavior; esp : LEWD, LASCIVIOUS — **li·cen·tious·ly** adv — **li·cen·tious·ness** n

li·chen \'lī-kən\ n [Gk leichēn] : any of numerous complex thallophytic plants (group Lichenes) made up of an alga and a fungus growing in symbiotic association on a solid surface (as a rock) — **li·chen·ous** \-kə-nəs\ adj

lic·it \'lis-ət\ adj [L licitus, fr. pp. of licēre to be permitted] : LAWFUL — **lic·it·ly** adv

¹lick \'lik\ vb [OE liccian] **1 a** : to draw the tongue over **b** : to flicker over like a tongue **2** : to lap up **3 a** : to strike repeatedly : THRASH **b** : DEFEAT — **lick·ing** n — **lick into shape** : to put into proper form or condition

²lick n **1 a** : an act or instance of licking **b** : a small amount : BIT ⟨haven't done a lick of work today⟩ **c** : a hasty careless effort **2 a** : a sharp hit : BLOW ⟨got in some licks for his side⟩ **b** : OPPORTUNITY, TURN — usu. used in pl. **3** : a place (as a spring) having a deposit of salt that animals regularly lick

lick·e·ty-split \ˌlik-ət-ē-'split\ adv : at great speed

lick·spit·tle \'lik-ˌspit-°l\ n : a fawning subordinate : TOADY

lic·o·rice \'lik-(ə)-rish, -rəs\ n [OF, fr. LL liquiritia, modif. of Gk glykyrrhiza, fr. glykys sweet + rhiza root] **1** : a European leguminous plant **2** : the dried root of licorice; also : an extract from it used esp. in medicine, brewing, and confectionery

lic·tor \ˌlik-tər\ n [L] : a Roman officer bearing the fasces as the insignia of his office with duties including attendance upon the chief magistrates in public appearances

lid \'lid\ n [OE hlid] **1** : a movable cover ⟨the lid of a box⟩ ⟨the lid of a saucepan⟩ **2** : EYELID — **lid·ded** \'lid-əd\ adj — **lid·less** \'lid-ləs\ adj

li·do \'lēd-ō\ n, pl **lidos** : a fashionable beach resort

¹lie \'lī\ vi **lay** \'lā\; **lain** \'lān\; **ly·ing** \'lī-iŋ\ [OE licgan] **1 a** : to be in, stay at rest in, or assume a horizontal position : RECLINE ⟨lie motionless⟩ ⟨lie asleep⟩ ⟨told him to lie down⟩ **b** archaic : LODGE **c** archaic : to have sexual intercourse **d** : to stay in concealment or secret readiness **2** : to be in a helpless or defenseless state ⟨lay in prison for years⟩ **3** : to have direction : EXTEND ⟨route lay to the west⟩ **4 a** : to occupy a certain relative place or position ⟨hills lie behind us⟩ **b** : to have an effect through mere presence, weight, or relative position ⟨remorse lay heavily on him⟩ **5 a** : EXIST **b** : REMAIN

²lie n **1** : the position in which something lies **2** : the haunt of an animal : COVERT

³lie vi **lied**; **ly·ing** \'lī-iŋ\ [OE lēogan] **1** : to make an untrue statement with intent to deceive ⟨had lied about his age⟩ **2** : to create a false impression ⟨statistics can sometimes lie⟩

⁴lie n **1** : an assertion of something known or believed by the speaker to be untrue with intent to deceive ⟨his story was a tissue of lies⟩ **2** : something that misleads or deceives ⟨her pose of innocence was a lie⟩

lied \'lēt\ n, pl **lie·der** \'lēd-ər\ [G, song] : a German art song esp. of the 19th century

lie detector n : an apparatus for detecting physical evidences of the tension that accompanies lying

¹lief \'lēf, 'lēv\ adj [OE lēof; akin to E love] archaic : DEAR, BELOVED

²lief \'lēv, 'lēf\ adv : GLADLY, WILLINGLY ⟨I had as lief go as not⟩

¹liege \'lēj\ adj [OF, fr. LL laeticus of serfs, fr. laetus serf, of Gmc origin] **1** : having the right to receive service and allegiance ⟨liege lord⟩ **2** : owing or giving service to a lord

²liege n **1** : VASSAL **2** : a feudal superior

liege man n **1** : VASSAL **2** : a devoted follower

lie in vi : to be confined to give birth to a child

lien \'lēn, 'lē-ən\ n [MF, tie, band, fr. L ligamen, fr. ligare to bind] : a legal claim on the real or personal property of another person until he has met a certain obligation (as a debt or the fulfillment of a duty)

lie to \(')lī-'tü\ vi : to stay stationary with head to windward ⟨the ship had to lie to because of fog⟩

lieu \'lü\ n [MF, fr. L locus] archaic : PLACE, STEAD — **in lieu of** : in the place of : instead of

lieu·ten·an·cy \lü-'ten-ən-sē\ n, pl **-cies** : the office, rank, or commission of a lieutenant

lieu·ten·ant \lü-'ten-ənt\ n [MF, fr. lieu + tenant holding] **1 a** : an officer empowered to act for a higher official **b** : a representative of another in the performance of duty **2 a** (1) : FIRST LIEUTENANT (2) : SECOND LIEUTENANT **b** : a commissioned officer in the navy ranking above a lieutenant junior grade and below a lieutenant commander **c** : a fire or police department officer ranking below a captain

lieutenant colonel n : a commissioned officer (as in the army) ranking above a major and below a colonel

lieutenant commander *n* : a commissioned officer in the navy ranking above a lieutenant and below a commander

lieutenant general *n* : a commissioned officer (as in the army) ranking above a major general and below a general

lieutenant governor *n* **1** : an elected official serving as deputy to the governor of an American state **2** : the formal head of the government of a Canadian province appointed by the federal government to represent the crown

lieutenant junior grade *n* : a commissioned officer in the navy ranking above an ensign and below a lieutenant

¹**life** \'līf\ *n, pl* **lives** \'līvz\ [OE *līf*] **1 a** : the quality that distinguishes a vital and functional being from a dead body or inanimate matter **b** : a principle or force held to underlie the distinctive quality of animate beings **c** : a state of an organism characterized esp. by capacity for metabolism, growth, reaction to stimuli, and reproduction **2** : the sequence of physical and mental experiences that make up the existence of an individual **3** : BIOGRAPHY 1 **4** : spiritual existence transcending physical death **5 a** : the period during which an organism lives **b** : a specific phase or aspect of such a life ⟨adult *life*⟩⟨sex *life*⟩ **6** : a way or manner of living **7** : a vital or living being; *esp* : PERSON **8** : an animating and shaping force or principle **9** : ANIMATION, SPIRIT ⟨eyes full of *life*⟩ **10** : the period of utility, continuance, or existence of something ⟨*life* of a car⟩ ⟨*life* of an insurance policy⟩ **11** : LIVELINESS **12** : living beings (as of a kind or place) ⟨forest *life*⟩ **13 a** : human activities **b** : animate activity and movement ⟨stirrings of *life*⟩ **14** : one providing interest and vigor ⟨*life* of the party⟩

²**life** *adj* **1** : of or relating to animate being ⟨the *life* force⟩ **2** : LIFELONG ⟨*life* tenure⟩ **3** : using a living model ⟨a *life* class⟩

life belt *n* : a life preserver in the form of a buoyant belt

life·blood \'līf-ˌbləd\ *n* : something that gives strength and energy : the vital force or essence ⟨freedom of inquiry is the *lifeblood* of a university⟩

life·boat \-ˌbōt\ *n* : a strong buoyant boat esp. designed for use in saving lives at sea

life buoy *n* : a float consisting of a ring of buoyant material to support a person who has fallen into the water

life cycle *n* **1** : the series of stages through which an organism passes between successive recurrences of a specified primary stage **2** : LIFE HISTORY 1a

life expectancy *n* : an expected number of years of life based on statistical probability

life·guard \'līf-ˌgärd\ *n* : a usu. expert swimmer employed to safeguard bathers

life history *n* **1 a** : a history of the changes through which an organism passes in its development from the primary stage to its natural death **b** : LIFE CYCLE 1 **2** : the history of an individual's development in his social environment

life insurance *n* : insurance providing for payment of a stipulated sum to a designated beneficiary upon death of the insured

life·less \'līf-ləs\ *adj* : having no life: **a** : DEAD **b** : INANIMATE ⟨*lifeless* as marble⟩ **c** : lacking qualities expressive of life and vigor : DULL ⟨*lifeless* voice⟩ **d** : destitute of living beings ⟨a *lifeless* desert⟩ — **life·less·ly** *adv* — **life·less·ness** *n*

life·like \'līf-ˌlīk\ *adj* : accurately representing or imitating real life — **life·like·ness** *n*

life·line \'līf-ˌlīn\ *n* **1 a** : a line to which persons may cling to save or protect their lives; *esp* : one stretched along the deck or from the yards of a ship **b** : a line attached to a diver's helmet by which he is lowered and raised **c** : a rope line for lowering a person to safety **2** : a land, sea, or air route regarded as indispensable

life·long \'līf-ˌlȯŋ\ *adj* : continuing through life ⟨a *lifelong* friendship⟩

life preserver *n* **1** : a device designed to save a person from drowning by buoying up the body while in the water **2** : BLACKJACK

lif·er \'lī-fər\ *n* : a person sentenced to life imprisonment

life raft *n* : a raft usu. made of wood or an inflatable material and designed for use by people forced into the water

life preserver

life·sav·ing \'līf-ˌsā-viŋ\ *n* : the art or practice of saving or protecting lives esp. of drowning persons — **life·sav·er** \-vər\ *n* — **lifesaving** *adj*

life–size \'līf-'sīz\ *or* **life–sized** \-'sīzd\ *adj* : of natural size : of the size of the original ⟨a *life-size* statue⟩

life·time \-ˌtīm\ *n* : the duration of an individual's existence

life vest *n* : a life preserver designed as a vest of buoyant or inflatable material — called also *life jacket*

life·work \'līf-'wərk\ *n* : the entire or principal work of one's lifetime; *also* : a work extending over a lifetime

life zone *n* : a biogeographic zone

¹**lift** \'lift\ *vb* [ME *liften*, fr. ON *lypta*; akin to E *loft*] **1** : to raise from a lower to a higher position, rate, or amount : ELEVATE **2** : to put an end to (a blockade or siege) by withdrawing investing forces **3** : REVOKE, RESCIND **4 a** : STEAL **b** : PLAGIARIZE **5** : to shift (artillery fire) usu. to a greater range **6** : to move from one place to another : TRANSPORT **7** : RISE, ASCEND **8 a** : to disperse upward ⟨until the fog *lifts*⟩ **b** : to stop temporarily — **lift·er** *n*

syn LIFT, RAISE, HOIST, HEAVE mean to move from a lower to a higher place or position. LIFT implies effort exerted to bring up from and esp. clear of the ground and may apply to immaterial as well as material things; RAISE often suggests bringing something to a vertical or high position for which it is suited or intended; HOIST implies lifting something very heavy by mechanical means; HEAVE implies lifting with great strain or convulsive effort

²**lift** *n* **1** : the amount that may be lifted at one time : LOAD **2 a** : the action or an instance of lifting **b** : elevated carriage ⟨the proud *lift* of her head⟩ **3 a** : ASSISTANCE, HELP **b** : a ride along one's way **4** : one of the layers forming the heel of a shoe **5** : a rise or advance in position or condition **6** : the distance or extent to which something rises ⟨the *lift* of a canal lock⟩ **7 a** *chiefly Brit* : ELEVATOR 1 **b** : an apparatus for raising an automobile (as for repair) **c** : a conveyor for carrying people up or down a mountain slope **8 a** : an elevating influence **b** : an elevation of the spirits **9** : the part of the total aerodynamic force acting on an airplane or airfoil that is upward and opposes the pull of gravity

lift–off \'lift-ˌȯf\ *n* : a takeoff by an airplane or rocket

lig·a·ment \'lig-ə-mənt\ *n* [L *ligamentum* bond, band, fr. *ligare* to bind] **1** : a tough band of tissue that holds bones together or keeps an organ in place in the body **2** : a connecting or unifying bond : TIE — **lig·a·men·tous** \ˌlig-ə-'ment-əs\ *adj*

li·gate \'lī-ˌgāt, lī-'\ *vt* : to tie with a ligature — **li·ga·tion** \lī-'gā-shən\ *n*

lig·a·ture \'lig-ə-ˌchu̇r, -chər\ *n* **1** : a binding or tying of something **2** : something that binds or connects : BAND, BOND **3** : a thread or filament used in surgery esp. for tying blood vessels **4** : a printed or written character consisting of two or more letters or characters united ⟨the *ligature* æ⟩

¹**light** \'līt\ *n* [OE *lēoht*] **1 a** : something that makes vision possible **b** : the sensation aroused by stimulation of the visual receptors **c** : an electromagnetic radiation in the wavelength range including infrared, visible, ultraviolet, and X rays and traveling in a vacuum with a speed of about 186,281 miles per second; *esp* : the part of this range that is visible to the human eye **2 a** : DAYLIGHT **b** : DAWN **3** : a source of light: as **a** : a heavenly body **b** : CANDLE **c** : an electric light ⟨turned on all the *lights*⟩ **4 a** : spiritual illumination **b** : INNER LIGHT **c** : ENLIGHTENMENT **d** : TRUTH **5 a** : public knowledge ⟨facts brought to *light*⟩ **b** : a particular aspect or appearance presented to view ⟨saw the matter in a false *light*⟩ **6** : a particular illumination ⟨by the *light* of the moon⟩ **7 a** : WINDOW **b** : SKYLIGHT **8** *pl* : philosophy of life : STANDARDS ⟨she was a good girl according to her *lights*⟩ **9** : a noteworthy person : LUMINARY ⟨one of the leading *lights* in the organization⟩ **10** : a particular expression of the eye **11 a** : LIGHTHOUSE, BEACON **b** : TRAFFIC SIGNAL **12** : a flame for lighting something

²**light** *adj* **1** : having light : BRIGHT ⟨a *light* room⟩ **2** : medium in saturation and high in lightness ⟨*light* blue⟩

³**light** *vb* **light·ed** *or* **lit** \'lit\; **light·ing 1** : to make or become light : BRIGHTEN **2** : to burn or cause to burn : KINDLE, IGNITE **3 a** : to conduct with a light : GUIDE

⟨*light* him to his room⟩ **b :** ILLUMINATE ⟨rockets *light* up the sky⟩
⁴light *adj* [OE *lēoht*] **1 a :** having little weight **:** not heavy **b :** designed to carry a comparatively small load ⟨*light* truck⟩ **c :** having relatively little weight in proportion to bulk ⟨aluminum is a *light* metal⟩ **d :** containing less than the legal, standard, or usual weight ⟨*light* coin⟩ **2 a :** of little importance or seriousness **:** TRIVIAL **b :** not abundant **:** SCANTY ⟨*light* rain⟩ ⟨*light* breakfast⟩ **3 a :** easily disturbed ⟨*light* sleeper⟩ **b :** exerting little force or pressure **:** GENTLE **c :** resulting from a very slight pressure **:** FAINT **4 :** requiring little effort ⟨*light* exercise⟩ **5 :** capable of moving swiftly or nimbly **6 a :** FRIVOLOUS ⟨*light* conduct⟩ **b :** sexually promiscuous **7 :** free from care **:** CHEERFUL **8 :** intended chiefly to entertain ⟨*light* reading⟩ **9 :** having a comparatively low alcoholic content ⟨*light* wines⟩ **10 :** well leavened ⟨*light* crust⟩ **11 :** lightly armed or equipped ⟨*light* cavalry⟩ **12 :** being coarse and sandy **:** easily reduced to dust ⟨*light* soil⟩ **13 :** DIZZY, GIDDY **14 :** producing goods for direct consumption by the consumer ⟨*light* industry⟩ **15 :** UNACCENTED ⟨*light* syllable⟩ **16 :** having a clear soft quality ⟨a *light* voice⟩
⁵light *adv* **1 :** LIGHTLY **2 :** with little baggage ⟨travels *light*⟩
⁶light *vi* **light·ed** *or* **lit** \'lit\; **light·ing 1 :** SETTLE, ALIGHT ⟨birds *lit* on the lawn⟩ **2 a :** to strike or fall unexpectedly ⟨the blow *lighted* on his arm⟩ **b :** to arrive by chance ⟨*lit* upon a solution⟩
light adaptation *n* **:** the whole process by which the eye adapts to seeing in strong light — **light-adapt·ed** \'līt-ə-,dap-təd\ *adj*
light bread \'līt-,bred\ *n, chiefly South & Midland* **:** wheat bread in loaves made from white flour leavened with yeast
¹light·en \'līt-ᵊn\ *vb* **light·ened; light·en·ing** \'līt-niŋ, -ᵊn-iŋ\ **1 :** to make or grow light or clear **:** BRIGHTEN **2 :** to make or become lighter **3 :** to give out flashes of lightning — **light·en·er** \'līt-nər, -ᵊn-ər\ *n*
²lighten *vb* **light·ened; light·en·ing** \'līt-niŋ, -ᵊn-iŋ\ **1 :** to relieve of a burden in whole or in part ⟨*lighten* the plane⟩ ⟨*lighten* his duties⟩ **2 :** CHEER, GLADDEN **3 :** to become lighter — **light·en·er** \'līt-nər, -ᵊn-ər\ *n*
¹ligh·ter \'līt-ər\ *n* [(assumed) MD *lichter*, fr. MD *lichten* to unload; akin to E **⁴light**] **:** a large usu. flat-bottomed barge used esp. in unloading or loading ships
²lighter *vt* **:** to convey by a lighter
³light·er \'līt-ər\ *n* **:** one that lights; *esp* **:** a device for lighting ⟨cigarette *lighter*⟩
ligh·ter·age \'līt-ə-rij\ *n* **1 :** a price paid for lightering **2 :** the process of lightering
lighter–than–air *adj* **:** of less weight than the air displaced — used of aircraft
light·face \'līt-,fās\ *n* **:** a type having light thin lines (as in this) — **light–faced** \-'fāst\ *adj*
light·fast \-'fast\ *adj* **:** resistant to light and esp. to sunlight; *esp* **:** colorfast to light — **light·fast·ness** \-,fas(t)-nəs\ *n*
light–fin·gered \-'fiŋ-gərd\ *adj* **1 :** adroit in stealing esp. by picking pockets **2 :** having a light and dexterous touch **:** NIMBLE — **light–fin·gered·ness** *n*
light–foot·ed \-'fut-əd\ *adj* **:** having a light and springy step or movement
light–hand·ed \-'han-dəd\ *adj* **:** having a light or delicate touch — **light–hand·ed·ness** *n*
light–head·ed \-'hed-əd\ *adj* **1 :** mentally disoriented **:** DIZZY **2 :** lacking in maturity or seriousness **:** FRIVOLOUS — **light–head·ed·ly** *adv* — **light–head·ed·ness** *n*
light–heart·ed \-'härt-əd\ *adj* **:** free from care or anxiety **:** GAY — **light·heart·ed·ly** *adv* — **light·heart·ed·ness** *n*
light heavyweight *n* **:** a boxer weighing more than 160 but not over 175 pounds
light·house \'līt-,haùs\ *n* **:** a structure (as a tower) with a powerful light for guiding navigators at night
light·ing \'līt-iŋ\ *n* **1 a :** ILLUMINATION **b :** IGNITION **2 :** an artificial supply of light or the apparatus providing it
light·ly \'līt-lē\ *adv* **1 :** with little weight or force **:** GENTLY **2 :** in a small degree or

lighthouse

amount ⟨sprinkle *lightly*⟩ **3 :** with little difficulty **:** EASILY ⟨let him off *lightly* with a warning⟩ **4 :** NIMBLY, SWIFTLY **5 :** UNCONCERNEDLY ⟨took the rebuff *lightly*⟩ **6 :** GAILY, FRIVOLOUSLY
light meter *n* **1 :** a small portable device for measuring illumination **2 :** a device for indicating correct photographic exposure under varying conditions of illumination
light–mind·ed \'līt-'mīn-dəd\ *adj* **:** lacking in seriousness **:** FRIVOLOUS — **light–mind·ed·ly** *adv*
¹light·ness \'līt-nəs\ *n* **1 :** the quality or state of being light or lighted **:** ILLUMINATION **2 :** the degree to which the achromatic element of a color is nearer white than black ⟨pink is high in *lightness*⟩
²lightness *n* **1 :** the quality or state of being light in weight **2 :** LEVITY **3 a :** NIMBLENESS **b :** an ease and gaiety of style or manner **4 :** DELICACY ⟨*lightness* of touch⟩
¹light·ning \'līt-niŋ\ *n* [ME, fr. gerund of *lightenen* to lighten] **:** the flashing of light produced by a discharge of atmospheric electricity from one cloud to another or between a cloud and the earth; *also* **:** the discharge itself
²lightning *adj* **:** moving or accomplished with the speed of lightning ⟨a *lightning* attack⟩
lightning arrester *n* **:** a device for protecting electrical apparatus and radio and television sets from injury from lightning by carrying the discharges to the ground
lightning bug *n* **:** FIREFLY
lightning rod *n* **:** a metal rod set up on a building or a ship and connected with the earth or water below to decrease the chances of damage from lightning
light opera *n* **:** OPERETTA
light out *vi* **:** to leave in a hurry ⟨*lit out* for home when it began to rain⟩
light·plane \'līt-'plān\ *n* **:** a small and comparatively lightweight airplane; *esp* **:** a privately owned passenger airplane
light·proof \'līt-'prüf\ *adj* **:** impenetrable by light
lights \'līts\ *n pl* [ME *lightes*, fr. **⁴light**] **:** the lungs esp. of a slaughtered animal
light·ship \'līt-,ship\ *n* **:** a ship equipped with a brilliant light and moored at a place dangerous to navigation
light·some \'līt-səm\ *adj* **1 :** AIRY, NIMBLE **2 :** free from care **:** CHEERFUL **3 :** FRIVOLOUS — **light·some·ly** *adv* — **light·some·ness** *n*
light–struck \'līt-,strək\ *adj* **:** fogged by accidental exposure to light — used of a photographic material
light–tight \'līt-,tīt\ *adj* **:** LIGHTPROOF
¹light·weight \'līt-,wāt\ *n* **1 :** one of less than average weight; *esp* **:** a boxer weighing more than 126 but not over 135 pounds **2 :** an ineffectual or poorly qualified person
²lightweight *adj* **1 :** of, relating to, or characteristic of a lightweight **2 :** having less than average weight **3 :** INCONSEQUENTIAL
light–year \'līt-,yi(ə)r\ *n* **:** a unit of length in astronomy equal to the distance that light travels in one year or 5,878,000,000,000 miles
lign- *or* **ligni-** *or* **ligno-** *comb form* [L *lignum*] **:** wood ⟨*lignin*⟩ ⟨*lignocellulose*⟩
lig·ne·ous \'lig-nē-əs\ *adj* [L *ligneus*, fr. *lignum* firewood, wood, fr. *legere* to gather] **:** of or resembling wood **:** WOODY
lig·ni·fy \'lig-nə-,fī\ *vb* **-fied; -fy·ing :** to convert into or become wood or woody tissue — **lig·ni·fi·ca·tion** \,lig-nə-fə-'kā-shən\ *n*
lig·nin \'lig-nən\ *n* **:** a substance related to cellulose that occurs in the woody cell walls of plants and in the cementing material between them
lig·nite \'lig-,nīt\ *n* **:** a usu. brownish black coal intermediate between peat and bituminous coal; *esp* **:** one in which the texture of the original wood is distinct
lig·no·cel·lu·lose \,lig-nō-'sel-yə-,lōs\ *n* **:** a material consisting of intimately associated lignin and cellulose and forming the essential part of woody cell walls — **lig·no·cel·lu·los·ic** \-,sel-yə-'lō-sik\ *adj*
lig·num vi·tae \,lig-nəm-'vīt-ē\ *n, pl* **lignum vitaes** [NL, lit., wood of life] **:** any of several tropical American trees or their very hard heavy wood
lig·u·la \'lig-yə-lə\ *n, pl* **-lae** \-,lē, -,lī\ *also* **-las** [NL] **:** the distal lobed part of the labium of an insect
lig·u·late \'lig-yə-lət\ *also* **lig·u·lat·ed** \-,lāt-əd\ *adj*

1 : shaped like a strap ⟨*ligulate* ray flowers⟩ **2** : having ligules

lig·ule \'lig-yül\ *n* [NL *ligula*, fr. L, small tongue, strap; akin to E *lick*] : an elongated flattened projection esp. on a plant: as **a** : an appendage of a leaf and esp. of the sheath of a blade of grass **b** : the limb of a ray flower

lik·a·ble *or* **like·a·ble** \'lī-kə-bəl\ *adj* : having qualities that bring about a favorable regard : PLEASANT, AGREEABLE — **lik·a·ble·ness** *n*

1like \'līk\ *vb* [OE *līcian* to be suitable, be pleasing; akin to E *like*] **1** : to feel attraction toward or take pleasure in : ENJOY ⟨*likes* baseball⟩ **2** : to feel toward : REGARD ⟨how would you *like* a change⟩ **3** : to wish to have : WANT ⟨would *like* a drink⟩ **4** : to feel inclined : CHOOSE ⟨allowed to do as he *liked*⟩

2like *n* : LIKING, PREFERENCE ⟨knows her husband's *likes* and dislikes⟩

3like *adj* [OE *gelīc*, fr. *līc* body] **1 a** : the same or nearly the same (as in appearance, character, or quantity) ⟨suits of *like* design⟩ **b** : resembling or characteristic of something — used after the word modified and in combination ⟨dog*like*⟩ ⟨bell-*like*⟩ **2 a** : LIKELY **b** : being about or as if about — used with an infinitive ⟨*like* to die⟩

4like *prep* **1 a** : similar to ⟨his house is *like* a barn⟩ **b** : typical of ⟨was *like* him to do that⟩ **2** : in the manner of : similarly to ⟨acts *like* a fool⟩ **3** : inclined to ⟨looks *like* rain⟩ **4** : such as ⟨a subject *like* physics⟩

5like *n* : one that is like another : COUNTERPART ⟨may never see his *like* again⟩

6like *adv* **1** : LIKELY, PROBABLY ⟨*like* enough, you will⟩ **2** : to some extent : SEEMINGLY ⟨came in nonchalantly *like*⟩

7like *conj* **1** : in the same way that : AS **2** : as if ⟨looked *like* he was scared⟩

like·li·hood \'lī-klē-,hùd\ *n* : PROBABILITY

1like·ly \'lī-klē\ *adj* **like·li·er; -est** **1** : being such as to make a certain happening or result probable ⟨that bomb is *likely* to explode any time⟩ **2** : seeming like the truth : BELIEVABLE ⟨a *likely* story⟩ **3** : PROMISING ⟨a *likely* place to fish⟩ **syn** see APT

2likely *adv* : in all probability : PROBABLY ⟨the dance was most *likely* her idea⟩

like-mind·ed \'līk-'mīn-dəd\ *adj* : of the same mind or habit of thought — **like-mind·ed·ly** *adv* — **like-mind·ed·ness** *n*

lik·en \'lī-kən\ *vt* **lik·ened; lik·en·ing** \'līk-(ə-)niŋ\ : to represent as like something : COMPARE

like·ness \'līk-nəs\ *n* **1** : the quality or state of being like : RESEMBLANCE **2** : APPEARANCE, SEMBLANCE ⟨in the *likeness* of a clown⟩ **3** : COPY, PORTRAIT

syn SIMILARITY, RESEMBLANCE: LIKENESS implies a closer correspondence than SIMILARITY, which often implies that things are only somewhat alike; RESEMBLANCE implies similarity chiefly in appearance or external qualities

like·wise \'līk-,wīz\ *adv* **1** : in like manner : SIMILARLY **2** : in addition : ALSO

lik·ing \'lī-kiŋ\ *n* : favorable regard : FONDNESS, TASTE

li·lac \'lī-lək, -,lak, -,läk\ *n* [obs. F, fr. Per *nīlak* bluish, fr. *nīl* blue, fr. Skt *nīla*] **1** : any of a genus of shrubs and trees of the olive family; *esp* : a European shrub widely grown for its showy panicles of fragrant pink, purple, or white flowers **2** : a variable color averaging a moderate purple

lil·i·a·ceous \,lil-ē-'ā-shəs\ *adj* : of or relating to lilies

lil·li·pu·tian \,lil-ə-'pyü-shən\ *adj* **1** *cap* : of, relating to, or characteristic of the island of Lilliput in Swift's *Gulliver's Travels* or its inhabitants who are six inches tall **2** *often cap* **a** : SMALL, MINIATURE **b** : PETTY — **Lilliputian** *n*

1lilt \'lilt\ *vb* [ME *lulten*] **1** : to sing or play in a lively cheerful manner **2** : to sing or speak rhythmically and with fluctuating pitch **3** : to move in a lively springy manner — **lilt·ing·ly** \'lil-tiŋ-lē\ *adv*

2lilt *n* **1** : a lively and usu. gay song or tune **2** : a rhythmical swing, flow, or cadence

1lily \'lil-ē\ *n, pl* **lil·ies** [L *lilium*] **1** : any of a genus of erect perennial leafy-stemmed bulbous herbs widely grown for their showy funnel-shaped flowers; *also* : any of various related monocotyledonous plants **2** : any of various plants with showy flowers

2lily *adj* : of, relating to, or resembling a lily

lily-liv·ered \,lil-ē-'liv-ərd\ *adj* : COWARDLY

lily of the valley : a low perennial herb of the lily family with usu. two large oblong leaves and a stalk of fragrant nodding bell-shaped flowers

lily pad *n* : a floating leaf of a water lily

1lily-white \,lil-ē-'hwīt\ *adj* **1** : white as a lily **2** : characterized by or favoring the exclusion of Negroes esp. from politics **3** : FAULTLESS, PURE

2lily-white *n* : a member of a lily-white political organization

li·ma bean \,lī-mə-\ *n* [*Lima*, Peru] : any of various bush or tall-growing beans widely grown for their flat edible usu. pale green or whitish seeds; *also* : this seed

lily of the valley

1limb \'lim\ *n* [OE *lim*] **1** : one of the projecting paired appendages (as wings) of an animal body used esp. for movement and grasping; *esp* : a leg or arm of a human being **2** : a large primary branch of a tree **3** : an active member or agent — **limbed** \'limd\ *adj*

2limb *vt* : to cut off the limbs of (a felled tree)

3limb *n* [L *limbus* border] **1** : the outer edge of the apparent disk of a celestial body ⟨the eastern *limb* of the sun⟩ **2** : the expanded portion of a bodily organ; *esp* : the spreading upper portion of a calyx or corolla that is not made up of separate petals

lim·bate \'lim-,bāt\ *adj* [L *limbus* border] : having a border of a different color ⟨a *limbate* leaf⟩

lim·beck \'lim-,bek\ *n* : ALEMBIC

1lim·ber \'lim-bər\ *adj* : bending easily : FLEXIBLE, SUPPLE ⟨a *limber* willow twig⟩ ⟨the *limber* body of an acrobat⟩ — **lim·ber·ly** *adv* — **lim·ber·ness** *n*

2limber *vb* **lim·bered; lim·ber·ing** \-b(ə-)riŋ\ : to become or cause to become limber ⟨*limbered* up by doing calisthenics⟩

limb·less \'lim-ləs\ *adj* : having no limbs

lim·bo \'lim-bō\ *n, pl* **limbos** [ML *in limbo* on the border] **1** *often cap* : an abode of souls (as of unbaptized infants) barred from heaven through no fault of their own **2 a** : a place or state of confinement or oblivion **b** : an intermediate or transitional place or state

Lim·burg·er \'lim-,bər-gər\ *n* [fr. *Limburg*, Belgium] : a semisoft surface-ripened cheese with a rind of pungent odor and a creamy-textured body

1lime \'līm\ *n* [OE *līm*] **1** : BIRDLIME **2 a** : a caustic highly infusible solid that consists of calcium oxide often together with magnesia, is obtained by calcining forms of calcium carbonate (as limestone or shells), and is used in mortar and plaster and in agriculture — called also *caustic lime* **b** : a dry white powder consisting essentially of calcium hydroxide that is made by treating lime with water — called also *slaked lime* **c** : CALCIUM ⟨carbonate of *lime*⟩

2lime *vt* : to treat or cover with lime

3lime *adj* : of, relating to, or containing lime or limestone

4lime *n* [alter. of earlier *line*, fr. OE *lind*] : a European linden tree

5lime *n* [F, fr. Ar *līm*] : a fruit like the lemon but smaller and with greenish yellow rind; *also* : the citrus tree that bears it

lime·ade \lī-'mād\ *n* : a drink made of lime juice, sugar, and water

lime·kiln \'līm-,kil(n)\ *n* : a kiln or furnace for reducing limestone or shells to lime by burning

lime·light \-,līt\ *n* **1** : a device formerly used for lighting of the stage producing light by means of a flame directed on a cylinder of lime; *also* : the light produced by this device **2** : the center of public attention

lim·er·ick \'lim-(ə-)rik\ *n* [*Limerick*, Ireland] : a light or humorous verse form that has 5 chiefly anapestic lines of which the 1st, 2d, and 5th are of 3 feet and the 3d and 4th of 2 feet and that has a rhyme scheme of *aabba*

lime·stone \'līm-,stōn\ *n* : a rock that is formed chiefly by accumulation of organic remains (as shells or coral), consists mainly of calcium carbonate, is extensively used in building, and yields lime when burned

lime·wa·ter \'līm-,wòt-ər, -,wät-\ *n* : an alkaline water solution of calcium hydroxide often used as an antacid

li·mic·o·line \lī-'mik-ə-,līn\ *adj* [L *limus* mud + *colere* to inhabit] **:** of or relating to the shorebirds; *also* **:** being a shorebird

¹lim·it \'lim-ət\ *n* [L *limit-, limes*] **1 a :** BOUNDARY **b** *pl* **:** BOUNDS **2 a :** something that bounds, restrains, or confines **b :** the utmost extent **3 :** LIMITATION **4 :** a prescribed maximum or minimum amount, quantity, or number **5 :** a fixed magnitude so related to a variable that the difference between them as the variable approaches the constant becomes and remains less than any assigned value

²limit *vt* **1 :** to set bounds or limits to **2 :** to curtail or reduce in quantity or extent — **lim·it·a·ble** \-ət-ə-bəl\ *adj* — **lim·it·er** *n*

lim·i·ta·tion \,lim-ə-'tā-shən\ *n* **1 :** an act or instance of limiting **2 :** the quality or state of being limited **3 :** something that limits **:** BOUNDARY, RESTRAINT — **lim·i·ta·tion·al** \-shnəl, -shən-ᵊl\ *adj*

lim·it·ed *adj* **1 a :** confined within limits **:** RESTRICTED **b :** having a limited number of passengers and offering superior and faster service and transportation **2 :** relating to or being a government in which constitutional limitations are placed upon the powers of one or more of its branches ⟨a *limited* monarchy⟩ — **lim·it·ed·ly** *adv* — **lim·it·ed·ness** *n*

limited war *n* **:** a war with an objective less than the total defeat of the enemy

lim·it·ing *adj* **1 :** functioning as a limit **:** RESTRICTIVE ⟨*limiting* value⟩ **2 :** serving to specify the application of the modified noun ⟨*this* in "this book" is a *limiting* word⟩

lim·it·less \'lim-ət-ləs\ *adj* **:** having no limits — **lim·it·less·ly** *adv* — **lim·it·less·ness** *n*

limn \'lim\ *vt* **limned**; **limn·ing** \'lim-(n)iŋ\ [ME *luminen, limnen* to illuminate, fr. L *illuminare*] **1 a :** DRAW **b :** PAINT **2 a :** to outline in clear sharp detail **:** DELINEATE **b :** DESCRIBE — **limn·er** \'lim-(n)ər\ *n*

lim·net·ic \lim-'net-ik\ *adj* [Gk *limnē* pool] **:** of, relating to, or inhabiting pelagic fresh water ⟨*limnetic* worms⟩

lim·nol·o·gy \lim-'näl-ə-jē\ *n* [Gk *limnē* pool] **:** the scientific study of fresh waters — **lim·no·log·i·cal** \,lim-nə-'läj-i-kəl\ *adj* — **lim·nol·o·gist** \lim-'näl-ə-jəst\ *n*

li·mo·nite \'lī-mə-,nīt\ *n* [G *limonit*, fr. Gk *leimōn* meadow] **:** an ore of iron consisting of a hydrous ferric oxide or a mixture of oxides — **li·mo·nit·ic** \,lī-mə-'nit-ik\ *adj*

lim·ou·sine \'lim-ə-,zēn, ,lim-ə-'\ *n* [F, lit., cloak, fr. *Limousin*, France] **:** any of various passenger vehicles; *esp* **:** a large luxurious often chauffeur-driven sedan

¹limp \'limp\ *vb* **1 :** to walk lamely **2 :** to proceed slowly or with difficulty ⟨the ship *limped* into port⟩ — **limp·er** *n*

²limp *n* **:** a limping movement or gait ⟨walked with a *limp*⟩

³limp *adj* **1 a :** having no defined shape **:** SLACK **b :** not stiff or rigid ⟨a *limp* bookbinding⟩ **2 a :** DROOPING, EXHAUSTED **b :** lacking in strength or firmness **:** SPIRITLESS — **limp·ly** *adv* — **limp·ness** *n*

syn LIMP, FLACCID, FLABBY mean lacking in firmness in texture or substance; LIMP implies a lack or loss of stiffness and a tendency to droop; FLACCID implies a loss of power to keep or return to shape ⟨*flaccid* muscles⟩ FLABBY implies hanging or sagging by its own weight as through loss of muscular tone ⟨*flabby* cheeks⟩

lim·pet \'lim-pət\ *n* [OE *lempedu*, fr. ML *lampreda*] **:** a marine gastropod mollusk with a low conical shell that browses over rocks or timbers and clings very tightly when disturbed

lim·pid \'lim-pəd\ *adj* [L *limpidus*, fr. *lympha* water] **1 :** TRANSPARENT ⟨a *limpid* pool⟩ **2 :** readily intelligible **:** CLEAR — **lim·pid·i·ty** \lim-'pid-ət-ē\ *n* — **lim·pid·ly** \'lim-pəd-lē\ *adv* — **lim·pid·ness** *n*

syn LIMPID, LUCID, PELLUCID mean clear and untroubled. LIMPID stresses freedom from murkiness or agitation and suggests the soft transparency of pure quiet water; LUCID implies being both clear and full of light; PELLUCID suggests unusual transparency or shining clearness as of crystal

limp·kin \'lim(p)-kən\ *n* **:** a large brown wading bird resembling a bittern but having longer bill, neck, and legs and white stripes on head and neck

lim·u·lus \'lim-yə-ləs\ *n*, *pl* **-li** \-,lī, -,lē\ [NL, fr. L *limus* sidelong] **:** KING CRAB 1

limy \'lī-mē\ *adj* **lim·i·er**; **-est** **:** containing lime or limestone

lin·age \'lī-nij\ *n* **1 :** the number of lines of printed or written matter **2 :** payment for literary matter at so much a line

linch·pin \'linch-,pin\ *n* [OE *lynis* linchpin] **:** a locking pin inserted crosswise (as through the end of an axle or shaft)

Lin·coln's Birthday \,liŋ-kənz-\ *n* **:** February 12 observed as a legal holiday in many of the states of the U.S.

lin·dane \'lin-,dān\ *n* [T. van der *Linden*, 20th cent. Dutch chemist] **:** an insecticide consisting of not less than 99 percent of an isomer of a chloride of benzene

lin·den \'lin-dən\ *n* [ME, of linden wood, fr. OE, fr. *lind* linden tree] **1 :** any of a genus of trees with large heart-shaped leaves and clustered yellowish flowers rich in nectar ⟨*esp* **:** BASSWOOD⟩ **2 :** the light fine-grained white wood of a linden; *esp* **:** BASSWOOD

¹line \'līn\ *vt* [ME *linen*, fr. *line* linen, fr. OE *līn*] **1 :** to cover the inner surface of ⟨*line* a box with paper⟩ **2 :** to put something in the inside of **:** SUPPLY **3 :** to serve as the lining of ⟨tapestries *lined* the walls⟩

²line *n* [partly fr. OF *ligne*, fr. L *linea*, fr. fem. of *lineus* of flax, fr. *linum* flax; partly fr. OE *līne*, fr. *līn* flax, linen] **1 :** THREAD, STRING, CORD, ROPE; *esp* **:** a comparatively strong slender cord ⟨a fishing *line*⟩ **2 :** a cord, wire, or tape used in measuring and leveling **3 a :** piping for conveying a fluid (as steam or oil) **b :** wire connecting one telegraph or telephone station with another or a whole system of such wires **c :** the principal circuits of an electric power system **4 a :** a horizontal row of written or printed characters **b :** a unit in the rhythmic structure of verse formed by the grouping of a number of the smallest units of the rhythm (as metrical feet) **c :** a short letter **:** NOTE ⟨drop me a *line*⟩ **d** *pl* **:** a certificate of marriage **e :** the words making up a part in a drama — usu. used in pl. ⟨she forgot her *lines*⟩ **5 a :** something (as a ridge or seam) that is distinct, elongated, and narrow **b :** a narrow crease (as on the face) **:** WRINKLE **c :** the course or direction of something in motion **:** ROUTE ⟨the *line* of flight of a bullet⟩ **d :** a boundary esp. of a plot of ground — usu. used in pl. **e :** the track and roadbed of a railway **6 :** a state of agreement ⟨bring ideas into *line*⟩ **7 a :** a course of conduct, action, or thought; *esp* **:** a publicly proclaimed policy or viewpoint ⟨a political *line*⟩ **b :** a field of activity or interest ⟨completely out of my *line*⟩ **c :** a glib often persuasive way of talking **8 a :** LIMIT, RESTRAINT ⟨overstep the *line* of good taste⟩ **b** (1) *archaic* **:** position in life **:** LOT (2) **:** FORTUNE, LUCK **9 :** any of various things arranged in or as if in a row or sequence: as **a :** FAMILY, LINEAGE ⟨descended from a noble *line*⟩ **b :** a strain produced and maintained by selective breeding ⟨a high-fat *line* of cattle⟩ **c** (1) **:** dispositions made to cover extended military positions and presenting a front to the enemy — usu. used in pl. (2) **:** a military formation in which the different elements are abreast of each other (3) **:** naval ships arranged in a regular order (4) **:** the combatant forces of an army distinguished from the staff corps and supply services (5) **:** the force of a regular navy (6) **:** officers of the navy eligible for command at sea (7) **:** officers of the army belonging to a combatant branch (8) **:** a set of objects (as goods for sale) of one general kind **d** (1) **:** a group of public conveyances plying regularly under one management over a route (2) **:** a system of transportation; *also* **:** the company owning or operating it **e :** a succession of musical notes esp. considered in melodic phrases **f :** an arrangement of manufacturing processes to permit sequentially various stages of production **g :** the football players who line up on or within one foot of the line of scrimmage **10 :** a narrow elongated mark (as one drawn by a pencil): as **a :** a circle of latitude or longitude on a map **b :** EQUATOR **c :** any of the horizontal parallel strokes on a music staff **d :** a division on a bridge score dividing the honors from the tricks **e :** LINE OF SCRIMMAGE **11 :** a geometric element that is generated by a moving point and that has length but no width or thickness; *esp* **:** a straight line **12 a :** a defining outline **:** CONTOUR ⟨a ship's *lines*⟩ **b :** a general plan ⟨a play along the same *lines* as a novel⟩ **13 :** an indication (as of intention) based on insight or investigation ⟨got a *line* on their

---

ə abut; ᵊ kitten; ər further; a back; ā bake; ä cot, cart; aù out; ch chin; e less; ē easy; g gift; i trip; ī life

plans⟩ **14 :** a complete game of 10 frames in bowling — called also *string* — **down the line :** all the way **:** FULLY — **in line for :** due or in a position to receive — **on the line 1 :** in full view and at hazard **2 :** on the border between two categories **3 :** IMMEDIATELY

³line *vb* **1 :** to mark or cover with a line **2 :** to depict by lines **:** DRAW **3 :** to place or form a line along ⟨pedestrians *line* the walks⟩ **4 a :** to form a line **:** form into lines **b :** ALIGN ⟨*line* up troops⟩ **c :** ORGANIZE ⟨*line* up votes⟩ **5 :** to hit a line drive

¹lin·e·age \'li-ē-ij\ *n* **1 :** lineal descent from a common progenitor **2 :** a group of persons tracing descent from a common ancestor regarded as its founder

²lineage \'li-ē-ij\ *var of* LINAGE

lin·e·al \'lin-ē-əl\ *adj* **1 :** LINEAR ⟨*lineal* measure⟩ **2 a :** consisting of or being in a direct line of ancestry or descent ⟨*lineal* descendants⟩ **b :** HEREDITARY **c :** of, relating to, or dealing with a lineage — **lin·e·al·ly** \-ē-ə-lē\ *adv*

lin·e·a·ment \'lin-ē-ə-mənt\ *n* **:** one of the outlines, features, or contours of a body or figure and esp. of the face

lin·e·ar \'lin-ē-ər\ *adj* **1 a :** relating to, consisting of, or resembling a line **:** STRAIGHT **b :** involving a single dimension **c :** characterized by an emphasis on line ⟨*linear* art⟩ **d** (1) **:** containing any number of variables all of which are of the first degree and represented graphically by a straight line ⟨*linear* equation⟩ ⟨*linear* function⟩ (2) **:** based on, involving, or expressed by linear functions or equations **2 :** long and uniformly narrow ⟨the *linear* leaf of the hyacinth⟩ — **lin·e·ar·i·ty** \,lin-ē-'ar-ət-ē\ *n* — **lin·e·ar·ly** \'lin-ē-ər-lē\ *adv*

linear accelerator *n* **:** a device in which charged particles are accelerated in a straight line by successive impulses from a series of electric fields

linear measure *n* **1 :** a measure of length **2 :** a system of measures of length

linear programming *n* **:** mathematical planning of industrial or military operations in terms of maximum or minimum values of linear functions in two or more variables subject to specific restrictions

lin·e·ation \,lin-ē-'ā-shən\ *n* **1 a :** the action of marking with lines **:** DELINEATION **b :** OUTLINE **2 :** an arrangement of lines

line·back·er \'līn-,bak-ər\ *n* **:** a defensive football player who lines up immediately behind the line of scrimmage and acts either as a lineman or as a pass defender

line·breed·ing \'līn-,brēd-iŋ\ *n* **:** the interbreeding of individuals within a particular line of descent usu. to perpetuate desirable characters — **line·breed** *vb*

line·cut \'līn-,kət\ *n* **:** a letterpress printing plate photoengraved from a line drawing — called also *line block*, *line engraving*

line drawing *n* **:** a drawing made in solid lines as copy for a linecut

line drive *n* **:** a batted baseball hit not far above the ground in a nearly straight line — called also *liner*

line engraving *n* **1 :** a metal plate for use in intaglio printing made by hand-engraving lines of different widths and closeness; *also* **:** a process involving such plates or a print made with them **2 :** LINECUT

line graph *n* **:** a graph in which the points representing specific values are connected by a broken line

line·man \'līn-mən\ *n* **1 :** one who sets up or repairs electric wire communication or power lines — called also *linesman* **2 :** a player in the line in football

lin·en \'lin-ən\ *n* [OE *līnen* of flax, fr. *līn* flax, fr. L *linum*] **1 a :** cloth made of flax and noted for its strength, coolness, and luster **b :** thread or yarn spun from flax **2 :** clothing or household articles made of linen cloth or a similar fabric **3 :** paper made from linen fibers or with a linen finish — **linen** *adj*

line of duty : all that is authorized, required, or normally associated with some field of responsibility

line of force : an imaginary line serving as a convenience in indicating the direction in space in which an electric or magnetic force acts

line of scrimmage : an imaginary line in football parallel to the goal lines and tangent to the nose of the ball laid on the ground preparatory to a scrimmage

line of sight 1 : a line from an observer's eye to a distant point toward which he is looking **2 :** the straight path between a radio transmitting antenna and receiving antenna when unobstructed by the horizon — **line-of-sight** *adj*

line out *vb* **1 :** to indicate with or as if with lines **:** OUTLINE ⟨*line out* a route⟩ **2 a :** to plant (young nursery stock) in rows for growing on **b :** to arrange in an extended line **3 :** to move rapidly ⟨*lined out* for home⟩

¹lin·er \'lī-nər\ *n* **1 :** one that makes, draws, or uses lines **2 :** something with which lines are made **3 a :** a ship belonging to a regular line of ships **b :** an airplane belonging to an airline **4 :** LINE DRIVE

²liner *n* **:** one that lines or is used to line or back something

line segment *n* **:** SEGMENT 2b

lines·man \'līnz-mən\ *n* **1 :** LINEMAN 1 **2 :** an official who assists a referee in an athletic game (as football)

line up \(')līn-'əp\ *vb* **1 :** to assume an orderly linear arrangement ⟨*line up* for inspection⟩ **2 :** to put into alignment

line-up \'līn-,əp\ *n* **1 :** a line of persons arranged esp. for identification by police **2 a :** a list of players taking part in a game (as of baseball); *also* **:** the players on such a list **b :** an alignment of persons or things having a common purpose or interest

¹ling \'liŋ\ *n* [ME; akin to E *long*] **1 :** any of various fishes (as a hake or burbot) of the cod family **2 :** LINGCOD

²ling *n* [ON *lyng*] **:** a heath plant; *esp* **:** a common Old World weather

¹-ling \liŋ\ *n suffix* [OE] **1 :** one connected with or having the quality of ⟨hireling⟩ **2 :** young, small, or inferior one ⟨duckling⟩

²-ling \liŋ\ *adv suffix* [ME -*ling*, -*linges*] **:** in (such) a direction or manner ⟨sideling⟩

ling·cod \'liŋ-,käd\ *n* **:** a large greenish-fleshed food fish of the Pacific coast of No. America related to the greenlings

lin·ger \'liŋ-gər\ *vi* **lin·gered**; **lin·ger·ing** \-g(ə-)riŋ\ [ME *lengeren*, freq. of *lengen*, fr. OE *lengan* to prolong; akin to E *long*] **1 :** to be slow in leaving or quitting a place or activity ⟨*lingered* at the dinner table⟩ **2 :** to remain alive although gradually dying ⟨*lingering* embers⟩ **3 :** to be slow to act **:** PROCRASTINATE **syn** see STAY — **lin·ger·er** \-gər-ər\ *n* — **lin·ger·ing·ly** \-g(ə-)riŋ-lē\ *adv*

lin·ge·rie \,län-jə-'rā, ,la²-zhə-, ,lan-jə-, -'rē\ *n* [F, fr. *linge* linen, fr. L *lineus* made of linen, fr. *linum* flax, linen] **:** women's intimate apparel (as nightclothes or underwear)

lin·go \'liŋ-gō\ *n*, *pl* **lingoes** [prob. fr. Prov, tongue, fr. L *lingua*] **1 :** strange or incomprehensible language or speech; *esp* **:** a foreign language **2 :** the special vocabulary of a particular field of interest **:** JARGON **3 :** language characteristic of an individual **syn** see DIALECT

lin·gua fran·ca \,liŋ-gwə-'fraŋ-kə\ *n*, *pl* **lingua francas** *or* **lin·guae fran·cae** \-,gwī-'fraŋ-,kī\ [It, lit., Frankish language] **1 :** a common language that consists of Italian mixed with French, Spanish, Greek, and Arabic and is spoken in Mediterranean ports **2 :** any of various languages used as common or commercial tongues among speakers of different languages

lin·gual \'liŋ-gwəl\ *adj* [L *lingua* tongue, language; akin to E *tongue*] **1 a :** of, relating to, or resembling a tongue **b :** lying near or next to the tongue **2 :** produced by the tongue ⟨*lingual* sounds such as \t\ or \l\⟩ — **lin·gual·ly** \-gwə-lē\ *adv*

lin·guist \'liŋ-gwəst\ *n* **1 :** a person skilled in languages **2 :** one who specializes in linguistics

lin·guis·tic \liŋ-'gwis-tik\ *adj* **:** of or relating to language or linguistics — **lin·guis·ti·cal·ly** \-ti-k(ə-)lē\ *adv*

lin·guis·tics \-tiks\ *n* **:** the study of human speech including the units, nature, structure, and development of language, languages, or a language

lin·i·ment \'lin-ə-mənt\ *n* [L *linere* to smear] **:** a liquid preparation rubbed on the skin esp. to relieve pain

li·nin \'lī-nən\ *n* [L *linum* flax, thread] **:** a feebly-staining part of the nuclear reticulum of a resting cell

lin·ing \'lī-niŋ\ *n* **1 :** material used to line esp. the inner surface of something (as a garment) **2 :** the act or process of providing something with a lining

¹link \'liŋk\ *n* [of Scand origin] **1 :** a connecting structure: as **a :** a single ring or division of a chain **b :** a division of a surveyor's chain that is 7.92 inches long and is used as a measure of length **c** : a usu. ornamental device for fastening a cuff **d** : BOND 3b **e** : an intermediate rod or piece for transmitting force or motion **2** : something analogous to a link of chain: as **a** : a segment of sausage in a chain **b** : a connecting element

²**link** *vb* : to couple or connect by a link : UNITE, JOIN — **link·er** *n*

³**link** *n* : a torch formerly used to light a person on his way through the streets

link·age \'liŋ-kij\ *n* **1** : the manner or style of being united: as **a** : the manner in which atoms or radicals are linked in a molecule **b** : BOND 3b **2** : the quality or state of being linked; *esp* : a relationship between genes that causes them to be manifested together in inheritance and that is usu. held to involve their location on the same chromosome **3** : a system of links; *esp* : a system of links or bars jointed together by means of which lines or curves may be traced

link·boy \'liŋk-,bȯi\ *n* : an attendant formerly employed to bear a light (as a torch) for a person abroad at night

linking verb *n* : a copulative verb

links \'liŋ(k)s\ *n pl* [OE *hlincas*, pl. of *hlinc* ridge] : COURSE 2d

links·man \-mən\ *n* : GOLFER

link·up \'liŋk-,əp\ *n* **1** : MEETING **2** : something that serves as a linking device or factor

Lin·nae·an *or* **Lin·ne·an** \lə-'nē-ən, 'lin-ē-\ *adj* [fr. Carolus *Linnaeus* (Carl von Linné)] : of, relating to, or following the method of the Swedish botanist Linné who established the system of binomial nomenclature

lin·net \'lin-ət\ *n* [MF *linette*, fr. *lin* flax, fr. L *linum*] : a common small Old World finch with variable plumage

lin·ole·ic acid \,lin-ə-,lē-ik-\ *n* [L *linum* flax + *oleum* oil] : a liquid unsaturated fatty acid found in various oils and held to be essential in animal nutrition

lin·ole·nic acid \-,lē-nik-\ *n* : a liquid unsaturated fatty acid found esp. in drying oils and held to be essential in animal nutrition

li·no·le·um \lə-'nō-lē-əm, -'nōl-yəm\ *n* [L *linum* flax + *oleum* oil] : a floor covering with a canvas back and a surface of hardened linseed oil and a filler (as cork dust)

Li·no·type \'lī-nə-,tīp\ *trademark* **1** — used for a keyboard-operated typesetting machine that uses circulating matrices and produces each line of type in the form of a solid metal slug **2** : matter produced by a Linotype machine or printing done from such matter

lin·seed \'lin-,sēd\ *n* [OE *linsǣd*, fr. *līn* flax + *sǣd* seed] : FLAXSEED

linseed oil *n* : a yellowish drying oil obtained from flax-seed and used esp. in paint, varnish, printing ink, and linoleum

lin·sey-wool·sey \,lin-zē-'wu̇l-zē\ *n* : a coarse sturdy fabric of wool and linen or cotton

lint \'lint\ *n* [ME] **1** : linen made into a soft fleecy substance for use in surgical dressings **2** : fine ravelings, fluff, or loose short fibers from yarn or fabrics **3** : fibers forming a close thick coating about cotton seeds and constituting the staple of cotton — **linty** \-ē\ *adj*

lin·tel \'lint-ᵊl\ *n* [MF, fr. LL *limitaris* threshold, fr. L *limit-, limes* limit] : a horizontal piece or part across the top of an opening (as of a door) that carries the weight of the structure above it

lint·er \'lint-ər\ *n* [*lint*] **1** : a machine for removing linters **2** *pl* : the fuzz of short fibers that adheres to cottonseed after ginning

li·on \'lī-ən\ *n, pl* **lion** *or* **lions** [OF, fr. L *leon-, leo*, fr. Gk *leōn*] **1 a** : a large tawny carnivorous chiefly nocturnal cat of open or rocky areas of Africa and esp. formerly southern Asia with a tufted tail and a shaggy mane in the male **b** : any of several large wildcats; *esp* : COUGAR **2 a** : a person resembling a lion (as in courage or ferocity) **b** : a person of outstanding interest or importance ⟨a literary *lion*⟩ **3** *cap* : a member of one of the major service clubs — **li·on·ess** \'lī-ə-nəs\ *n* — **li·on·like** \'lī-ən-,līk\ *adj*

li·on·heart·ed \,lī-ən-'härt-əd\ *adj* : having a courageous heart : BRAVE

li·on·ize \'lī-ə-,nīz\ *vt* : to treat as an object of great

lintel

interest or importance — **li·on·i·za·tion** \,lī-ə-nə-'zā-shən\ *n*

¹**lip** \'lip\ *n* [OE *lippa*] **1** : either of the two fleshy folds that surround the mouth **2** *slang* : an impudent, insolent, or argumentative reply **3 a** : a fleshy edge or margin ⟨*lips* of a wound⟩ **b** : LABIUM 2; *also* : the protruding part of an irregular corolla (as of a snapdragon or orchid) **4 a** : the edge of a hollow vessel or cavity esp. where it flares slightly **b** : a projecting edge (as of the mouth of an organ flue pipe or on the end of an auger) **c** : a short spout (as on a pitcher) **5** : EMBOUCHURE 1 — **lip·less** \-ləs\ *adj* — **lip·like** \-,līk\ *adj* — **lipped** \'lipt\ *adj*

²**lip** *adj* **1** : spoken with the lips only : INSINCERE ⟨*lip* praise⟩ **2** : produced with the participation of the lips : LABIAL ⟨*lip* consonants⟩

³**lip** *vt* **lipped**; **lip·ping** **1** : to touch with the lips; *esp* : KISS **2** : UTTER

lip- *or* **lipo-** *comb form* [Gk *lipos*] : fat : fatty tissue : fatty ⟨*lipoid*⟩ ⟨*lipoprotein*⟩

li·pase \'lī-,pās, 'lip-\ *n* : an enzyme that accelerates the hydrolysis or synthesis of fats or the breakdown of lipoproteins

lip·ide \'lip-,īd\ *or* **lip·id** \-əd\ *n* : any of various substances including fats, waxes, and phosphatides that with proteins and carbohydrates constitute the principal structural components of living cells

lip·oid \'lip-,ȯid, 'līp-\ *n* : a substance (as a fat or complex lipide) or mixture with the solubility characteristics of a lipide — **lipoid** *or* **li·poi·dal** \lip-'ȯid-ᵊl, lī-'pȯid-\ *adj*

li·pol·y·sis \lip-'äl-ə-səs, lī-'päl-\ *n* : the hydrolysis of fat — **lip·o·lyt·ic** \,lip-ə-'lit-ik, ,lī-pə-\ *adj*

li·po·ma \lip-'ō-mə, lī-'pō-\ *n, pl* **-mas** *or* **-ma·ta** \-mət-ə\ : a tumor of fatty tissue — **li·pom·a·tous** \lip-'äm-ət-əs, lī-'päm-\ *adj*

lip·o·phil·ic \,lip-ə-'fil-ik, ,līp-\ *adj* : having an affinity for lipides

lipo·pro·tein \,lip-ə-'prō-,tēn, ,līp-, -'prōt-ē-ən\ *n* : a protein containing a lipide group

lip·py \'lip-ē\ *adj* **lip·pi·er**; **-est** : given to back talk : IMPUDENT

lip·read·ing \'lip-,rēd-iŋ\ *n* : the interpreting of a speaker's words without hearing his voice by watching his lip and facial movements — **lip·read** *vb* — **lip·read·er** *n*

lip service *n* : an expression of allegiance (as to a rule) without corresponding action

lip·stick \-,stik\ *n* : a waxy solid colored cosmetic in stick form for the lips; *also* : a stick of such cosmetic with its case

liq·ue·fa·cient \,lik-wə-'fā-shənt\ *n* : something serving to liquefy or to promote liquefaction

liq·ue·fac·tion \,lik-wə-'fak-shən\ *n* **1** : the process of making or becoming liquid **2** : the state of being liquid

liquefied petroleum gas *n* : a compressed gas consisting of flammable light hydrocarbons and used esp. as fuel or as raw material for chemical synthesis

liq·ue·fy *also* **liq·ui·fy** \'lik-wə-,fī\ *vb* **-fied**; **-fy·ing** [L *liquefacere*, fr. *liquēre* to be fluid + *facere* to make] : to reduce to a liquid state : become liquid — **liq·ue·fi·a·ble** \-,fī-ə-bəl\ *adj* — **liq·ue·fi·er** \-,fī(-ə)r\ *n*

li·ques·cent \lik-'wes-ᵊnt\ *adj* : being or tending to become liquid — **li·ques·cence** \-²n(t)s\ *n*

li·queur \li-'kər, -'k(y)u̇(ə)r\ *n* [F, lit., liquor, liquid, fr. L *liquor*] : an alcoholic beverage flavored with aromatic substances and usu. sweetened

¹**liq·uid** \'lik-wəd\ *adj* [L *liquidus*, fr. *liquēre* to be fluid] **1** : flowing freely like water **2** : neither solid nor gaseous : characterized by free movement of the constituent molecules among themselves but without the tendency to separate characteristic of gases ⟨*liquid* mercury⟩ **3 a** : shining clear ⟨large *liquid* eyes⟩ **b** : being musical and free of harshness in sound **c** : smooth and unconstrained in movement **d** : that is without friction and like a vowel ⟨the *liquid* consonant \l\⟩ **4** : consisting of or capable of ready conversion into cash ⟨*liquid* assets⟩ — **li·quid·i·ty** \lik-'wid-ət-ē\ *n* — **liq·uid·ly** \'lik-wəd-lē\ *adv* — **liq·uid·ness** *n*

²**liquid** *n* **1** : a liquid substance **2** : a liquid consonant

liquid air *n* : air in the liquid state prepared by subjecting it to great pressure and then cooling it by its own expansion and used chiefly as a refrigerant

liq·ui·date \'lik-wə-ˌdāt\ vb **1 :** to pay off ⟨*liquidate* a debt⟩ **2 :** to settle the accounts of (as a business) and use the assets toward paying off the debts **:** close up a business **3 :** to do away with, get rid of, or destroy esp. a person or thing regarded as undesirable or dangerous; *esp* **:** to kill ruthlessly and in secret as a political measure — **liq·ui·da·tion** \ˌlik-wə-'dā-shən\ n — **liq·ui·da·tor** \'lik-wə-ˌdāt-ər\ n

liq·uid·ize \'lik-wə-ˌdīz\ vt **:** to cause to be liquid

liquid measure n **1 :** a unit or series of units for measuring liquid capacity — see MEASURE table, METRIC SYSTEM table **2 :** a measure for liquids

¹li·quor \'lik-ər\ n [L, fr. *liquēre* to be fluid] **:** a liquid substance or solution ⟨dye *liquor*⟩ ⟨the *liquor* from boiled meat⟩; *esp* **:** an alcoholic beverage distilled rather than fermented

²liquor vb **li·quored; li·quor·ing** \'lik-(ə-)riŋ\ **:** to make or become drunk with alcoholic liquor

li·quo·rice chiefly Brit var of LICORICE

li·ra \'lir-ə\ n [It, fr. L *libra* pound] **1** pl **li·re** \'lē-ˌrā\ or **liras a :** the basic monetary unit of Italy **b :** a coin or note representing one lira **2** pl **liras** also **lire** [Turk, fr. It] **:** a Turkish or Syrian pound **3** pl **li·roth** or **li·rot** \lē-ˌrōt(h)\ [NHeb, fr. It] **:** the Israeli pound

lisle \'līl\ n [*Lisle* Lille, France] **:** a smooth tightly twisted thread usu. made of long-staple cotton

¹lisp \'lisp\ vb [OE -*wlyspian*] **1 :** to pronounce *s* and *z* imperfectly esp. by giving them the sound of *th* **2 :** to speak falteringly, childishly, or with a lisp — **lisp·er** n

²lisp n **1 :** the habit or act of lisping **2 :** a sound resembling a lisp

lis·some also **lis·som** \'lis-əm\ adj [alter. of *lithesome*] **1 :** easily flexed **:** LITHE **2 :** NIMBLE — **lis·some·ly** adv — **lis·some·ness** n

¹list \'list\ vb [OE *lystan*; akin to E *lust*] **1 :** PLEASE, SUIT **2 :** WISH, CHOOSE

²list n, archaic **:** INCLINATION, CRAVING

³list vb **1 :** LISTEN **2** archaic **:** to listen to **:** HEAR

⁴list n [OE *līste* border] **1 a** obs **:** a strip of cloth **b :** SELVAGE **c :** a band or strip of any material (as wood) **2** pl **a :** an arena for jousting **b :** an arena for combat ⟨entered the *lists*⟩ **c :** a field of competition or controversy **3** obs **:** LIMIT, BOUNDARY **4 :** a streak of color (as on an animal's body) **:** STRIPE

⁵list n [F *liste*, fr. It *lista*, of Gmc origin] **1 a :** a simple series of names (as of persons or objects) ⟨guest *list*⟩ ⟨grocery *list*⟩ **b :** an official roster **:** ROLL **2 :** INDEX, CATALOG

⁶list vb **1 a :** to make a list of **:** ENUMERATE **b :** to include on a list **:** REGISTER ⟨securities *listed* on the exchange⟩ **2 a :** to put (oneself) down ⟨*lists* himself as a plumber⟩ **b :** to become entered in a catalog at a selling price ⟨the coat *lists* at $25⟩

⁷list vb **:** to lean or cause to lean to one side **:** TILT

⁸list n **:** a deviation from the vertical **:** TILT

lis·ten \'lis-ᵊn\ vi **lis·tened; lis·ten·ing** \'lis-niŋ, -ᵊn-iŋ\ [OE *hlysnan* to listen to; akin to E *loud*] **1 :** to pay attention in order to hear ⟨*listen* for a signal⟩ ⟨*listen* to a new record⟩ **2 :** to give heed **:** follow advice ⟨*listen* to a warning⟩ **syn** see HEAR — **lis·ten·er** \'lis-nər, -ᵊn-ər\ n

listen in vi **1 :** to tune in to or monitor a broadcast **2 :** to give ear to a conversation without participating in it; *esp* **:** EAVESDROP — **lis·ten·er-in** \ˌlis-nər-'in, -ᵊn-ər-\ n

list·er \'lis-tər\ n **:** a double-moldboard plow that throws up ridges of earth on both sides of the furrow

list·ing \'lis-tiŋ\ n **1 :** an act or instance of making or including in a list **2 :** something listed

list·less \'list-ləs\ adj **:** characterized by lack of inclination or impetus to exertion **:** LANGUID, SPIRITLESS — **list·less·ly** adv — **list·less·ness** n

list price n **:** the basic price of an item as published in a catalog, price list, or advertisement but subject to discounts or trade

lit past of LIGHT

lit·a·ny \'lit-ᵊn-ē\ n, pl **-nies** [Gk *litaneia* entreaty] **:** a prayer consisting of a series of supplications and responses said alternately by a leader and a group

li·tchi \'lē-(ˌ)chē, 'lē-\ n [Chin (Pek) *li⁴ chih¹*] **:** the oval fruit of an Asiatic tree having a hard outer covering and a seed surrounded by sweetish edible flesh that when dried is firm and black; *also* **:** the tree bearing this fruit

-lite \ˌlīt\ n comb form [F, fr. Gk *lithos* stone] **:** mineral **:** rock **:** fossil

li·ter \'lēt-ər\ n [F *litre*, fr. ML *litra*, a measure, fr. Gk, pound] **:** a metric unit of capacity equal to the volume of one kilogram of water at 4°C and at standard atmospheric pressure of 760 millimeters of mercury — see METRIC SYSTEM table

lit·er·a·cy \'lit-ə-rə-sē, 'li-trə-sē\ n **:** the state of being literate **:** ability to read and write

lit·er·al \'lit-ə-rəl, 'li-trəl\ adj [L *littera, litera* letter] **1 a :** according with the letter of the scriptures **b :** adhering to fact or to the ordinary or usual meaning of a term or expression **c :** PLAIN, UNADORNED **d :** characterized by a concern mainly with facts **:** PROSAIC **2 :** of, relating to, or expressed in letters ⟨*literal* equations⟩ **3 :** reproduced word for word **:** EXACT, VERBATIM — **lit·er·al·ly** \'lit-ər-(ə-)lē, 'li-trə-lē\ adv — **lit·er·al·ness** \'lit-ə-rəl-nəs, 'li-trəl-\ n

lit·er·al·ism \'lit-ə-rə-ˌliz-əm, 'li-trə-\ n **1 :** adherence to the explicit substance of an idea or expression **2 :** fidelity to observable fact — **lit·er·al·ist** \-ləst\ n — **lit·er·al·is·tic** \ˌlit-ə-rə-'lis-tik, ˌli-trə-\ adj

lit·er·ary \'lit-ə-ˌrer-ē\ adj [L *litterae, literae* letters, literature, pl. of *littera* letter] **1 a :** of, relating to, or having the characteristics of letters, humane learning, or literature **b :** BOOKISH **2 c :** of or relating to books **2 a :** well informed through reading **b :** of or relating to men of letters or writing as a profession — **lit·er·ar·i·ly** \ˌlit-ə-'rer-ə-lē\ adv — **lit·er·ar·i·ness** \'lit-ə-ˌrer-ē-nəs\ n

lit·er·ate \'lit-ə-rət, 'li-trət\ adj **1 a :** EDUCATED, CULTURED **b :** able to read and write **2 a :** versed in literature or creative writing **:** LITERARY **b :** POLISHED, LUCID — **literate** n — **lit·er·ate·ly** adv

lit·e·ra·ti \ˌlit-ə-'rät-(ˌ)ē\ n pl **1 :** the educated class **:** INTELLIGENTSIA **2 :** men of letters

lit·er·a·tim \ˌlit-ə-'rāt-əm, -'rät-\ adv (or adj) [ML, fr. L *littera* letter] **:** letter for letter

lit·er·a·ture \'lit-ə-rə-ˌchür, 'li-trə-, -chər\ n **1 :** the production of literary work esp. as an occupation **2 a :** writings in prose or verse; *esp* **:** writings having excellence of form or expression and expressing ideas of permanent or universal interest **b :** the body of writings on a particular subject **c :** printed matter (as leaflets or circulars) **3 :** the aggregate of musical compositions

lith- or **litho-** comb form [Gk *lithos*] **:** stone ⟨*lithology*⟩ **-lith** \ˌlith\ n comb form [Gk *lithos* stone] **1 :** structure or implement of stone ⟨mega*lith*⟩ **2 :** calculus ⟨uro*lith*⟩ **3 :** -LITE

li·tharge \'lith-ˌärj, lith-'\ n [MF, fr. Gk *lithargyros*, fr. *lithos* stone + *argyros* silver] **:** LEAD MONOXIDE

lithe \'līth, 'līth\ adj [OE *līthe* gentle] **1 :** easily bent **:** FLEXIBLE ⟨long *lithe* stems⟩ **2 :** marked by effortless grace **:** LIMBER ⟨*lithe* dancers⟩ — **lithe·ly** adv — **lithe·ness** n

lithe·some \'līth-səm, 'līth-\ adj **:** LISSOME

lith·ia \'lith-ē-ə\ n [NL, fr. Gk *lithos* stone] **:** an oxide of lithium occurring as a white crystalline substance

lithia water n **:** a mineral water containing lithium salts

lith·ic \'lith-ik\ adj [Gk *lithos* stone] **1 :** of, relating to, or made of stone **2 :** of or relating to lithium — **lith·i·cal·ly** \'lith-i-k(ə-)lē\ adv

-lith·ic \'lith-ik\ adj comb form **:** relating to or characteristic of a (specified) stage in man's use of stone as a cultural tool ⟨Neo*lithic*⟩

lith·i·um \'lith-ē-əm\ n [NL, fr. *lithia*] **:** a soft silvery-white univalent chemical element that is the lightest metal known and is used esp. in nuclear reactions and metallurgy — see ELEMENT table

¹litho·graph \'lith-ə-ˌgraf\ vt **:** to produce, copy, or portray by lithography — **li·thog·ra·pher** \lith-'äg-rə-fər, 'lith-ə-ˌgraf-ər\ n

²lithograph n **:** a print made by lithography — **litho·graph·ic** \ˌlith-ə-'graf-ik\ adj — **litho·graph·i·cal·ly** \-'graf-i-k(ə-)lē\ adv

li·thog·ra·phy \lith-'äg-rə-fē\ n **1 :** the process of printing from a plane surface (as a smooth stone or metal plate) on which the image to be printed is ink-receptive and the blank area ink-repellent **2 :** PLANOGRAPHY

li·thol·o·gy \lith-'äl-ə-jē\ n **1 :** the study of rocks **2 :** the character of a rock formation — **lith·o·log·ic**

\ˌlith-ə-'läj-ik\ *adj* — **lith·o·log·i·cal·ly** \-'läj-i-k(ə-)lē\ *adv*

lith·o·phyte \'lith-ə-ˌfīt\ *n* **1** : an organism (as a coral) with a hard stony skeleton **2** : a plant growing on the surface of rock — **lith·o·phyt·ic** \ˌlith-ə-'fit-ik\ *adj*

lith·o·pone \'lith-ə-ˌpōn\ *n* : a white pigment consisting essentially of zinc sulfide and barium sulfate

litho·print \'lith-ə-ˌprint\ *vt* : to print by offset or photo=offset

litho·sphere \-ˌsfi(ə)r\ *n* : the outer part of the solid earth

Lith·u·a·ni·an \ˌlith-(y)ə-'wā-nē-ən, -nyən\ *n* **1** : a native or inhabitant of Lithuania **2** : the Baltic language of the Lithuanian people — **Lithuanian** *adj*

lit·i·gant \'lit-i-gənt\ *n* : a party to a lawsuit

lit·i·gate \'lit-ə-ˌgāt\ *vb* [L *litigare*, fr. *lit-*, *lis* lawsuit] **1** : to carry on a legal contest by judicial process **2** : to contest in law — **lit·i·ga·tion** \ˌlit-ə-'gā-shən\ *n*

li·ti·gious \lə-'tij-əs\ *adj* **1 a** : DISPUTATIOUS, CONTENTIOUS **b** : prone to engage in lawsuits **2** : of or relating to litigation — **li·ti·gious·ly** *adv* — **li·ti·gious·ness** *n*

lit·mus \'lit-məs\ *n* [of Scand origin] : a coloring matter from lichens that turns red in acid solutions and blue in alkaline solutions and is used as an acid-base indicator

litmus paper *n* : paper impregnated with litmus

li·to·tes \'līt-ə-ˌtēz, 'lit-\ *n*, *pl* **litotes** [Gk *litotēs*, fr. *litos* simple] : understatement in which an affirmative is expressed by the negative of the contrary (as in "not a bad singer")

li·tre \'lēt-ər\ *var of* LITER

¹lit·ter \'lit-ər\ *n* [OF *litiere*, fr. *lit* bed, fr. L *lectus*; akin to E **¹lie**] **1 a** : a covered and curtained couch provided with shafts and used for carrying a single passenger **b** : a device (as a stretcher) for carrying a sick or injured person **2 a** : material used as bedding for animals **b** : the uppermost layer of organic debris on the forest floor **3** : the offspring of an animal at one birth **4** : an untidy accumulation of objects lying about : RUBBISH

²litter *vb* **1** : to give birth to young **2 a** : to strew with litter **b** : to scatter about in disorder

lit·ter·a·teur \ˌlit-ə-rə-'tər, ˌli-trə-\ *n* [F *littérateur*] : a literary man; *esp* : a professional writer

lit·ter·bug \'lit-ər-ˌbəg\ *n* : one that litters a public area

¹lit·tle \'lit-ᵊl\ *adj* **lit·tler** \'lit-ᵊl-ər, 'lit-lər\ *or* **less** \'les\ *or* **less·er** \'les-ər\; **lit·tlest** \'lit-ᵊl-əst, 'lit-ləst\ *or* **least** \'lēst\ [OE *lȳtel*] **1** : not big: as **a** : small in size or extent : TINY **b** : small in comparison with related forms ⟨*little* blue heron⟩ ⟨*little* celandine⟩ **c** : small in number **d** : small in condition, distinction, or scope **e** : NARROW, MEAN ⟨men of *little* natures⟩ **f** : pleasingly small **2** : not much: as **a** : existing only in a small amount or to a slight degree **b** : short in duration : BRIEF **3** : small in importance or interest : TRIVIAL **syn** see SMALL — **lit·tle·ness** \'lit-ᵊl-nəs\ *n*

²little *adv* **less** \'les\; **least** \'lēst\ **1 a** : in only a small quantity or degree : SLIGHTLY **b** : not at all ⟨he *little* knows or cares⟩ **2** : INFREQUENTLY, RARELY

³little *n* **1** : a small amount or quantity **2 a** : a short time **b** : a short distance — **in little** : on a small scale; *esp* : in miniature

Little Bear *n* : URSA MINOR

Little Dipper *n* : DIPPER 2b

Little Hours *n pl* : the offices of prime, terce, sext, and none

lit·tle·neck clam \ˌlit-ᵊl-ˌnek-\ *n* [*Littleneck* Bay, Long Island, N.Y.] : a young quahog suitable to be eaten raw

Little Office *n* : an office in honor of the Virgin Mary that resembles but is shorter than the Divine Office

little slam *n* : the winning of all tricks except one in bridge

little theater *n* : a small theater for low-cost experimental drama designed for a relatively limited audience

¹lit·to·ral \'lit-ə-rəl, ˌlit-ə-'ral, -'räl\ *adj* [L *litor-*, *litus* seashore] : of, relating to, or situated or growing on or near a shore esp. of the sea

²littoral *n* : a coastal region

li·tur·gi·cal \lə-'tər-ji-kəl\ *adj* **1** : of, relating to, or having the characteristics of liturgy **2** : using or favoring the use of liturgy — **li·tur·gi·cal·ly** \-k(ə-)lē\ *adv*

li·tur·gics \-jiks\ *n* : the study of formal public worship

lit·ur·gist \'lit-ər-jəst\ *n* **1** : one who adheres to, compiles, or leads a liturgy **2** : a specialist in liturgics

lit·ur·gy \'lit-ər-jē\ *n, pl* **-gies** [Gk *leitourgia* public service, divine service, fr. *laos*, *leōs* people + *ergon* work] **1** : a rite or body of rites prescribed for public worship **2** *often cap* : a eucharistic rite

liv·a·bil·i·ty \ˌliv-ə-'bil-ət-ē\ *n* **1** : survival expectancy : VIABILITY **2** : suitability for human living

liv·a·ble *also* **live·a·ble** \'liv-ə-bəl\ *adj* **1** : suitable for living in or with **2** : ENDURABLE — **liv·a·ble·ness** *n*

¹live \'liv\ *vb* [OE *libban*] **1** : to be or continue alive : have life **2** : to maintain oneself : SUBSIST ⟨*live* on fruits⟩ **3** : to conduct or pass one's life ⟨*lived* up to his principles⟩ **4** : DWELL, RESIDE **5** : to attain eternal life **6** : to remain in human memory or record **7** : to have a life rich in experience **8** : COHABIT **9** : to pass through or spend the duration of **10** : ENACT, PRACTICE ⟨*lives* what he preaches⟩ **11** : to exhibit vigor, gusto, or enthusiasm in

²live \'līv\ *adj* [short for *alive*] **1** : having life : LIVING **2** : abounding with life : VIVID **3** : exerting force or containing energy: as **a** : AFIRE, GLOWING ⟨*live* cigar⟩ **b** : carrying an electric current ⟨a *live* wire⟩ **c** : charged with explosives and containing shot or a bullet ⟨*live* ammunition⟩; *also* : UNEXPLODED ⟨*live* bomb⟩ **d** : rotating or imparting motion ⟨a *live* spindle⟩ **e** : power-driven ⟨a *live* axle⟩ **4** : of continuing or current interest : UNCLOSED ⟨*live* issue⟩ **5** : being in the native uncut state ⟨*live* rock⟩ **6** : of bright vivid color **7** : being in play ⟨a *live* ball⟩ **8 a** : of or involving the actual presence of real people ⟨*live* audience⟩ **b** : broadcast directly at the time of production instead of from recorded or filmed material ⟨a *live* radio program⟩

live-bear·ing \'līv-'ba(ə)r-iŋ, -'be(ə)r-\ *adj* : VIVIPAROUS — **live-bear·er** \-ˌbar-ər, -ˌber-\ *n*

lived \'līvd, 'livd\ *adj* : having a life of a specified kind or length ⟨long-*lived*⟩

live down *vt* : to live so as to wipe out the memory or effects of

live-for·ev·er \ˌliv-fə-ˌrev-ər\ *n* : SEDUM

live·li·hood \'līv-lē-ˌhud\ *n* : means of support or subsistence ⟨an honest *livelihood*⟩

live·long \ˌliv-ˌloŋ\ *adj* : WHOLE, ENTIRE ⟨all the *livelong* day⟩

live·ly \'līv-lē\ *adj* **live·li·er; -est** **1** : full of life : ACTIVE ⟨a *lively* puppy⟩ **2** : KEEN, VIVID ⟨a *lively* interest⟩ **3** : full of spirit or feeling : ANIMATED ⟨a *lively* debate⟩ **4** : showing activity or vigor ⟨a *lively* manner⟩ **5** : rebounding quickly ⟨a *lively* tennis ball⟩ — **live·li·ly** \'līv-lə-lē\ *adv* — **live·li·ness** \'līv-lē-nəs\ *n* — **lively** *adv*

syn LIVELY, ANIMATED, VIVACIOUS mean being keenly alive. LIVELY suggests briskness, alertness, or energy; ANIMATED applies to what is spirited, active, or vigorous ⟨an *animated* conversation⟩ VIVACIOUS suggests attractive gaiety and quickness of gesture and wit

liv·en \'lī-vən\ *vb* **liv·ened; liv·en·ing** \'līv-(ə-)niŋ\ : to make or become lively : ENLIVEN

live oak \'līv-ˌōk\ *n* : any of several American evergreen oaks

¹liv·er \'liv-ər\ *n* [OE *lifer*] **1 a** : a large vascular glandular organ of vertebrates that secretes bile and causes changes in the blood (as by converting sugars into glycogen) **b** : any of various large prob. digestive glands of invertebrate animals **2** : the tissue of the liver (as of a calf or pig) eaten as food — **liv·ered** \-ərd\ *adj*

²liv·er \'liv-ər\ *n* **1** : one that lives esp. in a specified way ⟨a fast *liver*⟩ **2** : RESIDENT

liver fluke *n* : any of various trematode worms that invade the liver of mammals

liv·er·ied \'liv-(ə-)rēd\ *adj* : wearing a livery ⟨a *liveried* footman at the door⟩

liv·er·ish \'liv-(ə-)rish\ *adj* **1** : suffering from liver disorder : BILIOUS **2** : CRABBED, MELANCHOLY — **liv·er·ish·ness** *n*

liv·er·wort \'liv-ər-ˌwərt, -ˌwort\ *n* : any of a class (Hepaticae) of bryophytes related to and resembling the mosses but differing esp. in reproduction and development

liv·er·wurst \'liv-ə(r)-ˌwərst, -ˌwurst\ *n* : a sausage consisting chiefly of liver

liv·ery \'liv-(ə-)rē\ *n, pl* **-er·ies** [OF *livree* allotment of provisions to servants, fr. *livrer* to deliver, fr. L *liberare* to liberate] **1** : a special uniform worn by the servants of a wealthy household ⟨a footman in *livery*⟩ **2** : distinctive dress ⟨the *livery* of a school⟩ **3 a** : the feeding, care, and stabling of horses for pay; *also* **:** the keeping of horses and vehicles for hire **b :** LIVERY STABLE

liv·ery·man \-mən\ *n* **:** the keeper of a livery stable

livery stable *n* **:** a stable where horses and vehicles are kept for hire and where stabling is provided

lives *pl of* LIFE

live steam *n* **:** steam direct from a boiler and under full pressure

live·stock \'līv-ˌstäk\ *n* **:** animals kept or raised for use or pleasure; *esp* **:** farm animals kept for use and profit

live wire *n* **:** an alert active aggressive person

liv·id \'liv-əd\ *adj* [L *lividus*] **1 :** discolored by bruising **:** BLACK-AND-BLUE **2 :** ASHEN, PALLID ⟨livid with rage⟩ — **li·vid·i·ty** \liv-'id-ət-ē\ *n* — **liv·id·ly** \'liv-əd-lē\ *adv* — **liv·id·ness** *n*

¹liv·ing \'liv-iŋ\ *adj* **1 a :** having life **b :** ACTIVE, FUNCTIONING ⟨a *living* faith⟩ **2 a :** exhibiting the life or motion of nature **:** NATURAL **b :** LIVE **3 a :** full of life or vigor ⟨made mathematics a *living* subject⟩ **b :** true to life **c :** suited for living ⟨the *living* area⟩ **4 :** VERY — used as an intensive

²living *n* **1 :** the condition of being alive **2 :** conduct or manner of life **3 a :** means of subsistence **:** LIVELIHOOD **b** *Brit* **:** BENEFICE

living room *n* **:** a room in a residence used for the common social activities of the occupants

living wage *n* **:** a wage sufficient to provide the necessities and comforts held to comprise an acceptable standard of living

liz·ard \'liz-ərd\ *n* [MF *laisarde*, fr. L *lacerta*] **:** any of a group (Lacertilia) of reptiles distinguished from the related snakes by a fused inseparable lower jaw, external ears, eyes with movable lids, and usu. two pairs of well differentiated functional limbs

typical lizard

'll \(ə)l, əl\ *vb* **:** WILL ⟨you'll be late⟩ **:** SHALL ⟨I'll be there⟩

lla·ma \'läm-ə\ *n* [Sp, fr. Quechua] **:** any of several wild and domesticated So. American ruminants related to the camels but smaller and without a hump

lla·no \'län-ō\ *n, pl* **llanos** [Sp, plain, fr. L *planum*] **:** an open grassy plain esp. of Spanish America

lo \'lō\ *interj* — used to call attention or to express wonder or surprise

loach \'lōch\ *n* [MF *loche*] **:** any of a family of small Old World freshwater fishes related to the carps

¹load \'lōd\ *n* [OE *lād* way, course, act of carrying] **1 a :** whatever is put on a man or pack animal to be carried **:** PACK **b :** whatever is put in a ship or vehicle or airplane for conveyance **:** CARGO; *esp* **:** a quantity of material assembled or packed as a shipping unit **c :** the quantity that can be carried at one time by a specified means; *esp* **:** a measured quantity of a commodity fixed for each type of carrier — often used in combination ⟨a boat*load* of tourists⟩ **2 :** a mass or weight supported by something **3 a :** something that weighs down the mind or spirits ⟨a *load* of care⟩ **b :** a burdensome or laborious responsibility **4 :** a large quantity **:** LOT — usu. used in pl. **5 a :** a charge for a firearm **b :** the quantity of material loaded into a device at one time **6 :** external resistance overcome by a machine **7 a :** power output (as of a power plant) **b :** a device to which power is delivered **8 a :** the amount of work that a person, department, or machine performs or is expected to perform **b :** the demand upon the operating resources of a system (as a telephone exchange or a refrigerating apparatus) **9** *slang* **:** EYEFUL ⟨get a *load* of her⟩

²load *vb* **1 a :** to put a load in or on; *also* **:** to receive a load **b :** to place in or on a means of conveyance or in a container **2 a :** to encumber or oppress with something heavy, laborious, or disheartening **:** BURDEN **b :** to place as a burden or obligation ⟨*load* more work on him⟩ **3 a** (1) **:** to increase the weight of by adding something heavy (2) **:** to weight (dice) to fall unfairly **b :** BIAS ⟨*loaded* questions⟩ **c :** to weight (as a test) with factors influencing validity or outcome **4 :** to supply in abundance or excess **:** HEAP **5 :** to place or insert a load or as a load ⟨*load* film in a camera⟩⟨*load* clothes into a washing

machine⟩⟨*load* a gun⟩ **6 :** to alter by adding an adulterant or drug — **load·er** *n*

load·ed *adj* **1** *slang* **:** DRUNK **2 :** having a large amount of money

load line *n* **:** the line on a ship indicating the depth to which it sinks in the water when properly loaded

load·star *var of* LODESTAR

load·stone *var of* LODESTONE

¹loaf \'lōf\ *n, pl* **loaves** \'lōvz\ [OE *hlāf*] **1 :** a shaped or molded mass of bread **2 :** a regularly molded often rectangular mass: as **a :** a conical mass of sugar **b :** a dish (as of seasoned meat or fish) baked in the form of a loaf

²loaf *vb* **1 :** to spend time in idleness **:** LOUNGE **2 :** to pass idly ⟨*loaf* the time away⟩

loaf·er \'lō-fər\ *n* **:** one that loafs **:** IDLER

Loaf·er \'lō-fər\ *trademark* — used for a low leather step-in shoe with an upper resembling the moccasin but with a broad flat heel

loam \'lōm, 'lüm\ *n* [OE *lām*] **:** SOIL; *esp* **:** a soil consisting of a friable mixture of varying proportions of clay, silt, and sand — **loamy** \'lō-mē, 'lü-\ *adj*

¹loan \'lōn\ *n* [ON *lān*; akin to E *lend*] **1 a :** money let out at interest **b :** something furnished for the borrower's temporary use **2 :** the grant of temporary use

²loan *vt* **:** to give for temporary possession or use **syn** see LEND

loan shark *n* **:** a person who lends money at excessive rates of interest

loan·word \'lōn-ˌwərd\ *n* **:** a word taken from another language and at least partly naturalized

loath \'lōth, 'lōth\ *adj* [OE *lāth* hateful, hostile] **:** unwilling to do something contrary to one's likes, sympathies, or ways of thinking **:** RELUCTANT ⟨was *loath* to run for office against his friend⟩

loathe \'lōth\ *vt* **:** to dislike greatly **:** feel extreme disgust for or at **:** DETEST ⟨*loathe* the smell of burning rubber⟩ **syn** see HATE

loath·ing \'lō-thiŋ\ *n* **:** extreme disgust **:** DETESTATION

¹loath·ly \'lōth-lē, 'lōth-\ *adj* **:** LOATHSOME, REPULSIVE

²loath·ly \'lōth-lē, 'lōth-\ *adv* **:** UNWILLINGLY

loath·some \'lōth-səm, 'lōth-\ *adj* **:** exciting loathing **:** DISGUSTING — **loath·some·ly** *adv* — **loath·some·ness** *n*

¹lob \'läb\ *vb* **lobbed**; **lob·bing** **1 :** to throw, hit, or propel slowly in or as if in a high arc; *esp* **:** to hit a tennis ball easily in a high arc **2 :** to move slowly and heavily

²lob *n* **:** a tennis ball hit slowly in a high arc

lo·ba·tion \lō-'bā-shən\ *n* **1 :** a lobed condition **2 :** a lobed part

¹lob·by \'läb-ē\ *n, pl* **lobbies** [ML *lobium* cloister, portico, of Gmc origin] **1 :** a corridor or hall connected with a larger room or series of rooms and used as a passageway or waiting room: as **a :** an anteroom of a legislative chamber **b :** a large hall serving as a foyer (as of a hotel or theater) **2 :** a group of persons engaged in lobbying esp. as representatives of a particular interest group

²lobby *vb* **lob·bied**; **lob·by·ing** **1 :** to try to influence public officials and esp. members of a legislative body **2 :** to promote or secure the passage of by influencing public officials — **lob·by·ist** \-ē-əst\ *n*

lobe \'lōb\ *n* [Gk *lobos*] **:** a curved or rounded projection or division; *esp* **:** such a subdivision of a bodily organ or part — **lo·bar** \'lō-bər, -ˌbär\ *adj* — **lo·bate** \-ˌbāt\ *or* **lo·bat·ed** \-ˌbāt-əd\ *adj* — **lobed** \'lōbd\ *adj*

lobe-fin \'lōb-ˌfin\ *n* **:** any of a large group (Crossopterygii) of mostly extinct fishes that have paired fins suggesting limbs and may be ancestral to the terrestrial vertebrates — compare LATIMERIA — **lobe-finned** \-'find\ *adj*

lo·be·lia \lō-'bēl-yə\ *n* [NL, fr. Matthias de *Lobel* d1616 Flemish botanist] **:** any of a genus of widely distributed herbs often grown for their terminal clusters of showy lipped flowers

lob·lol·ly pine \ˌläb-ˌläl-ē-\ *n* **:** a pine of the southern U.S. with thick flaky bark, long needles in threes, and spiny-tipped cones; *also* **:** its coarse-grained wood — called also **loblolly**

lob·ster \'läb-stər\ *n* [OE *loppestre*, fr. *loppe* spider] **:** any of several large edible marine crustaceans with stalked eyes, a pair of large claws, and a long abdomen; *also* : SPINY LOBSTER — **lobster** *adj*

lobster pot *n* : a trap for catching lobsters

lob·ule \'läb-yül\ *n* : a small lobe; *also* : a subdivision of a lobe — **lob·u·lar** \'läb-yə-lər\ *adj* — **lob·u·lar·ly** *adv* — **lob·u·late** \-ˌlāt\ *or* **lob·u·lose** \-ˌlōs\ *adj* — **lob·u·la·tion** \ˌläb-yə-'lā-shən\ *n*

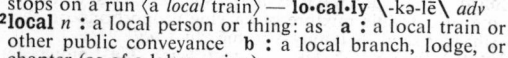

¹**lo·cal** \'lō-kəl\ *adj* [L *locus* place] **1** : characterized by or relating to position in space **2** : characterized by, relating to, or occupying a particular place ⟨*local* news⟩ **3** : not broad or general; *esp* : involving or affecting only a small part of the body ⟨a *local* infection⟩ **4 a** : primarily serving the needs of a particular limited district ⟨*local* government⟩ **b** : making all the stops on a run ⟨a *local* train⟩ — **lo·cal·ly** \-kə-lē\ *adv*

lobster

²**local** *n* : a local person or thing: as **a** : a local train or other public conveyance **b** : a local branch, lodge, or chapter (as of a labor union)

local color *n* : features and peculiarities used in a story or play that suggest a particular locality and its inhabitants

lo·cale \lō-'kal\ *n* **1** : a place or locality that is the setting for a particular event or characteristic **2** : SITE, SCENE

lo·cal·ism \'lō-kə-ˌliz-əm\ *n* **1** : the inclination to be esp. interested in the affairs of one's own locality **2** : a local manner of speech

lo·cal·i·ty \lō-'kal-ət-ē\ *n, pl* **-ties** : a particular spot, situation, or location : NEIGHBORHOOD

lo·cal·ize \'lō-kə-ˌlīz\ *vb* : to make or become local : fix in or assign or confine to a definite place or locality ⟨pain *localized* in a joint⟩ — **lo·cal·i·za·tion** \ˌlō-kə-lə-'zā-shən\ *n*

local option *n* : the power granted by a legislature to a political subdivision to determine by popular vote whether a law on a controversial issue is to apply locally

lo·cate \'lō-ˌkāt, lō-'\ *vb* [L *locare* to place, fr. *locus* place] **1** : to establish oneself or one's business : set or establish in a particular spot : STATION, SETTLE **2** : to determine or indicate the place, site, or limits of **3** : to find or fix the place of in a sequence — **lo·cat·er** *n*

lo·ca·tion \lō-'kā-shən\ *n* **1** : the process of locating **2** : SITUATION, PLACE; *esp* : a locality of or for a building **3** : a tract of land (as a mining claim) whose boundaries and purpose have been designated **4** : a place outside a studio where a motion picture is filmed ⟨on *location* in the desert⟩ — **lo·ca·tion·al** \-shnəl, -shən-°l\ *adj* — **lo·ca·tion·al·ly** \-ē\ *adv*

loc·a·tive \'läk-ət-iv\ *adj* : of, relating to, or constituting a grammatical case denoting place where — **locative** *n*

loch \'läk, 'läⱪ\ *n* [ScGael] **1** *Scot* : LAKE **2** *Scot* : a bay or arm of the sea esp. when nearly landlocked

loci *pl of* LOCUS

¹**lock** \'läk\ *n* [OE *locc*] : a tuft, strand, or ringlet of hair; *also* : a cohering bunch (as of wool, cotton, or flax)

²**lock** *n* [OE *loc*] **1 a** : a fastening (as for a door) in which a bolt is operated (as by a key) **b** : the mechanism for exploding the charge or cartridge of a firearm **2 a** : an enclosure (as in a canal) with gates at each end used in raising or lowering boats as they pass from level to level **b** : AIR LOCK **3** : a hold in wrestling secured on one part of the body ⟨a leg *lock*⟩

³**lock** *vb* **1 a** : to fasten the lock of **b** : to make or become fast with or as if with a lock ⟨*lock* up the house⟩ **2 a** : to make secure or inaccessible by means of locks : CONFINE **b** : to hold fast or inactive : FIX **3 a** : to make fast by the interlacing or interlocking of parts : INTERLACE, INTERLOCK **b** : to hold in a close embrace; *also* : to grapple in combat **4** : to move by raising or lowering in a lock : go or pass by means of a lock (as in a canal)

lock·age \'läk-ij\ *n* **1** : an act or the process of passing a ship through a lock **2** : a system of locks

lock·er \'läk-ər\ *n* **1 a** : a drawer, cabinet, compartment, or chest for personal use usu. with a lock **b** : a storage chest or compartment on shipboard **2** : an insulated compartment for storing frozen food at a low temperature **3** : one that locks

locker room *n* : a room devoted to storage lockers; *esp* : one in which participants in a sport have individual lockers for their clothes and special equipment and change into and out of sports costume

lock·et \'läk-ət\ *n* [MF *loquet* latch, fr. MD *loke*; akin to E ²*lock*] : a small case usu. of precious metal for a memento that is worn typically suspended from a chain or necklace

lock·jaw \'läk-ˌjó\ *n* : a symptom of tetanus characterized by spasm of the jaw muscles and inability to open the jaws; *also* : TETANUS

lock·nut \'läk-ˌnət\ *n* : a nut so constructed that it locks itself when screwed up tight; *also* : one so set as to hold another in place

lock out \(')läk-'aút\ *vt* : to subject (a body of employees) to a lockout

lock·out \'läk-ˌaút\ *n* : the suspension of work or closing of a plant by an employer during a labor dispute in order to make his employees accept his terms

lock·smith \'läk-ˌsmith\ *n* : one who makes or repairs locks

lock·step \'läk-ˌstep\ *n* : a mode of marching in step by a body of men moving in a very close single file

lock·stitch \'läk-ˌstich\ *n* : a sewing machine stitch formed by the looping together of two threads one on each side of the material being sewn

lock·up \'läk-ˌəp\ *n* : JAIL; *esp* : one where persons are detained prior to court hearing

¹**lo·co** \'lō-kō\ *n, pl* **locos** *or* **locoes** **1** : LOCOWEED **2** : LOCOISM

²**loco** *vt* : to poison with locoweed

³**loco** *adj* [Sp] *slang* : out of one's mind : CRAZY

lo·co·ism \'lō-kō-ˌiz-əm\ *n* : a nervous disease of horses, cattle, and sheep caused by chronic poisoning with locoweeds

lo·co·mo·tion \ˌlō-kə-'mō-shən\ *n* [L *loco* in place (fr. *locus* place) + E *motion*] **1** : the act or power of moving from place to place **2** : TRAVEL

¹**lo·co·mo·tive** \ˌlō-kə-'mōt-iv\ *adj* **1 a** : of, relating to, or functioning in locomotion **b** : having the ability to move independently from place to place **2** : of or relating to travel **3** : of, relating to, or being a machine that moves under its own power — **lo·co·mo·tive·ness** *n*

²**locomotive** *n* **1** : an engine that moves under its own power; *esp* : one that hauls cars on a railroad **2 a** : a school or college cheer characterized by a slow beginning and a progressive increase in speed

lo·co·mo·tor \ˌlō-kə-'mōt-ər\ *adj* **1** : LOCOMOTIVE 1 **2** : affecting or involving the locomotive organs

locomotor ataxia *n* : a syphilitic disorder of the nervous system marked esp. by disturbances of gait and difficulty in coordinating voluntary movements

lo·co·weed \'lō-kō-ˌwēd\ *n* : any of several leguminous plants of western No. America that cause locoism in livestock

loc·ule \'läk-yül\ *n* : LOCULUS; *esp* : any of the cells of a compound ovary of a plant — **loc·uled** \-yüld\ *adj*

loc·u·lus \'läk-yə-ləs\ *n, pl* **-li** \-ˌlī, -ˌlē\ [NL, fr. L, dim. of *locus* place] : a small chamber or cavity esp. in a plant or animal body — compare LOCULE — **loc·u·lar** \-lər\ *adj* — **loc·u·late** \-lət\ *adj* — **loc·u·la·tion** \ˌläk-yə-'lā-shən\ *n*

lo·cum te·nens \ˌlō-kəm-'tē-ˌnenz\ *n, pl* **locum te·nen·tes** \-tə-'nen-ˌtēz\ [ML, lit., one holding a place] : one filling an office for a time or temporarily taking the place of another — used esp. of a doctor or clergyman

lo·cus \'lō-kəs\ *n, pl* **lo·ci** \'lō-ˌsī\ [L] **1** : PLACE, LOCALITY **2** : the set of all points whose location is determined by stated conditions

lo·cus clas·si·cus \ˌlō-kəs-'klas-i-kəs\ *n, pl* **lo·ci clas·si·ci** \ˌlō-ˌsī-'klas-ə-ˌsī\ [L] : a standard passage important for the elucidation of a word or subject

lo·cust \'lō-kəst\ *n* [L *locusta*] **1 a** : SHORT-HORNED GRASSHOPPER; *esp* : a migratory grasshopper often traveling in vast swarms and stripping the areas passed of vegetation **b** : CICADA **2 a** : any of various hard-wooded leguminous trees **b** : the wood of a locust

lo·cu·tion \lō-'kyü-shən\ *n* [L *locut-, loqui* to speak] **1** : a particular form of expression or a peculiarity of phrasing ⟨involved *locutions*⟩ **2** : style of discourse : PHRASEOLOGY

lode \'lōd\ *n* [OE *lād* way, course] **1** : a mass or strip of a mineral (as gold or copper ore) that fills a crack in rock **2** : a mass of ore in the earth or among rocks

lode·star \-,stär\ *n* [ME *lode* way, course, fr. OE *lād*] **1** : a star that leads or guides; *esp* : NORTH STAR **2** : something that serves as a guiding star

lode·stone \-,stōn\ *n* **1** : magnetite having magnetic properties **2** : something that strongly attracts

¹lodge \'läj\ *vb* **1 a** : to provide temporary quarters for **b** : to establish or settle oneself in a place : SLEEP, DWELL **c** : to rent lodgings to **2** : to serve as a receptacle for : CONTAIN **3** : to bring (as by throwing or thrusting) to an intended or a fixed position : come to a rest and remain ⟨the bone *lodged* in his throat⟩ **4** : to deposit for safeguard or preservation **5** : to place or vest esp. in a source, means, or agent **6** : to lay (as a complaint) before a proper authority : FILE **7** : to fall or become beaten down ⟨the tall grass *lodged* in the storm⟩

²lodge *n* [OF *loge*, of Gmc origin] **1** *chiefly dial* : a rude shelter or abode **2 a** : a house set apart for residence in a special season ⟨hunting *lodge*⟩ **b** : an inn or resort hotel **3 a** : a house on an estate orig. for the use of a gamekeeper, caretaker, or porter **b** : a shelter for an employee (as a porter) of an institution **4** : a den or lair esp. of a group of gregarious animals **5** : the meeting place of a branch (as of a fraternal organization); *also* : the members of such a branch **6 a** : WIGWAM **b** : a family of No. American Indians

lodge·pole pine \,läj-,pōl-\ *n* : either of two western No. American pines with needles in pairs and short irregular cones

lodg·er \'läj-ər\ *n* : one that lodges; *esp* : one that occupies a rented room in another's house

lodg·ing \'läj-iŋ\ *n* **1** : DWELLING; *esp* : a temporary dwelling or sleeping place **2** : a room or suite of rooms in the house of another person rented as a dwelling place — usu. used in pl.

lodging house *n* : ROOMING HOUSE

lodg·ment *or* **lodge·ment** \'läj-mənt\ *n* **1 a** : a lodging place : SHELTER **b** : ACCOMMODATIONS, LODGINGS **2 a** : the act, fact, or manner of lodging **b** : a placing, depositing, or coming to rest **3 a** : an accumulation or collection of something deposited in a place ⟨a *lodgment* of leaves in a gutter⟩ **b** : a place of rest or deposit

loess \'les, 'lə(r)s, 'lō-əs\ *n* [G *löss*] : a usu. yellowish brown loamy deposit found in No. America, Europe, and Asia and believed to be chiefly deposited by the wind — **loess·ial** \'les-ē-əl, 'lə(r)s-, lō-'es-\ *adj*

¹loft \'loft\ *n* [ON *lopt* air, sky, loft] **1** : a room or floor above another : ATTIC **2 a** : a gallery in a church or hall ⟨organ *loft*⟩ **b** : an upper floor of a warehouse or business building esp. when not partitioned **c** : HAYLOFT **3 a** : the backward slant of the face of a golf-club head **b** : the act of lofting **c** : HEIGHT ⟨the ball had too much *loft* to reach the green⟩

²loft *vb* **1** : to place, house, or store in a loft **2** : to strike or throw a ball so that it rises high in the air ⟨*lofted* a high fly to center field⟩

lofty \'lof-tē\ *adj* **loft·i·er; -est 1** : having a haughty overbearing manner : SUPERCILIOUS ⟨a *lofty* air⟩ **2 a** : elevated in character and spirit : NOBLE ⟨*lofty* ideals⟩ **b** : elevated in position : SUPERIOR **3 a** : rising high in the air : TOWERING ⟨a *lofty* oak⟩ **b** : REMOTE, ESOTERIC — **loft·i·ly** \-tə-lē\ *adv* — **loft·i·ness** \-tē-nəs\ *n*

¹log \'log, 'läg\ *n* [ME *logge*] **1** : a bulky piece of unshaped timber; *esp* : a long piece of a tree trunk trimmed and ready for sawing **2** : an apparatus for measuring the rate of a ship's motion through the water that consists of a block fastened to a line and run out from a reel **3 a** : the daily record of a ship's speed and progress **b** : the full record of a ship's voyage or of an aircraft's flight **4** : a record of performance (as the operating history of an airplane or a piece of equipment, the flying time of a pilot, or a report on the construction of something) — **log** *adj*

²log *vb* **logged; log·ging 1** : to cut trees for lumber or to clear land of trees in lumbering **2** : to enter details of or about in a log **3 a** : to move (an indicated distance) or attain (an indicated speed) as noted in a log **b** (1) : to sail a ship or fly an airplane for (an indicated distance or an indicated period of time) ⟨the pilot *logged* thousands

of miles and hundreds of hours⟩ (2) : to have (an indicated record) to one's credit ⟨he *logged* many hours on combat missions⟩

³log *n* : LOGARITHM

lo·gan·ber·ry \'lō-gən-,ber-ē\ *n* [after James H. *Logan* d1928 American lawyer] : a red-fruited upright-growing and prob. hybrid dewberry; *also* : its berry

log·a·rithm \'log-ə-,rith-əm, 'läg-\ *n* [NL *logarithmus*, fr. Gk *logos* reckoning, ratio + *arithmos* number] : the exponent that indicates the power to which a number is raised to produce a given number ⟨the *logarithm* of 100 to the base 10 is 2⟩

log·a·rith·mic \,log-ə-'rith-mik, ,läg-\ *adj* : relating to, based on, or characteristic of logarithms ⟨*logarithmic* spiral⟩

log·book \'log-,bùk, 'läg-\ *n* : LOG 3, 4

loge \'lōzh\ *n* [F, lodge, loge] **1 a** : a small compartment : BOOTH **b** : a box in a theater **2 a** : a small partitioned area **b** : the forward section of a theater mezzanine

logged \'logd, 'lägd\ *adj* **1** : made heavy or sluggish so that movement is impossible or difficult **2** : made sodden; *esp* : WATERLOGGED

log·ger \'log-ər, 'läg-\ *n* : one engaged in logging

log·ger·head \'log-ər-,hed, 'läg-\ *n* **1** *chiefly dial* : BLOCKHEAD **2** : any of various very large turtles; *esp* : a carnivorous sea turtle of the warmer parts of the western Atlantic — **at loggerheads** : in or into a state of quarrelsome disagreement

log·gia \'läj-(ē-)ə\ *n* [It, fr. F *loge* lodge] : a roofed gallery open on at least one side

log·ic \'läj-ik\ *n* [Gk *logikē*, fr. *logos* speech, reason, reckoning, fr. *legein* to gather, speak] **1** : a science that deals with the rules and tests of sound thinking and proof by reasoning **2** : REASONING; *esp* : sound reasoning ⟨no *logic* in that remark⟩ **3** : connection (as of facts or events) in a way that seems reasonable ⟨the *logic* of a situation⟩ — **lo·gi·cian** \lō-'jish-ən\ *n*

log·i·cal \'läj-i-kəl\ *adj* **1** : of or relating to logic : used in logic **2** : conforming to or consistent with the rules of logic ⟨a *logical* argument⟩ **3** : skilled in logic ⟨a *logical* thinker⟩ **4** : being in accordance with what may be reasonably expected ⟨a *logical* result of an action⟩ — **log·i·cal·ly** \-k-(ə-)lē\ *adv* — **log·i·cal·ness** \-kəl-nəs\ *n*

lo·gis·tics \lō-'jis-tiks\ *n sing or pl* [F *logistique*, lit., art of calculating, fr. Gk *logizein* to calculate, fr. *logos* reckoning] : a branch of military science that deals with the transportation, quartering, and supplying of troops in military operations — **lo·gis·tic** \-tik\ *or* **lo·gis·ti·cal** \-ti-kəl\ *adj* — **lo·gis·ti·cal·ly** \-ti-k(ə-)lē\ *adv*

log·jam \'log-,jam, 'läg-\ *n* **1** : a deadlocked jumble of logs in a watercourse **2** : DEADLOCK

Lo·gos \'lō-,gäs\ *n* [Gk, speech, word, reason] : the divine wisdom manifest in the creation, government, and redemption of the world and often identified with the second person of the Trinity

log·roll·ing \'log-,rō-liŋ, 'läg-\ *n* **1** : the rolling of logs in water by treading; *also* : a sport in which men treading logs try to dislodge one another **2** : the exchanging of assistance or favors; *esp* : the trading of votes by legislators to secure favorable action on projects of interest to each one — **log·roll·er** \-,rō-lər\ *n*

-logue *or* **-log** \,log\ *n comb form* [OF *-logue*, fr. Gk *-logos*, fr. *legein* to speak] **1** : discourse : talk ⟨duo*logue*⟩ **2** : student : specialist ⟨sino*logue*⟩

log·wood \'log-,wùd, 'läg-\ *n* : a Central American and West Indian leguminous tree; *also* : its hard brown or brownish red heartwood used in dyeing or an extract of this

lo·gy \'lō-gē\ *adj* **lo·gi·er; -est** : marked by sluggishness and lack of vitality — **lo·gi·ly** \-gə-lē\ *adv* — **lo·gi·ness** \-gē-nəs\ *n*

-l·o·gy \l-ə-jē\ *n comb form* [Gk *-logia*, fr. *logos* speech, reason] **1** : oral or written expression ⟨phraseo*logy*⟩ **2** : doctrine : theory : science ⟨ethno*logy*⟩

Lo·hen·grin \'lō-ən-,grin\ *n* : a son of Parsifal and knight of the Holy Grail in German legend

loin \'loin\ *n* [MF *loigne*, fr. (assumed) VL *lumbea*, fr. L *lumbus*] **1 a** : the part of the body on each side of the spinal column and between the hip and the lower ribs **b** : a cut of meat comprising this part of one or both sides of a carcass with the adjoining half of the vertebrae included but without the flank **2** *pl* **a :** the pubic region **b :** the generative organs

loin·cloth \-,klòth\ *n* **:** a cloth worn about the loins often as the sole article of clothing in warm climates

loi·ter \'lóit-ǝr\ *vi* [ME *loiteren*] **1 :** to interrupt or delay an errand or a journey with aimless idle stops and pauses **:** LINGER **2 a :** to hang around idly **b :** to lag behind — **loi·ter·er** \-ǝr-ǝr\ *n*

loll \'läl\ *vb* [ME *lollen*] **1 :** to hang or let hang loosely or laxly **:** DROOP, DANGLE **2 :** to recline, lean, or move in a lax, lazy, or indolent manner **:** LOUNGE ⟨*loll* around in the sun⟩

Lol·lard \'läl-ǝrd\ *n* [MD *lollaert*, fr. *lollen* to mumble, doze] **:** a follower of Wycliffe in the 14th and 15th centuries — **Lol·lard·ism** \-ǝr-,diz-ǝm\ *n* — **Lol·lardy** \-ǝrd-ē\ *n*

lol·li·pop *or* **lol·ly·pop** \'läl-ē-,päp\ *n* **:** a lump of hard candy on the end of a stick

Lom·bard \'läm-,bärd, -bǝrd\ *n* **1 :** a member of a Teutonic people invading Italy in A.D. 568 and establishing a kingdom in the Po valley **2 :** a native of Lombardy or of the Kingdom of the Lombards

lo·ment \'lō-,ment, -mǝnt\ *n* **:** a fruit resembling a legume but breaking transversely into segments at maturity

lone \'lōn\ *adj* [ME, short for *alone*] **1 a :** having no company **:** SOLITARY ⟨a *lone* traveler⟩ **b :** preferring solitude ⟨*lone* hermits⟩ **2 :** ONLY, SOLE ⟨the *lone* theater in town⟩ **3 :** situated by itself **:** ISOLATED ⟨*lone* outpost⟩ — **lone·ness** \'lōn-nǝs\ *n*

lone·ly \'lōn-lē\ *adj* **lone·li·er; -est 1 :** being without company **:** LONE ⟨a *lonely* hiker⟩ **2 :** UNFREQUENTED, DESOLATE ⟨a *lonely* spot⟩ **3 :** LONESOME ⟨feeling *lonely*⟩ **syn** see ALONE — **lone·li·ness** *n*

lone·some \'lōn(t)-sǝm\ *adj* **1 :** sad from lack of companionship or separation from others **2 a :** REMOTE, UNFREQUENTED **b :** LONE **syn** see ALONE — **lone·some·ly** *adv* — **lone·some·ness** *n*

¹long \'lòŋ\ *adj* **long·er** \'lòŋ-gǝr\; **long·est** \'lòŋ-gǝst\ [OE *lang, long*] **1 a :** extending for a considerable distance **b :** having greater length than usual **c :** having greater height than usual **:** TALL **d :** having a greater length than breadth **:** ELONGATED **e :** having a greater length than desirable or necessary **2 a :** having a specified length **b :** forming the chief linear dimension **3 a :** extending over a considerable time **b :** having a specified duration **c :** prolonged beyond the usual time **:** TEDIOUS **4 a :** containing many items in a series **b :** having a specified number of units **c :** consisting of a greater number or amount than usual **:** LARGE **5 a :** being a syllable or speech sound of relatively great duration **b :** being the member of a pair of similarly spelled vowel or vowel-containing sounds that is descended from a vowel long in duration ⟨*long a* in *fate*⟩ ⟨*long i* in *sign*⟩ **6 :** having the capacity to reach or extend a considerable distance **7 :** larger or longer than the standard **8 a :** extending far into the future **b :** extending beyond what is known **9 :** strong in or well furnished with something **10 a :** of an unusual degree of difference between the amounts wagered on each side **b :** of or relating to the larger amount wagered **11 :** subject to great odds **12 :** holding securities or goods in anticipation of an advance in prices — **at long last :** after a long wait **:** FINALLY — **long in the tooth :** past one's best days **:** OLD

²long *adv* **1 :** for or during a long time **2 :** at or to a long distance **:** FAR ⟨*long*-traveled⟩ **3 :** for the duration of a specified period **4 :** at a point of time far before or after a specified moment or event **5 :** after or beyond a specified time — **as long as** *or* **so long as 1 :** in view of the fact that **:** SINCE **2 :** PROVIDED, IF — **so long :** GOOD-BYE

³long *n* **1 :** a long period of time **2 :** a long syllable **3 :** one who buys and holds goods or securities in anticipation of a rise in prices **4** *pl* **:** long trousers — **the long and short** *or* **the long and the short :** the sum and substance **:** GIST

⁴long *vi* **longed; long·ing** \'lòŋ-iŋ\ [OE *langian;* akin to E **¹long**] **:** to feel a strong desire or wish **:** YEARN

syn LONG, YEARN, HANKER, PINE mean to have a strong desire for something. LONG implies wishing with one's whole heart and often striving to attain; YEARN suggests an eager, restless, or painful longing ⟨*yearned* to be understood⟩ HANKER suggests somewhat disparagingly an uneasiness due to an unsatisfied and often unreasonable

appetite or desire ⟨*hankered* for fresh fruits⟩ PINE implies a languishing or fruitless longing

long·boat \'lòŋ-,bōt\ *n* **:** a large boat carried on a ship

long bone *n* **:** one of the bones supporting a vertebrate limb and consisting of a long nearly cylindrical shaft that contains marrow and ends in enlarged heads for articulation with other bones

long·bow \'lòŋ-,bō\ *n* **:** a wooden bow drawn by hand and usu. 5½ to 6 feet long

¹long–dis·tance \-'dis-tǝn(t)s\ *adj* **:** of or relating to telephone communication with a distant point

²long–distance *adv* **:** by long-distance telephone

long distance *n* **1 :** communication by long-distance telephone **2 :** a telephone operator or exchange that gives long-distance connections

long division *n* **:** arithmetical division in which the several steps corresponding to the division of parts of the dividend by the divisor are indicated in detail

lon·gev·i·ty \län-'jev-ǝt-ē, lòn-\ *n* [L *longaevus* long-lived, fr. *longus* long + *aevum* age] **1 :** a long duration of individual life **2 :** length of life

long·hair \'lòŋ-,ha(ǝ)r, -,he(ǝ)r\ *n* **1 :** a person of artistic gifts or interests; *esp* **:** a lover of classical music **2 :** an impractical intellectual — **long–hair** *or* **long–haired** \-'ha(ǝ)rd, -'he(ǝ)rd\ *adj*

long·hand \-,hand\ *n* **:** the characters used in ordinary writing **:** HANDWRITING

long–head·ed \-'hed-ǝd\ *adj* **1 :** having unusual foresight or wisdom **2 :** DOLICHOCEPHALIC — **long·head·ed·ness** *n*

long·horn \'lòŋ-,hòrn\ *n* **:** any of the long-horned cattle of Spanish derivation formerly common in southwestern U.S.

long–horned \-'hòrnd\ *adj* **:** having long horns or antennae

long·house \-,haùs\ *n* **:** a communal dwelling of the Iroquois

lon·gi·corn \'län-jǝ-,kòrn\ *adj* **:** having long antennae ⟨*longicorn* beetles⟩

long·ing \'lòŋ-iŋ\ *n* **:** an eager desire esp. for something unattainable **:** CRAVING ⟨had a *longing* to visit Europe⟩ — **long·ing·ly** \-iŋ-lē\ *adv*

long·ish \'lòŋ-ish\ *adj* **:** somewhat long

lon·gi·tude \'län-jǝ-,t(y)üd\ *n* [L *longitudin-, longitudo* length, fr. *longus* long; akin to E *long*] **:** distance measured by degrees or time east or west from the prime meridian ⟨the *longitude* of New York is 74 degrees or about five hours west of Greenwich⟩

lon·gi·tu·di·nal \,län-jǝ-'t(y)üd-nǝl, -°n-ǝl\ *adj* **1 :** of or relating to length or the lengthwise dimension **2 :** placed or running lengthwise — **lon·gi·tu·di·nal·ly** \-ē\ *adv*

long–leaf pine \,lòŋ-,lēf\ *also* **long–leaved pine** \-,lēv(d)-\ *n* **:** a large pine of the southern U.S. with long slim clustered needles and long cones that is a major timber tree; *also* **:** its tough coarse-grained durable wood

hemisphere marked with meridians of longitude

long–lived \'lòŋ-'līvd, -'livd\ *adj* **:** living or lasting long — **long–lived·ness** \-'līv(d)-nǝs, -'liv(d)-\ *n*

Lon·go·bard \'lòŋ-gǝ-,bärd, 'läŋ-\ *n, pl* **Longobards** *or* **Lon·go·bar·di** \,lòŋ-gǝ-'bär-,dī, ,läŋ-\ **:** LOMBARD — **Lon·go·bar·dic** \,lòŋ-gǝ-'bärd-ik, ,läŋ-\ *adj*

long–play·ing \'lòŋ-'plā-iŋ\ *adj* **:** of, relating to, or being an LP record

long–range \-'rānj\ *adj* **1 :** capable of traveling or shooting over great distances ⟨a *long-range* gun⟩ **2 :** lasting over or taking into account a long period **:** LONG-TERM 1 ⟨*long-range* planning⟩

long·shore·man \'lòŋ-'shòr-mǝn, -'shòr-\ *n* [*longshore* existing along the seacoast, short for *alongshore*] **:** a laborer at a wharf who loads and unloads cargo

long shot \'lòŋ-,shät\ *n* **1 :** an entry (as in a horse race) given little chance of winning **2 :** a bet in which the chances of winning are slight but the possible winnings great **3 :** a venture involving great risk but promising a great reward if successful — **by a long shot :** by a great deal

long·sight·ed \-'sīt-əd\ *adj* : FARSIGHTED — **long·sight·ed·ness** *n*

long·some \'loṅ-səm\ *adj* : tediously long — **long·some·ly** *adv* — **long·some·ness** *n*

long-suf·fer·ing \-'səf-(ə-)riṅ\ *or* **long-suf·fer·ance** \-(ə-)rən(t)s\ *n* : long and patient endurance of offense — **long-suffering** *adj* — **long-suf·fer·ing·ly** \-(ə-)riṅ-lē\ *adv*

long suit *n* **1** : a holding of more than the average number of cards in a suit **2** : the activity or quality in which a person excels

long-term \'loṅ-'tərm\ *adj* **1** : extending over or involving a long period of time **2** : constituting a financial obligation based on a term usu. of more than 10 years ⟨*long-term* mortgage⟩

lon·gueur \'lōⁿ-gœr\ *n, pl* **longueurs** \-gœr(z)\ [F, lit., length] : a dull and tedious passage or section

long-wind·ed \'loṅ-'win-dəd\ *adj* **1** : not easily subject to loss of breath **2** : tediously long in speaking or writing — **long-wind·ed·ly** *adv* — **long-wind·ed·ness** *n*

loo \'lü\ *n* **1** : an old card game **2** : money staked at loo

¹look \'luk\ *vb* [OE *lōcian*] **1** : to ascertain by the use of one's eyes **2** : to exercise the power of vision upon : EXAMINE, SEE **3** : EXPECT ⟨we *look* to see him soon⟩ **4** : to express by the eyes or facial expression **5** : to have an appearance that befits or accords with **6** : to have the appearance of being : SEEM **7** : to direct one's attention or eyes **8** : to have a specified outlook ⟨the house *looks* east⟩ **9** : to gaze in wonder or surprise : STARE **10** : to show a tendency ⟨the evidence *looks* to acquittal⟩ — **look after** : to take care of : attend to — **look for 1** : to await with hope or anticipation : EXPECT **2** : to search for : SEEK — **look on** *or* **look upon** : CONSIDER, REGARD ⟨*looked upon* him as a friend⟩

²look *n* **1 a** : the action of looking **b** : GLANCE **2 a** : the expression of the countenance **b** : physical appearance; *esp* : attractive physical appearance — usu. used in pl. **3** : the state or form in which something appears : ASPECT

look·er-on \ˌluk-ər-'ȯn, -'än\ *n, pl* **lookers-on** : ONLOOKER, SPECTATOR

looking glass *n* : MIRROR

look·out \'luk-ˌaut\ *n* **1** : a person engaged in watching; *esp* : one assigned to watch (as on a ship) **2** : an elevated place or structure affording a wide view for observation **3** : a careful looking or watching **4** : VIEW, OUTLOOK **5** : a matter of care or concern

¹loom \'lüm\ *n* [ME *lome*, fr. OE *gelōma* tool] : a frame or machine for weaving together threads or yarns into cloth

²loom *vi* **1** : to come into sight in an unnaturally large, indistinct, or distorted form ⟨*loomed* out of the fog⟩ **2 a** : to appear in an impressively great or exaggerated form **b** : to take shape as an impending occurrence

¹loon \'lün\ *n* [of Scand origin] : any of several fish-eating diving birds with webbed feet, black head, and white-spotted black back

²loon *n* : a person of dull or disordered mind : LUNATIC

loo·ny *or* **loo·ney** \'lü-nē\ *adj* **loo·ni·er; -est** [by shortening & alter. fr. *lunatic*] : CRAZY, FOOLISH — **loony** *n*

¹loop \'lüp\ *n* [ME *loupe*] **1** : a fold or doubling of a line leaving an aperture between the parts through which another line can be passed or into which a hook may be hooked; *also* : such a fold of cord or ribbon serving as an ornament **2** : a loop-shaped figure, bend, or course ⟨a *loop* in a river⟩ **3** : a circular airplane maneuver involving flying upside down **4 a** : the portion of a vibrating body between two nodes **b** : the middle point of such a portion **5** : a complete electric circuit — **for a loop** : into a state of amazement, confusion, or distress ⟨the news knocked her *for a loop*⟩

²loop *vb* **1** : to make or form a loop **2 a** : to make a loop in, on, or about **b** : to fasten with a loop **3** : to execute a loop in an airplane

loop·er \'lü-pər\ *n* **1** : any of numerous small hairless caterpillars that are mostly larvae of moths and move with a looping movement **2** : one that loops

loop·hole \'lüp-ˌhōl\ *n* **1 a** : a small opening in a wall through which small firearms may be discharged **b** : a small opening to admit light and air or to permit observation **2** : a means of escape; *esp* : an ambiguity or omission in the wording of a statute, contract, or obligation through which the statute, contract, or obligation may be evaded

¹loose \'lüs\ *adj* [ON *lauss*] **1 a** : not rigidly fastened or securely attached **b** (1) : having worked partly free from attachments (2) : having relative freedom of movement **c** : not tight-fitting **2 a** : free from a state of confinement, restraint, or obligation **b** : not brought together in a bundle, container, or binding **c** *archaic* : DISCONNECTED, DETACHED **3** : not dense or compact in structure or arrangement; *also* : marked by softness and moistness **4 a** : lacking in restraint or power of restraint **b** : LEWD, UNCHASTE **5 a** : not tightly drawn or stretched : SLACK **b** : having a flexible or relaxed character **6** : lacking in precision, exactness, or care — **loose·ly** *adv* — **loose·ness** *n*

²loose *vb* **1 a** : to let loose : RELEASE **b** : to free from restraint **2 a** : to make loose : UNTIE ⟨*loose* a knot⟩ **b** *archaic* : DISSOLVE **3** : to cast loose : DETACH **4** : to let fly : DISCHARGE, FIRE **5** : to make less rigid, tight, or strict : RELAX, SLACKEN

³loose *adv* : LOOSELY

loose constructionist *n* : one favoring a liberal interpretation of the U.S. Constitution as granting broad implied powers to the federal government

loose end *n* **1** : something left hanging loose **2** : a fragment of unfinished business — **at loose ends** : uncertain of one's future course of action : UNSETTLED

loose-joint·ed \'lüs-'jȯint-əd\ *adj* : having a flexibility or lack of rigidity suggesting the absence of rigid joints; *esp* : moving with unusual freedom or ease — **loose-joint·ed·ness** *n*

loos·en \'lüs-ᵊn\ *vb* **loos·ened; loos·en·ing** \'lüs-niṅ, -ᵊn-iṅ\ **1** : to release from restraint **2** : to make or become loose or looser **3** : to cause or permit to become less strict

loose sentence *n* : a sentence in which the principal clause comes first and the latter part contains subordinate modifiers or trailing elements

loose·strife \'lü(s)-ˌstrīf\ *n* **1** : any of a genus of plants of the primrose family with leafy stems and yellow or white flowers **2** : any of a genus of herbs including some with showy spikes of purple flowers

¹loot \'lüt\ *n* [Hindi *lūt*] **1** : goods taken in war : SPOILS, PLUNDER **2** : something stolen or taken by force or violence **3** : the action of looting

²loot *vb* **1** : to plunder or sack in war **2** : to rob or steal esp. on a large scale and by violence or corruption **3** : to seize and carry away by force esp. in war — **loot·er** *n*

¹lop \'läp\ *vt* **lopped; lop·ping** [ME *loppe* small branches and twigs cut from a tree] **1 a** : to cut branches or twigs from : TRIM ⟨*lop* a tree⟩ **b** : to cut or shear from a woody plant ⟨*lop* dead branches⟩ **2 a** : to remove superfluous parts from **b** : to eliminate as unnecessary or undesirable — usu. used with *off* — **lop·per** *n*

²lop *vi* **lopped; lop·ping** : to hang downward; *also* : to flop or sway loosely

¹lope \'lōp\ *n* [ON *hlaup;* akin to E *leap*] **1** : an easy natural gait of a horse resembling a canter **2** : an easy bounding gait (as of a wolf)

²lope *vi* : to go, move, or ride at a lope — **lop·er** *n*

lop-eared \'läp-ˌi(ə)rd\ *adj* : having ears that droop

loph·o·phore \'läf-ə-ˌfōr, -ˌfȯr\ *n* [Gk *lophos* crest] : a circular or horseshoe-shaped organ about the mouth of a brachiopod or bryozoan that bears tentacles and functions esp. in food-getting

lop·py \'läp-ē\ *adj* **lop·pi·er; -est** : hanging loose : LIMP

lop-sid·ed \'läp-'sīd-əd\ *adj* **1** : leaning to one side **2** : lacking in balance, symmetry, or proportion — **lop-sid·ed·ly** *adv* — **lop-sid·ed·ness** *n*

lo·qua·cious \lō-'kwā-shəs\ *adj* [L *loquac-, loquax,* fr. *loqui* to speak] : given to excessive talking : GARRULOUS — **lo·qua·cious·ly** *adv* — **lo·qua·cious·ness** *n* — **lo·quac·i·ty** \-'kwas-ət-ē\ *n*

lo·quat \'lō-ˌkwät\ *n* [Chin (Cant) *lō-kwat*] : a small Asiatic evergreen tree bearing a yellow plumlike fruit; *also* : its fruit used esp. in preserves

¹lord \'lȯrd\ *n* [OE *hlāford*, fr. *hlāf* loaf + *weard* keeper, ward] **1** : one having power and authority over others: **a** : a ruler to whom service and obedience are due **b** : a person from whom a feudal fee or estate is held **c** : HUSBAND **2** *cap* **a** : ²GOD **b** : CHRIST **3** : a man of rank or high position: as **a** : a feudal tenant holding directly of the king **b** : a British nobleman or a bishop in the Church of England entitled to sit in the House of Lords — used as a title **c** *pl, cap* : HOUSE OF LORDS

²**lord** *vi* : to play the lord — DOMINEER — used with *it*

lord chancellor *n, pl* **lords chancellor** : a British officer of state who presides over the House of Lords, serves as the head of the British judiciary, and is usu. a leading member of the cabinet

lord·ly \'lord-lē\ *adj* **lord·li·er; -est** **1 a** : of, relating to, or having the characteristics of a lord : DIGNIFIED **b** : GRAND, NOBLE **2** : exhibiting pride or superiority : HAUGHTY — **lord·li·ness** *n* — **lordly** *adv*

lord of misrule : a master of Christmas revels in England esp. in the 15th and 16th centuries

lor·do·sis \lor-'dō-səs\ *n* [Gk *lordos* curving forward] : abnormal curvature of the spine forward — **lor·dot·ic** \-'dät-ik\ *adj*

Lord's day *n, often cap D* : SUNDAY

lord·ship \'lord-,ship\ *n* **1** : the rank or dignity of a lord — used as a title ⟨his *Lordship* is not at home⟩ **2** : the authority, power, or territory of a lord

Lord's Prayer *n* : the prayer in Matthew 6:9–13 that Christ taught his disciples

Lord's Supper *n* : COMMUNION 2a

Lord's table *n, often cap T* : ALTAR 2

¹**lore** \'lō(ə)r, 'lȯ(ə)r\ *n* [OE *lār* teaching] **1** : something that is learned: **a** : knowledge gained through study or experience **b** : traditional knowledge or belief **2** : a particular body of knowledge or tradition ⟨forest *lore*⟩

²**lore** *n* [NL *lorum*, fr. L thong, rein] : the space between the eye and bill in a bird or the corresponding region in a reptile or fish — **lor·al** \'lōr-əl, 'lȯr-\ *or* **lo·re·al** \'lōr-ē-əl, 'lȯr-\ *adj*

Lo·re·lei \'lōr-ə-,lī, 'lȯr-\ *n* : a siren in German legend whose beauty and song lured sailors to destruction on a reef in the Rhine

lor·gnette \lȯrn-'yet\ *n* [F, fr. *lorgner* to take a sidelong look at, fr. *lorgne* cross-eyed] : a pair of eyeglasses or opera glasses with a handle

lo·ri·ca \lə-'rī-kə\ *n, pl* **-cae** \-,kē, -,sē\ *or* **-cas** \-kəz\ **1** : a Roman cuirass of leather or metal **2** : a hard protective case or shell (as of a rotifer) — **lor·i·cate** \'lȯr-i-kət, 'lȯr-ə-,kāt, 'lär-\ *or* **lor·i·cat·ed** \-ə-,kāt-əd\ *adj*

lor·i·keet \'lȯr-ə-,kēt, 'lär-\ *n* [*lory*, a parrot of Australia + *-keet* (as in *parrakeet*)] : any of numerous small arboreal parrots of Australasia that feed chiefly on nectar

lo·ris \'lōr-əs, 'lȯr-\ *n* [F] : either of two small nocturnal slow-moving lemurs

lorn \'lȯrn\ *adj* [ME, fr. *loren, lorn*, pp. of *lesen* to lose, fr. OE *lēosan;* akin to E *lose*] : FORSAKEN, DESOLATE — **lorn·ness** \'lȯrn-nəs\ *n*

lor·ry \'lȯr-ē, 'lär-\ *n, pl* **lorries** **1** : a large low horse-drawn wagon without sides **2** *Brit* : a motor truck esp. if open

lose \'lüz\ *vb* **lost** \'lȯst\; **los·ing** \'lü-ziŋ\ [OE *losian* to get lost, perish, lose] **1** : to bring to destruction ⟨ship was *lost* on the reef⟩ **2** : to miss from one's possession or customary place ⟨*lose* a billfold⟩ **3** : to suffer deprivation of esp. in an unforeseen or accidental manner ⟨*lose* his eyesight⟩ **4 a** : to suffer loss through the death or removal of or final separation from (a person) **b** : to fail to keep control of or allegiance of ⟨*lose* votes⟩ **5 a** : to fail to use : let slip by : WASTE ⟨*lose* the tide⟩ **b** : to fail to win, gain, or obtain ⟨*lose* a prize⟩ ⟨*lose* a contest⟩ : undergo defeat ⟨*lose* with good grace⟩ **c** : to fail to catch with the senses or the mind ⟨*lost* part of what he said⟩ **6** : to cause the loss of ⟨one careless statement *lost* him the election⟩ **7** : to fail to keep, sustain, or maintain ⟨*lost* his balance⟩ **8 a** : to cause to miss one's way or bearings ⟨*lost* himself in the maze of streets⟩ **b** : to make (oneself) withdraw from immediate reality ⟨*lost* himself in daydreaming⟩ **9 a** : to wander or go astray from ⟨*lost* his way⟩ **b** : OUTSTRIP ⟨*lost* his pursuers⟩ **10** : to fail to keep in sight or in mind **11** : to free oneself from : get rid of ⟨*dieting* to *lose* some weight⟩ — **lose ground** : to suffer loss or disadvantage : fail to advance or improve — **lose one's heart** : to fall in love

lose out *vi* : to fail to win in competition : fail to receive an expected reward or gain

los·er \'lü-zər\ *n* : one that loses

loss \'lȯs\ *n* [ME *los*] **1 a** : the act of losing **b** : the harm or privation resulting from losing ⟨her death was a *loss* to the community⟩ **c** : an instance of losing **2 a** : a person or thing or an amount that is lost **b** *pl* : killed, wounded, or captured soldiers **3** : failure to gain, win, obtain, or utilize : *esp* : an amount by which the cost of an article or service exceeds the selling price **4** : decrease in amount, magnitude, or degree **5** : DESTRUCTION, RUIN — **at a loss** : PUZZLED, UNCERTAIN — **for a loss** : into a state of distress

loss leader *n* : an article sold at a loss in order to draw customers

lost \'lȯst\ *adj* [fr. pp. of *lose*] **1** : not made use of, won, or claimed **2 a** : unable to find the way **b** : no longer visible **c** : lacking assurance or self-confidence : HELPLESS **3** : ruined or destroyed physically or morally : DESPERATE **4 a** : no longer possessed **b** : no longer known **5 a** : taken away or beyond reach or attainment : DENIED ⟨regions *lost* to the faith⟩ **b** : HARDENED, INSENSIBLE ⟨*lost* to shame⟩ **6** : ABSORBED, RAPT ⟨*lost* in revery⟩ — **lost·ness** \'lȯs(t)-nəs\ *n*

¹**lot** \'lät\ *n* [OE *hlot*] **1** : an object used as a counter in determining a question by chance **2 a** : the use of lots as a means of deciding something ⟨choose by *lot*⟩ **b** : the choice resulting from deciding by lot **3 a** : something that comes to one by or as if by lot : SHARE **b** : one's way of life or worldly fate : FORTUNE **4 a** : a piece or plot of land ⟨a building *lot*⟩ **b** : a motion-picture studio and its adjoining property **5** : a number of units of an article or a parcel of articles offered as one item (as in an auction sale) **6** : a number of associated persons : SET **7** : a considerable quantity — often used adverbially ⟨a *lot* worse⟩ **syn** see FATE

²**lot** *vb* **lot·ted; lot·ting** **1** : to cast or draw lots **2** : to form or divide into lots **3** : ALLOT, APPORTION

Lot \'lät\ *n* : a nephew of Abraham whose wife was turned into a pillar of salt for looking back during their flight from Sodom

loth \'lōth, 'lȯth\ *var of* LOATH

lo·thar·io \lō-'thar-ē-,ō, -'ther-\ *n, pl* **-i·os** *often cap* [*Lothario*, seducer in the play *The Fair Penitent* (1703) by Nicholas Rowe] : a gay seducer

lo·tion \'lō-shən\ *n* [L *lotion-, lotio* act of washing, fr. *lot-, lavere* to wash] : a liquid preparation for cosmetic and external medicinal use

lots \'läts\ *adv* [pl. of ¹*lot*] : MUCH ⟨feeling *lots* better⟩

lot·tery \'lät-ə-rē, 'lä-trē\ *n, pl* **-ter·ies** : a drawing of lots in which prizes are given to the winning names or numbers : a scheme for distributing prizes by chance

lot·to \'lät-ō\ *n* [It, lottery, fr. F *lot* lot, of Gmc origin; akin to E *lot*] : a game of chance played with cards having numbered squares corresponding with numbered counters drawn at random

lo·tus *or* **lo·tos** \'lōt-əs\ *n* [L *lotus*, fr. Gk *lōtos*] **1** : a fruit held in Greek legend to cause indolence and forgetfulness; *also* : a tree bearing this fruit **2** : any of various water lilies including several represented in ancient Egyptian and Hindu art and religious symbolism **3** : any of various erect leguminous plants including some used for hay and pasture

lo·tus–eat·er *or* **lo·tos–eat·er** \-,ēt-ər\ *n* **1** : one of a people described in the Odyssey of Homer as subsisting on the lotus and living in the dreamy indolence it induced **2** : IDLER, DREAMER

loud \'laüd\ *adj* [OE *hlūd*] **1 a** : marked by intensity or volume of sound **b** : producing a loud sound **2** : CLAMOROUS, NOISY **3** : obtrusive or offensive in color or pattern ⟨a *loud* suit⟩ — **loud** *adv* — **loud·ly** *adv* — **loud·ness** *n*

loud·en \'laüd-ºn\ *vb* **loud·ened; loud·en·ing** \'laüd-niŋ, -ºn-iŋ\ : to make or become loud

loud·mouthed \'laüd-'maüthd, -'maütht\ *adj* **1** : having an offensively loud voice or a noisy blustering manner **2** : TACTLESS, INDISCREET

loud·speak·er \'laüd-,spē-kər\ *n* : a device similar to a telephone receiver in operation but amplifying sound

lou·is d'or \,lü-ē-'dȯ(ə)r\ *n, pl* **louis d'or** [F, fr. *Louis* XIII *d*1643 king of France + *d'or* of gold] **1** : a French gold coin first struck in 1640 and issued up to the Revolution **2** : the French 20-franc gold piece issued after the Revolution

---

ə abut; ᵊ kitten; ər further; a back; ā bake; ä cot, cart; aú out; ch chin; e less; ē easy; g gift; i trip; ī life

Lou·is Qua·torze \,lü-ē-kə-'tȯrz\ *adj* [F, Louis XIV] : of, relating to, or characteristic of the architecture or furniture of the reign of Louis XIV of France

Louis Quinze \-'kaⁿz\ *adj* [F, Louis XV] : of, relating to, or characteristic of the architecture or furniture of the reign of Louis XV of France

Louis Seize \-'sāz, -'sez\ *adj* [F, Louis XVI] : of, relating to, or characteristic of the architecture or furniture of the reign of Louis XVI of France

Louis Treize \-'trāz, -'trez\ *adj* [F, Louis XIII] : of, relating to, or characteristic of the architecture or furniture of the reign of Louis XIII of France

¹lounge \'laúnj\ *vb* **1** : to move or act in a lazy, slow, or listless way : LOAF ⟨*lounge* away the afternoon⟩ **2** : to stand, sit, or lie in a slack manner — **loung·er** *n*

²lounge *n* **1 a** : a room with comfortable furniture : LIVING ROOM; *also* : LOBBY **b** : a room in a public building or vehicle often combining lounging, smoking, and toilet facilities **2** : a lounging gait or posture **3** : a long couch

lounge car *n* : a railroad passenger car with seats for lounging and facilities for serving refreshments

loup-ga·rou \,lü-gə-'rü\ *n*, *pl* **loups-garous** \,lü-gə-'rü(z)\ [MF] : WEREWOLF

lour \'laú-(ə)r\, **lour·ing, loury** \'laú-(ə)rē\ *var of* LOWER, LOWERING, LOWERY

louse \'laús\ *n* [OE *lūs*] **1** *pl* **lice** \'līs\ **a** : any of various small wingless usu. flat insects (orders Anoplura and Mallophaga) parasitic on warm-blooded animals **b** : any of several small arthropods **2** *pl* **lous·es** \'laú-səz\ **:** a contemptible person

louse up *vb* : to make a botch of something : BUNGLE, SPOIL

lousy \'laú-zē\ *adj* **lous·i·er; -est 1** : infested with lice **2 a** : MEAN, CONTEMPTIBLE **b** : miserably poor or inferior **c** : amply supplied ⟨*lousy* with money⟩ — **lous·i·ly** \-zə-lē\ *adv* — **lous·i·ness** \-zē-nəs\ *n*

lout \'laút\ *n* : a stupid, clownish, or awkward fellow — **lout·ish** \-ish\ *adj* — **lout·ish·ly** *adv* — **lout·ish·ness** *n*

lou·ver *or* **lou·vre** \'lü-vər\ *n* [MF *lover* dormer window] **1** : an opening provided with one or more slanted fixed or movable strips (as of metal or wood) to allow flow of air to exclude rain or sun or to provide privacy; *also* : a similar device with movable strips for controlling the passage of air or light **2** : one of the slanted strips of a louver — **lou·vered** \-vərd\ *adj*

lov·a·ble *also* **love·a·ble** \'ləv-ə-bəl\ *adj* : having qualities that tend to make one loved : worthy of love — **lov·a·ble·ness** *n* — **lov·a·bly** \-blē\ *adv*

lov·age \'ləv-ij\ *n* [AF *lovache*] : any of several aromatic perennial herbs of the carrot family

¹love \'ləv\ *n* [OE *lufu*] **1** : strong affection based on admiration or benevolence **2 a** : warm attachment, enthusiasm, or devotion ⟨*love* of the sea⟩ **b** : the object of attachment or devotion **3 a** : self-giving loyal concern that freely accepts another and seeks his good: (1) : the fatherly concern of God for man (2) : brotherly concern for others **b** : man's adoration of God **4 a** : attraction based on sexual desire : the ardent affection and tenderness felt by lovers **b** : an amorous episode **5** : a beloved person : DARLING **6** : a score of zero in tennis — **in love** : feeling love for and devotion toward someone

²love *vb* **1** : to hold dear : CHERISH **2 a** : to feel a lover's passion, devotion, or tenderness for **b** : CARESS **3** : to feel unselfish concern for **4** : to like or desire actively : take pleasure in ⟨*loved* to play the violin⟩ **5** : to thrive in ⟨the rose *loves* sunlight⟩ **6** : to feel affection or experience desire : be in love

love·bird \'ləv-,bərd\ *n* : any of various small usu. gray or green parrots that show great affection for their mates

love feast *n* **1** : a meal eaten in common by a Christian congregation in token of brotherly love **2** : a banquet or celebration held to reconcile differences and promote good feeling or show someone affectionate honor

love-in-a-mist \'ləv-ən-ə-,mist\ *n* : a European garden plant related to the buttercups that has flowers enveloped in finely dissected bracts

love knot *n* : a stylized knot sometimes used as an emblem of love

love·less \'ləv-ləs\ *adj* **1** : being without love ⟨a *loveless*

marriage⟩ **2** : UNLOVING **3** : UNLOVED — **love·less·ly** *adv* — **love·less·ness** *n*

love·lorn \'ləv-,lȯrn\ *adj* : deserted by one's love — **love·lorn·ness** \-,lȯrn-nəs\ *n*

love·ly \'ləv-lē\ *adj* **love·li·er; -est 1** : delicately beautiful ⟨a *lovely* dress⟩ **2** : beautiful in moral or spiritual character : GRACIOUS **3** : highly pleasing : FINE ⟨a *lovely* view⟩ **syn** see BEAUTIFUL — **love·li·ness** *n*

love·mak·ing \'ləv-,mā-kiŋ\ *n* **1** : WOOING, COURTSHIP **2** : sexual activity

lov·er \'ləv-ər\ *n* **1 a** : a person in love; *esp* : a man in love **b** *pl* : two persons in love with each other **2** : the male partner in a sexual relationship other than that of husband and wife **3** : one who greatly enjoys or admires something : DEVOTEE

lov·er·ly \-lē\ *adj* (*or adv*) : resembling or as a lover

love seat *n* : a double chair, sofa, or settee for two persons

love·sick \'ləv-,sik\ *adj* **1** : languishing with love : YEARNING **2** : expressing a lover's longing — **love·sick·ness** *n*

lov·ing \'ləv-iŋ\ *adj* : feeling or showing love : AFFECTIONATE ⟨*loving* care⟩ ⟨a *loving* glance⟩ — **lov·ing·ly** \-iŋ-lē\ *adv*

loving cup *n* [fr. its former use in ceremonial drinking] : a large ornamental drinking vessel with two or more handles; *esp* : one given as a prize or trophy

lov·ing–kind·ness \,ləv-iŋ-'kīn(d)-nəs\ *n* : tender and benevolent affection

¹low \'lō\ *vi* [OE *hlōwan*] : MOO

²low *n* : the deep sustained sound characteristic esp. of a cow

³low \'lō\ *adj* **low·er** \'lō-(ə)r\; **low·est** \'lō-əst\ [ME *lah, low*, fr. ON *lāgr*] **1 a** : not high or tall ⟨*low* wall⟩ ⟨*low* bridge⟩ **b** : cut far down at the neck : DÉCOLLETÉ **2 a** : situated or passing below the normal level, surface, or base of measurement ⟨*low* ground⟩ **b** : marking a nadir or bottom ⟨*low* point of his career⟩ **3** : STRICKEN, PROSTRATE ⟨laid *low*⟩ **4** : not loud : SOFT; *also* : FLAT **5 a** : being near the equator ⟨*low* northern latitudes⟩ **b** : being near the horizon ⟨the sun is *low*⟩ **6** : humble in status ⟨*low* birth⟩ **7 a** : lacking strength, health, or vitality : WEAK **b** : lacking spirit or vivacity : DEPRESSED **8 a** : of lesser degree, size, or amount than average or ordinary ⟨*low* pressure⟩ **b** : less than usual in number, amount, or value ⟨*low* price⟩ **9** : falling short of some standard: as **a** : lacking dignity or elevation ⟨*low* style of writing⟩ **b** : morally reprehensible : BASE ⟨*low* trick⟩ **c** : COARSE, VULGAR ⟨*low* language⟩ **10** : not advanced in complexity, development, or elaboration ⟨*low* organisms⟩ **11** : UNFAVORABLE, DISPARAGING ⟨*low* opinion of him⟩ **12** : pronounced with a wide opening between the relatively flat tongue and the palate ⟨the *low* vowel \ä\⟩ — **low** *adv* — **low·ness** *n*

⁴low *n* **1** : something that is low; *esp* : a region of low barometric pressure **2** : the arrangement of gears (as of an automobile) in a position to transmit the greatest power from the engine to the propeller shaft

low blood pressure *n* : HYPOTENSION

low-born \'lō-'bȯrn\ *adj* : born in a low condition or rank

low·boy \'lō-,bȯi\ *n* : a chest of drawers about three feet high with long legs

low-bred \'lō-'bred\ *adj* : RUDE, VULGAR

low·brow \'lō-,braú\ *n* : a person without intellectual interests or culture — **lowbrow** *adj*

Low Church *adj* : tending to minimize the priesthood, sacraments, and formal rites and often to emphasize evangelical principles — **Low Churchman** *n*

lowboy

low comedy *n* : comedy based on burlesque, horseplay, or slapstick rather than wit or satire

low-down \'lō-'daún\ *adj* : CONTEMPTIBLE, DESPICABLE

low-down \-,daún\ *n* : pertinent and esp. guarded information

¹low·er \'laú-(ə)r\ *vi* [ME *louren*] **1** : to look sullen : FROWN **2** : to become dark, gloomy, and threatening

²lower *n* : FROWN

³low·er \'lō-(ə)r\ *adj* **1** : relatively low in position, rank, or order ⟨*lower* court⟩ **2** : constituting the popular and more representative branch of a bicameral legislative body **3 a :** situated or held to be situated beneath the earth's surface **b** *cap* **:** of, relating to, or constituting an earlier geologic period or formation **4 :** SOUTHERN ⟨*lower* New York State⟩ **5 :** less advanced in the scale of evolutionary development ⟨*lower* animals⟩

⁴**low·er** \'lō(-ə)r\ *vb* **1 :** to move down **:** DROP; *also* **:** DIMINISH **2 a :** to let descend by its own weight **b :** to make the aim lower **c :** to reduce the height of **3 a :** to reduce in value or amount ⟨*lower* the price⟩ **b** (1) **:** to bring down **:** DEGRADE (2) **:** ABASE, HUMBLE **c :** to reduce the objective of — **lower the boom :** to crack down

low·er·case \,lō(-ə)r-'kās\ *adj* [fr. the printer's practice of keeping such letters in the lower of his pair of type cases] **:** being a letter that belongs to or conforms to the series a, b, c, etc. rather than A, B, C, etc. — **lowercase** *n*

lower class *n* **:** a social class occupying a position below the middle class and having the lowest status in a society

lower fungus *n* **:** a fungus with hyphae absent or rudimentary and without septa

low·er·ing \'laú-(ə-)riŋ\ *adj* **1 :** FROWNING, SCOWLING **2 :** OVERCAST, GLOOMY ⟨a *lowering* sky⟩

low·er·most \'lō(-ə)r-,mōst\ *adj* **:** LOWEST

low·er world \'lō(-ə)r-\ *n* **:** the world of the dead or of future punishment **:** HADES

low·ery \'laú-(ə-)rē\ *adj* **:** GLOOMY, LOWERING

lowest common denominator *n* **:** LEAST COMMON DENOMINATOR

lowest common multiple *n* **:** the smallest multiple common to two or more numbers

lowest terms *n pl* **:** the form of a fraction in which the numerator and denominator have no common divisor

low frequency *n* **:** a radio frequency in the range between 30 and 300 kilocycles — *abbr. lf*

Low German *n* **1 :** the German dialects of northern Germany esp. since the end of the medieval period **2 :** the Germanic languages other than High German

low-grade \'lō-'grād\ *adj* **1 :** being of a grade or quality rated as inferior **2 :** being nearer the lower extreme of the range in which it may occur ⟨a *low-grade* fever⟩ ⟨a *low-grade* imbecile⟩

low-key \'lō-'kē\ *adj* **:** of low intensity **:** RESTRAINED

low·land \'lō-lənd, -,land\ *n* **:** low and usu. level country — **lowland** *adj*

low·land·er \-lən-dər, -,lan-\ *n* **1 :** a native or inhabitant of a lowland region **2** *cap* **:** an inhabitant of the Lowlands of Scotland

¹**low·ly** \'lō-lē\ *adv* **1 :** HUMBLY, MEEKLY **2 :** in a low position, manner, or degree **3 :** not loudly

²**lowly** *adj* **low·li·er; -est 1 :** HUMBLE, MEEK **2 :** of or relating to a low social or economic rank **3 :** low in the scale of biological or cultural evolution **4 :** ranking low in some hierarchy — **low·li·ness** *n*

low mass *n, often cap L&M* **:** a mass that is said in the simplest ceremonial form

low-mind·ed \'lō-'mīn-dəd\ *adj* **:** inclined to low or unworthy things — **low-mind·ed·ly** *adv* — **low-mind·ed·ness** *n*

low-pres·sure \'lō-'presh-ər\ *adj* **1 a :** having, exerting, or operating under a relatively small pressure **b :** having or resulting from a low atmospheric pressure **2 :** EASY-GOING

low relief *n* **:** BAS-RELIEF

low-spir·it·ed \'lō-'spir-ət-əd\ *adj* **:** DEJECTED, DEPRESSED — **low-spir·it·ed·ly** *adv* — **low-spir·it·ed·ness** *n*

low-ten·sion \'lō-'ten-chən\ *adj* **1 :** having a low potential or voltage **2 :** constructed to be used at low voltage

low-test \-'test\ *adj* **:** having a low volatility ⟨*low-test* gasoline⟩

low tide *n* **:** the tide when the water is at its farthest ebb

¹**lox** \'läks\ *n* [*liquid oxygen*] **:** liquid oxygen

²**lox** *n, pl* **lox** *or* **lox·es** [Yiddish *laks*, fr. MHG *lahs* salmon] **:** smoked salmon

loy·al \'lói(-ə)l\ *adj* [MF, fr. OF *leial*, fr. L *legalis* legal] **1 a :** faithful in allegiance to one's lawful government **b :** faithful to a private person to whom fidelity is held to be due **2 :** faithful to a cause or ideal **syn** see FAITHFUL — **loy·al·ly** \'lói-ə-lē\ *adv*

loy·al·ist \'lói-ə-ləst\ *n* **:** one who is or remains loyal to a political cause, party, government, or sovereign; *esp* **:** TORY 2

loy·al·ty \'lói(-ə)l-tē\ *n, pl* **-ties :** the quality or state of being loyal **syn** see FIDELITY

loz·enge \'läz-ⁿj\ *n* [MF *losange*] **1 :** a figure with four equal sides and two acute and two obtuse angles **:** DIAMOND **2 :** something shaped like a lozenge; *esp* **:** a small often medicated candy

LP \(')el-'pē\ *trademark* — used for a microgroove phonograph record ordinarily having a diameter of 10 or 12 inches and turning at 33⅓ revolutions per minute

LSD \,el-,es-'dē\ *n* [*lysergic acid diethylamide*] **:** an organic compound that induces psychotic symptoms similar to those of schizophrenia

lu·au \'lü-,aú\ *n* [Hawaiian *lu'au*] **:** a Hawaiian feast

lub·ber \'ləb-ər\ *n* [ME *lobur*] **1 :** a big clumsy fellow **2 :** an unskilled seaman — **lub·ber·li·ness** \-lē-nəs\ *n* — **lub·ber·ly** \-lē\ *adj or adv*

lube \'lüb\ *n* **:** LUBRICANT

lu·bri·cant \'lü-bri-kənt\ *n* **:** something (as a grease or oil) capable of reducing friction when applied between moving parts — **lubricant** *adj*

lu·bri·cate \'lü-brə-,kāt\ *vb* [L *lubricare*, fr. *lubricus* slippery] **1 :** to make smooth or slippery **2 :** to apply a lubricant to ⟨*lubricate* a car⟩ **3 :** to act as a lubricant — **lu·bri·ca·tion** \,lü-brə-'kā-shən\ *n* — **lu·bri·ca·tive** \'lü-brə-,kāt-iv\ *adj* — **lu·bri·ca·tor** \-,kāt-ər\ *n*

lu·bri·cious \lü-'brish-əs\ *adj* [irreg. fr. L *lubricus*, slippery, easily led astray] **1 :** LECHEROUS; *also* **:** SALACIOUS **2 :** having a smooth or slippery quality ⟨a *lubricious* skin⟩ — **lu·bri·cious·ly** *adv* — **lu·bric·i·ty** \lü-'bris-ət-ē\ *n*

lu·bri·to·ri·um \,lü-brə-'tōr-ē-əm, -'tór-\ *n* **:** a station for lubricating motor vehicles

lu·cent \'lüs-ⁿt\ *adj* **1 :** glowing with light **:** LUMINOUS, BRIGHT **2 :** CLEAR, LUCID, TRANSLUCENT — **lu·cent·ly** *adv*

lu·cerne *also* **lu·cern** \lü-'sərn\ *n* [F *luzerne*, fr. Prov *luserno*] *chiefly Brit* **:** ALFALFA

lu·cid \'lü-səd\ *adj* [L *lucidus*, fr. *lucēre* to be light, fr. *luc-, lux* light; akin to E ¹*light*] **1 a :** suffused with light **:** LUMINOUS **b :** TRANSLUCENT **2 :** having full use of one's faculties **:** clear-minded **3 :** clear to the understanding **:** PLAIN **syn** see LIMPID — **lu·cid·i·ty** \lü-'sid-ət-ē\ *n* — **lu·cid·ly** *adv* — **lu·cid·ness** *n*

Lu·ci·fer \'lü-sə-fər\ *n* **:** DEVIL, SATAN

lu·cif·er·ase \lü-'sif-ə-,rās\ *n* **:** an enzyme that catalyzes the oxidation of luciferin

lu·cif·er·in \lü-'sif-ə-rən\ *n* [L *lucifer* light-bearing, fr. *luc-, lux* light + *ferre* to bear] **:** a component of luminescent organisms that furnishes practically heatless light in undergoing oxidation

Lu·cite \'lü-,sīt\ *trademark* — used for an acrylic resin or plastic consisting essentially of polymerized methyl methacrylate

luck \'lək\ *n* [MD *luc*] **1 :** whatever happens to a person apparently by chance **:** FORTUNE ⟨people who seem to have nothing but bad *luck*⟩ **2 :** the accidental way events occur ⟨happening by pure *luck*⟩ **3 :** good fortune **:** SUCCESS ⟨be out of *luck*⟩ — **luck·less** \'lək-ləs\ *adj*

luck·i·ly \'lək-ə-lē\ *adv* **:** by good luck **:** FORTUNATELY

luck·i·ness \'lək-ē-nəs\ *n* **:** the quality or state of being lucky

lucky \'lək-ē\ *adj* **luck·i·er; -est 1 :** favored by luck **:** FORTUNATE **2 :** producing a good result apparently by chance ⟨a *lucky* hit⟩ **3 :** seeming to have a good influence or to bring good luck ⟨a *lucky* coin⟩

syn FORTUNATE: LUCKY stresses the operation of pure chance in producing a favorable result; FORTUNATE suggests being rewarded beyond what one strictly deserves or succeeding beyond reasonable expectation

lu·cra·tive \'lü-krət-iv\ *adj* **:** producing wealth **:** PROFITABLE — **lu·cra·tive·ly** *adv* — **lu·cra·tive·ness** *n*

lu·cre \'lü-kər\ *n* [L *lucrum*] **:** monetary gain **:** PROFIT; *also* **:** MONEY

lu·cu·bra·tion \,lü-k(y)ə-'brā-shən\ *n* [L *lucubrare* to work by lamplight] **1 :** laborious study **:** MEDITATION **2 :** studied or pretentious expression in speech or writing

lu·di·crous \'lüd-ə-krəs\ *adj* [L *ludicrus*, fr. *ludus* play, sport] **1 :** amusing or laughable through obvious absurdity or incongruity **2 :** meriting derisive laughter or scorn as absurdly inept, false, or foolish **syn** see LAUGHABLE — **lu·di·crous·ly** *adv* — **lu·di·crous·ness** *n*

lu·es \'lü-(,)ēz\ *n, pl* **lues** [NL, fr. L, plague] **:** SYPHILIS

— **lu·et·ic** \lü-'et-ik\ *adj* — **lu·et·i·cal·ly** \-'et-i-k(ə-)lē\ *adv*

¹luff \'ləf\ *n* [MF *lof* weather side of a ship] : the act of sailing a ship closer to the wind

²luff *vi* : to sail nearer the wind

Luft·waf·fe \'lüft-‚väf-ə\ *n* [G, lit., air arm] : the German air force esp. in World War II

¹lug \'ləg\ *vb* **lugged**; **lug·ging** [ME *luggen*] **1** : DRAG, PULL **2** : to carry laboriously **3** : to introduce in a forced manner ⟨*lug* a story into the conversation⟩

²lug *n* : a box or basket for fruit or vegetables; *esp* : a shallow box of thin wood and standardized dimensions

³lug *n* **1** : a part (as a handle) that projects like an ear **2** : BLOCKHEAD, LOUT

lug·gage \'ləg-ij\ *n* **1** : a traveler's belongings : BAGGAGE **2** : containers (as suitcases and traveling bags) for carrying personal belongings

lug·ger \'ləg-ər\ *n* : a boat that carries one or more lugsails

lug·sail \'ləg-‚sāl, -səl\ *n* : a 4-sided sail fastened at the top to a yard that hangs obliquely across a mast and is raised and lowered with the sail

lu·gu·bri·ous \lu-'g(y)ü-brē-əs\ *adj* [L *lugubris*, fr. *lugēre* to mourn] : MOURNFUL; *esp* : exaggeratedly or affectedly mournful — **lu·gu·bri·ous·ly** *adv* — **lu·gu·bri·ous·ness** *n*

lugsail

lug·worm \'ləg-‚wərm\ *n* : any of a genus of marine annelid worms that have a row of tufted gills along each side of the back and are used for bait

Luke \'lük\ *n* **1** : a physician and companion of the apostle Paul held to be the author of the third Gospel in the New Testament and of the Book of Acts **2** — see BIBLE table

luke·warm \'lük-'wòrm\ *adj* [ME, fr. *luke* lukewarm] **1** : neither hot nor cold : moderately warm : TEPID ⟨*lukewarm* bath⟩ **2** : not enthusiastic : HALFHEARTED, INDIFFERENT ⟨his plan got a *lukewarm* reception⟩ — **luke·warm·ly** *adv* — **luke·warm·ness** *n*

¹lull \'ləl\ *vt* **1** : to cause to sleep or rest : SOOTHE **2** : to cause to relax vigilance

²lull *n* **1** : a temporary calm before or during a storm **2** : a temporary drop in activity

lul·la·by \'ləl-ə-‚bī\ *n*, *pl* **-bies** : a song to quiet children or lull them to sleep

lum·ba·go \‚ləm-'bā-gō\ *n* : usu. painful muscular rheumatism involving the lumbar region

lum·bar \'ləm-bər, -‚bär\ *adj* [L *lumbus* loin] : of, relating to, or adjacent to the loins or the vertebrae between the thoracic vertebrae and sacrum ⟨*lumbar* region⟩

¹lum·ber \'ləm-bər\ *vi* **lum·bered**; **lum·ber·ing** \-b(ə-)riŋ\ : to move heavily or clumsily; *also* : RUMBLE

²lumber *n* **1** : surplus or disused articles (as furniture) that are stored away **2** : timber or logs esp. when sawed up for use — **lumber** *adj*

³lumber *vb* **lum·bered**; **lum·ber·ing** \-b(ə-)riŋ\ **1** : to clutter with or as if with lumber : ENCUMBER **2** : to heap together in disorder **3** : to cut logs : saw logs into lumber — **lum·ber·er** \-bər-ər\ *n*

lum·ber·ing \'ləm-b(ə-)riŋ\ *adj* : heavy and awkward in movement — **lum·ber·ing·ly** \-b(ə-)riŋ-lē\ *adv*

lum·ber·jack \'ləm-bər-‚jak\ *n* : LOGGER

lum·ber·man \-mən\ *n* : one engaged in lumbering

lum·ber·yard \-‚yärd\ *n* : a place where a stock of lumber is kept for sale

lu·men \'lü-mən\ *n*, *pl* **lu·mi·na** \-mə-nə\ *or* **lumens** [NL *lumin-, lumen*, fr. L, light, airshaft] **1** : the cavity or bore of a tube or tubular organ ⟨*lumen* of a blood vessel⟩ ⟨*lumen* of a catheter⟩ **2** : a unit of luminous flux equal to the light on a unit surface all points of which are at a unit distance from a uniform point source of one candle — **lu·mi·nal** *also* **lu·men·al** \'lü-mən-ᵊl\ *adj*

lumin- *or* **lumini-** *or* **lumino-** *comb form* [L *lumin-, lumen*] : light ⟨*luminiferous*⟩

lu·mi·naire \‚lü-mə-'na(ə)r, -'ne(ə)r\ *n* : a complete lighting unit

Lu·mi·nal \'lü-mə-‚nal, -‚nòl\ *trademark* — used for phenobarbital

lu·mi·nance \'lü-mə-nən(t)s\ *n* : luminous intensity (as of a surface)

lu·mi·nary \'lü-mə-‚ner-ē\ *n*, *pl* **-nar·ies** **1** : a very famous person **2** : a source of light; *esp* : one of the heavenly bodies — **luminary** *adj*

lu·mi·nes·cence \‚lü-mə-'nes-ᵊn(t)s\ *n* : emission of light at low temperatures esp. as a by-product of physiological or other chemical processes; *also* : such light — **lu·mi·nesce** \-'nes\ *vi*

lu·mi·nes·cent \-'nes-ᵊnt\ *adj* : relating to, exhibiting, or adapted for the production of luminescence ⟨*luminescent* paint⟩

lu·mi·nif·er·ous \‚lü-mə-'nif-(ə-)rəs\ *adj* : transmitting, producing, or yielding light

lu·mi·nos·i·ty \‚lü-mə-'näs-ət-ē\ *n*, *pl* **-ties** **1** : the quality or state of being luminous : BRIGHTNESS **2** : something luminous

lu·mi·nous \'lü-mə-nəs\ *adj* **1** : emitting light : SHINING **2** : LIGHTED ⟨a public square *luminous* with sunlight⟩ **3** : CLEAR, INTELLIGIBLE — **lu·mi·nous·ly** *adv* — **lu·mi·nous·ness** *n*

luminous flux *n* : radiant flux in the visible-wavelength range

luminous paint *n* : a paint containing a phosphor (as zinc sulfide activated with copper) and so able to glow in the dark

lum·mox \'ləm-əks\ *n* : a clumsy person

¹lump \'ləmp\ *n* **1** : a piece or mass of irregular shape **2** : AGGREGATE, TOTALITY ⟨taken in the *lump*⟩ **3** : an abnormal swelling or growth **4** : a thickset heavy person; *esp* : one who is stupid or dull **5** *pl a* : BEATINGS **b** : COMEUPPANCE

²lump *adj* : not divided into parts : WHOLE ⟨*lump* sum⟩

³lump *vb* **1** : to group without discrimination **2** : to make into lumps **3** : to move noisily and clumsily **4** : to become formed into lumps

⁴lump *vt* : to put up with : TOLERATE ⟨like it or *lump* it⟩

lump·ish \'ləm-pish\ *adj* **1** : DULL, STUPID **2** : HEAVY, AWKWARD — **lump·ish·ly** *adv* — **lump·ish·ness** *n*

lumpy \'ləm-pē\ *adj* **lump·i·er**; **-est** **1** : having or full of lumps **2** : having a thickset clumsy appearance — **lump·i·ly** \-pə-lē\ *adv* — **lump·i·ness** \-pē-nəs\ *n*

lu·na·cy \'lü-nə-sē\ *n*, *pl* **-cies** **1** : unsoundness of mind : INSANITY **2** : great foolishness : extreme folly **syn** see INSANITY

luna moth \‚lü-nə-\ *n* : a large mostly pale green American moth with long tails on the hind wings

lu·nar \'lü-nər\ *adj* [L *luna* moon] **1** : of or relating to the moon **2** : measured by the moon's revolution ⟨*lunar* month⟩

lunar caustic *n* : silver nitrate fused and molded into sticks for use as a caustic

lunar eclipse *n* : an eclipse in which the moon passes partially or wholly through the umbra of the earth's shadow

lu·nate \'lü-‚nāt\ *adj* : shaped like a crescent — **lu·nate·ly** *adv*

lu·na·tic \'lü-nə-‚tik\ *adj* [LL *lunaticus*, fr. L *luna* moon; fr. the belief that lunacy fluctuated with the phases of the moon] **1 a** : INSANE **b** : designed for insane persons ⟨*lunatic* asylum⟩ **2** : wildly foolish : GIDDY — **lunatic** *n*

lunatic fringe *n* : the members of a political or social movement espousing extreme, eccentric, or fanatical views

¹lunch \'lənch\ *n* **1** : a light meal; *esp* : one eaten in the middle of the day **2** : the food prepared for a lunch

²lunch *vb* **1** : to eat lunch **2** : to provide lunch for — **lunch·er** *n*

lun·cheon \'lən-chən\ *n* : a light meal at midday; *esp* : a formal lunch

lun·cheon·ette \‚lən-chə-'net\ *n* : a place where light lunches are sold

lunch·room \'lənch-‚rüm, -‚rùm\ *n* **1** : a restaurant specializing in food that is ready to serve or that can be quickly prepared **2** : a room (as in a school) where lunches brought from home may be eaten

lune \'lün\ *n* [L *luna* moon] : a crescent-shaped figure on a plane surface or a sphere formed by two intersecting arcs of circles

lu·nette \lü-'net\ *n* : something (as a window or a space over a doorway) that is shaped like a crescent

lung \'ləŋ\ *n* [OE *lungen*] **1 a** : one of the usu. paired thoracic organs that form the special breathing apparatus of air-breathing vertebrates **b :** any of various respiratory organs **2 :** a device (as an iron lung) to promote and facilitate breathing

¹lunge \'lənj\ *vb* **1 :** to thrust or push with a lunge **2 :** to make a stretching thrust or a forceful forward movement

²lunge *n* **1 :** a sudden stretching thrust or pass (as with a sword or foil) **2 :** the act of striding or leaping suddenly forward

¹lung·er \'lən-jər\ *n* **:** one that lunges

²lung·er \'ləŋ-ər\ *n* **:** one suffering from a chronic disease of the lungs; *esp* **:** a tubercular person

lung·fish \'ləŋ-ˌfish\ *n* **:** any of various fishes (order Dipneusti or Cladistia) that breathe by a modified air bladder as well as gills

lung·wort \'ləŋ-ˌwərt, -ˌwȯrt\ *n* **:** any of several plants formerly used in the treatment of respiratory disorders; *esp* **:** a European herb of the borage family with bristly leaves and bluish flowers

lunk·head \'ləŋk-ˌhed\ *n* **:** a dull-witted person **:** DOLT — **lunk·head·ed** \-'hed-əd\ *adj*

lu·nu·late \'lü-nyə-ˌlāt\ *adj* **:** resembling a small crescent; *also* **:** having crescent-shaped markings

lu·nule \'lü-nyül\ *n* [L *lunula,* dim. of *luna* moon] **:** a crescent-shaped body part or marking; *esp* **:** the whitish mark at the base of a fingernail

Lu·per·ca·lia \ˌlü-pər-'kā-lē-ə\ *n* **:** an ancient Roman festival celebrated February 15 to ensure fertility for the people, fields, and flocks — **Lu·per·ca·li·an** \-lē-ən\ *adj*

lu·pine \'lü-pən\ *n* [L *lupinum,* fr. *lupus* wolf; akin to E *wolf*] **:** any of a genus of leguminous herbs some of which are poisonous and others grown for green manure, fodder, or their edible seeds

lu·pus \'lü-pəs\ *n* [ML, fr. L, wolf] **:** any of several diseases marked by skin lesions; *esp* **:** one of tuberculous origin

¹lurch \'lərch\ *n* [MF *lourche* defeated by a lurch, deceived] **:** a decisive defeat (as in cribbage) in which an opponent wins a game by more than double the defeated player's score — **in the lurch :** in a helpless or unsupported position

²lurch *n* **1 :** a sudden roll of a ship to one side **2 :** a sudden swaying or tipping movement ⟨the car gave a *lurch*⟩; *also* **:** a staggering gait

³lurch *vi* **:** to roll or tip abruptly **:** PITCH; *also* **:** STAGGER

lurch·er \'lər-chər\ *n, Brit* **:** a mongrel dog; *esp* **:** one used by poachers

¹lure \'lu̇(ə)r\ *n* [MF *loire,* a device used by a falconer to recall a hawk] **1 a :** an inducement to pleasure or gain **:** ENTICEMENT **b :** APPEAL, ATTRACTION **2 :** a decoy for attracting animals to capture; *esp* **:** an artificial bait used for catching fish

²lure *vt* **:** to tempt with a promise of pleasure or gain **:** ENTICE — **lur·er** *n*

lu·rid \'lu̇r-əd\ *adj* [L *luridus* pale yellow, sallow] **1 a :** wan and ghastly pale in appearance **:** LIVID **b :** of any of several light or medium grayish colors ranging in hue from yellow to orange **2 :** shining with the red glow of fire seen through smoke or cloud **3 a :** causing horror or revulsion **:** GRUESOME ⟨*lurid* tales of murder⟩ **b :** highly colored **:** SENSATIONAL **syn** see GHASTLY — **lu·rid·ly** *adv* — **lu·rid·ness** *n*

lurk \'lərk\ *vi* [ME *lurken*] **1 a :** to lie in ambush **:** SKULK **b :** to move furtively or inconspicuously **:** SNEAK **c :** to persist in staying **2 :** to lie concealed; *esp* **:** to constitute a latent threat — **lurk·er** *n*

lus·cious \'ləsh-əs\ *adj* **1 :** having a delicious taste or smell **:** SWEET ⟨*luscious* berries⟩ **2 :** having sensual appeal **:** SEDUCTIVE **3 :** richly luxurious or appealing to the senses; *also* **:** FLORID — **lus·cious·ly** *adv* — **lus·cious·ness** *n*

¹lush \'ləsh\ *adj* [ME *lusch* soft, tender] **1 :** producing or covered with luxuriant growth ⟨*lush* grass⟩ ⟨*lush* pastures⟩ **2 a :** THRIVING **b :** characterized by abundance **:** PLENTIFUL **3 a :** SAVORY, DELICIOUS **b :** OPULENT, SUMPTUOUS — **lush·ly** *adv* — **lush·ness** *n*

²lush *n* **1** *slang* **:** intoxicating liquor **:** DRINK **2 :** an habitual heavy drinker **:** DRUNKARD

¹lust \'ləst\ *n* [OE, pleasure, delight, lust] **1 a :** sexual desire **b :** intense or unrestrained sexual desire **:** LASCIVIOUSNESS **2 :** an intense longing **:** CRAVING

²lust *vi* **:** to have an intense desire or need **:** CRAVE; *esp* **:** to have a strong sexual desire

lus·ter *or* **lus·tre** \'ləs-tər\ *n* [MF *lustre,* fr. L *lustrare* to brighten] **1 :** a shine or sheen esp. from reflected light **:** GLOSS; *esp* **:** the appearance of the surface of a mineral with respect to its reflecting qualities ⟨a pearly *luster*⟩ **2 :** BRIGHTNESS, GLITTER **3 :** GLORY, SPLENDOR ⟨the *luster* of a famous name⟩ **4 :** a surface on pottery sometimes iridescent and always metallic in appearance — **lus·ter·less** \-tər-ləs\ *adj*

lus·ter·ware \-,wa(ə)r, -,we(ə)r\ *n* **:** pottery decorated by applying to the glaze metallic compounds which become iridescent metallic films in the process of firing

lust·ful \'ləst-fəl\ *adj* **:** excited by lust **:** LECHEROUS — **lust·ful·ly** \-fə-lē\ *adv* — **lust·ful·ness** *n*

lus·tral \'ləs-trəl\ *adj* **:** PURIFICATORY

lus·trate \'ləs-ˌtrāt\ *vt* **:** to purify ceremonially — **lus·tra·tion** \ˌləs-'trā-shən\ *n*

lus·trous \'ləs-trəs\ *adj* **1 :** having a gloss **:** SHINING **2 :** radiant in character or reputation **:** ILLUSTRIOUS — **lus·trous·ly** *adv* — **lus·trous·ness** *n*

lus·trum \'ləs-trəm\ *n, pl* **lustrums** *or* **lus·tra** \-trə\ [L] **1 a :** a purification of the whole Roman people made in ancient times after the census every five years **b :** the Roman census **2 :** a period of five years

lusty \'ləs-tē\ *adj* **lust·i·er; -est :** full of vitality **:** VIGOROUS, ROBUST — **lust·i·ly** \-tə-lē\ *adv* — **lust·i·ness** \-tē-nəs\ *n*

lu·ta·nist *or* **lu·te·nist** \'lüt-ᵊn-əst, 'lüt-nəst\ *n* **:** a lute player

¹lute \'lüt\ *n* [MF *lut,* fr. OProv *laut,* fr. Ar *al-ʽūd,* lit., the wood] **:** a stringed musical instrument with a pear-shaped body and a fretted fingerboard played by plucking the strings with the fingers

²lute *n* [L *lutum* mud] **:** material (as cement or clay) for packing a joint or coating a porous surface to make it impervious to fluid

³lute *vt* **:** to seal or cover with lute ⟨*lute* a joint⟩

lu·te·al \'lüt-ē-əl\ *adj* **:** of, relating to, or involving the corpus luteum

lu·tein·ize \'lüt-ē-ə-ˌnīz, 'lü-ˌtē-ˌnīz\ *vb* **:** to produce or become corpus luteum

lu·te·ous \'lüt-ē-əs\ *adj* **:** yellow tinged with green or brown

lu·te·tium *or* **lu·te·cium** \lü-'tē-sh(ē-)əm\ *n* [NL, fr. L *Lutetia,* ancient name of Paris] **:** a metallic chemical element — see ELEMENT table

¹Lu·ther·an \'lü-th(ə-)rən\ *n* **:** a member of a Lutheran church

²Lutheran *adj* **1 :** of or relating to Luther or his religious doctrines (as justification by faith alone) **2 :** of or relating to the Protestant churches adhering to Lutheran doctrines, liturgy, or polity — **Lu·ther·an·ism** \-ˌiz-əm\ *n*

lut·ing \'lüt-iŋ\ *n* **:** ²LUTE

lut·ist \'lüt-əst\ *n* **:** a lute player

lux·u·ri·ant \(ˌ)ləg-'zhur-ē-ənt, (ˌ)lək-'shur-\ *adj* **1 a :** yielding abundantly **:** PRODUCTIVE **b :** characterized by abundant growth **:** LUSH **2 a :** exuberantly rich and varied **:** PROFUSE **b :** excessively elaborate **:** FLORID — **lux·u·ri·ance** \-ən(t)s\ *n* — **lux·u·ri·ant·ly** *adv*

syn LUXURIOUS: LUXURIANT implies profuseness and rich abundance and suggests splendor of display ⟨a *luxuriant* bed of peonies⟩ ⟨*luxuriant* verbal facility⟩ LUXURIOUS applies to what is choice and costly and suggests the satisfactions of sensuous comforts and pleasures ⟨a *luxurious* apartment⟩

lux·u·ri·ate \-ē-ˌāt\ *vi* **1 :** to grow profusely **:** PROLIFERATE **2 :** to indulge oneself luxuriously **:** REVEL ⟨*luxuriating* in a soft bed after a week of camping⟩

lux·u·ri·ous \(ˌ)ləg-'zhur-ē-əs, (ˌ)lək-'shur-\ *adj* **1 :** of or relating to unrestrained gratification of the senses **:** VOLUPTUOUS **2 a :** fond of luxury or self-indulgence **:** SYBARITIC **b :** characterized by opulence or rich abundance; *esp* **:** excessively ornate **syn** see LUXURIANT — **lux·u·ri·ous·ly** *adv* — **lux·u·ri·ous·ness** *n*

lux·u·ry \'ləksh-(ə-)rē, 'ləgzh-\ *n, pl* **-ries** [L *luxuria* rankness, luxury, fr. *luxus* excess, luxury] **1 :** liberal use or possession of costly food, dress, or anything that pleases a person's appetite or desire **:** great ease or comfort **:** rich surroundings ⟨live in *luxury*⟩ **2 a :** something desirable but costly or hard to get ⟨a *luxury* few can

ə **abut;** ᵊ **kitten;** ər **further;** a **back;** ā **bake;** ä **cot, cart;** au̇ **out;** ch **chin;** e **less;** ē **easy;** g **gift;** i **trip;** ī **life**

afford⟩ **b :** something adding to pleasure or comfort but not absolutely necessary — **luxury** *adj*

¹-ly \lē\ *adj suffix* [OE -līc, -lic, fr. līc body] **1 :** like in appearance, manner, or nature **:** having the characteristics of ⟨queen*ly*⟩⟨father*ly*⟩ **2 :** characterized by regular recurrence in (specified) units of time **:** every ⟨hour*ly*⟩

²-ly *adv suffix* [OE -līce, -lice fr. -līc ¹-ly] **1 :** in a (specified) manner ⟨slow*ly*⟩ **2 :** from a (specified) point of view ⟨grammatical*ly*⟩

ly·cée \lē-'sā\ *n* [F, fr. MF, lyceum, fr. L *Lyceum*] **:** a French public secondary school that prepares for the university

ly·ce·um \lī-'sē-əm, 'lī-sē-\ *n* [L *Lyceum*, gymnasium near Athens where Aristotle taught, fr. Gk *Lykeion*, fr. *lykeios*, epithet of Apollo] **1 :** a hall for public lectures or discussions **2 :** an association providing public lectures, concerts, and entertainments

lych–gate \'lich-‚gāt\ *n* [ME *lich*, *lych* body, corpse, fr. OE *līc*] **:** a roofed gate in a churchyard under which a bier rests during the initial part of the burial service

lych·nis \'lik-nəs\ *n* **:** any of a genus of often sticky‑stemmed herbs of the pink family with usu. red or white flowers

ly·co·pod \'lī-kə-‚päd\ *n* **:** CLUB MOSS; *esp* **:** LYCOPODIUM 1

ly·co·po·di·um \‚lī-kə-'pōd-ē-əm\ *n* [Gk *lykos* wolf + *podion*, dim. of *pod-*, *pous* foot] **1 :** any of a large genus of erect or creeping club mosses with evergreen leaves in four to many ranks **2 :** a fine yellowish flammable powder of lycopodium spores used esp. in pharmacy and in fireworks

lye \'lī\ *n* [OE *lēag*] **1 :** a strong alkaline liquor rich in potassium carbonate leached from wood ashes and used esp. in making soap and in washing **2 :** any of various strong alkaline solutions; *also* **:** SODIUM HYDROXIDE **3 :** a solid caustic

ly·gus bug \'lī-gəs-\ *n* **:** any of several small sucking bugs of which some transmit virus diseases to plants

ly·ing \'lī-iŋ\ *adj* [fr. prp. of ³*lie*] **:** UNTRUTHFUL, FALSE

ly·ing–in \‚lī-iŋ-'in\ *n, pl* **lyings–in** *or* **lying–ins 1 :** the state attending and consequent to childbirth **:** CONFINEMENT — **lying–in** *adj*

lymph \'lim(p)f\ *n, pl* **lymphs** \'lim(p)fs, 'lim(p)s\ [L *lympha* water goddess, water, fr. Gk *nymphē* nymph] **1** *archaic* **:** a spring or stream of water; *also* **:** pure clear water **2 :** a pale coagulable fluid that consists of a liquid portion resembling blood plasma and containing white blood cells, circulates in lymphatic vessels, and bathes the cells of the body — **lymph** *adj*

lymph·ad·e·ni·tis \‚lim-‚fad-ᵊn-'īt-əs\ *n* [Gk *adēn* gland] **:** inflammation of lymph glands

¹lym·phat·ic \lim-'fat-ik\ *adj* **1 a :** of, relating to, or produced by lymph, lymphoid tissue, or lymphocytes **b :** conveying lymph **2 :** lacking physical or mental energy — **lym·phat·i·cal·ly** \-'fat-i-k(ə-)lē\ *adv*

²lymphatic *n* **:** a vessel that contains or conveys lymph

lymph gland *n* **:** one of the masses of lymphoid tissue occurring in association with the lymphatic vessels and giving rise to the lymphocytes — called also *lymph node*

lym·pho·cyte \'lim(p)-fə-‚sīt\ *n* **:** a colorless weakly motile cell produced in lymphoid tissue that is the typical cellular element of lymph and constitutes 20 to 30 percent of the leucocytes of normal human blood — **lym·pho·cyt·ic** \‚lim(p)-fə-'sit-ik\ *adj*

lym·phoid \'lim-‚fóid\ *adj* **1 :** of, relating to, or resembling lymph **2 :** of, relating to, or constituting the tissue characteristic of the lymph glands

lynch \'linch\ *vt* **:** to put to death by mob action without legal sanction or due process of law — **lynch·er** *n*

lynch law *n* **:** the punishment of presumed crimes or offenses usu. by death without due process of law

lynx \'liŋ(k)s\ *n, pl* **lynx** *or* **lynx·es** [Gk] **:** any of several wildcats with relatively long legs, short stubby tail, mottled coat, and often tufted ears; *esp* **:** a large No. American cat with soft fur and large padded feet — called also *Canada lynx*

lynx–eyed \'liŋ(k)s-'īd\ *adj* **:** having sharp sight

lyo·phile \'lī-ə-‚fīl\ *adj* **:** of, relating to, or obtained by freeze-drying

Ly·ra \'lī-rə\ *n* [L, lit., lyre] **:** a northern constellation representing the lyre of Orpheus or Mercury and containing Vega

ly·rate \'lī(ə)r-‚āt\ *or* **ly·rat·ed** \-‚āt-əd\ *adj* **:** having or suggesting the shape of a lyre — **ly·rate·ly** *adv*

lyre \'lī(ə)r\ *n* [L *lyra*, fr. Gk] **1 :** a stringed musical instrument of the harp class used by the ancient Greeks **2** *cap* **:** LYRA

lyre·bird \'lī(ə)r-‚bərd\ *n* **:** either of two Australian passerine birds of which the males have very long tail feathers displayed during courtship in the shape of a lyre

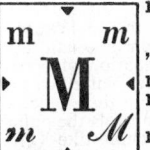
lyre

¹lyr·ic \'lir-ik\ *adj* **1 :** of or relating to a lyre **2 :** resembling a song in form, feeling, or literary quality **:** expressing a poet's own feeling **:** not narrative or dramatic ⟨*lyric* poetry⟩ **3 :** having a light flexible quality esp. adapted for singing songs ⟨a *lyric* tenor voice⟩

²lyric *n* **1 :** a lyric composition; *esp* **:** a lyric poem **2** *pl* **:** the words of a popular song or musical-comedy number

lyr·i·cal \'lir-i-kəl\ *adj* **1 :** resembling a song in mood or suggestion or emotional expression **2 :** EXUBERANT, RHAPSODIC — **lyr·i·cal·ly** \-k(ə-)lē\ *adv*

lyr·i·cism \'lir-ə-‚siz-əm\ *n* **1 :** the quality or character of being lyric **2 :** a style or quality expressing personal emotion in poetry or the other arts

lyr·i·cist \'lir-ə-səst\ *n* **:** a writer of lyrics

lyr·ist *n* **1** \'lī(ə)r-əst\ **:** a player on the lyre **2** \'lir-əst\ **:** LYRICIST

ly·sin \'līs-ᵊn\ *n* **:** a substance capable of causing lysis; *esp* **:** an antibody capable of causing disintegration of red blood cells or microorganisms

ly·sine \'lī-‚sēn\ *n* **:** a crystalline basic amino acid that is essential to animal nutrition

ly·sis \'lī-səs\ *n, pl* **ly·ses** \'lī-‚sēz\ [NL, fr. Gk, lit., act of loosening, breaking down, fr. *lyein* to loosen] **1 :** the gradual decline of a disease process (as fever) **2 :** a process of disintegration or dissolution (as of cells) — **lyt·ic** \'lit-ik\ *adj*

-ly·sis \l-ə-səs\ *n comb form, pl* **-ly·ses** \l-ə-‚sēz\ [NL, fr. L & Gk; L, fr. Gk, fr. *lysis*] **1 :** decomposition ⟨electro*lysis*⟩ **2 :** disintegration **:** breaking down ⟨auto*lysis*⟩ — **-lyt·ic** \'lit-ik\ *adj suffix*

ly·so·gen·e·sis \‚lī-sə-'jen-ə-səs\ *n* **:** a producing of lysins or of lysis — **ly·so·ge·net·ic** \-jə-'net-ik\ *adj*

ly·so·some \'lī-sə-‚sōm\ *n* **:** a saclike cellular organelle that contains hydrolytic enzymes

ly·so·zyme \'lī-sə-‚zīm\ *n* **:** a protein widely present in nature (as in egg white and saliva) that acts as an enzyme in destroying the capsules of certain bacteria

-lyze \‚līz\ *vb comb form* **:** produce or undergo (such) a lysis (sense 2) ⟨electro*lyze*⟩

m \'em\ *n, often cap* **1 :** the 13th letter of the English alphabet **2 :** the roman numeral 1000

'm *vb* **:** AM ⟨I'*m* going⟩

ma \'mä, 'mó\ *n, pl* **mas** **:** MOTHER

ma'am \'mam, *after* "yes" *often* əm\ *n* **:** MADAM

ma·ca·bre \mə-'käb(-rə)\ *adj* [F, fr. *danse macabre* dance of death, fr. MF *danse de Macabré*] **1 :** having death as a subject **:** including a representation of death personified **2 a :** dwelling on the gruesome **b :** tending to produce horror in a beholder — **ma·ca·bre·ly** \-'käb-rə-lē\ *adv*

mac·ad·am \mə-'kad-əm\ *n* [after John L. *McAdam* d1836 British engineer] **1 :** a roadway or pavement of small closely packed broken stone **2 :** the broken stone used in macadamizing

mac·a·da·mia nut \‚mak-ə-'dā-mē-ə-\ *n* **:** a hard-shelled nut produced by an Australian evergreen tree

mac·ad·am·ize \mə-'kad-ə-‚mīz\ *vt* **:** to construct or surface (as a road) by packing a layer of small broken stone on a well-drained earth roadbed

ma·caque \mə-'kak, -'käk\ *n* [F, fr. Pg *macaco*] **:** any of several short-tailed monkeys of Asia and the East Indies; *esp* **:** RHESUS MONKEY

mac·a·ro·ni \,mak-ə-'rō-nē\ *n, pl* **-nis** *or* **-nies** [It *maccheroni*, pl.] **1** : a food made chiefly of semolina paste dried in the form of slender tubes **2 a** : one of a class of young men in the 18th century who affected foreign ways **b** : DANDY, FOP

mac·a·roon \,mak-ə-'rün\ *n* [F *macaron*, fr. It dial. *macarone*] : a small cake made of egg whites, sugar, and ground almonds or coconut

ma·caw \mə-'kȯ\ *n* [Pg *macau*] : any of numerous parrots of South and Central America including some of the largest and showiest

Mac·ca·bees \'mak-ə-,bēz\ *n pl* : a priestly family who led a Jewish revolt against Hellenism and Syrian rule and governed Palestine from 142 B.C. to 63 B.C. — **Mac·ca·be·an** \,mak-ə-'bē-ən\ *adj*

Mc·Coy \mə-'kȯi\ *n* : something that is neither imitation nor substitute ⟨the real *McCoy*⟩

¹mace \'mās\ *n* [MF] **1** : a heavy spiked club used as a weapon in the Middle Ages for breaking armor **2** : an ornamental staff borne as a symbol of authority (as before a public official or a legislative body)

²mace *n* [MF *macis*] : a spice consisting of the dried outer fibrous covering of the nutmeg

mac·er·ate \'mas-ə-,rāt\ *vb* [L *macerare* to soften by steeping] **1** : to waste away or cause to waste away **2** : to cause to become soft or separated into constituent elements by or as if by steeping in fluid — **mac·er·a·tion** \,mas-ə-'rā-shən\ *n*

Mach \'mäk\ *n* : MACH NUMBER

ma·chete \mə-'shet-ē, -'chet-ē\ *n* [Sp] : a large heavy knife used for cutting sugarcane and underbrush and as a weapon

Ma·chi·a·vel·li·an \,mak-ē-ə-'vel-ē-ən, -'vel-yən\ *adj* **1** : of or relating to Niccolò Machiavelli or Machiavellianism **2** : suggesting the principles of conduct laid down by Machiavelli; *esp* : characterized by cunning, deceitfulness, or bad faith — **Machiavellian** *n*

Ma·chi·a·vel·li·an·ism \-ē-ə-,niz-əm, -yə-,niz-əm\ *n* : the political theory of Machiavelli; *esp* : the view that any means however unscrupulous can justifiably be used in gaining and maintaining political power

ma·chic·o·la·tion \mə-,chik-ə-'lā-shən\ *n* : an opening between the corbels of a projecting parapet (as of a medieval castle) or in the floor of a gallery or roof of a portal for discharging missiles upon assailants below

mach·i·nate \'mak-ə-,nāt, 'mash-ə-\ *vb* : CONTRIVE, PLOT; *esp* : to plot or scheme to do harm — **mach·i·na·tor** \-,nāt-ər\ *n*

mach·i·na·tion \,mak-ə-'nā-shən, ,mash-ə-\ *n* : a scheme or plot to accomplish some usu. evil end — usu. used in pl.

¹ma·chine \mə-'shēn\ *n* [MF, structure, contrivance, fr. L *machina*, fr. Gk *machana*, *mēchanē*] **1 a** : VEHICLE, CONVEYANCE; *esp* : AUTOMOBILE **b** : a combination of parts that transmit forces, motion, and energy in a way that accomplishes some desired work ⟨a sewing *machine*⟩ ⟨a hoisting *machine*⟩ **c** : an instrument (as a lever or pulley) designed to transmit or modify the application of power, force, or motion **2 a** : a person or organization that acts like a machine **b** : a combination of persons acting together for a common end together with the means they use; *esp* : a highly organized group that under the leadership of a boss or a small clique controls the policies and activities of a political party — **ma·chine·like** \-,līk\ *adj*

²machine *adj* **1** : characterized by the widespread use of machinery ⟨the *machine* age⟩ **2** : produced by or as if by machinery ⟨*machine* products⟩

³machine *vt* : to shape or finish by machine-operated tools — **ma·chin·a·ble** \-'shēn-ə-bəl\ *adj*

machine gun *n* : an automatic gun usu. having a cooling device and being capable of continuous firing — **ma·chine-gun** \mə-'shēn-,gən\ *vb* — **machine gunner** *n*

ma·chin·ery \mə-'shēn-(ə-)rē\ *n* **1** : MACHINES ⟨the *machinery* in a factory⟩ **2** : the working parts of a machine or instrument having moving parts ⟨the *machinery* of a watch⟩ **3** : the organization or system by which something is done or carried on ⟨the *machinery* of government⟩

machine shop *n* : a workshop in which metal articles are machined and assembled

machine tool *n* : a machine (as a lathe or drill) that is operated by power and is partly or wholly automatic

ma·chin·ist \mə-'shē-nəst\ *n* : a person who makes or works on machines and engines

Mach number \'mäk-\ *n* [after Ernst *Mach* d1916 Austrian physicist] : a number representing the ratio of the speed of a body to the speed of sound in the surrounding atmosphere ⟨a *Mach number* of 2 indicates a speed that is twice the speed of sound⟩

mack·er·el \'mak-(ə-)rəl\ *n, pl* **-el** *or* **-els** [OF *makerel*] : a No. Atlantic food fish that is green with blue bars above and silvery below; *also* : any of various usu. small or medium-sized related fishes

mackerel sky *n* : a sky covered with rows of clouds resembling the patterns on a mackerel's back

mack·i·naw \'mak-ə-,nȯ\ *n* **1** : a flat-bottomed boat with pointed prow and square stern formerly much used on the upper Great Lakes **2** : a short heavy woolen plaid coat reaching to about mid-thigh

mack·in·tosh *or* **mac·in·tosh** \'mak-ən-,täsh\ *n* **1** *chiefly Brit* : RAINCOAT **2** : a lightweight waterproof fabric

macr- *or* **macro-** *comb form* [Gk *makros* long] **1** : long ⟨*macro*diagonal⟩ **2** : large ⟨*macro*spore⟩

mac·ro·ceph·a·lous \,mak-rō-'sef-ə-ləs\ *or* **mac·ro·ce·phal·ic** \-sə-'fal-ik\ *adj* : having or being an exceptionally large head or cranium ⟨a *macrocephalic* idiot⟩ — **mac·ro·ceph·a·ly** \-'sef-ə-lē\ *n*

mac·ro·cosm \'mak-rə-,käz-əm\ *n* [Gk *kosmos* order, universe] : the great world : UNIVERSE — **mac·ro·cos·mic** \,mak-rə-'käz-mik\ *adj* — **mac·ro·cos·mi·cal·ly** \-mi-k(ə-)lē\ *adv*

mac·ro·ev·o·lu·tion \,mak-rō-,ev-ə-'lü-shən, -,ē-və-\ *n* : evolutionary change involving relatively large or complex steps

mac·ro·ga·mete \,mak-rō-gə-'mēt, -'gam-,ēt\ *n* : the larger and usu. female gamete of an organism with two kinds of gametes

mac·ro·mol·e·cule \,mak-rō-'mäl-i-,kyül\ *n* : a large molecule or a group of molecules — **mac·ro·mo·lec·u·lar** \,mak-rō-mə-'lek-yə-lər\ *adj*

ma·cron \'māk-,rän, 'mak-, -rən\ *n* : a mark ⁻ placed over a vowel (as in \mā̄k\) to show that the vowel is long

mac·ro·nu·cle·us \,mak-rō-'n(y)ü-klē-əs\ *n* : a large densely staining nucleus held to exert a controlling influence over the nutritional activities of most ciliated protozoans

mac·ro·nu·tri·ent \-'n(y)ü-trē-ənt\ *n* : a chemical element (as nitrogen) required in relatively large quantities in the nutrition of a plant — compare MICRONUTRIENT

mac·ro·phage \'mak-rə-,fāj, -,fäzh\ *n* : a large phagocyte — **mac·ro·phag·ic** \,mak-rə-'faj-ik\ *adj*

mac·ro·scop·ic \,mak-rə-'skäp-ik\ *adj* **1** : large enough to be observed by the naked eye **2** : considered in terms of large units or elements

mac·u·la \'mak-yə-lə\ *n, pl* **-lae** \-,lē, -,lī\ *also* **-las** [L, spot, stain] : an anatomical structure having the form of a spot differentiated from surrounding tissues — **mac·u·lar** \-lər\ *adj*

mac·u·la·tion \,mak-yə-'lā-shən\ *n* : the arrangement of spots and markings on an animal or plant

mac·ule \'mak-,yül\ *n* : a patch of skin altered in color but usu. not elevated that is a characteristic feature of various diseases (as smallpox)

mad \'mad\ *adj* **mad·der**; **mad·dest** [OE *gemǣd*] **1** : disordered in mind : INSANE **2** : being rash and foolish ⟨a *mad* promise⟩ **3** : FURIOUS, ENRAGED ⟨to make a bull *mad*⟩ **4** : FRANTIC ⟨*mad* with pain⟩ **5** : carried away by enthusiasm ⟨*mad* about dancing⟩ **6** : wildly gay ⟨a *mad* party⟩ **7** : affected with rabies : RABID ⟨a *mad* dog⟩ **8** : ANGRY, DISPLEASED **syn** see INSANE

mad·am \'mad-əm\ *n, pl* **mes·dames** \mā-'däm, -'dam\ — used as a form of polite address to a woman ⟨*Madam*, may I help you?⟩

ma·dame \mə-'dam, *before a surname also* ,mad-əm\ *n, pl* **mes·dames** \mā-'däm, -'dam\ [F, fr. OF *ma dame* my lady] : MISTRESS — used as a title equivalent to *Mrs.* for a married woman not of English-speaking nationality

mad·cap \'mad-,kap\ *adj* : WILD, RECKLESS — **madcap** *n*

mad·den \'mad-ᵊn\ *vt* : to make mad : ENRAGE

mad·den·ing \'mad-niŋ, -ᵊn-iŋ\ *adj* : INFURIATING, IRRI-

TATING ⟨a *maddening* habit⟩ — **mad·den·ing·ly** \-niŋ-lē, -ᵊn-iŋ-lē\ *adv*

mad·der \'mad-ər\ *n* [OE *mædere*] **1** : a Eurasian herb with spear-shaped leaves, small yellowish flowers followed by berries, and red fleshy roots used to make a dye; *also* : any of several related plants **2** : madder root or a dye prepared from it **3** : a moderate to strong red

mad·ding \'mad-iŋ\ *adj* **1** : acting as if mad : FRENZIED ⟨the *madding* crowd⟩ **2** : MADDENING

made *past of* MAKE

Ma·dei·ra \mə-'dir-ə, -'der-\ *n* : an amber-colored dessert wine of the Madeira islands; *also* : a similar wine made elsewhere

ma·de·moi·selle \,mad-(ə)-mə-'zel, -mwə-'zel; mam-'zel\ *n, pl* **ma·de·moi·selles** \-'zelz\ *or* **mes·de·moi·selles** \,mād-(ə)-mə-'zel, -mwə-'zel\ [F, fr. OF *ma damoisele* my young lady] : an unmarried girl or woman — used as a title equivalent to *Miss* for an unmarried woman not of English-speaking and esp. of French nationality

made-up \'mād-'əp\ *adj* **1** : marked by the use of make-up ⟨*made-up* eyelids⟩ **2** : fancifully conceived or falsely devised ⟨a *made-up* story⟩ **3** : fully manufactured

mad·house \'mad-,haús\ *n* **1** : a place where insane persons are detained and treated **2** : a place of bewildering uproar or confusion

mad·ly \'mad-lē\ *adv* : in a mad manner

mad·man \'mad-,man, -mən\ *n* : a man who is or acts as if insane : LUNATIC — **mad·wom·an** \'mad-,wúm-ən\ *n*

mad·ness \'mad-nəs\ *n* **1** : the quality or state of being mad: as **a** : INSANITY **b** : extreme folly **c** : FRENZY, RAGE **2** : any of several disorders of animals marked by frenzied behavior; *esp* : RABIES

Ma·don·na \mə-'dän-ə\ *n* [It, fr. earlier *ma donna* my lady] : Mary the mother of Jesus

Madonna lily *n* : a white-flowered lily often forced for spring bloom

ma·dras \mə-'dras, -'dräs; 'mad-rəs\ *n* [*Madras*, India] : a fine usu. corded or striped cotton fabric

mad·re·pore \'mad-rə-,pōr, -,pór\ *n* : any of various stony reef-building corals (order Madreporaria) of tropical seas — **mad·re·po·ri·an** \,mad-rə-'pōr-ē-ən, -'pór-\ *adj or n* — **mad·re·por·ic** \-'pōr-ik, -'pór-\ *adj*

mad·ri·gal \'mad-ri-gəl\ *n* [It *madrigale*] **1 a** : a short love poem suitable for a musical setting **b** : a musical setting for a madrigal **2** : a complex 16th century part-song — **mad·ri·gal·ist** \-gə-ləst\ *n*

ma·dro·na \mə-'drō-nə\ *n* [Sp *madroño*] : an evergreen heath of western No. America with shiny leaves and edible red berries

Mae·ce·nas \mi-'sē-nəs\ *n* [L, after Gaius *Maecenas* d8 B.C. patron of Horace and Vergil] : a generous patron esp. of literature or art

mael·strom \'māl-strəm\ *n* [obs. Dutch, fr. *malen* to grind + *strom* stream] **1** : a whirlpool of great force and violence dangerous to ships **2** : a great tumult : TURMOIL ⟨a *maelstrom* of emotions⟩

mae·nad \'mē-,nad\ *n* [Gk *mainad-, mainas*, fr. *mainesthai* to be mad] **1** : BACCHANTE **2** : an unnaturally excited or distraught woman — **mae·nad·ic** \mē-'nad-ik\ *adj*

mae·sto·so \mī-'stō-sō\ *adv (or adj)* [It, fr. *maestà* majesty, fr. L *majestat-, majestas*] : so as to be majestic and stately — used as a direction in music

mae·stro \'mī-strō\ *n, pl* **mae·stros** \-strōz\ *or* **mae·stri** \-,strē\ [It, lit., master, fr. L *magister*] : a master in an art; *esp* : an eminent composer, conductor, or teacher of music

Mae West \'mā-'west\ *n* [*Mae West* b1892 American actress noted for her full figure] : an inflatable life jacket

Ma·fia \'mäf-ē-ə, 'maf-\ *n* **1** : a Sicilian secret terrorist society **2** : a secret criminal organization held to control illicit activities (as racketeering) throughout the world

mag·a·zine \'mag-ə-,zēn, ,mag-ə-'\ *n* [MF, fr. Ar *makhzin*, pl. of *makhzan* storehouse] **1** : a storehouse or warehouse esp. for military supplies **2** : a place for keeping gunpowder in a fort or ship **3** : a publication usu. containing stories, articles, or poems and issued periodically (as weekly or monthly) **4** : a supply chamber: as **a** : a chamber in a gun for holding cartridges **b** : a chamber for film on a camera or motion-picture projector

ma·gen·ta \mə-'jent-ə\ *n* **1** : a deep red dye **2** : a deep purplish red

mag·got \'mag-ət\ *n* **1** : a soft-bodied legless grub that is the larva of a two-winged fly (as the housefly) **2** : a fantastic idea : WHIM — **mag·goty** \-ət-ē\ *adj*

ma·gi \'mā-,jī\ *n pl, often cap* : the three wise men from the East who paid homage to the infant Jesus

¹mag·ic \'maj-ik\ *n* [L *magice*, fr. Gk *magikē technē* art of sorcerers, fr. *magos* Persian wise man, sorcerer] **1** : the art of persons who claim to be able to do things by the help of supernatural creatures or by their own knowledge of nature's secrets **2 a** : something that charms ⟨the *magic* of his voice⟩ **b** : seemingly hidden or secret power ⟨the *magic* of a great name⟩ **3** : SLEIGHT OF HAND ⟨entertained the children with feats of *magic*⟩

²magic *adj* **1** : of or relating to magic **2 a** : having seemingly supernatural qualities or powers **b** : ENCHANTING — **mag·i·cal** \'maj-i-kəl\ *adj* — **mag·i·cal·ly** \-k(ə-)lē\ *adv*

ma·gi·cian \mə-'jish-ən\ *n* **1** : a person skilled in magic; *esp* : SORCERER **2** : a performer of sleight of hand

magic lantern *n* : an early type of slide projector

Ma·gi·not Line \,mazh-ə-,nō-, ,maj-\ *n* [after André *Maginot* d1932 French minister of war] : a line of defensive fortifications built before World War II to protect the eastern border of France but easily outflanked by German invaders

mag·is·te·ri·al \,maj-ə-'stir-ē-əl\ *adj* **1** : AUTHORITATIVE, COMMANDING ⟨a *magisterial* personality⟩ **2** : of or relating to a magistrate or his office or duties — **mag·is·te·ri·al·ly** \-ē-ə-lē\ *adv*

mag·is·tra·cy \'maj-ə-strə-sē\ *n, pl* **-cies** **1** : the state of being a magistrate **2** : the office, power, or dignity of a magistrate **3** : a body of magistrates

mag·is·tral \'maj-e-strəl\ *adj* : MAGISTERIAL 1 — **mag·is·tral·ly** \-strə-lē\ *adv*

mag·is·trate \'maj-ə-,strāt, -strət\ *n* [L *magistratus* magistracy, magistrate, fr. *magister* master] : an official entrusted with administration of the laws: as **a** : a principal official exercising executive powers over a major political unit **b** : a local official exercising administrative and often judicial functions **c** : a local judiciary official having jurisdiction in some criminal cases

mag·ma \'mag-mə\ *n* [Gk, pasty substance, fr. *massein* to knead] : molten rock material within the earth from which an igneous rock results by cooling — **mag·mat·ic** \mag-'mat-ik\ *adj*

Mag·na Char·ta *or* **Mag·na Car·ta** \,mag-nə-'kärt-ə\ *n* [ML, lit., great charter] **1** : a charter of civil liberties to which the English barons forced King John to give his assent in June 1215 at Runnymede **2** : a document constituting a fundamental guarantee of rights and privileges

mag·na cum lau·de \,mäg-nə-,kùm-'laùd-ə, -'laùd-ē; ,mag-nə-,kəm-'lòd-ē\ *adv (or adj)* [L, with great praise] : with great academic distinction ⟨graduated *magna cum laude*⟩

mag·na·nim·i·ty \,mag-nə-'nim-ət-ē\ *n, pl* **-ties** **1 a** : nobility of character : HIGH-MINDEDNESS **b** : GENEROSITY **2** : a magnanimous act

mag·nan·i·mous \mag-'nan-ə-məs\ *adj* [L *magnanimus*, fr. *magnus* great + *animus* spirit] **1** : showing or suggesting a lofty and courageous spirit : NOBLE **2** : GENEROUS, FORGIVING — **mag·nan·i·mous·ly** *adv* — **mag·nan·i·mous·ness** *n*

mag·nate \'mag-,nāt, -nət\ *n* : a person of rank, power, influence, or distinction (as in an industry)

mag·ne·sia \mag-'nē-shə, -'nē-zhə\ *n* [NL, fr. *magnes carneus*, a white earth, lit., flesh magnet] **1** : a white highly infusible earthy solid MgO that consists of magnesium and oxygen and is used in refractories, fertilizers, and rubber and as an antacid and mild laxative **2** : MAGNESIUM — **mag·ne·sian** \-shən, -zhən\ *adj*

mag·ne·sium \mag-'nē-zē-əm, -zhəm\ *n* : a silver-white metallic element that is lighter than aluminum, is easily worked, burns with a dazzling light, and is used in making lightweight alloys — see ELEMENT table

magnesium chloride *n* : a bitter deliquescent salt $MgCl_2$ that consists of magnesium and chlorine, occurs in sea-waters and underground brines, and is used in producing magnesium metal

mag·net \'mag-nət\ *n* [L *magnet-, magnes*, fr. Gk *magnēs lithos*, lit., stone of Magnesia, ancient city in Asia Minor] **1** : a piece of some material (as the mineral iron oxide) that is able to attract iron; *esp* : a mass of iron or steel so

---

j joke; **ŋ** sing; **ō** flow; **ò** flaw; **òi** coin; **th** thin; **th̲** this; **ü** loot; **ú** foot; **y** yet; **yü** few; **yú** furious; **zh** vision

treated that it has this property   **2** : something that attracts ⟨the *magnet* of fame⟩

magnet- *or* **magneto-** *comb form*   **1** : magnetism : magnetic ⟨*magneto*electric⟩   **2** : magnetoelectric ⟨*magneto*generator⟩

mag·net·ic \mag-'net-ik\ *adj*   **1 a** : of or relating to a magnet or magnetism   **b** : having the properties of a magnet   **2** : of or relating to the earth's magnetism ⟨the *magnetic* meridian⟩   **3** : capable of being magnetized   **4** : working by magnetic attraction   **5** : gifted with great power to attract ⟨a *magnetic* personality⟩ — **mag·net·i·cal·ly** \-'net-i-k(ə-)lē\ *adv*

magnetic compass *n* : COMPASS 2a

magnetic field *n* : the portion of space near a magnetic body or a body carrying an electric current within which forces due to the body or current can be detected

magnetic needle *n* : a narrow strip of magnetized steel that is free to swing horizontally or vertically to show the direction of the earth's magnetism and that is the essential part of a compass

magnetic north *n* : the northerly direction in the earth's magnetic field indicated by the north-seeking pole of the horizontal magnetic needle

magnetic pole *n*   **1** : either of the poles of a magnet   **2** : either of two small regions which are located respectively in the polar areas of the northern and southern hemispheres and toward which the compass needle points from any direction throughout adjacent regions

magnetic recording *n* : the process of recording sound, data, or a television program by producing varying local magnetization of a moving tape, wire, or disc

magnetic storm *n* : a marked temporary disturbance of the earth's magnetic field held to be related to sunspots

magnetic tape *n* : a ribbon of thin paper or plastic coated for use in magnetic recording

magnetic wire *n* : a thin wire used in magnetic recording

mag·ne·tism \'mag-nə-,tiz-əm\ *n*   **1 a** : the property of attracting certain metals or producing a magnetic field as shown by a magnet, a magnetized material, or a conductor carrying an electric current   **b** : the science that deals with magnetic occurrences or conditions   **2** : the power to attract or charm others

mag·ne·tite \'mag-nə-,tīt\ *n* : an iron ore Fe_3O_4 that is an oxide of iron, is strongly attracted by a magnet, and sometimes acts like a magnet

mag·ne·tize \'mag-nə-,tīz\ *vt*   **1** : to cause to be magnetic : make into a magnet   **2** : CHARM, CAPTIVATE — **mag·ne·tiz·a·ble** \-,tī-zə-bəl\ *adj* — **mag·ne·ti·za·tion** \,mag-nət-ə-'zā-shən\ *n* — **mag·ne·tiz·er** \'mag-nə-,tī-zər\ *n*

mag·ne·to \mag-'nēt-ō\ *n, pl* **-tos** [short for *magneto-electric machine*] : a small electric generator using permanent magnets; *esp* : one used to produce sparks in an internal-combustion engine

mag·ne·to·elec·tric \mag-,nēt-ō-ə-'lek-trik\ *adj* : relating to electromotive forces developed by magnetic means ⟨*magnetoelectric* induction⟩

mag·ne·tom·e·ter \,mag-nə-'täm-ət-ər\ *n* : an instrument for measuring magnetic intensity esp. of the earth's magnetic field

mag·ne·to·stric·tion \mag-'nēt-ō-,strik-shən\ *n* : the change in the dimensions of various magnetic bodies caused by a change in their state of magnetization — **mag·ne·to·stric·tive** \-,nēt-ō-'strik-tiv\ *adj*

Mag·nif·i·cat \mag-'nif-i-,kat, män-'yif-i-,kät\ *n* [L, magnifies, its first word] : the canticle of the Virgin Mary in Luke 1:46–55

mag·ni·fi·ca·tion \,mag-nə-fə-'kā-shən\ *n*   **1** : the act of magnifying : the state of being magnified   **2** : the apparent enlargement of an object by an optical instrument

mag·nif·i·cence \mag-'nif-ə-sən(t)s\ *n* [L *magnificentia*, fr. *magnificus* magnificent, fr. *magnus* great + *facere* to make, do] : the quality or state of being magnificent : SPLENDOR, GRANDEUR

mag·nif·i·cent \-sənt\ *adj*   **1** : having grandeur and beauty : SPLENDID ⟨*magnificent* palaces⟩ ⟨a *magnificent* view⟩   **2** : EXALTED, NOBLE ⟨a *magnificent* character⟩ *syn* see GRAND — **mag·nif·i·cent·ly** *adv*

mag·nif·i·co \mag-'nif-i-,kō\ *n, pl* **-coes** *or* **-cos**   **1** : a nobleman of Venice   **2** : a person of high position or distinguished appearance

mag·ni·fy \'mag-nə-,fī\ *vb* **-fied; -fy·ing** [L *magnificare*, fr. *magnificus* great, magnificent]   **1** : EXTOL, LAUD   **2** : to enlarge in fact or appearance ⟨a microscope *magnifies* an object seen through it⟩   **3** : to exaggerate in importance ⟨*magnify* a fault⟩ — **mag·ni·fi·er** \-,fī(-ə)r\ *n*

magnifying glass *n* : a lens that magnifies an object seen through it

mag·nil·o·quent \mag-'nil-ə-kwənt\ *adj* [L *magnus* big + *loqui* to speak] : speaking in a high-flown or bombastic manner : GRANDILOQUENT — **mag·nil·o·quence** \-kwən(t)s\ *n* — **mag·nil·o·quent·ly** *adv*

mag·ni·tude \'mag-nə-,t(y)üd\ *n* [L *magnitudo*, fr. *magnus* great, large; akin to E *much*]   **1 a** : greatness esp. in size or extent : BIGNESS   **b** : spatial quality : SIZE   **c** : QUANTITY, NUMBER   **d** : a numerical measure of size or quantity   **2** : greatness in influence or effect   **3** : degree of brightness; *esp* : a number representing the relative brightness of a star on a scale on which the lowest number represents the brightest star and on which 1 represents the brightness of a star that is 2.512+ times greater than that of a star of brightness 2 which in turn is 2.512+ times brighter than a star of brightness 3 and so on ⟨stars of *magnitudes* 1 to 6 are visible to the naked eye⟩

mag·no·lia \mag-'nōl-yə\ *n* [after Pierre *Magnol* d1715 French botanist] : any of a genus of No. American and Asiatic shrubs and trees with usu. showy white, yellow, rose, or purple flowers appearing in early spring

mag·num opus \,mag-nəm-'ō-pəs\ *n* [L] : a great work; *esp* : a literary or artistic masterpiece

magnolia blossom

mag·pie \'mag-,pī\ *n* [*Mag* (nickname for *Margaret*) + ¹*pie*]   **1** : any of numerous noisy birds related to the jays but having a long tapered tail and black-and-white plumage   **2** : a person who chatters constantly

ma·guey \mə-'gā\ *n, pl* **magueys**   **1** : any of various fleshy-leaved agaves or closely related fiber-yielding plants   **2** : any of several hard fibers derived from magueys

Mag·yar \'mag-,yär, 'mäg-; 'mäj-,är\ *n*   **1** : a member of the dominant people of Hungary   **2** : the language of the Magyars — called also *Hungarian* — **Magyar** *adj*

ma·ha·ra·ja *or* **ma·ha·ra·jah** \,mä-hə-'räj-ə, -'räzh-ə\ *n* [Sanskrit *mahārāja*, fr. *mahat* great + *rājan* raja; akin to E *much*] : a Hindu prince ranking above a raja

ma·ha·ra·ni *or* **ma·ha·ra·nee** \-'rän-ē\ *n*   **1** : the wife of a maharaja   **2** : a Hindu princess ranking above a rani

ma·hat·ma \mə-'hät-mə, -'hat-\ *n* [Sanskrit *mahātman* great-souled, fr. *mahat* great + *ātman* soul] : a person revered for high-mindedness, wisdom, and selflessness — used as a title of honor esp. by Hindus

Ma·ha·ya·na \,mä-hə-'yän-ə\ *n* [Skt *mahāyāna*, lit., great vehicle] : a theistic branch of Buddhism comprising sects chiefly in Tibet, China, and Japan, assimilating native language and culture, and teaching compassion and universal salvation — compare HINAYANA

Mah·di \'mäd-ē\ *n* [Ar *mahdīy*, lit., one rightly guided]   **1** : a messiah expected in Muslim tradition   **2** : a Muslim leader who assumes a messianic role — **Mah·dism** \'mäd-,iz-əm\ *n* — **Mah·dist** \'mäd-əst\ *n*

Ma·hi·can \mə-'hē-kən\ *n* : MOHICAN 1

ma·hog·a·ny \mə-'häg-ə-nē\ *n, pl* **-nies**   **1** : the wood of any of various chiefly tropical trees: as   **a** : the durable usu. reddish brown and moderately hard and heavy wood of a West Indian tree that is widely used for cabinetwork   **b** : any of several African woods that vary in color from pinkish to deep reddish brown   **2** : any of various woods resembling or substituted for true mahogany   **3** : a tree that yields mahogany   **4** : a moderate reddish brown

ma·ho·nia \mə-'hō-nē-ə\ *n* [NL, fr. Bernard Mc*Mahon* d1816 American botanist] : any of a genus of shrubs of the barberry family including one grown for its showy evergreen leaves that resemble holly

ma·hout \mə-'haut\ *n* [Hindu *mahāut*] : a keeper and driver of an elephant

maid \'mād\ *n* [ME, short for *maiden*]   **1** : an unmarried girl or woman; *esp* : a young unmarried woman   **2** : a female servant

¹**maid·en** \'mād-²n\ *n* [OE *mægden, mæden*]   **1** : a young unmarried girl or woman   **2** : VIRGIN

²**maiden** *adj*   **1 a** : UNMARRIED ⟨*maiden* aunt⟩   **b** : VIRGIN

2 : of, relating to, or befitting a maiden   **3** : FIRST, EARLIEST ⟨*maiden* voyage⟩   **4** : INTACT, FRESH

maid·en·hair \'mād-ᵊn-,ha(ə)r, -,he(ə)r\ *n* : a fern with slender stems and delicate much-divided often feathery leaves — called also *maidenhair fern*

maidenhair tree *n* : GINKGO

maid·en·hood \'mād-ᵊn-,hùd\ *n* : the condition or time of being a maiden

maid·en·ly \'mād-ᵊn-lē\ *adj* : of or relating to a maiden or maidenhood — **maid·en·li·ness** *n*

maiden name *n* : the surname of a woman before she is married

maid-in-wait·ing *n*, *pl* **maids-in-waiting** : a young woman of a queen's or princess's household appointed to attend her

maid of honor   **1** : an unmarried woman usu. of noble birth who attends a queen or princess   **2** : an unmarried woman serving as the principal female attendant of a bride at her wedding

maid·ser·vant \'mād-,sər-vənt\ *n* : a female servant

¹mail \'māl\ *n* [ME male bag, fr. OF, of Germanic origin]   **1** : matter (as letters or parcels) sent under public authority from one person to another through the agency of the post office   **2** : the whole system used in the public sending and delivery of letters and parcels ⟨do business by *mail*⟩   **3** : something that comes in the mail; *esp* : the contents of a single delivery   **4** : a conveyance that transports mail

²mail *vt* : to send by mail : POST — **mail·a·ble** \'mā-lə-bəl\ *adj* — **mail·er** *n*

³mail *n* [MF *maille*, fr. L *macula* spot, mesh] : a flexible network of small metal rings linked together for use as armor ⟨a coat of *mail*⟩

mail·box \'māl-,bäks\ *n*   **1** : a public box for the collection of mail   **2** : a private box for the delivery of mail

mail: fragment of a medieval hauberk

mailed \'māld\ *adj* : protected or armed with or as if with mail ⟨a *mailed* fist⟩

mail·man \'māl-,man\ *n* : a man who delivers mail or who collects mail from public mailboxes — called also *postman*

mail order *n* : an order for goods that is received and filled by mail — **mail-order** \'māl-,órd-ər\ *adj*

mail-order house *n* : a retail establishment whose business is conducted by mail

maim \'mām\ *vt* [ME *maynhen*, *maymen*, fr. OF *maynier*]   **1** : to commit mayhem upon   **2** : to mutilate, disfigure, or wound seriously : CRIPPLE — **maim·er** *n*

¹main \'mān\ *n* [OE *mægen*; akin to E *may*]   **1** : physical strength : FORCE — used in the phrase *with might and main*   **2 a** : MAINLAND   **b** : HIGH SEAS   **3** : a principal pipe, duct, or circuit of a utility system ⟨gas *main*⟩ ⟨water *main*⟩   **4 a** : MAINMAST   **b** : MAINSAIL — **in the main** : for the most part

²main *adj*   **1 a** : OUTSTANDING, CONSPICUOUS   **b** : CHIEF, PRINCIPAL   **2** : fully exerted : SHEER ⟨by *main* force⟩   **3** : connected with or located near the mainmast or mainsail   **4** : being a clause that is capable of standing alone as a simple sentence but actually is part of a larger sentence that includes also a subordinate clause or another main clause

³main *n* : a series of matches in cockfighting

main·land \'mān-,land, -lənd\ *n* : a continent or the main part of a continent as distinguished from an offshore island or sometimes from a cape or a peninsula — **main·land·er** \-,lan-dər, -lən-\ *n*

main·line \'mān-'līn\ *vi*, *slang* : to inject a narcotic drug (as heroin) into a principal vein

main·ly \'mān-lē\ *adv* : for the most part : CHIEFLY

main·mast \'mān-,mast, -məst\ *n* : the principal mast of a sailing ship

main·sail \'mān-,sāl, 'mān(t)-səl\ *n* : the principal sail on the mainmast

main·sheet \'mān-,shēt\ *n* : a rope by which the mainsail is trimmed and secured

main·spring \-,spriŋ\ *n*   **1** : the principal spring in a mechanism esp. of a watch or clock   **2** : the chief motive, cause, or force underlying or responsible for an action

main·stay \-,stā\ *n*   **1** : the large strong rope running from the maintop of a ship usu. to the foot of the foremast   **2** : a chief support ⟨the *mainstay* of the family⟩

main stem *n* : the main street of a city or town

main·stream \'mān-,strēm\ *n* : a prevailing current or direction of activity or influence

Main Street *n*   **1** : the principal street of a small town   **2** : the sections of a country centering about its small towns

main·tain \mān-'tān, mən-\ *vt* [OF *maintenir*, fr. L *manu tenēre* to hold with the hand]   **1** : to keep in an existing state; *esp* : to keep in a state of good repair or efficiency ⟨*maintain* one's health⟩ ⟨*maintain* machinery⟩   **2** : to uphold and defend against opposition or danger ⟨*maintain* a position by argument⟩   **3** : to continue in : carry on : keep up ⟨*maintain* his balance⟩⟨*maintain* a correspondence⟩   **4 a** : to provide for : SUPPORT ⟨*maintains* his family by working⟩   **b** : SUSTAIN ⟨enough food to *maintain* life⟩   **5** : to affirm in or as if in argument : ASSERT ⟨*maintained* that all men are not equal⟩ — **main·tain·a·ble** \-'tā-nə-bəl\ *adj* — **main·tain·er** *n*

syn MAINTAIN, ASSERT, VINDICATE, JUSTIFY mean to uphold as true, right, or just. MAINTAIN stresses firmness of conviction; ASSERT suggests vigor of statement and determination to make others accept one's claim; VINDICATE implies successfully defending what was under question or attack; JUSTIFY implies showing to be true or valid esp. by appeal to a standard or to precedent

main·te·nance \'mānt-nən(t)s, -ᵊn-ən(t)s\ *n*   **1** : the act of maintaining : the state of being maintained ⟨*maintenance* of law and order is the responsibility of the police⟩   **2** : something that maintains or supports; *esp* : a supply of necessities and conveniences   **3** : the upkeep of property or machinery ⟨workmen in charge of *maintenance*⟩

main·top \'mān-,täp\ *n* : a platform about the head of the mainmast of a square-rigged ship

mai·son·ette \,māz-ᵊn-'et\ *n* [F *maisonnette*, dim. of *maison* house]   **1** : a small house   **2** : an apartment often of two stories

maî·tre d'hô·tel \,mā-trə-(,)dō-'tel\ *n*, *pl* **maîtres d'hôtel** *same*\ [F, lit., master of house]   **1** : MAJORDOMO   **2** : HEADWAITER

maize \'māz\ *n* [Sp *maíz*, of AmerInd origin] : INDIAN CORN

ma·jes·tic \mə-'jes-tik\ *adj* : being stately and dignified : NOBLE **syn** see GRAND — **ma·jes·ti·cal·ly** \-ti-k(ə-)lē\ *adv*

maj·es·ty \'maj-ə-stē\ *n*, *pl* **-ties** [L *majestas*, fr. *major* greater]   **1** : sovereign power, authority, or dignity; *also* : the person of a sovereign — used as a title for a king, queen, emperor, or empress   **2 a** : royal bearing or quality : GRANDEUR   **b** : greatness of quality or character

ma·jol·i·ca \mə-'jäl-i-kə\ *n* [It *maiolica*, fr. ML *Majolica* Majorca] : any of several faiences; *esp* : an Italian tin-glazed pottery

¹ma·jor \'mā-jər\ *adj* [L *major*, compar. of *magnus* great]   **1 a** : greater in dignity, rank, or importance ⟨a *major* poet⟩   **b** : greater in number, quantity, or extent ⟨received the *major* part of the blame⟩   **2** : having attained majority   **3 a** : having half steps between the 3d and 4th and the 7th and 8th degrees ⟨*major* scale⟩   **b** : based on a major scale ⟨*major* key⟩ ⟨*major* chord⟩ ⟨*major* interval⟩   **4** : involving risk to life : SERIOUS ⟨*major* illness⟩   **5** : of or relating to an academic major

²major *n*   **1** : a person having attained majority   **2** : a major musical interval, scale, key, or mode   **3** : a commissioned officer (as in the army) ranking above a captain and below a lieutenant colonel   **4 a** : an academic subject chosen by a student as a field of specialization   **b** : a student specializing in such a field

³major *vi* **ma·jored**; **ma·jor·ing** \'māj-(ə-)riŋ\ : to pursue an academic major

ma·jor·do·mo \,mā-jər-'dō-mō\ *n*, *pl* **-mos** [Sp *mayordomo* or obs. It *maiordomo*, fr. ML *major domus*, lit., chief of the house]   **1** : a man in charge of a great household and esp. of a royal establishment : a head steward   **2** : BUTLER, STEWARD

majorette *n* : DRUM MAJORETTE

major general *n* : a commissioned officer (as in the army) ranking above a brigadier general and below a lieutenant general

ma·jor·i·ty \mə-'jór-ət-ē, -'jär-\ *n*, *pl* **-ties**   **1 a** : the age at which one is given full civil rights; *esp* : the age of 21   **b** : the status of one who has attained this age   **2 a** : a number greater than half of a total **b :** the amount by which such a greater number exceeds the smaller number ⟨won by a *majority* of seven⟩ **c :** the preponderant quantity or share **3 :** the group or party that makes up the greater part of a whole body of persons **4 :** the military office or rank of a major

syn MAJORITY, PLURALITY mean a winning margin of votes. MAJORITY specifically refers to the number in excess of half of all the votes cast ⟨270 votes gave him a *majority* of 20 out of the total of 500 votes⟩ PLURALITY refers to the number that is in excess of those of the nearest rival but may not be more than half of the total votes cast

majority rule *n* : a political principle providing that a majority of an organized group shall have the power to make decisions binding upon the whole group

major league *n* : a league in the highest class of U.S. professional baseball; *also* : a league of major importance in another sport (as hockey)

major order *n* **1 :** the order of priest, deacon, or subdeacon in the Roman Catholic Church **2 :** the order of bishop, priest, or deacon in the Eastern or Anglican Church

major party *n* : a political party strong enough to win control of a government periodically and when defeated to be the principal opposition to the party in power

major premise *n* : the premise of a syllogism containing the term that appears in the predicate of the conclusion

major seminary *n* : a Roman Catholic seminary giving usu. the entire six years of college and theological training

major suit *n* : hearts or spades in bridge

maj·us·cule \'maj-əs-ˌkyül, mə-'jəs-\ *n* [L *majusculus* rather large, dim. of *major*] : a large letter (as a capital) — **ma·jus·cu·lar** \mə-'jəs-kyə-lər\ *adj* — **majuscule** *adj*

¹make \'māk\ *vb* **made** \'mād\; **mak·ing** [OE *macian* to cause, perform, construct] **1 a :** to seem to begin an action ⟨he *made* as if to go⟩ **b :** to act so as to appear ⟨*make* merry⟩ **2 :** to cause to be undergone ⟨*made* trouble for us⟩ **b :** to cause to exist, occur, or appear : CREATE ⟨*make* a disturbance⟩ **c :** to create for some purpose or goal ⟨he was *made* to be an actor⟩ **3 a :** to form or shape out of material : FASHION ⟨*make* a dress⟩ **b :** to put together out of components : CONSTRUCT, BUILD ⟨*make* a table⟩ **c :** to comprise or become combined into a whole : CONSTITUTE ⟨a house *made* of stone⟩ ⟨five *make* a quorum⟩ **4 :** to frame or formulate in the mind ⟨*make* plans⟩ **5 a :** to decide by computation or estimation ⟨I *make* it an even $5⟩ **b :** to regard as being : CONSIDER ⟨he is not the fool you *make* him⟩ **c :** UNDERSTAND ⟨unable to *make* anything of the story⟩ **6 :** to set in order : PREPARE ⟨*make* a bed⟩ **7 :** to cut and spread for drying ⟨*make* hay⟩ **8 :** to cause to be or become ⟨*made* himself useful⟩ **9 a :** ENACT, ESTABLISH ⟨*make* laws⟩ **b :** to execute in an appropriate manner ⟨*make* a will⟩⟨*make* a novena⟩ **c :** SET, NAME ⟨*make* a price⟩⟨*make* clubs trump⟩ **10 :** to complete an electric circuit **11 a :** to carry out a specified action : UNDERTAKE, PERFORM ⟨*make* war⟩ ⟨*make* a curtsy⟩ **b :** FOLLOW, TRAVERSE ⟨the mailman *made* his rounds⟩ **12 :** to produce by action or effort expended on something ⟨*made* a mess of the job⟩ **13 :** to cause to act in some manner : COMPEL ⟨*made* him return home⟩ **14 :** to cause or assure the success of ⟨the first case *makes* or breaks a lawyer⟩ **15 :** to amount to in significance ⟨it *makes* a great difference⟩ **16 :** REACH, ATTAIN ⟨the ship *makes* port tonight⟩ ⟨he *made* corporal in 10 months⟩ ⟨*make* the first team⟩ **17 a :** to gain by or as if by working ⟨*makes* good money at the foundry⟩ **b :** to acquire by effort ⟨*makes* friends easily⟩ **c :** to score in a game or sport ⟨*make* a point after a touchdown⟩ **18 a :** CATCH ⟨*make* the train⟩ **b :** to set out in pursuit ⟨*made* after the fox⟩ — **make away with** **1 :** to carry off **2 :** KILL, DESTROY **3 :** CONSUME, EAT — **make believe :** FEIGN, PRETEND — **make good 1 :** to make complete : FULFILL ⟨*made good* his promise⟩ ⟨*make good* his escape⟩ **2 :** to make up for a deficiency ⟨*make good* the loss⟩ **3 :** SUCCEED ⟨*make good* as a salesman⟩ — **make head 1 :** to make progress : ADVANCE **2 :** to build up pressure (as in a steam boiler) — **make love 1 :** WOO, COURT — **make sail 1 :** to raise or spread sail **2 :** to set out on a voyage — **make time 1 :** to travel fast **2 :** to gain time — **make way 1 :** to open or give room for passing or entering

⟨the crowd *made way* for the injured man⟩ **2 :** to make progress

²make *n* **1 :** the way in which a thing is made : manner of construction ⟨the *make* was so poor the chair fell apart⟩ **2 :** the type or process of making or manufacturing ⟨the latest *make* of car⟩ **3 :** the completion of an electric circuit

¹make–be·lieve \'māk-bə-ˌlēv\ *n* : a pretending to believe (as in the play of children) : PRETENSE

²make–believe *adj* **1 :** PRETENDED, IMAGINARY ⟨a *make= believe* playmate⟩ **2 :** INSINCERE

make–do \'māk-ˌdü\ *adj* : MAKESHIFT — **make–do** *n*

make out *vb* **1 :** to draw up in writing ⟨*make out* a shopping list⟩ **2 :** to find or grasp the meaning of : UNDERSTAND ⟨how do you *make* that *out*⟩ **3 :** to represent as being ⟨*made* him *out* a hero⟩ **4 :** DISCERN ⟨*make out* a form in the fog⟩ **5 :** SUCCEED, PROSPER ⟨*make out* well in business⟩

make over *vt* **1 :** to transfer the title of : CONVEY **2 :** REMAKE, REMODEL

mak·er \'mā-kər\ *n* : one that makes: as **a** *cap* : ²GOD **b :** a person who makes a promissory note

make·ready \'māk-ˌred-ē\ *n* : final preparation (as of a form on a printing press) for running; *also* : material used in this preparation

make·shift \'māk-ˌshift\ *n* : a temporary expedient : SUBSTITUTE — **makeshift** *adj*

make up \(')māk-'əp\ *vb* **1 a :** CONSTRUCT, COMPOSE ⟨*make up* a poem⟩ **b :** to combine to produce a whole : COMPRISE ⟨nine players *make up* a team⟩ **2 :** INVENT, CONCOCT ⟨*make up* an excuse⟩ **3 :** to arrange type matter into columns or pages **4 :** to compensate for a deficiency **5 :** to become reconciled ⟨they quarreled and *made up*⟩ **6 a :** to put on costumes or makeup (as for a play) **b :** to apply cosmetics

make·up \'māk-ˌəp\ *n* **1 :** the way the parts or elements of something are put together : composition or manner of composition ⟨last-minute changes in the *makeup* of the book⟩ **2 :** materials (as wigs or cosmetics) used in making up or in special costuming ⟨put on *makeup* for a play⟩ ⟨a little girl too young to wear *makeup*⟩ **3 :** the arrangement (as in a newspaper or book) of printed matter and pictures

mak·ing \'mā-kiŋ\ *n* **1 :** the action of one that makes **2 :** a process or means of advancement or success ⟨misfortune is sometimes the *making* of a man⟩ **3 :** material from which something can be developed ⟨there is the *making* of a racehorse in this colt⟩ **4 :** *for cigarette materials usu* 'mā-kənz\ *pl* : the materials from which something can be made ⟨roll a cigarette from the *makings*⟩

mal- *comb form* [MF, fr. *mal* bad (fr. L *malus*) & *mal* badly, fr. L *male*] **1 a :** bad ⟨*mal*practice⟩ **b :** badly ⟨*mal*odorous⟩ **2 a :** abnormal ⟨*mal*formation⟩ **b :** abnormally ⟨*mal*formed⟩

ma·lac·ca cane \mə-ˌlak-ə-\ *n* [fr. *Malacca*, Malaya] : an often mottled cane from an Asiatic rattan palm used esp. for walking sticks and umbrella handles

Mal·a·chi \'mal-ə-ˌkī\ *n* **1 :** a Hebrew prophet of the 5th century B.C. **2 —** see BIBLE table

mal·a·chite \'mal-ə-ˌkīt\ *n* [Gk *molochites*, fr. *malachē*, *molochē* mallow] : a green mineral $Cu_2CO_3(OH)_2$ that consists of copper, carbon, oxygen, and hydrogen and is used as an ore of copper and for ornamental objects

mal·a·col·o·gy \ˌmal-ə-'käl-ə-jē\ *n* [Gk *malakos* soft] : a branch of zoology dealing with mollusks — **mal·a·col·o·gist** \-jəst\ *n*

mal·adapt·ed \ˌmal-ə-'dap-təd\ *adj* : poorly suited to a particular use, purpose, or situation

mal·ad·just·ed \ˌmal-ə-'jəs-təd\ *adj* : poorly or inadequately adjusted; *esp* : lacking harmony with one's environment — **mal·ad·just·ment** \-'jəs(t)-mənt\ *n*

mal·ad·min·is·ter \ˌmal-əd-'min-ə-stər\ *vt* : to administer badly — **mal·ad·min·is·tra·tion** \-ˌmin-ə-'strā-shən\ *n*

mal·adroit \ˌmal-ə-'drȯit\ *adj* : not adroit : AWKWARD, CLUMSY — **mal·adroit·ly** *adv* — **mal·adroit·ness** *n*

mal·a·dy \'mal-əd-ē\ *n, pl* **-dies** [OF *maladie*, fr. *malade* sick, fr. L *male habitus* in bad condition] : a disease or disorder of the body or mind : AILMENT

Mal·a·gasy \ˌmal-ə-'gas-ē\ *n* **1 :** a native or inhabitant of Madagascar or the Malagasy Republic **2 :** the language of the Malagasy people — **Malagasy** *adj*

ə abut; ᵊ kitten; ər further; a back; ā bake; ä cot, cart; aù out; ch chin; e less; ē easy; g gift; i trip; ī life

mal·aise \ma-'lāz\ *n* [F, fr. *mal-* + *aise* ease] **:** an indefinite feeling of bodily or mental disorder

mal·a·mute *or* **mal·e·mute** \'mal-ə-,myüt\ *n* **:** a sled dog of northern No. America; *esp* **:** ALASKAN MALAMUTE

mal·a·pert \,mal-ə-'pərt\ *adj* **:** impudently bold **:** SAUCY — **mal·a·pert·ly** *adv* — **mal·a·pert·ness** *n*

mal·a·prop·ism \'mal-ə-,präp-,iz-əm\ *n* [fr. Mrs. *Malaprop*, character in Sheridan's *The Rivals* (1775) given to misusing words] **1 :** a usu. humorous misuse of a word esp. for one of similar sound by someone unaware of the error **2 :** an example of malapropism — **mal·a·prop** \-,präp\ *or* **mal·a·prop·i·an** \,mal-ə-'präp-ē-ən\ *adj*

mal·ap·ro·pos \,mal-,ap-rə-'pō\ *adv* [F *mal à propos*, lit., badly (fitted) to the purpose] **:** in an inappropriate or inopportune way — **malapropos** *adj*

ma·lar \'mā-lər\ *adj* [L *mala* jawbone, cheek] **:** of or relating to the cheek or the side of the head

ma·lar·ia \mə-'ler-ē-ə\ *n* [It, fr. *mala aria* bad air] **:** a disease caused by protozoan parasites in the red blood cells, transmitted by the bite of mosquitoes, and characterized by periodic attacks of chills and fever — **ma·lar·i·al** \-ē-əl\ *adj* — **ma·lar·i·ous** \-ē-əs\ *adj*

Mal·a·thi·on \,mal-ə-'thī-,än\ *trademark* — used for an insecticide

Ma·lay \mə-'lā, 'mā-,lā\ *n* **1 :** a member of a people of the Malay peninsula and adjacent islands **2 :** the language of the Malay people — **Malay** *adj* — **Ma·lay·an** \mə-'lā-ən, 'mā-,lā-\ *adj or n*

mal·con·tent \,mal-kən-'tent\ *adj* **:** dissatisfied with the existing state of affairs **:** DISCONTENTED — **malcontent** *n*

mal de mer \,mal-də-'me(ə)r\ *n* [F] **:** SEASICKNESS

¹male \'māl\ *adj* [MF, fr. L *masculus*, dim. of *mas* male] **1 a :** of, relating to, or being the sex that fathers young **b :** STAMINATE; *esp* **:** having only staminate flowers and not producing fruit or seeds ⟨a *male* holly⟩ **2 a :** of, relating to, or characteristic of the male sex ⟨a deep *male* voice⟩ **b :** made up of males ⟨a *male* choir⟩ **3 :** designed for fitting into a corresponding hollow part — **male·ness** *n*

syn MANLY, MANFUL, MANNISH: MALE applies to animals and plants in a simple distinguishing of sex; MANLY suggests the characteristic qualities of a mature man and applies chiefly to youth; MANFUL is narrower in scope in stressing courage and resolution; MANNISH applies to women having or affecting male qualities

²male *n* **:** a male plant or animal

mal·e·dic·tion \,mal-ə-'dik-shən\ *n* [LL *maledict-, maledicere* to curse, fr. L, to speak evil of, fr. *male* badly + *dicere* to say] **:** a prayer for harm to befall someone **:** CURSE — **mal·e·dic·to·ry** \-'dik-t(ə-)rē\ *adj*

mal·e·fac·tion \-'fak-shən\ *n* **:** an evil deed **:** CRIME

mal·e·fac·tor \'mal-ə-,fak-tər\ *n* [L *malefact-, malefacere* to do evil, fr. *male* badly + *facere* to do] **1 :** one guilty of a crime or offense **2 :** EVILDOER

male fern *n* **:** a fern that yields a resinous substance used as a worm remedy

ma·lef·ic \mə-'lef-ik\ *adj* **1 :** BALEFUL **2 :** MALICIOUS

ma·lef·i·cent \mə-'lef-ə-sənt\ *adj* **:** working or productive of harm or evil **:** HARMFUL — **ma·lef·i·cence** \-sən(t)s\ *n*

ma·lev·o·lent \mə-'lev-ə-lənt\ *adj* [L *malevolent-, malevolens*, fr. *male* badly + *volens*, prp. of *velle* to wish] **:** having or showing ill will toward others **:** SPITEFUL — **ma·lev·o·lence** \-'lev-ə-lən(t)s\ *n* **syn** see MALICE — **ma·lev·o·lent·ly** *adv*

mal·fea·sance \(')mal-'fēz-ᵊn(t)s\ *n* **:** wrongful conduct esp. by a public official

mal·for·ma·tion \,mal-fȯr-'mā-shən, -fər-\ *n* **:** an irregular, anomalous, abnormal, or faulty formation or structure

mal·formed \(')mal-'fȯrmd\ *adj* **:** marked by malformation

mal·func·tion \(')mal-'fəŋ(k)-shən\ *vi* **:** to fail to operate in the normal or usual manner — **malfunction** *n*

mal·ic acid \,mal-ik-, ,mā-lik-\ *n* [L *malum* apple, fr. Gk *malon, mēlon*] **:** an acid $C_4H_6O_5$ found esp. in various plant juices

mal·ice \'mal-əs\ *n* [OF, fr. L *malitia*, fr. *malus* bad] **:** ILL WILL; *esp* **:** the deliberate intention of doing unjustified harm for the satisfaction of doing it

syn MALEVOLENCE, MALIGNITY: MALICE may range from

a passing mischievous impulse to a deep-seated unreasoning dislike and desire to cause harm and suffering; MALEVOLENCE stresses evil intent or influence rather than action; MALIGNITY stresses the intensity and driving force of malevolence and suggests a quality that is part of one's nature

ma·li·cious \mə-'lish-əs\ *adj* **1 :** feeling strong ill will **:** being mean and spiteful **2 :** done or carried on with malice or caused by malice ⟨*malicious* gossip⟩ — **ma·li·cious·ly** *adv* — **ma·li·cious·ness** *n*

¹ma·lign \mə-'līn\ *adj* [L *malignus*, lit., ill-natured, fr. *male* bad + *gignere* to beget] **1 :** moved by ill will toward others **:** MALEVOLENT **2 :** operating so as to injure or hurt ⟨hindered by *malign* influences⟩

²malign *vt* **:** to utter injurious or false reports about **:** speak evil of **:** DEFAME **syn** see SLANDER

ma·lig·nan·cy \mə-'lig-nən-sē\ *n, pl* **-cies 1 :** the quality or state of being malignant **2 :** a malignant tumor

ma·lig·nant \-nənt\ *adj* **1 a** *obs* **:** DISAFFECTED, MALCONTENT **b :** evil in influence or effect **:** INJURIOUS **c :** MALEVOLENT, MALICIOUS **2 :** tending or likely to produce death esp. through being dispersed and growing throughout the body ⟨*malignant* tumor⟩ — **ma·lig·nant·ly** *adv*

ma·lig·ni·ty \mə-'lig-nət-ē\ *n, pl* **-ties 1 :** the quality or state of being malignant **:** MALIGNANCY **2 :** something (as an act or an event) that is malignant **syn** see MALICE

ma·li·hi·ni \,mäl-ē-'hē-nē\ *n* [Hawaiian, stranger] **:** a newcomer to Hawaii

ma·lin·ger \mə-'liŋ-gər\ *vi* **ma·lin·gered; ma·lin·ger·ing** \-g(ə-)riŋ\ [F *malingre* sickly] **:** to pretend incapacity (as illness) so as to avoid duty or work — **ma·lin·ger·er** \-gər-ər\ *n*

mal·i·son \'mal-ə-sən, -zən\ *n* [OF *maleiçon*, fr. LL *malediction-, maledictio*] **:** MALEDICTION, CURSE

¹mall \'mȯl\ *var of* MAUL

²mall \'mȯl, 'mal\ *n* **1 :** a shaded walk **:** PROMENADE **2 :** a grassy strip between two roadways

mal·lard \'mal-ərd\ *n, pl* **mallard** *or* **mallards** [MF *mallart*] **:** a common and widely distributed wild duck of the northern hemisphere that is ancestral to the domestic ducks

mal·le·a·ble \'mal-ē-ə-bəl, 'mal-(y)ə-bəl\ *adj* [ML *malleare* to hammer, fr. L *malleus* hammer] **1 :** capable of being beaten out, extended, or shaped by hammer blows or by the pressure of rollers ⟨a *malleable* metal⟩ **2 :** ADAPTABLE, PLIABLE — **mal·le·a·bil·i·ty** \,mal-ē-ə-'bil-ət-ē, ,mal-(y)ə-'bil-\ *n*

mal·lee \'mal-ē\ *n* **:** a dense growth of shrubby eucalypts; *also* **:** Australian land covered with mallee

mal·let \'mal-ət\ *n* [MF *maillet*, dim. of *mail* hammer, fr. L *malleus*] **1 :** a hammer usu. having a barrel-shaped head of wood; *esp* **:** a tool with a short handle and a large head used for driving another tool (as a chisel) **2 :** a long-handled club with a cylindrical head used in playing croquet **3 :** a polo stick

mallet

mal·le·us \'mal-ē-əs\ *n, pl* **mal·lei** \-ē-,ī, -ē-,ē\ [NL, L, hammer] **:** the outermost of the three small bones of the mammalian ear — compare STAPES

mal·low \'mal-ō\ *n* [OE *mealwe*, fr. L *malva*] **:** any of a genus of herbs with lobed or dissected leaves, usu. showy flowers, and a disk-shaped fruit

malm·sey \'mä(l)m-zē\ *n, pl* **malmseys** *often cap* **:** a sweet aromatic wine orig. produced around Monemvasia in Greece

mal·nour·ished \(')mal-'nər-isht, -'nə-risht\ *adj* **:** poorly nourished

mal·nu·tri·tion \,mal-n(y)ù-'trish-ən\ *n* **:** faulty and esp. inadequate nutrition — **mal·nu·tri·tion·al** \-'trish-nəl, -ən-ᵊl\ *adj*

mal·oc·clu·sion \,mal-ə-'klü-zhən\ *n* **:** faulty coming together of teeth in biting

mal·odor·ous \(')mal-'ōd-ə-rəs\ *adj* **:** bad-smelling — **mal·odor·ous·ly** *adv* — **mal·odor·ous·ness** *n*

Mal·pigh·i·an corpuscle \(,)mal-,pig-ē-ən-, -,pē-gē-\ *n* [Marcello *Malpighi* d1694 Italian anatomist] **:** a kidney glomerulus with its membrane

Malpighian tubule *n* **:** any of a group of long blind vessels opening into the intestine in various arthropods and functioning in excretion

mal·prac·tice \(')mal-'prak-təs\ *n* **1** : violation of professional standards esp. by negligence or improper conduct **2** : an injurious, negligent, or improper practice — **mal·prac·ti·tion·er** \,mal-,prak-'tish-(ə-)nər\ *n*

¹malt \'mólt\ *n* [OE *mealt*; akin to E *melt*] **1** : grain and esp. barley softened by steeping in water, allowed to germinate, and used chiefly in brewing and distilling **2** : MALTED MILK — **malt** *adj* — **malty** \'mól-tē\ *adj*

²malt *vb* **1** : to convert into malt **2** : to make or treat with malt or malt extract **3** : to become malt

malt·ase \'mól-,tās\ *n* : an enzyme that accelerates the hydrolysis of maltose to glucose

malted milk *n* **1** : a soluble powder prepared from dried milk and malted cereals **2** : a beverage made by dissolving malted milk in a liquid (as milk)

Mal·tese \mól-'tēz\ *n, pl* **Maltese** **1** : a native or inhabitant of Malta **2** : the Semitic language of the Maltese people — **Maltese** *adj*

Maltese cat *n* : a bluish gray domestic short-haired cat

Maltese cross *n* : a cross with four arms of equal size that increase in width toward the outward ends — see CROSS illustration

Mal·thu·sian \mal-'th(y)ü-zhən, mól-\ *adj* : of or relating to Malthus or to his theory that population unless checked (as by war or disease) tends to increase at a faster rate than its means of subsistence — **Malthusian** *n* — **Mal·thu·sian·ism** \-zhə-,niz-əm\ *n*

malt·ose \'mól-,tōs\ *n* : a sugar formed esp. from starch by the action of enzymes and used in brewing and distilling

mal·treat \(')mal-'trēt\ *vt* : to treat unkindly or roughly : ABUSE ⟨*maltreat* animals⟩ — **mal·treat·ment** \-mənt\ *n*

mam·ba \'mäm-bə, 'mam-\ *n* [Zulu *im-amba*] : any of several African venomous snakes related to the cobras but lacking a hood

mam·bo \'mäm-bō\ *n, pl* **mambos** [AmerSp] : a dance of Haitian origin related to the rumba — **mambo** *vi*

¹mam·ma *or* **ma·ma** \'mäm-ə\ *n* [baby talk] : MOTHER

²mam·ma \'mam-ə\ *n, pl* **mam·mae** \'mam-,ē, -,ī\ : a mammary gland and its accessory parts — **mam·mate** \'mam-,āt\ *adj*

mam·mal \'mam-əl\ *n* [L *mamma* mother, breast] : any of a class (Mammalia) of higher vertebrates comprising man and all other animals that nourish their young with milk secreted by mammary glands and have the skin usu. more or less covered with hair — **mam·ma·li·an** \mə-'mā-lē-ən, ma-'mā-\ *adj or n*

mam·mal·o·gy \mə-'mal-ə-jē, ma-'mal-\ *n* : a branch of zoology dealing with mammals — **mam·mal·o·gist** \-jəst\ *n*

mam·ma·ry \'mam-ə-rē\ *adj* : of, relating to, or being one of the large compound sebaceous glands that in female mammals are modified to secrete milk and in males are usu. rudimentary, are situated ventrally in pairs, and usu. terminate in a nipple

mam·mil·la·ry \'mam-ə-,ler-ē, ma-'mil-ə-rē\ *adj* **1** : of, relating to, or resembling a breast **2** : studded with breast-shaped protuberances

mam·mil·late \'mam-ə-,lāt\ *or* **mam·mil·lat·ed** \-,lāt-əd\ *adj* : having or shaped like small bluntly rounded protuberances — **mam·mil·la·tion** \,mam-ə-'lā-shən\ *n*

mam·mon \'mam-ən\ *n, often cap* [LL *mammona*, fr. Gk *mamōna*, fr. Aramaic *māmōnā* riches] : an often personified devotion to material possessions; *also* : WEALTH

¹mam·moth \'mam-əth\ *n* [Russ *mamont, mamot*] **1** : any of numerous large hairy extinct elephants with very long upward-curving tusks **2** : something immense of its kind : GIANT

²mammoth *adj* : of very great size : GIGANTIC

mam·my \'mam-ē\ *n, pl* **mammies** **1** : MAMMA **2** : a Negro woman serving as a nurse to white children esp. formerly in the southern states of the U.S.

¹man \'man\ *n, pl* **men** \'men\ [OE] **1 a** : a human being; *esp* : an adult male human **b** : the human race : MANKIND **c** : HUSBAND, LOVER **d** : any member of the natural family to which human beings belong including both human beings and extinct related forms known only from fossils **e** : one possessing in high

degree the qualities considered distinctive of manhood **2 a** : VASSAL **b** : an adult male servant **c** *pl* : the working force as distinguished from the employer **3** : an indefinite person ⟨a *man* could easily be killed then⟩ **4** : one of the pieces with which various games (as chess) are played

²man *vt* **manned; man·ning** **1 a** : to supply with men (as for management or operation) ⟨*man* a fleet⟩ **b** : to station members of a ship's crew at ⟨*man* the capstan⟩ **2** : to furnish with strength : BRACE

ma·na \'män-ə\ *n* [of Melanesian & Polynesian origin] **1** : the power of the elemental forces of nature embodied in an object or person **2** : PRESTIGE

man-about-town \,man-ə-,baut-'taun\ *n, pl* **men-about-town** : a worldly and socially active man

¹man·a·cle \'man-i-kəl\ *n* [MF *manicle*, fr. L *manicula*, dim. of *manus* hand] **1** : a shackle for the hand or wrist : HANDCUFF — usu. used in pl. **2** : something that restrains or restricts

²manacle *vt* **-cled; -cling** \-k(ə-)liŋ\ **1** : to put manacles on **2** : RESTRAIN

¹man·age \'man-ij\ *vb* [It *maneggiare* to handle, fr. *mano* hand, fr. L *manus*] **1** : to oversee and make decisions about : DIRECT ⟨*manage* a factory⟩ **2** : to make responsive or submissive : HANDLE, MANIPULATE ⟨*manages* his skis well⟩ ⟨skill in *managing* problem children⟩ **3** : to treat with care : use to best advantage : HUSBAND ⟨there's enough food if it's *managed* well⟩ **4** : to succeed in one's purpose : get along : CONTRIVE ⟨*manages* despite a handicap⟩ ⟨always *manages* to win⟩ **syn** see CONDUCT

²manage *n* : MANEGE

man·age·a·ble \'man-ij-ə-bəl\ *adj* : capable of being managed — **man·age·a·bil·i·ty** \,man-ij-ə-'bil-ət-ē\ *n* — **man·age·a·ble·ness** \'man-ij-ə-bəl-nəs\ *n* — **man·age·a·bly** \-blē\ *adv*

man·age·ment \'man-ij-mənt\ *n* **1** : the act or art of managing : CONTROL, DIRECTION **2** : skillfulness in managing **3** : the collective body of those who manage an enterprise

man·ag·er \'man-ij-ər\ *n* : one that manages: as **a** : a person who conducts business or household affairs with economy and care **b** : a person whose work or profession is management **c** : a person who directs a team or an athlete **d** : a professional expert appointed to direct the administration of a municipal government ⟨city *manager*⟩ **e** : a legislator in charge of securing the enactment of a particular bill — **man·a·ge·ri·al** \,man-ə-'jir-ē-əl\ *adj* — **man·a·ge·ri·al·ly** \-ē-ə-lē\ *adv* — **man·ag·er·ship** \'man-ij-ər-,ship\ *n*

ma·ña·na \mən-'yän-ə\ *n* [Sp, lit., tomorrow] : an indefinite time in the future — **mañana** *adv*

man ape *n* **1** : GREAT APE **2** : any of various fossil primates intermediate in characters between recent man and the great apes

man-at-arms \,man-ət-'ärmz\ *n, pl* **men-at-arms** : SOLDIER; *esp* : a heavily armed mounted soldier

man·a·tee \'man-ə-,tē\ *n* [Sp *manaté*] : any of several chiefly tropical plant-eating aquatic mammals that differ from the related dugong esp. in having the tail broad and rounded

man·chi·neel \,man-chə-'nēl\ *n* [F *mancenille*, fr. Sp *manzanilla*, fr. dim. of *manzana* apple] : a tropical American tree with a blistering milky juice and poisonous apple-shaped fruit

Man·chu \'man-chü\ *n* **1** : a member of the native Mongolian race of Manchuria that conquered China and established a dynasty from 1644 **2** : the language of the Manchu people — **Manchu** *adj*

man·ci·ple \'man(t)-sə-pəl\ *n* [ML *mancipium* office of steward, fr. L *mancip-*, *manceps* purchaser, fr. *manus* hand + *capere* to take] : a steward or purveyor esp. for a college or monastery

-man·cy \,man(t)-sē\ *n comb form, pl* **-mancies** [Gk *manteia*, fr. *mantis* diviner, prophet] : divination ⟨necromancy⟩

man·da·mus \man-'dā-məs\ *n* [L, we enjoin, its first word] : a writ issued by a superior court commanding that a specified official act or duty be performed

¹man·da·rin \'man-d(ə-)rən\ *n* [Pg *mandarim*, fr. Malay *mĕntĕri*, fr. Skt *mantrin* counselor] **1** : a public official under the Chinese Empire of any of nine superior grades **2** *cap* **a** : the primarily northern dialect of China used by the court and the official classes under the Empire **b** : the chief dialect of China that is spoken in about four fifths of the country and has a standard variety centering about Peking **3** : a small spiny Chinese orange tree with yellow to reddish orange loose-skinned fruits; *also* : its fruit — compare TANGERINE — **man·da·rin·ate** \-,āt\ *n* — **man·da·rin·ism** \-,iz-əm\ *n*

²mandarin *adj* : of, relating to, or typical of a mandarin

man·da·tary \'man-də-,ter-ē\ *n, pl* **-tar·ies** : MANDATORY

¹man·date \'man-,dāt\ *n* [L *mandatum* command, fr. *mandare* to entrust, enjoin] **1** : a formal order from a superior court or official to an inferior one **2 a** : an authoritative command, instruction, or direction ⟨followed the constitutional *mandate*⟩ **b** : authorization or approval given to a representative esp. by voters **3 a** : a commission granted by the League of Nations to a member nation to administer a conquered territory as guardian on behalf of the League **b** : a mandated territory

²mandate *vt* : to administer or assign under a mandate

¹man·da·to·ry \'man-də-,tōr-ē, -,tȯr-\ *adj* **1** : containing or constituting a command : OBLIGATORY ⟨*mandatory* tasks⟩ ⟨attendance at the first meeting is *mandatory*⟩ **2** : of, relating to, or holding a League of Nations mandate ⟨a *mandatory* power⟩

²mandatory *n, pl* **-ries** : one given a mandate

man·di·ble \'man-də-bəl\ *n* [LL *mandibula*, fr. L *mandere* to chew; akin to E *mouth*] **1 a** : JAW 1a; *esp* : a lower jaw consisting of a single bone or completely fused bones **b** : the lower jaw with its surrounding soft parts **c** : either the upper or lower segment of the bill of a bird **2** : an invertebrate mouthpart that holds or bites food; *esp* : either member of the front pair of mouth appendages of an arthropod often forming strong biting jaws — **man·dib·u·lar** \man-'dib-yə-lər\ *adj*

man·do·lin \,man-də-'lin, 'man-d⁹l-ən\ *also* **man·do·line** \,man-də-'lēn, 'man-d⁹l-ən\ *n* [It *mandolino*] : a musical instrument of the lute family that has a pear-shaped body and fretted neck and four to six pairs of strings — **man·do·lin·ist** \,man-də-'lin-əst\ *n*

man·drag·o·ra \man-'drag-ə-rə\ *n* : MANDRAKE 1

man·drake \'man-,drāk\ *n* [alter. of OE *mandragora*, fr. L *mandragoras*, fr. Gk] **1** : a Mediterranean herb of the nightshade family with a large forked root superstitiously credited with human and medicinal attributes **2** : MAY-APPLE

man·drel \'man-drəl\ *n* **1** : an axle or spindle inserted into a hole in a piece of work to support it during machining **2** : a metal bar used as a core around which material may be cast, shaped, or molded

man·drill \'man-drəl\ *n* : a large fierce gregarious baboon of western Africa

mane \'mān\ *n* [OE *manu*] **1** : long heavy hair growing about the neck of some mammals (as a horse) **2** : long heavy hair on a person's head — **maned** \'mānd\ *adj*

man·eat·er \'man-,ēt-ər\ *n* : one (as a cannibal, shark, or tiger) that has or is thought to have an appetite for human flesh — **man-eat·ing** \-,ēt-iŋ\ *adj*

ma·nege *also* **ma·nège** \ma-'nezh\ *n* **1** : a school for teaching horsemanship **2** : the art of horsemanship or of training horses

ma·nes \'män-,ās, 'mä-,nēz\ *n pl, often cap* [L] : the spirits of the dead and gods of the lower world in ancient Roman belief

¹ma·neu·ver \mə-'n(y)ü-vər\ *n* [F *manœuvre*, fr. ML *manuopera* work done by hand, fr. L *manu operare* to work by hand] **1 a** : a planned movement of troops or ships **b** : an armed forces training exercise; *esp* : an extensive exercise involving large-scale deployment of military or naval forces **2 a** : a skillful physical movement or procedure ⟨avoided a collision by a quick *maneuver*⟩ **b** : a variation from the straight and level flight path of an airplane **3** : a clever often evasive move or action : a shift of position to gain a tactical end ⟨tried by various *maneuvers* to win support from both sides⟩

²maneuver *vb* **1** : to move (as troops or ships) in a maneuver **2** : to perform a maneuver **3** : to guide with adroitness and design : HANDLE, MANIPULATE **4** : to use stratagems : SCHEME — **ma·neu·ver·a·bil·i·ty** \-,n(y)üv-(ə-)rə-'bil-ət-ē\ *n* — **ma·neu·ver·a·ble** \-'n(y)üv-(ə-)rə-bəl\ *adj*

man Fri·day \'man-'frīd-ē\ *n* [fr. *Friday*, native servant

in Defoe's *Robinson Crusoe*] : a valued efficient aide or employee

man·ful \'man-fəl\ *adj* : showing courage and resolution : BRAVE **syn** see MALE — **man·ful·ly** \-fə-lē\ *adv* — **man·ful·ness** *n*

man·ga·nese \'maŋ-gə-,nēz, -,nēs\ *n* [F *manganèse* manganese dioxide, fr. It *manganese* magnesia, manganese dioxide, fr. ML *magnesia*] : a grayish white usu. hard and brittle metallic element that resembles iron but is not magnetic — see ELEMENT table

manganese dioxide *n* : a brown or gray-black insoluble compound MnO_2 that consists of manganese and oxygen and is used as an oxidizing agent, in making glass, and in ceramics

man·gan·ic \maŋ-'gan-ik\ *or* **man·ga·nous** \'maŋ-gə-nəs\ *adj* : of, relating to, or derived from manganese

mange \'mānj\ *n* : any of several persistent contagious skin diseases marked esp. by itching and loss of hair in domestic animals and sometimes man; *esp* : one caused by a minute parasitic mite

man·gel-wur·zel \'maŋ-gəl-,wər-zəl\ *n* [G, fr. *mangold* beet + *wurzel* root] : a large coarse yellow to reddish orange beet extensively grown as food for cattle

man·ger \'mān-jər\ *n* [MF *mangeure*, fr. *mangier* to eat] : a trough or open box for livestock feed or fodder

¹man·gle \'maŋ-gəl\ *vt* **man·gled**; **man·gling** \-g(ə-)liŋ\ [AF *mangler*] **1** : to cut, bruise, or hack with repeated blows or strokes **2** : to spoil or injure in making or performing — **man·gler** \-g(ə-)lər\ *n*

²mangle *n* [D *mangel*] : a machine for ironing laundry by passing it between heated rollers

³mangle *vt* **man·gled**; **man·gling** \-g(ə-)liŋ\ : to press or smooth with a mangle — **man·gler** \-g(ə-)lər\ *n*

man·go \'maŋ-gō\ *n, pl* **mangoes** *or* **mangos** [Pg *manga*, fr. Tamil *mān-kāy*] **1** : a yellowish red tropical fruit with a firm skin, hard central stone, and juicy aromatic mildly acid pulp; *also* : the evergreen tree of the sumac family that bears this fruit **2** : SWEET PEPPER

man·go·steen \'maŋ-gə-,stēn\ *n* : a dark reddish brown fruit with thick rind and juicy flesh having a flavor suggestive of both peach and pineapple; *also* : a resinous East Indian tree that bears this fruit

man·grove \'man-,grōv, 'maŋ-\ *n* : any of various tropical maritime trees or shrubs that throw out many prop roots and form dense masses

mangy \'mān-jē\ *adj* **mang·i·er; -est** **1** : affected with or resulting from mange **2** : having many worn-out or bare spots : SHABBY, SEEDY — **mang·i·ness** \'mān-jē-nəs\ *n*

man·han·dle \'man-,han-d⁹l\ *vt* **1** : to move or manage by human force **2** : to handle roughly

man·hat·tan \man-'hat-⁹n, mən-\ *n, often cap* : a cocktail consisting of sweet vermouth, rye or bourbon whiskey, and sometimes a dash of bitters

man·hole \'man-,hōl\ *n* : a hole (as in a pavement, tank, or boiler) through which a man may go

man·hood \'man-,hud\ *n* **1** : manly qualities : COURAGE, VIRILITY **2** : the condition of being an adult male **3** : adult males : MEN ⟨the nation's *manhood*⟩

man-hour *n* : a unit of one hour's work by one man used esp. as a basis for wages and cost accounting

man·hunt \'man-,hənt\ *n* : an organized hunt for a person and esp. for one charged with a crime

ma·nia \'mā-nē-ə, -nyə\ *n* [LL, fr. Gk, fr. *mainesthai* to be mad] **1** : MADNESS; *esp* : insanity characterized by uncontrollable emotion or excitement **2** : excessive or unreasonable enthusiasm : CRAZE **syn** see INSANITY

¹ma·ni·ac \'mā-nē-,ak\ *adj* **1** : affected with or suggestive of madness **2** : characterized by ungovernable excitement or frenzy : FRANTIC — **ma·ni·a·cal** \mə-'nī-ə-kəl\ *adj* — **ma·ni·a·cal·ly** \-k(ə-)lē\ *adv*

²maniac *n* **1** : LUNATIC, MADMAN **2** : a person characterized by an uncontrollable enthusiasm for something

man·ic \'man-ik\ *adj* : affected with, relating to, or resembling mania — **manic** *n*

man·ic-de·pres·sive \,man-ik-di-'pres-iv\ *adj* : characterized by alternating mania and depression — **manic-depressive** *n*

¹man·i·cure \'man-ə-,kyu(ə)r\ *n* [F, fr. L *manus* hand + *cura* care] **1** : MANICURIST **2** : a treatment for the care of the hands and nails

²manicure *vt* **1** : to give a manicure to ⟨had his nails *manicured*⟩ **2 :** to trim closely and evenly ⟨*manicured* his lawn⟩

man·i·cur·ist \-,kyùr-əst\ *n* **:** a person who gives manicures

¹**man·i·fest** \'man-ə-,fest\ *adj* [L *manifestus,* lit., hit by the hand] **:** readily perceived by the senses or by the mind **:** OBVIOUS ⟨heard the verdict with *manifest* relief⟩ ⟨the author's bias was *manifest*⟩ — **man·i·fest·ly** *adv*

²**manifest** *vt* **:** to show plainly **:** make evident **:** DISPLAY

³**manifest** *n* **:** a list (as of cargo or passengers) esp. for a ship or plane

man·i·fes·ta·tion \,man-ə-fə-'stā-shən, -,fes-'tā-\ *n* **1 a :** the act, process, or an instance of manifesting **:** EXPRESSION **b :** something that manifests **:** EVIDENCE **2 :** a public demonstration of power and purpose

manifest destiny *n, often cap M&D* **:** an ordering of human history regarded as obvious and inevitable that leads a people or race to expand to geographic limits held to be natural or to extend sovereignty over a usu. indefinite area; *esp* **:** the idea widespread during the 1840s and 1850s that the U.S. was destined to extend its boundaries to the Pacific

man·i·fes·to \,man-ə-'fes-tō\ *n, pl* **-tos** or **-toes** [It] **:** a public declaration of policy, purpose, or views

¹**man·i·fold** \'man-ə-,fōld\ *adj* **1 :** of many and various kinds ⟨*manifold* excuses⟩ **2 :** including or uniting various features **:** MULTIFARIOUS ⟨a *manifold* personality⟩ **3 :** consisting of or operating many of one kind joined together ⟨a *manifold* bellpull⟩ — **man·i·fold·ly** *adv* — **man·i·fold·ness** \-,fōl(d)-nəs\ *n*

²**manifold** *n* **:** something that is manifold: as **a :** a whole consisting of many diverse elements **b :** a pipe fitting having several outlets for connecting one pipe with others

³**manifold** *vb* **1 :** to make many or several copies ⟨*manifold* a manuscript⟩ **2 :** MULTIPLY

man·i·kin or **man·ni·kin** \'man-i-kən\ *n* **1 :** MANNEQUIN **2 :** a little man **:** DWARF, PYGMY

ma·nila also **ma·nil·la** \mə-'nil-ə\ *adj* **1 :** made of manila paper **2** *often cap* **:** made from Manila hemp

Manila hemp *n* [*Manila,* Philippines] **:** ABACA

manila paper *n, often cap M* **:** a tough brownish paper made orig. from Manila hemp and used esp. as a wrapping paper

man in the street : an average or ordinary man

man·i·oc \'man-ē-,äk\ or **man·i·o·ca** \,man-ē-'ō-kə\ *n* **:** CASSAVA

man·i·ple \'man-ə-pəl\ *n* **1 :** a long narrow band worn at mass over the left arm by clergymen or above the order of subdeacon **2 :** a subdivision of a Roman legion consisting of either 120 or 60 men

ma·nip·u·late \mə-'nip-yə-,lāt\ *vt* [L *manipulus* handful, fr. *manus* hand] **1 :** to treat or operate with the hands or by mechanical means esp. with skill ⟨*manipulate* the TV dials⟩ **2 a :** to manage or utilize skillfully ⟨*manipulate* masses of statistics⟩ **b :** to manage artfully or fraudulently ⟨*manipulate* accounts⟩ **c :** to influence (as prices of stocks) by artificial means **d :** to play upon or control by artful, unfair, or insidious means ⟨*manipulate* public opinion⟩ — **ma·nip·u·la·tion** \-,nip-yə-'lā-shən\ *n* — **ma·nip·u·la·tor** \-'nip-yə-,lāt-ər\ *n*

man·i·tou or **man·i·tu** \'man-ə-,tü\ also **man·i·to** \-,tō\ *n* [of Algonquian origin] **:** one of the Algonquian deities or spirits dominating the forces of nature

man·kind *n* **1** \'man-'kīnd, -,kīnd\ **:** the human race **:** the totality of human beings **2** \-,kīnd\ **:** men as distinguished from women

man·like \'man-,līk\ *adj* **:** resembling or characteristic of a man **:** MANNISH

man·li·ness \'man-lē-nəs\ *n* **:** manly conduct or character

man·ly \'man-lē\ *adj* **man·li·er; -est** **1 :** having qualities appropriate to a man **:** BRAVE, RESOLUTE **2 :** befitting a man ⟨*manly* sports⟩ syn see MALE

man–made \'man-'mād\ *adj* **:** made by man rather than nature ⟨*man-made* systems⟩; *also* **:** SYNTHETIC ⟨*man-made* fibers⟩

man·na \'man-ə\ *n* [OE, fr. LL, fr. Gk, fr. Heb *mān*] **1 :** food miraculously supplied to the Israelites in the wilderness **2 :** something likened to the biblical manna esp. in being much needed and joyfully received

manned \'mand\ *adj* **:** carrying or performed by a man ⟨*manned* spaceflight⟩

man·ne·quin \'man-i-kən\ *n* **1 :** an artist's, tailor's, or dressmaker's jointed figure of the human body; *also* **:** a form representing the human figure used esp. for displaying clothes **2 :** a woman who models clothing **:** MODEL

man·ner \'man-ər\ *n* [OF *maniere* way of acting, fr. L *manuarius* of the hand, fr. *manus* hand] **1 a :** KIND ⟨what *manner* of man is he⟩ **b :** SORTS ⟨all *manner* of information⟩ **2 a :** a way of acting or proceeding ⟨worked in a brisk *manner*⟩ **b :** HABIT, CUSTOM ⟨spoke bluntly as was his *manner*⟩ **c :** STYLE ⟨painted in the artist's early *manner*⟩ **3 a** *pl* **:** social conduct or rules of conduct as shown in the prevalent customs **:** MORES ⟨studied the *manners* of a primitive people⟩ ⟨a novel of *manners*⟩ **b** *pl* **:** characteristic or habitual deportment **:** BEHAVIOR ⟨taught the child good *manners*⟩ **c :** BEARING, AIR ⟨a *manner* suited to his status⟩

man·nered \'man-ərd\ *adj* **1 :** having manners of a specified kind ⟨well-*mannered*⟩ **2 :** having an artificial character ⟨a highly *mannered* style⟩

man·ner·ism \'man-ə-,riz-əm\ *n* **1 :** affected use of a particular style or manner **:** ARTIFICIALITY **2 :** a peculiarity of action, bearing, or treatment ⟨the *mannerism* of constantly smoothing her hair⟩ syn see AFFECTATION

man·ner·ly \'man-ər-lē\ *adj* **:** showing good manners **:** POLITE — **man·ner·li·ness** \-lē-nəs\ *n* — **mannerly** *adv*

man·nish \'man-ish\ *adj* **1 :** resembling or suggesting a man rather than a woman ⟨a *mannish* voice⟩ **2 :** suitable to or characteristic of a man rather than a woman ⟨her *mannish* clothes⟩ syn see MALE — **man·nish·ly** *adv* — **man·nish·ness** *n*

man·ni·tol \'man-ə-,tȯl, -,tōl\ *n* **:** a slightly sweet crystalline alcohol $C_6H_8(OH)_6$ found in many plants

ma·noeu·vre \mə-'n(y)ü-vər\ *var of* MANEUVER

man–of–war \,man-ə(v)-'wȯ(ə)r\ *n, pl* **men–of–war :** WARSHIP

ma·nom·e·ter \mə-'näm-ət-ər\ *n* [Gk *manos* sparse, loose, rare] **:** an instrument for measuring pressure (as of gases and vapors)

man·or \'man-ər\ *n* [OF *manoir* residence, fr. *manoir* to dwell, fr. L *manēre* to stay] **:** a usu. large landed estate; *esp* **:** one granted by a sovereign to a feudal lord with rights over land and tenants — **ma·no·ri·al** \mə-'nȯr-ē-əl, -'nȯr-\ *adj* — **ma·no·ri·al·ism** \-ē-ə-,liz-əm\ *n*

manor house *n* **:** the house of the lord of a manor

man–o'–war bird \,man-ə-'wȯr-,bərd\ *n* **:** any of several long-winged web-footed seabirds noted for their powers of flight and the habit of robbing other birds of fish

man power *n* **1 :** power available from or supplied by the physical effort of man **2** *usu* **manpower :** the total supply of persons available and fitted for service (as military or industrial)

man·qué \mä˜-'kā\ *adj* [F, fr. pp. of *manquer* to lack, fall short] **:** falling short of the fulfillment of one's aspirations or talents — used after the word modified ⟨a poet *manqué*⟩

man·rope \'man-,rōp\ *n* **:** a side rope (as to a ship's gangway or ladder) used as a handrail

man·sard \'man-,särd\ *n* [F *mansarde,* fr. François *Mansart* d1666 French architect] **:** a roof having two slopes on all sides with the lower slope steeper than the upper one — see ROOF illustration

manse \'man(t)s\ *n* **:** the residence of a clergyman; *esp* **:** the house of a Presbyterian clergyman

man·ser·vant \'man-,sər-vənt\ *n, pl* **men·ser·vants** \'men-,sər-vən(t)s\ **:** a male servant

man·sion \'man-chən\ *n* [L *mansion-, mansio* act of staying, lodging, fr. *mans-, manēre* to stay] **:** a large imposing residence

man–size \'man-,sīz\ or **man–sized** \-,sīzd\ *adj* **1 :** suitable for or requiring a man ⟨a *man-size* job⟩ **2 :** LARGE-SCALE ⟨a *man-size* model⟩

man·slaugh·ter \'man-,slȯt-ər\ *n* **:** the unlawful killing of a person without intent to do so

man·slay·er \-,slā-ər\ *n* **:** one who slays a man

man·sue·tude \'man(t)-swi-,t(y)üd, man-'sü-ə-,t(y)üd\ *n* **:** the quality or state of being gentle **:** MEEKNESS, TAMENESS

man·ta \'mant-ə\ *n* [Sp] **1 :** a square piece of cloth or blanket used in southwestern U.S. and Latin America as a cloak or shawl **2 :** DEVILFISH 1

man·teau \man-'tō\ *n* **:** a loose cloak, coat, or robe

man·tel \'mant-ᵊl\ *n* [MF, fr. OF, *mantle*] **1 :** the beam, stone, arch, or shelf above a fireplace **2 :** the finish covering the chimney around a fireplace

man·te·let \'mant-lət\ *n* **:** a very short cape or cloak

man·tel·piece \'mant-ᵊl-,pēs\ *n* **1 :** a mantel with its side elements **2 :** the shelf of a mantel

man·ti·core \'mant-i-,kō(ə)r, -,kȯ(ə)r\ *n* **:** a legendary animal with the head of a man, the body of a lion, and the tail of a dragon or scorpion

man·til·la \man-'tē-(y)ə, -'til-ə\ *n* [Sp, dim. of *manta*] **1 :** a light scarf worn over the head and shoulders esp. by Spanish and Latin American women **2 :** a short light cape or cloak

man·tis \'mant-əs\ *n, pl* **man·tis·es** *or* **man·tes** \'man-,tēz\ [Gk, lit., prophet] **:** any of various insects related to the grasshoppers and roaches that feed upon other insects and clasp the prey in forelimbs held up as if in prayer

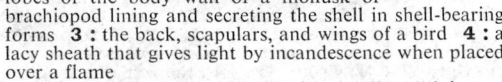
mantis

man·tis·sa \man-'tis-ə\ *n* [L *mantisa* something used to make up weight, fr. Etruscan] **:** the decimal part of a logarithm

¹**man·tle** \'mant-ᵊl\ *n* [OF *mantel*, fr. L *mantellum*] **1 :** a loose sleeveless outer garment **:** CLOAK **2 a :** something that covers or envelops **b :** a fold or lobe or pair of lobes of the body wall of a mollusk or brachiopod lining and secreting the shell in shell-bearing forms **3 :** the back, scapulars, and wings of a bird **4 a :** lacy sheath that gives light by incandescence when placed over a flame

²**mantle** *vt* **man·tled; man·tling** \'mant-liŋ, -ᵊl-iŋ\ **:** to cover or envelop with or as if with a mantle

man·tle·rock \'mant-ᵊl-,räk\ *n* **:** unconsolidated material that overlies the earth's solid rock

Man·toux test \,man-'tü-\ *n* [after Charles *Mantoux* d1947 French physician] **:** a serological test for past or present tuberculous infection

man·trap \'man-,trap\ *n* **:** a trap for catching men **:** SNARE

man·tua \'manch-(ə-)wə\ *n* **:** a usu. loose-fitting gown worn esp. in the 17th and 18th centuries

¹**man·u·al** \'man-yə(-wə)l\ *adj* [L *manus* hand] **1 a :** of, relating to, or involving the hands ⟨*manual* dexterity⟩ **b :** worked by hand ⟨*manual* choke⟩ **2 :** requiring or using physical skill and energy ⟨*manual* labor⟩ ⟨*manual* workers⟩ — **man·u·al·ly** \-ē\ *adv*

²**manual** *n* **1 :** a book capable of being conveniently handled; *esp* **:** HANDBOOK **2 :** the set movements in the handling of a weapon during a military drill or ceremony

manual alphabet *n* **:** an alphabet for deaf-mutes in which the letters are represented by finger positions

manual training *n* **:** a course of training to develop skill in using the hands and to teach arts (as woodworking) that serve ordinary or material needs

ma·nu·bri·um \mə-'n(y)ü-brē-əm\ *n, pl* **-bria** \-brē-ə\ *also* **-briums :** an anatomical part (as the upper end of the sternum) suggesting a handle

man·u·fac·to·ry \,man-(y)ə-'fak-t(ə-)rē\ *n, pl* **-ries :** FACTORY

¹**man·u·fac·ture** \,man-(y)ə-'fak-chər\ *n* [MF, fr. L *manu factus* made by hand] **1 :** something made from raw materials **2 :** the process of making wares by hand or by machinery esp. when carried on systematically with division of labor **3 :** the act or process of producing something

²**manufacture** *vt* **-fac·tured; -fac·tur·ing** \-'fak-chə-riŋ, -'fak-shriŋ\ **1 :** to make into a product suitable for use **2 :** to make from raw materials by hand or by machinery esp. systematically and with division of labor **3 :** INVENT, FABRICATE — **man·u·fac·tur·ing** *n*

man·u·fac·tur·er \-'fak-chər-ər, -'fak-shrər\ *n* **:** one that manufactures; *esp* **:** an employer of workers in manufacturing

man·u·mis·sion \,man-yə-'mish-ən\ *n* **:** emancipation from slavery

man·u·mit \,man-yə-'mit\ *vt* **-mit·ted; -mit·ting** [L *manumiss-, manumittere*, fr. *manus* hand + *mittere* to let go] **:** to set free; *esp* **:** to release from slavery

¹**ma·nure** \mə-'n(y)ù(ə)r\ *vt* [ME *manouren* to till, fr. MF *manouvrer*, lit., to work by hand, fr. L *manu operare*] **:** to enrich (land) by the application of manure — **ma·nur·er** \-'n(y)ùr-ər\ *n*

²**manure** *n* **:** material that fertilizes land; *esp* **:** refuse of stables and barnyards consisting of livestock excreta with or without litter — **ma·nu·ri·al** \mə-'n(y)ùr-ē-əl\ *adj*

¹**man·u·script** \'man-yə-,skript\ *adj* **:** written by hand or typed

²**manuscript** *n* **1 :** a written or typewritten composition or document **2 :** writing as opposed to print

Manx \'maŋ(k)s\ *n, pl* **Manx 1** *pl* **:** the people of the Isle of Man **2 :** the Celtic language formerly used on the Isle of Man — **Manx** *adj* — **Manx·man** \-mən\ *n*

Manx cat *n* **:** a short-haired domestic cat having no external tail

¹**many** \'men-ē\ *adj* **more** \'mō(ə)r, 'mȯ(ə)r\; **most** \'mōst\ [OE *manig*] **1 :** consisting of or amounting to a large but indefinite number ⟨worked for *many* years⟩ **2 :** being one of a large but indefinite number ⟨*many* a man⟩ — **as many :** the same in number ⟨saw three plays in *as many* days⟩

syn NUMEROUS, COUNTLESS: MANY implies a relatively large number usu. of like things in contrast with a few or several or with an exact number; NUMEROUS implies very many and often suggests crowding, thronging, or clustering; COUNTLESS may imply a number too great to count or apparently without limit

²**many** *pron* **:** a large number of persons or things ⟨*many* of them⟩

³**many** *n* **:** a large but indefinite number ⟨a good *many* of them⟩

many·fold \,men-ē-'fōld\ *adv* **:** by many times

many·sid·ed \,men-ē-'sīd-əd\ *adj* **1 :** having many sides or aspects **2 :** having many interests or aptitudes **:** VERSATILE — **many·sid·ed·ness** *n*

man·za·ni·ta \,man-zə-'nēt-ə\ *n* **:** any of various western No. American evergreen shrubs of the heath family

Mao·ism \'maù-,iz-əm\ *n* **:** the theory and practice of Marxism-Leninism developed in China chiefly by Mao Tse-tung — **Mao·ist** \'maù-əst\ *n or adj*

Mao·ri \'maù-rē\ *n* **1 :** a member of a Polynesian people native to New Zealand **2 :** the language of the Maori people — **Maori** *adj*

¹**map** \'map\ *n* [ML *mappa*, fr. L, napkin] **1 :** a drawing or picture showing features of the surface of the earth, another planet, or the moon **2 :** a drawing or picture of the sky showing the position of stars and planets

²**map** *vt* **mapped; map·ping 1 :** to study and make a map of ⟨*map* the heavens⟩ **2 :** to chart the course of **:** plan in detail ⟨*map* out a campaign⟩ — **map·per** *n*

ma·ple \'mā-pəl\ *n* [OE *mapul-*] **:** any of a genus of trees or shrubs with opposite leaves and a 2-winged dry fruit; *also* **:** the hard light-colored close-grained wood of a maple

maple sugar *n* **:** a brown sugar made by boiling maple syrup

maple syrup *n* **:** syrup made by concentrating the sap of maples and esp. the sugar maple

ma·quette \ma-'ket\ *n* **:** a usu. small preliminary model (as of a piece of sculpture)

ma·quis \ma-'kē, mä-\ *n, pl* **ma·quis** \-'kē(z)\ *often cap* [F] **:** a guerrilla fighter in the French underground during World War II

mar \'mär\ *vt* **marred; mar·ring** [OE *mierran* to waste] **1 :** to make a blemish on **:** DAMAGE, SPOIL **2 a** *archaic* **:** MANGLE, MUTILATE **b** *obs* **:** DESTROY

mar·a·bou *or* **mar·a·bout** \'mar-ə-,bü\ *n* **1 a :** a large Old World stork **b :** the long soft feathers from under the tail and wings of this bird used esp. formerly in millinery **2 a :** a thrown raw silk **b :** a fabric (as a feathery trimming material) made of this silk

mar·a·bout \'mar-ə-,bü\ *n, often cap* **:** a dervish in Muslim Africa credited with supernatural power

ma·ra·ca \mə-'räk-ə, -'rak-\ *n* [Pg *maracá*] **:** a dried gourd or a rattle like a gourd that contains dried seeds or pebbles and is used as a percussion instrument

mar·a·schi·no \,mar-ə-'skē-nō, -'shē-\ *n, often cap* [It, fr. *marasca* bitter wild cherry] **1 :** a sweet liqueur distilled from the fermented juice of a bitter wild cherry **2 :** a usu. large cherry preserved in true or imitation maraschino

ma·ras·mus \mə-'raz-məs\ *n* [LL, fr. Gk *marasmos*, fr. *marainein* to waste away] **:** a progressive wasting away usu. associated with faulty nutrition

mar·a·thon \'mar-ə-,thän\ *n* [fr. *Marathon*, Greece, site of a victory of Greeks over Persians in 490 B.C., the news

of which was carried to Athens by a long-distance runner]
1 : a long-distance race; *esp* **:** a footrace run on an open
course of 26 miles 385 yards **2 :** an endurance contest
— **marathon** *adj*
ma·raud \mə-'rȯd\ *vb* [F *marauder*] **:** to roam about and
raid in search of plunder — **ma·raud·er** *n*
¹mar·ble \'mär-bəl\ *n* [OF *marbre*, fr. L *marmor*, fr.
Gk *marmaros*] **1 a :** limestone that is more or less
crystallized by natural alteration, is capable of taking a
high polish, and is used in architecture and sculpture
b : something made from marble; *esp* **:** a piece of sculpture
2 a : a little ball (as of glass) used in various games **b** *pl*
: a children's game played with these little balls
²marble *vt* **mar·bled; mar·bling** \-b(ə-)liŋ\ **:** to give a
veined or mottled appearance to (as by staining) ⟨*marble*
the edges of a book⟩
³marble *adj* **:** made of, resembling, or suggestive of marble
mar·ble·ize \'mär-bə-,līz\ *vt* **:** MARBLE
mar·bling \'mär-b(ə-)liŋ\ *n* **1 :** coloration or markings
resembling or suggestive of marble **2 :** an intermixture
of fat through the lean of a cut of meat
mar·bly \'mär-b(ə-)lē\ *adj* **:** MARBLE
mar·ca·site \'mär-kə-,sīt, ,mär-kə-'zēt\ *n* **:** a mineral
FeS₂ consisting of iron and sulfur and having a metallic
luster
¹mar·cel \mär-'sel\ *n* **:** a deep soft wave made in the hair
by the use of a heated curling iron
²marcel *vt* **mar·celled; mar·cel·ling :** to make a marcel in
¹march \'märch\ *n* [OF *marche*, of Gmc origin; akin to
E *mark*] **1 :** a border region **:** FRONTIER **2** *pl* **:** the
borderlands between England and Scotland and between
England and Wales
²march *vi* **:** to have common borders or frontiers
³march *vb* [MF *marchier*] **1 :** to move along with a
steady regular stride esp. in step with others **2 a :** to
move in a direct purposeful manner **:** PROCEED **b :** AD-
VANCE — **march·er** *n*
⁴march *n* **1 a :** the action of marching **b :** the distance
covered within a specific period of time by marching
c : a regular even step used in marching **2 :** forward
movement **:** PROGRESS **3 :** a musical composition in
duple rhythm (as ¼ time) with a strongly accentuated
beat suitable to accompany marching
March \'märch\ *n* [OF, fr. L *Martius*, fr. *Mart-*, *Mars*
Mars] **:** the 3d month of the year
mär·chen \'me(ə)r-kən\ *n*, *pl* **märchen** [G] **:** TALE; *esp*
: FOLKTALE
mar·chio·ness \'mär-sh(ə-)nəs\ *n* **1 :** the wife or widow
of a marquess **2 :** a woman who holds the rank of a
marquess in her own right
march·pane \'märch-,pān\ *n* **:** MARZIPAN
march-past \'märch-,past\ *n* **:** a marching by esp. of
troops in review
Mar·di Gras \,märd-ē-'grä\ *n* [F, lit., fat Tuesday]
: Shrove Tuesday often observed with parades and
merrymaking
mare \'ma(ə)r, 'me(ə)r\ *n* [OE *mere*] **:** the female of a
member of the horse family
ma·re clau·sum \,mä-(,)rē-'klȯ-səm\ *n* [NL, lit., closed
sea] **:** a navigable body of water (as a sea) under the jurisdiction of one nation and closed to other nations
mare's nest *n* **1 :** something that is thought wonderful
at first but turns out to be imaginary or false **2 :** a
situation or condition of great confusion
mare's tail *n* **:** a cirrus cloud that has a long slender
flowing appearance
mar·ga·rine \'märj-(ə-)rən, 'märj-ə-,rēn\ *n* [Gk *margaron*
pearl] **:** a food product made from usu. vegetable oils
and skim milk often with vitamins A and D added and
used as a spread and a cooking fat
mar·gay \'mär-,gā\ *n* [F, of AmerInd origin] **:** a small
American spotted wildcat
marge \'märj\ *n*, *archaic* **:** MARGIN
mar·gent \'mär-jənt\ *n*, *archaic* **:** MARGIN
¹mar·gin \'mär-jən\ *n* [L *margin-*, *margo* border; akin to
E *mark*] **1 :** the part of a page outside the main body of
printed or written matter **2 :** BORDER, EDGE **3 a :** a
spare amount (as of time or money) allowed for use if
needed **b :** the limit below which economic activity cannot be continued under normal conditions **4 a :** the
difference which exists between net selling price and cost

b : cash or collateral deposited with a broker to secure
him from loss on a contract **c :** an allowance above or
below a certain figure within which a purchase or sale
is to be made **syn** see BORDER — **mar·gined** \-jənd\
adj
²margin *vt* **1 :** to provide with an edging or border
2 : BORDER
mar·gin·al \'märj-nəl, -ən-ᵊl\ *adj* **1 :** written or printed
in the margin of a page or sheet ⟨*marginal* notes⟩ **2 :** of,
relating to, or situated at a margin or border **3 a :** close
to the lower limit of qualification or acceptability ⟨*marginal* ability⟩ **b :** yielding a supply of goods which when
marketed at existing price levels will barely cover the cost
of production ⟨*marginal* land⟩; *also* **:** relating to or derived
from goods produced and marketed with such result
⟨*marginal* profits⟩ — **mar·gin·al·i·ty** \,märj-ə-'nal-ət-ē\ *n*
— **mar·gin·al·ly** \'märj-nə-lē, -ən-ᵊl-ē\ *adv*
mar·gi·na·lia \,märj-ə-'nā-lē-ə\ *n pl* **:** marginal notes
marginal utility *n* **:** the amount of additional utility to a
consumer provided by an additional unit of an economic
good or service
mar·gin·ate \'märj-ə-nət, -,nāt\ *or* **mar·gin·at·ed**
\-,nāt-əd\ *adj* **:** having a distinctive margin or border
⟨white-*marginate* leaves⟩
mar·grave \'mär-,grāv\ *n* **1 :** the military governor esp.
of a medieval German border province **2 :** a member of
the German nobility corresponding in rank to a British
marquess — **mar·gra·vate** \-grə-,vāt\ *or* **mar·gra·vi·ate**
\,mär-'grā-vē-ət, -vē-,āt\ — **mar·gra·vi·al** \-vē-əl\ *adj*
mar·gra·vine \'mär-grə-,vēn\ *n* **:** the wife of a margrave
mar·gue·rite \,mär-g(y)ə-'rēt\ *n* **1 :** DAISY 1a **2 :** any
of various single-flowered chrysanthemums **3 :** any of
several cultivated chamomiles
Mar·i·an \'mer-ē-ən, 'mar-\ *adj* **1 :** of or relating to
Mary Tudor or her reign (1553–58) **2 :** of or relating to
the Virgin Mary
Mar·i·an·ist \-ē-ə-nəst\ *n* **:** a priest or brother of the
Roman Catholic Society of Mary of Paris devoted esp.
to education
mari·gold \'mar-ə-,gōld, 'mer-\ *n* **1 :** POT MARIGOLD
2 : any of a genus of tropical American herbs related to
the daisies and grown for their showy yellow or red and
yellow flower heads
mar·i·jua·na *or* **mar·i·hua·na** \,mar-ə-'(h)wän-ə\ *n*
[MexSp *mariguana*] **:** a narcotic product of hemp
ma·rim·ba \mə-'rim-bə\ *n* [of African origin] **:** a primitive xylophone with resonators beneath each bar; *also*
: a modern form of this instrument
ma·ri·na \mə-'rē-nə\ *n* **:** a dock or basin providing secure
moorings for motorboats and yachts and often offering
other facilities
¹mar·i·nade \,mar-ə-'nād\ *vt* **:** MARINATE
²marinade *n* **:** a brine or pickle in which meat or fish is
soaked to enrich its flavor
mar·i·nate \'mar-ə-,nāt\ *vt* **:** to steep (as meat or fish)
in a marinade
¹ma·rine \mə-'rēn\ *adj* [L *mare* sea] **1 a :** of or relating
to the sea ⟨*marine* life⟩ **b :** of or relating to the navigation
of the sea **:** NAUTICAL ⟨*marine* chart⟩ **c :** of or relating to
the commerce of the sea **:** MARITIME ⟨*marine* insurance⟩
2 : of or relating to marines ⟨*marine* barracks⟩
²marine *n* **1 :** the mercantile and naval shipping of a
country **2 :** one of a class of soldiers serving on shipboard or in close association with a naval force; *esp*
: a member of the U.S. Marine Corps
marine glue *n* **:** a water-insoluble adhesive
mar·i·ner \'mar-ə-nər\ *n* **:** one who navigates or assists
in navigating a ship **:** SAILOR
Mar·i·ol·a·try \,mer-ē-'äl-ə-trē, ,mar-\ *n* **:** excessive
veneration of the Virgin Mary
mar·i·o·nette \,mar-ē-ə-'net, ,mer-\ *n* **:** a puppet moved
by strings or by hand
Mar·ist \'mar-əst, 'mer-\ *n* **:** a priest of the Roman
Catholic Society of Mary devoted to education
mar·i·tal \'mar-ət-ᵊl\ *adj* [L *maritus* married] **1 :** of or
relating to marriage **:** CONJUGAL **2** *archaic* **:** of or relating
to a husband **syn** see MATRIMONIAL — **mar·i·tal·ly**
\-ᵊl-ē\ *adv*
mar·i·time \'mar-ə-,tīm\ *adj* **1 :** of or relating to navigation or commerce on the sea ⟨*maritime* law⟩ **2 :** bordering on or living or situated near the ocean ⟨*maritime*

nations⟩ **3** : having characteristics controlled primarily by oceanic winds and air masses ⟨a *maritime* climate⟩

mar·jo·ram \'märj-(ə-)rəm\ *n* : any of various usu. fragrant and aromatic mints sometimes used in cookery

¹mark \'märk\ *n* [OE *mearc* boundary, march] **1** : a border territory : MARCH **2 a** (1) : something (as a line, notch, or fixed object) designed to record position ⟨high-water *mark*⟩ (2) : any of the bits of leather or bunting placed at intervals on a sounding line — see SOUNDING LINE illustration **b** : a conspicuous object serving as a guide for travelers **c** (1) : something aimed at : TARGET, GOAL (2) : the question under discussion ⟨a comment beside the *mark*⟩ **d** : an object of ridicule or abuse : BUTT **e** : the starting line or position in a track event **f** : a standard of performance, quality, or condition : NORM, RECORD **3 a** : SIGN, INDICATION **b** : a characteristic or distinguishing trait or quality **c** : a cross made in place of a signature **d** : a written or printed symbol — compare PUNCTUATION MARK **e** : a symbol (as a brand or label) used for identification or for indication of ownership or quality **f** : a symbol (as a number or letter) representing an estimation of the quality of work or conduct : GRADE **4** : an impression (as a scar, scratch, or stain) made on a surface **5** : a lasting or strong impression ⟨made his *mark* in the world⟩ **6** : ATTENTION, NOTICE ⟨nothing worthy of *mark*⟩ **7** : IMPORTANCE, DISTINCTION ⟨a man of *mark*⟩

²mark *vt* **1 a** : to fix or trace out the bounds of by or as if by a mark **b** : to set apart by a line or boundary ⟨*mark* off a tennis court⟩ **c** : CHART **2 a** : to designate as if by a mark ⟨*marked* for greatness⟩ **b** : to make a mark or notation on **c** : to furnish with natural marks **d** : to label so as to indicate price or quality **3 a** : to make note of in writing : JOT **b** : to indicate by a mark or symbol; *also* : RECORD **c** : to determine the value of by means of marks or symbols : GRADE **4** : CHARACTERIZE, DISTINGUISH **5** : to take notice of : OBSERVE — **mark time 1** : to keep the time of a marching step by moving the feet alternately without advancing **2** : to function or operate without making progress

³mark *n* **1** : the basic monetary unit of Germany **2** : a coin representing one mark

Mark \'märk\ *n* **1** : an evangelist held to be the author of the second Gospel in the New Testament **2** — see BIBLE table **3** : a king of Cornwall in Arthurian legend, uncle of Tristram, and husband of Isolde

mark down \(')märk-'daún\ *vt* : to put a lower price on

mark·down \'märk-,daún\ *n* **1** : a lowering of price **2** : the amount by which an original selling price is reduced

marked \'märkt\ *adj* **1** : having marks **2** : having a distinctive character : NOTICEABLE **3 a** : enjoying fame or notoriety **b** : being an object of attack, suspicion, or vengeance — **mark·ed·ly** \'mär-kəd-lē\ *adv*

mark·er \'mär-kər\ *n* **1** : one that marks **2** : something used for marking

¹mar·ket \'mär-kət\ *n* [ONF, fr. L *mercatus* trade, marketplace, fr. *merc-*, *merx* merchandise] **1 a** : a meeting together of people to buy and sell; *also* : the people at such a meeting **b** : a public place where a market is held; *esp* : a place where provisions are sold at wholesale **c** : a retail establishment usu. of a specified kind ⟨meat *market*⟩ **2 a** : a geographical area of demand for commodities ⟨our foreign *markets*⟩ ⟨the world *market*⟩ **b** : the course of commercial activity by which the exchange of commodities is effected ⟨the *market* is dull⟩ **c** : an opportunity for selling ⟨a good *market* for used cars⟩ **3** : the area of economic activity in which buyers and sellers come together and the forces of supply and demand affect prices

²market *vb* **1** : to deal in a market **2** : to offer for sale in a market : SELL — **mar·ke·teer** \,mär-kə-'ti(ə)r\ *or* **mar·ket·er** \'mär-kət-ər\ *n* — **mar·ket·ing** \'mär-kət-iŋ\ *n*

mar·ket·a·ble \'mär-kət-ə-bəl\ *adj* **1** : fit to be offered for sale in a market **2** : wanted by purchasers : SALABLE — **mar·ket·a·bil·i·ty** \,mär-kət-ə-'bil-ət-ē\ *n*

market garden *n* : a plot in which vegetables are raised for market — **market gardener** *n* — **market gardening** *n*

mar·ket·place \'mär-kət-,plās\ *n* **1** : an open square or place in a town where markets or public sales are held **2** : the world of trade or economic activity

market price *n* : a price actually given or obtainable in current market dealings

market research *n* : the gathering of factual information as to consumer preferences for goods and services

market value *n* : the value of a commodity determined by current market prices

mark·ing \'mär-kiŋ\ *n* **1** : the act, process, or an instance of making or giving a mark **2 a** : a mark made **b** : arrangement, pattern, or disposition of marks (as on the coat of a mammal)

mark·ka \'mär-,kä\ *n*, *pl* **mark·kaa** \-,kä\ *or* **mark·kas** \-,käs\ **1** : the basic monetary unit of Finland **2** : a coin representing one markka

marks·man \'märks-mən\ *n* : one that shoots at a mark; *esp* : a person skilled at target shooting — **marks·man·ship** \-,ship\ *n*

mark up \(')märk-'əp\ *vt* : to put a higher price on

mark·up \'märk-,əp\ *n* **1** : a raising of price **2** : an amount added to the cost price of an article to determine the selling price

¹marl \'märl\ *n* : a loose or crumbling earthy deposit that contains a substantial amount of calcium carbonate — **marly** \'mär-lē\ *adj*

²marl *vt* : to dress (land) with marl

mar·lin \'mär-lən\ *n* : any of several large oceanic sport fishes related to sailfishes

mar·line \'mär-lən\ *also* **mar·lin** *n* [D *marlijn*, fr. MD *marren* to moor, tie] : a small loosely twisted line of two strands used for seizing and as a covering for wire rope

mar·line·spike *also* **mar·lin·spike** \'mär-lən-,spīk\ *n* : a pointed iron tool used to separate strands of rope or wire (as in splicing)

marlinespike

mar·ma·lade \'mär-mə-,lād\ *n* [Pg *marmelada* quince conserve, fr. L *melimelum*, a sweet apple, fr. Gk *melimēlon*, fr. *meli* honey + *mēlon* apple] : a clear jelly holding in suspension pieces of fruit and fruit rind

mar·mo·re·al \mär-'mōr-ē-əl, mär-'mòr-\ *also* **mar·mo·re·an** \-ē-ən\ *adj* : of, relating to, or resembling marble or a marble statue — **mar·mo·re·al·ly** \-ē-ə-lē\ *adv*

mar·mo·set \'mär-mə-,set, -mə-,zet\ *n* : any of numerous soft-furred bushy-tailed So. and Central American monkeys with claws instead of nails except on the great toe

mar·mot \'mär-mət\ *n* : a stout-bodied short-legged burrowing rodent with coarse fur, a short bushy tail, and very small ears — compare WOODCHUCK

¹ma·roon \mə-'rün\ *vt* [AmerSp *cimarrón*, a fugitive Negro slave, fr. *cimarrón* wild] **1** : to put ashore and abandon on a desolate island or coast **2** : to leave isolated and helpless

²maroon *n* [F *marron* Spanish chestnut] : a variable color averaging a dark red

mar·plot \'mär-,plät\ *n* : one who frustrates or ruins a plan or undertaking by his meddling

mar·quee \mär-'kē\ *n* **1** : a large field tent set up for an outdoor party, reception, or exhibition **2** : a canopy usu. of metal and glass projecting over an entrance ⟨a theater *marquee*⟩

mar·quess \'mär-kwəs\ *n* [alter. of *marquis*] **1** : a nobleman of hereditary rank in Europe and Japan **2** : a member of the British peerage ranking below a duke and above an earl — **mar·quess·ate** \-kwə-sət\ *n*

mar·que·try \'mär-kə-trē\ *n*, *pl* **-tries** : decoration in which elaborate patterns are formed by the insertion of pieces of wood, shell, or ivory into a wood veneer that is then applied to a piece of furniture

mar·quis \'mär-kwəs, mär-'kē\ *n*, *pl* **mar·quises** \-kwə-səz, -'kēz\ [MF, alter. of OF *marchis*, fr. *marche* ¹march] : MARQUESS

mar·quise \mär-'kēz\ *n*, *pl* **mar·quises** \-'kēz(-əz)\ : MARCHIONESS

mar·qui·sette \,mär-k(w)ə-'zet\ *n* : a sheer meshed fabric used for clothing, curtains, and mosquito nets

mar·riage \'mar-ij\ *n* **1 a** : the state of being married **b** : the mutual relation of husband and wife : WEDLOCK **c** : the institution whereby a man and a woman are joined in a special social and legal relationship for the purpose of making a home and raising a family **2** : an act of marrying; *esp* : the wedding ceremony and attendant festivities or formalities **3** : an intimate or close union — **mar·riage·a·ble** \-ə-bəl\ *adj*

marriage of convenience : a marriage contracted for social, political, or economic advantage

mar·ried \'mar-ēd\ *adj* **1** : united in marriage : WEDDED ⟨a *married* couple⟩ **2** : of or relating to marriage : CONNUBIAL ⟨*married* life⟩

mar·ron \ma-'rōⁿ\ *n* [F] **1** : a Mediterranean chestnut or its large sweet nut **2** : a chestnut preserved in vanilla‑flavored syrup — usu. used in pl.

mar·row \'mar-ō\ *n* [OE *mearg*] **1 a** : a soft vascular tissue that fills the cavities of most bones **b** : the substance of the spinal cord **2** : the inmost, best, or essential part — **mar·row·less** \-ō-ləs\ *adj* — **mar·rowy** \'mar-ə-wē\ *adj*

marrow bean *n* : a bean grown primarily for its large white ripe seeds

mar·row·bone \'mar-ə-ˌbōn\ *n* **1** : a bone (as a shinbone) rich in marrow **2** *pl* : KNEES

mar·row·fat \'mar-ō-ˌfat\ *n* : any of several wrinkled‑seeded garden peas

¹mar·ry \'mar-ē\ *vb* **mar·ried; mar·ry·ing** [OF *marier*, fr. L *maritare*, fr. *maritus* married] **1 a** : to join as husband and wife according to law or custom ⟨were *married* yesterday⟩ **b** : to give in marriage ⟨*married* his daughter to a lawyer⟩ **c** : to take as husband or wife ⟨*married* his secretary⟩ **d** : to take a spouse : WED ⟨decided to *marry*⟩ **2** : to unite in close and usu. permanent relation

²marry *interj, archaic* — used to express agreement or surprise

Mars \'märz\ *n* **1** : the Roman god of war **2** : the planet 4th in order from the sun conspicuous for the redness of its light — see PLANET table

marsh \'märsh\ *n* [ME *mersh*, fr. OE *mersc*] : an area of soft wet land usu. overgrown by grasses and sedges — compare SWAMP

¹mar·shal \'mär-shəl\ *n* [OF *mareschal*, of Germanic origin] **1 a** : a high official in a medieval royal household **b** : a person who arranges and directs ceremonies **2** : a general officer of the highest rank in some military forces **3 a** : a federal official in a U.S. judicial district having duties similar to those of a sheriff **b** : a municipal official having similar duties — **mar·shal·cy** \-sē\ *n* — **mar·shal·ship** \-ˌship\ *n*

²marshal *vt* **-shaled** *or* **-shalled; -shal·ing** *or* **-shal·ling** \'märsh-(ə-)liŋ\ **1** : to arrange in proper position, rank, or order ⟨*marshaling* the troops⟩ ⟨*marshaling* his arguments⟩ **2** : to lead with ceremony : USHER

marsh gas *n* : METHANE

marsh hawk *n* : a common American hawk that feeds mostly on frogs and snakes and is closely related to the European hen harrier

marsh·mal·low \'märsh-ˌmel-ō, -ˌmal-\ *n* **1** : a pink‑flowered perennial herb related to the mallow that has a mucilaginous root sometimes used in confectionery and in medicine **2** : a sweetened pasty confection made from the root of the marshmallow or from corn syrup, sugar, albumen, and gelatin beaten to a light creamy consistency

marsh marigold *n* : a swamp herb having bright yellow flowers resembling those of the related buttercups — called also *cowslip*

marshy \'mär-shē\ *adj* **marsh·i·er; -est** **1** : resembling or constituting marsh **2** : of or relating to marshes — **marsh·i·ness** \-shē-nəs\ *n*

¹mar·su·pi·al \mär-'sü-pē-əl\ *adj* : of, relating to, or being a marsupial

²marsupial *n* : any of an order (Marsupialia) of lowly mammals comprising kangaroos, opossums, and related animals that have a pouch on the abdomen of the female containing the teats and serving to carry the young

mar·su·pi·um \-pē-əm\ *n, pl* **-pia** \-pē-ə\ [L, pouch, fr. Gk *marsypion*] **1** : the pouch of a female marsupial **2** : an analogous structure in which an invertebrate animal carries eggs or young

mart \'märt\ *n* : a trading place : MARKET

mar·ten \'märt-ᵊn\ *n, pl* **marten** *or* **martens** [MF *martrine* marten fur, fr. *martre* marten] : a slim flesh-eating mammal larger than the related weasels; *also* : its soft gray or brown fur

Mar·tha \'mär-thə\ *n* : a sister of Lazarus and Mary and friend of Jesus

mar·tial \'mär-shəl\ *adj* [L *Mart-, Mars* Mars] **1** : of, relating to, or suited for war or a warrior ⟨a *martial* stride⟩ **2** : of or relating to an army or to military life ⟨court-*martial*⟩ — **mar·tial·ly** \-shə-lē\ *adv*

syn MARTIAL, WARLIKE, MILITARY mean relating to or characteristic of war. MARTIAL suggests esp. the pomp and ceremony of war and preparation for war ⟨*martial* music⟩ WARLIKE implies the feeling or temper that leads to or accompanies war ⟨*warlike* mountain tribes⟩ MILITARY applies to anything pertaining to the art or conduct of organized warfare esp. on land ⟨*military* campaign⟩

martial law *n* **1** : the law applied in occupied territory by the military forces of the occupying power **2** : the established law of a country administered by military forces in an emergency when civilian law enforcement agencies are unable to maintain public order and safety

Mar·tian \'mär-shən\ *adj* : of or relating to the planet Mars or its hypothetical inhabitants — **Martian** *n*

mar·tin \'märt-ᵊn\ *n* : a small European swallow with a forked tail, bluish black head and back, and white rump and underparts; *also* : any of various swallows and flycatchers

mar·ti·net \ˌmärt-ᵊn-'et\ *n* : a strict disciplinarian

mar·tin·gale \'märt-ᵊn-ˌgāl\ *n* : a strap connecting a horse's girth to the bit or reins so as to hold down its head

mar·ti·ni \mär-'tē-nē\ *n* : a cocktail consisting of gin and dry vermouth

Mar·tin·mas \'märt-ᵊn-məs, -ˌmas\ *n* [St. *Martin* of Tours *d ab*399, whose festival is celebrated on that day] : November 11

¹mar·tyr \'märt-ər\ *n* [OE, fr. LL, fr. Gk *martyr-, martys*, lit., witness] **1** : a person who suffers death rather than give up his religion **2** : one who sacrifices his life or something of great value for the sake of principle or devotion to a cause **3** : a great or constant sufferer — **mar·tyr·i·za·tion** \ˌmärt-ə-rə-'zā-shən\ *n* — **mar·tyr·ize** \'märt-ə-ˌrīz\ *vb*

²martyr *vt* **1** : to put to death for adhering to a belief **2** : TORTURE

mar·tyr·dom \'märt-ər-dəm\ *n* **1** : the sufferings and death of a martyr **2** : TORTURE

¹mar·vel \'mär-vəl\ *n* [OF *merveille*, fr. LL *mirabilia* marvels, fr. L *mirari* to wonder] : something that causes wonder or astonishment

²marvel *vb* **mar·veled** *or* **mar·velled; mar·vel·ing** *or* **mar·vel·ling** \'märv-(ə-)liŋ\ : to become filled with surprise, wonder, or astonishment ⟨*marveled* at the magician's skill⟩

mar·vel·ous *or* **mar·vel·lous** \'märv-(ə-)ləs\ *adj* **1** : causing wonder : ASTONISHING **2** : having the characteristics of a miracle **3** : of the highest kind or quality : SPLENDID — **mar·vel·ous·ly** *adv* — **mar·vel·ous·ness** *n*

Marx·ian \'märk-sē-ən, 'märk-shən\ *adj* : of, developed by, or influenced by the doctrines of Marx ⟨*Marxian* socialism⟩

Marx·ism \'märk-ˌsiz-əm\ *n* : the political and economic doctrines developed by Karl Marx and Friedrich Engels including the labor theory of value, the theory of surplus value, dialectical materialism, the class struggle, and dictatorship of the proletariat until the establishment of a classless society and the withering away of the state and providing the basis for Marxian socialism and much of modern Communism — **Marx·ist** \'märk-səst\ *n or adj*

Marx·ism-Len·in·ism \-'len-ə-ˌniz-əm\ *n* : a theory and practice of Communism developed by Lenin from Marxism primarily to fit Russian conditions — **Marx·ist-Len·in·ist** \-'len-ə-nəst\ *n or adj*

Mary \'me(ə)r-ē, 'ma(ə)r-\ *n* **1** : the mother of Jesus **2** : a sister of Lazarus and Martha

Mary·knoll \-ˌnōl\ *adj* : of or relating to one of the institutes of priests, brothers, and sisters of the Catholic Foreign Mission Society of America organized in 1911

Mary Mag·da·lene \-'mag-də-ˌlēn, -ˌmag-də-'lē-nē\ *n* : a woman healed of evil spirits by Jesus — called also *the Magdalene*

mar·zi·pan \'märt-sə-ˌpän, 'mär-zə-ˌpan\ *n* [G, fr. It *marzapane*] : a confection of almond paste, sugar, and whites of eggs

mas·cara \ma-'skar-ə\ *n* [It *maschera, mascara* mask] : a cosmetic for coloring the eyelashes and eyebrows

---

ə abut; ᵊ kitten; ər further; a back; ā bake; ä cot, cart; aů out; ch chin; e less; ē easy; g gift; i trip; ī life

mas·cot \'mas-ˌkät, -kət\ n [F mascotte] : a person, animal, or object supposed to bring good luck

¹mas·cu·line \'mas-kyə-lən\ adj [L masculinus, fr. masculus, n., male, dim. of mas male] **1** : of the male sex **2** : characteristic of or belonging to men : MANLY ⟨a masculine voice⟩ **3** : of, relating to, or constituting the class of words that ordinarily includes most of those referring to males ⟨a masculine noun⟩ ⟨masculine gender⟩ **4** : having or occurring in a stressed final syllable ⟨masculine rhyme⟩ — **mas·cu·line·ly** adv — **mas·cu·line·ness** \-lən-nəs\ n — **mas·cu·lin·i·ty** \ˌmas-kyə-'lin-ət-ē\ n

²masculine n **1** : a word or form of the masculine gender **2** : the masculine gender

ma·ser \'mā-zər\ n [microwave amplification by stimulated emission of radiation] : a device that utilizes the natural oscillations of atoms or molecules for amplifying or generating electromagnetic waves

¹mash \'mash\ n [OE māx-] **1** : crushed malt or grain meal steeped and stirred in hot water to produce wort **2** : a mixture of ground feeds for livestock **3** : a soft pulpy mass

²mash vt **1** : to reduce to a soft pulpy state by beating or pressure : SMASH **2** : to subject (as crushed malt) to the action of water with heating and stirring in preparing wort — **mash·er** n

mash·ie \'mash-ē\ n : a golf iron with a somewhat sharply angled blade used for medium distance and loft — called also number five iron

mashie niblick n : a golf iron with more loft than a mashie — called also number six iron

¹mask \'mask\ n [MF masque, fr. It maschera] **1** : a cover for the face used for disguise or protection ⟨a Halloween mask⟩ ⟨a baseball catcher's mask⟩ **2** : a device usu. covering the mouth and nose either to aid in or prevent the inhaling of something (as a gas or spray) **3** : a covering (as of gauze) for the mouth and nose to prevent infective droplets from being blown into the air **4** : something that disguises or conceals : CLOAK, PRETENSE **5** : one that wears a mask : MASKER **6** : a sculptured face or face and neck or a copy of a face made by means of a mold in plaster or wax ⟨a death mask⟩ **7** : the face of a mammal (as a fox or dog) **8** : a dramatic entertainment : MASQUE syn see DISGUISE

ancient Greek masks used in 1 tragedy and 2 comedy

²mask vb **1** : to take part in a masquerade **2** : to put on or wear a mask **3** : CONCEAL, DISGUISE ⟨mask a gun battery⟩ ⟨masked his real purpose⟩ ⟨mask an undesirable flavor⟩ **4** : to cover for protection ⟨mask the glass before painting the windows⟩

masked \'maskt\ adj **1** : wearing or using a mask ⟨masked dancers⟩ ⟨masked bandit⟩ **2** : marked by or requiring the wearing of masks ⟨a masked ball⟩ **3** : CONCEALED, HIDDEN

mask·er \'mas-kər\ n : a person who wears a mask; esp : a participant in a masquerade

ma·son \'mās-ᵊn\ n [OF maçon] **1** : a person who builds or works with stone, brick, or cement **2** cap : FREEMASON

mason bee n : a solitary bee that constructs nests of hardened mud and sand

Ma·son–Dix·on line \ˌmās-ᵊn-'dik-sən-\ n : the southern boundary line of Pennsylvania important in U.S. history as being in part the boundary between the free and the slave states

Ma·son·ic \mə-'sän-ik\ adj : of, relating to, or characteristic of Freemasons or Freemasonry

Ma·son·ite \'mās-ᵊn-ˌīt\ trademark — used for a fiberboard made from steam-treated wood fiber

ma·son jar \ˌmās-ᵊn-\ n [after John L. Mason, 19th cent. American inventor] : a widemouthed jar used for home canning

ma·son·ry \'mās-ᵊn-rē\ n, pl -ries **1** : the art, trade, or occupation of a mason **2** : the work done by a mason ⟨good masonry⟩ **3** : something built of stone, brick, or concrete **4** cap : FREEMASONRY

mason wasp n : a solitary wasp that constructs nests of hardened mud

masque \'mask\ n [MF] **1** : MASQUERADE **2** : a short

allegorical dramatic entertainment of the 16th and 17th centuries performed by masked actors

masqu·er \'mas-kər\ n : MASKER

¹mas·quer·ade \ˌmas-kə-'rād\ n **1 a** : a social gathering of persons wearing masks and often fantastic costumes **b** : a costume for wear at such a gathering **2** : an action or appearance that is mere disguise or outward show : POSE

²masquerade vi **1 a** : to disguise oneself or go about disguised **b** : to take part in a masquerade **2** : to assume the appearance of something one is not : POSE ⟨was arrested for masquerading as a policeman⟩ — **masquer·ad·er** n

¹mass \'mas\ n [OE mæsse, fr. LL missa dismissal after a religious service, mass, fr. L miss-, mittere to send, let go] **1** cap : a sequence of prayers and ceremonies forming the eucharistic office esp. of the Roman Catholic Church **2** often cap : a celebration of the Eucharist **3** : a musical setting for parts of the Mass

²mass n [L massa, fr. Gk maza cake, mass, fr. massein to knead] **1 a** : a quantity of matter or the form of matter that holds or clings together in one body ⟨a mass of metal⟩ ⟨a great mass of water⟩ **b** : greatness of size : BULK, MAGNITUDE **c** : the principal part : main body **2** : the quantity of matter in a body as measured by its inertia ⟨mass is responsible for weight but is independent of gravity⟩ **3** : a large quantity, amount, or number **4 a** : a large body of persons in a compact group **b** pl : the body of ordinary or common people as contrasted with the elite syn see BULK

³mass vb : to form or collect into a mass

⁴mass adj **1 a** : of, relating to, or designed for the mass of the people ⟨mass market⟩ ⟨mass education⟩ **b** : participated in by or affecting a large number of individuals ⟨mass demonstrations⟩ **c** : LARGE-SCALE, WHOLESALE ⟨mass production⟩ **2** : viewed as a whole : TOTAL ⟨the mass effect of a design⟩

¹mas·sa·cre \'mas-i-kər, substand 'mas-ə-ˌkrē\ vt **-cred; -cring** \-k(ə-)riŋ, substand -ˌkrē-iŋ\ : to kill in a massacre : SLAUGHTER — **mas·sa·crer** \-i-kər-ər, -i-krər, substand -ə-ˌkrē-ər\ n

²mas·sa·cre n [MF] **1** : the violent, cruel, and indiscriminate killing of a number of persons **2** : a slaughter of animals in large numbers

¹mas·sage \mə-'säzh, -'säj\ n [F, fr. Arabic massa to stroke] : treatment for remedial or hygienic purposes by rubbing, stroking, kneading, or tapping

²massage vt : to subject to massage — **mas·sag·er** n

mas·sa·sau·ga \ˌmas-ə-'sȯ-gə\ n : any of several small rattlesnakes

mass–energy equation n : an equation for the conversion of mass and energy into one another: $E = MC^2$ where E is energy in ergs, M is mass in grams, and C is the velocity of light in centimeters per second — called also Einstein equation

mas·se·ter \mə-'sēt-ər\ n [Gk masē-, masasthai to chew] : a large muscle that raises the lower jaw and assists in chewing — **mas·se·ter·ic** \ˌmas-ə-'ter-ik\ adj

mas·seur \ma-'sər\ n : a man who practices massage

mas·seuse \-'sə(r)z, -'süz\ n : a woman who practices massage

mas·sif \ma-'sēf\ n [F] : a principal mountain mass

mas·sive \'mas-iv\ adj **1** : forming or consisting of a large mass: **a** : WEIGHTY, HEAVY ⟨massive walls⟩ ⟨a massive volume⟩ **b** : impressively large or ponderous **c** : having no regular form but not necessarily lacking crystalline structure ⟨massive sandstone⟩ **2 a** : large, solid, or heavy in structure ⟨massive jaw⟩ **b** : large in scope or degree ⟨massive effect⟩ ⟨massive retaliation⟩ — **mas·sive·ly** adv — **mas·sive·ness** n

mass medium n, pl **mass media** : a medium of communication (as newspapers, radio, or television) that is designed to reach the mass of the people

mass meeting n : a large or general assembly of people esp. for discussion of a public question

mass number n : an integer that expresses the mass of an isotope and designates the number of nucleons in the nucleus

mass–pro·duce \ˌmas-prə-'d(y)üs\ vt : to produce in quantity usu. by machinery — **mass production** n

mass spectrograph n : an apparatus that separates a

j joke; ŋ sing; ō flow; ȯ flaw; ȯi coin; th thin; th̲ this; ü loot; u̇ foot; y yet; yü few; yu̇ furious; zh vision

stream of charged particles into a spectrum according to their masses

massy \'mas-ē\ *adj* **mass·i·er; -est :** having bulk and weight or substance : MASSIVE

¹mast \'mast\ *n* [OE *mæst*] **1 :** a long pole or spar that rises from the keel or deck of a ship and supports the yards, booms, sails, and rigging **2 :** a vertical or nearly vertical tall pole (as a post on a lifting crane) — **mast·ed** \'mas-təd\ *adj* — **before the mast :** in the position of a common sailor

²mast *vt* **:** to furnish with a mast

³mast *n* **:** nuts (as acorns) accumulated on the forest floor and often serving as food for animals (as hogs)

¹mas·ter \'mas-tər\ *n* [OE *magister* & OF *maistre*, both fr. L *magister* superior, owner, teacher, lit., greater one, fr. *magnus* great] **1 a :** a male teacher **b :** a person holding an academic degree higher than a bachelor's but lower than a doctor's **c** *often cap* **:** a revered religious leader **d :** an independent workman of proved proficiency; *esp* **:** one employing journeymen and apprentices **e :** an artist or performer of consummate skill **2 a :** one having authority over another **b :** VICTOR, SUPERIOR **c :** a person licensed to command a merchant ship **d :** an owner esp. of a slave or animal **e :** EMPLOYER **f** *dial* **:** HUSBAND **g :** the male head of a household **3 a** *archaic* **:** MISTER **b :** a youth or boy too young to be called *mister* — used as a title **4 :** a presiding officer in an institution or society

²master *vt* **mas·tered; mas·ter·ing** \-t(ə-)riŋ\ **1 :** OVERCOME, SUBDUE **2 :** to become skilled or proficient in or in the use of ⟨*master* arithmetic⟩

³master *adj* **1 :** being a master ⟨a *master* carpenter⟩ **2 :** GOVERNING, MAIN, PRINCIPAL ⟨a *master* plan⟩ **3 :** controlling the operation of other mechanisms ⟨a *master* clock⟩ **4 :** establishing a standard (as of dimension or weight) for reference ⟨a *master* gauge⟩

mas·ter–at–arms \,mas-tər-ət-'ärmz\ *n, pl* **masters–at–arms :** a petty officer charged with maintaining discipline aboard ship

master chief petty officer *n* **:** a petty officer in the navy of the highest enlisted rank

mas·ter·ful \'mas-tər-fəl\ *adj* **1 :** inclined to take control or dominate **2 :** having or showing the technical or artistic skill of a master — **mas·ter·ful·ly** \-fə-lē\ *adv* — **mas·ter·ful·ness** *n*

syn DOMINEERING: MASTERFUL implies a strong virile personality and the ability to deal authoritatively with men and affairs; DOMINEERING suggests an overbearing or tyrannical manner and an obstinate attempt to enforce one's will

master key *n* **:** a key designed to open several different locks

mas·ter·ly \'mas-tər-lē\ *adj* **:** suitable to or resembling a master; *esp* **:** showing superior knowledge or skill — **mas·ter·li·ness** *n* — **masterly** *adv*

mas·ter·mind \-,mīnd\ *n* **:** a person who supplies the directing or creative intelligence for a project — **mastermind** *vt*

master of ceremonies 1 : a person who determines the forms to be observed on a public occasion or acts as host at a formal event **2 :** a person who acts as host for a variety program (as on television)

mas·ter·piece \'mas-tər-,pēs\ *n* **1 :** a piece of work presented by a journeyman to a guild as evidence of qualification for the rank of master **2 :** a work done with extraordinary skill; *esp* **:** a supreme intellectual or artistic achievement

master race *n* **:** a people held to be racially preeminent and hence fitted to rule or enslave other peoples

master sergeant *n* **:** a noncommissioned officer ranking in the army above a sergeant first class and below a sergeant major and in the air force above a technical sergeant and below a senior master sergeant

mas·ter·ship \'mas-tər-,ship\ *n* **1 :** the authority or control of a master **2 :** the office or position of a master **3 :** the proficiency of a master

mas·ter·stroke \-,strōk\ *n* **:** a masterly performance or move

mas·ter·work \-,wərk\ *n* **:** MASTERPIECE

mas·tery \'mas-t(ə-)rē\ *n, pl* **-ter·ies 1 :** the position or authority of a master : MASTERSHIP **2 :** VICTORY, ASCENDANCY, SUPERIORITY **3 :** skill or knowledge that makes

one master of something : COMMAND ⟨a *mastery* of French⟩

mast·head \'mast-,hed\ *n* **1 :** the top of a mast **2 a :** the printed matter in a newspaper or periodical that gives the title and pertinent details of ownership, advertising rates, and subscription rates **b :** the name of a newspaper displayed on the top of the first page

mas·tic \'mas-tik\ *n* **1 :** a yellowish to greenish resin of a small southern European tree used in varnish **2 :** a pasty material (as a preparation of asphalt) used as protective coating or cement

mas·ti·cate \'mas-tə-,kāt\ *vb* [Gk *mastichan* to gnash the teeth] **1 :** to grind or crush with or as if with the teeth in preparation for swallowing : CHEW **2 :** to soften or reduce to pulp by crushing or kneading — **mas·ti·ca·tion** \,mas-tə-'kā-shən\ *n* — **mas·ti·ca·tor** \'mas-tə-,kāt-ər\ *n* — **mas·ti·ca·to·ry** \'mas-ti-kə-,tōr-ē, -,tor-\ *adj*

mas·tiff \'mas-təf\ *n* **:** a large powerful deep-chested smooth-coated dog used chiefly as a watchdog and guard dog

mas·ti·tis \mas-'tīt-əs\ *n* **:** inflammation of the breast or udder usu. caused by infection

mas·to·don \'mas-tə-,dän, -dən\ *n* **:** any of numerous huge extinct mammals related to the mammoths and existing elephants — **mas·to·don·ic** \,mas-tə-'dän-ik\ *adj* — **mas·to·dont** \'mas-tə-,dänt\ *adj or n*

¹mas·toid \'mas-,tȯid\ *adj* [Gk *mastoeidēs*, lit., breast-shaped, fr. *mastos* breast] **:** of, relating to, or occurring in the region of a somewhat conical process of the temporal bone behind the ear

²mastoid *n* **1 :** a mastoid bone or process **2 :** MASTOIDITIS **b :** an operation for the relief of mastoiditis

mas·toid·ec·to·my \,mas-,tȯi-'dek-tə-mē\ *n, pl* **-mies :** surgical removal of all or part of the mastoid process

mas·toid·itis \,mas-,tȯi-'dīt-əs\ *n* **:** inflammation of the mastoid process

mas·tur·ba·tion \,mas-tər-'bā-shən\ *n* [L *masturbari* to masturbate] **:** erotic stimulation of the genital organs apart from sexual intercourse and esp. by use of the hand — **mas·tur·bate** \'mas-tər-,bāt\ *vb*

¹mat \'mat\ *n* [OE *meatte*, fr. LL *matta*] **1 a :** a piece of coarse fabric made of woven or braided rushes, straw, or wool **b :** a piece of material in front of a door to wipe the shoes on **c :** a piece of material (as leather, woven straw, or cloth) used under a dish or vase or as an ornament **d :** a pad or cushion for gymnastics or wrestling **2 :** something made up of many intertwined or tangled strands ⟨a thick *mat* of vegetation⟩

²mat *vb* **mat·ted; mat·ting 1 :** to provide with a mat or matting **2 :** to form into a tangled mass

³mat *adj* [F] **:** lacking or deprived of luster or gloss

⁴mat *vt* **mat·ted; mat·ting 1 :** to give a dull effect to **2 :** to provide (a picture) with a mat

⁵mat *n* **1 :** a border going around a picture between picture and serving as the frame **2 :** a dull finish or a roughened surface (as in gilding or painting)

mat·a·dor \'mat-ə-,dȯ(ə)r\ *n* [Sp, lit., killer, fr. *matar* to kill] **:** a bullfighter who finally kills the bull with a sword thrust

¹match \'mach\ *n* [ME *macche*, fr. OE *mæcca* mate] **1 a :** a person or thing that is equal or similar to another **b :** a thing that is exactly like another **c :** one that is able to cope with another ⟨a *match* for the enemy⟩ **2 :** two persons or things that go well together ⟨curtains and carpet are a good *match*⟩ **3 a :** MARRIAGE **b :** a person to be considered as a marriage partner **4 :** a contest between two or more parties ⟨a tennis *match*⟩

²match *vb* **1 :** to meet usu. successfully as a competitor **2 a :** to place in competition with **b :** to provide with a worthy competitor **3 :** to join or give in marriage **4 a :** to make or find the equal or the like of **b :** to make correspond **c :** to be the same or suitable to one another **:** be or make a match **5 a :** to flip or toss (coins) and compare exposed faces **b :** to toss coins with (another) — **match·er** *n*

³match *n* [ME *macche*, fr. MF *mesche*] **1 :** a wick or cord that is made to burn evenly and is used for igniting a charge of powder **2 :** a short slender piece of wood or other material tipped with a mixture that ignites when subjected to friction

match·board \'mach-,bȯrd, -,bȯrd\ *n* **:** a board with a groove cut along one edge and a tongue along the other

ə abut; ᵊ kitten; ər further; a back; ā bake; ä cot, cart; aů out; ch chin; e less; ē easy; g gift; i trip; ī life

so as to fit snugly with the edges of similarly cut boards — called also **matched board** \'mach(t)-\

match·book \'mach-,bůk\ *n* : a small folder containing rows of paper matches

match·less \'mach-ləs\ *adj* : having no equal : better than any other — **match·less·ly** *adv*

match·lock \'mach-,läk\ *n* : an old form of gunlock in which the charge was lighted by a cord match; *also* : a gun equipped with such a lock

match·mak·er \-,mā-kər\ *n* : one that arranges a match; *esp* : one that arranges marriages — **match·mak·ing** \-kiŋ\ *n*

match play *n* : golf competition in which the winner is the person or team winning the greater number of holes

match point *n* : the last point needed to win a match

match·wood \'mach-,wůd\ *n* : small pieces of wood : SPLINTERS

¹**mate** \'māt\ *vt* : CHECKMATE

²**mate** *n* : CHECKMATE

³**mate** *n* [ME] **1 a** : ASSOCIATE, COMPANION **b** : an assistant to a more skilled workman : HELPER ⟨plumber's *mate*⟩ **c** *archaic* : MATCH, PEER **2 a** : a deck officer on a merchant ship ranking below the captain **3** : one of a pair: as **a** : either member of a married couple **b** : either member of a breeding pair of animals ⟨a dove and his *mate*⟩ **c** : either of two matched objects ⟨couldn't find the *mate* to the glove⟩

⁴**mate** *vb* **1** *archaic* : MATCH **2** : to join or fit together **3 a** : to bring together as mates **b** : to provide a mate for

⁵**ma·té** *or* **má·te** \'mä-,tā\ *n* : an aromatic beverage made from the leaves and shoots of a So. American holly; *also* : these leaves and shoots

ma·ter \'māt-ər\ *n* [L] *chiefly Brit* : MOTHER

¹**ma·te·ri·al** \mə-'tir-ē-əl\ *adj* [L *materia* matter] **1 a** : relating to, derived from, or consisting of matter; *esp* : PHYSICAL ⟨*material* world⟩ **b** : BODILY ⟨*material* needs⟩ ⟨*material* comforts⟩ **2 a** : having real importance or great consequence **b** : ESSENTIAL, RELEVANT, PERTINENT **3** : relating to or concerned with physical rather than spiritual or intellectual things ⟨*material* progress⟩ **4** : of or relating to the production and distribution of economic goods and the social relationships of owners and laborers ⟨*material* factors⟩ — **ma·te·ri·al·i·ty** \-,tir-ē-'al-ət-ē\ *n* — **ma·te·ri·al·ly** \-'tir-ē-ə-lē\ *adv* — **ma·te·ri·al·ness** *n*
syn MATERIAL, PHYSICAL, CORPOREAL mean of or belonging to actuality. MATERIAL implies formation out of tangible matter; used in contrast with *spiritual* or *ideal* it suggests what is mundane, ignoble, or grasping; PHYSICAL applies to whatever is perceived by the senses and may contrast with *mental, spiritual,* or *imaginary;* CORPOREAL stresses having such tangible qualities of a body as fixed shape and size and resistance to force

²**material** *n* **1** : the elements, constituents, or substance of which something is composed or can be made ⟨dress *material*⟩ ⟨building *materials*⟩ **2 a** : apparatus necessary for doing or making something ⟨writing *materials*⟩ **b** : MATÉRIEL

ma·te·ri·al·ism \mə-'tir-ē-ə-,liz-əm\ *n* **1 a** : a theory that matter is the only reality and that everything can be explained as either being or coming from matter **b** : a doctrine that the only or the highest values lie in material well-being and material progress **c** : a Marxist doctrine that everything ultimately depends upon and esp. that economic and social change is caused by material factors — compare DIALECTICAL MATERIALISM, HISTORICAL MATERIALISM **2** : a preoccupation with material rather than intellectual or spiritual things — **ma·te·ri·al·ist** \-ē-ə-ləst\ *n or adj* — **ma·te·ri·al·is·tic** \-,tir-ē-ə-'lis-tik\ *adj* — **ma·te·ri·al·is·ti·cal·ly** \-'lis-ti-k(ə-)lē\ *adv*

ma·te·ri·al·ize \mə-'tir-ē-ə-,līz\ *vb* **1 a** : to make material : give form and substance to **b** : to cause to appear in bodily form ⟨*materialize* the spirits of the dead⟩ **2** : to assume bodily form **3 a** : to come into existence : become realized fact **b** : to put in an appearance; *esp* : to appear suddenly — **ma·te·ri·al·i·za·tion** \-,tir-ē-ə-lə-'zā-shən\ *n* — **ma·te·ri·al·iz·er** \-'tir-ē-ə-,lī-zər\ *n*

ma·te·ria med·i·ca \mə-,tir-ē-ə-'med-i-kə\ *n* [NL] **1** : material or substances used in medical remedies **2** : a branch of medical science that deals with the sources, nature, properties, and preparation of drugs

ma·té·ri·el *or* **ma·te·ri·el** \mə-,tir-ē-ə-'el\ *n* [F *matériel*]

material] : equipment, apparatus, and supplies used by an organization or institution

ma·ter·nal \mə-'tərn-ᵊl\ *adj* [L *maternus,* fr. *mater* mother; akin to E *mother*] **1** : of, relating to, or characteristic of a mother : MOTHERLY **2 a** : related through a mother ⟨*maternal* grandparents⟩ **b** : derived or received from a mother — **ma·ter·nal·ly** \-ᵊl-ē\ *adv*

ma·ter·ni·ty \mə-'tər-nət-ē\ *n, pl* **-ties** **1** : the state of being a mother : MOTHERHOOD **2** : motherly character or qualities : MOTHERLINESS

mat·ey \'māt-ē\ *adj, chiefly Brit* : COMPANIONABLE

math \'math\ *n* : MATHEMATICS

math·e·mat·i·cal \,math-ə-'mat-i-kəl\ *adj* [Gk *mathēmatikos,* fr. *mathēmata,* pl., mathematics, lit., objects of learning, fr. *math-, manthanein* to learn] **1** : of, relating to, or according with mathematics **2** : very exact : PRECISE ⟨*mathematical* accuracy⟩ **3** : possible but highly improbable ⟨only a *mathematical* chance⟩ — **math·e·mat·i·cal·ly** \-i-k(ə-)lē\ *adv*

math·e·ma·ti·cian \,math-(ə-)mə-'tish-ən\ *n* : a specialist or expert in mathematics

math·e·mat·ics \,math-ə-'mat-iks\ *n* : the science of numbers and their operations, interrelations, and combinations and of space configurations and their structure, measurement, and transformations

mat·i·nee *or* **mat·i·née** \,mat-ᵊn-'ā\ *n* [F *matinée,* lit., morning period or activity, fr. *matin* morning, fr. L *matutinum,* fr. *matutinus* of the morning] : a musical or dramatic performance or a social event ⟨as a reception⟩ held in the daytime and esp. in the afternoon

mat·ins \'mat-ᵊnz\ *n pl, often cap* [OF *matines,* fr. LL *matutinae,* fr. L *matutinus* of the morning] **1** : the office of prayer traditionally said with lauds between midnight and 4 a.m. as the first of the canonical hours **2** : the service of morning prayer in churches of the Anglican communion

ma·tri·arch \'mā-trē-,ärk\ *n* [L *matr-, mater* mother + Gk *archein* to rule] : a woman who rules a family, group, or state; *esp* : a mother who is head and ruler of her family and descendants — **ma·tri·ar·chal** \,mā-trē-'är-kəl\ *adj*

ma·tri·ar·chate \-,är-kət, -,kāt\ *n* : a family, group, or state governed by a matriarch

ma·tri·ar·chy \-,är-kē\ *n, pl* **-chies** **1** : MATRIARCHATE **2** : a system of social organization in which descent and inheritance are traced through the female line

mat·ri·cide \'ma-trə-,sīd, 'mā-\ *n* **1** : murder of a mother by her child **2** : one that murders his mother — **mat·ri·cid·al** \,ma-trə-'sīd-ᵊl, ,mā-\ *adj*

ma·tric·u·late \mə-'trik-yə-,lāt\ *vb* : to enroll as a member of a body and esp. of a college or university — **ma·tric·u·la·tion** \-,trik-yə-'lā-shən\ *n*

mat·ri·lin·e·al \,ma-trə-'lin-ē-əl, ,mā-\ *adj* : relating to, based on, or tracing descent through the maternal line ⟨*matrilineal* society⟩ — **mat·ri·lin·e·al·ly** \-ē-ə-lē\ *adv*

mat·ri·mo·ni·al \,ma-trə-'mō-nē-əl\ *adj* : of or relating to matrimony — **mat·ri·mo·ni·al·ly** \-nē-ə-lē\ *adv*
syn MARITAL, CONJUGAL, NUPTIAL: MATRIMONIAL may apply to whatever has to do with the married state or married persons; MARITAL may refer esp. to the husband's part in marriage but often equals MATRIMONIAL; CONJUGAL refers esp. to the relations and behavior of persons who are married; NUPTIAL applies to wedding rites and ceremonies

mat·ri·mo·ny \'ma-trə-,mō-nē\ *n, pl* **-nies** [L *matrimonium,* fr. *matr-, mater* mother, married woman] : the union of man and woman as husband and wife : MARRIAGE

matrimony vine *n* : a shrub or vine of the nightshade family with often showy flowers and bright berries

ma·trix \'mā-triks\ *n, pl* **ma·tri·ces** \'mā-trə-,sēz, 'ma-\ *or* **ma·trix·es** \'mā-trik-səz\ [L *matric-, matrix* womb, fr. *matr-, mater* mother] **1 a** : intercellular substance ⟨as of cartilage⟩ **b** : the thickened tissue at the base of a fingernail or toenail from which the nail grows **2 a** : a place or a surrounding or enclosing substance ⟨as a rock⟩ within which something ⟨as a mineral⟩ originates or develops **3** : something ⟨as a mold⟩ that gives form, foundation, or origin to something else ⟨as molten metal⟩ enclosed in it **4** : a rectangular array of mathematical elements that is subject to special algebraic laws

ma·tron \'mā-trən\ *n* **1** : a married woman usu. marked by dignified maturity or social distinction **2 a :** a woman who is in charge of the household affairs of an institution (as a hospital or a boarding school) **b :** a woman who supervises women prisoners in a police station or jail **c :** a woman attendant (as in a bathhouse or ladies' rest room)

ma·tron·ly \-lē\ *adj* : of or resembling a matron : suitable for a matron

matron of honor : a married woman serving as the principal wedding attendant of a bride

matt *or* **matte** \'mat\ *var of* MAT

¹mat·ter \'mat-ər\ *n* [OF *matere,* fr. L *materia* wood, matter] **1 a :** a subject of interest or concern (as a topic under consideration or a cause of disagreement or dispute) **b :** something to be dealt with : AFFAIR, CONCERN ⟨a few personal *matters* to take care of⟩ **c :** a condition affecting a person or thing usu unfavorably ⟨what's the *matter* with him⟩ **2 :** the material of thought or discourse esp. as contrasted with its form **3 a :** the substance of which a physical object is composed : something that occupies space and has weight **b :** material substance of a particular kind or function ⟨coloring *matter*⟩ ⟨the gray *matter* of the brain⟩ **c :** PUS **4 :** a more or less definite amount or quantity ⟨a *matter* of four miles to the next town⟩ **5 :** something written or printed **6 :** MAIL ⟨first≠ class *matter*⟩

²matter *vi* **1 :** to be of importance : SIGNIFY **2 :** to form or discharge pus : SUPPURATE ⟨*mattering* wound⟩

matter of course : something that may be expected as a natural or logical result of something else — **mat·ter-of-course** \,mat-ər-ə(v)-'kŏrs, -'kŏrs\ *adj*

mat·ter-of-fact \,mat-ər-ə-'fakt\ *adj* : adhering to or concerned with fact; *esp* : not fanciful or imaginative : PRACTICAL, COMMONPLACE — **mat·ter-of-fact·ly** *adv* — **mat·ter-of-fact·ness** \-'fak(t)-nəs\ *n*

mat·tery \'mat-ə-rē\ *adj* : producing or containing pus or material resembling pus

Mat·thew \'math-yü\ *n* **1 :** a customs collector chosen as one of the twelve apostles and held to be the author of the first Gospel in the New Testament **2** — see BIBLE table — **Mat·the·an** *or* **Mat·thae·an** \ma-'thē-ən\ *adj*

mat·ting \'mat-iŋ\ *n* **1 :** material for mats **2 :** MATS

mat·tins *chiefly Brit var of* MATINS

mat·tock \'mat-ək\ *n* [OE *mattuc*] : an implement for digging consisting of a long wooden handle and a steel head one end of which comes either to a point or to a cutting edge

mat·tress \'ma-trəs\ *n* [OF *materas,* fr. Arabic *maṭraḥ* place where something is thrown] **1 :** a fabric case filled with resilient material used either alone as a bed or on a bedstead **2 :** an inflatable airtight sack for use as a mattress

heads of mattocks

mat·u·rate \'mach-ə-,rāt\ *vb* : MATURE

mat·u·ra·tion \,mach-ə-'rā-shən\ *n* **1 :** the process of becoming mature **2 :** the process by which diploid cells are transformed into haploid gametes — **mat·u·ra·tion·al** \-shnəl, -shən-ᵊl\ *adj* — **ma·tu·ra·tive** \mə-'t(y)ür-ət-iv\ *adj*

¹ma·ture \mə-'t(y)ú(ə)r\ *adj* [L *maturus* ripe] **1 :** based on slow careful consideration **2 a :** fully grown and developed : ADULT, RIPE **b :** having attained a final or desired state ⟨*mature* wine⟩ **3 :** of or relating to a condition of full development ⟨*mature* outlook⟩ **4 :** due for payment (the note will become *mature* in 90 days) — **ma·ture·ly** *adv* — **ma·ture·ness** *n*

²mature *vb* **1 :** to bring to maturity or completion **2 :** to become fully developed or ripe **3 :** to become due ⟨when a bond *matures*⟩

ma·tu·ri·ty \mə-'t(y)ür-ət-ē\ *n* **1 :** the quality or state of being mature; *esp* : full development **2 :** the date when an obligation (as a bond or note) becomes due

ma·tu·ti·nal \,mach-ü-'tīn-ᵊl, mə-'t(y)üt-ᵊn-əl\ *adj* [L *matutinus* of the morning] : of, relating to, or occurring in the morning : EARLY — **ma·tu·ti·nal·ly** \-ē\ *adv*

mat·zo \'mät-sə, -,sō\ *n, pl* **mat·zoth** *or* **mat·zos** \-səz, -səs, -,sōz, -,sōs, -,sōth\ [Yiddish *matse,* fr. Heb *maṣṣāh*] **1 :** unleavened bread eaten at the Passover **2 :** a wafer of matzo

maud·lin \'mŏd-lən\ *adj* [fr. Mary *Magdalene;* fr. the

frequent depiction of her as a weeping penitent] **1 :** weakly and excessively sentimental **2 :** drunk enough to be tearfully silly

mau·gre \,mó-gər\ *prep, archaic* : in spite of

¹maul \'mól\ *n* [L *malleus*] : a heavy hammer often with a wooden head used esp. for driving wedges or posts

²maul *vt* **1 :** BEAT, BRUISE **2 :** to injure by beating : MANGLE **3 :** to handle roughly — **maul·er** *n*

maun·der \'món-dər, 'män-\ *vi* **maun·dered**; **maun·der·ing** \-d(ə)riŋ\ **1 :** to wander slowly and idly **2 :** to speak disconnectedly or without apparent plan or purpose — **maun·der·er** \-dər-ər\ *n*

syn MAUNDER, MEANDER mean to proceed without evident purpose or direction. MAUNDER suggests esp. aimlessness and futility in speech; MEANDER stresses leisurely digression and frequent change in direction rather than actual aimlessness

Maun·dy Thursday \,món-dē-, ,män-\ *n* : the Thursday before Easter

mau·so·le·um \,mó-sə-'lē-əm, ,mó-zə-\ *n, pl* **-le·ums** *or* **-lea** \-'lē-ə\ [Gk *Mausōleion,* tomb of Mausolus, fr. *Mausōlos* Mausolus *d*353 B.C. ruler of Caria] : a large tomb; *esp* : a usu. stone building for the entombment of the dead above ground

mauve \'mōv, 'móv\ *n* [F, mallow, fr. L *malva*] : a moderate purple, violet, or lilac color

mav·er·ick \'mav-(ə-)rik\ *n* [after Samuel A. *Maverick d*1870 American pioneer in Texas who did not brand his calves] **1 :** an unbranded range animal; *esp* : a motherless calf **2 :** a person who refuses to follow the leadership of his political party or conform with his group and sets an independent course

ma·vis \'mā-vəs\ *n* **1 :** SONG THRUSH 1 **2 :** a European thrush with spotted underparts — called also *mistle thrush*

ma·vour·neen *also* **ma·vour·nin** \mə-'vù(ə)r-,nēn\ *n, Irish* : my darling

maw \'mó\ *n* **1 :** the receptacle into which food is taken by swallowing : **a :** STOMACH **b :** CROP **2 :** the throat, gullet, or jaws **3 :** the gullet of a voracious carnivore

mawk·ish \'mó-kish\ *adj* [ME *mawke* maggot, fr. ON *mathkr*] **1 :** having an insipid often unpleasant taste **2 :** marked by sickly sentimentality — **mawk·ish·ly** *adv* — **mawk·ish·ness** *n*

max·il·la \mak-'sil-ə\ *n, pl* **max·il·lae** \-'sil-(,)ē, -'sil-,ī\ *or* **max·il·las** [L] **1 a :** JAW 1a **b :** an upper jaw esp. of a mammal **c :** either of two bones of the upper jaw that in higher vertebrates and man bear most of the teeth **2 :** one of the first or second pair of mouth appendages posterior to the mandibles in various arthropods — **max·il·lary** \'mak-sə-,ler-ē\ *adj or n*

max·il·li·ped \mak-'sil-ə-,ped\ *or* **max·il·li·pede** \-,pēd\ *n* : any of three pairs of appendages situated next behind the maxillae in a crustacean

max·im \'mak-səm\ *n* [ML *maxima,* fr. L, fem. of *maximus,* superl. of *magnus* great] **1 :** a general truth, fundamental principle, or rule of conduct **2 :** a proverbial saying

max·i·mal \'mak-s(ə-)məl\ *adj* : MAXIMUM ⟨*maximal* development⟩ ⟨*maximal* dose⟩ — **max·i·mal·ly** \-ē\ *adv*

max·i·mal·ist \'mak-s(ə)mə-ləst\ *n* : one who advocates immediate and direct action to accomplish the whole of a project; *esp* : a socialist advocating the immediate seizure of power by revolutionary means

max·i·mize \'mak-sə-,mīz\ *vb* **1 :** to raise to the highest degree **2 :** to assign maximum importance to **3 :** to interpret something in the broadest sense — **max·i·miz·er** *n*

max·i·mum \'mak-s(ə)məm\ *n, pl* **max·i·mums** *or* **max·i·ma** \-sə-mə\ [L, neuter of *maximus,* superl. of *magnus* great] **1 a :** the greatest quantity or value attainable or attained **b :** the period of highest, greatest, or utmost development **2 :** an upper limit allowed by authority — **maximum** *adj*

may \(')mā\ *auxiliary verb, past* **might** \(')mīt\; *pres sing & pl* **may** [OE *mæg* can, may] **1 a :** have permission to ⟨you *may* go now⟩ **b :** be in some degree likely to ⟨you *may* be right⟩ **2** — used to express a wish or desire ⟨long *may* he reign⟩ **3** — used to express purpose ⟨he laughed that he *might* not weep⟩, contingency ⟨he'll do his duty come what *may*⟩, or concession ⟨he *may* be slow but he is thorough⟩ **syn** see CAN

May \'mā\ *n* [L *Maius,* fr. *Maia,* Roman goddess] : the 5th month of the year

Ma·ya \'mī-ə\ *n* : a member of a group of peoples of the Yucatán peninsula and adjacent areas — **Ma·yan** \'mī-ən\ *adj*

may·ap·ple \'mā-,ap-əl\ *n* : a No. American woodland herb related to the barberries that has a poisonous rootstock, leaves up to one foot in diameter, and a single large waxy white flower followed by a yellow egg≈shaped berry; *also* : its edible but insipid fruit

may·be \'mā-bē, 'meb-ē\ *adv* : PERHAPS

May Day \'mā-,dā\ *n* : May 1 celebrated as a springtime festival in some countries as Labor Day

May·day \mā-'dā, 'mā-,\ [F *m'aider* help me] — an international radio telephone signal word used as a distress call

may·est *or* **mayst** \'mā-əst, (')māst\ *archaic pres 2d sing of* MAY

may·flow·er \'mā-,flau̇(-ə)r\ *n* : any of various spring≈blooming plants (as the trailing arbutus, hepatica, or several No. American anemones)

may·fly \-,flī\ *n* : a slender fragile-winged short-lived adult insect (order Plectophora)

may·hap \'mā-,hap, mā-'\ *adv* : PERHAPS

may·hem \'mā-,hem, 'mā-əm\ *n* [Anglo-French, fr. OF *maynier, mahaignier* to maim] **1** : willful and permanent crippling, mutilation, or disfigurement of any part of the body **2** : needless or willful damage

may·ing \'mā-iŋ\ *n, often cap* : the celebrating of May Day

mayn't \'mā-ənt, (')mānt\ : may not

may·on·naise \'mā-ə-,nāz, ,mā-ə-'\ *n* [F] : a dressing (as for salads) consisting chiefly of yolk of egg, vegetable oil, and vinegar or lemon juice

may·or \'mā-ər, 'me(-)ər\ *n* [OF *maire,* fr. L *major,* compar. of *magnus* great] : an official elected to act as chief executive or nominal head of a city or borough — **may·or·al** \'mā-ə-rəl, 'me-ə-\ *adj*

may·or·al·ty \'mā-ə-rəl-tē, 'mer-əl-\ *n, pl* **-ties** : the office or the term of office of a mayor

mayor–council *adj* : of, relating to, or being a method of municipal government in which a usu. elective mayor and council exercise both policy-making and administrative powers

mayor of the palace : the chief officer of the household of a Frankish king wielding practically supreme power under the later Merovingians

may·pole \'mā-,pōl\ *n, often cap* : a tall flower-wreathed pole forming a center for May Day sports and dances

may·pop \'mā-,päp\ *n* : a climbing perennial passion-flower of the southern U.S.; *also* : its ovoid yellow edible fruit

May queen *n* : a girl chosen queen of a May Day festival

May·tide \'mā-,tīd\ *or* **May·time** \-,tīm\ *n* : the month of May

maze \'māz\ *n* **1** : a confusing intricate network of passages : LABYRINTH **2** *chiefly dial* : a state of confusion or bewilderment

ma·zur·ka \mə-'zər-kə, -'zu̇(ə)r-\ *n* [Russ, fr. Polish *mazurek*] **1** : a Polish dance in moderate triple measure **2** : music for the mazurka usu. in moderate ¾ or ⅜ time

mazy \'mā-zē\ *adj* **maz·i·er; -est** : resembling a maze in confusing turns and windings

maze 1

maz·zard \'maz-ərd\ *n* : SWEET CHERRY; *esp* : wild or seedling sweet cherry used as a rootstock for grafting

me \(')mē\ *pron* [OE *mē*] *objective case of* I

¹mead \'mēd\ *n* [OE *medu*] : a fermented drink made of water, honey, malt, and yeast

²mead *n* [OE *mǣd*] *archaic* : MEADOW

mead·ow \'med-ō\ *n* [OE *mǣdwe,* oblique case form of *mǣd* meadow] : land in or mainly in grass; *esp* : a tract of moist low-lying usu. level grassland

meadow beauty *n* : any of a genus of low perennial American herbs with showy cymose flowers

meadow fescue *n* : a tall vigorous perennial fescue with broad flat leaves cultivated for pasture and hay

mead·ow·lark \'med-ō-,lärk\ *n* : any of several No.

American songbirds largely brown and buff above with a yellow breast bearing a black crescent

meadow mushroom *n* : a common edible fungus that is the chief mushroom of commerce

meadow saffron *n* : any of a genus of Old World flowers of the lily family with often autumn-borne flowers resembling crocuses and seeds and corms that yield colchicine — called also *autumn crocus*

mead·ow·sweet \'med-ō-,swēt\ *n* : any of several No. American native or naturalized spireas with pink or white fragrant flowers

mea·ger *or* **mea·gre** \'mē-gər\ *adj* [MF *maigre,* fr. L *macr-, macer*] **1** : having little flesh : THIN **2** : lacking richness, strength, or comparable qualities : INADEQUATE ⟨*meager* harvest⟩ — **mea·ger·ly** *adv* — **mea·ger·ness** *n* **syn** SCANTY, SPARSE: MEAGER implies lack of fullness, richness, or plenty ⟨*meager* diet⟩ SCANTY stresses insufficiency in quantity, degree, or extent ⟨*scanty* supply of fuel⟩ SPARSE implies a thin scattering of units ⟨*sparse* population⟩

¹meal \'mēl\ *n* [OE *mǣl* appointed time, meal] **1** : the food eaten or prepared for eating at one time **2** : the act or time of eating a meal

²meal *n* [OE *melu*] **1** : usu. coarsely ground seeds of a cereal grass or pulse; *esp* : CORNMEAL **2** : something like meal esp. in texture **syn** see FLOUR

meal·time \'mēl-,tīm\ *n* : the usual time at which a meal is served

meal·worm \-,wərm\ *n* : a small brownish worm that is the larva of various beetles and that lives in grain products and is often raised as food for insectivorous animals

mealy \'mē-lē\ *adj* **meal·i·er; -est 1** : being soft, dry, and crumbly **2** : containing meal **3** : covered with fine granules or with flecks (as of color) **4** : MEALYMOUTHED

mealy·bug \'mē-lē-,bəg\ *n* : any of numerous destructive scale insects with a white powdery covering

mealy-mouthed \,mē-lē-'mau̇thd, -'mau̇tht\ *adj* : smooth, plausible, and insincere in speech; *also* : affectedly unwilling to use strong or coarse language

¹mean \'mēn\ *adj* [ME *imene, mene,* fr. OE *gemǣne*] **1** : of low birth or station : HUMBLE **2** : ORDINARY, INFERIOR ⟨a man of no *mean* ability⟩ **3** : POOR, SHABBY ⟨live in *mean* surroundings⟩ **4** : not honorable or worthy : UNKIND, WICKED ⟨it is *mean* to take advantage of another's misfortunes⟩ **5** : STINGY, MISERLY **6** : SPITEFUL, MALICIOUS **7** : of a vicious or troublesome disposition ⟨a *mean* horse⟩ **8** : UNWELL, INDISPOSED ⟨wake up feeling *mean*⟩

²mean *vb* **meant** \'ment\; **mean·ing** \'mē-niŋ\ [OE *mǣnan*] **1 a** : to have in the mind as a purpose : INTEND ⟨I *mean* to go⟩ **b** : to intend for a particular purpose, use, or destination ⟨a book *meant* for children⟩ **2** : to serve to convey, show, or indicate : SIGNIFY ⟨what do his words *mean*⟩ ⟨those clouds *mean* rain⟩ **3** : to be of a specified degree of importance ⟨health *means* everything to him⟩ — **mean business** : to be in earnest

³mean \'mēn\ *n* [MF *meien,* fr. *meien,* adj., mean, median] **1** : a middle point between extremes **2 a** : a value that represents a range of values; *esp* : ARITHMETIC MEAN **b** : the arithmetic mean of the two extremes of a range of values **c** : either of the middle two terms of a proportion **3** *pl* : something by the use or help of which a desired end is accomplished or furthered ⟨*means* of production⟩ ⟨ready to use any *means* at his disposal⟩ **4** *pl* : resources available for disposal; *esp* : WEALTH ⟨a man of *means*⟩ **syn** see AVERAGE — **by all means** : without fail : CERTAINLY — **by any means** : in any way : at all — **by means of** : through the use of — **by no means** : not at all : certainly not

⁴mean \'mēn\ *adj* [MF *meien,* fr. L *medianus* median] **1** : holding a middle position : INTERMEDIATE **2 a** : lying about midway between extremes : being near the average **b** : being the mean of a set of values : AVERAGE ⟨*mean* temperature⟩

¹me·an·der \mē-'an-dər\ *n* [L *maeander,* fr. Gk *maiandros,* fr. *Maiandros* (now *Menderes*), river in Asia Minor] **1** : a turn or winding of a stream **2** : a winding path or course

²meander *vi* **-dered; -der·ing** \-d(ə-)riŋ\ **1** : to follow a winding or intricate course **2** : to wander aimlessly : RAMBLE **syn** see MAUNDER

¹mean·ing \'mē-niŋ\ *n* **1 a** : the sense one intends to convey esp. by language **:** PURPORT ⟨do not mistake my *meaning*⟩ **b :** the sense that is conveyed ⟨the poem's *meaning* to me⟩ **2 :** INTENT, PURPOSE **3 :** intent to convey information **:** SIGNIFICANCE ⟨a glance full of *meaning*⟩

syn MEANING, SENSE, SIGNIFICATION, SIGNIFICANCE denote the idea conveyed to the mind by a word, sign, or symbol. MEANING is the general term used of anything (as a word, poem, action) requiring or allowing interpretation; SENSE applies esp. to words or utterances and may denote one out of several meanings of any one word ⟨the word *charge* has many distinct *senses*⟩ SIGNIFICATION denotes the established meaning of a word, symbol, or written character; SIGNIFICANCE applies specifically to an underlying as distinguished from a surface meaning

²meaning *adj* **:** SIGNIFICANT, EXPRESSIVE ⟨gave him a *meaning* look⟩ — **mean·ing·ly** \-niŋ-lē\ *adv*

mean·ing·ful \-fəl\ *adj* **:** having a meaning or purpose; *esp* **:** full of meaning **:** SIGNIFICANT ⟨a *meaningful* experience⟩ — **mean·ing·ful·ly** \-fə-lē\ *adv* — **mean·ing·ful·ness** *n*

mean·ing·less \'mē-niŋ-ləs\ *adj* **1 :** lacking sense or significance **2 :** lacking motive — **mean·ing·less·ly** *adv* — **mean·ing·less·ness** *n*

mean·ly \'mēn-lē\ *adv* **1 :** in a poor, humble, or shabby manner ⟨*meanly* dressed⟩ **2 :** in an ungenerous or ignoble manner

mean·ness \'mēn-nəs\ *n* **1 :** the quality or state of being low in station or ignoble in conduct **2 :** a mean act

mean proportional *n* **1 :** GEOMETRIC MEAN 1 **2 :** MEAN 2c

means test \'mēnz-\ *n* **:** an examination of a person's financial state to determine his eligibility to receive unemployment insurance or public assistance benefits

meant *past of* MEAN

¹mean·time \'mēn-,tīm\ *n* **:** the intervening time

²meantime *adv* **:** MEANWHILE

¹mean·while \'mēn-,hwīl\ *n* **:** MEANTIME

²meanwhile *adv* **:** during the intervening time

mea·sle \'mē-zəl\ *n* [OF *mesel* leprous, infested with tapeworms, fr. ML *misellus* leper, fr. L *miser* miserable] **1 :** infestation with or disease caused by larval tapeworms in the muscles and tissues **2 :** a tapeworm larva in the muscles of a domesticated mammal — **mea·sled** \-zəld\ *adj*

mea·sles \'mē-zəlz\ *n sing or pl* [ME *meseles*, pl. of *mesel* measles, alteration of *masel*] **1 :** an acute contagious virus disease marked by fever and red spots on the skin; *also* **:** any of several similar diseases (as German measles)

mea·sly \'mēz-(ə-)lē\ *adj* **mea·sli·er; -est 1 :** infected or infested with measles or with trichina worms **2 :** contemptibly small or insignificant ⟨didn't even leave a *measly* dime for a tip⟩

mea·sur·a·ble \'mezh-(ə-)rə-bəl, 'mezh-ər-bəl, 'māzh-\ *adj* **:** capable of being measured — **mea·sur·a·bil·i·ty** \,mezh-(ə-)rə-'bil-ət-ē, ,māzh-\ *n* — **mea·sur·a·ble·ness** *n* — **mea·sur·a·bly** *adv*

¹mea·sure \'mezh-ər, 'māzh-\ *n* [OF *mesure*, fr. L *mensura*, fr. *mens-*, *metiri* to measure] **1 a :** a moderate extent or degree ⟨surprised beyond *measure*⟩ **b :** AMOUNT, EXTENT, DEGREE ⟨succeed in large *measure*⟩ **2 a :** the dimensions, capacity, or quantity of something as fixed by measuring ⟨give full *measure*⟩ **b :** something (as a yardstick or cup) used in measuring **c :** a unit used in measuring ⟨the foot is a *measure* of length⟩ **d :** a system of measuring ⟨metric *measure*⟩ **3 :** the act or process of measuring **4 a :** DANCE; *esp* **:** a stately dance **b :** rhythmic structure or movement in music or poetry **:** METER, CADENCE **c :** the part of a musical staff between two adjacent bars; *also* **:** the group or grouping of beats between these bars **5 :** a basis or standard of comparison **:** CRITERION **6 :** an action planned or taken as a means to an end; *esp* **:** a legislative bill or act

²measure *vb* **mea·sured; mea·sur·ing** \'mezh-(ə-)riŋ, 'māzh-\ **1 :** to select or regulate with caution **:** GOVERN ⟨*measures* his acts⟩ **2 a :** to mark or fix in multiples of a specific unit ⟨*measure* off three inches⟩ **b :** to allot or apportion in measured amounts ⟨*measure* out four cups⟩ **3 :** to determine the dimensions, extent, or amount of ⟨*measure* the walk of the house⟩ **4 a :** ESTIMATE ⟨*measure* the distance with his eye⟩ **b :** to bring into comparison ⟨*measure* one's skill against a rival⟩ **5 :** to serve as a measure of ⟨a thermometer *measures* temperature⟩ **6 :** to turn out to be of a certain measurement (as in length or

breadth) ⟨the cloth *measures* 3 yards⟩ — **mea·sur·er** \-ər-ər\ *n*

mea·sured \-ərd\ *adj* **1 a :** regulated or determined by a standard **b :** being slow and steady **:** EVEN ⟨walk with *measured* steps⟩ **2 :** DELIBERATE, CALCULATED ⟨speak with *measured* bluntness⟩ **3 :** RHYTHMICAL, METRICAL

mea·sure·less \-ər-ləs\ *adj* **:** being without measure **:** IMMEASURABLE

mea·sure·ment \'mezh-ər-mənt, 'māzh-\ *n* **1 :** the act or process of measuring **2 :** a figure, extent, or amount obtained by measuring **:** DIMENSION **3 :** a system of measures

measure up *vi* **1 :** to have necessary or fitting qualifications **2 :** to be the equal (as in ability) — used with *to*

measuring worm *n* **:** LOOPER 1

meat \'mēt\ *n* [OE *mete*] **1 a :** FOOD; *esp* **:** solid food as distinguished from drink **b :** the edible part of something as distinguished from the husk, shell, or other covering **2 :** animal and esp. mammal tissue used as food **3** *archaic* **:** MEAL 2; *esp* **:** DINNER

meat·ball \-,bȯl\ *n* **:** a small ball of chopped or ground meat ⟨spaghetti and *meatballs*⟩

meat·man \-,man\ *n* **:** BUTCHER

me·a·tus \mē-'āt-əs\ *n, pl* **me·a·tus·es** *or* **me·a·tus** \-'āt-əs, -'ā-,tüs\ [LL, fr. L *meat-*, *meare* to pass] **:** a natural body passage

meaty \'mēt-ē\ *adj* **meat·i·er; -est 1 :** full of meat **:** FLESHY **2 :** rich in matter for thought **:** SUBSTANTIAL ⟨a *meaty* book⟩ — **meat·i·ness** \'mēt-ē-nəs\ *n*

mec·ca \'mek-ə\ *n, often cap* [*Mecca*, birthplace of Muhammad and goal of Muslim pilgrimages] **:** a place considered extremely desirable esp. by a particular group of people ⟨the university is a *mecca* for chemistry students⟩

¹me·chan·ic \mi-'kan-ik\ *adj* [Gk *mēchanikos*, fr. *mēchanē* machine] **:** of or relating to manual work or skill ⟨*mechanic* arts⟩

²mechanic *n* **:** a manual worker **:** ARTISAN; *esp* **:** a repairer of machines

me·chan·i·cal \-'kan-i-kəl\ *adj* **1 a :** of or relating to machinery ⟨*mechanical* engineering⟩ **b :** made or operated by a machine or tool ⟨a *mechanical* concrete mixer⟩ ⟨a *mechanical* toy⟩ **2 :** of or relating to mechanics or artisans **3 :** done as if by machine **:** IMPERSONAL ⟨gave a *mechanical* reply⟩ **4 :** relating to or in accordance with the principles of mechanics **5 :** relating to a process that involves a purely physical change — **me·chan·i·cal·ly** \-i-k(ə-)lē\ *adv*

mechanical advantage *n* **:** the ratio of the force that performs the useful work of a machine to the force that is applied to the machine

mechanical drawing *n* **:** a method of drawing that makes use of such instruments as compasses, squares, and triangles in order to insure mathematical precision; *also* **:** a drawing made by this method

mech·a·ni·cian \,mek-ə-'nish-ən\ *n* **:** MECHANIC, MACHINIST

me·chan·ics \mi-'kan-iks\ *n sing or pl* **1 :** a branch of physical science that deals with energy and forces and their effect on bodies **2 :** the practical application of mechanics to the making or operation of machines **3 :** mechanical or functional details ⟨household *mechanics*⟩ ⟨the *mechanics* of running⟩ ⟨has a good command of the *mechanics* of writing plays⟩

mech·a·nism \'mek-ə-,niz-əm\ *n* **1 :** a machine or mechanical device **2 a :** the parts by which a machine operates as a mechanical unit ⟨the *mechanism* of a watch⟩ **b :** the parts or steps that make up a process or activity ⟨the *mechanism* of democratic government⟩ **3 :** the doctrine that natural processes (as of life) are orderly and wholly subject to natural law — compare VITALISM **4 :** the fundamental physical or chemical processes involved in or responsible for a natural phenomenon (as an action or reaction) — **mech·a·nist** \-nəst\ *n*

mech·a·nis·tic \,mek-ə-'nis-tik\ *adj* **1 :** mechanically determined ⟨*mechanistic* universe⟩ **2 :** of or relating to the doctrine of mechanism **3 :** MECHANICAL — **mech·a·nis·ti·cal·ly** \-ti-k(ə-)lē\ *adv*

mech·a·nize \'mek-ə-,nīz\ *vt* **1 :** to make mechanical; *esp* **:** to make automatic **2 a :** to equip with machinery esp. to replace human or animal labor **b :** to equip (a military force) with armed and armored motor-driven

---

ə **abut;** ə **kitten;** ər **further;** a **back;** ā **bake;** ä **cot, cart;** au̇ **out;** ch **chin;** e **less;** ē **easy;** g **gift;** i **trip;** ī **life**

MEASURES AND WEIGHTS

UNIT	ABBR. OR SYMBOL	EQUIVALENTS IN OTHER UNITS OF SAME SYSTEM	METRIC EQUIVALENT
length			
mile	mi	5280 feet, 320 rods, 1760 yards	1.609 kilometers
rod	rd	5.50 yards, 16.5 feet	5.029 meters
yard	yd	3 feet, 36 inches	0.914 meters
foot	ft or '	12 inches, 0.333 yards	30.480 centimeters
inch	in or "	0.083 feet, 0.027 yards	2.540 centimeters
area			
square mile	sq mi or mi²	640 acres, 102,400 square rods	2.590 square kilometers
acre	a or ac (seldom used)	4840 square yards, 43,560 square feet	0.405 hectares, 4047 square meters
square rod	sq rd or rd²	30.25 square yards, 0.006 acres	25.293 square meters
square yard	sq yd or yd²	1296 square inches, 9 square feet	0.836 square meters
square foot	sq ft or ft²	144 square inches, 0.111 square yards	0.093 square meters
square inch	sq in or in²	0.007 square feet, 0.00077 square yards	6.451 square centimeters
volume			
cubic yard	cu yd or yd³	27 cubic feet, 46,656 cubic inches	0.765 cubic meters
cubic foot	cu ft or ft³	1728 cubic inches, 0.0370 cubic yards	0.028 cubic meters
cubic inch	cu in or in³	0.00058 cubic feet, 0.000021 cubic yards	16.387 cubic centimeters
weight			
avoirdupois			
ton	tn (seldom used)		
short ton		20 short hundredweight, 2000 pounds	0.907 metric tons
long ton		20 long hundredweight, 2240 pounds	1.016 metric tons
hundredweight	cwt		
short hundredweight		100 pounds, 0.05 short tons	45.359 kilograms
long hundredweight		112 pounds, 0.05 long tons	50.802 kilograms
pound	lb or lb av also ♯	16 ounces, 7000 grains	0.453 kilograms
ounce	oz or oz av	16 drams, 437.5 grains	28.349 grams
dram	dr or dr av	27.343 grains, 0.0625 ounces	1.771 grams
grain	gr	0.036 drams, 0.002285 ounces	0.0648 grams
troy			
pound	lb t	12 ounces, 240 pennyweight, 5760 grains	0.373 kilograms
ounce	oz t	20 pennyweight, 480 grains	31.103 grams
pennyweight	dwt also pwt	24 grains, 0.05 ounces	1.555 grams
grain	gr	0.042 pennyweight, 0.002083 ounces	0.0648 grams
apothecaries'			
pound	lb ap	12 ounces, 5760 grains	0.373 kilograms
ounce	oz ap or ℥	8 drams, 480 grains	31.103 grams
dram	dr ap or ʒ	3 scruples, 60 grains	3.887 grams
scruple	s ap or ℈	20 grains, 0.333 drams	1.295 grams
grain	gr	0.05 scruples, 0.002083 ounces, 0.0166 drams	0.0648 grams
capacity			
U.S. liquid measure			
gallon	gal	4 quarts (231 cubic inches)	3.785 liters
quart	qt	2 pints (57.75 cubic inches)	0.946 liters
pint	pt	4 gills (28.875 cubic inches)	0.473 liters
gill	gi	4 fluidounces (7.218 cubic inches)	118.291 milliliters
fluidounce	fl oz or f ℥	8 fluidrams (1.804 cubic inches)	29.573 milliliters
fluidram	fl dr or f ʒ	60 minims (0.225 cubic inches)	3.696 milliliters
minim	min or ♏	⅟₆₀ fluidram (0.003759 cubic inches)	0.061610 milliliters
U.S. dry measure			
bushel	bu	4 pecks (2150.42 cubic inches)	35.238 liters
peck	pk	8 quarts (537.605 cubic inches)	8.809 liters
quart	qt	2 pints (67.200 cubic inches)	1.101 liters
pint	pt	½ quart (33.600 cubic inches)	0.550 liters

vehicles — **mech·a·ni·za·tion** \ˌmek-ə-nə-ˈzā-shən\ *n* — **mech·a·niz·er** \ˈmek-ə-ˌnī-zər\ *n*

me·co·ni·um \mi-ˈkō-nē-əm\ *n* : dark greenish matter in the bowel at birth

med·al \ˈmed-ᵊl\ *n* [MF *medaille*, fr. It *medaglia* coin worth half a denarius, medal, fr. (assumed) VL *medalis* half, fr. LL *medialis* medial] **1** : a metal disk bearing a religious emblem or picture **2** : a piece of metal often in the form of a coin issued to commemorate a person or event or as an award

med·al·ist *or* **med·al·list** \-ᵊl-əst\ *n* **1** : a

medal 2

designer or maker of medals **2** : a recipient of a medal

me·dal·lion \mə-ˈdal-yən\ *n* **1** : a large medal **2** : something (as a tablet or panel bearing a figure in relief or a design on wallpaper) resembling a large medal

medal play *n* : golf competition scored by total strokes

med·dle \ˈmed-ᵊl\ *vi* **med·dled** \-ᵊld\; **med·dling** \ˈmed-liŋ, -ᵊl-iŋ\ [OF *mesler, medler* to mix, fr. (assumed) VL *misculare*, fr. L *miscēre*] : to interfere without right or propriety ⟨*meddle* in another's business⟩ — **med·dler** \ˈmed-lər, -ᵊl-ər\ *n*

med·dle·some \ˈmed-ᵊl-səm\ *adj* : given to meddling : INTRUSIVE — **med·dle·some·ness** *n*

Mede \'mēd\ *n* : a native or inhabitant of ancient Media in northwestern Iran

Me·dea \mi-'dē-ə\ *n* : an enchantress noted in Greek legend for helping Jason to win the Golden Fleece and for killing her children, setting fire to the palace, and fleeing when he deserted her

medi- *or* **medio-** *comb form* [L, fr. *medius;* akin to E *mid*] : middle ⟨*medieval*⟩

media *pl of* MEDIUM

me·di·ae·val *var of* MEDIEVAL

me·di·al \'mēd-ē-əl\ *adj* **1 a :** MEDIAN **b :** extending toward the middle **2 :** situated between the beginning and the end of a word **3 :** ORDINARY, AVERAGE — **medial** *n* — **me·di·al·ly** \-ə-lē\ *adv*

¹me·di·an \'mēd-ē-ən\ *n* **1 :** a median part **2 :** a value in a series below and above which there are an equal number of values **3 a :** a line from a vertex of a triangle to the midpoint of the opposite side **b :** a line joining the midpoints of the nonparallel sides of a trapezoid **syn** see AVERAGE

²median *adj* **1 :** being in the middle or in an intermediate position **2 :** relating to or constituting a median

me·di·ant \'mēd-ē-ənt\ *n* [L *mediare* to be in the middle; fr. its being halfway between tonic and dominant] : the third tone above the tonic

me·di·as·ti·num \,mēd-ē-ə-'stī-nəm, -ē-a-'stī-\ *n, pl* **me·di·as·ti·na** \-nə\ : an irregular median partition of the chest formed of the opposing medial walls of the pleura — **me·di·as·ti·nal** \-'stīn-°l\ *adj*

¹me·di·ate \'mēd-ē-ət\ *adj* [LL *mediatus* intermediate, fr. pp. of *mediare* to be in the middle, fr. *medius* middle] : acting through an intermediate agent or agency : not direct or immediate — **me·di·ate·ly** *adv*

²me·di·ate \'mēd-ē-,āt\ *vb* **1 :** to intervene between conflicting parties or viewpoints to promote reconciliation, settlement, or compromise **2 a :** to bring about by mediation ⟨*mediate* a settlement⟩ **b :** to bring accord out of by mediation ⟨*mediate* a dispute⟩ **3 :** to transmit or act as an intermediate mechanism

me·di·a·tion \,mēd-ē-'ā-shən\ *n* : the act or process of mediating; *esp* : intervention by a third party in a dispute to promote reconciliation, settlement, or compromise between the conflicting parties

me·di·a·tor \'mēd-ē-,āt-ər\ *n* **1 :** one that mediates; *esp* : an impartial third party (as a person, group, or country) that acts as a go-between in a dispute in order to arrange a peaceful settlement **2 :** a mediating agent in a chemical or biological process — **me·di·a·to·ry** \'mēd-ē-ə-,tōr-ē, -,tor-\ *adj* — **me·di·a·tress** \'mēd-ē-,ā-trəs\ *n*

¹med·ic \'med-ik\ *n* [Gk *mēdikē*, fr. fem. of *mēdikos* of Media] : any of a genus of leguminous herbs resembling clovers and important for hay and forage

²medic *n* [L *medicus*, fr. *medicus* medical] : one (as a physician, a medical student, or a soldier or sailor assigned to the medical services) engaged in medical work

med·i·ca·ble \'med-i-kə-bəl\ *adj* : CURABLE, REMEDIABLE — **med·i·ca·bly** \-blē\ *adv*

med·ic·aid \'med-i-,kād\ *n* : a program of medical aid designed for those unable to afford regular medical service and financed jointly by the state and federal governments

med·i·cal \'med-i-kəl\ *adj* [L *medicus*, fr. *mederi* to heal] : of or relating to the science or practice of medicine or the treatment of disease — **med·i·cal·ly** \-k(ə-)lē\ *adv*

me·dic·a·ment \mi-'dik-ə-mənt\ *n* : a medicine or healing application

medi·care \'med-i-,ke(ə)r, -,ka(ə)r\ *n* : a government program of medical care esp. for the aged

med·i·cate \'med-ə-,kāt\ *vt* **1 :** to treat with medicine **2 :** to add a medicinal substance to ⟨*medicate* a soap⟩

med·i·ca·tion \,med-ə-'kā-shən\ *n* **1 :** the act or process of medicating **2 :** a medicinal substance : MEDICAMENT

me·dic·i·nal \mə-'dis-nəl, -°n-əl\ *adj* : tending or used to relieve or cure disease or pain — **me·dic·i·nal·ly** \-ē\ *adv*

medicinal leech *n* : a large European freshwater leech formerly used by physicians for bleeding patients

med·i·cine \'med-ə-sən\ *n* [L *medicina*, fr. *medicus* physician, fr. *mederi* to heal] **1 :** a substance or preparation used in treating disease **2 :** a science or art that deals with the prevention, cure, or easing of disease; *esp* : the part of this that is the business of the physician as dis-

tinguished from the surgeon **3 :** an object held to give control over natural or magical forces; *also* : a magical power or rite

medicine ball *n* : a large stuffed leather-covered ball used for conditioning exercises

medicine man *n* : a person among primitive peoples believed to be able to cure diseases by potions and charms

medicine show *n* : a traveling show using entertainers to attract a crowd that may buy remedies or nostrums

med·i·co \'med-i-,kō\ *n, pl* **-cos** : a medical practitioner : PHYSICIAN; *also* : a medical student

me·di·eval \,mēd-ē-'ē-vəl, ,med-\ *adj* [*medi-* + L *aevum* age] : of, relating to, or characteristic of the Middle Ages — **me·di·eval·ly** \-və-lē\ *adv*

me·di·eval·ism \-və-,liz-əm\ *n* **1 :** medieval quality, character, or state **2 :** devotion to the institutions, arts, and practices of the Middle Ages — **me·di·eval·ist** \-ləst\ *n*

Medieval Latin *n* : the Latin used esp. for liturgical and literary purposes from the 7th to the 15th centuries inclusive

medio- — see MEDI-

me·di·o·cre \,mēd-ē-'ō-kər\ *adj* [L *mediocris*, orig., halfway up a mountain, fr. *medi-* + *ocris* mountain] : of moderate or low quality : ORDINARY

me·di·oc·ri·ty \,mēd-ē-'äk-rət-ē\ *n, pl* **-ties** **1 :** the quality or state of being mediocre **2 :** a mediocre person

med·i·tate \'med-ə-,tāt\ *vb* [L *meditari*] **1 a :** to reflect on or muse over : CONTEMPLATE **b :** to engage in contemplation or reflection **2 :** INTEND, PURPOSE — **med·i·ta·tor** \-,tāt-ər\ *n*

med·i·ta·tion \,med-ə-'tā-shən\ *n* : the act or process of meditating : serious contemplation or reflection

med·i·ta·tive \'med-ə-,tāt-iv\ *adj* : inclined or given to meditation — **med·i·ta·tive·ly** *adv* — **med·i·ta·tive·ness** *n*

Med·i·ter·ra·ne·an \,med-ə-tə-'rā-nē-ən, -'rā-nyən\ *adj* : of or relating to the Mediterranean sea or to the lands or peoples around it

Mediterranean flour moth *n* : a common small largely gray and black moth with a larva that destroys processed grain products

Mediterranean fruit fly *n* : a widely distributed two-winged fly with black-and-white markings and a larva destructive to ripening fruit

¹me·di·um \'mēd-ē-əm\ *n, pl* **me·di·ums** *or* **me·dia** \'mēd-ē-ə\ [L, fr. neuter of *medium* middle] **1 :** something that is between or in the middle; *also* : a middle condition or degree **2 :** a means of effecting or conveying something; *esp* : a substance through which a force acts or through which something is transmitted (air is the common *medium* of sound) **3 :** a channel (as newspapers, radio, or television) of communication **4 a :** GO-BETWEEN, INTERMEDIARY **b :** a person through whom others seek to communicate with the spirits of the dead **5 a :** a surrounding substance **b :** a condition in which something may function or flourish (slums are a good *medium* for delinquency) **6 :** a nutrient system for the artificial cultivation of organisms (as bacteria) or cells **7 :** a liquid with which paint is mixed by a painter **8 :** a size of paper usu. 23 x 18 inches

²medium *adj* : intermediate in amount, quality, position, or degree

medium frequency *n* : a radio frequency in the range between 300 and 3000 kilocycles — abbr. *mf*

medium of exchange : something commonly accepted in exchange for goods and services and recognized as representing a standard of value

med·lar \'med-lər\ *n* [MF *medlier*] : a small hairy-leaved Eurasian tree related to the apples; *also* : its fruit that resembles a crab apple and is used esp. in preserves

med·ley \'med-lē\ *n, pl* **medleys** [MF *medlee*, fr. *mesler, medler* to mix] **1 :** MIXTURE; *esp* : a confused mixture **2 :** a musical composition made up of parts from other pieces

me·dul·la \mə-'dəl-ə\ *n, pl* **-dul·las** *or* **-dul·lae** \-'dəl-(,)ē, -,ī\ [L] **1 :** MARROW **2 :** the inner or deep part of an animal or plant structure — **med·ul·lary** \'med-°l-,er-ē, 'mej-ə-,ler-\ *adj*

medulla ob·lon·ga·ta \-,äb-,lȯŋ-'gät-ə\ *n* [NL, lit., oblong medulla] : the somewhat pyramidal last part of the vertebrate brain continuous posteriorly with the spinal cord

medullary ray *n* : one of the fine rays of woody tissue extending from the center of the stem toward the bark in plants having annual rings of growth

medullary sheath *n* : a layer of myelin about a nerve fiber

med·ul·lat·ed \'med-ᵊl-ˌāt-əd, 'mej-ə-ˌlāt-\ *adj* : having a medullary sheath; *also* : having a medulla

me·du·sa \mi-'d(y)ü-sə, -zə\ *n, pl* **-sae** \-ˌsē, -ˌzē\ *or* **-sas** 1 *cap* : a Gorgon slain by Perseus 2 : JELLYFISH — **me·du·san** \-'d(y)üs-ᵊn, -'d(y)üz-\ *adj or n* — **me·du·soid** \-'d(y)ü-ˌsȯid, -ˌzȯid\ *adj or n*

meed \'mēd\ *n* [OE *mēd*] : something deserved or earned : REWARD ⟨receive one's *meed* of praise⟩

meek \'mēk\ *adj* [of Scand origin] 1 : enduring injury with patience and without resentment : MILD 2 : lacking spirit or self-assurance : HUMBLE — **meek·ly** *adv* — **meek·ness** *n*

meer·schaum \'mi(ə)r-shəm, -ˌshȯm\ *n* [G, lit., sea-foam] : a soft white lightweight mineral resembling a very fine clay used esp. for tobacco pipes; *also* : a pipe made of this mineral

¹meet \'mēt\ *vb* **met** \'met\; **meet·ing** [OE *mētan*] 1 : to come upon or across ⟨*met* an old friend by chance⟩ 2 a : to approach from different directions ⟨the trains *meet* at the junction⟩ b : to come into contact and join or cross ⟨a fork where two roads *meet*⟩ 3 a : to go to the place where a person or thing is or will be ⟨agreed to *meet* her at school⟩ b : to become acquainted ⟨the couple *met* at a dance⟩ c : to make the acquaintance of ⟨*met* interesting people there⟩ 4 a : to come together as opponents ⟨the brothers *met* in the finals⟩ b : to struggle against : OPPOSE ⟨was chosen to *meet* the champion⟩ c : to cope with : MATCH ⟨tries to *meet* the competitor's price⟩ d : EXPERIENCE, ENDURE ⟨learned to *meet* defeat bravely⟩ 5 : to come together for a common purpose : ASSEMBLE ⟨*meet* weekly for discussion⟩ 6 : to become one : UNITE ⟨all the virtues *meet* in her⟩ 7 : to become noticed ⟨sounds of revelry *meet* the ear⟩ 8 a : to conform to or comply with : SATISFY ⟨*meets* all requirements⟩ b : to pay fully : DISCHARGE, FULFILL ⟨*meet* a financial obligation⟩

²meet *n* : an assembly or meeting esp. to engage in a competitive sport ⟨a track *meet*⟩

³meet *adj* [OE *gemǣte*; akin to E *mete*] : SUITABLE, PROPER — **meet·ly** *adv*

meet·ing \'mēt-iŋ\ *n* 1 : the act of persons or things that meet ⟨a chance *meeting* with a friend⟩ 2 : a coming together of a number of persons usu. at a stated time and place and for a known purpose : ASSEMBLY, GATHERING ⟨the monthly club *meeting*⟩⟨a *meeting* of Congress⟩ 3 : an assembly for religious worship ⟨a Quaker *meeting*⟩ 4 : the place where two things come together : JUNCTION

meet·ing·house \-ˌhaus\ *n* : a building used for public assembly and esp. for Protestant worship

mega- *or* **meg-** *comb form* [Gk *megal-, megas* large; akin to E *much*] 1 : great : large ⟨*megaspore*⟩ 2 : million : multiplied by one million ⟨*megohm*⟩ ⟨*megacycle*⟩

mega·cy·cle \'meg-ə-ˌsī-kəl\ *n* : one million cycles per second ⟨a radio frequency of 1.6 *megacycles*⟩

mega·ga·mete \ˌmeg-ə-gə-'mēt, -'gam-ˌēt\ *n* : MACROGAMETE

mega·lith \'meg-ə-ˌlith\ *n* [Gk *lithos* stone] : one of the huge stones used in various prehistoric monuments — **mega·lith·ic** \ˌmeg-ə-'lith-ik\ *adj*

meg·a·lo·ma·nia \ˌmeg-ə-lō-'mā-nē-ə, -nyə\ *n* [Gk *megal-, megas* large] : a disorder of mind marked by feelings of personal omnipotence and grandeur — **meg·a·lo·ma·ni·ac** \-'mā-nē-ˌak\ *adj or n* — **meg·a·lo·ma·ni·a·cal** \-mə-'nī-ə-kəl\ *or* **meg·a·lo·man·ic** \-'man-ik\ *adj*

meg·a·lop·o·lis \ˌmeg-ə-'läp-ə-ləs\ *n* [Gk *megal-, megas* large + *polis* city] 1 : a very large city 2 : a thickly populated region centering in a metropolis or embracing several metropolises — **meg·a·lo·pol·i·tan** \ˌmeg-ə-lō-'päl-ət-ᵊn\ *n or adj* — **meg·a·lo·pol·i·tan·ism** \-ᵊn-ˌiz-əm\ *n*

mega·phone \'meg-ə-ˌfōn\ *n* : a cone-shaped device used to intensify or direct the voice — **mega·phon·ic** \ˌmeg-ə-'fän-ik\ *adj*

mega·scop·ic \ˌmeg-ə-'skäp-ik\ *adj* [*mega-* + *-scopic* (as in *microscopic*)] : visible to the unaided eye

mega·spore \'meg-ə-ˌspō(ə)r, -ˌspȯ(ə)r\ *n* : a plant spore

that produces a female gametophyte — **mega·spor·ic** \ˌmeg-ə-'spōr-ik, -'spȯr-\ *adj*

mega·ton \'meg-ə-ˌtən\ *n* : an explosive force equal to that of one million tons of TNT

mega·watt \-ˌwät\ *n* : one million watts

meg·ohm \'meg-ˌōm\ *n* : one million ohms

¹me·grim \'mē-grəm\ *n* [MF *migraine*] 1 : a dizzy disordered state; *esp* : MIGRAINE 2 a : WHIM, FANCY b *pl* : low spirits : mental depression

²megrim *n* : any of several small flatfishes

mei·o·sis \mī-'ō-səs\ *n, pl* **-o·ses** \-'ō-ˌsēz\ [Gk *meiōsis* diminution, fr. *meioun* to diminish, fr. *meiōn* less] : the process by which the number of chromosomes in a cell that will produce gametes is reduced to one half — **mei·ot·ic** \mī-'ät-ik\ *adj* — **mei·ot·i·cal·ly** \-'ät-i-k(ə-)lē\ *adv*

Mei·ster·sing·er \'mī-stər-ˌsiŋ-ər, -stər-ˌziŋ-\ *n, pl* **-sing·er** \-ˌziŋ-ər\ *or* **-sing·ers** \-ˌsiŋ-ərz\ [G, lit., master singer] : a member of any of various German guilds formed chiefly in the 15th and 16th centuries by workingmen for the cultivation of poetry and music

mel·a·mine \'mel-ə-ˌmēn\ *n* : a synthetic resin composed of carbon, hydrogen, and nitrogen and used in molded products, adhesives, and coatings

mel·an·cho·lia \ˌmel-ən-'kō-lē-ə\ *n* : a mental condition characterized by extreme depression, bodily complaints, and often hallucinations and delusions — **mel·an·cho·li·ac** \-lē-ˌak\ *n*

mel·an·chol·ic \ˌmel-ən-'käl-ik\ *adj* 1 : inclined to or affected with melancholy 2 : affected with or relating to melancholia 3 : tending to depress the spirits — **mel·an·chol·i·cal·ly** \-'käl-i-k(ə-)lē\ *adv*

¹mel·an·choly \'mel-ən-ˌkäl-ē\ *n, pl* **-chol·ies** [Gk *melancholia*, fr. *melan-, melas* black + *cholē* bile; fr. the former belief that the condition was caused by an excess of black bile in the system] : depression of spirits : DEJECTION, SADNESS ⟨overtaken by a fit of *melancholy*⟩

syn SADNESS, DEJECTION: MELANCHOLY suggests a sad and serious pensiveness often without evident cause; SADNESS usu. suggests a mood of regret, longing, or disappointment without bitterness or anger; DEJECTION implies a usu. passing mood of discouragement or hopelessness

²melancholy *adj* 1 a : depressed in spirits : DEJECTED, SAD b : PENSIVE 2 a : DEPRESSING, DISMAL b : causing sadness : LAMENTABLE

Mel·a·ne·sian \ˌmel-ə-'nē-zhən, -shən\ *n* : a member of the dominant native group of Melanesia characterized by dark skin and frizzy hair — **Melanesian** *adj*

mé·lange \mā-'lä⁼zh, -'länj\ *n* [F, fr. MF, fr. *mesler, meler* to mix] : a mixture or medley esp. of incongruous elements

mel·a·nin \'mel-ə-nən\ *n* : a dark brown or black animal or plant pigment that in man makes some skins darker than others

mel·a·nism \'mel-ə-ˌniz-əm\ *n* [Gk *melan-, melas* black] : an exceptionally dark pigmentation (as of skin, feathers, or hair) of an individual or kind of organism — **mel·a·nis·tic** \ˌmel-ə-'nis-tik\ *adj*

mel·a·no·ma \ˌmel-ə-'nō-mə\ *n, pl* **-no·mas** *also* **-no·ma·ta** \-'nō-mət-ə\ : a usu. malignant tumor containing dark pigment

mel·a·not·ic \-'nät-ik\ *adj* : having or characterized by black pigmentation

mel·ba toast \ˌmel-bə-\ *n* [after Nellie *Melba* d1931 Australian soprano] : very thin bread toasted till crisp

Mel·chite *or* **Mel·kite** \'mel-ˌkīt\ *n* 1 : an Eastern Christian adhering to Chalcedonian orthodoxy 2 : a member of a Uniate body derived from the Melchites

Mel·chiz·e·dek \mel-'kiz-ə-ˌdek\ *adj* [after *Melchizedek*, king of Salem and priest in Genesis 14:18 & Psalms 110:4] : of or relating to the higher order of the Mormon priesthood

¹meld \'meld\ *vb* [G *melden* to announce] : to show or announce for a score in a card game

²meld *n* : a card or combination of cards that is or can be melded

Me·le·ager \'mel-ē-ˌā-jər\ *n* : an Argonaut and slayer of the Calydonian boar

me·lee \'mā-ˌlā, mā-'lā\ *n* [F *mêlée*, fr. OF *mesler, medler* to mix] : a confused fight or struggle; *esp* : a hand-to-hand fight among a number of persons

me·lio·rate \'mēl-yə-ˌrāt\ *vb* [L *melior* better] : to make or become better : IMPROVE — **me·lio·ra·tion** \,mēl-yə-'rā-shən\ *n* — **me·lio·ra·tive** \'mēl-yə-,rāt-iv\ *adj* — **me·lio·ra·tor** \-,rāt-ər\ *n*

mel·lif·lu·ous \me-'lif-lə-wəs, mə-\ *adj* [LL *mellifluus,* fr. L *mell-, mel* honey + *fluere* to flow] : smoothly or sweetly flowing ⟨*mellifluous* speech⟩ — **mel·lif·lu·ous·ly** *adv* — **mel·lif·lu·ous·ness** *n*

mel·lo·phone \'mel-ə-,fōn\ *n* : an althorn in circular form sometimes used as a substitute for the French horn

¹mel·low \'mel-ō\ *adj* [ME *melowe*] **1 a :** tender and sweet because of ripeness **b :** well aged and pleasingly mild ⟨a *mellow* wine⟩ **2 :** made gentle by age or experience **3 :** of soft and loamy consistency ⟨*mellow* soil⟩ **4 :** being clear, full, and pure : not coarse or rough ⟨a *mellow* sound⟩⟨a *mellow* color⟩ — **mel·low·ly** *adv* — **mel·low·ness** *n*

²mellow *vb* : to make or become mellow

me·lo·de·on \mə-'lōd-ē-ən\ *n* : a small reed organ in which a suction bellows draws air inward through the reeds

me·lod·ic \mə-'läd-ik\ *adj* : of or relating to melody : MELODIOUS — **me·lod·i·cal·ly** \-'läd-i-k(ə-)lē\ *adv*

me·lo·di·ous \mə-'lōd-ē-əs\ *adj* **1 :** pleasing to the ear because of a succession of sweet sounds : TUNEFUL ⟨*melodious* songs⟩ **2 :** of, relating to, or producing melody ⟨*melodious* birds⟩ — **me·lo·di·ous·ly** *adv* — **me·lo·di·ous·ness** *n*

mel·o·dist \'mel-əd-əst\ *n* : a composer or singer of melodies

melo·dra·ma \'mel-ə-,dräm-ə, -,dram-\ *n* [F *mélodrame* play with music, melodrama, fr. Gk *melos* song + *drama*] **1 a :** an extravagantly theatrical play in which action and plot predominate over characterization **b :** a dramatic category constituted by such plays **2 :** melodramatic events or behavior — **melo·dram·a·tist** \-'dram-ət-əst, -'dräm-\ *n*

melo·dra·mat·ic \-drə-'mat-ik\ *adj* **1 :** of or relating to melodrama **2 :** resembling or suitable for melodrama : SENSATIONAL ⟨made a *melodramatic* announcement of the discovery⟩ — **melo·dra·mat·i·cal·ly** \-i-k(ə-)lē\ *adv*

melo·dra·mat·ics \-'mat-iks\ *n sing or pl* : melodramatic conduct

mel·o·dy \'mel-əd-ē\ *n, pl* **-dies** [LL *melodia,* fr. Gk *melōidia* chanting, music, fr. *melos* song, tune + *aidein* to sing] **1 :** pleasing succession of sounds : TUNEFULNESS **2 :** a rhythmical series of musical tones of a given key so arranged as to make a pleasing effect **3 :** the leading part in a harmonic composition

mel·on \'mel-ən\ *n* [LL *melon-, melo,* short for *melopepon-, melopepo,* fr. Gk *mēlopepōn,* fr. *mēlon* apple + *pepōn,* an edible gourd] : any of certain gourds (as a muskmelon or watermelon) usu. eaten raw as fruits

Mel·pom·e·ne \mel-'päm-ə-(,)nē\ *n* : the Greek Muse of tragedy

¹melt \'melt\ *vb* [OE *meltan*] **1 :** to change from a solid to a liquid state usu. through the application of heat ⟨*melt* sugar⟩⟨snow *melts*⟩ **2 :** DISSOLVE ⟨sugar *melts* in the mouth⟩ **3 :** to grow less : disappear as if by dissolving ⟨clouds *melting* away⟩ **4 :** to make or become gentle : SOFTEN ⟨her warm smile *melts* the heart⟩ **5 :** to lose distinct outline or shape : BLEND, MERGE ⟨sky *melting* into sea⟩ — **melt·a·bil·i·ty** \,mel-tə-'bil-ət-ē\ *n* — **melt·a·ble** \'mel-tə-bəl\ *adj* — **melt·er** *n*

²melt *n* : a melted substance

³melt *n* [OE *milte*] : SPLEEN 1

melting point *n* : the temperature at which a solid melts

melting pot *n* **1 :** a container capable of withstanding great heat in which something is melted : CRUCIBLE **2 a :** a place (as a city or country) in which various nationalities or races live together and gradually blend into one community **b :** the population of such a place

mel·ton \'melt-ᵊn\ *n* : a smooth heavy woolen cloth with a short nap used for overcoats

melt·wa·ter \'melt-,wȯt-ər, -,wät-\ *n* : water derived from the melting of ice and snow

mem·ber \'mem-bər\ *n* [L *membrum*] **1 :** a part (as an arm, leg, leaf, or branch) of the body of a person, lower animal, or plant **2 :** one of the individuals or units belonging to or forming part of a group or organization ⟨a club *member*⟩ ⟨UN *members*⟩ **3 :** a part of a whole: as **a :** a part of a structure (as a building) ⟨a horizontal

member in a bridge⟩ **b :** either of the equated elements in a mathematical equation

mem·ber·ship \-,ship\ *n* **1 :** the state or status of being a member **2 :** the body of members

mem·brane \'mem-,brān\ *n* [L *membrana,* fr. *membrum* member] : a thin soft pliable sheet or layer esp. of animal or plant origin — **mem·bra·na·ceous** \,mem-brə-'nā-shəs\ *adj* — **mem·braned** \'mem-,brānd\ *adj* — **mem·bra·nous** \'mem-brə-nəs, mem-'brā-\ *adj* — **mem·bra·nous·ly** *adv*

me·men·to \mi-'ment-ō\ *n, pl* **-tos** *or* **-toes** [L, remember, fr. *meminisse* to remember] : something that serves as a reminder : SOUVENIR ⟨*mementos* of a trip to Europe⟩

me·men·to mo·ri \mi-,ment-ō-'mȯr-ē, -'mȯr-,ī, -'mȯr-\ *n, pl* **memento mori** [L, remember that you must die] : a reminder (as a death's-head) of mortality

memo \'mem-ō\ *n, pl* **mem·os** : MEMORANDUM

mem·oir \'mem-,wär, -,wȯr\ *n* [F *mémoire,* lit., memory, fr. L *memoria*] **1 a :** a narrative of a personal experience **b :** AUTOBIOGRAPHY — usu. used in pl. **c :** BIOGRAPHY **2 a :** ACCOUNT, REPORT **b** *pl* : the proceedings of a learned society

mem·o·ra·bil·ia \,mem-ə-rə-'bil-ē-ə\ *n pl* [L, fr. neut. pl. of *memorabilis* memorable] : things worthy of remembrance; *also* : a record of such things

mem·o·ra·ble \'mem-(ə-)rə-bəl\ *adj* [L *memorabilis,* fr. *memorare* to remember] : worth remembering : NOTABLE — **mem·o·ra·ble·ness** *n* — **mem·o·ra·bly** \-blē\ *adv*

mem·o·ran·dum \,mem-ə-'ran-dəm\ *n, pl* **-dums** *or* **-da** \-də\ [L, neuter of *memorandus* to be remembered, fr. *memorare* to remember, fr. *memor* mindful] **1 a :** an informal record or communication ⟨the state department sent *memoranda* to all embassies⟩ **b :** a written reminder **2 :** an informal written note of a transaction or proposed legal instrument

Me·mo·ra·re \,mem-ə-'rär-ē\ *n* : a prayer of intercession to the Virgin Mary

¹me·mo·ri·al \mə-'mōr-ē-əl, -'mȯr-\ *adj* : serving to preserve the memory of a person or an event ⟨a *memorial* service⟩ — **me·mo·ri·al·ly** \-ē-ə-lē\ *adv*

²memorial *n* **1 :** something that keeps alive the memory of a person or event; *esp* : MONUMENT **2 a :** RECORD, MEMOIR **b :** a statement of facts accompanying a petition or remonstrance to a government official

Memorial Day *n* : May 30 observed as a legal holiday in commemoration of dead servicemen

me·mo·ri·al·ize \mə-'mōr-ē-ə-,līz, -'mȯr-\ *vt* **1 :** to address or petition (as a government official) by a memorial **2 :** COMMEMORATE

mem·o·rize \'mem-ə-,rīz\ *vt* : to commit to memory : learn by heart — **mem·o·ri·za·tion** \,mem-(ə-)rə-'zā-shən\ *n* — **mem·o·riz·er** \'mem-ə-,rī-zər\ *n*

mem·o·ry \'mem-(ə-)rē\ *n, pl* **-ries** [L *memoria,* fr. *memor* mindful] **1 a :** the power or process of recalling what has been learned and retained **b :** the store of things learned and retained as evidenced by recall and recognition ⟨recite from *memory*⟩ **2 :** commemorative remembrance ⟨a monument in *memory* of a hero⟩ **3 a :** something remembered ⟨has pleasant *memories* of the trip⟩ **b :** the time within which past events can be or are remembered ⟨within the *memory* of living men⟩ **4 :** a part in an electronic computing machine into which information can be inserted and extracted when needed

syn REMEMBRANCE, RECOLLECTION, REMINISCENCE: MEMORY applies both to the ability to recall mentally and to what is recalled; REMEMBRANCE stresses the act of remembering or the fact of being remembered; RECOLLECTION adds an implication of deliberately recalling often with some effort; REMINISCENCE suggests the recalling of things, actions, and esp. of people from one's remote past

mem·sa·hib \'mem-,sä-,(h)ib\ *n* [Hindi *memsāhib,* fr. E ma'am + Hindi *sāhib* sahib] : a white foreign woman of some social status living in India; *esp* : the wife of a British official in India under British rule

men *pl of* MAN

¹men·ace \'men-əs\ *n* [MF, fr. L *minacia,* fr. *minari* to threaten] **1 :** a show of intention to inflict harm : THREAT **2 a :** someone or something that represents a threat : DANGER **b :** an annoying person : NUISANCE

²menace *vb* **1 :** to make a show of intention to harm **2 :** to appear likely to cause harm : ENDANGER ⟨*menacing*

overhanging cliffs⟩ **syn** see THREATEN — **men·ac·ing·ly**
\'men-ə-siŋ-lē\ *adv*
mé·nage \mā-'näzh\ *n* [F] **:** a domestic establishment
: HOUSEHOLD
me·nag·er·ie \mə-'naj-ə-rē\ *n* **1 :** a place where animals
are kept and trained esp. for exhibition **2 :** a collection of
wild or foreign animals kept esp. for exhibition
¹mend \'mend\ *vb* [ME *menden*, short for *amenden* to
amend] **1 a :** to improve in manners or morals **:** REFORM
b : to put into good shape or working order again **:** REPAIR
2 : to become corrected or improved **3 :** to improve in
health; *also* **:** HEAL — **mend·er** *n*
²mend *n* **1 :** an act of mending **:** REPAIR **2 :** a mended
place — **on the mend :** IMPROVING
men·da·cious \men-'dā-shəs\ *adj* [L *mendac-, mendax*
lying] **:** given to falsehood **:** LYING, UNTRUTHFUL; *also*
: FALSE — **men·da·cious·ly** *adv* — **men·da·cious·ness** *n*
men·dac·i·ty \men-'das-ət-ē\ *n, pl* **-ties :** the quality or
state of being mendacious; *also* **:** LIE
men·de·le·vi·um \,men-də-'lē-vē-əm\ *n* **:** a radioactive
element artificially produced — see ELEMENT table
Men·de·li·an \men-'dē-lē-ən\ *adj* **:** of, relating to, or according with Mendel's laws or Mendelism — **Mendelian** *n*
Men·del·ism \'men-d°l-,iz-əm\ *n* **:** the principles or the
operations of Mendel's laws
Men·del's law \,men-d°lz-\ *n* [after Gregor J. *Mendel*
*d*1884 Austrian monk and father of genetics] **:** any of three
principles in genetics that explain why an individual shows
a parental character wholly or not at all, why some parental
characters are not apparent in the offspring, and why such
characters tend to reappear in a predictable ratio in later
generations
men·di·can·cy \'men-di-kən-sē\ *n* **1 :** the condition of
being a beggar **2 :** the act or practice of begging
men·di·cant \-kənt\ *n* [L *mendicare* to beg, fr. *mendicus*
beggar] **1 :** BEGGAR; *esp* **:** one who lives by begging
2 : a member of a religious order (as the Franciscans)
combining monastic life and outside religious activity and
orig. owning neither personal nor community property
: FRIAR — **mendicant** *adj*
men·dic·i·ty \men-'dis-ət-ē\ *n* **:** MENDICANCY
Men·e·la·us \,men-°l-'ā-əs\ *n* **:** a king of Sparta, brother
of Agamemnon, and husband of Helen of Troy
men·folk \'men-,fōk\ *or* **men·folks** \-,fōks\ *n pl*
1 : men in general **2 :** the men of a family or community
men·ha·den \men-'hād-°n, mən-\ *n, pl* **-den** *also* **-dens**
[of Algonquian origin] **:** a fish of the herring family
found along the Atlantic coast of the U.S. and used for
bait or converted into oil and fertilizer
¹me·ni·al \'mē-nē-əl, -nyəl\ *adj* [ME *meynie* household,
fr. OF *mesnie*] **1 :** of, relating to, or suitable for servants
2 : HUMBLE, SERVILE — **me·ni·al·ly** \-ē\ *adv*
²menial *n* **:** a domestic servant or retainer
me·nin·geal \mə-'nin-j(ē-)əl, ,men-ən-'jē-əl\ *adj* **:** of, relating to, or affecting the meninges
men·in·gi·tis \,men-ən-'jīt-əs\ *n* **:** inflammation of the
meninges; *also* **:** a usu. bacterial disease in which this
occurs — **men·in·git·ic** \-'jit-ik\ *adj*
me·ninx \'mēn-iŋ(k)s, 'men-\ *n, pl* **me·nin·ges** \mə-
'nin-(,)jēz\ [Gk *mēning-, mēninx* membrane] **:** any of the
three membranes that envelop the brain and spinal cord
me·nis·cus \mə-'nis-kəs\ *n, pl* **me·nis·ci** \-'nis-,(k)ī,
-,kē\ *also* **me·nis·cus·es 1 :** a crescent-shaped body
: CRESCENT **2 :** a lens that is convex on one side and concave on the other **3 :** the curved upper surface of a liquid
column that is concave when the containing walls are
wetted by the liquid and convex when not
Men·no·nite \'men-ə-,nīt\ *n* [G *Mennonit*, fr. *Menno*
Simons *d*1559 Frisian religious reformer] **:** a member of
one of the Christian groups derived from the Anabaptist
movement in Holland and noted for simplicity of life and
rejection of oaths, public office, and military service
me·no mos·so \,mā-nō-'mó(ś)-sō\ *adv* [It] **:** less rapidly
— used as a direction in music
meno·pause \'men-ə-,póz\ *n* [F *ménopause*, fr. NL *meno-*
menses, fr. Gk *mēn* month; akin to E *moon*] **:** the period
of natural cessation of menstruation usu. between the
ages of 45 and 50 — **meno·paus·al** \,men-ə-'pó-zəl\ *adj*
me·no·rah \mə-'nōr-ə, -'nor-\ *n* [Heb *měnōrāh*] **:** a
candelabrum used in Jewish worship
menservants *pl of* MANSERVANT

men·ses \'men-,sēz\ *n pl* [L, fr. pl. of *mensis* month;
akin to E *moon*] **:** the menstrual flow
Men·she·vik \'men-chə-,vik, -,vēk\ *n, pl* **Men·she·viks**
or **Men·she·vi·ki** \,men-chə-'vik-ē, -'vē-kē\ [Russ *men'-*
shevik, fr. *men'she* less; fr. their forming the minority
group in the party in 1903] **:** a member of a wing of the
Russian Social Democratic party before and during the
Russian Revolution believing in the gradual achievement
of socialism by parliamentary methods in opposition to
the Bolsheviks — **Men·she·vism** \'men-chə-,viz-əm\ *n*
— **Men·she·vist** \-vəst\ *n or adj*
men·stru·al \'men(t)-strə(-wə)l\ *adj* [L *menstruus*
monthly, fr. *mensis* month] **1 :** of or relating to menstruation **2 :** MONTHLY
men·stru·ate \'men(t)-strə-,wāt, 'men-,strāt\ *vi* **:** to
undergo menstruation
men·stru·a·tion \,men(t)-strə-'wā-shən, men-'strā-shən\
n **:** a discharging of blood, secretions, and tissue debris
from the uterus that recurs at approximately monthly
intervals in breeding-age primate females that are not
pregnant; *also* **:** PERIOD 5c — **men·stru·ous** \'men(t)-
strə(-wə)s\ *adj*
men·stru·um \'men(t)-strə-wəm\ *n, pl* **men·stru·ums** *or*
men·strua \-strə-wə\ **:** a substance that dissolves a solid
or holds it in suspension **:** SOLVENT
men·su·ra·ble \'men(t)-sə-rə-bəl, 'men-chə-\ *adj* **:** MEA-
SURABLE — **men·su·ra·bil·i·ty** \,men(t)-sə-rə-'bil-ət-ē,
,men-chə-\ *n* — **men·su·ra·ble·ness** *n*
men·su·ra·tion \,men(t)-sə-'rā-shən, ,men-chə-\ *n* [LL
mensurare to measure, fr. L *mensura* measure] **1 :** the
process or art of measuring **2 :** the branch of mathematics that deals with the measurement of lengths, areas,
and volumes
-ment \mənt\ *n suffix* [L *-mentum*] **1 a :** concrete result,
object, or agent of a (specified) action ⟨embank*ment*⟩
⟨entangle*ment*⟩ **b :** concrete means or instrument of a
(specified) action ⟨entertain*ment*⟩ **2 a :** action **:** process
⟨encircle*ment*⟩ ⟨develop*ment*⟩ **b :** place of a (specified)
action ⟨encamp*ment*⟩ **3 :** state **:** condition ⟨amaze*ment*⟩
men·tal \'ment-°l\ *adj* [L *ment-, mens* mind; akin to E
mind] **1 a :** of or relating to the mind ⟨*mental* powers⟩
b : carried on or experienced in the mind ⟨*mental* arith-
metic⟩ **c :** relating to spirit or idea as opposed to matter
2 a : of, relating to, or affected by a disorder of the mind
⟨a *mental* patient⟩ **b :** intended for the care or treatment
of persons affected by mental disorders — **men·tal·ly**
\-°l-ē\ *adv*
syn INTELLECTUAL: MENTAL implies a contrast with what
is physically or materially caused, expressed, or performed
⟨make a *mental* note⟩ ⟨form a *mental* picture⟩ INTELLECTUAL
applies to the higher mental powers (as of generalizing or
discriminating abstractions) and often implies a contrast
with *moral, emotional,* or *practical* ⟨*intellectual* appreciation of musical form⟩ ⟨*intellectual* value of scientific study⟩
mental age *n* **:** a measure used in psychological testing
that expresses an individual's mental attainment in terms
of the number of years it takes an average child to reach
the same level
men·tal·i·ty \men-'tal-ət-ē\ *n, pl* **-ties 1 :** mental power
or capacity **:** INTELLIGENCE **2 :** mode of thinking
men·thol \'men-,thól, -,thôl\ *n* [L *mentha* mint] **:** a white
crystalline soothing substance from oils of mint
men·tho·lat·ed \'men(t)-thə-,lāt-əd\ *adj* **:** treated with or
containing menthol
¹men·tion \'men-chən\ *n* [L *mention-, mentio,* fr. *ment-,*
mens mind] **:** a brief reference to something **:** a passing remark ⟨made *mention* of the fact that he has been ill⟩
²mention *vt* **men·tioned; men·tion·ing** \'mench-(ə-)niŋ\
: to refer to **:** discuss or speak about briefly — **men·tion-**
a·ble \'mench-(ə-)nə-bəl\ *adj* — **men·tion·er** \-(ə-)nər\ *n*
men·tor \'men-,tó(ə)r, 'ment-ər\ *n* [after *Mentor,* adviser
of Telemachus in Homer's *Odyssey*] **:** a wise and faithful
adviser or teacher
menu \'men-yü, 'mān-\ *n* [F] **:** a list of dishes served at a
meal; *also* **:** the dishes served
me·ow \mē-'aù\ *n* **:** the cry of a cat — **meow** *vb*
Meph·is·toph·e·les \,mef-ə-'stäf-ə-,lēz\ *n* **:** one of the
seven chief devils in medieval demonology known esp. as
the cold scoffing relentless fiend in the Faust legend —
Me·phis·to·phe·lian *or* **Me·phis·to·phe·lean** \,mef-ə-
stə-'fēl-yən, mə,fis-tə-\ *adj*

me·phit·ic \mə-'fit-ik\ *adj* [L *mephitis* noxious odor] : foul-smelling

me·pro·ba·mate \me-'prō-bə-ˌmāt\ *n* : a bitter drug used as a tranquilizer

mer·can·tile \'mər-kən-ˌtēl, -ˌtīl\ *adj* [F, fr. It, fr. *mercante* merchant, fr. L *mercant-, mercans*, fr. prp. of *mercari* to trade, fr. *merc-, merx* merchandise] **1** : of or relating to merchants, trade, or commerce **2** : of, relating to, or having the characteristics of mercantilism ⟨*mercantile* system⟩ ⟨*mercantile* theory⟩

mer·can·til·ism \-ˌtēl-ˌiz-əm, -ˌtīl-\ *n* : an economic system developing during the 17th and 18th centuries to unify and increase the power and wealth of a nation by strict governmental regulation of the entire economy usu. through policies designed to secure an accumulation of bullion, a favorable balance of trade, the development of agriculture and manufactures, and the establishment of foreign trading monopolies — **mer·can·til·ist** \-əst\ *n or adj* — **mer·can·til·is·tic** \ˌmər-kən-ˌtē-'lis-tik, -kən-ˌtī-\ *adj*

Mer·ca·tor projection \ˌmər-ˌkāt-ər-\ *n* [after Gerhardus *Mercator d*1594 Flemish geographer] : a map projection in which the meridians are drawn parallel to each other and the parallels of latitude are straight lines whose distance from each other increases with their distance from the equator

1mer·ce·nary \'mərs-ᵊn-ˌer-ē\ *n, pl* **-nar·ies** [L *mercenarius*, fr. *merces* reward, wages, fr. *merc-, merx* merchandise] : one that serves merely for wages; *esp* : a soldier hired by a foreign country to fight in its army

2mercenary *adj* **1** : doing something only for the pay or reward **2** : greedy for money — **mer·ce·nar·i·ly** \ˌmərs-ᵊn-'er-ə-lē\ *adv* — **mer·ce·nar·i·ness** \'mərs-ᵊn-ˌer-ē-nəs\ *n*

mer·cer \'mər-sər\ *n, Brit* : a dealer in textile fabrics

mer·cer·ize \'mər-sə-ˌrīz\ *vt* [after John *Mercer d*1866 English calico printer] : to treat (cotton fiber or fabrics) with a chemical so that the fibers are strengthened, take dyes better, and often acquire a sheen

1mer·chan·dise \'mər-chən-ˌdīz, -ˌdīs\ *n* : the commodities or goods that are bought and sold in trade : WARES

2merchandise \-ˌdīz\ *vb* : to buy and sell : TRADE; *esp* : to try to further sales or the use of merchandise or services by attractive presentation and publicity — **mer·chan·dis·er** *n*

1mer·chant \'mər-chənt\ *n* [OF *marcheant*, fr. (assumed) VL *mercatant-, mercatans*, prp. of *mercatare*, freq. of L *mercari* to trade, fr. *merc-, merx* merchandise] **1** : a buyer and seller of commodities for profit; *esp* : one who carries on trade on a large scale or with foreign countries **2** : the operator of a retail business : STOREKEEPER

2merchant *adj* **1** : of, relating to, or used in commerce ⟨*merchant* ship⟩ **2** : of or relating to a merchant marine ⟨*merchant* seamen⟩

mer·chant·a·ble \-ə-bəl\ *adj* : of commercial quality : SALABLE ⟨*merchantable* goods⟩

mer·chant·man \-mən\ *n* : a ship used in commerce

merchant marine *n* **1** : the commercial shipping of a nation **2** : the personnel of a merchant marine

mer·ci·ful \'mər-si-fəl\ *adj* : having, showing, or disposed to mercy : COMPASSIONATE — **mer·ci·ful·ly** \-f(ə-)lē\ *adv* — **mer·ci·ful·ness** \-fəl-nəs\ *n*

mer·ci·less \'mər-si-ləs\ *adj* : having no mercy : PITILESS ⟨*merciless* slaughter⟩ — **mer·ci·less·ly** *adv* — **mer·ci·less·ness** *n*

1mer·cu·ri·al \(ˌ)mər-'kyur-ē-əl\ *adj* **1** : of or relating to the planet Mercury **2** : having qualities of eloquence, ingenuity, or thievishness attributed to the god Mercury or to the influence of the planet Mercury **3** : characterized by rapid and unpredictable changeableness of mood **4** : of, relating to, or containing the element mercury ⟨*mercurial* medical preparations⟩ ⟨a *mercurial* thermometer⟩ — **mer·cu·ri·al·ly** \-ē-ə-lē\ *adv* — **mer·cu·ri·al·ness** *n*

2mercurial *n* : a drug or chemical containing mercury

mer·cu·ric \(ˌ)mər-'kyur-ik\ *adj* : of, relating to, or containing mercury; *esp* : containing mercury that has a valence of two

mercuric chloride *n* : a heavy poisonous substance $HgCl_2$ used as a disinfectant and fungicide and in photography

mercuric oxide *n* : a fine yellow or coarse red poisonous powder HgO used in ointments and paints and in chemical synthesis

Mer·cu·ro·chrome \mər-'kyur-ə-ˌkrōm\ *trademark* — used for a red germicidal and antiseptic solution

mer·cu·rous \(ˌ)mər-'kyur-əs, 'mər-kyə-rəs\ *adj* : of, relating to, or containing mercury; *esp* : containing mercury that has a valence of one

mercurous chloride *n* : CALOMEL

mer·cu·ry \'mər-kyə-rē, -k(ə-)rē\ *n, pl* **-ries** **1** *cap* : a Roman god serving as herald and messenger of the other gods **2** : MESSENGER, GUIDE **3 a** : a heavy silver-white metallic element that is liquid at ordinary temperatures — called also *quicksilver;* see ELEMENT table **b** : the column of mercury in a thermometer or barometer **4** *cap* : the planet nearest the sun — see PLANET table

mercury fulminate *n* [*fulminate* salt of fulminic acid, fr. *fulminic acid* (CNOH), fr. L *fulmin-, fulmen* lightning] : a compound of mercury $Hg(ONC)_2$ that when dry explodes violently on percussion and is used in percussion caps and detonators

mer·cy \'mər-sē\ *n, pl* **mercies** [OF *merci*, fr. ML *merced-, merces* favor, mercy, fr. L, reward, wages, fr. *merc-, merx* merchandise] **1** : compassion or forbearance shown to one (as an offender or adversary) having no claim to kindness **2** : a fortunate circumstance ⟨it's a *mercy* that he arrived in time⟩ **3** : compassion shown to victims of misfortune

syn CLEMENCY, LENIENCY: MERCY implies kindness and compassion that withholds punishment even when justice demands it; CLEMENCY implies a mild or merciful disposition in one having the power or duty of punishing; LENIENCY suggests an easy or indulgent treatment of faults or misbehavior

mercy killing *n* : EUTHANASIA

1mere \'mi(ə)r\ *n* [OE] : a sheet of standing water : POOL

2mere *adj, superlative* **mer·est** [L *merus* pure, unmixed] : being only this and nothing else : nothing more than ⟨a *mere* whisper⟩ ⟨a *mere* child⟩ — **mere·ly** *adv*

-mere \ˌmi(ə)r\ *n comb form* [Gk *meros*] : part : segment ⟨arthro*mere*⟩

mer·e·tri·cious \ˌmer-ə-'trish-əs\ *adj* [L *meretricius* of a prostitute, fr. *meretric-, meretrix* prostitute, fr. *mereri* to earn] : attracting by a display of showy but superficial and tawdry charms : falsely attractive — **mer·e·tri·cious·ly** *adv* — **mer·e·tri·cious·ness** *n*

mer·gan·ser \(ˌ)mər-'gan(t)-sər\ *n, pl* **-sers** *or* **-ser** [L *mergus*, a waterfowl + *anser* goose] : a fish-eating wild duck with a slender hooked beak and a usu. crested head

merge \'mərj\ *vb* [L *mergere* to plunge] **1** : to be or cause to be swallowed up or absorbed in or within something else : MINGLE, BLEND ⟨*merging* traffic⟩ **2** : COMBINE, UNITE ⟨*merge* two business firms into one⟩

merg·er \'mər-jər\ *n* : the action or result of merging; *esp* : the combination of two or more business firms into one

hooded merganser

me·rid·i·an \mə-'rid-ē-ən\ *n* [L *meridianus* of noon, fr. *meridies* noon, irreg. fr. *medius* mid + *dies* day] **1** : the highest point attained : ZENITH, CULMINATION **2 a** : an imaginary great circle on the earth's surface passing through the north and south poles and any given place between **b** : the half of such a circle included between the poles **c** : a representation of such a circle or half circle on a globe or map : any of a series of lines drawn at intervals due north and south or in the direction of the poles and numbered according to the degrees of longitude — **meridian** *adj*

me·rid·i·o·nal \mə-'rid-ē-ən-ᵊl\ *adj* **1** : SOUTHERN **2** : of, relating to, or characteristic of people living in the south esp. of France **3** : of or relating to a meridian — **me·rid·i·o·nal·ly** \-ᵊl-ē\ *adv*

me·ringue \mə-'raŋ\ *n* [F] **1** : a mixture of beaten egg white and sugar put on pies or cakes and browned **2** : a shell of baked meringue filled with fruit or ice cream

me·ri·no \mə-'rē-nō\ *n, pl* **-nos** **1** : any of a breed of fine-wooled white sheep producing a heavy fleece of exceptional quality **2** : a soft wool or wool and cotton fabric resembling cashmere **3** : a fine wool and cotton yarn — **merino** *adj*

mer·i·stem \'mer-ə-ˌstem\ n : a formative plant tissue made up of unspecialized cells capable of dividing indefinitely and of producing cells that differentiate into the definitive tissues and organs — **mer·i·ste·mat·ic** \ˌmer-ə-stə-'mat-ik\ adj — **mer·i·ste·mat·i·cal·ly** \-'mat-i-k(ə-)lē\ adv

¹**mer·it** \'mer-ət\ n [L meritum, fr. pp. of mereri to earn, deserve] **1** : the condition or fact of deserving well or ill : DESERT **2** : WORTH, EXCELLENCE ⟨a suggestion having considerable merit⟩ **3** : a praiseworthy quality : VIRTUE ⟨an answer that at least had the merit of honesty⟩

²**merit** vb : to earn by service or performance : DESERVE

mer·i·to·ri·ous \ˌmer-ə-'tōr-ē-əs, -'tȯr-\ adj : deserving reward or honor : PRAISEWORTHY — **mer·i·to·ri·ous·ly** adv — **mer·i·to·ri·ous·ness** n

merit system n : a system by which appointments and promotions in the civil service are based on competence rather than political favoritism

merl or **merle** \'mərl\ n : BLACKBIRD a

mer·lin \'mər-lən\ n : a small European falcon; also : an American pigeon hawk

Mer·lin \'mər-lən\ n : a prophet and magician in Arthurian legend

mer·maid \'mər-ˌmād\ n [ME, fr. mere sea, mere] : an imaginary sea creature usu. represented with a woman's body and a fish's tail

mer·man \-ˌman, -mən\ n, pl **mer·men** \-ˌmen, -mən\ : an imaginary sea creature usu. represented with a man's body and a fish's tail

mer·o·crine \'mer-ə-krən, -ˌkrīn, -ˌkrēn\ adj [Gk meros part + krinein to separate] : producing a secretion that is discharged without major damage to the secreting cells

-m·er·ous \m-ə-rəs\ adj comb form [Gk meros part] : having (such or so many) parts ⟨dimerous⟩ ⟨polymerous⟩

Mer·o·vin·gian \ˌmer-ə-'vin-j(ē-)ən\ adj : of, relating to, or being the first Frankish dynasty reigning from about A.D. 500 to 751 — **Merovingian** n

mer·ri·ment \'mer-i-mənt\ n : GAIETY, MIRTH, FUN

mer·ry \'mer-ē\ adj **mer·ri·er; -est** [OE myrge, merge] **1** : full of good humor and good spirits : MIRTHFUL **2** : marked by gaiety or festivity ⟨a merry Christmas⟩ — **mer·ri·ly** \'mer-ə-lē\ adv — **mer·ri·ness** \'mer-ē-nəs\ n
   syn BLITHE, JOVIAL, JOLLY: MERRY suggests high spirits and unrestrained enjoyment of frolic or festivity; BLITHE implies lightheartedness as expressed in singing, skipping, and dancing; JOVIAL suggests behavior that stimulates conviviality and good-fellowship; JOLLY suggests often habitual good spirits expressed in laughing, bantering, and jesting

mer·ry-an·drew \ˌmer-ē-'an-ˌdrü\ n : CLOWN, BUFFOON

mer·ry-go-round \'mer-ē-gō-ˌraùnd\ n **1** : a circular revolving platform fitted with seats and figures of animals on which people sit for a ride **2** : a rapid round of activities : WHIRL ⟨a merry-go-round of parties⟩

mer·ry·mak·ing \-ˌmā-kiŋ\ n **1** : gay or festive activity : MERRIMENT, FESTIVITY **2** : a festive or convivial occasion — **mer·ry·mak·er** \-kər\ n

Mer·thi·o·late \(ˌ)mər-'thī-ə-ˌlāt\ trademark — used for an antiseptic, germicidal, and preservative compound

mes- or **meso-** comb form [Gk mesos; akin to E mid] **1** : mid : in the middle ⟨mesocarp⟩ **2** : intermediate (as in size or type) ⟨mesomorph⟩ ⟨meson⟩

me·sa \'mā-sə\ n [Sp, lit., table, fr. L mensa] : a flat‑topped hill or small plateau with steep sides

més·al·li·ance \ˌmā-ˌzal-'yäⁿs\ n, pl **-liances** \-'yäⁿs(-əz)\ [F] : a marriage with a person of inferior social position

mes·cal \me-'skal\ n [Sp mezcal, of AmerInd origin] **1** : a small cactus with rounded stems covered with jointed tubercles that are used as a stimulant and intoxicant esp. among the Mexican Indians **2 a** : a usu. colorless Mexican liquor distilled esp. from the central leaves of maguey plants **b** : a plant from which mescal is produced

mesdames pl of MADAM or of MADAME

mesdemoiselles pl of MADEMOISELLE

me·seems \mi-'sēmz\ vb impersonal, past **me·seemed** \-'sēmd\ archaic : seems to me

me·sem·bry·an·the·mum \mə-ˌzem-brē-'an(t)-thə-məm\ n [Gk mesēmbria midday (fr. mes- + hēmera day) + anthemon flower] : any of a genus of fleshy-leaved African plants sometimes grown as ornamentals

mes·en·ceph·a·lon \ˌmez-,en-'sef-ə-ˌlän, ˌmes-\ n : the middle division of the brain : MIDBRAIN — **mes·en·ce·phal·ic** \-,en(t)-sə-'fal-ik\ adj

mes·en·chyme \'mez-ən-ˌkīm, 'mes-\ n : a loosely organized mesodermal tissue that produces connective tissues, blood, lymphatics, bone, and cartilage — **mes·en·chy·mal** \məz-'eŋ-kə-məl, məs-; ˌmez-ən-'kī-məl, ˌmes-\ or **mes·en·chym·a·tous** \ˌmez-ən-'kim-ət-əs, ˌmes-\ adj

mes·en·tery \'mes-ən-ˌter-ē\ n, pl **-ter·ies** [Gk mes- + enteron intestine] : membranous tissue or one of the membranes that envelop and support visceral organs (as the intestines) — **mes·en·ter·ic** \ˌmes-ən-'ter-ik\ adj

¹**mesh** \'mesh\ n **1** : one of the open spaces formed by the threads of a net or the wires of a sieve or screen **2 a** : NET, NETWORK **b** : a fabric of open texture with evenly spaced small holes **3** : WEB, SNARE — usu. used in pl. ⟨caught in his own meshes⟩ **4** : the coming or fitting together of the teeth of two gears — **meshed** \'mesht\ adj

²**mesh** vb **1** : to catch in or as if in a mesh : ENTANGLE **2** : to make something into a net or network **3** : to fit together : INTERLOCK ⟨gear teeth that mesh⟩ ⟨he meshed the gears quietly⟩

mesh·work \'mesh-ˌwərk\ n : MESHES, NETWORK

mes·i·al \'mez-ē-əl, -'mēz-, 'mes-, 'mēs-\ adj : MIDDLE; esp : dividing something (as an animal body) into right and left halves — **mes·i·al·ly** \-ē-ə-lē\ adv

mes·mer·ism \'mez-mə-ˌriz-əm, 'mes-\ n [fr. F.A. Mesmer d1815 Austrian physician and proponent of a method of hypnotism] : HYPNOTISM — **mes·mer·ic** \mez-'mer-ik, me-'smer-\ adj — **mes·mer·ist** \'mez-mə-rəst, 'mes-\ n

mes·mer·ize \'mez-mə-ˌrīz, 'mes-\ vt **1** : HYPNOTIZE **2** : SPELLBIND, FASCINATE — **mes·mer·iz·er** n

meso·carp \'mez-ə-ˌkärp, 'mes-\ n : the often fleshy middle layer of the pericarp of a fruit — compare ENDOCARP, EPICARP — **meso·car·pic** \ˌmez-ə-'kär-pik, ˌmes-\ adj

meso·derm \'mez-ə-ˌdərm, 'mes-\ n : the middle of the three primary germ layers of an embryo from which most of the muscular, skeletal, and connective tissues develop; also : tissue derived from this layer — **meso·der·mal** \ˌmez-ə-'dər-məl, ˌmes-\ or **meso·der·mic** \-'dər-mik\ adj

meso·mor·phic \ˌmez-ə-'mȯr-fik, ˌmes-\ adj : characterized by predominance of the structures developed from the mesodermal layer of the embryo : of the muscular or athletic type of body-build — **meso·morph** \'mez-ə-ˌmȯrf, 'mes-\ n

mes·on \'mez-ˌän, 'mēz-, 'mes-, 'mēs-\ n [mes- + -on] : any of various particles that are smaller than the atom, have a mass between that of the electron and the proton, and are either charged positively or negatively or neutral

meso·phyll \'mez-ə-ˌfil, 'mes-\ n : the parenchyma of a foliage leaf

meso·phyte \-ˌfīt\ n : a plant that grows under medium conditions of moisture — **meso·phyt·ic** \ˌmez-ə-'fit-ik, ˌmes-\ adj

Meso·po·ta·mi·an \ˌmes-ə-pə-'tā-mē-ən\ adj : of or relating to Mesopotamia and esp. to the ancient civilization developed there as early as 4000 B.C. and characterized by the use of sun-dried brick for building and by the development of cuneiform writing — **Mesopotamian** n

mes·o·the·li·um \ˌmez-ə-'thē-lē-əm, ˌmes-\ n, pl **-lia** \-lē-ə\ : epithelium derived from mesoderm — **mes·o·the·li·al** \-lē-əl\ adj

Meso·zo·ic \ˌmez-ə-'zō-ik, ˌmes-\ n : the 4th of the five eras of geological history marked by the existence of dinosaurs, marine and flying reptiles, and evergreen trees; also : the corresponding system of rocks — see GEOLOGIC TIME table — **Mesozoic** adj

mes·quite \mə-'skēt, me-\ n [Sp] : a spiny deep-rooted leguminous tree or shrub of the southwestern U.S. and Mexico bearing pods rich in sugar and important as a livestock feed

¹**mess** \'mes\ n [OF mes, fr. LL missus course at a meal, fr. miss-, mittere to put, fr. L, to send] **1 a** : a quantity of food **b** : a dish of soft or liquid food ⟨a mess of porridge⟩ **2** : a group of people and esp. of military personnel who regularly eat together; also : the meal they eat or the place where they eat ⟨an officers' mess⟩ **3 a** : a confused heap **b** : a state of confusion or disorder ⟨left things in a mess⟩

²**mess** vb **1 a** : to supply with meals **b** : to take meals

with a mess **2 :** to make dirty or untidy **:** DISARRANGE; *also* **:** BUNGLE ⟨*messed* up the job⟩ **3 :** INTERFERE, MEDDLE **4 :** PUTTER ⟨likes to *mess* around the house on weekends⟩

mes·sage \'mes-ij\ *n* [OF, fr. ML *missaticum*, fr. L *miss-, mittere* to send] **1 :** a communication in writing, in speech, or by signals **2 :** a messenger's errand or function

messeigneurs *pl of* MONSEIGNEUR

mes·sen·ger \'mes-ᵊn-jər\ *n* **:** one who bears a message or does an errand: as **a** *obs* **:** FORERUNNER, HERALD **b :** a dispatch bearer esp. in military service **c :** an employee who carries messages

messenger RNA *n* **:** an RNA that carries the code for a particular protein from the nuclear DNA to the ribosome and acts as a template for the formation of that protein

mes·si·ah \mə-'sī-ə\ *n* [Heb *māshīaḥ* & Aram *mĕshīḥā*, lit., one anointed] **1** *cap* **a :** the expected king and deliverer of the Jews **b :** JESUS **2 :** a professed or accepted leader of some hope or cause — **mes·si·ah·ship** \-,ship\ *n* — **mes·si·an·ic** \,mes-ē-'an-ik\ *adj* — **mes·si·a·nism** \'mes-ē-ə-,niz-əm, mə-'sī-ə-\ *n*

Mes·si·as \mə-'sī-əs\ *n* **:** MESSIAH 1

messieurs *pl of* MONSIEUR

mess jacket *n* **:** a man's short tight jacket

mess kit *n* **:** a kit consisting of a metal dish and eating utensils for use by soldiers and campers

mess·mate \'mes-,māt\ *n* **:** a member of a group who eat regularly together (as in a ship's mess)

messy \'mes-ē\ *adj* **mess·i·er, -est :** marked by confusion, disorder, or dirt **:** UNTIDY — **mess·i·ly** \'mes-ə-lē\ *adv* — **mess·i·ness** \'mes-ē-nəs\ *n*

mes·ti·za \me-'stē-zə\ *n* **:** a female mestizo

mes·ti·zo \-zō\ *n, pl* **-zos** [Sp] **:** a person of mixed blood; *esp* **:** one of mixed European and American Indian ancestry

met *past of* MEET

meta- *or* **met-** *comb form* [Gk, among, with, after, change] **1 a :** occurring after **:** after ⟨*metestrus*⟩ **b :** situated behind or beyond ⟨*met*encephalon⟩ ⟨*meta*carpus⟩ **2 :** change **:** transformation ⟨*meta*morphosis⟩ **3 :** more comprehensive **:** transcending ⟨*meta*psychology⟩ — used with the name of a discipline to designate a new but related discipline designed to deal critically with the original one ⟨*meta*language⟩

me·tab·o·lism \mə-'tab-ə-,liz-əm\ *n* [Gk *metabolē* transformation, fr. *metaballein* to change, fr. *meta-* + *ballein* to throw] **1 a :** the sum of the processes in the building up and destruction of protoplasm incidental to life **b :** the sum of the processes by which a particular substance is handled in the living body **2 :** METAMORPHOSIS **3** — **met·a·bol·ic** \,met-ə-'bäl-ik\ *adj* — **me·tab·o·lize** \mə-'tab-ə-,līz\ *vb*

me·tab·o·lite \-,līt\ *n* **1 :** a product of metabolism **2 :** a substance essential to a metabolic process

meta·car·pal \,met-ə-'kär-pəl\ *n* **:** a metacarpal bone

meta·car·pus \-pəs\ *n* **:** the part of the hand or forefoot between the carpus and the phalanges — **meta·car·pal** \-pəl\ *adj*

meta·gal·axy \,met-ə-'gal-ək-sē\ *n* **:** the entire system of galaxies external to our own galaxy — **meta·ga·lac·tic** \-gə-'lak-tik\ *adj*

¹met·al \'met-ᵊl\ *n* [Gk *metallon* mine, metal] **1 :** any of various substances (as gold, tin, copper, or bronze) that have a more or less shiny appearance, are good conductors of electricity and heat, are opaque, can be melted, and are usu. capable of being drawn into a wire or hammered into a thin sheet **2 :** any of more than three fourths of the chemical elements that exhibit the properties of a metal, typically are crystalline solids, and have atoms that readily lose electrons **3 a :** METTLE **b :** the material or substance out of which a person or thing is made — **metal** *adj*

²metal *vt* **-aled** *or* **-alled; -al·ing** *or* **-al·ling :** to cover or furnish with metal

me·tal·lic \mə-'tal-ik\ *adj* **1 :** of, relating to, or being a metal **2 :** containing or made of metal **3 :** HARSH, GRATING ⟨a *metallic* voice⟩ — **me·tal·li·cal·ly** \-'tal-i-k(ə-)lē\ *adv*

met·al·lif·er·ous \,met-ᵊl-'if-(ə-)rəs\ *adj* **:** yielding or containing metal

met·al·lize *also* **met·al·ize** \'met-ᵊl-,īz\ *vt* **:** to treat or combine with a metal

met·al·log·ra·phy \,met-ᵊl-'äg-rə-fē\ *n* **:** a study of the structure of metals esp. with the microscope — **met·al·log·ra·pher** \-fər\ *n* — **me·tal·lo·graph·ic** \mə-,tal-ə-'graf-ik\ *adj*

met·al·loid \'met-ᵊl-,óid\ *n* **:** a chemical element intermediate in properties between the typical metals and other elements

met·al·lur·gy \'met-ᵊl-,ər-jē\ *n* [Gk *metallon* metal + *-ourgia* process of working, fr. *ergon* work] **:** the science of extracting metals from their ores, refining them, and preparing them for use — **met·al·lur·gi·cal** \,met-ᵊl-'ər-ji-kəl\ *adj* — **met·al·lur·gist** \'met-ᵊl-,ər-jəst\ *n*

met·al·ware \'met-ᵊl-,wa(ə)r, -,we(ə)r\ *n* **:** metal utensils for household use

met·al·work \'met-ᵊl-,wərk\ *n* **1 :** the process or occupation of making things from metal **2 :** work and esp. artistic work made of metal — **met·al·work·er** \-,wər-kər\ *n* — **met·al·work·ing** \-,kiŋ\ *n*

met·a·mere \'met-ə-,mi(ə)r\ *n* **:** any of a linear series of segments into which the body of a higher invertebrate or vertebrate is divisible — **met·a·mer·ic** \,met-ə-'mer-ik, -'mir-\ *adj* — **met·a·mer·i·cal·ly** \-i-k(ə-)lē\ *adv* — **me·tam·er·ism** \mə-'tam-ə-,riz-əm\ *n*

met·a·mor·phism \,met-ə-'mór-,fiz-əm\ *n* **1 :** METAMORPHOSIS **2 :** a change in the structure of rock; *esp* **:** a change to a more compact and more highly crystalline condition produced by such forces as pressure, heat, and water ⟨marble is produced by the *metamorphism* of limestone⟩ — **met·a·mor·phic** \-'mór-fik\ *adj*

met·a·mor·phose \-,fōz, -,fōs\ *vb* **:** to change or cause to change in form **:** undergo metamorphosis ⟨a rock that is a *metamorphosed* granite⟩ *syn* see TRANSFORM

met·a·mor·pho·sis \,met-ə-'mór-fə-səs\ *n, pl* **-pho·ses** \-fə-,sēz\ [L, fr. Gk *metamorphōsis*, fr. *metamorphoun* to transform, fr. *meta-* + *morphē* form] **1 :** a change of form, structure, or substance esp. by witchcraft or magic **2 :** a striking alteration in appearance, character, or circumstances **3 :** a fundamental and usu. rather abrupt change in the form and often the habits of an animal that occurs during the transformation of a larva into an adult

meta·phase \'met-ə-,fāz\ *n* **:** the stage of mitosis preceding the anaphase

met·a·phor \'met-ə-,fó(ə)r, -fər\ *n* [Gk *metaphora*, fr. *metapherein* to transfer, fr. *meta-* + *pherein* to carry, bear] **:** a figure of speech in which a word or phrase denoting one kind of object or idea is used in place of another to suggest a similarity between them (as in *the ship plows the sea*) — compare SIMILE — **met·a·phor·i·cal** \,met-ə-'fór-i-kəl, -'far-\ *adj* — **met·a·phor·i·cal·ly** \-i-k(ə-)lē\ *adv*

met·a·phys·i·cal \,met-ə-'fiz-i-kəl\ *adj* **1 :** of, relating to, or based on metaphysics **2 :** SUPERNATURAL **3 :** highly abstract or difficult to understand **4 :** of or relating to poetry esp. of the early 17th century that is marked by subtle and elaborate metaphors — **met·a·phys·i·cal·ly** \-'fiz-i-k(ə-)lē\ *adv*

met·a·phy·si·cian \-fə-'zish-ən\ *n* **:** a student of or specialist in metaphysics

met·a·phys·ics \,met-ə-'fiz-iks\ *n* [ML *Metaphysica*, title given to Aristotle's treatise on the subject, fr. Gk *(ta) meta (ta) physika* the (works) after the physical (works); fr. its position in his collected works] **:** the part of philosophy concerned with the study of the ultimate causes and the underlying nature of things; *also* **:** pure philosophy as distinguished from branches (as logic or ethics) of philosophy having a practical bearing

met·a·pla·sia \,met-ə-'plā-zh(ē-)ə\ *n* [NL, fr. Gk *meta-* + *plassein* to mold, form] **:** replacement of one kind of cell or tissue by another — **met·a·plas·tic** \-'plas-tik\ *adj*

meta·se·quoia \,met-ə-si-'kwói-ə\ *n* **:** any of a genus of fossil and living deciduous coniferous trees of the pine family

meta·sta·ble \,met-ə-'stā-bəl\ *adj* **:** marked by only a slight margin of stability ⟨a *metastable* chemical⟩

me·tas·ta·sis \mə-'tas-tə-səs\ *n, pl* **-ta·ses** \-tə-,sēz\ [Gk, transition, fr. *meta-* + *sta-, histanai* to stand] **:** transfer of a disease-producing agency from its original site to another part of the body; *also* **:** a secondary growth of a malignant tumor — **met·a·stat·ic** \,met-ə-'stat-ik\ *adj* — **met·a·stat·i·cal·ly** \-'stat-i-k(ə-)lē\ *adv*

me·tas·ta·size \mə-'tas-tə-,sīz\ *vi* **:** to spread by metastasis

ə abut; ᵊ kitten; ər further; a back; ā bake; ä cot, cart; aú out; ch chin; e less; ē easy; g gift; i trip; ī life

meta·tar·sal \,met-ə-'tär-səl\ *n* : a metatarsal bone

meta·tar·sus \-səs\ *n* : the part of the foot in man or of the hind foot in a quadruped between the tarsus and phalanges — **meta·tar·sal** \-səl\ *adj*

me·tath·e·sis \mə-'tath-ə-səs\ *n, pl* **-tath·e·ses** \-'tath-ə-,sēz\ [Gk, fr. *meta-* + *the-, tithenai* to put, place] : a change of place or condition; *esp* : transposition of two sounds or letters in a word (as in *emnity* for *enmity*)

met·a·zo·an \,met-ə-'zō-ən\ *or* **met·a·zo·on** \-'zō-,än\ *n* : any of a group (Metazoa) including all animals with a body composed of cells differentiated into tissues and organs — **met·a·zo·al** \-'zō-əl\ *or* **metazoan** *adj*

mete \'mēt\ *vt* [OE *metan* to measure] 1 *archaic* : MEASURE 2 : to assign by measure : ALLOT, APPORTION ⟨*mete* out punishment⟩ ⟨*mete* out rewards⟩

me·tem·psy·cho·sis \mə-,tem(p)-si-'kō-səs, ,met-əm-,sī-\ *n* [Gk *metempsychōsis*, fr. *meta-* + *en-* + *psychē* soul] : the passing of the soul at death into another body either human or animal

met·en·ceph·a·lon \,met-,en-'sef-ə-,län\ *n* : the anterior segment of the rhombencephalon — **met·en·ce·phal·ic** \,met-,en(t)-sə-'fal-ik\ *adj*

me·te·or \'mēt-ē-ər\ *n* [ML *meteorum*, fr. Gk *meteōron* phenomenon in the sky, fr. *meteōros* high in the air] : one of the small particles of matter in the solar system observable directly only when it falls into the earth's atmosphere where the heat of friction may cause it to glow brightly for a short time; *also* : the streak of light produced by the passage of a meteor

me·te·or·ic \,mēt-ē-'ȯr-ik, -'är-\ *adj* 1 : of or relating to a meteor ⟨a *meteoric* shower⟩ 2 : resembling a meteor in speed or in sudden and temporary brilliance ⟨a *meteoric* career⟩ — **me·te·or·i·cal·ly** \-i-k(ə-)lē\ *adv*

me·te·or·ite \'mēt-ē-ə-,rīt\ *n* : a meteor that reaches the surface of the earth

me·te·or·oid \-,rȯid\ *n* : a meteoric particle in interplanetary space

me·te·o·rol·o·gy \,mēt-ē-ə-'räl-ə-jē\ *n* : a science that deals with the atmosphere and its phenomena and with weather and weather forecasting — **me·te·o·ro·log·ic** \,mēt-ē-,ȯr-ə-'läj-ik, -ē-,är-, -ē-ər-\ *or* **me·te·o·ro·log·i·cal** \-'läj-i-kəl\ *adj* — **me·te·o·rol·o·gist** \,mēt-ē-ə-'räl-ə-jəst\ *n*

1me·ter \'mēt-ər\ *n* [OE *mēter*, fr. L *metrum*, fr. Gk *metron*, lit., measure] 1 : a systematically arranged and measured rhythm in verse 2 : the basic rhythmical pattern of note values, accents, and beats per measure in music

2meter *n* : a measure of length that is equal to 39.37 inches and is the basis of the metric system — see METRIC SYSTEM table

3meter *n* : an instrument for measuring and sometimes recording the amount of something ⟨gas *meter*⟩ ⟨electric light *meter*⟩

4meter *vt* 1 : to measure by means of a meter 2 : to supply in a measured or regulated amount

-me·ter \m-ət-ər, *in some words* ,mēt-ər\ *n comb form* : instrument or means for measuring ⟨baro*meter*⟩

meter–kilogram–second *adj* : of, relating to, or being a system of units based on the meter as the unit of length, the kilogram as the unit of mass, and the second as the unit of time — abbr. *mks*

meth·ac·ry·late \meth-'ak-rə-,lāt\ *n* : a light strong acrylic resin used esp. as a substitute for glass

meth·a·done \'meth-ə-,dōn\ *or* **meth·a·don** \-,dän\ *n* : a synthetic addictive narcotic drug used esp. as a substitute narcotic in the treatment of heroin addiction

meth·ane \'meth-,ān\ *n* [fr. *methyl*] : an odorless flammable gas CH_4 consisting of carbon and hydrogen produced by decomposition of organic matter in marshes and mines and by distillation

meth·a·nol \'meth-ə-,nȯl, -,nōl\ *n* : a volatile flammable poisonous liquid CH_3OH that consists of carbon, hydrogen, and oxygen and is used esp. as a solvent and antifreeze

me·thinks \mi-'thiŋ(k)s\ *vb impersonal, past* **me·thought** \-'thȯt\ *archaic* : seems to me

meth·od \'meth-əd\ *n* [Gk *methodos*, lit., pursuit after, fr. *meta-* after, in search of + *hodos* way] 1 a : a regular way of doing something b : a systematic plan or procedure for doing something ⟨developed a new *method* for

making cement⟩ 2 a : orderly arrangement b : REGULARITY, ORDERLINESS ⟨a pupil whose work lacks *method*⟩

me·thod·i·cal \mə-'thäd-i-kəl\ *adj* 1 : characterized by or performed or arranged by method or order 2 : habitually following a method : SYSTEMATIC — **me·thod·i·cal·ly** \-i-k(ə-)lē\ *adv* — **me·thod·i·cal·ness** \-kəl-nəs\ *n*

Meth·od·ist \'meth-əd-əst\ *n* : a member of one of the denominations deriving from the Wesleyan revival, having Arminian doctrine and often modified episcopal polity, and stressing personal and social morality — **Meth·od·ism** \-ə-,diz-əm\ *n* — **Methodist** *adj*

meth·od·ize \'meth-ə-,dīz\ *vt* : SYSTEMATIZE

meth·od·ol·o·gy \,meth-ə-'däl-ə-jē\ *n, pl* **-gies** 1 : a body of methods and rules followed in a science or discipline 2 : the study of the principles or procedures of inquiry in a particular field — **meth·od·o·log·i·cal** \,meth-əd-°l-'äj-i-kəl\ *adj* — **meth·od·ol·o·gist** \,meth-ə-'däl-ə-jəst\ *n*

Me·thu·se·lah \mə-'th(y)üz-(ə-)lə\ *n* : an Old Testament patriarch held to have lived 969 years

meth·yl \'meth-əl\ *n* [back-formation fr. *methylene* the radical CH_2, fr. F *méthylène*, fr. Gk *methy* wine (akin to E *1mead*) + *hylē* wood] : a chemical radical CH_3 consisting of carbon and hydrogen

methyl alcohol *n* : METHANOL

meth·y·lene blue \,meth-ə-,lēn-\ *n* : a basic dye used as a biological stain and as an antidote in cyanide poisoning

methyl orange *n* : a basic dye used as a chemical indicator that in dilute solution is yellow when neutral and pink when acid

met·ic \'met-ik\ *n* [Gk *metoikos*, fr. *meta-* + *oikos* house] : an alien resident having some civil rights but no part in the political life of an ancient Greek city

me·tic·u·lous \mə-'tik-yə-ləs\ *adj* [L *meticulus* timid, fr. *metus* fear] : extremely or excessively careful in small details syn see CAREFUL — **me·tic·u·lous·ly** *adv* — **me·tic·u·lous·ness** *n*

mé·tier \mā-'tyā\ *n* [F] : an area of activity in which one is expert or successful : FORTE

mé·tis \mā-'tē(s)\ *n, pl* **métis** \-'tē(s), -'tēz\ [F] : one of mixed blood; *esp* : the offspring of an American Indian and a white person

Me·tol \'mē-,tȯl, -,tōl\ *trademark* — used for a photographic developer

me·ton·y·my \mə-'tän-ə-mē\ *n, pl* **-mies** [Gk *metōnymia*, fr. *meta-* + *onoma, onyma* name] : a figure of speech in which the name of one thing is used for that of another of which it is an attribute or with which it is associated (as in "lands belonging to the *crown*")

me-too \'mē-'tü\ *adj* : marked by similarity to or acceptance of successful or persuasive policies or practices of a political rival ⟨a *me-too* policy⟩ — **me-too·ism** \-,iz-əm\ *n*

met·o·pon \'met-ə-,pän\ *n* : a narcotic drug derived from morphine

me·tre \'mēt-ər\ *chiefly Brit var of* METER

met·ric \'me-trik\ *adj* 1 : of or relating to measurement; *esp* : of, relating to, or based on the metric system 2 : of or relating to poetic or musical meter : METRICAL

-metric *or* **-metrical** *adj comb form* 1 : of, employing, or obtained by (such) a meter ⟨galvano*metric*⟩ 2 : of or relating to (such) an art, process, or science of measuring ⟨chrono*metric*⟩

met·ri·cal \'me-tri-kəl\ *adj* 1 a : of or relating to meter (as in poetry or music) b : arranged in meter ⟨*metrical* verse⟩ 2 : of or relating to measurement : METRIC — **met·ri·cal·ly** \-k(ə-)lē\ *adv*

met·rics \'me-triks\ *n* : a part of prosody that deals with metrical structure

metric system *n* : a decimal system of weights and measures in which the meter is the unit of length and the kilogram is the unit of weight

metric ton *n* : a weight of 1000 kilograms or 2204.6 pounds — see METRIC SYSTEM table

met·ro \'me-trō\ *n* [F *métro*, short for *chemin de fer métropolitain* metropolitan railroad] : SUBWAY

me·trol·o·gy \me-'träl-ə-jē\ *n* : the science of weights and measures or of measurement — **met·ro·log·i·cal** \,me-trə-'läj-i-kəl\ *adj*

met·ro·nome \'me-trə-,nōm\ *n* [Gk *metron* meter + *-nomos* controlling, fr. *nomos* law] : an instrument that produces a regularly repeated tick used esp. to help a

METRIC SYSTEM

LENGTH

unit	abbreviation	number of meters	approximate U.S. equivalent
myriameter	mym	10,000	6.2 miles
kilometer	km	1,000	0.62 mile
hectometer	hm	100	109.36 yards
dekameter	dkm	10	32.81 feet
meter	m	1	39.37 inches
decimeter	dm	0.1	3.94 inches
centimeter	cm	0.01	0.39 inch
millimeter	mm	0.001	0.04 inch

AREA

unit	abbreviation	number of square meters	approximate U.S. equivalent
square kilometer	sq km or km²	1,000,000	0.3861 square mile
hectare	ha	10,000	2.47 acres
are	a	100	119.60 square yards
centare	ca	1	10.76 square feet
square centimeter	sq cm or cm²	0.0001	0.155 square inch

VOLUME

unit	abbreviation	number of cubic meters	approximate U.S. equivalent
dekastere	dks	10	13.10 cubic yards
stere	s	1	1.31 cubic yards
decistere	ds	0.10	3.53 cubic feet
cubic centimeter	cu cm or cm³ also cc	0.000001	0.061 cubic inch

CAPACITY

unit	abbreviation	number of liters	approximate U.S. equivalent cubic	dry	liquid
kiloliter	kl	1,000	1.31 cubic yards		
hectoliter	hl	100	3.53 cubic feet	2.84 bushels	
dekaliter	dkl	10	0.35 cubic foot	1.14 pecks	2.64 gallons
liter	l	1	61.02 cubic inches	0.908 quart	1.057 quarts
deciliter	dl	0.10	6.1 cubic inches	0.18 pint	0.21 pint
centiliter	cl	0.01	0.6 cubic inch		0.338 fluid-ounce
milliliter	ml	0.001	0.06 cubic inch		0.27 fluidram

MASS AND WEIGHT

unit	abbreviation	number of grams	approximate U.S. equivalent
metric ton	MT or t	1,000,000	1.1 tons
quintal	q	100,000	220.46 pounds
kilogram	kg	1,000	2.2046 pounds
hectogram	hg	100	3.527 ounces
dekagram	dkg	10	0.353 ounce
gram	g or gm	1	0.035 ounce
decigram	dg	0.10	1.543 grains
centigram	cg	0.01	0.154 grain
milligram	mg	0.001	0.015 grain

music student play in exact time — **met·ro·nom·ic** \,me-trə-'näm-ik\ *adj* — **met·ro·nom·i·cal·ly** \-'näm-i-k(ə-)lē\ *adv*

me·trop·o·lis \mə-'träp-(ə-)ləs\ *n* [Gk *mētropolis*, fr. *mētr-*, *mētēr* mother (akin to E *mother*) + *polis* city] **1** : the mother city or country of a colony **2 a** : the chief or capital city of a country, state, or region **b** : a large or important city **3** : a principal seat or center of an activity

¹met·ro·pol·i·tan \,me-trə-'päl-ət-ᵊn\ *n* **1** : the primate of an ecclesiastical province **2** : one who lives in a metropolis or who exhibits metropolitan manners or customs

²metropolitan *adj* **1** : of or constituting a metropolitan or his see **2** : of, relating to, or characteristic of a metropolis **3** : of, relating to, or constituting a region made up of a city and the densely populated surrounding areas socially and economically integrated with it ⟨*metropolitan* area⟩

-m·e·try \m-ə-trē\ *n comb form, pl* **-metries** : art, process, or science of measuring (something specified) ⟨chronometry⟩ ⟨photometry⟩

met·tle \'met-ᵊl\ *n* [alteration of *metal*] **1** : quality of temperament or disposition **2 a** : SPIRIT, ARDOR ⟨the raw troops proved their *mettle* in the assault⟩ **b** : STAMINA — **on one's mettle** : aroused to do one's best

met·tle·some \-ᵊl-səm\ *adj* : full of mettle : SPIRITED, FIERY

¹mew \'myü\ *n* [OE *mǣw*] : GULL; *esp* : the common European gull

²mew *vi* : to utter a meow or similar sound

³mew *n* : MEOW

⁴mew *n* **1** *archaic* : a cage for hawks **2** *pl, chiefly Bri* **a** : stables usu. with living quarters built around a cour **b** : a street of stables

⁵mew *vt* : to shut up : CONFINE

mewl \'myül\ *vi* : to cry weakly : WHIMPER

Mex·i·can \'mek-si-kən\ *n* **1** : a native or inhabitant of Mexico **2** : a person of Mexican descent — **Mexican** *adj*

Mexican bean beetle *n* : a spotted ladybug that feeds on the leaves of beans

me·zu·zah *or* **me·zu·za** \mə-'zuz-ə\ *n* [Heb *mězūzāh* doorpost] : a small parchment scroll inscribed with Deuteronomy 6:4–9 and 11:13–21 and the divine name *Shaddai* (the Almighty) and placed in a case fixed to the doorpost by some Jewish families as a sign and reminder of their faith

mez·za·nine \'mez-ᵊn-,ēn\ *n* [It *mezzanino*, fr. *mezzano* middle, fr. L *medianus* middle, median] **1** : a low story between two main stories of a building often projecting in the form of a balcony **2** : the lowest balcony in a theater or its first few rows

mez·zo for·te \,met-sō-'fȯr-,tā, ,me(d)z-ō-, -'fȯrt-ē\ *adj (or adv)* [It, fr. *mezzo* middle, medium fr. L *medius*] : moderately loud — used as a direction in music

mez·zo·so·pra·no \-sə-'pran-ō, -'prän-\ *n* : a woman's voice having a full deep quality between that of the soprano and contralto; *also* : a singer having such a voice

mez·zo·tint \'met-sō-,tint, 'me(d)z-ō-\ *n* : a process of engraving on copper or steel by scraping or burnishing a roughened surface to produce light and shade; *also* : an engraving produced by this process

ə abut; ᵊ kitten; ər further; a back; ā bake; ä cot, cart; aú out; ch chin; e less; ē easy; g gift; i trip; ī life

mho \'mō\ *n* [backward spelling of *ohm*] : the unit of conductance equal to the reciprocal of the ohm

mi \'mē\ *n* [ML] : the 3d note of the diatonic scale

mi·as·ma \mī-'az-mə, mē-\ *n, pl* **-mas** *or* **-ma·ta** \-mət-ə\ [Gk, defilement, fr. *miainein* to pollute] **1** : a vaporous exhalation (as of a swamp) formerly believed to cause disease **2** : a harmful influence or atmosphere — **mi·as·mal** \-məl\ *or* **mi·as·mat·ic** \,mī-əz-'mat-ik\ *or* **mi·as·mic** \mī-'az-mik, mē-'az-\ *adj*

mi·ca \'mī-kə\ *n* [L, grain, crumb] : any of various silicon-containing minerals that may be separated easily into thin and often somewhat flexible and transparent sheets — **mi·ca·ceous** \mī-'kā-shəs\ *adj*

Mi·cah \'mī-kə\ *n* **1** : a Hebrew prophet of the 8th century B.C. **2** — see BIBLE table

mice *pl of* MOUSE

mi·celle \mī-'sel\ *also* **mi·cel·la** \-'sel-ə\ *n, pl* **micelles** \-'selz\ *also* **mi·cel·lae** \-'sel-(,)ē\ [NL *micella*, fr. dim. of L *mica* crumb, small bit] : a minute organized unit of matter (as a colloidal particle) — **mi·cel·lar** \-'sel-ər\ *adj*

Mi·chael \'mī-kəl\ *n* : one of the archangels

Mich·ael·mas \'mik-əl-məs\ *n* [St. *Michael* the Archangel, whose festival is celebrated on that day] : September 29

Michaelmas daisy *n* : a wild aster; *esp* : one blooming about Michaelmas

Mick·ey Finn \,mik-ē-'fin\ *n* : a drink of liquor doctored with a drug

mick·le \'mik-əl\ *adj, chiefly Scot* : GREAT, MUCH

micr- *or* **micro-** *comb form* [Gk *mikros*] **1 a** : small : minute ⟨*microfilm*⟩ **b** : enlarging : magnifying or amplifying ⟨*microphone*⟩ ⟨*microscope*⟩ **2** : one millionth part of a (specified) unit ⟨*microgram*⟩ ⟨*microhm*⟩ **3** : using or used in microscopy ⟨*microdissection*⟩

mi·cro \'mī-krō\ *adj* : MICROSCOPIC

mi·cro·am·pere \,mī-krō-'am-,pi(ə)r\ *n* : one millionth of an ampere

mi·crobe \'mī-,krōb\ *n* [*micr-* + Gk *bios* life] : MICROORGANISM, GERM — **mi·cro·bi·al** \mī-'krō-bē-əl\ *or* **mi·cro·bic** \-bik\ *adj*

mi·cro·bi·ol·o·gy \,mī-krō-bī-'äl-ə-jē\ *n* : a branch of biology dealing esp. with microscopic forms of life — **mi·cro·bi·o·log·i·cal** \-,bī-ə-'läj-i-kəl\ *also* **mi·cro·bi·o·log·ic** \-'läj-ik\ *adj* — **mi·cro·bi·o·log·i·cal·ly** \-i-k(ə-)lē\ *adv* — **mi·cro·bi·ol·o·gist** \-bī-'äl-ə-jəst\ *n*

Mi·cro·card \'mī-krō-,kärd\ *trademark* — used for a sensitized card on which printed matter is reproduced photographically in greatly reduced form

mi·cro·chem·is·try \,mī-krō-'kem-ə-strē\ *n* : chemistry dealing with very small quantities of substances — **mi·cro·chem·i·cal** \-'kem-i-kəl\ *adj*

mi·cro·cline \'mī-krō-,klīn\ *n* : a white to pale yellow, red, or green mineral that is like orthoclase in composition but has a different crystal form

mi·cro·coc·cus \,mī-krə-'käk-əs\ *n* : a small spherical bacterium

mi·cro·copy \'mī-krō-,käp-ē\ *n* : a photographic copy in which printed or drawn matter is reduced in size — **microcopy** *vb*

mi·cro·cosm \'mī-krə-,käz-əm\ *n* [Gk *mikros kosmos*] : a little world; *esp* : an individual man or a community that is a miniature universe or a world in itself — **mi·cro·cos·mic** \,mī-krə-'käz-mik\ *adj*

mi·cro·el·e·ment \,mī-krō-'el-ə-mənt\ *n* : TRACE ELEMENT

mi·cro·ev·o·lu·tion \-,ev-ə-'lü-shən, -,ē-və-\ *n* : evolutionary change involving selective accumulation of minute variations

mi·cro·far·ad \,mī-krō-'far-,ad, -'far-əd\ *n* : one millionth of a farad

mi·cro·film \'mī-krə-,film\ *n* : a film bearing a photographic record on a reduced scale of graphic matter (as printing) — **microfilm** *vb*

mi·cro·ga·mete \,mī-krō-gə-'mēt, -'gam-,ēt\ *n* : the smaller and usu. male gamete of an organism with two kinds of gametes

mi·cro·gram \'mī-krə-,gram\ *n* : one millionth of a gram

mi·cro·graph \-,graf\ *n* : a reproduction of the image of an object formed by a microscope

mi·cro·groove \-,grüv\ *n* : a minute closely spaced V-shaped groove used on long-playing phonograph records

mi·crom·e·ter \mī-'kräm-ət-ər\ *n* **1** : an instrument used with a telescope or microscope for measuring very small distances **2** : MICROMETER CALIPER

micrometer caliper *n* : a caliper having a spindle moved by a finely threaded screw for making precise measurements

mi·crom·e·try \mī-'kräm-ə-trē\ *n* : measurement with a micrometer

mi·cro·mi·cro·far·ad \,mī-krō-,mī-krō-'far-,ad, -'far-əd\ *n* : one millionth of a microfarad

micrometer caliper

mi·cro·mi·cron \,mī-krō-'mī-,krän\ *n* : one millionth of a micron

mi·cron \'mī-,krän\ *n* : one thousandth of a millimeter

mi·cron·ize \'mī-krə-,nīz\ *vt* [*micron*] : to pulverize extremely fine

mi·cro·nu·cleus \,mī-krō-'n(y)ü-klē-əs\ *n* : a minute nucleus held to be primarily concerned with reproductive and genetic functions in most ciliated protozoans

mi·cro·nu·tri·ent \-'n(y)ü-trē-ənt\ *n* **1** : TRACE ELEMENT **2** : an organic compound (as a vitamin) essential in minute amounts to the growth and welfare of an animal

mi·cro·or·gan·ism \,mī-krō-'ȯr-gə-,niz-əm\ *n* : an organism (as a bacterium) of microscopic or less than microscopic size

mi·cro·phone \'mī-krə-,fōn\ *n* : an instrument used in increasing or transmitting sounds; *esp* : one used in radio and television to receive sound and convert it into electrical waves

mi·cro·pho·to·graph \,mī-krə-'fōt-ə-,graf\ *n* **1** : a small photograph that is normally magnified for viewing **2** : PHOTOMICROGRAPH

mi·cro·print \'mī-krō-,print\ *n* : a photographic copy of printed or drawn matter in reduced size — **microprint** *vb*

mi·cro·pro·jec·tor \,mī-krō-prə-'jek-tər\ *n* : a projector using a compound microscope to throw a greatly enlarged image of a microscopic object on a screen

mi·cro·pyle \'mī-krə-,pīl\ *n* [Gk *pylē* gate] : a tiny opening in the integument of an ovule of a seed plant through which the pollen tube penetrates to the embryo sac — **mi·cro·py·lar** \,mī-krə-'pī-lər\ *adj*

mi·cro·scope \'mī-krə-,skōp\ *n* **1** : an optical instrument consisting of a lens or a combination of lenses for making enlarged or magnified images of minute objects **2** : an instrument using radiations other than light for making enlarged images of minute objects

mi·cro·scop·ic \,mī-krə-'skäp-ik\ *or* **mi·cro·scop·i·cal** \-'skäp-i-kəl\ *adj* **1** : of, relating to, or conducted with the microscope or microscopy ⟨a *microscopic* examination⟩ **2** : resembling a microscope : able to see very tiny objects ⟨some insects have *microscopic* vision⟩ **3** : able to be seen only through a microscope : very small ⟨a *microscopic* plant⟩ — **mi·cro·scop·i·cal·ly** \-'skäp-i-k(ə-)lē\ *adv*

mi·cros·co·py \mī-'kräs-kə-pē\ *n* : the use of the microscope : investigation with the microscope — **mi·cros·co·pist** \-pəst\ *n*

mi·cro·sec·ond \,mī-krō-'sek-ənd\ *n* : one millionth of a second

mi·cro·some \'mī-krə-,sōm\ *n* : a minute protoplasmic granule held to be a seat of protein formation — **mi·cro·so·mi·al** \,mī-krə-'sō-mē-əl\ *or* **mi·cro·so·mic** \-'sō-mik\ *adj*

mi·cro·spore \'mī-krə-,spō(ə)r, -,spȯ(ə)r\ *n* : a plant spore that produces a male gametophyte — **mi·cro·spor·ic** \,mī-krə-'spōr-ik, -'spȯr-\ *or* **mi·cro·spo·rous** \,mī-krə-'spōr-əs, -'spȯr-; mī-'kräs-pə-rəs\ *adj*

mi·cro·struc·ture \'mī-krō-,strək-chər\ *n* : the microscopic structure of a material

mi·cro·volt \'mī-krə-,vōlt\ *n* : one millionth of a volt

mi·cro·wave \-,wāv\ *n* : a radio wave between 1 and 100 centimeters in wavelength

mic·tu·rate \'mik-chə-,rāt, 'mik-tə-\ *vi* : URINATE

mic·tu·ri·tion \,mik-chə-'rish-ən, ,mik-tə-\ *n* : URINATION

¹mid \(')mid\ *adj* [OE *middle*] **1** : being the part in the middle or midst ⟨in *mid* ocean⟩ ⟨*mid*-August⟩ **2** : occupying a middle position ⟨the *mid* finger⟩ **3** : uttered with the tongue midway between its highest and its lowest elevation ⟨the *mid* vowel *e* in *pet*⟩

²mid \(,)mid\ *prep* : AMID

Mi·das \'mīd-əs\ *n* : a legendary king of Phrygia having the power to turn into gold everything he touched

mid·brain \'mid-,brān\ n : the middle division of the embryonic vertebrate brain or the parts developed from it

mid·day \'mid-,dā, -'dā\ n : the middle part of the day : NOON — **midday** adj

mid·den \'mid-°n\ n : a refuse heap; esp : KITCHEN MIDDEN

¹mid·dle \'mid-°l\ adj [OE middel; akin to E mid] 1 : equally distant from the extremes : CENTRAL ⟨the middle house in the row⟩ 2 : being at neither extreme : INTERMEDIATE ⟨of middle size⟩ 3 cap : constituting an intermediate division or period ⟨Middle Paleozoic⟩ ⟨Middle Dutch⟩ 4 : typically asserting that a person or thing both performs and is affected by the action represented ⟨the middle voice of a Greek verb⟩

²middle n 1 : a middle part, point, or position 2 : WAIST 3 : the position of being among or in the midst of something ⟨in the middle of the battle⟩

middle age n : the period of life from about 40 to about 60 — **mid·dle-aged** \,mid-°l-'ājd\ adj

Middle Ages n pl : the period of European history from about A.D. 500 to about 1500

mid·dle·brow \'mid-°l-,brau\ n : a person who is moderately but not highly cultivated — **middlebrow** adj

middle C n : the note designated by the first ledger line below the treble staff and the first above the bass staff

middle class n : a social class occupying a position between the upper class and the lower class: as a : a medieval class consisting of people (as artisans) between the hereditary nobility and the peasants b : a class between the aristocracy and the working class and consisting chiefly of merchants, manufacturers, and professional men c : a fluid grouping composed principally of business and professional people, bureaucrats, and some farmers and skilled workers sharing common social characteristics and values

middle-class adj : of or relating to the middle class; esp : characterized by a high material standard of living, sexual morality, and respect for property

middle distance n 1 : a part of a picture or scene between the foreground and the background 2 : any footrace distance from 400 meters and 440 yards to 1500 meters and one mile

middle ear n : a small membrane-lined cavity that is separated from the outer ear by the eardrum and that transmits sound waves from the eardrum to the partition between the middle and inner ears through a chain of tiny bones

Middle English n : the English language of the 12th to 15th centuries

Middle French n : the French language of the 14th to 16th centuries

Middle High German n : the High German in use from about 1100 to 1500

mid·dle·man \'mid-°l-,man\ n : an intermediary or agent between two parties; esp : a dealer or agent intermediate between the producer of goods and the retailer or the consumer

mid·dle·most \-,mōst\ adj : MIDMOST

mid·dle-of-the-road \,mid-°l-əv-thə-'rōd\ adj : standing for or following a course of action midway between extremes; esp : being neither liberal nor conservative in politics — **mid·dle-of-the-road·er** \-'rōd-ər\ n

middle term n : the term of a syllogism that occurs in both premises

mid·dle·weight \'mid-°l-,wāt\ n : one of average weight; esp : a boxer weighing more than 147 but not over 160 pounds

¹mid·dling \'mid-liŋ, -lən\ adj : of middle, medium, or moderate size, degree, or quality — **middling** adv

²middling n 1 : any of various commodities of medium quality or size 2 pl : a granular product of grain milling; esp : a wheat milling by-product used in animal feeds

mid·dy \'mid-ē\ n, pl **mid·dies** 1 : MIDSHIPMAN 2 : a loosely fitting blouse for women and children with a collar cut wide and square in the back

midge \'mij\ n [OE mycg] : a very small fly : GNAT

midg·et \'mij-ət\ n : an individual much smaller than the usual or typical — **midget** adj — **midg·et·ism** \-ət-,iz-əm\ n

mid·gut \'mid-,gət\ n : the middle part of the alimentary canal

mid·iron \'mid-,ī(-ə)rn\ n : a golf iron with a slightly angled blade — called also number two iron

mid·land \'mid-lənd, -,land\ n 1 : the interior or central region of a country 2 cap : the dialect of English spoken in parts of New Jersey and Delaware, northern Maryland, central and southern Pennsylvania, Ohio, Indiana, Illinois, the Appalachian Mountain area, West Virginia, Kentucky, and most of Tennessee — **midland** adj, often cap

mid·line \-,līn\ n : a median line

mid·most \'mid-,mōst\ adj 1 : being in the exact middle 2 : INNERMOST — **midmost** adv or n

mid·night \-,nīt\ n : the middle of the night; esp : 12 o'clock at night — **midnight** adj — **mid·night·ly** \-lē\ adv or adj

midnight sun n : the sun above the horizon at midnight in the arctic or antarctic summer

mid·point \'mid-,point\ n : a point at or near the center or middle

mid·rib \-,rib\ n : the central vein of a leaf — see LEAF illustration

mid·riff \-,rif\ n [OE midhrif, fr. midde mid + hrif belly] 1 : DIAPHRAGM 1 2 : the middle region of the human torso

mid·ship·man \'mid-,ship-mən, (')mid-'ship-\ n : a student naval officer ranking above a master chief petty officer and below a warrant officer

mid·ships \'mid-,ships\ adv : AMIDSHIPS

¹midst \'midst\ n 1 : the interior or central part or point : MIDDLE ⟨in the midst of the forest⟩ 2 : a position among the members of a group ⟨a visitor in our midst⟩ 3 : the condition of being surrounded or beset ⟨in the midst of his troubles⟩

²midst \(,)midst\ prep : AMID

mid·stream \'mid-'strēm\ n : the middle of a stream

mid·sum·mer \'mid-'səm-ər\ n 1 : the middle of summer 2 : the summer solstice

¹mid·way \'mid-,wā\ n : an avenue at a fair, carnival, or amusement park for concessions and light amusements

²mid·way \-,wā, -'wā\ adv (or adj) : in the middle of the way or distance : HALFWAY

mid·week \'mid-,wēk\ n : the middle of the week — **midweek** adj — **mid·week·ly** \-lē\ adj or adv

mid·wife \-,wīf\ n [ME, fr. mid with (fr. OE) + wife woman, wife] : a woman who helps other women in childbirth — **mid·wife·ry** \-,wī-f(ə-)rē\ n

mid·win·ter \'mid-'wint-ər\ n 1 : the middle of winter 2 : the winter solstice

mid·year \-,yi(ə)r\ n 1 a : the middle of a calendar year b : the middle of an academic year 2 : a midyear examination — **midyear** adj

mien \'mēn\ n : look, appearance, or bearing esp. as showing mood or personality : DEMEANOR ⟨a man of kindly mien⟩ ⟨a monster of frightful mien⟩

¹miff \'mif\ n 1 : a fit of ill humor 2 : a trivial quarrel

²miff vt : to put into an ill humor : OFFEND ⟨was miffed by his behavior⟩

¹might \(')mīt\ past of MAY — used as an auxiliary verb to express permission ⟨asked if she might leave⟩, probability ⟨she might go, if urged⟩, possibility in the past ⟨thought he might try⟩, or a present condition contrary to fact ⟨if you were older, you might understand⟩

²might \'mīt\ n [OE miht; akin to E may] : power to do something : FORCE ⟨hit the ball with all his might⟩ ⟨the nation's might⟩

might·i·ly \'mīt-°l-ē\ adv 1 : in a mighty manner : VIGOROUSLY 2 : very much

mightn't \'mīt-°nt\ : might not

¹mighty \'mīt-ē\ adj **might·i·er; -est** 1 : having might : POWERFUL, STRONG ⟨a mighty army⟩ 2 : done by might : showing great power ⟨mighty deeds⟩ 3 : great or imposing in size or extent ⟨a mighty famine⟩ — **might·i·ness** n

²mighty adv : VERY, EXTREMELY ⟨a mighty big man⟩

mi·gnon·ette \,min-yə-'net\ n [F] : a garden plant with long spikes of small fragrant greenish white flowers

mi·graine \'mī-,grān\ n [F, fr. LL hemicrania pain on one side of the head, fr. Gk hēmikrania, fr. hēmi- hemi- + kranion cranium] : a condition marked by recurrent severe headache often with nausea and vomiting — **mi·grain·ous** \-,grā-nəs\ adj

mi·grant \'mī-grənt\ *n* : a person, animal, or plant that migrates — **migrant** *adj*

mi·grate \'mī-,grāt\ *vi* [L *migrare*] **1** : to move from one country, place, or locality to another **2** : to pass usu. periodically from one region or climate to another for feeding or breeding **3** : to change position in an organism or substance — **mi·gra·tion** \mī-'grā-shən\ *n* — **mi·gra·tion·al** \-shnəl, -shən-°l\ *adj*

mi·gra·to·ry \'mī-grə-,tōr-ē, -,tȯr-\ *adj* : of, relating to, or characterized by migration ⟨*migratory* workers⟩ ⟨*migratory* birds⟩

mi·ka·do \mə-'käd-ō\ *n, pl* **-dos** [Jap] : an emperor of Japan

mike \'mīk\ *n* : MICROPHONE

mil \'mil\ *n* [L *mille* thousand] : a unit of length equal to ¹⁄₁₀₀₀ inch used esp. for the diameter of wire

mi·la·dy \mil-'ād-ē, mī-'lād-\ *n* [F, fr. E *my lady*] **1** : an Englishwoman of noble or gentle birth **2** : a woman of fashion

milch \'milk, 'milch, 'milks\ *adj* [OE *-milce;* akin to E ²*milk*] : giving milk : kept for milk production ⟨a *milch* cow⟩

mild \'mīld\ *adj* [OE *milde*] **1** : gentle in nature or behavior ⟨a *mild* man⟩ **2** : moderate in action or effect : not strong ⟨a *mild* drug⟩ **3** : TEMPERATE ⟨*mild* weather⟩ — **mild·ly** \'mīl(d)-lē\ *adv* — **mild·ness** \'mīl(d)-nəs\ *n*

¹**mil·dew** \'mil-,d(y)ü\ *n* [OE *meledēaw* honeydew] : a superficial usu. whitish growth produced on organic matter or living plants by fungi; *also* : a fungus producing mildew — **mil·dewy** \-,d(y)ü-ē\ *adj*

²**mildew** *vb* : to affect with or become affected with mildew

mile \'mīl\ *n* [OE *mīl,* fr. L *milia* miles, short for *milia passuum,* lit., thousands of paces] **1** : a unit of measure equal to 5280 feet — called also *statute mile;* see MEASURE table **2** : a unit of measure equal to about 6076 feet — called also *geographical mile, nautical mile*

mile·age \'mī-lij\ *n* **1** : an allowance for traveling expenses at a certain rate per mile **2** : distance or distance covered in miles **3 a** : the number of miles that something (as a car or tire) will travel before wearing out **b** : USEFULNESS, PROFIT

mile·post \'mīl-,pōst\ *n* : a post indicating the distance in miles to a stated place

mil·er \'mī-lər\ *n* : a man or a horse that competes in mile races

mile·stone \'mīl-,stōn\ *n* **1** : a stone serving as a milepost **2** : an important point in progress or development

mil·foil \'mil-,fȯil\ *n* **1** : YARROW **2** : WATER MILFOIL

mil·i·ar·ia \,mil-ē-'ar-ē-ə, -'er-\ *n* : PRICKLY HEAT

mi·lieu \mēl-'yə(r), -'yü\ *n* [F] : ENVIRONMENT, SETTING

mil·i·tant \'mil-ə-tənt\ *adj* **1** : engaged in warfare : FIGHTING **2** : aggressively active esp. in a cause ⟨a *militant* conservationist⟩ — **mil·i·tan·cy** \-tən-sē\ *n* — **militant** *n* — **mil·i·tant·ly** *adv* — **mil·i·tant·ness** *n*

mil·i·tar·i·ly \,mil-ə-'ter-ə-lē\ *adv* **1** : in a military manner **2** : from a military standpoint

mil·i·ta·rism \'mil-ə-tə-,riz-əm\ *n* **1 a** : control or domination by a military class **b** : exaltation of military virtues and ideals **2** : a policy of aggressive military preparedness — **mil·i·ta·rist** \-rəst\ *n* — **mil·i·ta·ris·tic** \,mil-ə-tə-'ris-tik\ *adj* — **mil·i·ta·ris·ti·cal·ly** \-'ris-ti-k(ə-)lē\ *adv*

mil·i·ta·rize \'mil-ə-tə-,rīz\ *vt* **1** : to equip with military forces and defenses **2** : to give a military character to — **mil·i·ta·ri·za·tion** \,mil-ə-t(ə-)rə-'zā-shən\ *n*

¹**mil·i·tary** \'mil-ə-,ter-ē\ *adj* [MF *militaire,* fr. L *militaris, militis, miles* soldier] **1** : of, relating to, or characteristic of soldiers, arms, or war ⟨*military* drill⟩ ⟨*military* discipline⟩ **2** : carried on or supported by armed force ⟨*military* government⟩ ⟨*military* dictatorship⟩ **3** : of or relating to the army ⟨*military* and naval affairs⟩ **syn** see MARTIAL

²**military** *n, pl* **military 1** : ARMED FORCES **2** : military persons; *esp* : army officers

military police *n* : a branch of an army that exercises guard and police functions

mil·i·tate \'mil-ə-,tāt\ *vi* [L *militare* to engage in warfare, fr. *milit-, miles* soldier] : to have weight or effect : OPERATE ⟨factors *militating* against the success of an enterprise⟩

mi·li·tia \mə-'lish-ə\ *n* : a body of citizens with some

military training who are called to active duty only in an emergency — **mi·li·tia·man** \-mən\ *n*

¹**milk** \'milk\ *n* [OE *meolc, milc*] **1** : a fluid secreted by the mammary glands of females for the nourishment of their young **2** : a liquid (as a plant juice) resembling milk

²**milk** *vb* **1** : to draw milk from the breasts or udder of **2** : to draw or yield milk **3** : to draw something from as if by milking; *esp* : to draw unreasonable or excessive profit or advantage from ⟨*milk* a business⟩ — **milk·er** *n*

milk-liv·ered \'milk-'liv-ərd\ *adj* : COWARDLY, TIMOROUS

milk·maid \'milk-,mād\ *n* : DAIRYMAID

milk·man \-,man, -mən\ *n* : a man who sells or delivers milk

milk of magnesia : a milk-white liquid preparation of magnesium in water used as a laxative and as a medicine to counteract acidity

milk shake *n* : a drink made of milk, a flavoring syrup, and sometimes ice cream shaken or mixed thoroughly

milk snake *n* : a common harmless gray or tan snake with black-bordered blotches and an arrow-shaped spot on the head

milk·sop \'milk-,säp\ *n* : a timid unmanly man or boy : MOLLYCODDLE

milk sugar *n* : LACTOSE

milk tooth *n* : one of the first temporary teeth of a young mammal that in man number 20

milk·weed \'milk-,wēd\ *n* : any of various related herbs and shrubs with milky juice and flowers usu. in dense clusters

milky \'mil-kē\ *adj* **milk·i·er; -est 1** : resembling milk in color or consistency **2** : MILD, TIMID **3** : consisting of, containing, or full of milk — **milk·i·ness** *n*

milky disease *n* : a destructive bacterial disease of some beetle larvae used esp. in the control of Japanese beetles

Milky Way *n* **1** : a broad luminous irregular band of light that stretches across the sky and is caused by the light of a vast multitude of faint stars **2** : MILKY WAY GALAXY **3** : GALAXY

Milky Way galaxy *n* : the galaxy of which the sun and the solar system are a part and which contains the myriads of stars that comprise the Milky Way

¹**mill** \'mil\ *n* [OE *mylen,* fr. LL *molinum, molina,* fr. L *mola* millstone] **1** : a building with machinery for grinding grain into flour **2** : a machine used in treating (as by grinding, crushing, stamping, cutting, or finishing) raw material **3** : a building or group of buildings with machinery for manufacturing

²**mill** *vb* **1** : to subject to an operation or process in a mill: as **a** : to grind into flour, meal, or powder **b** : to shape or dress by means of a rotary cutter **c** : to mix and condition (as rubber) by passing between rotating rolls **2** : to give a raised rim to (a coin) **3** : to hit out hard with the fists : SLUG **4** : to move about in a circle or in a disorderly eddying mass **5** : to undergo milling

³**mill** *n* [L *mille* thousand] : one tenth of a cent

mill·dam \'mil-,dam\ *n* : a dam to make a millpond; *also* : MILLPOND

mil·le·nar·i·an \,mil-ə-'ner-ē-ən\ *adj* **1** : of or relating to 1000 years **2** : of or relating to belief in the millennium — **millenarian** *n* — **mil·le·nar·i·an·ism** \-ē-ə-,niz-əm\ *n*

¹**mil·le·nary** \'mil-ə-,ner-ē, mə-'len-ə-rē\ *n, pl* **-nar·ies 1** : a thousand units or things **2** : 1000 years : MILLENNIUM

²**millenary** *adj* : relating to or consisting of 1000

mil·len·ni·al·ism \mə-'len-ē-ə-,liz-əm\ *n* : MILLENARIANISM — **mil·len·ni·al·ist** \-ē-ə-ləst\ *n*

mil·len·ni·um \mə-'len-ē-əm\ *n, pl* **-nia** \-ē-ə\ *or* **-niums** [NL, fr. L *mille* thousand + *-ennium* (as in *biennium*)] **1 a** : a period of 1000 years **b** : a 1000th anniversary or its celebration **2 a** : the thousand years mentioned in Revelation 20 during which holiness is to prevail and Christ is to reign on earth **b** : a period of great happiness or of perfection in human existence — **mil·len·ni·al** \-ē-əl\ *adj*

mill·er \'mil-ər\ *n* **1** : one that operates a mill; *esp* : one that grinds grain into flour **2** : a moth whose wings are covered with powdery dust

mil·let \'mil-ət\ *n* [MF *milet,* dim. of *mil* millet, fr. L *milium*] **1** : any of several small-seeded annual cereal and forage grasses; *esp* : one with small shiny whitish seeds **2** : the seed of a millet

milli- *comb form* [L *mille* thousand] **:** thousandth ⟨*milli-ampere*⟩

mil·li·am·pere \,mil-ē-'am-,pi(ə)r\ *n* **:** one thousandth of an ampere

mil·liard \'mil-,yärd, 'mil-ē-,ärd\ *n, Brit* **:** a thousand millions — see NUMBER table

mil·li·bar \'mil-ə,bär\ *n* [*bar* unit of pressure equal to 1,000,000 dynes per sq. cm., fr. Gk *baros* weight] **:** a unit used in measuring atmospheric pressure and in reading the barometer equal to a force of 1000 dynes acting on a square centimeter ⟨an atmospheric pressure of 1013 *millibars* is commonly referred to as a standard⟩

mil·li·gram \'mil-ə,gram\ *n* **:** a weight equal to ⅟₁₀₀₀ gram — see METRIC SYSTEM table

mil·li·li·ter \'mil-ə-,lēt-ər\ *n* **:** a measure of capacity equal to ⅟₁₀₀₀ liter — see METRIC SYSTEM table

mil·li·me·ter \'mil-ə-,mēt-ər\ *n* **:** a measure of length equal to ⅟₁₀₀₀ meter — see METRIC SYSTEM table

mil·li·mi·cron \'mil-ə-'mī-,krän\ *n* **:** a unit of length equal to ⅟₁₀₀₀ micron or one millionth of a millimeter

mil·li·ner \'mil-ə-nər\ *n* [irreg. fr. *Milan,* Italy; so called fr. the importation of women's finery into England from Italy in the 16th century] **:** a person who designs, makes, trims, or sells women's hats

mil·li·nery \'mil-ə-,ner-ē\ *n* **1 :** women's hats **2 :** the business or work of a milliner

mill·ing \'mil-iŋ\ *n* **:** a corrugated edge on a coin

milling machine *n* **:** a machine tool on which work usu. of metal secured to a carriage is shaped by being fed against rotating cutters

mil·lion \'mil-yən\ *n, pl* **millions** *or* **million** [MF *milion,* fr. It *milione,* fr. aug. of *mille* thousand, fr. L] **1** — see NUMBER table **2 :** a very large or indefinitely great number ⟨*millions* of mosquitoes⟩ — **million** *adj* — **mil·lionth** \-yən(t)th\ *adj or n*

mil·lion·aire \,mil-yə-'na(ə)r, -'ne(ə)r, 'mil-yə-,\ *n* **:** one whose wealth is estimated at a million or more (as of dollars)

mil·li·pede *or* **mil·le·pede** \'mil-ə-,pēd\ *n* **:** any of numerous myriopods (class Diplopoda) having a long segmented body with a hard covering, two pairs of legs on most apparent segments, and no poison fangs — compare CENTIPEDE

millipede

mil·li·sec·ond \'mil-ə-,sek-ənd\ *n* **:** one thousandth of a second

mil·li·volt \-,vōlt\ *n* **:** one thousandth of a volt

mill·pond \'mil-,pänd\ *n* **:** a pond produced by damming a stream to produce a head of water for operating a mill

mill·race \-,rās\ *n* **:** a canal in which water flows to and from a mill wheel; *also* **:** the current that drives the wheel

mill·stone \-,stōn\ *n* **1 :** either of two circular stones used for grinding a substance (as grain) **2 a :** something that grinds or crushes **b :** a heavy burden

mill·stream \-,strēm\ *n* **1 :** a stream whose flow is utilized to run a mill **2 :** the stream in a millrace

mill wheel *n* **:** a waterwheel that drives a mill

mill·wright \'mil-,rīt\ *n* **:** one whose occupation is planning and building mills or setting up their machinery

mi·lo \'mī-lō\ *n* [of Bantu origin] **:** a small usu. early and drought-resistant grain sorghum

mi·lord \mil-'ó(ə)r, -'órd\ *n* **:** an Englishman of noble or gentle birth

milt \'milt\ *n* **:** the male reproductive glands of fishes when filled with secretion; *also* **:** the secretion itself

Mil·ton·ic \mil-'tän-ik\ *or* **Mil·to·ni·an** \mil-'tō-nē-ən\ *adj* **:** of, relating to, or characteristic of John Milton or his work

¹mime \'mīm, 'mēm\ *n* [Gk *mimos*] **1 :** MIMIC 2 **2 a :** an ancient play or skit representing scenes from life usu. in a ridiculous manner **b :** an actor in such a performance **3 :** the art of portraying a character or of narration by body movement **:** PANTOMIME

²mime *vb* **1 :** to act a part with mimic gesture and action usu. without words **2 :** to imitate closely **:** MIMIC **3 :** to act out in the manner of a mime — **mim·er** *n*

mim·e·o·graph \'mim-ē-ə-,graf\ *n* **:** a machine for making copies of typewritten or written matter by means of a stencil — **mimeograph** *vb*

mi·me·sis \mə-'mē-səs, mī-'mē-\ *n* **:** IMITATION, MIMICRY

mi·met·ic \-'met-ik\ *adj* **1 :** IMITATIVE **2 :** relating to, characterized by, or exhibiting mimicry ⟨*mimetic* coloring of a butterfly⟩ — **mi·met·i·cal·ly** \-'met-i-k(ə-)lē\ *adv*

¹mim·ic \'mim-ik\ *adj* **1 a :** IMITATIVE **b :** IMITATION, MOCK ⟨*mimic* battle⟩ **2 :** of or relating to mime or mimicry

²mimic *n* **1 :** MIME 2b **2 :** one that mimics

³mimic *vt* **mim·icked** \-ikt\; **mim·ick·ing 1 :** to imitate closely **:** APE **2 :** to ridicule by imitation **3 :** SIMULATE **4 :** to resemble by biological mimicry **syn** see IMITATE

mim·ic·ry \'mim-i-krē\ *n, pl* **-ries 1 :** the action, art, or an instance of mimicking **2 :** a superficial resemblance of one organism to another or to a natural objects among which it lives that secures it concealment, protection, or other advantage

mi·mo·sa \mə-'mō-sə, mī-, -zə\ *n* [L *mimus* mime, fr. Gk *mimos*] **:** any of a genus of leguminous trees, shrubs, and herbs of warm regions with small white or pink flowers in ball-shaped heads

mi·na \'mī-nə\ *n* [L, fr. Gk *mna,* of Sem origin] **:** an ancient unit of weight and value equal to ⅟₆₀ talent

min·a·ret \,min-ə-'ret\ *n* [F, fr. Turk *minare,* fr. Arabic *manārah* lighthouse] **:** a tall slender tower of a mosque from a balcony of which the people are called to prayer

min·a·to·ry \'min-ə-,tōr-ē, 'mī-nə-, -,tór-\ *adj* [L *minari* to threaten] **:** THREATENING, MENACING

¹mince \'min(t)s\ *vb* [MF *mincer,* fr. L *minutia* smallness, fr. *minutus* minute] **1 :** to cut into very small pieces **:** HASH **2 :** to utter with affectation **3 a** *archaic* **:** MINIMIZE **b :** to restrain (words) within the bounds of politeness or decorum **4 :** to walk with short steps in a prim affected manner — **minc·er** *n*

²mince *n* **:** small bits into which something is chopped; *esp* **:** MINCEMEAT

mince·meat \'min(t)s-,mēt\ *n* **1 :** minced meat **2 :** a finely chopped mixture of ingredients (as raisins, apples, or spices) with or without meat

mince pie *n* **:** a pie made of mincemeat

minc·ing \'min(t)-siŋ\ *adj* **:** affectedly dainty or delicate — **minc·ing·ly** \-siŋ-lē\ *adv*

¹mind \'mīnd\ *n* [OE *gemynd*] **1 :** MEMORY, RECOLLECTION ⟨out of sight, out of *mind*⟩ **2 :** the element or complex of elements in an individual that feels, perceives, thinks, wills, and esp. reasons **3 :** INTENTION, DESIRE ⟨changed his *mind*⟩ **4 :** the normal or healthy condition of the mental faculties ⟨lost her *mind*⟩ **5 :** OPINION, VIEW ⟨spoke his *mind*⟩ **6 :** CHOICE, LIKING ⟨the decision was not at all to his *mind*⟩

²mind *vb* **1** *chiefly dial* **:** REMIND **2** *chiefly dial* **:** REMEMBER **3 a :** to attend to closely ⟨*minds* his own business⟩ **b :** to pay attention to **:** HEED ⟨*mind* what you're doing⟩ **c :** OBEY ⟨*minds* her parents⟩ **4 a :** NOTICE **b** *chiefly dial* **:** INTEND **5 a :** to be bothered about ⟨never *mind* your mistake⟩ **b :** DISLIKE ⟨doesn't *mind* the cold⟩ **6 a :** to be careful **:** SEE ⟨*mind* you finish it⟩ **b :** to be cautious about **:** watch out for ⟨*mind* the broken rung⟩ **7 :** to take charge of **:** TEND ⟨*minded* the children⟩ — **mind·er** *n*

mind·ed \'mīn-dəd\ *adj* **1 :** having a specified kind of mind — usu. used in combination ⟨narrow-*minded*⟩ **2 :** DISPOSED, INCLINED

mind·ful \'mīn(d)-fəl\ *adj* **:** bearing in mind **:** AWARE, HEEDFUL — **mind·ful·ly** \-fə-lē\ *adv* — **mind·ful·ness** *n*

mind·less \'mīn-(d)ləs\ *adj* **:** lacking mind or consciousness; *esp* **:** UNINTELLIGENT — **mind·less·ly** *adv* — **mind·less·ness** *n*

mind reader *n* **:** one who professes or is held to be able to perceive another's thought without normal means of communication — **mind reading** *n*

mind's eye *n* **:** the mental faculty of conceiving imaginary or recollected scenes

¹mine \(')mīn\ *adj* [OE *mīn* my] *archaic* **:** MY — used before a word beginning with a vowel or *h* ⟨*mine* eyes⟩ ⟨*mine* host⟩ or sometimes as a modifier of a preceding noun ⟨mother *mine*⟩

²mine \'mīn\ *pron* **:** my one **:** my ones — used without a following noun as a pronoun equivalent in meaning to the adjective *my*

³mine \'mīn\ *n* [MF] **1 :** a pit or tunnel from which minerals (as coal, gold, or diamonds) are taken **2 :** a deposit of ore **3** : a subterranean passage under an enemy position **4 a** : a charge buried in the ground and set to explode when disturbed (as by an enemy soldier) **b** : an explosive charge placed in a case and sunk in the water to sink enemy ships **5** : a rich source of supply

⁴mine \'mīn\ *vb* **1** : to dig a mine **2** : to obtain from a mine ⟨*mine* coal⟩ **3** : to work in a mine **4 a** : to burrow in the earth : dig or form mines under a place **b** : to lay military mines in or under ⟨*mine* a harbor⟩

mine·lay·er \'mīn-,lā-ər\ *n* : a naval vessel for laying underwater mines

min·er \'mī-nər\ *n* : one that mines; *esp* : a person who works in a mine

¹min·er·al \'min-(ə-)rəl\ *n* [ML *minerale*, fr. neuter of *mineralis* of a mine, fr. *minera* ore, mine, fr. OF *miniere*, fr. *mine* mine] **1** : a naturally occurring crystalline element or compound (as diamond or quartz) that has a definite chemical composition and results from processes other than those of plants and animals ⟨most rocks are composed of more than one *mineral*⟩ **2** : any of various naturally occurring substances (as ore, coal, salt, sand, stone, petroleum, natural gas, or water) obtained for man's use usu. from the ground **3 a** : a natural substance that is neither plant nor animal **b** : an inorganic substance

²mineral *adj* **1** : of, relating to, or having the characteristics of a mineral : INORGANIC **2** : containing mineral salts or gases

min·er·al·ize \'min-(ə-)rə-,līz\ *vb* **1** : to transform a metal into an ore **2** : PETRIFY ⟨*mineralized* bones⟩ **3 a** : to impregnate or supply with minerals **b** : to change into mineral form — **min·er·al·i·za·tion** \,min-(ə-)rə-lə-'zā-shən\ *n*

min·er·al·o·gy \,min-ə-'räl-ə-jē, -'ral-\ *n* : a science that collects and studies facts about minerals — **min·er·al·og·i·cal** \,min-(ə-)rə-'läj-i-kəl\ *adj* — **min·er·al·o·gist** \,min-ə-'räl-ə-jəst, -'ral-\ *n*

mineral oil *n* **1** : an oil (as petroleum) of mineral origin **2** : a refined petroleum oil having no color, odor, or taste that is used as a laxative

mineral water *n* : water naturally or artificially impregnated with mineral salts or gases

mineral wool *n* : any of various lightweight materials that resemble wool in texture, are made from slag, rock, or glass, and are used esp. in heat and sound insulation

Mi·ner·va \mə-'nər-və\ *n* : the Roman goddess of wisdom

min·e·stro·ne \,min-ə-'strō-nē, -'strōn\ *n* [It] : a rich thick vegetable soup with dried beans, macaroni, vermicelli, or similar ingredients

mine·sweep·er \'mīn-,swē-pər\ *n* : a warship designed for removing or neutralizing mines by dragging

Ming \'miŋ\ *n* : a Chinese dynasty dated 1368–1644 and noted for restoration of earlier traditions and in the arts for perfection of established techniques

min·gle \'miŋ-gəl\ *vb* **min·gled; min·gling** \-g(ə-)liŋ\ [ME *menglen*, freq. of *mengen* to mix, fr. OE *mengan*] **1 a** : to bring or combine together or with something else : MIX ⟨*mingled* fact with fancy⟩ **b** : to become mingled **2** : to come in contact : ASSOCIATE ⟨*mingles* with all sorts of people⟩ **syn** see MIX

ming tree \'miŋ-\ *n* : a dwarfed usu. evergreen tree grown in a pot; *also* : an artificial imitation of this made from plant materials

mini- *comb form* [*miniature*] : miniature : of small dimensions ⟨*minibike*⟩ ⟨*minicomputer*⟩

¹min·i·a·ture \'min-ē-ə-,chur, 'min-i-,chur, -chər\ *n* [It *miniatura* illumination of a manuscript, picture in an illuminated manuscript, fr. ML, fr. L *miniare* to color with red lead, fr. *minium* red lead] **1** : something much smaller than the usual size; *esp* : a copy on a much reduced scale **2** : a painting in an illuminated book or manuscript **3** : the art of painting miniatures **4** : a very small portrait or painting (as on ivory or metal) — **min·i·a·tur·ist** \-,chùr-əst\ *n*

²miniature *adj* : very small : represented on a small scale **syn** see LESSEN

min·i·a·tur·ize \-,chùr-,īz, -chər-\ *vt* : to design or construct in small size — **min·i·a·tur·i·za·tion** \,min-ē-ə-,chùr-ə-'zā-shən, ,min-i-,chùr-, -chər-\ *n*

min·i·fy \'min-ə-,fī\ *vt* **-fied; -fy·ing** : to make small or smaller : LESSEN

min·im \'min-əm\ *n* [L *minimus* least] **1** : HALF NOTE **2** : something very minute **3** : a single downward stroke in penmanship **4** : either of two units of liquid capacity equal to ⅟₆₀ fluidram — see MEASURE table

min·i·mal \'min-ə-məl\ *adj* : relating to or being a minimum : LEAST — **min·i·mal·ly** \-mə-lē\ *adv*

min·i·mize \'min-ə-,mīz\ *vt* **1** : to make as small as possible : reduce to a minimum ⟨*minimize* the chance of error⟩ **2 a** : to place a low estimate on ⟨*minimized* his losses⟩ **b** : BELITTLE, DISPARAGE ⟨*minimize* the achievements of a rival⟩ — **min·i·mi·za·tion** \,min-ə-mə-'zā-shən\ *n*

syn MINIMIZE and DIMINISH both mean to reduce in size, amount, or rate, but MINIMIZE stresses the positive attainment of the smallest possible amount or lowest possible rate, DIMINISH implies only the fact of being less than or lower than an earlier or original amount or rate

min·i·mum \'min-ə-məm\ *n, pl* **-ma** \-mə\ *or* **-mums** [L, neuter of *minimus*, superlative of *minor* smaller, less] **1** : the least quantity assignable, admissible, or possible **2** : the lowest degree or amount reached or recorded — **minimum** *adj*

minimum wage *n* : a wage fixed by legal authority or by contract as the least that will provide the minimum standard of living necessary for employee health, well-being, and efficiency

min·ing \'mī-niŋ\ *n* : the process or business of working mines

min·ion \'min-yən\ *n* [MF *mignon* darling] **1** : a servile dependent : CREATURE **3 2** : FAVORITE, IDOL **3** : a subordinate official

min·is·cule \'min-əs-,kyül\ *var of* MINUSCULE

¹min·is·ter \'min-ə-stər\ *n* [L, servant, fr. *minus* less] **1** : AGENT **2 a** : one officiating or assisting at the administration of a sacrament **b** : a Protestant clergyman **c** : a person exercising the functions of a clergyman **3** : a high government official entrusted with the management of a division of governmental activities **4 a** : a diplomatic representative (as an ambassador) accredited to the court or seat of government of a foreign state **b** : a diplomatic representative ranking below an ambassador and usu. accredited to states of less importance

²minister *vi* **min·is·tered; min·is·ter·ing** \-st(ə-)riŋ\ : to give aid : SERVE ⟨*minister* to the sick⟩

min·is·te·ri·al \,min-ə-'stir-ē-əl\ *adj* **1** : of or relating to a minister or ministry **2 a** : prescribed by law as part of the duties of an administrative office **b** : done in obedience to a legal order without exercise of personal judgment or discretion — **min·is·te·ri·al·ly** \-ē-ə-lē\ *adv*

min·is·trant \'min-ə-strənt\ *adj* : serving as a minister — **ministrant** *n*

min·is·tra·tion \,min-ə-'strā-shən\ *n* : the act or process of ministering

min·is·try \'min-ə-strē\ *n, pl* **-tries 1** : MINISTRATION **2** : the office, duties, or functions of a minister ⟨study for the *ministry*⟩ **3** : the body of ministers of religion : CLERGY **4** : AGENCY 2, INSTRUMENTALITY **5** : the period of service or office of a minister or ministry **6** *often cap* **a** : the body of ministers governing a nation or state from which a smaller cabinet is sometimes selected ⟨a responsible *ministry*⟩ **b** : the group of ministers constituting a cabinet **7 a** : a government department presided over by a minister ⟨*ministry* of foreign affairs⟩ **b** : the building in which the business of a ministry is transacted

min·i·ver \'min-ə-vər\ *n* [OF *menu vair* small fur] : a white fur worn orig. by medieval nobles and now used chiefly for robes of state

mink \'miŋk\ *n, pl* **mink** *or* **minks** \'miŋ(k)s\ [ME] : any of several slender-bodied mammals resembling the related weasels, having partially webbed feet and a somewhat bushy tail, and living near water; *also* : the soft typically dark brown fur of this animal

min·ne·sing·er \'min-i-,siŋ-ər, 'min-ə-,ziŋ-\ *n* [G, fr. *minne* love + *singer* singer] : one of a class of German lyric poets and musicians of the 12th to the 14th centuries

min·now \'min-ō\ *n, pl* **minnows** *or* **minnow** [ME *menawe*] : any of various small freshwater bottom-feeding fish (as the dace or shiner) related to the carps; *also* : any of various similar small fishes

¹Mi·no·an \mə-'nō-ən, mī-\ *adj* [L *minous*, fr. Gk *minōios*, fr. *Minōs* Minos] : of or relating to a Bronze Age culture centered in Crete (3000 B.C.–1100 B.C.)

²Minoan *n* : a native or inhabitant of ancient Crete

---

j joke; **ŋ** sing; **ō** flow; **ȯ** flaw; **ȯi** coin; **th** thin; **th̲** this; **ü** loot; **u̇** foot; **y** yet; **yü** few; **yu̇** furious; **zh** vision

¹mi·nor \'mī-nər\ *adj* [L, smaller, lesser] **1 a :** inferior in dignity, rank, or importance ⟨a *minor* poet⟩ **b :** inferior in number, quantity, or extent ⟨received a *minor* share of the blame⟩ **2 :** not having attained majority **3 a :** having the 3d, 6th, and sometimes the 7th degrees lowered a semitone ⟨*minor* scale⟩ **b :** based on a minor scale ⟨*minor* key⟩ **c :** less by a semitone than the corresponding major interval ⟨*minor* third⟩ **4 :** not involving risk to life **:** not serious ⟨*minor* illness⟩ **5 :** of or relating to an academic minor

²minor *n* **1 :** a person who has not attained majority **2 :** a minor musical interval, scale, key, or mode **3 :** an academic subject chosen by a student as a secondary field of specialization; *also* **:** a student specializing in such a field

³minor *vi* **:** to pursue an academic minor

mi·nor·i·ty \mə-'nȯr-ət-ē, mī-, -'när-\ *n, pl* **-ties 1 a :** the period before attainment of majority **b :** the state of being a legal minor **2 :** the smaller in number of two groups constituting a whole; *esp* **:** a group having less than the number of votes necessary for control **3 :** a part of a population differing from other groups in some characteristics and often subjected to differential treatment

minor league *n* **:** a league of professional clubs in a sport (as baseball) other than the recognized major leagues

minor order *n* **:** one of the four lower clerical orders; *esp* **:** one conferred on candidates for the Roman Catholic priesthood for nominal service as a doorkeeper, lector, exorcist, or acolyte

minor party *n* **:** a political party whose strength in elections is so small as to prevent its gaining control of a government except in rare and exceptional circumstances

minor premise *n* **:** the premise of a syllogism containing the term that forms the subject of the conclusion

minor seminary *n* **:** a Roman Catholic seminary giving all or part of high school and junior college training

minor suit *n* **:** clubs or diamonds in bridge

Mi·nos \'mī-nəs\ *n* **:** a king and lawgiver of Crete, son of Zeus and Europa, and after death a judge in Hades

Min·o·taur \'min-ə-,tȯ(ə)r, 'mī-nə-\ *n* [Gk *minōtauros*, fr. *Minōs* Minos + *tauros* bull] **:** a monster of Greek legend shaped half like a man and half like a bull and given a periodical tribute of seven youths and seven maidens until slain by Theseus

min·ster \'min(t)-stər\ *n* [OE *mynster* monastery, minster, fr. LL *monasterium* monastery] **1 :** a church attached to a monastery **2 :** a large or important church

min·strel \'min(t)-strəl\ *n* [OF *menestrel* servant, minstrel, fr. L *ministerium* service, fr. *minister* servant] **1 :** a medieval musical entertainer; *esp* **:** a singer of verses to the accompaniment of a harp **2 a :** MUSICIAN **b :** POET **3 a :** one of a troupe of performers typically giving a program of Negro melodies and jokes and usu. blacked in imitation of Negroes **b :** a performance by a troupe of minstrels

min·strel·sy \-sē\ *n, pl* **-sies 1 :** the singing and playing of a minstrel **2 :** a body of minstrels **3 :** a collection of songs or verse

¹mint \'mint\ *n* [OE *mynet* coin, fr. L *moneta* mint, coin, fr. *Moneta*, epithet of Juno; so called fr. the Roman use of the temple of Juno Moneta as a mint] **1 :** a place where coins are made **2 :** a place where something is manufactured **3 :** a vast sum or amount

²mint *vt* **1 a :** to make (money) out of metal **:** COIN **b :** to convert (a metal) into coin **2 :** FABRICATE, INVENT — **mint·er** *n*

³mint *adj* **:** unmarred as if fresh from a mint ⟨*mint* coins⟩

⁴mint *n* [OE *minte*, fr. L *mentha*] **1 :** any of a family of herbs and shrubs (as basil, rosemary, and salvia) with square stems, opposite aromatic leaves, commonly 2-lipped flowers; *esp* **:** one (as peppermint or spearmint) that is fragrant and yields a flavoring oil **2 :** a piece of candy flavored with mint

mint·age \'mint-ij\ *n* **1 :** the action or process of minting coins **2 :** coins produced by minting **3 :** the cost of manufacturing coins

min·u·end \'min-yə-,wend\ *n* [L *minuendus* to be lessened, fr. *minuere* to lessen] **:** a number from which another number is to be subtracted — compare SUBTRAHEND

min·u·et \,min-yə-'wet\ *n* [F *menuet*, fr. OF *menu* small, fr. L *minutus*] **1 :** a slow graceful dance consisting of

forward balancing, bowing, and toe pointing **2 :** music for or in the rhythm of a minuet

¹mi·nus \'mī-nəs\ *prep* [L *minus*, adv., less, fr. neuter of *minor*] **1 :** diminished by ⟨seven *minus* four is three⟩ **2 :** deprived of **:** WITHOUT ⟨*minus* his hat⟩

²minus *n* **1 :** a negative quantity **2 :** DEFICIENCY, DEFECT

³minus *adj* **1 :** algebraically negative ⟨*minus* quantity⟩ **2 :** falling low in a specified range ⟨a grade of C *minus*⟩

¹min·us·cule \'min-əs-,kyül, min-'əs-\ *n* **:** a lowercase letter

²minuscule *adj* **:** very small

minus sign *n* **:** a sign — used esp. in mathematics to indicate subtraction (as in $8 - 6 = 2$) or a negative quantity (as in $-10°$)

¹min·ute \'min-ət\ *n* [LL *minuta*, fr. L, fem. of *minutus*, adj., minute] **1 :** the 60th part of an hour of time or of a degree **2 :** the distance one can cover in a minute ⟨10 *minutes* from home to office⟩ **3 :** MOMENT **4 a :** a brief note of instructions or recommendations written on a document **b :** an official memorandum authorizing or recommending some action **5** *pl* **:** a series of brief notes taken to provide a record of the proceedings of a meeting

²minute *vt* **1 a :** to write in or in the form of a minute ⟨*minuted* instructions⟩ **b :** to write a minute on ⟨*minute* a dispatch⟩ **2 :** to make notes or a brief summary of ⟨*minute* a meeting⟩

³mi·nute \mī-'n(y)üt, mə-\ *adj* [L *minutus*, fr. pp. of *minuere* to lessen, make small] **1 :** very small **:** INFINITESIMAL **2 :** of small importance **:** TRIFLING **3 :** marked by close attention to details ⟨*minute* description⟩ **syn** see CIRCUMSTANTIAL — **mi·nute·ness** *n*

mi·nute·ly \mī-'n(y)üt-lē, mə-\ *adv* **1 :** into very small pieces **2 :** in a minute manner or degree

min·ute·man \'min-ət-,man\ *n* **:** a member of a group of armed men pledged to take the field at a minute's notice during and immediately before the American Revolution

mi·nu·tia \mə-'n(y)ü-sh(ē-)ə, mī-\ *n, pl* **-ti·ae** \-shē-,ē, -shē-,ī\ [L, fr. *minutus* minute] **:** a minute or minor detail — usu. used in pl.

minx \'min(k)s\ *n* **1 :** a pert girl **2** *obs* **:** a wanton woman

Mio·cene \'mī-ə-,sēn\ *n* [Gk *meiōn* less + *kainos* new] **:** the epoch of the Tertiary between the Oligocene and Pliocene; *also* **:** the corresponding system of rocks — **Miocene** *adj*

mir \'mi(ə)r\ *n* [Russ] **:** a village community common in czarist Russia in which the land was owned jointly by the peasants and cultivable land was redistributed among the individual families at regular intervals

mir·a·cle \'mir-i-kəl\ *n* [L *miraculum*, fr. *mirari* to wonder at] **1 :** an extraordinary event taken to manifest a supernatural work of God **2 :** an extremely outstanding or unusual event, thing, or accomplishment

miracle play *n* **:** a medieval play presenting episodes from the life of a miracle-working saint or martyr

mi·rac·u·lous \mə-'rak-yə-ləs\ *adj* **1 :** of the nature of a miracle **:** SUPERNATURAL **2 :** resembling a miracle **:** MARVELOUS **3 :** working or able to work miracles — **mi·rac·u·lous·ly** *adv* — **mi·rac·u·lous·ness** *n*

mi·rage \mə-'räzh\ *n* [F, fr. *mirer* to look at] **1 :** an optical effect that sometimes seen at sea, in the desert, or over a hot pavement, that may have the appearance of a pool of water or a mirror in which distant objects are seen inverted, and that is caused by the bending or reflection of rays of light by a layer of heated air of varying density **2 :** something illusory like a mirage

¹mire \'mī(ə)r\ *n* [ON *mȳrr*] **1 :** MARSH, BOG **2 :** heavy often deep mud, slush, or dirt

²mire *vb* **1 a :** to sink or stick fast in mire **b :** ENTANGLE, INVOLVE **2 :** to soil with mud, slush, or dirt

mirk, mirky *var of* MURK, MURKY

¹mir·ror \'mir-ər\ *n* [OF *miror*, fr. *mirer* to look at, fr. L *mirari* to wonder at] **1 :** a glass backed with a reflecting substance (as mercury) **2 :** a smooth or polished surface that reflects an image **3 :** something that reflects a true likeness or gives a true description **:** PATTERN, MODEL

²mirror *vt* **:** to reflect in or as if in a mirror

mirth \'mərth\ *n* [OE *myrgth*, fr. *myrge* merry] **:** gladness or gaiety as shown by or accompanied with laughter **syn** GLEE, HILARITY **:** MIRTH implies generally lightness of heart and love of gaiety and specif. denotes laughter ⟨trying to suppress his *mirth*⟩ GLEE suggests an exulting sometimes malicious delight expressed in laughter or cries of joy; HILARITY implies loud or irrepressible laughter or boisterousness

mirth·ful \-fəl\ *adj* : full of, expressing, or producing mirth — **mirth·ful·ly** \-fə-lē\ *adv* — **mirth·ful·ness** *n*

miry \'mī(ə)r-ē\ *adj* **mir·i·er; -est** **1** : MARSHY, BOGGY **2** : MUDDY, SLUSHY

mis- *prefix* [OE; akin to E **¹miss**] **1 a** : badly : wrongly ⟨*misjudge*⟩ **b** : unfavorably ⟨*misesteem*⟩ **c** : in a suspicious manner ⟨*misdoubt*⟩ **2** : bad : wrong ⟨*misdeed*⟩ **3** : opposite or lack of ⟨*mistrust*⟩ **4** : not ⟨*misknow*⟩

mis·ad·ven·ture \,mis-əd-'ven-chər\ *n* : MISFORTUNE, MISHAP

mis·al·li·ance \,mis-ə-'lī-ən(t)s\ *n* : an improper or unsuitable alliance esp. in marriage

mis·an·thrope \'mis-ᵊn-,thrōp\ *n* [Gk *misanthrōpos* hating mankind, fr. *misein* to hate + *anthrōpos* man] : a person who dislikes and distrusts mankind

mis·an·thro·py \mis-'an(t)-thrə-pē\ *n* : a dislike or hatred of mankind — **mis·an·throp·ic** \,mis-ᵊn-'thräp-ik\ *adj* syn see CYNICAL — **mis·an·throp·i·cal·ly** \-'thräp-i-k(ə-)lē\ *adv*

mis·ap·ply \,mis-ə-'plī\ *vt* : to apply wrongly — **mis·ap·pli·ca·tion** \,mis-,ap-lə-'kā-shən\ *n*

mis·ap·pre·hend \,mis-,ap-ri-'hend\ *vt* : MISUNDERSTAND — **mis·ap·pre·hen·sion** \-'hen-chən\ *n*

mis·ap·pro·pri·ate \,mis-ə-'prō-prē-,āt\ *vt* : to appropriate wrongly; *esp* : to take dishonestly for one's own use — **mis·ap·pro·pri·a·tion** \-,prō-prē-'ā-shən\ *n*

mis·be·got·ten \,mis-bi-'gät-ᵊn\ *adj* : unlawfully or irregularly begotten : ILLEGITIMATE

mis·be·have \,mis-bi-'hāv\ *vi* : to behave badly — **mis·be·hav·ior** \-'hā-vyər\ *n*

mis·be·lief \,mis-bə-'lēf\ *n* : a mistaken or false belief

mis·be·liev·er \-'lē-vər\ *n* : one who is held to have false beliefs esp. in religion

mis·brand \(')mis-'brand\ *vt* : to brand falsely or in a misleading way

mis·cal·cu·late \(')mis-'kal-kyə-,lāt\ *vb* : to calculate wrongly — **mis·cal·cu·la·tion** \,mis-,kal-kyə-'lā-shən\ *n*

mis·call \(')mis-'kol\ *vt* : to call by a wrong name

mis·car·riage \mis-'kar-ij\ *n* **1** : MISMANAGEMENT; *esp* : a failure or blunder in the administration of justice **2 a** : a failure (as of a letter) to arrive **b** : a failure (as of goods) to carry properly **3** : the accidental separation of an unborn child from the body of its mother before it is capable of living independently : loss of a child through premature birth — compare ABORTION

mis·car·ry \mis-'kar-ē\ *vi* **1** : to have a miscarriage : give birth prematurely **2** : to fail of the intended purpose : go wrong or go amiss ⟨the plan *miscarried*⟩

mis·cast \(')mis-'kast\ *vt* : to cast in an unsuitable role

mis·ceg·e·na·tion \(,)mis-,ej-ə-'nā-shən, ,mis-i-jə-'nā-\ *n* [L *miscēre* to mix + *genus* kind, race] : a mixture of races; *esp* : marriage or cohabitation between a white person and a member of another race

mis·cel·la·ne·ous \,mis-ə-'lā-nē-əs\ *adj* [L *miscellaneus*, fr. *miscellus* mixed] **1** : consisting of numerous things of different sorts : MIXED **2 a** : marked by an interest in unrelated topics or subjects **b** : having the characteristics of a patchwork syn see INDISCRIMINATE — **mis·cel·la·ne·ous·ly** *adv* — **mis·cel·la·ne·ous·ness** *n*

mis·cel·la·nist \'mis-ə-,lā-nəst\ *n* : a writer of miscellanies

mis·cel·la·ny \-nē\ *n, pl* **-nies** **1** : a mixture of various things **2** *pl* : separate studies or writings collected in one book

mis·chance \(')mis-'chan(t)s\ *n* **1** : bad luck **2** : a piece of bad luck : MISHAP syn see MISFORTUNE

mis·chief \'mis-chəf\ *n* [OF *meschief* calamity, fr. *meschever* to be unsuccessful, fr. *mes-* mis- (of Gmc origin; akin to E *mis-*) + *chief* head, end, fr. L *caput*] **1** : injury or damage caused by a human agency **2** : a source of harm, evil, or irritation; *esp* : a person who causes mischief **3** : action that annoys ⟨that child is always in *mischief*⟩ **b** : mischievous quality ⟨he has *mischief* in his eyes⟩

mis·chie·vous \'mis-chə-vəs\ *adj* **1** : causing mischief : intended to do harm ⟨*mischievous* gossip⟩ **2 a** : causing

or tending to cause petty injury or annoyance **b** : irresponsibly playful **3** : showing a spirit of mischief ⟨*mischievous* behavior⟩ — **mis·chie·vous·ly** *adv* — **mis·chie·vous·ness** *n*

mis·ci·ble \'mis-ə-bəl\ *adj* [L *miscēre* to mix] : capable of being mixed; *esp* : soluble in each other ⟨alcohol and water are *miscible*⟩ — **mis·ci·bil·i·ty** \,mis-ə-'bil-ət-ē\ *n*

mis·con·ceive \,mis-kən-'sēv\ *vt* : to interpret incorrectly : MISJUDGE — **mis·con·ceiv·er** *n* — **mis·con·cep·tion** \-'sep-shən\ *n*

¹mis·con·duct \(')mis-'kän-(,)dəkt\ *n* **1** : bad management **2** : improper or unlawful behavior

²mis·con·duct \,mis-kən-'dəkt\ *vt* **1** : MISMANAGE **2** : to behave (oneself) badly

mis·con·struc·tion \,mis-kən-'strək-shən\ *n* : the act, the process, or an instance of misconstruing

mis·con·strue \,mis-kən-'strü\ *vt* : to construe wrongly : MISINTERPRET

mis·count \(')mis-'kaunt\ *vb* : to count incorrectly : MISCALCULATE — **miscount** *n*

mis·cre·ant \'mis-krē-ənt\ *n* [ME, infidel, fr. MF *mescreant*, prp. of *mescroire* to disbelieve] : VILLAIN, SCOUNDREL, RASCAL — **miscreant** *adj*

¹mis·cue \(')mis-'kyü\ *n* **1** : a stroke (as in billiards) in which the cue slips **2** : MISTAKE, SLIP

²miscue *vi* **1** : to make a miscue **2 a** : to miss a stage cue **b** : to answer a wrong cue

mis·deal \(')mis-'dēl\ *vb* **-dealt** \-'delt\; **-deal·ing** \-'dē-liŋ\ : to deal wrongly ⟨*misdeal* cards⟩ — **misdeal** *n*

mis·deed \(')mis-'dēd\ *n* : a wrong deed; *esp* : an immoral or criminal action

mis·de·mean·or \,mis-di-'mē-nər\ *n* **1** : a crime less serious than a felony **2** : MISDEED

mis·di·rect \,mis-də-'rekt, -dī-\ *vt* : to direct incorrectly — **mis·di·rec·tion** \-'rek-shən\ *n*

mis·do·ing \(')mis-'dü-iŋ\ *n* **1** : WRONGDOING **2** : MISDEED — **mis·do·er** \-'dü-ər\ *n*

mis·doubt \(')mis-'daut\ *vt* **1** : to doubt the reality or truth of **2** : SUSPECT, FEAR — **misdoubt** *n*

mise–en–scène \,mē-,zä°-'sen, -'san\ *n, pl* **mise–en–scènes** \-'sen(z)\ [F, putting on the stage] **1** : the setting of a play **2** : physical setting : ENVIRONMENT

mi·ser \'mī-zər\ *n* [L, wretched, miserable] : a mean grasping person; *esp* : one who lives miserably in order to hoard his wealth

mis·er·a·ble \'miz-ər-bəl, 'miz-(ə)rə-bəl\ *adj* [L *miserabilis* pitiable, wretched, fr. *miserari* to pity, fr. *miser* wretched] **1 a** : wretchedly deficient or meager ⟨a *miserable* hovel⟩ **b** : causing great discomfort or unhappiness ⟨a *miserable* cold⟩ **2** : extremely poor or unhappy : WRETCHED **3** : PITIFUL, LAMENTABLE **4** : SHAMEFUL, DISCREDITABLE — **miserable** *n* — **mis·er·a·ble·ness** *n* — **mis·er·a·bly** \-blē\ *adv*

Mi·se·re·re \,miz-ə-'re)r-ē, -'re(ə)r-\ *n* [L, be merciful (first word of the Psalm), fr. *misereri* to be merciful, fr. *miser* wretched] : the 50th Psalm in the Vulgate

mi·ser·ly \'mī-zər-lē\ *adj* : of, relating to, or characteristic of a miser : GRASPING syn see STINGY — **mi·ser·li·ness** *n*

mis·ery \'miz-(ə)rē\ *n, pl* **-er·ies** [L *miseria*, fr. *miser* wretched] **1** : a state of great suffering and want due to poverty or affliction **2** : a circumstance, thing, or place that causes suffering or discomfort ⟨the *miseries* of life in prison⟩ **3** : a state of great unhappiness and emotional distress syn see DISTRESS

mis·es·ti·mate \(')mis-'es-tə-,māt\ *vt* : to estimate falsely — **mis·es·ti·ma·tion** \,mis-,es-tə-'mā-shən\ *n*

mis·fea·sance \mis-'fēz-ᵊn(t)s\ *n* [MF *mesfaisance*, fr. *mesfaire* to do wrong, fr. *mes-* mis- + *faire* to do, fr. L *facere*] : the performance of a lawful action in an illegal or improper manner

mis·file \(')mis-'fīl\ *vt* : to file in an inappropriate place

mis·fire \(')mis-'fī(ə)r\ *vi* **1** : to have the explosive or propulsive charge fail to ignite at the proper time ⟨the engine *misfired*⟩ **2** : to fail to fire ⟨the gun *misfired*⟩ **3** : to miss an intended effect — **misfire** *n*

mis·fit \'mis-,fit, (')mis-'fit\ *n* **1** : something that fits badly **2** : a person poorly adjusted to his environment

mis·for·tune \mis-'for-chən\ *n* **1** : bad fortune : ill luck **2** : an unfortunate condition or event : DISASTER, MISHAP

syn MISCHANCE: MISFORTUNE is a general term for bad luck; applied to a single instance it implies resulting distress usu. of some considerable duration; MISCHANCE emphasizes the immediate practical inconvenience or disruption of plans resulting from a chance happening or fall of circumstances

mis·give \(')mis-'giv\ *vb* **-gave** \'gāv\; **-giv·en** \-'giv-ən\; **-giv·ing** **1** : to suggest doubt or fear to ⟨his mind *misgave* him⟩ **2** : to be fearful or apprehensive

mis·giv·ing \-'giv-iŋ\ *n* : a feeling of doubt or suspicion esp. concerning a future event

mis·gov·ern \-'gəv-ərn\ *vt* : to govern badly — **mis·gov·ern·ment** \-ər(n)-mənt\ *n*

mis·guide \(')mis-'gīd\ *vt* : to lead astray : MISDIRECT ⟨well-meaning but *misguided* benefactors⟩ — **mis·guid·ance** \-'gīd-ⁿ(t)s\ *n* — **mis·guid·er** *n*

mis·han·dle \(')mis-'han-dᵊl\ *vt* **1** : to treat roughly : MALTREAT **2** : to manage wrongly

mis·hap \'mis-,hap, mis-'\ *n* **1** *archaic* : bad luck : MISFORTUNE **2** : an unfortunate accident

mish·mash \'mish-,mash, -,mäsh\ *n* : HODGEPODGE, JUMBLE

Mish·nah *or* **Mish·na** \'mish-nə\ *n* [LHeb *mishnāh* instruction] : the collection of Jewish halakic traditions compiled about A.D. 200 and made the basic half of the Talmud

mis·in·form \,mis-ⁿn-'fȯrm\ *vt* : to give untrue or misleading information to — **mis·in·for·ma·tion** \,mis-,in-fər-'mā-shən\ *n*

mis·in·ter·pret \,mis-ⁿn-'tər-prət, *rapid* -pət\ *vt* : to understand or explain wrongly — **mis·in·ter·pre·ta·tion** \-,tər-prə-'tā-shən, *rapid* -pə-'tā-\ *n*

mis·judge \(')mis-'jəj\ *vb* : to judge wrongly or unjustly — **mis·judg·ment** \-'jəj-mənt\ *n*

mis·lay \(')mis-'lā\ *vt* **-laid** \-'lād\; **-lay·ing** : to put in a place later forgotten : LOSE

mis·lead \(')mis-'lēd\ *vt* **-led** \-'led\; **-lead·ing** : to lead in a wrong direction or into a mistaken action or belief **syn** see DECEIVE — **misleading** *adj*

mis·like \(')mis-'līk\ *vt* : DISLIKE — **mislike** *n*

mis·man·age \(')mis-'man-ij\ *vt* : to manage badly or improperly — **mis·man·age·ment** \-mənt\ *n*

mis·match \(')mis-'mach\ *vt* : to match (as in marriage) unsuitably or badly — **mismatch** *n*

mis·mate \(')mis-'māt\ *vt* : to mate unsuitably

mis·name \(')mis-'nām\ *vt* : to name incorrectly : MISCALL

mis·no·mer \(')mis-'nō-mər\ *n* [Anglo-French, the misnaming of a person, fr. MF *mesnommer* to misname] : a wrong or unsuitable name

mi·sog·a·mist \mə-'säg-ə-məst\ *n* [Gk *misein* to hate + *gamos* marriage] : one who hates marriage — **mi·sog·a·my** \-'säg-ə-mē\ *n*

mi·sog·y·nist \mə-'säj-ə-nəst\ *n* : one who hates or distrusts women — **mis·o·gyn·ic** \,mis-ə-'jin-ik, -ə-'gī-nik\ *adj*

mi·sog·y·ny \mə-'säj-ə-nē\ *n* [Gk *misogynia*, fr. *misein* to hate + *gynē* woman] : a hatred of women

mis·place \(')mis-'plās\ *vt* **1** : to put in a wrong place ⟨*misplaced* a comma⟩ **2** : MISLAY — **mis·place·ment** \-mənt\ *n*

mis·play \(')mis-'plā\ *n* : a wrong or unskillful play — **misplay** *vt*

mis·print \(')mis-'print\ *vt* : to print incorrectly — **misprint** \'mis-,print, (')mis-'\ *n*

mis·prize \(')mis-'prīz\ *vt* **1** : SCORN, DESPISE **2** : UNDERVALUE

mis·pro·nounce \,mis-prə-'naun(t)s\ *vt* : to pronounce incorrectly or in a way regarded as incorrect — **mis·pro·nun·ci·a·tion** \-,nən(t)-sē-'ā-shən\ *n*

mis·quote \(')mis-'kwōt\ *vt* : to quote incorrectly — **mis·quo·ta·tion** \,mis-kwō-'tā-shən\ *n*

mis·read \(')mis-'rēd\ *vt* **-read** \-'red\; **-read·ing** \-'rēd-iŋ\ **1** : to read incorrectly **2** : to misinterpret in or as if in reading

mis·rep·re·sent \,mis-,rep-ri-'zent\ *vt* : to give a false or misleading representation of — **mis·rep·re·sen·ta·tion** \,(,)mis-,rep-ri-,zen-'tā-shən\ *n*

¹mis·rule \(')mis-'rül\ *vt* : to rule or govern badly

²misrule *n* **1** : the action of misruling : the state of being misruled **2** : DISORDER, ANARCHY

¹miss \'mis\ *vb* [OE *missan*] **1** : to fail to hit, catch, reach, or get ⟨*miss* a target⟩ **2** : ESCAPE, AVOID ⟨*missed* being hurt by a narrow margin⟩ **3** : to leave out : OMIT ⟨*missed* his lunch⟩ **4** : to discover or feel the absence of ⟨*miss* an absent friend⟩ **5** : to fail to understand, sense, or experience ⟨*missed* his meaning⟩ ⟨don't *miss* that movie⟩ **6** : MISFIRE ⟨the engine *missed*⟩

²miss *n* **1 a** : a failure to reach a desired goal (as a target) **b** : a failure to attain a result **2** : MISFIRE

³miss *n* [short for *mistress*] **1 a** — used as a title before the name of an unmarried woman or girl **b** — used before the name of a place or of a line of activity or before some epithet to form a title for a girl who represents the thing indicated ⟨*Miss* America⟩ **2** : young lady — used without a name as a conventional term of address to a young woman **3** : a young unmarried woman or girl

mis·sal \'mis-əl\ *n* [LL *missa* mass] : a book containing the prayers to be said or sung in the Mass during the year

mis·send \(')mis-'send\ *vt* : to send incorrectly ⟨*missent* mail⟩

mis·shape \(')mis(h)-'shāp\ *vt* : to shape badly : DEFORM — **mis·shap·en** \-'shā-pən\ *adj*

mis·sile \'mis-əl\ *n* [L, fr. neuter of *missilis* capable of being thrown, fr. *miss-, mittere* to let go, send] : an object (as a stone, arrow, artillery shell, bullet, or rocket) that is thrown or projected usu. so as to strike something at a distance; *esp* : GUIDED MISSILE

mis·sile·man \-mən\ *n* : one who helps to design, build, or operate guided missiles

mis·sile·ry \-rē\ *n* **1** : MISSILES; *esp* : GUIDED MISSILES **2** : the science dealing with the design, manufacture, and use of guided missiles

miss·ing \'mis-iŋ\ *adj* : ABSENT; *also* : LOST

missing link *n* **1** : an absent member needed to complete a series **2** : a hypothetical intermediate form between man and his presumed simian progenitors

mis·sion \'mish-ən\ *n* [L *mission-, missio* act of sending, fr. *miss-, mittere* to send] **1 a** : a ministry commissioned by a religious organization to propagate its faith or carry on humanitarian work **b** : assignment to or work in a field of missionary enterprise **c** (1) : a mission establishment (2) : a local church or parish dependent on a larger religious organization for direction or financial support **d** *pl* : organized missionary work **e** : a course of sermons and services given to convert to or quicken Christian faith **2** : a group of persons sent to perform a service or carry on an activity: as **a** : a group sent to a foreign country to conduct diplomatic or political negotiations **b** : a permanent embassy or legation **c** : a team of military or technical specialists or cultural leaders sent to a foreign country **3** : a task or function assigned or undertaken; *esp* : an official assignment ⟨his *mission* was to recover the stolen plans⟩ — **mission** *adj*

¹mis·sion·ary \'mish-ə-,ner-ē\ *adj* **1** : relating to, engaged in, or devoted to missions **2** : characteristic of a missionary

²missionary *n, pl* **-ar·ies** : one sent to spread a religious faith among unbelievers

mis·sion·er \'mish-ə-nər\ *n* : MISSIONARY

Mis·sis·sip·pi·an \,mis-ə-'sip-ē-ən\ *adj* **1** : of or relating to Mississippi, its people, or the Mississippi river **2** : of, relating to, or being the period of the Paleozoic era between the Devonian and Pennsylvanian or the corresponding system of rocks — **Mississippi** *n*

mis·sive \'mis-iv\ *n* [L *miss-, mittere* to send] : a written communication : LETTER

mis·spell \(')mis-'spel\ *vt* : to spell incorrectly

mis·spell·ing \-'spel-iŋ\ *n* : an incorrect spelling

mis·spend \(')mis-'spend\ *vt* **-spent** \-'spent\; **-spend·ing** : WASTE, SQUANDER ⟨a *misspent* youth⟩

mis·state \(')mis-'stāt\ *vt* : to state incorrectly — **mis·state·ment** \-mənt\ *n*

mis·step \(')mis-'step\ *n* **1** : a wrong step **2** : a mistake in judgment or action : BLUNDER

missy \'mis-ē\ *n* : a young girl : MISS

¹mist \'mist\ *n* [OE] **1** : water in the form of particles floating in the air or falling as fine rain **2** : something that blurs or hinders vision : HAZE, FILM **3** : a cloud of small particles or objects suggestive of a mist — **mist·like** \-,līk\ *adj*

²**mist** *vb* **1** : to be or become misty **2** : to become dim or blurred **3** : to cover with mist

mis·tak·a·ble \mə-'stā-kə-bəl\ *adj* : capable of being misunderstood or mistaken

¹**mis·take** \mə-'stāk\ *vb* **mis·took** \-'stùk\; **mis·tak·en** \-'stā-kən\; **mis·tak·ing** **1** : to choose wrongly **2 a** : to understand wrongly : MISINTERPRET **b** : to estimate incorrectly 〈*mistook* the strength of the enemy〉 **3** : to identify wrongly 〈*mistook* him for another〉 — **mis·tak·en·ly** *adv* — **mis·tak·er** *n*

²**mistake** *n* **1** : a wrong judgment : MISUNDERSTANDING **2** : a wrong action or statement : BLUNDER **syn** see ERROR

mis·ter \'mis-tər\ *n* [alter. of *master*] **1 a** — used sometimes in writing instead of the usual *Mr.* **b** — used before the name of a place or of a line of activity or before some epithet to form a title for a male representing the thing indicated 〈*Mr.* Conservative〉 **2** : SIR — used without a name as a conventional term of address of a man who is a stranger 〈hey, *mister*, do you want to buy a newspaper〉

mis·time \(')mis-'tīm\ *vt* : to time wrongly

mis·tle thrush \'mis-əl-\ *n* : MAVIS 2

mis·tle·toe \'mis-əl-ˌtō\ *n* [OE *misteltān*, fr. *mistel* mistletoe + *tān* twig] : a green plant with yellowish flowers and waxy white berries that grows on the branches and trunks of trees

mis·tral \'mis-trəl, mi-'sträl\ *n* [F, fr. Prov. fr. *mistral* masterful] : a violent cold dry northerly wind of southern Europe

mis·treat \(')mis-'trēt\ *vt* : to treat badly : ABUSE — **mis·treat·ment** \-mənt\ *n*

mis·tress \'mis-trəs; *in contracted form* "Mrs." ˌmis-əz, -əs, *esp South* ˌmiz-əz, -əs, (ˌ)miz *or before given names* (ˌ)mis\ *n* [ME *maistresse*, fr. MF, fem. of *maistre* master, fr. L *magister*] **1** : a woman (as the head of a household or school) who has power, authority, or ownership like that of a master **2** : something personified as female that rules or directs **3** : a woman with whom a man habitually fornicates **4** — used formerly as a title before the name of a woman

mis·tri·al \(')mis-'trī(-ə)l\ *n* : a trial that is void because of some error or serious prejudicial misconduct in the proceedings

¹**mis·trust** \(')mis-'trəst\ *n* : a lack of confidence : DISTRUST — **mis·trust·ful** \-fəl\ *adj* — **mis·trust·ful·ly** \-fə-lē\ *adv* — **mis·trust·ful·ness** *n*

²**mistrust** *vb* **1** : SUSPECT 〈I *mistrust* his motives〉 **2** : to lack confidence in 〈*mistrusts* his own ability〉

misty \'mis-tē\ *adj* **mist·i·er; -est** **1** : full of mist 〈a *misty* valley〉 **2** : blurred by or as if by mist 〈through *misty* eyes〉 **3** : VAGUE, INDISTINCT 〈a *misty* memory〉 — **mist·i·ly** \-tə-lē\ *adv* — **mist·i·ness** \-tē-nəs\ *n*

mis·un·der·stand \ˌ(ˌ)mis-ˌən-dər-'stand\ *vt* **-stood** \-'stùd\; **-stand·ing** **1** : to fail to understand **2** : to interpret incorrectly

mis·un·der·stand·ing \-'stan-diŋ\ *n* **1** : a failure to understand **2** : QUARREL

mis·us·age \(')mis-'yü-sij, -'yü-zij, mish-'ü-\ *n* **1** : bad treatment : ABUSE **2** : wrong or improper use

¹**mis·use** \(')mis-'yüz, mish-'üz\ *vt* **1** : to use incorrectly : MISAPPLY **2** : ABUSE, MISTREAT

²**mis·use** \(')mis-'yüs, mish-'üs\ *n* : incorrect or improper use : MISAPPLICATION 〈*misuse* of public funds〉

mite \'mīt\ *n* [OE *mīte*] **1** : any of various tiny animals that are related to the ticks and spiders, often live on plants, animals, and stored foods, and include important disease vectors **2** : a very small coin or sum of money **3** : a very small object or creature

¹**mi·ter** *or* **mi·tre** \'mīt-ər\ *n* [MF *mitre*, fr. L *mitra* turban, headband, fr. Gk] **1** : a high pointed headdress worn by a bishop or abbot in church ceremonies — see COPE illustration **2** : MITER JOINT

²**miter** *or* **mitre** *vt* **mi·tered** *or* **mi·tred**; **mi·ter·ing** *or* **mi·tring** \'mīt-ə-riŋ\ **1** : to match or fit together in a miter joint **2** : to bevel the ends of for making a miter joint

miter box *n* : a device for guiding a handsaw at the proper angle in making a miter joint in wood

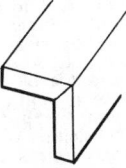

miter joint

miter joint *n* : the joint or corner made by cutting the square edges of two boards at an angle and fitting them together

Mith·ras \'mith-rəs\ *n* : the savior hero of an oriental mystery cult for men flourishing in the late Roman empire — **Mith·ra·ic** \mith-'rā-ik\ *adj* — **Mith·ra·ism** \'mith-rə-ˌiz-əm\ *n* — **Mith·ra·ist** \mith-'rā-əst, 'mith-rā-ˌist\ *n*

mit·i·gate \'mit-ə-ˌgāt\ *vt* [L *mitigare*, fr. *mitis* mild] **1** : to make less severe 〈*mitigate* a punishment〉 〈*mitigate* pain〉 — **mit·i·ga·ble** \'mit-i-gə-bəl\ *adj* — **mit·i·ga·tion** \ˌmit-ə-'gā-shən\ *n* — **mit·i·ga·tor** \'mit-ə-ˌgāt-ər\ *n* — **mit·i·ga·to·ry** \'mit-i-gə-ˌtōr-ē, -ˌtòr-\ *adj*

mi·to·chon·dri·on \ˌmīt-ə-'kän-drē-ən\ *n, pl* **-dria** \-drē-ə\ [Gk *mitos* thread + *chondrion* granule] : any of various round or long bodies found in cells that are rich in fats, proteins, and enzymes and are held to be centers of cellular respiration — **mi·to·chon·dri·al** \-drē-əl\ *adj*

mi·to·sis \mī-'tō-səs\ *n, pl* **-to·ses** \-'tō-ˌsēz\ [NL, fr. Gk *mitos* thread] **1** : a process taking place in the nucleus of a dividing cell that results in the formation of two new nuclei having each the same number of chromosomes as the parent nucleus **2** : a cell division in which mitosis occurs — **mi·tot·ic** \-'tät-ik\ *adj* — **mi·tot·i·cal·ly** \-'tät-i-k(ə-)lē\ *adv*

mi·tral valve \ˌmī-trəl-\ *n* [fr. its resemblance in shape to a miter] : BICUSPID VALVE

mitt \'mit\ *n* [short for *mitten*] **1 a** : a woman's glove that leaves the fingers uncovered **b** : MITTEN **c** : a baseball catcher's or first baseman's glove **2** *slang* : HAND

mit·ten \'mit-ᵊn\ *n* [MF *mitaine*] : a covering for the hand and wrist having a separate section for the thumb only

mitz·vah \'mits-və\ *n, pl* **mitz·voth** \-ˌvōth\ *or* **mitz·vahs** [Heb *miṣwāh*] **1** : a commandment of the Jewish law **2** : a meritorious act

¹**mix** \'miks\ *vb* [ME *mixen*, back-formation fr. *mixte* mixed, fr. MF, fr. L *mixtus*, pp. of *miscēre* to mix] **1** : to make into one mass by stirring together : BLEND **2** : to make by blending different things 〈*mix* a salad dressing〉 **3** : to become one mass through blending 〈oil will not *mix* with water〉 **4** : to associate with others on friendly terms 〈*mixes* well in any company〉 **5** : CONFUSE 〈*mix* up facts〉 — **mix·er** *n*

syn MIX, MINGLE, BLEND, COALESCE mean to put or come together into one mass. MIX may or may not imply loss of each element's separate identity; MINGLE suggests that the elements are still somewhat distinguishable or separately active; BLEND implies that the elements lose some or all of their individuality; COALESCE stresses the action or process of like things growing into an organic unity

²**mix** *n* : MIXTURE; *esp* : a commercially prepared mixture of food ingredients

mixed \'mikst\ *adj* **1** : combining characteristics of more than one kind; *esp* : combining features of two or more systems 〈a *mixed* government〉 〈a *mixed* economy〉 **2** : made up of or involving individuals or items of more than one kind: as **a** : made up of or involving persons differing in race, national origin, religion, or class 〈*mixed* marriage〉 **b** : made up of or involving individuals of both sexes 〈*mixed* company〉 〈*mixed* chorus〉 **3** : including or accompanied by inconsistent or incompatible elements 〈a *mixed* blessing〉 〈a *mixed* reaction〉 〈a *mixed* metaphor〉 **4** : CROSSBRED

mixed bud *n* : a plant bud that produces a branch and leaves as well as flowers

mixed nerve *n* : a nerve containing both sensory and motor fibers

mixed number *n* : a number (as 5⅔) composed of an integer and a fraction

mix·ture \'miks-chər\ *n* [L *mixt-, miscēre* to mix] **1** : the act, the process, or an instance of mixing **2 a** : something mixed or being mixed : a product of mixing 〈add eggs to the *mixture*〉 **b** : a cloth made of thread of different colors **c** : a preparation consisting of two or more ingredients or kinds 〈a smoking *mixture*〉 **3** : the relative proportion of the elements in a mixture 〈the choke controls the *mixture* of fuel and air in the carburetor〉 **4** : two or more substances mixed together but not chemically united and not necessarily present in definite proportions ⟨sand mixed with sugar forms a *mixture*⟩

mix-up \'miks-,əp\ *n* **1** : an instance of confusion ⟨a *mix-up* about who was to meet the train⟩ **2** : CONFLICT, FIGHT

¹**miz·zen** *or* **miz·en** \'miz-ᵊn\ *n* [ME *meseyn, meson*] **1** : a fore-and-aft sail set on the mizzenmast **2** : MIZZENMAST

²**mizzen** *or* **mizen** *adj* : of or relating to the mizzenmast ⟨*mizzen* shrouds⟩

miz·zen·mast \-,mast, -məst\ *n* : the mast aft or next aft of the mainmast in a ship

mne·mon·ic \ni-'män-ik\ *adj* [Gk *mnēmōn* mindful, remembering, fr. *mimnēskesthai* to remember] **1** : assisting or intended to assist memory ⟨*mnemonic* devices⟩ **2** : of or relating to memory — **mne·mon·i·cal·ly** \-'män-i-k(ə-)lē\ *adv*

Mne·mos·y·ne \ni-'mäs-ᵊn-ē\ *n* : the Greek goddess of memory and mother of the Muses by Zeus

-mo \(,)mō\ *n suffix, pl* **-mos** [fr. *duodecimo* size of page produced by dividing a large sheet into twelve leaves, fr. L, abl. of *duodecimus* twelfth] — after numerals or their names to indicate the number of leaves made by folding a sheet of paper ⟨sixteen*mo*⟩ ⟨16*mo*⟩

moa \'mō-ə\ *n* [Maori] : any of various extinct flightless ratite birds of New Zealand

Mo·ab·ite \'mō-ə-,bīt\ *n* : a member of an ancient Semitic people related to the Hebrews — **Moabite** *or* **Mo·ab·it·ish** \-,bīt-ish\ *adj* — **Mo·ab·it·ess** \-,bīt-əs\ *n*

¹**moan** \'mōn\ *n* [ME *mone*] **1** : a low drawn-out sound indicative of pain or grief **2** : a sound like a moan

²**moan** *vb* **1** : to utter a moan **2** : COMPLAIN, LAMENT ⟨*moaned* about their troubles⟩ **3** : to utter with moans

moat \'mōt\ *n* [ME *mote*] : a deep wide trench around the walls of a castle or fortress that is usu. filled with water : DITCH

¹**mob** \'mäb\ *n* [L *mobile vulgus* vacillating crowd] **1** : the common usu. uncultured mass of people; *esp* : the lower classes of a city **2** : a large disorderly crowd often tending to violent and illegal action **3 a** : a criminal gang **b** : SET 3

²**mob** *vt* **mobbed; mob·bing** : to crowd about and attack or annoy

¹**mo·bile** \'mō-bəl, -,bēl, -,bīl\ *adj* [L *mobilis*, fr. *movēre* to move] **1** : MOVABLE **2** : changing quickly in expression ⟨a *mobile* face⟩ **3** : capable of being readily moved ⟨*mobile* troops⟩ **4** : MIGRATORY ⟨*mobile* workers⟩ **5** : providing opportunity for or characterized by movement from one class or group to another ⟨a *mobile* society⟩ — **mo·bil·i·ty** \mō-'bil-ət-ē\ *n*

²**mo·bile** \-,bēl\ *n* : an artistic structure (as of cardboard or sheet metal) that has parts moved by a current of air or by machinery or that is itself suspended (as by a wire) so as to move in a current of air

mo·bi·lize \'mō-bə-,līz\ *vb* **1** : to put into movement or circulation **2** : to assemble and make ready for action : MARSHAL ⟨*mobilize* army reserves⟩ — **mo·bi·li·za·tion** \,mō-b(ə-)lə-'zā-shən\ *n*

mob·oc·ra·cy \mä-'bäk-rə-sē\ *n* **1** : rule by the mob **2** : the mob as a ruling class **3** : rule by gangsters — **mob·o·crat** \'mäb-ə-,krat\ *n* — **mob·o·crat·ic** \,mäb-ə-'krat-ik\ *adj*

mob·ster \'mäb-stər\ *n* : a member of a criminal gang

moc·ca·sin \'mäk-ə-sən\ *n* [of Algonquian origin] **1** : a soft leather shoe without a heel and with the sole and sides made of one piece joined on top by a seam to a U-shaped piece across the front **2** : WATER MOCCASIN

moccasin flower *n* : any of several lady's slippers; *esp* : a woodland orchid of eastern No. America with usu. pink flowers

mo·cha \'mō-kə\ *n* [*Mocha*, seaport in Arabia] **1** : choice coffee with small green or yellowish beans grown in Arabia **2** : a pliable suede-finished glove leather from African sheepskins

¹**mock** \'mäk, 'mók\ *vb* [MF *mocquer*] **1** : to laugh at scornfully : RIDICULE **2** : DEFY, DISREGARD **3** : to make fun of by mimicking **syn** see IMITATE, RIDICULE — **mock·er** *n* — **mock·ing·ly** \-iŋ-lē\ *adv*

²**mock** *n* **1** : an act of mocking : JEER **2** : an object of ridicule

³**mock** *adj* : not real : SHAM ⟨*mock* grief⟩ ⟨a *mock* battle⟩

⁴**mock** *adv* : in an insincere or counterfeit manner — usu. used in combination

mock·ery \'mäk-(ə-)rē, 'mók-\ *n, pl* **-er·ies** **1** : insulting or contemptuous action or speech ⟨the odd-looking invention drew forth a good deal of *mockery* from the townspeople⟩ **2** : someone or something that is laughed at **3** : an insincere or a poor imitation ⟨his acting was a *mockery* of his former greatness⟩ **4** : something ridiculously or impudently unsuitable

mock-he·ro·ic \,mäk-hi-'rō-ik, ,mók-\ *adj* : ridiculing or burlesquing the heroic style or heroic character or action ⟨a *mock-heroic* poem⟩

mock·ing·bird \'mäk-iŋ-,bərd, 'mók-\ *n* : a songbird of the southern U.S. remarkable for its exact imitations of the notes of other birds

mock orange *n* : a hardy white-flowered shrub; *esp* : PHILADELPHUS

mock turtle soup *n* : a soup made of meat (as calf's head or veal) in imitation of soup made from a green turtle

mock-up \'mäk-,əp, 'mók-\ *n* : a full-sized structural model built accurately to scale chiefly for study, testing, or display ⟨a *mock-up* of an airplane⟩

mod \'mäd\ *adj* : MODERN; *esp* : bold, free, and unconventional in style, behavior, or dress

mod·al \'mōd-ᵊl\ *adj* **1** : of or relating to a mode or to form as opposed to substance **2** : relating to or constituting a unit of speech characteristically entering into expressions that state a point of view (as concerning desirability, possibility, or necessity) regarding the being or occurrence of something — **mo·dal·i·ty** \mō-'dal-ət-ē\ *n* — **mo·dal·ly** \'mōd-ᵊl-ē\ *adv*

modal auxiliary *n* : a verb (as *can, must, might, may*) that is characteristically used with a verb of predication and expresses a modal modification

¹**mode** \'mōd\ *n* [L *modus* measure, manner, musical mode; akin to E *mete*] **1** : an arrangement of the eight tones of an octave according to one of several fixed schemes of their intervals **2** : ²MOOD **3 a** : a particular form or variety of something **b** : a form or manner of expression : STYLE **c** : a manner of doing something ⟨*mode* of travel⟩ **4** : the most frequent value of a frequency distribution

²**mode** *n* [F, lit., manner, fr. L *modus*] : a prevailing fashion or style of dress or behavior **syn** see FASHION

¹**mod·el** \'mäd-ᵊl\ *n* [MF *modelle*, fr. It *modello*, fr. L *modulus*, dim. of *modus* measure] **1 a** : a small but exact copy of something ⟨a *model* of a ship⟩ **b** : a pattern or figure of something to be made ⟨clay *models* for a statue⟩ **2** : a person who sets a good example ⟨a *model* of politeness⟩ **3 a** : a person or thing that serves as an artist's pattern; *esp* : a person who poses for an artist **b** : a person who wears in the presence of customers garments that are for sale : MANNEQUIN **4** : a type or design of product (as a car or airplane) **5 a** : a description or analogy used to help visualize something (as an atom) that cannot be directly observed **b** : a system of assumptions, data, and inferences used to describe mathematically an object or state of affairs **6** : a description of a possible or imaginary system

²**model** *vb* **mod·eled** *or* **mod·elled; mod·el·ing** *or* **mod·el·ling** \-ᵊl-iŋ, 'mäd-liŋ\ **1** : to plan or shape after a pattern ⟨a sports car *modeled* on a racing car⟩ **2** : to make a model : MOLD ⟨*model* a dog in clay⟩ **3** : to act or serve as a model ⟨*model* for an artist⟩ — **mod·el·er** *or* **mod·el·ler** \-ᵊl-ər, 'mäd-lər\ *n*

³**model** *adj* **1** : serving as or worthy of being a pattern ⟨a *model* student⟩ **2** : being a miniature representation of something ⟨a *model* airplane⟩

¹**mod·er·ate** \'mäd-(ə-)rət\ *adj* [L *moderatus*, fr. pp. of *moderare* to moderate] **1** : being neither too much nor too little : not extreme ⟨*moderate* heat⟩ **2** : avoiding extremes of behavior ⟨tried to be *moderate* in everything he did⟩ **3** : REASONABLE, CALM ⟨was *moderate* in his protests⟩ **4 a** : avoiding extremes of view, program, and tactics esp. in politics and usu. inclined to compromise ⟨*moderate* groups⟩ **b** : not extremely partisan ⟨*moderate* views⟩ **5** : neither very good nor very bad : MEDIOCRE, ORDINARY ⟨*moderate* success⟩ **6** : not expensive : reasonable in price ⟨*moderate* rates⟩ **7** : of medium lightness and medium saturation ⟨a *moderate* blue⟩ — **mod·er·ate·ly**

ə abut; ᵊ kitten; ər further; a back; ā bake; ä cot, cart; aú out; ch chin; e less; ē easy; g gift; i trip; ī life

\'mäd-ərt-lē, 'mäd-(ə-)rət-\ *adv* — **mod·er·ate·ness**
\'mäd-(ə-)rət-nəs\ *n*
syn MODERATE, TEMPERATE mean being neither very much
nor very little. MODERATE implies absence or avoidance
of excess ⟨*moderate* prices⟩ ⟨*moderate* liking for candy⟩
TEMPERATE suggests the exercise of restraint ⟨*temperate*
use of alcohol⟩
²**mod·er·ate** \'mäd-ə-,rāt\ *vb* **1** : to make or become
less violent, severe, or intense **2** : to preside over or
act as chairman of a meeting
³**mod·er·ate** \'mäd-(ə-)rət\ *n* : one holding moderate
views or belonging to a moderate group (as in politics or
religion)
mod·er·a·tion \,mäd-ə-'rā-shən\ *n* **1** : the action of
moderating **2** : the quality or state of being moderate
: an avoidance of extremes ⟨do everything in *moderation*⟩
mod·er·a·to \,mäd-ə-'rät-ō\ *adv (or adj)* [It, fr. L *moderatus*] : MODERATE — used as a direction in music to
indicate tempo
mod·er·a·tor \'mäd-ə-,rāt-ər\ *n* **1** : one that moderates
2 : a presiding officer (as of a Presbyterian governing
body, a town meeting, or a discussion group) **3** : a
substance (as graphite) used for slowing down neutrons
in a nuclear reactor — **mod·er·a·tor·ship** \-,ship\ *n*
¹**mod·ern** \'mäd-ərn\ *adj* [LL *modernus*, fr. L *modo* just
now, fr. *modus* measure] **1** : of, relating to, or characteristic of the present or the immediate past : CON-
TEMPORARY **2** : of or relating to the period from about
1500 to the present ⟨*modern* history⟩ **syn** see RECENT
— **mo·der·ni·ty** \mə-'dər-nət-ē, mä-\ *n* — **mod·ern·ly**
\'mäd-ərn-lē\ *adv* — **mod·ern·ness** \-ərn-nəs\ *n*
²**modern** *n* : a person of modern times or with modern
views
Modern Hebrew *n* : the Hebrew used in present-day
Israel
mod·ern·ism \'mäd-ər-,niz-əm\ *n* **1** : a modern practice;
esp : a modern usage, expression, or characteristic **2** : a
movement to adapt religion to modern science, culture,
and ideals of social reform: as **a** : a movement in Roman
Catholicism condemned by Pope Pius X in 1907 for basing
religious belief on human aspiration and experience rather
than supernatural revelation **b** : Protestant liberalism
3 : the theory and practices of modern art; *esp* : a
deliberate breaking from past practices and a search for
new forms of expression — **mod·ern·ist** \-nəst\ *n or adj*
— **mod·ern·is·tic** \,mäd-ər-'nis-tik\ *adj*
mod·ern·ize \'mäd-ər-,nīz\ *vb* : to make or become modern : make conform to present usage, style, or taste
⟨*modernize* an old house⟩ — **mod·ern·i·za·tion** \,mäd-ər-
nə-'zā-shən\ *n* — **mod·ern·iz·er** \'mäd-ər-,nī-zər\ *n*
mod·est \'mäd-əst\ *adj* [L *modestus* moderate] **1** : having a moderate opinion of one's own good qualities and
abilities : not boastful ⟨a *modest* winner⟩ **2** : showing
moderation in size, scope, or aim : not excessive ⟨a
modest request⟩ ⟨a *modest* cottage⟩ **3** : pure in thought,
conduct, and dress : DECENT ⟨a *modest* girl⟩ **syn** see
CHASTE, SHY — **mod·est·ly** *adv*
mod·es·ty \'mäd-ə-stē\ *n* : the quality of being modest;
esp : freedom from conceit or impropriety
mod·i·cum \'mäd-i-kəm, 'mōd-\ *n* [L, neut. of *modicus*
moderate, fr. *modus* measure] : a limited quantity : a
small amount ⟨an explanation that anyone with a *modicum*
of intelligence should understand⟩
mod·i·fi·ca·tion \,mäd-ə-fə-'kā-shən\ *n* **1** : the act of
modifying : the state of being modified **2** : QUALIFICA-
TION, LIMITATION ⟨a *modification* of a statement made in
haste⟩ **3** : partial alteration ⟨*modification* of plans⟩ **4** : a
change in an organism caused by environmental factors
mod·i·fi·er \'mäd-ə-,fī(-ə)r\ *n* : one that modifies; *esp*
: a word (as an adjective or adverb) joined to another
word to limit or qualify its meaning
mod·i·fy \'mäd-ə-,fī\ *vb* **-fied; -fy·ing** [L *modificare* to
limit, moderate, fr. *modus* measure] **1 a** : to make
changes in : ALTER ⟨*modify* a plan⟩ **b** : to become modified
2 : to lower or reduce in extent or degree : MODERATE
⟨*modify* a punishment⟩ **3** : to limit in meaning : QUALIFY
⟨in the phrase "green gloves" "green" *modifies* "gloves"⟩
syn see CHANGE — **mod·i·fi·a·ble** \-,fī-ə-bəl\ *adj* —
mod·i·fi·a·ble·ness *n*
mod·ish \'mōd-ish\ *adj* : FASHIONABLE, STYLISH — **mod-
ish·ly** *adv* — **mod·ish·ness** *n*

mo·diste \mō-'dēst\ *n* [F, fr. *mode* mode, fashion] : a
fashionable dressmaker
Mo·dred \'mō-drəd, 'mäd-rəd\ *n* : a knight of the Round
Table and rebellious nephew of King Arthur
mod·u·lar \'mäj-ə-lər\ *adj* : of, relating to, or based on
a module or a modulus
modular arithmetic *n* : arithmetic that deals only with
remainders left over after all the numbers considered are
divided by a fixed number
mod·u·late \'mäj-ə-,lāt\ *vb* [L *modulari*, fr. *modulus*,
dim. of *modus* measure] **1** : to adjust or regulate to
a certain proportion; *esp* : to soften or tone down
⟨*modulated* his voice⟩ **2** : to tune to a key or pitch
3 : to vary a quality of an electric wave in radio and
television in accordance with a quality of another electric
wave; *esp* : to vary the frequency or amplitude of the
carrier wave in accordance with the electric wave that
carries the sound or picture **4** : to pass from one musical
key to another usu. in a gradual movement and esp. by
a melodious progression of chords — **mod·u·la·tor**
\-,lāt-ər\ *n* — **mod·u·la·to·ry** \-lə-,tōr-ē, -,tór-\ *adj*
mod·u·la·tion \,mäj-ə-'lā-shən\ *n* **1** : an action of
modulating : the extent or degree by which something is
modulated **2** : variation of some quality (as the frequency
or amplitude) of the carrier wave in radio or television
in accordance with the sound or picture that is to be
transmitted
mod·ule \'mäj-ül\ *n* [L *modulus*, dim. of *modus* measure]
1 : a standard or unit of measurement **2** : a usu. packaged
functional subassembly of parts (as for an electronic
device) **3** : an independent unit that is a part of the total
structure of a space vehicle
mod·u·lo \'mäj-ə-,lō\ *prep* [NL, ablative of *modulus*] : with
respect to a modulus of
mod·u·lus \'mäj-ə-ləs\ *n, pl* **-li** \-,lī, -,lē\ [NL, fr. L,
dim. of *modus* measure] **1** : a number that expresses
the degree in which a property (as elasticity) is possessed
by a substance or body **2 a** : ABSOLUTE VALUE 2 **b** : an
integer that when divided into the difference of two numbers leaves no remainder
mo·dus ope·ran·di \,mōd-əs-,äp-ə-'ran-dē\ *n, pl* **mo·di
operandi** \,mō-,dē-,äp-\ [NL] : a method of procedure
mo·dus vi·ven·di \,mō-dəs-vi-'ven-dē\ *n* [NL, manner of
living] : a usu. temporary working arrangement or compromise pending or in place of a permanent settlement of
matters in dispute
mo·gul \'mō-(,)gəl, mō-'gəl\ *n* [Persian *mughul*, fr.
Mongolian *Mongol* Mongol] **1** *or* **moghul** *cap* : a member
of a Muslim dynasty of Turkish and Mongolian origin
conquering and ruling India from the 16th to the 18th
century **2** : a great personage : MAGNATE — **mogul** *adj*
mo·hair \'mō-,ha(ə)r, -,he(ə)r\ *n* [obs. It *mocaiarro*, fr.
Ar *mukhayyar*] : a fabric or yarn made wholly or in part
of the long silky hair of the Angora goat; *also* : the hair
of this goat
Mo·ham·med·an *var of* MUHAMMADAN
Mo·hawk \'mō-,hók\ *n* : a member of an Iroquoian
people of the Mohawk river valley, New York
Mo·hi·can \mō-'hē-kən\ *n* **1** : a member of an Indian
people of the upper Hudson river valley **2** *or* **Mo·he·gan**
\-'hē-gən\ : a member of an Indian people of southeastern Connecticut
Mohs' scale \'mōz-, 'mōs-, ,mō-səz-\ *n* [Friedrich *Mohs*
d1839 German mineralogist] : a scale of hardness for
minerals ranging from 1 for the softest to 10 for the hardest
in which 1 represents the hardness of talc; 2, gypsum; 3,
calcite; 4, fluorite; 5, apatite; 6, orthoclase; 7, quartz;
8, topaz; 9, corundum; and 10, diamond
moi·e·ty \'mói-ət-ē\ *n, pl* **-ties** [MF *moité*, fr. LL *medi-
etat-, medietas*, fr. L *medius* middle] **1** : one of two equal
parts : HALF **2** : approximately a half
¹**moil** \'móíl\ *vi* [ME *moillen* to wet, dirty, fr. MF
moillier to wet, fr. L *mollis* soft] : to work hard : DRUDGE
— **moil·er** *n*
²**moil** *n* **1** : DRUDGERY **2** : CONFUSION, TURMOIL
moi·ré \mó-'rā, mwä-\ *or* **moire** *same, or* 'mói(ə)r,
'mwär\ *n* [F *moiré*, fr. *moire* watered mohair, fr. E
mohair] : a fabric (as silk) having a watered appearance
— **moiré** *adj*
moist \'móíst\ *adj* [MF *moiste*, modif. of L *mucidus*
slimy, fr. *mucus*] : slightly wet : not completely dry

: DAMP ⟨*moist* earth⟩ — **moist·ly** *adv* — **moist·ness** \'mȯis(t)-nəs\ *n*

moist·en \'mȯis-ᵊn\ *vb* **moist·ened**; **moist·en·ing** \-ᵊn-iŋ, 'mȯis-niŋ\ : to make or become moist — **moist·en·er** \'mȯis-ᵊn-ər, 'mȯis-nər\ *n*

mois·ture \'mȯis-chər\ *n* : the small amount of liquid that causes moistness : dampness in the air or on a surface

mol·al \'mō-ləl\ *adj* : of, relating to, or containing one mole of solute per 1000 grams of solvent

mo·lal·i·ty \mō-'lal-ət-ē\ *n, pl* **-ties** : the concentration of a solution expressed by the number of moles of solute per 1000 grams of solvent

¹mo·lar \'mō-lər\ *n* [L *molaris,* fr. *mola* millstone] : a tooth with a rounded or flattened surface adapted for grinding : a cheek tooth behind the premolars of a mammal — see DENTITION illustration, TOOTH illustration

²molar *adj* **1** : able or fitted to grind **2** : of or relating to a molar

³molar *adj* **1** : of or relating to a molecule or mole **2** : of, relating to, or containing one mole of solute per liter of solution

mo·lar·i·ty \mō-'lar-ət-ē\ *n, pl* **-ties** : the concentration of a solution expressed by the number of moles of solute per liter of solution

mo·las·ses \mə-'las-əz\ *n* [Pg *melaço,* fr. LL *mellaceum* must, fr. L *mell-, mel* honey] : a thick brown syrup that is separated from raw sugar in sugar manufacture

¹mold \'mōld\ *n* [OE *molde*] : light rich crumbly earth containing decayed organic matter (as leaves or manure)

²mold *n* [OF *modle,* fr. L *modulus,* dim. of *modus* measure] **1** : distinctive nature or character : TYPE ⟨a man of austere *mold*⟩ **2** : the frame on or around which an object is constructed **3 a** : a cavity in which something is shaped ⟨a candle *mold*⟩ ⟨a *mold* for metal type⟩ ⟨a *mold* for jelly⟩ **b** : something shaped in a mold ⟨a *mold* of ice cream⟩

³mold *vb* **1** : to knead into shape ⟨*mold* loaves of bread⟩ **2** : to form or become formed in or as if in a mold ⟨*mold* butter⟩ ⟨his character was *molded* by his early life⟩ — **mold·a·ble** \'mōl-də-bəl\ *adj* — **mold·er** *n*

⁴mold *n* [ME *mowlde*] : an often woolly surface growth of fungus esp. on damp or decaying organic matter; *also* : a fungus that produces mold

⁵mold *vi* : to become moldy

mold·board \'mōl(d)-ˌbȯrd, -ˌbȯrd\ *n* : a curved iron plate attached above the plowshare of a plow to lift and turn the soil

mol·der \'mōl-dər\ *vi* **mol·dered**; **mol·der·ing** \-d(ə-)riŋ\ : to crumble into particles

mold·ing \'mōl-diŋ\ *n* **1** : the act or work of a person who molds **2** : an object produced by molding **3** : a strip of material having a shaped surface and used (as on a wall or the edge of a table) as a decoration

moldy \'mōl-dē\ *adj* **mold·i·er**; **-est** **1** : of, resembling, or covered with a mold **2 a** : being old and moldering : CRUMBLING **b** : ANTIQUATED, FUSTY — **mold·i·ness** *n*

¹mole \'mōl\ *n* [OE *māl*] : a small usu. brown and sometimes protruding permanent spot on the skin

²mole *n* [ME] : any of numerous burrowing insectivores with tiny eyes, concealed ears, and soft fur

³mole *n* [MF, fr. It *molo,* fr. LGk *mōlos,* fr. L *moles,* lit., mass] **1** : a heavy masonry structure built in the sea as a breakwater or pier **2** : the harbor formed by a mole

⁴mole *also* **mol** \'mōl, 'mäl\ *n* [G *mol,* short for *molekulargewicht* molecular weight] : GRAM MOLECULE

mo·lec·u·lar \mə-'lek-yə-lər\ *adj* **1** : relating to molecules **2** : produced by or consisting of molecules

molecular formula *n* : a chemical formula that gives the total number of atoms of each element present in a molecule

molecular weight *n* : the weight of a molecule equal to the sum of the weights of the atoms contained in it

mol·e·cule \'mäl-i-ˌkyül\ *n* [F *molécule,* fr. NL *molecula,* dim. of L *moles* mass] **1** : the smallest portion of a substance retaining all the properties of the substance in a mass ⟨a *molecule* of water⟩ ⟨a *molecule* of oxygen⟩ **2** : a very small bit : PARTICLE

mole·hill \'mōl-ˌhil\ *n* **1** : a little ridge of earth thrown up by a mole **2** : an unimportant obstacle

mole·skin \-ˌskin\ *n* **1** : the skin of the mole used as fur **2 a** : a heavy cotton fabric with a velvety nap on one side **b** : a garment made of moleskin — usu. used in pl.

mo·lest \mə-'lest\ *vt* [L *molestare,* fr. *molestus* burdensome, fr. *moles* mass, burden] **1** : to annoy, disturb, or persecute esp. with hostile intent or injurious effect **2** : to take indecent liberties with — **mo·les·ta·tion** \ˌmōl-ˌes-'tā-shən, ˌmäl-\ *n* — **mo·lest·er** \mə-'les-tər\ *n*

moll \'mäl\ *n* : a girl friend esp. of a gangster

mol·lie \'mäl-ē\ *n* : any of several brightly colored topminnows often kept in a tropical aquarium

mol·li·fy \'mäl-ə-ˌfī\ *vt* **-fied**; **-fy·ing** [L *mollis* soft; akin to E *melt*] **1** : CALM, QUIET **2** : APPEASE, PACIFY — **mol·li·fi·ca·tion** \ˌmäl-ə-fə-'kā-shən\ *n*

mol·lusk *or* **mol·lusc** \'mäl-əsk\ *n* [F *mollusque,* fr. NL *Mollusca,* phylum name, fr. L, neut. pl. of *molluscus* soft, fr. *mollis*] : any of a large phylum (Mollusca) of invertebrate animals (as snails or clams) with a soft body lacking segments and usu. enclosed in a calcareous shell — **mol·lus·can** *also* **mol·lus·kan** \mə-'ləs-kən, mä-\ *adj*

¹mol·ly·cod·dle \'mäl-ē-ˌkäd-ᵊl\ *n* : a person who is used to being coddled or petted; *esp* : a pampered man or boy

²mollycoddle *vt* **-cod·dled**; **-cod·dling** \-ˌkäd-liŋ, -ᵊl-iŋ\ : CODDLE, PAMPER — **mol·ly·cod·dler** \-ˌkäd-lər, -ᵊl-ər\ *n*

Mol·och \'mäl-ək, 'mō-ˌläk\ *or* **Mol·ech** \'mäl-ək, 'mō-ˌlek\ *n* : a Semitic deity worshiped through the sacrifice of children

Mol·o·tov cocktail \ˌmäl-ə-ˌtȯf-, ˌmō-lə-\ *n* [Vyacheslav M. *Molotov* b1890 Russian statesman] : a crude hand grenade made of a bottle filled with a flammable liquid (as gasoline) and fitted with a wick or saturated rag taped to the bottom and ignited at the moment of hurling

¹molt \'mōlt\ *vb* [ME *mouten,* fr. (assumed) OE *mūtian* to change, fr. L *mutare*] : to shed hair, feathers, outer skin, or horns periodically with the cast-off parts being replaced by a new growth — **molt·er** *n*

²molt *n* : the act or process of molting

mol·ten \'mōlt-ᵊn\ *adj* [ME, fr. pp. of *melten* to melt] **1** *obs* : made by melting and casting **2** : melted esp. by intense heat ⟨*molten* metal⟩⟨*molten* rock⟩

mol·to \'mȯl-tō, 'mōl-\ *adv* [It, fr. L *multum,* fr. *multus,* adj., much] : MUCH, VERY — used in music directions ⟨*molto* adagio⟩ ⟨*molto* sostenuto⟩

mo·ly \'mō-lē\ *n* [Gk *mōly*] : a mythical herb with black root, white flowers, and magic powers

mo·lyb·de·nite \mə-'lib-də-ˌnīt\ *n* : a soft lead-gray mineral MoS_2 consisting of molybdenum and sulfur and constituting a source of molybdenum

mo·lyb·de·num \-də-nəm\ *n* [NL, fr. Gk *molybdaina* galena, fr. *molybdos* lead] : a white metallic element used in steel alloys to give greater strength and hardness — see ELEMENT table

mo·ment \'mō-mənt\ *n* [L *momentum* movement, particle sufficient to turn the scales, moment, fr. *movēre* to move] **1** : a minute portion or point of time : INSTANT **2** : a time of importance or conspicuousness ⟨he has his *moments*⟩ **3** : IMPORTANCE, CONSEQUENCE ⟨a matter of great *moment*⟩ **4 a** : tendency to produce motion esp. about a point or axis **b** : the product of a force and the perpendicular distance from the axis to the line of action of the force

mo·men·tar·i·ly \ˌmō-mən-'ter-ə-lē\ *adv* **1** : for a moment ⟨the pain eased *momentarily*⟩ **2** : INSTANTLY ⟨he was stunned by the blow but recovered *momentarily*⟩ **3** : at any moment ⟨we expect him *momentarily*⟩

mo·men·tary \'mō-mən-ˌter-ē\ *adj* : lasting only a moment : SHORT-LIVED, TRANSITORY — **mo·men·tar·i·ness** \'mō-mən-ˌter-ē-nəs\ *n*

mo·ment·ly \'mō-mənt-lē\ *adv* : MOMENTARILY

mo·men·tous \mō-'ment-əs\ *adj* : very important : CONSEQUENTIAL ⟨a *momentous* decision⟩ — **mo·men·tous·ly** *adv* — **mo·men·tous·ness** *n*

mo·men·tum \mō-'ment-əm\ *n, pl* **-men·ta** \-'ment-ə\ *or* **-men·tums** [NL, fr. L, movement, moment] : a property of a moving body that determines the length of time required to bring it to rest when under the action of a constant force or moment : the product of the mass of a body and its velocity; *also* : IMPETUS

mon- *or* **mono-** *comb form* [Gk, fr. *monos* alone, single] **1** : one : single : alone ⟨*mono*plane⟩ ⟨*mono*drama⟩ ⟨*mono*phobia⟩ **2** : one atom or group ⟨*mono*xide⟩

mon·an·drous \mə-'nan-drəs, mä-\ *adj* [Gk *mon-* + *andr-, anēr* man, male] **1** : having a single stamen or flowers with a single stamen **2** : of, relating to, or being

ə abut; ᵊ kitten; ər further; a back; ā bake; ä cot, cart; au̇ out; ch chin; e less; ē easy; g gift; i trip; ī life

a marriage form in which a woman has but one husband at a time — **mon·an·dry** \'män-,an-drē\ n

mon·arch \'män-ərk, -,ärk\ n [Gk *monarchos,* fr. *mon-* + *archein* to rule] **1 :** a person who reigns over a kingdom or empire usu. for life and by hereditary succession: **a :** one having sovereign power and exercising effective control over the government 〈an absolute *monarch*〉 **b :** one acting primarily as chief of state and exercising only limited powers 〈a constitutional *monarch*〉 — compare CZAR, EMPEROR, KAISER, KING, QUEEN **2 :** someone or something holding preeminent position or power **3 :** a large orange and black migratory American butterfly — **mo·nar·chal** \mə-'när-kəl, mä-\ or **mo·nar·chi·al** \-kē-əl\ adj

mo·nar·chi·cal \mə-'när-ki-kəl, mä-\ or **mo·nar·chic** \-'när-kik\ adj **1 :** of, resembling, or having the powers of a monarch **2 :** having the form of a monarchy 〈*monarchical* government〉 **3 :** favoring monarchism — **mo·nar·chi·cal·ly** \-ki-k(ə-)lē\ adv

mon·ar·chism \'män-ər-,kiz-əm\ n **1 :** the principles of monarchical government **2 :** belief in or support of the principles of monarchical government — **mon·ar·chist** \-kəst\ n

mon·ar·chy \'män-ər-kē\ n, pl **-chies 1 :** undivided or absolute rule by one person **2 :** a nation or country having a monarch as chief of state **3 :** a form of government characterized by a usu. hereditary chief of state with life tenure and powers varying from nominal to absolute

mo·nar·da \mə-'närd-ə\ n : any of a genus of coarse No. American mints with whorls of showy flowers

mon·as·tery \'män-ə-,ster-ē\ n, pl **-ter·ies** [LGk *monastērion,* fr. Gk, hermit's cell, fr. *monazein* to live alone, fr. *monos* alone] : an establishment in which a community of religious persons and esp. monks live and carry on their work — **mon·as·te·ri·al** \,män-ə-'stir-ē-əl\ adj

mo·nas·tic \mə-'nas-tik\ adj **1 :** of or relating to monks or monasteries **2 :** separated from worldly affairs 〈a *monastic* life〉 — **monastic** n — **mo·nas·ti·cal·ly** \-ti-k(ə-)lē\ adv

mo·nas·ti·cism \mə-'nas-tə-,siz-əm\ n : the life or state of monks : the system or practice of living apart from the rest of the world for religious reasons esp. as members of a secluded community

mon·atom·ic \,män-ə-'täm-ik\ adj : consisting of one atom; *esp :* having but one atom in the molecule

mon·au·ral \(')män-'ȯ-rəl\ adj : MONOPHONIC 2 — **mon·au·ral·ly** \-rə-lē\ adv

mon·ax·i·al \(')män-'ak-sē-əl\ adj : having or based on a single axis 〈*monaxial* symmetry〉

Mon·day \'mən-dē\ n [OE *mōnandæg,* lit., day of the moon] : the 2d day of the week

mon·ecious *var of* MONOECIOUS

mon·e·tary \'män-ə-,ter-ē, 'mən-\ adj [L *moneta* mint, money] **1 :** of or relating to coinage or currency 〈*monetary* policy〉 **2 :** of or relating to money : PECUNIARY 〈*monetary* gifts〉 **syn** see FINANCIAL

monetary unit n : the standard unit of value of a currency

mon·e·tize \'män-ə-,tīz, 'mən-\ vt **1 a :** to establish as the standard of a national currency **b :** to establish as legal tender **2 :** to coin into money — **mon·e·ti·za·tion** \,män-ət-ə-'zā-shən, ,mən-\ n

mon·ey \'mən-ē\ n, pl **mon·eys** or **mon·ies** \-ēz\ [MF *moneie,* fr. L *moneta* mint, money] **1 :** something generally accepted as a medium of exchange, a measure of value, or a means of payment: as **a :** officially coined or stamped metal currency **b :** PAPER MONEY **c :** an amount or a sum of money **2 :** wealth reckoned in terms of money **3 :** a form or denomination of coin or paper money **4 :** the 1st, 2d, and 3d place in a horse or dog race 〈finished in the *money*〉 **5 :** persons or interests possessing or controlling great wealth — **mon·ey·lend·er** \'mən-ē-,len-dər\ n

mon·ey·bags \'mən-ē-,bagz\ n sing or pl : a wealthy person

money changer n : one whose business is the exchanging of kinds or denominations of currency

mon·eyed or **mon·ied** \'mən-ēd\ adj **1 :** having money : WEALTHY **2 :** consisting in or derived from money

mon·ey·mak·er \'mən-ē-,mā-kər\ n **1 :** one who accumulates wealth **2 :** a plan or product that produces profit — **mon·ey·mak·ing** \-kiŋ\ adj or n

money order n : an order purchased at a post office, bank, or express or telegraph office directing another office to pay to a named payee a specified sum of money equal to the purchaser's deposit at the issuing office

mon·ger \'məŋ-gər, 'mäŋ-\ n [OE *mangere,* fr. L *mangon-, mango*] **1 :** a dealer in some commodity — usu. used in combination 〈fish*monger*〉 **2 :** one dealing in or promoting something petty or discreditable 〈hate *monger*〉

Mon·gol \'mäŋ-gəl, 'män-,gōl\ n **1 a :** a member of one of the chiefly pastoral Mongoloid peoples of Mongolia **b :** MONGOLOID **2 :** MONGOLIAN 2

Mon·go·lian \män-'gōl-yən\ n **1 :** a native or inhabitant of Mongolia **2 :** the Mongolic language of the Mongol people — **Mongolian** adj

Mon·gol·ic \män-'gäl-ik\ n : a subfamily of Altaic languages including Mongolian and Kalmuck — **Mongolic** adj

mon·gol·ism \'mäŋ-gə-,liz-əm\ also **mon·go·lian·ism** \män-'gōl-yə-,niz-əm\ n : a congenital idiocy in which a child is born with slanting eyes, a broad short skull, and broad hands with short fingers

mon·gol·oid \'mäŋ-gə-,lȯid\ adj **1** cap **:** of or relating to a major racial stock native to Asia and considered to comprise peoples of northern and eastern Asia, Malaysians, Eskimos, and often American Indians **2 :** affected with mongolism — **mongoloid** n, often cap

mon·goose \'mäŋ-,güs, 'mäŋ-\ n, pl **mon·goos·es** [Hindi *māgūs*] : an agile grizzled Indian mammal that is related to the civets, is about the size of a ferret, and feeds on snakes and rodents

mon·grel \'mäŋ-grəl, 'mäŋ-\ n **1 :** the offspring of parents of different breeds (as of dogs); *esp :* one of uncertain ancestry **2 :** a person or thing of mixed origin — **mongrel** or **mon·grel·ly** \-grə-lē\ adj — **mon·grel·ism** \-grə-,liz-əm\ n — **mon·grel·i·za·tion** \,mäŋ-grə-lə-'zā-shən, ,mäŋ-\ n — **mon·grel·ize** \'məŋ-grə-,līz, 'mäŋ-\ vt

mo·nism \'mō-,niz-əm, 'män-,iz-\ n : a view that a complex entity (as the universe) is basically one — **mo·nist** \'mō-nəst, 'män-əst\ n — **mo·nis·tic** \mō-'nis-tik, mä-\ or **mo·nis·ti·cal** \-ti-kəl\ adj

¹mon·i·tor \'män-ət-ər\ n [L, one that warns, overseer, fr. *monēre* to warn] **1 a :** a student appointed to assist a teacher **b :** a person or thing that warns or instructs **c :** one that monitors or is used in monitoring; *esp :* a receiver used to view the picture being picked up by a television camera **2 :** any of various large tropical Old World lizards closely related to the iguanas **3 :** [after the *Monitor* (1862), first ship of the type] : a heavily armored warship formerly used in coastal operations that has a very low freeboard and one or more revolving gun turrets — **mon·i·to·ri·al** \,män-ə-'tōr-ē-əl, -'tȯr-\ adj — **mon·i·tor·ship** \'män-ət-ər-,ship\ n — **mon·i·tress** \'män-ə-trəs\ n

²monitor vt **mon·i·tored; mon·i·tor·ing** \'män-ət-ə-riŋ, 'män-ə-triŋ\ : to watch, observe, or check esp. for a special purpose: as **a :** to check (a radio or television signal or program) by means of a receiver for quality of transmission **b :** to check (a radio or television broadcast or a telephone conversation) for military, political, or criminal significance **c :** to test for intensity of radioactivity

mon·i·to·ry \'män-ə-,tōr-ē, -,tȯr-\ adj : giving admonition : WARNING

monk \'məŋk\ n [OE *munuc,* fr. LL *monachus,* fr. LGk *monachos,* fr. Gk *monos* alone] **1 :** a member of a religious order of men taking vows of poverty, chastity, and obedience and living in community under a rule — compare FRIAR **2 :** a member of a religious community of men **3 :** a man who renounces the world for ascetic reasons — **monk·hood** \-,hu̇d\ n

¹mon·key \'məŋ-kē\ n, pl **monkeys 1 :** a primate mammal other than man and usu. also the lemurs and tarsiers; *esp :* any of the smaller longer-tailed primates as contrasted with the apes **2 a :** a mischievous child : IMP **b :** a ludicrous figure : DUPE — **mon·key·ish** \-kē-ish\ adj

²monkey vi **mon·keyed; mon·key·ing 1 :** to act in a grotesque or mischievous manner **2 :** TRIFLE, MEDDLE

mon·key·shine \'məŋ-kē-,shīn\ n : a mischievous trick : PRANK

monkey wrench n **1 :** a wrench with one fixed and one

adjustable jaw at right angles to a straight handle — see WRENCH illustration **2 :** something that disrupts ⟨his last-minute proposal threw a *monkey wrench* into the negotiations⟩

monk·ish \'məŋ-kish\ *adj* **1 :** of or relating to monks **2 :** having features attributed to a monk or monasticism ⟨lived in *monkish* retirement⟩ — **monk·ish·ly** *adv* — **monk·ish·ness** *n*

monks·hood \'məŋ(k)s-,hùd\ *n* **:** a poisonous Eurasian herb related to the buttercups and often cultivated for its showy hood-shaped white or purplish flowers

mono- — see MON-

mono·ba·sic \,män-ə-'bā-sik\ *adj* **:** having only one hydrogen atom replaceable by an atom or radical ⟨*monobasic* acid⟩

mono·car·pel·lary \-'kär-pə-,ler-ē\ *adj* **:** consisting of a single carpel

mono·car·pic \-'kär-pik\ *adj* [Gk *karpos* fruit] **:** bearing fruit but once and dying

mono·chla·myd·e·ous \-klə-'mid-ē-əs\ *adj* [Gk *chlamyd-*, *chlamys* cloak] **:** lacking petals or sepals but not both; *also* **:** having monochlamydeous flowers

mono·chro·mat·ic \-krō-'mat-ik\ *adj* **1 :** having or consisting of one color **2 :** consisting of radiation (as light) of a single wavelength — **mono·chro·mat·i·cal·ly** \-'mat-i-k(ə-)lē\ *adv* — **mono·chro·ma·tic·i·ty** \-,krō-mə-'tis-ət-ē\ *n*

mono·chro·ma·tism \-'krō-mə-,tiz-əm\ *n* **:** complete color blindness in which all colors appear as shades of gray

mono·chrome \'män-ə-,krōm\ *n* **:** a painting, drawing, or photograph in a single hue — **monochrome** *adj*

mon·o·cle \'män-i-kəl\ *n* [F, fr. LL *monoculus* one-eyed, fr. Gk *mon-* + L *oculus* eye] **:** an eyeglass for one eye — **mon·o·cled** \-kəld\ *adj*

mono·clin·ic \,män-ə-'klin-ik\ *adj* **:** being a crystal in which the three axes are of unequal length with two of them at right angles to each other and the third perpendicular to only one of the other two

mono·cli·nous \-'klī-nəs\ *adj* [Gk *klinē* couch, fr. *klinein* to lean, recline] **:** having both stamens and pistils in the same flower — compare DICLINOUS

mon·o·cot \,män-ə-,kät\ *also* **mon·o·cot·yl** \-,kät-ⁱl\ *n* **:** MONOCOTYLEDON — **monocot** *adj*

mono·cot·y·le·don \,män-ə-,kät-ⁱl-'ēd-ⁿn\ *n* **:** any of a group (Monocotyledoneae) of seed plants having an embryo with a single cotyledon and usu. parallel-veined leaves and flower parts in groups of three — **mono·cot·y·le·don·ous** \-'n-əs\ *adj*

¹**mon·oc·u·lar** \mä-'näk-yə-lər, mə-\ *adj* **:** of, relating to, or suitable for use with only one eye

²**monocular** *n* **:** a monocular device (as a microscope)

mono·cul·ture \'män-ə-,kəl-chər\ *n* **:** the cultivation of a single product to the exclusion of all other uses of land

mono·cyte \'män-ə-,sīt\ *n* **:** a large phagocytic white blood cell — **mono·cyt·ic** \,män-ə-'sit-ik\ *adj* — **mono·cyt·oid** \-'sīt-,óid\ *adj*

mon·o·dy \'män-əd-ē\ *n, pl* **-dies** [Gk *monōidia* lyric sung by one voice, fr. *mon-* + *aidein* to sing] **1 :** ELEGY **2 :** a style of musical composition in which one voice part carries the melody; *also* **:** a composition in this style — **mo·nod·ic** \mə-'näd-ik\ *adj* — **mon·o·dist** \'män-əd-əst\ *n*

mon·oe·cious \mə-'nē-shəs, (')män-'ē-\ *adj* [Gk *mon-* + *oikos* house] **1 :** having male and female sex organs in the same individual **:** HERMAPHRODITIC **2 :** having pistillate and staminate flowers on the same plant — **mon·oe·cious·ly** *adv* — **mon·oe·cism** \mə-'nē-,siz-əm, (')män-'ē-\ *or* **mon·oe·cy** \'män-,ē-sē\ *n*

mo·nog·a·mous \mə-'näg-ə-məs\ *adj* **:** of, relating to, or practicing monogamy — **mo·nog·a·mous·ly** *adv* — **mo·nog·a·mous·ness** *n*

mo·nog·a·my \mə-'näg-ə-mē\ *n* **:** marriage with but one person at a time — **mo·nog·a·mist** \-'näg-ə-məst\ *n*

mono·gen·ic \,män-ə-'jen-ik\ *adj* **:** of, relating to, or controlled by a single gene and esp. by either of an allelic pair — **mono·gen·i·cal·ly** \-'jen-i-k(ə-)lē\ *adv*

mono·gram \'män-ə-,gram\ *n* **:** an identifying symbol made up of the combined initials of a person's name — **monogram** *vt* — **mono·grammed** \-,gramd\ *adj*

mono·graph \'män-ə-,graf\ *n* **:** a learned treatise on a

particular subject; *esp* **:** a scholarly or scientific paper printed in a journal or as a pamphlet

mo·nog·y·nous \mə-'näj-ə-nəs\ *adj* [Gk *gynē* woman, wife] **1 :** having a single pistil or flowers with a single pistil **2 :** of, relating to, or being a marriage form in which a man has but one wife at a time — **mo·nog·y·ny** \-'näj-ə-nē\ *n*

mono·hy·brid \,män-ə-'hī-brəd\ *adj* **:** heterozygous in respect to a single gene pair — **monohybrid** *n*

mono·lay·er \'män-ə-,lā-ər, -,le(-)ər\ *n* **:** a layer one molecule in thickness

mono·lin·gual \,män-ə-'liŋ-gwəl\ *adj* **:** expressed in or knowing or using only one language

mon·o·lith \'män-ⁱl-,ith\ *n* [Gk *monolithos* consisting of a single stone, fr. *mon-* + *lithos* stone] **1 :** a single great stone often in the form of a monument or column **2 :** something (as a political organization or a social structure) held to be a single massive whole exhibiting solid uniformity — **mon·o·lith·ic** \,män-ⁱl-'ith-ik\ *adj*

mon·o·logue *or* **mon·o·log** \'män-ⁱl-,óg, \'man-ⁱl-,äg\ *n* [F *monologue*, fr. *mon-* + *-logue* (as in *dialogue*)] **1 :** a dramatic scene in which one person speaks alone **2 :** a drama performed by one actor **3 :** a literary composition (as a poem) in the form of a soliloquy **4 :** a long speech monopolizing a conversation — **mon·o·logu·ist** \'män-ⁱl-,óg-əst\ *n*

mono·ma·nia \,män-ə-'mā-nē-ə, -'mā-nyə\ *n* **1 :** mental derangement restricted to one idea or group of ideas **2 :** excessive concentration on a single object or idea — **mono·ma·ni·ac** \-'mā-nē-,ak\ *n or adj*

mon·o·mer \'män-ə-mər\ *n* **:** one of the molecular units of a polymer — **mon·o·mer·ic** \,män-ə-'mer-ik\ *adj*

mo·nom·e·ter \mə-'näm-ət-ər\ *n* [Gk *monometros*, fr. *mon-* + *metron* measure] **:** a line consisting of one metrical foot

mo·no·mi·al \mä-'nō-mē-əl, mə-'nō-\ *n* [*mon-* + *-nomial* (as in *binomial*)] **:** an expression (as in mathematics) consisting of a single term — **monomial** *adj*

mono·mo·lec·u·lar \,män-ō-mə-'lek-yə-lər\ *adj* **:** being only one molecule thick ⟨a *monomolecular* film⟩ — **mono·mo·lec·u·lar·ly** *adv*

mono·nu·cle·ar \,män-ō-'n(y)ü-klē-ər\ *adj* **:** having only one nucleus — **mononuclear** *n*

mo·noph·a·gous \mə-'näf-ə-gəs\ *adj* **:** feeding on a single kind of plant or animal — **mo·noph·a·gy** \-'näf-ə-jē\ *n*

mono·phon·ic \,män-ə-'fän-ik\ *adj* **1 :** having a single melodic line with little or no accompaniment **2 :** of or relating to sound transmission, recording, or reproduction involving a single transmission path — compare STEREOPHONIC

mon·oph·thong \'män-ə(f)-,thóŋ\ *n* [Gk *phthongos* sound] **:** a vowel sound that throughout its duration has a single constant articulatory position — **mon·oph·thon·gal** \,män-ə(f)-'thóŋ-(g)əl\ *adj*

mono·phy·let·ic \,män-ō-fī-'let-ik\ *adj* **:** of or relating to a single stock; *esp* **:** developed from a single common parent form — **mono·phy·let·i·cal·ly** \-'let-i-k(ə-)lē\ *adv* — **mono·phy·le·tism** \,män-ō-'fī-lə-,tiz-əm\ *n* — **mono·phy·le·ty** \-,lət-ē\ *n*

mono·plane \'män-ə-,plān\ *n* **:** an airplane with only one main supporting surface

mono·ploid \'män-ə-,plóid\ *adj* [*mon-* + *-ploid* (as in *diploid*)] **:** having or being a chromosome set comprising a single genome — **monoploid** *n*

mo·nop·o·list \mə-'näp-ə-ləst\ *n* **:** one who has a monopoly or favors monopoly

mo·nop·o·lis·tic \mə-,näp-ə-'lis-tik\ *adj* **:** tending toward or having the characteristics of monopoly — **mo·nop·o·lis·ti·cal·ly** \-'lis-ti-k(ə-)lē\ *adv*

mo·nop·o·lize \mə-'näp-ə-,līz\ *vt* **:** to acquire or have a monopoly of — **mo·nop·o·li·za·tion** \-,näp-ə-lə-'zā-shən\ *n* — **mo·nop·o·liz·er** \-'näp-ə-,lī-zər\ *n*

mo·nop·o·ly \mə-'näp-(ə-)lē\ *n, pl* **-lies** [Gk *monopōlion*, fr. *mon-* + *pōlein* to sell] **1 a :** exclusive ownership or control through legal privilege, command of supply, or concerted action **b :** exclusive possession **2 :** an instance of monopoly **3 :** a commodity controlled by one party **4 :** a person or group having a monopoly

syn TRUST, SYNDICATE, CARTEL: MONOPOLY implies exclusive power to buy or sell in a specified market; TRUST applies specif. to a merger of corporations by which control is given to trustees and the individual owners are compensated by shares of stock; SYNDICATE applies to a group organized to carry out an enterprise or purchase a property requiring large capital outlay; CARTEL commonly implies an international combination of firms for controlling production and control of products in one field or division of industry

mono·rail \'män-ə-ˌrāl\ *n* : a single rail serving as a track for cars that are balanced upon it or suspended from it

mono·sac·cha·ride \ˌmän-ə-'sak-ə-ˌrīd\ *n* : a sugar not decomposable to simpler sugars by hydrolysis

mono·so·mic \ˌmän-ə-'sō-mik\ *adj* : having one less than the diploid number of chromosomes — **monosomic** *n*

mono·syl·la·ble \'män-ə-ˌsil-ə-bəl, ˌmän-ə-'\ *n* : a word of one syllable — **mono·syl·lab·ic** \ˌmän-ə-sə-'lab-ik\ *adj* — **mono·syl·lab·i·cal·ly** \-'lab-i-k(ə-)lē\ *adv*

mono·the·ism \'män-ə-(ˌ)thē-ˌiz-əm\ *n* : a doctrine or belief that there is only one deity — **mono·the·ist** \-ˌthē-əst\ *n* — **mono·the·is·tic** \-thē-'is-tik\ *adj*

mono·tone \'män-ə-ˌtōn\ *n* 1 : a succession of syllables, words, or sentences on one unvaried key or pitch ⟨speak in a *monotone*⟩ 2 : a single unvaried musical tone 3 a : tedious sameness of tone or style ⟨a poem written in *monotone*⟩ b : sameness of color ⟨engravings in *monotone*⟩ 4 : a person not able to produce musical intervals properly with the voice — **monotone** *adj* — **mono·ton·ic** \ˌmän-ə-'tän-ik\ *adj* — **mono·ton·i·cal·ly** \-'tän-i-k(ə-)lē\ *adv*

mo·not·o·nous \mə-'nät-ᵊn-əs, -'nät-nəs\ *adj* 1 : uttered or sounded in one unvarying tone 2 : tediously uniform or unvarying ⟨a *monotonous* voice⟩ — **mo·not·o·nous·ly** *adv* — **mo·not·o·nous·ness** *n*

mo·not·o·ny \mə-'nät-ᵊn-ē, -'nät-nē\ *n, pl* **-nies** 1 : sameness of tone or sound 2 : lack of variety; *esp* : tiresome sameness ⟨the *monotony* of the empty landscape⟩

mono·treme \'män-ə-ˌtrēm\ *n* [Gk *trēma* hole] : any of an order (Monotremata) of lowly egg-laying mammals comprising the duckbills and echidnas

Mono·type \'män-ə-ˌtīp\ *trademark* — used for a keyboard typesetting machine that casts and sets type in separate characters

mono·typ·ic \ˌmän-ə-'tip-ik\ *adj* : including a single representative — used esp. of a genus with only one species

mono·va·lent \ˌmän-ə-'vā-lənt\ *adj* : UNIVALENT

mon·ovu·lar \(')män-'ō-vyə-lər\ *adj* [L *ovum* egg] : derived from a single egg ⟨*monovular* twins⟩

mon·ox·ide \mə-'näk-ˌsīd\ *n* : an oxide containing only one oxygen atom in the molecule

mono·zy·got·ic \ˌmän-ə-zī-'gät-ik\ *adj* : MONOVULAR

Mon·roe Doctrine \mən-ˌrō-\ *n* : a statement of U.S. foreign policy proclaimed in 1823 by President James Monroe expressing opposition to extension of European control or influence in the western hemisphere

mon·sei·gneur \ˌmōⁿ-ˌsān-'yər\ *n, pl* **mes·sei·gneurs** \ˌmā-ˌsān-'yər(z)\ [F, lit., my lord] : a French dignitary — used as a title preceding a title of office or rank ⟨*Monseigneur* the Archbishop⟩

mon·sieur \məs(h)-'yə(r), mə-'si(ə)r\ *n, pl* **mes·sieurs** \same, *or with* z *added*\ [F, lit., my lord] — used as a title equivalent to *Mister* and prefixed to the name of a Frenchman

mon·si·gnor \män-'sē-nyər\ *n, pl* **mon·si·gnors** *or* **mon·si·gno·ri** \ˌmän-ˌsēn-'yōr-ē, -'yȯr-\ [It *monsignore*, fr. F *monseigneur*, lit., my lord] : a Roman Catholic clergyman with the office of vicar-general or one of several papal offices or titular distinctions — used as a title prefixed to the surname or to the given name and surname — **mon·si·gno·ri·al** \ˌmän-ˌsēn-'yōr-ē-əl, -'yȯr-\ *adj*

mon·soon \män-'sün\ *n* [obs. D *monssoen*, fr. Pg *monção*, fr. Ar *mawsim* time, season] 1 : a wind in the Indian ocean and southern Asia that blows from the southwest from April to October and from the northeast from October to April 2 : the rainy season that accompanies the southwest monsoon in India and adjacent areas

¹**mon·ster** \'män(t)-stər\ *n* [L *monstrum* portent, monster] 1 : an animal or plant of abnormal form or structure 2 : a creature of strange or horrible form 3 : one unusually large for its kind 4 : an extremely wicked or cruel person

²**monster** *adj* : very large : ENORMOUS

mon·strance \'män(t)-strən(t)s\ *n* [ML *monstrantia*, fr.

L *monstrare* to show] : a vessel in which the consecrated Host is exposed for the adoration of the faithful

mon·stros·i·ty \män-'sträs-ət-ē\ *n, pl* **-ties** 1 : the condition of being monstrous 2 : something monstrous : MONSTER

mon·strous \'män(t)-strəs\ *adj* 1 : being great or overwhelming in size : GIGANTIC 2 : having the qualities or appearance of a monster 3 a : very ugly or vicious : HORRIBLE b : shockingly wrong or ridiculous 4 : deviating greatly from the natural form or character — **mon·strous·ly** *adv* — **mon·strous·ness** *n*

monstrance

syn MONSTROUS, PRODIGIOUS, TREMENDOUS, STUPENDOUS mean extremely impressive in size. MONSTROUS further implies ugliness or abnormality; PRODIGIOUS suggests a marvelousness that strains belief; TREMENDOUS implies an awe-inspiring or terrifying effect; STUPENDOUS suggests a power to stun or astound

mon·tage \män-'täzh\ *n* [F, fr. *monter* to mount] 1 : a composite photograph made by combining several separate pictures 2 : an artistic composition made up of several different kinds of items (as strips of newspaper, pictures, bits of wood) arranged together

month \'mən(t)th\ *n, pl* **months** \'mən(t)s, 'mən(t)ths\ [OE *mōnath*; akin to E *moon*] 1 : one of the 12 portions into which the year is divided 2 : MOON 2; *also* : a period of 28 days regarded as the period of revolution of the moon

¹**month·ly** \'mən(t)th-lē\ *adj* 1 : occurring, done, produced, or issued every month 2 : computed in terms of one month 3 : lasting a month — **monthly** *adv*

²**monthly** *n, pl* **monthlies** 1 : a monthly periodical 2 *pl* : a menstrual period

month's mind *n* : a Roman Catholic requiem mass for a person a month after his death

mon·u·ment \'män-yə-mənt\ *n* [L *monumentum*, fr. *monēre* to remind, warn] 1 : something that serves as a memorial; *esp* : a building, pillar, stone, or statue provided in memory of a person or event 2 : a work, saying, or deed that lasts or that is worth preserving ⟨the book is a *monument* of scholarship⟩ 3 : a boundary marker (as a stone) 4 : a natural feature or historic site set aside and maintained by the government as public property

mon·u·men·tal \ˌmän-yə-'ment-ᵊl\ *adj* 1 : serving as or resembling a monument : MASSIVE; *also* : OUTSTANDING 2 : of, relating to, or suitable for a monument 3 : very great : COLOSSAL ⟨*monumental* stupidity⟩ — **mon·u·men·tal·ly** \-ᵊl-ē\ *adv*

moo \'mü\ *vi* : to make the natural throat noise of a cow : LOW — **moo** *n*

¹**mood** \'müd\ *n* [OE *mōd* mind, mood] : a state or frame of mind : HUMOR, DISPOSITION ⟨in a good *mood*⟩

syn MOOD, HUMOR, TEMPER mean a state of mind in which one emotion or desire temporarily has control. MOOD implies a pervasiveness and compelling quality of the emotion ⟨he could write only when in the *mood* for it⟩ HUMOR implies a mood resulting from one's special temperament or present physical condition ⟨a good dinner put him in a better *humor*⟩ TEMPER suggests the domination of a single strong emotion such as anger ⟨quick *temper* over trifles⟩

²**mood** *n* [alter. of ¹*mode*] : a set of inflectional forms of a verb that show whether the action or state expressed is to be thought of as a fact, a command, or a wish or possibility — compare IMPERATIVE, INDICATIVE, SUBJUNCTIVE

moody \'müd-ē\ *adj* **mood·i·er; -est** 1 : subject to moods; *esp* : subject to fits of depression or bad temper 2 : expressing a moody state of mind ⟨a *moody* face⟩ — **mood·i·ly** \'müd-ᵊl-ē\ *adv* — **mood·i·ness** \'müd-ē-nəs\ *n*

¹**moon** \'mün\ *n* [OE *mōna*] 1 a : the earth's natural satellite shining by the sun's reflected light, revolving about the earth from west to east in about 29½ days, and having a diameter of 2160 miles and a mean distance from the earth of about 238,857 miles and a volume about one forty-ninth that of the earth b : SATELLITE 2a 2 : the average period of revolution of the moon about the earth equal to about 29½ days 3 : MOONLIGHT

²**moon** *vb* : to spend time in idle thought : DREAM ⟨*moon* away the hours⟩

moon·beam \'mün-ˌbēm\ *n* : a ray of light from the moon

j joke; **ŋ** sing; **ō** flow; **ȯ** flaw; **ȯi** coin; **th** thin; **t͟h** this; **ü** loot; **u̇** foot; **y** yet; **yü** few; **yu̇** furious; **zh** vision

moon blindness n **1** : a recurrent eye disorder of the horse **2** : NIGHT BLINDNESS — **moon–blind** \-,blīnd\ adj
moon·calf \-,kaf, -,kȧf\ n **1** : MONSTER 1 **2** : a foolish or absentminded person : SIMPLETON
moon·fish \-,fish\ n : any of various compressed often short deep-bodied silvery or yellowish marine fishes
moon-flow·er \-,flaů(-ə)r\ n : a tropical American morning glory with fragrant night-blooming flowers; also : any of several related plants
moon·let \'mün-lət\ n : a small natural or artificial satellite
moon·light \-,līt\ n : the light of the moon
moon·light·er \-,līt-ər\ n : a person holding two jobs at the same time — **moon·light·ing** \-,līt-iŋ\ n
moon·lit \-,lit\ adj : lighted by the moon ⟨a moonlit night⟩
moon·scape \'mün-,skāp\ n : the surface of the moon as seen or as pictured
moon·shine \-,shīn\ n **1** : MOONLIGHT **2** : empty talk : NONSENSE **3** : intoxicating liquor; esp : illegally distilled corn whiskey — **moon·shin·er** \-,shī-nər\ n
moon·stone \-,stōn\ n : a transparent or translucent mineral with a pearly greenish or bluish luster that is a variety of feldspar and is used in jewelry
moon·struck \-,strək\ adj **1** : mentally unbalanced **2** : romantically sentimental
¹moor \'mů(ə)r\ n [OE mōr] : an area of open wasteland that is usu. infertile or wet and peaty
²moor vb [ME moren] : to secure or fasten with cables, lines, or anchors ⟨moor a boat⟩ — **moor·age** \-ij\ n
Moor \'mů(ə)r\ n : one of a No. African people of mixed Arab and Berber ancestry conquering Spain in the 8th century and ruling until 1492 — **Moor·ish** \-ish\ adj
moor·hen \'mů(ə)r-,hen\ n : GALLINULE
moor·ing \'mů(ə)r-iŋ\ n **1 a** : a place where or an object to which a craft can be made fast **b** : a device (as a chain or line) by which an object is moored **2** : moral or spiritual resources — usu. used in pl.
moor·land \'mů(ə)r-lənd, -,land\ n : land consisting of moors
moose \'müs\ n, pl **moose** [of Algonquian origin] **1** : a large ruminant mammal related to the typical deers and found in forested parts of Canada and the northern U.S. **2** : ELK 1
¹moot \'müt\ vt [obs. moot discussion, fr. OE mōt assembly; akin to E meet] **1** : to bring up for discussion : BROACH **2** : DEBATE
²moot adj : subject to argument or discussion : DEBATABLE ⟨a moot question⟩
moot court n : a mock court in which students of law argue hypothetical cases for practice
¹mop \'mäp\ n [ME mappe] **1 a** : an implement for cleaning made of a bundle of cloth or yarn fastened to a handle **b** : a device consisting of a sponge fastened to a handle **2** : something resembling a mop ⟨a tangled mop of hair⟩
²mop vb **mopped; mop·ping** : to wipe or clean with or as if with a mop ⟨mop the floor⟩ ⟨mopped his brow with a handkerchief⟩ — **mop·per** n
¹mope \'mōp\ vb : to be or pass in a dull and dispirited state — **mop·er** n
²mope n **1** : a dull listless person **2** pl : low spirits : BLUES ⟨a fit of the mopes⟩
mop·pet \'mäp-ət\ n [obs. mop fool, child] : a young child
mop up \(')mäp-'əp\ vb **1** : to clean up by or as if by mopping ⟨mop up spilt milk⟩ **2** : to eliminate remaining resistance ⟨mop up an area⟩ ⟨mop up enemy forces⟩ **3** : to finish a task
mop–up \'mäp-,əp\ n : a final clearance or disposal
mo·raine \mə-'rān\ n [F] : an accumulation of earth and stones deposited by a glacier — **mo·rain·al** \-'rān-ᵊl\ adj — **mo·rain·ic** \-'rā-nik\ adj
¹mor·al \'mȯr-əl, 'mär-\ adj [L moralis, fr. mor-, mos custom, pl., mores character, morals] **1 a** : of or relating to principles of right and wrong in behavior : ETHICAL **b** : expressing or teaching a conception of right behavior ⟨a moral poem⟩ **c** : conforming to a standard of right behavior : VIRTUOUS, GOOD ⟨moral conduct⟩ ⟨a moral man⟩ **d** : capable of right and wrong action ⟨man is a moral being⟩ **2** : probable but not proved : VIRTUAL ⟨a moral certainty⟩ — **mor·al·ly** \-ə-lē\ adv
syn ETHICAL: MORAL and ETHICAL are both concerned

with rightness or wrongness of actions and conduct, but MORAL is more often applied to the practice or acts of individuals, now esp. in sexual relations, ETHICAL more often to theoretical or general questions of rightness, fairness, or equity
²moral n **1** : the inner meaning of or lesson to be learned from a story or an experience **2** pl : moral conduct ⟨men of bad morals⟩ **3** pl : moral teachings or principles
mo·rale \mə-'ral\ n [F moral, fr. moral, adj., moral] : the mental and emotional condition (as of enthusiasm, spirit, loyalty) of an individual or a group with regard to the function or tasks at hand
mor·al·ist \'mȯr-ə-ləst, 'mär-\ n **1** : one who moralizes; esp : a person who teaches, studies, or points out morals **2** : one who leads a moral life
mor·al·is·tic \,mȯr-ə-'lis-tik, ,mär-\ adj **1** : teaching or pointing out morals : MORALIZING ⟨a moralistic story⟩ **2** : narrowly conventional in morals ⟨a moralistic attitude towards the problems of youth⟩ — **mor·al·is·ti·cal·ly** \-'lis-ti-k(ə-)lē\ adv
mo·ral·i·ty \mə-'ral-ət-ē\ n, pl **-ties** **1** : moral quality or character : VIRTUE ⟨judge the morality of an action⟩ **2** : moral conduct : MORALS ⟨standards of morality⟩ **3** : a system of morals : principles of conduct
morality play n : an allegorical play esp. of the 15th and 16th centuries in which the characters personify moral qualities or abstractions
mor·al·ize \'mȯr-ə-,līz, 'mär-\ vb **1** : to explain in a moral sense : draw a moral from **2** : to make moral or morally better **3** : to make moral reflections : talk or write in a moralistic way — **mor·al·i·za·tion** \,mȯr-ə-lə-'zā-shən, ,mär-\ n — **mor·al·iz·er** \'mȯr-ə-,lī-zər, 'mär-\ n
mo·rass \mə-'ras\ n [D moeras] : MARSH, SWAMP — **mo·rassy** \-'ras-ē\ adj
mor·a·to·ri·um \,mȯr-ə-'tōr-ē-əm, ,mär-, -'tȯr-\ n, pl **-ri·ums** or **-ria** \-ē-ə\ [NL, fr. L morari to delay, fr. mora delay] **1** : a legally authorized period of delay in the performance of a legal obligation and esp. the payment of a debt ⟨a moratorium on war debt payments⟩ **2** : a temporary ban or suspension ⟨a moratorium on atomic testing⟩
Mo·ra·vi·an \mə-'rā-vē-ən\ n **1** : a member of a Christian denomination that traces its history back through the evangelical movement in Moravia and Bohemia to the doctrines of John Huss **2 a** : a native or inhabitant of Moravia **b** : the group of Czech dialects spoken by the Moravian people — **Moravian** adj
mo·ray \mə-'rā, 'mȯr-,ā\ n [Pg moréia, fr. L muraena, fr. Gk myraina] : any of numerous often brightly colored savage voracious eels occurring in warm seas
mor·bid \'mȯr-bəd\ adj [L morbidus, fr. morbus disease] **1 a** : of, relating to, or characteristic of disease ⟨morbia anatomy⟩ **b** : not healthful : DISEASED ⟨morbid condition⟩ **2** : characterized by gloomy or unwholesome ideas or feelings ⟨takes a morbid interest in funerals⟩ — **mor·bid·ly** adv — **mor·bid·ness** n
mor·bid·i·ty \mȯr-'bid-ət-ē\ n, pl **-ties** **1** : the quality or state of being morbid **2** : the relative incidence of disease
¹mor·dant \'mȯrd-ᵊnt\ adj [MF, prp. of mordre to bite, fr. L mordēre] : biting and caustic in thought, manner, or style : INCISIVE ⟨mordant criticism⟩ — **mor·dan·cy** \-ᵊn-sē\ n — **mor·dant·ly** adv
²mordant n **1** : a chemical that fixes a dye in or on a substance by combining with the dye to form an insoluble compound **2** : a corroding substance used in etching
³mordant vt : to treat with a mordant
Mor·de·cai \'mȯrd-i-,kī\ n : a cousin of Esther who saved the Jews from the destruction planned by Haman
mor·dent \'mȯrd-ᵊnt, mȯr-'dent\ n [It mordente] : a musical ornament made by a quick alternation of a principal tone with the tone below
¹more \'mō(ə)r, 'mȯ(ə)r\ adj [OE māra] **1** : greater in amount or degree ⟨felt more pain⟩ **2** : ADDITIONAL, FURTHER ⟨bought more apples⟩
²more adv **1 a** : in addition **b** : MOREOVER **2** : to a greater or higher degree — often used with an adjective or adverb to form the comparative ⟨more active⟩ ⟨more actively⟩
³more n **1** : a greater amount or number ⟨got more than

he expected⟩ **2 a :** an additional amount ⟨too full to eat *more*⟩ **b :** additional persons or things ⟨the *more* the merrier⟩

mo·rel \mə-'rel\ *n* [F *morille*] **:** any of several large pitted edible fungi

mo·rel·lo \mə-'rel-ō\ *n* **:** a cultivated sour cherry with dark red fruit

more·over \mōr-'ō-vər, mòr-\ *adv* **:** in addition to what has been said **:** BESIDES

mo·res \'mó(ə)r-,āz, 'mō(ə)r-, -,ēz\ *n pl* [L, pl. of *mor-, mos* custom] **1 :** the fixed morally binding customs of a particular group **2 :** CUSTOMS, CONVENTIONS

Mor·gan \'mòr-gən\ *n* [after Justin *Morgan* d1798 American teacher] **:** any of an American breed of light horses originated in Vermont

mor·ga·nat·ic marriage \,mòr-gə-,nat-ik-\ *n* [ML *morganaticum* morning gift (given by the husband to the wife on the morning after consummation of the marriage), fr. Old High German *morgan* morning] **:** a marriage between a person of royal or noble rank and a commoner who does not assume the superior partner's rank and whose children do not succeed to the title or inheritance of the parent of superior rank

morgue \'mòrg\ *n* [F] **1 :** a place where the bodies of persons found dead are kept usu. for identification until released for burial **2 :** a department of a newspaper where reference material is filed

mor·i·bund \'mòr-ə-(,)bənd, 'mär-\ *adj* [L *moribundus*, fr. *mori* to die] **:** being in a dying state — **mor·i·bun·di·ty** \,mòr-ə-'bən-dət-ē, ,mär-\ *n*

mo·ri·on \'mōr-ē-,än, 'mòr-\ *n* **:** a high-crested helmet with no visor

Mo·ris·co \mə-'ris-kō\ *n, pl* **-cos** *or* **-coes :** MOOR; *esp* **:** a Spanish Moor — **Morisco** *adj*

Mor·mon \'mòr-mən\ *n* **:** LATTER-DAY SAINT; *esp* **:** a member of the Church of Jesus Christ of Latter-Day Saints — **Mormon** *adj* — **Mor·mon·ism** \'mòr-mə-,niz-əm\ *n*

morn \'mòrn\ *n* [OE *morgen*] **1 :** DAWN **2 :** MORNING

morn·ing \'mòr-niŋ\ *n* [ME, fr. *morn* + *-ing* (as in *evening*)] **1 a :** DAWN **b :** the time from sunrise to noon **c :** the time from midnight to noon **2 :** the first or early part ⟨the *morning* of life⟩

morning glory *n* **:** any of various usu. twining plants with showy trumpet-shaped flowers that usu. close when the sun is high; *also* **:** any of various related plants including herbs, vines, shrubs, or trees with alternate leaves and regular usu. funnel-shaped flowers

Morning Prayer *n* **:** a morning service of the Anglican communion

morn·ings \'mòr-niŋz\ *adv* **:** in the morning repeatedly ⟨he only works *mornings*⟩

morning sickness *n* **:** nausea on arising usu. associated with early pregnancy

morning star *n* **:** any of the planets Venus, Jupiter, Mars, Mercury, and Saturn when it rises before the sun; *esp* **:** VENUS

Mo·ro \'mōr-ō, 'mòr-\ *n* **:** a member of any of several Muslim peoples of the southern Philippines — **Moro** *adj*

mo·roc·co \mə-'räk-ō\ *n* [*Morocco*, Africa] **:** a fine leather made of goat skins tanned with sumac

mo·ron \'mōr-,än, 'mòr-\ *n* [Gk *mōros* foolish, stupid] **1 :** a feebleminded person having a potential mental age of between eight and twelve years and being capable of doing routine work under supervision **2 :** a very stupid person **syn** see IDIOT — **mo·ron·ic** \mə-'rän-ik, mò-\ *adj* — **mo·ron·i·cal·ly** \-'rän-i-k(ə-)lē\ *adv*

mo·rose \mə-'rōs\ *adj* [L *morosus*, lit., capricious, fr. *mor-, mos* custom, habit] **1 :** having a sullen and gloomy disposition **2 :** marked by or expressive of gloom — **mo·rose·ly** *adv* — **mo·rose·ness** *n*

mor·pheme \'mòr-,fēm\ *n* **:** a meaningful linguistic unit that contains no smaller meaningful parts

Mor·pheus \'mòr-fē-əs, -,fyüs\ *n* **:** the Greek god of dreams

mor·phia \'mòr-fē-ə\ *n* **:** MORPHINE

mor·phine \'mòr-,fēn\ *n* [F, fr. *Morpheus*] **:** a bitter white crystalline habit-forming drug made from opium and used to deaden pain and to induce sleep

mor·pho·gen·e·sis \,mòr-fə-'jen-ə-səs\ *n, pl* **-gen·e·ses** \-'jen-ə-,sēz\ **1 :** BIOGENESIS 2 **2 :** ORGANOGENESIS —

mor·pho·ge·net·ic \,mòr-fə-jə-'net-ik\ *adj* — **mor·pho·gen·ic** \-fə-'jen-ik\ *adj*

mor·phol·o·gy \mòr-'fäl-ə-jē\ *n* [Gk *morphē* form] **1 a :** a branch of biology that deals with the form and structure of animals and plants **b :** the form and structure of an organism or any of its parts **2 :** the part of grammar dealing with word formation and including inflection, derivation, and the formation of compounds **3 a :** a study of structure or form **b :** STRUCTURE, FORM ⟨the *morphology* of rocks⟩ — **mor·pho·log·i·cal** \,mòr-fə-'läj-i-kəl\ *adj* — **mor·pho·log·i·cal·ly** \-i-k(ə-)lē\ *adv* — **mor·phol·o·gist** \mòr-'fäl-ə-jəst\ *n*

-mor·phous \'mòr-fəs\ *adj comb form* [Gk *-morphos*, fr. *morphē* form] **:** having (such) a form ⟨isomorphous⟩

mor·ris \'mòr-əs, 'mär-\ *n* [ME *moreys* Moorish] **:** a vigorous English dance performed by men wearing costumes and bells

Mor·ris chair *n* [after William *Morris* d1896 English poet and artist] **:** an easy chair with adjustable back and removable cushions

mor·row \'mär-ō, 'mòr-\ *n* [ME *morwen, morwe*, fr. OE *morgen*] **1** *archaic* **:** MORNING **2 :** the next following day

Morse code \'mòrs-\ *n* [after Samuel F. B. *Morse* d1872 American inventor] **:** either of two codes consisting of dots and dashes or long and short sounds used for transmitting messages by audible or visual signals

MORSE CODE

AMERICAN MORSE CODE[1]

A ·—	K —·—	U ··—			5 ———		
B —···	L ——	V ···—			6 ·····—		
C ·· ·	M ——	W ·——			7 ——··		
D —··	N —·	X ·—··			8 —····		
E ·	O · ·	Y ·· ··			9 —··—		
F ·—·	P ·····	Z ··· ·			0 —		
G ——·	Q ··—·				(comma) ·—·—		
H ····	R · ···	2 ··—··					
I ··	S ···	3 ···—			& ·—··		
J —·—·	T —	4 ···—					

INTERNATIONAL CODE[2]

A ·—	N —·	Á ·——·—	8 —····
B —···	O ———	Ä ·—·—	9 ——··—
C —·—·	P ·——·	É ··—··	0 —————
D —··	Q ——·—	Ñ ——·——	, (comma) ——··——
E ·	R ·—·	Ö ———·	
F ··—·	S ···	Ü ··——	? ··——··
G ——·	T —	1 ·————	; —·—·—·
H ····	U ··—	2 ··———	' (apostrophe) ·————·
I ··	V ···—	3 ···——	' ·——·—·
J ·———	W ·——	4 ····—	- (hyphen) —····—
K —·—	X —··—	5 ·····	/ —··—·
L ·—··	Y —·——	6 —····	parenthesis —·——·—
M ——	Z ——··	7 ——···	underline ··——·—

[1]Formerly used on overland telegraph lines in the U.S. and Canada but largely out of use

[2]Often called the continental code; a modification of this code, with dots only, is used on ocean cables

mor·sel \'mòr-səl\ *n* [OF, dim. of *mors* bite, fr. L *morsus*, fr. *mors-, mordēre* to bite] **1 :** a small piece of food **:** BITE **2 :** a small quantity **:** a little piece

¹mor·tal \'mòrt-°l\ *adj* [L *mortalis*, fr. *mort-, mors* death; akin to E *murder*] **1 :** capable of causing death **:** FATAL ⟨a *mortal* wound⟩ **2 a :** subject to death ⟨*mortal* man⟩ **b :** very tedious or prolonged ⟨three *mortal* hours⟩ **3 :** unrelentingly hostile **:** IMPLACABLE ⟨a *mortal* enemy⟩ **4 a :** committed in a grave matter with awareness of guilt and full consent and held in Roman Catholicism to bring eternal punishment ⟨*mortal* sin⟩ — compare VENIAL **b :** very great, intense, or severe ⟨in *mortal* fear⟩ **5 :** HUMAN ⟨*mortal* limitations⟩ **6 :** of, relating to, or connected with death ⟨*mortal* agony⟩ **syn** see DEADLY — **mor·tal·ly** \-°l-ē\ *adv*

²mortal *n* **:** a human being

mor·tal·i·ty \mòr-'tal-ət-ē\ *n, pl* **-ties** **1 :** the quality or state of being mortal **2 :** the death of large numbers **3 :** the human race **:** MANKIND **4 a :** the number of deaths in a given time or place   **b :** the ratio of deaths to population   **5 a :** failure in and withdrawal or elimination from an activity ⟨*mortality* among college students⟩   **b :** the rate of failure and withdrawal from an activity

mortality table *n* : a table of mortality statistics over a number of years used chiefly by insurance companies in computing premiums

¹mor·tar \'mȯrt-ər\ *n* [MF *mortier*, fr. L *mortarium*]   **1 :** a strong bowl-shaped container in which substances are pounded or rubbed with a pestle   **2 :** a muzzle-loading cannon that has a tube short in relation to its caliber and is used to throw projectiles at high angles

mortar with pestle

²mortar *n* : a plastic building material (as one made of lime and cement mixed with sand and water) that hardens and is spread between bricks or stones to hold them together — **mortar** *vt*

mor·tar·board \'mȯrt-ər-ˌbȯrd, -ˌbȯrd\ *n*   **1 :** a board for holding mortar while it is being applied   **2 :** an academic cap with a broad projecting square top

¹mort·gage \'mȯr-gij\ *n* [MF, fr. *mort* dead + *gage* pledge, gage]   **1 :** a conditional conveyance of rights to a piece of property usu. as security for the payment of a loan or debt and with the rights reverting to the mortgagor upon payment or performance according to stipulated terms   **2 :** the formal document by which a mortgage is made

²mortgage *vt* : to subject to or as if to a mortgage ⟨*mortgage* a farm⟩

mort·gag·ee \ˌmȯr-gi-'jē\ *n* : a person to whom property is mortgaged

mort·ga·gor \ˌmȯr-gi-'jȯ(ə)r\ *also* **mort·gag·er** \'mȯr-gi-jər\ *n* : a person who mortgages his property

mor·ti·cian \mȯr-'tish-ən\ *n* [L *mort-, mors* death] : UNDERTAKER

mor·ti·fi·ca·tion \ˌmȯrt-ə-fə-'kā-shən\ *n*   **1 :** the overcoming or disciplining of bodily passions and appetites through penance and self-denial   **2 :** humiliation or shame caused by something that wounds one's pride   **3 :** NECROSIS, GANGRENE

mor·ti·fy \'mȯrt-ə-ˌfī\ *vb* **-fied; -fy·ing** [MF *mortifier*, fr. LL *mortificare*, fr. L *mort-, mors* death]   **1 :** to subdue or deaden the body or bodily appetites through mortification   **2 :** to subject to humiliation or shame   **3 :** to become necrotic or gangrenous

¹mor·tise *also* **mor·tice** \'mȯrt-əs\ *n* [MF *mortaise*] : a hole cut in a piece of wood or other material into which another piece fits so as to form a joint — compare TENON

²mortise *also* **mortice** *vt*   **1 :** to join or fasten securely esp. by a tenon and mortise   **2 :** to cut a mortise in — **mor·tised** \-əst\ *adj*

¹mor·tu·ary \'mȯr-chə-ˌwer-ē\ *n, pl* **-ar·ies** [ML *mortuarium*, fr. L *mortuus* dead] : a place in which dead bodies are kept until burial; *esp* : FUNERAL HOME

²mortuary *adj* : of or relating to death or the burial of the dead

mor·u·la \'mȯr-(y)ə-lə, 'mär-\ *n, pl* **-lae** \-ˌlē, -ˌlī\ *or* **-las** [NL, fr. L *morum* mulberry] : an early embryo that is a solid mass of cleavage cells and typically precedes the blastula — **mor·u·lar** \-lər\ *adj* — **mor·u·la·tion** \ˌmȯr-(y)ə-'lā-shən, ˌmär-\ *n*

mo·sa·ic \mō-'zā-ik\ *n* [It *mosaico*, fr. ML *musaicum*, alteration of LL *musivum*, fr. *musivus* artistic, fr. L *Musa* Muse]   **1 :** a surface decoration made by inlaying small pieces of variously colored material to form pictures or patterns; *also* : the process of making it   **2 :** a picture or design made in mosaic   **3 :** something resembling a mosaic; *esp* : a virus disease of plants characterized by mottling of the foliage   **4 :** the part of a television camera tube consisting of many minute particles that convert light to an electric charge — **mosaic** *adj* — **mo·sa·i·cal·ly** \-'zā-i-k(ə-)lē\ *adv*

mo·sa·i·cist \-'zā-ə-səst\ *n* : one who makes mosaics

mosaic vision *n* : vision characteristic of a compound eye in which many minute images combine to form a visual mosaic

mos·co·vite \'mäs-kə-ˌvīt, -(ˌ)kō-\ *var of* MUSCOVITE

Mo·ses \'mō-zəz, -zəs\ *n* : a Hebrew prophet and law-

giver and liberator of the Israelites from Egypt — **Mo·sa·ic** \mō-'zā-ik\ *adj*

Mos·lem \'mäz-ləm, 'mäs-\ *var of* MUSLIM

mosque \'mäsk\ *n* [MF *mosquee*, fr. It *moschea*, fr. Sp *mezquita*, fr. Ar *masjid*] : a Muslim place of worship

mos·qui·to \mə-'skēt-ō\ *n, pl* **-toes** *also* **-tos** [Sp, fr. *mosca* fly, fr. L *musca*] : any of numerous two-winged flies having females with a proboscis adapted to puncture the skin of animals and suck the blood — **mos·qui·to·ey** \-'skēt-ə-wē\ *adj*

mosquito net *n* : a net for keeping out mosquitoes

moss \'mȯs\ *n* [OE *mōs* bog, swamp]   **1 :** any of a class (Musci) of plants without flowers but with small leafy often tufted stems growing in patches and bearing sex organs at the tip   **2 :** any of various plants (as lichens) resembling mosses — **moss·like** \-ˌlīk\ *adj*

moss animal *n* : BRYOZOAN

moss·back \'mȯs-ˌbak\ *n* : one who is far behind the times : an extremely conservative person : FOGY — **moss·backed** \-ˌbakt\ *adj*

moss pink *n* : a low tufted perennial phlox widely cultivated for its abundant usu. pink or white flowers

mossy \'mȯ-sē\ *adj* **moss·i·er; -est**   **1 :** covered with moss or something like moss ⟨a *mossy* grave⟩   **2 :** resembling moss ⟨*mossy* strands⟩

¹most \'mōst\ *adj* [OE *mǣst*, superl. of *māra* more]   **1 :** the majority of ⟨*most* men⟩   **2 :** greatest in quantity, extent, or degree ⟨the *most* ability⟩

²most *adv*   **1 :** to the greatest or highest degree — often used with an adjective or adverb to form the superlative ⟨*most* active⟩ ⟨*most* actively⟩   **2 :** to a very great degree ⟨a *most* careful driver⟩

³most *n* : the greatest amount, number, or part

⁴most *adv* : ALMOST

-most \ˌmōst\ *adj suffix* [ME, alter. of OE *-mest* (as in *formest* foremost)] : most ⟨inner*most*⟩ : most toward ⟨head*most*⟩

most·ly \'mōst-lē\ *adv* : for the greatest part : MAINLY

Most Reverend — used as a title for an archbishop or a Roman Catholic bishop

mot \'mō\ *n, pl* **mots** \'mō(z)\ [F, word, saying] : a pithy or witty saying

mote \'mōt\ *n* [OE *mot*] : a small particle : SPECK

mo·tel \mō-'tel\ *n* [blend of *motor* and *hotel*] : a building or group of buildings used as a hotel in which the rooms are directly accessible from an outdoor parking area for automobiles

mo·tet \mō-'tet\ *n* [MF, fr. dim. of *mot* word] : a polyphonic choral composition on a sacred text usu. without accompaniment

moth \'mȯth\ *n, pl* **moths** \'mȯthz, 'mȯths\ [OE *moththe*]   **1 :** CLOTHES MOTH   **2 :** a usu. night-flying insect (order Lepidoptera) with mostly feathery antennae and a stouter body, duller coloring, and proportionately smaller wings than the related butterflies

moth·ball \'mȯth-ˌbȯl\ *n*   **1 :** a ball (as of naphthalene) used to keep moths out of clothing   **2 pl :** protective storage ⟨a fleet put in *mothballs* after the war⟩

moth-eat·en \'mȯth-ˌēt-ⁿn\ *adj*   **1 :** eaten into by moths   **2 :** resembling cloth eaten into by moths

¹moth·er \'məth-ər\ *n* [OE *mōdor*]   **1 a :** a female parent   **b (1) :** a woman in authority; *esp* : the superior of a religious community of women   **(2) :** an old or elderly woman   **2 :** SOURCE, ORIGIN ⟨necessity is the *mother* of invention⟩ — **moth·er·hood** \-ˌhu̇d\ *n* — **moth·er·less** \-ləs\ *adj* — **moth·er·less·ness** *n*

²mother *adj*   **1 a :** of, relating to, or being a mother   **b :** being in the relation of a mother to others ⟨a *mother* church⟩ ⟨a *mother* country⟩   **2 :** derived from or as if from one's mother   **3 :** acting as or providing parental stock — used without reference to sex

³mother *vt* **moth·ered; moth·er·ing** \'məth-(ə-)riŋ\ : to be or act as mother to

⁴mother *n* : a slimy mass of yeast cells and bacteria that forms on the surface of fermenting alcoholic liquids and is added to wine or cider to produce vinegar

Mother Car·ey's chicken \ˌməth-ər-ˌkar-ēz, -ˌker-\ *n* : any of several small petrels; *esp* : STORM PETREL

moth·er·house \'məth-ər-ˌhau̇s\ *n*   **1 :** the convent in which the superior of a religious community resides   **2 :** the original convent of a religious community

Mother Hub·bard \,məth-ər-'həb-ərd\ *n* : a loose usu. shapeless dress

moth·er-in-law \'məth-ər(-ə)n-,lò\ *n, pl* **moth·ers-in-law** \-ər-zən-,lò\ : the mother of one's husband or wife

moth·er·land \'məth-ər-,land\ *n* **1** : the land of origin of something **2** : FATHERLAND

moth·er·ly \'məth-ər-lē\ *adj* **1** : of, relating to, or characteristic of a mother ⟨*motherly* affection⟩ **2** : resembling a mother : MATERNAL ⟨a *motherly* old lady⟩ — **moth·er·li·ness** \-lē-nəs\ *n*

moth·er-of-pearl \,məth-ər-ə(v)-'pərl\ *n* : the hard pearly iridescent substance forming the inner layer of a mollusk shell

Mother's Day *n* : the 2d Sunday in May appointed for the honoring of mothers

mother tongue *n* **1** : one's native language **2** : a language from which another language derives

mother wit *n* : natural wit or intelligence

mo·tif \mō-'tēf\ *n* [F, motive, motif] **1** : a usu. recurring element in a work of art; *esp* : a dominant idea or central theme **2** : a feature in a decoration or design ⟨a flower *motif* in wallpaper⟩

mo·tile \'mōt-°l, 'mō-,tīl\ *adj* : exhibiting or being capable of movement — **mo·til·i·ty** \mō-'til-ət-ē\ *n*

¹mo·tion \'mō-shən\ *n* [L *mot-, movēre* to move] **1** : a formal proposal for action made in a deliberative assembly ⟨a *motion* to adjourn⟩ **2** : an act, process, or instance of changing place : MOVEMENT — **mo·tion·less** \-ləs\ *adj* — **mo·tion·less·ly** *adv* — **mo·tion·less·ness** *n*

²motion *vb* **mo·tioned; mo·tion·ing** \'mō-sh(ə-)niŋ\ : to direct or signal by a movement or gesture ⟨*motioned* him to come forward⟩

motion picture *n* **1** : a series of pictures projected on a screen in rapid succession with objects shown in successive positions slightly changed so as to produce the optical effect of a continuous picture in which the objects move **2** : a representation of a story or other subject matter by means of motion pictures

motion sickness *n* : sickness induced by motion (as in travel by air, car, or ship) and characterized by nausea

mo·ti·vate \'mōt-ə-,vāt\ *vt* : to provide with a motive : INDUCE — **mo·ti·va·tion** \,mōt-ə-'vā-shən\ *n* — **mo·ti·va·tion·al** \-shnəl, -shən-°l\ *adv* — **mo·ti·va·tive** \'mōt-ə-,vāt-iv\ *adj*

¹mo·tive \'mōt-iv, *2 is also* mō-'tēv\ *n* **1** : something (as a need or desire) that leads or influences a person to do something ⟨his *motive* in running away was to avoid trouble⟩ **2** : a fragment of a musical theme recurring again and again and often elaborated or developed — **mo·tive·less** \-ləs\ *adj*

   syn MOTIVE, IMPULSE, INCENTIVE, INDUCEMENT mean a stimulus to action. MOTIVE implies a desire or emotion causing the will to act; IMPULSE suggests a driving power arising from personal temperament often without explainable cause; INCENTIVE suggests a hope or expectation of reward that incites to effort; INDUCEMENT implies an attempt to urge to action by deliberate allurement or enticement **syn** see in addition CAUSE

²motive *adj* : of or relating to motion or the causing of motion ⟨*motive* power⟩

mot juste \mō-zhūest\ *n, pl* **mots justes** *same*\ [F] : the exactly right word

¹mot·ley \'mät-lē\ *adj* [ME] **1** : having various colors **2** : of various mixed kinds or parts ⟨a *motley* crowd⟩ ⟨a *motley* collection of junk⟩

²motley *n* **1** : an old English woolen fabric of mixed colors **2 a** : a garment of motley constituting the characteristic dress of a court jester **b** : JESTER, FOOL **3** : a mixture of diverse elements

mo·to·neu·ron \,mōt-ə-'n(y)ü-,rän, -'n(y)ù(ə)r-,än\ *n* : a motor nerve cell with its processes

¹mo·tor \'mōt-ər\ *n* [L, one that moves, fr. *mot-, movēre* to move] **1** : a small compact engine **2** : INTERNAL-COMBUSTION ENGINE; *esp* : a gasoline engine **3** : MOTOR VEHICLE; *esp* : AUTOMOBILE **4** : a rotating machine that transforms electrical energy into mechanical energy

²motor *adj* **1** : causing or imparting motion ⟨*motor* power⟩ **2 a** : of, relating to, or being a nerve or nerve fiber that conducts an impulse to a muscle or gland which results in functional activity ⟨*motor* nerves⟩ **b** : concerned with or involving muscular movement ⟨*motor* areas of the brain⟩

⟨a *motor* reaction⟩ **3 a** : equipped with or driven by a motor **b** : of, in, or relating to an automobile **c** : designed for motor vehicles or motorists

³motor *vi* : to travel by automobile

mo·tor·boat \'mōt-ər-,bōt\ *n* : a boat propelled by a motor

motor bus *n* : BUS 1a

mo·tor·cade \'mōt-ər-,kād\ *n* [*motor* + *-cade* (as in *cavalcade*)] : a procession of motor vehicles

mo·tor·car \-,kär\ *n* : AUTOMOBILE

motor court *n* : MOTEL

mo·tor·cy·cle \'mōt-ər-,sī-kəl\ *n* : a 2-wheeled motor vehicle having one or two saddles and sometimes a third wheel for the support of a sidecar — **motorcycle** *vi* — **mo·tor·cy·clist** \-,sī-k(ə-)ləst\ *n*

mo·tor·ist \'mōt-ə-rəst\ *n* : a person who travels by automobile; *esp* : one who drives an automobile

mo·tor·ize \'mōt-ə-,rīz\ *vt* **1** : to equip with a motor **2** : to equip with motor-driven vehicles for transportation ⟨*motorized* troops⟩ — **mo·tor·i·za·tion** \,mōt-ə-rə-'zā-shən\ *n*

mo·tor·man \'mōt-ər-mən\ *n* : an operator of a motor-driven vehicle (as a streetcar or a subway train)

motor pool *n* : a group of governmental motor vehicles controlled by a single agency and dispatched for use as needed

motor scooter *n* : a low 2- or 3-wheeled automotive vehicle resembling a child's scooter but having a seat

motor torpedo boat *n* : a high-speed 60- to 100-foot motorboat usu. equipped with torpedoes, machine guns, and depth charges

mo·tor·truck \'mōt-ər-,trək\ *n* : an automotive truck for transporting freight

motor vehicle *n* : an automotive vehicle not operated on rails; *esp* : one with rubber tires for use on highways

mot·tle \'mät-°l\ *n* [prob. back-formation fr. ¹*motley*] **1** : a colored spot **2** : a pattern of colored spots or blotches — **mottle** *vt* — **mot·tled** \-°ld\ *adj* — **mot·tler** \'mät-lər, -°l-ər\ *n*

mot·to \'mät-ō\ *n, pl* **mottoes** *also* **mottos** [It, saying, motto, fr. L *muttum* grunt, fr. *muttire* to mutter] **1** : a sentence, phrase, or word inscribed on something as suitable to its character or use ⟨a *motto* on a sundial⟩ **2** : a short expression of a guiding rule of conduct : MAXIM

moue \'mü\ *n* [F] : a little grimace : POUT

mou·flon *or* **mouf·lon** \'mü-,flōⁿ\ *n* : a wild sheep of the mountains of Sardinia and Corsica with large curling horns in the male; *also* : a wild sheep with large horns

mou·jik \'mü-'zhēk, -'zhik\ *var of* MUZHIK

mould \'mōld\ *var of* MOLD

moult \'mōlt\ *var of* MOLT

¹mound \'maùnd\ *n* **1** : a small hill or heap of dirt (as made by man to mark a grave or to serve as a fort) **2** : the slightly elevated ground on which a baseball pitcher stands

²mound *vt* : to form into a mound

Mound Builder *n* : a member of a prehistoric Indian people of central No. America whose extensive earthworks are found esp. around the Great Lakes and in the Mississippi valley region

¹mount \'maùnt\ *n* [ME, fr. OE *munt* & OF *mont*; both fr. L *mont-, mons*] : a high hill : MOUNTAIN — used esp. before a proper name ⟨*Mount* Everest⟩

²mount *vb* **1** : RISE, ASCEND; *also* : CLIMB ⟨*mount* a ladder⟩ **2** : to get up onto something ⟨*mount* a platform⟩; *esp* : to get astride a horse **3** : to furnish (as troops) with riding animals or vehicles ⟨*mounted* infantry⟩ **4** : to increase rapidly in amount ⟨*mounting* debts⟩ **5 a** : to prepare for use or display by fastening in proper position on a support ⟨*mount* a picture on cardboard⟩ ⟨*mount* an engine⟩ **b** : to prepare (a specimen) for examination or display **6** : to furnish with scenery, properties, and costumes ⟨*mount* a play⟩ **7** : to post as a means of defense or observation ⟨*mount* guard⟩ **8** : to place (as artillery) in position **syn** see ASCEND — **mount·er** *n*

³mount *n* **1** : something upon which a person or thing is mounted : SUPPORT: as **a** : a jewelry setting **b** : a glass slide with its accessories on which objects are placed for examination with a microscope **2** : a means of conveyance; *esp* : SADDLE HORSE — **mount·a·ble** \'maùnt-ə-bəl\ *adj*

moun·tain \'maùnt-°n\ *n* [OF *montaigne*, fr. (assumed) VL *montanea*, fr. L *mont-, mons* mount] **1** : a land mass

---

that is higher than a hill **2** : a great mass or vast number 〈a *mountain* of mail〉

Moun·tain \'maůnt-ᵊn\ *n* : an extreme revolutionary faction in the French National Convention (1792–94) — compare GIRONDIST, JACOBIN

mountain ash *n* : any of various trees of the rose family with pinnate leaves and red fruits

moun·tain·eer \,maůnt-ᵊn-'i(ə)r\ *n* **1** : a person who lives in the mountains **2** : a mountain climber — **mountaineer** *vi*

mountain goat *n* : an antelope of the mountains of western No. America that has a thick white hairy coat and slightly curved black horns and closely resembles a goat

mountain laurel *n* : a No. American evergreen shrub of the heath family with glossy leaves and pink or white cup-shaped flowers

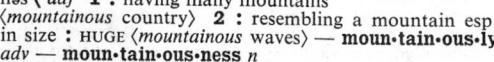

mountain goat

mountain lion *n* : COUGAR

moun·tain·ous \'maůnt-ᵊn-əs, 'maůnt-nəs\ *adj* **1** : having many mountains 〈*mountainous* country〉 **2** : resembling a mountain esp. in size : HUGE 〈*mountainous* waves〉 — **moun·tain·ous·ly** *adv* — **moun·tain·ous·ness** *n*

mountain range *n* : a series of mountains or mountain ridges closely related in direction and position

mountain sheep *n* : any of various wild sheep inhabiting high mountains

moun·tain·side \'maůnt-ᵊn-,sīd\ *n* : the side of a mountain

Mountain standard time *n* : the time of the 7th time zone west of Greenwich that includes the west central U.S.

moun·tain·top \'maůnt-ᵊn-,täp\ *n* : the summit of a mountain

moun·te·bank \'maůnt-i-,baŋk\ *n* [It *montimbanco*, fr. *montare in banco* to mount on a bench] **1** : a person who sells quack medicines from a platform (as at fairs and carnivals) **2** : a boastful pretender : CHARLATAN — **moun·te·bank·ery** \-,baŋ-k(ə)rē\ *n*

Mount·ie \'maůnt-ē\ *n* : a member of the Royal Canadian Mounted Police

mount·ing \'maůnt-iŋ\ *n* **1** : the act of a person who mounts **2** : something that serves as a mount : SUPPORT 〈a *mounting* for an engine〉〈a *mounting* for a diamond〉

mourn \'mōrn, 'mȯrn\ *vb* [OE *murnan*] : to feel or show grief or sorrow; *esp* : to grieve over someone's death — **mourn·er** *n* — **mourn·ing·ly** \-iŋ-lē\ *adv*

mourn·ful \'mōrn-fəl, 'mȯrn-\ *adj* **1** : expressing sorrow : SORROWFUL 〈a *mournful* face〉 **2** : full of sorrow : SAD **3** : causing sorrow : SADDENING 〈a *mournful* story〉 — **mourn·ful·ly** \-fə-lē\ *adv* — **mourn·ful·ness** *n*

mourn·ing \'mōr-niŋ, 'mȯr-\ *n* **1** : the act of sorrowing **2 a** : an outward sign (as black clothes, a veil, or an arm band) of grief for a person's death 〈to wear *mourning*〉 **b** : a period of time during which signs of grief are shown — **in mourning** : showing the outward signs and observing the conventions of mourning

mourning cloak *n* : a blackish brown butterfly of Europe and No. America having a broad yellow border on the wings

mourning dove *n* : a wild dove of the U.S. with a mournful cry

¹mouse \'maůs\ *n*, *pl* **mice** \'mīs\ [OE *mūs*] **1** : any of numerous small rodents with pointed snout, rather small ears, elongated body, and slender tail **2** : a person without spirit or courage **3** : a dark-colored swelling caused by a blow; *esp* : BLACK EYE

²mouse \'maůz\ *vb* **1** : to hunt for mice **2** : to search or move slyly **3** : to move about softly like a mouse **4** : to discover by painstaking search

mouse–ear \'maůs-,i(ə)r\ *n* : any of several plants with soft, hairy, and usu. small leaves

mous·er \'maů-zər\ *n* : a catcher of mice and rats; *esp* : a cat proficient at mousing

mousse \'müs\ *n* [F, lit., froth, fr. LL *mulsa* mixture of honey and water] : a light spongy food; *esp* : a dessert of sweetened and flavored whipped cream or thin cream and gelatin frozen without stirring

mous·tache \'məs-,tash, (,)məs-'\ *n* [MF, fr. It *mustacchio*, fr. Gk *mystak-, mystax*] **1** : the hair growing on the human upper lip **2** : hair or bristles about the mouth of a lower animal

mous·ta·chio *var of* MUSTACHIO

mousy *or* **mous·ey** \'maů-sē, -zē\ *adj* **mous·i·er; -est** : of, relating to, or suggestive of mice: as **a** : QUIET **b** : TIMID, COLORLESS

¹mouth \'maůth\ *n*, *pl* **mouths** \'maůthz, 'maůths\ [OE *mūth*] **1 a** : the opening through which food passes into the body of an animal **b** : the cavity that encloses in the typical vertebrate the tongue, gums, and teeth **2** : GRIMACE 〈make a *mouth*〉 **3** : something that resembles a mouth esp. in affording entrance or exit 〈the *mouth* of a cave〉 **4** : the place where a stream enters a larger body of water — **mouthed** \'maůthd, 'maůtht\ *adj* — **mouth·like** \'maůth-,līk\ *adj*

²mouth \'maůth\ *vb* **1 a** : SPEAK, UTTER **b** : to utter loudly or pompously : RANT **c** : to repeat without comprehension or sincerity 〈*mouth* platitudes〉 **2** : to take into the mouth — **mouth·er** \'maů-thər\ *n*

mouth·breed·er \'maůth-,brēd-ər\ *n* : a fish that carries its eggs and young in the mouth

mouth·ful \'maůth-,fůl\ *n* **1** : as much as the mouth will hold; *also* : the amount put into the mouth at one time **2** : a word or phrase that is very long or difficult to say

mouth organ *n* : HARMONICA

mouth·part \'maůth-,pärt\ *n* : a structure or appendage near the mouth

mouth·piece \-,pēs\ *n* **1** : something placed at or held in the mouth **2** : a part (as of an instrument) to which the mouth is held 〈the *mouthpiece* of a trumpet〉〈the *mouthpiece* of a telephone〉 **3 a** : one that expresses another's views : SPOKESMAN **b** *slang* : a usu. unscrupulous criminal lawyer

mouth·wash \-,wȯsh, -,wäsh\ *n* : a usu. antiseptic liquid preparation for cleaning the mouth and teeth

mou·ton \'mü-,tän\ *n* [F, sheep, mutton] : processed sheepskin that has been sheared and dyed to resemble beaver or seal

¹mov·a·ble *or* **move·a·ble** \'mü-və-bəl\ *adj* **1** : capable of being moved : not fixed 〈*movable* property〉 **2** : changing from one date to another 〈Easter is a *movable* holiday〉 — **mov·a·bil·i·ty** \,mü-və-'bil-ət-ē\ *n* — **mov·a·ble·ness** *n* — **mov·a·bly** \'mü-və-blē\ *adv*

²movable *or* **moveable** *n* : a piece of property (as an article of furniture) that can be moved

¹move \'müv\ *vb* [L *movēre*] **1** : to change the place or position of 〈*move* the chair closer to the window〉 **2** : to go or shift continuously from one place to another 〈*move* into the shade〉〈*move* the pulley up and down〉 **3** : to set in motion 〈*moved* his head〉 **4 a** : to cause a person to act or decide : PERSUADE 〈*moved* him to change his mind〉 **b** : to take action : ACT **5** : to affect the feelings of 〈the sad story *moved* the children to tears〉 **6 a** : to propose something formally in a deliberative assembly 〈*move* that the meeting adjourn〉 **b** : to present a motion or make an appeal **7** : to change hands or cause to change hands through sale or rental 〈the store's stock must be *moved*〉 **8 a** : to change residence 〈*move* to California〉 **b** : to change place or position : STIR 〈*moved* around in his chair〉 **9** : to cause to operate or function : ACTUATE 〈*move* the handle to increase pressure〉 **10** : PROGRESS, ADVANCE **11** : to carry on one's way of life or activity 〈he *moves* in high circles〉 **12** : to go away : DEPART 〈police made the crowd *move* on〉 **13** : to transfer a piece in a game (as chess or checkers) from one place to another **14** : to evacuate or cause to evacuate 〈the medicine *moved* the bowels〉

syn MOVE, ACTUATE, DRIVE, IMPEL mean to set or keep in motion. MOVE is very general and implies no more than the fact of changing position; ACTUATE stresses the transmission of power so as to work or set in motion; DRIVE implies imparting continuous forward motion and often stresses the effect rather than the impetus; IMPEL implies a greater impetus producing more headlong action

²move *n* **1 a** : the act of moving a piece in a game **b** : the turn of a player to move **2 a** : a step taken to gain an objective : MANEUVER **b** : the action of moving : MOVEMENT **c** : a change of residence or location

move·less \'müv-ləs\ *adj* : MOTIONLESS, FIXED — **move·less·ly** *adv* — **move·less·ness** *n*

move·ment \'müv-mənt\ *n* **1 a** : the act or process of moving **:** an instance or manner of moving ⟨observe the *movement* of a star⟩ **b :** ACTION, ACTIVITY ⟨a great deal of *movement* in the crowd⟩ **2 :** TENDENCY, TREND ⟨a *movement* of prices upward⟩ **3 a :** a series of actions taken by a body of persons to bring about an objective ⟨a *movement* for political reform⟩ **b :** the body of persons taking part in a series of actions ⟨joined the *movement*⟩ **4 :** a mechanical arrangement (as of wheels) for causing a particular motion (as in a clock or watch) **5 a :** RHYTHM, METER; *also* **:** CADENCE, TEMPO **b :** a section of a longer piece of music ⟨a *movement* in a symphony⟩ **6 :** an emptying of the bowels or the matter emptied

mov·er \'mü-vər\ *n* **:** one that moves or sets in motion; *esp* **:** a person or company that moves the belongings of others from one home or place of business to another

mov·ie \'mü-vē\ *n* [*moving picture*] **1 :** MOTION PICTURE **2** *pl* **:** a showing of a motion picture **3** *pl* **:** the motion⹀ picture industry

mov·ing \'mü-viŋ\ *adj* **1 :** changing place or position **2 :** causing motion or action **3 :** having the power to affect feelings or sympathies — **mov·ing·ly** \-viŋ-lē\ *adv*

moving picture *n* **:** MOTION PICTURE

moving staircase *n* **:** ESCALATOR

¹mow \'maů\ *n* [OE *müga* heap, stack] **:** the part of a barn where hay or straw is stored

²mow \'mō\ *vb* **mowed; mowed** *or* **mown** \'mōn\; **mow·ing** [OE *māwan*] **1 :** to cut down with a scythe or machine ⟨*mow* hay⟩ **2 :** to cut the standing herbage from ⟨*mow* a lawn⟩ **3 :** to kill or destroy in great numbers ⟨machine guns *mowed* down the attackers⟩ **4 :** to overcome decisively **:** ROUT — **mow·er** \'mō-(ə)r\ *n*

mow·ing ma·chine *n* **:** an implement with blades for cutting standing grass or grain

Mr. \,mis-tər\ *n, pl* **Messrs.** \,mes-ərz\ [*Mr.* fr. ME, abbr. of *maister* master; *Messrs.* abbr. of *Messieurs*, fr. F, pl. of *Monsieur*] **1** — used as a conventional title of courtesy before a man's surname **2** — used in direct address as a conventional title of respect before a man's title of office

Mrs. \,mis-əz, -əs, *esp South* ,miz-\ *n, pl* **Mes·dames** \mā-,däm, -,dam\ [*Mrs.* abbr. of *mistress; Mesdames* fr. F, pl. of *Madame*] — used as a conventional title of courtesy before a married woman's surname

Ms. \(,)miz\ *n* — used instead of *Miss* or *Mrs.* (as when the marital status of a woman is unknown) ⟨*Ms.* Mary Smith⟩

mu \'myü\ *n* **:** the 12th letter of the Greek alphabet — M or μ

¹much \'məch\ *adj* **more** \'mō(ə)r, 'mȯ(ə)r\; **most** \'mōst\ [ME *michel, muchel, muche* large, much, fr. OE *micel, mycel*] **:** great in quantity, amount, extent, or degree ⟨has *much* money⟩ ⟨takes too *much* time⟩

²much *adv* **more; most 1 a :** to a great degree or extent **:** CONSIDERABLY ⟨*much* happier⟩ **b** (1) **:** FREQUENTLY, OFTEN (2) **:** LONG (3) **:** APPROXIMATELY ⟨*much* the same⟩

³much *n* **1 :** a great quantity, amount, extent, or degree **2 :** something considerable or impressive

mu·cif·er·ous \myü-'sif-(ə-)rəs\ *adj* **:** producing or filled with mucus

mu·ci·lage \'myü-s(ə-)lij\ *n* [LL *mucilagin-, mucilago* musty juice, mucus] **1 :** a gelatinous substance esp. from seaweeds that contains protein and carbohydrates and is similar to plant gums **2 :** an aqueous solution of a gum or similar substance used esp. as an adhesive

mu·ci·lag·i·nous \,myü-sə-'laj-ə-nəs\ *adj* **1 :** STICKY, VISCID **2 :** producing or full of mucilage — **mu·ci·lag·i·nous·ly** *adv*

mu·cin \'myüs-ᵊn\ *n* [*mucus*] **:** any of various complex proteins found as viscid solutions in animal secretions and tissues — **mu·cin·oid** \-,ȯid\ *adj* — **mu·cin·ous** \-əs\ *adj*

muck \'mək\ *n* [ME *muk*] **1 :** soft moist barnyard manure **2 :** DIRT, FILTH **3 a :** dark highly organic soil **b :** MIRE, MUD — **mucky** \'mək-ē\ *adj*

muck·rak·er \'mək-,rā-kər\ *n* **:** one of a group of writers noted for seeking out and exposing real or alleged abuses in American business, government, and society at the beginning of the 20th century — **muck·rake** \-,rāk\ *vb*

mu·co·cu·ta·ne·ous \,myü-kō-kyü-'tā-nē-əs\ *adj* **:** of, relating to, or involving both mucous membrane and typical skin

mu·co·sa \myü-'kō-zə\ *n, pl* **-sae** \-(,)zē, -,zī\ *or* **-sas** [NL, fr. L, fem. of *mucosus* mucous] **:** MUCOUS MEMBRANE — **mu·co·sal** \-zəl\ *adj*

mu·cous \'myü-kəs\ *adj* [L *mucosus*, fr. *mucus*] **1 :** of, relating to, or resembling mucus ⟨*mucous* discharges⟩ **2 :** secreting or containing mucus ⟨a *mucous* gland⟩

mucous membrane *n* **:** a membrane rich in mucous glands; *esp* **:** one that lines body passages and cavities which communicate directly or indirectly with the exterior

mu·cro \'myü-,krō\ *n, pl* **mu·cro·nes** \myü-'krō-(,)nēz\ [L *mucron-, mucro*] **:** an abrupt sharp terminal point (as of a leaf) — **mu·cro·nate** \'myü-krə-,nāt\ *adj* — **mu·cro·na·tion** \,myü-krə-'nā-shən\ *n*

mu·cus \'myü-kəs\ *n* [L, nasal mucus] **:** a viscid slippery animal secretion rich in mucins produced esp. by mucous membranes which it moistens and protects — **mu·coid** \-,kȯid\ *adj*

mud \'məd\ *n* [ME *mudde*] **:** soft wet earth

¹mud·dle \'məd-ᵊl\ *vb* **mud·dled; mud·dling** \'məd-liŋ, -ᵊl-iŋ\ **1 :** CONFUSE, STUPEFY ⟨*muddled* by too much advice⟩ **2 :** to mix up confusedly ⟨*muddle* the household accounts⟩ **3 :** to think or act in a confused way **:** BUNGLE ⟨*muddle* through a task⟩ — **mud·dler** \'məd-lər, -ᵊl-ər\ *n*

²muddle *n* **1 :** a state of confusion **2 :** a confused mess

mud·dle·head·ed \,məd-ᵊl-'hed-əd\ *adj* **1 :** mentally confused **2 :** BUNGLING, INEPT — **mud·dle·head·ed·ness** *n*

¹mud·dy \'məd-ē\ *adj* **mud·di·er; -est 1 :** filled or covered with mud **2 :** resembling mud **3 :** not clear or bright **:** DULL, CLOUDY ⟨*muddy* varnish⟩ ⟨a *muddy* complexion⟩ **4 :** CONFUSED, MUDDLED ⟨*muddy* thinking⟩ — **mud·di·ly** \'məd-ᵊl-ē\ *adv* — **mud·di·ness** \'məd-ē-nəs\ *n*

²muddy *vt* **mud·died; mud·dy·ing 1 :** to soil or stain with or as if with mud **2 :** to make turbid **3 :** to make cloudy or dull **4 :** CONFUSE

mud·guard \'məd-,gärd\ *n* **:** a guard over a wheel of a vehicle to catch or deflect mud

mud puppy *n* **:** any of several large American salamanders; *esp* **:** HELLBENDER

mud·sling·ing \'məd-,sliŋ-iŋ\ *n* **:** the use of abusive tactics (as invective or slander) esp. in a political campaign — **mud·sling·er** \-,sliŋ-ər\ *n*

mud·stone \'məd-,stōn\ *n* **:** a hardened shale produced by the consolidation of mud

mud turtle *n* **:** a bottom-dwelling freshwater turtle (as a musk turtle)

mu·ez·zin \m(y)ü-'ez-ᵊn\ *n* [Ar *mu'adhdhin*] **:** a Muslim crier who calls the hours of daily prayers

¹muff \'məf\ *n* [Dutch *mof*, fr. MF *moufle* mitten] **:** a soft thick cover into which both hands may be thrust for protection from cold

²muff *n* **:** a bungling performance; *esp* **:** a failure to hold a ball in attempting a catch — **muff** *vb*

muf·fin \'məf-ən\ *n* **:** a bread made of egg batter or yeast dough and baked in a small cup-shaped container

muf·fle \'məf-əl\ *vt* **muf·fled; muf·fling** \'məf-(ə-)liŋ\ **1 :** to wrap up so as to conceal or protect or to prevent seeing, hearing, or speaking **2 :** to deaden the sound of

muf·fler \'məf-lər\ *n* **1 :** a scarf for the neck **2 :** something that deadens noises; *esp* **:** a device attached to the exhaust system of an automobile

¹muf·ti \'məf-tē\ *n* [Ar *muftī*] **:** a professional jurist who interprets Muslim law

²mufti *n* **:** ordinary clothes when worn by one usu. dressed in a uniform

¹mug \'məg\ *n* **1 :** a usu. large metal or earthenware cylindrical drinking cup **2 :** the face or mouth of a person **3 :** PUNK, THUG

²mug *vb* **mugged; mug·ging 1 :** to make faces esp. in order to attract the attention of an audience **2 :** PHOTOGRAPH; *esp* **:** to take a photograph of

³mug *vb* **:** to assault with intent to rob

¹mug·ger \'məg-ər\ *n* **:** a common usu. harmless freshwater crocodile of southeastern Asia

²mugger *n* **:** a person who attacks from behind

mug·gy \'məg-ē\ *adj* **mug·gi·er; -est** [E dial. *mug* drizzle] **:** being warm, damp, and stifling — **mug·gi·ly** \'məg-ə-lē\ *adv* — **mug·gi·ness** \'məg-ē-nəs\ *n*

mu·gho pine \,m(y)ü-(,)gō-\ *n* **:** a shrubby spreading pine widely grown as an ornamental

mug

---

j joke; ŋ sing; ō flow; ȯ flaw; ȯi coin; th thin; t͟h this; ü loot; ů foot; y yet; yü few; yů furious;· zh vision

mug·wump \'məg-ˌwəmp\ *n* [obs. slang, chief, kingpin, of Algonquian origin] **1** : a bolter from the Republican party in 1884 **2** : a person who is undecided or neutral in politics often because he cannot make up his mind

Mu·ham·mad·an \mō-'ham-əd-ən, mü-\ *n* : MUSLIM — **Muhammadan** *adj* — **Mu·ham·mad·an·ism** \-əd-ə-ˌniz-əm\ *n*

mu·jik \mü-'zhēk, -'zhik\ *var of* MUZHIK

muk·luk \'mək-ˌlək\ *n* [Eskimo *muklok* large seal] **1** : an Eskimo boot of sealskin or reindeer skin **2** : a boot with a soft leather sole worn over several pairs of socks

mu·lat·to \m(y)ù-'lat-ō\ *n, pl* **-toes** *or* **-tos** [Sp *mulato*, fr. *mulo* mule, fr. L *mulus*] **1** : a person with one Negro and one white parent **2** : a person of mixed white and Negro descent

mul·ber·ry \'məl-ˌber-ē\ *n* [ME *murberie, mulberie,* fr. OF *moure* mulberry, fr. L *morum,* fr. Gk *moron*] **1** : any of a genus of trees with edible usu. purple fruits resembling berries; *also* : the fruit **2** : a dark purple or a purplish black

mulch \'məlch\ *n* : a protective covering (as of sawdust, compost, or paper) used on the ground esp. to reduce evaporation, prevent erosion, control weeds, or enrich the soil; *also* : the material used — **mulch** *vt*

¹**mulct** \'məlkt\ *n* [L *multa, mulcta*] : a fine imposed as a punishment

²**mulct** *vt* **1** : to punish by a fine **2 a** : to defraud esp. of money : SWINDLE **b** : to obtain (as money) by fraud, duress, or theft

¹**mule** \'myül\ *n* [L *mulus*] **1 a** : a hybrid between a horse and a donkey; *esp* : the offspring of a male donkey and a mare **b** : a usu. sterile hybrid plant or animal **2** : a very stubborn person **3** : a machine for drawing and twisting fiber into yarn or thread and winding it onto spindles

²**mule** *n* [MF, fr. L *mulleus* shoe worn by magistrates] : a slipper whose upper does not extend around the heel of the foot

mule deer *n* : a long-eared deer of western No. America that is larger and more heavily built than the common white-tailed deer

mule skinner *n* : a driver of mules

mu·le·teer \ˌmyü-lə-'ti(ə)r\ *n* : a driver of mules

mu·ley *also* **mul·ley** \'myü-lē, 'mùl-ē\ *adj* [of Celtic origin] : HORNLESS; *esp* : naturally hornless ⟨a *muley* cow⟩

mul·ish \'myü-lish\ *adj* : STUBBORN, INFLEXIBLE — **mul·ish·ly** *adv* — **mul·ish·ness** *n*

¹**mull** \'məl\ *vb* [ME *mullen* to grind, pulverize, fr. *mul* dust] : to consider at length : PONDER ⟨*mull* over an idea⟩

²**mull** *vt* : to sweeten, spice, and heat ⟨*mulled* wine⟩

³**mull** *n* [G] : granular forest humus with a layer of mixed organic matter and mineral soil merging gradually into the mineral soil beneath

mul·lah \'məl-ə, 'mùl-ə\ *n* [Hindi *mulla,* fr. Ar *mawlā*] : a Muslim of a class trained in traditional law and doctrine; *esp* : one who is head of a mosque

mul·lein *also* **mul·len** \'məl-ən\ *n* [AF *moleine*] : a tall herb having coarse woolly leaves and spikes of usu. yellow flowers

mul·let \'məl-ət\ *n, pl* **mullet** *or* **mullets** [MF *mulet,* fr. L *mullus* red mullet, fr. Gk *myllos*] **1** : any of a family of largely gray food fishes — called also *gray mullet* **2** : any of a family of moderate-sized usu. red or golden fishes with two barbels on the chin

mul·li·gan \'məl-i-gən\ *n* : a stew basically of vegetables and meat or fish

mul·li·ga·taw·ny \ˌməl-i-gə-'tó-nē\ *n* [Tamil *milakutaṇṇi,* lit., pepper water] : a soup usu. of chicken stock seasoned with curry

mul·lion \'məl-yən\ *n* : a slender vertical bar between units of windows, doors, or screens — **mullion** *vt*

multi- *comb form* [L *multus* much, many] **1 a** : many : multiple : much ⟨*multivalent*⟩ **b** : more than two ⟨*multilateral*⟩ ⟨*multiparty*⟩ ⟨*multiracial*⟩ **2** : many times over ⟨*multimillionaire*⟩

mul·ti·cel·lu·lar \ˌməl-ti-'sel-yə-lər, -ˌtī-\ *adj* : having or consisting of many cells — **mul·ti·cel·lu·lar·i·ty** \-ˌsel-yə-'lar-ət-ē\ *n*

mul·ti·col·ored \ˌməl-ti-'kəl-ərd\ *adj* : having many colors

mul·ti·far·i·ous \ˌməl-tə-'far-ē-əs, -'fer-\ *adj* : of various

kinds : being many and varied ⟨the *multifarious* complexities of language⟩ — **mul·ti·far·i·ous·ly** *adv* — **mul·ti·far·i·ous·ness** *n*

mul·ti·fid \'məl-ti-ˌfid\ *adj* [L *multifidus,* fr. *findere* to split, cleave] : cleft into several parts ⟨a *multifid* leaf⟩

mul·ti·flo·ra rose \ˌməl-tə-ˌflōr-ə-, -ˌflór-\ *n* : a vigorous thorny rose with clusters of small flowers that is used for hedges

mul·ti·fold \'məl-ti-ˌfōld\ *adj* : MANIFOLD

mul·ti·form \'məl-tə-ˌfórm\ *adj* : having many forms, shapes, or appearances

mul·ti·graph \'məl-tə-ˌgraf\ *vt* : to print on a Multigraph machine

Multigraph *trademark* — used for a machine consisting essentially of a cylinder with grooves into which type or electrotypes are inserted

mul·ti·lat·er·al \ˌməl-ti-'lat-ə-rəl, -'la-trəl\ *adj* **1** : having many sides **2** : participated in by more than two nations or parties — **mul·ti·lat·er·al·ly** \-ē\ *adv*

mul·ti·lith \'məl-tə-ˌlith\ *vt* : to print on a Multilith machine

Multilith *trademark* — used for a small offset press used typically for duplicating office forms

mul·ti·mil·lion·aire \ˌməl-ti-ˌmil-yə-'na(ə)r, -'ne(ə)r, -'mil-yə-,\ *n* : a person worth several million dollars

mul·ti·nu·cle·ate \ˌməl-ti-'n(y)ü-klē-ət, -ˌtī-\ *adj* : having more than two nuclei

mul·tip·a·rous \ˌməl-'tip-ə-rəs\ *adj* [NL *multiparus,* fr. L *multus* + *parere* to produce] **1** : producing many or more than one at a birth **2** : having experienced one or more previous parturitions

mul·ti·par·tite \ˌməl-ti-'pär-ˌtīt\ *adj* : having numerous members or signatories ⟨*multipartite* treaty⟩

¹**mul·ti·ple** \'məl-tə-pəl\ *adj* [F, fr. L *multiplex,* fr. *multus* many + *-plex* -fold] : containing or consisting of more than one : MANIFOLD ⟨*multiple* ideas⟩ ⟨*multiple* copies⟩

²**multiple** *n* **1** : the product of a quantity by an integer ⟨35 is a *multiple* of 7⟩ **2** : a group with respect to its divisions or parts ⟨lay mines in *multiple*⟩

multiple–choice *adj* : having several answers given from which the correct one is to be chosen ⟨*multiple-choice* examination⟩

multiple factor *n* : one of a group of nonallelic genes held to control various quantitative hereditary characters

multiple fruit *n* : a fruit (as a mulberry) formed from a cluster of flowers

multiple sclerosis *n* : a disease marked by patches of hardened tissue in the brain or spinal cord resulting in partial or complete paralysis and muscular twitching

mul·ti·plex \'məl-tə-ˌpleks\ *adj* [L] **1** : MANIFOLD, MULTIPLE **2** : being or relating to a system of transmitting several messages simultaneously on the same circuit or channel

mul·ti·pli·cand \ˌməl-tə-pli-'kand\ *n* [L *multiplicandus* to be multiplied, fr. *multiplicare* to multiply] : the number that is to be multiplied by another

mul·ti·pli·ca·tion \ˌməl-tə-plə-'kā-shən\ *n* **1** : the act or process of multiplying **2** : a mathematical operation that consists of adding an integer to itself a specified number of times — **mul·ti·plic·a·tive** \ˌməl-tə-'plik-ət-iv, 'məl-tə-plə-ˌkāt-\ *adj* — **mul·ti·plic·a·tive·ly** *adv*

multiplicative inverse *n* : the reciprocal of a given number

mul·ti·plic·i·ty \ˌməl-tə-'plis-ət-ē\ *n, pl* **-ties 1** : the quality or state of being multiple or various **2** : a great number ⟨a *multiplicity* of ideas⟩

mul·ti·pli·er \'məl-tə-ˌplī(-ə)r\ *n* : one that multiplies: as **a** : a number by which another number is multiplied **b** : a device for multiplying or for intensifying some effect

mul·ti·ply \'məl-tə-ˌplī\ *vb* **-plied; -ply·ing** [OF *multiplier,* fr. L *multiplicare,* fr. *multiplic-, multiplex* multiple] **1 a** : to increase in number : make or become more numerous **b** : BREED, PROPAGATE **2** : to find the product of numbers by means of multiplication : perform the operation of multiplication ⟨*multiply* 7 by 8⟩

mul·ti·ra·cial \ˌməl-ti-'rā-shəl, -ˌtī-\ *adj* : composed of, relating to, or representing various races

mul·ti·stage \ˌməl-ti-ˌstāj\ *adj* : operating in or involving two or more steps or stages ⟨a *multistage* rocket⟩

mul·ti·tude \'məl-tə-ˌt(y)üd\ *n* : a countless number of

things or people : HOST ⟨starving *multitudes*⟩ ⟨a *multitude* of reasons⟩
syn CROWD, THRONG: MULTITUDE implies great numbers ⟨*multitude* of stars⟩ CROWD stresses packing together and loss of individuality ⟨*crowd* of onlookers⟩ THRONG suggests a crowd in motion ⟨people came to the fair in *throngs*⟩
mul·ti·tu·di·nous \,məl-tə-'t(y)üd-nəs, -ᵊn-əs\ *adj* : consisting of a great multitude ⟨a *multitudinous* gathering⟩ — **mul·ti·tu·di·nous·ly** *adv* — **mul·ti·tu·di·nous·ness** *n*
mul·ti·va·lent \,məl-ti-'vā-lənt, -,tī-\ *adj* 1 : POLYVALENT 2 : represented more than twice in the somatic chromosome number ⟨*multivalent* chromosomes⟩ — **multivalent** *n*
mul·ti·vi·ta·min \,məl-ti-'vīt-ə-mən\ *adj* : containing several vitamins and esp. all known to be essential to health ⟨a *multivitamin* formula⟩
mul·ti·vol·ume \,məl-ti-'väl-yəm, -,tī-\ *or* **mul·ti·vol·umed** \-yəmd\ *adj* : comprising several volumes
¹mum \'məm\ *adj* : SILENT ⟨keep *mum*⟩ — often used interjectionally
²mum *n* : CHRYSANTHEMUM
mum·ble \'məm-bəl\ *vb* **mum·bled**; **mum·bling** \-b(ə-)liŋ\ 1 : to speak indistinctly usu. with lips partly closed : MUTTER ⟨*mumble* one's words⟩ 2 : to chew gently with closed lips or with little use of the lips ⟨a baby *mumbling* its food⟩ — **mumble** *n* — **mum·bler** \-b(ə-)lər\ *n* — **mum·bling·ly** \-bliŋ-lē\ *adv*
mum·ble·ty·peg \'məm-bəl-(tē-),peg\ *n* : a game in which the players try to flip a knife from various positions so that the blade will stick into the ground
mum·bo jum·bo \,məm-bō-'jəm-bō\ *n* [*Mumbo Jumbo*, an idol or deity held to have been worshiped in Africa] 1 : an object of superstitious homage and fear 2 a : a complicated ritual with elaborate trappings b : complicated activity or language that obscures and confuses
mum·mer \'məm-ər\ *n* [F *momeur*, fr. *momer* to go masked] 1 : a person who masks and engages in merry-making (as at Christmastide) 2 : an actor esp. in a pantomime
mum·mery \'məm-ə-rē\ *n, pl* **-mer·ies** 1 : a performance by mummers 2 : a ridiculous or pompous ceremony
mum·mi·fy \'məm-i-,fī\ *vb* **-fied**; **-fy·ing** 1 : to embalm and dry as a mummy 2 : to dry up like the skin of a mummy : SHRIVEL — **mum·mi·fi·ca·tion** \,məm-i-fə-'kā-shən\ *n*
mum·my \'məm-ē\ *n, pl* **mummies** [ML *mumia*, fr. Ar *mūmiyah*, fr. Per *mūm* wax] 1 : a body embalmed for burial in the manner of the ancient Egyptians 2 : an unusually well-preserved body
mumps \'məm(p)s\ *n sing or pl* [pl. of obs. *mump* grimace] : an acute contagious virus disease marked by fever and by swelling esp. of salivary glands
munch \'mənch\ *vb* : to chew with a crunching sound ⟨*munch* on hard candy⟩ — **munch·er** *n*
mun·dane \,mən-'dān, 'mən-,\ *adj* [LL *mundanus*, fr. L *mundus* world] : of or relating to the world : WORLDLY ⟨concerned with *mundane* affairs⟩ **syn** see EARTHLY — **mun·dane·ly** *adv*
mu·nic·i·pal \myu̇-'nis-ə-pəl\ *adj* [L *municipalis* of a municipality, fr. *municip-, municeps* inhabitant of a municipality, fr. *munus* duty + *capere* to take] 1 : of or relating to the internal affairs of a nation 2 : of or relating to a municipality ⟨*municipal* government⟩ — **mu·nic·i·pal·ly** \-p(ə-)lē\ *adv*
mu·nic·i·pal·i·ty \myu̇-,nis-ə-'pal-ət-ē\ *n, pl* **-ties** : a primarily urban political unit (as a city or town) having corporate status and usu. powers of self-government
mu·nif·i·cent \myu̇-'nif-ə-sənt\ *adj* [L *munus* service, gift + *facere* to make, do] : extremely liberal in giving : very generous **syn** see GENEROUS — **mu·nif·i·cence** \-sən(t)s\ *n* — **mu·nif·i·cent·ly** *adv*
mu·ni·tions \myu̇-'nish-ənz\ *n pl* [L *munition-, munitio* fortification, fr. *munire* to fortify] : military supplies, equipment, or provisions; *esp* : AMMUNITION — **mu·ni·tion** \-'nish-ən\ *vt*
mun·tin \'mənt-ᵊn\ *or* **munt·ing** \-ᵊn, -iŋ\ *n* : a strip separating panes of glass in a sash
¹mu·ral \'myu̇r-əl\ *adj* [L *murus* wall] 1 : of or relating to a wall 2 : applied to and made a part of a wall surface ⟨a *mural* painting⟩
²mural *n* : a mural painting — **mu·ral·ist** \-ə-ləst\ *n*

¹mur·der \'mərd-ər\ *n* [partly fr. ME *murther*, fr. OE *morthor*; partly fr. ME *murdre*, fr. OF, of Gmc origin] : the crime of unlawfully killing a person esp. with deliberate intent or design
²murder *vb* **mur·dered**; **mur·der·ing** \'mərd-(ə-)riŋ\ 1 : to kill a human being unlawfully and esp. with deliberate intent or design : commit murder 2 : to spoil by performing in a wretched manner : MANGLE ⟨*murder* a song⟩ **syn** see KILL — **mur·der·er** \'mərd-ər-ər\ *n* — **mur·der·ess** \'mərd-ə-rəs\ *n*
mur·der·ous \'mərd-(ə-)rəs\ *adj* 1 : characterized by or causing murder or bloodshed ⟨*murderous* machine-gun fire⟩ ⟨a *murderous* act⟩ 2 : having or appearing to have the purpose of murder ⟨with *murderous* intent⟩ ⟨gave him a *murderous* glance⟩ — **mur·der·ous·ly** *adv* — **mur·der·ous·ness** *n*
mu·rex \'myu̇(ə)r-,eks\ *n, pl* **mu·ri·ces** \'myu̇r-ə-,sēz\ *or* **mu·rex·es** [L *muric-, murex*] : any of a genus of sea snails that yield a purple dye
mu·ri·ate \'myu̇r-ē-,āt\ *n* [back-formation fr. *muriatic acid*] : CHLORIDE
mu·ri·at·ic acid \,myu̇r-ē-,at-ik-\ *n* [L *muria* brine] : HYDROCHLORIC ACID
mu·rid \'myu̇r-əd\ *adj* : of, relating to, or being typical mice and rats — **murid** *n*
mu·rine \'myu̇(ə)r-,īn\ *adj* [L *mur-, mus* mouse] : of or relating to the common house mouse or closely related rodents ⟨*murine* typhus⟩
murk \'mərk\ *n* [ME *mirke*] : DARKNESS, GLOOM; *also* : FOG
murky \'mər-kē\ *adj* 1 : marked by darkness, gloominess, or obscurity 2 : FOGGY, MISTY — **murk·i·ly** \-kə-lē\ *adv* — **murk·i·ness** \-kē-nəs\ *n*
mur·mur \'mər-mər\ *n* [L] 1 : a muttered complaint : GRUMBLE 2 : a low indistinct sound ⟨the *murmur* of the wind⟩ 3 : an abnormal heart sound occurring when the heart is disordered in function or structure — **murmur** *vb* — **mur·mur·er** \'mər-mər-ər\ *n*
mur·mur·ous \'mərm-(ə-)rəs\ *adj* : filled with or characterized by murmurs — **mur·mur·ous·ly** *adv*
mur·rain \'mər-ən, 'mə-rən\ *n* [MF *morine*, fr. *morir* to die, fr. L *mori*] : a pestilence or plague esp. of domestic animals
murre \'mər\ *n* : any of several guillemots
mur·ther \'mər-thər\ *chiefly dial var of* MURDER
mus·ca·dine \'məs-kə-,dīn\ *n* : a grape of the southern U.S. with musky fruits in small clusters
mus·cari \(,)məs-'ka(ə)r-ē, -'ke(ə)r-ē\ *n, pl* **-cari** *or* **-car·is** : GRAPE HYACINTH
mus·cat \'məs-,kat, -kət\ *n* [Prov, fr. *muscat* musky] : any of several cultivated grapes used in making wine and raisins
mus·ca·tel \,məs-kə-'tel\ *n* : a sweet wine made from muscat grapes
¹mus·cle \'məs-əl\ *n* [MF, fr. L *musculus*, dim. of *mus* mouse, muscle; akin to E *mouse*] 1 a : a body tissue consisting of long cells that contract when stimulated and produce motion b : an organ that is essentially a mass of muscle tissue attached at either end to a fixed point and that by contracting moves or checks the movement of a body part 2 a : muscular strength : BRAWN b : effective strength : POWER
²muscle *vi* **mus·cled**; **mus·cling** \'məs-(ə-)liŋ\ : to force one's way ⟨*muscle* in on another racketeer⟩
mus·cle-bound \'məs-əl-,bau̇nd\ *adj* : having some of the muscles abnormally enlarged and lacking in elasticity (as from excessive athletic exercise)
mus·co·vite \'məs-kə-,vīt\ *n* 1 *cap* a : a native or resident of the ancient principality of Moscow or of the city of Moscow b : RUSSIAN 2 : a mineral that consists of a colorless to pale brown potassium-containing mica — **Muscovite** *adj*
Mus·co·vy duck \,məs-,kō-vē-\ *n* : a large crested tropical American duck widely kept in domestication
mus·cu·lar \'məs-kyə-lər\ *adj* 1 a : of, relating to, or constituting muscle b : performed by the muscles 2 a : having well-developed muscles b : of or relating to physical strength : STRONG — **mus·cu·lar·i·ty** \,məs-kyə-'lar-ət-ē\ *n* — **mus·cu·lar·ly** \'məs-kyə-lər-lē\ *adv*
muscular dystrophy *n* : a disease characterized by progressive wasting of muscles

mus·cu·la·ture \'məs-kyə-lə-,chù(ə)r\ *n* : the muscles of the body or of one of its parts

mus·cu·lo·skel·e·tal \,məs-kyə-lō-'skel-ət-ʔl\ *adj* : of, relating to, or involving both musculature and skeleton

¹muse \'myüz\ *vb* [MF *muser* to gape, muse, fr. *muse* mouth of an animal] : to consider carefully : PONDER, MEDITATE — **mus·er** *n* — **mus·ing·ly** \'myü-ziŋ-lē\ *adv*

²muse *n* [L *Musa*, fr. Gk *Mousa*] **1** *cap* : any of the nine sister goddesses in Greek mythology presiding over song and poetry and the arts and sciences **2** : a source of inspiration; *esp* : a guiding genius

mu·sette \myù-'zet\ *n* [F, lit., small bagpipe] : a small knapsack with a shoulder strap used esp. by soldiers for carrying provisions and personal belongings — called also *musette bag*

mu·se·um \myù-'zē-əm, 'myü-,\ *n* [L, place for learned occupation, fr. Gk *Mouseion*, fr. *Mousa* Muse] : a building or part of a building in which are displayed objects of permanent interest in one or more of the arts or sciences

¹mush \'məsh\ *n* **1** : cornmeal boiled in water **2** : something soft and spongy or shapeless **3** : insipid sentimentality or courting

²mush *vi* : to travel over snow with a sled drawn by dogs — often used as a command to a dog team — **mush·er** *n*

³mush *n* : a hike across snow with a dog team

¹mush·room \'məsh-,rüm, -,rúm\ *n* [MF *mousseron*] **1** : a fleshy aerial fruiting body of a fungus that consists typically of a stem bearing a flattened cap; *esp* : one that is edible **2** : FUNGUS 1

²mushroom *adj* **1** : springing up suddenly or multiplying rapidly ⟨*mushroom* growth of new agencies⟩ **2** : having the shape of a mushroom

³mushroom *vi* : to spring up suddenly or multiply rapidly

mushy \'məsh-ē\ *adj* **mush·i·er; -est** **1** : soft like mush **2** : weakly sentimental — **mush·i·ly** \'məsh-ə-lē\ *adv* — **mush·i·ness** \'məsh-ē-nəs\ *n*

mu·sic \'myü-zik\ *n* [L *musica*, fr. Gk *mousikē* art presided over by the Muses, fr. *Mousa* Muse] **1 a** : the art of combining tones so that they are pleasing, expressive, or intelligible **b** : compositions made according to the rules of music **c** : the score of music compositions inscribed on paper ⟨did you bring your *music* with you?⟩ **2** : sounds that have rhythm, harmony, and melody; *also* : an agreeable sound ⟨the *music* of a brook⟩ **3** : punishment for a misdeed ⟨must face the *music*⟩

¹mu·si·cal \'myü-zi-kəl\ *adj* **1 a** : of or relating to music ⟨*musical* instruments⟩ **b** : having the pleasing harmonious qualities of music : MELODIOUS ⟨a *musical* voice⟩ **2** : having an interest in or talent for music ⟨a *musical* family⟩ **3** : set to or accompanied by music **4** : of or relating to musicians or music lovers — **mu·si·cal·i·ty** \,myü-zi-'kal-ət-ē\ *n* — **mu·si·cal·ly** \'myü-zi-k(ə-)lē\ *adv*

²musical *n* : a film or theatrical production consisting of musical numbers and dialogue that develop the plot of an underlying story — called also *musical comedy;* compare REVUE

mu·si·cale \,myü-zi-'kal\ *n* : a usu. private social gathering featuring a concert of music

music box *n* : a box or case enclosing an apparatus that reproduces music mechanically when activated by clockwork

music hall *n* : a vaudeville theater

mu·si·cian \myù-'zish-ən\ *n* : one skilled in music; *esp* : a composer or professional performer of music — **mu·si·cian·ly** \-lē\ *adj* — **mu·si·cian·ship** \-,ship\ *n*

mu·si·col·o·gy \,myü-zi-'käl-ə-jē\ *n* : a study of music as a branch of knowledge or field of research — **mu·si·co·log·i·cal** \-zi-kə-'läj-i-kəl\ *adj* — **mu·si·col·o·gist** \-zi-'käl-ə-jəst\ *n*

mus·ing \'myü-ziŋ\ *n* : MEDITATION ⟨considered it in his *musings*⟩ — **musing** *adj* — **mus·ing·ly** \-ziŋ-lē\ *adv*

musk \'məsk\ *n* [LL *muscus*, fr. Gk *moschos*, fr. Per *mushk*, fr. Skt *muṣka* testicle, fr. dim. of *mūṣ* mouse; akin to E *mouse*] **1** : a substance of penetrating persistent odor obtained usu. from the male musk deer and used as a perfume fixative; *also* : an odor of or resembling that of musk **2** : any of various plants with musky odors

musk deer *n* : a small hornless deer about 3 feet long and 20 inches tall that lives in the high regions of central Asia

mus·keg \'məs-,keg\ *n* : BOG; *esp* : a dense sphagnum bog of northern No. America

mus·kel·lunge \'məs-kə-,lənj\ *n*, *pl* **muskellunge** [of Algonquian origin] : a large No. American pike prized as a sport fish

mus·ket \'məs-kət\ *n* [MF *mousquet*, fr. It *moschetto* arrow for a crossbow, musket, fr. dim. of *mosca* fly, fr. L *musca*] : a large-caliber usu. muzzle-loading military shoulder firearm with smooth bore

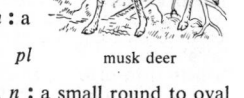
musk deer

mus·ke·teer \,məs-kə-'ti(ə)r\ *n* : a soldier armed with a musket

mus·ket·ry \'məs-kə-trē\ *n*, *pl* **-ries** : small-arms fire

musk·mel·on \'məsk-,mel-ən\ *n* : a small round to oval and sometimes ridged melon that is related to the cucumber and has usu. sweet edible green or orange flesh — compare CANTALOUPE

Mus·ko·gee \(,)məs-'kō-gē\ *n* : a member of an Indian people of Georgia and eastern Alabama forming the nucleus of the Creek Confederacy

musk-ox \'məsk-,äks\ *n* : a heavy-set shaggy-coated wild ox confined to Greenland and the barren lands of northern No. America

musk·rat \'məs-,krat\ *n*, *pl* **muskrat** *or* **muskrats** : a No. American aquatic rodent with a long scaly tail, webbed hind feet, and dark glossy brown fur; *also* : its fur or pelt

musk turtle *n* : any of several small American freshwater turtles with a strong musky odor

musky \'məs-kē\ *adj* **musk·i·er; -est** : having an odor of or resembling musk — **musk·i·ness** *n*

Mus·lim \'məz-ləm, 'mús-\ *n* [Ar, lit., one who surrenders (to God)] : an adherent of Islam — **Muslim** *adj*

mus·lin \'məz-lən\ *n* [F *mousseline*, fr. It *mussolina*, fr. Ar *mawṣilīy* of Mosul] : a cotton fabric of plain weave

mus·quash \'məs-,kwäsh\ *n* : MUSKRAT

¹muss \'məs\ *n* : DISORDER, CONFUSION

²muss *vt* : to make untidy : RUMPLE ⟨*mussed* his hair⟩

mus·sel \'məs-əl\ *n* [OE *muscelle*, fr. L *musculus* muscle, mussel] **1** : an edible saltwater 2-valved mollusk with a long dark shell **2** : any of numerous 2-valved freshwater mollusks of the central U.S. having shells with pearly inner linings

Mus·sul·man *also* **Mus·sal·man** \'məs-əl-mən\ *n*, *pl* **-men** *or* **-mans** : MUSLIM

mussy \'məs-ē\ *adj* **muss·i·er; -est** : DISORDERED, SOILED, RUMPLED — **muss·i·ly** \'məs-ə-lē\ *adv* — **muss·i·ness** \'məs-ē-nəs\ *n*

¹must \məs(t), 'məst\ *auxiliary verb, pres & past all persons* **must** [ME *moste*, fr. OE *mōste* was allowed to, had to, past of *mōt* is allowed to, has to] **1 a** : is commanded or requested to ⟨the train *must* stop⟩ **b** : is urged to ⟨*must* read that book⟩ **2 a** : is compelled, required, or obliged to ⟨one *must* eat to live⟩ ⟨*must* be quiet⟩ ⟨*must* accept your reasoning⟩ **b** : is determined to ⟨if he *must* go⟩ **3** : is inferred by reasoning or supposed to ⟨it *must* be time⟩ ⟨if he had been there I *must* have seen him⟩

²must \'məst\ *n* : something necessary, required, or indispensable ⟨new shoes are a *must*⟩

³must *n* [OE, fr. L *mustum*] : the expressed juice of fruit (as grapes) before and during fermentation

mus·tache *var of* MOUSTACHE

mus·ta·chio \(,)məs-'tash-ō, -'täsh-, -ē-,ō\ *n*, *pl* **-chios** : MOUSTACHE; *esp* : a large moustache — **mus·ta·chioed** \-,ōd, -ē-,ōd\ *adj*

mus·tang \'məs-,taŋ\ *n* [AmerSp *mestengo*, fr. Sp, stray, fr. *mesta* annual roundup of stray cattle, fr. ML *animalia mixta* mixed animals] : the small hardy naturalized horse of the western plains directly descended from horses brought in by the Spaniards; *also* : BRONCO

mus·tard \'məs-tərd\ *n* [OF *mostarde*, fr. *moust* must, fr. L *mustum*] **1** : a pungent yellow powder of the seeds of a common mustard used as a condiment or in medicine **2** : any of several yellow-flowered herbs related to the turnips and cabbages

mustard gas *n* : a poisonous oily liquid $C_4H_8Cl_2S$ consisting of carbon, hydrogen, chlorine, and sulfur and having violent irritating and esp. blistering effects

mustard plaster *n* : a counterirritant medicinal plaster containing powdered mustard

---

ə abut; ᵊ kitten; ər further; a back; ā bake; ä cot, cart; aù out; ch chin; e less; ē easy; g gift; i trip; ī life

¹mus·ter \'məs-tər\ vb **mus·tered**; **mus·ter·ing** \-t(ə-)riŋ\ [ME mustren to show, muster, fr. OF monstrer to show, fr. L monstrare, fr. monstrum sign, portent, monster] **1** : to enlist or enroll a person in military service **2 a** : to assemble (as troops or a ship's company) for roll call or inspection **b** : ASSEMBLE, CONGREGATE **3** : to collect and display ⟨all the strength he could muster⟩ **4** : to amount to : COMPRISE ⟨the company musters 200 men⟩

²muster n **1 a** : an act of assembling; esp : a formal military inspection **b** : critical examination ⟨slipshod work that would never pass muster⟩ **2** : an assembled group : COLLECTION

muster out vt : to discharge from service

mustn't \'məs-ᵊnt\ : must not

musty \'məs-tē\ adj **must·i·er**; **-est** **1 a** : impaired by damp or mildew : MOLDY **b** : tasting or smelling of damp and decay **2 a** : TRITE, STALE **b** : OUT-OF-DATE, ANTIQUATED — **must·i·ly** \-tə-lē\ adv — **must·i·ness** \-tē-nəs\ n

mu·ta·ble \'myüt-ə-bəl\ adj **1** : prone to change : INCONSTANT **2 a** : capable of change in form or nature **b** : capable of or liable to mutation — **mu·ta·bil·i·ty** \,myüt-ə-'bil-ət-ē\ n — **mu·ta·ble·ness** \'myüt-ə-bəl-nəs\ n — **mu·ta·bly** \-blē\ adv

mu·ta·gen \'myüt-ə-jən, -,jen\ n : an agent inducing mutation — **mu·ta·gen·ic** \,myüt-ə-'jen-ik\ adj — **mu·ta·gen·i·cal·ly** \-'jen-i-k(ə-)lē\ adv

mu·tant \'myüt-ᵊnt\ adj : of, relating to, or produced by mutation — **mutant** n

mu·tate \'myü-,tāt\ vb : to undergo or cause to undergo mutation

mu·ta·tion \myü-'tā-shən\ n [L mutare to change] **1** : a basic alteration : CHANGE **2 a** : a relatively permanent change in hereditary material involving either a physical change in chromosome relations or a fundamental change in genes **b** : an individual or strain resulting from mutation — **mu·ta·tion·al** \-shnəl, -shən-ᵊl\ adj — **mu·ta·tion·al·ly** \-ē\ adv — **mu·ta·tive** \'myü-,tāt-iv, 'myüt-ət-iv\ adj

mutation theory n : a theory that views evolution as the result of accumulation of useful mutations

mu·ta·tis mu·tan·dis \mü-,tät-əs-mù-'tän-dəs\ adv [NL] : with the necessary changes having been made

¹mute \'myüt\ adj [L mutus] **1** : unable to speak : DUMB **2** : marked by absence of speech ⟨a mute appeal for help⟩ **3** : not pronounced : SILENT ⟨the mute b in thumb⟩ **syn** see DUMB — **mute·ly** adv — **mute·ness** n — **mut·ism** \'myüt-,iz-əm\ n

²mute n **1 a** : a person who cannot or does not speak **b** : a person employed by undertakers to attend a funeral as a mourner **2** : a device on a musical instrument that deadens, softens, or muffles its tone **3** : STOP 8

³mute vt **1** : to muffle or reduce the sound of **2** : to tone down (a color)

mu·ti·late \'myüt-ᵊl-,āt\ vt [L mutilare] **1 a** : to deprive of an essential part (as a limb) : CRIPPLE, MAIM **b** : to cut off or permanently destroy the use of (as a limb) **2** : to cut up or alter radically so as to make imperfect ⟨mutilate a document⟩ — **mu·ti·la·tion** \,myüt-ᵊl-'ā-shən\ n — **mu·ti·la·tor** \'myüt-ᵊl-,āt-ər\ n

mu·ti·neer \,myüt-ᵊn-'i(ə)r\ n : one that mutinies

mu·ti·nous \'myüt-ᵊn-əs, 'myüt-nəs\ adj **1 a** : disposed to or in a state of mutiny : REBELLIOUS ⟨a mutinous crew⟩ **b** : TURBULENT, UNRULY **2** : of, relating to, or constituting mutiny ⟨mutinous acts⟩ — **mu·ti·nous·ly** adv — **mu·ti·nous·ness** n

mu·ti·ny \'myüt-ᵊn-ē, 'myüt-nē\ n, pl **-nies** [obs. mutine to rebel, fr. MF se mutiner, fr. meute revolt, fr. L movēre to move] **1** : willful refusal to obey constituted authority; esp : revolt by a military group against a superior officer **2** : an act or instance of mutiny — **mutiny** vi

mutt \'mət\ n : MONGREL, CUR

mut·ter \'mət-ər\ vb **1** : to utter indistinctly or with a low voice and lips partly closed **2** : to murmur complainingly or angrily : GRUMBLE — **mutter** n — **mut·ter·er** \'mət-ər-ər\ n

mut·ton \'mət-ᵊn\ n [OF moton sheep] : the flesh of a mature sheep — **mut·tony** \-ē\ adj

mut·ton·chops \-,chäps\ n pl : side-whiskers that are narrow at the temple and broad and round by the lower jaws — called also muttonchop whiskers

mu·tu·al \'myü-chə-wəl, -chəl\ adj [MF mutuel, fr. L mutuus] **1 a** : given and received in equal amount ⟨mutual favors⟩ **b** : having the same feelings one for the other ⟨mutual enemies⟩ **2** : participated in, shared, or enjoyed by two or more at the same time : JOINT ⟨our mutual friend⟩ ⟨mutual defense⟩ **3** : organized in such a way that the members share in the profits, benefits, expenses, and liabilities ⟨mutual savings bank⟩ ⟨mutual life insurance company⟩ **syn** see RECIPROCAL — **mu·tu·al·i·ty** \,myü-chə-'wal-ət-ē\ n — **mu·tu·al·ly** \'myü-chə-(wə-)lē\ adv

mutual fund n : an investment company that invests money of its shareholders in a usu. diversified group of securities of other corporations

mu·tu·al·ism \'myü-chə-wə-,liz-əm, -chə-,liz-\ n : mutually beneficial association between different kinds of organisms — **mu·tu·al·ist** \-chə-wə-ləst, -chə-ləst\ n — **mu·tu·al·is·tic** \,myü-chə-wə-'lis-tik, -chə-'lis-\ adj — **mu·tu·al·is·ti·cal·ly** \-'lis-ti-k(ə-)lē\ adv

muu-muu \'mü-mü\ n [Hawaiian mu'umu'u] : a loose dress of Hawaiian origin for informal wear

mu·zhik \mü-'zhēk, -'zhik\ n [Russ] : a Russian peasant

¹muz·zle \'məz-əl\ n [MF musel, fr. dim. of muse mouth of an animal] **1** : the projecting jaws and nose of an animal : SNOUT **2** : a fastening or covering for the mouth of an animal used to prevent eating or biting **3** : the open end of a weapon from which the missile is discharged

²muzzle vt **muz·zled**; **muz·zling** \'məz-(ə-)liŋ\ **1** : to fit with a muzzle **2** : to prevent free or normal expression by : GAG ⟨the dictator muzzled the press⟩ — **muz·zler** \'məz-(ə-)lər\ n

muz·zle-load·er \,məz-ə(l)-'lōd-ər\ n : a gun that is loaded through the muzzle — **muz·zle-load·ing** \-'lōd-iŋ\ adj

muz·zy \'məz-ē\ adj **muz·zi·er**; **-est** **1** : muddled or confused in mind : DULL **2** : BLURRED — **muz·zi·ly** \'məz-ə-lē\ adv — **muz·zi·ness** \'məz-ē-nəs\ n

my \(')mī, mə\ adj [OE mīn] : of or relating to me or myself esp. as possessor ⟨my head⟩, agent ⟨kept my promise⟩, or object of an action ⟨my injuries⟩

my·as·the·nia \,mī-əs-'thē-nē-ə\ n [NL, fr. Gk mys mouse, muscle] : abnormal muscular weakness — **my·as·then·ic** \-'then-ik\ adj

myc- or **myco-** comb form [Gk mykēt-, mykēs] : fungus ⟨mycology⟩ ⟨mycosis⟩

my·ce·li·um \mī-'sē-lē-əm\ n, pl **-lia** \-lē-ə\ also **-li·ums** : the vegetative part of the body of a fungus typically consisting of a mass of interwoven hyphae and often being submerged in another body (as of soil, organic matter, or the tissues of a plant or animal host) — **my·ce·li·al** \-lē-əl\ adj

My·ce·nae·an \,mī-sə-'nē-ən\ adj : of or relating to the Bronze Age culture of the eastern Mediterranean area centering in Mycenae esp. from 1600 to 1100 B.C.

my·ce·toph·a·gous \,mī-sə-'täf-ə-gəs\ adj [Gk mykēt-, mykēs fungus] : feeding on fungi

my·ce·to·zo·an \(,)mī-,sēt-ə-'zō-ən\ n : SLIME MOLD — **mycetozoan** adj

my·co·bac·te·ri·um \,mī-kō-bak-'tir-ē-əm\ n : any of a genus of bacteria that includes the causers of tuberculosis and of leprosy as well as harmless saprophytes

my·col·o·gy \mī-'käl-ə-jē\ n **1** : a branch of botany dealing with fungi **2** : fungal life — **my·co·log·i·cal** \,mī-kə-'läj-i-kəl\ adj — **my·col·o·gist** \mī-'käl-ə-jəst\ n

my·cor·rhi·za \,mī-kə-'rī-zə\ n, pl **-zae** \-,zē\ or **-zas** [NL, fr. myc- + Gk rhiza root] : a symbiotic association of the mycelium of a fungus with the roots of a seed plant — **mycorrhizal** adj

my·co·sis \mī-'kō-səs\ n, pl **-co·ses** \-'kō-,sēz\ : infection with or disease caused by a fungus — **my·cot·ic** \-'kät-ik\ adj

my·e·lin \'mī-ə-lən\ n [Gk myelos marrow] : a soft white somewhat fatty material that forms a thick sheath about certain nerve fibers — **my·e·lin·at·ed** \-lə-,nāt-əd\ adj — **my·e·lin·ic** \,mī-ə-'lin-ik\ adj

my·e·li·tis \,mī-ə-'līt-əs\ n : inflammation of the spinal cord or of the bone marrow

my·i·a·sis \mī-'ī-ə-səs\ n, pl **-a·ses** \-ə-,sēz\ [Gk myia fly] : infestation (as of tissue) with fly maggots

my·na or **my·nah** \'mī-nə\ n [Hindi mainā] : any of

---

j joke; ŋ sing; ō flow; o flaw; oi coin; th thin; th this; ü loot; ù foot; y yet; yü few; yù furious; zh vision

various Asiatic starlings; *esp* **:** a dark brown slightly crested bird of southeastern Asia

myo·car·di·um \ˌmī-ə-'kärd-ē-əm\ *n* [Gk *mys* mouse, muscle (akin to E *mouse*) + *kardia* heart] **:** the middle muscular layer of the heart wall — **myo·car·di·al** \-ē-əl\ *adj*

myo·fi·bril \ˌmī-ō-'fīb-rəl, -'fib-\ *n* **:** one of the long thin intracellular bodies that are the contractile elements of muscle

my·o·gen·ic \ˌmī-ə-'jen-ik\ *adj* [Gk *mys* mouse, muscle] **:** originating in muscle

myo·neu·ral \ˌmī-ō-'n(y)uṙ-əl\ *adj* **:** of, relating to, or involving both muscle and nerve

my·o·pia \mī-'ō-pē-ə\ *n* [Gk *myōpia*, fr. *myein* to be closed + *ōps* eye, face] **:** NEARSIGHTEDNESS, SHORT-SIGHTEDNESS — **my·o·pic** \-'ōp-ik, -'äp-\ *adj* — **my·o·pi·cal·ly** \-i-k(ə-)lē\ *adv*

my·o·sin \'mī-ə-sən\ *n* [Gk *myos*, gen. of *mys* muscle] **:** a protein of muscle that with actin is active in muscular contraction

¹myr·i·ad \'mir-ē-əd\ *n* [Gk *myriad-, myrias*, fr. *myrioi*, pl., countless, ten thousand] **1 :** ten thousand **2 :** an indefinitely large number ⟨the *myriads* of stars of the Milky Way⟩

²myriad *adj* **:** consisting of a very great but indefinite number ⟨the *myriad* grains of sand in a single handful⟩

myr·ia·me·ter \'mir-ē-ə-ˌmēt-ər\ *n* — see METRIC SYSTEM table

myr·io·pod *or* **myr·ia·pod** \'mir-ē-ə-ˌpäd\ *n* **:** any of a former group (Myriopoda) of arthropods including the millipedes and centipedes — **myriopod** *adj*

myr·me·coph·a·gous \ˌmər-mə-'käf-ə-gəs\ *adj* [Gk *myrmēk-, myrmēx* ant] **:** feeding on ants

myr·me·co·phile \'mər-mi-kə-ˌfīl\ *n* **:** an organism that habitually shares an ant nest — **myr·me·coph·i·lous** \ˌmər-mə-'käf-ə-ləs\ *adj* — **myr·me·coph·i·ly** \-lē\ *n*

myr·mi·don \'mər-mə-ˌdän, 'mər-məd-ən\ *n* **1** *cap* **:** one of a legendary Thessalian people following Achilles to the Trojan war **2 a :** a loyal follower or retainer **b :** a subordinate who unquestioningly or pitilessly executes orders

myrrh \'mər\ *n* [OE *myrre*, fr. L *myrrha*, fr. Gk, of Semitic origin] **:** a brown slightly bitter aromatic gum resin obtained from African and Arabian trees and used esp. in perfumes or formerly in incense

myr·tle \'mərt-ᵊl\ *n* [L *myrtus*, fr. Gk *myrtos*] **1 :** a common evergreen bushy shrub of southern Europe with oval to lance-shaped shining leaves, fragrant white or rosy flowers, and black berries **2 a :** any of the family of chiefly tropical shrubs or trees to which the common myrtle belongs **b :** any of several plants of other families; *esp* **:** the common periwinkle

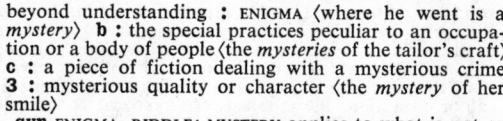

myrtle

my·self \mī-'self, mə-\ *pron* **1 :** that identical one that is I — used reflexively ⟨I'm going to get *myself* a new suit⟩, for emphasis ⟨I *myself* will go⟩, or in absolute constructions ⟨*myself* a tourist, I nevertheless avoided other tourists⟩ **2 :** my normal, healthy, or sane condition or self ⟨didn't feel *myself* yesterday⟩

mys·te·ri·ous \mis-'tir-ē-əs\ *adj* **:** of or relating to mystery **:** containing, suggesting, or implying a mystery **:** SECRET ⟨the *mysterious* ways of nature⟩ — **mys·te·ri·ous·ly** *adv* — **mys·te·ri·ous·ness** *n*

mys·tery \'mis-t(ə-)rē\ *n, pl* **-ter·ies** [L *mysterium*, fr. Gk *mystērion*, fr. *myein* to be closed (of eyes or lips)] **1 a :** a religious truth that man can know by revelation alone and cannot fully understand **b** (1) **:** any of the 15 events (as the Nativity, the Crucifixion, or the Assumption) serving as a subject for meditation during the saying of the rosary (2) *cap* **:** a Christian sacrament; *esp* **:** EUCHARIST **c** (1) **:** a secret religious rite believed (as in the Eleusinian cult) to impart enduring bliss to the initiate (2) **:** a cult devoted to such rites **2 a :** something not understood or

beyond understanding **:** ENIGMA ⟨where he went is a *mystery*⟩ **b :** the special practices peculiar to an occupation or a body of people ⟨the *mysteries* of the tailor's craft⟩ **c :** a piece of fiction dealing with a mysterious crime **3 :** mysterious quality or character ⟨the *mystery* of her smile⟩

syn ENIGMA, RIDDLE: MYSTERY applies to what is not or cannot be fully understood or explained ⟨the disappearance of the money remained a *mystery*⟩ ENIGMA applies to words or actions very difficult to interpret correctly; RIDDLE suggests esp. a problem or enigma involving paradox or apparent contradiction

mystery play *n* **:** a medieval play based on scriptural incidents (as the life, death, and resurrection of Christ)

¹mys·tic \'mis-tik\ *adj* **1 :** MYSTICAL 1 **2 :** of or relating to mysteries or magical rites **:** OCCULT **3 :** of or relating to mysticism or mystics **4 a :** MYSTERIOUS **b :** AWESOME **c :** MAGICAL

²mystic *n* **:** a person who seeks direct knowledge of God through contemplation and prayer

mys·ti·cal \'mis-ti-kəl\ *adj* **1 :** having a spiritual meaning or reality that is neither apparent to the senses nor obvious to the intelligence **2 :** of, relating to, or resulting from an individual's direct communion with God or ultimate reality **3 :** MYSTIC 2 — **mys·ti·cal·ly** \-ti-k(ə-)lē\ *adv*

mys·ti·cism \'mis-tə-ˌsiz-əm\ *n* **1 :** the experience of mystical union or direct communion with ultimate reality reported by mystics **2 :** the belief that direct knowledge of God or of spiritual truth can be achieved by personal insight and inspiration **3 :** vague guessing or speculation; *also* **:** a belief without a sound basis **:** GUESS

mys·ti·fy \'mis-tə-ˌfī\ *vb* **-fied; -fy·ing 1 :** to make obscure or difficult to understand **2 :** PERPLEX, BEWILDER ⟨strange actions that *mystified* everyone⟩ **syn** see PUZZLE — **mys·ti·fi·ca·tion** \ˌmis-tə-fə-'kā-shən\ *n*

mys·tique \mi-'stēk\ *n* **:** a set of beliefs and attitudes developing around an object or associated with a particular group **:** CULT ⟨the *mystique* of mountain climbing⟩

myth \'mith\ *n* [Gk *mythos*] **1 :** a usu. legendary narrative that presents part of the beliefs of a people or explains a practice, belief, or natural phenomenon **2 :** PARABLE, ALLEGORY **3 a :** a person or thing having only an imaginary existence ⟨the griffin is a *myth*⟩ **b :** a belief that supports the practices and institutions of a group and is held uncritically by its members ⟨a *myth* of racial superiority⟩ **c :** a belief concerning a visionary ideal ⟨the *myth* of a classless society⟩ **4 :** the whole body of myths

syn LEGEND, FABLE: a MYTH is a story dealing with gods or personifications of natural phenomena; a LEGEND may include supernatural incidents but deals with human beings and is attached to definite places; a FABLE is an invented story in which talking animals or things illustrate human follies and weaknesses

myth·i·cal \'mith-i-kəl\ *also* **myth·ic** \-ik\ *adj* **1 :** based on, described in, or constituting a myth ⟨Hercules is a *mythical* hero⟩ **2 :** IMAGINARY, INVENTED ⟨a person dreaming of his *mythical* castle⟩ **syn** see FABULOUS — **myth·i·cal·ly** \-i-k(ə-)lē\ *adv*

my·thol·o·gy \mith-'äl-ə-jē\ *n, pl* **-gies 1 :** a body of myths; *esp* **:** the myths dealing with the gods and heroes of a people ⟨Greek *mythology*⟩ **2 :** a branch of knowledge that deals with myth — **myth·o·log·i·cal** \ˌmith-ə-'läj-i-kəl\ *adj* — **myth·o·log·i·cal·ly** \-k(ə-)lē\ *adv* — **my·thol·o·gist** \mith-'äl-ə-jəst\ *n*

my·thos \'mī-ˌthäs, 'mith-ˌäs\ *n* **:** a pattern of beliefs expressing often symbolically the characteristic or prevalent attitudes in a group or culture

myx·ede·ma \ˌmik-sə-'dē-mə\ *n* **:** a disorder caused by deficient thyroid secretion and marked by puffy swelling, dry skin and hair, and loss of mental and physical vigor — **myx·ede·ma·tous** \-'dem-ət-əs, -'dē-mət-\ *adj*

myxo·my·cete \ˌmik-sō-'mī-ˌsēt, -mī-'sēt\ *n* [Gk *myxa* mucus, slime + *mykēt-, mykēs* fungus] **:** SLIME MOLD — **myxo·my·ce·tous** \-mī-'sēt-əs\ *adj*

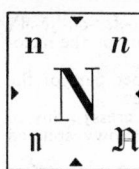

n \'en\ *n, often cap* **1** : the 14th letter of the English alphabet **2** : an unspecified quantity ⟨of any *n* samples 0.1*n* may be expected to be defective⟩

-n — see -EN

nab \'nab\ *vt* **nabbed; nab·bing** **1** : to seize and take into custody : ARREST, APPREHEND **2** : to seize suddenly : snatch away

na·bob \'nā-ˌbäb\ *n* [Hindi *nawwāb*] **1** : a provincial governor of the Mogul empire in India **2** : a man of great wealth or prominence

na·celle \nə-'sel\ *n* [F, lit., small boat, fr. LL *navicella*, dim. of L *navis* ship] : an enclosed shelter on an aircraft for an engine or sometimes for crew

na·cre \'nā-kər\ *n* [MF, fr. It *naccara* drum, nacre, fr. Ar *naqqārah* drum made of two small concave pieces] : MOTHER-OF-PEARL — **na·cred** \-kərd\ *adj* — **na·cre·ous** \-krē-əs, -k(ə)rəs\ *adj*

na·dir \'nā-ˌdi(ə)r, 'nād-ər\ *n* [MF, fr. Ar *naẓīr* opposite] **1** : the point of the celestial sphere that is directly opposite the zenith and vertically downward from the observer **2** : the lowest point ⟨we were desperate; our hopes had reached their *nadir*⟩

¹nag \'nag\ *n* [ME *nagge*] : HORSE; *esp* : one that is old or in poor condition

²nag *vb* **nagged; nag·ging** **1** : to find fault incessantly : COMPLAIN **2** : to irritate by constant scolding or urging **3** : to be a continuing source of annoyance ⟨a *nagging* toothache⟩ — **nag·ger** *n*

Na·huatl \'nä-ˌwät-ᵊl\ *n* **1** : a group of peoples of southern Mexico and Central America **2** : the language of the Nahuatl people — **Na·huat·lan** \-ˌwät-lən\ *adj or n*

Na·hum \'nā-(h)əm\ *n* **1** : a Hebrew prophet of the 7th century B.C. **2** — see BIBLE table

na·iad \'nā-əd, 'nī-, -ˌad\ *n, pl* **na·iads** *or* **na·ia·des** \-ə-ˌdēz\ [L *naiad-, naias*, fr. Gk, fr. *nan* to flow] **1** : one of the nymphs in ancient mythology living in and giving life to lakes, rivers, springs, and fountains **2** : the aquatic young of a mayfly, dragonfly, damselfly, or stone fly **3** : MUSSEL 2

na·if \nä-'ēf\ *adj* [F] : NAÏVE

¹nail \'nāl\ *n* [OE *nægl*] **1 a** : a horny sheath protecting the end of each finger and toe in man and most other primates **b** : a corresponding structure (as a claw) terminating a digit **2** : a slender usu. pointed and headed fastener to be pounded in

²nail *vt* **1** : to fasten with or as if with a nail **2** : to fix (as the eyes) in steady attention **3** : CATCH, TRAP ⟨*nail* a thief⟩; *esp* : to detect and expose so as to discredit ⟨*nail* a lie⟩ — **nail·er** *n*

nail·brush \'nāl-ˌbrəsh\ *n* : a small firm-bristled brush for cleaning the hands and esp. the fingernails

nail down *vt* : to settle or establish clearly and unmistakably

nain·sook \'nān-ˌsu̇k\ *n* [Hindi *nainsukh*, fr. *nain* eye + *sukh* delight] : a soft lightweight muslin

na·ïve *also* **na·ive** \nä-'ēv\ *adj* [F *naïve*, fem. of *naïf*, fr. L *nativus* native] **1** : marked by unaffected simplicity : ARTLESS, INGENUOUS **2** : showing lack of informed judgment; *esp* : CREDULOUS — **na·ïve·ly** *adv* — **na·ïve·ness** *n*

na·ïve·té *also* **na·ive·té** \(ˌ)nä-ˌē-və-'tā, nä-'ē-və-ˌ\ *n* [F *naïveté*, fr. *naïf*] **1** : the quality or state of being naïve **2** : a naïve remark or action

na·ive·ty *also* **na·ïve·ty** \nä-'ē-vət-ē, -'ēv-tē\ *n* : NAÏVETÉ

na·ked \'nā-kəd, *esp South* 'nek-əd\ *adj* [OE *nacod*] **1** : having no clothes on : NUDE **2** : lacking a usual or natural covering (as of foliage or feathers) ⟨*naked* hills⟩: as **a** : UNSHEATHED ⟨a *naked* sword⟩ **b** : lacking protective enveloping parts (as membranes, scales, or shells) ⟨a *naked* seed⟩⟨slugs and other *naked* mollusks⟩ **3** : lacking embellishment of any kind : PLAIN, UNADORNED ⟨the *naked* truth⟩ **4** : not aided by artificial means ⟨seen by the *naked* eye⟩ — **na·ked·ly** *adv* — **na·ked·ness** *n*

nam·by-pam·by \ˌnam-bē-'pam-bē\ *adj* [*Namby Pamby*, nickname given to Ambrose Philips to ridicule the style

nails 2

of his poetry] **1** : lacking in character or substance : INSIPID **2** : WEAK, INDECISIVE — **namby-pamby** *n*

¹name \'nām\ *n* [OE *nama*] **1** : a word or combination of words by which a person or thing is regularly known **2** : a descriptive often disparaging epithet ⟨call someone *names*⟩ **3** : REPUTATION; *esp* : a distinguished reputation ⟨made a *name* for himself⟩ **4** : FAMILY, CLAN ⟨was a disgrace to his *name*⟩ **5** : semblance as opposed to reality ⟨a friend in *name* only⟩

²name *vt* **1** : to give a name to : CALL **2 a** : to mention or identify by name **b** : to accuse by name **3** : to nominate for office : APPOINT **4** : to decide upon : CHOOSE **5** : to speak about : MENTION ⟨*name* a price⟩ — **nam·er** *n*

³name *adj* **1** : of, relating to, or bearing a name ⟨*name* tag⟩ **2** : having an established reputation ⟨a hotel featuring only *name* bands⟩ ⟨*name* brands⟩

name·a·ble *also* **nam·a·ble** \'nā-mə-bəl\ *adj* **1** : capable of being named : IDENTIFIABLE **2** : worthy of being named : MEMORABLE

name day *n* : the day of the saint whose name one bears

name·less \'nām-ləs\ *adj* **1** : having no name **2** : not marked with a name ⟨a *nameless* grave⟩ **3** : not known by name : UNKNOWN, ANONYMOUS ⟨a *nameless* hero⟩ ⟨a *nameless* sculptor⟩ **4** : not to be described ⟨*nameless* fears⟩ ⟨*nameless* indignities⟩ — **name·less·ly** *adv* — **name·less·ness** *n*

name·ly \'nām-lē\ *adv* : that is to say ⟨the cat family, *namely*, lions, tigers, and similar animals⟩

name·plate \-ˌplāt\ *n* : a plate or plaque bearing a name (as of a resident)

name·sake \'nām-ˌsāk\ *n* : one that has the same name as another; *esp* : one named after another

nan·keen \nan-'kēn\ *also* **nan·kin** \-'kēn, -'kin\ *n* [fr. *Nanking*, China] : a durable brownish yellow cotton fabric orig. woven by hand in China

nan·ny goat \'nan-ē-\ *n* : a female domestic goat

nano- \'nan-ō, -ə\ *comb form* [Gk *nanos* dwarf] : one billionth part of ⟨*nano*second⟩

Na·o·mi \nā-'ō-mē\ *n* : the mother-in-law of the Old Testament heroine Ruth

¹nap \'nap\ *vi* **napped; nap·ping** [OE *hnappian*] **1** : to sleep briefly esp. during the day : DOZE **2** : to be off guard ⟨was caught *napping*⟩

²nap *n* : a short sleep esp. during the day : SNOOZE ⟨takes a *nap* every day after lunch⟩

³nap *n* [MD *noppe* tuft of wool, nap] : a hairy or downy surface on a woven fabric — **nap·less** \'nap-ləs\ *adj* — **napped** \'napt\ *adj* — **nap·py** \'nap-ē\ *adj*

⁴nap *vt* **napped; nap·ping** : to raise a nap on ⟨fabric or leather⟩

na·palm \'nā-ˌpäm, -ˌpälm\ *n* **1** : a thickener used in jelling gasoline esp. for incendiary bombs and flamethrowers **2** : fuel jelled with napalm

nape \'nāp, 'nap\ *n* [ME] : the back of the neck

na·pery \'nā-p(ə-)rē\ *n* [MF *naperie*, fr. *nappe, nape* tablecloth] : household linen esp. for the table

naph·tha \'naf-thə, 'nap-\ *n* [L, fr. Gk, of Iranian origin] **1** : PETROLEUM **2** : any of various volatile often flammable liquid hydrocarbon mixtures used chiefly as solvents and diluents

naph·tha·lene \-ˌlēn\ *n* : a crystalline hydrocarbon usu. obtained by distillation of coal tar and used in chemical manufacture and as a moth repellent — **naph·tha·le·nic** \ˌnaf-thə-'lēn-ik, -nap-, -'len-\ *adj*

naph·thol \'naf-ˌthȯl, 'nap-, -ˌthōl\ *n* : either of two derivatives of naphthalene found in coal tar or made synthetically and used as antiseptics and in the manufacture of dyes

nap·kin \'nap-kən\ *n* [ME *nappekin*, fr. *nappe* tablecloth, fr. MF, fr. L *mappa* napkin] **1** : a piece of material (as cloth or paper) used at table to wipe the lips or fingers and protect the clothes **2** : a small cloth or towel

na·po·leon \nə-'pōl-yən, -'pō-lē-ən\ *n* [F *napoléon*, fr. *Napoléon* Napoleon] **1** : a French 20-franc gold coin **2** : an oblong pastry consisting of layers of puff paste with a filling of cream, custard, or jelly

Na·po·le·on·ic \nə-ˌpō-lē-'än-ik\ *adj* : of, relating to, or characteristic of Napoleon I or his family — **Na·po·le·on·i·cal·ly** \-'än-i-k(ə-)lē\ *adv*

nappe \'nap\ *n* : one of the two similar parts of a conical surface on either side of the vertex

nar·cis·sism \'när-sə-,siz-əm\ *n* : undue dwelling on one's own self or attainments — **nar·cis·sist** \'när-sə-səst\ *n or adj* — **nar·cis·sis·tic** \,när-sə-'sis-tik\ *adj*

nar·cis·sus \när-'sis-əs\ *n, pl* **-cissus** *or* **-cis·sus·es** \-'sis-ə-səz\ *or* **-cis·si** \-'sis-,ī, -,(,)ē\ **1** *cap* : a beautiful youth in Greek legend punished by being made to pine away for love of his own image and transformed into the narcissus **2** : DAFFODIL; *esp* : one whose flowers have a short corona and are usu. borne separately

nar·co·sis \när-'kō-səs\ *n, pl* **-co·ses** \-'kō-,sēz\ : a state of stupor, unconsciousness, or arrested activity produced by the influence of chemicals (as narcotics)

narcissus

¹nar·cot·ic \när-'kät-ik\ *n* [Gk *narkoun* to benumb, fr. *narkē* numbness] **1** : a drug (as opium) that in moderate doses dulls the senses, relieves pain, and induces sleep but in excessive doses causes stupor, coma, or convulsions **2** : something that soothes, relieves, or lulls

²narcotic *adj* **1** : having the properties of or yielding a narcotic **2** : of or relating to narcotics or to their use or addicts — **nar·cot·i·cal·ly** \-'kät-i-k(ə-)lē\ *adv*

nar·co·tize \'när-kə-,tīz\ *vt* **1 a** : to treat with or subject to a narcotic **b** : to put into a state of narcosis **2** : to soothe to unconsciousness or unawareness

nard \'närd\ *n* [Gk *nardos*, of Sem origin] : SPIKENARD 1b

na·ris \'nar-əs, 'ner-\ *n, pl* **na·res** \'na(ə)r-(,)ēz, 'ne(ə)r-\ [L] : any of the openings of the nose or nasal cavity of a vertebrate

nark \'närk\ *n, Brit* : a spy employed by the police

nar·rate \'nar-,āt, na-'rāt\ *vt* [L *narrare*] : to recite the details of (as a story) : give an account of : RELATE, TELL — **nar·ra·tor** *or* **nar·rat·er** \'nar-,āt-ər, na-'rāt-\ *n*

nar·ra·tion \na-'rā-shən, nə-\ *n* **1** : the act or process or an instance of narrating **2** : STORY, NARRATIVE — **nar·ra·tion·al** \-shnəl, -shən-ᵊl\ *adj*

nar·ra·tive \'nar-ət-iv\ *n* **1** : something (as a story or an account of a series of events) that is narrated **2** : the art or practice of narration — **narrative** *adj* — **nar·ra·tive·ly** *adv*

¹nar·row \'nar-ō\ *adj* [OE *nearu*] **1 a** : of slender width **b** : of less than standard width **2** : limited in size or scope **:** RESTRICTED **3 a** : not liberal in views or disposition **:** PREJUDICED **b** : interpreted or interpreting strictly ⟨a *narrow* view⟩ **4 a** : barely sufficient : CLOSE ⟨a *narrow* escape⟩ **b** : barely successful ⟨won by a *narrow* margin⟩ **5** : minutely precise : METICULOUS ⟨a *narrow* inspection⟩ — **nar·row·ly** *adv* — **nar·row·ness** *n*

²narrow *n* : a narrow part or passage; *esp* : a strait connecting two bodies of water — usu. used in pl.

³narrow *vb* : to lessen in width or extent : CONTRACT, RESTRICT

nar·row-mind·ed \,nar-ō-'mīn-dəd\ *adj* : lacking in tolerance or breadth of vision : ILLIBERAL, BIGOTED — **nar·row-mind·ed·ly** *adv* — **nar·row-mind·ed·ness** *n*

nar·thex \'när-,theks\ *n* [LGk *narthēx*, fr. Gk, giant fennel, cane, casket] **1** : the portico of an ancient church **2** : a vestibule leading to the nave of a church — see BASILICA illustration

nar·whal \'när-,(h)wäl, 'när-wəl\ *n* : an arctic sea animal about 20 feet long that is related to the dolphin and in the male has a long twisted ivory tusk

nary \'na(ə)r-ē, 'ne(ə)r-\ *adj, dial* : not one

¹na·sal \'nā-zəl\ *n* **1** : a nasal part **2** : a nasal consonant or vowel

²nasal *adj* [L *nasus* nose] **1** : of or relating to the nose **2 a** : uttered with the mouth passage closed and the nose passage open ⟨the *nasal* consonants \m\, \n\, and \ŋ\⟩ **b** : uttered with the nose passage as well as the mouth passage open ⟨the *nasal* vowels in French⟩ **c** : characterized by resonance produced through the nose ⟨speaking in a *nasal* tone⟩ — **na·sal·i·ty** \nā-'zal-ət-ē\ *n* — **na·sal·ly** \'nā-zə-lē\ *adv*

na·sal·ize \'nā-zə-,līz\ *vb* **1** : to make nasal **2** : to speak in a nasal manner — **na·sal·i·za·tion** \,nā-zə-lə-'zā-shən\ *n*

nas·cent \'nas-ᵊnt, 'nās-\ *adj* [L *nascent-, nascens*, fr. prp. of *nasci* to be born] : coming into existence : beginning to develop — **nas·cence** \-ᵊn(t)s\ *also* **nas·cen·cy** \-ᵊn-sē\ *n*

na·so·pha·ryn·geal \,nā-zō-fə-'rin-j(ē-)əl, -,far-ən-'jē-əl\ *adj* : of or relating to the nose and pharynx or the nasopharynx

na·so·phar·ynx \-'far-in(k)s\ *n* : the upper part of the pharynx continuous with the nasal passages

nas·tur·tium \nə-'stər-shəm, na-\ *n* [L, a cress] : any of a genus of watery-stemmed herbs with showy spurred flowers and pungent seeds

nas·ty \'nas-tē\ *adj* **nas·ti·er; -est** [ME] **1** : very dirty or foul : FILTHY **2** : INDECENT, VILE **3** : DISAGREEABLE ⟨*nasty* weather⟩ **4** : MEAN, ILL-NATURED ⟨a *nasty* temper⟩ **5** : DISHONORABLE ⟨a *nasty* trick⟩ **6** : HARMFUL, DANGEROUS ⟨a *nasty* fall on the ice⟩ **syn** see DIRTY — **nas·ti·ly** \-tə-lē\ *adv* — **nas·ti·ness** \-tē-nəs\ *n*

na·tal \'nāt-ᵊl\ *adj* [L *natalis*, fr. *natus* birth, fr. *nat-, nasci* to be born] **1** : NATIVE **2** : of or relating to birth ⟨his *natal* day⟩

na·tal·i·ty \nā-'tal-ət-ē, nə-\ *n* : BIRTHRATE

na·ta·tion \,nā-'tā-shən, na-\ *n* : the action or art of swimming

na·ta·to·ri·al \,nāt-ə-'tōr-ē-əl, ,nat-, -'tȯr-\ *or* **na·ta·to·ry** \'nāt-ə-,tōr-ē, 'nat-, -,tȯr-\ *adj* **1** : of or relating to swimming **2** : adapted to or characterized by swimming

na·ta·to·ri·um \,nāt-ə-'tōr-ē-əm, ,nat-, -'tȯr-\ *n* [LL, fr. L *natare* to swim] : a swimming pool esp. indoors

na·tes \'nā-,tēz\ *n pl* [L, pl. of *natis* buttock] : BUTTOCKS

nathe·less \'nāth-ləs\ *or* **nath·less** \'nath-\ *adv* [OE *nā thē læs* not the less] *archaic* : NEVERTHELESS, NOTWITHSTANDING

na·tion \'nā-shən\ *n* [L *nation-, natio* birth, race, nation, fr. *nat-, nasci* to be born; akin to E *kin*] **1 a** : NATIONALITY 4a **b** : a politically organized nationality **c** : a community of people composed of one or more nationalities with its own territory and government **d** : a usu. large and independent territorial division containing a body of people of one or more nationalities **2** : a tribe or federation of tribes (as of American Indians)

¹na·tion·al \'nash-nəl, -ən-ᵊl\ *adj* **1** : of or relating to a nation **2** : comprising or characteristic of a nationality **3** : FEDERAL 1c

²national *n* **1** : one who is under the protection of a nation without regard to the more formal status of citizen or subject **2** : an organization (as a labor union) having local units throughout a nation **syn** see CITIZEN

national anthem *n* : a song or hymn officially adopted and played or sung on formal occasions as a mark of loyalty to the nation

national bank *n* **1** : a bank associated with the finances of a nation **2** : a commercial bank organized under laws passed by Congress and chartered and supervised by the national government

National Guard *n* : a militia force recruited by each state, equipped by the federal government, and jointly maintained subject to the call of either

national income *n* : the total earnings from a nation's current production including wages of employees, interest, rental income, and business profits after taxes

na·tion·al·ism \'nash-nəl-iz-əm, -ən-ᵊl-\ *n* : loyalty and devotion to a nation esp. as expressed in an exalting of one nation above all others with primary emphasis on promotion of its culture and interests

na·tion·al·ist \-nəl-əst, -ən-ᵊl-əst\ *n* **1** : an advocate of or believer in nationalism **2** *cap* : a member of a political party or group advocating national independence or strong national government — **nationalist** *adj, often cap* — **na·tion·al·is·tic** \,nash-nəl-'is-tik, -ən-ᵊl-'is-\ *adj* — **na·tion·al·is·ti·cal·ly** \-ti-k(ə-)lē\ *adv*

na·tion·al·i·ty \,nash-(ə-)'nal-ət-ē\ *n, pl* **-ties** **1** : national character **2 a** : national status; *esp* : a legal relationship involving allegiance of an individual and his protection by the state **b** : membership in a particular nation **3** : political independence or existence as a separate nation **4 a** : a people having a common origin, tradition, and language and capable of forming or actually constituting a state **b** : an ethnic group within a larger unit (as a nation)

na·tion·al·ize \'nash-nəl-,īz, -ən-ᵊl-\ *vt* **1** : to make national : make a nation of **2** : to remove from private ownership and place under government control ⟨*nationalize* railroads⟩ — **na·tion·al·i·za·tion** \,nash-nəl-ə-'zā-shən, ,nash-ən-ᵊl-\ *n* — **na·tion·al·iz·er** *n*

na·tion·al·ly \'nash-nəl-ē, -ən-ᵊl-ē\ *adv* : by or with regard to a nation as a whole : throughout a nation

national park *n* : an area of special scenic, historical, or scientific importance set aside and maintained by a national government esp. for recreation or study

national socialism *n* : NAZISM — **national socialist** *adj*

na·tion·hood \'nā-shən-,hùd\ *n* : the quality or state of being a nation

na·tion·wide \,nā-shən-'wīd\ *adj* : extending throughout a nation

¹na·tive \'nāt-iv\ *adj* [L *nativus*, fr. *nat-, nasci* to be born] **1** : INBORN, NATURAL ⟨*native* shrewdness⟩ **2** : born in a particular place or country ⟨*native* Americans⟩ **3** : belonging to a person because of the place or circumstances of his birth ⟨his *native* language⟩ **4** : grown, produced, or having its origin in a particular region : INDIGENOUS ⟨*native* art⟩ **5** : occurring in nature : not artificially prepared ⟨*native* salt⟩ — **na·tive·ly** *adv* — **na·tive·ness** *n*
syn NATIVE, INDIGENOUS, ABORIGINAL mean belonging to a locality. NATIVE implies birth or origin in a place or region and may suggest special compatibility with it; INDIGENOUS applies to species or races and adds an implication of not having been introduced from elsewhere; ABORIGINAL implies having no known predecessor in occupying a region

²native *n* **1** : one born or reared in a particular place **2 a** : an original or indigenous inhabitant **b** : something indigenous to a particular locality **3** : a local resident; *esp* : a person who has lived all his life in a place

na·tiv·i·ty \nə-'tiv-ət-ē, nā-\ *n, pl* **-ties 1** *cap* : the birth of Christ **2** *cap* : CHRISTMAS 1 **3** : the process or circumstances of being born : BIRTH **4** : a horoscope at or of the time of one's birth

nat·ty \'nat-ē\ *adj* **nat·ti·er; -est** : trimly neat and tidy : SMART — **nat·ti·ly** \'nat-ᵊl-ē\ *adv* — **nat·ti·ness** \'nat-ē-nəs\ *n*

¹nat·u·ral \'nach-(ə-)rəl\ *adj* **1** : born in or with one : INNATE ⟨*natural* ability⟩ **2** : being such by nature : BORN ⟨a *natural* fool⟩ **3** : born of unmarried parents : ILLEGITIMATE ⟨a *natural* son⟩ **4** : existing or used in or produced by nature ⟨the *natural* woodland flora⟩ ⟨meat is the *natural* food of dogs⟩ **5** : having or showing qualities held to be part of the nature of man : HUMAN ⟨it is not *natural* to hate your son⟩ **6** : of or relating to nature : conforming to the laws of nature or of the physical world ⟨*natural* causes⟩ ⟨*natural* history⟩ **7** : not made or altered by man ⟨*natural* silk⟩ ⟨a person's *natural* complexion⟩ **8** : marked by simplicity and sincerity : not affected ⟨*natural* manners⟩ **9** : closely resembling the object imitated : LIFELIKE ⟨the people in the picture look *natural*⟩ **10** : having neither sharps nor flats in the key signature or having a sharp or a flat changed in pitch by a natural sign — **nat·u·ral·ness** *n*

²natural *n* **1** : IDIOT **2 a** : a character ♮ placed on a line or space of the musical staff to nullify the effect of a preceding sharp or flat **b** : a note or tone affected by the natural sign **3 a** : one having natural skills, talents, or abilities **b** : one obviously suitable for a specific purpose

natural gas *n* : gas issuing from the earth's crust through natural openings or bored wells; *esp* : a combustible mixture of hydrocarbons and esp. methane used chiefly as a fuel and raw material

natural history *n* : the study of natural objects esp. from an amateur or popular point of view

nat·u·ral·ism \'nach-(ə-)rə-,liz-əm\ *n* **1** : action, inclination, or thought based only on natural desires and instincts **2** : a theory denying a supernatural explanation of the origin and development of the universe and holding that scientific laws account for everything in nature **3** : realism in art or literature; *esp* : a theory in literature emphasizing scientific observation of life without idealization or the avoidance of the ugly

nat·u·ral·ist \-ləst\ *n* **1** : one that advocates or practices naturalism **2** : a student of natural history; *esp* : a field biologist — **naturalist** *adj*

nat·u·ral·is·tic \,nach-(ə-)rə-'lis-tik\ *adj* : of, characterized by, or according with naturalism — **nat·u·ral·is·ti·cal·ly** \-ti-k(ə-)lē\ *adv*

nat·u·ral·ize \'nach-(ə-)rə-,līz\ *vb* **1** : to introduce into common use or into the vernacular ⟨*naturalize* a foreign word⟩ **2** : to become or cause to become established as if native ⟨*naturalized* weeds⟩ **3** : to bring into conformity with nature **4** : to confer the rights of a national on; *esp* : to admit to citizenship — **nat·u·ral·i·za·tion** \,nach-(ə-)rə-lə-'zā-shən\ *n*

natural law *n* : a body of law or a specific principle held to be derived from nature and binding upon human society in the absence of or in addition to positive law

natural logarithm *n* : a logarithm in a system that uses as a base the transcendental number *e* whose value is approximately 2.71828

nat·u·ral·ly \'nach-(ə-)rə-lē, 'nach-ər-lē\ *adv* **1** : by nature : by natural character or ability ⟨*naturally* timid⟩ **2** : according to the usual course of things : as might be expected ⟨we *naturally* dislike being hurt⟩ **3 a** : without artificial aid ⟨hair that curls *naturally*⟩ **b** : without affectation ⟨speak *naturally*⟩ **4** : with truth to nature : REALISTICALLY ⟨paints flowers *naturally*⟩

natural number *n* : the number 1 or any number (as 3, 12, or 432) obtained by repeatedly adding 1 to this number

natural philosophy *n* : NATURAL SCIENCE; *esp* : PHYSICAL SCIENCE

natural resource *n* : something (as a mineral, water-power source, forest, or kind of animal) that occurs in nature and is of value to human life ⟨pure water is a precious and limited *natural resource*⟩

natural science *n* : a science (as physics, chemistry, or biology) that deals with matter, energy, and their interrelations and transformations or with objectively measurable phenomena

natural selection *n* : a natural process that tends to cause the survival of individuals or groups best adjusted to the conditions under which they live and that is equally important for the perpetuation of desirable genetic qualities and for the elimination of those that are undesirable

na·ture \'nā-chər\ *n* [L *natura*, fr. *nat-, nasci* to be born] **1** : the peculiar quality or character or basic constitution of a person or thing ⟨the *nature* of steel⟩ **2** : general character : KIND, SORT ⟨and things of that *nature*⟩ **3** : DISPOSITION, TEMPERAMENT ⟨behavior quite contrary to his *nature*⟩ **4** *often cap* : a power or set of forces thought of as controlling the universe ⟨Mother *Nature*⟩ **5** : natural feeling esp. as shown in one's attitude toward others ⟨his good *nature* is well known⟩ **6** : man's native state : primitive life ⟨return to *nature*⟩ **7** : the whole physical universe ⟨the study of *nature*⟩ **8** : the physical workings or drive of an organism ⟨sex is a part of *nature*⟩ **9** : natural scenery ⟨the beauties of *nature*⟩

¹naught \'nòt, 'nät\ *pron* [OE *nāwiht*, fr. *nā* no + *wiht* creature, thing] : NOTHING

²naught *n* **1 a** : NOTHING **b** : NOTHINGNESS, NONEXISTENCE **2** : the arithmetical symbol 0 — see NUMBER table

³naught *adj* : of no importance : INSIGNIFICANT

naugh·ty \'nòt-ē, 'nät-\ *adj* **naugh·ti·er; -est** [fr. *naught*] **1 a** *archaic* : vicious in moral character : WICKED **b** : guilty of disobedience or misbehavior **2** : lacking in taste or propriety — **naugh·ti·ly** \'nòt-ᵊl-ē, 'nät-\ *adv* — **naugh·ti·ness** \'nòt-ē-nəs, 'nät-\ *n*

nau·pli·us \'nò-plē-əs\ *n, pl* **-plii** \-plē-,ī, -,ē\ [Gk *nauplios*, a shellfish] : an early crustacean larva with three pairs of appendages and a median eye

nau·sea \'nò-zē-ə, -shə\ *n* [Gk *nautia, nausia* seasickness, nausea, fr. *nautēs* sailor] **1** : a stomach distress with distaste for food and an urge to vomit **2** : extreme disgust

nau·se·ate \'nò-z(h)ē-,āt, -s(h)ē-\ *vb* : to affect or become affected with nausea — **nau·se·at·ing** \-,āt-iŋ\ *adj* — **nau·se·at·ing·ly** \-iŋ-lē\ *adv*

nau·seous \'nò-shəs, 'nò-zē-əs\ *adj* **1** : NAUSEATED ⟨feel *nauseous*⟩ **2** : NAUSEATING ⟨a *nauseous* odor⟩ — **nau·seous·ly** *adv* — **nau·seous·ness** *n*

nautch \'nòch\ *n* [Hindi *nāc*] : an entertainment in India consisting chiefly of dancing by professional dancing girls

nau·ti·cal \'nòt-i-kəl\ *adj* [Gk *nautikos*, fr. *nautēs* sailor, fr. *naus* ship] : of or relating to seamen, navigation, or ships — **nau·ti·cal·ly** \-k(ə-)lē\ *adv*

nautical mile *n* : MILE 2

nau·ti·loid \'nòt-ᵊl-,óid\ *n* : any of an ancient group (Nautiloidea) of cephalopods represented in the recent fauna by the nautiluses — **nautiloid** *adj*

---

j joke; ŋ sing; ō flow; ȯ flaw; ȯi coin; th thin; th this; ü loot; ù foot; y yet; yü few; yù furious; zh vision

nau·ti·lus \'nȯt-ᵊl-əs\ *n, pl* **-lus·es** *or* **-li** \-ᵊl-ˌī, -ˌē\ [Gk *nautilos* paper nautilus, lit., sailor, fr. *naus* ship] **1** : any of a genus of cephalopod mollusks of the So. Pacific and Indian oceans having a spiral chambered shell pearly on the inside **2** : a cephalopod whose female has a delicate papery shell — called also *paper nautilus*

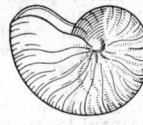

nautilus 1

Na·va·ho *or* **Na·va·jo** \'nav-ə-ˌhō, 'näv-\ *n* **1** : a member of an Indian people of northern New Mexico and Arizona **2** : the language of the Navaho people

na·val \'nā-vəl\ *adj* **1** : of or relating to a navy or warships ⟨*naval* shipyard⟩⟨*naval* officer⟩ **2** : possessing a navy ⟨a *naval* power⟩

naval stores *n pl* : products (as pitch, turpentine, or rosin) obtained from resinous conifers (as pines)

¹**nave** \'nāv\ *n* [OE *nafu*] : the hub of a wheel

²**nave** *n* [ML *navis*, fr. L, ship] : the main part of the interior of a church; *esp* : the long central hall in a cruciform church that rises higher than the aisles flanking it to form a clerestory — see BASILICA illustration

na·vel \'nā-vəl\ *n* [OE *nafela*] **1** : a depression in the middle of the abdomen marking the point of attachment of the umbilical cord or yolk stalk **2** : the central point : MIDDLE

navel orange *n* : a seedless orange having a pit at the apex where the fruit encloses a small secondary fruit

na·vic·u·lar \nə-'vik-yə-lər\ *adj* : shaped like a boat ⟨a *navicular* bone⟩

nav·i·ga·ble \'nav-i-gə-bəl\ *adj* **1** : deep enough and wide enough to afford passage to ships **2** : capable of being steered — **nav·i·ga·bil·i·ty** \ˌnav-i-gə-'bil-ət-ē\ *n* — **nav·i·ga·ble·ness** \'nav-i-gə-bəl-nəs\ *n* — **nav·i·ga·bly** \-blē\ *adv*

nav·i·gate \'nav-ə-ˌgāt\ *vb* [L *navigare*, fr. *navis* ship + -*igare* (fr. *agere* to drive)] **1 a** : to travel by water **b** : to sail over, on, or through **2 a** : to direct one's course in a ship or aircraft **b** : to steer, direct, or control the course of (as a boat or aircraft) **3 a** : to get about : MOVE; *esp* : WALK **b** : to make one's way on, about, or through

nav·i·ga·tion \ˌnav-ə-'gā-shən\ *n* **1** : the act or practice of navigating **2** : the science of getting ships or airplanes from place to place; *esp* : the method of determining position, course, and distance traveled **3** : ship traffic or commerce — **nav·i·ga·tion·al** \-shnəl, -shən-ᵊl\ *adj* — **nav·i·ga·tion·al·ly** \-ē\ *adv*

nav·i·ga·tor \'nav-ə-ˌgāt-ər\ *n* : one that navigates or is qualified to navigate: as **a** : an officer on a ship or airplane responsible for its navigation **b** : one who explores by ship

nav·vy \'nav-ē\ *n, pl* **navvies** [by shortening & alter. fr. *navigator* construction worker on a canal, navvy] *Brit* : an unskilled laborer

na·vy \'nā-vē\ *n, pl* **navies** [MF *navie*, fr. L *navigia* ships, fr. *navigare* to navigate] **1** : a group of ships : FLEET **2** : a nation's ships of war **3** *often cap* : the complete naval establishment of a nation including yards, stations, ships, and personnel **4** : a variable color averaging a grayish purplish blue

navy bean *n* : a kidney bean grown esp. for its small white nutritious seeds

navy yard *n* : a naval shore station with facilities for building, equipping, and repairing warships

na·wab \nə-'wäb\ *n* [Hindi *nawwāb, nawāb*] **1** : NABOB 1 **2** : any of various Muslim princes of India

¹**nay** \'nā\ *adv* [ON *nei*, fr. *ne* not + *ei* ever] **1** : NO **2** : not merely this but also : not only so but ⟨the letter made him happy, *nay*, ecstatic⟩

²**nay** *n* **1** : DENIAL, REFUSAL **2 a** : a negative reply or vote **b** : one who votes no

Naz·a·rene \ˌnaz-ə-'rēn\ *n* **1 a** : a native or resident of Nazareth **b** : JESUS **2** : a member of the Church of the Nazarene organized in 1908 and characterized by Wesleyan doctrines and polity — **Nazarene** *adj*

na·zi \'nät-sē, 'nat-\ *n* [G, by shortening & alter. fr. *Nationalsozialist* National Socialist] **1** *cap* : a member of a German fascist party controlling Germany from 1933 to 1945 under Adolf Hitler **2** *often cap* : one held to resemble a German Nazi — **nazi** *adj, often cap* — **na·zi-**

fi·ca·tion \ˌnät-si-fə-'kā-shən, ˌnat-\ *n, often cap* — **na·zi·fy** \'nät-si-ˌfī, 'nat-\ *vt, often cap* — **Na·zism** \'nät-ˌsiz-əm, 'nat-\ *or* **Na·zi·ism** \-sē-ˌiz-əm\ *n*

ne- *or* **neo-** *comb form* [Gk *neos*; akin to E *new*] **1** : new : recent ⟨*Neocene*⟩ ⟨*Neoplatonism*⟩ **2** : New World ⟨*Neotropical*⟩

Ne·an·der·thal \nē-'an-dər-ˌt(h)ȯl, nā-'än-dər-ˌtäl\ *adj* **1** : being, relating to, or resembling Neanderthal man **2** : suggesting a caveman in appearance or behavior — **Ne·an·der·thal·er** \-ər\ *or* **Neanderthal** *n*

Neanderthal man *n* [fr. *Neanderthal*, valley in western Germany] : a prehistoric man known from skeletal remains and artifacts and intermediate in some respects between modern man and pithecanthropus — **Ne·an·der·thal·oid** \-ˌȯid\ *adj or n*

neap \'nēp\ *adj* [OE *nēp*] being at the stage of neap tide] : of, relating to, or constituting a neap tide

Ne·a·pol·i·tan ice cream \ˌnē-ə-ˌpäl-ət-ᵊn-\ *n* : a brick of from two to four layers of ice cream of different flavors sometimes including an ice

neap tide *n* : a tide of minimum range occurring at the first and the third quarters of the moon

¹**near** \'ni(ə)r\ *adv* [partly fr. OE *nēar* nearer, compar. of *nēah* nigh; partly fr. ON *nær* nearer, near, fr. compar. of *nā-* nigh] **1** : at, within, or to a short distance or time **2** : ALMOST, NEARLY ⟨*near* dead⟩ **3** : CLOSELY ⟨*near* related⟩

²**near** *prep* : close to ⟨standing *near* the door⟩

³**near** *adj* **1** : closely related or associated **2 a** : not far distant in time, place, or degree **b** : barely avoided ⟨a *near* disaster⟩ **c** : coming close : failing or missing by very little ⟨a *near* miss⟩ **3 a** : being the closer of two ⟨*near* side of a hill⟩ **b** : being the left-hand one of a pair ⟨*near* wheel of a cart⟩ **4** : DIRECT, SHORT ⟨*nearest* route⟩ **5** : STINGY **6 a** : closely resembling a prototype **b** : approximating the genuine ⟨*near* silk⟩ — **near·ly** *adv* — **near·ness** *n*

  syn NEAR, CLOSE mean not distant or not much removed in space, time, or resemblance. NEAR implies that the space, interval, or degree of difference though small is none the less distinct and real; CLOSE implies virtual or approximate contact, coincidence, or identity

⁴**near** *vb* : to draw near : APPROACH

near·by \ˌni(ə)r-'bī, 'ni(ə)r-ˌ\ *adv (or adj)* : close at hand

near point *n* : the point nearest the eye at which an object can be accurately focused on the retina — compare FAR POINT

near·sight·ed \'ni(ə)r-'sīt-əd\ *adj* : able to see near things more clearly than distant ones : MYOPIC — **near·sight·ed·ly** *adv* — **near·sight·ed·ness** *n*

¹**neat** \'nēt\ *n, pl* **neat** [OE *nēat*] : the common domestic bovine (as a cow, bull, or ox)

²**neat** *adj* [MF *net*, fr. L *nitidus* bright, neat, fr. *nitēre* to shine] **1** : not mixed or diluted : STRAIGHT ⟨*neat* brandy⟩ **2** : marked by tasteful simplicity **3 a** : PRECISE, SYSTEMATIC **b** : marked by skill or ingenuity : ADROIT **4** : being orderly and clean : TIDY **5** : CLEAR, NET ⟨*neat* profit⟩ **6** *slang* : FINE, ADMIRABLE — **neat·ly** *adv* — **neat·ness** *n*

neat·herd \'nēt-ˌhərd\ *n* : COWHERD, HERDSMAN

neat's-foot oil \ˌnēts-ˌfut-\ *n* : a pale yellow fatty oil made esp. from the bones of cattle and used chiefly as a leather dressing

neb \'neb\ *n* [OE] **1 a** : the beak of a bird or tortoise : BILL **b** : NOSE, SNOUT **2** : NIB, TIP

Neb·u·chad·nez·zar \ˌneb-(y)ə-kəd-'nez-ər, -ˌkad-\ *also* **Neb·u·chad·rez·zar** \-'rez-\ *n* : king of Babylon from 605 to 562 B.C. and conqueror of Jerusalem

neb·u·la \'neb-yə-lə\ *n, pl* **-las** *or* **-lae** \-ˌlē, -ˌlī\ [L, mist, cloud] **1** : any of many immense bodies of highly rarefied gas or dust in interstellar space **2** : GALAXY — **neb·u·lar** \-lər\ *adj*

nebular hypothesis *n* : a hypothesis in astronomy: the solar system has evolved from a hot gaseous nebula

neb·u·lize \'neb-yə-ˌlīz\ *vt* : to reduce to a fine spray — **neb·u·liz·er** *n*

neb·u·los·i·ty \ˌneb-yə-'läs-ət-ē\ *n, pl* **-ties** **1** : the quality or state of being nebulous **2** : nebulous matter : NEBULA

neb·u·lous \'neb-yə-ləs\ *adj* **1** : HAZY, INDISTINCT, VAGUE **2** : of, relating to, or resembling a nebula : NEBULAR — **neb·u·lous·ly** *adv* — **neb·u·lous·ness** *n*

¹nec·es·sary \'nes-ə-,ser-ē\ adj [L necessarius, fr. necesse necessity, fr. ne- not + cess-, cedere to withdraw] **1 a** : of an inevitable nature : INESCAPABLE **b** : logically unavoidable : CERTAIN **c** : PREDETERMINED **d** : COMPULSORY **2** : positively needed : INDISPENSABLE — **nec·es·sar·i·ly** \,nes-ə-'ser-ə-lē\ adv
syn REQUISITE, ESSENTIAL : NECESSARY applies to what cannot be done without or avoided and may stress lack of choice or uselessness of wishing or resisting; REQUISITE implies being needful esp. for fulfillment or attainment of a set purpose or standard; ESSENTIAL implies being absolutely or urgently necessary
²necessary n, pl **-sar·ies** : an indispensable item : ESSENTIAL ⟨supplied with the necessaries of life⟩
ne·ces·si·tate \ni-'ses-ə-,tāt\ vt : to make necessary : make inevitable or unavoidable : DEMAND, REQUIRE, COMPEL ⟨the overwhelming attack necessitated a withdrawal by our troops⟩ ⟨was sick enough to necessitate his staying home from school⟩ — **ne·ces·si·ta·tion** \-,ses-ə-'tā-shən\ n
ne·ces·si·tous \ni-'ses-ət-əs\ adj **1** : hard up : NEEDY **2** : forced by necessity : NECESSARY ⟨necessitous bargaining⟩ — **ne·ces·si·tous·ly** adv — **ne·ces·si·tous·ness** n
ne·ces·si·ty \ni-'ses-ət-ē, -'ses-tē\ n, pl **-ties 1** : very great need of help or relief ⟨call in case of necessity⟩ **2** : a very necessary thing : something badly needed **3** : lack of necessary things : WANT, POVERTY **4** : conditions that cannot be changed ⟨compelled by necessity⟩ **syn** see NEED
¹neck \'nek\ n [OE hnecca] **1** : the part of the body connecting the head and the trunk **2** : the part of a garment covering or nearest to the neck **3** : something like a neck in shape or position : a relatively narrow part ⟨neck of a bottle⟩⟨neck of a guitar⟩⟨neck of land⟩ **4** : a narrow margin esp. of victory ⟨won by a neck⟩ — **necked** \'nekt\ adj — **neck and neck** : so nearly equal (as in a race) that one cannot be said to be ahead of the other : very close
²neck vb : to kiss and caress amorously
neck·band \'nek-,band\ n **1** : a band worn around the neck **2 a** : a part of a garment that encircles the neck **b** : a part of a shirt to which the collar is attached
neck·er·chief \'nek-ər-chəf, -(,)chif, -,chēf\ n, pl **-chiefs** also **-chieves** ⟨see HANDKERCHIEF pl\ [ME nekkerchef, fr. nekke neck + kerchef kerchief] : a square of cloth worn folded about the neck like a scarf
neck·lace \'nek-ləs\ n : an ornament (as a string of beads) worn around the neck
neck·line \-,līn\ n : the outline of the neck opening of a garment
neck·piece \-,pēs\ n : an article of apparel (as a fur scarf) worn about the neck
neck·tie \-,tī\ n : a narrow length of material worn about the neck and tied in front; esp : FOUR-IN-HAND
neck·wear \-,wa(ə)r, -,we(ə)r\ n : articles (as scarves or neckties) for wear around the neck
necr- or **necro-** comb form [Gk nekros dead body] **1** : those that are dead ⟨necrology⟩ **2** : dead body ⟨necropsy⟩
ne·crol·o·gy \nə-'kräl-ə-jē, ne-\ n, pl **-gies 1** : a list of the recently dead **2** : OBITUARY — **nec·ro·log·i·cal** \,nek-rə-'läj-i-kəl\ adj — **ne·crol·o·gist** \nə-'kräl-ə-jəst, ne-\ n
nec·ro·man·cer \'nek-rə-,man(t)-sər\ n : one that practices necromancy : MAGICIAN, SORCERER, WIZARD
nec·ro·man·cy \-sē\ n **1** : the art or practice of conjuring up the spirits of the dead for purposes of magically revealing the future or influencing the course of events **2** : MAGIC, SORCERY — **nec·ro·man·tic** \,nek-rə-'mant-ik\ adj — **nec·ro·man·ti·cal·ly** \-'mant-i-k(ə-)lē\ adv
ne·crop·o·lis \nə-'kräp-ə-ləs, ne-\ n, pl **-lis·es** or **-les** \-,lēz\ [Gk nekropolis city of the dead, fr. nekros dead body + -polis] : CEMETERY; esp : a large elaborate cemetery of an ancient city
nec·rop·sy \'nek-,räp-sē\ n, pl **-sies** : POSTMORTEM EXAMINATION
ne·cro·sis \nə-'krō-səs, ne-\ n, pl **-cro·ses** \-'krō-,sēz\ [Gk nekroun to make dead, fr. nekros dead body] : usu. local death of body tissue — **ne·crot·ic** \-'krät-ik\ adj
nec·ro·tize \'nek-rə-,tīz\ vb : to undergo or cause necrosis
nec·tar \'nek-tər\ n [L, fr. Gk nektar] **1 a** : the drink of the Greek and Roman gods **b** : a delicious drink **2** : a sweet liquid secreted by plants that is the chief raw material of honey — **nec·tar·ous** \-t(ə-)rəs\ adj

nec·tar·ine \,nek-tə-'rēn\ n : a smooth-skinned peach; also : a tree producing this fruit
nec·tary \'nek-t(ə-)rē\ n, pl **-tar·ies** : a plant gland that secretes nectar
née or **nee** \'nā\ adj [F née, fem. of né born, pp. of naître to be born, fr. L nat-, nasci] : BORN — used to identify a woman by her maiden family name ⟨Mrs. Jane Doe, née Roe⟩
¹need \'nēd\ n [OE nīed, nēd] **1** : necessary duty : OBLIGATION **2** : a lack of something requisite, desirable, or useful **3** : a condition requiring supply or relief **4** : want of the means of subsistence : POVERTY
syn NEED, NECESSITY, EXIGENCY mean a lack of something essential. NEED implies urgency and may suggest distress ⟨helped him in his hour of need⟩ NECESSITY stresses imperative demand or compelling cause ⟨oxygen is a necessity of animal life⟩ EXIGENCY implies unusual or special difficulty ⟨deprivations caused by the exigencies of war⟩
²need vb **1** : to be in want **2** : to have cause or occasion for : REQUIRE ⟨he needs advice⟩ **3 a** : to be under obligation or necessity ⟨we need to look at the facts⟩ **b** — used as an auxiliary verb ⟨you need not answer⟩
need·ful \'nēd-fəl\ adj : NECESSARY, REQUISITE — **need·ful·ly** \-fə-lē\ adv — **need·ful·ness** n
¹nee·dle \'nēd-ᵊl\ n [OE nǣdl] **1 a** : a small slender usu. steel instrument having an eye for thread at one end and used for sewing **b** : a device for carrying thread and making stitches (as in suturing a wound) **c** : a slender hollow instrument for introducing material into or removing material from the body **2** : a slender usu. sharp-pointed indicator on a dial; esp : MAGNETIC NEEDLE **3 a** : a slender pointed object resembling a needle (as a pointed crystal or a sharp rock) **b** : OBELISK **c** : a needle-shaped leaf (as of a pine) **d** : a slender piece of jewel, steel, wood, or fiber with a rounded tip used in a phonograph to transmit vibrations from the record **e** : a slender pointed rod controlling a fine inlet or outlet (as in a valve) — **nee·dle·like** \'nēd-ᵊl-,(l)īk\ adj
²needle vb **nee·dled; nee·dling** \'nēd-liŋ, -ᵊl-iŋ\ **1** : to sew with or as if with a needle **2** : to pierce with or as if with a needle **3** : PROD, GOAD; esp : to incite to action by repeated gibes — **nee·dler** \'nēd-lər, -ᵊl-ər\ n — **nee·dling** n
nee·dle·point \'nēd-ᵊl-,point\ n **1** : lace worked with a needle in buttonhole stitch over a paper pattern **2** : embroidery done on canvas usu. in simple even stitches across counted threads — **needlepoint** adj
need·less \'nēd-ləs\ adj : UNNECESSARY — **need·less·ly** adv — **need·less·ness** n
nee·dle·wom·an \'nēd-ᵊl-,wùm-ən\ n : a woman who does needlework; esp : SEAMSTRESS
nee·dle·work \-,wərk\ n : work done with a needle; esp : work (as embroidery) other than plain sewing — **nee·dle·work·er** n
needn't \'nēd-ᵊnt\ : need not
needs \'nēdz\ adv [OE nēdes, fr. gen. of nēd need] : of necessity : NECESSARILY ⟨must needs be recognized⟩
needy \'nēd-ē\ adj **need·i·er; -est** : being in want : very poor — **need·i·ness** n
ne'er \(')ne(ə)r, (')na(ə)r\ adv : NEVER
ne'er-do-well \'ne(ə)rd-ù-,wel, 'na(ə)rd-\ n : an idle worthless person — **ne'er-do-well** adj
ne·far·i·ous \ni-'far-ē-əs, -'fer-\ adj [L nefarius, fr. nefas wickedness, fr. ne- not + fas right] : flagrantly wicked or impious : EVIL — **ne·far·i·ous·ly** adv — **ne·far·i·ous·ness** n
ne·gate \ni-'gāt\ vt [L negare to deny, fr. neg- no, not] **1** : to deny the existence or truth of **2** : to cause to be ineffective or invalid **syn** see NULLIFY — **ne·ga·tor** or **ne·gat·er** \-'gāt-ər\ n
ne·ga·tion \ni-'gā-shən\ n **1 a** : the action of negating : DENIAL **b** : a negative doctrine or statement **2** : something that is the opposite of something positive : CONTRADICTION — **ne·ga·tion·al** \-shnəl, -shən-ᵊl\ adj
¹neg·a·tive \'neg-ət-iv\ adj **1** : marked by denial, prohibition, or refusal ⟨a negative reply⟩ **2 a** : lacking positive qualities **b** : opposing constructive treatment or development ⟨a negative attitude⟩ **3** : less than zero and opposite in sign to a positive number of like absolute value **b** : taken in a direction opposite to one chosen as positive ⟨negative angle⟩ **4 a** : of, being, or relating to

electricity of a kind of which the electron is the elementary unit and which predominates in a hard rubber rod after being rubbed with wool ⟨a *negative* charge⟩ **b** : having more electrons than protons ⟨a *negative* particle⟩ **c** : being the part toward which the electric current flows from the external circuit ⟨the *negative* pole of a discharging storage battery⟩ **d** : electron-emitting — used of an electrode in an electron tube **5 a** : not affirming the presence of what is sought or suspected to be present ⟨a *negative* TB test⟩ **b** : directed or moving away from a source of stimulation ⟨*negative* tropism⟩ **6** : having the light and dark parts in approximately inverse order to those of the original photographic subject — **neg·a·tive·ly** *adv* — **neg·a·tive·ness** *n* — **neg·a·tiv·i·ty** \,neg-ə-'tiv-ət-ē\ *n*
²**negative** *n* **1 a** : a proposition by which something is denied or contradicted **b** : a reply that indicates the withholding of assent : REFUSAL **2** : something that is the opposite or negation of something else **3 a** : an expression (as the word *no*) of negation or denial **b** : a negative number **4** : the side that upholds the contradictory proposition in a debate **5** : a negative photographic image on transparent material used for printing positive pictures; *also* : the material that carries such an image
³**negative** *vt* **1 a** : to refuse to accept or approve **b** (1) : to vote against (2) : VETO **2** : DISPROVE **3** : DENY, CONTRADICT
neg·a·tiv·ism \'neg-ət-iv-,iz-əm\ *n* : an attitude of skepticism and denial of nearly everything affirmed or suggested by others — **neg·a·tiv·ist** \-iv-əst\ *n* — **neg·a·tiv·is·tic** \,neg-ət-iv-'is-tik\ *adj*
¹**ne·glect** \ni-'glekt\ *vt* [L *neglect-, neglegere,* fr. *neg-* not + *legere* to gather] **1** : to give little attention or respect to : DISREGARD **2** : to leave undone or unattended to esp. through carelessness — **ne·glect·er** *n*
²**neglect** *n* **1** : an act or instance of neglecting something **2** : the condition of being neglected
ne·glect·ful \ni-'glekt-fəl\ *adj* : given to neglecting : CARELESS, HEEDLESS **syn** see NEGLIGENT — **ne·glect·ful·ly** \-fə-lē\ *adv* — **ne·glect·ful·ness** *n*
neg·li·gee *also* **neg·li·gé** \,neg-lə-'zhā\ *n* [F *négligé,* fr. pp. of *négliger* to neglect, fr. L *neglegere*] **1** : a woman's long flowing dressing gown **2** : carelessly informal or incomplete attire
neg·li·gence \'neg-li-jən(t)s\ *n* **1 a** : the quality or state of being negligent **b** : failure to exercise the care that a prudent person usu. exercises **2** : an act or instance of negligence
neg·li·gent \-jənt\ *adj* [L *neglegent-, neglegens,* prp. of *neglegere* to neglect] **1 a** : marked by or given to neglect **b** : chargeable with negligence **2** : marked by a carelessly easy manner : NONCHALANT — **neg·li·gent·ly** *adv*
syn NEGLECTFUL, REMISS: NEGLIGENT implies inattention to one's duty or business; NEGLECTFUL adds a stronger implication of laziness or callousness; REMISS implies carelessness or forgetfulness in performance of duty
neg·li·gi·ble \'neg-li-jə-bəl\ *adj* : fit to be neglected or disregarded : TRIFLING — **neg·li·gi·bil·i·ty** \,neg-li-jə-'bil-ət-ē\ *n* — **neg·li·gi·bly** \'neg-li-jə-blē\ *adv*
ne·go·tia·ble \ni-'gō-sh(ē-)ə-bəl\ *adj* : capable of being negotiated; *esp* : transferable from one person to another in return for equivalent value by delivery with or without endorsement in a manner that passes title — **ne·go·tia·bil·i·ty** \-,gō-sh(ē-)ə-'bil-ət-ē\ *n*
ne·go·tiant \ni-'gō-sh(ē-)ənt\ *n* : NEGOTIATOR
ne·go·ti·ate \ni-'gō-shē-,āt\ *vb* [L *negotiari* to transact business, fr. *negotium* business, fr. *neg-* not + *otium* leisure] **1** : to confer with another so as to arrive at the settlement of some matter; *also* : to arrange for or bring about by such conference ⟨*negotiate* a treaty⟩ **2** : to transfer to another by delivery or endorsement in return for equivalent value ⟨*negotiate* a check⟩ **3** : to get through, around, or over successfully ⟨*negotiate* a turn⟩ — **ne·go·ti·a·tion** \-,gō-s(h)ē-'ā-shən\ *n* — **ne·go·ti·a·tor** \-'gō-shē-,āt-ər\ *n* — **ne·go·tia·to·ry** \-sh(ē-)ə-,tōr-ē, -,tōr-\ *adj*
Ne·gril·lo \ni-'gril-ō, -'grē-(y)ō\ *n, pl* **-los** *or* **-loes** [Sp, dim. of *negro*] : a member of a people (as Pygmies) belonging to a group of negroid peoples of small stature found in Africa
Ne·gri·to \nə-'grēt-ō\ *n, pl* **-tos** *or* **-toes** [Sp, dim. of *negro*] : a member of a people (as the Andamanese) be-

longing to a group of negroid peoples of small stature found in Oceania and southeastern Asia
Ne·gro \'nē-grō, *esp South* 'nig-rō\ *n, pl* **Negroes** [Sp *or* Pg, fr. *negro,* adj., black, fr. L *nigr-, niger*] **1** : a member of the black race of mankind distinguished from members of other races by classification according to physical features but without regard to language or culture; *esp* : a member of a people belonging to the African branch of the black race **2** : a person of Negro ancestry — **Negro** *adj* — **ne·groid** \'nē-,gròid\ *n or adj, often cap*
ne·gus \'nē-gəs\ *n* [after Francis *Negus* d1732 English colonel] : a beverage of wine, hot water, sugar, lemon juice, and nutmeg
Ne·he·mi·ah \,nē-(h)ə-'mī-ə\ *n* **1** : a Hebrew leader of the 5th century B.C. **2** — see BIBLE table
neigh \'nā\ *vi* [OE *hnǣgan*] : to make the loud prolonged cry of a horse — **neigh** *n*
¹**neigh·bor** \'nā-bər\ *n* [OE *nēahgebūr,* fr. *nēah* near + *gebūr* dweller] **1** : one living or located near another **2** : FELLOWMAN — often used as a term of address
²**neighbor** *vt* **neigh·bored**; **neigh·bor·ing** \-b(ə-)riη\ : to be next to or near to : border on ⟨the U.S. *neighbors* northern Mexico⟩
neigh·bor·hood \'nā-bər-,hùd\ *n* **1** : the quality or state of being neighbors : NEARNESS **2 a** : a place or region near : VICINITY **b** : an approximate amount, extent, or degree ⟨cost in the *neighborhood* of $10⟩ **3 a** : the people living near one another **b** : a section lived in by neighbors and usu. having distinguishing characteristics ⟨an older *neighborhood*⟩
neigh·bor·ly \'nā-bər-lē\ *adj* : of, relating to, or characteristic of congenial neighbors; *esp* : FRIENDLY — **neigh·bor·li·ness** *n*
¹**nei·ther** \'nē-thər, 'nī-\ *pron* [ME, alter. of *nauther,* fr. OE *nāhwæther,* fr. *nā* not + *hwæther* which of two, whether] : not the one and not the other ⟨*neither* of the two⟩
²**neither** *conj* **1** : both not : equally not ⟨*neither* black nor white⟩ **2** : not either ⟨*neither* did I⟩
³**neither** *adj* : not either ⟨*neither* hand⟩
nek·ton \'nek-tən, -,tän\ *n* [G, fr. Gk *nēkton,* neut. of *nēktos* swimming, fr. *nēchein* to swim] : free-swimming aquatic animals whose distribution is essentially independent of wave and current action — compare PLANKTON — **nek·ton·ic** \nek-'tän-ik\ *adj*
nel·son \'nel-sən\ *n* : a wrestling hold marked by the application of leverage against an opponent's arm, neck, and head
ne·ma \'nē-mə\ *n* : NEMATODE
nem·a·to·cid·al \,nem-ət-ə-'sīd-ᵊl, nə-,mat-ə-\ *adj* : capable of destroying nematodes — **nem·a·to·cide** \'nem-ət-ə-,sīd, nə-'mat-ə-\ *n*
nem·a·to·cyst \'nem-ət-ə-,sist, nə-'mat-ə-\ *n* [Gk *nēmat-, nēma* thread] : one of the minute stinging organs of various coelenterates — **nem·a·to·cys·tic** \,nem-ət-ə-'sis-tik, nə-,mat-ə-\ *adj*
nem·a·tode \'nem-ə-,tōd\ *n* [NL *Nematoda,* class name, fr. Gk *nēmat-, nēma* thread] : any of a class or phylum (Nematoda) of elongated cylindrical worms parasitic in animals or plants or free-living in soil or water — **nema·tode** *adj*
Nem·bu·tal \'nem-byə-,tòl\ *trademark* — used for the sodium salt of pentobarbital
ne·mer·te·an \ni-'mərt-ē-ən\ *n* : any of a class (Nemertea) of often vividly colored marine worms most of which burrow in the mud or sand along seacoasts — **nemertean** *adj* — **nem·er·tine** \'nem-ər-,tīn\ *or* **nem·er·tin·e·an** \,nem-ər-'tin-ē-ən\ *adj or n*
nem·e·sis \'nem-ə-səs\ *n, pl* **-e·ses** \-ə-,sēz\ **1** *cap* : the Greek goddess who punished men according to their deserts **2 a** : one that inflicts retribution or vengeance **b** : a formidable and usu. victorious rival **3** [Gk, righteous indignation, retribution] **a** : an act or effect of retribution **b** : BANE 2, CURSE
ne·moph·i·la \ni-'mäf-ə-lə\ *n* [NL, fr. Gk *nemos* wooded pasture + *-philos* loving] : any of a genus of American herbs widely grown for their showy blue usu. spotted flowers
neo- — see NE-
neo·clas·sic \,nē-ō-'klas-ik\ *adj* : of or relating to a revival or adaptation of the classical style esp. in literature,

ə abut; ᵊ kitten; ər further; a back; ā bake; ä cot, cart; aù out; ch chin; e less; ē easy; g gift; i trip; ī life

art, or music — **neo·clas·si·cal** \-'klas-i-kəl\ *adj* — **neo·clas·si·cism** \-'klas-ə-,siz-əm\ *n*

neo–Dar·win·ism \-'där-wə-,niz-əm\ *n* : a theory that holds natural selection to be the chief factor in evolution and specif. denies the possibility of inheriting acquired characters — **neo–Dar·win·i·an** \-där-'win-ē-ən\ *adj* — **neo–Dar·win·ist** \-'där-wə-nəst\ *n*

neo·dym·i·um \,nē-ō-'dim-ē-əm\ *n* [NL, fr. *ne-* + *-dymium* (fr. *didymium*)] : a metallic chemical element — see ELEMENT table

neo–im·pres·sion·ism \-im-'presh-ə-,niz-əm\ *n*, *often cap N&I* : a late 19th century French art theory and practice characterized by an attempt to make impressionism more precise in form and the use of a pointillist painting technique — **neo–im·pres·sion·ist** \-'presh-(ə-)nəst\ *adj or n*, *often cap N&I*

Ne·o·lith·ic \,nē-ə-'lith-ik\ *adj* : of or relating to the latest period of the Stone Age characterized by polished stone implements

ne·ol·o·gism \nē-'äl-ə-,jiz-əm\ *n* : a new word or expression — **ne·ol·o·gist** \-jəst\ *n* — **ne·ol·o·gis·tic** \-,äl-ə-'jis-tik\ *adj*

ne·ol·o·gy \-jē\ *n* : the use of a new word or expression or of an established word in a new or different sense

ne·o·my·cin \,nē-ə-'mīs-ᵊn\ *n* : a broad-spectrum antibiotic or mixture of antibiotics produced by a soil actinomycete

ne·on \'nē-,än\ *n* [Gk, neut. of *neos* new] **1** : a colorless odorless inert gaseous chemical element found in minute amounts in air and used in electric lamps — see ELEMENT table **2 a** : a discharge lamp in which the gas contains a large amount of neon **b** : a sign composed of such lamps

neo·na·tal \,nē-ō-'nāt-ᵊl\ *adj* : of, relating to, or affecting the newborn — **neo·na·tal·ly** \-ᵊl-ē\ *adv* — **neo·nate** \'nē-ə-,nāt\ *n*

neo·or·tho·dox \,nē-ō-'ȯr-thə-,däks\ *adj* : of or relating to a 20th century movement in Protestant theology characterized by a reaction against liberalism and emphasis on various Reformation doctrines — **neo·or·tho·doxy** \-,däk-sē\ *n*

ne·o·phyte \'nē-ə-,fīt\ *n* [Gk *neophytos*, fr. *neophytos* newly planted, fr. *neos* new + *phyein* to bring forth] **1** : a new convert : PROSELYTE **2** : BEGINNER, NOVICE

ne·o·plasm \'nē-ə-,plaz-əm\ *n* : a new growth of tissue serving no physiologic function : TUMOR — **ne·o·plas·tic** \,nē-ə-'plas-tik\ *adj*

ne·o·prene \'nē-ə-,prēn\ *n* : a synthetic rubber made by the polymerization of a substance derived from acetylene and hydrochloric acid

ne·o·te·ny \'nē-ə-,tē-nē\ *n* : attainment of sexual maturity during the larval stage; *also* : retention of immature characters in adulthood — **ne·o·te·nic** \,nē-ə-'tē-nik, -'ten-ik\ *adj*

ne·pen·the \nə-'pen(t)-thē\ *n* [Gk *nēpenthes*, neut. of *nēpenthēs* banishing sorrow, fr. *nē-* not + *penthos* sorrow] **1** : a potion used by the ancients to dull pain and sorrow **2** : something capable of making one forget grief or suffering — **ne·pen·the·an** \-thē-ən\ *adj*

neph·e·line \'nef-ə-,lēn\ *or* **neph·e·lite** \-,līt\ *n* [Gk *nephelē* cloud] : a usu. glassy silicate mineral common in igneous rocks

neph·ew \'nef-yü\ *n* [OF *neveu*, fr. L *nepot-, nepos* grandson, nephew] : a son of one's brother, sister, brother-in-law, or sister-in-law

neph·o·scope \'nef-ə-,skōp\ *n* [Gk *nephos* cloud] : an instrument for observing the direction of motion and velocity of clouds

neph·ric \'nef-rik\ *adj* : RENAL

ne·phrid·i·um \ni-'frid-ē-əm\ *n, pl* **-ia** \-ē-ə\ [NL, fr. Gk *nephros* kidney] **1** : a tubular excretory organ of various invertebrates **2** : a primarily excretory structure; *esp* : NEPHRON — **ne·phrid·i·al** \-ē-əl\ *adj*

ne·phri·tis \ni-'frīt-əs\ *n* [Gk, fr. *nephros* kidney] : inflammation of the kidneys — **ne·phrit·ic** \-'frit-ik\ *adj*

neph·ro·gen·ic \,nef-rə-'jen-ik\ *adj* : originating in the kidney

neph·ron \'nef-,rän\ *n* : a single excretory unit esp. of the vertebrate kidney

ne plus ul·tra \,nē-,pləs-'əl-trə\ *n* [NL, no further] : the highest point capable of being attained : ACME ⟨a hotel that is the *ne plus ultra* of elegance⟩

nep·man \'nep-mən\ *n* [Russ, fr. *Novaya Ekonomicheskaya Politika* New Economic Policy] : a small private trader in the U.S.S.R. during the period of the New Economic Policy

nep·o·tism \'nep-ə-,tiz-əm\ *n* [L *nepot-, nepos* grandson, nephew] : favoritism (as in the distribution of political offices) shown to a relative

Nep·tune \'nep-,t(y)ün\ *n* **1** : the Roman god of the sea **2** : the planet 8th in order from the sun — see PLANET table — **Nep·tu·ni·an** \nep-'t(y)ü-nē-ən\ *adj*

nep·tu·ni·um \nep-'t(y)ü-nē-əm\ *n* [NL, fr. L *Neptunus* Neptune] : a radioactive metallic chemical element that is similar to uranium and is obtained in nuclear reactors as a by-product in the production of plutonium — see ELEMENT table

Ne·re·id \'nir-ē-əd\ *n* : any of the sea nymphs held in Greek mythology to be the daughters of the sea-god Nereus

ne·re·is \'nir-ē-əs\ *n, pl* **ne·re·ides** \nə-'rē-ə-,dēz\ : any of a genus of usu. large greenish marine annelid worms

ne·rit·ic \nə-'rit-ik\ *adj* : of, relating to, or being the shallow water adjoining the seacoast

ner·va·tion \,nər-'vā-shən\ *n* : an arrangement or system of nerves; *also* : VENATION

¹nerve \'nərv\ *n* [L *nervus* sinew, nerve] **1** : SINEW, TENDON ⟨strain every *nerve*⟩ **2** : one of the filamentous bands of nervous tissue connecting parts of the nervous system with the other organs and conducting nervous impulses **3 a** : power of endurance or control **b** (1) : BOLDNESS, DARING (2) : BRASS, GALL **4 a** : a sore or sensitive point **b** *pl* : nervous disorganization or collapse : HYSTERIA **5** : VEIN 2b, 2c **6** : the sensitive pulp of a tooth — **nerved** *adj* — **nerved** \'nərvd\ *adj*

²nerve *vt* : to give strength or courage to

nerve cell *n* : NEURON; *also* : a nerve cell body exclusive of its processes

nerve center *n* **1** : CENTER 2b **2** : a source of leadership, control, or energy

nerve fiber *n* : AXON, DENDRITE

nerve gas *n* : a war gas damaging esp. to the nervous and respiratory systems

nerve impulse *n* : the progressive alteration in the protoplasm of a nerve fiber that follows stimulation and serves to transmit a record of sensation from a receptor or an instruction to act to an effector

nerve·less \'nərv-ləs\ *adj* **1** : destitute of strength or courage : FEEBLE **2** : showing control : not nervous : POISED — **nerve·less·ly** *adv* — **nerve·less·ness** *n*

nerve net *n* : a network of nerve cells apparently continuous one with another and conducting impulses in all directions; *also* : a nervous system (as in a jellyfish) consisting of such a network

nerve–rack·ing *or* **nerve–wrack·ing** \'nərv-,rak-iŋ\ *adj* : extremely trying on the nerves

nerv·ous \'nər-vəs\ *adj* **1** *archaic* : SINEWY, STRONG **2** : marked by vigor of thought, feeling, or style **3 a** : of, relating to, or composed of neurons **b** : of or relating to the nerves; *also* : originating in or affected by the nerves **4 a** : easily excited or irritated : JUMPY **b** : TIMID, APPREHENSIVE ⟨*nervous* smile⟩ **5** : UNEASY, UNSTEADY — **nerv·ous·ly** *adv* — **nerv·ous·ness** *n*

nervous breakdown *n* **1** : NEURASTHENIA **2** : a case of neurasthenia

nervous system *n* : the bodily system that receives and interprets stimuli and transmits impulses to the effector organs and that in vertebrates is made up of brain and spinal cord, nerves, ganglia, and parts of the receptor organs

ner·vure \'nər-vyər\ *n* : VEIN 2b, c

nervy \'nər-vē\ *adj* **nerv·i·er; -est 1 a** : showing calm courage : BOLD **b** : marked by impudence or presumption : BRASH ⟨a *nervy* salesman⟩ **2** : EXCITABLE, NERVOUS — **nerv·i·ness** *n*

ne·science \'nesh-(ē-)ən(t)s, 'nēsh-\ *n* [L *nescire* to be ignorant, fr. *ne-* not + *scire* to know] : lack of knowledge or awareness : IGNORANCE — **ne·scient** *adj*

ness \'nes\ *n* : CAPE, PROMONTORY

-ness \nəs\ *n suffix* [OE *-nes*] : state : condition : quality : degree ⟨good*ness*⟩

Nes·sel·rode \'nes-əl-,rōd\ *n* [after Count Karl R. Nesselrode d1862 Russian statesman] : a mixture of

j joke; ŋ sing; ō flow; ȯ flaw; ȯi coin; th thin; <u>th</u> this; ü loot; u̇ foot; y yet; yü few; yu̇ furious; zh vision candied fruits, nuts, and maraschino used in puddings, pies, and ice cream

Nes·sus \'nes-əs\ *n* : a centaur shot by Hercules with a poisoned arrow for attempting to carry away his wife

¹**nest** \'nest\ *n* [OE] **1 a** : a bed or receptacle prepared by a bird for its eggs and young **b** : a place where eggs are laid and hatched **2 a** : a place of rest, retreat, or lodging **b** : DEN, HANGOUT **3** : the occupants or frequenters of a nest **4 a** : a group of similar things : AGGREGATION **b** : HOTBED 2 **5** : a group of objects made to fit close together or one within another

nest of measuring spoons

²**nest** *vb* **1** : to build or occupy a nest ⟨robins *nested* in the underbrush⟩ **2** : to fit compactly together or within one another ⟨crockery wrapped in tissue and *nested* in a barrel⟩

nest egg *n* **1** : a natural or artificial egg left in a nest to induce a fowl to continue to lay there **2** : a fund of money accumulated as a reserve

nest·er \'nes-tər\ *n* **1** : one that nests **2** *West* : a homesteader or squatter who takes up open range for a farm

nes·tle \'nes-əl\ *vb* **nes·tled; nes·tling** \'nes-(ə-)liŋ\ [OE *nestlian*, fr. *nest*] **1** : to settle snugly or comfortably **2 a** : to settle, shelter, or house as if in a nest **b** : to press closely and affectionately : CUDDLE — **nes·tler** \-(ə-)lər\ *n*

nest·ling \'nest-liŋ\ *n* : a young bird not yet able to leave the nest

Nes·tor \'nes-tər\ *n* : an aged and wise counselor of the Greeks in the Trojan War

¹**net** \'net\ *n* [OE *nett*] **1 a** : a meshed fabric twisted, knotted, or woven together at regular intervals **b** : something made of net; *esp* : a device for catching fish, birds, or insects **2** : an entrapping situation **3** : a network of lines, fibers, or figures **4 a** : a ball that during play in a racket game is hit into the net for loss of a point **b** : a let ball — **net·like** \-ˌlīk\ *adj* — **net·ty** \'net-ē\ *adj*

²**net** *vt* **net·ted; net·ting** **1** : to cover or enclose with or as if with a net **2** : to catch in or as if in a net **3** : to hit (the ball) into the net in a racket game — **net·ter** *n*

³**net** *adj* [MF, clean, neat] : free from all charges or deductions ⟨*net* profit⟩⟨*net* price⟩

⁴**net** *vt* **net·ted; net·ting** : to gain or produce as profit : CLEAR ⟨*net* ten cents⟩

⁵**net** *n* **1** : a net amount, profit, weight, or price **2** : the score of a golfer in a handicap match after deducting his handicap from his gross

neth·er \'neth-ər\ *adj* [OE *nithera*, fr. *nither* down] **1** : situated down or below : LOWER **2** : situated beneath the earth's surface ⟨the *nether* regions⟩

neth·er·most \-ˌmōst\ *adj* : LOWEST

neth·er·world \-ˌwərld\ *n* **1** : the world of the dead **2** : UNDERWORLD 4

net·ting \'net-iŋ\ *n* **1** : NETWORK **2** : the act or process of making a net or network **3** : the act, process, or right of fishing with a net

¹**net·tle** \'net-ᵊl\ *n* [OE *netel*] : any of various coarse dicotyledonous herbs with stinging hairs

²**nettle** *vt* **net·tled; net·tling** \'net-liŋ, -ᵊl-iŋ\ **1** : to strike or sting with or as if with nettles **2** : PROVOKE, VEX

nettle rash *n* : an eruption on the skin caused by or resembling the condition produced by stinging with nettles

net·tle·some \'net-ᵊl-səm\ *adj* : causing vexation : IRRITATING

net-veined \'net-ˌvānd\ *adj* : having veins that branch and interlace to form a network ⟨dicotyledons have *net-veined* leaves⟩ — compare PARALLEL-VEINED

net-winged \-ˌwiŋd\ *adj* : having wings with a fine network of veins

net·work \'net-ˌwərk\ *n* **1** : a fabric or structure of cords or wires that cross at regular intervals and are knotted or secured at the crossings **2** : a system of lines, channels, or other elements resembling a network **3** : an interconnected or interrelated chain, group, or system; *esp* : a group of radio or television stations linked by wire or radio relay

neur- *or* **neuro-** *comb form* [Gk *neuron* sinew, nerve] : nerve ⟨*neural*⟩ ⟨*neurology*⟩

neu·ral \'n(y)ur-əl\ *adj* **1** : of, relating to, or involving a nerve or the nervous system **2** : DORSAL — **neu·ral·ly** \-ə-lē\ *adv*

neu·ral·gia \n(y)u-'ral-jə\ *n* : acute pain that follows the course of a nerve; *also* : a condition marked by such pain — **neu·ral·gic** \-jik\ *adj*

neural tube *n* : a hollow longitudinal tube produced from dorsal ectodermal folds and giving rise to the central nervous system of a vertebrate embryo

neur·as·the·nia \ˌn(y)ur-əs-'thē-nē-ə\ *n* : a state in which one is tense and irritable, esp. subject to fatigue, and troubled by headache and often ill-defined circulatory or digestive distress — **neur·as·then·ic** \-'then-ik\ *adj or n* — **neur·as·then·i·cal·ly** \-'then-i-k(ə-)lē\ *adv*

neu·ri·lem·ma \ˌn(y)ur-ə-'lem-ə\ *n* [NL, alter. of *neurilema*, fr. Gk *neuron* nerve + *eilēma* covering, coil, fr. *eilein* to wind] : the outer sheath of a nerve fiber — **neu·ri·lem·mal** \-'lem-əl\ *adj* — **neu·ri·lem·mat·ic** \-le-'mat-ik\ *adj* — **neu·ri·lem·ma·tous** \-'lem-ət-əs\ *adj*

neu·ri·tis \n(y)u-'rīt-əs\ *n* : inflammation of a nerve — **neu·rit·ic** \-'rit-ik\ *adj or n*

neu·ro·crine \'n(y)ur-ə-krən, -ˌkrīn, -ˌkrēn\ *adj* [*neur-* + *endocrine*] : of, relating to, or being a hormonal substance that influences the activity of nerves

neu·ro·fi·bril \ˌn(y)ur-ō-'fīb-rəl, -'fib-\ *n* : a filament (as in a protozoan or a neuron) believed to be a conducting element — **neu·ro·fi·bril·lar** \-rə-lər\ *or* **neu·ro·fi·bril·lary** \-rə-ˌler-ē\ *adj*

neu·ro·gen·ic \ˌn(y)ur-ə-'jen-ik\ *adj* **1** : originating in nervous tissue **2** : induced or altered by nervous factors

neu·rog·lia \n(y)u-'räg-lē-ə, ˌn(y)ur-ə-'glī-ə\ *n* [MGk *glia* glue] : supporting tissue of the brain, spinal cord, and ganglia — **neu·rog·li·al** \-əl\ *or* **neu·rog·li·ar** \-ər\ *adj*

neu·ro·hu·mor \ˌn(y)ur-ō-'hyü-mər, -'yü-\ *n* : a substance released at a nerve ending that plays a part in transmitting a nerve impulse — **neu·ro·hu·mor·al** \-'hyüm-(ə-)rəl, -'yüm-\ *adj*

neu·rol·o·gy \n(y)u-'räl-ə-jē\ *n* : the scientific study of the nervous system — **neu·ro·log·i·cal** \ˌn(y)ur-ə-'läj-i-kəl\ *or* **neu·ro·log·ic** \-'läj-ik\ *adj* — **neu·rol·o·gist** \n(y)u-'räl-ə-jəst\ *n*

neu·ro·mo·tor \ˌn(y)ur-ə-'mōt-ər\ *adj* : relating to efferent nervous impulses

neu·ro·mus·cu·lar \ˌn(y)ur-ō-'məs-kyə-lər\ *adj* : of or relating to nerves and muscles; *esp* : jointly involving nervous and muscular elements

neu·ron \'n(y)ü-ˌrän, 'n(y)ù(ə)r-ˌän\ *also* **neu·rone** \-ˌrōn, -ˌōn\ *n* : a grayish or reddish granular cell with specialized processes that is the fundamental functional unit of nervous tissue — **neu·ro·nal** \'n(y)ùr-ən-ᵊl, n(y)ù-'rōn-ᵊl\ *or* **neu·ron·ic** \n(y)ù-'rän-ik\ *adj*

neu·rop·ter·an \n(y)ù-'räp-tə-rən\ *n* [Gk *neuron* sinew + *pteron* wing] : any of an order (Neuroptera) of usu. net-winged insects that include the lacewings and ant lions — **neuropteran** *adj* — **neu·rop·ter·ous** \-rəs\ *adj*

neu·ro·sis \n(y)ù-'rō-səs\ *n, pl* **-ro·ses** \-'rō-ˌsēz\ : a functional nervous disorder without demonstrable physical lesion

neu·ros·po·ra \n(y)ù-'räs-pə-rə\ *n* : any of a genus of often pink-spored ascomycetous fungi that are destructive in bakeries but important tools of genetic research

¹**neu·rot·ic** \n(y)ù-'rät-ik\ *adj* : of, relating to, constituting, or affected with neurosis — **neu·rot·i·cal·ly** \-'rät-i-k(ə-)lē\ *adv*

²**neurotic** *n* : an emotionally unstable person or one affected with a neurosis

neu·ro·tox·ic \ˌn(y)ur-ə-'täk-sik\ *adj* : poisonous to nervous tissue

¹**neu·ter** \'n(y)üt-ər\ *adj* [L, lit., neither, fr. *ne-* not + *uter* which of two; akin to E *whether*] **1** : of, relating to, or constituting the class of words that ordinarily includes most of those referring to things that are neither male nor female ⟨a *neuter* noun⟩ ⟨the *neuter* gender⟩ **2** : lacking sex organs; *also* : having imperfectly developed sex organs

²**neuter** *n* **1 a** : a word or form of the neuter gender **b** : the neuter gender **2** : one that is neutral **3 a** : WORKER 2 **b** : a spayed or castrated animal

³**neuter** *vt* : CASTRATE, ALTER

¹**neu·tral** \'n(y)ü-trəl\ *adj* [L *neuter* neither] **1** : not

engaged on either side; *esp* : not aligned with a political or ideological grouping **2** : of or relating to a neutral state or power **3 a** : neither one thing nor the other : MIDDLING **b** (1) : ACHROMATIC (2) : not decided in color : nearly achromatic **c** : neither acid nor basic **d** : not electrically charged **4** : produced with the tongue in the position it has when at rest ⟨the *neutral* vowels of \ə-'bəv\ *above*⟩ — **neu·tral·ly** \-trə-lē\ *adv* — **neu·tral·ness** *n*

²**neutral** *n* **1** : one that is neutral **2** : a neutral color **3** : a position of disengagement (as of gears)

neu·tral·ism \'n(y)ü-trə-,liz-əm\ *n* : a policy or the advocacy of neutrality — **neu·tral·ist** \-ləst\ *n* — **neu·tral·is·tic** \,n(y)ü-trə-'lis-tik\ *adj*

neu·tral·i·ty \n(y)ü-'tral-ət-ē\ *n* **1** : the quality or state of being neutral **2** : immunity from invasion or from use by belligerents

neu·tral·ize \'n(y)ü-trə-,līz\ *vt* **1** : to make chemically neutral **2** : to destroy the effectiveness of : NULLIFY ⟨*neutralize* an opponent's move⟩ **3** : to make electrically inert by combining equal positive and negative quantities **4** : to invest with neutrality under international law ⟨*neutralize* a country⟩ — **neu·tral·i·za·tion** \,n(y)ü-trə-lə-'zā-shən\ *n* — **neu·tral·iz·er** \'n(y)ü-trə-,lī-zər\ *n*

neutral spirits *n pl* : ethyl alcohol of 190 or higher proof used esp. for blending other alcoholic liquors

neu·tri·no \n(y)ü-'trē-nō\ *n, pl* **-nos** [It, dim. of *neutrone* neutron] : an uncharged elementary particle having a mass less than ⅟₁₀ that of the electron

neu·tron \'n(y)ü-,trän\ *n* [prob. fr. *neutral* + *-on*] : an uncharged elementary particle that has a mass nearly equal to that of the proton and is present in all known atomic nuclei except the hydrogen nucleus

neutron star *n* [fr. the hypothesis that the cores of such stars are composed entirely of neutrons] : any of various hypothetical dense celestial objects that consist of closely packed nuclear particles resulting from the collapse of a much larger stellar body

neu·tro·phil \'n(y)ü-trə-,fil\ *or* **neu·tro·phile** \-,fīl\ *n* [L *neuter* neuter; fr. its staining indifferently with acid or basic dyes] : a finely granular cell that is the chief phagocytic white blood cell

né·vé \nā-'vā\ *n* [F *névé*, fr. L *niv-*, *nix* snow] : the partially compacted granular snow that forms the surface part of the upper end of a glacier; *also* : a field of granular snow

nev·er \'nev-ər\ *adv* [ME, fr. OE *næfre*, fr. *ne* not + *æfre* ever] **1** : not ever : at no time ⟨*never* saw him before⟩ **2** : not in any degree, way, or condition ⟨had *never* a cent in those days⟩

nev·er·more \,nev-ər-'mō(ə)r, -'mȯ(ə)r\ *adv* : never again

nev·er–nev·er land \,nev-ər-'nev-ər-\ *n* : an ideal or imaginary place

nev·er·the·less \,nev-ər-thə-'les\ *adv* : in spite of that : HOWEVER **syn** see BUT

ne·vus \'nē-vəs\ *n, pl* **ne·vi** \-,vī\ [NL, fr. L *naevus*] : a congenital pigmented area on the skin : BIRTHMARK

¹**new** \'n(y)ü\ *adj* [OE *nīwe*] **1** : not old : RECENT, MODERN **2** : not the same as the former : taking the place of one that came before ⟨a *new* teacher⟩ **3** : recently discovered, recognized, or learned about ⟨*new* lands⟩ **4** : not formerly known or experienced ⟨*new* feelings⟩ **5** : not accustomed ⟨*new* to her work⟩ **6** : beginning as a repetition of some previous act or thing **7** : REFRESHED, REGENERATED **8** : being in a position or place for the first time ⟨a *new* member⟩ **9** *cap* : having been in use after medieval times : MODERN ⟨*New* Latin⟩ — **new·ness** *n*

syn NEW, NOVEL, FRESH mean having recently come into existence or use. NEW may apply to what is freshly made and unused ⟨*new* bricks⟩ or has not been known before ⟨*new* design⟩ or not experienced before ⟨started his *new* job today⟩ NOVEL applies to what is not only new but strange and unprecedented ⟨*novel* hair styles⟩ FRESH applies to what has not yet had time to grow dim, soiled, or stale ⟨put on a *fresh* shirt⟩⟨offering *fresh* ideas⟩

²**new** *adv* : NEWLY, RECENTLY ⟨*new*-mown hay⟩

new·born \-'bȯrn\ *adj* **1** : recently born **2** : REBORN

new·com·er \'n(y)ü-,kəm-ər\ *n* **1** : one recently arrived **2** : BEGINNER, NOVICE

New Deal *n* **1** : the legislative and administrative program of President F. D. Roosevelt designed to promote

economic recovery and social reform during the 1930s **2** : the period of the New Deal — **New Deal·er** \-'dē-lər\ *n*

New Economic Policy *n* : a relaxation of restrictions on private business and on the individual peasant in the U.S.S.R. during the 1920s

new·el \'n(y)ü-əl\ *n* [MF *nouel* stone of a fruit, fr. LL *nucalis* like a nut, fr. L *nuc-*, *nux* nut] **1** : an upright post about which the steps of a circular staircase wind **2** : a post at the foot of a straight stairway or one at a landing

New English Bible *n* : a translation of the Bible by a British interdenominational committee first published in its entirety in 1970

new·fan·gled \'n(y)ü-'faŋ-gəld\ *adj* **1** : attracted to novelty **2** : of the newest style : NOVEL

new–fash·ioned \-'fash-ənd\ *adj* **1** : made in a new fashion or form **2** : UP-TO-DATE   *newel*

new·found \-'faȯnd\ *adj* : newly found

New·found·land \'n(y)ü-fən-(d)lənd, -,(d)land; n(y)ü-'faȯn-(d)lənd\ *n* : any of a breed of very large usu. black dogs developed in Newfoundland

New Greek *n* : Greek as used by the Greeks since the end of the medieval period

New Hamp·shire \n(y)ù-'ham(p)-shər, -,shi(ə)r\ *n* : any of a breed of single-combed domestic fowls developed chiefly in New Hampshire and noted for heavy winter egg production

New Hebrew *n* : MODERN HEBREW

new·ish \'n(y)ü-ish\ *adj* : rather new

New Latin *n* : Latin as used since the end of the medieval period esp. in scientific description and classification

new·ly \'n(y)ü-lē\ *adv* **1** : LATELY, RECENTLY ⟨*newly* married⟩ **2** : ANEW, AFRESH ⟨a *newly* furnished house⟩

new·ly·wed \-,wed\ *n* : one recently married

new math *n* : mathematics that is based on set theory esp. as taught in elementary and secondary school — called also *new mathematics*

new moon *n* **1** : the moon's phase when it is in conjunction with the sun so that its dark side is toward the earth; *also* : the thin crescent moon seen shortly after sunset a few days after the actual occurrence of the new moon phase **2** : the 1st day of the Jewish month

news \'n(y)üz\ *n* **1** : a report of recent events : TIDINGS ⟨brought him the office *news*⟩ **2 a** : material reported in a newspaper or news periodical or on a newscast **b** : matter that is newsworthy

news agency *n* : an organization that supplies news to subscribing newspapers, periodicals, and newscasters

news·boy \-,bȯi\ *n* : a person who delivers or sells newspapers

news·cast \-,kast\ *n* [*news* + broad*cast*] : a radio or television news broadcast — **news·cast·er** \-,kas-tər\ *n*

news conference *n* : PRESS CONFERENCE

news–let·ter \'n(y)üz-,let-ər\ *n* : a newspaper containing news or information of interest chiefly to a special group

news·man \-mən, -,man\ *n* : one who gathers, reports, or comments on the news : REPORTER, CORRESPONDENT

news·mon·ger \-,məŋ-gər, -,mäŋ-\ *n* : GOSSIP

news·pa·per \'n(y)üz-,pā-pər\ *n* **1** : a paper that is printed and distributed usu. daily or weekly and contains news, articles of opinion, features, and advertising **2** : an organization publishing a newspaper **3** : the paper making up a newspaper

news·pa·per·man \-,man\ *n* : one who owns or is employed by a newspaper; *esp* : one who writes or edits copy for a newspaper

news·print \'n(y)üz-,print\ *n* : cheap machine-finished paper made chiefly from wood pulp and used mostly for newspapers

news·reel \-,rēl\ *n* : a short motion picture dealing with current events

news·stand \'n(y)üz-,stand\ *n* : a place where newspapers and periodicals are sold

New Style *adj* : using or according to the Gregorian calendar

news·wor·thy \'n(y)üz-,wər-thē\ *adj* : sufficiently interesting to the general public to warrant reporting (as in a newspaper)

newsy \'n(y)ü-zē\ *adj* **news·i·er**; **-est** : filled with news; *esp* : CHATTY ⟨a *newsy* letter⟩

newt \'n(y)üt\ *n* [ME *newte*, the phrase *an ewte* (fr. OE *efete* eft) being understood as *a newte*] **:** any of various small salamanders that live mostly in water

New Testament *n* **:** the second of the two chief divisions of the Bible consisting of the books dealing with Christ's life and death and the work done by his apostles after his death — see BIBLE table

new·ton \'n(y)üt-ᵊn\ *n* [after Sir Isaac *Newton* d1727 English physicist] **:** a unit of force in the mks system of such size that under its influence a body whose mass is one kilogram would experience an acceleration of one meter per second per second

New·to·ni·an \n(y)ü-'tō-nē-ən\ *adj* **:** of, relating to, or characteristic of Sir Isaac Newton, his discoveries, or his doctrines

New World *n* **:** the western hemisphere; *esp* **:** the continental landmass of No. and So. America

New Year \'n(y)ü-ˌyi(ə)r\ *n* **1 :** NEW YEAR'S DAY; *also* **:** the first days of the year **2 :** ROSH HASHANAH

New Year's Day *n* **:** January 1 observed as a legal holiday

¹next \'nekst\ *adj* [OE *nīehst*, superl. of *nēah* nigh] **:** immediately preceding or following **:** NEAREST ⟨turn to the *next* page⟩ ⟨the house *next* to ours⟩

²next *adv* **1 :** in the time, place, or order nearest or immediately succeeding ⟨open this package *next*⟩ **2 :** on the first occasion to come ⟨when *next* we meet⟩

³next *prep* **:** next to

next of kin : one or more persons in the nearest degree of relationship to another person

¹next to *prep* **:** immediately following **:** adjacent to ⟨*next to* the head of his class⟩

²next to *adv* **:** very nearly **:** ALMOST ⟨*next to* impossible to win⟩

nex·us \'nek-səs\ *n, pl* **nex·us·es** \-sə-səz\ *or* **nex·us** \-səs, -ˌsüs\ [L, fr. *nectere* to bind] **:** CONNECTION, LINK

Nez Percé \'nez-'pərs, F nā-per-sā\ *n* [F, lit., pierced nose] **:** a member of an Indian people of central Idaho and adjacent parts of Washington and Oregon

ni·a·cin \'nī-ə-sən\ *n* [*nicotinic acid* + *-in*] **:** NICOTINIC ACID

Ni·ag·a·ra \nī-'ag-(ə-)rə\ *n* [*Niagara* Falls, waterfall of the Niagara river] **:** an overwhelming flood **:** TORRENT ⟨a *Niagara* of protests⟩

nib \'nib\ *n* **1 :** BILL, BEAK **2 a :** the sharpened point of a quill pen **b :** a pen point **3 :** a small pointed or projecting part

¹nib·ble \'nib-əl\ *vb* **nib·bled; nib·bling** \'nib-(ə-)liŋ\ **1 :** to bite or chew gently or bit by bit **2 :** to make cautious attempts — **nib·bler** \-(ə-)lər\ *n*

²nibble *n* **1 :** an act of nibbling; *esp* **:** a small or cautious bite **2 :** a very small quantity

Ni·be·lung \'nē-bə-ˌlu̇ŋ\ *n* [G] **:** a member of a race of dwarfs in Germanic legend owning a hoard and ring taken from them by Siegfried

nib·lick \'nib-lik\ *n* **:** a golf iron with a sharply angled blade used for maximum loft and least distance — called also *number nine iron*

nibs \'nibz\ *n sing or pl* **:** an important or self-important person — used chiefly in the phrase *his nibs*

nice \'nīs\ *adj* [ME, foolish, wanton, fr. OF, fr. L *nescius* ignorant, fr. *nescire* not to know, fr. *ne-* not + *scire* to know] **1 :** showing fastidious or finicky tastes **:** REFINED **2 :** marked by or demanding delicate discrimination or treatment ⟨*nice* distinction⟩ **3 a :** PLEASING, AGREEABLE ⟨*nice* time⟩ ⟨*nice* person⟩ **b :** well-executed ⟨*nice* shot⟩ **4 a :** socially acceptable **:** WELL-BRED ⟨offensive to *nice* people⟩ **b :** VIRTUOUS, RESPECTABLE ⟨*nice* girl⟩ — **nice·ly** *adv* — **nice·ness** *n*

Ni·cene Creed \ˌnī-ˌsēn\ *n* **:** a Christian creed issued by the first Council of Nicaea in A.D. 325 and later expanded that begins "I believe in one God"

nice-nel·ly \'nīs-'nel-ē\ *adj, often cap 2d N* **1 :** PRUDISH **2 :** EUPHEMISTIC — **nice nelly** *n, often cap 2d N* — **nice-nel·ly·ism** \-ˌiz-əm\ *n, often cap 2d N*

ni·ce·ty \'nī-sət-ē, -stē\ *n, pl* **-ties** **1 :** a dainty, delicate, or elegant thing ⟨enjoy the *niceties* of life⟩ **2 :** a small point **:** a fine detail ⟨the *niceties* of table manners⟩ **3 :** careful attention to details **:** EXACTNESS ⟨the greatest *nicety* is needed in making watches⟩ **4 :** the point at which a thing is at its best ⟨roasted to a *nicety*⟩

¹niche \'nich\ *n* [F, fr. MF *nicher* to nest, fr. L *nidus* nest] **1 a :** a recess in a wall esp. for a statue **b :** something

that resembles a niche **2 :** a place, use, or work for which a person is best fitted **3 :** a habitat supplying the factors necessary for the existence of an organism or species

²niche *vt* **:** to place in a niche

¹nick \'nik\ *n* **1 :** a small groove **:** NOTCH ⟨file a *nick* in steel⟩ **2 :** CHIP ⟨a *nick* in a cup⟩ **3 :** the final critical moment ⟨in the *nick* of time⟩

²nick *vb* **1 :** to make a nick in **:** NOTCH, CHIP **2 :** to make petty attacks **:** SNIPE **3 :** to complement one another genetically and produce superior offspring

¹nick·el \'nik-əl\ *n* [G *kupfernickel* nickel arsenide ore, prob. fr. *kupfer* copper + *nickel* goblin; fr. the deceptive copper color of the ore] **1 :** a silver-white hard malleable ductile metallic chemical element that is capable of a high polish, resistant to corrosion, and used chiefly in alloys and as a catalyst — see ELEMENT table **2 a** *also* **nick·le** **:** the U.S. 5-cent piece regularly containing 25 percent nickel and 75 percent copper **b :** five cents

²nick·el *vt* **-eled** *or* **-elled; -el·ing** *or* **-el·ling** \'nik-(ə-)liŋ\ **:** to plate with nickel

nick·el·ic \nik-'el-ik\ *adj* **:** of, relating to, or containing nickel esp. with a higher valence than two

nick·el·if·er·ous \ˌnik-ə-'lif-(ə-)rəs\ *adj* **:** containing nickel

nick·el·ode·on \ˌnik-ə-'lōd-ē-ən\ *n* **1 :** a theater presenting entertainment for an admission price of five cents **2 :** JUKEBOX

nick·el·ous \'nik-ə-ləs\ *adj* **:** of, relating to, or containing nickel esp. with a valence of two

nickel silver *n* **:** a silver-white alloy of copper, zinc, and nickel

nick·er \'nik-ər\ *vi* **nick·ered; nick·er·ing** \'nik-(ə-)riŋ\ **:** NEIGH, WHINNY — **nicker** *n*

nicknack *var of* KNICKKNACK

¹nick·name \'nik-ˌnām\ *n* [ME *nekename* additional name, the phrase *an ekename* (fr. *eke* + *name*) being understood as *a nekename*] **1 :** a usu. descriptive name given instead of or in addition to the one belonging to an individual **2 :** a familiar form of a proper name

²nickname *vt* **1 :** MISNAME, MISCALL **2 :** to give a nickname to — **nick·nam·er** *n*

ni·co·ti·ana \nik-ə-ˌtō-shē-'an-ə, -'än-ə, -'ā-nə\ *n* **:** any of several tobaccos grown for their showy flowers

nic·o·tin·amide \ˌnik-ə-'tē-nə-ˌmīd\ *n* **:** a compound of the vitamin B complex found esp. as a constituent of coenzymes and used similarly to nicotinic acid

nic·o·tine \'nik-ə-ˌtēn\ *n* [F, fr. Jean *Nicot* d1600 F diplomat and scholar who introduced tobacco into France] **:** a poisonous alkaloid that is the chief active principle of tobacco and is used as an insecticide

nic·o·tin·ic \ˌnik-ə-'tē-nik, -'tin-ik\ *adj* **:** of or relating to nicotine or nicotinic acid

nicotinic acid *n* **:** an organic acid of the vitamin B complex found widely in animals and plants and used esp. against pellagra

nic·ti·tate \'nik-tə-ˌtāt\ *vi* [alter. of earlier *nictate*, fr. L *nictare*] **:** WINK — **nic·ti·ta·tion** \ˌnik-tə-'tā-shən\ *n*

nic·ti·tat·ing membrane \ˌnik-tə-ˌtāt-iŋ-\ *n* [NL *nictitare*, freq. of L *nictare* to wink] **:** a thin membrane found in many animals at the inner angle or beneath the lower lid of the eye and capable of extending across the eyeball

niece \'nēs\ *n* [OF, fr. LL *neptia*, fr. L *neptis* granddaughter] **:** a daughter of one's brother, sister, brother-in-law, or sister-in-law

nif·ty \'nif-tē\ *adj* **nif·ti·er; -est :** FINE, SWELL — **nifty** *n*

nig·gard \'nig-ərd\ *n* [ME, of Scand origin] **:** a meanly covetous and stingy person **:** MISER — **niggard** *adj*

nig·gard·li·ness \'nig-ərd-lē-nəs\ *n* **:** the quality or state of being niggardly

nig·gard·ly \-lē\ *adj* **1 :** grudgingly reluctant to spend or grant **:** STINGY **2 :** characteristic of a niggard **:** SCANTY — **niggardly** *adv*

nig·gling \'nig-(ə-)liŋ\ *adj* [fr. earlier *niggle* to carp] **1 :** PETTY **2 :** demanding meticulous care — **niggling** *n* — **nig·gling·ly** \-(ə-)lē\ *adv*

¹nigh \'nī\ *adv* [OE *nēah*] **1 :** near in place, time, or relationship **2 :** NEARLY, ALMOST

²nigh *adj* **1 :** CLOSE, NEAR **2 :** being on the left side ⟨the *nigh* horse⟩

³nigh *prep* **:** NEAR

⁴nigh *vb* **:** to draw near **:** APPROACH

ə abut; ᵊ kitten; ər further; a back; ā bake; ä cot, cart; au̇ out; ch chin; e less; ē easy; g gift; i trip; ī life

night \'nīt\ *n* [OE *niht*] **1 :** the time between dusk and dawn when there is no sunlight **2 :** the beginning of darkness **: NIGHTFALL 3 :** the darkness of night — **night** *adj*

night-blind \-,blīnd\ *adj* **:** afflicted with night blindness

night blindness *n* **:** reduced visual capacity in faint light (as at night)

night-blooming cereus *n* **:** any of several night-blooming cacti; *esp* **:** a slender sprawling or climbing cactus often grown for its large showy fragrant white flowers

night-cap \'nīt-,kap\ *n* **1 :** a cloth cap worn with night-clothes **2 :** a usu. alcoholic drink taken at bedtime **3 :** the final race or contest of a day's sports; *esp* **:** the final game of a baseball doubleheader

night-clothes \-,klō(th)z\ *n pl* **:** garments worn in bed

night-club \-,kləb\ *n* **:** a place of entertainment open at night usu. serving food and liquor, having a floor show, and providing music and space for dancing

night crawler *n* **: EARTHWORM;** *esp* **:** a large earthworm found on the soil surface at night

night-dress \'nīt-,dres\ *n* **1 : NIGHTGOWN 2 : NIGHT-CLOTHES**

night-fall \-,fol\ *n* **:** the coming of night

night-gown \-,gaun\ *n* **:** a long loose garment worn in bed

night-hawk \-,hok\ *n* **1 :** any of several goatsuckers that resemble the related whippoorwill **2 :** a person who habitually stays up late at night

night-ie \'nīt-ē\ *n* [by shortening & alter. fr. *nightgown*] **:** a nightgown for a woman or a child

night-in-gale \'nīt-ᵊn-,gāl\ *n* [OE *nihtegale*, fr. *niht* night + *galan* to sing] **:** any of several Old World thrushes noted for the sweet usu. nocturnal song of the male

night-jar \'nīt-,jär\ *n* [fr. its harsh sound] **:** a common grayish brown European nightsucker; *also* **: GOATSUCKER**

night latch *n* **:** a door lock having a spring bolt operated from the outside by a key and from the inside by a knob

night letter *n* **:** a telegram sent at night at a reduced rate per word for delivery the following morning

¹night-long \'nīt-,lon\ *adj* **:** lasting the whole night

²night-long \-'lon\ *adv* **:** through the whole night

night-ly \'nīt-lē\ *adj* **1 :** of or relating to the night or every night **2 :** happening, done, or produced by night or every night — **nightly** *adv*

night-mare \-,ma(ə)r, -,me(ə)r\ *n* [ME, fr. *night* + *mare* incubus] **1 :** an evil spirit formerly thought to oppress people during sleep **2 :** a frightening dream accompanied by a sense of oppression or suffocation that usu. awakens the sleeper **3 :** an experience, situation, or object having the monstrous character of a nightmare or producing a feeling of anxiety or terror — **night-mar-ish** \-ish\ *adj*

night owl *n* **:** a person who keeps late hours at night

night raven *n* **:** a bird that cries at night

night rider *n* **:** a member of a secret band who ride masked at night doing acts of violence for the purpose of punishing or terrorizing

night-robe \'nīt-,rōb\ *n* **: NIGHTGOWN**

nights \'nīts\ *adv* **:** in the nighttime repeatedly ⟨getting a degree by going to school *nights*⟩

night-shade \'nīt-,shād\ *n* **:** any of a family of herbs, shrubs, and trees having alternate leaves, cymes of usu. white, yellow, or purple flowers, and fruits that are berries and including many poisonous forms (as bella-donna and henbane) and important food plants (as the potato, tomato, and eggplant)

night-shirt \-,shərt\ *n* **:** a nightgown resembling a shirt

night-stick \-,stik\ *n* **:** a policeman's club

night-tide \'nīt-,tīd\ *n* **: NIGHTTIME**

night-time \'nīt-,tīm\ *n* **:** the time from dusk to dawn

night-walk-er \-,wo-kər\ *n* **:** a person who roves about at night esp. with criminal or immoral intent

ni-gres-cence \nī-'gres-ᵊn(t)s\ *n* [L *nigrescere* to become black, fr. *niger* black] **:** a process of becoming black or dark — **ni-gres-cent** \-ᵊnt\ *adj*

ni-gri-tude \'nī-grə-,t(y)üd\ *n* **:** intense darkness **: BLACK-NESS**

ni-hil-ism \'nī-ə-,liz-əm\ *n* [L *nihil* nothing] **1 :** a doctrine or belief that conditions in the social organization are so bad as to make destruction desirable for its own sake independent of any constructive program or possibility **2** *cap* **:** the program of a 19th century Russian party advocating revolutionary reform and using terrorism and assassination — **ni-hil-ist** \-ə-ləst\ *n* — **nihilist** *or* **ni-hil-is-tic** \,nī-ə-'lis-tik\ *adj*

ni-hil-i-ty \nī-'hil-ət-ē\ *n* **: NOTHINGNESS**

ni-hil ob-stat \,nī-,hil-'äb-,stät, -,nīl-,jil-\ *n* [L, nothing hinders] **1 :** the certification by an official censor of the Roman Catholic Church that a book has been examined and found to contain nothing opposed to faith and morals **2 :** authoritative or official approval

-nik \nik\ *n suffix* [Yiddish, fr. Russ & Pol] **:** one connected with or characterized by being ⟨beat*nik*⟩

Ni-ke \'nī-kē\ *n* **:** the Greek goddess of victory usu. represented as winged and as carrying a wreath and a palm branch

nil \'nil\ *n* [L, contr. of *nihil*] **: NOTHING, ZERO** — **nil** *adj*

nile green \'nīl-\ *n, often cap N* [fr. *Nile* river, Africa] **:** a variable color averaging a pale yellow green

Ni-lot-ic \nī-'lät-ik\ *adj* **:** of or relating to the Nile or the peoples of the Nile basin

nim-ble \'nim-bəl\ *adj* **nim-bler** \-b(ə-)lər\; **-blest** \-b(ə-)ləst\ [OE *numol* holding much] **1 :** quick and light in motion **: AGILE** ⟨a *nimble* dancer⟩ **2 :** quick in understanding and learning **: CLEVER** ⟨a *nimble* mind⟩ — **nim-ble-ness** \-bəl-nəs\ *n* — **nim-bly** \-blē\ *adv*

nim-bo-stra-tus \,nim-bō-'strāt-əs, -'strat-\ *n* **:** a low dark gray rainy cloud layer

nim-bus \'nim-bəs\ *n, pl* **nim-bi** \-,bī, -,bē\ *or* **nim-bus-es** [L, rainstorm, cloud] **1 :** a luminous vapor, cloud, or atmosphere about a god or goddess when on earth **2 :** an indication (as a circle) of radiant light or glory about the head of a drawn or sculptured divinity, saint, or sovereign **3 a :** a rain cloud that is of uniform grayness and extends over the entire sky **b :** a cloud from which rain is falling

Nim-rod \'nim-,räd\ *n* **1 :** a mighty hunter and great-grandson of Noah **2** *often not cap* **: HUNTER**

nin-com-poop \'nin-kəm-,püp, 'niŋ-\ *n* **: FOOL, SIMPLETON**

nine \'nīn\ *n* [OE *nigon*] **1** — see NUMBER table **2 :** the ninth in a set or series **3 :** something having nine units or members; *esp* **:** a baseball team — **nine** *adj or pron* — **to the nines :** to the highest point **:** to perfection ⟨dressed *to the nines*⟩

nine days' wonder *n* **:** something that creates a short-lived sensation

nine-pence \'nīn-pən(t)s, *US also* -,pen(t)s\ *n* **:** the sum of nine usu. British pennies

nine-pin \'nīn-,pin\ *n* **1 :** a pin used in ninepins **2** *pl* **:** tenpins played without the headpin

nine-teen \(')nīn(t)-'tēn\ *n* — see NUMBER table — **nine-teen** *adj or pron* — **nine-teenth** \-'tēn(t)th\ *adj or n*

nine-ty \'nīnt-ē\ *n, pl* **nineties** — see NUMBER table — **nine-ti-eth** \-ē-əth\ *adj or n* — **ninety** *adj or pron*

nin-ny \'nin-ē\ *n, pl* **ninnies** **: FOOL, SIMPLETON**

nin-ny-ham-mer \'nin-ē-,ham-ər\ *n* **: NINNY**

ninth \'nīn(t)th\ *n, pl* **ninths** \'nīn(t)s, 'nīn(t)ths\ **1** — see NUMBER table **2 a :** a musical interval embracing an octave and a second **b :** a chord containing a ninth — **ninth** *adj or adv*

Ni-o-be \'nī-ə-bē\ *n* **:** a daughter of Tantalus held in Greek legend to have been turned into stone while weeping for her slain children and to continue weeping her loss

ni-o-bi-um \nī-'ō-bē-əm\ *n* [NL, fr. *Niobe*; fr. its occurrence in ores with tantalum] **:** a lustrous platinum-gray ductile metallic chemical element that is used in alloys — see ELEMENT table

¹nip \'nip\ *vb* **nipped; nip-ping** [ME *nippen*] **1 :** to catch hold of and squeeze tightly between two surfaces, edges, or points ⟨the dog *nipped* his ankle⟩ **2 a :** to sever by or as if by pinching sharply **: CLIP b :** to destroy the growth, progress, maturing, or fulfillment of ⟨*nipped* in the bud⟩ **3 :** to injure or make numb with cold **: CHILL 4 : SNATCH, STEAL 5** *chiefly Brit* **:** to move briskly, nimbly, or quickly

²nip *n* **1 :** something that nips: as **a :** a sharp stinging cold **b :** a biting or pungent flavor **: TANG 2 :** the act of nipping **: PINCH, BITE 3 :** a small portion **: BIT**

³nip *n* **:** a small quantity of liquor ⟨takes a *nip* now and then⟩

⁴nip *vi* **nipped; nip-ping :** to take liquor in nips **: TIPPLE**

ni-pa \'nē-pə\ *n* [Malay *nipah* nipa palm] **1 :** an alcoholic drink made from the juice of an Australasian creeping palm; *also* **:** this palm **2 :** thatch made of nipa leaves

nip and tuck \,nip-ən-'tək\ *adj (or adv)* **:** so close that the lead or advantage shifts rapidly from one contestant to another

nip·per \\'nip-ər\\ *n* **1** : a device (as pincers) for nipping — usu. used in pl. **2 a** : an incisor of a horse **b** : CHELA **3** *chiefly Brit* : CHILD; *esp* : a small boy

nippers

nip·ple \\'nip-əl\\ *n* **1** : the protuberance of a mammary gland upon which the ducts open and from which milk is drawn **2** : something resembling a nipple; *esp* : the rubber mouthpiece of a baby's nursing bottle

Nip·pon·ese \\,nip-ə-'nēz, -'nēs\\ *adj* : JAPANESE — **Nipponese** *n*

nip·py \\'nip-ē\\ *adj* **nip·pi·er; -est** **1** : brisk, quick, or nimble in movement **2** : CHILLY, CHILLING ⟨a *nippy* day⟩

nir·va·na \\nir(ə)r-'vän-ə, nər-\\ *n, often cap* [Skt *nirvāṇa*, lit., act of extinguishing] **1** : the final beatitude that transcends suffering, karma, and samsara and is sought in Hinduism and Buddhism through the extinction of desire and individual consciousness **2** : a place or state of oblivion to care, pain, or external reality

ni·sei \\(')nē-'sā\\ *n, pl* **nisei** *also* **niseis** [Jap, lit., second generation] : a son or daughter of immigrant Japanese parents who is born and educated in America

Nis·sen hut \\,nis-°n-\\ *n* : a prefabricated shelter of corrugated iron with cement floor shaped like a cylinder on edge

nit \\'nit\\ *n* [OE *hnitu*] : the egg of a louse or similar insect; *also* : the insect itself when young

ni·ter *also* **ni·tre** \\'nīt-ər\\ *n* [ME *nitre* sodium carbonate, fr. MF, fr. L *nitrum*, fr. Gk *nitron*, fr. Egypt *nṯry*] **1** : POTASSIUM NITRATE **2** : SODIUM NITRATE

nitr- *or* **nitro-** *comb form* [*niter*] **1** : nitrate ⟨*nitro*bacteria⟩ **2 a** : nitrogen ⟨*nitr*ide⟩ **b** *usu* **nitro-** : containing the univalent group —NO₂ composed of one nitrogen and two oxygen atoms ⟨*nitro*benzene⟩

¹ni·trate \\'nī-,trāt, -trət\\ *n* **1** : a salt or ester of nitric acid **2** : sodium nitrate or potassium nitrate used as a fertilizer

²ni·trate \\-,trāt\\ *vt* : to treat or combine with nitric acid or a nitrate — **ni·tra·tion** \\nī-'trā-shən\\ *n* — **ni·tra·tor** \\'nī-,trāt-ər\\ *n*

nitrate bacterium *n* : a bacterium functioning in the nitrogen cycle to convert nitrites to nitrates — compare NITRITE BACTERIUM

ni·tric \\'nī-trik\\ *adj* : of, relating to, or containing nitrogen esp. with a higher valence than in corresponding nitrous compounds

nitric acid *n* : a corrosive liquid acid HNO₃ used esp. as an oxidizing agent, in nitrations, and in making fertilizers, explosives, and dyes

nitric oxide *n* : a colorless poisonous gas NO obtained by oxidation of nitrogen or ammonia

ni·tride \\'nī-,trīd\\ *n* : a compound of nitrogen with a more electropositive element

ni·tri·fi·ca·tion \\,nī-trə-fə-'kā-shən\\ *n* : the process of nitrifying; *esp* : the oxidation (as by bacteria) of ammonium salts to nitrites and the further oxidation of nitrites to nitrates

ni·tri·fy \\'nī-trə-,fī\\ *vb* **-fied; -fy·ing** **1** : to combine or impregnate with nitrogen or a nitrogen compound **2** : to subject to or produce by nitrification **3** : to engage or be active in nitrification ⟨*nitrifying* bacteria⟩ — **ni·tri·fi·er** \\-,fī(-ə)r\\ *n*

ni·trite \\'nī-,trīt\\ *n* : a salt or ester of nitrous acid

nitrite bacterium *n* : a bacterium functioning in the nitrogen cycle to convert ammonium compounds to nitrites — compare NITRATE BACTERIUM

ni·tro \\'nī-trō\\ *n* : any of various nitrated products; *esp* : NITROGLYCERIN

ni·tro·ben·zene \\,nī-trō-'ben-,zēn, -,ben-'\\ *n* : a poisonous insoluble oil made by nitration of benzene and used as a solvent, oxidizing agent, and source of aniline

ni·tro·cel·lu·lose \\-'sel-yə-,lōs\\ *n* : nitrated cellulose — **ni·tro·cel·lu·los·ic** \\-,sel-yə-'lō-sik\\ *adj*

ni·tro·gen \\'nī-trə-jən\\ *n* [F *nitrogène*, fr. *nitre* niter + *-gène* -gen] : a colorless tasteless odorless gaseous chemical element that usu. has a valence of 3 or 5, constitutes 78 percent of the atmosphere by volume, and is a constituent

of all living tissues — see ELEMENT table — **ni·trog·e·nous** \\nī-'träj-ə-nəs\\ *adj*

nitrogen balance *n* : the ratio between nitrogen intake and nitrogen loss of the body or the soil

nitrogen cycle *n* : a continuous series of natural processes by which nitrogen passes successively from air to soil to organisms and back involving principally nitrogen fixation, nitrification, decay, and denitrification

nitrogen dioxide *n* : a brownish to yellowish poisonous gas NO₂ that is used esp. in making nitric acid and in nitration

nitrogen fixation *n* : the conversion of free nitrogen into combined forms; *esp* : metabolic assimilation of atmospheric nitrogen by microorganisms in soil and root nodules and its subsequent release in a form fit for plant use

nitrogen–fixing *adj* : capable of nitrogen fixation ⟨*nitrogen–fixing* bacteria⟩

ni·trog·e·nize \\nī-'träj-ə-,nīz\\ *vt* : to combine or impregnate with nitrogen or one of its compounds

nitrogen mustard *n* : any of various toxic blistering compounds analogous to mustard gas but with nitrogen replacing sulfur

ni·tro·glyc·er·in *or* **ni·tro·glyc·er·ine** \\,nī-trō-'glis-(ə-)rən\\ *n* : a heavy oily explosive poisonous liquid obtained by nitrating glycerol and used chiefly in making dynamites and in medicine as a vasodilator

ni·tro·so·bac·te·ri·um \\nī-,trō-sō-bak-'tir-ē-əm\\ *n* : NITRITE BACTERIUM

ni·trous \\'nī-trəs\\ *adj* **1** : of, relating to, or containing niter **2** : of, relating to, or containing nitrogen esp. with a lower valence than in corresponding nitric compounds

nitrous acid *n* : an unstable acid HNO₂ known only in solution or in the form of its salts

nitrous oxide *n* : a colorless gas N₂O that when inhaled produces loss of sensibility to pain preceded by exhilaration and sometimes laughter and is used esp. as an anesthetic in dentistry — called also *laughing gas*

nit·ty-grit·ty \\'nit-ē-,grit-ē, ,nit-ē-'grit-ē\\ *n* : the actual state of things : what is ultimately essential and true — **nitty-gritty** *adj*

nit·wit \\'nit-,wit\\ *n* : a scatterbrained or stupid person

¹nix \\'niks\\ *n* [G] : a water sprite of Germanic folklore usu. having the form of a woman or a half human and half fish — called also *nixie*

²nix *adv* [G *nichts* nothing] *slang* : NO — used to express disagreement or the withholding of permission

³nix *vt, slang* : VETO, FORBID

ni·zam \\ni-'zäm\\ *n* [Hindi *nizām* order, governor] : one of a line of sovereigns of Hyderabad from 1713 to 1950 — **ni·zam·ate** \\-,āt\\ *n*

¹no \\(')nō\\ *adv* [OE *nā*, fr. *ne* not + *ā* always] **1 a** *chiefly Scot* : NOT **b** — used as a function word to express the negative of an alternative choice or possibility ⟨shall we continue or *no*⟩ **2** : in no respect or degree — used in comparisons ⟨he is *no* better than he should be⟩ **3** : not so — used to express negation, dissent, denial, or refusal ⟨*no*, I'm not hungry⟩ **4** — used with a following adjective to imply a meaning expressed by the opposite positive statement ⟨*no* uncertain terms⟩ **5** — used as a function word to emphasize a following negative or to introduce a more emphatic, explicit, or comprehensive statement ⟨has the right, *no*, the duty, to continue⟩ **6** — used as an interjection to express surprise, doubt, or incredulity ⟨*no* — you don't say⟩

²no *adj* **1 a** : not any ⟨he has *no* money⟩ **b** : hardly any : very little ⟨finished in *no* time⟩ **2** : not a : quite other than a ⟨he's *no* expert⟩ ⟨this is certainly *no* place to be hanging around⟩

³no \\'nō\\ *n, pl* **noes** *or* **nos** \\'nōz\\ **1** : an act or instance of refusing or denying by the use of the word *no* : DENIAL **2 a** : a negative vote or decision **b** *pl* : persons voting in the negative

No·ah \\'nō-ə\\ *n* : an Old Testament patriarch and builder of the ark in which he, his family, and living creatures of every kind survived the flood

nob \\'näb\\ *n, chiefly Brit* : one in a superior position in life

nob·by \\'näb-ē\\ *adj* **nob·bi·er; -est** : of the first quality or style : SMART

no·bel·i·um \\nō-'bel-ē-əm\\ *n* [after Alfred B. *Nobel*] : a radioactive chemical element produced artificially — see ELEMENT table

No·bel prize \(,)nō-,bel-\ *n* : any of various annual prizes (as in peace, literature, medicine) established by the will of Alfred Nobel for the encouragement of persons who work for the interests of humanity

no·bil·i·ary \nō-'bil-ē-,er-ē\ *adj* : of or relating to the nobility

no·bil·i·ty \nō-'bil-ət-ē\ *n, pl* **-ties 1** : the quality or state of being noble ⟨*nobility* of character⟩ **2** : noble rank ⟨confer *nobility* on a person⟩ **3** : the class or group of nobles ⟨a member of the *nobility*⟩

¹**no·ble** \'nō-bəl\ *adj* **no·bler** \-b(ə-)lər\; **no·blest** \-b(ə-)ləst\ [OF, fr. L *nobilis* knowable, noble, fr. *noscere* to come to know] **1 a** : possessing outstanding qualities : ILLUSTRIOUS ⟨a *noble* warrior⟩ **b** : FAMOUS, NOTABLE ⟨*noble* deed⟩ **2** : of high birth or exalted rank : ARISTOCRATIC **3 a** : possessing very high or excellent qualities or properties ⟨*noble* hawk⟩ **b** : very good or excellent **4** : grand or impressive esp. in appearance ⟨*noble* edifice⟩ **5** : possessing, characterized by, or arising from superiority of mind or character : MAGNANIMOUS ⟨*noble* nature⟩ **6** : chemically inert or inactive esp. toward oxygen ⟨*noble* metal⟩ — **no·ble·ness** \-bəl-nəs\ *n* — **no·bly** \-blē\ *adv*

²**noble** *n* **1** : a person of noble rank or birth **2** : an old English gold coin equivalent to 8*s* 6*d*

no·ble·man \'nō-bəl-mən\ *n* : a member of the nobility : PEER — **no·ble·wom·an** \-,wùm-ən\ *n*

no·blesse oblige \nō-,bles-ə-'blēzh\ *n* [F, lit., nobility obligates] : the obligation of honorable, generous, and responsible behavior associated with high rank or birth

¹**no·body** \'nō-,bäd-ē, -,bəd-ē\ *pron* : no person : not anybody

²**nobody** *n* : a person of no influence, importance, or worth ⟨they're a bunch of *nobodies*⟩

no·ci·cep·tive \,nō-si-'sep-tiv\ *adj* [L *nocēre* to harm + E *-i-* + *receptive*] : being, receiving, or responding to a painful or harmful stimulus ⟨a *nociceptive* reflex⟩

¹**nock** \'näk\ *n* : a notch on the end of a bow or in an arrow for the bowstring

²**nock** *vt* : to make a notch in or fit into or by means of a notch

noct·am·bu·la·tion \(,)näk-,tam-byə-'lā-shən\ *or* **noct·am·bu·lism** \näk-'tam-byə-,liz-əm\ *n* : SOMNAMBULISM — **noct·am·bu·list** \-ləst\ *n*

noc·ti·lu·ca \,näk-tə-'lü-kə\ *n* [L, something that shines by night, fr. *noct-, nox* night + *lucēre* to shine] : any of a genus of marine luminescent flagellates that often cause phosphorescence of the sea

noc·tur·nal \näk-'tərn-ᵊl\ *adj* [L *nocturnus*, fr. *noct-, nox* night; akin to E *night*] **1** : of, relating to, or occurring in the night ⟨a *nocturnal* journey⟩ **2** : active at night ⟨*nocturnal* insects⟩ — **noc·tur·nal·ly** \-ᵊl-ē\ *adv*

noc·turne \'näk-,tərn\ *n* [F, nocturnal, fr. L *nocturnus*] : a work of art dealing with night; *esp* : a dreamy pensive composition for the piano

noc·u·ous \'näk-yə-wəs\ *adj* [L *nocuus*, fr. *nocēre* to harm] : likely to cause injury : HARMFUL — **noc·u·ous·ly** *adv*

¹**nod** \'näd\ *vb* **nod·ded; nod·ding** [ME *nodden*] **1** : to bend the head downward or forward (as in bowing or going to sleep or as a way of answering "yes"); *also* : to cause (the head) to move in this way **2** : to move up and down ⟨the tulips *nodded* in the breeze⟩ **3** : to show by a nod of the head ⟨*nod* agreement⟩ **4** : to let one's attention lapse for a moment : make a slip or an error — **nod·der** *n*

²**nod** *n* : the action of nodding

nod·dle \'näd-ᵊl\ *n* [ME *nodle* back of the head or neck] : HEAD

nod·dy \'näd-ē\ *n, pl* **noddies 1** : a stupid person **2** : any of several stout-bodied terns of warm seas

node \'nōd\ *n* [L *nodus* knot, node] **1** : an entangling complication (as in a drama) : PREDICAMENT **2 a** : a thickened or swollen enlargement (as of a rheumatic joint) **b** : a discrete mass of one kind of tissue enclosed in tissue of a different kind **3** : either of the two points where the orbit of a planet or comet intersects the ecliptic **4 a** : a point at which subsidiary parts originate or center **b** : a point on a stem at which a leaf is inserted **5** : a part of a vibrating body marked by absolute or relative freedom from vibratory motion — **nod·al** \'nōd-ᵊl\ *adj* — **nod·ed** \'nōd-əd\ *adj*

nod·i·cal \'nōd-i-kəl, 'näd-\ *adj* : of or relating to astronomical nodes

no·dose \'nō-,dōs\ *adj* : having numerous or conspicuous protuberances — **no·dos·i·ty** \nō-'däs-ət-ē\ *n*

nod·u·lar \'näj-ə-lər\ *adj* : of, relating to, characterized by, or occurring in the form of nodules

nod·ule \'näj-ül\ *n* : a small mass of rounded or irregular shape: as **a** : a small rounded lump of a mineral or mineral aggregate **b** : a swelling on the root of a legume that contains nitrogen-fixing bacteria

nod·u·lose \'näj-ə-,lōs\ *also* **nod·u·lous** \-ləs\ *adj* : having minute nodules : finely knobby

no·el \nō-'el\ *n* [F *noël* Christmas, carol, fr. L *natalis* birthday, fr. *natalis* natal] **1** : a Christmas carol **2** *cap* : the Christmas season

nog \'näg\ *n* **1** : a strong ale formerly brewed in Norfolk, England **2** : EGGNOG **3** : an often alcoholic drink containing beaten egg, milk, or broth

nog·gin \'näg-ən\ *n* **1** : a small mug or cup **2** : a small quantity of drink usu. equivalent to a gill **3** : a person's head

¹**no-good** \,nō-'gúd\ *adj* : having no worth, use, or chance of success

²**no-good** \'nō-,gúd\ *n* : a no-good person or thing

¹**noise** \'nóiz\ *n* [OF, strife, noise, fr. L *nausea* nausea] **1** : loud, confused, or senseless shouting or outcry **2 a** : SOUND; *esp* : one that lacks agreeable musical quality or is noticeably loud, harsh, or discordant **b** : an unwanted signal in an electronic communication system

²**noise** *vt* : to spread by rumor or report ⟨*noised* it about that the troops would be home by Christmas⟩

noise·less \'nóiz-ləs\ *adj* : making or causing no noise ⟨kittens on *noiseless* feet⟩ — **noise·less·ly** *adv* — **noise·less·ness** *n*

noise·mak·er \-,mā-kər\ *n* : one that makes noise; *esp* : a device used to make noise at parties

noi·some \'nói-səm\ *adj* [ME *noy* annoyance, fr. OF *enui*] **1** : NOXIOUS, UNWHOLESOME **2** : offensive to the senses (as smell) : DISGUSTING — **noi·some·ly** *adv* — **noi·some·ness** *n*

noisy \'nói-zē\ *adj* **nois·i·er; -est 1** : making noise **2** : full of or characterized by noise — **nois·i·ly** \-zə-lē\ *adv* — **nois·i·ness** \-zē-nəs\ *n*

nol·le pro·se·qui \,näl-ē-'präs-ə-,kwī\ *n* [L, to be unwilling to pursue] : an entry on the record of a legal action that the prosecutor or plaintiff will proceed no further in his action or suit

no·lo con·ten·de·re \,nō-lō-kən-'ten-də-rē\ *n* [L, I do not wish to contend] : a plea by the defendant in a criminal prosecution that without admitting guilt subjects him to conviction but does not preclude him from denying the charges in another proceeding

nol-pros \'näl-'präs\ *vt* **nol-prossed; nol-pros·sing** : to discontinue by entering a nolle prosequi

no·mad \'nō-,mad\ *n* [Gk *nomad-, nomas*, fr. *nemein* to pasture] **1** : a member of a people that has no fixed residence but wanders from place to place **2** : an individual who roams about aimlessly — **nomad** *or* **no·mad·ic** \nō-'mad-ik\ *adj* — **no·mad·ism** \'nō-,mad-,iz-əm\ *n*

no-man's-land \'nō-,manz-,land\ *n* **1** : an area of unowned, unclaimed, or uninhabited land **2** : an unoccupied area between opposing troops **3** : an area of anomalous, ambiguous, or indefinite character

nom de guerre \,näm-di-'ge(ə)r\ *n, pl* **noms de guerre** \,näm(z)-di-\ [F, lit., war name] : PSEUDONYM

nom de plume \,näm-di-'plüm\ *n, pl* **noms de plume** \,näm(z)-di-\ [F *nom* name + *de* of + *plume* pen] : PEN NAME

nome \'nōm\ *n* [Gk *nomos* district] : a province of ancient Egypt

no·men \'nō-mən\ *n, pl* **nom·i·na** \'näm-ə-nə, 'nō-mə-\ [L *nomin-, nomen*, lit., name] : the second of the three usual names of an ancient Roman

no·men·cla·ture \'nō-mən-,klā-chər\ *n* [L *nomenclatura* calling by name, list of names, fr. *nomen* name + *calare* to call] **1** : NAME, DESIGNATION **2** : a system of terms used in a particular science, discipline, or art; *esp* : the standardized New Latin names used in biology — **no·men·cla·tur·al** \,nō-mən-'klāch-(ə-)rəl\ *adj*

nom·i·nal \'näm-ən-ᵊl\ *adj* [L *nomin-, nomen* name, noun; akin to E *name*] **1** : of, relating to, or being a noun or a word or expression taking a noun construction **2 a :** of, relating to, or constituting a name **b :** bearing the name of a person **3 a :** existing in name or form only ⟨*nominal* head of his party⟩ **b :** very small **:** TRIFLING, INSIGNIFICANT ⟨a *nominal* price⟩ — **nom·i·nal·ly** \-ᵊl-ē\ *adv*

nom·i·nate \'näm-ə-,nāt\ *vt* **:** to choose as a candidate for election, appointment, or honor; *esp* **:** to propose for office ⟨*nominate* a man for president⟩ — **nom·i·na·tor** \-,nāt-ər\ *n*

nom·i·na·tion \,näm-ə-'nā-shən\ *n* **1 :** the act, process, or an instance of nominating **2 :** the state of being nominated

nom·i·na·tive \'näm-(ə-)nət-iv\ *adj* **:** of, relating to, or constituting a grammatical case marking typically the subject of a verb esp. in languages that have relatively full inflection — **nominative** *n*

nom·i·nee \,näm-ə-'nē\ *n* **:** a person nominated for an office, duty, or position

non- \('\)nän, ,nän\ *prefix* [L *non*] **:** not **:** reverse of **:** absence of

non·age \'nän-ij, 'nō-nij\ *n* [MF, fr. *non-* + *age*] **1 :** MINORITY 1 **2 a :** a period of youth **b :** IMMATURITY

no·na·ge·nar·i·an \,nō-nə-jə-'ner-ē-ən, ,nän-ə-\ *n* [L *nonaginta* ninety] **:** a person who is 90 or more but less than 100 years old — **nonagenarian** *adj*

no·na·gon \'nō-nə-,gän, 'nän-ə-\ *n* [L *nonus* ninth] **:** a polygon of nine angles and nine sides

non·al·le·lic \,nän-ᵊl-'ē-lik, -'el-ik\ *adj* **:** not behaving as alleles toward one another ⟨*nonallelic* genes⟩

non·as·sim·i·la·tion \,nän-ə-,sim-ə-'lā-shən\ *n* **:** failure or absence of assimilation ⟨*nonassimilation* of fat⟩ — **non·as·sim·i·la·ble** \-'sim-ə-lə-bəl\ *adj*

nonagon

non·cal·car·e·ous \,nän-kal-'kar-ē-əs, -'ker-\ *adj* **:** not calcareous; *esp* **:** lacking or deficient in lime ⟨*noncalcareous* soils⟩

¹nonce \'nän(t)s\ *n* [ME *nanes*, fr. incorrect division of *then anes* in such phrases as *to then anes* for the one purpose] **:** the one, particular, or present occasion, purpose, or use ⟨for the *nonce*⟩

²nonce *adj* **:** occurring, used, or made only once or for a special occasion ⟨*nonce* word⟩

non·cha·lance \,nän-shə-'län(t)s\ *n* **:** the state of being nonchalant

non·cha·lant \-'länt\ *adj* [F, fr. OF, fr. prp. of *nonchaloir* to disregard, fr. L *non* not + *calēre* to be warm, be troubled] **:** having a confident and easy manner; *esp* **:** unconcerned about drawing attention to oneself ⟨face an unfriendly crowd with *nonchalant* ease⟩ — **non·cha·lant·ly** *adv*

non·com \'nän-,käm\ *n* **:** NONCOMMISSIONED OFFICER

non·com·bat·ant \,nän-kəm-'bat-ᵊnt, (')nän-'käm-bət-ᵊnt\ *n* **:** a member (as a chaplain) of the armed forces whose duties do not include fighting; *also* **:** CIVILIAN — **noncombatant** *adj*

non·com·mis·sioned officer \,nän-kə-,mish-ənd-\ *n* **:** a subordinate officer in a branch of the armed forces appointed from enlisted personnel and holding one of various grades (as staff sergeant)

non·com·mit·tal \,nän-kə-'mit-ᵊl\ *adj* **:** not telling or showing what a person thinks or has decided ⟨a *noncommittal* answer⟩ — **non·com·mit·tal·ly** \-ᵊl-ē\ *adv*

non com·pos men·tis \,nän-,käm-pəs-'ment-əs, ,nōn-\ *adj* [L, lit., not having control of one's mind] **:** not of sound mind

non·con·duc·tor \,nän-kən-'dək-tər\ *n* **:** a substance that conducts heat, electricity, or sound only in very small degree

non·con·form·ist \,nän-kən-'fȯr-məst\ *n* **1** *often cap* **:** a person who does not conform to an established church and esp. the Church of England **2 :** a person who does not conform to a generally accepted pattern of thought or action — **nonconformist** *adj, often cap*

non·con·for·mi·ty \-'fȯr-mət-ē\ *n* **1 a :** failure or refusal to conform to an established church **b** *often cap* **:** the movement or principles of English Protestant dissent **c** *often cap* **:** the body of English Nonconformists **2 :** refusal to conform to conventional rules or customs

non·con·trib·u·to·ry \,nän-kən-'trib-yə-,tōr-ē, -,tȯr-\ *adj* **:** paid for entirely by an employer **:** not involving payments by employees ⟨*noncontributory* pension plan⟩

non·co·op·er·a·tion \,nän-kō-,äp-ə-'rā-shən\ *n* **:** failure or refusal to cooperate; *esp* **:** refusal through civil disobedience of a people to cooperate with the government of a country — **non·co·op·er·a·tive** \-'äp-(ə-)rət-iv, -ə-,rāt-\ *adj*

non·de·script \,nän-di-'skript\ *adj* [L *descriptus*, pp. of *describere* to describe] **:** belonging or appearing to belong to no particular class or kind **:** not easily described — **nondescript** *n*

non·dis·junc·tion \,nän-dis-'jəŋ(k)-shən\ *n* **:** the failure of two homologous chromosomes to separate during meiosis — **non·dis·junc·tion·al** \-shnəl, -shən-ᵊl\ *adj*

non·du·ra·ble goods \(,)nän-,d(y)ùr-ə-bəl-\ *n pl* **:** articles (as clothing or food) usable only for a short time or usable only once

¹none \'nən\ *pron* [OE *nān*, fr. *ne* not + *ān* one] **1 :** not any ⟨*none* of them went⟩⟨*none* of it is needed⟩ **2 :** not one ⟨*none* of the family⟩ **3 :** not any such thing or person ⟨half a loaf is better than *none*⟩

²none *adj, archaic* **:** not any **:** NO

³none *adv* **1 :** by no means **:** not at all ⟨he finally got there, and *none* too soon⟩ **2 :** in no way **:** to no extent

⁴none \'nōn\ *n, often cap* [LL *nona*, fr. L, 9th hour of the day, fr. *nonus* ninth] **:** the fifth of the canonical hours

non·elec·tro·lyte \,nän-ə-'lek-trə-,līt\ *n* **:** a substance (as

See *non-* and 2d element				
nonabasive	nonautomotive	noncommunicable	noncontradictory	nondevelopment
nonabsorbent	nonbasic	noncompensating	noncontributing	nondifferentiation
nonabstainer	nonbearing	noncompetent	noncontrolled	nondiffusible
nonacademic	nonbeing	noncompeting	noncontrolling	nondigestible
nonacceptance	nonbeliever	noncompetitive	noncontroversial	nondirectional
nonacid	nonbelligerent	noncomplementary	nonconvertible	nondirective
nonactive	nonbiting	noncompliance	noncorporate	nondisclosure
nonadaptive	nonbreakable	noncompound	noncorrodible	nondiscriminatory
nonadherence	nonbusiness	noncompressible	noncorrosive	nondiscursive
nonadhesive	noncaking	nonconclusive	noncovered	nondisqualifying
nonadjacent	noncanonical	nonconcurrent	noncreative	nondistinctive
nonadjustable	noncarbohydrate	noncondensable	noncriminal	nondistribution
nonadministrative	noncarnivorous	noncondensing	noncritical	nondivided
nonadmission	noncash	nonconditioned	noncrystalline	nondocumentary
nonaggression	noncellular	nonconducting	noncultivated	nondollar
nonagreement	nonchargeable	nonconfidence	noncumulative	nondomesticated
nonagricultural	non-Christian	nonconflicting	noncurrent	nondramatic
nonalcoholic	noncitizen	nonconformance	noncyclic	nondrying
nonalphabetic	nonclassical	nonconforming	nondeductible	nondurable
nonanalytic	nonclerical	noncongenital	nondeferrable	nondynastic
nonappearance	nonclinical	nonconscious	nondefining	nonecclesiastical
nonaquatic	nonclotting	nonconstitutional	nondegenerate	noneconomic
nonaqueous	noncoagulable	nonconstructive	nondelivery	noneducational
nonaromatic	noncoercive	nonconsumable	nondemocratic	noneffective
nonassessable	noncollapsible	noncontact	nondenominational	noneffervescent
nonathletic	noncollectible	noncontagious	nondepartmental	nonelastic
nonattendance	noncollegiate	noncontemporary	nondeposition	nonelective
nonattributive	noncombining	noncontentious	nonderivative	nonelectric
nonauthoritative	noncombustible	noncontiguous	nondestructive	noneligible
nonautomatic	noncommercial	noncontinuous	nondeteriorative	nonemotional
		noncontraband	nondetonating	

sugar) that does not ionize in water and is therefore a poor conductor of electricity

non·en·ti·ty \nä-'nent-ət-ē\ *n, pl* **-ties 1 :** something that does not exist or exists only in the imagination **2 :** one of no consequence or significance

nones \'nōnz\ *n pl* [L *nonus* ninth] **:** the 9th day before the ides according to ancient Roman reckoning

non·es·sen·tial \,nän-ə-'sen-chəl\ *adj* **:** not fundamentally needed or indispensable — **nonessential** *n*

none·such \'nən-,səch\ *n* **:** a person or thing without an equal — **nonesuch** *adj*

none·the·less \,nən-thə-'les\ *adv* **:** NEVERTHELESS

non–eu·clid·e·an \,nän-yü-'klid-ē-ən\ *adj, often cap* E **:** not assuming or in accordance with all the postulates of Euclid's *Elements* ⟨*non-euclidean* geometry⟩

non·fea·sance \(')nän-'fēz-²ns\ *n* **:** omission to do esp. what ought to be done

non·flow·er·ing \(')nän-'flaù-(ə-)riŋ\ *adj* **:** lacking a flowering stage in the life cycle

non·ho·mol·o·gous \,nän-hō-'mäl-ə-gəs, -hə-\ *adj* **:** of unlike genic constitution ⟨*nonhomologous* chromosomes⟩

no·nil·lion \nō-'nil-yən\ *n* — see NUMBER table

non·in·ter·ven·tion \,nän-,int-ər-'ven-chən\ *n* **:** the state or habit of not intervening **:** refusal or failure to intervene — **non·in·ter·ven·tion·ist** \-'vench-(ə-)nəst\ *n or adj*

non·in·tox·i·cant \,nän-in-'täk-si-kənt\ *adj* **:** not intoxicating — **nonintoxicant** *n*

non·ir·ri·gat·ed \(')nän-'ir-ə-,gāt-əd\ *adj* **:** not irrigated

non·ju·ror \(')nän-'jür-ər\ *n* **:** a person refusing to take an oath esp. of allegiance, supremacy, or abjuration — **non·jur·ing** \-'jù(ə)r-iŋ\ *adj*

non·lin·e·ar \(')nän-'lin-ē-ər\ *adj* **:** not linear **:** represented by or being a curve ⟨*nonlinear* equations⟩

non·liv·ing \(')nän-'liv-iŋ\ *adj* **:** not having or characterized by life

non·met·al \(')nän-'met-²l\ *n* **:** a chemical element (as carbon or nitrogen) that lacks metallic properties

non·me·tal·lic \,nän-mə-'tal-ik\ *adj* **1 :** not metallic **2 :** of, relating to, or being a nonmetal

non·met·a·mer·ic \,nän-,met-ə-'mer-ik, -'mir-\ *adj* **:** not made up of linear segments

non·ob·jec·tive \,nän-əb-'jek-tiv\ *adj* **:** representing or intended to represent no concrete object of nature or natural appearance **:** ABSTRACT

¹non·pa·reil \,nän-pə-'rel\ *adj* [MF, fr. *non-* + *pareil* equal] **:** having no equal **:** PEERLESS

²nonpareil *n* **1 :** an individual of unequaled excellence

: PARAGON 2 : 6-point interlinear space in printing **3 a :** a small flat disk of chocolate covered with white sugar pellets **b :** small sugar pellets of various colors

non·par·ti·san \(')nän-'pärt-ə-zən\ *adj* **:** not partisan; *esp* **:** free from party affiliation, bias, or designation ⟨*nonpartisan* ballot⟩ ⟨a *nonpartisan* committee⟩ — **non·par·ti·san·ship** \-,ship\ *n*

non·pas·ser·ine \(')nän-'pas-ə-,rīn\ *adj* **:** not passerine; *esp* **:** belonging to the order (Coraciiformes) that includes the kingfishers and related birds

¹non·plus \(')nän-'pləs\ *n, pl* **non·plus·es** *or* **non·plus·ses** [L *non plus* no more] **:** a state of bafflement or perplexity **:** QUANDARY

²nonplus *vt* **non·plussed** *also* **non·plused; non·plus·sing** *also* **non·plus·ing :** to cause to be at a loss as to what to say, think, or do **:** PERPLEX

non·po·lar \(')nän-'pō-lər\ *adj* **1 :** lacking electrical poles ⟨a *nonpolar* molecule⟩ **2 :** of or characterized by covalency ⟨*nonpolar* liquid⟩

non·pro·duc·tive \,nän-prə-'dək-tiv\ *adj* **1 :** failing to produce or yield **:** UNPRODUCTIVE ⟨a *nonproductive* oil well⟩ **2 :** not directly productive ⟨*nonproductive* labor⟩ — **non·pro·duc·tive·ness** *n*

non·prof·it \(')nän-'präf-ət\ *adj* **:** not conducted or maintained for the purpose of making a profit ⟨a *nonprofit* organization⟩

non·ran·dom \(')nän-'ran-dəm\ *adj* **:** not governed by chance **:** following a definite pattern or plan

non·rep·re·sen·ta·tion·al \,nän-,rep-ri-,zən-'tā-shnəl, -shən-²l\ *adj* **:** not representing an object of nature **:** ABSTRACT

non·res·i·dent \(')nän-'rez-əd-ənt, -ə-,dent\ *adj* **:** not living in a specified or implied place — **non·res·i·dence** \-əd-ən(t)s, -ə-,den(t)s\ *n* — **nonresident** *n*

non·re·sis·tance \,nän-ri-'zis-tən(t)s\ *n* **:** the principles or practice of passive submission to authority even when unjust or oppressive — **non·re·sis·tant** \-tənt\ *adj*

non·re·stric·tive \,nän-ri-'strik-tiv\ *adj* **1 :** not serving or tending to restrict **2 :** not limiting the reference of the word or phrase modified ⟨a *nonrestrictive* clause⟩

non·rig·id \(')nän-'rij-əd\ *adj* **:** maintaining form by pressure of contained gas ⟨a *nonrigid* airship⟩

non·sched·uled \(')nän-'skej-üld, -əld\ *adj* **:** licensed to carry passengers or freight by air without a regular schedule ⟨*nonscheduled* airline⟩

non·sec·tar·i·an \,nän-sek-'ter-ē-ən\ *adj* **:** not having a sectarian character

See *non-* and 2d element	nonfreezing	nonlethal	nonofficial	nonracial
nonempirical	nonfulfillment	nonlife	nonoily	nonradical
nonenforceable	nonfunctional	nonliquid	nonoperating	nonradioactive
nonentanglement	non-Gaelic	nonliterary	nonorganic	nonrated
nonepiscopal	nongame	nonliterate	nonorthodox	nonrational
noneruptive	nongaseous	nonliturgical	nonparallel	nonreactive
nonethical	nongenetic	nonlocal	nonparalytic	nonreader
nonexclusive	nongovernmental	nonlogical	nonparasitic	nonrealistic
nonexempt	non-Greek	nonluminous	nonparticipant	nonreciprocal
nonexistence	nongregarious	nonmagnetic	nonparty	nonrecognition
nonexistent	nonhardy	nonmailable	nonpaternity	nonrecourse
nonexpendable	nonharmonic	nonmalignant	nonpathogenic	nonrecoverable
nonexpert	nonhereditary	nonmalleable	nonpayment	nonrecurrent
nonexplosive	nonhistorical	nonman	nonpecuniary	nonreducing
nonexportation	nonhomogeneous	nonmarketable	nonperformance	nonrefillable
nonextant	nonhuman	nonmaterial	nonperishable	nonregistered
nonfarm	nonidentical	nonmechanical	nonpermanent	nonregulation
nonfat	nonidentity	nonmechanistic	nonpersistent	nonreligious
nonfatal	nonimmigrant	nonmember	nonpersonal	nonremovable
nonfattening	nonimmune	nonmembership	nonphysical	nonrenewable
nonfebrile	nonimportation	nonmetered	nonpoisonous	nonrepayable
nonfederal	non-Indo-European	nonmetrical	nonpolar	nonrepresentative
nonfederated	nonindustrial	nonmigratory	nonpolitical	nonresidential
nonfeeding	noninfectious	nonmilitary	nonporous	nonrestraint
nonferrous	noninflammable	nonmoney	nonpossession	nonrestricted
nonfiction	noninflammatory	nonmoral	nonpractical	nonretractile
nonfictional	noninflationary	nonmotile	nonpredicative	nonretroactive
nonfigurative	noninstitutional	nonmoving	nonpregnant	nonreturnable
nonfilamentous	noninstructional	nonmutant	nonprinting	nonrevenue
nonfilterable	nonintegrated	nonnational	nonproducer	nonreversible
nonfinancial	nonintellectual	nonnative	nonprofessional	nonrhetorical
nonfissionable	nonintercourse	nonnatural	nonprogressive	nonrotating
nonflagellated	noninterference	nonnecessity	nonproprietary	nonruminant
nonflammable	nonintersecting	nonnegotiable	nonprotein	nonsalable
nonflowering	nonintoxicating	nonnitrogenous	nonproven	nonscientific
nonfluency	noninvolvement	nonnormative	nonpublic	nonscientist
nonflying	nonionized	nonobligatory	nonpungent	nonseasonal
nonforfeiture	nonirritating	nonobservance	nonquota	nonsecret
nonfraternal	nonlegal	nonoccurrence	nonrabbinic	nonsecretory

---

j joke; ŋ sing; ō flow; ȯ flaw; ȯi coin; th thin; th this; ü loot; ù foot; y yet; yü few; yù furious; zh vision

non·sense \'nän-,sen(t)s, 'nän(t)-sən(t)s\ *n* **1** : foolish or meaningless words or actions **2** : things of no importance or value : TRIFLES ⟨the children were told not to spend their money for *nonsense*⟩ — **non·sen·si·cal** \(')nän-'sen(t)-si-kəl\ *adj* — **non·sen·si·cal·ly** \-k(ə-)lē\ *adv* — **non·sen·si·cal·ness** \-kəl-nəs\ *n*

non se·qui·tur \(')nän-'sek-wət-ər\ *n* [L, it does not follow] : an inference that does not follow from the premises

non·sig·ni·fi·cant \,nän(t)-sig-'nif-i-kənt\ *adj* : not significant: as **a** : INSIGNIFICANT **b** : MEANINGLESS

non·sked \(')nän-'sked\ *n* : a nonscheduled airline or transport plane

non·skid \(')nän-'skid\ *adj* : having the tread corrugated or specially constructed to resist skidding

non·sport·ing \(')nän-'spōrt-iŋ, -'spȯrt-\ *adj* **1** : lacking the qualities characteristic of a hunting dog **2** : not subject to frequent mutation

non·stan·dard \(')nän-'stan-dərd\ *adj* **1** : not standard **2** : not conforming in pronunciation, grammatical construction, idiom, or choice of word to the usage generally characteristic of educated native speakers of the language

non·stop \(')nän-'stäp\ *adj* : done or made without a stop ⟨a *nonstop* flight to Chicago⟩ — **nonstop** *adv*

non·such \'nən-,səch, 'nän-\ *var of* NONESUCH

non·suit \(')nän-'süt\ *n* [AF *nounsuyte*, fr. *noun-* non- + OF *siute* following, pursuit] : a judgment against a plaintiff for his failure to prosecute his case or his inability to establish a prima facie case — **nonsuit** *vt*

non·sup·port \,nän(t)-sə-'pōrt, -'pȯrt\ *n* : failure to support; *esp* : failure on the part of one under obligation to provide maintenance

non·syl·lab·ic \,nän(t)-sə-'lab-ik\ *adj* : not constituting a syllable or the nucleus of a syllable

non·sym·bi·ot·ic \,nän-,sim-,bī-'ät-ik, -bē-\ *adj* : not symbiotic

non trop·po \(')nän-'trȯ-pō, (')nōn-\ *adv (or adj)* [It, lit., not too much] : not too much so : moderately so — used as a direction in music

non·union \(')nän-'yü-nyən\ *adj* **1** : not belonging to a trade union ⟨*nonunion* carpenters⟩ **2** : not recognizing or favoring trade unions or their members ⟨*nonunion* employers⟩

non·vi·a·ble \(')nän-'vī-ə-bəl\ *adj* : not capable of living, growing, or developing and functioning successfully

non·vi·o·lence \(')nän-'vī-ə-lən(t)s\ *n* : abstention on principle from violence; *also* : the principle of such abstention — **non·vi·o·lent** \-lənt\ *adj*

non·vol·a·tile \(')nän-'väl-ət-ªl\ *adj* : not volatile : not volatilizing readily

non·ze·ro \(')nän-'zē-rō, -'zi(ə)r-ō\ *adj* : not zero : either positive or negative

¹noo·dle \'nüd-ªl\ *n* : a stupid person : SIMPLETON

²noodle *n* [G *nudel*] : a food like macaroni but shaped into long flat strips and made with egg — usu. used in pl.

nook \'nuk\ *n* [ME *noke, nok*] **1** : an interior angle or corner formed usu. by two walls ⟨a chimney *nook*⟩ **2** : a sheltered or hidden place : a corner set apart from its surroundings ⟨a shady *nook*⟩

noon \'nün\ *n* [OE *nōn* ninth hour from sunrise, fr. L *nona*, fr. fem. of *nonus* ninth; akin to E *nine*] : the middle of the day : 12 o'clock in the daytime — **noon** *adj*

noon·day \-,dā\ *n* : MIDDAY

no one *pron* : NOBODY

noon·ing \'nü-niŋ, -nən\ *n, chiefly dial* : a midday meal; *also* : a period at noon for eating or resting

noon·tide \'nün-,tīd\ *n* **1** : the time of noon **2** : the highest or culminating point

noon·time \-,tīm\ *n* : NOONTIDE

¹noose \'nüs\ *n* : a loop with a running knot that binds closer the more it is drawn

²noose *vt* : to catch or fasten with or as if with a noose

no-par *adj* : having no face value ⟨*no-par* stock⟩

nor \nər, (')nō(ə)r\ *conj* [ME, contraction of *nother* neither, nor] : and not ⟨the book is too long; *nor* is the style easy⟩ ⟨not for you *nor* for me *nor* for him⟩ — used esp. to introduce and negate the second member and each later member of a series of items of which the first is preceded by *neither* ⟨neither here *nor* there⟩

nor·adren·a·lin \,nȯr-ə-'dren-ªl-ən\ *n* : NOREPINEPHRINE

¹Nor·dic \'nȯrd-ik\ *adj* [F *nordique*, fr. *nord* north, fr. OE *north*] **1** : of or relating to the Germanic peoples of northern Europe and esp. of Scandinavia **2** : of or relating to a physical type characterized by tall stature, long head, light skin and hair, and blue eyes

²Nordic *n* **1** : a native of northern Europe **2** : a person of Nordic physical type or of a hypothetical Nordic division of the Caucasian race **3** : a member of any of the peoples of Scandinavia

nor·epi·neph·rine \,nō(ə)r-,ep-ə-'nef-,rēn, -rən\ *n* [*normal* + *epinephrine*] : a compound that occurs with epinephrine, has a strong vasoconstrictor action, and is held to mediate the transmission of sympathetic nerve impulses

Nor·folk jacket \,nȯr-fək-, -,fȯk-\ *n* [*Norfolk*, county in England] : a loose-fitting belted single= breasted jacket with box pleats

norm \'nȯrm\ *n* [L *norma*, lit., carpenter's square] : AVERAGE, STANDARD; *esp* : a set standard of development or achievement usu. derived from the average or median achievement of a large group

¹nor·mal \'nȯr-məl\ *adj* [L *normalis*, fr. *norma* carpenter's square] **1** : forming a right angle; *esp* : perpendicular to a tangent at a point of tangency **2** : constituting or not deviating from a norm, rule, or principle : REGULAR **3** : occurring naturally **4 a** : of, relating to, or characterized by average intelligence or development **b** : free from disorder of body or mind : SOUND, SANE **5 a** : having a concentration of one gram equivalent of solute per liter ⟨a *normal* salt solution⟩ **b** : containing neither basic hydroxyl nor acid hydrogen ⟨a *normal* salt⟩ **c** : having a straight-chain structure ⟨a *normal* alcohol⟩ **syn** see REGULAR — **nor·mal·cy** \-sē\ *n* — **nor·mal·i·ty** \nȯr-'mal-ət-ē\ *n* — **nor·mal·ly** \'nȯr-mə-lē\ *adv*

Norfolk jacket

²normal *n* **1** : one (as a line or person) that is normal **2** : the usual condition, level, or quantity : AVERAGE

normal distribution *n* : a frequency distribution whose graph is a symmetrical bell-shaped curve

nor·mal·ize \'nȯr-mə-,līz\ *vt* : to make normal or average — **nor·mal·i·za·tion** \,nȯr-mə-lə-'zā-shən\ *n*

normal school *n* : a usu. two-year school for training chiefly elementary teachers

Nor·man \'nȯr-mən\ *n* **1** : one of the Scandinavians who conquered Normandy in the 10th century **2** : one of the people of mixed Norman and French blood who conquered England in 1066 **3** : a native or inhabitant of the province of Normandy — **Norman** *adj*

Norman-French *n* : the French language of the medieval Normans

nor·ma·tive \'nȯr-mət-iv\ *adj* : of, relating to, or prescribing norms — **nor·ma·tive·ly** *adv* — **nor·ma·tive·ness** *n*

Norn \'nȯrn\ *n* : any of the three Norse goddesses of fate

Norse \'nȯrs\ *n* **1** *pl* **Norse a** : SCANDINAVIANS **b** : NORWEGIANS **2 a** : NORWEGIAN **2 b** : any of the western

See *non-* and 2d element			
nonsegregated	nonspecialized	nonsuccess	nontraditional	nonvegetative
nonselective	nonspecific	nonsurgical	nontransferable	nonvenomous
non-self-governing	nonspectacular	nonsymbolic	nontransparent	nonvibratory
nonsensitive	nonspectral	nonsymmetrical	nontransposing	nonviolation
nonsensuous	nonspeculative	nontarnishable	nontropical	nonviscous
nonseptate	nonstaining	nontaxable	nontuberculous	nonvisual
nonsexual	nonstarter	nontechnical	nontypical	nonvocal
nonshrinkable	nonstationary	nontemporal	nonunderstandable	nonvocational
nonsinkable	nonstatistical	nonterritorial	nonuniform	nonvoluntary
nonsmoker	nonstellar	nontheatrical	nonuniformity	nonvoting
nonsocial	nonstrategic	nontheistic	nonuser	nonwhite
nonsolid	nonstriated	nonthermal	nonutilitarian	nonworker
nonspatial	nonstriker	nontidal	nonvariant	nonwoven
nonspeaking	nonstructural	nontoxic	nonvascular	nonzero
	nonsubscriber			

ə abut; ª kitten; ər further; a back; ā bake; ä cot, cart; aů out; ch chin; e less; ē easy; g gift; i trip; ī life

Scandinavian dialects or languages **c** : the Scandinavian group of Germanic languages — **Norse** *adj*

Norse·man \-mən\ *n* : one of the ancient Scandinavians

¹north \'nȯrth; *in compounds, as "northeast", also* (')nȯr *esp by seamen*\ *adv* [OE] : to or toward the north

²north *adj* **1** : situated toward or at the north **2** : coming from the north

³north *n* **1 a** : the direction to the left of one facing east **b** : the compass point directly opposite to south — see COMPASS CARD **2** *cap* : regions or countries north of a specified or implied point

north·bound \'nȯrth-ˌbau̇nd\ *adj* : headed north

north by east : one point east of due north : N 11° 15′ E

north by west : one point west of due north : N 11° 15′ W

¹north·east \nȯrth-'ēst\ *adv* : to or toward the northeast

²northeast *n* **1 a** : the general direction between north and east **b** : the compass point midway between north and east — see COMPASS CARD **2** *cap* : regions or countries northeast of a specified or implied point

³northeast *adj* **1** : situated toward or at the northeast **2** : coming from the northeast

northeast by east : one point east of due northeast : N 56° 15′ E

northeast by north : one point north of due northeast : N 33° 45′ E

north·east·er \nȯrth-'ē-stər\ *n* **1** : a strong northeast wind **2** : a storm with northeast winds

north·east·er·ly \-lē\ *adv (or adj)* **1** : from the northeast **2** : toward the northeast

north·east·ern \nȯrth-'ē-stərn\ *adj* **1** *often cap* : of, relating to, or characteristic of a region conventionally designated Northeast **2** : lying toward or coming from the northeast — **north·east·ern·most** \-ˌmōst\ *adj*

North·east·ern·er \-stə(r)-nər\ *n* : a native or inhabitant of a northeastern region (as of the U.S.)

¹north·east·ward \nȯrth-'ēs-twərd\ *adv (or adj)* : toward the northeast — **north·east·wards** \-twərdz\ *adv*

²northeastward *n* : NORTHEAST

north·er \'nȯr-thər\ *n* **1** : a strong north wind **2** : a storm with north winds

¹north·er·ly \-lē\ *adv (or adj)* **1** : from the north **2** : toward the north

²northerly *n, pl* **-lies** : a wind from the north

north·ern \'nȯr-tha(r)n\ *adj* **1** *often cap* : of, relating to, or characteristic of a region conventionally designated North **2** : lying toward or coming from the north — **north·ern·most** \-ˌmōst\ *adj*

Northern Cross *n* : a cross formed by six stars in Cygnus

Northern Crown *n* : CORONA BOREALIS

North·ern·er \'nȯr-tha(r)-nər\ *n* : a native or inhabitant of the North (as of the U.S.)

northern hemisphere *n* : the half of the earth that lies north of the equator

northern lights *n pl* : AURORA BOREALIS

north·ing \'nȯr-thiŋ, -thiŋ\ *n* **1** : difference in latitude to the north from the last preceding point of reckoning **2** : northerly progress

north·land \'nȯrth-ˌland, -lənd\ *n, often cap* : land in the north : the north of a country or region

North·man \-mən\ *n* : NORSEMAN

north–northeast *n* — see COMPASS CARD

north–northwest *n* — see COMPASS CARD

north pole *n* **1** *often cap N&P* : the northernmost point of the earth : the northern end of the earth's axis **2** : the pole of a magnet that points toward the north

North Star *n* : the star toward which the northern end of the earth's axis very nearly points — called also *polestar*

¹north·ward \'nȯrth-wərd\ *adv (or adj)* : toward the north — **north·wards** \-wərdz\ *adv*

²northward *n* : northward direction or part ⟨sail to the *northward*⟩

¹north·west \nȯrth-'west\ *adv* : to or toward the north-west

²northwest *n* **1 a** : the general direction between north and west **b** : the compass point midway between north and west — see COMPASS CARD **2** *cap* : regions or countries northwest of a specified or implied point

³northwest *adj* **1** : situated toward or at the northwest **2** : coming from the northwest

northwest by north : one point north of due northwest : N 33° 45′ W

northwest by west : one point west of due northwest : N 56° 15′ W

north·west·er \nȯrth-'wes-tər\ *n* : a strong northwest wind

north·west·er·ly \-lē\ *adv (or adj)* **1** : from the north-west **2** : toward the northwest

north·west·ern \nȯrth-'wes-tərn\ *adj* **1** *often cap* : of, relating to, or characteristic of a region conventionally designated Northwest **2** : lying toward or coming from the northwest

North·west·ern·er \-tə(r)-nər\ *n* : a native or inhabitant of a northwestern region (as of the U.S.)

¹north·west·ward \nȯrth-'wes-twərd\ *adv (or adj)* : toward the northwest — **north·west·wards** \-twərdz\ *adv*

²northwestward *n* : NORTHWEST

Norway pine \ˌnȯr-ˌwā-\ *n* : a No. American pine with reddish bark and hard but not durable wood; *also* : its wood

Nor·we·gian \nȯr-'wē-jən\ *n* **1 a** : a native or inhabitant of Norway **b** : a person of Norwegian descent **2** : the Germanic language of the Norwegian people — **Norwegian** *adj*

nos *pl of* NO

¹nose \'nōz\ *n* [OE *nosu*] **1 a** : the part of the face that bears the nostrils and covers the anterior part of the nasal cavity; *also* : this part together with the nasal cavity **b** : the vertebrate olfactory organ **2** : the sense of smell : OLFACTION **3** : something (as a point, edge, or projecting front part) that resembles a nose ⟨the *nose* of a plane⟩ — **nosed** \'nōzd\ *adj*

²nose *vb* **1** : to detect by or as if by smell : SCENT **2 a** : to push or move with the nose **b** : to touch or rub with the nose : NUZZLE **3** : to defeat by a narrow margin in a contest ⟨the home team barely *nosed* out the visitors⟩ **4** : to search impertinently : PRY **5** : to move ahead slowly or cautiously ⟨the ship *nosed* into her berth⟩

nose·band \'nōz-ˌband\ *n* : the part of a headstall that passes over a horse's nose

nose·bleed \-ˌblēd\ *n* : a bleeding from the nose

nose cone *n* : a protective cone constituting the forward end of a rocket or missile

nose dive *n* **1** : the downward nose-first plunge of a flying object (as an airplane) **2** : a sudden extreme drop — **nose-dive** \'nōz-ˌdīv\ *vi*

nose·gay \'nōz-ˌgā\ *n* [¹*nose* + E dial. *gay* ornament] : a small bunch of flowers : POSY

nose·piece \-ˌpēs\ *n* **1** : a piece of armor for protecting the nose **2** : a fitting at the lower end of a microscope tube to which the objectives are attached

no-show \nō-'shō\ *n* : a person who reserves space esp. on an airplane but neither uses nor cancels the reservation

no·sol·o·gy \nō-'säl-ə-jē\ *n* [Gk *nosos* disease] : a branch of medicine dealing with the classification of diseases — **no·so·log·ic** \ˌnō-sə-'läj-ik\ *or* **no·so·log·i·cal** \-'läj-i-kəl\ *adj*

nos·tal·gia \nä-'stal-jə, nə-\ *n* [NL, fr. Gk *nostos* return home + *algos* grief, pain] : a wistful yearning for something past or irrecoverable — **nos·tal·gic** \-jik\ *adj* — **nos·tal·gi·cal·ly** \-ji-k(ə-)lē\ *adv*

nos·toc \'näs-ˌtäk\ *n* : any of a genus of blue-green algae able to use atmospheric nitrogen

nos·tril \'näs-trəl\ *n* [OE *nosthyrl*, fr. *nosu* nose + *thyrel* hole] : an external naris ou. with the adjoining passage on the same side of the nasal septum; *also* : either fleshy lateral wall of the nose

nos·trum \'näs-trəm\ *n* [L, neut. of *noster* our, ours, fr. *nos* we; akin to E *us*] **1** : a medicine of secret composition recommended esp. by its preparer **2** : a questionable remedy or scheme : PANACEA

nosy *or* **nos·ey** \'nō-zē\ *adj* **nos·i·er;** **-est** : of prying or inquisitive disposition or quality : INTRUSIVE — **nos·i·ly** \-zə-lē\ *adv* — **nos·i·ness** \-zē-nəs\ *n*

not \(')nät\ *adv* [ME, alter. of *nought*, fr. *nought*, pron.] **1** — used as a function word to make negative a group of words or a word ⟨the books are *not* here⟩ **2** — used as a function word to stand for the negative of a preceding group of words ⟨is sometimes hard to see and sometimes *not*⟩

no·ta be·ne \ˌnōt-ə-'ben-ē, -'bē-nē\ [L, mark well] — used to call attention to something important

---

j joke; ŋ sing; ō flow; ȯ flaw; ȯi coin; th thin; th this; ü loot; u̇ foot; y yet; yü few; yu̇ furious; zh vision

no·ta·bil·i·ty \ˌnōt-ə-'bil-ət-ē\ n, pl **-ties** **1** : the quality or state of being notable **2** : a notable or prominent person

¹no·ta·ble \'nōt-ə-bəl\ adj **1** : worthy of note : RE-MARKABLE **2** : DISTINGUISHED, PROMINENT — **no·ta·bly** \-blē\ adv

²notable n : a person of note or of great reputation : NOTABILITY

no·tar·i·al \nō-'ter-ē-əl\ adj : of, relating to, or done by a notary public — **no·tar·i·al·ly** \-ē-ə-lē\ adv

no·ta·rize \'nōt-ə-ˌrīz\ vt : to make legally authentic through the use of the powers granted to a notary public — **no·ta·ri·za·tion** \ˌnōt-ə-rə-'zā-shən\ n

no·ta·ry public \ˌnōt-ə-rē-\ n, pl **notaries public** or **notary publics** [L notarius clerk, secretary, fr. nota note] : a public officer who attests or certifies writings (as deeds) as authentic and takes affidavits, depositions, and pro-tests of negotiable paper — called also **notary**

no·tate \'nō-ˌtāt\ vt : to put into notation

no·ta·tion \nō-'tā-shən\ n **1** : the act of noting ⟨careful notation of the foibles of his time⟩ **2** : ANNOTATION, NOTE ⟨make notations for corrections in the margin⟩ **3** : the act, process, or method of representing data symbolically by marks, signs, figures, or characters; also : a system of symbols (as letters, numerals, or musical notes) used in such notation — **no·ta·tion·al** \-shnəl, -shən-°l\ adj

¹notch \'näch\ n **1 a** : a V-shaped indentation **b** : any of several rounded indentations cut symmetrically on the fore edge of a book to facilitate reference — called also **thumb notch 2** : a narrow pass between mountains : GAP **3** : DEGREE, STEP

²notch vt **1** : to cut or make notches in **2** : to score or record by or as if by cutting a series of notches ⟨notch up points for the team⟩

¹note \'nōt\ vt [L notare to mark, note, fr. nota note] **1 a** : to notice or observe with care **b** : to record or preserve in writing **2** : to make special mention of : REMARK — **not·er** n

²note n [L nota mark, character, written note] **1 a** : a musical sound **b** : a cry, call, or sound esp. of an animal ⟨a bird's note⟩ **c** : a special and often emotional tone of voice ⟨a note of fear⟩ **2 a** : MEMORANDUM **b** : a brief and informal record **c** : a written or printed comment or explanation ⟨notes in the back of the book⟩ **d** : a short in-formal letter **e** : a formal diplomatic or official communi-cation **f** (1) : a written promise to pay — called also promissory note (2) : a piece of paper money **3** : a character in music that by its shape shows the length of time a tone is to be held and by its place on the staff shows the pitch of a tone **4** : MOOD, QUALITY, CHARAC-TERISTIC ⟨a note of optimism⟩ **5 a** : REPUTATION, DIS-TINCTION ⟨a man of note⟩ **b** : NOTICE, HEED, OBSERVATION ⟨take note of the exact time⟩

note·book \'nōt-ˌbuk\ n : a book for notes or memoranda

note·case \-ˌkās\ n, Brit : WALLET

not·ed \'nōt-əd\ adj : specially marked or noticed : well-known and highly regarded : FAMOUS ⟨a noted scientist⟩ — **not·ed·ly** adv

syn NOTORIOUS: NOTED implies being singled out for public attention for excellence of achievement; NOTORIOUS stresses being widely known for certain acts or qualities that are nearly always evil or questionable

note·less \'nōt-ləs\ adj **1** : not noticed : UNDISTINGUISHED **2** : UNMUSICAL, VOICELESS

note·wor·thy \'nōt-ˌwər-thē\ adj : worthy of note : REMARKABLE — **note·wor·thi·ly** \-thə-lē\ adv — **note·wor·thi·ness** \-thē-nəs\ n

¹noth·ing \'nəth-iŋ\ pron [OE nān thing, nāthing, fr. nān no + thing] **1** : not anything ⟨there's nothing in the box⟩ **2** : one of no interest, value, or consequence ⟨she's nothing to me⟩ — **nothing doing** : by no means : definitely no

²nothing adv : not at all : in no degree

³nothing n **1 a** : something that does not exist **b** : ab-sence of magnitude : ZERO **2** : something of little or no worth or importance — **noth·ing·ness** n

¹no·tice \'nōt-əs\ n [L notitia knowledge, fr. notus known, fr. pp. of noscere to come to know; akin to E know] **1 a** : warning or intimation of something : AN-NOUNCEMENT **b** : notification by one of the parties to an agreement usu. of intent to terminate it at a specified time **c** : the condition of being warned or notified ⟨the

tenant was on notice to vacate the premises⟩ **2 a** : ATTEN-TION, HEED **b** : polite or favorable attention : CIVILITY **3** : a written or printed announcement **4** : a short criti-cal account

²notice vt **1** : to make mention of : remark on **2** : to take notice or note of : OBSERVE, MARK ⟨notice even the smallest details⟩

no·tice·a·ble \'nōt-ə-sə-bəl\ adj **1** : worthy of notice ⟨noticeable for its fine coloring⟩ **2** : capable of being or likely to be noticed ⟨a slight but noticeable taste⟩ — **no·tice·a·bly** \-blē\ adv

no·ti·fi·ca·tion \ˌnōt-ə-fə-'kā-shən\ n **1** : the act or an instance of notifying; esp : the act of giving official notice or information **2** : written or printed matter that gives notice

no·ti·fy \'nōt-ə-ˌfī\ vt **-fied; -fy·ing** [MF notifier to make known, fr. LL notificare, fr. L notus known] **1** : to give notice of : report the occurrence of **2** : to give notice to — **no·ti·fi·er** \-ˌfī-(-ə)r\ n

no·tion \'nō-shən\ n [L not-, noscere to know] **1 a** : IDEA, CONCEPTION ⟨have a notion of a poem's meaning⟩ **b** : a belief held : OPINION, VIEW ⟨it was his notion that everyone else was wasteful⟩ **c** : WHIM, FANCY ⟨a sudden notion to go home⟩ **2** pl : small useful articles (as pins, needles, or thread)

no·tion·al \'nō-shnəl, -shən-°l\ adj **1** : existing in idea only : IMAGINARY, UNREAL ⟨a plan that never got beyond the notional stage⟩ **2** : inclined to foolish or visionary fancies or moods ⟨a notional man⟩

no·to·chord \'nōt-ə-ˌkórd\ n [Gk nōton back + chordē cord] : a longitudinal flexible rod of cells that in the lowest chordates (as lancelets and the lampreys) and in the em-bryos of the higher vertebrates forms the supporting axis of the body — **no·to·chord·al** \ˌnōt-ə-'kórd-°l\ adj

no·to·ri·e·ty \ˌnōt-ə-'rī-ət-ē\ n, pl **-ties** **1** : the quality or state of being notorious **2** : a notorious person

no·to·ri·ous \nō-'tōr-ē-əs, -'tór-\ adj [ML notorius, fr. L not-, noscere to come to know] : generally known and talked of; esp : widely and unfavorably known — **syn** see NOTED — **no·to·ri·ous·ly** adv — **no·to·ri·ous·ness** n

not·or·nis \nō-'tór-nəs\ n, pl **notornis** [Gk notos south + ornis bird] : any of a genus of flightless New Zealand birds

no-trump \'nō-ˌtrəmp\ adj : being a bid, contract, or hand suitable to play (as in bridge) without any suit being trumps — **no-trump** n

¹not·with·stand·ing \ˌnät-with-'stan-diŋ, -with-\ prep : in spite of ⟨he failed notwithstanding his skill⟩

²notwithstanding adv : NEVERTHELESS, HOWEVER

³notwithstanding conj : ALTHOUGH

nou·gat \'nü-gət\ n [F, fr. Prov, fr. OProv nogat, fr. noga nut, fr. L nuc-, nux] : a confection of nuts or fruit pieces in a sugar paste

nought \'nót, 'nät\ var of NAUGHT

noun \'naun\ n [AF, name, noun, fr. OF nom, fr. L nomen] : a word that is the name of something that can be talked about (as a person, animal, plant, place, thing, substance, quality, idea, action, or state) and that is typically used in a sentence as subject or object of a verb or as object of a preposition

nour·ish \'nər-ish, 'nə-rish\ vt [OF norriss-, norrir, fr. L nutrire] : to cause to grow or to survive in a healthy state: as **a** : to provide with nutriment : FEED ⟨plants nourished by rain and soil⟩ **b** : SUPPORT, CHERISH, MAINTAIN ⟨nourished a faint hope of getting home for Christmas⟩ ⟨a friendship nourished by respect and trust⟩ — **nour·ish·er** n

nour·ish·ing adj : giving nourishment : NUTRITIOUS ⟨nourishing food⟩

nour·ish·ment \'nər-ish-mənt, 'nə-rish-\ n **1** : something that nourishes : NUTRIMENT **2** : the act of nourishing : the state of being nourished

nou·veau riche \ˌnü-ˌvō-'rēsh\ n, pl **nou·veaux riches** \same\ [F, lit., new rich] : a person newly rich : PARVENU

no·va \'nō-və\ n, pl **novas** or **no·vae** \-(ˌ)vē, -ˌvī\ [NL, fr. L, feminine of novus new] : a star that suddenly in-creases greatly in brightness and then within a few months or years grows dim again

¹nov·el \'näv-əl\ adj [L novellus, fr. dim. of novus new] **1** : having no precedent **2** : STRANGE, UNUSUAL **syn** see NEW

²novel *n* : a prose narrative longer than a short story that usu. portrays imaginary characters and events — **nov·el·is·tic** \ˌnäv-ə-'lis-tik\ *adj*
nov·el·ette \ˌnäv-ə-'let\ *n* : a brief novel or long short story
nov·el·ist \'näv-(ə-)ləst\ *n* : a writer of novels
nov·el·ize \'näv-ə-ˌlīz\ *vt* : to convert into the form of a novel — **nov·el·i·za·tion** \ˌnäv-ə-lə-'zā-shən\ *n*
no·vel·la \nō-'vel-ə\ *n, pl* **no·vel·le** \-'vel-ē\ [It, fr. fem. of *novello* new, fr. L *novellus*] : a story with a compact and pointed plot
nov·el·ty \'näv-əl-tē\ *n, pl* **-ties** **1** : something new or unusual **2** : the quality or state of being novel : NEWNESS **3** : a small manufactured article intended mainly for personal or household adornment — usu. used in pl.
No·vem·ber \nō-'vem-bər\ *n* [L, fr. *novem* nine; akin to E *nine*; fr. its having been orig. the ninth month of the Roman calendar] : the 11th month of the year
no·ve·na \nō-'vē-nə\ *n, pl* **-nas** *or* **-nae** \-(ˌ)nē\ [ML, fr. L, fem. of *novenus* nine each, fr. *novem* nine] : a Roman Catholic devotion in which prayers are said for the same intention on nine successive days
nov·ice \'näv-əs\ *n* [L *novicius* inexperienced, fr. *novus* new] **1** : a new member of a religious order who is preparing to take the vows of religion **2** : one who has no previous training or experience in a specific field or activity : BEGINNER
   syn TYRO: NOVICE implies inexperience in something to be done ⟨a *novice* in writing⟩ TYRO suggests a beginner in something to be learned ⟨a *tyro* in politics⟩
no·vi·ti·ate \nō-'vish-ət\ *n* **1** : the period or state of being a novice **2** : NOVICE **3** : a house where novices are trained
No·vo·cain \'nō-və-ˌkān\ *trademark* — used for the hydrochloride of procaine
¹now \('nau)\ *adv* [OE *nū*] **1 a** : at the present time or moment ⟨he is busy *now*⟩ **b** : in the time immediately before the present ⟨he left just *now*⟩ **c** : in the time immediately to follow : FORTHWITH ⟨he will leave *now*⟩ **2** — used with the sense of present time weakened or lost (as to express command, introduce an important point, or indicate a transition) ⟨*now* this would imply a deliberate act⟩ **3** : SOMETIMES ⟨*now* one and *now* another⟩ **4** : under the present circumstances ⟨*now* what can we do⟩ **5** : at the time referred to ⟨*now* the trouble began⟩
²now *conj* : seeing that at or by this time : SINCE ⟨*now* we are here⟩
³now \'nau\ *n* : the present time or moment : PRESENT
⁴now \'nau\ *adj* : of or relating to the present time : EXISTING ⟨the *now* president⟩
now·a·days \'nau-(ə-)ˌdāz\ *adv* : at the present time
no·way \'nō-ˌwā\ *or* **no·ways** \-ˌwāz\ *adv* : NOWISE
no·where \'nō-ˌhwe(ə)r, -ˌhwa(ə)r, -ˌhwər\ *adv* **1** : not in or at any place **2** : to no place — **nowhere** *n*
nowhere near *adv* : not nearly
no·wise \'nō-ˌwīz\ *adv* : in no way : not at all
nox·ious \'näk-shəs\ *adj* [L *noxius*, fr. *noxa* harm] : harmful or injurious esp. to health or morals : UNWHOLESOME, PERNICIOUS ⟨*noxious* fumes⟩ ⟨a *noxious* doctrine⟩ — **nox·ious·ly** *adv* — **nox·ious·ness** *n*
noz·zle \'näz-əl\ *n* [dim. of *nose*] : a projecting part with an opening that usu. serves as an outlet ⟨the *nozzle* of a gun⟩⟨the *nozzle* of a bellows⟩; *esp* : a short tube with a taper or constriction used on a hose or pipe to direct or speed up a flow of fluid
-n't \(°)nt\ *adv comb form* : not ⟨*isn't*⟩
nth \'en(t)th\ *adj* [*n* + *-th*] **1** : numbered with an unspecified or indefinitely large ordinal number **2** : EXTREME, UTMOST ⟨to the *nth* degree⟩

nozzles

nu \'n(y)ü\ *n* : the 13th letter of the Greek alphabet — N or ν
nu·ance \'n(y)ü-ˌän(t)s, -ˌä^ⁿs, n(y)ü-'-\ *n* [F, fr. *nuer* to make shades of color, fr. *nue* cloud, fr. L *nubes*] : a shade of difference : a delicate gradation or variation (as in color, tone, or meaning)
nub \'nəb\ *n* **1** : KNOB, LUMP **2** : GIST, POINT ⟨the *nub* of the story⟩
nub·bin \'nəb-ən\ *n* **1** : a small or imperfect ear of

Indian corn; *also* : any small shriveled or undeveloped fruit **2** : a small and usu. projecting part or bit ⟨the horns were mere *nubbins*⟩ **3** : NUB 2
nub·ble \'nəb-əl\ *n* : a small knob or lump : a projecting bit — **nub·bly** \'nəb-(ə-)lē\ *adj*
nu·bile \'n(y)ü-bəl, -ˌbīl\ *adj* [L *nubilis*, fr. *nubere* to be married] : of marriageable condition or age ⟨*nubile* girls⟩ — **nu·bil·i·ty** \n(y)ü-'bil-ət-ē\ *n*
nu·cel·lus \n(y)ü-'sel-əs\ *n, pl* **-cel·li** \-'sel-ˌī\ [NL, dim. of L *nuc-, nux* nut] : the central and chief part of a plant ovule containing the embryo sac — **nu·cel·lar** \-'sel-ər\ *adj*
nu·chal \'n(y)ü-kəl\ *adj* [ML *nucha* nape, fr. Ar *nukhā'* spinal cord] : of, relating to, or lying in the region of the nape — **nuchal** *n*
nucle- *or* **nucleo-** *comb form* [NL *nucleus*] **1** : nucleus ⟨*nucleon*⟩ **2** : nucleic acid ⟨*nucleoprotein*⟩
nu·cle·ar \'n(y)ü-klē-ər\ *adj* **1** : of, relating to, or constituting a nucleus (as of a cell) **2** : of, relating to, or utilizing the atomic nucleus, atomic energy, the atom bomb, or atomic power
nuclear energy *n* : ATOMIC ENERGY
nuclear membrane *n* : the boundary of a nucleus
nuclear reactor *n* : REACTOR 2b
nuclear sap *n* : the ground substance of a cell nucleus
nu·cle·ase \'n(y)ü-klē-ˌās\ *n* : an enzyme that promotes hydrolysis of nucleic acids
¹nu·cle·ate \'n(y)ü-klē-ˌāt\ *vb* **1** : to gather about or into a center; *also* : to act as a nucleus for or provide with a nucleus **2** : to form, act as, or have a nucleus — **nu·cle·a·tion** \ˌn(y)ü-klē-'ā-shən\ *n*
²nu·cle·ate \'n(y)ü-klē-ət\ *adj* : having a nucleus or nuclei ⟨*nucleate* cells⟩
nu·cle·ic acid \n(y)ü-ˌklē-ik-, -ˌklā-\ *n* : any of various acids composed of a sugar or derivative of a sugar, phosphoric acid, and a base and found esp. in cell nuclei
nu·cle·o·lus \n(y)ü-'klē-ə-ləs\ *n, pl* **-li** \-ˌlī\ [NL, fr. L, dim. of *nucleus*] : a body in a cell nucleus usu. held to be a center of synthetic activity or storage — **nu·cle·o·lar** \-lər\ *adj*
nu·cle·on \'n(y)ü-klē-ˌän\ *n* : a proton or a neutron esp. as part of the atomic nucleus
nu·cle·on·ics \ˌn(y)ü-klē-'än-iks\ *n* : a branch of physical science that deals with nucleons or with all phenomena of the atomic nucleus
nu·cleo·plasm \'n(y)ü-klē-ə-ˌplaz-əm\ *n* : the protoplasm of a nucleus; *esp* : NUCLEAR SAP — **nu·cleo·plas·mat·ic** \ˌn(y)ü-klē-ō-ˌplaz-'mat-ik\ *or* **nu·cleo·plas·mic** \-ˌklē-ə-'plaz-mik\ *adj*
nu·cleo·pro·tein \ˌn(y)ü-klē-ō-'prō-ˌtēn, -'prōt-ē-ən\ *n* : any of the proteins conjugated with nucleic acid that occur esp. in the nuclei of living cells and are an essential constituent of genes and viruses
nu·cle·o·side \'n(y)ü-klē-ə-ˌsīd\ *n* : a compound that is formed by partial hydrolysis of a nucleic acid or a nucleotide and contains a purine or pyrimidine base
nu·cle·o·tide \-ˌtīd\ *n* : a phosphoric ester of a nucleoside
nu·cle·us \'n(y)ü-klē-əs\ *n, pl* **-clei** \-klē-ˌī\ *also* **-cle·us·es** [NL, fr. L, kernel, fr. dim. of *nuc-, nux* nut] : a central point, group, or mass of something: as **a** : the small, brighter, and denser part of a galaxy or of the head of a comet **b** : a part of cell protoplasm held to be essential to vital phenomena and heredity, rich in nucleoproteins from which chromosomes and nucleoli arise, and bounded by a nuclear membrane **c** : a mass of gray matter or group of nerve cells in the central nervous system **d** : a characteristic and stable complex of atoms or groups in a molecule **e** : the positively charged central part of an atom that comprises nearly all of the atomic mass and that consists of protons and neutrons except in hydrogen which consists of one proton only
nu·clide \'n(y)ü-ˌklīd\ *n* [*nucleus* + *-ide* (fr. Gk *eidos* form)] : a species of atom characterized by the constitution of its nucleus — **nu·clid·ic** \n(y)ü-'klid-ik\ *adj*
¹nude \'n(y)üd\ *adj* [L *nudus*; akin to E *naked*] **1** : lacking an essential particular **2** : NAKED; *esp* : having no clothes on — **nude·ly** *adv* — **nude·ness** *n* — **nu·di·ty** \'n(y)üd-ət-ē\ *n*
²nude *n* **1** : a nude human figure esp. as depicted in art **2** : the condition of being nude ⟨in the *nude*⟩
nudge \'nəj\ *vt* : to touch or push gently; *esp* : to seek

the attention of by a push of the elbow — **nudge** *n* — **nudg·er** *n*

nu·di·branch \'n(y)üd-ə-ˌbraŋk\ *n, pl* **-branchs** \-ˌbraŋ(k)s\ [L *nudus* nude + *branchia* gill] : any of a group (Nudibranchia) of marine gastropod mollusks without a shell as adults and without true gills — **nudibranch** *adj* — **nu·di·bran·chi·ate** \ˌn(y)üd-ə-'braŋ-kē-ət\ *adj or n*

nud·ism \'n(y)ü-ˌdiz-əm\ *n* : the cult or practice of living unclothed — **nud·ist** \'n(y)üd-əst\ *n*

nu·ga·to·ry \'n(y)ü-gə-ˌtōr-ē, -ˌtōr-\ *adj* [L *nugari* to trifle, fr. *nugae* trifles] **1** : INCONSEQUENTIAL, WORTHLESS **2** : having no force : INOPERATIVE

nug·get \'nəg-ət\ *n* **1** : a solid lump usu. of precious metal **2** : something like a gold nugget ⟨*nuggets* of wisdom⟩

nui·sance \'n(y)üs-ᵊn(t)s\ *n* [OF *nuisir* to harm, fr. L *nocēre*] : an annoying or troublesome person or thing; *also* : an act or practice that constitutes a continuous invasion of the legal rights of another

nuisance tax *n* : an excise tax collected in small amounts directly from the consumer

¹null \'nəl\ *adj* [MF *nul*, lit., not any, fr. L *nullus*, fr. *ne-* not + *ullus* any] **1** : having no legal or binding force : INVALID, VOID **2** : amounting to nothing : NIL **3** : having no value : INSIGNIFICANT **4** : having no members ⟨*null* set⟩

²null *n* : ZERO

null and void *adj* : having no force, binding power, or validity

nul·li·fi·ca·tion \ˌnəl-ə-fə-'kā-shən\ *n* **1** : the act of nullifying : the state of being nullified **2** : the action of a state impeding or attempting to prevent the operation and enforcement within its territory of a law of the U.S. — **nul·li·fi·ca·tion·ist** \-sh(ə-)nəst\ *n*

nul·li·fi·er \'nəl-ə-ˌfī(-ə)r\ *n* **1** : one that nullifies **2** : one maintaining the right of nullification against the U.S. government

nul·li·fy \'nəl-ə-ˌfī\ *vt* **-fied; -fy·ing** : to make null or valueless; *also* : ANNUL

syn NULLIFY, NEGATE, ANNUL, INVALIDATE mean to deprive of effective or continued existence. NULLIFY implies counteracting completely the force, effectiveness, or value of something ⟨all his work *nullified* by one act of carelessness⟩ NEGATE implies the destruction or canceling out of each of two things by the other ⟨slavery *negates* freedom⟩ ANNUL suggests making ineffective by legal or official action ⟨the treaty *annuls* all previous agreements⟩ INVALIDATE implies a legal or moral flaw that makes something not acceptable or not valid ⟨his conclusions are *invalidated* by the fallaciousness of his argument⟩

nul·li·ty \'nəl-ət-ē\ *n, pl* **-ties 1** : the quality or state of being null; *esp* : legal invalidity **2** : something null; *esp* : an act with no legal effect

numb \'nəm\ *adj* [ME *nomen*, fr. pp. of *nimen* to take, seize] **1** : devoid of sensation esp. from cold **2** : devoid of emotion : INDIFFERENT — **numb** *vt* — **numb·ly** *adv* — **numb·ness** *n*

¹num·ber \'nəm-bər\ *n* [OF *nombre*, fr. L *numerus*] **1 a** : the sum of units : total of individual items ⟨the *number* of people in the room⟩ **b** : a group or aggregate not specifically enumerated — used collectively with a singular or distributively with a plural verb ⟨a small *number* of heaters is still available⟩ ⟨a *number* of accidents occur on wet roads⟩ **2 a** : numerable state : the possibility of being counted ⟨times without *number*⟩ ⟨mosquitoes in swarms beyond *number*⟩ **b** : the characteristic common to all collections whose members can be matched unit by unit : the property involved in seeing things as units subject to separating ⟨observing the difference between few and many and calling it *number*⟩ **3 a** : a unit belonging to a mathematical system and subject to its laws **b** *pl* : ARITHMETIC **4** : a distinction of word form to denote reference to one or more than one ⟨a verb agrees in *number* with its subject⟩; *also* : a form or group of forms so distinguished — compare PLURAL, SINGULAR **5** : a symbol (as a character, letter, or word) used to represent a mathematical number; *also* : such a number used to identify or designate ⟨*number* one on the list⟩ ⟨a phone *number*⟩ **6** *pl* : regular count esp. of syllables in poetry : METER; *also* : metrical verse **7** : a member of a sequence or series ⟨the best *number* on the program⟩ ⟨lost

the last *number* of the magazine⟩ **8** *pl* : a form of lottery in which bets are placed on numbers regularly published for other purposes **syn** see AMOUNT — **by the numbers 1** : in unison to a specific count or cadence **2** : in a systematic, routine, or mechanical manner

²number *vb* **num·bered; num·ber·ing** \-b(ə-)riŋ\ **1** : COUNT, ENUMERATE **2** : to claim as part of a total : INCLUDE **3** : to restrict to a definite number **4** : to assign a number to **5** : to comprise in number ⟨our group *numbered* 10 in all⟩ **6** : to comprise a total number ⟨his fans *number* in the millions⟩ — **num·ber·a·ble** \'nəm-b(ə-)rə-bəl\ *adj* — **num·ber·er** \-bər-ər\ *n*

num·ber·less \'nəm-bər-ləs\ *adj* : too many to count : INNUMERABLE ⟨the *numberless* stars in the sky⟩

Num·bers \'nəm-bərz\ *n* — see BIBLE table

numb·ing \'nəm-iŋ\ *adj* : causing numbness — **numb·ing·ly** \-iŋ-lē\ *adv*

numb·skull *var of* NUMSKULL

nu·mer·a·ble \'n(y)üm-(ə-)rə-bəl\ *adj* : capable of being counted

nu·mer·al \'n(y)üm-(ə-)rəl\ *n* [L *numerus* number] **1** : a symbol representing a number **2** *pl* : numbers designating by year a school or college class that are awarded for distinction in an extracurricular activity

nu·mer·ate \'n(y)ü-mə-ˌrāt\ *vt* [L *numerare* to count, fr. *numerus* number] : ENUMERATE

nu·mer·a·tion \ˌn(y)ü-mə-'rā-shən\ *n* **1** : the act or process or a system or instance of enumeration **2** : the reading in words of numbers expressed by numerals

nu·mer·a·tor \'n(y)ü-mə-ˌrāt-ər\ *n* **1** : the part of a fraction written above the line that signifies the number of parts of the denominator taken **2** : one that counts something

nu·mer·i·cal \n(y)ù-'mer-i-kəl\ *adj* : of or relating to number : denoting a number or expressed in numbers — **nu·mer·i·cal·ly** \-k(ə-)lē\ *adv*

nu·mer·ol·o·gy \ˌn(y)ü-mə-'räl-ə-jē\ *n* : the study of the occult significance of numbers — **nu·mer·ol·o·gist** \-jəst\ *n*

nu·mer·ous \'n(y)üm-(ə-)rəs\ *adj* **1** : consisting of or including a great number ⟨a *numerous* group of people⟩ **2** : of or relating to a great number : MANY ⟨late on *numerous* occasions⟩ **syn** see MANY — **nu·mer·ous·ly** *adv* — **nu·mer·ous·ness** *n*

nu·mis·mat·ic \ˌn(y)ü-məz-'mat-ik, -məs-\ *adj* [F *numismatique*, fr. Gk *nomismat-, nomisma* coin] **1** : of or relating to numismatics **2** : of or relating to coins — **nu·mis·mat·i·cal·ly** \-'mat-i-k(ə-)lē\ *adv*

nu·mis·mat·ics \-iks\ *n* : the study or collection of monetary objects (as coins, tokens, medals, or paper money) — **nu·mis·ma·tist** \n(y)ü-'miz-mət-əst\ *n*

num·mu·lar \'nəm-yə-lər\ *adj* [L *nummulus*, dim. of *nummus* coin] : circular or oval in shape

num·skull \'nəm-ˌskəl\ *n* [*numb* + *skull*] : a stupid person : DUNCE

nun \'nən\ *n* [OE *nunne*, fr. LL *nonna*] : a woman belonging to a religious order; *esp* : one under solemn vows of poverty, chastity, and obedience

Nunc Di·mit·tis \ˌnəŋk-də-'mit-əs\ *n* [L, now lettest thou depart; fr. the first words of the canticle] : the prayer of Simeon in Luke 2:29–32 used as a canticle

nun·ci·a·ture \'nən(t)-sē-ə-ˌchùr, 'nùn(t)-, -chər\ *n* **1** : the office or period of office of a nuncio **2** : a papal delegation headed by a nuncio

nun·cio \'nən(t)-sē-ˌō, 'nùn(t)-\ *n, pl* **-ci·os** [It, fr. L *nuntius* messenger] : a papal legate of the highest rank permanently accredited to a civil government

nun·cu·pa·tive \'nən-kyù-ˌpāt-iv, ˌnən-'kyü-pət-\ *adj* [ML *nuncupativus*, fr. LL, so-called, fr. L *nuncupare* to name, call, fr. *nomen* name + *capere* to take] : not written : ORAL ⟨a *nuncupative* will⟩

nun·nery \'nən-(ə-)rē\ *n, pl* **-ner·ies** : a convent of nuns

¹nup·tial \'nəp-shəl\ *adj* [L *nuptiae*, pl., wedding, fr. *nupt-, nubere* to be married] **1** : of or relating to marriage or a wedding **2** : characteristic of the breeding season **syn** see MATRIMONIAL

²nuptial *n* : MARRIAGE, WEDDING — usu. used in pl.

¹nurse \'nərs\ *n* [OF *nurice*, fr. LL *nutricia*, fr. L, fem. of *nutricius* nutritious] **1 a** : a woman who has the care of a young child **b** : one that fosters or advises **2** : one skilled or trained in caring for the sick or infirm esp.

TABLE OF NUMBERS

CARDINAL NUMBERS[1]			ORDINAL NUMBERS[4]	
NAME[2]	SYMBOL		NAME[5]	SYMBOL[6]
	arabic	roman[3]		
naught *or* zero *or* cipher	0		first	1st
one	1	I	second	2d *or* 2nd
two	2	II	third	3d *or* 3rd
three	3	III	fourth	4th
four	4	IV	fifth	5th
five	5	V	sixth	6th
six	6	VI	seventh	7th
seven	7	VII	eighth	8th
eight	8	VIII	ninth	9th
nine	9	IX	tenth	10th
ten	10	X	eleventh	11th
eleven	11	XI	twelfth	12th
twelve	12	XII	thirteenth	13th
thirteen	13	XIII	fourteenth	14th
fourteen	14	XIV	fifteenth	15th
fifteen	15	XV	sixteenth	16th
sixteen	16	XVI	seventeenth	17th
seventeen	17	XVII	eighteenth	18th
eighteen	18	XVIII	nineteenth	19th
nineteen	19	XIX	twentieth	20th
twenty	20	XX	twenty-first	21st
twenty-one	21	XXI	twenty-second	22d *or* 22nd
twenty-two	22	XXII	twenty-third	23d *or* 23rd
twenty-three	23	XXIII	twenty-fourth	24th
twenty-four	24	XXIV	twenty-fifth	25th
twenty-five	25	XXV	twenty-sixth	26th
twenty-six	26	XXVI	twenty-seventh	27th
twenty-seven	27	XXVII	twenty-eighth	28th
twenty-eight	28	XXVIII	twenty-ninth	29th
twenty-nine	29	XXIX	thirtieth	30th
thirty	30	XXX	thirty-first *etc*	31st
thirty-one *etc*	31	XXXI	fortieth	40th
forty	40	XL	fiftieth	50th
fifty	50	L	sixtieth	60th
sixty	60	LX	seventieth	70th
seventy	70	LXX	eightieth	80th
eighty	80	LXXX	ninetieth	90th
ninety	90	XC	hundredth *or* one hundredth	100th
one hundred	100	C	hundred and first *or*	101st
one hundred and one *or*	101	CI	one hundred and first *etc*	
one hundred one *etc*			two hundredth	200th
two hundred	200	CC	three hundredth	300th
three hundred	300	CCC	four hundredth	400th
four hundred	400	CD	five hundredth	500th
five hundred	500	D	six hundredth	600th
six hundred	600	DC	seven hundredth	700th
seven hundred	700	DCC	eight hundredth	800th
eight hundred	800	DCCC	nine hundredth	900th
nine hundred	900	CM	thousandth *or* one thousandth	1,000th
one thousand *or* ten hundred *etc*	1,000	M	two thousandth *etc*	2,000th
			five thousandth	5,000th
two thousand *etc*	2,000	MM	ten thousandth	10,000th
five thousand	5,000	$\overline{\text{V}}$	hundred thousandth *or*	100,000th
ten thousand	10,000	$\overline{\text{X}}$	one hundred thousandth	
one hundred thousand	100,000	$\overline{\text{C}}$	millionth *or* one millionth	1,000,000th
one million	1,000,000	$\overline{\text{M}}$	(continued on next page)	

[1]The cardinal numbers are used in simple counting or in answer to "how many?" The words for these numbers may be used as nouns (he counted to *twelve*), as pronouns (*twelve* were found), or as adjectives (*twelve* boys).
[2]In formal contexts the numbers one to one hundred and in less formal contexts the numbers one to nine are commonly written out, while larger numbers are given in numerals. In nearly all contexts a number occurring at the beginning of a sentence is usually written out. Except in very formal contexts numerals are invariably used for dates. Arabic numerals from 1,000 to 9,999 are often written without commas (1000; 9999). Year numbers are always written without commas (1783).
[3]The roman numerals are written either in capitals or in lowercase letters.
[4]The ordinal numbers are used to show the order of succession in which such items as names, objects, and periods of time are considered (the *twelfth* month; the *fourth* row of seats; the *18th* century).
[5]Each of the terms for the ordinal numbers excepting *first* and *second* is used in designating one of a number of parts into which a whole may be divided (a *fourth;* a *sixth;* a *tenth*) and as the denominator in fractions designating the number of such parts constituting a certain portion of a whole (*one fourth; three fifths*). When used as nouns the fractions are usually written as two words, although they are regularly hyphenated as adjectives (a *two-thirds* majority). When fractions are written in numerals, the cardinal symbols are used (¼, ⅗, ⅚).
[6]The arabic symbols for the cardinal numbers may be read as ordinals in certain contexts (January 1 = January first; 2 Samuel = Second Samuel). The roman numerals are sometimes read as ordinals (Henry IV = Henry the Fourth); sometimes they are written with the ordinal suffixes (XIXth Dynasty).

---

j joke; ŋ sing; ō flow; ȯ flaw; ȯi coin; th thin; t̲h̲ this; ü loot; u̇ foot; y yet; yü few; yu̇ furious; zh vision

DENOMINATIONS ABOVE ONE MILLION

American system[1]				British system[1]			
NAME	VALUE IN POWERS OF TEN	NUMBER OF ZEROS[2]	NUMBER OF GROUPS OF THREE 0's AFTER 1,000	NAME	VALUE IN POWERS OF TEN	NUMBER OF ZEROS[2]	POWERS OF 1,000,000
billion	10^9	9	2	milliard	10^9	9	—
trillion	10^{12}	12	3	billion	10^{12}	12	2
quadrillion	10^{15}	15	4	trillion	10^{18}	18	3
quintillion	10^{18}	18	5	quadrillion	10^{24}	24	4
sextillion	10^{21}	21	6	quintillion	10^{30}	30	5
septillion	10^{24}	24	7	sextillion	10^{36}	36	6
octillion	10^{27}	27	8	septillion	10^{42}	42	7
nonillion	10^{30}	30	9	octillion	10^{48}	48	8
decillion	10^{33}	33	10	nonillion	10^{54}	54	9
				decillion	10^{60}	60	10

[1]The American system of numeration for denominations above one million is the same as the French system, and the British system corresponds to the German. In the American system each of the denominations above 1,000 millions (the American *billion*) is 1,000 times the one preceding (one trillion = 1,000 billions; one quadrillion = 1,000 trillions). In the British system the first denomination above 1,000 millions (the British *milliard*) is 1,000 times the preceding one, but each of the denominations above 1,000 milliards (the British *billion*) is 1,000,000 times the preceding one (one trillion = 1,000,000 billions; one quadrillion = 1,000,000 trillions).
[2]For convenience in reading large numerals the thousands, millions, etc., are usually separated by commas (21,530; 1,155,465) or by half spaces (1 155 465). Serial numbers (as a social security number or the engine number of a car) are often written with hyphens (583-695-20).

under the supervision of a physician **3** : a worker of a social insect that cares for the young
²nurse *vb* **1** : to feed at the breast : SUCKLE **2** : REAR, EDUCATE **3 a** : to manage with care or economy **b** : to take charge of and watch over **4** : to care for as a nurse **5** : to hold in one's memory or consideration 〈*nurse* a grudge〉 **6** : to treat with special care 〈*nursed* his car over the rough road〉 **7** : to act or serve as a nurse — **nurs·er** *n*
nurse·maid \'nərs-ˌmād\ *n* : a girl employed to look after children
nurs·ery \'nərs-(ə-)rē\ *n, pl* **-er·ies 1 a** : a child's bedroom **b** : a place where children are temporarily cared for in their parents' absence **c** : DAY NURSERY **2** : something that fosters, develops, or promotes **3** : a place where plants (as trees or shrubs) are grown for transplanting, for use as stocks in grafting, or for sale
nurs·ery·maid \-(ə-)rē-ˌmād\ *n* : NURSEMAID
nurs·ery·man \-mən\ *n* : a man who keeps or works in a plant nursery
nursery rhyme *n* : a tale in rhymed verse for children
nursery school *n* : a school for children usu. under five years of age
nursing bottle *n* : a bottle with a rubber nipple used for feeding a baby
nurs·ling \'nərs-liŋ\ *n* **1** : one that is solicitously cared for **2** : a nursing child
¹nur·ture \'nər-chər\ *n* [MF *norriture*, fr. LL *nutritura* act of nursing, fr. L *nutrire* to nourish, nurse] **1** : TRAINING, UPBRINGING **2** : something that nourishes : FOOD **3** : the influences that modify the expression of the genetic potentialities of an organism
²nurture *vt* **nur·tured; nur·tur·ing** \'nərch-(ə-)riŋ\ **1** : to supply with nourishment **2** : EDUCATE **3** : to further the development of : FOSTER — **nur·tur·er** \'nər-chər-ər\ *n*
¹nut \'nət\ *n* [OE *hnutu*] **1 a** : a hard-shelled dry fruit or seed with a separable kernel and an inner kernel; *also* : this kernel **b** : a dry indehiscent one-seeded fruit with a woody outer layer **2 a** : a perforated block usu. of metal that has an internal screw thread and is used on a bolt or screw for tightening or holding something **3** : the ridge in a stringed musical instrument over which the strings pass on the upper end of the fingerboard **4 a** : a foolish, eccentric, or crazy person **b** : ENTHUSIAST — **nut·like** \-ˌlīk\ *adj*

nuts 2

²nut *vi* **nut·ted; nut·ting** : to gather or seek nuts
nut·crack·er \'nət-ˌkrak-ər\ *n* **1** : an instrument for cracking the shells of nuts **2** : a bird related to the crows that lives largely on seeds from the cones of the pine tree
nut·hatch \'nət-ˌhach\ *n* [ME *notehache*, fr. *note* nut + *hache* ax, fr. OF] : any of various small birds intermediate in appearance and habits between the titmice and creepers

nut·let \'nət-lət\ *n* **1 a** : a small nut **b** : a small fruit similar to a nut **2** : the stone of a drupelet
nut·meg \'nət-ˌmeg\ *n* **1** : the aromatic seed of a tree grown in the East and West Indies and Brazil; *also* : this tree **2** : a spice consisting of ground nutmeg seeds
nut·pick \-ˌpik\ *n* : a small sharp-pointed table implement for extracting the kernels from nuts
nu·tria \'n(y)ü-trē-ə\ *n* [Sp, otter, modif. of L *lutra*] **1** : COYPU **2** : the durable usu. light brown fur of the coypu
¹nu·tri·ent \'n(y)ü-trē-ənt\ *adj* [L *nutrire* to nourish] : furnishing nourishment
²nutrient *n* : a nutritive substance or ingredient
nu·tri·ment \'n(y)ü-trə-mənt\ *n* : something that nourishes or promotes growth and repairs the natural wastage of organic life
nu·tri·tion \n(y)u̇-'trish-ən\ *n* : the act or process of nourishing or being nourished; *esp* : the processes by which an animal or plant takes in and utilizes food substances — **nu·tri·tion·al** \-'trish-nəl, -ən-ᵊl\ *adj* — **nu·tri·tion·al·ly** \-ē\ *adv*
nu·tri·tion·ist \-'trish-(ə-)nəst\ *n* : a specialist in the study of nutrition
nu·tri·tious \n(y)u̇-'trish-əs\ *adj* : NOURISHING — **nu·tri·tious·ly** *adv* — **nu·tri·tious·ness** *n*
nu·tri·tive \'n(y)ü-trət-iv\ *adj* **1** : of or relating to nutrition **2** : NUTRITIOUS — **nu·tri·tive·ly** *adv*
nuts \'nəts\ *adj* **1** : ENTHUSIASTIC, KEEN **2** : CRAZY, DEMENTED
nut·shell \'nət-ˌshel\ *n* : the shell of a nut — **in a nutshell** : in a small compass
nut·ty \'nət-ē\ *adj* **nut·ti·er; -est 1** : containing or suggesting nuts (as in flavor) **2** : CRACKBRAINED, ECCENTRIC; *also* : mentally unbalanced — **nut·ti·ness** *n*
nux vom·i·ca \(')nəks-'väm-i-kə\ *n, pl* **nux vomica** [NL, lit., emetic nut] : the poisonous seed of an Asiatic tree that contains medically important alkaloids; *also* : this tree
nuz·zle \'nəz-əl\ *vb* **nuz·zled; nuz·zling** \'nəz-(ə-)liŋ\ [ME *noselen*, fr. *nose*] **1** : to push or rub with the nose **2** : to lie close : NESTLE
ny·lon \'nī-ˌlän\ *n* **1** : any of numerous strong tough elastic synthetic materials used esp. in textiles and plastics **2** *pl* : stockings made of nylon — **nylon** *adj*
nymph \'nim(p)f\ *n, pl* **nymphs** \'nim(p)fs, 'nim(p)s\ [Gk *nymphē* bride, nymph] **1** : one of the minor divinities of nature in ancient mythology represented as beautiful maidens dwelling in the mountains, forests, meadows, and waters **2** : any of various immature insects; *esp* : a larval insect that differs chiefly in size and degree of differentiation from the adult — **nymph·al** \'nim(p)-fəl\ *adj*
nys·tag·mus \nis-'tag-məs\ *n* [Gk *nystagmos* drowsiness, fr. *nystazein* to doze] : a rapid involuntary oscillation (as from dizziness) of the eyeballs — **nys·tag·mic** \-mik\ *adj*

ə abut; ᵊ kitten; ər further; a back; ā bake; ä cot, cart; au̇ out; ch chin; e less; ē easy; g gift; i trip; ī life

o \'ō\ *n, often cap* **1** : the 15th letter of the English alphabet **2** : ZERO

O *var of* OH

o- *or* **oo-** *comb form* [Gk *ōion*] : egg : ovum ⟨*oology*⟩ ⟨*oogonium*⟩

-o- [Gk, stem vowel of certain nouns and adjectives] — used as a connective vowel orig. to join word elements of Greek origin and now also to join word elements of Latin or other origin ⟨drunkometer⟩ ⟨speedometer⟩

o' *also* **o** \ə\ *prep* **1** *chiefly dial* : ON **2** : OF ⟨one o'clock⟩

oaf \'ōf\ *n* [of Scand origin; akin to E *elf*] : a stupid or awkward person — **oaf·ish** \'ō-fish\ *adj* — **oaf·ish·ly** *adv* — **oaf·ish·ness** *n*

oak \'ōk\ *n, pl* **oaks** *or* **oak** [OE *āc*] **1** : any of various trees or shrubs closely related to the beech and chestnut and having a rounded one-seeded thin-shelled nut **2** : the usu. tough hard durable wood of the oak much used for furniture and flooring — **oak** *adj* — **oak·en** \'ō-kən\ *adj*

oak apple *n* : a large round gall produced on oak leaves by a small wasp

oa·kum \'ō-kəm\ *n* [OE *ācumba*] : hemp or jute fiber impregnated with tar or a tar derivative and used in caulking seams and packing joints

oar \'ō(ə)r, 'o(ə)r\ *n* [OE *ār*] **1** : a long slender broad-bladed wooden implement for propelling or steering a boat **2** : OARSMAN — **oared** \'ō(ə)rd, 'o(ə)rd\ *adj*

oar·lock \'ō(ə)r-,läk, 'o(ə)r-\ *n* : a usu. U-shaped device for holding an oar in place

oars·man \'ō(ə)rz-mən, 'o(ə)rz-\ *n* : one who rows esp. in a racing crew

oa·sis \ō-'ā-səs\ *n, pl* **oa·ses** \-'ā-,sēz\ [Gk] : a fertile or green area in an arid region

oat \'ōt\ *n* [OE *āte*] **1** : a cereal grass with long spikelets in loose clusters that is widely grown for its seed which is used for human food and livestock feed **2** *pl* : a crop or plot of the oat; *also* : oat seed

oat·cake \-,kāk\ *n* : a thin flat oatmeal cake

oat·en \'ōt-ᵊn\ *adj* : of or relating to oats, oat straw, or oatmeal

oath \'ōth\ *n, pl* **oaths** \'ōthz, 'ōths\ [OE *āth*] **1** : a solemn appeal to God or to some revered person or thing to bear witness to the truth of one's word or the sacredness of a promise ⟨under *oath* to tell the truth⟩ **2** : a careless or profane use of a sacred name

oat·meal \'ōt-,mēl, ōt-'\ *n* : oats husked and crushed into coarse meal or flattened into flakes; *also* : porridge made from such meal or flakes

ob- *prefix* [NL, fr. L, in the way, in front, towards] : inversely ⟨obovate⟩ ⟨obcordate⟩

Oba·di·ah \,ō-bə-'dī-ə\ *n* **1** : a Hebrew prophet of Old Testament times **2** — see BIBLE table

¹ob·bli·ga·to \,äb-lə-'gät-ō\ *adj* [It, obligatory, fr. pp. of *obbligare* to oblige, fr. L *obligare*] : not to be omitted : OBLIGATORY — used as a direction in music

²obbligato *n, pl* **-gatos** *also* **-ga·ti** \-'gät-ē\ : a prominent accompanying part usu. played by a solo instrument ⟨a violin *obbligato*⟩; *also* : any accompanying part

ob·con·ic \(')äb-'kän-ik\ *adj* : conical with the apex below or forming the point of attachment

ob·cor·date \-'kor-,dāt\ *adj* : heart-shaped with the notch apical ⟨*obcordate* leaf⟩

ob·du·ra·cy \'äb-d(y)ə-rə-sē, äb-'d(y)ùr-ə-\ *n, pl* **-cies** : the quality or state or an instance of being obdurate

ob·du·rate \'äb-d(y)ə-rət, äb-'d(y)ùr-ət\ *adj* [L *obduratus*, pp. of *obdurare* to harden, fr. *ob-* in the way + *durus* hard] **1 a** : hardened in feelings **b** : stubbornly persistent in wrongdoing **2** : resisting change : UNYIELDING ⟨*obdurate* materials⟩ — **ob·du·rate·ly** *adv* — **ob·du·rate·ness** *n*

obe·di·ence \ō-'bēd-ē-ən(t)s, ə-\ *n* **1** : an act or instance of obeying **2** : the quality or state of being obedient

obe·di·ent \-ənt\ *adj* [L *oboedient-, oboediens*, fr. prp. of *oboedire* to obey] : submissive to the restraint or command of authority — **obe·di·ent·ly** *adv*

obei·sance \ō-'bās-ᵊn(t)s, -'bēs-\ *n* [MF *obeissance* obedience, obeisance, fr. *obeiss-, obeir* to obey] **1** : a movement of the body made in token of respect or submission : BOW **2** : DEFERENCE, HOMAGE — **obei·sant** \-ᵊnt\ *adj*

obe·lia \ō-'bēl-yə\ *n* : any of a genus of small colonial marine hydroids with colonies branched like trees

ob·e·lisk \'äb-ə-,lisk\ *n* [Gk *obeliskos*, fr. dim. of *obelos* spit] : a 4-sided pillar that tapers toward the top and ends in a pyramid

Ober·on \'ō-bə-,rän\ *n* : king of the fairies in medieval folklore

obese \ō-'bēs\ *adj* [L *obesus*] : excessively fat — **obe·si·ty** \ō-'bē-sət-ē\ *n*

obey \ō-'bā, ə-\ *vb* **obeyed; obey·ing** [OF *obeir*, fr. L *oboedire*] **1** : to follow the commands or guidance of **2** : to comply with : EXECUTE ⟨*obey* an order⟩ **3** : to behave obediently — **obey·er** *n*

ob·fus·cate \'äb-fə-,skāt, äb-'fəs-,kāt\ *vt* [LL *obfuscare*, fr. L *ob-* in the way + *fuscus* dark brown] **1** : to make dark or obscure **2** : CONFUSE — **ob·fus·ca·tion** \,äb-(,)fəs-'kā-shən\ *n* — **ob·fus·ca·to·ry** \äb-'fəs-kə-,tōr-ē, -,tor-\ *adj*

obi \'ō-bē\ *n* [Jap] : a broad sash worn with a Japanese kimono

obelisk

obit \ō-'bit, 'ō-bət\ *n* : OBITUARY

obi·ter dic·tum \,ō-bət-ər-'dik-təm\ *n, pl* **obiter dic·ta** \-tə\ [LL, lit., something said in passing] : an incidental remark or observation

obit·u·ary \ə-'bich-ə-,wer-ē\ *n, pl* **-ar·ies** [L *obitus* decease, fr. *obire* to go to meet, die, fr. *ob-* in the way + *ire* to go] : a notice of a person's death usu. with a short biographical account — **obituary** *adj*

¹ob·ject \'äb-jikt\ *n* [ML *objectum*, fr. L, neut. of *objectus*, pp. of *obicere* to throw in the way, present, object] **1 a** : something that may be seen or felt ⟨tables and chairs are *objects*⟩ **b** : something that may be perceived or examined mentally ⟨an *object* of study⟩ **2** : something that arouses an emotional response (as of affection, hatred, or pity) ⟨he is an *object* of envy⟩ **3** : AIM, PURPOSE ⟨the *object* is to raise money⟩ **4 a** : a noun or noun equivalent denoting someone or something that the action of a verb is directed toward **b** : a noun or noun equivalent in a prepositional phrase — **ob·ject·less** \'äb-jik-tləs\ *adj*

²ob·ject \əb-'jekt\ *vb* [L *object-, obicere* to throw in the way, object, fr. *ob-* in the way + *jacere* to throw] **1** : to offer or cite as an objection **2** : to state one's opposition to or oppose something **3** : to feel distaste for or disapproval of something — **ob·jec·tor** \-'jek-tər\ *n*

object ball \'äb-jik(t)-\ *n* : the ball first struck by the cue ball in pool or billiards; *also* : a ball hit by the cue ball

ob·jec·ti·fy \əb-'jek-tə-,fī\ *vt* **-fied; -fy·ing** : to make objective — **ob·jec·ti·fi·ca·tion** \-,jek-tə-fə-'kā-shən\ *n*

ob·jec·tion \əb-'jek-shən\ *n* **1** : an act of objecting **2** : a reason for or feeling of disapproval

ob·jec·tion·a·ble \-sh(ə-)nə-bəl\ *adj* : arousing objection : DISPLEASING, OFFENSIVE ⟨was written in *objectionable* language⟩ — **ob·jec·tion·a·ble·ness** *n* — **ob·jec·tion·a·bly** \-blē\ *adv*

¹ob·jec·tive \əb-'jek-tiv\ *adj* **1** : of or relating to an object or end ⟨reach our *objective* point⟩ **2** : existing outside and independent of the mind ⟨dragons have no *objective* existence⟩ **3** : treating or dealing with facts without distortion by personal feelings or prejudices ⟨an *objective* editorial⟩ ⟨an *objective* study⟩ **4** : of, relating to, or constituting a grammatical case marking typically the object of a verb or preposition — compare ACCUSATIVE — **ob·jec·tive·ly** *adv* — **ob·jec·tive·ness** *n* — **ob·jec·tiv·i·ty** \(,)äb-,jek-'tiv-ət-ē, əb-\ *n*

²objective *n* **1** : something toward which effort is directed : an aim or end of action : GOAL **2** : the objective case; *also* : a word in the objective case **3** : a lens or system of lenses (as in a microscope) that forms an image of an object

objective complement *n* : a noun, adjective, or pronoun used in the predicate as complement to a verb and as qualifier of its direct object ⟨*green* in "paint the wall green" is an *objective complement*⟩

object lesson \'äb-jikt-\ *n* : a lesson taught by means of illustrative objects or concrete examples; *also* : something that teaches by a concrete example

ob·jet d'art \,ōb-,zhä-'där\ *n, pl* **ob·jets d'art** *same*\ [F, lit., art object] : an article of artistic worth; *also* : CURIO

ob·jur·gate \'äb-jər-,gāt\ *vt* [L *objurgare*, fr. *ob-* toward + *jurgare* to quarrel, lit., to take to law, fr. *jur-, jus* law] : to denounce or reproach harshly — **ob·jur·ga·tion**

---

j joke; ŋ sing; ō flow; o̊ flaw; o̊i coin; th thin; t͟h this; ü loot; u̇ foot; y yet; yü few; yu̇ furious; zh vision

\ˌäb-jər-'gā-shən\ *n* — **ob·jur·ga·to·ry** \əb-'jər-gə-ˌtȯr-ē, -ˌtȯr-\ *adj*

ob·lan·ce·o·late \(')äb-'lan(t)-sē-ə-ˌlāt\ *adj* : inversely lanceolate ⟨an *oblanceolate* leaf⟩

oblast \'ȯ-ˌblast\ *n, pl* **oblasts** *or* **obla·sti** \-ˌblə-stē\ [Russ *oblast'*] : a political subdivision of a republic in the U.S.S.R.

¹ob·late \äb-ˌlāt, 'äb-ˌ\ *adj* [NL *oblatus*, fr. *ob-* + *-latus* (as in *prolatus* elongated in the direction of the poles, fr. L, used as pp. of *proferre* to extend, fr. *pro-* + *ferre* to carry)] : flattened or depressed at the poles ⟨the *oblate* shape of the earth⟩

²ob·late \'äb-ˌlāt\ *n* [ML *oblatus*, lit., one offered up, fr. L, pp. of *offerre* to offer] **1** : a layman living in a monastery under a modified rule and without vows **2** *cap* : a member of one of several Roman Catholic communities of men or women

obla·tion \ə-'blā-shən\ *n* [LL *oblation-, oblatio*, fr. *oblat-*, used as stem of *offerre* to offer] : a religious offering

¹ob·li·gate \'äb-li-gət, -lə-ˌgāt\ *adj* **1** : restricted to a particular mode of life ⟨an *obligate* parasite⟩ **2** : ESSENTIAL, NECESSARY — **ob·li·gate·ly** *adv*

²ob·li·gate \äb-lə-ˌgāt\ *vt* [L *obligare*, fr. *ob-* toward + *ligare* to bind] : to bring under obligation : bind legally or morally ⟨*obligated* to pay taxes⟩

ob·li·ga·tion \ˌäb-lə-'gā-shən\ *n* **1** : an act of obligating oneself to a course of action **2 a** : something (as the constraining power of a promise or contract) that binds one to a course of action **b** : something one is bound to do : DUTY **3 a** : INDEBTEDNESS **b** : money committed to a particular purpose : LIABILITY

oblig·a·to·ry \ə-'blig-ə-ˌtȯr-ē, 'äb-li-gə-, -ˌtȯr-\ *adj* : legally or morally binding : REQUIRED ⟨a meeting at which attendance was *obligatory*⟩ — **oblig·a·to·ri·ly** \ə-ˌblig-ə-'tȯr-ə-lē, ˌäb-li-gə-, -ˌtȯr-\ *adv*

oblige \ə-'blīj\ *vb* [OF *obliger*, fr. L *obligare* to obligate] **1** : FORCE, COMPEL ⟨laws *oblige* citizens to pay taxes⟩ **2 a** : to bind by a favor ⟨*oblige* an acquaintance by lending him money⟩ **b** : to do a favor for or do something as a favor ⟨a man always willing to *oblige*⟩ — **oblig·er** *n*

oblig·ing \ə-'blī-jiŋ\ *adj* : willing to do favors : ACCOMMODATING — **oblig·ing·ly** \-jiŋ-lē\ *adv* — **oblig·ing·ness** *n*

¹oblique \ō-'blēk, ə-, -'blīk; *military usu* ī\ *adj* [L *obliquus*] **1** : neither perpendicular nor parallel : INCLINED **2** : not straightforward : INDIRECT, DEVIOUS ⟨*oblique* accusations⟩ — **oblique·ly** *adv* — **oblique·ness** *n*

²oblique *n* **1** : something that is oblique **2** : any of several obliquely placed muscles; *esp* : one of the thin flat diagonal muscles of the abdominal wall

³oblique *adv* : at a 45 degree angle ⟨to the right *oblique*, march⟩

oblique angle *n* : an acute or obtuse angle

oblique case *n* : a grammatical case other than the nominative or vocative

obliq·ui·ty \ō-'blik-wət-ē, ə-\ *n, pl* **-ties** : the quality or state of being oblique: as **a** : deviation from what is proper or right : CROOKEDNESS, PERVERSITY **b** : deviation from a parallel or perpendicular condition : SLANT; *also* : the amount of this **c** : usu. deliberate obscurity of speech or conduct

oblit·er·ate \ə-'blit-ə-ˌrāt, ō-\ *vt* [L *oblitterare*, fr. *ob* in the way of + *littera* letter] **1** : to make undecipherable or imperceptible by wiping out or covering over **2** : to remove from recognition or memory : destroy all trace of **3** : CANCEL **syn** see ERASE — **oblit·er·a·tion** \-ˌblit-ə-'rā-shən\ *n* — **oblit·er·a·tive** \-'blit-ə-ˌrāt-iv\ *adj*

obliv·i·on \ə-'bliv-ē-ən\ *n* [L *oblivion-, oblivio*, fr. *oblivisci* to forget] **1** : an act or instance of forgetting **2** : the quality or state of being forgotten

obliv·i·ous \-ē-əs\ *adj* : lacking memory or mindful attention : FORGETFUL, UNAWARE — **obliv·i·ous·ly** *adv* — **obliv·i·ous·ness** *n*

ob·long \'äb-ˌlȯŋ\ *adj* [L *oblongus*, fr. *ob-* toward + *longus* long] : longer in one direction than in the other with opposite sides parallel : RECTANGULAR — **oblong** *n*

ob·lo·quy \'äb-lə-kwē\ *n, pl* **-quies** [LL *obloquium*, fr. *obloqui* to speak against, fr. *ob-* against + *loqui* to speak] **1** : strongly condemnatory utterance or language **2** : bad repute : DISGRACE

ob·nox·ious \äb-'näk-shəs, əb-\ *adj* [L *obnoxius*, fr. *ob* in the way of, exposed to + *noxa* harm] **1** : liable esp. to a hurtful influence — used with *to* **2** : OFFENSIVE, REPUGNANT — **ob·nox·ious·ly** *adv* — **ob·nox·ious·ness** *n*

oboe \'ō-bō\ *n* [It, fr. F *hautbois*, lit., high wood] : a woodwind musical instrument in the form of a slender cone-shaped tube with holes and keys that is played by blowing into a reed mouthpiece — **obo·ist** \-(ˌ)bō-əst\ *n*

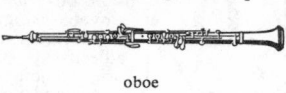

oboe

obol \'äb-əl, 'ō-bəl\ *n* [Gk *obolos*] : an ancient Greek coin or weight equal to ⅙ drachma

ob·ovate \(')äb-'ō-ˌvāt\ *adj* : ovate with the base narrower ⟨an *obovate* leaf⟩

ob·ovoid \-ˌvȯid\ *adj* : ovoid with the broad end toward the apex ⟨an *obovoid* fruit⟩

ob·scene \äb-'sēn, əb-\ *adj* [L *obscenus*] **1** : disgusting to the senses : REPULSIVE **2** : deeply offensive to morality or decency; *esp* : designed to incite to lust or depravity **syn** see COARSE — **ob·scene·ly** *adv*

ob·scen·i·ty \-'sen-ət-ē\ *n, pl* **-ties 1** : the quality or state of being obscene **2** : something that is obscene

ob·scur·ant \äb-'skyúr-ənt, əb-\ *or* **ob·scu·ran·tic** \ˌäb-skyə-'rant-ik\ *adj* : tending to make obscure — **ob·scu·ra·tion** \ˌäb-skyə-'rā-shən\ *n*

ob·scu·ran·tism \äb-'skyúr-ən-ˌtiz-əm, əb-; ˌäb-skyù-'ran-\ *n* **1** : opposition to the spread of knowledge **2 a** : deliberate vagueness or abstruseness **b** : an act or instance of obscurantism — **ob·scu·ran·tist** \-ən-təst, -'rant-əst\ *n or adj*

¹ob·scure \äb-'skyú(ə)r, əb-\ *adj* [L *obscurus*] **1** : lacking or inadequately supplied with light : DIM, GLOOMY **2 a** : withdrawn from the centers of human activity : REMOTE ⟨*obscure* country village⟩ **b** : not readily understood or not clearly expressed : ABSTRUSE **c** : lacking showiness or prominence : HUMBLE ⟨an *obscure* poet⟩ **d** : not distinct : FAINT **3** : constituting the unstressed vowel \ə\ or having unstressed \ə\ as its value — **ob·scure·ly** *adv* — **ob·scure·ness** *n*

syn OBSCURE, DARK, VAGUE mean not clearly understandable. OBSCURE implies a veiling of meaning through defective expression or a withholding of full knowledge; DARK implies an imperfect revelation often with ominous or sinister suggestion ⟨*dark* prophecies⟩ VAGUE implies lacking clarity because imperfectly conceived, grasped, or thought out

²obscure *vt* **1** : to make dark, dim, or indistinct **2** : to conceal or hide by or as if by covering **3** : to use the unstressed vowel \ə\ as the sound of

ob·scu·ri·ty \-'skyúr-ət-ē\ *n, pl* **-ties 1** : the quality or state of being obscure **2** : one that is obscure

ob·se·qui·ous \əb-'sē-kwē-əs, äb-\ *adj* [L *obsequi* to comply, fr. *ob-* toward + *sequi* to follow] : humbly or excessively attentive (as to a person in authority) : FAWNING, SERVILE — **ob·se·qui·ous·ly** *adv* — **ob·se·qui·ous·ness** *n*

ob·se·quy \'äb-sə-kwē\ *n, pl* **-quies** [ML *obsequiae*, pl., alter. of L *exsequiae*, fr. *exsequi* to follow out, fr. *ex-* + *sequi* to follow] : a funeral or burial rite — usu. used in pl.

ob·serv·a·ble \əb-'zər-və-bəl\ *adj* **1** : necessarily or customarily observed ⟨forms *observable* in social intercourse⟩ **2** : capable of being observed : DETECTABLE, NOTICEABLE ⟨an *observable* change⟩ ⟨*observable* distress⟩ — **ob·serv·a·bly** \-blē\ *adv*

ob·serv·ance \əb-'zər-vən(t)s\ *n* **1** : a customary practice or ceremony **2** : an act or instance of following a custom, rule, or law **3** : an act or instance of noticing : OBSERVATION

ob·serv·ant \-vənt\ *adj* **1** : paying strict attention : WATCHFUL **2** : careful in observing : MINDFUL **3** : quick to observe : KEEN — **ob·serv·ant·ly** *adv*

ob·ser·va·tion \ˌäb-sər-'vā-shən, -zər-\ *n* **1** : an act or the power of seeing or fixing the mind upon something **2** : the gathering of information (as for scientific studies) by noting facts or occurrences ⟨weather *observations*⟩ **3 a** : a conclusion drawn from observing : VIEW **b** : REMARK, COMMENT **4** : the fact of being observed — **obser·vation·al** \-shnəl, -shən-ᵊl\ *adj*

ob·serv·a·to·ry \əb-'zər-və-ˌtȯr-ē, -ˌtȯr-\ *n, pl* **-ries 1** : a place or institution given over to or equipped for observation of natural phenomena (as in astronomy) **2** : a place or structure commanding a wide view

ob·serve \əb-'zərv\ *vb* [L *observare* to guard, watch, observe, fr. *ob-* in front + *servare* to keep] **1** : to conform one's action or practice to ⟨*observe* rules⟩ **2** : CELEBRATE 1 **3** : to see or sense esp. through directed careful analytic attention : WATCH **4** : to come to realize or know esp. through consideration of noted facts : PERCEIVE **5** : to utter as a remark **6** : to make a scientific observation of syn see KEEP — **ob·serv·ing·ly** \-'zər-viṇ-lē\ *adv*

ob·serv·er \əb-'zər-vər\ *n* : one that observes; *esp* : a representative sent to observe but not participate officially in an activity

ob·sess \əb-'ses, äb-\ *vt* [L *obsess-, obsidēre* to besiege, fr. *ob-* + *sedēre* to sit] : to preoccupy intensely or abnormally

ob·ses·sion \äb-'sesh-ən, əb-\ *n* : a persistent disturbing preoccupation with an often unreasonable idea or feeling; *also* : an emotion or idea causing such a preoccupation — **ob·ses·sion·al** \-'sesh-nəl, -ən-°l\ *adj* — **ob·ses·sion·al·ly** \-ē\ *adv* — **ob·ses·sive** \-'ses-iv\ *adj* — **ob·ses·sive·ly** *adv*

ob·sid·i·an \əb-'sid-ē-ən\ *n* : a dark-colored natural glass formed by the cooling of molten lava

ob·so·les·cent \,äb-sə-'les-°nt\ *adj* : going out of use : becoming obsolete — **ob·so·lesce** \-'les\ *vi* — **ob·so·les·cence** \-'les-°n(t)s\ *n* — **ob·so·les·cent·ly** *adv*

ob·so·lete \,äb-sə-'lēt\ *adj* [L *obsoletus*, fr. pp. of *solescere* to grow old, become disused] : no longer in use : DISUSED ⟨an *obsolete* word⟩: **a** : OUTMODED ⟨*obsolete* machinery⟩ **b** : VESTIGIAL ⟨the appendix is an *obsolete* organ in man⟩ — **ob·so·lete·ly** *adv* — **ob·so·lete·ness** *n*

ob·sta·cle \'äb-sti-kəl\ *n* [L *obstaculum*, fr. *obstare* to stand in the way, fr. *ob-* in the way + *stare* to stand] : something that stands in the way or opposes : HINDRANCE, OBSTRUCTION

ob·stet·ri·cal \əb-'ste-tri-kəl\ *also* **ob·stet·ric** \-trik\ *adj* [L *obstetric-, obstetrix* midwife, fr. *obstare* to stand in front, fr. *ob-* in front + *stare* to stand] : of or relating to childbirth or obstetrics — **ob·stet·ri·cal·ly** \-tri-k(ə-)lē\ *adv*

ob·ste·tri·cian \,äb-stə-'trish-ən\ *n* : a physician specializing in obstetrics

ob·stet·rics \əb-'ste-triks\ *n* : a branch of medical science that deals with childbirth and with the care of women before, during, and after this

ob·sti·na·cy \'äb-stə-nə-sē\ *n, pl* **-cies** **1** : the quality or state of being obstinate **2** : an instance of being obstinate

ob·sti·nate \'äb-stə-nət\ *adj* [L *obstinatus*, fr. pp. of *obstinare* to be firm] **1** : clinging to an opinion, purpose, or course in spite of reason, arguments, or persuasion **2** : not easily subdued, remedied, or removed ⟨*obstinate* fever⟩ — **ob·sti·nate·ly** *adv* — **ob·sti·nate·ness** *n*

syn OBSTINATE, DOGGED, STUBBORN, PERTINACIOUS mean fixed and unyielding in course or purpose. OBSTINATE implies a persistent adherence and suggests unreasonableness and perversity ⟨too *obstinate* to take advice⟩ DOGGED suggests a tenacious sometimes sullen persistence ⟨shoveled with a *dogged* regularity⟩ STUBBORN implies sturdiness in resisting changes to change or abandon a course or opinion ⟨met persuasion with *stubborn* resistance⟩ PERTINACIOUS suggests an annoying persistence ⟨a *pertinacious* beggar⟩

ob·strep·er·ous \əb-'strep-(ə-)rəs, äb-\ *adj* [L *obstrepere* to clamor against, fr. *ob-* in front + *strepere* to make a noise] **1** : uncontrollably noisy : CLAMOROUS **2** : stubbornly defiant : UNRULY — **ob·strep·er·ous·ly** *adv* — **ob·strep·er·ous·ness** *n*

ob·struct \əb-'strəkt\ *vt* [L *obstruct-, obstruere*, fr. *ob-* in the way + *struere* to build] **1** : to block or close up by an obstacle **2** : to hinder from passage, action, or operation : IMPEDE **3** : to cut off from sight ⟨a wall *obstructing* the view⟩ — **ob·struc·tive** \-'strək-tiv\ *adj or n* — **ob·struc·tor** \-tər\ *n*

ob·struc·tion \əb-'strək-shən\ *n* **1** : an act of obstructing : the state of being obstructed **2** : something that obstructs : HINDRANCE

ob·struc·tion·ist \əb-'strək-sh(ə-)nəst\ *n* : a person who hinders progress esp. in a legislative body — **ob·struc·tion·ism** \-shə-,niz-əm\ *n* — **ob·struc·tion·is·tic** \-,strək-shə-'nis-tik\ *adj*

ob·tain \əb-'tān\ *vb* [MF *obtenir*, fr. L *obtinēre* to hold on to, possess, obtain, fr. *ob-* in the way + *tenēre* to hold]

1 : to gain or attain usu. by planning or effort **2** : to be generally recognized or established : PREVAIL — **ob·tain·a·ble** \-'tā-nə-bəl\ *adj* — **ob·tain·er** *n* — **ob·tain·ment** \-'tān-mənt\ *n*

ob·trude \əb-'trüd\ *vb* [L *obtrus-, obtrudere* to thrust at, fr. *ob-* in the way + *trudere* to thrust] **1** : to thrust out ⟨the tortoise *obtruded* his head⟩ **2** : to thrust forward or call to notice without warrant or request **3** : to thrust oneself upon attention syn see INTRUDE — **ob·trud·er** *n* — **ob·tru·sion** \-'trü-zhən\ *n*

ob·tru·sive \-'trü-siv, -ziv\ *adj* : inclined to obtrude : FORWARD, PUSHING — **ob·tru·sive·ly** *adv* — **ob·tru·sive·ness** *n*

ob·tuse \äb-'t(y)üs\ *adj* [L *obtusus* blunt, dull, fr. pp. of *obtundere* to blunt, fr. *ob-* in front + *tundere* to pound] **1** : lacking sharpness or quickness of wit : DULL, INSENSITIVE **2 a** (1) : exceeding 90 degrees but less than 180 degrees ⟨*obtuse* angle⟩ (2) : having an obtuse angle — see TRIANGLE illustration **b** : not pointed or acute : BLUNT ⟨an *obtuse* leaf⟩ syn see BLUNT — **ob·tuse·ly** *adv* — **ob·tuse·ness** *n*

¹ob·verse \äb-'vərs, 'äb-,\ *adj* [L *obversus*, fr. pp. of *obvertere* to turn toward, fr. *ob-* toward + *vertere* to turn] **1** : facing the observer or opponent **2** : having the base narrower than the top **3** : being a counterpart or complement — **ob·verse·ly** *adv*

²ob·verse \'äb-,vərs, äb-'\ *n* **1** : the side of something (as a coin or medal) bearing the principal design or lettering **2** : a front or principal surface **3** : COUNTERPART

ob·vi·ate \'äb-vē-,āt\ *vt* [LL *obviare* to meet, withstand, fr. L *obviam* in the way] : to anticipate and dispose of beforehand : make unnecessary ⟨*obviate* an objection⟩ — **ob·vi·a·tion** \,äb-vē-'ā-shən\ *n*

ob·vi·ous \'äb-vē-əs\ *adj* [L *obvius* being in the way, fr. *obviam* in the way, fr. *ob viam*] : easily discovered, seen, or understood : PLAIN ⟨an *obvious* mistake⟩ ⟨an *obvious* place to put it⟩ — **ob·vi·ous·ly** *adv* — **ob·vi·ous·ness** *n*

oc·a·ri·na \,äk-ə-'rē-nə\ *n* [It, fr. *oca* goose, fr. LL *auca*, fr. L *avis* bird] : a simple wind instrument usu. of terra-cotta having an oval body with finger holes and a projecting mouthpiece and giving soft flutelike tones — called also *sweet potato*

ocarina

¹oc·ca·sion \ə-'kā-zhən\ *n* [L *occasion-, occasio*, fr. *occidere* to fall, fall down, fr. *ob-* toward + *cadere* to fall] **1** : a favorable opportunity or circumstance **2** : a state of affairs that provides a ground or reason **3** : an occurrence or condition that brings something about; *esp* : the immediate inciting circumstance as distinguished from fundamental cause **4** : a time at which something happens **5** : a need arising from a particular circumstance : EXIGENCY **6** *pl* : AFFAIRS, BUSINESS **7** : a special event or ceremony : CELEBRATION

²occasion *vt* **oc·ca·sioned**; **oc·ca·sion·ing** \-'kāzh-(ə-)niṇ\ : to give occasion to : CAUSE

oc·ca·sion·al \ə-'kāzh-nəl, -ən-°l\ *adj* **1** : happening or met with now and then ⟨made *occasional* references to the war⟩ **2** : used or meant for a special occasion ⟨*occasional* verse⟩ — **oc·ca·sion·al·ly** \-ē\ *adv*

Oc·ci·dent \'äk-səd-ənt, -sə-,dent\ *n* [L *occident-, occidens*, fr. prp. of *occidere* to fall, set (of heavenly bodies), fr. *ob-* toward + *cadere* to fall] : WEST 2

oc·ci·den·tal \,äk-sə-'dent-°l\ *adj, often cap* **1** : of, relating to, or situated in the Occident : WESTERN **2** : of or relating to Occidentals — **oc·ci·den·tal·ly** \-°l-ē\ *adv*

Occidental *n* : a member of one of the indigenous peoples of the Occident

Oc·ci·den·tal·ism \-°l-,iz-əm\ *n* : the characteristic features of occidental peoples or culture — **Oc·ci·den·tal·ist** \-°l-əst\ *n*

oc·ci·den·tal·ize \-°l-,īz\ *vt, often cap* : to make occidental in standards or culture

oc·cip·i·tal \äk-'sip-ət-°l\ *adj* : of or relating to the occiput or the occipital bone — **occipital** *n* — **oc·cip·i·tal·ly** \-°l-ē\ *adv*

occipital bone *n* : a compound bone that forms the posterior part of the skull and articulates with the atlas

oc·ci·put \'äk-sə-(,)pət\ *n, pl* **occiputs** *or* **oc·cip·i·ta** \äk-'sip-ət-ə\ [L *occipit-, occiput*, fr. *ob-* toward + *capit-, caput* head] : the back part of the head or skull

---

j joke; ŋ sing; ō flow; ȯ flaw; ȯi coin; th thin; th̲ this; ü loot; u̇ foot; y yet; yü few; yu̇ furious; zh vision

oc·clude \ə-'klüd, ä-\ *vb* [L *occlus-, occludere,* fr. *ob-* in the way + *claudere* to shut, close] **1 :** to stop up **:** OBSTRUCT **2 :** to shut in or out **3 :** to take up and hold by absorption or adsorption **4 :** to come together with opposing surfaces in contact ⟨his teeth do not *occlude* properly⟩ — **oc·clud·ent** \-'klüd-ᵊnt\ *adj* — **oc·clu·sive** \-'klü-siv, -ziv\ *adj*

oc·clu·sion \ə-'klü-zhən\ *n* **:** the act of occluding **:** the state of being occluded

oc·cult \ə-'kəlt, ä-\ *adj* [L *occultus,* fr. pp. of *occulere* to cover up, hide] **1 :** not revealed **:** SECRET, HIDDEN **2 :** ABSTRUSE, MYSTERIOUS **3 :** of or relating to supernatural agencies, their effects, or knowledge of them — **oc·cult·ly** *adv*

oc·cul·ta·tion \,äk-(,)əl-'tā-shən\ *n* **1 :** the state of being hidden from view or lost to notice **2 :** the shutting out of the light of one celestial body by the intervention of another; *esp* **:** an eclipse of a star or planet by the moon

oc·cult·ism \ə-'kəl-,tiz-əm, ä-\ *n* **:** a belief in or study of supernatural powers and the possibility of subjecting them to human control — **oc·cult·ist** \-tƏst\ *n*

oc·cu·pan·cy \'äk-yə-pən-sē\ *n, pl* **-cies :** the act of occupying **:** the state of being occupied

oc·cu·pant \'äk-yə-pənt\ *n* **:** one that occupies something or takes or has possession of it

oc·cu·pa·tion \,äk-yə-'pā-shən\ *n* **1 :** an activity in which one engages; *esp* **:** one's business or vocation **2 a :** the taking possession of property **:** OCCUPANCY **b :** the taking possession or holding and controlling of an area by a foreign military force; *also* **:** such a military force — **oc·cu·pa·tion·al** \-shnəl, -shən-ᵊl\ *adj* — **oc·cu·pa·tion·al·ly** \-ē\ *adv*

occupational therapy *n* **:** therapy by means of activity; *esp* **:** creative activity prescribed for its effect in promoting recovery or rehabilitation — **occupational therapist** *n*

oc·cu·py \'äk-yə-,pī\ *vt* **-pied; -py·ing** [modif. of MF *occuper* to take possession of, fr. L *occupare,* fr. *ob-* in front + *-cupare* (fr. *capere* to take)] **1 a :** to engage the attention or energies of ⟨*occupy* oneself with reading⟩ **b :** to fill up (an extent in space or time) ⟨sports *occupied* his spare time⟩ ⟨a liter of water *occupies* 1000 cubic centimeters of space⟩ **2 :** to take or hold possession of **3 :** to reside in as an owner or tenant — **oc·cu·pi·er** \-,pī-(-ə)r\ *n*

oc·cur \ə-'kər\ *vi* **oc·curred; oc·cur·ring** \-'kər-iŋ\ [L *occurrere* to meet, occur, fr. *ob-* in the way + *currere* to run] **1 :** to be found or met with **:** APPEAR **2 :** to take place **3 :** to come to mind **:** suggest itself **syn** see HAPPEN

oc·cur·rence \ə-'kər-ən(t)s, -'kə-rən(t)s\ *n* **1 :** something that takes place; *esp* **:** something that happens unexpectedly **2 a :** the action or process of taking place **b :** the action or process of coming into view **:** APPEARANCE **syn** OCCURRENCE, EVENT, INCIDENT, EPISODE mean something that happens or takes place. OCCURRENCE suggests a happening without plan, intent, or volition; EVENT usu. implies a significant occurrence and frequently one resulting from or giving rise to another ⟨Columbus' voyage was one of the great *events* of history⟩ INCIDENT suggests an occurrence of brief duration or secondary importance ⟨the plot of the play is strung with amusing *incidents*⟩ or a minor but unusual happening of consequence ⟨the death of the little-known general was one of those *incidents* that pass unnoticed⟩ EPISODE stresses the distinctiveness or apartness of an incident ⟨a memorable *episode* in his life was his trip to Africa⟩

ocean \'ō-shən\ *n* [L *oceanus,* fr. Gk *ōkeanos*] **1 :** the whole body of salt water that covers nearly three fourths of the surface of the earth **2 :** one of the large bodies of water into which the great ocean is divided **3 :** an unlimited space or quantity — **ocean·ic** \,ō-shē-'an-ik\ *adj*

ocean·ar·i·um \,ō-shə-'nar-ē-əm, -'ner-\ *n, pl* **-i·ums** *also* **-ia** \-ē-ə\ **:** a large marine aquarium

ocean·go·ing \'ō-shən-,gō-iŋ\ *adj* **:** of, relating to, or suitable for travel on the ocean

ocean·og·ra·phy \,ō-shə-'näg-rə-fē\ *n* **:** a science that deals with the ocean and its phenomena — **ocean·og·ra·pher** \-fər\ *n* — **ocean·o·graph·ic** \,ō-shə-nə-'graf-ik\ *adj* — **ocean·o·graph·i·cal·ly** \-'graf-i-k(ə-)lē\ *adv*

Oce·anus \ō-'sē-ə-nəs\ *n* **:** the god of the great outer sea held in Greek mythology to encircle the earth

ocel·lus \ō-'sel-əs\ *n, pl* **ocel·li** \-'sel-,ī, -(,)ē\ [NL, fr. L, dim. of *oculus* eye] **1 :** a minute simple eye or eyespot of an

invertebrate **2 :** a spot of color encircled by a band of another color — **ocel·lar** \ō-'sel-ər\ *adj* — **ocel·lat·ed** \'ō-sə-,lāt-əd\ *adj* — **ocel·la·tion** \,ō-sə-'lā-shən\ *n*

oc·e·lot \'äs-ə-,lät, 'ō-sə-\ *n* [F, fr. Nahuatl *ocelotl* jaguar] **:** a medium-sized American wildcat ranging from Texas to Patagonia and having a tawny yellow or grayish coat marked with black

ocher *or* **ochre** \'ō-kər\ *n* [Gk *ōchra,* fr. fem. of *ōchros* yellow] **1 :** an earthy usu. red or yellow and often impure iron ore used as a pigment **2 :** the color of ocher and esp. of yellow ocher — **ocher·ous** \'ō-k(ə-)rəs\ *or* **ochre·ous** \'ō-k(ə-)rəs, -krē-əs\ *adj*

-ock \ək, ik, ,äk\ *n suffix* [OE *-oc*] **:** small one ⟨hill*ock*⟩

o'clock \ə-'kläk\ *adv* [contr. of *of the clock*] **1 :** according to the clock ⟨the time is three *o'clock*⟩ **2 :** — used for indicating position or direction as if on a clock dial ⟨an airplane approaching at eleven *o'clock*⟩

oco·ti·llo \,ō-kə-'tē-(y)ō\ *n* **:** a thorny scarlet-flowered shrub of the southwestern U.S. and Mexico

octa- *or* **octo-** *also* **oct-** *comb form* [Gk *oktō* & L *octo;* akin to E *eight*] **:** eight ⟨*octa*merous⟩ ⟨*oct*ane⟩ ⟨*octo*roon⟩

oc·ta·gon \'äk-tə-,gän\ *n* **:** a polygon of eight angles and eight sides — **oc·tag·o·nal** \äk-'tag-ən-ᵊl\ *adj* — **oc·tag·o·nal·ly** \-ᵊl-ē\ *adv*

oc·ta·he·dron \,äk-tə-'hē-drən\ *n, pl* **-drons** *or* **-dra** \-drə\ **:** a solid bounded by eight plane faces — **oc·ta·he·dral** \-drəl\ *adj*

oc·tam·e·ter \äk-'tam-ət-ər\ *n* **:** a line consisting of eight metrical feet

oc·tane \'äk-,tān\ *n* **:** any of several isomeric liquid hydrocarbons C_8H_{18}

octane number *n* **:** a number that is used to measure or indicate the antiknock properties of a liquid motor fuel and that increases as the likelihood of a knocking decreases — called also *octane rating*

oc·tant \'äk-tənt\ *n* [L *octant-, octans* eighth of a circle, fr. *octo* eight] **1 :** an instrument for observing altitudes of a celestial body from a moving ship or aircraft **2 :** any group of eight similar units or parts ⟨an *octant* of spores⟩

oc·tave \'äk-tiv, -,tāv\ *n* [L *octavus* eighth, fr. *octo* eight] **1 :** an 8-day period of observances beginning with the festival day **2 :** a stanza or poem of eight lines; *esp* **:** the first eight lines of an Italian sonnet — compare SESTET **3 a :** a musical interval embracing eight degrees **b :** a tone or note at this interval **c :** the whole series of notes, tones, or keys within this interval **4 :** a group of eight

oc·ta·vo \äk-'tā-vō, -'täv-ō\ *n, pl* **-vos** [L, abl. of *octavus* eighth] **:** the size of a piece of paper cut eight from a sheet; *also* **:** a book, a page, or paper of this size

oc·tet \äk-'tet\ *n* **1 :** a musical composition for eight voices or eight instruments; *also* **:** the performers of such a composition **2 :** a group or set of eight

oc·til·lion \äk-'til-yən\ *n* — see NUMBER table

Oc·to·ber \äk-'tō-bər\ *n* [L, fr. *octo* eight; fr. its having been orig. the 8th month of the Roman calendar] **:** the 10th month of the year

oc·to·dec·i·mo \,äk-tə-'des-ə-,mō\ *n, pl* **-mos** [L *octodecimus* eighteenth] **:** EIGHTEENMO

oc·to·ge·nar·i·an \,äk-tə-jə-'ner-ē-ən\ *n* [L *octogeni* eighty each, fr. *octoginta* eighty, fr. *octo* eight] **:** a person who is 80 or more but less than 90 years old

oc·to·pod \'äk-tə-,päd\ *n* **:** any of an order (Octopoda) of cephalopod mollusks comprising the octopuses, argonauts, and related 8-armed mollusks — **octopod** *adj* — **oc·top·o·dan** \äk-'täp-əd-ən\ *adj or n* — **oc·top·o·dous** \-əd-əs\ *adj*

oc·to·pus \'äk-tə-pəs\ *n, pl* **-pus·es** *or* **-pi** \-,pī, -,pē\ [Gk *oktōpod-, oktōpus* having eight feet, fr. *oktō* eight + *pod-, pous* foot] **1 :** any of various cephalopod sea mollusks having round the front of the head eight muscular arms with two rows of suckers which hold objects (as its prey) **2 :** something suggestive of an octopus; *esp* **:** a powerful grasping organization with many branches

oc·to·roon \,äk-tə-'rün\ *n* **:** a person of one-eighth Negro ancestry

oc·to·syl·lab·ic \,äk-tə-sə-'lab-ik\ *adj* **:** having eight syllables **:** composed of verses having eight syllables — **octosyllabic** *n*

¹oc·u·lar \'äk-yə-lər\ *adj* [L *oculus* eye; akin to E *eye*] **1 :** of or relating to the eye or the eyesight **2 :** obtained or perceived by the sight **:** VISUAL ⟨*ocular* proof⟩

octagon

²ocular *n* : EYEPIECE

oc·u·list \'äk-yə-ləst\ *n* **1** : OPHTHALMOLOGIST **2** : OPTOMETRIST

oc·u·lo·mo·tor \,äk-yə-lə-'mōt-ər\ *adj* **1** : moving or acting to move the eyeball **2** : of or relating to the oculomotor nerve

oculomotor nerve *n* : either of a pair of chiefly motor cranial nerves that arise from the midbrain and supply most muscles of the eye

odd \'äd\ *adj* [ON *oddi* point of land, triangle, odd number] **1** : being only one of a pair or set ⟨an *odd* shoe⟩ ⟨an *odd* chair⟩ **2 a** : not divisible by two without leaving a remainder ⟨1, 3, 5, and 7 are *odd* numbers⟩ **b** : numbered with an odd number ⟨an *odd* year⟩ **c** : somewhat more than the number mentioned ⟨fifty *odd* years ago⟩ **3** : additional to or apart from what is usual, planned on, or taken into account : RANDOM, CASUAL, OCCASIONAL ⟨*odd* jobs⟩ ⟨done at *odd* moments⟩⟨*odd* bits of material⟩ **4** : not usual or conventional : STRANGE ⟨an *odd* way of behaving⟩ — **odd·ly** *adv* — **odd·ness** *n*

odd·ball \-,bȯl\ *n* : one whose behavior is eccentric

Odd Fellow *n* : a member of one of the major benevolent and fraternal orders

odd·i·ty \'äd-ət-ē\ *n, pl* **-ties** **1** : one that is odd : ECCENTRICITY **2** : the quality or state of being odd ⟨the *oddity* of his behavior⟩

odd·ment \'äd-mənt\ *n* : something left over : REMNANT

odds \'ädz\ *n pl* **1** *archaic* : unequal things or conditions **2** : DIFFERENCE ⟨made little *odds* whether they stayed⟩; *esp* : a difference by which one thing is favored over another ⟨the *odds* are in favor of our side⟩ **3** : an equalizing allowance made to a bettor or contestant believed to have a smaller chance of winning **4** : DISAGREEMENT, QUARRELING ⟨the brothers were at *odds*⟩

odds and ends *n pl* : miscellaneous things or matters : ODDMENTS, REMNANTS

odds-on \'äd-'zȯn, -'zän\ *adj* : having or viewed as having a better than even chance to win

ode \'ōd\ *n* [LL, fr. Gk *ōidē*, lit., song, fr. *aidein* to sing] : a lyric poem characterized usu. by elevation of feeling and style, varying length of line, and complexity of stanza forms

-ode \,ōd\ *n comb form* [Gk *hodos*] **1** : way : path ⟨electr*ode*⟩ **2** : electrode ⟨di*ode*⟩

Odin \'ōd-ᵊn\ *n* : the chief god in Germanic mythology

odi·ous \'ōd-ē-əs\ *adj* : causing or deserving hatred or repugnance — **odi·ous·ly** *adv* — **odi·ous·ness** *n*

odi·um \'ōd-ē-əm\ *n* [L, hatred, fr. *odisse* to hate] **1** : the condition of being generally hated and condemned usu. for despicable conduct : merited loathing **2** : the disgrace or shame attached to something considered hateful or low

odom·e·ter \ō-'däm-ət-ər\ *n* [Gk *hodos* way, road] : an instrument for measuring the distance traversed (as by a vehicle)

odo·nate \'ōd-ᵊn-,āt\ *n* : any of an order (Odonata) of predacious insects comprising the dragonflies and damselflies — **odonate** *adj*

odon·toid \ō-'dän-,tȯid\ *adj* : shaped like a tooth

odon·tol·o·gy \(,)ō-,dän-'täl-ə-jē\ *n* [Gk *odont-, odous* tooth; akin to E *tooth*] : a science dealing with the teeth, their structure and development, and their diseases — **odon·tol·o·gist** \-jəst\ *n*

odor \'ōd-ər\ *n* [OF *odour*, fr. L *odor*] **1** : a quality of something that stimulates the nasal sensory organs that receive smell : SCENT; *also* : the resulting sensation : SMELL **2 a** : a predominant quality : FLAVOR **b** : REPUTE, ESTIMATION ⟨in bad *odor*⟩ **syn** see SMELL — **odored** \-ərd\ *adj* — **odor·less** \-ər-ləs\ *adj*

odor·ant \'ōd-ə-rənt\ *n* : an odorous substance

odor·if·er·ous \,ōd-ə-'rif-(ə-)rəs\ *adj* **1 a** : producing an odorous substance **b** : ODOROUS **2** : morally offensive — **odor·if·er·ous·ly** *adv* — **odor·if·er·ous·ness** *n*

odor·ous \'ōd-ə-rəs\ *adj* : having an odor : SCENTED: as **a** : FRAGRANT **b** : MALODOROUS — **odor·ous·ly** *adv* — **odor·ous·ness** *n*

odour \'ōd-ər\ *chiefly Brit var of* ODOR

Odys·seus \ō-'dish-,üs, -'dis-ē-əs\ *n* : a king of Ithaca and Greek leader in the Trojan War whose ten-year wanderings after the war are related in Homer's *Odyssey*

od·ys·sey \'äd-ə-sē\ *n, pl* **-seys** [the *Odyssey*, epic poem attributed to Homer recounting the long wanderings of

Odysseus] : a long wandering usu. marked by many changes of fortune

Oe·di·pus \'ed-ə-pəs, 'ēd-\ *n* : a son of the king and queen of Thebes who according to Greek legend unwittingly kills his father and marries his mother as foretold by an oracle

Oedipus complex *n* : a positive sexual orientation of a child toward the parent of the opposite sex that may persist as a source of adult personality disorder — **oe·di·pal** \'ed-ə-pəl, 'ēd-\ *adj*

oe·do·go·ni·um \,ēd-ə-'gō-nē-əm\ *n* : any of a genus of filamentous green algae often studied in the laboratory

Oe·no·ne \ē-'nō-nē\ *n* : a nymph of Mount Ida and wife of Paris who abandons her for Helen of Troy

¹o'er \'ō(ə)r, 'ȯ(ə)r\ *adv* : OVER

²o'er \'(')ō(ə)r, '(')ȯ(ə)r\ *prep* : OVER

oer·sted \'ər-stəd\ *n* [Hans Christian *Oersted* d1851 Danish physicist] : a unit of magnetic intensity equal to the intensity of a magnetic field in a vacuum in which a unit magnetic pole experiences a mechanical force of one dyne in the direction of the field

oe·soph·a·gus *var of* ESOPHAGUS

oestr- *or* **oestro-** — see ESTR-

of \əv, 'əv, 'äv\ *prep* [OE, off, adv. & prep., from, of] **1** : from as a point of reckoning ⟨*north of* the lake⟩ **2 a** : from by origin or derivation ⟨a man *of* noble birth⟩ **b** : from as a consequence ⟨died *of* flu⟩ **c** : by as author or doer ⟨plays *of* Shakespeare⟩ **d** : as experienced or performed by ⟨love *of* a parent for his child⟩ **3** : having as its material, parts, or contents ⟨throne *of* gold⟩⟨cup *of* water⟩ **4** — used as a function word to indicate the whole that includes the part denoted by the preceding word ⟨most *of* the army⟩ **5 a** : CONCERNING ⟨stories *of* his travels⟩ **b** : in respect to ⟨slow *of* speech⟩ **6** : possessed by : belonging to ⟨courage *of* the pioneers⟩ **7** — used as a function word to indicate separation ⟨eased *of* pain⟩ **8** : specified as ⟨the city *of* Rome⟩ **9** : having as its object ⟨love *of* nature⟩ **10** : having as a distinctive quality or possession ⟨a man *of* courage⟩

¹off \'ȯf\ *adv* [OE *of*] **1 a** (1) : from a place or position ⟨march *off*⟩ (2) : away from land ⟨ship stood *off* to sea⟩ **b** : so as to prevent close approach ⟨drove the dogs *off*⟩ **c** (1) : from a course : ASIDE ⟨turned *off* into a bypath⟩ (2) : away from the wind **d** : into an unconscious state ⟨dozed *off*⟩ **2 a** : so as not to be supported ⟨rolled to the edge of the table and *off*⟩ or covering or enclosing ⟨blew the lid *off*⟩ or attached ⟨the handle came *off*⟩ **b** : so as to be divided ⟨surface marked *off* into squares⟩ **3** : to a state of discontinuance ⟨shut *off* an engine⟩ or exhaustion ⟨drink *off* a glass⟩ or completion ⟨coat of paint to finish it *off*⟩ **4** : in absence from or suspension of regular work or service ⟨take time *off* for lunch⟩ **5** : at a distance in space or time ⟨stood 10 paces *off*⟩

²off \(')ȯf\ *prep* **1** : away from; *esp* : from a place or situation on ⟨take it *off* the table⟩ **2** : at the expense of ⟨lived *off* his sister⟩ **3** : to seaward of ⟨two miles *off* shore⟩ **4 a** : not now engaged in ⟨*off* duty⟩ **b** : below the usual standard or level of ⟨*off* his game⟩ ⟨a dollar *off* the list price⟩ **5 a** : diverging or opening from ⟨a path *off* the main walk⟩ **b** : being or occurring away or apart from ⟨a shop just *off* the main street⟩

³off \(')ȯf\ *adj* **1 a** : more removed or distant ⟨the *off* side of the building⟩ **b** : SEAWARD **c** : RIGHT **2 a** : started on the way ⟨*off* on a spree⟩ **b** : CANCELED **c** : not operating **d** : not placed so as to permit operation **3 a** : not corresponding to fact : INCORRECT ⟨*off* in his reckoning⟩ **b** : POOR, SUBNORMAL **c** : not entirely sane : ECCENTRIC **d** : REMOTE, SLIGHT ⟨an *off* chance⟩ **4 a** : spent off duty ⟨reading on his *off* days⟩ **b** : SLACK ⟨*off* season⟩ **5 a** : OFF-COLOR **b** : INFERIOR ⟨*off* grade of oil⟩ **c** : DOWN 1c ⟨stocks were *off*⟩ **6** : CIRCUMSTANCED ⟨well *off*⟩

of·fal \'ȯ-fəl, 'äf-əl\ *n* **1** : the waste or by-product of a process: as **a** : trimmings of a hide **b** : the by-products of milling used esp. for stock feeds **c** : the viscera and trimmings of a butchered animal removed in dressing **2** : RUBBISH

¹off·beat \'ȯf-,bēt\ *n* : the unaccented part of a musical measure

²offbeat *adj* : ECCENTRIC, UNCONVENTIONAL ⟨offers *offbeat* entertainment⟩

off-col·or \'ȯf-'kəl-ər\ *or* **off-col·ored** \-ərd\ *adj* **1** : not having the right or standard color **2 :** of doubtful propriety **: RISQUÉ**

of·fend \ə-'fend\ *vb* [L *offens-, offendere* to strike against, offend, fr. *ob-* in the way + *-fendere* to strike] **1 a :** to transgress the moral or divine law **: SIN b :** to violate the law **:** do wrong ⟨*offend* against the law⟩ **2 a :** to cause difficulty or discomfort or injury **b :** to cause dislike, anger, or vexation **3 :** to cause pain to **4 :** to cause to feel vexed or resentful esp. by hurting pride or self-respect — **of·fend·er** *n*

syn OFFEND, OUTRAGE, INSULT, AFFRONT mean to cause hurt feelings or deep resentment. OFFEND may suggest a violating of ideas of what is right or proper without implying intent ⟨sounds that *offend* the sensitive ear⟩ OUTRAGE implies offending beyond endurance and calling forth extreme feelings ⟨*outraged* by the vandalism⟩ INSULT suggests deliberately and insolently causing humiliation, hurt pride, or shame; AFFRONT implies treating with deliberate rudeness or contempt ⟨*affronted* by his insinuations of the inferiority of their product⟩

of·fense *or* **of·fence** \ə-'fen(t)s, *esp for 2* 'äf-,en(t)s\ *n* **1 :** something that outrages the moral or physical senses **: NUISANCE 2 a :** the act of attacking **: ASSAULT b :** the side that is attacking in a contest or battle **3 a :** the act of displeasing or affronting **b :** the state of being insulted or morally outraged **4 a :** SIN, MISDEED **b :** an infraction of law **: CRIME** — **of·fense·less** \-ləs\ *adj*

¹of·fen·sive \ə-'fen(t)-siv\ *adj* **1 :** relating to or made or suited for attack ⟨*offensive* weapons⟩ **2 :** causing unpleasant sensations ⟨*offensive* smells⟩ **3 :** causing displeasure or resentment **: INSULTING** ⟨an *offensive* remark⟩ — **of·fen·sive·ly** *adv* — **of·fen·sive·ness** *n*

²offensive *n* **1 :** the act, attitude, or position of an attacking party ⟨on the *offensive*⟩ **2 :** ATTACK ⟨launch an *offensive*⟩

¹of·fer \'ôf-ər, 'äf-\ *vb* **of·fered; of·fer·ing** \-(ə-)riŋ\ [L *offerre* to present, fr. *ob-* toward + *ferre* to carry] **1 :** to present as an act of worship **: SACRIFICE 2 a :** to present for acceptance or rejection **: TENDER b :** to propose as payment **: BID 3 a :** PROPOSE, SUGGEST **b :** to declare one's readiness or willingness ⟨*offered* to help me⟩ **4 a :** to put up ⟨*offered* stubborn resistance⟩ **b :** THREATEN ⟨*offered* to strike him with his cane⟩ **5 :** to place (merchandise) on sale

²offer *n* **1 a :** PROPOSAL **b :** an undertaking to do an act or give something on condition that the party to whom the proposal is made do some specified act or make a return promise **2 :** a price named by one proposing to buy **: BID 3 a :** ATTEMPT, TRY **b :** an action or movement indicating a purpose or intention

of·fer·ing *n* **1 a :** the act of one who offers **b :** something offered; *esp :* a sacrifice ceremonially offered as a part of worship **c :** a contribution to the support of a church **2 :** something offered for sale **3 :** a course of instruction or study

of·fer·to·ry \'ôf-ə(r)-,tōr-ē, 'äf-, -,tôr-\ *n, pl* **-ries 1** *often cap* **a :** the offering of the sacramental bread and wine to God before they are consecrated **b :** a verse from a psalm said or sung at the beginning of the offertory **2 a :** the presentation of the offerings of the congregation at public worship **b :** the musical accompaniment played or sung during an offertory

off·hand \'ôf-'hand\ *adv (or adj)* **1 :** without previous thought or preparation **: EXTEMPORE 2 :** from a standing position without a support or rest ⟨*offhand* shooting⟩ **off·hand·ed** \-'han-dəd\ *adj* **: OFFHAND** — **off·hand·ed·ly** *adv* — **off·hand·ed·ness** *n*

of·fice \'ôf-əs, 'äf-\ *n* [L *officium* service, duty, fr. *opus* work + *facere* to do] **1 a :** a special duty, charge, or position; *esp :* a position of authority in government ⟨hold public *office*⟩ **b :** a position of responsibility or some degree of executive authority ⟨the *office* of chairman⟩ **2 :** a prescribed form or service of worship; *esp, cap :* DIVINE OFFICE **3 :** RITE **4 a :** an assigned or assumed duty, task, or role **b :** FUNCTION **5 :** a place where a business is transacted or a service is supplied ⟨ticket *office*⟩: as **a :** a place in which record keeping and clerical work are performed **b :** the directing headquarters of an enterprise or organization **c :** the place in which a professional man (as a physician or lawyer) conducts his business **6 a :** a major administrative unit in some governments ⟨British

Foreign *Office*⟩ **b :** a subdivision of some government departments ⟨Patent *Office*⟩

office boy *n* **:** a boy employed for odd jobs in a business office

of·fice·hold·er \-,hōl-dər\ *n* **:** one holding a public office

¹of·fi·cer \'ôf-ə-sər, 'äf-\ *n* **1 :** a policeman or other person charged with the enforcement of law **2 :** one who holds an office of trust, authority, or command **3 a :** one who holds a commission in the armed forces **b :** the master or mate of a merchant or passenger ship

²officer *vt* **1 :** to furnish with officers **2 :** to command or direct as an officer

¹of·fi·cial \ə-'fish-əl\ *n* **:** one who holds an office **: OFFICER**

²official *adj* **1 :** of or relating to an office, position, or trust ⟨*official* duties⟩ **2 :** holding an office ⟨an *official* referee⟩ **3 a :** AUTHORIZED, AUTHORITATIVE **b :** prescribed by authority **:** recognized as authorized **4 :** befitting or characteristic of a person in office **: FORMAL** ⟨an *official* greeting⟩ — **of·fi·cial·ly** \-'fish-(ə-)lē\ *adv*

of·fi·cial·dom \ə-'fish-əl-dəm\ *n* **:** officials as a class

of·fi·cial·ism \-'fish-ə-,liz-əm\ *n* **:** lack of flexibility and initiative combined with excessive adherence to regulations (as in the behavior of government officials)

of·fi·ci·ant \ə-'fish-ē-ənt\ *n* **:** an officiating clergyman

of·fi·ci·ate \ə-'fish-ē-,āt\ *vi* **1 :** to perform a ceremony, function, or duty **2 :** to act in an official capacity; *esp :* to preside as an officer — **of·fi·ci·a·tion** \-,fish-ē-'ā-shən\ *n*

of·fic·i·nal \ə-'fis-ªn-əl, ,ō-fə-'sīn-ºl\ *adj* [ML *officina* storeroom, fr. L, workshop, fr. *opific-, opifex* workman, fr. *opus* work + *facere* to do] **1 :** kept in stock and ready for dispensing without special compounding ⟨an *officinal* remedy⟩; *also :* OFFICIAL 3b ⟨*officinal* drugs⟩ **2 :** MEDICINAL ⟨*officinal* herbs⟩

of·fi·cious \ə-'fish-əs\ *adj* [L *officiosus* obliging, helpful, fr. *officium* service, office] **:** volunteering one's services where they are neither asked nor needed **: MEDDLESOME** — **of·fi·cious·ly** *adv* — **of·fi·cious·ness** *n*

off·ing \'ôf-iŋ, 'äf-\ *n* **1 :** the part of the deep sea seen from the shore **2 :** the near or foreseeable future or distance (sees trouble in the *offing*)

off·ish \'ôf-ish\ *adj* **:** inclined to be formal, stiff, or aloof in manner — **off·ish·ly** *adv* — **off·ish·ness** *n*

off·print \'ôf-,print\ *n* **:** a separately printed excerpt (as from a magazine)

¹off·set \'ôf-,set\ *n* **1 a :** a short prostrate shoot arising from the base of a plant **b :** OFFSHOOT 2b **2 :** a horizontal ledge on the face of a wall formed by a diminution of its thickness above **3 :** an abrupt bend in an object by which one part is turned aside out of line **4 :** something that serves to counterbalance or to compensate for something else **5 a :** unintentional transfer of ink (as on a freshly printed sheet) **b :** a printing process in which an inked impression is first made on a rubber-blanketed cylinder and then transferred to the paper being printed

²off·set \'ôf-,set, *1 is also* ôf-'\ *vb* **-set; -set·ting 1 a :** to place over against **: BALANCE** ⟨credits *offset* debits⟩ **b :** to compensate for **: COUNTERBALANCE 2 :** to form an offset in ⟨*offset* a wall⟩ **syn** see COMPENSATE

off·shoot \'ôf-,shüt\ *n* **1 :** a branch of a main stem esp. of a plant **2 a :** a lateral branch (as of a mountain range) **b :** a collateral or derived branch, descendant, or member

¹off·shore \'ôf-'shō(ə)r, -'shó(ə)r\ *adv* **:** from the shore **:** at a distance from the shore

²off·shore \'ôf-,\ *adj* **1 :** coming or moving away from the shore ⟨an *offshore* breeze⟩ **2 a :** situated off the shore and esp. within a zone extending three miles from low-water line ⟨*offshore* fisheries⟩ **b :** distant from the shore

off side *adv (or adj)* **:** illegally in advance of the ball or puck

off·spring \'ôf-,spriŋ\ *n, pl* **offspring** *also* **offsprings :** the progeny of an animal or plant **: YOUNG**

off·stage \-'stāj\ *adv (or adj)* **:** off or away from the stage

off-the-rec·ord *adj* **:** given or made in confidence and not for publication ⟨*off-the-record* remarks⟩

off-white \'ôf-'hwīt\ *n* **:** a yellowish or grayish white

off year *n* **1 :** a year in which no major election is held **2 :** a year of diminished activity or production

oft \'ôft\ *adv* **:** OFTEN ⟨an *oft* neglected factor⟩

of·ten \'ô-fən, 'ôf-tən\ *adv* [ME, alter. of *oft, ofte,* fr. OE *oft*] **:** many times **: FREQUENTLY**

of·ten·times \-,tīmz\ *or* **oft·times** \'ôf(t)-,tīmz\ *adv* **:** OFTEN

ə abut; ᵊ kitten; ər further; a back; ā bake; ä cot, cart; aù out; ch chin; e less; ē easy; g gift; i trip; ī life

ogee *also* **OG** \'ō-,jē\ *n* **1** : a molding with an S-shaped profile **2** : a pointed arch having on each side a reversed curve near the apex — see ARCH illustration

¹ogle \'ō-gəl\ *vb* **ogled; ogling** \-g(ə-)liŋ\ : to glance or stare in a flirtatious way : eye amorously — **ogler** \-g(ə-)lər\ *n*

²ogle *n* : an amorous or coquettish glance

ogre \'ō-gər\ *n* [F] **1** : a hideous giant of fairy tales and folklore that feeds on human beings : MONSTER **2** : a dreaded person or object — **ogre·ish** \'ō-g(ə-)rish\ *adj* — **ogress** \'ō-g(ə-)rəs\ *n*

¹oh \(')ō\ *interj* **1** — used to express various emotions (as astonishment, pain, or desire) **2** — used in direct address ⟨*Oh* sir, you forgot your change⟩

²oh \'ō\ *n* : ZERO

ohm \'ōm\ *n* [after G. S. *Ohm* d1854 German physicist] : the mks unit of electric resistance equal to the resistance of a circuit in which a potential difference of one volt produces a current of one ampere — **ohm·ic** \'ō-mik\ *adj*

ohm·age \'ō-mij\ *n* : the ohmic resistance of a conductor

ohm·me·ter \'ō(m)-,mēt-ər\ *n* : an instrument for indicating resistance in ohms directly

¹-oid \,oid\ *n suffix* : something resembling a (specified) object or having a (specified) quality ⟨planet*oid*⟩

²-oid *adj suffix* [L *-oïdes*, fr. Gk *-oeidēs*, fr. *-o-* + *eidos* appearance, form] : resembling : having the form or appearance of ⟨petal*oid*⟩

¹oil \'òil\ *n* [OF *oile*, fr. L *oleum* olive oil, fr. Gk *elaion*, fr. *elaia* olive] **1 a** : any of numerous greasy combustible and usu. liquid substances from plant, animal, or mineral sources that are soluble in ether but not in water **b** : PETROLEUM **2** : a substance of oily consistency **3 a** : an oil color used by an artist **b** : a painting done in oil colors — **oil** *adj*

²oil *vt* : to treat, furnish, or lubricate with oil

oil·cloth \'òil-,klòth\ *n* : cloth treated with oil or paint and used for table and shelf coverings

oil color *n* : a pigment used for oil paint

oil·er \'òi-lər\ *n* : one that oils; *esp* : a receptacle or device for applying oil

oil field *n* : a region rich in petroleum deposits

oil gland *n* : a gland (as of the skin) that produces an oily secretion

oil of vitriol : concentrated sulfuric acid

oil of wintergreen : the methyl ester of salicylic acid used as a flavoring

oil paint *n* : paint in which a drying oil is the vehicle

oil painting *n* **1 a** : the act or art of painting in oil colors **b** : a picture painted in oils **2** : painting that uses pigments ground in oil

oil·seed \'òil-,sēd\ *n* : a seed or crop (as linseed) grown largely for oil

oil·skin \-,skin\ *n* **1** : an oiled waterproof cloth used for coverings and garments **2** : an oilskin raincoat **3** *pl* : an oilskin suit of coat and trousers

oil slick *n* : a film of oil floating on water

oil·stone \'òil-,stōn\ *n* : a whetstone for use with oil

oil well *n* : a well from which petroleum is obtained

oily \'òi-lē\ *adj* **oil·i·er; -est** **1** : of, relating to, or consisting of oil **2** : covered or impregnated with oil : GREASY **3** : excessively smooth or suave in manner : UNCTUOUS — **oil·i·ness** *n*

oint·ment \'òint-mənt\ *n* [OF *oignement*, fr. *oign-*, *oindre* to anoint, fr. L *unguere*] : a semisolid usu. greasy and medicated preparation for application to the skin

Ojib·wa *or* **Ojib·way** \ō-'jib-wä\ *n* : a member of an Indian people of the region around Lake Superior

¹OK *or* **okay** \ō-'kā\ *adv* (*or adj*) [abbr. of *oll korrect*, alter. of *all correct*] : all right

²OK *or* **okay** *vt* **OK'd** *or* **okayed; OK'·ing** *or* **okay·ing** : APPROVE, AUTHORIZE

³OK *or* **okay** *n* : APPROVAL, ENDORSEMENT

oka·pi \ō-'käp-ē\ *n* [of African origin] : an African mammal closely related to the giraffe but lacking the long neck

okapi

okra \'ō-krə\ *n* [of African origin] : a tall annual plant related to the hollyhocks and grown for its edible green pods which are used esp. in soups and stews; *also* : these pods

-ol \,ȯl, ,ōl\ *n suffix* [*alcohol*] : chemical compound containing hydroxyl ⟨glycer*ol*⟩ ⟨creos*ol*⟩

¹old \'ōld\ *adj* [OE *eald*] **1 a** : dating from the remote past : ANCIENT ⟨*old* traditions⟩ **b** : persisting from an earlier time : of long standing ⟨an *old* friend⟩ **2** *cap* : belonging to an early period in the development of a language ⟨*Old* Irish⟩ **3** : having existed for a specified period of time ⟨a girl three years *old*⟩ **4** : of, relating to, or originating in a past era : ANTIQUE ⟨the *old* chronicles⟩ **5 a** : advanced in years or age ⟨an *old* man⟩ **b** : showing the characteristics of age ⟨looked *old* at 20⟩ **6** : FORMER ⟨his *old* students⟩ **7 a** : showing the effects of time or use : WORN, AGED ⟨*old* shoes⟩ **b** : no longer in use : DISCARDED ⟨*old* rags⟩

syn ANCIENT, ANTIQUE, ARCHAIC: OLD may imply actual or relative length of existence ⟨*old* castles⟩ ⟨*old* dogs⟩ ANCIENT implies occurrence, existence, or use in the distant past ⟨*ancient* history⟩ ANTIQUE is a close synonym of ANCIENT, though it suggests something old-fashioned that has acquired value through rarity and sentimental associations ⟨a collector of *antique* clocks⟩ ARCHAIC implies having the characteristics of an earlier period ⟨an *archaic* chivalry⟩ ⟨*methinks* is an *archaic* construction⟩

²old *n* : old or earlier time ⟨days of *old*⟩

Old Church Slavonic *n* : the Slavic language used in the Bible translation of Cyril and Methodius and as the liturgical language of several Eastern churches — called also *Old Church Slavic*

old country *n* : an emigrant's country of origin; *esp* : EUROPE

old·en \'ōl-dən\ *adj* : of or relating to a bygone era : ANCIENT

Old English *n* **1** : the language of the English people from the time of the earliest documents in the 7th century to about 1100 **2** : English of any period before Modern English

old–fash·ioned \'ōl(d)-'fash-ənd\ *adj* **1** : of, relating to, or characteristic of a past era : ANTIQUATED **2** : adhering to customs of a past era : CONSERVATIVE

Old French *n* : the French language from the 9th to the 16th century; *esp* : French from the 9th to the 13th century

Old Glory *n* : the flag of the U.S.

old guard *n*, *often cap O & G* : the conservative or reactionary members esp. of a political party

old hand *n* : VETERAN

Old High German *n* : High German exemplified in documents prior to the 12th century

old·ish \'ōl-dish\ *adj* : somewhat old or elderly

old–line \'ōl-'(d)līn\ *adj* **1** : ORIGINAL, ESTABLISHED ⟨an *old-line* business⟩ **2** : adhering to old policies or practices : CONSERVATIVE

old maid *n* **1** : SPINSTER 2 **2** : a prim nervous fussy person **3** : a simple card game in which the player holding the odd queen at the end is an "old maid" — **old–maid·ish** \'ōl(d)-'mād-ish\ *adj*

old man *n* **1 a** : HUSBAND **b** : FATHER **2** *cap* : one in authority; *esp* : COMMANDING OFFICER

old master *n* **1** : a superior artist or craftsman of established reputation; *esp* : a distinguished painter of the 16th, 17th, or early 18th century **2** : a work by an old master

Old Nick \'ōl(d)-'nik\ *n* : DEVIL, SATAN

Old Norse *n* : the Germanic language of the Scandinavian peoples prior to about 1350

Old North French *n* : the northern dialects of Old French including esp. those of Normandy and Picardy

Old Regime *n* : the political and social system of France prior to the revolution of 1789; *also* : a system no longer prevailing

old school *n* : adherents to the policies and practices of the past

old–squaw \'ōl(d)-'skwȯ\ *n* : a common sea duck of the more northern parts of the northern hemisphere

old·ster \'ōl(d)-stər\ *n* : an old or elderly person

Old Style *n* : a style of reckoning time used before the adoption of the Gregorian calendar

Old Testament *n* : the first of the two chief divisions of the

Bible consisting of the books dealing with the history of the Hebrews before the time of Christ — see BIBLE table

old–time \'ōl(d)-ˌtīm\ *adj* : of, relating to, or characteristic of an earlier period

old–tim·er \-'tī-mər\ *n* **1 a** : VETERAN **b** : OLDSTER **2** : something that is old-fashioned : ANTIQUE

old wives' tale *n* : a traditional tale or bit of lore (as a superstitious notion)

Old World *n* : EASTERN HEMISPHERE; *esp* : the continent of Europe

old–world \'ōl-'(d)wərld\ *adj* : OLD-FASHIONED, PICTURESQUE

ole·ag·i·nous \ˌō-lē-'aj-ə-nəs\ *adj* [MF *oleagineux*, fr. L *oleagineus* of an olive tree, fr. *olea* olive tree] **1** : resembling or having the properties of oil; *also* : containing or producing oil **2** : UNCTUOUS — **ole·ag·i·nous·ly** *adv* — **ole·ag·i·nous·ness** *n*

ole·an·der \'ō-lē-ˌan-dər\ *n* [ML] : a poisonous evergreen shrub of the dogbane family often grown for its showy fragrant white to red flowers

ole·as·ter \-ˌas-tər\ *n* [L, fr. *olea* olive tree] : any of a genus of trees and shrubs with usu. silvery foliage and fruits suggesting small olives

ole·cra·non \ō-'lə-'krā-ˌnän\ *n* [Gk *ōlekranon*, fr. *ōlenē* elbow + *kranion* skull] : a process of the ulna that projects behind the elbow joint

ole·ic \ō-'lē-ik\ *adj* [L *oleum* oil] **1** : relating to, derived from, or contained in oil **2** : of or relating to oleic acid

oleic acid *n* : an unsaturated fatty acid $C_{18}H_{34}O_2$ found as glycerides in natural fats and oils

oleo \'ō-lē-ˌō\ *n, pl* **ole·os** : MARGARINE

oleo·mar·ga·rine \ˌō-lē-ō-'märj-(ə-)rən, -'märj-ə-ˌrēn\ *n* [L *oleum* oil] : MARGARINE

oleo·res·in \-'rez-ᵊn\ *n* : a plant product (as a turpentine) containing chiefly essential oil and resin — **oleo·res·in·ous** \-'rez-ᵊn-əs, -'rez-nəs\ *adj*

ole·um \'ō-lē-əm\ *n, pl* **oleums** [L, oil] : a heavy oily fuming strongly corrosive solution of sulfur trioxide in anhydrous sulfuric acid

ol·fac·tion \äl-'fak-shən, ōl-\ *n* : the sense of smell : the act or process of smelling

ol·fac·to·ry \äl-'fak-t(ə-)rē, ōl-\ *adj* [L *olfact-, olfacere* to smell, fr. *olēre* to have odor + *facere* to make] : of, relating to, or concerned with the sense of smell

olfactory lobe *n* : an anterior projection of each cerebral hemisphere that is continuous anteriorly with the olfactory nerve

olfactory nerve *n* : either of a pair of sensory cranial nerves that arise in the sensory membranes of the nose and conduct olfactory stimuli to the brain

ol·i·garch \'äl-ə-ˌgärk\ *n* : a member of an oligarchy

ol·i·gar·chy \-ˌgär-kē\ *n, pl* **-chies** [Gk *oligos* little in amount, few] **1** : a government in which the power is in the hands of a few persons **2** : a state having an oligarchy; *also* : the group of persons holding power in such a state — **ol·i·gar·chic** \ˌäl-ə-'gär-kik\ *or* **ol·i·gar·chi·cal** \-ki-kəl\ *adj*

Ol·i·go·cene \'äl-i-gō-ˌsēn\ *n* [Gk *oligos* little] : the epoch of the Tertiary between the Eocene and Miocene; *also* : the corresponding system of rocks — **Oligocene** *adj*

ol·i·go·chaete \'äl-i-gō-ˌkēt\ *n* [Gk *oligos* little + *chaitē* hair] : any of a class or order (Oligochaeta) of annelid worms lacking a specialized head and including the earthworms — **oligochaete** *or* **ol·i·go·chae·tous** \ˌäl-i-gō-'kēt-əs\ *adj*

ol·i·gop·o·ly \ˌäl-i-'gäp-ə-lē\ *n, pl* **-lies** [Gk *oligos* few + *pōlein* to sell] : a market situation in which a few producers control the demand from a large number of buyers

olio \'ō-lē-ˌō\ *n, pl* **oli·os** [modif. of Sp *olla*, a kind of stew, lit., pot, fr. L] : HODGEPODGE, MEDLEY

¹ol·ive \'äl-iv\ *n* [L *oliva*, fr. Gk *elaia*] **1** : an Old World evergreen tree grown for its fruit that is an important food and source of oil; *also* : this fruit **2** : any of several colors resembling that of the unripe olive that are yellow to yellow green in hue, of medium to low lightness, and of moderate to low saturation

olive: *1* flowering branch, *2* fruit

²olive *adj* **1** : of the color olive or olive green **2** : approaching olive in color or complexion

olive branch *n* **1** : a branch of the olive tree esp. when used as a symbol of peace **2** : an offer or gesture of conciliation or goodwill

olive drab *n* **1** : a variable color averaging a grayish olive **2 a** : a wool or cotton fabric of an olive drab color **b** : a uniform of this fabric

olive green *n* : a variable color that is greener, lighter, and stronger than average olive color

ol·iv·ine \'äl-i-ˌvēn\ *n* : a mineral $(Mg,Fe)_2SiO_4$ that is a complex silicate of magnesium and iron

ol·la po·dri·da \ˌäl-ə-pə-'drēd-ə\ *n, pl* **olla podridas** \-'drēd-əz\ *also* **ollas podridas** \ˌäl-ə(z)-pə-drēd-əz\ [Sp, a kind of stew, lit., rotten pot] : OLIO

olym·pi·ad \ə-'lim-pē-ˌad, ō-\ *n, often cap* **1** : one of the four-year intervals between Olympic Games by which time was reckoned in ancient Greece **2** : a quadrennial celebration of the modern Olympic Games

¹Olym·pi·an \-pē-ən\ *adj* **1** : of or relating to the ancient Greek region of Olympia **2** : of, relating to, or constituting the Olympic Games

²Olympian *n* : a participant in Olympic Games

³Olympian *adj* **1** : of or relating to Mount Olympus in Thessaly **2** : befitting or characteristic of the gods of Olympus : LOFTY

⁴Olympian *n* **1** : one of the Greek deities of highest rank dwelling on Olympus **2** : a being of lofty detachment or superior attainments

Olym·pic \ə-'lim-pik, ō-\ *adj* : ³OLYMPIAN

Olympic Games *n pl* **1** : an ancient Panhellenic festival held at Olympia every 4th year and made up of contests in sports, music, and literature with the victor's prize a crown of wild olive **2** : a revival of the Olympic Games held once every four years and made up of international athletic contests — called also *Olympics* \-'lim-piks\

Olym·pus \ə-'lim-pəs, ō-\ *n* : a mountain in Thessaly held to be the abode of the Greek gods

-o·ma \'ō-mə\ *n suffix, pl* **-o·mas** \-məz\ *or* **-o·ma·ta** \-mət-ə\ [Gk *-ōmat-, -ōma* ending of nouns denoting result formed fr. causative verbs in *-oun*] : tumor ⟨*lipoma*⟩

Oma·ha \'ō-mə-ˌhȯ, -ˌhä\ *n* : a member of a Siouan people of northeastern Nebraska

oma·sum \ō-'mā-səm\ *n, pl* **-sa** \-sə\ [NL, fr. L, fat tripe] : the division between the reticulum and the abomasum in the stomach of a ruminant

om·buds·man \'äm-ˌbu̇dz-mən, äm-'bu̇dz-\ *n* [Sw, lit., representative, fr. ON *umbothsmathr*, fr. *umboth* commission + *mathr* man] **1** : a government appointee who receives and investigates complaints made by individuals against public officials **2** : one that investigates and helps settle reported complaints (as from students or consumers)

omega \ō-'meg-ə, -'mē-gə\ *n* **1** : the 24th and last letter of the Greek alphabet — Ω *or* ω **2** : LAST, ENDING

om·elet *also* **om·elette** \'äm-(ə-)lət\ *n* [F *omelette*, fr. OF *lemelle* thin plate, fr. L *lamella*, dim. of *lamina*] : eggs beaten with milk or water, cooked without stirring until set, and folded over

omen \'ō-mən\ *n* [L *omin-, omen*] : an event or phenomenon believed to be a sign or warning of some future occurrence : PORTENT

omen·tum \ō-'ment-əm\ *n, pl* **-ta** \-ə\ *or* **-tums** [L] : a fold of peritoneum usu. connecting or supporting viscera or other abdominal structures — **omen·tal** \-'ment-ᵊl\ *adj*

omer \'ō-mər\ *n* [Heb *ōmer*] **1** : an ancient Hebrew unit of dry capacity equal to ¹⁄₁₀ ephah **2** *often cap* : a 7-week period in the Jewish year between Passover and Shabuoth

om·i·cron \'äm-ə-ˌkrän\ *n* : the 15th letter of the Greek alphabet — O *or* ο

om·i·nous \'äm-ə-nəs\ *adj* : being or showing an omen; *esp* : foretelling evil : THREATENING ⟨*ominous* events leading to war⟩ — **om·i·nous·ly** *adv* — **om·i·nous·ness** *n*

omis·si·ble \ō-'mis-ə-bəl, ə-\ *adj* : that may be omitted

omis·sion \ō-'mish-ən, ə-\ *n* **1** : something neglected or left undone **2** : the act of omitting : the state of being omitted

omis·sive \ō-'mis-iv, ə-\ *adj* : failing or neglecting to do : OMITTING — **omis·sive·ly** *adv*

omit \ō-'mit, ə-\ *vt* **omit·ted; omit·ting** [L *omiss-, omittere*, fr. *ob-* toward + *mittere* to let go, send] **1** : to leave out or leave unmentioned ⟨*omitted* his name from the list⟩ **2 :** to fail to perform **:** leave undone **:** NEGLECT ⟨*omitted* to write in her diary that day⟩

om·ma·tid·i·um \ˌäm-ə-'tid-ē-əm\ *n, pl* **-ia** \-ē-ə\ [NL, fr. Gk ommat-, omma eye] **:** one of the elements corresponding to a small simple eye that make up the compound eye of an arthropod — **om·ma·tid·i·al** \-ē-əl\ *adj*

omni- *comb form* [L omnis] **:** all **:** universally ⟨*omni*directional⟩

¹om·ni·bus \'äm-ni-(ˌ)bəs\ *n* [L, for all, dat. pl. of omnis all] **1 :** a usu. automotive public vehicle designed to carry a comparatively large number of passengers **:** BUS **2 :** a book containing reprints of a number of works

²omnibus *adj* **:** of, relating to, or providing for many things or classes at once ⟨an *omnibus* legislative bill⟩

om·ni·di·rec·tion·al \ˌäm-ni-də-'rek-shnəl, -dī-, -shən-ᵊl\ *adj* **:** receiving or sending radiations equally well in all directions ⟨*omnidirectional* antenna⟩

om·ni·far·i·ous \ˌäm-nə-'far-ē-əs, -'fer-\ *adj* **:** of all varieties, forms, or kinds

om·nip·o·tence \äm-'nip-ət-ən(t)s\ *n* **:** the quality or state of being omnipotent

om·nip·o·tent \-ət-ənt\ *adj* [L omnipotent-, omnipotens, fr. omnis all + potens powerful, potent] **1** *often cap* **:** ALMIGHTY 1 **2 :** having virtually unlimited authority or influence — **omnipotent** *n* — **om·nip·o·tent·ly** *adv*

om·ni·pres·ent \ˌäm-ni-'prez-ᵊnt\ *adj* **:** present in all places at all times — **om·ni·pres·ence** \-ᵊn(t)s\ *n*

om·ni·range \'äm-ni-ˌrānj\ *n* **:** a system of radio navigation in which any bearing relative to a special radio transmitter on the ground may be chosen and flown by an airplane pilot

om·ni·scient \äm-'nish-ənt\ *adj* [L omnis all + scient-, sciens, prp. of scire to know] **1 :** having infinite awareness, understanding, and insight **2 :** possessed of universal or complete knowledge — **om·ni·science** \-ən(t)s\ *n* — **om·ni·scient·ly** *adv*

om·ni·um-gath·er·um \ˌäm-nē-əm-'gath-ə-rəm\ *n* **:** a miscellaneous collection of a variety of things or persons **:** HODGEPODGE

om·niv·o·ra \äm-'niv-ə-rə\ *n pl* [NL, fr. L, neut. pl. of omnivorus omnivorous, fr. omnis all + vorare to devour] **:** omnivorous animals

om·ni·vore \'äm-ni-ˌvōr, -ˌvȯr\ *n* **:** one that is omnivorous

om·niv·o·rous \äm-'niv-(ə-)rəs\ *adj* **1 :** feeding on both animal and vegetable substances **2 :** avidly taking in everything as if devouring or consuming — **om·niv·o·rous·ly** *adv* — **om·niv·o·rous·ness** *n*

¹on \(')ȯn, (')än\ *prep* [OE an, on] **1 a (1) :** over and in contact with or supported by ⟨the book *on* the table⟩⟨stand *on* one foot⟩ **(2) :** in contact or juxtaposition with ⟨a fly *on* the wall⟩⟨a town *on* the river⟩ **(3) :** in the direction of or area of ⟨*on* the right⟩ **b (1) :** to a position over and in contact with ⟨jumped *on* the horse⟩ **(2) :** into contact with ⟨put the notice *on* the bulletin board⟩ **2** — used as a function word to indicate someone or something that action or feeling is directed against or toward ⟨crept up *on* him⟩ ⟨have pity *on* me⟩⟨paid *on* account⟩ **3** — used as a function word to indicate the basis or source (as of an action, opinion, or computation) ⟨know it *on* good authority⟩⟨ten cents *on* the dollar⟩ **4 :** with respect to ⟨agreed *on* a price⟩ ⟨a satire *on* society⟩ **5 a :** in connection, association, or activity with or with regard to ⟨*on* a committee⟩⟨*on* tour⟩ **b :** in a state or process of ⟨*on* fire⟩⟨*on* the increase⟩ **6 a** — used as a function word to indicate occurrence within the limits of a specified day or at a set time ⟨came *on* Monday⟩⟨every hour *on* the hour⟩ **b :** at the time of ⟨cash *on* delivery⟩ **7 :** through the means or agency of ⟨talking *on* the telephone⟩ **8 :** following in series ⟨loss *on* loss⟩

²on \'ȯn, 'än\ *adv* **1 a :** in or into a position of contact with an upper surface ⟨put the plates *on*⟩ **b :** in or into a position of being attached to or covering a surface ⟨has new shoes *on*⟩ **2 a :** forward in space, time, or action **:** ONWARD ⟨went *on* home⟩ **b :** in continuance or succession ⟨and so *on*⟩ **3 :** into operation or a position permitting operation ⟨turn the light *on*⟩

on \'ȯn, 'än\ *adj* **1 :** engaged in an activity or function (as a dramatic role) **2 a (1) :** OPERATING ⟨the radio is *on*⟩ **(2) :** placed so as to permit operation ⟨the switch is *on*⟩ **b :** taking place ⟨the game is *on*⟩ **3 :** PLANNED ⟨has nothing *on* for tonight⟩

-on \ˌän\ *n suffix* [ion] **:** elementary particle ⟨nucle*on*⟩

on·a·ger \'än-i-jər\ *n* [L, wild ass, fr. Gk onagros, fr. onos ass + agros field] **1 :** an Asiatic wild ass **2 :** an ancient and medieval heavy catapult

¹once \'wən(t)s\ *adv* [ME ones, fr. gen. of on one] **1 :** one time and no more ⟨will repeat the question *once*⟩ **2 :** at any one time **:** under any circumstances **:** EVER ⟨if he *once* hesitates, he's lost⟩ **3 :** at some indefinite time in the past **:** FORMERLY ⟨*once* lived in luxury⟩ **4 :** by one degree of relationship ⟨cousin *once* removed⟩

²once *n* **:** one single time **:** one time at least ⟨just this *once*⟩ — **at once 1 :** at the same time **:** SIMULTANEOUSLY **2 :** IMMEDIATELY

³once *conj* **:** at the moment when **:** as soon as ⟨*once* that is done, all will be well⟩

once-over \'wən(t)s-ˌō-vər\ *n* **:** a swift examination or survey

on·col·o·gy \än-'käl-ə-jē, äŋ-\ *n* [Gk onkos mass] **:** the study of tumors — **on·co·log·ic** \ˌäŋ-kə-'läj-ik\ *adj*

on·com·ing \'ȯn-ˌkəm-iŋ, 'än-\ *adj* **:** coming on **:** APPROACHING ⟨*oncoming* traffic⟩⟨*oncoming* generations⟩

¹one \'wən\ *adj* [ME on, one, fr. OE ān] **1 :** being a single unit or thing ⟨*one* man went⟩ — see NUMBER table **2 a :** being one in particular ⟨early *one* morning⟩ **b :** being preeminently what is indicated ⟨*one* fine person⟩ **3 a :** being the same in kind or quality ⟨both of *one* race⟩ **b :** not divided **:** UNITED **4 :** existing or occurring as something not definitely fixed or placed ⟨will see you again *one* day⟩

²one *pron* **1 a :** a single member or specimen of a usu. specified class or group ⟨saw *one* of his friends⟩ **b :** a person in general **:** SOMEBODY ⟨*one* never knows⟩ **2** — used for I or we ⟨*one* hopes to see you there⟩

³one *n* **1 :** the number denoting unity **2 :** the first in a set or series **3 :** a single person or thing

one another *pron* **:** EACH OTHER

one-base hit \ˌwən-ˌbās-\ *n* **:** a base hit that enables a batter to reach first base safely — called also *one-bag·ger* \'wən-'bag-ər\, *single*

one-horse \ˌwən-ˌhȯrs\ *adj* **1 :** drawn or operated by one horse **2 :** small in scope or importance ⟨*one-horse* town⟩

Onei·da \ō-'nīd-ə\ *n* **:** a member of an Iroquoian people orig. living near Oneida Lake in New York

onei·ric \ō-'nī(ə)r-ik\ *adj* [Gk oneiros dream] **:** of or relating to dreams **:** DREAMY

one·ness \'wən-nəs\ *n* **:** the quality or state or fact of being one: as **a :** SINGLENESS **b :** WHOLENESS, INTEGRITY **c :** HARMONY **d :** SAMENESS, IDENTITY **e :** UNITY, UNION

on·er·ous \'än-ə-rəs, 'ō-nə-\ *adj* [L oner-, onus burden] **:** involving, imposing, or constituting a burden **:** TROUBLESOME ⟨an *onerous* task⟩ — **on·er·ous·ly** *adv* — **on·er·ous·ness** *n*

one·self \(ˌ)wən-'self\ *also* **one's self** \(ˌ)wən-, ˌwənz-\ *pron* **1 :** a person's self **:** one's own self — used reflexively as object of a preposition or verb or for emphasis in various constructions **2 :** one's normal, healthy, or sane condition or self

one-sid·ed \'wən-'sīd-əd\ *adj* **1 a :** having or occurring on one side only ⟨a *one-sided* argument⟩ **b :** having one side prominent or more developed **c :** UNEQUAL ⟨a *one-sided* game⟩ **2 :** limited to or favoring one side **:** PARTIAL ⟨a *one-sided* view of the case⟩— **one-sid·ed·ly** *adv* — **one-sid·ed·ness** *n*

one-step \'wən-ˌstep\ *n* **:** a ballroom dance marked by quick walking steps backward and forward in ¾ time — **one-step** *vi*

one·time \'wən-ˌtīm\ *adj* **:** FORMER, SOMETIME

one-to-one \ˌwən-tə-'wən\ *adj* **:** pairing each element of a class uniquely with an element of another class

one-way \'wən-'wā\ *adj* **:** that moves in, allows movement in, or functions in only one direction ⟨*one-way* traffic⟩ ⟨*one-way* ticket⟩

on·go·ing \'ȯn-ˌgō-iŋ, 'än-\ *adj* **:** continuously moving forward **:** GROWING

on·ion \'ən-yən\ *n* [MF oignon, fr. L union-, unio] **:** a widely grown Asiatic herb of the lily family with pungent edible bulbs; *also* **:** its bulb

on·ion·skin \-ˌskin\ *n* **:** a thin strong translucent paper of very light weight

on·look·er \'ȯn-ˌlu̇k-ər, 'än-\ *n* **:** one that looks on **:** SPECTATOR — **on·look·ing** \-ˌlu̇k-iŋ\ *adj*

---

j joke; ŋ sing; ō flow; ȯ flaw; ȯi coin; th thin; th̶ this; ü loot; u̇ foot; y yet; yü few; yu̇ furious; zh vision

¹on·ly \'ōn-lē\ *adj* [OE *ānlīc*, fr. *ān* one + *-līc* -ly] **1** : unquestionably the best : PEERLESS ⟨the *only* girl for me⟩ **2** : alone in its class or kind : SOLE ⟨the *only* survivor of the crash⟩

²only *adv* **1 a** : as a single fact or instance and nothing more or different : MERELY ⟨worked *only* in the mornings⟩ **b** : EXCLUSIVELY, SOLELY ⟨known *only* to him⟩ **2** : at the very least ⟨it was *only* too true⟩ **3 a** : in the final outcome ⟨will *only* make you sick⟩ **b** : with nevertheless the final result ⟨won the battles, *only* to lose the war⟩ **4** : as recently as ⟨*only* last week⟩ : in the immediate past ⟨*only* just talked to her⟩

³only *conj* **1** : with this sole restriction ⟨you may go, *only* come back early⟩ **2** : were it not that ⟨might play tennis, *only* I'm too tired⟩

on·o·mat·o·poe·ia \,än-ə-,mat-ə-'pē-(y)ə\ *n* [Gk *onomatopoiia*, fr. *onomat-, onoma* name (akin to E *name*) + *poiein* to make] **1** : formation of words in imitation of natural sounds (as *buzz* or *hiss*) **2** : the use of words whose sound suggests the sense — **on·o·mat·o·poe·ic** \-'pē-ik\ *or* **on·o·mat·o·po·et·ic** \-pō-'et-ik\ *adj* — **on·o·mat·o·poe·i·cal·ly** \-'pē-ə-k(ə-)lē\ *or* **on·o·mat·o·po·et·i·cal·ly** \-pō-'et-i-k(ə-)lē\ *adv*

On·on·da·ga \,än-ə(n)-'dô-gə\ *n* : a member of an Iroquoian people of central New York

on·rush \'ón-,rəsh, 'än-\ *n* **1** : a rushing forward or onward **2** : ONSET

on·set \-,set\ *n* **1** : ATTACK **2** : BEGINNING

on·shore \'ón-,shōr, 'än-, -,shór\ *adj* : moving toward the shore ⟨*onshore* winds⟩ — **on·shore** \'ón-, 'än-\ *adv*

on side *adv (or adj)* : not off side : in a position legally to receive the ball or puck

on·slaught \'än-,slôt, 'ón-\ *n* [modif. of D *aanslag* act of striking] : an esp. fierce attack

on-stream \-'strēm, 'än-\ *adv* : in or into operation ⟨a new plant will go *on-stream*⟩

on·to \'ón-tə, 'än-, -,tü\ *prep* : to a position or point on ⟨climbed *onto* the roof⟩

on·tog·e·ny \än-'täj-ə-nē\ *n, pl* **-nies** [Gk *ont-, on* existing thing, fr. neut. of *ōn,* prp. of *einai* to be] : the development or course of development of an individual organism — compare PHYLOGENY — **on·to·ge·net·ic** \,än-tə-jə-'net-ik\ *adj* — **on·to·ge·net·i·cal·ly** \-'net-i-k(ə-)lē\ *adv*

onus \'ō-nəs\ *n* [L] **1 a** : BURDEN **b** : a disagreeable necessity : OBLIGATION **2** : BLAME

¹on·ward \'ón-wərd, 'än-\ *also* **on·wards** \-wərdz\ *adv* : toward or at a point lying ahead in space or time : FORWARD ⟨kept moving *onward*⟩

²onward *adj* : directed or moving onward : FORWARD ⟨the *onward* march of time⟩

on·y·choph·o·ran \,än-i-'käf-ə-rən\ *n* : PERIPATUS — **onychophoran** *adj*

on·yx \'än-iks\ *n* [Gk *onych-, onyx,* lit., toenail or fingernail] : chalcedony with straight parallel alternating bands of color

oo- — see O-

oo·cyte \'ō-ə-,sīt\ *n* : an immature ovum

oo·dles \'üd-ºlz\ *n pl* : a great quantity : LOT

oog·a·mous \ō-'äg-ə-məs\ *adj* : reproducing by egg and sperm : HETEROGAMETIC — **oog·a·my** \-mē\ *n*

oo·gen·e·sis \,ō-ə-'jen-ə-səs\ *n, pl* **-gen·e·ses** \-ə-,sēz\ : formation and maturation of the egg — **oo·ge·net·ic** \-jə-'net-ik\ *adj*

oo·go·ni·um \,ō-ə-'gō-nē-əm\ *n, pl* **-nia** \-nē-ə\ **1** : a female sexual organ in various algae and fungi **2** : a cell that gives rise to oocytes — **oo·go·ni·al** \-nē-əl\ *adj*

oo·lite \'ō-ə-,līt\ *n* : a rock consisting of small round grains usu. of calcium carbonate cemented together — **oo·lit·ic** \,ō-ə-'lit-ik\ *adj*

ool·o·gy \ō-'äl-ə-jē\ *n* : a branch of ornithology dealing with birds' eggs — **oo·log·i·cal** \,ō-ə-'läj-i-kəl\ *adj* — **oo·log·i·cal·ly** \-k(ə-)lē\ *adv* — **ool·o·gist** \ō-'äl-ə-jəst\ *n*

oo·long \'ü-,lón\ *n* [Chin (Pek) *wu¹ lung²,* lit., black dragon] : a tea partially fermented before drying that combines characteristics of black and green teas

oo·mi·ak *var of* UMIAK

oomph \'úm(p)f\ *n* **1** : personal charm or magnetism : GLAMOUR **2** : SEX APPEAL **3** : VITALITY, ENTHUSIASM

oo·spore \'ō-ə-,spōr, -,spór\ *n* : ZYGOTE; *esp* : a spore produced by heterogamous fertilization that yields a sporophyte — compare ZYGOSPORE — **oo·spor·ic** \,ō-ə-'spōr-ik, -'spór-\ *adj* — **oo·spo·rous** \,ō-ə-'spōr-əs, -'spór-; ō-'äs-pə-rəs\ *adj*

oo·tid \'ō-ə-,tid\ *n* : an egg cell after meiosis

¹ooze \'üz\ *n* [OE *wāse* mire] **1** : a soft deposit (as of mud, slime, or shells) esp. on the bottom of a body of water **2** : soft wet plastic ground : MUD, SLIME

²ooze *vb* [ME *wosen,* fr. *wose* juice, fr. OE *wōs*] **1** : to pass or flow slowly through or as if through small openings ⟨sap *oozed* from the tree⟩ **2** : to move slowly or imperceptibly **3** : to give off : EXUDE ⟨her manner *oozed* confidence⟩

³ooze *n* **1** : the action of oozing **2** : something that oozes

oozy \'ü-zē\ *adj* **ooz·i·er; -est** **1** : containing or composed of ooze **2** : exuding moisture : SLIMY

opac·i·ty \ō-'pas-ət-ē\ *n, pl* **-ties** [L *opacus* shaded, dark] **1** : the quality or state of being opaque to radiant energy **2** : obscurity of meaning **3** : mental dullness **4** : an opaque spot on an otherwise or normally transparent structure

opal \'ō-pəl\ *n* [L *opalus,* fr. Skt *upala* stone, jewel] : a mineral that is a hydrated amorphous silica softer and less dense than quartz and typically with an iridescent play of colors

opal·es·cent \,ō-pə-'les-ºnt\ *adj* : having a play of colors like an opal — **opal·esce** \-'les\ *vi* — **opal·es·cence** \-'les-ºn(t)s\ *n*

opal·ine \'ō-pə-,līn, -,lēn\ *adj* : resembling opal : OPALESCENT

¹opaque \ō-'pāk\ *adj* [L *opacus* shaded, dark] **1 a** : not transmitting light rays : being neither transparent nor translucent **b** : impervious to other forms of radiant energy (as heat or X rays) **2 a** : not easily understood : OBSCURE **b** : lacking mental clarity : OBTUSE **3** : neither reflecting nor giving off light : DARK — **opaque·ly** *adv* — **opaque·ness** *n*

²opaque *n* : something that is opaque

ope \'ōp\ *vb* : OPEN

¹open \'ō-pən, 'óp-ºm\ *adj* **open·er** \'ōp-(ə-)nər\; **open·est** \-(ə-)nəst\ [OE; akin to E *up*] **1 a** : permitting passage or access : not shut or shut up : not stopped or clogged ⟨an *open* door⟩ ⟨*open* books⟩ ⟨*open* pores⟩ **b** : having openings or spaces ⟨an *open* soil⟩ ⟨*open* type⟩ **2 a** : not enclosed or covered : BARE ⟨an *open* boat⟩ ⟨*open* fire⟩ ⟨*open* wounds⟩ **b** : not protected against something : LIABLE ⟨*open* to challenge⟩ ⟨*open* to infection⟩ **c** : not secret : exposed to general knowledge : PUBLIC ⟨*open* dislike⟩; *also* : not secretive ⟨*open* about his plans⟩ **3 a** : free to the use, entry, or participation of all ⟨an *open* meeting⟩ ⟨*open* classes in a fair⟩ **b** : easy to enter, get through, or see ⟨*open* country⟩ ⟨an *open* woodland⟩; *also* : free from hampering restraints or controls ⟨an *open* economy⟩ ⟨*open* gambling⟩ **c** : available or ready for use or operation ⟨keep an hour *open* for our meeting⟩ ⟨the store was still *open*⟩ **4** : not snowy or stormy ⟨an *open* winter⟩ **5** : not drawn together : not folded or contracted : spread out ⟨an *open* flower⟩ ⟨*open* umbrellas⟩ **6 a** : not finally decided or settled ⟨an *open* question⟩ **b** : receptive to appeals or ideas : RESPONSIVE ⟨an *open* mind⟩ ⟨*open* to suggestion⟩ **7** : having components separated by a space in writing and printing ⟨the name *Spanish mackerel* is an *open* compound⟩ **syn** see FRANK — **open·ly** \'ō-pən-lē\ *adv* — **open·ness** \'ō-pən-nəs\ *n*

²open *vb* **opened** \'ō-pənd\; **open·ing** \'ōp-(ə-)niŋ\ **1 a** : to change or move from a shut condition : UNFASTEN, UNCLOSE ⟨*open* a book⟩ ⟨*open* a switch⟩ ⟨the door *opened* slowly⟩ **b** : to make or become open by or as if by clearing away obstacles ⟨*open* a road blocked with snow⟩ ⟨the clouds *opened*⟩ **c** : to make an opening or openings in ⟨*open* a boil⟩ **2** : to spread out : UNFOLD ⟨an *opening* flower⟩ ⟨*open* a napkin⟩ **2** : to make or become functional ⟨*open* a new store⟩ ⟨the office *opens* early⟩ **3** : to give access ⟨the rooms *open* onto a hall⟩ **4** : to enter upon : BEGIN, START ⟨*open* fire⟩ ⟨*open* talks⟩ **5** : to speak out — **open·er** \'ōp-(ə-)nər\ *n*

³open *n* **1** : OPENING **2 a** : open and unobstructed space or water **b** : OUTDOORS **3** : an open contest, competition, or tournament

open air *n* : space where air is unconfined; *esp* : OUT-OF-DOORS

open-air *adj* : OUTDOOR ⟨pleasures of *open-air* life⟩ ⟨*open-air* theaters⟩

open-and-shut *adj* : perfectly simple : OBVIOUS

open circuit *n* : an electrical circuit in which current does not flow because of an interruption (as by the opening of a switch) of continuity

open door *n* : a policy giving opportunity for commercial relations with a country to all nations on equal terms — **open-door** *adj*

open-end *adj* : organized to allow for contingencies; *esp* : offering for sale capital shares redeemable on demand

open-eyed \ˌō-pən-ˈīd\ *adj* 1 : having the eyes open 2 : WATCHFUL, DISCERNING, ALERT

open-hand·ed \ˌō-pən-ˈhan-dəd\ *adj* : generous in giving : LIBERAL — **open-hand·ed·ly** *adv* — **open-hand·ed·ness** *n*

open-heart·ed \-ˈhärt-əd\ *adj* : FRANK, GENEROUS — **open-heart·ed·ly** *adv* — **open-heart·ed·ness** *n*

open-hearth *adj* : being or relating to a process of making steel from pig iron in a furnace that reflects heat from the roof onto the material

open house *n* : ready and usu. informal hospitality or entertainment for all comers; *also* : an occasion devoted to this

open·ing \ˈōp-(ə-)niŋ\ *n* 1 : an act or instance of making or becoming open 2 : an open place or span : HOLE 3 : something that constitutes a beginning: as **a** : a planned series of moves made at the start of a game of chess or checkers **b** : a first performance 4 **a** : OCCASION, CHANCE **b** : an opportunity for employment

open letter *n* : a letter of protest or appeal intended for the general public and printed in a newspaper or periodical

open-mind·ed \ˌō-pən-ˈmīn-dəd\ *adj* : receptive of arguments or ideas : not prejudiced — **open-mind·ed·ly** *adv* — **open-mind·ed·ness** *n*

open-mouthed \ˌō-pən-ˈmau̇t͟hd, -ˈmau̇t͟ht\ *adj* 1 : having the mouth wide open 2 : struck with amazement or wonder — **open-mouthed·ly** \-ˈmau̇-t͟hə-lē, -ˈmau̇th-tlē\ *adv* — **open-mouthed·ness** \-ˈmau̇-t͟hə-nəs, -ˈmau̇th(t)-nəs\ *n*

open-pol·li·nat·ed *adj* : pollinated by natural agencies without human interference

open sea *n* : the part of the sea not enclosed between headlands or included in narrow straits : the main sea

open secret *n* : something supposedly secret but in fact generally known

open sentence *n* : an equation that contains one or more unknown quantities and is in itself is neither true nor false ⟨the *open sentence* X + 3 = 5⟩

open ses·a·me \ˌō-pən-ˈses-ə-mē\ *n* [fr. *open sesame*, the magical command used by Ali Baba to open the door of the robbers' den in *Ali Baba and the Forty Thieves*] : something that unfailingly brings about a desired end

open shop *n* : an establishment employing and retaining on the payroll both members and nonmembers of a labor union

open·work \ˈō-pən-ˌwərk\ *n* : something made or work done so as to show openings through the substance — **openwork** *or* **open-worked** \ˌō-pən-ˈwərkt\ *adj*

¹**opera** *pl of* OPUS

²**op·era** \ˈäp-(ə-)rə\ *n* [It, lit., work, fr. L, work, pains] : a drama set to music and made up of vocal pieces with orchestral accompaniment and orchestral overtures and interludes; *also* : a performance of an opera or a house where operas are performed

op·er·a·ble \ˈäp-(ə-)rə-bəl\ *adj* 1 : fit, possible, or desirable to use : PRACTICABLE 2 : suitable for surgical treatment ⟨an *operable* cancer⟩ — **op·er·a·bly** \-blē\ *adv*

opé·ra bouffe \ˌäp-(ə-)rə-ˈbüf\ *n* [F] : farcical comic opera

opé·ra co·mique \ˌäp-(ə-)rə-(ˌ)käm-ˈēk\ *n* [F] : an opera in which spoken dialogue is interspersed between the parts sung

opera glass *n* : a small binocular similar to a field glass and adapted for use at the opera — often used in pl.

opera hat *n* : a man's collapsible top hat consisting usu. of a dull silky fabric stretched over a steel frame

op·er·ate \ˈäp-ə-ˌrāt\ *vb* [L *operari*, fr. *oper-*, *opus* work] 1 : to perform or cause to perform an appointed function ⟨the switch *operates* easily⟩ ⟨learn to *operate* a car safely⟩ 2 : to produce an effect ⟨a drug that *operates* quickly⟩ 3 : to carry on the activities of ⟨*operate*

opera glass

a farm⟩; *esp* : MANAGE ⟨*operate* a business⟩ 4 : to perform surgery ⟨*operate* on a tumor⟩

op·er·at·ic \ˌäp-ə-ˈrat-ik\ *adj* [*opera* + *-tic* (as in *dramatic*)] : of, relating to, resembling, or suitable to opera — **op·er·at·i·cal·ly** \-ˈrat-i-k(ə-)lē\ *adv*

op·er·a·tion \ˌäp-ə-ˈrā-shən\ *n* 1 : the act, process, method, or result of operating 2 : a functioning; *esp* : the quality or state of being functional or operative 3 : a surgical procedure 4 : a process (as addition or multiplication) of deriving one mathematical expression from others according to a rule 5 **a** : a military or naval action, mission, or maneuver including its planning and execution **b** *pl* : the office of an airfield which controls flying from the field — **op·er·a·tion·al** \-shnəl, -shən-ᵊl\ *adj*

¹**op·er·a·tive** \ˈäp-(ə-)rət-iv, ˈäp-ə-ˌrāt-\ *adj* 1 : producing an appropriate effect : EFFICACIOUS ⟨an *operative* penalty⟩ 2 : exerting force or influence : OPERATING ⟨an *operative* force⟩ 3 **a** : having to do with physical operations ⟨*operative* costs⟩ **b** : WORKING ⟨an *operative* craftsman⟩ 4 : based on or consisting of operation ⟨*operative* dentistry⟩ — **op·er·a·tive·ly** *adv* — **op·er·a·tive·ness** *n*

²**operative** *n* : OPERATOR: as **a** : ARTISAN, MECHANIC **b** (1) : a secret agent (2) : DETECTIVE

op·er·a·tor \ˈäp-ə-ˌrāt-ər\ *n* 1 : one that operates: as **a** : one that operates a machine or device **b** : one that operates a business **c** : one that deals in stocks or commodities 2 : a shrewd person who knows how to circumvent restrictions or difficulties

oper·cu·lum \ō-ˈpər-kyə-ləm\ *n*, *pl* **-la** \-lə\ *also* **-lums** [L, cover, fr. *operire* to shut, cover] 1 : a lid or covering flap (as of a moss capsule) 2 : a body part that suggests a lid: as **a** : a plate on the foot of a gastropod mollusk that closes the shell **b** : the covering of the gills of a fish — **oper·cu·lar** \-lər\ *adj* — **oper·cu·late** \-lət\ *adj*

op·er·et·ta \ˌäp-ə-ˈret-ə\ *n* [It, dim. of *opera*] : a light musical-dramatic production having usu. a romantic plot and containing spoken dialogue and dancing scenes — **op·er·et·tist** \-ˈret-əst\ *n*

ophid·i·an \ō-ˈfid-ē-ən\ *adj* [Gk *ophis* snake] : of, relating to, or resembling snakes — **ophidian** *n*

ophi·uroid \ˌäf-ē-ˈ(y)u̇(ə)r-ˌȯid\ *n* [Gk *ophis* snake + *oura* tail] : BRITTLE STAR — **ophiuroid** *adj*

oph·thal·mia \äf-ˈthal-mē-ə, äp-\ *n* : inflammation of the conjunctiva or eyeball

oph·thal·mic \-mik\ *adj* [Gk *ophthalmos* eye] : of, relating to, or situated near the eye : OCULAR

oph·thal·mol·o·gist \ˌäf-thal-ˈmäl-ə-jəst, ˌäp-\ *n* : a physician specializing in ophthalmology — compare OPTICIAN

oph·thal·mol·o·gy \-jē\ *n* : a branch of medical science dealing with the structure, functions, and diseases of the eye — **oph·thal·mo·log·ic** \(ˌ)äf-ˌthal-mə-ˈläj-ik, (ˌ)äp-\ *or* **oph·thal·mo·log·i·cal** \-ˈläj-i-kəl\ *adj* — **oph·thal·mo·log·i·cal·ly** \-i-k(ə-)lē\ *adv*

-opia \ˈō-pē-ə\ *n comb form* [Gk *ōps* eye] : condition of having (such) vision ⟨dipl*opia*⟩ ⟨hyper*opia*⟩

¹**opi·ate** \ˈō-pē-ət, -ˌāt\ *adj* 1 : containing or mixed with opium 2 **a** : inducing sleep : NARCOTIC **b** : causing dullness or inaction

²**opiate** *n* 1 : a preparation or derivative of opium; *also* : NARCOTIC 1 2 : something that induces rest or inaction or quiets uneasiness

opine \ō-ˈpīn\ *vb* [MF *opiner*, fr. L *opinari* to have an opinion] 1 : to state as an opinion 2 : to form or express opinions

opin·ion \ə-ˈpin-yən\ *n* [L *opinion-*, *opinio*] 1 : a belief stronger than an impression but less strong than positive knowledge 2 : a judgment about a person or thing ⟨has a high *opinion* of his doctor⟩ 3 : a formal statement by an expert after careful study

syn OPINION, BELIEF, CONVICTION mean a judgment one holds as true. OPINION implies a conclusion still open to dispute ⟨a dissenting *opinion* by a Supreme Court justice⟩ BELIEF implies deliberate acceptance and intellectual assent ⟨firm in his religious *beliefs*⟩ CONVICTION applies to a firm, unshakable belief

opin·ion·at·ed \-yə-ˌnāt-əd\ *adj* : adhering unduly to personal opinions or preconceived notions — **opin·ion·at·ed·ly** *adv* — **opin·ion·at·ed·ness** *n*

opin·ion·a·tive \-ˌnāt-iv\ *adj* 1 : of, relating to, or consisting of opinion 2 : OPINIONATED

opi·um \'ō-pē-əm\ *n* [L, fr. Gk *opion*] **1** : a bitter brownish addictive narcotic drug that is the dried juice of the opium poppy **2** : something having an effect like that of opium — **opium** *adj*

opium poppy *n* : an annual Eurasian poppy grown since antiquity for opium, for its edible oily seeds, and for its showy flowers

opos·sum \(ə-)'päs-əm\ *n, pl* **-sums** *also* **-sum** [of AmerInd origin] : any of various American marsupials; *esp* : a common omnivorous largely nocturnal and arboreal mammal of the eastern U.S.

¹op·po·nent \ə-'pō-nənt\ *n* [L *opponent-, opponens,* prp. of *opponere* to oppose] **1** : a person or thing that opposes another person or thing : RIVAL, ANTAGONIST **2** : a muscle that counteracts and restricts the action of another
   syn ANTAGONIST, ADVERSARY, ENEMY: OPPONENT implies a position on the other side as in a debate, election, or conflict; ANTAGONIST implies sharper opposition in a struggle for supremacy; ADVERSARY suggests active hostility; ENEMY usu. adds to the idea of opposition or contention the element of wishing to injure or destroy (as in military warfare)

²opponent *adj* **1** : ANTAGONISTIC **2** : OPPOSITE

op·por·tune \,äp-ər-'t(y)ün\ *adj* [L *opportunus,* fr. *ob* towards + *portus* port, harbor] : SUITABLE, TIMELY (an *opportune* moment to act) — **op·por·tune·ly** *adv* — **op·por·tune·ness** \-'t(y)ün-nəs\ *n*

op·por·tun·ism \-'t(y)ü-,niz-əm\ *n* : the art, policy, or practice of taking advantage of opportunities or circumstances esp. with little regard for principles or ultimate consequences — **op·por·tun·ist** \-nəst\ *n or adj* — **op·por·tu·nis·tic** \-t(y)ü-'nis-tik\ *adj*

op·por·tu·ni·ty \,äp-ər-'t(y)ü-nət-ē\ *n, pl* **-ties 1** : a favorable juncture of circumstances, time, and place **2** : a chance for advancement or progress

op·pos·a·ble \ə-'pō-zə-bəl\ *adj* **1** : capable of being resisted **2** : capable of being placed opposite something else and esp. in a position for grasping (the *opposable* human thumb) — **op·pos·a·bil·i·ty** \ə-,pō-zə-'bil-ət-ē\ *n*

op·pose \ə-'pōz\ *vt* [F *opposer,* irreg. fr. L *opponere,* fr. *ob-* in the way + *ponere* to put, place] **1** : to place opposite or against something esp. so as to provide resistance, counterbalance, or contrast **2** : to offer resistance to : strive against — **op·pos·er** *n*
   syn RESIST: OPPOSE may apply to an act or attitude ranging from mild objection to bitter hostility or warfare; RESIST implies a recognition of a hostile or threatening force and a positive effort to counteract it (*resist* temptation)

¹op·po·site \'äp-ə-zət\ *adj* [L *oppositus,* pp. of *opponere* to oppose] **1 a** : set over against something that is at the other end or side (*opposite* ends of a diameter) **b** : attached to a stem or axis in exactly opposite pairs (*opposite* leaves) — compare ALTERNATE **2 a** : OPPOSED, HOSTILE (*opposite* sides of the question) **b** : diametrically different : CONTRARY (*opposite* meanings) **3** : contrarily turned or moving (go in *opposite* directions) **syn** see CONTRARY — **op·po·site·ly** *adv* — **op·po·site·ness** *n*

²opposite *adv* : on opposite sides

³opposite *n* : something that is opposed or contrary

op·po·si·tion \,äp-ə-'zish-ən\ *n* **1** : a setting opposite or being set opposite; *also* : a configuration in which the difference in celestial longitude of two heavenly bodies is 180° **2** : resistant or contrary action or condition (offer *opposition* to a plan) (the *opposition* of two forces) **3 a** : something that opposes; *esp* : a body of persons opposing something **b** *often cap* : a political party opposing and prepared to replace the party in power — **op·po·si·tion·al** \-'zish-nəl, -ən-ᵊl\ *adj*

op·press \ə-'pres\ *vt* [L *oppress-, opprimere,* fr. *ob-* in the way + *premere* to press] **1** : to weigh down : burden in spirit as if with weight (*oppressed* by debts) **2** : to crush by harsh rule : treat cruelly or with too great severity (a country *oppressed* by a dictator's rule) **syn** see DEPRESS — **op·pres·sor** \-'pres-ər\ *n*

op·pres·sion \ə-'presh-ən\ *n* **1 a** : unjust or cruel exercise of authority or power **b** : something that so oppresses **2** : a sense of heaviness or obstruction in the body or mind : DEPRESSION

op·pres·sive \ə-'pres-iv\ *adj* **1** : unreasonably burdensome or severe (*oppressive* legislation) **2** : TYRANNICAL

(*oppressive* rulers) **3** : overpowering or depressing to the spirit or senses (an *oppressive* silence) — **op·pres·sive·ly** *adv* — **op·pres·sive·ness** *n*

op·pro·bri·ous \ə-'prō-brē-əs\ *adj* **1** : expressive of opprobrium : SCURRILOUS (*opprobrious* language) **2** : deserving of opprobrium — **op·pro·bri·ous·ly** *adv* — **op·pro·bri·ous·ness** *n*

op·pro·bri·um \-brē-əm\ *n* [L, fr. *opprobrare* to reproach, fr. *ob* in the way of + *probrum* reproach] **1** : something that brings disgrace **2** : public disgrace or ill repute that follows from conduct considered grossly wrong or vicious : INFAMY

op·so·nin \'äp-sə-nən\ *n* [L *opsonium* relish, fr. Gk *opsōnion* victuals] : a constituent of blood serum that makes foreign cells more susceptible to the action of the phagocytes — **op·son·ic** \äp-'sän-ik\ *adj*

-op·sy \,äp-sē, əp-\ *n comb form, pl* **-opsies** [Gk *opsis* appearance] : examination (necr*opsy*)

opt \'äpt\ *vi* [F *opter,* fr. L *optare*] : to make a choice

op·ta·tive \'äp-tət-iv\ *adj* **1** : of, relating to, or constituting a grammatical mood expressive of wish or desire **2** : expressing desire or wish — **optative** *n* — **op·ta·tive·ly** *adv*

op·tic \'äp-tik\ *adj* [Gk *optikos,* fr. *op-,* used as stem of *horan* to see; akin to E *eye*] : of or relating to vision or the eye

op·ti·cal \'äp-ti-kəl\ *adj* **1** : relating to optics **2** : OPTIC — **op·ti·cal·ly** \-k(ə-)lē\ *adv*

op·ti·cian \äp-'tish-ən\ *n* **1** : a maker of or dealer in optical items and instruments **2** : one that grinds spectacle lenses to prescription and dispenses spectacles — compare OPHTHALMOLOGIST, OPTOMETRIST

optic nerve *n* : either of a pair of sensory cranial nerves that arise from the ventral part of the diencephalon, supply the retina, and conduct visual stimuli to the brain

op·tics \'äp-tiks\ *n* : a science that deals with the nature and properties of light and the effects that it undergoes and produces

op·ti·mal \'äp-tə-məl\ *adj* : most desirable or satisfactory : OPTIMUM — **op·ti·mal·ly** \-mə-lē\ *adv*

op·ti·mism \'äp-tə-,miz-əm\ *n* [F *optimisme,* fr. L *optimus* best] **1** : a doctrine that this world is the best possible world **2** : an inclination to put the most favorable construction on actions and happenings or to anticipate the best possible outcome — **op·ti·mist** \-məst\ *n or adj* — **op·ti·mis·tic** \,äp-tə-'mis-tik\ *or* **op·ti·mis·ti·cal** \-ti-kəl\ *adj* — **op·ti·mis·ti·cal·ly** \-ti-k(ə-)lē\ *adv*

op·ti·mum \'äp-tə-məm\ *n, pl* **-ma** \-mə\ *also* **-mums** [L] **1** : the amount or degree of something that is most favorable to some end **2** : greatest degree attained under implied or specified conditions — **optimum** *adj*

op·tion \'äp-shən\ *n* [L *option-, optio*] **1 a** : the power or right to choose **b** : a right to buy or sell something at a specified price during a specified period **c** : a right of an insured person to choose the form in which payments due him are to be made **2** : something offered for choice **syn** see CHOICE

op·tion·al \'äp-shnəl, -shən-ᵊl\ *adj* : permitting a choice : not compulsory — **op·tion·al·ly** \-ē\ *adv*

op·tom·e·trist \äp-'täm-ə-trəst\ *n* : a specialist in optometry — compare OPTICIAN

op·tom·e·try \-trē\ *n* [Gk *op-,* used as stem of *horan* to see] : the art or profession of examining the eye for defects and faults of refraction and prescribing correctional lenses or exercises but not drugs or surgery — **op·to·met·ric** \,äp-tə-'me-trik\ *or* **op·to·met·ri·cal** \-tri-kəl\ *adj*

op·u·lence \'äp-yə-lən(t)s\ *n* **1** : WEALTH, RICHES **2** : PLENTY, PROFUSION

op·u·lent \-lənt\ *adj* [L *opulentus,* fr. *ops* power, wealth] : marked by opulence: as **a** : WEALTHY **b** : richly abundant : PROFUSE (*opulent* harvests) (*opulent* foliage); *also* : amply fashioned : LUSH — **op·u·lent·ly** *adv*

opun·tia \ō-'pən-ch(ē-)ə\ *n* : PRICKLY PEAR

opus \'ō-pəs\ *n, pl* **opera** \'ō-pə-rə, 'äp-ə-\ *also* **opus·es** \'ō-pə-səz\ [L *oper-, opus* work] : WORK; *esp* : a musical composition or set of compositions

¹or \ər, (,)ȯ(ə)r\ *conj* [ME *other, or,* fr. OE *oththe*] — used as a function word to indicate an alternative (coffee *or* tea) (sink *or* swim)

²or *prep* [ON *ār,* adv., early, before] *archaic* : BEFORE

³or *conj, archaic* : BEFORE

⁴or \'ȯ(ə)r\ *n* [MF, gold, fr. L *aurum*] : the heraldic color gold or yellow

-or \ər, ‚ȯ(ə)r, 'ȯ(ə)r\ *n suffix* [L] : one that does a (specified) thing ⟨grant*or*⟩ ⟨elevat*or*⟩

ora *pl of* OS

or·a·cle \'ȯr-ə-kəl, 'är-\ *n* [L *oraculum*, fr. *orare* to speak] **1 a** : a person (as a priestess of ancient Greece) through whom a deity is held to speak **b** : a shrine in which a deity so reveals hidden knowledge or the divine purpose **c** : an answer or revelation given by an oracle **2 a** : a person giving wise or authoritative decisions or opinions **b** : an authoritative or wise expression or answer

orac·u·lar \ȯ-'rak-yə-lər, ə-\ *adj* **1** : of, relating to, or being an oracle **2** : resembling an oracle in wisdom, solemnity, or obscurity — **orac·u·lar·i·ty** \-‚rak-yə-'lar-ət-ē\ *n* — **orac·u·lar·ly** \-'rak-yə-lər-lē\ *adv*

oral \'ōr-əl, 'ȯr-, 'är-\ *adj* [L *or-, os* mouth] **1 a** : uttered by the mouth or in words : SPOKEN ⟨*oral* agreement⟩ **b** : using speech or the lips ⟨*oral* reading⟩ **2** : of, relating to, given through, or situated near the mouth ⟨*oral* hygiene⟩ ⟨the *oral* surface of a starfish⟩ — **oral·ly** \-ə-lē\ *adv*

syn VERBAL : ORAL applies to what is spoken rather than written ⟨*oral* traditions⟩ VERBAL applies to words whether oral or written and stresses the use of words in contrast to other forms of communication or expression ⟨*verbal* facility⟩ ⟨*verbal* difficulties⟩

or·ange \'ȯr-inj, 'är-\ *n* [MF, fr. OProv *auranja*, fr. Ar *nāranj*, fr. Per *nārang*] **1 a** : a globose berry with a reddish yellow rind and a sweet edible pulp **b** : any of various rather small evergreen citrus trees whose fruits are oranges **2** : any of a group of colors that lie midway between red and yellow in hue and are of medium lightness and moderate to high saturation — **orange** *adj*

or·ange·ade \‚ȯr-inj-'ād, ‚är-\ *n* : a drink made of orange juice, sugar, and water

Or·ange·man \'ȯr-inj-mən, 'är-\ *n* [fr. William III *d*1702 king of England and prince of *Orange*] **1** : a member of a secret society organized in the north of Ireland in 1795 to defend the British sovereign and to support the Protestant religion **2** : a Protestant Irishman esp. of Ulster

orange pekoe *n* : a tea formerly made from the tiny leaf and end bud of the spray; *also* : India or Ceylon tea of good quality

or·ange·ry \'ȯr-inj-(ə-)rē, 'är-\ *n, pl* **-ries** : a protected place (as a greenhouse) for raising oranges in cool climates

or·ange·wood \-inj-‚wu̇d\ *n* : the wood of the orange tree used esp. in turnery and carving

orang·u·tan *or* **orang·ou·tan** \ə-'raŋ-ə-‚taŋ, -‚tan\ *n* [Malay *orang hutan*, lit., man of the forest] : a largely herbivorous and arboreal anthropoid ape of Borneo and Sumatra about two thirds as large as the gorilla

orate \ȯ-'rāt\ *vi* [back-formation fr. *oration*] : to speak in a declamatory or grandiloquent manner : HARANGUE

ora·tion \ə-'rā-shən, ȯ-\ *n* [L *oration-, oratio*, fr. *orare* to speak, pray] : an elaborate discourse delivered in a formal and dignified manner usu. on some special occasion

or·a·tor \'ȯr-ət-ər, 'är-\ *n* [L, speaker, fr. *orare* to speak] : one that delivers an oration; *also* : a public speaker noted for skill and power in speaking

Or·a·to·ri·an \‚ȯr-ə-'tōr-ē-ən, ‚är-, -'tȯr-\ *n* : a member of the Congregation of the Oratory of St. Philip Neri originating in Rome in 1564 and comprising independent communities of secular priests under obedience but without vows — **Oratorian** *adj*

or·a·tor·i·cal \‚ȯr-ə-'tȯr-i-kəl, ‚är-ə-'tär-\ *adj* : of, relating to, or characteristic of an orator or oratory — **or·a·tor·i·cal·ly** \-k(ə-)lē\ *adv*

or·a·to·rio \‚ȯr-ə-'tōr-ē-‚ō, ‚är-, -'tȯr-\ *n, pl* **-ri·os** [It, fr. the *Oratorio* di San Filippo Neri (Oratory of St. Philip Neri) in Rome] : a vocal and orchestral work on a usu. scriptural subject consisting chiefly of recitatives, arias, and choruses without action or scenery

¹or·a·to·ry \'ȯr-ə-‚tōr-ē, 'är-, -‚tȯr-\ *n, pl* **-ries** [LL *oratorium*, fr. L *orare* to speak, pray] : a place of prayer; *esp* : a private or institutional chapel

²oratory *n* [L *oratoria*, fr. fem. of *oratorius* of an orator, fr. *orator*] **1** : the art of an orator **2** : oratorical language or presentations

¹orb \'ȯrb\ *n* [L *orbis* circle, disk, orbit] : a spherical body : as **a** : a heavenly body (as a planet) **b** : EYE **c** : a sphere

surmounted by a cross symbolizing kingly power and justice

²orb *vt* **1** : to form into a disk or circle **2** *archaic* : ENCIRCLE, ENCLOSE

or·bic·u·lar \ȯr-'bik-yə-lər\ *adj* : SPHERICAL, CIRCULAR — **or·bic·u·lar·i·ty** \-‚bik-yə-'lar-ət-ē\ *n* — **or·bic·u·lar·ly** \-'bik-yə-lər-lē\ *adv*

or·bic·u·late \ȯr-'bik-yə-lət\ *adj* : ORBICULAR ⟨an *orbiculate* leaf⟩

¹or·bit \'ȯr-bət\ *n* [L *orbita* wheel track, orbit, fr. *orbis* circle] **1** : the bony socket of the eye **2** : a path described by one body or object in its revolution about another ⟨the *orbit* of the earth about the sun⟩ **3** : range or sphere of activity — **or·bit·al** \-ᵊl\ *adj*

²orbit *vb* **1** : to revolve in an orbit around : CIRCLE **2** : to send up and make revolve in an orbit ⟨*orbit* a satellite⟩ **3** : to travel in circles — **or·bit·er** *n*

or·chard \'ȯr-chərd\ *n* [OE *ortgeard*, fr. L *hortus* garden (akin to E *yard*) + OE *geard* yard] : a planting of fruit trees or nut trees; *also* : the trees of such a planting — **or·chard·ist** \-əst\ *n* — **or·chard·man** \-mən, -‚man\ *n*

or·ches·tra \'ȯr-kə-strə\ *n* [Gk *orchēstra* space occupied by the chorus in the Greek theater, fr. *orcheisthai* to dance] **1** : a group of instrumentalists including esp. string players organized to perform ensemble music **2** : a front part of a theater : as **a** : the space in front of the stage in a modern theater that is used by an orchestra **b** : the forward section of seats on the main floor of a theater

or·ches·tral \ȯr-'kes-trəl\ *adj* **1** : of, relating to, or composed for an orchestra **2** : suggestive of an orchestra or its musical qualities ⟨a poem of *orchestral* sweep⟩ — **or·ches·tral·ly** \-trə-lē\ *adv*

or·ches·trate \'ȯr-kə-‚strāt\ *vt* : to compose or arrange (music) for an orchestra; *also* : to provide (as a ballet) with such music — **or·ches·tra·tion** \‚ȯr-kə-'strā-shən\ *n* — **or·ches·tra·tor** *also* **or·ches·trat·er** \'ȯr-kə-‚strāt-ər\ *n*

or·chid \'ȯr-kəd\ *n* [NL *orchid-, orchis*, fr. L *orchi-, orchis*, fr. Gk, testicle, orchid] **1** : any of a large family of perennial monocotyledonous plants that have usu. showy 3-petaled flowers with the middle petal enlarged into a lip and differing from the others in shape and color; *also* : its flower **2** : a variable color averaging a light purple

or·chis \'ȯr-kəs\ *n* [L] : ORCHID; *esp* : a woodland plant having fleshy roots and flowers with the lip spurred

or·dain \ȯr-'dān\ *vb* [OF *ordener*, fr. L *ordinare* to put in order, appoint, fr. *ordin-, ordo* order] **1** : to admit to the Christian ministry or priesthood by the ritual of a church : confer holy orders upon **2** : to establish or order by appointment, decree, or law : ENACT, DECREE; *esp* : DESTINE — **or·dain·er** *n* — **or·dain·ment** \-'dān-mənt\ *n*

or·deal \ȯr-'dēl\ *n* [OE *ordāl*] **1** : a primitive method of determining guilt or innocence by submitting the accused to dangerous or painful tests believed to be under supernatural control ⟨*ordeal* by fire⟩ **2** : a severe trial or experience

¹or·der \'ȯrd-ər\ *n* [MF *ordre*, fr. L *ordin-, ordo* arrangement, group, class] **1 a** : a group of people united in some way (as by living under the same religious rules, by having won the same distinction, or by loyalty to common interests and obligations) ⟨an *order* of monks⟩ ⟨an *order* of knighthood⟩ **b** : the badge or insignia of such an order **c** : a military decoration **2 a** : any of the several grades of the Christian ministry **b** *pl* : ORDINATION **3 a** : a rank, class, or special group in a community or society **b** : a class grouped according to quality, value, or natural characteristics; *esp* : a category of taxonomic classification ranking above the family and below the class **4 a** : the arrangement or sequence of objects in position or of events in time **b** : the prevailing mode or arrangement of things ⟨the old *order*⟩ **c** : regular or harmonious arrangement ⟨the *order* of nature⟩; *also* : a condition characterized by such an arrangement **5 a** : a customary or prescribed mode of procedure (as in debate or religious ritual) **b** : the rule of law or

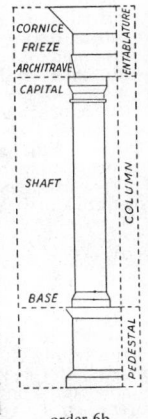

order 6b

proper authority ⟨*order* was restored⟩ **c** : a specific rule, regulation, or authoritative direction : COMMAND **6 a** : a style of building **b** : an architectural column with its related structures forming the unit of a style **7** : state or condition esp. with regard to functioning or repair ⟨out of *order*⟩ **8 a** : a written direction to pay money to someone **b** : a commission to purchase, sell, or supply goods or to perform work **c** : goods or items bought or sold — **in order to** : for the purpose of

²**order** *vb* **or·dered; or·der·ing** \'órd-(ə-)riŋ\ **1** : to put in order : ARRANGE; *also* : REGULATE **2** : to give an order to or for ⟨*order* troops to the front⟩ ⟨*order* groceries⟩ **3** : to give or place an order — **or·der·er** \'órd-ər-ər\ *n*

order arms — used as a command in the manual of arms to bring the rifle to a vertical position by the right side with its butt on the ground

¹**or·der·ly** \'órd-ər-lē\ *adj* **1 a** : arranged or disposed according to some order or pattern : REGULAR **b** : not marked by disorder : TIDY; *also* : METHODICAL **c** : governed by law or system : REGULATED ⟨an *orderly* universe⟩ **2** : well behaved : PEACEFUL ⟨an *orderly* crowd⟩ — **or·der·li·ness** \-lē-nəs\ *n* — **orderly** *adv*

²**orderly** *n, pl* **-lies** **1** : a soldier who attends a superior officer to convey messages and perform various services **2** : a hospital attendant who does general work

¹**or·di·nal** \'órd-nəl, -°n-əl\ *adj* [L *ordin-, ordo* order] : of a specified order or rank (as sixth) in a series

²**ordinal** *n* **1** *cap* : a collection of forms to be used in ordination **2** : ORDINAL NUMBER

ordinal number *n* : a number designating the place (as first, second, third) occupied by an item in an ordered sequence — see NUMBER table

or·di·nance \'órd-nən(t)s, 'órd-°n-ən(t)s\ *n* [MF *ordenance*, lit., art of arranging, fr. L *ordinant-, ordinans*, prp. of *ordinare* to put in order] **1** : an authoritative decree or direction : ORDER **2** : a law enacted by governmental authority; *esp* : a municipal regulation **3** : a prescribed usage, practice, or ceremony **syn** see LAW

or·di·nand \,órd-°n-'and\ *n* : a person being ordained esp. into holy orders

¹**or·di·nary** \'órd-°n-,er-ē\ *n, pl* **-nar·ies** [ML *ordinarius*, fr. L *ordinarius*, adj., ordinary] **1** : a prelate (as the bishop of a diocese) exercising jurisdiction over a territory or group by virtue of his office **2** *often cap* : the parts of the mass that do not vary from day to day **3** : regular or customary condition or course of things ⟨nothing out of the *ordinary*⟩ **4 a** *Brit* : a meal served at a fixed price **b** *chiefly Brit* : a tavern or eating house serving regular meals

²**ordinary** *adj* [L *ordinarius*, fr. *ordin-, ordo* order] **1** : to be expected : ROUTINE, NORMAL **2 a** : of common quality, rank, or ability **b** : POOR, INFERIOR **c** : lacking in refinement — **or·di·nar·i·ly** \,órd-°n-'er-ə-lē\ *adv* — **or·di·nar·i·ness** \'órd-°n-ē-nəs\ *n*

or·di·nate \'órd-nət, -°n-ət\ *n* : the distance of a point on a graph above or below the axis commonly labeled *x* : the vertical coordinate in a plane coordinate system

or·di·na·tion \,órd-°n-'ā-shən\ *n* : the act of ordaining : the state of being ordained

ord·nance \'órd-nən(t)s\ *n* **1 a** : military supplies including weapons, ammunition, vehicles, and equipment **b** : a service of the army in charge of ordnance **2** : CANNON, ARTILLERY

Or·do·vi·cian \,órd-ə-'vish-ən\ *n* : the period of the Paleozoic era between the Cambrian and Silurian; *also* : the corresponding system of rocks — **Ordovician** *adj*

or·dure \'ór-jər\ *n* [MF, fr. *ord* filthy, fr. L *horridus* horrid] **1** : EXCREMENT **2** : something morally degrading or depraving

¹**ore** \'ō(ə)r, 'ó(ə)r\ *n* [OE *ār* brass, copper, ore] : a mineral containing a constituent for which it is mined and worked ⟨get iron from its *ore*⟩

²**öre** \'ər-ə\ *n, pl* **öre** [Sw *öre* & Dan & Norw *øre*] **1** : a unit of value equal to ¹⁄₁₀₀ krona or ¹⁄₁₀₀ krone **2** : a coin representing one öre

ore·ad \'ōr-ē-,ad, 'ór-\ *n* [Gk *ereiad-, oreias*, fr. *oros* mountain] : one of the nymphs of mountains and hills

oreg·a·no \ə-'reg-ə-,nō\ *n, pl* **-nos** [Sp *orégano*, fr. L *origanum*] : a bushy perennial mint used as a seasoning and a source of aromatic oil — called also *wild marjoram*

Or·e·gon grape \,ór-i-gən-, ,är-, -,gän-\ *n* : a yellow-

flowered mahonia of the northwestern U.S. sometimes grown as an ornamental

Ores·tes \ó-'res-(,)tēz\ *n* : a son of Agamemnon and Clytemnestra who avenges his father's murder by slaying his mother and her lover

or·gan \'ór-gən\ *n* [OE & OF *organe*, fr. L *organum*, fr. Gk *organon*, lit., tool, instrument; akin to E *work*] **1 a** : a wind instrument consisting of sets of pipes made to sound by compressed air and controlled by keyboards and producing a variety of musical effects — called also *pipe organ* **b** : REED ORGAN **c** : an instrument in which the sounds of the pipe organ are approximated by means of electronic devices **d** : any of various similar cruder instruments **2** : a differentiated animal or plant structure consisting of cells and tissues and performing some specific function — compare SYSTEM **3** : a means of performing some function or accomplishing some end ⟨the courts and other *organs* of government⟩ **4** : a publication (as a newspaper or magazine) expressing the opinions or serving the interests of a special group

organ- or **organo-** *comb form* **1** : organ ⟨*organo*genesis⟩ **2** : organic ⟨*organo*mercurial⟩

or·gan·dy *also* **or·gan·die** \'ór-gən-dē\ *n, pl* **-dies** [F *organdi*] : a very fine transparent muslin with a stiff finish

or·gan·elle \,ór-gə-'nel\ *n* : a specialized part of a cell analogous to an organ

organ-grind·er \'ór-gən-,grīn-dər\ *n* : one that cranks a hand organ; *esp* : an itinerant street musician who grinds a barrel organ

or·gan·ic \ór-'gan-ik\ *adj* **1 a** : of, relating to, or arising in a bodily organ **b** : affecting the structure of the organism **2 a** : of, relating to, or derived from living organisms **b** (1) : of, relating to, or containing carbon compounds (2) : of, relating to, or dealt with by a branch of chemistry concerned with the carbon compounds of living beings and most other carbon compounds **3 a** : forming an integral element of a whole **b** : having systematic coordination of parts : ORGANIZED ⟨an *organic* whole⟩ **c** : developing in the manner of a living plant or animal ⟨society is *organic*⟩ — **or·gan·i·cal·ly** \-i-k(ə-)lē\ *adv*

or·gan·ism \'ór-gə-,niz-əm\ *n* **1** : an individual constituted to carry on the activities of life by means of organs separate in function but mutually dependent : a living person, plant, or animal **2** : a complex structure (as society) like a living organism in having many interdependent parts — **or·gan·is·mal** \,ór-gə-'niz-məl\ *or* **or·gan·is·mic** \-mik\ *adj* — **or·gan·is·mi·cal·ly** \-mi-k(ə-)lē\ *adv*

or·gan·ist \'ór-gə-nəst\ *n* : one who plays an organ

or·ga·ni·za·tion \,órg-(ə-)nə-'zā-shən\ *n* **1** : the act or process of organizing or of being organized **2** : the condition or manner of being organized **3 a** : ASSOCIATION, SOCIETY **b** : an administrative body or its personnel : MANAGEMENT; *also* : such a body with other groups directed and supervised by it — **or·ga·ni·za·tion·al** \-shnəl, -shən-°l\ *adj* — **or·ga·ni·za·tion·al·ly** \-ē\ *adv*

organization man *n* : a man who subordinates individualism to conformity with the standards and requirements of an organization

or·ga·nize \'ór-gə-,nīz\ *vb* **1** : to develop an organic structure : undergo or cause to undergo organization **2** : to arrange or form into a complete and functioning whole **3 a** : to set up an administrative structure for ⟨*organize* a business⟩ **b** : to persuade to associate in an organization; *esp* : UNIONIZE **4** : to arrange by systematic planning and united effort ⟨*organize* a prom⟩ **5** : to form or join into an organization; *esp* : to join in a union

or·ga·niz·er \-,nī-zər\ *n* **1** : one that organizes **2** : INDUCTOR 3

or·gan·o·gen·e·sis \,ór-gə-nō-'jen-ə-səs\ *n, pl* **-gen·e·ses** \-ə-,sēz\ : the origin and development of bodily organs — **or·gan·o·ge·net·i·cal·ly** \-i-k(ə-)lē\ *adv* — **or·gan·o·ge·net·ic** \-jə-'net-ik\ *adj*

or·gan·ol·o·gy \,ór-gə-'näl-ə-jē\ *n* : the study of bodily organs — **or·gan·o·log·ic** \-nə-'läj-ik\ *adj*

or·gan·o·ther·a·py \-nō-'ther-ə-pē\ *n* : the use of animal organs or their extracts in the treatment of disease

or·gan·za \ór-'gan-zə\ *n* : a sheer dress fabric resembling organdy and usu. made of silk, rayon, or nylon

or·gasm \'ór-,gaz-əm\ *n* [Gk *orgasmos*, fr. *organ* to grow ripe, be lustful] : the climax of sexual excitement in coitus

— or·gas·mic \ȯr-'gaz-mik\ *or* or·gas·tic \-'gas-tik\ *adj*

or·gi·as·tic \ˌȯr-jē-'as-tik\ *adj* : of, relating to, or marked by orgies — or·gi·as·ti·cal·ly \-ti-k(ə-)lē\ *adv*

or·gu·lous \'ȯr-gyə-ləs\ *adj* [OF *orgueil* pride] : PROUD, HAUGHTY

or·gy \'ȯr-jē\ *n, pl* orgies [Gk *orgia*, pl.] 1 : secret ceremonial rites held in honor of an ancient Greek or Roman deity and usu. characterized by ecstatic singing and dancing 2 : drunken revelry 3 : an excessive indulgence in an activity

ori·el \'ȯr-ē-əl, 'ȯr-\ *n* [ME, porch, oriel, fr. MF *oriol* porch] : a large bay window projecting from a wall and supported by a corbel or bracket

Ori·ent \'ȯr-ē-ənt, 'ȯr-, -ˌent\ *n* [L *orient-, oriens*, fr. prp. of *oriri* to rise] : EAST; *esp* : the countries of eastern Asia

¹orient *adj* 1 *archaic* : ORIENTAL 2 : LUSTROUS, SPARKLING ⟨*orient* gems⟩ 3 *archaic* : RISING

²ori·ent \-ˌent\ *vt* 1 a : to cause to face or point toward the east; *esp* : to build (as a church) with the longitudinal axis pointing eastward and the chief altar at the eastern end b : to set or arrange in a definite position esp. in relation to the points of the compass 2 a : to set right by adjusting to facts or principles b : to acquaint with an existing situation or environment

oriel

ori·en·tal \ˌȯr-ē-'ent-ºl, ˌȯr-\ *adj, often cap* : of or relating to the Orient — ori·en·tal·ly \-ºl-ē\ *adv*

Oriental *n* : a member of one of the indigenous peoples of the Orient; *esp* : a Chinese, Japanese, or other Mongoloid

ori·en·tal·ism \-ºl-ˌiz-əm\ *n, often cap* 1 : a trait, custom, or habit of expression characteristic of oriental peoples 2 : learning in oriental subjects — ori·en·tal·ist \-ºl-əst\ *n, often cap*

ori·en·tal·ize \-ºl-ˌīz\ *vb* : to make or become oriental

Oriental poppy *n* : an Asiatic perennial poppy widely grown for its very large showy flowers

Oriental rug *n* : a handwoven or hand-knotted one-piece rug or carpet made in the Orient

ori·en·tate \'ȯr-ē-ən-ˌtāt, 'ȯr-, -ˌen-\ *vb* 1 : ORIENT 2 : to face east

ori·en·ta·tion \ˌȯr-ē-ən-'tā-shən, ˌȯr-, -ˌen-\ *n* 1 : the act or process of orienting : the state of being oriented 2 : change of position by a protoplasmic body in response to external stimulus — ori·en·ta·tion·al \-shnəl, -shən-ºl\ *adj*

or·i·fice \'ȯr-ə-fəs, 'är-\ *n* [LL *orificium*, fr. L *or-, os* mouth + *facere* to make] : an opening (as a vent, mouth, hole, or aperture) through which something may pass — or·i·fi·cial \ˌȯr-ə-'fish-əl, ˌär-\ *adj*

ori·flamme \'ȯr-ə-ˌflam, 'är-\ *n* [MF *oriflambe*, fr. ML *aurea flamma*, lit., golden flame] 1 : a brightly colored banner used as a standard or ensign in battle 2 : something suggestive of an oriflamme in its power to inspire devotion or courage

ori·ga·mi \ˌȯr-ə-'gäm-ē\ *n* [Jap] : the art or process of Japanese paper folding

orig·a·num \ə-'rig-ə-nəm\ *n* [L, wild marjoram, fr. Gk *origanon*] : any of various fragrant aromatic plants of the mint or vervain families used as seasonings

or·i·gin \'ȯr-ə-jən, 'är-\ *n* [L *origin-, origo*, fr. *oriri* to rise] 1 : ANCESTRY, PARENTAGE 2 a : rise, beginning, or derivation from a source b : primary source or cause 3 : the more fixed, more central, or larger attachment of a muscle 4 : the intersection of the axes in a coordinate system

syn ORIGIN, SOURCE, INCEPTION, ROOT mean the point at which something begins its course or existence. ORIGIN applies to the things or persons from which something is ultimately derived and often to the causes operating before the thing itself comes into being; SOURCE stresses the point from which something springs into being ⟨an insect bite was the *source* of the infection⟩ INCEPTION stresses the beginning point without implying causes ⟨a member from the *inception* of the club⟩ ROOT suggests a first, ultimate, or fundamental source not always discernible ⟨their quarrel had *roots* deep in the past⟩

¹orig·i·nal \ə-'rij-ən-ºl, -'rij-nəl\ *n* 1 *archaic* : the source or cause from which something arises 2 a : that from which a copy, reproduction, or translation is made b : a

work composed firsthand 3 a : a person who is original in thought or action b *archaic* : ECCENTRIC 2

²original *adj* 1 : of or relating to the origin or beginning : FIRST, EARLIEST ⟨the *original* part of an old house⟩ ⟨*original* inhabitants⟩ 2 a : having spontaneous origin : not copied, reproduced, or translated ⟨*original* paintings⟩ ⟨an *original* idea⟩ b : constituting that from which a copy, reproduction, or translation is made 3 : independent and creative in thought or action : INVENTIVE — orig·i·nal·ly \-ē\ *adv*

orig·i·nal·i·ty \ə-ˌrij-ə-'nal-ət-ē\ *n* 1 : the quality or state of being original 2 : FRESHNESS, NOVELTY 3 : the power or ability to think, to act, or to do something in ways that are new ⟨an artist of great *originality*⟩

original sin *n* : sinfulness often held in Christian theology to be transmitted from generation to generation and inherited by each person as a consequence of the original sinful choice made by Adam

orig·i·nate \ə-'rij-ə-ˌnāt\ *vb* 1 : to bring into existence : cause to be : give rise to : INITIATE 2 : to take or have origin : come into existence — orig·i·na·tion \ə-ˌrij-ə-'nā-shən\ *n* — orig·i·na·tor \ə-'rij-ə-ˌnāt-ər\ *n*

orig·i·na·tive \ə-'rij-ə-ˌnāt-iv\ *adj* : having ability to originate : CREATIVE — orig·i·na·tive·ly *adv*

ori·ole \'ȯr-ē-ˌōl, 'ȯr-\ *n* [F *oriol*, fr. L *aureolus*, dim. of *aureus* golden, fr. *aurum* gold] 1 : any of a family of usu. brightly colored Old World passerine birds related to the crows 2 : any of a family of New World passerine birds of which the males are usu. black and yellow or orange and the females chiefly greenish or yellowish

Ori·on \ə-'rī-ən, ȯ-\ *n* : a constellation on the equator east of Taurus represented on charts by the figure of a hunter with belt and sword

or·i·son \'ȯr-ə-sən, 'är-\ *n* [ME, fr. OF, fr. LL *oration-, oratio*, fr. L *orare* to speak, pray] : PRAYER

Or·lean·ist \'ȯr-lē-ə-nəst, ȯr-'lē-(ə-)nəst\ *n* : a supporter of the Orleans family in its claim to the throne of France by descent from a younger brother of Louis XIV

Or·lon \'ȯr-ˌlän\ *trademark* 1 — used for a synthetic fiber typically of high bulk and soft warm hand 2 : yarn or fabric made of Orlon fiber

or·mo·lu \'ȯr-mə-ˌlü\ *n* [F *or moulu*, lit., ground gold] : a brass made to imitate gold and used for decorative purposes

¹or·na·ment \'ȯr-nə-mənt\ *n* [L *ornare* to adorn] 1 : something that adorns or adds beauty : DECORATION, EMBELLISHMENT 2 : the act of adorning : addition or inclusion of something that beautifies : ORNAMENTATION 3 : an embellishing note in music that does not belong to the essential harmony or melody

²or·na·ment \-ˌment\ *vt* : to provide with ornament : EMBELLISH, ADORN, DECORATE

¹or·na·men·tal \ˌȯr-nə-'ment-ºl\ *adj* : of, relating to, or serving as ornament — or·na·men·tal·ly \-ºl-ē\ *adv*

²ornamental *n* : a decorative object; *esp* : a plant cultivated for its beauty rather than for use

or·na·men·ta·tion \ˌȯr-nə-mən-'tā-shən, -ˌmen-\ *n* 1 : the act or process of ornamenting : the state of being ornamented 2 : a decorative device; *also* : ORNAMENTS

or·nate \ȯr-'nāt\ *adj* 1 : marked by elaborate rhetoric or florid style 2 : elaborately or excessively decorated — or·nate·ly *adv* — or·nate·ness *n*

or·nery \'ȯrn-(ə-)rē, 'än-\ *adj* or·ner·i·er; -est [E dial., common, alter. of *ordinary*] : having an irritable disposition : CANTANKEROUS — or·ner·i·ness *n*

ornith- *or* ornitho- *comb form* [Gk *ornith-, ornis;* akin to E *erne*] : bird ⟨*ornithology*⟩

or·ni·this·chi·an \ˌȯr-nə-'this-kē-ən\ *n* : any of an order (Ornithischia) of dinosaurs having a pelvis like that of a bird — ornithischian *adj*

or·ni·thol·o·gy \ˌȯr-nə-'thäl-ə-jē\ *n* : a branch of zoology dealing with birds — or·ni·tho·log·i·cal \ˌȯr-nith-ə-'läj-i-kəl\ *or* or·ni·tho·log·ic \-'läj-ik\ *adj* — or·ni·tho·log·i·cal·ly \-i-k(ə-)lē\ *adv* — or·ni·thol·o·gist \ˌȯr-nə-'thäl-ə-jəst\ *n*

or·ni·tho·sis \ˌȯr-nə-'thō-səs\ *n, pl* -tho·ses \-'thō-ˌsēz\ : PSITTACOSIS

orog·e·ny \ȯ-'räj-ə-nē\ *n, pl* -nies [Gk *oros* mountain] : the process of mountain formation — oro·gen·ic \ˌȯr-ə-'jen-ik, ˌär-\ *adj*

oro·tund \'ȯr-ə-ˌtənd, 'är-\ *adj* [modif. of L *ore rotundo*, lit., with round mouth] 1 : marked by fullness, strength, and clarity of sound **:** SONOROUS **2 :** POMPOUS, BOMBASTIC — **oro·tun·di·ty** \,ȯr-ə-'tän-dət-ē, ,är-\ *n*

¹or·phan \'ȯr-fən\ *n* [Gk *orphanos*] **1 :** a child deprived by death of one or usu. both parents **2 :** a motherless young animal — **orphan** *adj* — **or·phan·hood** \-,hud\ *n*

²orphan *vt* **or·phaned; or·phan·ing** \'ȯrf-(ə-)niŋ\ **:** to cause to become an orphan **:** deprive of parents

or·phan·age \'ȯrf-(ə-)nij\ *n* **:** an institution for the care of orphans

Or·pheus \'ȯr-fē-əs, -,fyüs\ *n* **:** a musician in Greek legend who descended to Hades after the death of his wife Eurydice and by his music obtained her release on condition that he not look back at her until reaching the upper world

or·phic \'ȯr-fik\ *adj* **1** *cap* **:** of or relating to Orpheus or to mystic rites or doctrines ascribed to him **2 :** MYSTIC, ORACULAR **3 :** resembling the music of Orpheus **:** ENTRANCING — **or·phi·cal·ly** \-fi-k(ə-)lē\ *adv*

or·pi·ment \'ȯr-pə-mənt\ *n* [MF, fr. L *auripigmentum*, fr. *aurum* gold + *pigmentum* pigment] **:** a yellow to orange sulfide of arsenic used as a pigment

or·pine \'ȯr-pən\ *n* **:** a sedum with pink or purple flowers used in folk medicine

or·ris \'ȯr-əs, 'är-\ *n* **:** a European iris with a fragrant rootstock used esp. in perfume and sachet powder; *also* **:** its rootstock

or·ris·root \-,rüt, -,rut\ *n* **:** the rootstock of an orris

orth- *or* **ortho-** *comb form* [Gk *orthos* straight, right] **1 :** straight **:** upright **:** vertical ⟨*orth*opteran⟩ **2 :** correct **:** corrective ⟨*ortho*dontia⟩

or·tho·cen·ter \'ȯr-thə-,sent-ər\ *n* **:** the point of intersection of the altitudes of a triangle

or·tho·chro·mat·ic \,ȯr-thə-krō-'mat-ik\ *adj* **:** sensitive to all colors except red ⟨an *orthoch*romatic film⟩

or·tho·clase \'ȯr-thə-,klās\ *n* [G *orthoklas*, fr. Gk *orthos* straight + *klas-, klan* to break] **:** a mineral KAlSi₃O₈ consisting of common potassium feldspar often with sodium in place of some of the potassium

orth·odon·tia \,ȯr-thə-'dän-ch(ē-)ə\ *n* **:** ORTHODONTICS

orth·odon·tics \-'dänt-iks\ *n* [Gk *odont-, odous* tooth] **:** a branch of dentistry dealing with irregularities of the teeth and their correction — **orth·odon·tic** \-'dänt-ik\ *adj* — **orth·odon·tist** \-'dänt-əst\ *n*

or·tho·dox \'ȯr-thə-,däks\ *adj* [LGk *orthodoxos*, fr. Gk *orthos* right + *doxa* opinion] **1 :** holding established beliefs esp. in religion ⟨an *orthodox* Christian⟩ **2 :** approved as measuring up to some standard **:** USUAL, CONVENTIONAL ⟨*orthodox* dress for a church wedding⟩ **3 :** EASTERN ORTHODOX

Orthodox Judaism *n* **:** Judaism that adheres to biblical law as interpreted in the authoritative rabbinic tradition and seeks to observe all the practices commanded in it

or·tho·doxy \'ȯr-thə-,däk-sē\ *n*, *pl* **-dox·ies 1 :** the quality or state of being orthodox **2 :** an orthodox belief or practice

or·tho·epy \'ȯr-thə-,wep-ē, ȯr-'thō-ə-pē\ *n* [Gk *epos* word] **:** the customary pronunciation of a language — **or·tho·ep·ic** \,ȯr-thə-'wep-ik\ *adj* — **or·tho·ep·i·cal·ly** \-'wep-i-k(ə-)lē\ *adv* — **or·tho·ep·ist** \'ȯr-thə-,wep-əst, ȯr-'thō-ə-pəst\ *n*

or·tho·gen·e·sis \,ȯr-thə-'jen-ə-səs\ *n*, *pl* **-gen·e·ses** \-ə-,sēz\ **:** variation of organisms held to occur in successive generations along a predestined line resulting in progressive evolutionary trends independent of external factors — **or·tho·ge·net·ic** \-jə-'net-ik\ *adj* — **or·tho·ge·net·i·cal·ly** \-'net-i-k(ə-)lē\ *adv*

or·thog·o·nal \ȯr-'thäg-ən-ᵊl\ *adj* [Gk *orthogōnios*, fr. *orthos* upright + *gōnia* angle] **:** mutually perpendicular — **or·thog·o·nal·ly** \ȯr-'thäg-nə-lē, -ən-ᵊl-ē\ *adv*

or·tho·grade \'ȯr-thə-,grād\ *adj* **:** walking with the body upright or vertical

or·tho·graph·ic \,ȯr-thə-'graf-ik\ *or* **or·tho·graph·i·cal** \-'graf-i-kəl\ *adj* **1 :** ORTHOGONAL **2** a **:** of or relating to orthography b **:** correct in spelling — **or·tho·graph·i·cal·ly** \-i-k(ə-)lē\ *adv*

or·thog·ra·phy \ȯr-'thäg-rə-fē\ *n*, *pl* **-phies 1** a **:** the writing of words with the proper letters according to standard usage b **:** a manner of representing the sounds of a language by written or printed symbols ⟨17th century *orthography*⟩ **2 :** the study of letters and spelling

or·tho·pe·dic \,ȯr-thə-'pēd-ik\ *adj* [Gk *paid-, pais* child]

1 : of or relating to orthopedics **2 :** marked by deformities or crippling — **or·tho·pe·di·cal·ly** \-'pēd-i-k(ə-)lē\ *adv*

or·tho·pe·dics \-'pēd-iks\ *n* **:** the correction or prevention of skeletal deformities — **or·tho·pe·dist** \-'pēd-əst\ *n*

or·thop·ter·an \ȯr-'thäp-tə-rən\ *n* [Gk *pteron* wing] **:** any of an order (Orthoptera) comprising insects with biting mouthparts, two pairs of wings or none, and an incomplete metamorphosis and usu. including the grasshoppers, mantises, and crickets — **orthopteran** *or* **or·thop·ter·al** \-rəl\ *or* **or·thop·ter·ous** \-rəs\ *adj* — **or·thop·ter·oid** \-,rȯid\ *n or adj* — **or·thop·ter·on** \-,rän\ *n*

or·tho·rhom·bic \,ȯr-thə-'räm-bik\ *adj* **:** of, relating to, or constituting a system of crystallization characterized by three unequal axes at right angles to each other

or·to·lan \'ȯrt-ᵊl-ən\ *n* [It *ortolano*, lit., gardener, fr. L *hortulanus*, fr. *hortus* garden] **1 :** a European bunting valued as a table delicacy **2** a **:** SORA b **:** BOBOLINK

¹-o·ry \,ȯr-ē, ,ȯr-ē, (ə-)rē\ *n suffix, pl* **-ories** [L *-orium*, fr. neut. of *-orius* -ory] **1 :** place of or for ⟨observat*ory*⟩ **2 :** something that serves for ⟨cremat*ory*⟩

²-ory *adj suffix* [L *-orius*] **1 :** of, relating to, or characterized by ⟨gustat*ory*⟩ **2 :** serving for, producing, or maintaining ⟨exculpat*ory*⟩

oryx \'ȯr-iks, 'ȯr-, 'är-\ *n*, *pl* **oryx·es** *or* **oryx** [Gk] **:** a large straight-horned African antelope

¹os \'äs\ *n*, *pl* **os·sa** \'äs-ə\ [L *oss-, os*] **:** BONE

²os \'ōs\ *n*, *pl* **ora** \'ȯr-ə, 'ȯr-ə\ [L *or-, os*] **:** MOUTH, ORIFICE

Osage \ō-'sāj\ *n* **:** a member of a Siouan people of Missouri

Osage orange *n* **:** an ornamental American tree of the mulberry family with shiny ovate leaves and hard bright orange wood; *also* **:** its yellowish fruit

Os·can \'äs-kən\ *n* **1 :** one of a people of ancient Italy occupying Campania **2 :** the language of the Oscan people

Os·car \'äs-kər\ *n* [after *Oscar* Pierce, 20th cent. American wheat grower] **:** a golden statuette awarded for achievement in motion pictures; *also* **:** any similar award

os·cil·late \'äs-ə-,lāt\ *vi* [L *oscillare*, fr. *oscillum* swing] **1** a **:** to swing backward and forward like a pendulum **:** VIBRATE b **:** to move or travel back and forth between two points **2 :** to vary between opposing beliefs, feelings, or theories **3 :** to vary above and below a mean value **4** a **:** to increase and decrease in magnitude or reverse direction periodically ⟨an *oscillating* electric current⟩ b **:** to generate or maintain an alternating current ⟨an *oscillating* circuit⟩ **syn** see SWAY — **os·cil·la·to·ry** \-ə-,tōr-ē, -,tȯr-\ *adj*

os·cil·la·tion \,äs-ə-'lā-shən\ *n* **1 :** the act or fact of oscillating **:** VIBRATION **2 :** VARIATION, FLUCTUATION **3 :** a flow of electricity changing periodically from a maximum to a minimum; *esp* **:** a flow periodically changing direction **4 :** a single swing or change (as of an oscillating body) from one extreme limit to the other — **os·cil·la·tion·al** \-shnəl, -shən-ᵊl\ *adj*

os·cil·la·tor \'äs-ə-,lāt-ər\ *n* **1 :** one that oscillates **2 :** a device for producing alternating current; *esp* **:** a radio-frequency or audio-frequency generator

os·cil·la·to·ria \ä-,sil-ə-'tōr-ē-ə, -'tȯr-\ *n* **:** any of a genus of filamentous blue-green algae growing in soil or water and exhibiting oscillatory movement

os·cil·lo·scope \ä-'sil-ə-,skōp, ə-\ *n* **:** an instrument in which the variations in a fluctuating electrical quantity appear temporarily as visible waves of light on the fluorescent screen of a cathode-ray tube

os·cine \'äs-,īn\ *adj* [L *oscin-, oscen* bird used in divination, fr. *obs-* in front of + *canere* to sing] **:** PASSERINE 2 — **oscine** *n*

os·cu·late \'äs-kyə-,lāt\ *vb* [L *osculari*, fr. *osculum* kiss, fr. dim. of *os* mouth] **:** KISS — **os·cu·la·tion** \,äs-kyə-'lā-shən\ *n* — **os·cu·la·to·ry** \'äs-kyə-lə-,tōr-ē, -,tȯr-\ *adj*

os·cu·lum \'äs-kyə-ləm\ *n*, *pl* **-la** \-lə\ **:** an excurrent opening of a sponge

¹-ose \,ōs, 'ōs\ *adj suffix* [L *-osus* -ous] **:** having, being, or possessing the qualities of ⟨cym*ose*⟩

²-ose \,ōs\ *n suffix* [F, fr. *glucose*] **1 :** carbohydrate; *esp* **:** sugar ⟨pent*ose*⟩ **2 :** primary hydrolysis product ⟨prot*ose*⟩

osier \'ō-zhər\ *n* [MF, fr. ML *auseria* osier bed] **1 :** any of various willows with pliable twigs used for furniture and basketry **2 :** a willow rod used in basketry **3 :** any of several American dogwoods — **osier** *adj*

Osi·ris \ō-'sī-rəs\ *n* **:** the Egyptian god of the Nile and judge of the dead

-o·sis \'ō-səs\ *n suffix, pl* **-o·ses** \'ō-ˌsēz\ *or* **-o·sis·es** [Gk *-ōsis*, fr. *-ō-* (stem of causative verbs in *-oun*) + *-sis*] **1 :** action **:** process **:** condition ⟨hypn*osis*⟩ **2 :** abnormal or diseased condition ⟨leuk*osis*⟩ ⟨leukocyt*osis*⟩ — **-ot·ic** \'ät-ik\ *adj suffix*

Os·man·li \äz-'man-lē\ *n* **1 :** a Turk of the western branch of the Turkish peoples **2 :** TURKISH — **Osmanli** *adj*

os·mat·ic \äz-'mat-ik\ *adj* [Gk *osmē* smell + E *-atic* (as in *aquatic*)] **:** depending primarily on the sense of smell for orientation

os·mic acid \ˌäz-mik-\ *n* **:** a crystalline compound OsO_4 that is an oxide of osmium, has a poisonous irritating vapor, and is used as a catalyst, oxidizing agent, and biological stain

os·mi·um \'äz-mē-əm\ *n* [NL, fr. Gk *osmē* odor] **:** a hard brittle blue-gray or blue-black metallic element with a high melting point that is the heaviest metal known and that is used esp. as a catalyst and in hard alloys — see ELEMENT table

os·mom·e·ter \äs-'mäm-ət-ər, äz-\ *n* **:** an apparatus for measuring the pressure produced by osmosis

os·mose \'äs-ˌmōs, 'äz-\ *vb* **1 :** to subject to osmosis **2 :** to diffuse by osmosis

os·mo·sis \äs-'mō-səs, äz-\ *n* [NL, fr. E *osmose*, fr. Gk *ōsmos* act of thrusting, fr. *ōthein* to push] **1 :** a diffusion through a semipermeable membrane typically separating a solvent and a solution that tends to equalize their concentrations; *esp* **:** the passage of solvent in distinction from the passage of solute **2 :** a process of absorption or diffusion suggestive of the flow of osmotic action ⟨a knowledge of human nature acquired largely by *osmosis*⟩ — **os·mot·ic** \-'mät-ik\ *adj* — **os·mot·i·cal·ly** \-'mät-i-k(ə-)lē\ *adv*

os·prey \'äs-prē\ *n, pl* **ospreys** [(assumed) MF *osfraie*, fr. L *ossifraga*, lit., bonebreaker] **1 :** a large brown and white hawk that feeds on fish **2 :** a feather trimming (as an aigrette) used for millinery

os·se·ous \'äs-ē-əs\ *adj* [L *osseus*, fr. *oss-*, *os* bone] **:** BONY 1 — **os·se·ous·ly** *adv*

os·si·cle \'äs-i-kəl\ *n* **:** a small bone or bony structure — **os·sic·u·lar** \ä-'sik-yə-lər\ *adj* — **os·sic·u·late** \-lət\ *adj*

os·si·fi·ca·tion \ˌäs-ə-fə-'kā-shən\ *n* **1 a :** formation of or conversion into bone or a bony substance **b :** an area of ossified tissue **2 :** a state of being callous or conventional in outlook — **os·sif·i·ca·to·ry** \ä-'sif-i-kə-ˌtōr-ē, -ˌtȯr-\ *adj*

os·si·fy \'äs-ə-ˌfī\ *vb* **-fied; -fy·ing** **1 :** to become or change into bone or bony tissue **2 :** to become or make callous or conventional

os·su·ary \'äsh-ə-ˌwer-ē\ *n, pl* **-ar·ies** **:** a depository for the bones of the dead

oste- *or* **osteo-** *comb form* [Gk *osteon*] **:** bone ⟨*oste*al⟩ ⟨*osteo*myelitis⟩

os·te·ich·thy·an \ˌäs-tē-'ik-thē-ən\ *n* **:** any of a large group (Osteichthyes) of fishes comprising the higher fishes with bony skeletons as distinguished from cartilaginous forms (as sharks) — **osteichthyan** *adj*

os·ten·si·ble \ä-'sten(t)-sə-bəl\ *adj* [L *ostens-*, *ostendere* to show, fr. *obs-* in front + *tendere* to stretch] **:** open to view **:** shown outwardly **:** DECLARED, PROFESSED, APPARENT ⟨his *ostensible* and possibly real motive⟩ — **os·ten·si·bly** \-blē\ *adv*

os·ten·so·ri·um \ˌäs-tən-'sōr-ē-əm, -'sȯr-\ *n, pl* **-ria** \-ē-ə\ **:** MONSTRANCE

os·ten·ta·tion \ˌäs-tən-'tā-shən\ *n* [L *ostentare* to show off, freq. of *ostendere* to show] **:** pretentious or excessive display **:** unnecessary show

os·ten·ta·tious \-shəs\ *adj* **:** marked by or fond of unnecessary display — **os·ten·ta·tious·ly** *adv* — **os·ten·ta·tious·ness** *n*

os·teo·ar·thri·tis \ˌäs-tē-ō-ˌär-'thrīt-əs\ *n* **:** degenerative arthritis

os·te·o·blast \'äs-tē-ə-ˌblast\ *n* [Gk *blastos* bud, embryo] **:** a cell that produces bone

os·te·o·clast \-ˌklast\ *n* [Gk *klan* to break] **:** a cell believed to break down unwanted bone

os·te·oid \'äs-tē-ˌȯid\ *adj* **:** resembling bone

os·teo·my·e·li·tis \ˌäs-tē-ō-ˌmī-ə-'līt-əs\ *n* [Gk *myelos* marrow] **:** an infectious inflammatory disease of bone marked by local death and separation of tissue

os·te·o·path \'äs-tē-ə-ˌpath\ *n* **:** a practitioner of osteopathy

os·te·op·a·thy \ˌäs-tē-'äp-ə-thē\ *n* **:** a system of treating diseases that places emphasis on manipulation esp. of bones but does not exclude other treatment (as the use of medicine and surgery) — **os·te·o·path·ic** \ˌäs-tē-ə-'path-ik\ *adj* — **os·te·o·path·i·cal·ly** \-'path-i-k(ə-)lē\ *adv*

os·ti·ole \'äs-tē-ˌōl\ *n* **:** a small opening

os·ti·um \'äs-tē-əm\ *n, pl* **ostia** \-tē-ə\ [NL, fr. L, door, mouth of a river] **:** an opening resembling a mouth

ostler *var of* HOSTLER

os·tra·cism \'äs-trə-ˌsiz-əm\ *n* **1 :** a method of temporary banishment by popular vote without trial or special accusation practiced in ancient Greece **2 :** exclusion by general consent from common privileges or social acceptance

os·tra·cize \'äs-trə-ˌsīz\ *vt* [Gk *ostrakizein*, fr. *ostrakon* shell, potsherd; fr. the use of potsherds as ballots in the voting] **1 :** to exile by ostracism **2 :** to exclude from a group by common consent

os·tra·cod \'äs-trə-ˌkäd\ *n* **:** any of a group (Ostracoda) of small mostly freshwater crustaceans — **os·tra·co·dan** \ˌäs-trə-'kōd-ᵊn\ *adj* — **os·tra·co·dous** \-'kōd-əs\ *adj*

os·tra·co·derm \ä-'strak-ə-ˌdərm, 'äs-trə-kō-\ *n* **:** any of an order (Ostracodermi) of primitive fossil armored fishes

os·trich \'äs-trich, 'ȯs-\ *n* [OF *ostruce*, fr. L *avis* bird + LL *struthio* ostrich, fr. Gk *strouthos* sparrow, ostrich] **1 :** a swift-footed 2-toed flightless bird of Africa and Arabia with valuable wing and tail plumes that is the largest of existing birds **2 :** one who attempts to avoid danger by refusing to face it

Os·tro·goth \'äs-trə-ˌgäth\ *n* **:** a member of the eastern division of the Goths — called also *East Goth;* compare VISIGOTH

Os·we·go tea \ä-ˌswē-gō-\ *n* **:** a No. American mint with showy bright scarlet irregular flowers

ot- *or* **oto-** *comb form* [Gk *ōt-*, *ous*; akin to E *ear*] **:** ear ⟨*otitis*⟩

¹oth·er \'əth-ər\ *adj* [OE *ōther*] **1 a :** being the one (as of two or more) left ⟨held his *other* arm straight⟩ **b :** being the ones distinct from those first mentioned ⟨thought the *other* members dull⟩ **c :** SECOND ⟨every *other* day⟩ **2 :** not the same **:** DIFFERENT ⟨*other* times and customs⟩ **3 :** ADDITIONAL ⟨some *other* guests are coming⟩ **4 :** recently past ⟨the *other* evening⟩

²other *pron* **1 :** remaining one **:** remaining ones ⟨lift one foot and then the *other*⟩ **2 :** a different or additional one ⟨something or *other*⟩

³other *adv* **:** OTHERWISE

oth·er·wise \-ˌwīz\ *adv* [OE *on ōthre wīsan* in another manner] **1 :** in a different way **:** DIFFERENTLY ⟨could not do *otherwise*⟩ **2 :** in different circumstances ⟨*otherwise* he might have won⟩ **3 :** in other respects ⟨the *otherwise* busy street⟩ — **otherwise** *adj*

oth·er·world \'əth-ər-ˌwərld\ *n* **:** a world beyond death or beyond present reality

oth·er·world·ly \-ˌwərl-(d)lē\ *adj* **1 a :** of or relating to a world other than the actual world **b :** concerned with or devoted to preparing for a world to come **2 :** devoted to highly intellectual, imaginative, or idealistic pursuits — **oth·er·world·li·ness** *n*

otic \'ōt-ik\ *adj* [Gk *ōt-*, *ous* ear] **:** of, relating to, or located near the ear

oti·ose \'ō-shē-ˌōs, 'ōt-ē-\ *adj* [L *otium* leisure] **1 :** being at leisure **:** IDLE **2 :** STERILE **3 :** USELESS, FUNCTIONLESS — **oti·ose·ly** *adv* — **oti·ose·ness** *n*

oti·tis \ō-'tīt-əs\ *n* **:** inflammation of the ear

oto·lar·yn·gol·o·gy \ˌōt-ō-ˌlar-ən-'gäl-ə-jē\ *n* **:** a branch of medicine dealing with the ear, nose, and throat

oto·lith \'ōt-ə-ˌlith\ *n* **:** a calcareous concretion in the inner ear — **oto·lith·ic** \ˌōt-ə-'lith-ik\ *adj*

ostrich

---

j joke; ŋ sing; ō flow; ȯ flaw; ȯi coin; th thin; th̲ this; ü loot; u̇ foot; y yet; yü few; yu̇ furious; zh vision

Ot·ta·wa \\'ät-ə-wə, -ˌwä, -ˌwȯ\\ *n* : a member of an Algonquian people of southern Ontario and Michigan

ot·ter \\'ät-ər\\ *n, pl* **otter** *or* **otters** [OE *otor*] **1** : any of several aquatic fish-eating mammals that are related to the weasels and minks and that have webbed and clawed feet and dark brown fur **2** : the fur or pelt of an otter

ot·to·man \\'ät-ə-mən\\ *n, pl* **-mans 1** *cap* : TURK — called also *Ottoman Turk* **2 a** : an upholstered often overstuffed seat or couch usu. without a back **b** : an overstuffed footstool — **Ottoman** *adj*

ou·bli·ette \\ˌü-blē-'et\\ *n* [F, fr. *oublier* to forget, fr. L *oblit-, oblivisci*] : a dungeon with an opening only at the top

ouch \\'aúch\\ *interj* — used to express sudden pain or displeasure

¹ought \\'ȯt\\ *auxiliary verb* [ME *oughte*, fr. *oughte*, past of *owen* to owe] — used to express moral obligation ⟨*ought* to pay our debts⟩, advisability ⟨*ought* to take care of yourself⟩, natural expectation ⟨*ought* to be here by now⟩, or logical consequence ⟨the result *ought* to be infinity⟩

²ought \\'ȯt, 'ät\\ *var of* AUGHT

oughtn't \\'ȯt-ᵊnt\\ : ought not

¹ounce \\'aún(t)s\\ *n* [MF *unce*, fr. L *uncia* twelfth part, ounce, inch] **1 a** : a unit of weight equal to ¹⁄₁₂ troy pound — see MEASURE table **b** : a unit of weight equal to ¹⁄₁₆ avoirdupois pound **c** : a small portion or quantity **2** : FLUIDOUNCE

²ounce *n* [OF *once* wildcat, alter. of *lonce*, fr. L *lync-, lynx lynx*] : SNOW LEOPARD

our \\är, (')aú(ə)r\\ *adj* [OE *ūre;* akin to E *us*] : of or relating to us or ourselves or ourself esp. as possessors or possessor ⟨*our* throne⟩, agents or agent ⟨*our* actions⟩, or objects or object of an action ⟨*our* being chosen⟩

Our Father *n* : LORD'S PRAYER

ours \\(')aú(ə)rz, ärz\\ *pron* : our one : our ones — used without a following noun as a pronoun equivalent in meaning to the adjective *our*

our·self \\är-'self, aú(ə)r-\\ *pron* : MYSELF — used (as by a sovereign or writer) to refer to the single-person subject when *we* is used instead of *I*

our·selves \\-'selvz\\ *pron* **1** : those identical ones that are we — compare WE **1** ; used reflexively ⟨we're doing it solely for *ourselves*⟩, for emphasis ⟨we *ourselves* will never go⟩, or in absolute constructions ⟨*ourselves* no longer young, we can sympathize with those who are old⟩ **2** : our normal, healthy, or sane condition or selves ⟨we weren't feeling like *ourselves* that day⟩

-ous \\əs\\ *adj suffix* [ME, partly fr. OF *-ous, -eus, -eux*, fr. L *-osus;* partly fr. L *-us*, nom. sing. masc. ending of many adjectives] **1** : full of : abounding in : having : possessing the qualities of ⟨clamor*ous*⟩ ⟨poison*ous*⟩ **2** : having a valence lower than in compounds or ions named with an adjective ending in *-ic* ⟨mercur*ous*⟩

ou·sel *var of* OUZEL

oust \\'aúst\\ *vt* [AF *ouster*, fr. OF *oster*, fr. L *ob-* against + *stare* to stand] : to force or drive out (as from office or from possession of something) : EXPEL ⟨*oust* a corrupt official⟩

oust·er \\'aús-tər\\ *n* : the act or an instance of ousting : EXPULSION

¹out \\'aút\\ *adv* [OE *ūt*] **1 a** : in a direction away from the inside or the center ⟨look *out* of a window⟩ **b** : from among others ⟨picked *out* a hat⟩ **2** : away from home, business, or usual or proper place ⟨*out* to lunch⟩ ⟨left a word *out*⟩ **3** : into a state of loss or deprivation ⟨vote the party *out* of office⟩ **4** : beyond control, possession, or occupation ⟨let a secret *out*⟩ ⟨lent *out* money⟩ **5** : into a state of vexation or disagreement ⟨friends fall *out*⟩ **6 a** : beyond the limits of existence, continuance, or supply ⟨the food ran *out*⟩ **b** : to extinction, exhaustion, or completion ⟨burn *out*⟩ **7 a** : in or into the open ⟨the sun came *out*⟩ **b** : ALOUD ⟨cried *out*⟩ **8** — used as an intensive with numerous verbs ⟨sketch *out* the plans⟩ **9 a** : so as to retire a batter or base runner ⟨the catcher threw *out* the runner trying to steal second base⟩ **b** : so as to be retired ⟨grounded *out* to the shortstop⟩

²out *vi* : to become known ⟨the truth will *out*⟩

³out *adj* **1** : situated outside : EXTERNAL ⟨the *out* edge⟩ **2** : situated at a distance : OUTLYING ⟨the *out* islands⟩ **3 a** : not being in power ⟨the *out* party⟩ **b** : not successful in reaching base ⟨the batter was *out*⟩ **4** : directed outward

or serving to direct something outward : OUTGOING ⟨put the letter in the *out* basket⟩

⁴out \\(')aút\\ *prep* **1** : out through ⟨ran *out* the door⟩ **2** : outward along or on ⟨drive *out* the old road⟩

⁵out \\'aút\\ *n* **1** : one who is out of power **2 a** : the retiring of a batter or base runner in baseball **b** : a player so retired **3** : a ball hit out-of-bounds in tennis or squash **4** : an item that is out of stock **5** : a way of escaping from an embarrassing situation or a difficulty

out- *prefix* [*¹out*] : in a manner that goes beyond, surpasses, or excels ⟨*out*maneuver⟩

out-and-out \\ˌaút-ᵊn-'(d)aút\\ *adj* **1** : OPEN, UNDISGUISED **2** : COMPLETE, THOROUGHGOING

out-and-out·er \\-ər\\ *n* : EXTREMIST

out·bal·ance \\(')aút-'bal-ən(t)s\\ *vt* : OUTWEIGH

out·bid \\-'bid\\ *vt* **-bid; -bid·ding** : to make a higher bid than

¹out·board \\'aút-ˌbȯrd, -ˌbȯrd\\ *adj* **1** : situated outboard **2** : having, using, or limited to the use of an outboard motor

²outboard *adv* **1** : outside the line of a ship's bulwarks or hull : away from the center line of a ship **2** : in a position closer or closest to either of the wing tips of an airplane

outboard motor *n* : a small internal-combustion engine with propeller attached for mounting at the stern of a small boat

out·bound \\'aút-ˌbaúnd\\ *adj* : outward bound ⟨*outbound* traffic⟩

out·brave \\(')aút-'brāv\\ *vt* **1** : to face or resist defiantly **2** : to exceed in courage

out·break \\'aút-ˌbrāk\\ *n* **1** : a sudden or violent breaking out : a sudden increase of activity or currency ⟨the *outbreak* of war⟩ ⟨an *outbreak* of bizarre hat styles⟩ **2** : something that breaks out: as **a** : EPIDEMIC ⟨an *outbreak* of measles⟩ **b** : INSURRECTION, REVOLT

out·breed \\-'brēd\\ *vt* **-breed·ing** **1** \\'aút-ˌbrēd\\ : to subject to outbreeding **2** \\(')aút-'\\ : to breed faster than

out·breed·ing \\'aút-ˌbrēd-iŋ\\ *n* : the interbreeding of relatively unrelated individuals

out·build·ing \\'aút-ˌbil-diŋ\\ *n* : a building separate from and smaller than the main one

out·burst \\-ˌbərst\\ *n* **1** : ERUPTION; *esp* : a violent expression of feeling **2** : a surge of activity or growth

out·cast \\-ˌkast\\ *n* : one who is cast out by society : PARIAH — **outcast** *adj*

out·caste \\-ˌkast\\ *n* : a Hindu who has been ejected from his caste for violation of its customs or rules; *also* : one who has no caste

out·class \\(')aút-'klas\\ *vt* : to excel or surpass so decisively as to appear of a higher class

out·come \\'aút-ˌkəm\\ *n* : final consequence : RESULT

¹out·crop \\'aút-ˌkräp\\ *n* **1** : a coming out of bedrock or of an unconsolidated deposit to the surface of the ground **2** : the part of a rock formation that appears at the surface of the ground

²out·crop \\'aút-'kräp\\ *vi* : to come to the surface : APPEAR ⟨granite *outcropping* through softer rocks⟩

out·cross·ing \\'aút-ˌkrȯ-siŋ\\ *n* : interbreeding of individuals of different strains but usu. the same breed — **out·cross** \\-ˌkrȯs\\ *vt or n*

out·cry \\'aút-ˌkrī\\ *n* **1** : a loud cry : CLAMOR **2** : a vehement protest

out·dat·ed \\(')aút-'dāt-əd\\ *adj* : OBSOLETE

out·dis·tance \\(')aút-'dis-tən(t)s\\ *vt* : to go far ahead of (as in a race) : OUTSTRIP

out·do \\(')aút-'dü\\ *vt* **-did** \\-'did\\; **-done** \\-'dən\\; **-do·ing** \\-'dü-iŋ\\ : to go beyond in action or performance : EXCEL, SURPASS

out·door \\ˌaút-ˌdȯr, -ˌdȯr\\ *also* **out·doors** \\-ˌdȯrz, -ˌdȯrz\\ *adj* **1** : of or relating to the outdoors ⟨an *outdoor* setting⟩ **2** : performed outdoors ⟨*outdoor* games⟩ **3** : not enclosed : having no roof ⟨an *outdoor* theater⟩

¹out·doors \\(')aút-'dō(ə)rz, -'dȯ(ə)rz\\ *adv* : outside a building : in or into the open air

²outdoors *n* **1** : the open air **2** : the world away from human habitations

out·er \\'aút-ər\\ *adj* **1** : EXTERNAL, OBJECTIVE ⟨*outer* appearance⟩ **2 a** : situated farther out ⟨the *outer* wall⟩ **b** : being away from a center ⟨the *outer* solar planets⟩

outer ear *n* : the outer visible portion of the ear that collects and directs sound waves toward the eardrum by way of a canal which extends inward through the temporal bone

out·er·most \'aut-ər-‚mōst\ *adj* : farthest out

outer space *n* : SPACE; *esp* : the region beyond the solar system

out·face \(')aut-'fās\ *vt* **1** : to stare down **2** : to confront unflinchingly : DEFY

out·fall \'aut-‚fól\ *n* : the outlet of a river, stream, lake, drain, or sewer

out·field \-‚fēld\ *n* **1** : the part of a baseball field beyond the infield and between the foul lines **2** : the baseball defensive positions comprising right field, center field, and left field — **out·field·er** \-‚fēl-dər\ *n*

out·fight \(')aut-'fīt\ *vt* **-fought** \-'fót\; **-fight·ing** : to surpass in fighting : DEFEAT

¹out·fit \'aut-‚fit\ *n* **1** : the articles forming the equipment or apparel for some purpose or occasion ⟨a camping *outfit*⟩ ⟨a sports *outfit*⟩ **2** : a group of persons working together or associated in the same undertaking ⟨soldiers belonging to the same *outfit*⟩

²outfit *vt* **1** : to furnish with an outfit : EQUIP ⟨*outfit* an expedition⟩ **2** : SUPPLY — **out·fit·ter** *n*

out·flank \(')aut-'flaŋk\ *vt* : to get around the flank of (an opposing force)

out·flow \'aut-‚flō\ *n* **1** : a flowing out **2** : something that flows out

out·foot \(')aut-'fut\ *vt* : to outdo in speed : OUTSTRIP

out·fox \(')aut-'fäks\ *vt* : OUTSMART

out·gen·er·al \-'jen-(ə-)rəl\ *vt* **-gen·er·aled** *or* **-gen·er·alled**; **-gen·er·al·ing** *or* **-gen·er·al·ling** : to surpass in generalship : OUTMANEUVER

out·go \'aut-‚gō\ *n, pl* **outgoes** : EXPENDITURE, OUTLAY

out·go·ing \'aut-‚gō-iŋ\ *adj* **1 a** : going out : DEPARTING ⟨*outgoing* tide⟩ **b** : retiring or withdrawing from a place or position ⟨the *outgoing* governor⟩ **2** : FRIENDLY, RESPONSIVE ⟨an *outgoing* person⟩

out·grow \(')aut-'grō\ *vt* **-grew** \-'grü\; **-grown** \-'grōn\; **-grow·ing** **1** : to grow faster than **2** : to grow too large or too mature for ⟨*outgrew* his clothes⟩

out·growth \'aut-‚grōth\ *n* **1** : a product of growing out : PROCESS 4, OFFSHOOT **2** : CONSEQUENCE, BY-PRODUCT

out·guess \(')aut-'ges\ *vt* : ANTICIPATE, OUTWIT

out·house \'aut-‚haus\ *n* : OUTBUILDING; *esp* : an outdoor toilet

out·ing \'aut-iŋ\ *n* **1** : an excursion usu. with a picnic ⟨hired buses for the club *outing* at the seashore⟩ **2** : a brief stay or trip in the open ⟨took the baby for an *outing*⟩

out·land·er \'aut-‚lan-dər\ *n* : FOREIGNER, ALIEN, STRANGER

out·land·ish \(')aut-'lan-dish\ *adj* **1** : of or relating to another country **2** : of foreign appearance or manner : BIZARRE **3** : remote from civilization ⟨lived in *outlandish* places⟩ **syn** see STRANGE — **out·land·ish·ly** *adv* — **out·land·ish·ness** *n*

out·last \(')aut-'last\ *vt* : to last longer than : SURVIVE

¹out·law \'aut-‚ló\ *n* [OE *ūtlaga*, fr. ON *ūtlagi*, fr. *ūt* out + *lag-*, *lög* law] **1** : a person excluded from the benefit or protection of the law **2 a** : a lawless person or a fugitive from the law **b** : a person or organization under a ban or disability — **outlaw** *adj*

²outlaw *vt* **1 a** : to deprive of the benefit and protection of law **b** : to make illegal **2** : to place under a ban or disability — **out·law·ry** \'aut-‚ló-rē\ *n*

out·lay \'aut-‚lā\ *n* **1** : the act of laying out or spending **2** : EXPENDITURE, PAYMENT

out·let \'aut-‚let, -lət\ *n* **1** : a place or opening through which something is let out : EXIT, VENT **2** : a means of release or satisfaction for an emotion or impulse **3** : a place (as in a wall) at which an electrical device can be plugged into the wiring system **4** : a market for a product : an agency (as a store or a dealer) through which a product is marketed

¹out·line \'aut-‚līn\ *n* **1** : a line that traces or forms the outer limits of an object or figure and shows its shape **2** : a drawing or picture giving only the outlines of something; *also* : this method of drawing **3 a** : a summary statement of information often in the form of numbered heads and subheads **b** : a preliminary account of a project **4** : a condensed treatment of a subject : DIGEST

²outline *vt* **1** : to draw the outline of **2** : to indicate the principal features or different parts of

out·live \(')aut-'liv\ *vt* : to live longer than : SURVIVE, OUTLAST

out·look \'aut-‚luk\ *n* **1 a** : a place offering a view **b** : a view from a particular place **2** : POINT OF VIEW **3** : the prospect for the future

out·ly·ing \'aut-‚lī-iŋ\ *adj* : remote from a center or main body ⟨an *outlying* suburb⟩

out·ma·neu·ver \‚aut-mə-'n(y)ü-vər\ *vt* **1** : to defeat by more skillful maneuvering **2** : to surpass in maneuvering

out·match \(')aut-'mach\ *vt* : to prove superior to : OUTDO

out·mod·ed \(')aut-'mōd-əd\ *adj* **1** : not in style ⟨an *outmoded* dress⟩ **2** : no longer acceptable or usable ⟨*outmoded* beliefs⟩ ⟨*outmoded* equipment⟩

out·most \'aut-‚mōst\ *adj* : farthest out : OUTERMOST

out·num·ber \(')aut-'nəm-bər\ *vt* : to exceed in number ⟨girls *outnumber* boys in the class⟩

out of *prep* **1 a** (1) : from within to the outside of ⟨walked *out of* the room⟩ (2) — used as a function word to indicate a change in quality, state, or form ⟨woke up *out of* a deep sleep⟩ **b** (1) : beyond the range or limits of ⟨*out of* sight⟩ (2) : from among ⟨one *out of* four survived⟩ **2** : in or into a state of deprivation or lack of ⟨cheated him *out of* his savings⟩ **3** : because of : FROM ⟨came *out of* curiosity⟩ **4** — used as a function word to indicate the constituent material, basis, or source ⟨built *out of* old lumber⟩

out-of-bounds \‚aut-ə(v)-'baun(d)z\ *adv (or adj)* : outside the prescribed area of play

out-of-date \‚aut-ə(v)-'dāt\ *adj* : OUTMODED, OBSOLETE

out-of-door \‚aut-ə(v)-'dō(ə)r, -'dó(ə)r\ *or* **out-of-doors** \-'dō(ə)rz, -'dó(ə)rz\ *adj* : OUTDOOR

out-of-doors *n* : OUTDOORS

out-of-the-way \‚aut-ə(v)-thə-'wā\ *adj* **1** : being off the beaten track ⟨an *out-of-the-way* restaurant⟩ **2** : not commonly found or met : UNUSUAL ⟨the bookstore specializes in *out-of-the-way* titles⟩

out·pa·tient \'aut-‚pā-shənt\ *n* : a patient not an inmate of a hospital who visits it for diagnosis or treatment — **outpatient** *adj*

out·play \(')aut-'plā\ *vt* : to play more skillfully than : EXCEL

out·point \-'póint\ *vt* : to win more points than

out·post \'aut-‚pōst\ *n* **1** : a soldier or group of soldiers stationed at some distance from a military force or a camp as a guard against enemy attack **2** : the position occupied by an outpost **3** : a settlement on a frontier; *also* : an outlying settlement

out·pour \aut-'pō(ə)r, -'pó(ə)r\ *vt* : to pour out — **out·pour** \'aut-‚\ *n*

out·pour·ing \'aut-‚pōr-iŋ, -‚pór-\ *n* **1** : the act of pouring out **2** : something that pours out or is poured out : OUTFLOW **3** : OUTBURST

out·put \-‚put\ *n* **1** : the amount produced or able to be produced usu. in a stated time by a man, machine, factory, or industry : PRODUCTION, YIELD ⟨daily *output* of a factory⟩ **2 a** : power or energy delivered by a machine or system **b** : a point at which something (as power, an electronic signal, or data) comes out

¹out·rage \'aut-‚rāj\ *n* [OF, excess, outrage, fr. *outre* beyond, in excess, fr. L *ultra*] **1** : an act of violence or brutality **2** : INJURY, INSULT **3** : the resentment aroused by injury or insult

²outrage *vt* **1 a** : RAPE **b** : to subject to violent injury or gross insult **2** : to arouse anger or extreme resentment in **syn** see OFFEND

out·ra·geous \aut-'rā-jəs\ *adj* : being beyond all bounds of decency or justice : extremely offensive, insulting, or shameful : SHOCKING — **out·ra·geous·ly** *adv* — **out·ra·geous·ness** *n*

syn OUTRAGEOUS, ATROCIOUS mean flagrantly bad or horrible. OUTRAGEOUS implies exceeding the limits of what is tolerable or decent ⟨*outrageous* manners⟩ ATROCIOUS implies merciless cruelty, savagery, or contempt of ordinary values ⟨*atrocious* killings by the invaders⟩

out·rank \(')aut-'raŋk\ *vt* : to rank higher than : exceed in importance

ou·tré \ü-'trā\ *adj* [F] : violating convention or propriety : BIZARRE

out·reach \(')aut-'rēch\ *vb* **1** : to surpass in reach : EXCEED **2** : to get the better of by trickery : OVERREACH

---

j joke; **ŋ** sing; **ō** flow; **ȯ** flaw; **ȯi** coin; **th** thin; **th** this; **ü** loot; **u̇** foot; **y** yet; **yü** few; **yu̇** furious; **zh** vision

out·ride \(')aut-'rīd\ *vt* **-rode** \-'rōd\; **-rid·den** \-'rid-ʰn\; **-rid·ing** \-'rīd-iŋ\ : to ride better, faster, or farther than : OUTSTRIP

out·rid·er \'aut-ˌrīd-ər\ *n* **1** : a mounted attendant **2** : FORERUNNER, HARBINGER

out·rig·ger \'aut-ˌrig-ər\ *n* **1 a** : a projecting frame on a float attached to the side of a canoe or boat to prevent upsetting **b** : a projecting beam run out from a ship's side to help secure the masts or from a mast to extend a rope or sail **c** : a projecting support for an oarlock; *also* : a boat so equipped **2** : a projecting frame to support the elevator or tail planes of an airplane or the rotor of a helicopter

¹out·right \(')aut-'rīt\ *adv* **1 a** : in entirety : COMPLETELY (sold *outright*) **b** : UNRESERVEDLY (laughed *outright*) **2** : on the spot : INSTANTANEOUSLY (killed *outright*)

²out·right \'aut-ˌrīt\ *adj* **1** : going to the full extent : THOROUGHGOING (*outright* persecution) **2** : given without reservation (an *outright* gift)

out·run \(')aut-'rən\ *vt* **-ran** \-'ran\; **-run; -run·ning** : to run faster than; *also* : EXCEED

out·sell \-'sel\ *vt* **-sold** \-'sōld\; **-sell·ing 1** : to exceed in sales (cigarettes far *outsold* cigars) **2** : to surpass in selling

out·set \'aut-ˌset\ *n* : BEGINNING, START

out·shine \(')aut-'shīn\ *vt* **-shone** \-'shōn\; **-shin·ing 1 a** : to shine brighter than **b** : to exceed in splendor or showiness **2** : OUTDO, SURPASS

out·shoot \(')aut-'shüt\ *vt* **-shot** \-'shät\; **-shoot·ing 1** : to surpass in shooting or making shots **2** : to shoot or go beyond

¹out·side \(')aut-'sīd, 'aut-ˌ\ *n* **1** : a place or region beyond an enclosure or boundary **2** : an outer side or surface **3** : the utmost limit or extent (would sell 500 copies at the *outside*)

²outside *adj* **1** : of, relating to, or being on or toward the outer side or surface (the *outside* edge) **2 a** : situated or performed outside a particular place (*outside* noises) **b** : connected with or giving access to the outside (*outside* telephone line) **3** : MAXIMUM **4 a** : not included or originating in a particular group or organization (*outside* influences) **b** : not belonging to one's regular occupation or duties (*outside* activities) (*outside* reading) **5** : barely possible : REMOTE (an *outside* chance)

³outside *adv* : on or to the outside : OUTDOORS

⁴outside *prep* **1** : on or to the outside of (*outside* the house) **2** : beyond the limits of (*outside* the law) **3** : EXCEPT 1 (nobody *outside* a few close friends)

outside of *prep* **1** : OUTSIDE **2** : BESIDES

out·sid·er \(')aut-'sīd-ər\ *n* : a person who does not belong to a particular group

out·sit \-'sit\ *vt* **-sat** \-'sat\; **-sit·ting** : to remain sitting or in session longer than or beyond the time of

¹out·size \'aut-ˌsīz\ *n* : an unusual size; *esp* : a size larger than the standard

²outsize *also* **out·sized** \-ˌsīzd\ *adj* **1** : unusually large or heavy **2** : too large

out·skirts \'aut-ˌskərts\ *n pl* : the outlying parts of a place or town : BORDERS

out·smart \(')aut-'smärt\ *vt* : to get the better of; *esp* : OUTWIT

out·soar \-'sō(ə)r, -'so(ə)r\ *vt* : to soar beyond or above

out·sole \'aut-ˌsōl\ *n* : the outside sole of a boot or shoe

out·spo·ken \aut-'spō-kən\ *adj* : direct and open in speech or expression : FRANK (an *outspoken* person) (*outspoken* criticism) — **out·spo·ken·ness** \-kən-nəs\ *n*

out·spread \aut-'spred\ *vt* **-spread; -spread·ing** : to spread out : EXTEND — **outspread** \'aut-ˌspred\ *adj*

out·stand·ing \aut-'stan-diŋ\ *adj* **1 a** : UNPAID (*outstanding* bills) **b** : CONTINUING, UNRESOLVED (problems *outstanding*) **c** : publicly issued and sold (20,000 shares *outstanding*) **2 a** : standing out from a group : CONSPICUOUS (*outstanding* talent) **b** : DISTINGUISHED, EMINENT (*outstanding* scholar) — **out·stand·ing·ly** \aut-'stan-diŋ-lē\ *adv*

out·sta·tion \'aut-ˌstā-shən\ *n* : a remote or outlying station

out·stay \(')aut-'stā\ *vt* **1** : to stay beyond or longer than (*outstayed* his welcome) **2** : to surpass in staying power (*outstayed* the early leaders to win at the finish)

out·stretch \aut-'strech\ *vt* : to stretch out : EXTEND

out·strip \aut-'strip\ *vt* [*out-* + obs. *strip* to move fast] **1** : to go faster or farther than (*outstripped* the other runners) **2 a** : EXCEL (*outstripped* all rivals) **b** : EXCEED (demand *outstrips* supply)

¹out·ward \'aut-wərd\ *adj* **1** : moving or directed toward the outside or away from a center (the *outward* journey) **2** : showing outwardly : EXTERNAL, VISIBLE (*outward* optimism) (the *outward* pattern of his life)

²outward *or* **out·wards** \-wərdz\ *adv* **1** : toward the outside (the city stretches *outward* for miles) (fold it *outward*) **2** *obs* : EXTERNALLY

out·ward·ly \'aut-wərd-lē\ *adv* : on the outside : in outward appearance : SUPERFICIALLY (*outwardly* calm)

out·ward·ness \-nəs\ *n* **1** : the quality or state of being existent or external **2** : concern with or responsiveness to outward things

out·wear \(')aut-'wa(ə)r, -'we(ə)r\ *vt* **-wore** \-'wō(ə)r, -'wo(ə)r\; **-worn** \-'wōrn, -'worn\; **-wear·ing** : to wear or last longer than (a fabric that *outwears* most others)

out·weigh \-'wā\ *vt* : to exceed in weight, value, or importance

out·wit \aut-'wit\ *vt* : to get the better of by superior cleverness : OUTSMART

¹out·work \(')aut-'wərk\ *vt* : to outdo in working

²out·work \'aut-ˌwərk\ *n* : a minor defensive position constructed outside a fortified area

out·worn \(')aut-'wōrn, -'worn\ *adj* : no longer useful or accepted : OUT-OF-DATE (an *outworn* system)

ou·zel \'ü-zəl\ *n* [OE *ōsle*] : a European blackbird or a related bird

ov- *or* **ovi-** *or* **ovo-** *comb form* [L *ovum*] : egg (*oviform*) (*ovocyte*)

ova *pl of* OVUM

¹oval \'ō-vəl\ *adj* : having the shape of an egg; *also* : broadly elliptical

²oval *n* : an oval figure or object

oval

ova·ry \'ōv-(ə-)rē\ *n, pl* **-ries** [L *ovum* egg] **1** : the typically paired essential female reproductive organ that produces eggs and in vertebrates female sex hormones **2** : the enlarged rounded part of the pistil or gynoecium of a flowering plant that bears the ovules and consists of one or more carpels — see FLOWER illustration — **ovar·i·an** \ō-'var-ē-ən, -'ver-\ *adj*

ovate \'ō-ˌvāt\ *adj* : shaped like an egg esp. with the basal end broader (*ovate* leaves)

ova·tion \ō-'vā-shən\ *n* [L *ovare* to exult] **1** : a ceremony honoring a Roman general who had won a victory less important than one for which a triumph was granted **2** : an expression or demonstration of popular acclaim (received a standing *ovation* at the end of the concert)

ov·en \'əv-ən\ *n* [OE *ofen*] : a heated chamber (as in a stove) for baking, heating, or drying

ov·en·bird \-ˌbərd\ *n* [fr. the shape and structural details of its nest] : an American warbler that builds a dome-shaped nest on the ground

¹over \'ō-vər\ *adv* [OE *ofer*, adv. & prep.] **1 a** : across a barrier or intervening space (fly *over* to London) **b** : in a direction down or forward and down (fell *over*) **c** : across the brim (soup boiled *over*) **d** : so as to bring the underside up (turned his cards *over*) **e** : from a vertical to a prone or inclined position (knocked him *over*) **f** : from one person or side to another (hand it *over*) **2 a** : ACROSS (got his point *over*) **b** : to agreement or concord (won them *over*) **3** : beyond some quantity, limit, or norm often by a specified amount or to a specified degree (show ran a minute *over*) (so glad you could stay *over*); *also* : in or to excess : EXCESSIVELY **4** : so as to cover the whole surface (windows boarded *over*) **5 a** : at an end (the day is *over*) **b** — used on a two-way radio circuit to indicate that a message is complete and a reply is expected **6 a** : THROUGH (read it *over*); *also* : THOROUGHLY **b** : once more : AGAIN (do it *over*)

²over *prep* **1** : higher than : ABOVE (towered *over* his mother) **2 a** : having authority, power, or jurisdiction in regard to (respected those *over* him) **b** : having superiority, advantage, or preference in comparison to (a big lead *over* the others) **3** : more than (cost *over* $5) **4 a** : upon or down upon esp. so as to cover (laid a blanket *over* the child) **b** : throughout the area of (all *over* town) **c** : along the length of (*over* the road) **d** : through a review or examination of (went *over* his notes) **5 a** : moving above and across (jump *over* a stream) **b** : to or on the other side of ⟨climb *over* the fence⟩ ⟨lives *over* the way⟩ **c** : off or down from ⟨fell *over* a cliff⟩ **6** : THROUGHOUT, DURING ⟨*over* the past 25 years⟩ **7 a** — used as a function word to indicate an object of concern ⟨the Lord watches *over* his own⟩ or an activity ⟨an hour *over* cards⟩ **b** : on account of ⟨trouble *over* money⟩ **8** : by or through the medium of ⟨heard the news *over* TV⟩

³over *adj* **1** : COVERING, OUTER **2 a** : EXCESSIVE ⟨*over* imagination⟩ **b** : having or showing an excess or surplus usu. of a specified amount or degree ⟨the cash was $3 *over* in his books⟩

over- *prefix* **1** : so as to exceed or surpass **2** : excessive
over·abun·dance \ˌō-vər-ə-'bən-dən(t)s\ *n* : EXCESS, SURFEIT

over·act \ˌō-vər-'akt\ *vb* **1** : to exaggerate or overdo in acting **2** : to act more than is necessary — **over·ac·tion** \-'ak-shən\ *n*
over·ac·tive \-'ak-tiv\ *adj* : excessively or abnormally active ⟨an *overactive* thyroid⟩
over against *prep* : opposed to : contrasted with
¹over·age \ˌō-vər-'āj\ *adj* [²*over* + *age*] **1** : too old to be useful **2** : older than is normal for one's position, function, or grade ⟨*overage* students⟩
²over·age \'ōv-(ə-)rij\ *n* [³*over* + *-age*] : SURPLUS, EXCESS
¹over·all \ˌō-vər-'ol\ *adv* : as a whole : GENERALLY ⟨we find his work satisfactory, *overall*⟩
²overall *adj* : including everything ⟨*overall* expenses⟩
over·alls \'ō-vər-ˌolz\ *n pl* : loose trousers made of strong material usu. with a bib and shoulder straps and worn esp. by workmen
over·arm \'ō-vər-ˌärm\ *adj* : done with the arm raised above the shoulder ⟨*overarm* pitching⟩
over·awe \ˌō-vər-'o\ *vt* : to restrain or subdue by awe ⟨a mob *overawed* by troops⟩
over·bal·ance \ˌō-vər-'bal-ən(t)s\ *vb* **1** : to have greater weight or importance than ⟨in his friend's opinion his good qualities more than *overbalanced* his shortcomings⟩ **2** : to lose or cause to lose balance ⟨a boat *overbalanced* by shifting cargo⟩
over·bear \ˌō-vər-'ba(ə)r, -'be(ə)r\ *vb* **-bore** \-'bō(ə)r, -'bo(ə)r\; **-borne** \-'bōrn, -'bórn\ *also* **-born** \-'bórn\; **-bear·ing** **1** : to bear or carry down (as by too much weight) : OVERBURDEN **2** : to domineer over **3** : to bear fruit or offspring to excess
over·bear·ing \-'ba(ə)r-iŋ, -'be(ə)r-\ *adj* : acting in a proud or domineering way toward other people : ARROGANT — **over·bear·ing·ly** \-iŋ-lē\ *adv*
over·bid \ˌō-vər-'bid\ *vb* **-bid**; **-bid·ding** : to bid too high; *esp* : to bid more than the value of (one's hand at cards) — **over·bid** \'ō-vər-ˌbid\ *n*
¹over·blown \ˌō-vər-'blōn\ *adj* **1** : excessively large of girth **2** : INFLATED, PRETENTIOUS ⟨*overblown* oratory⟩
²overblown *adj* : past the prime of bloom ⟨*overblown* roses⟩
over·board \'ō-vər-ˌbōrd, -ˌbórd\ *adv* **1** : over the side of a ship into the water **2** : to extremes of enthusiasm ⟨go *overboard* for a new fad⟩ **3** : into discard : ASIDE ⟨threw the rules *overboard*⟩
over·build \ˌō-vər-'bild\ *vb* **-built** \-'bilt\; **-build·ing** : to build beyond the actual demand
¹over·bur·den \ˌō-vər-'bərd-°n\ *vt* : to burden too heavily
²over·bur·den \'ō-vər-ˌbərd-°n\ *n* : material overlying a deposit of useful geological materials
over·buy \ˌō-vər-'bī\ *vb* **-bought** \-'bót\; **-buy·ing** : to buy beyond need or ability to pay
over·call \ˌō-vər-'kol\ *vb* **1** : to make a higher bridge bid than (the previous bid or player) **2** : to bid over an opponent's bid in bridge when one's partner has not bid or doubled — **over·call** \'ō-vər-ˌkol\ *n*
over·cap·i·tal·ize \ˌō-vər-'kap-ət-°l-ˌīz\ *vt* : to capitalize (a business) beyond what assets or profit-making prospects warrant — **over·cap·i·tal·i·za·tion** \-ˌkap-ət-°l-ə-'zā-shən\ *n*
¹over·cast *vt* **-cast**; **-cast·ing** **1** \ˌō-vər-'kast, 'ō-vər-ˌ\ : DARKEN, OVERSHADOW **2** \'ō-vər-ˌ\ : to sew (raw edges of a seam) with long slanting widely spaced stitches to prevent raveling

²over·cast *adj* **1** \'ō-vər-ˌkast, ˌō-vər-'\ : clouded over : GLOOMY ⟨an *overcast* night⟩ **2** \'ō-vər-ˌ\ : made with overcast stitches
³over·cast \'ō-vər-ˌkast\ *n* : COVERING; *esp* : a covering of clouds over the sky
over·cast·ing \'ō-vər-ˌkas-tiŋ\ *n* : the act of stitching raw edges of fabric to prevent raveling; *also* : the stitching so done
over·charge \ˌō-vər-'chärj\ *vb* **1** : to charge too much **2** : to fill or load too full ⟨an old cannon *overcharged* with powder and shot⟩ **3** : EXAGGERATE, OVERDRAW — **over·charge** \'ō-vər-ˌchärj\ *n*
over·clothes \'ō-vər-ˌklō(th)z\ *n pl* : outer garments
over·cloud \ˌō-vər-'klaúd\ *vt* : to overspread with clouds : DARKEN
over·coat \'ō-vər-ˌkōt\ *n* : a warm coat worn over indoor clothing
over·come \ˌō-vər-'kəm\ *vt* **-came** \-'kām\; **-come**; **-com·ing** **1** : to get the better of : CONQUER ⟨*overcome* an enemy⟩ ⟨*overcome* temptation⟩ **2** : to make helpless or exhausted ⟨was *overcome* by gas⟩
over·com·pen·sa·tion \-ˌkäm-pən-'sā-shən, -ˌpen-\ *n* : excessive compensation; *esp* : excessive reaction to a feeling of inferiority, guilt, or inadequacy — **over·com·pen·sa·to·ry** \-kəm-'pen(t)-sə-ˌtōr-ē, -ˌtór-\ *adj*
over·de·vel·op \ˌō-vər-di-'vel-əp\ *vt* : to develop excessively; *esp* : to subject (an exposed photographic plate or film) too long to the developing process — **over·de·vel·op·ment** \-mənt\ *n*
over·do \ˌō-vər-'dü\ *vb* **-did** \-'did\; **-done** \-'dən\; **-do·ing** \-'dü-iŋ\ **1 a** : to do too much ⟨as for housework, she *overdoes* it⟩ **b** : to tire oneself **2** : EXAGGERATE ⟨*overdo* praise⟩ **3** : to cook too long ⟨meat that is *overdone*⟩
¹over·dose \'ō-vər-ˌdōs\ *n* : too great a dose — **over·dos·age** \ˌō-vər-'dō-sij\ *n*
²over·dose \ˌō-vər-'dōs\ *vt* : to give an overdose or too many doses to
over·draft \'ō-vər-ˌdraft, -ˌdráft\ *n* : an overdrawing of a bank account; *also* : the amount overdrawn
over·draw \ˌō-vər-'dró\ *vb* **-drew** \-'drü\; **-drawn** \-'drón\; **-draw·ing** **1** : to draw checks on (a bank account) for more than the balance **2** : EXAGGERATE, OVERSTATE ⟨*overdrew* the dangers in the task⟩ **3** : to make an overdraft
¹over·dress \ˌō-vər-'dres\ *vb* : to dress too richly for an occasion
²over·dress \'ō-vər-ˌdres\ *n* : a dress worn over another
over·drive \'ō-vər-ˌdrīv\ *n* : an automotive gear mechanism so arranged as to provide a higher car speed for a specific engine speed than that provided by ordinary high gear
over·due \ˌō-vər-'d(y)ü\ *adj* **1 a** : unpaid when due ⟨*overdue* bills⟩ **b** : delayed beyond an appointed time ⟨an *overdue* train⟩ **2** : more than ready ⟨a country *overdue* for governmental reform⟩
over·es·ti·mate \ˌō-vər-'es-tə-ˌmāt\ *vt* : to estimate too highly — **over·es·ti·mate** \-mət\ *n* — **over·es·ti·ma·tion** \-ˌes-tə-'mā-shən\ *n*
over·ex·pose \ˌō-vər-ik-'spōz\ *vt* : to expose excessively; *esp* : to expose (photographic material) for a longer time than is needed — **over·ex·po·sure** \-'spō-zhər\ *n*
over·ex·tend \-'stend\ *vt* : to extend or expand beyond a safe or reasonable point
over·fill \ˌō-vər-'fil\ *vb* : to fill to overflowing
over·flight \'ō-vər-ˌflīt\ *n* : a passage over an area in an airplane — **over·fly** \ˌō-vər-'flī\ *vt*
¹over·flow \ˌō-vər-'flō\ *vb* **1** : to cover with or as if with water : INUNDATE **2** : to flow over the brim or top of ⟨the river *overflowed* its banks⟩ **3** : to flow over bounds ⟨the creek *overflows* every spring⟩
²over·flow \'ō-vər-ˌflō\ *n* **1** : a flowing over : FLOOD **2** : something that flows over : SURPLUS **3** : an outlet or receptacle for surplus liquid
over·gar·ment \'ō-vər-ˌgär-mənt\ *n* : an outer garment
over·glaze \-ˌglāz\ *adj* : applied or suitable for use over a fired glaze ⟨*overglaze* decoration on china⟩

j joke; **ŋ** sing; **ō** flow; **ó** flaw; **ói** coin; **th** thin; **th̲** this; **ü** loot; **ú** foot; **y** yet; **yü** few; **yú** furious; **zh** vision

over·graze \,ō-vər-'grāz\ *vt* : to allow animals to graze to the point of damaging the vegetational cover

over·grow \,ō-vər-'grō\ *vb* **-grew** \-'grü\; **-grown** \-'grōn\; **-grow·ing** 1 : to grow over so as to cover 2 : to grow beyond or rise above : OUTGROW 3 : to grow excessively 4 : to become grown over — **over·growth** \'ō-vər-,grōth\ *n*

over·grown \,ō-vər-'grōn\ *adj* : grown unusually or too big ⟨*overgrown* boys⟩ ⟨*overgrown* cities⟩

¹over·hand \'ō-vər-,hand\ *adj* 1 : made with the hand brought down from above ⟨an *overhand* blow⟩ 2 : played with the hand downward or inward toward the body ⟨an *overhand* tennis stroke⟩ — **overhand** *adv* — **over·hand·ed** \,ō-vər-'han-dəd\ *adv*

²overhand *n* : an overhand stroke (as in tennis)

³overhand *vt* : to sew with short vertical stitches

overhand knot \,ō-vər-,han(d)-\ *n* : a small knot often used to prevent the end of a cord from fraying

¹over·hang \'ō-vər-,haŋ, ,ō-vər-'\ *vb* **-hung** \-,həŋ, -'həŋ\; **-hang·ing** \-,haŋ-iŋ, -'haŋ-\ 1 : to jut, project, or be suspended over 2 : to hang over threateningly

²over·hang \'ō-vər-,haŋ\ *n* : a part that overhangs ⟨the *overhang* of a roof⟩

over·haul \,ō-vər-'hȯl\ *vt* 1 : to make a thorough examination of and the necessary repairs and adjustments on (as a car) 2 : OVERTAKE ⟨the refugees' skiff was *overhauled* by a gunboat⟩ — **over·haul** \'ō-vər-,hȯl\ *n*

¹over·head \,ō-vər-'hed\ *adv* : above one's head : ALOFT

²over·head \'ō-vər-,hed\ *adj* 1 : operating or lying above ⟨an *overhead* door⟩ 2 : of or relating to business expense

³over·head \'ō-vər-,hed\ *n* 1 : business expenses not chargeable to a particular part of the work or product 2 : a stroke in a racket game made above head height : SMASH

over·hear \,ō-vər-'hi(ə)r\ *vb* **-heard** \-'hərd\; **-hear·ing** \-'hi(ə)r-iŋ\ : to hear without the speaker's knowledge or intention

over·heat \,ō-vər-'hēt\ *vb* : to heat too much

over·is·sue \-'ish-(,)ü\ *n* : an issue exceeding the limit of capital, credit, or authority — **overissue** *vt*

over·joy \,ō-vər-'jȯi\ *vt* : to fill with great joy

over·kill \'ō-vər-'kil\ *vt* : to obliterate (a target) with more nuclear force than required — **over·kill** \'ō-vər-,kil\ *n*

over·land \'ō-vər-,land, -lənd\ *adv (or adj)* : by, on, or across land

over·lap \,ō-vər-'lap\ *vb* 1 : to lap over 2 : to have something in common or in common with — **over·lap** \'ō-vər-,lap\ *n*

¹over·lay \,ō-vər-'lā\ *vt* **-laid** \-'lād\; **-lay·ing** 1 a : to lay or spread over or across something : SUPERIMPOSE ⟨*overlay* silver on gold⟩ b : to lay or spread something over or across : COVER ⟨*overlay* silver with gold⟩ 2 : OVERLIE ⟨silver *overlaying* gold⟩

²over·lay \'ō-vər-,lā\ *n* : something (as a veneer on wood) that is overlaid

over·leap \,ō-vər-'lēp\ *vt* 1 : to leap over or across ⟨*overleap* a ditch⟩ 2 : to defeat (oneself) by going too far

over·lie \,ō-vər-'lī\ *vt* **-lay** \-'lā\; **-lain** \-'lān\; **-ly·ing** \-'lī-iŋ\ 1 : to lie over or upon 2 : to cause the death of by lying upon

¹over·load \,ō-vər-'lōd\ *vt* : to load to excess

²over·load \'ō-vər-,lōd\ *n* : an excessive load; *also* : the amount that is beyond the proper load

over·look \,ō-vər-'lük\ *vt* 1 : to look over : INSPECT 2 a : to look down upon from above b : to rise above or afford a view of 3 a : to fail to see : MISS b : to pass over : IGNORE ⟨*overlook* his insolence⟩ c : EXCUSE ⟨*overlook* a beginner's mistakes⟩ 4 : to watch over : SUPERVISE

over·lord \'ō-vər-,lȯrd\ *n* 1 : a lord who has supremacy over other lords 2 : an absolute or supreme ruler — **over·lord·ship** \-,ship\ *n*

over·ly \'ō-vər-lē\ *adv* : EXCESSIVELY, TOO

over·man \,ō-vər-'man\ *vt* : to have or get too many men for the needs of ⟨*overman* a ship⟩

over·mas·ter \,ō-vər-'mas-tər\ *vt* : OVERPOWER, SUBDUE

over·match \,ō-vər-'mach\ *vt* 1 : to be more than a match for : DEFEAT ⟨our troops *overmatched* the enemy⟩ 2 : to match with a superior opponent ⟨a boxer who was badly *overmatched*⟩

¹over·much \,ō-vər-'məch\ *adj (or adv)* : too much

²over·much \'ō-vər-,məch\ *n* : too great an amount

¹over·night \,ō-vər-'nīt\ *adv* 1 : on or during the evening or night ⟨stayed away *overnight*⟩ 2 : SUDDENLY ⟨became famous *overnight*⟩

²overnight *adj* : of, lasting, or staying the night ⟨*overnight* trip⟩ ⟨*overnight* guests⟩

¹over·pass \,ō-vər-'pas\ *vt* 1 : to pass across, over, or beyond : CROSS; *also* : SURPASS 2 : TRANSGRESS 3 : DISREGARD, IGNORE

²over·pass \'ō-vər-,pas\ *n* : a crossing (as by means of a bridge) of two highways or of a highway and pedestrian path or railroad at different levels; *also* : the upper level of such a crossing

over·per·suade \,ō-vər-pər-'swād\ *vt* : to persuade to act contrary to conviction or preference — **over·per·sua·sion** \-'swā-zhən\ *n*

over·play \,ō-vər-'plā\ *vt* 1 a : to present (as a dramatic role) extravagantly : EXAGGERATE b : OVEREMPHASIZE 2 : to rely too much on the strength of ⟨*overplayed* his hand⟩

over·plus \'ō-vər-,pləs\ *n* : SURPLUS

over·pop·u·la·tion \,ō-vər-,päp-yə-'lā-shən\ *n* : the condition of having a population so dense as to cause environmental deterioration, a reduced qualify of life, or a population crash — **over·pop·u·lat·ed** \-'päp-yə-,lāt-əd\ *adj*

over·pow·er \,ō-vər-'pau̇(-ə)r\ *vt* 1 : to overcome by superior force : DEFEAT 2 : OVERWHELM ⟨*overpowered* by hunger⟩ — **over·pow·er·ing·ly** \-'pau̇r-iŋ-lē\ *adv*

¹over·print \,ō-vər-'print\ *vt* : to print over with something additional

²over·print \'ō-vər-,print\ *n* : something added by overprinting; *esp* : a printed marking added to a postage or revenue stamp esp. to alter the original or to commemorate a special event

over·pro·por·tion \,ō-vər-prə-'pōr-shən, -'pȯr-\ *vt* : to make disproportionately large — **overproportion** *n* — **over·pro·por·tion·ate** \-sh(ə-)nət\ *adj* — **over·pro·por·tion·ate·ly** *adv*

over·pro·tect \,ō-vər-prə-'tekt\ *vt* : to protect too much — **over·pro·tec·tion** \-'tek-shən\ *n* — **over·pro·tec·tive** \-'tek-tiv\ *adj*

over·proud \,ō-vər-'prau̇d\ *adj* : excessively proud

over·rate \,ō-və(r)-'rāt\ *vt* : to rate too highly

over·reach \,ō-və(r)-'rēch\ *vb* 1 : to reach above or beyond : OVERTOP 2 : to defeat (oneself) by seeking to do or gain too much 3 : OUTWIT, TRICK 4 a : to go to excess b : EXAGGERATE — **over·reach·er** *n*

over·ride \,ō-və(r)-'rīd\ *vt* **-rode** \-'rōd\; **-rid·den** \-'rid-°n\; **-rid·ing** \-'rīd-iŋ\ 1 a : to ride over or across b : TRAMPLE 2 : to ride (as a horse) too much or too hard 3 a : to prevail over : DOMINATE b : to set aside : annul by a contrary decision ⟨Congress *overrode* the president's veto⟩ 4 : to extend or pass over; *esp* : OVERLAP

over·ripe \,ō-və(r)-'rīp\ *adj* : passed beyond maturity or ripeness toward decay

over·rule \,ō-və(r)-'rül\ *vt* 1 : to decide against ⟨the chairman *overruled* the suggestion⟩ 2 : to reverse or set aside (a decision or ruling made by a lesser authority)

¹over·run \,ō-və(r)-'rən\ *vt* **-ran** \-'ran\; **-run; -run·ning** 1 : to run over : OVERSPREAD ⟨a garden *overrun* with weeds⟩ 2 : to trample down ⟨the escaped cattle *overran* the field of wheat⟩ 3 : INFEST ⟨rats *overran* the ship⟩ 4 : to win over and occupy the positions of ⟨the outpost was *overrun* by the enemy⟩ 5 : to run further than : go beyond : EXCEED ⟨*overrun* a base⟩ ⟨*overran* the allotted time⟩

²over·run \'ō-və(r)-,rən\ *n* : an act or instance of overrunning; *also* : the amount by which something overruns

over·sea \,ō-vər-'sē, 'ō-vər-,\ *adj (or adv)* : OVERSEAS

over·seas \-'sēz, -,sēz\ *adv* : beyond or across the sea : ABROAD — **overseas** *adj*

over·see \,ō-vər-'sē\ *vt* **-saw** \-'sȯ\; **-seen** \-'sēn\; **-see·ing** 1 : SURVEY, WATCH 2 a : INSPECT, EXAMINE b : SUPERINTEND, SUPERVISE, MANAGE

See *over-* and 2d element				
overhasty	overindulgent	overlong	overpopulate	overprice
overindulge	overlarge	overmodest	overpopulation	overproduce
overindulgence	overlearn	overnice	overpraise	overproduction
	overliberal	overpay		

over·seer \'ō-və(r)-ˌsi(ə)r, -ˌsē-ər, ˌō-və(r)-'\ *n* : SUPERIN- TENDENT, SUPERVISOR

over·sell \ˌō-vər-'sel\ *vt* **-sold** \-'sōld\; **-sell·ing 1** : to sell too much to **2** : to sell too much of

over·set \ˌō-vər-'set\ *vt* **-set**; **-set·ting 1** : to turn or tip over : OVERTURN **2** : OVERTHROW — **over·set** \'ō-vər-ˌset\ *n*

over·sexed \ˌō-vər-'sekst\ *adj* : exhibiting an excessive or unhealthful sexual drive or interest

over·shad·ow \ˌō-vər-'shad-ō\ *vt* **1** : to cast a shadow over : DARKEN **2** : to exceed in importance : OUTWEIGH ⟨the excitement of winning *overshadowed* everything else⟩

over·shoe \'ō-vər-ˌshü\ *n* : a protective outer shoe; *esp* : GALOSH

over·shoot \ˌō-vər-'shüt\ *vt* **-shot** \-'shät\; **-shoot·ing 1** : to pass swiftly beyond ⟨the train *overshot* the platform⟩; *also* : to miss by going beyond ⟨the plane *overshot* the field⟩ **2** : to shoot over or beyond so as to miss ⟨*overshot* his target⟩

over·shot \'ō-vər-ˌshät\ *adj* **1** : having the upper jaw extending beyond the lower **2** : moved by water shooting over from above ⟨an *overshot* waterwheel⟩

over·sight \'ō-vər-ˌsīt\ *n* **1** : the act or duty of overseeing : SUPERVISION ⟨have the *oversight* of a piece of work⟩ **2** : an omission or error resulting from carelessness or haste

¹over·size \'ō-vər-ˌsīz\ *n* : a size larger than the usual or normal size

²over·size \ˌō-vər-'sīz\ *or* **over·sized** \-'sīzd\ *adj* : being of more than ordinary size

over·skirt \'ō-vər-ˌskərt\ *n* : a skirt worn over another skirt

over·sleep \ˌō-vər-'slēp\ *vi* **-slept** \-'slept\; **-sleep·ing** : to sleep beyond the usual time for waking or beyond the time set for getting up

over·spend \-'spend\ *vb* **-spent** \-'spent\; **-spend·ing 1** : to spend beyond one's means or to excess **2** : to exceed in expenditure

over·spread \ˌō-vər-'spred\ *vt* **-spread**; **-spread·ing** : to spread over or above ⟨branches *overspreading* a garden path⟩ — **over·spread** \'ō-vər-ˌspred\ *n*

over·state \ˌō-vər-'stāt\ *vt* : to state in too strong terms : EXAGGERATE — **over·state·ment** \-mənt\ *n*

over·stay \ˌō-vər-'stā\ *vt* : to stay beyond the time or the limits of ⟨*overstayed* his leave⟩

over·step \ˌō-vər-'step\ *vt* : to step over or beyond : EX- CEED ⟨*overstepped* his authority⟩

over·stock \ˌō-vər-'stäk\ *vb* : to stock beyond require- ments or facilities ⟨*overstock* on canned goods⟩ — **over·stock** \'ō-vər-ˌstäk\ *n*

over·strew \ˌō-vər-'strü\ *vt* **-strewed**; **-strewed** *or* **-strewn** \-'strün\; **-strew·ing 1** : to strew or scatter about ⟨leaves *overstrewn* on a forest path⟩ **2** : to cover here and there ⟨a forest path *overstrewn* with leaves⟩

over·strung \ˌō-vər-'strəŋ\ *adj* : too highly strung : too sensitive

over·stuffed \ˌō-vər-'stəft\ *adj* **1** : stuffed too full **2** : covered completely and deeply with upholstery ⟨an *overstuffed* chair⟩

over·sub·scribe \ˌō-vər-səb-'skrīb\ *vt* : to subscribe for more of than is available, asked for, or offered for sale ⟨*oversubscribe* a stock issue⟩ — **over·sub·scrip·tion** \-'skrip-shən\ *n*

over·sub·tle \ˌō-vər-'sət-ᵊl\ *adj* : excessively or impracti- cably subtle

over·sup·ply \ˌō-vər-sə-'plī\ *n* : an excessive supply — **oversupply** *vt*

overt \ō-'vərt, 'ō-(ˌ)vərt\ *adj* [MF, fr. pp. of *ouvrir* to open, modif. of L *aperire*] : open to view : not secret — **overt·ly** *adv*

over·take \ˌō-vər-'tāk\ *vt* **-took** \-'tùk\; **-tak·en** \-'tā- kən\; **-tak·ing 1 a** : to catch up with **b** : to catch up with and pass by **2** : to come upon suddenly ⟨a blizzard *overtook* the hunting party⟩

over-the-count·er \ˌō-vər-thə-'kaùnt-ər\ *adj* **1** : sold otherwise than on an organized securities exchange : UN- LISTED **2** : sold lawfully without prescription

over·throw \ˌō-vər-'thrō\ *vt* **-threw** \-'thrü\; **-thrown** \-'thrōn\; **-throw·ing 1** : to thrust or knock over : UP-

SET ⟨lawn chairs *overthrown* by the gale⟩ **2** : to bring down : DEFEAT ⟨a government *overthrown* by rebels⟩ — **over·throw** \'ō-vər-ˌthrō\ *n*

¹over·time \'ō-vər-ˌtīm\ *n* **1** : time in excess of a set limit; *esp* : working time in excess of a standard day or week **2** : the wage paid for overtime work — **overtime** *adv (or adj)*

²over·time \ˌō-vər-'tīm\ *vt* : to exceed the proper limit in timing (as a photographic exposure)

over·tone \'ō-vər-ˌtōn\ *n* **1** : one of the higher tones that with the fundamental comprise a musical tone : HARMONIC 1a **2** : a secondary effect, quality, or meaning : SUGGES- TION ⟨the words carried an *overtone* of menace⟩

over·top \ˌō-vər-'täp\ *vt* **1** : to rise above the top of : surpass in height ⟨*overtopped* his brother by 6 inches⟩ **2** : to rise above in power ⟨a tyrant who *overtopped* the laws⟩ **3** : SURPASS

over·trick \'ō-vər-ˌtrik\ *n* : a card trick won in excess of the number bid

over·trump \ˌō-vər-'trəmp\ *vb* : to trump with a higher trump card than the highest previously played to the same trick

over·ture \'ō-və(r)-ˌchùr, -chər\ *n* [ME, lit., opening, fr. MF *ouverture*, modif. of L *apertura* aperture] **1** : an open- ing offer : a first proposal ⟨the enemy made *overtures* for peace⟩ **2** : an orchestral composition that is the intro- duction to an oratorio, opera, or dramatic work; *also* : a composition in this style for concert performance

over·turn \ˌō-vər-'tərn\ *vb* **1** : to turn over : UPSET **2** : OVERTHROW, DESTROY — **over·turn** \'ō-vər-ˌtərn\ *n*

¹over·use \ˌō-vər-'yüz\ *vt* : to use too much ⟨an *overused* phrase⟩

²over·use \ˌō-vər-'yüs\ *n* : too much use

over·view \'ō-vər-ˌvyü\ *n* : an overall view

over·watch \ˌō-vər-'wäch\ *vt* **1** *archaic* : to weary or exhaust by keeping awake **2** : to watch over

over·ween·ing \ˌō-vər-'wē-niŋ\ *adj* **1** : ARROGANT, PRESUMPTUOUS **2** : EXAGGERATED, IMMODERATE — **over·ween·ing·ly** \-niŋ-lē\ *adv*

over·weigh \ˌō-vər-'wā\ *vt* **1** : to exceed in weight : OVERBALANCE **2** : to weigh down : OPPRESS

¹over·weight \'ō-vər-ˌwāt, *2 is usu* ˌō-vər-'\ *n* **1** : weight over and above what is required or allowed **2** : excessive or burdensome weight; *esp* : bodily weight in excess of what is held normal to one's age, height, and build — **over·weight** \ˌō-vər-'\ *adj*

²over·weight \ˌō-vər-'wāt\ *vt* **1** : to give too much weight or consideration to ⟨he *overweights* her opinion⟩ **2** : to weight excessively ⟨*overweighted* prose⟩ **3** : to exceed in weight : OVERBALANCE

over·whelm \ˌō-vər-'hwelm\ *vt* [ME *overwhelmen*, fr. *over* + *whelmen* to turn upside down] **1** : OVERTHROW, UPSET **2 a** : to cover over completely : SUBMERGE ⟨a boat *overwhelmed* by a wave⟩ **b** : to overcome completely : CRUSH ⟨*overwhelmed* by superior numbers⟩ ⟨*overwhelmed* by grief⟩ — **over·whelm·ing·ly** \-'hwel-miŋ-lē\ *adv*

over·wind \ˌō-vər-'wīnd\ *vt* **-wound** \-'waùnd\; **-wind· ing** : to wind too much

over·win·ter \ˌō-vər-'wint-ər\ *vi* : to spend or survive the winter

over·work \ˌō-vər-'wərk\ *vb* **1** : to work or cause to work too hard or long or to exhaustion ⟨*overworked* his horses⟩ **2** : to decorate all over ⟨a granite tombstone *over- worked* with flowery designs⟩ **3 a** : to work too much on : OVERDO **b** : to make excessive use of ⟨*overworked* phrases⟩ — **overwork** *n*

over·write \ˌō-vər-'rīt\ *vb* **-wrote** \-'rōt\; **-writ·ten** \-'rit-ᵊn\; **-writ·ing** \-'rīt-iŋ\ **1** : to write over the sur- face of **2** : to write in inflated or pretentious style ⟨*over- written* accounts of simple events⟩ **3** : to write too much

over·wrought \ˌō-və(r)-'rôt\ *adj* [fr. pp. of *overwork*] **1** : extremely excited : AGITATED ⟨*overwrought* feelings⟩ **2** : elaborated to excess : OVERDONE

ovi- *or* **ovo-** — see OV-

ovi·cid·al \ˌō-və-'sīd-ᵊl\ *adj* : capable of killing eggs — **ovi·cide** \'ō-və-ˌsīd\ *n*

ovi·duct \'ō-və-ˌdəkt\ *n* : a tube for the passage of eggs from the ovary of an animal

See *over*- and 2d element	oversimplification	overspecialize	overtired	overvalue
oversensitive	oversimplify	overstrict	overtrain	overzealous
oversensitiveness	overspecialization	overtax		

ovine \'ō-ˌvīn\ *adj* [L *ovis* sheep; akin to E *ewe*] **:** of or relating to sheep — **ovine** *n*

ovi·pa·rous \ō-'vip-(ə-)rəs\ *adj* [L *ovum* egg + *parere* to produce] **:** producing eggs that develop and hatch outside the maternal body — **ovip·a·rous·ly** *adv*

ovi·pos·it \'ō-və-ˌpäz-ət\ *vi* **:** to lay eggs — used esp. of insects — **ovi·po·si·tion** \ˌō-və-pə-'zish-ən\ *n*

ovi·pos·i·tor \'ō-və-ˌpäz-ət-ər\ *n* [L *ovum* egg + *posit-, ponere* to place] **:** a specialized organ (as of an insect) for depositing eggs

ovoid \'ō-ˌvoid\ *or* **ovoi·dal** \ō-'void-ᵊl\ *adj* **:** shaped like an egg **:** OVATE — **ovoid** *n*

ovo·vi·vip·a·rous \ˌō-vō-ˌvī-'vip-(ə-)rəs\ *adj* **:** producing eggs that develop within the maternal body and hatch within or immediately after extrusion from the parent — **ovo·vi·vip·a·rous·ly** *adv*

ov·u·late \'äv-yə-ˌlāt, 'ō-vyə-\ *vi* **:** to produce eggs or discharge them from an ovary — **ov·u·la·tion** \ˌäv-yə-'lā-shən, ˌō-vyə-\ *n*

ovule \'ō-vyül\ *n* **1 :** an outgrowth of the ovary of a seed plant that encloses an embryo sac within a nucellus and after fertilization develops into a seed **2 :** a small egg; *esp* **:** one in an early stage of growth — **ov·u·lar** \'äv-yə-lər, 'ō-vyə-\ *adj*

ovum \'ō-vəm\ *n, pl* **ova** \-və\ [L, egg] **:** a female gamete **:** an egg cell **:** MACROGAMETE

owe \'ō\ *vb* [ME *owen* to possess, own, owe, fr. OE *āgan*] **1 a** *archaic* **:** POSSESS, OWN **b :** to have or bear (an emotion or attitude) to someone or something ⟨*owes* the boss a grudge⟩ **2 a** (1) **:** to be under obligation to pay or repay in return for something received **:** be indebted in the sum of ⟨*owes* me $5⟩ (2) **:** to be under obligation to render (as duty or service) **b :** to be indebted to or for ⟨*owes* the grocer for supplies⟩ **c :** to be in debt ⟨*owes* for his house⟩

ow·ing \'ō-iŋ\ *adj* **:** due to be paid **:** OWED ⟨have bills *owing*⟩⟨claim no more than is *owing*⟩

owing to *prep* **:** because of ⟨delayed *owing to* a crash⟩

owl \'aul\ *n* [OE *ūle*] **:** any of an order (Strigiformes) of birds of prey with large head and eyes, short hooked bill, strong talons, and more or less nocturnal habits

owl·et \'au-lət\ *n* **:** a young or small owl

owl·ish \'au-lish\ *adj* **:** resembling or suggesting an owl (as in solemnity or appearance of wisdom) — **owl·ish·ly** *adv* — **owl·ish·ness** *n*

¹own \'ōn\ *adj* [OE *āgen*; akin to E *owe*] **:** belonging to oneself or itself — usu. used following a possessive case or pronoun ⟨wanted his *own* room⟩

²own *vb* **1 a** **:** to have or hold as property **:** POSSESS **b :** to have legal title to **2 :** ACKNOWLEDGE, ADMIT ⟨*own* a debt⟩ ⟨*owned* him to be their master⟩ **3 :** CONFESS — used with *to* or *up* ⟨*owned* to being scared⟩⟨if you break a window, *own* up⟩ ⟨hates to *own* up to his mistakes⟩ — **own·er** \'ō-nər\ *n* — **own·er·ship** \-ˌship\ *n*

³own *pron* **:** one or ones belonging to oneself — used after a possessive and without a following noun as a pronoun equivalent in meaning to the adjective *own* ⟨wants a room of his *own*⟩ — **on one's own** **1 :** being without outside help or control **:** INDEPENDENT ⟨he's *on his own* now⟩ **2 :** on one's own initiative **:** INDEPENDENTLY ⟨did the whole thing *on his own*⟩

ox \'äks\ *n, pl* **ox·en** \'äk-sən\ *also* **ox** [OE *oxa*] **1 :** the common large domestic bovine mammal kept for milk, draft, and meat; *esp* **:** an adult castrated male **2 :** any of the larger hollow-horned ruminant mammals (as the domestic ox, buffaloes, and the yak) with even-toed hoofs as distinguished from similar and related but smaller forms (as sheep and goats)

ox- *or* **oxo-** *comb form* [F, fr. *oxygène*] **:** oxygen ⟨*oxi*meter⟩

ox·a·late \'äk-sə-ˌlāt\ *n* **:** a salt or ester of oxalic acid

ox·al·ic acid \(ˌ)äk-ˌsal-ik-\ *n* [F *acide oxalique*, fr. L *oxalis* wood sorrel] **:** a poisonous strong acid (COOH)₂ that occurs in various plants as oxalates and is used esp. as a bleaching or cleaning agent and in making dyes

ox·al·is \äk-'sal-əs\ *n* [L, fr. Gk, fr. *oxys* sharp] **:** WOOD SORREL

ox·blood \'äks-ˌbləd\ *n* **:** a moderate reddish brown

ox·bow \'äks-ˌbō\ *n* **1 :** a U-shaped collar worn by a draft ox **2 :** a U-shaped bend in a river — **oxbow** *adj*

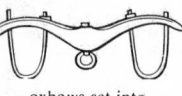
oxbows set into an ox yoke

ox·cart \'äks-ˌkärt\ *n* **:** a cart drawn by oxen

ox·eye \'äk-ˌsī\ *n* **:** any of several composite plants having heads with both disk and ray flowers

ox·ford \'äks-fərd\ *n* [fr. *Oxford*, England] **:** a low shoe laced or tied over the instep

ox·heart \'äks-ˌhärt\ *n* **:** any of various large sweet cherries

ox·i·dant \'äk-səd-ənt\ *n* **:** OXIDIZING AGENT

ox·i·dase \'äk-sə-ˌdās\ *n* **:** any of various enzymes that catalyze oxidations — **ox·i·da·sic** \ˌäk-sə-'dā-sik\ *adj*

ox·i·da·tion \ˌäk-sə-'dā-shən\ *n* **1 :** the process of oxidizing **2 :** the state or result of being oxidized — **ox·i·da·tive** \'äk-sə-ˌdāt-iv\ *adj*

oxidation–reduction *n* **:** a chemical reaction in which one or more electrons are transferred from one atom or molecule to another

oxidation state *or* **oxidation number** *n* **:** the degree of oxidation of an atom (as in a compound) that is usu. expressed as a positive or negative number representing the ionic charge or effective charge of the atom ⟨the usual *oxidation state* of hydrogen is +1 and of oxygen −2⟩

ox·ide \'äk-ˌsīd\ *n* [F, fr. *ox-* + *-ide*, fr. *acide* acid] **:** a compound of oxygen with an element or radical

ox·i·dize \'äk-sə-ˌdīz\ *vb* **1 :** to combine with oxygen **2 :** to dehydrogenate esp. by the action of oxygen **3 :** to remove one or more electrons from (an atom, ion, or molecule) **4 :** to become oxidized — **ox·i·diz·er** *n*

oxidizing agent *n* **:** a substance (as oxygen or nitric acid) that oxidizes by taking up electrons

Ox·o·ni·an \äk-'sō-nē-ən\ *n* [ML *Oxonia* Oxford] **1 :** a native or resident of Oxford, England **2 :** a student or graduate of Oxford University — **Oxonian** *adj*

ox·o·ni·um \äk-'sō-nē-əm\ *n* **:** HYDRONIUM

ox·tail \'äks-ˌtāl\ *n* **:** the tail of cattle; *esp* **:** the skinned tail used for soup

oxy- *comb form* [F, fr. *oxygène*] **1 :** oxygen **:** containing oxygen or additional oxygen ⟨*oxy*hemoglobin⟩ **2 :** of oxygen and ⟨*oxy*hydrogen⟩ — **oxy** \'äk-sē\ *adj*

oxy·acet·y·lene \ˌäk-sē-ə-'set-ᵊl-ən, -ᵊl-ˌēn\ *adj* **:** of, relating to, or utilizing a mixture of oxygen and acetylene ⟨*oxyacetylene* torch⟩

ox·y·gen \'äk-si-jən\ *n* [F *oxygène*, fr. Gk *oxys* sharp, acid + F *-gène* -gen] **:** a chemical element that is found free as a colorless tasteless odorless gas in the atmosphere of which it forms about 21 percent or combined in water, that is capable of combining with all elements except the inert gases, that is active in physiological processes, and that is involved in combustion processes — see ELEMENT table — **ox·y·gen·ic** \ˌäk-si-'jen-ik\ *adj*

ox·y·gen·ate \'äk-si-jə-ˌnāt, äk-'sij-ə-\ *vt* **:** to impregnate, combine, or supply with oxygen — **ox·y·gen·a·tion** \ˌäk-si-jə-'nā-shən, (ˌ)äk-ˌsij-ə-\ *n*

oxygen debt *n* **:** a cumulative oxygen deficit that develops during periods of intense bodily activity and must be made good when the body returns to rest

oxygen mask *n* **:** a device worn over the nose and mouth (as by airmen at high altitudes) through which oxygen is supplied from a storage tank

oxygen tent *n* **:** a canopy which can be placed over a bedfast person and within which a flow of oxygen can be maintained

oxy·he·mo·glo·bin \ˌäk-si-'hē-mə-ˌglō-bən, -'hem-ə-\ *n* **:** hemoglobin loosely combined with oxygen that it can release to the tissues

oxy·hy·dro·gen \ˌäk-si-'hī-drə-jən\ *adj* **:** of, relating to, or utilizing a mixture of oxygen and hydrogen ⟨*oxyhydrogen* torch⟩

oxy·to·cin \ˌäk-si-'tōs-ᵊn\ *n* [Gk *oxys* sharp + *tok-, tiktein* to bear] **:** a pituitary hormone that stimulates esp. the contraction of uterine muscle — **oxy·to·cic** \-'tō-sik\ *adj*

oyez \ō-'yā, -'yes, -'yez\ *imperative verb* [AF, hear ye, fr. *oïr* to hear, fr. L *audire*] — used by a court or public crier to gain attention before a proclamation

oys·ter \'oi-stər\ *n* [MF *oistre*, fr. L *ostrea*, fr. Gk *ostreon*] **:** any of various marine bivalve mollusks having a rough irregular shell closed by a single adductor muscle and including important edible shellfish

oyster bed *n* **:** a place where oysters grow or are cultivated

oyster catcher *n* **:** any of a genus of wading birds with stout legs and heavy wedge-shaped bill and often black and white plumage

---

oyster cracker *n* : a small salted cracker

oys·ter·man \-mən\ *n* : a gatherer, opener, breeder, or seller of oysters

oyster plant *n* : SALSIFY

ozone \'ō-,zōn\ *n* [G *ozon*, fr. Gk *ozōn*, prp. of *ozein* to smell] **1** : a form O₃ of oxygen that has three atoms in the molecule, is a faintly blue irritating gas with a pungent odor, is generated usu. in dilute form by a silent electric discharge in oxygen or air, and is used esp. in disinfection and deodorization and in oxidation and bleaching **2** : pure and refreshing air — **ozo·nic** \ō-'zō-nik\ *adj* — **ozo·nif·er·ous** \,ō-(,)zō-'nif-(ə-)rəs\ *adj*

ozon·ide \'ō-(,)zō-,nīd\ *n* : a compound of ozone

ozo·no·sphere \ō-'zō-nə-,sfi(ə)r\ *n* : an atmospheric layer at heights of approximately 20 to 30 miles characterized by high ozone content

p \'pē\ *n, often cap* : the 16th letter of the English alphabet

pa \'pä, 'pȯ\ *n* [short for *papa*] : FATHER

PABA \'pab-ə, ,pē-,ā-'bē-,ā\ *n* [*para*≠*aminobenzoic acid*] : PARA-AMINOBENZOIC ACID

pab·u·lum \'pab-yə-ləm\ *n* [L, food, fodder] : FOOD; *esp* : a suspension or solution of nutrients suitable for absorption

pa·ca \'päk-ə\ *n* [Pg & Sp, of AmerInd origin] : any of a genus of large So. and Central American rodents

¹pace \'pās\ *n* [OF *pas* step, fr. L *passus*, fr. *pandere* to spread] **1** : rate of moving or progressing esp. on foot **2 a** : a manner of walking : TREAD **b** : GAIT; *esp* : a fast 2-beat gait of a horse in which the legs move in lateral pairs and support the animal alternately on the right and left legs **3** : a single step or a measure based on the length of a human step

²pace *vb* **1 a** : to walk with slow or measured tread **b** : to move along : PROCEED **2** : to go or cover at a pace — used of a horse **3** : to measure by or in paces **4** : to set or regulate the pace of; *also* : LEAD, PRECEDE — **pac·er** *n*

pace·mak·er \'pās-,mā-kər\ *n* : one that sets the pace for another

pa·chi·si \pə-'chē-zē\ *n* [Hindi *pacīsī*] : an ancient board game

pach·y·derm \'pak-i-,dərm\ *n* [Gk *pachydermos* thick≠skinned, fr. *pachys* thick + *derma* skin] : any of various thick-skinned hoofed mammals (as an elephant or a rhinoceros) — **pach·y·der·mal** \,pak-i-'dər-məl\ *adj* — **pach·y·der·ma·tous** \-mət-əs\ *adj*

pach·ys·an·dra \,pak-ə-'san-drə\ *n* : any of a genus of evergreen woody trailing plants of the box family often used as a ground cover

pa·cif·ic \pə-'sif-ik\ *adj* **1** : making or suitable to make peace ⟨*pacific* words to end a quarrel⟩ **2** : having a mild and calm nature : PEACEABLE ⟨a quiet *pacific* people⟩ — **pa·cif·i·cal·ly** \-'sif-i-k(ə-)lē\ *adv*

pac·i·fi·ca·tion \,pas-ə-fə-'kā-shən\ *n* : the act or process of pacifying : the state of being pacified

Pacific standard time *n* : the time of the 8th time zone west of Greenwich that includes the Pacific coastal region of the U.S. and Juneau, Alaska

pac·i·fi·er \'pas-ə-,fī(-ə)r\ *n* **1** : one that pacifies **2** : a usu. nipple-shaped device for babies to suck or bite upon

pac·i·fism \'pas-ə-,fiz-əm\ *n* : opposition to war or violence as a means of settling disputes; *esp* : refusal to bear arms on moral or religious grounds — **pac·i·fist** \-fəst\ *n* — **pacifist** *or* **pac·i·fis·tic** \,pas-ə-'fis-tik\ *adj*

pac·i·fy \'pas-ə-,fī\ *vt* **-fied; -fy·ing** [L *pacificare*, fr. *pac-*, *pax* peace] **1** : to ease the anger, agitation, or distress of : SOOTHE ⟨*pacify* a crying child⟩ **2** : to restore to a peaceful state : SETTLE, SUBDUE ⟨*pacify* a country⟩ — **pac·i·fi·a·ble** \-,fī-ə-bəl\ *adj*

syn APPEASE, PLACATE: PACIFY may imply a soothing or calming of anger or agitation or the forceful quelling of insurrection; APPEASE implies quieting anger or averting threats by making concessions often to unreasonable demands; PLACATE suggests changing resentment or bitterness to goodwill

¹pack \'pak\ *n* [MLG or MD *pak*] **1 a** : a bundle arranged for convenience in carrying esp. on the back **b** : a group or pile of related objects or these together with their container ⟨a *pack* of cards⟩ **2** : a large amount or number : HEAP **3** : an act or instance or a method of packing; *also* : arrangement in a pack **4 a** : a group of often predatory animals of the same kind **b** : a set of persons with a common interest : CLIQUE **5** : a concentrated mass or group; *esp* : a mass of ice chunks floating on the sea **6** : absorbent material used therapeutically (as for checking bleeding or applying medication or moisture) **7 a** : a cosmetic paste for the face **b** : an application or treatment of oils or creams for conditioning the scalp and hair **8** : material used as packing — **pack** *adj*

²pack *vb* **1 a** : to place articles in (as for transportation or storage) ⟨*pack* a suitcase⟩ ⟨*pack* jars with beans⟩ **b** : to arrange closely and securely in a container or bundle ⟨*pack* goods⟩ **2 a** : to crowd together so as to fill full : CRAM ⟨the crowd *packed* the hall⟩ **b** : to force into a smaller volume : COMPRESS; *also* : to form into a pack or packs ⟨the ice is *packing* in the gorge⟩ **3** : to fill or cover so as to prevent passage (as of air or steam) ⟨*pack* a joint in a pipe⟩ **4** : to send or go away without ceremony ⟨*pack* a boy off to school⟩ **5** : to transport in packs (as on the back of an animal) **6** : to wear or have in one's possession ⟨*pack* a gun⟩ **7** : to process (foodstuffs) for use or storage usu. on a wholesale scale — **pack·a·bil·i·ty** \,pak-ə-'bil-ət-ē\ *n* — **pack·a·ble** \'pak-ə-bəl\ *adj*

³pack *vt* : to bring together or make up fraudulently to secure a favorable vote ⟨*pack* a jury⟩

¹pack·age \'pak-ij\ *n* **1 a** : a small or moderate-sized pack : PARCEL **b** : a single item or set of a product uniformly wrapped or sealed for sale **2** : a covering wrapper or container **3** : something (as a package deal) that in unified and integrated state is felt to resemble a package of merchandise

²package *vt* : to make into or enclose in a package — **pack·ag·er** *n*

package deal *n* : an offer or agreement involving more than one item or making acceptance of one item dependent on the acceptance of another

package store *n* : a store that sells alcoholic beverages only in containers that may not lawfully be opened on the premises

pack animal *n* : an animal (as a horse or donkey) used for carrying packs

pack·er \'pak-ər\ *n* : one that packs: as **a** : a dealer who prepares and packs foods for the market ⟨a meat *packer*⟩ **b** : ²PORTER 1 **c** : one that conveys goods on pack animals

pack·et \'pak-ət\ *n* [MF *pacquet*, of Gmc origin] **1 a** : a small group, cluster, or mass **b** : a small bundle or parcel **2** : a passenger boat carrying mail and cargo on a regular schedule

pack·ing·house \'pak-iŋ-,haůs\ *n* : an establishment for processing and packing foodstuffs and esp. meat and its by-products — called also *packing plant*

pack rat *n* : WOOD RAT; *esp* : a large bushy-tailed rodent of the Rocky Mountain area that hoards food and miscellaneous objects

pack·sack \'pak-,sak\ *n* : a case used to carry gear on the back when traveling on foot

pack·sad·dle \'pak-,sad-ᵊl\ *n* : a saddle that supports the load on the back of a pack animal

pack·thread \-,thred\ *n* : strong thread or small twine used esp. for sewing or tying packs or parcels

pact \'pakt\ *n* [L *pactum*, fr. neut. of *pactus*, pp. of *pacisci* to agree, contract] : ⁴COMPACT; *esp* : an international treaty

¹pad \'pad\ *n* **1 a** : a cushioned or cushioning part or thing : CUSHION **b** : a piece of material saturated with ink for inking the surface of a rubber stamp **2 a** : the hairy foot of some mammals **b** : the cushioned thickening of the underside of the toes of some mammals **3** : a floating leaf of a water plant **4** : TABLET 1b **5** : LAUNCHING PAD

²pad *vt* **pad·ded; pad·ding 1** : to furnish with a pad or padding **2** : to expand with superfluous or insignificant matter ⟨*pad* a short speech⟩

³pad *vb* **pad·ded; pad·ding 1** : to traverse or go on foot **2** : to move along with a muffled step

---

j joke; ŋ sing; ō flow; ȯ flaw; ȯi coin; th thin; th this; ü loot; ů foot; y yet; yü few; yů furious; zh vision

⁴pad *n* : a soft muffled or slapping sound

pad·ding \'pad-iŋ\ *n* : material with which something is padded

¹pad·dle \'pad-ᵊl\ *n* [ME *padell*] **1 a** : an implement with a flat blade to propel and steer a small craft (as a canoe) **b** : something (as the flipper of a seal) suggesting a paddle in appearance or action **2** : an implement used for stirring, mixing, or beating **3** : one of the broad boards at the circumference of a paddle wheel or waterwheel

²paddle *vb* **pad·dled; pad·dling** \'pad-liŋ, -ᵊl-iŋ\ **1** : to go, propel, or transport by or as if by means of a paddle or paddle wheel **2** : to beat, stir, or punish by or as if by a paddle

³paddle *vi* **pad·dled; pad·dling** \'pad-liŋ, -ᵊl-iŋ\ **1** : to move the hands or feet about in shallow water **2** : TODDLE

pad·dle·fish \'pad-ᵊl-,fish\ *n* : a ganoid fish of the Mississippi valley about four feet long with a paddle-shaped snout

pad·dler \'pad-lər, -ᵊl-ər\ *n* : one that paddles

paddle wheel *n* : a wheel with paddles, floats, or boards around its circumference used to propel a vessel

pad·dock \'pad-ək, -ik\ *n* [alter. of ME *parrok*, fr. OE *pearroc*] : a usu. enclosed area used esp. for pasturing or exercising animals; *esp* : an enclosure where racehorses are saddled and paraded before a race

pad·dy \'pad-ē\ *n*, *pl* **paddies** [Malay *padi*] **1** : RICE; *esp* : threshed unmilled rice **2** : wet land in which rice is grown

pad·dy wagon \'pad-ē-\ *n* : PATROL WAGON

pad·lock \'pad-,läk\ *n* : a removable lock with a hinged bow-shaped piece attached at one end so that the other end can be passed through a staple (as on a hasp) and then snapped into a catch in the lock — **padlock** *vt*

pa·dre \'päd-(,)rā, -rē\ *n* [Sp or It or Pg, lit., father, fr. L *pater*] **1** : PRIEST **2** : a military chaplain

padlock

pa·dro·ne \pə-'drō-nē\ *n* [It, protector, owner, fr. L *patronus* patron] **1** : an Italian innkeeper **2** : one that secures employment for immigrants esp. of Italian extraction

pae·an \'pē-ən\ *n* [Gk *paian* hymn of thanksgiving esp. addressed to Apollo, fr. *Paian*, epithet of Apollo] : a joyously exultant song or hymn of praise, tribute, thanksgiving, or triumph

paed- *or* **paedo-** *or* **ped-** *or* **pedo-** *comb form* [Gk *paid-*, *pais* child, boy] : child ⟨*pediatric*⟩ ⟨*paedogenesis*⟩

pae·do·gen·e·sis \,pēd-ō-'jen-ə-səs\ *n*, *pl* **-gen·e·ses** \-ə-,sēz\ : reproduction by young or larval animals — **pae·do·ge·net·ic** \-jə-'net-ik\ *adj* — **pae·do·ge·net·i·cal·ly** \-'net-i-k(ə-)lē\ *adv*

pa·gan \'pā-gən\ *n* [ME, fr. LL *paganus*, fr. L, country dweller, fr. *pagus* country district] **1** : HEATHEN 1 **2** : an irreligious person — **pagan** *adj* — **pa·gan·ish** \-gə-nish\ *adj* — **pa·gan·ize** \-gə-,nīz\ *vt*

pa·gan·ism \'pā-gə-,niz-əm\ *n* **1 a** : pagan beliefs or practices **b** : a pagan religion **2** : the quality or state of being a pagan

¹page \'pāj\ *n* [OF, fr. It *paggio*] **1** : a youth being trained for the medieval rank of knight and in the personal service of a knight; *also* : a youth attendant on a person of rank **2** : one employed (as by a hotel) esp. to deliver messages or perform personal services for patrons

²page *vt* **1** : to serve in the capacity of a page **2** : to summon by repeatedly calling out the name of

³page *n* [MF, fr. L *pagina*] **1 a** : one side of a printed or written leaf; *also* : the entire leaf ⟨a *page* torn from a book⟩ **b** : the matter printed or written on a page ⟨set several *pages* of type⟩ **2 a** : a written record ⟨the *pages* of history⟩ **b** : an event or circumstance worth recording ⟨an exciting *page* in his life⟩

⁴page *vt* : to number or mark the pages of

pag·eant \'paj-ənt\ *n* [ME *padgeant*, lit., scene of a play, fr. ML *pagina*, fr. L, page] **1** : an elaborate exhibition or spectacle **2** : an entertainment consisting of loosely linked scenes or tableaux based on history or legend ⟨a Christmas *pageant*⟩ **3** : ostentatious pomp and display

pag·eant·ry \'paj-ən-trē\ *n*, *pl* **-ries** **1** : pageants and the presentation of pageants **2** : splendid or ostentatious display : SPECTACLE

page boy *n* **1** : a boy serving as a page **2** *usu* **page·boy** : a woman's often shoulder-length bob with the ends of the hair turned under in a smooth roll

pag·i·nal \'paj-ən-ᵊl\ *adj* : of, relating to, or consisting of pages

pag·i·nate \'paj-ə-,nāt\ *vt* : ⁴PAGE

pag·i·na·tion \,paj-ə-'nā-shən\ *n* [L *pagina* page] **1** : the paging of written or printed matter **2** : the number and arrangement of pages (as of a book) or an indication of these

pa·go·da \pə-'gōd-ə\ *n* [Pg *pagode* oriental idol, temple, fr. a Dravidian source, fr. Skt *bhagavatī*, epithet of Hindu goddesses, feminine of *bhagavat* blessed one] : a Far Eastern tower esp. with roofs curving upward at the division of each of several stories and erected as a temple or memorial

paid *past of* PAY

pail \'pāl\ *n* [ME *payle*, *paille*] **1** : a usu. cylindrical vessel with a handle : BUCKET **2** : PAILFUL

pail·ful \-,fúl\ *n*, *pl* **pailfuls** \-,fúlz\ *or* **pails·ful** \'pālz-,fúl\ : the quantity held by a pail

¹pain \'pān\ *n* [OF *peine*, fr. L *poena*, fr. Gk *poinē* payment, penalty] **1** : PUNISHMENT ⟨prescribed *pains* and penalties⟩ ⟨forbidden on *pain* of death⟩ **2 a** : usu. localized physical suffering associated with disease, injury, or other bodily disorder ⟨the *pain* of a boil⟩ ⟨a *pain* in his back⟩ ⟨in constant *pain*⟩; *also* : a basic bodily sensation induced by a noxious stimulus, received by naked nerve endings, characterized by physical discomfort (as pricking, throbbing, or aching), and typically leading to evasive action **b** : acute mental or emotional distress : GRIEF **3** *pl* : the throes of childbirth **4** *pl* : care or effort taken for the accomplishment of something ⟨took *pains* with his work⟩ — **pain** *adj* — **pain·less** \-ləs\ *adj* — **pain·less·ly** *adv* — **pain·less·ness** *n*

pagoda

²pain *vb* **1** : to cause pain in or to : HURT **2** : to give or experience pain

pain·ful \'pān-fəl\ *adj* **1 a** : feeling or giving pain **b** : ANNOYING, IRKSOME, VEXATIOUS ⟨a *painful* interview⟩ **2** : requiring or involving effort or careful diligence ⟨a *painful* task⟩ — **pain·ful·ly** \-fə-lē\ *adv* — **pain·ful·ness** *n*

pains·tak·ing \'pānz-,tā-kiŋ\ *adj* : marked by diligent care and effort — **pains·tak·ing·ly** \-kiŋ-lē\ *adv*

¹paint \'pānt\ *vb* [OF *peint* painted, pp. of *peindre* to paint, fr. L *pingere*] **1** : to apply paint or a comparable covering or coloring substance to ⟨*paint* a wall⟩ ⟨*paint* the wound with iodine⟩ **2 a** : to represent in lines and colors on a surface by applying pigments ⟨*paint* a picture⟩ ⟨*painted* the scene from memory⟩ **b** : to produce or evoke as if by painting ⟨*paints* glowing pictures of a promised utopia⟩ **3** : to practice the art of painting **4** : to use cosmetics

²paint *n* **1** : MAKEUP; *esp* : a cosmetic to add color **2 a** : a mixture of a pigment and a suitable liquid to form a thin closely adherent coating when spread on a surface in a thin coat **b** : an applied coating of paint ⟨scrape old *paint* from woodwork⟩

paint·brush \'pānt-,brəsh\ *n* **1** : a brush for applying paint **2** : any of several plants with showy tufted flowers

painted bunting *n* : a brightly colored finch of the southern U.S.

¹paint·er \'pānt-ər\ *n* : one that paints; *esp* : an artist who paints — **paint·er·ly** \-lē\ *adj*

²paint·er \'pānt-ər\ *n* [ME *paynter*, prob. fr. MF *pendoir*, *pentoir* clothesline, fr. *pendre* to hang] : a line used for securing or towing a boat

³paint·er \alter. of *panther*] : COUGAR

paint·ing \'pānt-iŋ\ *n* **1** : a product of painting; *esp* : a painted work of art **2** : the art or occupation of painting

¹pair \'pa(ə)r, 'pe(ə)r\ *n*, *pl* **pairs** *also* **pair** [OF *paire*, fr. L *paria* equal things, fr. neut. pl. of *par* equal] **1** : two corresponding things either naturally matched or intended to be used together ⟨a *pair* of muscular hands⟩ ⟨a *pair* of gloves⟩ **2** : a single thing composed of two connected corresponding parts ⟨a *pair* of scissors⟩ **3** : a set of two: as **a** : two mated animals ⟨a *pair* of robins⟩ **b** : two persons in love, engaged, or married   **c** : two individuals who belong to opposing parties or hold opposed opinions and agree not to vote on a specific issue before a deliberative body (as a legislature)   **4** *chiefly dial* : a set or series of usu. small objects ⟨climbed two *pair* of stairs⟩

²pair *vb* **1** : to make a pair of or arrange in pairs ⟨*paired* her guests⟩   **2** : to become grouped or separated into pairs ⟨*paired* off for the next dance⟩

pais·ley \'pāz-lē\ *adj, often cap* [*Paisley,* Scotland] : made typically of soft wool with colorful curved abstract figures ⟨a *paisley* shawl⟩ — **paisley** *n*

Pai·ute \'pī-,(y)üt\ *n* : a member of an Indian people of Utah, Arizona, Nevada, and California

pa·ja·mas \pə-'jäm-əz, -'jam-\ *n pl* [Hindi *pājāma,* sing., loose lightweight trousers, fr. Per *pā* leg + *jāma* garment] : a loose usu. 2-piece lightweight suit designed for sleeping or lounging

¹pal \'pal\ *n* [Romany *phral, phal* brother, friend, fr. Skt *bhrātṛ* brother; akin to E *brother*] : PARTNER; *esp* : a close friend

²pal *vi* **palled; pal·ling** : to be or become pals

pal·ace \'pal-əs\ *n* [OF *palais,* fr. L *palatium,* fr. *Palatium,* hill in Rome where the emperors' residences were built]   **1 a** : the official residence of a sovereign   **b** *chiefly Brit* : the official residence of an archbishop or bishop   **2 a** : a large stately house   **b** : a large public building (as for a legislature, court, or governor)   **c** : a showy place for public amusement or refreshment

pal·a·din \'pal-əd-ən\ *n* [F, fr. It *paladino,* fr. ML *palatinus* courtier, fr. L, palatine]   **1** : a knightly supporter of a medieval prince   **2** : an outstanding protagonist of a cause

pa·laes·tra \pə-'les-trə\ *n, pl* **-trae** \-(,)trē\ [Gk *palaistra,* fr. *palaiein* to wrestle]   **1** : a school in ancient Greece or Rome for sports (as wrestling)   **2** : GYMNASIUM

pal·an·quin \,pal-ən-'kēn\ *n* [Pg *palanquim,* fr. Jav *pĕlaṅki*] : a conveyance usu. for one person consisting of an enclosed litter carried on the shoulders of men by means of poles and used formerly esp. in eastern Asia

pal·at·a·ble \'pal-ət-ə-bəl\ *adj* **1** : agreeable to the taste : SAVORY   **2** : agreeable to the mind : ACCEPTABLE — **pal·at·a·bil·i·ty** \,pal-ət-ə-'bil-ət-ē\ *n* — **pal·at·a·ble·ness** \'pal-ət-ə-bəl-nəs\ *n* — **pal·at·a·bly** \-blē\ *adv*

pal·a·tal \'pal-ət-ᵊl\ *adj* **1** : of or relating to the palate   **2** : pronounced with the front or blade of the tongue near or touching the hard palate ⟨the \y\ in *yeast* and the \sh\ in *she* are *palatal* sounds⟩ — **palatal** *n* — **pal·a·tal·ly** \-ᵊl-ē\ *adv*

pal·a·tal·ize \'pal-ət-ᵊl-,īz\ *vt* : to pronounce as or change into a palatal sound — **pal·a·tal·i·za·tion** \,pal-ət-ᵊl-ə-'zā-shən\ *n*

pal·ate \'pal-ət\ *n* [L *palatum*]   **1** : the roof of the mouth separating the mouth from the nasal cavity   **2 a** : the sense of taste   **b** : intellectual relish or taste

pa·la·tial \pə-'lā-shəl\ *adj* **1** : of, relating to, or being a palace   **2** : suitable to a palace : MAGNIFICENT — **pa·la·tial·ly** \-shə-lē\ *adv* — **pa·la·tial·ness** *n*

pa·lat·i·nate \pə-'lat-ᵊn-ət\ *n* : the territory of a palatine

¹pal·a·tine \'pal-ə-,tīn\ *adj* [L *palatinus,* fr. *palatium* palace]   **1 a** : of or relating to a palace esp. of a Roman or Holy Roman emperor   **b** : PALATIAL   **2 a** : possessing royal privileges   **b** : of or relating to a palatine or a palatinate

²palatine *n* **1 a** : a high officer of an imperial palace   **b** : a feudal lord having sovereign power within his domains   **2** *cap* : a native or inhabitant of the Palatinate

³palatine *adj* : of, relating to, or lying near the palate

⁴palatine *n* : a palatine bone

¹pa·lav·er \pə-'lav-ər, -'läv-\ *n* [Pg *palavra* word, speech, fr. LL *parabola* parable, speech]   **1** : a long parley usu. between persons of different levels of culture or sophistication   **2 a** : idle talk : CHATTER   **b** : misleading or beguiling speech

²palaver *vi* : to talk at length and usu. obscurely or idly

¹pale \'pāl\ *adj* [MF, fr. L *pallidus* pallid]   **1 a** : lacking color or intensity of color   **b** : not vivid in hue or luster; *esp* : low in saturation and high in lightness ⟨a *pale* pink⟩   **c** : not having the warm skin color of a person in good health : PALLID, WAN ⟨became *pale*⟩   **2** : not bright or brilliant : DIM ⟨a *pale* moon⟩ — **pale·ly** \'pāl-lē\ *adv* — **pale·ness** \'pāl-nəs\ *n* — **pal·ish** \'pā-lish\ *adj*

²pale *vb* : to make or become pale

³pale *vt* [MF *paler,* fr. *pal* stake, fr. L *palus*] : to enclose with pales : FENCE

⁴pale *n* **1** : a stake or picket of a fence or palisade   **2** : an enclosed place; *also* : territory within clearly marked bounds or under a particular jurisdiction   **3** : limits within which one is protected or privileged ⟨behavior outside the *pale* of common decency⟩

pale- *or* **paleo-** *or* **palae-** *or* **palaeo-** *comb form* [Gk *palaios* ancient, fr. *palai* long ago]   **1** : involving or dealing with ancient forms or conditions ⟨*paleo*botany⟩   **2** : early : primitive : archaic ⟨*Paleo*lithic⟩

pa·lea \'pā-lē-ə\ *n, pl* **-le·as** *or* **-le·ae** \-lē-,ē\ [NL, fr. L, chaff]   **1** : a chaffy scale on the receptacle of a composite flower head   **2** : the upper bract of a grass flower — **pa·le·a·ceous** \,pā-lē-'ā-shəs\ *adj* — **pa·le·al** \'pā-lē-əl\ *adj*

pale·face \'pāl-,fās\ *n* : a white person : CAUCASIAN

pa·le·o·bot·a·ny \,pā-lē-ō-'bät-ᵊn-ē, -'bät-nē\ *n* : a branch of botany dealing with fossil plants — **pa·le·o·bo·tan·i·cal** \-bə-'tan-i-kəl\ *adj* — **pa·le·o·bo·tan·i·cal·ly** \-k(ə-)lē\ *adv* — **pa·le·o·bot·a·nist** \-'bät-ᵊn-əst, -'bät-nəst\ *n*

Pa·le·o·cene \'pā-lē-ə-,sēn\ *n* : the earliest epoch of the Tertiary; *also* : the corresponding system of rocks — **Paleocene** *adj*

pa·le·og·ra·phy \,pā-lē-'äg-rə-fē\ *n* **1 a** : an ancient manner of writing   **b** : ancient writings   **2** : the study of ancient writings and inscriptions — **pa·le·og·ra·pher** \-fər\ *n* — **pa·le·o·graph·ic** \,pā-lē-ə-'graf-ik\ *adj* — **pa·le·o·graph·i·cal·ly** \-'graf-i-k(ə-)lē\ *adv*

pa·le·o·lith \'pā-lē-ə-,lith\ *n* : a Paleolithic stone implement

Pa·le·o·lith·ic \,pā-lē-ə-'lith-ik\ *adj* : of, relating to, or being the 2d period of the Stone Age which is characterized by rough or crudely chipped stone implements

pa·le·on·tol·o·gy \,pā-lē-än-'täl-ə-jē\ *n* [Gk *palaios* ancient + *onta* existing things, fr. neut. pl. of *ont-, ōn,* prp. of *einai* to be] : a science dealing with the life of past geological periods as known esp. from fossil remains — **pa·le·on·to·log·i·cal** \-,änt-ᵊl-'äj-i-kəl\ *or* **pa·le·on·to·log·ic** \-'äj-ik\ *adj* — **pa·le·on·tol·o·gist** \-än-'täl-ə-jəst\ *n*

Pa·le·o·zo·ic \,pā-lē-ə-'zō-ik\ *n* : the 3d of the five eras of geological history which is marked by the culmination of nearly all classes of invertebrates except the insects and in the later epochs of which seed-bearing plants, amphibians, and reptiles first appeared; *also* : the corresponding system of rocks — see GEOLOGIC TIME table — **Paleozoic** *adj*

pa·le·o·zo·ol·o·gy \,pā-lē-ō-zō-'äl-ə-jē\ *n* : a branch of zoology dealing with fossil animals — **pa·le·o·zo·o·log·i·cal** \-,zō-ə-'läj-i-kəl\ *adj* — **pa·le·o·zo·ol·o·gist** \-zō-'äl-ə-jəst\ *n*

pal·et \pā-'let, 'pā-lət\ *n* : PALEA

pal·ette \'pal-ət\ *n* [MF, dim. of *pale* spade, shovel, fr. L *pala*]   **1** : a thin oval or rectangular board or tablet with a hole for the thumb at one end by which a painter holds it and on which he lays and mixes pigments   **2** : the set of colors put on the palette

palette knife *n* : a knife with a flexible steel blade and no cutting edge used to mix colors

pal·frey \'pól-frē\ *n, pl* **palfreys** [OF *palefrei,* fr. ML *palafredus,* alter. of LL *paraveredus* post-horse for secondary roads] : a saddle horse formerly used for the road as distinguished from a war-horse; *esp* : one suitable for a lady

Pa·li \'päl-ē\ *n* : an Indic language used as the liturgical and scholarly language of Hinayana Buddhism

pal·imp·sest \'pal-əm(p)-,sest\ *n* [Gk *palimpsēstos* scraped again, fr. *palin* back, again + *psēn* to scrape] : writing material (as a parchment) used again after earlier writing has been erased

pal·in·drome \'pal-ən-,drōm\ *n* [Gk *palindromos* running back again, fr. *palin* back, again + *dramein* to run] : a word, verse, or sentence (as "Able was I ere I saw Elba") that reads the same backward or forward

pal·ing \'pā-liŋ\ *n* **1** : PALE, PICKET   **2 a** : material for pales   **b** : a fence of pales

pal·in·ode \'pal-ə-,nōd\ *n* [Gk *palinōidia,* fr. *palin* back, re- + *aeidein* to sing]   **1** : an ode or song recanting or retracting something in a former one   **2** : a usu. formal retraction

---

j joke;   ŋ sing;   ō flow;   ȯ flaw;   ȯi coin;   th thin;   th this;   ü loot;   u̇ foot;   y yet;   yü few;   yu̇ furious;   zh vision

¹pal·i·sade \‚pal-ə-'sād\ *n* [F *palissade*] **1 a :** a stout high fence of stakes esp. for defense **b :** a long strong stake pointed at the top and set close with others as a defense **2 :** a line of bold cliffs **3 :** PALISADE PARENCHYMA

²palisade *vt* **:** to surround or fortify with palisades

palisade parenchyma *n* **:** a layer of columnar chlorophyll-rich cells just under the upper epidermis of a leaf — called also *palisade mesophyll;* compare SPONGY PARENCHYMA

¹pall \'pól\ *n* [L *pallium* cloak, coverlet] **1 :** a heavy cloth covering for a coffin, hearse, or tomb **2 :** a chalice cover made of a square piece of stiffened linen **3 :** something that covers, darkens, or produces a gloomy effect ⟨a *pall* of smoke⟩⟨a *pall* of silence⟩

²pall *vi* [ME *pallen*, short for *appallen* to become pale, make pale] **1 :** to become dull or uninteresting **:** lose the ability to give pleasure

¹pal·la·di·um \pə-'lād-ē-əm\ *n, pl* **-dia** \-ē-ə\ [L, fr. Gk *palladion*, fr. *Pallad-, Pallas* Pallas] **1** *cap* **:** a statue of Pallas Athena whose preservation was held to ensure the safety of Troy **2 :** SAFEGUARD

²palladium *n* [NL, fr. *Pallad-, Pallas*, the asteroid] **:** a silver-white ductile malleable metallic chemical element that is used esp. as a catalyst and in alloys — see ELEMENT table

Pal·las \'pal-əs\ *n* **1 :** ATHENA — called also *Pallas Athena* **2 :** one of the asteroids

pall·bear·er \'pól-‚bar-ər, -‚ber-\ *n* **:** a person who attends the coffin at a funeral

¹pal·let \'pal-ət\ *n* [ME *pailet*, fr. MF *paille* straw, fr. L *palea* chaff, straw] **:** a straw-filled tick or mattress; *also* **:** any small, hard, or temporary bed

²pallet *n* [MF *palette*, fr. dim. of *pale* spade, fr. L *pala*] **1 :** a flat-bladed implement for forming, beating, or rounding clay or glass **2 :** PALETTE 1 **3 :** a lever or surface in a timepiece that receives an impulse from the escapement wheel and imparts motion to a balance or pendulum

pal·li·al \'pal-ē-əl\ *adj* [L *pallium* cloak] **1 :** of or relating to the cerebral cortex **2 :** of or relating to the mantle of a mollusk

pal·li·ate \'pal-ē-‚āt\ *vt* [LL *palliare* to cloak, conceal, fr. L *pallium* cloak] **1 :** to make less intense or severe **:** ABATE **2 :** to cover by excuses and apologies **:** EXCUSE — **pal·li·a·tion** \‚pal-ē-'ā-shən\ *n* — **pal·li·a·tor** \'pal-ē-‚āt-ər\ *n*

pal·li·a·tive \'pal-ē-‚āt-iv, 'pal-yət-\ *adj* **:** serving to palliate — **palliative** *n* — **pal·li·a·tive·ly** *adv*

pal·lid \'pal-əd\ *adj* [L *pallidus*, fr. *pallēre* to be pale] **:** deficient in color **:** WAN — **pal·lid·i·ty** \pa-'lid-ət-ē\ *n* — **pal·lid·ly** \'pal-əd-lē\ *adv* — **pal·lid·ness** *n*

pal·li·um \'pal-ē-əm\ *n, pl* **-lia** \-ē-ə\ *or* **-li·ums** [L] **1 a :** a draped rectangular cloak worn by men of ancient Greece and Rome **b :** a white woolen band with pendants in front and back worn over the chasuble by a pope or archbishop **2 :** an anatomical covering or enfolding layer; *esp* **:** MANTLE 2b

pal·lor \'pal-ər\ *n* [L, fr. *pallēre* to be pale] **:** deficiency of color esp. of the face **:** PALENESS

pal·ly \'pal-ē\ *adj* **:** sharing the relationship of pals **:** INTIMATE

¹palm \'päm, 'pälm\ *n* [OE, fr. L *palma*, fr. *palma* palm of the hand; fr. the resemblance of the tree's leaves to an outstretched hand] **1 :** any of a family of mostly tropical or subtropical monocotyledonous trees, shrubs, or vines usu. with a simple but often tall stem topped by a crown of huge feathery or fan-shaped leaves **2 a :** a palm leaf esp. when carried as a symbol of victory or rejoicing **b :** an emblem of success or triumph; *also* **:** VICTORY, HONORS ⟨our team carried off the *palm*⟩ — **palm·like** \-‚līk\ *adj*

²palm *n* [MF *paume*, fr. L *palma*] **1 :** the under part of the hand between the fingers and the wrist **2 :** a rough measure of length based on the width or length of the palm **3 :** something (as the blade of an oar or paddle) resembling or corresponding to the palm of the hand

³palm *vt* **1 :** to conceal in or pick up stealthily with the hand **2 :** to impose by fraud ⟨trash *palmed* off on the unwary⟩

pal·mar \'pal-mər, 'pä(l)m-ər\ *adj* **:** of, relating to, situated in, or involving the palm of the hand

pal·mate \'pal-‚māt, 'pä(l)m-‚āt\ *also* **pal·mat·ed** \-əd\ *adj* **:** resembling a hand with the fingers spread: **a :** having lobes or veins radiating from a common point ⟨*palmate* leaf⟩ **b :** having the anterior toes united by a web ⟨*palmate* birds⟩ **c :** having the distal portion broad, flat, and lobed ⟨a *palmate* antler⟩ — **pal·mate·ly** *adv* — **pal·ma·tion** \pal-'mā-shən, pä(l)-'mā-\ *n*

palm·er \'päm-ər, 'päl-mər\ *n* **:** a person wearing two crossed palm leaves as a sign of his pilgrimage to the Holy Land

pal·met·to \pal-'met-ō\ *n, pl* **-tos** *or* **-toes** [modif. of Sp *palmito*] **:** any of several usu. low-growing palms with fan-shaped leaves

palm·ist·ry \'päm-ə-strē, 'päl-mə-\ *n* [ME *pawmestry*, prob. fr. *paume* palm + *maistrie* mastery] **:** the art or practice of reading a person's character or future from the markings on his palms — **palm·ist** \'päm-əst, 'päl-məst\ *n*

pal·mit·ic acid \(‚)pal-‚mit-ik-, (‚)pä(l)-\ *n* **:** a waxy fatty acid occurring free or esp. in the form of glycerides in most fats and fatty oils

pal·mi·tin \'pal-mət-ən, 'pä(l)m-ət-\ *n* **:** an ester of glycerol and palmitic acid

palm oil *n* **:** an edible fat obtained from the flesh of the fruit of several palms and used esp. in soap, candles, and lubricating greases

Palm Sunday *n* **:** the Sunday before Easter celebrated in commemoration of Christ's triumphal entry into Jerusalem

palmy \'päm-ē, 'päl-mē\ *adj* **palm·i·er; -est 1 :** abounding in or bearing palms **2 :** FLOURISHING, PROSPEROUS

pal·my·ra \pal-'mī-rə\ *n* [Pg *palmeira*, fr. *palma* palm, fr. L] **:** an African palm cultivated in tropical regions for its decay-resistant wood, its sugar-rich sap, its large edible fruits, and its leaves which are used in thatching and as a source of coarse fibers

pal·o·mi·no \‚pal-ə-'mē-nō\ *n, pl* **-nos** [AmerSp, fr. Sp, like a dove, fr. L *palumbinus*, fr. *palumbes* wood pigeon] **:** a slender-legged short-bodied horse of a light tan or cream color with lighter mane and tail

palp \'palp\ *n* **:** PALPUS — **pal·pal** \'pal-pəl\ *adj*

pal·pa·ble \'pal-pə-bəl\ *adj* [L *palpare* to stroke; akin to E *feel*] **1 :** capable of being touched or felt **:** TANGIBLE **2 :** easily perceptible **:** NOTICEABLE **3 :** easily understood or recognized **:** MANIFEST — **pal·pa·bil·i·ty** \‚pal-pə-'bil-ət-ē\ *n* — **pal·pa·bly** \'pal-pə-blē\ *adv*

pal·pate \'pal-‚pāt\ *vt* **:** to examine by touch esp. medically — **pal·pa·tion** \pal-'pā-shən\ *n*

pal·pe·bral \'pal-pə-brəl, pal-'pē-brəl\ *adj* [L *palpebra* eyelid] **:** of, relating to, or located on or near the eyelids

pal·pi·tate \'pal-pə-‚tāt\ *vi* [L *palpitare*, freq. of *palpare* to stroke] **:** to beat rapidly and strongly **:** THROB, QUIVER ⟨*palpitating* with excitement⟩ — **pal·pi·tant** \-pət-ənt\ *adj*

pal·pi·ta·tion \‚pal-pə-'tā-shən\ *n* **:** an act or instance of palpitating; *esp* **:** an abnormally rapid beating (as from violent exertion or strong emotion) of the heart

pal·pus \'pal-pəs\ *n, pl* **pal·pi** \-‚pī, -pē\ [NL, fr. L, caress, soft palm of the hand] **:** a segmented sensory process on an arthropod mouthpart — **pal·pate** \'pal-‚pāt\ *adj*

pal·sy \'pól-zē\ *n* [MF *paralisie*, fr. L *paralysis*] **1 :** PARALYSIS **2 :** a condition marked by uncontrollable tremor of the body or a part — **palsy** *vt*

pal·ter \'pól-tər\ *vi* **pal·tered; pal·ter·ing** \-t(ə-)riŋ\ **1 :** to act insincerely **:** EQUIVOCATE **2 :** HAGGLE, CHAFFER — **pal·ter·er** \-tər-ər\ *n*

pal·try \'pól-trē\ *adj* **pal·tri·er; -est 1 :** INFERIOR, TRASHY **2 :** MEAN, DESPICABLE **3 :** TRIVIAL — **pal·tri·ness** *n*

pal·y·nol·o·gy \‚pal-ə-'näl-ə-jē\ *n* **:** a branch of science dealing with pollen and spores

p-ami·no·ben·zo·ic acid \‚pē-ə-‚mē-nō-ben-‚zō-ik-, ‚pē-‚am-ə-‚nō-\ *n* **:** PARA-AMINOBENZOIC ACID

pam·pa \'pam-pə\ *n, pl* **pampas** \-pəz, -pəs\ [AmerSp, fr. Quechua] **:** an extensive generally grass-covered plain of So. America — **pam·pe·an** \'pam-pē-ən, pam-'\ *adj*

pam·per \'pam-pər\ *vt* **pam·pered; pam·per·ing** \'pam-p(ə-)riŋ\ [ME *pamperen*] **:** to treat with extreme or excessive care and attention — **pam·per·er** \-pər-ər\ *n*

pam·phlet \'pam(p)-flət\ *n* [ME *pamflet* unbound booklet, fr. *Pamphilus seu De Amore* Pamphilus or On Love, popular Latin love poem of the 12th cent.] **:** an unbound printed publication with no cover or a paper cover

¹**pam·phle·teer** \‚pam(p)-flə-'ti(ə)r\ *n* **:** a writer of pamphlets usu. attacking something or urging a cause

²**pamphleteer** *vi* **:** to write and publish pamphlets

¹**pan** \'pan\ *n* [OE *panne*, fr. L *patina*, fr. Gk *patanē*] **1 a** **:** a usu. broad, shallow, and open container for domestic use **b :** a broad shallow open vessel: as (1) **:** either of the receptacles of a pair of scales (2) **:** a round shallow metal container used to wash waste from metal (as gold) **2 :** a basin or depression in the earth ⟨a salt *pan*⟩ **3 :** HARDPAN 1

²**pan** *vb* **panned**; **pan·ning** **1 :** to wash earthy material in a pan to concentrate bits of native metal; *also* **:** to separate (metal) from debris by panning **2 a :** to yield precious metal in panning **b :** to turn out; *esp* **:** SUCCEED ⟨a visit that *panned* out⟩ **3 :** to criticize severely

Pan \'pan\ *n* **:** the Greek god of forests, pastures, flocks, and shepherds represented as having the legs and sometimes the ears and horns of a goat

pan- *comb form* [Gk, fr. *pan*, neut. of *pant-*, *pas* all, every] **1 :** all **:** completely ⟨*panchromatic*⟩ **2 a :** involving all of a (specified) group ⟨*Pan*-American⟩ **b :** advocating or involving the union of a (specified) group ⟨*Pan*-Asian⟩ **3 :** total **:** general ⟨*panleucopenia*⟩

pan·a·cea \‚pan-ə-'sē-ə\ *n* [Gk *panakeia*, fr. *pan*- + *akeisthai* to heal] **:** a remedy for all ills or difficulties **:** CURE-ALL — **pan·a·ce·an** \-'sē-ən\ *adj*

pa·nache \pə-'nash\ *n* [MF *pennache*] **1 :** an ornamental tuft (as of feathers) esp. on a helmet **2 :** dash or flamboyance in style and action **:** VERVE

pan·a·ma \'pan-ə-‚mä, -‚mȯ\ *n*, *often cap* [AmerSp *panamá*, fr. *Panama*, Central America] **:** a lightweight hat hand-plaited of narrow strips from the young leaves of a tropical American tree

Pan–Amer·i·can \‚pan-ə-'mer-ə-kən\ *adj* **:** of, relating to, or involving the independent republics of No. and So. America

Pan American Day *n* **:** April 14 observed as the anniversary of the founding of the Pan American Union in 1890

Pan–Amer·i·can·ism \-kə-‚niz-əm\ *n* **:** a movement for greater cooperation among the Pan-American nations esp. in defense, commerce, and cultural relations

pan·a·tela \‚pan-ə-'tel-ə\ *n* [Sp, fr. AmerSp, a long thin biscuit] **:** a long slender cigar with straight sides rounded off at the sealed end

¹**pan·cake** \'pan-‚kāk\ *n* **:** GRIDDLE CAKE

²**pancake** *vb* **:** to make or cause to make a pancake landing

pancake landing *n* **:** a landing in which an airplane is leveled off higher than for a normal landing causing it to stall and drop in an approximately horizontal position with little forward motion

pan·chax \'pan-‚kaks\ *n* **:** any of a genus of brightly colored Old World killifishes often kept in the tropical aquarium

Pan·chen Lama \‚pän-chən-\ *n* **:** the lama next in rank to the Dalai Lama

pan·chro·mat·ic \‚pan-krō-'mat-ik\ *adj* **:** sensitive to light of all colors in the visible spectrum ⟨*panchromatic* film⟩

pan·cre·as \'pan-krē-əs, 'pan-\ *n* [Gk *pankreas*, fr. *pan*- + *kreas* flesh, meat; akin to E *raw*] **:** a large compound gland of vertebrates that lies near the stomach and secretes digestive enzymes and the hormone insulin — **pan·cre·at·ic** \‚pan-krē-'at-ik, ‚pan-\ *adj*

pancreatic juice *n* **:** a clear alkaline secretion of pancreatic enzymes that is poured into the duodenum and acts on food already partly digested by the gastric juice and saliva

pan·da \'pan-də\ *n* **:** a large black-and-white mammal of Tibet that suggests a bear but is related to the raccoon; *also* **:** a smaller reddish related animal that resembles the raccoon

pan·da·nus \pan-'dā-nəs, -'dan-əs\ *n* **:** SCREW PINE

Pan·da·rus \'pan-d(ə-)rəs\ *n* **:** the procurer of Cressida for Troilus in medieval legend

pan·dem·ic \pan-'dem-ik\ *n* [Gk *pan-* + *dēmos* people] **:** an outbreak of disease occurring over a wide area and affecting many people ⟨an influenza *pandemic*⟩ — **pandemic** *adj*

pan·de·mo·ni·um \‚pan-də-'mō-nē-əm\ *n* **1** *cap* **:** the capital of Hell in Milton's *Paradise Lost* **2 :** a wild uproar **:** TUMULT; *also* **:** a wildly riotous place

¹**pan·der** \'pan-dər\ *or* **pan·der·er** \-dər-ər\ *n* [*Pandarus*] **1 a :** a go-between in love intrigues **b :** a man who solicits clients for a prostitute **2 :** someone who caters to or exploits the weaknesses of others

²**pander** *vi* **pan·dered**; **pan·der·ing** \-d(ə-)riŋ\ **:** to act as a pander

Pan·do·ra \pan-'dōr-ə, -'dȯr-\ *n* **:** a woman to whom Zeus gave a box enclosing all human ills which escaped when she opened it

pan·dow·dy \pan-'daud-ē\ *n*, *pl* **-dies :** a deep-dish apple dessert spiced, sweetened, and covered with a rich crust

pane \'pān\ *n* [MF, strip of cloth, pane, fr. L *pannus* cloth] **1 a :** a section or side of something (as a facet of a gem) **b :** one of the sections into which a sheet of postage stamps is divided for distribution and which in the U.S. usu. contains 100 stamps **2 :** one of the compartments of a window or door consisting of a sheet of glass in a frame; *also* **:** the sheet of glass in such a frame

pan·e·gyr·ic \‚pan-ə-'jir-ik, -'jī-rik\ *n* [Gk *panēgyrikos* for a festival, fr. *panēgyris* festival assembly, fr. *pan*- + *agyris* assembly] **:** a formal speech or writing in praise of someone or something; *also* **:** formal or elaborate praise — **pan·e·gyr·i·cal** \-'jir-i-kəl, -'jī-ri-\ *adj* — **pan·e·gyr·i·cal·ly** \-k(ə-)lē\ *adv*

pan·e·gyr·ist \‚pan-ə-'jir-əst, -'jī-rəst\ *n* **:** EULOGIST

¹**pan·el** \'pan-ᵊl\ *n* [ME, piece of cloth, slip of parchment, jury schedule, fr. MF, piece of cloth, dim. of *pan* cloth, fr. L *pannus*] **1 a :** a schedule containing names of persons summoned as jurors; *also* **:** JURY 1 **b :** a group of persons who discuss before an audience a topic of usu. political or social interest **c :** a group of entertainers or guests engaged as players in a quiz or guessing game on a radio or television program **2 :** a separate or distinct part of a surface: as **a :** a usu. rectangular and sunken or raised section of a surface (as of a door, wall, or ceiling) set off by a margin **b :** a unit of construction material (as plywood) made to form part of a surface (as of a wall or an airplane wing) **c :** a vertical section (as a gore) of cloth **d :** a section of a switchboard; *also* **:** a mount for controls (as of an electrical device) **3 :** a thin flat piece of wood on which a picture is painted; *also* **:** a painting on such a surface

²**panel** *vt* **-eled** *or* **-elled**; **-el·ing** *or* **-el·ling :** to furnish or decorate with panels

panel heating *n* **:** space heating by means of wall, floor, baseboard, or ceiling panels with embedded electric conductors or hot-air or hot-water pipes

pan·el·ing \'pan-ᵊl-iŋ\ *n* **:** panels joined in a continuous surface; *esp* **:** decorative wood panels so combined

pan·el·ist \'pan-ᵊl-əst\ *n* **:** a member of a panel for discussion or entertainment

panel truck *n* **:** a small light motortruck with a fully enclosed body used chiefly for delivery service

pan·e·tela *or* **pan·e·tel·la** *var of* PANATELA

pan·fish \'pan-‚fish\ *n* **:** a small food fish (as a sunfish) usu. taken with hook and line and not available on the market

pang \'paŋ\ *n* **:** a sudden sharp attack or spasm (as of pain or emotional distress) ⟨hunger *pangs*⟩

pan·go·lin \pan-'gō-lən\ *n* [Malay *pĕngguling*] **:** any of several Asiatic and African edentate mammals having the body covered with large overlapping horny scales

¹**pan·han·dle** \'pan-‚han-dᵊl\ *n* **:** a narrow projection of a larger territory (as a state) ⟨the Texas *Panhandle*⟩

²**panhandle** *vb* **-dled**; **-dling** \-dliŋ, -dᵊl-iŋ\ **:** to approach people on the street and beg for money — **pan·han·dler** \-dlər\ *n*

Pan·hel·len·ic \‚pan-hə-'len-ik\ *adj* **1 :** of or relating to all Greece or all the Greeks **2 :** of or relating to the Greek-letter sororities or fraternities in American colleges and universities or to an association representing them

¹**pan·ic** \'pan-ik\ *n* [*panic*, adj., fr. Gk *panikos*, lit., of Pan, fr. *Pan*, who was believed to inspire panic] **1 :** a sudden overpowering fright; *esp* **:** a sudden unreasoning terror causing headlong flight **2 :** a sudden widespread fright concerning financial affairs that induces hurried selling resulting in a sharp fall in prices **syn** see FEAR — **panic** *adj* — **pan·icky** \'pan-i-kē\ *adj* — **pan·ic·strick·en** \'pan-ik-‚strik-ən\ *adj*

²**panic** *vb* **pan·icked** \-ikt\; **pan·ick·ing** **1 :** to affect or be affected with panic **2 :** to produce demonstrative appreciation on the part of ⟨*panic* an audience with a gag⟩

pan·i·cle \'pan-i-kəl\ *n* [L *panicula*, dim. of *panus* swelling] **:** a loosely branched often pyramidal flower cluster (as of the oat) that is usu. technically a raceme — see INFLORESCENCE illustration — **pan·i·cled** \-kəld\ *adj* — **pa·nic·u·late** \pa-'nik-yə-lət\ *adj*

Pan·ja·bi \‚pən-'jäb-ē, -'jab-\ *n* **1 :** an Indic language of the Punjab region of the Indian subcontinent **2 :** PUNJABI 1

pan·jan·drum \pan-'jan-drəm\ *n* **:** a powerful personage or pretentious official

pan·leu·co·pe·nia \‚pan-‚lü-kə-'pē-nē-ə\ *n* **:** an acute usu. fatal viral disease of cats characterized by fever, diarrhea and dehydration, and extensive destruction of white blood cells

pan·nier \'pan-yər\ *n* [MF *panier,* fr. L *panarium,* fr. *panis* bread] **1 :** a large basket; *esp* **:** one of wicker carried on the back of an animal or the shoulder of a person **2 a :** either of a pair of hoops formerly used by women to expand their skirts at the hips **b :** an overskirt draped and puffed out at the sides

pannier 1

pan·ni·kin \'pan-i-kən\ *n, chiefly Brit* **:** a small pan or cup

pa·no·cha \pə-'nō-chə\ *or* **pa·no·che** \-chē\ *var of* PENUCHE

pan·o·ply \'pan-ə-plē\ *n, pl* **-plies** [Gk *panoplia,* fr. *pan-* + *hopla* arms, armor] **1 a :** a full suit of armor **b :** ceremonial attire **2 :** something forming a protective covering **3 :** a magnificently impressive array or display — **pan·o·plied** \-plēd\ *adj*

pan·o·rama \‚pan-ə-'ram-ə, -'räm-\ *n* [*pan-* + Gk *horama* sight, fr. *horan* to see; akin to E *wary*] **1 a :** CYCLORAMA **b :** a picture exhibited a part at a time by being unrolled before the spectator **2 a :** a full and unobstructed view in every direction **b :** a comprehensive presentation of a subject **3 :** a mental picture of a series of images or events — **pan·o·ram·ic** \'ram-ik\ *adj*

pan·pipe \'pan-‚pīp\ *n* [after *Pan,* its traditional inventor] **:** a primitive wind instrument consisting of a graduated series of short vertical pipes bound together with the mouthpieces in an even row — often used in pl.

pan·sy \'pan-zē\ *n, pl* **pansies** [MF *pensée,* fr. *pensée* thought; fr. its being a symbol of remembrance] **:** a garden plant originated by hybridization of various violets and violas; *also* **:** its showy velvety 5-petaled flower

panpipe

¹pant \'pant\ *vb* [ME *panten,* fr. MF *pantaisier,* fr. Gk *phantasioun* to have hallucinations, fr. *phantasia* imagination] **1 a :** to breathe hard or quickly **:** GASP **b :** to make a throbbing or puffing sound **c :** to progress with panting ⟨the car *panted* up the hill⟩ **2 :** to long eagerly **:** YEARN **3 :** to utter with panting ⟨ran up and *panted* out the message⟩

²pant *n* **1 :** a panting breath **2 :** a throbbing or puffing sound

pan·ta·lets *or* **pan·ta·lettes** \‚pant-ᵊl-'ets\ *n pl* **:** long drawers with a ruffle at the bottom of each leg usu. showing below the skirt and formerly worn by women and girls

pan·ta·loon \‚pant-ᵊl-'ün\ *n* **1 a** *or* **pan·ta·lo·ne** \‚pant-ᵊl-'ō-nē\ *cap* **:** a character in old Italian comedies that is usu. a lean old dotard in tight-fitting trousers and stockings **b :** a buffoon in pantomimes **2** *pl* **a :** BREECHES **b :** TROUSERS

pan·the·ism \'pan(t)-thē-‚iz-əm\ *n* **:** a doctrine that equates God with the forces and laws of the universe — **pan·the·ist** \-thē-əst\ *n* — **pan·the·is·tic** \‚pan(t)-thē-'is-tik\ *adj* — **pan·the·is·ti·cal** \-ti-kəl\ *adj* — **pan·the·is·ti·cal·ly** \-k(ə-)lē\ *adv*

pan·the·on \'pan(t)-thē-‚än\ *n* **1 :** a temple dedicated to all the gods **2 :** a building serving as the burial place of or containing memorials to famous dead **3 :** the gods of a people; *esp* **:** the gods officially recognized

pan·ther \'pan(t)-thər\ *n, pl* **panthers** *also* **panther** [Gk *panthēr*] **1 :** LEOPARD **2 :** COUGAR **3 :** JAGUAR

pant·ie *or* **panty** \'pant-ē\ *n, pl* **pant·ies** **:** a woman's or

child's undergarment covering the lower trunk and made with closed crotch and short legs — usu. used in pl.

pan·to·graph \'pant-ə-‚graf\ *n* [F *pantographe,* fr. Gk *pant-, pas* all + *-graphe* -graph] **:** an instrument for copying a figure (as a map or plan) to scale — **pan·to·graph·ic** \‚pant-ə-'graf-ik\ *adj*

pan·to·mime \'pant-ə-‚mīm\ *n* [L *pantomimus,* fr. Gk *pant-, pas* all + *mimos* mime] **1 :** PANTOMIMIST **2 :** a dramatic or dancing performance in which a story is told primarily by expressive bodily or facial movements of the performers **3 :** conveyance of information by bodily or facial movements — **pantomime** *vb* — **pan·to·mim·ic** \‚pant-ə-'mim-ik\ *adj*

pan·to·mim·ist \'pant-ə-‚mim-əst, -‚mīm-\ *n* **:** an actor or dancer in or a composer of pantomimes

pan·to·then·ic acid \‚pant-ə-‚then-ik-\ *n* [Gk *pantothen* from all sides, fr. *pant-, pas* all] **:** a viscous oily acid of the vitamin B complex found in all living tissues

pan·trop·ic \(')pan-'träp-ik\ *or* **pan·trop·i·cal** \-'träp-i-kəl\ *adj* **:** occurring or growing throughout the tropics

pan·try \'pan-trē\ *n, pl* **pantries** [MF *paneterie,* fr. *panetier* servant in charge of the pantry, fr. *pan* bread, fr. L *panis*] **:** a small room in which food and dishes are kept or from which food is brought to the table

pants \'pan(t)s\ *n pl* [short for *pantaloons*] **1 :** TROUSERS **2 :** UNDERPANTS; *esp* **:** PANTIE

panty hose *n pl* **:** a one-piece undergarment for women that consists of hosiery combined with panties

panty·waist \'pant-ē-‚wāst\ *n* **1 :** a child's garment consisting of short pants buttoned to a waist **2 :** SISSY

pan·zer \'pan-zər, 'pän(t)-sər\ *adj* **:** of or relating to a panzer division or similar armored unit

panzer division *n* **:** a German armored division

¹pap \'pap\ *n* [ME *pappe*] **1** *chiefly dial* **:** NIPPLE, TEAT **2 :** something shaped like a nipple

²pap *n* [ME] **:** soft or bland food for infants or invalids

pa·pa \'päp-ə\ *n* **:** FATHER

pa·pa·cy \'pā-pə-sē\ *n, pl* **-cies** **1 :** the office of pope **2 :** a line of popes **3 :** the term of a pope's reign **4** *cap* **:** the government of the Roman Catholic Church

pa·pa·in \pə-'pā-ən, -'pī-ən\ *n* **:** a proteinase in papaya juice used esp. as a meat tenderizer and in medicine

pa·pal \'pā-pəl\ *adj* [LL *papa* pope, fr. L, father] **:** of or relating to the pope or the papacy — **pa·pal·ly** \-pə-lē\ *adv*

pa·paw *n* **1** \pə-'pó\ **:** PAPAYA **2** \'päp-ò, 'póp-\ **:** a No. American tree of the custard-apple family with purple flowers and a yellow edible fruit; *also* **:** its fruit

pa·pa·ya \pə-'pī-ə\ *n* [Sp, of AmerInd origin] **:** a tropical American tree with large lobed leaves and oblong yellow black-seeded edible fruit; *also* **:** its fruit

¹pa·per \'pā-pər\ *n* [MF *papier,* fr. L *papyrus* papyrus, fr. Gk *papyros*] **1 a :** a felted sheet of usu. vegetable fibers laid down on a fine screen from a water suspension **b :** a sheet or piece of paper **2 a :** a piece of paper containing a written or printed statement; *esp* **:** a document of identification or authorization **b :** a written composition (as a piece of schoolwork) **3 :** a paper container or wrapper **4 :** NEWSPAPER **5 :** instruments (as negotiable notes) of credit **6 :** WALLPAPER

²paper *vb* **pa·pered; pa·per·ing** \'pā-p(ə-)riŋ\ **1 :** to cover or line with paper; *esp* **:** to apply wallpaper to **2 :** to hang wallpaper — **pa·per·er** \-pər-ər\ *n*

³paper *adj* **1 a :** of, relating to, or made of paper or a related composition **b :** resembling paper **:** PAPERY **2 :** of or relating to clerical work or written communication **3 :** NOMINAL 3a

pa·per·back \'pā-pər-‚bak\ *n* **:** a paper-covered book — **paperback** *adj*

pa·per·board \-‚bōrd, -‚bórd\ *n* **:** a board made from cellulose fiber and used esp. for packaging

paper cutter *n* **1 :** PAPER KNIFE **2 :** a machine for simultaneous cutting of many sheets of paper

pa·per·hang·er \-‚haŋ-ər\ *n* **:** one that applies wallpaper — **pa·per·hang·ing** \-‚haŋ-iŋ\ *n*

paper knife *n* **1 :** a knife for slitting envelopes or uncut pages **2 :** the knife of a paper cutter

paper money *n* **:** money consisting of government notes and bank notes

paper mulberry *n* **:** an Asiatic tree related to the mulberries and widely grown as a shade tree

paper profit *n* : a profit that can be realized by selling

pa·per·weight \'pā-pər-‚wāt\ *n* : an object used to hold down loose papers by its weight

paper work *n* : routine clerical or record-keeping work often incidental to a more important task

pa·pery \'pā-p(ə-)rē\ *adj* : resembling paper in thinness or consistency — **pa·per·i·ness** *n*

pa·pier-mâ·ché \‚pā-pər-mə-'shā, -ma-\ *n* [F, lit., chewed paper] : a light strong molding material of wastepaper pulped with glue and other additives — **papier-mâché** *adj*

pa·pil·i·o·na·ceous \pə-‚pil-ē-ə-'nā-shəs\ *adj* [L *papilion-, papilio* butterfly] : resembling a butterfly esp. in irregular shape ⟨the *papilionaceous* flowers of many legumes⟩

pa·pil·la \pə-'pil-ə\ *n, pl* **-pil·lae** \-'pil-(‚)ē, -‚ī\ [L, nipple] : a small projecting bodily structure that suggests a nipple — **pap·il·la·ry** \'pap-ə-‚ler-ē, pə-'pil-ə-rē\ *adj* — **pap·il·late** \'pap-ə-‚lāt, pə-'pil-ət\ *adj* — **pap·il·lose** \'pap-ə-‚lōs, pə-'pil-‚ōs\ *adj*

pap·il·lo·ma \‚pap-ə-'lō-mə\ *n, pl* **-mas** *or* **-ma·ta** \-mət-ə\ : a usu. benign epithelial tumor

pa·pil·lote \‚päp-ē-'(y)ōt\ *n* [F, fr. *papillon* butterfly] : a greased paper wrapper in which food is cooked

pa·pist \'pā-pəst\ *n, often cap* [LL *papa* pope] : ROMAN CATHOLIC — usu. used disparagingly — **papist** *adj* — **pa·pist·ry** \-pə-strē\ *n*

pa·poose \pa-'püs, pə-\ *n* [of AmerInd origin] : a No. American Indian infant

pap·pus \'pap-əs\ *n, pl* **pap·pi** \'pap-‚ī, -ē\ [Gk *pappos*] : a downy or bristly appendage or tuft of appendages crowning the seed or fruit of some seed plants and functioning in its dispersal — **pap·pose** \'pap-‚ōs\ *also* **pap·pous** \'pap-əs\ *adj*

pa·pri·ka \pə-'prē-kə, pa-\ *n* [Hung, fr. Serb, fr. *papar* pepper, fr. Gk *peperi*] : a mild red condiment consisting of the dried finely ground pods of various cultivated sweet peppers; *also* : a sweet pepper used for making paprika

pap·ule \'pap-yül\ *n* [L *papula*] : a small solid usu. conical lesion of the skin — **pap·u·lar** \-yə-lər\ *adj*

pa·py·rus \pə-'pī-rəs\ *n, pl* **-rus·es** *or* **-ri** \-(‚)rē, -‚rī\ [L, fr. Gk *papyros*] **1** : a tall sedge of the Nile valley **2** : the pith of the papyrus plant esp. when cut in strips and pressed into a writing material **3** : a writing on or written scroll of papyrus

par \'pär\ *n* [L, an equal, fr. *par*, adj., equal] **1 a** : the established value of the monetary unit of one country expressed in terms of the monetary unit of another country using the same metal as the standard of value **b** : the face value or issuing price of a security ⟨stocks that sell near *par*⟩ **2** : common level : EQUALITY ⟨boys with abilities on a *par*⟩ **3** : an accepted standard (as of physical condition or health) ⟨not feeling up to *par*⟩ **4** : the score standard set for each hole of a golf course — **par** *adj*

¹para- *or* **par-** *prefix* [Gk; akin to E *for*] **1 a** : beside or alongside of ⟨*para*thyroid⟩ **b** : beyond or outside of ⟨*par*enteral⟩ **2 a** : closely related to or resembling ⟨*par*aldehyde⟩⟨*para*typhoid⟩ **b** : associated in a subsidiary or accessory capacity ⟨*para*military⟩ **3** : faulty : abnormal ⟨*para*esthesia⟩

²para- *comb form* [*parachute*] **1** : parachute ⟨*para*trooper⟩ **2** : parachutist ⟨*para*spotter⟩

para-ami·no·ben·zo·ic acid \'par-ə-ə-‚mē-nō-ben-‚zō-ik-, 'par-ə‚am-ə-‚nō-\ *n* : a colorless organic acid that is a derivative of benzoic acid and is a growth factor of the vitamin B complex

para·bi·o·sis \‚par-ə-bī-'ō-səs, -bē-\ *n* [Gk *para-* side by side + *biōsis* way of life] : anatomical and physiological union of two organisms — **para·bi·ot·ic** \-'ät-ik\ *adj* — **para·bi·ot·i·cal·ly** \-'ät-i-k(ə-)lē\ *adv*

par·a·ble \'par-ə-bəl\ *n* [LL *parabola*, fr. Gk *parabolē*, fr. *paraballein* to compare, fr. *para-* + *ballein* to throw] : a short simple story illustrating a moral or spiritual truth

pa·rab·o·la \pə-'rab-ə-lə\ *n* [Gk *parabolē* parable, parabola] **1** : the curve formed by the intersection of a cone with a plane parallel to one of its sides; *also* : a curve resembling this one ⟨a ball thrown high into the air will form a *parabola* in its flight⟩ — see CONIC SECTION illustration **2** : something bowl-shaped — **par·a·bol·ic** \‚par-ə-'bäl-ik\ *adj* — **par·a·bol·i·cal·ly** \-'bäl-i-k(ə-)lē\ *adv*

pa·rab·o·loid \pə-'rab-ə-‚lȯid\ *n* : a surface all of whose intersections by planes are either parabolas and ellipses or parabolas and hyperbolas

¹par·a·chute \'par-ə-‚shüt\ *n* [F, fr. *para-* (as in *parasol*) + *chute* fall] **1** : a folding umbrella-shaped device of light fabric used esp. for making a safe descent from an airplane **2** : something suggestive of a parachute in form, use, or operation

²parachute *vb* : to convey or descend by means of a parachute

par·a·chut·ist \'par-ə-‚shüt-əst\ *n* : one that descends by parachute

Par·a·clete \'par-ə-‚klēt\ *n* [Gk *Paraklētos*, lit., comforter, fr. *parakalein* to comfort, fr. *para-* + *kalein* to call] : HOLY SPIRIT

¹pa·rade \pə-'rād\ *n* [F, fr. *parer* to prepare, fr. L *parare*] **1** : pompous show or display **2 a** : a ceremonial formation of a body of troops before a superior officer **b** : a place where troops assemble regularly for parade **3** : a public procession **4** : a place of promenade; *also* : those who promenade

²parade *vb* **1 a** : to cause to maneuver or march **b** : to march in a procession **2** : PROMENADE **3** : to exhibit ostentatiously : show off — **pa·rad·er** *n*

para·di·chlo·ro·ben·zene \‚par-ə-‚dī-‚klōr-ə-'ben-‚zēn, -‚klȯr-, -‚ben-\ *n* : a white crystalline chlorinated benzene used chiefly as a fumigant

par·a·digm \'par-ə-‚dīm, -‚dim\ *n* [Gk *paradeigmat-, paradeigma*, fr. *paradeiknynai* to show side by side, fr. *para-* + *deiknynai* to show] **1** : MODEL, PATTERN ⟨an essay that is a *paradigm* of clear writing⟩ **2** : an example of a conjugation or declension showing a word in all its inflectional forms — **par·a·dig·mat·ic** \‚par-ə-dig-'mat-ik\ *adj*

par·a·dise \'par-ə-‚dīs, -‚dīz\ *n* [LL *paradisus*, fr. Gk *paradeisos*, lit., enclosed park, of Iranian origin] **1** : the garden of Eden **2** : HEAVEN **3** : a place or state of bliss — **par·a·di·si·a·cal** \‚par-ə-də-'sī-ə-kəl\ *or* **par·a·dis·i·ac** \-'diz-ē-‚ak\ *adj* : of, relating to, or resembling paradise — **par·a·di·si·a·cal·ly** \-də-'sī-ə-k(ə-)lē\ *adv*

par·a·dox \'par-ə-‚däks\ *n* [Gk *paradoxos* contrary to opinion, fr. *para* beside, contrary to + *doxa* opinion] **1 a** : a statement that seems to contradict common sense and yet is perhaps true **b** : a self-contradictory statement that at first seems true **2** : something (as a person, condition, or act) with seemingly contradictory qualities or phases — **par·a·dox·i·cal** \‚par-ə-'däk-si-kəl\ *adj* — **par·a·dox·i·cal·ly** \-k(ə-)lē\ *adv* — **par·a·dox·i·cal·ness** \-kəl-nəs\ *n*

¹par·af·fin \'par-ə-fən\ *n* [G, fr. L *parum* too little + *affinis* bordering on, associated with; so called fr. the small affinity it possesses for other bodies] **1** : a flammable waxy crystalline mixture of hydrocarbons obtained esp. from distillates of wood, coal, or petroleum and used chiefly in coating and sealing, in candles, and in drugs and cosmetics **2** : a hydrocarbon of the methane series **3** *chiefly Brit* : KEROSENE — **par·af·fin·ic** \‚par-ə-'fin-ik\ *adj*

²paraffin *vt* : to coat or saturate with paraffin

par·a·gon \'par-ə-‚gän, -gən\ *n* [MF, fr. It *paragone*, lit., touchstone, fr. *paragonare* to test on a touchstone, fr. Gk *parakonan* to sharpen, fr. *para-* + *akonē* whetstone] : a model of excellence or perfection

¹par·a·graph \'par-ə-‚graf\ *n* [Gk *paragraphos* marginal sign used to mark change of speakers in a dialogue, fr. *para-* + *graphein* to write] **1 a** : a subdivision of a piece of writing or a speech that consists of one or more sentences and develops in an organized manner one point of a subject or gives the words of one speaker **b** : a short written article (as in a newspaper) that is complete in one undivided section **2** : a character ¶ used as a reference mark or to indicate the beginning of a paragraph — **par·a·graph·ic** \‚par-ə-'graf-ik\ *adj*

²paragraph *vb* **1** : to divide into paragraphs **2** : to write paragraphs esp. as a paragrapher

par·a·graph·er \'par-ə-‚graf-ər\ *n* : a writer of paragraphs esp. for the editorial page of a newspaper

Par·a·guay tea \‚par-ə-‚gwī-, -‚gwä-\ *n* : MATÉ

par·a·keet *var of* PARRAKEET

par·al·de·hyde \pa-'ral-də-‚hīd\ *n* : a liquid derivative of acetaldehyde used as a hypnotic

par·al·lax \'par-ə-‚laks\ *n* [Gk *parallaxis*, fr. *parallassein*

parachute

to cause to alternate, change, fr. *para-* + *allassein* to change] **:** the apparent displacement or the difference in apparent direction of an object as seen from two different points not on a straight line with the object; *esp* **:** the difference in direction of a celestial body as measured from two points on the earth or from opposite points on the earth's orbit — **par·al·lac·tic** \,par-ə-'lak-tik\ *adj*

¹**par·al·lel** \'par-ə-,lel\ *adj* [Gk *parallēlos*, fr. *para* beside + *allēlōn* of one another] **1 a :** extending in the same direction, everywhere equidistant, and not meeting ⟨*parallel* rows of trees⟩ **b :** everywhere equally distant ⟨concentric spheres are *parallel*⟩ **2 a :** marked by likeness or correspondence **:** SIMILAR, ANALOGOUS ⟨*parallel* situations⟩ **b :** having corresponding syntactical elements ⟨*parallel* clauses⟩ **syn** see SIMILAR

²**parallel** *n* **1 a :** a parallel line, curve, or surface **b** (1) **:** one of the imaginary circles on the surface of the earth paralleling the equator and marking the latitude (2) **:** the corresponding line on a globe or map **c :** a character ‖ used as a reference mark **2 a :** something equal or similar in all essential particulars **:** COUNTERPART **b :** SIMILARITY, ANALOGUE **3 :** a tracing of similarity ⟨draw a *parallel* between two eras⟩ **4 a :** the state of being physically parallel **:** PARALLELISM **b :** the arrangement of electrical devices in which all positive poles, electrodes, and terminals are joined to one conductor and all negative ones to another

³**parallel** *vt* **1 :** to indicate similarity or analogy of **:** COMPARE **2 a :** to show something equal to **:** MATCH **b :** to correspond to **3 :** to place so as to be parallel in direction with something **4 :** to extend, run, or move in a direction parallel to ⟨the highway *parallels* the river⟩

⁴**parallel** *adv* **:** in a parallel manner — often used with *with* or *to*

parallel bars *n pl* **:** a pair of bars on a support adjustable in height and spacing that are parallel to each other and are used for gymnastic exercises

par·al·lel·e·pi·ped \,par-ə-,lel-ə-'pī-pəd, -'pip-əd\ *n* [Gk *epipedon* plane surface, fr. *epi-* + *pedon* ground] **:** a prism whose bases are parallelograms

par·al·lel·ism \'par-ə-,lel-,iz-əm\ *n* **1 :** the quality or state of being parallel **2 :** RESEMBLANCE, CORRESPONDENCE **3 :** similarity of syntactical construction of adjacent word groups esp. for rhetorical effect or rhythm **4 :** the development of similar new characters by two or more related organisms in response to similarity of environment

par·al·lel·o·gram \,par-ə-'lel-ə-,gram\ *n* **:** a quadrilateral whose opposite sides are parallel and equal

par·al·lel–veined \,par-ə-,lel-'vānd\ *adj* **:** having linear veins that do not branch and interlace ⟨monocotyledons have *parallel-veined* leaves⟩ — compare NET‑VEINED

pa·ral·y·sis \pə-'ral-ə-səs\ *n, pl* **-y·ses** \-ə-,sēz\ [Gk, fr. *paralyein* to loosen, disable, fr. *para-* + *lyein* to loosen] **1 :** complete or partial loss of function esp. when involving motion or sensation in a part of the body **2 :** loss of the ability to move or act ⟨*paralysis* of highway traffic⟩ — **par·a·lyt·ic** \,par-ə-'lit-ik\ *adj or n*

par·a·lyze \'par-ə-,līz\ *vt* **1 :** to affect with paralysis **2 :** to make powerless, ineffective, or unable to act or function ⟨a labor dispute that *paralyzed* the industry⟩ — **par·a·ly·za·tion** \,par-ə-lə-'zā-shən\ *n* — **par·a·lyz·er** \'par-ə-,lī-zər\ *n*

para·mag·net·ic \,par-ə-mag-'net-ik\ *adj* **:** being or relating to a magnetizable substance that has small susceptibility varying but little with magnetizing force — **para·mag·ne·tism** \-'mag-nə-,tiz-əm\ *n*

par·a·me·cium \,par-ə-'mē-sh(ē-)əm, -sē-əm\ *n, pl* **-cia** \-sh(ē-)ə, -sē-ə\ *also* **-ciums** [NL, fr. Gk *paramēkēs* oblong, fr. *para-* + *mēkos* length] **:** any of a genus of somewhat slipper-shaped ciliate protozoans

para·med·ic \'par-ə-,med-ik\ *n* **:** one who assists a physician (as by giving injections and taking X rays)

pa·ram·e·ter \pə-'ram-ət-ər\ *n* **1 :** an arbitrary constant each of whose values characterizes a member of a system (as a family of curves) **2 :** a characteristic element or constant factor — **para·met·ric** \,par-ə-'me-trik\ *adj*

par·am·ne·sia \,par-,am-'nē-zhə\ *n* [*para-* + *-mnesia* (as

in *amnesia*)] **:** a disorder of memory; *esp* **:** an illusion of remembering something when experienced for the first time

par·a·mount \'par-ə-,maunt\ *adj* [AF *paramont*, fr. OF *par* by (fr. L *per*) + *amont* up, above, fr. L *ad montem* to the mountain] **:** superior to all others **:** SUPREME

par·amour \'par-ə-,mùr\ *n* **:** an illicit lover; *esp* **:** MISTRESS

par·a·noia \,par-ə-'nói-ə\ *n* [Gk, madness, fr. *paranous* demented, fr. *para-* + *nous* mind] **1 :** a psychosis marked by delusions of persecution or of grandeur usu. without hallucinations **2 :** a tendency toward excessive or irrational suspiciousness and distrustfulness of others — **par·a·noi·ac** \-'nói-,ak, -'nói-ik\ *adj or n*

par·a·noid \'par-ə-,nóid\ *adj* **1 :** resembling paranoia **2 :** characterized by suspiciousness, persecutory trends, or megalomania — **paranoid** *n*

par·a·pet \'par-ə-pət, -,pet\ *n* [It *parapetto*, fr. *parare* to shield (fr. L, to prepare) + *petto* chest, fr. L *pectus*] **1 :** a wall of earth or stone to protect soldiers **:** BREASTWORK **2 :** a low wall or railing to protect the edge of a platform, roof, or bridge

par·aph \'par-əf\ *n* **:** a flourish at the end of a signature sometimes meant to safeguard against forgery

par·a·pher·na·lia \,par-ə-fə(r)-'nāl-yə\ *n sing or pl* [Gk *parapherna* goods a bride brings over and above the dowry, fr. *para-* + *phernē* dowry, fr. *pherein* to bear] **1 :** personal belongings **2 :** FURNISHINGS, APPARATUS

¹**par·a·phrase** \'par-ə-,frāz\ *n* **:** a restatement of a text, passage, or work giving the meaning in another form

²**paraphrase** *vb* **:** to make a paraphrase of **:** give the meaning of something in different words — **par·a·phras·er** *n*

par·a·ple·gia \,par-ə-'plē-j(ē-)ə\ *n* [NL, fr. Gk *paraplēgiē* hemiplegia, fr. *para-* + *plēg-*, *plēssein* to strike] **:** paralysis of the lower half of the body with involvement of both legs — **par·a·ple·gic** \-jik\ *adj or n*

para·po·di·um \,par-ə-'pōd-ē-əm\ *n, pl* **-dia** \-ē-ə\ **:** either of a pair of fleshy lateral processes borne by most segments of a polychaete worm — **para·po·di·al** \-ē-əl\ *adj*

para·pro·fes·sion·al \-prə-'fesh-nəl, -ən-ᵊl\ *n* **:** a trained aide who assists a professional person; *esp* **:** a teacher's aide

para·psy·chol·o·gy \,par-ə-sī-'käl-ə-jē\ *n* **:** a branch of study involving the investigation of telepathy and related subjects

par·a·site \'par-ə-,sīt\ *n* [Gk *parasitos* one habitually dining at the tables of others, fr. *para-* + *sitos* grain, food] **1 :** a person who lives at the expense of another **2 :** an organism living in or on another organism in parasitism **3 :** something that resembles a biological parasite in dependence on something else for existence or support without making a useful or adequate return — **par·a·sit·ic** \,par-ə-'sit-ik\ *also* **par·a·sit·i·cal** \-'sit-i-kəl\ *adj* — **par·a·sit·i·cal·ly** \-i-k(ə-)lē\ *adv*

par·a·sit·i·cid·al \,par-ə-,sit-ə-'sīd-ᵊl\ *adj* **:** destructive to parasites — **par·a·sit·i·cide** \-'sit-ə-,sīd\ *n*

par·a·sit·ism \'par-ə-,sīt-,iz-əm\ *n* **1 :** an intimate association between organisms of two or more kinds; *esp* **:** one in which a parasite obtains benefits from a host which it usu. injures **2 :** PARASITOSIS

par·a·sit·ize \'par-ə-sə-,tīz, -,sīt-,īz\ *vt* **:** to infest or live on or with as a parasite

par·a·si·tol·o·gy \,par-ə-sə-'täl-ə-jē, -,sīt-'äl-\ *n* **:** a branch of biology dealing with parasites and parasitism esp. among animals — **par·a·si·tol·o·gist** \-jəst\ *n*

par·a·sol \'par-ə-,sól\ *n* [It *parasole*, fr. *parare* to shield, ward off (fr. L *parare* to prepare) + *sole* sun, fr. L *sol*] **:** a lightweight umbrella used as a protection against the sun

para·sym·pa·thet·ic \,par-ə-,sim-pə-'thet-ik\ *adj* **:** of, relating to, being, or acting on the parasympathetic nervous system — **parasympathetic** *n*

parasympathetic nervous system *n* **:** the part of the autonomic nervous system that tends to induce secretion, increase the tone and contractility of smooth muscle, and cause the dilatation of blood vessels — compare SYMPATHETIC NERVOUS SYSTEM

para·thi·on \,par-ə-'thī-ən, -,än\ *n* **:** an extremely toxic insecticide that is a derivative of a sulfur-containing phosphoric acid

par·a·thor·mone \,par-ə-'thor-,mōn\ *n* **:** the parathyroid hormone

parallelograms

ə abut; ᵊ kitten; ər further; a back; ā bake; ä cot, cart; aú out; ch chin; e less; ē easy; g gift; i trip; ī life

para·thy·roid \-'thī-,róid\ *adj* : of, relating to, or produced by the parathyroid glands — **parathyroid** *n*
parathyroid gland *n* : any of usu. four small endocrine glands adjacent to or embedded in the thyroid gland that produce a hormone concerned with calcium metabolism
para·troops \'par-ə-,trüps\ *n pl* : troops trained and equipped to parachute from an airplane — **para·troop** \-,trüp\ *adj* — **para·troop·er** \-,trü-pər\ *n*
¹para·ty·phoid \,par-ə-'tī-,fóid, -tī-'\ *adj* **1** : resembling typhoid fever **2** : of or relating to paratyphoid or its causative organisms 〈*paratyphoid* infection〉
²paratyphoid *n* : a salmonellosis resembling typhoid fever and occurring as a food poisoning
par·boil \'pär-,bóil\ *vt* [ME *parboilen*, fr. MF *parboillir* to boil thoroughly, fr. LL *perbullire*, fr. L *per-* + *bullire* to boil] **1** : to boil briefly usu. before cooking in another manner **2** : OVERHEAT
Par·cae \'pär-,kī, -,sē\ *n pl* : the three Fates of Roman mythology
¹par·cel \'pär-səl\ *n* [MF, fr. (assumed) VL *particella*, dim. of L *particula* particle] **1** : FRAGMENT, PORTION **2** : a tract or plot of land **3** : a company, collection, or group of persons, animals, or things : LOT **4** : a wrapped bundle : PACKAGE
²parcel *vt* **par·celed** *or* **par·celled**; **par·cel·ing** *or* **par·cel·ling** \'pär-s(ə-)liŋ\ **1** : to divide into parts : DISTRIBUTE **2** : to make up into a parcel : WRAP
parcel post *n* **1** : a mail service handling parcels **2** : packages handled by parcel post
parch \'pärch\ *vb* [ME *parchen*] **1** : to toast under dry heat **2** : to dry up : shrivel with heat
Par·chee·si \pär-'chē-zē\ *trademark* — used for a board game adapted from an ancient game resembling backgammon
parch·ment \'pärch-mənt\ *n* [OF *parchemin*, modif. of L *pergamena*, fr. Gk *pergamēnē*, fr. *Pergamon* Pergamum] **1** : the skin of a sheep or goat prepared for use as a writing material **2** : a paper made to resemble parchment **3** : a parchment manuscript; *also* : an academic diploma
¹pard \'pärd\ *n* [L *pardus*, fr. Gk *pardos*] *archaic* : LEOPARD
²pard *n*, *chiefly dial* : PARTNER, CHUM
pard·ner \'pärd-nər\ *n*, *chiefly dial* : PARTNER, CHUM
¹par·don \'pärd-ᵊn\ *n* [MF, fr. *pardoner* to pardon, fr. LL *perdonare* to grant freely, fr. L *per-* thoroughly + *donare* to give] **1 a** : the excusing of an offense without exacting a penalty **b** : remission of the legal penalties of an offense **2** : INDULGENCE 1 **3** : excuse for a fault or discourtesy — **par·don·a·ble** \'pärd-nə-bəl, -ᵊn-ə-bəl\ *adj* — **par·don·a·bly** \-blē\ *adv*
²pardon *vt* **par·doned**; **par·don·ing** \'pärd-niŋ, -ᵊn-iŋ\ **1** : to free from penalty **2** : to allow (an offense) to pass without punishment : FORGIVE *syn* see EXCUSE
par·don·er \'pärd-nər, -ᵊn-ər\ *n* : a medieval preacher delegated to raise money for religious works by soliciting offerings and granting indulgences
pare \'pa(ə)r, 'pe(ə)r\ *vt* [MF *parer* to prepare, adorn, trim, fr. L *parare* to prepare, acquire] **1** : to cut or shave off the outside or the ends of 〈*pare* an apple〉〈*paring* his nails〉 **2** : to diminish gradually by or as if by paring 〈*pare* expenses〉
par·e·go·ric \,par-ə-'gór-ik, -'gōr-, -'gär-\ *n* [Gk *parēgorein* to talk over, comfort, fr. *para-* + *agora* assembly] : camphorated tincture of opium used esp. to relieve pain
pa·ren·chy·ma \pə-'reŋ-kə-mə\ *n* [Gk, tissue of the viscera, fr. *perenchein* to pour in beside, fr. *para-* + *en-* + *chein* to pour] **1** : a tissue of higher plants consisting of thin-walled living cells that remain capable of cell division even when mature, are agents of photosynthesis and storage, and make up much of the substance of leaves and roots and the pulp of fruits as well as parts of stems and supporting structures **2** : the distinctive functional tissue of an animal organ (as a gland) as distinguished from its supporting tissue or framework — **par·en·chym·a·tous** \,par-ən-'kim-ət-əs\ *also* **pa·ren·chy·mal** \pə-'reŋ-kə-məl\ *adj* — **par·en·chym·a·tous·ly** \,par-ən-'kim-ət-əs-lē\ *adv*
par·ent \'par-ənt, 'per-\ *n* [L *parent-*, *parens*, fr. prp. of *parere* to give birth to] **1 a** : one that begets or brings forth offspring **b** : an animal or plant regarded in relation to its offspring **2** : the material, source, or originator of something — **parent** *adj*

par·ent·age \-ənt-ij\ *n* **1** : descent from parents or ancestors : LINEAGE 〈a man of noble *parentage*〉 **2** : DERIVATION, ORIGIN
pa·ren·tal \pə-'rent-ᵊl\ *adj* : of, typical of, or being parents 〈*parental* affection〉〈a *parental* generation〉— **pa·ren·tal·ly** \-ᵊl-ē\ *adv*
par·en·ter·al \pə-'rent-ə-rəl\ *adj* [Gk *enteron* intestine] : situated or occurring outside the intestine; *esp* : introduced otherwise than by way of the digestive system — **par·en·ter·al·ly** \-rə-lē\ *adv*
pa·ren·the·sis \pə-'ren(t)-thə-səs\ *n*, *pl* **-the·ses** \-thə-,sēz\ [Gk, fr. *parentithenai* to insert, fr. *para-* + *en-* + *tithenai* to place] **1 a** : an amplifying or explanatory word, phrase, or sentence inserted in a passage from which it is usu. set off by punctuation **b** : DIGRESSION **2** : one of a pair of marks ( ) used to enclose a parenthetic expression or to group a symbolic unit in a mathematical expression — **par·en·thet·ic** \,par-ən-'thet-ik\ *or* **par·en·thet·i·cal** \-'thet-i-kəl\ *adj* — **par·en·thet·i·cal·ly** \-i-k(ə-)lē\ *adv*
pa·ren·the·size \pə-'ren(t)-thə-,sīz\ *vt* : to make a parenthesis of
par·ent·hood \'par-ənt-,hùd, 'per-\ *n* : the position, function, or standing of a parent
pa·re·sis \pə-'rē-səs, 'par-ə-\ *n*, *pl* **-re·ses** \-'rē-,sēz, -ə-,sēz\ [Gk, fr. *parienai* to relax, fr. *para-* + *hienai* to let go, send] : a usu. partial paralysis; *also* : a syphilitic disorder in which spirochetes invade the brain and ultimately produce dementia and paralysis — **pa·ret·ic** \pə-'ret-ik\ *adj or n*
par ex·cel·lence \,pär-,ek-sə-'läⁿs\ *adv* (*or adj*) [F, lit., by excellence] : in the highest degree : PREEMINENTLY
par·fait \pär-'fā\ *n* [F, fr. *parfait* perfect, fr. L *perfectus*] **1** : a flavored custard containing whipped cream and syrup frozen without stirring **2** : a cold dessert made of layers of fruit, syrup, ice cream, and whipped cream
par·he·lion \pär-'hēl-yən\ *n*, *pl* **-lia** \-yə\ [Gk *parēlion*, fr. *para-* beside + *hēlios* sun] : any one of several bright spots often tinged with color that often appear on both sides of the sun and at the same altitude as the sun
pa·ri·ah \pə-'rī-ə\ *n* [Tamil *paraiyan*, lit., drummer] **1** : a member of a low caste of southern India and Burma **2** : a person despised or rejected by society : OUTCAST
pa·ri·e·tal \pə-'rī-ət-ᵊl\ *adj* [L *pariet-*, *paries* wall] : of, relating to, or forming the walls of a part or cavity and esp. the upper posterior wall of the head
parietal bone *n* : either of a pair of bones of the roof of the skull between the frontal bones and the occipital bones
pari–mu·tu·el \,par-i-'myü-chə-wəl, -chəl\ *n* [F *pari mutuel*, lit., mutual stake] : a system of betting on a race in which those who bet on the winners of the first three places share the total stakes minus a percentage for the management
par·ing \'pa(ə)r-iŋ, 'pe(ə)r-\ *n* **1** : the act of cutting away an edge or surface **2** : something pared off 〈apple *parings*〉
pa·ri pas·su \,par-ē-'pas-ü\ *adv* (*or adj*) [L, with equal step] : at an equal rate or pace
Par·is \'par-əs\ *n* : a son of Priam whose abduction of Helen led to the Trojan War
Paris green \,par-əs-\ *n* : a poisonous bright green powder containing copper and arsenic that is used as a pigment and as an insecticide
par·ish \'par-ish\ *n* [MF *paroisse*, *paroche*, fr. LL *parochia*, modif. of LGk *paroikia* diocese, parish, fr. Gk *paroikos* stranger, fr. *para-* + *oikos* house] **1 a** : a section of a diocese in charge of a priest or minister **b** : the persons who live in such a section and attend the parish church **2** : a British unit of local government often coinciding with an original ecclesiastical parish **3** : the members of any church **4** : a civil division of the state of Louisiana corresponding to a county in other states
parish house *n* : a building for the educational and social activities of a church
pa·rish·io·ner \pə-'rish-(ə-)nər\ *n* : a member or resident of a parish
par·i·ty \'par-ət-ē\ *n*, *pl* **-ties** [L *par* equal] **1** : the quality or state of being equal or equivalent **2** : equality of purchasing power established by law between different kinds of money at a given ratio **3** : an equivalence of the price of an agricultural commodity to its price in a year taken as the base and usu. designated 100 that is designed

---

j joke; ŋ sing; ō flow; ó flaw; ói coin; th thin; th̲ this; ü loot; ù foot; y yet; yü few; yù furious; zh vision

to maintain the farmers' current purchasing power at the level of the base period

¹park \'pärk\ *n* [OF *parc*] **1 :** a tract of land attached to a country house and used for recreation (as hunting or riding) **2 a :** a piece of ground in or near a city or town kept as a place of beauty and recreation **b :** an area maintained in its natural state as a public property **3 a :** a space occupied by military animals, vehicles, or materials **b :** PARKING LOT **4 :** an enclosed arena or stadium used esp. for ball games

²park *vb* **1 a :** to leave a vehicle temporarily on a public way or in a parking lot or garage **b :** to land or leave an airplane **2 :** to set and leave temporarily

par·ka \'pär-kə\ *n* [Aleut, skin, outer garment, fr. Russ, pelt, of Uralic origin] **:** a hooded fur pullover garment for arctic wear; *also* **:** a garment of similar style made of windproof fabric for sports or military wear

parking lot *n* **:** an outdoor area for the parking of motor vehicles

park·way \'pärk-,wā\ *n* **:** a broad landscaped thoroughfare

par·lance \'pär-lən(t)s\ *n* [MF, fr. *parler* to speak] **:** manner or mode of speech **:** IDIOM

¹par·lay \'pär-,lā, -lē\ *vt* **:** to bet in a parlay; *esp* **:** to multiply by or as if by so betting

²parlay *n* [F *paroli*, fr. It dial.] **:** a series of bets in which the original stake plus its winnings are risked on the successive wagers

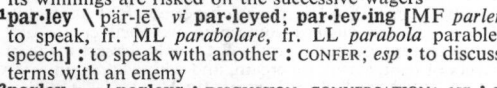

parka

¹par·ley \'pär-lē\ *vi* **par·leyed; par·ley·ing** [MF *parler* to speak, fr. ML *parabolare*, fr. LL *parabola* parable, speech] **:** to speak with another **:** CONFER; *esp* **:** to discuss terms with an enemy

²parley *n, pl* **parleys :** DISCUSSION, CONVERSATION; *esp* **:** a conference with an enemy

par·lia·ment \'pär-lə-mənt, 'pärl-yə-\ *n* [OF *parlement*, fr. *parler* to speak] **1 :** a formal conference on public affairs; *esp* **:** a council of state in early medieval England **2 a :** an assemblage of the nobility, clergy, and commons called together by the British sovereign as the supreme legislative body in the United Kingdom **b :** a similar assemblage in another nation or state **3 a :** the supreme legislative body of a political unit comprising a series of successive parliaments **b :** the British House of Commons **4 :** one of several principal courts of justice existing in France before the revolution of 1789

par·lia·men·tar·i·an \,pär-lə-,men-'ter-ē-ən, -mən-, ,pärl-yə-\ *n* **1** *often cap* **:** an adherent of the parliament in opposition to the king during the English Civil War **2 :** an expert in parliamentary procedure

par·lia·men·ta·ry \-'ment-ə-rē, -'men-trē\ *adj* **1 :** of, relating to, or enacted by a parliament **2 :** adhering to the parliament as opposed to the king during the English Civil War **3 :** of or relating to a system of government in which executive power is vested in a cabinet whose members belong to and are individually and collectively responsible to the legislature **4 :** of, relating to, or in accordance with the rules and precedents governing the proceedings of a parliament or other deliberative body

par·lor \'pär-lər\ *n* [OF *parlour*, fr. *parler* to speak] **1 :** a room used primarily for conversation or the reception of guests: as **a :** a room in a private dwelling for the entertainment of guests **b :** a semiprivate room in an inn, hotel, or club **2 :** any of various business places ⟨funeral *parlor*⟩ ⟨beauty *parlor*⟩

parlor car *n* **:** an extra-fare railroad passenger car for day travel equipped with individual chairs

par·lor·maid \-,mād\ *n* **:** a maid in a private home who attends to the parlor, the table, and the door

par·lous \'pär-ləs\ *adj* [ME, alter. of *perilous*] **1 :** full of danger or risk **:** PRECARIOUS ⟨*parlous* state of a country's finances⟩ **2 :** SHOCKING — **par·lous·ly** *adv*

Par·nas·si·an \pär-'nas-ē-ən\ *adj* [fr. the belief that Mount Parnassus was a home of the Muses] **:** of or relating to the Muses or to poetry

pa·ro·chi·al \pə-'rō-kē-əl\ *adj* [LL *parochia* parish] **1 :** of or relating to a parish **2 :** confined as if within the borders of a parish **:** NARROW, PROVINCIAL ⟨a *parochial*

attitude⟩ — **pa·ro·chi·al·ism** \-kē-ə-,liz-əm\ *n* — **pa·ro·chi·al·ly** \-kē-ə-lē\ *adv*

parochial school *n* **:** a school maintained by a religious body

par·o·dy \'par-əd-ē\ *n, pl* **-dies** [Gk *parōidia*, fr. *para-* + *aidein* to sing] **1 :** a literary or musical work in which the style of an author or work is closely imitated for comic effect or in ridicule **2 :** a feeble or ridiculous imitation **syn** see CARICATURE — **par·o·dist** \-əd-əst\ *n* — **parody** *vt*

¹pa·role \pə-'rōl\ *n* [F, speech, parole, fr. LL *parabola* parable, speech] **1 :** a promise confirmed by a pledge; *esp* **:** the promise of a prisoner of war to fulfill stated conditions in consideration of his release **2 :** a conditional release of a prisoner before his sentence has expired

²parole *vt* **:** to release (a prisoner) on parole — **pa·rol·ee** \pə-,rō-'lē, ,par-ə-'lē\ *n*

par·o·no·ma·sia \,par-ə-nō-'mā-zh(ē-)ə\ *n* [Gk, fr. *para-* + *onoma* name] **:** a play on words **:** PUN — **par·o·no·mas·tic** \-'mas-tik\ *adj*

pa·rot·id \pə-'rät-əd, -'rōt-\ *adj* [Gk *para-* + *ōt-, ous* ear] **:** of or relating to the parotid gland

parotid gland *n* **:** either of a pair of large salivary glands situated below and in front of the ear

par·o·ti·tis \,par-ə-'tīt-əs\ *n* **:** inflammation of the parotid glands; *also* **:** MUMPS

par·ox·ysm \'par-ək-,siz-əm\ *n* [Gk *paroxysmos*, fr. *par-oxynein* to irritate, fr. *para-* + *oxys* sharp, acute] **1 :** a fit, attack, or sudden increase of violence of a disease that occurs at intervals ⟨a *paroxysm* of coughing⟩ **2 :** a sudden violent emotion or action ⟨*paroxysms* of rage⟩ — **par·ox·ys·mal** \,par-ək-'siz-məl\ *adj*

par·quet \'pär-'kā\ *n* [F, lit., small enclosure, fr. dim. of *parc* park] **1 :** a flooring of parquetry **2 :** the lower floor of a theater esp. in front of the balcony

par·que·try \'pär-kə-trē\ *n, pl* **-tries :** a patterned wood inlay used esp. for floors

parr \'pär\ *n, pl* **parr** *also* **parrs :** a young salmon actively feeding in fresh water

par·ra·keet \'par-ə-,kēt\ *n* [Sp *peri-quito*, fr. MF *perroquet* parrot] **:** any of numerous usu. small slender parrots with a long graduated tail

par·ri·cide \'par-ə-,sīd\ *n* **1** [L *par-ricida*] **:** one that murders his father or mother or a close relative **2** [L *parricidium*] **:** the act of a parricide — **par·ri·cid·al** \,par-ə-'sīd-ᵊl\ *adj*

parquetry

¹par·rot \'par-ət\ *n* **1 :** a bright-colored tropical bird of a family characterized by a strong hooked bill, by toes arranged in pairs with two in front and two behind, and often by the ability to mimic speech **2 :** a person who repeats words mechanically and without understanding

²parrot *vt* **:** to repeat by rote

parrot disease *n* **:** PSITTACOSIS — called also *parrot fever*

parrot fish *n* **:** any of various sea fishes related to the perches that have the teeth fused into a cutting plate resembling a beak

par·ry \'par-ē\ *vb* **par·ried; par·ry·ing 1 :** to ward off a weapon or blow **:** turn aside skillfully **2 :** to evade esp. by an adroit answer ⟨*parry* an embarrassing question⟩ — **parry** *n*

parse \'pärs, 'pärz\ *vb* [L *pars orationis* part of speech] **1 :** to analyze a sentence by naming its parts and their relations to each other **2 :** to give the part of speech of a word and explain its relation to other words in a sentence

par·sec \'pär-,sek\ *n* [*parallax* + *second*] **:** a unit of measure equal to 19.2 trillion miles

Par·si *also* **Par·see** \'pär-,sē\ *n* **:** a Zoroastrian descended from Persian refugees settled principally at Bombay

Par·si·fal \'pär-zi-,fäl, -sə-,fól\ *n* **:** a knight of the Holy Grail

par·si·mo·ni·ous \,pär-sə-'mō-nē-əs\ *adj* **:** excessively frugal **:** STINGY, NIGGARDLY — **par·si·mo·ni·ous·ly** *adv* — **par·si·mo·ni·ous·ness** *n*

par·si·mo·ny \'pär-sə-,mō-nē\ *n* [L *parsimonia*, fr. *pars-, parcere* to spare] **:** extreme frugality **:** STINGINESS

pars·ley \'pär-slē\ *n, pl* **parsleys** [OE *petersilie*, fr. L *petroselinum*, fr. Gk *petroselinon*, fr. *petros* stone + *selinon* celery] **:** a southern European herb of the carrot family widely grown for its finely divided leaves which are used as a flavoring or garnish

pars·nip \'pär-snəp\ *n* [ME *pasnepe*, modif. of MF *pasnaie*, fr. L *pastinaca*] **:** a European biennial herb of the carrot family grown for its long white root used as a vegetable; *also* **:** this root

par·son \'pärs-°n\ *n* [ME *persone*, fr. ML *persona*, lit., person, fr. L] **1 :** a minister in charge of a parish **:** RECTOR **2 :** CLERGYMAN; *esp* **:** a Protestant pastor

par·son·age \'pär-snij, 'pärs-°n-ij\ *n* **:** the house provided by a church for its pastor

¹part \'pärt\ *n* [L *part-, pars*] **1 a :** one of the portions into which something is divisible and which together constitute the whole **b :** one of several or many equal units of which something is composed ⟨a fifth *part* for each⟩ **c :** a portion of a plant or animal body **:** MEMBER, ORGAN ⟨wash the injured *part*⟩ **d :** a vocal or instrumental line or melody in concerted music or in harmony; *also* **:** the score for it **e :** a constituent member of a machine or apparatus; *also* **:** a spare piece or member **2 :** something falling to one in a division or apportionment **:** SHARE **3 :** DUTY, FUNCTION **4 :** one of the opposing sides in a conflict ⟨take someone's *part* in a quarrel⟩ **5 :** DISTRICT, REGION — usu. used in pl. **6 :** a function or course of action performed **7 a :** an actor's lines in a play **b :** the role of a character in a play **8** *pl* **:** a constituent of character or capacity **:** TALENT ⟨a man of *parts*⟩ **9 :** the line where the hair is divided in combing

syn PART, PORTION, PIECE, SEGMENT mean something less than the whole. PART is the general term and is interchangeable with any of the others; PORTION suggests an assigned or allotted part ⟨*portion* of the voting population⟩ ⟨read the middle *portion* of the book⟩ PIECE applies to a separate or detached part ⟨*piece* of pie⟩ SEGMENT applies to a part separated or marked out by natural lines of cleavage ⟨*segments* of an orange⟩

²part *vb* [OF *partir*, fr. L *partire* to divide, fr. *part-, pars* part] **1 a :** to separate from or take leave of someone **b :** to take leave of one another **2 :** to go away **:** DEPART **3 :** to become separated, detached, or broken **4 :** to give up possession or control ⟨wouldn't *part* with his old car⟩ **5 a :** to divide into parts or shares **b :** to separate by combing on each side of a line **6 a :** SEPARATE, SUNDER **b :** to hold apart **:** intervene between ⟨the referee *parts* the fighters⟩

³part *adv* **:** in a measure **:** PARTLY ⟨he was only *part* right⟩

par·take \pär-'tāk, pər-\ *vi* **par·took** \-'tȯk\; **par·tak·en** \-'tā-kən\; **par·tak·ing** **1 a :** to take a part or share ⟨*partake* of a meal⟩ **b :** PARTICIPATE ⟨all may *partake* in the ceremony⟩ **2 :** to have some of the qualities or attributes of something ⟨the story *partook* of the nature of fantasy⟩ — **par·tak·er** *n*

part·ed \'pärt-əd\ *adj* **1 :** divided into parts **2 :** cleft so that the divisions reach nearly but not quite to the base ⟨3-*parted* corolla⟩

par·terre \pär-'te(ə)r\ *n* [F, fr. *par terre* on the ground] **1 :** an ornamental garden with paths between the beds **2 :** the part of the floor of a theater behind the orchestra

par·the·no·car·py \'pär-thə-nō-,kär-pē\ *n* **:** the production of fruits without fertilization — **par·the·no·car·pic** \,pär-thə-nō-'kär-pik\ *adj*

par·the·no·gen·e·sis \,pär-thə-nō-'jen-ə-səs\ *n, pl* **-gen·e·ses** \-ə-,sēz\ [Gk *parthenos* virgin] **:** reproduction esp. among lower plants and invertebrate animals in which an unfertilized gamete develops into a new individual — **par·the·no·ge·net·ic** \-jə-'net-ik\ *adj* — **par·the·no·ge·net·i·cal·ly** \-'net-i-k(ə-)lē\ *adv*

par·tial \'pär-shəl\ *adj* **1 :** inclined to favor one side or party over another **:** BIASED ⟨a *partial* judge⟩ **2 :** markedly or excessively fond of someone or something ⟨*partial* to double milk shakes⟩ **3 :** of or relating to a part rather than the whole ⟨a *partial* eclipse⟩ — **par·tial·ly** \'pärsh-(ə-)lē\ *adv*

partial denture *n* **:** an often removable artificial replacement of one or more teeth

par·ti·al·i·ty \,pär-shē-'al-ət-ē, pär-'shal-\ *n, pl* **-ties** **1 :** the quality or state of being partial **:** BIAS **2 :** a special taste or liking

partial product *n* **:** one of the products obtained by multiplying successively the multiplicand by each digit of the multiplier

part·i·ble \'pärt-ə-bəl\ *adj* **:** capable of being parted **:** DIVISIBLE

par·tic·i·pant \pər-'tis-ə-pənt, pär-\ *n* **:** one that participates

par·tic·i·pate \pär-'tis-ə-,pāt, pər-\ *vi* [L *participare*, fr. *particip-, particeps* participant, fr. *part-, pars* part + *capere* to take] **:** to take part or have a share in something (as an activity) usu. in common with others — **par·tic·i·pa·tion** \-,tis-ə-'pā-shən\ *n* — **par·tic·i·pa·tor** \-'tis-ə-,pāt-ər\ *n*

par·ti·cip·i·al \,pärt-ə-'sip-ē-əl\ *adj* **:** of, relating to, or formed with or from a participle ⟨*participial* phrase⟩ — **par·ti·cip·i·al·ly** \-ē-ə-lē\ *adv*

par·ti·ci·ple \'pärt-ə-,sip-əl\ *n* [MF, modif. of L *participium*, fr. *particip-, particeps* participant] **:** a word having the characteristics of both verb and adjective; *esp* **:** an English verbal form that has the function of an adjective and at the same time shows such verbal features as tense and voice and capability of taking an object

par·ti·cle \'pärt-i-kəl\ *n* [L *particula*, fr. dim. of *part-, pars*] **1 :** one of the minute subdivisions of matter (as a molecule, atom, electron) — compare ELEMENTARY PARTICLE **2 a :** a minute quantity or fragment **b :** the smallest possible portion or amount of something **3 a :** a word (as an article, preposition, or conjunction) expressing some general meaning or some connective or limiting relation **b :** a derivational affix

par·ti·col·ored \,pärt-ē-'kəl-ərd\ *adj* **:** showing different colors or tints

¹par·tic·u·lar \pə(r)-'tik-yə-lər\ *adj* [L *particula* small part] **1 :** of or relating to a single person or thing **2 :** of or relating to details **:** MINUTE **3 :** distinctive among others **:** SPECIAL **4 a :** attentive to details **:** EXACT **b :** hard to please **:** EXACTING, FASTIDIOUS **syn** see CIRCUMSTANTIAL

²particular *n* **:** an individual fact, detail, or item — **in particular 1 :** ESPECIALLY, PARTICULARLY **2 :** in detail **:** INDIVIDUALLY

par·tic·u·lar·i·ty \-,tik-yə-'lar-ət-ē\ *n, pl* **-ties 1 a :** a minute detail **:** PARTICULAR **b :** an individual characteristic **:** PECULIARITY **2 :** the quality or state of being particular as opposed to universal **3 :** attentiveness to detail **:** EXACTNESS, FASTIDIOUSNESS

par·tic·u·lar·ize \-'tik-yə-lə-,rīz\ *vb* **:** to go into details **:** state in detail **:** SPECIFY — **par·tic·u·lar·i·za·tion** \-,tik-yə-lə-rə-'zā-shən\ *n*

par·tic·u·lar·ly \-'tik-yə-lər-lē\ *adv* **1 :** in a particular manner **2 :** to an unusual degree **:** ESPECIALLY

par·tic·u·late \-'tik-yə-lət\ *adj* **:** relating to or existing as minute separate particles

particulate inheritance *n* **:** inheritance of characters specif. transmitted by genes in accord with Mendel's laws

¹part·ing \'pärt-iŋ\ *n* **1 :** SEPARATION, DIVISION **2 :** a place where a division or separation occurs ⟨the *parting* of the ways⟩ **3 :** LEAVE-TAKING ⟨shake hands at *parting*⟩

²parting *adj* **1 :** DEPARTING ⟨*parting* day⟩ **2 :** serving to divide **:** SEPARATING ⟨the *parting* strip of a window sash⟩ **3 :** given, taken, or performed at parting ⟨a *parting* kiss⟩

par·ti·san \'pärt-ə-zən\ *n* [MF *partisan*, fr. It *partigiano*, fr. *parte* part, fr. L *part-, pars*] **1 :** a person who takes the part of another; *esp* **:** a devoted adherent to the cause of another **2 :** a member of a guerrilla force within enemy lines who impedes the enemy by sabotage and raids — **partisan** *adj* — **par·ti·san·ship** \-,ship\ *n*

par·tite \'pär-,tīt\ *adj* [L *partitus*, fr. pp. of *partire* to divide, fr. *part-, pars* part] **:** divided into a usu. specified number of parts

par·ti·tion \pər-'tish-ən, pär-\ *n* **1 a :** the action of parting **:** DIVISION **b :** separation of a class or whole into constituent elements; *esp* **:** the division of a united territory among two or more governments **2 :** an interior dividing wall **3 :** PART, SECTION — **partition** *vt* — **par·ti·tion·er** \-'tish-(ə-)nər\ *n*

par·ti·tive \'pärt-ət-iv\ *adj* **1 :** of, relating to, or denoting a part ⟨a *partitive* construction⟩ **2 :** serving to indicate that of which a part is specified ⟨*partitive* genitive⟩ — **partitive** *n* — **par·ti·tive·ly** *adv*

part·ly \'pärt-lē\ *adv* **:** in some measure or degree **:** PARTIALLY

part music *n* **:** vocal music for several voices in independent parts usu. without accompaniment

¹part·ner \'pärt-nər\ *n* [ME alter. of *parcener* sharer, fr.

---

j joke; **ŋ** sing; **ō** flow; **ȯ** flaw; **ȯi** coin; **th** thin; **th̲** this; **ü** loot; **u̇** foot; **y** yet; **yü** few; **yu̇** furious; **zh** vision

OF *parçonier*, fr. *parçon* division, share, fr. L *partition-, partitio*] **1 a :** one that is associated in action with another **:** COLLEAGUE **b :** either of a couple who dance together **c :** one of two or more persons who play together in a game against an opposing side **d :** HUSBAND, WIFE **2 :** a member of a partnership

²partner *vt* **:** to join as partner **:** act as partner to

part·ner·ship \'pärt-nər-,ship\ *n* **1 :** the state of being a partner **:** PARTICIPATION **2 :** a form of business organization formed, owned, and managed by two or more persons who agree to share the profits and usu. are individually liable for losses

part of speech : a traditional class of words distinguished according to the kind of idea denoted and the function performed in a sentence — compare ADJECTIVE, ADVERB, CONJUNCTION, INTERJECTION, NOUN, PREPOSITION, PRONOUN, VERB

partook *past of* PARTAKE

par·tridge \'pär-trij\ *n, pl* **partridge** *or* **par·tridg·es** [OF *perdris*, fr. L *perdic-, perdix*, fr. Gk *perdix*] **:** any of several stout-bodied Old World game birds related to the common domestic fowl; *also* **:** any of various similar and related American birds (as a bobwhite or ruffed grouse)

par·tridge·ber·ry \-,ber-ē\ **:** an American trailing evergreen plant of the madder family with insipid scarlet berries

part–song \'pärt-,sóŋ\ *n* **:** a song consisting of two or more voice parts

par·tu·ri·ent \pär-'t(y)ùr-ē-ənt\ *adj* [L *parturire* to be in labor, fr. *parere* to bring forth] **:** bringing forth or about to bring forth young; *also* **:** of or relating to parturition

par·tu·ri·tion \,pärt-ə-'rish-ən\ *n* **:** the act or process of giving birth to offspring

par·ty \'pärt-ē\ *n, pl* **parties** [OF *partie* part, party, fr. fem. of *parti*, pp. of *partir* to part] **1 :** a person or group taking one side of a question, dispute, or contest **2 :** a group of persons usu. agreeing on fundamental principles that is organized for the purpose of influencing or directing the policies of a government or of overthrowing an established government **3 :** a person or group participating in an action, affair, or transaction ⟨*party* to a lawsuit⟩ **4 :** a particular individual **:** PERSON ⟨get the right *party* on the telephone⟩ **5 :** a detail of soldiers ⟨work *party*⟩ **6 :** a social gathering; *also* **:** the entertainment provided for it — **party** *adj*

party line *n* **1 :** a single telephone circuit connecting two or more subscribers with the exchange — called also *party wire* **2 :** the principles or policies of an individual or organization; *esp* **:** the official policies of a Communist party — **par·ty·lin·er** \,pärt-ē-'lī-nər\ *n*

par·ve·nu *also* **par·ve·nue** \'pär-və-,n(y)ü\ *n* [F, fr. pp. of *parvenir* to arrive, fr. L *pervenire*, fr. *per-* + *venire* to come] **:** one who has recently or suddenly risen to wealth or power and has not yet secured the social position appropriate to it **:** UPSTART — **parvenu** *also* **parvenue** *adj*

Pasch \'pask\ *n* [Gk *pascha*, fr. Heb *pesaḥ*] **1 :** PASSOVER **2 :** EASTER — **pas·chal** \'pas-kəl\ *adj*

paschal lamb *n* **1 :** a lamb slain and eaten at the Passover **2** *cap P&L* **:** CHRIST

pas de deux \,päd-ə-'də(r)\ *n, pl* **pas de deux** \-'dər(z), -'də(z)\ [F, lit., step for two] **:** a dance or figure for two performers

pas de trois \-'trwä\ *n, pl* **pas de trois** \-'trwä(z)\ [F, lit., step for three] **:** a dance or figure for three performers

pa·sha \'päsh-ə, pə-'shä\ *n* [Turk *paşa*] **:** a Middle Eastern man (as a governor of the Ottoman Empire) of high rank

Pash·to \'pəsh-tō\ *n* **:** the Iranian language of the Pathan people which is the chief vernacular of eastern Afghanistan and adjacent parts of West Pakistan

pasque–flow·er \'pask-,flaù(-ə)r\ *n* **:** any of several low perennial herbs related to the buttercups that have palmately compound leaves and large usu. white or purple flowers in early spring

¹pass \'pas\ *vb* [OF *passer*, fr. L *passus* step, pace] **1 :** MOVE, PROCEED **2 a :** to go away **:** DEPART **b :** DIE — often used with *on* or *away* **3 :** to go by or move past **4 a :** to go across, over, or through **b :** to go unchallenged ⟨let his remark *pass*⟩ **5 a :** to change or transfer ownership **b :** to go from the control or possession of one person or group to that of another ⟨throne *passed* to his son⟩ **6 a :** HAPPEN, OCCUR **b :** to take place as a mutual

exchange or transaction ⟨words *passed*⟩ **7 a :** to secure the approval of a legislative body **b :** to go through or allow to go through an inspection, test, or course of study successfully **8 a :** to serve as a medium of exchange **b :** to be held or regarded ⟨*passed* for an honest man⟩ **9 :** to execute a pass (as in football) **10 :** to decline to bid, bet, or draw an additional card in a card game **11 :** to go beyond; *esp* **:** SURPASS **12 :** to leave out in an account or narration **13 a :** UNDERGO **b :** to cause or permit to elapse **:** SPEND ⟨*pass* time⟩ **14 :** to secure the approval of **15 a :** to give official sanction or approval to ⟨*pass* a new law⟩ **b :** OVERLOOK **16 a :** to put in circulation ⟨*pass* bad checks⟩ **b :** to transfer from one person to another **c :** to take a turn with (as a rope) around something **d :** to transfer (as a ball) to another player on the same team **17 a :** to pronounce judicially ⟨*pass* sentence⟩ **b :** UTTER **18 a :** to cause or permit to go over, past, or through **b :** to cause to march or go by in order ⟨*pass* the troops in review⟩ **19 :** to emit or discharge from the bowels **20 :** to permit to reach first base by giving a base on balls — **pass·er** *n* — **pass muster :** to pass an inspection or examination — **pass the buck :** to shift a responsibility to someone else — **pass the hat :** to take up a collection of money

²pass *n* **1 :** an opening or way for passing along or through **2 :** a gap in a mountain range

³pass *n* **1 :** the act or an instance of passing **:** PASSAGE **2 :** ACCOMPLISHMENT **3 :** a state of affairs **:** CONDITION **4 a :** a written permission to move about freely in a particular place or to leave or enter it **b :** a written leave of absence from a military post or station for a brief period **c :** a ticket allowing one free transportation or free admission **5 :** a thrust or lunge in fencing **6 a :** a transference of objects by sleight of hand **b :** a moving of the hands over or along something **7 :** a transfer of a ball or a puck from one player to another on the same team; *esp* **:** FORWARD PASS **8 :** BASE ON BALLS **9 :** a refusal to bid, bet, or draw an additional card in a card game **10 :** EFFORT, TRY; *esp* **:** an amorous approach

pass·a·ble \'pas-ə-bəl\ *adj* **1 :** capable of being passed, crossed, or traveled on ⟨*passable* roads⟩ **2 :** barely good enough **:** TOLERABLE ⟨a *passable* imitation⟩ — **pass·a·bly** \-blē\ *adv*

pas·sage \'pas-ij\ *n* **1 :** the action or process of passing from one place or condition to another **2 a :** a road, path, channel, or course by which something can pass **b :** a corridor or lobby giving access to the different rooms or parts of a building or apartment **3 a :** VOYAGE, JOURNEY **b :** a privilege of conveyance as a passenger **4 :** the passing of a legislative measure or law **:** ENACTMENT **5 a :** INCIDENT **b :** a mutual transaction or exchange ⟨a *passage* at arms⟩⟨a *passage* of wit⟩ **6 a :** a usu. brief portion of a written work or speech that is relevant to a point under discussion or noteworthy for content or style **b :** a phrase or short section of a musical composition

pas·sage·way \-,wā\ *n* **:** a road or way by which a person or thing may pass **:** PASSAGE ⟨a dark *passageway* between two cellar rooms⟩ ⟨a *passageway* between buildings⟩

pass·book \'pas-,bùk\ *n* **:** BANKBOOK

pas·sé \pa-'sā\ *adj* [F, fr. pp. of *passer* to pass] **:** behind the times **:** OUTMODED

passed ball *n* **:** a pitched ball that passes the catcher when he should have stopped it and that allows a base runner to advance

pas·sen·ger \'pas-ᵊn-jər\ *n* [MF *passager*, fr. *passage*] **1 :** PASSERBY, WAYFARER **2 :** a traveler in a public or private conveyance

passenger pigeon *n* **:** an extinct but formerly abundant No. American migratory pigeon

passe–par·tout \,pas-pər-'tü\ *n* [F, fr. *passe partout* pass everywhere] **1 :** something that passes or enables one to pass everywhere **:** MASTER KEY **2 :** a strong paper gummed on one side and used esp. for mounting pictures

pass·er·by \,pas-ər-'bī\ *n, pl* **pass·ers·by** \-ərz-\ **:** one who passes by

pas·ser·ine \'pas-ə-,rīn\ *adj* [L *passer* sparrow] **1 :** of or relating to the largest order (Passeriformes) of birds including more than half of all living birds and consisting chiefly of songbirds of perching habits **2 :** of or relating to the group (Passeres) comprising true songbirds with specialized vocal apparatus — **passerine** *n*

ə *abut;* ᵊ *kitten;* ər *further;* a *back;* ā *bake;* ä *cot, cart;* aù *out;* ch *chin;* e *less;* ē *easy;* g *gift;* i *trip;* ī *life*

pas seul \pä-'sə(r)l\ *n* [F, lit., solo step] **:** a solo dance or dance figure

pas·sim \'pas-əm\ *adv* [L, fr. *passus* scattered, fr. pp. of *pandere* to spread] **:** here and there **:** THROUGHOUT — used to indicate that something (as a phrase) is to be found at many places in the same book or work

¹**pass·ing** *n* **:** the act of one that passes or causes to pass; *esp* **:** DEATH — **in passing :** by the way **:** PARENTHETICALLY

²**passing** *adj* **1 :** going by or past ⟨the *passing* crowd⟩ **2 :** having a brief duration ⟨a *passing* interest⟩ **3 :** marked by haste or inattention **:** SUPERFICIAL ⟨a *passing* glance⟩ **4 :** given on satisfactory completion of an examination or course of study ⟨a *passing* grade⟩

³**passing** *adv* **:** to a surpassing degree **:** EXCEEDINGLY ⟨*passing* fair⟩

pas·sion \'pash-ən\ *n* [L *pass-, pati* to suffer] **1** *often cap* **:** the sufferings of Christ between the night of the Last Supper and his death **2 a** *pl* **:** the emotions as distinguished from reason **b :** violent, intense, or overmastering feeling **3 a :** ardent affection **:** LOVE **b :** a strong liking for some activity, object, or concept **c :** sexual desire **d :** an object of desire or deep interest ⟨bowling is his *passion* at the present time⟩ — **pas·sion·al** \-ᵊl\ *adj* — **pas·sion·less** \-ləs\ *adj*

syn PASSION, FERVOR, ARDOR mean intense emotion compelling action. PASSION implies an emotion that is deeply stirring or ungovernable ⟨stalked out of the room in a towering *passion*⟩ FERVOR implies a strong, steadily glowing emotion ⟨sang their hymns with deep *fervor*⟩ ARDOR suggests a warm excited feeling likely to be fitful or short-lived ⟨dampened their *ardor* for reform⟩

pas·sion·ate \'pash-(ə-)nət\ *adj* **1 a :** easily aroused to anger **b :** filled with anger **:** ANGRY **2 :** capable of, affected by, or expressing intense feeling **3 :** strongly affected with sexual desire **syn** see IMPASSIONED — **pas·sion·ate·ly** *adv* — **pas·sion·ate·ness** *n*

pas·sion·flow·er \'pash-ən-ˌflaü(-ə)r\ *n* [fr. the fancied resemblance of parts of the flower to the cross, nails, and crown of thorns used in Christ's crucifixion] **:** any of a genus of chiefly tropical climbing vines or erect herbs having showy symmetrical flowers and pulpy often edible fruits

passionflower

Pas·sion·ist \'pash-(ə-)nəst\ *n* **:** a priest of a Roman Catholic mendicant order founded in Italy in 1720 and devoted chiefly to missionary work and retreats

passion play *n, often cap 1st P* **:** a play representing scenes connected with Christ's suffering and crucifixion

Passion Sunday *n* **:** the 5th Sunday in Lent

Pas·sion·tide \'pash-ən-ˌtīd\ *n* **:** the last two weeks of Lent

Passion Week *n* **1 :** HOLY WEEK **2 :** the 2d week before Easter

¹**pas·sive** \'pas-iv\ *adj* [L *pass-, pati* to be acted upon, suffer] **1 a :** not active but acted upon **:** receptive to or affected by outside force, agency, or influence ⟨*passive* spectators⟩ ⟨play a *passive* role⟩ **b :** of, relating to, or constituting a verb form or voice indicating that the person or thing represented by the grammatical subject is subjected to or affected by the action represented by the verb ⟨*was hit* in "he was hit by the ball" is *passive*⟩ **2 :** receiving or enduring without resistance **:** SUBMISSIVE ⟨*passive* surrender to fate⟩ — **pas·sive·ly** *adv* — **pas·sive·ness** *n* — **pas·siv·i·ty** \pa-'siv-ət-ē\ *n*

²**passive** *n* **:** the passive voice; *also* **:** a verb form in the passive voice

passive immunity *n* **:** immunity acquired by transfer (as by injection of serum from an individual with active immunity) of antibodies

passive resistance *n* **:** resistance esp. to a government or an occupying power characterized mainly by failure to cooperate rather than by violence or active measures of opposition

pass·key \'pas-ˌkē\ *n* **1 :** a key for opening two or more locks **2 :** SKELETON KEY

pass off *vt* **1 :** to make public or offer for sale with intent to deceive **2 :** to give a false identity or character to

pass out *vi* **1 :** to lose consciousness **2 :** DIE

Pass·over \'pas-ˌō-vər\ *n* [fr. the Lord's passing over the houses of the Israelites when he smote the firstborn in Egypt] **:** a Jewish holiday celebrated in March or April in commemoration of the liberation of the Hebrews from slavery in Egypt

pass·port \'pas-ˌpōrt, -ˌpȯrt\ *n* **1 a :** an official document issued to a citizen about to travel abroad that requests protection for him in foreign countries and is usu. necessary for exit from and reentry into his own country **b :** a similar document required by law to be carried by persons residing or traveling within a country **2 :** something that secures admission or acceptance ⟨his musical talent was his *passport* in that society⟩

pass up *vt* **:** DECLINE, REJECT

pass·word \'pas-ˌwərd\ *n* **1 :** a word or phrase that must be spoken by a person before he is allowed to pass a guard **2 :** WATCHWORD 1

¹**past** \'past\ *adj* [ME, fr. pp. of *passen* to pass] **1 a :** AGO ⟨10 years *past*⟩ **b :** just gone by or elapsed ⟨for the *past* few months⟩ **2 :** having existed or taken place in a period before the present **:** BYGONE **3 :** of, relating to, or constituting a verb tense that in English is usu. formed by internal vowel change (as in *sang*) or by the addition of a suffix (as in *laughed*) and that expresses elapsed time **4 :** having served as a specified officer in an organization ⟨*past* president⟩

²**past** *prep* **1 a :** beyond the age for or of **b :** AFTER ⟨half *past* two⟩ **2 a :** at the farther side of **:** BEYOND **b :** in a course or direction going close to and then beyond ⟨the road goes *past* the house⟩ **3 :** beyond the range, scope, or sphere of ⟨*past* belief⟩

³**past** *n* **1 a :** time gone by **b :** something that happened or was done in the past **2 a :** PAST TENSE **b :** a verb form in the past tense **3 :** a past life, history, or course of action; *esp* **:** a past life that is secret or questionable

⁴**past** *adv* **:** so as to reach and go beyond a point near at hand

pas·ta \'päs-tə\ *n* [It, fr. LL, paste, dough] **1 :** a paste in processed form (as spaghetti) or in the form of fresh dough (as ravioli) **2 :** a dish of cooked pasta

¹**paste** \'pāst\ *n* [LL *pasta* dough, paste] **1 a :** a dough rich in fat that is used for pastry crust or fancy rolls **b :** a confection made by evaporating fruit with sugar or by flavoring a gelatin, starch, or gum arabic preparation ⟨almond *paste*⟩ **c :** a smooth food product made by evaporation or grinding **d :** a shaped dough (as spaghetti or ravioli) prepared from semolina, farina, or wheat flour **2 :** a preparation of flour and water or starch and water used for sticking things together **3 :** a soft doughy mixture (as of wet clay) used in making china **4 :** a very brilliant glass used for the manufacture of artificial gems

²**paste** *vt* **1 :** to cause to adhere by paste **:** STICK **2 :** to cover with or as if with something pasted on ⟨*paste* a wall with advertising⟩

³**paste** *vt* [alter. of *baste*] **:** to hit hard

paste·board \'pās(t)-ˌbōrd, -ˌbȯrd\ *n* **1 :** a stiff material made of sheets of paper pasted together **2 :** cardboard of medium thickness

¹**pas·tel** \pa-'stel\ *n* [F] **1 :** a paste made of ground color and used for making crayons; *also* **:** a crayon made of such paste **2 :** a drawing in pastel **3 :** any of various pale or light colors

²**pastel** *adj* **1 a :** of or relating to a pastel **b :** made with pastels **2 :** pale and light in color

pas·tern \'pas-tərn\ *n* [MF *pasturon*, fr. *pasture* pasture, tether attached to the foot of a horse at pasture] **:** the part of the foot of a horse between the fetlock and the joint at the hoof; *also* **:** the corresponding part of some other quadrupeds — see FETLOCK illustration

pas·teur·i·za·tion \ˌpas-chə-rə-'zā-shən, ˌpas-tə-\ *n* **:** partial sterilization of a substance and esp. a fluid (as milk) at a temperature and period of exposure that destroys objectionable organisms without major chemical alteration of the substance

pas·teur·ize \'pas-chə-ˌrīz, 'pas-tə-\ *vt* [Louis *Pasteur* *d*1895 French chemist] **:** to subject to pasteurization — **pas·teur·iz·er** *n*

Pas·teur treatment \pa-'stər-\ *n* [after Louis *Pasteur*

---

j joke;   **ŋ** sing;   **ō** flow;   **ȯ** flaw;   **ȯi** coin;   **th** thin;   **th̲** this;   **ü** loot;   **u̇** foot;   **y** yet;   **yü** few;   **yu̇** furious;   **zh** vision

: a method of aborting rabies by stimulating production of antibodies through successive inoculations with attenuated virus of gradually increasing strength

pas·tiche \pa-'stēsh\ *n* [F, fr. It *pasticcio*, lit., pasty] : a composition (as in literature or music) made up of selections from different works : POTPOURRI

pas·tille \pa-'stēl\ *also* **pas·til** \'pas-t°l\ *n* [F *pastille*, fr. L *pastillus* small loaf, lozenge] 1 : a small mass of aromatic paste for fumigating or scenting the air of a room 2 : an aromatic or medicated lozenge : TROCHE

pas·time \'pas-,tīm\ *n* : something that serves to make time pass agreeably : DIVERSION

past·i·ness \'pā-stē-nəs\ *n* : the quality or state of being pasty

past master *n* 1 : one who has held the office of master (as in a lodge of Freemasons) 2 : one who is expert : ADEPT — **past mistress** *n*

pas·tor \'pas-tər\ *n* [L, herdsman, shepherd, fr. *past-*, *pascere* to feed] : a minister or priest in charge of a church or parish — **pas·tor·ship** \-,ship\ *n*

¹pas·to·ral \'pas-t(ə-)rəl\ *adj* 1 a : of or relating to shepherds or rural life b : devoted to or based on livestock raising c : RURAL d : portraying the life of shepherds or country people esp. in an idealized and conventionalized manner (*pastoral* poetry) 2 : of or relating to spiritual care or to the pastor of a church — **pas·to·ral·ly** \-t(ə-)rə-lē\ *adv* — **pas·to·ral·ness** *n*

²pas·to·ral \'pas-t(ə-)rəl, *2d is often* ,pas-tə-'räl, -'ral\ *n* 1 : a letter of a spiritual overseer; *esp* : one addressed by a bishop to his diocese 2 a : a literary work dealing with shepherds or rural life in a usu. artificial manner b : pastoral poetry or drama c : a rural picture or scene d : PASTORALE

pas·to·rale \,pas-tə-'räl, -'ral\ *n* [It, fr. *pastorale* pastoral] : an instrumental or vocal composition having a pastoral theme

pas·tor·ate \'pas-t(ə-)rət\ *n* 1 : the office, duties, or term of service of a pastor 2 : a body of pastors (as of a denomination or a region)

past participle *n* : a participle that expresses completed action, that is traditionally one of the principal parts of the verb, and that is used in English in the formation of perfect tenses in the active voice and of all tenses in the passive voice

past perfect *adj* : of, relating to, or constituting a verb tense formed in English with *had* and expressing an action or state completed at or before a past time spoken of — **past perfect** *n*

pas·tra·mi \pə-'sträm-ē\ *n* [Yiddish, fr. Romanian *pastramă*] : a highly seasoned smoked beef prepared esp. from shoulder cuts

pas·try \'pā-strē\ *n, pl* **pastries** [¹*paste*] 1 : sweet baked goods (as cakes, puffs, or tarts) made of dough or having a crust made of enriched dough 2 : a piece of pastry

past tense *n* : a verb tense expressing action or state in the past

pas·tur·age \'pas-chə-rij\ *n* : PASTURE

¹pas·ture \'pas-chər\ *n* [L *past-*, *pascere* to feed] 1 : plants (as grass) for the feeding esp. of grazing animals 2 : land or a plot of land used for grazing

²pasture *vb* 1 : GRAZE 2 : to feed (as cattle) on pasture 3 : to use as pasture — **pas·tur·er** *n*

¹pas·ty \'pas-tē\ *n, pl* **pasties** [MF *pasté*, fr. *paste* dough, paste] ; ²PIE 1; *esp* : a meat pie

²pasty \'pā-stē\ *adj* **past·i·er; -est** : resembling paste; *esp* : pallid and unhealthy in appearance

PA system \pē-'ā-\ *n* : PUBLIC-ADDRESS SYSTEM

¹pat \'pat\ *n* [ME *patte*] 1 : a light blow esp. with the hand or a flat instrument 2 : a light tapping often rhythmical sound 3 : something (as butter) shaped into a small flat usu. square individual portion

²pat *vb* **pat·ted; pat·ting** 1 : to strike lightly with a flat instrument : strike or beat gently 2 : to flatten, smooth, or put into place or shape with light blows (as of the hand) 3 : to stroke or tap gently with the hand to soothe, caress, or show approval 4 : to walk or run with a light beating sound

³pat *adv* : in a pat manner : APTLY, PROMPTLY

⁴pat *adj* **pat·ter; pat·test** 1 a : exactly suited to the purpose or occasion : APT, OPPORTUNE (a *pat* answer) b : too exactly suitable : CONTRIVED 2 : learned, mastered, or

memorized exactly (have a lesson down *pat*) 3 : FIRM, UNYIELDING (stand *pat*)

¹patch \'pach\ *n* [ME *pacche*] 1 : a piece of material used to mend or cover a hole, a torn place, or a weak spot 2 : a small piece (as of cloth) worn on the face to cover a defect or to attract attention 3 : a small piece : SCRAP 4 a : a small area or plot distinguished from its surroundings (a *patch* of oats) (a *patch* of blistered skin) b : a spot of color : BLOTCH (a *patch* of white on a dog's head) 5 : a piece of cloth sewed on a garment as an ornament or insignia; *esp* : SHOULDER PATCH

²patch *vt* 1 : to mend, cover, or fill up a hole or weak spot in 2 : to provide with a patch 3 a : to make of patches or fragments c : to mend or put together esp. hastily or clumsily c : SETTLE, ADJUST — usu. used with *up* (*patched* up their differences)

pa·tchou·li *or* **pa·tchou·ly** \'pach-ə-lē, pə-'chü-lē\ *n, pl* **-lis** *or* **-lies** [Tamil *pacculi*] 1 : an East Indian shrubby mint that yields a fragrant essential oil 2 : a heavy perfume made from patchouli

patch pocket *n* : a flat pocket applied to the outside of a garment

patch test *n* : a test for determining allergic sensitivity made by applying to the unbroken skin small pads soaked with the allergen in question

patch·work \'pach-,wərk\ *n* 1 : something composed of miscellaneous or incongruous parts : HODGEPODGE 2 : pieces of cloth of various colors and shapes sewed together usu. in a pattern (a covering of *patchwork*) — **patch·work** *adj*

patchy \'pach-ē\ *adj* **patch·i·er; -est** : consisting of or marked by patches : resembling patchwork : SPOTTY

¹pate \'pāt\ *n* [ME] : HEAD; *esp* : the crown of the head — **pat·ed** \'pāt-əd\ *adj*

²pâ·té \pä-'tā\ *n* [F, fr. OF *pasté*, fr. *paste* dough, paste] 1 : a meat or fish pie or patty 2 : a spread of finely mashed seasoned and spiced meat

pâ·té de foie gras \pä-,tād-ə-,fwä-'grä\ *n, pl* **pâtés de foie gras** \-,tā(z)d-ə-\ [F] : a paste of fat goose liver and truffles

pa·tel·la \pə-'tel-ə\ *n, pl* **-tel·lae** \-'tel-(,)ē, -,ī\ *or* **-tellas** [L, fr. dim. of *patina* shallow dish] : a thick flat triangular movable bone that forms the anterior point of the knee and protects the front of the joint — called also *kneecap* — **pa·tel·lar** \-'tel-ər\ *adj*

pat·en \'pat-°n\ *n* [OF *patene*, fr. L *patina* shallow dish, fr. Gk *patanē*] 1 : a plate of precious metal for the eucharistic bread 2 : PLATE 3 : a thin disk (as of metal)

¹pat·ent \5, 6 *are* 'pat-°nt, 'pāt-; *1-4 are* 'pat-, *Brit also* 'pāt-\ *adj* [L *patēre* to lie open; akin to E *fathom*] 1 : open to public inspection — used chiefly in the phrase *letters patent* 2 : PATENTED 3 : of, relating to, or concerned with the granting of patents esp. for inventions (a *patent* lawyer) 4 : marketed as a proprietary commodity (a *patent* can opener) 5 : OPEN, UNOBSTRUCTED 6 : EVIDENT, OBVIOUS (a *patent* lie) — **pat·en·cy** \-°n-sē\ *n* — **pat·ent·ly** *adv*

²pat·ent \'pat-°nt, *Brit also* 'pāt-\ *n* 1 : an official document conferring a right or privilege 2 a : a writing securing to an inventor for a term of years the exclusive right to make, use, or sell his invention b : the right so granted 3 : PRIVILEGE, LICENSE

³pat·ent *vt* 1 : to grant a privilege, right, or license to by patent 2 : to obtain or secure by patent; *esp* : to secure by letters patent exclusive right to make, use, or sell 3 : to obtain or grant a patent right to — **pat·ent·a·ble** \-ə-bəl\ *adj*

pat·en·tee \,pat-°n-'tē, *Brit also* ,pāt-\ *n* : one to whom a grant is made or a privilege secured by patent

patent leather \,pat-°n(t)-, *Brit usu* ,pāt-\ *n* : a leather with a hard smooth glossy surface

patent medicine *n* : PROPRIETARY 3

patent office *n* : a government office for examining claims to patents and granting patents

pat·en·tor \'pat-°n-tər, ,pat-°n-'tȯ(ə)r, *Brit also* 'pāt-, ,pāt-\ *n* : one that grants a patent

patent right *n* : a right granted by letters patent; *esp* : the exclusive right to an invention

pa·ter *n* 1 *often cap* \'pä-,te(ə)r\ : PATERNOSTER 2 \'pāt-ər\ [L] *chiefly Brit* : FATHER

pa·ter·fa·mil·i·as \,pāt-ər-fə-'mil-ē-əs\ *n* [L, fr. *pater* father + *familias*, old gen. of *familia* family] **1** : the male head of a household **2** : the father of a family

pa·ter·nal \pə-'tərn-°l\ *adj* [L *paternus*, fr. *pater* father; akin to E *father*] **1** : of or relating to a father : FATHERLY **2** : received or inherited from one's father **3** : related through the father ⟨a *paternal* grandfather⟩ — **pa·ter·nal·ly** \-°l-ē\ *adv*

pa·ter·nal·ism \-°l-,iz-əm\ *n* : the principle or practice of governing or of exercising authority (as over a group of employees) in a manner suggesting the care and control exercised by a father over his children — **pa·ter·nal·ist** \-°l-əst\ *adj or n* — **pa·ter·nal·is·tic** \-,tərn-°l-'is-tik\ *adj*

pa·ter·ni·ty \pə-'tər-nət-ē\ *n* **1** : the quality or state of being a father **2** : origin or descent from a father

pat·er·nos·ter \'pat-ər-,näs-tər\ *n* [L *pater noster* our father] **1** *often cap* : LORD'S PRAYER **2** : a word formula repeated as a prayer or magical charm

path \'path, 'pȧth\ *n, pl* **paths** \'pathz, 'paths, 'pȧthz, 'pȧths\ [OE *pæth*] **1** : a trodden way **2** : a track specially constructed for a particular use (as walking or horseback riding) **3 a** : the way traversed by something : COURSE, ROUTE **b** : a way of life, conduct, or thought ⟨*paths* of glory⟩

path- *or* **patho-** *comb form* [Gk *pathos*, lit., suffering] : pathological state : DISEASE ⟨*pathogen*⟩

-path \,path\ *n comb form* **1** : practitioner of a (specified) system of medicine that emphasizes one aspect of disease or its treatment ⟨osteo*path*⟩ **2** : one suffering from (such) an ailment ⟨psycho*path*⟩

Pa·than \pə-'tän\ *n* : a member of the principal ethnic group of Afghanistan

pa·thet·ic \pə-'thet-ik\ *adj* [Gk *pathētikos* capable of feeling, pathetic, fr. *path-*, *paschein* to experience, suffer] **1** : evoking tenderness, pity, or sorrow : PITIABLE **2** : marked by sorrow or melancholy : SAD ⟨a *pathetic* lament⟩ — **pa·thet·i·cal·ly** \-'thet-i-k(ə-)lē\ *adv*

path·find·er \'path-,fīn-dər, 'pȧth-\ *n* : one that discovers a way; *esp* : one that explores untraveled regions to mark out a new route

path·less \-ləs\ *adj* : UNTROD, TRACKLESS

path·o·gen \'path-ə-jən\ *n* : a specific cause (as a bacterium or virus) of disease — **path·o·gen·e·sis** \,path-ə-'jen-ə-səs\ — **path·o·ge·net·ic** \-jə-'net-ik\ *adj* — **path·o·gen·ic** \-'jen-ik\ *adj* — **path·o·gen·i·cal·ly** \-'jen-i-k(ə-)lē\ *adv* — **path·o·ge·nic·i·ty** \-jə-'nis-ət-ē\ *n*

path·o·log·i·cal \,path-ə-'läj-i-kəl\ *or* **path·o·log·ic** \-ik\ *adj* **1** : of or relating to pathology **2** : altered or caused by disease — **path·o·log·i·cal·ly** \-'läj-i-k(ə-)lē\ *adv*

pa·thol·o·gist \pə-'thäl-ə-jəst, pa-\ *n* : a specialist in pathology and esp. in tissue pathology

pa·thol·o·gy \-jē\ *n* **1** : the study of the essential nature of diseases and esp. of the structural and functional changes produced by them **2** : something abnormal; *esp* : the structural and functional deviations from the normal that constitute disease or characterize a particular disease

pa·thos \'pā-,thäs\ *n* [Gk, suffering, experience, emotion, fr. *path-*, *paschein* to suffer] **1** : an element in experience or in artistic representation evoking pity or compassion **2** : an emotion of sympathetic pity

path·way \'path-,wā, 'pȧth-\ *n* : PATH, COURSE

-pa·thy \p-ə-thē\ *n comb form, pl* **-pathies** **1** : feeling : suffering ⟨em*pathy*⟩ ⟨tele*pathy*⟩ **2** : disease of (such) a part or kind ⟨neuro*pathy*⟩ **3** : system of medicine based on (such) a factor ⟨osteo*pathy*⟩

pa·tience \'pā-shən(t)s\ *n* **1** : the capacity, habit, or fact of being patient **2** *chiefly Brit* : SOLITAIRE 2

¹pa·tient \'pā-shənt\ *adj* [L *pati* to suffer, submit] **1** : bearing pains or trials calmly or without complaint **2** : manifesting forbearance under provocation or strain **3** : not hasty or impetuous **4** : steadfast despite opposition, difficulty, or adversity ⟨took years of *patient* labor to carve his masterpiece⟩ — **pa·tient·ly** *adv*

²patient *n* : an individual awaiting or under medical care and treatment

pat·i·na \'pat-ə-nə, pə-'tē-nə\ *n, pl* **patinas** *or* **pat·i·nae** \'pat-ə-,nē, -,nī\ [NL, fr. L, shallow dish] **1 a** : a usu. green film formed on copper and bronze by long exposure or by chemicals and often valued aesthetically **b** : a surface appearance (as a coloring or mellowing) of something grown beautiful esp. with age or use **2** : PATEN 1

pat·io \'pat-ē-,ō, 'pät-\ *n, pl* **-i·os** [Sp] **1** : COURTYARD;

esp : an inner court open to the sky **2** : an often paved recreation area that adjoins a dwelling

pa·tois \'pa-,twä\ *n, pl* **patois** \-,twäz\ [F] **1 a** : a dialect other than the standard or literary dialect **b** : illiterate or provincial speech **2** : JARGON 2

pa·tri·arch \'pā-trē-,ärk\ *n* [Gk *patriarchēs*, fr. *patria* lineage (fr. *patēr* father) + *-archēs* -arch] **1 a** : one of the Old Testament fathers of the human race or of the Hebrew people **b** : a man who is father or founder **c** (1) : the oldest member or representative of a group (2) : a venerable old man **2 a** : a bishop of the leading ancient sees of Constantinople, Alexandria, Antioch, Jerusalem, and Rome **b** : the head of any of various Eastern churches **c** : a Roman Catholic bishop next in rank to the pope — **pa·tri·ar·chal** \,pā-trē-'är-kəl\ *adj*

pa·tri·arch·ate \'pā-trē-,är-kət\ *n* **1 a** : the office, jurisdiction, or time in office of a patriarch **b** : the residence or headquarters of a patriarch **2** : PATRIARCHY

pa·tri·ar·chy \-,är-kē\ *n, pl* **-chies** **1** : social organization marked by the supremacy of the father in the clan or family and the reckoning of descent and inheritance in the male line **2** : a society organized according to the principles of patriarchy

pa·tri·cian \pə-'trish-ən\ *n* [L *patricius*, fr. *patres* senators, fr. pl. of *pater* father] **1** : a member of one of the original citizen families of ancient Rome **2 a** : a person of high birth : ARISTOCRAT **b** : a person of breeding and cultivation — **patrician** *adj* — **pa·tri·ci·ate** \-'trish-ē-ət\ *n*

pat·ri·cide \'pa-trə-,sīd\ *n* **1** [L *pater* father] : one who murders his own father **2** : the murder of one's own father — **pat·ri·cid·al** \,pa-trə-'sīd-°l\ *adj*

pat·ri·mo·ny \'pa-trə-,mō-nē\ *n, pl* **-nies** [L *patrimonium*, fr. *pater* father] **1 a** : an estate inherited from one's father or ancestors **b** : something derived from one's father or ancestors : HERITAGE **2** : an estate or endowment belonging to an ancient right to a church — **pat·ri·mo·ni·al** \,pa-trə-'mō-nē-əl\ *adj*

pa·tri·ot \'pā-trē-ət\ *n* [Gk *patriōtēs* compatriot, fr. *patrios* of one's father, fr. *patēr* father; akin to E *father*] : a person who loves his country and zealously supports it

pa·tri·ot·ic \,pā-trē-'ät-ik\ *adj* **1** : inspired by patriotism **2** : befitting or characteristic of a patriot — **pa·tri·ot·i·cal·ly** \-'ät-i-k(ə-)lē\ *adv*

pa·tri·ot·ism \'pā-trē-ə-,tiz-əm\ *n* : love of one's own country and devotion to its welfare

Patriots' Day *n* : April 19 observed as a legal holiday in Maine and Massachusetts in commemoration of the battles of Lexington and Concord in 1775

pa·tris·tic \pə-'tris-tik\ *adj* [Gk *patēr* father] : of or relating to the church fathers or their writings — **pa·tris·ti·cal** \-ti-kəl\ *adj*

Pa·tro·clus \pə-'trō-kləs, -'träk-ləs\ *n* : a Greek slain in the Trojan War by Hector and avenged by his friend Achilles

¹pa·trol \pə-'trōl\ *n* [F *patrouille*, fr. *patrouiller* to patrol, fr. MF, to tramp around in the mud, fr. *patte* paw] **1 a** : the action of traversing a district or beat or of going the rounds along a chain of guards for the purpose of observation or of the maintenance of security **b** : the person performing such an action **c** : a detachment of men employed for reconnaissance, security, or combat **2 a** : a subdivision of a boy scout troop made up of two or more boys **b** : a subdivision of a girl scout troop usu. composed of from six to eight girls

²patrol *vb* **pa·trolled**; **pa·trol·ling** : to carry out a patrol or a patrol of — **pa·trol·ler** *n*

pa·trol·man \pə-'trōl-mən\ *n* : one who patrols; *esp* : a policeman assigned to a beat

patrol wagon *n* : an enclosed police truck used to carry prisoners

pa·tron \'pā-trən\ *n* [L *patronus*, fr. *pater* father] **1** : a person chosen as a special guardian, protector, or supporter ⟨a *patron* of poets⟩ **2** : one who gives of his means or uses his influence to help an individual, an institution, or a cause ⟨a *patron* of the arts⟩ **3** : a regular client or customer — **pa·tron·ess** \-trə-nəs\ *n*

pat·ron·age \'pa-trə-nij, 'pā-\ *n* **1** : the support or influence of a patron **2** : the trade of customers **3 a** : the power to distribute government jobs on a basis other than

---

j joke; **ŋ** sing; **ō** flow; **ȯ** flaw; **ȯi** coin; **th** thin; **th̲** this; **ü** loot; **u̇** foot; **y** yet; **yü** few; **yu̇** furious; **zh** vision

merit alone **b : the distribution of jobs on this basis
c :** the jobs so distributed

pa·tron·ize \'pā-trə-ˌnīz, 'pa-\ *vt* **1 :** to act as a patron
to or of **: FAVOR, SUPPORT** ⟨*patronize* the arts⟩ **2 :** to treat
with a superior air **:** be condescending toward **3 :** to do
business with ⟨*patronize* a neighborhood store⟩ — **pa·tron·iz·ing·ly** \-ˌnī-ziŋ-lē\ *adv*

patron saint *n* **:** a saint to whose protection and intercession a person, a society, a church, ɒr a place is dedicated

pat·ro·nym·ic \ˌpa-trə-'nim-ik\ *n* [Gk *patēr* father +
onyma name] **:** a name derived from that of the father or a
paternal ancestor usu. by the addition of a prefix or suffix
(as in *MacDonald*, son of Donald, or *Johnson*, son of
John) — **patronymic** *adj*

pa·troon \pə-'trün\ *n* [D, lit., boss, superior, fr. F *patron*,
fr. L *patronus* patron] **:** the proprietor of a manorial
estate esp. in New York or New Jersey granted by the
Dutch

pat·sy \'pat-sē\ *n, pl* **patsies :** one who is duped or
victimized **: SUCKER**

pat·ten \'pat-ᵊn\ *n* [MF *patin*, fr. *patte* paw, hoof] **:** a
clog, sandal, or overshoe often with a wooden sole or
metal device to elevate the foot and increase the wearer's
height or aid in walking in mud

¹pat·ter \'pat-ər\ *vb* [ME *patren*, fr. *paternoster*] **1 a :** to
say or speak in a rapid or mechanical manner **b :** to talk
glibly and volubly **2 :** to recite prayers (as paternosters)
rapidly or mechanically — **pat·ter·er** *n*

²patter *n* **1 :** a specialized lingo **: CANT**; *esp* **:** the jargon
of criminals (as thieves) **2 :** the spiel of a street hawker
or of a circus barker **3 :** empty chattering talk **4 a** (1)
: the rapid-fire talk of a comedian (2) **:** the talk with
which any of various entertainers accompanies his routine
b : the words of a comic song or of a rapidly spoken usu.
humorous monologue introduced into such a song

³patter *vb* **1 :** to strike or pat rapidly and repeatedly ⟨rain
pattering on a roof⟩ **2 :** to run with quick light-sounding
steps

⁴patter *n* **:** a quick succession of light sounds or pats
⟨the *patter* of little feet⟩

¹pat·tern \'pat-ərn\ *n* [ME *patron*, fr. MF, fr. ML *patronus* patron saint, pattern, fr. L, patron] **1 :** a form or
model proposed for imitation **: EXEMPLAR** **2 :** something
designed or used as a model for making things ⟨a dressmaker's *pattern*⟩ **3 :** a model for making a mold into
which molten metal is poured to form a casting **4 : SPECI-
MEN, SAMPLE 5 a :** an artistic or mechanical design ⟨chintz
with a small *pattern*⟩ **b :** form or style in literary or musical composition **6 :** a natural or chance configuration
⟨frost *patterns*⟩ **7 :** a length of fabric sufficient for an
article **8 :** a reliable sample of observable features (as
traits or acts) characterizing an individual or group
⟨behavior *patterns*⟩ ⟨the *pattern* of American industry⟩

²pattern *vt* **:** to make or fashion according to a pattern
⟨he *patterned* himself after his hero⟩

pat·ty *also* **pat·tie** \'pat-ē\ *n, pl* **patties** [F *pâté*] **1 :** a
little pie **2 a :** a small flat cake of chopped food ⟨a fish
patty⟩ **b :** a small flat candy ⟨mint *patties*⟩

pat·u·lous \'pach-ə-ləs\ *adj* **:** spreading widely from a
center ⟨a tree with *patulous* branches⟩ — **pat·u·lous·ly**
adv — **pat·u·lous·ness** *n*

pau·ci·ty \'pó-sət-ē\ *n* [L *paucus* little; akin to E *few*]
1 : smallness of number **: FEWNESS** ⟨a *paucity* of tenor
voices⟩ **2 :** smallness of quantity **: DEARTH** ⟨a *paucity* of
experience⟩

Paul \'pól\ *n* **:** an early Christian missionary and author
of several New Testament epistles — **Paul·ine** \'pó-ˌlīn\
adj

Paul Bun·yan \'pól-'bən-yən\ *n* **:** a lumberjack in American folklore noted for his ability to perform superhuman
feats

Paul·ist \'pó-ləst\ *n* **:** a member of the Roman Catholic
Congregation of the Missionary Priests of St. Paul the
Apostle founded in the U.S. in 1858

pau·low·nia \pó-'lō-nē-ə\ *n* [NL, fr. Anna *Paulovna*
*d*1865 Russian princess] **:** a Chinese tree widely grown in
warm regions for its showy clusters of fragrant violet
flowers

paunch \'pónch, 'pänch\ *n* [MF *panche*, fr. L *pantic-,
pantex*] **1 a :** the belly together with its contents **b
: POTBELLY 2 : RUMEN**

paunchy \'pón-chē\ *adj* **:** having a potbelly — **paunch·i-
ness** *n*

pau·per \'pó-pər\ *n* [L, poor; akin to E *few*] **:** a very poor
person; *esp* **:** one supported by charity — **pau·per·ism**
\-pə-ˌriz-əm\ *n* — **pau·per·ize** \-ˌrīz\ *vt*

¹pause \'póz\ *n* [L *pausa*, fr. Gk *pausis*, fr. *pauein* to stop]
1 : a temporary stop **2 a :** a break in a verse **b :** a brief
suspension of the voice to indicate the limits and relations
of sentences and their parts **3 :** temporary inaction often
because of doubt or uncertainty **4 a :** the sign ⌢ or ⌣
placed over or under a musical note, chord, or rest to
indicate that it is to be prolonged **b :** a mark (as a period
or comma) used in writing or printing to indicate or correspond to a pause of voice **5 :** a reason or cause for
pausing ⟨a thought that should give *pause*⟩

²pause *vi* **1 :** to stop temporarily **: HESITATE 2 :** to linger
for a time ⟨*pause* on a high note⟩

pa·vane \pə-'vän, -'van\ *also* **pa·van** \-'vän, -'van\ *or*
pav·in \'pav-ən\ *n* [MF *pavane*, fr. Sp *pavana*, fr. It]
1 : a stately court dance by couples that was introduced
from southern Europe into England in the 16th century
2 : music for the pavane

pave \'pāv\ *vt* [MF *paver*, fr. L *pavire* to strike, stamp]
1 : to lay or cover with material (as stone or concrete)
that makes a firm level surface for travel **2 :** to cover
firmly and solidly as if with paving material — **pave the
way :** to prepare a smooth easy way **:** facilitate the development ⟨*pave the way* for those who come after⟩

pave·ment \'pāv-mənt\ *n* **1 :** a paved surface (as of a
street) **2 :** the material with which something is paved

pa·vil·ion \pə-'vil-yən\ *n* [OF *paveillon*, fr. L *papilion-,
papilio* butterfly] **1 :** a usu. large tent with a peaked or
rounded top **2 :** a lightly constructed ornamented building serving as a shelter in a park, garden, or athletic field
3 : a part of a building projecting from the main body of
the structure **4 :** a building either partly or completely
detached from the main building or main group of buildings

pav·ing \'pā-viŋ\ *n* **: PAVEMENT**

¹paw \'pó\ *n* [MF *poue*] **1 :** the foot of a quadruped (as
a lion or dog) having claws; *also* **:** the foot of an animal
2 : a human hand esp. when large or clumsy

²paw *vb* **1 :** to feel or touch clumsily, amorously, or
rudely ⟨merchandise *pawed* by customers⟩ **2 :** to touch or
strike with a paw **3 :** to scrape or beat upon with a hoof
4 : to flail at or grab for wildly ⟨hands *pawing* the air⟩

pawl \'pól\ *n* **:** a pivoted tongue or sliding bolt on one
part of a machine that is adapted to fall into notches on
another part (as a ratchet wheel) so as to permit motion
in only one direction

¹pawn \'pón, 'pän\ *n* [MF *pan*] **1 :** something deposited
with another as security for a loan **: PLEDGE 2 :** the state
of being pledged ⟨the watch was in *pawn*⟩

²pawn *vt* **:** to deposit in pledge or as security **: STAKE** —
pawn·er *n*

³pawn *n* [MF *peon*, fr. ML *pedon-, pedo* foot soldier, fr.
L *ped-, pes* foot] **1 :** one of the chessmen of least value
that can move only one square forward at a time or at
option two on its first move and can capture an enemy
only on either of the two squares diagonally forward
2 : one used to further the purposes of another

pawn·bro·ker \'pón-ˌbrō-kər, 'pän-\ *n* **:** one who loans
money on the security of personal property pledged in his
keeping — **pawn·bro·king** \-kiŋ\ *n*

Paw·nee \pó-'nē, pä-\ *n* **:** a member of an Indian people
of Nebraska and Kansas

pawn·shop \'pón-ˌshäp, 'pän-\ *n* **:** a pawnbroker's shop

paw-paw *var of* **PAPAW**

¹pay \'pā\ *vb* **paid** \'pād\ *also in sense 7* **payed; paid;
pay·ing** [OF *paier*, fr. L *pacare* to pacify, fr. *pac-, pax*
peace] **1 :** to give money esp. in return for services received or for something bought ⟨*pay* the taxi driver⟩ ⟨*pay*
for a ticket⟩ **2 :** to discharge a debt ⟨*pay* a tax⟩ **3 :** to get
even with ⟨*pay* someone back for an injury⟩ **4 :** to give
or offer freely ⟨*pay* a compliment⟩ ⟨*pay* attention⟩ **5 :** to
return value or profit ⟨an investment *paying* 5 percent⟩
6 : to make or secure suitable return for expense or
trouble **:** be worth the effort or pains required ⟨it *pays* to
drive carefully⟩ **7 :** to make slack (as a rope) and allow
to run out — usu. used with *out*

syn PAY, COMPENSATE, REMUNERATE mean to give money

or its equivalent in return for something. PAY implies the discharge of an obligation incurred ⟨*pay* the man's wages⟩ COMPENSATE implies making up for services rendered or help given or loss suffered ⟨gave $10 more to *compensate* her for her trouble⟩ REMUNERATE suggests paying for services rendered often more generously than contracted for

²pay *n* **1 a :** the act or fact of paying or being paid **:** PAYMENT **b :** the status of being paid by an employer **:** EMPLOY **2 :** something paid; *esp* **:** WAGES, SALARY

³pay *adj* **1 :** containing or leading to something precious or valuable (as gold or oil) ⟨*pay* rock⟩ **2 :** equipped with a coin slot for receiving a fee for use ⟨*pay* phone⟩ **3 :** requiring payment ⟨*pay* TV⟩

pay·a·ble \'pā-ə-bəl\ *adj* **:** that may, can, or must be paid; *esp* **:** DUE ⟨accounts *payable*⟩

pay·check \'pā-,chek\ *n* **1 :** a check in payment of wages or salary **2 :** WAGES, SALARY

pay dirt *n* **1 :** earth or ore that yields a profit to a miner **2 :** a useful or remunerative discovery or object ⟨really hit *pay dirt* with his invention⟩

pay·ee \pā-'ē\ *n* **:** one to whom money is or is to be paid

pay·er \'pā-ər\ *also* **pay·or** \'pā-ər, pā-'ò(ə)r\ *n* **:** one that pays; *esp* **:** the maker of a bill or note

pay·load \'pā-,lōd\ *n* **:** something (as cargo, passengers, instruments, or explosives) carried by a vehicle, missile, or rocket in addition to what is necessary for its operation

pay·mas·ter \-,mas-tər\ *n* **:** an officer or agent of an employer whose duty it is to pay salaries or wages

pay·ment \'pā-mənt\ *n* **1 :** the act of paying **2 :** money given to discharge a debt ⟨monthly *payments* on a car⟩ **3 :** PAY ⟨*payment* for a day's work⟩

pay·nim \'pā-nəm\ *n* [OF *paienime* paganism, territory of the pagans, fr. LL *paganismus*] *archaic* **:** PAGAN, INFIDEL; *esp* **:** MUSLIM

pay off \(')pā-'òf\ *vt* **1 :** to pay in full often through small payments made at intervals ⟨*pay off* a mortgage⟩ **2 :** to take revenge on ⟨*pay off* an enemy⟩

pay·off \'pā-,òf\ *n* **1 :** payment at the outcome of an enterprise ⟨a big *payoff* from an investment⟩ **2 :** the climax of an incident or enterprise ⟨the *payoff* of a story⟩

pay·roll \'pā-,rōl\ *n* **:** a list of persons entitled to receive pay with the amounts due to each; *also* **:** the amount of money necessary to pay those on such a list

pay station *n* **:** a pay telephone or a booth containing a pay telephone

pay up *vb* **:** to pay in full esp. debts that are overdue

PCB \,pē-,sē-'bē\ *n* **:** POLYCHLORINATED BIPHENYL

PDQ \,pē-,dē-'kyü\ *adv, often not cap* [abbr. of *pretty damned quick*] **:** IMMEDIATELY

pea \'pē\ *n, pl* **peas** *also* **pease** \'pēz\ [back-formation fr. ME *pease*, taken as a pl., fr. OE *pise*, fr. LL *pisa*, fr. L *pisum*, fr. Gk *pison*] **1 a :** a variable annual leguminous vine grown for its rounded smooth or wrinkled edible protein-rich seeds **b :** the seed of the pea **c** *pl* **:** the immature pods of the pea with their included seeds **2 :** any of various leguminous plants related to or resembling the pea

peace \'pēs\ *n* [OF *pais*, fr. L *pac-, pax*] **1 :** a state of tranquillity or quiet: as **a :** freedom from civil disturbance or foreign war **b :** a state of security or order within a community protected by law or custom ⟨breach of the *peace*⟩ **2 :** freedom from disquieting or oppressive thoughts or emotions **3 :** harmony in personal relations **4 a :** a state or period of concord between governments **b :** a pact or agreement between combatants to end hostilities

peace·a·ble \'pē-sə-bəl\ *adj* **1 :** inclined toward peace **:** not quarrelsome **2 :** PEACEFUL; *esp* **:** not disturbing the public peace — **peace·a·bly** \-blē\ *adv*

peace corps *n* **:** a body of trained personnel sent out as volunteers to assist underdeveloped nations

peace·ful \'pēs-fəl\ *adj* **1 :** PEACEABLE 1 ⟨a *peaceful* man⟩ **2 :** untroubled by conflict, agitation, or commotion **:** QUIET, TRANQUIL ⟨a *peaceful* countryside⟩ **3 :** devoid of violence or force ⟨settled the conflict by *peaceful* means⟩ — **peace·ful·ly** \-fə-lē\ *adv* — **peace·ful·ness** *n*

peace·mak·er \'pēs-,mā-kər\ *n* **:** a person who arranges a peace **:** one who settles an argument or stops a fight — **peace·mak·ing** \-kiŋ\ *n or adj*

peace offering *n* **:** a gift or service to procure peace or reconciliation

peace officer *n* **:** a civil officer (as a policeman, constable, or sheriff) whose duty it is to preserve the public peace

peace pipe *n* **:** CALUMET

peace sign *n* **:** a sign made by holding the palm outward and forming a V with the index and middle fingers and used to indicate the desire for peace

peace·time \'pēs-,tīm\ *n* **:** a time when a nation is not at war

¹peach \'pēch\ *n* [MF *peche* peach fruit, fr. LL *persica*, fr. L *persicum*, fr. neut. of *persicus* Persian, fr. *Persia*] **1 :** a low spreading Chinese tree related to the plums and cherries that is grown in most temperate areas for its sweet juicy fruit with pulpy white or yellow flesh, thin downy skin, and single rough hard stone; *also* **:** its fruit **2 :** a variable color averaging a moderate yellowish pink **3 :** one likened to a peach in sweetness, beauty, or excellence

²peach *vi* [ME *pechen*, short for *apechen* to impeach, fr. (assumed) AF *apecher*, fr. LL *impedicare* to entangle] **:** to turn informer **:** BLAB

peachy \'pē-chē\ *adj* **peach·i·er; -est** **1 :** resembling a peach **2 :** unusually fine **:** DANDY

¹pea·cock \'pē-,käk\ *n* [ME *pecok*, fr. OE *pēa* peafowl (fr. L *pavo* peacock) + *cocc* cock] **1 :** a male peafowl distinguished by a small upright crest and by greatly elongated loosely webbed upper tail coverts mostly tipped with ocellated spots and erected and spread at will in a fan shimmering with iridescent color; *also* **:** PEAFOWL **2 :** one making a proud display of himself

²peacock *vi* **:** to make a vainglorious display **:** STRUT

peacock blue *n* **:** a variable color averaging a moderate greenish blue

pea·fowl \'pē-,faul\ *n* **:** a very large terrestrial pheasant of southeastern Asia and the East Indies that is often kept as an ornamental fowl

pea green *n* **:** a variable color averaging a moderate yellow-green

pea·hen \'pē-,hen, -'hen\ *n* **:** a female peafowl

pea jacket \'pē-\ *n* **:** a heavy woolen double-breasted jacket worn chiefly by sailors

¹peak \'pēk\ *n* **1 :** a pointed or projecting part (as of a garment); *esp* **:** the visor of a cap or hat **2 :** PROMONTORY **3 :** a sharp or pointed ridge or end ⟨the *peak* of a roof⟩ **4 a :** the top of a hill or mountain ending in a point **b :** a whole hill or mountain esp. when isolated **5 :** the narrow part of a ship's bow or stern or the part of the hold in it **6 :** the highest level or greatest degree of development esp. as represented on a graph **7 :** a point formed by the hair on the forehead **syn** see SUMMIT

²peak *vb* **:** to come or cause to come to a peak, point, or maximum

³peak *adj* **:** being at or reaching the maximum

peaked *adj* **1** \'pēkt, 'pē-kəd\ **:** having a peak **:** POINTED **2** \'pē-kəd\ **:** sharp and lean in figure or features **:** THIN, SICKLY — **peaked·ness** \'pēk(t)-nəs, 'pē-kəd-nəs\ *n*

¹peal \'pēl\ *n* [ME, appeal, summons to church, short for *appel* appeal] **1 a :** the loud ringing of bells **b :** a complete set of changes on a given number of bells **c :** a set of bells tuned to the tones of the major scale for change ringing **2 :** a loud sound or succession of sounds ⟨a *peal* of laughter⟩⟨a *peal* of thunder⟩

²peal *vb* **:** to give out peals or in peals ⟨bells *pealing* in the distance⟩⟨an organ *pealing* anthems⟩

pea·like \'pē-,līk\ *adj* **1 :** resembling a garden pea (as in firmness or shape) **2 :** being showy and resembling a butterfly in shape ⟨*pealike* flowers⟩

pea·nut \'pē-(,)nət\ *n* **1 :** a low-branching widely cultivated leguminous annual herb with showy yellow flowers and pods that ripen underground; *also* **:** this pod or one of the oily edible seeds it contains **2 :** an insignificant or tiny person **3** *pl* **:** a trifling amount

peanut butter *n* **:** a paste made by grinding roasted skinned peanuts

pear \'pa(ə)r, 'pe(ə)r\ *n* [OE *peru*, fr. L *pirum*] **:** a fleshy pome fruit that usu. tapers toward the stem end; *also* **:** a tree related to the apple that bears pears

¹pearl \'pərl\ *n* [MF *perle*, fr. (assumed) VL *pernula*, dim. of L *perna* mussel] **1 a :** a dense usu. lustrous body formed of concentric layers of nacre as an abnormal growth within the shell of some mollusks and used as a gem **b :** MOTHER-OF-PEARL **2 :** something resembling a pearl (as in shape, color, or value) **3** : a nearly neutral slightly bluish medium gray

²pearl vb **1** : to set or adorn with pearls **2** : to sprinkle or bead with pearly drops **3** : to form into drops or beads like pearls or into small round grains **4** : to give a pearly color or luster to **5** : to fish or search for pearls

³pearl adj **1 a** : of, relating to, or resembling pearl **b** : made of or adorned with pearls **2** : having grains of medium size ⟨*pearl* barley⟩

pearl·er \'pər-lər\ n **1** : a person who dives for pearls or who employs pearl divers **2** : a boat used in pearl fishing

pearl gray n **1** : a yellowish to light gray **2** : a variable color averaging a pale blue

pearly \'pər-lē\ adj **pearl·i·er; -est** : resembling, containing, or adorned with pearls or mother-of-pearl

peart \'pi(ə)rt\ adj, chiefly South & Midland : in good spirits : LIVELY

peas·ant \'pez-ᵊnt\ n [MF paisant, fr. païs country, fr. L pagensis inhabitant of a district, fr. L pagus country district] **1** : a European small farmer or farm laborer; also : a member of a similar agricultural class elsewhere **2** : an uncouth person or one of low social status

peas·ant·ry \'pez-ᵊn-trē\ n : a body of peasants ⟨a nation's peasantry⟩ ⟨the local peasantry⟩

pease pl of PEA

pease·cod or **peas·cod** \'pēz-ˌkäd\ n : a pea pod

pea·shoot·er \'pē-ˈshüt-ər\ n : a toy blowgun for shooting peas

pea soup n **1** : a thick soup made of dried peas usu. pureed **2** : a heavy fog

peat \'pēt\ n [ML peta] **1** : TURF 2b **2** : partially carbonized vegetable matter resulting from partial decomposition in water of various plants and esp. some mosses — **peaty** \'pēt-ē\ adj

peat moss n : SPHAGNUM

pea·vey or **pea·vy** \'pē-vē\ n, pl **peaveys** or **peavies** : a lever like a cant hook but with the end armed with a strong sharp spike

¹peb·ble \'peb-əl\ n [ME pobble, fr. OE papolstān] **1** : a small usu. round stone esp. when worn by the action of water **2** : an irregular, crinkled, or grainy surface — **peb·bly** \'peb-(ə-)lē\ adj

peavey

²pebble vt **peb·bled; peb·bling** \'peb-(ə-)liŋ\ **1** : to pelt with pebbles **2** : to pave or cover with pebbles or something resembling pebbles **3** : to treat (as leather) so as to produce a rough and irregularly indented surface

pe·can \pi-ˈkän, -ˈkan\ n [of Algonquian origin] : a large hickory of the south central U.S.; also : its edible oblong nut

pec·ca·dil·lo \ˌpek-ə-ˈdil-(ˌ)ō\ n, pl **-loes** or **-los** [Sp pecadillo, dim. of pecado sin, fr. L peccatum, fr. peccare to sin] : a slight offense or fault

pec·ca·ry \'pek-ə-rē\ n, pl **-ries** [of AmerInd origin] : either of two largely nocturnal gregarious American chiefly tropical mammals resembling but smaller than the related pigs

¹peck \'pek\ n [OF pek] **1** — see MEASURE table **2** : a large quantity : great deal ⟨a peck of trouble⟩

²peck vb [ME pecken] **1** : to strike with the bill : thrust the beak into ⟨a woodpecker pecking a tree⟩ **2** : to strike (as in breaking up earth or ice) with a sharp instrument (as a pick) **3** : to pick up with the bill ⟨a chicken pecking corn⟩ **4** : to strike at or pick up something with or as if with a bill **5** : to bite daintily : NIBBLE ⟨pecked at his food⟩

³peck n **1** : an impression or hole made by pecking **2** : a quick sharp stroke

peck·er \'pek-ər\ n **1** : one that pecks **2** chiefly Brit : COURAGE ⟨keep your pecker up⟩

peck order n : a basic pattern of social organization within a flock of poultry in which each bird pecks another lower in the scale without fear of retaliation and submits to pecking by one of higher rank — called also pecking order

pec·ten \'pek-tən\ n [L, comb, scallop] : ¹SCALLOP 1a

pec·tic \'pek-tik\ adj : of, relating to, or derived from pectin

pec·tin \'pek-tən\ n [F pectine, fr. Gk pēkt-, pēgnynai to fix, coagulate] : any of various water-soluble substances in plant tissues that yield a gel which is the basis of fruit jellies; also : a commercial product rich in pectins — **pec·tin·ous** \-tə-nəs\ adj

pec·ti·nate \'pek-tə-ˌnāt\ also **pec·ti·nat·ed** \-ˌnāt-əd\ adj [L pectin-, pecten comb] : having narrow parallel projections or divisions suggestive of the teeth of a comb — **pec·ti·na·tion** \ˌpek-tə-ˈnā-shən\ n

pec·to·ral \'pek-t(ə-)rəl\ adj [L pector-, pectus breast] **1** : of, relating to, or situated in, near, or on the chest **2** : coming from the breast or heart as the seat of emotion : SUBJECTIVE

pectoral cross n : a cross worn on the breast esp. by a prelate

pectoral fin n : either of a pair of fins that correspond in a fish to the forelimbs of a quadruped — compare PELVIC FIN; see FIN illustration

pectoral girdle n : the bony or cartilaginous arch supporting the forelimbs of a vertebrate

pec·u·late \'pek-yə-ˌlāt\ vt : EMBEZZLE — **pec·u·la·tion** \ˌpek-yə-ˈlā-shən\ n — **pec·u·la·tor** \'pek-yə-ˌlāt-ər\ n

pe·cu·liar \pi-ˈkyül-yər\ adj [ME peculier, fr. L peculiaris of private property, special, fr. peculium private property, fr. pecu cattle; akin to E fee] **1** : belonging exclusively to one person or group **2** : characteristic of one only : DISTINCTIVE **3** : different from the usual or normal: **a** : SPECIAL, PARTICULAR **b** : ODD, CURIOUS, ECCENTRIC syn see STRANGE — **pe·cu·liar·ly** adv

pe·cu·li·ar·i·ty \pi-ˌkyü-lē-ˈar-ət-ē, -ˌkyül-ˈyar-\ n, pl **-ties** **1** : the quality or state of being peculiar **2** : a distinguishing characteristic **3** : ODDITY, QUIRK

pe·cu·ni·ary \pi-ˈkyü-nē-ˌer-ē\ adj [L pecunia money, fr. pecu cattle; akin to E fee] **1** : consisting of money : taken or given in money ⟨pecuniary aid⟩ **2** : of or relating to money : MONETARY ⟨pecuniary policies⟩ syn see FINANCIAL — **pe·cu·niar·i·ly** \-ˌkyün-ˈyer-ə-lē, -ˌkyü-nē-ˈer-\ adv

ped- — see PAED-

-ped \ˌped\ or **-pede** \ˌpēd\ n comb form [L ped-, pes; akin to E foot] : foot ⟨maxilliped⟩ ⟨maxillipede⟩

ped·a·gog·ics \ˌped-ə-ˈgäj-iks\ n : PEDAGOGY

ped·a·gogue also **ped·a·gog** \'ped-ə-ˌgäg\ n [Gk paidagōgos, fr. paid-, pais child + agein to lead] **1** : a teacher of children : SCHOOLMASTER **2** : a dull, formal, and pedantic teacher

ped·a·go·gy \'ped-ə-ˌgō-jē, -ˌgäj-ē\ n : the art, science, or profession of teaching; esp : EDUCATION 2 — **ped·a·gog·ic** \ˌped-ə-ˈgäj-ik\ or **ped·a·gog·i·cal** \-ˈgäj-i-kəl\ adj — **ped·a·gog·i·cal·ly** \-i-k(ə-)lē\ adv

¹ped·al \'ped-ᵊl\ n **1** : a lever acted on by the foot in the playing of musical instruments **2** : a foot lever or treadle by which a part is activated in a mechanism

²pedal adj [L ped-, pes foot] : of or relating to the foot

³pedal vb **ped·aled** also **ped·alled; ped·al·ing** also **ped·al·ling** \'ped-ᵊl-iŋ, 'ped-liŋ\ **1** : to use or work the pedals of something **2** : to ride a bicycle

pedal point n : a single tone usu. the tonic or dominant that is normally sustained in the bass and sounds against changing harmonies in the other parts

pedal pushers n pl : women's and girls' calf-length trousers

ped·ant \'ped-ᵊnt\ n [MF, fr. It pedante] **1** : a person who shows off his learning **2** : a formal unimaginative teacher who emphasizes petty details — **pe·dan·tic** \pə-ˈdant-ik\ adj — **pe·dan·ti·cal·ly** \-ˈdant-i-k(ə-)lē\ adv

ped·ant·ry \'ped-ᵊn-trē\ n, pl **-ries** **1** : pedantic presentation or application of knowledge or learning **2** : an instance of pedantry

ped·ate \'ped-ˌāt\ adj : palmate with the lateral lobes cleft into two or more segments — **ped·ate·ly** adv

ped·dle \'ped-ᵊl\ vb **ped·dled; ped·dling** \'ped-liŋ, -ᵊl-iŋ\ [back-formation fr. peddler, fr. ME pedlere] **1** : to travel about esp. from house to house with wares for sale **2** : to sell or offer for sale from place to place usu. in small quantities : HAWK **3** : to seek to disseminate ⟨peddle scandal⟩ — **ped·dler** or **ped·lar** \'ped-lər\ n

ped·es·tal \'ped-əst-ᵊl\ n [MF piedestal, fr. It piedestallo, fr. pie di stallo foot of a stall] **1** : the support or foot of a column; also : the base of any upright structure (as a vase, lamp, or statue)—see ORDER illustration **2** : a position of high regard : the state of being held in exceptionally high esteem ⟨had been placed on a pedestal by his children⟩

¹pe·des·tri·an \pə-ˈdes-trē-ən\ adj [L pedester, lit., going

on foot, fr. *ped-, pes* foot] **1** : UNIMAGINATIVE, COMMON-PLACE **2 a** : going or performed on foot **b** : of or relating to walking
²pedestrian *n* : a person going on foot : WALKER
pe·des·tri·an·ism \-,iz-əm\ *n* **1 a** : the practice of walking **b** : fondness for walking **2** : the quality or state of being unimaginative or commonplace
pe·di·a·tri·cian \,pēd-ē-ə-'trish-ən\ *n* : a specialist in pediatrics
pe·di·at·rics \,pēd-ē-'a-triks\ *n* : a branch of medicine dealing with the child, its development, care, and diseases — **pe·di·at·ric** \-'trik\ *adj*
pedi·cab \'ped-i-,kab\ *n* : a small 3-wheeled hooded passenger vehicle that is pedaled
ped·i·cel \'ped-ə-,sel\ *n* : a slender basal part of an organism; *esp* : a stalk that supports a single flower — compare PEDUNCLE; see CORYMB illustration — **ped·i·cel·late** \,ped-ə-'sel-ət\ *adj*
pe·dic·u·lar \pi-'dik-yə-lər\ *adj* [L *pediculus* louse] : of or relating to lice
pe·dic·u·lo·sis \pi-,dik-yə-'lō-səs\ *n* [L *pediculus* louse] : infestation with lice — called also *lousiness* — **pe·dic·u·lous** \-'dik-yə-ləs\ *adj*
ped·i·cure \'ped-i-,kyùr\ *n* [F *pédicure*, fr. L *ped-, pes* foot + *curare* to take care] **1** : CHIROPODIST **2 a** : care of the feet, toes, and nails **b** : a single treatment of these parts — **ped·i·cur·ist** \-,kyùr-əst\ *n*
ped·i·gree \'ped-ə-,grē\ *n* [ME *pedegru*, fr. MF *pie de grue* crane's foot; fr. the shape made by the lines of a genealogical chart] **1** : a register of a line of ancestors **2 a** : an ancestral line : LINEAGE **b** : the origin and history of something (as a document, a collector's coin or stamp) **3 a** : distinguished ancestry **b** : recorded purity of breed of an individual or strain — **ped·i·greed** \-,grēd\ *adj*
ped·i·ment \'ped-ə-mənt\ *n* : a triangular space forming the gable of a 2-pitched roof in classic architecture; *also* : a similar form used as a decoration (as over a door or a window) — **ped·i·men·tal** \,ped-ə-'ment-°l\ *adj*
pedi·palp \'ped-ə-,palp\ *n* : either of the second pair of appendages of an arachnid (as a spider) borne near the mouth and often modified for a special (as sensory) function

P pediment

pedo- — see PAED-
pedo·gen·e·sis \,ped-ə-'jen-ə-səs\ *n* [Gk *pedon* ground, earth] : the formation and development of soil — **pedo·ge·net·ic** \-jə-'net-ik\ *adj*
¹pe·dol·o·gy \pē-'däl-ə-jē\ *n* : the scientific study of the life and development of children — **pe·do·log·i·cal** \,pēd-°l-'äj-i-kəl\ *adj* — **pe·dol·o·gist** \pē-'däl-ə-jəst\ *n*
²pe·dol·o·gy \pi-'däl-ə-jē, pe-\ *n* [Gk *pedon* ground, earth] : a science dealing with soils — **pe·do·log·i·cal** \,ped-°l-'äj-i-kəl\ *adj* — **pe·dol·o·gist** \pi-'däl-ə-jəst, pe-\ *n*
pe·dom·e·ter \pi-'däm-ət-ər\ *n* [L *ped-, pes* foot] : an instrument that measures the distance one covers in walking
pe·dun·cle \'pē-,dəŋ-kəl, pi-'\ *n* [NL *pedunculus*, dim. of L *ped-, pes* foot] : a narrow part by which some larger part or the body of an organism is attached; *esp* : a stalk that supports a flower cluster — compare PEDICEL; see CORYMB illustration — **pe·dun·cled** \-kəld\ *adj* — **pe·dun·cu·lar** \pi-'dəŋ-kyə-lər\ *adj* — **pe·dun·cu·late** \-lət\ *or* **pe·dun·cu·lat·ed** \-,lāt-əd\ *adj*
¹peek \'pēk\ *vi* [ME *piken*] **1 a** : to look furtively **b** : to peer through a crack or hole or from a place of concealment **2** : to take a brief look : GLANCE
²peek *n* : a brief or surreptitious look
¹peel \'pēl\ *vb* [MF *peler*, fr. L *pilare* to depilate, fr. *pilus* hair] **1** : to strip off the skin, bark, or rind of ⟨peel an apple⟩ **2** : to strip or tear off ⟨peeled off his coat⟩ **3 a** : to come off ⟨the paint is peeling⟩ **b** : to lose the skin, bark, or rind ⟨his face is peeling⟩ — **peel·er** *n*
²peel *n* : a skin or rind esp. of a fruit
³peel *n* : a usu. long-handled spade-shaped instrument used chiefly by bakers
peel·ing \'pē-liŋ\ *n* : a peeled-off piece or strip (as of skin or rind)
peel off *vi* : to veer away from an airplane formation esp. for diving or landing

peen \'pēn\ *n* : the usu. hemispherical or wedge-shaped end of the head of a hammer opposite the face
¹peep \'pēp\ *vi* **1** : to utter a feeble shrill sound as of a bird newly hatched : CHEEP **2** : to speak with a small weak voice : utter the slightest sound
²peep *n* **1** : a feeble shrill sound : CHEEP **2** : a slight utterance esp. of complaint or protest ⟨don't let me hear another peep out of you⟩
³peep *vb* [ME *pepen*] **1 a** : to peer through a crevice **b** : to look cautiously or slyly **2** : to begin to emerge from concealment : show slightly **3** : to cause (as the head of one peeping) to protrude slightly
⁴peep *n* **1** : the first glimpse or faint appearance ⟨at the peep of dawn⟩ **2** : a brief or furtive look
¹peep·er \'pē-pər\ *n* : one that peeps; *esp* : any of various small frogs that peep shrilly in spring
²peeper *n* **1** : one that peeps; *esp* : PEEPING TOM **2** : EYE
peep·hole \'pēp-,hōl\ *n* : a hole or crevice to peep through
Peeping Tom \-'täm\ *n* **1** : a tailor of Coventry held to have peeped at Lady Godiva **2** *often not cap* : a person who spies into the windows of private dwellings : one who furtively watches others
peep show *n* : an entertainment suggesting a stage show and consisting of a display of objects or pictures viewed through a small hole usu. fitted with a lens
peep sight *n* : a rear sight for a gun having an adjustable metal piece pierced with a small hole to look through in aiming
¹peer \'pi(ə)r\ *n* [OF *per*, fr. *per*, adj., equal, fr. L *par*] **1** : one that is of equal standing with another : EQUAL **2** *archaic* : COMPANION, FELLOW **3 a** : a member (as a duke, marquess, earl, viscount, or baron) of one of the five ranks of the British peerage **b** : NOBLE 1
²peer *vi* **1** : to look narrowly or curiously; *esp* : to look searchingly at something difficult to discern **2** : to come slightly into view
peer·age \'pi(ə)r-ij\ *n* **1** : the body of peers **2** : the rank or dignity of a peer **3** : a book containing a list of peers
peer·ess \'pir-əs\ *n* **1** : the wife or widow of a peer **2** : a woman who holds the rank of a peer in her own right
peer·less \'pi(ə)r-ləs\ *adj* : having no equal : MATCHLESS, INCOMPARABLE — **peer·less·ly** *adv* — **peer·less·ness** *n*
¹peeve \'pēv\ *vt* [back-formation fr. *peevish*, fr. ME *pevish* spiteful] : to make peevish or resentful : ANNOY, IRRITATE
²peeve *n* **1** : a peevish mood : a feeling of resentment **2** : a particular grievance : GRUDGE
pee·vish \'pē-vish\ *adj* **1** : cross and complaining in temperament or mood : FRETFUL, IRRITABLE **2** : perversely obstinate : CONTRARY **3** : marked by ill temper — **pee·vish·ly** *adv* — **pee·vish·ness** *n*
pee·wee \'pē-(,)wē\ *n* : something or someone diminutive or tiny — **peewee** *adj*
¹peg \'peg\ *n* [ME *pegge*] **1** : a small usu. cylindrical pointed or tapered piece (as of wood) used esp. to pin down or fasten things or to fit into or close holes : PIN, PLUG ⟨clothes *peg*⟩ **2** : a projecting piece used as a support or boundary marker ⟨a tent *peg*⟩ **3 a** : one of the pins of a stringed musical instrument that are turned to regulate the pitch of the strings **b** : a step or degree esp. in estimation (took him down a *peg*) **4** : a pointed prong or claw for catching or tearing **5** *Brit* : a small drink (as of whiskey) **6** : THROW ⟨a quick *peg* to first base⟩
²peg *vb* **pegged**; **peg·ging** **1 a** : to fasten or mark with pegs **b** : to pin down : RESTRICT **c** : to fix or hold (as prices) at a predetermined level **2** : to place in a definite category **2** : THROW **3** : to work steadily and diligently **4** : to move along vigorously or hastily : HUSTLE
Peg·a·sus \'peg-ə-səs\ *n* **1** : a winged horse in Greek mythology **2** : poetic inspiration **3** : a northern constellation near the vernal equinoctial point
peg·board \'peg-,bōrd, -,bòrd\ *n* : paneling punched at regular intervals with small holes into which holders (as for tools or utensils) may be inserted
peg·ma·tite \'peg-mə-,tīt\ *n* : a coarse variety of granite occurring in dikes or veins
peg top *n* **1** : a pear-shaped top with a sharp metal peg spun by a string as it is thrown from the hand **2** *pl* : **peg-top** trousers
peg-top \'peg-'täp\ *or* **peg-topped** \-'täpt\ *adj* : wide at the top and narrow at the bottom ⟨peg-top trousers⟩

---

j joke; **ŋ** sing; **ō** flow; **ȯ** flaw; **ȯi** coin; **th** thin; **th̲** this; **ü** loot; ** u̇** foot; **y** yet; **yü** few; **yu̇** furious; **zh** vision

pei·gnoir \pān-'wär\ *n* [F, fr. *peigner* to comb the hair] : a woman's loose negligee or dressing gown

pe·jor·a·tive \pi-'jör-ət-iv, -'jär-; 'pej-(ə-)rət-\ *adj* [LL *pejorare* to make or become worse, fr. L *pejor* worse] : having a tendency to make or become worse : DEPRECIATORY, DISPARAGING — **pe·jor·a·tive·ly** *adv*

Pe·kin \pi-'kin, 'pē-\ *n* : any of a breed of large white ducks of Chinese origin used for meat production

Pe·king·ese or **Pe·kin·ese** \,pē-kən-'ēz, -kiŋ-, -'ēs\ *n, pl* **Pekingese** or **Pekinese** 1 a : a native or resident of Peking   b : the Chinese dialect of Peking   2 : any of a Chinese breed of small short-legged dogs with a broad flat face and a profuse long soft coat

Pe·king man \,pē-kiŋ-\ *n* : an extinct Pleistocene man known from skeletal and cultural remains in cave deposits at Choukoutien, China that is more advanced in some details than the pithecanthropus of Java but nearer to him than to recent man and is usu. included in the same genus

pe·koe \'pē-kō\ *n* : a black tea made from small-sized tea leaves esp. in India and Ceylon

pel·age \'pel-ij\ *n* [F, fr. MF, fr. *poil* hair, fr. L *pilus*] : the hairy covering of a mammal

pe·lag·ic \pə-'laj-ik\ *adj* [Gk *pelagos* sea] : of, relating to, or living or occurring in the open sea : OCEANIC

pel·ar·go·ni·um \,pel-är-'gō-nē-əm\ *n* [NL, genus name, irreg. fr. Gk *pelargos* stork] : any of a genus of southern African herbs of the geranium family that include the garden geraniums

Pe·las·gian \pə-'laz-j(ē-)ən, -'laz-gē-ən\ *n* : one of an ancient people mentioned by classical writers as early inhabitants of Greece and the eastern islands of the Mediterranean — **Pelasgian** *adj*

pe·lecy·pod \pə-'les-ə-,päd\ *adj or n* [Gk *pelekys* ax + *pod-, pous* foot] : LAMELLIBRANCH

pelf \'pelf\ *n* [MF *pelfre* booty] : MONEY, RICHES

pel·i·can \'pel-i-kən\ *n* [OE *pellican*, fr. LL *pelecanus*, fr. Gk *pelekan*] : any of a genus of large web-tooted birds with a very large bill bearing a pouch in which fish are caught

pe·lisse \pə-'lēs\ *n* [F, fr. LL *pellicia*, fr. L *pellis* skin] 1 : a long cloak or coat made of fur or lined or trimmed with fur   2 : a woman's loose lightweight cloak with wide collar and fur trimming

pel·la·gra \pə-'lag-rə, -'lāg-\ *n* : a disease marked by dermatitis, gastrointestinal disorders, and central nervous symptoms and associated with a diet deficient in niacin and protein — **pel·lag·rous** \-rəs\ *adj*

¹pel·let \'pel-ət\ *n* [ME *pelote*, fr. MF, fr. (assumed) VL *pilota*, dim. of L *pila* ball] 1 : a little ball (as of food, medicine, or debris)   2 a : a usu. stone ball used as a missile in medieval times   b : BULLET   c : a piece of small shot

²pellet *vt* 1 : to form into pellets   2 : to strike with pellets

pel·li·cle \'pel-i-kəl\ *n* [L *pellicula*, dim. of *pellis* skin] : a thin skin or film — **pel·lic·u·lar** \pə-'lik-yə-lər\ *adj* — **pel·lic·u·late** \-lət\ *adj*

pell-mell \'pel-'mel\ *adv* [MF *pelemele*] 1 : in confusion or disorder   2 : in confused or headlong haste — **pell-mell** *adj or n*

pel·lu·cid \pə-'lü-səd\ *adj* [L *pellucidus*, fr. *perlucēre*, *pellucēre* to shine through] 1 : admitting maximum passage of light without diffusion or distortion   2 : reflecting light evenly from all surfaces   3 : extremely easy to understand   **syn** see LIMPID — **pel·lu·cid·i·ty** \,pel-yü-'sid-ət-ē\ *n* — **pel·lu·cid·ly** \pə-'lü-səd-lē\ *adv* — **pel·lu·cid·ness** *n*

pe·lo·rus \pə-'lōr-əs, -'lòr-\ *n* : a navigational instrument having a disk marked in degrees and two sights by which bearings are taken

pe·lo·ta \pə-'lōt-ə\ *n* [Sp, fr. OF *pelote* little ball] : any of various Basque, Spanish, or Spanish-American games played in a court with a ball and a wickerwork racket; *esp* : JAI ALAI

¹pelt \'pelt\ *n* [ME] : a usu. undressed skin with its hair, wool, or fur

²pelt *vt* : to strip off the skin of

³pelt *vb* [ME *pelten*] 1 : to strike with or deliver a succession of blows or missiles ⟨*pelted* him with snowballs⟩⟨was *pelted* with questions by the reporters⟩   2 : HURL, THROW ⟨*pelting* snowballs⟩   3 : to beat or dash repeatedly against something ⟨hail *pelting* against a window⟩   4 : to move

rapidly and vigorously or with pounding blows or thuds — **pelt·er** *n*

⁴pelt *n* 1 : a persistent falling or beating (as of rain, hail, or sleet)   2 : a rapid pace or speed — used esp. in the phrase *full pelt*

pel·tate \'pel-,tāt\ *adj* [Gk *peltē* small shield] : shaped like a shield ⟨a *peltate* leaf⟩ — **pel·tate·ly** *adv*

pelt·ry \'pel-trē\ *n, pl* **peltries** : PELTS, FURS; *esp* : raw undressed skins

pel·vic \'pel-vik\ *adj* : of, relating to, or located in or near the pelvis — **pelvic** *n*

pelvic fin *n* : either of a pair of fins that correspond in a fish to the hind limbs of a quadruped — compare PECTORAL FIN; see FIN illustration

pelvic girdle *n* : a bony or cartilaginous arch that supports the hind limbs of a vertebrate

pel·vis \'pel-vəs\ *n, pl* **pel·vis·es** or **pel·ves** \'pel-,vēz\ [NL, fr. L, basin] 1 : a basin-shaped structure in the skeleton of many vertebrates formed by the pelvic girdle and adjoining bones of the spine; *also* : its cavity   2 : the funnel-shaped cavity of the kidney into which urine is discharged

Pem·broke \'pem-,brōk, -,bruk\ *n* : a Welsh corgi of a variety characterized by pointed erect ears, straight legs, and short tail

pem·mi·can \'pem-i-kən\ *n* : a concentrated food used by No. American Indians consisting of dried lean meat pounded fine and mixed with melted fat

¹pen \'pen\ *n* [OE *penn*] 1 : a small enclosure for animals; *also* : a small group of animals handled as a unit   2 : a small place of confinement or storage

²pen *vt* **penned**; **pen·ning** : to shut in a pen

³pen *n* [MF *penne* feather, pen, fr. L *penna*, *pinna* feather] 1 : an implement for writing or drawing with ink or a similar fluid: as   a : QUILL   b : a small thin convex metal device tapering to a split point and fitting into a holder   c : a penholder containing a pen; *also* : a similar implement (as a fountain pen or ball-point pen)   2 a : a writing instrument regarded as a means of expression ⟨lives by his *pen*⟩   b : WRITER   3 : the internal horny feather-shaped shell of a squid

⁴pen *vt* **penned**; **pen·ning** : WRITE, INDITE

⁵pen *n* : a female swan

⁶pen *n, slang* : PENITENTIARY

pe·nal \'pēn-ᵊl\ *adj* [L *poena* punishment, fr. Gk *poinē* penalty] : of, relating to, or involving punishment, penalties, or punitive institutions ⟨*penal* laws⟩ ⟨a *penal* colony⟩ — **pe·nal·ly** \-ᵊl-ē\ *adv*

penal code *n* : a code of laws concerning crimes and offenses and their punishment

pe·nal·ize \'pēn-ᵊl-,īz, 'pen-\ *vt* 1 : to subject to a penalty ⟨*penalize* an athlete for a foul⟩   2 : to place at a disadvantage : HANDICAP ⟨*penalized* in the business world by his youth⟩ — **pe·nal·i·za·tion** \,pēn-ᵊl-ə-'zā-shən, ,pen-\ *n*

pen·al·ty \'pen-ᵊl-tē\ *n, pl* **-ties** 1 : punishment for a crime or offense   2 : something forfeited when a person fails to do what he agreed to do   3 : disadvantage, loss, or hardship due to some action or condition   4 : a punishment or handicap imposed for breaking a rule in a sport or game

pen·ance \'pen-ən(t)s\ *n* [OF, fr. ML *poenitentia* penitence] 1 : an act of self-abasement, mortification, or devotion performed to show sorrow or repentance for sin   2 : a sacrament in the Roman Catholic and Eastern churches consisting in repentance or contrition for sin, confession to a priest, satisfaction as imposed by the confessor, and absolution

pe·na·tes \pə-'nāt-ēz\ *n pl* : the Roman gods of the household worshiped in close connection with Vesta and with the lares and household genius

pence \'pen(t)s\ *pl of* PENNY

pen·chant \'pen-chənt\ *n* [F, fr. prp. of *pencher* to lean] : a strong leaning : LIKING

syn FLAIR: PENCHANT may imply a decided taste and strong inclination for ⟨a decided *penchant* for gardening⟩ FLAIR implies instinctive ability or perception and acumen ⟨a real *flair* for cooking⟩

¹pen·cil \'pen(t)-səl\ *n* [MF *pincel*, fr. L *penicillus*, fr. dim. of *penis* tail] 1 *archaic* : an artist's brush   2 : an artist's individual skill or style   3 a : an implement for writing, drawing, or marking consisting of or containing a slender cylinder or strip of a solid marking substance **b :** a small medicated or cosmetic roll or stick **4 :** an aggregate of rays of light esp. when diverging from or converging to a point **5 :** something long and thin like a pencil

²pencil vt **-ciled** or **-cilled; -cil·ing** or **-cil·ling** \-s(ə-)liŋ\ **:** to mark, draw, or write with or as if with a pencil — **pen·cil·er** \-s(ə-)lər\ n

pen·dant also **pen·dent** \'pen-dənt\ n [MF pendant, fr. prp. of pendre to hang, fr. L pendēre] **:** something that hangs down esp. as an ornament

pen·den·cy \'pen-dən-sē\ n **:** the state of being pending

pen·dent or **pen·dant** \'pen-dənt\ adj **1 :** supported from above **:** SUSPENDED **2 :** jutting or leaning over **:** OVERHANGING **3 :** remaining undetermined **:** PENDING — **pen·dent·ly** adv

¹pend·ing \'pen-diŋ\ prep [F pendant, fr. prp. of pendre to hang] **1 :** DURING **2 :** while awaiting ⟨pending a reply⟩

²pending adj **:** not yet decided

pen·drag·on \pen-'drag-ən\ n [W, fr. pen chief + dragon leader] **:** head of all the chiefs among the ancient Britons **:** KING

pen·du·lar \'pen-jə-lər, -dyə-lər, -dʼl-ər\ adj **:** being or resembling the movement of a pendulum

pen·du·lous \'pen-jə-ləs\ adj [L pendulus, fr. pendēre to hang] **1 :** suspended so as to swing freely **2 :** inclined or hanging downward **:** DROOPING — **pen·du·lous·ly** adv — **pen·du·lous·ness** n

pen·du·lum \'pen-jə-ləm, -dyə-ləm, -dʼl-əm\ n [NL, fr. L, neut. of pendulus pendulous] **:** a body suspended from a fixed point so as to swing freely to and fro under the action of gravity ⟨the pendulum of a clock⟩

pe·ne·plain also **pe·ne·plane** \'pēn-i-,plān, 'pen-\ n [L paene almost] **:** a land surface of considerable area and slight relief shaped by erosion

pen·e·tra·bil·i·ty \,pen-ə-trə-'bil-ət-ē\ n **:** the quality or state of being penetrable or being able to penetrate

pen·e·tra·ble \'pen-ə-trə-bəl\ adj **:** capable of being penetrated — **pen·e·tra·ble·ness** n — **pen·e·tra·bly** \-blē\ adv

pen·e·trate \'pen-ə-,trāt\ vb [L penetrare] **1 a :** to pass into or through **b :** to enter by overcoming resistance **:** PIERCE **2 a :** to see into or through **b :** to discover the inner contents or meaning of **3 :** to affect deeply the senses or feelings **4 :** to diffuse through **:** PERMEATE **syn** see ENTER

pen·e·trat·ing adj **1 :** BITING, SHARP ⟨penetrating cold⟩ **2 :** ACUTE, DISCERNING ⟨a penetrating mind⟩ — **pen·e·trat·ing·ly** \-,trāt-iŋ-lē\ adv

pen·e·tra·tion \,pen-ə-'trā-shən\ n **1 :** the act or process of penetrating **2 a :** the depth to which something penetrates **b :** the power to penetrate; esp **:** the ability to discern deeply and acutely

pen·e·tra·tive \'pen-ə-,trāt-iv\ adj **:** tending or able to penetrate — **pen·e·tra·tive·ly** adv — **pen·e·tra·tive·ness** n

pen·guin \'peŋ-gwən, 'pen-\ n **:** any of various erect short-legged aquatic birds of the southern hemisphere with the wings reduced to flippers and used in swimming

pen·hold·er \'pen-,hōl-dər\ n **:** a holder or handle for a pen

pen·i·cil·late \,pen-ə-'sil-ət\ adj [L penicillus brush] **:** furnished with a tuft of fine filaments — **pen·i·cil·late·ly** adv

pen·i·cil·lin \,pen-ə-'sil-ən\ n **:** any of several antibiotics or a mixture of these produced by penicillia or synthetically and used esp. against cocci

pen·i·cil·li·um \-'sil-ē-əm\ n, pl **-lia** \-ē-ə\ [NL, fr. L penicillus brush, pencil] **:** any of a genus of fungi comprising mostly blue molds found chiefly on moist nonliving organic matter — compare PENICILLIN

pen·in·su·la \pə-'nin(t)-sə-lə, -'nin-chə-lə\ n [L paeninsula, fr. paene almost + insula island] **:** a portion of land nearly surrounded by water; also **:** a piece of land jutting out into the water — **pen·in·su·lar** \-lər\ adj

pe·nis \'pē-nəs\ n, pl **pe·nes** \'pē-,nēz\ or **pe·nis·es** [L, penis, tail] **:** a male organ of copulation — **pe·ni·al** \-nē-əl\ adj — **pe·nile** \-,nīl\ adj

¹pen·i·tence \'pen-ə-tən(t)s\ n **:** sorrow for one's sins or faults **:** REPENTANCE

syn PENITENCE, REPENTANCE, CONTRITION mean regret for sin or wrongdoing: PENITENCE implies humble realization of and regret for one's wrongdoings; REPENTANCE emphasizes the change of mind of one who not only

regrets his errors but abandons them for a new standard; CONTRITION suggests penitence shown by signs of grief or pain

¹pen·i·tent \-tənt\ adj [L paenitēre to be sorry] **:** feeling or expressing pain or sorrow for sins or offenses **:** REPENTANT — **pen·i·tent·ly** adv

²penitent n **1 :** a person who repents of sin **2 :** a person under church censure but admitted to penance esp. under the direction of a confessor

pen·i·ten·tial \,pen-ə-'ten-chəl\ adj **:** of or relating to penitence or penance — **pen·i·ten·tial·ly** \-'tench-(ə-)lē\ adv

¹pen·i·ten·tia·ry \,pen-ə-'tench-(ə-)rē\ n, pl **-ries** [ME penitenciary, fr. ML poenitentiarius, fr. poenitentia penitence] **:** a public institution in which criminals are confined; esp **:** a state or federal prison in the U.S.

²penitentiary adj **:** of, relating to, or incurring confinement in a penitentiary

pen·knife \'pen-,nīf\ n [fr. its original use for mending quill pens] **:** a small pocketknife

pen·man \'pen-mən\ n **1 a :** COPYIST, SCRIBE **b :** one who is expert in penmanship **2 :** AUTHOR

pen·man·ship \'pen-mən-,ship\ n **1 :** the art or practice of writing with the pen **2 :** quality or style of handwriting

pen name n **:** an author's pseudonym

pen·nant \'pen-ənt\ n [alter. of pendant] **1 a :** any of various nautical flags tapering usu. to a point or swallowtail and used for identification or signaling **b :** a long narrow flag or banner that tapers to a point **2 :** a flag emblematic of championship

pen·nate \'pen-,āt\ also **pen·nat·ed** \-,āt-əd\ adj **:** PINNATE

pen·ner \'pen-ər\ n **:** one that pens a document **:** WRITER

pen·ni·less \'pen-i-ləs, 'pen-ʼl-əs\ adj **:** having no money at all **:** very poor

pen·non \'pen-ən\ n [MF penon, aug. of penne feather] **1 a :** a long usu. triangular or swallow-tailed streamer typically attached to the head of a lance as an ensign **b :** PENNANT 1a **2 :** a flag of any shape **:** BANNER **3 :** WING, PINION

Penn·syl·va·nia Dutch \,pen(t)-səl-,vā-nyə-\ n **1 :** a people living mostly in eastern Pennsylvania whose characteristic cultural traditions go back to the German migrations of the 18th century **2 :** a German dialect spoken by the Pennsylvania Dutch — **Pennsylvania Dutchman** n

Penn·syl·va·nian \-'vā-nyən\ adj **1 :** of or relating to Pennsylvania or its people **2 :** of, relating to, or being the period of the Paleozoic era between the Mississippian and Permian or the corresponding system of rocks — **Pennsylvanian** n

pen·ny \'pen-ē\ n, pl **pen·nies** \-ēz\ or **pence** \'pen(t)s\ [OE penning] **1 a :** a British monetary unit equal to ¹⁄₂₄₀ pound or ¹⁄₁₂ shilling **b :** a coin representing this unit **2 :** a coin of small denomination: as **a :** DENARIUS **b** pl **pennies :** a cent of the U.S. or Canada **3 :** a piece or sum of money ⟨earn an honest penny⟩

penny ante n **:** poker played for very low stakes

penny arcade n **:** an amusement center where each device for entertainment may be operated for a small sum and orig. for a penny

penny dreadful n **:** a novel of violent adventure or crime orig. costing one penny

pen·ny pinch·er \'pen-ē-,pin-chər\ n **:** a stingy person — **pen·ny-pinch·ing** \-chiŋ\ adj or n

pen·ny·roy·al \,pen-ē-'rȯi-(ə)l, 'pen-i-,rīl\ n **:** a European perennial mint with small aromatic leaves; also **:** a similar American mint that yields an oil used in folk medicine or to drive away mosquitoes

pen·ny·weight \'pen-ē-,wāt\ n — see MEASURE table

pen·ny-wise \-,wīz\ adj **:** wise or prudent only in small matters

pen·ny·wort \-,wort, -,wȯrt\ n **:** any of several plants with round leaves

pen·ny·worth \'pen-ē-,wərth\ n, pl **-worth** or **-worths :** a penny's worth **:** as much as a penny will buy

pe·nol·o·gy \pi-'näl-ə-jē\ n [Gk poinē penalty] **:** a branch of criminology dealing with prison management and the treatment of offenders — **pe·no·log·i·cal** \,pēn-ʼl-'äj-i-kəl\ adj — **pe·nol·o·gist** \pi-'näl-ə-jəst\ n

pen pal n **:** a friend made and kept through correspondence

---

j joke; ŋ sing; ō flow; ȯ flaw; ȯi coin; th thin; th̲ this; ü loot; u̇ foot; y yet; yü few; yu̇ furious; zh vision

often without any face-to-face acquaintance — called also *pen-friend* \'pen-,frend\

pen·sile \'pen-,sīl\ *adj* [L *pens-, pendēre* to hang] : HANGING, PENDENT

1pen·sion *n* [L *pens-, pendēre* to weigh, pay] **1** \'pen-chən\ : a fixed sum paid regularly to a person; *esp* : one paid to a person following his retirement or to his surviving dependents **2** \päⁿ's-yōⁿ\ **a** : payment for board and room **b** : a boardinghouse esp. in continental Europe — **pen·sion·less** \'pen-chən-ləs\ *adj*

2pension \'pen-chən\ *vt* **pen·sioned; pen·sion·ing** \'pench-(ə-)niŋ\ : to grant or pay a pension to

pen·sion·er \'pench-(ə-)nər\ *n* **1** : a person who receives or lives on a pension **2** : a mercenary dependent : HIRELING

pen·sive \'pen(t)-siv\ *adj* [MF *pensif*, fr. *penser* to think, fr. L *pensare* to ponder, freq. of *pendere* to weigh] **1** : musingly or dreamily thoughtful **2** : suggestive of sad thoughtfulness : MELANCHOLY — **pen·sive·ly** *adv* — **pen·sive·ness** *n*

pen·stock \'pen-,stäk\ *n* **1** : a sluice or gate for regulating a flow (as of water) **2** : a conduit or pipe for conducting water

pent \'pent\ *adj* : shut up : CONFINED ⟨*pent*-up feelings⟩

penta- *or* **pent-** *comb form* [Gk, fr. *pente;* akin to E *five*] : five ⟨*penta*hedron⟩

pen·ta·dac·tyl \,pent-ə-'dak-t°l\ *also* **pen·ta·dac·ty·late** \-tə-lət, -,lāt\ *adj* : having five fingers or toes or five digitate parts — **pen·ta·dac·tyl·ism** \-tə-,liz-əm\ *n*

pen·ta·gon \'pent-i-,gän\ *n* : a polygon of five angles and five sides — **pen·tag·o·nal** \pen-'tag-ən-°l\ *adj*

Pentagon *n* : a pentagonal building near Washington, D.C., housing the U.S. Department of Defense

pen·tam·er·ous \pen-'tam-ə-rəs\ *adj* : divided into or consisting of five parts

pen·tam·e·ter \pen-'tam-ət-ər\ *n* : a line consisting of five metrical feet

pen·tane \'pen-,tān\ *n* : any of three isomeric hydrocarbons C_5H_{12} occurring in petroleum and natural gas

pentagon

Pen·ta·teuch \'pent-ə-,t(y)ük\ *n* [Gk *Pentateuchos*, fr. *penta-* + *teuchos* tool, vessel, book] : the first five books of the Old Testament

pen·tath·lon \pen-'tath-lən\ *n* [Gk, fr. *penta-* + *athlon* contest] : an athletic contest in which each contestant participates in five different events

Pen·te·cost \'pent-i-,kost, -,käst\ *n* [Gk *pentēkostē*, lit., fiftieth (day), fr. *pentēkonta* 50] **1** : SHABUOTH **2** : the 7th Sunday after Easter observed as a church festival in commemoration of the descent of the Holy Spirit on the apostles

Pen·te·cos·tal \,pent-i-'käst-°l, -'kost-\ *adj* **1** : of, relating to, or suggesting Pentecost **2** : of, relating to, or constituting any of various usu. fundamentalist sects that employ revivalistic methods — **Pentecostal** *n* — **Pen·te·cos·tal·ism** \-,iz-əm\ *n*

pent·house \'pent-,haús\ *n* [ME *pentis*, fr. MF *appentis*] **1** : a roof or a shed attached to and sloping from a wall or building **2** : a structure (as an apartment) built on the roof of a building

pent·land·ite \'pent-lən-,dīt\ *n* : a bronzy yellow mineral $(Fe,Ni)_9S_8$ that is a nickel iron sulfide and the principal ore of nickel

pen·to·bar·bi·tal \,pent-ə-'bär-bə-,tol\ *n* : a barbiturate used esp. in the form of its sodium or calcium salt chiefly as a sedative and hypnotic

pen·tode \'pen-,tōd\ *n* : a vacuum tube with five electrodes

pen·tom·ic \pen-'täm-ik\ *adj* **1** : made up of five battle groups ⟨*pentomic* division⟩ **2** : organized into pentomic divisions ⟨*pentomic* army⟩

pen·tose \'pen-,tōs\ *n* : any of various sugars $C_5H_{10}O_5$ containing five carbon atoms in the molecule

Pen·to·thal \'pent-ə-,thol\ *trademark* — used for a substance that is used as an intravenous anesthetic of short duration and as a hypnotic

pent·ox·ide \'pent-'äk-,sīd\ *n* : an oxide containing five atoms of oxygen in the molecule

pent·ste·mon *or* **pen·ste·mon** \pen(t)-'stē-mən, 'pent)-

stə-\ *n* : any of a genus of chiefly American herbs of the figwort family with showy blue, purple, red, yellow, or white flowers

pe·nu·che \pə-'nü-chē\ *n* [MexSp *panocha* raw sugar, fr. dim. of Sp *pan* bread, fr. L *panis*] : fudge made usu. of brown sugar, butter, cream or milk, and nuts

pe·nult \'pē-,nəlt\ *n* [L *paene* almost + *ultimus* last] : the next to the last syllable of a word

pen·ul·ti·mate \pi-'nəl-tə-mət\ *adj* **1** : next to the last **2** : of or relating to a penult — **penultimate** *n* — **pen·ul·ti·mate·ly** *adv*

pen·um·bra \pə-'nəm-brə\ *n, pl* **-brae** \-(,)brē, -,brī\ *or* **-bras** [L *paene* almost + *umbra* shadow] **1** : the partial shadow surrounding a perfect shadow (as in an eclipse) **2** : the shaded region around the dark central portion of a sunspot — **pen·um·bral** \-brəl\ *adj*

pe·nu·ri·ous \pə-'n(y)ur-ē-əs\ *adj* **1** : marked by or suffering from penury **2** : given to or marked by extreme stinting frugality — **pe·nu·ri·ous·ly** *adv* — **pe·nu·ri·ous·ness** *n*

pen·u·ry \'pen-yə-rē\ *n* [L *penuria* want] **1** : extreme poverty : PRIVATION **2** : absence of resources : SCANTINESS

pe·on \'pē-,än, -ən\ *n* [Pg *peão* & F *pion*, fr. ML *pedon-, pedo* foot soldier, fr. L *ped-, pes* foot] **1** : a member of the landless laboring class in Spanish America **2** : a person held in compulsory servitude to work out an indebtedness **3** : DRUDGE, MENIAL

pe·on·age \'pē-ə-nij\ *n* **1** : the condition of a peon **2** : the use of laborers bound in servitude because of debt

pe·o·ny \'pē-ə-nē, 'pī-nē\ *n, pl* **-nies** [Gk *paiōnia*, fr. *Paiōn* Paeon, physician of the gods] : any of a genus of perennial plants related to the buttercups and widely grown for their large usu. double flowers of red, pink, or white

1peo·ple \'pē-pəl\ *n, pl* **people** [OF *peuple* body of citizens, populace, fr. L *populus*] **1** *pl* : human beings **2** *pl* : the members of a family : KINDRED; *also* : ANCESTORS **3** *pl* : the mass of a community as distinguished from a special class **4** *pl* **peoples** : a body of persons united by a common culture, tradition, or sense of kinship, typically having common language, institutions, and beliefs, and often politically organized **5** : a body of enfranchised citizens : ELECTORATE

2people *vt* **peo·pled; peo·pling** \'pē-p(ə-)liŋ\ **1** : to supply or fill with people **2** : to dwell in : INHABIT

1pep \'pep\ *n* : brisk energy or initiative and high spirits : LIVELINESS

2pep *vt* **pepped; pep·ping** : to inject pep into : STIMULATE ⟨*pep* him up⟩

pep·lum \'pep-ləm\ *n* [L, woman's upper garment, fr. Gk *peplos*] : a short section attached to the waistline of a blouse, jacket, or dress

pe·po \'pē-pō\ *n* [L, melon] : an indehiscent fleshy many-seeded berry (as a pumpkin, squash, melon, or cucumber) that is the characteristic fruit of the gourd family

1pep·per \'pep-ər\ *n* [OE *pipor*, fr. L *piper*, fr. Gk *peperi*] **1 a** : a pungent product from the fruit of an East Indian climbing shrub used as a condiment and in medicine and consisting of (1) the entire dried berry or (2) the dried seeds divested of membranes and pulp — called also (1) *black pepper*, (2) *white pepper* **b** : the plant that yields pepper **c** : any of several somewhat

1 sweet pepper 2 pepper 1b

similar products obtained from other plants **2** : CAPSICUM; *esp* : a New World capsicum whose fruits are hot peppers or sweet peppers — **pepper** *adj*

2pepper *vt* **pep·pered; pep·per·ing** \-(ə-)riŋ\ **1 a** : to sprinkle or season with or as if with pepper **b** : to shower with missiles (as shot) **2** : to hit with rapid repeated blows **3** : to sprinkle as pepper is sprinkled

pepper–and–salt *adj* : having black and white or dark and light color intermingled in small flecks ⟨a *pepper-and-salt* overcoat⟩

pep·per·box \'pep-ər-,bäks\ *n* : a small box or bottle with a perforated top used for sprinkling ground pepper on food

pep·per·corn \'pep-ər-,kȯrn\ *n* **1** : a dried berry of the East Indian pepper **2** : a trifling or nominal return by way of acknowledgment

pep·per·mint \-(,)mint\ *n* **1** : a pungent and aromatic mint with dark green lanceolate leaves and whorls of small pink flowers in spikes **2** : candy flavored with peppermint

pep·pery \'pep-(ə-)rē\ *adj* **1** : of, relating to, or having the qualities of pepper : HOT, PUNGENT **2** : having a hot temper : TOUCHY **3** : FIERY, STINGING ⟨*peppery* words⟩

pep·py \'pep-ē\ *adj* **pep·pi·er; -est** : full of pep — **pep·pi·ness** *n*

pep·sin \'pep-sən\ *n* [G, fr. Gk *pepsis* digestion, fr. *pessein* to cook, digest] **1** : a proteinase of the stomach that begins the digestion of most proteins **2** : a preparation of pepsin obtained esp. from the stomach of the hog and used medicinally

pep·sin·o·gen \pep-'sin-ə-jən\ *n* : a granular product of gastric glands that is converted into pepsin in the acid medium of the stomach

pep talk *n* : a usu. brief, high-pressure, and emotional utterance designed to influence or encourage an audience ⟨the coach gave the team a *pep talk* before the game⟩

pep·tic \'pep-tik\ *adj* [Gk *pep-*, *pessein* to cook, digest] **1** : relating to or promoting digestion **2** : of, relating to, producing, or caused by pepsin ⟨*peptic* digestion⟩ **3** : resulting from the action of digestive juices ⟨a *peptic* ulcer⟩

pep·ti·dase \'pep-tə-,dās\ *n* : an enzyme that hydrolyzes simple peptides or their derivatives

pep·tide \'pep-,tīd\ *n* : any of various amides derived from two or more amino acids by combination of the amino group of one acid with the carboxyl group of another and usu. obtained by partial hydrolysis of proteins

peptide bond *n* : the bond between carbon and nitrogen in the amide group that unites the amide residues in a peptide — called also *peptide linkage*

pep·tone \'pep-,tōn\ *n* : any of various water-soluble products of partial hydrolysis of proteins

Pe·quot \'pē-,kwät\ *n* : a member of an Algonquian people of southeastern Connecticut

per \(')pər\ *prep* [L, through, by] **1** : by the means or agency of ⟨*per* bearer⟩ **2** : to or for each ⟨$10 *per* day⟩ **3** : as indicated by : according to ⟨*per* list price⟩

per- *prefix* [L, through, throughout, thoroughly, to destruction] **1** : throughout : thoroughly ⟨*perchlorinate*⟩ **2 a** : the largest possible or a relatively large proportion of a (specified) chemical element ⟨*perchloride*⟩ **b** : an element in its highest or a high oxidation state ⟨*perchloric* acid⟩

¹per·ad·ven·ture \'pər-əd-,ven-chər, 'per-\ *adv* [OF *per aventure* by chance] *archaic* : PERHAPS, POSSIBLY

²peradventure *n* : DOUBT, CHANCE

per·am·bu·late \pə-'ram-byə-,lāt\ *vb* [L *perambulare*, fr. *per-* + *ambulare* to walk] **1** : to travel over or through esp. on foot : TRAVERSE **2** : STROLL, RAMBLE — **per·am·bu·la·tion** \-,ram-byə-'lā-shən\ *n*

per·am·bu·la·tor \pə-'ram-byə-,lāt-ər\ *n* **1** : one that perambulates **2** *chiefly Brit* : a baby carriage — **per·am·bu·la·to·ry** \-lə-,tōr-ē, -,tȯr-\ *adj*

per an·num \(,)pər-'an-əm\ *adv* [ML] : in or for each year : ANNUALLY

per·cale \(,)pər-'kāl, -'kal\ *n* [Per *pargālah*] : a fine closely woven cotton cloth variously finished for clothing, sheeting, and industrial uses

per cap·i·ta \(,)pər-'kap-ət-ə\ *adv (or adj)* [ML, by heads] : per unit of population : by or for each person ⟨*per capita* income⟩

per·ceiv·a·ble \pər-'sē-və-bəl\ *adj* : PERCEPTIBLE, INTELLIGIBLE — **per·ceiv·a·bly** \-blē\ *adv*

per·ceive \pər-'sēv\ *vt* [OF *perceivre*, fr. L *percipere*, fr. *per-* thoroughly + *capere* to take] **1** : to attain awareness or understanding of **2** : to become aware of through the senses and esp. through sight — **per·ceiv·er** *n*

¹per·cent \pər-'sent\ *adv* [*per* + L *centum* hundred] : in the hundred : of each hundred

²percent *n*, *pl* **percent 1** : one part in a hundred : HUNDREDTH **2** : PERCENTAGE

³percent *adj* : reckoned on the basis of a whole divided into one hundred parts

per·cent·age \pər-'sent-ij\ *n* **1** : a part of a whole expressed in hundredths **2** : a share of winnings or profits **3** : an indeterminate part : PROPORTION **4 a** : PROBABILITY ⟨a gambler who plays the *percentages*⟩ **b** : favorable odds

per·cen·tile \pər-'sen-,tīl\ *n* : a measure widely used in educational testing that expresses an individual's standing in terms of the percentage of people falling below him ⟨a person with a *percentile* of 75 has done as well as or better than 75 percent of the people with whom he is being compared⟩

per cen·tum \pər-'sent-əm\ *n* : PERCENT

per·cep·ti·ble \pər-'sep-tə-bəl\ *adj* : capable of being perceived ⟨a *perceptible* change⟩ — **per·cep·ti·bil·i·ty** \-,sep-tə-'bil-ət-ē\ *n* — **per·cep·ti·bly** \-'sep-tə-blē\ *adv*

per·cep·tion \pər-'sep-shən\ *n* [L *percept-*, *percipere* to perceive] **1 a** : a result of perceiving : OBSERVATION, DISCERNMENT **b** : a mental image : CONCEPT **2** : awareness of the elements of environment through physical sensation ⟨color *perception*⟩ **3 a** : INSIGHT **b** : a capacity for comprehension — **per·cep·tion·al** \-shnəl, -shən-ᵊl\ *adj*

per·cep·tive \pər-'sep-tiv\ *adj* **1** : responsive to sensory stimulus : DISCERNING **2 a** : capable of or exhibiting keen perception : OBSERVANT **b** : characterized by sympathetic understanding or insight — **per·cep·tive·ly** *adv* — **per·cep·tive·ness** *n* — **per·cep·tiv·i·ty** \(,)pər-,sep-'tiv-ət-ē\ *n*

per·cep·tu·al \(,)pər-'sep-chə-wəl\ *adj* : of, relating to, or involving sensory stimulus as opposed to abstract concept — **per·cep·tu·al·ly** \-wə-lē\ *adv*

¹perch \'pərch\ *n* [OF *perche*, fr. L *pertica* pole] **1** : a bar or peg on which something is hung **2** : a roost for a bird **3 a** : a resting place or vantage point : SEAT **c** : EMINENCE **3** : a measure of length equal to a rod or in square measure to a square rod

²perch *vb* **1** : to place on a perch, a height, or precarious spot ⟨*perched* himself on the table⟩ **2** : to alight, settle, or rest on or as if on a perch

³perch *n*, *pl* **perch** *or* **perch·es** [MF *perche*, fr. L *perca*, fr. Gk *perkē*] **1** : a small largely olive-green and yellow European freshwater spiny-finned fish; *also* : a closely related American fish **2** : any of numerous teleost fishes related to or resembling the true perches : a percoid fish

per·chance \pər-'chan(t)s\ *adv* : PERHAPS, POSSIBLY

per·chlo·rate \(,)pər-'klōr-,āt, -'klȯr-\ *n* : a salt or ester of perchloric acid

per·chlo·ric acid \(,)pər-,klōr-ik-, -,klȯr-\ *n* : a fuming corrosive strong acid $HClO_4$ that is a powerful oxidizing agent when heated

per·cip·i·ent \pər-'sip-ē-ənt\ *adj* [L *percipere* to perceive] : capable of or characterized by perception : DISCERNING — **per·cip·i·ence** \-ē-ən(t)s\ *n* — **percipient** *n*

Per·ci·vale \'pər-sə-,val, -,väl\ *n* : an Arthurian knight who wins a sight of the Holy Grail

per·coid \'pər-,kȯid\ *adj* [L *perca* perch] : of or relating to a very large suborder (Percoidea) of spiny-finned fishes including the true perches, sunfishes, sea basses, and sea breams — **percoid** *n*

per·co·late \'pər-kə-,lāt\ *vb* [L *percolare*, fr. *per-* through + *colare* to sieve] **1 a** : to pass or cause to pass through a permeable substance (as a powdered drug) esp. for extracting a soluble constituent : FILTER, SEEP **b** : to prepare (coffee) in a percolator **2** : to be or become diffused through : PENETRATE **3 a** : to become percolated **b** : to become lively or effervescent — **per·co·la·tion** \,pər-kə-'lā-shən\ *n*

per·co·la·tor \'pər-kə-,lāt-ər\ *n* : one that percolates; *esp* : a coffeepot in which boiling water rising through a tube is repeatedly deflected downward through a perforated basket containing the ground coffee beans to extract their essence

per·cuss \pər-'kəs\ *vt* : to tap sharply; *esp* : to practice percussion on

¹per·cus·sion \pər-'kəsh-ən\ *n* [L *percuss-*, *percutere* to beat, fr. *per-* thoroughly + *quatere* to shake] **1** : the act of tapping sharply: as **a** : the striking of a percussion cap so as to set off the charge in a firearm **b** : the beating or striking of a musical instrument **c** : the act or technique of tapping the surface of a body part to learn the condition of the parts beneath by the resultant sound **2** : the striking of sound sharply on the ear **3** : percussion instruments esp. as forming a section of a band or orchestra

²per·cus·sion *adj* : PERCUSSIVE ⟨a *percussion* drill⟩

percussion cap *n* : a small cap or container of explosive to be fired by a sharp forceful blow

percussion instrument *n* : a musical instrument sounded by striking

per·cus·sion·ist \pər-'kəsh-(ə-)nəst\ *n* : one skilled in the playing of percussion instruments

per·cus·sive \pər-'kəs-iv\ *adj* : of or relating to percussion; *esp* : operative or operated by striking — **per·cus·sive·ly** *adv* — **per·cus·sive·ness** *n*

per·cu·ta·ne·ous \,pər-kyù-'tā-nē-əs\ *adj* : effected or performed through the skin — **per·cu·ta·ne·ous·ly** *adv*

¹per di·em \(')pər-'dē-əm\ *adv* [ML] : by the day : for each day — **per diem** *adj*

²per diem *n* : a sum (as for traveling expenses) computed by the day

per·di·tion \pər-'dish-ən\ *n* [L *perdit-*, *perdere* to destroy, fr. *per-* to destruction + *dare* to give] **1** *archaic* : utter destruction **2 a** : eternal damnation **b** : HELL

per·du·ra·bil·i·ty \(,)pər-,d(y)ùr-ə-'bil-ət-ē\ *n* : the quality or state of being perdurable : PERSISTENCE, PERMANENCE

per·du·ra·ble \(,)pər-'d(y)ùr-ə-bəl\ *adj* : very durable — **per·du·ra·bly** \-blē\ *adv*

per·e·gri·nate \'per-ə-grə-,nāt\ *vb* : to travel esp. on foot : WALK, TRAVERSE — **per·e·gri·na·tion** \,per-ə-grə-'nā-shən\ *n*

¹per·e·grine \'per-ə-grən, -,grēn\ *adj* [L *peregrinus* foreign] : having a tendency to wander : ROVING

²peregrine *n* : a dark swift nearly cosmopolitan falcon much used in falconry

pe·remp·to·ry \pə-'rem(p)-t(ə-)rē\ *adj* [L *perempt-*, *perimere* to take entirely, destroy, fr. *per-* + *emere* to take] **1 a** : putting an end to or precluding a right of action, debate, or delay **b** : ABSOLUTE, FINAL **2** : expressive of urgency or command : IMPERATIVE ⟨*peremptory* tone⟩ **3 a** : marked by self-assurance : POSITIVE **b** : DECISIVE **4** : HAUGHTY, DICTATORIAL, MASTERFUL — **pe·remp·to·ri·ly** \-t(ə-)rə-lē\ *adv* — **pe·remp·to·ri·ness** \-t(ə-)rē-nəs\ *n*

pe·ren·ni·al \pə-'ren-ē-əl\ *adj* [L *perennis*, fr. *per-* throughout + *annus* year] **1** : present at all seasons of the year ⟨*perennial* springs⟩ **2** : persisting for several years usu. with new herbaceous growth from a basal crown ⟨*perennial* asters⟩ **3 a** : PERSISTENT, ENDURING **b** : continuing without interruption : CONSTANT **c** : regularly repeated : RECURRENT — **perennial** *n* — **pe·ren·ni·al·ly** \-ē-ə-lē\ *adv*

¹per·fect \'pər-fikt\ *adj* [L *perfectus*, fr. pp. of *perficere* to carry out, perfect, fr. *per-* thoroughly + *facere* to make, do] **1 a** : being entirely without fault or defect : FLAWLESS **b** : satisfying all requirements : ACCURATE **c** : corresponding to an ideal standard **2** : faithfully reproducing the original **3 a** : PURE, TOTAL ⟨*perfect* stillness⟩ **b** : lacking in no essential detail : COMPLETE **c** : of an extreme kind : UNMITIGATED ⟨*perfect* fool⟩ **4** : of, relating to, or constituting a verb form or verbal that expresses an action or state completed at the time of speaking or at a time spoken of **5** : belonging to the musical consonances unison, fourth, fifth, and octave **6** : MONOCLINOUS **syn** see WHOLE — **per·fect·ness** \-fik(t)-nəs\ *n*

²per·fect \pər-'fekt, 'pər-fikt\ *vt* **1** : to make perfect : IMPROVE, REFINE **2** : to bring to final form : COMPLETE — **per·fect·er** *n*

³per·fect \'pər-fikt\ *n* **1** : the perfect tense **2** : a verb form in the perfect tense

perfect flower *n* : a flower with both stamens and pistils

per·fect·i·ble \pər-'fek-tə-bəl, 'pər-fik-\ *adj* : capable of improvement or perfection — **per·fect·i·bil·i·ty** \pər-,fek-tə-'bil-ət-ē, ,pər-fik-\ *n*

per·fec·tion \pər-'fek-shən\ *n* **1** : the quality or state of being perfect: as **a** : FLAWLESSNESS **b** : COMPLETENESS **c** : MATURITY **d** : SAINTLINESS **2 a** : an exemplification of supreme excellence **b** : an unsurpassable degree of accuracy or excellence **3** : the act or process of perfecting

per·fec·tion·ist \pər-'fek-sh(ə-)nəst\ *n* : a person who will not accept or be content with anything less than perfection — **perfectionist** *or* **per·fec·tion·is·tic** \-,fek-shə-'nis-tik\ *adj*

per·fect·ly \'pər-fik-(t)lē\ *adv* **1** : in a perfect manner ⟨understand *perfectly*⟩ **2** : to an adequate extent : QUITE ⟨he was *perfectly* willing⟩

perfect number *n* : an integer that is equal to the sum of all its divisors except itself ⟨28 is a *perfect number* because it is the sum of $1 + 2 + 4 + 7 + 14$⟩

per·fec·to \pər-'fek-tō\ *n*, *pl* **-tos** [Sp, perfect, fr. L *perfectus*] : a cigar that is thick in the middle and tapers almost to a point at each end

perfect participle *n* : PAST PARTICIPLE

perfect square *n* : an integer whose square root is an integer ⟨9 is a *perfect square* because it is the square of 3⟩

perfect year *n* **1** : a common year of 355 days in the Jewish calendar **2** : a leap year of 385 days in the Jewish calendar

per·fer·vid \,pər-'fər-vəd\ *adj* : extremely fervent

per·fid·i·ous \(,)pər-'fid-ē-əs\ *adj* : of, relating to, or characterized by perfidy — **per·fid·i·ous·ly** *adv* — **per·fid·i·ous·ness** *n*

per·fi·dy \'pər-fəd-ē\ *n*, *pl* **-dies** [L *perfidia*, fr. *per fidem decipere* to betray, lit., to deceive by trust] : the quality or state of being faithless or disloyal : TREACHERY

per·fo·rate \'pər-fə-,rāt\ *vb* [L *perforare*, fr. *per-* through + *forare* to bore] **1** : to make a hole through : PIERCE; *esp* : to make a line of holes to facilitate separation (as in sheets of postage stamps) **2** : to pass through or into by or as if by making a hole — **per·fo·rate** \'pər-f(ə-)rət, -fə-,rāt\ *adj* — **per·fo·ra·tor** \-fə-,rāt-ər\ *n*

per·fo·ra·tion \,pər-fə-'rā-shən\ *n* **1** : the act or process of perforating **2 a** : a hole or pattern made by or as if by piercing or boring **b** : one of the series of holes made between rows of postage stamps in a sheet

per·force \pər-'fōrs, -'fórs\ *adv* [MF *par force* by force] : by force of circumstances or of necessity : WILLY-NILLY ⟨he went *perforce*⟩

per·form \pər-'fórm\ *vb* [AF *performer*, alter. of OF *parfournir*, fr. *per-* thoroughly + *fournir* to complete] **1** : to adhere to the terms of : FULFILL ⟨*perform* a contract⟩ **2 a** : to carry out : DO **b** : ACT, FUNCTION **3 a** : to do in a formal manner or according to prescribed ritual **b** : to give a performance or a rendition of : PRESENT, PLAY ⟨the first time he had *performed* Hamlet⟩ — **per·form·a·ble** \-'fór-mə-bəl\ *adj* — **per·form·er** *n*

per·form·ance \pər-'fór-mən(t)s\ *n* **1 a** : the execution of an action **b** : something accomplished : DEED, FEAT **2** : the fulfillment of an obligation, claim, promise, or request : IMPLEMENTATION **3 a** : the action of representing a character in a play **b** : a public presentation or exhibition **4 a** : the ability to perform : EFFICIENCY **b** : the manner in which a mechanism performs — **per·form·a·to·ry** \-mə-,tōr-ē, -,tór-\ *adj*

per·form·ing *adj* : of, relating to, or constituting an art that involves public performance

¹per·fume \'pər-,fyüm, (,)pər-'\ *n* [MF *perfum*] **1** : the scent of something usu. sweet-smelling **2** : a substance that emits a pleasant odor; *esp* : a fluid preparation of floral essences or synthetics and a fixative used for scenting

²per·fume \(,)pər-'fyüm, 'pər-,\ *vt* : to fill or impregnate with an odor (as of flowers) : SCENT

per·fum·er \pə(r)-'fyü-mər\ *n* : one that makes or sells perfumes

per·fum·ery \pə(r)-'fyüm-(ə-)rē\ *n*, *pl* **-er·ies** **1 a** : the art or process of making perfume **b** : the products made by a perfumer **2** : a perfume establishment

per·func·to·ry \pər-'fəŋ(k)-t(ə-)rē\ *adj* [L *perfunct-*, *perfungi* to accomplish, get through with, fr. *per-* through + *fungi* to perform] **1** : characterized by routine or superficiality : MECHANICAL **2** : lacking in interest or enthusiasm : APATHETIC, INDIFFERENT — **per·func·to·ri·ly** \-t(ə-)rə-lē\ *adv* — **per·func·to·ri·ness** \-t(ə-)rē-nəs\ *n*

per·fuse \pər-'fyüz\ *vt* **1** : SUFFUSE **2 a** : to cause to flow or spread : DIFFUSE **b** : to force a fluid through (an organ or tissue) esp. by way of the blood vessels — **per·fu·sion** \-'fyü-zhən\ *n* — **per·fu·sive** \-'fyü-siv, -ziv\ *adj*

per·go·la \'pər-gə-lə, pər-'gō-\ *n* [It] : a structure consisting of posts supporting an open roof in the form of a trellis

per·haps \pər-'(h)aps, 'praps\ *adv* : possibly but not certainly : MAYBE

pe·ri \'pi(ə)r-ē\ *n*, *pl* **peris** [Per *perī*] : a supernatural being in Persian folklore descended from fallen angels and excluded from paradise until penance is accomplished

peri- *prefix* [Gk, around, in excess] **1** : all around : about

⟨*peri*scope⟩ **2** : near ⟨*peri*helion⟩ **3** : enclosing : surrounding ⟨*peri*odontal⟩

per·i·anth \'per-ē-,an(t)th\ *n* : the external envelope of a flower esp. when not differentiated into calyx and corolla — see FLOWER illustration

per·i·car·di·um \,per-ə-'kärd-ē-əm\ *n, pl* **per·i·car·dia** \-ē-ə\ : the conical sac of serous membrane that encloses the heart and the roots of the great blood vessels of vertebrates — **per·i·car·di·al** \-ē-əl\ *adj*

per·i·carp \'per-ə-,kärp\ *n* : the ripened and variously modified walls of a plant ovary that form the substance of a fruit and enclose the seeds — **per·i·car·pi·al** \,per-ə-'kär-pē-əl\ *or* **per·i·car·pic** \-'kär-pik\ *adj*

per·i·chon·dri·um \,per-ə-'kän-drē-əm\ *n, pl* **-dria** \-drē-ə\ [NL, fr. Gk *peri* around + *chondros* cartilage] : a sheath of fibrous tissue enclosing a cartilage — **per·i·chon·dri·al** \-drē-əl\ *adj*

per·i·cy·cle \'per-ə-,sī-kəl\ *n* : a thin layer of parenchymatous or sclerenchymatous cells surrounding the stele in most vascular plants

per·i·derm \'per-ə-,dərm\ *n* : an outer layer of tissue; *esp* : a cortical protective layer of many roots and stems — **per·i·der·mal** \,per-ə-'dər-məl\ *or* **per·i·der·mic** \-mik\ *adj*

per·i·gee \'per-ə-(,)jē\ *n* [Gk *gē* earth] : the point in the orbit of a satellite of the earth or of a vehicle orbiting the earth that is nearest to the center of the earth; *also* : the point nearest a planet or a satellite (as the moon) reached by any object orbiting it — compare APOGEE

pe·rig·y·nous \pə-'rij-ə-nəs\ *adj* **1** : growing from a ring or cup of the receptacle surrounding a pistil ⟨*perigynous* petals⟩ **2** : having perigynous floral organs — **pe·rig·y·ny** \-nē\ *n*

per·i·he·lion \,per-ə-'hēl-yən\ *n* [Gk *hēlios* sun] : the point in the path of a celestial body (as a planet) that is nearest to the sun

¹per·il \'per-əl\ *n* [OF, fr. L *periculum;* akin to E *fear*] **1** : exposure to the risk of being injured, destroyed, or lost ⟨fire put the city in *peril* of destruction⟩ **2** : something that imperils : RISK ⟨*perils* of the highway⟩ **syn** see DANGER

²peril *vt* **-iled** *also* **-illed; -il·ing** *also* **-il·ling** : to expose to danger : HAZARD

per·il·ous \'per-ə-ləs\ *adj* : full of or involving peril : HAZARDOUS — **per·il·ous·ly** *adv* — **per·il·ous·ness** *n*

pe·rim·e·ter \pə-'rim-ət-ər\ *n* **1** : the boundary of a closed plane figure; *also* : the length of this boundary **2** : a line or strip bounding or protecting an area **3** : outer limits

per·i·my·si·um \,per-ə-'miz(h)-ē-əm\ *n, pl* **-sia** \-ē-ə\ [NL, fr. *peri* around + *mys* muscle] : the connective tissue sheath of a muscle

per·i·ne·um \,per-ə-'nē-əm\ *n, pl* **-nea** \-'nē-ə\ [NL, fr. Gk *perinaion*] : an area between the thighs marking the approximate lower pelvic boundary and giving passage to the urinary and genital ducts and rectum — **per·i·ne·al** \-'nē-əl\ *adj*

¹pe·ri·od \'pir-ē-əd\ *n* [Gk *periodos* circuit, period of time, rhetorical period, fr. *peri-* + *hodos* way] **1 a** : an utterance from one full stop to another : SENTENCE **b** : PERIODIC SENTENCE **2 a** : the full pause with which a sentence closes **b** : END, STOP **3** : a punctuation mark . used chiefly to mark the end of a declarative sentence or an abbreviation **4** : the completion of a cycle, a series of events, or a single action : CONCLUSION **5 a** : a portion of time determined by some recurring phenomenon **b** : the interval of time required for a motion or phenomenon to complete a cycle and begin to repeat itself ⟨the *period* of a pendulum⟩ **c** : a single cyclic occurrence of menstruation **6 a** : a chronological division : STAGE **b** : a division of geologic time longer than an epoch and shorter than an era **c** : a stage of culture having a definable place in time and space ⟨the colonial *period*⟩ **7 a** : one of the divisions of the academic year **b** : one of the divisions of the playing time of a game **8** : one of the stages or the number of units in a stage of a periodic function **9** : a series of elements of increasing atomic number as listed in horizontal rows in the periodic table

syn PERIOD, EPOCH, ERA, AGE mean a division of time. PERIOD may designate any extent of time; EPOCH applies to a period begun by some striking or significant event ⟨the steam engine marked a new *epoch* in industry⟩ ERA

suggests a period in history marked by a new or distinct order ⟨*era* of exploration⟩ AGE is applied to a fairly definite period strongly dominated by a central figure ⟨*age* of Jackson⟩ or by a prominent feature ⟨nuclear *age*⟩

²period *adj* : of, relating to, or representing a particular historical period ⟨*period* furniture⟩

pe·ri·od·ic \,pir-ē-'äd-ik\ *adj* **1 a** : occurring at regular intervals **b** : happening repeatedly : RECURRENT **2** : consisting of or containing a series of repeated stages : CYCLIC ⟨*periodic* vibrations⟩ **3** : of or relating to a period

¹pe·ri·od·i·cal \,pir-ē-'äd-i-kəl\ *adj* **1** : PERIODIC 1 **2 a** : published with a fixed interval between the issues or numbers **b** : published in, characteristic of, or connected with a periodical — **pe·ri·od·i·cal·ly** \-k(ə-)lē\ *adv*

²periodical *n* : a periodical publication

periodic function *n* : a mathematical function any value of which recurs at regular intervals

pe·ri·od·ic·i·ty \,pir-ē-ə-'dis-ət-ē\ *n, pl* **-ties** : the quality, state, or fact of being regularly recurrent

periodic law *n* : a law in chemistry: the elements when arranged in the order of their atomic numbers show a periodic variation in most of their properties

periodic motion *n* : a recurrent motion in which the intervals of time required to complete each cycle are equal

periodic sentence *n* : a sentence that has no subordinate or trailing elements following full grammatical statement of the essential idea (as in "yesterday, in broad daylight while I was walking down the street, I saw him")

periodic table *n* : an arrangement of chemical elements based on the periodic law

per·i·odon·tal \,per-ē-ō-'dänt-ᵊl\ *adj* [*peri-* + Gk *odont-, odous* tooth] : surrounding or occurring about the teeth

per·i·os·te·um \,per-ē-'äs-tē-əm\ *n, pl* **-tea** \-tē-ə\ [NL, fr. Gk *osteon* bone] : the membrane of connective tissue that covers all bones except at the surfaces in a joint — **per·i·os·te·al** \-tē-əl\ *adj*

per·i·pa·tet·ic \,per-ə-pə-'tet-ik\ *adj* [Gk *peripatein* to walk about, fr. *peri-* + *patein* to walk] : moving about from place to place : ITINERANT ⟨a *peripatetic* preacher⟩ — **per·i·pa·tet·i·cal·ly** \-'tet-i-k(ə-)lē\ *adv*

pe·rip·a·tus \pə-'rip-ət-əs\ *n* : any of a class (Onychophora) of primitive tropical arthropods in some respects intermediate between annelid worms and typical arthropods

pe·riph·er·al \pə-'rif-(ə-)rəl\ *adj* : of, relating to, located in, or forming a periphery ⟨*peripheral* vision⟩ — **pe·riph·er·al·ly** \-ē\ *adv*

pe·riph·ery \pə-'rif-(ə-)rē\ *n, pl* **-er·ies** [Gk *peripheria,* fr. *peripherein* to carry around, fr. *peri-* + *pherein* to carry] **1** : the perimeter of a closed curve; *also* : the perimeter of a polygon **2** : the external boundary or surface of a body **3 a** : the outer or outermost part of something as distinguished from its more internal regions or center **b** : an area lying beyond the strict limits of a thing

pe·riph·ra·sis \pə-'rif-rə-səs\ *n, pl* **-ra·ses** \-rə-,sēz\ [Gk, fr. *periphrazein* to express periphrastically, fr. *peri-* + *phrazein* to tell] : use of a longer phrasing in place of a possible shorter and plainer form of expression : CIRCUMLOCUTION

per·i·phras·tic \,per-ə-'fras-tik\ *adj* **1** : of, relating to, or characterized by periphrasis **2** : formed by the use of function words or auxiliaries instead of by inflection ⟨*more fair* is a *periphrastic* comparative⟩ — **per·i·phras·ti·cal·ly** \-ti-k(ə-)lē\ *adv*

pe·rique \pə-'rēk\ *n* : a strong-flavored Louisiana tobacco used in smoking mixtures

peri·scope \'per-ə-,skōp\ *n* : a tubular optical instrument containing lenses and mirrors by which an observer (as on a submerged submarine) obtains an otherwise obstructed field of view — **peri·scop·ic** \,per-ə-'skäp-ik\ *adj*

per·ish \'per-ish\ *vi* [OF *periss-, perir,* fr. L *perire,* fr. *per-* to destruction + *ire* to go] : to pass away completely : become destroyed or ruined : DIE

per·ish·a·bil·i·ty \,per-ish-ə-'bil-ət-ē\ *n* : the quality or condition of being perishable

per·ish·a·ble \'per-ish-ə-bəl\ *adj* : liable to spoil or decay ⟨such *perishable* products as fruit, vegetables, butter, and eggs⟩ — **perishable** *n*

pe·ris·so·dac·tyl \pə-,ris-ə-'dak-tᵊl\ *n* [Gk *perissos* excessive, odd + *daktylos* finger, toe] **:** any of an order (Perissodactyla) of hoofed mammals (as the horse or rhinoceros) with an odd number of functional toes on each foot — **perissodactyl** *or* **pe·ris·so·dac·ty·lous** \-tə-ləs\ *adj*

per·i·stal·sis \,per-ə-'stȯl-səs, -'stal-\ *n, pl* **-stal·ses** \-,sēz\ [NL, fr. Gk *peristellein* to wrap around, fr. *peri-* + *stellein* to place] **:** successive waves of involuntary contraction passing along the walls of a hollow muscular structure (as the intestine) and forcing the contents onward — **per·i·stal·tic** \-'stȯl-tik, -'stal-\ *adj* — **per·i·stal·ti·cal·ly** \-ti-k(ə-)lē\ *adv*

per·i·stome \'per-ə-,stōm\ *n* [Gk *stoma* mouth] **1 :** the fringe of teeth surrounding the orifice of a moss capsule **2 :** the region around the mouth in various invertebrates — **per·i·sto·mi·al** \,per-ə-'stō-mē-əl\ *adj*

per·i·style \'per-ə-,stīl\ *n* [Gk *stylos* pillar] **1 :** a row of columns surrounding a building or court **2 :** an open space enclosed by a row of columns

per·i·the·ci·um \,per-ə-'thē-s(h)ē-əm\ *n, pl* **-cia** \-s(h)ē-ə\ [NL, fr. Gk *thēkion*, dim. of *thēkē* case, fr. *tithenai* to place] **:** a hollow fruiting body in various ascomycetous fungi that contains the asci and usu. opens by a terminal pore — **per·i·the·cial** \-sh(ē-)əl, -sē-əl\ *adj*

per·i·to·ne·um \,per-ət-ᵊn-'ē-əm\ *n, pl* **-ne·ums** *or* **-nea** \-'ē-ə\ [Gk *peritonaion*, fr. *peri-* + *ton-, teinein* to stretch] **:** the smooth transparent serous membrane that lines the cavity of the abdomen and encloses the abdominal and pelvic viscera — **per·i·to·ne·al** \-'ē-əl\ *adj*

per·i·to·ni·tis \,per-ət-ᵊn-'īt-əs\ *n* **:** inflammation of the peritoneum

peri·wig \'per-i-,wig\ *n* [by folk etymology fr. MF *perruque*] **:** WIG

¹per·i·win·kle \'per-i-,wiŋ-kəl\ *n* [OE *perwince*, fr. L *pervinca*] **:** any of several trailing or woody evergreen herbs of the dogbane family; *esp* **:** a European creeper widely grown as a ground cover and for its usu. blue flowers

²periwinkle *n* [alter. of OE *pīnewincle*] **:** any of various gastropod mollusks; *esp* **:** any of numerous small edible littoral marine snails

per·jure \'per-jər\ *vt* **per·jured; per·jur·ing** \'pərj-(ə-)riŋ\ [L *perjurare*, fr. *per-* to destruction, to the bad + *jurare* to swear] **:** to make (oneself) guilty of perjury

per·jur·er \'per-jər-ər\ *n* **:** a person guilty of perjury

per·ju·ri·ous \(,)pər-'jur-ē-əs\ *adj* **:** marked by perjury — **per·ju·ri·ous·ly** *adv*

per·ju·ry \'pərj-(ə-)rē\ *n, pl* **-ries :** violation of an oath by knowingly swearing to what is untrue **:** false swearing

perk \'pərk\ *vb* [ME *perken* to be jaunty] **1 :** to lift quickly, saucily, or alertly ⟨a dog *perking* its ears⟩ **2 :** to smarten one's appearance — **perk up :** to be or become lively **:** regain vigor or cheerfulness

perky \'pər-kē\ *adj* **perk·i·er; -est :** JAUNTY, SAUCY, LIVELY — **perk·i·ly** \-kə-lē\ *adv* — **perk·i·ness** \-kē-nəs\ *n*

per·lite \'per-,līt\ *n* **:** glassy cooled volcanic lava of shelly structure that when expanded by heat forms a lightweight material used esp. in concrete and plaster

per·ma·frost \'pər-mə-,frȯst\ *n* **:** a permanently frozen layer at variable depth below the earth's surface in frigid regions

per·ma·nence \'pər-mə-nən(t)s\ *n* **:** the quality or state of being permanent

per·ma·nen·cy \-nən-sē\ *n, pl* **-cies :** PERMANENCE

¹per·ma·nent \'pər-mə-nənt\ *adj* [L *permanēre* to endure, fr. *per-* + *manēre* to remain] **:** lasting or intended to last for a very long time **:** not temporary **:** not changing ⟨a *permanent* address⟩ ⟨the *permanent* population of a city⟩ **syn** see LASTING — **per·ma·nent·ly** *adv* — **per·ma·nent·ness** *n*

²permanent *n* **:** a long-lasting hair wave produced by mechanical and chemical means

permanent magnet *n* **:** a magnet that retains its magnetism after removal of the magnetizing force

permanent tooth *n* **:** one of the second set of teeth of a mammal that follow the milk teeth, typically persist into old age, and in man are 32 in number

per·man·ga·nate \(,)pər-'maŋ-gə-,nāt\ *n* **:** POTASSIUM PERMANGANATE

per·me·a·bil·i·ty \,pər-mē-ə-'bil-ət-ē\ *n, pl* **-ties 1 :** the quality or state of being permeable **2 :** the property of a magnetizable substance that determines the degree to which it will conduct magnetic lines of force usu. as compared with air taken as 1

per·me·a·ble \'pər-mē-ə-bəl\ *adj* **:** having pores or openings that permit liquids or gases to pass through ⟨a *permeable* membrane⟩ ⟨*permeable* limestone⟩ — **per·me·a·ble·ness** *n* — **per·me·a·bly** \-blē\ *adv*

per·me·ance \'pər-mē-ən(t)s\ *n* **:** PERMEATION

per·me·ate \'pər-mē-,āt\ *vb* [L *permeare*, fr. *per-* through + *meare* to pass] **1 :** to pass through something which has pores or small openings or is of loose texture **:** seep through ⟨water *permeates* sand⟩ **2 :** to spread throughout **:** PERVADE ⟨a room *permeated* with the odor of tobacco⟩ — **per·me·a·tion** \,pər-mē-'ā-shən\ *n* — **per·me·a·tive** \'pər-mē-,āt-iv\ *adj*

Perm·ian \'pər-mē-ən\ *n* **:** the most recent period of the Paleozoic era; *also* **:** the corresponding system of rocks — **Permian** *adj*

per·mis·si·ble \pər-'mis-ə-bəl\ *adj* **:** that may be permitted **:** ALLOWABLE — **per·mis·si·bil·i·ty** \-,mis-ə-'bil-ət-ē\ *n* — **per·mis·si·ble·ness** \-'mis-ə-bəl-nəs\ *n* — **per·mis·si·bly** \-blē\ *adv*

per·mis·sion \pər-'mish-ən\ *n* **1 :** the act of permitting **2 :** the consent of a person in authority **:** LEAVE, AUTHORIZATION

per·mis·sive \pər-'mis-iv\ *adj* **1 :** granting or tending to grant permission **:** ALLOWING **2 :** not forbidden **:** ALLOWABLE, OPTIONAL — **per·mis·sive·ly** *adv* — **per·mis·sive·ness** *n*

¹per·mit \pər-'mit\ *vb* **per·mit·ted; per·mit·ting** [L *permiss-, permittere*, fr. *per-* through + *mittere* to let go, send] **1 :** to consent to expressly or formally **:** give permission **2 :** to make possible **:** give an opportunity **:** ALLOW ⟨if time *permits*⟩ ⟨made himself as comfortable as the cold ground would *permit*⟩ — **per·mit·ter** *n*

²per·mit \'pər-,mit, pər-'\ *n* **:** a written statement of permission given by one having authority **:** LICENSE ⟨a *permit* to keep a dog⟩

per·mu·ta·tion \,pər-myu-'tā-shən\ *n* [L *permutare* to change completely, fr. *per-* + *mutare* to change] **1 :** a thorough change in character or condition **:** TRANSFORMATION **2 a :** the act or process of changing the order of a set of objects **b :** an ordered arrangement of a set of objects — **per·mu·ta·tion·al** \-shnəl, -shən-ᵊl\ *adj*

per·ni·cious \pər-'nish-əs\ *adj* [L *pernicies* destruction, fr. *per-* + *nec-, nex* violent death] **:** very destructive or injurious ⟨a *pernicious* disease⟩ ⟨a *pernicious* habit⟩ — **per·ni·cious·ly** *adv* — **per·ni·cious·ness** *n*

pernicious anemia *n* **:** a severe anemia in which the red blood cells progressively decrease in number and increase in size and various systemic symptoms occur and which is associated with a deficiency of vitamin B_{12}

per·nick·e·ty \pər-'nik-ət-ē\ *var of* PERSNICKETY

per·o·ra·tion \,per-ər-'ā-shən\ *n* **1 :** the concluding part of a discourse and esp. an oration **2 :** a highly rhetorical speech — **per·orate** \'per-ər-,āt\ *vi* — **per·ora·tion·al** \,per-ər-'ā-shnəl, -shən-ᵊl\ *adj*

¹per·ox·ide \pə-'räk-,sīd\ *n* **1 :** an oxide containing a high proportion of oxygen; *esp* **:** a compound (as hydrogen peroxide H_2O_2) in which oxygen is held to be joined to oxygen **2 :** HYDROGEN PEROXIDE

²peroxide *vt* **:** to bleach (hair) with hydrogen peroxide

¹per·pen·dic·u·lar \,pər-pən-'dik-yə-lər\ *adj* [L *perpendiculum* plumb line, fr. *per-* + *pendēre* to hang] **1 a :** exactly vertical or upright **b :** being at right angles to a given line or plane **2 :** extremely steep **:** PRECIPITOUS **syn** see VERTICAL — **per·pen·dic·u·lar·i·ty** \-,dik-yə-'lar-ət-ē\ *n* — **per·pen·dic·u·lar·ly** \-'dik-yə-lər-lē\ *adv*

²perpendicular *n* **:** a line at right angles to the plane of the horizon or to another line or surface

per·pe·trate \'pər-pə-,trāt\ *vt* [L *perpetrare*, fr. *per-* + *patrare* to accomplish] **:** to be guilty of doing or performing ⟨*perpetrate* a crime⟩ **:** COMMIT — **per·pe·tra·tion** \,pər-pə-'trā-shən\ *n* — **per·pe·tra·tor** \'pər-pə-,trāt-ər\ *n*

per·pet·u·al \pər-'pech-(ə-w)əl\ *adj* [L *perpetuus*, fr. *per-* + *petere* to go to] **1 a :** continuing forever **:** EVERLASTING **b (1) :** valid for all time **(2) :** holding for life or for an unlimited time **2 :** occurring continually **:** indefinitely long-continued

d

b ───── *c*

    a

bc horizontal,
ad perpendicular

: CONSTANT **3** : blooming continuously throughout the season — **per·pet·u·al·ly** \-ē\ *adv*

perpetual calendar *n* : a table for finding the day of the week for any one of a wide range of dates

per·pet·u·ate \par-'pech-ə-,wāt\ *vt* : to make perpetual or cause to last indefinitely — **per·pet·u·a·tion** \-,pech-ə-'wā-shən\ *n* — **per·pet·u·a·tor** \-'pech-ə-,wāt-ər\ *n*

per·pe·tu·i·ty \,pər-pə-'t(y)ü-ət-ē\ *n, pl* **-ties** **1** : perpetual existence or duration ⟨bequeathed to them in *perpetuity*⟩ **2** : endless time : ETERNITY

per·plex \par-'pleks\ *vt* [L *perplexus* involved, confused, fr. *per-* thoroughly + *plexus* involved, fr. pp. of *plectere* to braid] **1** : to disturb mentally; *esp* : CONFUSE, BEWILDER **2** : to make intricate or involved : COMPLICATE **syn** see PUZZLE

per·plexed \-'plekst\ *adj* **1** : filled with uncertainty : PUZZLED **2** : full of difficulty : COMPLICATED — **per·plexed·ly** \-'plek-səd-lē, -'pleks-tlē\ *adv*

per·plex·i·ty \par-'plek-sət-ē\ *n, pl* **-ties** **1** : the state of being perplexed : BEWILDERMENT **2** : something that perplexes **3** : ENTANGLEMENT

per·qui·site \'pər-kwə-zət\ *n* [ML *perquisitum* property acquired by other means than inheritance, fr. neut. of *perquisitus*, pp. of *perquirere* to acquire, fr. L, to search out, fr. *per-* + *quaerere* to seek] **1** : a profit made from one's employment in addition to one's regular pay; *esp* : such a profit when expected or promised **2** : TIP

per·ry \'per-ē\ *n* : the expressed juice of pears often made alcoholic by fermentation

per se \(,)pər-'sā\ *adv* [L] : by, of, or in itself or oneself or themselves : as such : INTRINSICALLY

per second per second *adv* : per second every second — used of a rate of acceleration over an indefinite period

per·se·cute \'pər-si-,kyüt\ *vt* [LL *persecut-, persequi*, fr. L, to pursue, fr. *per-* through + *sequi* to follow] **1** : to harass in a manner to injure, grieve, or afflict; *esp* : to cause to suffer because of belief **2** : to annoy with persistent or urgent approaches : PESTER — **per·se·cu·tor** \-,kyüt-ər\ *n* — **per·se·cu·to·ry** \-kyü-,tōr-ē, -,tôr-\ *adj*

per·se·cu·tion \,pər-si-'kyü-shən\ *n* **1** : the act or practice of persecuting esp. those who differ in origin, religion, or social outlook **2** : the condition of being persecuted, harassed, or annoyed

Per·seph·o·ne \pər-'sef-ə-nē\ *n* : a daughter of Zeus and Demeter abducted by Pluto and made his wife and queen

Per·seus \'pər-,süs, -sē-əs\ *n* **1** : a son of Zeus and Danaë and slayer of Medusa **2** : a northern constellation between Taurus and Cassiopeia

per·se·ver·ance \,pər-sə-'vir-ən(t)s\ *n* : the action, condition, or an instance of persevering : STEADFASTNESS

per·se·vere \,pər-sə-'vi(ə)r\ *vi* [L *perseverare*, fr. *per-* throughout + *severus* severe] : to keep at something in spite of difficulties, opposition, or discouragement

per·se·ver·ing \-'vi(ə)r-iŋ\ *adj* : showing perseverance : PERSISTENT — **per·se·ver·ing·ly** \-iŋ-lē\ *adv*

Per·sian \'pər-zhən\ *n* **1** : one of the people of Persia: as **a** : one of the ancient Iranian Caucasians who under Cyrus and his successors dominated western Asia **b** : a member of one of the peoples forming the modern Iranian nation **2** : the modern language of Iran and western Afghanistan used also in Pakistan and by Indian Muslims as a literary language **3** : a thin soft silk formerly used esp. for linings — **Persian** *adj*

Persian cat *n* : a stocky round-headed domestic cat with long and silky fur that is the long-haired cat of shows and fanciers

Persian lamb *n* : a pelt obtained from karakul lambs older than those yielding broadtail and characterized by very silky tightly curled fur

per·si·flage \'pər-sə-,fläzh, 'per-\ *n* [F, fr. *persifler* to banter, fr. *per-* + *siffler* to whistle, hiss, boo, fr. L *sibilare*] : frivolous or lightly derisive talk or manner of treating a subject

per·sim·mon \pər-'sim-ən\ *n* [of Algonquian origin] **1** : any of a genus of trees of the ebony family with hard fine wood, oblong leaves, and small bell-shaped white flowers **2** : the usu. orange several-seeded berry of a persimmon that resembles a plum and is edible when fully ripe

per·sist \pər-'sist, -'zist\ *vi* [L *persistere*, fr. *per-* + *sistere* to take a stand, stand firm] **1** : to go on resolutely in spite of opposition, warnings, or pleas : PERSEVERE **2** : to last on and on : continue to exist ⟨rain *persisting* for days⟩ — **per·sist·er** *n*

per·sist·ence \pər-'sis-tən(t)s, -'zis-\ *n* **1** : the act or fact of persisting **2** : the quality of being persistent : the power of going on in spite of difficulties : PERSEVERANCE

per·sist·en·cy \-tən-sē\ *n* : PERSISTENCE, LASTINGNESS

per·sist·ent \-tənt\ *adj* **1** : continuing, existing, or acting for a long or longer than usual time ⟨a *persistent* cough⟩ ⟨*persistent* gills⟩⟨a *persistent* drug⟩ **2** : DOGGED, TENACIOUS ⟨a *persistent* salesman⟩ — **per·sist·ent·ly** *adv*

per·snick·e·ty \pər-'snik-ət-ē\ *adj* : fussy about small details : FASTIDIOUS

per·son \'pərs-°n\ *n* [L *persona* actor's mask, character in a play, person] **1** : a human being : INDIVIDUAL **2** : CHARACTER, GUISE **3** : one of the three modes of being in the Godhead as understood by Trinitarians **4 a** : bodily appearance **b** : the body of a human being **5 a** : the individual personality of a human being : SELF **b** : bodily presence ⟨appear in *person*⟩ **6** : an entity (as a human being or corporation) recognized by law as having rights and duties **7** : reference of a segment of discourse to the speaker, to one spoken to, or to one spoken of as indicated by means of certain pronouns or in many languages by verb inflection

per·son·a·ble \'pərs-nə-bəl, -°n-ə-bəl\ *adj* : pleasing in appearance : attractive in looks and manner — **per·son·a·ble·ness** *n*

per·son·age \'pərs-nij, -°n-ij\ *n* **1** : a person of rank or distinction : a famous person **2** : a character in a book or play

¹**per·son·al** \'pərs-nəl, -°n-əl\ *adj* **1** : of, relating to, or belonging to a person : PRIVATE **2 a** : done in person or proceeding from a single person **b** : carried on between individuals directly **3** : relating to the person or body **4** : closely related to an individual : INTIMATE **5** : denoting grammatical person

²**personal** *n* : a short newspaper paragraph relating to a person or group or to personal matters

personal effects *n pl* : possessions having a close relationship to one's person

personal equation *n* : variation (as in scientific observation) due to the personal peculiarities of an individual; *also* : a correction or allowance made for such variation

per·son·al·i·ty \,pərs-°n-'al-ət-ē\ *n, pl* **-ties** **1** : the state of being a person **2** : the totality of characteristics or traits of a person that makes him different from other persons : INDIVIDUALITY **3** : pleasing qualities of character ⟨lack *personality*⟩ **4** : a person who has strongly marked qualities ⟨a great stage *personality*⟩ **5** : a personal remark : a slighting reference to a person ⟨use *personalities* in an argument⟩

per·son·al·ize \'pərs-nə-,līz, -°n-ə-\ *vt* **1** : PERSONIFY **2** : to make personal or individual; *esp* : to mark as belonging to a particular person ⟨*personalized* shirts⟩⟨*personalized* stationery⟩

per·son·al·ly \'pərs-nə-lē, -°n-ə-\ *adv* **1** : in person ⟨attend to the matter *personally*⟩ **2** : as a person : in personality ⟨*personally* attractive but not very trustworthy⟩ **3** : for oneself : as far as oneself is concerned ⟨*personally*, I am against it⟩

personal pronoun *n* : a pronoun (as *I, you,* or *they*) expressing a distinction of person

personal property *n* : movable property (as money, clothing, furnishings, or automobiles) other than real property : CHATTELS

per·son·al·ty \'pərs-nəl-tē, -°n-əl-\ *n, pl* **-ties** : PERSONAL PROPERTY

per·so·na non gra·ta \pər-,sō-nə-,nän-'grat-ə, -'grät-\ *n, pl* **per·so·nae non gra·tae** \-nē-,nän-'grat-ē, -,nī-,nän-'grat-,ī, -'grät-\ [NL] : an unacceptable person; *esp* : a diplomat who is personally not acceptable to a foreign government to which he is accredited

per·son·ate \'pərs-°n-āt\ *vt* **1** : IMPERSONATE, REPRESENT **2** : to invest with personality or personal characteristics — **per·son·a·tion** \,pərs-°n-'ā-shən\ *n* — **per·son·a·tive** \'pərs-°n-,āt-iv\ *adj* — **per·son·a·tor** \-,āt-ər\ *n*

per·son·i·fi·ca·tion \pər-,sän-ə-fə-'kā-shən\ *n* **1** : the act of personifying **2** : an imaginary being thought of as representing a thing or an idea **3** : EMBODIMENT, INCARNATION ⟨he is the *personification* of generosity⟩ **4** : a figure

j joke; ŋ sing; ō flow; ô flaw; ȯi coin; th thin; t͟h this; ü loot; u̇ foot; y yet; yü few; yu̇ furious; zh vision

of speech in which a lifeless object or abstract quality is spoken of as if alive

per·son·i·fi·er \pər-'sän-ə-,fī(-ə)r\ *n* : one that personifies

per·son·i·fy \-,fī\ *vt* **-fied;** **-fy·ing** **1** : to think of or represent as a person ⟨*personify* the forces of nature⟩ ⟨in "Justice is blind", *justice is personified*⟩ **2** : to represent in a physical form ⟨the law was *personified* in the sheriff⟩ **3** : to serve as the perfect type or example of ⟨a man who *personified* kindness⟩

per·son·nel \,pərs-ᵊn-'el\ *n* [F] : a group of persons employed (as in a public service, a factory, or an office)

¹per·spec·tive \pər-'spek-tiv\ *n* [MF, prob. modif. of It *prospettiva,* fr. *prospetto* view, prospect, fr. L *prospectus*] **1** : the art or technique of painting or drawing a scene so that objects in it have apparent depth and distance **2** : the power to see or think of things in their true relationship to each other **3** : the true relationship of objects or events to one another ⟨view the events of the last year in *perspective*⟩ **4 a** : a visible scene; *esp* : one giving a definite impression of distance **b** : a mental view or prospect **5** : the appearance to the eye of objects in respect to their relative distance and positions

²perspective *adj* : of, relating to, or seen in perspective — **per·spec·tive·ly** *adv*

per·spi·ca·cious \,pər-spə-'kā-shəs\ *adj* [L *perspicac-, perspicax,* fr. *perspicere* to see through, see clearly, fr. *per-* through + *specere* to see] : having or showing keen understanding or discernment — **per·spi·ca·cious·ly** *adv* — **per·spi·ca·cious·ness** *n*

per·spi·cac·i·ty \,pər-spə-'kas-ət-ē\ *n* : the quality or state of being perspicacious : acuteness of understanding or discernment

per·spi·cu·i·ty \,pər-spə-'kyü-ət-ē\ *n* : the quality of being easily understandable : clearness of expression or thought

per·spic·u·ous \pər-'spik-yə-wəs\ *adj* [L *perspicuus,* lit., transparent, fr. *perspicere* to see through] **1** : plain to the understanding : CLEAR **2** : expressing oneself clearly — **per·spic·u·ous·ly** *adv* — **per·spic·u·ous·ness** *n*

per·spi·ra·tion \,pər-spə-'rā-shən\ *n* **1** : the act or process of perspiring **2** : a saline fluid secreted by the sweat glands : SWEAT — **per·spi·ra·to·ry** \pər-'spī-rə-,tōr-ē, -,tór-\ *adj*

per·spire \pər-'spī(ə)r\ *vi* [F *perspirer,* fr. L *per-* through + *spirare* to blow, breathe] : to secrete and emit perspiration : SWEAT

per·suad·a·ble \pər-'swäd-ə-bəl\ *adj* : capable of being persuaded

per·suade \pər-'swäd\ *vt* [L *persuas-, persuadēre,* fr. *per-* + *suadēre* to urge] : to win over to a belief or to a course of action by argument or earnest request : induce to do or believe something — **per·suad·er** *n*

per·sua·si·ble \pər-'swä-zə-bəl\ *adj* : PERSUADABLE

per·sua·sion \pər-'swā-zhən\ *n* **1** : the act of persuading **2** : the power or ability to persuade : persuasive quality **3** : the state of being persuaded **4** : a way of believing : BELIEF; *esp* : a system of religious beliefs **5** : a group having the same religious beliefs

per·sua·sive \pər-'swā-siv, -ziv\ *adj* : tending to persuade : having the power or effect of persuading ⟨a *persuasive* speech⟩ — **per·sua·sive·ly** *adv* — **per·sua·sive·ness** *n*

pert \'pərt\ *adj* [ME, open, bold, pert, modif. of OF *apert,* fr. L *apertus* open, fr. pp. of *aperire* to open] **1 a** : saucily free and forward : IMPUDENT **b** : being trim and chic : JAUNTY **c** : piquantly stimulating **2** : LIVELY, VIVACIOUS — **pert·ly** *adv* — **pert·ness** *n*

per·tain \pər-'tān\ *vi* [MF *partenir,* fr. L *pertinēre* to hold out, reach to, pertain, fr. *per-* through + *tenēre* to hold] **1** : to belong to a person or thing as a part, quality, or function ⟨duties that *pertain* to an office⟩ **2** : to refer or relate to a person or thing ⟨books *pertaining* to birds⟩

per·ti·na·cious \,pərt-ᵊn-'ā-shəs\ *adj* [L *pertinac-, pertinax,* fr. *pertinēre* to hold out] **1** : holding strongly to an opinion, purpose, or course of action **2** : stubbornly or annoyingly persistent **syn** see OBSTINATE — **per·ti·na·cious·ly** *adv* — **per·ti·na·cious·ness** *n* — **per·ti·nac·i·ty** \,pərt-ᵊn-'as-ət-ē\ *n*

per·ti·nent \'pərt-ᵊn-ənt\ *adj* [L *pertinēre* to pertain] : having to do with the subject or matter that is being considered : being to the point ⟨a *pertinent* suggestion⟩ — **per·ti·nence** \-ᵊn-ən(t)s\ *or* **per·ti·nen·cy** \-ᵊn-ən-sē\ *n* — **per·ti·nent·ly** *adv*

per·turb \pər-'tərb\ *vt* [L *perturbare* to throw into confusion, fr. *per-* + *turbare* to disturb] **1** : to disturb greatly in mind : DISQUIET **2** : to throw into confusion : AGITATE **syn** see DISTURB — **per·turb·a·ble** \-'tər-bə-bəl\ *adj*

per·tur·ba·tion \,pərt-ər-'bā-shən, ,pər-,tər-\ *n* **1** : the action of perturbing : the state of being perturbed **2** : a cause of worry or disquiet **3** : a disturbance of the regular motion of a celestial body produced by some force additional to that which causes its regular motion — **per·tur·ba·tion·al** \-shnəl, -shən-ᵊl\ *adj*

per·tus·sis \pər-'təs-əs\ *n* [NL, fr. L *per-,* intensive prefix + *tussis* cough] : WHOOPING COUGH

Pe·ru current \pə-,rü-\ *n* : a cold current of the south Pacific flowing north and northwest along the coast of northern Chile, Peru, and Ecuador — called also *Humboldt current*

pe·ruke \pə-'rük\ *n* [MF *perruque,* fr. It *parrucca*] : WIG

pe·rus·al \pə-'rü-zəl\ *n* : the action of perusing

pe·ruse \pə-'rüz\ *vt* [ME *perusen*] : READ; *esp* : to read carefully or thoroughly — **pe·rus·er** *n*

Pe·ru·vi·an bark \pə-,rü-vē-ən-\ *n* : CINCHONA 2

per·vade \pər-'vād\ *vt* [L *pervas-, pervadere,* fr. *per-* through + *vadere* to go] : to spread or become diffused throughout every part of — **per·va·sion** \-'vā-zhən\ *n* — **per·va·sive** \-'vā-siv, -ziv\ *adj* — **per·va·sive·ly** *adv* — **per·va·sive·ness** *n*

per·verse \(,)pər-'vərs, 'pər-\ *adj* [L *perversus,* fr. pp. of *pervertere* to pervert] **1** : turned away from what is right or good : CORRUPT **2 a** : obstinate in opposing what is right, reasonable, or accepted : WRONGHEADED **b** : arising from or showing stubbornness or obstinacy **3** : marked by peevishness or petulance : CRANKY — **per·verse·ly** *adv* — **per·verse·ness** *n*

per·ver·sion \pər-'vər-zhən\ *n* **1** : the action of perverting : the condition of being perverted **2** : a perverted form **3** : abnormal sexual behavior

per·ver·si·ty \pər-'vər-sət-ē\ *n, pl* **-ties** : the quality, state, or an instance of being perverse

¹per·vert \pər-'vərt\ *vt* [L *pervertere* to overturn, corrupt, pervert, fr. *per-* + *vertere* to turn] **1 a** : to cause to turn aside or away from what is good or true or morally right : CORRUPT **b** : to cause to turn aside or away from what is generally done or accepted : MISDIRECT **2 a** : to divert to a wrong end or purpose : MISUSE **b** : to twist the meaning or sense of : MISINTERPRET — **per·ver·sive** \-'vər-siv, -ziv\ *adj* — **per·vert·er** *n*

²per·vert \'pər-,vərt\ *n* : one that is perverted; *esp* : one given to some form of sexual perversion

per·vert·ed \pər-'vərt-əd\ *adj* **1** : TWISTED, CORRUPT **2** : marked by perversion — **per·vert·ed·ly** *adv* — **per·vert·ed·ness** *n*

per·vi·ous \'pər-vē-əs\ *adj* [L *pervius,* fr. *per-* through + *via* way] : allowing entrance or passage : PERMEABLE ⟨*pervious* rock⟩ — **per·vi·ous·ness** *n*

Pe·sach \'pä-,säk\ *n* [Heb *pesaḥ*] : PASSOVER

pe·se·ta \pə-'sāt-ə\ *n* [Sp, fr. dim. of *peso*] **1** : the basic monetary unit of Spain **2** : a coin or note representing one peseta

pes·ky \'pes-kē\ *adj* **pes·ki·er; -est** : ANNOYING, TROUBLESOME, VEXATIOUS — **pes·ki·ly** \-kə-lē\ *adv* — **pes·ki·ness** \-kē-nəs\ *n*

pe·so \'pā-sō\ *n, pl* **pesos** [Sp, lit., weight, fr. L *pensum,* fr. *pendere* to weigh] **1** : an old silver coin of Spain or Spanish America equal to eight reals **2 a** : the basic monetary unit of any of several countries (as Argentina, Mexico, the Republic of the Philippines) **b** : a coin or note representing one peso

pes·si·mism \'pes-ə-,miz-əm\ *n* [L *pessimus* worst] **1** : an inclination to emphasize adverse aspects, conditions, and possibilities or to expect the worst possible outcome **2** : a belief that evil is more common or powerful than good — **pes·si·mist** \-məst\ *n*

pes·si·mis·tic \,pes-ə-'mis-tik\ *adj* **1** : lacking in hope that one's troubles will end or that success or happiness will come : GLOOMY ⟨*pessimistic* about the stock market⟩ **2** : having the belief that evil is more common or powerful than good **syn** see CYNICAL — **pes·si·mis·ti·cal·ly** \-ti-k(ə-)lē\ *adv*

pest \'pest\ *n* [L *pestis*] **1** : an epidemic disease with a high mortality; *esp* : PLAGUE **2** : something resembling

ə abut; ə kitten; ər further; a back; ā bake; ä cot, cart; aù out; ch chin; e less; ē easy; g gift; i trip; ī life

a pest in destructiveness; *esp* : a plant or animal detrimental to man **3** : one that pesters or annoys : NUISANCE

pes·ter \'pes-tər\ *vt* **pes·tered; pes·ter·ing** \-t(ə-)riŋ\ [MF *empestrer* to hobble (a horse), embarrass] : ANNOY, BOTHER

pest·hole \'pest-‚hōl\ *n* : a place in which pestilences are common

pest·house \-‚haús\ *n* : a shelter or hospital for those infected with a contagious or epidemic disease

pes·ti·cide \'pes-tə-‚sīd\ *n* : an agent used to destroy pests — **pes·ti·cid·al** \‚pes-tə-'sīd-ᵊl\ *adj*

pes·tif·er·ous \pe-'stif-(ə-)rəs\ *adj* **1** : dangerous to society : PERNICIOUS **2** : carrying or propagating infection **3** : ANNOYING, TROUBLESOME — **pes·tif·er·ous·ly** *adv* — **pes·tif·er·ous·ness** *n*

pes·ti·lence \'pes-tə-lən(t)s\ *n* : a contagious or infectious epidemic disease that is virulent and devastating; *esp* : BUBONIC PLAGUE

pes·ti·lent \-lənt\ *adj* [L *pestilent-, pestilens* pestilential, fr. *pestis* plague] **1** : dangerous or destructive to life : DEADLY ⟨a *pestilent* drug⟩; *also* : being or conveying a pestilence ⟨a *pestilent* disease⟩ ⟨*pestilent* infections⟩ **2** : harmful or dangerous to society : PERNICIOUS ⟨the *pestilent* influence of the slums⟩ **3** : VEXING, IRRITATING ⟨a *pestilent* child⟩ — **pes·ti·lent·ly** *adv*

pes·ti·len·tial \‚pes-tə-'len-chəl\ *adj* : causing or likely to cause pestilence : PESTILENT — **pes·ti·len·tial·ly** \-'lench-(ə-)lē\ *adv*

pes·tle \'pes-əl\ *n* [MF *pestel*, fr. L *pistillum*, fr. *pist-, pinsere* to pound] : a usu. club-shaped implement for pounding or grinding substances in a mortar — **pestle** *vt*

¹pet \'pet\ *n* **1** : a domesticated animal kept for pleasure rather than utility **2 a** : a pampered and usu. spoiled child **b** : a person who is treated with unusual kindness or consideration : DARLING

²pet *adj* **1** : kept or treated as a pet **2** : expressing fondness or endearment **3** : FAVORITE

³pet *vb* **pet·ted; pet·ting 1** : to stroke in a gentle or loving manner **2** : to treat with unusual kindness and consideration : PAMPER **3** : to engage in amorous embracing, caressing, and kissing — **pet·ter** *n*

⁴pet *n* : a fit of peevishness, sulkiness, or anger

pet·al \'pet-ᵊl\ *n* [NL *petalum*, fr. Gk *petalon*] : one of the often brightly colored modified leaves making up the corolla of a flower — see FLOWER illustration — **pet·aled** *or* **pet·alled** \-ᵊld\ *adj* — **pet·al·less** \-ᵊl-(l)əs\ *adj* — **pet·al·like** \-ᵊl-‚(l)īk\ *adj*

pet·al·oid \'pet-ᵊl-‚óid\ *adj* : resembling a flower petal

pe·tard \pə-'tär(d)\ *n* [MF] : a case containing an explosive to break down a door or gate or breach a wall

pet cock \'pet-‚käk\ *n* : a small cock, faucet, or valve for letting out air, releasing compression, or draining

pe·te·chia \pə-'tē-kē-ə\ *n, pl* **-chi·ae** \-kē-‚ī, -kē-‚ē\ : one of the tiny purple or hemorrhagic spots appearing in skin or mucous membrane esp. in some diseases — **pe·te·chi·al** \-kē-əl\ *adj* — **pe·te·chi·ate** \-kē-ət\ *adj*

pe·ter \'pēt-ər\ *vi* : to diminish gradually and come to an end : give out ⟨the stream *peters* out⟩

Pe·ter \'pēt-ər\ *n* **1** : a fisherman of Galilee chosen as one of the twelve apostles **2** — see BIBLE table

Pe·ter's pence \‚pēt-ərz-\ *n* [fr. the tradition that St. Peter founded the papal see] **1** : an annual tribute of a penny formerly paid by each householder in England to the papal see **2** : a voluntary annual contribution made by Roman Catholics to the pope

pet·i·ole \'pet-ē-‚ōl\ *n* [L *petiolus*] **1** : the stem of a leaf — see LEAF illustration **2** : STALK; *esp* : a narrow segment joining the abdomen and thorax in some insects (as wasps) — **pet·i·o·lar** \‚pet-ē-'ō-lər\ *adj* — **pet·i·o·late** \'pet-ē-ə-‚lāt\ *or* **pet·i·oled** \'pet-ē-‚ōld\ *adj*

pet·it \'pet-ē, 'pet-ət\ *adj* [ME, small, minor, fr. MF, small] : PETTY **1** — chiefly in legal compounds

pe·tite \pə-'tēt\ *adj* [F, fem. of *petit* small] : small and trim of figure : LITTLE ⟨a *petite* young lady⟩ — **pe·tite·ness** *n*

pe·tit four \‚pet-ē-'fō(ə)r, -'fó(ə)r\ *n, pl* **petits fours** *or* **petit fours** \-ē-'fō(ə)rz, -'fó(ə)rz\ [F, lit., small oven] : a small frosted and ornamented cake cut from pound or sponge cake

¹pe·ti·tion \pə-'tish-ən\ *n* [L *petit-, petere* to seek, request] **1** : an earnest request : ENTREATY **2** : a formal written request made to a superior or authority **3** : something asked or requested — **pe·ti·tion·ary** \-'tish-ə-‚ner-ē\ *adj*

²petition *vb* **pe·ti·tioned; pe·ti·tion·ing** \-'tish-(ə-)niŋ\ : to make a request to or for : SOLICIT; *esp* : to make a formal written request — **pe·ti·tion·er** \-'tish-(ə-)nər\ *n*

petit jury *n* : a jury of twelve persons impaneled to try and decide the facts at issue in causes for trial in a court

pe·tit mal \pə-‚tē-'mäl\ *n* [F, lit., little illness] : a mild form of epilepsy

pe·tit point \'pet-ē-‚póint\ *n* [F, lit., small point] : TENT STITCH; *also* : embroidery made with this stitch

petr- *or* **petri-** *or* **petro-** *comb form* [Gk *petros* stone & *petra* rock] : stone : rock ⟨*petrology*⟩

Pe·trar·chan \pi-'trär-kən, pe-\ *adj* : of, relating to, or characteristic of Petrarch or his writings

pet·rel \'pe-trəl\ *n* **1** : any of various small long-winged seabirds that fly far from land **2** : STORM PETREL

Pe·tri dish \‚pē-trē-\ *n* [after Julius R. *Petri* d1921 German bacteriologist] : a small shallow dish of thin glass with a loose cover used esp. for cultures in bacteriology

pet·ri·fac·tion \‚pe-trə-'fak-shən\ *n* **1** : the process of petrifying or state of being petrified **2** : something that is petrified — **pet·ri·fac·tive** \-'fak-tiv\ *adj*

pet·ri·fi·ca·tion \‚pe-trə-fə-'kā-shən\ *n* : PETRIFACTION

pet·ri·fy \'pe-trə-‚fī\ *vb* **-fied; -fy·ing 1** : to convert (an organic object) into stony material **2** : to make or become rigid or inert like stone: **a** : to make lifeless or inactive : DEADEN **b** : to confound with fear, amazement, or awe : PARALYZE

Pe·trine \'pē-‚trīn\ *adj* : of, relating to, or characteristic of the apostle Peter or the doctrines associated with his name

pet·ro·chem·i·cal \‚pe-trō-'kem-i-kəl\ *n* : a chemical isolated or derived from petroleum or natural gas

pe·trog·ra·phy \pə-'träg-rə-fē\ *n* : the description and systematic classification of rocks — compare PETROLOGY — **pe·trog·ra·pher** \-fər\ *n* — **pet·ro·graph·ic** \‚pe-trə-'graf-ik\ *or* **pet·ro·graph·i·cal** \-'graf-i-kəl\ *adj*

pet·rol \'pe-trəl, -‚träl\ *n* [F *essence de pétrole*, lit., essence of petroleum] *Brit* : GASOLINE

pet·ro·la·tum \‚pe-trə-'lāt-əm\ *n* : a tasteless, odorless, and oily or greasy substance from petroleum that is used esp. in ointments and dressings

pe·tro·le·um \pə-'trō-lē-əm, -'trōl-yəm\ *n* [ML, fr. Gk *petra* rock + L *oleum* oil] : an oily flammable liquid widely distributed in the upper strata of the earth that is a complex mixture mostly of hydrocarbons and is the source of gasoline and lubricants and a major industrial raw material

pe·trol·o·gy \pə-'träl-ə-jē\ *n* : a science that deals with the origin, history, occurrence, structure, chemical composition, and classification of rocks — compare PETROGRAPHY — **pet·ro·log·ic** \‚pe-trə-'läj-ik\ *or* **pet·ro·log·i·cal** \-'läj-i-kəl\ *adj* — **pet·ro·log·i·cal·ly** \-i-k(ə-)lē\ *adv* — **pe·trol·o·gist** \pə-'träl-ə-jəst\ *n*

pe·trous \'pe-trəs\ *adj* : resembling stone esp. in hardness : ROCKY; *also* : of, relating to, or being the very hard dense part of the temporal bone that contains the inner ear

¹pet·ti·coat \'pet-ē-‚kōt\ *n* **1 a** : an outer skirt formerly worn by women and small children **b** : a skirt worn under a dress or outer skirt **2 a** : a garment characteristic or typical of women **b** : WOMAN **3** : something (as a valance) resembling a petticoat

²petticoat *adj* : FEMALE ⟨*petticoat* government⟩

pet·ti·fog \'pet-ē-‚fóg, -‚fäg\ *vi* **-fogged; -fog·ging 1** : to engage in legal trickery **2** : to quibble over insignificant details : CAVIL — **pet·ti·fog·ger** *n* — **pet·ti·fog·gery** \-‚fóg-(ə-)rē, -‚fäg-\ *n*

pet·tish \'pet-ish\ *adj* : FRETFUL, PEEVISH — **pet·tish·ly** *adv* — **pet·tish·ness** *n*

pet·ty \'pet-ē\ *adj* **pet·ti·er; -est** [ME *pety* small, minor, alter. of *petit*, fr. MF, small] **1** : having secondary rank or importance : MINOR, SUBORDINATE ⟨a *petty* prince⟩ **2** : having little or no importance or significance **3** : marked by or reflective of narrow interests and sympathies : SMALL-MINDED — **pet·ti·ly** \'pet-ᵊl-ē\ *adv* — **pet·ti·ness** \'pet-ē-nəs\ *n*

petty cash *n* : cash kept on hand for payment of minor items

petty officer *n* **:** an enlisted man in the navy of a rank corresponding to a noncommissioned officer in the army; *esp* **:** one in one of the three lowest grades (as petty officer second class)

pet·u·lant \'pech-ə-lənt\ *adj* [L *petulant-, petulans*] **:** characterized by temporary or capricious ill humor **:** PEEVISH — **pet·u·lance** \-lən(t)s\ *n* — **pet·u·lant·ly** *adv*

pe·tu·nia \pə-'t(y)ü-nyə\ *n* [NL, fr. obs. F *petun* tobacco, fr. Tupi *petyn*] **:** any of a genus of tropical American herbs related to the potato and widely grown for their showy funnel-shaped flowers

pew \'pyü\ *n* [MF *puie* balustrade, fr. L *podium* parapet, podium] **1 :** a compartment in the auditorium of a church providing seats for several persons **2 :** one of the benches with backs and sometimes doors fixed in rows in a church

pe·wee \'pē-(,)wē\ *n* **:** any of various small olive greenish flycatchers

pe·wit \'pē-,wit, 'pyü-ət\ *n* **:** any of several birds: as **a :** LAPWING **b :** a small black-headed European gull **c :** PEWEE

pew·ter \'pyüt-ər\ *n* [MF *peutre*] **1 :** any of various tin⸗based alloys usu. with lead and sometimes also with varying amounts of copper or antimony **2 :** wares (as table utensils) of pewter — **pewter** *adj*

pew·ter·er \'pyüt-ər-ər\ *n* **:** one that makes pewter wares

pey·o·te \pā-'ōt-ē\ *or* **pey·otl** \-'ōt-ᵊl\ *n* [MexSp *peyote,* fr. Nahuatl *peyotl*] **:** any of a genus of American cacti including the mescal; *also* **:** a drug obtained from mescal tops

pfen·nig \'fen-ig, -ik\ *n, pl* **pfennigs** *or* **pfen·ni·ge** \'fen-i-gə\ [G; akin to E *penny*] **1 :** a unit of value equal to ¹⁄₁₀₀ deutsche mark **2 :** a coin representing one pfennig

pH \pē-'āch\ *n* **:** the negative logarithm of the effective hydrogen-ion concentration used in expressing both acidity and alkalinity on a scale whose values run from 0 to 14 with 7 representing neutrality, numbers less than 7 increasing acidity, and numbers greater than 7 increasing alkalinity; *also* **:** the condition with respect to acidity or alkalinity

Pha·ë·thon \'fā-ə-,thän\ *n* **:** a son of Helios permitted for a day to drive the chariot of the sun and struck down with a thunderbolt by Zeus to keep the world from being set on fire

pha·e·ton \'fā-ət-ᵊn\ *n* [after *Phaëthon*] **1 :** any of various light four-wheeled horse-drawn vehicles **2 :** TOURING CAR

phage \'fāj, 'fäzh\ *n* **:** BACTERIOPHAGE

-phage \,fāj, ,fäzh\ *n comb form* **:** one that eats ⟨bacterio*phage*⟩

-pha·gia \'fā-j(ē-)ə\ *n comb form* [NL, fr. Gk *phagein* to eat] **:** eating of a (specified) type or substance ⟨dys*phagia*⟩

phago·cyte \'fag-ə-,sīt\ *n* [Gk *phagein* to eat] **:** a cell and esp. a white blood cell that takes in and consumes debris and foreign bodies — **phago·cyt·ic** \,fag-ə-'sit-ik\ *adj*

phago·cy·to·sis \,fag-ə-sī-'tō-səs\ *n* **:** the taking and usu. the destruction of particulate matter by phagocytes — **phago·cy·tot·ic** \-'tät-ik\ *adj*

-ph·a·gous \f-ə-gəs\ *adj comb form* [Gk *phagein* to eat] **:** eating ⟨sapro*phagous*⟩

pha·lan·ger \fə-'lan-jər\ *n* **:** any of various marsupial mammals of the Australian region ranging in size from a mouse to a large cat

pha·lanx \'fā-,laŋ(k)s\ *n, pl* **pha·lanx·es** *or* **pha·lan·ges** \fə-'lan-(,)jēz, fā-\ [Gk *phalang-, phalanx,* lit., log; akin to E *balk*] **1 :** a body of heavily armed infantry formed in close deep ranks and files; *also* **:** a body of troops in close array **2** *pl* **phalanges :** one of the bones of a finger or toe **3** *pl usu* **phalanxes a :** a massed arrangement of persons, animals, or things **b :** an organized body of persons — **pha·lan·geal** \fə-'lan-j(ē-)əl\ *adj*

phal·a·rope \'fal-ə-,rōp\ *n* [F, fr. NL *phalaropod-, phalaropus,* fr. Gk *phalaris* coot + *pod-, pous* foot] **:** any of various small shorebirds that resemble sandpipers but have lobed toes and are good swimmers

phal·lus \'fal-əs\ *n, pl* **phal·li** \'fal-,ī, -,ē\ *or* **phal·lus·es** [Gk *phallos*] **1 :** a symbol or representation of the male organ of generation **2 :** PENIS — **phal·lic** \'fal-ik\ *adj*

phan·er·o·gam \'fan-ə-rə-,gam, fə-'ner-ə-\ *n* [Gk *phaneros* visible + *gamos* marriage] **:** SEED PLANT, SPERMATOPHYTE — **phan·er·o·gam·ic** \,fan-ə-rə-'gam-ik, fə-,ner-ə-\ *adj* — **phan·er·og·a·mous** \,fan-ə-'räg-ə-məs\ *adj*

phan·tasm \'fan-,taz-əm\ *n* [Gk *phantasma,* fr. *phantazein* to present to the mind, fr. *phainein* to show] **1 :** a product of fantasy: as **a :** delusive appearance **:** ILLUSION **b :** GHOST, SPECTER **c :** a figment of the imagination **:** FANTASY **2 :** a deceptive or illusory appearance of a thing — **phan·tas·mal** \fan-'taz-məl\ *adj* — **phan·tas·mic** \-'taz-mik\ *adj*

phan·tas·ma·go·ria \(,)fan-,taz-mə-'gōr-ē-ə, -'gór-\ *n* **1 :** an optical effect by which figures on a screen appear to dwindle into the distance or to rush toward the observer with enormous increase of size **2 a :** a constantly shifting complex succession of things seen or imagined **b :** a scene that constantly changes or fluctuates — **phan·tas·ma·go·ric** \-'gōr-ik, -'gór-, -'gär-\ *adj*

phantasy *var of* FANTASY

¹phan·tom \'fant-əm\ *n* **1 a :** something (as a specter) apparent to sense but with no substantial existence **:** APPARITION **b :** something elusive or visionary **:** WILL-O'⸗THE-WISP **c :** an object of continual dread or abhorrence **:** BUGBEAR **2 :** something existing in appearance only **3 :** a representation of something abstract, ideal, or incorporeal

²phantom *adj* **1 :** of the nature of, suggesting, or being a phantom **2 :** FICTITIOUS, DUMMY ⟨*phantom* voters⟩

phar·aoh \'fe(ə)r-ō, 'fā-rō\ *n, often cap* [Gk *pharaō,* fr. Heb *par'ōh,* fr. Egypt *pr-';*] **:** a ruler of ancient Egypt — **phar·a·on·ic** \,fer-ā-'än-ik, ,far-\ *adj, often cap*

pharaoh ant *n* **:** a little red ant that is a common household pest

phar·i·sa·ic \,far-ə-'sā-ik\ *adj* **1** *cap* **:** of or relating to the Pharisees **2 :** PHARISAICAL

phar·i·sa·i·cal \-'sā-ə-kəl\ *adj* **:** marked by hypocritical censorious self-righteousness — **phar·i·sa·i·cal·ly** \-k(ə-)lē\ *adv* — **phar·i·sa·i·cal·ness** \-kəl-nəs\ *n*

phar·i·sa·ism \'far-ə-(,)sā-,iz-əm\ *n* **1** *cap* **:** the doctrines or practices of the Pharisees **2** *often cap* **:** pharisaical character, spirit, or attitude

phar·i·see \'far-ə-(,)sē\ *n* [Gk *pharisaios,* fr. Aram *pĕrī-shayyā,* pl. of *pĕrīshā,* lit., separated] **1** *cap* **:** a member of a Jewish sect of New Testament times noted for strict observance of rites and ceremonies of the written law and for insistence on the validity of the oral tradition **2 :** a pharisaical person

¹phar·ma·ceu·ti·cal \,fär-mə-'süt-i-kəl\ *or* **phar·ma·ceu·tic** \-'süt-ik\ *adj* **1 :** of or relating to pharmacy or pharmacists **2 :** MEDICINAL — **phar·ma·ceu·ti·cal·ly** \-i-k(ə-)lē\ *adv*

²pharmaceutical *n* **:** a pharmaceutical preparation **:** a medicinal material or product

phar·ma·cist \'fär-mə-səst\ *n* **:** one skilled or engaged in pharmacy

pharmaco- *comb form* [Gk *pharmakon*] **:** medicine **:** drug ⟨*pharmaco*logy⟩

phar·ma·cog·no·sy \,fär-mə-'käg-nə-sē\ *n* [Gk *gnōsis* knowledge, fr. *gignōskein* to know] **:** descriptive pharmacology dealing esp. with the identification of crude drugs

phar·ma·col·o·gy \,fär-mə-'käl-ə-jē\ *n* **1 :** the science of drugs esp. as related to their use in medicine **2 :** the properties and reactions of drugs esp. with relation to their therapeutic value — **phar·ma·co·log·i·cal** \-kə-'läj-i-kəl\ *or* **phar·ma·co·log·ic** \-'läj-ik\ *adj* — **phar·ma·co·log·i·cal·ly** \-i-k(ə-)lē\ *adv* — **phar·ma·col·o·gist** \-'käl-ə-jəst\ *n*

phar·ma·co·pe·ia *or* **phar·ma·co·pe·ia** \,fär-mə-kə-'pē-(y)ə\ *n* [LGk *pharmakopoiia* preparation of drugs, fr. Gk *pharmakon* drug + *poiein* to make] **1 :** a book describing drugs, chemicals, and medicinal preparations **2 :** a collection or stock of drugs — **phar·ma·co·poe·ial** \-(y)əl\ *adj*

phar·ma·cy \'fär-mə-sē\ *n, pl* **-cies** [Gk *pharmakeia,* fr. *pharmakon* magic charm, drug] **1 :** the art, practice, or profession of preparing, preserving, compounding, and dispensing drugs **2 a :** a place where medicines are compounded or dispensed **b :** DRUGSTORE **3 :** PHARMACOPEIA 2

phar·os \'fa(ə)r-,äs, 'fe(ə)r-\ *n* [Gk, fr. *Pharos,* island in the bay of Alexandria, Egypt, famous for its lighthouse] **:** a lighthouse or beacon to guide seamen

phar·yn·gi·tis \,far-ən-'jīt-əs\ *n* **:** inflammation of the pharynx

phar·ynx \'far-iŋ(k)s\ *n, pl* **pha·ryn·ges** \fə-'rin-(,)jēz\

also **phar·ynx·es** [Gk *pharyng-, pharynx* throat, pharynx] : the space in a vertebrate just behind the cavity of the mouth into which the nostrils, Eustachian tubes, esophagus, and trachea open; *also* : a corresponding part of an invertebrate — **pha·ryn·geal** \fə-'rin-j(ē-)əl, ‚far-ən-'jē-əl\ *adj*

phase \'fāz\ *n* [Gk *phasis* appearance of a star, phase of the moon, fr. *phainesthai* to appear] **1** : the apparent shape of the moon or a planet at any time in its series of changes with respect to illumination ⟨the new moon and the full moon are *phases* of the moon⟩ **2 a** : a stage or interval in a development or cycle **b** : an aspect or part under consideration **3** : the stage of progress in a regularly recurring motion or a cyclic process ⟨as a wave or vibration⟩ in relation to a reference point **4** : a homogeneous physically distinct portion of matter present in a nonhomogeneous system ⟨the three *phases* ice, water, and steam⟩ — **pha·sic** \'fā-zik\ *adj*

phase microscope *n* : a microscope that translates differences in phase of the light transmitted through or reflected by the object into differences of intensity in the image

pheas·ant \'fez-°nt\ *n, pl* **pheasant** *or* **pheasants** [OF *fesan,* fr. L *phasianus,* fr. Gk *phasianos,* fr. *Phasis,* river in Colchis] : any of numerous large long-tailed brilliantly colored Old World birds related to the domestic fowl many of which are reared as ornamental or game birds

pheasant

phel·lem \'fel-‚em\ *n* [Gk *phellos* cork] : CORK 1b

phel·lo·gen \'fel-ə-jən\ *n* : cork cambium — **phel·lo·ge·net·ic** \‚fel-ə-jə-'net-ik\ *adj* — **phel·lo·gen·ic** \-'jen-ik\ *adj*

phen- *or* **pheno-** *comb form* [F *phène* benzene, fr. Gk *phainein* to show; fr. its occurrence in illuminating gas] : related to or derived from benzene ⟨*phenol*⟩ : containing phenyl ⟨*pheno*barbital⟩

phe·no·bar·bi·tal \‚fē-nō-'bär-bə-‚tȯl\ *n* : a crystalline barbituric acid drug used as a hypnotic and sedative

phe·no·copy \'fē-nə-‚käp-ē\ *n* [*phenotype* + *copy*] : a phenotype that mimics the expression of a genotype other than its own

phe·nol \'fē-‚nōl, fi-'\ *n* **1** : a caustic poisonous crystalline acidic compound C_6H_5OH present in coal tar and wood tar that in dilute solution is used as a disinfectant **2** : any of various acidic compounds analogous to phenol and regarded as hydroxyl derivatives of aromatic hydrocarbons — **phe·no·lic** \fi-'nō-lik, -'näl-ik\ *adj*

phe·no·lic \fi-'nō-lik, -'näl-ik\ *n* : a resin or plastic made by condensation of a phenol with an aldehyde and used esp. for molding and insulating and in coatings and adhesives

phe·nol·o·gy \fi-'näl-ə-jē\ *n* [*phenomena* + *-logy*] : a branch of science dealing with the relation of climate to periodically recurring biological phenomena — **phe·no·log·i·cal** \‚fēn-°l-'äj-i-kəl\ *adj*

phe·nol·phtha·lein \‚fē-‚nōl-'thal-ē-ən, -'thal-‚ēn, -'thāl-\ *n* : a white or yellowish white crystalline compound used as a laxative and as an acid-base indicator because its solution is brilliant red in alkalies and is decolorized by acids

phe·nom·e·nal \fi-'näm-ən-°l\ *adj* **1** : of, relating to, or being a phenomenon **2** : EXTRAORDINARY, REMARKABLE — **phe·nom·e·nal·ly** \-°l-ē\ *adv*

phe·nom·e·non \fi-'näm-ə-‚nän, -nən\ *n, pl* **-na** \-nə, -‚nä\ *or* **-nons** [Gk *phainomenon,* fr. neut. of *phainomenos,* prp. of *phainesthai* to appear] **1** : an observable fact or event **2** : a fact or feature characteristic of something **3** : a fact or event that can be scientifically described and explained **4 a** : a rare or significant fact or event **b** *pl* **phenomenons** : an exceptional person, thing, or event : PRODIGY

phe·no·type \'fē-nə-‚tīp\ *n* [Gk *phainesthai* to appear] **1** : the visible characters of an organism resulting from the interaction of genotype and environment **2** : a group of organisms sharing a particular phenotype — **phe·no-**

typ·ic \‚fē-nə-'tip-ik\ *or* **phe·no·typ·i·cal** \-'tip-i-kəl\ *adj* — **phe·no·typ·i·cal·ly** \-i-k(ə-)lē\ *adv*

phen·yl \'fen-°l, 'fēn-\ *n* : a univalent radical C_6H_5 derived from benzene by removal of one hydrogen atom — **phe·nyl·ic** \fi-'nil-ik\ *adj*

phen·yl·al·a·nine \‚fen-°l-'al-ə-‚nēn, ‚fēn-\ *n* : an essential amino acid $C_9H_{11}NO_2$ obtained by the hydrolysis of proteins

phi \'fī\ *n, pl* **phis** \'fīz\ : the 21st letter of the Greek alphabet — Φ *or* φ

phi·al \'fī(-ə)l\ *n* [Gk *phialē*] : VIAL

phil- *or* **philo-** *comb form* [Gk, fr. *philos* dear, friendly] : loving : having an affinity for ⟨*philo*-Russian⟩

-phil \‚fil\ *or* **-phile** \‚fīl\ *n comb form* [Gk *philos* dear, friendly] : lover : one having an affinity for or a strong attraction to ⟨Franco*phil*⟩ ⟨Germano*phile*⟩ — **-phil** *or* **-phile** *adj comb form*

phil·a·del·phus \‚fil-ə-'del-fəs\ *n* : any of a genus of shrubs of the saxifrage family including several widely grown for their showy white flowers

phi·lan·der \fə-'lan-dər\ *vi* **phi·lan·dered; phi·lan·der·ing** \-d(ə-)riŋ\ : to make love frivolously : FLIRT — **phi·lan·der·er** \-dər-ər\ *n*

phil·an·throp·ic \‚fil-ən-'thräp-ik\ *adj* : of, relating to, or characterized by philanthropy : BENEVOLENT, CHARITABLE — **phil·an·throp·i·cal** \-'thräp-i-kəl\ *adj* — **phil·an·throp·i·cal·ly** \-i-k(ə-)lē\ *adv*

phi·lan·thro·pist \fə-'lan(t)-thrə-pəst\ *n* : one who practices philanthropy

phi·lan·thro·py \-pē\ *n, pl* **-pies** [Gk *anthrōpos* man] **1** : goodwill to fellowmen; *esp* : active effort to promote human welfare **2** : a philanthropic act or gift or an organization distributing or supported by philanthropic funds

phil·a·tel·ic \‚fil-ə-'tel-ik\ *adj* : of or relating to philately — **phil·a·tel·i·cal·ly** \-'tel-i-k(ə-)lē\ *adv*

phi·lat·e·ly \fə-'lat-°l-ē\ *n* [F *philatélie,* fr. *phil-* + Gk *ateleia* tax exemption, fr. *a-* + *telos* tax; fr. the fact that a stamped letter frees the recipient from paying the mailing charges] : the collection and study of postage and imprinted stamps — **phi·lat·e·list** \-°l-əst\ *n*

Phi·le·mon \fə-'lē-mən, fī-\ *n* **1** : a friend and probable convert of the apostle Paul **2** — see BIBLE table

¹phil·har·mon·ic \‚fil-ər-'män-ik, ‚fil-(h)är-\ *adj* : of or relating to a musical organization and esp. a symphony orchestra

²philharmonic *n* : a musical organization

-philic \'fil-ik\ *adj comb form* : having an affinity for : loving ⟨photo*philic*⟩

Phi·lip·pi·ans \fə-'lip-ē-ənz\ *n* — see BIBLE table

phi·lip·pic \fə-'lip-ik\ *n* [Gk *philippikoi logoi,* speeches of Demosthenes against Philip II of Macedon, lit., speeches relating to Philip] : a discourse or declamation full of acrimonious invective : TIRADE

Phil·ip·pine mahogany \‚fil-ə-‚pēn-\ *n* : any of several Philippine timber trees with wood resembling that of the true mahoganies; *also* : this wood

phil·is·tine \'fil-ə-‚stēn; fə-'lis-tən, -‚tēn\ *n* **1** *cap* : a member of an ancient race that lived in the coastal regions of Palestine and conducted many raids against the Israelites **2** *often cap* : a person who takes an attitude of smug indifference to art and literature and the cultural values they represent **3** : one who shows antagonism to any creative intellectual activity having no clear practical application — **philistine** *adj* — **phil·is·tin·ism** \-‚iz-əm\ *n*

phil·o·den·dron \‚fil-ə-'den-drən\ *n, pl* **-drons** *or* **-dra** \-drə\ : any of various arums grown for their showy often variegated foliage

phi·lol·o·gy \fə-'läl-ə-jē\ *n* [Gk *philologia* love of learning and literature] **1** : the study of literature and of relevant disciplines **2** : LINGUISTICS; *esp* : historical and comparative linguistics — **phil·o·log·i·cal** \‚fil-ə-'läj-i-kəl\ *adj* — **phil·o·log·i·cal·ly** \-'läj-i-k(ə-)lē\ *adv* — **phi·lol·o·gist** \fə-'läl-ə-jəst\ *n*

phi·los·o·pher \fə-'läs-ə-fər\ *n* **1 a** : SCHOLAR, THINKER **b** : a student of philosophy **2** : a person whose philosophical perspective enables him to meet trouble with fortitude and resignation

philosophers' stone *n* : an imaginary stone, substance, or chemical preparation believed to have the power of transmuting base metals into gold and sought for by alchemists

phil·o·soph·ic \,fil-ə-'säf-ik\ *adj* **1** : of, relating to, or based on philosophy **2** : characterized by the attitude of a philosopher; *esp* : calm in face of trouble : TEMPERATE — **phil·o·soph·i·cal** \-'säf-i-kəl\ *adj* — **phil·o·soph·i·cal·ly** \-i-k(ə-)lē\ *adv*

phi·los·o·phize \fə-'läs-ə-,fīz\ *vi* **1** : to reason in the manner of a philosopher **2** : to expound a superficial philosophy : MORALIZE — **phi·los·o·phiz·er** *n*

phi·los·o·phy \fə-'läs-ə-fē\ *n, pl* **-phies** [Gk *philosophia*, fr. *phil-* + *sophia* wisdom] **1** : the study of the nature of knowledge and existence and the principles of moral and esthetic value **2** : the philosophical teachings or principles of a man or group of men ⟨Greek *philosophy*⟩ **3** : the general principles of a field of study ⟨*philosophy* of history⟩ **4** : wisdom or insight applied to life itself **5** : sciences and liberal arts exclusive of medicine, law, and theology ⟨doctor of *philosophy*⟩

-ph·i·lous \f-(ə-)ləs\ *adj comb form* : -PHILIC ⟨hygroph*ilous*⟩

phil·ter *or* **phil·tre** \'fil-tər\ *n* [Gk *philtron*] **1** : a potion, drug, or charm held to have the power to excite sexual passion **2** : a potion credited with magical power

phiz \'fiz\ *n* [by shortening & alter. fr. *physiognomy*] : FACE

phle·bi·tis \fli-'bīt-əs\ *n* [Gk *phleb-, phleps* vein] : inflammation of a vein

phle·bot·o·my \fli-'bät-ə-mē\ *n* : the letting of blood in the treatment of disease — **phle·bot·o·mist** \-məst\ *n* — **phle·bot·o·mize** \-,mīz\ *vt*

Phleg·e·thon \'fleg-ə-,thän\ *n* : a river of Hades held in Greek mythology to contain fire instead of water

phlegm \'flem\ *n* [Gk *phlegmat-, phlegma* inflammation, phlegm, fr. *phlegein* to burn; akin to E *black*] **1** : viscid mucus secreted in abnormal quantity in the respiratory passages **2 a** : dull or apathetic coldness or indifference **b** : intrepid coolness : CALMNESS — **phlegmy** \'flem-ē\ *adj*

phleg·mat·ic \fleg-'mat-ik\ *adj* : not easily excited or aroused : slow to respond **syn** see IMPASSIVE — **phleg·mat·i·cal·ly** \-i-k(ə-)lē\ *adv*

phlo·em \'flō-,em\ *n* [Gk *phloios* bark] : a vascular tissue of higher plants that transports dissolved food material, contains sieve tubes, and lies mostly external to the cambium — compare XYLEM

phlo·gis·ton \flō-'jis-tən\ *n* : the hypothetical principle of fire regarded formerly as a material substance

phlox \'fläks\ *n, pl* **phlox** *or* **phlox·es** [Gk, flame, wallflower] : any of a genus of American annual or perennial herbs with showy red, purple, white, or variegated flowers

-phobe \,fōb\ *n comb form* [Gk *phobos* fear] : one fearing or averse to (something specified) ⟨Franco*phobe*⟩ — **-pho·bic** \'fō-bik, 'fäb-ik\ *adj comb form*

pho·bia \'fō-bē-ə\ *n* [Gk *-phobia*, fr. *phobos* fear] : an unreasonable persistent fear of a particular thing — **pho·bic** \'fō-bik, 'fäb-ik\ *adj*

phoe·be \'fē-bē\ *n* [alter. of *pewee*] : any of several American flycatchers; *esp* : one of the eastern U.S. that has a slight crest and is plain grayish brown above and yellowish white below

Phoe·be \'fē-bē\ *n* : ARTEMIS

Phoe·bus \'fē-bəs\ *n* : APOLLO

Phoe·ni·cian \fi-'nish-ən\ *n* **1** : a native or inhabitant of ancient Phoenicia **2** : the Semitic language of ancient Phoenicia : Phoenician — **Phoenician** *adj*

phoebe

phoe·nix \'fē-niks\ *n* [OE *fenix*, fr. L *phoenix*, fr. Gk *phoinix*] : a legendary bird represented by ancient Egyptians as living five or six centuries, being consumed in fire by its own act, and rising in youthful freshness from its own ashes

phon- *or* **phono-** *comb form* [Gk *phōnē* voice, fr. *phanai* to speak] : sound : voice : speech ⟨*phonate*⟩ ⟨*phono*graph⟩

pho·na·tion \fō-'nā-shən\ *n* : the act or process of producing speech sounds ⟨organs of *phonation*⟩ — **pho·nate** \'fō-,nāt\ *vi*

¹phone \'fōn\ *n* **1** : EARPHONE **2** : TELEPHONE

²phone *vb* : TELEPHONE

³phone *n* : a speech sound considered as a physical event without regard to its place in the structure of a language

-phone \,fōn\ *n comb form* [Gk *phōnē* voice] : sound ⟨homo*phone*⟩ — often in names of musical instruments and sound-transmitting devices ⟨radio*phone*⟩ ⟨xylo*phone*⟩

pho·neme \'fō-,nēm\ *n* [Gk *phōnēmat-, phōnēma* speech sound, fr. *phōnein* to utter] : a member of the set of the smallest units of speech that serve to distinguish one utterance from another in all the variations that a speech sound undergoes (as in the speech of a single person or a particular dialect) chiefly as a result of the modifying influence of neighboring sounds ⟨\p\ and \f\ in *pin* and *fin*, \i\ and \a\ in *pin* and *pan*, and \n\ and \t\ in *pin* and *pit* are different *phonemes*⟩ — compare ALLOPHONE

pho·ne·mic \fə-'nē-mik\ *adj* **1** : of, relating to, or having the characteristics of a phoneme **2** : constituting different phonemes ⟨in English \n\ and \ŋ\ are *phonemic*⟩ — **pho·ne·mi·cal·ly** \-mi-k(ə-)lē\ *adv*

pho·net·ic \fə-'net-ik\ *adj* [Gk *phōnein* to utter, fr. *phōnē* voice] **1 a** : of or relating to spoken language or speech sounds **b** : of or relating to the science of phonetics **2** : representing the phenomena of speech — **pho·net·i·cal** \-'net-i-kəl\ *adj* — **pho·net·i·cal·ly** \-i-k(ə-)lē\ *adv*

phonetic alphabet *n* : a set of symbols used for phonetic transcription

pho·ne·ti·cian \,fō-nə-'tish-ən\ *n* : a specialist in phonetics

pho·net·ics \fə-'net-iks\ *n* **1** : the study and systematic classification of the sounds made in spoken utterance **2** : the system of speech sounds of a language or group of languages

phon·ic \'fän-ik\ *adj* **1** : of, relating to, or producing sound **2** : of or relating to the sounds of speech or to phonics — **phon·i·cal·ly** \-i-k(ə-)lē\ *adv*

phon·ics \'fän-iks\ *n* : a method of teaching beginners to read and pronounce words by learning the phonetic value of letters, letter groups, and esp. syllables

pho·no·gram \'fō-nə-,gram\ *n* : a character or symbol used to represent a word, syllable, or phoneme

pho·no·graph \'fō-nə-,graf\ *n* : an instrument for reproducing sounds by means of the vibration of a stylus or needle following a spiral groove on a revolving disc

pho·no·graph·ic \,fō-nə-'graf-ik\ *adj* **1** : of or relating to phonography **2** : of or relating to a phonograph — **pho·no·graph·i·cal·ly** \-i-k(ə-)lē\ *adv*

pho·nog·ra·phy \fō-'näg-rə-fē\ *n* : spelling based on pronunciation

pho·nol·o·gy \fō-'näl-ə-jē\ *n* : the science of speech sounds including esp. the history and theory of sound changes in a language or in two or more related languages — **pho·no·log·i·cal** \,fōn-ᵊl-'äj-i-kəl\ *adj* — **pho·no·log·i·cal·ly** \-k(ə-)lē\ *adv* — **pho·nol·o·gist** \fō-'näl-ə-jəst\ *n*

pho·no·re·cep·tion \,fō-nō-ri-'sep-shən\ *n* : the perception of vibratory motion of relatively high frequency; *esp* : HEARING — **pho·no·re·cep·tor** \-'sep-tər\ *n*

¹pho·ny *or* **pho·ney** \'fō-nē\ *adj* **pho·ni·er; -est** : FALSE, SPURIOUS, COUNTERFEIT; *esp* : falsely pretentious ⟨the *phony* elegance of the decorations⟩ — **pho·ni·ly** \'fōn-ᵊl-ē\ *adv* — **pho·ni·ness** \'fō-nē-nəs\ *n*

²phony *or* **phoney** *n, pl* **phonies** *or* **phoneys** : one that is fraudulent or spurious : FAKE

-phore \,fōr, ,fȯr\ *n comb form* [Gk *phor-, pherein* to carry] : carrier ⟨sema*phore*⟩

phos·gene \'fäz-,jēn\ *n* [Gk *phōs* light; fr. its originally having been obtained by the action of sunlight] : a colorless gas of unpleasant odor that is a severe respiratory irritant and used as a war gas

phosph- *or* **phospho-** *comb form* : phosphorus ⟨*phos*phide⟩ ⟨*phospho*protein⟩

phos·pha·gen \'fäs-fə-jən\ *n* [*phosphat*e + *-gen* (as in *glycogen*)] : any of several organic phosphorus-containing compounds occurring esp. in muscle and releasing energy on hydrolysis

phos·pha·tase \'fäs-fə-,tās\ *n* : any of various enzymes that accelerate the hydrolysis and synthesis of organic phosphates or the transfer of phosphate groups

phos·phate \'fäs-,fāt\ *n* **1** : a salt or ester of a phosphoric acid **2** : an effervescent drink of carbonated water with a small amount of phosphoric acid or an acid phosphate flavored with fruit syrup **3** : a phosphatic material used for fertilizers

phos·phat·ic \fäs-'fat-ik, -'fāt-\ *adj* : of, relating to, or containing phosphoric acid or phosphates

phos·pha·tide \'fäs-fə-,tīd\ *n* : a complex phosphoric ester lipide found in all living cells in association with stored fats — **phos·pha·tid·ic** \,fäs-fə-'tid-ik\ *adj*

phos·phide \'fäs-,fīd\ *n* : a compound of phosphorus usu. with a more electropositive element or radical

phos·phite \-,fīt\ *n* : a salt or ester of phosphorous acid

phos·pho·lip·ide \,fäs-fō-'lip-,īd\ *n* : PHOSPHATIDE

phos·phor \'fäs-fər, -,fȯr\ *n* [L *phosphorus,* fr. Gk *phōsphoros,* lit., light bringer, fr. *phōs* light + *pherein* to carry, bring] **1** *cap* : MORNING STAR; *esp* : Venus as morning star **2** *also* **phos·phore** \-fər, -,fȯr, -,fȯr\ : a phosphorescent substance; *esp* : one that emits light when excited by radiation

phosphor bronze *n* : a bronze of great hardness, elasticity, and toughness that contains a small amount of phosphorus

phos·pho·resce \,fäs-fə-'res\ *vi* : to exhibit phosphorescence

phos·pho·res·cence \,fäs-fə-'res-ᵊn(t)s\ *n* **1** : the property of emitting light without easily perceptible heat shown by phosphorus or living organisms (as various bacteria and fungi); *also* : the light so produced **2** : luminescence caused by the absorption of radiations (as X rays or ultraviolet light) and continuing for a noticeable time after these radiations have stopped — **phos·pho·res·cent** \-ᵊnt\ *adj*

phos·phor·ic \fäs-'fȯr-ik, -'fär-\ *adj* : of, relating to, or containing phosphorus esp. with a valence higher than in phosphorous compounds

phosphoric acid *n* : an oxygen-containing acid of phosphorus; *esp* : a syrupy or crystalline acid H_3PO_4 used in making fertilizers and as a flavoring in soft drinks

phos·pho·rous \'fäs-f(ə-)rəs; fäs-'fȯr-əs, -'fȯr-\ *adj* : of, relating to, or containing phosphorus esp. with a valence lower than in phosphoric compounds

phosphorous acid *n* : a deliquescent crystalline acid H_3PO_3 used esp. as a reducing agent and in making phosphites

phos·pho·rus \'fäs-f(ə-)rəs\ *n* [NL, fr. Gk *phōsphoros* light-bearing, fr. *phōs* light + *phor-, pherein* to carry] **1** : a phosphorescent substance; *esp* : one that glows in the dark **2** : a poisonous active chemical element usu. obtained in the form of waxy disagreeable-smelling crystals that glow in moist air — see ELEMENT table — **phosphorus** *adj*

phos·pho·ryl·ate \'fäs-fə-rə-,lāt\ *vt* : to cause (an organic compound) to take up or combine with phosphoric acid or a phosphorus-containing group — **phos·pho·ryl·a·tion** \,fäs-fə-rə-'lā-shən\ *n*

phot- *or* **photo-** *comb form* [Gk *phōt-, phōs*] **1** : light ⟨*photon*⟩ ⟨*photo*graphy⟩ **2** : photograph : photographic ⟨*photo*engraving⟩ **3** : photoelectric ⟨*photo*cell⟩

pho·tic \'fōt-ik\ *adj* **1** : of, relating to, or involving light esp. in relation to organisms ⟨a *photic* response⟩ **2** : penetrated by light esp. of the sun ⟨*photic* layers of the sea⟩

pho·to \'fōt-ō\ *n, pl* **photos** : PHOTOGRAPH — **photo** *vb* — **photo** *adj*

pho·to·cell \'fōt-ə-,sel\ *n* : PHOTOELECTRIC CELL

pho·to·chem·is·try \,fōt-ō-'kem-ə-strē\ *n* : a branch of chemistry that deals with the effect of radiant energy in producing chemical changes — **pho·to·chem·i·cal** \-'kem-i-kəl\ *adj*

pho·to·com·pose \-kəm-'pōz\ *vt* : to compose (reading matter) for reproduction by means of characters photographed on film in the preparation of a printing surface — **pho·to·com·po·si·tion** \-,käm-pə-'zish-ən\ *n*

pho·to·con·duc·tive cell \-kən-,dək-tiv-\ *n* : a photoelectric cell containing a substance whose electrical resistance decreases as the amount of light falling on it increases

pho·to·copy \'fōt-ə-,käp-ē\ *n* : a photographic reproduction of graphic matter — **photocopy** *vb*

pho·to·du·pli·cate \,fōt-ō-'d(y)ü-plə-,kāt\ *vb* : PHOTOCOPY — **pho·to·du·pli·cate** \-pli-kət\ *n*

pho·to·elec·tric \,fōt-ō-ə-'lek-trik\ *adj* : relating to or utilizing any of various electrical effects due to the interaction of light with matter

photoelectric cell *n* : a cell in which variations of light are converted into corresponding variations in an electric current

photoelectric effect *n* : the emission of free electrons from a metal surface when light strikes it

pho·to·elec·tron \,fōt-ō-ə-'lek-,trän\ *n* : an electron released in the photoelectric effect

pho·to·emis·sive \,fōt-ō-i-'mis-iv\ *adj* : emitting electrons when exposed to radiation (as light)

pho·to·en·grave \,fōt-ō-in-'grāv\ *vt* : to make a photoengraving of — **pho·to·en·grav·er** *n*

pho·to·en·grav·ing \-'grā-viŋ\ *n* **1** : a process for making linecuts and halftone cuts by photographing an image on a metal plate and then etching **2 a** : a plate made by photoengraving **b** : a print made from such a plate

photo finish *n* **1** : a race finish in which contestants are so close that a photograph of them as they cross the finish line has to be examined to determine the winner **2** : a close contest

pho·to·flash \'fōt-ə-,flash\ *n* : FLASHBULB

pho·to·flood \-,fləd\ *n* : an electric lamp using excess voltage to give intense sustained illumination for taking photographs

pho·to·gen·ic \,fōt-ə-'jen-ik, -'jēn-\ *adj* **1** : produced or precipitated by light **2** : producing or generating light : PHOSPHORESCENT **3** : suitable for being photographed esp. from the artistic point of view : photographing well ⟨*photogenic* hands⟩ ⟨a movie starlet, not very talented but very *photogenic*⟩ — **pho·to·gen·i·cal·ly** \-i-k(ə-)lē\ *adv*

pho·to·gram·me·try \,fōt-ə-'gram-ə-trē\ *n* : the science of making reliable measurements by the use of usu. aerial photographs in surveying and map making

¹pho·to·graph \'fōt-ə-,graf\ *n* : a picture or likeness obtained by photography

²photograph *vb* **1** : to take a photograph of **2** : to take photographs **3** : to undergo being photographed

pho·tog·ra·pher \fə-'täg-rə-fər\ *n* : one that practices or is skilled in photography; *esp* : one who takes photographs as a business

pho·to·graph·ic \,fōt-ə-'graf-ik\ *adj* **1** : relating to, obtained by, or used in photography ⟨*photographic* supplies⟩ **2** : representing nature and human beings with the exactness of a photograph ⟨a painter with a *photographic* technique⟩ **3** : capable of retaining vivid impressions ⟨a *photographic* mind⟩ — **pho·to·graph·i·cal·ly** \-i-k(ə-)lē\ *adv*

pho·tog·ra·phy \fə-'täg-rə-fē\ *n* : the art or process of producing images on a sensitized surface (as a film or plate) by the action of light or other radiant energy

pho·to·gra·vure \,fōt-ə-grə-'vyü(ə)r\ *n* : a process for making prints from an intaglio plate prepared by photographic methods; *also* : a print produced by photogravure — **photogravure** *vt*

pho·tol·y·sis \fō-'täl-ə-səs\ *n* : chemical decomposition by the action of radiant energy and esp. light

pho·tom·e·ter \fō-'täm-ət-ər\ *n* : an instrument for measuring luminous intensity, illumination, or brightness

pho·to·met·ric \,fōt-ə-'me-trik\ *adj* : of or relating to photometry or the photometer — **pho·to·met·ri·cal·ly** \-tri-k(ə-)lē\ *adv*

pho·tom·e·try \fō-'täm-ə-trē\ *n* : a branch of science that deals with measurement of the intensity of light

pho·to·mi·cro·graph \,fōt-ə-'mī-krə-,graf\ *n* : a photograph of a magnified image of a small object — **pho·to·mi·cro·graph·ic** \-,mī-krə-'graf-ik\ *adj* — **pho·to·mi·crog·ra·phy** \-,mī-'kräg-rə-fē\ *n*

pho·to·mon·tage \-män-'täzh\ *n* : montage using photographic images; *also* : a picture made by photomontage

pho·to·mu·ral \-'myür-əl\ *n* : an enlarged photograph usu. several yards long used on walls esp. as decoration

pho·ton \'fō-,tän\ *n* : a quantum of radiant energy

pho·to·off·set \,fōt-ō-'ȯf-,set\ *n* : offset using a photographically prepared planographic printing plate

pho·to·pe·ri·od \,fōt-ə-'pir-ē-əd\ *n* : the relative lengths of alternating periods of lightness and darkness as they affect the growth and maturity of an organism — **pho·to·pe·ri·od·ic** \-,pir-ē-'äd-ik\ *or* **pho·to·pe·ri·od·i·cal** \-'äd-i-kəl\ *adj* — **pho·to·pe·ri·od·i·cal·ly** \-i-k(ə-)lē\ *adv* — **pho·to·pe·ri·od·ic·i·ty** \-,pir-ē-ə-'dis-ət-ē\ *n* — **pho·to·pe·ri·od·ism** \-,pir-ē-ə-,diz-əm\ *n*

pho·to·phil·ic \,fōt-ə-'fil-ik\ *adj* : thriving in or requiring abundant light ⟨*photophilic* plants⟩ — **pho·toph·i·ly** \fō-'täf-ə-lē\ *n*

pho·to·pho·bic \,fōt-ə-'fō-bik, -'fäb-ik\ *adj* **1** : shunning or avoiding light **2** : growing best under reduced illumination

pho·to·pia \fō-'tō-pē-ə\ *n* : vision in bright light with light-adapted eyes believed to be mediated by the retinal cones — **pho·to·pic** \fō-'tō-pik, -'täp-ik\ *adj*

pho·to·play \'fōt-ə-,plā\ *n* : MOTION PICTURE 2

pho·to·pos·i·tive \,fōt-ə-'päz-ət-iv, -'päz-tiv\ *adj* : exhibiting positive phototaxis or phototropism

pho·to·re·cep·tion \,fōt-ə-ri-'sep-shən\ *n* : perception of waves in the range of visible light; *esp* : VISION — **pho·to·re·cep·tive** \-'sep-tiv\ *adj* — **pho·to·re·cep·tor** \-tər\ *n*

pho·to·sen·si·tive \-'sen(t)-sət-iv, -'sen(t)-stiv\ *adj* : sensitive or sensitized to the action of radiant energy and esp. light — **pho·to·sen·si·tiv·i·ty** \-,sen(t)-sə-'tiv-ət-ē\ *n*

pho·to·sen·si·ti·za·tion \-,sen(t)-sət-ə-'zā-shən\ *n* : the process of photosensitizing : the condition of being photosensitized

pho·to·sen·si·tize \-'sen(t)-sə-,tīz\ *vt* : to make photosensitive

pho·to·sphere \'fōt-ə-,sfi(ə)r\ *n* **1** : a sphere of light **2** : the luminous surface of the sun or a star — **pho·to·spher·ic** \,fōt-ə-'sfi(ə)r-ik, -'sfer-\ *adj*

pho·to·stat \'fōt-ə-,stat\ *vb* : to copy by a Photostat device — **pho·to·stat·ic** \,fōt-ə-'stat-ik\ *adj*

Pho·to·stat \'fōt-ə-,stat\ *trademark* **1** — used for a device for making a photographic copy of graphic matter directly upon the surface of prepared paper with the image in correct position **2** : a copy made by a Photostat device

pho·to·syn·the·sis \,fōt-ə-'sin(t)-thə-səs\ *n* : synthesis of chemical compounds with the aid of radiant energy; *esp* : formation of carbohydrates in the chlorophyll-containing tissues of plants exposed to light — **pho·to·syn·the·size** \-,sīz\ *vi* — **pho·to·syn·thet·ic** \-sin-'thet-ik\ *adj* — **pho·to·syn·thet·i·cal·ly** \-'thet-i-k(ə-)lē\ *adv*

pho·to·tax·is \,fōt-ə-'tak-səs\ *n* : a taxis in which light is the directive factor — **pho·to·tac·tic** \-'tak-tik\ *adj*

pho·tot·ro·pism \fō-'tä-trə-,piz-əm\ *n* : a tropism in which light is the orienting stimulus — **pho·to·trop·ic** \,fōt-ə-'träp-ik\ *adj*

pho·to·vol·ta·ic cell \,fōt-ə-,väl-,tā-ik-, -,vōl-\ *n* : a cell in which an electromotive force is generated when light falls on the boundary between dissimilar substances

phras·al \'frā-zəl\ *adj* : of, relating to, or consisting of a phrase ⟨*phrasal* prepositions⟩ — **phras·al·ly** \-zə-lē\ *adv*

¹phrase \'frāz\ *n* [Gk *phrasis*, fr. *phrazein* to point out, tell] **1** : a characteristic manner of expression : DICTION **2** : a brief expression; *esp* : one commonly used **3** : a musical thought typically two to four measures long and closing with a cadence **4** : a group of two or more grammatically related words that form a sense unit expressing a thought either in a fragmentary manner or as a sentence element not containing a subject and predicate but having the force of a single part of speech

²phrase *vt* **1 a** : to express in words or in appropriate or telling terms : WORD **b** : to designate by a descriptive word or phrase : TERM **2** : to divide into melodic phrases

phra·se·ol·o·gy \,frā-zē-'äl-ə-jē\ *n* **1** : manner of organizing words and phrases into longer elements : DICTION, STYLE **2** : choice of words : VOCABULARY

phras·ing \'frā-ziŋ\ *n* **1** : style of expression : PHRASEOLOGY **2** : the act, method, or result of grouping notes into musical phrases

phre·net·ic \fri-'net-ik\ *adj* : FRENETIC

phren·ic \'fren-ik\ *adj* [Gk *phrēn* diaphragm] : of or relating to the diaphragm ⟨*phrenic* nerves⟩

phre·nol·o·gy \fri-'näl-ə-jē\ *n* [Gk *phrēn* diaphragm, heart, mind] : the study of the conformation of the skull as indicative of mental faculties and character — **phren·o·log·i·cal** \,fren-ᵊl-'äj-i-kəl, ,frēn-\ *adj* — **phre·nol·o·gist** \fri-'näl-ə-jəst\ *n*

phthi·sis \'thī-səs\ *n, pl* **phthi·ses** \'thī-,sēz\ [Gk, fr. *phthinein* to waste away] : a progressively wasting or consumptive condition; *esp* : pulmonary tuberculosis — **phthis·ic** \'tiz-ik\ *or* **phthis·i·cal** \'tiz-i-kəl\ *adj* — **phthis·icky** \-i-kē\ *adj*

phy·co·cy·a·nin \,fī-kō-'sī-ə-nən\ *n* : any of the bluish green protein pigments of blue-green algae

phy·co·er·y·thrin \,fī-kō-'er-ə-thrən\ *n* : any of the red protein pigments of red algae

phy·co·my·cete \-'mī-,sēt, -,mī-'sēt\ *n* [Gk *phykos* seaweed] : any of a large class (Phycomycetes) of highly variable lower fungi in many respects similar to algae — **phy·co·my·ce·tous** \-,mī-'sēt-əs\ *adj*

phyl- *or* **phylo-** *comb form* [Gk *phylē*, *phylon*, fr. *phyein* to bring forth] : tribe : race : phylum ⟨*phylogeny*⟩

phy·lac·tery \fə-'lak-t(ə-)rē\ *n, pl* **-ter·ies** [Gk *phylaktērion*, fr. *phylassein* to guard] **1** : one of two small square leather boxes containing slips inscribed with scripture passages and traditionally worn on the left arm and forehead by Jewish men during morning weekday prayers **2** : AMULET

phy·le·sis \fī-'lē-səs\ *n* : the course of evolutionary or phylogenetic development — **phy·let·ic** \-'let-ik\ *adj* — **phy·let·i·cal·ly** \-'let-i-k(ə-)lē\ *adv*

-phyll \,fil\ *n comb form* [Gk *phyllon* leaf; akin to E *blade*] : leaf ⟨sporo*phyll*⟩

phyl·lo·clade \'fil-ə-,klād\ *n* [Gk *phyllon* leaf + *klados* branch, twig] : a flattened stem that functions as a leaf

phyl·lode \'fil-,ōd\ *n* [NL *phyllodium*, fr. Gk *phyllōdēs* like a leaf, fr. *phyllon* leaf] : a flat expanded petiole that functionally replaces a leaf — **phyl·lo·di·al** \fə-'lōd-ē-əl\ *adj*

phyl·lo·taxy \'fil-ə-,tak-sē\ *also* **phyl·lo·tax·is** \,fil-ə-'tak-səs\ *n* : the arrangement of leaves on a stem and in relation to one another — **phyl·lo·tac·tic** \,fil-ə-'tak-tik\ *adj*

-phyl·lous \'fil-əs\ *adj comb form* [Gk *phyllon* leaf] : having (such or so many) leaves, leaflets, or leaflike parts ⟨di*phyllous*⟩

phyl·lox·e·ra \,fil-,äk-'sir-ə, fə-'läk-sə-rə\ *n* : any of various wholly oviparous plant lice; *esp* : one destructive to grapevines — **phyl·lox·e·ran** \-'sir-ən, -sə-rən\ *adj or n*

phy·lo·ge·net·ic \,fī-lō-jə-'net-ik\ *adj* : of or relating to phylogeny; *also* : acquired in the course of phylogenetic development — **phy·lo·ge·net·i·cal·ly** \-'net-i-k(ə-)lē\ *adv*

phy·log·e·ny \fī-'läj-ə-nē\ *n, pl* **-nies** : the racial history of a kind of organism; *also* : the evolutionary development of a group as distinguished from the individual development of an organism — compare ONTOGENY

phy·lum \'fī-ləm\ *n, pl* **phy·la** \-lə\ [NL, fr. Gk *phylon* tribe, race] **1** : a direct line of descent within a group **2** : a group that constitutes or has the unity of a phylum; *esp* : one of the usu. primary divisions of the animal kingdom ⟨the *phylum* Arthropoda⟩ — **phy·lar** \-lər\ *adj*

physi- *or* **physio-** *comb form* [Gk *physis*] **1** : nature ⟨*physio*graphy⟩ **2** : physical ⟨*physio*therapy⟩

¹phys·ic \'fiz-ik\ *n* **1** *archaic* : the profession of a physician : medical science **2** : a remedy for disease; *esp* : CATHARTIC, PURGATIVE

²physic *vt* **phys·icked** \-ikt\; **phys·ick·ing** \-i-kiŋ\; **phys·ics** *or* **phys·icks** : to treat with or administer medicine to; *esp* : PURGE

phys·i·cal \'fiz-i-kəl\ *adj* [Gk *physikos*, fr. *physis* nature] **1** : of or relating to nature or the laws of nature **2** : of or relating to material things : not mental or spiritual **3** : of or relating to natural science **4** : of or relating to physics **5** : of or relating to the body : BODILY; *also* : preoccupied with the body or its needs **syn** see MATERIAL — **phys·i·cal·ly** \-k(ə-)lē\ *adv*

physical education *n* : instruction in the care and development of the body ranging from simple calisthenic exercises to a course of study providing training in hygiene, gymnastics, and the performance and management of athletic games

physical geography *n* : geography that deals with the exterior physical features and changes of the earth

physical science *n* : the natural sciences (as mineralogy or astronomy) that deal primarily with nonliving materials

physical therapy *n* : the treatment of disease by physical and mechanical means (as massage, exercise, water, or heat) — **physical therapist** *n*

phy·si·cian \fə-'zish-ən\ *n* : a person skilled in the art of healing; *esp* : a doctor of medicine

phys·i·cist \'fiz-ə-səst\ *n* : a specialist in the science of physics

phys·i·co·chem·i·cal \,fiz-i-kō-'kem-i-kəl\ *adj* **1** : being physical and chemical **2** : relating to chemistry that deals with the physicochemical properties of substances — **phys·i·co·chem·i·cal·ly** \-k(ə-)lē\ *adv*

phys·ics \'fiz-iks\ *n* [Gk *physika*, fr. neut. pl. of *physikos* of nature, fr. *physis* nature, lit., growth, fr. *phyein* to bring forth, *phyesthai* to grow; akin to E *be*] **1** : a science that deals with the phenomena of inanimate matter and motion and includes consideration of mechanics, heat, light, electricity, sound, and nuclear phenomena **2** : physical composition, properties, or processes ⟨the *physics* of sound⟩

phys·i·og·no·my \,fiz-ē-'ä(g)-nə-mē\ *n, pl* **-mies** [Gk *physis* nature, physique + *gnōmōn* interpreter, fr. *gignōskein* to know] **1** : the art of discovering temperament and character from outward appearance **2** : the facial features held to show qualities of mind or character **3** : external aspect; *also* : inner character or quality revealed outwardly — **phys·i·og·nom·ic** \-ē-ə(g)-'näm-ik\ *or* **phys·i·og·nom·i·cal** \-'näm-i-kəl\ *adj* — **phys·i·og·nom·i·cal·ly** \-i-k(ə-)lē\ *adv*

phys·i·og·ra·phy \,fiz-ē-'äg-rə-fē\ *n* : PHYSICAL GEOGRAPHY — **phys·i·og·ra·pher** \-rə-fər\ *n* — **phys·io·graph·ic** \,fiz-ē-ə-'graf-ik\ *adj*

phys·i·o·log·i·cal \,fiz-ē-ə-'läj-i-kəl\ *or* **phys·i·o·log·ic** \-'läj-ik\ *adj* **1** : of, relating to, or affecting physiology **2** : characteristic of healthy or normal physiology — **phys·i·o·log·i·cal·ly** \-i-k(ə-)lē\ *adv*

physiological saline *n* : a solution of a salt or salts that is essentially isotonic with tissue fluids or blood

phys·i·ol·o·gy \,fiz-ē-'äl-ə-jē\ *n* **1** : a branch of biology dealing with the processes, activities, and phenomena incidental to and characteristic of life or of living matter **2** : the organic processes and phenomena of an organism or any of its parts or of a particular bodily process — **phys·i·ol·o·gist** \-jəst\ *n*

phys·io·ther·a·py \,fiz-ē-ō-'ther-ə-pē\ *n* : PHYSICAL THERAPY

phy·sique \fə-'zēk\ *n* [F, fr. *physique* physical] : the build of a person's body : physical constitution

phyt- *or* **phyto-** *comb form* [Gk *phyton*, fr. *phyein* to bring forth] : plant ⟨*phytophagous*⟩

-phyte \,fīt\ *n comb form* [Gk *phyton* plant] **1** : plant having a (specified) characteristic or habitat ⟨xero*phyte*⟩ **2** : pathological growth ⟨osteo*phyte*⟩

-phyt·ic \'fit-ik\ *adj comb form* : resembling a plant ⟨holo*phytic*⟩

phy·to·ge·og·ra·phy \,fīt-ō-jē-'äg-rə-fē\ *n* : the biogeography of plants

phy·tog·ra·phy \fī-'täg-rə-fē\ *n* : descriptive botany sometimes including plant taxonomy

phy·tol·o·gy \fī-'täl-ə-jē\ *n* : BOTANY — **phy·to·log·ic** \,fīt-ºl-'äj-ik\ *adj*

phy·ton \'fī-,tän\ *n* [Gk, plant] : a structural unit of a plant consisting of a leaf and the associated part of a stem; *also* : the smallest part of a plant capable of developing into a new plant when isolated

phy·to·pa·thol·o·gy \,fīt-ə-pə-'thäl-ə-jē, -pa-\ *n* : the study of plant diseases — **phy·to·path·o·log·ic** \-,path-ə-'läj-ik\ *or* **phy·to·path·o·log·i·cal** \-'läj-i-kəl\ *adj*

phy·to·plank·ton \,fīt-ō-'plaŋ(k)-tən, -,tän\ *n* : planktonic plant life — **phy·to·plank·ton·ic** \-plaŋ(k)-'tän-ik\ *adj*

phy·to·tox·ic \,fīt-ə-'täk-sik\ *adj* : poisonous to plants — **phy·to·tox·ic·i·ty** \-,täk-'sis-ət-ē\ *n*

¹pi \'pī\ *n, pl* **pis** \'pīz\ **1** : the 16th letter of the Greek alphabet — II or π **2 a** : the symbol π denoting the ratio of the circumference of a circle to its diameter **b** : the ratio itself having a value to eight decimal places of 3.14159265

²pi *n, pl* **pies** : type or type matter that is spilled, mixed, or incorrectly distributed

³pi *vb* **pied; pi·ing 1** : to spill or throw (type or type matter) into disorder **2** : to become pied

pia ma·ter \'pī-ə-,māt-ər\ *n* [L, tender mother] : the innermost and thin vascular membrane investing the brain and spinal cord — **pi·al** \'pī-əl\ *adj*

pi·a·nis·si·mo \,pē-ə-'nis-ə-,mō\ *adv (or adj)* [It, fr. *piano* softly] : very softly — used as a direction in music

pi·an·ist \pē-'an-əst, 'pē-ə-nəst\ *n* : a person who plays the piano

¹pi·a·no \pē-'än-ō\ *adv (or adj)* [It, soft, softly, fr. LL *planus* smooth, fr. L, level] : SOFTLY, QUIETLY — used as a direction in music

²pi·ano \pē-'an-ō\ *n, pl* **-an·os** [It, short for *pianoforte*, fr. *piano e forte* soft and loud; fr. the fact that its tones could be varied in loudness] : a stringed percussion instrument having steel-wire strings that sound when struck by felt-covered hammers operated by a keyboard

pi·an·o·forte \pē-'an-ə-,fōrt, -,fórt, -,fórt-ē\ *n* : PIANO

pi·as·ter *or* **pi·as·tre** \pē-'as-tər\ *n* **1** : a Spanish dollar : PIECE OF EIGHT **2 a** : any of several monetary units of some Middle Eastern countries (as Egypt) equal to ¹⁄₁₀₀ pound **b** : a coin representing one piaster

pi·az·za \pē-'az-ə, *1 is usu* -'at-sə, -'ät-sə\ *n, pl* **piazzas** *or* **pi·az·ze** \-'at-(,)sā, -'ät-\ [It, fr. L *platea* broad street, fr. Gk *plateia*, fr. fem. of *platys* broad] **1** : an open square esp. in an Italian town **2 a** : an arcaded and roofed gallery **b** *chiefly North & Midland* : VERANDA, PORCH

pi·broch \'pē-,bräk\ *n* [ScGael *piobaireachd* pipe music] : a set of martial or mournful variations for the Scottish bagpipe

pi·ca \'pī-kə\ *n* **1** : 12-point type **2** : a unit of ⅙ inch used in measuring typographical material **3** : a typewriter type providing 10 characters to the inch

pic·a·dor \'pik-ə-,dór\ *n, pl* **picadors** \-,dórz\ *or* **pic·a·do·res** \,pik-ə-'dōr-ēz, -'dór-\ [Sp, fr. *picar* to prick] : a horseman in a bullfight who prods the bull with a lance to weaken its neck and shoulder muscles

pic·a·resque \,pik-ə-'resk\ *adj* [Sp *picaresco*, fr. *pícaro* rogue] : of or relating to rogues or rascals; *also* : of or relating to a type of fiction of Spanish origin dealing with rogues and vagabonds

¹pic·a·yune \,pik-ē-'(y)ün\ *n* [F *picaillon* halfpenny] **1** : a small coin of Spanish origin formerly circulated in the southern U.S. **2** : something trivial

²picayune *adj* : having little value : PALTRY; *also* : PETTY, SMALL-MINDED

pic·ca·lil·li \,pik-ə-'lil-ē\ *n* : a pungent relish of chopped vegetables and spices

pic·co·lo \'pik-ə-,lō\ *n, pl* **-los** [It, short for *piccolo flauto* small flute] : a small shrill flute pitched an octave higher than the ordinary flute — **pic·co·lo·ist** \-əst\ *n*

pi·ce·ous \'pī-sē-əs\ *adj* [L *piceus* like pitch, fr. *pic-, pix* pitch] : glossy brownish black in color

¹pick \'pik\ *vb* [partly fr. (assumed) OE *pīcian* to prick; partly fr. MF *piquer* to prick, fr. (assumed) VL *piccare*, fr. L *picus* woodpecker] **1** : to strike or work on (as for piercing, breaking, or denting) with a pointed tool; *also* : to move, alter, or form by such action **2 a** : to clear away (something) or free from something by or as if by plucking ⟨*pick* meat from a bone⟩⟨*picked* the bone clean⟩ ⟨*pick* a chicken⟩ **b** : to gather or move by plucking ⟨*pick* berries⟩⟨*picked* the dish from the table⟩ **c** : to handle or operate by plucking something ⟨*pick* a guitar⟩; *also* : to pluck at **3** : to look over and choose or separate : CULL, SELECT ⟨*picked* over the apples and threw away the spoiled ones⟩⟨*picked* out a red dress⟩⟨*pick* a book⟩ **4** : to steal or pilfer from ⟨*pick* a purse⟩ **5** : PROVOKE ⟨*pick* a quarrel⟩ **6** : to eat sparingly or in a finicky manner **7** : to unlock without a key ⟨*pick* a lock⟩ — **pick·er** *n* — **pick on 1** : TEASE, HARASS **2** : to single out esp. for some unpleasant task

²pick *n* **1** : a blow or stroke with a pointed instrument **2 a** : the act or privilege of choosing or selecting : CHOICE ⟨take your *pick*⟩ **b** : the best or choicest one ⟨took only the *pick* of the crop⟩

³pick *n* **1** : PICKAX **2** : any of several slender pointed implements for picking or chipping ⟨an ice *pick*⟩ **3** : PLECTRUM

pick·a·back \'pig-ē-,bak, 'pik-ə-\ *var of* PIGGYBACK

pick·a·nin·ny *or* **pic·a·nin·ny** \'pik-ə-,nin-ē, ,pik-ə-'\ *n, pl* **-nies** : a Negro child

pick·ax *or* **pick·axe** \'pik-,aks\ *n* : a heavy tool with a wooden handle and a curved or straight blade pointed at one or both ends that is used esp. in loosening or breaking up soil or rock

heads of pickaxes

picked \'pikt\ *adj* : fit or ready for use : CHOICE ⟨a team of *picked* men⟩

pick·er·el \'pik-(ə-)rəl\ *n, pl* **pickerel** *or* **pickerels** [ME *pikerel*, dim. of *pike*] : any of several comparatively small pikes; *also* : WALLEYE 2

pick·er·el·weed \-,wēd\ *n* : any of various monocotyledonous aquatic plants; *esp* : a blue-flowered American shallow-water herb

¹pick·et \'pik-ət\ *n* [F *piquet*, fr. *piquer* to prick] **1** : a pointed stake or post (as for a fence) **2** : a soldier or a detachment of soldiers posted to guard an army from

surprise attack **3 :** a person posted by a labor organization at a place of work where there is a strike
²picket vb **1 :** to enclose, fence, or fortify with pickets **2 :** to guard or post as a picket **3 :** TETHER **4 a :** to post pickets or act as a picket at ⟨*picket* a factory⟩ **b :** to serve as a picket — **pick·et·er** n
pick·ings \'pik-iŋz, -ənz\ n pl **1 :** something available or left over; esp **:** eatable remains **2 :** yield or return for effort expended
¹pick·le \'pik-əl\ n [ME pekille] **1 :** a bath for preserving or cleaning; esp **:** a brine or vinegar solution in which foods are preserved **2 :** a difficult situation **:** PLIGHT **3 :** an article of food (as a cucumber) preserved in brine or vinegar
²pickle vt **pick·led; pick·ling** \'pik-(ə-)liŋ\ **:** to treat, preserve, or clean in or with a pickle
pick·lock \'pik-,läk\ n **1 :** a tool for picking locks **2 :** BURGLAR, THIEF
pick off vt **1 :** to shoot or bring down one by one **2 :** to catch (a base runner) off base with a quick throw by the pitcher or catcher
pick out vt **1 a :** SELECT, CHOOSE **b :** DISTINGUISH **2 :** to play the notes of by ear or one by one
pick over vt **:** to examine in order to select the best or remove the unwanted
pick·pock·et \'pik-,päk-ət\ n **:** one who steals from pockets
pick up \(')pik-'əp\ vb **1 a :** to take hold of and lift ⟨*pick up* your clothes⟩ **b :** to take in or into a vehicle ⟨the bus *picked up* passengers⟩ **2 :** to acquire casually, irregularly, or at a bargain ⟨*pick up* a bad habit⟩ ⟨*picked up* some shirts at the sale⟩ **b :** to strike up a casual acquaintance with and persuade to accompany esp. for purposes of lovemaking **3 :** to bring within range of sight or hearing **4 :** to gather or regain speed, vigor, or activity ⟨failed to *pick up* after his illness⟩ ⟨the market is expected to *pick up* soon⟩
pick·up \'pik-,əp\ n **1 a :** a revival of activity ⟨a business pickup⟩ **b :** ACCELERATION **2 :** a temporary chance acquaintance **3 :** the conversion of mechanical movements into electrical impulses in the reproduction of sound; also **:** a device (as on a phonograph) for making such conversion **4 a :** the reception of sound or an image into a radio or television transmitting apparatus for conversion into electrical signals **b :** a device (as a microphone or a television camera) for converting sound or the image of a scene into electrical signals **c :** the place where a broadcast originates **5 :** a light truck having an open body with low sides
picky \'pik-ē\ adj **:** FUSSY, FINICKY
¹pic·nic \'pik-(,)nik\ n [F pique-nique] **1 :** an excursion or outing with food usu. taken along and eaten in the open **2 :** something pleasant or easy **3 :** a shoulder of pork with much of the butt removed
²picnic vi **pic·nicked; pic·nick·ing :** to go on a picnic **:** eat in picnic fashion — **pic·nick·er** n
pi·co- \'pē-kō\ comb form **:** one trillionth part of ⟨picogram⟩
¹pi·cot \'pē-kō, pē-'\ n [F, lit., small point, fr. piquer to prick] **:** one of a series of small ornamental loops forming an edging on ribbon or lace
²picot vt **pi·coted** \-(')kōd\; **pi·cot·ing** \-(')kō-iŋ\ **:** to finish with a picot
pic·ric acid \,pik-rik-\ n [Gk pikros bitter] **:** a bitter toxic explosive yellow crystalline strong acid used esp. in high explosives, as a dye, or in medicine
Pict \'pikt\ n **:** one of a possibly non-Celtic people who once occupied Great Britain, were in many places displaced by the Britons, carried on continual border wars with the Romans, and about the 9th century became amalgamated with the Scots — **Pict·ish** \'pik-tish\ adj or n
pic·to·gram \'pik-tə-,gram\ n **:** PICTOGRAPH 3
pic·to·graph \-,graf\ n **1 :** an ancient or prehistoric drawing or painting on a rock wall **2 :** one of the symbols belonging to a pictorial graphic system **3 :** a diagram representing statistical data by pictorial forms — **pic·to·graph·ic** \,pik-tə-'graf-ik\ adj
pic·tog·ra·phy \pik-'täg-rə-fē\ n **:** use of pictographs **:** PICTURE WRITING 1
pic·to·ri·al \pik-'tōr-ē-əl, -'tòr-\ adj [L pictor painter, fr.

pict-, pingere to paint] **1 :** of or relating to a painter, a painting, or the painting or drawing of pictures ⟨*pictorial* art⟩ **2 a :** consisting of pictures ⟨*pictorial* records⟩ **b :** illustrated by pictures ⟨*pictorial* magazines⟩ **3 :** having the qualities of a picture ⟨*pictorial* reporting⟩ — **pic·to·ri·al·ly** \-ē-ə-lē\ adv — **pic·to·ri·al·ness** n
¹pic·ture \'pik-chər\ n [L pict-, pingere to paint] **1 :** a representation made on a surface (as by painting, drawing, or photography) **2 a :** a very vivid or graphic description **b :** a presentation of a problem or situation or the matter presented ⟨a worsening of the economic *picture*⟩ **3 a :** an exact likeness **:** SEMBLANCE ⟨the *picture* of his father⟩ **b :** a tangible or visible representation **:** EMBODIMENT ⟨the very *picture* of health⟩ **4 a :** a transitory visible image (as on a television screen) **b :** MOTION PICTURE — **picture** adj
²picture vt **pic·tured; pic·tur·ing** \'pik-chə-riŋ, 'pik-shriŋ\ **1 :** to make a picture of (as by drawing) **:** DEPICT **2 :** to describe vividly **3 :** to form a mental image of **:** IMAGINE
picture hat n **:** a woman's dressy hat with a broad brim
pic·tur·esque \,pik-chə-'resk\ adj **1 :** resembling a picture **:** suggesting or suitable for a painted scene **2 :** CHARMING, QUAINT ⟨*picturesque* customs⟩ **syn** see GRAPHIC — **pic·tur·esque·ly** adv — **pic·tur·esque·ness** n
picture tube n **:** KINESCOPE 1
picture window n **:** an outsize window designed to frame a desirable exterior view
picture writing n **1 :** the recording of events or expression of messages by pictures representing actions or facts **2 :** the record or message represented by picture writing
pid·dle \'pid-ᵊl\ vi **pid·dled; pid·dling** \'pid-liŋ, -ᵊl-iŋ\ **:** to act or work idly **:** DAWDLE
pid·dling \'pid-lən, -ᵊl-ən, -liŋ, -ᵊl-iŋ\ adj **:** TRIVIAL, PALTRY
pid·dock \'pid-ək\ n **:** a marine bivalve mollusk that bores in stone, wood, or clay
pid·gin \'pij-ən\ n [short for pidgin English, an English-based pidgin, fr. pidgin E pidgin business, modif. of E business] **:** a simplified speech used for communication between people with different languages; esp **:** an English-based pidgin used in the Orient
¹pie \'pī\ n [OF, fr. L pica] **1 :** MAGPIE **2 :** a parti-colored animal
²pie n [ME] **1 :** a dish consisting of a pastry crust and a filling (as of fruit or meat) **2 :** a layer cake with a thick filling (as of jam or custard)
³pie var of PI
¹pie·bald \'pī-,bòld\ adj [¹pie] **:** of two colors; esp **:** spotted or blotched with black and white ⟨a *piebald* horse⟩
²piebald n **:** a piebald animal (as a horse)
¹piece \'pēs\ n [OF, fr. (assumed) VL pettia, of Gaulish origin] **1 :** a part cut, torn, or broken from a thing **:** FRAGMENT ⟨a *piece* of string⟩ **2 :** one of a group, set, or mass of things ⟨a *piece* of mail⟩ ⟨a 3-*piece* suite of furniture⟩ ⟨a chess *piece*⟩ **3 :** a portion marked off ⟨a *piece* of land⟩ **4 :** a single item, example, or instance ⟨a *piece* of news⟩ **5 :** a definite quantity or size in which an article is made for sale or use (buy lumber by the *piece*) **6 :** a finished product **:** something made, composed, or written ⟨a *piece* of music⟩ ⟨a sculptor's most famous *piece*⟩ **7 :** COIN **8 :** FIREARM **syn** see PART — **of a piece :** ALIKE, UNIFORM, CONSISTENT
²piece vt **1 :** to repair, renew, or complete by adding pieces **:** PATCH **2 :** to join into a whole ⟨*pieced* their stories together⟩ — **piec·er** n
pièce de ré·sis·tance \pē-,es-də-rə-,zē-'stän(t)s\ n, pl **pièces de ré·sis·tance** \same\ [F, lit., piece of resistance] **1 :** the chief dish of a meal **2 :** an outstanding item
piece goods n pl **:** cloth fabrics sold from the bolt at retail in lengths specified by the customer
¹piece·meal \'pēs-,mēl\ adv **1 :** one piece at a time **:** GRADUALLY **2 :** in pieces or fragments **:** APART
²piecemeal adj **:** done, made, or accomplished piece by piece or in a fragmentary way **:** GRADUAL
piece of eight n **:** an old Spanish peso of eight reals
piece·work \'pēs-,wərk\ n **:** work paid for at a rate based on the number of articles made rather than the time spent in making them — **piece·work·er** \-,wər-kər\ n
pie chart n **:** a circular chart that illustrates quantities or frequencies by radial segments

---

ə abut; ᵊ kitten; ər further; a back; ā bake; ä cot, cart; aů out; ch chin; e less; ē easy; g gift; i trip; ī life

pied \'pīd\ *adj* [¹*pie*] **:** of two or more colors in blotches **:** PARTI-COLORED

pied-à-terre \pē-ˌād-ə-'te(ə)r\ *n, pl* **pieds-à-terre** *same*\ [F, lit., foot to the ground] **:** a temporary or second lodging

pied·mont \'pēd-ˌmänt\ *adj* [Piedmont, region of Italy] **:** lying or formed at the base of mountains — **piedmont** *n*

pie·plant \'pī-ˌplant\ *n* **:** garden rhubarb

pier \'pi(ə)r\ *n* [OE *per*, fr. ML *pera*] **1 :** a support for a bridge span **2 :** a structure built out into the water for use as a landing place or walk or to protect or form a harbor **3 :** a single pillar or a structure used to support something **4 :** a mass of masonry (as a buttress) used to strengthen a wall

pierce \'pi(ə)rs\ *vb* [OF *percer*] **1 :** to run into or through as a pointed weapon does **:** STAB **2 :** to make a hole through **:** PERFORATE **3 :** to force or make a way into or through something **4 :** to penetrate with the eye or mind **:** DISCERN **5 :** to penetrate so as to move or touch the emotions of **syn** see ENTER — **pierc·ing·ly** \'pir-siŋ-lē\ *adv*

pier glass *n* **:** a tall mirror; *esp* **:** one designed to occupy the wall space between windows

Pi·eri·an \pī-'ir-ē-ən, -'er-\ *adj* **:** of or relating to the region of Pieria in ancient Macedonia or to the Muses as early worshiped there

Pier·rot \'pē-ə-ˌrō\ *n* **:** a standard comic character of old French pantomime usu. with whitened face and loose white clothes

pier table *n* **:** a table to be placed under a pier glass

pies *pl of* PI *or of* PIE

pie·tà \ˌpē-ā-'tä\ *n, often cap* [It, lit., pity, fr. L *pietat-*, *pietas*] **:** a representation of the Virgin Mary mourning over the dead body of Christ

pi·e·tism \'pī-ə-ˌtiz-əm\ *n* **1** *cap* **:** a 17th century religious movement originating in Germany and stressing Bible study and personal religious experience **2 a :** emphasis on devotional experience and practices **b :** affected piety — **pi·e·tist** \'pī-ət-əst\ *n, often cap* — **pi·e·tis·tic** \ˌpī-ə-'tis-tik\ *adj* — **pi·e·tis·ti·cal·ly** \-'tis-ti-k(ə-)lē\ *adv*

pi·e·ty \'pī-ət-ē\ *n, pl* **-ties** [L *pietas*, fr. *pius* pious] **1 :** the quality or state of being pious: as **a :** fidelity to natural obligations (as to parents) **b :** dutifulness in religion **:** DEVOUTNESS **2 :** an act inspired by piety

pi·ezo·elec·tric·i·ty \pē-ˌā-zō-ə-ˌlek-'tris-ət-ē, -ˌāt-sō-, -'tris-tē\ *n* [Gk *piezein* to press] **:** electricity or electric polarity due to pressure esp. in a crystalline substance — **pi·ezo·elec·tric** \-'lek-trik\ *adj* — **pi·ezo·elec·tri·cal·ly** \-'lek-tri-k(ə-)lē\ *adv*

¹pif·fle \'pif-əl\ *vi* **pif·fled**; **pif·fling** \'pif-(ə-)liŋ\ **:** to talk or act in a trivial, inept, or ineffective way **:** TRIFLE

²piffle *n* **:** trifling talk or action

¹pig \'pig\ *n* [ME *pigge*] **1 a :** a young swine not yet sexually mature **b :** a wild or domestic swine **2 a :** PORK **b :** the dressed carcass of a young swine weighing less than 130 pounds **c :** PIGSKIN **3 :** one resembling a pig **4 :** a casting of metal (as iron or lead) run directly from the smelting furnace into a mold — *adj*

²pig *vb* **pigged**; **pig·ging** **1 :** FARROW **2 :** to live like a pig ⟨*pig* it⟩

pi·geon \'pij-ən\ *n* [MF *pijon*, fr. LL *pipion-*, *pipio* young bird, fr. L *pipire* to chirp] **1 :** any of numerous birds (order Columbiformes) with a stout body, usu. short legs, and smooth and compact plumage; *esp* **:** a domesticated bird derived from the rock pigeon **2 :** an easy mark **:** DUPE

pigeon breast *n* **:** a chest deformity marked by a sharp protrusion of the sternum that is typical of rickets

pigeon hawk *n* **:** any of several small hawks; *esp* **:** a small American falcon related to the European merlin

pi·geon·heart·ed \ˌpij-ən-'härt-əd\ *adj* **:** COWARDLY

¹pi·geon·hole \'pij-ən-ˌhōl\ *n* **1 :** a hole or small place for pigeons to nest **2 :** a small open compartment (as in a desk or cabinet) for keeping letters or papers

²pigeonhole *vt* **:** to place in or as if in the pigeonhole of a desk: as **a :** to lay aside **:** SHELVE **b :** to assign to a category **:** CLASSIFY

pi·geon-toed \ˌpij-ən-'tōd\ *adj* **:** having the toes turned in

pig·gery \'pig-(ə-)rē\ *n, pl* **-ger·ies :** a place where swine are kept

pig·gish \'pig-ish\ *adj* **:** resembling a pig esp. in greed, dirtiness, or stubbornness — **pig·gish·ly** *adv*

pig·gy·back \'pig-ē-ˌbak\ *adv (or adj)* **1 :** on the back or shoulders **2 :** on a railroad flatcar

piggy bank *n* **:** a coin bank often in the shape of a pig

pig·head·ed \'pig-'hed-əd\ *adj* **:** OBSTINATE, STUBBORN

pig iron *n* **:** iron that is the direct product of the blast furnace and is refined to produce steel, wrought iron, or ingot iron

¹pig·ment \'pig-mənt\ *n* [L *pigmentum*, fr. *pingere* to paint] **1 :** a substance that imparts black or white or a color to other materials; *esp* **:** a powdered substance mixed with a liquid in which it is relatively insoluble to impart color **2 a :** a natural coloring matter in animals and plants **b :** any of various related colorless substances — **pig·men·tary** \-mən-ˌter-ē\ *adj*

²pig·ment \-mənt, -ˌment\ *vt* **:** to color with or as if with pigment

pig·men·ta·tion \ˌpig-mən-'tā-shən, -ˌmen-\ *n* **:** coloration with or deposition of pigment; *esp* **:** an excessive deposition of bodily pigment

pigmy *var of* PYGMY

pig·nut \'pig-ˌnət\ *n* **:** any of several bitter-flavored hickory nuts or a tree bearing these

pig·pen \-ˌpen\ *n* **1 :** PIGSTY **2 :** a dirty place

pig·skin \-ˌskin\ *n* **1 :** the skin of a swine or leather made of it **2 a :** a jockey's saddle **b :** FOOTBALL 2

pig·sty \'pig-ˌstī\ *n* **:** a pen for pigs

pig·tail \-ˌtāl\ *n* **1 :** tobacco in small twisted strands or rolls **2 :** a tight braid of hair

pig-tailed \-ˌtāld\ *adj* **:** wearing a pigtail ⟨a *pig-tailed* little girl⟩

pig·weed \-ˌwēd\ *n* **:** any of various strongly growing weedy plants esp. of the goosefoot or amaranth families

pi·ka \'pē-kə\ *n* **:** any of various small short-eared mammals of rocky uplands of Asia and western No. America that are related to the rabbits

¹pike \'pīk\ *n* [OE *pīc* pickax] **1 :** PIKESTAFF 1 **2 :** a sharp point or spike; *also* **:** the tip of a spear — **piked** \'pīkt\ *adj*

²pike *n, pl* **pike** *or* **pikes** [ME, fr. ¹*pike*] **:** a large long-bodied and long-snouted gluttonous freshwater fish valued for food and sport and widely distributed in cool northern waters; *also* **:** any of various related or similar fishes

³pike *n* [MF *pique*, fr. *piquer* to prick, fr. (assumed) VL *piccare*, fr. L *picus* woodpecker] **:** a long wooden shaft with a pointed steel head formerly used as a weapon by infantry

⁴pike *n* **:** TURNPIKE

pike perch *n* **:** a fish (as a walleye) of the perch group that resembles the pike

pik·er \'pī-kər\ *n* **1 :** one who does things in a small way or on a small scale **2 :** TIGHTWAD, CHEAPSKATE, CHISELER

pike·staff \'pīk-ˌstaf\ *n* **1 :** a spiked staff for use on slippery ground **2 :** the shaft of a soldier's pike

pi·laf *or* **pi·laff** \pi-'läf\ *or* **pi·lau** \pi-'lō, -'lȯ, South often 'pər-lü, -lō\ *n* [Per & Turk *pilāu*] **:** a dish made of rice with meat and seasoning

pi·las·ter \'pī-ˌlas-tər\ *n* [It *pilastro*] **:** an upright rectangular slightly projecting architectural member that ornaments or helps to support a wall

Pilate *n* **:** PONTIUS PILATE

pil·chard \'pil-chərd\ *n* **:** a fish resembling the related herring and occurring in great schools along the coasts of Europe; *also* **:** any of several related fishes — compare SARDINE

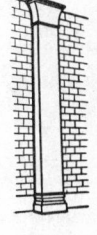

pilaster

¹pile \'pīl\ *n* [OE *pīl* dart, stake, fr. L *pilum* javelin] **:** a long slender column usu. of timber, steel, or reinforced concrete driven into the ground to carry a vertical load

²pile *vt* **:** to equip or support with piles

³pile *n* [L *pila* pillar, mole of stone] **1 a :** a quantity of things heaped together **b :** a heap of wood for burning a corpse or a sacrifice **:** PYRE **2 :** a great amount (as of money) **3 a :** a vertical series of alternate disks of two dissimilar metals (as copper and zinc) with disks of cloth or paper moistened with an electrolyte between them

for producing a current of electricity   **b** : a battery made up of cells similarly constructed   **4** : REACTOR 2b
⁴pile *vb*   **1** : to lay or place something in a pile : STACK   **2** : to heap in abundance : LOAD   **3** : to move or press forward in or as if in a mass : CROWD ⟨*piled* into a car⟩
⁵pile *n* [L *pilus* hair]   **1** : a coat or surface of usu. short close fine furry hairs   **2** : a velvety surface produced on textile by an extra set of filling yarns that form raised loops which are cut and sheared
⁶pile *n* [L *pila* ball]   **1** : a single hemorrhoid   **2** *pl* : HEMORRHOIDS
pi·le·ate \'pī-lē-ˌāt\ *or* **pi·le·at·ed** \-ˌāt-əd\ *adj* [L *pilleus, pileus* felt cap] : having a cap or crest ⟨a *pileated* woodpecker⟩⟨*pileate* fungi⟩
piled \'pīld\ *adj* : having a pile
pile driver *n* : a machine for driving or hammering piles into place
pi·le·us \'pī-lē-əs\ *n, pl* **-lei** \-lē-ˌī\ [NL, fr. L *pilleus* felt cap]   CAP 3a
pil·fer \'pil-fər\ *vb* **pil·fered; pil·fer·ing** \-f(ə-)riŋ\ [MF *pelfrer,* fr. *pelfre* booty] : to steal articles of small value or in small amounts at a time — **pil·fer·age** \-f(ə-)rij\ *n* — **pil·fer·er** \-fər-ər\ *n*
pil·grim \'pil-grəm\ *n* [OF *peligrin,* fr. LL *pelegrinus,* alter. of L *peregrinus* foreigner, fr. *pereger* being abroad, fr. *per* through + *ager* land]   **1** : one who journeys in alien lands : WAYFARER   **2** : one who travels to a shrine or holy place as a devotee   **3** *cap* : one of the English colonists founding the first permanent settlement in New England at Plymouth in 1620
pil·grim·age \'pil-grə-mij\ *n* : a journey of a pilgrim esp. to a shrine or a sacred place — **pilgrimage** *vi*
pil·ing \'pī-liŋ\ *n* : a structure of piles; *also* : PILES
pill \'pil\ *n* [L *pilula,* dim. of *pila* ball]   **1 a** : medicine in a small rounded mass to be swallowed whole   **b** : an oral contraceptive — usu. used with *the*   **2** : something resembling a pill (as in distasteful quality or globular form)
¹pil·lage \'pil-ij\ *n* [MF, fr. *piller* to plunder, fr. *peille* rag, fr. L *pilleus* felt cap] : the act of looting or plundering esp. in war
²pillage *vb* : to take booty : PLUNDER, LOOT — **pil·lag·er** *n*
pil·lar \'pil-ər\ *n* [OF *piler,* fr. ML *pilare,* fr. L *pila* pillar]   **1** : a comparatively slender upright support (as for a roof)   **2** : a column or shaft standing alone (as for a monument)   **3** : something suggesting a pillar : a main support ⟨a *pillar* of local society⟩ — **pil·lared** \-ərd\ *adj* — **from pillar to post** : from one place or one situation to another
pil·lar–box \'pil-ər-ˌbäks\ *n, Brit* : a pillar⸗shaped mailbox
pill·box \'pil-ˌbäks\ *n*   **1** : a small usu. shallow round box for pills   **2** : a small low concrete emplacement for machine guns and antitank weapons   **3** : a small round hat without a brim; *esp* : a woman's shallow hat with a flat crown and straight sides
pill bug *n* : WOOD LOUSE
¹pil·lion \'pil-yən\ *n* [ScGael *pillean*]   **1** : a cushion or pad placed behind a saddle for an extra rider   **2** : a passenger's saddle (as on a motorcycle)
²pillion *adv* : on or as if on a pillion ⟨ride *pillion*⟩
pil·lo·ry \'pil-(ə-)rē\ *n, pl* **-ries** [OF *pilori*]   **1** : a device for publicly punishing offenders that consists of a wooden frame with holes in which the head and hands can be locked — compare STOCK   **2** : a means for exposing to public scorn or ridicule — **pillory** *vt*
¹pil·low \'pil-ō\ *n* [OE *pyle, pylu,* fr. L *pulvinus*] : a support for the head of a person lying down that consists usu. of a bag filled with resilient material (as feathers or sponge rubber)
²pillow *vb*   **1** : to rest or lay on or as if on a pillow   **2** : to serve as a pillow for
pil·low·case \-ˌkās\ *n* : a removable covering for a pillow — called also *pillow slip*
pi·lose \'pī-ˌlōs\ *adj* [L *pilus* hair] : covered with usu. soft hair — **pi·los·i·ty** \pī-'läs-ət-ē\ *n*

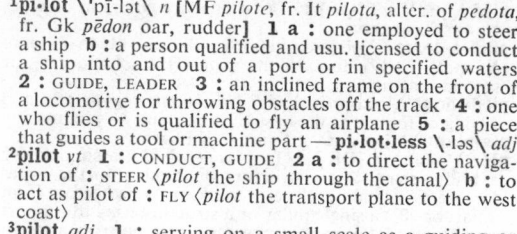

pillar 1

pillory

¹pi·lot \'pī-lət\ *n* [MF *pilote,* fr. It *pilota,* alter. of *pedota,* fr. Gk *pēdon* oar, rudder]   **1 a** : one employed to steer a ship   **b** : a person qualified to conduct a ship into and out of a port or in specified waters   **2** : GUIDE, LEADER   **3** : an inclined frame on the front of a locomotive for throwing obstacles off the track   **4** : one who flies or is qualified to fly an airplane   **5** : a piece that guides a tool or machine part — **pi·lot·less** \-ləs\ *adj*
²pilot *vt*   **1** : CONDUCT, GUIDE   **2 a** : to direct the navigation of : STEER ⟨*pilot* the ship through the canal⟩   **b** : to act as pilot of : FLY ⟨*pilot* the transport plane to the west coast⟩
³pilot *adj*   **1** : serving on a small scale as a guiding or tracing device or an activating or auxiliary unit ⟨a *pilot* parachute⟩   **2** : serving on a small scale as a testing or trial device or unit ⟨a *pilot* factory⟩
pi·lot·age \'pī-lət-ij\ *n*   **1** : the act or business of piloting   **2** : the compensation paid to a pilot
pilot balloon *n* : a small unmanned balloon sent up to show the direction and speed of the wind
pilot biscuit *n* : HARDTACK — called also *pilot bread*
pilot burner *n* : a small burner kept lighted to rekindle the principal burner
pilot engine *n* : a locomotive going in advance of a train to make sure that the way is clear
pi·lot·house \-ˌhaus\ *n* : an enclosed place forward on the upper deck of a ship that shelters the steering gear and the helmsman
pilot light *n*   **1** : a light indicating the location (as of a switch) or the operational state (as of a motor)   **2** : a small permanent flame used to ignite gas at a burner
Pilt·down man \ˌpilt-ˌdaun-\ *n* : a supposedly very early primitive modern man based on skull fragments uncovered in a gravel pit at Piltdown, England, and used in combination with comparatively recent skeletal remains of various animals in the development of an elaborate fraud
pi·ma cotton \ˌpē-mə-, ˌpim-ə-\ *n* [*Pima* county, Arizona] : an American cotton with fiber of exceptional strength and firmness derived from Egyptian cottons
pi·men·to \pə-'ment-ō\ *n, pl* **-tos** *or* **-to** [Sp *pimiento,* fr. *pimienta* allspice, pepper, fr. LL *pigmenta,* pl. of *pigmentum* plant juice, fr. L, pigment]   **1** : PIMIENTO   **2** : ALLSPICE
pi·mien·to \pə-'ment-ō, pəm-'yent-\ *n, pl* **-tos** [Sp] : any of various thick-fleshed sweet peppers of mild flavor used esp. as a source of paprika
¹pimp \'pimp\ *n* : PROCURER, PANDER
²pimp *vi* : to act as a pimp
pim·per·nel \'pim-pər-ˌnel\ *n* [MF *pimprenelle,* fr. LL *pimpinella,* a medicinal herb] : any of a genus of herbs of the primrose family; *esp* : one whose scarlet, white, or purplish flowers close at the approach of rainy or cloudy weather — called also *scarlet pimpernel*
pim·ple \'pim-pəl\ *n* [ME *pinple*] : a small inflamed swelling of the skin often containing pus : PUSTULE — **pim·pled** \-pəld\ *adj* — **pim·ply** \-p(ə-)lē\ *adj*
¹pin \'pin\ *n* [OE *pinn*]   **1 a** : a piece of wood or metal used esp. for fastening separate articles together or as a support by which one article may be suspended from another   **b** : one of the pieces constituting the target in various games (as bowling)   **c** : the staff of the flag marking a hole on a golf course   **d** : a peg for regulating the tension of the strings of a musical instrument   **2 a** : a small pointed piece of wire with a head used esp. for fastening cloth or paper   **b** : an ornament or emblem fastened to clothing with a pin   **c** : any of several devices for fastening (as a hairpin or safety pin)   **3** : LEG ⟨wobbly on his *pins*⟩   **4** : something of small value : TRIFLE ⟨doesn't care a *pin* for her⟩
²pin *vt* **pinned; pin·ning**   **1 a** : to fasten, join, or pierce with a pin   **b** : to hold or fix as if with a pin ⟨*pinned* his opponent against the wall⟩   **2 a** : ATTACH, HANG ⟨*pinned* his hopes on a miracle⟩   **b** : to assign the blame or responsibility ⟨*pin* the robbery on him⟩
pin·a·fore \'pin-ə-ˌfōr, -ˌfȯr\ *n* : a low-necked sleeveless apron worn esp. by children
pi·ña·ta \pēn-'yät-ə\ *n* [Sp, lit., pot] : a decorated pottery jar filled with candies, fruits, and gifts and hung from the ceiling to be broken as part of Mexican Christmas festivities
pin·ball machine \'pin-ˌbȯl-\ *n* : an amusement device

in which a ball propelled by a plunger scores points as it rolls down a slanting surface among pins and targets

pin·bone \'pin-ˌbōn, -ˌbȯn\ *n* : the hipbone esp. of a quadruped

pince-nez \paⁿs-ˈnā, pan(t)s-\ *n, pl* **pince-nez** \-ˈnā(z)\ [F, fr. *pincer* to pinch + *nez* nose] : eyeglasses clipped to the nose by a spring

pin·cer \'pin-chər, 'pin(t)-sər\ *n* [ME *pinceour*, fr. MF *pincier* to pinch] **1 a** *pl* : an instrument having two short handles and two grasping jaws working on a pivot and used for gripping things **b** : CHELA **2** : one of two attacking forces advancing one on each side of an enemy position so as to surround and destroy it — **pin·cer·like** \-ˌlīk\ *adj*

¹pinch \'pinch\ *vb* [ME *pinchen*, fr. (assumed) ONF *pinchier*] **1 a** : to squeeze between the finger and thumb or between the jaws of an instrument **b** : to squeeze or compress painfully **c** : to cause to appear thin or shrunken **2** : to subject to or practice strict economy **3** *slang* **a** : STEAL **b** : ARREST **4** : NARROW, TAPER

²pinch *n* **1 a** : a critical time or point : EMERGENCY **b** : a hurtful pressure or stress : HARDSHIP ⟨the *pinch* of hunger⟩ **2 a** : an act of pinching : SQUEEZE **b** : as much as may be taken between the finger and thumb ⟨a *pinch* of salt⟩ **3** *slang* **a** : THEFT **b** : a police raid : ARREST

pinch bar *n* : a lever with a pointed projection at one end that is used esp. to roll heavy wheels

pinch·beck \'pinch-ˌbek\ *n* [after Christopher *Pinchbeck* d1732 English watchmaker] **1** : an alloy of copper and zinc used esp. to imitate gold in cheap jewelry **2** : something counterfeit or spurious — **pinchbeck** *adj*

pinch·cock \-ˌkäk\ *n* : a clamp used on a flexible tube to regulate the flow of a fluid through the tube

pinch·er \'pin-chər\ *n* **1** : one that pinches **2** : PINCER — usu. used in pl.

pinch hitter *n* **1** : a baseball player sent in to bat for another esp. in an emergency when a hit is much needed **2** : a person called upon to do another's work in an emergency — **pinch-hit** \'pinch-ˈhit\ *vi*

pin curl *n* : a curl made usu. by dampening a strand of hair with water or lotion, coiling it, and securing it by a hairpin or clip

pin·cush·ion \'pin-ˌkush-ən\ *n* : a small cushion in which pins may be stuck

Pin·dar·ic \pin-ˈdar-ik\ *adj* : of or relating to or written in a manner or style characteristic of the poet Pindar

¹pine \'pīn\ *vi* [OE *pīnian*, fr. (assumed) OE *pīn* punishment, pain, fr. L *poena*] **1** : to lose vigor, health, or weight through grief, worry, or other distress ⟨*pine* away⟩ **2** : to have a continuing fruitless desire : YEARN ⟨*pine* for home⟩ **syn** see LONG

²pine *n* [OE *pin*, fr. L *pinus*] **1** : any of a genus of coniferous evergreen trees having slender elongated needles and including valuable timber trees as well as many ornamentals **2** : the straight-grained white or yellow usu. durable and resinous wood of a pine **3** : any of various Australian coniferous trees — **piny** *or* **pin·ey** \'pī-nē\ *adj*

pin·e·al \'pin-ē-əl, 'pī-nē-\ *adj* : of, relating to, or being the pineal body

pineal body *n* [L *pinea* pine cone, fr. *pinus* pine] : a small usu. conical appendage of the brain of most vertebrates that in a few reptiles has the essential structure of an eye and that is variously held to be a vestigial third eye, an endocrine organ, or the seat of the soul

pine·ap·ple \'pīn-ˌap-əl\ *n* : a tropical monocotyledonous plant with stiff spiny sword-shaped leaves and a short flowering stalk that develops into a fleshy edible fruit; *also* : this fruit

pine nut *n* : the edible seed of any of several chiefly western No. American pines

pine tar *n* : tar obtained by distillation of pinewood and used esp. in roofing and soaps and in the treatment of skin diseases

pine·wood \'pīn-ˌwu̇d\ *n* **1** : a wood or growth of pines **2** : PINE 2

pin·feath·er \'pin-ˌfeth-ər\ *n* : an incompletely developed feather just breaking through the skin — **pin·feath·ered** \-ərd\ *adj* — **pin·feath·ery** \-(ə-)rē\ *adj*

ping \'piŋ\ *n* **1** : a sharp sound like that of a bullet striking **2** : ignition knock ⟨kept hearing a *ping* in his automobile engine⟩ — **ping** *vi*

Ping–Pong \'piŋ-ˌpäŋ, -ˌpȯŋ\ *trademark* — used for table tennis

pin·head·ed \'pin-ˈhed-əd\ *adj* : lacking intelligence or understanding : DULL, STUPID — **pin·head·ed·ness** *n*

pin·hole \-ˌhōl\ *n* : a small hole made by, for, or as if by a pin

¹pin·ion \'pin-yən\ *n* [MF *pignon*] **1** : the terminal section of a bird's wing; *also* : WING **2** : FEATHER, QUILL — **pinioned** \-yənd\ *adj*

²pinion *vt* **1** : to restrain (a bird) from flight esp. by cutting off the pinion of one wing **2 a** : to disable or restrain by binding the arms **b** : to bind fast : SHACKLE

³pinion *n* [F *pignon*, fr. *peigne* comb, fr. L *pecten*] **1** : a gear with a small number of teeth designed to mesh with a larger wheel or rack **2** : the smallest of a train or set of gear wheels

¹pink \'piŋk\ *vt* [ME *pinken*] **1** : PIERCE, STAB **2 a** : to perforate in an ornamental pattern **b** : to cut a saw-toothed edge on

²pink *n* **1** : any of a genus of annual or perennial herbs with thick-noded stems often grown for their showy flowers borne singly or in clusters **2** : the highest degree ⟨*pink* of condition⟩

³pink *adj* **1** : of the color pink **2** : holding moderately radical and usu. socialistic political or economic views — **pink·ly** *adv* — **pink·ness** *n*

⁴pink *n* **1** : any of a group of colors bluish red to red in hue, of medium to high lightness, and of low to moderate saturation **2 a** : the scarlet color of a fox hunter's coat; *also* : a coat of this color **b** *pl* : light-colored trousers formerly worn by army officers **3** [fr. the viewing of pink as a weak form of red] : a person who holds moderately radical political or economic views

pink·eye \'piŋk-ˌī\ *n* : an acute highly contagious conjunctivitis of man and various domestic animals

pin·kie *or* **pin·ky** \'piŋ-kē\ *n, pl* **pinkies** : a little finger

pinking shears *n pl* : shears with a saw-toothed inner edge on the blades for making a zigzag cut

pink·ish \'piŋ-kish\ *adj* : somewhat pink — **pink·ish·ness** *n*

pin money *n* **1** : money given by a man to his wife for her own use **2** : money for incidental expenses

pin·na \'pin-ə\ *n, pl* **pin·nae** \-ˌnē, -ˌī\ *or* **pinnas** [NL, fr. L, feather, wing] **1** : a primary division of a pinnate leaf or frond **2** : a feather, wing, fin, or similar part **3** : the largely cartilaginous projecting portion of the external ear — **pin·nal** \'pin-ᵊl\ *adj*

pin·nace \'pin-əs\ *n* [MF *pinace*] **1** : a light sailing ship used largely as a tender **2** : any of various ship's boats

pin·na·cle \'pin-i-kəl\ *n* [LL *pinnaculum* gable, fr. diminutive of L *pinna* wing, battlement] **1** : an upright structure (as on a tower) generally ending in a small spire **2** : a lofty peak : a pointed summit **3** : the summit or highest point of achievement or development **syn** see SUMMIT

pin·nate \'pin-ˌāt\ *adj* [L *pinna* feather; akin to E *feather*] : resembling a feather esp. in having similar parts arranged on opposite sides of an axis ⟨a *pinnate* leaf⟩ — **pin·nate·ly** *adv* — **pin·na·tion** \pin-ˈā-shən\ *n*

pin-
nacle 1

pin·nat·i·fid \pə-ˈnat-ə-fəd, -ˌfid\ *adj* [L *-fidus* split, fr. *findere* to split] : cleft in a pinnate manner ⟨a *pinnatifid* leaf⟩ — **pin·nat·i·fid·ly** *adv*

pin·ni·ped \'pin-ə-ˌped\ *n* : any of a group (Pinnipedia) of aquatic carnivorous mammals including the seals and the walruses — **pin·niped** *adj*

pin·nule \'pin-ˌyül\ *n* [NL *pinnula*, fr. dim. of L *pinna* feather] **1** : a secondary branch of a plumose organ **2** : one of the ultimate divisions of a twice-pinnate leaf — **pin·nu·late** \'pin-yə-ˌlāt\ *adj* — **pin·nu·lat·ed** \-ˌlāt-əd\ *adj*

pi·noch·le \'pē-ˌnək-əl\ *n* : a card game played with a 48-card pack containing two of each suit of A, K, Q, J, 10, 9; *also* : the combination of queen of spades and jack of diamonds which scores 40 points in this game

pi·ñon \'pin-yən\ *n, pl* **piñons** *or* **pi·ño·nes** \pin-ˈyō-nēz\ [AmerSp *piñón*, fr. Sp, pine nut, fr. *piña* pine cone, fr. L *pinea*, fr. *pinus* pine] : any of various low-growing pines of western No. America with seeds that are pine nuts

¹pin·point \'pin-ˌpȯint\ *vt* **1** : to locate or determine

---

with precision **2** : to cause to stand out conspicuously : HIGHLIGHT

²**pinpoint** *adj* **1** : extremely fine or precise **2** : located, fixed, or directed with extreme precision

pin·prick \'pin-ˌprik\ *n* **1** : a small puncture made by or as if by a pin **2** : a petty irritation or annoyance — **pinprick** *vb*

pins and needles *n pl* : a pricking tingling sensation in a limb recovering from numbness — **on pins and needles** : in a nervous or jumpy state of anticipation

pin·set·ter \'pin-ˌset-ər\ *n* : an employee or a mechanical device that spots pins in a bowling alley — called also *pin·spot·ter* \-ˌspät-ər\

pin·stripe \'pin-ˌstrīp\ *n* : a fine stripe on a fabric — **pin-striped** \-ˌstrīpt\ *adj*

pint \'pīnt\ *n* [MF *pinte*, fr. VL *pincta*] **1** — see MEASURE table **2** : a pint vessel

pin·tail \'pin-ˌtāl\ *n, pl* **pintail** *or* **pintails** : a bird (as a duck or grouse) with long central tail feathers — **pin-tailed** \-ˌtāld\ *adj*

¹**pin·to** \'pin-tō\ *n, pl* **pintos** *also* **pintoes** [AmerSp, fr. obs. Sp *pinto* painted, fr. (assumed) VL *pinctus*, pp. of L *pingere* to paint] : a spotted horse or pony

²**pinto** *adj* : MOTTLED, PIED

pint-size \'pīnt-ˌsīz\ *or* **pint-sized** \-ˌsīzd\ *adj* : SMALL, DIMINUTIVE

pin·up \'pin-ˌəp\ *n* **1** : a photograph of a pinup girl **2** : an accessory (as a lamp) attached to a wall

pinup girl *n* : a girl whose glamorous qualities make her a suitable subject for a display photograph

pin·wale \'pin-ˌwāl\ *adj* : made with narrow wales ⟨*pinwale* corduroy⟩

pin·wheel \-ˌhwēl\ *n* **1** : a toy consisting of lightweight vanes that revolve at the end of a stick **2** : a fireworks device in the form of a revolving wheel of colored fire

pin·worm \-ˌwərm\ *n* : any of numerous small nematode worms that infest the intestines and usu. the cecum of various vertebrates; *esp* : one parasitic in man

¹**pi·o·neer** \ˌpī-ə-'ni(ə)r\ *n* [MF *pionier*, fr. *peon* foot soldier, fr. ML *pedon-, pedo*, fr. *ped-, pes* foot] **1** : a member of a unit of military engineers **2 a** : a person who goes before opening up new ways (as of thought or activity) ⟨*pioneers* of American medicine⟩ **b** : one of the first to settle in an area : COLONIST **3** : a plant or animal capable of establishing itself in a bare or barren area — **pioneer** *adj*

²**pioneer** *vb* **1** : to act as a pioneer **2** : to open or prepare for others to follow; *esp* : SETTLE **3** : to originate or take part in the development of something new

pi·os·i·ty \ˌpī-'äs-ət-ē\ *n, pl* **-ties** : an exaggerated or superficial piousness

pi·ous \'pī-əs\ *adj* [L *pius*] **1 a** : showing reverence for deity and devotion to divine worship : DEVOUT **b** : marked by conspicuous display of religion **2** : SACRED, RELIGIOUS ⟨a *pious* opinion⟩ **3** : showing loyal reverence for a person or thing : DUTIFUL **4 a** : marked by sham or hypocrisy **b** : marked by self-conscious virtue **syn** see DEVOUT — **pi·ous·ly** *adv* — **pi·ous·ness** *n*

¹**pip** \'pip\ *n* [MD *pippe*, fr. (assumed) VL *pipita*, alter. of L *pituita* phlegm, pip] **1** : a disorder of a bird marked by formation of a scale or crust on the tongue; *also* : this scale or crust **2** : any of various human ailments; *esp* : a slight unidentified disorder

²**pip** *n* **1** : a dot or spot (as on dice or playing cards) to indicate numerical value **2** : SPOT, SPECK

³**pip** *n* [short for *pippin*, fr. OF *pepin*] **1** : a small fruit seed ⟨orange *pips*⟩ **2** *slang* : something extraordinary of its kind

⁴**pip** *vb* **pipped; pip·ping 1** : ¹PEEP 1 **2 a** : to break the shell of the egg in hatching **b** : to be broken by a pipping bird

⁵**pip** *n* : a short high-pitched tone ⟨broadcast six *pips* as a time signal⟩

pi·pal \'pē-pəl\ *n* [Hindi *pīpal*, fr. Skt *pippala*] : a large Indian fig tree yielding a product like lac

¹**pipe** \'pīp\ *n* [OE *pipa*, fr. L *pipare* to peep] **1 a** : a musical instrument consisting of a tube of reed, wood, or metal that is played by blowing **b** : a tube producing a musical sound ⟨an organ *pipe*⟩ **c** : BAGPIPE — usu. used in pl. **d** : the whistle, call, or note esp. of a bird or an insect **2 a** : a long tube or hollow body used esp.

to conduct a substance (as water, steam, or gas) **b** : a cylindrical object, part, or passage **3 a** : a tube with a small bowl at one end used for smoking tobacco **b** : a toy pipe for blowing bubbles **4 a** : a large cask used esp. for wine and oil **b** : any of various units of liquid capacity based on the size of a pipe; *esp* : a unit of liquid capacity equal to 2 hogsheads — **pipe·less** \-ləs\ *adj*

²**pipe** *vb* **1 a** : to play on a pipe **b** : to convey orders or direct by signals on a boatswain's pipe **2** : to speak in or have a high shrill tone **3** : to furnish or trim with piping **4** : to convey by or as if by pipes — **pip·er** *n*

pipe cleaner *n* : a piece of flexible wire in which tufted fabric is twisted and which is used to clean the stem of a tobacco pipe

pipe down *vi* : to become quiet : stop talking

pipe dream *n* : an illusory or fantastic plan, hope, or story

pipe·fish \'pīp-ˌfish\ *n* : any of various long slender fishes that are related to the sea horses and have a tube-shaped snout and an angular body covered with bony plates

pipe fitter *n* : one who installs and repairs piping

pipe fitting *n* **1** : a piece (as a coupling, elbow, or valve) used to connect pipe or as accessory to a pipe **2** : the work of a pipe fitter

pipe·ful \'pīp-ˌfùl\ *n* : a quantity of tobacco smoked in a pipe at one time

pipe·line \'pīp-ˌlīn\ *n* **1** : a line of pipe with pumps, valves, and control devices for conveying liquids, gases, or finely divided solids **2** : a direct channel for information

pi·pette *also* **pi·pet** \pī-'pet\ *n* : a device for measuring and transferring small volumes of liquid that typically consists of a narrow glass tube into which the liquid is drawn by suction and retained by closing the upper end

pipe up *vi* : to begin to play or to sing or speak

pip·ing \'pī-piŋ\ *n* **1 a** : the music of a pipe **b** : the producing of or a calling in shrill pipes ⟨the *piping* of frogs⟩ **2** : a quantity or system of pipes **3** : a narrow decorative fold stitched in seams or along edges (as of clothing or slipcovers)

piping hot *adj* : very hot

pip·is·trelle \ˌpip-ə-'strel\ *n* : any of a genus of blunt-nosed mostly small and brown bats

pip·it \'pip-ət\ *n* : any of various small singing birds resembling the lark

pip·kin \'pip-kən\ *n* : a small earthenware or metal pot usu. with a horizontal handle

pip·pin \'pip-ən\ *n* [ONF *pepin* seedling apple tree] **1** : any of numerous apples of superior dessert quality with usu. yellow or greenish yellow skins strongly flushed with red **2** : a highly admired or very admirable person or thing

pip·sis·se·wa \pip-'sis-ə-ˌwȯ\ *n* [of AmerInd origin] : a low evergreen herb related to the wintergreens that has astringent leaves used medicinally

pip-squeak \'pip-ˌskwēk\ *n* : a small or insignificant person

pi·quant \'pē-kənt\ *adj* [F, fr. prp. of *piquer* to prick] **1** : agreeably stimulating to the palate : PUNGENT **2** : engagingly provocative; *also* : having a lively arch charm ⟨*piquant* face⟩ — **pi·quan·cy** \-kən-sē\ *n* — **pi·quant·ly** *adv* — **pi·quant·ness** *n*

¹**pique** \'pēk\ *n* : offense taken by one slighted or disdained; *also* : a fit of resentment

²**pique** *vt* [F *piquer*, lit., to prick] **1** : to arouse anger or resentment in : IRRITATE; *esp* : to offend by slighting **2** : to excite or arouse by a provocation, challenge, or rebuff

³**pi·qué** *or* **pi·que** \pi-'kā, 'pē-, -ˌ\ *n* [F *piqué*, fr. pp. of *piquer* to prick, quilt] : a durable ribbed fabric of cotton, rayon, or silk

pi·quet \pi-'kā\ *n* [F] : a two-handed card game played with 32 cards

pi·ra·cy \'pī-rə-sē\ *n, pl* **-cies 1** : robbery on the high seas **2** : the unauthorized use of another's production or invention esp. in infringement of a copyright

pi·ra·nha \pə-'rän-yə\ *n* [Pg, of AmerInd origin] : CARIBE

¹**pi·rate** \'pī-rət\ *n* [L *pirata*, fr. Gk *peiratēs*, fr. *peiran* to attempt] : a person who commits piracy and esp. robbery on the high seas — **pi·rat·i·cal** \pə-'rat-i-kəl, pī-\ *adj* — **pi·rat·i·cal·ly** \-'rat-i-k(ə-)lē\ *adv*

²pirate vt : to take or appropriate by piracy ⟨*pirate* an invention⟩

pi·rogue \'pē-ˌrōg\ n [F, fr. Sp *piragua*, of AmerInd origin] **1** : DUGOUT 1 **2** : a boat like a canoe

pir·ou·ette \ˌpir-ə-'wet\ n [F] : a rapid whirling about of the body; *esp* : a full turn on the toe or ball of one foot in ballet — **pirouette** vi

pis pl of PI

pis·ca·to·ry \'pis-kə-ˌtōr-ē, -ˌtor-\ adj [L *piscari* to fish, fr. *piscis* fish] : of, relating to, or dependent on fishermen or fishing — **pis·ca·to·ri·al** \ˌpis-kə-'tōr-ē-əl, -'tor-\ adj — **pis·ca·to·ri·al·ly** \-ē-ə-lē\ adv

Pi·sces \'pī-(ˌ)sēz, 'pis-ˌēz\ n [L, fr. pl. of *piscis* fish] **1** : a zodiacal constellation directly south of Andromeda **2** : the 12th sign of the zodiac — see ZODIAC table

pi·scine \'pī-ˌsēn, 'pis-ˌ(k)īn\ adj [L *piscis* fish; akin to E *fish*] : of, relating to, or characteristic of fish

pis·mire \'pis-ˌmī(ə)r, 'piz-\ n [ME *pissemire*, fr. *pisse* urine + *mire* ant, of Scand origin] : ANT

pi·so·lite \'pī-sə-ˌlīt\ n : a limestone made up of small concretions — **pi·so·lit·ic** \ˌpī-sə-'lit-ik\ adj

pis·tach·io \pə-'stash-(ē-)ō, -'stäsh-\ n, pl **-chios** [It *pistacchio*] : a small tree of the sumac family whose fruit contains a greenish edible seed; *also* : its seed

pis·til \'pist-ᵊl\ n [L *pistillum* pestle] : the seed-producing part and female reproductive organ of a flower consisting usu. of stigma, style, and ovary — see FLOWER illustration

pis·til·late \'pis-tə-ˌlāt\ adj : having pistils; *esp* : having pistils but no stamens

pis·tol \'pist-ᵊl\ n [MF *pistole*, fr. G, fr. Czech *pištal*, lit., pipe] : a short firearm intended to be aimed and fired with one hand — **pistol** vt

pis·tole \pis-'tōl\ n : an old gold 2-escudo piece of Spain or any of several old gold coins of Europe of approximately the same value

pis·tol-whip \'pist-ᵊl-ˌhwip\ vt : to beat with a pistol

pis·ton \'pis-tən\ n [F, fr. It *pistone* pestle, fr. *pistare* to pound, fr. ML, freq. of L *pinsere* to crush] **1** : a sliding piece moved by or moving against fluid pressure that usu. consists of a short cylinder fitting within a cylindrical vessel along which it moves back and forth **2** : a valve sliding in a cylinder in a brass wind instrument and serving when pressed down to lower its pitch

piston ring n : a springy split metal ring around a piston for making a tight fit

piston rod n : a rod by which a piston is moved or by which it communicates motion

¹pit \'pit\ n [OE *pytt*] **1** : a hole, shaft, or cavity in the ground ⟨gravel *pit*⟩ **2** : an area set off from and often sunken below adjacent areas: as **a** : an enclosure where animals (as cocks) are set to fight **b** : the space occupied by an orchestra in a theater **c** : the area where members of an exchange actually trade **3 a** : a hollowed or indented area esp. in the surface of the body ⟨the *pit* of the stomach⟩ **b** : an indented scar (as from a boil) **c** : a thin area in a plant cell wall through which dissolved materials can pass

²pit vb **pit·ted; pit·ting 1 a** : to put into or store in a pit **b** : to make pits in; *esp* : to scar with pits **2** : to set (as gamecocks) into or as if into a pit to fight; *also* : to set into opposition or rivalry **3** : to become marked with pits

³pit n [D; akin to E *pith*] : the stone of a fruit (as the cherry) that is a drupe

⁴pit vt **pit·ted; pit·ting** : to remove the pit from

pit-a-pat \ˌpit-i-'pat\ adv (or adj) : PITTER-PATTER — **pit-a-pat** n — **pit-a-pat** vi

¹pitch \'pich\ n [OE *pic*, fr. L *pic-, pix*] **1** : a dark sticky substance obtained as a residue in the distillation of organic materials (as tars) **2** : resin from various conifers

²pitch vt : to cover, smear, or treat with or as if with pitch

³pitch vb [ME *pichen*] **1** : to erect and fix firmly in place ⟨*pitch* a tent⟩ **2** : THROW, TOSS, FLING ⟨*pitch* hay⟩; *also* : to deliver a baseball to a batter **3** : to sell or advertise esp. by high-pressure methods **4 a** : to cause to be at a particular pitch or level ⟨*pitch* a tune too high⟩ **b** : to incline or cause to incline at a particular angle **5 a** : to fall precipitately or headlong **b** : to have the bow alternately plunge precipitately down and rise abruptly up ⟨a ship *pitching* in heavy seas⟩ **c** : BUCK 1a ⟨a *pitching*

horse⟩ **6** : to play ball as a pitcher ⟨*pitched* for fourteen years in the minor leagues⟩

⁴pitch n **1** : the action or a manner of pitching **2 a** : SLOPE; *also* : degree of slope **b** (1) : distance between one point on a gear tooth and the corresponding point on the next tooth (2) : distance from any point on the thread of a screw to the corresponding point on an adjacent thread measured parallel to the axis **c** : the distance advanced by a propeller in one revolution **3 a** : a high point : ZENITH **4 a** : the property of a tone that is determined by the frequency of the sound waves producing it : highness or lowness of sound **b** : a standard frequency for tuning instruments **c** : the difference in the relative vibration frequency of the human voice that contributes to the total meaning of speech **5** : a high-pressure sales talk **6 a** : the delivery of a baseball by a pitcher to a batter **b** : a baseball so thrown — **pitched** \'picht\ adj

pitch-black \'pich-'blak\ adj : extremely dark or black

pitch·blende \'pich-ˌblend\ n [G *pechblende*, fr. *pech* pitch + *blende* sphalerite] : a brown to black mineral that consists essentially of an oxide of uranium, often contains radium, and is a source of uranium

pitch-dark \-'därk\ adj : extremely dark

pitched battle \'pich(t)-\ n : an intensely fought battle in which the opposing forces are locked in close combat

¹pitch·er \'pich-ər\ n [OF *pichier*, fr. ML *bicarius* goblet, fr. Gk *bikos* earthen jug] : a container for holding and pouring liquids that usu. has a lip or spout and a handle

²pitcher n : one that pitches: as **a** : a baseball player who pitches **b** : a broad-faced golf iron with more loft than a mashie niblick — called also *number seven iron*

pitcher plant n : any of various plants with leaves modified into pitchers in which insects are trapped and digested by the plant

pitch·fork \'pich-ˌfork\ n : a usu. long-handled fork used in pitching hay or grain — **pitchfork** vt

pitchfork

pitch in vi **1** : to begin to work energetically **2** : to contribute to a common endeavor

pitching niblick n : a golf iron with more loft than a pitcher — called also *number eight iron*

pitch·man \'pich-mən\ n : SALESMAN; *esp* : one who vends novelties or similar articles on the streets or from a concession

pitch·out \'pich-ˌaut\ n **1** : a pitch in baseball deliberately out of reach of the batter to enable the catcher to check or put out a base runner **2** : a lateral pass in football between two backs behind the line of scrimmage

pitch pipe n : a small pipe blown to indicate musical pitch esp. for singers or for tuning an instrument

pitchy \'pich-ē\ adj **pitch·i·er; -est 1 a** : full of pitch **: TARRY b** : of, relating to, or having the qualities of pitch **2** : PITCH-BLACK

pit·e·ous \'pit-ē-əs\ adj : arousing or deserving pity or compassion — **pit·e·ous·ly** adv — **pit·e·ous·ness** n

pit·fall \'pit-ˌfol\ n **1** : TRAP, SNARE; *esp* : a pit flimsily covered or camouflaged and used to capture and hold animals or men **2** : a hidden or not easily recognized danger or difficulty

pith \'pith\ n [OE *pitha*] **1 a** : a central strand of spongy tissue in the stems of most vascular plants that prob. functions chiefly in storage **b** : any of various loose spongy internal tissues or parts ⟨the *pith* of a feather⟩ **2** : the essential part : CORE — **pith** adj

pith·e·can·thro·pus \ˌpith-i-'kan(t)-thrə-pəs, -kan-'thrō-\ n, pl **-thro·pi** \-ˌpī, -ˌpē\ [NL, fr. Gk *pithēkos* ape + *anthrōpos* man] : any of several primitive extinct men known esp. from skeletal remains from Javanese Pliocene gravels — compare PEKING MAN — **pith·e·can·thro·pi·an** \-kan-'thrō-pē-ən\ adj or n — **pith·e·can·thro·pine** \-'kan(t)-thrə-ˌpīn\ n — **pith·e·can·thro·poid** \-ˌpoid\ adj or n

pith ray n : MEDULLARY RAY

pithy \'pith-ē\ adj **pith·i·er; -est 1** : consisting of or filled with pith **2** : having substance and point : tersely cogent — **pith·i·ly** \'pith-ə-lē\ adv — **pith·i·ness** \'pith-ē-nəs\ n

piti·a·ble \'pit-ē-ə-bəl\ adj **1** : deserving or exciting pity **: LAMENTABLE 2** : pitifully insignificant or scanty — **piti·a·ble·ness** n — **piti·a·bly** \-blē\ adv

---

j joke; ŋ sing; ō flow; ȯ flaw; ȯi coin; th thin; t̲h̲ this; ü loot; u̇ foot; y yet; yü few; yu̇ furious; zh vision

pit·i·ful \'pit-i-fəl\ *adj* **1** : arousing pity or sympathy ⟨a *pitiful* orphan⟩ **2** : deserving pitying contempt : PITI-ABLE ⟨a *pitiful* excuse⟩ **syn** see CONTEMPTIBLE — **pit·i·ful·ly** \-f(ə-)lē\ *adv*

pit·i·less \'pit-i-ləs, 'pit-ʾl-əs\ *adj* : devoid of pity : MERCI-LESS — **pit·i·less·ly** *adv* — **pit·i·less·ness** *n*

pi·ton \'pē-,tän\ *n* [F] : a spike, wedge, or peg that can be driven into a rock or ice surface as a support often with an eye through which a rope may pass

pit·tance \'pit-ʾn(t)s\ *n* [ML *pietantia* donation to a religious house to provide an extra allowance of food, fr. *pietare* to be charitable, fr. L *pietas* pity] : a small portion, amount, or allowance

pit·ter-pat·ter \'pit-ər-,pat-ər, 'pit-ē-,pat-\ *n* : a rapid succession of light sounds or beats — **pit·ter-pat·ter** \,pit-ər-', ,pit-ē-'\ *adv* (*or adj*) — **pitter-patter** *like adv*\ *vi*

pi·tu·i·tary \pə-'t(y)ü-ə-,ter-ē\ *adj* [L *pituita* phlegm; fr. the former belief that the pituitary body secreted phlegm] : of, relating to, or being the pituitary body — **pituitary** *n*

pituitary body *n* : a small oval endocrine organ attached to the base of the brain that consists of an epithelial anterior lobe joined by an intermediate part to a posterior lobe of nervous origin and that produces various internal secretions with a direct or indirect regulatory relation to most basic body functions and esp. to growth and reproduction — called also *pituitary gland*

Pi·tu·i·trin \pə-'t(y)ü-ə-trən\ *trademark* — used for an extract of cattle pituitary bodies

pit viper *n* : any of a family of mostly New World venomous snakes with a sensory pit on each side of the head and hollow perforated fangs

¹pity \'pit-ē\ *n* [OF *pité*, fr. L *pietat-, pietas* piety, pity, fr. *pius* pious] **1 a** : sympathetic sorrow for one suffering, distressed, or unhappy : COMPASSION **b** : capacity to feel pity **2** : something to be regretted

²pity *vb* **pit·ied**; **pity·ing** : to feel pity or pity for — **pit·i·er** *n*

pity·ing *adj* : expressing or feeling pity ⟨a *pitying* glance⟩ — **pity·ing·ly** \-iŋ-lē\ *adv*

¹piv·ot \'piv-ət\ *n* [F] **1** : a shaft or pin on which something turns **2** : something upon which something else turns or depends : a central member, part, or point

²pivot *vb* **1** : to turn on or as if on a pivot **2** : to provide with, mount on, or attach by a pivot **3** : to cause to pivot

piv·ot·al \'piv-ət-ʾl\ *adj* **1** : of, relating to, or functioning as a pivot **2** : vitally important : CRUCIAL — **piv·ot·al·ly** \-ʾl-ē\ *adv*

pix·ie *or* **pixy** \'pik-sē\ *n, pl* **pix·ies** : a mischievous sprite or fairy — **pix·ie·ish** \-sē-ish\ *adj*

piz·za \'pēt-sə\ *n* [It] : an open pie made typically of thinly rolled bread dough spread with a spiced mixture (as of tomatoes, cheese, and ground meat) and baked

piz·ze·ria \,pēt-sə-'rē-ə\ *n* : an establishment where pizzas are made or sold

piz·zi·ca·to \,pit-si-'kät-ō\ *adv* (*or adj*) [It, lit., plucked] : by means of plucking by the fingers instead of bowing — used as a direction in music

plac·a·ble \'plak-ə-bəl, 'plā-kə-\ *adj* : easily placated : TOLERANT, TRACTABLE — **plac·a·bil·i·ty** \,plak-ə-'bil-ət-ē, ,plā-kə-\ *n* — **plac·a·bly** \'plak-ə-blē, 'plā-kə-\ *adv*

¹plac·ard \'plak-,ärd, -ərd\ *n* [MF *placquart*, fr. *plaquier* to plate, plaster] : a notice posted or carried in a public place : POSTER

²placard *vt* **1** : to post placards on or in **2** : to announce by or as if by posting

pla·cate \'plā-,kāt, 'plak-,āt\ *vt* [L *placare*] : to calm the anger of esp. by concessions : SOOTHE, APPEASE **syn** see PACIFY — **pla·ca·tion** \plā-'kā-shən, pla-\ *n* — **pla·ca·tive** \'plā-,kāt-iv, 'plak-,āt-\ *adj* — **pla·ca·to·ry** \'plā-kə-,tōr-ē, 'plak-ə-, -,tōr-\ *adj*

¹place \'plās\ *n* [MF, open space, fr. L *platea* broad street, fr. Gk *plateia*, fr. fem. of *platys* broad] **1 a** : physical extension : SPACE ⟨considerations of time and *place*⟩ **b** : a particular but often unspecified location in space : LOCALITY ⟨stopped several days at each *place*⟩; *also* : an inhabited area (as a city or village) ⟨her native *place*⟩ **2 a** : a building in which people live : a dwelling or residence often together with its grounds : HOMESTEAD **b** : a building or part of a building or sometimes an outside area designed for or devoted to a particular purpose ⟨amusement *places*⟩⟨a *place* of resort⟩⟨a *place* of worship⟩ **3** : an identifiable or differentiated part of something : SPOT ⟨a sore *place* on his shoulder⟩⟨a wet *place* in the driveway⟩⟨lost his *place* in the book⟩ **4** : position in some ordering ⟨in the first *place*⟩: as **a** : relative position in a scale or sequence : DEGREE **b** : a leading position at the conclusion of a competition **c** : the position of a figure in relation to others in a row or series; *esp* : that of one to the right of a decimal point **5** : suitable or assigned location or situation ⟨not the *place* for an active man⟩: as **a** : accommodation occupied by or available for occupancy of one person ⟨took 2 *places* on the coach⟩⟨set 12 *places* at table⟩ **b** : space or situation customarily or formerly occupied ⟨paper towels taking the *place* of linen⟩ **c** : a situation of employment : JOB ⟨lost her *place* at the office⟩; *also* : official position ⟨had a *place* in the treasury⟩ — **place·less** \'plās-ləs\ *adj*

²place *vb* **1** : to distribute in an orderly manner : ARRANGE **2 a** : to put in or direct to a particular place **b** : to present for consideration ⟨a question *placed* before the group⟩ **c** : to put in a particular state **3** : to appoint to a position; *esp* : to find employment or a home for **4 a** : to assign to or hold a position in a series : RANK **b** : ESTIMATE ⟨*placed* the value of the estate too high⟩ **c** : to identify by association ⟨could not *place* the girl when he met her again⟩ **5** : to give an order for ⟨*place* a bet⟩ **6** : to come in second in a horse race — **place·a·ble** \'plā-sə-bəl\ *adj*

pla·ce·bo \plə-'sē-bō\ *n, pl* **-bos** [L, I shall please] : an inert medication used for psychological reasons or as a control

place hitter *n* : a baseball player who is able to hit a pitched ball to a chosen part of the playing field

place·hold·er \'plās-,hōl-dər\ *n* : a symbol used in mathematics in the place of a numeral not yet determined

place-kick \'plās-,kik\ *n* : the kicking of a football placed or held in a stationary position on the ground — **place-kick** *vb*

place·ment \'plās-mənt\ *n* : an act or instance of placing: as **a** : the position of a ball for a place-kick **b** : PLACE-KICK **c** : the assignment of a person to a suitable place (as a class in school or a job)

place-name \-,nām\ *n* : the name of a geographical locality

pla·cen·ta \plə-'sent-ə\ *n* [L, flat cake, fr. Gk *plakount-, plakous*] **1** : the vascular organ in most mammals by which the fetus is joined to the maternal uterus and nourished; *also* : an analogous organ in another animal **2** : the part of a carpel that bears ovules — **pla·cen·tal** \-'sent-ʾl\ *adj or n* — **plac·en·ta·tion** \,plas-ʾn-'tā-shən\ *n*

plac·er \'plas-ər\ *n* [Sp, fr. Catal, submarine plain, fr. *plaça* plaza] : an alluvial or glacial deposit containing particles of valuable mineral (as gold) — **placer miner** *n* — **placer mining** *n*

place setting *n* : a table service for one person ⟨a set of china with four *place settings*⟩

plac·id \'plas-əd\ *adj* [L *placidus*, fr. *placēre* to please] **1** : UNDISTURBED, PEACEFUL **2** : COMPLACENT **syn** see CALM — **pla·cid·i·ty** \pla-'sid-ət-ē, plə-\ *n* — **plac·id·ly** \'plas-əd-lē\ *adv* — **plac·id·ness** *n*

plack·et \'plak-ət\ *n* : a slit or opening in a garment (as a skirt) often forming the closure

plac·o·derm \'plak-ə-,dərm\ *n* : any of a class (Placodermi) of extinct Paleozoic armored and jawed fishes

plac·oid \'plak-,ȯid\ *adj* [Gk *plak-, plax* flat surface, tablet] : of, relating to, or being a fish scale of dermal origin with an enamel-tipped spine

pla·gia·rism \'plā-jə-,riz-əm\ *n* [L *plagiarius* plunderer, plagiarist, fr. *plagium* hunting net, fr. *plaga* net] **1** : an act of plagiarizing **2** : something plagiarized — **pla·gia·rist** \-rəst\ *n* — **pla·gia·ris·tic** \,plā-jə-'ris-tik\ *adj*

pla·gia·rize \'plā-jə-,rīz\ *vb* : to steal and pass off as one's own the work of another — **pla·gia·riz·er** *n*

pla·gio·clase \'plā-j(ē-)ə-,klās\ *n* [Gk *plagios* oblique + *klas-, klan* to break] : a feldspar having calcium or sodium in its composition

¹plague \'plāg\ *n* [LL *plaga*, fr. L, blow] **1** : a disastrous evil or destructively numerous influx ⟨*plague* of locusts⟩; *also* : a cause or occasion of annoyance **2** : an epidemic disease causing a high rate of mortality : PESTILENCE;

esp : a virulent contagious bacterial disease occurring in several forms (as bubonic plague)

²**plague** *vt* **1** : to strike or afflict with or as if with disease, calamity, or natural evil **2** : TEASE, TORMENT — **plagu·er** *n*

plague·some \'plāg-səm\ *adj* **1** : TROUBLESOME **2** : PESTILENTIAL

plagu·ey *or* **plaguy** \'plā-gē, 'pleg-ē\ *adj, chiefly dial* : causing irritation or annoyance : TROUBLESOME — **plaguey** *adv* — **plagu·i·ly** \'plā-gə-lē, 'pleg-ə-\ *adv*

plaice \'plās\ *n, pl* **plaice** [OF *plaïs*, fr. LL *platensis*] : any of several flatfishes; *esp* : a large European flounder

plaid \'plad\ *n* [ScGael *plaide*] **1** : a rectangular length of tartan worn over the left shoulder by men and women as part of the Scottish national costume **2 a** : TARTAN 2 **b** : a fabric with a pattern of tartan or imitative of tartan **3 a** : TARTAN 1 **b** : a pattern of unevenly spaced repeated stripes crossing at right angles — **plaid** *adj* — **plaid·ed** \-əd\ *adj*

¹**plain** \'plān\ *n* [OF, fr. L *planum*, fr. neut. of *planus* flat, plain] : an extensive area of level or rolling treeless country; *also* : a broad unbroken expanse

²**plain** *adj* [L *planus* flat, level, clear; akin to E *floor*] **1 a** : lacking ornament : UNDECORATED ⟨her dress was *plain*⟩ **b** : having no pattern **2** : free of added or extraneous matter : PURE ⟨a glass of *plain* water⟩ **3** : free of impediments to view : UNOBSTRUCTED **4 a** : clear to the mind or senses ⟨the trouble was *plain* to the mechanic⟩ **b** : marked by candor : BLUNT ⟨*plain* speaking⟩ **5 a** : of common or average attainments or status : neither notable nor lowly : ORDINARY ⟨*plain* people⟩ **b** : free from complexity : SIMPLE ⟨a *plain* explanation⟩; *also* : containing or using only simple wholesome ingredients ⟨*plain* food⟩ ⟨*plain* cooking⟩ **c** : lacking beauty or ugliness : HOMELY — **plain·ly** *adv* — **plain·ness** \'plān-nəs\ *n*

³**plain** *adv* : in a plain manner

plain·clothes·man \'plān-'klō(th)z-mən, -,man\ *n* : a police officer who does not wear a uniform while on duty : DETECTIVE

plain sailing *n* : easy progress over an unobstructed course

plains·man \'plānz-mən\ *n* : an inhabitant of plains

plain·song \'plān-,sȯŋ\ *n* : rhythmic but not metrical liturgical chant sung in unison in various Christian rites; *esp* : GREGORIAN CHANT

plain·spo·ken \'plān-'spō-kən\ *adj* : speaking or spoken plainly and esp. bluntly ⟨a *plainspoken* man⟩ ⟨his words were very *plainspoken*⟩ — **plain·spo·ken·ness** \-kən-nəs\ *n*

plaint \'plānt\ *n* [MF, fr. L *planctus*, fr. *plangere* to strike, beat one's breast, lament] **1** : LAMENTATION, WAIL **2** : PROTEST, COMPLAINT

plaint·ful \'plānt-fəl\ *adj* : MOURNFUL

plain·tiff \'plānt-əf\ *n* [MF *plaintif*, fr. *plaintif* complaining, plaintive] : the complaining party in a lawsuit : one who begins a lawsuit to enforce his claims — compare DEFENDANT

plain·tive \'plānt-iv\ *adj* : expressive of suffering or woe : MELANCHOLY — **plain·tive·ly** *adv* — **plain·tive·ness** *n*

plain weave *n* : a weave in which the threads interlace alternately

¹**plait** \'plāt, 'plat\ *n* [MF *pleit*, fr. L *plicare* to fold] **1** : PLEAT 2 **a** : a usu. flat braid (as of hair or straw)

²**plait** *vt* **1** : PLEAT 1 **2 a** : to interweave the strands or locks of : BRAID **b** : to make by plaiting — **plait·er** *n*

¹**plan** \'plan\ *n* [F, plane, foundation, ground plan; partly fr. L *planum* plain, plane; partly fr. LL *plantare* to plant] **1** : a drawing or diagram showing the parts or outline of something **2** : a method or scheme of acting, doing, or arranging ⟨a civil defense *plan*⟩ ⟨vacation *plans*⟩ **3** : INTENT, AIM ⟨his *plan* was to stop them at the bridge⟩
syn PLAN, DESIGN, PLOT, SCHEME mean a method of making or doing something or achieving an end. PLAN implies mental formulation and often graphic representation ⟨studied the *plans* for the stage sets⟩ DESIGN suggests a pattern and a degree of order or harmony ⟨*designs* for three new gowns⟩ PLOT implies a laying out in clearly distinguished sections with attention to their relations and proportions ⟨outlined the *plot* of his new play⟩ SCHEME stresses systematic choice and ordering of detail for the end in view and may suggest a plan motivated by craftiness and self-seeking

²**plan** *vb* **planned; plan·ning 1** : to form a plan of or for

: arrange the parts or details of in advance ⟨*plan* a church⟩ ⟨*plan* a party⟩ **2** : to have in mind : INTEND; *also* : to make plans — **plan·ner** *n*

plan- *or* **plano-** *comb form* : flat and ⟨*plano*-concave⟩

pla·nar \'plā-nər\ *adj* : of, relating to, or lying in a plane

pla·nar·ia \plə-'nar-ē-ə, -'ner-\ *n* : PLANARIAN; *esp* : one of a common freshwater genus

pla·nar·i·an \-ē-ən\ *n* : any of an order (Tricladida) of small soft-bodied ciliated mostly aquatic turbellarian worms — **planarian** *adj*

¹**plane** \'plān\ *vt* [LL *planare*, fr. L *planus* level] : to make smooth or even esp. with a plane; *also* : to remove by planing — **plan·er** *n*

²**plane** *n* [MF, fr. L *platanus*, fr. Gk *platanos*] : any of a genus of trees with large palmately lobed leaves and flowers in globose heads — called also *sycamore*

³**plane** *n* : a tool for smoothing or shaping a wood surface

⁴**plane** *n* [L *planum*, fr. neut. of *planus* level] **1 a** : a surface such that any two included points can be joined by a straight line lying wholly within the surface **b** : a flat or level material surface **2** : a level of existence, consciousness, or development **3 a** : one of the main supporting surfaces of an airplane **b** : AIRPLANE

plane

⁵**plane** *adj* [L *planus*] **1** : lacking elevations or depressions : FLAT, LEVEL **2** : of, relating to, or dealing with planes ⟨*plane* curve⟩

plane angle *n* : a measure of the difference of direction of two straight lines lying in a plane

plane geometry *n* : a branch of elementary geometry that deals with plane figures

plan·et \'plan-ət\ *n* [L *planeta*, mod. of Gk *planēt-*, *planēs*, lit., wanderer, fr. *planasthai* to wander] **1** : a heavenly body except a comet or meteor that revolves about the sun; *also* : such a body revolving about the sun of another solar system **2** : a heavenly body held to influence the fate of human beings

PLANETS

SYMBOL	NAME	MEAN DISTANCE FROM THE SUN		PERIOD IN DAYS OR YEARS	DIAMETER IN MILES
		astronomical units	million miles		
♃	Jupiter	5.20	483	12 years	86,800
♄	Saturn	9.54	886	29 years	71,500
♅	Uranus	19.19	1782	84 years	29,400
♆	Neptune	30.07	2793	165 years	28,000
♁	Earth	1.00	93	365¼ days	7,913
♀	Venus	0.72	67	225 days	7,600
♂	Mars	1.52	142	687 days	4,200
♇	Pluto	39.46	3670	248 years	4,000?
☿	Mercury	0.39	36	88 days	2,900

plan·e·tar·i·um \,plan-ə-'ter-ē-əm\ *n, pl* **-i·ums** *or* **-ia** \-ē-ə\ **1** : a model or representation of the solar system **2 a** : an optical device to project various celestial images and effects **b** : a building or room housing such a device

plan·e·tary \'plan-ə-,ter-ē\ *adj* **1 a** : of or relating to a planet **b** : having a motion like that of a planet ⟨*planetary* electrons of the atomic nucleus⟩ **2** : GLOBAL, WORLDWIDE ⟨a matter of *planetary* concern⟩

plan·e·tes·i·mal \,plan-ə-'tes-ə-məl\ *n* [*planet* + -*esimal* (as in *infinitesimal*)] : one of numerous small solid heavenly bodies which may have existed at an early stage of the development of the solar system and from which the planets may have been formed

plan·e·toid \'plan-ə-,tȯid\ *n* : a body resembling a planet; *esp* : ASTEROID

plan·gent \'plan-jənt\ *adj* [L *plangere* to strike, beat the breast, lament] **1** : having a loud reverberating sound **2** : having an expressive esp. plaintive quality — **plan·gen·cy** *n* — **plan·gent·ly** *adv*

¹**plank** \'plaŋk\ *n* [ONF *planke*, fr. L *planca*] **1** : a heavy thick board usu. 2 to 4 inches thick and at least 8 inches wide **2** : an article in the platform of a political party

²**plank** *vt* **1** : to cover or floor with planks **2** : to set down forcefully ⟨*planked* the book onto the shelf⟩ **3** : to cook and serve on a board usu. with an elaborate garnish

plank·ing *n* : a quantity or covering of planks ⟨worn deck *planking*⟩

plank·ter \'plaŋ(k)-tər\ *n* [Gk *planktēr* wanderer, fr. *plankt-, plazesthai* to wander] **:** a planktonic organism

plank·ton \'plaŋ(k)-tən, -,tän\ *n* [G, fr. Gk *plankt-, plazesthai* to wander, drift] **:** the passively floating or weakly swimming animal and plant life of a body of water — compare NEKTON '— **plank·ton·ic** \plaŋ(k)-'tän-ik\ *adj*

plan·less \'plan-ləs\ *adj* **:** functioning or taking place without a plan or set goal — **plan·less·ly** *adv* — **plan·less·ness** *n*

pla·no-con·cave \,plā-nō-kän-'kāv, -'kän-,\ *adj* **:** flat on one side and concave on the other

pla·no-con·vex \-'kän-'veks, -'kän-, , -kən-'\ *adj* **:** flat on one side and convex on the other

pla·nog·ra·phy \plā-'näg-rə-fē, plə-\ *n* **:** a process (as lithography) for printing from a plane surface — **pla·no·graph·ic** \,plā-nə-'graf-ik, ,plan-ə-\ *adj*

¹plant \'plant\ *vb* [OE *plantian*, fr. LL *plantare* to plant, fix in place, fr. L *planta* plant] **1 a :** to put or set in the ground to grow ⟨*plant* seeds⟩ **b :** IMPLANT ⟨*plant* good habits⟩ **2 a :** to cause to become established ⟨*plant* colonies⟩ **b :** to stock or provide with something usu. to grow or increase ⟨*plant* fields to corn⟩ ⟨*plant* a stream with trout⟩ **3 a :** to place or fix in the ground ⟨*planted* stakes to hold the vines⟩ **b :** to place firmly or forcibly ⟨*planted* a blow on his opponent's nose⟩ ⟨*planted* the book with a thud⟩ ⟨*planting* herself in his path⟩ **4 :** to hide, place secretly, or prearrange with intent to mislead ⟨*planted* nuggets in a worthless mine⟩ ⟨*plant* a spy in an office⟩ ⟨*planted* a rumor about the senator⟩ **5 :** to plant something — **plant·a·ble** \-ə-bəl\ *adj*

²plant *n* [L *planta*] **1 :** any of a kingdom (Plantae) of living beings typically lacking locomotive movement or obvious nervous or sensory organs and possessing cellulose cell walls and capacity for indefinite growth — compare ANIMAL **2 a :** the land, buildings, and equipment esp. of an industrial business ⟨the college *plant*⟩ **b :** a factory or workshop for the manufacture of a product ⟨automobile *plant*⟩ **3 :** an act of planting **4 :** something or someone planted — **plant·like** \-,līk\ *adj*

Plan·tag·e·net \plan-'taj-ə-nət\ *adj* **:** of or relating to an English royal house furnishing sovereigns from 1154 to 1399 — **Plantagenet** *n*

¹plan·tain \'plant-ᵊn\ *n* [OF, fr. L *plantagin-, plantago*] **:** any of several common short-stemmed or stemless weedy herbs with parallel-veined leaves and a long spike of tiny greenish flowers

²plantain *n* [Sp *plántano*, plane tree, plantain, fr. ML *plantanus* plane tree, alter. of L *platanus*] **:** a banana plant with large greenish starchy fruit that is eaten cooked and is a staple food in the tropics; *also* **:** this fruit

plantain lily *n* **:** a plant of the lily family with ribbed basal leaves and racemes of white or lilac flowers

plan·tar \'plant-ər, 'plan-,tär\ *adj* [L *planta* sole] **:** of or relating to the sole of the foot

plan·ta·tion \plan-'tā-shən\ *n* **1 :** a usu. large group of plants and esp. trees under cultivation **2 :** a settlement in a new country or region **:** COLONY **3 :** a planted area; *esp* **:** an agricultural estate worked by resident labor

plant·er \'plant-ər\ *n* **1 :** one that plants or cultivates ⟨a mechanical *planter*⟩; *esp* **:** an owner or operator of a plantation **2 :** one who settles or founds a colony **3 :** a container in which ornamental plants are grown

plant food *n* **1 :** FOOD 1b **2 :** FERTILIZER

plant hormone *n* **:** an organic substance other than a nutrient that in minute amounts modifies a plant physiological process; *esp* **:** one produced by a plant and active elsewhere than at the site of production

plan·ti·grade \'plant-ə-,grād\ *adj* [L *planta* sole + *gradi* to step] **:** walking on the sole with the heel touching the ground ⟨man is a *plantigrade* animal⟩ — **plantigrade** *n*

plantlike flagellate *n* **:** any of a major group (Phytomastigina) of organisms that have many characteristics in common with typical algae and are considered as protozoans or as algae — compare ZOOFLAGELLATE

plant louse *n* **:** an aphid or a related insect

plan·u·la \'plan-yə-lə\ *n, pl* **-u·lae** \-yə-,lē, -,lī\ **:** the young usu. flattened oval or oblong free-swimming ciliated larva of some coelenterates — **plan·u·lar** \-lər\ *adj* — **plan·u·loid** \-,lȯid\ *adj*

plaque \'plak\ *n* [F, fr. MF, metal sheet, fr. *plaquier* to

plate, fr. MD *placken* to piece, patch] **1 :** an ornamental brooch; *esp* **:** the badge of an honorary order **2 :** a flat thin piece (as of metal) used for decoration; *also* **:** a commemorative or identifying inscribed tablet

plash \'plash\ *n* **:** SPLASH — **plash** *vb*

-pla·sia \'plā-zh(ē-)ə\ *or* **-pla·sy** \,plā-sē, ,plas-ē, p-lə-sē\ *n comb form, pl* **-plasias** *or* **-plasies** [NL *-plasia*, fr. Gk *plassein* to mold] **:** development **:** formation ⟨hyperplasia⟩ ⟨homoplasy⟩

-plasm \,plaz-əm\ *n comb form* [Gk *plasma* something molded] **:** formative or formed material (as of a cell or tissue) ⟨endoplasm⟩

plas·ma \'plaz-mə\ *n* [Gk, something molded, fr. *plassein* to mold] **1 a :** the fluid part of blood, lymph, or milk as distinguished from suspended material **b :** PROTOPLASM **2 :** a gas in a highly ionized condition — **plas·mat·ic** \plaz-'mat-ik\ *adj*

plas·ma·gel \'plaz-mə-,jel\ *n* **:** firm gelated protoplasm

plas·ma·lem·ma \,plaz-mə-'lem-ə\ *n* [Gk *lemma* husk, rind] **:** PLASMA MEMBRANE

plasma membrane *n* **:** a semipermeable limiting layer of cell protoplasm

plas·ma·sol \'plaz-mə-,säl, -,sȯl\ *n* **:** fluid solated protoplasm

plas·mo·di·um \plaz-'mōd-ē-əm\ *n, pl* **-dia** \-ē-ə\ **1 :** a multinucleate mass of protoplasm **2 :** an individual malaria parasite — **plas·mo·di·al** \-ē-əl\ *adj*

plas·mol·y·sis \plaz-'mäl-ə-səs\ *n* **:** shrinking of the cytoplasm away from the wall of a living cell — **plas·mo·lyt·ic** \,plaz-mə-'lit-ik\ *adj* — **plas·mo·lyt·i·cal·ly** \-'lit-i-k(ə-)lē\ *adv* — **plas·mo·lyze** \'plaz-mə-,līz\ *vb*

¹plas·ter \'plas-tər\ *n* [OE, fr. L *emplastrum*, fr. Gk *emplastron*, fr. *emplassein* to plaster on, fr. *en-* + *plassein* to mold, plaster] **1 :** a medicated or protective dressing consisting of a film (as of cloth or plastic) spread with an often medicated substance that clings to the skin ⟨adhesive *plaster*⟩ **2 :** a pasty composition (as of lime, water, and sand) that hardens on drying and is used for coating walls, ceilings, and partitions **3 :** PLASTER OF PARIS — **plas·tery** \-t(ə-)rē\ *adj*

²plaster *vb* **plas·tered; plas·ter·ing** \-t(ə-)riŋ\ **1 :** to apply or to overlay or cover with plaster **2 :** to apply a plaster to **3 :** to cover over or conceal as if with a coat of plaster **4 :** to fasten with or as if with paste **:** stick tightly **5 :** to affix to or place upon esp. conspicuously or in quantity — **plas·ter·er** \-tər-ər\ *n*

plas·ter·board \'plas-tər-,bȯrd, -,bȯrd\ *n* **:** a board used in large sheets as a backing or as a substitute for plaster in walls and consisting of several plies of fiberboard, paper, or felt usu. bonded to a hardened gypsum plaster core

plaster cast *n* **:** a rigid dressing of gauze impregnated with plaster of paris

plaster of par·is \-'par-əs\ *often cap 2d P* **:** a white powdery slightly hydrated calcium sulfate made by calcining gypsum and used chiefly for casts and molds in the form of a quick-setting paste with water

¹plas·tic \'plas-tik\ *adj* [Gk *plastikos* of molding, fr. *plassein* to mold, form] **1 :** FORMATIVE, CREATIVE ⟨*plastic* forces in nature⟩ **2 a :** capable of being molded or modeled ⟨*plastic* clay⟩ **b :** capable of usu. adaptive change ⟨*plastic* species⟩ ⟨a *plastic* tissue⟩ **3 :** characterized by or using modeling ⟨*plastic* arts⟩ **4 :** SCULPTURAL **5 :** made or consisting of a plastic **6 :** capable of being deformed continuously and permanently in any direction without rupture — **plas·ti·cal·ly** \-ti-k(ə-)lē\ *adv* — **plas·tic·i·ty** \plas-'tis-ət-ē\ *n*

syn PLIABLE, PLIANT: PLASTIC applies to substances soft enough to mold into any desired form; PLIABLE implies lack of resistance to bending, folding, or manipulating; PLIANT may stress flexibility and springiness and so suggest ready responsiveness rather than the submissiveness implied by PLIABLE

²plastic *n* **:** a plastic substance; *esp* **:** any of numerous organic synthetic or processed materials that can be formed into objects, films, or filaments

Plas·ti·cine \'plas-tə-,sēn\ *trademark* — used for a modeling paste

plas·ti·ciz·er \'plas-tə-,sī-zər\ *n* **:** a chemical added to rubbers and resins to impart flexibility, workability, or stretchability

---

ə abut; ᵉ kitten; ər further; a back; ā bake; ä cot, cart; au̇ out; ch chin; e less; ē easy; g gift; i trip; ī life

plastic surgery _n_ : surgery concerned with the repair or restoration of lost, injured, or deformed parts of the body — **plastic surgeon** _n_

plas·tid \'plas-təd\ _n_ : any of various small bodies of specialized protoplasm in a cell — **plas·tid·i·al** \pla-'stid-ē-əl\ _adj_

plas·tron \'plas-trən\ _n_ **1 a** : a metal breastplate **b** : a quilted chest protector worn in fencing **2** : the ventral part of the shell of a turtle **3** : a trimming like a bib for a woman's dress — **plas·tral** \-trəl\ _adj_

-plas·ty \ˌplas-tē\ _n comb form, pl_ **-plasties** : plastic surgery ⟨osteo_plasty_⟩

¹plat \'plat\ _n_ **1** : a small piece of ground : PLOT **2** : a plan or map of a piece of land (as a town) with lots and landmarks marked out

²plat _vt_ **plat·ted; plat·ting** : to make a plat of

¹plate \'plāt\ _n_ [OF, fr. fem. of _plat_ flat, fr. (assumed) VL _plattus_] **1** : a flat, thin, and usu. smooth piece of material ⟨mica splits easily into _plates_⟩: as **a** : metal in sheets usu. thicker than ¼ inch ⟨steel _plate_⟩ **b** : a thin layer of one metal deposited on another usu. by electrical means **c** : one of the broad metal pieces used in medieval armor; _also_ : armor made of plates **d** : a usu. flat bony or horny outgrowth forming part of a covering of an animal (as some fishes or reptiles) **e** : HOME PLATE **f** : a rubber slab from which a baseball pitcher delivers the ball **g** : the thin fatty underpart of a forequarter of beef or the back part of this cut **2** : precious metal; _esp_ : silver bullion **3** [MF _plat_ dish, plate, fr. _plat_ flat] **a** : domestic hollow ware usu. of or plated with precious metal (as silver) **b** : a shallow usu. circular dish **c** : a main food course served on a plate ⟨a _plate_ of beans⟩ ⟨chose the vegetable _plate_⟩; _also_ : food and service for one person ⟨a dinner at ten dollars a _plate_⟩ **d** : a dish or pouch used in taking a collection (as in a church) **4 a** : a flat piece or surface on which something (as letters or a design) is or is to be embossed or incised ⟨license _plates_⟩ **b** : PRINTING SURFACE **c** : a sheet of material (as glass) coated with a light-sensitive photographic emulsion **5** : a horizontal truss that supports the roof trusses or rafters of a building **6 a** : the electrode to which the electrons flow in an electron tube **b** : a metallic grid with its interstices filled with active material that forms one of the structural units of a storage cell or battery **7** : the part of a denture that bears the teeth and fits to the mouth **8** : a full-page illustration often on special paper

²plate _vt_ **1** : to cover or equip with plate: as **a** : to arm with armor plate **b** : to cover with an adherent layer (as of metal) ⟨had the teapot _plated_ with silver⟩ **c** : to deposit (as a layer of metal) on a surface ⟨_plate_ silver onto copper⟩ **2** : to make a printing surface from or for

pla·teau \pla-'tō, 'pla-\ _n, pl_ **plateaus** _or_ **plateaux** \-'tōz, -ˌtōz\ [F, fr. MF, platter, fr. _plat_ flat] **1** : a usu. large relatively level land area raised above adjacent land on at least one side : TABLELAND **2** : a relatively stable level, period, or condition

plate·ful \'plāt-ˌful\ _n, pl_ **platefuls** \-ˌfulz\ _also_ **plates·ful** \'plāts-ˌful\ : a quantity to fill a plate

plate glass _n_ : fine rolled, ground, and polished sheet glass

plate·let \'plāt-lət\ _n_ : a tiny flat body; _esp_ : BLOOD PLATELET

plate·like \-ˌlīk\ _adj_ : resembling a plate esp. in smooth flat form

plat·en \'plat-ᵊn\ _n_ **1** : a flat plate of metal that exerts or receives pressure; _esp_ : one in some printing presses that presses the paper against the type **2** : the roller of a typewriter

plat·er \'plāt-ər\ _n_ **1** : one that plates **2** : an inferior racehorse

plat·form \'plat-ˌform\ _n_ [MF _plate-forme_ diagram, map, lit., flat form] **1** : a declaration of principles; _esp_ : a declaration of principles and policies adopted by a political party or a candidate **2** : a horizontal flat surface usu. higher than the adjoining area; _esp_ : a raised flooring (as for speakers or performers) **3** : a thick layered sole for a shoe usu. having its edges covered with the material used in the upper; _also_ : a shoe with such a sole

platform rocker _n_ : a chair that rocks on a stable platform

platform scale _n_ : a weighing machine with a flat platform on which objects are weighed

plat·ing _n_ **1** : the act or process of covering esp. with

metal plate **2** : a coating of metal plates or plate ⟨the _plating_ of a ship⟩ ⟨the _plating_ wore off the spoons⟩

pla·tin·ic \pla-'tin-ik\ _adj_ : of, relating to, or containing platinum esp. with a valence of four — compare PLATINOUS

plat·i·nous \'plat-nəs, -ᵊn-əs\ _adj_ : of, relating to, or containing platinum esp. with a valence of two — compare PLATINIC

plat·i·num \'plat-nəm, -ᵊn-əm\ _n_ [NL, fr. Sp _platina_, fr. dim. of _plata_ silver] **1** : a heavy precious grayish white ductile malleable metallic element that is used esp. in chemical ware and apparatus, as a catalyst, and in jewelry — see ELEMENT table **2** : a moderate gray

platinum blonde _n_ : a pale silvery blonde color usu. produced in human hair by bleach and a bluish rinse; _also_ : a person with such hair

plat·i·tude \'plat-ə-ˌt(y)üd\ _n_ [F, fr. _plat_ flat, dull] **1** : the quality or state of being dull or insipid : TRITENESS **2** : a flat, trite, or weak remark — **plat·i·tu·di·nous** \ˌplat-ə-'t(y)üd-nəs, -ᵊn-əs\ _adj_

pla·ton·ic \plə-'tän-ik, plā-\ _adj_ **1** _cap_ : of, relating to, or characteristic of Plato or Platonism **2** : of or relating to love freed from sexual desire — **pla·ton·i·cal·ly** \-'tän-i-k(ə-)lē\ _adv_

Pla·to·nism \'plāt-ᵊn-ˌiz-əm\ _n_ : the philosophy of Plato stressing esp. that actual things and ideas (as of truth or beauty) are only copies of transcendent ideas which are the objects of true knowledge — **Pla·to·nist** \-ᵊn-əst\ _n_

pla·toon \plə-'tün\ _n_ [F _peloton_ small detachment, fr. _pelote_ little ball, pellet] **1** : a subdivision of a military company normally consisting of a headquarters and two or more squads **2** : a group of football players trained either for offense or defense and sent into or withdrawn from the game as a body

platoon sergeant _n_ **1** : a noncommissioned officer in charge of an army platoon **2** : SERGEANT FIRST CLASS

plat·ter \'plat-ər\ _n_ [AF _plater_, fr. MF _plat_ plate] **1** : a large plate used esp. for serving meat **2** : a phonograph record

platy \'plat-ē\ _n, pl_ **platy** _or_ **plat·ys** _or_ **plat·ies** : any of various small variably but brightly colored Mexican topminnows highly favored for the tropical aquarium

plat·y·pus \'plat-i-pəs, -ˌpùs\ _n, pl_ **-pus·es** _also_ **-pi** \-ˌpī, -ˌpē\ [Gk _platypous_ flat-footed, fr. _platys_ broad, flat + _pous_ foot] : a small aquatic egg-laying mammal of southern and eastern Australia and Tasmania with a fleshy bill resembling that of a duck, webbed feet, and a broad flattened tail

plau·dit \'plòd-ət\ _n_ [L _plaudite_ applaud, pl. imper. of _plaudere_ to applaud] **1** : an act or round of applause **2** : enthusiastic approval

plau·si·bil·i·ty \ˌplò-zə-'bil-ət-ē\ _n, pl_ **-ties** **1** : the quality or state of being plausible **2** : something plausible

plau·si·ble \'plò-zə-bəl\ _adj_ [L _plausibilis_ worthy of applause, fr. _plaus-, plaudere_ to applaud] **1** : apparently reasonable or worthy of belief ⟨a _plausible_ explanation⟩ **2** : seemingly trustworthy : inspiring confidence : PERSUASIVE ⟨a very _plausible_ liar⟩ — **plau·si·bly** \'plò-zə-blē\ _adv_

syn PLAUSIBLE, CREDIBLE, SPECIOUS mean outwardly acceptable as true or genuine. PLAUSIBLE implies reasonableness at first sight or hearing usu. with a hint of a possibility of being deceived ⟨a _plausible_ excuse⟩ CREDIBLE stresses worthiness of belief ⟨testimony given by a _credible_ witness⟩ SPECIOUS stresses surface plausibility usu. with the implication of deceit or fraud ⟨_specious_ reasoning⟩ ⟨_specious_ claims for damage⟩

¹play \'plā\ _n_ [OE _plega_] **1 a** : a brisk handling or using (as of a weapon) **b** : the conduct, course, or action of or a particular act or maneuver in a game; _also_ : one's turn to participate in a game **c** : recreational activity; _esp_ : the spontaneous activity of children **d** : JEST ⟨said it in _play_⟩; _also_ : a playing on words **e** : GAMBLING, GAMING **2 a** : a way or manner of acting or proceeding ⟨fair _play_⟩ ⟨a poor _play_ for such a situation⟩ **b** : OPERATION, ACTIVITY ⟨the normal _play_ of economic pressures⟩ **c** : brisk, fitful, or light movement ⟨the light _play_ of a breeze through the room⟩ **d** : free or unimpeded motion (as of a part of a machine); _also_ : freedom for such motion ⟨a jacket that gave _play_ to his shoulders⟩ **e** : scope or opportunity for action ⟨the new job gave _play_ to his talents⟩ **3 a** : the stage representation of an action or story **b** : a dramatic composition : DRAMA — **in play** : in condition or position to be legitimately played

²play *vb* **1 a** : to move swiftly, aimlessly, or lightly ⟨shadows *playing* on the wall⟩; *also* : to move freely ⟨the shaft *played* in its housing⟩ **b** : to treat or behave frivolously or lightly or without due consideration or respect sometimes with an ulterior motive ⟨*play* with a new idea⟩ ⟨*play* a person for a fool⟩ **c** : to make use of double meaning or of the similarity of sound of two words usu. for humorous effect **d** : to take advantage ⟨were *playing* upon fears⟩ **e** : to finger or trifle with something ⟨*played* with his pencil⟩ **f** : to discharge in a stream ⟨hoses *playing* on the fire⟩ **2 a** : to engage in sport or recreation and esp. in spontaneous activity for amusement ⟨children *playing*⟩ **b** : to imitate in playing **c** : to take part or engage in ⟨as a game⟩ ⟨*play* cards⟩ ⟨*play* ball⟩ **d** : to contend against in a game **e** : to bet on : WAGER **3 a** : to perform on a musical instrument ⟨*play* the piano⟩ ⟨*play* waltzes⟩ **b** : to produce music ⟨listen to an organ *playing*⟩ **4** : to be performed ⟨a new show *playing* for one week⟩ ⟨the music began to *play*⟩ **5 a** : ACT, BEHAVE; *esp* : to conduct oneself in a particular way ⟨*play* safe⟩ **b** : to perform on or as if on the stage ⟨*play* a part⟩; *also* : to act the part of ⟨*play* the fool⟩ **c** : to put or keep in action ⟨*play* a card in a game⟩ ⟨*play* a fish on a line⟩ ⟨*play* a hose on a fire⟩ **d** : to do for amusement or from mischief ⟨*play* a trick on someone⟩; *also* : to bring about : WREAK ⟨the wind *played* havoc with the garden⟩ — **play·a·ble** \-ə-bəl\ *adj* — **play ball** : COOPERATE

pla·ya \'plī-ə\ *n* [Sp, lit., beach] : the flat-floored bottom of an undrained desert basin that becomes a shallow lake

play·act·ing \'plā-,ak-tiŋ\ *n* **1** : performance in theatrical productions **2** : insincere or artificial behavior

play back \(')plā-'bak\ *vt* : to run through (a disc or tape) recently recorded

play·back \'plā-,bak\ *n* : an act of reproducing a sound recording often immediately after recording

play·bill \-,bil\ *n* : a poster advertising the performance of a play and usu. the cast of players; *also* : a theater program

play·boy \-,bȯi\ *n* : a man whose chief interest is the pursuit of pleasure

play–by–play \,plā-bə-,plā, -bī-\ *adj* **1** : being a running commentary on a sports event **2** : circumstantially related : DETAILED

play down *vt* : to refrain from emphasizing

played out *adj* **1** : worn out or used up **2** : tired out : SPENT

play·er \'plā-ər\ *n* : one that plays: as **a** : a person who plays a game **b** : MUSICIAN **c** : ACTOR **d** : a mechanical device for reproducing music (as from a phonograph record)

player piano *n* : a piano containing a mechanical player

play·fel·low \'plā-,fel-ō\ *n* : PLAYMATE

play·ful \-fəl\ *adj* **1** : full of play : SPORTIVE **2** : HUMOROUS, JOCULAR — **play·ful·ly** \-fə-lē\ *adv* — **play·ful·ness** *n*

play·go·er \-,gō(-ə)r\ *n* : a person who frequently attends plays

play·ground \-,graùnd\ *n* : a piece of ground used for games and recreation esp. by children

play·house \-,haùs\ *n* **1** : THEATER **2** : a small house for children to play in

playing card *n* : one of a set of cards marked to show its rank and suit (as spades, hearts, diamonds, or clubs) and used in playing various games

playing field *n* : a field for various games; *esp* : the part of a field officially marked off for play

play·let \'plā-lət\ *n* : a short play

play·mate \-,māt\ *n* : a companion in play

play off \(')plā-'óf\ *vt* **1** : to complete the playing of (an interrupted contest) **2** : to break (a tie) by a play-off

play–off \'plā-,óf\ *n* **1** : a final contest or series of contests to determine the winner between contestants or teams that have tied **2** : a series of contests played after the end of the regular season to determine a championship

play out *vb* **1** : to perform to the end **2** : to use up or become used up : FINISH, EXHAUST **3** : UNREEL, UNFOLD

play·pen \'plā-,pen\ *n* : a portable enclosure in which a baby or young child may play

play·suit \-,süt\ *n* : a sports and play outfit for women and children

play·thing \-,thiŋ\ *n* : TOY

play·time \-,tīm\ *n* : a time for play or diversion

play up *vt* : to give emphasis or prominence to — **play up to** \plā-'əp-tü\ : to support or flatter by eager agreement

play·wright \'plā-,rīt\ *n* [obs. *wright* maker, fr. OE *wryhta*] : a person who writes plays

plaza \'plaz-ə, 'pläz-\ *n* [Sp, fr. L *platea* broad street, fr. Gk *plateia*, fr. fem. of *platys* broad] : a public square in a city or town

plea \'plē\ *n* [ME *plaid*, *plai*, fr. OF *plaid* lawsuit, fr. ML *placitum*, fr. L, decision, decree, fr. neut. of *placitus*, pp. of *placēre* to please, be decided] **1** : a defendant's answer to a plaintiff's declaration or to a criminal charge ⟨a *plea* of insanity⟩ ⟨a *plea* of guilty⟩ **2** : something offered as an excuse **3** : an earnest entreaty : APPEAL

plead \'plēd\ *vb* **plead·ed** \'plēd-əd\ *or* **pled** \'pled\; **plead·ing** [OF *plaidier*, fr. *plaid* lawsuit] **1** : to argue a case in a court of law **2** : to answer the other party in a court of law by denying facts stated or by alleging new facts **3** : to make a plea of a specified nature ⟨*plead* not guilty⟩ **4 a** : to argue for or against a claim **b** : to entreat or appeal earnestly : IMPLORE **5** : to offer in defense, apology, or excuse — **plead·a·ble** \'plēd-ə-bəl\ *adj* — **plead·er** *n*

plead·ing *n* **1** : advocacy of a cause in a court of law **2** *pl* : one of the formal usu. written statements of the plaintiff and defendant in a legal action ⟨a case decided on the *pleadings*⟩

pleas·ance \'plez-ᵊn(t)s\ *n* **1** : a feeling of pleasure **2** : a pleasing place (as a charming vista); *esp* : a private formal garden attached to a mansion

pleas·ant \'plez-ᵊnt\ *adj* **1** : giving pleasure : AGREEABLE **2** : having or characterized by pleasing manners, behavior, or appearance — **pleas·ant·ly** *adv* — **pleas·ant·ness** *n*

pleas·ant·ry \-ᵊn-trē\ *n*, *pl* **-ries** **1** : agreeable playfulness esp. in conversation **2 a** : a humorous act or speech : JEST **b** : a light or casual polite remark

please \'plēz\ *vb* [MF *plaisir*, fr. L *placēre*] **1** : to afford or give pleasure or satisfaction : GRATIFY **2** : to feel the desire or inclination : LIKE **3** : to be willing to — usu. used in the imperative to express a polite command or request ⟨*please* come in⟩

pleas·ing \'plē-ziŋ\ *adj* : giving pleasure : AGREEABLE — **pleas·ing·ly** \-ziŋ-lē\ *adv* — **pleas·ing·ness** *n*

plea·sur·a·ble \'plezh-(ə-)rə-bəl, 'plāzh-\ *adj* : GRATIFYING, PLEASANT — **plea·sur·a·bil·i·ty** \,plezh-(ə-)rə-'bil-ət-ē, ,plāzh-\ *n* — **plea·sur·a·ble·ness** \'plezh-(ə-)rə-bəl-nəs, 'plāzh-\ *n* — **plea·sur·a·bly** \-blē\ *adv*

plea·sure \'plezh-ər, 'plāzh-\ *n* **1** : DESIRE, INCLINATION **2** : a state of gratification : ENJOYMENT **3** : a source of delight or joy

¹pleat \'plēt\ *vt* **1** : FOLD; *esp* : to arrange in pleats **2** : PLAIT 2 — **pleat·ed** *adj* — **pleat·er** *n*

²pleat *n* [MF *pleit*, fr. L *plicare* to fold] : a fold (as in cloth) made by doubling material over on itself

pleb \'pleb\ *n* : PLEBEIAN

plebe \'plēb\ *n* [obs. *plebe* common people, fr. L *plebs*] : a freshman at a military or naval academy

¹ple·be·ian \pli-'bē-(y)ən\ *n* [L *plebeius* of the common people, fr. *plebs* common people] **1** : a member of the Roman plebs **2** : one of the common people — **ple·be·ian·ism** \-(y)ə-,niz-əm\ *n*

²plebeian *adj* **1** : of or relating to plebeians **2** : crude or coarse in manner or style : COMMON — **ple·be·ian·ly** *adv*

pleb·i·scite \'pleb-ə-,sīt, -sət\ *n* [L *plebis scitum* decree of the common people] : a popular vote by which the people of an entire country or a district indicate their wishes on a measure officially submitted to them

plebs \'plebz\ *n*, *pl* **ple·bes** \'plē-bēz\ [L] **1** : the common people of ancient Rome **2** : the general populace

plec·trum \'plek-trəm\ *n*, *pl* **plec·tra** \-trə\ *or* **plec·trums** [L, fr. Gk *plēktron*, fr. *plēssein* to strike] : a small thin piece (as of ivory or metal) used to pluck a stringed instrument

¹pledge \'plej\ *n* [MF *plege* security, fr. LL *plebium*] **1 a** : the handing over of a chattel to another as security for an obligation without transfer of title;

plectra

also : the chattel so delivered **b** : the state of being held as a security or guaranty ⟨given in *pledge*⟩ **2 a** : something given as security for the performance of an act **b** : a token, sign, or earnest of something else **3 a** : TOAST 3 **b** : a binding promise or agreement **4 a** : a person pledged to join an organization (as a fraternity) **b** : a gift pledged (as to a charity)

²pledge *vt* **1** : to make a pledge of; *esp* : to deposit in pledge or pawn **2** : to drink the health of : TOAST **3** : to bind by a pledge ⟨*pledge* oneself⟩ **4** : to promise by a pledge ⟨*pledge* money to charity⟩ — **pledg·ee** \ple-'jē\ *n* — **pledg·er** \'plej-ər\ *n* — **pledg·or** \'plej-ər, ple-'jȯ(ə)r\ *n*

Ple·iad \'plē-əd\ *n* : any of the Pleiades

Ple·ia·des \'plē-ə-,dēz\ *n pl* **1** : the seven daughters of Atlas transformed according to Greek mythology into a group of stars **2** : a conspicuous loose cluster of stars in the constellation Taurus consisting of six stars visible to the average eye

plei·o·trop·ic \,plī-ə-'träp-ik\ *adj* [Gk *pleiōn* more + *tropos* way, manner] : having more than one effect ⟨*pleiotropic* genes⟩ — **plei·o·trop·i·cal·ly** \-'träp-i-k(ə-)lē\ *adv*

Pleis·to·cene \'plī-stə-,sēn\ *n* [Gk *pleistos* most] : the earlier epoch of the Quaternary; *also* : the corresponding system of rocks — **Pleistocene** *adj*

ple·na·ry \'plē-nə-rē, 'plen-ə-\ *adj* [L *plenus* full; akin to E *full*] **1** : COMPLETE, FULL ⟨*plenary* powers⟩ **2** : including all entitled to attend ⟨a *plenary* session of an assembly⟩

plenary indulgence *n* : a remission of the entire temporal punishment due to sin

plen·i·po·ten·tia·ry \,plen-ə-pə-'tench-(ə-)rē, -'ten-chē-,er-ē\ *n, pl* **-ries** [L *plenus* full + *potentia* power] : a person and esp. a diplomatic agent invested with full power to transact any business — **plenipotentiary** *adj*

plen·i·tude \'plen-ə-,t(y)üd\ *or* **plent·i·tude** \'plen(t)-ə-\ *n* [L *plenus* full] : the quality or state of being full; *also* : ABUNDANCE

plen·te·ous \'plent-ē-əs\ *adj* **1** : ABUNDANT, PLENTIFUL **2** : yielding abundantly : FRUITFUL ⟨the *plenteous* earth⟩ — **plen·te·ous·ly** *adv* — **plen·te·ous·ness** *n*

plen·ti·ful \'plent-i-fəl\ *adj* **1** : containing or yielding plenty : FRUITFUL **2** : characterized by, constituting, or existing in plenty : NUMEROUS, ABUNDANT — **plen·ti·ful·ly** \-fə-lē\ *adv* — **plen·ti·ful·ness** *n*

syn PLENTIFUL, AMPLE, ABUNDANT, COPIOUS mean more than sufficient yet not in excess. PLENTIFUL suggests a great or rich supply ⟨eggs are cheap when *plentiful*⟩ AMPLE implies a generous sufficiency to satisfy a particular requirement ⟨an income *ample* for his needs⟩ ABUNDANT suggests an even greater or richer supply than does PLENTIFUL ⟨*abundant* harvests⟩ COPIOUS stresses largeness in quantity or number rather than fullness or richness ⟨shed *copious* tears⟩ ⟨took *copious* notes at the lecture⟩

¹plen·ty \'plent-ē\ *n* [LL *plenitas*, fr. L, fullness, fr. *plenus* full] **1** : a full or abundant supply : a sufficient number or amount ⟨there will be *plenty* of things to choose from⟩ ⟨got there in *plenty* of time⟩ **2** : PLENTIFULNESS, ABUNDANCE ⟨in times of *plenty*⟩

²plenty *adj* : PLENTIFUL, ABUNDANT, AMPLE ⟨food was not too plenty⟩ ⟨had *plenty* help⟩

³plenty *adv* : ABUNDANTLY, QUITE ⟨a *plenty* exciting trip⟩

plen·um \'plen-əm, 'plēn-əm\ *n, pl* **plenums** *or* **ple·na** \-ə\ [NL, fr. L, neut. of *plenus*] : a general assembly of all members of a public body

ple·o·mor·phism \,plē-ə-'mȯr-,fiz-əm\ *n* [Gk *pleiōn*, *pleōn* more + *morphē* form] : the occurrence of more than one distinct form esp. in the life cycle of a plant — **ple·o·mor·phic** \-fik\ *adj*

ple·o·nasm \'plē-ə-,naz-əm\ *n* [Gk *pleonasmos*, fr. *pleonazein* to be excessive, fr. *pleiōn*, *pleōn* more] : the use of more words than those necessary to denote mere sense (as in *the man he said*) : REDUNDANCY; *also* : an instance or example of this — **ple·o·nas·tic** \,plē-ə-'nas-tik\ *adj* — **ple·o·nas·ti·cal·ly** \-ti-k(ə-)lē\ *adv*

ple·si·o·saur \'plē-sē-ə-,sȯr\ *n* [Gk *plēsios* close] : any of a group (Plesiosauria) of Mesozoic marine reptiles

pleth·o·ra \'pleth-ə-rə\ *n* [ML, fr. Gk *plēthōra*, lit., fullness, fr. *plēthein* to be full; akin to E *full*] **1** : a bodily condition characterized by an excess of blood **2** : SUPERFLUITY, EXCESS — **ple·thor·ic** \plə-'thȯr-ik, -'thär-\ *adj*

pleu·ra \'plur-ə\ *n, pl* **pleu·rae** \'plu̇(ə)r-,ē, -,ī\ *or* **pleuras** [NL, fr. Gk, rib, side] : the delicate serous membrane lining each half of the chest of mammals and folded back over the surface of the lung of the same side — **pleu·ral** \'plur-əl\ *adj*

pleu·ri·sy \'plur-ə-sē\ *n* : inflammation of the pleura usu. with fever, painful breathing, and coughing — **pleu·rit·ic** \plu̇-'rit-ik\ *adj*

pleu·ro·coc·cus \,plur-ə-'käk-əs\ *n, pl* **-coc·cus·es** *or* **-coc·ci** \-'käk-,(s)ī, -'käk-(,)sē\ : PROTOCOCCUS

pleu·ro·pneu·mo·nia \,plur-ō-n(y)u̇-'mō-nyə\ *n* : combined inflammation of the lungs and pleura; *also* : a disease (as of cattle) marked by this

plex·us \'plek-səs\ *n, pl* **plex·us·es** *or* **plex·us** \-səs, -,süs\ [L, fr. *plectere* to braid] : an interlacing network esp. of blood vessels or nerves

pli·a·ble \'plī-ə-bəl\ *adj* [MF, fr. *plier* to bend, fr. L *plicare* to fold] **1** : capable of being bent or folded without damage : FLEXIBLE **2** : easily influenced ⟨a boy too *pliable* for his own good⟩ *syn* see PLASTIC — **pli·a·bil·i·ty** \,plī-ə-'bil-ət-ē\ *n* — **pli·a·ble·ness** \'plī-ə-bəl-nəs\ *n* — **pli·a·bly** \-blē\ *adv*

pli·an·cy \'plī-ən-sē\ *n* : the quality or state of being pliant

pli·ant \'plī-ənt\ *adj* **1** : readily yielding without breaking : FLEXIBLE ⟨*pliant* willow twigs⟩ **2** : easily influenced : PLIABLE, YIELDING ⟨a *pliant* will⟩ **3** : ADAPTABLE *syn* see PLASTIC — **pli·ant·ly** *adv*

pli·cate \'plī-,kāt\ *adj* [L *plicatus*, pp. of *plicare* to fold] : having lengthwise folds or ridges ⟨a *plicate* leaf⟩ — **pli·cate·ly** *adv*

pli·ers \'plī-(ə)rz\ *n pl* : a small pincers with long jaws for holding small objects or for bending and cutting wire

¹plight \'plīt\ *vt* [OE *plihtan* to endanger, fr. *pliht* danger] : to put or give in pledge : ENGAGE — **plight·er** *n*

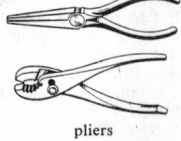

pliers

²plight *n* [AF *plit*, fr. (assumed) VL *plictus* fold, fr. L *plicare* to fold] : CONDITION, STATE; *esp* : bad state or condition ⟨a man in a sorry *plight*⟩

Plim·soll mark \,plim(p)-səl-, -,sȯl-\ *n* [after Samuel *Plimsoll* d1898 English shipping reformer] : a load line or a set of load-line markings on an oceangoing cargo ship — called also **Plimsoll line**

plink \'plink\ *vb* **1** : to make or cause to make a tinkling sound **2** : to shoot at esp. in a casual manner — **plink** *n*

plinth \'plin(t)th\ *n* [Gk *plinthos*] **1** : the lowest part of the base of an architectural column **2** : a block used as a base (as for a statue or vase)

Pli·o·cene \'plī-ə-,sēn\ *n* [Gk *pleiōn* more] : the latest epoch of the Tertiary; *also* : the corresponding system of rocks — **Pliocene** *adj*

Plio·film \'plī-ə-,film\ *trademark* — used for a glossy membrane used esp. for raincoats and packaging material

plod \'pläd\ *vi* **plod·ded**; **plod·ding** **1** : to walk heavily or slowly : TRUDGE **2** : to work or study laboriously : DRUDGE — **plod** *n* — **plod·der** *n* — **plod·ding·ly** \-in-lē\ *adv*

ploi·dy \'plȯid-ē\ *n* [fr. such words as *diploidy*, *triploidy*] : degree of replication of chromosomes or genomes

plop \'pläp\ *vb* **plopped**; **plop·ping** **1** : to make or move with a sound like that of something dropping into water **2** : to allow the body to drop heavily **3** : to set, drop, or throw heavily — **plop** *n*

¹plot \'plät\ *n* [OE] **1** : a small area of ground : LOT **2** : GROUND PLAN **3** : the plan or main story of a literary work **4** : a secret plan for accomplishing a usu. evil or unlawful end : INTRIGUE **5** : a graphic representation : CHART, DIAGRAM

syn PLOT, INTRIGUE, CONSPIRACY mean a plan secretly devised to accomplish an evil purpose. PLOT implies careful foresight in planning positive action; INTRIGUE suggests secret maneuvering; CONSPIRACY implies a secret agreement among a number of persons not necessarily for positive action ⟨*conspiracy* in restraint of trade⟩ ⟨*conspiracy* of silence⟩ *syn* see in addition PLAN

²plot *vb* **plot·ted**; **plot·ting** **1 a** : to make a plot, map, or plan of **b** : to mark or note on or as if on a map or chart **2 a** : to locate (a point) by means of coordinates **b** : to locate (a curve) by plotted points **3 :** to plan or contrive esp. secretly **:** CONSPIRE, SCHEME — **plot·ter** *n*

plov·er \'pləv-ər, 'plō-vər\ *n, pl* **plover** *or* **plovers** [MF] **:** any of numerous shorebirds differing from the related sandpipers in having shorter and stouter bills

¹**plow** *or* **plough** \'plaù\ *n* [OE *plōh* plowland] **1 :** an implement used to cut, lift, and turn over soil esp. in preparing a seedbed **2 :** any of various devices (as for spreading or opening something) that operate like a plow; *esp :* SNOWPLOW

²**plow** *or* **plough** *vb* **1 :** to open, break up, or work with a plow ⟨*plow* a straight furrow⟩⟨*plow* the soil⟩⟨*plow* a road out with a snowplow⟩ **2 a :** to cleave the surface of or move through like a plow cutting the soil ⟨a ship *plowing* the waves⟩ **b :** to proceed steadily and laboriously **:** PLOD ⟨*plow* through a report⟩ — **plow·a·ble** \-ə-bəl\ *adj* — **plow·er** \'plaù(-ə)r\ *n*

plow back *vt* **:** to reinvest (profits) in a business

plow·boy \'plaù-,bói\ *n* **:** a boy who guides a plow or leads the horse drawing it

plow·man \-mən\ *n* **1 :** a man who guides a plow **2 :** a farm laborer

plow·share \-,she(ə)r, -,sha(ə)r\ *n* **:** the part of a plow that cuts the earth

plow sole *n* **:** a layer of earth at the bottom of the furrow compacted by repeated plowing at the same depth

plow under *vt* **:** to cause to disappear **:** BURY, OVERWHELM

ploy \'plói\ *n* **:** a tactic intended to embarrass or frustrate an opponent

¹**pluck** \'plək\ *vt* [OE *pluccian*] **1 a :** to pull or pick off or out ⟨*pluck* a flower⟩⟨*plucked* a bill from his wallet⟩ **b :** to remove something and esp. hair or feathers from by or as if by plucking ⟨*pluck* a fowl⟩ **2 :** ROB, FLEECE **3 :** to move or separate forcibly **:** TUG, SNATCH ⟨*plucked* the child from danger⟩ **4 :** to pick, pull, or grasp at; *also* **:** to play (an instrument) in this manner — **pluck·er** *n*

²**pluck** *n* **1 :** an act or instance of plucking **:** a sharp pull **:** TUG **2 :** the heart, liver, lungs, and windpipe of a slaughtered animal **3 :** SPIRIT, COURAGE, RESOLUTION

plucky \'plək-ē\ *adj* **pluck·i·er; -est :** COURAGEOUS, RESOLUTE — **pluck·i·ly** \'plək-ə-lē\ *adv* — **pluck·i·ness** \'plək-ē-nəs\ *n*

¹**plug** \'pləg\ *n* [D] **1 a :** a piece (as of wood or metal) used to stop or fill a hole **:** STOPPER **b :** an obtruding or obstructing mass of material (as in rock or tissue) felt to resemble a stopper **2 :** a poor or worn-out horse **3 a :** FIREPLUG **b :** SPARK PLUG **c :** a device for making an electrical connection by insertion into an interrupted circuit **5 :** a flat cake of tightly pressed tobacco leaves **6 :** an angling lure with several hooks used in casting for fish **7 :** a piece of favorable publicity usu. placed in general material

²**plug** *vb* **plugged; plug·ging 1 :** to stop, make tight, or secure with or as if with a plug **2 :** to hit with a bullet **:** SHOOT **3 :** to advertise or publicize insistently **4 :** to become plugged — usu. used with *up* — **plug·ger** *n*

plug hat *n* **:** a man's stiff hat (as a bowler or top hat)

plug in *vb* **:** to establish or connect to an electric circuit by inserting a plug

plum \'pləm\ *n* [OE *plūme*, fr. L *prunum* fruit of the plum, fr. Gk *proumnon*] **1 a :** any of numerous trees and shrubs related to the peach and cherries and having globular to oval smooth-skinned fruits with oblong seeds **b :** the edible fruit of a plum **2 a :** a raisin for use in cooking **b :** SUGARPLUM **3 :** something excellent or superior; *esp* **:** something given as recompense for service **4 :** a variable color averaging a dark reddish purple — **plum·like** \-,līk\ *adj*

plum·age \'plü-mij\ *n* **:** the entire clothing of feathers of a bird

plu·mate \'plü-,māt\ *adj* **:** having a main shaft that bears fine filaments

¹**plumb** \'pləm\ *n* [L *plumbum* lead] **:** a weight often of lead used on a line esp. to determine a vertical direction or distance — **out of plumb** *or* **off plumb :** out of vertical or true

²**plumb** *adv* **1 :** straight down or up **:** VERTICALLY **2 :** DIRECTLY, EXACTLY **3** *chiefly dial* **:** COMPLETELY, ABSOLUTELY

³**plumb** *vb* **1 :** to sound, adjust, or test with a plumb ⟨*plumb* a wall⟩⟨*plumb* the depth of the

plumb

well⟩ **2 :** to examine and determine hidden aspects of **:** FATHOM ⟨*plumbed* their motives⟩ **3 :** to supply with or install as plumbing; *also* **:** to work as a plumber

⁴**plumb** *also* **plum** *adj* **1 :** exactly vertical or true **2 :** DOWNRIGHT, COMPLETE **syn** see VERTICAL

plum·ba·go \,pləm-'bā-gō\ *n* [L, galena, fr. *plumbum* lead] **:** GRAPHITE

plumb bob *n* **:** the metal bob of a plumb line

plumb·er \'pləm-ər\ *n* [L *plumbum* lead] **:** one that installs, repairs, and maintains piping, fittings, and fixtures involved in the distribution and use of water in a building

plum·bic \'pləm-bik\ *adj* **:** of, relating to, or containing lead esp. with a valence of four

plumb·ing \'pləm-iŋ\ *n* **1 :** a plumber's occupation or trade **2 :** the apparatus (as pipes and fixtures) concerned in the distribution and use of water in a building ⟨brand-new *plumbing* in the house⟩

plum·bism \'pləm-,biz-əm\ *n* **:** lead poisoning esp. when chronic

plumb line *n* **:** a line or cord having at one end a weight (as a plumb bob) and serving esp. to determine whether something is vertical or to measure depth

plum·bous \'pləm-bəs\ *adj* **:** of, relating to, or containing lead esp. with a valence of two

¹**plume** \'plüm\ *n* [ME, fr. MF, fr. L *pluma* small soft feather, down; akin to E *fleece*] **1 :** a feather of a bird; *esp* **:** a large conspicuous or showy feather **2 a :** a feather, cluster of feathers, tuft of hair, or similar matter worn as an ornament **b :** a token of honor or prowess **:** PRIZE **3 :** a plumose appendage (as a bushy tail) of a plant or animal — **plumy** \'plü-mē\ *adj*

²**plume** *vt* **1 :** to provide or deck with plumes ⟨*plume* a hat⟩ **2 :** to pride (oneself) on something **3 :** to dress the feathers of **:** PREEN ⟨a bird *pluming* itself⟩

¹**plum·met** \'pləm-ət\ *n* **:** PLUMB BOB; *also* **:** PLUMBLINE

²**plummet** *vi* **:** to fall perpendicularly or sharply and abruptly

plu·mose \'plü-,mōs\ *adj* **:** FEATHERED, FEATHERY — **plu·mose·ly** *adv*

¹**plump** \'pləmp\ *vb* [ME *plumpen*] **1 :** to drop, sink, or come in contact suddenly or heavily ⟨*plumped* down into the chair⟩⟨*plumping* his books on the table⟩ **2 :** to favor someone or something strongly — used with *for*

²**plump** *adv* **1 :** with a sudden or heavy drop **2 :** STRAIGHT, DIRECTLY ⟨ran *plump* into the wall⟩

³**plump** *n* **:** a sudden plunge, fall, or blow; *also* **:** the sound accompanying such an act

⁴**plump** *adj* [ME, dull, blunt] **:** having a full rounded usu. pleasing form — **plump·ness** *n*

⁵**plump** *vb* **:** to make or become plump

plum pudding *n* **:** a boiled or steamed pudding containing fruits (as raisins) and usu. rich in fat

plu·mule \'plü-myül\ *n* [L *plumula*, dim. of *pluma* feather, down] **1 :** the primary bud of a plant embryo **2 :** a down feather

¹**plun·der** \'plən-dər\ *vb* **plun·dered; plun·der·ing** \-d(ə-)riŋ\ [G *plündern*] **:** to rob esp. openly and by force (as in an invasion or raid) **:** PILLAGE — **plun·der·er** \-dər-ər\ *n*

²**plunder** *n* **1 :** an act of plundering **:** PILLAGING **2 :** something taken by force or theft **:** LOOT

¹**plunge** \'plənj\ *vb* [MF *plonger*, fr. (assumed) VL *plumbicare*, fr. L *plumbum* plumb] **1 :** to cause to penetrate or enter something quickly and forcibly ⟨*plunged* her hands into the washtub⟩⟨*plunging* a knife into the roast⟩ **2 :** to thrust or cast oneself into or as if into water **:** DIVE **3 a :** to throw oneself or move suddenly and sharply forward and downward ⟨a *plunging* horse⟩ ⟨the ship *plunged* through the rough seas⟩ **b :** to move rapidly or suddenly downward ⟨the market *plunged* after war was declared⟩ **4 a :** to rush or act with reckless haste ⟨*plunged* into debt⟩; *also* **:** to bring to a usu. unpleasant state or course of action suddenly or unexpectedly ⟨*plunged* his family into disorder⟩ ⟨the president's illness *plunged* the nation into gloom⟩ **b :** to speculate or gamble recklessly

²**plunge** *n* **:** an act or instance of plunging **:** a sudden dive, leap, or rush

plung·er \'plən-jər\ *n* **1 :** a person (as a diver or a reckless gambler) that plunges **2 a :** a device (as a piston in a pump) that acts with a plunging motion **b :** a rubber suction cup on a handle used to free plumbing traps and waste outlets of obstructions

plunk \'pləŋk\ vb 1 : to make or cause to make a hollow metallic sound ⟨*plunk* the strings of a banjo⟩ 2 : to drop heavily or suddenly ⟨*plunk* a suitcase on the bench⟩ 3 : to publicly favor someone or something — used with *for* — **plunk** n

plu·per·fect \plü-'pər-fikt\ adj [modif. of LL *plusquamperfectus*, lit., more than perfect] : PAST PERFECT — **pluperfect** n

plu·ral \'plür-əl\ adj [L *plur-*, *plus* more] 1 : of, relating to, or constituting a class of grammatical forms used to denote more than one ⟨*plural* nouns⟩ 2 : relating to, consisting of, or containing more than one — **plural** n — **plu·ral·ly** \-ə-lē\ adv

plu·ral·i·ty \plü-'ral-ət-ē\ n, pl **-ties** 1 : the state of being plural or numerous 2 : the greater number or part ⟨a *plurality* of the nations want peace⟩ 3 a : the fact of being chosen by the voters out of three or more candidates or measures when no one of them obtains more than half the total vote b : the excess of the number of votes received by one candidate over another; *esp* : that of the highest over the next highest ⟨win by a *plurality* of 4000 votes⟩ **syn** see MAJORITY

plu·ral·ize \'plür-ə-,līz\ vt : to make plural or express in the plural form — **plu·ral·i·za·tion** \,plür-ə-lə-'zā-shən\ n

pluri- comb form [L *plur-*, *plus* more] : having or being more than one : MULTI- ⟨*pluri*axial⟩

¹plus \'pləs\ prep [L, adv., more, fr. neut. of *plur-*, *plus*, adj., more; akin to E *full*] 1 : increased by ⟨four *plus* five is nine⟩ ⟨the debt *plus* interest⟩ 2 : WITH

²plus n 1 : an added quantity 2 : a positive factor or quality : ADVANTAGE 3 : SURPLUS

³plus adj 1 : requiring addition 2 : having, receiving, or being in addition 3 a : falling high in a specified range ⟨a grade of C *plus*⟩ b : greater than that specified 4 : electrically positive

¹plush \'pləsh\ n [MF *peluche*] : a fabric with an even pile longer and less dense than velvet pile — **plushy** \-ē\ adj

²plush adj 1 : relating to, resembling, or made of plush 2 : notably luxurious or satisfactory

plus sign n : a sign + used esp. in mathematics to indicate addition (as in $8 + 6 = 14$) or a positive quantity (as in $+10°$)

Plu·to \'plüt-ō\ n 1 : the god of the dead and the lower world in classical mythology 2 : the planet most remote from the sun — see PLANET table

plu·toc·ra·cy \plü-'täk-rə-sē\ n, pl **-cies** [Gk *ploutos* wealth] 1 : government by the wealthy 2 : a controlling class of rich men — **plu·to·crat** \'plüt-ə-,krat\ n — **plu·to·crat·ic** \,plüt-ə-'krat-ik\ adj — **plu·to·crat·i·cal·ly** \-'krat-i-k(ə-)lē\ adv

plu·ton·ic \plü-'tän-ik\ adj [L *Pluton-*, *Pluto* god of the lower world] : formed by solidification of a molten magma deep within the earth and crystalline throughout ⟨*plutonic* rock⟩

plu·to·ni·um \plü-'tō-nē-əm\ n [NL, fr. *Pluton-*, *Pluto*, the planet Pluto] : a radioactive metallic chemical element that is formed by decay of neptunium and found in minute quantities in pitchblende and that is fissionable to yield atomic energy — see ELEMENT table

plu·vi·al \'plü-vē-əl\ adj [L *pluvia* rain, fr. *pluere* to rain; akin to E *flow*] 1 : of or relating to rain 2 : characterized by or resulting from the action of abundant rain ⟨a *pluvial* period⟩

¹ply \'plī\ vt **plied**; **ply·ing** [MF *plier*, fr. L *plicare* to fold, braid] : to twist together ⟨*ply* yarns⟩

²ply n, pl **plies** : one of the folds, thicknesses, layers, or strands of which something (as yarn or plywood) is made up

³ply vb **plied**; **ply·ing** [ME *plien*, short for *applien* to apply] 1 a : to use or wield diligently ⟨*plied* an ax⟩ b : to practice or perform diligently ⟨*plied* his trade⟩ 2 : to keep supplying to ⟨*ply* a guest with delicacies⟩; *also* : to press or harass with something ⟨*plied* her with questions⟩ 3 : to go or travel regularly

Plym·outh Rock \,plim-əth-\ n : a bird of an American breed of medium-sized single-combed dual-purpose domestic fowls

ply·wood \'plī-,wùd\ n : a structural material consisting of thin sheets of wood glued or cemented together under heat and pressure with the grains of adjacent layers arranged at right angles or at a wide angle

-pnea or **-pnoea** \(p)-(')nē-ə\ n comb form [Gk *-pnoia*, fr. *pnein* to breathe] : breath : breathing ⟨hyper*pnea*⟩⟨ap*noea*⟩

pneu·mat·ic \n(y)ù-'mat-ik\ adj [Gk *pneumat-*, *pneuma* air, breath, spirit, fr. *pnein* to breathe; akin to E *sneeze*] 1 : of, relating to, or using air, wind, or other gas 2 : moved or worked by air pressure ⟨a *pneumatic* drill⟩ 3 : adapted for holding or inflated with compressed air ⟨*pneumatic* tires⟩— **pneu·mat·i·cal·ly** \-'mat-i-k(ə-)lē\ adv

pneu·mat·ics \n(y)ù-'mat-iks\ n : a branch of physics that deals with the mechanical properties of gases

pneu·mo·coc·cus \,n(y)ù-mə-'käk-əs\ n, pl **-coc·ci** \-'käk-,(s)ī, -'käk-(,)ī(s)ē\ also **-coc·cus·es** : the bacterium that causes lobar pneumonia — **pneu·mo·coc·cal** \-'käk-əl\ or **pneu·mo·coc·cic** \-'käk-(s)ik\ adj

pneu·mo·nia \n(y)ù-'mō-nyə\ n [Gk, fr. *pneumōn* lung, alter. of *pleumōn*] : a disease of the lungs characterized by inflammation and consolidation of tissue followed by resolution and caused by infection or irritants

pneu·mon·ic \n(y)ù-'män-ik\ adj 1 : of or relating to the lungs 2 : of, relating to, or affected with pneumonia

pneu·mo·tho·rax \,n(y)ù-mə-'thōr-,aks, -'thòr-\ n : a state in which gas is present in the pleural cavity and which may occur in disease or injury or be induced surgically to collapse a lung for therapeutic reasons

¹poach \'pōch\ vt [MF *pocher*, lit., to put into a bag, fr. *poche* bag, pocket, of Gmc origin] : to cook in simmering liquid ⟨*poached* egg⟩

²poach vb [MF *pocher* to push, poke] : to hunt or fish unlawfully usu. on private property — **poach·er** n

po·chard \'pō-chərd\ n : any of several large-bodied large-headed diving ducks

pock \'päk\ n [OE *pocc*] : a small swelling on the skin similar to a pimple (as in chicken pox or smallpox); *also* : the scar it leaves — **pock** vt — **pocky** \-ē\ adj

¹pock·et \'päk-ət\ n [ONF *pokete*, dim. of *poke* bag, of Gmc origin] 1 a : a small bag carried by a person : PURSE b : a small bag open at the top or side inserted in a garment 2 : supply of money : MEANS ⟨out of *pocket*⟩ 3 : RECEPTACLE, CONTAINER; *esp* : a bag at the corner or side of a billiard table 4 : a small isolated area or group: a : a cavity containing a deposit (as of gold or water) b : a small body of ore c : AIR HOLE

²pocket vt 1 a : to put or enclose in or as if in one's pocket ⟨*pocketed* his change⟩ b : to appropriate to one's own use esp. dishonestly ⟨*pocket* the profits⟩ 2 : to put up with : ACCEPT ⟨*pocket* an insult⟩ 3 : to set aside : SUPPRESS ⟨*pocket* his pride⟩ 4 a : to hem in b : to drive (a ball) into a pocket of a pool table 5 : to cover or supply with pockets

³pocket adj 1 a : small enough to be carried in the pocket ⟨a *pocket* dictionary⟩ b : SMALL, MINIATURE 2 : MONETARY 3 : carried in or paid from one's own pocket in or for small cash outlays ⟨*pocket* money⟩

pocket battleship n : a small battleship built so as to come within treaty limitations of tonnage and armament

pocket billiards n : POOL 2

pock·et·book \'päk-ət-,bùk\ n 1 usu **pocket book** : a small esp. paperback book that can be carried in the pocket 2 a (1) : a pocket-size container for money and personal papers : WALLET (2) : PURSE b : HANDBAG 2 3 a : financial resources : INCOME b : economic interests

pocket edition n 1 : POCKETBOOK 1 2 : a miniature form of something

pock·et·ful \'päk-ət-,fùl\ n, pl **pocketfuls** \-,fùlz\ or **pock·ets·ful** \-əts-,fùl\ : as much or as many as the pocket will contain

pocket gopher n : any of various stocky burrowing No. American rodents with fur-lined cheek pouches

pock·et·knife \'päk-ət-,nīf\ n : a knife with a folding blade to be carried in the pocket — see KNIFE illustration

pocket veto n : an indirect veto of a legislative bill by an executive through retention of the bill unsigned until after adjournment of the legislature

pock·mark \'päk-,märk\ n : the depressed scar left by a pock esp. of smallpox — **pockmark** vt

po·co \'pō-kō, -pò-\ adv [It, little] : SOMEWHAT — used to qualify an adverb or adjective used as a direction in music

---

po·co a po·co \ˌpō-kō-ä-ˈpō-kō, ˌpȯ·kō-ä-ˈpȯ-kō\ *adv* [It] : little by little : GRADUALLY — used as a direction in music

po·co·sin \pə-ˈkōs-ᵊn\ *n* [of AmerInd origin] : an upland swamp of the coastal plain of the southeastern U.S.

pod \ˈpäd\ *n* **1** : a dry dehiscent fruit; *esp* : LEGUME **2** : an anatomical pouch **3** : a stream-lined compartment under the wings or fuselage of an airplane used as a container (as for fuel or a jet engine)

-pod \ˌpäd\ *n comb form* [Gk *pod-, pous* foot; akin to E *foot*] : foot : part resembling a foot ⟨*uropod*⟩

podgy \ˈpäj-ē\ *adj* **podg·i·er; -est** : PUDGY

po·di·a·try \pə-ˈdī-ə-trē\ *n* : CHIROPODY — **po·di·a·trist** \-trəst\ *n*

pod·ite \ˈpäd-ˌīt\ *n* [Gk *pod-, pous* foot] : a limb segment of an arthropod — **po·dit·ic** \pä-ˈdit-ik\ *adj*

pod

po·di·um \ˈpōd-ē-əm\ *n, pl* **-di·ums** *or* **-dia** \-ē-ə\ [L, fr. Gk *podion*, dim. of *pod-, pous* foot] **1** : a low wall serving as a foundation or terrace wall: as **a** : one around the arena of an ancient amphitheater serving as a base for the tiers of seats **b** : the masonry under the stylobate of a temple **2 a** : a dais esp. for an orchestral conductor **b** : LECTERN

Po·dunk \ˈpō-ˌdəŋk\ *n* [*Podunk*, village in Mass. or locality in Conn.] : a small, unimportant, and isolated town

po·em \ˈpō-əm, -ˌem\ *n* [L *poema*, fr. Gk *poiēma*, fr. *poiein* to make, create] **1** : a composition in verse **2** : a piece of poetry communicating to the reader the sense of a complete experience **3** : a creation, experience, or object likened to a poem

po·e·sy \ˈpō-ə-zē, -sē\ *n, pl* **-sies 1 a** : a body of poems : POEM **b** : POETRY **2** : poetic inspiration

po·et \ˈpō-ət\ *n* [L *poeta*, fr. Gk *poiētēs* maker, poet, fr. *poiein* to make, create] **1** : one who writes poetry **2** : a creative artist of great imaginative and expressive gifts and special sensitivity to his medium

po·et·as·ter \ˈpō-ət-ˌas-tər\ *n* [L *poeta* poet + *-aster*, suffix denoting partial resemblance] : an inferior poet : VERSIFIER

po·et·ess \ˈpō-ət-əs\ *n* : a female poet

po·et·ic \pō-ˈet-ik\ *adj* **1 a** : of, relating to, or characteristic of poets or poetry ⟨*poetic* words⟩ **b** : given to writing poetry **2** : written in verse

po·et·i·cal \pō-ˈet-i-kəl\ *adj* **1** : POETIC **2** : beyond or above the truth of history or nature : IDEALIZED — **po·et·i·cal·ly** \-k(ə-)lē\ *adv* — **po·et·i·cal·ness** \-kəl-nəs\ *n*

poetic justice *n* : an outcome in which vice is punished and virtue rewarded usu. in a manner peculiarly or ironically appropriate

poetic license *n* : LICENSE 4

po·et·ics \pō-ˈet-iks\ *n* **1 a** : a treatise on poetry or aesthetics **b** : poetic theory or practice **2** : poetic feelings or utterances

poet laureate *n, pl* **poets laureate** *or* **poet laureates 1** : a poet honored for achievement in his art **2** : a poet appointed by an English sovereign as a member of the royal household to write poems for state occasions **3** : one regarded by a country or region as its most eminent or representative poet

po·et·ry \ˈpō-ə-trē\ *n* **1 a** : VERSE **b** : the productions of a poet : POEMS **2** : writing in language chosen and arranged to create a specific emotional response through meaning, sound, and rhythm **3 a** : a quality that stirs the imagination **b** : a quality of spontaneity and grace ⟨her dancing is pure *poetry*⟩

po·go stick \ˈpō-gō-\ *n* [fr. *Pogo*, a trademark] : a pole with two footrests and a strong spring at the bottom propelled along the ground by jumping

po·grom \pō-ˈgräm, ˈpō-grəm\ *n* [Yiddish, fr. Russ. lit., massacre] : an organized massacre of helpless people and esp. of Jews

po·gy \ˈpō-gē\ *n, pl* **pogies** : MENHADEN

poi \ˈpȯi\ *n, pl* **poi** *or* **pois** [Hawaiian] : a Hawaiian food made of cooked taro root pounded to a paste and often fermented

poi·gnant \ˈpȯi-nyənt\ *adj* [MF *poignant*, prp. of *poindre* to prick, fr. L *pungere*] **1** : PUNGENT **2 a** (1) : painfully affecting the feelings : PIERCING ⟨*poignant* grief⟩ (2)

: deeply affecting : TOUCHING **b** : CUTTING, INCISIVE ⟨*poignant* satire⟩ **3 a** : pleasurably stimulating **b** : being to the point : APT ⟨*poignant* remarks⟩ — **poi·gnan·cy** \-nyən-sē\ *n* — **poi·gnant·ly** *adv*

poi·kilo·therm \ˈpȯi-ˈkil-ə-ˌthərm\ *n* [Gk *poikilos* variegated + *thermē* heat] : a cold-blooded organism — **poi·kilo·ther·mic** \ˌ(ˌ)pȯi-ˌkil-ə-ˈthər-mik\ *or* **poi·kilo·ther·mous** \-məs\ *adj* — **poi·kilo·ther·mism** \-ˈthər-ˌmiz-əm\ *n*

poin·ci·ana \ˌpȯin(t)-sē-ˈan-ə\ *n* [after De *Poinci*, 17th cent. governor of part of the French West Indies] : any of several showy tropical leguminous trees or shrubs with bright orange or red flowers

poin·set·tia \pȯin-ˈset-ē-ə, -ˈset-ə\ *n* [after Joel R. Poinsett *d*1851 American diplomat] : a showy Mexican and So. American spurge with tapering scarlet bracts that grow like petals about its small yellow flowers

¹point \ˈpȯint\ *n* [OF, puncture, small spot, point in time or space, fr. L *punctum*, fr. *punct-, pungere* to prick] **1 a** (1) : an individual detail : ITEM (2) : a distinguishing detail : CHARACTERISTIC **b** : the most important essential in a discussion or matter ⟨*point* of the joke⟩ ⟨*point* at issue in a court of law⟩ **c** : EFFECTIVENESS, COGENCY, FORCE **2** : an end or object to be achieved : PURPOSE ⟨there's no *point* in continuing⟩ **3 a** (1) : an undefined geometric element of which it is postulated that at least two exist and that two suffice to determine a line (2) : a geometric element determined by an ordered set of coordinates **b** (1) : a narrowly localized place having a precisely indicated position (2) : a particular place : LOCALITY ⟨visited many *points* of interest⟩ **c** (1) : an exact moment (2) : a time interval immediately before something indicated : VERGE ⟨at the *point* of death⟩ **d** (1) : a particular step, stage, or degree in development ⟨at the *point* of departure⟩ (2) : a definite position in a scale **4 a** : the terminal usu. sharp or narrowly rounded part of something (as a fin, sword, or pencil) : TIP **b** : a weapon or tool having such a part and used for stabbing or piercing **c** : either of two metal pieces in a distributor through which the circuit is made or broken **5 a** : a projecting usu. tapering piece of land or a sharp prominence **b** (1) : the tip of a projecting body part (2) *pl* : terminal bodily projections esp. when differing from the rest of the body in color **6** : a short musical phrase; *esp* : a phrase in contrapuntal music **7 a** : a very small mark **b** (1) : PUNCTUATION MARK; *esp* : PERIOD (2) : DECIMAL POINT **8** : a lace like a shoelace for tying parts of a garment together used esp. in the 16th and 17th centuries **9 a** : one of the 32 pointed marks indicating direction on a mariner's compass **b** : the difference of 11¼ degrees between two such adjacent points **10 a** : NEEDLEPOINT 1 **b** : lace made with a bobbin **11** : one of 12 spaces marked off on each side of a backgammon board **12** : a unit in a scale of measurement: as **a** : a unit of counting in the scoring of a game or contest **b** : a unit used in evaluating the strength of a bridge hand **c** : a unit of academic credit **d** : a unit of about ½ inch used to measure the belly-to-back dimension of printing type **13** : the action of pointing: as **a** : the action in dancing of extending one leg so that only the tips of the toes touch the floor **b** : a thrust or lunge in fencing **14** : a position of a player in various games (as lacrosse); *also* : the player of such a position — **in point** : RELEVANT, PERTINENT ⟨a case *in point*⟩ — **to the point** : RELEVANT, PERTINENT, APT ⟨a remark that was quite *to the point*⟩

²point *vb* **1 a** : to furnish with a point **b** : to give added force, emphasis, or piquancy to ⟨*point* up a remark⟩ **2** : to scratch out the old mortar from the joints of (as a brick wall) and fill in with new material **3 a** (1) : PUNCTUATE (2) : to separate (a decimal fraction) from an integer by a decimal point ⟨*point* off three decimal places⟩ **b** : to mark the vowels in (as Hebrew words) **4 a** : to direct someone's attention to ⟨*point* out a mistake⟩ **b** : to indicate the position or direction of something (as by the finger or by the nose of a dog) ⟨*point* out a house⟩ **5 a** : to turn, face, or cause to be turned in a particular direction : AIM ⟨*point* a gun⟩ **b** : to extend (a leg) in executing a point in dancing **6** : to indicate the fact or probability of something specified ⟨everything *points* to a bright future for the hardworking boy⟩

point-blank \ˈpȯint-ˈblaŋk\ *adj* **1 a** : marked by no appreciable drop below initial horizontal line of flight **b** : so close to a target that a missile fired will travel in a straight line to the mark ⟨fired from *point-blank* range⟩ **2** : DIRECT, BLUNT ⟨a *point-blank* refusal⟩ — **point-blank** *adv*

pointe \'pwaⁿ(n)t\ *n* [F, lit., point] : a position of balance in ballet on the extreme tip of the toe

point·ed \'pȯint-əd\ *adj* **1 a** : having a point **b** : having a crown tapering to a point ⟨the *pointed* arch of Gothic architecture⟩ **2 a** : PERTINENT, TERSE **b** : aimed at a particular person or group ⟨*pointed* remarks⟩ **3** : CONSPICUOUS, MARKED ⟨*pointed* indifference⟩ — **point·ed·ly** *adv* — **point·ed·ness** *n*

point·er \'pȯint-ər\ *n* **1** : one that furnishes with points **2 a** : one that points out; *esp* : a rod used to direct attention **b** *pl, cap* : the two stars in the Great Bear a line through which points to the North Star **3** : a large strong slender smooth-haired hunting dog that hunts by scent and indicates the presence of game by pointing **4** : a useful suggestion or hint : TIP ⟨gave a few *pointers* on how to study⟩

poin·til·lism \'pwaⁿ(n)-tē-,iz-əm\ *n* : the practice or technique of applying dots of color to a surface so that from a distance they blend together — **poin·til·list** \-tē-əst\ *n* — **poin·til·lis·tic** \,pwaⁿ(n)-tē-'is-tik\ *adj*

point·less \'pȯint-ləs\ *adj* **1** : without a point **2** : devoid of meaning : SENSELESS ⟨a *pointless* remark⟩ **3** : devoid of effectiveness : FLAT — **point·less·ly** *adv* — **point·less·ness** *n*

point of honor : a matter seriously affecting one's honor

point of view : a position from which something is considered or evaluated : STANDPOINT

¹poise \'pȯiz\ *vb* [MF *pois-, peser* to ponder, fr. L *pensare*, freq. of *pendere* to weigh] **1 a** : BALANCE; *esp* : to hold or carry in equilibrium **b** : to hold or be supported or suspended without motion in a steady position ⟨a bird *poised* in the air⟩ **2** : to hold or carry (the head) in a particular way **3** : to put into readiness : BRACE ⟨*poised* for action⟩ **4** : HOVER

²poise *n* **1** : BALANCE, EQUILIBRIUM **2 a** (1) : self-possessed composure, assurance, and dignity (2) : TRANQUILLITY, CALM, SERENITY **b** : a particular way of carrying oneself : BEARING, CARRIAGE

¹poi·son \'pȯiz-ⁿn\ *n* [OF, drink, poisonous drink, poison, fr. L *potion-, potio* drink, potion] **1 a** : a substance that through its chemical action is able to kill, injure, or impair an organism **b** (1) : something destructive or harmful (2) : an object of aversion or abhorrence **2** : a substance that inhibits the activity of another substance or the course of a reaction or process ⟨a catalyst *poison*⟩

²poison *vb* **poi·soned; poi·son·ing** \'pȯiz-niŋ, -ⁿn-iŋ\ **1 a** : to injure or kill with poison **b** : to treat, taint, or impregnate with poison ⟨*poisoned* the air with its fumes⟩ **2** : to exert a baneful influence on : CORRUPT ⟨*poisoned* their minds⟩ **3** : to inhibit the activity, course, or occurrence of — **poi·son·er** \'pȯiz-nər, -ⁿn-ər\ *n*

³poison *adj* **1** : POISONOUS ⟨a *poison* plant⟩ : VENOMOUS ⟨a *poison* tongue⟩ **2** : POISONED ⟨*poison* arrow⟩

poison gas *n* : a poisonous gas or a liquid or a solid giving off poisonous vapors designed (as in chemical warfare) to kill, injure, or disable by inhalation or contact

poison hemlock *n* **1** : a biennial poisonous herb of the carrot family with finely divided leaves and white flowers **2** : WATER HEMLOCK

poison ivy *n* : a usu. climbing plant of the sumac family mostly with three leaflets, greenish flowers and berries, and foliage and stems that when bruised and touched may cause an itching rash on the skin

poison oak *n* : a shrubby poison ivy; *esp* : POISON SUMAC

poi·son·ous \'pȯiz-nəs, -ⁿn-əs\ *adj* : having the properties or effects of poison : VENOMOUS — **poi·son·ous·ly** *adv*

poison sumac *n* : a shrubby swamp poison ivy with 7 to 13 leaflets

¹poke \'pōk\ *n* [ONF] *chiefly South & Midland* : BAG, SACK

²poke *vb* [ME *poken*] **1 a** (1) : PROD, JAB, THRUST (2) : to urge or stir by prodding or jabbing **b** (1) : PIERCE, STAB (2) : to produce by piercing, stabbing, or jabbing ⟨*poke* a hole⟩ **c** (1) : HIT, PUNCH (2) : to deliver (a blow) with the fist **2 a** : to cause to project forward

obtrusively or suddenly ⟨*poked* his nose into our affairs⟩ **3 a** : to look about or through something without system : RUMMAGE **b** : MEDDLE **4** : to move or act slowly or aimlessly : DAWDLE ⟨*poke* along⟩ — **poke fun at** : RIDICULE, MOCK

³poke *n* **1 a** : a quick thrust : JAB **b** : a blow with the fist : PUNCH **2** : a projecting brim on the front of a woman's bonnet

poke·ber·ry \'pōk-,ber-ē\ *n* : the berry of the pokeweed; *also* : POKEWEED

poke bonnet *n* : a woman's bonnet with a projecting brim at the front

¹pok·er \'pō-kər\ *n* : one that pokes; *esp* : a metal rod for stirring a fire

²po·ker \'pō-kər\ *n* : any of several card games in which a player bets on the value of his hand to win a pool

poker face *n* : an immobile inscrutable face characteristic of an expert poker player — **po·ker-faced** \-,pō-kər-'fāst\ *adj*

poke·weed \'pō-,kwēd\ *n* : a coarse American perennial herb with racemes of white flowers, dark purple juicy berries, a poisonous root, and young shoots sometimes used as potherbs

poke bonnet

poky *or* **pok·ey** \'pō-kē\ *adj* **pok·i·er; -est** [²*poke*] **1** : being small and cramped ⟨a *poky* room⟩ **2** : SHABBY, DULL ⟨a *poky* way of writing⟩ **3** : annoyingly slow ⟨a *poky* horse⟩ — **pok·i·ly** \-kə-lē\ *adv* — **pok·i·ness** \-kē-nəs\ *n*

po·lar \'pō-lər\ *adj* **1** : of or relating to a geographical pole or the region around it; *also* : coming from or having the characteristics of such a region **2 a** : of or relating to one or more poles (as of a magnet) **b** : having a dipole or characterized by molecules having dipoles ⟨a *polar* molecule⟩ **3** : serving as a guide **4** : diametrically opposite **5** : resembling a pole or axis around which all else revolves : PIVOTAL

polar bear *n* : a large creamy-white bear of arctic regions

polar body *n* : one of the minute bodies or cells cast off during maturation of an ovum

polar circle *n* : one of the two parallels of latitude each at a distance from a pole of the earth equal to about 23 degrees 27 minutes

polar coordinate *n* : either of two numbers that locate a point in a plane by its distance from a fixed point on a line and the angle this line makes with a fixed line

Po·lar·is \pə-'lar-əs\ *n* [NL, fr. *polaris* polar] : NORTH STAR

po·lari·scope \pō-'lar-ə-,skōp\ *n* : an instrument for studying the properties of substances in polarized light

po·lar·i·ty \pō-'lar-ət-ē, pə-\ *n, pl* **-ties 1** : the quality or condition of being polar : having poles **2** : attraction toward a particular object or in a specific direction **3** : the particular state either positive or negative with reference to magnetic or electrical poles **4 a** : diametrical opposition **b** : an instance of diametrical opposition

po·lar·i·za·tion \,pō-lə-rə-'zā-shən\ *n* **1** : the action of polarizing or state of being polarized: as **a** : the action of affecting radiation (as light) so that the vibrations of the wave assume a definite form (as in one plane) **b** : the deposition of gas on one or both electrodes of an electrolytic cell increasing the resistance and setting up a counter electromotive force **c** : MAGNETIZATION **2 a** : division into two opposites **b** : concentration about opposing extremes of groups or interests formerly ranged on a continuum

po·lar·ize \'pō-lə-,rīz\ *vb* **1** : to cause to undergo polarization **2** : to give polarity to **3** : to become polarized — **po·lar·iz·a·ble** \-,rī-zə-bəl\ *adj* — **po·lar·iz·er** *n*

polar nucleus *n* : either of the two nuclei of a seed plant embryo sac that are destined to form endosperm — compare DOUBLE FERTILIZATION

Po·lar·oid \'pō-lə-,rȯid\ *trademark* — used for a light-polarizing material used esp. in eyeglasses and lamps to prevent glare

pol·der \'pōl-dər, 'päl-\ *n* [D] : a tract of low land reclaimed from a body of water (as the sea)

¹pole \'pōl\ *n* [OE *pāl* stake, pole, fr. L *palus* stake] **1** : a long slender usu. cylindrical piece of material (as wood or metal) ⟨telephone *poles*⟩ **2 a** : a unit of length equal to 16½ feet **b** : a unit of area equal to a square

rod or perch **3** : a tree with a breast-high diameter of from 4 to 12 inches **4** : the inside position on a racetrack
²pole *vb* **1** : to act upon, impel, or push with a pole **2 a** : to propel a boat with a pole **b** : to use ski poles to gain speed — **pol·er** *n*
³pole *n* [Gk *polos* pivot, pole] **1** : either end of an axis of a sphere and esp. of the earth's axis **2 a** : either of two related opposites **b** : a point of guidance or attraction **3 a** : one of the two terminals of an electric cell, battery, or dynamo **b** : one of two or more regions in a magnetized body at which the magnetism seems to be concentrated **4** : either of two structurally or functionally differentiated areas at opposite ends of an axis in an organism or cell **5** : the vertex of the angle coordinate in a polar coordinate system
Pole \'pōl\ *n* **1** : a native or inhabitant of Poland **2** : a person of Polish descent
pole·ax \'pōl-,aks\ *n* [ME *pollax*, fr. *polle* poll + *ax*] : a battle-ax with short handle and cutting edge or point opposite the blade; *also* : one with a long handle used as an ornamental weapon
pole bean *n* : a cultivated bean having long internodes and twining stems and usu. trained to grow upright on supports
pole·cat \'pōl-,kat\ *n, pl* **polecats** *or* **polecat** **1** : a European carnivorous mammal of which the ferret is considered a domesticated variety **2** : SKUNK
pole horse *n* : the horse having a starting position next to the inside rail in a harness race
po·lem·ic \pə-'lem-ik\ *n* [Gk *polemos* war] **1 a** : an aggressive attack on or refutation of the opinions or principles of another **b** : the art or practice of disputation or controversy — usu. used in pl. **2** : an aggressive controversialist : DISPUTANT **3** *pl* : the branch of Christian theology devoted to the refutation of errors — **polemic** *or* **po·lem·i·cal** \-'lem-i-kəl\ *adj* — **po·lem·i·cal·ly** \-i-k(ə-)lē\ *adv* — **po·lem·i·cist** \-'lem-ə-səst\ *n*
pole·star \'pōl-,stär\ *n* **1** : NORTH STAR **2 a** : a directing principle : GUIDE **b** : a center of attraction
pole vault *n* : a vault with the aid of a pole; *esp* : a field event consisting of a vault for height over a crossbar — called also *pole jump* — **pole-vault** \'pōl-,vólt\ *vi* — **pole-vault·er** *n*
¹po·lice \pə-'lēs\ *n, pl* **police** [MF, fr. LL *politia* government, administration, fr. Gk *politeia*, fr. *politeuein* to be a citizen, engage in political activity, fr. *polites* citizen, fr. *polis* city] **1** : control and regulation of affairs affecting the general order and welfare of a political unit esp. with respect to general comfort, health, morals, safety, or prosperity **2 a** : the department of government concerned primarily with maintenance of public order, safety, and health and enforcement of laws **b** : the department of government charged with prevention, detection, and prosecution of public nuisances and crimes **3** *pl* : POLICEMEN **4** : a private organization resembling a police force ⟨railroad *police*⟩ **5 a** : the action or process of cleaning and putting in order **b** : military personnel detailed to perform this function
²police *vt* **1** : to control, regulate, or keep in order by use of or as of police **2** : to make clean and put in order : clean up ⟨*police* the area⟩ **3** : to supervise the operation, execution, or administration of
police action *n* : a localized military action undertaken without formal declaration of war by regular forces against persons held to be violators of international peace and order
police court *n* : a court having jurisdiction over various minor offenses and authority to send cases involving serious offenses to a superior court
police dog *n* **1** : a dog trained to assist police esp. in tracking criminals **2** : GERMAN SHEPHERD
police force *n* : a body of trained officers and men entrusted by a government with maintenance of public peace and order, enforcement of laws, and prevention and detection of crime
po·lice·man \pə-'lēs-mən\ *n* : a member of a police force — **po·lice·wom·an** \-,wùm-ən\ *n*
police power *n* : the inherent power of a government to exercise reasonable control over persons and property within its jurisdiction in the interest of the general security, health, safety, morals, and welfare

police reporter *n* : a reporter assigned to cover news resulting from the operation of the police force
police state *n* : a state in which the social, economic, and political activities of the people are under the arbitrary power of the government often acting through a secret police force
police station *n* : the headquarters of the police for a particular locality
pol·i·clin·ic \,päl-i-'klin-ik\ *n* [G *poliklinik*, fr. Gk *polis* city + G *klinik* clinic] : a dispensary or department of a hospital where outpatients are treated — compare POLYCLINIC
¹pol·i·cy \'päl-ə-sē\ *n, pl* **-cies** **1 a** : prudence or wisdom in the management of affairs : SAGACITY **b** : management or procedure based primarily on material interest **2** : a course of action selected in light of given conditions to guide and determine decisions
²policy *n, pl* **-cies** [modif. of MF *police* certificate, fr. It *polizza*, modif. of ML *apodixa* receipt, fr. Gk *apodeixis* proof] **1** : a writing embodying a contract of insurance **2 a** : a daily lottery in which participants bet that certain numbers will be drawn from a lottery wheel **b** : NUMBER 8
pol·i·cy·hold·er \-,hōl-dər\ *n* : one granted an insurance policy
po·lio \'pō-lē-,ō\ *n* : POLIOMYELITIS — **polio** *adj*
po·lio·my·e·li·tis \,pō-lē-,ō-,mī-ə-'līt-əs\ *n* [NL, fr. Gk *polios* gray + *myelos* marrow] : an acute infectious virus disease marked by inflammation of nerve cells in the spinal cord accompanied by fever and often paralysis and atrophy of muscles — called also *infantile paralysis* — **po·lio·my·e·lit·ic** \-'lit-ik\ *adj*
¹pol·ish \'päl-ish\ *vb* [OF *poliss-*, *polir*, fr. L *polire*] **1** : to make smooth and glossy usu. by friction **2** : to smooth or refine in manners or condition **3** : to bring to a highly developed, finished, or refined state : PERFECT **syn** see BURNISH — **pol·ish·er** *n*
²polish *n* **1 a** : a smooth glossy surface : LUSTER **b** : REFINEMENT, CULTURE **c** : a state of high development or refinement **2** : the action or process of polishing **3** : a preparation used in polishing
¹Pol·ish \'pō-lish\ *adj* : of, relating to, or characteristic of Poland, the Poles, or Polish
²Polish *n* : the Slavic language of the Poles
polish off *vt* : to dispose of rapidly or completely
pol·it·bu·ro *also* **pol·it·bu·reau** \'päl-ət-,byùr-ō\ *n* [Russ *politbyuro*, fr. *politicheskoe byuro* political bureau] : the principal policy-making and executive committee of a Communist party
po·lite \pə-'līt\ *adj* [L *politus*, fr. pp. of *polire* to polish] **1** : of, relating to, or having the characteristics of advanced culture ⟨customs of *polite* society⟩ **2 a** : showing or characterized by correct social usage ⟨*polite* forms of address⟩ **b** : marked by consideration, tact, deference, or courtesy : COURTEOUS **syn** see CIVIL — **po·lite·ly** *adv* — **po·lite·ness** *n*
po·li·tesse \,päl-ē-'tes\ *n* [F] : formal politeness : DECOROUSNESS
pol·i·tic \'päl-ə-,tik\ *adj* [Gk *politikos* political, fr. *politēs* citizen, fr. *polis* city] **1** : characterized by shrewdness **2** : sagacious in promoting a policy **3** : shrewdly tactful ⟨a *politic* answer⟩ **syn** see EXPEDIENT
po·lit·i·cal \pə-'lit-i-kəl\ *adj* **1** : of or relating to government, a government, or the conduct of government **2** : of or relating to politics **3** : organized in governmental terms ⟨*political* units⟩ **4** : involving or charged or concerned with acts against a government or a political system ⟨*political* crimes⟩⟨*political* police⟩ — **po·lit·i·cal·ly** \-k(ə-)lē\ *adv*
political economy *n* : a modern social science dealing with the interrelationship of political and economic processes
political science *n* : a social science concerned chiefly with the description and analysis of political institutions and processes — **political scientist** *n*
pol·i·ti·cian \,päl-ə-'tish-ən\ *n* **1** : one experienced in the art or science of government; *esp* : one actively conducting governmental affairs **2** : one engaged in party politics as a profession
pol·i·tick \'päl-ə-,tik\ *vi* : to engage in political discussion or activity — **pol·i·tick·er** *n*
po·lit·i·co \pə-'lit-i-,kō\ *n, pl* **-cos** *also* **-coes** : POLITICIAN 2
pol·i·tics \'päl-ə-,tiks\ *n sing or pl* **1 a** : the art or science

of government   **b** : the art or science of guiding or influencing governmental policy   **c** : the art or science of winning and holding control over a government   **2 a** : political affairs or business; *esp* : competition between groups or individuals for power and leadership   **b** : political life esp. as a profession   **3** : political opinions

pol·i·ty \ˈpäl-ət-ē\ *n, pl* **-ties**   **1** : political organization   **2** : a form of political organization ⟨a republican *polity*⟩   **3** : a politically organized unit   **4** : the form of government of a religious denomination

pol·ka \ˈpōl-kə\ *n* [Czech, fr. Pol *Polka* Polish woman]   **1** : a vivacious couple dance of Bohemian origin with three steps and a hop in duple time   **2** : a lively Bohemian dance tune in ¾ time — **polka** *vi*

pol·ka dot \ˈpō-kə-ˌdät\ *n* : a dot in a pattern of regularly distributed dots in textile design

¹poll \ˈpōl\ *n* [MLG *polle*]   **1 a** : HEAD   **b** : the prominent hairy top or back of the head   **c** : NAPE   **2** : the broad or flat end of a hammer or similar tool   **3 a** : the casting or recording of the votes of a body of persons   **b** : the place where votes are cast or recorded — usu. used in pl.   **4 a** : a questioning or canvassing of persons to obtain information or opinions   **b** : the information so obtained

²poll *vb*   **1 a** : to cut off or cut short a growth or part of : CROP, SHEAR   **b** : to cut off or cut short (as wool)   **2 a** : to receive and record the votes of   **b** : to request each member of to declare his vote individually ⟨*poll* a jury⟩   **3** : to receive (as votes) in an election   **4** : to question or canvass in a poll   **5** : to cast one's vote at a poll — **poll·ee** \pō-ˈlē\ *n* — **poll·er** \ˈpō-lər\ *n*

pol·lack *or* **pol·lock** \ˈpäl-ək\ *n, pl* **pollack** *or* **pollacks** *or* **pollock** *or* **pollocks** [Sc *podlok*] : a commercially important north Atlantic food fish resembling the related cods but darker

polled \ˈpōld\ *adj* : having no horns

pol·len \ˈpäl-ən\ *n* [L *pollin-, pollen* fine flour]   **1** : a mass of microspores in a seed plant appearing usu. as a fine dust   **2** : a dusty bloom on the body of an insect — **pollen** *adj* — **pol·lin·ic** \pä-ˈlin-ik\ *adj*

pollen basket *n* : a flat or hollow area bordered with stiff hairs on the hind leg of a bee in which it carries pollen to the nest

pollen grain *n* : one of the granular microspores occurring in pollen and giving rise to the male gametophyte of a seed plant

pol·len·iz·er \ˈpäl-ə-ˌnī-zər\ *n*   **1** : a plant that is a source of pollen   **2** : POLLINATOR 1

pollen sac *n* : one of the pouches of a seed plant anther in which pollen is formed

pollen tube *n* : a tube formed by the pollen grain that passes down the style and conveys the sperm nuclei to the embryo sac of a flower

pol·lex \ˈpäl-ˌeks\ *n, pl* **pol·li·ces** \ˈpäl-ə-ˌsēz\ [L *pollic-, pollex*] : THUMB — **pol·li·cal** \ˈpäl-i-kəl\ *adj*

pol·li·nate \ˈpäl-ə-ˌnāt\ *vt* : to place pollen on the stigma of — **pol·li·na·tion** \ˌpäl-ə-ˈnā-shən\ *n*

pol·li·na·tor \ˈpäl-ə-ˌnāt-ər\ *n*   **1** : an agent that pollinates flowers   **2** : POLLENIZER 2

pol·li·no·sis *or* **pol·len·osis** \ˌpäl-ə-ˈnō-səs\ *n* : an acute recurrent allergic respiratory disorder caused by sensitivity to particular pollens

pol·li·wog *or* **pol·ly·wog** \ˈpäl-ē-ˌwäg\ *n* [ME *polwigle*] : TADPOLE

poll·ster \ˈpōl-stər\ *n* : one that conducts a poll or compiles data obtained by a poll

poll tax *n* : a tax of a fixed amount per person levied on adults and often payable as a requirement for voting

pol·lu·tant \pə-ˈlüt-ᵊnt\ *n* : something that pollutes

pol·lute \pə-ˈlüt\ *vt* [L *pollut-, polluere*] : to make impure : CONTAMINATE — **pol·lu·tion** \pə-ˈlü-shən\ *n*

Pol·lux \ˈpäl-əks\ *n*   **1** : the immortal twin of Castor — compare DIOSCURI   **2** : a first-magnitude star in the constellation Gemini

Pol·ly·an·na \ˌpäl-ē-ˈan-ə\ *n* [after *Pollyanna*, heroine of Eleanor Porter's novel *Pollyanna*] : one characterized by irrepressible optimism and a tendency to find good in everything

po·lo \ˈpō-lō\ *n* [of Tibetan origin]   **1** : a game played by teams of players on horseback using mallets with long flexible handles to drive a wooden ball   **2** : WATER POLO — **po·lo·ist** \ˈpō-lə-wəst\ *n*

polo coat *n* : a tailored overcoat for casual wear often of tan camel's hair

pol·o·naise \ˌpäl-ə-ˈnāz, ˌpō-lə-\ *n* [F, fr. fem. of *polonais* Polish]   **1** : an elaborate 18th century overdress with short-sleeved fitted waist and draped cutaway overskirt   **2 a** : a stately 19th century Polish processional dance   **b** : music for this dance in moderate ¾ time

po·lo·ni·um \pə-ˈlō-nē-əm\ *n* : a radioactive metallic chemical element that emits a helium nucleus to form an isotope of lead — see ELEMENT table

polo shirt *n* : a close-fitting pullover shirt of knitted cotton with a turnover collar or round banded neck

pol·ter·geist \ˈpōl-tər-ˌgīst\ *n* [G, fr. *poltern* to knock + *geist* spirit] : a noisy usu. mischievous ghost held to be responsible for unexplained noises (as rappings)

¹pol·troon \päl-ˈtrün\ *n* [MF *poultron*, fr. It *poltrone*, fr. aug. of *poltro* colt] : a spiritless coward : CRAVEN

²poltroon *adj* : characterized by cowardice : cowardly

pol·troon·ery \-ˈtrün-(ə-)rē\ *n* : COWARDICE

poly- *comb form* [Gk, fr. *polys*; akin to E *full*]   **1 a** : many : much : MULTI- ⟨*poly*gyny⟩   **b** : excessive : HYPER- ⟨*poly*phagia⟩   **2 a** : more than one of a (specified) substance ⟨*poly*sulfide⟩   **b** : polymeric ⟨*poly*ethylene⟩

pol·y·an·drous \ˌpäl-ē-ˈan-drəs\ *adj* [Gk *andr-, anēr* male, husband]   **1** : having many usu. free hypogynous stamens   **2** : of, relating to, or being a marriage form in which a woman has more than one husband at a time — **pol·y·an·dry** \ˈpäl-ē-ˌan-drē\ *n*

pol·y·an·thus \-ˈan(t)-thəs\ *n, pl* **-an·thus·es** *or* **-an·thi** \-ˈan-ˌthī, -ˌthē\ [Gk *anthos* flower]   **1** : any of various hybrid primroses   **2** : a narcissus with umbels of small white or yellow flowers with spreading perianths

pol·y·ba·sic \ˌpäl-i-ˈbā-sik\ *adj* : having more than one hydrogen atom replaceable by basic atoms or radicals — used of acids

pol·y·chaete \ˈpäl-i-ˌkēt\ *n* [Gk *chaitē* long hair] : any of a class (Polychaeta) of annelid worms including most of the common marine worms and usu. having paired segmental appendages — **polychaete** *adj*

poly·chlo·ri·nat·ed biphenyl \ˌpäl-i-ˈklōr-ə-ˌnāt-əd-, -ˈklôr-\ *n* : any of several compounds that have various industrial applications and are poisonous environmental pollutants which tend to accumulate in animal tissues

poly·chro·mat·ic \ˌpäl-i-krō-ˈmat-ik\ *adj* : showing a variety or a change of colors : MULTICOLORED

poly·chrome \ˈpäl-i-ˌkrōm\ *adj* : relating to, made with, or decorated in several colors ⟨*polychrome* pottery⟩

poly·clin·ic \ˌpäl-i-ˈklin-ik\ *n* : a clinic or hospital treating diseases of many sorts — compare POLICLINIC

poly·dac·tyl \ˌpäl-i-ˈdak-tᵊl\ *adj* [Gk *daktylos* digit] : having several to many and esp. abnormally many digits — **poly·dac·ty·lous** \-tə-ləs\ *adj* — **poly·dac·ty·ly** \-lē\ *n*

poly·es·ter \ˈpäl-ē-ˌes-tər\ *n* : a complex ester formed by polymerization or condensation and used esp. in making fibers

poly·eth·yl·ene \ˌpäl-ē-ˈeth-ə-ˌlēn\ *n* : one of various lightweight plastics resistant to chemicals and moisture that are used in packaging

po·lyg·a·mous \pə-ˈlig-ə-məs\ *adj*   **1 a** : of, relating to, or being a marriage form in which a spouse of either sex has more than one mate at one time   **b** : having more than one spouse or mate at one time   **2** : bearing both hermaphroditic and unisexual flowers on the same plant — **po·lyg·a·mist** \-məst\ *n* — **po·lyg·a·mous·ly** *adv* — **po·lyg·a·my** \-mē\ *n*

poly·gen·ic \ˌpäl-i-ˈjen-ik\ *adj* : of, relating to, or controlled by several usu. nonallelic genes

pol·y·glot \ˈpäl-i-ˌglät\ *adj* [Gk *glōtta* language]   **1** : speaking or writing several languages   **2** : containing matter in or composed of elements from several languages — **polyglot** *n*

pol·y·gon \ˈpäl-i-ˌgän\ *n*   **1** : a closed plane figure bounded by straight lines   **2** : a closed figure on a sphere bounded by arcs of great circles — **po·lyg·o·nal** \pə-ˈlig-ən-ᵊl\ *adj*

poly·graph \ˈpäl-i-ˌgraf\ *n* : an instrument for recording tracings of several different pulsations simultaneously; *also* : LIE DETECTOR — **poly·graph·ic** \ˌpäl-i-ˈgraf-ik\ *adj*

po·lyg·y·nous \pə-ˈlij-ə-nəs\ *adj*   **1** : relating to or practicing polygyny   **2** : having many pistils

po·lyg·y·ny \-nē\ *n* : the practice of having more than one wife at one time

pol·y·he·dron \,päl-i-'hē-drən\ *n, pl* **-drons** *or* **-dra** \-drə\ : a solid formed by plane faces — **pol·y·he·dral** \-drəl\ *adj*

Pol·y·hym·nia \,päl-i-'him-nē-ə\ *n* : the Greek Muse of sacred lyric poetry

pol·y·math \'päl-i-,math\ *n* [Gk *math-, manthanein* to learn] : one of encyclopedic learning

pol·y·mer \'päl-ə-mər\ *n* [Gk *meros* part] : a chemical compound or mixture of compounds that is formed by polymerization and consists essentially of repeating structural units

pol·y·mer·ic \,päl-ə-'mer-ik\ *adj* : of, relating to, or consisting of a polymer

po·lym·er·i·za·tion \pə-,lim-ə-rə-'zā-shən, ,päl-ə-mə-rə-\ *n* : a chemical reaction in which two or more small molecules combine to form larger molecules

po·lym·er·ize \pə-'lim-ə-,rīz, 'päl-ə-mə-\ *vb* : to subject to or undergo polymerization

poly·morph \'päl-i-,mórf\ *n* : a polymorphic organism or one of the several forms of such an organism

poly·mor·phic \,päl-i-'mór-fik\ *or* **poly·mor·phous** \-fəs\ *adj* : having, assuming, or occurring in various forms, characters, or styles — **poly·mor·phism** \-,fiz-əm\ *n*

poly·mor·pho·nu·cle·ar \-,mór-fə-'n(y)ü-klē-ər\ *adj* : having the nucleus complexly lobed ⟨*polymorphonuclear* leucocytes⟩ — **polymorphonuclear** *n*

Pol·y·ne·sian \,päl-ə-'nē-zhən, -shən\ *n* **1** : a member of any of the native peoples of Polynesia **2** : a group of Austronesian languages spoken in Polynesia — **Polynesian** *adj*

pol·y·no·mi·al \,päl-i-'nō-mē-əl\ *n* [*poly-* + *-nomial* (as in *binomial*)] : an algebraic expression having two or more terms ⟨the *polynomial* a² + 2ab — b²⟩

poly·nu·cle·o·tide \,päl-i-'n(y)ü-klē-ə-,tīd\ *n* : an organic compound consisting of complex phosphoric acid‑containing esters usu. arranged in long chains

pol·yp \'päl-əp\ *n* [Gk *polypous* octopus, nasal tumor, fr. *poly-* + *pous* foot] **1** : a coelenterate (as a sea anemone) having a hollow cylindrical body closed and attached at one end and opening at the other by a central mouth surrounded by tentacles armed with nematocysts **2** : a projecting mass of swollen and hypertrophied or tumorous membrane — **pol·yp·oid** \'päl-ə-,póid\ *adj*

poly·pep·tide \,päl-i-'pep-,tīd\ *n* : a compound that yields amino acids on hydrolysis but has a lower molecular weight than a protein

pol·y·pha·gia \-'fā-j(ē-)ə\ *n* [Gk, fr. *poly-* +*phagein* to eat] : excessive appetite or eating

po·lyph·a·gous \pə-'lif-ə-gəs\ *adj* : feeding on or utilizing many kinds of food

poly·phase \'päl-i-,fāz\ *or* **poly·pha·sic** \,päl-i-'fā-zik\ *adj* : having or producing two or more phases ⟨a *polyphase* machine⟩ ⟨a *polyphase* current⟩

Pol·y·phe·mus \,päl-ə-'fē-məs\ *n* : a Cyclops blinded by Odysseus in order to escape from his cave

pol·y·phon·ic \,päl-i-'fän-ik\ *adj* : of, relating to, or marked by polyphony — **pol·y·phon·i·cal·ly** \-'fän-i-k(ə-)lē\ *adv*

po·lyph·o·ny \pə-'lif-ə-nē\ *n* [Gk *phōnē* voice] : music consisting of two or more melodically independent but harmonizing voice parts

poly·phy·let·ic \,päl-i-fī-'let-ik\ *adj* [Gk *phylē* tribe] : of or relating to more than one stock; *esp* : derived from more than one ancestral line — **poly·phy·let·i·cal·ly** \-'let-i-k(ə-)lē\ *adv* — **poly·phy·let·i·cism** \-'let-ə-,siz-əm\ *n*

pol·y·ploid \'päl-i-,plóid\ *adj* [*poly-* +*-ploid* (as in *diploid*)] : manifold in appearance or arrangement; *esp* : having or being a chromosome number that is a multiple greater than two of the monoploid number — **polyploid** *n* — **pol·y·ploi·dic** \,päl-i-'plóid-ik\ *adj* — **pol·y·ploi·dy** \'päl-i-,plóid-ē\ *n*

pol·y·po·dy \'päl-ə-,pōd-ē\ *n, pl* **-dies** [Gk*polypodion*, fr. *poly-* + *pod-, pous* foot] : a widely distributed fern with creeping rootstocks and pinnately cleft fronds

poly·sac·cha·ride \,päl-i-'sak-ə-,rīd\ *n* : a carbohydrate that can be decomposed by hydrolysis into two or more molecules of monosaccharides; *esp* : one of the more complex carbohydrates

poly·sty·rene \,päl-i-'stī(ə)r-,ēn\ *n* : a rigid transparent plastic of good physical and electrical insulating properties

poly·syl·lab·ic \,päl-i-sə-'lab-ik\ *adj* : having many syllables; *esp* : having more than three syllables — **poly·syl·lab·i·cal·ly** \-'lab-i-k(ə-)lē\ *adv* — **poly·syl·la·ble** \'päl-i-,sil-ə-bəl, ,päl-i-'\ *n*

pol·y·syn·de·ton \,päl-i-'sin-də-,tän\ *n* [LGk *polysyndetos* using many conjunctions, fr. Gk *poly-* + *syndetos* bound together] : repetition of conjunctions in close succession (as in "paper and pencils and books")

pol·y·tech·nic \,päl-i-'tek-nik\ *adj* [Gk *technē* art] : relating to or devoted to instruction in many technical arts or applied sciences ⟨a *polytechnic* school⟩

poly·the·ism \'päl-i-(,)thē-,iz-əm\ *n* : belief in or worship of more than one god — **poly·the·ist** \-,thē-əst\ *adj or n* — **poly·the·is·tic** \,päl-i-thē-'is-tik\ *also* **poly·the·is·ti·cal** \-'is-ti-kəl\ *adj*

poly·ton·al \,päl-i-'tōn-ᵊl\ *adj* : of or relating to polytonality

poly·to·nal·i·ty \-tō-'nal-ət-ē\ *n* : the simultaneous use of two or more musical keys

poly·un·sat·u·rat·ed \,päl-ē-,ən-'sach-ə-,rāt-əd\ *adj* : rich in unsaturated chemical bonds ⟨a *polyunsaturated* oil⟩

poly·va·lent \,päl-i-'vā-lənt\ *adj* **1 a** : having a valence greater usu. than two **b** : having variable valence **2** : effective against or sensitive toward more than one exciting agent — **poly·va·lence** \-lən(t)s\ *n*

pol·y·zo·an \,päl-i-'zō-ən\ *adj or n* **1** : BRYOZOAN **2** : CESTODE

pom·ace \'pəm-əs, 'päm-\ *n* **1** : the substance of fruit (as apples) crushed or ground or the residue remaining after pressing wine grapes **2** : a substance crushed to a pulpy mass (as for the extraction of oil)

po·ma·ceous \pō-'mā-shəs\ *adj* [LL *pomum* apple, fr. L, fruit] : of, resembling, or related to apples

po·made \pō-'mād, -'mäd\ *n* [MF *pommade* ointment formerly made from apples, fr. LL *pomum* apple] : a perfumed unguent esp. for the hair or scalp — **pomade** *vt*

po·man·der \'pō-,man-dər, pō-'\ *n* [MF *pome d'ambre*, lit., apple or ball of amber] : a mixture of aromatic substances enclosed in a perforated bag or box and formerly carried as a guard against infection

po·ma·tum \pō-'māt-əm, -'mät-\ *n* : OINTMENT; *esp* : POMADE

pome \'pōm\ *n* [L *pomum* fruit] : a fleshy fruit (as an apple) consisting of a central core with usu. five seeds enclosed in a capsule and surrounded by a thick fleshy outer layer derived from the receptacle — **po·mif·er·ous** \pō-'mif-(ə-)rəs\ *adj*

pome·gran·ate \'päm-(ə-),gran-ət, 'pəm-,gran-\ *n* [MF *pomme grenate*, lit., seedy apple] : a thick-skinned reddish berry about the size of an orange having many seeds in a crimson pulp of agreeable acid flavor; *also* : a tropical Old World tree bearing pomegranates

Pom·er·a·ni·an \,päm-ə-'rā-nē-ən, -nyən\ *n* **1** : a native or inhabitant of Pomerania **2** : any of a breed of very small compact long-haired dogs of the spitz type — **Pomeranian** *adj*

¹pom·mel \'pəm-əl, 'päm-\ *n* [MF *pomel*, fr. LL *pomum* apple] **1** : the knob on the hilt of a sword or saber **2** : the protuberance at the front and top of a saddlebow

²pom·mel \'pəm-əl\ *vt* **-meled** *or* **-melled; -mel·ing** *or* **-mel·ling** \'pəm-(ə-)liŋ\ : PUMMEL

po·mol·o·gy \pō-'mäl-ə-jē\ *n* [L *pomum* fruit] : the science and practice of fruit growing — **po·mo·log·i·cal** \,pō-mə-'läj-i-kəl\ *adj* — **po·mol·o·gist** \pō-'mäl-ə-jəst\ *n*

Po·mo·na \pə-'mō-nə\ *n* : the ancient Italian goddess of fruit trees

pomp \'pämp\ *n* [Gk *pompē*] **1** : a show of magnificence : SPLENDOR ⟨the *pomp* of a coronation ceremony⟩ **2** : an ostentatious act or display ⟨a person who loves *pomp*⟩

pom·pa·dour \'päm-pə-,dōr, -,dór\ *n* [after Marquise de *Pompadour* d1764 mistress of Louis XV of France] : a style of dressing the hair high over the forehead; *also* : hair dressed in this style

pom·pa·no \'päm-pə-,nō, 'pəm-\ *n, pl* **-nos** [Sp *pámpano*] : a spiny-finned food fish of the southern Atlantic and Gulf coasts having a narrow body and forked tail; *also* : any of several related or similar fishes

pom-pom \'päm-,päm\ *n* : an automatic gun of 20 to 40 millimeters mounted on ships in pairs, fours, or eights

pom·pon \'päm-,pän\ *n* **1** : an ornamental ball or tuft used on clothing, caps, and fancy costumes **2** : a chrysanthemum or dahlia with small rounded flower heads

pom·pos·i·ty \päm-'päs-ət-ē\ *n, pl* **-ties** **1** : POMPOUSNESS **2** : a pompous gesture, habit, or action

pomp·ous \'päm-pəs\ *adj* **1** : making an appearance of importance or dignity ⟨a *pompous* manner⟩ **2** : SELF= IMPORTANT ⟨a very *pompous* little man⟩ **3** : excessively elevated or ornate ⟨*pompous* rhetoric⟩ — **pomp·ous·ly** *adv* — **pomp·ous·ness** *n*

pon·cho \'pän-chō\ *n, pl* **ponchos** [AmerSp, of AmerInd origin] **1** : a cloak resembling a blanket with a slit in the middle for the head **2** : a waterproof garment resembling a poncho worn chiefly as a raincoat

pond \'pänd\ *n* [ME, artificially confined body of water, alter. of ⁴*pound*] : a body of standing water usu. smaller than a lake

pon·der \'pän-dər\ *vb* **pon·dered; pon·der·ing** \'pänd(ə-)riŋ\ [L *ponderare* to weigh, ponder, fr. *ponder-, pondus* weight] : to consider carefully — **pon·der·er** \-dər-ər\ *n*

pon·der·a·ble \'pän-d(ə-)rə-bəl\ *adj* : capable of being weighed or appraised : APPRECIABLE

pon·der·o·sa pine \,pän-də-,rō-sə-, -zə-\ *n* : a tall timber pine of western No. America with long needles in bundles of 2 to 5; *also* : its strong straight-grained wood

pon·der·ous \'pän-d(ə-)rəs\ *adj* **1** : very heavy **2** : heavy because of weight and size ⟨a *ponderous* weapon⟩ **3** : not light or lively : DULL ⟨*ponderous* words⟩ — **pon·der·ous·ly** *adv* — **pon·der·ous·ness** *n*

pond lily *n* : WATER LILY

pond scum *n* **1** : SPIROGYRA; *also* : any of various related algae **2** : a mass of tangled algal filaments in stagnant water

pond·weed \'pänd-,wēd\ *n* : any of several water plants with both submerged and floating leaves and spikes of greenish flowers

pone \'pōn\ *n* [of Algonquian origin] *South & Midland* : a cornmeal cake shaped into an oval in the palms and baked, fried, or boiled; *also* : corn bread in the form of pones

pon·gee \pän-'jē, 'pän-,\ *n* [Chin (Pek) *pen³ chi¹*] : a thin soft ecru or tan fabric of Chinese origin woven from raw silk; *also* : an imitation of this fabric in cotton or rayon

¹pon·iard \'pän-yərd\ *n* [MF *poignard*, fr. *poing* fist, fr. L *pugnus*] : a slender dagger

²poniard *vt* : to stab with a poniard

pons \'pänz\ *n, pl* **pon·tes** \'pän-,tēz\ : a broad mass of nerve fibers on the ventral surface of the brain at the anterior end of the medulla oblongata — called also *pons Va·ro·lii* \,pänz-və-'rō-lē-,ī, -lē-,ē\

pon·ti·fex \'pänt-ə-,feks\ *n, pl* **pon·tif·i·ces** \pän-'tif-ə-,sēz\ : a member of the Roman council of priests

pon·tiff \'pänt-əf\ *n* [F *pontif*, fr. L *pontific-, pontifex*, fr. *pont-, pons* bridge + *facere* to make] **1** : PONTIFEX **2** : BISHOP; *esp* : POPE

poniard

¹pon·tif·i·cal \pän-'tif-i-kəl\ *adj* **1** : of or relating to a pontiff or pontifex **2** : celebrated by a prelate of episcopal rank with distinctive ceremonies ⟨*pontifical* mass⟩ — **pon·tif·i·cal·ly** \-k(ə-)lē\ *adv*

²pontifical *n* **1** : episcopal attire; *esp* : the insignia of the episcopal order worn by a prelate when celebrating a pontifical service — usu. used in pl. **2** : a book containing the forms for sacraments and rites performed by a bishop

¹pon·tif·i·cate \pän-'tif-i-kət, -'tif-ə-,kāt\ *n* : the office or term of office of a pontiff

²pon·tif·i·cate \-'tif-ə-,kāt\ *vi* **1** : to officiate with pontifical authority or ceremony **2** : to speak pompously or dogmatically ⟨*pontificating* on the subject of fishing⟩ — **pon·tif·i·ca·tor** \-,kāt-ər\ *n*

Pon·tius Pi·late \,pän-chəs-'pī-lət, ,pän-\ *n* : the Roman procurator of Judea under whom Jesus was crucified

pon·toon \pän-'tün\ *n* [F *ponton* floating bridge, punt, fr. L *ponton-, ponto*, fr. *pont-, pons* bridge] **1** : a flat-bottomed boat; *esp* : a flat-bottomed boat or portable float used

in building a floating temporary bridge **2** : a float of an airplane

pontoon bridge *n* : a bridge whose deck is supported on pontoons

po·ny \'pō-nē\ *n, pl* **ponies** **1** : a small-horse; *esp* : one of any of several breeds of very small stocky animals **2** : a small glass for an alcoholic drink or the amount it will hold **3** : a literal translation of a foreign language text; *esp* : one used illegitimately by students in preparing or reciting lessons

Pony Express *n* : a rapid postal and express system across the western U.S. in 1860–61 operating by relays of horses

po·ny·tail \'pō-nē-,tāl\ *n* : a style of arranging hair to resemble the tail of a pony; *also* : hair arranged in this style

po·ny up \,pō-nē-'əp\ *vb* : to pay esp. in settlement of an account

pooch \'püch\ *n, slang* : DOG

pood \'püd, 'püt\ *n* [Russ *pud*, fr. ON *pund* pound] : a Russian unit of weight equal to about 36.11 pounds

poo·dle \'püd-ʼl\ *n* [G *pudel*, short for *pudelhund*, fr. *pudel* puddle + *hund* dog] : any of an old breed of active intelligent heavy-coated solid-colored dogs

pooh \'pü, 'pu\ *interj* — used to express contempt, disapproval, or impatience

pooh-bah \'pü-,bä\ *n, often cap P&B* [*Pooh-Bah*, character in Gilbert and Sullivan's opera *The Mikado* bearing the title Lord-High-Everything-Else] : one in high position

pooh-pooh \'pü-pü, pü-'pü\ *also* **pooh** \'pü\ *vb* **1** : to express contempt or impatience **2** : DERIDE, SCORN ⟨*pooh-pooh* the idea that a house is haunted⟩

¹pool \'pül\ *n* [OE *pōl*] **1** : a small and rather deep natural or artificial body of usu. fresh water **2** : a small body of standing liquid : PUDDLE

²pool *n* [F *poule*, lit., hen] **1 a** : a stake to which each player of a game has contributed **b** : all the money bet by a number of persons on an event **2** : a game of billiards played on a pool table having 6 pockets with usu. 15 object balls **3 a** : a common fund for buying or selling; *esp* : one for speculating in or manipulating the market price of securities or commodities (as grain) **b** : a combination between competing firms for the control of business by removing competition **4 a** : a readily available supply, aggregation, or group ⟨a *pool* of talent⟩ ⟨a stenographic *pool*⟩ ⟨a car *pool*⟩ **b** : the whole quantity of a particular material present in the body and available for function or the satisfying of metabolic demands

³pool *vt* : to contribute to a common fund or effort ⟨*pooled* their resources⟩

pool·room \'pül-,rüm, -,rùm\ *n* **1** : a room in which bookmaking is carried on **2** : a room for the playing of pool

¹poop \'püp\ *n* **1** *obs* : STERN **2** : an enclosed superstructure at the stern of a ship above the main deck

²poop *vt* **1** : to break over the stern of **2** : to ship (a sea or wave) over the stern

poop deck *n* : a partial deck above a ship's main afterdeck

¹poor \'pù(ə)r, 'pō(ə)r\ *adj* [OF *povre*, fr. L *pauper*] **1** : lacking riches : NEEDY **2** : SCANTY, INSUFFICIENT ⟨a *poor* crop⟩ **3** : not good in quality or workmanship **4** : FEEBLE ⟨*poor* health⟩ **5** : lacking fertility ⟨*poor* land⟩ **6** : UNFAVORABLE, UNCOMFORTABLE ⟨the patient had a *poor* day⟩ **7** : lacking in signs of wealth or good taste ⟨*poor* furnishings⟩ **8** : not efficient or capable : not satisfactory ⟨a *poor* carpenter⟩ **9** : worthy of pity or sympathy ⟨the *poor* child hurt herself⟩ — **poor·ness** *n*

²poor *n pl* : the class of poor people ⟨charity for the *poor*⟩

poor box *n* : a box for alms for the poor; *esp* : one placed near the door of a church

Poor Clare \-'kla(ə)r, -'kle(ə)r\ *n* : a nun of an order founded early in the 13th century at Assisi by St. Clare under the direction of St. Francis

poor farm \'pù(ə)r-,färm, 'pō(ə)r-\ *n* : a farm maintained at public expense for the support and employment of needy or dependent persons

poor·house \-,hàus\ *n* : a place maintained at public expense to house needy or dependent persons

poor·ish \'pù(ə)r-ish, 'pō(ə)r-\ *adj* : rather poor

poor law \'pù(ə)r-,lò, 'pō(ə)r-\ *n* : a law providing for or regulating the public relief or support of the poor

poor·ly \-lē\ *adj* : somewhat ill : INDISPOSED

---

j joke; ŋ sing; ō flow; ȯ flaw; ȯi coin; th thin; t͟h this; ü loot; ù foot; y yet; yü few; yù furious; zh vision

poor-spir·it·ed \-'spir-ət-əd\ *adj* : lacking zest, confidence, or courage — **poor-spir·it·ed·ly** *adv* — **poor-spir·it·ed·ness** *n*

¹pop \'päp\ *vb* **popped; pop·ping 1** : to burst or cause to burst with a pop ⟨the balloon *popped*⟩ **2** : to go, come, push, or enter quickly or unexpectedly ⟨*pop* into bed⟩ ⟨*popped* a candy into her mouth⟩ **3** : to shoot with a gun ⟨*pop* at a bird⟩ ⟨tried to *pop* some rabbits in the woods⟩ **4** : to stick out ⟨eyes *popping* with surprise⟩ **5** : to cause to burst open ⟨*pop* corn⟩ **6** : to hit a pop fly — **pop the question** : to propose marriage

²pop *n* **1** : a sharp explosive sound **2** : a shot from a gun **3** : a flavored carbonated beverage

³pop *adv* : like or with a pop : SUDDENLY

pop·corn \'päp-,kȯrn\ *n* : an Indian corn whose kernels burst open to form a white starchy mass when heated

pope \'pōp\ *n, often cap* [OE *pāpa,* fr. LL *papa,* fr. Gk *pappas,* title of bishops, lit., papa] : the head of the Roman Catholic Church

pop·ery \'pō-p(ə-)rē\ *n* : ROMAN CATHOLICISM — usu. used disparagingly

pop-eyed \'päp-'īd\ *adj* : having eyes that bulge (as from disease or excitement)

pop fly *n* : a short high fly in baseball

pop·gun \'päp-,gən\ *n* : a toy gun for shooting pellets with compressed air

pop·in·jay \'päp-ən-,jā\ *n* [ME *papejay* parrot, fr. MF *papegai,* fr. Ar *babghā'*] : a vain talkative thoughtless person

pop·ish \'pō-pish\ *adj* : Roman Catholic — often used disparagingly — **pop·ish·ly** *adv*

pop·lar \'päp-lər\ *n* [MF *pouplier,* fr. *pouple* poplar, fr. L *populus*] **1 a** : any of a genus of slender quick-growing trees (as an aspen or cottonwood) of the willow family **b** : TULIP TREE **2** : the wood of a poplar

pop·lin \'päp-lən\ *n* : a strong fabric in plain weave with crosswise ribs

pop off \(')päp-'ȯf\ *vi* **1 a** : to leave suddenly **b** : to die unexpectedly **2** : to talk thoughtlessly and often loudly or angrily

pop–off \'päp-,ȯf\ *n* : one who talks loosely or loudly

pop·over \'päp-,ō-vər\ *n* : a quick bread made from a thin batter of eggs, milk, and flour which bakes into a hollow shell

pop·per \'päp-ər\ *n* : one that pops; *esp* : a utensil for popping corn

pop·pet \'päp-ət\ *n* [ME *popet* doll, puppet] **1** *chiefly Brit* : DEAR **2** *Midland* : DOLL

pop·ple \'päp-əl\ *n, chiefly dial* : POPLAR 1a

pop·py \'päp-ē\ *n, pl* **poppies** [OE *popæg,* modif. of L *papaver*] **1** : any of a genus of chiefly annual or perennial herbs with milky juice, showy regular flowers, and capsular fruits including one that is the source of opium and several that are grown as ornamentals **2** : a strong reddish orange

pop·py·cock \'päp-ē-,käk\ *n* [D dial. *pappekak*] : empty talk : NONSENSE

pop·u·lace \'päp-yə-ləs\ *n* **1** : the common people : MASSES **2** : POPULATION

pop·u·lar \'päp-yə-lər\ *adj* [L *populus* the people, a people] **1** : of, relating to, or coming from the whole body of people ⟨*popular* government⟩ ⟨*popular* opinion⟩ **2** : suitable to the majority: as **a** : easy to understand ⟨*popular* science⟩ **b** : suited to the means of the majority : INEXPENSIVE ⟨*popular* prices⟩ **3** : having general currency : PREVALENT ⟨*popular* opinion⟩ **4** : commonly liked or approved ⟨voted the most *popular* girl in the class⟩ — **pop·u·lar·ly** *adv*

pop·u·lar·i·ty \,päp-yə-'lar-ət-ē\ *n* : the quality or state of being popular

pop·u·lar·i·za·tion \,päp-yə-lə-rə-'zā-shən\ *n* **1** : the act of popularizing : the state of being popularized **2** : something that is popularized

pop·u·lar·ize \'päp-yə-lə-,rīz\ *vt* : to make popular — **pop·u·lar·iz·er** *n*

popular song *n* : a song of wide appeal that is easily learned and performed

popular sovereignty *n* : a pre-Civil War doctrine asserting the right of the people living in a newly organized territory to decide by vote of their territorial legislature whether or not slavery would be permitted in the territory

pop·u·late \'päp-yə-,lāt\ *vt* : to furnish or provide with inhabitants : PEOPLE

pop·u·la·tion \,päp-yə-'lā-shən\ *n* **1** : the whole number of people or inhabitants in a country or region **2** : the act or process of populating **3 a** : the organisms inhabiting a particular area or habitat **b** : a group of interbreeding biotypes **4** : a group of items from which samples are taken for statistical measurement

pop·u·list \'päp-yə-ləst\ *n* **1** *cap* : a member of a U.S. political party formed in 1891 primarily to represent agrarian interests and to advocate the free coinage of silver and government control of monopolies **2** : a member of any of various popular or agrarian political parties — **pop·u·lism** \-,liz-əm\ *n, often cap* — **populist** *adj, often cap*

pop·u·lous \'päp-yə-ləs\ *adj* : densely populated — **pop·u·lous·ly** *adv* — **pop·u·lous·ness** *n*

por·bea·gle \'pȯr-,bē-gəl\ *n* [Corn *porgh-bugel*] : a small greedy viviparous shark of northern seas

por·ce·lain \'pȯr-s(ə-)lən, 'pȯr-\ *n* [MF *porcelaine,* fr. It *porcellana*] : a fine ceramic ware that is hard, translucent, white, and nonporous, usu. consists essentially of kaolin, quartz, and feldspar, and is used for dishes, dentures, and chemical utensils — **por·ce·lain·like** \-,līk\ *adj*

por·ce·lain·ize \-s(ə-)lə-,nīz\ *vt* : to fire a vitreous coating on (as steel)

porch \'pȯrch, 'pȯrch\ *n* [OF *porche,* fr. L *porticus* portico, fr. *porta* gate] **1** : a covered entrance to a building usu. with a separate roof **2** : VERANDA 2

por·cine \'pȯr-,sīn\ *adj* [L *porcus* pig] : of, relating to, or suggesting swine

por·cu·pine \'pȯr-kyə-,pīn\ *n* [MF *porc espin,* lit., spiny pig] : any of various rather large rodents with stiff sharp erectile bristles mingled with the hair

¹pore \'pō(ə)r, 'pȯ(ə)r\ *vi* [ME *pouren*] : to gaze, study, or think long or earnestly ⟨*pore* over a book⟩

²pore *n* [L *poros* passage, pore; akin to E *fare*] : a tiny opening or space (as in the skin or the soil) often giving passage to a fluid — **pored** \'pōrd, 'pȯrd\ *adj*

pore fungus *n* : a fungus having the spore-bearing surface within tubes or pores

por·gy \'pȯr-gē\ *n, pl* **porgies** *also* **porgy** : a blue-spotted crimson food fish of the coasts of Europe and America; *also* : any of various other fishes

po·rif·er·an \pə-'rif-(ə-)rən\ *n* : any of a phylum (Porifera) of lowly invertebrate animals comprising the sponges — **poriferan** *or* **po·rif·er·al** \-(ə-)rəl\ *adj*

pork \'pȯrk, 'pȯrk\ *n* [OF *porc* pig, fr. L *porcus;* akin to E *farrow*] : the fresh or salted flesh of swine dressed for food

pork barrel *n* : a government project or appropriation yielding rich patronage benefits

pork·er \'pȯr-kər, 'pȯr-\ *n* : HOG; *esp* : a young pig suitable for use as fresh pork

pork·pie hat \,pȯrk-,pī-, ,pȯrk-\ *n* : a felt, straw, or cloth hat with a low crown and flat top

por·nog·ra·phy \pȯr-'näg-rə-fē\ *n* [Gk *pornographos,* adj., writing of harlots, fr. *pornē* harlot + *graphein* to write] : pictures or writings describing erotic behavior and intended to cause sexual excitement — **por·nog·ra·pher** \-fər\ *n* — **por·no·graph·ic** \,pȯr-nə-'graf-ik\ *adj* — **por·no·graph·i·cal·ly** \-'graf-i-k(ə-)lē\ *adv*

po·ros·i·ty \pə-'räs-ət-ē, pȯr-'äs-, pȯ-'räs-\ *n, pl* **-ties 1** : the quality or state of being porous **2** : PORE

po·rous \'pōr-əs, 'pȯr-\ *adj* **1** : full of pores **2** : capable of absorbing liquids : permeable to fluids — **po·rous·ly** *adv* — **po·rous·ness** *n*

por·phy·ry \'pȯr-f(ə-)rē\ *n, pl* **-ries** [Gk *porphyritēs* (*lithos*), lit., purple-colored stone, fr. *porphyra* purple] **1** : a rock consisting of feldspar crystals embedded in a compact dark red or purple groundmass **2** : an igneous rock having distinct crystals in a relatively fine-grained base — **por·phy·rit·ic** \,pȯr-fə-'rit-ik\ *adj*

por·poise \'pȯr-pəs\ *n* [MF *porpois,* fr. L *porcus* pig + *piscis* fish] **1** : any of several small gregarious blunt-snouted toothed whales **2** : DOLPHIN 1a

por·ridge \'pȯr-ij, 'pär-\ *n* : a soft food made by boiling meal of grains or legumes in milk or water until thick ⟨oatmeal *porridge*⟩

por·rin·ger \'pȯr-ən-jər, 'pär-\ *n* : a low one-handled metal bowl or cup for children

¹port \'pōrt, 'pȯrt\ *n* [OE & OF, both fr. L *portus* house door, port] **1 :** a place where ships may ride secure from storms **2 a :** a harbor town or city where ships may take on or discharge cargo **b :** AIRPORT

²port *n* [L *porta* passage, gate] **1 :** an opening (as in machinery) for intake or exhaust of a fluid **2 :** PORTHOLE

³port *n* [L *portare* to carry] **:** the manner in which one bears himself

⁴port *n* **:** the left side of a ship or airplane looking forward — called also *larboard;* compare STARBOARD — **port** *adj*

⁵port *vt* **:** to turn or put (the helm) to the left — used chiefly as a command

⁶port *n* [fr. *Oporto*, Portugal] **:** a fortified sweet wine of rich taste and aroma

por·ta·ble \'pōrt-ə-bəl, 'pȯrt-\ *adj* [L *portare* to carry] **:** capable of being carried : easily moved from one place to another — **por·ta·bil·i·ty** \ˌpōrt-ə-'bil-ət-ē, ˌpȯrt-\ *n*

¹por·tage \'pōrt-ij, 'pȯrt-, 2 *is also* pȯr-'täzh\ *n* **1 :** the labor of carrying or transporting **2 :** the carrying of boats or goods overland from one body of water to another; *also* **:** a regular route for such carrying

²portage *vb* **1 :** to carry over a portage ⟨a canoe light enough to *portage*⟩ **2 :** to move gear over a portage ⟨we *portaged* around the falls⟩

¹por·tal \'pōrt-ᵊl, 'pȯrt-\ *n* **1 :** DOOR, GATE, ENTRANCE; *esp* **:** a grand or imposing one **2 :** the point at which something enters the body of an organism ⟨infection *portals*⟩

²portal *adj* **:** of, relating to, or being a portal vein

portal–to–portal *adj* **:** of or relating to the time spent by a workman in traveling from the entrance to his employer's property to his actual working place (as in a mine) and in returning after the work shift

portal vein *n* **:** a vein that collects blood from one part of the body and distributes it in another through capillaries **:** a vein that begins and ends in capillaries; *esp* **:** one carrying blood from the digestive organs and spleen to the liver

por·ta·men·to \ˌpōrt-ə-'men-tō, ˌpȯrt-\ *n, pl* **-ti** \-(ˌ)tē\ [It, lit., act of carrying] **:** a continuous glide effected by the voice, a trombone, or a bowed stringed musical instrument in passing from one tone to another

port arms — used as a command in the manual of arms to bring the rifle to a position in which it is held diagonally in front of the body with the muzzle pointing upward toward the left

port·cul·lis \pōrt-'kəl-əs, pȯrt-\ *n* [MF *porte coleïce*, lit., sliding door] **:** a grating at the gateway of a castle or fortress that can be lowered to prevent entrance

porte co·chere \ˌpōrt-kō-'she(ə)r, ˌpȯrt-\ *n* **:** a roofed structure extending from the entrance of a building over an adjacent driveway and sheltering those getting in or out of vehicles

portcullis

porte–mon·naie \'pōrt-ˌmən-ē\ *n* [F] **:** a small pocketbook or purse

por·tend \pȯr-'tend, pōr-\ *vt* [L *por-* forward + *tendere* to stretch] **:** to give a sign or warning of beforehand ⟨the distant thunder *portended* a storm⟩

por·tent \'pō(ə)r-ˌtent, 'pȯ(ə)r-\ *n* **1 :** a sign or warning that foreshadows something usu. evil **2 :** prophetic indication or significance

por·ten·tous \pȯr-'tent-əs, pōr-\ *adj* **1 :** of, relating to, or constituting a portent **3 :** THREATENING **2 :** eliciting amazement or wonder **3 :** self-consciously weighty **:** POMPOUS — **por·ten·tous·ly** *adv* — **por·ten·tous·ness** *n*

¹por·ter \'pōrt-ər, 'pȯrt-\ *n* [L *porta* gate] *chiefly Brit* **:** a person stationed at a door or gate to admit or assist those entering

²porter *n* [L *portare* to carry] **1 :** one who carries burdens; *esp* **:** one employed to carry baggage for patrons at a hotel or transportation terminal **2 :** a parlor-car or sleeping-car attendant **3** [short for *porter's beer*] **:** a dark heavy ale that is weaker than stout

por·ter·house \-ˌhaus\ *n* **:** a choice beefsteak with a large piece of tenderloin on a T-shaped bone

port·fo·lio \pōrt-'fō-lē-ˌō, pȯrt-\ *n, pl* **-lios** [It *portafoglio,* fr. *portare* to carry + *foglio* leaf, sheet, fr. L *folium*] **1 :** a case for carrying papers or drawings **2** [fr. the use

of such a case to carry documents of state] **:** the office and functions of a minister of state or member of a cabinet **3 :** the securities held by an investor or a financial house

port·hole \'pōrt-ˌhōl, 'pȯrt-\ *n* **1 :** an opening (as a window) in the side of a ship or airplane **2 :** an opening (as in a wall) to shoot through **3 :** ²PORT 1

por·ti·co \'pōrt-i-ˌkō, 'pȯrt-\ *n, pl* **-coes** *or* **-cos 1 :** a covered walk **2 :** a row of columns supporting a roof around or at the entrance of a building

por·ti·ere \ˌpōrt-ē-'e(ə)r, ˌpȯrt-; pōr-'ti(ə)r, pȯr-\ *n* **:** a curtain hanging across a doorway

¹por·tion \'pōr-shən, 'pȯr-\ *n* [L *portion-, portio*] **1 :** an individual's share of something: as **a :** a share received by gift or inheritance **b :** DOWRY **c :** a helping of food **2 :** one's lot, fate, or fortune **3 a :** a part of a whole **b :** a limited amount or quantity syn see PART

²portion *vt* **por·tioned; por·tion·ing** \-sh(ə-)niŋ\ **1 :** to divide into portions **:** DISTRIBUTE **2 :** to allot or give as a portion **:** DOWER

por·tion·less \-shən-ləs\ *adj* **:** having no portion

port·land cement \ˌpōrt-lən(d)-, ˌpȯrt-\ *n* **:** a cement made by burning and grinding a mixture of clay and limestone or a mixture of similar materials

port·ly \'pōrt-lē, 'pȯrt-\ *adj* **port·li·er; -est** [³port] **1** *chiefly dial* **:** DIGNIFIED, STATELY **2 :** heavy or rotund of body **:** CORPULENT — **port·li·ness** *n*

¹port·man·teau \pōrt-'man-tō, pȯrt-\ *n, pl* **-teaus** *or* **-teaux** \-ˌtōz\ [MF *portemanteau*, fr. *porter* to carry + *manteau* mantle] **:** TRAVELING BAG, SUITCASE

²portmanteau *adj* **:** combining more than one use or quality

port of call : an intermediate port where ships customarily stop for supplies, repairs, or transshipment of cargo

port of entry 1 : a place where foreign goods may be cleared through a customhouse **2 :** a place where an alien may enter a country

por·trait \'pōr-trət, 'pȯr-, -ˌtrāt\ *n* [MF, fr. pp. of *portraire* to portray] **1 :** a pictorial representation (as a painting) of a person usu. showing his face **2 :** a graphic portrayal in words

por·trait·ist \-əst\ *n* **:** a maker of portraits

por·trai·ture \'pōr-trə-ˌchùr, 'pȯr-, -chər\ *n* **1 :** the making of portraits **:** PORTRAYAL **2 :** PORTRAIT

por·tray \pōr-'trā, pȯr-\ *vt* [MF *portraire*, fr. L *protrahere* to draw forth, reveal, fr. *pro-* forth + *trahere* to draw, drag] **1 :** to make a picture of **2 a :** to describe in words **b :** to play the role of **:** ENACT — **por·tray·er** *n*

por·tray·al \-'trā(-ə)l\ *n* **1 :** the act or process of portraying **:** REPRESENTATION **2 :** PORTRAIT

Por·tu·guese \ˌpōr-chə-'gēz, ˌpȯr-, -'gēs\ *n, pl* **Portuguese 1 a :** a native or inhabitant of Portugal **b :** a person of Portuguese descent **2 :** the Romance language of Portugal and Brazil — **Portuguese** *adj*

Portuguese man-of-war *n* **:** any of several large colonial coelenterates having a large crested bladder by means of which the colony floats at the surface of the sea

por·tu·laca \ˌpōr-chə-'lak-ə, ˌpȯr-\ *n* [L, purslane] **:** any of a genus of mostly tropical succulent herbs of the purslane family; *esp* **:** one cultivated for its showy flowers

¹pose \'pōz\ *vb* [MF, *poser* to put, place, fr. LL *pausare* to stop, rest, pause, fr. L *pausa* pause] **1 a :** to hold or cause to hold a special posture or attitude usu. for artistic purposes ⟨*posed* for fashion photographers⟩ **b :** to affect an attitude or character ⟨*pose* as a hero⟩ **2 :** to put forth **:** PROPOUND ⟨*posed* a question for the group to answer⟩

²pose *n* **1 :** a sustained posture; *esp* **:** one assumed for artistic effect **2 :** an assumed attitude; *esp* **:** AFFECTATION ⟨a *pose* of innocence⟩

Po·sei·don \pə-'sīd-ᵊn\ *n* **:** the Greek god of the sea

¹pos·er \'pō-zər\ *n* **:** a puzzling or baffling question

²poser *n* **:** a person who poses

po·seur \pō-'zər\ *n* [F, fr. *poser* to put, pose] **:** one who habitually pretends to be what he is not **:** an affected person

posh \'päsh\ *adj* **:** ELEGANT, FASHIONABLE

pos·it \'päz-ət\ *vt* **pos·it·ed; pos·it·ing** [L *posit-, ponere* to put, assume] **:** to assume the existence of **:** POSTULATE

¹po·si·tion \pə-'zish-ən\ *n* [L *posit-, ponere* to lay down, put, place, fr. *po-* away + *sinere* to lay, leave] **1 a :** an arranging in order **b :** the manner in which something is placed or arranged **c :** POSTURE **2 :** the stand taken on a question **3 a :** the point or area occupied by a physical object **b** : situation in an ordered arrangement **4 a** : social or official rank or status **b** : EMPLOYMENT, JOB **c** : a situation that confers advantage or preference ⟨jockeyed for *position* in the race⟩ — **po·si·tion·al** \-'zish-nəl, -ən-°l\ *adj*

²**position** *vt* **po·si·tioned; po·si·tion·ing** \-'zish-(ə-)niŋ\ : to put in proper position

¹**pos·i·tive** \'päz-ət-iv, 'päz-tiv\ *adj* **1 a** : formally laid down or imposed : PRESCRIBED ⟨*positive* laws⟩ **b** : expressed clearly or definitely : PEREMPTORY ⟨*positive* orders⟩ **c** : fully assured : CONFIDENT ⟨was *positive* he'd win⟩ **2 a** : of the degree of comparison expressed by the unmodified and uninflected form of an adjective or adverb **b** : definite, accurate, or certain in its action ⟨*positive* traction of a sprocket chain⟩ **c** : INCONTESTABLE, UNQUALIFIED **3 a** : not fictitious : REAL ⟨a *positive* influence for good⟩ **b** : active in the social or economic sphere ⟨*positive* government⟩ **4 a** : having or expressing actual existence or quality as distinguished from deprivation or deficiency ⟨*positive* change in temperature⟩ **b** : having rendition of light and shade similar in tone to the tones of the original subject ⟨a *positive* photographic image⟩ **c** : being real and numerically greater than zero ⟨+2 is a *positive* integer⟩ **d** (1) : reckoned or proceeding in a direction taken as that of increase or progression (2) : directed or moving toward a source of stimulation ⟨a *positive* taxis⟩ **5 a** : of, being, or relating to electricity of a kind that predominates in a glass rod after being rubbed with silk ⟨a *positive* charge⟩ **b** : charged with positive electricity : having a deficiency of electrons ⟨a *positive* particle⟩ **c** : being the part from which the current flows to the external circuit ⟨the *positive* pole of a discharging storage battery⟩ **d** : electron-collecting — used of an electrode in an electron tube **6 a** : marked by or indicating agreement or affirmation ⟨a *positive* response⟩ **b** : affirming the presence of what is sought or suspected to be present ⟨*positive* test for blood⟩ **syn** see SURE — **pos·i·tive·ness** *n*

²**positive** *n* : something positive: as **a** : the positive degree or a positive form in a language **b** : a positive photograph or a print from a negative

pos·i·tive·ly \-lē, 2 *is often* ‚päz-ə-'tiv-lē\ *adv* **1** : in a positive manner : so as to be positive **2** : EXTREMELY, CERTAINLY, ABSOLUTELY

pos·i·tron \'päz-ə-‚trän\ *n* [*positive* + *-tron* (as in *electron*)] : a positively charged particle having the same mass and magnitude of charge as the electron

pos·se \'päs-ē\ *n* [ML *posse comitatus*, lit., power of the county] **1** : a force of men called upon by a sheriff to aid him in his duty (as pursuit of a criminal) **2** : a number of people temporarily organized to make a search (as for a lost child)

pos·sess \pə-'zes\ *vt* [L *possess-, possidēre* to have or take possession of, fr. *potis* able, in power + *sedēre* to sit] **1 a** : to give legal possession to **b** : to have possession of **2 a** : to have and hold as property : OWN **b** : to have as an attribute, knowledge, or skill ⟨*possesses* a keen wit⟩ **3 a** : to take into one's possession ⟨*possessed* the land by force⟩ **b** : to enter into and control firmly : DOMINATE ⟨*possessed* by a demon⟩ ⟨whatever *possessed* you to do such a stupid thing as that⟩

pos·ses·sion \pə-'zesh-ən\ *n* **1 a** : the act of possessing or holding as one's own : OWNERSHIP **b** : control or occupancy of property without regard to ownership **2 a** : something that is held as one's own property **b** : an area under the control of but not formally part of a nation ⟨island *possessions* of the U.S.⟩ **3** : domination by an idea or influence from outside oneself — **pos·ses·sion·al** \-'zesh-nəl, -ən-°l\ *adj*

¹**pos·ses·sive** \pə-'zes-iv\ *adj* **1** : of, relating to, or constituting a grammatical case that denotes ownership or a relation analogous to ownership — compare GENITIVE **2** : showing possession or the desire to possess or keep ⟨took a *possessive* attitude toward him⟩ — **pos·ses·sive·ly** *adv* — **pos·ses·sive·ness** *n*

²**possessive** *n* **1** : the possessive case **2** : a word in the possessive case

possessive adjective *n* : a pronominal adjective expressing possession

possessive pronoun *n* : a pronoun that derives from a personal pronoun and denotes possession

pos·ses·sor \pə-'zes-ər\ *n* : one that possesses

pos·set \'päs-ət\ *n* [ME *poshet, possot*] : a hot drink of sweetened and spiced milk curdled with ale or wine

pos·si·bil·i·ty \‚päs-ə-'bil-ət-ē\ *n, pl* **-ties** **1** : the condition or fact of being possible **2** : something possible

pos·si·ble \'päs-ə-bəl\ *adj* [L *possibilis*, fr. *posse* to be able, fr. *potis* able + *esse* to be] **1** : being within the limits of one's ability : being something that can be done or brought about ⟨a task *possible* only to skilled workmen⟩ **2** : being something that may or may not occur ⟨plan against *possible* dangers⟩ **3** : ALLOWABLE, PERMITTED ⟨*possible* to see the patient only during visiting hours⟩ **4** : able or fitted to be or to become ⟨a *possible* site for a camp⟩

syn POSSIBLE, PRACTICABLE, FEASIBLE mean capable of being realized. POSSIBLE implies that a thing may exist or occur when the proper conditions meet; PRACTICABLE implies that something may be easily or readily put into operation by current available means ⟨when television at last became *practicable*⟩ FEASIBLE applies to what is likely to work or be useful in attaining an end ⟨commercially *feasible* for mass production⟩ **syn** see in addition PROBABLE

pos·si·bly \-blē\ *adv* **1** : by possible means : by any possibility ⟨not *possibly* true⟩ **2** : PERHAPS, MAYBE ⟨may *possibly* recover⟩

pos·sum \'päs-əm\ *n* : OPOSSUM

¹**post** \'pōst\ *n* [OE, fr. L *postis*] **1** : a piece of timber or metal fixed firmly in an upright position esp. as a stay or support : PILLAR, COLUMN **2** : a pole or stake set up to mark or indicate something ⟨starting *post*⟩

²**post** *vt* **1** : to fasten to a place (as a post) used for public notices : PLACARD **2 a** : to fix (public notices) to or on **b** : to publish or announce by or as if by a notice **3** : to forbid persons from entering or using by putting up warning notices ⟨*post* a trout stream⟩ **4 a** : to enter on a list put up on a bulletin board ⟨*post* all arrivals and departures⟩ **b** : SCORE ⟨*posted* a 72 for the round⟩

³**post** *n* [MF *poste* relay station, courier, fr. It *posta* relay station, fr. *porre* to place, fr. L *ponere*] **1** *obs* : COURIER **2** *archaic* : one of a series of stations for keeping horses for relays **3** *chiefly Brit* **a** : a nation's organization for handling mail; *also* : the mail handled by a single dispatch of mail

⁴**post** *vb* **1** : to ride or travel with haste : HURRY **2** : MAIL **3 a** : to transfer from a book of original entry to a ledger **b** : to make transfer entries in **4** : to make familiar with a subject : INFORM ⟨kept *posted* on the latest developments⟩ **5** : to rise and sink in the saddle in accordance with the motion of the horse

⁵**post** *adv* : with post-horses : EXPRESS

⁶**post** *n* [MF *poste*, fr. It *posto*, fr. pp. of *porre* to place] **1 a** : the place at which a soldier is stationed; *esp* : a sentry's beat or station **b** : a station or task to which anyone is assigned **c** : a place to which troops are assigned : CAMP **d** : a local subdivision of a veterans' organization **2** : an office or position to which a person is appointed **3** : TRADING POST, SETTLEMENT

⁷**post** *vt* **1 a** : to station in a given place ⟨*post* a guard⟩ **b** : to carry ceremoniously to a position ⟨*posting* the colors⟩ **2** : to put up as security ⟨*post* a bond⟩

post- *prefix* [L] **1 a** : after : subsequent : later ⟨*post*paid⟩ **b** : behind : posterior : following after ⟨*post*consonantal⟩ **2 a** : subsequent to : later than ⟨*post*operative⟩ ⟨*post*-Pleistocene⟩ **b** : posterior to ⟨*post*orbital⟩

post·age \'pō-stij\ *n* : the charge fixed by law for carrying something (as a letter or parcel) by mail

postage meter *n* : a machine that prints postal indicia on pieces of mail, records the amount of postage given in the indicia, and subtracts it from a total amount which has been paid at a post office and for which the machine has been set

postage stamp *n* : a government stamp for use on mail as evidence of payment of postage

post·al \'pōst-°l\ *adj* : of or relating to the mails or to the post office

postal card *n* : POSTCARD; *esp* : one bearing a government imprinted stamp and sold by a post office

postal union *n* : an association of governments setting up uniform regulations and practices for international mail

post·boy \'pōs(t)-‚bȯi\ *n* : POSTILION

post·card \'pōs(t)-‚kärd\ *n* : a card on which a message may be written for mailing without an envelope

post·ca·va \(')pōs(t)-'kāv-ə, -'kā-və\ *n* [NL] : the inferior vena cava of vertebrates above the fishes — **post·ca·val** \-'kāv-əl, -'kā-vəl\ *adj*

post chaise *n* [³*post*] : a carriage usu. having a closed body on four wheels and seating two to four persons

post·clas·si·cal \(')pōs(t)-'klas-i-kəl\ *adj* : of or relating to a period following the classical

post–com·mu·nion \,pōs(t)-kə-'myü-nyən\ *n, often cap P & C* : a prayer following the communion of the people at Mass

post·con·so·nan·tal \,pōs(t)-,kän(t)-sə-'nant-ᵊl\ *adj* : immediately following a consonant

post·date \(')pōs(t)-'dāt\ *vt* **1** : to date with a date later than that of execution ⟨*postdate* a check⟩ **2** : to follow in time ⟨the text changes *postdated* the first production of the play⟩

post·doc·tor·al \(')pōs(t)-'däk-t(ə-)rəl\ *adj* : of, relating to, or engaged in advanced academic or professional work beyond a doctor's degree

post·er \'pō-stər\ *n* **1** : a notice or advertisement to be posted in a public place **2** : a person who posts such notices ⟨a bill *poster*⟩

poste res·tante \,pōst-,res-'tä(ⁿ)nt\ *n* [F, lit., waiting mail] : GENERAL DELIVERY

¹pos·te·ri·or \pō-'stir-ē-ər, pä-\ *adj* [L, compar. of *posterus* coming after, fr. *post* after] **1** : later in time : SUBSEQUENT **2 a** : situated behind or toward the back **b** : ADAXIAL — **pos·te·ri·or·ly** *adv*

²posterior *n* : the hinder parts of the body; *esp* : BUTTOCKS

pos·ter·i·ty \pä-'ster-ət-ē\ *n* **1** : the offspring of one progenitor to the furthest generation : DESCENDANTS **2** : all future generations : future time ⟨leave a record for *posterity*⟩

pos·tern \'pōs-tərn, 'päs-\ *n* [OF *posterne*, modif. of LL *posterula*, dim. of *postera* back door] **1** : a back door or gate **2** : a private or side entrance or way — **postern** *adj*

post exchange *n* : a store at a military post that sells to military personnel and authorized civilians

post·gan·gli·on·ic \,pōs(t)-,gaŋ-glē-'än-ik\ *adj* : distal to a ganglion; *also* : of, relating to, or being an axon arising from a cell body within an autonomic ganglion

post·gla·cial \(')pōs(t)-'glā-shəl\ *adj* : coming or occurring after a period of glaciation

¹post·grad·u·ate \-'graj-ə-wət, -,wāt\ *adj* : GRADUATE 2

²postgraduate *n* : a student continuing his education after graduation from high school or college

post·haste \'pōst-'hāst\ *adv* [³*post*] : with great speed : in great haste ⟨sent *posthaste* for the doctor⟩

post·hole \'pōst-,hōl\ *n* : a hole for a post and esp. a fence post

post–horse \-,hórs\ *n* : a horse for use esp. by couriers or mail carriers

post·hu·mous \'päs-chə-məs\ *adj* [L *posthumus*, alter. of *postumus* late-born, posthumous, fr. superl. of *posterus* coming after] **1** : born after the death of the father ⟨*posthumous* son⟩ **2** : published after the death of the author ⟨*posthumous* novel⟩ **3** : following or occurring after one's death ⟨*posthumous* fame⟩ ⟨*posthumous* award of a medal⟩ — **post·hu·mous·ly** *adv*

post·hyp·not·ic \,pōst-(h)ip-'nät-ik\ *adj* : of, relating to, or characteristic of the period following a hypnotic trance

pos·til·ion *or* **pos·til·lion** \pō-'stil-yən\ *n* [MF *postillon* mail carrier using post-horses, fr. It *postiglione*, fr. *posta* post] : one who rides as a guide on the near horse of one of the pairs attached to a coach or post chaise esp. without a coachman

Post·im·pres·sion·ism \,pō-stim-'presh-ə-,niz-əm\ *n* : a theory or practice originating among French artists (as Cézanne, Matisse, and Derain) in the last quarter of the 19th century that in revolt against impressionism stresses variously volume, picture structure, or expressionism

post·lude \'pōst-,lüd\ *n* [*post-* + *-lude* (as in *prelude*)] : a closing piece of music; *esp* : an organ voluntary at the end of a church service

post·man \'pōs(t)-mən, -,man\ *n* : MAILMAN

¹post·mark \-,märk\ *n* : a mark officially put on a piece of mail; *esp* : one canceling the postage stamp and giving the date and place of sending

²postmark *vt* : to put a postmark on

post·mas·ter \-,mas-tər\ *n* : one who has charge of a post office

postmaster general *n, pl* **postmasters general** : an official in charge of a national post office department

post·me·rid·i·an \,pōs(t)-mə-'rid-ē-ən\ *adj* : occurring after noon

post me·ri·di·em \-'rid-ē-əm\ *adj* [L, after midday] : POSTMERIDIAN

post·mis·tress \'pōs(t)-,mis-trəs\ *n* : a woman in charge of a post office

post·mor·tem \pōs(t)-'mórt-əm\ *adj* [L *post mortem* after death] **1 a** : occurring after death **b** : of or relating to a postmortem examination **2** : following the event ⟨*postmortem* analysis of the unsuccessful advertising campaign⟩ — **postmortem** *n*

postmortem examination *n* : an examination of a dead body esp. to determine the cause of death

post·na·sal \(')pōs(t)-'nā-zəl\ *adj* : lying or occurring posterior to the nose ⟨*postnasal* drip⟩ — **postnasal** *n*

post·na·tal \(')pōs(t)-'nāt-ᵊl\ *adj* : subsequent to birth; *also* : of or relating to a newborn child ⟨*postnatal* care⟩ — **post·na·tal·ly** \-ᵊl-ē\ *adv*

post office *n* **1** : a government department handling the transmission of mail **2** : a local branch of a post office department handling the mail for a particular place

post·op·er·a·tive \(')pōst-'äp-(ə-)rət-iv, -'äp-ə-,rāt-\ *adj* : following a surgical operation ⟨*postoperative* care⟩ — **post·op·er·a·tive·ly** *adv*

post·or·bit·al \(')pōst-'ór-bət-ᵊl\ *adj* : situated behind the eye socket

post·paid \'pōs(t)-'pād\ *adv* : with postage paid by the sender and not chargeable to the receiver

post·par·tum \'pōs(t)-'pärt-əm\ *adj* [NL *post partum* after giving birth] : following parturition

post·pone \pōs(t)-'pōn\ *vt* [L *postponere*, lit., to place after, fr. *post-* + *ponere* to place] : to hold back to a later time : put off **syn** see DEFER — **post·pone·ment** \-mənt\ *n* — **post·pon·er** *n*

post road *n* : a road over which mail is carried

post·script \'pō(s)-,skript\ *n* [L *postscriptus*, pp. of *postscribere* to write after, fr. *post-* + *scribere* to write] : a note or series of notes added at the end of a letter, article, or book

post·syn·ap·tic \,pōs(t)-sə-'nap-tik\ *adj* : occurring after synapsis ⟨a *postsynaptic* chromosome⟩

post·trau·mat·ic \,pōs(t)-trə-'mat-ik, -tró-, -traù-\ *adj* : following or resulting from trauma

pos·tu·lant \'päs-chə-lənt\ *n* [F, petitioner, candidate, postulant, fr. prp. of *postuler* to demand, solicit, fr. L *postulare*] **1** : a person admitted to a religious house as a probationary candidate for membership **2** : a person on probation before being admitted as a candidate for holy orders in the Episcopal Church — **pos·tu·lan·cy** \-lən-sē\ *n*

¹pos·tu·late \'päs-chə-,lāt\ *vt* [L *postulare* to demand, fr. *poscere* to ask] : to claim as true : assume as a postulate or axiom ⟨*postulates* that power corrupts⟩ — **pos·tu·la·tion** \,päs-chə-'lā-shən\ *n*

²pos·tu·late \-lət, -,lāt\ *n* **1** : a hypothesis advanced as an essential basis of a system of thought or premise of a train of reasoning **2** : a statement (as in logic or mathematics) that is assumed and therefore requires no proof of its validity : AXIOM 2a

¹pos·ture \'päs-chər\ *n* [F, fr. It *postura*, fr. L *positura* position, fr. *posit-*, *ponere* to place] **1** : the position or bearing of the body or of a body part ⟨erect *posture*⟩ **2** : relative place or position : SITUATION **3** : state or condition at a given time esp. in relation to other persons or things ⟨the *posture* of affairs⟩ **4** : frame of mind : ATTITUDE — **pos·tur·al** \-chə-rəl\ *adj*

²posture *vb* : to assume or cause to assume a given posture; *esp* : to strike a pose for effect — **pos·tur·er** *n*

post·vo·cal·ic \,pōst-vō-'kal-ik\ *adj* : immediately following a vowel

post·war \'pōst-'wó(ə)r\ *adj* : of, relating to, or being a period after a war

po·sy \'pō-zē\ *n, pl* **posies** [alter. of *poesy*] **1** : a brief sentiment, motto, or legend **2** : a bunch of flowers : FLOWER, BOUQUET, NOSEGAY

¹pot \'pät\ *n* [OE *pott*] **1 a** : a rounded metal or earthen container used chiefly for domestic purposes **b** : the quantity held by a pot **2** : an enclosed framework for catching fish or lobsters **3 a** : a large quantity or sum

b : the total of the bets at stake at one time **4 :** RUIN, DETERIORATION ⟨business went to *pot*⟩ **5 :** MARIJUANA
²pot *vt* **pot·ted; pot·ting 1 a :** to preserve in a sealed pot, jar, or can ⟨*potted* chicken⟩ **b :** to make an entertaining but superficial digest of ⟨*potted* history⟩ **2 :** to plant or grow in a pot ⟨*potted* plants⟩ **3 :** to shoot with a potshot ⟨*pot* a rabbit⟩
po·ta·ble \'pōt-ə-bəl\ *adj* [L *potare* to drink] **:** suitable for drinking — **po·ta·bil·i·ty** \,pōt-ə-'bil-ət-ē\ *n* — **po·ta·ble·ness** \'pōt-ə-bəl-nəs\ *n*
po·tage \pō-'tāzh\ *n* [MF, fr. *pot* pot] **:** a thick soup
pot·ash \'pät-,ash\ *n* [*pot* + *ash*] **1 a :** potassium carbonate esp. from wood ashes **b :** POTASSIUM HYDROXIDE **2 :** potassium or a potassium compound esp. as used in agriculture or industry
po·tas·si·um \pə-'tas-ē-əm\ *n* [NL, fr. *potassa* potash, fr. E *potash*] **:** a silver-white soft light low-melting univalent metallic chemical element that occurs abundantly in nature esp. combined in minerals — see ELEMENT table
potassium bromide *n* **:** a crystalline salt KBr with a saline taste used as a sedative and in photography
potassium carbonate *n* **:** a white salt K_2CO_3 that forms a strongly alkaline solution and is used in making glass and soap
potassium chlorate *n* **:** a crystalline salt $KClO_3$ that is used as an oxidizing agent in matches, fireworks, and explosives
potassium chloride *n* **:** a crystalline salt KCl that occurs as a mineral and in natural waters and is used as a fertilizer
potassium cyanide *n* **:** a very poisonous crystalline salt KCN used in electroplating
potassium dichromate *n* **:** a soluble salt $K_2Cr_2O_7$ forming large orange-red crystals used in dyeing, in photography, and as an oxidizing agent
potassium hydroxide *n* **:** a white deliquescent solid KOH that dissolves in water with much heat to form a strongly alkaline and caustic liquid and is used in making soap and as a reagent
potassium iodide *n* **:** a crystalline salt KI that is soluble in water and used in photographic emulsions and in medicine
potassium nitrate *n* **:** a crystalline salt KNO_3 that occurs as a product of nitrification in soil, is a strong oxidizer, and is used in making gunpowder, in preserving meat, and in medicine
potassium permanganate *n* **:** a dark purple salt $KMnO_4$ used as an oxidizer and disinfectant
po·ta·tion \pō-'tā-shən\ *n* [L *potare* to drink] **1 :** a usu. alcoholic drink or brew **2 a :** the act of drinking **b :** DRAFT 4a
po·ta·to \pə-'tāt-ō\ *n, pl* **-toes** [Sp *batata*, of AmerInd origin] **1 :** SWEET POTATO **2 a :** an erect American herb of the nightshade family widely cultivated as a vegetable crop **b :** its edible starchy tuber — called also *white potato*
potato beetle *n* **:** a black-and-yellow striped beetle that feeds on the leaves of the potato — called also *potato bug*
potato blight *n* **:** any of several destructive fungus diseases of the potato
potato chip *n* **:** a thin slice of potato that has been fried crisp in deep fat
pot·bel·ly \'pät-,bel-ē\ *n* **1 :** an enlarged, swollen, or protruding abdomen **2 :** a stove with a bulging body — **pot·bel·lied** \-,ēd\ *adj*
pot·boil·er \-,bȯi-lər\ *n* **:** a usu. inferior work of art or literature produced only to earn money
pot·boy \-,bȯi\ *n* **:** a boy who serves drinks in a tavern
pot cheese *n* **:** COTTAGE CHEESE
po·teen \pə-'tēn\ *n* [IrGael *poitín*] **:** illicitly distilled whiskey of Ireland
po·ten·cy \'pōt-ə n-sē\ *n, pl* **-cies :** the quality or condition of being potent; *esp* **:** power to bring about a certain result
po·tent \'pōt-ə nt\ *adj* [ME (Sc), fr. L *potent-*, *potens*, fr. *potis*, *pote* able] **1 :** having or wielding force, authority, or influence **:** POWERFUL **2 :** producing an effect **3 a :** chemically or medicinally effective ⟨a *potent* vaccine⟩ **b :** rich in a characteristic constituent **:** STRONG ⟨*potent* tea⟩ **4 :** able to copulate — **po·tent·ly** *adv*
po·ten·tate \'pōt-ə n-,tāt\ *n* **:** one who wields controlling power **:** SOVEREIGN

¹po·ten·tial \pə-'ten-chəl\ *adj* [L *potentia* power, fr. *potent-*, *potens* potent] **:** capable of becoming real **:** POSSIBLE ⟨aware of the *potential* dangers in a scheme⟩ — **po·ten·tial·ly** \-'tench-(ə-)lē\ *adv*
²potential *n* **1 :** something that can develop or become actual **:** POSSIBILITY **2 :** the degree of electrification with reference to a standard (as that of the earth)
potential difference *n* **:** the difference in electrical potential between two points that represents the work involved or the energy released in the transfer of a unit quantity of electricity from one point to the other
potential energy *n* **:** the amount of energy a thing (as a weight raised to a height or a coiled spring) has because of its position or because of the arrangement of its parts
po·ten·ti·al·i·ty \pə-,ten-chē-'al-ət-ē\ *n, pl* **-ties 1 :** the ability to develop or to come into existence **2 :** POTENTIAL 1
po·ten·ti·ate \pə-'ten-chē-,āt\ *vt* **:** to make potent; *esp* **:** to augment (as a drug) synergistically — **po·ten·ti·a·tion** \-,ten-chē-'ā-shən\ *n* — **po·ten·ti·a·tor** \-'ten-chē-,āt-ər\ *n*
po·ten·ti·om·e·ter \pə-,ten-chē-'äm-ət-ər\ *n* **1 :** an instrument for measuring electromotive forces **2 :** VOLTAGE DIVIDER
pot·ful \'pät-,fúl\ *n* **:** the quantity held by a pot
¹poth·er \'päth-ər\ *n* **1 a :** a noisy disturbance **b :** FUSS **2 :** a choking cloud of dust or smoke **3 :** mental turmoil
²pother *vb* **poth·ered; poth·er·ing** \'päth-(ə-)riŋ\ **:** to put into or be in a pother
pot·herb \'pät-,(h)ərb\ *n* **:** an herb whose leaves or stems are boiled for use as greens; *also* **:** one (as mint) used to season food
pot·hole \-,hōl\ *n* **:** a large pit or hole (as in the bed of a river or in a road surface)
pot·hook \-,húk\ *n* **1 :** an S-shaped hook for hanging pots and kettles over an open fire **2 :** a stroke in writing resembling a pothook
pot·hunt·er \-,hənt-ər\ *n* **:** one who hunts game for food — **pot·hunt·ing** \-,hənt-iŋ\ *n*
po·tion \'pō-shən\ *n* [L *potion-*, *potio* drink, potion, fr. *potare* to drink] **:** DRINK, DOSE; *esp* **:** a dose of a liquid medicine or poison
pot·latch \'pät-,lach\ *n* [of AmerInd origin] **1 :** a ceremonial feast of northwest coast Indians in which the host distributes gifts lavishly and the guests must reciprocate **2** *Northwest* **:** a social event or celebration
pot liquor *n* **:** the liquid left in a pot after cooking meat or vegetables
pot·luck \'pät-'lək\ *n* **:** the regular meal available to a guest for whom no special preparations have been made
pot marigold *n* **:** a variable hardy calendula widely grown esp. for ornament
pot·pie \'pät-'pī\ *n* **:** meat or fowl stew served with a crust or dumplings
pot·pour·ri \,pō-pú-'rē\ *n* [F *pot pourri*, lit., rotten pot] **1 :** a jar of flower petals and spices used for scent **2 :** a miscellaneous collection **:** MEDLEY
pot roast *n* **:** a piece of meat (as beef) cooked by braising usu. on top of the stove
pot·sherd \'pät-,shərd\ *n* **:** a pottery fragment
pot·shot \-,shät\ *n* [fr. the sportsman's feeling that such shots were worthy only of pothunters] **1 :** a shot taken in a casual manner or at an easy target **2 :** a critical remark made in a random or sporadic manner — **pot·shot** *vb*
pot·tage \'pät-ij\ *n* **:** a thick soup of vegetables or vegetables and meat
¹pot·ter \'pät-ər\ *n* **:** one that makes pottery
²potter *vi* **:** PUTTER — **pot·ter·er** *n*
potter's clay *n* **:** a plastic clay suitable for modeling or throwing pottery — called also *potter's earth*
potter's field *n* [fr. the mention in Matthew 27:7 of the purchase of a potter's field for use as a graveyard] **:** a public burial place for paupers, unknown persons, and criminals
potter's wheel *n* **:** a horizontal disk revolving on a spindle and carrying the clay being shaped by a potter

potter's wheel

ə **abut;** ⁹ **kitten;** ər **further;** a **back;** ā **bake;** ä **cot, cart;** au̇ **out;** ch **chin;** e **less;** ē **easy;** g **gift;** i **trip;** ī **life**

pot·tery \'pät-ə-rē\ *n, pl* **-ter·ies** **1** : a place where earthen vessels are made **2** : the art of the potter : CERAMICS **3** : ware made usu. from clay that is shaped while moist and soft and hardened by heat; *esp* : coarser ware so made

¹**pot·ty** \'pät-ē\ *adj, slang chiefly Brit* : slightly crazy

²**potty** *n, pl* **potties** : a small child's pot for urinating or defecating

pot·ty-chair \-,che(ə)r, -,cha(ə)r\ *n* : a small chair with an open seat under which a potty is placed for use by a small child

¹**pouch** \'pauch\ *n* [MF *pouche*, of Gmc origin] **1** : a small drawstring bag carried on the person **2** : a bag of small or moderate size for storing or transporting goods; *esp* : a bag with a lock for first class mail or diplomatic dispatches **3** : an anatomical structure in the form of a bag or sac; *esp* : one for carrying the young on the abdomen of a female marsupial (as a kangaroo or opossum) — **pouched** \'paucht\ *adj*

²**pouch** *vb* : to put or form into or as if into a pouch

pouchy \'pau-chē\ *adj* : having, tending to have, or resembling a pouch

poult \'pōlt\ *n* [ME *polet, pulte* young fowl] : a young fowl; *esp* : a young turkey

poul·ter·er \'pōl-tər-ər\ *n* : one that deals in poultry

poul·ter's measure \-pōl-tərz-\ *n* [fr. obs. *poulter* poulterer; fr. the former practice of occasionally giving one or two extra when counting eggs by dozens] : a meter in which lines of 12 and 14 syllables alternate

poul·tice \'pōl-təs\ *n* [ML *pultes* pap, fr. L, pl. of *pult-, puls* porridge] : a soft usu. heated and often medicated mass spread on cloth and applied to sores or other lesions — **poultice** *vt*

poul·try \'pōl-trē\ *n* [MF *pouleterie*, fr. *pouletier* poulterer, fr. *polet* pullet] : domesticated birds kept for eggs or meat

poul·try·man \-mən\ *n* **1** : one that raises domestic fowls esp. on a commercial scale **2** : a dealer in poultry or poultry products

¹**pounce** \'paun(t)s\ *vi* [ME *pounce*, n., talon] **1** : to swoop down on and seize something with or as if with talons ⟨a cat waiting to *pounce*⟩ **2** : to make an abrupt assault or approach

²**pounce** *n* : an act of pouncing : a sudden swoop or spring

³**pounce** *n* [F *pounce* pumice, fr. L *pumic-, pumex*] **1** : a fine powder formerly used to prevent ink from spreading **2 a** : a fine powder for making stenciled patterns **b** : a perforated pattern

⁴**pounce** *vt* : to dust, rub, finish, or stencil with pounce

¹**pound** \'paund\ *n, pl* **pounds** *also* **pound** [OE *pund*, fr. L *pondo* pound, fr. *pondo* by weight] **1** : any of various units of mass and weight; *esp* : a unit in general use among English-speaking peoples equal to 16 ounces — see MEASURE table **2 a** : the basic monetary unit of the United Kingdom — called also *pound sterling* **b** : a basic monetary unit of a country (as Australia, Turkey, or Israel) outside the United Kingdom

²**pound** *vb* [ME *pounen*, fr. OE *pūnian*] **1** : to reduce to powder or pulp by beating **2 a** : to strike heavily or repeatedly ⟨*pound* the piano⟩ **b** : to produce by means of repeated vigorous strokes ⟨*pound* out a tune on the piano⟩ **c** : DRIVE **3** : to move along heavily or persistently ⟨the horses *pounded* along the lane⟩

³**pound** *n* : an act or sound of pounding

⁴**pound** *n* [ME, enclosure, fr. OE *pund-*] **1** : an enclosure for animals; *esp* : a public enclosure for stray or unlicensed animals **2 a** : a confine for fish; *esp* : the inner compartment of a fish trap **b** : an establishment selling live lobsters

pound·al \'paun-d°l\ *n* [*pound* + *-al* (as in *quintal*)] : a unit of force equal to the force that would give a free mass of one pound an acceleration of one foot per second per second

pound cake *n* : a rich cake made with a large amount of eggs and shortening in proportion to the flour used

¹**pound·er** \'paun-dər\ *n* : one that pounds

²**pounder** *n* **1** : one having a specified weight or value in pounds **2** : a gun throwing a projectile of a specified weight in pounds

pound-fool·ish \'paun(d)-'fü-lish\ *adj* [fr. the phrase *penny-wise and pound-foolish*] : imprudent in dealing with large sums or large matters

¹**pour** \'pō(ə)r, 'po(ə)r\ *vb* [ME *pouren*] **1** : to flow or to cause to flow in a stream ⟨*pour* the tea⟩ ⟨tears *pouring* down her cheeks⟩ **2 a** : to let loose something without restraint : express freely **b** : to supply or produce copiously **3** : to rain very hard — **pour·a·ble** \-ə-bəl\ *adj* — **pour·er** *n*

²**pour** *n* : the action of pouring; *esp* : a heavy fall of rain

pour·boire \pùrb-'wär\ *n* [F, fr. *pour boire* for drinking] : TIP, GRATUITY

pour·par·ler \,pùr-pär-'lā\ *n* : a discussion preliminary to negotiations

¹**pout** \'paut\ *n, pl* **pout** *or* **pouts** [OE *-pūte*] : any of several large-headed fishes (as a bullhead)

²**pout** *vb* [ME *pouten*] **1 a** : to show displeasure by thrusting out the lips **b** : SULK **2** : to swell out or cause to protrude

³**pout** *n* **1** : a protrusion of the lips expressive of displeasure **2** *pl* : a fit of bad humor

pout·er \'paut-ər\ *n* **1** : one that pouts **2** : a domestic pigeon of erect carriage with a distensible crop

pouty \'paut-ē\ *adj* : SULKY

pov·er·ty \'päv-ərt-ē\ *n* [OF *poverté*, fr. L *paupertat-, paupertas*, fr. *pauper* poor] **1** : the state of being poor : lack of money or material possessions : WANT **2** : SCARCITY, DEARTH **3 a** : debility due to malnutrition **b** : lack of fertility ⟨*poverty* of the soil⟩

pov·er·ty-strick·en \-,strik-ən\ *adj* : afflicted with poverty : very poor : DESTITUTE

¹**pow·der** \'paud-ər\ *n* [OF *poudre* dust, powder, fr. L *pulver-, pulvis*] **1** : dry material made up of fine particles; *also* : a medicinal or cosmetic preparation in this form **2** : any of various solid explosives used chiefly in gunnery and blasting — see SHELL illustration

²**powder** *vb* **1** : to sprinkle or cover with or as if with powder **2** : to reduce to powder or become powder **3** : to apply cosmetic powder — **pow·der·er** \-ər-ər\ *n*

powder blue *n* : a variable color averaging a pale blue

powder horn *n* : a flask for carrying gunpowder; *esp* : one made of the horn of an ox or cow

powder keg *n* **1** : a small usu. metal cask for holding gunpowder or blasting powder **2** : something (as an unstable political situation) liable to explode

powder puff *n* : a soft or fluffy pad for applying cosmetic powder

powder room *n* : a rest room for women

pow·dery \'paud-ə-rē\ *adj* **1 a** : resembling or consisting of powder **b** : easily reduced to powder : CRUMBLING **2** : covered with or as if with powder : DUSTY

powdery mildew *n* : a parasitic fungus producing abundant powdery conidia on the host; *also* : a plant disease caused by such a fungus

¹**pow·er** \'pau(-ə)r\ *n* [OF *poeir*, fr. *poeir* to be able, fr. (assumed) L *potēre*, fr. L *potis, pote* able] **1 a** : possession of control, authority, or influence over others **b** : one having such power; *esp* : a sovereign state **2 a** : ability to act or do ⟨lose the *power* of speech⟩ **b** : legal or official authority, capacity, or right **3 a** : physical might **b** : mental or moral efficacy **4** : the number of times as indicated by an exponent a number is to be multiplied by itself **5 a** : force or energy that is or can be applied to work; *esp* : mechanical or electrical force or energy **b** : the time rate at which work is done or energy emitted or transferred **6** : MAGNIFICATION 2

syn POWER, FORCE, ENERGY, STRENGTH mean the ability to exert effort. POWER may imply latent or exerted physical, mental, or spiritual ability to act or be acted upon; FORCE implies the actual effective exercise of power ⟨pushed with enough *force* to overturn the chair⟩ ⟨a wind of intense *force*⟩ ENERGY applies to power expended or capable of being transformed into work ⟨a crusader of untiring *energy*⟩ STRENGTH applies to the quality or characteristic that enables one to exert force or withstand pressure or attack ⟨a mind of *strength* and decisiveness⟩

²**power** *adj* : relating to, supplying, or utilizing power ⟨a *power* play in football⟩; *esp* : utilizing mechanical or electrical energy ⟨*power* drill⟩ ⟨*power* steering⟩

³**power** *vt* : to supply with power

pow·er·boat \-,bōt\ *n* : MOTORBOAT

power dive *n* : a dive of an airplane accelerated by the power of the engine — **power-dive** *vb*

---

j joke; ŋ sing; ō flow; ȯ flaw; ȯi coin; th thin; th this; ü loot;   u̇ foot; y yet; yü few; yu̇ furious; zh vision

pow·er·ful \'paů(-ə)r-fəl\ *adj* : full of or having power, strength, or influence : STRONG, MIGHTY, EFFECTIVE — **pow·er·ful·ly** \-f(ə-)lē\ *adv*

pow·er·house \'paů(-ə)r-,haůs\ *n* **1** : a building in which electric power is generated **2** : a source of power, energy, or influence **3** : one having unusual strength or energy

pow·er·less \'paů(-ə)r-ləs\ *adj* **1** : lacking power, force, or energy : unable to produce an effect **2** : lacking authority to act — **pow·er·less·ly** *adv* — **pow·er·less·ness** *n*

power mower *n* : a motor-driven lawn mower

power of attorney : a legal instrument authorizing a person to act as the attorney or agent of another

power pack *n* : a unit for converting a power supply to a voltage suitable for an electronic device

power plant *n* **1** : POWERHOUSE 1 **2** : an engine and related parts supplying the motive power of a self-propelled vehicle

power shovel *n* : a power-operated excavating machine consisting of a boom or crane that supports a dipper handle with a dipper at the end of it

¹pow·wow \'paů-,waů\ *n* [of Algonquian origin] **1** : a No. American Indian medicine man **2 a** : a No. American Indian ceremony (as for victory in war) **b** : a conference with an Indian leader or group **3 a** : a noisy gathering **b** : a meeting for discussion

²powwow *vi* : to hold a powwow

pox \'päks\ *n* [alter. of *pocks*, pl. of *pock*] : any of various usu. virus diseases (as smallpox or syphilis) that cause eruptions on the skin

prac·ti·ca·ble \'prak-ti-kə-bəl\ *adj* **1** : capable of being done, put into practice, or accomplished : FEASIBLE ⟨an interesting but not *practicable* idea⟩ **2** : USABLE ⟨a *practicable* weapon⟩ — **prac·ti·ca·bil·i·ty** \,prak-ti-kə-'bil-ət-ē\ *n* — **prac·ti·ca·ble·ness** \'prak-ti-kə-bəl-nəs\ *n* — **prac·ti·ca·bly** \-blē\ *adv*

syn PRACTICABLE, PRACTICAL both mean relating to practice or use but they are not interchangeable. PRACTICABLE applies to what seems feasible but has not been tested in use; PRACTICAL applies to things and to persons and implies success in meeting the demands made by actual use or living **syn** see in addition POSSIBLE

prac·ti·cal \'prak-ti-kəl\ *adj* [Gk *praktikos*, fr. *prassein* to do, act; akin to E *fare*] **1** : actively engaged in an action or occupation **2 a** : of, relating to, or manifested in practice or action ⟨for *practical* purposes⟩ **b** : being such in practice or effect : VIRTUAL ⟨a *practical* failure⟩ **3** : capable of being put to use or account : USEFUL **4 a** : disposed to action as opposed to speculation or theorizing ⟨a *practical* mind⟩ **b** (1) : qualified by practice or practical training (2) : designed to supplement theoretical training by experience **syn** see PRACTICABLE — **prac·ti·cal·i·ty** \,prak-ti-'kal-ət-ē\ *n* — **prac·ti·cal·ness** \'prak-ti-kəl-nəs\ *n*

practical joke *n* : a joke turning on something done rather than said; *esp* : a trick played on a person — **practical joker** *n*

prac·ti·cal·ly \'prak-ti-k(ə-)lē\ *adv* **1** : REALLY, ACTUALLY ⟨a clever but *practically* worthless scheme⟩ **2** : by experience or experiment **3** : to all practical purposes though not absolutely ⟨a *practically* inert gas⟩ **4** : NEARLY, ALMOST ⟨*practically* friendless⟩ **5** : within limits of usefulness

practical nurse *n* : a nurse that cares for the sick professionally without having the training or experience required of a registered nurse

¹prac·tice *or* **prac·tise** \'prak-təs\ *vb* [MF *practiser*, fr. *practique*, n., practice, fr. LL *practice*, fr. Gk *praktikē* practical knowledge, fr. fem. of *praktikos* practical] **1 a** : to perform or work at repeatedly so as to become proficient ⟨*practice* his act⟩ **b** : to train by repeated exercises ⟨*practice* pupils in penmanship⟩ **2 a** : to carry out : APPLY ⟨*practices* what he preaches⟩ **b** : to do or perform often, customarily, or habitually ⟨*practice* politeness⟩ **c** : to be professionally engaged in ⟨*practice* medicine⟩ — **prac·tic·er** *n*

²practice *also* **practise** *n* **1 a** : actual performance or application **b** : a repeated or customary action **c** : the usual way of doing something ⟨local *practice*⟩ **d** : an established manner of conducting legal proceedings **2 a** : systematic exercise for proficiency ⟨*practice* makes perfect⟩ **b** : the condition of being proficient through systematic exercise ⟨get in *practice*⟩ **3 a** : the exercise of a profession ⟨the *practice* of law⟩ **b** : a professional business ⟨the doctor sold his *practice*⟩ **syn** see HABIT

prac·ticed *or* **prac·tised** \'prak-təst\ *adj* **1** : EXPERIENCED, SKILLED **2** : learned by practice

prac·tice-teach \,prak-təs-'tēch\ *vi* : to engage in practice teaching

practice teaching *n* : teaching by a student preparing for a teaching career for the purpose of practicing educational skills and methods under the supervision of an experienced teacher — **practice teacher** *n*

prac·ti·tio·ner \prak-'tish-(ə-)nər\ *n* **1** : a person who practices a profession and esp. law or medicine **2** : a Christian Scientist who is an authorized healer

prae·no·men \prē-'nō-mən\ *n*, *pl* **-nomens** *or* **-no·mi·na** \-'näm-ə-nə, -'nō-mə-\ [L, fr. *prae-* pre- + *nomen* name] : the first of the usual three names of an ancient Roman

prae·tor \'prēt-ər\ *n* [L] : an ancient Roman magistrate ranking below a consul and having chiefly judicial functions

¹prae·to·ri·an \prē-'tōr-ē-ən, -'tȯr-\ *adj* **1** : of or relating to a Roman praetor **2** *often cap* : of, relating to, or constituting the bodyguard of a Roman emperor ⟨the *praetorian* guard⟩

²praetorian *n*, *often cap* : a member of the praetorian guard

prag·mat·ic \prag-'mat-ik\ *also* **prag·mat·i·cal** \-'mat-i-kəl\ *adj* [Gk *pragmatikos* skilled in affairs, fr. *pragmat-*, *pragma* action, affair, fr. *prassein* to do] **1 a** : concerned with practical affairs often to the exclusion of intellectual or artistic matters **b** : PRACTICAL **2** : relating to or in accordance with pragmatism — **prag·mat·i·cal·ly** \-i-k(ə-)lē\ *adv*

pragmatic sanction *n* : a solemn decree of a sovereign on a matter of primary importance and with the force of fundamental law

prag·ma·tism \'prag-mə-,tiz-əm\ *n* **1** : a practical approach to problems and affairs **2** : an American movement in philosophy holding that the meaning of an idea is to be sought in its practical bearings, that the function of thought is to guide action, and that truth is to be tested by the practical consequences of belief — **prag·ma·tist** \-mət-əst\ *adj or n* — **prag·ma·tis·tic** \,prag-mə-'tis-tik\ *adj*

prai·rie \'pre(ə)r-ē\ *n* [F, fr. (assumed) VL *prataria*, fr. L *pratum* meadow] : a tract of grassland; *esp* : a large area of level or rolling land (as in the central U.S.) with deep fertile soil, a cover of tall coarse grasses, and few trees

prairie chicken *n* : a grouse of the Mississippi valley with a patch of bare inflatable skin on the neck

prairie dog *n* : a colonial buff or grayish American burrowing rodent related to the marmots

prairie schooner *n* : a covered wagon used by pioneers in cross-country travel — called also *prairie wagon*

prairie wolf *n* : COYOTE

¹praise \'prāz\ *vb* [MF *preisier* to prize, praise, fr. LL *pretiare* to prize, fr. L *pretium* price] **1** : to express approval : COMMEND **2** : to glorify esp. by ascription of perfections : WORSHIP — **prais·er** *n*

²praise *n* **1** : an act of praising : COMMENDATION **2** : WORSHIP

praise·wor·thy \-,wər-thē\ *adj* : worthy of praise : LAUDABLE — **praise·wor·thi·ly** \-thə-lē\ *adv* — **praise·wor·thi·ness** \-thē-nəs\ *n*

Pra·krit \'präk-,rit\ *n* [Skt *prākṛta*, fr. *prākṛta* natural, vulgar] **1** : any or all of the ancient Indic languages or dialects other than Sanskrit **2** : any of the modern Indic languages

pra·line \'prä-,lēn, 'prā-\ *n* [F, after Count Plessy-*Praslin* d1675 French soldier] : a candy of nut kernels embedded in boiled brown sugar or maple sugar

pram \'pram\ *n* [by shortening & alter. fr. *perambulator*] *chiefly Brit* : a baby carriage

prance \'pran(t)s\ *vi* [ME *prauncen*] **1** : to spring from the hind legs or move by so doing **2** : to ride on a prancing horse **3 a** : SWAGGER **b** : CAPER — **prance** *n* — **pranc·er** \'pran(t)-sər\ *n* — **pranc·ing·ly** \-siŋ-lē\ *adv*

¹prank \'praŋk\ *n* : a playful or mischievous act : PRACTICAL JOKE, TRICK ⟨Halloween *pranks*⟩ — **prank·ish** \'praŋ-kish\ *adj* — **prank·ish·ly** *adv* — **prank·ish·ness** *n*

ə *abut*; ə *kitten*; ər *further*; a *back*; ā *bake*; ä *cot, cart*; aů *out*; ch *chin*; e *less*; ē *easy*; g *gift*; i *trip*; ī *life*

²**prank** *vt* : to dress or adorn (oneself) gaily or showily
prank·ster \'praŋ(k)-stər\ *n* : a player of pranks
pra·seo·dym·i·um \,prā-zē-ō-'dim-ē-əm\ *n* : a yellowish white metallic chemical element used chiefly in the form of its salts in coloring glass greenish yellow — see ELEMENT table
¹**prate** \'prāt\ *vb* [MD *praten*] : to talk long and idly : speak foolishly : CHATTER, BABBLE — **prat·er** *n* — **prat·ing·ly** \'prāt-iŋ-lē\ *adv*
²**prate** *n* : an act of prating : idle or foolish talk
prat·fall \'prat-,fόl\ *n* : a fall on the buttocks
pra·tique \pra-'tēk\ *n* [F, lit., practice] : clearance given an incoming ship by the health authority of a port
¹**prat·tle** \'prat-ᵊl\ *vb* **prat·tled**; **prat·tling** \'prat-liŋ, -ᵊl-iŋ\ [LG *pratelen*] **1** : PRATE **2** : to utter meaningless sounds suggestive of the chatter of children **3** : BABBLE — **prat·tler** \'prat-lər, -ᵊl-ər\ *n* — **prat·tling·ly** \'prat-liŋ-lē\ *adv*
²**prattle** *n* **1** : trifling or empty talk **2** : a sound that is meaningless, repetitive, and suggestive of the chatter of children
prau \'praú\ *n* [Malay *pĕrahu*] : any of several usu. undecked Indonesian boats propelled by sails, oars, or paddles
prawn \'prόn, 'prän\ *n* [ME *prane*] : any of numerous widely distributed edible decapod crustaceans resembling shrimps with large compressed abdomens; *also* : SHRIMP

prawn

pray \'prā\ *vb* [OF *preier*, fr. L *precari*, fr. *prec-*, *prex* request, prayer] **1** : ENTREAT, IMPLORE ⟨*prayed* the king for land⟩ ⟨*pray* tell me the time⟩ **2** : to get or bring by praying **3** : to make entreaty or supplication : PLEAD **4** : to address God with adoration, confession, supplication, or thanksgiving
¹**prayer** \'pra(ə)r, 'pre(ə)r\ *n* [OF *preiere*, fr. ML *precaria*, fr. L *prec-*, *prex* prayer] **1** : the act or practice of praying to God ⟨a moment of silent *prayer*⟩ **2 a** : a supplication or expression addressed to God ⟨a *prayer* of thanksgiving⟩ **b** : an earnest request or wish : PLEA **3** : a religious service consisting chiefly of prayers ⟨had regular family *prayers*⟩ **4** : a set form of words used in praying ⟨a book of *prayers*⟩
²**pray·er** \'prā-ər\ *n* : one that prays : SUPPLIANT
prayer book *n* : a book containing prayers and often other forms and directions for worship
prayer·ful \'pra(ə)r-fəl, 'pre(ə)r-\ *adj* **1** : given to or characterized by prayer : DEVOUT **2** : EARNEST — **prayer·ful·ly** \-fə-lē\ *adv* — **prayer·ful·ness** *n*
prayer meeting *n* : a Protestant Christian service of evangelical worship usu. held regularly on a week night — called also *prayer service*
praying mantis *n* : MANTIS
pre- *prefix* [L *prae-*; akin to E *for*] **1 a** (1) : earlier than : prior to : before ⟨*Precambrian*⟩ ⟨*pre*historic⟩ ⟨*pre*-English⟩ (2) : preparatory or prerequisite to ⟨*pre*medical⟩ **b** : in advance : beforehand ⟨*pre*cancel⟩ ⟨*pre*pay⟩ **2 a** : in front of : anterior to ⟨*pre*axial⟩ ⟨*pre*molar⟩ **b** : front : anterior ⟨*pre*abdomen⟩
preach \'prēch\ *vb* [OF *prechier*, fr. LL *praedicare*, fr. L, to proclaim publicly, fr. *prae-* pre- + *dicare* to proclaim] **1 a** : to deliver a sermon : utter publicly **b** : to set forth in a sermon ⟨*preach* the gospel⟩ **2** : to urge acceptance or abandonment of an idea or course of action : ADVOCATE ⟨*preach* patience⟩; *esp* : to exhort in an officious or tiresome manner **3** : to bring, put, or affect by preaching — **preach·er** *n* — **preach·ing·ly** \'prē-chiŋ-lē\ *adv*
preach·ify \'prē-chə-,fī\ *vi* **-fied**; **-fy·ing** : to preach ineptly or tediously
preach·ment \'prēch-mənt\ *n* **1** : the act or practice of preaching **2** : SERMON, EXHORTATION; *esp* : a tedious or unwelcome exhortation
preachy \'prē-chē\ *adj* : marked by obvious moral exhortation : DIDACTIC — **preach·i·ly** \-chə-lē\ *adv* — **preach·i·ness** \-chē-nəs\ *n*
pre·ad·o·les·cence \,prē-,ad-ᵊl-'es-ᵊn(t)s\ *n* : the period of human development just preceding adolescence — **pre·ad·o·les·cent** \-ᵊnt\ *adj or n*
pre·am·ble \'prē-,am-bəl\ *n* [ML *praeambulum*, fr. LL, neut. of *praeambulus* walking in front, fr. L *prae-* pre- + *ambulare* to walk] **1** : an introductory statement; *esp* : the introductory part of a constitution or statute that usu. states the reasons for and intent of the law **2** : an introductory fact or circumstance : PRELIMINARY; *esp* : one indicating what is to follow
pre·ar·range \,prē-ə-'rānj\ *vt* : to arrange beforehand — **pre·ar·range·ment** \-mənt\ *n*
pre·as·signed \,prē-ə-'sīnd\ *adj* : assigned beforehand
preb·end \'preb-ənd\ *n* [ML *praebenda*, fr. LL, subsistence allowance granted by the state, fr. L *praebēre* to offer, fr. *prae-* + *habēre* to have, hold] **1 a** : an endowment held by a cathedral or collegiate church for the maintenance of a prebendary **b** : the stipend paid from this endowment **2** : PREBENDARY
preb·en·dary \'preb-ən-,der-ē\ *n, pl* **-dar·ies 1** : a clergyman receiving a prebend for officiating and serving in the church **2** : an honorary canon
Pre·cam·bri·an \(')prē-'kam-brē-ən\ *n* : the earliest era of geological history equivalent to the Archeozoic and Proterozoic; *also* : the corresponding system of rocks — **Precambrian** *adj*
pre·can·cel \(')prē-'kan(t)-səl\ *vt* : to cancel (a postage stamp) in advance of use — **pre·can·cel·la·tion** \,prē-,kan(t)-sə-'lā-shən\ *n*
pre·can·cer·ous \(')prē-'kan(t)s-(ə-)rəs\ *adj* : likely to become cancerous ⟨a *precancerous* lesion⟩
pre·car·i·ous \pri-'kar-ē-əs, -'ker-\ *adj* [L *precarius* obtained by entreaty, uncertain, fr. *prec-*, *prex* entreaty] **1** : DUBIOUS **2 a** : dependent on chance circumstances, unknown conditions, or uncertain developments **b** : characterized by a lack of security or stability that threatens with danger ⟨a *precarious* state of health⟩ — **pre·car·i·ous·ly** *adv* — **pre·car·i·ous·ness** *n*
pre·cau·tion \pri-'kό-shən\ *n* **1** : care taken in advance : FORESIGHT **2** : a measure taken beforehand to prevent harm or secure good : SAFEGUARD ⟨take *precautions* against fire⟩ — **pre·cau·tion·ary** \-shə-,ner-ē\ *adj*
pre·ca·va \(')prē-'kāv-ə, -'kā-və\ *n, pl* **-ca·vae** \-'kāv-,ī, -'kā-(,)vē\ [NL] : a superior vena cava — **pre·ca·val** \-'kāv-əl, -'kā-vəl\ *adj*
pre·cede \pri-'sēd\ *vb* [L *praecedere*, fr. *prae-* pre- + *cedere* to go] **1** : to surpass in rank, dignity, or importance **2** : to be, go, or come before or in front of in position or time **3** : to cause to be preceded : PREFACE ⟨*preceded* his speech with a welcome to the visitors⟩
prec·e·dence \'pres-əd-ən(t)s, pri-'sēd-ᵊn(t)s\ *or* **prec·e·den·cy** \-ən-sē, -ᵊn-sē\ *n* **1** : the act or fact of preceding (as in time, importance, or position) **2** : PRIORITY, PREFERENCE
¹**prec·e·dent** \pri-'sēd-ᵊnt, 'pres-əd-ənt\ *adj* : prior in time, order, arrangement, or significance
²**prec·e·dent** \'pres-əd-ənt\ *n* **1** : an earlier occurrence of something similar **2** : something that may serve as an example or rule to authorize or justify a similar future act or statement
pre·ced·ing \pri-'sēd-iŋ\ *adj* : going before : PREVIOUS
syn PRECEDING, ANTECEDENT, FOREGOING mean being before. PRECEDING implies being immediately before in time or place ⟨on the *preceding* day⟩ ⟨last line in the *preceding* stanza⟩ ANTECEDENT applies to order in time and may suggest a causal relation ⟨*antecedent* symptoms of the disease⟩ FOREGOING applies to what has preceded esp. in a discourse ⟨the *foregoing* phrase⟩
pre·cen·tor \pri-'sent-ər\ *n* [LL *praecentor*, fr. L *praecent-*, *praecinere* to sing before, fr. *prae-* + *canere* to sing] : a leader of the singing of a choir or congregation — **pre·cen·to·ri·al** \,prē-,sen-'tōr-ē-əl, -'tόr-\ *adj* — **pre·cen·tor·ship** \pri-'sent-ər-,ship\ *n*
pre·cept \'prē-,sept\ *n* [L *praeceptum*, fr. neut. of *praeceptus*, pp. of *praecipere* to take beforehand, instruct, fr. *prae-* + *capere* to take] : a command or principle intended as a general rule of action
pre·cep·tor \pri-'sep-tər, 'prē-,\ *n* **1** : TEACHER, TUTOR **2** : the headmaster or principal of a school — **pre·cep·to·ri·al** \pri-,sep-'tōr-ē-əl, ,prē-, -'tόr-\ *adj* — **pre·cep·tor·ship** \pri-'sep-tər-,ship, 'prē-,\ *n* — **pre·cep·tress** \-trəs\ *n*
pre·ces·sion \prē-'sesh-ən\ *n* [L *praecess-*, *praecedere* to precede, go ahead] : a comparatively slow circling of the rotation axis of a spinning body about another line intersecting it

pre·cinct \'prē-,siŋ(k)t\ *n* [ML *praecinctum* bounded district, fr. L, neut. of *praecinctus*, pp. of *praecingere* to gird about, fr. *prae-* pre- + *cingere* to gird] **1 :** an administrative subdivision of a territory **:** DISTRICT: as **a :** a subdivision of a county, town, city, or ward for election purposes **b :** a division of a city for police control **2 :** the enclosure bounded by the walls or limits of a building or place ⟨within the *precincts* of the college⟩ **3** *pl* **:** the region immediately surrounding a place **:** ENVIRONS ⟨the *precincts* of the city⟩ **4 :** BOUNDARY

pre·ci·os·i·ty \,pres(h)-ē-'äs-ət-ē\ *n*, *pl* **-ties :** fastidious refinement esp. in language

¹pre·cious \'presh-əs\ *adj* [OF *precios*, fr. L *pretiosus*, fr. *pretium* price] **1 :** of great value or high price ⟨diamonds, emeralds, and other *precious* stones⟩ **2 :** highly esteemed or cherished ⟨*precious* memories⟩ **3 :** excessively refined **:** AFFECTED ⟨*precious* language⟩ **4 :** GREAT, THOROUGH-GOING ⟨a *precious* scoundrel⟩ — **pre·cious·ly** *adv* — **pre·cious·ness** *n*

²precious *adv* **:** EXTREMELY, VERY ⟨they had *precious* little to say⟩

prec·i·pice \'pres-ə-pəs\ *n* [L *praecipitium*, fr. *praecipit-*, *praeceps* headlong, fr. *prae-* + *caput* head] **1 :** a very steep or overhanging place (as the face of a cliff) **2 :** the brink of disaster

pre·cip·i·tance \pri-'sip-ət-ən(t)s\ *n* **:** rash haste **:** PRECIPITANCY

pre·cip·i·tan·cy \-ən-sē\ *n*, *pl* **-cies :** precipitate action **:** PRECIPITATION

pre·cip·i·tant \-ənt\ *adj* **:** PRECIPITATE — **pre·cip·i·tant·ly** *adv* — **pre·cip·i·tant·ness** *n*

¹pre·cip·i·tate \pri-'sip-ə-,tāt\ *vb* [L *praecipitatus*, pp. of *praecipitare*, fr. *praecipit-*, *praeceps* headlong] **1 a :** to throw violently **:** HURL **b :** to fall headlong **c :** to fall or come suddenly into some condition **2 a :** to move, urge, or press on with haste or violence **b :** to bring on abruptly **3 a :** to separate or cause to separate from solution or suspension **b :** to cause (vapor) to condense and fall or deposit or to condense from a vapor and fall as rain or snow — **pre·cip·i·ta·tor** \-,tāt-ər\ *n*

²pre·cip·i·tate \pri-'sip-ət-ət, -ə-,tāt\ *n* **:** a usu. solid substance separated from a solution or suspension by chemical or physical change

³pre·cip·i·tate \pri-'sip-ət-ət\ *adj* **1 :** exhibiting violent or unwise speed **:** RASH ⟨a *precipitate* attack⟩ **2 a :** falling, flowing, or rushing with steep descent **b :** PRECIPITOUS — **pre·cip·i·tate·ly** *adv* — **pre·cip·i·tate·ness** *n*

pre·cip·i·ta·tion \pri-,sip-ə-'tā-shən\ *n* **1 :** the quality or state of being precipitate **:** HASTE **2 :** the process of precipitating or of forming a precipitate **3 a :** a deposit on the earth of hail, mist, rain, sleet, or snow; *also* **:** the quantity of water deposited **b :** PRECIPITATE

pre·cip·i·tin \pri-'sip-ət-ən\ *n* **:** an antibody that forms an insoluble precipitate when it unites with its antigen

pre·cip·i·tin·o·gen \pri-,sip-ə-'tin-ə-jən\ *n* **:** an antigen that stimulates the production of a corresponding precipitin

pre·cip·i·tous \pri-'sip-ət-əs\ *adj* **1 a :** steep like a precipice **b :** having precipices ⟨a *precipitous* trail⟩ **2 :** falling very quickly **:** very rapid ⟨*precipitous* rush of water⟩ **3 :** SUDDEN, RASH ⟨a *precipitous* act⟩ **syn** see STEEP — **pre·cip·i·tous·ly** *adv* — **pre·cip·i·tous·ness** *n*

pré·cis \prā-'sē, 'prā-(,)sē\ *n*, *pl* **pré·cis** \-'sēz, -(,)sēz\ [F, fr. *précis* precise] **:** a concise summary of essential points, statements, or facts

pre·cise \pri-'sīs\ *adj* [MF *precis*, fr. L *praecisus*, pp. of *praecidere* to cut off, fr. *prae-* + *caedere* to cut] **1 :** exactly or sharply defined or stated **2 :** very exact **:** ACCURATE ⟨*precise* scales⟩⟨*precise* time of arrival⟩ **3 :** clear and sharp in enunciation **:** DISTINCT ⟨a low *precise* voice⟩ **4 :** strictly conforming to rule or convention ⟨*precise* daily habits⟩ **5 :** distinguished from every other **:** VERY ⟨at just that *precise* moment⟩ **syn** see CORRECT — **pre·cise·ly** *adv* — **pre·cise·ness** *n*

pre·ci·sian \pri-'sizh-ən\ *n* **:** a person who stresses or practices scrupulous adherence to a strict standard esp. of religious observance or morality

¹pre·ci·sion \pri-'sizh-ən\ *n* **:** the quality or state of being precise **:** EXACTNESS; *esp* **:** the degree of refinement with which an operation is performed or a measurement stated — **pre·ci·sion·ist** \-'sizh-(ə-)nəst\ *n*

²precision *adj* **1 :** adapted for extremely accurate measurement or operation ⟨a *precision* gauge⟩ **2 :** marked by precision of execution ⟨*precision* bombing⟩

pre·clin·i·cal \(')prē-'klin-i-kəl\ *adj* **:** of or relating to the period preceding clinical manifestations ⟨*preclinical* infection⟩

pre·clude \pri-'klüd\ *vt* [L *praeclus-*, *praecludere*, lit., to shut out, fr. *prae-* pre- + *claudere* to close] **:** to make impossible or ineffectual **:** keep from taking place **:** PREVENT ⟨his actions *precluded* him from winning⟩ ⟨*preclude* escape⟩ — **pre·clu·sion** \-'klü-zhən\ *n* — **pre·clu·sive** \-'klü-siv, -ziv\ *adj* — **pre·clu·sive·ly** *adv*

pre·co·cial \pri-'kō-shəl\ *adj* **:** capable of a high degree of independent activity from birth ⟨*precocial* birds⟩ — compare ALTRICIAL

pre·co·cious \pri-'kō-shəs\ *adj* [L *praecoc-*, *praecox*, lit., early ripening, fr. *prae-* pre- + *coquere* to cook] **1 :** exceptionally early in development or occurrence **2 :** exhibiting mature qualities at an unusually early age ⟨a *precocious* child⟩ — **pre·co·cious·ly** *adv* — **pre·co·cious·ness** *n* — **pre·coc·i·ty** \pri-'käs-ət-ē\ *n*

pre·con·ceive \,prē-kən-'sēv\ *vt* **:** to form an opinion of prior to actual knowledge or experience ⟨*preconceived* ideas about foreign lands⟩ — **pre·con·cep·tion** \-'sep-shən\ *n*

pre·con·cert·ed \,prē-kən-'sərt-əd\ *adj* **:** arranged or agreed upon in advance ⟨following a *preconcerted* plan of attack⟩

pre·con·di·tion \,prē-kən-'dish-ən\ *vt* **:** to put in proper or desired condition or frame of mind in advance

pre·con·scious \(')prē-'kän-chəs\ *adj* **:** not present in consciousness but capable of being readily recalled — **pre·con·scious·ly** *adv*

pre·cook \(')prē-'kük\ *vt* **:** to cook partially or entirely before final cooking or reheating

pre·cur·sor \pri-'kər-sər, 'prē-\ *n* [L *praecurs-*, *praecurrere* to run before, fr. *prae-* pre- + *currere* to run] **1 :** one that precedes and indicates the approach of another **:** FORERUNNER **2 :** PREDECESSOR

pre·cur·so·ry \pri-'kərs-(ə-)rē\ *adj* **:** having the character of a precursor **:** PRELIMINARY, PREMONITORY ⟨*precursory* symptoms of a fever⟩

pre·da·cious *or* **pre·da·ceous** \pri-'dā-shəs\ *adj* **:** living by preying on others **:** PREDATORY — **pre·da·cious·ness** *n* — **pre·dac·i·ty** \-'das-ət-ē\ *n*

pre·date \(')prē-'dāt\ *vt* **:** ANTEDATE

pre·da·tion \pri-'dā-shən\ *n* **1 :** the act of preying or plundering **:** DEPREDATION **2 :** a mode of life in which food is primarily obtained by killing and consuming animals — **pred·a·tor** \'pred-ət-ər\ *n*

pred·a·to·ry \'pred-ə-,tōr-ē, -,tòr-\ *adj* [L *praedari* to prey upon, fr. *praeda* prey] **1 :** of, relating to, or marked by plundering ⟨*predatory* raids⟩ **2 :** living by predation **:** PREDACIOUS; *also* **:** adapted to predation — **pred·a·to·ri·ly** \,pred-ə-'tōr-ə-lē, -'tòr-\ *adv*

pre·de·cease \,prēd-i-'sēs\ *vb* **:** to die before another person

pred·e·ces·sor \'pred-ə-,ses-ər, 'prēd-\ *n* [LL *praedecessor*, fr. L *prae-* pre- + *decessor* retiring governor, fr. *decess-*, *decedere* to depart, retire from office, fr. *de-* + *cedere* to go] **1 :** one that precedes; *esp* **:** a person who has held a position or office before another **2** *archaic* **:** ANCESTOR

pre·des·ig·nate \(')prē-'dez-ig-,nāt\ *vt* **:** to designate beforehand — **pre·des·ig·na·tion** \,prē-,dez-ig-'nā-shən\ *n*

pre·des·ti·nate \prē-'des-tə-,nāt\ *vt* **1 :** to foreordain to an earthly or eternal destiny by divine decree **2** *archaic* **:** PREDETERMINE

pre·des·ti·na·tion \(,)prē-,des-tə-'nā-shən\ *n* **:** the act of predestinating **:** the state of being predestinated

pre·des·tine \(')prē-'des-tən\ *vt* **:** to destine, decree, determine, appoint, or settle beforehand; *esp* **:** PREDESTINATE 1

pre·de·ter·mine \,prēd-i-'tər-mən\ *vt* **1 a :** FOREORDAIN, PREDESTINE **b :** to determine or settle beforehand ⟨meet at a *predetermined* place⟩ **2 :** to impose a direction or tendency on beforehand — **pre·de·ter·mi·na·tion** \-,tər-mə-'nā-shən\ *n*

pred·i·ca·ble \'pred-i-kə-bəl\ *adj* **:** capable of being predicated or affirmed

pre·dic·a·ment \pri-'dik-ə-mənt\ *n* [ME, that which is predicated, category, fr. LL *praedicamentum*, fr. *praedicare* to predicate] **:** a difficult, perplexing, or trying situation **:** FIX

syn DILEMMA, QUANDARY: PREDICAMENT suggests a difficult situation offering no satisfactory solution ⟨increased leisure poses a *predicament* for our society⟩ DILEMMA implies the need to choose between two alternatives offering essentially equal advantages or disadvantages ⟨in a *dilemma* about a choice of careers⟩ QUANDARY stresses puzzlement and perplexity ⟨in a *quandary* as to what excuse to make⟩

¹**pred·i·cate** \'pred-i-kət\ *n* [LL *praedicatum*, fr. neuter of *praedicatus*, pp. of *praedicare* to assert, predicate, preach, fr. L *prae-* pre- + *dicare* to proclaim] **1 :** something that is affirmed or denied of the subject in a proposition in logic ⟨in "paper is white", whiteness is the *predicate*⟩ **2 :** the part of a sentence or clause that expresses what is said of the subject and that usu. consists of a verb with or without objects, complements, or adverbial modifiers — **pred·i·ca·tive** \'pred-i-kət-iv, 'pred-ə-ˌkāt-\ *adj* — **pred·i·ca·tive·ly** *adv*

²**predicate** *adj* **:** belonging to the predicate; *esp* **:** completing the meaning of a linking verb ⟨*hot* in "the sun is hot" is a *predicate* adjective⟩ — compare ATTRIBUTIVE

³**pred·i·cate** \'pred-ə-ˌkāt\ *vt* **1 :** AFFIRM, DECLARE **2 a :** to assert as a predicate in a proposition **b :** to assert to be a quality or property ⟨*predicate* sweetness of sugar⟩ **3 :** BASE, FOUND ⟨a proposal *predicated* upon the belief that sufficient support could be obtained⟩ **4 :** IMPLY

predicate nominative *n* **:** a noun or pronoun in the nominative case completing the meaning of a linking verb

pred·i·ca·tion \ˌpred-ə-'kā-shən\ *n* **:** an act or instance of predicating; *esp* **:** the expression of action, state, or quality by a grammatical predicate

pre·dict \pri-'dikt\ *vt* [L *praedict-, praedicere*, fr. *prae-* pre- + *dicere* to say] **:** to declare in advance **:** foretell on the basis of observation, experience, or scientific reasoning syn see FORETELL — **pre·dict·a·ble** \-'dik-tə-bəl\ *adj* — **pre·dict·a·bly** \-blē\ *adv*

pre·dic·tion \pri-'dik-shən\ *n* **1 :** an act of predicting **2 :** something that is predicted **:** FORECAST — **pre·dic·tive** \-'dik-tiv\ *adj* — **pre·dic·tive·ly** *adv*

pre·di·gest \ˌprēd-ī-'jest, ˌprēd-ə-\ *vt* **:** to subject to predigestion

pre·di·ges·tion \-'jes(h)-chən\ *n* **:** artificial partial digestion of food for use in illness or impaired digestion

pred·i·lec·tion \ˌpred-ᵊl-'ek-shən, ˌprēd-\ *n* [ML *praedilect-, praediligere* to prefer, fr. L *prae-*, pre- + *diligere* to love, fr. *dis-* apart + *legere* to pick, choose] **:** an inclination in favor of something in advance of knowledge of it **:** PREFERENCE, PARTIALITY

pre·dis·pose \ˌprēd-is-'pōz\ *vt* **:** to dispose in advance **:** make susceptible **:** INCLINE ⟨an inherited weakness *predisposing* one to certain diseases⟩

pre·dis·po·si·tion \ˌprē-ˌdis-pə-'zish-ən\ *n* **:** a condition of being predisposed **:** INCLINATION

pre·dom·i·nance \pri-'däm-ə-nən(t)s\ *also* **pre·dom·i·nan·cy** \-nən-sē\ *n* **:** the quality or state of being predominant **:** PREVALENCE

pre·dom·i·nant \-nənt\ *adj* **:** having superior strength, influence, or authority **:** PREVAILING ⟨the *predominant* color in a painting⟩ — **pre·dom·i·nant·ly** *adv*

pre·dom·i·nate \pri-'däm-ə-ˌnāt\ *vb* **1 :** to exert controlling power or influence **:** PREVAIL, DOMINATE **2 :** to hold advantage in numbers or quantity **:** PREPONDERATE ⟨cottages *predominated*⟩ — **pre·dom·i·na·tion** \-ˌdäm-ə-'nā-shən\ *n*

pre·em·i·nence \prē-'em-ə-nən(t)s\ *n* **:** the quality or state of being preeminent **:** SUPERIORITY

pre·em·i·nent \-nənt\ *adj* **:** having paramount rank, dignity, or importance **:** OUTSTANDING, SUPREME — **pre·em·i·nent·ly** *adv*

pre·empt \prē-'em(p)t\ *vt* [ML *praeempt-, praeemere* to buy before, fr. L *prae-* pre- + *emere* to buy] **1 :** to settle upon (as public land) with the right to purchase before others; *also* **:** to take by such a right **2 :** to take before someone else can **:** APPROPRIATE ⟨*preempt* a seat at the stadium⟩ — **pre·emp·tion** \-'em(p)-shən\ *n* — **pre·emp·tive** \-'em(p)-tiv\ *adj* — **pre·emp·tive·ly** *adv* — **pre·emp·tor** \-tər\ *n*

preen \'prēn\ *vb* [ME *preinen*] **1 :** to trim or dress with the bill **2 :** to dress or smooth oneself up **:** PRIMP **3 :** to

indulge oneself in pride **:** congratulate oneself **:** GLOAT — **preen·er** *n*

pre·ex·ist \ˌprē-ig-'zist\ *vb* **:** to exist earlier or before something

pre·ex·ist·ence \-'zis-tən(t)s\ *n* **:** existence in a former state or previous to something else; *esp* **:** existence of the soul before its union with the body — **pre·ex·ist·ent** \-tənt\ *adj*

pre·fab \(')prē-'fab, 'prē-ˌ\ *n* **:** a prefabricated structure

pre·fab·ri·cate \(')prē-'fab-ri-ˌkāt\ *vt* **1 :** to fabricate the parts of at a factory so that construction consists mainly of assembling and uniting standardized parts **2 :** to produce synthetically or artificially — **pre·fab·ri·ca·tion** \ˌprē-ˌfab-ri-'kā-shən\ *n*

¹**pref·ace** \'pref-əs\ *n* [MF, fr. L *praefation-, praefatio* foreword, fr. *praefari* to say beforehand, fr. *prae-* pre- + *fari* to say] **1** *often cap* **:** a prayer introducing the central part of the eucharistic office **2 :** the introductory remarks of a speaker or author **:** PROLOGUE **3 :** PRELIMINARY

²**preface** *vb* **1 :** to make introductory remarks **:** say or write as a preface ⟨a note *prefaced* to the manuscript⟩ **2 :** PRECEDE, HERALD **3 :** to introduce by or begin with a preface ⟨*preface* a speech with a few jokes⟩ **4 :** to locate in front of **5 :** to be a preliminary to — **pref·ac·er** *n*

pref·a·to·ri·al \ˌpref-ə-'tōr-ē-əl, -'tòr-\ *adj* **:** PREFATORY — **pref·a·to·ri·al·ly** \-ē-ə-lē\ *adv*

pref·a·to·ry \'pref-ə-ˌtōr-ē, -ˌtòr-\ *adj* **:** of, relating to, or constituting a preface **:** INTRODUCTORY, PRELIMINARY ⟨*prefatory* remarks⟩

pre·fect \'prē-ˌfekt\ *n* [L *praefectus*, fr. pp. of *praeficere* to place at the head of, fr. *prae-* + *facere* to make] **1 :** a high official or magistrate (as of ancient Rome or France) **2 :** a presiding or chief officer or magistrate **3 :** a student monitor in some usu. private schools

prefect apostolic *n* **:** a Roman Catholic priest with quasi-episcopal jurisdiction over a district of a missionary territory

pre·fec·ture \'prē-ˌfek-chər\ *n* **1 :** the office or term of office of a prefect **2 :** the district governed by a prefect — **pre·fec·tur·al** \prē-'fek-chə-rəl\ *adj*

pre·fer \pri-'fər\ *vt* **pre·ferred; pre·fer·ring** [L *praeferre* to put before, prefer, fr. *prae-* + *ferre* to carry] **1 :** to choose or esteem above another ⟨*prefer* dark clothes⟩ **2** *archaic* **:** to put or set forward or before someone **:** RECOMMEND **3 :** to present for action or consideration ⟨*prefer* charges against a person⟩ — **pre·fer·rer** *n*

pref·er·a·ble \'pref-(ə-)rə-bəl, 'pref-ər-bəl\ *adj* **:** worthy to be preferred **:** more desirable — **pref·er·a·bil·i·ty** \ˌpref-(ə-)rə-'bil-ət-ē\ *n* — **pref·er·a·ble·ness** \'pref-(ə-)rə-bəl-nəs, -ər-bəl-nəs\ *n* — **pref·er·a·bly** \-blē\ *adv*

pref·er·ence \'pref-ərn(t)s, 'pref-(ə-)rən(t)s\ *n* **1 a :** the act of preferring **:** the state of being preferred **2 :** the power or opportunity of choosing ⟨gave him his *preference*⟩ **2 :** one that is preferred **:** FAVORITE, CHOICE **3 :** the act, fact, or principle of giving advantages to some over others ⟨show *preference*⟩

pref·er·en·tial \ˌpref-ə-'ren-chəl\ *adj* **1 :** of or relating to preference **2 :** showing preference ⟨*preferential* treatment⟩ **3 :** creating or employing preference ⟨a *preferential* tariff⟩ **4 :** permitting the showing of preference or order of choice (as of candidates in an election) ⟨a *preferential* ballot⟩ **5 :** giving preference in hiring to union members ⟨*preferential* shop⟩ — **pref·er·en·tial·ly** \-'rench-(ə-)lē\ *adv*

pre·fer·ment \pri-'fər-mənt\ *n* **1 a :** advancement or promotion in dignity, office, or station **b :** a position or office of honor or profit **2 :** the act of bringing forward (as charges)

preferred stock *n* **:** stock guaranteed priority by a corporation's charter over common stock in the payment of dividends and usu. in the distribution of assets

pre·fig·ure \(')prē-'fig-yər, *esp Brit* -'fig-ər\ *vt* **1 :** to show, suggest, or announce by an antecedent type, image, or likeness ⟨other religions *prefigured* the Christian Easter⟩ **2 :** to picture or imagine beforehand **:** FORESEE ⟨*prefigure* the outcome of a ball game⟩ — **pre·fig·u·ra·tion** \(ˌ)prē-ˌfig-(y)ə-'rā-shən\ *n* — **pre·fig·u·ra·tive** \(')prē-'fig-(y)ə-rət-iv, -'fig-(y)ərt-iv\ *adj* — **pre·fig·u·ra·tive·ly** *adv* — **pre·fig·u·ra·tive·ness** — **pre·fig·ure·ment** \(')prē-'fig-yər-mənt, *esp Brit* -'fig-ər-\ *n*

¹**pre·fix** *vt* **1** \(')prē-'fiks\ *archaic* **:** to fix or appoint

beforehand **2** \'prē-,, prē-'\ : to place in front : add as a prefix ⟨*prefix* a syllable to a word⟩

²pre·fix \'prē-,fiks\ *n* [NL *praefixum,* fr. L, neut. of *praefixus,* pp. of *praefigere* to fasten before, fr. *prae-* pre- + *figere* to fasten] : a sound or sequence of sounds or in writing a letter or sequence of letters occurring as a bound form attached to the beginning of a word and serving to produce a derivative word — **pre·fix·al** \'prē-,fik-səl, prē-'\ *adj* — **pre·fix·al·ly** \-sə-lē\ *adv*

pre·flight \'prē-'flīt\ *adj* : preparing for or preliminary to airplane flight ⟨*preflight* training⟩

pre·form \'prē-'fȯrm\ *vt* : to form or shape beforehand

pre·for·ma·tion \,prē-fȯr-'mā-shən\ *n* **1** : previous formation **2** : a discredited theory holding that every germ cell contains the organism of its kind fully formed and that development consists merely in increase in size — **pre·for·ma·tion·ist** \-sh(ə-)nəst\ *n*

pre·fron·tal \(')prē-'frənt-ᵊl\ *adj* : anterior to or involving the anterior part of a frontal structure ⟨a *prefrontal* bone⟩

pre·gan·gli·on·ic \,prē-,gaŋ-glē-'än-ik\ *adj* : proximal to a ganglion; *also* : of, relating to, or being an axon passing from the central nervous system into an autonomic ganglion

preg·na·ble \'preg-nə-bəl\ *adj* [alter. of ME *prenable,* fr. MF, fr. *prendre* to take, fr. L *prehendere*] : capable of being taken or captured : VULNERABLE ⟨a *pregnable* fort⟩ — **preg·na·bil·i·ty** \,preg-nə-'bil-ət-ē\ *n*

preg·nan·cy \'preg-nən-sē\ *n, pl* **-cies** : the condition or quality of being pregnant : GESTATION

preg·nant \'preg-nənt\ *adj* [L *praegnant-, praegnans,* alter. of *praegnas,* fr. *prae-* pre- + *gnat-, gignere* to produce] **1 a** : containing unborn young within the uterus : GRAVID **b** : capable of producing **2** : abounding in fancy, wit, or resourcefulness : INVENTIVE ⟨a *pregnant* mind⟩ **3** : rich in significance or implication : MEANINGFUL ⟨*pregnant* ideas⟩ **4** : containing the germ or shape of future events ⟨*pregnant* years⟩ **5** : exhibiting fertility : TEEMING ⟨nature was *pregnant* with life⟩ — **preg·nant·ly** *adv*

pre·heat \(')prē-'hēt\ *vt* : to heat beforehand; *esp* : to heat (an oven) to a designated temperature before placing food therein

pre·hen·sile \prē-'hen(t)-səl\ *adj* [L *prehens-, prehendere* to grasp] : adapted for grasping esp. by wrapping around ⟨a *prehensile* tail⟩

pre·hen·sion \-'hen-chən\ *n* : the act of taking hold, seizing, or grasping

pre·his·tor·ic \,prē-(h)is-'tȯr-ik, -'tär-\ *adj* : of, relating to, or existing in times antedating written history ⟨*prehistoric* man⟩ — **pre·his·tor·i·cal** \-i-kəl\ *adj* — **pre·his·tor·i·cal·ly** \-i-k(ə-)lē\ *adv*

pre·his·to·ry \(')prē-'his-t(ə-)rē\ *n* **1** : the study of prehistoric man **2** : a history of the antecedents of an event or situation — **pre·his·to·ri·an** \,prē-(h)is-'tȯr-ē-ən, -'tȯr-\ *n*

pre·judge \(')prē-'jəj\ *vt* : to judge before hearing or before full and sufficient examination : pass judgment on beforehand — **pre·judg·ment** \-'jəj-mənt\ *n*

¹prej·u·dice \'prej-əd-əs\ *n* [L *praejudicium* previous judgment, damage, fr. *prae-* + *judicium* judgment] **1** : injury or damage due to a judgment or action of another in disregard of one's rights; *esp* : detriment to one's legal rights **2 a** (1) : preconceived judgment or opinion (2) : a favoring or dislike of something without just grounds or before sufficient knowledge **b** : an irrational attitude of hostility directed against an individual, a group, or a race

syn BIAS: PREJUDICE implies usu. but not always an unfavorable view or fixed dislike and suggests a feeling rooted in suspicion, fear, or intolerance; BIAS implies partiality or distortion of individual judgments owing to a consistent mental leaning in favor of or against persons or things of certain kinds or classes

²prejudice *vt* **1** : to injure or damage by some judgment or action esp. at law **2** : to cause to have prejudice : BIAS ⟨the incident *prejudiced* them against her⟩

prej·u·di·cial \,prej-ə-'dish-əl\ *adj* **1** : tending to injure or impair : DETRIMENTAL **2** : leading to premature judgment or unwarranted opinion — **prej·u·di·cial·ly** \-'dish-(ə-)lē\ *adv* — **prej·u·di·cial·ness** \-'dish-əl-nəs\ *n*

prej·u·di·cious \,prej-ə-'dish-əs\ *adj* : PREJUDICIAL — **prej·u·di·cious·ly** *adv*

prel·a·cy \'prel-ə-sē\ *n, pl* **-cies** **1** : the office or dignity of a prelate **2** : the whole body of prelates **3** : episcopal church government

prel·ate \'prel-ət\ *n* [ML *praelatus,* lit., one receiving preferment, fr. L *praelatus,* used as pp. of *praeferre* to prefer] : a high-ranking clergyman (as a bishop)

prelate nul·li·us \-nü-'lē-əs\ *n* [*nullius* fr. NL *nullius dioecesis* of no diocese] : a Roman Catholic prelate usu. a titular bishop with ordinary jurisdiction over a district independent of any diocese

prel·a·ture \'prel-ə-,chu̇r, -chər\ *n* **1** : PRELACY 1, 2 **2** : the jurisdiction of a prelate

pre·lim \'prē-,lim, pri-'\ *n or adj* : PRELIMINARY

¹pre·lim·i·nary \pri-'lim-ə-,ner-ē\ *n, pl* **-nar·ies** [L *prae-* pre- + *limin-, limen* threshold] : something that precedes or is introductory or preparatory: as **a** : a preliminary scholastic examination ⟨he passed the *preliminaries*⟩ **b** : a minor match preceding the main event

²preliminary *adj* : preceding the main discourse or business : INTRODUCTORY — **pre·lim·i·nar·i·ly** \-,lim-ə-'ner-ə-lē\ *adv*

¹prel·ude \'prel-,yüd, 'prā-,lüd\ *n* [ML *praeludium,* fr. L *praeludere* to play beforehand, fr. *prae-* + *ludere* to play] **1** : an introductory performance, action, or event preceding and preparing for the principal or a more important matter : INTRODUCTION, PREFACE ⟨the wind was a *prelude* to the storm⟩ **2 a** : a musical section or movement introducing the theme or chief subject (as of a fugue) or serving as an introduction to an opera or oratorio **b** : a short musical piece (as an organ solo) played at the beginning of a church service **c** : a separate concert piece usu. for piano or orchestra and based entirely on a short motive

²prelude *vb* **1** : to give, play, or serve as a prelude; *esp* : to play a musical introduction **2** : FORESHADOW — **prel·ud·er** *n*

pre·man \'prē-'man\ *n* : a hypothetical ancient primate immediately ancestral to man

pre·ma·ture \,prē-mə-'t(y)u̇(ə)r, -'chu̇(ə)r\ *adj* : happening, arriving, existing, or performed before the proper or usual time; *esp* : born after a gestation period of less than 37 weeks ⟨*premature* babies⟩ — **premature** *n* — **pre·ma·ture·ly** *adv* — **pre·ma·ture·ness** *n* — **pre·ma·tu·ri·ty** \-'t(y)u̇r-ət-ē, -'chu̇r-\ *n*

pre·med \'prē-'med\ *adj* : PREMEDICAL — **premed** *n*

pre·med·i·cal \(')prē-'med-i-kəl\ *adj* : preceding and preparing for the professional study of medicine

pre·med·i·tate \pri-'med-ə-,tāt, 'prē-\ *vt* : to think about and plan beforehand ⟨*premeditated* murder⟩ — **pre·med·i·tat·ed·ly** \-,tāt-əd-lē\ *adv* — **pre·med·i·ta·tion** \pri-,med-ə-'tā-shən, ,prē-\ *n*

¹pre·mier \pri-'m(y)i(ə)r; 'prē-mē-ər, 'prem-ē-\ *adj* [MF, fr. L *primarius* of the first rank, fr. *primus* first] **1** : first in position, rank, or importance : PRINCIPAL **2** : first in time : EARLIEST

²premier *n* : the chief minister of government : PRIME MINISTER — **pre·mier·ship** \-,ship\ *n*

¹pre·miere \pri-'mye(ə)r, -'mi(ə)r\ *n* [F *première,* fr. fem. of *premier* first] : a first performance or exhibition ⟨*premiere* of a play⟩

²premiere *vb* : to present or appear in a first public performance

³premiere *adj* : OUTSTANDING, CHIEF ⟨the nation's *premiere* author⟩

¹prem·ise \'prem-əs\ *n* [ML *praemissa,* fr. L, fem. of *praemissus,* pp. of *praemittere* to place ahead, fr. *prae-* pre- + *mittere* to send] **1** : a proposition assumed as a basis of argument or inference; *esp* : either of the first two propositions of a syllogism from which the conclusion is drawn **2** *pl* : matters previously stated **3** *pl* : a tract of land with the buildings thereon **b** : a building or part of a building usu. with its grounds or other appurtenances

²premise *vt* **1** : to set forth beforehand as introductory or as postulated : POSTULATE **2** : to offer as a premise in an argument

¹pre·mi·um \'prē-mē-əm\ *n* [L *praemium* booty, reward, recompense, fr. *prae-* pre- + *emere* to take, buy] **1 a** : a reward or recompense for a particular act **b** : a sum over and above a regular price or a face or par value **c** : something given free or at a reduced price with the purchase of a product or service **2** : the amount paid for a contract of insurance **3** : a high value or a value in excess of that normally or usu. expected ⟨put a *premium* on accuracy⟩

— **at a premium** : above par : unusually valuable esp. because of demand ⟨housing was *at a premium*⟩

²**premium** *adj* : of exceptional quality, value, or price

pre·mix \(')prē-'miks\ *vt* : to mix before use

pre·mo·lar \(')prē-'mō-lər\ *adj* : situated in front of or preceding the molar teeth; *also* : being or relating to those teeth of a mammal in front of the true molars and behind the canines when the latter are present — **premolar** *n*

pre·mo·ni·tion \,prē-mə-'nish-ən, ,prem-ə-\ *n* [L *praemonit-, praemonēre* to warn in advance, fr. *prae-* + *monēre* to warn] **1** : previous warning or notice : FOREWARNING **2** : anticipation of an event without conscious reason : PRESENTIMENT — **pre·mon·i·to·ry** \prē-'män-ə-,tōr-ē, -,tȯr-\ *adj*

Pre·mon·stra·ten·sian \,prē-,män(t)-strə-'ten-chən\ *n* : a member of an order of regular canons founded by St. Norbert at Prémontré near Laon, France, in 1119

pre·name \'prē-,nām\ *n* : FORENAME

pre·na·tal \(')prē-'nāt-ᵊl\ *adj* : occurring or existing before birth ⟨*prenatal* care⟩ — **pre·na·tal·ly** \-ᵊl-ē\ *adv*

pren·tice \'prent-əs\ *n* : APPRENTICE 1, LEARNER — **prentice** *adj*

pre·oc·cu·pied \prē-'äk-yə-,pīd\ *adj* **1** : lost in thought : ENGROSSED ⟨too much *preoccupied* with his own thoughts to notice⟩ **2** : already occupied

pre·oc·cu·py *vt* **-pied; -py·ing** **1** \prē-'äk-yə-,pī\ : to engage or engross the attention of beforehand or preferentially **2** \(')prē-\ : to take possession of or fill beforehand or before another — **pre·oc·cu·pa·tion** \(,)prē-,äk-yə-'pā-shən\ *n*

pre·op·er·a·tive \(')prē-'äp-(ə-)rət-iv, -'äp-ə-,rāt-\ *adj* : occurring during the period preceding a surgical operation — **pre·op·er·a·tive·ly** *adv*

pre·or·dain \,prē-ȯr-'dān\ *vt* : to decree in advance : FOREORDAIN — **pre·or·di·na·tion** \(,)prē-,ȯrd-ᵊn-'ā-shən\ *n*

¹**prep** \'prep\ *n* : PREPARATORY SCHOOL

²**prep** *vb* **prepped; prep·ping** **1** : to attend preparatory school **2** : to engage in preparatory study or training **3** : to get ready : PREPARE ⟨*prepped* the patient for the operation⟩

prep·a·ra·tion \,prep-ə-'rā-shən\ *n* **1** : the action or process of making something ready for use or service or of getting ready for some occasion, test, or duty **2** : a state of being prepared : READINESS **3** : a preparatory act or measure **4** : something that is prepared; *esp* : a medicinal material made ready for use

pre·par·a·to·ry \pri-'par-ə-,tōr-ē, -,tȯr-\ *adj* : preparing or serving to prepare for something : INTRODUCTORY, PRELIMINARY — **pre·par·a·to·ri·ly** \-,par-ə-'tōr-ə-lē, -'tȯr-\ *adv*

preparatory school *n* **1** : a usu. private school preparing students primarily for college **2** *Brit* : a private elementary school preparing students primarily for public schools

pre·pare \pri-'pa(ə)r, -'pe(ə)r\ *vb* [L *praeparare*, fr. *prae-* + *parare* to procure, prepare] **1** : to make or get ready ⟨*prepared* her for the shocking news⟩ ⟨*prepare* for a test⟩ **2** : to put together : COMPOUND ⟨*prepare* a vaccine⟩ ⟨*prepare* a prescription⟩ — **pre·par·er** *n*

pre·par·ed·ness \pri-'par-əd-nəs, -'per-; -'pa(ə)rd-nəs, -'pe(ə)rd-\ *n* : the quality or state of being prepared; *esp* : a state of adequate preparation for war

pre·pay \(')prē-'pā\ *vt* **pre·paid; pre·pay·ing** : to pay or pay the charge on in advance — **pre·pay·ment** \-'pā-mənt\ *n*

pre·pon·der·ance \pri-'pän-d(ə-)rən(t)s\ *n* **1** : a superiority in weight or in power, importance, or strength ⟨the *preponderance* of the evidence⟩ **2** : a superiority or excess in number or quantity ⟨the *preponderance* of lawyers in the legislature⟩

pre·pon·der·ant \pri-'pän-d(ə-)rənt\ *adj* **1** : outweighing others : PREDOMINANT **2** : having greater frequency or prevalence — **pre·pon·der·ant·ly** *adv*

pre·pon·der·ate \pri-'pän-də-,rāt\ *vi* [L *praeponderare*, lit., to outweigh, fr. *prae-* + *ponder-, pondus* weight] **1** : to exceed in weight, power, or importance : PREDOMINATE **2** : to exceed in numbers — **pre·pon·der·a·tion** \-,pän-də-'rā-shən\ *n*

prep·o·si·tion \,prep-ə-'zish-ən\ *n* [L *praeposit-, praeponere* to put in front, fr. *prae-* pre- + *ponere* to put] : a linguistic form that combines with a noun or pronoun to form a phrase that typically has an adverbial, adjectival, or substantival relation to some other word — **prep·o·si·tion·al** \-'zish-nəl, -ən-ᵊl\ *adj* — **prep·o·si·tion·al·ly** \-ē\ *adv*

pre·pos·sess \,prē-pə-'zes\ *vt* **1** : to cause to be preoccupied with an idea, belief, or attitude **2** : to influence beforehand; *esp* : to move to a favorable opinion beforehand

pre·pos·sess·ing *adj* : tending to create a favorable impression : ATTRACTIVE ⟨a *prepossessing* appearance⟩ — **pre·pos·sess·ing·ly** \-iŋ-lē\ *adv* — **pre·pos·sess·ing·ness** *n*

pre·pos·ses·sion \,prē-pə-'zesh-ən\ *n* **1** : an attitude, belief, or impression formed beforehand : PREJUDICE **2** : an exclusive concern with one idea or object : PREOCCUPATION

pre·pos·ter·ous \pri-'päs-t(ə-)rəs\ *adj* [L *praeposterus*, lit., with the hindside in front, fr. *prae-* pre- + *posterus* hinder, posterior] : contrary to nature, reason, or common sense : ABSURD — **pre·pos·ter·ous·ly** *adv* — **pre·pos·ter·ous·ness** *n*

pre·po·tent \(')prē-'pōt-ᵊnt\ *adj* **1** : PREEMINENT, SUPERIOR **2** : having an unusual ability to transmit characters to offspring ⟨a *prepotent* sire⟩ — **pre·po·ten·cy** \-ᵊn-sē\ *n*

pre·pu·ber·ty \(')prē-'pyü-bərt-ē\ *n* : the period immediately preceding puberty — **pre·pu·ber·tal** \-bərt-ᵊl\ *adj*

pre·puce \'prē-,pyüs\ *n* [MF, fr. L *praeputium*] : FORESKIN — **pre·pu·tial** \prē-'pyü-shəl\ *n*

pre·re·cord \,prē-ri-'kȯrd\ *vt* : to record (as a radio or television program) in advance of presentation or use

pre·req·ui·site \(')prē-'rek-wə-zət\ *n* : something that is required beforehand or is necessary as a preliminary to something else ⟨the course is a *prerequisite* for more advanced study⟩ — **prerequisite** *adj*

pre·rog·a·tive \pri-'räg-ət-iv\ *n* [L *praerogativus* voting first, fr. *praerogare* to ask for an opinion before another, fr. *prae-* pre- + *rogare* to ask] : a superior privilege or advantage; *esp* : a right attached to an office, rank, or status ⟨a royal *prerogative*⟩ ⟨a woman's *prerogative* to change her mind⟩

¹**pres·age** \'pres-ij\ *n* [L *praesagium*, fr. *praesagire* to forebode, fr. *prae-* pre- + *sagire* to perceive keenly] **1** : something that foreshadows or portends a future event : OMEN **2** : FOREBODING, PRESENTIMENT — **pre·sage·ful** \pri-'sāj-fəl\ *adj*

²**presage** \'pres-ij, pri-'sāj\ *vt* **1** : to give an omen or warning of : FORESHADOW, PORTEND **2** : FORETELL, PREDICT

pre·sanc·ti·fied \(')prē-'saŋ(k)-ti-,fīd\ *adj* : consecrated at a previous service — used of eucharistic elements

pres·by·o·pia \,prez-bē-'ō-pē-ə, ,pres-\ *n* [Gk *presbys* old man] : a visual condition of old age in which loss of elasticity of the lens of the eye causes defective accommodation and inability to focus sharply for near vision — **pres·by·op·ic** \-'äp-ik, -'ō-pik\ *adj or n*

pres·by·ter \'prez-bət-ər, 'pres-\ *n* [LL, elder, priest, fr. Gk *presbyteros*, fr. compar. of *presbys* old man] **1** : a member of the governing body of an early Christian church **2** : a Christian priest **3** : ELDER 4b — **pres·byt·er·ate** \prez-'bit-ə-rət, pres-\ *n*

Pres·by·te·ri·an \,prez-bə-'tir-ē-ən, ,pres-\ *adj* **1** *often not cap* : characterized by a system of representative governing councils of ministers and elders **2** : of, relating to, or constituting a Protestant Christian church that is presbyterian in government and traditionally Calvinistic in doctrine — **Presbyterian** *n* — **Pres·by·te·ri·an·ism** \-ē-ə-,niz-əm\ *n*

pres·by·tery \'prez-bə-,ter-ē, 'pres-\ *n, pl* **-ter·ies** **1** : the part of a church reserved for the officiating clergy **2** : a ruling body in presbyterian churches consisting of the ministers and representative elders from congregations within a district **3** : the territorial jurisdiction of a presbytery **4** : the house of a Roman Catholic parish priest

pre·school \'prē-'skül\ *adj* : of, relating to, or constituting the period in a child's life from infancy to the age of five or six that ordinarily precedes attendance at elementary school

pre·science \'prēsh-(ē-)ən(t)s, 'presh-\ *n* [LL *praescientia*, fr. L *praescient-, praesciens*, prp. of *praescire* to know beforehand, fr. *prae-* pre- + *scire* to know] **:** foreknowledge of events: **a :** omniscience with regard to the future **b :** FORESIGHT — **pre·scient** \-(ē-)ənt\ *adj* — **pre·scient·ly** *adv*

pre·scribe \pri-'skrīb\ *vb* [L *praescript-*, *praescribere* to write at the beginning, dictate, fr. *prae-* pre- + *scribere* to write] **1 a :** to lay down as a guide, direction, or rule of action : ORDAIN⟨*prescribed* a way of life⟩ **b :** to specify with authority ⟨*prescribed* the courses for freshmen⟩ **2 :** to order or direct the use of something as a remedy ⟨the doctor *prescribed* rest⟩ — **pre·scrib·er** *n*

pre·script \'prē-,skript\ *n* **:** something prescribed — **prescript** *adj*

pre·scrip·tion \pri-'skrip-shən\ *n* **1 a :** the establishment of a claim of title to something usu. by use and enjoyment for a fixed period **b :** the right or title acquired by possession **2 :** the action of laying down authoritative rules or directions **3 :** a written direction or order for the preparation and use of a medicine; *also* **:** a medicine prescribed — **pre·scrip·tive** \-'skrip-tiv\ *adj* — **pre·scrip·tive·ly** *adv*

pres·ence \'prez-ᵊn(t)s\ *n* **1 :** the fact or condition of being present ⟨no one noticed his *presence*⟩ **2 a :** the part of space within one's immediate vicinity ⟨felt awkward in her *presence*⟩ **b :** the neighborhood of one of superior esp. royal rank **3 :** one that is present ⟨influential as an impressive *presence* in the group⟩ **4 :** the bearing or air of a person; *esp* **:** stately or distinguished bearing **5 :** something held to be present ⟨an eerie sense of some *presence* guiding him⟩

presence chamber *n* **:** the room where a dignitary receives those entitled to come into his presence

presence of mind : self-control in an emergency such that one can say and do the right thing

¹pres·ent \'prez-ᵊnt\ *n* [OF, fr. *presenter* to present] **:** something presented : GIFT

²pre·sent \pri-'zent\ *vt* [OF *presenter*, fr. L *praesentare*, fr. *praesent-*, *praesens*, adj., present] **1 a :** to bring or introduce into the presence of someone **b :** to bring (as a play) before the public **c :** to introduce (one person) formally to another **2 :** to make a gift to **3 :** to give or bestow formally **4 :** to lay (a charge) against a person **5 :** to offer to view : DISPLAY, SHOW **6 :** to aim, point, or direct (as a weapon) so as to face something or in a particular direction **syn** see GIVE — **pre·sent·er** *n*

³pres·ent \'prez-ᵊnt\ *adj* [L *praesent-*, *praesens*, fr. prp. of *praeesse* to be before one, fr. *prae-* pre- + *esse* to be] **1 :** now existing or in progress **2 a :** being in view or at hand **b :** existing in something mentioned or under consideration **3 :** of, relating to, or constituting a verb tense that expresses present time or the time of speaking

⁴pres·ent \'prez-ᵊnt\ *n* **1** *pl* **:** the present words or statements; *esp* **:** the legal instrument in which these words are used ⟨know all men by these *presents*⟩ **2 a :** PRESENT TENSE **b :** a verb form in the present tense **3 :** the present time

pre·sent·a·ble \pri-'zent-ə-bəl\ *adj* **1 :** capable of being presented ⟨whipped the speech into *presentable* form⟩ **2 :** being in condition to be seen or inspected esp. by the critical ⟨made the room *presentable*⟩ — **pre·sent·a·bil·i·ty** \-,zent-ə-'bil-ət-ē\ *n* — **pre·sent·a·ble·ness** \-'zent-ə-bəl-nəs\ *n* — **pre·sent·a·bly** \-blē\ *adv*

present arms \pri-,zent-\ — used as a command in the manual of arms to bring the rifle to a position in which it is held perpendicularly in front of the body

pre·sen·ta·tion \,prē-,zen-'tā-shən, ,prez-ᵊn-\ *n* **1 :** the act of presenting **2 :** something presented: as **a :** something offered or given : GIFT **b :** something set forth for the attention of the mind — **pre·sen·ta·tion·al** \-shnəl, -shən-ᵊl\ *adj*

pres·ent-day \,prez-ᵊnt-,dā\ *adj* **:** now existing or occurring : CURRENT

pre·sen·ti·ment \pri-'zent-ə-mənt\ *n* [F *pressentiment*, fr. *pressentir* to have a presentiment, fr. L *praesentire*, fr. *prae-* pre- + *sentire* to feel] **:** a feeling that something will or is about to happen : PREMONITION

pres·ent·ly \'prez-ᵊnt-lē\ *adv* **1** *archaic* **:** at once **2 :** before long : SOON ⟨*presently* they arrived⟩ **3 :** at the present time : NOW ⟨*presently* we have none⟩

pre·sent·ment \pri-'zent-mənt\ *n* **1 :** the act of presenting; *esp* **:** the act of offering a draft or a promissory note at the proper time and place to be paid by another

2 a : the act of presenting to view or consciousness **b :** something set forth, presented, or exhibited

present participle *n* **:** a participle that expresses present action in relation to the time expressed by the finite verb in its clause and that in English is formed with the suffix *-ing* and is used in the formation of the progressive tenses

present perfect *adj* **:** of, relating to, or constituting a verb tense formed in English with *have* and expressing action or state completed at the time of speaking — **present perfect** *n*

present tense *n* **:** the tense of a verb that expresses action or state in the present time and is used of what occurs or is true at the time of speaking and of what is habitual or characteristic or is always or necessarily true and that is sometimes used to refer to action in the past (as in the historical present)

pres·er·va·tion \,prez-ər-'vā-shən\ *n* **:** the act of preserving **:** the state of being preserved

¹pre·ser·va·tive \pri-'zər-vət-iv\ *adj* **:** having the power of preserving

²preservative *n* **:** something that preserves; *esp* **:** an additive used to protect against decay, discoloration, or spoilage

¹pre·serve \pri-'zərv\ *vt* [ML *praeservare*, fr. L *prae-* pre- + *servare* to keep, guard] **1 :** to keep safe from harm or destruction : PROTECT ⟨*preserve* the republic⟩ **2 a :** to keep alive, intact, or free from decay or decomposition ⟨*preserve* laboratory specimens⟩ **b :** to keep up : MAINTAIN, RETAIN **3 :** to prepare (as by canning or pickling) for future use ⟨*preserve* beets⟩ — **pre·serv·a·ble** \-'zər-və-bəl\ *adj* — **pre·serv·er** *n*

²preserve *n* **1 :** fruit canned or made into jams or jellies or cooked whole or in large pieces with sugar so as to keep its shape — often used in pl. ⟨strawberry *preserves*⟩ **2 :** an area restricted for the protection and preservation of natural resources (as animals and trees); *esp* **:** one used primarily for regulated hunting or fishing **3 :** something regarded as reserved for certain persons

pre·set \('prē-'set\ *vt* **:** to set beforehand

pre·shrunk \'prē-'shrəŋk\ *adj* **:** of, relating to, or constituting a fabric subjected to a shrinking process during manufacture usu. to reduce later shrinking

pre·side \pri-'zīd\ *vi* [L *praesidēre*, lit., to sit at the head of, fr. *prae-* pre- + *sedēre* to sit] **1 a :** to occupy the place of authority **:** act as chairman ⟨the senior committee member *presides*⟩ **b :** to occupy a position similar to that of a president or chairman ⟨*presided* over the ceremonies⟩ **2 :** to exercise guidance or control ⟨*presided* over the destinies of the empire⟩ **3 :** to occupy a position of featured instrumental performer ⟨*presided* at the organ⟩ — **pre·sid·er** *n*

pres·i·den·cy \'prez-əd-ən-sē, 'prez-dən-; 'prez-ə-,den(t)-sē\ *n, pl* **-cies** **1 a :** the office or term of a president **b :** the jurisdiction or function of a president **2 :** one of three major divisions of British India **3 :** an executive council in the Mormon Church

pres·i·dent \'prez-əd-ənt, 'prez-dənt, 'prez-ə-,dent\ *n* **1 :** one who presides over a meeting or assembly **2 :** an appointed governor of a subordinate political unit **3 :** the chief officer of a corporation, institution, or organization **4 :** the presiding officer of a governmental body **5 a :** an elected official serving as both chief of state and chief political executive in a republic **b :** an elected official having the position of chief of state but usu. only minimal political powers in a republic having a parliamentary government — **pres·i·den·tial** \,prez-ə-'den-chəl\ *adj*

pre·si·dio \pri-'sēd-ē-,ō, -'sid-\ *n, pl* **-di·os** [Sp, fr. L *praesidium*] **:** a garrisoned place; *esp* **:** a military post or fortified settlement in areas currently or orig. under Spanish control

pre·sid·i·um \pri-'sid-ē-əm, -'zid-\ *n, pl* **-ia** \-ē-ə\ *or* **-i·ums :** a permanent executive committee selected in Communist countries to act for a larger body

¹press \'pres\ *n* [OF *presse*, fr. *presser* to press] **1 :** a crowded condition : CROWD, THRONG **2 :** an apparatus or machine for exerting pressure (as for shaping material, extracting liquid, drilling, or preventing something from warping) **3 :** CLOSET **4 :** an act of pressing

press 2

or pushing : PRESSURE **5** : the properly smoothed and creased condition of a freshly pressed garment **6 a** : PRINTING PRESS **b** : the act or the process of printing **c** : a printing or publishing establishment **7 a** : the gathering and publishing of news : JOURNALISM **b** : newspapers, periodicals, and often radio and television news broadcasting **c** : comment or notice in newspapers and periodicals

²**press** *vb* [MF *presser*, fr. L *pressare*, freq. of *premere* to press] **1** : to act upon through steady pushing or thrusting force exerted in contact : SQUEEZE **2 a** : ASSAIL **b** : OPPRESS **3 a** : to squeeze so as to force out the juice or contents of ⟨*press* oranges⟩ **b** : to squeeze out ⟨*press* juice from grapes⟩ **4 a** : to flatten out or smooth by bearing down upon; *esp* : to smooth by ironing ⟨*press* a tie⟩ **b** : to squeeze with an apparatus into a desired shape **5** : to urge strongly or forcefully : CONSTRAIN ⟨*pressed* him to attend⟩ **6 a** : to present earnestly or insistently : STRESS ⟨*presses* his claim⟩ **b** : to follow through (a course of action) **7** : to clasp in affection or courtesy : EMBRACE **8 a** : to crowd closely : MASS ⟨reporters *pressed* around the celebrity⟩ **b** : to force or push one's way ⟨*presses* forward through the throng⟩ **9** : to seek urgently : CONTEND ⟨*pressed* for higher salaries⟩ — **press·er** *n*

³**press** *vt* [alter. of obs. *prest* to enlist by giving pay in advance] : to force into service esp. in the army or navy : IMPRESS

press agent *n* : an agent employed to establish and maintain good public relations through publicity

press box *n* : a space reserved for reporters (as at a baseball or football game)

press conference *n* : an interview given by a public figure to newsmen by appointment

press-gang \'pres-,gaŋ\ *n* : a detachment of men empowered to force men into military or naval service

press·ing *adj* **1** : urgently important : CRITICAL ⟨the *pressing* national interest⟩ **2** : EARNEST, WARM ⟨a *pressing* invitation⟩ — **press·ing·ly** \-iŋ-lē\ *adv*

press·man \'pres-mən, -,man\ *n* **1** : an operator of a press; *esp* : the operator of a printing press **2** *Brit* : NEWSPAPERMAN

pres·sor \'pres-,òr, -ər\ *adj* [LL, one that presses, fr. L *press-, premere* to press] : raising or tending to raise blood pressure

press release *n* : material given in advance to a newspaper for publication at a future date

press·room \'pres-,rüm, -,rùm\ *n* : a room in a printing plant containing the printing presses

press·run \-,rən\ *n* : a continuous operation of a printing press producing a specified number of copies; *also* : the number of copies printed

¹**pres·sure** \'presh-ər\ *n* **1 a** : the action of pressing ⟨done by slow steady *pressure*⟩ **b** : the condition of being pressed ⟨kept under *pressure*⟩ **2 a** : a painful feeling of weight or burden : OPPRESSION, DISTRESS **b** : a burdensome or restricting force or influence ⟨the *pressure* of taxes⟩⟨the constant *pressures* of modern life⟩ **3 a** : the action of a force against an opposing force : the force exerted over a surface divided by its area **c** : ELECTROMOTIVE FORCE **4** : the stress of matters demanding attention : URGENCY **5** : atmospheric pressure

²**pressure** *vt* **pres·sured; pres·sur·ing** \'presh-(ə-)riŋ\ **1** : to apply pressure to : CONSTRAIN **2** : PRESSURIZE **3** : to cook in a pressure cooker

pressure cooker *n* : a utensil for quick cooking or preserving of foods by means of steam under pressure — **pressure-cook** \,presh-ər-'kùk\ *vb*

pressure group *n* : a group that seeks to influence governmental policy but not to elect candidates to office

pressure point *n* : a point where a blood vessel runs near a bone and can be compressed (as to check bleeding) by pressure against the bone

pressure suit *n* : an inflatable suit for protection (as of an aviator) against low pressure

pres·sur·ize \'presh-ə-,rīz\ *vt* **1** : to maintain near-normal atmospheric pressure in (as an airplane cabin) during high-level flight **2** : to apply pressure to **3** : to design to withstand pressure — **pres·sur·i·za·tion** \,presh-ə-rə-'zā-shən\ *n* — **pres·sur·iz·er** *n*

Pres·ter John \,pres-tər-'jän\ *n* : a legendary medieval Christian priest and king

pre·ster·num \(')prē-'stər-nəm\ *n* : the anterior segment of the sternum of a mammal : MANUBRIUM

pres·ti·dig·i·ta·tion \,pres-tə-,dij-ə-'tā-shən\ *n* [F, fr. *preste* nimble, quick (fr. It *presto*) + L *digitus* finger] : SLEIGHT OF HAND, LEGERDEMAIN — **pres·ti·dig·i·ta·tor** \-'dij-ə-,tāt-ər\ *n*

pres·tige \pre-'stēzh, -'stēj\ *n* [F, fr. MF, illusion, fr. L *praestigia*, irreg. fr. *praestringere* to blindfold, fr. *prae-* pre- + *stringere* to bind tight] **1** : importance or estimation in the eyes of people : high standing : REPUTE **2** : commanding position in men's minds : ASCENDANCY **syn** see INFLUENCE — **pres·ti·gious** \-'stij-əs\ *adj* — **pres·ti·gious·ly** *adv* — **pres·ti·gious·ness** *n*

pres·to \'pres-tō\ *adv* (*or adj*) [It, quick, quickly, fr. L *praesto*, adv., on hand] **1** : at once : QUICKLY ⟨a wave of the hand and, *presto*, it's gone⟩ **2** : at a rapid tempo — used as a direction in music

pre·sume \pri-'züm\ *vb* [LL *praesumpt-, praesumere*, fr. L, to take in advance, fr. *prae-* pre- + *sumere* to take] **1** : to undertake without leave or clear justification : DARE, VENTURE ⟨*presume* to question the authority of a superior⟩ **2** : to suppose to be true without proof ⟨our law *presumes* all persons charged with crime to be innocent until they are proved guilty⟩ **3** : to act or behave boldly without reason for doing so; *esp* : to take liberties ⟨*presume* upon a brief acquaintance to ask favors⟩ **syn** see ASSUME — **pre·sum·a·ble** \-'zü-mə-bəl\ *adj* — **pre·sum·a·bly** \-blē\ *adv* — **pre·sum·er** *n*

pre·sum·ing *adj* : PRESUMPTUOUS — **pre·sum·ing·ly** \-'zü-miŋ-lē\ *adv*

pre·sump·tion \pri-'zəm(p)-shən\ *n* **1** : presumptuous attitude or conduct : AUDACITY **2 a** : strong grounds for believing something to be so in spite of lack of proof **b** : a conclusion reached on strong grounds of belief : something believed to be so but not proved

pre·sump·tive \-'zəm(p)-tiv\ *adj* **1** : giving grounds for reasonable opinion or belief ⟨*presumptive* evidence⟩ **2** : based on probability or presumption ⟨heir *presumptive*⟩ — **pre·sump·tive·ly** *adv*

pre·sump·tu·ous \pri-'zəm(p)-ch(ə-w)əs\ *adj* : overstepping due bounds : taking liberties : OVERWEENING — **pre·sump·tu·ous·ly** *adv* — **pre·sump·tu·ous·ness** *n*

pre·sup·pose \,prē-sə-'pōz\ *vt* **1** : to suppose beforehand **2** : take for granted ⟨a book that *presupposes* wide knowledge in its readers⟩ — **pre·sup·po·si·tion** \(,)prē-,səp-ə-'zish-ən\ *n*

pre·tend \pri-'tend\ *vb* [L *praetendere* to allege as an excuse, fr. *prae-* pre- + *tendere* to stretch] **1** : to hold out the appearance of being, possessing, or performing : PROFESS **2 a** : to make believe : feign an action, part, or role in a play **b** : to hold out, represent, or assert falsely **3** : to put in a claim (as to a throne or title)

pre·tend·ed *adj* : professed or avowed but not genuine — **pre·tend·ed·ly** *adv*

pre·tend·er \pri-'ten-dər\ *n* : one that pretends; *esp* : a claimant to a throne who has no just title

pre·tense *or* **pre·tence** \'prē-,ten(t)s, pri-'\ *n* [LL *praetensus*, pp. of L *praetendere* to allege as an excuse] **1** : a claim made or implied and usu. not supported by fact **2 a** : mere ostentation : PRETENTIOUSNESS **b** : a pretentious act or assertion **3** : an attempt to attain a condition or quality **4** : professed rather than real intention or purpose : PRETEXT **5** : MAKE-BELIEVE, FICTION **6** : false show : SIMULATION ⟨made a *pretense* of searching his pockets for a dime to lend⟩

pre·ten·sion \pri-'ten-chən\ *n* **1** : PRETEXT **2** : PRETENSE 1; *also* : an effort to establish a claim made or implied **3** : a claim for or right to attention or honor because of merit **4** : PRETENTIOUSNESS, VANITY — **pre·ten·sion·less** \-ləs\ *adj*

pre·ten·tious \-chəs\ *adj* [L *praetentus*, pp. of *praetendere* to allege as an excuse] **1** : making or having claims esp. as to excellence or worth : SHOWY, OSTENTATIOUS ⟨living in a *pretentious* style⟩ **2** : making demands on one's skill, ability, or means : AMBITIOUS ⟨*pretentious* plans⟩ — **pre·ten·tious·ly** *adv* — **pre·ten·tious·ness** *n*

pret·er·it *or* **pret·er·ite** \'pret-ə-rət\ *adj* [L *praeteritus*, fr. pp. of *praeterire* to pass, fr. *praeter* beyond, past + *ire* to go] : of, relating to, or constituting a verb tense that indicates action in the past without reference to duration, continuance, or repetition — **preterit** *n*

---

j joke; ŋ sing; ō flow; ò flaw; òi coin; th thin; th̲ this; ü loot; ù foot; y yet; yü few; yù furious; zh vision

pre·ter·mi·nal \(')prē-'tər-mən-°l\ *adj* : occurring before death

pre·ter·mit \,prēt-ər-'mit\ *vt* -**mit·ted**; -**mit·ting** [L *praeter* by, past + *mittere* to let go, send] **1** : to let pass without mention or notice : OMIT **2** : to leave undone : NEGLECT **3** : to break off : SUSPEND — **pre·ter·mis·sion** \-'mish-ən\ *n*

pre·ter·nat·u·ral \,prēt-ər-'nach-(ə-)rəl\ *adj* [L *praeter naturam* beyond nature] **1** : not conforming to what is natural or regular in nature : ABNORMAL **2** : inexplicable by ordinary means — **pre·ter·nat·u·ral·ly** \-'nach-(ə-)rə-lē, -'nach-ər-lē\ *adv* — **pre·ter·nat·u·ral·ness** \-'nach-(ə-)rəl-nəs\ *n*

pre·test \'prē-,test, (')prē-'\ *n* : a preliminary test serving for exploration rather than evaluation — **pretest** *vt*

pre·text \'prē-,tekst\ *n* [L *praetextus*, fr. *praetext-, praetexere* to assign as a pretext, lit., to weave in front, fr. *prae-* pre- + *texere* to weave] : something (as a claimed intent or motive) put forward in order to conceal a real intent, motive, or state of affairs

pret·ti·fy \'prit-i-,fī, 'purt-\ *vt* -**fied**; -**fy·ing** : to make pretty — **pret·ti·fi·ca·tion** \,prit-i-fə-'kā-shən, ,purt-\ *n*

¹pret·ty \'prit-ē, 'purt-\ *adj* **pret·ti·er**; -**est** [OE *prættig* tricky, fr. *prætt* trick] **1 a** : ARTFUL, CLEVER **b** : PAT, APT **2** : pleasing by delicacy or grace esp. of appearance or sound : conventionally attractive but without elements of grandeur, stateliness, and excellence usu. associated with true beauty ⟨a *pretty* face⟩ ⟨light *pretty* tunes⟩ ⟨a *pretty* manner⟩ **3** : FINE, GOOD — often used ironically **4** : moderately large : CONSIDERABLE — **pret·ti·ly** \'prit-°l-ē, 'purt-\ *adv* — **pret·ti·ness** \'prit-ē-nəs, 'purt-\ *n* — **pret·ty·ish** \-ē-ish\ *adj*

²pret·ty \,purt-ē, pərt-ē (*unstressed* pərt-), ,prit-ē\ *adv* : in some degree : MODERATELY

³pretty *like* ¹\ *n, pl* **pretties 1** : a pretty person or thing **2** *pl* : dainty clothes

pre·tu·ber·cu·lous \,prē-t(y)ü-'bər-kyə-ləs\ *or* **pre·tu·ber·cu·lar** \-lər\ *adj* **1** : preceding the development of identifiable tuberculosis **2** : likely to develop tuberculosis

pret·zel \'pret-səl\ *n* [G *brezel*] : a brittle, glazed and salted, and usu. twisted cracker

pre·vail \pri-'vāl\ *vi* [L *praevalēre*, fr. *prae-* pre- + *valēre* to be strong] **1** : to gain ascendancy through strength or superiority : TRIUMPH **2** : to be or become effective or effectual **3** : to urge successfully ⟨was *prevailed* upon to sing⟩ **4** : to be frequent : PREDOMINATE ⟨the west winds that *prevail* in the mountains⟩ **5** : to be or continue in use or fashion : PERSIST ⟨studying the customs that *prevail* among mountain people⟩

pre·vail·ing *adj* **1** : having superior force or influence **2 a** : most frequent ⟨*prevailing* winds⟩ **b** : generally current : COMMON — **pre·vail·ing·ly** \-'vā-liŋ-lē\ *adv*

syn PREVAILING, PREVALENT, CURRENT mean generally circulated, accepted, or used in a certain time or place. PREVAILING applies esp. to something that is predominant ⟨*prevailing* opinion⟩ PREVALENT implies widespread frequency ⟨*prevalent* custom⟩ ⟨a disease that is *prevalent* in many countries⟩ CURRENT applies to things subject to change and implies prevalence at the present time ⟨*current* fashions⟩ ⟨*current* scientific trends⟩

prev·a·lent \'prev-(ə-)lənt\ *adj* **1** : being in ascendancy : DOMINANT **2** : generally or widely accepted, practiced, or favored : WIDESPREAD **syn** see PREVAILING — **prev·a·lence** \-(ə-)lən(t)s\ *n* — **prev·a·lent·ly** *adv*

pre·var·i·cate \pri-'var-ə-,kāt\ *vi* [L *praevaricari*, lit., to walk crookedly, fr. *prae-* + *varicus* having the feet spread apart, fr. *varus* bent] : to deviate from the truth : EQUIVOCATE — **pre·var·i·ca·tion** \-,var-ə-'kā-shən\ *n* — **pre·var·i·ca·tor** \-'var-ə-,kāt-ər\ *n*

pre·vent \pri-'vent\ *vt* [L *praevent-, praevenire* to come before, anticipate, forestall, fr. *prae-* pre- + *venire* to come] : to keep from happening, acting, or succeeding : HINDER, STOP ⟨*prevent* accidents⟩ ⟨rain *prevented* the plane from taking off⟩ — **pre·vent·a·ble** *also* **pre·vent·i·ble** \-ə-bəl\ *adj* — **pre·vent·er** *n*

syn PREVENT, AVERT, FORESTALL mean to stop something from coming or occurring. PREVENT implies placing an insurmountable obstacle or impediment ⟨took measures to *prevent* an epidemic⟩ AVERT implies taking immediate or effective measures to force back, avoid, or counteract a threatening evil ⟨efforts to *avert* a revolution⟩ FORESTALL

implies forehanded action to stop or interrupt something in its course ⟨radar helped *forestall* surprise attacks⟩

pre·ven·ta·tive \-'vent-ət-iv\ *adj or n* : PREVENTIVE

pre·ven·tion \pri-'ven-chən\ *n* : the act of preventing or hindering

¹pre·ven·tive \-'vent-iv\ *n* : something that prevents; *esp* : something used to prevent disease

²preventive *adj* : devoted to, concerned with, or undertaken for prevention — **pre·ven·tive·ly** *adv* — **pre·ven·tive·ness** *n*

¹pre·view \'prē-,vyü\ *vt* : to view or to show in advance

²preview *n* : an advance showing or viewing ⟨invited to a *preview* of the art exhibition⟩: as **a** *also* **pre·vue** \-,vyü\ : a showing of snatches from a motion picture advertised for appearance in the near future **b** : a statement giving advance information **c** : a preliminary survey

pre·vi·ous \'prē-vē-əs\ *adj* [L *praevius* leading the way, fr. *prae* pre- + *via* way] **1** : going before in time or order : PRECEDING ⟨the *previous* lesson⟩ **2** : acting too soon : PREMATURE ⟨was a bit *previous* with his answer⟩ — **pre·vi·ous·ly** *adv* — **pre·vi·ous·ness** *n*

previous question *n* : a parliamentary motion that the pending question be put to an immediate vote without further debate or amendment

previous to *prep* : prior to : BEFORE

¹pre·vi·sion \prē-'vizh-ən\ *n* **1** : FORESIGHT, PRESCIENCE **2** : FORECAST, PREDICTION — **pre·vi·sion·al** \-'vizh-nəl, -ən-°l\ *adj* — **pre·vi·sion·ary** \-'vizh-ə-,ner-ē\ *adj*

²prevision *vt* : FORESEE

pre·vo·cal·ic \,prē-vō-'kal-ik\ *adj* : immediately preceding a vowel

pre·war \'prē-'wò(ə)r\ *adj* : occurring or existing before a war

¹prey \'prā\ *n* [OF *preie* booty, prey, fr. L *praeda*] **1** : an animal taken by a predator as food **2** : a person that is helpless or unable to resist attack : VICTIM **3** : the act or habit of preying

²prey *vi* **1** : to raid for booty **2** : to seize and devour something as prey **3** : to have an injurious, destructive, or wasting effect ⟨fears that *prey* on the mind⟩ — **prey·er** *n*

Pri·am \'prī-əm, -,am\ *n* : the father of Hector and Paris and king of Troy during the Trojan War

¹price \'prīs\ *n* [OF *pris*, fr. L *pretium* price, money] **1 a** : the quantity of one thing that is exchanged or demanded in barter or sale for another **b** : the amount of money given or demanded for a specified thing **2** : the terms for the sake of which something is done or undertaken: as **a** : an amount sufficient to bribe one **b** : a reward for the apprehension or death of a person **3** : the cost at which something is obtainable **syn** see WORTH

²price *vt* **1** : to set a price on **2** : to ask the price of **3** : to drive by raising prices excessively ⟨*priced* themselves out of the market⟩ — **pric·er** *n*

price–cut·ter \'prīs-,kət-ər\ *n* : one that reduces prices esp. to a level designed to cripple competition

price·less \'prīs-ləs\ *adj* **1** : having a value beyond any price : INVALUABLE **2** : surprisingly amusing, odd, or absurd

price support *n* : artificial maintenance of prices of a commodity at a level usu. fixed through government action

price tag *n* **1** : a tag on merchandise showing the price at which it is offered for sale **2** : PRICE, COST

price war *n* : a period of commercial competition in which prices are repeatedly cut by the competitors

¹prick \'prik\ *n* [OE *prica*] **1** : a mark or shallow hole made by a pointed instrument **2** : a pointed instrument or part **3** : an instance of pricking : the sensation of being pricked

²prick *vb* **1 a** : to pierce slightly with a sharp point **b** : to have or cause a pricking sensation **2** : to cause to feel anguish, grief, or remorse ⟨his conscience *pricked* him⟩ **3** : to urge on a horse with spurs **4** : to mark or outline with or as if with pricks ⟨*prick* a design on paper⟩ **5** : to direct forward or upward : make or become erect ⟨the dog's ears *pricked* toward the sound⟩ — **prick up one's ears** : to listen intently

prick·er \'prik-ər\ *n* **1** : one that pricks **2** : BRIAR, PRICKLE, THORN

¹prick·le \'prik-əl\ *n* **1** : a fine sharp projection; *esp* : a sharp pointed process of the epidermis or bark of a plant **2** : a prickling sensation

²**prickle** *vb* **prickled; prick·ling** \'prik-(ə-)liŋ\ **1** : to prick lightly **2** : TINGLE

prick·ly \'prik-lē\ *adj* **prick·li·er; -est 1** : full of or covered with prickles ⟨*prickly* plants⟩ **2** : PRICKING, STINGING ⟨a *prickly* sensation⟩ — **prick·li·ness** *n*

prickly heat *n* : an inflammation around the sweat ducts with pimples, itching, and tingling

prickly pear *n* **1** : any of numerous flat-jointed often prickly cacti **2** : the pear-shaped edible pulpy fruit of a prickly pear

¹**pride** \'prīd\ *n* [OE *prȳde*, fr. *prūd* proud] **1** : the quality or state of being proud: as **a** : excessive self-esteem : CONCEIT **b** : a reasonable or justifiable self-respect **c** : delight or elation arising from some act or possession **2** : proud or disdainful behavior or treatment : DISDAIN **3 a** : the best part or condition : PRIME **b** : something that is or is fit to be a source of pride ⟨this pup is the *pride* of the litter⟩⟨his car is his chief *pride*⟩ **4** : a company of lions

prickly pear

²**pride** *vt* : to indulge in pride : PLUME ⟨*pride* oneself on one's skill⟩

pride·ful \'prīd-fəl\ *adj* : full of pride: as **a** : HAUGHTY **b** : ELATED — **pride·ful·ly** \-fə-lē\ *adv* — **pride·ful·ness** *n*

prie-dieu \prēd-'yə(r)\ *n, pl* **prie-dieux** \-'yə(r)(z)\ [F, fr. *prier* to pray + *Dieu* God] : a small kneeling bench designed for use by a person at prayer and fitted with a raised shelf on which the elbows or a book may be rested

priest \'prēst\ *n* [OE *prēost*, modif. of LL *presbyter* elder, priest, fr. Gk *presbyteros*, fr. compar. of *presbys* old man] : a person who has the authority to conduct religious rites; *esp* : a clergyman ranking below a bishop and above a deacon — **priest·ess** \'prē-stəs\ *n*

priest·hood \'prēst-,hud, 'prē-,stud\ *n* **1** : the office, dignity, or status of a priest **2** : the whole group of priests

priest·ly \'prēst-lē\ *adj* **priest·li·er; -est 1** : of or relating to a priest or the priesthood **2** : characteristic of or befitting a priest — **priest·li·ness** *n*

prig \'prig\ *n* : a person who offends or irritates others by a too careful or rigid observance of niceties and proprieties (as of speech or manners) — **prig·gery** \'prig-ə-rē\ *n* — **prig·gish** \'prig-ish\ *adj* — **prig·gish·ly** *adv* — **prig·gish·ness** *n*

prim \'prim\ *adj* **prim·mer; -mest** : very or excessively formal and precise (as in conduct or dress) ⟨a *prim* old lady⟩ ⟨*prim* remarks⟩ — **prim·ly** *adv* — **prim·ness** *n*

pri·ma·cy \'prī-mə-sē\ *n, pl* **-cies 1** : the condition of being first (as in time, place, or rank) **2** : the office, status, or dignity of a bishop of the highest rank

pri·ma don·na \,prim-ə-'dän-ə, ,prē-mə-\ *n, pl* **prima donnas** [It, lit., first lady] **1** : a principal female singer (as in an opera) **2** : an extremely sensitive, vain, or undisciplined person

¹**pri·ma fa·cie** \,prī-mə-'fā-shə, -s(h)ē\ *adv* [L] : at first view : on the first appearance

²**prima facie** *adj* **1** : APPARENT, EVIDENT ⟨a *prima facie* responsibility⟩ **2** : legally sufficient to establish a fact or a case unless disproved

¹**pri·mal** \'prī-məl\ *adj* **1** : ORIGINAL, PRIMITIVE **2** : first in importance : CHIEF

pri·mar·i·ly \prī-'mer-ə-lē\ *adv* **1** : FUNDAMENTALLY **2** : in the first place : ORIGINALLY

¹**pri·mary** \'prī-,mer-ē, 'prīm-(ə-)rē\ *adj* [L *primus* first] **1 a** : first in order of time or development : INITIAL, PRIMITIVE ⟨a *primary* lesion of disease⟩ ⟨the *primary* stages of a process⟩ **b** : not derived from or dependent on something else ⟨a *primary* source of information⟩ **c** : coming before and usu. preparatory for something else ⟨*primary* school⟩ **2 a** : of first rank, importance, or value : CHIEF ⟨the *primary* elective officer is the president⟩ **b** : BASIC, FUNDAMENTAL ⟨man's *primary* duty⟩ **c** : of, relating to, or constituting the strongest of the three or four degrees of stress ⟨the first syllable of *basketball* carries *primary* stress⟩ **d** : not derivable from other colors ⟨*primary* colors⟩ **e** : of, relating to, or being one of the principal quills of a bird's wing borne on the outer joint **3** : expressive of present or future time ⟨*primary* tense⟩ **4** : of, relating to, or being the inducing current or its circuit in an induction coil or transformer

²**primary** *n, pl* **-mar·ies 1** : something that is primary: as **a** : a planet as distinguished from its satellites **b** : a primary quill or feather — see BIRD illustration **c** : any of a set of colors (as red, yellow, or blue) from which all other colors may be derived — called also *primary color* **2** : an election in which voters select party candidates for political office, choose party officials, or select delegates for a party convention **3** : PRIMARY COIL

primary atypical pneumonia *n* : a usu. mild pneumonia believed to be caused by a virus

primary cell *n* : a cell that converts chemical energy into electrical energy by irreversible chemical reactions

primary coil *n* : the coil through which the inducing current passes in an induction coil or transformer

primary road *n* : a principal usu. state-maintained road in a recognized system of highways

pri·mate \'prī-,māt *or esp for 1* -mət\ *n* [L *primat-, primas* leader, one of the first, fr. *primus* first] **1** : a bishop or archbishop governing or having highest status in a district, nation, or church **2** : any of an order (Primates) of mammals comprising man together with the apes, monkeys, and related forms (as lemurs and tarsiers)

¹**prime** \'prīm\ *n* [L *primus* first] **1** [OE *prīm*, fr. L *prima hora* first hour] *often cap* : the second of the canonical hours **2** : the first part : earliest stage **3** : the most active, thriving, or successful stage or period (as of one's life) **4** : the chief or best individual or part : PICK ⟨the *prime* of the flock⟩ **5** : a prime number **6** : the symbol '

²**prime** *adj* **1** : first in time : ORIGINAL **2 a** : having no factor except itself and one ⟨3 is a *prime* number⟩ **b** : having no common factor except one ⟨12 and 25 are relatively *prime*⟩ **3 a** : first in rank, authority, or significance : PRINCIPAL **b** : first in excellence, quality, or value **c** : of the highest grade regularly marketed — used of meat and esp. beef — **prime·ly** *adv* — **prime·ness** *n*

³**prime** *vt* **1** : to prepare for firing by supplying with priming or a primer **2** : to apply (as in painting) a first color, coating, or preparation to **3** : to put into working order by filling or charging with something ⟨*prime* a pump with water⟩ **4** : to instruct beforehand : COACH

prime meridian *n* : the meridian of 0° longitude which runs through the original site of the Royal Observatory at Greenwich, England, and from which other longitudes are reckoned east and west

prime minister *n* **1** : the chief minister of a ruler or state **2** : the head of a cabinet or ministry; *esp* : the chief executive of a parliamentary government — **prime ministry** *n*

¹**prim·er** \'prim-ər, *esp Brit* 'prī-mər\ *n* **1** : a small book for teaching children to read **2** : a small introductory book on a subject

²**prim·er** \'prī-mər\ *n* **1** : a device (as a cap, tube, or wafer) containing a substance that ignites an explosive charge and that is itself ignited by friction, percussion, or electricity **2** : PRIMING

pri·me·val \prī-'mē-vəl\ *adj* [L *primus* first + *aevum* age] : of or relating to the earliest ages : PRIMITIVE — **pri·me·val·ly** \-və-lē\ *adv*

prim·ing *n* **1** : the explosive used in priming a charge **2** : the material used in priming a surface

¹**prim·i·tive** \'prim-ət-iv\ *adj* [L *primitivus*, fr. *primus* first] **1** : not derived : ORIGINAL, PRIMARY ⟨nature, the *primitive* source of art⟩ **2 a** : of or relating to the earliest age or period : PRIMEVAL ⟨*primitive* forests⟩⟨the *primitive* church⟩ **b** : little evolved and closely approximating an early ancestral type ⟨a *primitive* fish⟩ **3 a** : of or relating to a relatively simple people or culture ⟨*primitive* society⟩ **b** : marked by the style, simplicity, or crudity held to characterize simple people ⟨*primitive* building techniques⟩ **c** : lacking formal or technical training : SELF-TAUGHT ⟨a *primitive* craftsman⟩; *also* : produced by a self-taught artist — **prim·i·tive·ly** *adv* — **prim·i·tive·ness** *n*

²**primitive** *n* **1 a** : something primitive; *esp* : a primitive idea, term, or proposition **b** : a root word **2 a** (1) : an artist of an early period of a culture or artistic movement (2) : a later imitator or follower of such an artist **b** : a work of art produced by a primitive artist **3** : a member of a primitive people

pri·mo·gen·i·tor \,prī-mō-'jen-ət-ər\ *n* [LL, fr. L *primus* first + *genit-, gignere* to beget] : ANCESTOR, FOREFATHER

pri·mo·gen·i·ture \-'jen-ə-,chur, -'jen-i-chər\ *n* **1** : the state of being the firstborn among the children of a pair of parents **2 :** an exclusive right of inheritance belonging to the eldest son

pri·mor·di·al \prī-'mȯrd-ē-əl\ *adj* [L *primordius* original, fr. *primus* first + *ordiri* to begin] **1 a :** first created or developed : PRIMEVAL **b :** earliest formed in the growth of an individual or organ : PRIMITIVE **2 :** FUNDAMENTAL, PRIMARY — **pri·mor·di·al·ly** \-ē-ə-lē\ *adv*

pri·mor·di·um \-ē-əm\ *n, pl* **-dia** \-ē-ə\ **:** the first-formed rudiment of a part or organ

primp \'primp\ *vb* **:** to dress, adorn, or arrange in a careful or finicky manner

prim·rose \'prim-,rōz\ *n* [MF *primerose*] **:** any of a genus of perennial herbs with large tufted basal leaves and showy variously colored flowers borne in clusters on leafless stalks

primrose path *n* **:** a path of ease or pleasure and esp. sensual pleasure

primrose yellow *n* **1 :** a light to moderate greenish yellow **2 :** a light to moderate yellow

prim·u·la \'prim-yə-lə\ *n* **:** PRIMROSE

prince \'prin(t)s\ *n* [OF, fr. L *princip-, princeps,* lit., one who is taken as first, fr. *primus* first + *capere* to take] **1 a :** MONARCH, KING **b :** the ruler of a principality or state **2 :** a male member of a royal family; *esp* **:** a son of the king **3 :** a nobleman of varying rank **4 :** a person of high standing in his class or profession — **prince·dom** \-dəm\ *n* — **prince·ship** \-,ship\ *n*

Prince Al·bert \-'al-bərt\ *n* **:** a long double-breasted frock coat

prince charming *n* [after *Prince Charming,* hero of the fairy tale *Cinderella*] **:** a suitor who fulfills the dreams of his beloved; *also* **:** a man of often specious affability and charm toward women

prince consort *n, pl* **princes consort :** the husband of a reigning female sovereign

prince·ling \'prin(t)s-liŋ\ *n* **:** a petty prince

prince·ly \'prin(t)s-lē\ *adj* **prince·li·er; -li·est 1 :** of or relating to a prince : ROYAL **2 :** befitting a prince : NOBLE, MAGNIFICENT ⟨*princely* manners⟩⟨a *princely* sum⟩ — **prince·li·ness** *n*

Prince of Wales \-'wālz\ **:** the male heir apparent to the British throne — used as a title only after it has been specif. conferred by the sovereign

prince's-feath·er \'prin(t)-səz-,feth-ər\ *n* **:** a showy annual amaranth often grown for its dense usu. red spikes of bloom

¹prin·cess \'prin(t)-səs, 'prin-,ses, prin-'ses\ *n* **1** *archaic* **:** a woman having sovereign power **2 :** a female member of a royal family; *esp* **:** a daughter or granddaughter of a sovereign **3 :** the consort of a prince

²princess \like ¹\ *or* **prin·cesse** \prin-'ses\ *adj* **:** close-fitting and usu. with gores from neck to flaring hemline ⟨*princess* gown⟩

princess royal *n, pl* **prin·cess·es royal :** the eldest daughter of a sovereign

¹prin·ci·pal \'prin(t)-sə-pəl\ *adj* [L *princip-, princeps* one who is taken as first] **1 :** most important, consequential, or influential : CHIEF **2 :** of, relating to, or constituting principal or a principal — **prin·ci·pal·ly** \-pə-lē\ *adv*

²principal *n* **1 a :** a chief or head man or woman **b :** the head of a school **c :** one who employs another to act for him **d :** an actual participant in a crime **e :** the person primarily liable on a legal obligation **f :** a leading performer : STAR **2 a :** a capital sum placed at interest, due as a debt, or used as a fund **b :** the main body of an estate or bequest left by will — **prin·ci·pal·ship** \-,ship\ *n*

prin·ci·pal·i·ty \,prin(t)-sə-'pal-ət-ē\ *n, pl* **-ties 1 :** the office or position of a prince or principal **2 :** the territory or jurisdiction of a prince : the country that gives his title to a prince

principal parts *n pl* **:** a series of verb forms from which all the other forms of a verb can be derived including in English the present infinitive, the past tense, and the past participle

prin·ci·pate \'prin(t)-sə-,pāt\ *n* **:** princely power; *also* **:** the early Roman Empire or the jurisdiction of an early Roman emperor when the senate and people still retained some formal authority

prin·ci·ple \'prin(t)-sə-pəl\ *n* [L *principium* beginning, fr. *princip-, princeps* one taken as first] **1 a :** a comprehensive and fundamental law, doctrine, or assumption **b :** a rule

or code of conduct; *also* **:** habitual devotion to right principles **c :** the laws or facts of nature underlying the working of an artificial device **2 a :** a primary source : ORIGIN **b :** an underlying faculty or endowment ⟨such *principles* of human nature as greed and curiosity⟩ **3 :** a constituent that exhibits or imparts a characteristic quality ⟨quinine is the active *principle* of cinchona bark⟩

prin·ci·pled \-pəld\ *adj* **:** exhibiting, based on, or characterized by principle ⟨high-*principled*⟩

prink \'priŋk\ *vb* **:** PRIMP — **prink·er** *n*

¹print \'print\ *n* [OF *preinte,* fr. pp. of *preindre* to press, fr. L *premere*] **1 a :** a mark made by pressure : IMPRESSION **b :** something impressed with a print or formed in a mold ⟨a *print* of butter⟩ **2 :** a device or instrument for impressing or forming a print **3 a :** printed state or form ⟨put a manuscript into *print*⟩ **b :** printed matter **c :** printed letters : TYPE **4 a :** a copy made by printing (as from a photographic negative) **b :** cloth with a pattern applied by printing; *also* **:** an article of such cloth — **in print :** procurable from the publisher — **out of print :** not procurable from the publisher

²print *vb* **1 a :** to make an impression in or on **b :** to cause (as a mark) to be stamped **c :** to produce impressions with a relief surface (as type or a plate) **d :** to impress (a surface) with a design by pressure ⟨*print* wallpaper⟩ **2 :** to publish in printed form ⟨*print* a newspaper⟩ **3 :** to write in unconnected letters like those made by a printing press **4 :** to make (a positive picture) on a sensitized photographic surface **5 :** to reproduce by printing ⟨a negative that *prints* well⟩

print·a·ble \'print-ə-bəl\ *adj* **1 :** capable of being printed or of being printed from **2 :** worthy or fit to be published — **print·a·bil·i·ty** \,print-ə-'bil-ət-ē\ *n*

printed circuit *n* **:** a circuit for electronic apparatus made by depositing conductive material on an insulating surface

printed matter *n* **:** matter printed by any of various mechanical processes that is eligible for mailing at a special rate

print·er \'print-ər\ *n* **:** one that prints: as **a :** a person whose business or occupation is printing; *esp* **:** a setter of type **b :** a device used for printing esp. from photographic negatives

printer's devil *n* **:** an apprentice in a printing office

print·ery \'print-ə-rē\ *n, pl* **-er·ies :** an establishment where printing is done

print·ing *n* **1 :** reproduction in printed form **2 :** the art, practice, or business of a printer **3 :** IMPRESSION 4b

printing press *n* **:** a machine that produces printed copies (as by letterpress); *esp* **:** one that is power driven

printing surface *n* **:** a prepared surface from which printing is done

print·out \'print-,aut\ *n* **:** a printed record produced automatically (as by a computer)

¹pri·or \'prī-(ə)r\ *n* [OE & MF, both fr. ML, fr. L, former, superior] **1 :** the deputy head of an abbey **2 :** the head of a monastic house, province, or order — **pri·or·ate** \'prī-ə-rət\ *n* — **pri·or·ship** \'prī-ər-,ship\ *n*

²prior *adj* **1 :** earlier in time or order **2 :** taking precedence logically or in importance or value ⟨a *prior* responsibility⟩ — **pri·or·ly** *adv*

pri·or·ess \'prī-ə-rəs\ *n* **:** a nun corresponding in rank to a prior

pri·or·i·ty \prī-'ȯr-ət-ē, -'är-\ *n, pl* **-ties :** the quality or state of coming before another in time or importance: as **a :** superiority in rank, position, or privilege **b :** order of preference usu. based on urgency, importance, or merit; *esp* **:** a preferential rating that allocates rights to goods and services in limited supply

prior to *prep* **:** in advance of : BEFORE

pri·o·ry \'prī-(ə-)rē\ *n, pl* **-ries :** a religious house under a prior or prioress

prise \'prīz\ *chiefly Brit var of* ⁵PRIZE

prism \'priz-əm\ *n* [Gk *prismat-, prisma,* lit., something sawed, fr. *priein* to saw] **1 :** a solid whose ends are similar, equal, and parallel polygons and whose faces are parallelograms **2 a :** a transparent body bounded in part by two plane faces that are not parallel used to deviate or disperse a beam of light **b :** a prism-shaped decorative glass pendant

prisms

pris·mat·ic \priz-'mat-ik\ *adj* **1** : relating to, resembling, or constituting a prism **2** : formed by refraction of light through a transparent prism ⟨*prismatic* colors⟩ **3** : highly colored : BRILLIANT — **pris·mat·i·cal·ly** \-'mat-i-k(ə-)lē\ *adv*

pris·ma·toid \'priz-mə-,tȯid\ *n* : a polyhedron in which every vertex lies in one or the other of two parallel planes

pris·on \'priz-ᵊn\ *n* [OF, fr. L *prehension-, prehensio* act of seizing, fr. *prehens-, prehendere* to seize] **1** : a state of confinement esp. for criminals ⟨sentenced to *prison*⟩ **2** : a building or group of buildings with its appurtenances in which persons are confined while awaiting or on trial or as punishment after conviction; *esp* : PENITENTIARY

pris·on·er \'priz-nər, -ᵊn-ər\ *n* : a person kept under involuntary restraint, confinement, or custody; *esp* : one in prison

prisoner of war : a person captured in war; *esp* : a member of the armed forces of a nation taken by the enemy during combat

prisoner's base *n* : a game in which players of one team seek to tag and imprison players of the other team who have ventured out of their home territory

pris·sy \'pris-ē\ *adj* **pris·si·er; -est** : being prim and precise : FINICKY — **pris·si·ly** \'pris-ə-lē\ *adv* — **pris·si·ness** \'pris-ē-nəs\ *n*

pris·tine \'pris-,tēn\ *adj* [L *pristinus*] : of or relating to the earliest period or condition : ORIGINAL, PRIMITIVE; *esp* : having the purity or freshness of the original state — **pris·tine·ly** *adv*

prith·ee \'prith-ē, 'prith-\ *interj* [alter. of *I pray thee*] *archaic* — used to express a wish or request

pri·va·cy \'prī-və-sē\ *n, pl* **-cies** **1** : the condition of being apart from company or observation : SECLUSION ⟨lodgings desirable because of their *privacy*⟩ **2** : SECRECY ⟨talk together in *privacy*⟩

¹pri·vate \'prī-vət\ *adj* [L *privatus* not holding public office, fr. pp. of *privare* to deprive] **1** : belonging to, concerning, or reserved for the use of a particular person or group : not public ⟨*private* property⟩ ⟨a *private* park⟩ **2 a** : offering privacy : SECLUDED ⟨a *private* office⟩ **b** : not publicly known : SECRET ⟨*private* agreements⟩ **3** : not holding public office or employment ⟨a *private* citizen⟩ **4** : not under public control ⟨a *private* school⟩ — **pri·vate·ly** *adv* — **pri·vate·ness** *n*

²private *n* : a person of low or lowest rank in an organized group (as a police or fire department); *esp* : an enlisted man in the army ranking above a recruit and below a private first class — **in private** : PRIVATELY, SECRETLY

private enterprise *n* : FREE ENTERPRISE

¹pri·va·teer \,prī-və-'ti(ə)r\ *n* **1** : an armed private ship commissioned to cruise against the commerce or warships of an enemy **2** : the commander or one of the crew of a privateer — **pri·va·teers·man** \-'ti(ə)rz-mən\ *n*

²privateer *vi* : to cruise in or as a privateer

private first class *n* : an enlisted man in the army ranking above a private and below a corporal

pri·va·tion \prī-'vā-shən\ *n* [L *privare* to deprive] **1** : an act or instance of depriving : DEPRIVATION **2** : the state of being deprived esp. of what is needed for existence : WANT

¹priv·a·tive \'priv-ət-iv\ *n* : a privative term, expression, or proposition; *also* : a privative prefix or suffix

²privative *adj* : constituting or predicating privation or absence of a quality ⟨*a-, un-, non-* are *privative* prefixes⟩ — **priv·a·tive·ly** *adv*

priv·et \'priv-ət\ *n* : a half-evergreen shrub of the olive family with small white flowers that is widely used for hedges

¹priv·i·lege \'priv(-ə)-lij\ *n* [L *privilegium* law for a private person, fr. *privus* private + *leg-, lex* law] : a right or immunity granted as a benefit, advantage, or favor; *esp* : one attached specif. to a position or an office

²privilege *vt* : to grant a privilege to

priv·i·leged \-lijd\ *adj* **1** : having or enjoying one or more privileges ⟨*privileged* classes⟩ **2** : not subject to disclosure in a court of law ⟨a *privileged* communication⟩

priv·i·ly \'priv-ə-lē\ *adv* : PRIVATELY, SECRETLY

¹priv·y \'priv-ē\ *adj* [OF *privé*, fr. L *privatus* private] **1** : belonging or relating to a person in his individual rather than his official capacity **2** : WITHDRAWN, PRIVATE ⟨a *privy* place⟩ **3** : sharing in a secret ⟨*privy* to the conspiracy⟩

²privy *n, pl* **priv·ies** : a small building without plumbing that is used as a toilet; *also* : TOILET 2b

privy council *n* **1** *cap P & C* : an advisory council to the British crown usu. functioning through its committees **2** : a usu. appointive advisory council to an executive — **privy councillor** *n*

privy purse *n, often cap both Ps* : an allowance for the private expenses of the British sovereign

¹prize \'prīz\ *n* [ME *pris* prize, price, fr. MF, price] **1** : something won or to be won in competition or in contests of chance; *also* : a premium given as an inducement to buy **2** : something exceptionally desirable

²prize *adj* **1 a** : awarded a prize **b** : awarded as a prize **2** : outstanding of its kind ⟨a *prize* idiot⟩ ⟨raised *prize* hogs⟩

³prize *vt* [MF *prisier*, fr. LL *pretiare*, fr. L *pretium* price, value] **1** : to estimate the value of : RATE **2** : to value highly : ESTEEM

⁴prize *n* [OF *prise* act of taking, fr. *prendre* to take, fr. L *prehendere*] **1** : something taken by force, stratagem, or threat; *esp* : property lawfully captured in time of war **2** : an act of capturing or taking; *esp* : the wartime capture of a ship and its cargo at sea

⁵prize *vt* : to press, force, or move with or as if with a lever : PRY

prize·fight \'prīz-,fīt\ *n* : a contest between professional boxers for pay — **prize·fight·er** \-ər\ *n* — **prize·fight·ing** \-iŋ\ *n*

prize ring *n* : a ring for a prizefight

prize·win·ner \-,win-ər\ *n* : a winner of a prize — **prize·win·ning** \-,win-iŋ\ *adj*

¹pro \'prō\ *n, pl* **pros** \'prōz\ [L, prep., for; akin to E *for*] **1** : a favorable argument or piece of evidence ⟨*pros* and cons⟩ **2** : the affirmative position or one holding it

²pro *adv* : on the affirmative side

³pro *n or adj* : PROFESSIONAL

¹pro- *prefix* [Gk, before, forward, forth, for; akin to E *for*] **1 a** : prior to : prior ⟨*provitamin*⟩ **b** : rudimentary : PROT- 2 ⟨*pronucleus*⟩ **2** : located in front of or at the front of : anterior to ⟨*procephalic*⟩ **3** : projecting ⟨*prognathous*⟩

²pro- *prefix* [L, before, forward, forth, for] **1** : taking the place of : substituting for ⟨*procathedral*⟩ **2** : favoring : supporting : championing ⟨*pro*-American⟩

prob·a·bil·i·ty \,präb-ə-'bil-ət-ē\ *n, pl* **-ties** **1** : the quality, state, or degree of being probable **2** : something probable **3** : a measure of the likelihood of an outcome or event expressed as the ratio of the number of times it occurs in a test series to the total number of trials in the series

prob·a·ble \'präb-ə-bəl\ *adj* [L *probare* to test, approve, fr. *probus* good, honest, fr. *pro* for, in favor of] **1** : supported by evidence strong enough to make it likely though not certain to be true ⟨a *probable* explanation⟩ **2** : likely to happen or to have happened : being such as may or might be real or true ⟨*probable* outcome of the game⟩ ⟨*probable* story⟩ — **prob·a·bly** \'präb-ə-blē, 'präb-lē\ *adv*

syn PROBABLE, POSSIBLE mean such as may be or may become true or actual. PROBABLE applies to what is supported by strong but not necessarily conclusive evidence ⟨*probable* cause of the accident⟩ POSSIBLE refers to that which is within the limit of what may happen or of what a person or thing may do regardless of the chances for or against its actuality

probable cause *n* : a reasonable ground for supposing that a criminal charge is well-founded

¹pro·bate \'prō-,bāt\ *n* [L *probare* to test, prove, approve] **1** : proof before a probate court that the last will and testament of a deceased person is genuine **2** : judicial determination of the validity of a will

²probate *vt* : to establish (a will) by probate as genuine and valid

probate court *n* : a court having jurisdiction chiefly over the probate of wills and the administration of estates of deceased persons

pro·ba·tion \prō-'bā-shən\ *n* **1** : critical examination and evaluation or subjection to such examination and evaluation **2 a** : subjection of an individual to a period of testing and trial to ascertain fitness (as for a job or school) **b** : the suspending of a convicted offender's sentence during good behavior under the supervision of a probation officer **c** : the state or a period of being subject to proba-

---

j joke; ŋ sing; ō flow; ȯ flaw; ȯi coin; th thin; th this; ü loot; u̇ foot; y yet; yü few; yu̇ furious; zh vision

tion — **pro·ba·tion·al** \-shnəl, -shən-ºl\ *adj* — **pro·ba·tion·al·ly** \-ē\ *adv* — **pro·ba·tion·ary** \-shə-ner-ē\ *adj*
pro·ba·tion·er \prō-'bā-sh(ə-)nər\ *n* : a person (as a new student nurse or a convict on a suspended sentence) who is undergoing probation
probation officer *n* : an officer appointed to investigate, report on, and supervise the conduct of convicted offenders on probation
pro·ba·tive \'prō-bət-iv\ *adj* **1** : serving to test or try **2** : serving to prove
pro·ba·to·ry \'prō-bə-ˌtōr-ē\ *adj* : PROBATIVE
¹probe \'prōb\ *n* [ML *proba* examination, fr. L *probare* to test, prove] **1** : a slender instrument for examining a cavity (as a wound) **2 a** : a pointed metal tip for making electrical contact with a circuit element being checked **b** : a device used to penetrate or send back information from outer space **3** : a searching examination; *esp* : an inquiry to discover evidence of wrongdoing ⟨a legislative *probe*⟩
²probe *vb* **1** : to examine with or as if with a probe **2** : to investigate thoroughly **3** : to make an exploratory investigation — **prob·er** *n*
pro·bi·ty \'prō-bət-ē, 'präb-ət-\ *n* [L *probus* honest] : adherence to the highest principles and ideals : UPRIGHTNESS
¹prob·lem \'präb-ləm\ *n* [Gk *problēma*, lit., something thrown forward, fr. *proballein* to throw forward, fr. *pro-* forward + *ballein* to throw] **1 a** : a question raised for inquiry, consideration, or solution **b** : a proposition in mathematics or physics stating something to be done **2 a** : an intricate unsettled question **b** : a source of perplexity or vexation
²problem *adj* **1** : dealing with a problem of human conduct or social relationship ⟨a *problem* play⟩ **2** : difficult to deal with ⟨a *problem* child⟩
prob·lem·at·ic \ˌpräb-lə-'mat-ik\ *or* **prob·lem·at·i·cal** \-'mat-i-kəl\ *adj* : having the nature of a problem : difficult and uncertain : PUZZLING — **prob·lem·at·i·cal·ly** \-i-k(ə-)lē\ *adv*
pro·bos·ci·de·an \prə-ˌbäs-ə-'dē-ən\ *or* **pro·bos·cid·i·an** \prə-ˌbäs-'id-ē-ən\ *n* [L *proboscid-, proboscis* proboscis] : any of an order (Proboscidea) of large mammals comprising the elephants and extinct related forms — **proboscidean** *adj*
pro·bos·cis \prə-'bäs-əs\ *n, pl* **-bos·cis·es** *also* **-bos·ci·des** \-'bäs-ə-ˌdēz\ [Gk *proboskis*, fr. *pro-* + *boskein* to feed] **1** : the trunk of an elephant; *also* : a long, flexible, or prominent nose or snout **2** : an elongated or extensible tubular process (as the sucking organ of a mosquito) of the oral region of an invertebrate
pro·caine \'prō-ˌkān\ *n* [*pro-* + *cocaine*] : a drug resembling cocaine and used as a local anesthetic
pro·cam·bi·um \(')prō-'kam-bē-əm\ *n* : the part of a plant meristem that forms cambium and primary vascular tissues — **pro·cam·bi·al** \-bē-əl\ *adj*
pro·ca·the·dral \ˌprō-kə-'thē-drəl\ *n* : a parish church used as a cathedral
pro·ce·dure \prə-'sē-jər\ *n* **1** : a particular often prescribed manner or method of proceeding in a process or a course of action ⟨observance of legal *procedure*⟩ **2** : an action or series of actions : the continuance or progress of a process or action ⟨climbing high mountains is a slow *procedure*⟩ — **pro·ce·dur·al** \prə-'sēj-(ə-)rəl\ *adj* — **pro·ce·dur·al·ly** \-ē\ *adv*
pro·ceed \prō-'sēd, prə-\ *vi* [L *procedere*, fr. *pro-* + *cedere* to go] **1** : to come forth from a source : ISSUE **2 a** : to continue after a pause or interruption **b** : to go on in an orderly regulated way **3 a** : to begin and carry on an action, process, or movement **b** : to be in the process of being accomplished **4** : to move along a course **syn** see ADVANCE
pro·ceed·ing *n* **1** : PROCEDURE **2** *pl* : EVENTS, HAPPENINGS ⟨talked over the day's *proceedings*⟩ **3 a** *pl* : legal action : LITIGATION ⟨divorce *proceedings*⟩ **b** : a suit or action at law **4** : AFFAIR, TRANSACTION **5** *pl* : an official record of things said or done
pro·ceeds \'prō-ˌsēdz\ *n pl* : the total amount or the profit arising from an investment, transaction, tax, or business : RETURN
¹proc·ess \'präs-ˌes, 'prōs-, -əs\ *n, pl* **proc·ess·es** \-ˌes-əz, -ə-səz, -ə-ˌsēz\ [L *processus*, fr. *process-, procedere* to proceed] **1 a** : PROGRESS, ADVANCE ⟨things will come right

in the *process* of time⟩ **b** : something going on : PROCEEDING **2 a** : a natural phenomenon marked by gradual changes that lead toward a particular result ⟨*process* of growth⟩ **b** : a series of actions, operations, or changes conducing to an end ⟨education is a *process* that takes years⟩ **3 a** : the proceedings or manner of proceeding in a legal action ⟨due *process* of law⟩ **b** : a legal summons or writ used by a court to compel the appearance of the defendant or compliance with its orders **4** : a prominent or projecting bodily part : OUTGROWTH ⟨a bony *process*⟩
²process *vt* : to subject to a special process or treatment (as in the course of manufacture) — **proc·es·sor** \-ˌes-ər, -ə-sər, -ə-ˌsór\ *n*
³process *adj* : treated or made by a special process esp. when involving synthesis or artificial modification
pro·ces·sion \prə-'sesh-ən\ *n* **1** : continuous forward movement : PROGRESSION **2** : a group of individuals moving along in an orderly often ceremonial way ⟨a funeral *procession*⟩
¹pro·ces·sion·al \prə-'sesh-nəl, -ən-ºl\ *n* : a hymn sung during a procession (as of a choir entering the church at the beginning of a service); *also* : a ceremonial procession
²processional *adj* : of, relating to, or moving in a procession — **pro·ces·sion·al·ly** \-ē\ *adv*
pro·claim \prō-'klām\ *vt* [L *proclamare*, fr. *pro-* before + *clamare* to cry out] : to announce publicly : DECLARE ⟨*proclaim* a holiday⟩ ⟨the prince was *proclaimed* king⟩ — **pro·claim·er** *n*
proc·la·ma·tion \ˌpräk-lə-'mā-shən\ *n* **1** : the action of proclaiming : an official publication ⟨*proclamation* of a new law⟩ **2** : something proclaimed
pro·cliv·i·ty \prō-'kliv-ət-ē\ *n, pl* **-ties** [L *proclivis* sloping, prone, fr. *pro-* forward + *clivus* hill] : a tendency or inclination of the mind or temperament : DISPOSITION ⟨a boy with a marked *proclivity* toward laziness⟩ ⟨a *proclivity* for being snobbish⟩
¹pro·con·sul \(')prō-'kän(t)-səl\ *n* **1** : a governor or military commander of an ancient Roman province **2** : an administrator in a modern colony, dependency, or occupied area — **pro·con·su·lar** \-s(ə-)lər\ *adj* — **pro·con·sul·ate** \-s(ə-)lət\ *n* — **pro·con·sul·ship** \-səl-ˌship\ *n*
²proconsul *n* [after *Consul*, chimpanzee in the London Zoo] : an African Miocene fossil ape possibly ancestral to the anthropoid apes and man
pro·cras·ti·nate \prə-'kras-tə-ˌnāt\ *vb* [L *procrastinare*, fr. *pro-* + *crastinus* of tomorrow, fr. *cras* tomorrow] **1** : to put off repeatedly **2** : to keep postponing something supposed to be done — **pro·cras·ti·na·tion** \-ˌkras-tə-'nā-shən\ *n* — **pro·cras·ti·na·tor** \-'kras-tə-ˌnāt-ər\ *n*
pro·cre·ate \'prō-krē-ˌāt\ *vb* [L *procreare*, fr. *pro-* forth + *creare* to create] : to beget or bring forth offspring : REPRODUCE — **pro·cre·a·tion** \ˌprō-krē-'ā-shən\ *n* — **pro·cre·a·tive** \'prō-krē-ˌāt-iv\ *adj* — **pro·cre·a·tor** \-ˌāt-ər\ *n*
pro·crus·te·an \prə-'krəs-tē-ən\ *adj, often cap* **1** : of, relating to, or typical of Procrustes **2** : marked by arbitrary often ruthless disregard of individual differences or special circumstances
procrustean bed *n, often cap P* : a scheme or pattern into which someone or something is arbitrarily forced
Pro·crus·tes \prə-'krəs-(ˌ)tēz\ *n* : a robber of ancient Greek legend noted for stretching or cutting off the legs of his victims to fit them to the length of his bed
proc·to·dae·um \ˌpräk-tə-'dē-əm\ *n, pl* **-daea** \-'dē-ə\ *or* **-dae·ums** : the posterior ectodermal part of the alimentary canal formed in the embryo by invagination of the outer body wall
proc·tor \'präk-tər\ *n* [alter. of ME *procuratour* procurator, proctor] : SUPERVISOR, MONITOR; *esp* : one appointed to supervise students (as at an examination) — **proctor** *vb* — **proc·to·ri·al** \präk-'tōr-ē-əl, -'tór-\ *adj* — **proc·tor·ship** \'präk-tər-ˌship\ *n*
pro·cum·bent \prō-'kəm-bənt\ *adj* [L *procumbent-, procumbens*, prp. of *procumbere* to fall or lean forward] **1** : being or having stems that trail along the ground without rooting **2** : lying face down
pro·cur·a·ble \prə-'kyúr-ə-bəl\ *adj* : capable of being procured
proc·u·ra·tor \'präk-yə-ˌrāt-ər\ *n* **1** : one that manages another's affairs : AGENT **2** : a Roman provincial administrator and financial manager **3** : a criminal

ə **abut**; ⁹ **kitten**; ər **further**; a **back**; ā **bake**; ä **cot, cart**; aú **out**; ch **chin**; e **less**; ē **easy**; g **gift**; i **trip**; ī **life**

prosecutor in various countries — **proc·u·ra·to·ri·al** \ˌpräk-yə-rə-ˈtōr-ē-əl, -ˈtȯr-\ *adj*

pro·cure \prə-ˈkyu̇(ə)r\ *vb* [LL *procurare*, fr. L, to take care of, fr. *pro-* for + *cura* care] **1 a** : to get possession of : OBTAIN **b** : to make women available for promiscuous sexual intercourse **2** : to bring about : ACHIEVE — **pro·cure·ment** \-mənt\ *n*

pro·cur·er \-ˈkyu̇r-ər\ *n* : one that procures; *esp* : PANDER — **pro·cur·ess** \-ˈkyu̇r-əs\ *n*

Pro·cy·on \ˈprō-sē-ˌän, ˈpräs-ē-\ *n* [Gk *Prokyōn*, lit., fore-dog; fr. its rising before the Dog Star] : a first-magnitude star in Canis Minor

¹prod \ˈpräd\ *vt* **prod·ded; prod·ding 1 a** : to thrust a pointed instrument into : PRICK **b** : to incite to action : STIR **2** : to poke or stir as if with a prod — **prod·der** *n*

²prod *n* **1** : a pointed instrument used to prod **2** : an incitement to act

¹prod·i·gal \ˈpräd-i-gəl\ *adj* [L *prodigere* to drive away, squander, fr. *pro-*, *prod-* forth + *agere* to drive] **1** : recklessly extravagant ⟨a *prodigal* spender⟩ **2** : WASTEFUL, LAVISH ⟨*prodigal* entertainment⟩ — **prod·i·gal·i·ty** \ˌpräd-ə-ˈgal-ət-ē\ *n* — **prod·i·gal·ly** \ˈpräd-i-g(ə-)lē\ *adv*

²prodigal *n* : a person who spends prodigally : SPENDTHRIFT

pro·di·gious \prə-ˈdij-əs\ *adj* **1** : exciting amazement or wonder **2** : extraordinary in bulk, quantity, or degree : ENORMOUS **syn** see MONSTROUS — **pro·di·gious·ly** *adv* — **pro·di·gious·ness** *n*

prod·i·gy \ˈpräd-ə-jē\ *n, pl* **-gies** [L *prodigium* omen, monster] **1** : something that is out of the ordinary course of nature; *esp* : a marvel or wonder taken as an omen ⟨comets and other *prodigies* of nature⟩ **2** : an amazing instance, deed, or performance ⟨an exhibition of weight lifting that was a *prodigy* of strength and skill⟩ **3** : a highly gifted or precocious person ⟨a child *prodigy*⟩

¹pro·duce \prə-ˈd(y)üs\ *vb* [L *producere*, fr. *pro-* forward + *ducere* to lead] **1** : to offer to view or notice : EXHIBIT ⟨*produce* evidence⟩ **2** : to give birth or rise to : YIELD ⟨a tree *producing* good fruit⟩ **3** : to extend in length, area, or volume ⟨*produce* a side of a triangle⟩ **4** : to present to the public on the stage or screen or over radio or television ⟨*produce* a play⟩ **5** : to give being, form, or shape to : MAKE; *esp* : MANUFACTURE **6** : to accrue or cause to accrue ⟨income-*producing* investments⟩ **7** : to produce something

²prod·uce \ˈpräd-,üs, ˈprōd-, -,yüs\ *n* **1** : something produced **2** : agricultural products; *esp* : fresh fruits and vegetables as distinguished from staple crops (as grain)

pro·duced \prə-ˈd(y)üst\ *adj* : disproportionately elongated ⟨a *produced* leaf⟩

pro·duc·er \prə-ˈd(y)ü-sər\ *n* **1** : one that produces; *esp* : one that grows agricultural products or manufactures articles **2** : a person who supervises or finances a stage or screen production or radio or television program **3** : an organism (as a green plant) which produces its own organic compounds from simple precursors (as carbon dioxide and inorganic nitrogen) and many of which are food sources for other organisms

producer gas *n* : a manufactured fuel gas consisting chiefly of carbon monoxide, hydrogen, and nitrogen

producer goods *n pl* : goods (as tools) that are used to produce other goods

pro·duc·i·ble \prə-ˈd(y)ü-sə-bəl\ *adj* : capable of being produced

prod·uct \ˈpräd-(,)əkt\ *n* [L *productum* thing produced, fr. neut. of pp. of *producere* to produce] **1** : the number or expression resulting from the multiplication of two or more numbers or expressions **2** : something produced **3** : the amount, quantity, or total produced

pro·duc·tion \prə-ˈdək-shən\ *n* **1 a** : something produced : PRODUCT **b** (1) : a literary or artistic work (2) : a work presented on the stage or screen or over the air **2 a** : the act or process of producing **b** : the making of goods available for human wants **3** : total output

pro·duc·tive \prə-ˈdək-tiv\ *adj* **1** : having the power to produce esp. in abundance ⟨*productive* fishing waters⟩ **2** : effective in or bringing about a production ⟨an age *productive* of great men⟩ ⟨an investigation *productive* of nothing⟩ **3** : yielding or furnishing results, benefits, or profits **4 a** : effecting or contributing to effect production **b** : yielding or devoted to the satisfaction of wants or the creation of utilities **5** : continuing to be used in the

formation of new words or constructions ⟨*un-* is a *productive* English prefix⟩ — **pro·duc·tive·ly** *adv* — **pro·duc·tive·ness** *n* — **pro·duc·tiv·i·ty** \(,)prō-,dək-ˈtiv-ət-ē, ,präd-(,)ək-\ *n*

pro·em \ˈprō-,em\ *n* [L *prooemium*, fr. Gk *prooimion*, fr. *pro-* + *oimē* song] **1** : preliminary comment : PREFACE **2** : PRELUDE

prof \ˈpräf\ *n, slang* : PROFESSOR

prof·a·na·tion \ˌpräf-ə-ˈnā-shən, ˌprō-fə-\ *n* : the act of profaning

pro·fan·a·to·ry \prō-ˈfan-ə-ˌtōr-ē, -ˈfā-nə-, -ˌtȯr-\ *adj* : tending to profane : DESECRATING

¹pro·fane \prō-ˈfān\ *vt* [L *profanus* profane, fr. *pro* before + *fanum* temple] **1** : to violate or treat with irreverence, abuse, or contempt : DESECRATE **2** : to put to a wrong, unworthy, or vulgar use : DEBASE — **pro·fan·er** *n*

²profane *adj* **1** : not concerned with religion or religious purposes : SECULAR **2** : not holy because unconsecrated, impure, or defiled : UNSANCTIFIED **3** : serving to debase or defile what is holy : IRREVERENT — **pro·fane·ly** *adv* — **pro·fane·ness** \-ˈfān-nəs\ *n*

pro·fan·i·ty \prō-ˈfan-ət-ē\ *n, pl* **-ties 1 a** : the quality or state of being profane **b** : the use of profane language **2** : profane language **syn** see BLASPHEMY

pro·fess \prə-ˈfes\ *vt* [L *profess-, profiteri* to profess, confess, fr. *pro-* before + *fateri* to acknowledge] **1 a** : to receive formally into a religious community following a novitiate by acceptance of the required vows **b** : to take (vows) as a member of a religious community or order **2 a** : to declare openly or freely ⟨*profess* confidence in a friend's honesty⟩ **b** : PRETEND, CLAIM **3** : to confess one's faith in or allegiance to ⟨*profess* Christianity⟩ **4** : to practice or claim to be versed in (a calling or profession)

pro·fessed \-ˈfest\ *adj* **1** : openly declared whether truly or falsely ⟨a *professed* hater of jazz⟩ **2** : having taken the vows of a religious order

pro·fess·ed·ly \prə-ˈfes-əd-lē, -ˈfest-lē\ *adv* **1** : AVOWEDLY **2** : ALLEGEDLY

pro·fes·sion \prə-ˈfesh-ən\ *n* **1** : the act of taking the vows of a religious community **2** : an act of openly declaring or publicly claiming a belief, faith, or opinion : PROTESTATION **3** : an avowed religious faith **4 a** : a calling requiring specialized knowledge and academic preparation **b** : a principal calling, vocation, or employment **c** : the whole body of persons engaged in a calling

¹pro·fes·sion·al \prə-ˈfesh-nəl, -ən-ᵊl\ *adj* **1 a** : of, relating to, or characteristic of a profession ⟨his work had a *professional* polish⟩ **b** : engaged in one of the learned professions **2 a** : participating for gain or livelihood in an activity or field of endeavor often engaged in by amateurs **b** : engaged in by persons receiving financial return ⟨*professional* football⟩ **3** : following a line of conduct as though it were a profession ⟨a *professional* patriot⟩ — **pro·fes·sion·al·ly** \-ē\ *adv*

²professional *n* : one that engages in a pursuit or activity professionally

pro·fes·sion·al·ism \-ˌiz-əm\ *n* **1** : the conduct, aims, or qualities that characterize or mark a profession or a professional person **2** : the following of a profession (as athletics) for gain or livelihood

pro·fes·sion·al·ize \-ˌīz\ *vt* : to give a professional character to

pro·fes·sor \prə-ˈfes-ər\ *n* **1** : one that professes, avows, or declares **2 a** : a faculty member of the highest academic rank at an institution of higher education **b** : a teacher at a university, college, or sometimes secondary school — **pro·fes·so·ri·al** \ˌprō-fə-ˈsōr-ē-əl, ˌpräf-ə-, -ˈsȯr-\ *adj* — **pro·fes·so·ri·al·ly** \-ē-ə-lē\ *adv*

pro·fes·sor·ate \prə-ˈfes-ə-rət\ *n* : the office, term of office, or position of a professor

pro·fes·sor·ship \prə-ˈfes-ər-ˌship\ *n* : the office, duties, or position of an academic professor

¹prof·fer \ˈpräf-ər\ *vt* **prof·fered; prof·fer·ing** \ˈpräf-(ə-)riŋ\ [AF *profrer*, fr. OF *porofrir*, fr. *por-* forth + *offrir* to offer] : to present for acceptance : TENDER, OFFER

²proffer *n* : OFFER, SUGGESTION

pro·fi·cien·cy \prə-ˈfish-ən-sē\ *n, pl* **-cies 1** : advancement in knowledge or skill **2** : the quality or state of being proficient

pro·fi·cient \prə-ˈfish-ənt\ *adj* [L *proficient-, proficiens*, prp. of *proficere* to go forward, accomplish, fr. *pro-* for-

---

j joke; ŋ sing; ō flow; ȯ flaw; ȯi coin; th thin; t͟h this; ü loot; u̇ foot; y yet; yü few; yu̇ furious; zh vision

ward + *facere* to make] : well advanced in an art, occupation, or branch of knowledge : ADEPT

syn PROFICIENT, ADEPT, SKILLFUL, EXPERT mean having great knowledge and experience in a trade or profession. PROFICIENT stresses competence derived from training and practice ⟨an eminently *proficient* typist⟩ ADEPT adds to proficiency the implication of aptitude or cleverness ⟨*adept* writer of dialogue⟩ SKILLFUL stresses dexterity in execution or performance ⟨*skillful* juggler⟩ EXPERT implies extraordinary proficiency and often connotes knowledge and technical skill ⟨*expert* in accountancy⟩ ⟨*expert* mimicry⟩ — **pro·fi·cient·ly** *adv*

¹pro·file \'prō-ˌfīl\ *n* [It *profilo*, fr. *profilare* to draw in outline, fr. *pro-* forward + *filare* to spin]
1 : a representation of something in outline; *esp* : a human head or face represented or seen in a side view **2** : an outline seen or represented in sharp relief : CONTOUR **3** : a side or sectional elevation (as of a building)
4 : a concise biographical sketch

²profile *vt* **1** : to represent in profile : draw or write a profile of **2** : to shape the outline of by passing a cutter around

¹prof·it \'präf-ət\ *n* [MF, fr. L *profectus* advance, profit, fr. *profect-*, *proficere* to go forward] **1** : a valuable return : GAIN **2** : the excess of returns over expenditure; *esp* : the excess of the selling price of goods over their cost **3** : the compensation accruing to entrepreneurs as distinguished from wages or rent — **prof·it·less** \-ləs\ *adj*

²profit *vb* **1** : to be of service or advantage : AVAIL **2** : to derive benefit : GAIN ⟨*profit* by experience⟩ **3** : BENEFIT ⟨a business deal that *profited* no one⟩

prof·it·a·ble \'präf-ət-ə-bəl, 'präf-tə-bəl\ *adj* : affording profits : USEFUL, LUCRATIVE **syn** see BENEFICIAL — **prof·it·a·bil·i·ty** \ˌpräf-ət-ə-'bil-ət-ē, ˌpräf-tə-'bil-\ *n* — **prof·it·a·ble·ness** \'präf-ət-ə-bəl-nəs, 'präf-tə-bəl-\ *n* — **prof·it·a·bly** \-blē\ *adv*

prof·it·eer \ˌpräf-ə-'ti(ə)r\ *n* : one who makes an unreasonable profit esp. on the sale of essential goods during an emergency — **profiteer** *vi*

profit sharing *n* : the sharing with employees of a part of the profits of an enterprise

prof·li·ga·cy \'präf-li-gə-sē\ *n* : the quality or state of being profligate

prof·li·gate \'präf-li-gət\ *adj* [L *profligatus*, fr. pp. of *profligare* to strike down, destroy] **1** : completely given up to dissipation and licentiousness **2** : wildly extravagant : PRODIGAL — **profligate** *n* — **prof·li·gate·ly** *adv*

pro for·ma \(ˈ)prō-'fȯr-mə\ *adj* [L] : for the sake of or as a matter of form

pro·found \prə-'faȯnd\ *adj* [L *profundus* deep, fr. *pro-* before + *fundus* bottom] **1 a** : having intellectual depth and insight ⟨a *profound* scholar⟩ **b** : difficult to fathom or understand ⟨a *profound* work⟩ **2 a** : extending far below the surface **b** : coming from, reaching to, or situated at a depth : DEEP-SEATED ⟨*profound* sigh⟩ **3 a** : characterized by intensity of feeling or quality ⟨*profound* passion⟩ **b** : all encompassing : COMPLETE ⟨*profound* sleep⟩ — **pro·found·ly** *adv* — **pro·found·ness** \-'faȯn(d)-nəs\ *n*

pro·fun·di·ty \prə-'fən-dət-ē\ *n, pl* **-ties** [L *profundus* deep, profound] **1 a** : intellectual depth **b** : something profound or abstruse **2** : the quality or state of being very profound or deep

pro·fuse \prə-'fyüs\ *adj* [L *profusus*, pp. of *profundere* to pour forth, fr. *pro-* forth + *fundere* to pour] **1** : pouring forth liberally ⟨*profuse* in their thanks⟩ **2** : exhibiting great abundance — **pro·fuse·ly** *adv* — **pro·fuse·ness** *n*

pro·fu·sion \prə-'fyü-zhən\ *n* **1** : profuse or lavish expenditure **2** : lavish display ⟨*profusion* of flowers⟩

pro·gen·i·tor \prō-'jen-ət-ər\ *n* [L, fr. *progenit-*, *progignere* to beget] **1 a** : a direct ancestor : FOREFATHER **b** : a biologically ancestral form **2** : ORIGINATOR, PRECURSOR

prog·e·ny \'präj-ə-nē\ *n, pl* **-nies** [L *progenies*, fr. *progignere* to beget, fr. *pro-* forth + *gignere* to beget] : DESCENDANTS, CHILDREN, OFFSPRING

pro·ges·ta·tion·al \ˌprō-ˌjes-'tā-shnəl, -shən-ᵊl\ *adj* : preceding pregnancy or gestation; *also* : associated with ovulation

pro·ges·ter·one \prō-'jes-tə-ˌrōn\ *n* : a steroid progestational hormone

pro·glot·tid \(ˈ)prō-'glät-əd\ *n* [Gk *proglōttis* tip of the tongue, fr. *pro-* before + *glōtta* tongue] : a segment of a tapeworm containing both male and female reproductive organs — **pro·glot·ti·de·an** \ˌprō-ˌglät-ə-'dē-ən\ *adj*

pro·glot·tis \(ˈ)prō-'glät-əs\ *n, pl* **-glot·ti·des** \-'glät-ə-ˌdēz\ : PROGLOTTID

prog·na·thous \'präg-nə-thəs, präg-'nā-\ *adj* [*pro-* + Gk *gnathos* jaw] : having the jaws projecting beyond the upper part of the face — **prog·na·thism** \-ˌthiz-əm\ *n*

prog·no·sis \präg-'nō-səs\ *n, pl* **-no·ses** \-'nō-ˌsēz\ [Gk *prognōsis*, lit., foreknowledge, fr. *progignōskein* to know before, fr. *pro-* + *gignōskein* to know] **1** : a forecast of the course of a disease; *also* : the outlook given by such a forecast **2** : FORECAST, PROGNOSTICATION

prog·nos·tic \präg-'näs-tik\ *n* [Gk *prognōstikon*, fr. neut. of *prognōstikos* prophetic, fr. *progignōskein* to know beforehand] **1** : something that foretells : OMEN **2** : PROGNOSTICATION, PROPHECY — **prognostic** *adj*

prog·nos·ti·cate \präg-'näs-tə-ˌkāt\ *vt* **1** : to foretell from signs or symptoms : PREDICT, PROPHESY **2** : FORESHOW, PRESAGE — **prog·nos·ti·ca·tive** \-ˌkāt-iv\ *adj* — **prog·nos·ti·ca·tor** \-ˌkāt-ər\ *n*

prog·nos·ti·ca·tion \(ˌ)präg-ˌnäs-tə-'kā-shən\ *n* **1** : an indication in advance : FORETOKEN **2** : FORECAST

¹pro·gram *or* **pro·gramme** \'prō-ˌgram, -grəm\ *n* [Gk *programma*, fr. *prographein* to write before, fr. *pro-* + *graphein* to write] **1** : a brief statement or written outline of something (as a concert or play) **2** : PERFORMANCE ⟨a television *program*⟩ **3** : a plan of action **4** : a sequence of coded instructions for a computer

²program *also* **pro·gramme** *vt* **pro·grammed** *or* **pro·gramed** \-ˌgramd, -grəmd\; **pro·gram·ming** *or* **pro·gram·ing** **1 a** : to arrange or furnish a program of or for : BILL **b** : to enter in a program **2** : to provide (an electronic computer) with a program — **pro·gram·mer** *n*

programmed instruction *n* : instruction through information given in small steps with each requiring a correct response by the learners before going on to the next step

¹prog·ress \'präg-rəs, -ˌres, *chiefly Brit* 'prō-ˌgres\ *n* [L *progressus* advance, fr. *progress-*, *progredi* to go forth, fr. *pro-* forward + *gradi* to go] **1 a** : a royal journey or tour **b** : an official journey or circuit **c** : a journeying forward **2** : a forward movement : ADVANCE **3** : gradual betterment; *esp* : the progressive development of mankind

²pro·gress \prə-'gres\ *vi* **1** : to move forward : PROCEED **2** : to develop to a higher, better, or more advanced stage **syn** see ADVANCE

pro·gres·sion \prə-'gresh-ən\ *n* **1** : the action of progressing or moving forward ⟨a snail's manner of *progression*⟩ **2** : a continuous and connected series ⟨the rapid *progression* of incidents in a play⟩ **3** : a sequence of numbers in which each term is related to its predecessor by a uniform law **4 a** : succession of chords **b** : the movement of voice parts in harmony — **pro·gres·sion·al** \-'gresh-nəl, -ən-ᵊl\ *adj*

¹pro·gres·sive \prə-'gres-iv\ *adj* **1 a** : of, relating to, or characterized by progress or progression **b** : gradually increasing : GRADUATED ⟨*progressive* income tax⟩ **2** : of, relating to, or constituting an educational theory marked by emphasis on the individual child, informal classroom procedure, and encouragement of self-expression **3** : moving forward or onward : ADVANCING ⟨the *progressive* movements of the hands of a clock⟩ **4** : increasing in extent or severity ⟨a *progressive* disease⟩ **5** *often cap* : of or relating to political Progressives **6** : of, relating to, or constituting a verb form that expresses action or state in progress at the time of speaking or a time spoken of — **pro·gres·sive·ly** *adv* — **pro·gres·sive·ness** *n*

²progressive *n* **1 a** : one that is progressive **b** : one believing in moderate political change and social improvement by governmental action **2** *cap* **a** : a member of a minor U.S. political party split off from the Republicans about 1912 : BULL MOOSE **b** : a follower of Robert M. La Follette in the presidential campaign of 1924 **c** : a follower of Henry A. Wallace in the presidential campaign of 1948

progressive jazz *n* : jazz of the 1950s characterized by harmonic, contrapuntal, and rhythmic experimentation

pro·gres·siv·ism \prə-'gres-i-ˌviz-əm\ *n* **1** *often cap* : the principles or beliefs of progressives or of Progressives

---

2 : the theories of progressive education — **pro·gres·siv·ist** \-vəst\ *n or adj*

pro·hib·it \prō-'hib-ət\ *vt* [L *prohibit-, prohibēre* to hold away, fr. *pro-* forward + *habēre* to hold] **1** : to forbid by authority ⟨*prohibit* all-day parking⟩ **2 a** : to prevent from doing something **b** : to make impossible ⟨the high walls *prohibit* escape⟩ **syn** see FORBID

pro·hi·bi·tion \ˌprō-ə-'bish-ən\ *n* **1** : the act of prohibiting **2** : an order to restrain or stop **3** : the forbidding by law of the sale and sometimes the manufacture and transportation of alcoholic liquors as beverages

pro·hi·bi·tion·ist \-'bish-(ə-)nəst\ *n* : a person who is in favor of prohibiting the manufacture and sale of alcoholic liquors as beverages

pro·hib·i·tive \prō-'hib-ət-iv\ *adj* : serving or tending to prohibit ⟨*prohibitive* prices⟩ — **pro·hib·i·tive·ly** *adv*

pro·hib·i·to·ry \prō-'hib-ə-ˌtōr-ē, -ˌtor-\ *adj* : PROHIBITIVE ⟨*prohibitory* legislation⟩

1proj·ect \'präj-ˌekt, -ikt\ *n* [L *projectus,* pp. of *proicere* to throw forward, fr. *pro-* + *jacere* to throw] **1** : a specific plan or design : SCHEME **2** : a planned undertaking: as **a** : a definitely formulated piece of research **b** : a large usu. government-supported undertaking **c** : a task or problem engaged in usu. by a group of students to supplement and apply classroom studies **3** : a group of houses or apartment buildings constructed and arranged according to a single plan; *esp* : one built with government help to provide low-cost housing

2pro·ject \prə-'jekt\ *vb* **1** : to devise in the mind : DESIGN ⟨*project* civic improvements⟩ **2** : to throw or cast forward **3** : to stick out or cause to protrude ⟨a stone jetty *projecting* into the bay⟩ **4** : to cause (light or shadow) to fall into space or (an image) upon a surface ⟨*project* a beam of light⟩ ⟨*project* motion pictures on a screen⟩ **5** : to reproduce (as a point, line, or area) on a surface by motion in a prescribed direction

pro·ject·a·ble \prə-'jek-tə-bəl\ *adj* : capable of being projected

1pro·jec·tile \prə-'jek-t⁹l\ *n* **1** : a body projected by external force and continuing in motion by its own inertia; *esp* : a missile for a weapon (as a firearm or cannon) **2** : a self-propelling weapon (as a guided missile)

2projectile *adj* **1** : projecting or impelling forward ⟨a *projectile* force⟩ **2** : capable of being thrust forward

pro·jec·tion \prə-'jek-shən\ *n* **1 a** : a systematic presentation of intersecting coordinate lines on a flat surface upon which features from the curved surface of the earth or the celestial sphere may be mapped **b** : the process of reproducing a spatial object upon a surface by projecting its points; *also* : the graphic reproduction so formed **2** : the act of throwing or shooting forward **3** : the forming of a plan : SCHEMING **4 a** : a jutting out **b** : a part that juts out **5** : the act of objectifying what is primarily subjective **6** : the display of motion pictures by projecting an image from them upon a screen **7** : an estimate of future possibilities based on a current trend — **pro·jec·tion·al** \-shnəl, -shən-⁹l\ *adj*

syn PROJECTION, PROTRUSION mean extension beyond a normal line or surface. PROJECTION implies a jutting out esp. at a sharp angle; PROTRUSION suggests a thrusting or bulging out so as to seem a deformity

pro·jec·tion·ist \-sh(ə-)nəst\ *n* : one that makes projections; *esp* : one that operates a motion-picture projector or television equipment

pro·jec·tive \prə-'jek-tiv\ *adj* **1** : relating to, produced by, or involving geometric projection ⟨*projective* geometry⟩ **2** : jutting out : PROJECTING

pro·jec·tor \prə-'jek-tər\ *n* **1** : one that plans a project; *esp* : PROMOTER **2** : one that projects: as **a** : a device for projecting a beam of light **b** : an optical instrument or machine for projecting an image or pictures upon a surface

pro·lac·tin \prō-'lak-tən\ *n* : a pituitary lactogenic hormone

pro·lapse \prō-'laps\ *n* [L *prolaps-, prolabi* to fall or slide forward, fr. *pro-* forward + *labi* to slide] : the slipping of a body part from its usual position or relations — **pro·lapse** *vi*

pro·leg \'prō-ˌleg\ *n* : a fleshy leg on an abdominal segment of some insect larvae

pro·le·gom·e·non \ˌprō-li-'gäm-ə-ˌnän\ *n, pl* **-na** \-nə\ [Gk, neut. pres. pass. part. of *prolegein* to say beforehand,

fr. *pro-* before + *legein* to say] **:** prefatory remarks; *esp* : a formal essay or critical discussion serving to introduce and interpret an extended work — **pro·le·gom·e·nous** \-nəs\ *adj*

1pro·le·tar·i·an \ˌprō-lə-'ter-ē-ən\ *n* [L *proletarius,* fr. *proles* progeny; fr. the fact that their chief contribution to the state was progeny rather than property] : a member of the proletariat

2proletarian *adj* : of, relating to, or representative of the proletariat

pro·le·tar·i·at \ˌprō-lə-'ter-ē-ət, -'tar-\ *n, pl* **proletariat** **1** : the lowest social or economic class of a community **2** : industrial workers who sell their labor to live

pro·lif·er·ate \prə-'lif-ə-ˌrāt\ *vi* : to grow or increase by rapid production of new units (as cells or offspring) — **pro·lif·er·a·tion** \-ˌlif-ə-'rā-shən\ *n* — **pro·lif·er·a·tive** \-'lif-ə-ˌrāt-iv\ *adj*

pro·lif·ic \prə-'lif-ik\ *adj* [F *prolifique,* fr. L *proles* offspring] **1** : producing young or fruit abundantly : REPRODUCTIVE ⟨*prolific* orchard⟩ **2** : highly inventive : PRODUCTIVE ⟨*prolific* brain⟩ **3** : causing fruitfulness : characterized by fruitfulness ⟨*prolific* growing season⟩ **syn** see FERTILE — **pro·lif·i·cal·ly** \-'lif-i-k(ə-)lē\ *adv* — **pro·lif·ic·ness** *n*

pro·lix \prō-'liks, 'prō-(ˌ)liks\ *adj* [L *prolixus* extended, fr. *pro-* forward + *liquēre* to be fluid] : continued or drawn out too long (as by too many words) : WORDY, LONG-WINDED — **pro·lix·i·ty** \prō-'lik-sət-ē\ *n* — **pro·lix·ly** \prō-'liks-lē, 'prō-(ˌ)\ *adv*

pro·logue \'prō-ˌlȯg\ *n* [Gk *pro-* + *log-, legein* to speak] **1** : the preface or introduction to a literary work **2 a** : a speech often in verse addressed to the audience by an actor at the beginning of a play **b** : the actor speaking such a prologue **3** : an introductory or preceding event or development

pro·long \prə-'lȯŋ\ *vt* **1** : to make longer than usual : continue or lengthen in time ⟨*prolonged* whistle of a train⟩ **2** : to lengthen in extent or range ⟨*prolong* a boundary line⟩

pro·lon·ga·tion \(ˌ)prō-ˌlȯŋ-'gā-shən\ *n* **1** : a lengthening in space or time **2** : something that prolongs or is prolonged

prom \'präm\ *n* [short for *promenade*] : an often formal dance given by a high school or college class

1prom·e·nade \ˌpräm-ə-'nād, -'näd\ *n* [F, fr. *promener* to take for a walk, fr. L *prominare* to drive forward, fr. *pro-* forward + *minare* to drive] **1** : a leisurely walk or ride esp. in a public place for pleasure or display **2** : a place for strolling **3 a** : a ceremonious opening of a formal ball consisting of a grand march of all the guests **b** : PROM

2promenade *vb* **1** : to take or go on a promenade **2** : to walk about in or on ⟨*promenading* the sun deck⟩ — **prom·e·nad·er** *n*

promenade deck *n* : an upper deck or an area on a deck of a passenger ship where passengers promenade

Pro·me·the·an \prə-'mē-thē-ən\ *adj* : of, relating to, or resembling Prometheus; *esp* : daringly original or creative

Pro·me·theus \-ˌth(y)üs, -thē-əs\ *n* : a Titan noted in Greek legend for stealing fire from heaven as a gift for man

pro·me·thi·um \-thē-əm\ *n* [NL, fr. *Prometheus*] : a metallic chemical element obtained as a fission product of uranium or from neutron-irradiated neodymium — see ELEMENT table

prom·i·nence \'präm-ə-nən(t)s\ *n* **1** : the quality, state, or fact of being prominent or conspicuous ⟨a person of *prominence*⟩ **2** : something prominent : PROJECTION **3** : a mass of gas resembling a cloud that arises from the chromosphere of the sun

prom·i·nent \-nənt\ *adj* [L *prominent-, prominens,* fr. prp. of *prominēre* to jut forward] **1** : standing out or projecting beyond a surface or line : PROTUBERANT **2** : readily noticeable : CONSPICUOUS **3** : NOTABLE, EMINENT — **prom·i·nent·ly** *adv*

prom·is·cu·i·ty \ˌpräm-is-'kyü-ət-ē, (ˌ)prō-ˌmis-\ *n, pl* **-ties** **1** : a miscellaneous mixture or mingling of persons or things **2** : promiscuous sexual behavior

pro·mis·cu·ous \prə-'mis-kyə-wəs\ *adj* [L *promiscuus,* fr. *pro-* forth + *miscēre* to mix] **1** : composed of all sorts of persons and things ⟨*promiscuous* crowd of onlookers⟩ **2** : not restricted to one person or class ⟨give *promiscuous* praise⟩; *esp* : not restricted to one sexual partner **3** : HAP-

---

j joke; ŋ sing; ō flow; ȯ flaw; ȯi coin; th thin; th this; ü loot; u̇ foot; y yet; yü few; yu̇ furious; zh vision

HAZARD, IRREGULAR ⟨*promiscuous* eating habits⟩ **syn** see INDISCRIMINATE — **pro·mis·cu·ous·ly** *adv* — **pro·mis·cu·ous·ness** *n*

¹prom·ise \'präm-əs\ *n* [L *promissum*, fr. neut. of *promissus*, pp. of *promittere* to send forth, promise, fr. *pro-* forth + *mittere* to send] **1** : a statement assuring someone that the person making the statement will do or not do something : PLEDGE ⟨a *promise* to pay⟩ **2** : something promised **3** : a cause or ground for hope or expectation esp. of success or distinction ⟨give *promise* of success⟩⟨the boy shows *promise*⟩

²promise *vb* **1 a** : to engage to do, bring about, or provide ⟨*promise* aid⟩ ⟨*promise* to pay⟩ **b** : to tell as a promise ⟨*promised* her he'd be on time⟩ **c** : to make a promise **2** *archaic* : WARRANT, ASSURE **3** : to suggest beforehand : FORETOKEN ⟨dark clouds *promising* rain⟩ — **prom·is·er** \'präm-ə-sər\ *or* **prom·i·sor** \,präm-ə-'sȯ(ə)r\ *n*

promised land *n* **1** : the land of Canaan that Jehovah promised to Abraham and his descendants **2** : a better place that one hopes to reach or a better condition that one hopes to attain

prom·is·ing *adj* : full of promise : giving hope or assurance (as of success) ⟨a very *promising* pupil⟩ — **prom·is·ing·ly** \-ə-siŋ-lē\ *adv*

prom·is·so·ry \'präm-ə-,sōr-ē, -,sȯr-\ *adj* : containing or conveying a promise or assurance ⟨*promissory* oath⟩

promissory note *n* : NOTE 2f(1)

prom·on·to·ry \'präm-ən-,tōr-ē, -,tȯr-\ *n, pl* **-ries** [L *promunturium*] **1** : a high point of land or rock jutting out into a body of water : HEADLAND **2** : a bodily prominence

pro·mot·a·ble \prə-'mōt-ə-bəl\ *adj* : likely or deserving to be advanced in rank or position

pro·mote \prə-'mōt\ *vt* [L *promot-, promovēre*, lit., to move forward] **1** : to advance in position, rank, or honor : ELEVATE ⟨*promote* pupils to a higher grade⟩ ⟨was *promoted* to sergeant⟩ **2** : to contribute to the growth, success, or development of : FURTHER ⟨good food *promotes* health⟩ **3** : to take the first steps in organizing (as a business)

pro·mot·er \prə-'mōt-ər\ *n* : one that promotes: as **a** : one who assumes the financial responsibilities of a sporting event **b** : a person who alone or with others organizes a business undertaking

pro·mo·tion \prə-'mō-shən\ *n* **1** : the act or fact of being raised in position or rank **2** : the act of furthering the growth or development of something — **pro·mo·tion·al** \-shnəl, -shən-ºl\ *adj*

¹prompt \'präm(p)t\ *vt* [ML *promptare*, fr. L *promptus* ready, prompt] **1** : to move to action : CAUSE ⟨curiosity *prompted* him to ask the question⟩ **2** : to remind of something forgotten or poorly learned (as by suggesting the next few words in a speech) ⟨*prompt* an actor⟩ **3** : SUGGEST, INSPIRE ⟨pride *prompted* the act⟩

²prompt *adj* [L *promptus*, fr. pp. of *promere* to bring forth, fr. *pro-* forth + *emere* to take] **1 a** : being ready and quick as occasion demands ⟨*prompt* to answer⟩ **b** : PUNCTUAL ⟨*prompt* in arriving⟩ **2** : performed readily or immediately ⟨*prompt* assistance⟩ — **prompt·ly** *adv* — **prompt·ness** *n*

prompt·book \'präm(p)t-,bu̇k\ *n* : a copy of a play with directions for performance used by a theater prompter

prompt·er \'präm(p)-tər\ *n* : a person who reminds another of the words to be spoken next (as in a play)

promp·ti·tude \'präm(p)-tə-,t(y)üd\ *n* : the quality or habit of being prompt : PROMPTNESS

prom·ul·gate \'präm-əl-,gāt; prō-'məl-\ *vt* [L *promulgare*] **1** : to make known by open declaration : PROCLAIM **2 a** : to make public the terms of (a proposed law) **b** : to issue or give out (a law) by way of putting into execution — **prom·ul·ga·tion** \,präm-əl-'gā-shən, ,prō-(,)məl-\ *n* — **prom·ul·ga·tor** \'präm-əl-,gāt-ər, prō-'məl-\ *n*

pro·nate \'prō-,nāt\ *vt* [L *pronus* bent forward] : to rotate (the hand or forearm) so as to bring the palm facing downward or backward; *also* : to rotate (a joint or part) forward and toward the midline — **pro·na·tion** \prō-'nā-shən\ *n*

pro·na·tor \'prō-,nāt-ər\ *n* : a muscle that produces pronation

prone \'prōn\ *adj* [L *pronus* bent forward, tending] **1** : having a tendency or inclination : DISPOSED ⟨*prone* to laziness⟩ **2 a** : lying belly or face downward ⟨shoot from

a *prone* position⟩ **b** : not erect : lying flat or prostrate ⟨the wind blew the trees *prone*⟩ — **prone·ness** \'prōn-nəs\ *n* **syn** PRONE, PROSTRATE, SUPINE mean lying down. PRONE implies a position with the front of the body turned toward the supporting surface ⟨lying *prone* on the deck⟩ PROSTRATE implies lying at full length as in submission or physical collapse ⟨found the body *prostrate* on the floor⟩ SUPINE implies lying on one's back and may connote abjectness or moral cowardice **syn** see in addition APT

¹prong \'prȯŋ, 'präŋ\ *n* [ME *pronge*] **1** : a tine of a fork **2** : a slender pointed or projecting part (as of a tooth or an antler) — **pronged** \'prȯŋd, 'präŋd\ *adj*

²prong *vt* : to stab, pierce, or break up with a pronged device

prong·horn \'prȯŋ-,hȯrn, 'präŋ-\ *n, pl* **pronghorn** *also* **pronghorns** : a ruminant mammal of treeless parts of western No. America resembling an antelope

pro·nom·i·nal \prō-'näm-ən-ºl\ *adj* **1** : of, relating to, or constituting a pronoun **2** : resembling a pronoun in identifying or specifying without describing ⟨the *pronominal* adjective *this* in "this dog"⟩ — **pronominal** *n* — **pro·nom·i·nal·ly** \-ºl-ē\ *adv*

pro·noun \'prō-,nau̇n\ *n* [L *pro-nomin-, pronomen*, fr. *pro-* for + *nomen* name] : a word that is used as a substitute for a noun, takes noun constructions, and refers to persons or things named, asked for, or understood in the context

pronghorn

pro·nounce \prə-'nau̇n(t)s\ *vb* [MF *prononcier*, fr. L *pronuntiare*, fr. *pro-* forth + *nuntiare* to report, fr. *nuntius* messenger] **1** : to declare officially or solemnly ⟨the minister *pronounced* them man and wife⟩ ⟨the judge *pronounced* sentence⟩ **2** : to assert as an opinion ⟨*pronounce* the book a success⟩ **3** : to utter the sounds of : speak aloud ⟨ practice *pronouncing* foreign words⟩; *esp* : to say or speak correctly ⟨she can't *pronounce* his name⟩ — **pronounce·a·ble** \-'nau̇n(t)-sə-bəl\ *adj* — **pro·nounc·er** *n*

pro·nounced \-'nau̇n(t)st\ *adj* : strongly marked : DECIDED ⟨a *pronounced* change for the better⟩ — **pro·nounc·ed·ly** \-'nau̇n(t)-səd-lē\ *adv*

pro·nounce·ment \prə-'nau̇n(t)s-mənt\ *n* **1** : a usu. formal declaration of opinion **2** : an authoritative announcement

pron·to \'prän-,tō\ *adv* [Sp, fr. L *promptus* prompt] : QUICKLY, PROMPTLY

pro·nu·cle·us \(')prō-'n(y)ü-klē-əs\ *n* : either gamete nucleus after completion of maturation and entry of a sperm into the egg — **pro·nu·cle·ar** \-klē-ər\ *adj*

pro·nun·ci·a·men·to \prō-,nən(t)-sē-ə-'ment-ō\ *n, pl* **-tos** *or* **-toes** [Sp *pronunciamiento*] : PROCLAMATION, MANIFESTO

pro·nun·ci·a·tion \prə-,nən(t)-sē-'ā-shən\ *n* : the act or manner of pronouncing something — **pro·nun·ci·a·tion·al** \-shnəl, -shən-ºl\ *adj*

¹proof \'prüf\ *n* [OF *preuve*, fr. LL *proba*, fr. L *probāre* to prove] **1 a** : evidence of truth or correctness ⟨gave *proof* of his statement⟩ **b** : a test to find out or show the essential facts or truth ⟨put his theory to the *proof*⟩⟨the *proof* of the pudding is in the eating⟩ **2 a** : an impression (as from type) taken for correction or examination **b** : a test photographic print made from a negative **3** : alcoholic content (as of a beverage) indicated by a number that is about twice the percent by volume of alcohol present ⟨whiskey of 90 *proof* is about 45% alcohol⟩

²proof *adj* **1** : designed for or successful in repelling, resisting, or withstanding ⟨*proof* against tampering⟩ — usu. used in combination ⟨bombproof⟩ ⟨waterproof⟩ **2** : used in proving or testing or as a standard of comparison ⟨use only *proof* loads in a gun⟩

proof·read \'prüf-,rēd\ *vb* : to read and make corrections (as in printer's proof) ⟨*proofread* a composition⟩

proof·read·er \-,rēd-ər\ *n* : a person who reads and makes corrections in printer's proof

¹prop \'präp\ *n* [MD *proppe* stopper] : something that props or sustains : SUPPORT

²prop *vt* **propped; prop·ping 1 a** : to hold up or keep from falling or slipping by placing something under or against ⟨*prop* the limb up until the apples are picked⟩ **b** : to support by placing against something ⟨*propped* his

rake against the tree⟩ **2** : SUSTAIN, STRENGTHEN ⟨*propped up by his faith in times of crisis*⟩
³prop *n* : PROPERTY 5
⁴prop *n* : PROPELLER
prop·a·gan·da \,präp-ə-'gan-də, ,prō-pə-\ *n* [NL. fr. *Congregatio de propaganda fide* congregation for propagating the faith, an organization established by Pope Gregory XV] **1** *cap* : a congregation of the Roman curia having jurisdiction over missionary territories and related institutions **2** : the spreading of ideas, information, or rumor for the purpose of helping or injuring a cause or the ideas, facts, or allegations so spread — **prop·a·gan·dist** \-dəst\ *n* — **prop·a·gan·dis·tic** \-,gan-'dis-tik\ *adj* — **prop·a·gan·dis·ti·cal·ly** \-ti-k(ə-)lē\ *adv*
prop·a·gan·dize \-'gan-,dīz\ *vb* **1** : to spread propaganda **2** : to influence or attempt to influence by propaganda
prop·a·gate \'präp-ə-,gāt\ *vb* [L *propagare* to set slips, propagate, fr. *propages* slip, offspring, fr. *pro-* before + *pangere* to fasten] **1** : to reproduce or increase by sexual or asexual means : MULTIPLY ⟨*propagate* an apple by grafting⟩ **2** : to pass along to offspring **3** a : to cause to spread out and affect a greater number or greater area **b** : PUBLICIZE **c** : TRANSMIT **4** : INCREASE, EXTEND — **prop·a·ga·ble** \-gə-bəl\ *adj* — **prop·a·ga·tive** \-,gāt-iv\ *adj* — **prop·a·ga·tor** \-,gāt-ər\ *n*
prop·a·ga·tion \,präp-ə-'gā-shən\ *n* : the act or process of propagating: as **a** : an increasing (as of a kind of organism) numerically **b** : the spreading of something (as a belief) abroad or into new regions : DISSEMINATION ⟨*propagation* of a faith⟩ — **prop·a·ga·tion·al** \-shnəl, -shən-ᵊl\ *adj*
pro·pane \'prō-,pān\ *n* [*prop*ionic acid + *-ane*] : a heavy flammable gaseous hydrocarbon C_3H_8 found in crude petroleum and natural gas and used esp. as fuel and in chemical synthesis
pro·pa·nol \'prō-pə-,nȯl, -,nōl\ *n* : PROPYL ALCOHOL
pro·pel \prə-'pel\ *vt* **pro·pelled**; **pro·pel·ling** [L *propro-* forward + *pellere* to drive] **1** : to push or drive usu. forward or onward ⟨a bicycle is *propelled* by pedals⟩ **2** : to give an impelling motive to : urge ahead ⟨a man *propelled* by ambition⟩
¹pro·pel·lant *or* **pro·pel·lent** \-'pel-ənt\ *adj* : capable of propelling
²propellant *also* **propellent** *n* : something that propels: as **a** : an explosive for propelling projectiles **b** : fuel plus oxidizer used by a rocket engine **c** : a gas in a specially made bottle for expelling the contents when the pressure is released
pro·pel·ler *also* **pro·pel·lor** \prə-'pel-ər\ *n* : one that propels; *esp* : SCREW PROPELLER
pro·pen·si·ty \prə-'pen(t)-sət-ē\ *n, pl* **-ties** [L *propens-, propendēre* to incline, fr. *pro-* before + *pendēre* to hang] : a natural inclination or liking : BENT ⟨a *propensity* for drawing⟩
¹prop·er \'präp-ər\ *adj* [L *proprius* own] **1** : marked by suitability, rightness, or appropriateness : FIT **2 a** : appointed for the liturgy of a particular day **b** : belonging to one : OWN **3** : belonging characteristically to a species or individual : PECULIAR **4** : strictly limited to a specified thing, place, or idea ⟨outside the city *proper*⟩ **5 a** : strictly accurate : CORRECT **b** : strictly decorous : GENTEEL **syn** see FIT
²proper *n, often cap* : the parts of the mass or Divine Office that vary according to the day or feast
proper adjective *n* : an adjective formed from a proper noun
proper fraction *n* : a fraction in which the numerator is less or of lower degree than the denominator
prop·er·ly \'präp-ər-lē\ *adv* **1** : in a suitable or fit manner ⟨behave *properly* in church⟩ **2** : strictly in accordance with fact : CORRECTLY ⟨goods not *properly* labeled⟩ ⟨*properly* speaking, whales are not fish⟩
proper noun *n* : a noun that designates a particular being or thing and does not take a limiting modifier — called also *proper name*
proper subset *n* : a subset containing fewer elements than the set to which it belongs
prop·er·tied \'präp-ərt-ēd\ *adj* : owning property and esp. much property
prop·er·ty \'präp-ərt-ē\ *n, pl*-**ties** [MF *proprieté, propreté*, fr. L *proprietat-, proprietas*, fr. *proprius* own] **1** : a special

quality or characteristic of a thing : a quality or attribute common to all things called by the same name ⟨sweetness is a *property* of sugar⟩ **2** : anything that is owned (as land, goods, or money) **3** : a piece of real estate with or without a structure on it ⟨a business *property*⟩ **4** : the legal right to property : OWNERSHIP **5** : an article to be used on the stage during a play or on the set of a motion picture except artificial scenery or actors' costumes **syn** see QUALITY
prop·er·ty·less \-ləs\ *adj* : lacking property
property man *n* : one who is in charge of theater or motion-picture stage properties
pro·phase \'prō-,fāz\ *n* : the initial phase of mitosis in which chromosomes are condensed from the resting form and split into paired chromatids — **pro·pha·sic** \(')prō-'fā-zik\ *adj*
proph·e·cy \'präf-ə-sē\ *n, pl* **-cies 1** : the work or revelation of an inspired prophet **2** : the foretelling of the future ⟨the gift of *prophecy*⟩ **3** : something foretold of the future : PREDICTION
proph·e·si·er \-,sī-(-ə)r\ *n* : one that prophesies
proph·e·sy \'präf-ə-,sī\ *vb* **-sied**; **-sy·ing** [MF *prophesier*, fr. *prophecie* prophecy] **1 a** : to speak or write as a prophet **b** : to utter by divine inspiration **2** : FORETELL, PREDICT ⟨*prophesy* bad weather⟩
proph·et \'präf-ət\ *n* [Gk *prophētēs*, fr. *pro-* before, forth + *phanai* to speak] **1** : a person who declares publicly a message that he believes has been divinely inspired; *esp, often cap* : the writer of one of the prophetic books of the Old Testament **2** : one gifted with more than ordinary spiritual and moral insight; *esp* : an inspired poet **3** : one who foretells future events **4** : an effective or leading spokesman for a cause, doctrine, or group ⟨a *prophet* of the revolution⟩ — **proph·et·ess** \-ət-əs\ *n*
pro·phet·ic \prə-'fet-ik\ *adj* **1** : of, relating to, or characteristic of a prophet or prophecy ⟨*prophetic* insight⟩ **2** : foretelling events : PREDICTIVE ⟨a *prophetic* statement⟩ — **pro·phet·i·cal** \-'fet-i-kəl\ *adj* — **pro·phet·i·cal·ly** \-i-k(ə-)lē\ *adv*
Proph·ets \'präf-əts\ *n pl* : the second part of the Jewish scriptures — compare HAGIOGRAPHA, LAW
pro·phy·lac·tic \,prō-fə-'lak-tik\ *adj* [Gk *pro-* before + *phylak-, phylax* guard] **1** : guarding from or preventing disease **2** : tending to prevent or ward off : PREVENTIVE — **pro·phy·lac·ti·cal·ly** \-ti-k(ə-)lē\ *adv*
pro·phy·lax·is \-'lak-səs\ *n, pl* **-lax·es** \-'lak-,sēz\ : measures designed to preserve health and prevent the spread of disease
pro·pin·qui·ty \prō-'piŋ-kwət-ē\ *n* [L *propinquus* near, akin, fr. *prope* near] **1** : nearness of blood : KINSHIP **2** : nearness in place or time
pro·pi·on·ic acid \,prō-pē-,än-ik-\ *n* [*pro-* + Gk *piōn* fat] : a liquid sharp-odored fatty acid $C_3H_6O_2$ found in milk and distillates of wood, coal, and petroleum
pro·pi·ti·ate \prō-'pish-ē-,āt\ *vt* : to gain or regain the favor or goodwill of : APPEASE, CONCILIATE ⟨*propitiate* the angry gods with sacrifices⟩ — **pro·pi·ti·a·tion** \-,pish-ē-'ā-shən\ *n* — **pro·pi·ti·a·tor** \-'pish-ē-,āt-ər\ *n* — **pro·pi·tia·to·ry** \-'pish-(ē-)ə-,tōr-ē, -,tȯr-\ *adj*
pro·pi·tious \prə-'pish-əs\ *adj* [L *propitius*, fr. *pro-* before + *petere* to seek] **1** : favorably disposed ⟨the fates are *propitious*⟩ **2** : of good omen : PROMISING ⟨*propitious* signs⟩ **3** : likely to produce good results : OPPORTUNE ⟨the *propitious* moment for asking a favor⟩ — **pro·pi·tious·ly** *adv* — **pro·pi·tious·ness** *n*
prop·jet engine \'präp-,jet-\ *n* : TURBO-PROPELLER ENGINE
prop·man \'präp-,man\ *n* : PROPERTY MAN
prop·o·lis \'präp-ə-ləs\ *n* [Gk, fr. *pro-* + *polis* city] : a brownish waxy resinous material collected by bees from the buds of trees and used as a cement
pro·po·nent \prə-'pō-nənt\ *n* [L *proponent-, proponens*, prp. of *proponere* to propound] : one who argues in favor of something : ADVOCATE
¹pro·por·tion \prə-'pōr-shən, -'pȯr-\ *n* **1** : the size, number, or amount of one thing or group of things as compared to the size, number, or amount of another thing or group of things ⟨the *proportion* of boys to girls in our class is three to one⟩ **2** *pl* : the length and width or length, breadth, and height : DIMENSIONS ⟨the *proportions* of this room are very good⟩ **3** : a balanced or pleasing arrangement ⟨out of *proportion*⟩ **4** : fair or just share ⟨each did his

proportion of the work⟩ **5 :** a statement of the equality of two ratios (as ½ = ¹⁰⁄₈)

²**proportion** _vt_ **-tioned; -tion·ing** \-sh(ə-)niŋ\ **1 :** to adjust (a part or thing) in size relative to other parts or things **2 :** to make the parts of harmonious or symmetrical

¹**pro·por·tion·al** \prə-'pōr-shnəl, -'pȯr-, -shən-ᵊl\ _adj_ **1 a :** being in proportion **:** PROPORTIONATE ⟨wages _proportional_ to ability⟩ **b :** having the same or a constant ratio **2 :** regulated or determined in size or degree with reference to proportions — **pro·por·tion·al·i·ty** \-,pōr-shə-'nal-ət-ē, -,pȯr-\ _n_ — **pro·por·tion·al·ly** \-'pōr-shnə-lē, -'pȯr-,- shən-ᵊl-ē\ _adv_

²**proportional** _n_ **:** a number or quantity in a proportion

proportional parts _n pl_ **:** fractional parts of the difference between successive entries in a table for use in linear interpolation

proportional representation _n_ **:** an electoral system in which each political group is represented in a legislative body in proportion to its actual voting strength in the electorate

¹**pro·por·tion·ate** \prə-'pōr-sh(ə-)nət, -'pȯr-\ _adj_ **:** being in proportion ⟨did not receive returns _proportionate_ to his efforts⟩ — **pro·por·tion·ate·ly** _adv_

²**pro·por·tion·ate** \-shə-,nāt\ _vt_ **:** to make proportionate **:** PROPORTION

pro·pos·al \prə-'pō-zəl\ _n_ **1 :** an act of putting forward or stating something for consideration **2 a :** something proposed **:** SUGGESTION **b :** OFFER; _esp_ **:** an offer of marriage

pro·pose \prə-'pōz\ _vb_ [MF _proposer,_ irregular fr. L _proponere_ to propound] **1 :** to offer for consideration or discussion **:** SUGGEST ⟨_propose_ terms of peace⟩ **2 :** to make plans **:** INTEND ⟨_propose_ to buy a new house⟩ **3 :** to offer as a toast **:** suggest drinking to ⟨_propose_ a toast⟩ **4 :** NAME, NOMINATE ⟨_proposed_ him for membership⟩ **5 :** to make an offer of marriage — **pro·pos·er** _n_

prop·o·si·tion \,präp-ə-'zish-ən\ _n_ **1 a :** something proposed or offered for consideration or acceptance **:** PROPOSAL **b :** a theorem or problem to be demonstrated or performed **2 :** an expression in language or signs of something that can be either true or false **3 :** a project or situation requiring action **:** AFFAIR, UNDERTAKING — **prop·o·si·tion·al** \-'zish-nəl, -ən-ᵊl\ _adj_

pro·pound \prə-'paȯnd\ _vt_ [alter. of earlier _propone,_ fr. L _proponere_ to display, propound, fr. _pro-_ before + _ponere_ to put] **:** to offer for consideration **:** PROPOSE — **pro·pound·er** _n_

¹**pro·pri·e·tary** \prə-'prī-ə-,ter-ē\ _n, pl_ **-tar·ies 1 :** one to whom a proprietary colony is granted **2 :** a body of proprietors **3 :** a drug that is protected by secrecy, patent, or copyright against free competition **:** a proprietary medicine

²**proprietary** _adj_ [L _proprietas_ property] **1 :** of, relating to, or characteristic of a proprietor ⟨_proprietary_ rights⟩ **2 :** made and marketed by one having the exclusive right to manufacture and sell **3 :** privately owned and managed ⟨a _proprietary_ clinic⟩

proprietary colony _n_ **:** a colony granted to a proprietor with full prerogatives of government

pro·pri·e·tor \prə-'prī-ət-ər\ _n_ **1 :** one who holds something as his property or possession **:** OWNER **2 :** PROPRIETARY 1 — **pro·pri·e·tor·ship** \-,ship\ _n_ — **pro·pri·e·tress** \-'prī-ə-trəs\ _n_

pro·pri·e·ty \prə-'prī-ət-ē\ _n, pl_ **-ties** [MF _propriété_ property] **1 :** the quality or state of being proper **2 :** correctness in manners or behavior **:** POLITENESS **3 pl :** the rules and customs of polite society **syn** see DECORUM

pro·prio·cep·tive \,prō-prē-ō-'sep-tiv\ _adj_ [L _proprius_ own + E _-ceptive_ (as in _receptive_)] **:** of, relating to, or being stimuli arising within the organism — **pro·prio·cep·tor** \-tər\ _n_

prop root _n_ **:** a root that braces or supports a plant

pro·pul·sion \prə-'pəl-shən\ _n_ [L _propuls-, propellere_ to propel] **1 :** the action or process of propelling **2 :** something that propels

pro·pul·sive \-'pəl-siv\ _adj_ **:** tending or having power to propel

pro·pyl alcohol \,prō-pəl-\ _n_ [_propionic_ acid + _-yl_] **:** a usu. synthesized alcohol C_3H_7OH used as a solvent and in chemical manufacture

pro·pyl·ene gly·col \,prō-pə-,lēn-'glī-,kȯl, -,kōl\ _n_ **:** a

sweet viscous liquid $C_3H_8O_2$ used as an antifreeze, solvent, and preservative

pro ra·ta \(')prō-'rāt-ə, -'rät-ə\ _adv_ [L _pro rata parte_ according to a calculated part] **:** according to share or liability **:** PROPORTIONATELY — **pro rata** _adj_

pro·rate \(')prō-'rāt\ _vb_ **:** to divide, distribute, or assess proportionately — **pro·ra·tion** \-'rā-shən\ _n_

pro·rogue \prə-'rōg\ _vb_ [L _prorogare_ to prolong, put off, fr. _pro-_ forward + _rogare_ ask] **:** to suspend or end a legislative session — **pro·ro·ga·tion** \,prȯr-ō-'gā-shən, ,prȯr-\ _n_

pro·sa·ic \prō-'zā-ik\ _adj_ **1 a :** characteristic of prose as distinguished from poetry **:** FACTUAL **b :** DULL, UNIMAGINATIVE **2 :** belonging to the everyday world **:** COMMONPLACE — **pro·sa·i·cal·ly** \-'zā-ə-k(ə-)lē\ _adv_

pro·sce·ni·um \prō-'sē-nē-əm\ _n_ [L, fr. Gk _proskēnion_ front of the building forming the background for a dramatic performance, stage, fr. _pro-_ + _skēnē_ building forming the background for a dramatic performance] **1 :** the stage of an ancient theater **2 :** the part of a modern stage in front of the curtain **3 :** the wall that separates the stage from the auditorium and provides the arch that frames it

pro·scribe \prō-'skrīb\ _vt_ **1 :** to put outside the protection of the law **:** OUTLAW **2 :** to condemn or forbid as harmful **:** PROHIBIT — **pro·scrib·er** _n_ — **pro·scrip·tion** \-'skrip-shən\ _n_ — **pro·scrip·tive** \-'skrip-tiv\ _adj_ — **pro·scrip·tive·ly** _adv_

¹**prose** \'prōz\ _n_ [L _prosa,_ fr. fem. of _prorsus, prosus,_ straightforward, contr. of _proversus,_ pp. of _provertere_ to turn forward, fr. _pro-_ forward + _vertere_ to turn] **1 a :** the ordinary language of men in speaking or writing **b :** a literary medium distinguished from poetry esp. by its greater irregularity and variety of rhythm and its closer correspondence to the patterns of everyday speech **2 :** a prosaic style, quality, character, or condition **:** ORDINARINESS, MATTER-OF-FACTNESS ⟨the _prose_ of everyday life⟩ — **prose** _adj_

²**prose** _vi_ **1 :** to write prose **2 :** to write or speak in a dull prosy manner

pros·e·cute \'präs-i-,kyüt\ _vb_ [L _prosecut-, prosequi_ to follow after, fr. _pro-_ forward + _sequi_ to follow] **1 :** to follow up to the end **:** keep at **:** persist in ⟨_prosecute_ a war⟩ **2 :** to seek to punish through an appeal to the courts **:** carry on a legal action against an accused person to prove his guilt — **pros·e·cut·a·ble** \-,kyüt-ə-bəl\ _adj_

prosecuting attorney _n_ **:** DISTRICT ATTORNEY

pros·e·cu·tion \,präs-i-'kyü-shən\ _n_ **1 :** the act or process of prosecuting; _esp_ **:** the institution and continuance of a criminal suit in court **2 :** the party by whom criminal proceedings are instituted or conducted

pros·e·cu·tor \'präs-i-,kyüt-ər\ _n_ **1 :** a person who institutes an official prosecution before a court **2 :** an attorney who conducts proceedings in a court on behalf of the government **:** DISTRICT ATTORNEY

¹**pros·e·lyte** \'präs-ə-,līt\ _n_ [Gk _prosēlytos_ alien resident, proselyte] **:** a new convert **:** NEOPHYTE **syn** see CONVERT

²**proselyte** _vb_ **1 :** to convert from one religion, belief, or party to another **2 :** to recruit members esp. by the offer of special inducements — **pros·e·ly·tism** \-,līt-,iz-əm, -lə-,tiz-\ _n_

pros·e·ly·tize \-lə-,tīz\ _vb_ **:** PROSELYTE

pros·en·ceph·a·lon \,präs-,en-'sef-ə-,län\ _n_ [NL, fr. Gk _pros-_ near] **:** FOREBRAIN — **pros·en·ce·phal·ic** \,präs-,en(t)-sə-'fal-ik\ _adj_

pros·en·chy·ma \prä-'seŋ-kə-mə\ _n, pl_ **pros·en·chym·a·ta** \,präs-ᵊn-'kim-ət-ə\ _or_ **prosenchymas** [NL, fr. Gk _pros-_ near, in addition + NL _-enchyma_ (as in _parenchyma_)] **:** a tissue of higher plants specialized for conduction and support — **pros·en·chym·a·tous** \,präs-ᵊn-'kim-ət-əs\ _adj_

Pro·ser·pi·na \prə-'sər-pə-nə\ _or_ **Pros·er·pine** \'präs-ər-,pīn\ _n_ **:** PERSEPHONE

pro·sim·i·an \(')prō-'sim-ē-ən\ _n_ **:** a lower primate (as a lemur) — **prosimian** _adj_

pros·i·ness \'prō-zē-nəs\ _n_ **:** the quality or state of being prosy

pro·sit \'prō-zət, -sət\ _or_ **prost** \'prōst\ _interj_ [G, fr. L _prosit_ may it be beneficial] — used to wish good health esp. before drinking

pros·o·dist \'präs-əd-əst\ _n_ **:** a specialist in prosody

pros·o·dy \'präs-əd-ē\ _n, pl_ **-dies** [Gk _prosōidia_ accent, fr.

pros in addition to + *ōidē* song\ 1 : the study of versifica-tion; *esp* : METRICS 2 : a particular system, theory, or style of versification — **pro·sod·ic** \prə-'säd-ik\ *adj* — **pro·sod·i·cal·ly** \-i-k(ə-)lē\ *adv*

¹pros·pect \'präs-,pekt\ *n* [L *prospectus,* fr. *prospicere* to look forward, fr. *pro-* forward + *specere* to look] 1 a : an extensive view   b : SURVEY 2 : something extended to the view : SCENE 3 a : act of looking forward : ANTICIPATION   b : a mental picture of something to come : VISION   c : something that is awaited or expected : POSSIBILITY 4 a : a potential buyer or customer   b : a candidate or a person likely to become a candidate ⟨presidential *prospect*⟩

²prospect *vb* : to explore an area esp. for mineral deposits — **pros·pec·tor** \-,pek-tər\ *n*

pro·spec·tive \prə-'spek-tiv, 'präs-,pek-\ *adj* 1 : likely to come about : EXPECTED ⟨the *prospective* benefits of a law⟩ 2 : likely to be or become ⟨a *prospective* bride⟩— **pro·spec·tive·ly** *adv*

pro·spec·tus \prə-'spek-təs, prä-\ *n, pl* **pro·spec·tus·es** [L, prospect] : a printed statement describing an enterprise and distributed to prospective investors

pros·per \'präs-pər\ *vb* **pros·pered; pros·per·ing** \-p(ə-)riŋ\ [L *prosperare* to cause to succeed, fr. *prosperus* favorable] 1 : SUCCEED; *esp* : to succeed financially 2 : FLOURISH, THRIVE 3 : to cause to succeed or thrive

pros·per·i·ty \prä-'sper-ət-ē\ *n* : the condition of being successful or thriving; *esp* : economic well-being

pros·per·ous \'präs-p(ə-)rəs\ *adj* 1 : marked by success or economic well-being 2 : FLOURISHING — **pros·per·ous·ly** *adv* — **pros·per·ous·ness** *n*

pros·ta·glan·din \,präs-tə-'glan-dən\ *n* [*prosta*te *gland* + *-in;* fr. its occurrence in the sexual glands of animals] : any of various fatty acids of animals that may perform a variety of hormonelike actions (as in controlling blood pressure or smooth muscle contraction)

pros·tate \'präs-,tāt\ *also* **pros·tat·ic** \prä-'stat-ik\ *adj* [NL *prostata* prostate gland, fr. Gk *prostatēs,* fr. *proïs-tasthai* to stand in front, fr. *pro-* + *histasthai* to stand] : of or relating to or being the prostate gland

prostate gland *n* : a firm partly muscular partly glandular body about the base of the mammalian male urethra

pros·the·sis \präs-'thē-səs, 'präs-thə-\ *n, pl* **-the·ses** \-,sēz\ [Gk, addition, fr. *prostithenai* to add to, fr. *pros-* in addition to + *tithenai* to put] : an artificial device to replace a missing part of the body — **pros·thet·ic** \präs-'thet-ik\ *adj* — **pros·thet·i·cal·ly** \-'thet-i-k(ə-)lē\ *adv*

prosthetic group *n* : a nonprotein group of a conjugated protein

¹pros·ti·tute \'präs-tə-,t(y)üt\ *vt* [L *prostituere* to offer for prostitution, fr. *pro-* forth + *statuere* to cause to stand, fr. *status* standing] : to devote to corrupt or unworthy pur-poses : DEBASE ⟨*prostitute* one's talent⟩

²prostitute *n* : a woman who engages in promiscuous sexual intercourse esp. for money : WHORE

pros·ti·tu·tion \,präs-tə-'t(y)ü-shən\ *n* 1 : the acts or practices of a prostitute 2 : the state of being prostituted

pro·sto·mi·um \prō-'stō-mē-əm\ *n, pl* **-mia** \-mē-ə\ [NL, fr. Gk *stoma* mouth] : the portion of the head of various worms and mollusks situated in front of the mouth and usu. held not to be a true segment — **pro·sto·mi·al** \-mē-əl\ *adj*

¹pros·trate \'präs-,trāt\ *adj* [L *prostratus,* pp. of *proster-nere* to prostrate, fr. *pro-* forward + *sternere* to spread out flat] 1 a : stretched out with face on the ground (as in adoration or submission)   b : extended in a horizontal position : FLAT 2 : lacking in vitality or will : OVERCOME **syn** see PRONE

²prostrate *vt* 1 : to throw or put into a prostrate position 2 : to reduce to submission, helplessness, or exhaustion : OVERCOME

pros·tra·tion \prä-'strā-shən\ *n* 1 : the act of assuming or state of being in a prostrate position 2 : complete physical or mental exhaustion : COLLAPSE

prosy \'prō-zē\ *adj* **pros·i·er; -est** 1 : PROSAIC 2 : TE-DIOUS

prot- *or* **proto-** *comb form* [Gk *prōtos* foremost, first] 1 : first in time ⟨*proto*lithic⟩ 2 : first formed : primary ⟨*proto*xylem⟩ 3 *cap* : relating to or constituting the re-corded or assumed language that is ancestral to a language or to a group of related languages or dialects ⟨*Proto*-Indo-European⟩

prot·ac·tin·i·um \,prōt-,ak-'tin-ē-əm\ *n* : a shiny metallic radioactive chemical element of relatively short life — see ELEMENT table

pro·tag·o·nist \prō-'tag-ə-nəst\ *n* [Gk *prōtagōnistēs,* fr. *prōtos* first + *agōnistēs* competitor at games, actor, fr. *agōn* contest] 1 : one who takes the leading part in a drama, novel, or story 2 : the leader of a cause : CHAM-PION 3 : a muscle that by its contraction actually causes a particular movement

prot·amine \'prōt-ə-,mēn\ *n* : any of various simple strongly basic proteins that are not coagulable by heat but are soluble in water and dilute ammonia

pro·te·an \'prōt-ē-ən\ *adj* [*Proteus*] : readily assuming different shapes or roles ⟨the *protean* amoeba⟩ ⟨a *protean* actor⟩

pro·te·ase \'prōt-ē-,ās\ *n* : PROTEINASE, PEPTIDASE

pro·tect \prə-'tekt\ *vt* [L *protect-, protegere,* fr. *pro-* in front + *tegere* to cover] 1 : to cover or shield from injury or destruction : GUARD 2 : to save from contingent financial loss **syn** see DEFEND

pro·tec·tion \prə-'tek-shən\ *n* 1 : the act of protecting : the state of being protected 2 a : one that protects   b : the oversight or support of one that is smaller and weaker 3 : the freeing of the producers of a country from foreign competition by high duties on foreign goods 4 : money extorted by racketeers threatening violence 5 : COVERAGE 2b — **pro·tec·tive** \-'tek-tiv\ *adj* — **pro·tec·tive·ly** *adv*

pro·tec·tion·ist \-sh(ə-)nəst\ *n* : an advocate of govern-ment economic protection for domestic producers through restrictions on foreign competitors — **pro·tec·tion·ism** \-shə-,niz-əm\ *n* — **protectionist** *adj*

protective tariff *n* : a tariff intended primarily to protect domestic producers rather than to yield revenue

pro·tec·tor \prə-'tek-tər\ *n* 1 a : one that protects : GUARDIAN   b : a device used to prevent injury : GUARD 2 : one having the care of a kingdom during the king's minority : REGENT — **pro·tec·tor·ship** \-,ship\ *n* — **pro·tec·tress** \-'tek-trəs\ *n*

pro·tec·tor·ate \prə-'tek-t(ə-)rət\ *n* 1 a : government by a protector; *esp* : the government of England (1653–59) under the Cromwells   b : the rank, office, or period of rule of a protector 2 a : the relationship of superior authority assumed by one state over a dependent one   b : the de-pendent state in such a relationship

pro·té·gé \'prōt-ə-,zhā\ *n* [F, fr. pp. of *protéger* to protect, fr. L *protegere*] : a person under the care and protection of someone influential who intends to further his career

pro·té·gée \-,zhā\ *n* : a female protégé

pro·tein \'prō-,tēn, 'prōt-ē-ən\ *n* [F *protéine,* fr. Gk *prōtos* first] 1 : any of numerous naturally occurring combinations of amino acids that contain esp. the elements carbon, hydrogen, nitrogen, oxygen, usu. sulfur, occas. phosphorus or iron, are essential constituents of all living cells, and are synthesized from raw materials by plants but assimilated as separate amino acids by animals 2 : the total nitrogenous material in plant or animal substances — **pro·tein·a·ceous** \,prō-,tē-'nā-shəs, ,prōt-ē-ə-'nā-\ *adj*

pro·tein·ase \'prō-,tē-,nās, 'prōt-ē-ə-\ *n* : an enzyme that hydrolyzes proteins esp. to peptides

pro tem \prō-'tem\ *adv* : pro tempore

pro tem·po·re \prō-'tem-pə-rē\ *adv* [L] : for the present : TEMPORARILY ⟨chairman *pro tempore*⟩

pro·te·ol·y·sis \,prōt-ē-'äl-ə-səs\ *n* : hydrolysis of proteins or peptides to simpler and soluble products — **pro·teo·lyt·ic** \,prōt-ē-ə-'lit-ik\ *adj*

pro·te·ose \'prōt-ē-,ōs\ *n* : any of various water-soluble protein derivatives formed by partial hydrolysis

Prot·ero·zo·ic \,prät-ə-rə-'zō-ik, ,prōt-\ *n* [Gk *proteros* former, earlier, fr. *pro* before] : the 2d of the five eras of geological history that perhaps exceeds in length all of subsequent geological time and is marked by rocks that contain a few fossils indicating the existence of annelid worms and algae; *also* : the corresponding system of rocks — see GEOLOGIC TIME table — **Proterozoic** *adj*

¹pro·test \'prō-,test\ *n* 1 : a formal declaration of opinion and usu. of objection or complaint 2 : a declaration that payment of a note or bill has been refused and that all endorsers are liable for damages 3 : a complaint, objec-tion, or display of unwillingness or disapproval

²pro·test \prə-'test\ *vb* [L *protestari,* fr. *pro-* forth +

testari to call to witness] **1 a :** to make solemn declaration of : ASSERT ⟨*protested* his innocence⟩ **b :** to make a protestation **2 a :** to make a protest against ⟨*protested* the higher tax rate⟩ **b :** to object strongly ⟨*protest* against an arbitrary ruling⟩

prot·es·tant \'prät-əs-tənt, *2 is also* prə-'tes-\ *n* **1** *cap* **a :** one of a group of German princes and cities presenting a defense of freedom of conscience against an edict of the Diet of Spires in 1529 intended to suppress the Lutheran movement **b :** a member or adherent of one of the Christian churches deriving from the Reformation and affirming justification by faith, the priesthood of all believers, and the primacy of the Bible **c :** a Christian not of a Catholic or Eastern church **2 :** one who makes or enters a protest — **protestant** *adj, often cap* — **Prot·es·tant·ism** \'prät-əs-tənt-,iz-əm\ *n*

prot·es·ta·tion \,prät-əs-'tā-shən, ,prō-,tes-\ *n* : the act of protesting : a solemn declaration or avowal

Pro·teus \'prō-,t(y)üs, 'prōt-ē-əs\ *n* : a sea-god in Greek mythology capable of assuming different forms

pro·tha·la·mi·on \,prō-thə-'lā-mē-ən\ *or* **pro·tha·la·mi·um** \-mē-əm\ *n, pl* **pro·tha·la·mia** \-mē-ə\ [NL, fr. Gk *pro- -thalamion* + (as in *epithalamion*)] : a song in celebration of a marriage

pro·thal·li·um \(')prō-'thal-ē-əm\ *or* **pro·thal·lus** \-'thal-əs\ *n, pl* **-lia** \-ē-ə\ *or* **-li** \-,ī, -,ē\ [NL, fr. *pro-* + *thallus*] : a small flat green thallus attached to the soil by rhizoids that is the gametophyte of a pteridophyte (as a fern) — **pro·thal·li·al** \-ē-əl\ *adj*

pro·tho·rax \(')prō-'thō(ə)r-,aks, -'thò(ə)r-\ *n* : the anterior segment of the thorax of an insect — **pro·tho·rac·ic** \,prō-thə-'ras-ik\ *adj*

pro·throm·bin \(')prō-'thräm-bən\ *n* : a plasma protein produced in the liver in the presence of vitamin K and converted into thrombin in the clotting of blood

pro·tist \'prōt-əst\ *n* [Gk *prōtistos* very first, primal, fr. superl. of *prōtos* first] : any of a kingdom or group (Protista) of unicellular or noncellular organisms comprising bacteria, protozoans, various algae and fungi, and sometimes viruses — **pro·tis·tan** \prō-'tis-tən\ *adj or n*

pro·ti·um \'prōt-ē-əm, 'prō-shē-\ *n* [NL, fr. Gk *prōtos* first] : the ordinary light hydrogen isotope of atomic mass 1

proto- — SEE PROT-

pro·to·ac·tin·i·um \,prōt-ō-,ak-'tin-ē-əm\ *var of* PROTACTINIUM

pro·to·coc·cus \,prōt-ə-'käk-əs\ *n* : any of a genus of globose and mostly terrestrial green algae

pro·to·col \'prōt-ə-,kól\ *n* [LGk *prōtokollon* first sheet of a papyrus roll bearing data of manufacture, fr. Gk *prōtos* first + *kollan* to glue] **1 :** an original draft, minute, or record of a document or transaction : MEMORANDUM **2 :** a code of diplomatic or military etiquette and precedence

pro·to·his·to·ry \,prōt-ō-'his-t(ə-)rē\ *n* : the study of man in the times that just antedate recorded history — **pro·to·his·tor·ic** \-his-'tór-ik, -'tär-\ *adj*

pro·to·hu·man \-'hyü-mən, -'yü-\ *adj* : of, relating to, or being an early primitive human or manlike primate

pro·to·mar·tyr \'prōt-ō-,märt-ər\ *n* : the first martyr in a cause or region

pro·ton \'prō-,tän\ *n* [Gk *prōton*, neut. of *prōtos* first] : an elementary particle identical with the nucleus of the hydrogen atom that along with neutrons is a constituent of all other atomic nuclei and carries a positive charge numerically equal to the negative charge of an electron — **pro·ton·ic** \prō-'tän-ik\ *adj*

pro·to·ne·ma \,prōt-ə-'nē-mə\ *n, pl* **-ne·ma·ta** \-'nē-mət-ə, -'nem-ət-\ [Gk *nēmat-, nēma* thread] : the primary usu. filamentous stage of the gametophyte in mosses and some liverworts that is comparable to the fern prothallium — **pro·to·ne·mal** \-'nē-məl\ *adj* — **pro·to·ne·ma·tal** \-'nē-mət-ᵊl, -'nem-ət-\ *adj*

pro·to·plasm \'prōt-ə-,plaz-əm\ *n* **1 :** a colloidal complex of protein, various organic and inorganic substances, and water that constitutes the living nucleus, cytoplasm, plastids, and mitochondria of the cell and is held to be the only form of matter in which the vital phenomena are manifested **2 :** CYTOPLASM — **pro·to·plas·mic** \,prōt-ə-'plaz-mik\ *adj*

pro·to·plast \'prōt-ə-,plast\ *n* : the nucleus, cytoplasm, and plasma membrane of a cell constituting a living unit

distinct from inert walls and inclusions — **pro·to·plas·tic** \,prōt-ə-'plas-tik\ *adj*

pro·to·troph·ic \,prōt-ə-'träf-ik\ *adj* : deriving nutriment from inorganic sources

pro·to·type \'prōt-ə-,tīp\ *n* **1 :** an original model on which something is patterned **2 :** an individual that exhibits the essential features of a later type — **pro·to·typ·al** \,prōt-ə-'tī-pəl\ *adj* — **pro·to·typ·ic** \-'tip-ik\ *adj*

pro·to·zo·an \,prōt-ə-'zō-ən\ *n* [NL *protozoon*, fr. Gk *zōion* animal] : any of a phylum or group (Protozoa) of minute protoplasmic animals that are not divided into cells and have varied morphology and physiology and often complex life cycles — **protozoan** *or* **pro·to·zo·al** \-'zō-əl\ *adj* — **pro·to·zo·ic** \-'zō-ik\ *adj*

pro·to·zo·ol·o·gy \-zō-'äl-ə-jē\ *n* : a branch of zoology dealing with protozoans — **pro·to·zo·ol·o·gist** \-jəst\ *n*

pro·to·zo·on \-'zō-,än\ *n, pl* **-zoa** \-'zō-ə\ : PROTOZOAN

pro·tract \prō-'trakt\ *vt* [L *protract-, protrahere*, lit., to draw forward, fr. *pro-* forward + *trahere* to draw] **1 :** to prolong in time or space **2 :** to lay down the lines and angles of with scale and protractor : PLOT **syn** see EXTEND — **pro·trac·tion** \-'trak-shən\ *n* — **pro·trac·tive** \-'trak-tiv\ *adj*

pro·trac·tor \prō-'trak-tər\ *n* **1 a :** one that protracts, prolongs, or delays **b :** a muscle that extends a part — compare RETRACTOR **2 :** an instrument for laying down and measuring angles that is used in drawing and plotting

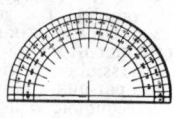

protractor 2

pro·trude \prō-'trüd\ *vb* [L *protrus-, protrudere* to thrust forward, fr. *pro-* + *trudere* to thrust] **1 :** to stick out or cause to stick out : PROJECT **2 :** to jut out from the surroundings — **pro·tru·si·ble** \-'trü-sə-bəl, -zə-\ *adj*

pro·tru·sile \prō-'trü-səl, -zəl\ *adj* : capable of being protruded

pro·tru·sion \prō-'trü-zhən\ *n* **1 :** the act of protruding : the state of being protruded **2 :** something that protrudes **syn** see PROJECTION

pro·tu·ber·ance \prō-'t(y)ü-b(ə-)rən(t)s\ *n* **1 :** the quality or state of being protuberant **2 :** something that is protuberant : BULGE

pro·tu·ber·ant \-b(ə-)rənt\ *adj* [LL *protuberare* to bulge out, fr. L *pro-* forward + *tuber* hump, swelling] : bulging beyond the surrounding surface : PROMINENT — **pro·tu·ber·ant·ly** *adv*

proud \'praud\ *adj* [OE *prūd*] **1 :** feeling or showing pride: as **a :** having or displaying excessive self-esteem ⟨*proud* ladies⟩ **b :** much pleased : EXULTANT ⟨*proud* parents of the valedictorian⟩ **c :** having proper self-respect ⟨too *proud* to beg⟩ **2 :** MAGNIFICENT, GLORIOUS ⟨a *proud* record⟩ **3 :** VIGOROUS, SPIRITED ⟨a *proud* steed⟩ — **proud·ly** *adv*

proud flesh *n* : an excessive growth of granulation tissue (as in a wound)

prove \'prüv\ *vb* **proved; proved** *or* **prov·en** \'prü-vən\; **prov·ing** [OF *prover*, fr. L *probare* to test, approve, demonstrate, fr. *probus* good, honest] **1 :** to try or ascertain by an experiment or a standard **2 a :** to establish the truth or validity of by evidence or demonstration **b :** to check the correctness of (as an arithmetic operation) **3 :** to ascertain the genuineness of : VERIFY; *esp* : to obtain probate of (a will) **4 :** to turn out esp. after trial or test ⟨the new automobile engine *proved* to be impractical⟩ — **prov·a·ble** \'prü-və-bəl\ *adj*

prov·e·nance \'präv-(ə-)nən(t)s\ *n* [F, fr. *provenir* to come forth, originate, fr. L *provenire*, fr. *pro-* + *venire* to come] : ORIGIN, SOURCE

Pro·ven·çal \,präv-ən-'säl\ *n* **1 :** a native or inhabitant of Provence **2 :** a Romance language spoken in southeastern France — **Provençal** *adj*

prov·en·der \'präv-ən-dər\ *n* [MF *provende, provendre*, fr. ML *provenda*, alter. of *praebenda* prebend, provender] **1 :** dry food for domestic animals : FEED **2 :** FOOD, VICTUALS

pro·ve·nience \prə-'vē-nyən(t)s\ *n* [alter. of *provenance*] : ORIGIN, SOURCE

pro·ven·tric·u·lus \,prō-ven-'trik-yə-ləs\ *n, pl* **-li** \-,lī, -,lē\ [NL] : a pouch of the digestive tract (as of an insect), *esp* : the glandular stomach of a bird situated between the crop and gizzard

prov·erb \'präv-,ərb\ *n* [L *proverbium*, fr. *pro-* + *verbum* word] : a brief popular saying or maxim : ADAGE

pro·ver·bi·al \prə-'vər-bē-əl\ *adj* 1 : of, relating to, or resembling a proverb ⟨*proverbial* wisdom⟩ 2 : commonly spoken of ⟨the *proverbial* beginner's luck⟩ — **pro·ver·bi·al·ly** \-bē-ə-lē\ *adv*

Prov·erbs \'präv-,ərbz\ *n* — see BIBLE table

pro·vide \prə-'vīd\ *vb* [L *providēre*, lit., to see ahead, fr. *pro-* forward + *vidēre* to see] 1 : to take precautionary measures ⟨*provide* against a possible scarcity⟩ 2 : to make a proviso or condition : STIPULATE ⟨the contract *provided* for 10 paid holidays⟩ 3 : to supply what is needed for sustenance or support ⟨*provides* for a large family⟩ 4 a : OUTFIT, EQUIP b : to supply for use : YIELD ⟨cows *provide* milk⟩ — **pro·vid·er** *n*

pro·vid·ed *conj* : on condition : IF — sometimes followed by *that*

prov·i·dence \'präv-əd-ən(t)s, -ə-,den(t)s\ *n* 1 a *often cap* : divine guidance or care b *cap* : God conceived as the power sustaining and guiding human destiny 2 : the quality or state of being provident : PRUDENCE

prov·i·dent \-əd-ənt,-ə-,dent\ *adj* 1 : making provision for the future : PRUDENT 2 : FRUGAL, SAVING — **prov·i·dent·ly** *adv*

prov·i·den·tial \,präv-ə-'den-chəl\ *adj* 1 : of, relating to, or determined by Providence ⟨a *providential* plan⟩ 2 : occurring by or as if by an intervention of Providence : FORTUNATE ⟨*providential* escape⟩ — **prov·i·den·tial·ly** \-'dench-(ə-)lē\ *adv*

pro·vid·ing \prə-'vīd-iŋ\ *conj* : PROVIDED

prov·ince \'präv-ən(t)s\ *n* [L *provincia*] 1 a : a country or region brought under the control of the ancient Roman government b : a usu. large administrative district or division of a country c *pl* : all of a country except the metropolis 2 : a division of a country forming the jurisdiction of an archbishop or metropolitan or of a religious provincial 3 : proper or appropriate business or scope : SPHERE ⟨a legal question outside the physician's *province*⟩

¹**pro·vin·cial** \prə-'vin-chəl\ *n* 1 : the superior of a province of a religious order 2 : one living in or coming from a province 3 a : a person of local or restricted outlook b : a person lacking urban polish or refinement

²**provincial** *adj* 1 : of, relating to, or coming from a province 2 a : limited in outlook : SECTIONAL, NARROW b : lacking the polish of urban society : UNSOPHISTICATED 3 : of or relating to a decorative style (as in furniture and architecture) characterized by simplicity of design and relative plainness of decoration — **pro·vin·ci·al·i·ty** \-,vin-chē-'al-ət-ē\ *n* — **pro·vin·cial·ly** \-'vinch-(ə-)lē\ *adv*

pro·vin·cial·ism \prə-'vin-chə-,liz-əm\ *n* 1 : a dialectal or local word, phrase, or idiom 2 : the quality or state of being provincial

proving ground *n* : a place for scientific experimentation or testing; *esp* : an area used for testing weapons

¹**pro·vi·sion** \prə-'vizh-ən\ *n* [L, *provis-, providēre* to provide] 1 a : the act or process of providing ⟨*provision* of transportation for the trip⟩ b : a measure taken beforehand : PREPARATION ⟨make *provision* for emergencies⟩ 2 : a stock of needed materials or supplies; *esp* : a stock of food — usu. used in pl. 3 : STIPULATION, PROVISO ⟨a constitutional *provision*⟩

²**provision** *vt* **pro·vi·sioned; pro·vi·sion·ing** \-'vizh-(ə-)niŋ\ : to supply with provisions ⟨*provision* a military garrison⟩

pro·vi·sion·al \prə-'vizh-nəl, -ən-°l\ *adj* : serving for the time being : TEMPORARY, TENTATIVE ⟨a *provisional* government⟩ ⟨*provisional* arrangements⟩ — **pro·vi·sion·al·ly** \-ē\ *adv*

pro·vi·so \prə-'vī-zō\ *n, pl* **-sos** *or* **-soes** [ML *proviso quod* provided that] 1 : a sentence or clause in a legal document in which a condition is stated 2 : a conditional stipulation : PROVISION ⟨given a bicycle with the *proviso* that it be kept in good repair⟩

pro·vi·ta·min \(')prō-'vīt-ə-mən\ *n* : a precursor of a vitamin convertible into the vitamin in an organism

prov·o·ca·tion \,präv-ə-'kā-shən\ *n* : the act of provoking : INCITEMENT; *also* : something that provokes, arouses, or stimulates

pro·voc·a·tive \prə-'väk-ət-iv\ *adj* : serving or tending to provoke, excite, or stimulate ⟨*provocative* comments⟩ — **pro·voc·a·tive·ly** *adv* — **pro·voc·a·tive·ness** *n*

pro·voke \prə-'vōk\ *vt* [L *provocare*, fr. *pro-* forth + *vocare* to call] 1 : to arouse to action or feeling; *esp* : to excite to anger 2 : to bring about : stir up : EVOKE ⟨*provoke* a response from a nerve⟩

syn PROVOKE, EXCITE, STIMULATE mean to arouse as if by pricking. PROVOKE directs attention to the response called forth ⟨a joke that failed to *provoke* laughter⟩ ⟨such diplomatic moves as *provoke* nations to war⟩ EXCITE implies a stirring up or moving profoundly ⟨*exciting* admiration by his performance⟩ STIMULATE suggests a rousing out of lethargy, quiescence, or indifference ⟨the need to *stimulate* the economy⟩

pro·vok·ing \-'vō-kiŋ\ *adj* : causing mild anger : ANNOYING ⟨a *provoking* delay⟩ — **pro·vok·ing·ly** \-kiŋ-lē\ *adv*

pro·vost \'prō-,vōst, 'präv-əst, *before* "marshal" *often* 'prō-vō\ *n* [OE *profost* & OF *provost*, fr. ML *propositus*, alter. of L *praepositus* one in charge, fr. pp. of *praeponere* to place at the head] 1 : the chief dignitary of a collegiate or cathedral chapter 2 : a chief magistrate or a high-ranking administrative officer (as in a university)

provost marshal *n* : the head of the military police of a command

prow \'prau̇\ *n* [MF *proue*, fr. It dial. *prua*, fr. L *prora*, fr. Gk *prōira*] 1 : the bow of a ship : STEM 2 : a pointed projecting front part

prow·ess \'prau̇-əs\ *n* [OF *proesse*, fr. *prou* valiant] 1 : distinguished bravery; *esp* : military valor and skill 2 : extraordinary ability

prowl \'prau̇l\ *vb* [ME *prollen*] 1 : to move about or wander stealthily in the manner of a wild beast seeking prey 2 : to roam over in a predatory manner ⟨*prowled* the streets⟩ — **prowl** *n* — **prowl·er** *n*

prowl car *n* : SQUAD CAR

prox·i·mal \'präk-sə-məl\ *adj* 1 : NEAREST, PROXIMATE 2 : near or next to the point of attachment or origin — compare DISTAL — **prox·i·mal·ly** \-mə-lē\ *adv*

prox·i·mate \-mət\ *adj* [L *proximus*, superl. of *prope* near] 1 a : very near : CLOSE b : soon forthcoming 2 : next preceding or following : DIRECT ⟨the *proximate* cause⟩ — **prox·i·mate·ly** *adv* — **prox·i·mate·ness** *n*

prox·im·i·ty \präk-'sim-ət-ē\ *n* : the quality or state of being proximate

prox·i·mo \'präk-sə-,mō\ *adj* [L *proximo mense* in the next month] : of or occurring in the next month after the present

proxy \'präk-sē\ *n, pl* **prox·ies** [AF *procuracie*, fr. ML *procuratia*, alter. of L *procuratio* procuration] 1 : authority held by one person to act for another (as in voting) 2 a : a person holding authority to act for another b : a written paper giving a person such authority — **proxy** *adj*

prude \'prüd\ *n* [F, good woman, prudish woman, short for *prudefemme* good woman] : a person and esp. a woman who is exaggeratedly or affectedly modest in speech, behavior, and dress and is oversensitive to slight violations of accepted rules of decorous behavior — **prud·ish** \'prüd-ish\ *adj* — **prud·ish·ly** *adv* — **prud·ish·ness** *n*

pru·dence \'prüd-°n(t)s\ *n* 1 : the ability to govern and discipline oneself by the use of reason 2 : sagacity or shrewdness in the management of affairs : DISCRETION 3 : skill and good judgment in the use of resources : ECONOMY, FRUGALITY 4 : CAUTION, CIRCUMSPECTION

pru·dent \-°nt\ *adj* [L *prudent-, prudens*, contr. of *providens* provident] 1 : FORESIGHTED, WISE 2 : shrewd in the management of practical affairs 3 : CIRCUMSPECT, DISCREET 4 : PROVIDENT, FRUGAL — **pru·dent·ly** *adv*

pru·den·tial \prü-'den-chəl\ *adj* 1 : of, relating to, or resulting from prudence 2 : using prudence — **pru·den·tial·ly** \-chə-lē\ *adv*

prud·ery \'prüd-(ə-)rē\ *n, pl* **-er·ies** 1 : the quality or state of being prudish : exaggerated or priggish modesty 2 : a prudish remark or act

pru·inose \'prü-ə-,nōs\ *adj* [L *pruina* hoarfrost] : covered with whitish dust or bloom

¹**prune** \'prün\ *n* [L *prunum* plum] 1 : a plum dried or capable of drying without fermentation 2 : a dull or unattractive person

²**prune** *vb* [MF *proignier*] 1 : to cut off the dead or unwanted parts of a usu. woody plant ⟨*prune* the hedge⟩

---

j joke; ŋ sing; ō flow; ȯ flaw; ȯi coin; th thin; th͟ this; ü loot; u̇ foot; y yet; yü few; yu̇ furious; zh vision

2 a : to cut down or reduce by eliminating superfluous or unwanted matter : RETRENCH 〈*prune* an essay〉 〈*prune* a budget〉 **b :** to remove as superfluous — **prun·er** *n*

pruning hook *n* : a pole bearing a curved blade for pruning plants

pru·ri·ent \'prŭr-ē-ənt\ *adj* [L *prurire* to itch] : having or revealing indecent desires or thoughts : LEWD — **pru·ri·ence** \-ē-ən(t)s\ *n* — **pru·ri·ent·ly** *adv*

pru·ri·go \prŭ-'rī-gō, -'rē-\ *n* [L *prurigin-, prurigo* itch, fr. *prurire* to itch] : a chronic inflammatory skin disease marked by itching papules

pru·ri·tus \prŭ-'rīt-əs, -'rēt-\ *n* : ITCHING — **pru·rit·ic** \-'rit-ik\ *adj*

prus·sic acid \,prəs-ik-\ *n* : HYDROCYANIC ACID

¹pry \'prī\ *vi* **pried; pry·ing** [ME *prien*] : to look closely or inquisitively : PEER; *esp* : to make a presumptuous inquiry 〈*pry* into other people's affairs〉

²pry *vt* **pried; pry·ing** [alter. of ⁵*prize*] **1 :** to raise, move, or pull apart with a pry or lever **2 :** to extract, detach, or open with difficulty 〈*pry* a secret out of a person〉

³pry *n* **1 :** a tool for prying **2 :** LEVERAGE

pry·ing *adj* : impertinently or officiously inquisitive or interrogatory   **syn** see CURIOUS — **pry·ing·ly** \-iŋ-lē\ *adv*

psalm \'säm, 'sälm\ *n* [OE *psealm*, fr. LL *psalmus*, fr. Gk *psalmos*, lit., twanging of a harp, fr. *psallein* to pluck] **1 :** a sacred song or poem **2** *cap* : one of the hymns that make up the Old Testament Book of Psalms

psalm·book \-,bùk\ *n* **1 :** PSALTER **2 :** a book of sacred poems or songs for use in public worship

psalm·ist \-əst\ *n* : a writer or composer of psalms

psalm·o·dy \-əd-ē\ *n, pl* **-dies 1 :** the art or practice of singing psalms in worship **2 :** a collection of psalms

Psalms \'sämz, 'sälmz\ *n* — see BIBLE table

Psal·ter \'sòl-tər\ *n* [OE *psalter*, fr. LL *psalterium*, fr. LGk *psaltērion*, fr. Gk, psaltery] : the Book of Psalms; *also* : a collection of Psalms for liturgical or devotional use

psal·te·ri·um \sòl-'tir-ē-əm\ *n, pl* **-ria** \-ē-ə\ [LL, psalter; fr. the resemblance of the folds to the pages of a book] : OMASUM

psal·tery *also* **psal·try** \'sòl-t(ə-)rē\ *n, pl* **-ter·ies** *also* **-tries** [Gk *psaltērion*, fr. *psallein* to play on a stringed instrument] : an ancient stringed musical instrument resembling the zither

pseud- *or* **pseudo-** *comb form* [Gk *pseudēs*] : false : sham : spurious 〈*pseudaxis*〉〈*pseudoclassic*〉〈*pseudopodium*〉

pseu·do \'süd-ō\ *adj* : SHAM, FEIGNED, SPURIOUS

pseu·do·coel \'süd-ə-,sēl\ *n* : a body cavity of an invertebrate that is not structurally or in origin a true coelom — **pseu·do·coe·lo·mate** \,süd-ə-'sē-lə-,māt\ *adj or n*

pseu·do·nym \'süd-°n-,im\ *n* [Gk *onyma, onoma* name] : a fictitious name; *esp* : PEN NAME

pseu·do·pod \'süd-ə-,päd\ *n* : PSEUDOPODIUM — **pseu·dop·o·dal** \sü-'däp-əd-°l\ *adj*

pseu·do·po·di·um \,süd-ə-'pōd-ē-əm\ *n, pl* **pseu·do·po·dia** \-ē-ə\ [NL, fr. Gk *podion*, dim. of *pod-, pous* foot] : a part of a cell that is temporarily protruded by moving cytoplasm (as in the amoeba) and that helps to move the cell and to take in its food — **pseu·do·po·di·al** \-ē-əl\ *adj*

psi \'sī\ *n* : the 23d letter of the Greek alphabet — Ψ *or* ψ

psi·lop·sid \sī-'läp-səd\ *n* : any of a major group (Psilopsida) of primitive rootless and often leafless vascular plants — **psilopsid** *adj*

psit·ta·cine \'sit-ə-,sīn\ *adj* [Gk *psittakos* parrot] : of or relating to the parrots — **psittacine** *n*

psit·ta·co·sis \,sit-ə-'kō-səs\ *n* : an infectious disease of birds caused by a rickettsia, marked by diarrhea and wasting, and transmissible to man in whom it usu. occurs as an atypical pneumonia accompanied by high fever

pso·ri·a·sis \sə-'rī-ə-səs\ *n* [Gk *psōriasis*, fr. *psōrian* to have the itch, fr. *psōra* itch] : a chronic skin disease characterized by circumscribed red patches covered with white scales — **pso·ri·at·ic** \,sōr-ē-'at-ik, ,sòr-\ *adj or n*

psych- *or* **psycho-** *comb form* [Gk *psychē* principle of life, soul] **1 :** mind : mental processes and activities 〈*psycho*dynamic〉〈*psychology*〉〈*psycho*analysis〉 **2 :** brain 〈*psycho*surgery〉 **3 :** mental and 〈*psycho*somatic〉

psych·as·the·nia \,sī-kəs-'thē-nē-ə\ *n* : a psychoneurotic state marked by inability to face reality or to resist phobias, obsessions, or compulsions that one knows are irrational — **psych·as·then·ic** \-'then-ik\ *adj or n*

psy·che \'sī-kē\ *n* **1** *cap* : a beautiful princess of classical mythology loved by Cupid **2 :** SOUL, SELF; *also* : MIND

¹psy·che·del·ic \,sī-kə-'del-ik\ *adj* [Gk *psychē* soul + *dēloun* to show] **1 a :** of, relating to, or being a drug (as LSD) that radically alters the mind or mental processes usu. only temporarily **b :** relating to the taking of psychedelic drugs 〈a *psychedelic* experience〉 **2 a :** imitating the effect of psychedelic drugs 〈*psychedelic* art〉 **b :** very bright; *esp* : FLUORESCENT 〈*psychedelic* colors〉

²psychedelic *n* : a psychedelic drug

psy·chi·a·try \sə-'kī-ə-trē, sī-\ *n* : a branch of medicine that deals with mental, emotional, or behavioral disorders — **psy·chi·at·ric** \,sī-kē-'a-trik\ *adj* — **psy·chi·at·ri·cal·ly** \-tri-k(ə-)lē\ *adv* — **psy·chi·a·trist** \sə-'kī-ə-trəst, sī-\ *n*

¹psy·chic \'sī-kik\ *adj* **1 :** of or relating to the psyche; *also* : PSYCHOGENIC **2 :** not physical; *esp* : not to be explained by knowledge of natural laws **3 :** sensitive to influences or forces supposedly exerted from beyond the natural world — **psy·chi·cal** \-ki-kəl\ *adj* — **psy·chi·cal·ly** \-ki-k(ə-)lē\ *adv*

²psychic *n* : a person (as a medium) apparently sensitive to nonphysical forces

psy·cho·anal·y·sis \,sī-kō-ə-'nal-ə-səs\ *n, pl* **-y·ses** \-,sēz\ : a method of explaining and treating psychic and esp. emotional disorders that emphasizes the importance of the patient's talking freely about himself while under treatment and esp. about early childhood memories and experiences and about his dreams — **psy·cho·an·a·lyst** \-'an-°l-əst\ *n* — **psy·cho·an·a·lyt·ic** \-,an-°l-'it-ik\ *or* **psy·cho·an·a·lyt·i·cal** \-'it-i-kəl\ *adj* — **psy·cho·an·a·lyt·i·cal·ly** \-'it-i-k(ə-)lē\ *adv* — **psy·cho·an·a·lyze** \-'an-°l-,īz\ *vb*

psy·cho·gen·ic \,sī-kə-'jen-ik\ *adj* : originating in the mind or in mental or emotional conflict

psy·cho·log·i·cal \,sī-kə-'läj-i-kəl\ *also* **psy·cho·log·ic** \-'läj-ik\ *adj* **1 a :** of or relating to psychology **b :** MENTAL **2 :** directed toward or intended to influence the will or mind 〈*psychological* warfare〉 — **psy·cho·log·i·cal·ly** \-i-k(ə-)lē\ *adv*

psy·chol·o·gy \sī-'käl-ə-jē\ *n, pl* **-gies 1 :** the science or study of mind and behavior **2 :** the mental or behavioral characteristics of an individual or group — **psy·chol·o·gist** \-jəst\ *n*

psy·cho·neu·ro·sis \,sī-kō-n(y)ù-'rō-səs\ *n* **1 :** a neurosis based on emotional conflict in which a blocked impulse seeks expression in a disguised response or symptom **2 :** NEUROSIS — **psy·cho·neu·rot·ic** \-'rät-ik\ *adj or n*

psy·cho·path \'sī-kə-,path\ *n* : a person lacking in mental strength and stability and defective in social orientation often to the point of delinquency

psy·cho·pa·thol·o·gy \,sī-kō-pə-'thäl-ə-jē\ *n* : the study of mental disorders and of the associated psychologic and behavioral alterations and anomalies; *also* : such disordered state — **psy·cho·path·o·log·i·cal** \-,path-ə-'läj-i-kəl\ *adj* — **psy·cho·pa·thol·o·gist** \-pə-'thäl-ə-jəst\ *n*

psy·chop·a·thy \sī-'käp-ə-thē\ *n* : mental disorder; *esp* : disorder of mind typical of a psychopath and marked usu. by egocentric and antisocial activity — **psy·cho·path·ic** \,sī-kə-'path-ik\ *adj or n*

psy·cho·sis \sī-'kō-səs\ *n, pl* **-cho·ses** \-'kō-,sēz\ : fundamental lasting mental derangement characterized by defective or lost contact with reality — **psy·chot·ic** \-'kät-ik\ *adj or n* — **psy·chot·i·cal·ly** \-'kät-i-k(ə-)lē\ *adv*

psy·cho·so·mat·ic \,sī-kə-sə-'mat-ik\ *adj* : of, relating to, or resulting from the interaction and interdependence of mental and bodily phenomena

psy·cho·sur·gery \,sī-kō-'sərj-(ə-)rē\ *n* : cerebral surgery employed in treating psychic symptoms — **psy·cho·sur·geon** \-'sər-jən\ *n* — **psy·cho·sur·gi·cal** \-'sər-ji-kəl\ *adj*

psy·cho·ther·a·py \,sī-kō-'ther-ə-pē\ *n* : treatment of mental or emotional disorder or of related bodily ills by psychological means — **psy·cho·ther·a·pist** \-pəst\ *n*

Psy·cho·zo·ic \,sī-kə-'zō-ik\ *adj* : QUATERNARY

psy·chrom·e·ter \sī-'kräm-ət-ər\ *n* [Gk *psychros* cold] : an instrument for measuring the water vapor in the atmosphere by means of the difference in the readings of two thermometers when one of them is kept wet so that it is cooled by evaporation — **psy·chro·met·ric** \,sī-krō-'me-trik\ *adj*

psy·chro·phil·ic \,sī-krō-'fil-ik\ *adj* [Gk *psychros* cold]

: thriving at relatively low temperatures ⟨*psychrophilic* bacteria⟩ — **psy·chro·phile** \'sī-krō-,fīl\ *n*

psyl·la \'sil-ə\ *n* [Gk, flea] : any of a family of plant lice including many economic pests — **psyl·lid** \-əd\ *adj or n*

ptar·mi·gan \'tär-mi-gən\ *n, pl* **ptarmigans** *or* **ptarmigan** [ScGael *tàrmachan*] : any of various grouses of northern regions with completely feathered feet

P T boat \(')pē-'tē-\ *n* [*patrol torpedo*] : MOTOR TORPEDO BOAT

pter·an·odon \tə-'ran-ə-,dän\ *n* : any of a genus of Cretaceous flying reptiles with a wingspread of 25 feet

pte·rid·o·phyte \tə-'rid-ə-,fīt\ *n* [Gk *pterid-*, *pteris* fern, fr. *pteron* wing, feather] : any of a division (Pteridophyta) of vascular plants that have roots, stems, and leaves, lack flowers or seeds, and comprise the ferns and related forms — **pte·rid·o·phyt·ic** \tə-,rid-ə-'fit-ik\ *or* **pter·i·doph·y·tous** \,ter-ə-'däf-ət-əs\ *adj*

pter·o·dac·tyl \,ter-ə-'dak-t°l\ *n* [Gk *pteron* wing (akin to E *feather*) + *daktylos* finger] : an extinct flying reptile having a featherless membrane extending from the body along the arms and forming the supporting surface of the wings

ptero·saur \'ter-ə-,sòr\ *n* : PTERODACTYL

pter·y·la \'ter-ə-lə\ *n, pl* **-lae** \-,lē, -,lī\ : one of the definite areas of the skin of a bird on which feathers grow

Ptol·e·ma·ic \,täl-ə-'mā-ik\ *adj* [Gk *Ptolemaikos*, fr. *Ptolemaios* Ptolemy] : of, relating to, or characteristic of Ptolemy

Ptolemaic system *n* [after *Ptolemy*, 2d cent. A.D. Greek astronomer] : the system of planetary motions according to which the earth is at the center with the sun, moon, and planets revolving around it

pto·maine \'tō-,mān, tō-'\ *n* [It *ptomaina*, fr. Gk *ptōma* fall, fallen body, corpse, fr. *piptein* to fall] : any of various organic compounds formed by the action of putrefactive bacteria on nitrogenous matter

ptomaine poisoning *n* : food poisoning caused usu. by bacteria or bacterial products

pty·a·lin \'tī-ə-lən\ *n* [Gk *ptyalon* saliva, fr. *ptyein* to spit; akin to E *spew*] : an amylase found in the saliva of many animals

pub \'pəb\ *n, chiefly Brit* : PUBLIC HOUSE

pub crawler *n* : one that goes from bar to bar

pu·ber·ty \'pyü-bərt-ē\ *n* [L *pubertas*, fr. *puber* pubescent] **1** : the condition of being or the period of becoming first capable of reproducing sexually **2** : the age at which puberty occurs often construed legally as at 14 in boys and 12 in girls — **pu·ber·tal** \-bərt-°l\ *adj*

pu·ber·u·lent \pyü-'ber-(y)ə-lənt\ *adj* : covered with fine pubescence

pu·bes·cent \pyü-'bes-°nt\ *adj* **1** : arriving at or having reached puberty **2** : covered with fine soft short hairs — compare VILLOUS — **pu·bes·cence** \-°n(t)s\ *n*

pu·bic \'pyü-bik\ *adj* [L *pubes* pubic hair, pubic region] : of, relating to, or situated near the pubis

pu·bis \'pyü-bəs\ *n, pl* **pu·bes** \-(,)bēz\ [NL *os pubis*, lit., bone of the pubic region] : the ventral and anterior of the three principal bones composing each hipbone

¹pub·lic \'pəb-lik\ *adj* [L *publicus*] **1 a** : of, relating to, or affecting all the people ⟨*public* law⟩ **b** : GOVERNMENTAL **c** : relating to or engaged in the service of the community or nation ⟨*public* life⟩ **2 a** : of or relating to mankind in general : UNIVERSAL **b** : GENERAL, POPULAR **3** : of or relating to business or community interests as opposed to private affairs : SOCIAL **4** : devoted to the general welfare : HUMANITARIAN ⟨his *public* spirit⟩ **5** : accessible to or shared by all members of the community **6 a** : exposed to general view : OPEN **b** : WELL-KNOWN, PROMINENT ⟨*public* figure⟩ **c** : PERCEPTIBLE, MATERIAL — **pub·lic·ly** *adv* — **pub·lic·ness** *n*

²public *n* **1** : a place accessible or visible to the public ⟨seen together in *public*⟩ **2** : the people as a whole : POPULACE ⟨a lecture open to the *public*⟩ **3** : a particular group of people ⟨a writer's *public*⟩

public address system *n* : an apparatus including one or more loudspeakers for reproducing sound so that it may be heard by a large audience in an auditorium or out of doors

pub·li·can \'pəb-li-kən\ *n* [L *publicanus*, fr. *publicum* public revenue, fr. neut. of *publicus* public] **1** : a provincial tax collector for the ancient Romans **2** *chiefly Brit* : a keeper of a public house

pub·li·ca·tion \,pəb-lə-'kā-shən\ *n* **1** : the act or process or an instance of publishing **2** : a published work

public domain *n* **1** : land owned directly by the government **2** : the property rights that belong to the community at large, are unprotected by copyright or patent, and may be used by anyone

public house *n* **1** : INN, HOSTELRY **2** *chiefly Brit* : a licensed saloon or bar

pub·li·cist \'pəb-lə-səst\ *n* **1 a** : an expert in international law **b** : an expert or commentator on public affairs **2** : one that publicizes; *esp* : PRESS AGENT

pub·lic·i·ty \(,)pə-'blis-ət-ē\ *n* **1** : the condition of being public or publicly known **2** : ADVERTISING; *esp* : information with a news value designed to further the interests of a place, person, or cause **3** : an action that gains public attention; *also* : the attention so gained ⟨he likes *publicity*⟩

pub·li·cize \'pəb-lə-,sīz\ *vt* : to give publicity to : ADVERTISE

public opinion *n* : the general attitude of the public on some issue or the expression of this attitude ⟨*public opinion* favored the government's policy⟩

public relations *n* : the business of inducing the public to have understanding and goodwill for a person, firm, or institution; *also* : the degree of understanding and goodwill achieved

public school *n* **1** : any of various select endowed British schools that give a liberal education and prepare students for the universities **2** : an elementary or secondary school maintained by a local government

public servant *n* : a governmental official or employee

public service *n* **1** : the business of supplying a commodity (as electricity or gas) or service (as transportation) to any or all members of a community **2** : governmental employment; *esp* : CIVIL SERVICE

public speaking *n* **1** : the act or process of making speeches in public **2** : the art or science of effective oral communication with an audience ⟨took a course in *public speaking*⟩

pub·lic-spir·it·ed \,pəb-lik-'spir-ət-əd\ *adj* : motivated by devotion to the general or national welfare — **pub·lic-spir·it·ed·ness** *n*

public utility *n* : a business organization performing a public service and subject to special governmental regulation

public works *n pl* : works (as schools, highways, or docks) constructed for public use or enjoyment and financed and owned by the government

pub·lish \'pəb-lish\ *vb* [ME *publishen*, modif. of MF *publier*, fr. L *publicare*, fr. *publicus* public] **1** : to make generally known : make public announcement of ⟨*publish* a libel⟩ **2 a** : to produce or release for publication; *esp* : PRINT **b** : to issue the work of (an author) **3** : to have one's work accepted for publication ⟨a *publishing* scholar⟩ *syn* see DECLARE — **pub·lish·a·ble** \-ə-bəl\ *adj*

pub·lish·er \-ər\ *n* : one that publishes; *esp* : one that issues and offers for sale printed matter (as books, periodicals, or newspapers)

puc·coon \pə-'kün\ *n* [of AmerInd origin] : any of several American plants (as the bloodroot) that yield a red or yellow pigment

¹puck \'pək\ *n* [OE *pūca*] **1** *archaic* : an evil spirit : DEMON **2** : a mischievous sprite : HOBGOBLIN

²puck *n* [E dial. *puck* to poke, alter. of E ²*poke*] : a vulcanized rubber disk used in ice hockey

pucka *var of* PUKKA

¹puck·er \'pək-ər\ *vb* **puck·ered; puck·er·ing** \'pək-(ə-)riŋ\ : to contract into folds or wrinkles ⟨*puckered* his brow⟩ ⟨the cloth *puckered* in shrinking⟩

²pucker *n* : a fold or wrinkle in a normally even surface — **puck·ery** \'pək-(ə-)rē\ *adj*

puck·ish \'pək-ish\ *adj* : IMPISH, WHIMSICAL — **puck·ish·ly** *adv* — **puck·ish·ness** *n*

pud·ding \'pùd-iŋ\ *n* [ME] **1** : a boiled or baked soft food usu. with a cereal base ⟨corn *pudding*⟩ **2** : a dessert of a soft, spongy, or thick creamy consistency ⟨bread *pudding*⟩ **3** : a dish often containing suet or having a suet crust and orig. boiled in a bag ⟨kidney *pudding*⟩ ⟨makes a fig *pudding* every Christmas⟩

pudding stone *n* : CONGLOMERATE

¹pud·dle \'pəd-°l\ *n* [ME *podel*] **1** : a very small pool of usu. dirty or muddy water **2** : an earthy mixture (as of clay, sand, and gravel) worked while wet into a compact mass that becomes impervious to water when dry

²puddle *vt* **pud·dled; pud·dling** \'pəd-liŋ, -'l-iŋ\ **1** : to make muddy or turbid : MUDDLE **2 a** : to make a puddle of (as clay) **b** : to convert (melted pig iron) into wrought iron by stirring in the presence of an oxidizer **3** : to strew with puddles — **pud·dler** \-lər, -'l-ər\ *n*

pu·den·cy \'pyüd-°n-sē\ *n* : MODESTY, PRUDISHNESS

pu·den·dum \pyü-'den-dəm\ *n, pl* **-da** \-'den-də\ [L, neut. of *pudendus* shameful, fr. *pudēre* to be ashamed] : the external genital organs esp. of a woman — **pu·den·dal** \-'den-d°l\ *adj*

pudgy \'pəj-ē\ *adj* **pudg·i·er; -est** : short and plump : CHUBBY — **pudg·i·ness** *n*

pueb·lo \pü-'eb-lō, pyü-\ *n, pl* **pueblos** [Sp, people, village, fr. L *populus* people] **1** : an Indian village of Arizona or New Mexico consisting of flat-roofed stone or adobe houses joined in groups sometimes several stories high **2** *cap* : a member of any of several Indian peoples of Arizona and New Mexico

pu·er·ile \'pyù-(-ə)r-əl, -,īl\ *adj* [L *puer* boy, child] **1** : JUVENILE **2** : CHILDISH, SILLY ⟨*puerile* remarks⟩ — **pu·er·il·i·ty** \,pyü-(-ə)r-'il-ət-ē\ *n*

pu·er·per·al \pyü-'ər-p(ə-)rəl\ *adj* [L *puerpera* woman in childbirth, fr. *puer* child + *parere* to give birth to] : of or relating to parturition ⟨*puerperal* infection⟩

¹puff \'pəf\ *vb* [OE *pyffan*] **1 a** (1) : to blow in short gusts (2) : to exhale forcibly **b** : to breathe hard : PANT ⟨*puffed* as he climbed the hill⟩ **c** : to emit, propel, blow, or expel by or as if by small whiffs or clouds (as of smoke) : WAFT ⟨*puffed* at his pipe⟩⟨a brisk breeze *puffed* the clouds away⟩ **2 a** : to speak or act in a scornful, conceited, or exaggerated manner **b** : to make proud or conceited : ELATE **c** : to praise extravagantly; *esp* : ADVERTISE **3 a** : to distend or become distended with or as if with air or gas : SWELL, INFLATE ⟨the sprained ankle *puffed* up⟩ **b** : to open or appear in or as if in a puff

²puff *n* **1 a** : an act or instance of puffing : WHIFF, GUST **b** : a slight explosive sound accompanying a puff ⟨*c* : a perceptible cloud (as of smoke or steam) emitted in a puff **2** : a light pastry that rises high in baking **3 a** : a slight swelling : PROTUBERANCE **b** : a fluffy mass: as (1) : a small fluffy pad for applying cosmetic powder (2) : a soft loose roll of hair (3) : a quilted bed covering **4** : a commendatory notice or review — **puff·i·ness** \'pəf-ē-nəs\ *n* — **puffy** \'pəf-ē\ *adj*

puff adder *n* : HOGNOSE SNAKE

puff·ball \'pəf-,bol\ *n* : any of various mostly edible globose fungi that discharge ripe spores in a cloud resembling smoke when they are disturbed

puff·er \'pəf-ər\ *n* **1** : one that puffs **2** : any of various fishes that can inflate their bodies with air

puf·fin \'pəf-ən\ *n* [ME *pophyn*] : any of several short-necked seabirds related to the auk that have a deep grooved bill marked with different colors

puff paste *n* : dough used in making light flaky pastries

pug \'pəg\ *n* **1** : a small sturdy compact dog of Asiatic origin with a close coat, tightly curled tail, and broad wrinkled face **2 a** : PUG NOSE **b** : a close knot or coil of hair : BUN

pu·gi·list \'pyü-jə-ləst\ *n* [L *pugil* boxer] : FIGHTER; *esp* : a professional boxer — **pu·gi·lism** \-,liz-əm\ *n* — **pu·gi·lis·tic** \,pyü-jə-'lis-tik\ *adj*

pug·na·cious \,pəg-'nā-shəs\ *adj* [L *pugnac-, pugnax*, fr. *pugnare* to fight] : having a quarrelsome or belligerent nature : TRUCULENT, COMBATIVE — **pug·na·cious·ly** *adv* — **pug·na·cious·ness** *n* — **pug·nac·i·ty** \-'nas-ət-ē\ *n*

pug nose *n* : a nose having a slightly concave bridge and flattened nostrils — **pug-nosed** \'pəg-'nōzd\ *adj*

puis·ne \'pyü-nē\ *adj* [MF *puisné* younger, lit., born after] *chiefly Brit* : inferior in rank ⟨*puisne* judge⟩

puis·sance \'pwis-°n(t)s, 'pyü-ə-sən(t)s\ *n* [MF, fr. *puissant* powerful, fr. prp. of *poeir* to be able, be powerful] : STRENGTH, POWER ⟨bowed to the *puissance* of the emperor⟩ — **puis·sant** \-°nt, -sənt\ *adj* — **puis·sant·ly** *adv*

puk·ka \'pək-ə\ *adj* [Hindi *pakkā* cooked, ripe, solid] : GENUINE, AUTHENTIC; *also* : FIRST-CLASS, COMPLETE

pul·chri·tude \'pəl-krə-,t(y)üd\ *n* [L *pulchritudin-, pulchritudo*, fr. *pulcher* beautiful] : physical comeliness : BEAUTY — **pul·chri·tu·di·nous** \,pəl-krə-'t(y)üd-°n-əs\ *adj*

pule \'pyül\ *vi* : WHINE, WHIMPER ⟨a *puling* infant⟩

¹pull \'púl\ *vb* [OE *pullian*] **1 a** : to separate forcibly from a natural or firm attachment : PLUCK, EXTRACT ⟨*pull* a tooth⟩⟨*pulled* feathers from the rooster's tail⟩⟨*pull* carrots⟩ **b** : to remove something by or as if by pulling **2 a** : to exert force upon so as to cause or tend to cause motion toward the force **b** : to stretch (cooling candy) repeatedly **c** : to strain by stretching abnormally ⟨*pull* a tendon⟩ **d** (1) : to use force in drawing, dragging, or tugging (2) : MOVE ⟨the car *pulled* out of the driveway⟩ (3) : to take a drink (4) : to draw hard in smoking ⟨*pulled* at his pipe⟩ **e** : to work (an oar) by drawing back strongly **3** : to hit (a ball) toward the left from a right-handed swing **4** : to draw apart : REND, TEAR **5** : to print a proof from by impression **6** : REMOVE ⟨*pull* a crankshaft⟩⟨*pulled* the pitcher in the third inning⟩ **7** : to bring (a weapon) into the open ⟨*pulled* a knife⟩ **8** : to carry out with skill or daring : COMMIT **9** : to draw the support or attention of : ATTRACT ⟨*pull* votes⟩ **10** : to feel or express strong sympathy : ROOT ⟨*pulling* for his team to win⟩ — **pull·er** *n* — **pull oneself together** : to regain one's self-possession — **pull one's leg** : to deceive someone playfully : HOAX — **pull stakes** *or* **pull up stakes** : to move out : LEAVE — **pull strings** *or* **pull wires** : to exert secret influence or control — **pull together** : to work in harmony : COOPERATE

²pull *n* **1 a** : the act or an instance of pulling **b** : a draft of liquid : an inhalation of smoke **c** : the effort expended in moving ⟨a long *pull* uphill⟩ **d** : force required to overcome resistance to pulling **2 a** : ADVANTAGE **b** : special influence ⟨got his job through *pull*⟩ **3** : PROOF 2a **4** : a device for pulling something or for operating by pulling **5** : a force that attracts, compels, or influences : ATTRACTION ⟨the *pull* of gravity⟩

pull away *vi* : to draw oneself back or away : WITHDRAW, ESCAPE

pull·back \'púl-,bak\ *n* : a pulling back; *esp* : an orderly withdrawal of troops from a position

pull down *vt* **1** : DEMOLISH, DESTROY **2 a** : to bring to a lower level : REDUCE **b** : to depress in health, strength, or spirits **3** : to draw as wages or salary

pul·let \'púl-ət\ *n* [ME *polet* young fowl, fr. MF *poulet*, dim. of *poul* fowl, fr. L *pullus*] : a young hen; *esp* : a hen of the common fowl less than a year old

pul·ley \'púl-ē\ *n, pl* **pulleys** [MF *poulie*] **1** : a small wheel with a grooved rim used singly with a rope or chain to change the direction and point of application of a pulling force and in combinations to increase the applied force esp. for lifting weights; *also* : the simple machine constituted by such a pulley with ropes **2** : a wheel used to transmit power by means of a band, belt, cord, rope, or chain

pulleys

pull in *vb* **1** : CHECK, RESTRAIN ⟨*pull* a horse *in*⟩ **2** : ARREST **3** : to arrive at a destination : come to a stop ⟨train *pulled in* on time⟩

Pull·man \'púl-mən\ *n* [George M. *Pullman* d1897 American inventor] : a railroad passenger car with specially comfortable furnishings; *esp* : SLEEPING CAR

pull off *vt* : to accomplish successfully esp. against odds

pull out \(')púl-'aút\ *vi* **1** : LEAVE, DEPART **2** : WITHDRAW

pull·out \'púl-,aút\ *n* **1** : something that can be pulled out **2** : the action in which an airplane goes from a dive to horizontal flight **3** : PULLBACK

pull over \(')púl-'ō-vər\ *vi* : to steer one's vehicle to the side of the road

¹pull·over \,púl-,ō-vər\ *adj* : put on by being pulled over the head

²pull·over \'púl-,ō-vər\ *n* : a pullover garment

pull through *vb* : to help through or to survive a dangerous or difficult period or situation

pull up *vb* **1** : CHECK, REBUKE **2** : to bring or come to a stop : HALT ⟨*pulled* the car *up* in front of the hotel⟩ **3** : to draw even with others in a race

pul·mo·nary \'púl-mə-,ner-ē, 'pəl-\ *adj* [L *pulmon-, pulmo* lung] **1** : relating to or associated with the lungs **2** : carried on by the lungs

pulmonary artery *n* : an artery that conveys venous blood from the heart to the lungs

pulmonary vein *n* : a vein that returns oxygenated blood from the lungs to the heart

pul·mo·nate \'pûl-mə-ˌnāt, 'pəl-\ *adj* : having lungs or organs resembling lungs; *also* : air-breathing ⟨*pulmonate* snails⟩

pul·mo·tor \'pûl-ˌmōt-ər, 'pəl-\ *n* [fr. *Pulmotor*, a trademark] : a respiratory apparatus for pumping oxygen or air into and out of the lungs (as of an asphyxiated person)

¹pulp \'pəlp\ *n* [L *pulpa*] **1 a** : the soft juicy or fleshy part of a fruit or vegetable ⟨the *pulp* of an apple⟩ **b** : a mass of vegetable matter from which the moisture has been pressed **2** : the soft sensitive tissue that fills the central cavity of a tooth **3** : a material prepared by chemical or mechanical means chiefly from wood but also from other materials (as rags) and used in making paper and cellulose products **4 a** : pulpy condition **b** : something in a pulpy condition **5** : a magazine or book using rough-surfaced paper made of wood pulp and often dealing with sensational material

²pulp *vb* : to form into a pulp : make or become pulpy — **pulp·er** *n*

pul·pit \'pûl-ˌpit, 'pəl-, -pət\ *n* [L *pulpitum* staging, platform] **1** : an elevated platform or high reading desk used in preaching or conducting a worship service **2** : the preaching profession; *also* : a post in it

pulp·wood \'pəlp-ˌwùd\ *n* : a wood (as of aspen, hemlock, pine, or spruce) used in making pulp for paper

pulpy \'pəl-pē\ *adj* **pulp·i·er; -est** : resembling or consisting of pulp — **pulp·i·ness** *n*

pul·que \'pûl-ˌkā\ *n* [MexSp] : a fermented drink made in Mexico from the juice of a maguey

pul·sar \'pəl-ˌsär\ *n* [*pulse* + *-ar* (as in *quasar*)] : a celestial source of pulsating radio waves characterized by a short interval (as .033 or 3.5 seconds) between pulses and uniformity of the repetition rate of the pulses

pul·sate \'pəl-ˌsāt\ *vi* [L *pulsare*, freq. of *pellere* to drive, beat] : to expand and contract in a rhythmic manner : throb rhythmically : BEAT

pul·sa·tile \'pəl-sət-ᵊl, -sə-ˌtīl\ *adj* : PULSATING

pul·sa·tion \ˌpəl-'sā-shən\ *n* : pulsating movement or action (as of an artery); *also* : a single throb of such movement

¹pulse \'pəls\ *n* [OF *pouls* porridge, fr. L *pult-, puls*] : the edible seeds of several leguminous crops (as peas, beans, or lentils); *also* : a plant yielding pulse

²pulse *n* [L *pulsus*, lit., beating, fr. *pellere* to drive, beat] **1** : a regular throbbing caused in the arteries by the contractions of the heart **2 a** : rhythmical beating, vibrating, or sounding **b** : BEAT, THROB **3 a** : a transient variation of a quantity (as electrical current or voltage) whose value is normally constant **b** : an electromagnetic wave or a sound wave of brief duration

³pulse *vb* **1** : to exhibit a pulse or pulsation : THROB **2** : to drive by or as if by a pulsation **3** : to cause to pulsate **4** : to produce or modulate (as electromagnetic waves) in the form of pulses ⟨*pulsed* waves⟩

pul·ver·ize \'pəl-və-ˌrīz\ *vb* [L *pulver-, pulvis* dust, powder] **1** : to reduce or become reduced (as by beating or grinding) into a powder or dust **2** : to demolish as if by pulverizing : SMASH, ANNIHILATE — **pul·ver·iz·er** *n*

pu·ma \'p(y)ü-mə\ *n, pl* **pumas** *also* **puma** [Sp, fr. Quechua] : COUGAR

pum·ice \'pəm-əs\ *n* [L *pumic-, pumex;* akin to E *foam*] : a volcanic glass full of cavities and very light in weight used esp. in powder form for smoothing and polishing — called also *pumice stone*

pum·ic·ite \'pəm-ə-ˌsīt\ *n* : PUMICE

pum·mel \'pəm-əl\ *vb* **-meled** *or* **-melled; -mel·ing** *or* **-mel·ling** : POUND, BEAT, THUMP

¹pump \'pəmp\ *n* [ME *pumpe, pompe,* fr. MLG *pumpe* or MD *pompe*] : a device that raises, transfers, or compresses fluids or that reduces the density of gases esp. by suction or pressure or both ⟨a water *pump*⟩

²pump *vb* **1** : to raise, transfer, or compress by means of a pump ⟨*pump* up water⟩ **2** : to free (as from water or air) by the use of a pump ⟨*pump* a boat dry⟩ **3** : to fill by means of a pump ⟨*pump* up a tire⟩ **4** : to draw, force, or drive onward in the manner of a pump ⟨the heart *pumps* blood into the arteries⟩ **5** : to move up and down like a

pump handle ⟨*pump* the hand of a friend⟩ **6** : to spurt out intermittently **7** : to subject to persistent questioning to find out something; *also* : to draw out by such questioning — **pump·er** *n*

³pump *n* : a low shoe not fastened on and gripping the foot chiefly at the toe and heel

pum·per·nick·el \'pəm-pər-ˌnik-əl\ *n* [G] : a dark coarse somewhat sour rye bread

pump·kin \'pəŋ-kən, 'pəm(p)-kən\ *n* [modif. of F *pompon* melon, pumpkin, fr. L *pepon-, pepo,* fr. Gk *pepōn,* fr. *pep-, pessein* to cook, ripen] **1** : the usu. round deep yellow fruit of a vine of the gourd family widely used as food; *also* : a fruit (as a crookneck squash) of a closely related vine **2** : a usu. hairy prickly vine that produces pumpkins

pumpkin·seed \-ˌsēd\ *n* : a small brilliantly colored No. American freshwater sunfish or the related bluegill

¹pun \'pən\ *n* : the humorous use of a word in such a way as to suggest different meanings or applications or of words having the same or nearly the same sound but different meanings

²pun *vi* **punned; pun·ning** : to make puns

¹punch \'pənch\ *vb* [MF *poinçonner* to prick, stamp, fr. *poinçon* puncheon] **1 a** : PROD, POKE **b** : to drive or herd (cattle) **2 a** : to strike with a forward thrust of the fist **b** : to drive or push forcibly by or as if by a punch; *esp* : to press so as to activate ⟨*punch* a time clock⟩ **3** : to emboss, cut, perforate, or make with a punch **4** : to strike or press sharply — **punch·er** *n*

²punch *n* **1** : the action of punching **2** : a quick blow with or as if with the fist **3** : energy that commands attention : effective force

³punch *n* **1** : a tool or machine for piercing, cutting (as a hole or notch), forming, driving the head of a nail below a surface or a bolt out of a hole, or impressing a design in a softer material **2** : a hole or notch resulting from a perforating operation

⁴punch *n* : a drink made of various and usu. many ingredients and often flavored with wine or distilled liquor

Punch-and-Judy show \ˌpən-chən-'jüd-ē-\ *n* : a puppet show in which a little hook-nosed humpback Punch quarrels ludicrously with his wife Judy

punch bowl *n* : a large bowl from which a beverage (as punch) is served

punch-drunk \'pənch-ˌdrəŋk\ *adj* **1** : suffering from brain injury received in prizefighting **2** : GROGGY, DAZED

punched card *or* **punch card** *n* : a data card with holes punched in particular positions each with its own significance for use in electrically operated tabulating or accounting equipment or computers

¹pun·cheon \'pən-chən\ *n* [MF *poinçon*] **1** : a pointed tool for piercing **2 a** : a short upright framing timber **b** : a split log or slab with the face smoothed **3** : a figured stamp or punch used esp. by goldsmiths and engravers

²puncheon *n* [MF *ponchon*] **1** : a large cask of varying capacity **2** : any of various units of liquid capacity

punch in *vi* : to record the time of one's arrival or beginning work by punching a time clock

pun·chi·nel·lo \ˌpən-chə-'nel-ō\ *n, pl* **-los** *or* **-loes** [modif. of It dial. *polecenella*] **1** : a fat short humpbacked clown or buffoon in Italian puppet shows **2** : a squat grotesque person

punching bag *n* : a usu. suspended stuffed or inflated bag to be punched for exercise or for training in boxing

punch line *n* : a sentence, statement, or phrase (as in a humorous story) that makes the point

punch out *vi* : to record the time of one's stopping work or departure by punching a time clock

punch press *n* : a press for working on material (as metal) by the use of cutting, shaping, or combination dies

punchy \'pən-chē\ *adj* **punch·i·er; -est** : PUNCH-DRUNK

punc·tate \'pəŋ(k)-ˌtāt\ *adj* [L *punctum* point] **1** : ending in or resembling a point **2** : marked with minute spots or depressions ⟨a *punctate* leaf⟩ — **punc·ta·tion** \ˌpəŋ(k)-'tā-shən\ *n*

punc·til·io \ˌpəŋ(k)-'til-ē-ˌō\ *n, pl* **-i·os** [It *puntiglio* point of honor, scruple, fr. Sp. *puntillo,* fr. dim. of *punto* point, fr. L *punctum*] **1** : a nice detail of conduct in a ceremony or in observance of a code **2** : careful observance of forms (as in social conduct)

punc·til·i·ous \-ē-əs\ *adj* : marked by precise exact accordance with the details of codes or conventions — **punc·til·i·ous·ly** *adv* — **punc·til·i·ous·ness** *n*

punc·tu·al \'pəŋk-chə-wəl\ *adj* [L *punctus* pricking, point, fr. *pungere* to prick] **1** : PUNCTILIOUS **2** : acting or habitually acting at an appointed time or at a regularly scheduled time : PROMPT — **punc·tu·al·i·ty** \,pəŋk-chə-'wal-ət-ē\ *n* — **punc·tu·al·ly** \'pəŋk-chə-wə-lē\ *adv* — **punc·tu·al·ness** \-wəl-nəs\ *n*

punc·tu·ate \'pəŋk-chə-,wāt\ *vb* [ML *punctuare*, fr. L *punctus* point] **1** : to mark or divide with punctuation marks **2** : to break into or interrupt at intervals ⟨a speech *punctuated* by a harsh cough⟩ — **punc·tu·a·tor** \-,wāt-ər\ *n*

punc·tu·a·tion \,pəŋk-chə-'wā-shən\ *n* : the act, practice, or system of inserting standardized marks or signs in written matter to clarify the meaning and separate structural units

punctuation mark *n* : any of various standardized marks or signs used in punctuation

punc·tu·late \'pəŋk-chə-,lāt\ *adj* : minutely punctate — **punc·tu·la·tion** \,pəŋk-chə-'lā-shən\ *n*

¹punc·ture \'pəŋk(k)-chər\ *n* [L *punct-*, *pungere* to prick] **1** : the act of puncturing **2** : a hole or a narrow wound resulting from puncturing ⟨a *puncture* of the abdomen⟩ ⟨a tire with a *puncture*⟩ **3** : a minute depression

²puncture *vb* **punc·tured; punc·tur·ing** \'pəŋ(k)-chə-riŋ, 'pəŋ(k)-shriŋ\ **1** : to pierce with a pointed instrument or object **2** : to suffer a puncture of **3** : to become punctured **4** : to make useless or absurd as if by a puncture ⟨*puncture* an argument⟩

pun·dit \'pən-dət\ *n* [Hindi *paṇḍit*, fr. Skt *paṇḍita*] : a wise or learned man : AUTHORITY

pun·gen·cy \'pən-jən-sē\ *n* : the quality or state of being pungent

pun·gent \'pən-jənt\ *adj* [L *pungere* to prick, sting] **1** : having a stiff and sharp point ⟨*pungent* leaves⟩ **2** : sharply stimulating to the mind ⟨*pungent* criticism⟩ ⟨*pungent* wit⟩ **3** : causing a sharp or irritating sensation; *esp* : ACRID — **pun·gent·ly** *adv*

Pu·nic \'pyü-nik\ *adj* [L *punicus*, fr. *Poenus* inhabitant of Carthage, modif. of Gk *Phoinix* Phoenician] : of or relating to Carthage or the Carthaginians

pun·ish \'pən-ish\ *vb* [MF *puniss-*, *punir*, fr. L *punire*, *poena* penalty, pain] **1** : to cause to suffer pain or loss of freedom or privileges for an offense committed : CHASTISE ⟨*punish* criminals with imprisonment⟩ **2** : to inflict punishment for (as a crime) ⟨*punish* treason with death⟩ **3** : to deal with or handle severely or roughly ⟨badly *punished* by his opponent⟩ **4** : to inflict punishment — **pun·ish·a·bil·i·ty** \,pən-ish-ə-'bil-ət-ē\ *n* — **pun·ish·a·ble** \'pən-ish-ə-bəl\ *adj* — **pun·ish·er** *n*

syn CHASTISE, DISCIPLINE: PUNISH implies subjection to penalty for wrongdoing; CHASTISE implies corporal punishment; DISCIPLINE may involve punishment but suggests action with the intent of bringing under control ⟨a temper that had never been *disciplined*⟩

pun·ish·ment \'pən-ish-mənt\ *n* **1** : the act of punishing : the state or fact of being punished ⟨persons undergoing *punishment*⟩ **2** : the penalty for a fault or crime ⟨the *punishment* for speeding⟩ **3** : severe, rough, or disastrous treatment ⟨trees showing the effects of *punishment* by a heavy storm⟩

pu·ni·tive \'pyü-nət-iv\ *adj* **1** : of or relating to punishment or penalties ⟨*punitive* law⟩ **2** : intended to inflict punishment ⟨a *punitive* expedition against outlaws⟩ — **pu·ni·tive·ly** *adv* — **pu·ni·tive·ness** *n*

Pun·jabi \,pən-'jäb-ē, -'jab-\ *n* **1** : a native or inhabitant of the Punjab region of the Indian subcontinent **2** : PANJABI 1 — **Punjabi** *adj*

¹punk \'pəŋk\ *n* : a young inexperienced man; *esp* : a young hoodlum

²punk *adj* : very poor in quality : BAD, MISERABLE

³punk *n* **1** : wood so decayed as to be dry, crumbly, and useful for tinder **2** : a dry spongy substance prepared from fungi and used to ignite fuses esp. of fireworks

pun·kah \'pəŋ-kə\ *n* [Hindi *pākhā*] : a large fan or a canvas-covered frame suspended from the ceiling and used esp. in India for fanning a room

pun·kie *also* **pun·ky** \'pəŋ-kē\ *n, pl* **punkies** [D dial. *punki*, of AmerInd origin] : a tiny biting fly : MIDGE

pun·kin *var of* PUMPKIN

pun·ster \'pən(t)-stər\ *n* : one who is given to making puns

¹punt \'pənt\ *n* [OE, fr. L *ponton-*, *ponto*, fr. *pont-*, *pons* bridge] : a long narrow flat-bottomed boat with square ends usu. propelled with a pole

²punt *vb* **1** : to propel by pushing with a pole against the bottom of a body of water **2** : to go boating in a punt

³punt *vi* : to play at a gambling game against the banker

⁴punt *vb* **1** : to kick (a football) before the ball touches the ground when let fall from the hands **2** : to punt a ball ⟨*punted* on fourth down⟩

⁵punt *n* : the act or an instance of punting a ball

punt·er \'pənt-ər\ *n* : one that punts

punt formation *n* : an offensive football formation in which a back making a punt stands approximately 10 yards behind the line and the other backs are in blocking position close to the line of scrimmage

pun·ty \'pənt-ē\ *n, pl* **punties** : a metal rod used for fashioning hot glass

pu·ny \'pyü-nē\ *adj* **pu·ni·er; -est** [MF *puisné* younger, fr. *puis* afterward + *né* born] : slight or inferior in power, size, or importance : WEAK — **pu·ni·ness** *n*

¹pup \'pəp\ *n* : a young dog; *also* : one of the young of various animals (as seals)

²pup *vi* **pupped; pup·ping** : to give birth to pups

pu·pa \'pyü-pə\ *n, pl* **pu·pae** \-(,)pē, -,pī\ *or* **pupas** [L, girl, doll] : an intermediate usu. quiescent form of a metamorphic insect (as a bee, moth, or beetle) that occurs between the larva and the imago, is usu. enclosed in a cocoon or case, and undergoes internal changes by which larval structures are replaced by those typical of the imago — **pu·pal** \'pyü-pəl\ *adj*

pu·pate \'pyü-,pāt\ *vi* : to become a pupa : pass through a pupal stage — **pu·pa·tion** \pyü-'pā-shən\ *n*

¹pu·pil \'pyü-pəl\ *n* [L *pupillus* ward, fr. dim. of *pupus* boy] **1** : a child or young person in school or in the charge of a tutor : STUDENT **2** : one who has been taught or influenced by a person of fame or distinction : DISCIPLE **syn** see SCHOLAR

²pupil *n* [L *pupilla*, fr. dim. of *pupa* girl, doll; fr. the tiny image of oneself seen reflected in another's eye] : the contractile usu. round aperture in the iris of the eye — **pu·pil·ar** \-pə-lər\ *adj* — **pu·pil·lary** \-,ler-ē\ *adj*

pu·pil·age *or* **pu·pil·lage** \'pyü-pə-lij\ *n* : the state or period of being a pupil

pup·pet \'pəp-ət\ *n* [MF *poupette*, fr. L *pupa* doll] **1** : a small-scale figure of a living being (as a human) often made with jointed limbs and moved by hand or by strings or wires **2** : DOLL 1 **3** : one (as a person or a government) whose acts are controlled by an outside force or influence

pup·pe·teer \,pəp-ə-'ti(ə)r\ *n* : one who manipulates puppets or marionettes

pup·pe·try \'pəp-ə-trē\ *n* : the production or creation of puppets or puppet shows

pup·py \'pəp-ē\ *n, pl* **puppies** [MF *poupée* doll, toy, fr. L *pupa* doll] **1** : a young domestic dog; *esp* : one less than a year old **2** : a silly or ill-bred young man — **pup·py·ish** \-ē-ish\ *adj*

pup tent *n* : a wedge-shaped tent usu. consisting of two shelter halves

pur·blind \'pər-,blīnd\ *adj* **1 a** *obs* : wholly blind **b** : partly blind **2** : lacking in vision, insight, or understanding : OBTUSE — **pur·blind·ly** *adv* — **pur·blind·ness** \-,blīn(d)-nəs\ *n*

¹pur·chase \'pər-chəs\ *vt* [OF *purchacier* to seek to obtain, fr. *pur-* forward (modif. of L *pro-*) + *chacier* to chase] **1 a** : to obtain by paying money or its equivalent : BUY ⟨*purchase* a house⟩ **b** : to obtain by labor, danger, or sacrifice : EARN **2** : to apply a device for obtaining a mechanical advantage to (as something to be moved); *also* : to move by a purchase — **pur·chas·a·ble** \-chə-sə-bəl\ *adj* — **pur·chas·er** *n*

²purchase *n* **1** : an act or instance of purchasing **2** : something purchased **3 a** : a mechanical hold or advantage applied to the raising or moving of heavy bodies **b** : an apparatus or device by which advantage is gained **4** : a secure hold, grasp, or place to stand ⟨could not get a *purchase* on the ledge⟩

pur·dah \'pərd-ə\ *n* [Hindi *parda*, lit., screen, veil] : seclusion of women from public observation among Muslims and some Hindus esp. in India

pure \'pyü(ə)r\ *adj* [L *purus*] **1** : not mixed with anything else : free from everything that might taint, alter, or lower the quality ⟨*pure* water⟩ ⟨*pure* food⟩ ⟨*pure* French⟩ **2** : free from sin or moral guilt; *esp* : marked by chastity **3** : nothing other than : MERE, SHEER, ABSOLUTE ⟨*pure* nonsense⟩ **4** : ABSTRACT, THEORETICAL ⟨*pure* science⟩ ⟨*pure* mathematics⟩ **5 a** : of pure blood and unmixed ancestry **b** : homozygous in and breeding true for one or more characters **syn** see CHASTE — **pure·ness** *n*

pure·blood \-,bləd\ *or* **pure-blood·ed** \-'bləd-əd\ *adj* : of unmixed ancestry : PUREBRED — **pureblood** *n*

pure·bred \-'bred\ *adj* : bred from members of a recognized breed, strain, or kind without admixture of other blood over many generations — **pure·bred** \-,bred\ *n*

¹**pu·ree** \pyü-'rā, -'rē\ *n* [F, fr. fem. of *puré*, pp. of *purer* to purify, strain] **1** : a paste or thick liquid suspension usu. produced by rubbing cooked food through a sieve **2** : a thick soup having pureed vegetables as a base

²**puree** *vt* **pu·reed**; **pu·ree·ing** : to boil soft and then rub through a sieve

pure line *n* : an essentially homozygous strain (as of corn plants) usu. formed by repeated selfing; *also* : CLONE — **pure–line** *adj*

pure·ly \'pyu̇(ə)r-lē\ *adv* **1** : without admixture of anything injurious or foreign **2** : MERELY, SOLELY **3** : CHASTELY, INNOCENTLY **4** : COMPLETELY

pur·ga·tion \,pər-'gā-shən\ *n* : the act or result of purging

¹**pur·ga·tive** \'pər-gət-iv\ *adj* : purging or tending to purge; *esp* : causing a usu. marked looseness of the bowels ⟨the *purgative* effect of green apples⟩

²**purgative** *n* : a purgative medicine

pur·ga·to·ri·al \,pər-gə-'tōr-ē-əl, -'tȯr-\ *adj* **1** : cleansing of sin : EXPIATORY **2** : of or relating to purgatory

pur·ga·to·ry \'pər-gə-,tōr-ē, -,tȯr-\ *n, pl* **-ries** **1** : an intermediate state after death in which according to Roman Catholic doctrine the souls of those who die in God's grace but without having made full satisfaction for their sins are purified by suffering **2** : a place or state of temporary punishment

¹**purge** \'pərj\ *vb* [OF *purgier*, fr. L *purgare*, fr. *purus* pure] **1** : to cleanse or purify by separating and carrying off impurities; *esp* : to remove sin or guilt from **2** : to become free of impurities or excess matter through a cleansing process **3** : to remove by cleansing **4** : to have or cause vigorous and usu. repeated evacuation of the bowels ⟨*purged* him with drugs⟩ **5** : to get rid of (as disloyal or suspect elements) by a purge — **purg·er** *n*

²**purge** *n* **1 a** : an act or instance of purging **b** : a ridding of persons regarded as treacherous or disloyal **2** : something that purges; *esp* : PURGATIVE

pu·ri·fi·ca·tion \,pyu̇r-ə-fə-'kā-shən\ *n* : an act or instance of purifying or of being purified

pu·ri·fi·ca·tor \'pyu̇r-ə-fə-,kāt-ər\ *n* **1** : PURIFIER **2** : a linen cloth used to wipe the chalice after celebration of the Eucharist

pu·rif·i·ca·to·ry \pyu̇r-'if-i-kə-,tōr-ē, 'pyu̇r-ə-fə-kə-, -,tȯr-\ *adj* : serving, tending, or intended to purify

pu·ri·fy \'pyu̇r-ə-,fī\ *vb* **-fied**; **-fy·ing** **1** : to make pure : free from anything alien, extraneous, improper, corrupting, or damaging **2** : to grow or become pure or clean — **pu·ri·fi·er** \-,fī(-ə)r\ *n*

Pu·rim \'pu̇r-(,)im, pu̇r-'\ *n* : a Jewish holiday celebrated in February or March in commemoration of the deliverance of the Jews from the massacre plotted by Haman

pu·rine \'pyu̇(ə)r-,ēn\ *n* : a crystalline organic base $C_5H_4N_4$ that is made from uric acid and is the parent of many compounds; *also* : a derivative of this

pur·ism \'pyu̇(ə)r-,iz-əm\ *n* : rigid adherence to or insistence on nicety esp. in use of words — **pur·ist** \-əst\ *n* — **pu·ris·tic** \pyu̇r-'is-tik\ *adj*

pu·ri·tan \'pyu̇r-ət-°n\ *n* **1** *cap* : a member of a 16th and 17th century Protestant group in England and New England opposing as unscriptural many traditional customs of the Church of England **2** : one who practices or preaches or follows a stricter moral code than that which prevails — **puritan** *adj, often cap* — **pu·ri·tan·i·cal** \,pyu̇r-ə-'tan-i-kəl\ *adj* — **pu·ri·tan·i·cal·ly** \-k(ə-)lē\ *adv* — **pu·ri·tan·ism** \'pyu̇r-ət-°n-,iz-əm\ *n, often cap*

pu·ri·ty \'pyu̇r-ət-ē\ *n* : the quality or state of being pure: as **a** : freedom from impurities : CLEANNESS **b** : freedom from guilt or sin **c** : freedom from all elements considered linguistically or stylistically inappropriate ⟨was admired for the *purity* of his English⟩

¹**purl** \'pərl\ *n* [obs. *pirl* to twist] **1** : gold or silver thread or wire for embroidering or edging **2** : the intertwist of thread knotting a stitch usu. along an edge

²**purl** *vb* **1 a** : to embroider with gold or silver thread **b** : to edge or border with gold or silver embroidery **2** : to knit in purl stitch

³**purl** *n* **1** : a purling or swirling stream or rill **2** : a gentle murmur or movement (as of purling water)

⁴**purl** *vi* **1** : EDDY, SWIRL **2** : to make a soft murmuring sound like that of a purling stream

pur·lieu \'pərl-,yü\ *n* **1 a** : a place of resort : HAUNT **b** *pl* : BOUNDS **2 a** : an outlying or adjacent district **b** *pl* : ENVIRONS

pur·lin \'pər-lən\ *n* : a horizontal member in a roof supporting the rafters

pur·loin \(,)pər-'lȯin, 'pər-,\ *vb* [AF *purloigner* to put away, fr. OF *pur-* forward (fr. L *pro-*) + *loing* at a distance, fr. L *longe*, fr. *longus* long] : STEAL, FILCH — **pur·loin·er** *n*

purl stitch *n* : a knitting stitch usu. made with the yarn at the front of the work by inserting the right needle into the front of a loop on the left needle from the right, catching the yarn with the right needle, and bringing it through to form a new loop — compare KNIT STITCH

¹**pur·ple** \'pər-pəl\ *adj* [OE *purple*, alter. of *purpuran*, gen. of *purpure* purple color, fr. L *purpura*, fr. Gk *porphyra*] **1** : of the color purple **2** : highly rhetorical : ORNATE ⟨*purple* prose⟩

²**purple** *n* **1 a** : TYRIAN PURPLE **b** : any of various colors that fall about midway between red and blue in hue **2 a** : cloth dyed purple **b** : a garment of purple cloth; *esp* : a robe worn as an emblem of rank or authority **3** : a mollusk yielding a purple dye and esp. the Tyrian purple of ancient times **4** : a pigment or dye that colors purple **5** : imperial or regal rank or power : exalted station

³**purple** *vb* **pur·pled**; **pur·pling** \'pər-p(ə-)liŋ\ : to turn purple

pur·plish \'pər-p(ə-)lish\ *adj* : somewhat purple

¹**pur·port** \'pər-,pōrt, -,pȯrt\ *n* [AF, content, tenor, fr. OF *porporter* to convey, fr. *por-* forward + *porter* to carry] : meaning conveyed, professed, or implied : IMPORT; *also* : SUBSTANCE, GIST

²**pur·port** \(,)pər-'pōrt, -'pȯrt\ *vt* : to give the impression of being : CLAIM, PROFESS ⟨a medicine *purporting* to cure all ills⟩

pur·port·ed *adj* : REPUTED, RUMORED ⟨saw the *purported* spies⟩ — **pur·port·ed·ly** *adv*

¹**pur·pose** \'pər-pəs\ *n* [OF *purpos*, fr. *purposer* to purpose, irreg. fr. L *proponere* to propose] **1 a** : something set up as an end to be attained : INTENTION **b** : RESOLUTION, DETERMINATION **2** : an object or result aimed at or achieved **3** : a subject under discussion **syn** see INTENTION — **pur·pose·ful** \-fəl\ *adj* — **pur·pose·ful·ly** \-fə-lē\ *adv* — **pur·pose·ful·ness** \-fəl-nəs\ *n* — **pur·pose·less** \-ləs\ *adj* — **on purpose** : by intent : INTENTIONALLY

²**purpose** *vt* : to propose as an aim to oneself : INTEND

pur·pose·ly \'pər-pəs-lē\ *adv* : with a deliberate or express purpose : INTENTIONALLY

pur·pos·ive \'pər-pə-siv\ *adj* **1** : serving or effecting a useful end though not clearly as a result of design **2** : having or tending to fulfill a conscious purpose or design : PURPOSEFUL — **pur·pos·ive·ly** *adv* — **pur·pos·ive·ness** *n*

purr \'pər\ *n* : a low vibratory murmur typical of a cat apparently contented or pleased — **purr** *vb*

¹**purse** \'pərs\ *n* [OE *purs*, modif. of ML *bursa*, fr. Gk *byrsa* oxhide] **1 a** : a small receptacle (as a wallet) esp. to carry money **b** : a receptacle (as a pouch) shaped like a purse **2 a** : RESOURCES, FUNDS **b** : a sum of money offered as a prize or present

²**purse** *vt* **1** : to put into a purse **2** : PUCKER, KNIT ⟨*pursed* lips⟩

purse–proud \-,prau̇d\ *adj* : proud because of one's wealth

purs·er \'pər-sər\ *n* : an official on a ship who keeps accounts and attends to the comfort and welfare of passengers

purs·lane \'pər-slən, -,slān\ *n* [MF *porcelaine*, fr. LL *porcillagin-, porcillago*] : a fleshy-leaved trailing plant with tiny bright yellow flowers that is a common troublesome weed but is sometimes eaten as a potherb or in salads

---

j joke; ŋ sing; ō flow; ȯ flaw; ȯi coin; th thin; th̲ this; ü loot; u̇ foot; y yet; yü few; yu̇ furious; zh vision

pur·su·ance \pər-'sü-ən(t)s\ *n* : the act of pursuing or carrying out ⟨in *pursuance* of his plans⟩

pur·su·ant to \-ənt-\ *prep* : in carrying out : in conformance to : according to

pur·sue \pər-'sü\ *vb* [OF *poursuir*, fr. L *prosequi*, fr. *pro-* forward + *sequi* to follow] **1** : to follow in order to overtake and capture or destroy **2** : to try to obtain or accomplish : SEEK ⟨*pursue* pleasure⟩ **3** : to proceed along : FOLLOW ⟨*pursue* a northerly course⟩ **4** : to engage in : PRACTICE ⟨*pursue* a hobby⟩ **5** : HARASS, HAUNT ⟨*pursued* by fears of bankruptcy⟩ **6** : COURT, WOO **syn** see CHASE — **pur·su·er** *n*

pur·suit \pər-'süt\ *n* **1** : the act of pursuing **2** : an activity that one engages in esp. as a vocation : OCCUPATION

pur·sui·vant \'pər-s(w)i-vənt\ *n* [MF *poursuivant* attendant of a herald, fr. prp. of *poursuir*, *poursuivre* to pursue] **1** : an officer of arms ranking below a herald but having similar duties **2** : FOLLOWER, ATTENDANT

pur·sy \'pəs-ē, 'pər-sē\ *adj* **pur·si·er**; -est **1** : shortwinded esp. because of corpulence **2** : too fat esp. from self-indulgent or luxurious living — **pur·si·ness** *n*

pu·ru·lent \'pyùr-(y)ə-lənt\ *adj* [L *purulentus*, fr. *pur-*, *pus* pus] : containing, consisting of, or accompanied by the formation of pus ⟨a *purulent* fever⟩ — **pu·ru·lence** \-lən(t)s\ *n*

pur·vey \(,)pər-'vā, 'pər-,\ *vt* [MF *porveeir*, fr. L *providēre* to provide] : to supply (as provisions) usu. as a business — **pur·vey·ance** \-ən(t)s\ *n*

pur·vey·or \-ər\ *n* : a person who supplies esp. provisions : CATERER

pur·view \'pər-,vyü\ *n* [ME *purveu* provision of a statute, fr. AF *purveu est* it is provided (opening phrase of a statute)] **1** : the range or limit of authority, competence, responsibility, concern, or intention **2** : range of vision, understanding, or cognizance

pus \'pəs\ *n* [L *pur-*, *pus*; akin to E *foul*] : thick opaque usu. yellowish white fluid matter formed by suppuration (as in an abscess) and containing white blood cells, tissue debris, and microorganisms

¹push \'pùsh\ *vb* [OF *poulser*, fr. L *pulsare*, freq. of *pellere* to drive, strike] **1 a** : to press against with force in order to drive or impel **b** : to move away or ahead by pressure without striking **2** : to thrust forward, downward, or outward **3 a** : to press or urge forward **b** : to prosecute with vigor or effectiveness **4** : to bear hard upon so as to involve in difficulty ⟨was *pushed* for money⟩ **5** : to exert oneself continuously, vigorously, or obtrusively to gain an end (as social advancement) — **push·er** *n*

syn PUSH, SHOVE, THRUST mean to cause to move ahead or aside by force. PUSH implies application of force by a body already in contact with the body to be moved; SHOVE implies a fast or rough pushing of something usu. along a surface; THRUST suggests less steadiness and greater violence than PUSH ⟨*thrust* his hand into his pocket⟩ ⟨*thrust* her grievance out of her mind⟩

²push *n* **1** : a vigorous advance against obstacles (as a military offensive) **2** : a condition or occasion of stress : EMERGENCY **3** : an act of pushing: as **a** : a sudden thrust : SHOVE **b** : a steady application of physical force in a direction away from the body exerting it **c** : a stimulating effect or action ⟨the holiday business gave retail trade a *push*⟩

push button *n* : a small button or knob that when pushed operates something esp. by closing an electric circuit

push-but·ton \,pùsh-,bət-³n\ *adj* : using or dependent on complex and more or less automatic mechanisms ⟨*push= button* warfare⟩ ⟨a *push-button* civilization⟩

push·cart \'pùsh-,kärt\ *n* : a cart or barrow pushed by hand

push·ing *adj* **1** : ENTERPRISING, ENERGETIC **2** : tactlessly forward or officious

push off *vi* : to set out

push·over \'pùsh-,ō-vər\ *n* **1** : an opponent easy to defeat or a victim capable of no effective resistance **2** : someone unwilling or unable to resist the power of a particular attraction or appeal **3** : something accomplished without difficulty : SNAP

Push·tu \'pəsh-tü\ *var of* PASHTO

push-up \'pùsh-,əp\ *n* : an exercise for strengthening arm and shoulder muscles by bending and extending the elbows

with the body in a prone position supported by the hands and toes

pushy \'pùsh-ē\ *adj* **push·i·er**; -est : aggressive often to an objectionable degree : FORWARD — **push·i·ly** \'pùsh-ə-lē\ *adv* — **push·i·ness** \'pùsh-ē-nəs\ *n*

pu·sil·la·nim·i·ty \,pyü-sə-lə-'nim-ət-ē\ *n* : the quality or state of being pusillanimous : COWARDLINESS

pu·sil·lan·i·mous \,pyü-sə-'lan-ə-məs\ *adj* [L *pusillus* very small + *animus* spirit] **1** : lacking in manly strength or spirit : COWARDLY **2** : indicative of or resulting from lack of courage and weakness of spirit ⟨a *pusillanimous* retreat⟩ — **pu·sil·lan·i·mous·ly** *adv*

puss \'pùs\ *n* **1** : CAT **2** : GIRL

puss·ley \'pəs-lē\ *n* : PURSLANE

¹pussy \'pùs-ē\ *n*, *pl* **puss·ies 1** : PUSS **2** : a catkin of the pussy willow

²pus·sy \'pəs-ē\ *adj* **pus·si·er**; -est : full of or resembling pus

³pus·sy \'pəs-ē\ *var of* PURSY

pussy·foot \'pùs-ē-,fùt\ *vi* **1** : to tread or move warily or stealthily **2** : to refrain from committing oneself : HEDGE

pussy willow \,pùs-ē-\ *n* : a willow having large cylindrical silky catkins

pus·tu·lar \'pəs-chə-lər\ *adj* **1** : of, relating to, marked by, or resembling pustules ⟨a *pustular* eruption⟩ **2** : covered with pustular prominences

pus·tule \'pəs-chül\ *n* [L *pustula*] **1** : a small elevation of the skin having an inflamed base and containing pus **2** : a small elevation resembling a pimple or blister

¹put \'pùt\ *vb* **put**; **put·ting** [ME *putten*] **1 a** : to place in or move into a particular position or relationship ⟨*put* the book down⟩ **b** : to throw with an overhand pushing motion ⟨*put* the shot⟩ **c** : to bring into a specified state or condition ⟨*put* it to use⟩ ⟨*put* the matter right⟩ **2 a** : to cause to endure or suffer something ⟨*put* him to death⟩ **b** : IMPOSE, INFLICT ⟨*put* a special tax on luxuries⟩ **c** : to apply to some end ⟨*put* their skills to use⟩ **3** : to see before one for judgment or decision (as by a formal vote) ⟨*put* the motion⟩ **4** : to give expression to esp. in intelligible language : TRANSLATE ⟨*put* his feelings in words⟩ ⟨*put* the poem into English⟩ **5 a** : to devote or urge to an activity or end ⟨*put* his mind to the problem⟩ ⟨*put* them to work⟩ **b** : INVEST ⟨*put* his money in the company⟩ **6 a** : to give as an estimate ⟨*put* the time at about eleven⟩ **b** : ATTACH, ATTRIBUTE ⟨*puts* a high value on friendship⟩ **c** : IMPUTE ⟨*put* the blame on his partner⟩ **7** : to commence a voyage ⟨the ship *put* to sea shorthanded⟩; *also* : to take a course ⟨the stream *puts* into a larger river⟩ ⟨*put* into a sheltered bay to escape the storm⟩ — **put forth 1** : to bring into action : EXERT **2** : to produce or send out by growth ⟨*put forth* leaves⟩ **3** : to start out — **put forward** : PROPOSE ⟨*put forward* a theory⟩ — **put in mind** : REMIND — **put to it** : to give difficulty to ⟨had been *put to it* to keep up⟩

²put *n* : a throw made usu. with an overhand pushing motion

³put *adj* : being in place : FIXED, SET ⟨stay *put*⟩

put about *vb* : to change or cause to change course or direction

put across *vt* : to achieve or convey successfully ⟨*put across* a plan⟩

pu·ta·tive \'pyüt-ət-iv\ *adj* [L *putare* to think] : commonly accepted or supposed : REPUTED — **pu·ta·tive·ly** *adv*

put away *vt* **1** : DISCARD, RENOUNCE **2** : to consume by eating or drinking **3** : to confine esp. in a mental institution

put by *vt* : to lay aside : SAVE ⟨had some money *put by*⟩

put down *vt* **1** : to bring to an end by force : SUPPRESS, CRUSH ⟨*put down* a riot⟩ **2 a** : DEPOSE, DEGRADE **b** : DISPARAGE, BELITTLE ⟨mentioned his poetry only to *put it down*⟩ **c** : DISAPPROVE, CRITICIZE ⟨was *put down* for the way she dressed⟩ **d** : HUMILIATE, SQUELCH ⟨*put* him *down* with a sharp retort⟩ **3** : to make ineffective : CHECK **4 a** : to write down (as in a list) **b** : to assign to a particular category or cause **5** : to preserve for future use ⟨*put down* a cask of pickles⟩

put in *vb* **1** : to make or make as a request, offer, or declaration ⟨*put in* a plea of guilty⟩ ⟨*put in* for a job at the store⟩ **2** : to spend (time) at some activity or place ⟨*put in* six hours at the office⟩ **3** : PLANT ⟨*put in* a crop⟩ **4** : to call at or enter a place; *esp* : to enter a harbor or port

put off *vt* **1** : DISCONCERT, REPEL   **2 a** : to hold back to a later time : DEFER ⟨*put off* his visit to the dentist⟩ **b** : to induce to wait ⟨*put* the bill collector *off*⟩ **3** : to rid oneself of

put on *vt* **1 a** : to dress oneself in : DON   **b** : to assume as if a garment : ADOPT ⟨*put on* airs⟩; *also* : FEIGN ⟨*put on* a show of anger⟩ **2** : EXAGGERATE, OVERSTATE ⟨he's *putting it on* when he makes such claims⟩ **3** : PERFORM, PRODUCE ⟨*put on* an entertaining act⟩ **4** : to mislead deliberately esp. for amusement — **put-on** *adj*

put out \(')pùt-'aùt\ *vb* **1** : EXERT, USE ⟨*put out* all his strength to move the piano⟩ **2** : EXTINGUISH ⟨*put* the fire *out*⟩ **3** : PRODUCE   **4** : IRRITATE, PROVOKE, INCONVENIENCE ⟨his father was *put out* by his failure⟩ **5** : to cause to be out (as in baseball) **6** : to set out from shore

put-out \'pùt-,aùt\ *n* : the retiring of a base runner or batter in baseball

put over *vt* : to put across ⟨*put over* a deliberate deception⟩ ⟨*put* his talk *over* very well⟩

pu·tre·fac·tion \,pyü-trə-'fak-shən\ *n* **1** : the decomposing of organic matter; *esp* : an anaerobic splitting of proteins by bacteria and fungi with the formation of foul-smelling incompletely oxidized products **2** : the state of being putrefied : CORRUPTION — **pu·tre·fac·tive** \-'fak-tiv\ *adj*

pu·tre·fy \'pyü-trə-,fī\ *vb* **-fied; -fy·ing** [L *putrefacere*, fr. *putrēre* to be rotten + *facere* to make] : to make or become putrid : DECOMPOSE, ROT

pu·tres·cent \pyü-'tres-ᵊnt\ *adj* : becoming putrid : ROTTING — **pu·tres·cence** \-ᵊn(t)s\ *n*

pu·trid \'pyü-trəd\ *adj* [L *putridus*, fr. *putrēre* to be rotten] **1 a** : being in a state of putrefaction : ROTTEN ⟨*putrid* meat⟩ **b** : characteristic of putrefaction : FOUL ⟨a *putrid* odor⟩ **2 a** : morally corrupt **b** : totally disagreeable or objectionable : VILE — **pu·trid·i·ty** \pyü-'trid-ət-ē\ *n* — **pu·trid·ly** \'pyü-trəd-lē\ *adv* — **pu·trid·ness** *n*

putsch \'pùch\ *n* [G] : a secretly plotted and suddenly executed attempt to overthrow a government

putt \'pət\ *n* : a golf stroke made on a putting green to cause the ball to roll into or near the hole — **putt** *vb*

put·tee \,pə-'tē, pù-; 'pət-ē\ *n* [Hindi *paṭṭī* strip of cloth] **1** : a cloth strip wrapped around the leg from ankle to knee **2** : a leather legging secured by a strap or catch or by laces

¹put·ter \'pùt-ər\ *n* : one that puts

²put·ter \'pət-ər\ *n* : a golf club used in putting

³put·ter \'pət-ər\ *vi* [alter. of *potter*] **1** : to move or act aimlessly or idly : DAWDLE **2** : to work at random : TINKER — **put·ter·er** \-ər-ər\ *n*

put through *vt* : to carry to a successful conclusion ⟨*put through* a number of reforms⟩

putt·ing green \'pət-iŋ-\ *n* : a smooth usu. grassy area around the hole into which the ball must be played in golf

put to *vi* : to put in to shore (as for shelter)

¹put·ty \'pət-ē\ *n*, *pl* **putties** [F *potée*, lit., potful, fr. *pot*] : a cement usu. made of whiting and boiled linseed oil beaten or kneaded to the consistency of dough and used in fastening glass in sashes and stopping crevices in woodwork; *also* : any of various substances resembling such cement in appearance, consistency, or use

²putty *vt* **put·tied; put·ty·ing** : to cement or seal up with putty

put up \(')pùt-'əp\ *vb* **1 a** : to prepare for later use ⟨*put up* a lunch⟩; *esp* : CAN ⟨*put up* peaches⟩ **b** : to put away out of use ⟨*put up* your sword⟩ **2** : to start (game) from cover **3** : to nominate for election **4** : to offer for public sale ⟨*puts* his possessions *up* for auction⟩ **5** : to give or obtain food and shelter : LODGE ⟨*put* him *up* overnight⟩ **6** : BUILD, ERECT **7** : to carry on ⟨*put up* a bluff⟩ ⟨*put up* a struggle against odds⟩ **8** : to make available : PAY ⟨*put up* a prize for the best essay⟩ — **put up to** : INCITE, INSTIGATE — **put up with** : TOLERATE, ENDURE

put-up \,pùt-,əp\ *adj* : arranged secretly beforehand ⟨a *put-up* job⟩

¹puz·zle \'pəz-əl\ *vb* **puz·zled; puz·zling** \'pəz-(ə-)liŋ\ **1** : to confuse the understanding of : PERPLEX, BEWILDER **2** : to solve with difficulty or ingenuity ⟨*puzzled* out the mystery⟩ **3** : to be uncertain as to action or choice **4** : to attempt a solution of a puzzle — **puz·zler** \-(ə-)lər\ *n*

syn PERPLEX, MYSTIFY: PUZZLE suggests some complication or contradiction difficult to understand or explain

and causing mental confusion; PERPLEX usu. adds an implication of causing worry and uncertainty in making a decision; MYSTIFY implies puzzling or perplexing thoroughly esp. by playing on one's credulity

²puzzle *n* **1** : the state of being puzzled : PERPLEXITY **2 a** : something that puzzles **b** : a question, problem, or contrivance designed for testing ingenuity

puz·zle·ment \'pəz-əl-mənt\ *n* **1** : the state of being puzzled : PERPLEXITY **2** : PUZZLE 2

py- *or* **pyo-** *comb form* [Gk *pyon* pus; akin to E *foul*] : pus ⟨*pyemia*⟩⟨*pyorrhea*⟩

pyc·nom·e·ter \pik-'näm-ət-ər\ *n* [Gk *pyknos* thick, dense] : a standard vessel for measuring and comparing the densities of liquids or solids

py·emia \pī-'ē-mē-ə\ *n* : a septicemia caused by pus-forming bacteria and accompanied by multiple abscesses — **py·emic** \-mik\ *adj*

py·gid·i·um \pī-'jid-ē-əm\ *n*, *pl* **-ia** \-ē-ə\ [NL, fr. Gk *pygidion*, dim. of *pygē* rump] : a tail or terminal body region of an invertebrate — **py·gid·i·al** \-ē-əl\ *adj*

Pyg·ma·lion \pig-'māl-yən, -'mā-lē-ən\ *n* : a sculptor and king of Cyprus — compare GALATEA

pyg·my \'pig-mē\ *n*, *pl* **pygmies** [Gk *pygmaios*, fr. *pygmē*, a measure of length, lit., fist] **1** *often cap* : one of a race of dwarfs described by ancient Greek authors **2** *cap* : one of a small people of equatorial Africa ranging under five feet in height **3** : a person or thing very small for its kind : DWARF — **pygmy** *adj*

py·ja·mas \pə-'jä-məz\ *chiefly Brit var of* PAJAMAS

py·lon \'pī-,län, -lən\ *n* [Gk *pylōn*, fr. *pylē* gate] **1** : a usu. massive gateway; *esp* : an ancient Egyptian one composed of two flat-topped pyramids and a crosspiece **2** : a tower for supporting either end of a wire over a long span **3** : a projection (as a post or tower) marking a prescribed course of flight for an airplane

py·lo·ric \pī-'lȯr-ik, pə-, -'lȯr-\ *adj* : of or relating to the pylorus; *also* : of, relating to, or situated in or near the posterior part of the stomach

py·lo·rus \-'lȯr-əs, -'lȯr-\ *n*, *pl* **-lo·ri** \-'lȯr-,ī, -'lȯr-, -,ē\ [Gk *pylōros*, lit., gatekeeper, fr. *pylē* gate] : the opening in a vertebrate from the stomach into the intestine

pyo·gen·ic \,pī-ə-'jen-ik\ *adj* : producing pus : marked by pus production

pyo·or·rhea \,pī-ə-'rē-ə\ *n* : a pussy inflammation of the sockets of the teeth leading usu. to loosening of the teeth — **py·or·rhe·al** \-'rē-əl\ *adj*

pyr- *or* **pyro-** *comb form* [Gk; akin to E *fire*] : fire : heat ⟨*pyrotechnic*⟩

¹pyr·a·mid \'pir-ə-,mid\ *n* [Gk *pyramid-, pyramis*] **1** : a massive structure built esp. in ancient Egypt that usu. has a square base and four triangular faces meeting at a point and contains tombs **2 a** : something felt to resemble a pyramid (as in shape or in broad-based organization) ⟨the social *pyramid*⟩ **b** : one of the conical masses that project from the medulla into the cavity of the kidney pelvis **3** : a polyhedron having for its base a plane figure with three or more angles and for its sides three or more triangles that meet to form the vertex — **py·ram·i·dal** \pə-'ram-əd-ᵊl, ,pir-ə-'mid-ᵊl\ *adj* — **py·ram·i·dal·ly** \-ē\ *adv* — **pyr·a·mid·i·cal** \,pir-ə-'mid-i-kəl\ *adj*

pyramids 3

²pyramid *vt* **1** : to increase rapidly and progressively step by step on a broad base **2** : to arrange or build up as if on the base of a pyramid

Pyr·a·mus \'pir-ə-məs\ *n* : a legendary Babylonian and lover of Thisbe

pyre \'pī(ə)r\ *n* [Gk *pyra*, fr. *pyr* fire] : a combustible heap for burning a dead body as a funeral rite; *also* : a pile of material to be burned

py·re·noid \pī-'rē-,nȯid\ *n* [Gk *pyrēn* stone of a fruit] : one of the protein bodies in the chromatophores of various low organisms that act as centers for starch deposition

py·re·thrin \pī-'rē-thrən, -'reth-rən\ *n* : either of two oily liquid esters having high insecticidal properties and occurring esp. in pyrethrum flowers

py·re·thrum \-'rē-thrəm, -'reth-rəm\ *n* [Gk *pyrethron*, a plant resembling yarrow, fr. *pyr* fire] **1** : any of several chrysanthemums with finely divided often aromatic leaves including ornamentals as well as important sources of insecticides **2 :** an insecticide consisting of the dried heads of some Old World pyrethrums

Py·rex \'pī-ˌreks\ *trademark* — used for glass and glass-ware resistant to heat, chemicals, or electricity

py·rex·ia \pī-'rek-sē-ə\ *n* [NL, fr. Gk *pyressein* to be feverish, fr. *pyretos* fever, fr. *pyr* fire] **:** FEVER — **py·ret·ic** \-'ret-ik\ *also* **py·rex·i·al** \-'rek-sē-əl\ *adj*

pyr·i·dine \'pir-ə-ˌdēn\ *n* **:** a toxic water-soluble flammable liquid organic base C_5H_5N of pungent odor used as a solvent and in the manufacture of pharmaceuticals

pyr·i·dox·ine *also* **pyr·i·dox·in** \ˌpir-ə-'däk-ˌsēn, -sən\ *n* **:** a crystalline alcohol of the vitamin B_6 group found esp. in cereals and convertible in the organism into phosphate compounds that are essential coenzymes

pyr·i·form \'pir-ə-ˌform\ *adj* [ML *pyrum* pear, alter. of L *pirum*] **:** having the form of a pear

py·rim·i·dine \pī-'rim-ə-ˌdēn\ *n* **1 :** a feeble organic base of penetrating odor **2 :** a derivative of pyramidine; *esp* **:** a base that is an important component of nucleotides

py·rite \'pī-ˌrīt\ *n* **:** a common mineral FeS_2 that consists of iron disulfide, has a pale brass-yellow color and metallic luster, and is burned in making sulfur dioxide and sulfuric acid

py·rites \pə-'rīt-ēz, pī-; 'pī-ˌrīts\ *n, pl* **pyrites** [L, flint, fr. Gk *pyritēs* of fire, fr. *pyr* fire] **:** any of various metallic-looking sulfides of which pyrite is the commonest

py·ro·gal·lol \ˌpī-rō-'gal-ˌol, -ˌōl\ *n* **:** a poisonous acidic bitter crystalline organic compound used esp. as a photographic developer

py·ro·lu·site \ˌpī-rō-'lü-ˌsīt\ *n* **:** a mineral MnO_2 consisting of manganese dioxide that is of an iron-black or dark steel-gray color and metallic luster, is usu. soft, and is the most important ore of manganese

py·rol·y·sis \pī-'räl-ə-səs\ *n* **:** chemical change brought about by the action of heat

py·ro·ma·nia \ˌpī-rō-'mā-nē-ə, -nyə\ *n* **:** a compulsive urge to start fires — **py·ro·ma·ni·ac** \-nē-ˌak\ *n*

py·rom·e·ter \pī-'räm-ət-ər\ *n* **:** an instrument for measuring temperatures esp. when beyond the range of mercurial thermometers — **py·ro·met·ric** \ˌpī-rə-'me-trik\ *adj* — **py·ro·met·ri·cal·ly** \-tri-k(ə-)lē\ *adv* — **py·rom·e·try** \pī-'räm-ə-trē\ *n*

py·rope \'pī-ˌrōp\ *n* **:** a magnesium-aluminum garnet that is deep red in color and is frequently used as a gem

py·ro·phor·ic \ˌpī-rə-'fōr-ik, -'fär-\ *adj* [Gk *phor-, pherein* to bear] **1 :** igniting spontaneously **2 :** emitting sparks when scratched or struck esp. with steel

py·ro·tech·nic \ˌpī-rə-'tek-nik\ *n* **1** *pl* **:** the art of making or the manufacture and use of fireworks **2** *pl* **:** materials (as fireworks) for flares or signals **b :** a display of fireworks **3 :** a spectacular display (as of oratory) — usu. used in pl. — **py·ro·tech·ni·cal** \-ni-kəl\ *or* **pyrotechnic** *adj* — **py·ro·tech·ni·cal·ly** \-ni-k(ə-)lē\ *adv* — **py·ro·tech·nist** \-'tek-nəst\ *n*

py·rox·ene \pī-'räk-ˌsēn\ *n* [F *pyroxène*, fr. Gk *pyr* fire + *xenos* stranger] **:** any of various silicate minerals that usu. contain magnesium or iron — **py·rox·e·nic** \ˌpī-ˌräk-'sē-nik\ *adj*

py·rox·y·lin \pī-'räk-sə-lən\ *n* **:** a flammable substance resembling cotton that is produced chemically from cellulose and used in the manufacture of various products (as celluloid, lacquer, and some explosives)

Pyr·rhic victory \ˌpir-ik-\ *n* [after *Pyrrhus* d272 B.C. king of Epirus who sustained heavy losses in defeating the Romans] **:** a victory won at excessive cost

pyr·uvate \pī-'rü-ˌvāt\ *n* **:** a salt or ester of pyruvic acid

pyr·uvic acid \(ˌ)pī-ˌrü-vik-\ *n* [*pyr-* + L *uva* grape] **:** a liquid organic acid that smells like acetic acid and is an important intermediate in metabolism and fermentation

Py·thag·o·re·an \pə-ˌthag-ə-'rē-ən, (ˌ)pī-\ *adj* **:** of, relating to, or associated with the Greek philosopher Pythagoras ⟨*Pythagorean* theorem⟩⟨*Pythagorean* numbers⟩

Pyth·i·an \'pith-ē-ən\ *adj* [Gk *pythios* of Delphi, fr. *Pythō* Pytho, former name of Delphi] **1 :** of or relating to the ancient Greek god Apollo esp. as patron deity of Delphi **2 :** of or relating to games celebrated at Delphi every four years

Pyth·i·as \'pith-ē-əs\ *n* **:** a friend of Damon condemned to death by Dionysius of Syracuse

py·thon \'pī-ˌthän, -thən\ *n* [Gk *Pythōn*, a monstrous serpent killed by Apollo] **:** a large constricting snake (as a

boa); *esp* **:** any of an Old World genus including the largest recent snakes — **py·tho·nine** \'pī-thə-ˌnīn\ *adj*

py·tho·ness \'pī-thə-nəs, 'pith-ə-\ *n* [LL *pythonissa*, fr. Gk *Pythōn*, spirit of divination, fr. *Pythō*, seat of the Delphic oracle] **:** a woman supposed to have a spirit of divination; *esp* **:** a priestess of Apollo held to have prophetic powers — **py·thon·ic** \pī-'thän-ik\ *adj*

pyx \'piks\ *n* [Gk *pyxis* box] **:** a small round case used to carry the Eucharist to the sick

pyx·id·i·um \pik-'sid-ē-əm\ *n, pl* **-ia** \-ē-ə\ [NL, fr. Gk *pyxidion*, dim. of *pyxis* box] **:** a capsular fruit that splits at maturity so that the upper part falls off like a cap

q \'kyü\ *n, often cap* **:** the 17th letter of the English alphabet

Q fever \'kyü-\ *n* [query] **:** a disease marked by high fever, chills, and muscular pains, caused by a rickettsia, and transmitted by raw milk, by contact, or by ticks

¹quack \'kwak\ *vi* **:** to make the characteristic cry of a duck

²quack *n* **:** a cry made by or as if by quacking

³quack *n* [short for *quacksalver*] **1 :** a pretender to medical skill **2 :** CHARLATAN — **quack·ery** \'kwak-(ə-)rē\ *n*

⁴quack *adj* **:** of, relating to, or characteristic of a quack; *esp* **:** pretending to cure diseases

quack grass *n* **:** COUCH GRASS

quack·sal·ver \'kwak-ˌsal-vər\ *n* [obs. D] **:** ³QUACK

¹quad \'kwäd\ *n* **:** QUADRANGLE

²quad *n* [short for earlier *quadrat*, alter. of ²*quadrate*] **:** a type-metal space that is 1 en or more in width

³quad *n* **:** QUADRUPLET

quad·ran·gle \'kwäd-ˌraŋ-gəl\ *n* **1 :** QUADRILATERAL **2 a :** a quadrilateral enclosure esp. when surrounded by buildings **b :** the buildings enclosing a quadrangle — **qua·dran·gu·lar** \kwä-'draŋ-gyə-lər\ *adj*

quad·rant \'kwäd-rənt\ *n* [L *quadrant-, quadrans* fourth part] **1 :** an instrument for measuring altitudes (as in astronomy or surveying) **2 a :** an arc of 90° **:** one quarter of a circle **b :** the area bounded by a quadrant and two radii **c :** a device shaped like the quadrant of a circle **3 :** any of the four quarters into which something is divided by two real or imaginary lines that intersect each other at right angles — **qua·dran·tal** \kwä-'drant-ʾl\ *adj*

qua·draph·o·ny \kwä-'draf-ə-nē\ *n* **:** the transmission, recording, or reproduction of sound by techniques that utilize four transmission channels — **quad·ra·phon·ic** \ˌkwädrə-'fän-ik\ *adj*

quad·rat \'kwäd-rət, -ˌrat\ *n* **:** a usu. rectangular plot used for ecological or population studies

¹quad·rate \'kwäd-ˌrāt, -rət\ *adj* [L *quadratus*, fr. pp. of *quadrare* to make square, fr. *quadrum* square; akin to E *four*] **1 :** square or approximately square **2 :** of, relating to, or being a bony or cartilaginous element of each side of the skull to which the lower jaw is attached in most lower vertebrates

²quadrate *n* **1 :** an approximately square or cubical area, space, or body **2 :** a quadrate bone

qua·drat·ic \kwä-'drat-ik\ *adj* **:** involving terms of second degree at most ⟨*quadratic* function⟩; *also* **:** based on or derivable from a quadratic equation ⟨*quadratic* figures such as the sphere⟩ — **quadratic** *n*

quadratic equation *n* **:** an equation containing one term in which the unknown is squared and no term in which it is raised to a higher power

qua·drat·ics \kwä-'drat-iks\ *n* **:** a branch of algebra dealing with quadratic equations

quad·ra·ture \'kwäd-rə-ˌchür, -chər\ *n* **1 :** the process of finding a square equal in area to a given area ⟨*quadrature* of the circle is impossible with ruler and compass⟩ **2 :** a configuration in which two celestial bodies have a separation of 90 degrees

qua·dren·ni·al \kwä-'dren-ē-əl\ *adj* [L *quadrennium* period of four years, fr. *quadri-* + *annus* year] **1 :** consisting of or lasting for four years **2 :** occurring or being done every four years — **qua·dren·ni·al·ly** \-ē-ə-lē\ *adv*

quadri- *or* **quadr-** *or* **quadru-** *comb form* [L; akin to E *four*] **1 :** four ⟨*quadri*lingual⟩ **2 :** fourth ⟨*quadri*centennial⟩

quad·ri·ceps \'kwäd-rə-,seps\ *n* [NL, fr. *quadri-* + *-ceps* (as in *biceps*)] **:** the great extensor muscle of the front of the thigh

quad·ri·fid \-fəd, -,fid\ *adj* [L *quadrifidus*, fr. *quadri-* + *findere* to split] **:** divided or deeply cleft into four parts ⟨*quadrifid* petals⟩

¹**quad·ri·lat·er·al** \,kwäd-rə-'lat-ə-rəl, -'la-trəl\ *adj* [L *later-, latus* side] **:** having four sides

²**quadrilateral** *n* **:** a plane figure of four sides and four angles

quadrilaterals

qua·drille \kwä-'dril, k(w)ə-\ *n* **:** a square dance for four couples or music for this dance

qua·dril·lion \kwä-'dril-yən\ *n* — see NUMBER table

quad·ri·par·tite \,kwäd-rə-'pär-,tīt\ *adj* [L *quadri-* + *part-, pars* part] **1 :** consisting of four parts ⟨a *quadripartite* vault⟩ **2 :** shared by four parties or persons ⟨a *quadripartite* agreement⟩

qua·driv·i·um \kwä-'driv-ē-əm\ *n* [LL, fr. L *quadri-* + *via* way] **:** a group of studies consisting of arithmetic, music, geometry, and astronomy and forming the course for the three years of study between the B.A. and M.A. degrees in a medieval university

qua·droon \kwä-'drün\ *n* [modif. of Sp *cuarterón*, fr. *cuarto* fourth, fr. L *quartus*] **:** a person of quarter Negro ancestry

quad·ru·ped \'kwäd-rə-,ped\ *n* **:** an animal having four feet — **quadruped** *or* **qua·dru·pe·dal** \kwä-'drü-pəd-ᵊl, ,kwäd-rə-'ped-\ *adj*

¹**qua·dru·ple** \kwä-'drüp-əl, -'drəp-; 'kwäd-rəp-\ *vb* **qua·dru·pled; qua·dru·pling** \-(ə-)liŋ\ **:** to make or become four times as great or as many

²**quadruple** *adj* [L *quadruplus*, fr. *quadri-* + *-plus* multiplied by] **1 :** having four units or members **2 :** being four times as great or as many **3 :** marked by four beats per measure ⟨*quadruple* meter⟩ — **quadruple** *n*

qua·drup·let \kwä-'drəp-lət, -'drüp-; 'kwäd-rəp-\ *n* **1 :** one of four offspring born at one birth **2 :** a combination of four of a kind

¹**qua·dru·pli·cate** \kwä-'drü-pli-kət\ *adj* [L *quadruplic-, quadruplex* fourfold] **1 :** repeated four times **2 :** FOURTH

²**qua·dru·pli·cate** \-plə-,kāt\ *vt* **1 :** QUADRUPLE **2 :** to provide in quadruplicate — **qua·dru·pli·ca·tion** \(,)kwä-,drü-plə-'kā-shən\ *n*

³**qua·dru·pli·cate** \kwä-'drü-pli-kət\ *n* **1 :** one of four like things **2 :** four copies all alike ⟨typed in *quadruplicate*⟩

quaes·tor \'kwes-tər\ *n* [L, fr. *quaest-, quaerere* to seek, ask] **:** one of numerous ancient Roman officials concerned chiefly with financial administration

¹**quaff** \'kwäf, 'kwaf\ *vb* **:** to drink deeply or repeatedly

²**quaff** *n* **:** a deep drink

quag \'kwag, 'kwäg\ *n* **:** MARSH, BOG

quag·ga \'kwag-ə, 'kwäg-\ *n* [obs. Afrik] **:** an extinct wild ass of southern Africa related to the zebras

quag·gy \'kwag-ē, 'kwäg-\ *adj* **quag·gi·er; -est 1 :** BOGGY, MARSHY **2 :** FLABBY, YIELDING

quag·mire \'kwag-,mī(ə)r, 'kwäg-\ *n* **1 :** soft miry land that shakes or yields under the foot **2 :** a complex or precarious position

qua·hog \'kwò-,hòg, 'kwō-, -,häg\ *n* [of AmerInd origin] **:** a round thick-shelled American clam

quai \'kā\ *n* **:** QUAY

¹**quail** \'kwāl\ *n, pl* **quail** *or* **quails** [MF *quaille*, fr. ML *quaccula*] **:** any of various game birds related to the common fowl: as **a :** a stocky short-winged Old World migratory bird occurring in many varieties **b :** any of various small American birds; *esp* **:** BOBWHITE

²**quail** *vi* [MF *quailler* to curdle, fr. L *coagulare*] **:** to lose courage **:** shrink fearfully **:** COWER

quaint \'kwānt\ *adj* [OF *cointe* skilled, fr. L *cognitus*, pp. of *cognoscere* to know] **:** unusual or different in character or appearance **:** ODD; *esp* **:** pleasingly old-fashioned or unfamiliar — **quaint·ly** *adv* — **quaint·ness** *n*

¹**quake** \'kwāk\ *vi* [OE *cwacian*] **1 :** to shake or vibrate

usu. from shock or instability **2 :** to tremble or shudder usu. from cold or fear

²**quake** *n* **:** a shaking or trembling; *esp* **:** EARTHQUAKE

quak·er \'kwā-kər\ *n* **:** one that quakes **2** *cap* **:** FRIEND 4 — **Quak·er·ism** \-kə-,riz-əm\ *n*

Quaker meeting *n* **1 :** a meeting of Friends for worship marked often by long periods of silence **2 :** a social gathering marked by many periods of silence

qual·i·fi·ca·tion \,kwäl-ə-fə-'kā-shən\ *n* **1 :** the act or an instance of qualifying **2 :** the state of being qualified **3 a :** a special skill, knowledge, or ability that fits a person for a particular work or position **:** FITNESS **b :** a condition that must be complied with (as for the attainment of a privilege) **4 :** something that qualifies **:** LIMITATION ⟨agree without *qualification*⟩

qual·i·fied \'kwäl-ə-,fīd\ *adj* **1 :** having the necessary skill, knowledge, or ability to do something **:** FITTED ⟨*qualified* to lead men⟩ **2 :** limited or modified in some way ⟨*qualified* agreement⟩ — **qual·i·fied·ly** \-,fī(-ə)d-lē\ *adv*

qual·i·fi·er \-,fī(-ə)r\ *n* **:** one that qualifies: as **a :** one that satisfies specified requirements **b :** a word or word group that limits the meaning of another word or word group **:** MODIFIER

qual·i·fy \'kwäl-ə-,fī\ *vb* **-fied; -fy·ing** [ML *qualificare* to attribute a quality to, fr. L *qualis* of what kind] **1 a :** to reduce from a general to a particular or restricted form **:** MODIFY **b :** to make less harsh or strict **:** MODERATE **c :** to alter the strength or flavor of ⟨*qualify* a liquor⟩ **d :** to limit the meaning of (as a noun) **2 :** to characterize by naming an attribute **:** DESCRIBE **3 a :** to fit by training, skill, or ability for a special purpose **b :** to declare competent or adequate **:** CERTIFY, LICENSE **4 :** to be fit (as for an office); *also* **:** to demonstrate the skill or ability required for an end (as an award or the right to membership on a team)

qual·i·ta·tive \'kwäl-ə-,tāt-iv\ *adj* **:** of, relating to, or involving quality or kind — **qual·i·ta·tive·ly** *adv*

qualitative analysis *n* **:** chemical analysis designed to identify the components of a substance or mixture

qual·i·ty \'kwäl-ət-ē\ *n, pl* **-ties** [L *qualitas*, fr. *qualis* of what kind] **1 a :** peculiar and essential character **:** NATURE **b :** an inherent feature **:** PROPERTY **2 a :** degree of excellence **:** GRADE **b :** superiority in kind **3 :** social status **:** RANK **4 :** a distinguishing attribute **:** CHARACTERISTIC **5 a :** vividness of hue **b :** TIMBRE **c :** the identifying character of a vowel sound

syn PROPERTY, ATTRIBUTE: QUALITY is a very general term applying to any trait, mark, or character of an individual or of a type; PROPERTY applies to a quality belonging to a thing's essential nature and helping to distinguish and identify its type or species; ATTRIBUTE is a quality ascribed to a thing or being often through lack of definite knowledge of it ⟨the *attributes* of God⟩

qualm \'kwäm, 'kwälm, 'kwòm\ *n* **1 :** a sudden attack of illness, faintness, or nausea **2 :** a sudden fear or misgiving **3 :** a feeling of doubt or hesitation in matters of conscience **:** SCRUPLE — **qualmy** \-ē\ *adj*

syn QUALM, SCRUPLE, COMPUNCTION mean a misgiving about what one is doing or going to do. QUALM implies an uneasy fear that one is not following one's conscience or better judgment; SCRUPLE implies doubt of the rightness of an act on grounds of principle; COMPUNCTION implies a spontaneous feeling that one is inflicting a wrong or injustice on someone

qualm·ish \-ish\ *adj* **1 a :** feeling qualms **:** NAUSEATED **b :** overly scrupulous **:** SQUEAMISH **2 :** of, relating to, or producing qualms — **qualm·ish·ly** *adv* — **qualm·ish·ness** *n*

quan·da·ry \'kwän-d(ə-)rē\ *n, pl* **-ries** **:** a state of perplexity or doubt **:** DILEMMA **syn** see PREDICAMENT

quan·ti·fi·er \'kwänt-ə-,fī(-ə)r\ *n* **:** a term (as *two, all, most,* or *no*) expressive of quantity; *esp* **:** one that binds the variables in a logical formula

quan·ti·ta·tive \'kwän(t)-ə-,tāt-iv\ *adj* **:** of, relating to, expressible in terms of, or involving the measurement of quantity — **quan·ti·ta·tive·ly** *adv* — **quan·ti·ta·tive·ness** *n*

quantitative analysis *n* **:** chemical analysis designed to determine the amounts or proportions of the components of a substance or mixture

---

j joke; ŋ sing; ō flow; ò flaw; òi coin; th thin; th̲ this; ü loot;   u̇ foot; y yet; yü few; yu̇ furious; zh vision

quantitative inheritance n : particulate inheritance of a character (as height or skin color in man) controlled by multiple factors each allelic pair of which adds to or subtracts from the end result

quan·ti·ty \'kwän(t)-ət-ē\ n, pl **-ties** [L quantitas amount, extent, fr. quantus how much, how large] **1 a :** an indefinite amount or number **b :** a determinate or estimated amount **c :** a considerable amount or number — often used in pl. **2 a :** the aspect in which a thing is measurable in terms of degree or magnitude **b :** the subject of a mathematical operation **3 a :** duration of a speech sound as distinct from individual quality **b :** the relative length or brevity of a prosodic syllable in some languages (as Greek and Latin) **syn** see AMOUNT

quan·tize \'kwän-,tīz\ vt **1 :** to subdivide (as energy) into small units or amounts **2 :** to calculate or express in terms of quantum mechanics — **quan·ti·za·tion** \,kwänt-ə-'zā-shən\ n

quan·tum \'kwänt-əm\ n, pl **quan·ta** \'kwänt-ə\ [L, neut. of quantus how large] **1 :** QUANTITY, AMOUNT **2 :** one of the very small parcels into which many forms of energy are subdivided

quantum mechanics n : a general mathematical theory dealing with the interactions of matter and radiation in terms of observable quantities only — **quantum mechanical** adj

quantum theory n : a branch of physical theory based on the concept of the subdivision of radiant energy into finite quanta and applied to numerous processes involving transference or transformation of energy on an atomic or molecular scale

¹quar·an·tine \'kwȯr-ən-,tēn, 'kwär-\ n [It quarantina, fr. MF quarantaine, fr. quarante forty, fr. L quadraginta] **1 :** a period of 40 days **2 a :** a term during which a ship arriving in port and suspected of carrying contagious disease is forbidden contact with the shore **b :** a restraint upon the activities or movements of persons or the transport of goods designed to prevent the spread of disease or pests; also : the period during which a person with a contagious disease is under quarantine **3 :** a place (as a hospital) where individuals under quarantine are kept **4 :** a state of enforced isolation — **quar·an·tin·a·ble** \-,tē-nə-bəl\ adj

²quarantine vt **1 :** to detain in or exclude by quarantine **2 :** to isolate from normal relations or intercourse (quarantine an aggressor)

¹quar·rel \'kwȯr-(ə)l, 'kwär-(ə)l\ n [OF, fr. (assumed) VL quadrellum, dim. of L quadrum square] : a square-headed bolt or arrow esp. for a crossbow

²quarrel n [MF querele complaint, fr. L querela, fr. queri to complain] **1 :** a ground of dispute or complaint **2 :** DISAGREEMENT, ALTERCATION; esp : an angry dispute

³quarrel vi **-reled** or **-relled; -rel·ing** or **-rel·ling 1 :** to find fault : CAVIL (quarrel with his lot) **2 :** to contend or dispute actively : SQUABBLE — **quar·rel·er** or **quar·rel·ler** n

quar·rel·some \'kwȯr-(ə)l-səm, 'kwär-(ə)l-\ adj : apt or disposed to quarrel : CONTENTIOUS — **quar·rel·some·ly** adv — **quar·rel·some·ness** n

¹quar·ry \'kwȯr-ē, 'kwär-\ n, pl **quarries** [ME querre entrails of game given to the hounds, fr. MF cuiriee] **1 :** the object of a chase : GAME; esp : game hunted with hawks **2 :** PREY

²quarry n, pl **quarries** [MF quarriere, fr. (assumed) OF quarre squared stone, fr. L quadrum square] : an open excavation usu. for obtaining building stone, slate, or limestone

³quarry vt **quar·ried; quar·ry·ing 1 :** to dig or take from or as if from a quarry **2 :** to make a quarry in — **quar·ri·er** n

quart \'kwȯrt\ n [MF quarte one fourth of a gallon, fr. L quartus fourth] **1 —** see MEASURE table **2 :** a vessel or measure having a capacity of one quart

¹quar·tan \'kwȯrt-ᵊn\ adj : occurring every fourth day reckoning inclusively

²quartan n : an intermittent fever recurring at approximately 72-hour intervals; esp : a quartan malaria

¹quar·ter \'kwȯrt-ər\ n [OF quartier, fr. L quartarius, fr. quartus fourth; akin to E four] **1 :** one of four equal parts into which something is divisible **2 :** a unit (as of weight or length) that equals one fourth of some larger unit

3 : something that is or approximates one fourth of something else: as **a :** any of four 3-month divisions of a year; also : a school term of about 12 weeks **b :** a coin worth a fourth of a dollar; also : the sum of 25 cents **c :** one limb of a 4-limbed animal or carcass with the parts near it (a quarter of beef) **d :** a fourth part of the moon's period (a moon in its first quarter) **e :** any of four parts into which a heraldic shield is divided by perpendicular and horizontal lines **f :** one of the four parts into which the horizon may be divided; also : a region or direction under such a part **g :** one of the four cardinal points corresponding to the four parts of the horizon; also : a compass point **h :** one of the four equal parts into which the playing time of some games is divided **i :** one side of the upper of a shoe or boot from heel to vamp **4 :** someone or something (as a place, direction, or group) not definitely or implicitly specified (expecting trouble from another quarter) **5 a :** a particular division or district of a city (the foreign quarter) **b :** an assigned place or duty station esp. of a member of a naval crew (call to quarters) **c** pl : living accommodations : LODGING **6 :** MERCY; esp : a refraining from destroying a defeated enemy **7 a :** the stern area of a ship's side **b :** the part of the yardarm outside the slings — **at close quarters :** at close range or in immediate contact

²quarter vb **1 a :** to divide into four essentially equal parts **b :** to separate into more or fewer than four parts (peel and quarter an orange) **c :** DISMEMBER **2 :** to provide with or occupy a lodging **3 :** to crisscross an area in many directions (a dog quartering a field in search of game) **4 :** to add (a coat of arms) to others on one escutcheon **5 :** to strike on a ship's quarter (the wind quarters)

³quarter adj : consisting of or equal to a quarter

¹quar·ter·back \-,bak\ n : an offensive football back who calls the signals and directs the offensive play of his team

²quarterback vb **1 :** to act as quarterback of (a football team) **2 :** to play quarterback

quarter day n, chiefly Brit : the day which begins a quarter of the year and on which a quarterly payment falls due

quar·ter·deck \-,dek\ n **1 :** the stern area of a ship's upper deck **2 :** a part of a naval vessel set aside for ceremonial and official use

quarter horse n : an alert stocky muscular horse capable of high speed for short distances and of great endurance under the saddle

quarter hour n **1 :** 15 minutes **2 :** any of the quarter points of an hour

quar·ter·ing adj **1 :** coming from a point well abaft the beam of a ship but not directly astern (quartering waves) **2 :** lying at right angles (quartering cranks of a locomotive)

¹quar·ter·ly \'kwȯrt-ər-lē\ adv : at 3-month intervals (interest compounded quarterly)

²quarterly adj : coming during or at the end of each 3-month interval (quarterly premium) (quarterly meeting)

³quarterly n, pl **-lies :** a periodical published four times a year

quar·ter·mas·ter \'kwȯrt-ər-,mas-tər\ n **1 :** a petty officer who attends to a ship's steering and signals **2 :** an army officer responsible for the clothing and subsistence of a body of troops

quar·tern \'kwȯrt-ərn\ n : a fourth part : QUARTER

quarter note n : a musical note equal in time value to a fourth of a whole note — called also crotchet

quar·ter·saw \'kwȯrt-ər-,sȯ\ vt **-sawed; -sawed** or **-sawn** \-,sȯn\; **-saw·ing :** to saw (a log) into quarters and then into planks in which the annual rings are nearly at right angles to the wide face

quarter section n : a tract of land that is half a mile square and contains 160 acres in the U.S. government system of land surveying

quarter sessions n pl : a local court with criminal jurisdiction and sometimes civil or administrative functions in England and in some states of the U.S.

quar·ter·staff \'kwȯrt-ər-,staf\ n : a long stout staff formerly used as a weapon

quarter tone n : an interval of one half a semitone

quar·tet also **quar·tette** \kwȯr-'tet\ n [It quartetto, fr. quarto fourth, fr. L quartus] **1 :** a musical composition for four instruments or voices **2 :** a group or set of four

quar·tile \'kwȯr-,tīl, 'kwȯrt-ᵊl\ n : one of three values

that divide a frequency distribution into four equal intervals
quar·to \'kwȯrt-ō\ *n, pl* **quartos** [L, abl. of *quartus*
fourth] **1** : the size of a piece of paper cut four from a
sheet; *also* : paper or a page of this size **2** : a book
printed on quarto pages
quartz \'kwȯrts\ *n* [G *quarz*] : a common mineral SiO₂
consisting of silica often found in the form of colorless
transparent crystals but sometimes (as in amethysts,
agates, and jaspers) brightly colored
quartz glass *n* : vitreous silica prepared from pure quartz
and noted for its transparency to ultraviolet radiation
quartz·ite \'kwȯrt-ˌsīt\ *n* : a compact granular rock composed of quartz and derived from sandstone
quartz·ose \-ˌsōs\ *adj* : containing, consisting of, or
resembling quartz
qua·sar \'kwā-ˌzär, -ˌsär\ *n* [*quasi*-stell*ar* radio source]
: any of various distant celestial objects that resemble
stars but emit unusually bright blue and ultraviolet light
and radio waves
¹quash \'kwäsh, 'kwȯsh\ *vt* [ME *quassen*, fr. MF *casser*,
quasser, fr. LL *cassare*, fr. L *cassus* void] : to set aside or
make void by judicial action ⟨*quash* an indictment⟩
²quash *vt* [ME *quashen* to smash, fr. MF *quasser*, *casser*,
fr. L *quassare*, intens. of *quatere* to shake] : to suppress or
extinguish completely : QUELL ⟨*quash* a rebellion⟩
¹qua·si \'kwā-ˌzī, -ˌsī; 'kwäz-ē\ *adv* [L, as if, as it were,
approximately, fr. *quam* as + *si* if] : in some sense or
degree : SEEMINGLY ⟨*quasi*-historical⟩ ⟨*quasi*-officially⟩
²quasi *adj* : having or legally regarded as having a likeness
to something else ⟨a *quasi* contract⟩
quas·sia \'kwäsh-ə\ *n* [NL, genus name, fr. *Quassi* 18th
cent. Surinam Negro slave who discovered its medicinal
value] : a bitter tonic drug from the heartwood of several
tropical trees sometimes used as a mild vermifuge or as an
insecticide
qua·ter·na·ry \'kwät-ər-ˌner-ē, kwə-'tər-nə-rē\ *adj* [L
quaternarius, fr. *quaterni* four each; akin to E *four*] **1** : of,
relating to, or consisting of four units or members : QUA-
DRUPLE **2** *cap* : of, relating to, or being the geological
period from the end of the Tertiary to the present time or
the corresponding system of rocks — **quaternary** *n, often
cap*
qua·train \'kwä-ˌtrān\ *n* [F, fr. *quatre* four, fr. L *quattuor*;
akin to E *four*] : a unit or group of four lines of verse
qua·tre·foil \'kat-ər-ˌfȯil, 'ka-trə-\ *n* [ME
quaterfoil, fr. MF *quatre* + ME *-foil* (as
in *trefoil*)] **1** : a conventionalized representation of a flower with four petals or
of a leaf with four leaflets **2** : a 4-lobed
foliation in architecture

quatrefoil

¹qua·ver \'kwā-vər\ *vb* **qua·vered; qua-
ver·ing** \'kwāv-(ə-)riŋ\ [ME *quaveren*]
1 : TREMBLE, SHAKE ⟨*quavering* inwardly⟩
2 : TRILL **3** : to utter sound in tremulous
uncertain tones ⟨a voice that *quavered*⟩
4 : to utter quaveringly — **qua·ver·ing·ly** \'kwāv-
(ə-)riŋ-lē\ *adv* — **qua·very** \'kwāv-(ə-)rē\ *adj*
²quaver *n* **1** : EIGHTH NOTE **2** : TRILL 1 **3** : a tremulous
sound
quay \'kē, 'k(w)ā\ *n* [alter. of earlier *key*, fr. MF *cai*] : a
paved bank or a solid artificial landing place beside
water for convenience in loading and unloading ships
quean \'kwēn\ *n* : a disreputable woman
quea·sy *also* **quea·zy** \'kwē-zē\ *adj* **quea·si·er; -est** [ME
coysy, qwesye] **1** : full of doubt : HAZARDOUS **2 a** : causing nausea ⟨*queasy* motion⟩ **b** : NAUSEATED **3 a** : causing
uneasiness **b** (1) : DELICATE, SQUEAMISH ⟨a *queasy* con-
science⟩ (2) : ill at ease ⟨*queasy* about his debts⟩ — **quea-
si·ly** \-zə-lē\ *adv* — **quea·si·ness** \-zē-nəs\ *n*
que·bra·cho \kā-'bräch-ō\ *n, pl* **-chos** : a So. American
tree of the sumac family with dense wood rich in tannins;
also : its wood or a tannin-rich extract of this used in
tanning
Que·chua \'kech(-ə)-wə\ *n* **1 a** : a member of a people
of central Peru **b** : a member of a group of peoples constituting the dominant element of the Inca Empire **2** : the
language of the Quechua people widely spoken by other
Indian peoples of Peru, Bolivia, Ecuador, Chile, and Argentina — **Que·chu·an** \-wən\ *adj or n*
¹queen \'kwēn\ *n* [OE *cwēn* woman, queen] **1** : the wife

or widow of a king **2** : a female monarch **3 a** : a woman
eminent in rank, power, or attractions ⟨a society *queen*⟩
b : a goddess or a thing personified as female and having
supremacy in a specified realm ⟨*queen* of the ocean liners⟩
c : an attractive girl or woman; *esp* : a beauty contest
winner **4** : a chess piece that can move as either a rook
or a bishop and is the most privileged piece in the set
5 : a playing card bearing the stylized figure of a queen
6 a : the fertile fully developed female of social bees, ants,
and termites whose function is to lay eggs **b** : a mature
female cat — **queen·like** \-ˌlīk\ *adj* — **queen·li·ness**
\-lē-nəs\ *n* — **queen·ly** \-lē\ *adv or adj*
²queen *vb* **1** : to act like a queen **b** : to put on airs
2 : to become or promote to a queen in chess
Queen Anne \kwēn-'an\ *adj* [*Queen Anne* of England
*d*1714] **1** : of or relating to an early 18th century style of
furniture characterized by extensive use of upholstery,
marquetry, and Oriental fabrics **2** : of or relating to an
early 18th century English style of building characterized
by unpretentious design, modified classic ornament, and
red brickwork in which relief ornament is carved
Queen Anne's lace *n* : WILD CARROT
queen consort *n, pl* **queens consort** : the wife of a reigning king
queen mother *n* : a dowager queen who is mother of the
reigning sovereign
queen post *n* : one of two vertical tie posts in a truss (as
of a roof)
¹queer \'kwi(ə)r\ *adj* **1 a** : differing from what is usual
or normal : ODD **b** (1) : ECCENTRIC, UNCONVENTIONAL
(2) : mildly insane : TOUCHED **2 a** *slang* : WORTHLESS,
COUNTERFEIT ⟨*queer* money⟩ **b** : QUESTIONABLE, SUSPICIOUS
3 : not quite well : QUEASY **syn** see STRANGE — **queer·ish**
\-ish\ *adj* — **queer·ly** *adv* — **queer·ness** *n*
²queer *adv* : QUEERLY
³queer *vt* **1** : to spoil the effect or success of : DISRUPT
2 : to put or get into an embarrassing or disadvantageous
situation
quell \'kwel\ *vt* [OE *cwellan* to kill] **1** : to put down
: SUPPRESS ⟨*quell* a riot⟩ **2** : QUIET, PACIFY ⟨*quell* fears⟩ —
quell·er *n*
quench \'kwench\ *vt* [OE *-cwencan*] **1 a** : to put out
: EXTINGUISH **b** : to put out the fire or light of ⟨*quench* a
lamp⟩ **2** : SUBDUE, OVERCOME ⟨*quench* hatred⟩ **3** : DE-
STROY ⟨*quench* rebellion⟩ **4** : SLAKE, SATISFY ⟨*quench* thirst⟩
5 : to cool (as heated steel) suddenly by immersion esp. in
water or oil **6** : SUPPRESS, INHIBIT ⟨a love easily *quenched*⟩
— **quench·a·ble** \'kwen-chə-bəl\ *adj* — **quench·er** *n* —
quench·less \'kwench-ləs\ *adj*
quer·ci·tron \'kwər-sə-trən, ˌkwər-'si-\ *n* [blend of L
quercus oak and E *citron*] : an American deciduous oak
whose bark yields tannin and a yellow dye; *also* : its
bark or an extract used in tanning and dyeing
quern \'kwərn\ *n* [OE *cweorn*] : a primitive hand mill for
grinding grain
quer·u·lous \'kwer-(y)ə-ləs\ *adj* [L *querulus*, fr. *queri* to
complain; akin to E *wheeze*] **1** : habitually complaining
: CAPTIOUS **2** : FRETFUL, WHINING ⟨a *querulous* voice⟩ —
quer·u·lous·ly *adv* — **quer·u·lous·ness** *n*
¹que·ry \'kwi(ə)r-ē, 'kwe(ə)r-\ *n, pl* **queries** [L *quaere*,
imper. of *quaerere* to ask] **1** : QUESTION, INQUIRY **2** : a
question in the mind : DOUBT **3** : QUESTION MARK
²query *vt* **que·ried; que·ry·ing** **1** : to put as a question
⟨*queried* the matter to his teacher⟩ **2** : to ask questions
about esp. in order to resolve a doubt ⟨*queried* a statement⟩
3 : to ask questions of esp. with a desire for authoritative
information ⟨*queried* the professor⟩ **4** : to mark with a
query
¹quest \'kwest\ *n* [MF *queste* search, pursuit, fr. *quaest-*,
quaerere to seek, ask] **1** : an act or instance of seeking
2 a : PURSUIT, SEARCH ⟨in *quest* of game⟩ **b** : a chivalrous
enterprise in medieval romance ⟨*quest* of the Holy Grail⟩
3 *obs* : ones who search or make inquiry
²quest *vb* **1** : to go on a quest : SEEK **2** : to search for
: PURSUE **3** : to ask for : DEMAND
¹ques·tion \'kwes-chən\ *n* [L *quaest-*, *quaerere* to seek,
ask] **1 a** (1) : an interrogative expression often used to
test knowledge (2) : an interrogative sentence or clause
b : a subject or aspect in dispute or open for discussion
: ISSUE; *also* : PROBLEM, MATTER **c** (1) : a subject or point
of debate or a proposition to be voted on in a meeting

⟨put the *question* to the members⟩ (2) **:** the bringing of this to a vote **d :** the specific point at issue **2 a :** an act or instance of asking **:** INQUIRY **b** (1) **:** OBJECTION, DISPUTE (2) **:** room for doubt or objection (3) **:** CHANCE, POSSIBILITY ⟨no *question* of escape⟩

²question *vb* **1 a :** to ask questions of or about **b :** INQUIRE ⟨a *questioning* mind⟩ **2 :** CROSS-EXAMINE ⟨*question* a witness⟩ **3 a :** DOUBT, DISPUTE ⟨*question* a decision⟩ **b :** to subject to analysis **:** EXAMINE — **ques·tion·er** *n* — **ques·tion·ing·ly** \-chə-niŋ-lē\ *adv*

ques·tion·a·ble \ʹkwes-chə-nə-bəl\ *adj* **1 :** affording reason for being doubted, questioned, or challenged **:** not certain or exact **:** PROBLEMATIC ⟨milk of *questionable* purity⟩ ⟨a *questionable* decision⟩ **2 :** attended by well-grounded suspicions of being immoral, crude, false, or unsound **:** DUBIOUS ⟨*questionable* motives⟩ — **ques·tion·a·bly** \-blē\ *adv*

question mark *n* **:** a punctuation mark ? used chiefly at the end of a sentence to indicate a direct question

ques·tion·naire \ˌkwes-chə-ʹna(ə)r, -ʹne(ə)r\ *n* **:** a set of questions to be asked of a number of persons usu. in order to gather statistics (as on opinions, facts, or knowledge)

quet·zal \ket-ʹsäl, -ʹsal\ *n, pl* **quet·zals** *or* **quet·za·les** \-ʹsäl-ās\ [AmerSp *quetzal,* fr. Nahuatl *quetzaltototl,* fr. *quetzalli* brilliant tail feather + *tototl* bird] **1 :** a Central American bird with narrow crest and brilliant plumage and in the male tail feathers often over two feet in length **2** *pl usu* **quetzales :** the basic monetary unit of Guatemala; *also* **:** a silver coin representing this unit

¹queue \ʹkyü\ *n* [F, lit., tail, fr. L *cauda*] **1 :** a taillike braid of hair usu. worn hanging at the back of the head **2 :** a line esp. of persons or vehicles ⟨a *queue* waiting at a ticket window⟩

²queue *vb* **queued; queu·ing** *or* **queue·ing 1 :** to arrange or form in a queue **2 :** to line up or wait in a queue ⟨the crowd *queued* up for tickets⟩ — **queu·er** *n*

¹quib·ble \ʹkwib-əl\ *n* **1 :** an evasion of or shift from the point **:** EQUIVOCATION **2 :** a minor objection or criticism

²quibble *vi* **quib·bled; quib·bling** \ʹkwib-(ə-)liŋ\ **1 :** to evade the issue **:** EQUIVOCATE **2 a :** CAVIL, CARP **b :** BICKER — **quib·bler** \-(ə-)lər\ *n*

¹quick \ʹkwik\ *adj* [OE *cwic*] **1** *archaic* **:** not dead **:** LIVING, ALIVE **2 :** RAPID, SPEEDY: as **a :** fast in understanding, thinking, or learning **:** mentally agile **b :** reacting with speed and sensitivity **c :** aroused immediately and intensely ⟨*quick* temper⟩ **d :** fast in development or occurrence ⟨a *quick* succession of events⟩ ⟨gave them a *quick* look⟩ **e :** marked by speed, readiness, or promptness of physical movement ⟨walked with *quick* steps⟩ **3 :** turning or bending at a sharp angle ⟨a *quick* turn in the road⟩ — **quick·ly** *adv* — **quick·ness** *n*

syn SPEEDY: QUICK stresses the shortness of time in which response, movement, or action takes place ⟨saved by *quick* thinking⟩ ⟨a *quick* answer⟩ SPEEDY implies quickness of successful accomplishment ⟨found a *speedy* solution of his problems⟩ or unusual velocity ⟨*speedy* runner⟩

²quick *adv* **:** QUICKLY

³quick *n* **1 :** a very sensitive area of flesh (as under a fingernail) **2 :** the inmost sensibilities ⟨hurt to the *quick* by the remark⟩ **3 :** the very center of something **:** HEART ⟨the *quick* of the matter⟩

quick bread *n* **:** a bread made with a leavening agent that permits immediate baking of the dough or batter mixture

quick·en \ʹkwik-ən\ *vb* **quick·ened; quick·en·ing** \ʹkwik-(ə-)niŋ\ **1 a :** to make or become alive **:** REVIVE **b :** to cause to be enlivened **:** STIMULATE ⟨curiosity *quickened* her interest⟩ **2 :** to make or become more rapid **:** HASTEN, ACCELERATE ⟨*quickened* her steps⟩ ⟨her pulse *quickened* at the sight⟩ **3 :** to show vitality or animation: as **a :** to commence active growth and development ⟨seeds *quickening* in the soil⟩ **b :** to reach the stage of fetal growth at which motion is felt **4 :** to shine more brightly ⟨watched the dawn *quickening* in the east⟩ — **quick·en·er** \-(ə-)nər\ *n*

quick-freeze \ʹkwik-ʹfrēz\ *vt* **-froze** \-ʹfrōz\; **-fro·zen** \-ʹfrōz-ᵊn\; **-freez·ing :** to freeze (food) for preservation so rapidly that ice crystals formed are too small to rupture the cells and the natural juices and flavor are preserved

quick·ie \ʹkwik-ē\ *n* **:** something done or made in a hurry or in less than the usual time

quick·lime \ʹkwik-ˌlīm\ *n* **:** the first solid product that is obtained by calcining limestone and consists essentially

of calcium oxide and that develops great heat and becomes crumbly when treated with water

quick·sand \-ˌsand\ *n* **:** a deep mass of loose sand mixed with water into which heavy objects sink

quick·sil·ver \-ˌsil-vər\ *n* **:** MERCURY 3a

quick·step \-ˌstep\ *n* **:** a spirited march tune esp. accompanying a march in quick time

quick-tem·pered \ʹkwik-ʹtem-pərd\ *adj* **:** easily angered **:** IRASCIBLE

quick time *n* **:** a rate of marching in which 120 steps each 30 inches in length are taken in one minute

quick-wit·ted \-ʹwit-əd\ *adj* **:** quick in perception and understanding **:** mentally alert — **quick-wit·ted·ness** *n*

¹quid \ʹkwid\ *n, pl* **quid** *also* **quids** *slang Brit* **:** a pound sterling **:** SOVEREIGN

²quid *n* [OE *cwidu* cud] **:** a cut or wad of something chewable ⟨a *quid* of tobacco⟩

quid pro quo \ˌkwid-ˌprō-ʹkwō\ *n* [NL, something for something] **:** an equivalent something (as a gift, privilege, or action) in return

qui·es·cent \kwī-ʹes-ᵊnt, kwē-\ *adj* **1 :** being at rest **:** INACTIVE, MOTIONLESS **2 :** causing no trouble or symptoms **syn** see LATENT — **qui·es·cence** \-ᵊn(t)s\ *n* — **qui·es·cent·ly** *adv*

¹qui·et \ʹkwī-ət\ *n* [L *quiet-, quies* rest, quiet] **:** the quality or state of being quiet **:** TRANQUILLITY — **on the quiet :** in a secretive manner

²quiet *adj* [L *quietus,* fr. pp. of *quiescere* to come to rest, fr. *quies* rest, quiet] **1 a :** marked by little or no motion or activity **:** CALM **b :** GENTLE, EASYGOING ⟨*quiet* temperament⟩ **c :** UNDISTURBED ⟨*quiet* reading⟩ **d :** enjoyed in peace and relaxation ⟨a *quiet* cup of tea⟩ **2 a :** free from noise or uproar **:** STILL **b :** UNOBTRUSIVE, CONSERVATIVE ⟨*quiet* clothes⟩ **3 :** RETIRED, SECLUDED ⟨*quiet* nook⟩ — **qui·et·ly** *adv* — **qui·et·ness** *n*

³quiet *adv* **:** QUIETLY ⟨*quiet*-running engine⟩

⁴quiet *vb* **1 :** to cause to be quiet **:** CALM **2 :** to become quiet ⟨the audience *quieted* down when the curtain rose⟩ — **qui·et·er** *n*

qui·e·tude \ʹkwī-ə-ˌt(y)üd\ *n* **:** TRANQUILLITY, QUIETNESS, REPOSE

qui·e·tus \kwī-ʹēt-əs\ *n* [ME *quietus est,* fr. ML, he is quit, formula of discharge from obligation] **1 :** a final freeing from something (as a debt, an office or duty, or life itself) **2 :** something that quiets or represses **3 :** a state of inactivity

¹quill \ʹkwil\ *n* [ME *quil* hollow reed, bobbin] **1 a :** a bobbin, spool, or spindle on which filling yarn is wound **b :** a hollow shaft often surrounding another shaft and used in various mechanical devices **2 a :** the hollow horny barrel of a feather; *also* **:** one of the large stiff feathers of the wing or tail **b :** one of the hollow sharp spines of a porcupine or hedgehog **3 :** an article made from or resembling the quill of a feather: as **a :** a writing implement formed by cutting a nib on the base of the quill of a stiff feather **b :** a roll of dried bark (as of cinnamon) **c :** a float for a fishing line

²quill *vt* **:** to pierce or wound with quills ⟨a dog badly *quilled* by a porcupine⟩

¹quilt \ʹkwilt\ *n* [OF *cuilte* mattress, quilt, fr. L *culcita* mattress] **1 :** a bed coverlet having two layers of cloth filled with wool, cotton, or down held in place by usu. patterned stitching **2 :** something that is quilted or resembles a quilt

²quilt *vb* **1 a :** to fill, pad, or line like a quilt **b :** to stitch, sew, or cover with lines or patterns like those used in quilts **c :** to fasten between two pieces of material **2 :** to stitch or sew in layers with padding in between **3 a :** to make quilts **b :** to do quilted work **4 :** COMPILE ⟨*quilted* together a collection of verse⟩ — **quilt·er** *n*

quilt·ing *n* **1 :** the process of quilting **2 :** material that is quilted or used for making quilts

quince \ʹkwin(t)s\ *n* [ME *quynce* quinces, pl. of *quyn* quince, fr. MF *coin,* fr. L *cydonium,* fr. Gk *kydōnion*] **:** the fruit of an Asiatic tree of the rose family that resembles a hard-fleshed yellow apple and is used esp. for marmalade, jelly, and preserves; *also* **:** this tree

qui·nine \ʹkwī-ˌnīn, *Brit* kwin-ʹēn\ *n* [Sp *quina* cinchona, short for *quinaquina,* fr. Quechua] **:** a bitter crystalline alkaloid from cinchona bark used in medicine esp. against malaria; *also* **:** a salt of this

---

ə abut; ᵊ kitten; ər further; a back; ā bake; ä cot, cart; aú out; ch chin; e less; ē easy; g gift; i trip; ī life

quinine water *n* : a carbonated beverage flavored with a small amount of quinine, lemon, and lime

Quin·qua·ge·si·ma \ˌkwin-kwə-'jes-ə-mə, -'jā-zə-\ *n* [ML, fr. L *quinquagesimus* fiftieth, fr. *quinquaginta* fifty] : the Sunday before Lent

quin·quen·ni·al \kwin-'kwen-ē-əl\ *adj* [L *quinque* five (akin to E *five*) + *annus* year] **1** : consisting of or lasting for five years **2** : occurring or being done every five years — **quinquennial** *n* — **quin·quen·ni·al·ly** \-ē-ə-lē\ *adv*

quin·sy \'kwin-zē\ *n* [MF *quinancie*, fr. LL *cynanche*, fr. Gk *kynanchē*, fr. *kyn-*, *kyōn* dog + *anchein* to choke] : a severe inflammation of the throat or adjacent parts with swelling and fever

quint \'kwint\ *n* : QUINTUPLET

quin·tain \'kwint-ᵊn\ *n* : a device used in training medieval youths in skill with the lance consisting typically of a crude figure (as of a Saracen) having the arms pivoted in such a manner that failure to deliver a well-centered blow causes them to whirl and strike the tilter with a sandbag

quin·tal \'kwint-ᵊl\ *n* [ML *quintale*, fr. Ar *qinṭār*, fr. LL *centenarium*] **1** : HUNDREDWEIGHT **2** — see METRIC SYSTEM table

quin·tes·sence \kwin-'tes-ᵊn(t)s\ *n* [ML *quinta essentia* fifth essence, supposed fifth element more subtle than earth, air, fire, or water] **1** : the purest form of something **2** : the most highly perfected type or example ⟨manners were the *quintessence* of courtesy⟩ — **quin·tes·sen·tial** \ˌkwint-ə-'sen-chəl\ *adj*

quin·tet *also* **quin·tette** \kwin-'tet\ *n* [It *quintetto*, fr. *quinto* fifth, fr. L *quintus*] **1** : a musical composition or movement for five instruments or voices **2** : a group or set of five

quin·til·lion \kwin-'til-yən\ *n* — see NUMBER table

¹**quin·tu·ple** \kwin-'t(y)üp-əl, -'təp-; 'kwint-əp-\ *adj* **1** : having five units or members **2** : being five times as great or as many — **quintuple** *n*

²**quintuple** *vb* **quin·tu·pled**; **quin·tu·pling** \-(ə-)liŋ\ : to make or become five times as great or as many

quin·tup·let \kwin-'təp-lət, -'t(y)üp-; 'kwint-əp-\ *n* **1** : a combination of five of a kind **2** : one of five offspring born at one birth

¹**quin·tu·pli·cate** \kwin-'t(y)ü-pli-kət\ *adj* **1** : repeated five times **2** : FIFTH ⟨the *quintuplicate* copy⟩

²**quin·tu·pli·cate** \-plə-ˌkāt\ *vt* **1** : QUINTUPLE **2** : to provide in quintuplicate

³**quin·tu·pli·cate** \-pli-kət\ *n* **1** : one of five like things **2** : five copies all alike ⟨typed in *quintuplicate*⟩

¹**quip** \'kwip\ *n* **1** : a clever usu. taunting remark : GIBE **2** : a witty or funny observation or response **3** : something strange or eccentric : ODDITY **syn** see JEST — **quip·ster** \-stər\ *n*

²**quip** *vb* **quipped**; **quip·ping** **1** : to make quips : GIBE **2** : to jest or gibe at

¹**quire** \'kwī(ə)r\ *n* [ME *quair* four sheets of paper folded once, collection of sheets, fr. MF *quaer*, fr. L *quaterni* four each] : a collection of 24 or sometimes 25 sheets of paper of the same size and quality : ¹⁄₂₀ ream

²**quire** *var of* CHOIR

quirk \'kwərk\ *n* **1** : an abrupt turn, twist, or curve (as a flourish in writing) **2** : a peculiar trait : MANNERISM, IDIOSYNCRASY — **quirk·i·ly** \'kwər-kə-lē\ *adv* — **quirk·i·ness** \-kē-nəs\ *n* — **quirky** \-kē\ *adj*

quirt \'kwərt\ *n* [MexSp *cuarta*] : a riding whip with a short handle and a rawhide lash

quis·ling \'kwiz-liŋ\ *n* [Vidkun *Quisling* d1945 Norwegian politician] : a traitor who collaborates with the invaders of his country esp. by serving in a puppet government

¹**quit** \'kwit\ *adj* [ME *quite*, fr. MF, lit., at rest, fr. L *quietus* quiet] : released from obligation, charge, or penalty : ABSOLVED; *esp* : FREE ⟨*quit* of unnecessary fears⟩

²**quit** *vb* **quit** *also* **quit·ted**; **quit·ting** **1** : to make full payment to or for : REPAY ⟨*quit* a debt⟩ **2** : ACQUIT ⟨the youths *quit* themselves like men⟩ **3 a** : to depart from or out of **b** : to bring (as a way of thought, acting, or living) to an end : RELINQUISH, ABANDON, FORSAKE **c** : to give up (an action, activity, or employment) : LEAVE ⟨*quit* a job⟩ **4** : to admit defeat : SURRENDER **syn** see STOP

quit·claim \'kwit-ˌklām\ *vt* : to release or relinquish a legal claim to esp. by a quitclaim deed — **quitclaim** *n*

quitclaim deed *n* : a legal instrument used to release or transfer a right, title, or interest in property to another without warranting the title

quite \'kwīt\ *adv* [ME, fr. *quite* free, quit] **1** : COMPLETELY, WHOLLY ⟨not *quite* all⟩ **2** : to an extreme : POSITIVELY ⟨not *quite* sure⟩ **3** : to a considerable extent : RATHER ⟨*quite* near⟩

quit·rent \'kwit-ˌrent\ *n* : a fixed rent; *esp* : one payable to a feudal superior in commutation of services

quits \'kwits\ *adj* : even or equal with another (as by repaying a debt, returning a favor, or retaliating for an injury)

quit·tance \'kwit-ᵊn(t)s\ *n* **1 a** : discharge from a debt or an obligation **b** : a document evidencing quittance **2** : RECOMPENSE, REQUITAL

quit·ter \'kwit-ər\ *n* : one that shirks or gives up too easily; *esp* : COWARD, DEFEATIST

¹**quiv·er** \'kwiv-ər\ *n* [OF *quivre*, of Gmc origin] **1** : a case for carrying arrows **2** : the arrows in a quiver

²**quiver** *vb* **quiv·ered**; **quiv·er·ing** \'kwiv-(ə-)riŋ\ [ME *quiveren*] : to move with a slight trembling motion ⟨tall grass *quivering* in the breeze⟩

³**quiver** *n* : the act or action of quivering : TREMOR

qui vive \(')kē-'vēv\ *n* [F *qui vive?* long live who?, challenge of a French sentry] **1** : CHALLENGE **2** : ALERT, LOOKOUT ⟨on the *qui vive* for prowlers⟩

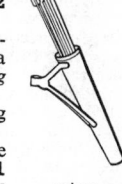
quiver

quix·ot·ic \kwik-'sät-ik\ *adj* [Don *Quixote*, hero of the novel *Don Quixote de la Mancha* by Cervantes] : idealistic to an impractical degree; *esp* : marked by rash lofty romantic ideas or extravagantly chivalrous action — **quix·ot·i·cal·ly** \-'sät-i-k(ə-)lē\ *adv* — **quix·o·tism** \'kwik-sə-ˌtiz-əm\ *n*

¹**quiz** \'kwiz\ *n, pl* **quiz·zes** **1 a** : an eccentric person **b** : a person who ridicules or mocks **2** : PRACTICAL JOKE **3** : the act or action of quizzing; *esp* : a short oral or written test

²**quiz** *vt* **quizzed**; **quiz·zing** **1** : to make fun of : MOCK **2** : to look at inquisitively **3** : to question closely : EXAMINE — **quiz·zer** *n*

quiz·zi·cal \'kwiz-i-kəl\ *adj* **1** : slightly eccentric : ODD **2** : BANTERING, TEASING **3** : QUESTIONING, INQUISITIVE — **quiz·zi·cal·ly** \-k(ə-)lē\ *adv*

quoin \'k(w)oin\ *n* [alter. of earlier *coin* corner, coin] : a solid exterior angle (as of a building); *also* : one of the blocks forming it

quoit \'kwāt, 'k(w)oit\ *n* **1** : a flattened ring of iron or circle of rope used in a throwing game to encircle a fixed peg **2** *pl* : a game played with quoits

quoins

quon·dam \'kwän-dəm, -ˌdam\ *adj* [L, at one time, formerly] : FORMER, SOMETIME ⟨a *quondam* friend⟩

Quon·set \'kwän-sət\ *trademark* — used for a prefabricated shelter set on a foundation of steel trusses and built of a semicircular arching roof of corrugated metal

quo·rum \'kwōr-əm, 'kwor-\ *n* [L, of whom] : the number of officers or members of a body that when duly assembled is legally competent to transact business

quo·ta \'kwōt-ə\ *n* [ML, fr. L *quota pars* how great a part] **1** : a proportional part or share; *esp* : the share or proportion assigned to each member of a body **2** : the number or amount constituting a proportional share

quot·a·ble \'kwōt-ə-bəl\ *adj* : fit for or worth quoting

quo·ta·tion \kwō-'tā-shən\ *n* **1** : something that is quoted; *esp* : a passage referred to or repeated **2 a** : the act or process of quoting **b** : the naming or publishing of current bids and offers or prices of securities or commodities; *also* : the bids, offers, or prices so named or published

quotation mark *n* : one of a pair of punctuation marks " " or '' '' or ' ' used chiefly to indicate the beginning and the end of a quotation in which the exact phraseology of another or of a text is directly cited

¹**quote** \'kwōt\ *vb* [ML *quotare* to mark the number of, number references, fr. L *quot* how many] **1 a** : to speak or write (a passage) from another usu. with credit ac-

knowledgment ⟨*quote* Shakespeare⟩ **b :** to repeat a passage from esp. as authority or illustration **2 :** to cite in illustration ⟨*quote* cases⟩ **3 a :** to name (the current price) of a commodity, stock, or bond **b :** to give exact information on **4 :** to set off by quotation marks **5 :** to inform a hearer or reader that matter following is quoted

²**quote** *n* **1 :** QUOTATION **2 :** QUOTATION MARK

quoth \(')kwōth\ *vb past* [OE *cwæth,* past of *cwethan* to say] *archaic* : SAID — used chiefly in the first and third persons with a postpositive subject

quo·tha \'kwō-thə\ *interj* [alter. of *quoth he*] *archaic* — used esp. to express surprise or contempt

quo·tid·i·an \kwō-'tid-ē-ən\ *adj* [L *quotidianus,* fr. *quotidie* every day, fr. *quot* (as) many as + *dies* day] **1 :** DAILY **2 :** COMMONPLACE, ORDINARY

quo·tient \'kwō-shənt\ *n* [L *quotiens* how many times, fr. *quot* how many] **1 :** the number resulting from the division of one number by another **2 :** the numerical ratio usu. multiplied by 100 between a test score and a measurement on which that score might be expected largely to depend ⟨accomplishment *quotient*⟩

quo war·ran·to \ˌkwō-wə-'ränt-ō\ *n* [ML, by what warrant; fr. the wording of the writ] **1 a :** an English writ formerly requiring a person to show by what authority he exercises a public office, franchise, or liberty **b :** a legal proceeding begun by an information requiring a person to justify an act **2 :** the legal action begun by a quo warranto

r \'är\ *n, often cap* **:** the 18th letter of the English alphabet

Ra \'rä\ *n* **:** the great god of the sun and the chief deity of ancient Egypt

rab·at \'rab-ē, 'rab-ət\ *n* [MF] **:** a black shirtfront often worn with a clerical collar

¹**rab·bet** \'rab-ət\ *n* [MF *rabat* act of beating down, fr. *rabattre* to beat down] **:** a groove or recess cut in the edge or face of a surface esp. to receive the edge of another surface (as a panel)

²**rabbet** *vt* **1 :** to cut a rabbet in **2 :** to join the edges of (as boards) by a rabbet

rab·bi \'rab-ˌī\ *n* [LHeb *rabbī* my master, fr. *rabh* master + *-ī* my] **1 :** MASTER, TEACHER — used as a term of address for Jewish religious leaders **2** *often cap* **:** one of the scholars who developed the Talmudic basis of orthodox Judaism during the first centuries of the Christian era **3 :** a Jew trained professionally and ordained as the official leader of a Jewish congregation

rab·bin·ate \'rab-ə-nət, -ˌnāt\ *n* **1 :** the office or tenure of a rabbi **2 :** a group of rabbis

rab·bin·ic \ra-'bin-ik, ra-\ *adj* **1** *often cap* **:** of or relating to rabbis or their writings **2 :** of or preparing for the rabbinate — **rab·bin·i·cal** \-'bin-i-kəl\ *adj* — **rab·bin·i·cal·ly** \-i-k(ə)lē\ *adv*

rab·bin·ism \'rab-ə-ˌniz-əm\ *n* **:** rabbinic teachings and traditions

rab·bit \'rab-ət\ *n, pl* **rabbits** *also* **rabbit** [ME *rabet*] **:** a small long-eared burrowing mammal differing from the related hares esp. in producing naked young; *also* **:** its pelt — **rabbit** *vi*

rab·bit·eye \'rab-ət-ˌī\ *n* **:** a blueberry of the southeastern U.S. grown commercially esp. for canning

rabbit fever *n* **:** TULAREMIA

rabbit punch *n* **:** a short chopping blow delivered to the back of the neck or the base of the skull

rab·ble \'rab-əl\ *n* [ME *rabel* pack, string (of animals)] **1 :** a noisy and unruly crowd **:** MOB **2 :** a body of people looked down upon as ignorant and disorderly

rab·ble-rous·er \-ˌraù-zər\ *n* **:** one that stirs up the masses of the people esp. to hatred or violence

Ra·be·lai·sian \ˌrab-ə-'lā-zhən, -zē-ən\ *adj* **1 :** of, relating to, or characteristic of Rabelais or his works **2 :** marked by gross robust humor or extravagance of caricature

rab·id \'rab-əd\ *adj* [L *rabidus* mad, fr. *rabere* to rage, rave] **1 :** extremely violent **:** FURIOUS **2 :** going to extreme lengths in expressing or pursuing a feeling, interest, stock, or opinion ⟨a *rabid* sports fan⟩ **3 :** affected with rabies ⟨a *rabid* dog⟩ — **rab·id·ly** *adv* — **rab·id·ness** *n*

ra·bies \'rā-bēz\ *n* [L, madness, fr. *rabere* to rage, rave] **:** an acute virus disease of the central nervous system of warm-blooded animals transmitted by the bite of a rabid animal and always fatal when untreated — called also *hydrophobia* — **ra·bic** \-bik\ *adj*

rac·coon \ra-'kün\ *n, pl* **raccoon** *or* **raccoons** [of Algonquian origin] **:** a small flesh-eating mammal of No. America that is chiefly gray, has a bushy ringed tail, and lives chiefly in trees; *also* **:** its pelt

¹**race** \'rās\ *n* [ON *rās*] **1 :** a strong or rapid current of water or the channel or passage for such a current; *esp* **:** a current of water used for industrial purposes (as in mining or for turning the wheel of a mill) **2 a :** a set course or duration of time **b :** the course of life **3 a :** a running in competition **b** *pl* **:** a meeting for contests in the running esp. of horses ⟨off to the *races*⟩ **c :** a contest involving progress toward a goal ⟨the *race* for the governorship⟩ **4 :** a track or channel in which something rolls or slides; *esp* **:** a groove for the balls in a bearing

²**race** *vb* **1 :** to run in a race **2 :** to go, move, or drive at top speed or out of control **3 a :** to engage in a race with ⟨*race* the champion⟩ **b :** to enter in a race ⟨had a new horse to *race*⟩ **4 :** to speed (as an engine) without a load or with the transmission disengaged

³**race** *n* [MF, generation, fr. It *razza*] **1 a :** a group of people of common ancestry or stock ⟨scion of a noble *race*⟩; *also* **:** one unified by community of interests, habits, or characteristics as if by ancestry ⟨the English *race*⟩ **b :** one of the three, four, or five primary divisions commonly recognized in mankind and based on readily observed traits (as skin color) that are transmitted by heredity ⟨the Caucasian *race*⟩ **c :** MANKIND ⟨the human *race*⟩ **2 :** an actually or potentially interbreeding group of individuals within a species; *also* **:** a taxonomic category (as a subspecies or breed) held to represent such a group **3** *obs* **:** inherited temperament or disposition

race·course \'rās-ˌkōrs, -ˌkȯrs\ *n* **:** a course for racing; *esp* **:** a turf course for steeplechase or cross-country racing

race·horse \-ˌhȯrs\ *n* **:** a horse bred or kept for racing

ra·ceme \rā-'sēm\ *n* [L *racemus* bunch of grapes] **:** a simple inflorescence with a long axis bearing flowers on short stems in succession toward the apex — see INFLORESCENCE illustration — **rac·e·mose** \'ras-ə-ˌmōs, rā-'sē-\ *adj*

racemose gland *n* **:** a compound gland of freely branching ducts that end in acini

rac·er \'rā-sər\ *n* **1 :** one that races **2 :** any of various slender active American snakes; *esp* **:** a common blacksnake

race runner *n* **:** a long-tailed active No. American lizard

race·track \'rās-ˌtrak\ *n* **:** a usu. oval course on which races are run

Ra·chel \'rā-chəl\ *n* **:** one of the wives of Jacob

ra·chis \'rā-kəs, 'rak-əs\ *n, pl* **ra·chis·es** *also* **rach·i·des** \'rak-ə-ˌdēz, 'rā-kə-\ [NL *rachid-, rachis,* modif. of Gk *rhachis*] **1 :** SPINAL COLUMN **2 :** an axial structure: as **a :** the axis of an inflorescence **b :** an extension of the petiole of a compound leaf that bears the leaflets **c :** the distal part of the shaft of a feather

ra·chi·tis \rə-'kīt-əs\ *n* [NL, fr. Gk *rhachitis* disease of the spine, fr. *rhachis* spine] **:** RICKETS — **ra·chit·ic** \-'kit-ik\ *adj*

ra·cial \'rā-shəl\ *adj* **1 :** of, relating to, or based on race **2 :** existing or occurring between human races ⟨*racial* tensions⟩ — **ra·cial·ly** \-shə-lē\ *adv*

ra·cial·ism \'rā-shə-ˌliz-əm\ *n* **:** RACISM — **ra·cial·ist** \'rāsh-(ə-)ləst\ *n* — **ra·cial·is·tic** \ˌrā-shə-'lis-tik\ *adj*

rac·i·ly \'rā-sə-lē\ *adv* **:** in a racy manner

rac·i·ness \-sē-nəs\ *n* **:** the quality or state of being racy

racing form *n* **:** an information sheet giving data about horse races and racehorses

rac·ism \'rā-ˌsiz-əm\ *n* **1 :** belief that certain races of men are by birth and nature superior to others **2 a :** discrimination against the members of one or more races based upon racism **b :** race hatred and discrimination — **rac·ist** \'rā-səst\ *n*

¹**rack** \'rak\ *n* [ME] **1 :** a framework for holding fodder for livestock; *also* **:** one fitted on a vehicle for carrying loose produce (as hay or grain) **2 :** an instrument of torture on which a body is stretched **3 :** STRAIN, STRESS **4 :** a framework, stand, or grating on or in which articles are placed ⟨clothes *rack*⟩ ⟨bicycle *rack*⟩ ⟨baggage *rack*⟩ **5 :** a bar with teeth on one face for gearing with a pinion or worm gear — **on the rack :** under great mental or emotional stress

²**rack** *vt* **1 :** to torture on the rack **2 :** to cause to suffer torture, pain, or anguish ⟨*racked* by a cough⟩ **3 :** to stretch or strain violently **4 :** to place (as pool balls) in a rack

³**rack** *vi* **:** to go at a rack

⁴**rack** *n* **:** either of two gaits of a horse: **a :** PACE 2b **b :** a fast showy usu. artificial 4-beat gait

⁵**rack** *n* [alter. of *wrack*] **:** DESTRUCTION ⟨went to *rack* and ruin⟩

¹**rack·et** *also* **rac·quet** \'rak-ət\ *n* [MF *raquette*, fr. Ar *rāḥah* palm of the hand] **1 :** a light bat that consists of a netting (as of nylon) stretched in an oval open frame ⟨a tennis *racket*⟩ **2 :** a small round paddle with a short handle used in table tennis

²**racket** *n* **1 :** confused clattering noise **:** DIN **2 a :** a dishonest scheme; *esp* **:** one for obtaining money by cheating or through threats of violence **b** *slang* **:** OCCUPATION

rackets: *1* badminton, *2* racquets, *3* tennis, *4* court tennis

³**racket** *vi* **1 :** to engage in active social life **2 :** to move with or make a racket

¹**rack·e·teer** \,rak-ə-'ti(ə)r\ *n* **:** one who extorts money or advantages by threats of violence, by blackmail, or by unlawful interference with business or employment

²**racketeer** *vi* **:** to carry on a racket

rack up *vt* **:** SCORE ⟨*racked up* 30 points in the first half⟩

ra·con·teur \,rak-,än-'tər\ *n* [F, fr. *raconter* to tell, recount] **:** one who excels in telling anecdotes

ra·coon *var of* RACCOON

rac·quets \'rak-əts\ *n* **:** a game for two or four played with ball and racket on a 4-walled court

¹**racy** \'rā-sē\ *adj* **rac·i·er; -est** [³*race*] **1 :** having the distinctive quality of something in its original or most characteristic form ⟨peasants *racy* of the soil⟩ ⟨the *racy* vernacular of the region⟩ **2 a :** full of zest or vigor **:** LIVELY ⟨brisk, *racy* prose⟩ **b :** PIQUANT, PUNGENT ⟨*racy* satire⟩ **c :** RISQUÉ, SUGGESTIVE ⟨*racy* stories⟩

²**racy** *adj* **:** being long-bodied and lean ⟨a *racy* whippet⟩

ra·dar \'rā-,där\ *n* [*radio detecting and ranging*] **:** a device that sends out a powerful beam of radio waves that when reflected back to it from a distant object indicate the position and direction of motion of the object — **ra·dar·man** \-mən, -,man\ *n*

ra·dar·scope \-,skōp\ *n* **:** the part of a radar apparatus on which the spots of light appear that indicate the position and direction of motion of a distant object

¹**ra·di·al** \'rād-ē-əl\ *adj* [L *radius* spoke, radius, ray] **1 :** arranged or having parts arranged like rays coming from a common center **2 :** relating to, placed like, or moving along a radius **3 :** of, relating to, or adjacent to a bodily radius — **ra·di·al·ly** \-ē-ə-lē\ *adv*

²**radial** *n* **:** a radial part

radial engine *n* **:** a usu. internal-combustion engine with cylinders arranged radially like the spokes of a wheel

radial symmetry *n* **:** the condition of having similar parts regularly arranged around a central axis ⟨*radial symmetry* of the starfish⟩ — compare BILATERAL SYMMETRY

ra·di·an \'rād-ē-ən\ *n* **:** the measure of a central angle of a circle subtended by an arc equal in length to the radius

ra·di·ance \'rād-ē-ən(t)s\ *also* **ra·di·an·cy** \-ən-sē\ *n, pl* **-anc·es** *or* **-an·cies** **:** the quality or state of being radiant **:** SPLENDOR

ra·di·ant \'rād-ē-ənt\ *adj* **1 a :** giving out or reflecting rays of light ⟨the *radiant* sun⟩ ⟨a *radiant* jewel⟩ **b :** vividly bright and shining **:** GLOWING ⟨*radiant* eyes⟩ **2 :** marked by or expressive of love, confidence, or happiness ⟨a *radiant* bride⟩ **3 a :** emitted or transmitted by radiation

⟨*radiant* heat from the sun⟩ **b :** emitting or relating to radiant heat ⟨a *radiant* lamp⟩ — **ra·di·ant·ly** *adv*

radiant energy *n* **:** energy transmitted in the form of electromagnetic waves (as heat waves, light waves, radio waves, X rays)

radiant flux *n* **:** the rate of emission or transmission of radiant energy

radiant heating *n* **:** PANEL HEATING

¹**ra·di·ate** \'rād-ē-,āt\ *vb* [L *radiare*, fr. *radius* ray] **1 :** to send out rays of light or as if of light **:** shine brightly **2 :** to issue in rays or be sent out as if from a center **3 :** to proceed in a direct line from or toward a center; *also* **:** to spread out from a point of origin **4 :** to send out in rays or as if in rays ⟨stars *radiate* energy⟩ **5 :** IRRADIATE, ILLUMINATE **6 :** to spread abroad or around as if from a center

²**ra·di·ate** \-ē-ət\ *adj* **:** having rays or radial parts: as **a :** having ray flowers **b :** having radial symmetry

ra·di·a·tion \,rād-ē-'ā-shən\ *n* **1 :** the action or process of radiating; *esp* **:** the process of emitting radiant energy in the form of waves or particles **2 :** something that is radiated: as **a :** energy radiated in the form of waves or particles **b :** the spread of organisms by natural processes into new habitats and there adapted to new ways of life ⟨the Devonian *radiation* of fishes⟩ — **ra·di·a·tion·al** \-shnəl, -shən-ᵊl\ *adj* — **ra·di·a·tive** \'rād-ē-,āt-iv\ *adj*

ra·di·a·tor \'rād-ē-,āt-ər\ *n* **:** one that radiates: as **a :** a device consisting of a nest of pipes through which hot water or steam circulates for heating a room **b :** a device for cooling by radiation the water (as of an automobile engine) that circulates through a nest of tubes

¹**rad·i·cal** \'rad-i-kəl\ *adj* [L *radic-, radix* root; akin to E *wort*] **1 :** of, relating to, or proceeding from a root **2 :** of or relating to the origin **:** FUNDAMENTAL **3 a :** marked by a sharp departure from the usual or traditional **:** EXTREME **b :** tending or disposed to make extreme changes in existing views, habits, conditions, or institutions **c :** of, relating to, or constituting a political group associated with views, practices, and policies of extreme change **syn** see LIBERAL — **rad·i·cal·ness** *n*

²**radical** *n* **1 :** ROOT 5 **2 :** one who is radical **3 :** a group of atoms that is replaceable by a single atom and is capable of remaining unchanged during a series of reactions **4 a :** the indicated root of a mathematical expression **b :** RADICAL SIGN

radical expression *n* **:** a mathematical expression involving radical signs

rad·i·cal·ism \'rad-i-kə-,liz-əm\ *n* **1 :** the quality or state of being radical **2 :** the doctrines or principles of radicals

rad·i·cal·ize \-kə-,līz\ *vt* **:** to make radical esp. in politics — **rad·i·cal·iza·tion** \,rad-i-kə-lə-'zā-shən\ *n*

rad·i·cal·ly \'rad-i-k(ə-)lē\ *adv* **1 :** in origin or essence **2 :** in a radical or extreme manner

radical sign *n* **:** the sign √ placed before an expression in mathematics to indicate that its root is to be extracted

rad·i·cand \,rad-ə-'kand\ *n* [L *radic-, radix* root + E *-and* (as in *multiplicand*)] **:** the expression under a radical sign

rad·i·cle \'rad-i-kəl\ *n* [L *radicula*, dim. of *radic-, radix* root] **1 :** the lower part of the axis of a plant embryo or seedling **:** the growing tip of the hypocotyl **:** HYPOCOTYL **2 :** the rootlike beginning of an anatomical vessel or part — **ra·dic·u·lar** \ra-'dik-yə-lər\ *adj*

radii *pl of* RADIUS

¹**ra·dio** \'rād-ē-,ō\ *n, pl* **ra·di·os** [short for *radiotelegraphy*] **:** the sending or receiving of messages or effects and esp. sound by means of electric waves without a connecting wire ⟨*radio* includes television and radar⟩ **2 :** a radio message **3 :** a radio receiving set **4 a :** a radio transmitting station **b :** a radio broadcasting organization **c :** the radio broadcasting industry

²**radio** *adj* **1 :** of, relating to, or operated by radiant energy **2 :** of or relating to electric currents or phenomena of frequencies between about 15,000 and (10)¹¹ per second **3 a :** of, relating to, or used in radio or a radio set **b :** controlled or directed by radio

³**radio** *vb* **1 :** to send or communicate by radio **2 :** to send a radio message to

radio- *comb form* [F, fr. L *radius* spoke, radius, ray] **1 :** radial **:** radially ⟨*radio*symmetrical⟩ **2 a :** radiant

energy : radiation ⟨*radio*active⟩ ⟨*radio*dermatitis⟩ **b** : radioactive ⟨*radio*iodine⟩ ⟨*radio*carbon⟩
ra·dio·ac·tive \,rād-ē-ō-'ak-tiv\ *adj* : of, caused by, or exhibiting radioactivity — **ra·dio·ac·tive·ly** *adv*
ra·dio·ac·tiv·i·ty \-,ak-'tiv-ət-ē\ *n* : the property possessed by some elements (as uranium) of spontaneously emitting alpha or beta rays and sometimes also gamma rays by the disintegration of the nuclei of atoms
radio astronomy *n* : astronomy dealing with electromagnetic radiations of radio frequency received from outside the earth's atmosphere — **radio astronomer** *n*
ra·dio·au·to·graph \,rād-ē-ō-'ȯt-ə-,graf\ *n* : AUTORADIOGRAPH — **ra·dio·au·tog·ra·phy** \-ō-'täg-rə-fē\ *n*
radio beacon *n* : a radio transmitting station that transmits special radio signals for use (as on a landing field) in determining the direction or position of those receiving them
ra·dio·bi·ol·o·gy \,rād-ē-ō-bī-'äl-ə-jē\ *n* : a branch of biology dealing with the interaction of living systems with radiant energy and radioactive materials — **ra·dio·bi·o·log·i·cal** \-,bī-ə-'läj-i-kəl\ *or* **ra·dio·bi·o·log·ic** \-'läj-ik\ *adj*
ra·dio·broad·cast \,rād-ē-ō-'brȯd-,kast\ *vt* : BROADCAST 3a — **ra·dio·broad·cast·er** *n*
radio car *n* : an automobile equipped with radio communication
ra·dio·car·bon \-'kär-bən\ *n* : radioactive carbon; *esp* : CARBON 14
ra·dio·cast \'rād-ē-ō-,kast\ *vt* : BROADCAST 3a — **ra·dio·cast·er** *n*
ra·dio·el·e·ment \,rād-ē-ō-'el-ə-mənt\ *n* : a radioactive element
radio frequency *n* : any of the electromagnetic wave frequencies intermediate between audio frequencies and infrared frequencies used esp. in radio and television transmission
ra·dio·gen·ic \,rād-ē-ō-'jen-ik\ *adj* : produced by radioactivity
ra·dio·gram \'rād-ē-ō-,gram\ *n* **1** : RADIOGRAPH **2** : a message transmitted by radiotelegraphy
¹**ra·dio·graph** \-,graf\ *n* : a picture produced on a sensitive surface by a form of radiation other than light; *esp* : X-RAY PHOTOGRAPH — **ra·dio·graph·ic** \,rād-ē-ō-'graf-ik\ *adj* — **ra·dio·graph·i·cal·ly** \-'graf-i-k(ə-)lē\ *adv*
²**radiograph** *vt* : to make a radiograph of
³**radiograph** *vt* : to send a radiogram to
ra·di·og·ra·phy \,rād-ē-'äg-rə-fē\ *n* : the art or process of making radiographs
ra·dio·iso·tope \,rād-ē-ō-'ī-sə-,tōp\ *n* : a radioactive isotope
ra·di·o·lar·i·an \,rād-ē-ō-'lar-ē-ən, -'ler-\ *n* [LL *radiolus*, dim. of L *radius* ray] : any of a large order (Radiolaria) of marine protozoans with radiating threadlike pseudopodia and a siliceous skeleton
ra·di·ol·o·gy \,rād-ē-'äl-ə-jē\ *n* : the science of radioactive substances and high-energy radiations; *esp* : the use of radiant energy in medicine — **ra·dio·log·ic** \,rād-ē-ə-'läj-ik\ *adj* — **ra·dio·log·i·cal** \-'läj-i-kəl\ *adj* — **ra·di·ol·o·gist** \,rād-ē-'äl-ə-jəst\ *n*
ra·di·om·e·ter \,rād-ē-'äm-ət-ər\ *n* : an instrument for measuring the intensity of radiant energy — **ra·dio·met·ric** \,rād-ē-ō-'me-trik\ *adj* — **ra·di·om·e·try** \-'äm-ə-trē\ *n*
ra·dio·phone \'rād-ē-ə-,fōn\ *n* : RADIOTELEPHONE
ra·dio·pho·to \,rād-ē-ō-'fōt-ō\ *n* **1** : a picture transmitted by radio — called also *ra·dio·pho·to·graph* \-'fōt-ə-,graf\ **2** : the process of transmitting a picture by radio
ra·dio·sonde \'rād-ē-ō-,sänd\ *n* [F *sonde* sounding line] : a miniature radio transmitter that is carried (as by a balloon) aloft with instruments for broadcasting data on the humidity, temperature, and pressure
ra·dio·sym·met·ri·cal \,rād-ē-ō-sə-'me-tri-kəl\ *adj* : exhibiting radial symmetry
ra·dio·tel·e·graph \,rād-ē-ō-'tel-ə-,graf\ *n* : WIRELESS TELEGRAPHY — **ra·dio·te·leg·ra·phy** \-tə-'leg-rə-fē\ *n*
ra·dio·tel·e·phone \-'tel-ə-,fōn\ *n* : a telephone that utilizes radio waves wholly or partly instead of connecting wires — **ra·dio·te·leph·o·ny** \-tə-'lef-ə-nē, -'tel-ə-,fō-nē\ *n*
radio telescope *n* : a radio receiver-antenna combination used for observation in radio astronomy

ra·dio·ther·a·py \,rad-ē-ō-'ther-ə-pē\ *n* : the treatment of disease by means of X rays or radioactive substances — **ra·dio·ther·a·pist** \-pəst\ *n*
radio tube *n* : a vacuum tube used in radio
ra·dio·ul·na \,rād-ē-ō-'əl-nə\ *n* : a bone of some lower vertebrates (as the toad) equivalent to the combined radius and ulna of higher forms
radio wave *n* : an electromagnetic wave with radio frequency used in radio, television, or radar communication
rad·ish \'rad-ish, 'red-\ *n* [OE *rædic*, fr. L *radic-, radix*, lit., root] : a pungent fleshy root usu. eaten raw; *also* : a plant of the mustard family whose roots are radishes
ra·di·um \'rād-ē-əm\ *n* [NL, fr. L *radius* ray] : an intensely radioactive shining white metallic chemical element that occurs in combination in minute quantities in minerals (as pitchblende), emits alpha particles and gamma rays to form radon, and is used chiefly in luminous materials and in the treatment of cancer — see ELEMENT table
ra·di·us \'rād-ē-əs\ *n, pl* **-dii** \-ē-,ī\ *also* **-di·us·es** [L, spoke, ray, radius] **1 a** : the anterior and thicker and shorter bone of the human forearm or of the corresponding part of the forelimb of vertebrates above fishes **b** : the 3d and usu. largest vein of an insect's wing **2 a** : a line segment extending from the center of a circle or sphere to the curve or surface — see CIRCLE illustration **b** : a circular area defined by a radius ⟨deer may wander within a *radius* of several miles⟩ **3** : a radial part or plane
radius vector *n* : a line segment or its length from a fixed point to a variable point; *also* : the polar coordinate of the variable point
ra·dix \'rād-iks\ *n, pl* **rad·i·ces** \'rad-ə-,sēz, 'rād-\ *or* **ra·dix·es** [L *radic-, radix*] : ROOT, RADICLE
ra·dome \'rā-,dōm\ *n* [*radar dome*] : a plastic housing sheltering the antenna assembly of a radar set
ra·don \'rā-,dän\ *n* [fr. *radium*] : a heavy radioactive gaseous chemical element formed by disintegration of radium — see ELEMENT table
rad·u·la \'raj-ə-lə\ *n, pl* **-lae** \-,lē, -,lī\ *also* **-las** [NL, fr. L, scraper, fr. *radere* to scrape] : a toothed horny band in mollusks other than bivalves used to tear up and draw food into the mouth — **rad·u·lar** \-lər\ *adj*
raf·fia \'raf-ē-ə\ *n* [Malagasy *rafia*] : fiber from a pinnate-leaved palm of Madagascar used esp. for baskets and hats
raff·ish \'raf-ish\ *adj* **1** : vulgarly crude or flashy **2** : carelessly unconventional — **raff·ish·ly** *adv* — **raff·ish·ness** *n*
¹**raf·fle** \'raf-əl\ *n* [ME *rafle*, a dice game, fr. MF] : a lottery in which the prize is won by one of numerous persons buying chances
²**raffle** *vt* **raf·fled; raf·fling** \'raf-(ə-)liŋ\ : to dispose of by a raffle ⟨*raffle* off a turkey⟩
³**raffle** *n* : RUBBISH; *esp* : a jumble or tangle of nautical material
¹**raft** \'raft\ *n* [ME *rafte* rafter, raft, fr. ON *raptr* rafter; akin to E *rafter*] **1** : a collection of logs or timber fastened together for conveyance by water **2** : a flat structure for support or transportation on water; *also* : a floating cohesive mass
²**raft** *vb* **1** : to transport or move in or by means of a raft **2** : to make into a raft
³**raft** *n* : a large amount
raf·ter \'raf-tər\ *n* [OE *ræfter*] : one of the usu. sloping timbers that support a roof
¹**rag** \'rag\ *n* [ON *rögg* tuft, shagginess] **1 a** : a waste or worn piece of cloth **b** *pl* : shabby or tattered clothing ⟨dressed in *rags*⟩ **2** : something felt to resemble a rag of cloth ⟨cloud *rags* swept before the wind⟩
²**rag** *vt* **ragged** \'ragd\; **rag·ging** **1** : to rail at : SCOLD **2** : TEASE, HARASS

a rafters, *b* ridgepole

rag·a·muf·fin \'rag-ə-,məf-ən\ *n* : a ragged often disreputable person; *esp* : a poorly clothed often dirty child
rag·bag \'rag-,bag\ *n* **1** : a bag for scraps **2** : a miscellaneous collection
¹**rage** \'rāj\ *n* [MF, fr. L *rabies* madness, rage, fr. *rabere* to be mad] **1 a** : violent and uncontrolled anger : FURY

b : a fit of violent wrath **2** : violent action (as of wind or sea) **3** : CRAZE, VOGUE ⟨was all the *rage*⟩ **syn** see ANGER

²rage *vi* **1** : to be in a rage **2** : to be in tumult **3** : to prevail uncontrollably ⟨*raging* epidemic⟩

rag·ged \'rag-əd\ *adj* **1** : roughly unkempt : STRAGGLY ⟨a *ragged* lawn⟩ **2** : having an irregular edge or outline : JAGGED ⟨*ragged* cliffs⟩ **3 a** : torn or worn to or as if to tatters ⟨a *ragged* dress⟩⟨run *ragged*⟩ **b** : wearing tattered clothes **4** : executed in an irregular or uneven manner — **rag·ged·ly** *adv* — **rag·ged·ness** *n*

rag·ge·dy \-əd-ē\ *adj* : somewhat ragged

rag·gle–tag·gle \'rag-əl-,tag-əl\ *adj* : MOTLEY

rag·ing \'rā-jiŋ\ *adj* **1** : causing great pain or distress **2** : VIOLENT, WILD

rag·lan \'rag-lən\ *n* [Baron *Raglan* d1855 British field marshal] : a loose overcoat having sleeves that extend to the neckline with slanted seams from the underarm to the neck

rag·man \'rag-,man\ *n* : a collector of or dealer in rags and waste

ra·gout \ra-'gü\ *n* [F *ragoût*] : a highly seasoned meat stew with vegetables

rag·tag and bob·tail \,rag-,tag-ən-'bäb-,tāl\ *n* : RABBLE

rag·time \'rag-,tīm\ *n* **1** : musical rhythm in which the melody has the accented notes falling on beats that are not usu. accented **2** : music with ragtime rhythm

rag·weed \'rag-,wēd\ *n* : any of various chiefly No. American weedy herbs related to the daisies that produce highly allergenic pollen

rah \'rä, 'rö\ *interj* : HURRAH — used esp. to cheer a team on ⟨*rah, rah,* team⟩

¹raid \'rād\ *n* [Sc dial., fr. OE *rād* ride, raid; akin to E *ride*] **1 a** : a hostile or predatory incursion **b** : a surprise attack by a small force **2** : a sudden invasion by officers of the law **3** : a daring or sudden or sometimes stealthy act or procedure designed to gain something usu. by taking it from another ⟨a *raid* on the icebox⟩

²raid *vt* : to make a raid on — **raid·er** *n*

¹rail \'rāl\ *n* [MF *reille* ruler, bar, fr. L *regula* ruler, fr. *regere* to keep straight, rule] **1 a** : a bar extending from one post or support to another and serving as a guard or barrier **b** : RAILING **2 a** : a bar of rolled steel forming a track for wheeled vehicles **b** : TRACK 1c(2) **c** : RAILROAD

²rail *vt* : to provide with a railing : FENCE

³rail *n, pl* **rails** *or* **rail** [MF *raale*] : any of a family of small wading birds related to the cranes

⁴rail *vi* [MF *railler* to mock, rally] : to revile or scold in harsh, insolent, or abusive language — **rail·er** *n*

rail·ing \'rā-liŋ\ *n* **1** : a barrier (as a fence or balustrade) consisting of rails and their supports **2** : material for making rails : RAILS

rail·lery \'rā-lə-rē\ *n, pl* **-ler·ies** **1** : good-natured ridicule : BANTER **2** : JEST

¹rail·road \'rāl-,rōd\ *n* : a permanent road having a line of rails fixed to ties and laid on a roadbed and providing a track for rolling stock drawn by locomotives or propelled by self-contained motors; *also* : such a road and its assets constituting a single property

²railroad *vb* **1 a** : to transport by railroad **b** : to work for a railroad company **2 a** : to push through hastily or without due consideration **b** : to convict with undue haste and by means of false charges or insufficient evidence — **rail·road·er** *n*

rail·road·ing *n* : construction or operation of a railroad

rail·way \'rāl-,wā\ *n* **1** : RAILROAD; *esp* : a railroad operating with light equipment or within a small area **2** : a line of track providing a runway for wheels ⟨a cash or parcel *railway* in a department store⟩

rai·ment \'rā-mənt\ *n* [ME *rayment*, short for *arrayment*, fr. *arrayen* to array] : CLOTHING, GARMENTS

¹rain \'rān\ *n* [OE *regn*] **1** : water falling in drops condensed from vapor in the atmosphere; *also* : the descent of such water **2 a** : a fall of rain : RAINSTORM **b** *pl* : the rainy season **3** : rainy weather **4** : a heavy fall of particles or bodies — **rain·less** \-ləs\ *adj*

²rain *vb* **1** : to fall as water in drops from the clouds **2** : to send down rain **3** : to fall like rain ⟨ashes *rained* from the volcano⟩ **4** : to bestow abundantly

rain·bird \'rān-,bərd\ *n* : any of various birds (as a cuckoo) whose cries are popularly believed to augur rain

rain·bow \-,bō\ *n* **1** : an arc or circle that exhibits in concentric bands the colors of the spectrum and that is formed opposite the sun by the refraction and reflection of the sun's rays in raindrops, spray, or mist **2** : a multi-colored array

rainbow runner *n* : a large brightly marked blue and yellow food and sport fish of warm seas

rainbow trout *n* : a large stout-bodied usu. brightly marked trout native to western No. America — compare STEELHEAD

rain·coat \'rān-,kōt\ *n* : a coat of waterproof or water-resistant material

rain·drop \-,dräp\ *n* : a drop of rain

rain·fall \-,fol\ *n* **1** : RAIN 2a **2** : amount of precipitation ⟨our annual *rainfall* of 20 inches⟩

rain forest *n* : a usu. tropical woodland with a high annual rainfall and lofty trees forming a continuous canopy

rain gauge *n* : an instrument for measuring rainfall

rain·mak·ing \'rān-,mā-kiŋ\ *n* : the act or process of attempting to produce rain by artificial means — **rain·mak·er** \-kər\ *n*

rain·proof \'rān-'prüf\ *adj* : impervious to rain

rain·storm \-,storm\ *n* : a storm of or with rain

rain·wa·ter \-,wot-ər, -,wät-\ *n* : water falling or fallen as rain

rainy \'rā-nē\ *adj* **rain·i·er; -est** : having much rain : SHOWERY ⟨a *rainy* season⟩

rainy day *n* : a period of want or need ⟨set a little aside for a *rainy day*⟩

rai·on \rī-'ön\ *n, pl* **raions** *or* **rai·o·ni** \-'ō-nē\ [Russ *raĭon,* fr. F *rayon* honeycomb, department in a store] : a subdivision of an oblast or of a republic not divided into oblasts in the U.S.S.R.

¹raise \'rāz\ *vb* [ON *reisa;* akin to E **¹rear**] **1** : to cause to rise : LIFT ⟨*raise* a window⟩⟨*raise* dust⟩ **2 a** : AWAKEN, AROUSE **b** : to stir up : INCITE ⟨*raise* a rebellion⟩ **c** : to establish radio communication with **3 a** : to set upright by lifting or building **b** : to place higher in rank or dignity : ELEVATE **c** : HEIGHTEN, INVIGORATE **d** : to end or suspend the operation or validity of ⟨*raise* a siege⟩ **4** : COLLECT ⟨*raise* funds⟩ **5 a** : to foster the growth and development of : GROW, REAR ⟨*raise* a crop for market⟩⟨*raise* pigs on slop⟩ **b** : to bring up (a child) ⟨boys *raised* in the city⟩ **6 a** : to give rise to : PROVOKE **b** : to give voice to ⟨*raise* a cheer⟩ **7** : to bring up for consideration or debate ⟨*raise* an issue⟩ **8 a** : to increase the strength, intensity, or pitch of **b** : to increase the degree or rate of ⟨*raise* the rent⟩ **c** : to multiply (a quantity) by itself a specified number of times **d** : to increase the amount of a poker bet or a partner's bridge bid **9** : to make light and porous ⟨*raise* dough⟩ **10** : to bring in sight on the horizon by approaching ⟨*raise* land⟩ **11** : to cause (an elevated injury) to form on the skin ⟨the blow *raised* a welt⟩ **12** : to increase the nominal value of fraudulently ⟨*raise* a check⟩ **syn** see LIFT — **rais·er** *n*

²raise *n* **1** : an act of raising or lifting **2** : an upward grade : RISE **3 a** : an increase in amount (as of a bet or bid) **b** : an increase in pay

rai·sin \'rāz-ʰn\ *n* [MF, grape, fr. L *racemus* cluster of grapes or berries] : a grape usu. of a special type dried for food

rai·son d'être \,rā-,zōⁿ-'detr°\ *n* [F] : reason or justification for existence

ra·ja *or* **ra·jah** \'räj-ə\ *n* [Hindi *rājā,* fr. Skt *rājan* king] : an Indian or Malay prince or chief

Raj·put *or* **Raj·poot** \'räj-,put\ *n* [Hindi *rājpūt,* fr. Skt *rājaputra* king's son] : a member of an Indo-Aryan dominant military caste of northern India

¹rake \'rāk\ *n* [OE *racu*] : a long-handled garden tool having a bar with teeth or prongs; *also* : a machine for gathering hay

²rake *vt* **1** : to gather, loosen, or smooth with or as if with a rake **2** : SCRATCH **3 a** : to search through : RANSACK **b** : to search out and gather together ⟨*rake* up the money for the rent⟩ ⟨*raked* together a small stock of goods⟩⟨*rake* up old scandals⟩ **4** : to sweep the length of esp. with gunfire : ENFILADE **5** : to glance over rapidly — **rak·er** *n*

³rake *vi* : to incline from the perpendicular : SLANT

⁴rake *n* : a slant or slope away from the perpendicular ⟨the *rake* of a mast⟩

⁵rake *n* : a dissolute person : LIBERTINE

---

j joke; **ŋ** sing; **ō** flow; **o** flaw; **oi** coin; **th** thin; **th** this; **ü** loot; **u** foot; **y** yet; **yü** few; **yu** furious; **zh** vision

rake-off \'rāk-,óf\ *n* : an often unlawful commission or profit received by one party in a business deal

¹**rak·ish** \'rā-kish\ *adj* : of, relating to, or characteristic of a rake : DISSOLUTE, PROFLIGATE — **rak·ish·ly** *adv* — **rak·ish·ness** *n*

²**rakish** *adj* **1** : having a smart stylish appearance suggestive of speed ⟨a *rakish* ship⟩ **2** : negligent of convention or formality : JAUNTY ⟨*rakish* clothes⟩ — **rak·ish·ly** *adv* — **rak·ish·ness** *n*

rale \'ral, 'räl\ *n* [F *râle*] : an abnormal sound accompanying breathing (as in pneumonia)

ral·len·tan·do \,räl-ən-'tän-dō\ *adv (or adj)* [It, lit., slowing down] : with a gradual decrease in tempo — used as a direction in music

¹**ral·ly** \'ral-ē\ *vb* **ral·lied; ral·ly·ing** [F *rallier*, fr. OF *ralier*, fr. re- + *alier* to unite, ally] **1 a** : to bring together for a common purpose **b** : to bring back to order ⟨a leader *rallying* his forces⟩ **2** : to rouse for action or from depression or weakness ⟨*rallied* his strength for a second try⟩ ⟨the medicine *rallied* the fainting girl⟩ **3** : to come together to renew an effort : join in a common cause **4** : RECOVER, REBOUND ⟨the market *rallied* after a slump⟩ **5** : to engage in a rally (as in tennis)

²**rally** *n, pl* **rallies 1** : the action of rallying **2** : a mass meeting intended to arouse group enthusiasm **3** : a series of strokes interchanged between players (as in tennis) before a point is won

³**rally** *vt* **ral·lied; ral·ly·ing** [F *railler*] : to attack with raillery : BANTER

¹**ram** \'ram\ *n* [OE *ramm*] **1** : a male sheep **2** : BATTERING RAM **3** : a pointed beak on the prow of a ship for piercing an enemy ship **4** : a guided piece (as the plunger of a force pump) for exerting pressure or for driving or forcing something by impact

²**ram** *vb* **rammed; ram·ming 1** : to strike or strike against with violence : CRASH **2** : to rush violently or forcibly ⟨*ram* through traffic⟩ **3** : to force in, down, or together by or as if by driving or pressing **4** : to force passage or acceptance of ⟨*ram* a bill through congress⟩ — **ram·mer** *n*

Ram·a·dan \'ram-ə-,dän\ *n* [Ar *Ramaḍān*] : the 9th month of the Muhammadan year observed with daily fasting from dawn to sunset

ra·mate \'rā-,māt\ *adj* : having branches

¹**ram·ble** \'ram-bəl\ *vb* **ram·bled; ram·bling** \-b(ə-)liŋ\ **1 a** : to move aimlessly from place to place : WANDER, ROAM **b** : to explore idly **2** : to talk or write in a desultory fashion **3** : to grow or extend irregularly

²**ramble** *n* : a leisurely excursion for pleasure; *esp* : an aimless walk

ram·bler \'ram-blər\ *n* **1** : one that rambles **2** : a climbing rose with rather small often double flowers in large clusters

ramb·ling \'ram-bliŋ\ *adj* : DISCURSIVE — **ram·bling·ly** \-bliŋ-lē\ *adv*

ram·bouil·let \,ram-bə-'lā\ *n, often cap* : a large sturdy sheep developed in France for mutton and wool

ram·bunc·tious \ram-'bəŋ(k)-shəs\ *adj* : marked by uncontrollable exuberance : UNRULY — **ram·bunc·tious·ly** *adv* — **ram·bunc·tious·ness** *n*

ram·e·kin or **ram·e·quin** \'ram-i-kən\ *n* [F *ramequin*, fr. LG *ramken*, dim. of *ram* cream] **1** : a savory dish of cheese usu. with bread crumbs or eggs baked in a mold or shell **2** : an individual baking dish

ram·ie \'ram-ē, 'rä-mē\ *n* [Malay *rami*] : an Asian perennial plant of the nettle family; *also* : its strong lustrous bast fiber used as a textile fiber

ram·i·fi·ca·tion \,ram-ə-fə-'kā-shən\ *n* **1 a** : the act or process of branching **b** : arrangement of branches (as on a plant) **2 a** : BRANCH, OFFSHOOT **b** : a branched structure **3** : OUTGROWTH, CONSEQUENCE ⟨the *ramifications* of a problem⟩

ram·i·form \'ram-ə-,form\ *adj* : resembling or constituting branches : BRANCHED

ram·i·fy \'ram-ə-,fī\ *vb* **-fied; -fy·ing** [MF *ramifier*, fr. ML *ramificare*, fr. L *ramus* branch] : to spread out or split up into branches or divisions

ram·jet engine \,ram-,jet-\ *n* : a jet engine having in its forward end a continuous inlet of air so that there is a compressing effect produced on the air taken in while the engine is in motion

ra·mose \'rā-,mōs\ *adj* [L *ramus* branch] : BRANCHED — **ra·mose·ly** *adv*

ra·mous \'rā-məs\ *adj* **1** : BRANCHED **2** : resembling branches

¹**ramp** \'ramp\ *vi* [OE *ramper* to crawl, rear] **1** : to stand or advance menacingly with forelegs or with arms raised **2** : to move or act furiously : STORM

²**ramp** *n* [F *rampe*, fr. *ramper* to crawl, rear] : a sloping passage or roadway connecting different levels

¹**ram·page** \'ram-,pāj, (')ram-'\ *vi* : to rush wildly about : STORM

²**ram·page** \'ram-,pāj\ *n* : a course of violent, riotous, or reckless action or behavior — **ram·pa·geous** \ram-'pā-jəs\ *adj* — **ram·pa·geous·ly** *adv* — **ram·pa·geous·ness** *n*

ram·pant \'ram-pənt, -,pant\ *adj* [MF, prp. of *ramper* to crawl, rear] **1** : rearing upon one or both hind legs with forelegs extended **2 a** : marked by a menacing wildness, extravagance, or absence of restraint **b** : unchecked in growth or spread — **ram·pan·cy** \-pən-sē\ *n* — **ram·pant·ly** *adv*

ram·part \'ram-,pärt, -pərt\ *n* [MF] **1** : a broad embankment raised as a fortification or protective barrier : BULWARK **2** : a ridge (as of rock fragments or earth) that suggests a wall

¹**ram·rod** \'ram-,räd\ *n* **1** : a rod for ramming home the charge in a muzzle-loading firearm **2** : a cleaning rod for small arms

²**ramrod** *adj* : marked by rigidity, severity, or stiffness

ram·shack·le \'ram-,shak-əl\ *adj* : appearing ready to collapse: as **a** : DILAPIDATED **b** : carelessly or loosely constructed

ra·mus \'rā-məs\ *n, pl* **ra·mi** \-,mī\ [NL, fr. L, branch] : a projecting part or elongated process : BRANCH ⟨the *rami* of the lower jaw⟩

ran *past of* RUN

¹**ranch** \'ranch\ *n* [MexSp *rancho*, fr. Sp *ranchearse* to settle, fr. MF *se ranger* to arrange oneself] **1** : an establishment for the grazing and rearing of horses, cattle, or sheep **2** : a farm devoted to a specialty ⟨a fruit *ranch*⟩

²**ranch** *vb* : to live or work or raise livestock on a ranch

ranch·er \'ran-chər\ *n* : one who owns or operates or works on a ranch

ran·che·ro \ran-'che(ə)r-ō, rän-\ *n, pl* **-ros** [MexSp, fr. *rancho* ranch] : RANCHER

ranch house *n* : a one-story house typically with a low-pitched roof

ranch·man \'ranch-mən\ *n* : RANCHER

ran·cho \'ran-chō, 'rän-\ *n, pl* **ranchos** : RANCH 1

ran·cid \'ran(t)-səd\ *adj* [L *rancidus*] **1** : having a rank smell or taste typical of decomposed oil or fat ⟨*rancid* butter⟩ **2** : RANK, ROTTEN — **ran·cid·i·ty** \ran-'sid-ət-ē\ *n* — **ran·cid·ness** \'ran(t)-səd-nəs\ *n*

ran·cor \'raŋ-kər\ *n* [L, lit., rancidity] : strong ill will : intense hatred or spite — **ran·cor·ous** \-k(ə-)rəs\ *adj* — **ran·cor·ous·ly** *adv*

¹**ran·dom** \'ran-dəm\ *n* [ME, impetuosity, fr. MF *randon*, fr. *randir* to run, of Gmc origin; akin to E *run*] : a haphazard course — **at random** : without definite aim, direction, rule, or method

²**random** *adj* **1** : lacking a definite plan, purpose, or pattern **2** : having a definite and esp. an equal probability of occurring ⟨*random* number⟩; *also* : consisting of or relating to such elements selected independently ⟨*random* sample⟩ — **ran·dom·ly** *adv* — **ran·dom·ness** *n*

syn RANDOM, HAPHAZARD mean determined by accident rather than design. RANDOM stresses lack of definite aim or fixed goal or avoidance of regular procedure ⟨*random* collection of furniture⟩ HAPHAZARD applies to what is done without regard for regularity or fitness or ultimate consequences ⟨*haphazard* arrangement of furniture⟩

³**random** *adv* : in a random manner

ran·dom·ize \'ran-də-,mīz\ *vt* : to make random ⟨carefully *randomized* sampling⟩ — **ran·dom·i·za·tion** \,ran-də-mə-'zā-shən\ *n*

rang *past of* RING

¹**range** \'rānj\ *n* [OF *renge*, fr. *rengier* to set in a row, fr. *renc, reng* rank, row] **1 a** : a series of things in a line : ROW ⟨*range* of mountains⟩ **b** : an aggregate of individuals in one rank : CLASS, ORDER **2 a** : a cooking stove that has a flat top with plates or racks to hold utensils over flames or coils and an oven **3 a** : a place that may

be ranged over **b :** open land over which livestock may roam and feed **c :** the region throughout which a kind of organism or ecological community naturally occurs **4 :** the act of ranging about **5 a** (1) **:** the horizontal distance to which a projectile can be propelled (2) **:** the maximum distance a vehicle can travel without refueling **b :** a place where shooting is practiced; *also* **:** a special course (as over water) over which missiles are tested **6 a :** the space or extent included, covered, or used **:** SCOPE **b :** the extent of pitch covered by a voice or a melody **7 a :** a sequence, series, or scale between limits **b :** the difference between the least and greatest of a set of values **8 :** the set of values a function may take on; *esp* **:** the set of values that the dependent variable may take on

²**range** *vb* **1 a :** to set in a row or in the proper order **b :** to place among others in a position or situation **c :** to assign to a category **:** CLASSIFY **2 a :** to rove over or through **:** roam at large or freely **b :** to sail or pass along **3 :** to raise (livestock) on a range **4 :** to determine or give the elevation necessary for (a gun) to propel a projectile to a given distance **5 :** to take a position **6 a :** to correspond in direction or line **:** ALIGN **b :** to extend in a particular direction **7 :** to vary within limits **8 :** to live or occur in or be native to a region

range finder *n* **1 :** an instrument used in gunnery to determine the distance of a target **2 :** a camera attachment for measuring the distance between the camera and an object

rang·er \'rān-jər\ *n* **1 a :** the keeper of a British royal park or forest **b :** an officer charged with patrolling and protecting a forest **2 :** one that ranges **3 a :** one of a body of organized armed men who range over a region **b :** a soldier trained in close-range fighting and raiding tactics

rangy \'rān-jē\ *adj* **rang·i·er; -est 1 :** able to range for considerable distances **2 :** being long-limbed and long≠bodied **:** being tall and slender ⟨*rangy* cattle⟩ **3 :** having room for ranging **4 :** having great scope — **rang·i·ness** *n*

ra·ni *or* **ra·nee** \rä-'nē\ *n* [Hindi *rānī*, fr. Skt *rājñī*, fem. of *rājan* king] **:** a Hindu queen **:** a raja's wife

¹**rank** \'raŋk\ *adj* [OE *ranc* strong, overbearing] **1 :** strong and vigorous and usu. coarse in growth ⟨*rank* weeds⟩ ⟨*rank* meadows⟩ **2 :** offensively gross or coarse **3 :** unpleasantly strong-smelling **:** RANCID, FOUL **4 :** EXTREME, UTTER — **rank·ly** *adv* — **rank·ness** *n*

²**rank** *n* [MF *renc, reng*, of Gmc origin] **1 :** ROW, SERIES ⟨*ranks* of houses⟩ **2 :** a line of soldiers ranged side by side **3** *pl* **:** a group of individuals classed together ⟨in the *ranks* of the unemployed⟩ **4 :** relative position or order **:** STANDING ⟨his *rank* was fifth in number of points scored⟩ **5 :** official grade or status (as in the army or navy) ⟨the *rank* of general⟩ **6 :** position in regard to merit ⟨a musician of the highest *rank*⟩ **7 :** high social position **8** *pl* **:** the body of enlisted men in an army

³**rank** *vb* **1 :** to arrange in lines or in a regular formation **2 :** to determine the relative position of **:** RATE **3 :** to take precedence of ⟨a captain *ranks* a lieutenant⟩ **4 :** to take or have a position in relation to others **:** be in a class

rank and file *n* **1 :** the enlisted men of an armed force **2 :** the ordinary body of an organization or society as distinguished from the leaders

rank·er \'raŋ-kər\ *n* **:** one who serves or has served in the ranks; *esp* **:** a commissioned officer promoted from the ranks

rank·ing *adj* **:** having a high position: as **a :** FOREMOST ⟨*ranking* poet⟩ **b :** being next to the chairman in seniority ⟨*ranking* committee member⟩

ran·kle \'raŋ-kəl\ *vb* **ran·kled; ran·kling** \-k(ə-)liŋ\ [MF *rancler* to fester] **1 :** to cause anger, irritation, or deep bitterness **2 :** to cause resentment or bitterness in **:** irritate deeply

ran·sack \'ran-,sak, (')ran-'\ *vt* [ON *rannsaka*] **:** to search thoroughly **:** RUMMAGE; *esp* **:** to search through and rob — **ran·sack·er** *n*

¹**ran·som** \'ran(t)-səm\ *n* [OF *rançon*, fr. L *redemption-, redemptio* redemption] **1 :** a consideration (as money) paid or demanded for the freedom of a captured person **2 :** the act of ransoming

²**ransom** *vt* **1 :** to deliver esp. from sin or its penalty **2 :** to free from captivity or punishment by paying a price **syn** see RESCUE — **ran·som·er** *n*

¹**rant** \'rant\ *vb* [obs. D *ranten*] **1 :** to talk noisily, excitedly, or wildly ⟨*rant* and rave in anger⟩ **2 :** to scold violently **3 :** to declaim noisily ⟨an actor who *rants* blank verse⟩ — **rant·er** *n*

²**rant** *n* **:** ranting speech **:** bombastic extravagant language

¹**rap** \'rap\ *n* [ME *rappe*] **1 :** a sharp blow or knock **2** *slang* **a :** the blame for an action **b :** a criminal charge

²**rap** *vb* **rapped; rap·ping 1 :** to give a quick sharp blow **:** KNOCK ⟨*rap* on the door⟩ **2 :** to utter suddenly with force ⟨*rap* out an order⟩

³**rap** *n* **:** the least bit ⟨don't care a *rap*⟩

⁴**rap** *n* **:** TALK, CONVERSATION

⁵**rap** *vi* **rapped; rap·ping :** to talk freely and frankly

ra·pa·cious \rə-'pā-shəs\ *adj* [L *rapac-, rapax*, fr. *rapere* to seize] **1 :** excessively grasping or covetous **2 :** living on prey **:** PREDATORY **3 :** RAVENOUS, VORACIOUS — **ra·pa·cious·ly** *adv* — **ra·pa·cious·ness** *n* — **ra·pac·i·ty** \-'pas-ət-ē\ *n*

¹**rape** \'rāp\ *n* [L *rapa, rapum* turnip, rape] **:** a European herb of the mustard family grown as a forage crop and for its seeds which are used as a source of oil and as a bird food

²**rape** *vt* [L *rapere*] **1** *archaic* **:** to seize and take away by force **2 :** to commit rape on **:** RAVISH — **rap·er** *n* — **rap·ist** \'rā-pəst\ *n*

³**rape** *n* **1 :** a seizing by force **2 :** sexual intercourse with a woman carried out without her consent and esp. by force

Raph·a·el \'raf-ē-əl, 'rā-fē-\ *n* **:** one of the archangels

ra·phe \'rā-(,)fē\ *n* [Gk *rhaphē* seam, fr. *rhaptein* to sew] **:** a seam or ridge (as at the union of the two lateral halves of an organ or on a seed)

ra·phide \'rā-fəd\ *n, pl* **ra·phides** \-fədz, -fə-,dēz\ [Gk *rhaphid-, rhaphis* needle, fr. *rhaptein* to sew] **:** a needlelike crystal (as of calcium oxalate) in a plant cell

¹**rap·id** \'rap-əd\ *adj* [L *rapidus*, fr. *rapere* to seize, sweep away] **:** marked by a fast rate of motion, activity, succession, or occurrence **:** SWIFT **syn** see FAST — **rap·id·ly** *adv* — **rap·id·ness** *n*

²**rapid** *n* **:** a part of a river where the current is fast and the surface is usu. broken by obstructions — usu. used in pl.

rap·id-fire \,rap-əd-'fī(ə)r\ *adj* **1 :** firing or adapted for firing shots in rapid succession **2 :** marked by rapidity, liveliness, or sharpness ⟨*rapid-fire* questions⟩

ra·pid·i·ty \rə-'pid-ət-ē, ra-\ *n* **:** SWIFTNESS, SPEED

rapid transit *n* **:** fast public passenger transportation (as by subway) in urban areas

ra·pi·er \'rā-pē-ər\ *n* [MF *rapiere*] **:** a straight 2-edged sword with a narrow pointed blade

rap·ine \'rap-ən\ *n* **:** the seizing and carrying away of something by force **:** PILLAGE, PLUNDER

rap·i·ni \ra-'pē-nē\ *n pl* [It *rapini*, pl. of *rapino*, dim. of *rapo* turnip, fr. L *rapum*] **:** leafy young turnip plants for use as greens

rap·port \ra-'pō(ə)r, -'pö(ə)r\ *n* [F] **:** harmonious accord or relation that makes communication possible or easy ⟨an actor able to establish *rapport* with his audience⟩

rap·proche·ment \,rap-,rōsh-'mäⁿ\ *n* [F, fr. *rapprocher* to bring together, fr. *re-* + *approcher* to approach] **:** the establishment or a state of cordial relations

rap·scal·lion \rap-'skal-yən\ *n* **:** RASCAL, SCAMP

rapt \'rapt\ *adj* [L *raptus*, pp. of *rapere* to seize, sweep away] **1 :** carried away with emotion **:** ENRAPTURED **2 :** wholly absorbed **:** ENGROSSED — **rapt·ly** *adv* — **rapt·ness** \'rap(t)-nəs\ *n*

rap·tor \'rap-tər, -,tȯr\ *n* [L, plunderer, fr. *rapere* to seize] **:** a bird of prey

rap·to·ri·al \rap-'tȯr-ē-əl, -'tȯr-\ *adj* **1 :** adapted to seize prey **2 :** of, relating to, or being a bird of prey

rap·ture \'rap-chər\ *n* **1 :** a state of being carried away by joy or delight or love **2 :** an expression or manifestation of ecstasy or passion — **rap·tur·ous** \'rap-chə-rəs, 'rap-shrəs\ *adj* — **rap·tur·ous·ly** *adv* — **rap·tur·ous·ness** *n*

ra·ra avis \,rar-ə-'ā-vəs, ,rer-; ,rär-ə-'ä-wəs\ *n, pl* **ra·ra avis·es** \-'ā-və-səz\ *or* **ra·rae aves** \,rär-,ī-'ä-,wās\ [L, rare bird] **:** a rare person or thing **:** RARITY

¹**rare** \'ra(ə)r, 're(ə)r\ *adj* [OE *hrēre*] **:** cooked a short time **:** UNDERDONE ⟨*rare* roast beef⟩

rapier

²rare *adj* [L *rarus*] **1** : not thick or dense : THIN ⟨*rare* atmosphere at high altitudes⟩ **2** : unusually fine : EXCELLENT, SPLENDID ⟨a woman of *rare* charm⟩ **3** : seldom occurring or found : very uncommon : INFREQUENT **4** : valuable because of scarcity ⟨a collection of *rare* books⟩ — **rare·ness** *n*

rare·bit \'ra(ə)r-bət, 're(ə)r-\ *n* : WELSH RABBIT

rare earth *n* : any of a series of metallic elements that includes the elements with atomic numbers 58 through 71, usu. lanthanum, and sometimes yttrium and scandium, that have similar properties — called also *rare-earth element*

rar·e·fac·tion \,rar-ə-'fak-shən, ,rer-\ *n* : the act or process of rarefying : the state of being rarefied — **rar·e·fac·tion·al** \-shnəl, -shən-°l\ *adj*

rar·e·fy *also* **rar·i·fy** \'rar-ə-,fī, 'rer-\ *vb* **-fied; -fy·ing** [MF *rarefier*, modif. of L *rarefacere*, fr. *rarus* rare + *facere* to make] **1** : to make or become thin, porous, or less dense **2** : to make or become more spiritual, refined, tenuous, or abstruse

rare·ly \'ra(ə)r-lē, 're(ə)r-\ *adv* **1** : not often : SELDOM **2** : with rare skill : EXCELLENTLY **3** : UNUSUALLY ⟨a *rarely* beautiful girl⟩

rare·ripe \-,rīp\ *adj* : early ripe — **rareripe** *n*

rar·ing \-iŋ\ *adj* : full of enthusiasm or eagerness

rar·i·ty \'rar-ət-ē, 'rer-\ *n, pl* **-ties 1** : the quality, state, or fact of being rare : THINNESS **2** : SCARCITY **3** : someone or something rare ⟨black pearls are *rarities*⟩

ras·cal \'ras-kəl\ *n* [ME *rascaile* rabble, one of the rabble] **1** : a mean, unprincipled, or dishonest person : ROGUE **2** : a mischievous person : IMP

ras·cal·i·ty \ra-'skal-ət-ē\ *n, pl* **-ties** : the act, actions, or character of a rascal

ras·cal·ly \'ras-kə-lē\ *adj* : of or characteristic of a rascal ⟨a *rascally* trick⟩ — **rascally** *adv*

¹rash \'rash\ *adj* [ME *rasch* quick] **1** : being too hasty in speech or action or in making decisions : RECKLESS ⟨a *rash* act⟩ ⟨regret a *rash* promise⟩ **syn** see DARING — **rash·ly** *adv* — **rash·ness** *n*

²rash *n* [obs. F *rache* scurf, fr. L *rasicare* to scratch, fr. *ras-, radere* to scrape, shave] : a breaking out of the skin with red spots (as in measles) : ERUPTION

rash·er \'rash-ər\ *n* : a thin slice of bacon or ham cut for broiling or frying

¹rasp \'rasp\ *vb* **1** : to rub with or as if with a rough file ⟨*rasp* off a rough edge⟩ ⟨snails *rasping* at leaves⟩ **2** : to grate harshly upon : IRRITATE ⟨a *rasping* voice⟩ **3** : to speak or utter in a grating tone **4** : to produce a grating sound — **rasp·er** *n*

²rasp *n* **1** : a coarse file with cutting points instead of lines **2 a** : an act of rasping **b** : a rasping sound, sensation, or effect

rasp·ber·ry \'raz-,ber-ē, -b(ə-)rē\ *n* **1 a** : any of various black or red edible berries that consist of numerous small drupes on a fleshy receptacle and are rounder and smaller than the related blackberries **b** : a bramble that bears raspberries **2** : a sound of contempt made by trilling the tongue between protruded lips

raspy \'ras-pē\ *adj* **rasp·i·er; -est 1** : GRATING, HARSH **2** : IRRITABLE

¹rat \'rat\ *n* [OE *ræt*] **1** : a scaly-tailed gnawing rodent distinguished from the mouse chiefly by its larger size and by differences in the teeth **2** : a person who deserts a cause or betrays his fellows

²rat *vi* **rat·ted; rat·ting 1** : to desert or inform on one's associates **2** : to catch or hunt rats

rat·a·ble *or* **rate·a·ble** \'rāt-ə-bəl\ *adj* : capable of being rated, estimated, or apportioned — **rat·a·bly** \-blē\ *adv*

rat·a·fia \,rat-ə-'fē-ə\ *n* [F] **1** : a liqueur flavored with fruit kernels and bitter almonds **2** : a sweet biscuit made of almond paste

ratch \'rach\ *n* [G *ratsche*, fr. *ratschen* to rattle] **1** : RATCHET **2** : a notched bar with which a pawl or detent works to prevent reversal of motion

rat cheese *n* : CHEDDAR

ratch·et \'rach-ət\ *n* [alter. of earlier *rochet*, fr. F] **1** : a mechanism that consists of a bar or wheel having inclined teeth into which a pawl drops so as to allow motion in one direction only **2** : a pawl or detent for holding or propelling a ratchet wheel

ratchet wheel *n* : a toothed wheel held in position or turned by an engaging pawl

¹rate \'rāt\ *vt* [ME *raten*] : to scold violently : BERATE

²rate *n* [MF, fr. ML *rata*, fr. L *pro rata parte* according to a fixed proportion] **1** : reckoned value : VALUATION **2 a** : a fixed ratio between two things ⟨a *rate* of exchange⟩ **b** : a charge, payment, or price fixed according to a ratio, scale, or standard ⟨tax *rate*⟩ **3 a** : a quantity, amount, or degree of something measured per unit of something else **b** : an amount of payment or charge based on another amount ⟨interest at the rate of six percent⟩ **4** : relative condition or quality : CLASS — **at any rate** : in any case : at least

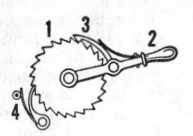

ratchet wheel: *1* wheel, *2* reciprocating lever, *3* pawl for communicating motion, *4* pawl for preventing backward motion

³rate *vb* **1** : CONSIDER, REGARD ⟨*rated* a good pianist⟩ **2** : to set an estimate or value on ⟨*rate* houses for tax purposes⟩ **3** : to determine the rank, class, or position of : assign to a rank or class : GRADE ⟨*rate* a seaman⟩ ⟨*rate* a ship⟩ **4** : to have a rating or rank : be classed ⟨*rate* high⟩ **5** : to set a rate on **6** : to be qualified for ⟨*rate* a promotion⟩

rate·pay·er \'rāt-,pā-ər\ *n, Brit* : TAXPAYER

rat·er \'rāt-ər\ *n* **1** : one that rates; *esp* : a person who estimates or determines a rating **2** : one having a specified rating or class — usu. used in combination ⟨first-rater⟩

rath·er \'rath-ər, 'roth-, 'räth-\ *adv* [OE *hrathor*, fr. compar. of *hrathe* quickly] **1** : more willingly : PREFERABLY ⟨I would *rather* not go⟩ **2** : on the contrary : INSTEAD ⟨things did not turn out well; *rather*, they turned out very badly⟩ **3** : more exactly : more properly : with better reason ⟨my father, or, *rather*, my stepfather⟩ ⟨to be pitied *rather* than blamed⟩ **4** : SOMEWHAT ⟨*rather* cold today⟩

raths·kel·ler \'räts-,kel-ər, 'rat(h)s-\ *n* [obs. G (now *ratskeller*), city-hall basement restaurant, lit., council cellar] : a restaurant patterned after the cellar of a German city hall where beer is sold

rat·i·fy \'rat-ə-,fī\ *vt* **-fied; -fy·ing** [MF *ratifier*, fr. ML *ratificare*, fr. L *ratus* determined, fr. pp. of *reri* to calculate] : to approve and sanction formally : CONFIRM ⟨*ratify* a treaty⟩ ⟨*ratify* the decision of a subordinate⟩ — **rat·i·fi·ca·tion** \,rat-ə-fə-'kā-shən\ *n* — **rat·i·fi·er** \'rat-ə-,fī(-ə)r\ *n*

rat·ing \'rāt-iŋ\ *n* **1 a** : a classification according to grade or rank **b** : a naval specialist classification **2** *chiefly Brit* : a naval enlisted man **3** : a relative estimate or evaluation ⟨credit rating⟩

ra·tio \'rā-shō, -shē-,ō\ *n, pl* **ra·tios** [L, computation, relation, fr. *rat-, reri* to calculate] **1** : a fixed or approximate relation in number, quantity, or degree between things or one thing to another thing ⟨the *ratio* of eggs to butter in a cake⟩ ⟨women outnumbered men in the *ratio* of three to one⟩ **2** : the quotient of one quantity divided by another ⟨the *ratio* of 6 to 3 may be expressed as 6:3, ⅔, and 2⟩

ra·ti·o·ci·na·tion \,rat-ē-,ōs-°n-'ā-shən, ,rash-ē-, -ē-,äs-\ *n* [L *ratiocinari* to reckon, reason, fr. *ratio* computation, reason] **1** : the process of exact thinking : REASONING **2** : a reasoned train of thought — **ra·ti·o·ci·nate** \-'ōs-°n-,āt, -'äs-\ *vi* — **ra·ti·o·ci·na·tive** \-,āt-iv\ *adj* — **ra·ti·o·ci·na·tor** \-,āt-ər\ *n*

¹ra·tion \'rash-ən, 'rā-shən\ *n* [L *ration-, ratio* computation] **1 a** : a food allowance for one day **b** : FOOD, PROVISIONS, DIET — usu. used in pl. ⟨a salt-free *ration*⟩ ⟨had to pack supplies and *rations* on their backs⟩ **2** : a share esp. as determined by supply or allotment by authority

²ration *vt* **ra·tioned; ra·tion·ing** \'rash-(ə-)niŋ, 'rāsh-\ **1** : to supply with rations ⟨*ration* cattle⟩ **2 a** : to distribute or allot as a ration ⟨the government *rationed* gas⟩ **b** : to use or allot sparingly ⟨her doctor *rationed* her sugar intake⟩

¹ra·tio·nal \'rash-nəl, -ən-°l\ *adj* [L *rationalis*, fr. *ration-, ratio* computation, reason, fr. *rat-, reri* to calculate, reason] **1 a** : having reason or understanding ⟨*rational* beings⟩ **b** : relating to, based on, or agreeable to reason; *also* : SANE ⟨*rational* behavior⟩ **2** : relating to or involving rational numbers ⟨a *rational* fraction⟩ — **ra·tio·nal·i·ty**

\‚rash-ə-'nal-ət-ē\ *n* — **ra·tio·nal·ly** \'rash-nə-lē, -ən-°l-ē\ *adv*

²**rational** *n* : something rational; *esp* : a rational number or fraction

ra·tio·nale \‚rash-ə-'nal\ *n* [L, neut. of *rationalis* rational] : a fundamental explanation or underlying reason : BASIS ⟨the *rationale* of a law⟩

ra·tio·nal·ism \'rash-nə-‚liz-əm, -ən-°l-‚iz-\ *n* **1** : a theory that reason is a source of knowledge superior to and independent of sense perceptions **2** : a view that reason is the final judge of truth — **ra·tio·nal·ist** \-nə-ləst, -ən-°l-əst\ *n* — **rationalist** *or* **ra·tio·nal·is·tic** \‚rash-nə-'lis-tik, -ən-°l-'is-\ *adj* — **ra·tio·nal·is·ti·cal·ly** \-ti-k(ə-)lē\ *adv*

ra·tio·nal·ize \'rash-nə-‚līz, -ən-°l-‚īz\ *vb* **1** : to free (a mathematical equation) from irrational expressions **2** : to bring into accord with reason or cause something to seem reasonable: as **a** : to account for on the basis of known phenomena ⟨*rationalize* a myth⟩ **b** : to attribute rational and creditable motives to (as actions or beliefs) without analyzing underlying motives ⟨*rationalized* his dislike of his brother⟩ — **ra·tio·nal·i·za·tion** \‚rash-nə-lə-'zā-shən, -ən-°l-ə-\ *n*

rational number *n* : a number expressible as an integer or the quotient of two integers

rat·ite \'ra-‚tīt, 'rā-\ *n* [NL *ratitus*, fr. L *ratis* raft, ship] : a bird with a flat breastbone — **ratite** *adj*

rat·like \'rat-‚līk\ *adj* : of, relating to, or resembling a rat

rat·line \'rat-lən\ *n* : one of the small transverse ropes attached to the shrouds of a ship so as to form the steps of a rope ladder

rat mite *n* : a widely distributed mite that usu. feeds on rodents but may cause dermatitis in or transmit typhus to man

rat snake *n* : any of various large harmless rat-eating snakes

rat·tan \ra-'tan, rə-\ *n* [Malay *rotan*] **1 a** : a climbing palm with very long tough stems **b** : a part of one of these stems used esp. for walking sticks and wickerwork **2** : a rattan cane or switch

rat·ter \'rat-ər\ *n* : one that catches rats; *esp* : a rat-catching dog or cat

ratlines and shrouds

¹**rat·tle** \'rat-°l\ *vb* **rat·tled; rat·tling** \'rat-liŋ, -°l-iŋ\ **1** : to make or cause to make a rapid succession of short sharp noises **2** : to chatter incessantly and aimlessly **3 a** : to move with a clatter or rattle **b** : to say, perform, or affect in a brisk lively fashion **4** : to disturb the composure of : UPSET ⟨*rattled* his mother with questions⟩

²**rattle** *n* **1** : a series of short sharp sounds : CLATTER ⟨the *rattle* of hail on a roof⟩ **2** : a device (as a toy) for making a rattling sound **3** : a rattling organ at the end of a rattlesnake's tail made up of horny joints **4** : a noise in the throat caused by air passing through mucus esp. at the approach of death

rat·tle·brain \'rat-°l-‚brān\ *n* : a flighty or thoughtless person — **rat·tle·brained** \‚rat-°l-'brānd\ *adj*

rat·tler \'rat-lər, -°l-ər\ *n* : one that rattles; *esp* : RATTLESNAKE

rat·tle·snake \'rat-°l-‚snāk\ *n* : any of various venomous American snakes having at the end of the tail horny interlocking joints that rattle when shaken

rat·tle·trap \-‚trap\ *n* : something rattly or rickety; *esp* : an old car — **rattletrap** *adj*

rat·tling \'rat-liŋ, -°l-iŋ\ *adj* **1** : LIVELY, BRISK **2** : extraordinarily good : SPLENDID — **rat·tling·ly** \'rat-liŋ-lē\ *adv*

rat·tly \'rat-lē, -°l-ē\ *adj* : likely to rattle : making a rattle ⟨a *rattly* old car⟩

rat·ty \'rat-ē\ *adj* **rat·ti·er; -est** **1** : infested with or suggestive of rats **2** : resembling a rat esp. in shabbiness or meanness

rat unit *n* : a bioassay unit equal to the amount of a material just sufficient to produce a response in rats under standardized conditions

rau·cous \'ro-kəs\ *adj* [L *raucus* hoarse] **1** : disagreeably harsh or strident **2** : boisterously disorderly — **rau·cous·ly** *adv* — **rau·cous·ness** *n*

rau·wol·fia \raù-'wùl-fē-ə, ró-\ *n* [NL, genus of trees, fr. Leonhard *Rauwolf* d1596 German botanist] : a medicinal extract from the root of an Indian tree of the dogbane family used in the treatment of hypertension and mental disorders; *also* : this tree

¹**rav·age** \'rav-ij\ *n* [F, fr. *ravir* to ravish] **1** : an act or practice of ravaging **2** : damage resulting from ravaging

²**ravage** *vb* **1** : to lay waste : PLUNDER **2** : DESTROY, RUIN ⟨body *ravaged* by disease⟩ — **rav·ag·er** *n*
syn RAVAGE, DEVASTATE mean to lay waste by plundering or destroying. RAVAGE suggests violent often repeated or continuing depredation and destruction; DEVASTATE implies causing complete ruin and desolation over a wide area

¹**rave** \'rāv\ *vb* [ME *raven*] **1 a** : to talk irrationally in or as if in delirium **b** : to speak or utter with extreme enthusiasm or violence ⟨*raved* out his denunciation⟩ **2** : to move or advance violently : RAGE ⟨the wind *raved* through the treetops⟩ — **rav·er** *n*

²**rave** *n* : an extravagantly favorable criticism

¹**rav·el** \'rav-əl\ *vb* **-eled** *or* **-elled; -el·ing** *or* **-el·ling** \'rav-(ə-)liŋ\ [D *rafelen*, fr. *rafel* loose thread] **1 a** : to separate or undo the texture of : UNRAVEL, FRAY **b** : to undo the intricacies of : DISENTANGLE **2** : ENTANGLE, CONFUSE — **rav·el·er** *or* **rav·el·ler** \-(ə-)lər\ *n*

²**ravel** *n* : something that is raveled

rav·el·ing *or* **rav·el·ling** \'rav-(ə-)liŋ, -(ə-)lən\ *n* : something raveled or frayed; *esp* : a thread raveled out of a fabric

¹**ra·ven** \'rā-vən\ *n* [OE *hræfn*] : a glossy black bird about two feet long of northern regions that is related to the crow and has pointed throat feathers

²**raven** *adj* : of the color or glossy sheen of the raven

³**rav·en** \'rav-ən\ *vb* **rav·ened; rav·en·ing** \'rav-(ə-)niŋ\ [MF *raviner* to take by force, fr. *ravine* rapine] **1** : to devour greedily **2** : to feed greedily **3** : to prowl for food : PREY **4** : PLUNDER — **rav·en·er** \-(ə-)nər\ *n*

rav·en·ing \'rav-(ə-)niŋ\ *adj* : GREEDY, RAPACIOUS

rav·en·ous \'rav-ə-nəs\ *adj* **1** : RAPACIOUS, VORACIOUS **2** : very eager for food, satisfaction, or gratification — **rav·en·ous·ly** *adv* — **rav·en·ous·ness** *n*

ra·vine \rə-'vēn\ *n* [F, mountain torrent, fr. MF, rapine, rush, fr. L *rapina* rapine] : a small narrow steep-sided valley larger than a gully, smaller than a canyon, and usu. worn by running water

rav·i·o·li \‚rav-ē-'ō-lē\ *n pl* [It] : little cases of dough containing a savory filling that are usu. boiled and served with a spicy tomato sauce

rav·ish \'rav-ish\ *vt* [MF *raviss-, ravir*, fr. L *rapere*] **1** : to seize and take away by violence **2** : to transport with emotion **3** : RAPE **4** : PLUNDER, ROB — **rav·ish·er** *n*

rav·ish·ing \'rav-i-shiŋ\ *adj* : unusually attractive, pleasing, or striking — **rav·ish·ing·ly** \-shiŋ-lē\ *adv*

¹**raw** \'ró\ *adj* **raw·er** \'ró(-ə)r\; **raw·est** \'ró-əst\ [OE *hrēaw*] **1** : not cooked **2 a** : being in or nearly in the natural state ⟨*raw* furs⟩ : not processed or manufactured ⟨*raw* milk⟩ ⟨*raw* data⟩ **b** : not diluted or blended ⟨*raw* spirits⟩ **3 a** : having the surface abraded or chafed ⟨a *raw* wound⟩; *also* : irritated as if by chafing ⟨a *raw* sore throat⟩ **b** : lacking covering : NAKED **4 a** : lacking experience or understanding : GREEN **b** : lacking comforts or refinements ⟨a *raw* frontier village⟩ **c** : VULGAR, COARSE ⟨a *raw* story⟩ **5** : disagreeably damp or cold ⟨a *raw* blustery November day⟩ — **raw·ly** \'ró-lē\ *adv* — **raw·ness** *n*

²**raw** *n* : a raw place or state; *esp* : NUDITY ⟨slept in the *raw*⟩

raw·boned \'ró-'bōnd\ *adj* : having little flesh : GAUNT

raw deal *n* : an instance of unfair treatment

¹**raw·hide** \'ró-‚hīd\ *n* **1** : untanned cattle skin **2** : a whip of untanned hide

²**rawhide** *vt* **-hid·ed; -hid·ing** : to whip or drive with or as if with a rawhide

raw material *n* : natural resources in an unprocessed state : material (as wood, petroleum, or grain) from which useful things can be produced

¹**ray** \'rā\ *n* [MF *raie*, fr. L *raia*] : any of numerous flat broad elasmobranch fishes (as a skate) that live on the sea bottom and have their eyes on the upper surface of their bodies and the tail long and narrow

²**ray** *n* [MF *rai*, fr. L *radius* rod, spoke, ray] **1 a** : one of the lines of light that appear to radiate from a bright ob-

---

j joke;   **ŋ** sing;   **ō** flow;   **ó** flaw;   **ói** coin;   **th** thin;   **th** this;   **ü** loot;   **ù** foot;   **y** yet;   **yü** few;   **yù** furious;   **zh** vision

ject **b :** a thin beam of radiant energy (as light) **c :** a stream of particles traveling (as in radioactive phenomena) in the same line **2 a :** light cast by rays **:** RADIANCE **b :** a moral or intellectual light **3 :** a thin line suggesting a ray: as **a :** any of a group of lines diverging from a common center **b :** HALF LINE **4 :** a plant or animal structure felt to resemble a ray: as **a :** one of the bony rods that support the fin of a fish **b :** one of the radiating divisions of the body of a radially symmetrical animal **c :** a band of tissue extending radially in a woody plant stem and usu. storing food or conducting raw material **d :** RAY FLOWER **5 :** PARTICLE, TRACE

³ray *vb* **:** to extend like the radii of a circle; *also* **:** RADIATE

rayed \'rād\ *adj* **:** having ray flowers

ray flower *n* **:** one of the marginal flowers of the head in a composite plant (as the aster) that also has disk flowers; *also* **:** any flower in the head of a plant (as chicory) that lacks disk flowers — called also *ray floret*

ray·less \'rā-ləs\ *adj* **:** lacking ray flowers — **ray·less·ness** *n*

ray·on \'rā-,än\ *n* **1 :** a smooth textile fiber made from cellulosic material by extrusion through minute holes **2 :** a rayon yarn, thread, or fabric

raze \'rāz\ *vt* [ME *rasen* to erase, fr. MF *raser* to scrape, erase] **:** to utterly destroy by or as if by laying level with the ground **:** DEMOLISH, OBLITERATE

ra·zor \'rā-zər\ *n* [OF *raseor*, fr. *raser* to scrape, shave, fr. L *ras-*, *radere*] **:** a sharp cutting instrument used esp. to shave off hair — **razor** *adj*

ra·zor·back \-,bak\ *n* **:** a thin-bodied long-legged half=wild mongrel hog chiefly of the southeastern U.S.

ra·zor·backed \,rā-zər-'bakt\ *or* **ra·zor·back** \'rā-zər-,bak\ *adj* **:** having a sharp narrow back ⟨a *razor-backed* horse⟩

razz \'raz\ *vt* [*raspberry*] **:** to banter mockingly **:** RIDICULE, TEASE, KID

¹re \'rā\ *n* [ML] **:** the 2d note of the diatonic scale

²re \(')rā, (')rē\ *prep* [L, abl. of *res* thing, matter] **:** with regard to **:** in re

re- \(')rē *before* '-stressed *syll*, (,)rē *before* ,-stressed *syll*, ,rē *before unstressed syll*\ *prefix* [L *re-*, *red-* back, again, against] **1 :** again **:** anew ⟨*retell*⟩ **2 :** back **:** backward ⟨*recall*⟩

Re \'rā\ *var of* RA

're \(ə)r\ *vb* **:** ARE ⟨what'*re* you doing⟩ ⟨they'*re* very nice children⟩

re·ab·sorb \,rē-əb-'sȯrb, -'zȯrb\ *vt* **:** to absorb again; *esp* **:** RESORB — **re·ab·sorp·tion** \-'sȯrp-shən, -'zȯrp-\ *n*

¹reach \'rēch\ *vb* [OE *rǣcan*] **1 a :** to stretch out **:** EXTEND ⟨*reached* out his arms⟩ **b :** to attempt to grasp something with or as if with the hand ⟨*reached* for a knife⟩ **c :** to touch or grasp by extending a part of the body or an object ⟨couldn't *reach* the apple on the tree⟩ **2 a :** to go as far as ⟨the shadow *reached* the wall⟩ **b :** to extend continuously ⟨his field *reaches* to the highway⟩ **c :** to go or function effectively ⟨as far as the eye can *reach*⟩ **3 a :** to arrive at **:** come to ⟨*reached* home late⟩; *also* **:** ACHIEVE ⟨*reached* an understanding⟩ **b :** to get or be delivered to ⟨your message *reached* me⟩ **4 :** to communicate with ⟨tried to *reach* you by phone⟩; *also* **:** to make an impression on **:** INFLUENCE ⟨cou!dn't *reach* his own son⟩ **5 :** to hand over **:** PASS ⟨*reach* me the salt⟩ **6 :** to sail on a reach — **reach·a·ble** \'rē-chə-bəl\ *adj* — **reach·er** *n*

²reach *n* **1 a** (1) **:** the action or an act of reaching (2) **:** an individual part of a progression or journey **b :** the distance or extent of reaching or of ability to reach **c :** COMPREHENSION, RANGE ⟨the subject was beyond his *reach*⟩ **2 :** a continuous unbroken stretch or expanse; *esp* **:** a straight portion of a stream or river **3 :** the tack sailed by a ship with the wind coming just forward of the beam or with the wind directly abeam or abaft the beam

re·act \rē-'akt\ *vb* **1 :** to exert a reciprocal or counter-acting force or influence — often used with *on* or *upon* **2 :** to act or behave in response ⟨*reacted* violently to his suggestion⟩; *also* **:** to respond to a stimulus **3 :** to act in opposition to a force or influence — usu. used with *against* **4 :** to move or tend in a reverse direction **5 :** to undergo or make undergo chemical reaction

re–act \(')rē-'akt\ *vt* **:** to act or perform a second time

re·ac·tance \rē-'ak-tən(t)s\ *n* **:** the part of the impedance of an alternating-current circuit due to capacitance or inductance or both and expressed in ohms

re·ac·tant \-tənt\ *n* **:** a chemically reacting substance

re·ac·tion \rē-'ak-shən\ *n* **1 a :** the act or process or an instance of reacting **b :** tendency toward a former esp. outmoded political or social order or policy **2 :** bodily response to or activity aroused by a stimulus: as **a :** the response of tissues to a foreign substance (as an allergen or infective agent) **b :** mental or emotional response (as to exhausting effort or one's life situation) **3 :** the force that a body subjected to the action of a force from another body exerts in the opposite direction **4 a :** chemical transformation or change **:** the action between atoms or molecules to form one or more new substances **b :** a process involving change in atomic nuclei — **re·ac·tion·al** \-shnəl, -shən-°l\ *adj* — **re·ac·tion·al·ly** \-ē\ *adv*

¹re·ac·tion·ary \rē-'ak-shə-,ner-ē\ *adj* **:** relating to, marked by, or favoring esp. political reaction

²reactionary *n*, *pl* **-aries :** a reactionary person

reaction time *n* **:** the time between the beginning of a stimulus and an individual's reaction to it

re·ac·ti·vate \(')rē-'ak-tə-,vāt\ *vb* **:** to make or become activated again — **re·ac·ti·va·tion** \(,)rē-,ak-tə-'vā-shən\ *n*

re·ac·tive \rē-'ak-tiv\ *adj* **1 :** of or relating to reaction or reactance **2 :** reacting or tending to react — **re·ac·tive·ly** *adv* — **re·ac·tive·ness** *n* — **re·ac·tiv·i·ty** \(,)rē-,ak-'tiv-ət-ē\ *n*

re·ac·tor \rē-'ak-tər\ *n* **1 :** one that reacts; *esp* **:** one that reacts positively to a foreign substance (as in a test for hypersensitivity or a disease) **2 a :** a vat for an industrial chemical reaction **b :** an apparatus in which a chain reaction of fissionable material is initiated and controlled — called also *nuclear reactor*

¹read \'rēd\ *vb* **read** \'red\; **read·ing** \'rēd-iŋ\ [OE *rǣdan* to advise, interpret, read] **1 a** (1) **:** to go over systematically by sight or touch to take in and understand the meaning of (as letters or symbols); *esp* **:** to perform such an action with written matter (2) **:** to study the movements of (a speaker's lips) and so understand what is being said (3) **:** to utter aloud the words represented by ⟨written matter⟩ (4) **:** to understand the written form of ⟨*reads* French⟩ **b :** to learn from what one has seen or found in writing or printing ⟨*read* that she got married⟩ ⟨*read* about his promotion⟩ **c :** to deliver aloud by or as if by reading; *esp* **:** to utter interpretatively **d :** to make a study of ⟨*read* law⟩ **e :** to take in and get the meaning of ⟨a transmitted message⟩ **2 a :** to interpret the meaning or significance of ⟨*read* palms⟩ **b :** FORETELL, PREDICT **3 :** to discover or perceive by interpreting outward expression or signs ⟨*read* guilt in his manner⟩ **4 a :** to attribute meaning or interpretation to **:** UNDERSTAND ⟨how do you *read* this passage⟩ **b :** to put or attribute as an assumption or conjecture ⟨*read* a nonexistent meaning into her words⟩ **5 :** to use as a substitute for or in preference to another word or phrase in a particular passage, text, or version ⟨*read* "hurry" for "harry"⟩ **6 :** INDICATE ⟨thermometer *reads* zero⟩ **7 :** to interpret (a musical work) in performance **8 :** to pursue a course of study **9 :** to yield a particular meaning or impression when read **10 :** to consist of specific words, phrases, or symbols ⟨the passage *reads* differently in older versions⟩ — **read·a·bil·i·ty** \,rēd-ə-'bil-ət-ē\ *n* — **read·a·ble** \'rēd-ə-bəl\ *adj* — **read·a·ble·ness** *n* — **read·a·bly** \-blē\ *adv* — **read between the lines :** to understand more than is directly stated — **read the riot act 1 :** to give an order or warning to cease something **2 :** to give a severe reprimand

²read \'red\ *adj* **:** taught or informed by reading ⟨a well=*read* man⟩ ⟨widely *read* in history⟩

read·er \'rēd-ər\ *n* **1 :** one that reads **2 :** one appointed to read to others: as **a :** LECTOR **b :** one chosen to read aloud selected material in a Christian Science church or society **3 :** a book for instruction and practice esp. in reading

read·er·ship \-,ship\ *n* **1 :** the office or position of a reader **2 :** the mass or a particular group of readers

read·i·ly \'red-°l-ē\ *adv* **:** in a ready manner: as **a :** WILLINGLY **b :** SPEEDILY **c :** EASILY

| See *re-* and 2d element | reacquire | reactuate | readapt | readdress |
| reaccommodate | | | | |

read·i·ness \'red-ē-nəs\ *n* : the quality or state of being ready

read·ing \'rēd-iŋ\ *n* **1 a** : material read or for reading **b** : extent of material read **2 a** : a particular version **b** : something that is registered (as on a gauge) ⟨the thermometer *reading* was 70 degrees⟩ **3** : a particular interpretation or performance **4** : the introduction of a proposed bill to a legislative body by reading aloud all or a part of it

reading desk *n* : a desk to support a book in a convenient position for a standing reader

reading glass *n* : a magnifying glass usu. on a handle used esp. for reading fine print

read out \(')rēd-'aút\ *vt* : to drive out officially : EXPEL

read·out \'rēd-,aút\ *n* : a device that displays data (as in a computer)

¹ready \'red-ē\ *adj* **read·i·er** \-ē-ər\; **-est** [ME *redy*] **1** : prepared for use or action ⟨dinner is *ready*⟩ **2** : APT, LIKELY ⟨*ready* to cry⟩ **3** : WILLING ⟨*ready* to give aid⟩ **4** : notably dexterous, adroit, or skilled **5** : PROMPT ⟨a *ready* answer⟩ **6** : AVAILABLE, HANDY ⟨*ready* money⟩

²ready *vt* **read·ied**; **ready·ing** : to make ready

³ready *n* : the state of being ready; *esp* : preparation of a gun for immediate aiming or firing

ready-made \,red-ē-'mād\ *adj* **1** : made beforehand for general sale ⟨*ready-made* suit⟩ **2** : lacking individuality : COMMONPLACE

ready room *n* : a room in which pilots are briefed and await takeoff orders

ready-to-wear \,red-ē-tə-'wa(ə)r, -'we(ə)r\ *adj* : READY-MADE 1

ready-wit·ted \,red-ē-'wit-əd\ *adj* : QUICK-WITTED

re·agent \rē-'ā-jənt\ *n* : one that reacts or induces a reaction; *esp* : a substance that takes part in or brings about a particular chemical reaction ⟨a fixing *reagent* for tissues⟩ ⟨a *reagent* for etching steel⟩

re·agin \rē-'ā-jən\ *n* [*reagent* + *-in*] : an antibody in the blood of some allergic individuals that can passively sensitize the skin of normal individuals — **re·agin·ic** \,rē-ə-'jin-ik\ *adj* — **re·agin·i·cal·ly** \-'jin-i-k(ə-)lē\ *adv*

¹re·al \'rē(-ə)l\ *adj* [LL *realis* actual & ML *realis* of property, fr. L *res* thing, fact, property] **1** : of, relating to, or constituting fixed, permanent, or immovable things (as lands, houses, or fixtures) ⟨*real* property⟩ **2 a** : not artificial, fraudulent, illusory, or apparent : GENUINE ⟨*real* gold⟩ **b** : occurring in fact **c** (1) : necessarily existent (2) : FUNDAMENTAL, ESSENTIAL **d** : measured by purchasing power rather than by money received ⟨*real* income⟩ — **re·al·ness** *n*

syn REAL, ACTUAL, TRUE mean corresponding to known facts. REAL implies an agreement between what a thing seems to be and what it is ⟨this is a *real* diamond⟩ ACTUAL stresses occurrence or existence as action or fact ⟨the *actual* temperature today is higher than predicted⟩ TRUE implies conforming to what is real or actual ⟨a *true* account of the incident⟩ or to a model or standard ⟨proved himself a *true* friend⟩

²real *n* : a real thing; *esp* : REAL NUMBER

³real *adv* : VERY ⟨we had a *real* good time⟩

⁴re·al \rā-'äl\ *n, pl* **re·als** *or* **re·ales** \-'äl-ās\ [Sp, fr. *real* royal, fr. L *regalis*] : the chief former monetary unit of Spain

real estate *n* : property in houses and land

re·al·gar \rē-'al-,gär, -gər\ *n* [Ar *rahj al-ghār* powder of the mine] : an orange-red mineral As_4S_4 or AsS consisting of a sulfide of arsenic and having a resinous luster

real image *n* : an image of an object formed by rays of light coming to a focus (as after passing through a lens or after being reflected by a concave mirror)

re·al·ism \'rē-ə-,liz-əm\ *n* **1** : the belief that objects we perceive through our senses are real and have an existence outside our own minds **2** : the disposition to see situations or difficulties in the light of facts and to deal with them practically **3** : the representation in literature and art of things as they are in life — **re·al·ist** \-ləst\ *n*

re·al·is·tic \,rē-ə-'lis-tik\ *adj* **1** : true to life or nature ⟨a *realistic* painting⟩ **2** : having or showing an inclination to face facts and to deal with them sensibly — **re·al·is·ti·cal·ly** \-ti-k(ə-)lē\ *adv*

re·al·i·ty \rē-'al-ət-ē\ *n, pl* **-ties** **1** : actual existence : GENUINENESS ⟨doubt the *reality* of sea serpents⟩ **2** : someone or something real or actual ⟨the *realities* of life⟩ **3** : the characteristic of being true to life or to fact

re·al·ize \'rē-ə-,līz\ *vt* **1** : to make actual : ACCOMPLISH ⟨*realize* a lifelong ambition⟩ **2** : to convert into money ⟨*realized* his assets⟩ **3** : to bring or get by sale, investment, or effort : GAIN ⟨*realize* a large profit⟩ **4** : to be aware of : UNDERSTAND ⟨*realized* his danger⟩ — **re·al·iz·a·ble** \'rē-ə-,lī-zə-bəl\ *adj* — **re·al·i·za·tion** \,rē-ə-lə-'zā-shən\ *n* — **re·al·iz·er** *n*

re·al·ly \'rē-(ə)lē\ *adv* **1 a** : in reality : ACTUALLY **b** : UNQUESTIONABLY, TRULY **2** : INDEED

realm \'relm\ *n* [OF *realme*, modif. of L *regimen* rule] **1** : KINGDOM **2** : SPHERE, DOMAIN ⟨the *realm* of fancy⟩

real number *n* : any number (as −2, 3, ⅞, .25, √2, π) which is not an imaginary number

Re·al·tor \'rē(-ə)l-tər\ *n* : a real estate agent who is a member of the National Association of Real Estate Boards

re·al·ty \'rē(-ə)l-tē\ *n, pl* **-ties** [*real* + *-ty* (as in *property*)] : REAL ESTATE

¹ream \'rēm\ *n* [MF *raime*, a quantity of paper, fr. Ar *rizmah*, lit., bundle] **1** : a quantity of paper being 20 quires or variously 480, 500, or 516 sheets **2** : a great amount — usu. used in pl.

²ream *vt* **1** : to widen the opening of (a hole) : COUNTERSINK **2** : to shape, enlarge, or dress (a hole) with a reamer **3** : to remove by reaming

ream·er \'rē-mər\ *n* **1** : a rotating tool with cutting edges for enlarging or shaping a hole **2** : a juice extractor with a ridged and pointed center rising from a shallow dish

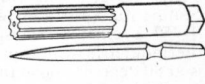
reamers 1

re·an·i·mate \(')rē-'an-ə-,māt\ *vb* : to give life to anew : REVIVE

reap \'rēp\ *vb* [OE *repan*] **1 a** (1) : to cut with a sickle, scythe, or reaping machine (2) : to clear of a crop by so cutting **b** : to gather by so cutting : HARVEST **2** : to gain as a reward ⟨*reap* the benefit of many years of hard work⟩

reap·er \'rē-pər\ *n* : one that reaps; *esp* : a machine for reaping grain

re·ap·pear \,rē-ə-'pi(ə)r\ *vi* : to appear again — **re·ap·pear·ance** \-'pir-ən(t)s\ *n*

¹rear \'ri(ə)r\ *vb* [OE *rǣran*; akin to E *rise*] **1** : to erect by building : CONSTRUCT **2 a** : to raise upright **b** : to rise high ⟨skyscrapers *rearing* above the city⟩ **c** : to rise up on the hind legs ⟨the horse *reared* in fright⟩ **3 a** : to undertake the breeding and raising of ⟨*rear* cattle⟩ **b** : to bring up (a person)

²rear *n* [prob. fr. MF *rere-* backward, behind, fr. L *retro*] **1** : the back part of something: as **a** : the unit (as of an army) or area farthest from the enemy **b** : BUTTOCKS **2** : the space or position at the back ⟨the *rear* of a building⟩

³rear *adj* : being at the back

rear admiral *n* : a commissioned officer in the navy ranking above a captain and below a vice admiral

rear guard *n* : a military detachment detailed to bring up and protect the rear of a main body or force

re·arm \(')rē-'ärm\ *vb* : to arm again esp. with new or better weapons — **re·ar·ma·ment** \-'är-mə-mənt\ *n*

rear·most \'ri(ə)r-,mōst\ *adj* : farthest in the rear

re·ar·range \,rē-ə-'rānj\ *vt* : to arrange again esp. in a different way

¹rear·ward \'ri(ə)r-wərd\ *adj* **1** : located at, near, or toward the rear **2** : directed toward the rear : BACKWARD — **rear·ward·ly** *adv*

²rearward *also* **rear·wards** \-wərdz\ *adv* : at, near, or toward the rear : BACKWARD

¹rea·son \'rēz-ⁿn\ *n* [OF *raison*, fr. L *ration-*, *ratio* com-

---

---

j joke;   ŋ sing;   ō flow;   ȯ flaw;   ȯi coin;   th thin;   th this;   ü loot;   u̇ foot;   y yet;   yü few;   yu̇ furious;   zh vision

putation, reason, fr. *reri* to calculate, think] **1 a :** a statement offered in explanation or justification ⟨asked to give a *reason* for his absence⟩ **b :** a rational ground or motive ⟨*reasons* for thinking life may exist on Mars⟩ **c :** the thing that makes some fact intelligible **:** CAUSE **2 a :** the power of comprehending, inferring, or thinking esp. in orderly logical ways see INTELLIGENCE **b :** SANITY **syn** see CAUSE — **in reason :** with reason **:** JUSTIFIABLY, RIGHTLY — **within reason :** within reasonable limits **with reason :** with good cause **:** JUSTIFIABLY

²reason *vb* **rea·soned; rea·son·ing** \'rēz-niŋ, -°n-iŋ\ **1 :** to talk persuasively or to present reasons in order to cause a change of mind ⟨*reason* with someone for hours⟩ **2 a :** to use one's reason or to think in a logical way or manner **b :** to state, formulate, or conclude by use of reason ⟨*reasoned* that both statements couldn't be true⟩ **syn** see THINK

rea·son·a·ble \'rēz-nə-bəl, -°n-ə-bəl\ *adj* **1 a :** agreeable to reason ⟨a *reasonable* theory⟩ **b :** not extreme or excessive **:** MODERATE **c :** INEXPENSIVE **2 a :** having the faculty of reason **:** RATIONAL **b :** possessing sound judgment — **rea·son·a·bil·i·ty** \ˌrēz-nə-'bil-ət-ē, -°n-ə-\ *n* — **rea·son·a·ble·ness** \'rēz-nə-bəl-nəs, -°n-ə-\ *n* — **rea·son·a·bly** \-blē\ *adv*

rea·son·ing *n* **1 :** the use of reason; *esp* **:** the drawing of inferences or conclusions through the use of reason **2 :** the reasons used in and the proofs that result from thought **:** ARGUMENT

re·as·sur·ance \ˌrē-ə-'shùr-ən(t)s\ *n* **:** the action of reassuring **:** the state of being reassured

re·as·sure \ˌrē-ə-'shù(ə)r\ *vt* **1 :** to assure anew **2 :** to restore to confidence **3 :** to insure anew

re·ata \rē-'at-ə, -'ät-\ *n* [AmerSp] **:** LARIAT

Re·au·mur \ˌrā-ō-'myü(ə)r\ *adj* [after R.A.F. de *Réaumur* d1757 French physicist] **:** relating or conforming to a thermometric scale on which the boiling point of water is at 80 degrees above the zero of the scale and the freezing point is at zero

reave \'rēv\ *vb* **reaved** *or* **reft** \'reft\; **reav·ing** [OE *rēafian*] *archaic* **:** PLUNDER, ROB — **reav·er** *n*

reb \'reb\ *n* **:** JOHNNY REB

¹re·bate \'rē-ˌbāt, ri-'\ *vt* [MF *rabattre* to beat down again, fr. OF, fr. *re-* + *abattre* to beat down] **:** to make a rebate of **:** give as a rebate — **re·bat·er** *n*

²re·bate \'rē-ˌbāt\ *n* **:** a return of a portion of a payment **:** ABATEMENT

re·bec *or* **re·beck** \'rē-ˌbek\ *n* [MF *rebec*, alter. of OF *rebebe*, fr. OProv *rebeb*, fr. Ar *rebāb*] **:** an old bowed usu. 3-stringed musical instrument with a pear-shaped body and slender neck

Re·bek·ah *or* **Re·bec·ca** \ri-'bek-ə\ *n* **:** the wife of Isaac

¹reb·el \'reb-əl\ *adj* [ME, fr. OF *rebelle*, fr. L *rebellis*, fr. *re-* re-, against + *bellum* war] **1 a :** opposing or taking arms against the government or ruler **b :** of or relating to rebels **2 :** DISOBEDIENT, REBELLIOUS

²rebel *n* **:** one who rebels or participates in a rebellion

³re·bel \ri-'bel\ *vi* **re·belled; re·bel·ling 1 a :** to oppose or resist authority or control **b :** to renounce and resist by force the authority of one's government **2 :** to feel or exhibit anger or revulsion

re·bel·lion \ri-'bel-yən\ *n* **1 :** opposition to one in authority or dominance **2 a :** open defiance of or resistance to an established government **b :** an instance of such defiance or resistance **:** REVOLT, UPRISING

syn REVOLT, REVOLUTION: REBELLION implies open, organized, often armed resistance to authority; REVOLT suggests an armed uprising that quickly succeeds or fails; REVOLUTION applies to a successful rebellion resulting in a change of government and often of social structure

re·bel·lious \ri-'bel-yəs\ *adj* **1 :** engaged in rebellion **2 :** inclined to resist or disobey authority **:** INSUBORDINATE — **re·bel·lious·ly** *adv* — **re·bel·lious·ness** *n*

re·bind \(')rē-'bīnd\ *vt* **-bound** \-'baùnd\; **-bind·ing :** to bind anew or again

re·birth \(')rē-'bərth\ *n* **1 :** a new or second birth **2 :** RENAISSANCE, REVIVAL

re·born \(')rē-'bórn\ *adj* **:** born again **:** REVIVED

¹re·bound \ri-'baùnd\ *vi* **1 :** to spring back on striking something **2 :** to recover from setback or frustration

²re·bound \'rē-ˌbaùnd, ri-'\ *n* **1 a :** the action of rebounding **:** RECOIL **b :** an upward leap or movement **2 a :** a basketball or hockey puck that rebounds **b :** the act of taking a basketball rebound **3 :** an immediate spontaneous reaction to setback, frustration, or crisis

re·branch \(')rē-'branch\ *vi* **:** to form secondary branches

re·broad·cast \(')rē-'bród-ˌkast\ *vt* **-cast** *also* **-cast·ed; -cast·ing 1 :** to broadcast again (a radio or television program being simultaneously received from another source) **2 :** to repeat (a broadcast) at a later time — **rebroadcast** *n*

¹re·buff \ri-'bəf\ *vt* [MF *rebuffer*, fr. obs. It *ribuffare*] **1 :** SNUB **2 :** to drive or beat back

²rebuff *n* **1 :** an abrupt refusal to meet an advance or offer **:** SNUB **2 :** a sharp check **:** REPULSE

re·build \(')rē-'bild\ *vb* **-built** \-'bilt\; **-build·ing 1 a :** to make extensive repairs to **b :** to restore to a previous state **2 :** to make extensive changes in **:** REMODEL **3 :** to build again ⟨planned to *rebuild* after the fire⟩

¹re·buke \ri-'byük\ *vt* [ONF *rebuker*] **:** to scold or criticize sharply **:** REPRIMAND **syn** see REPROVE — **re·buk·er** *n*

²rebuke *n* **:** REPRIMAND, REPROOF

re·bus \'rē-bəs\ *n* [L, by things, abl. pl. of *res* thing] **:** a representation of words or syllables by pictures of objects whose names resemble the intended words or syllables in sound; *also* **:** a riddle made up of such pictures or symbols

re·but \ri-'bət\ *vt* **re·but·ted; re·but·ting** [OF *reboter* to drive back, fr. *re-* + *boter* to butt] **1 :** to contradict or oppose by formal argument, plea, or contrary proof **2 :** to expose the falsity of **:** REFUTE ⟨*rebuts* a long-accepted dictum⟩ — **re·but·ta·ble** \-'bət-ə-bəl\ *adj*

re·but·tal \ri-'bət-°l\ *n* **:** the act of rebutting; *also* **:** argument or proof that rebuts

re·cal·ci·trance \ri-'kal-sə-trən(t)s\ *or* **re·cal·ci·tran·cy** \-trən-sē\ *n* **:** the state of being recalcitrant

re·cal·ci·trant \ri-'kal-sə-trənt\ *adj* [L *recalcitrare* to kick back, fr. *re-* + *calc-, calx* heel] **1 :** obstinately defiant of authority or restraint **2 :** not responsive to handling or treatment — **recalcitrant** *n*

¹re·call \ri-'kól\ *vt* **1 a :** to ask or order to come back **b :** to bring back to mind **2 :** CANCEL, REVOKE **3 :** RESTORE, REVIVE **syn** see REMEMBER — **re·call·a·ble** \-'kó-lə-bəl\ *adj*

²re·call \ri-'kól, 'rē-ˌ\ *n* **1 :** a summons to return **2 :** the right or procedure by which an official may be removed by vote of the people on petition **3 :** remembrance of what has been learned or experienced **4 :** the act of revoking; *also* **:** the possibility of being revoked ⟨the matter is beyond *recall*⟩

re·cant \ri-'kant\ *vb* [L *recantare*, fr. *re-* + *cantare* to sing] **:** to withdraw or repudiate a statement of opinion or belief formally and publicly **:** RENOUNCE, DISCLAIM — **re·can·ta·tion** \ˌrē-ˌkan-'tā-shən\ *n*

syn RECANT, RETRACT mean to withdraw publicly something declared or professed. RECANT implies admission of error in something one has openly professed or taught; RETRACT applies to the withdrawing of a promise, an accusation, or an offer

¹re·cap \(')rē-'kap\ *vt* **re·capped; re·cap·ping :** to cement, mold, and vulcanize a strip of rubber upon the surface of the tread of (a worn automobile tire)

²re·cap \'rē-ˌkap\ *n* **:** a recapped tire

³re·cap \ri-'kap, 'rē-ˌ\ *vt* **re·capped; re·cap·ping :** RECAPITULATE ⟨now, to *recap* the news⟩

⁴re·cap \'rē-ˌkap, ri-'\ *n* **:** RECAPITULATION ⟨a *recap* of the news highlights⟩

re·ca·pit·u·late \ˌrē-kə-'pich-ə-ˌlāt\ *vb* [LL *recapitulare*,

---

See *re-* and 2d element	reassess	reassume	reattainment	rebaptize
reassail	reassessment	reassumption	reattempt	rebid
reassemble	reassign	reattach	reauthorize	reboil
reassembly	reassignment	reattachment	reawake	reburial
reassert	reassort	reattack	reawaken	rebury
reassertion	reassortment	reattain	rebaptism	

fr. L *re-* + *capitulum* heading, fr. *capit-*, *caput* head]
: to repeat briefly : SUMMARIZE
re·ca·pit·u·la·tion \-ˌpich-ə-'lā-shən\ *n* **1** : a concise
summary **2** : the supposed repetition in an individual of
the phylogenetic history of its group — **re·ca·pit·u·la·to·ry** \-'pich-ə-lə-ˌtōr-ē, -ˌtȯr-\ *adj*
re·cap·ture \(')rē-'kap-chər\ *n* : the act of retaking : the
fact of being retaken : RECOVERY — **recapture** *vt*
re·cast \(')rē-'kast\ *vt* -cast; -cast·ing : to cast again
⟨*recast* a cannon⟩ ⟨*recast* a play⟩ — **re·cast** \(')rē-'kast, 're-\ *n*
re·cede \ri-'sēd\ *vi* [L *recedere*, fr. *re-* + *cedere* to go]
1 a : to move back or away : WITHDRAW ⟨the *receding*
tide⟩ **b** : to slant backward ⟨a *receding* forehead⟩ **2** : to
grow less : CONTRACT
¹**re·ceipt** \ri-'sēt\ *n* [ONF *receite*, fr. ML *recepta*, fr. L
recept-, *recipere* to receive] **1** : RECIPE **2** : the act or
process of receiving **3** : something received — usu. used
in pl. **4** : a writing acknowledging the receiving of
goods or money
²**receipt** *vt* **1** : to give a receipt for or acknowledge the
receipt of **2** : to mark as paid
re·ceiv·a·ble \ri-'sē-və-bəl\ *adj* **1** : capable of being
received **2** : subject to call for payment ⟨accounts
receivable⟩
re·ceiv·a·bles \-bəlz\ *n pl* : amounts of money receivable
re·ceive \ri-'sēv\ *vb* [ONF *receivre*, fr. L *recipere*, fr.
re- + *capere* to take] **1** : to take or get something that is
given, paid, or sent ⟨*receive* the money⟩ ⟨*receive* a letter⟩ **2**
: to permit to enter one's household or company : WELCOME,
GREET ⟨*receive* friends⟩ **3** : to hold a reception ⟨*receive* from
four to six o'clock⟩ **4** : to undergo or be subjected to ⟨an
experience or treatment⟩ ⟨*receive* a shock⟩ **5** : to change
incoming radio waves into sounds or pictures
syn ACCEPT, TAKE: RECEIVE normally implies passiveness
but usu. suggests physical contact or presence; ACCEPT
implies some element of consent or approval but a minimum of physical activity ⟨he *accepted* the award and
attended a dinner where he was to *receive* it⟩ TAKE may
imply seizing or picking up what is offered ⟨*take* a bribe⟩
⟨*take* a hint⟩ or enduring what is inflicted ⟨*took* his
opponent's best blows and came on to win⟩
re·ceiv·er \ri-'sē-vər\ *n* : one that receives: as **a** : a
person appointed to take control of property that is involved in a lawsuit or of a business that is bankrupt or is
being reorganized **b** (1) : an apparatus for receiving radio
or television broadcasts (2) : the portion of a telegraphic or
telephonic apparatus that converts the electric currents
or waves into visible or audible signals **c** : an offensive
football player who may catch a forward pass
re·ceiv·er·ship \-ˌship\ *n* **1** : the office or function of a
receiver **2** : the state of being in the hands of a receiver
receiving set *n* : an apparatus for receiving radio or television signals
re·cen·cy \'rēs-ᵊn-sē\ *n* : the quality or state of being
recent : RECENTNESS
re·cent \'rēs-ᵊnt\ *adj* [L *recent-*, *recens*] **1 a** : of or relating to a time not long past **b** : having lately appeared or
come into existence : NEW, FRESH **2** *cap* : of, relating to,
or being the present epoch of the Quaternary which is
dated from the close of the Pleistocene — **re·cent·ly** *adv*
— **re·cent·ness** *n*
syn MODERN, LATE: RECENT suggests comparative nearness to the present ⟨*recent* discoveries in nuclear physics⟩
MODERN implies being characteristic of the present age
⟨*modern* methods of teaching⟩ LATE applies to what has
recently ceased to exist or is no longer what it was ⟨his
late father's estate⟩ ⟨his *late* residence⟩
re·cep·ta·cle \ri-'sep-ti-kəl\ *n* [L *receptaculum*, fr.
receptare, freq. of *recipere* to receive] **1** : something used
to receive and contain smaller objects : CONTAINER
2 : the enlarged end of the flower stalk upon which the
floral organs are borne **3** : an electrical fitting (as a
socket) into which another fitting may be pushed or
screwed for making an electrical connection
re·cep·tion \ri-'sep-shən\ *n* [L *recept-*, *recipere* to receive]
: the act or process of receiving: as **a** : RECEIPT **b** : AD-
MISSION **c** (1) : WELCOME, RESPONSE (2) : a social gathering **d** : the receiving of a radio or television broadcast

re·cep·tion·ist \ri-'sep-sh(ə-)nəst\ *n* : an office employee
who is usu. a woman and who greets callers, answers
questions, and arranges appointments
re·cep·tive \ri-'sep-tiv\ *adj* **1** : able or inclined to receive
ideas **2** : able to receive and transmit stimuli : SENSORY
— **re·cep·tive·ly** *adv* — **re·cep·tive·ness** *n* — **re·cep·tiv·i·ty** \ˌrē-ˌsep-'tiv-ət-ē, ri-\ *n*
re·cep·tor \ri-'sep-tər\ *n* : a cell or group of cells that
receives stimuli : SENSE ORGAN
¹**re·cess** \'rē-ˌses, ri-'\ *n* [L *recessus*, fr. *recedere* to recede]
1 : a hidden, secret, or secluded place **2** **a** : a space or
little hollow set back (as from the main line of a coast
or mountain range) : INDENTATION **b** : ALCOVE **3** : a
suspension of business or procedure; *esp* : a brief period
for relaxation between class or study periods of a school
day
²**recess** *vb* **1** : to put into a recess ⟨*recessed* lighting⟩
2 : to make a recess in **3** : to interrupt for or take a recess
re·ces·sion \ri-'sesh-ən\ *n* **1** : the act or fact of receding
or withdrawing **2** : a departing procession (as of clergy
and choir at the end of a church service) **3** : a downward
turn in business activity; *also* : the period of such a downward turn
re·ces·sion·al \ri-'sesh-nəl, -ən-ᵊl\ *n* : a hymn or musical
piece at the conclusion of a service or program; *also*
: RECESSION 2
¹**re·ces·sive** \ri-'ses-iv\ *adj* **1** : tending to go back
: RECEDING **2** : subordinate to a contrasting allele in
manifestation — compare DOMINANT — **re·ces·sive·ly**
adv — **re·ces·sive·ness** *n*
²**recessive** *n* : a recessive character or factor or an organism
possessing one or more such characters
re·cher·ché \rə-ˌsher-'shā\ *adj* [F, fr. pp. of *rechercher*
to seek with care, research] **1** : CHOICE, RARE **2** : excessively refined : PRECIOUS
rec·i·pe \'res-ə-(ˌ)pē\ *n* [L, take, imper. of *recipere* to take,
receive] **1** : PRESCRIPTION 3 **2** : a set of instructions for
making something (as a food dish) from various ingredients
3 : method of procedure ⟨a *recipe* for happiness⟩
re·cip·i·ent \ri-'sip-ē-ənt\ *n* [L *recipient-*, *recipiens*, prp.
of *recipere* to receive] : one that receives ⟨the *recipient* of
many honors⟩ — **recipient** *adj*
¹**re·cip·ro·cal** \ri-'sip-rə-kəl\ *adj* [L *reciprocus* returning
the same way, alternating, irreg. fr. *re-* back + *pro-*
forward] **1** : done or felt equally by both sides ⟨*reciprocal*
affection⟩ **2** : related to each other in such a way that
one completes the other or is the equivalent of the other
: mutually corresponding — **re·cip·ro·cal·ly** \-k(ə-)lē\
adv
syn RECIPROCAL, MUTUAL, COMMON mean shared or experienced by each. RECIPROCAL implies an equal return or
counteraction by each of two sides ⟨*reciprocal* lowering
of tariffs⟩ MUTUAL applies to feelings or effects shared by
two jointly ⟨*mutual* affection⟩ ⟨*mutual* admirers⟩ COMMON
implies only being shared by others ⟨united in a *common*
purpose⟩
²**reciprocal** *n* **1** : something in a reciprocal relationship
to another **2** : one of a pair of numbers (as 9, ⅑; ⅔, 3/2)
whose product is one
re·cip·ro·cate \ri-'sip-rə-ˌkāt\ *vb* **1** : to give and take
mutually : EXCHANGE **2** : to make a return for something
3 : to move forward and backward alternately ⟨a *reciprocating* mechanical part⟩ — **re·cip·ro·ca·tion** \-ˌsip-
rə-'kā-shən\ *n* — **re·cip·ro·ca·tor** \-'sip-rə-ˌkāt-ər\ *n*
reciprocating engine *n* : an engine in which the to-and-fro
motion of a piston is transformed into circular motion of
the crankshaft
rec·i·proc·i·ty \ˌres-ə-'präs-ət-ē\ *n, pl* -ties **1** : mutual
dependence, cooperation, or exchange between persons,
groups, or states **2** : international policy by which special
commercial advantages are granted to one country in
return for special advantages granted by another
re·cit·al \ri-'sīt-ᵊl\ *n* **1** : a reciting of something; *esp*
: a story told in detail ⟨the *recital* of his troubles⟩ **2** : a
program of one kind of music ⟨a piano *recital*⟩ **3** : a
public performance by pupils (as music or dancing pupils)
— **re·cit·al·ist** \-ᵊl-əst\ *n*
rec·i·ta·tion \ˌres-ə-'tā-shən\ *n* **1** : an enumeration or
telling in detail **2** : the act or an instance of reading or

See *re-* and 2d element				
recarbonize	rechannel	recharter	recheck	rechristen
	recharge			

repeating aloud esp. publicly **3 a** : a student's oral reply to questions **b** : a class period

rec·i·ta·tive \,res-(ə-)tə-'tēv\ n [It *recitativo*, fr. *recitare* to recite, fr. L] : a rhythmically free declamatory vocal style used for dialogue and narrative in operas and oratorios; *also* : a passage in this style — **recitative** *adj*

re·cite \ri-'sīt\ vb [L *recitare*, fr. *re-* + *citare* to summon] **1** : to repeat from memory or read aloud publicly ⟨*recite* a poem⟩ **2 a** : to give a detailed narration of **b** : STATE **3** : to answer (as to a teacher) questions about a lesson — **re·cit·er** n

reck \'rek\ vi [OE *reccan*] **1** : CARE, MIND **2** : to be of interest : MATTER

reck·less \'rek-ləs\ adj **1 a** : marked by lack of caution : RASH **b** : IRRESPONSIBLE, WILD **2** : CARELESS, NEGLIGENT **syn** see DARING — **reck·less·ly** adv — **reck·less·ness** n

reck·on \'rek-ən\ vb **reck·oned; reck·on·ing** \'rek-(ə-)niŋ\ [OE *-recnian*] **1 a** : COUNT, COMPUTE ⟨*reckon* the days till Christmas⟩ **b** : to estimate by calculation ⟨*reckon* the height of a building⟩ **2** : CONSIDER, REGARD ⟨was *reckoned* among the leaders⟩ **3** *chiefly dial* : THINK, SUPPOSE ⟨*reckoned* he hadn't a chance to win⟩ **4** : to make up or settle an account **5** : to count on : DEPEND ⟨*reckon* on support⟩ — **reck·on·er** \-(ə-)nər\ n — **reckon with** : to take into account — **reckon without** : to fail to take into account

reck·on·ing n **1** : the act or an instance of reckoning: as **a** : ACCOUNT, BILL **b** : COMPUTATION **c** : calculation of a ship's position **2** : a settling of accounts ⟨day of *reckoning*⟩ **3** : APPRAISAL

re·claim \ri-'klām\ vt [OF *reclamer* to call back, fr. *re-* + *clamer* to call out, claim] **1** : to recall from wrong or improper conduct : REFORM **2** : to alter from an undesirable or uncultivated state ⟨*reclaim* swampland for agriculture⟩ **3** : to obtain from a waste product or by-product : RECOVER ⟨*reclaimed* wool⟩ — **re·claim·a·ble** \-'klā-mə-bəl\ adj — **re·claim·er** n

rec·la·ma·tion \,rek-lə-'mā-shən\ n : the act or process of reclaiming : the state of being reclaimed

re·cline \ri-'klīn\ vb [L *reclinare*, fr. *re-* + *clinare* to bend] **1** : to lean or cause to lean backwards **2** : REPOSE, LIE ⟨*reclining* on the sofa⟩

¹rec·luse \'rek-,lüs, ri-'klüs\ adj [LL *reclusus*, pp. of *recludere* to shut up, fr. L *re-* + *claudere* to close] : marked by withdrawal from society : SOLITARY — **re·clu·sive** \ri-'klü-siv, -ziv\ adj

²recluse n : a person (as a hermit) who lives away from others

rec·og·ni·tion \,rek-ig-'nish-ən, ,rek-əg-\ n [L *recognit-*, *recognoscere* to recognize] **1** : the act of recognizing ⟨her *recognition* of the old man⟩ **2** : special attention or notice **3** : acknowledgment of something done or given (as by making an award) ⟨got a medal in *recognition* of bravery⟩ **4** : formal acknowledgment of the political existence of a government or nation

rec·og·niz·a·ble \'rek-ig-,nī-zə-bəl, 'rek-əg-\ adj : capable of being recognized — **rec·og·niz·a·bil·i·ty** \,rek-ig-,nī-zə-'bil-ət-ē, ,rek-əg-\ n — **rec·og·niz·a·bly** adv

re·cog·ni·zance \ri-'käg-nə-zən(t)s, -'kän-ə-\ n : a recorded legal promise to do something (as to appear in court or to keep the peace)

rec·og·nize \'rek-ig-,nīz, 'rek-əg-\ vt [modif. of MF *reconoiss-, reconoistre*, fr. L *recognoscere*, fr. *re-* + *cognoscere* to know, fr. *co-* + *gnoscere, noscere* to know] **1** : to know and remember upon seeing ⟨*recognize* a person⟩ **2** : to consent to admit : ACKNOWLEDGE ⟨*recognized* her own faults⟩ **3** : to take approving notice of ⟨*recognize* an act of bravery by the award of a medal⟩ **4** : to acknowledge acquaintance with ⟨*recognize* someone with a nod⟩ **5** : to acknowledge as entitled to be heard at a meeting ⟨the chair *recognizes* the delegate from Illinois⟩ **6** : to grant diplomatic recognition to ⟨*recognized* the new government⟩

¹re·coil \ri-'kȯil\ vi [OF *reculer*, fr. *re-* + *cul* backside, fr. L *culus*] **1 a** : to fall back under pressure ⟨the soldiers

recoiled before the savage attack of the enemy⟩ **b** : to shrink back ⟨*recoil* in horror at the sight of blood⟩ **2** : to spring back to or as if to a starting point ⟨the compressed spring *recoiled* upon release⟩ ⟨the big gun *recoiled* upon firing⟩

²re·coil \ri-'kȯil, 'rē-,\ n **1** : the act or action of recoiling : REBOUND **2** : a springing back (as of a discharged gun or a spring) **3** : the distance through which something (as a spring) recoils

re·coil·less \ri-'kȯil-ləs, 'rē-,\ adj : having a minimum of recoil ⟨a *recoilless* gun⟩

re·col·lect \,rē-kə-'lekt\ vt : to collect again; *esp* : RALLY, RECOVER

rec·ol·lect \,rek-ə-'lekt\ vb **1** : to recall to mind : REMEMBER **2** : to remind (oneself) of something temporarily forgotten **syn** see REMEMBER

rec·ol·lec·tion \,rek-ə-'lek-shən\ n **1** : the action or power of recalling to mind : REMEMBRANCE **2** : something recalled to the mind **syn** see MEMORY

re·com·bi·nant \(')rē-'käm-bə-nənt\ n : an individual exhibiting genetic recombination

re·com·bi·na·tion \,rē-,käm-bə-'nā-shən\ n : the formation of new combinations of genes either by normal union in fertilization or by crossing-over — **re·com·bi·na·tion·al** \-shnəl, -shən-ᵊl\ adj

rec·om·mend \,rek-ə-'mend\ vt **1** : to make a statement in praise of; *esp* : to endorse as fit, worthy, or competent ⟨*recommend* a person for a position⟩ **2** : to put forward or suggest as one's advice, as one's choice, or as having one's support ⟨*recommend* that the matter be dropped⟩ **3** : to cause to receive favorable attention ⟨a man *recommended* by his good manners⟩ — **rec·om·mend·a·ble** \-'men-də-bəl\ adj — **rec·om·mend·er** n

rec·om·men·da·tion \,rek-ə-mən-'dā-shən, -,men-\ n **1** : the act of recommending **2** : something that recommends ⟨a written *recommendation*⟩ **3** : a thing or course of action recommended

re·com·mit \,rē-kə-'mit\ vt **1** : to refer (as a bill) again to a committee **2** : to commit again — **re·com·mit·ment** \-mənt\ n — **re·com·mit·tal** \-'mit-ᵊl\ n

¹rec·om·pense \'rek-əm-,pen(t)s\ vt [LL *recompensare*, fr. L *re-* + *compensare* to compensate] **1** : to give compensation to or for : REPAY, PAY

²recompense n : an equivalent or return for something done, suffered, or given : COMPENSATION

rec·on·cil·a·bil·i·ty \,rek-ən-,sī-lə-'bil-ət-ē\ n : the quality or state of being reconcilable

rec·on·cil·a·ble \,rek-ən-'sī-lə-bəl\ adj : capable of being reconciled — **rec·on·cil·a·ble·ness** n

rec·on·cile \'rek-ən-,sīl\ vt [L *reconciliare*, fr. *re-* + *conciliare* to conciliate] **1** : to make friendly again ⟨*reconcile* friends who have quarreled⟩ **2** : SETTLE, ADJUST ⟨*reconcile* differences of opinion⟩ **3** : to make agree ⟨a story that cannot be *reconciled* with the facts⟩ **4** : to cause to submit or to accept : make content ⟨*reconciled* himself to the loss⟩ — **rec·on·cile·ment** \-mənt\ n — **rec·on·cil·er** n — **rec·on·cil·i·a·tion** \,rek-ən-,sil-ē-'ā-shən\ n — **rec·on·cil·ia·to·ry** \,rek-ən-'sil-yə-,tōr-ē, -,tȯr-\ adj

rec·on·dite \'rek-ən-,dīt, ri-'kän-\ adj [L *reconditus*, pp. of *recondere* to put away, conceal, fr. *re-* + *condere* to store up, fr. *re-* + *-dere* to put] **1** *archaic* : hidden from sight : CONCEALED **2** : incomprehensible to one of ordinary understanding or knowledge : DEEP ⟨a *recondite* subject⟩ **3** : of, relating to, or dealing with something little known or obscure — **rec·on·dite·ly** adv — **rec·on·dite·ness** n

re·con·di·tion \,rē-kən-'dish-ən\ vt : to restore to good condition (as by repairing or replacing parts) ⟨a *reconditioned* used car⟩

re·con·firm \,rē-kən-'fərm\ vt : to confirm again; *also* : to establish more strongly — **re·con·fir·ma·tion** \(,)rē-,kän-fər-'mā-shən\ n

re·con·nais·sance \ri-'kän-ə-zən(t)s\ n [F, lit., recognition, fr. MF *reconoissance*, fr. *reconoiss-*, *reconoistre* to

ə abut; ᵊ kitten; ər further; a back; ā bake; ä cot, cart; aů out; ch chin; e less; ē easy; g gift; i trip; ī life

recognize] **:** a preliminary survey to gain information; *esp* **:** an exploratory military survey of enemy territory

re·con·noi·ter \ˌrē-kə-'nȯit-ər, ˌrek-ə-\ *vb* [obs. F *reconnoître*, lit., to recognize, fr. MF *reconnoistre*] **:** to make a reconnaissance; *esp* **:** to survey in preparation for military action ⟨*reconnoiter* enemy territory⟩

re·con·sid·er \ˌrē-kən-'sid-ər\ *vb* **:** to consider again esp. with a view to change or reversal — **re·con·sid·er·a·tion** \-ˌsid-ə-'rā-shən\ *n*

re·con·sti·tute \(')rē-'kän(t)-stə-ˌt(y)üt\ *vt* **:** to restore to a former condition by adding water ⟨*reconstitute* powdered milk⟩

re·con·struct \ˌrē-kən-'strəkt\ *vt* **:** to construct again **:** REBUILD, REMODEL

re·con·struc·tion \ˌrē-kən-'strək-shən\ *n* **1 a :** the action of reconstructing **:** the state of being reconstructed **b** *often cap* **:** the reorganization and reestablishment of the seceded states in the Union after the American Civil War **2 :** something reconstructed

re·con·ver·sion \ˌrē-kən-'vər-zhən\ *n* **:** conversion back to a previous state

re·con·vert \ˌrē-kən-'vərt\ *vb* **:** to convert back

¹re·cord \ri-'kȯrd\ *vb* [OF *recorder* to recall to mind, fr. L *recordari*, fr. *re-* + *cord-, cor* heart] **1 a** (1) **:** to set down in writing (2) **:** to deposit an authentic official copy of ⟨*record* a deed⟩ **b** (1) **:** to register permanently (2) **:** INDICATE, READ ⟨the thermometer *recorded* 90°⟩ **2 :** to cause (as sound or visual images) to be registered (as on a phonograph disc or magnetic tape) in reproducible form **3 :** to admit of being recorded or reproduced ⟨a voice that *records* well⟩ **4 :** to give evidence of

²rec·ord \'rek-ərd, -ˌȯrd\ *n* **1 :** the state or fact of being recorded ⟨on *record*⟩ ⟨a matter of *record*⟩ **2 :** something that records: as **a :** something that recalls or relates past events **b :** an official writing that records the proceedings or acts of a group, organization, or official **c :** an authentic official copy of a document **3 a :** the known or recorded facts regarding something or someone ⟨his school *record* is good⟩ **b :** an attested top performance ⟨broke the broad jump *record*⟩ **4 :** something on which sound or visual images have been recorded for later reproduction; *esp* **:** a disc with a spiral groove carrying recorded sound for phonograph reproduction

³rec·ord \'rek-ərd\ *adj* **:** setting a record **:** outstanding among other like things ⟨a *record* crop⟩ ⟨*record* prices⟩

rec·or·da·tion \ˌrek-ˌȯr-'dā-shən, ˌrē-ˌkȯr-\ *n* **:** the action or process of recording

re·cord·er \ri-'kȯrd-ər\ *n* **1 :** a person or device that records **2 :** a municipal judge with criminal and sometimes limited civil jurisdiction **3 :** a fipple flute with eight finger holes

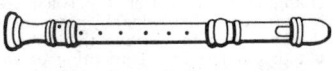

recorder 3

re·cord·ing \ri-'kȯrd-iŋ\ *n* **:** RECORD 4

re·cord·ist \ri-'kȯrd-əst\ *n* **:** one who records sound esp. on film

rec·ord player \'rek-ərd-\ *n* **:** an electronic instrument for playing phonograph records through a usu. incorporated loudspeaker

¹re·count \ri-'kaůnt\ *vt* [MF *reconter*, fr. *re-* + *conter* to count, relate] **:** to relate in detail **:** NARRATE ⟨*recount* an adventure⟩

²re·count \(')rē-'kaůnt\ *vt* **:** to count again

³re·count \(')rē-'kaůnt, 'rē-ˌ\ *n* **:** a second or fresh count (as of election votes)

re·coup \ri-'küp\ *vt* [F *recouper* to cut back, fr. *re-* + *couper* to cut] **1 :** to make up for **:** RECOVER ⟨*recoup* a loss⟩ **2 :** REIMBURSE, COMPENSATE ⟨*recoup* a person for losses⟩ — **re·coup·a·ble** \-'kü-pə-bəl\ *adj* — **re·coup·ment** \-'küp-mənt\ *n*

re·course \'rē-ˌkōrs, -ˌkȯrs, ri-'\ *n* [MF *recours*, fr. LL *recursus*, fr. L, act of running back, fr. *re-* + *curs-, currere* to run] **1 :** a turning for assistance or protection

⟨have *recourse* to the law⟩ **2 :** a source of help or strength **:** RESORT

re·cov·er \ri-'kəv-ər\ *vb* **-cov·ered; -cov·er·ing** \-'kəv-(ə-)riŋ\ [MF *recoverer*, fr. L *recuperare*] **1 :** to get back **:** REGAIN ⟨*recover* a lost wallet⟩ ⟨*recovered* his breath⟩ **2 :** to bring back to normal position or condition ⟨stumbled, then *recovered* himself⟩ **3 a :** to make up for ⟨*recover* lost time⟩ **b :** to gain by legal process ⟨*recover* damages⟩; *also* **:** to recover damages at law **4** *archaic* **:** REACH **5 :** RECLAIM ⟨*recover* gold from ore⟩ **6 :** to regain health, consciousness, or self-control — **re·cov·er·a·ble** \-'kəv-(ə-)rə-bəl\ *adj*

re·cov·er \(')rē-'kəv-ər\ *vt* **:** to cover again or anew

re·cov·ery \ri-'kəv-(ə-)rē\ *n*, *pl* **-er·ies :** the act or process or an instance of recovering; *esp* **:** return to a former normal state (as of health or spirits)

recovery room *n* **:** a hospital room equipped for meeting emergencies following surgery or childbirth

¹rec·re·ant \'rek-rē-ənt\ *adj* [MF, fr. prp. of *recroire* to renounce one's cause in a trial by battle, fr. *re-* + *croire* to believe, fr. L *credere*] **1 :** crying for mercy **:** COWARDLY **2 :** unfaithful to duty or allegiance

²recreant *n* **1 :** COWARD **2 :** DESERTER, APOSTATE

rec·re·ate \'rek-rē-ˌāt\ *vt* **:** to give new life or freshness to — **rec·re·a·tive** \-ˌāt-iv\ *adj*

re·cre·ate \ˌrē-krē-'āt\ *vt* **:** to create anew esp. in the imagination — **re·cre·a·tion** \-'ā-shən\ *n* — **re·cre·a·tive** \-'āt-iv\ *adj*

rec·re·a·tion \ˌrek-rē-'ā-shən\ *n* [L *recreare* to restore, refresh, fr. *re-* + *creare* to create] **:** refreshment of strength and spirits after toil **:** DIVERSION; *also* **:** a means of refreshment or diversion (as a game or exercise) — **rec·re·a·tion·al** \-shnəl, -shən-ᵊl\ *adj*

re·crim·i·nate \ri-'krim-ə-ˌnāt\ *vi* **1 :** to make a retaliatory charge against an accuser **2 :** to retort bitterly — **re·crim·i·na·tion** \-ˌkrim-ə-'nā-shən\ *n* — **re·crim·i·na·to·ry** \-'krim-ə-nə-ˌtōr-ē, -ˌtȯr-\ *adj*

re·cru·desce \ˌrē-krü-'des\ *vi* **:** to break out or become active again

re·cru·des·cence \ˌrē-krü-'des-ᵊn(t)s\ *n* [L *recrudescere* to become raw again, fr. *re-* + *crudus* raw, crude] **:** a renewal or breaking out again esp. of something unhealthful or dangerous ⟨*recrudescence* of an epidemic⟩ — **re·cru·des·cent** \-ᵊnt\ *adj*

¹re·cruit \ri-'krüt\ *n* [F *recrute, recrue* fresh growth, new levy of soldiers, fr. MF, fr. *recroistre* to grow up again, fr. L *recrescere*, fr. *re-* + *crescere* to grow] **1 :** a newcomer to a field or activity; *esp* **:** a newly enlisted or drafted member of the armed forces **2 :** an enlisted man of the lowest rank in the army

²recruit *vb* **1 a :** to fill up the number of (as an army) with new members **:** REINFORCE **b :** to enlist new members **:** RAISE **c :** to secure the services of **:** ENGAGE **2 :** REPLENISH **3 :** to restore or increase the health, vigor, or intensity of — **re·cruit·er** *n* — **re·cruit·ment** \-'krüt-mənt\ *n*

rect·an·gle \'rek-ˌtaŋ-gəl\ *n* [ML *rectangulum* having a right angle, fr. L *rectus* right + *angulus* angle] **:** a parallelogram all of whose angles are right angles

rect·an·gu·lar \rek-'taŋ-gyə-lər\ *adj* **1 :** having a flat surface shaped like a rectangle **2 a :** crossing, lying, or meeting at a right angle **b :** having lines or surfaces that meet at right angles ⟨*rectangular* coordinates⟩ — **rect·an·gu·lar·i·ty** \(ˌ)rek-ˌtaŋ-gyə-'lar-ət-ē\ *n* — **rect·an·gu·lar·ly** \rek-'taŋ-gyə-lər-lē\ *adv*

rectangle

rec·ti·fi·a·ble \'rek-tə-ˌfī-ə-bəl\ *adj* **:** capable of being rectified

rec·ti·fi·er \'rek-tə-ˌfī(-ə)r\ *n* **:** one that rectifies; *esp* **:** a device for converting alternating current into direct current

rec·ti·fy \'rek-tə-ˌfī\ *vt* **-fied; -fy·ing** [MF *rectifier*, fr. ML *rectificare*, fr. L *rectus* right, fr. pp. of *regere* to lead straight, direct; akin to E *right*] **1 :** to set right **:** REMEDY **2 :** to purify (as alcohol) esp. by repeated or fractional

See *re-* and 2d element	reconsecration	reconsult	recontract	recouple
reconnect	reconsign	reconsultation	reconvene	recross
reconquer	reconsignment	recontact	recook	recrystallization
reconquest	reconstructible	recontaminate	recopy	recrystallize
reconsecrate	reconstructive	recontamination		

distillation **3 :** to correct by removing errors **:** ADJUST ⟨*rectify* the calendar⟩ **4 :** to convert (an alternating current) into a direct current **syn** see CORRECT — **rec·ti·fi·ca·tion** \,rek-tə-fə-'kā-shən\ *n*

rec·ti·lin·e·ar \,rek-tə-'lin-ē-ər\ *adj* **1 :** moving in, being in, or forming a straight line⟨*rectilinear* motion⟩ **2 :** characterized by straight lines — **rec·ti·lin·e·ar·ly** *adv*

rec·ti·tude \'rek-tə-,t(y)üd\ *n* [LL *rectitudo*, fr. L *rectus* straight, right] **1 :** STRAIGHTNESS **2 :** moral integrity **:** RIGHTEOUSNESS

rec·to \'rek-tō\ *n, pl* **rectos** [NL *recto folio* the page being straight] **:** a right-hand page — compare VERSO

rec·tor \'rek-tər\ *n* [L, guide, director, fr. *rect-, regere* to lead straight, direct] **1 :** a clergyman in charge of a church or parish **2 :** the priest in charge of certain Roman Catholic religious houses for men **3 :** the head of a university or school

rec·to·ry \'rek-t(ə-)rē\ *n, pl* **-ries :** a rector's residence

rec·trix \'rek-triks\ *n, pl* **rec·tri·ces** \'rek-trə-,sēz\ [NL, fr. L, fem. of *rector* one that directs] **:** one of the stiff quill feathers of a bird's tail that are important in controlling flight direction

rec·tum \'rek-təm\ *n, pl* **rectums** *or* **rec·ta** \-tə\ [NL, fr. *rectum intestinum*, lit., straight intestine] **:** the last part of the intestine linking the colon to the anus — **rec·tal** \-t⁰l\ *adj*

rec·tus \'rek-təs\ *n, pl* **rec·ti** \-,tī, -,tē\ [L *rectus* straight] **:** any of several straight muscles (as of the abdomen)

re·cum·ben·cy \ri-'kəm-bən-sē\ *n* **:** recumbent position **:** REPOSE

re·cum·bent \-bənt\ *adj* [L *recumbere* to recline, fr. *re- + -cumbere* to lie down] **1 :** RESTING **2 :** lying down — **re·cum·bent·ly** *adv*

re·cu·per·ate \ri-'k(y)ü-pə-,rāt\ *vb* [L *recuperare*] **:** to get back **:** RECOVER; *esp* **:** to regain health or strength — **re·cu·per·a·tion** \-,k(y)ü-pə-'rā-shən\ *n*

re·cu·per·a·tive \ri-'k(y)ü-pə-,rāt-iv, -p(ə-)rət-\ *adj* **:** of, relating to, or promoting recuperation ⟨*recuperative* powers⟩

re·cur \ri-'kər\ *vi* **re·curred; re·cur·ring** [L *recurrere*, lit., to run back, return, fr. *re- + currere* to run] **1 :** to go or come back in thought or discussion ⟨*recur* to the subject of an earlier conversation⟩ **2 :** to come again into the mind ⟨a childhood memory that *recurred* over and over again⟩ **3 :** to occur or appear again ⟨a fever that *recurred*⟩ — **re·cur·rence** \-'kər-ən(t)s, -'kə-rən(t)s\ *n*

re·cur·rent \ri-'kər-ənt, -'kə-rənt\ *adj* **1 :** returning from time to time **:** RECURRING ⟨a *recurrent* fever⟩ **2 :** running or turning back in direction ⟨a *recurrent* vein⟩ — **re·cur·rent·ly** *adv*

re·curve \(')rē-'kərv\ *vb* **:** to curve backward or inward

¹**red** \'red\ *adj* **red·der; red·dest** [OE *rēad*] **1 a :** of the color red **b :** having red as a distinguishing color **2 a** (1) **:** FLUSHED (2) **:** RUDDY, FLORID (3) **:** BLOODSHOT **b :** of a coppery hue **c :** in the color range between a moderate orange and russet or bay **d :** REDDISH **3 a :** inciting or endorsing radical social or political change esp. by force **b :** COMMUNIST **c :** of or relating to the U.S.S.R. or a Communist country — **red·ly** *adv* — **red·ness** *n*

²**red** *n* **1 :** a color whose hue resembles that of blood or the ruby or is that of the long-wave extreme of the visible spectrum **2 :** one that is of a red or reddish color **3 :** a pigment or dye that colors red **4 a :** REVOLUTIONARY **b** *cap* **:** COMMUNIST **5** [fr. the bookkeeping practice of entering debit items in red ink] **:** the condition of showing a loss ⟨in the red⟩

re·dact \ri-'dakt\ *vt* **1 :** to put in writing **:** FRAME **2 :** EDIT — **re·dac·tor** \-'dak-tər\ *n*

re·dac·tion \ri-'dak-shən\ *n* [L *redact-, redigere* to bring back, reduce, fr. *re-, red-* re- + *agere* to lead] **1 :** an act or instance of redacting **2 :** EDITION — **re·dac·tion·al** \-shnəl, -shən-⁰l\ *adj*

red alga *n* **:** an alga (division Rhodophyta) having predominantly red pigmentation

red·bird \'red-,bərd\ *n* **:** any of several birds (as a cardinal, several tanagers, or the bullfinch) with predominantly red plumage

red blood cell *n* **:** one of the hemoglobin-containing cells that carry oxygen to the tissues and are responsible for the red color of vertebrate blood — called also *red blood corpuscle*

red-blood·ed \'red-'bləd-əd\ *adj* **:** VIGOROUS, LUSTY

red·bone \'red-,bōn\ *n* **:** a speedy medium-sized dark red or red and tan American hound

red·breast \'red-,brest\ *n* **:** a bird (as a robin) with a reddish breast

red·cap \-,kap\ *n* **:** a baggage porter (as at a railroad station)

red–car·pet \'red-'kär-pət\ *adj* [fr. the traditional laying down of a red carpet for important guests to walk on] **:** marked by ceremonial courtesy ⟨*red-carpet* treatment⟩

red cedar *n* **:** an American juniper with fragrant close=grained red wood; *also* **:** its wood

red cell *n* **:** RED BLOOD CELL — called also *red corpuscle*

red clover *n* **:** a Eurasian clover with globose heads of reddish purple flowers widely grown as a hay, forage, and cover crop

red·coat \'red-,kōt\ *n* **:** a British soldier esp. during the Revolutionary War

red cross *n* **:** a red-colored cross on a white background used as a badge for hospitals and for members of an international organization that helps the suffering esp. in war or disaster areas

¹**redd** \'red\ *vb* **redd·ed** *or* **redd; redd·ing** [ME *redden* to clear] **1** *chiefly dial* **:** to set in order **2** *chiefly dial* **:** to make things tidy

²**redd** *n* **:** the spawning place or nest of a fish

red deer *n* **:** the common deer of temperate Europe and Asia related to but smaller than the elk

red·den \'red-⁰n\ *vb* **red·dened; red·den·ing** \'red-niŋ, -⁰n-iŋ\ **:** to make or become red or reddish; *esp* **:** BLUSH

red·dish \'red-ish\ *adj* **:** somewhat red — **red·dish·ness** *n*

red·dle \'red-⁰l\, **red·dle·man** \-mən\ *var of* RUDDLE, RUDDLEMAN

rede \'rēd\ *vt* [OE *rēdan* to advise, explain, read] **1** *dial* **:** to give counsel to **:** ADVISE **2** *dial* **:** INTERPRET, EXPLAIN

red·ear \'red-,i(ə)r\ *n* **:** a common American sunfish with orange-red marks on the gill cover

re·dec·o·rate \(')rē-'dek-ə-,rāt\ *vb* **1 :** to freshen or change in appearance **:** REFURBISH **2 :** to freshen or change a decorative scheme — **re·dec·o·ra·tion** \(,)rē-,dek-ə-'rā-shən\ *n*

re·deem \ri-'dēm\ *vt* [MF *redimer*, fr. L *redimere*, fr. *re-, red-* re- + *emere* to take, buy] **1 a :** to buy back **:** REPURCHASE **b :** to get or win back **2 a :** RANSOM **b :** LIBERATE **c :** to free from the bondage of sin **3 :** to change for the better **4 :** REPAIR, RESTORE **5 a :** to regain (a pledge) by payment of an amount secured thereby **b :** to remove the obligation of by payment **c :** to convert into something of value **6 a :** to atone for **:** EXPIATE **b :** to offset the bad effect of **:** RETRIEVE **7 :** to make good **:** FULFILL ⟨*redeem* a promise⟩ **syn** see RESCUE — **re·deem·a·ble** \-'dē-mə-bəl\ *adj*

re·deem·er \ri-'dē-mər\ *n* **:** a person who redeems; *esp, cap* **:** JESUS

red eft *n* **:** an individual of the reddish terrestrial phase of a common American newt that has also a spotted aquatic phase

re·demp·tion \ri-'dem(p)-shən\ *n* [L *redempt-, redimere* to redeem] **:** the act or process or an instance of redeeming — **re·demp·tion·al** \-shnəl, -shən-⁰l\ *adj* — **re·demp·tive** \-'dem(p)-tiv\ *adj*

Re·demp·tor·ist \ri-'dem(p)-t(ə-)rəst\ *n* **:** a member of the Roman Catholic Congregation of the Most Holy Redeemer

re·de·sign \,rēd-i-'zīn\ *vt* **:** to revise in appearance, function, or content — **redesign** *n*

re·de·vel·op·ment \,rēd-i-'vel-əp-mənt\ *n* **:** the act or process of redeveloping; *esp* **:** renovation of a blighted area

red–eye \'red-,ī\ *n* **:** cheap whiskey

red·fish \'red-,fish\ *n* **:** any of various reddish to bright red fishes

red fox *n* **:** a common fox with orange-red to dusky reddish brown fur — see FOX illustration

See *re-* and 2d element				
recut	rededicate	redefinition	redemand	redeposit
recycle	rededication	redeliver	redemandable	redevelop
	redefine	redelivery	redeploy	redeveloper

ə abut; ⁰ kitten; ər further; a back; ā bake; ä cot, cart; aů out; ch chin; e less; ē easy; g gift; i trip; ī life

red gum *n* : an American timber tree with palmately lobed leaves and hard reddish wood; *also* : its wood

red-hand·ed \'red-'han-dəd\ *adv* (*or adj*) : in the act of committing a crime or misdeed

red·head \'red-,hed\ *n* **1** : a person having red hair **2** : an American duck related to the canvasback but having in the male a brighter rufous head and shorter bill

red heat *n* : the state of being red-hot; *also* : the temperature at which a substance is red-hot

red herring *n* **1** : a herring cured by salting and slow smoking to a dark brown color **2** [fr. the practice of drawing a red herring across a trail to confuse hunting dogs] : a diversion intended to distract attention from the real issue

red-hot \'red-'hät\ *adj* **1** : glowing red with heat **2** : exhibiting or marked by intense emotion, enthusiasm, or energy ⟨a *red-hot* political campaign⟩ **3** : FRESH, NEW

re·dia \'rēd-ē-ə\ *n, pl* **re·di·ae** \-ē-,ē\ *also* **re·di·as** : a larva produced within the sporocyst of many trematodes that produces another generation of rediae or develops into a cercaria — **re·di·al** \-ē-əl\ *adj*

Red Indian *n* : INDIAN 2a — called also *Red Man*

red·in·gote \'red-iŋ-,gōt\ *n* [F, fr. E *riding coat*] : a fitted outer garment: as **a** : a woman's lightweight coat open at the front **b** : a dress with a front gore of contrasting material

red·in·te·grate \ri-'dint-ə-,grāt, re-\ *vt* [L *redintegrare*, fr. *re-, red-* re- + *integrare* to integrate] *archaic* : to restore to a former or sound state — **red·in·te·gra·tion** \-,dint-ə-'grā-shən, ,rē-, (,)re-\ *n*

re·di·rect \,rēd-ə-'rekt, ,red-(,)dī-\ *vt* : to change the course or direction of — **re·di·rec·tion** \-'rek-shən\ *n*

¹re·dis·count \(')rē-'dis-,kaunt, ,rē-dis-'\ *vt* : to discount again (as commercial paper) — **re·dis·count·a·ble** \-ə-bəl\ *adj*

²re·dis·count \(')rē-'dis-,kaunt\ *n* : the act or process of rediscounting

re·dis·trict \(')rē-'dis-(,)trikt\ *vt* : to divide anew into districts; *esp* : to revise the legislative districts of

red jasmine *n* : a widely cultivated frangipani with large terminal cymes of pink, red, or purple fragrant flowers

red lead *n* : a red lead oxide Pb_3O_4 used in storage-battery plates, in glass and ceramics, and as a paint pigment

red-let·ter \'red-'let-ər\ *adj* [fr. the practice of marking holy days in red letters in church calendars] : memorable esp. in a happy or joyful way ⟨a *red-letter* day⟩

red maple *n* : a common American maple with reddish twigs and rather soft wood

red marrow *n* : reddish bone marrow that is the seat of blood-cell production

red mass *n, often cap R & M* : a votive mass of the Holy Ghost celebrated in red vestments esp. at the opening of courts and congresses

red-neck \'red-,nek\ *n* : a member of the Southern rural laboring class

re·do \(')rē-'dü\ *vt* **-did** \-'did\; **-done** \-'dən\; **-do·ing** : to do over or again; *esp* : REDECORATE ⟨*redid* the bedroom in blue⟩

red oak *n* : any of numerous American oaks with acorns that take two years to mature

red ocher *n* : a red earthy hematite used as a pigment

red·o·lence \'red-ºl-ən(t)s\ *n* **1** : the quality or state of being redolent **2** : SCENT, AROMA

red·o·lent \-ənt\ *adj* [L *redolēre* to emit a scent, fr. *re-, red-* re- + *olēre* to smell] **1** : exuding fragrance : AROMATIC **2 a** : full of a specified fragrance : SCENTED ⟨a room *redolent* of tobacco smoke⟩ **b** : EVOCATIVE, REMINISCENT — **red·o·lent·ly** *adv*

re·dou·ble \(')rē-'dəb-əl\ *vb* **1** : to make or become doubled (as in size, amount, or degree) ⟨*redoubled* his efforts⟩ **2** : to double back ⟨the fox *redoubled* on his tracks⟩ **3** : to double again; *esp* : to double an opponent's double in bridge

re·doubt \ri-'daut\ *n* [F *redoute*, fr. It *ridotto*, fr. ML *reductus* secret place, fr. L, withdrawn, fr. pp. of *reducere* to lead back] : a small often temporary fortification (as for defending a hilltop)

re·doubt·a·ble \ri-'daut-ə-bəl\ *adj* [MF, fr. *redouter* to dread, fr. *re-* + *douter* to doubt] : arousing fear or dread : FORMIDABLE ⟨a *redoubtable* warrior⟩ — **re·doubt·a·bly** \-blē\ *adv*

re·dound \ri-'daund\ *vi* [MF *redonder*, fr. L *redundare* to overflow, fr. *re-, red-* re- + *unda* wave] **1** : to become reflected back esp. so as to bring credit or discredit : have a result or effect ⟨actions that *redound* to a man's credit⟩

re·dox \'rē-,däks\ *n* : OXIDATION-REDUCTION

red pepper *n* : CAYENNE PEPPER

red·poll \'red-,pōl\ *n* : any of several small finches which resemble siskins and in which the males usu. have a red or rosy crown

¹re·dress \ri-'dres\ *vt* [MF *redresser*, fr. *re-* + *dresser* to straighten, dress] **1** : to set (as a wrong) right : make amends for : REMEDY, RELIEVE **2** : to correct or amend the faults of

²re·dress \ri-'dres, 'rē-,\ *n* **1 a** : relief from distress **b** : means or possibility of seeking a remedy **2** : compensation for wrong or loss **3 a** : an act or instance of redressing **b** : CORRECTION, RETRIBUTION

red siskin *n* : a So. American finch that is scarlet with black head, wings, and tail and is often kept as a cage bird

red·skin \'red-,skin\ *n* : a No. American Indian

red snapper *n* : any of several reddish sea fishes including some esteemed for food or sport

red snow *n* : snow reddened by various airborne dusts or esp. by a growth of reddish algae

red spider *n* : any small web-spinning mite that attacks forage and crop plants

red·start \'red-,stärt\ *n* [obs. *start* tail, fr. OE *steort*] **1** : a small red-tailed European thrush **2** : an American fly-catching warbler

red tape *n* [fr. the red tape formerly used to bind legal documents in England] : official routine or procedure esp. as marked by delay or inaction

red tide *n* : seawater discolored and made toxic by the presence of large numbers of dinoflagellates — compare GYMNODINIUM

red·top \'red-,täp\ *n* : any of several grasses with reddish panicles including an important forage and lawn grass of eastern No. America

re·duce \ri-'d(y)üs\ *vb* [L *reducere* to lead back, fr. *re-* + *ducere* to lead] **1 a** : to draw together or cause to converge : CONSOLIDATE **b** : to diminish in size, amount, extent, or number ⟨*reduce* the number of accidents⟩; *esp* : to lose weight by dieting **c** : to undergo meiosis **2** : to bring to a specified state or condition ⟨*reduce* anarchy to order⟩ **3** : to force to surrender **4 a** : to bring to a systematic form or character ⟨*reduce* language to writing⟩ ⟨*reduced* his observations to a theorem⟩ **b** : to become converted or equated ⟨their differences *reduced* to a question of semantics⟩ **5** : to correct (as a fracture) by bringing displaced or broken parts back into normal position **6 a** : to lower in grade or rank : DEMOTE **b** : to lower in condition or status ⟨*reduced* to panhandling⟩ **c** : to diminish in strength or intensity **d** : to diminish in value **7 a** : to change the denominations or form of without changing the value **b** : to transpose from one form into another **8** : to break down (as by crushing or grinding) ⟨*reduce* metal from its ore⟩ **9 a** : to bring to the metallic state by removal of nonmetallic elements **b** : DEOXIDIZE **c** : to combine with or subject to the action of hydrogen **d** (1) : to change (an element or ion) from a higher to a lower oxidation state (2) : to add one or more electrons to (an atom or ion or molecule) — **re·duc·er** *n* — **re·duc·i·bil·i·ty** \-,d(y)ü-sə-'bil-ət-ē\ *n* — **re·duc·i·ble** \-'d(y)ü-sə-bəl\ *adj* — **re·duc·i·bly** \-blē\ *adv*

reducing agent *n* : a substance that reduces; *esp* : a substance (as hydrogen or sodium) that donates electrons to another substance

re·duc·tase \ri-'dək-,tās\ *n* : an enzyme that catalyzes a chemical reduction

re·duc·tio ad ab·sur·dum \ri-'dək-tē-,ō-,ad-əb-'sərd-əm, -'zərd-\ *n* [LL, reduction to the absurd] : disproof of a proposition by showing that it contradicts accepted propositions when carried to its logical conclusion

See *re-* and 2d element				
redifferentiation	redip	redisposition	redistribute	redraft
redigest	rediscover	redissolve	redistribution	redraw
redigestion	rediscovery	redistill	redomesticate	redrawer
	redispose	redistillation		

re·duc·tion \ri-'dək-shən\ *n* **1** : the act or process of reducing : the state of being reduced **2 a** : the amount by which something is reduced in price **b** : something made by reducing **3** : a So. American Indian settlement directed by Spanish missionaries **4** : MEIOSIS; *esp* : halving of the chromosome number in the first meiotic division — **re·duc·tion·al** \-shnəl, -shən-ᵊl\ *adj* — **re·duc·tive** \-'dək-tiv\ *adj*

reduction division *n* : the first division of meiosis in which chromosome reduction occurs; *also* : MEIOSIS

re·dun·dan·cy \ri-'dən-dən-sē\ *n, pl* **-cies** **1** : the quality or state of being redundant : SUPERFLUITY **2** : PROFUSION, ABUNDANCE **3 a** : superfluous repetition : PROLIXITY **b** : an act or instance of needless repetition

re·dun·dant \ri-'dən-dənt\ *adj* [L *redundare* to overflow, fr. *re-, red-* re- + *unda* wave] **1 a** : exceeding what is necessary or normal **b** : characterized by or containing more words than necessary : REPETITIOUS **2** : PROFUSE, LAVISH — **re·dun·dant·ly** *adv*

re·du·pli·cate \ri-'d(y)ü-pli-ˌkāt, 'rē-\ *vt* **1** : to make or perform again : COPY **2** : to form (a word) by reduplication — **re·du·pli·cate** \-kət\ *adj*

re·du·pli·ca·tion \ri-ˌd(y)ü-pli-'kā-shən, ˌrē-\ *n* **1** : an act or instance of doubling or reiterating : DUPLICATION **2** : repetition of a radical element or a part of it occurring usu. at the beginning of a word and often accompanied by change of the radical vowel — **re·du·pli·ca·tive** \ri-'d(y)ü-pli-ˌkāt-iv, 'rē-\ *adj* — **re·du·pli·ca·tive·ly** *adv*

red·wing \'red-ˌwiŋ\ *n* **1** : a red-winged European thrush **2** : REDWING BLACKBIRD

red·wing blackbird *or* **red–winged blackbird** \ˌred-ˌwiŋ(d)-\ *n* : a No. American blackbird of which the adult male is black with a patch of bright scarlet on the wing

red·wood \'red-ˌwùd\ *n* **1** : a tree yielding a red dye or having red or reddish wood **2** : a tall coniferous timber tree of California; *also* : its light durable brownish red wood

re·echo \(')rē-'ek-ō\ *vb* : to echo back : REVERBERATE ⟨thunder *reechoed* through the valley⟩

reed \'rēd\ *n* [OE *hrēod*] **1 a** : any of various tall grasses having slender often prominently jointed stems and growing esp. in wet areas **b** : a stem or a growth or mass of reeds **2** : ARROW **3** : a musical instrument made of the hollow joint of a plant **4** : an ancient Hebrew unit of length equal to 6 cubits **5 a** : a thin elastic tongue (as of cane, wood, metal, or plastic) fastened at one end to the mouthpiece of a musical instrument (as a clarinet) or to a fixture (as a reed block) over an air opening (as in an accordion) and set in vibration by an air current (as the breath) **b** : a reed instrument ⟨the *reeds* of an orchestra⟩ **6** : a device on a loom resembling a comb and used to space warp yarns evenly

reed·bird \'rēd-ˌbərd\ *n, chiefly South* : BOBOLINK

reed·buck \-ˌbək\ *n, pl* **reedbuck** *also* **reedbucks** : any of several fawn-colored African antelopes with hornless females

reed organ *n* : a keyboard wind instrument in which the wind acts on a set of metal reeds

re·ed·u·cate \(')rē-'ej-ə-ˌkāt\ *vt* : to train again; *esp* : to rehabilitate through education — **re·ed·u·ca·tion** \(ˌ)rē-ˌej-ə-'kā-shən\ *n* — **re·ed·u·ca·tive** \(')rē-'ej-ə-ˌkāt-iv\ *adj*

reedy \'rēd-ē\ *adj* **reed·i·er; -est** **1** : abounding in or covered with reeds ⟨a *reedy* marsh⟩ **2** : made of or resembling reeds; *esp* : SLENDER, FRAIL ⟨*reedy* arms⟩ ⟨the *reedy* stem of a goblet⟩ **3** : having the tone quality of a reed instrument ⟨a *reedy* tenor voice⟩ — **reed·i·ly** \'rēd-ᵊl-ē\ *adv* — **reed·i·ness** \'rēd-ē-nəs\ *n*

¹reef \'rēf\ *n* [ON *rif*] **1** : a part of a sail taken in or let out in regulating size **2** : the reduction in sail area made by reefing

²reef *vt* **1** : to reduce the area of (a sail) by rolling or folding a portion **2** : to lower or bring inboard (a spar) wholly or partially

³reef *n* [D *rif*] **1** : a chain of rocks or ridge of sand at or near the surface of water **2** : VEIN, LODE

¹reef·er \'rē-fər\ *n* **1** : one that reefs **2** : a close-fitting usu. double-breasted jacket of thick cloth

²reefer *n* : a marijuana cigarette

³ree·fer \'rē-fər\ *n* : REFRIGERATOR; *also* : a refrigerator car, truck, trailer, or ship

reef knot *n* : a square knot used in reefing a sail

¹reek \'rēk\ *n* [OE *rēc* smoke] **1** : VAPOR, FOG **2** : a strong or disagreeable fume or odor

²reek *vi* **1** : to emit smoke or vapor **2 a** : to have a strong or unpleasant smell ⟨his clothes *reeked* of tobacco smoke⟩ **b** : to be unpleasantly or strongly permeated ⟨the room *reeked* with the smell of boiled cabbage⟩ **3** : to give a strong impression ⟨an old lady *reeking* of gentility⟩ — **reeky** \'rē-kē\ *adj*

¹reel \'rēl\ *n* [OE *hrēol*] **1** : a revolvable device on which something flexible is wound: as **a** : a small windlass at the butt of a fishing rod for the line **b** : a flanged spool for photographic film **2** : a quantity of something wound on a reel **3** : a frame for drying clothes usu. having radial arms on a vertical pole

²reel *vb* **1** : to wind upon or as if upon a reel **2** : to draw (as a fish) by reeling a line **3** : to wind or turn a reel — **reel·a·ble** \'rē-lə-bəl\ *adj* — **reel·er** *n*

³reel *vi* **1 a** : to whirl around ⟨*reeling* in a dance⟩ **b** : to be in a whirl ⟨heads *reeling* with excitement⟩ **2** : to give way : fall back : WAVER ⟨soldiers *reeling* in defeat⟩ **3** : to stagger or sway dizzily

⁴reel *n* : a reeling motion

⁵reel *n* : a lively Scottish-Highland dance or its music

re·elect \ˌrē-ə-'lekt\ *vt* : to elect for another term in office — **re·elec·tion** \-'lek-shən\ *n*

reel off *vt* **1** : to recite fluently ⟨*reeled off* some impressive statistics⟩ **2** : to cover or traverse with seeming ease ⟨*reeled off* a four-minute mile⟩

re·en·act \ˌrē-ə-'nakt\ *vt* **1** : to enact again **2** : to perform again — **re·en·act·ment** \-'nak(t)-mənt\ *n*

re·en·force \ˌrē-ən-'fōrs, -'fôrs\ *var of* REINFORCE

re·en·trance \(')rē-'en-trən(t)s\ *n* : REENTRY

re·en·trant \-trənt\ *n* : one that reenters

re·en·try \(')rē-'en-trē\ *n* **1** : a retaking possession esp. from a tenant **2** : a second or new entry **3** : the action of reentering the earth's atmosphere after travel in space

¹reeve \'rēv\ *n* [OE *gerēfa*] : a medieval English manor officer responsible chiefly for enforcing the discharge of feudal obligations

²reeve *vt* **rove** \'rōv\ *or* **reeved; reev·ing** **1** : to pass (as a rope) through a hole or opening **2** : to rig for operation by passing a rope through ⟨*reeve* up a set of blocks⟩

³reeve *n* : the female of the ruff

ref \'ref\ *n* : REFEREE 2

re·fash·ion \(')rē-'fash-ən\ *vt* : to make over : ALTER

re·fec·tion \ri-'fek-shən\ *n* [L *refect-, reficere* to restore, fr. *re-* + *facere* to make] **1** : refreshment of mind, spirit, or body; *esp* : NOURISHMENT **2 a** : the taking of refreshment **b** : food and drink together : REPAST

re·fec·to·ry \ri-'fek-t(ə-)rē\ *n, pl* **-ries** : a dining hall esp. in a monastery

refectory table *n* : a long narrow table with heavy legs

re·fer \ri-'fər\ *vb* **re·ferred; re·fer·ring** [L *referre* to bring back, report, refer, fr. *re-* + *ferre* to carry] **1** : to place in a certain class so far as cause, relationship, or source is concerned ⟨*referred* the defeat to poor training⟩ **2** : to send or direct to some person or place for treatment, help, or information ⟨*refer* a boy to a dictionary⟩ **3** : to go for information, advice, or aid ⟨*refer* to the dictionary for the meaning of a word⟩ **4** : to have relation or connection : RELATE ⟨the asterisk *refers* to a footnote⟩ **5** : to submit or hand over to someone else ⟨*refer* a patient to a specialist⟩ **6** : to direct attention : make reference — **ref·er·a·ble** \'ref-(ə-)rə-bəl, ri-'fər-ə-\ *adj* — **re·fer·rer** \ri-'fər-ər\ *n*

syn REFER, ALLUDE mean to direct attention to something. REFER implies intentional introduction and distinct

ə **abut;** ᵊ **kitten;** ər **further;** a **back;** ā **bake;** ä **cot, cart;** aù **out;** ch **chin;** e **less;** ē **easy;** g **gift;** i **trip;** ī **life**

mention as by direct naming; ALLUDE suggests such indirect mention as is conveyed in a hint, a figure of speech, or other roundabout expression

¹**ref·er·ee** \,ref-ə-'rē\ *n* **1** : a person to whom a legal matter is referred for investigation and report or for settlement **2** : a sports official usu. having final authority in administering a game

²**referee** *vb* **-eed; -ee·ing** : to act or supervise as a referee

ref·er·ence \'ref-ərn(t)s, 'ref-(ə-)rən(t)s\ *n* **1** : the act of referring or consulting **2** : a bearing on a matter : RELATION ⟨with *reference* to what was said⟩ **3** : something that refers: as **a** : ALLUSION, MENTION ⟨made *reference* to our agreement⟩ **b** : a sign or indication referring a reader to another passage or book **c** : consultation of sources of information **4** : one referred to: as **a** : a person to whom inquiries as to character or ability can be made **b** : a statement of the qualifications of a person seeking employment or appointment given by someone familiar with them **c** : a book, passage, or document to which a reader is referred

reference book *n* : a book (as a dictionary, encyclopedia, almanac, or yearbook) containing useful facts or information

reference mark *n* : a conventional mark (as *, †, or ‡) used in printing or writing to mark a reference

ref·er·en·dum \,ref-ə-'ren-dəm\ *n, pl* **-da** \-də\ *or* **-dums** [NL, fr. L, neut. of *referendus* to be referred, fr. *referre* to refer] : the principle or practice of submitting to popular vote a measure passed upon or proposed by a legislative body or by popular initiative; *also* : a vote on a measure so submitted

re·fer·ent \'ref-(ə-)rənt, ri-'fər-ənt\ *n* : something that refers or is referred to; *esp* : the thing a word stands for — **referent** *adj*

re·fer·ral \ri-'fər-əl\ *n* **1** : the act or an instance of referring **2** : one that is referred

¹**re·fill** \(')rē-'fil\ *vb* : to fill or become filled again — **re·fill·a·ble** \-'fil-ə-bəl\ *adj*

²**re·fill** \'rē-,fil\ *n* **1** : a new or fresh supply of something for a device ⟨a *refill* for a ball-point pen⟩ **2** : something provided again; *esp* : a second filling of a medical prescription

re·fine \ri-'fīn\ *vb* **1** : to come or bring to a pure state ⟨*refine* sugar⟩ **2** : to make or become improved or perfected esp. by pruning or polishing **3** : to free from what is coarse, vulgar, or uncouth **4** : to make improvement by introducing subtleties or distinctions ⟨*refined* upon the older methods⟩ — **re·fin·er** *n*

re·fined \ri-'fīnd\ *adj* **1** : freed from impurities : PURE ⟨*refined* gold⟩ ⟨*refined* sugar⟩ **2** : WELL-BRED, CULTURED ⟨very *refined* manners⟩ **3** : carried to a fine point : SUBTLE ⟨*refined* cruelty⟩ ⟨*refined* measurements⟩

re·fine·ment \ri-'fīn-mənt\ *n* **1** : the action or process of refining **2** : the quality or state of being refined : CULTIVATION **3 a** : a refined feature or method **b** : SUBTLETY **c** : a contrivance or device intended to improve or perfect

re·fin·ery \ri-'fīn-(ə-)rē\ *n, pl* **-er·ies** : a building and equipment for refining or purifying metals, oil, or sugar

re·fin·ish \(')rē-'fin-ish\ *vt* : to give (as furniture) a new surface — **re·fin·ish·er** *n*

re·fit \(')rē-'fit\ *vb* **re·fit·ted; re·fit·ting** : to get ready for use again : fit out or equip again ⟨*refit* a ship for service⟩ — **re·fit** \'rē-,fit, (')rē-'\ *n*

re·flect \ri-'flekt\ *vb* [L *reflectere* to bend back, fr. *re-* + *flectere* to bend] **1** : to bend or throw back waves of light, sound, or heat ⟨a polished surface *reflects* light⟩ **2** : to give back an image or likeness of as if by a mirror **3** : to bring as a result ⟨the boy's scholarship *reflects* credit on his school⟩ **4** : to cast reproach or blame ⟨our bad conduct *reflects* upon our training⟩ **5** : to think seriously and carefully : MEDITATE **syn** see THINK

re·flect·ance \ri-'flek-tən(t)s\ *n* : the fraction of the light falling upon a surface that is reflected

reflecting telescope *n* : REFLECTOR 2

re·flec·tion \ri-'flek-shən\ *n* **1** : an instance of reflecting; *esp* : the return of light or sound waves from a surface **2** : the production of an image by or as if by a mirror **3 a** : the action of bending or folding back **b** : a reflected

part : FOLD **4** : something produced by reflecting; *esp* : an image given back by a reflecting surface **5** : REPROACH, CENSURE **6** : a thought, idea, or opinion formed or a remark made as a result of meditation **7** : consideration of some subject matter, idea, or purpose ⟨lost in sober *reflection*⟩ — **re·flec·tion·al** \-shnəl, -shən-°l\ *adj*

re·flec·tive \ri-'flek-tiv\ *adj* **1** : capable of reflecting light, images, or sound waves **2** : marked by reflection : THOUGHTFUL **3** : of, relating to, or caused by reflection — **re·flec·tive·ly** *adv* — **re·flec·tive·ness** *n* — **re·flec·tiv·i·ty** \,rē-,flek-'tiv-ət-ē, ri-\ *n*

re·flec·tor \ri-'flek-tər\ *n* **1** : one that reflects; *esp* : a polished surface for reflecting light or heat **2** : a telescope in which the principal focusing element is a mirror

¹**re·flex** \'rē-,fleks\ *n* [L *reflexus*, pp. of *reflectere* to bend back] **1 a** : reflected heat, light, or color **b** : a mirrored image **c** : a copy exact in essential or peculiar features **2 a** : an automatic and usu. inborn response to a stimulus in which a nerve impulse passes inward from a receptor to a nerve center and thence outward to an effector (as a muscle or gland) without reaching the level of consciousness — compare HABIT **b** *pl* : the power of acting or responding with adequate speed

²**reflex** *adj* **1** *or* **re·flexed** \-,flekst\ : bent, turned, or directed back : REFLECTED **2** : produced in reaction, resistance, or return **3** *of an angle* : being between 180° and 360° **4** : of, relating to, or produced by a neural reflex ⟨*reflex* action⟩ — **re·flex·ly** *adv*

reflex arc *n* : the complete nervous path involved in a reflex

reflex camera *n* : a camera in which the image formed by the lens is reflected onto a screen for focusing and composition

re·flex·ion \ri-'flek-shən\ *chiefly Brit var of* REFLECTION

¹**re·flex·ive** \ri-'flek-siv\ *adj* **1** : directed or turned back upon itself **2** : of, relating to, or constituting an action directed back upon the agent or the grammatical subject ⟨*myself* in "I hurt myself" is a *reflexive* pronoun⟩ — **re·flex·ive·ly** *adv* — **re·flex·ive·ness** *n* — **re·flex·iv·i·ty** \,rē-,flek-'siv-ət-ē, ri-\ *n*

²**reflexive** *n* : a reflexive pronoun or verb

re·flux \'rē-,fləks\ *n* : a flowing back : EBB

re·for·est \(')rē-'fòr-əst, -'fär-\ *vt* : to renew forest cover on by seeding or planting — **re·for·es·ta·tion** \(,)rē-,fòr-ə-'stā-shən, -,fär-\ *n*

¹**re·form** \ri-'fòrm\ *vb* **1** : to make better or improve by removal of faults ⟨*reform* a prisoner⟩ **2** : to correct or improve one's own character or habits — **re·form·a·ble** \-'fòr-mə-bəl\ *adj*

²**reform** *n* **1** : amendment of what is bad or corrupt **2** : a removal or correction of an abuse, a wrong, or errors

ref·or·ma·tion \,ref-ər-'mā-shən\ *n* **1** : the act of reforming : the state of being reformed **2** *cap* : a 16th century religious movement marked by rejection or modification of much of Roman Catholic doctrine and practice and establishment of the Protestant churches — **ref·or·ma·tion·al** \-shnəl, -shən-°l\ *adj*

re·for·ma·tive \ri-'fòr-mət-iv\ *adj* : tending or disposed to reform

¹**re·for·ma·to·ry** \ri-'fòr-mə-,tōr-ē, -,tòr-\ *adj* : REFORMATIVE ⟨*reformatory* measures⟩

²**reformatory** *n, pl* **-ries** : a penal institution to which young or first offenders or women are committed for training and reformation

re·formed *adj* **1** : restored to purity or excellence : CORRECTED **2** *cap* **a** : PROTESTANT **b** : of or relating to the Calvinist churches of continental Europe

reformed spelling *n* : any of several methods of spelling English words that use letters with more phonetic consistency than conventional spelling and usu. discard some silent letters (as in *thoro* for *thorough*)

re·form·er \ri-'fòr-mər\ *n* **1** : one that works for or urges reform **2** *cap* : a leader of the Protestant Reformation

re·form·ism \ri-'fòr-,miz-əm\ *n* : a doctrine, policy, or movement of reform — **re·form·ist** \-məst\ *n*

Reform Judaism *n* : a 19th and 20th century development of Judaism marked by rationalization of belief, simplifica-

---

See *re-* and 2d element

refight	refilm	refind	reflourish	refocus
refigure	refilter	refix	reflower	refold
	refinance	refloat	refly	

j joke;   ŋ sing;   ō flow;   ȯ flaw;   ȯi coin;   th thin;   t̲h̲ this;   ü loot;   u̇ foot;   y yet;   yü few;   yu̇ furious;   zh vision

tion of many observances, and affirmation of the religious rather than national character of Judaism

reform school *n* : a reformatory for boys or girls

re·fract \ri-'frakt\ *vt* [L *refract-, refringere* to break open, break up, refract, fr. *re-* + *frangere* to break] : to subject to refraction

refracting telescope *n* : REFRACTOR

re·frac·tion \ri-'frak-shən\ *n* : the bending of a ray when it passes slantwise from one medium into another in which its speed is different (as when light passes from air into water)

re·frac·tive \ri-'frak-tiv\ *adj* : of, relating to, or active in refraction — **re·frac·tiv·i·ty** \ˌrē-ˌfrak-'tiv-ət-ē, ri-\ *n*

refractive index *n* : INDEX OF REFRACTION

re·frac·tor \ri-'frak-tər\ *n* : a telescope whose principal focusing element is usu. an achromatic lens

refraction: ray of light *sp* passing from air into water at *p* is refracted from *pl* to *pr*

¹**re·frac·to·ry** \ri-'frak-t(ə-)rē\ *adj* [modif. of L *refractarius*, irreg. fr. *refragari* to oppose] **1** : resisting control or authority : STUBBORN ⟨a *refractory* boy⟩ **2 a** : resistant to treatment **b** : unresponsive to stimulus **3** : difficult to fuse, corrode, or draw out; *esp* : capable of enduring high temperature — **re·frac·to·ri·ly** \-t(ə-)rə-lē\ *adv* — **re·frac·to·ri·ness** \-t(ə-)rē-nəs\ *n*

²**refractory** *n*, *pl* **-ries** : something refractory; *esp* : a heat-resisting ceramic material

¹**re·frain** \ri-'frān\ *vi* [MF *refraindre* to restrain, fr. L *refringere* to break up, check, refract] : to hold oneself back : restrain oneself ⟨must *refrain* from doing things like that⟩ — **re·frain·ment** \-mənt\ *n*

syn REFRAIN, ABSTAIN mean to keep oneself from doing or indulging in something. REFRAIN suggests the checking of a momentary impulse or inclination ⟨*refrain* from smiling⟩ ABSTAIN implies deliberate renunciation or self-denial on principle ⟨*abstained* from alcohol in any form⟩

²**refrain** *n* [MF, fr. *refraindre* to resound, fr. L *refringere* to break up, refract] : a regularly recurring phrase or verse esp. at the end of each stanza of a poem or song : CHORUS; *also* : the melody of a refrain

re·fran·gi·ble \ri-'fran-jə-bəl\ *adj* : capable of being refracted — **re·fran·gi·bil·i·ty** \-ˌfran-jə-'bil-ət-ē\ *n* — **re·fran·gi·ble·ness** *n*

re·fresh \ri-'fresh\ *vb* **1** : to restore strength and animation to : REVIVE ⟨sleep *refreshes* the body⟩ ⟨*refreshing* his memory by looking at his notes⟩ **2** : to restore or maintain by renewing supply : REPLENISH **3** : to restore water to **4** : to take refreshment **syn** see RENEW

re·fresh·en \-'fresh-ən\ *vt* : REFRESH

re·fresh·er \ri-'fresh-ər\ *n* **1** : something that refreshes **2** : REMINDER **3** : review or instruction designed esp. to keep one abreast of professional developments

re·fresh·ing *adj* : serving to refresh; *esp* : agreeably stimulating because of freshness or newness ⟨her sense of humor is very *refreshing*⟩

re·fresh·ment \ri-'fresh-mənt\ *n* **1** : the act of refreshing : the state of being refreshed **2 a** : something that refreshes **b** *pl* : a light meal : LUNCH ⟨*refreshments* will be served after the meeting⟩

¹**re·frig·er·ant** \ri-'frij-(ə-)rənt\ *adj* : COOLING

²**refrigerant** *n* : a substance (as ice, ammonia, or carbon dioxide) used in refrigeration

re·frig·er·ate \ri-'frij-ə-ˌrāt\ *vt* [L *refrigerare*, fr. *re-* + *frigor-, frigus* cold] : to make or keep cold or cool; *esp* : to freeze or chill (food) for preservation — **re·frig·er·a·tion** \ri-ˌfrij-ə-'rā-shən\ *n*

re·frig·er·a·tor \ri-'frij-ə-ˌrāt-ər\ *n* : a cabinet or room for keeping articles (as food) cool esp. by means of ice or a mechanical device

reft *past of* REAVE

re·fu·el \(')rē-'fyü(-ə)l\ *vb* : to provide with or take on fresh fuel

ref·uge \'ref-(ˌ)yüj\ *n* [L *refugium*, fr. *refugere* to take refuge, fr. *re-* + *fugere* to flee] **1** : shelter or protection from danger or distress **2** : a place that provides shelter or protection ⟨wildlife *refuges*⟩

ref·u·gee \ˌref-yu̇-'jē\ *n* : a person who flees for safety esp. to a foreign country

re·ful·gence \ri-'fu̇l-jən(t)s, -'fəl-\ *n* [L *refulgēre* to shine brightly, fr. *re-* + *fulgēre* to shine] : a radiant or resplendent quality or state : BRILLIANCE — **re·ful·gent** \-jənt\ *adj*

¹**re·fund** \ri-'fənd, 'rē-ˌfənd\ *vt* [L *refundere*, lit., to pour back, fr. *re-* + *fundere* to pour] : to return (money) in restitution or repayment — **re·fund·a·ble** \-ə-bəl\ *adj*

²**re·fund** \'rē-ˌfənd\ *n* **1** : the act of refunding **2** : a sum refunded

³**re·fund** \(')rē-'fənd\ *vt* : to fund (a debt) again or anew

re·fur·bish \(')rē-'fər-bish\ *vt* : to brighten or freshen up : RENOVATE — **re·fur·bish·ment** \-mənt\ *n*

re·fus·al \ri-'fyü-zəl\ *n* **1** : the act of refusing or denying **2** : the opportunity or right of refusing or taking before others

¹**re·fuse** \ri-'fyüz\ *vb* [MF *refuser*, fr. L *refus-, refundere* to pour back, fr. *re-* + *fundere* to pour] **1** : to decline to accept : REJECT ⟨*refused* the money⟩ **2 a** : to show or express positive unwillingness : fail deliberately ⟨*refused* to act⟩ **b** : DENY ⟨was *refused* entrance⟩ **3** : to withhold acceptance, compliance, or permission — **re·fus·er** *n*

²**ref·use** \'ref-ˌyüs, -ˌyüz\ *n* **1** : the worthless or useless part of something : TRASH, GARBAGE

re·fut·a·ble \ri-'fyüt-ə-bəl, 'ref-yət-\ *adj* : capable of being refuted — **re·fut·a·bly** \-blē\ *adv*

ref·u·ta·tion \ˌref-yu̇-'tā-shən\ *n* : the act or process of refuting : DISPROOF

re·fute \ri-'fyüt\ *vt* [L *refutare*, lit., to drive back] : to prove wrong by argument or evidence : show to be false ⟨*refute* the testimony of a witness⟩ — **re·fut·er** *n*

re·gain \(')rē-'gān\ *vt* **1** : to gain or get again : get back ⟨*regained* his health⟩ **2** : to get back to : reach again ⟨*regain* the shore⟩

re·gal \'rē-gəl\ *adj* [L *regalis*, fr. *reg-, rex* king] **1** : of, relating to, or suitable for a king **2** : of notable excellence or magnificence : SPLENDID — **re·gal·i·ty** \ri-'gal-ət-ē\ *n* — **re·gal·ly** \'rē-gə-lē\ *adv*

re·gale \ri-'gāl\ *vb* [F *régaler*, fr. MF *rigale, regale* party, fr. *re-* + *galer* to have a good time] **1** : to treat or entertain sumptuously or agreeably **2** : to feast oneself : FEED — **re·gale·ment** \-mənt\ *n*

re·ga·lia \ri-'gāl-yə\ *n sing or pl* [ML, fr. L, neut. pl. of *regalis* regal] **1** : the emblems and symbols (as the crown and scepter) of royalty **2** : the insignia of an office or order **3** : special dress : FINERY

¹**re·gard** \ri-'gärd\ *n* [MF, fr. *regarder* to look back at, regard, fr. *re-* + *garder* to guard, look at] **1 a** : CONSIDERATION, HEED **b** : LOOK, GAZE **2 a** : the worth or estimation in which something is held **b** (1) : a feeling of respect and affection : ESTEEM (2) *pl* : friendly greetings implying such feeling ⟨give him my *regards*⟩ **3** : REFERENCE, RESPECT ⟨this is in *regard* to your unpaid balance⟩ **4** : an aspect to be taken into consideration : a particular matter or point ⟨there's nothing to worry about in that *regard*⟩

²**regard** *vt* **1** : to pay attention to **2 a** : to show respect or consideration for **b** : to hold in high esteem **3** : to look at steadily or attentively **4** : to take into consideration or account **5** : to relate to **6** : to think of : look upon ⟨*regarded* him as a friend⟩

syn REGARD, RESPECT, ESTEEM, ADMIRE mean to recognize the worth of. REGARD is formal and requires some qualification ⟨he is highly *regarded* in banking circles⟩ RESPECT implies having a good opinion of without suggesting real liking or warmth of feeling; ESTEEM implies high evaluation together with warmth of feeling; ADMIRE implies enthusiastic and often uncritical appreciation

— **as regards** : with respect to : REGARDING

re·gard·ful \ri-'gärd-fəl\ *adj* **1** : HEEDFUL, OBSERVANT **2** : full or expressive of regard or respect : RESPECTFUL — **re·gard·ful·ly** \-fə-lē\ *adv* — **re·gard·ful·ness** *n*

re·gard·ing *prep* : CONCERNING

¹**re·gard·less** \ri-'gärd-ləs\ *adj* : having or taking no regard or heed : HEEDLESS, CARELESS ⟨plunge ahead *regardless* of consequences⟩ — **re·gard·less·ly** *adv* — **re·gard·less·ness** *n*

²**regardless** *adv* : despite everything ⟨are going ahead with their plans *regardless*⟩

ə abut; ᵊ kitten; ər further; a back; ā bake; ä cot, cart; au̇ out; ch chin; e less; ē easy; g gift; i trip; ī life

re·gat·ta \ri-'gät-ə, -'gat-\ *n* [It] **:** a rowing, speedboat, or sailing race or a series of such races

¹re·gen·cy \'rē-jən-sē\ *n, pl* **-cies** **1 :** the office, jurisdiction, or government of a regent or body of regents **2 :** the period of rule of a regent or body of regents

²regency *adj* **:** of, relating to, or resembling the furniture or the dress of the regency (1811–20) of George, Prince of Wales

re·gen·er·a·cy \ri-'jen-(ə-)rə-sē\ *n* **:** the state of being regenerated

¹re·gen·er·ate \ri-'jen-(ə-)rət\ *adj* **:** REGENERATED; *esp* **:** spiritually reborn or converted — **re·gen·er·ate·ly** *adv* — **re·gen·er·ate·ness** *n*

²re·gen·er·ate \ri-'jen-ə-,rāt\ *vb* **1 :** to cause to be reborn spiritually **2 :** to reform completely in character and habits ⟨the difficulty of *regenerating* criminals⟩ **3 :** to generate or produce anew; *esp* **:** to renew (a lost or damaged body part) by a new growth of tissue **4 :** to give new life to **:** REVIVE ⟨land *regenerated* by rotation of crops⟩ **5 :** to increase the amplification of (radio signals) by electron tubes in which a part of the outgoing current acts upon the incoming signal so as to increase the amplification — **re·gen·er·a·tor** \-,rāt-ər\ *n*

re·gen·er·a·tion \ri-,jen-ə-'rā-shən, ,rē-\ *n* **:** an act or the process of regenerating **:** the state of being regenerated; *esp* **:** spiritual renewal or revival

re·gen·er·a·tive \ri-'jen-ə-,rāt-iv\ *adj* **1 :** of, relating to, or marked by regeneration **2 :** tending to regenerate

re·gent \'rē-jənt\ *n* [L *regent-, regens,* prp. of *regere* to lead straight, direct, rule; akin to E *right*] **1 :** one who governs a kingdom during the minority, absence, or disability of the sovereign **2 :** a member of a governing board (as of a state university) — **regent** *adj*

reg·i·cide \'rej-ə-,sīd\ *n* [L *reg-, rex* king] **1 :** one who kills a king or assists in his death **2 :** the killing of a king — **reg·i·cid·al** \,rej-ə-'sīd-ᵊl\ *adj*

re·gime *also* **ré·gime** \rā-'zhēm, ri-\ *n* [F *régime,* fr. L *regimen*] **1 a :** REGIMEN 1 **b :** a regular pattern of occurrence or action **2 a :** mode of rule or management **b :** a form of government or administration; *esp* **:** a governmental or social system ⟨a totalitarian *regime*⟩ **c :** a period of rule of a regime ⟨during the last *regime*⟩

reg·i·men \'rej-ə-mən, -,men\ *n* [L, rule, fr. *regere* to rule] **1 :** a systematic course of treatment ⟨a strict dietary *regimen*⟩ **2 :** GOVERNMENT, RULE

¹reg·i·ment \'rej-(ə-)mənt\ *n* [LL *regimentum* rule, government, fr. L *regere* to rule] **:** a military unit consisting of a variable number of units (as battalions) — **reg·i·men·tal** \,rej-ə-'ment-ᵊl\ *adj* — **reg·i·men·tal·ly** \-ᵊl-ē\ *adv*

²reg·i·ment \'rej-ə-,ment\ *vt* **1 :** to organize rigidly esp. for the sake of regulation or control **2 :** to subject to order or uniformity — **reg·i·men·ta·tion** \,rej-ə-mən-'tā-shən, -,men-\ *n*

reg·i·men·tals \,rej-ə-'ment-ᵊlz\ *n pl* **1 :** a regimental uniform **2 :** military dress

re·gion \'rē-jən\ *n* [L *region-, regio* direction, district, fr. *regere* to lead straight] **1 :** an administrative area, division, or district **2 a :** an often indefinitely bounded part, portion, or area ⟨the darker *regions* of the night sky⟩; *also* **:** VICINITY ⟨had a pain in the *region* of the heart⟩ **b :** a broad, continuous, and usu. homogeneous area (as of the earth) ⟨arctic *regions*⟩ **3 :** a sphere of activity or interest **:** FIELD

re·gion·al \'rēj-nəl, -ən-ᵊl\ *adj* **1 :** of, relating to, or characteristic of a region ⟨a *regional* turn of speech⟩ **2 :** affecting a particular region **:** LOCALIZED ⟨*regional* pain⟩ — **re·gion·al·ly** \-ē\ *adv*

re·gion·al·ism \'rēj-nəl-,iz-əm, -ən-ᵊl-\ *n* **1 :** consciousness of and loyalty to a distinct region **2 :** emphasis on regional locale and characteristics in art or literature — **re·gion·al·ist** \-əst\ *n or adj* — **re·gion·al·is·tic** \,rēj-nəl-'is-tik, -ən-ᵊl-\ *adj*

¹reg·is·ter \'rej-ə-stər\ *n* [ML *registrum,* alter. of LL *regesta,* pl., lit., things recorded, fr. L, pp. of *regerere* to carry back, record, fr. *re-* + *gerere* to carry] **1 a :** a written record or list containing regular entries of items or details **b :** a book for such a record ⟨a *register* of deeds⟩ ⟨*register* of voters⟩ **2 :** a device (as in a floor or wall) usu. with a grille and shutters that regulates the flow of heated air from a furnace **3 a :** a set of organ pipes of like quality **:** STOP **b :** a part of the range of a human voice or a musical instrument comprising tones similarly produced or of the same quality **4 :** REGISTRATION, REGISTRY **5 a :** an automatic device registering a number or a quantity **b :** a number or quantity so registered **6 :** a condition of correct alignment or proper relative position

²register *vb* **reg·is·tered; reg·is·ter·ing** \-st(ə-)riŋ\ **1 a :** to make or secure official entry of in a register ⟨*register* a will⟩ **b :** to enroll formally esp. as a voter or student **c :** to record automatically **:** INDICATE ⟨the thermometer *registered* zero⟩ **2 :** to make or adjust so as to correspond exactly **3 :** to secure special protection for (a piece of mail) by prepayment of a fee **4 :** to convey by expression and bodily movements alone **5 :** to be in correct alignment or register **6 :** to make or convey an impression

³register *n* **:** REGISTRAR

reg·is·tered *adj* **:** having the owner's name entered in a register ⟨*registered* security⟩

registered nurse *n* **:** a graduate trained nurse who has been licensed to practice by a state authority

reg·is·tra·ble \'rej-ə-strə-bəl\ *adj* **:** capable of being registered

reg·is·trant \-strənt\ *n* **:** one that registers or is registered

reg·is·trar \'rej-ə-,strär\ *n* **:** an official recorder or keeper of records

reg·is·tra·tion \,rej-ə-'strā-shən\ *n* **1 :** an act or the fact of registering **2 :** an entry in a register **3 :** the number of individuals registered **:** ENROLLMENT **4 :** a document certifying an act of registering ⟨automobile *registration*⟩

reg·is·try \'rej-ə-strē\ *n, pl* **-tries** **1 :** ENROLLMENT, REGISTRATION **2 :** a ship's nationality as proved by its entry in a register **3 :** a place of registration **4 :** an official record book or an entry in one

reg·nal \'reg-nᵊl\ *adj* **:** of or relating to a king or his reign; *esp* **:** calculated from a monarch's accession to the throne ⟨*regnal* year⟩

reg·nant \'reg-nənt\ *adj* [L *regnare* to reign, fr. *regnum,* n., reign] **1 :** exercising rule **:** REIGNING **2 :** having the chief power **:** DOMINANT

reg·o·lith \'reg-ə-,lith\ *n* [Gk *rhēgos* blanket] **:** MANTLEROCK

¹re·gress \'rē-,gres\ *n* [L *regressus,* fr. *regredi* to go back, fr. *re-* + *gradi* to go] **1 a :** an act or the privilege of going or coming back **:** WITHDRAWAL **b :** REENTRY 1 **2 :** RETROGRESSION, RETROGRADATION

²re·gress \ri-'gres\ *vb* **:** to go or cause to go back esp. to a former level or condition — **re·gres·sor** \-'gres-ər\ *n*

re·gres·sion \ri-'gresh-ən\ *n* **:** an act or the fact of regressing **:** RETROGRESSION: as **a :** progressive decline of something (as a manifestation of disease) **b :** gradual loss of differentiation and function by a body part **c :** reversion to an earlier mental or behavioral level

re·gres·sive \ri-'gres-iv\ *adj* **1 :** of, relating to, or tending toward regression **2 :** decreasing in rate as the base increases ⟨*regressive* tax⟩ — **re·gres·sive·ly** *adv* — **re·gres·sive·ness** *n*

¹re·gret \ri-'gret\ *vb* **re·gret·ted; re·gret·ting** [MF *regreter*] **1 a :** to mourn the loss or death of **b :** to miss poignantly **2 :** to be keenly sorry for **3 :** to experience regret — **re·gret·ta·ble** \-'gret-ə-bəl\ *adj* — **re·gret·ta·bly** \-blē\ *adv* — **re·gret·ter** *n*

²regret *n* **1 :** sorrow aroused by circumstances beyond one's power to remedy **2 a :** an expression of distressing emotion (as sorrow or disappointment) **b** *pl* **:** a note politely declining an invitation — **re·gret·ful** \-'gret-fəl\ *adj* — **re·gret·ful·ly** \-fə-lē\ *adv* — **re·gret·ful·ness** *n*

re·group \(')rē-'grüp\ *vb* **:** to form into a new grouping — **re·group·ment** \-mənt\ *n*

¹reg·u·lar \'reg-yə-lər\ *adj* [L *regula* straightedge, norm, rule, fr. *regere* to lead straight, rule] **1 :** belonging to a religious order ⟨*regular* clergy⟩ **2 a :** formed, built, arranged, or ordered according to an established rule, law, principle, or type **b** (1) **:** being both equilateral and equi-

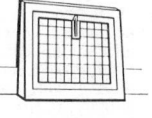

register 2

See *re-* and 2d element			
regild	regive	reglow	regrade	regrow
	reglaze	reglue	regrind	regrowth

j joke;   **ŋ** sing;   **ō** flow;   **ȯ** flaw;   **ȯi** coin;   **th** thin;   **th̲** this;   **ü** loot;   **u̇** foot;   **y** yet;   **yü** few;   **yu̇** furious;   **zh** vision

angular ⟨a *regular* polygon⟩ (2) **:** having faces that are congruent regular polygons and all the polyhedral angles congruent ⟨a *regular* polyhedron⟩ **c :** perfectly symmetrical or even; *esp* **:** radially symmetrical ⟨*regular* flowers⟩ **d :** having or constituting an isometric system ⟨*regular* crystals⟩ **3 a :** ORDERLY, METHODICAL **b :** recurring or functioning at fixed or uniform intervals **4 a :** following or conforming to established or prescribed usages, rules, or discipline ⟨a *regular* Democrat⟩ **b :** NORMAL, CORRECT: as (1) **:** undeviating in conformance to a set standard (2) **:** COMPLETE, UNMITIGATED ⟨a *regular* scoundrel⟩ **c :** conforming to the normal or usual manner of inflection **5 :** of, relating to, or constituting a permanent standing army — **reg·u·lar·i·ty** \ˌreg-yə-'lar-ət-ē\ *n* — **reg·u·lar·ly** \'reg-yə-lər-lē\ *adv*

syn NORMAL, TYPICAL: REGULAR stresses conformity to a rule, standard, or pattern; NORMAL implies lack of deviation from what has been established as the most usual or expected; TYPICAL implies showing all the important traits of a type, class, or group and may suggest lack of strong individuality

²regular *n* **:** one who is regular: as **a :** one of the regular clergy **b :** a soldier in a regular army **c :** a player on an athletic team who usu. starts every game

regular army *n* **:** a permanently organized body constituting the standing army of a state

reg·u·lar·ize \'reg-yə-lə-ˌrīz\ *vt* **:** to make regular — **reg·u·lar·iz·er** *n*

reg·u·late \'reg-yə-ˌlāt\ *vt* [LL *regulare*, fr. L *regula* rule] **1 a :** to govern or direct according to rule **b :** to bring under the control of law or constituted authority **2 :** to reduce to order, method, or uniformity ⟨*regulated* his habits⟩ **3 :** to adjust so as to work accurately or regularly ⟨*regulate* a clock⟩ — **reg·u·la·tive** \-ˌlāt-iv\ *adj* — **reg·u·la·tor** \-ˌlāt-ər\ *n* — **reg·u·la·to·ry** \-lə-ˌtōr-ē, -ˌtòr-\ *adj*

¹reg·u·la·tion \ˌreg-yə-'lā-shən\ *n* **1 :** the act of regulating **:** the state of being regulated **2 a :** an authoritative rule dealing with details of procedure **b :** a rule or order having the force of law issued by an executive authority **syn** see LAW

²regulation *adj* **:** prescribed by regulations ⟨*regulation* cap of a nurse⟩

Reg·u·lus \'reg-yə-ləs\ *n* [L, dim. of *reg-*, *rex* king] **:** a first-magnitude star in the constellation Leo

re·gur·gi·tate \(')rē-'gər-jə-ˌtāt\ *vb* [ML *regurgitare*, fr. L *re-* + *gurgit*, *gurges* whirlpool] **:** to throw or be thrown back or out again ⟨*regurgitate* undigested food⟩ — **re·gur·gi·ta·tion** \(ˌ)rē-ˌgər-jə-'tā-shən\ *n*

re·ha·bil·i·tate \ˌrē-(h)ə-'bil-ə-ˌtāt\ *vt* [ML *rehabilitare*, fr. L *re-* + *habilitas* aptness, ability, fr. *habilis* handy, apt, fr. *habēre* to have, hold] **1 a :** to restore to a former capacity **:** REINSTATE **b :** to restore to good repute by vindicating **2 a :** to restore to a state of efficiency, good management, or repair **b :** to restore to a condition of health or useful and constructive activity — **re·ha·bil·i·ta·tion** \-ˌbil-ə-'tā-shən\ *n* — **re·ha·bil·i·ta·tive** \-'bil-ə-ˌtāt-iv\ *adj*

re·hash \(')rē-'hash\ *vt* **:** to present or use (as an argument) again in another form without substantial change or improvement — **re·hash** \'rē-ˌhash\ *n*

re·hears·al \ri-'hər-səl\ *n* **:** a rehearsing of something: as **a :** a private performance or practice session preparatory to a public appearance **b :** a practice exercise **:** TRIAL

re·hearse \ri-'hərs\ *vb* [MF *rehercier*, lit., to harrow again, fr. *re-* + *hercier* to harrow, fr. *herce* harrow, fr. L *hirpic-*, *hirpex*] **1 a :** to say again **:** REPEAT **b :** to recount in order **:** ENUMERATE **2 a :** to practice (a play or scene) for public performance **b :** to train or make proficient (as actors) by rehearsal **3 :** to engage in a rehearsal — **re·hears·er** *n*

re·hy·drate \(')rē-'hī-ˌdrāt\ *vt* **:** to restore fluid lost in dehydration to — **re·hy·dra·tion** \ˌrē-ˌhī-'drā-shən\ *n*

reichs·mark \'rīks-ˌmärk\ *n*, *pl* **reichsmarks** *also* **reichs·mark** [G, fr. *reich* empire] **:** the German mark from 1925 to 1948

Reichs·tag \'rīks-ˌtäg, -ˌtäk\ *n* [G, fr. *reich* empire + *tag* diet, council] **:** the lower house of the legislature of the German Empire and of the succeeding Republic

¹reign \'rān\ *n* [OF *regne*, fr. L *regnum*, fr. *reg-*, *rex* king] **1 :** the authority or rule of a sovereign **2 :** the time during which a sovereign reigns

²reign *vi* **1 a :** to possess or exercise sovereign power **:** RULE **b :** to hold office as chief of state with slight powers of governing **2 :** to exercise authority or hold sway in the manner of a monarch **3 :** to be predominant or prevalent

reign of terror : a period marked by violence usu. committed by those in power that produces terror among the people involved

re·im·burse \ˌrē-əm-'bərs\ *vt* [*re-* + obs. *imburse* to put in one's purse, fr. MF *embourser*, fr. *en-* + *bourse* purse, fr. ML *bursa*] **:** to pay back **:** REPAY — **re·im·burs·a·ble** \-'bər-sə-bəl\ *adj* — **re·im·burse·ment** \-'bərs-mənt\ *n*

¹rein \'rān\ *n* [MF *rene*, fr. L *retinēre* to hold back, fr. *re-* + *tenēre* to hold] **1 :** a line or strap fastened to a bit on each side for controlling an animal — usu. used in pl. **2 a :** a restraining influence **:** CHECK ⟨kept his son under a tight *rein*⟩ **b :** controlling or guiding power ⟨seized the *reins* of government⟩ **3 :** complete freedom **:** SCOPE — usu. used in the phrase *give rein to*

²rein *vb* **:** to check, control, or stop by or as if by reins

re·in·car·nate \ˌrē-ən-'kär-ˌnāt\ *vt* **:** to incarnate again or anew

re·in·car·na·tion \(ˌ)rē-ˌin-ˌkär-'nā-shən\ *n* **1 :** the action of reincarnating **:** the state of being reincarnated **2 :** rebirth in new bodies or forms of life; *esp* **:** a rebirth of a soul in a new human body

rein·deer \'rān-ˌdi(ə)r\ *n*, *pl* **reindeer** *also* **reindeers** [ME *reindere*, fr. ON *hreinn* reindeer + ME *dere* deer] **:** any of several large deer of northern regions having antlers in both sexes and including some used as meat and draft animals

reindeer moss *n* **:** a gray, erect, tufted, and much-branched lichen of northern and arctic regions important as reindeer food

re·in·fec·tion \ˌrē-ən-'fek-shən\ *n* **:** infection following another infection of the same type

re·in·force \ˌrē-ən-'fōrs, -'fòrs\ *vt* **1 :** to strengthen with new force, assistance, material, or support ⟨*reinforce* a wall⟩ ⟨*reinforce* an argument⟩ **2 :** to strengthen with additional troops or ships — **re·in·forc·er** *n*

reinforced concrete *n* **:** concrete in which metal is embedded for strengthening

re·in·force·ment \ˌrē-ən-'fōrs-mənt, -'fòrs-\ *n* **1 :** the action of reinforcing **:** the state of being reinforced **2 :** something that reinforces

reins \'rānz\ *n pl* [MF, fr. L *renes*] **1 :** the kidneys or the region thereof **2 :** the seat of the feelings or passions

re·in·state \ˌrē-ən-'stāt\ *vt* **:** to place again in possession or in a former position, condition, or capacity ⟨*reinstate* an official⟩ — **re·in·state·ment** \-mənt\ *n*

re·in·ter·pret \ˌrē-ən-'tər-prət\ *vt* **:** to interpret again; *esp* **:** to give a new or different interpretation to — **re·in·ter·pre·ta·tion** \-ˌtər-prə-'tā-shən\ *n*

re·in·vest \ˌrē-ən-'vest\ *vt* **1 :** to invest again or anew **2 a :** to invest (as income from investments) in additional securities **b :** to invest in a business rather than distribute as dividends or profits — **re·in·vest·ment** \-'ves(t)-mənt\ *n*

re·is·sue \(')rē-'ish-ü, -ˌü\ *vb* **:** to issue again ⟨*reissued* the book in one volume⟩ — **reissue** *n*

re·it·er·ate \rē-'it-ə-ˌrāt\ *vt* **:** to say or do over again or repeatedly **syn** see REPEAT — **re·it·er·a·tion** \(ˌ)rē-ˌit-ə-'rā-shən\ *n* — **re·it·er·a·tive** \rē-'it-ə-ˌrāt-iv, -rət-\ *adj* — **re·it·er·a·tive·ly** *adv* — **re·it·er·a·tive·ness** *n*

¹re·ject \ri-'jekt\ *vt* [L *reject-*, *reicere*, fr. *re-* + *jacere* to throw] **1 :** to refuse to acknowledge, believe, or receive **2 :** to throw away as useless or unsatisfactory **3 :** to refuse to grant or consider

syn REJECT, REPUDIATE, SPURN mean to refuse to accept or receive something proposed or offered. REJECT stresses a throwing away or abandoning and implies firmness and finality ⟨*rejected* all proposals for a truce⟩ REPUDIATE implies a usu. scornful and public thrusting away as unworthy, untrue, or unjustified ⟨now *repudiates* his former friends⟩ SPURN implies disdain or contempt more strongly

See *re-* and 2d element	rehear	reimpose	reincorporate	reintroduce
rehammer	rehearing	reimposition	reinsert	reinvasion
rehandle	reheat			

than REJECT ⟨*spurned* all her suitors⟩ **syn** see in addition DISCARD

²re·ject \'rē-.jekt\ *n* : a rejected person or thing

re·jec·tion \ri-'jek-shən\ *n* **1** : the action of rejecting : the state of being rejected **2** : something rejected

re·joice \ri-'jȯis\ *vb* [MF *rejoiss-, rejoir*, fr. *re-* + *joir* to rejoice, fr. L *gaudēre*] **1** : to give joy to : GLADDEN ⟨news that *rejoices* the heart⟩ **2** : to feel joy or great delight ⟨*rejoice* over a friend's good fortune⟩ — **re·joic·er** *n* — **re·joic·ing·ly** \-'jȯi-siŋ-lē\ *adv*

re·joic·ing \-'jȯi-siŋ\ *n* **1** : the action of one that rejoices **2** : an instance, occasion, or expression of joy : FESTIVITY

re·join *vt* **1** \(')rē-'jȯin\ : to join again : return to ⟨*rejoined* his family after a week in camp⟩ **2** \ri-\ : to say as an answer : REPLY

re·join·der \ri-'jȯin-dər\ *n* [ME *rejoiner*, fr. MF *rejoindre* to rejoin, fr. *re- + joindre* to join] : REPLY; *esp* : an answer to a reply

re·ju·ve·nate \ri-'jü-və-.nāt\ *vt* [*re-* + L *juvenis* young] : to make young or youthful again : give new vigor to — **re·ju·ve·na·tion** \-.jü-və-'nā-shən\ *n* — **re·ju·ve·na·tor** \-'jü-və-.nāt-ər\ *n*

re·kin·dle \(')rē-'kin-dᵊl\ *vb* : to kindle again

¹re·lapse \ri-'laps\ *n* : a relapsing; *esp* : a recurrence of illness after a period of improvement

²relapse *vi* **1** : to slip or fall back into a former worse state **2** : SINK, SUBSIDE **3** : BACKSLIDE — **re·laps·er** *n*

relapsing fever *n* : an epidemic disease marked by recurring high fever lasting five to seven days and caused by a spirochete transmitted by the bites of lice or ticks

re·lat·a·ble \ri-'lāt-ə-bəl\ *adj* : capable of being related

re·late \ri-'lāt\ *vb* [L *relat-*, used as stem of *referre* to carry back, report, refer, fr. *re- + ferre* to carry] **1** : to give an account of : NARRATE ⟨*relate* a story⟩ **2** : to show or establish a relationship between ⟨*relate* cause and effect⟩ **3** : to have relationship or connection : REFER **4** : to have meaningful social relationships — **re·lat·er** *n*

re·lat·ed *adj* : belonging to the same group on the basis of known or determinable qualities ⟨*related* phenomena⟩ ⟨pneumonia and *related* diseases⟩: as **a** : having a common ancestry ⟨bees and the *related* wasps⟩; *also* : belonging to the same family by blood or marriage ⟨*related* to the queen⟩ **b** : having close harmonic connection ⟨*related* keys⟩

re·la·tion \ri-'lā-shən\ *n* **1** : the act of telling or recounting : ACCOUNT **2** : an aspect or quality (as resemblance) that connects two or more things or parts as being or belonging or working together or as being of the same kind **3** : a related person : RELATIVE **4** : relationship by blood or marriage : KINSHIP **4** : REFERENCE, RESPECT ⟨in *relation* to⟩ **5 a** : the state of being mutually or reciprocally interested (as in social or commercial matters) **b** *pl* (1) : DEALINGS, AFFAIRS (2) : INTERCOURSE **6** : a set of ordered pairs in mathematics — compare FUNCTION — **re·la·tion·al** \-shnəl, -shən-ᵊl\ *adj*

re·la·tion·ship \-shən-.ship\ *n* **1** : the state or character of being related or interrelated **2** : KINSHIP; *also* : a specific instance or type of this

¹rel·a·tive \'rel-ət-iv\ *n* **1** : a word referring grammatically to an antecedent **2** : a thing having a relation to or connection with or necessary dependence upon another thing **3** : an individual connected with another by ancestry or affinity

²relative *adj* **1** : introducing a subordinate clause that qualifies an expressed or implied antecedent ⟨*relative* pronoun⟩; *also* : introduced by such a connective ⟨*relative* clause⟩ **2** : RELATIVE, PERTINENT **3** : not absolute or independent : COMPARATIVE **4** : having the same key signature — used of major and minor keys and scales — **rel·a·tive·ness** *n*

relative humidity *n* : the ratio of the amount of water vapor actually present in the air to the greatest amount possible at the same temperature

rel·a·tive·ly \'rel-ət-iv-lē\ *adv* : in relation or respect to something else : COMPARATIVELY

rel·a·tiv·i·ty \.rel-ə-'tiv-ət-ē\ *n* **1** : the quality or state of being relative; *esp* : dependence on something else **2 a** : a theory formulated by Albert Einstein and leading to the assertion of the equivalence of mass and energy and of the increase of the mass of a body with increased

velocity and based on the two postulates that if two systems are in relative motion with uniform linear velocity it is impossible for observers in either system by observation and measurement of phenomena in the other to learn more about the motion than the fact that it is relative motion **b** : an extension of the theory to include a discussion of gravitation and related phenomena — **rel·a·tiv·ist** \'rel-ət-iv-əst\ *n* — **rel·a·tiv·is·tic** \.rel-ət-iv-'istik\ *adj* — **rel·a·tiv·is·ti·cal·ly** \-ti-k(ə-)lē\ *adv*

re·la·tor \ri-'lāt-ər\ *n* : one that relates : NARRATOR

re·lax \ri-'laks\ *vb* [L *relaxare*, fr. *re- + laxare* to loosen, fr. *laxus* loose, lax] **1** : to make or become less tense or rigid : SLACKEN, EASE **2** : to make or become less severe or stringent **3** : to make soft or enervated **4** : to cast off social restraint, nervous tension, or attitude of anxiety or suspicion **5** : to seek rest or recreation **6** : to relieve constipation — **re·lax·er** *n*

¹re·lax·ant \-'lak-sənt\ *adj* : producing relaxation

²relaxant *n* : a relaxing agent; *esp* : a drug that induces muscular relaxation

re·lax·a·tion \.rē-.lak-'sā-shən, ri-\ *n* : the act or fact of relaxing : the state of being relaxed; *esp* : the lengthening that characterizes inactive muscle

re·laxed \ri-'lakst\ *adj* **1** : lacking in precision or strictness **2** : set at rest or at ease **3** : easy of manner : INFORMAL — **re·laxed·ly** \-'lak-səd-lē, -'laks-tlē\ *adv* — **re·laxed·ness** \-'lak-səd-nəs, -'laks(t)-nəs\ *n*

re·lax·in \ri-'lak-sən\ *n* : a hormone of the corpus luteum that relaxes pelvic ligaments and facilitates childbirth

¹re·lay \'rē-.lā\ *n* [MF *relais*] **1** : a fresh supply (as of horses or men) arranged to relieve others at various stages esp. of a journey or race **2 a** : a race between teams in which each team member covers a specified portion of the course **b** : one of the divisions of such a race **3 a** : an electromagnetic device for remote or automatic control actuated by variation in conditions of an electric circuit and operating in turn other devices (as switches) in the same or a different circuit **b** : SERVOMOTOR **4** : the act of passing along by stages; *also* : one of such stages

²relay \'rē-.lā, ri-'lā\ *vt* **re·layed; re·lay·ing 1 a** : to place or dispose in relays **b** : to provide with relays **2** : to pass along by relays

³re·lay \(')rē-'lā\ *vt* **-laid** \-'lād\; **-lay·ing** : to lay again ⟨had to take up the flagstones and *relay* them⟩

¹re·lease \ri-'lēs\ *vt* [OF *relaissier*, fr. L *relaxare* to relax] **1** : to set free from restraint, confinement, or servitude **2** : to relieve from something that holds, burdens, or oppresses **3** : to give up in favor of another : RELINQUISH ⟨*release* a claim to property⟩ **4** : to give permission for publication, performance, exhibition, or sale of at a specified date **syn** see FREE — **re·leas·a·bil·i·ty** \-.lē-sə'bil-ət-ē\ *n* — **re·leas·a·ble** \-'lē-sə-bəl\ *adj* — **releas·er** *n*

²release *n* **1** : relief or deliverance from sorrow, suffering, or trouble **2 a** : a discharge from an obligation (as a debt) **b** : a relinquishment of a right or claim; *esp* : a conveyance of a right in real property to another **c** : a document embodying a release **3 a** : the act or an instance of liberating or freeing : a letting go (as from physical restraint) **b** : the act or manner of ending a speech sound **4** : the state of being freed **5** : a device adapted to hold or release a mechanism as required **6 a** : the act of permitting performance or publication **b** : the matter released

released time *n* : a scheduled time when children are dismissed from public school to receive religious instruction

rel·e·gate \'rel-ə-.gāt\ *vt* [L *relegare*, fr. *re- + legare* to send with a commission] **1** : EXILE, BANISH **2** : to remove or dismiss to a less important or prominent place ⟨*relegate* some old books to the attic⟩ **3** : to refer or hand over for decision or carrying out — **rel·e·ga·tion** \.rel-ə-'gā-shən\ *n*

re·lent \ri-'lent\ *vi* [L *re- + lentus* flexible, slow] **1** : to become less severe, harsh, or strict **2** : to let up : SLACKEN

re·lent·less \-ləs\ *adj* : mercilessly hard or harsh — **relent·less·ly** *adv* — **re·lent·less·ness** *n*

rel·e·vance \'rel-ə-vən(t)s\ *also* **rel·e·van·cy** \-vən-sē\ *n*, *pl* **-vanc·es** *also* **-van·cies** : relation to the matter at hand : PERTINENCE

rel·e·vant \-vənt\ *adj* [ML *relevant-, relevans*, fr. L, prp. of *relevare* to lift up, relieve] : having something to do

---

See *re-* and 2d element |rejudge |relearn |relet |reletter

j joke; **ŋ** sing; **ō** flow; **ȯ** flaw; **ȯi** coin; **th** thin; **th̲** this; **ü** loot; **u̇** foot; **y** yet; **yü** few; **yu̇** furious; **zh** vision

with the case being considered : PERTINENT ⟨a *relevant* question⟩ — **rel·e·vant·ly** *adv*

re·li·a·bil·i·ty \ri-,lī-ə-'bil-ət-ē\ *n* : the quality or state of being reliable

re·li·a·ble \ri-'lī-ə-bəl\ *adj* : suitable or fit to be relied on : DEPENDABLE — **re·li·a·ble·ness** *n* — **re·li·a·bly** \-blē\ *adv*

re·li·ance \ri-'lī-ən(t)s\ *n* **1** : the act of relying **2** : the condition or attitude of one who relies : DEPENDENCE **3** : something or someone relied on

re·li·ant \-ənt\ *adj* : having reliance on something or someone : TRUSTING — **re·li·ant·ly** *adv*

rel·ic \'rel-ik\ *n* [LL *reliquiae* remains of a martyr, fr. L, remains, fr. *relinquere* to leave behind] **1 a** : an object venerated because of association with a saint or martyr **b** : SOUVENIR, MEMENTO **2** *pl* : REMAINS, CORPSE **3** : something left behind after decay, disintegration, or disappearance **4** : a trace of some past or outmoded practice, custom, or belief : VESTIGE

rel·ict \'rel-ikt\ *n* [L *relictus,* pp. of *relinquere* to leave behind] **1** : WIDOW **2** : a persistent remnant of an otherwise extinct flora or fauna

re·lief \ri-'lēf\ *n* **1 a** : removal or lightening of something oppressive, painful, or distressing **b** : aid in the form of money or necessities for the indigent, aged, or handicapped **c** : military assistance to a post or force in extreme danger **d** : means of breaking monotony or boredom : DIVERSION **2 a** : release from sentry or other duty **b** : one that takes the place of another on duty **3** : legal remedy or redress **4 a** : projection from the background (as of figures in sculpture or of mountains on a relief map) : sharpness of outline **b** : a work of art with such raised figures **c** : the appearance of projection above the background given in drawing and painting by lines and shading **5** : the elevations or inequalities of a land surface

relief map *n* : a map representing topographic relief

relief pitcher *n* : a baseball pitcher who takes over for another during a game

re·lieve \ri-'lēv\ *vb* [MF *relever* to raise up, relieve, fr. L *relevare,* fr. *re-* + *levare* to raise] **1** : to bring or give relief wholly or partly from a burden, pain, discomfort, or trouble ⟨*relieve* the distress of the poor⟩ **2** : to release from a post or duty esp. by taking the place of ⟨*relieve* a sentry⟩ **3** : to take away the sameness or monotony of ⟨black dress *relieved* by a white collar⟩ **4** : to put or stand out in relief : give prominence to or set off by contrast (as in sculpture or painting) — **re·liev·er** *n*

syn RELIEVE, ALLEVIATE mean to make something less grievous or burdensome. RELIEVE implies either removing entirely or lifting enough of a burden to make it tolerable; ALLEVIATE suggests temporary or partial lessening of pain or distress

re·li·gion \ri-'lij-ən\ *n* [L *religion-, religio*] **1 a** (1) : the service and worship of God or the supernatural (2) : belief in or devotion to religious faith or observance **b** : the state of a religious **2** : a set or system of religious attitudes, beliefs, and practices **3** : a cause, principle, or system of beliefs held to with ardor and faith

re·li·gion·ist \-'lij-(ə-)nəst\ *n* : a person adhering to a religion

re·li·gi·ose \ri-'lij-ē-,ōs\ *adj* : excessively, obtrusively, or sentimentally religious — **re·li·gi·os·i·ty** \-,lij-ē-'äs-ət-ē\ *n*

¹re·li·gious \ri-'lij-əs\ *adj* **1 a** : devoted to God or to the powers or principles believed to govern life ⟨a very *religious* person⟩ **b** : belonging to a religious order ⟨a *religious* house⟩ **2** : of or relating to religion ⟨*religious* beliefs⟩ **syn** see DEVOUT — **re·li·gious·ly** *adv* — **re·li·gious·ness** *n*

²religious *n, pl* **religious** : a member of a religious order

re·lin·quish \ri-'liŋ-kwish\ *vt* [MF *relinquiss-, relinquir,* fr. L *relinquere* to leave behind, fr. *re-* + *linquere* to leave] **1** : to withdraw or retreat from : ABANDON **2 a** : to desist from **b** : to release a claim to or possession or control of : RENOUNCE **3** : to let go of : RELEASE — **re·lin·quish·ment** \-mənt\ *n*

rel·i·quary \'rel-ə-,kwer-ē\ *n, pl* **-quar·ies** : a small box or shrine in which sacred relics are kept

¹rel·ish \'rel-ish\ *n* [alter. of ME *reles* aftertaste, taste, fr. OF *relais* something left behind, fr. *relaissier* to leave

behind, fr. *re-* + *laissier* to leave] **1** : a pleasing appetizing taste **2** : a small bit added for flavor : DASH **3** : personal liking ⟨have no *relish* for hard work⟩ **4** : keen enjoyment of food or of anything ⟨eat with *relish*⟩ **5** : a highly seasoned sauce (as of pickles or mustard) eaten with other food to add flavor **syn** see TASTE

²relish *vt* **1** : to add relish to **2** : to be pleased or gratified by : ENJOY **3** : to eat or drink with pleasure — **rel·ish·a·ble** \-ə-bəl\ *adj*

re·live \(')rē-'liv\ *vb* : to live again or over again; *esp* : to experience again in imagination

re·lo·cate \(')rē-'lō-,kāt, ,rē-lō-'kāt\ *vb* **1** : to locate again **2** : to move to a new location ⟨*relocate* a factory⟩ — **re·lo·ca·tion** \,rē-lō-'kā-shən\ *n*

re·luc·tance \ri-'lək-tən(t)s\ *n* **1** : the quality or state of being reluctant **2** : the opposition offered by a magnetic substance to magnetic flux; *also* : the ratio of the magnetic potential difference to the corresponding flux

re·luc·tan·cy \-tən-sē\ *n, pl* **-cies** : RELUCTANCE 1

re·luc·tant \ri-'lək-tənt\ *adj* [L *reluctari* to struggle against, fr. *re-* re-, against + *luctari* to struggle] **1** : UNWILLING ⟨*reluctant* to answer⟩ **2** : showing hesitation or unwillingness ⟨*reluctant* obedience⟩ — **re·luc·tant·ly** *adv*

re·ly \ri-'lī\ *vi* **re·lied; re·ly·ing** [ME *relien* to rally, fr. MF *relier* to connect, rally, fr. L *religare* to tie back, fr. *re-* + *ligare* to tie] **1** : to have confidence : TRUST **2** : to be dependent : COUNT ⟨a man you can *rely* on⟩

¹re·main \ri-'mān\ *vi* [MF *remaindre,* fr. L *remanēre,* fr. *re-* + *manēre* to stay, remain] **1 a** : to be a part not destroyed, taken, or used up ⟨little *remained* after the fire⟩ **b** : to be something yet to be shown, done, or treated : have yet ⟨that *remains* to be proved⟩ **2** : to stay in the same place or with the same person or group; *esp* : to stay behind **3** : to continue unchanged ⟨the weather *remained* cold⟩ **syn** see STAY

²remain *n* **1** : a remaining part or trace — usu. used in pl. **2** *pl* : writings left unpublished at a writer's death **3** *pl* : a dead body

¹re·main·der \ri-'mān-dər\ *n* [AF, fr. MF *remaindre* to remain] **1 a** : a remaining group, part, or trace **b** (1) : the number left after a subtraction (2) : the final undivided part after division that is less than the divisor **2** : a book sold at a reduced price by the publisher after sales have slowed **syn** see BALANCE

²remainder *vt* **re·main·dered; re·main·der·ing** \-d(ə-)riŋ\ : to dispose of as remainders

re·make \(')rē-'māk\ *vt* **-made** \-'mād\; **-mak·ing** : to make anew or in a different form — **re·make** \'rē-,māk\ *n*

¹re·mand \ri-'mand\ *vt* [LL *remandare* to send back word, fr. L *re-* + *mandare* to entrust, order] : to order back: as **a** : to send back (a case) to a lower court for further action **b** : to return to custody pending trial or for further detention

²remand *n* : the act of remanding : the state of being remanded ⟨sent back on *remand*⟩

¹re·mark \ri-'märk\ *vb* [F *remarquer,* fr. *re-* + *marquer* to mark] **1** : to take notice of : OBSERVE ⟨*remarked* her strange manner⟩ **2** : to express as an observation or comment : SAY **3** : to make an observation or comment

²remark *n* **1** : the act of remarking : NOTICE **2** : mention of that which deserves attention or notice **3** : an expression of opinion or judgment

re·mark·a·ble \ri-'mär-kə-bəl\ *adj* **1** : worthy of being or likely to be noticed **2** : UNCOMMON, EXTRAORDINARY — **re·mark·a·ble·ness** *n* — **re·mark·a·bly** \-blē\ *adv*

re·mar·riage \(')rē-'mar-ij\ *n* : a second or later marriage

re·match \(')rē-'mach, 'rē-,\ *n* : a second match between the same contestants or teams

re·me·di·a·ble \ri-'mēd-ē-ə-bəl\ *adj* : capable of being remedied — **re·me·di·a·ble·ness** *n* — **re·me·di·a·bly** \-blē\ *adv*

re·me·di·al \ri-'mēd-ē-əl\ *adj* : intended to remedy or improve ⟨*remedial* measures⟩ ⟨*remedial* reading courses⟩ — **re·me·di·al·ly** \-ē-ə-lē\ *adv*

¹rem·e·dy \'rem-əd-ē\ *n, pl* **-dies** [L *remedium,* fr. *re-* + *mederi* to treat, heal] **1** : a medicine or treatment that cures or relieves **2** : something that corrects an evil, rights a wrong, or makes up for a loss

See *re-* and 2d element **relight**	**reload**	**reloader**	**remanufacture**	**remarry**

²**remedy** *vt* **-died; -dy·ing** : to provide or serve as a remedy for : RELIEVE

re·mem·ber \ri-'mem-bər\ *vb* **-bered; -ber·ing** \-b(ə-)riŋ\ [MF *remembrer*, fr. LL *rememorari*, fr. *re-* + LL *memorari* to be mindful of, fr. L *memor* mindful] **1** : to bring to mind or think of again **2 a** : to keep in mind for attention or consideration **b** : REWARD **3** : to retain in the memory **4** : to convey greetings from **5** : COMMEMORATE — **re·mem·ber·a·ble** \-b(ə-)rə-bəl\ *adj* — **re·mem·ber·er** \-bər-ər\ *n*
    syn RECOLLECT, RECALL: REMEMBER may apply to an effortless or involuntary keeping in memory; RECOLLECT implies bringing back to mind what is lost or scattered; RECALL suggests an effort to bring back to mind and often to recreate in speech

re·mem·brance \ri-'mem-brən(t)s\ *n* **1** : the act of remembering **2** : something remembered ⟨a vivid *remembrance*⟩ **3** : something (as a souvenir) that brings to mind **4** *pl* : GREETINGS **syn** see MEMORY

re·mex \'rā-,meks, 'rē-\ *n, pl* **re·mi·ges** \'rā-mə-,gās, 'rem-ə-,jēz\ [NL *remig-, remex*, fr. L, oarsman, fr. *remus* oar + *agere* to drive] : a quill feather of the wing of a bird — **re·mi·gial** \ri-'mij-(ē-)əl\ *adj*

re·mind \ri-'mīnd\ *vt* : to put in mind of something : cause to remember ⟨*remind* a child that it is bedtime⟩ — **re·mind·er** *n*

rem·i·nisce \,rem-ə-'nis\ *vi* : to indulge in reminiscence

rem·i·nis·cence \,rem-ə-'nis-°n(t)s\ *n* **1** : a recalling or telling of a past experience ⟨a *reminiscence* of early childhood⟩ **2** *pl* : an account of one's memorable experiences **syn** see MEMORY

rem·i·nis·cent \-°nt\ *adj* [L *reminiscent-, reminiscens*, prp. of *reminisci* to remember] **1** : of or relating to reminiscence : indulging in reminiscence **2** : that reminds one (as of something seen or known before) ⟨a city *reminiscent* of one's home⟩

re·miss \ri-'mis\ *adj* [L *remissus*, fr. pp. of *remittere* to remit, relax] **1** : negligent in the performance of work or duty : CARELESS **2** : showing neglect or inattention : LAX **syn** see NEGLIGENT — **re·miss·ly** *adv* — **re·miss·ness** *n*

re·mis·si·ble \ri-'mis-ə-bəl\ *adj* : that may be forgiven ⟨*remissible* sins⟩ — **re·mis·si·bly** \-blē\ *adv*

re·mis·sion \ri-'mish-ən\ *n* : the act or process of remitting

re·mit \ri-'mit\ *vb* **re·mit·ted; re·mit·ting** [L *remiss-, remittere*, lit., to send back, fr. *re-* + *mittere* to send] **1 a** : to release from the guilt or penalty of : PARDON ⟨*remit* sins⟩ **b** : to refrain from exacting **c** : to give relief from (suffering) **2 a** : to lay aside (a mood or disposition) partly or wholly **b** : to desist from **c** : to let slacken : RELAX **3** : to submit or refer for consideration, judgment, decision, or action **4** : to restore or consign to a former status or condition **5** : POSTPONE, DEFER **6** : to send (money) esp. in payment **7** : to abate in intensity or severity often temporarily ⟨the fever had *remitted*⟩ — **remit** *n* — **re·mit·ment** \-'mit-mənt\ *n* — **re·mit·ta·ble** \-'mit-ə-bəl\ *adj* — **re·mit·ter** *n*

re·mit·tal \ri-'mit-°l\ *n* : REMISSION

re·mit·tance \ri-'mit-°n(t)s\ *n* **1** : a sending (as of money or bills) esp. to a distance **2** : money sent esp. in payment

remittance man *n* : a person living abroad on remittances from home

re·mit·tent \ri-'mit-°nt\ *adj* : marked by alternating periods of abatement and increase of symptoms ⟨a *remittent* fever⟩ — **re·mit·tent·ly** *adv*

rem·nant \'rem-nənt\ *n* [MF *remenant*, fr. prp. of *remenoir* to remain, fr. L *remanēre*] **1** : something that remains or is left over ⟨a *remnant* of cloth⟩ **2** : a surviving trace ⟨the *remnants* of a great civilization⟩

re·mod·el \(')rē-'mäd-°l\ *vt* : to alter the structure of : partly rebuild : RECONSTRUCT

re·mon·strance \ri-'män(t)-strən(t)s\ *n* : an act or instance of remonstrating : EXPOSTULATION

re·mon·strant \-strənt\ *adj* : vigorously objecting or opposing — **remonstrant** *n* — **re·mon·strant·ly** *adv*

re·mon·strate \ri-'män-,strāt\ *vb* [ML *remonstrare* to demonstrate, fr. L *re-* + *monstrare* to show] : to plead in opposition to something : speak in reproof : OBJECT, PROTEST ⟨*remonstrate* with a pupil for behaving disorderly⟩

rem·o·ra \'rem-ə-rə\ *n* [L, lit., delay] : a fish having the anterior dorsal fin converted into a disk on the head by means of which it clings to other fishes and to ships — **rem·o·rid** \-rəd\ *adj*

re·morse \ri-'mȯrs\ *n* [ML *remorsus*, fr. L *remors-, remordēre* to bite again, fr. *re-* + *mordēre* to bite] : a gnawing distress arising from a sense of guilt for past wrongs : SELF-REPROACH

re·morse·ful \-fəl\ *adj* : springing from or marked by remorse — **re·morse·ful·ly** \-fə-lē\ *adv* — **re·morse·ful·ness** *n*

re·morse·less \-ləs\ *adj* : being without remorse : MERCILESS — **re·morse·less·ly** *adv* — **re·morse·less·ness** *n*

re·mote \ri-'mōt\ *adj* [L *remotus*, fr. pp. of *removēre* to remove] **1** : far off in place or time : not near or recent ⟨*remote* countries⟩ ⟨*remote* ages⟩ **2** : OUT-OF-THE-WAY, SECLUDED ⟨*remote* valley⟩ **3** : not closely connected or related **4** : not obvious or striking : SLIGHT ⟨*remote* likeness⟩ **5** : APART, ALOOF ⟨kept himself *remote* from the dispute⟩ **6** : operated or operating from a distance ⟨*remote* control⟩ **syn** see DISTANT — **re·mote·ly** *adv* — **re·mote·ness** *n*

¹**re·mount** \(')rē-'maȯnt\ *vb* : to mount again

²**re·mount** \'rē-,maȯnt, (')rē-'\ *n* : a fresh horse to take the place of one disabled or exhausted

re·mov·a·bil·i·ty \ri-,mü-və-'bil-ət-ē\ *n* : the quality or state of being removable

re·mov·a·ble \ri-'mü-və-bəl\ *adj* : capable of being removed — **re·mov·a·ble·ness** *n* — **re·mov·a·bly** \-blē\ *adv*

re·mov·al \ri-'mü-vəl\ *n* : the act of removing : the fact of being removed

¹**re·move** \ri-'müv\ *vb* [L *removēre*, fr. *re-* + *movēre* to move] **1 a** : to change or cause to change to another location, position, station, or residence **b** : to go away **2** : to move by lifting, pushing aside, or taking away or off; *also* : to yield to being so moved ⟨this cap should *remove* easily⟩ **3** : to dismiss from office **4** : ELIMINATE — **re·mov·er** *n*

²**remove** *n* **1** : REMOVAL; *esp* : MOVE 2c **2 a** : a distance or interval separating one thing from another **b** : a degree or stage of separation ⟨at one *remove*⟩

re·moved \ri-'müvd\ *adj* **1** : far away : DISTANT ⟨a town far *removed* from cities⟩ **2** : distant in relationship ⟨the children of your first cousin are your first cousins once *removed*⟩

re·mu·da \ri-'müd-ə\ *n* [AmerSp, relay of horses, fr. Sp, exchange, fr. *remudar* to exchange, fr. *re-* + *mudar* to change, fr. L *mutare*] : a herd of horses from which those to be used (as on a ranch) for the day are drawn

re·mu·ner·ate \ri-'myü-nə-,rāt\ *vt* [L *remunerare*, fr. *re-* + *muner-, munus* gift] : to pay an equivalent to for a service, loss, or expense : RECOMPENSE **syn** see PAY — **re·mu·ner·a·tor** \-,rāt-ər\ *n* — **re·mu·ner·a·to·ry** \ri-'myü-nə-rə-,tōr-ē, -,tȯr-\ *adj*

re·mu·ner·a·tion \ri-,myü-nə-'rā-shən\ *n* **1** : an act or fact of remunerating **2** : something that remunerates : RECOMPENSE

re·mu·ner·a·tive \ri-'myü-nə-,rāt-iv\ *adj* **1** : serving to remunerate **2** : affording remuneration : PROFITABLE ⟨made a highly *remunerative* investment⟩ — **re·mu·ner·a·tive·ly** *adv* — **re·mu·ner·a·tive·ness** *n*

Re·mus \'rē-məs\ *n* : the twin brother of Romulus

Re·nais·sance \,ren-ə-'sän(t)s, -'zän(t)s\ *n* [F, fr. MF, rebirth, fr. *renaistre* to be born again, fr. L *renasci*, fr. *re-* + *nasci* to be born] **1 a** : the movement or period in Europe between the 14th and 17th centuries marked by a humanistic revival of classical influence in the arts and literature and the beginnings of modern science **b** : the neoclassic style of architecture prevailing during the Renaissance **2** *often not cap* : a movement or period marked by a revival of vigorous artistic and intellectual activity

re·nal \'rēn-°l\ *adj* [L *renes* kidneys] : of, relating to, or located in or near the kidneys

renal artery *n* : either of the paired arteries that arise from the dorsal aorta and supply blood to the kidneys

renal vein *n* : either of the paired veins that drain blood from the kidneys into the vena cava

See *re-* and 2d element	remigrate	remilitarization	remix	remonetization
remelt	remigration	remilitarize	remold	rename

re·nas·cence \ri-'nas-ᵊn(t)s, -'nās-\ *n, often cap* : RENAIS-
SANCE — **re·nas·cent** \-ᵊnt\ *adj*

rend \'rend\ *vb* **rent** \'rent\ *also* **rend·ed; rend·ing** [OE
rendan] **1** : to remove from place by violence : WREST
2 : to split or tear apart or in pieces by violence **3** : to
tear (the hair or clothing) as a sign of anger, grief, or
despair **4 a** : to lacerate with painful feelings **b** : to
pierce with sound **c** : to divide (as a nation) into parties

ren·der \'ren-dər\ *vt* **ren·dered; ren·der·ing** \-d(ə-)riŋ\
[MF *rendre* to give back, deliver, cause to become, modif.
of L *reddere*, partly fr. *re-*, *red-* re- + *dare* to give & partly
fr. *re-*, *red-* + *-dere* to put] **1** : DELIVER, GIVE (render
judgment) **2** : to melt down : extract by heating (render
lard) **3** : to give up : SURRENDER (rendered his life) **4** : to
give in return (render thanks) **5** : to present a statement of
: bring to one's attention (render a bill) **6** : to cause to
be or become : MAKE (render a person helpless) **7** : FUR-
NISH, CONTRIBUTE (render aid) **8** : PRESENT, PERFORM
(render a song) (render a salute) **9** : TRANSLATE (render
Latin into English) — **ren·der·a·ble** \-d(ə-)rə-bəl\ *adj* —
ren·der·er \-dər-ər\ *n*

¹ren·dez·vous \'rän-di-ˌvü, -dā-\ *n, pl* **ren·dez·vous**
\-ˌvüz\ [MF, fr. *rendez vous* present yourselves] **1 a** : a
place appointed for assembling or meeting **b** : a place
of popular resort : HAUNT **2** : an appointed meeting

²rendezvous *vb* **ren·dez·voused** \-ˌvüd\; **ren·dez·vous·
ing** \-ˌvü-iŋ\; **ren·dez·vouses** \-ˌvüz\ : to come or
bring together at a rendezvous

ren·di·tion \ren-'dish-ən\ *n* : the act or result of rendering: as **a** : SURRENDER **b** : TRANSLATION **c** : PERFOR-
MANCE, INTERPRETATION

¹ren·e·gade \'ren-i-ˌgād\ *n* [Sp *renegado*, fr. ML *renegatus*, fr. pp. of *renegare* to deny, fr. L *re-* + *negare* to
deny] : a deserter from one faith, cause, or allegiance
to another

²renegade *vi* : to become a renegade

³renegade *adj* : TRAITOROUS, APOSTATE

ren·e·ga·do \ren-i-'gäd-ō, -'gād-\ *n, pl* **-does** : RENEGADE

re·nege \ri-'nig, -'neg, -'nēg, -'nāg\ *vi* [ML *renegare* to
deny] **1** : to violate a rule in a card game by failing to
follow suit when able **2** : to go back on a promise or
commitment — **re·neg·er** *n*

re·ne·go·ti·ate \rē-ni-'gō-shē-ˌāt\ *vt* : to negotiate again;
esp : to readjust by negotiation to eliminate or recover
excessive profits — **re·ne·go·tia·ble** \-sh(ē-)ə-bəl\ *adj*
— **re·ne·go·ti·a·tion** \-ˌgō-s(h)ē-'ā-shən\ *n*

re·new \ri-'n(y)ü\ *vt* **1** : to make new again : restore to
freshness or vigor (strength renewed by a night's rest)
2 : to restore to existence : REESTABLISH, RE-CREATE
(renew the splendor of a palace) **3** : to do or make again
: REPEAT (renew a complaint) **4** : to begin again : RESUME
(renewed efforts to make peace) **5** : to put in a fresh
supply of : REPLACE (renew the water in a tank) **6** : to
grant or obtain an extension of : continue in force for a
fresh period (renew a lease) (renew a subscription) — **re-
new·a·bil·i·ty** \-ˌn(y)ü-ə-'bil-ət-ē\ *n* — **re·new·a·ble**
\-'n(y)ü-ə-bəl\ *adj* — **re·new·a·bly** \-blē\ *adv* — **re-
new·er** *n*

syn RENEW, RESTORE, REFRESH, RENOVATE mean to make
like new. RENEW implies a replacing of parts or of used-up
materials or supplies; RESTORE suggests a returning to an
original state of soundness or wholeness; REFRESH implies restoring qualities of liveliness or zest (refreshed by a
short nap) RENOVATE applies chiefly to material things and
suggests making like new but not necessarily like the original (renovate the upstairs rooms)

re·new·al \ri-'n(y)ü-əl\ *n* **1** : the act of renewing : the
state of being renewed **2** : something renewed

re·ni·form \'ren-ə-ˌförm, 'rē-nə-\ *adj* [L *renes* kidneys]
: suggesting a kidney in outline (a reniform leaf)

ren·net \'ren-ət\ *n* [ME, fr. OE *gerennan* to cause to run
together, coagulate; akin to E *run*] **1** : the contents of the
stomach of an unweaned calf or other animal or the lining
membrane of the stomach used for curdling milk **2** : ren-
nin or a substitute used to curdle milk

ren·nin \'ren-ən\ *n* : a stomach enzyme that coagulates
casein and is used commercially to curdle milk in the
making of cheese

re·nom·i·nate \(')rē-'näm-ə-ˌnāt\ *vt* : to nominate again

esp. for a succeeding term — **re·nom·i·na·tion** \(ˌ)rē-
ˌnäm-ə-'nā-shən\ *n*

re·nounce \ri-'naün(t)s\ *vt* [MF *renoncer*, fr. L *renuntiare*,
fr. *re-* + *nuntiare* to report, announce, fr. *nuntius* messen-
ger] **1** : to give up, abandon, or resign usu. by formal
declaration (renounced the throne) (renounce his errors)
2 : to refuse further to follow, obey, or recognize : RE-
PUDIATE (renounced his allegiance) — **re·nounce·ment**
\-mənt\ *n* — **re·nounc·er** *n*

ren·o·vate \'ren-ə-ˌvāt\ *vt* [L *renovare*, fr. *re-* + *novus*
new] : to make like new again : restore to a former state
or to good condition **syn** see RENEW — **ren·o·va·tion**
\ˌren-ə-'vā-shən\ *n* — **ren·o·va·tor** \'ren-ə-ˌvāt-ər\ *n*

re·nown \ri-'naün\ *n* [MF *renon*, fr. *renomer* to celebrate,
fr. *re-* + *nomer* to name, fr. L *nominare*] : a state of being
widely acclaimed and highly honored : FAME

re·nowned \-'naünd\ *adj* : having renown : CELEBRATED
syn see FAMOUS

¹rent \'rent\ *n* [OF *rente* income from a property, fr.
rendre to render, yield] **1** : property (as a house) rented
or for rent **2** : money paid for the use of property : a
periodic payment made by a tenant to the owner for the
possession and use of real property **3** : the portion of
the national income attributable to land as a factor of
production — **for rent** : available for use or service at a
price

²rent *vb* **1** : to take and hold property under an agreement
to pay rent **2** : to grant the possession and enjoyment of
for rent : LET **3** : to be for rent **syn** see HIRE — **rent·a·ble**
\-ə-bəl\ *adj*

³rent *past of* REND

⁴rent *n* **1** : an opening made by or as if by rending **2**
: an act or instance of rending

¹rent·al \'rent-ᵊl\ *n* **1** : an amount paid or collected as
rent **2** : an act of renting

²rental *adj* **1** : of, relating to, or available for rent **2**
: dealing in rental property

rental library *n* : a commercially operated library (as in a
store) that lends books at a fixed charge per book per day

rent·er \'rent-ər\ *n* : one that rents; *esp* : TENANT

ren·tier \rän-'tyā\ *n* [F, fr. *rente* income from a property]
: a person who receives a fixed income from investments

re·num·ber \(')rē-'nəm-bər\ *vt* : to number again or
differently

re·nun·ci·a·tion \ri-ˌnən(t)-sē-'ā-shən\ *n* [L *renuntiare* to
renounce] : the act or practice of renouncing — **re·nun-
ci·a·tive** \-'nən(t)-sē-ˌāt-iv\ *adj* — **re·nun·ci·a·to·ry**
\-sē-ə-ˌtör-ē, -ˌtor-\ *adj*

re·open \(')rē-'ō-pən, -'öp-ᵊm\ *vb* **1** : to open again
2 : to take up again : RESUME

¹re·or·der \(')rē-'örd-ər\ *vb* **1** : REORGANIZE **2** : to
place a reorder

²reorder *n* : an order like a previous order from the same
supplier

re·or·ga·ni·za·tion \(ˌ)rē-ˌörg-(ə-)nə-'zā-shən\ *n* : the act
of reorganizing : the state of being reorganized; *esp* : the
financial reconstruction of a business concern

re·or·ga·nize \(')rē-'ör-gə-ˌnīz\ *vb* : to organize again or
anew; *esp* : to bring about a reorganization (as of a
business concern) — **re·or·ga·niz·er** *n*

rep \'rep\ *n* [F *reps*, modif. of E *ribs*, pl. of *rib*] : a plain-
weave fabric with prominent rounded crosswise ribs

re·pack·age \(')rē-'pak-ij\ *vt* : to package again or anew;
esp : to put into a more efficient or attractive form

¹re·pair \ri-'pa(ə)r, -'pe(ə)r\ *vi* [MF *repairier* to go back
to one's country, fr. LL *repatriare*, fr. L *re-* + *patria* native
country] : to betake oneself : GO (repair to an inner office)

²repair *vb* [MF *reparer*, fr. L *reparare*, fr. *re-* + *parare* to
prepare] **1 a** : to restore by replacing a part or putting
together what is torn or broken : MEND **b** : to restore to
a sound or healthy state : RENEW **2** : to make good
: REMEDY **3** : to make up for : compensate for **syn** see
FIX — **re·pair·a·ble** \-'par-ə-bəl, -'per-\ *adj* — **re·pair·er**
\-ər\ *n*

³repair *n* **1** : the action or process of repairing (make
repairs) **2** : the result of repairing (a tire with three
repairs) **3** : good or sound condition (a house in repair)
4 : condition with respect to soundness or need of repairing (a house in bad repair)

ə abut; ᵊ kitten; ər further; a back; ā bake; ä cot, cart; aü out; ch chin; e less; ē easy; g gift; i trip; ī life

re·pair·man \-'pa(ə)r-mən, -'pe(ə)r-, -,man\ *n* : one whose occupation is making repairs ⟨TV *repairman*⟩

re·pand \ri-'pand\ *adj* [L *repandus* bent backward] : having a slightly undulating margin ⟨a *repand* leaf⟩

rep·a·ra·ble \'rep-(ə-)rə-bəl\ *adj* : capable of being repaired

rep·a·ra·tion \,rep-ə-'rā-shən\ *n* **1** : the action or process of repairing or restoring : the state of being repaired or restored **2** : a making amends for a wrong or injury done : COMPENSATION **3** : the amends made for a wrong or injury; *esp* : money paid (as by one country to another) in compensation (as for damages in war)

re·par·a·tive \ri-'par-ət-iv\ *adj* **1** : of, relating to, or effecting repair **2** : serving to make amends

rep·ar·tee \,rep-ər-'tē\ *n* [F *repartie*, fr. *repartir* to retort] : a clever witty reply; *also* : the making of such replies

re·pass \(')rē-'pas\ *vb* **1** : to pass again esp. in the opposite direction : RETURN **2** : to cause to pass again **3** : to adopt again — **re·pas·sage** \-'pas-ij\ *n*

re·past \ri-'past\ *n* [MF, fr. *repaistre* to feed, fr. *re-* + *paistre* to feed, fr. L *pascere*] : MEAL, FEAST

re·pa·tri·ate \(')rē-'pā-trē-,āt, -'pa-\ *vt* [LL *repatriare* to go back to one's country, fr. *re-* + *patria* native land] : to send or bring back to one's own country or to the country of which one is a citizen ⟨*repatriate* prisoners of war⟩ — **re·pa·tri·ate** \-trē-ət, -trē-,āt\ *n* — **re·pa·tri·a·tion** \(,)rē-,pā-trē-'ā-shən, -,pa-\ *n*

re·pay \(')rē-'pā\ *vb* **-paid**; **-pay·ing** **1** : to pay back ⟨he's already been *repaid*⟩ ⟨*repay* a loan⟩ **2** : to make return payment or requital ⟨a lending bank requires proof of ability to *repay*⟩ — **re·pay·a·ble** \-ə-bəl\ *adj* — **re·pay·ment** \-mənt\ *n*

re·peal \ri-'pēl\ *vt* [MF *repeler*, fr. *re-* + *apeler* to call, appeal] : REVOKE, ANNUL; *esp* : to do away with by legislative enactment — **repeal** *n* — **re·peal·a·ble** \-'pē-lə-bəl\ *adj* — **re·peal·er** *n*

¹re·peat \ri-'pēt\ *vt* [L *repetere*, fr. *re-* + *petere* to go to, seek] **1 a** : to say or state again : REITERATE **b** : to say over from memory : RECITE **c** : to say after another **d** : to tell to others ⟨*repeat* gossip⟩ **2** : to make, do, or perform again ⟨*repeat* a mistake⟩ — **re·peat·a·ble** \-ə-bəl\ *adj*
syn REPEAT, REITERATE mean to do or say again. REPEAT is the general term and may apply to one or many actions or utterances; REITERATE stresses exact repetition of something said and may be stronger in implying multiple repetition
— **repeat oneself** : to say or do the same thing more than once

²re·peat \ri-'pēt, 'rē-,\ *n* **1** : the act of repeating **2 a** : something repeated **b** (1) : a musical passage to be repeated in performance (2) : a sign consisting of vertical dots placed before and after a passage to be repeated

re·peat·ed \ri-'pēt-əd\ *adj* : done or happening again and again : FREQUENT — **re·peat·ed·ly** *adv*

re·peat·er \ri-'pēt-ər\ *n* : one that repeats: as **a** : a watch that strikes the time when a spring is pressed **b** : a firearm that fires several times without reloading **c** : an habitual violator of the laws **d** : a student repeating a class or course

repeating decimal *n* : a decimal in which after a certain point a particular digit or sequence of digits repeats itself indefinitely

re·pel \ri-'pel\ *vb* **re·pelled**; **re·pel·ling** [L *repellere*, fr. *re-* + *pellere* to drive] **1 a** : to drive back : REPULSE **b** : to fight against : RESIST **2** : to turn away : REJECT ⟨*repelled* the insinuation⟩ **3 a** : to drive away : DISCOURAGE **b** : to be incapable of adhering to, mixing with, taking up, or holding **c** : to force away or apart or tend to do so by mutual action at a distance **4** : to cause aversion : DISGUST — **re·pel·ler** *n*

re·pel·lant \ri-'pel-ənt\ *adj or n* : REPELLENT

¹re·pel·lent \-ənt\ *adj* **1** : serving or tending to drive away or ward off **2** : arousing aversion or disgust : REPULSIVE **syn** see REPUGNANT — **re·pel·len·cy** \-ən-sē\ *n* — **re·pel·lent·ly** *adv*

²repellent *n* : something that repels; *esp* : a substance employed to prevent insect attacks

re·pent \ri-'pent\ *vb* [OF *repentir*, fr. *re-* + *pentir* to be sorry, fr. L *paenitēre*] **1** : to feel sorrow for one's sin and determine to do what is right **2** : to feel sorry for or dis-

satisfied with something one has done : REGRET ⟨*repent* a rash decision⟩ — **re·pent·er** *n*

re·pent·ance \ri-'pent-ᵊn(t)s\ *n* : a feeling of regret for something done or said; *esp* : regret or sorrow for sin **syn** see PENITENCE

re·pent·ant \ri-'pent-ᵊnt\ *adj* : feeling or showing repentance — **re·pent·ant·ly** *adv*

re·peo·ple \(')rē-'pē-pəl\ *vt* **1** : to people anew **2** : to stock again (as with animals)

re·per·cus·sion \,rē-pər-'kəsh-ən, ,rep-ər-\ *n* **1** : REFLECTION, REVERBERATION **2 a** : a reciprocal action or effect **b** : a widespread, indirect, or unforeseen effect of an act, action, or event — **re·per·cus·sive** \-'kəs-iv\ *adj*

rep·er·toire \'rep-ə(r)-,twär\ *n* [F *répertoire*, lit., repertory, fr. LL *repertorium*] **1 a** : a list or supply of dramas, operas, pieces, or parts that a company or person is prepared to perform **b** : a supply of skills, devices, or expedients possessed by a person **2 a** : the complete list or supply of dramas, operas, or musical works available for performance **b** : the complete list or supply of skills, devices, or ingredients used in a particular field, occupation, or practice

rep·er·to·ry \'rep-ə(r)-,tōr-ē, -,tȯr-\ *n, pl* **-ries** [LL *repertorium* list, catalog, fr. L *reperire* to find, fr. *re-* + *parere* to produce] **1** : a stock or store of something : COLLECTION ⟨a *repertory* of unusual skills⟩ **2** : REPERTOIRE

rep·e·ti·tion \,rep-ə-'tish-ən\ *n* [L *repetit-, repetere* to repeat] **1** : the act or an instance of repeating **2** : the fact of being repeated **3** : something repeated

rep·e·ti·tious \-'tish-əs\ *adj* : marked by repetition; *esp* : tediously repeating — **rep·e·ti·tious·ly** *adv* — **rep·e·ti·tious·ness** *n*

re·pet·i·tive \ri-'pet-ət-iv\ *adj* : REPETITIOUS — **re·pet·i·tive·ly** *adv* — **re·pet·i·tive·ness** *n*

re·phrase \(')rē-'frāz\ *vt* : to phrase over again in a different form

re·pine \ri-'pīn\ *vi* **1** : to feel or express dejection or discontent : COMPLAIN **2** : to wish discontentedly — **re·pin·er** *n*

re·place \ri-'plās\ *vt* **1** : to put back in a proper or former place ⟨*replace* a card in a file⟩ **2** : to take the place of : SUPPLANT ⟨paper money has *replaced* gold coins⟩ **3** : to fill the place of : supply an equivalent for ⟨*replace* a broken dish⟩ — **re·place·a·ble** \-'plā-sə-bəl\ *adj*
syn REPLACE, SUPPLANT, SUPERSEDE mean to put out of place or into the place of another. REPLACE implies a filling of a place once occupied by one now lost, destroyed, or no longer usable or adequate; SUPPLANT implies taking the place of one forced out by craft or fraud; SUPERSEDE implies taking the place of one that has become outmoded, obsolete, or inferior

re·place·ment \-mənt\ *n* **1** : the act of replacing : the state of being replaced **2** : that which replaces another

re·plant \(')rē-'plant\ *vt* **1** : to set (a plant) to grow again or anew **2** : to provide with new plants ⟨*replanted* the park⟩

re·plen·ish \ri-'plen-ish\ *vt* [MF *repleniss-, replenir* to fill up, fr. *re-* + *plein* full, fr. L *plenus*] : to fill again : bring back to a condition of being full or complete — **re·plen·ish·er** *n* — **re·plen·ish·ment** \-ish-mənt\ *n*

re·plete \ri-'plēt\ *adj* [L *repletus*, pp. of *replēre* to fill up, fr. *re-* + *plēre* to fill] **1** : filled to capacity : FULL; *esp* : full of food **2** : fully supplied or provided ⟨a book *replete* with illustrations⟩ **3** : COMPLETE — **re·plete·ness** *n*

re·ple·tion \ri-'plē-shən\ *n* **1** : the act of eating to excess : the state of being fed to excess : SURFEIT **2** : the condition of being filled up or overcrowded **3** : fulfillment of a need or desire : SATISFACTION

rep·li·ca \'rep-li-kə\ *n* [It, repetition, fr. *replicare* to repeat, fr. LL, fr. L, to fold back] **1** : a close reproduction or facsimile esp. by the maker of the original **2** : COPY, DUPLICATE

¹rep·li·cate \'rep-lə-,kāt\ *vt* : DUPLICATE, REPEAT

²rep·li·cate \-li-kət\ *n* : one of several identical experiments, procedures, or samples

³rep·li·cate \-li-kət\ *adj* **1** : folded over, backward, or upon itself **2** : MANIFOLD, REPEATED

rep·li·ca·tion \,rep-lə-'kā-shən\ *n* **1** : ANSWER, REPLY **2** : precise copying or reproduction; *also* : an act or process of this

¹re·ply \ri-'plī\ *vb* **re·plied; re·ply·ing** [MF *replier* to fold again, fr. L *replicare* to fold back, fr. *re-* + *plicare* to fold] **1 a** : to respond in words or writing : make answer **b** : to give as an answer **2** : to do something in response; *esp* : to return an attack — **re·pli·er** \-'plī(-ə)r\ *n*

²reply *n, pl* **replies** : something said, written, or done in answer or response

¹re·port \ri-'pōrt, -'pȯrt\ *n* [MF, fr. *reporter* to report, fr. L *reportare*, fr. *re-* + *portare* to carry] **1 a** : common talk : an account spread by common talk : RUMOR **b** : FAME, REPUTATION **2** : a usu. detailed account or statement (as of a judicial decision or of the proceedings of a meeting or session) **3** : an explosive noise ⟨the *report* of a gun⟩

²report *vb* **1** : to give an account (as of an incident or of one's activities) **2** : to give an account of in a newspaper article ⟨*report* a baseball game⟩ **3** : to make a charge of misconduct against ⟨*report* a schoolmate⟩ **4** : to present oneself ⟨*report* for duty⟩ ⟨*report* at the office⟩ **5** : to make known to the proper authorities ⟨*report* a fire⟩ **6** : to return or present (as a matter officially referred to a committee) with conclusions and recommendations — **re·port·a·ble** \-ə-bəl\ *adj*

re·port·age \ri-'pōrt-ij, -'pȯrt-, *esp for 2* ,rep-ər-'täzh\ *n* **1** : the act or process of reporting news **2** : writing intended to give an account of observed or documented events

report card *n* : a report on a student's grades that is periodically submitted by a school to the student's parents or guardian

re·port·ed·ly \ri-'pōrt-əd-lē, -'pȯrt-\ *adv* : according to report

re·port·er \ri-'pōrt-ər, -'pȯrt-\ *n* : one that reports: as **a** : one that makes authorized statements of law decisions or legislative proceedings **b** : one employed by a newspaper or magazine to gather and write news **c** : one that broadcasts news — **rep·or·to·ri·al** \,rep-ə(r)-'tōr-ē-əl, ,rēp-, -'tȯr-\ *adj* — **rep·or·to·ri·al·ly** \-ē-ə-lē\ *adv*

¹re·pose \ri-'pōz\ *vt* [irreg. fr. L *reponere* to put back, put away, place, fr. *re-* + *ponere* to put] **1** : to place unquestioningly : SET ⟨*repose* trust in a friend⟩ **2** : to place for control, management, or use

²repose *vb* [MF *reposer*, fr. LL *repausare*, fr. *re-* + *pausare* to pause, rest] **1** : to lay at rest : put in a restful position ⟨*reposed* his head on a cushion⟩ **2** : to lie at rest : take rest ⟨*reposing* on the couch⟩

³repose *n* **1** : a state of resting after exertion or strain; *esp* : rest in sleep **2** : CALM, PEACE **3** : cessation or absence of activity, movement, or animation ⟨a face in *repose*⟩

re·pose·ful \ri-'pōz-fəl\ *adj* : full of repose : QUIET — **re·pose·ful·ly** \-fə-lē\ *adv* — **re·pose·ful·ness** *n*

re·po·si·tion \,rē-pə-'zish-ən\ *vt* : to change or restore the position of

re·pos·i·to·ry \ri-'päz-ə-,tōr-ē, -,tȯr-\ *n, pl* **-ries** [L *repositorium*, fr. *reposit-, reponere* to put away, repose] **1** : a place or container where something is deposited or stored **2** : a side altar in a Roman Catholic church where the consecrated host is reserved from Holy Thursday until Good Friday **3** : one that contains or stores something nonmaterial **4** : a person to whom something is confided or entrusted

re·pos·sess \,rē-pə-'zes\ *vt* **1 a** : to regain possession of **b** : to retake possession of in default of the payment of installments due **2** : to restore to possession — **re·pos·ses·sion** \-'zesh-ən\ *n*

re·pous·sé \rə-,pü-'sā\ *adj* [F, lit., pushed back] **1** : shaped or ornamented with patterns in relief made by hammering or pressing on the reverse side — used of metal **2** : formed in relief

repp *var of* REP

rep·re·hend \,rep-ri-'hend\ *vt* [ME *reprehenden*, fr. L *reprehens-, reprehendere*, lit., to hold back by grasping, fr. *re-* + *prehendere* to grasp] : to voice disapproval of : CENSURE

rep·re·hen·si·ble \,rep-ri-'hen(t)-sə-bəl\ *adj* : worthy of or deserving censure or reprehension : CULPABLE — **rep·re·hen·si·ble·ness** *n* — **rep·re·hen·si·bly** \-blē\ *adv*

rep·re·hen·sion \-'hen-chən\ *n* : the act of reprehending : REPROOF — **rep·re·hen·sive** \-'hen(t)-siv\ *adj*

rep·re·sent \,rep-ri-'zent\ *vt* **1** : to present a picture, image, or likeness of : PORTRAY ⟨this picture *represents* a scene at King Arthur's court⟩ **2** : to serve as a sign or symbol of ⟨the flag *represents* our country⟩ **3 a** : to take the place of in some respect **b** : to act for or in the place of (as in a legislative body) ⟨*represents* his constituents in the Senate⟩ **4** : to describe as having a specified character or quality ⟨*represented* himself as a friend of the people⟩ **5** : to serve as a specimen, example, or instance of — **rep·re·sent·a·ble** \-ə-bəl\ *adj* — **rep·re·sent·er** *n*

rep·re·sen·ta·tion \,rep-ri-,zen-'tā-shən\ *n* **1** : one that represents: as **a** : an artistic likeness or image **b** : a sign or symbol of something **c** : a statement or account of an opinion or of a fact made to influence opinion or action **d** : a dramatic production or performance **2** : a usu. formal protest **3** : the act or action of representing or state of being represented (as in a legislative body) **4** : the body of persons representing a constituency — **rep·re·sen·ta·tion·al** \-shnəl, -shən-°l\ *adj*

¹rep·re·sen·ta·tive \,rep-ri-'zent-ət-iv\ *adj* **1** : serving to represent ⟨a painting *representative* of a battle⟩ **2** : standing or acting for another esp. through delegated authority **3** : of, based upon, or constituting a government in which the many are represented by persons chosen from among them usu. by election **4** : serving as a typical or characteristic example ⟨a *representative* housewife⟩ — **rep·re·sen·ta·tive·ly** *adv* — **rep·re·sen·ta·tive·ness** *n*

²representative *n* **1** : a typical example of a group, class, or quality : SPECIMEN **2** : one that represents another or others : DELEGATE, AGENT; *esp* : a member of the house of representatives of the U.S. Congress or a state legislature

re·press \ri-'pres\ *vt* [L *repress-, reprimere*, fr. *re-* + *premere* to press] **1** : to check by or as if by pressure : CURB **2** : to hold in by self-control **3** : to put down by force : SUBDUE **4** : to prevent the natural or normal expression, activity, or development of **5** : to exclude from consciousness — **re·pres·sive** \-'pres-iv\ *adj* — **re·pres·sive·ly** *adv* — **re·pres·sive·ness** *n* — **re·pres·sor** \-'pres-ər\ *n*

re·pressed *adj* **1** : subjected to or marked by usu. excessive repression **2** : characterized by restraint

re·pres·sion \ri-'presh-ən\ *n* **1** : the act of repressing : the state of being repressed **2** : a psychological process by which unacceptable wishes or impulses are kept from conscious awareness

¹re·prieve \ri-'prēv\ *vt* **1** : to delay the punishment of (as a condemned prisoner) : RESPITE **2** : to give relief or deliverance to for a time

²reprieve *n* **1 a** : the act of reprieving : the state of being reprieved **b** : a formal temporary suspension of the execution of a sentence **2** : a temporary respite

¹rep·ri·mand \'rep-rə-,mand\ *n* [F *réprimande*, fr. L *reprimendus* to be checked, fr. *reprimere* to repress] : a severe or formal reproof

²reprimand *vt* : to reprove severely and esp. officially **syn** see REPROVE

¹re·print \(')rē-'print\ *vt* : to print again — **re·print·er** *n*

²re·print \'rē-,print\ *n* **1** : a subsequent printing of a book already published having the identical text of the previous printing **2** : a separately printed text or excerpt : OFFPRINT

re·pri·sal \ri-'prī-zəl\ *n* [MF *reprisaille*, fr. obs. It *ripresaglia*, fr. *ripres-, riprendere* to take back, fr. *ri-, re-* + *prendere* to take, fr. L *prehendere*] **1** : the use of force short of war by one nation against another in retaliation for damage or loss suffered ⟨economic *reprisals*⟩ **2** : an act of retaliation esp. in war

re·prise \ri-'prēz\ *n* [MF, fr. *reprendre* to take back, fr. *re-* + *prendre* to take, fr. L *prehendere*] : a recurrence, renewal, or resumption of an action or a musical passage

re·pro \'rē-prō\ *n, pl* **repros** [short for *reproduction*] : a clear sharp proof made esp. from a letterpress printing surface to serve as photographic copy for a printing plate

¹re·proach \ri-'prōch\ *n* [MF *reproche*] **1 a** : a cause or occasion of blame, discredit, or disgrace **b** : DISCREDIT, DISGRACE **2** : the act or action of reproaching : REBUKE — **re·proach·ful** \-fəl\ *adj* — **re·proach·ful·ly** \-fə-lē\ *adv* — **re·proach·ful·ness** *n*

²reproach *vt* **1** : to utter a reproach to : find fault with : blame for a mistake or failure ⟨*reproached* him for his cowardice⟩ **2** : to bring into discredit **syn** see REPROVE

See *re-* and 2d element | **reprice**

ə abut; ə kitten; ər further; a back; ā bake; ä cot, cart; aů out; ch chin; e less; ē easy; g gift; i trip; ī life

— **re·proach·a·ble** \-'prō-chə-bəl\ *adj* — **re·proach·er** *n* — **re·proach·ing·ly** \-'prō-chiŋ-lē\ *adv*

¹**rep·ro·bate** \'rep-rə-,bāt\ *vt* [LL *reprobare*, fr. L *re-* + *probare* to test, approve] **1** : to condemn as unworthy or evil **2** : to foreordain to damnation — **rep·ro·ba·tion** \,rep-rə-,'bā-shən\ *n* — **rep·ro·ba·tive** \'rep-rə-,bāt-iv\ *adj* — **rep·ro·ba·to·ry** \-bə-,tōr-ē, -,tór-\ *adj*

²**reprobate** *adj* **1** : foreordained to damnation **2** : morally abandoned : DEPRAVED

³**reprobate** *n* : a reprobate person

re·pro·duce \,rē-prə-'d(y)üs\ *vb* **1** : to produce again: as **a** : to give rise to (new individuals of the same kind) **b** : to cause to exist again or anew ⟨*reproduce* water from steam⟩ **c** : to imitate closely ⟨sound-effects men can *reproduce* the sound of thunder and footsteps⟩ **d** : to present again **e** : to make an image or copy of **f** : to revive mentally **g** : to translate (a recording) into sound **2** : to undergo reproduction ⟨her voice *reproduces* well⟩ **3** : to produce offspring — **re·pro·duc·er** *n* — **re·pro·duc·i·bil·i·ty** \-,d(y)ü-sə-'bil-ət-ē\ *n* — **re·pro·duc·i·ble** \-'d(y)ü-sə-bəl\ *adj*

re·pro·duc·tion \,rē-prə-'dək-shən\ *n* **1** : the act or process of reproducing; *esp* : the process by which plants and animals give rise to offspring **2** : something reproduced : COPY **syn** see DUPLICATE

re·pro·duc·tive \,rē-prə-'dək-tiv\ *adj* : of, relating to, capable of, or concerned with reproduction — **re·pro·duc·tive·ly** *adv* — **re·pro·duc·tive·ness** *n* — **re·pro·duc·tiv·i·ty** \-,dək-'tiv-ət-ē\ *n*

re·proof \ri-'prüf\ *n* [MF *reprove*, fr. *reprover* to reprove] : censure for a fault : REBUKE

re·prove \ri-'prüv\ *vt* [MF *reprover*, fr. LL *reprobare* to reprobate] **1** : to administer a rebuke to : SCOLD **2** : to express disapproval of : CENSURE, CONDEMN — **re·prov·er** *n* **syn** REPROVE, REBUKE, REPRIMAND, REPROACH mean to criticize for faulty behavior. REPROVE may imply a kindly intent and lack of harshness; REBUKE implies a stern or sharp reproving; REPRIMAND implies a severe, formal, often public or official rebuke; REPROACH often suggests displeasure or disappointment expressed in mild scolding.

rep·tant \'rep-tənt\ *adj* : CREEPING, PROSTRATE

¹**rep·tile** \'rep-t'l, -,tīl\ *n* [LL, fr. neut. of *reptilis* creeping, fr. *repere* to creep] **1** : any of a class (Reptilia) of air-breathing vertebrates comprising the alligators and crocodiles, lizards, snakes, turtles, and extinct related forms and having a bony skeleton and a body usu. covered with scales or bony plates **2** : a groveling or despicable person

²**reptile** *adj* : characteristic of a reptile : REPTILIAN

¹**rep·til·i·an** \rep-'til-ē-ən\ *adj* : of, relating to, or resembling reptiles

²**reptilian** *n* : REPTILE 1

re·pub·lic \ri-'pəb-lik\ *n* [F *république*, fr. L *res publica*, lit., public thing, commonwealth] **1 a** (1) : a government having a chief of state who is not a monarch and who is usu. a president (2) : a political unit having such a form of government **b** (1) : a government in which supreme power resides in a body of citizens entitled to vote and is exercised by elected officers and representatives responsible to them (2) : a political unit (as a nation) having such a form of government **2** : a constituent political and territorial unit of the U.S.S.R. or Yugoslavia **syn** see DEMOCRACY

¹**re·pub·li·can** \ri-'pəb-li-kən\ *adj* **1 a** : of, relating to, or having the characteristics of a republic **b** : favoring, supporting, or advocating a republic **2** *cap* **a** : DEMOCRATIC-REPUBLICAN **b** : of, relating to, or constituting a political party in the U.S. evolving in the mid-19th century and usu. associated with business, financial, and some agricultural interests and with favoring a restricted governmental role in social and economic life

²**republican** *n* **1** : one that favors or supports a republican form of government **2** *cap* **a** : a member of a political party advocating republicanism **b** : a member of the Republican party of the U.S.

re·pub·li·can·ism \-kə-,niz-əm\ *n* **1** : adherence to or sympathy for a republican form of government **2** : the principles or theory of republican government **3** *cap* : the principles, policy, or practices of the Republican party of the U.S.

re·pub·li·ca·tion \(,)rē-,pəb-lə-'kā-shən\ *n* **1** : the act or action of republishing : the state of being republished **2** : something republished

re·pub·lish \(')rē-'pəb-lish\ *vt* **1** : to publish again or anew **2** : to execute (a will) anew — **re·pub·lish·er** *n*

re·pu·di·ate \ri-'pyüd-ē-,āt\ *vt* [L *repudiare*, fr. *repudium* divorce] **1** : to divorce or separate formally from (a woman) **2** : to refuse to have anything to do with : DISOWN ⟨*repudiated* his son and heir⟩ **3 a** : to refuse to accept; *esp* : to reject as unauthorized or as having no binding force **b** : to reject as untrue or unjust ⟨*repudiate* a charge of favoritism⟩ **4** : to refuse to acknowledge or pay **syn** see REJECT — **re·pu·di·a·tion** \-,pyüd-ē-'ā-shən\ *n* — **re·pu·di·a·tor** \-'pyüd-ē-,āt-ər\ *n*

re·pug·nance \ri-'pəg-nən(t)s\ *n* : deep-rooted dislike : AVERSION, LOATHING

re·pug·nant \-nənt\ *adj* [MF, opposed, incompatible, fr. L *repugnant-*, *repugnans*, prp. of *repugnare* to fight against, fr. *re-* + *pugnare* to fight] **1** : CONTRARY, INCOMPATIBLE ⟨punishments *repugnant* to the spirit of the law⟩ **2** : DISTASTEFUL, REPULSIVE — **re·pug·nant·ly** *adv* **syn** REPELLENT, ABHORRENT: REPUGNANT implies arousing one's resistance or loathing through being alien to one's ideas, principles, or tastes; REPELLENT suggests a generally forbidding or unlovely quality that makes one back away; ABHORRENT adds to REPUGNANT an implication of stronger resistance or profound antagonism ⟨police methods *abhorrent* to a free people⟩

¹**re·pulse** \ri-'pəls\ *vt* [L *repuls-*, *repellere*] **1** : to drive or beat back : REPEL ⟨*repulse* an attack⟩ **2** : to repel by discourtesy, coldness, or denial : REBUFF ⟨*repulsed* his advances⟩ **3** : to cause repulsion in : DISGUST ⟨*repulsed* at the sight⟩

²**repulse** *n* **1** : REBUFF, REJECTION **2** : the action of repelling an attacker : the fact of being repelled

re·pul·sion \ri-'pəl-shən\ *n* **1** : the action of repulsing : the state of being repulsed **2** : the action of repelling : the force with which bodies, particles, or like forces repel one another **3** : a feeling of aversion : REPUGNANCE

re·pul·sive \ri-'pəl-siv\ *adj* **1** : tending or serving to repulse **2** : arousing aversion or disgust — **re·pul·sive·ly** *adv* — **re·pul·sive·ness** *n*

rep·u·ta·ble \'rep-yət-ə-bəl\ *adj* : having a good reputation : RESPECTED — **rep·u·ta·bil·i·ty** \,rep-yət-ə-'bil-ət-ē\ *n* — **rep·u·ta·bly** \-'rep-yət-ə-blē\ *adv*

rep·u·ta·tion \,rep-yə-'tā-shən\ *n* **1** : overall quality or character as seen or judged by people in general ⟨he's got a bad *reputation*⟩ **2** : recognition by other people of some characteristic or ability ⟨has the *reputation* of being clever⟩ **3** : good name : a place in public esteem ⟨lost her *reputation*⟩ **4** : FAME ⟨a worldwide *reputation*⟩

¹**re·pute** \ri-'pyüt\ *vt* [L *reputare* to reckon up, think over, fr. *re-* + *putare* to reckon] : SUPPOSE, BELIEVE, CONSIDER ⟨a man *reputed* to be a millionaire⟩

²**repute** *n* **1** : the character or status commonly ascribed to one : REPUTATION ⟨know a man by *repute*⟩ **2** : FAME, NOTE ⟨a scientist of *repute*⟩

re·put·ed \ri-'pyüt-əd\ *adj* **1** : having repute ⟨a highly *reputed* lawyer⟩ **2** : popularly supposed ⟨a *reputed* success⟩ — **re·put·ed·ly** *adv*

¹**re·quest** \ri-'kwest\ *n* [MF *requeste*, fr. (assumed) VL *requaesta*, fr. *requaest-*, *requaerere* to require, request] **1** : an asking for something : PETITION, ENTREATY **2** : something asked for ⟨grant every *request*⟩ **3** : the condition of being requested ⟨tickets are available upon *request*⟩ **4** : DEMAND ⟨that book is in great *request*⟩

²**request** *vt* **1** : to make a request to or of **2** : to ask for **syn** see ASK — **re·quest·er** *n*

req·ui·em \'rek-wē-əm, 'rā-kwē-\ *n* [L, accus. of *requies* rest; first word of the introit of the requiem mass] **1** : a mass for a dead person; *also* : a musical setting for such a mass **2** : a musical service or hymn in honor of the dead

req·ui·es·cat \,rek-wē-'es-,kät, ,rā-kwē-\ *n* [L, may he (or she) rest, fr. *requiescere* to rest, fr. *re-* + *quiescere* to be quiet, fr. *quies* quiet] : a prayer for the repose of a dead person

re·quin \rə-'kan\ *n* [F] : any of several voracious sharks

re·quire \ri-'kwī(ə)r\ *vt* [MF *requerre*, fr. (assumed) VL *requaerere* to request, require, fr. L *re-* + *quaerere* to seek, ask] **1** : ORDER, COMMAND ⟨the law *requires* drivers to

j joke; **ŋ** sing; **ō** flow; **ó** flaw; **ói** coin; **th** thin; **th** this; **ü** loot; **ù** foot; **y** yet; **yü** few; **yù** furious; **zh** vision

observe traffic lights⟩ **2 :** to call for **:** NEED ⟨a trick that *requires* skill⟩ **syn** see DEMAND

re·quire·ment \-mənt\ *n* **1 :** something (as a condition or quality) required ⟨comply with all *requirements*⟩ **2 :** NECESSITY, NEED ⟨sleep is a *requirement* for health⟩

req·ui·site \'rek-wə-zət\ *adj* [L *requisitus*, pp. of *requirere* to require, fr. *re-* + *quaerere* to seek, ask] **:** REQUIRED, NEEDFUL **syn** see NECESSARY — **requisite** *n* — **req·ui·site·ness** *n*

¹req·ui·si·tion \,rek-wə-'zish-ən\ *n* **1 :** the act of requiring or demanding **2 :** an authoritative or formal demand or application ⟨a *requisition* for army supplies⟩ **3 :** the condition of being demanded or put into use ⟨every car was in *requisition*⟩

²requisition *vt* **-si·tioned; -si·tion·ing** \-'zish-(ə-)niŋ\ **:** to make a requisition for ⟨*requisition* fresh supplies⟩

re·quit·al \ri-'kwīt-ᵊl\ *n* **1 :** the act or action of requiting **:** the state of being requited **2 :** something given in requital

re·quite \ri-'kwīt\ *vt* [*re-* + obs. *quite* to quit, pay] **1 a :** to make return for **:** REPAY **b :** to make retaliation for **:** AVENGE **2 :** to make return to for a benefit or service or for an injury — **re·quit·er** *n*

rer·e·dos \'rer-ə-,däs\ *n* [AF *areredos*, fr. MF *arrere* behind + *dos* back] **:** a usu. ornamental wood or stone screen or partition wall behind and altar

rere·mouse \'ri(ə)r-,maús\ *n, chiefly dial* **:** BAT

¹re·run \(')rē-'rən\ *vt* **:** to run again or anew

²re·run \'rē-,rən, (')rē-'\ *n* **:** the act or action or an instance of rerunning; *esp* **:** presentation of a motion-picture film or television program after its first run

re·sale \'rē-,sāl, (')rē-'\ *n* **:** the act or an instance of selling again

re·scind \ri-'sind\ *vt* [L *resciss-, rescindere* to cut apart, annul, fr. *re-* + *scindere* to cut] **1 :** to make void **:** ANNUL, CANCEL ⟨*rescind* a contract⟩ **2 :** REPEAL — **re·scind·er** *n*

re·scis·sion \ri-'sizh-ən\ *n* **:** an act of rescinding

re·script \'rē-,skript\ *n* [L *rescriptum*, fr. neut. of *rescriptus*, pp. of *rescribere* to write in reply, fr. *re-* + *scribere* to write] **1 :** a written answer of a Roman emperor or of a pope to a legal inquiry or petition **2 :** an official or authoritative order, decree, edict, or announcement **3 :** an act or instance of rewriting

res·cue \'res-kyü\ *vt* [MF *rescourre*, fr. *re-* + *escourre* to shake out, wrest away, fr. L *excutere*, fr. *ex-* + *quatere* to shake] **:** to free from confinement, danger, or evil **:** SAVE — **rescue** *n* — **res·cu·er** *n*

syn DELIVER, REDEEM, RANSOM: RESCUE implies freeing from imminent danger by prompt or vigorous action; DELIVER implies releasing from confinement, temptation, slavery, or suffering; REDEEM implies releasing from bondage or penalties by giving what is demanded or necessary; RANSOM applies specifically to buying out of captivity

rescue mission *n* **:** a city religious mission seeking to convert and rehabilitate human derelicts

re·search \ri-'sərch, 'rē-,\ *n* [MF *recerche*, fr. *recerchier* to investigate thoroughly, fr. *re-* + *cerchier* to search] **1 :** careful or diligent search **2 :** studious inquiry or examination; *esp* **:** investigation or experimentation aimed at the discovery and interpretation of facts, revision of accepted theories or laws in the light of new facts, or practical application of such new or revised theories or laws — **research** *vb* — **re·search·er** *n*

re·sec·tion \ri-'sek-shən\ *n* [L *resect-, resecare* to cut off, fr. *re-* + *secare* to cut] **:** the surgical removal of part of an organ or structure — **re·sect** \-'sekt\ *vt* — **re·sect·a·ble** \-'sek-tə-bəl\ *adj*

re·seed \(')rē-'sēd\ *vb* **1 :** to sow seed on again or anew **2 :** to maintain itself by self-sown seed

re·sem·blance \ri-'zem-blən(t)s\ *n* **1 :** the quality or state of resembling **:** SIMILARITY; *also* **:** a point of likeness **2 :** REPRESENTATION, IMAGE **syn** see LIKENESS

re·sem·ble \ri-'zem-bəl\ *vt* **-bled; -bling** \-b(ə-)liŋ\ [MF *resembler*, fr. *re-* + *sembler* to be like, seem, fr. L *similare* to copy, fr. *similis* like] **:** to be like or similar to ⟨he *resembles* his father⟩

re·sent \ri-'zent\ *vt* [F *ressentir*, fr. *re-* + *sentir* to feel] **:** to feel or express annoyance or ill will over ⟨*resent* all criticism⟩

re·sent·ful \-fəl\ *adj* **1 :** full of resentment **:** inclined to resent **2 :** caused or marked by resentment — **re·sent·ful·ly** \-fə-lē\ *adv* — **re·sent·ful·ness** *n*

re·sent·ment \ri-'zent-mənt\ *n* **:** a feeling of indignant displeasure at something regarded as a wrong, insult, or injury

re·ser·pine \ri-'sər-pən, -'zər-\ *n* [G *reserpin*, prob. irreg. fr. NL *Rauwolfia serpentina*, a species of rauwolfia] **:** a drug obtained esp. from rauwolfia and used similarly

res·er·va·tion \,rez-ər-'vā-shən\ *n* **1 :** the act of reserving **2 :** an arrangement to have something (as a hotel room or train seat) held for one's use **3 :** something reserved for a special use; *esp* **:** a tract of public lands so reserved ⟨an Indian *reservation*⟩ **4 :** a limiting condition **:** EXCEPTION ⟨agree without *reservations*⟩

¹re·serve \ri-'zərv\ *vt* [L *reservare*, lit., to keep back, fr. *re-* + *servare* to keep, save] **1 :** to keep in store for future or special use **2 :** to retain or hold over to a future time or place **:** DEFER **3 :** to arrange to have set aside and held for one's use ⟨*reserve* a hotel room⟩ **4 :** to set or have set aside or apart

²reserve *n* **1 :** something stored or available for future use **:** STOCK ⟨oil *reserves*⟩ **2 :** something reserved for a particular use: as **a :** military forces withheld or available for later decisive use — usu. used in pl. **b :** the military forces of a country not part of the regular services; *also* **:** RESERVIST **c :** a tract set apart **:** RESERVATION **3 :** an act of reserving **:** EXCEPTION **4 a :** restraint, closeness, or caution in one's words and bearing **b :** forbearance from making a full explanation, complete disclosure, or free expression of one's mind **5 a :** money or its equivalent kept in hand or set apart usu. to meet liabilities **b :** the liquid resources of a nation for meeting international payments **6 :** SUBSTITUTE

reserve bank *n* **:** a central bank holding reserves of other banks

re·served \ri-'zərvd\ *adj* **1 :** restrained in words and actions ⟨very *reserved* in public⟩ **2 :** kept or set apart or aside for future or special use — **re·serv·ed·ly** \-'zər-vəd-lē\ *adv* — **re·serv·ed·ness** \-'zər-vəd-nəs, -'zərv(d)-nəs\ *n*

re·serv·ist \ri-'zər-vəst\ *n* **:** a member of a military reserve

res·er·voir \'rez-ə(r)v-,wär, -ə(r)v-,(w)ôr\ *n* [F *réservoir*, fr. *réserver* to reserve] **1 :** a place where something is kept in store; *esp* **:** an artificial lake where water is collected and kept in quantity for use **2 :** an extra supply **:** RESERVE **3 :** an organism in which a parasite that is harmful to some other species lives and multiplies

re·shape \(')rē-'shāp\ *vt* **:** to give a new form or orientation to

re·ship \(')rē-'ship\ *vb* **:** to ship again; *esp* **:** to put on board a second time — **re·ship·ment** \-mənt\ *n* — **re·ship·per** *n*

re·shuf·fle \(')rē-'shəf-əl\ *vt* **1 :** to shuffle again **2 :** to reorganize usu. by redistribution of existing elements — **reshuffle** *n*

re·side \ri-'zīd\ *vi* [L *residēre* to sit back, abide, fr. *re-* + *sedēre* to sit] **1 :** to dwell permanently or continuously **:** have a fixed abode ⟨*reside* in St. Louis⟩ **2 :** to be present as an element, quality, or right ⟨the power of veto *resides* in the president⟩ — **re·sid·er** *n*

res·i·dence \'rez-əd-ən(t)s\ *n* **1 :** the act or fact of residing in a place as a dweller or in discharge of a duty ⟨physicians in *residence* in a hospital⟩ ⟨*residence* abroad⟩ **2 a :** the place where one actually lives as distinguished from a place of temporary sojourn **b :** the place where a corporation is actually or officially established **c :** the status of a legal resident **3 a :** DWELLING **b :** a unit of housing provided for students **4 a :** the period or duration of abode in a place **b :** a period of active study, research, or teaching at a college or university

res·i·den·cy \'rez-əd-ən-sē, -ə-,den(t)-\ *n, pl* **-cies 1 :** a usu. official place of residence **2 :** a territorial unit in which a political resident exercises authority **3** : a period of advanced resident training esp. in a medical specialty

¹res·i·dent \'rez-əd-ənt, -ə-,dent\ *adj* [L *resident-, residens,* prp. of *residēre* to sit back, abide] **1** : living in a place for some length of time : RESIDING **2** : living in a place while discharging official duties ⟨a *resident* physician of a hospital⟩ **3** : PRESENT, INHERENT **4** : not migratory ⟨*resident* birds⟩

²resident *n* **1** : one who resides in a place **2** : a diplomatic agent exercising authority in a protected state **3** : one (as a physician) serving a residency

res·i·den·tial \,rez-ə-'den-chəl\ *adj* **1** : used as a residence or by residents ⟨a *residential* hotel⟩ **2** : adapted to or occupied by residences ⟨a *residential* section⟩ **3** : of or relating to residence or residences — **res·i·den·tial·ly** \-'dench-(ə-)lē\ *adv*

¹re·sid·u·al \ri-'zij-(ə-w)əl\ *adj* : being or active as a residue : left over — **re·sid·u·al·ly** \-ē\ *adv*

²residual *n* : a residual product, substance, or result : REMAINDER

residual power *n* : a power held to be reserved to the states if the constitution does not forbid it to them or specifically delegate it to the federal government ⟨supervision of education is a *residual power*⟩

re·sid·u·ary \ri-'zij-ə-,wer-ē\ *adj* : of, relating to, disposing of, or constituting a residue ⟨a *residuary* clause in a will⟩

res·i·due \'rez-ə-,d(y)ü\ *n* [MF *residu,* fr. L *residuum,* fr. neut. of *residuus* left over, fr. *residēre* to sit back, remain] : whatever remains after a part is taken, set apart, or lost : REMNANT, REMAINDER: as **a** : the part of an estate remaining after the payment of all debts and specific devises and bequests **b** : the remainder after subtracting a multiple of a modulus from an integer

re·sid·u·um \ri-'zij-ə-wəm\ *n, pl* **-ua** \-wə\ [L] : something residual : RESIDUE, REMAINDER

re·sign \ri-'zīn\ *vb* [L *resignare,* to unseal, cancel, resign, fr. *re-* + *signare* to seal, sign] **1** : to give up by a formal or official act ⟨*resign* an office⟩ **2** : to give up an office or position **3** : to commit or give over or up : submit or yield deliberately ⟨*resigned* herself to a disappointment⟩ — **re·sign·er** *n*

res·ig·na·tion \,rez-ig-'nā-shən\ *n* **1 a** : an act of resigning **b** : a letter or written statement that gives notice of this act **2** : the quality or the feeling of a person who is resigned : quiet or patient submission or acceptance

re·signed \ri-'zīnd\ *adj* : submitting patiently (as to loss, sorrow, or misfortune) : SUBMISSIVE, UNCOMPLAINING — **re·sign·ed·ly** \-'zī-nəd-lē\ *adv* — **re·sign·ed·ness** \-'zī-nəd-nəs\ *n*

re·sil·ience \ri-'zil-yən(t)s\ *or* **re·sil·ien·cy** \-yən-sē\ *n* **1** : the ability of a body to rebound, recoil, or resume its original size and shape after being compressed, bent, or stretched : ELASTICITY ⟨the *resilience* of rubber⟩ ⟨the *resiliency* of arteries⟩ **2** : the ability to recover from or adjust to misfortune or change

re·sil·ient \-yənt\ *adj* [L *resilient-, resiliens,* prp. of *resilire* to jump back, recoil, fr. *re-* + *salire* to leap] : having resilience: as **a** : capable of withstanding shock without permanent deformation or rupture **b** : SPRINGY ⟨*resilient* turf⟩ **c** : tending to recover readily from fatigue or depression **syn** see ELASTIC — **re·sil·ient·ly** *adv*

res·in \'rez-²n\ *n* [L *resina,* fr. Gk *rhētinē* pine resin] **1 a** : any of various solid or semisolid fusible natural organic substances that are usu. transparent or translucent and yellowish to brown, are formed esp. in plant secretions, are soluble in organic solvents but not in water, are electrical nonconductors, and are used chiefly in varnishes, printing inks, plastics, and sizes and in medicine **b** : ROSIN **2** : any of a large class of synthetic products that have some of the physical properties of natural resins but are different chemically and are used chiefly as plastics — **res·in·ous** \-əs\ *adj*

res·in·oid \-,óid\ *n* **1** : a somewhat resinous substance; *esp* : a thermosetting synthetic resin **2** : a mixture of gum and resin obtained by allowing the juice from an incision in a plant to solidify

¹re·sist \ri-'zist\ *vb* [L *resistere,* fr. *re-* re-, against + *sistere* to take a stand] **1** : to withstand the force or effect of ⟨*resist* disease⟩ ⟨silver *resists* acids⟩ **2** : to exert oneself to

check or defeat **3** : to exert force in opposition **syn** see OPPOSE — **re·sist·er** *n*

²resist *n* : something (as a coating) that resists or prevents a particular action

re·sist·ance \ri-'zis-tən(t)s\ *n* **1 a** : an act or instance of resisting : OPPOSITION **b** : a means of resisting **2** : the ability to resist **3** : an opposing or retarding force **4 a** : the opposition offered by a body or substance to the passage through it of a steady electric current **b** : a source of resistance **5** *often cap* : an underground organization of a conquered country engaging in sabotage and secret operations against occupation forces and collaborators

re·sist·ant \-tənt\ *adj* : giving or capable of resistance

re·sist·i·bil·i·ty \ri-,zis-tə-'bil-ət-ē\ *n* **1** : the quality or state of being resistible **2** : the ability to resist

re·sist·i·ble \ri-'zis-tə-bəl\ *adj* : capable of being resisted

re·sis·tive \ri-'zis-tiv\ *adj* : marked by resistance

re·sis·tiv·i·ty \ri-,zis-'tiv-ət-ē\ *n, pl* **-ties** **1** : capacity for resisting : RESISTANCE **2** : the longitudinal electrical resistance of a uniform rod of unit length and unit cross-sectional area : the reciprocal of conductivity

re·sist·less \ri-'zist-ləs\ *adj* **1** : IRRESISTIBLE **2** : offering no resistance — **re·sist·less·ly** *adv* — **re·sist·less·ness** *n*

re·sis·tor \ri-'zis-tər\ *n* : a device offering electrical resistance

re·sol·u·ble \ri-'zäl-yə-bəl\ *adj* : SOLUBLE

res·o·lute \'rez-ə-,lüt\ *adj* [L *resolutus,* pp. of *resolvere* to resolve] **1** : marked by firm determination : RESOLVED **2** : BOLD, STEADY — **res·o·lute·ly** *adv* — **res·o·lute·ness** *n*

res·o·lu·tion \,rez-ə-'lü-shən\ *n* **1** : the act or process of reducing to simpler form: as **a** : the act of analyzing a complex notion into simpler ones **b** : the act of answering : SOLVING **c** : the act of determining **2** : the progression of a chord from dissonance to consonance **3** : the process or capability of making distinguishable individual parts, closely adjacent optical images, or sources of light **4** : the subsidence of inflammation esp. in a lung **5 a** : something that is resolved **b** : firmness of resolve **6** : a formal expression of the opinion, will, or intent of an official body or assembled group **7** : the point in a work of literature (as a play) at which the chief dramatic complication is worked out

¹re·solve \ri-'zälv, -'zólv\ *vb* [L *resolvere* to unloose, break up, fr. *re-* + *solvere* to loosen] **1 a** : to break up or separate into component parts; *also* : to change by disintegration **b** : to reduce by analysis **c** : to distinguish between or make independently visible adjacent parts of **2 a** : to clear up : DISPEL ⟨*resolve* doubts⟩ **b** : to find an answer or solution to **3** : to reach a decision about : DETERMINE, DECIDE **4** : to declare or decide by a formal resolution and vote **5** : to work out the resolution of (as a play) **6** : to progress or cause to progress from dissonance to consonance — **re·solv·a·ble** \-'zäl-və-bəl, -'zól-\ *adj* — **re·solv·er** *n*

²resolve *n* **1** : something resolved : DETERMINATION, RESOLUTION **2** : fixity of purpose

re·solved \ri-'zälvd, -'zólvd\ *adj* : DETERMINED, RESOLUTE — **re·solv·ed·ly** \-'zäl-vəd-lē, -'zól-\ *adv*

res·o·nance \'rez-°n-ən(t)s\ *n* **1 a** : the quality or state of being resonant **b** (1) : a vibration of large amplitude in a mechanical or electrical system caused by a relatively small periodic stimulus of the same or nearly the same period as the natural vibration period of the system (as when a radio receiving circuit is tuned to a broadcast frequency) (2) : the state of adjustment that produces resonance in a mechanical or electrical system ⟨two circuits in *resonance* with each other⟩ **2 a** : the intensification and enriching of a musical tone by supplementary vibration **b** : a quality imparted to voiced sounds by the configuration of the mouth and pharynx and in some cases also of the nostrils **3** : a phenomenon that is shown by a molecule, ion, or radical to which two or more structures differing only in the distribution of electrons can be assigned and that gives rise to stabilization of the structure

res·o·nant \-°n-ənt\ *adj* [L *resonare* to resound] **1** : continuing to sound : ECHOING **2** : of, relating to, or showing resonance **3** : intensified and enriched by resonance — **res·o·nant·ly** *adv*

res·o·nate \'rez-°n-,āt\ *vi* **1** : to produce or exhibit resonance **2** : REECHO, RESOUND

res·o·na·tor \-,āt-ər\ *n* : something (as a device for increasing the resonance of a musical instrument) that resounds or resonates

re·sorb \(')rē-'sórb, -'zórb\ *vt* [L *resorbēre* to swallow again, fr. *re-* + *sorbēre* to suck up] : to break down and assimilate (something previously produced) ⟨the tadpole's tail is gradually *resorbed*⟩ — **re·sorp·tion** \-'sórp-shən, -'zórp-\ *n*

¹re·sort \ri-'zórt\ *n* [MF, resource, recourse, fr. *resortir* to rebound, resort, fr. *re-* + *sortir* to escape] **1 a** : one that is looked to for help : REFUGE, RESOURCE **b** : RECOURSE ⟨have *resort* to force⟩ **2 a** : frequent, habitual, or general visiting **b** (1) : a frequently visited place (2) : a place providing recreation and entertainment esp. to vacationers **syn** see RESOURCE

²resort *vi* **1** : to go esp. frequently or habitually : REPAIR **2** : to have recourse ⟨*resort* to violence⟩

re·sort·er \ri-'zórt-ər\ *n* : one that resorts; *esp* : a frequenter of resorts

re·sound \ri-'zaúnd\ *vb* [MF *resoner*, fr. L *resonare*, fr. *re-* + *sonare* to sound] **1** : to become filled with sound : REVERBERATE **2 a** : to sound loudly **b** : to sound or utter in full resonant tones **3** : to become renowned **4** : to extol loudly or widely : CELEBRATE

re·sound·ing *adj* **1** : RESONATING, RESONANT **2 a** : impressively sonorous ⟨*resounding* name⟩ **b** : EMPHATIC, UNEQUIVOCAL ⟨a *resounding* success⟩ — **re·sound·ing·ly** \-'zaún-diŋ-lē\ *adv*

re·source \'rē-,sórs, -,zórs, -,sórs, -,zórs, ri-'\ *n* [F *ressource*, fr. OF *ressourse*, fr. *resourdre* to relieve, lit., to rise again, fr. L *resurgere*] **1** : a new or a reserve source of supply or support **2** *pl* : a usable stock or supply (as of money, products, power, or energy) ⟨America has great natural *resources*⟩ **3** : the possibility of relief or recovery ⟨left helpless without *resource*⟩ **4** : the ability to meet and handle situations : RESOURCEFULNESS **5** : a means of handling a situation or of getting out of difficulty : EXPEDIENT

syn RESORT: RESOURCE applies to anything one falls back upon in the absence or failure of usual means; RESORT implies usu. one final resource called upon or used only under compulsion or in desperation ⟨using his gun only as a last *resort*⟩

re·source·ful \-fəl\ *adj* : able to meet situations : capable of devising ways and means — **re·source·ful·ly** \-fə-lē\ *adv* — **re·source·ful·ness** *n*

¹re·spect \ri-'spekt\ *n* [L *respectus*, lit., act of looking back, fr. *respicere* to look back at, regard, fr. *re-* + *specere* to look] **1** : a relation to or concern with something usu. specified : REFERENCE ⟨with *respect* to your last letter⟩ **2** : an act of giving particular attention : CONSIDERATION **3 a** : deferential regard : ESTEEM **b** : the quality or state of being esteemed : HONOR **c** *pl* : expressions of respect or deference **4** : PARTICULAR, DETAIL ⟨perfect in all *respects*⟩ **syn** see DEFERENCE

²respect *vt* **1 a** : to consider worthy of high regard : ESTEEM **b** : to refrain from interfering with ⟨*respected* their privacy⟩ **2** : to have reference to : CONCERN **syn** see REGARD — **re·spect·er** *n*

re·spect·a·bil·i·ty \ri-,spek-tə-'bil-ət-ē\ *n* **1** : the quality or state of being respectable **2 a** : respectable persons **b** : a respectable convention

re·spect·a·ble \ri-'spek-tə-bəl\ *adj* **1** : worthy of respect : ESTIMABLE **2** : decent or correct in character or behavior : PROPER ⟨a *respectable* woman⟩ **3 a** : fair in size or quantity ⟨*respectable* amount⟩ **b** : moderately good : TOLERABLE **4** : fit to be seen : PRESENTABLE ⟨*respectable* clothes⟩ — **re·spect·a·ble·ness** *n* — **re·spect·a·bly** \-blē\ *adv*

re·spect·ful \ri-'spekt-fəl\ *adj* : marked by or showing respect or deference — **re·spect·ful·ly** \-fə-lē\ *adv* — **re·spect·ful·ness** *n*

re·spect·ing *prep* : CONCERNING

re·spec·tive \ri-'spek-tiv\ *adj* **1** : PARTIAL, DISCRIMINATIVE **2** : PARTICULAR, SEVERAL ⟨their *respective* homes⟩ — **re·spec·tive·ness** *n*

re·spec·tive·ly \ri-'spek-tiv-lē\ *adv* : as relating to each : each in the order given

re·spell \(')rē-'spel\ *vt* : to spell again or in another way; *esp* : to spell out according to a phonetic system ⟨*respelled* pronunciations⟩

re·spi·ra·ble \'res-p(ə-)rə-bəl, ri-'spī-rə-\ *adj* : fit for breathing

res·pi·ra·tion \,res-pə-'rā-shən\ *n* **1 a** : the placing (as by breathing) of air or dissolved gases in intimate contact with the circulating medium of a multicellular organism **b** : a single complete act of breathing **2** : the physical and chemical processes by which an organism supplies its cells and tissues with the oxygen needed for metabolism and relieves them of the carbon dioxide formed **3** : an energy-yielding oxidative reaction in living matter — **res·pi·ra·tion·al** \-shnəl, -shən-ᵊl\ *adj*

res·pi·ra·tor \'res-pə-,rāt-ər\ *n* **1** : a device covering the mouth or nose esp. to prevent the inhalation of harmful vapors **2** : a device used in artificial respiration

res·pi·ra·to·ry \'res-p(ə-)rə-,tōr-ē, ri-'spī-rə-, -,tór-\ *adj* : of or relating to respiration or the organs of respiration ⟨*respiratory* diseases⟩ ⟨*respiratory* enzymes⟩

respiratory pigment *n* : any of various permanently or intermittently colored complex proteins that function in the transfer of oxygen in cellular respiration

respiratory quotient *n* : a ratio indicating the relation of the volume of carbon dioxide given off in respiration to that of the oxygen consumed

re·spire \ri-'spī(ə)r\ *vb* [L *respirare*, fr. *re-* + *spirare* to blow, breathe] : to engage in respiration; *esp* : BREATHE

¹res·pite \'res-pət\ *n* [OF *respit*, fr. ML *respectus*, fr. L, act of looking back] **1** : a temporary delay : POSTPONEMENT; *esp* : REPRIEVE 1b **2** : an interval of rest or relief ⟨a *respite* from toil⟩

²respite *vt* **1** : to grant a respite to **2** : to put off : DELAY

re·splen·dence \ri-'splen-dən(t)s\ *n* : the quality or state of being resplendent : SPLENDOR — **re·splen·den·cy** \-dən-sē\ *n*

re·splen·dent \-dənt\ *adj* [L *resplendēre* to shine back, fr. *re-* + *splendēre* to shine] : shining brilliantly : LUSTROUS — **re·splen·dent·ly** *adv*

re·spond \ri-'spänd\ *vi* [L *respondēre* to promise in return, answer, fr. *re-* + *spondēre* to promise] **1** : to say something in return : make an answer **2** : to react esp. favorably in response ⟨*respond* to surgery⟩ **3** : to be answerable ⟨*respond* in damages⟩

¹re·spon·dent \ri-'spän-dənt\ *n* : one who responds: as **a** : one who maintains a thesis in reply **b** : one who answers in various legal proceedings (as in equity or to an appeal)

²respondent *adj* : RESPONSIVE; *esp* : being a respondent at law

re·sponse \ri-'spän(t)s\ *n* [L *responsum*, fr. neut. of *responsus*, pp. of *respondēre* to respond] **1** : the act of replying : ANSWER **2** : words said or sung by the people or choir in a religious service **3** : a reaction of an organism to stimulation

re·spon·si·bil·i·ty \ri-,spän(t)-sə-'bil-ət-ē\ *n, pl* **-ties** **1** : the quality or state of being responsible : ACCOUNTABILITY **2** : RELIABILITY, TRUSTWORTHINESS **3** : something for which one is responsible : BURDEN

re·spon·si·ble \ri-'spän(t)-sə-bəl\ *adj* **1** : liable to be called upon to give satisfaction (as for losses or misdeeds) : ANSWERABLE ⟨*responsible* for the damage⟩ **2** : able to fulfill one's obligations : TRUSTWORTHY, RELIABLE ⟨he proved *responsible*⟩ **3** : requiring a person to take charge of or be trusted with important matters ⟨a *responsible* job⟩ **4** : able to choose for oneself between right and wrong — **re·spon·si·ble·ness** *n* — **re·spon·si·bly** \-blē\ *adv*

re·spon·sive \ri-'spän(t)-siv\ *adj* **1** : giving response : ANSWERING ⟨*responsive* glance⟩ **2** : quick to respond or react sympathetically : SENSITIVE **3** : using responses ⟨*responsive* worship⟩ — **re·spon·sive·ly** *adv* — **re·spon·sive·ness** *n*

¹rest \'rest\ *n* [OE] **1** : REPOSE, SLEEP; *esp* : a bodily state characterized by minimal functional and metabolic activities **2 a** : freedom from activity **b** : a state of motion-

rests: *w* whole, *h* half, *q* quarters, *e* eighth, *s* sixteenth, *t* thirty-second

---

See *re-* and 2d element | **resow** | **respell** | **respring**

ə abut; ᵊ kitten; ər further; a back; ā bake; ä cot, cart; aü out; ch chin; e less; ē easy; g gift; i trip; ī life

lessness or inactivity   **c** : the repose of death **3** : a place for resting or lodging **4** : peace of mind or spirit **5 a** (1) : a silence in music equivalent in duration to a note of the same name (2) : a character representing such a silence **b** : a brief pause in reading **6** : something used for support ⟨a chin *rest* for a violin⟩

²rest *vb* **1 a** : to get rest by lying down : SLEEP; *also* : to give rest to ⟨*rest* yourself on the couch⟩ **b** : to lie dead **2** : to refrain from work or activity **3** : to place or be placed for or as if for support ⟨*rested* his foot on the rail⟩ ⟨his hand *resting* on the gun butt⟩ **4 a** : to remain for action or accomplishment ⟨the determination of the outcome *rests* with him alone⟩ **b** : DEPEND ⟨the success of the flight *rests* on the wind⟩ **c** : to fix or be fixed in trust or confidence ⟨she *rested* her hopes on his promise⟩ **5** : to stop voluntarily the introduction of evidence in a law case ⟨the defense *rests*⟩

³rest *n* [MF *reste*, fr. *rester* to remain, fr. L *restare*, lit., to stand back, fr. *re-* + *stare* to stand] : something that is left over or behind : REMAINDER — used with *the*   **syn** see BALANCE

re·state \(')rē-'stāt\ *vt* : to state again or in another way — **re·state·ment** \-mənt\ *n*

res·tau·rant \'res-t(ə-)rənt, -tə-,ränt\ *n* [F, fr. prp. of *restaurer* to rebuild, restore, fr. L *restaurare*] : a public eating place

res·tau·ra·teur \,res-tə-rə-'tər\ *also* **res·tau·ran·teur** \-,rän-\ *n* [F *restaurateur*, fr. LL *restaurator* restorer, fr. L *restaurare* to restore] : the operator or proprietor of a restaurant

rest·ful \'rest-fəl\ *adj* **1** : giving rest ⟨a *restful* chair⟩ **2** : giving a feeling of rest : QUIET ⟨a *restful* scene⟩ — **rest·ful·ly** \-fə-lē\ *adv* — **rest·ful·ness** *n*

rest home *n* : SANATORIUM

rest house *n* : a building used for shelter by travelers

rest·ing *adj* **1** : DORMANT ⟨a *resting* spore⟩ **2** : VEGETATIVE 1a ⟨a *resting* nucleus⟩

res·ti·tu·tion \,res-tə-'t(y)ü-shən\ *n* [L *restituere* to restore, fr. *re-* + *statuere* to set up, fr. *status* condition of standing, status] : the restoring of something to its rightful owner or the giving of an equivalent (as for loss or damage) ⟨make *restitution* for personal injuries⟩

res·tive \'res-tiv\ *adj* [*rester* to stop behind, remain, fr. L *restare*] **1** : stubbornly resisting control : BALKY **2** : fidgeting about : UNEASY — **res·tive·ly** *adv* — **res·tive·ness** *n*

  syn RESTIVE, RESTLESS mean showing signs of unrest. RESTIVE implies impatience under attempts to restrain or coerce ⟨the colonies were becoming increasingly *restive*⟩ RESTLESS implies constant, aimless activity as from anxiety, boredom, discontent, or discomfort ⟨*restless* children in rainy weather⟩

rest·less \'rest-ləs\ *adj* **1** : being without rest : giving no rest **2** : finding no rest or sleep : UNEASY ⟨a *restless* night⟩ **3** : never resting or settled : always moving   **syn** see RESTIVE — **rest·less·ly** *adv* — **rest·less·ness** *n*

rest mass *n* : the mass of a body exclusive of additional mass acquired by the body when in motion according to the theory of relativity

re·stor·a·ble \ri-'stōr-ə-bəl, -'stȯr-\ *adj* : fit for restoring or reclaiming

res·to·ra·tion \,res-tə-'rā-shən\ *n* **1** : an act of restoring or the condition of being restored: as **a** : a bringing back to a former position or condition : REINSTATEMENT **b** : RESTITUTION **c** : a restoring to an unimpaired or improved condition **2** : something that is restored; *esp* : a representation or reconstruction of the original form (as of a fossil or a building) **3** *cap* : the reestablishment of the monarchy in England in 1660 under Charles II; *also* : the period in English history following this Restoration

¹re·stor·a·tive \ri-'stōr-ət-iv, -'stȯr-\ *adj* : of or relating to restoration; *esp* : having power to restore — **re·stor·a·tive·ly** *adv* — **re·stor·a·tive·ness** *n*

²restorative *n* : something that serves to restore to consciousness or health

re·store \ri-'stō(ə)r, -'stȯ(ə)r\ *vt* [OF *restorer*, fr. L *restaurare* to renew, rebuild] **1** : to give back : RETURN

⟨*restored* the purse to its owner⟩ **2** : to put or bring back into existence or use ⟨*restore* harmony to the club⟩ **3** : to bring back or put back into a former or original state : RENEW; *esp* : RECONSTRUCT **4** : to put again in possession of something ⟨*restore* the king to the throne⟩   **syn** see RENEW — **re·stor·er** *n*

re·strain \ri-'strān\ *vt* [MF *restraindre*, fr. L *restringere* fr. *re-* + *stringere* to bind tight] **1 a** (1) : to prevent from doing something (2) : CURB, REPRESS ⟨*restrain* anger⟩ **b** : to limit, restrict, or keep under control ⟨*restrain* trade⟩ **2** : to deprive of liberty; *esp* : to place under arrest or restraint — **re·strain·a·ble** \-'strā-nə-bəl\ *adj* — **re·strain·er** \-'strā-nər\ *n*

re·strained \ri-'strānd\ *adj* : marked by restraint : being without excess or extravagance : DISCIPLINED — **re·strain·ed·ly** \-'strā-nəd-lē\ *adv*

re·straint \ri-'strānt\ *n* **1** : the act of restraining : the state of being restrained ⟨held in *restraint*⟩ **2** : a means of restraining : a restraining force or influence **3** : control over one's thoughts or feelings : RESERVE, CONSTRAINT ⟨shows *restraint* in his manner⟩

re·strict \ri-'strikt\ *vt* [L *restrict-, restringere* to restrain, restrict] **1** : to confine within bounds : RESTRAIN **2** : to place under restrictions as to use — **re·strict·ed** *adj* — **re·strict·ed·ly** *adv*

re·stric·tion \ri-'strik-shən\ *n* **1** : something (as a law or rule) that restricts **2** : an act of restricting : the condition of being restricted

re·stric·tive \ri-'strik-tiv\ *adj* **1** : serving or tending to restrict **2** : limiting the reference of a modified word or phrase ⟨*restrictive* clause⟩ — **restrictive** *n* — **re·stric·tive·ly** *adv* — **re·stric·tive·ness** *n*

rest room *n* : a room or suite of rooms providing personal facilities (as toilets)

¹re·sult \ri-'zəlt\ *vi* [L *resultare* to rebound, fr. *re-* + *saltare* to leap, freq. of *salire* to jump] **1** : to come about as an effect ⟨disease *results* from infection⟩ **2** : to end as an effect : FINISH ⟨the disease *results* in death⟩

²result *n* : something that results as a consequence, issue, or conclusion; *also* : beneficial or tangible effect ⟨this method gets *results*⟩   **syn** see EFFECT — **re·sult·ful** \-fəl\ *adj* — **re·sult·less** \-ləs\ *adj*

¹re·sult·ant \ri-'zəlt-ᵊnt\ *adj* : derived from or resulting from something else — **re·sult·ant·ly** *adv*

²resultant *n* **1** : something that results : OUTCOME **2 a** : a single force equal to two or more other forces and therefore exerting an effect on a body equivalent to that which would be produced by the joint action of the forces that it equals **b** : a vector equal to a given set of vectors

¹re·sume \ri-'züm\ *vb* [L *resumere*, fr. *re-* + *sumere* to take] **1** : to take again : occupy again ⟨*resume* your seats⟩ **2** : to begin again or go back to (as after an interruption) ⟨*resume* a game⟩

²ré·su·mé *or* **re·su·me** \'rez-ə-,mā\ *n* [F *résumé*, fr. pp. of *résumer* to resume, summarize] : a summing up : SUMMARY ⟨a *résumé* of the news⟩; *esp* : a short account of one's career and qualifications prepared typically by an applicant for a position

re·sump·tion \ri-'zəm(p)-shən\ *n* [L *resumpt-, resumere* to resume] : the action of resuming ⟨*resumption* of work⟩

re·su·pi·nate \ri-'sü-pə-nət\ *adj* [L *resupinatus*, pp. of *resupinare* to bend back to a supine position, fr. *re-* + *supinus* supine] : inverted or appearing inverted in position ⟨*resupinate* flowers⟩ — **re·su·pi·na·tion** \ri-,sü-pə-'nā-shən\ *n*

re·sur·gence \ri-'sər-jən(t)s\ *n* [L *resurgere* to rise again] : a rising again into life, activity, or prominence — **re·sur·gent** \-jənt\ *adj*

res·ur·rect \,rez-ə-'rekt\ *vt* [back-formation fr. *resurrection*] **1** : to raise from the dead : bring back to life **2** : to bring to view or into use again ⟨*resurrect* an old song⟩

res·ur·rec·tion \,rez-ə-'rek-shən\ *n* [L *resurrect-, resurgere* to rise again, fr. *re-* + *surgere* to rise] **1 a** *cap* : the rising of Christ from the dead **b** *often cap* : the rising again to life of all the human dead before the final judgment **2** : RESURGENCE, REVIVAL — **res·ur·rec·tion·al** \-shnəl, -shən-ᵊl\ *adj*

See *re-* and 2d element				
restaff	restock	restring	restyle	resupply
restage	restraighten	restructure	resubmission	resurface
restimulate	restrengthen	restudy	resubmit	resurvey
	restrike	restuff	resummon	

re·sus·ci·tate \ri-'səs-ə-ˌtāt\ vb [L resuscitare, fr. re- + suscitare to stir up, fr. sub-, sus- up + citare to put in motion] : to revive from apparent death or from unconsciousness; also : REVITALIZE — **re·sus·ci·ta·tion** \-ˌsəs-ə-'tā-shən\ n — **re·sus·ci·ta·tive** \-'səs-ə-ˌtāt-iv\ adj

re·sus·ci·ta·tor \ri-'səs-ə-ˌtāt-ər\ n : one that resuscitates; esp : an apparatus used to relieve asphyxiation

ret \'ret\ vb **ret·ted**; **ret·ting** [MD reten] : to soak so as to loosen the fiber from the woody tissue ⟨ret flax⟩

¹re·tail \'rē-ˌtāl, esp for 2 also ri-'\ vb [MF retaillier to cut back, divide into pieces, fr. re- + taillier to cut] **1 a** : to sell in small quantities **b** : to sell directly to the ultimate consumer ⟨retail groceries⟩ ⟨these shoes retail for $20⟩ **2** : TELL, RETELL — **re·tail·er** n

²re·tail \'rē-ˌtāl\ n : the sale of commodities or goods in small quantities directly to consumers — **at retail 1** : at a retailer's price **2** : ⁴RETAIL

³re·tail \'rē-ˌtāl\ adj : of, relating to, or engaged in the sale of commodities at retail ⟨retail trade⟩

⁴re·tail \'rē-ˌtāl\ adv **1** : in small quantities **2** : from a retailer

re·tain \ri-'tān\ vt [MF retenir, fr. L retinēre to hold back, keep, fr. re- + tenēre to hold] **1 a** : to keep in possession or use ⟨retain knowledge⟩ **b** : to keep in pay or in one's service; esp : to employ by paying a retainer **2** : to hold secure or intact ⟨lead retains heat⟩

retained object n : an object in a passive construction ⟨me in a book was given me and book in I was given a book are retained objects⟩

¹re·tain·er \ri-'tā-nər\ n : a fee paid (as to a lawyer) for advice or services or for a claim upon his services in case of need

²retainer n **1** : one that retains **2** : a servant or follower in a wealthy household

¹re·take \'rē-'tāk\ vt **-took** \-'tůk\; **-tak·en** \-'tā-kən\; **-tak·ing** : to take again; esp : to photograph again

²re·take \'rē-ˌtāk\ n : a second photographing or photograph

re·tal·i·ate \ri-'tal-ē-ˌāt\ vi [LL retaliare, fr. L re- + talio punishment in kind] : to return like for like; esp : to get revenge — **re·tal·i·a·tion** \-ˌtal-ē-'ā-shən\ n — **re·tal·i·a·tive** \-'tal-ē-ˌāt-iv\ adj — **re·tal·i·a·to·ry** \-'tal-yə-ˌtōr-ē, -ˌtór-\ adj

re·tard \ri-'tärd\ vt [L retardare, fr. re- + tardus slow] : to slow up : keep back : HINDER, DELAY — **re·tard·er** n

re·tard·ant \ri-'tärd-ᵊnt\ adj : serving or tending to retard — **retardant** n

re·tard·ate \ri-'tär-ˌdāt\ n : one who is mentally retarded

re·tar·da·tion \ˌrē-ˌtär-'dā-shən\ n **1** : an act or instance of retarding **2** : the extent to which something is retarded **3** : an abnormal slowness esp. of mental or bodily development

re·tard·ed \ri-'tärd-əd\ adj : showing developmental retardation

retch \'rech, Brit 'rēch\ vb [OE hrǣcan to clear the throat] : VOMIT; also : to try to vomit

re·te \'rēt-ē\ n, pl **re·tia** \-ē-ə\ [NL, fr. L, net] : an anatomical network (as of nerves or blood vessels)

re·ten·tion \ri-'ten-chən\ n [L retent-, retinēre to retain] **1** : the act of retaining : the state of being retained **2** : power of retaining : RETENTIVENESS **3** : something retained

re·ten·tive \ri-'tent-iv\ adj : having ability to retain; esp : having a good memory — **re·ten·tive·ly** adv — **re·ten·tive·ness** n

re·ten·tiv·i·ty \ˌrē-ˌten-'tiv-ət-ē\ n : the power of retaining; esp : the capacity for retaining magnetism after the action of the magnetizing force has ceased

ret·i·cence \'ret-ə-sən(t)s\ n : the quality or state of being secretive or reticent

ret·i·cen·cy \-sən-sē\ n, pl **-cies** : RETICENCE

ret·i·cent \-sənt\ adj [L reticēre to keep silent, fr. re- + tacēre to be silent] **1** : inclined to be silent or secretive : UNCOMMUNICATIVE **2** : restrained in expression or presentation **syn** see SILENT — **ret·i·cent·ly** adv

re·tic·u·lar \ri-'tik-yə-lər\ adj : RETICULATE; also : of, relating to, or being a reticulum

¹re·tic·u·late \-lət\ adj [L reticulatus, fr. reticulum network, fr. dim. of rete net] : resembling a net; esp : having

veins, fibers, or lines crossing ⟨a reticulate leaf⟩ — **re·tic·u·late·ly** adv

²re·tic·u·late \-ˌlāt\ vb **1** : to divide, mark, or construct so as to form network **2** : to distribute by a network **3** : to become reticulated

re·tic·u·la·tion \ri-ˌtik-yə-'lā-shən\ n : a reticulate formation : NETWORK

ret·i·cule \'ret-i-ˌkyül\ n [F réticule, fr. L reticulum network, network bag, fr. dim. of rete net] : a woman's drawstring bag used esp. as a carryall

re·tic·u·lo·en·do·the·li·al \ri-ˌtik-yə-lō-ˌen-də-'thē-lē-əl\ adj : of, relating to, or being a system of scattered phagocytic cells derived from mesenchyme

re·tic·u·lum \ri-'tik-yə-ləm\ n, pl **-la** \-lə\ [NL, fr. L, network] **1** : the second stomach of a ruminant mammal **2** : NETWORK

ret·i·na \'ret-ᵊn-ə\ n, pl **retinas** or **ret·i·nae** \-ᵊn-ˌē, -ᵊn-ˌī\ [ML] : the sensory membrane that lines the eye, receives the image formed by the lens, is the immediate instrument of vision, and is connected with the brain by the optic nerve — **ret·i·nal** \-ᵊn-əl\ adj

ret·i·nene \'ret-ᵊn-ˌēn\ n : either a yellowish or an orange aldehyde derived from vitamin A that in combination with proteins forms the visual pigments of the retinal rods and cones

ret·i·nue \'ret-ᵊn-ˌ(y)ü\ n [MF retenue, fr. fem. of retenu, pp. of retenir to retain] : the body of retainers who follow a distinguished person : SUITE

re·tire \ri-'tī(ə)r\ vb [MF retirer, fr. re- + tirer to draw] **1** : to withdraw or cause to withdraw from action or danger : RETREAT **2** : to withdraw esp. for privacy **3** : to withdraw or cause to withdraw from one's position or occupation **4** : to go to bed **5 a** : to withdraw from circulation : RECALL **b** : to withdraw (as obsolete equipment) from usual use or service **6** : to put out (a batter or side) in baseball

re·tired \ri-'tī(ə)rd\ adj **1** : QUIET, HIDDEN, SECRET ⟨a retired spot in the woods⟩ **2** : withdrawn from active duties or business **3** : received by or due to a person who has retired ⟨retired pay⟩ — **re·tired·ly** \-'tī-rəd-lē, -'tī(ə)rd-\ adv — **re·tired·ness** \-'tī(ə)rd-nəs\ n

re·tire·ment \ri-'tī(ə)r-mənt\ n : an act of retiring : the state of being retired; esp : withdrawal from one's position or occupation

re·tir·ing \ri-'tī(ə)r-iŋ\ adj : RESERVED, SHY — **re·tir·ing·ly** \-iŋ-lē\ adv — **re·tir·ing·ness** n

re·tool \(')rē-'tül\ vt : to equip anew with new or different tools ⟨retool a factory for making a new product⟩

¹re·tort \ri-'tórt\ vb [L retort-, retorquēre, lit., to twist back, hurl back, fr. re- + torquēre to twist] **1** : to answer back : to reply angrily or sharply **2** : to reply (as to an argument) with a counter argument

²retort n : a quick, witty, or cutting reply; esp : one that turns the first speaker's words against him

³re·tort \ri-'tórt, 'rē-\ n [ML retorta, fr. L, fem. of retortus, pp. of retorquēre to twist back; fr. its shape] : a vessel in which substances are distilled or decomposed by heat

retorts: 1 plain, 2 with receiver, R

re·touch \(')rē-'təch\ vt : to touch up; esp : to alter (as a photographic negative) in order to produce a more desirable appearance — **re·touch** \'rē-ˌtəch, (')rē-'\ n — **re·touch·er** \(')rē-'təch-ər\ n

re·trace \(')rē-'trās\ vt : to trace again or back

re·tract \ri-'trakt\ vt [L retract-, retrahere, fr. re- + trahere to draw] **1** : to draw or pull back or in ⟨a cat can retract its claws⟩ **2** : to take back (as an offer, a statement, or an accusation) : WITHDRAW, DISAVOW **syn** see RECANT — **re·tract·a·ble** \-'trak-tə-bəl\ adj

re·trac·tile \ri-'trak-tᵊl, -ˌtīl\ adj : capable of being drawn back or in ⟨the retractile claws of a cat⟩ — **re·trac·til·i·ty** \ˌrē-ˌtrak-'til-ət-ē\ n

re·trac·tion \ri-'trak-shən\ n **1** : RECANTATION; esp : a statement made by one retracting **2** : an act of retracting : the state of being retracted **3** : the ability to retract

re·trac·tor \ri-'trak-tər\ n : one that retracts; esp : a

See re- and 2d element **resynthesis**	**resynthesize** **retaste**	**retell** **rethink**		**retrack** **retrain**	**retransmission** **retransmit**

muscle that draws an organ or part in or back — compare ABDUCTOR, ADDUCTOR, PROTRACTOR

¹re·tread \(')rē-'tred\ *vt* **re·tread·ed; re·tread·ing** : to cement, mold, and vulcanize a new tread of camelback upon the bare cord fabric of (a worn pneumatic tire)

²re·tread \'rē-,tred\ *n* **1 a** : a new tread on a tire **b** : a retreaded tire **2** : one pressed into service again; *also* : REMAKE

¹re·treat \ri-'trēt\ *n* [MF *retrait*, fr. *retraire* to withdraw, fr. L *retrahere* to retract] **1 a** : an act or process of withdrawing esp. from what is difficult, dangerous, or disagreeable **b** (1) : the usu. forced withdrawal of troops from an enemy or from an advanced position (2) : a signal for retreating **c** (1) : a signal given by bugle at the beginning of a military flag-lowering ceremony (2) : a military flag-lowering ceremony **2** : a place of privacy or safety : REFUGE **3** : a period of group withdrawal for prayer, meditation, and instruction under a director

²retreat *vi* **1** : to make a retreat **2** : to slope backward

re·trench \ri-'trench\ *vb* [obs. F *retrencher*, fr. MF *retrenchier*, fr. re- + *trenchier* to cut] **1** : to cut down (as expenses) : REDUCE **2** : to reduce expenses : ECONOMIZE — **re·trench·ment** \-mənt\ *n*

re·tri·al \(')rē-'trī(-ə)l\ *n* : a second trial, experiment, or test

ret·ri·bu·tion \,re-trə-'byü-shən\ *n* [L *retribuere* to pay back, fr. re- + *tribuere* to pay] : something given in payment for an offense : PUNISHMENT

re·trib·u·tive \ri-'trib-yət-iv\ *adj* : of, relating to, or marked by retribution — **re·trib·u·tive·ly** *adv*

re·trib·u·to·ry \-yə-,tōr-ē, -,tòr-\ *adj* : RETRIBUTIVE

re·triev·al \ri-'trē-vəl\ *n* **1** : an act or process of retrieving **2** : possibility of being retrieved or recovering

¹re·trieve \ri-'trēv\ *vb* [ME *retreven*, modif. of MF *retrouver* to find again, fr. re- + *trouver* to find] **1** : to find and bring in killed or wounded game (a dog that *retrieves* well) **2** : to recover, restore, repair, or make good (as a loss or damage) (*retrieve* a damaged reputation) — **re·triev·a·ble** \-'trē-və-bəl\ *adj*

²retrieve *n* **1** : RETRIEVAL **2** : the successful return of a ball that is difficult to reach or control (as in tennis)

re·triev·er \ri-'trē-vər\ *n* : one that retrieves; *esp* : a vigorous active medium-sized dog with heavy water-resistant coat developed by crossbreeding and used esp. for retrieving game

retro- *prefix* [L, fr. *retro*, adv.] **1** : backward : back (*retro*rocket) **2** : situated behind (*retro*choir)

ret·ro·ac·tive \,re-trō-'ak-tiv\ *adj* : intended to apply or take effect at a date in the past (a *retroactive* pay raise) — **ret·ro·ac·tive·ly** *adv*

ret·ro·cede \,re-trō-'sēd\ *vb* [L *retrocess-, retrocedere* to go backward, fr. *retro-* + *cedere* to go] **1** : to go back : RECEDE **2** : to cede back (as a territory or jurisdiction) — **ret·ro·ces·sion** \-'sesh-ən\ *n*

ret·ro·flex \'re-trə-,fleks\ *or* **ret·ro·flexed** \-,flekst\ *adj* [NL *retroflexus*, fr. retro- + *flexus*, pp. of *flectere* to bend] **1** : turned or bent abruptly backward **2** : articulated with or involving the participation of the tongue tip turned up or curled back just under the hard palate

ret·ro·flex·ion *or* **ret·ro·flec·tion** \,re-trə-'flek-shən\ *n* : the act or process of bending back : the state of being bent back

ret·ro·gra·da·tion \,re-trō-grā-'dā-shən, -grə-\ *n* : the act or process of retrograding

¹ret·ro·grade \'re-trə-,grād\ *adj* [L *retrogradus* moving backward, fr. *retrogradi* to retrogress] **1** : going or inclined to go from a better to a worse state : DEGENERATING **2** : having a backward direction, motion, or tendency

²retrograde *vi* **1** : to go back : RETREAT (a glacier *retrogrades*) **2** : to decline to a worse condition

ret·ro·gress \,re-trə-'gres\ *vi* [L *retrogress-, retrogradi*, fr. *retro-* + *gradi* to step, go] : to move backward; *esp* : to revert to an earlier, lower, or less specialized state or condition — **ret·ro·gres·sion** \-'gresh-ən\ *n*

ret·ro·gres·sive \-'gres-iv\ *adj* : characterized by or tending to retrogression — **ret·ro·gres·sive·ly** *adv*

ret·ro·rock·et \'re-trō-,räk-ət\ *n* : an auxiliary rocket on an airplane, missile, or space vehicle that produces thrust in a direction opposite to or at an oblique angle to the motion of the object for deceleration

re·trorse \'rē-,tròrs\ *adj* [L *retrorsus*, contr. of *retroversus*, pp. of *retrovertere* to turn back, fr. retro- + *vertere* to turn] : bent backward or downward — **re·trorse·ly** *adv*

ret·ro·spect \'re-trə-,spekt\ *n* [retro- + -spect (as in prospect)] : a looking back on things past : a thinking of past events

ret·ro·spec·tion \,re-trə-'spek-shən\ *n* **1** : the act or power of recalling the past **2** : a review of past events

ret·ro·spec·tive \-'spek-tiv\ *adj* **1** : of, relating to, characteristic of, or given to retrospection **2** : affecting things past : RETROACTIVE — **ret·ro·spec·tive·ly** *adv*

re·trous·sé \rə-,trü-'sā\ *adj* [F, fr. pp. of *retrousser* to tuck up] : turned up (*retroussé* nose)

¹re·turn \ri-'tərn\ *vb* [MF *retourner*, fr. re- + *tourner* to turn] **1** : to come or go back **2** : REPLY, ANSWER **3** : to make (as a report) officially by submitting a statement (the jury *returned* a verdict) **4** : to elect to office (a candidate *returned* by a large majority) **5** : to bring, carry, send, or put back : RESTORE (*return* a book to the library) **6** : to bring in (as profit) : YIELD **7** : REPAY (*return* borrowed money) **8** : to send or say in response or reply (*return* thanks) — **re·turn·er** *n*

²return *n* **1 a** : the act of coming back to or from a place or condition **b** : a regular or frequent returning : RECURRENCE (the *return* of spring) **2 a** : a report of the results of balloting — usu. used in pl. (election *returns*) **b** : a formal statement on a required legal form showing taxable income, allowable deductions and exemptions, and the computation of the tax due **3** : a means for conveying something (as water) back to its starting point **4 a** : the profit from labor, investment, or business : YIELD **b** : the rate of profit per unit of cost **5 a** : the act of returning something to a former place, condition, or ownership **b** : something returned **6 a** : something given in repayment or reciprocation **b** : ANSWER, RETORT **c** : an answering or retaliatory play: as (1) : the act of returning a ball to an opponent (2) : the run of a football after a kick by the other team

³return *adj* : played, delivered, or given in return (a *return* call) (a *return* game)

re·turn·a·ble \ri-'tər-nə-bəl\ *adj* **1** : that may be returned (*returnable* bottles) **2** : that must be returned (a library book *returnable* in two weeks)

re·turn·ee \ri-,tər-'nē\ *n* : one who returns; *esp* : one returning to the U.S. after military service abroad

re·tuse \ri-'t(y)üs\ *adj* [L *retusus* blunted, fr. pp. of *retundere* to blunt, fr. re- + *tundere* to beat, pound] : having the apex rounded or obtuse with a slight notch (a *retuse* leaf)

re·uni·fi·ca·tion \(,)rē-,yü-nə-fə-'kā-shən\ *n* : the act or process of reunifying : the state of being reunified

re·uni·fy \(')rē-'yü-nə-,fī\ *vt* : to restore unity to

re·union \(')rē-'yü-nyən\ *n* **1** : the act of reuniting : the state of being reunited **2** : a reuniting of persons after separation (a class *reunion*)

re·unite \,rē-yü-'nīt\ *vb* : to come or bring together again after a separation

re·use \(')rē-'yüz\ *vt* : to use again — **re·us·a·ble** \-'yü-zə-bəl\ *adj* — **re·use** \-'yüs\ *n*

¹rev \'rev\ *n* : a revolution of a motor

²rev *vb* **revved; rev·ving** : to operate or cause to operate at an increasing speed of revolution (*rev* up a motor)

re·val·u·ate \(')rē-'val-yə-,wāt\ *vt* : REVALUE — **re·val·u·a·tion** \(,)rē-,val-yə-'wā-shən\ *n*

re·val·ue \(')rē-'val-yü\ *vt* : to make a new valuation of : REAPPRAISE

re·vamp \(')rē-'vamp\ *vt* **1** : RENOVATE, RECONSTRUCT **2** : to work over : REVISE

re·veal \ri-'vēl\ *vt* [MF *reveler*, fr. L *revelare* to uncover, reveal, fr. re- + *velare* to cover, fr. *velum* veil] **1** : to make known : DIVULGE (*reveal* a secret) **2** : to show plainly : DISPLAY — **re·veal·a·ble** \-'vē-lə-bəl\ *adj* — **re·veal·er** *n*

re·veal·ment \-'vēl-mənt\ *n* : an act of revealing : REVELATION

rev·eil·le \'rev-ə-lē\ *n* [modif. of F *réveillez*, imper. pl. of *réveiller* to wake up, fr. re- + *éveiller* to wake] : a signal sounded at about sunrise on a bugle or drum to call soldiers or sailors to duty

¹rev·el \'rev-əl\ *vi* **-eled** *or* **-elled; -el·ing** *or* **-el·ling**

j joke; ŋ sing; ō flow; ò flaw; òi coin; th thin; th this; ü loot; u̇ foot; y yet; yü few; yu̇ furious; zh vision

\'rev-(ə-)liŋ\ [MF *reveler*, lit., to rebel, fr. L *rebellare*] **1** : to take part in a revel : ROISTER **2** : to take intense satisfaction 〈*reveling* in success〉 — **rev·el·er** or **rev·el·ler** \-(ə-)lər\ *n*

²revel *n* : a noisy or merry celebration

rev·e·la·tion \,rev-ə-'lā-shən\ *n* [LL *revelation-, revelatio,* fr. L *revelare* to reveal] **1** : an act of revealing or communicating divine truth **2 a** : an act of revealing to view **b** : something that is revealed; *esp* : an enlightening or astonishing disclosure

Rev·e·la·tion \,rev-ə-'lā-shən\ *n* — see BIBLE table

re·vel·a·to·ry \ri-'vel-ə-,tōr-ē, -,tȯr-\ *adj* : of, relating to, or characteristic of revelation

rev·el·ry \'rev-əl-rē\ *n, pl* **-ries** : boisterous merrymaking : REVELING

¹re·venge \ri-'venj\ *vt* [MF *revengier,* fr. re- + *vengier* to avenge, fr. L *vindicare*] **1** : to inflict injury in return for **2** : to avenge for a wrong done 〈able to *revenge* himself on his former persecutors〉 **syn** see AVENGE — **re·veng·er** *n*

²revenge *n* **1** : an act or instance of revenging **2** : a desire to repay injury for injury **3** : an opportunity for getting satisfaction

re·venge·ful \-fəl\ *adj* : full of or prone to revenge : VINDICTIVE — **re·venge·ful·ly** \-fə-lē\ *adv* — **re·venge·ful·ness** *n*

rev·e·nue \'rev-ə-,n(y)ü\ *n* [MF, fr. *revenir* to return, fr. L *revenire,* fr. re- + *venire* to come] **1** : the income from an investment **2** : the income that a government collects for public use **3** : the income produced by a given source

rev·e·nu·er \-,n(y)ü-ər\ *n* : a revenue officer or boat

revenue stamp *n* : a stamp (as on a cigar box) for use as evidence of payment of a tax

re·ver·ber·ant \ri-'vər-b(ə-)rənt\ *adj* : REVERBERATING — **re·ver·ber·ant·ly** *adv*

re·ver·ber·ate \ri-'vər-bə-,rāt\ *vi* [L *reverberare* to cause to rebound, fr. re- + *verberare* to lash, fr. *verber* rod] : RESOUND, ECHO 〈the shot *reverberated* among the hills〉 — **re·ver·ber·a·tion** \-,vər-bə-'rā-shən\ *n* — **re·ver·ber·a·tive** \-'vər-bə-,rāt-iv\ *adj*

¹re·ver·ber·a·to·ry \ri-'vər-b(ə-)rə-,tōr-ē, -,tȯr-\ *adj* : acting by reverberation

²reverberatory *n, pl* **-tories** : a furnace or kiln in which heat is radiated from the roof onto the material treated

¹re·vere \ri-'vi(ə)r\ *vt* [L *revereri,* fr. re- + *vereri* to fear, respect; akin to E *wary*] : to show devotion and honor to : regard with reverence

syn REVERE, REVERENCE, VENERATE, WORSHIP mean to hold in profound respect and honor. REVERE further implies deference and tenderness of feeling 〈*revered* his grandfather〉 REVERENCE suggests a self-denying acknowledging of what has a deep and inviolate claim to respect 〈*reverence* truth〉 VENERATE implies regarding as holy or sacrosanct esp. because of age; WORSHIP implies paying homage to or as if to a divine being 〈*worship* idols〉

²revere *n* : REVERS

¹rev·er·ence \'rev-(ə-)rən(t)s, 'rev-ərn(t)s\ *n* **1 a** : honor or respect felt or shown : DEFERENCE **b** : a feeling of worshipful respect : VENERATION **2** : a gesture of respect (as a bow) **3** : the state of being revered or honored **4** : one held in reverence — used as a title for a clergyman **syn** see DEFERENCE

²reverence *vt* : to regard or treat with reverence **syn** see REVERE

¹rev·er·end \'rev-(ə-)rənd, 'rev-ərnd\ *adj* [L *reverendus* worthy of reverence, fr. *revereri* to revere] **1** : worthy of reverence : REVERED 〈these *reverend* halls〉 **2** — used as a title for clergymen and some female religious usu. preceded by *the* and followed by a title or a full name 〈the *Reverend* Mr. Doe〉〈the *Reverend* John Doe〉〈the *Reverend* Mother Superior〉

²reverend *n* : a member of the clergy 〈the *reverend* spoke at the meeting〉

rev·er·ent \'rev-(ə-)rənt, 'rev-ərnt\ *adj* : very respectful : showing reverence — **rev·er·ent·ly** *adv*

rev·er·en·tial \,rev-ə-'ren-chəl\ *adj* **1** : proceeding from or expressing reverence 〈*reverential* awe〉 **2** : inspiring reverence — **rev·er·en·tial·ly** \-'rench-(ə-)lē\ *adv*

rev·er·ie or **rev·ery** \'rev-(ə-)rē\ *n, pl* **-er·ies** [F *rêverie,* fr. MF, delirium, fr. *rever* to wander, be delirious] **1** : DAYDREAM **2** : the condition of being lost in thought

See re- and 2d element | **reverification** | **reverify**

re·vers \ri-'vi(ə)r, -'ve(ə)r\ *n, pl* **revers** \-'vi(ə)rz, -'ve(ə)rz\ [F, fr. MF *revers,* adj., turned back, reversed] : a lapel esp. on a woman's garment

re·ver·sal \ri-'vər-səl\ *n* : an act or the process of reversing

¹re·verse \ri-'vərs\ *adj* [L *reversus,* pp. of *revertere* to turn back] **1** : opposite or contrary to a previous or normal condition 〈*reverse* order〉 **2** : acting or operating in a manner contrary to the usual **3** : effecting reverse movement 〈*reverse* gear〉 — **re·verse·ly** *adv*

revers

²reverse *vb* **1** : to turn completely about or upside down or inside out **2** : ANNUL: as **a** : to overthrow or set aside (a legal decision) by a contrary decision **b** : to cause to take an opposite point of view **c** : to change to the contrary 〈*reverse* a policy〉 **3 a** : to go or cause to go in the opposite direction **b** : to put (as a car) into reverse — **re·vers·er** *n*

syn REVERSE, INVERT mean to change to the opposite position. REVERSE may imply change in order, direction of motion, or meaning; INVERT applies chiefly to turning upside down or inside out, less often end for end

³reverse *n* **1** : something directly contrary to something else : OPPOSITE **2** : an act or instance of reversing; *esp* : a change for the worse **3** : the back part of something; *esp* : VERSO **4 a** (1) : a gear that reverses something; *also* : the whole mechanism brought into play when such a gear is used (2) : movement in reverse **b** : an offensive play in football in which a back moving in one direction gives the ball to a player moving in the opposite direction

re·vers·i·bil·i·ty \ri-,vər-sə-'bil-ət-ē\ *n* : the quality or state of being reversible

¹re·vers·i·ble \ri-'vər-sə-bəl\ *adj* : capable of being reversed or of reversing: as **a** : having two finished usable sides 〈*reversible* fabric〉 **b** : wearable with either side out 〈*reversible* coat〉 — **re·vers·i·bly** \-blē\ *adv*

²reversible *n* : a reversible cloth or garment

re·ver·sion \ri-'vər-zhən\ *n* **1** : a right of future possession (as of property or a title) **2 a** : an act or the process of returning (as to a former condition); *also* : a product of reversion **b** : return toward some ancestral type; *also* : an atavistic individual : THROWBACK **3** : an act or instance of turning the opposite way : the state of being so turned

re·ver·sion·ary \-zhə-,ner-ē\ *adj* : of, relating to, constituting, or involving esp. a legal reversion

re·vert \ri-'vərt\ *vi* [L *revertere* to turn back, fr. re- + *vertere* to turn] **1** : to come or go back 〈many *reverted* to savagery〉 **2** : to undergo reversion — **re·vert·er** *n* — **re·vert·i·ble** \-'vərt-ə-bəl\ *adj*

re·vet \ri-'vet\ *vt* **re·vet·ted; re·vet·ting** [F *revêtir,* lit., to clothe again, dress up, fr. L *revestire,* fr. re- + *vestire* to clothe] : to face (as an embankment) with a revetment

re·vet·ment \-mənt\ *n* **1** : a facing (as of stone) to sustain an embankment **2** : EMBANKMENT; *esp* : a protective barricade (as against bomb splinters)

re·vic·tual \(')rē-'vit-ᵊl\ *vb* : to victual again

¹re·view \ri-'vyü\ *n* [MF *revue,* fr. *revoir* to look over, fr. re- + *voir* to see, fr. L *vidēre*] **1 a** : a formal military inspection **b** : a military ceremony honoring a person or an event **2** : a general survey **3** : an act of inspecting or examining **4** : judicial reexamination of the proceedings of a lower court **5 a** : a critical evaluation (as of a book or play) **b** : a magazine devoted chiefly to reviews and essays **6 a** : a retrospective view or survey **b** (1) : renewed study of material previously studied (2) : an exercise facilitating such study **7** : REVUE

²review *vb* **1** : to look at a thing again : study or examine again 〈*review* a lesson〉; *esp* : to reexamine judicially **2** : to make a formal inspection of (as troops) **3** : to give a criticism of (as a book or play) **4** : to look back on 〈*review* accomplishments〉 — **re·view·er** *n*

re·vile \ri-'vīl\ *vb* [MF *reviler* to despise, fr. re- + *vil* vile] **1** : to subject to verbal abuse **2** : to use abusive language : RAIL — **re·vile·ment** \-mənt\ *n* — **re·vil·er** *n*

re·vis·a·ble \ri-'vī-zə-bəl\ *adj* : capable of being revised

re·vis·al \-zəl\ *n* : an act of revising : REVISION

¹re·vise \ri-'vīz\ *vt* [L *revisere* to look at again, fr. re- +

visere to look at, visit, fr. *vis-*, *vidēre* to see] **1** : to look over again in order to correct or improve ⟨*revise* a manuscript⟩ **2** : to make a new, amended, improved, or up-to-date version or arrangement of ⟨*revise* a dictionary⟩ ⟨*revising* the alpine ferns⟩ — **re·vis·er** *or* **re·vi·sor** \-'vī-zər\ *n*

²**re·vise** \'rē-,vīz, ri-'\ *n* **1** : an act of revising : REVISION **2** : a printing proof taken from matter that incorporates changes marked in a previous proof

Revised Standard Version *n* : a revision of the American Standard Version of the Bible published in 1946 and 1952

Revised Version *n* : a British revision of the Authorized Version of the Bible published in 1881 and 1885

re·vi·sion \ri-'vizh-ən\ *n* **1** : an act of revising (as a manuscript) **2** : a revised version — **re·vi·sion·ary** \-'vizh-ə-,ner-ē\ *adj*

re·vi·sion·ism \ri-'vizh-ə-,niz-əm\ *n* : a movement in revolutionary Marxian socialism favoring an evolutionary spirit — **re·vi·sion·ist** \-'vizh-(ə-)nəst\ *adj or n*

re·vi·so·ry \ri-'vīz-(ə-)rē\ *adj* : having the power or purpose to revise ⟨*revisory* body⟩ ⟨a *revisory* function⟩

re·vi·tal·i·za·tion \(,)rē-,vīt-ºl-ə-'zā-shən\ *n* **1** : an act or instance of revitalizing **2** : something revitalized

re·vi·tal·ize \(')rē-'vīt-ºl-,īz\ *vt* : to give new life or vigor to

re·viv·al \ri-'vī-vəl\ *n* **1** : a reviving of interest (as in art, literature, or religion) **2** : a new publication or presentation (as of a book or play) **3** : a renewed flourishing ⟨a *revival* of business⟩ **4** : a meeting or series of meetings conducted by a preacher to arouse religious emotions or to make converts

re·viv·al·ism \-'vī-və-,liz-əm\ *n* : the often highly emotional spirit or methods characteristic of religious revivals

re·viv·al·ist \ri-'vī-və-ləst\ *n* : one who conducts revivals — **re·viv·al·is·tic** \-,vī-və-'lis-tik\ *adj*

re·vive \ri-'vīv\ *vb* [L *revivere*, fr. *re-* + *vivere* to live] **1** : to bring back or come back to life, consciousness, or activity : make or become fresh or strong again **2** : to bring back into use ⟨trying to *revive* an old fashion⟩ — **re·viv·er** *n*

re·viv·i·fy \rē-'viv-ə-,fī\ *vt* **-fied**; **-fy·ing** : to give new life to : REVIVE — **re·viv·i·fi·ca·tion** \-,viv-ə-fə-'kā-shən\ *n*

rev·o·ca·ble \'rev-ə-kə-bəl\ *adj* : capable of being revoked

rev·o·ca·tion \,rev-ə-'kā-shən\ *n* : an act or instance of revoking

¹**re·voke** \ri-'vōk\ *vb* [MF *revoquer*, fr. L *revocare*, lit., to call back, fr. *re-* + *vocare* to call] **1** : to put an end to (as a law, order, or privilege) by withdrawing, repealing, or canceling : ANNUL ⟨*revoke* a driver's license for speeding⟩ **2** : to renege in cards — **re·vok·a·ble** \-'vō-kə-bəl\ *adj* — **re·vok·er** *n*

²**revoke** *n* : an act or instance of revoking in a card game

¹**re·volt** \ri-'vōlt\ *vb* [MF *revolter*, fr. It *rivoltare* to overthrow, fr. (assumed) VL *revolvitare*, freq. of L *revolvere* to revolve, roll back] **1** : to renounce allegiance or subjection (as to a government) : REBEL **2** : to experience or cause to experience disgust or shock ⟨his nature *revolts* against such treatment⟩ — **re·volt·er** *n*

²**revolt** *n* **1** : an act or instance of revolting **2** : a renunciation of allegiance to a government or other legitimate authority; *esp* : INSURRECTION **syn** see REBELLION

re·volt·ing \ri-'vōl-tiŋ\ *adj* : extremely offensive : NAUSEATING — **re·volt·ing·ly** \-'vōl-tiŋ-lē\ *adv*

rev·o·lute \'rev-ə-,lüt\ *adj* : rolled backward or downward ⟨*revolute* margins⟩

rev·o·lu·tion \,rev-ə-'lü-shən\ *n* [L *revolut-*, *revolvere* to revolve, roll back] **1** : the action by a celestial body of going round in an orbit or elliptic course; *also* : the time taken to complete one such circuit **2** : completion of a course (as of years) : CYCLE, EPOCH **3 a** : the action or motion of revolving : a turning round a center or axis : ROTATION **b** : a single complete turn (as of a wheel or a phonograph record) **4 a** : a sudden, radical, or complete change **b** : a fundamental change in political organization; *esp* : the overthrow of one government and the substitution of another by the governed **syn** see REBELLION

¹**rev·o·lu·tion·ary** \-shə-,ner-ē\ *adj* **1 a** : of, relating to, or constituting a revolution ⟨*revolutionary* war⟩ **b** (1) : tending to or promoting revolution (2) : RADICAL,

EXTREMIST **2** *cap* : of or relating to the American Revolution

²**revolutionary** *n*, *pl* **-ar·ies** : REVOLUTIONIST

rev·o·lu·tion·ist \,rev-ə-'lü-sh(ə-)nəst\ *n* **1** : one engaged in a revolution **2** : an adherent or advocate of revolutionary doctrines — **revolutionist** *adj*

rev·o·lu·tion·ize \-shə-,nīz\ *vt* **1** : to overthrow the established government of **2** : to imbue with revolutionary doctrines **3** : to change fundamentally or completely (as by a revolution) — **rev·o·lu·tion·iz·er** *n*

re·volve \ri-'välv, -'vólv\ *vb* [L *revolvere* to roll back, cause to return, fr. *re-* + *volvere* to roll] **1** : to turn over at length in the mind ⟨*revolved* the story while he waited⟩ **2 a** : to go round or cause to go round in an orbit **b** : to turn round on or as if on an axis : ROTATE **3** : RECUR **4** : to move in response to or dependence on a specified agent ⟨whole household *revolves* about the baby⟩ — **re·volv·a·ble** \-'väl-və-bəl, -'vól-\ *adj*

re·volv·er \ri-'väl-vər, -'vól-\ *n* : a handgun with a cylinder of several chambers brought successively into line with the barrel and discharged with the same hammer

re·volv·ing *adj* : tending to revolve or recur; *esp* : recurrently available ⟨*revolving* credit⟩

re·vue \ri-'vyü\ *n* [F, lit., review] : a theatrical production consisting typically of brief often satirical sketches and songs — compare MUSICAL

re·vul·sion \ri-'vəl-shən\ *n* [L *revuls-*, *revellere* to tear away, fr. *re-* + *vellere* to pluck] **1** : a strong pulling or drawing away : WITHDRAWAL **2 a** : a sudden or strong reaction or change **b** : a sense of utter repugnance : REPULSION — **re·vul·sive** \-'vəl-siv\ *adj*

re·wake \(')rē-'wāk\ *or* **re·wak·en** \-'wā-kən\ *vb* : to waken again or anew

¹**re·ward** \ri-'word\ *vt* [ONF *rewarder* to regard, reward, fr. *re-* + *warder* to watch, ward, guard] **1** : to give a reward to or for **2** : RECOMPENSE — **re·ward·a·ble** \-ə-bəl\ *adj* — **re·ward·er** *n*

²**reward** *n* : something given or offered in return for a service; *esp* : money offered for the return of something lost or stolen or for the capture of a criminal

re·word \(')rē-'wərd\ *vt* : to state in different words ⟨*reword* a question⟩

re·work \(')rē-'wərk\ *vt* : to work again or anew

¹**re·write** \(')rē-'rīt\ *vt* **-wrote** \-'rōt\; **-writ·ten** \-'rit-ºn\ *also* **-writ** \-'rit\; **-writ·ing** **1** : to write over again esp. in a different form **2** : to put (material turned in by a reporter) into form for publication in a newspaper — **re·writ·er** *n*

²**re·write** \'rē-,rīt\ *n* : something (as a newspaper article) rewritten

rex \'reks\ *n*, *pl* **rex·es** *or* **rex** [F *castorex*, a variety of rabbit, fr. L *castor* beaver + *rex* king] : a mammal of a genetically variant strain characterized by a coat in which the normally longer and coarser guard hairs are shorter than the undercoat or lacking entirely

rey·nard \'rān-ərd, 'ren-\ *n*, *often cap* [Renard, the fox who is hero of the French beast epic *Roman de Renart*] : FOX

re·zone \(')rē-'zōn\ *vt* : to alter the zoning of

rhad·a·man·thine \,rad-ə-'man(t)-thən\ *adj*, *often cap* [fr. *Rhadamanthus*, mythical judge in the lower world] : rigorously strict or just

Rhae·to·Ro·man·ic \,rēt-ō-rō-'man-ik\ *n* [L *rhaetus* of Rhaetia, ancient Roman province + E *Romanic* Romance] : a Romance language of eastern Switzerland, northeastern Italy, and adjacent parts of Austria

rhap·so·dize \'rap-sə-,dīz\ *vi* : to speak or write rhapsodically ⟨*rhapsodize* about a new book⟩ — **rhap·so·dist** \-səd-əst\ *n*

rhap·so·dy \'rap-səd-ē\ *n*, *pl* **-dies** [Gk *rhapsōidia* recitation of selections from epic poetry, fr. *rhaptein* to sew, stitch together + *aidein* to sing] **1** : a written or spoken expression of extravagant praise or ecstasy **2** : a musical composition of irregular form — **rhap·sod·ic** \rap-'säd-ik\ *or* **rhap·sod·i·cal** \-i-kəl\ *adj* — **rhap·sod·i·cal·ly** \-i-k(ə-)lē\ *adv*

rhea \'rē-ə\ *n* : any of several large tall flightless three-toed So. American birds that resemble but are smaller than the ostrich

See *re-* and 2d element	rewarm	rewater	rewed	reweld
revisit	rewash	reweave	reweigh	rewind

j joke;   ŋ sing;   ō flow;   ȯ flaw;   ȯi coin;   th thin;   th̲ this;   ü loot;   u̇ foot;   y yet;   yü few;   yu̇ furious;   zh vision

rhe·ni·um \'rē-nē-əm\ n [NL, fr. L *Rhenus* Rhine river] : a rare heavy hard silvery white metallic chemical element that is used in catalysts and thermocouples — see ELEMENT table

rhe·o·phile \'rē-ə-‚fīl\ adj [Gk *rhein* to flow] : preferring or living in flowing water ⟨*rheophile* fishes⟩

rhe·o·stat \'rē-ə-‚stat\ n [Gk *rhein* to flow + -*states* one that stops or steadies, fr. *histanai* to cause to stand] : a resistor for regulating an electric current by means of variable resistances — **rhe·o·stat·ic** \‚rē-ə-'stat-ik\ adj

rhe·sus monkey \‚rē-səs-\ n : a pale brown Indian monkey often kept in zoos and frequently used in medical research

rhet·o·ric \'ret-ə-rik\ n [Gk *rhētorikē*, fr. *rhētōr* orator, rhetorician, fr. *rhē-*, *eirein* to say, speak; akin to E *word*] **1** : the art of speaking or writing effectively; *also* : the study or application of the principles and rules of composition **2 a** : skill in the effective use of speech **b** : insincere or grandiloquent language

rhe·tor·i·cal \ri-'tór-i-kəl, -'tär-\ adj **1 a** : of, relating to, or dealing with rhetoric ⟨*rhetorical* studies⟩ **b** : used solely for rhetorical effect ⟨a *rhetorical* question⟩ **2** : using rhetoric; *esp* : GRANDILOQUENT — **rhe·tor·i·cal·ly** \-k(ə-)lē\ adv — **rhe·tor·i·cal·ness** \-kəl-nəs\ n

rhet·o·ri·cian \‚ret-ə-'rish-ən\ n **1 a** : a master or teacher of rhetoric **b** : ORATOR **2** : an eloquent or grandiloquent writer or speaker

rheum \'rüm\ n [Gk *rheumat-*, *rheuma*, lit., flow, flux, fr. *rhein* to flow; akin to E *stream*] **1** : a watery discharge from the mucous membranes **2** : of the eyes or nose **2** : a condition (as a cold) marked by a rheum — **rheumy** \'rü-mē\ adj

¹rheu·mat·ic \rù-'mat-ik\ adj : of, relating to, characteristic of, or affected with rheumatism — **rheu·mat·i·cal·ly** \-'mat-i-k(ə-)lē\ adv

²rheumatic n : one affected with rheumatism

rheumatic fever n : an acute disease esp. of young people characterized by fever, by inflammation and pain in and around the joints, and by inflammation of the pericardium and heart valves

rheu·ma·tism \'rü-mə-‚tiz-əm\ n : any of various conditions characterized by inflammation or pain in muscles, joints, or fibrous tissue ⟨muscular *rheumatism*⟩ — compare RHEUMATOID ARTHRITIS

rheu·ma·toid arthritis \‚rü-mə-‚tóid-\ n : a disease of unknown cause and progressive course characterized by inflammation and swelling of joint structures

Rh factor \‚är-'āch-\ n [*rhesus* monkey, in which it was first detected] : a substance present in the red blood cells inherited according to Mendelian principles and capable of inducing intense antigenic reactions

rhin·en·ceph·a·lon \‚rī-‚nen-'sef-ə-‚län\ n [Gk *rhin-*, *rhis* nose] : the part of the forebrain concerned mostly with the sense of smell — **rhin·en·ce·phal·ic** \‚rī-‚nen(t)-sə-'fal-ik\ adj

rhine·stone \'rīn-‚stōn\ n : a brilliant colorless imitation diamond made usu. of glass or paste

Rhine wine \'rīn-\ n : a typically light-bodied dry white wine produced in the Rhine valley; *also* : a similar wine made elsewhere

rhi·ni·tis \rī-'nīt-əs\ n [NL, fr. Gk *rhin-*, *rhis* nose] : inflammation of the mucous membrane of the nose

rhi·no \'rī-nō\ n, pl **rhino** or **rhinos** : RHINOCEROS

rhi·noc·er·os \rī-'näs-(ə-)rəs\ n, pl **-er·os·es** or **-er·os** [Gk *rhinokerōs*, fr. *rhin-*, *rhis* nose + *keras* horn] : a large thick-skinned three-toed plant-eating mammal of Africa and Asia that is related to the horse and has one or two heavy upright horns on the snout

rhiz- or **rhizo-** comb form [Gk *rhiza*; akin to E *root*] : root ⟨*rhizo*carpous⟩

rhi·zo·bi·um \rī-'zō-bē-əm\ n, pl **-bia** \-bē-ə\ : any of a genus of small soil bacteria capable of forming symbiotic nodules on the roots of leguminous plants and of there fixing atmospheric nitrogen

rhi·zoid \'rī-‚zóid\ n : a structure (as a fungal hypha) that functions like a root in absorption or support — **rhi·zoi·dal** \rī-'zóid-°l\ adj

rhi·zom·a·tous \rī-'zäm-ət-əs, -'zōm-\ adj : having, resembling, or being a rhizome

rhi·zome \'rī-‚zōm\ n : a somewhat elongate, often thickened, and usu. horizontal underground plant stem that produces shoots above and roots below — **rhi·zo·mic** \rī-'zō-mik\ adj

rhi·zo·pod \'rī-zə-‚päd\ n : any of a group (Rhizopoda) of usu. creeping protozoans having lobate or rootlike pseudopods and including the typical amoebas and related forms — **rhi·zop·o·dal** \rī-'zäp-əd-°l\ adj — **rhi·zop·o·dous** \-əd-əs\ adj

rhi·zo·pus \'rī-zə-pəs\ n : any of a genus of mold fungi including economic pests (as the common black mold of bread) causing decay

rhi·zo·sphere \-‚sfi(ə)r\ n : the soil immediately about and influenced by plant roots : the rooting zone of a soil

Rh-negative \‚är-‚āch-'neg-ət-iv\ adj : lacking Rh factor in the red blood cells

rho \'rō\ n : the 17th letter of the Greek alphabet — P or ρ

Rhode Is·land Red \rō-‚dī-lən(d)-\ n : any of an American breed of general-purpose domestic fowls with rich brownish red plumage

Rho·de·sian man \rō-‚dē-zh(ē-)ən-\ n : an extinct African man with prominent brow ridges and large face but human palate and dentition

rho·di·um \'rōd-ē-əm\ n [NL, fr. Gk *rhodon* rose] : a white hard ductile metallic chemical element used in alloys with platinum — see ELEMENT table

rho·do·den·dron \‚rōd-ə-'den-drən\ n [Gk, fr. *rhodon* rose + *dendron* tree] : any of a genus of the heath family of widely grown shrubs and trees with alternate leaves and showy flowers; *esp* : one with leathery evergreen leaves as distinguished from a deciduous azalea

rho·dop·sin \rō-'däp-sən\ n [Gk *rhodon* rose + *opsis* vision] : a red photosensitive pigment in the retinal rods of marine fishes and most higher vertebrates that is important in vision in dim light — called also *visual purple*; compare IODOPSIN

rho·do·ra \rō-'dōr-ə, -'dór-\ n : any of a genus of low shrubs of the heath family that occur in New England and Canada and bear their delicate rosy flowers in early spring often before the leaves appear

rhomb·en·ceph·a·lon \‚räm-‚ben-'sef-ə-‚län\ n : the parts of the vertebrate brain that develop from the embryonic hindbrain

rhom·bic \'räm-bik\ adj **1** : having the form of a rhombus **2** : ORTHORHOMBIC

rhom·bo·he·dron \‚räm-bō-'hē-drən\ n, pl **-drons** or **-dra** \-drə\ : a parallelepiped whose faces are rhombuses — **rhom·bo·he·dral** \-drəl\ adj

rhom·boid \'räm-‚bóid\ n : a parallelogram in which the angles are oblique and adjacent sides are unequal — **rhomboid** adj — **rhom·boi·dal** \räm-'bóid-°l\ adj

rhom·bus \'räm-bəs\ n, pl **rhom·bus·es** or **rhom·bi** \-‚bī, -‚bē\ [Gk *rhombos*] : a parallelogram having the sides equal and the angles usu. oblique

Rh-pos·i·tive \‚är-‚āch-'päz-ət-iv, -'päz-tiv\ adj : containing Rh factor in the red blood cells

rhu·barb \'rü-‚bärb\ n [ML *reubarbarum*, alter. of *rha barbarum*, lit., barbarian rhubarb] **1** : a plant related to buckwheat that has broad green leaves borne on thick juicy pinkish stems often used for food **2** : a heated dispute or controversy ⟨the pitcher got into a *rhubarb* with the umpire⟩

rhombus

rhumba var of RUMBA

rhumb line \'rəm-\ n [Sp *rumbo*] : a line on the surface of the earth that makes equal oblique angles with all meridians

¹rhyme \'rīm\ n [alter. of ME *rime*, fr. OF] **1 a** : correspondence in terminal sounds of two or more words or lines of verse **b** : one of two or more words thus corresponding in sound **2 a** : rhyming verse **b** : a composition in verse that rhymes

²rhyme vb **1** : to make rhymes : put into rhyme; *also* : to compose rhyming verse **2** : to end in syllables that rhyme ⟨*rhymed* verse⟩ **3** : to be in accord : HARMONIZE ⟨colors that *rhyme* well⟩ **4** : to cause to rhyme : use as rhyme ⟨*rhymed* "moon" with "June"⟩ — **rhym·er** n

rhyme scheme n : the arrangement of rhymes in a stanza or a poem

rhyme·ster \'rīm-stər\ n : an inferior poet : a maker of poor verse

rhyn·cho·ce·pha·lian \ˌriŋ-kō-sə-'fāl-yən\ *n* : the tuatara or a related extinct reptile

rhy·o·lite \'rī-ə-ˌlīt\ *n* [Gk *rhyax* stream, stream of lava, fr. *rhein* to flow] : a very acid, volcanic rock that is the lava form of granite — **rhy·o·lit·ic** \ˌrī-ə-'lit-ik\ *adj*

rhythm \'rith-əm\ *n* [Gk *rhythmos*, fr. *rhy-, rhein* to flow] **1 a** : a flow of rising and falling sounds in language that is produced in verse by a regular recurrence of stressed and unstressed syllables : CADENCE **b** : a particular example or form of rhythm ⟨iambic *rhythm*⟩ **2 a** : a flow of sound in music marked by accented beats coming at regular intervals **b** : a particular or characteristic pattern of rhythm ⟨waltz *rhythm*⟩ **3** : a movement or activity in which some action or element recurs regularly ⟨the *rhythm* of breathing⟩⟨the daily *rhythm* of waking and sleeping⟩ — **rhyth·mic** \'rith-mik\ *or* **rhyth·mi·cal** \-mi-kəl\ *adj* — **rhyth·mi·cal·ly** \-mi-k(ə-)lē\ *adv*

ri·al·to \rē-'al-tō\ *n, pl* **-tos** [*Rialto*, island and district in Venice] **1** : EXCHANGE, MARKETPLACE **2** : a theater district

ri·ata \rē-'at-ə, -'ät-\ *n* [modif. of AmerSp *reata*] : LARIAT

¹rib \'rib\ *n* [OE] **1 a** : one of the paired curved bony or partly cartilaginous rods that are joined to the spinal column, stiffen the walls of the body of most vertebrates, and protect the viscera **b** : a cut of meat including a rib **2** : something (as a structural member of a ship or airplane) resembling a rib in shape or function **3** : an elongated ridge: as **a** : a major vein of an insect's wing or of a leaf **b** : one of the ridges in some knitted or woven fabrics

²rib *vt* **ribbed; rib·bing** **1** : to furnish or enclose with ribs **2** : to form ribs in (a fabric) in knitting or weaving — **rib·ber** *n*

³rib *vt* **ribbed; rib·bing** : to poke fun at : KID — **rib·ber** *n*

rib·ald \'rib-əld\ *adj* [ME, n., rascal, wanton, fr. OF *ribauld*] **1** : CRUDE, OFFENSIVE ⟨*ribald* language⟩ **2** : characterized by or using broad indecent humor **syn** see COARSE — **rib·ald·ry** \-əl-drē\ *n*

rib·and \'rib-ənd\ *n* : a ribbon used esp. as a decoration

rib·bon \'rib-ən\ *n* [MF *riban, ruban*] **1 a** : a narrow usu. closely woven strip of decorative fabric (as silk) used esp. for trimming or for tying or ornamenting packages **b** : a piece of usu. multicolored ribbon worn as a military decoration or as a symbol of a medal **c** : a strip of colored ribbon given as a token of a place won in competition **2** : a long narrow strip resembling a ribbon: as **a** : a board framed into the studs to support the ceiling or floor joists **b** : a strip of inked fabric (as in a typewriter) **3** : TATTER, SHRED — usu. used in pl. — **rib·bon·like** \-ˌlīk\ *adj*

rib·bon·fish \-ˌfish\ *n* : any of various very long and greatly compressed sea fishes

ribbon worm *n* : NEMERTEAN

rib·by \'rib-ē\ *adj* : having prominent ribs; *also* : GAUNT

rib cage *n* : the bony enclosing wall of the chest consisting chiefly of the ribs and their connectives

ri·bo·fla·vin \ˌrī-bə-'flā-vən\ *n* [*ribose* + L *flavus* yellow] : a yellow crystalline compound that is a growth-promoting member of the vitamin B complex occurring both free (as in milk) and combined (as in liver)

ri·bo·nu·cle·ic acid \ˌrī-bō-n(y)ù-ˌklē-ik-, -ˌklā-\ *n* : any of various nucleic acids that contain ribose and uracil as structural components, are associated esp. with protein synthesis in the cell, and are the molecular basis of heredity in some viruses

ri·bose \'rī-ˌbōs\ *n* : a pentose sugar found in the nucleotides of nucleic acids

ribose nucleic acid *n* : RIBONUCLEIC ACID

ri·bo·some \'rī-bə-ˌsōm\ *n* : a protoplasmic granule containing ribonucleic acid and held to be a center of protein synthesis

rice \'rīs\ *n, pl* **rice** [OF *ris*, fr. It *riso*, fr. Gk *oryza*] : an annual cereal grass widely grown in warm wet areas for its seed that is used esp. for food; *also* : this seed

rice·bird \'rīs-ˌbərd\ *n* : any of several small birds common in rice fields; *esp* : BOBOLINK

rice polishings *n pl* : the inner bran layer of rice rubbed off in milling

ric·er \'rī-sər\ *n* : a kitchen utensil in

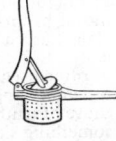

ricer

which soft foods (as boiled potatoes) are pressed through a perforated container in slender strings

rich \'rich\ *adj* [OE *rīce*] **1** : possessing or controlling great wealth : WEALTHY **2** : having high value ⟨a *rich* harvest⟩; *also* : COSTLY, SUMPTUOUS ⟨*rich* robes⟩ **3** : abundantly supplied with some usu. desirable quality or thing ⟨a land *rich* in resources⟩: as **a** : of pleasingly strong odor ⟨*rich* perfumes⟩ **b** : highly productive : FRUITFUL, FERTILE ⟨a *rich* mine⟩ **c** : containing much seasoning, fat, or sugar ⟨*rich* food⟩ **d** : high in combustible content ⟨a *rich* fuel mixture⟩ **4 a** : vivid and deep in color ⟨*rich* red⟩ **b** : full and mellow in tone and quality ⟨*rich* voice⟩ **5** : AMUSING; *also* : LAUGHABLE — **rich·ness** *n*

rich·en \'rich-ən\ *vt* **rich·ened; rich·en·ing** \'rich-(ə-)niŋ\ : to make rich or richer

rich·es \'rich-əz\ *n pl* [ME, fr. OF *richesse*, sing., lit., richness, fr. *riche* rich, of Gmc origin; akin to E *rich*] : things that make one rich : WEALTH

rich·ly \'rich-lē\ *adv* **1** : in a rich manner **2** : in full measure : AMPLY ⟨praise *richly* deserved⟩

¹rick \'rik\ *n* [OE *hrēac*] : a stack or pile (as of hay or grain) in the open air

²rick *vt* : to pile (as hay) in ricks

rick·ets \'rik-əts\ *n* : a children's disease marked esp. by soft and deformed bones due to failure to assimilate and use calcium and phosphorus normally and caused by inadequate vitamin D

rick·ett·sia \rik-'et-sē-ə\ *n, pl* **-si·as** *or* **-si·ae** \-sē-ˌē, -sē-ˌī\ [NL, genus of microorganisms, fr. Howard T. *Ricketts* d1910 American pathologist] : any of various microorganisms sometimes held to be intermediate between bacteria and true viruses that live in cells and include causers of serious diseases (as typhus) — **rick·ett·si·al** \-sē-əl\ *adj*

rick·ety \'rik-ət-ē\ *adj* **1** : affected with rickets **2** : feeble in the joints ⟨a *rickety* old man⟩ **3** : DILAPIDATED, SHAKY ⟨a *rickety* wagon⟩

rick·ey \'rik-ē\ *n, pl* **rickeys** : a drink containing liquor, lime juice, sugar, and soda water; *also* : a similar drink without liquor

rick·rack *or* **ric·rac** \'rik-ˌrak\ *n* : a flat braid woven to form zigzags and used esp. as trimming on clothing

rick·sha *or* **rick·shaw** \'rik-ˌshò\ *n* : JINRIKISHA

¹ric·o·chet \'rik-ə-ˌshā, *Brit also* -ˌshet\ *n* [F] : a glancing rebound (as of a bullet off a flat surface); *also* : an object that ricochets

²ricochet *vi* **-cheted** \-ˌshād\ *or* **-chet·ted** \-ˌshet-əd\; **-chet·ing** \-ˌshā-iŋ\ *or* **-chet·ting** \-ˌshet-iŋ\ : to skip with or as if with glancing rebounds

ric·tus \'rik-təs\ *n, pl* **ric·tus** \-təs, -ˌtüs\ *or* **ric·tus·es** \-tə-səz\ [NL, fr. L, open mouth, fr. *ringi* to gape] **1** : GAPE **2** **2** : gaping grin or grimace

rid \'rid\ *vt* **rid** *also* **rid·ded; rid·ding** [ME *ridden* to clear, fr. ON *rythja*] : to make free : RELIEVE — often used in the phrase *be rid of* or *get rid of*

rid·a·ble *or* **ride·a·ble** \'rīd-ə-bəl\ *adj* **1** : fit for riding **2** : fit for riding over (as a road)

rid·dance \'rid-ᵊn(t)s\ *n* : the act of ridding : the state of being rid of

¹rid·dle \'rid-ᵊl\ *n* [OE *rǣdelse* opinion, conjecture, riddle; akin to E *read*] **1** : a mystifying, misleading, or puzzling question posed as a problem to be solved or guessed : CONUNDRUM **2** : something or someone difficult to understand **syn** see MYSTERY

²riddle *vb* **rid·dled; rid·dling** \'rid-liŋ, -ᵊl-iŋ\ **1** : to find the solution of a riddle or mystery **2** : to set a riddle for : MYSTIFY **3** : to speak in riddles or set forth a riddle — **rid·dler** \-lər, -ᵊl-ər\ *n*

³riddle *n* [OE *hriddel*] : a coarse sieve (as for ashes)

⁴riddle *vt* **1** : to sift or separate with or as if with a riddle **2 a** : to fill full of holes ⟨a boat *riddled* with shot⟩ **b** : to damage or corrupt as if by filling with holes

¹ride \'rīd\ *vb* **rode** \'rōd\; **rid·den** \'rid-ᵊn\; **rid·ing** \'rīd-iŋ\ [OE *rīdan*] **1 a** : to go or be carried along on an animal's back or on or in a conveyance (as a boat, automobile, or airplane) **b** : to sit on and control so as to be carried along ⟨*ride* a bicycle⟩ **2 a** : to be supported and usu. carried along by ⟨a ship *riding* the waves⟩⟨the bearings *ride* on a cushion of grease⟩ **b** : to float at anchor **c** : to remain afloat through : SURVIVE ⟨*ride* out a storm⟩ **3 a** : to convey in or as if in a vehicle : give a ride to ⟨*rode* the child on his back⟩ **b :** to function as a means of conveyance ⟨the car *rides* well⟩ **4 a :** to torment by constant nagging or teasing **:** HARASS ⟨*ride* a man over harmless faults⟩ **b :** OBSESS, OPPRESS ⟨*ridden* by nameless fears⟩ **5 a :** to depend on something and esp. on the outcome of some event ⟨all our hopes *ride* on his success⟩ **b :** to become or remain wagered ⟨had all his money *riding* on the favorite⟩

syn DRIVE: RIDE stresses being borne along on the back of an animal or in a conveyance and implies control only when the rider is mounted astride ⟨*ride* a bicycle⟩ ⟨*ride* in a train⟩ DRIVE implies the action of controlling the movements of an animal or a powered vehicle whether or not the agent is borne along ⟨*drive* a herd of sheep⟩ ⟨*drive* a bus⟩ — **ride for a fall :** to court disaster — **ride roughshod over :** to treat with disdain or abuse

2ride *n* **1 :** an act of riding; *esp* **:** a trip on horseback or by vehicle ⟨a *ride* in the country⟩ **2 :** a way (as a road or path) for riding **3 :** a mechanical device (as at an amusement park) for riding on **4 :** a means of transportation ⟨needs a *ride* to work⟩

rid·er \ˈrīd-ər\ *n* **1 :** one that rides **2 a :** an addition to a document often attached on a separate piece of paper **b :** an additional clause often dealing with an unrelated subject attached to a bill during its passage through a lawmaking body — **rid·er·less** \-ləs\ *adj*

1ridge \ˈrij\ *n* [OE *hrycg*] **1 :** a raised body part (as along the backbone) **2 :** a range of hills or mountains **3 :** a raised strip (as of plowed ground) **4 :** the line made where two sloping surfaces come together ⟨the *ridge* of a roof⟩

2ridge *vb* **:** to form into or extend in ridges

ridge·ling *or* **ridg·ling** \ˈrij-liŋ\ *n* **:** a male domestic animal that is imperfectly developed sexually or imperfectly castrated

ridge·pole \ˈrij-ˌpōl\ *n* **1 :** the highest horizontal timber in a sloping roof to which the upper ends of the rafters are fastened — see RAFTER illustration **2 :** a horizontal support for the top of a tent

ridgy \ˈrij-ē\ *adj* **:** having or rising in ridges

1rid·i·cule \ˈrid-ə-ˌkyül\ *n* [L *ridiculum* jest, fr. neut. of *ridiculus* laughable, fr. *ridēre* to laugh] **:** the act of exposing to laughter **:** DERISION, MOCKERY

2ridicule *vt* **:** to make fun of **:** DERIDE — **rid·i·cul·er** *n*

syn RIDICULE, DERIDE, MOCK mean to make an object of laughter or scorn. RIDICULE implies an often malicious belittling; DERIDE suggests contemptuous and often bitter ridicule; MOCK implies scorn often expressed ironically as by mimicry or sham deference

ri·dic·u·lous \rə-ˈdik-yə-ləs\ *adj* **:** arousing or deserving ridicule **:** ABSURD, LAUGHABLE — **ri·dic·u·lous·ly** *adv* — **ri·dic·u·lous·ness** *n*

1ri·ding \ˈrīd-iŋ\ *n* [ME, alter. of (assumed) OE *thriding*, fr. ON *thrithjungr* third part; akin to E *third*] **:** one of the three administrative jurisdictions into which Yorkshire, England, is divided

2rid·ing \ˈrīd-iŋ\ *n* **:** the act or state of one that rides

3rid·ing *adj* **1 :** used for or when riding ⟨*riding* horse⟩ **2 :** operated by a rider ⟨*riding* plow⟩

rid·ley \ˈrid-lē\ *n* **:** a large sea turtle of the western Atlantic

rife \ˈrīf\ *adj* [OE *rȳfe*] **1 :** WIDESPREAD, PREVALENT ⟨lands where famine is *rife*⟩ **2 :** ABOUNDING ⟨the air was *rife* with rumors⟩ — **rife·ly** *adv*

1riff \ˈrif\ *vb* **:** RIFFLE, SKIM ⟨*riff* pages⟩

2riff *n* **:** a repeated figure in jazz typically supporting a solo improvisation

3riff *vi* **:** to perform a jazz riff

Riff \ˈrif\ *n* **:** a Berber of the Rif in northern Morocco

1rif·fle \ˈrif-əl\ *n* **1 a :** a shallow extending across a stream bed and causing broken water **b :** a stretch of water flowing over a riffle **2 :** a small wave or succession of small waves **:** RIPPLE **3 :** the act or process of shuffling (as cards)

2riffle *vb* **rif·fled; rif·fling** \ˈrif-(ə-)liŋ\ **1 :** to form, flow over, or move in riffles **2 :** to ruffle slightly **:** RIPPLE **3 a :** to flip or leaf through hastily; *esp* **:** to leaf (as a stack of paper) by sliding a thumb along the edge of the leaves **b :** to shuffle (playing cards) by separating the deck into two parts and riffling with the thumbs so the cards intermix

riff·raff \ˈrif-ˌraf\ *n* **1 a :** disreputable persons **b :** RABBLE **2 :** REFUSE, RUBBISH — **riffraff** *adj*

1ri·fle \ˈrī-fəl\ *vb* **ri·fled; ri·fling** \-f(ə-)liŋ\ [MF *rifler* to scratch, file, plunder, of Gmc origin] **1 :** to ransack esp. with the intent to steal ⟨*rifle* the mail⟩ **2 :** to steal and carry away **3 :** to engage in ransacking or pillaging — **ri·fler** \-f(ə-)lər\ *n*

2rifle *vt* **ri·fled; ri·fling** \-f(ə-)liŋ\ [F *rifler* to scratch, file] **:** to cut spiral grooves into the bore of ⟨*rifled* arms⟩ ⟨*rifled* pipe⟩

3rifle *n* **1 a :** a weapon with a rifled bore intended to be fired from the shoulder **b :** a rifled artillery piece **2** *pl* **:** a body of soldiers armed with rifles

4rifle *vt* **ri·fled; ri·fling** \-f(ə-)liŋ\ **:** to hit or throw (a ball) with great force

ri·fle·man \ˈrī-fəl-mən\ *n* **1 :** a soldier armed with a rifle **2 :** a person skilled in shooting with a rifle

ri·fle·ry \ˈrī-fəl-rē\ *n* **1 :** rifle fire **2 :** rifle shooting esp. at targets

ri·fling \ˈrī-f(ə-)liŋ\ *n* **1 :** the act or process of making spiral grooves **2 :** a system of spiral grooves in the bore of a gun causing a projectile when fired to rotate about its longer axis

1rift \ˈrift\ *n* [of Scand origin] **1 a :** an opening made by splitting or separation **:** CLEFT, FISSURE, CREVASSE **b :** a normal geological fault **2 :** ESTRANGEMENT, BREACH

2rift *vb* **:** CLEAVE, DIVIDE, SPLIT

1rig \ˈrig\ *vt* **rigged; rig·ging** [ME *riggen*] **1 :** to fit out (as a ship) with rigging **2 :** CLOTHE, DRESS ⟨was *rigged* out in his Sunday clothes⟩ **3 :** to furnish with special gear **:** EQUIP **4 :** to set up or fit up often as a makeshift ⟨*rig* up a temporary shelter⟩

2rig *n* **1 :** the distinctive shape, number, and arrangement of sails and masts of a ship ⟨a schooner *rig*⟩ **2 :** EQUIPAGE; *esp* **:** a carriage with its horse **3 :** DRESS, CLOTHING **4 :** tackle, equipment, or machinery fitted for a specified pupose ⟨oil-drilling *rig*⟩

3rig *vt* **rigged; rig·ging 1 :** to manipulate or control usu. by deceptive or dishonest means ⟨*rig* an election⟩ **2 :** to fix in advance for a desired result ⟨*rig* a quiz⟩

rig·a·doon \ˌrig-ə-ˈdün\ *or* **ri·gau·don** \ˌrē-gō-ˈdōⁿ\ *n* [F *rigaudon*] **:** a lively dance of the 17th and 18th centuries; *also* **:** the music for this

Ri·gel \ˈrī-jəl, -gəl\ *n* [Ar *Rijl*, lit., foot] **:** a first-magnitude star in the left foot of the constellation Orion

rig·ger \ˈrig-ər\ *n* **1 :** one that rigs **2 :** a ship of a specified rig ⟨square-*rigger*⟩

rig·ging \ˈrig-iŋ, -ən\ *n* **1 a :** the lines and chains used aboard a ship esp. in working sail and supporting masts and spars **b :** a similar network (as in theater scenery) used for support and manipulation **2 :** TACKLE, GEAR

1right \ˈrīt\ *adj* [OE *riht*] **1 :** RIGHTEOUS, UPRIGHT **2 :** being in accordance with what is just, good, or proper ⟨*right* conduct⟩ **3 a :** agreeable to a standard **b :** conforming to facts or truth **:** CORRECT ⟨*right* answer⟩ **4 :** SUITABLE, APPROPRIATE ⟨*right* man for the job⟩ ⟨*right* tool⟩ **5 :** STRAIGHT ⟨*right* line⟩ **6 :** GENUINE, REAL **7 a :** of, relating to, situated on, or being the side of the body which is away from the heart and on which the hand is stronger and more skilled in most people ⟨*right* arm⟩ **b :** located in the same relative position as the right of the body when facing in the same direction as the observer **:** RIGHT-HAND ⟨the *right* side of the road⟩ **8 :** having its axis perpendicular to the base ⟨*right* cone⟩ **9 :** of, relating to, or constituting the principal or more prominent side of an object ⟨*right* side out⟩ **10 :** acting or judging in accordance with truth or fact ⟨time proved him *right*⟩ **11 a :** physically or mentally well ⟨did not feel *right*⟩ **b :** being in a correct or proper state ⟨put things *right*⟩ **12 :** most favorable or desired **:** PREFERABLE **13** *often cap* **:** of or adhering to the Right in politics — **right·ness** *n*

2right *n* **1 :** qualities (as adherence to duty and obedience to lawful authority) that together constitute the ideal of moral propriety **2 :** something to which one has a just claim: as **a :** a power or privilege to which one is justly entitled **b :** an interest that one has in a piece of property — often used in pl. ⟨mineral *rights*⟩ ⟨film *rights* of the novel⟩ **3 :** something that one may properly claim as due **4 :** the cause of truth or justice **5 :** the location or direction of or something situated on or toward the right side ⟨the woods on his *right*⟩ **6 a :** the true account or correct interpretation **b** : the quality or state of being factually correct **7** *often cap* **a** : the part of a legislative chamber located to the right of the presiding officer **b** : the members of a continental European legislative body occupying the right and holding more conservative political views than other members **8 a** *cap* : individuals sometimes professing opposition to change in the established order and favoring traditional attitudes and practices and sometimes advocating the forced establishment of an authoritarian political order **b** *often cap* : a conservative position — **by rights** : with reason or justice : PROPERLY — **to rights** : into proper order

³**right** *adv* **1** : according to right ⟨live *right*⟩ **2** : EXACTLY, PRECISELY ⟨*right* at his fingertips⟩ **3** : in a suitable, proper, or desired manner ⟨hold your pen *right*⟩ **4** : in a direct line or course ⟨go *right* home⟩ **5** : according to fact or truth : TRULY ⟨guess *right*⟩⟨heard *right*⟩ **6 a** : all the way ⟨windows *right* to the floor⟩ **b** : COMPLETELY **7** : IMMEDIATELY ⟨*right* after lunch⟩ **8** : EXTREMELY, VERY ⟨*right* pleasant day⟩ **9** : on or to the right ⟨looked *right* and left⟩

⁴**right** *vb* **1 a** : to relieve from wrong **b** : JUSTIFY, VINDICATE **2 a** : to adjust or restore to the proper state or condition **b** : to bring or restore to an upright position **3** : to become upright — **right·er** *n*

right angle *n* : the angle bounded by two lines perpendicular to each other — **right–an·gled** \ˈrīt-ˈaŋ-gəld\ *or* **right–an·gle** \-gəl\ *adj*

right·eous \ˈrī-chəs\ *adj* [alter. of earlier *rightuous*, fr. OE *rihtwīs*, fr. *riht*, n., right + *wīs* wise] **1** : acting rightly : UPRIGHT **2 a** : according to what is right ⟨*righteous* actions⟩ **b** : arising from an outraged sense of justice or morality ⟨*righteous* indignation⟩ — **right·teous·ly** *adv* — **righ·teous·ness** *n*

right field *n* **1** : the part of the baseball outfield to the right looking out from the home plate **2** : the position of the player defending right field — **right fielder** *n*

right·ful \ˈrīt-fəl\ *adj* **1** : JUST, EQUITABLE **2** : having a just or legally enforceable claim : LEGITIMATE ⟨*rightful* owner⟩ **3** : FITTING, PROPER **4** : held by right or just claim : LEGAL ⟨*rightful* authority⟩ — **right·ful·ly** \-fə-lē\ *adv* — **right·ful·ness** *n*

right hand *n* **1 a** : the hand on a person's right side **b** : a reliable or indispensable person **2 a** : the right side **b** : a place of honor

right–hand \ˌrīt-ˌhand\ *adj* **1** : situated on the right **2** : RIGHT-HANDED **3** : chiefly relied on ⟨*right-hand* man⟩

right–hand·ed \ˈrīt-ˈhan-dəd\ *adj* **1** : using the right hand more skillfully or freely than the left **2** : done or made with or for the right hand **3** : having or moving with a clockwise turn or twist — **right–hand·ed·ly** *or* **right–hand·ed** *adv* — **right–hand·ed·ness** *n*

right–hand·er \-ˈhan-dər\ *n* **1** : a blow struck with the right hand **2** : a right-handed person

right·ist \ˈrīt-əst\ *n, often cap* : an advocate or adherent of the doctrines of the Right — **rightist** *adj, often cap*

right·ly \ˈrīt-lē\ *adv* **1** : FAIRLY, JUSTLY **2** : PROPERLY, FITLY **3** : CORRECTLY, EXACTLY

right–of–way \ˌrīt-ə(v)-ˈwā\ *n* **1** : a legal right of passage over another person's ground **2 a** : the area over which a right-of-way exists **b** : the strip of land over which is built a public road **c** : the land occupied by a railroad esp. for its main line **d** : the land used by a public utility (as for a transmission line) **3** : the right of traffic to take precedence over other traffic

Right Reverend — used as a title for high ecclesiastical officials (as Episcopal bishops and some monsignors)

right shoulder arms — used as a command in the manual of arms to bring the rifle to a position in which the butt is held in the right hand, the barrel rests on the right shoulder, and the muzzle is inclined to the rear

right–to–work law \ˌrī(t)-tə-ˈwərk-\ *n* : a law that prohibits the union shop in its jurisdiction

right triangle *n* : a triangle having a right angle

right·ward \-wərd\ *also* **right·wards** \-wərdz\ *adv* : toward or on the right — **rightward** *adj*

right whale *n* : a large whalebone whale with no dorsal fin, a very large head, and small eyes near the angles of the mouth

right wing *n* **1** : the rightist division of a group **2** : RIGHT **8** — **right–wing·er** \ˈrīt-ˈwiŋ-ər\ *n*

rig·id \ˈrij-əd\ *adj* [L *rigidus*, fr. *rigēre* to be stiff] **1** : lack-

ing flexibility : STIFF, HARD **2 a** : inflexibly set : UNYIELDING **b** : strictly observed : SCRUPULOUS **3** : HARSH, SEVERE ⟨*rigid* treatment⟩ **4** : precise and accurate in procedure — **ri·gid·i·ty** \rə-ˈjid-ət-ē\ *n* — **rig·id·ly** \ˈrij-əd-lē\ *adv* — **rig·id·ness** *n*

syn RIGID, RIGOROUS, STRICT, STRINGENT mean very severe or stern. RIGID implies uncompromising inflexibility ⟨*rigid* arbitrary rules⟩ RIGOROUS implies the imposing of hardship and difficulty ⟨*rigorous* training⟩ STRICT emphasizes close conformity to rules, standards, or requirements ⟨*strict* discipline⟩ STRINGENT suggests restrictions or limitations that curb or coerce ⟨*stringent* punishment⟩

rig·ma·role \ˈrig-ə-mə-ˌrōl, ˈrig-mə-\ *n* **1** : confused or meaningless talk **2** : a complex and ritualistic procedure

rig·or \ˈrig-ər, 2 is also ˈrī-ˌgòr\ *n* [L, lit., stiffness, fr. *rigēre* to be stiff] **1 a** : harsh inflexibility : the quality of being unyielding : SEVERITY, STRICTNESS **b** : an act or instance of strictness or severity **2** : a tremor caused by a chill **3** : a condition that makes life difficult or uncomfortable; *esp* : extremity of cold **4** : strict precision : EXACTNESS ⟨logical *rigor*⟩ **5** *obs* : RIGIDITY, STIFFNESS

rig·or mor·tis \ˌrig-ər-ˈmòrt-əs\ *n* [NL, lit., stiffness of death] : transitory rigidity of muscles occurring after death

rig·or·ous \ˈrig-(ə-)rəs\ *adj* **1** : exercising or favoring rigor : very strict **2** : marked by extremes of temperature or climate : HARSH, SEVERE **3** : scrupulously accurate : PRECISE **syn** see RIGID — **rig·or·ous·ly** *adv* — **rig·or·ous·ness** *n*

rile \ˈrīl\ *vt* **1** : ROIL 1 **2** : to make angry

¹**rill** \ˈril\ *n* [D *ril* or LG *rille*] : a very small brook

²**rill** \ˈril\ *or* **rille** \ˈril, ˈril-ə\ *n* : any of several long narrow valleys on the moon's surface

¹**rim** \ˈrim\ *n* [OE *rima*] **1 a** : the outer often curved or circular edge or border of something **b** : BRINK **2** : the outer part of a wheel joined to the hub usu. by spokes — **rim·less** \-ləs\ *adj*

syn BRIM: RIM applies to the edge of something circular or curving ⟨*rim* of a plate⟩ BRIM applies to the upper inside rim of something hollow ⟨fill the cup to the *brim*⟩

²**rim** *vb* **rimmed; rim·ming** **1** : to furnish with a rim : serve as a rim for : BORDER **2** : to run around the rim of ⟨putts that *rim* the cup⟩ **3** : to form or show a rim

¹**rime** \ˈrīm\ *n* [OE *hrim*] **1** : FROST 1c **2** : an accumulation of granular ice tufts on objects that resembles frost in appearance but is formed from supercooled fog or cloud **3** : CRUST 3a, INCRUSTATION

²**rime** *vt* : to cover with or as if with rime

³**rime, rimer, rimester** *var of* RHYME, RHYMER, RHYMESTER

rimy \ˈrī-mē\ *adj* **rim·i·er; -est** : covered with rime : FROSTY

rind \ˈrīnd\ *n* [OE] : the bark of a tree; *also* : a usu. hard or tough outer layer (as the skin of a fruit) — **rind·ed** \ˈrīn-dəd\ *adj*

rin·der·pest \ˈrin-dər-ˌpest\ *n* [G, fr. *rinder* cattle + *pest* pestilence] : an acute virus disease of cattle and sometimes sheep and goats

¹**ring** \ˈriŋ\ *n* [OE *hring*] **1** : a circular band for holding, connecting, hanging, or pulling ⟨curtain *ring*⟩ ⟨key *ring*⟩ ⟨towel *ring*⟩ or for packing or sealing **2** : a circlet usu. of precious metal worn on the finger **3 a** : a circular line, figure, or object **b** : an encircling arrangement **c** : a circular or spiral course **4 a** : an often circular space for exhibitions or competitions; *esp* : such a space at a circus **b** : a square enclosure in which boxers or wrestlers contest; *also* : PRIZEFIGHTING **5** : ANNUAL RING **6** : a combination of persons for a selfish and often corrupt purpose (as to control a market) **7** : an arrangement of atoms represented in formulas or models as a ring **8** : a figure bounded by two concentric circles — **ringed** \ˈriŋd\ *adj* — **ring·like** \ˈriŋ-ˌlīk\ *adj*

²**ring** *vb* **1** : to place or form a ring around : ENCIRCLE **2** : to provide with a ring **3** : GIRDLE 3 **4** : to throw a ring over (the mark) in a game where curved objects (as horseshoes) are tossed at a mark **5** : to form or take the shape of a ring

³**ring** *vb* **rang** \ˈraŋ\; **rung** \ˈrəŋ\; **ring·ing** \ˈriŋ-iŋ\ [OE *hringan*] **1** : to sound clearly and resonantly when struck ⟨church bells *ringing*⟩ ⟨swords *rang* on helmets⟩ **2** : to cause (as a metallic body) to sound esp. by striking ⟨*rang* the dinner bell⟩ ⟨*ring* a coin⟩ **3** : to cause something (as a bell) to ring ⟨*rang* for the waiter⟩⟨*ring* and enter⟩ **4 a** : to make

(a sound) by ringing ⟨*ring* a wedding peal⟩ **b** : to announce by or as if by ringing ⟨*ring* an alarm⟩ ⟨*ring* in the new year⟩ **5** : to sound loudly ⟨cheers *rang* out⟩ ⟨his voice *rang* with indignation⟩ **6 a** : to be filled with reverberating sound : RESOUND ⟨the whole hall *rang* with their cheers⟩ **b** : to have a sensation of being filled with a humming sound ⟨his ears were *ringing*⟩ **7** : to be filled with talk or report ⟨the whole land *rang* with his fame⟩ **8** : to repeat often or loudly or earnestly ⟨everywhere men *rang* his praises⟩ **9** : to have a sound or character expressive of some quality ⟨a story that *rings* true⟩ **10 a** : to summon esp. by bell **b** : to call on the telephone — **ring a bell** : to arouse a response ⟨no, that name doesn't *ring a bell*⟩ — **ring the changes** : to run through a whole range of possible variations

⁴**ring** *n* **1** : a set of bells **2** : a clear resonant sound made by or as if by vibrating metal **3** : resonant tone : SONORITY **4** : a loud sound continued, repeated, or reverberated **5** : a sound or character expressive of some particular quality ⟨a story with the *ring* of truth⟩ **6 a** : the act or an instance of ringing **b** : a telephone call

ring·bolt \'riŋ-ˌbōlt\ *n* : a bolt with a ring through a loop at one end

rin·gent \'rin-jənt\ *adj* [L *ringi* to gape] : GAPING; *esp* : having lips separated like an open mouth ⟨a *ringent* corolla⟩

¹**ring·er** \'riŋ-ər\ *n* **1** : one that sounds esp. by ringing **2 a** : one that enters a competition under false representations **b** : one that strongly resembles another

²**ringer** *n* : one (as a quoit or horseshoe) that encircles or puts a ring around a peg

ring finger *n* : the third finger of the left hand

ring·lead·er \'riŋ-ˌlēd-ər\ *n* : a leader of a group engaged esp. in improper or unlawful activities

ring·let \'riŋ-lət\ *n* **1** *archaic* : a small ring or circle **2** : CURL; *esp* : a long curl of hair

ring·mas·ter \'riŋ-ˌmas-tər\ *n* : one in charge of performances in a ring (as of a circus)

ring·neck \-ˌnek\ *n* : a ring-necked animal (as a bird)

ring–necked \'riŋ-ˈnek(t), ˌriŋ-\ *or* **ring–neck** \'riŋ-ˌnek\ *adj* : having a ring of color about the neck

ring–necked pheasant *n* : an Old World pheasant with white neck ring widely introduced in temperate regions as a game bird

ring·side \'riŋ-ˌsīd\ *n* **1** : the area just outside a ring esp. in which a contest occurs **2** : a place from which one may have a close view — **ringside** *adj*

ring stand *n* : a metal stand consisting of an upright rod on a rectangular base used with rings and clamps for supporting laboratory apparatus

ring–tailed \'riŋ-ˈtāld\ *adj* : having a tail marked with rings of differing colors

ring·toss \-ˌtos, -ˌtäs\ *n* : a game the object of which is to toss a ring so that it will fall over an upright stick

ring·worm \-ˌwərm\ *n* : a contagious skin disease caused by fungi and characterized by ring-shaped discolored patches

rink \'riŋk\ *n* [ME *rinc* area for a contest, fr. MF *renc* row, rank, place] **1 a** : a sheet of ice marked off for curling or ice hockey **b** : a usu. artificial sheet of ice for ice-skating **c** : an enclosure for roller-skating **2** : a division of a bowling green large enough for a match **3** : a team in bowls or curling

¹**rinse** \'rin(t)s\ *vt* [MF *rincer*, fr. (assumed) VL *recentiare*, fr. L *recent-, recens* fresh, recent] **1** : to cleanse by introduction of a liquid (as water) **2 a** : to cleanse (as from soap used in washing) by clear water **b** : to treat (hair) with a rinse **3** : to remove (as dirt or impurities) by washing lightly or in water only — **rins·er** *n*

²**rinse** *n* **1** : the act or process of rinsing **2 a** : liquid used for rinsing **b** : a solution that temporarily tints hair

rins·ing *n* **1** : water that has been used for rinsing — usu. used in pl. **2** : DREGS, RESIDUE — usu. used in pl.

¹**ri·ot** \'rī-ət\ *n* [OF, quarrel, dispute] **1** *archaic* : DEBAUCHERY **b** : unrestrained revelry **2 a** : public violence, tumult, or disorder **b** : a tumultuous disturbance of the public peace by three or more persons assembled together **3** : a random or disorderly profusion esp. of color **4** : something or someone wildly amusing

²**riot** *vb* **1** : REVEL **2** : to create or engage in a riot **3** : to waste or spend recklessly — **ri·ot·er** *n*

riot act *n* [the *Riot Act*, English law of 1715 providing for the dispersal of riots upon command of legal authority] : a vigorous reproof, reprimand, or warning — used in the phrase *read the riot act*

riot gun *n* : a small arm used to disperse rioters rather than to inflict serious injury; *esp* : a short-barreled shotgun

ri·ot·ous \'rī-ət-əs\ *adj* **1** : ABUNDANT, EXUBERANT **2 a** : of the nature of a riot : TURBULENT **b** : participating in riot — **ri·ot·ous·ly** *adv* — **ri·ot·ous·ness** *n*

¹**rip** \'rip\ *vb* **ripped**; **rip·ping** **1** : to tear or split apart or open **2** : to saw or split (wood) with the grain **3** : to slash or slit with or as if with a sharp blade **4** : to rush headlong — **rip·per** *n*

²**rip** *n* : a rent made by ripping : TEAR

³**rip** *n* : a body of water made rough by the meeting of opposing currents or by passing over an irregular bottom

⁴**rip** *n* **1** : a worn-out worthless horse **2** : a dissolute person : LIBERTINE

ri·par·i·an \rə-'per-ē-ən, rī-\ *adj* [L *ripa* bank] : relating to or living or located on the bank of a natural watercourse (as a stream or river) or sometimes of a lake or a tidewater

rip cord *n* : a cord or wire pulled in making a descent to release the pilot parachute which lifts the main parachute out of its container

rip current *n* : a strong surface current flowing outward from a shore

ripe \'rīp\ *adj* [OE *rīpe*; akin to E *reap*] **1** : fully grown and developed : MATURE **2** : having mature knowledge, understanding, or judgment **3 a** : far advanced in years ⟨a *ripe* old age⟩ **b** : fully arrived : SUITABLE ⟨the time seemed *ripe*⟩ **4** : fully prepared : READY ⟨*ripe* for action⟩ **5** : brought by aging to full flavor or the best state : MELLOW ⟨*ripe* cheese⟩ **6** : ruddy, plump, or full like ripened fruit — **ripe·ly** *adv* — **ripe·ness** *n*

rip·en \'rī-pən\ *vb* **rip·ened**; **rip·en·ing** \'rīp-(ə-)niŋ\ : to grow or make ripe — **rip·en·er** \'rīp-(ə-)nər\ *n*

rip off \(')rip-'of\ *vb* : ROB; *also* : STEAL

rip–off \'rip-ˌof\ *n* : an act or instance of stealing : THEFT; *also* : a financial exploitation

ri·poste \ri-'pōst\ *n* [F, modif. of It *risposta*, lit., answer, fr. *rispondere* to answer, fr. L *respondēre*] **1** : a fencer's quick return thrust following a parry **2** : a quick retort **3** : a retaliatory maneuver or measure — **riposte** *vi*

rip·ping \'rip-iŋ\ *adj* : EXCELLENT, SWELL

¹**rip·ple** \'rip-əl\ *vb* **rip·pled**; **rip·pling** \'rip-(ə-)liŋ\ **1 a** : to become lightly ruffled or covered with small waves **b** : to flow in small waves **c** : to fall in soft undulating folds **2** : to stir up small waves on ⟨wind *rippling* water⟩ **3** : to flow with a light rise and fall of sound or inflection **4** : to impart a wavy motion or appearance to ⟨the athlete *rippled* his arm muscles⟩ — **rip·pler** \-(ə-)lər\ *n*

²**ripple** *n* **1 a** : the ruffling of the surface of water **b** : a small wave **2** : a sound like that of rippling water **3 a** : a fluctuation in the intensity of a steady electrical current **b** : an alternating-current component in a direct-current supply

¹**rip·rap** \'rip-ˌrap\ *n* **1** : a foundation or sustaining wall of stones thrown together without order (as in deep water or on an embankment slope to prevent erosion) **2** : stone used for riprap

²**riprap** *vt* **rip·rapped**; **rip·rap·ping** **1** : to form a riprap in or upon **2** : to strengthen or support with a riprap

rip–roar·ing \'rip-'rōr-iŋ, -'ror-\ *adj* : noisily excited or exciting : HILARIOUS

rip·saw \'rip-ˌso\ *n* : a coarse-toothed saw for cutting wood in the direction of the grain — see SAW illustration

rip·tide \'rip-ˌtīd\ *n* : RIP CURRENT

¹**rise** \'rīz\ *vi* **rose** \'rōz\; **ris·en** \'riz-ᵊn\; **ris·ing** \'rī-ziŋ\ [OE *rīsan*] **1 a** : to get up esp. from lying, kneeling, or sitting **b** : to get up from sleep or from one's bed **2** : to return from death **3** : to take up arms ⟨*rise* in rebellion⟩ **4** : to end a session : ADJOURN ⟨the house *rose* at noon⟩ **5** : to appear above the horizon ⟨sun *rises* at six⟩ ⟨land *rose* to starboard⟩ **6 a** : to move upward : ASCEND ⟨smoke *rises*⟩ **b** : to extend upward ⟨hill *rises* to a great height⟩ **7** : to swell in size or volume ⟨the river was *rising*⟩ ⟨bread dough *rises*⟩ **8 a** : to become heartened or elated ⟨their spirits *rose*⟩ **b** : to increase in intensity ⟨felt his anger *rise*⟩ **9 a** : to attain a higher rank or position ⟨*rose* to colonel⟩ **b** : to increase in quantity or number

⟨steel production *rose* sharply⟩ **c** : to increase in price or be marked by increasing prices ⟨*rising* costs⟩⟨a *rising* stock market⟩ **10 a** : to come about : HAPPEN ⟨an ugly rumor had *risen*⟩ **b** : to have a source : ORIGINATE ⟨river *rises* in the hills⟩ **11** : to exert oneself to meet a challenge ⟨always *rose* to the occasion⟩

²**rise** \'rīz\ *n* **1** : an act of rising : a state of being risen **2** : BEGINNING, ORIGIN **3** : the distance or elevation of one point above another **4** : the amount of an increase (as in number, volume, price, value, or rate) **5 a** : an upward slope **b** : a spot higher than surrounding ground **6** : an irritated or angry reaction ⟨got a *rise* out of him⟩

ris·er \'rī-zər\ *n* **1** : one that rises (as from sleep) ⟨an early *riser*⟩ **2** : the upright member between two stair treads

ris·i·bil·i·ty \,riz-ə-'bil-ət-ē\ *n, pl* -ties **1** : the ability or inclination to laugh — often used in pl. **2** : LAUGHTER, MERRIMENT

ris·i·ble \'riz-ə-bəl\ *adj* [L *ris-*, *ridēre* to laugh] **1** : able or disposed to laugh **2** : arousing laughter : FUNNY **3** : relating to or used in laughter ⟨*risible* muscles⟩

¹**risk** \'risk\ *n* [F *risque*, fr. It *risco*] **1** : possibility of loss or injury : PERIL **2 a** : the chance of loss or the perils to a person or thing that is insured **b** : a person or thing that is a hazard to an insurer ⟨a poor *risk*⟩⟨a good *risk*⟩

²**risk** *vt* **1** : to expose to hazard or danger ⟨*risked* his life⟩ **2** : to incur the risk or danger of ⟨*risked* breaking his neck⟩ — **risk·er** *n*

risky \'ris-kē\ *adj* **risk·i·er**; **-est** : attended with risk or danger : HAZARDOUS — **risk·i·ness** *n*

ris·qué \ri-'skā\ *adj* [F, fr. pp. of *risquer* to risk, fr. *risque* risk] : verging on impropriety or indecency : OFF-COLOR

ri·tar·dan·do \ri-,tär-'dän-dō, ,rē-\ *adv* (*or adj*) [It, lit., retarding] : with a gradual slackening in tempo — used as a direction in music — **ritardando** *n*

rite \'rīt\ *n* [L *ritus*] **1 a** : a prescribed form for a ceremony **b** : LITURGY **2** : a ceremonial act or action **3** : a group marked by a characteristic set of rites; *esp* : a division of the Christian church using a distinctive liturgy

¹**rit·u·al** \'rich-(ə-w)əl\ *adj* **1** : of or relating to rites or a ritual ⟨a *ritual* dance⟩ **2** : according to religious law or social custom ⟨*ritual* purity⟩ — **rit·u·al·ly** \-ē\ *adv*

²**ritual** *n* **1** : an established form for a ceremony **2 a** : ritual observance; *esp* : a system of rites **b** : a ceremonial act or action **c** : a formal and customarily repeated act or series of acts

rit·u·al·ism \-,iz-əm\ *n* **1** : the use of ritual **2** : excessive devotion to ritual — **rit·u·al·ist** \-əst\ *n* — **rit·u·al·is·tic** \,rich-(ə-w)əl-'is-tik\ *adj* — **rit·u·al·is·ti·cal·ly** \-ti-k(ə-)lē\ *adv*

ritzy \'rit-sē\ *adj* **ritz·i·er**; **-est** [*Ritz* hotels, noted for their opulence] **1** : ostentatiously smart : FASHIONABLE **2** : SNOBBISH

¹**ri·val** \'rī-vəl\ *n* [L *rivalis* one using the same stream as another, rival in love, fr. *rivus* stream] **1 a** : one of two or more striving to reach or obtain that which only one can possess **b** : one who tries to excel **2** : one that equals another in desired qualities : PEER

²**rival** *adj* : having the same pretensions or claims : COMPETING

³**rival** *vt* -valed *or* -valled; -val·ing *or* -val·ling \'rīv-(ə-)liŋ\ **1** : to be in competition with **2** : to strive to equal or excel **3** : EQUAL, MATCH

ri·val·ry \'rī-vəl-rē\ *n, pl* -ries : the act of rivaling : the state of being a rival : COMPETITION

rive \'rīv\ *vb* **rived** \'rīvd\; **riv·en** \'riv-ən\ *also* **rived**; **riv·ing** \'rī-viŋ\ [ON *rīfa*] **1 a** : to tear apart : REND **b** : SPLIT, CLEAVE **2 a** : to divide into pieces : SHATTER **b** : FRACTURE

riv·er \'riv-ər\ *n* [OF *rivere*, fr. L *riparius* of a bank, fr. *ripa* bank] **1** : a natural stream of water larger than a brook or creek **2** : a large stream : copious flow ⟨a *river* of oil⟩⟨shed *rivers* of blood⟩

riv·er·bed \-,bed\ *n* : the channel occupied or formerly occupied by a river

riv·er·boat \-,bōt\ *n* : a boat for use on a river

river horse *n* : HIPPOPOTAMUS

riv·er·ine \'riv-ə-,rīn, -,rēn\ *adj* **1** : relating to, formed by, or resembling a river **2** : living or situated on the banks of a river

riv·er·side \'riv-ər-,sīd\ *n* : the side or bank of a river

¹**riv·et** \'riv-ət\ *n* [MF, fr. *river* to attach, clinch] : a headed pin or bolt of metal used for uniting two or more pieces by passing the shank through a hole in each piece and then beating or pressing down the plain end so as to make a second head

²**rivet** *vt* **1** : to fasten with or as if with rivets **2** : to beat or press the end or point of (as a metallic pin, rod, or bolt) so as to form a head **3** : to attract and hold (as the attention) completely — **riv·et·er** *n*

rivets

riv·i·era \,riv-ē-'er-ə\ *n, often cap* [fr. the *Riviera*, France and Italy] : a coastal region frequented as a resort area and usu. marked by a mild climate

riv·u·let \'riv-(y)ə-lət\ *n* : a small stream

riv·u·lose \'riv-yə-,lōs\ *adj* [L *rivulus* rivulet, dim. of *rivus* stream] : marked with irregular, narrow, or crooked lines

RNA \,är-,en-'ā\ *n* : RIBONUCLEIC ACID

¹**roach** \'rōch\ *n, pl* **roach** *also* **roach·es** [MF *roche*] : a silver-white greenish-backed European freshwater fish related to the carp; *also* : any of several similar or related fishes

²**roach** *vt* **1** : to brush the hair into an arched roll **2** : to cut (as a horse's mane) so that the part left stands upright

³**roach** *n* : COCKROACH

road \'rōd\ *n* [OE *rād* ride, journey; akin to E *ride*] **1** : a place less enclosed than a harbor where ships may ride at anchor — often used in pl. **2 a** : an open way for vehicles, persons, and animals; *esp* : one lying outside an urban district **b** : ROADBED 2 **3** : ROUTE, PATH **4** : RAILWAY

road·a·bil·i·ty \,rōd-ə-'bil-ət-ē\ *n* : the qualities (as steadiness and balance) desirable in an automobile on the road

road·a·ble \'rōd-ə-bəl\ *adj* : capable of being driven along roads like an automobile

road·bed \'rōd-,bed\ *n* **1** : the foundation of a road or railroad **2** : the part of the surface of a road traveled by vehicles

road·block \-,bläk\ *n* **1 a** : a barricade for holding up an enemy at a point on a road covered by fire **b** : a road barricade set up by law-enforcement officers **2** : an obstruction in a road

road hog *n* : a driver of an automotive vehicle who obstructs others esp. by occupying part of another's traffic lane

road·house \-,haus\ *n* : an inn usu. outside city limits providing liquor and usu. meals, dancing, and often gambling

road metal *n* : broken stone or cinders used in making and repairing roads or ballasting railroads

road·run·ner \'rōd-,rən-ər\ *n* : a swift-running long-tailed cuckoo of the southwestern U.S.

¹**road·side** \'rōd-,sīd\ *n* : the strip of land along a road : the side of a road

²**roadside** *adj* : situated at the side of a road

road·stead \'rōd-,sted\ *n* : ROAD 1

road·ster \'rōd-stər\ *n* **1** : a light horse for driving or riding **2** : an open automobile with one cross seat

road·way \'rōd-,wā\ *n* **1 a** : the strip of land over which a road passes **b** : ROAD; *esp* : ROADBED 2 **2** : a railroad right-of-way **3** : the part of a bridge used by vehicles

road·work \-,wərk\ *n* : conditioning for an athletic contest (as a boxing match) consisting mainly of long runs

roam \'rōm\ *vb* [ME *romen*] **1** : to go or go over from place to place with no fixed purpose or direction : WANDER ⟨*roam* the hills⟩ ⟨cattle *roaming* in search of water⟩ — **roam·er** *n*

¹**roan** \'rōn\ *adj* [MF, fr. Sp *roano*] : of a base color (as black, red, or brown) muted and lightened by white hairs

²**roan** *n* **1** : an animal (as a horse) with a roan coat **2** : the color of a roan horse

¹**roar** \'rō(ə)r, 'ro(ə)r\ *vb* [OE *rārian*] **1** : to utter or emit a loud prolonged sound **2 a** : to make or emit a loud confused sound ⟨the wind *roared* through the trees⟩ **b** : to laugh loudly **3** : to be boisterous or disorderly **4** : to cause to roar ⟨*roar* a motor⟩ — **roar·er** \'rōr-ər, 'ror-\ *n*

²**roar** *n* **1 a** : the deep cry of a wild beast **b** : a loud deep cry (as of pain or anger) **2** : a loud continuous confused sound ⟨the *roar* of the crowd⟩

roar·ing *adj* : THRIVING, BOOMING

---

j joke; **ŋ** sing; **ō** flow; **ȯ** flaw; **ȯi** coin; **th** thin; **th** this; **ü** loot; **u̇** foot; **y** yet; **yü** few; **yu̇** furious; **zh** vision

¹roast \'rōst\ *vb* [OF *rostir*, of Gmc origin] **1 a :** to cook by exposing to dry heat (as in an oven or before a fire) ⟨*roast* a potato in ashes⟩ **b :** to dry and parch by exposure to heat ⟨*roast* coffee⟩ ⟨*roast* chestnuts⟩ **2 :** to heat (inorganic material) with access of air and without fusing to effect change (as expulsion of volatile matter) ⟨*roast* a sulfide ore⟩ **3 :** to criticize severely **4 :** to be in the process of being roasted

²roast *n* **1 :** a piece of meat roasted or suitable for roasting **2 :** an outing at which food is roasted (as before an open fire)

³roast *adj* : ROASTED ⟨*roast* beef⟩

roast·er \'rō-stər\ *n* **1 :** one that roasts; *esp* : a usu. covered pan for roasting meat **2 :** something (as a chicken) of a size or kind suitable for roasting

rob \'räb\ *vb* **robbed; rob·bing** [OF *rober*, of Gmc origin] **1 a :** to take something away from a person or place by force, threat, stealth, or trickery ⟨*rob* a store⟩ ⟨*rob* a safe⟩ ⟨*rob* an old woman⟩ **b :** to commit robbery : STEAL **2 a :** to deprive of something due, expected, or desired **b :** to withhold unjustly or injuriously — **rob·ber** *n*

robber fly *n* : any of various predaceous flies that usu. resemble bumblebees

rob·bery \'räb-(ə-)rē\ *n, pl* **-ber·ies :** the act or practice of robbing; *esp* : larceny from the person or presence of another by violence or threat

¹robe \'rōb\ *n* [ME, fr. OF, plunder, robe, of Gmc origin] **1 :** a long loose or flowing garment: as **a :** one used for ceremonial occasions or as a symbol of office or profession **b :** an easy garment (as a dressing gown) replacing outer garments for informal wear **2 :** a covering or wrap for the lower body ⟨wrapped their legs in a *robe* at the game⟩

²robe *vb* **1 :** to clothe, invest, or cover with or as if with a robe **2 :** to put on a robe; *also* : DRESS

rob·in \'räb-ən\ *n* [short for ME *Robin redbreast*, fr. *Robin*, nickname for Robert] **1 :** a small European thrush with yellowish red throat and breast **2 :** a large No. American thrush with grayish upperparts, streaked throat, and chiefly dull reddish breast and underparts

Rob·in Good·fel·low \,räb-ən-'gùd-,fel-ō\ *n* : a mischievous sprite in English folklore

Rob·in Hood \,räb-ən-'hùd\ *n* : a legendary English outlaw noted for his skill in archery and for his robbing the rich to help the poor

ro·ble \'rō-blā\ *n* [AmerSp, fr. Sp, oak, fr. L. *robur*] : any of several oaks of the southwestern U.S. and Mexico

ro·bot \'rō-,bät\ *n* [Czech, fr. *robota* work] **1 a :** a machine that looks like a human being and performs various complex acts (as walking or talking) of a human being; *also* : a similar but fictional machine whose lack of capacity for human emotions is often emphasized **b :** an efficient, insensitive, often brutalized person **2 :** an automatic apparatus that performs functions ordinarily ascribed to human beings or operates with what appears to be almost human intelligence **3 :** something guided by automatic controls ⟨a *robot* airplane⟩ ⟨a *robot* factory⟩

ro·bust \rō-'bəst, 'rō-,\ *adj* [L *robustus*, fr. *robur* oak, strength] **1 :** being strong and vigorously healthy : STURDY **2 :** ROUGH, RUDE ⟨*robust* humor⟩ **3 :** requiring strength or vigor ⟨*robust* work⟩ — **ro·bust·ly** *adv* — **ro·bust·ness** *n*

roc \'räk\ *n* [Ar *rukhkh*] : a fabulous bird of oriental folklore so huge that it carries off elephants to feed its young

Ro·chelle salt \rō-,shel-\ *n* [La *Rochelle*, France] : a hydrated crystalline salt of potassium and sodium that is a mild purgative

roch·et \'räch-ət\ *n* [MF] : a white linen ceremonial vestment resembling a surplice worn by bishops and privileged prelates

¹rock \'räk\ *vb* [OE *roccian*] **1 :** to move back and forth as in a cradle **2 a :** to sway or cause to sway back and forth **b** (1) : DAZE, STUN (2) : DISTURB, UPSET **syn** see SHAKE

²rock *n* : a rocking movement

³rock *n* [ONF *roque*] **1 :** a large mass of stone forming a cliff, promontory, or peak **2 :** consolidated or unconsolidated solid mineral matter; *also* : a particular mass of it **3 :** something (as a support or refuge) like a rock in firmness — **on the rocks 1 :** in or into a state of destruction or wreckage **2 :** on ice cubes ⟨bourbon *on the rocks*⟩

rock bottom *n* : the lowest or most fundamental part or level — **rock-bottom** *adj*

rock·bound \'räk-'baùnd\ *adj* : fringed, surrounded, or covered with rocks : ROCKY

rock candy *n* : sugar crystallized in large masses

rock crystal *n* : transparent quartz

rock·er \'räk-ər\ *n* **1 a :** a curving piece of wood or metal on which an object (as a cradle) rocks **b :** a structure or device (as a chair) that rocks upon rockers **2 :** a mechanism that works with a rocking motion

¹rock·et \'räk-ət\ *n* [It *rocchetta*, fr. dim. of *rocca* distaff] **1 :** a firework consisting of a case containing a combustible composition fastened to a guiding stick and projected through the air by the reaction resulting from the rearward discharge of the gases liberated by combustion **2 :** a jet engine that operates on the same principle as the firework rocket, carries the fuel and oxygen needed for combustion and thus makes the engine independent of the oxygen of the air, and is used esp. for the propulsion of a missile or a vehicle (as an airplane) — called also *rocket engine* **3 :** a rocket-propelled bomb, missile, or projectile

²rocket *vb* **1 :** to convey by means of a rocket ⟨*rocket* a satellite into orbit⟩ **2 :** to rise up swiftly, spectacularly, and with force **3 :** to travel rapidly in or as if in a rocket

rock·e·teer \,räk-ə-'ti(ə)r\ *n* **1 :** one who fires, pilots, or rides in a rocket **2 :** a scientist who specializes in rocketry

rocket plane *n* : an airplane propelled by rockets or armed with rocket launchers

rock·et·ry \'räk-ə-trē\ *n* : the study of, experimentation with, or use of rockets

rocket ship *n* : a rocket-propelled spaceship

rock·fish \'räk-,fish\ *n* : any of various valuable market and sport fishes (as a greenling or striped bass) that live among rocks or on rocky bottoms

rock garden *n* : a garden laid out among rocks or decorated with rocks and adapted for the growth of particular kinds of plants (as alpines)

rocking chair *n* : a chair mounted on rockers

rocking horse *n* : a toy horse mounted on rockers — called also *hobbyhorse*

rock·ling \'räk-lin\ *n* : any of several rather small slender cods

rock lobster *n* : SPINY LOBSTER

rock 'n' roll \,räk-ən-'rōl\ *n* : jazz characterized by a strong beat and much repetition; *also* : improvisational popular dancing associated with this music

rock pigeon *n* : a wild bluish gray Old World pigeon

rock-ribbed \'räk-'ribd\ *adj* **1 :** ROCKY **2 :** firmly inflexible (as in doctrine)

rock salt *n* : common salt in large crystals or masses

rock·weed \'räk-,wēd\ *n* : FUCUS

rock wool *n* : mineral wool made by blowing a jet of steam through molten rock or through slag and used chiefly for heat and sound insulation

¹rocky \'räk-ē\ *adj* **rock·i·er; -est 1 :** abounding in or consisting of rocks **2 :** difficult to impress or affect: as **a :** INSENSITIVE ⟨his *rocky* heart⟩ **b :** STEADFAST — **rock·i·ness** *n*

²rocky *adj* **rock·i·er; -est 1 :** UNSTABLE, WOBBLY **2 :** physically upset : UNWELL — **rock·i·ness** *n*

Rocky Mountain sheep *n* : BIGHORN

Rocky Mountain spotted fever *n* : an acute rickettsial disease marked by chills, fever, prostration, pains in muscles and joints, and a red to purple eruption and transmitted by the bite of a tick

ro·co·co \rə-'kō-kō\ *adj* [F slang, fr. *rocaille*, ornamentation based on rock and shell forms, fr. *roc* rock] : of or relating to a style of artistic expression esp. of the 18th century characterized by fanciful curved spatial forms and ornament of pierced shellwork — **rococo** *n*

rod \'räd\ *n* [OE *rodd*] **1 :** a straight slender stick or bar ⟨a curtain *rod*⟩: as **a :** a stick used to punish; *also* : PUNISHMENT **b :** a pole with a line and usu. a reel attached for fishing **c :** a bar for measuring **d :** a staff carried as a badge of office (as of marshal) **2 a :** a unit of length — see MEASURE table **b :** a square rod **3 :** any of the rod-shaped sensory bodies in the retina responsive to faint light **4 :** a bacterium shaped like a rod **5** *slang* : PISTOL — **rod·less** \-ləs\ *adj* — **rod·like** \-,līk\ *adj*

rode *past of* RIDE

ro·dent \'rōd-ᵊnt\ *n* [deriv. of L *rodent- rodens*, prp. of *rodere* to gnaw; akin to E *rat*] **:** any of an order (Rodentia) of relatively small gnawing mammals (as mice, squirrels, or beavers) having a single pair of upper incisors with a chisel-shaped edge — compare LAGOMORPH — **rodent** *adj*

ro·den·ti·cide \rō-'dent-ə-ˌsīd\ *n* **:** an agent that kills or repels rodents — **ro·den·ti·cid·al** \-ˌdent-ə-'sīd-ᵊl\ *adj*

ro·deo \'rōd-ē-ˌō, rə-'dā-ō\ *n, pl* **-de·os** [Sp, fr. *rodear* to surround, fr. L *rota* wheel] **1 :** ROUNDUP l **2 :** an exhibition featuring cowboy skills (as riding and roping)

rod·o·mon·tade \ˌräd-ə-mən-'tād, ˌrōd-\ *n* [MF, fr. *Rodomonte*, character in *Orlando Innamorato* by Matteo M. Boiardo] **:** vain boasting or bluster — **rodomontade** *adj*

¹roe \'rō\ *n, pl* **roe** *or* **roes** [OE *rā*] **:** DOE

²roe *n* [ME *roughe, row*] **:** the eggs of a fish esp. while still bound together in a membrane

roe·buck \'rō-ˌbək\ *n, pl* **roebuck** *or* **roebucks :** ROE DEER; *esp* **:** the male roe deer

roe deer *n* **:** a small active deer of Europe and Asia that has erect antlers forked at the tip and is reddish brown in summer and grayish in winter

¹roent·gen \'rent-gən, 'rənt-, -jən\ *adj* [after Wilhelm *Röntgen* d1923 German physicist] **:** of or relating to X rays ⟨*roentgen* examinations⟩

²roentgen *n* **:** the international unit of X-radiation or gamma radiation equal to the amount of radiation that produces in one cubic centimeter of dry air ionization equal to one electrostatic unit of charge

roent·gen·o·gram \-ə-ˌgram\ *n* **:** a photograph made with X rays

roent·gen·ol·o·gy \ˌrent-gən-'äl-ə-jē, ˌrent-jən-, ˌrənt-\ *n* **:** a branch of radiology that deals with the use of X rays for diagnosis or treatment of disease — **roent·gen·o·log·ic** \-ə-'läj-ik\ *or* **roent·gen·o·log·i·cal** \-'läj-i-kəl\ *adj* — **roent·gen·o·log·i·cal·ly** \-i-k(ə-)lē\ *adv* — **roent·gen·ol·o·gist** \-gən-'äl-ə-jəst, -jən-\ *n*

roentgen ray *n, often cap 1st R* **:** X RAY

Ro·ga·tion Day \rō-'gā-shən-\ *n* [L *rogation-, rogatio* act of asking, fr. *rogare* to ask] **:** one of the days of prayer esp. for the harvest observed on the three days before Ascension Day and by Roman Catholics also on April 25

rogations *n pl* **:** the ceremonies of the Rogation Days

rog·er \'räj-ər\ *interj* [fr. *Roger*, communications code word for *r*, initial letter of *received*] — used esp. in radio and signaling to indicate that a message has been received and understood

¹rogue \'rōg\ *n* **1 a :** an idle, wandering, or disorderly person (as a vagabond) **b :** a worthless, dishonest, or unprincipled person **:** KNAVE, SCOUNDREL **c :** a pleasantly mischievous individual **:** SCAMP **2 :** a vicious or lazy animal **3 :** an individual with a chance and usu. inferior biological variation — **rogu·ish** \'rō-gish\ *adj* — **rogu·ish·ly** *adv* — **rogu·ish·ness** *n*

²rogue *vi* **rogued; rogu·ing** *or* **rogue·ing :** to weed out inferior individuals from a crop

³rogue *adj* **:** being vicious and destructive ⟨*rogue* elephants⟩

rogu·ery \'rō-g(ə-)rē\ *n, pl* **-er·ies :** the practices of a rogue: as **a :** CHEATING, FRAUD **b :** playful trickery **:** MISCHIEVOUSNESS

rogues' gallery *n* **:** a file kept by the police of photographs of persons arrested as criminals

roil \'rȯil, 2 is also 'rīl\ *vt* **1 :** to make cloudy or muddy by stirring up sediment ⟨*roil* the water of a brook⟩ **2 :** to rouse the temper of **:** stir up **:** VEX

roily \'rȯi-lē\ *adj* **roil·i·er; -est 1 :** full of sediment or dregs **:** MUDDY **2 :** TURBULENT

rois·ter \'rȯi-stər\ *vi* **rois·tered; rois·ter·ing** \-st(ə-)riŋ\ **:** to engage in noisy revelry — **rois·ter·er** \-stər-ər\ *n*

Ro·land \'rō-lənd\ *n* **:** a stalwart defender of the Christians against the Saracens in French romance killed at Roncesvalles in 778

role *also* **rôle** \'rōl\ *n* [F *rôle* actor's part, lit., roll, fr. OF *rolle*; so called fr. the roll on which the actor's part was written] **1 a :** a character assigned or assumed **b :** a part played by an actor or singer **2 :** FUNCTION ⟨the *role* of enzymes in digestion⟩

¹roll \'rōl\ *n* [OF *rolle*, fr. L *rotula*, dim. of *rota* wheel] **1 a :** a written document that may be rolled up **:** SCROLL **b :** an official list esp. of members of a body (as a legislative body) ⟨call the *roll*⟩ **2 :** something that is rolled or rounded: as **a :** a quantity (as of fabric or paper) rolled

up to form a single package **b :** a food preparation rolled up for cooking or serving; *esp* **:** a small piece of baked bread dough **c :** paper money folded or rolled; *also* **:** MONEY, FUNDS **3 :** something that rolls **:** ROLLER

²roll *vb* **1 a :** to move by turning over and over on a surface without sliding **b :** to turn over and over **c :** to move about or as if about an axis or point ⟨clouds *rolling* by⟩ **2 a :** to put a wrapping around **b :** to form into a ball or roll **3 :** to make smooth, even, or compact with or as if with a roller **4 a :** to move on rollers or wheels **b :** to begin operating or moving ⟨the new shop finally got *rolling*⟩ **5 a :** to sound with a full reverberating tone or with a continuous beating sound ⟨*roll* a drum⟩ ⟨thunder *rolled*⟩ **b :** to utter with a trill ⟨*rolled* his *r*'s⟩ **6 :** to luxuriate in an abundant supply ⟨*rolling* in money⟩ **7 :** ELAPSE, PASS ⟨time *rolled by*⟩ **8 :** to flow in a continuous stream ⟨money was *rolling* in⟩ **9 :** to have an undulating contour ⟨*rolling* prairie⟩ **10 :** to move with a side-to-side sway **:** ROCK ⟨the ship heaved and *rolled*⟩ **11 :** to respond to rolling in a specified way ⟨a paper that *rolls* easily⟩ ⟨a good paint should *roll* perfectly smooth⟩ **12 :** to move forward **:** develop and maintain impetus

³roll *n* **1 a :** a sound produced by rapid strokes on a drum **b :** a sonorous and often rhythmical flow of speech **c :** a heavy reverberatory sound ⟨the *roll* of cannon⟩ **2 :** a rolling movement or an action or process involving such movement; *esp* **:** a swaying or side-to-side movement

roll bar *n* **:** an overhead metal bar on an automobile that is designed to protect the occupant in case of a turnover

roll call *n* **:** the act of calling off a list of names (as for checking attendance); *also* **:** a time for a roll call

¹roll·er \'rō-lər\ *n* **1 a :** a revolving cylinder over or on which something is moved or which is used to press, shape, or smooth something **b :** a rod on which something (as a map) is rolled up **c :** a small wheel (as of a roller skate) **2 :** a long heavy wave on the sea

²roll·er \'rō-lər\ *n* [G, fr. *rollen* to roll, reverberate] **1 :** any of numerous mostly brightly colored Old World nonpasserine birds **2 :** a canary with a soft trilling song

roller bearing *n* **:** a bearing in which a revolving part turns on rollers held in a circular frame or cage

roll·er coast·er \'rō-lər-ˌkō-stər, 'rō-lē-ˌkō-\ *n* **:** an elevated railway (as in an amusement park) constructed with sharp curves and steep inclines on which cars roll

roll·er skate *n* **:** a skate that has wheels instead of a runner — **roller–skate** *vi*

rol·lick \'räl-ik\ *vi* **:** to move or behave in a carefree joyous manner **:** FROLIC — **rollick** *n* — **rol·lick·ing** *adj*

rolling mill *n* **:** an establishment where metal is rolled into plates and bars

rolling pin *n* **:** a cylinder (as of wood) for rolling out dough

rolling stock *n* **:** wheeled vehicles owned or used by a railroad or motor carrier

roll·top desk \ˌrōl-ˌtäp-\ *n* **:** a writing desk with a cover that rolls back into the frame

roller skate

ro·ly–po·ly \ˌrō-lē-'pō-lē\ *n, pl* **-lies 1 :** a pudding made of rolled-out dough spread with a filling, rolled up into a cylinder shape, and baked or steamed **2 :** a short stout person or thing — **roly–poly** *adj*

ro·maine \rō-'mān\ *n* [F, fr. fem. of *romain* Roman, fr. L *romanus*] **:** a lettuce with long spoon-shaped leaves and columnar heads

¹Ro·man \'rō-mən\ *n* **1 a :** a native or resident of Rome **b :** a citizen of the Roman Empire **2 :** ROMAN CATHOLIC — often taken to be offensive **3** *not cap* **:** roman letters or type

²Roman *adj* **1 a :** of or relating to ancient or modern Rome, the people of Rome, or the empire of which Rome was the original capital ⟨*Roman* law⟩ **b :** characteristic of the ancient Romans ⟨*Roman* fortitude⟩ **2 :** LATIN **3** *not cap* **:** UPRIGHT — used of numbers and letters whose capital forms are modeled on ancient Roman inscriptions **4 :** of or relating to the see of Rome or the Roman Catholic Church **5 :** having a prominent slightly aquiline bridge ⟨*Roman* nose⟩

ro·man à clef \rō-ˌmä(ⁿ)n-ä-'klä\ *n, pl* **ro·mans à clef** *same or* -ˌmä(ⁿ)z-ä-\ [F, lit., novel with a key] **:** a novel in which real persons or actual events figure under disguise

Roman candle *n* : a cylindrical firework that discharges at intervals balls or stars of fire

Roman Catholic *adj* : of or relating to the body of Christians in communion with the pope having a hierarchy under the pope, a chiefly Latin liturgy centered in the Mass, and a body of dogma formulated by the church as the infallible interpreter of revealed truth — **Roman Catholic** *n* — **Roman Catholicism** *n*

¹**ro·mance** \rō-'man(t)s, 'rō-,\ *n* [OF *romans* French, something written in French, romance, fr. L *romanice* in the Roman manner, fr. *romanus* Roman] **1 a** : a medieval tale based on legend, chivalric love and adventure, and the supernatural **b** : a prose narrative dealing with imaginary characters involved in heroic, adventurous, or mysterious events remote in time or place **c** : a love story **2** : something suggesting romantic fiction: as **a** : an often intricate untruth **b** : a love affair **3** : an emotional attraction or aura belonging to an esp. heroic era, adventure, or calling **4** *cap* : the Romance languages

²**romance** *vb* **1** : to exaggerate or invent detail or incident **2 a** : to entertain romantic thoughts or ideas **b** : to carry on a love affair with

Ro·mance \rō-'man(t)s, 'rō-,\ *adj* : of, relating to, or constituting the languages (as French, Italian, or Spanish) developed from Latin

Roman collar *n* : CLERICAL COLLAR

Ro·man·esque \,rō-mə-'nesk\ *adj* : of or relating to a style of architecture developed in Italy and western Europe and characterized in its development after 1000 A.D. by the use of the round arch and vault, decorative use of arcades, and profuse ornament — **Romanesque** *n*

Ro·ma·ni·an \ru̇-'mā-nē-ən, rō-\ *n* **1** : a native or inhabitant of Romania **2** : the Romance language of the Romanians — **Romanian** *adj*

Ro·man·ic \rō-'man-ik\ *adj* : ROMANCE — **Romanic** *n*

Ro·man·ism \'rō-mə-,niz-əm\ *n* : ROMAN CATHOLICISM — often taken to be offensive — **Ro·man·ist** \-nəst\ *n*

roman numeral *n, often cap R* : a numeral in a system of notation based on the ancient Roman system — see NUMBER table

Ro·mans \'rō-mənz\ *n* — see BIBLE table

Ro·mansh *or* **Ro·mansch** \rō-'mänch\ *n* : the Rhaeto-Romanic dialects spoken in the Grisons, Switzerland, and adjacent parts of Italy

¹**ro·man·tic** \rō-'mant-ik\ *adj* [F *romantique*, fr. obs. *romant* romance, alter. of OF *romans*] **1 a** : of, relating to, or resembling a romance ⟨*romantic* writing⟩ **b** : not factual : IMAGINARY ⟨a too *romantic* report of his adventure⟩ **2 a** : IMPRACTICAL, VISIONARY **b** *often cap* : of, relating to, or exhibiting romanticism **3** : having a strong emotional or imaginative appeal or association ⟨a *romantic* spot⟩ **4** : of, relating to, or associated with love ⟨*romantic* episodes in her past⟩ — **ro·man·ti·cal·ly** \-i-k(ə-)lē\ *adv*

²**romantic** *n* **1** : a romantic person, trait, or component **2** *often cap* : ROMANTICIST

ro·man·ti·cism \rō-'mant-ə-,siz-əm\ *n* **1** : the quality or state of being romantic **2** *often cap* : a literary, artistic, and philosophical movement characterized chiefly by an emphasis on the imagination and emotions and marked esp. by an exaltation of the primitive and the common man, an appreciation of external nature, and an interest in the remote or melancholy — **ro·man·ti·cist** \-səst\ *n, often cap*

ro·man·ti·cize \rō-'mant-ə-,sīz\ *vb* **1** : to make romantic : present romantically **2** : to hold romantic ideas — **ro·man·ti·ci·za·tion** \-,mant-ə-sə-'zā-shən\ *n*

Rom·a·ny \'räm-ə-nē, 'rō-\ *n* [Romany *romani*, adj., gypsy, fr. *rom* gypsy man] **1** : GYPSY 1 **2** : the Indic language of the Gypsies — **Romany** *adj*

Rom·ish \'rō-mish\ *adj* : Roman Catholic — usu. used disparagingly — **Rom·ish·ly** *adv* — **Rom·ish·ness** *n*

¹**romp** \'rämp\ *n* **1** : one that romps; *esp* : a romping girl or woman **2** : boisterous play : FROLIC

²**romp** *vi* : to play in a boisterous manner : FROLIC

romp·er \'räm-pər\ *n* **1** : one that romps **2** : a child's one-piece garment with the lower part shaped like bloomers — usu. used in pl.

Rom·u·lus \'räm-yə-ləs\ *n* : the legendary founder and first king of Rome

ron·deau \'rän-dō\ *n, pl* **ron·deaux** \-,dōz\ [MF *rondel, rondeau,* fr. dim. of *rond* round] : a poem consisting usu.

of 15 lines divided into three stanzas with the unrhymed refrain of the second and third stanzas formed from the beginning of the first line of the poem

ron·do \'rän-dō\ *n, pl* **rondos** [It *rondò,* fr. MF *rondeau* song with frequent repetitions of its two themes, rondeau] : a musical composition or movement in which the principal theme recurs several times with contrasting themes in between

röntgen *var of* ROENTGEN

rood \'rüd\ *n* [OE *rōd* rod, rood] **1** : CROSS, CRUCIFIX **2** : any of various units of land area; *esp* : a British unit equal to ¼ acre

¹**roof** \'rüf, 'ru̇f\ *n, pl* **roofs** \'rüfs, 'ru̇fs, 'rüvz, 'ru̇vz\

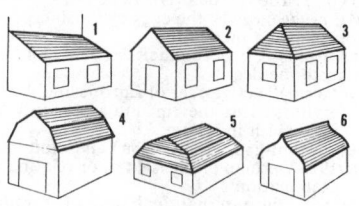

roofs: *1* lean-to, *2* saddle, *3* hip, *4* gambrel, *5* mansard, *6* ogee

[OE *hrōf*] **1** : the upper covering part of a building; *also* : ROOFING **2** : something (as the vaulted upper boundary of the mouth) resembling a roof in form, position, or function — **roof·less** \-ləs\ *adj* — **roof·like** \-,līk\ *adj*

²**roof** *vt* **1** : to cover with or as if with a roof **2** : to provide (a roof) with a protective exterior — **roof·er** *n*

roof·ing *n* : material for a roof

roof·top \'rüf-,täp, 'ru̇f-\ *n* : ROOF; *esp* : the outer surface of a usu. flat roof ⟨sunning themselves on the *rooftop*⟩

roof·tree \-,trē\ *n* : RIDGEPOLE

¹**rook** \'ru̇k\ *n* [OE *hrōc*] : a common Old World gregarious bird about the size and color of the related American crow

²**rook** *vt* : to defraud by cheating or swindling

³**rook** *n* [MF *roc,* fr. Ar *rukhkh,* fr. Per *rukh*] : a chess piece that can move parallel to the sides of the board across any number of unoccupied squares — called also *castle*

rook·ery \'ru̇k-ə-rē\ *n, pl* **-er·ies** **1** : the breeding place of a colony of rooks or of some other gregarious birds or mammals; *also* : the colony itself **2** : a crowded dilapidated tenement or group of dwellings : WARREN

rook·ie \'ru̇k-ē\ *n* : RECRUIT; *also* : NOVICE

¹**room** \'rüm, 'ru̇m\ *n* [OE *rūm*] **1** : unoccupied area : SPACE ⟨*room* to turn the car⟩ **2** : a delimited space : COMPASS **3 a** : a partitioned part of the inside of a building **b** : the people in a room **c** *pl* : LODGINGS, APARTMENT **4** : opportunity or occasion for something : CHANCE ⟨*room* for improvement⟩

²**room** *vb* : to provide with or occupy lodgings

room·er \'rü-mər, 'ru̇m-ər\ *n* : LODGER

room·ette \rü-'met, ru̇m-'et\ *n* : a small private single room on a railroad sleeping car

room·ful \'rüm-,fu̇l, 'ru̇m-\ *n, pl* **roomfuls** \-,fu̇lz\ *or* **rooms·ful** \'rümz-,fu̇l, 'ru̇mz-\ : as much or as many as a room will hold; *also* : the persons or objects in a room

rooming house *n* : a house where rooms are provided and let

room·mate \'rüm-,māt, 'ru̇m-\ *n* : one of two or more persons occupying the same room

roomy \'rü-mē, 'ru̇m-ē\ *adj* **room·i·er; -est** : having plenty of room : SPACIOUS — **room·i·ness** *n*

¹**roost** \'rüst\ *n* [OE *hrōst*] **1** : PERCH **2** : a place where birds customarily roost

²**roost** *vb* : to settle on or as if on a roost : PERCH

roost·er \'rü-stər\ *n* : an adult male domestic fowl : an adult male bird

¹**root** \'rüt, 'ru̇t\ *n* [OE *rōt,* fr. ON; akin to E *wort*] **1 a** : the usu. underground part of a seed plant body that functions as an organ of absorption, aeration, and food storage or as a means of anchorage and support, and differs from a stem esp. in lacking nodes, buds, and leaves **b** : a subterranean plant part esp. when fleshy and edible **2 a** : the part of a tooth within the socket **b** : the enlarged

basal part of a hair within the skin **c :** the basal or central part of a bodily structure or that by which it is attached ⟨nerve *roots*⟩ ⟨the *root* of a fingernail⟩ **3 a :** an original cause or quality **: SOURCE** **b :** an underlying support **: BASIS** **c :** the essential core **: HEART** **4 a :** a number that when taken as a factor an indicated number of times gives a specified number ⟨2 is a 4th *root* of 16⟩ **b :** a solution of a polynomial equation in one unknown **5 :** a word or part of a word from which other words are derived by adding a prefix or suffix **6 :** the lowest tone of a chord in normal position — compare INVERSION **syn** see ORIGIN — **root·ed** \-əd\ *adj* — **root·less** \-ləs\ *adj* — **root·like** \-,līk\ *adj*

²root *vb* **1 a :** to form or enable to form roots **b :** to fix or become fixed by or as if by roots : take root **2 :** to remove altogether often by force ⟨*root* out dissenters⟩

³root *vb* [OE *wrōtan*] **1 :** to turn up or dig in the earth with the snout **2 :** to poke or dig about

⁴root \'rút\ *vi* **1 :** to applaud noisily : CHEER **2 :** to encourage or lend support to someone or something ⟨*rooted* for the reform candidate⟩ — **root·er** *n*

root beer *n* **:** a sweetened effervescent or carbonated beverage flavored with extracts of roots and herbs

root cap *n* **:** a protective cap of parenchyma cells that covers the terminal meristem in most root tips

root cellar *n* **:** a pit or compartment used for the storage of root crops or other vegetables

root crop *n* **:** a crop (as turnips or sweet potatoes) grown for its enlarged roots

root hair *n* **:** one of the filamentous outgrowths near the tip of a rootlet that function in absorption of water and minerals

root·let \'rüt-lət, 'rút-\ *n* **:** a small root

root pressure *n* **:** the chiefly osmotic pressure by which water rises through the stem of a plant

root·stock \'rüt-,stäk, 'rút-\ *n* **1 :** a rhizomatous underground part of a plant **2 :** a stock for grafting consisting of a root or a piece of root

rooty \'rüt-ē, 'rút-\ *adj* **root·i·er; -est :** full or consisting of roots ⟨*rooty* soil⟩

¹rope \'rōp\ *n* [OE *rāp*] **1 a :** a large stout cord of strands (as of fiber or wire) twisted or braided together **b :** a length of material (as rope or rawhide) suitable for a use; *esp* **: LARIAT** **c :** a hangman's noose **2 :** a row or string consisting of things united by or as if by braiding, twining, or threading ⟨a *rope* of daisies⟩

²rope *vb* **1 a :** to bind, fasten, or tie with a rope or cord **b :** to set off or divide by a rope ⟨*rope* off the street⟩ ⟨*rope* back a crowd⟩ **c : LASSO** **2 :** to draw as if with a rope **: LURE** **3 :** to take the form of or twist in the manner of rope — **rop·er** *n*

rope·danc·er \'rōp-,dan(t)-sər\ *n* **:** one that dances, walks, or performs acrobatic feats on a rope high in the air — **rope·danc·ing** \-siŋ\ *n*

rope·walk \-,wók\ *n* **:** a place where rope is made

rope·walk·er \-,wó-kər\ *n* **:** an acrobat that walks on a rope high in the air

ropy \'rō-pē\ *adj* **rop·i·er; -est** **1 :** capable of being drawn into a sticky thread **: VISCOUS** **2 :** resembling rope **: STRINGY, SINEWY** ⟨*ropy* muscles⟩ — **rop·i·ness** *n*

ror·qual \'rór-kwəl, -,kwól\ *n* [F, fr. Norw *rørhval*, fr. ON *reytharhvalr*, fr. *reythr* rorqual + *hvalr* whale] **:** a large whalebone whale having the skin of the throat marked with deep longitudinal furrows

Ror·schach test \,rór-,shäk-, ,rōr-\ *n* [after Hermann *Rorschach* d1922 Swiss psychiatrist] **:** a personality and intelligence test in which a subject interprets inkblot designs in terms that reveal intellectual and emotional factors

ro·sar·i·an \rō-'zar-ē-ən, -'zer-\ *n* **:** a grower or fancier of roses

ro·sa·ry \'rōz-(ə-)rē\ *n, pl* **-ries** [L *rosarium* rose garden, fr. *rosa* rose] **1 :** a string of beads used in counting prayers esp. of the Roman Catholic rosary **2** *often cap* **:** a Roman Catholic devotion consisting of meditation on usu. five sacred mysteries during recitation of five decades of Hail Marys of which each is preceded by the Lord's Prayer and followed by the Gloria Patri

¹rose *past of* RISE

²rose \'rōz\ *n* [OE, fr. L *rosa*] **1 a :** any of a genus of usu. prickly dicotyledonous shrubs with pinnate leaves

and showy flowers having five petals in the wild state but being often double in cultivation **b :** the flower of a rose **2 :** something resembling a rose in form: as **a : COMPASS CARD** **b :** a form in which gems (as diamonds) are cut that usu. has a flat circular base and facets rising to a point; *also* **:** a gem cut in this form **3 :** a variable color averaging a moderate purplish red — **rose·like** \-,līk\ *adj*

³rose *adj* **1 :** of, relating to, resembling, or used for the rose **2 :** of the color rose

ro·se·ate \'rō-zē-ət, -zē-,āt\ *adj* **1 :** resembling a rose esp. in color **2 :** overly optimistic : viewed favorably — **ro·se·ate·ly** *adv*

rose·bay \'rōz-,bā\ *n* **1 : OLEANDER** **2 : RHODODENDRON;** *esp* **:** one of eastern No. America with rosy bell-shaped flowers

rose–col·ored \'rōz-,kəl-ərd\ *adj* **1 :** having a rose color **2 :** seeing or seen in a promising light **: OPTIMISTIC**

rose fever *n* **:** hay fever occurring in the spring or early summer

rose·fish \'rōz-,fish\ *n* **:** a marine food fish of northern Atlantic coasts that is usu. rosy red when adult

rose mallow *n* **:** a usu. rosy-flowered hibiscus or hollyhock

rose·mary \'rōz-,mer-ē\ *n* [ME *rosmarine*, fr. L *rosmarinus*, fr. *ros*, *ros* dew + *marinus* of the sea] **:** a fragrant shrubby mint of southern Europe and Asia Minor used in cookery and in perfumery

ro·se·o·la \rō-'zē-ə-lə, ,rō-zē-'ō-\ *n* **:** a spotty rose-colored eruption or a condition marked by this; *esp* **: GERMAN MEASLES** — **ro·se·o·lar** \-lər\ *adj*

rose pink *n* **:** a variable color averaging a moderate pink

ro·sette \rō-'zet\ *n* **1 :** an ornament resembling a rose usu. gathered or pleated and worn as a badge of office, as evidence of having won a decoration, or as trimming **2 :** a disk of foliage or a floral design used as a decorative motif **3 :** one of the groups of spots on a leopard or similar cat **4 :** a cluster of leaves developed on a plant in crowded whorls either basally (as in a dandelion) or at the apex (as in palms)

rosette 2

rose water *n* **:** a watery solution of the fragrant constituents of the rose used as a perfume

rose window *n* **:** a circular window that is filled with tracery or ornamental work radiating from the center

rose·wood \'rōz-,wúd\ *n* **1 :** any of various tropical trees yielding valuable cabinet woods of a dark red or purplish color streaked and variegated with black **2 :** the wood of a rosewood

Rosh Ha·sha·nah \,rōsh-(h)ə-'shō-nə\ *n* [LHeb *rōsh hashshānāh*, lit., beginning of the year] **:** the Jewish New Year observed as a religious holiday in September or October

rose window

Ro·si·cru·cian \,rō-zə-'krü-shən, ,räz-ə-\ *n* [Christian *Rosenkreutz* (NL *Rosae Crucis*) reputed 15th cent. founder of the movement] **1 :** an adherent of a 17th and 18th century movement devoted to esoteric wisdom **2 :** a member of one of several organizations held to be descended from the Rosicrucians — **Rosicrucian** *adj* — **Ro·si·cru·cian·ism** \-shə-,niz-əm\ *n*

¹ros·in \'räz-ʰn, 'róz-\ *n* [modif. of MF *resine* resin] **:** a translucent amber-colored to almost black brittle resin that is obtained by chemical means from pine trees or from tall oil and is used in making varnish, paper size, soap, and soldering flux and on violin bows

²rosin *vt* **:** to rub (as the bow of a violin) with rosin

ros·in·ous \-əs\ *adj* **:** containing or resembling rosin

ros·tel·lum \rä-'stel-əm\ *n* [NL, fr. L, dim. of *rostrum* beak] **:** a small anatomical process (as the sucking organ of a louse or a beaked process on an orchid flower) resembling a beak — **ros·tel·lar** \-'stel-ər\ *adj* — **ros·tel·late** \'räs-tə-,lāt, rä-'stel-ət\ *adj*

ros·ter \'räs-tər\ *n* [D *rooster*, lit., gridiron, fr. *roosten* to roast; fr. the parallel lines] **:** a list usu. of personnel **: ROLL;** *esp* **:** one assigning duties

ros·trum \\'räs-trəm\\ *n, pl* **rostrums** *or* **ros·tra** \\-trə\\ [L, beak, ship's beak, fr. *rodere* to gnaw] **1** [L *Rostra*, speakers' platform in the Roman Forum, fr. pl. of *rostrum* beak; so called because it was decorated with the beaks of captured ships] **a :** an ancient Roman platform for public orators **b :** a stage or platform for public speaking **2 :** the curved end of a ship's prow; *esp :* the beak of a war galley **3 :** a bodily part or process (as a snout or median projection) suggesting a bird's bill — **ros·tral** \\-trəl\\ *adj* — **ros·trate** \\-ˌtrāt\\ *adj*
rosy \\'rō-zē\\ *adj* **ros·i·er; -est 1 a :** of the color rose **b :** having a rosy complexion **:** BLOOMING **c :** BLUSHING **2 :** characterized by or tending to promote optimism ⟨*rosy* prospects⟩ — **ros·i·ly** \\-zə-lē\\ *adv* — **ros·i·ness** \\-zē-nəs\\ *n*
¹rot \\'rät\\ *vb* **rot·ted; rot·ting** [OE *rotian*] **1 a :** to undergo decomposition from the action of bacteria or fungi **b :** to become unsound or weak (as from use or chemical action) **2 a :** to go to ruin **:** DETERIORATE **b :** to become morally corrupt **:** DEGENERATE **3 :** to cause to decompose or deteriorate with rot **syn** see DECAY
²rot *n* **1 a :** the process of rotting **:** the state of being rotten **b :** something rotten or rotting **2 :** a disease of plants or animals marked by the breaking down of tissue; *also* **:** an area of broken-down tissue ⟨pruned the *rot* from the tree trunk⟩ **3 :** NONSENSE — often used interjectionally
Ro·ta \\'rōt-ə\\ *n* [ML, fr. L, wheel] **:** a tribunal of the papal curia exercising jurisdiction esp. in matrimonial cases appealed from diocesan courts
Ro·tar·i·an \\rō-'ter-ē-ən\\ *n* **:** a member of one of the major service clubs
¹ro·ta·ry \\'rōt-ə-rē\\ *adj* [L *rota* wheel] **1 a :** turning on an axis like a wheel ⟨a *rotary* blade⟩ **b :** taking place about an axis ⟨*rotary* motion⟩ **2 :** having an important part that turns on an axis ⟨*rotary* cutter⟩ **3 :** characterized by rotation
²rotary *n, pl* **-ries 1 :** a rotary machine **2 :** a road junction formed around a central circle about which traffic moves in one direction only
rotary engine *n* **1 :** any of various engines (as a turbine) in which power is applied to vanes or similar parts that move in a circular path **2 :** a radial engine in which the cylinders revolve about a stationary crankshaft
rotary-wing aircraft *n* **:** an aircraft supported in flight partially or wholly by rotating airfoils
ro·tat·a·ble \\'rō-ˌtāt-ə-bəl\\ *adj* **:** capable of being rotated
ro·tate \\'rō-ˌtāt\\ *vb* [L *rotare*, fr. *rota* wheel] **1 :** to turn or cause to turn about an axis or a center **:** REVOLVE ⟨the earth *rotates*⟩ **2 a :** to do or cause to do something in turn **:** ALTERNATE ⟨*rotate* on the night shift⟩ **b :** to pass in a series ⟨the seasons *rotate*⟩ **3 :** to cause to grow in rotation ⟨*rotate* alfalfa and corn⟩
ro·ta·tion \\rō-'tā-shən\\ *n* **1 a :** the act of rotating esp. on or as if on an axis **b :** one complete turn **2 :** return or succession in a series (as of different successive crops on one field) — **ro·ta·tion·al** \\-shnəl, -shən-°l\\ *adj*
ro·ta·tor \\'rō-ˌtāt-ər\\ *n* **:** one that rotates or causes rotation; *esp* **:** a muscle that partially rotates a part on its axis
ro·ta·to·ry \\'rōt-ə-ˌtōr-ē, -ˌtor-\\ *adj* **1 :** of, relating to, or producing rotation **2 :** occurring in rotation
rote \\'rōt\\ *n* [ME] **1 :** the use of memory usu. with little intelligence ⟨learn by *rote*⟩ **2 :** routine or repetition carried out mechanically or without understanding
ro·te·none \\'rōt-°n-ˌōn\\ *n* [Jap *roten* derris plant] **:** a crystalline insecticide obtained from plants (as derris) that is of low toxicity for warm-blooded animals and is used esp. in home gardens
ro·ti·fer \\'rōt-ə-fər\\ *n* [L *rota* wheel + *ferre* to bear, carry] **:** any of a class (Rotifera) of minute aquatic animals having at one end a disk with circles of cilia which in motion look like revolving wheels — **ro·tif·er·an** \\rō-'tif-ə-rən\\ *adj or n*
ro·tis·ser·ie \\rō-'tis-(ə-)rē\\ *n* [F *rôtisserie*, fr. MF *rostisserie*, fr. *rostir* to roast] **1 :** a restaurant specializing in broiled and barbecued meats **2 :** an appliance fitted with a spit on which food is rotated before or over a source of heat
ro·to \\'rōt-ō\\ *n, pl* **rotos :** ROTOGRAVURE
ro·to·gra·vure \\ˌrōt-ə-grə-'vyü(ə)r\\ *n* **1 a :** a photo-

gravure process in which the impression is produced by a rotary press **b :** a print made by rotogravure **2 :** a section of a newspaper devoted to rotogravure pictures
ro·tor \\'rōt-ər\\ *n* [contr. of *rotator*] **1 :** a part that revolves in a stationary part (as in an electrical machine) **2 :** a complete system of more or less horizontal rotating blades that supplies all or a major part of the force supporting an aircraft in flight ⟨the *rotor* of a helicopter⟩
rot·ten \\'rät-°n\\ *adj* **1 :** having rotted **:** PUTRID, UNSOUND ⟨*rotten* wood⟩ **2 :** morally corrupt **3 :** extremely unpleasant or inferior — **rot·ten·ly** *adv* — **rot·ten·ness** \\-°n-(n)əs\\ *n*
rotten borough *n* **:** an election district that has many fewer inhabitants than other election districts with the same voting power
rot·ten·stone \\'rät-°n-ˌstōn\\ *n* **:** a decomposed siliceous limestone used for polishing
rot·ter \\'rät-ər\\ *n* **:** a thoroughly objectionable person
ro·tund \\rō-'tənd, 'rō-ˌ\\ *adj* [L *rotundus* round] **1 :** marked by roundness **:** ROUNDED **2 :** FULL, SONOROUS ⟨*rotund* voices⟩ **3 :** PLUMP, CHUBBY — **ro·tun·di·ty** \\rō-'tən-dət-ē\\ *n* — **ro·tund·ly** \\rō-'tən-dlē, 'rō-ˌ\\ *adv* — **ro·tund·ness** \\rō-'tən(d)-nəs, 'rō-ˌ\\ *n*
ro·tun·da \\rō-'tən-də\\ *or* **ro·ton·da** \\-'tän-\\ *n* [It *rotonda*, fr. L *rotunda*, fem. of *rotundus* round] **1 a :** a round building; *esp* **:** one covered by a dome **2 a :** a large round room **b :** a large central area (as in a hotel)
rou·ble *var of* RUBLE
roué \\rü-'ā\\ *n* [F, lit., broken on the wheel, fr. pp. of *rouer* to break on the wheel, fr. ML *rotare*, fr. L, to rotate; fr. the feeling that such a person deserves this punishment] **:** DEBAUCHEE, RAKE
¹rouge \\'rüzh, *esp South* 'rüj\\ *n* [F, fr. *rouge* red, fr. L *rubeus* reddish] **1 :** any of various cosmetics to color the cheeks or lips red **2 :** a red powder consisting essentially of ferric oxide used in polishing glass, metal, or gems and as a pigment
²rouge *vb* **1 :** to apply rouge to **2 :** to use rouge
¹rough \\'rəf\\ *adj* [OE *rūh*] **1 a :** marked by inequalities or projections on the surface **:** COARSE **b :** covered with or made up of coarse and often shaggy hair or bristles ⟨a *rough*-coated terrier⟩ ⟨a *rough* unshaven face⟩ **c (1) :** having an uneven or bumpy surface **(2) :** difficult to travel over or penetrate **:** WILD **2 a :** TURBULENT, TEMPESTUOUS **b (1) :** characterized by harshness, violence, or force **(2) :** DIFFICULT, TRYING **3 :** coarse or rugged in character or appearance: as **a :** harsh to the ear **b :** crude in style or expression **c :** marked by a lack of refinement or grace **:** UNCOUTH **4 a :** CRUDE, UNFINISHED **b :** executed hastily, tentatively, or imperfectly ⟨a *rough* draft⟩ ⟨*rough* estimate⟩ — **rough·ly** *adv* — **rough·ness** *n*
syn ROUGH, HARSH, RUGGED mean not smooth or even. ROUGH implies having points, bristles, ridges, or projections on the surface; HARSH implies having a surface or texture that is unpleasant to the touch; RUGGED implies irregularity or unevenness of land surface and connotes difficulty of travel
²rough *n* **1 :** uneven ground covered with high grass, brush, and stones; *esp* **:** such ground bordering a golf fairway **2 :** the disagreeable side or aspect ⟨take the *rough* with the smooth⟩ **3 a :** something in a crude, unfinished, or preliminary state; *also* **:** such a state **b :** broad outline **:** general terms ⟨discussed in the *rough*⟩ **c :** a hasty preliminary drawing or layout **4 :** ROWDY, TOUGH ⟨a gang of *roughs*⟩
³rough *vt* **1 :** ROUGHEN **2 a :** MANHANDLE, BEAT ⟨*roughed* up by hoodlums⟩ **b :** to subject to unnecessary and intentional violence in a sport **3 a :** to shape, make, or dress in a rough or preliminary way **b :** to indicate the chief lines of ⟨*rough* out the structure of a building⟩ — **rough·er** *n* — **rough it :** to live under primitive conditions
rough·age \\'rəf-ij\\ *n* **:** coarse bulky food (as bran) that is relatively high in fiber and low in digestible nutrients and that by its bulk stimulates peristalsis
rough-and-ready \\ˌrəf-ən-'red-ē\\ *adj* **:** crude in nature, method, or manner but effective in action or use
rough-and-tum·ble \\-ən-'təm-bəl\\ *n* **:** a rough disorderly unrestrained struggle — **rough-and-tumble** *adj*
¹rough·cast \\'rəf-ˌkast\\ *n* **1 :** a rough model **2 :** a

plaster of lime mixed with shells or pebbles used for covering buildings

²**roughcast** *vt* **-cast; -cast·ing 1 :** to plaster (as a wall) with roughcast **2 :** to shape or form roughly

rough·dry \-'drī\ *vt* **:** to dry (laundry) without smoothing or ironing — **roughdry** *adj*

rough·en \'rəf-ən\ *vb* **rough·ened; rough·en·ing** \'rəf-(ə-)niŋ\ **:** to make or become rough

rough fish *n* **:** a fish that is neither a sport fish nor an important food for sport fishes

rough·hew \'rəf-'hyü\ *vt* **-hewed; -hewed** *or* **-hewn** \-'hyün\; **-hew·ing 1 :** to hew (as timber) coarsely without smoothing or finishing **2 :** to form crudely **:** ROUGHCAST

rough·house \'rəf-,haùs\ *n* **:** violence or rough boisterous play esp. among occupants of a room — **rough·house** \-,haùs, -,haùz\ *vb* — **rough·house** \-,haùs\ *adj*

rough·ish \'rəf-ish\ *adj* **:** somewhat rough

rough·neck \'rəf-,nek\ *n* **:** a rough or uncouth person; *esp* **:** ROWDY, TOUGH

rough·rid·er \'rəf-'rīd-ər\ *n* **1 :** one who breaks horses to the saddle or who rides little-trained horses **2** *cap* **:** a member of the 1st U.S. Volunteer Cavalry regiment in the Spanish-American War commanded by Theodore Roosevelt

rough·shod \-'shäd\ *adj* **:** shod with calked shoes

rou·lade \rü-'läd\ *n* [F, fr. *rouler* to roll] **:** a slice of meat rolled with or without a stuffing

rou·lette \rü-'let\ *n* [F, fr. OF *roelete*, dim. of *roele* wheel, fr. LL *rotella*, dim. of L *rota* wheel] **1 :** a gambling game in which players bet on which compartment of a revolving wheel a small ball will come to rest in **2 a :** a toothed wheel or disk (as for producing rows of dots on engraved plates or for making short consecutive incisions in paper to facilitate subsequent division) **b :** tiny slits in a sheet of stamps made by a roulette — **roulette** *vt*

Rou·ma·ni·an \rü-'mā-nē-ən\ *var of* ROMANIAN

¹**round** \'raùnd\ *adj* [OF *roont*, fr. L *rotundus*] **1 a :** having every part of the surface or circumference equidistant from the center **:** SPHERICAL, CIRCULAR **b :** CYLINDRICAL **c :** having a curved outline **2 :** PLUMP, SHAPELY **3 a :** COMPLETE, FULL ⟨a *round* dozen⟩ ⟨a *round* ton⟩ **b :** approximately correct; *esp* **:** exact only to a specific decimal **c :** AMPLE, LARGE ⟨a good *round* sum⟩ **4 :** BLUNT, OUTSPOKEN **5 :** moving in or forming a circle **6 a :** brought to completion or perfection **:** FINISHED **b :** presented with lifelike fullness or vividness **7 a :** having full or unimpeded resonance or tone **:** SONOROUS **b :** pronounced with rounded lips **8 :** of or relating to handwriting predominantly curved rather than angular ⟨in *round* schoolboy hand⟩ — **round·ly** *adv* — **round·ness** \'raùn(d)-nəs\ *n*

²**round** *adv* **:** AROUND

³**round** \(')raùnd\ *prep* **1 :** AROUND **2 :** all during **:** THROUGHOUT ⟨*round* the year⟩

⁴**round** \'raùnd\ *n* **1 a :** something (as a circle, globe, or ring) round **b :** a knot or circle of people or things ⟨a *round* of politicians⟩ **2 :** ROUND DANCE 1 **3 :** a vocal composition in which three or four voices follow each other around and sing the same melody and words **4 a :** a rung of a ladder or a chair **b :** a rounded molding **5 a :** a circling or circuitous path or course **b :** motion in a circle or a curving path **6 :** a route or circuit habitually covered **:** a series of customary calls or stops ⟨the watchman made his *rounds*⟩ **7 :** a drink or allowance apiece served at one time to each person in a group **8 :** a sequence of recurring routine or repetitive actions or events ⟨a *round* of parties⟩ **9 :** a period of time that recurs in a fixed pattern **10 a :** one shot fired by a weapon or by each man in a military unit **b :** a unit of ammunition consisting of the parts necessary to fire one shot **11 :** a unit of play in a contest or game which occupies a stated period, covers a prescribed distance, includes a specified number of plays, or gives each player one turn **12 :** an outburst of applause **13 :** a cut of beef esp. between the rump and the lower leg **14 :** a rounded or curved part — **in the round 1 :** in full sculptured form unattached to a background **:** FREESTANDING — compare RELIEF **2 :** with an inclusive or comprehensive view or representation **3 :** with a center stage surrounded by an audience on all sides ⟨theater *in the round*⟩

⁵**round** \'raùnd\ *vb* **1 a :** to make round **b :** to become

round, plump, or shapely **c :** to pronounce (a sound) with rounding of the lips **2 a :** to go around **b :** to pass part way around **3 :** ENCIRCLE, ENCOMPASS **4 a :** to bring to completion **:** FINISH ⟨*round* out a career⟩ **b :** to become complete **c :** to bring to perfection of style **:** POLISH **5 :** to express as a round number ⟨*round* off to three decimal places⟩ **6 :** to follow a winding course **:** BEND ⟨jockeys *rounding* into the homestretch⟩ — **round on :** to turn against **:** ASSAIL

¹**round·about** \'raùn-də-,baùt\ *n* **1 :** a circuitous route **:** DETOUR **2** *Brit* **:** MERRY-GO-ROUND **3 :** a short close-fitting jacket worn by men and boys esp. in the 19th century

²**round·about** \,raùn-də-'baùt\ *adj* **:** CIRCUITOUS, INDIRECT

round clam *n* **:** QUAHOG

round dance *n* **1 :** a folk dance in which participants form a ring and move in a prescribed direction **2 :** a ballroom dance in which couples progress around the room

roun·del \'raùn-d⁴l\ *n* [OF *rondel*, fr. *roont* round] **1 :** a round figure or object; *esp* **:** a circular panel, window, or niche **2 :** an English modified rondeau

roun·de·lay \'raùn-də-,lā\ *n* [modif. of MF *rondelet*, dim. of *rondel*] **1 :** a simple song with refrain **2 :** a poem with a refrain recurring frequently or at fixed intervals

round·er \'raùn-dər\ *n* **1 :** a dissolute person **:** WASTREL **2** *pl* **:** an English game played with ball and bat somewhat resembling baseball **3 a :** one that rounds by hand or by machine **b :** a tool for making an edge or a surface round **4 :** a boxing match lasting a specified number of rounds ⟨a 10-*rounder* between two welterweight contenders⟩

Round·head \'raùnd-,hed\ *n* **:** a Puritan or member of the parliamentary party in England at the time of Charles I and Oliver Cromwell

round·head·ed \-'hed-əd\ *adj* **:** having a round head; *esp* **:** BRACHYCEPHALIC — **round·head·ed·ness** *n*

round·house \'raùnd-,haùs\ *n* **1 :** a circular building for housing and repairing locomotives **2 :** a cabin or apartment on the stern of a quarterdeck **3 :** a blow in boxing delivered with a wide swing **4 :** a slow wide curve in baseball

round·ish \'raùn-dish\ *adj* **:** somewhat round

round robin *n* **1 a :** a written petition or protest whose signers affix their signatures in a circle so as not to indicate who signed first **b :** a letter sent in turn to the members of a group each of whom signs and forwards it sometimes after adding comment **2 :** a tournament in which every contestant meets every other contestant in turn **3 :** SERIES, ROUND

round–shoul·dered \'raùn(d)-'shōl-dərd\ *adj* **:** having the shoulders stooping or rounded

round steak *n* **:** a steak cut from the whole round

round table *n* **1** *cap R & T a* **:** a large circular table for King Arthur and his knights **b :** the knights of King Arthur **2 :** a meeting of a group of persons for discussion of questions of mutual interest; *also* **:** the persons meeting for such a purpose

round trip *n* **:** a trip to a place and back usu. over the same route

round up \(')raùn-'dəp\ *vt* **1 :** to collect (cattle) by means of a roundup **2 :** to gather in or bring together

round·up \'raùn-,dəp\ *n* **1 :** the gathering together of cattle on the range by riding around them and driving them in **2 :** a gathering together of scattered persons or things **3 :** SUMMARY, RÉSUMÉ ⟨a *roundup* of the day's news⟩

round·worm \'raùnd-,wərm\ *n* **:** a nematode worm; *also* **:** a related round-bodied unsegmented worm as distinguished from a flatworm

¹**rouse** \'raùz\ *vb* [ME *rousen*] **1 :** to arouse or become aroused from or as if from sleep **:** AWAKEN **2 :** to become stirred **3 :** to stir up **:** EXCITE

²**rouse** *n* **:** an act or instance of rousing; *esp* **:** an excited stir

³**rouse** *n, archaic* **:** CAROUSE

rous·ing \'raù-ziŋ\ *adj* **1 a :** EXCITING, STIRRING **b :** BRISK, LIVELY ⟨a *rousing* cheer⟩ **2 :** EXCEPTIONAL, SUPERLATIVE

roust·about \'raù-stə-,baùt\ *n* **:** one who does heavy unskilled labor (as a deckhand or longshoreman, a laborer in an oil field, or a circus worker who erects and dismantles tents)

¹rout \'raut\ *n* [MF *route* division, troop, fr. (assumed) VL *rupta*, fr. L, fem. of *ruptus*, pp. of *rumpere* to break] **1** : MOB, THRONG; *esp* : RABBLE **2** : DISTURBANCE **3** : a fashionable gathering : RECEPTION

²rout *vb* [alter. of *³root*] **1** : to poke around with the snout : ROOT; *also*, *archaic* : to dig up with the snout **2** : to search haphazardly : RUMMAGE **3** : to find or bring to light esp. with difficulty : DISCOVER **4** : to gouge out or make a furrow in (as wood or metal); *esp* : to cut away (as blank parts) from a printing surface (as an engraving or electrotype) **5 a** : to expel by force : EJECT (*routed* out of their homes) **b** : to cause to emerge from bed : ROUSE

³rout *n* [MF *route*, fr. L *rupt-*, *rumpere* to break] **1** : a state of wild confusion and disorderly retreat **2 a** : a disastrous defeat : DEBACLE **b** : an act or instance of routing

⁴rout *vt* **1** : to disorganize or defeat completely; *esp* : to put to precipitate flight **2** : to drive out : DISPEL

¹route \'rüt, 'raut\ *n* [OF, fr. (assumed) VL *rupta via*, lit., broken way] **1** : a means of access : CHANNEL **2** : an established, selected, or assigned course of travel (a mailman's *route*)

²route *vt* **1** : to send, forward, or transport by a certain route (*route* traffic around the city) **2** : to arrange and direct the course of procedure of (as a series of operations in a factory)

route·man \-mən, -,man\ *n* : one who sells or makes deliveries on an assigned route

route march *n* : a practice march in which troops maintain prescribed interval and distance but are not required to keep step or maintain silence

¹rou·tine \rü-'tēn\ *n* [F, fr. *route* route] **1** : a regular or customary course of procedure **2** : a reiterated speech or formula **3** : a fixed piece of entertainment often repeated : ACT; *esp* : a theatrical number

²routine *adj* **1** : COMMONPLACE, UNINSPIRED **2** : of, relating to, or in accordance with established procedure (*routine* inspection) — **rou·tine·ly** *adv*

¹rove \'rōv\ *vb* [ME *roven* to shoot arrows at a mark chosen at random] **1** : to move aimlessly : ROAM (*rove* about the country) **2** : to wander through or over (*rove* the seas)

²rove *past of* REEVE

rove beetle *n* : any of numerous often predatory active beetles with a long body and very short wing cases

¹ro·ver \'rō-vər\ *n* [MD, fr. *roven* to rob] : PIRATE

²rov·er \'rō-vər\ *n* **1** : a random or long-distance mark in archery — usu. used in pl. **2** : WANDERER, ROAMER

¹row \'rō\ *vb* [OE *rōwan*] **1** : to propel a boat by means of oars **2** : to move by or as if by the propulsion of oars **3** : to be equipped with (a specifed number of oars) **4 a** : to participate in (a rowing match) **b** : to compete against in rowing **c** : to pull (an oar) in a crew **5** : to transport in or as if in a boat propelled by oars — **row·er** \'rō(-ə)r\ *n*

²row *n* : an act or instance of rowing

³row *n* [OE *rǣw*, *rāw*] **1** : a number of objects in an orderly series or sequence **2 a** : WAY, STREET **b** : a street or area dominated by a specific kind of enterprise or occupancy **3 a** : a continuous strip usu. running horizontally or parallel to a base line **b** : a horizontal arrangement of items **c** : a line of cultivated plants

⁴row \'rau\ *n* : a noisy disturbance or quarrel : BRAWL

⁵row \'rau\ *vi* : to engage in a row : FIGHT, QUARREL

row·an \'rau-ən, 'rō-ən\ *n* [of Scand origin] **1** : a Eurasian tree of the rose family with flat clusters of white flowers followed by small red pomes; *also* : the closely related American mountain ash **2** *or* **row·an·ber·ry** \-,ber-ē\ : the fruit of a rowan

row·boat \'rō-,bōt\ *n* : a boat designed to be rowed by oars

¹row·dy \'raud-ē\ *adj* **row·di·er; -est** : coarse or boisterous in behavior : ROUGH — **row·di·ness** *n* — **row·dy·ish** \-ē-ish\ *adj* — **row·dy·ism** \-ē-,iz-əm\ *n*

²rowdy *n*, *pl* **rowdies** : a rowdy person : TOUGH

¹row·el \'rau-(ə)l\ *n* [MF *rouelle* small

rowel, R

wheel, fr. LL *rotella*, dim. of L *rota* wheel] : a revolving disk at the end of a spur with sharp marginal points for goading a horse

²rowel *vt* **-eled** *or* **-elled; -el·ing** *or* **-el·ling** : to goad with or as if with a rowel : SPUR

row·en \'rau-ən\ *n* **1** : a stubble field left unplowed for late grazing **2** : AFTERMATH 1 — often used in pl.

row house \'rō-\ *n* : one of a series of houses connected by common sidewalls and forming a continuous group

row·lock \'räl-ək, 'rō-,läk\ *n*, *chiefly Brit* : OARLOCK

¹roy·al \'rȯi-(ə)l\ *adj* [MF, fr. L *regalis*, fr. *reg-*, *rex* king] **1 a** : of kingly ancestry **b** : of, relating to, or subject to the crown **c** : being in the Crown's service (*Royal* Navy) **2 a** : suitable for royalty : MAGNIFICENT (a *royal* welcome) **b** : requiring no exertion : EASY (no *royal* road to victory) **3 a** : of superior size, magnitude, or quality **b** : established or chartered by the Crown (a *royal* colony) — **roy·al·ly** \'rȯi-ə-lē\ *adv*

²royal *n* **1** : a small sail on the mast immediately above the topgallant sail **2** : a size of paper typically 20 x 25 inches

royal blue *n* : a variable color averaging a vivid purplish blue

roy·al·ist \'rȯi-ə-ləst\ *n* **1** : a supporter (as during a time of civil war) of a king **2** : an adherent or advocate of monarchy — **royalist** *adj*

royal jelly *n* : a highly nutritious secretion of the pharyngeal glands of the honeybee that is fed to all very young larvae and continuously to queen larvae

royal palm *n* : a tall graceful American palm widely planted as an ornamental tree in tropical regions

royal poinciana *n* : a showy tropical tree widely planted for its immense racemes of scarlet and orange flowers

roy·al·ty \'rȯi-(ə)l-tē\ *n*, *pl* **-ties** **1 a** : royal status or power : SOVEREIGNTY **b** : a right or privilege of a sovereign (as a percentage of gold or silver taken from mines) **2** : regal character or bearing : NOBILITY **3 a** : persons of royal lineage **b** : a person of royal rank **c** : a privileged class **4 a** : a share of the product or profit reserved by the grantor esp. of an oil or mining lease **b** : a payment made to the owner of a patent or copyright for the use of it

-r·rhea *also* **-r·rhoea** \'rē-ə\ *n comb form* [Gk *-rrhoia*, fr. *rhoia*, fr. *rhein* to flow] : flow : discharge (leukorrhea)

¹rub \'rəb\ *vb* **rubbed; rub·bing** [ME *rubben*] **1 a** : to move along the surface of a body with pressure : GRATE **b** (1) : to fret or chafe with friction (the new shoes *rubbed*) (2) : to cause discontent, irritation, or anger : ANNOY, IRRITATE (*rubbed* me the wrong way) **2 a** : to admit of being rubbed (as for erasure or obliteration) **b** : to treat in any of various ways by rubbing (*rub* out an error) **c** : to bring into reciprocal back-and-forth or rotary contact

²rub *n* **1 a** : OBSTRUCTION, DIFFICULTY (that's the *rub*) **b** : something grating to the feelings (as a gibe, sarcasm, or harsh criticism) **c** : something that mars or upsets serenity **2** : the application of friction with pressure : RUBBING (an alcohol *rub*)

ru·ba·to \rü-'bät-ō\ *n*, *pl* **-tos** [It, lit., robbed, stolen] : fluctuation of speed within a musical phrase typically against a rhythmically steady accompaniment

¹rub·ber \'rəb-ər\ *n* **1 a** : one that rubs **b** : an instrument or object (as a rubber eraser) used in rubbing, polishing, scraping, or cleaning **c** : something that prevents rubbing or chafing **2** [fr. its use in erasers] **a** : an elastic substance obtained by coagulating the milky juice of various tropical plants **b** : any of various synthetic rubberlike substances **c** : natural or synthetic rubber modified by chemical treatment to increase its useful properties (as toughness and resistance to wear) and used in tires, electrical insulation, and waterproof materials **3** : something made of or resembling rubber: as **a** : a rubber overshoe **b** : PLATE 1f — **rub·ber·like** \-,līk\ *adj* — **rub·bery** \'rəb-(ə-)rē\ *adj*

²rubber *n* **1** : a contest that consists of an odd number of games and is won by the side that takes a majority (as two out of three) **2** : an odd game played to determine the winner of a tie

rub·ber·ize \'rəb-ə-,rīz\ *vt* : to coat or impregnate with rubber or a rubber preparation (*rubberized* raincoats)

rub·ber·neck \'rəb-ər-,nek\ *n* **1** : an inquisitive person **2** : TOURIST; *esp* : one on a guided tour — **rubberneck** *vi*

rubber plant *n* : a tall tropical Asian fig tree that is often dwarfed in pots as a house plant

rub·ber-stamp \,rəb-ər-'stamp\ *vt* : to approve, endorse, or dispose of as a matter of routine usu. without exercise of judgment or at the command of another

rub·bing \'rəb-iŋ\ *n* : an image of a raised, indented, or textured surface obtained by placing paper over it and rubbing the paper

rubbing alcohol *n* : a watery solution of denatured alcohol or a propyl alcohol used externally esp. to soothe or refresh

rub·bish \'rəb-ish\ *n* [ME *robys*] : useless waste or rejected matter : TRASH — **rub·bishy** \'rəb-i-shē\ *adj*

rub·ble \'rəb-əl\ *n* [ME *robyl*] **1** : rough stone as it comes from the quarry **2** : waterworn or rough broken stones or bricks used in coarse masonry or in filling courses of walls; *also* : RUBBLEWORK **3** : a mass made up of rough irregular pieces ⟨a town bombed to *rubble*⟩

rub·ble·work \'rəb-əl-,wərk\ *n* : masonry of unsquared or rudely squared stones that are irregular in size and shape

rub·down \'rəb-,daủn\ *n* : a brisk rubbing of the body (as after a bath)

rube \'rüb\ *n* [fr. *Rube*, nickname for *Reuben*] : an awkward unsophisticated person : RUSTIC

¹ru·be·fa·cient \,rü-bə-'fā-shənt\ *adj* [L *rubefacere* to make red, fr. *rubēre* to be red] : causing redness (as of the skin)

²rubefacient *n* : a substance for external application that produces redness of the skin — **ru·be·fac·tion** \-'fak-shən\ *n*

ru·bel·la \rü-'bel-ə\ *n* : GERMAN MEASLES

ru·be·o·la \rü-'bē-ə-lə, ,rü-bē-'ō-\ *n* [NL, fr. neut. pl. of (assumed) NL *rubeolus* reddish, fr. L *rubeus* reddish] : MEASLES — **ru·be·o·lar** \-lər\ *adj*

Ru·bi·con \'rü-bi-,kän\ *n* [L *Rubicon-*, *Rubico*, river of northern Italy forming part of the boundary between Cisalpine Gaul and Italy whose crossing by Julius Caesar in 49 B.C. was regarded by the Senate as an act of war] : a line that when crossed by a person commits him irrevocably to a course of action

ru·bi·cund \'rü-bi-(,)kənd\ *adj* [L *rubicundus*, fr. *rubēre* to be red] : RED, RUDDY — **ru·bi·cun·di·ty** \,rü-bi-'kən-dət-ē\ *n*

ru·bid·i·um \rü-'bid-ē-əm\ *n* [NL, fr. L *rubidus* red, fr. *rubēre* to be red] : a soft silvery metallic chemical element that decomposes water with violence and bursts into flame spontaneously in air — see ELEMENT table

ru·big·i·nous \rü-'bij-ə-nəs\ *adj* [L *rubigin-*, *rubigo* rust, fr. *rubēre* to be red] : of a rusty red color

ru·ble \'rü-bəl\ *n* [Russ *rubl'*] **1** : the basic monetary unit of the U.S.S.R. **2** : a coin representing one ruble

ru·bric \'rü-brik\ *n* [L *rubrica*, lit., red ocher, fr. *ruber* red; akin to E *red*] **1** : a heading of a part of a book or manuscript done or underlined in a color (as red) different from the rest **2 a** : NAME, TITLE; *esp* : the title of a statute **b** : an authoritative rule; *esp* : a rule for conduct of a liturgical service **c** : an explanatory or introductory commentary or gloss; *esp* : an editorial interpolation **3** : an established rule or custom — **rubric** *or* **ru·bri·cal** \-bri-kəl\ *adj*

¹ru·by \'rü-bē\ *n*, *pl* **rubies** [MF *rubi*, irreg. fr. L *rubeus* reddish] **1** : a precious stone that is a deep red corundum **2 a** : the dark red color of the ruby **b** : something resembling a ruby in color

²ruby *adj* : of the color ruby

ruby glass *n* : glass of a deep red color containing selenium, an oxide of copper, or chloride of gold

ruck \'rək\ *n* [ME *ruke* pile of combustible material] : the usual run of persons or things : GENERALITY

ruck·sack \'rək-,sak, 'rủk-\ *n* [G] : KNAPSACK

ruck·us \'rək-əs, 'rü-kəs\ *n* : ROW, DISTURBANCE

ruc·tion \'rək-shən\ *n* **1** : a noisy fight **2** : DISTURBANCE, UPROAR

rudd \'rəd, 'rủd\ *n* : a freshwater European fish resembling the related roach

rud·der \'rəd-ər\ *n* [OE *rōther* paddle; akin to E **¹row**] : a flat piece of wood or metal attached to the stern of a boat for steering it; *also* : a similar piece attached to the rear of an aircraft

rud·dle \'rəd-ºl\ *n* [dim. of *rud* red ocher] : RED OCHER

rud·dle·man \-mən\ *n* : a dealer in red ocher

rud·dy \'rəd-ē\ *adj* **rud·di·er**; **-est** [OE *rudig*, fr. *rudu* redness] **1** : having a healthy reddish color **2** : RED, REDDISH — **rud·di·ly** \'rəd-ºl-ē\ *adv* — **rud·di·ness** \'rəd-ē-nəs\ *n*

rude \'rüd\ *adj* [L *rudis*] **1** : being in a rough or unfinished state : CRUDE **2** : lacking refinement, delicacy, or culture : UNCOUTH **3** : offensive in manner or action : DISCOURTEOUS **4** : FORCEFUL, ABRUPT ⟨a *rude* awakening⟩ — **rude·ly** *adv* — **rude·ness** *n*

ru·der·al \'rüd-ə-rəl\ *adj* [L *ruder-*, *rudus* rubble, rubbish] : growing where the natural vegetative cover has been disturbed by man ⟨*ruderal* weeds⟩

ru·di·ment \'rüd-ə-mənt\ *n* [L *rudimentum* first attempt, beginning, fr. *rudis* rude] **1 a** : a basic principle or element or a fundamental skill — usu. used in pl. ⟨the *rudiments* of chess⟩ **2 a** : something unformed or undeveloped : BEGINNING — usu. used in pl. **b** : a body part so deficient in size or structure as to prevent its performing its normal function — **ru·di·men·tal** \,rüd-ə-'ment-ºl\ *adj* — **ru·di·men·ta·ri·ness** \-'ment-ə-rē-nəs, -'men-trē-\ *n* — **ru·di·men·ta·ry** \,rüd-ə-'ment-ə-rē, -'men-trē\ *adj*

¹rue \'rü\ *vt* **rued**; **ru·ing** [OE *hrēowan*] : to feel penitence, remorse, or regret for

²rue *n* : REGRET, SORROW

³rue *n* [MF, fr. L *ruta*, fr. Gk *rhytē*] : a woody perennial herb with yellow flowers, a strong smell, and bitter-tasting leaves

rue·ful \'rü-fəl\ *adj* **1** : exciting pity or sympathy : PITIABLE ⟨a *rueful* tale⟩ **2** : MOURNFUL, REGRETFUL ⟨*rueful* over lost chances⟩ ⟨took defeat with a *rueful* smile⟩ — **rue·ful·ly** \-fə-lē\ *adv* — **rue·ful·ness** *n*

ru·fes·cent \rü-'fes-ºnt\ *adj* [L *rufescere* to become red, fr. *rufus* red] : REDDISH

¹ruff \'rəf\ *n* **1** : a wheel-shaped stiff collar worn by men and women of the late 16th and early 17th centuries **2 a** : a fringe of long hairs or feathers growing around or on the neck **b** : a common Eurasian sandpiper whose male during the breeding season has a large ruff — **ruffed** \'rəft\ *adj*

²ruff *n* [MF *roffle*] : the act of trumping

³ruff *vb* : TRUMP

ruffed grouse *n* : a No. American grouse with tufts of shiny black feathers on the sides of the neck

ruff 1

ruf·fi·an \'rəf-ē-ən\ *n* [MF, fr. It *ruffiano*] : a brutal cruel fellow — **ruffian** *adj* — **ruf·fi·an·ism** \-ē-ə-,niz-əm\ *n* — **ruf·fi·an·ly** \-ē-ən-lē\ *adj*

¹ruf·fle \'rəf-əl\ *vb* **ruf·fled**; **ruf·fling** \'rəf-(ə-)liŋ\ [ME *ruffelen*] **1 a** : to disturb the smoothness of : ROUGHEN ⟨*ruffle* the waters of a pond⟩ **b** : TROUBLE, VEX ⟨*ruffled* her composure⟩ **2** : to erect (as feathers) in or like a ruff **3** : RIFFLE, SHUFFLE **4** : to make into a ruffle

²ruffle *n* **1** : a state or cause of irritation **2** : an unevenness or disturbance of surface : RIPPLE **3 a** : a strip of fabric gathered or pleated on one edge **b** : **¹RUFF 2a** — **ruf·fly** \'rəf-(ə-)lē\ *adj*

³ruffle *n* : a low vibrating drumbeat that is less loud than a roll

ru·fous \'rü-fəs\ *adj* [L *rufus* red; akin to E *red*] : REDDISH

rug \'rəg\ *n* [of Scand origin] **1** : a piece of thick heavy fabric usu. with a nap or pile used as a floor covering **2** : a floor mat of an animal pelt ⟨bearskin *rug*⟩ **3** : a lap robe

ru·ga \'rü-gə\ *n*, *pl* **ru·gae** \-,gī, -,gē, -,jē\ [L, wrinkle; akin to E *rough*] : a visceral fold or wrinkle — used chiefly in pl. — **ru·gate** \'rü-,gāt\ *adj*

rug·by \'rəg-bē\ *n*, *often cap* [after *Rugby* School, Rugby, Warwickshire, England] : a football game played by teams of 15 players and marked by continuous play featuring kicking, dribbling, and lateral passing

rug·ged \'rəg-əd\ *adj* **1** : having a rough uneven surface : JAGGED ⟨*rugged* mountains⟩ **2** : TURBULENT, STORMY **3** : showing signs of strength : STURDY ⟨*rugged* pioneers⟩ **4 a** : AUSTERE, STERN **b** : COARSE, RUDE **5** : presenting a severe test of ability, stamina, or resolution ⟨*rugged* course of training⟩ **syn** see ROUGH — **rug·ged·ly** *adv* — **rug·ged·ness** *n*

rug·ged·ize \'rəg-ə-,dīz\ *vt* : to make (as a machine) stronger — **rug·ged·i·za·tion** \,rəg-əd-ə-'zā-shən\ *n*

ru·gose \'rü-ˌgōs\ *adj* : full of folds or wrinkles ⟨*rugose* leaves⟩ — **ru·gose·ly** *adv* — **ru·gos·i·ty** \rü-'gäs-ət-ē\ *n*

¹ru·in \'rü-ən\ *n* [L *ruina* collapse, fr. *ruere* to rush, fall] **1** : physical, moral, economic, or social collapse **2 a** *archaic* : the state of being ruined **b** : the remains of something destroyed — usu. used in pl. ⟨the *ruins* of a city⟩ **3** : a cause of destruction ⟨drink was his *ruin*⟩ **4** : the action of destroying, laying waste, or wrecking **5** : a ruined building, person, or object

²ruin *vt* **1** : to reduce to ruins : DEVASTATE **2 a** : to damage irreparably **b** : BANKRUPT, IMPOVERISH — **ru·in·er** *n*

ru·in·a·tion \ˌrü-ə-'nā-shən\ *n* : RUIN, DESTRUCTION

ru·in·ous \'rü-ə-nəs\ *adj* **1** : RUINED, DILAPIDATED **2** : causing or tending to cause ruin : DESTRUCTIVE — **ru·in·ous·ly** *adv*

¹rule \'rül\ *n* [OF *reule*, fr. L *regula* straightedge, norm, rule, fr. *regere* to lead straight, rule] **1 a** : a prescribed guide for conduct or action **b** : the laws laid down by the founder of a religious order **c** : an accepted procedure, custom, or habit **d** : a legal precept or doctrine **e** : REGULATION, BYLAW **2 a** : a usu. valid generalization **b** : a generally prevailing quality, state, or mode **c** : a regulating principle ⟨the *rules* of harmony⟩ **3 a** : the exercise of authority or control : DOMINION **b** : a period of such rule : REIGN ⟨during the *rule* of King George III⟩ **4 a** : a strip of material marked off in units used for measuring or ruling off lengths **b** (1) : a metal strip that prints a linear design (2) : the linear design printed by this strip

²rule *vb* **1 a** : CONTROL, DIRECT **b** : GUIDE, MANAGE **2 a** : to exercise authority or power over : GOVERN **b** : to be preeminent in : DOMINATE **3** : to declare authoritatively; *esp* : to lay down a legal rule **4** : to mark with lines drawn along or as if along the straight edge of a ruler **5 a** : to exercise supreme authority **b** : PREDOMINATE, PREVAIL **syn** see GOVERN

rule·less \'rül-ləs\ *adj* : not restrained or regulated by law

rule of thumb 1 : a rough measurement or calculation **2** : a judgment based on practical experience rather than on scientific knowledge

rule out *vt* **1** : EXCLUDE, ELIMINATE **2** : to make impossible : PREVENT

rul·er \'rü-lər\ *n* **1** : one that rules; *esp* : SOVEREIGN **2** : a smooth-edged strip (as of wood or metal) used as a guide in drawing lines or for measuring

¹rul·ing \'rü-liŋ\ *n* : an official or authoritative decision or interpretation (as by a judge on a point of law)

²ruling *adj* **1** : exerting power or authority **2** : CHIEF, PREDOMINATING ⟨his *ruling* ambition⟩

rum \'rəm\ *n* **1** : an alcoholic liquor distilled from a fermented cane product (as molasses) **2** : alcoholic liquor

Ru·ma·ni·an \ru-'mā-nē-ən\ *var of* ROMANIAN

rum·ba \'rəm-bə, 'rüm-\ *n* [AmerSp] **1** : a Cuban Negro dance marked by violent movements **2** : an American ballroom dance imitative of the Cuban rumba

¹rum·ble \'rəm-bəl\ *vb* **rum·bled**; **rum·bling** \-b(ə-)liŋ\ [ME *rumblen*] **1** : to make a low heavy rolling sound **2** : to travel with a low reverberating sound **3** : to speak or utter in a low rolling tone

²rumble *n* : a low heavy continuous reverberating often muffled sound

rumble seat *n* : a folding seat in the back of an automobile (as a coupe or roadster) not covered by the top

ru·men \'rü-mən\ *n*, *pl* **ru·mi·na** \-mə-nə\ *or* **rumens** [L *rumin-*, *rumen* gullet] : the large first compartment of the stomach of a ruminant in which cellulose is broken down by the action of symbionts — **ru·mi·nal** \-mən-ᵊl\ *adj*

¹ru·mi·nant \'rü-mə-nənt\ *n* : a ruminant mammal

²ruminant *adj* [L *ruminare* to chew the cud, muse upon, fr. *rumin-*, *rumen* gullet] **1 a** : chewing the cud **b** : of or relating to a group (Ruminantia) of even-toed hoofed mammals (as sheep, giraffes, deer, and camels) that chew the cud and have a complex 3- or 4-chambered stomach **2** : given to or engaged in contemplation : MEDITATIVE — **ru·mi·nant·ly** *adv*

ru·mi·nate \'rü-mə-ˌnāt\ *vb* **1** : to engage in contemplation : MUSE, MEDITATE **2** : to chew the cud : bring up and chew again what has been chewed slightly and

swallowed — **ru·mi·na·tion** \ˌrü-mə-'nā-shən\ *n* — **ru·mi·na·tive** \'rü-mə-ˌnāt-iv\ *adj* — **ru·mi·na·tive·ly** *adv* — **ru·mi·na·tor** \-ˌnāt-ər\ *n*

¹rum·mage \'rəm-ij\ *n* [MF *arrimage* act of packing cargo] : a thorough search esp. among a confusion of objects or into every section

²rummage *vb* **1** : to make a thorough or active search esp. by moving about, turning over, or looking through the contents of a place or receptacle ⟨*rummage* through an attic⟩ **2** : to discover by searching : hunt out ⟨*rummaged* up what they needed for costumes⟩

rummage sale *n* : a sale of donated articles usu. by a church or charitable organization

rum·my \'rəm-ē\ *n* : a card game in which each player tries to be the first to assemble all of his cards in groups of three or more

¹ru·mor \'rü-mər\ *n* [L] **1** : talk or opinion widely current but having no known source : HEARSAY **2** : a statement or report current without known authority for its truth

²rumor *vt* **ru·mored**; **ru·mor·ing** \'rüm-(ə-)riŋ\ : to tell or spread by rumor

ru·mor·mon·ger \'rü-mər-ˌməŋ-gər, -ˌmäŋ-\ *n* : one who spreads rumors

rump \'rəmp\ *n* [of Scand origin] **1** : the back part of an animal's body where the hips and thighs join generally including the buttocks **2** : a cut of beef between the loin and round **3** : a small fragment remaining after the separation of the larger part of a group or an area; *esp* : a group (as a parliament) carrying on in the name of the original body after the departure or expulsion of a large number of its members — **rumped** \'rəm(p)t\ *adj*

rum·ple \'rəm-pəl\ *vt* **rum·pled**; **rum·pling** \-p(ə-)liŋ\ [D *rompelen*] **1** : WRINKLE, CRUMPLE ⟨*rumple* the bedclothes⟩ **2** : to make unkempt : TOUSLE ⟨*rumpled* his hair⟩

rum·pus \'rəm-pəs\ *n* : DISTURBANCE, FRACAS

rumpus room *n* : a room usu. in the basement of a home set apart for games, parties, and recreation

¹run \'rən\ *vb* **ran** \'ran\; **run**; **run·ning** [ME *rinnen*, v.i. (partly fr. OE *rinnan*, partly fr. ON *rinna*) & *rennen*, v.t., fr. ON *renna*] **1 a** : to go faster than a walk; *esp* : to go steadily by springing steps so that both feet leave the ground for an instant in each step **b** : to move at a fast gallop ⟨*running* horses⟩ **c** : FLEE, RETREAT, ESCAPE ⟨dropped his gun and *ran*⟩ **2 a** : to move freely about at will ⟨let his chickens *run* loose⟩ **b** : to sail in the same direction as the wind blows **c** : ROAM, ROVE **3 a** : to go or cause to go rapidly or hurriedly : HASTEN **b** : to do or accomplish something by or as if by running ⟨*run* errands⟩ **4 a** : to contend in a race **b** : to enter or put forward as a contestant in an election contest **5 a** : to move on or as if on wheels : GLIDE ⟨file drawers *running* on ball bearings⟩ **b** : to roll forward rapidly or freely **c** : to ravel lengthwise **6** : to sing or play a musical passage quickly ⟨*run* up the scale⟩ **7 a** : to go back and forth **: PLY b** : to migrate or move in schools; *esp* : to ascend a river to spawn ⟨shad are *running* in the river⟩ **8** : FUNCTION, OPERATE **9 a** : to continue in force or operation ⟨the contract has two years to *run*⟩ **b** : to accompany as an obligation or right **10** : to pass into a specified condition ⟨*run* into debt⟩ **11 a** : to move as a fluid : FLOW **b** : MELT, FUSE **c** : to spread out : DISSOLVE ⟨colors guaranteed not to *run*⟩ **d** : to discharge a fluid ⟨a *running* sore⟩ **12 a** : to develop rapidly in a specific direction **b** : to tend to develop a specified quality or feature ⟨they *run* to big noses in that family⟩ **13 a** : EXTEND ⟨the boundary line *runs* east⟩ **b** : to go back **c** : to be in a certain form or expression ⟨the letter *runs* as follows⟩ or order of succession ⟨house numbers *run* in odd numbers from 3 to 57⟩ **14 a** : to occur persistently : RECUR **b** : to exist or occur in a continuous range of variation **c** : to play on a stage a number of successive days or nights ⟨the play *ran* for six months⟩ **15 a** : to spread or pass quickly from point to point ⟨chills *ran* up his spine⟩ **b** : to be current : CIRCULATE ⟨speculation *ran* rife on who the candidate would be⟩ **16 a** : to bring to a specified condition by or as if by running ⟨*ran* himself to death⟩ **b** : TRACE ⟨*ran* the rumor to its source⟩ **c** : to keep or maintain (livestock) on or as if on pasturage **17 a** : to pass over or traverse ⟨*ran* the whole range of emotions⟩ **b** : to slip through or past ⟨*run* a blockade⟩ **18 a** : to cause to penetrate or enter : THRUST ⟨*ran* a splinter into his toe⟩   **b** : STITCH   **c** : to cause to pass : LEAD ⟨*run* a wire in from the antenna⟩   **d** : to cause to collide ⟨*ran* his head into a post⟩   **e** : SMUGGLE   **19** : to cause to pass lightly or quickly over, along, or into something ⟨*ran* his eye down the list⟩   **20 a** : to cause or allow to go in a specified manner or direction ⟨*ran* his car off the road⟩ ⟨*run* out the beam from the ship's side⟩   **b** : to carry on : MANAGE ⟨*run* a factory⟩   **21 a** : to flow with ⟨streets *ran* blood⟩   **b** : CONTAIN, ASSAY ⟨the ore *runs* high in silver⟩   **22** : to make oneself liable to ⟨*ran* the risk of discovery⟩   **23** : to mark out ⟨*run* a contour line on a map⟩ : DRAW   **24** : to permit charges to accumulate before settling ⟨*run* an account⟩   **25** : PRINT ⟨a book to be *run* on lightweight paper⟩ ⟨*run* the advertisement for three days⟩   **26 a** : to make (a series of counts) without a miss ⟨*run* 19 in an inning in billiards⟩   **b** : to lead winning cards of (a suit) successively — **run across** : to meet with or discover by chance — **run a fever** *or* **run a temperature** : to have a fever — **run foul of** : to collide with ⟨*ran* *foul of* a hidden reef⟩ : run into conflict with or hostility to ⟨*run* *foul of* the law⟩ — **run into   1** : to mount up to ⟨a boat like that one *runs into* money⟩   **2 a** : to collide with   **b** : ENCOUNTER, MEET — **run riot   1** : to act wildly or without restraint   **2** : to occur in profusion — **run short** : to become insufficient — **run to seed** : to exhaust vitality in or as if in producing seed

²**run** *n*   **1 a** : an act or the action of running : continued rapid movement ⟨broke into a *run*⟩   **b** : a fast gallop   **c** : a migrating of fish; *also* : fish migrating esp. to spawn   **d** : a running race ⟨a mile *run*⟩   **e** : a score made in baseball by a base runner reaching home plate   **2 a** *chiefly Midland* : CREEK   2   **b** : something that flows in the course of an operation or during a particular time ⟨the first *run* of maple sap⟩   **3 a** : the horizontal distance from one point to another   **b** : general tendency or direction   **4** : a continuous series esp. of things of identical or similar sort: as   **a** : a rapid scale passage in vocal or instrumental music   **b** : the act of making successively a number of successful shots or strokes ⟨a *run* of 20 in billiards⟩   **c** : an unbroken course of theatrical performances   **d** : sudden heavy demands from depositors, creditors, or customers ⟨a *run* on a bank⟩ : SEQUENCE 1b   **5** : the quantity of work turned out in a continuous operation   **6** : the usual or normal kind ⟨average *run* of college graduates⟩   **7 a** : the distance covered in a period of continuous traveling or sailing ⟨logged the day's *run*⟩   **b** : regular course : TRIP ⟨the bus makes four *runs* daily⟩   **c** : freedom of movement in or access to a place or area ⟨has the *run* of his friend's house⟩   **8 a** : a way, track, or path frequented by animals   **b** : an enclosure for livestock where they may feed or exercise   **9 a** : an inclined course (as for skiing)   **b** : a track or guide on which something runs   **10** : a ravel in a knitted fabric (as in hosiery) caused by the breaking of stitches — **run·less** \-ləs\ *adj*

run·about \'rən-ə-ˌbaut\ *n*   **1** : one who wanders about : STRAY   **2** : a light open wagon, roadster, or motorboat
run·a·gate \'rən-ə-ˌgāt\ *n* [alter. of obs. *renegate* renegade, fr. ML *renegatus*]   **1** : FUGITIVE, RUNAWAY   **2** : VAGABOND
run·around \'rən-ə-ˌraund\ *n* : deceptive or delaying action esp. in response to a request
run away \ˌrən-ə-'wā\ *vi*   **1** : FLEE, DESERT   **2** : to leave home; *esp* : ELOPE   **3** : to run out of control : STAMPEDE, BOLT
¹**run·away** \'rən-ə-ˌwā\ *n*   **1** : FUGITIVE   **2** : the act of running away out of control; *also* : a horse that is running out of control
²**runaway** *adj*   **1** : running away : FUGITIVE   **2** : accomplished by elopement or during flight ⟨a *runaway* marriage⟩   **3** : won by or having a long lead   **4** : subject to uncontrolled changes ⟨*runaway* inflation⟩
run·ci·nate \'rən(t)-sə-ˌnāt\ *adj* [L *runcinare* to plane off, fr. *runcina* plane] : pinnately incised with the lobes pointing toward the base ⟨a *runcinate* leaf of a dandelion⟩
run down \'rən-'daun, ˌrən-\ *vb*   **1 a** : to collide with and knock down   **b** : to run against and cause to sink   **2 a** : to chase until exhausted or captured   **b** : to find by search : trace the source of   **3** : DISPARAGE   **4** : to cease to operate because of the exhaustion of motive power   **5** : to deteriorate in physical condition
run-down \'rən-ˌdaun\ *adj*   **1** : being in poor repair

: DILAPIDATED   **2** : being in poor health   **3** : completely unwound ⟨a *run-down* clock⟩
run-down \'rən-ˌdaun\ *n* : an item-by-item report : SUMMARY
rune \'rün\ *n* [ON & OE *rūn* mystery, runic character]   **1** : one of the characters of an alphabet used by the Germanic peoples from about the 3d to the 13th centuries   **2** : mystic utterance or inscription   **3** [Finn *runo*, of Gmc origin] : a Finnish or Old Norse poem — **ru·nic** \'rü-nik\ *adj*
¹**rung** *past part of* RING
²**rung** \'rəŋ\ *n* [OE *hrung* crossbar, spoke]   **1 a** : a rounded part placed as a crosspiece between the legs of a chair   **b** : one of the crosspieces of a ladder   **2** : a stage in an ascent : DEGREE
run-in \'rən-ˌin\ *n* : ALTERCATION, QUARREL
run·let \'rən-lət\ *n* : RUNNEL
run·nel \'rən-ᵊl\ *n* [OE *rynel*] : RIVULET, STREAMLET
run·ner \'rən-ər\ *n*   **1 a** : one that runs : RACER   **b** : a football player in possession of a live ball   **2** : MESSENGER   **3** : any of various large active sea fishes   **4 a** : either of the longitudinal pieces on which a sled or sleigh slides   **b** : the part of a skate that slides on the ice : BLADE   **c** : the support of a drawer or a sliding door   **5 a** : a slender creeping branch of a plant; *esp* : STOLON   **b** : a plant that forms or spreads by runners   **6 a** : a long narrow carpet for a hall or staircase   **b** : a narrow decorative cloth cover for a table or dresser top

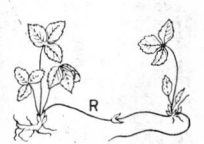

R runner 5a

run·ner-up \'rən-ər-ˌəp\ *n* : the competitor in a contest that finishes next to the winner
¹**run·ning** *adj*   **1** : FLUID, RUNNY   **2** : INCESSANT, CONTINUOUS ⟨a *running* battle⟩   **3** : measured in a straight line ⟨cost of lumber per *running* foot⟩   **4** : FLOWING, CURSIVE ⟨a *running* hand in writing⟩   **5** : initiated or performed while running or with a running start ⟨a *running* leap⟩   **6** : fitted or trained for running ⟨*running* track⟩ ⟨*running* horse⟩
²**running** *adv* : in succession : CONSECUTIVELY
running board *n* : a footboard esp. at the side of an automobile
running knot *n* : a knot that slips along the line round which it is tied
running light *n* : one of the lights carried by a ship under way at night or on the wing and fuselage of an airplane
running mate *n* : a candidate running for a subordinate office (as of vice-president) who is paired with the candidate for the top office on the same ticket
running title *n* : the title of a volume printed at the top of left-hand text pages or sometimes of all text pages
run·ny \'rən-ē\ *adj* **run·ni·er; -est** : having a tendency to run ⟨watery eyes and *runny* nose⟩
run off \'rən-'óf, ˌrən-\ *vb*   **1** : to produce by a printing press   **2** : to cause to be run or played to a finish   **3** : to steal (as cattle) by driving away   **4** : to run away — **run off with** : to carry off : STEAL
run·off \'rən-ˌóf\ *n*   **1** : water that is removed from soil by natural drainage   **2** : a final contest to decide a previous indecisive contest or series of contests
run-of-the-mill \ˌrən-ə(v)-thə-'mil\ *adj* : not outstanding in quality or rarity : AVERAGE
run on \'rən-'ón, ˌrən-, -'än\ *vb*   **1** : CONTINUE   **2** : to talk or narrate at length   **3** : to continue (matter in type) without a break or a new paragraph   **4** : to place or add (as an entry in a dictionary) at the end of a paragraphed item
¹**run-on** \'rən-ˌón, -ˌän\ *adj* : continuing without rhetorical pause from one line of verse into another
²**run-on** \-ˌón, -ˌän\ *n* : something (as a dictionary entry) that is run on
run-on sentence *n* : a sentence formed with a comma fault
run out *vi*   **1** : to come to an end : EXPIRE   **2** : to become exhausted or used up : FAIL — **run out of** : to use up the available supply of
run over *vb*   **1** : OVERFLOW   **2** : to exceed a limit   **3** : to go over, examine, repeat, or rehearse quickly   **4** : to

collide with, knock down, and often drive over ⟨*run over* a dog in the road⟩

runt \'rənt\ *n* : an unusually small person or animal — **runt·i·ness** \-ē-nəs\ *n* — **runty** \-ē\ *adj*

run through *vt* **1** : PIERCE **2** : to spend or consume wastefully and rapidly

run·way \'rən-ˌwā\ *n* **1** : RUN 8 **2** : an artificially surfaced strip of ground on a landing field for the landing and takeoff of airplanes **3** : a support (as a track, pipe, or trough) on which something runs

ru·pee \rü-'pē, 'rü-(ˌ)pē\ *n* [Hindi *rūpaiyā*, fr. Skt *rūpya* coined silver, fr. neut. of *rūpya* well-shaped, impressed, fr. *rūpa* shape, beauty] **1** : the basic monetary unit of India, Pakistan, and Ceylon **2** : a coin representing one rupee

¹rup·ture \'rəp-chər\ *n* [L *rupt-*, *rumpere* to break] **1** : breach of peace or concord; *esp* : open hostility or war between nations **2** : a breaking or tearing apart (as of body tissue) or the resulting state **3** : HERNIA **syn** see FRACTURE

²rupture *vb* **rup·tured**; **rup·tur·ing** \-chə-riŋ, -shriŋ\ **1** : to part by violence : BREAK **2** : to produce a rupture in **3** : to have a rupture

ru·ral \'rur-əl\ *adj* [L *rur-*, *rus* open land, country] : of or relating to the country, country people or life, or agriculture

rural free delivery *n* : the free delivery of mail on routes in country districts — called also *rural delivery*

rural route *n* : a mail-delivery route in a rural free delivery area

rur·ban \'rər-bən, 'rur-\ *adj* [blend of *rural* and *urban*] : of, relating to, or constituting an area which is chiefly residential but where some farming is carried on

ruse \'rüs, 'rüz\ *n* [F, fr. MF *ruser* to retreat, dodge, deceive] : a deceptive stratagem : ARTIFICE, SUBTERFUGE **syn** see TRICK

¹rush \'rəsh\ *n* [OE *risc*, *rysc*] : any of various monocotyledonous often tufted marsh plants with cylindrical often hollow stems used in chair seats and mats — **rushy** \-ē\ *adj*

²rush *vb* [MF *ruser* to retreat, dodge, put to flight, fr. L *recusare* to refuse] **1** : to move forward, progress, or act with haste or eagerness or without preparation **2** : to act as carrier of a football in a running play **3** : to push or impel on or forward with speed or violence **4** : to perform in a short time or at high speed **5** : ATTACK, CHARGE **6** : to lavish attention on : COURT — **rush·er** *n*

³rush *n* **1 a** : a violent forward motion ⟨a *rush* of wind⟩ **b** : ATTACK, ONSET **2** : a burst of activity, productivity, or speed **3** : a thronging of people usu. to a new place and in search of wealth ⟨gold *rush*⟩ **4** : the act of carrying a football during a game : running play **5** : a round of attention usu. involving extensive social activity

⁴rush *adj* : requiring or marked by special speed or urgency ⟨*rush* orders⟩ ⟨*rush* season⟩

rusk \'rəsk\ *n* [Sp & Pg *rosca* coil, twisted roll] : a sweet or plain bread baked, sliced, and baked again until dry and crisp

Russ \'rəs\ *n*, *pl* **Russ** *or* **Russ·es** : RUSSIAN — **Russ** *adj*

rus·set \'rəs-ət\ *n* [OF *rousset*, adj., reddish brown, dim. of *rous*, fr. L *russus* red] **1** : coarse homespun usu. reddish brown cloth **2** : a variable color averaging a strong brown **3** : any of various winter apples with rough russet skins — **russet** *adj*

Rus·sian \'rəsh-ən\ *n* **1 a** : one of the people of Russia; *esp* : a member of the dominant Slavic-speaking Great Russian ethnic group of Russia **b** : a person of Russian descent **2** : a Slavic language of the Russian people that is the official language of the U.S.S.R. — **Russian** *adj*

Russian olive *n* : a small Eurasian tree or shrub with usu. silvery leaves widely grown in dry windy regions as a hedge and shelter plant

Russian thistle *n* : a prickly European herb that is a serious weed in No. America

Russian wolfhound *n* : BORZOI

Rus·so- *comb form* **1** \ˌrəs-ə, 'rəs-, -ō\ : Russia

: Russians ⟨*Russo*phobia⟩ **2** \'rəs(h)-ō, ˌrəs(h)-\ : Russian and ⟨*Russo*-Japanese⟩

¹rust \'rəst\ *n* [OE *rūst*; akin to E *red*] **1 a** : the reddish brittle coating chiefly of ferric oxide formed on iron esp. when chemically attacked by moist air **b** : a comparable coating produced on other metals by corrosion **2** : corrosive or injurious influence or effect **3 a** : any of numerous destructive diseases of plants caused by fungi and marked by reddish brown pustular lesions **b** : any of an order (Uredinales) of parasitic fungi that cause plant rusts — compare WHITE RUST **4** : a strong reddish brown

²rust *vb* **1** : to form or cause to form rust : become oxidized ⟨iron *rusts*⟩ **2** : to weaken or degenerate or cause to degenerate esp. from inaction, lack of use, or passage of time : CORRODE ⟨his diplomatic skill had not *rusted*⟩ **3** : to turn the color of rust

¹rus·tic \'rəs-tik\ *adj* [L *rusticus*, fr. *rus* open land, country] **1** : of, relating to, or suitable for the country : RURAL ⟨*rustic* sports⟩ **2** : made of the rough limbs of trees ⟨*rustic* furniture⟩ **3** : AWKWARD, BOORISH ⟨*rustic* manners⟩ **4** : PLAIN, SIMPLE — **rus·ti·cal·ly** \-ti-k(ə-)lē\ *adv* — **rus·tic·i·ty** \ˌrəs-'tis-ət-ē\ *n*

²rustic *n* : an inhabitant of a rural area; *esp* : an unsophisticated one

rus·ti·cate \'rəs-ti-ˌkāt\ *vb* **1** : to go into or reside in the country **2** : to suspend from school or college — **rus·ti·ca·tion** \ˌrəs-ti-'kā-shən\ *n* — **rus·ti·ca·tor** \'rəs-ti-ˌkāt-ər\ *n*

¹rus·tle \'rəs-əl\ *vb* **rus·tled**; **rus·tling** \'rəs-(ə-)liŋ\ [ME *rustelen*] **1** : to make or cause to make a rustle ⟨*rustled* the papers in his hand⟩ **2** : to act or move with energy or speed **3** : to get by rustling ⟨*rustle* up some food⟩; *esp* : FORAGE **4** : to steal (as cattle) from the range — **rus·tler** \'rəs-(ə-)lər\ *n*

²rustle *n* : a quick succession or confusion of small sounds ⟨the *rustle* of leaves⟩ ⟨the *rustle* among a theater audience⟩

rust·proof \'rəst-'prüf\ *adj* : incapable of rusting

rusty \'rəs-tē\ *adj* **rust·i·er**; **-est** **1** : affected by or as if by rust; *esp* : stiff with or as if with rust **2** : inept and slow through lack of practice or old age **3 a** : of the color rust **b** : dulled in color or appearance by age and use — **rust·i·ly** \'rəs-tə-lē\ *adv* — **rust·i·ness** \-tē-nəs\ *n*

¹rut \'rət\ *n* [MF *ruit*, *rut* roar, fr. LL *rugitus*, fr. L *rugire* to roar] : a state of sexual excitement esp. in the male deer

²rut *vi* **rut·ted**; **rut·ting** : to be in or enter into a state of rut

³rut *n* **1** : a track worn by a wheel or by habitual passage **2** : a usual or fixed practice : a regular course; *esp* : a monotonous routine ⟨his teaching has fallen into a *rut*⟩ — **rut·ty** \'rət-ē\ *adj*

⁴rut *vt* **rut·ted**; **rut·ting** : to make a rut in : FURROW

ru·ta·ba·ga \ˌrüt-ə-'bā-gə, ˌrüt-\ *n* [Sw dial. *rotabagge*, fr. Sw *rot* root + *bagge* bag] : a turnip with a very large yellowish root

ruth \'rüth\ *n* [ME *ruthe*, fr. *ruen* to rue] **1** : compassion for the misery of another : PITY **2** : sorrow for one's own faults : REMORSE

Ruth \'rüth\ *n* **1** : a Moabite woman who became the wife of Boaz and ancestress of David **2** — see BIBLE table

ru·the·ni·um \rü-'thē-nē-əm\ *n* [NL, fr. ML *Ruthenia* Russia] : a hard brittle grayish rare metallic chemical element used in hardening platinum alloys — see ELEMENT table

ruth·less \'rüth-ləs\ *adj* : having no ruth : MERCILESS, CRUEL — **ruth·less·ly** *adv* — **ruth·less·ness** *n*

ru·tile \'rü-ˌtēl\ *n* [L *rutilus* reddish] : a mineral that consists of titanium dioxide usu. with a little iron, is mostly of a reddish brown color, and is a major source of titanium

-ry \rē\ *n suffix*, *pl* **-ries** [OF *-erie*, *-rie* *-ery*] : -ERY ⟨wizard*ry*⟩ ⟨citizen*ry*⟩ ⟨ancient*ry*⟩

rye \'rī\ *n* [OE *ryge*] **1** : a hardy annual cereal grass widely grown for grain and as a cover crop; *also* : its seeds **2** : whiskey distilled from rye or from rye and malt

rye bread *n* : bread made wholly or partly from rye flour

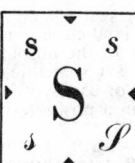

s \'es\ *n, often cap* **1** : the 19th letter of the English alphabet **2** : a grade rating a student's work as satisfactory

¹-s \s *after a voiceless consonant sound,* z *after a voiced consonant sound or a vowel sound*\ *n pl suffix* [OE *-as,* nom. & acc. pl. ending of some masc. nouns] **1** — used to form the plural of most nouns that do not end in *s, z, sh, ch,* or postconsonantal *y* ⟨heads⟩⟨books⟩⟨boys⟩ ⟨beliefs⟩, to form the plural of proper nouns that end in postconsonantal *y* ⟨Marys⟩, and with or without a preceding apostrophe to form the plural of abbreviations, numbers, letters, and symbols used as nouns ⟨MCs⟩ ⟨4s⟩ ⟨#s⟩ ⟨B's⟩ — compare ¹-ES 1 **2** — used to form adverbs denoting usual or repeated action or state ⟨always at home Sundays⟩ ⟨mornings he stops by the newsstand⟩ ⟨goes to school nights⟩

²-s *vb suffix* [OE (Northumbrian dial.) *-es, -as*] — used to form the third person singular present of most verbs that do not end in *s, z, sh, ch,* or postconsonantal *y* ⟨falls⟩ ⟨takes⟩ ⟨plays⟩ — compare ²-ES

-'s \s *after voiceless consonant sounds other than* s, sh, ch; z *after vowel sounds and voiced consonant sounds other than* z, zh, j; əz *after* s, sh, ch, z, zh, j\ *n suffix or pron suffix* [OE *-es,* gen. sing. ending] — used to form the possessive of singular nouns ⟨boy's⟩, of plural nouns not ending in *s* ⟨children's⟩, of some pronouns ⟨anyone's⟩, and of word groups functioning as nouns ⟨the man in the corner's hat⟩ or pronouns ⟨someone else's⟩

¹'s \like -'s\ *vb* [contr. of *is, has, does*] **1** : IS ⟨she's here⟩ ⟨she's talking now⟩ **2** : HAS ⟨he's seen them⟩ **3** : DOES ⟨what's he want?⟩

²'s \s\ *pron* : US — used with *let* ⟨let's⟩

sab·a·dil·la \,sab-ə-'dil-ə, -'dē-(y)ə\ *n* : a Mexican plant of the lily family; *also* : its seeds used as a source of veratrine and in insecticides

Sab·ba·tar·i·an \,sab-ə-'ter-ē-ən\ *n* **1** : one who keeps the 7th day of the week as holy **2** : one who favors strict observance of the Sabbath — **Sabbatarian** *adj* — **Sab·ba·tar·i·an·ism** \-ē-ə-,niz-əm\ *n*

Sab·bath \'sab-əth\ *n* [L *sabbatum,* fr. Gk *sabbaton,* fr. Heb *shabbāth,* lit., rest] **1** : the 7th day of the week observed from Friday evening to Saturday evening as a day of rest and worship by Jews and some Christians **2** : the day of the week (as among Christians) set aside in a religion for rest and worship SYN see SUNDAY

sab·bat·i·cal \sə-'bat-i-kəl\ *or* **sab·bat·ic** \-'bat-ik\ *adj* **1** : of or relating to the Sabbath **2** : being a recurring period of rest or renewal

sabbatical year *n* : a leave granted (as to a college professor) usu. every 7th year for rest, travel, or research — called also *sabbatical leave*

¹sa·ber *or* **sa·bre** \'sā-bər\ *n* [F *sabre,* modif. of G dial. *sabel,* of Slav origin] **1** : a cavalry sword with a curved blade, thick back, and guard **2** : a light fencing or dueling sword

²saber *or* **sabre** *vt* **sa·bered** *or* **sa·bred;** **sa·ber·ing** *or* **sa·bring** \-b(ə-)riŋ\ : to strike, cut, or kill with a saber

saber rattling *n* : ostentatious display of military power

sa·ber-toothed tiger \,sā-bər-,tüth(t)-'tī-gər\ *n* : any of various large prehistoric cats with long curved upper canine teeth — called also *saber-toothed cat*

Sa·bine \'sā-,bīn\ *n* : a member of an ancient people of the Apennines northeast of Latium conquered by Rome in 290 B.C. — **Sabine** *adj*

Sa·bin vaccine \'sā-bən-\ *n* [after Albert B. *Sabin* b1906 American virologist] : a polio vaccine that contains living attenuated virus and is taken by mouth — compare SALK VACCINE

¹sa·ble \'sā-bəl\ *n, pl* **sable** *or* **sables** [MF, sable or its fur, the heraldic color black, fr. MLG *sabel,* of Slav origin] **1 a** : the color black **b** : black clothing worn in mourning — usu. used in pl. **2 a** : a carnivorous mammal of northern Europe and Asia related to the martens and valued for its soft rich brown fur; *also* : a related animal **b** : the fur or pelt of a sable

²sable *adj* **1** : of the color black **2** : DARK

sa·ble·fish \'sā-bəl-,fish\ *n* : a large dark spiny-finned fish of the Pacific coast that is a leading market fish with a liver rich in vitamins — called also *black cod*

sa·bot \sa-'bō, 'sab-ō\ *n* [F] : a wooden shoe worn in various European countries

¹sab·o·tage \'sab-ə-,täzh\ *n* [F, fr. *saboter* to clatter with sabots, botch, sabotage, fr. *sabot*] **1** : destruction of an employer's property (as tools or materials) or the hindering of manufacturing by discontented workmen **2** : destructive or obstructive action carried on by enemy agents or sympathizers to hinder a nation's war or defense effort

²sabotage *vt* : to practice sabotage on : WRECK, DESTROY

sab·o·teur \,sab-ə-'tər, -'tür\ *n* : a person who commits sabotage

sab·u·lous \'sab-yə-ləs\ *adj* [L *sabulum* sand] : SANDY, GRITTY

sac \'sak\ *n* [F, lit., bag, fr. L *saccus*] : a pouch within an animal or plant often containing a fluid ⟨a synovial *sac*⟩ — **sac·cate** \'sak-,āt\ *adj* — **sac·like** \'sak-,līk\ *adj*

sac·cha·ride \'sak-ə-,rīd\ *n* : a simple sugar, combination of sugars, or polymerized sugar

sac·cha·rim·e·ter \,sak-ə-'rim-ət-ər\ *n* : a device for measuring the amount of sugar in a solution

sac·cha·rin \'sak-(ə-)rən\ *n* : a very sweet white coal tar derivative that is used as a calorie-free sweetener

sac·cha·rine \'sak-ə-rən\ *adj* [Gk *sakcharon* sugar, fr. Skt *śarkarā* gravel, sugar] **1 a** : of, relating to, or resembling that of sugar ⟨*saccharine* taste⟩ ⟨*saccharine* fermentation⟩ **b** : yielding or containing sugar ⟨*saccharine* fluids⟩ **2** : overly or ingratiatingly sweet ⟨a *saccharine* smile⟩ — **sac·cha·rin·i·ty** \,sak-ə-'rin-ət-ē\ *n*

sac·cha·ro·my·cete \,sak-ə-rō-'mī-,sēt, -mī-'sēt\ *n* : a yeast fungus

sac·cu·lat·ed \'sak-yə-,lāt-ad\ *adj* : having or formed of a series of saclike expansions — **sac·cu·la·tion** \,sak-yə-'lā-shən\ *n*

sac·cule \'sak-yül\ *n* [NL *sacculus,* fr. L, dim. of *saccus* bag] : a little sac; *esp* : the smaller chamber of the membranous labyrinth of the ear — compare UTRICLE

sac·cu·lus \'sak-yə-ləs\ *n, pl* **-li** \-,lī, -,lē\ : SACCULE

sac·er·do·tal \,sas-ər-'dōt-ᵊl, ,sak-ər-\ *adj* [L *sacerdot-, sacerdos* priest, fr. *sacer* sacred] : PRIESTLY — **sac·er·do·tal·ly** \-ᵊl-ē\ *adv*

sac·er·do·tal·ism \-ᵊl-,iz-əm\ *n* : religious belief emphasizing the powers of priests as essential mediators between God and man — **sac·er·do·tal·ist** \-ᵊl-əst\ *n*

sac fungus *n* : ASCOMYCETE

sa·chem \'sā-chəm\ *n* [of Algonquian origin] : a No. American Indian chief; *esp* : an Algonquian chief — **sa·chem·ic** \sā-'chem-ik\ *adj*

sa·chet \sa-'shā\ *n* [F, dim. of *sac* bag] : a small bag that contains a perfumed powder and is used to scent clothes and linens

¹sack \'sak\ *n* [OE *sacc* bag, fr. L *saccus,* fr. Gk *sakkos,* of Sem origin] **1 a** : a large bag made of coarse strong material **b** : a small container made of light material (as paper) **2** : the amount contained in a sack **3 a** : a woman's loose-fitting dress **b** : a short usu. loose-fitting coat for women and children **4** : DISMISSAL — usu. used with *get* or *give* **5** : BUNK, BED

²sack *vt* **1** : to put in a sack **2** : to dismiss esp. in a summary manner

³sack *n* [MF *vin sec* dry wine] : a usu. dry and strong white wine imported to England from the south of Europe esp. during the 16th and 17th centuries

⁴sack *n* [MF *sac,* fr. It *sacco,* lit., bag, fr. L *saccus*] : the plundering of a captured town

⁵sack *vt* **1** : to plunder after capture **2** : PILLAGE, LOOT

sack·but \'sak-(,)bət\ *n* [MF *saqueboute* hooked lance, sackbut] : a medieval trombone

sack·cloth \'sak-,klòth\ *n* **1** : a coarse cloth suitable for sacks : SACKING **2** : a garment of sackcloth worn as a sign of mourning or penitence

sack coat *n* : a man's jacket with a straight unfitted back

sack·ful \'sak-,fùl\ *n, pl* **sackfuls** \-,fùlz\ *or* **sacks·ful** \'saks-,fùl\ : the quantity that fills a sack

sack·ing \'sak-iŋ\ *n* : strong coarse cloth (as burlap) from which sacks are made

sack race *n* : a race run by persons each with his legs in a sack

sacque \'sak\ *n* [alter. of ¹*sack*] : a loose lightweight jacket; *esp* : an infant's short jacket fastened at the neck

sac·ral \'sak-rəl, 'sā-krəl\ *adj* : of, relating to, or lying near the sacrum

sac·ra·ment \'sak-rə-mənt\ n [LL sacramentum, fr. L, oath of allegiance, obligation, fr. sacrare to consecrate, fr. sacer sacred] **1** : a formal religious act that is sacred as a sign or symbol of a spiritual reality; esp : one instituted by Jesus Christ as a means of grace **2** cap : BLESSED SACRAMENT — **sac·ra·men·tal** \,sak-rə-'ment-°l\ adj — **sac·ra·men·tal·ly** \-°l-ē\ adv

sac·ra·men·tal \,sak-rə-'ment-°l\ n : something (as a rite or object) related to or resembling a sacrament but held to be of ecclesiastical origin rather than to have been instituted by Jesus Christ

sac·ra·men·tal·ism \-°l-,iz-əm\ n : belief in or use of sacramental rites, acts, or objects; esp : belief that the sacraments are inherently efficacious and necessary for salvation — **sac·ra·men·tal·ist** \-°l-əst\ n

sa·cred \'sā-krəd\ adj [ME, fr. pp. of sacren to consecrate, fr. L sacrare, fr. sacer sacred] **1** : set apart in honor of someone (as a god) ⟨a mountain sacred to Jupiter⟩ ⟨a monument sacred to the memory of our heroes⟩ **2** : HOLY ⟨the sacred name of Jesus⟩ **3** : RELIGIOUS ⟨sacred songs⟩ **4** : requiring or deserving to be held in highest esteem and protected from violation or encroachment ⟨a sacred right⟩ ⟨his sacred word⟩ — **sa·cred·ly** adv — **sa·cred·ness** n

sacred cow n [so called fr. the veneration of cows in India] : a person or thing immune from criticism

¹sac·ri·fice \'sak-rə-,fīs, -fəs\ n [L sacrificium, fr. sacer sacred + facere to make] **1** : an act of offering to deity something precious; esp : the killing of a victim on an altar **2** : something offered in sacrifice **3** : a destroying or yielding of something for the sake of something else; also : something so given up ⟨the sacrifices made by parents⟩ **4** : loss of something and esp. of a profit ⟨sell goods at a sacrifice⟩

²sac·ri·fice \-,fīs\ vb **1** : to offer as a sacrifice or perform sacrificial rites **2** : to give up for the sake of something else ⟨sacrificed his free time to help his sister⟩ ⟨sacrificed everything to win the election⟩ **3** : to sell at a loss **4** : to make a sacrifice hit — **sac·ri·fic·er** n

sacrifice fly n : an outfield fly in baseball caught by a fielder after which a base runner scores

sacrifice hit n : a bunt in baseball that allows a runner to advance one base while the batter is put out

sac·ri·fi·cial \,sak-rə-'fish-əl\ adj : of or relating to sacrifice — **sac·ri·fi·cial·ly** \-'fish-ə-lē\ adv

sac·ri·lege \'sak-rə-lij\ n [L sacrilegium, fr. sacer sacred + legere to gather, steal] **1** : theft or violation of something consecrated to God **2** : gross misuse or disrespect of something sacred or precious ⟨would be a sacrilege to cut such splendid trees⟩ — **sac·ri·le·gious** \,sak-rə-'lij-əs, -'lē-jəs\ adj — **sac·ri·le·gious·ly** adv — **sac·ri·le·gious·ness** n

sac·ris·tan \'sak-rə-stən\ n : an officer of a church in charge of the sacristy and ceremonial equipment; also : SEXTON

sac·ris·ty \-rə-stē\ n, pl -ties [ML sacristia, fr. sacrista sacristan, fr. L sacer sacred] : a room in a church where sacred utensils and vestments are kept : VESTRY

¹sac·ro·il·i·ac \,sak-rō-'il-ē-,ak, ,sā-krō-\ adj : of, relating to, or being the region in which the sacrum and ilium join **²sacroiliac** n : the sacroiliac region

sac·ro·sanct \'sak-rō-,san(k)t\ adj : SACRED, INVIOLABLE — **sac·ro·sanc·ti·ty** \,sak-rō-'san(k)-tət-ē\ n

sac·rum \'sak-rəm, 'sāk-\ n, pl **sac·ra** \-rə\ [NL, fr. LL os sacrum last bone of the spine, lit., sacred bone] : the part of the vertebral column that is directly connected with or forms a part of the pelvis and in man consists of five united vertebrae

sad \'sad\ adj **sad·der**; **sad·dest** [OE sæd sated] **1** : affected with or expressive of grief or unhappiness ⟨sad at the loss of his dog⟩ ⟨sad songs⟩ **2 a** : causing or associated with grief or unhappiness : DEPRESSING ⟨sad news⟩ **b** : DISMAYING, DEPLORABLE ⟨a sad result⟩ — **sad·ly** adv

sad·den \'sad-°n\ vb **sad·dened**; **sad·den·ing** \'sad-niŋ, -°n-iŋ\ : to make or become sad

¹sad·dle \'sad-°l\ n [OE sadol] **1 a** : a girthed usu. padded and leather-covered seat for a rider on horseback; also : a

saddle (English)

comparable part of a driving harness **b** : a seat esp. on a bicycle **2** : a ridge connecting two higher land elevations **3** : a cut of meat consisting of both sides of the unsplit back of a carcass including both loins **4** : something that resembles a saddle in shape, position, or use; esp : a support for an object — **in the saddle** : in a position to control or command

²saddle vb **sad·dled**; **sad·dling** \'sad-liŋ, -°l-iŋ\ **1** : to put on a saddle or put a saddle on **2** : ENCUMBER, BURDEN

sad·dle·bag \'sad-°l-,bag\ n : a large pouch carried hanging from one side of a saddle or over the rear wheel of a bicycle or motorcycle and used. one of a pair

sad·dle·bow \-,bō\ n : the arch in or the pieces forming the front of a saddle

sad·dle·cloth \-,klóth\ n : a cloth placed under or over a saddle

saddle horse n : a horse suited for or trained for riding

saddle leather n : vegetable-tanned leather from cattle hide that is used for saddlery; also : smooth polished leather simulating this

sad·dler \'sad-lər\ n : one that makes, repairs, or sells horse equipment (as saddles)

saddle roof n : a roof (as of a tower) having two gables and one ridge — see ROOF illustration

sad·dlery \'sad-lə-rē, 'sad-°l-rē\ n, pl -dler·ies : the trade, articles of trade, or shop of a saddler

saddle shoe n : an oxford-style shoe having a saddle of contrasting color or leather

saddle soap n : a mild oily soap used for cleansing and conditioning leather

saddle sore n **1** : a sore on the back of a horse from an ill≈ fitting saddle **2** : an irritation or sore on parts of the rider's body chafed by the saddle

sad·dle·tree \'sad-°l-,trē\ n : the frame of a saddle

Sad·du·cee \'saj-ə-,sē\ n : a member of a Jewish party of Jesus' day consisting largely of the priestly aristocracy and rejecting doctrines (as resurrection) not in the Law — **Sad·du·ce·an** \,saj-ə-'sē-ən\ adj — **Sad·du·cee·ism** \-,iz-əm\ n

sa·dhu or **sad·dhu** \'säd-ü\ n [Skt sādhu, fr. sādhu good] : a Hindu mendicant ascetic

sad·iron \'sad-,ī-(ə)rn\ n : a flatiron pointed at both ends and having a removable handle

sad·ism \'sād-,iz-əm, 'sad-\ n [Marquis de Sade d1814 French author] **1** : an abnormal condition in which a person takes pleasure in hurting another; also : an unwholesome love of cruelty **2** : excessive cruelty — **sad·ist** \-əst\ n — **sa·dis·tic** \sə-'dis-tik, sā-\ adj — **sa·dis·ti·cal·ly** \-ti-k(ə-)lē\ adv

sad·ness \'sad-nəs\ n : the quality, state, or fact of being sad syn see MELANCHOLY

sad sack n : an extremely inept person; esp : a meek inept serviceman

sa·fa·ri \sə-'fär-ē, -'far-\ n, pl -ris [Ar safarīy of a trip] **1** : the caravan and equipment of a hunting expedition esp. in eastern Africa **2 a** : a hunting expedition in eastern Africa **b** : JOURNEY, TRIP

¹safe \'sāf\ adj [OF sauf, fr. L salvus] **1** : freed from harm or risk : UNHURT **2 a** : secure from threat of danger, harm, or loss **b** : successful in reaching base in baseball **3** : affording safety from danger **4** : not threatening danger : HARMLESS ⟨safe medicine⟩ **5 a** : CAUTIOUS ⟨a safe policy⟩ **b** : TRUSTWORTHY, RELIABLE ⟨a safe guide⟩ — **safe·ly** adv — **safe·ness** n

syn SAFE, SECURE mean free from danger. SAFE often implies danger successfully avoided or risk run without harm ⟨arrived safe on the other bank of the river⟩ and always suggests present or immediate freedom from threatening harm ⟨stayed safe at home⟩ SECURE implies freedom from anxiety or apprehension of loss or danger ⟨felt secure in his parents' affection⟩

²safe n : a place or receptacle to keep articles (as provisions or valuables) safe

safe-con·duct \'sāf-'kän-(,)dəkt\ n **1** : protection given a person passing through a military zone or occupied area **2** : a document authorizing safe-conduct

safe-crack·er \'sāf-,krak-ər\ n : one that breaks open safes to steal

safe-de·pos·it box \,sāf-di-'päz-ət-\ n : a box (as in the vault of a bank) for the safe storage of valuables

¹safe·guard \'sāf-ˌgärd\ *n* : something that protects and gives safety : DEFENSE

²safeguard *vt* : to make safe or secure : PROTECT ⟨rights *safeguarded* by the constitution⟩

safe·keep·ing \'sāf-'kē-piŋ\ *n* : a keeping or being kept in safety : PROTECTION, CARE, CUSTODY

safe·light \'sāf-ˌlīt\ *n* : a darkroom lamp with a filter to screen out rays that are harmful to sensitive film or paper

safe·ty \'sāf-tē\ *n, pl* **safeties** [ME *saufte*, fr. OF *sauveté*, fr. *sauf* safe, fr. L *salvus*] **1** : the condition of being safe from hurt, injury, or loss : SECURITY **2** : a protective device to prevent inadvertent or hazardous operation of something (as a pistol or a machine) **3 a** : a football play in which the ball is downed by the offensive team behind its own goal line and which counts two points for the defensive team — compare TOUCHBACK **b** : a defensive football back who plays the deepest position in the secondary

safety belt *n* : a belt fastening a person to an object to prevent falling or injury

safety glass *n* : glass that resists shattering and is formed of two sheets of glass with a sheet of transparent plastic between them

safety island *n* : an area within a roadway from which vehicular traffic is excluded

safety lamp *n* : a miner's lamp constructed to avoid explosion in an atmosphere containing flammable gas usu. by enclosing the flame in fine wire gauze

safety match *n* : a match that can be ignited only by striking on a specially prepared surface

safety pin *n* : a pin made in the form of a clasp with a guard covering its point

safety razor *n* : a razor provided with a guard for the blade to prevent deep cuts in the skin

safety valve *n* **1** : a valve that opens automatically to prevent accident (as when steam pressure becomes too great) **2** : an outlet for pent-up energy or emotion

safety zone *n* : a safety island for pedestrians or for streetcar or bus passengers

saf·flow·er \'saf-ˌlaú(-ə)r\ *n* : a widely grown Old World herb related to the daisies that has large orange or red flower heads yielding a dyestuff and seeds rich in edible oil

saf·fron \'saf-rən\ *n* [OF *safran*, fr. ML *safranum*, fr. Ar *za'farān*] **1 a** : a purple-flowered crocus whose deep orange aromatic pungent dried stigmas are used esp. to color and flavor foods **b** : these dried usu. powdered stigmas **2** : a moderate orange to orange yellow

saf·ra·nine *or* **saf·ra·nin** \'saf-rə-ˌnēn, -nən\ *n* : any of various usu. red synthetic dyes

¹sag \'sag\ *vi* **sagged**; **sag·ging** [ME *saggen*] **1** : to droop, sink, or settle from or as if from pressure or loss of tautness **2** : to lose firmness, resiliency, or vigor ⟨spirits *sagging* from overwork⟩ **3** : to fall from a thriving state ⟨*sagging* industrial production⟩

²sag *n* : a sagging part or area ⟨the *sag* in a rope⟩; *also* : an instance or amount of sagging ⟨*sag* is inevitable in a heavy unsupported span⟩

sa·ga \'säg-ə\ *n* [ON; akin to E *say*] **1** : an Icelandic prose narrative of historic or legendary figures and events of Norway and Iceland **2** : a modern heroic narrative resembling the Icelandic saga

sa·ga·cious \sə-'gā-shəs\ *adj* [L *sagac-, sagax*] : of keen and farsighted understanding and judgment : DISCERNING ⟨*sagacious* judge of character⟩ **syn** see SHREWD — **sa·ga·cious·ly** *adv* — **sa·ga·cious·ness** *n* — **sa·gac·i·ty** \-'gas-ət-ē\ *n*

sag·a·more \'sag-ə-ˌmōr, -ˌmór\ *n* [of Algonquian origin] **1** : an Algonquian Indian chief subordinate to a sachem **2** : SACHEM

¹sage \'sāj\ *adj* [OF, fr. (assumed) VL *sapius*, fr. L *sapere* to taste, be wise] : WISE, PRUDENT ⟨*sage* advice⟩ — **sage·ly** *adv* — **sage·ness** *n*

²sage *n* : a man of profound and scholarly wisdom; *also* : a mature or venerable man of sound judgment

³sage *n* [MF *sauge*, fr. L *salvia*] **1** : a mint with grayish green aromatic leaves used esp. in flavoring meats; *also* : a plant belonging to the same genus as this mint and including several grown as ornamentals for their showy flowers — compare SALVIA **2** : SAGEBRUSH

sage·brush \'sāj-ˌbrəsh\ *n* : any of several low shrubby

No. American plants related to the daisies; *esp* : a common plant with a bitter juice and an odor like a sage that is widespread on alkaline plains of the western U.S.

sag·it·tal \'saj-ət-ᵊl, sə-'jit-\ *adj* [L *sagitta* arrow] : of, relating to, or being the median longitudinal plane of the body — **sag·it·tal·ly** \-ᵊl-ē\ *adv*

Sag·it·tar·i·us \ˌsaj-ə-'ter-ē-əs, ˌsag-\ *n* [L, lit., archer, fr. *sagitta* arrow] **1** : a southern constellation pictured as a centaur shooting an arrow **2** : the 9th sign of the zodiac — see ZODIAC table

sag·it·tate \'saj-ə-ˌtāt\ *adj* : shaped like an arrowhead ⟨*sagittate* leaf⟩

sa·go \'sā-gō\ *n, pl* **sagos** [Malay *sagu* sago palm] : a dry granulated or powdered starch prepared from the pith of a sago palm

sago palm *n* : a palm or cycad that yields sago; *esp* : any of a genus of tall pinnate-leaved East Indian palms

sa·gua·ro \sə-'(g)wär-ō\ *n, pl* **-ros** : a cactus of desert regions of the southwestern U.S. and Mexico that has a columnar spiny sparsely branched trunk of up to 60 feet and bears white flowers and edible fruit

sa·hib \'sä-,(h)ib\ *n* [Hindi *ṣāhib*, lit., lord, master, fr. Ar] : SIR, MASTER — used esp. among Hindus and Muslims in colonial India when addressing or speaking of a European of some social or official status

said \'sed\ *adj* [fr. pp. of *say*] : AFOREMENTIONED

¹sail \'sāl, *as last element in compounds often* səl\ *n* [OE *segl*] **1 a** : a usu. rectangular or triangular piece of fabric (as canvas) by means of which wind is used to propel a ship through water; *also* : the sails of a ship **b** *pl usu* **sail** : a ship equipped with sails **2** : something like a sail in function or form ⟨the *sail* of an iceboat⟩ **3** : a passage by a sailing ship

²sail *vb* **1 a** : to travel on water by sailboat ⟨*sail* about the bay⟩; *also* : to travel or begin a journey by water ⟨*sailed* for England on the first steamer⟩ **b** : to move or pass over by ship ⟨*sail* the seas⟩ **c** : to function in sailing ⟨a boat that *sails* well⟩; *also* : to handle or manage the sailing of ⟨experienced in *sailing* small craft⟩ **2** : to move or cause to move in a manner suggesting a ship under sail ⟨*sail* into a roomful of people⟩ ⟨*sail* a ball toward the dog⟩ **3** : to attack something with gusto ⟨*sailed* into his dinner⟩ ⟨*sailed* through his work⟩

sail·boat \'sāl-ˌbōt\ *n* : a boat equipped with sails

sail·cloth \-ˌklóth\ *n* : a heavy canvas used esp. for sails and tents

sail·er \'sā-lər\ *n* : a ship or boat esp. having specified sailing qualities

sail·fish \'sāl-ˌfish\ *n* : any of a genus of large sea fishes related to the swordfish but having teeth, scales, and a very large dorsal fin

sail·ing \'sā-liŋ\ *n* **1** : the technical skill of managing a ship : NAVIGATION **2** : the sport of navigating or riding in a sailboat

sail·or \'sā-lər\ *n* **1** : one that sails: as **a** : a member of a ship's crew **b** : SEAMAN 2 **c** : a traveler by water **2** : a stiff straw hat with a low flat crown and straight circular brim

sail·plane \'sāl-ˌplān\ *n* : a glider designed to rise in an upward current of air

¹saint \'sānt; *when a name follows* (ˌ)sānt *or* (*not shown below*) sənt\ *n* [MF, fr. L *sanctus* holy, sacred, fr. pp. of *sancire* to hallow, ordain, sanction] **1** : a holy and godly person; *esp* : one who is canonized **2** : a person who is sweet-tempered, self-sacrificing, and righteous **3** *cap* : LATTER-DAY SAINT

²saint \'sānt\ *vt* : to recognize or designate as a saint; *esp* : CANONIZE

Saint Ag·nes's Eve \ˌsānt-ˌag-nə-səz-'ēv\ *n* : the night of January 20 when a woman is traditionally held to have a revelation of her future husband

Saint An·drew's cross \-ˌan-ˌdrüz-\ *n* : a cross having the form of two intersecting oblique bars — see CROSS illustration

Saint An·tho·ny's fire \-ˌan(t)-thə-nēz-\ *n* : an inflammatory or gangrenous skin condition (as erysipelas); *esp* : one usu. caused by eating rye (as in bread) infected with a particular fungus

Saint Ber·nard \ˌsānt-bə(r)-'närd\ *n* : any of a Swiss alpine breed of tall powerful dogs used esp. formerly in aiding lost travelers

saint·dom \'sānt-dəm\ *n* : the quality or state of being a saint

saint·ed \'sānt-əd\ *adj* **1** : befitting or relating to a saint **2** : attained to or worthy of sainthood

Saint El·mo's fire \sānt-,el-mōz-\ *n* : a luminous discharge of electricity sometimes seen in stormy weather at prominent points on an airplane or ship

saint·hood \'sānt-,hủd\ *n* **1** : the quality or state of being a saint **2** : SAINTHOOD 1

Saint–John's–wort \sānt-'jänz-,wort, -,wȯrt\ *n* : any of a large genus of mostly weedy herbs and shrubs with showy yellow flowers

saint·ly \'sānt-lē\ *adj* **saint·li·er; -est** : relating to, resembling, or befitting a saint : HOLY — **saint·li·ness** *n*

Saint Mar·tin's summer \sānt-,märt-°n(z)-'sȯm-ər\ *n* [*Saint Martin's Day*, November 11] : Indian summer when occurring in November

Saint Pat·rick's Day \sānt-'pa-triks-\ *n* : March 17 celebrated in honor of St. Patrick and observed as a legal holiday in Ireland in commemoration of his death

saint·ship \'sānt-,ship\ *n* : SAINTHOOD 1

Saint Val·en·tine's Day \-'val-ən-,tīnz-\ *n* : February 14 observed as a time for sending valentines

Saint Vi·tus's dance \-,vīt-əs-, -əs-əz-\ *n* : CHOREA

saith \(')seth, 'sā-əth\ *archaic pres 3d sing of* SAY

¹sake \'sāk\ *n* [ME, fr. OE *sacu* dispute, action at law; akin to E *seek*] **1** : END, PURPOSE ⟨for the *sake* of argument⟩ **2** : GOOD, ADVANTAGE ⟨the *sake* of his country⟩

²sa·ke *or* **sa·ki** \'säk-ē\ *n* [Jap *sake*] : a Japanese alcoholic beverage of fermented rice usu. served hot

sa·ker \'sā-kər\ *n* : an Old World falcon used in falconry

sal \'sal\ *n* [L] : SALT

sa·laam \sə-'läm\ *n* [Ar *salām*, lit., peace] **1** : a salutation or ceremonial greeting in the East **2** : an obeisance performed by bowing very low and placing the right palm on the forehead — **salaam** *vb*

sal·a·ble *or* **sale·a·ble** \'sā-lə-bəl\ *adj* **1** : fit to be sold **2** : likely to be bought : easy to sell — **sal·a·bil·i·ty** \,sā-lə-'bil-ət-ē\

sa·la·cious \sə-'lā-shəs\ *adj* [L *salac-, salax*] **1** : arousing sexual desire or imagination : LASCIVIOUS **2** : LECHEROUS, LUSTFUL — **sa·la·cious·ly** *adv* — **sa·la·cious·ness** *n*

sal·ad \'sal-əd\ *n* [MF *salade*, fr. OProv *salada*, fr. pp. of *salar* to salt] **1 a** : a cold dish usu. of raw green vegetables served with oil, vinegar, and seasonings **b** : a cold dish (as of meat, shellfish, fruit, or vegetables served singly or in combinations) with a dressing **2** : a green vegetable or herb grown for salad

salad days *n pl* : time of youthful inexperience or indiscretion

salad dressing *n* : a savory sauce (as mayonnaise) for a salad

sal·a·man·der \'sal-ə-,man-dər\ *n* [Gk *salamandra*] **1** : a mythical being having the power to endure fire without harm **2** : any of an order (Caudata) of amphibians superficially resembling lizards but scaleless and covered with a soft moist skin **3** : something (as a utensil for browning pastry or a portable stove or incinerator) used in connection with fire — **sal·a·man·drine** \,sal-ə-'man-drən\ *adj*

sa·la·mi \sə-'läm-ē\ *n* [It, pl. of *salame* salami, fr. *salare* to salt] : highly seasoned sausage of pork and beef often dried for storage

sal am·mo·ni·ac \,sal-ə-'mō-nē-,ak\ *n* : AMMONIUM CHLORIDE

sal·a·ried \'sal-(ə-)rēd\ *adj* : receiving or yielding a salary ⟨a *salaried* position⟩

sal·a·ry \'sal-(ə-)rē\ *n, pl* **-ries** [L *salarium* money allowed to soldiers for salt, salary] : fixed compensation paid regularly for work or services : STIPEND **syn** see WAGE

sale \'sāl\ *n* [ON *sala*; akin to E *sell*] **1** : the act of selling; *esp* : the transfer of ownership of property from one person to another for a price **2** : availability for purchase — usu. used in the phrases *for sale* and *on sale* **3** : public disposal to the highest bidder : AUCTION **4** : a selling of goods at bargain prices **5** *pl* **a** : the business of selling **b** : gross receipts

sal·e·ra·tus \,sal-ə-'rāt-əs\ *n* [NL *sal aeratus* aerated salt] : SODIUM BICARBONATE

sales \'sālz\ *adj* : of, relating to, or used in selling ⟨*sales* manager⟩

sales check *n* : a strip or piece of paper that is used by retail stores as a memorandum, record, or receipt of a purchase

sales·clerk \-,klərk\ *n* : a salesman or saleswoman in a store

Sa·le·sian \sə-'lē-zhən\ *n* : a member of the Society of St. Francis de Sales founded as a Roman Catholic religious congregation in the 19th century by St. John Bosco in Turin and devoted chiefly to education

sales·man \'sālz-mən\ *n* : one that sells either in a territory or in a store — **sales·man·ship** \-,ship\ *n* — **sales·wom·an** \'sālz-,wủm-ən\ *n*

sales promotion *n* : activities and devices designed to create goodwill and sell a product

sales register *n* : CASH REGISTER

sales·room \'sālz-,rüm, -,rùm\ *n* : a place where goods are displayed for sale

sales talk *n* : argument often accompanied by demonstration used to persuade others to buy a product or service or to accept an idea or proposal

sales tax *n* : a tax levied on the sale of goods and services that is usu. calculated as a percentage of the purchase price and collected by the seller

Sa·lic \'sā-lik, 'sal-ik\ *adj* : of, relating to, or being a Frankish people settling early in the 4th century on the Ijssel river

Salic law *n* **1** : the legal code of the Salic Franks **2** : a rule held to derive from the Salic code excluding females from the line of succession to a throne

sa·lic·y·late \sə-'lis-ə-,lāt\ *n* : a salt or ester of salicylic acid; *also* : SALICYLIC ACID

sal·i·cyl·ic acid \,sal-ə-,sil-ik-\ *n* [L *salic-, salix* willow; akin to E ¹*sallow*] : a crystalline organic acid $C_7H_6O_3$ used esp. in the form of salts as an analgesic and antipyretic and in the treatment of rheumatism

sa·lience \'sāl-yən(t)s, 'sā-lē-ən(t)s\ *or* **sa·lien·cy** \-yən-sē, -lē-ən-\ *n, pl* **sa·lienc·es** *or* **sa·lien·cies** **1** : the quality or state of being salient **2** : a striking point or feature : HIGHLIGHT

¹sa·lient \'sāl-yənt, 'sā-lē-ənt\ *adj* [L *salire* to leap] **1** : moving by leaps or springs : JUMPING **2** : jetting upward ⟨*salient* fountain⟩ **3 a** : projecting beyond a line, surface, or level : PROTUBERANT ⟨a *salient* angle⟩ **b** : standing out conspicuously : PROMINENT, STRIKING ⟨*salient* traits⟩ — **sa·lient·ly** *adv*

²salient *n* : something that projects outward or upward from its surroundings; *esp* : an outwardly projecting part of a fortification, trench system, or line of defense

sa·li·en·tian \,sā-lē-'en-chən\ *n* : any of an order (Salientia) of amphibians comprising the frogs, toads, and tree toads all of which lack a tail in the adult stage and have long strong hind limbs suited to leaping and swimming — **salientian** *adj*

¹sa·line \'sā-,lēn, -,līn\ *adj* [L *sal* salt; akin to E *salt*] **1** : consisting of or containing salt ⟨a *saline* solution⟩ **2** : of, relating to, or resembling salt : SALTY ⟨a *saline* taste⟩ ⟨*saline* compounds⟩ — **sa·lin·i·ty** \sā-'lin-ət-ē, sə-\ *n*

²sa·line *l usu* sə-'lēn, *2 & 3 usu* 'sā-,lēn *or* 'sā-,līn\ *n* **1** : a natural deposit of common salt or other soluble salt **2** : a metallic salt; *esp* : a salt of potassium, sodium, or magnesium with a cathartic action **3** : a saline solution

sal·i·nom·e·ter \,sal-ə-'näm-ət-ər\ *n* : an instrument for measuring the amount of salt in a solution

Salis·bury steak \,sȯlz-,ber-ē-\ *n* : ground beef mixed with egg, milk, bread crumbs, and seasonings and formed into patties

sa·li·va \sə-'lī-və\ *n* [L] : a slightly alkaline secretion of water, mucin, protein, salts, and often a starch-splitting enzyme secreted into the mouth by salivary glands

sal·i·vary \'sal-ə-,ver-ē\ *adj* : of or relating to saliva or the glands that secrete it; *esp* : producing or carrying saliva ⟨*salivary* glands⟩

sal·i·vate \'sal-ə-,vāt\ *vi* : to secrete saliva esp. in large amounts — **sal·i·va·tion** \,sal-ə-'vā-shən\ *n*

Salk vaccine \'sȯ(l)k-\ *n* [after Jonas *Salk* b1914 American physician] : a polio vaccine that contains virus inactivated with formaldehyde and is administered by injection — compare SABIN VACCINE

¹sal·low \'sal-ō\ *n* [OE *sealh*] : any of various Old World broad-leaved willows used esp. as sources of charcoal and tanbark

²sallow *adj* [OE *salu*] **:** of a grayish greenish yellow color ⟨*sallow* complexion⟩ — **sal·low·ish** \'sal-ə-wish\ *adj* — **sal·low·ness** \'sal-ō-nəs\ *n*

³sallow *vt* **:** to make sallow

¹sal·ly \'sal-ē\ *n, pl* **sallies** [MF *saillie*, fr. *saillir* to rush forward, fr. L *salire* to leap] **1 :** an action of rushing or bursting forth; *esp* **:** a sortie of besieged troops upon the attackers **2 a :** a brief outbreak **:** OUTBURST **b :** a witty or imaginative saying **:** QUIP **3 :** an excursion usu. off the beaten track **:** JAUNT

²sally *vi* **sal·lied; sal·ly·ing 1 :** to leap out or burst forth suddenly **2 :** to set out **:** DEPART ⟨*sallied* forth to see the town⟩

Sal·ly Lunn \,sal-ē-'lən\ *n* [after *Sally Lunn*, 18th cent. English baker] **:** a slightly sweetened cake often eaten hot with butter

sally port *n* **:** a gate or passage in a fortified place for use of troops making a sortie

sal·ma·gun·di \,sal-mə-'gən-dē\ *n* [F *salmigondis*] **1 :** a salad plate of chopped meats, anchovies, eggs, and vegetables arranged in rows for contrast and dressed with a salad dressing **2 :** a heterogeneous mixture **:** POTPOURRI

salm·on \'sam-ən\ *n, pl* **salmon** *also* **salmons** [L *salmon-, salmo*] **1 a :** a large soft-finned anadromous game fish of the northern Atlantic related to the trouts and chars and noted as a table fish **b :** any of various related anadromous fishes; *esp* **:** any of a genus of fishes that breed in rivers tributary to the northern Pacific **2 :** a variable color that resembles that of the flesh of some salmons and averages a strong yellowish pink — **salmon** *adj* — **salm·on·oid** \'sam-ə-,nȯid\ *adj or n*

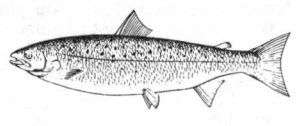

salmon 1a

salm·on·ber·ry \-,ber-ē\ *n* **:** a showy red-flowered raspberry of the Pacific coast; *also* **:** its edible salmon‑colored fruit

sal·mo·nel·la \,sal-mə-'nel-ə\ *n, pl* **-nellas** *or* **-nella** *also* **-nel·lae** \-'nel-(,)ē, -,ī\ [NL, fr. Daniel E. *Salmon* d1914 American veterinarian] **:** any of a genus of rod‑shaped bacteria that cause food poisoning, gastrointestinal inflammation, or diseases of the genital tract of warm-blooded animals

sal·mo·nel·lo·sis \,sal-mə-,nel-'ō-səs\ *n* **:** infection with or disease caused by salmonellas

salmon pink *n* **:** a strong yellowish pink

Sa·lo·me \sə-'lō-mē\ *n* **:** a niece of Herod Antipas given the head of John the Baptist as a reward for her dancing

sa·lon \sa-'lōⁿ, sə-'län\ *n* [F] **1 :** an elegant apartment or living room (as in a fashionable French home) **2 :** a fashionable assemblage of notables held by custom at the home of a prominent person **3 a :** a hall for exhibition of art **b :** an annual exhibition of such works **4 :** a stylish business establishment or shop

sa·loon \sə-'lün\ *n* [F *salon*, fr. It *salone*, aug. of *sala* hall, of Gmc origin] **1 :** SALON 1 **2 :** SALON 2 **3 a :** an elaborately decorated public apartment or hall (as a large cabin for social use of a ship's passengers) **b :** SALON 3 **c :** a place in which alcoholic beverages are sold and consumed **:** BARROOM

sal·pa \'sal-pə\ *n* [NL, fr. Gk *salpē*, a sea fish] **:** a transparent free-swimming often barrel-shaped tunicate of warm seas

sal·pi·glos·sis \,sal-pə-'gläs-əs\ *n* [NL, fr. Gk *salpinx* trumpet + *glōssa* tongue] **:** any of a genus of Chilean herbs related to the potato that are sometimes grown for their large multicolored funnel-shaped flowers

sal·pinx \'sal-(,)piŋ(k)s\ *n, pl* **sal·pin·ges** \sal-'pin-(,)jēz\ [NL *salping-, salpinx*, fr. Gk, trumpet] **1 :** EUSTACHIAN TUBE **2 :** FALLOPIAN TUBE

sal·si·fy \'sal-sə-fē, -,fī\ *n, pl* **-fies** [F *salsifis*] **:** a purple‑flowered herb related to the daisies that is grown for its long fleshy edible root — called also *oyster plant*

sal soda \'sal-'sōd-ə\ *n* **:** a transparent crystalline hydrated sodium carbonate $Na_2CO_3.10H_2O$ used in washing and bleaching textiles

¹salt \'sȯlt\ *n* [OE *sealt*] **1 a :** a crystalline compound NaCl that is the chloride of sodium, abundant in nature, and used esp. for seasoning or preserving food — called also *common salt* **b** *pl* (1) **:** a mineral or saline mixture (as Epsom salts) used as a laxative or cathartic (2) **:** SMELLING SALTS **c :** a compound formed by replacement of part or all of the acid hydrogen of an acid by a metal or radical acting like a metal **2 a :** an element that gives savor, piquancy, or zest **:** FLAVOR **b :** sharpness of wit **:** PUNGENCY **c :** EARTHINESS **d :** RESERVE, SKEPTICISM — often used in the phrase *with a grain of salt* **e :** the sprinkling of people thought to set a model of excellence for or to give tone to the rest — usu. used in the phrase *salt of the earth* **3 :** SAILOR

²salt *vt* **1 :** to treat, preserve, flavor, or supply with salt ⟨*salt* a dish to taste⟩ ⟨*salt* down meat for winter use⟩; *esp* **:** to sprinkle with or as if with salt **2 :** to give flavor or piquancy to **3 :** to enrich (as a mine) artificially by secretly placing valuable mineral in some of the working places

³salt *adj* **1 a :** SALINE, SALTY ⟨*salt* water⟩ **b :** being or inducing one of the four basic taste sensations **2 :** cured or seasoned with salt **:** SALTED ⟨*salt* pork⟩ **3 :** overflowed with salt water **4 :** SHARP, PUNGENT — **salt·ness** *n*

sal·ta·tion \sal-'tā-shən, sȯl-\ *n* [L *saltare* to leap, dance, freq. of *salire* to leap] **1 a :** the action of leaping or jumping **b :** DANCING **2 :** an abrupt change esp. in the course of evolution

sal·ta·to·ry \'sal-tə-,tȯr-ē, 'sȯl-, -,tōr-\ *adj* **1 :** of or relating to dancing ⟨the *saltatory* art⟩ **2 :** proceeding by leaps rather than by gradual transitions **:** DISCONTINUOUS — compare SALTATION 2

salt away *vt* **:** to lay away safely **:** SAVE ⟨*salt away* a little of their income for retirement⟩

salt·box \'sȯlt-,bäks\ *n* **:** a frame dwelling with two stories in front and one behind and a roof with a long rear slope

salt·cel·lar \-,sel-ər\ *n* **:** a small vessel for holding salt at table

salt·er \'sȯlt-ər\ *n* **1 :** one that manufactures or deals in salt **2 :** one that salts something (as meat, fish, or hides)

salt·ern \'sȯlt-ərn\ *n* **:** a place where salt is made by boiling or evaporation

saltbox

sal·tine \sȯl-'tēn\ *n* **:** a thin crisp cracker sprinkled with salt

salt·ish \'sȯl-tish\ *adj* **:** somewhat salty

salt lick *n* **:** LICK 3

salt marsh *n* **:** flat land subject to overflow by salt water — **salt-marsh** *adj*

salt out *vb* **:** to precipitate, coagulate, or separate (a dissolved substance or sol) from a solution by the addition of salt

salt·pe·ter \'sȯlt-'pēt-ər\ *n* [ML *sal petrae*, lit., salt of the rock] **1 :** POTASSIUM NITRATE **2 :** CHILE SALTPETER

salt·shak·er \-,shā-kər\ *n* **:** a container with a perforated top for sprinkling salt

salt·wa·ter \,sȯlt-,wȯt-ər, -,wät-\ *adj* **:** relating to, living in, or consisting of salt water

salt·works \'sȯlt-,wərks\ *n sing or pl* **:** a plant where salt is made on a commercial scale

salty \'sȯl-tē\ *adj* **salt·i·er; -est 1 :** of, seasoned with, or containing salt **:** tasting of or like salt **2 :** smacking of the sea or nautical life **3 a :** PIQUANT **b :** EARTHY, RACY ⟨*salty* talk⟩ — **salt·i·ness** *n*

sa·lu·bri·ous \sə-'lü-brē-əs\ *adj* [L *salubris*] **:** favorable to or promoting health **:** HEALTHFUL — **sa·lu·bri·ous·ly** *adv* — **sa·lu·bri·ous·ness** *n* — **sa·lu·bri·ty** \-'brət-ē\ *n*

sal·u·tary \'sal-yə-,ter-ē\ *adj* [L *salutaris*, fr. *salut-, salus* health] **1 :** promoting health **:** CURATIVE **2 :** producing a beneficial effect ⟨*salutary* advice⟩ **syn** see HEALTHFUL — **sal·u·tar·i·ly** \,sal-yə-'ter-ə-lē\ *adv* — **sal·u·tar·i·ness** \'sal-yə-,ter-ē-nəs\ *n*

sal·u·ta·tion \,sal-yə-'tā-shən\ *n* **1 a :** an expression of greeting, goodwill, or courtesy by word, gesture, or ceremony **b** *pl* **:** REGARDS **2 :** the word or phrase of greeting (as *Gentlemen* or *Dear Sir*) that conventionally comes immediately before the body of a letter — **sal·u·ta·tion·al** \-shnəl, -shən-°l\ *adj*

sa·lu·ta·to·ri·an \sə-,lüt-ə-'tōr-ē-ən, -'tȯr-\ *n* **:** the graduating student usu. second highest in rank who pronounces the salutatory oration

¹sa·lu·ta·to·ry \sə-'lüt-ə-ˌtōr-ē, -ˌtȯr-\ *adj* **:** expressing salutations or welcome

²salutatory *n, pl* **-ries :** a salutatory oration delivered at the commencement exercises of an educational institution

¹sa·lute \sə-'lüt\ *vb* [L *salutare,* fr. *salut-, salus* health, greeting] **1 :** to address with expressions of kind wishes, courtesy, or honor or with a sign of respect, courtesy, or goodwill **:** GREET **2 a :** to honor by a conventional military or naval ceremony **b :** to show respect and recognition to (a military superior) by assuming a prescribed position **c :** PRAISE — **sa·lut·er** *n*

²salute *n* **1 :** GREETING, SALUTATION **2 a :** a sign, token, or ceremony (as a kiss or a bow) expressing goodwill, compliment, or respect **b :** the position of the hand or weapon or the entire attitude of a person saluting a superior

sal·u·tif·er·ous \ˌsal-yə-'tif-(ə-)rəs\ *adj* **:** SALUTARY

salv·a·ble \'sal-və-bəl\ *adj* **:** capable of being saved or salvaged

¹sal·vage \'sal-vij\ *n* **1 :** money paid for saving a wrecked or endangered ship or its cargo or passengers **2 a :** the act of saving a ship **b :** the saving of possessions in danger of being lost **3 :** something that is saved or recovered (as from a wreck or fire)

²salvage *vt* **:** to rescue or save esp. from wreckage or ruin — **sal·vage·a·ble** \-ə-bəl\ *adj* — **sal·vag·er** *n*

Sal·var·san \'sal-vər-ˌsan\ *trademark* — used for arsphenamine

sal·va·tion \sal-'vā-shən\ *n* [L *salvare* to save, fr. *salvus* safe, in good health] **1 :** the saving of a person from the power and effects of sin **2 :** the saving from danger or evil (the *salvation* of a country) **3 :** something that saves (he believed medicine was his *salvation*) — **sal·va·tion·al** \-shnəl, -shən-ᵊl\ *adj*

¹salve \'sav, 'sav\ *n* [OE *sealf*] **1 :** a healing ointment **2 :** an influence or agency that remedies or soothes **3 :** something (as praise or flattery) laid on like a salve

²salve *vt* **:** to ease or soothe with or as if with a salve

sal·ver \'sal-vər\ *n* **:** a tray esp. for serving food or beverages

sal·via \'sal-vē-ə\ *n* [L] **:** SAGE 1 ; *esp* **:** a scarlet-flowered sage widely grown for ornament

sal·vo \'sal-vō\ *n, pl* **salvos** *or* **salvoes** [It *salva,* fr. F *salve,* fr. L, hail!, fr. imper. of *salvēre* to be well] **1 :** a discharge of one gun after another in an artillery battery **2 a :** a simultaneous discharge of two or more guns at the same target or as a salute **b :** the release all at one time of a rack of bombs or rockets (as from an airplane); *also* **:** the bombs or projectiles so released **3 :** SALUTE, TRIBUTE **4 :** a sudden burst (as of cheers)

sal vo·la·ti·le \ˌsal-və-'lat-ᵊl-ē\ *n* [NL, lit., volatile salt] **:** an aromatic solution of ammonium carbonate in alcohol or ammonia water or both

sam·a·ra \'sam-ə-rə, sə-'mar-ə\ *n* [L, elm seed] **:** a dry indehiscent usu. one-seeded winged fruit (as of an ash or elm tree) — called also *key*

Sa·mar·i·tan \sə-'mar-ət-ᵊn, -'mer-\ *n* **1 :** a member of a sect in Samaria of ancient Jewish and foreign origin **2** *often not cap* [fr. the parable of the good Samaritan, Luke 10:30–37] **:** one ready and generous in helping those in distress — **samaritan** *adj, often cap*

sa·mar·i·um \sə-'mer-ē-əm, -'mar-\ *n* **:** a pale gray lustrous metallic chemical element — see ELEMENT table

sam·ba \'sam-bə, 'säm-\ *n* [Pg] **:** a Brazilian dance characterized by a dip and spring upward with a bending of the knee at each beat of the music — **samba** *vi*

Sam Browne belt \ˌsam-'braȯn-\ *n* **:** a leather belt for a dress uniform supported by a light strap passing over the right shoulder

¹same \'sām\ *adj* [ON *samr*] **1 a :** resembling in every relevant respect **b :** conforming in every respect (gave him the *same* answer as before) **2 a :** being one without addition, change, or discontinuance **:** IDENTICAL **b :** being the one under discussion or already referred to (quoted from this *same* book) **3 :** corresponding so closely as to be indistinguishable **:** COMPARABLE (on the *same* day last year)

²same *pron* **1 :** something identical with or similar to another **2 :** something previously defined or described

³same *adv* **:** in the same manner (spelled differently but pronounced the *same*)

same·ness \'sām-nəs\ *n* **1 :** the quality or state of being the same **:** IDENTITY **2 :** MONOTONY, UNIFORMITY

sam·i·sen \'sam-ə-ˌsen\ *n* **:** a 3-stringed Japanese musical instrument resembling a banjo

sam·ite \'sam-ˌīt, 'sā-ˌmīt\ *n* [MGk *hexamiton,* fr. Gk *hexamitos* of six threads] **:** a rich medieval silk fabric interwoven with gold or silver

sam·o·var \'sam-ə-ˌvär\ *n* [Russ, fr. *samo-* self + *varit'* to boil] **1 :** an urn with a spigot at its base used esp. in Russia to boil water for tea **2 :** an urn similar to a Russian samovar with a device for heating the contents

samp \'samp\ *n* [of Algonquian origin] **:** coarse hominy or a boiled cereal made from it

sam·pan \'sam-ˌpan\ *n* [Chin (Pek) *san¹ pan³,* fr. *san¹* three + *pan³* plank] **:** a flat-bottomed Chinese skiff usu. propelled by two short oars

¹sam·ple \'sam-pəl\ *n* [MF *essample* example, sample, fr. L *exemplum*] **1 :** a representative part or a single item from a larger whole or group presented for inspection or shown as evidence of quality **:** SPECIMEN **2 :** a part of a statistical population whose properties are studied to gain information about the whole

²sample *vt* **sam·pled; sam·pling** \-p(ə-)liŋ\ **1 :** to take a sample of; *esp* **:** to judge the quality of by a sample **:** TEST (*sampled* her jams) **2 :** to present a sample of

¹sam·pler \'sam-plər\ *n* **:** a decorative piece of needlework typically having letters or verses embroidered on it in various stitches as an example of skill

²sampler *n* **1 :** one that collects or examines samples **2 :** something containing representative specimens or selections

sample room *n* **:** a room (as in a hotel) in which samples are displayed for the inspection of buyers for retail stores

sam·pling *n* **1** \'sam-pliŋ\ **:** a small part selected as a sample for inspection or analysis **2** \-p(ə-)liŋ\ **:** the act, process, or technique of selecting a suitable sample

sam·sa·ra \səm-'sär-ə\ *n* [Skt *saṃsāra*] **:** the indefinitely repeated cycles of birth, misery, and death caused by karma

Sam·son \'sam(p)-sən\ *n* **:** an Israelite judge of great physical strength

Sam·u·el \'sam-yə(-wə)l\ *n* **1 :** an early Hebrew judge and prophet **2** — see BIBLE table

sam·u·rai \'sam-(y)ə-ˌrī\ *n, pl* **samurai** [Jap] **1 :** a military feudal retainer of a Japanese daimyo **2 :** the warrior aristocracy of Japan

san·a·tar·i·um \ˌsan-ə-'ter-ē-əm\ *n, pl* **-i·ums** *or* **-ia** \-ē-ə\ **:** SANATORIUM

san·a·tive \'san-ət-iv\ *adj* **:** CURATIVE, RESTORATIVE

san·a·to·ri·um \ˌsan-ə-'tōr-ē-əm, -'tȯr-\ *n, pl* **-ri·ums** *or* **-ria** \-ē-ə\ [L *sanare* to heal, cure, fr. *sanus* healthy] **:** an establishment for the care and treatment esp. of convalescents or the chronically ill

sanc·ti·fy \'saŋ(k)-ti-ˌfī\ *vt* **-fied; -fy·ing** [MF *sanctifier,* fr. LL *sanctificare,* fr. L *sanctus* holy, fr. pp. of *sancire* to hallow] **1 :** to set apart as sacred **:** CONSECRATE **2 :** to make free from sin **:** PURIFY **3 :** to give moral or social sanction to — **sanc·ti·fi·ca·tion** \ˌsaŋ(k)-ti-fə-'kā-shən\ *n* — **sanc·ti·fi·er** \'saŋ(k)-ti-ˌfī(-ə)r\ *n*

sanc·ti·mo·ni·ous \ˌsaŋ(k)-tə-'mō-nē-əs\ *adj* **:** affecting piousness **:** hypocritically devout — **sanc·ti·mo·ni·ous·ly** *adv* — **sanc·ti·mo·ni·ous·ness** *n*

sanc·ti·mo·ny \'saŋ(k)-tə-ˌmō-nē\ *n* **:** assumed or hypocritical holiness

¹sanc·tion \'saŋ(k)-shən\ *n* [L *sanct-, sancire* to hallow, ordain, sanction] **1 a :** a binding or compelling force; *esp* **:** one that determines action in accordance with morality **b :** an economic or military measure adopted usu. by several nations against a nation violating international law **2 :** explicit or official permission or ratification **:** APPROBATION

²sanction *vt* **sanc·tioned; sanc·tion·ing** \-sh(ə-)niŋ\ **1 :** RATIFY, VALIDATE **2 :** to give effective approval or consent to **:** PERMIT **syn** see APPROVE

sanc·ti·ty \'saŋ(k)-tət-ē\ *n, pl* **-ties 1 :** HOLINESS, GODLINESS **2 a :** INVIOLABILITY, SACREDNESS (the *sanctity* of an oath) **b** *pl* **:** sacred objects, obligations, or rights

sanc·tu·ary \'saŋ(k)-chə-ˌwer-ē\ *n, pl* **-ar·ies 1 :** a holy or sacred place **2 :** a building or room for religious worship **3** : the most sacred part (as near the altar) of a place of worship **4** : a refuge for wildlife where predators are controlled and hunting is illegal **5 a** : a place of refuge and protection **b** : safety or protection afforded by a sanctuary

sanc·tum \'saŋ(k)-təm\ *n, pl* **sanctums** *also* **sanc·ta** \-tə\ [LL, fr. L, neut. of *sanctus* holy] **1** : a sacred place **2** : a study, office, or place where one is free from intrusion ⟨an editor's *sanctum*⟩

sanc·tum sanc·to·rum \ˌsaŋ-təm-ˌsaŋ(k)-'tōr-əm, -'tòr-\ *n* [LL] **1** : HOLY OF HOLIES **2** : SANCTUM 2

Sanc·tus \'saŋ(k)-təs, 'sän(k)-\ *n* : an ancient Christian hymn closing the preface of most Christian liturgies and commencing with the words *Sanctus, sanctus, sanctus* or *Holy, holy, holy*

¹sand \'sand\ *n* [OE] **1 a** : a loose granular material resulting from the disintegration of rocks **b** : soil containing 85 percent or more of sand and a maximum of 10 percent of clay **2** : a tract, region, or deposit of sand : BEACH — often used in pl. **3** : the sand in an hourglass; *also* : the moments of a lifetime — usu. used in pl. **4** : firm resolution : COURAGE, BOLDNESS ⟨hasn't the *sand* to talk back to her⟩

²sand *vt* **1** : to sprinkle with sand **2** : to add sand to **3** : to smooth by grinding or rubbing with an abrasive and esp. with sandpaper

san·dal \'san-dəl\ *n* [Gk *sandalon*] **1** : a shoe consisting of a sole strapped to the foot **2** : a low-cut shoe that fastens by an ankle strap **3** : a strap to hold on a slipper or low shoe **4** : a rubber overshoe cut very low — **san·daled** *or* **san·dalled** \-dəld\ *adj*

san·dal·wood \'san-dəl-ˌwùd\ *n* [ML *sandalum*, fr. LGk *santalon*] : the close-grained fragrant yellowish heartwood of an Indo-Malayan tree much used in ornamental carving and cabinetwork; *also* : the tree that yields this wood

¹sand·bag \'san(d)-ˌbag\ *n* **1** : a bag filled with sand and used as ballast or as part of a fortification wall or of a temporary dam **2** : a small bag of sand used as a weapon

²sandbag *vt* **1** : to bank, stop up, or weight with sandbags **2** : to hit or stun with a sandbag — **sand·bag·ger** *n*

sand·bank \-ˌbaŋk\ *n* : a deposit of sand in a mound, hillside, bar, or shoal

sand·bar \-ˌbär\ *n* : a ridge of sand formed in water by tides or currents

¹sand·blast \-ˌblast\ *n* : a stream of sand projected by air or steam for engraving, cutting, or cleaning glass or stone or for removing scale from metals

²sandblast *vt* : to engrave, cut, or clean with a high-velocity stream of sand — **sand·blast·er** *n*

sand–blind \'san(d)-ˌblīnd\ *adj* [prob. fr. OE *sam*- half] : having poor eyesight

sand·box \'san(d)-ˌbäks\ *n* : a box for holding sand

sand·bur \-ˌbər\ *n* : any of several weeds of waste places with burry fruit

sand dollar *n* : a flat circular sea urchin that lives chiefly in shallow water and on sandy bottoms

sand·er \'san-dər\ *n* : one that sands

sand·er·ling \'san-dər-liŋ\ *n* : a small largely gray and white sandpiper

sand flea *n* **1** : a flea found in sandy places **2** : BEACH FLEA

sand fly *n* : any of various small biting two-winged flies

sand·glass \'san(d)-ˌglas\ *n* : an instrument like an hourglass for measuring time by the running of sand

sand·hog \'sand-ˌhóg, -ˌhäg\ *n* : a laborer who works in a caisson in driving underwater tunnels

sand·i·ness \'san-dē-nəs\ *n* : the quality or state of being sandy

sanding machine *n* : a machine for smoothing, polishing, or scouring with an abrasive disk or belt

sand·lot \'san-ˌdlät\ *n* : a vacant lot esp. when used for the unorganized sports of boys from city streets — **sandlot** *adj* — **sand·lot·ter** *n*

sand·man \'san(d)-ˌman\ *n* : the genie of folklore who makes children sleepy supposedly by sprinkling sand in their eyes

¹sand·pa·per \-ˌpā-pər\ *n* : paper covered on one side with abrasive material (as sand) glued fast and used for smoothing and polishing

²sandpaper *vt* : to rub with sandpaper

sand·pile \-ˌpīl\ *n* : a pile of sand; *esp* : sand for children to play in

sand·pip·er \-ˌpī-pər\ *n* : any of numerous small shorebirds distinguished from the related plovers chiefly by the longer and soft-tipped bill

sand·stone \'san(d)-ˌstōn\ *n* : a sedimentary rock consisting of usu. quartz sand united by a natural cement

sand·storm \-ˌstòrm\ *n* : a storm of wind (as in a desert) that drives clouds of sand

sand table *n* : a table with raised edges to hold sand (as for molding)

sand trap *n* : an artificial hazard on a golf course consisting of a depression containing sand

¹sand·wich \'san-,(d)wich\ *n* [John Montagu, 4th Earl of *Sandwich* d1792 English diplomat] **1** : two or more slices of bread with a filling (as of meat, cheese, or savory mixture) spread between them **2** : something resembling a sandwich

²sandwich *vt* **1** : to insert between two or more things ⟨plastic *sandwiched* between layers of glass to make safety glass⟩ **2** : to make a place for : CROWD ⟨*sandwich* another activity into a busy schedule⟩

sandwich board *n* : two usu. hinged boards designed for hanging from the shoulders with one board before and one behind and used esp. for advertising

sandwich man *n* : one who advertises or pickets a place of business by wearing a sandwich board

sand·worm \'san-,(d)wərm\ *n* : any of various sand-dwelling polychaete worms; *esp* : any of several large burrowing worms often used as bait

sand·wort \'san-,(d)wərt, -,(d)wórt\ *n* : any of various low tufted chickweeds growing in sandy or gritty soil

sandy \'san-dē\ *adj* **sand·i·er; -est 1** : consisting of, containing, or sprinkled with sand **2** : of a yellowish gray color

sandy loam *n* : a loam low in clay and high in sand

sane \'sān\ *adj* [L *sanus* healthy, sane] : mentally sound and healthy; *also* : RATIONAL, SENSIBLE — **sane·ly** *adv* — **sane·ness** \'sān-nəs\ *n*

sang *past of* SING

sang·froid \'sä n-'frwä\ *n* [F *sang-froid*, lit., cold blood] : self-possession or imperturbability esp. under strain

san·gui·nary \'saŋ-gwə-ˌner-ē\ *adj* [L *sanguin-, sanguis* blood] **1** : BLOODTHIRSTY, MURDEROUS **2** : attended by bloodshed ⟨BLOODY ⟨a *sanguinary* battle⟩ — **san·gui·nar·i·ly** \ˌsaŋ-gwə-'ner-ə-lē\ *adv*

san·guine \'saŋ-gwən\ *adj* [L *sanguineus*, fr. *sanguin-, sanguis* blood] **1 a** : BLOODRED **b** : RUDDY ⟨a *sanguine* complexion⟩ **2** : SANGUINARY 1 **3** : having a bodily conformation and temperament marked by sturdiness, high color, and cheerfulness ⟨a *sanguine* disposition⟩ **4** : CONFIDENT, OPTIMISTIC ⟨*sanguine* of success⟩ — **san·guine·ly** *adv* — **san·guine·ness** \-gwən-nəs\ *n* — **san·guin·i·ty** \san-'gwin-ət-ē\ *n*

san·guin·e·ous \san-'gwin-ē-əs\ *adj* **1** : BLOODRED **2** : of, relating to, or involving bloodshed : BLOODTHIRSTY **3** : of, relating to, or containing blood

San·he·drin \san-'hēd-rən, -'hed-\ *n* [LHeb *sanhedhrīn gĕdhōlāh* great council] : the supreme council and religious, civil, and criminal court of the Jews in New Testament times

san·i·cle \'san-i-kəl\ *n* [ML *sanicula*, prob. fr. L *sanus* healthy] : any of several plants held to have healing powers

san·i·tar·i·an \ˌsan-ə-'ter-ē-ən\ *n* : a specialist in sanitary science and public health ⟨milk *sanitarian*⟩

san·i·tar·i·um \ˌsan-ə-'ter-ē-əm\ *n, pl* **-i·ums** *or* **-ia** \-ē-ə\ [L *sanitas* health, sanity] : SANATORIUM

san·i·tary \'san-ə-ˌter-ē\ *adj* [F *sanitaire*, fr. L *sanitas* health] **1** : of or relating to health : HYGIENIC ⟨*sanitary* laws⟩ **2** : free from filth, infection, or dangers to health — **san·i·tar·i·ly** \ˌsan-ə-'ter-ə-lē\ *adv*

sanitary napkin *n* : a disposable absorbent pad in a gauze covering used to absorb uterine flow (as during menstruation)

san·i·tate \'san-ə-ˌtāt\ *vt* : to provide with sanitary appliances or facilities

san·i·ta·tion \ˌsan-ə-'tā-shən\ *n* **1** : the act or process of making sanitary **2** : the promotion of hygiene and prevention of disease by maintenance of sanitary conditions

san·i·tize \'san-ə-ˌtīz\ *vt* : to make sanitary (as by cleaning or sterilizing)

---

j joke; ŋ sing; ō flow; ò flaw; òi coin; th thin; th this; ü loot; ù foot; y yet; yü few; yù furious; zh vision

san·i·ty \'san-ət-ē\ *n* [L *sanitas* health, sanity, fr. *sanus* healthy, sane] **:** the quality or state of being sane

San Jo·se scale \,san-ə-,zā-\ *n* [*San Jose,* Calif.] **:** a prob. Asiatic scale insect naturalized in the U.S. and a most damaging pest to fruit trees

sank *past of* SINK

sans \(,)sanz\ *prep* [MF, modif. of L *sine*] **:** WITHOUT

sans·cu·lotte \,san-skyu̇-'lät\ *n* [F *sans-culotte,* lit., without breeches] **1 :** an extreme radical republican in France at the time of the Revolution **2 :** a radical or violent extremist

san·sei \(')sän-'sā\ *n, pl* **sansei** *also* **sanseis** *often cap* [Jap *san* third + *sei* generation] **:** a son or daughter of nisei parents

San·skrit \'san-,skrit\ *n* **:** an ancient Indic language that is the classical language of India and of Hinduism — **Sanskrit** *adj*

sans ser·if *or* **san·ser·if** \san-'ser-əf\ *n* **:** a letter or typeface with no serifs

San·ta Claus \'sant-ə-,klȯz, 'sant-ē-\ *n* [modif. of D *Sinterklaas,* alter. of *Sint Nikolaas* Saint Nicholas] **:** the gift₌ giving and holiday spirit of Christmas personified as a fat, jolly old man in a red suit who distributes toys to children at Christmas

san·ton·i·ca \san-'tän-i-kə\ *n* **:** the dried unopened flower heads of a wormwood sometimes used as a worm remedy

¹sap \'sap\ *n* [OE *sæp*] **1 :** the fluid part of a plant; *esp* **:** a watery solution that circulates through a vascular plant **2 :** VITALITY **3 :** a foolish gullible person

²sap *n* [MF *sappe* spade, hoe, fr. It *zappa*] **:** a trench built out to a point beneath an enemy's fortifications

³sap *vt* **sapped; sap·ping 1 a :** to attack, pierce, or undermine by a sap **b :** to destroy by undermining ⟨heavy tides *sapped* the seawall⟩ **2 :** to weaken gradually ⟨the heat *sapped* his strength⟩

sap·head \-,hed\ *n* **:** a weak-minded or foolish person **:** SAP — **sap·head·ed** \-'hed-əd\ *adj*

sap·id \'sap-əd\ *adj* [L *sapidus* tasty, fr. *sapere* to taste] **1 :** affecting the organs of taste **:** possessing flavor and esp. a strong agreeable flavor **2 :** agreeable to the mind — **sa·pid·i·ty** \sə-'pid-ət-ē, sa-\ *n*

sa·pi·ence \'sā-pē-ən(t)s, 'sap-ē-\ *n* **:** WISDOM, SAGENESS

sap·i·ens \'sap-ē-ənz, 'sā-pē-\ *adj* [NL, fr. *Homo sapiens*] **:** of, relating to, or being recent man as distinguished from various fossil men

sa·pi·ent \'sā-pē-ənt, 'sap-ē-\ *adj* [L *sapient-, sapiens,* fr. prp. of *sapere* to taste, be wise] **:** WISE, DISCERNING — **sa·pi·ent·ly** *adv*

sap·less \'sap-ləs\ *adj* **1 :** destitute of sap **:** DRY **2 :** lacking vitality or vigor **:** FEEBLE — **sap·less·ness** *n*

sap·ling \'sap-liŋ\ *n* **:** a young tree usu. not over four inches in diameter at breast height

sap·o·dil·la \,sap-ə-'dil-ə\ *n* [Sp *zapotillo*] **:** a tropical American evergreen tree with hard reddish wood, an edible brownish berry, and a latex that yields chicle

sap·o·na·ceous \,sap-ə-'nā-shəs\ *adj* [L *sapon-, sapo* soap, of Gmc origin; akin to E *soap*] **:** resembling or having the qualities of soap **:** SOAPY — **sap·o·na·ceous·ness** *n*

sa·pon·i·fi·ca·tion \sə-,pän-ə-fə-'kā-shən\ *n* **1 :** the hydrolysis of a fat by alkali with formation of a soap together with glycerol **2 :** the hydrolysis by alkali of an ester into the corresponding alcohol and acid

sa·pon·i·fy \sə-'pän-ə-,fī\ *vb* **-fied; -fy·ing :** to subject to or undergo saponification — **sa·pon·i·fi·a·ble** \-,fī-ə-bəl\ *adj* — **sa·pon·i·fi·er** \-,fī-(-ə)r\ *n*

sa·por \'sā-pər\ *n* [L] **:** the property of something that stimulates the sense of taste **:** FLAVOR — **sa·por·ous** \-pə-rəs\ *adj*

sap·per \'sap-ər\ *n* **1 :** a military engineer who constructs field fortifications **2 :** an engineer who lays, detects, and disarms mines

sap·phire \'saf-,ī(ə)r\ *n* [Gk *sappheiros,* fr. Heb *sappīr,* fr. Skt *śanipriya,* lit., dear to the planet Saturn] **1 :** a gem variety of corundum occurring in transparent or translucent colorless or colored forms except red; *esp* **:** a transparent rich blue gemstone **2 :** a variable color averaging a deep purplish blue — **sapphire** *adj*

sap·py \'sap-ē\ *adj* **sap·pi·er; -est 1 :** abounding with sap **2 :** containing much sapwood **3 a :** foolishly sentimental **:** MAWKISH **b :** lacking in good sense **:** SILLY — **sap·pi·ness** *n*

sapr- *or* **sapro-** *comb form* [Gk *sapros,* fr. *sap-, sēpein* to rot] **1 :** rotten **:** putrid ⟨*sapremia*⟩ **2 :** dead or decaying organic matter ⟨*sapro*phyte⟩

sap·robe \'sap-,rōb\ *or* **sap·ro·bi·ont** \,sap-rō-'bī-,änt\ *n* **:** a saprobic organism

sa·pro·bic \sa-'prō-bik\ *adj* [Gk *bios* life] **:** SAPROPHYTIC; *also* **:** living in or being an environment rich in organic matter and relatively free from oxygen — **sa·pro·bi·cal·ly** \-bi-k(ə-)lē\ *adv*

sa·proph·a·gous \sa-'präf-ə-gəs\ *adj* **:** feeding on decaying matter

sap·ro·phyte \'sap-rə-,fīt\ *n* **:** a plant living on dead or decaying organic matter; *also* **:** any saprophytic organism

sap·ro·phyt·ic \,sap-rə-'fit-ik\ *adj* **:** obtaining food by absorbing dissolved organic material and esp. the products of organic breakdown and decay — **sap·ro·phyt·i·cal·ly** \-'fit-i-k(ə-)lē\ *adv*

sap·suck·er \'sap-,sək-ər\ *n* **:** any of various small American woodpeckers reputed to feed on sap

sap·wood \-,wu̇d\ *n* **:** the younger softer physiologically active outer portion of wood that lies between the cambium and the heartwood and is more permeable, less durable, and usu. lighter in color than the heartwood

sar·a·band *or* **sar·a·bande** \'sar-ə-,band\ *n* [F *sarabande,* fr. Sp *zarabanda*] **1 :** a stately court dance of the 17th and 18th centuries **2 :** the music for the saraband in slow triple time

Sar·a·cen \'sar-ə-sən\ *n* **1 :** a member of a nomadic people of the deserts of Syria and northern Arabia **2 :** ARAB **3 :** one of the Muslim opponents of the Crusaders — **Saracen** *adj* — **Sar·a·cen·ic** \,sar-ə-'sen-ik\ *adj*

Sar·ah \'ser-ə, 'sar-ə\ *n* **:** the wife of Abraham and mother of Isaac

sa·ran \sə-'ran\ *n* **:** a tough flexible thermoplastic that can be formed into waterproof and chemically resistant products (as filaments, tubing, and coating)

sa·ra·pe \sə-'räp-ē\ *n* [MexSp] **:** a woolen blanket worn by Spanish-American men as a cloak or poncho

Sar·a·to·ga trunk \,sar-ə-,tō-gə-\ *n* **:** a large traveling trunk usu. with a rounded top

sarc- *or* **sarco-** *comb form* [Gk *sark-, sarx*] **:** flesh ⟨*sarcous*⟩

sar·casm \'sär-,kaz-əm\ *n* [Gk *sarkasmos,* fr. *sarkazein* to tear flesh, bite the lips, sneer, fr. *sark-, sarx* flesh] **1 a :** a cutting remark **:** a bitter rebuke **2 :** the use of sharp, stinging remarks expressing contempt and often made in the form of irony

sar·cas·tic \sär-'kas-tik\ *adj* **1 :** having the habit of sarcasm **2 :** containing sarcasm ⟨a *sarcastic* remark⟩ — **sar·cas·ti·cal·ly** \-ti-k(ə-)lē\ *adv*

sarce·net *or* **sarse·net** \'sär-snət\ *n* **:** a soft thin silk fabric

sar·co·lem·ma \,sär-kə-'lem-ə\ *n* [Gk *lemma* husk, fr. *lepein* to peel] **:** the thin sheath of a muscle fiber

sar·co·ma \sär-'kō-mə\ *n* **:** a malignant tumor arising in tissue of mesodermal origin (as connective tissue or striated muscle) — **sar·com·a·tous** \sär-'käm-ət-əs, -'kōm-\ *adj*

sar·coph·a·gous \sär-'käf-ə-gəs\ *or* **sar·co·phag·ic** \,sär-kə-'faj-ik\ *adj* **:** CARNIVOROUS — **sar·coph·a·gy** \sär-'käf-ə-jē\ *n*

sar·coph·a·gus \sär-'käf-ə-gəs\ *n, pl* **-gi** \-,gī, -,jī\ *or* **-gus·es** [Gk *sarkophagos,* fr. *sark-, sarx* flesh + *phagein* to eat] **:** a stone coffin; *esp* **:** one exposed to view in the open air or in a tomb

sar·dine \sär-'dēn\ *n, pl* **sardines** *also* **sardine** [L *sardina,* fr. *sardus* Sardinian] **1 :** any of several small or immature fishes of the herring family; *esp* **:** the young of the European pilchard when of a size suitable for preserving for food **2 :** any of various small fishes (as an anchovy) resembling the true sardines or similarly preserved for food

sar·don·ic \sär-'dän-ik\ *adj* [Gk *sardonios*] **:** bitterly scornful **:** MOCKING, SNEERING — **sar·don·i·cal·ly** \-'dän-i-k(ə-)lē\ *adv*

sard·on·yx \sär-'dän-iks, 'särd-°n-\ *n* [Gk, fr. *sardion* carnelian + *onyx*] **:** onyx having layers of carnelian

sar·gas·so \sär-'gas-ō\ *n, pl* **-sos** [Pg *sargaço*] **1 :** GULFWEED, SARGASSUM **2 :** a mass of floating vegetation and esp. sargassums

sar·gas·sum \sär-'gas-əm\ *n* **:** any of a genus of branching brown algae with lateral outgrowths differentiated as leafy segments, air bladders, or spore-bearing structures

sa·ri *or* **sa·ree** \'sär-ē\ *n* [Hindi *sāṛī,* fr. Skt *śāṭī*] **:** a garment of Hindu women that consists of a long cloth draped so that one end forms a skirt and the other a head or shoulder covering

sar·men·tose \sär-'men-ˌtōs, 'sär-mən-\ *adj* [L *sarmentum* twig] : producing slender prostrate branches or runners

sa·rong \sə-'róŋ, -'räŋ\ *n* [Malay *kain sarong* cloth sheath] : a loose skirt made of a long strip of cloth wrapped loosely around the body and worn by men and women of the Malay archipelago and the Pacific islands

sar·sa·pa·ril·la \ˌsas-(ə-)pə-'ril-ə, ˌsärs-\ *n* [Sp *zarzaparilla*] **1 a** : any of various tropical American smilaxes **b** : the dried roots of a sarsaparilla plant used esp. as a flavoring **2** : a sweetened carbonated beverage flavored chiefly with birch oil and sassafras

sar·to·ri·al \sär-'tōr-ē-əl, -'tór-\ *adj* [L *sartor* tailor, fr. *sart-, sarcire* to mend] : of or relating to a tailor or tailored clothes and esp. men's clothes — **sar·to·ri·al·ly** \-ē-ə-lē\ *adv*

sar·to·ri·us \-ē-əs\ *n* [NL, fr. L *sartor* tailor] : a muscle that crosses the front of the thigh obliquely and assists in rotating the leg outward to the position assumed in sitting cross-legged

¹sash \'sash\ *n* [Ar *shāsh* muslin] : a broad band (as of silk) worn around the waist or over the shoulder

²sash *n, pl* **sash** *or* **sash·es** : the framework in which panes of glass are set in a window or door; *also* : the movable part of a window ⟨raised the *sash* to let in air⟩

sa·shay \sa-'shā, sī-\ *vi* **1** : to strut or move about in an ostentatious manner **2** : to proceed in a diagonal or sideways manner

¹sass \'sas\ *n* : impudent speech

²sass *vt* : to talk impudently or disrespectfully to

sas·sa·fras \'sas-(ə-)ˌfras\ *n* [Sp *sasafrás*] : a tall eastern No. American tree of the laurel family with mucilaginous twigs and leaves; *also* : its dried root bark used esp. in medicine or as a flavoring agent

sassy \'sas-ē\ *adj* **sass·i·er; -est** : SAUCY, IMPUDENT

sassafras: leaves and berries

sat *past of* SIT

Sa·tan \'sāt-ᵊn\ *n* : DEVIL 1 — **sa·tan·ic** \sə-'tan-ik, sā-\ *adj* — **sa·tan·i·cal·ly** \-'tan-i-k(ə-)lē\ *adv*

satch·el \'sach-əl\ *n* [MF *sachel*, fr. L *sacellus*, dim. of *saccus* bag] : a small bag of leather or heavy cloth for carrying clothes or books

sate \'sāt\ *vt* **1** : to cloy with overabundance : GLUT **2** : to appease (as a thirst or violent emotion) by indulging to the full

sa·teen \sa-'tēn\ *n* : a cotton fabric finished with a glossy surface to resemble satin

sat·el·lite \'sat-ᵊl-ˌīt\ *n* [L *satellit-, satelles* bodyguard, attendant] **1** : an obsequious follower or dependent **2 a** : a celestial body orbiting another of larger size **b** : a man-made object or vehicle intended to orbit the earth, the moon, or another celestial body **3** : someone or something attendant, subordinate, or dependent; *esp* : a country politically and economically dominated or controlled by another more powerful country — **satellite** *adj*

sa·tia·ble \'sā-shə-bəl\ *adj* : capable of being appeased or satisfied

¹sa·tiate \'sā-sh(ē-)ət\ *adj* : SATIATED

²sa·ti·ate \'sā-shē-ˌāt\ *vt* [L *satiare*, fr. *satis* enough; akin to E *sad*] **1** : to satisfy fully **2** : GLUT, SURFEIT — **sa·ti·a·tion** \ˌsā-s(h)ē-'ā-shən\ *n*

sa·ti·e·ty \sə-'tī-ət-ē\ *n* **1** : FULLNESS, REPLETION **2** : the revulsion or disgust of overindulgence or excess

sat·in \'sat-ᵊn\ *n* [MF] : a fabric (as of silk) with smooth lustrous face and dull back — **satin** *adj*

sat·in·et *or* **sat·in·ette** \ˌsat-ᵊn-'et\ *n* : a usu. thin silk satin

satin stitch *n* : an embroidery stitch nearly alike on both sides and worked so closely as to resemble satin

satin weave *n* : a weave in which warp threads interlace with filling threads to produce a smooth-faced fabric

sat·in·wood \'sat-ᵊn-ˌwùd\ *n* **1** : a hard yellowish brown wood with a satiny luster **2** : a tree yielding satinwood; *esp* : an East Indian tree of the mahogany family

sat·iny \'sat-ᵊn-ē\ *adj* : having the soft lustrous smoothness of satin : resembling satin ⟨*satiny* skin⟩

sat·ire \'sa-ˌtī(ə)r\ *n* [L *satura, satira*, fr. *lanx satura* full plate, medley] **1** : a literary work holding up human vices and follies to ridicule or scorn **2** : biting wit, irony, or sarcasm used to expose and discredit vice or folly — **sa·tir·ic** \sə-'tir-ik\ *or* **sa·tir·i·cal** \-'tir-i-kəl\ *adj* — **sa·tir·i·cal·ly** \-i-k(ə-)lē\ *adv*

sat·i·rist \'sat-ə-rəst\ *n* : one that satirizes; *esp* : a satirical writer

sat·i·rize \-ˌrīz\ *vb* **1** : to utter or write satires **2** : to censure or ridicule by means of satire

sat·is·fac·tion \ˌsat-əs-'fak-shən\ *n* **1** : the payment through penance of the temporal punishment incurred by a sin **2 a** : fulfillment of a need or want **b** : the quality or state of being satisfied : CONTENTMENT **c** : a cause or means of enjoyment : GRATIFICATION **3** : compensation for a loss or injury : RESTITUTION **4** : convinced assurance or certainty

sat·is·fac·to·ry \ˌsat-əs-'fak-t(ə-)rē\ *adj* : sufficient or adequate to satisfy : meeting what is asked or demanded — **sat·is·fac·to·ri·ly** \-t(ə-)rə-lē\ *adv* — **sat·is·fac·to·ri·ness** \-t(ə-)rē-nəs\ *n*

sat·is·fi·a·ble \'sat-əs-ˌfī-ə-bəl\ *adj* : capable of being satisfied

sat·is·fy \'sat-əs-ˌfī\ *vb* **-fied; -fy·ing** [MF *satisfier*, modif. of L *satisfacere*, fr. *satis* enough + *facere* to do] **1 a** : to carry out the terms of (as a contract) : DISCHARGE **b** : to meet a financial obligation to : PAY **2** : INDEMNIFY **3 a** : to make happy : PLEASE **b** : to gratify to the full : APPEASE ⟨*satisfied* his hunger⟩ **4 a** : CONVINCE ⟨*satisfied* that he is innocent⟩ **b** : to put an end to : DISPEL ⟨*satisfied* all their objections⟩ **5 a** : FULFILL, MEET ⟨*satisfy* the requirements for graduation⟩ **b** : to make true by fulfilling a condition ⟨values that *satisfy* an equation⟩ ⟨*satisfy* a hypothesis⟩ — **sat·is·fy·ing·ly** \-ˌfī-iŋ-lē\ *adv*

sa·trap \'sā-ˌtrap, 'sa-\ *n* [Gk *satrapēs*, fr. OPer *xshathrapāvan*, lit., protector of the dominion] **1** : the governor of a province in ancient Persia **2 a** : a subordinate ruler; *esp* : a petty tyrant **b** : HENCHMAN

sa·tra·py \'sā-trə-pē, 'sa-, -ˌtrap-ē\ *n, pl* **-pies** : the territory or jurisdiction of a satrap

sat·u·ra·ble \'sach-(ə-)rə-bəl\ *adj* : capable of saturation — **sat·u·ra·bil·i·ty** \ˌsach-(ə-)rə-'bil-ət-ē\ *n*

sat·u·rant \'sach-ə-rənt\ *n* : something that saturates

sat·u·rate \'sach-ə-ˌrāt\ *vt* [L *saturare*, fr. *satur* full, sated] **1** : to treat, furnish, or charge with something to the point where no more can be absorbed, dissolved, or retained ⟨water *saturated* with salt⟩ ⟨air *saturated* with water vapor⟩ **2 a** : to infuse thoroughly or cause to be pervaded : STEEP **b** : to fill completely : IMBUE — **sat·u·ra·tor** \-ˌrāt-ər\ *n*

sat·u·rat·ed \'sach-ə-ˌrāt-əd\ *adj* **1** : steeped in moisture : SOAKED **2 a** : being the most concentrated solution that can remain in the presence of an excess of the dissolved substance **b** : being a compound that does not tend to unite directly with another compound — used esp. of organic compounds containing no double or triple bonds **3** : not diluted with white ⟨a *saturated* color⟩

sat·u·ra·tion \ˌsach-ə-'rā-shən\ *n* **1** : the act of saturating : the state of being saturated **2** : magnetization to the point beyond which a further increase in the magnetizing force will produce no further magnetization **3 a** : chromatic purity : freedom from dilution with white **b** (1) : degree of difference from the gray having the same lightness — used of an object color (2) : degree of difference from the achromatic light-source color of the same brightness — used of a light-source color **4** : an overwhelming concentration of military forces or firepower

Sat·ur·day \'sat-ərd-ē\ *n* [OE *sæterndæg*, lit., Saturn's day, fr. L *Saturnus* Saturn + OE *dæg* day] : the 7th day of the week

Sat·urn \'sat-ərn\ *n* **1** : an ancient Roman god of agriculture held to have reigned during a golden age **2** : the planet 6th in order from the sun — see PLANET table — **Sa·tur·ni·an** \sə-'tər-nē-ən\ *adj*

sat·ur·na·lia \ˌsat-ər-'nāl-yə\ *n sing or pl* **1** *cap* : the festival of Saturn in ancient Rome beginning on Dec. 17 **2** : an unrestrained often licentious celebration : ORGY — **sat·ur·na·lian** \-yən\ *adj*

sat·ur·nine \'sat-ər-ˌnīn\ *adj* [L *Saturnus* Saturn; fr. the supposed character conferred by Saturn as a natal planet] : having a sullen or sardonic aspect : GLOOMY, GRAVE — **sat·ur·nine·ly** *adv*

---

sa·tyr \'sāt-ər, 'sat-\ *n* [Gk *satyros*] **1 :** a forest god in Greek mythology often represented as having the ears and tail of a horse or goat and given to boisterous pleasures **2 :** a man of lustful or lecherous habits **3 :** any of a family of usu. brown and gray butterflies often with ocelli on the wings — **sa·tyr·ic** \sa-'tir-ik, sə-, sa-\ *adj*

¹sauce \'sós, *4 is usu* 'sas\ *n* [MF, fr. L *salsa*, fem. of *salsus* salted, fr. pp. of *sallere* to salt, fr. *sal* salt] **1 :** a condiment or relish for food; *esp* **:** a fluid or semisolid accompaniment of food **:** DRESSING **2 :** something that adds zest or piquancy **3 :** stewed or canned fruit eaten with other food or as a dessert **4 :** pert or impudent language or actions

²sauce \'sós, *2 usu* 'sas\ *vt* **1 a :** to add relish or seasoning to **b :** to give zest or piquancy to **2 :** to be rude or impudent to

sauce·pan \'sós-,pan\ *n* **:** a small deep cooking pan with a handle

sau·cer \'sò-sər\ *n* [ME, dish for sauce, fr. MF *saucier*, fr. *sauce*] **1 :** a small round shallow dish in which a cup is set at table **2 :** something like a saucer esp. in shape

saucy \'sas-ē *also* 'sós-ē\ *adj* **sauc·i·er; -est 1 :** BOLD, IMPUDENT **2 :** IRREPRESSIBLE, PERT **3 :** SMART, TRIM ⟨a *saucy* ship⟩ — **sauc·i·ly** \-ə-lē\ *adv* — **sauc·i·ness** \-ē-nəs\ *n*

sau·er·bra·ten \'saú(-ə)r-,brät-ⁿn\ *n* [G, lit., sour roast] **:** pot-roasted beef marinated in vinegar with seasonings before cooking

sau·er·kraut \'saú(-ə)r-,kraút\ *n* [G, lit., sour cabbage] **:** finely cut cabbage fermented in brine

sau·ger \'sò-gər\ *n* **:** a pike perch similar to the walleye but smaller; *also* **:** WALLEYE

Saul \'sòl\ *n* **1 :** the first king of Israel **2 :** the apostle Paul — called also *Saul of Tarsus*

sau·na \'saú-nə\ *n* [Finn] **:** a Finnish steam bath; *also* **:** the bathhouse with steam provided by water thrown on hot stones

saun·ter \'sónt-ər, 'sänt-\ *vi* **:** to walk along in an idle or leisurely manner **:** STROLL — **saunter** *n* — **saun·ter·er** \-ər-ər\ *n*

sau·ri·an \'sòr-ē-ən\ *n* [Gk *sauros* lizard] **:** any of a group (Sauria) of reptiles including the lizards and in older classifications the crocodiles and various extinct forms (as the dinosaurs) suggesting lizards — **saurian** *adj*

saur·is·chi·an \sò-'ris-kē-ən\ *n* **:** any of an order (Saurischia) of quadrupedal dinosaurs with a typically reptilian pelvic girdle — **saurischian** *adj*

sau·ro·pod \'sòr-ə-,päd\ *n* **:** any of a group (Sauropoda) of large long-necked herbivorous saurischian dinosaurs — **sauropod** *adj* — **sau·rop·o·dous** \sò-'räp-əd-əs\ *adj*

sau·sage \'só-sij\ *n* [ONF *saussiche*, fr. LL *salsicia*, fr. L *salsus* salted] **:** highly seasoned minced meat (as pork) usu. stuffed in casings; *also* **:** a roll of such meat in a casing

¹sau·té \sò-'tā, sō-\ *n* [F, sautéed, fr. pp. of *sauter* to jump, fr. L *saltare*] **:** a sautéed dish — **sauté** *adj*

²sauté *vt* **sau·téed** *or* **sau·téd; sau·té·ing :** to fry quickly in shallow fat

sau·terne \sō-'tərn, só-, -'te(ə)rn\ *n* [F *sauternes*, fr. *Sauternes*, France] **:** a semisweet golden-colored table wine

¹sav·age \'sav-ij\ *adj* [MF *sauvage*, fr. L *silvaticus*, lit., of the woods, fr. *silva* wood] **1 a :** not domesticated or not under human control ⟨a *savage* bull⟩ **b :** FERAL, WILD **2 :** CRUEL, FEROCIOUS **3 a :** PRIMITIVE **b :** UNCIVILIZED, RUDE **syn** see BARBARIAN — **sav·age·ly** *adv* — **sav·age·ness** *n*

²savage *n* **1 :** a person belonging to a primitive society **2 :** a brutal person **3 :** a rude or unmannerly person

³savage *vt* **:** to attack or treat violently or brutally

sav·age·ry \'sav-ij-(ə-)rē\ *n, pl* **-ries 1 :** savage disposition or action **:** CRUELTY **2 :** the state or condition of being savage

sav·ag·ism \-ij-,iz-əm\ *n* **:** SAVAGERY

sa·van·na *or* **sa·van·nah** \sə-'van-ə\ *n* [Sp *sabana*, of AmerInd origin] **:** a tropical or subtropical grassland containing scattered trees

sa·vant \sa-'vänt, -'väⁿ; 'sav-ənt\ *n* [F, fr. prp. of *savoir* to know, fr. L *sapere* to taste, be wise] **:** a man of learning **:** SCHOLAR

¹save \'sāv\ *vb* [OF *sauver* to make or keep safe, fr. LL *salvare*, fr. L *salvus* safe] **1 a :** to deliver from sin **b :** to rescue or deliver from danger or harm **c :** to preserve or guard from injury, destruction, or loss **2 :** to put by as a store or reserve **:** ACCUMULATE **3 a :** to make unnecessary **:** AVOID ⟨*saves* an hour's waiting⟩ **b :** to prevent an opponent from scoring or winning **:** MAINTAIN, PRESERVE ⟨*save* appearances⟩ **5 a :** to put by money **b :** ECONOMIZE — **sav·a·ble** *or* **save·a·ble** \'sā-və-bəl\ *adj* — **sav·er** *n*

²save *n* **:** a play that prevents an opponent from scoring or winning ⟨the goalie made 20 *saves* in the hockey game⟩; *also* **:** a game that has been saved ⟨a relief pitcher with several *saves*⟩

³save \(,)sāv\ *prep* **:** EXCEPT ⟨no hope *save* one⟩

⁴save \(,)sāv\ *conj* **1 :** BUT **2b 2 :** UNLESS

sav·in *or* **sav·ine** \'sav-ən\ *n* **:** any of several mostly low-growing junipers

¹sav·ing \'sā-viŋ\ *n* **1 :** the act of rescuing ⟨the *saving* of lives⟩ **2 a :** something saved ⟨made a *saving* of 50 percent⟩ **b** *pl* **:** money saved over a period of time

²saving *adj* **1 :** ECONOMICAL, THRIFTY **2 :** making up for something **:** COMPENSATING ⟨a *saving* sense of humor⟩

³saving *prep* **1 :** EXCEPT, SAVE **2 :** without disrespect to

⁴saving *conj* **:** EXCEPT, SAVE

savings account *n* **:** an account (as in a bank) on which interest is usu. paid and from which withdrawals can be made usu. only by presentation of a passbook or by written authorization on a prescribed form — compare CHECKING ACCOUNT

savings and loan association *n* **:** a cooperative association that solicits savings in the form of share capital and invests its funds in mortgages

savings bank *n* **:** a bank that receives and invests savings accounts and pays interest to depositors

savings bond *n* **:** a nontransferable registered U.S. bond issued in denominations of $25 to $1000

sav·ior *or* **sav·iour** \'sāv-yər\ *n* [MF *saveour*, fr. LL *salvator*, fr. *salvare* to save] **1 :** one that saves from danger or destruction **2** *cap* **:** one who brings salvation; *esp* **:** JESUS

sa·voir faire \,sav-,wär-'fa(ə)r, -'fe(ə)r\ *n* [F *savoir-faire*, lit., knowing how to do] **:** ability to do or say the right or graceful thing **:** TACT

¹sa·vor \'sā-vər\ *n* [OF, fr. L *sapor*, fr. *sapere* to taste] **1 :** the taste and odor of something ⟨the *savor* of roast meat⟩ **2 :** a distinctive quality **:** SMACK — **sa·vor·less** \-ləs\ *adj*

²savor *vb* **sa·vored; sa·vor·ing** \'sāv-(ə-)riŋ\ **1 :** to have a specified smell or quality **:** SMACK **2 :** to give flavor to **:** SEASON **3 a :** to have experience of **:** TASTE **b :** to taste or smell with pleasure **:** RELISH **c :** to delight in **:** ENJOY — **sa·vor·er** \'sā-vər-ər\ *n*

¹sa·vory \'sāv-(ə-)rē\ *adj* **sa·vor·i·er; -est :** pleasing to the taste or smell **:** APPETIZING ⟨*savory* sausages⟩ — **sa·vor·i·ness** *n*

²savory *n, pl* **-vor·ies** *Brit* **:** a dish of stimulating flavor served usu. at the end of dinner

³sa·vo·ry \'sāv-(ə-)rē\ *n, pl* **-ries :** any of a genus of aromatic mints used in cookery as seasonings

Sa·voy·ard \sə-'vói-,ärd\ *n* [fr. *Savoy* Theatre, London, built for the presentation of Gilbert and Sullivan operas] **:** a devotee, performer, or producer of Gilbert and Sullivan comic operas

¹sav·vy \'sav-ē\ *vb* **sav·vied; sav·vy·ing** [Sp *sabe* he knows, fr. *saber* to know, fr. L *sapere* to taste, be wise] *slang* **:** COMPREHEND, UNDERSTAND

²savvy *n, slang* **:** practical grasp **:** SHREWDNESS ⟨political *savvy*⟩

¹saw *past of* SEE

²saw \'só\ *n* [OE *sagu*] **1 :** a hand or power tool used to cut hard material (as wood, metal, or bone) and made of a toothed blade or disk **2 :** a machine mounting a saw (as a band saw or circular saw)

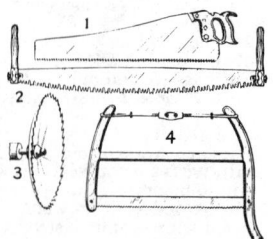

³saw *vb* **sawed** \'sòd\; **sawed** *or* **sawn** \'són\; **saw·ing :** to cut or form by cutting with a saw **2 :** to slice as though with a saw **3 :** to

saws: *1* ripsaw, *2* two-man saw, *3* concave circular saw, *4* bucksaw make motions as though using a saw ⟨*sawed* at the reins⟩ — **saw·er** \'sȯ(-ə)r\ *n*

⁴saw *n* [OE *sagu* talk; akin to E *say*] **:** a common saying **:** PROVERB

saw·buck \'sȯ-ˌbək\ *n* **1 :** SAWHORSE **2** *slang* **:** a 10-dollar bill

saw·dust \'sȯ-(ˌ)dəst\ *n* **:** dust or fine particles of wood made by a saw in cutting

saw–edged \'sȯ-ˈejd\ *adj* **:** having a toothed or badly nicked edge

sawed–off \'sȯd-ˈȯf\ *adj* **1 :** having an end sawed off ⟨a *sawed-off* shotgun⟩ **2 :** being of less than average height

saw–fish \'sȯ-ˌfish\ *n* **:** any of several mostly tropical rays with a long flattened snout bearing a row of stout toothlike structures along each edge

saw·fly \-ˌflī\ *n* **:** any of numerous insects that are related to the wasps and bees and usu. have in the female a pair of organs for making slits in leaves or stems into which she lays her eggs

saw grass *n* **:** a sedge with sharply toothed leaves

saw·horse \-ˌhȯrs\ *n* **:** a frame or rack on which wood is rested while being sawed by hand

saw·log \-ˌlȯg, -ˌläg\ *n* **:** a log of suitable size for sawing into lumber

saw·mill \-ˌmil\ *n* **:** a mill or machine for sawing logs

saw·tim·ber \'sȯ-ˌtim-bər\ *n* **:** timber suitable for sawing into lumber

saw·tooth \-ˌtüth\ *adj* **:** SAW-TOOTHED

saw–toothed \-'tütht\ *adj* **:** having an edge or outline like the teeth of a saw

saw–whet \-ˌhwet\ *n* **:** a very small harsh-voiced No. American owl largely dark brown above and white beneath

saw·yer \'sȯ-yər\ *n* **1 :** one that saws something and esp. timber **2 :** any of several large beetles whose larvae bore large holes in timber

sax \'saks\ *n* **:** SAXOPHONE

sax·horn \'saks-ˌhȯrn\ *n* [fr. A. J. *Sax* d1894 Belgian maker of musical instruments] **:** one of a family of valved conical-bore brass-wind instruments of full even tone and large compass

sax·ic·o·lous \sak-'sik-ə-ləs\ *adj* [L *saxum* rock + E -*i*- + -*colous*] **:** living or growing among rocks

sax·i·frage \'sak-sə-frij, -ˌfrāj\ *n* [LL *saxifraga*, fr. L *saxum* rock + *frangere* to break] **:** any of a genus of plants with showy 5-parted flowers and usu. with leaves growing in tufts close to the ground

Sax·on \'sak-sən\ *n* **1 a :** a member of a Germanic people invading and conquering England with the Angles and Jutes in the 5th century A.D. and merging with them to form the Anglo-Saxon people **b :** an Englishman or Lowlander as distinguished from a Welshman, Irishman, or Highlander **2 :** a native or inhabitant of Saxony — **Saxon** *adj*

sax·o·phone \'sak-sə-ˌfōn\ *n* [fr. A. J. *Sax* d1894 Belgian maker of musical instruments] **:** a wind instrument with reed mouthpiece, curved conical metal tube, and finger keys — **sax·o·phon·ic** \ˌsak-sə-'fän-ik\ *adj* — **sax·o·phon·ist** \'sak-sə-ˌfō-nəst\ *n*

sax·tu·ba \'saks-'t(y)ü-bə\ *n* **:** a bass saxhorn

¹say \'sā\ *vt* said \'sed\; **say·ing** \'sā-iŋ\; **says** \'sez\ [OE *secgan*] **1 a :** to express in words **:** STATE **b :** to state as opinion or belief **:** DECLARE **2 a :** UTTER, PRONOUNCE **b :** RECITE, REPEAT ⟨*said* his prayers⟩ **3 :** INDICATE, SHOW ⟨the clock *says* five minutes after twelve⟩ ⟨a glance that *said* all that was necessary⟩ — **say·er** \'sā-ər\ *n*

²say *n* **1 :** an expression of opinion ⟨had his *say*⟩ **2 :** the power to decide or help decide

³say *adv* **1 :** ABOUT, APPROXIMATELY ⟨the property is worth, *say*, four million dollars⟩ **2 :** for example **:** AS ⟨if we compress any gas, *say* oxygen⟩

say·able \'sā-ə-bəl\ *adj* **1 :** capable of being said **2 :** capable of being spoken effectively or easily

say·ing \'sā-iŋ\ *n* **:** something frequently said **:** PROVERB, SAW

say–so \'sā-ˌsō\ *n* **1 a :** one's bare word or assurance **b :** an authoritative pronouncement **:** DICTUM **2 :** a right of final decision **:** AUTHORITY

¹scab \'skab\ *n* [of Scand origin] **1 a :** scabies of domestic animals **b :** any of various plant diseases characterized by crusted spots **2 :** a crust of hardened blood

and serum over a wound **3 a :** a contemptible person **b :** a worker who replaces a union worker during a strike

²scab *vi* **scabbed; scab·bing 1 :** to become covered with a scab **2 :** to act as a scab

scab·bard \'skab-ərd\ *n* [AF *escauberz* scabbards, of Gmc origin] **:** a sheath for a sword, dagger, or bayonet — **scabbard** *vt*

scab·by \'skab-ē\ *adj* **scab·bi·er; -est 1 a :** covered with or full of scabs ⟨*scabby* skin⟩ **b :** diseased with scab ⟨a *scabby* animal⟩⟨*scabby* potatoes⟩ **2 :** MEAN, CONTEMPTIBLE ⟨a *scabby* trick⟩

sca·bies \'skā-bēz\ *n, pl* **scabies** [L] **:** an itch or mange caused by mites living as parasites under the skin

scab·rous \'skab-rəs, 'skāb-\ *adj* [L *scaber* rough, scurfy] **1 :** DIFFICULT, KNOTTY ⟨a *scabrous* problem⟩ **2 :** rough to the touch **:** SCALY, SCURFY ⟨a *scabrous* leaf⟩ **3 :** dealing with suggestive, indecent, or scandalous themes **:** SALACIOUS; *also* **:** SQUALID — **scab·rous·ly** *adv* — **scab·rous·ness** *n*

¹scad \'skad\ *n, pl* **scad** *also* **scads :** any of several mostly small sea fishes related to the pompanos

²scad *n* **1 :** a large number or quantity **2** *pl* **:** a great abundance ⟨*scads* of money⟩

scaf·fold \'skaf-əld, -ˌōld\ *n* [ONF *escafaut*] **1 a :** a temporary or movable platform for workmen (as bricklayers, painters, or miners) **b :** a platform on which a criminal is executed (as by hanging or beheading) **c :** a platform at a height above ground or floor level **2 :** a supporting framework

scaf·fold·ing \-əl-diŋ, -ˌōl-\ *n* **:** a system of scaffolds; *also* **:** materials for scaffolds

scal·a·ble \'skā-lə-bəl\ *adj* **:** capable of being scaled

scal·age \'skā-lij\ *n* **:** the act or result of scaling in weight, quantity, or dimensions

sca·lar \'skā-lər\ *adj* [L *scalae* stairs, ladder] **1 :** arranged like a ladder **:** GRADUATED ⟨*scalar* chain of authority⟩ ⟨*scalar* cells⟩ **2 :** that can be represented by a point on a scale ⟨*scalar* quantity⟩

sca·lare \skə-'la(ə)r-ē, -'le(ə)r-\ *n* **:** a black and silver laterally compressed So. American fish popular in aquariums

scal·a·tion \skā-'lā-shən\ *n* **:** arrangement of scales (as on a fish)

scal·a·wag \'skal-i-ˌwag\ *n* **1 :** SCAMP, REPROBATE **2 :** a white Southerner acting as a Republican in the time of reconstruction after the Civil War

¹scald \'skȯld\ *vb* [ONF *escalder*, fr. LL *excaldare* to wash in warm water, fr. L *ex*- + *calidus* warm] **1 :** to burn with or as if with hot liquid or steam **2 a :** to subject to the action of boiling water or steam ⟨*scald* dishes⟩ **b :** to bring to a temperature just below the boiling point ⟨*scald* milk⟩ **3 :** SCORCH

²scald *n* **1 :** an injury to the body caused by scalding **2 :** an act or process of scalding **3 :** a plant disease marked esp. by discoloration suggesting injury by heat

³scald \'skȯld, 'skäld\ *var of* SKALD

scald·ing \'skȯl-diŋ\ *adj* **1 :** causing the sensation of scalding or burning **2 :** BOILING **3 :** SCORCHING, ARDENT ⟨the *scalding* sun⟩ **4 :** BITING, SCATHING ⟨a series of *scalding* editorials⟩

¹scale \'skāl\ *n* [ON *skāl* bowl, scale; akin to E *shell*] **1 a :** either pan of a balance **b :** BALANCE — usu. used in pl. **2 :** a device for weighing ⟨a bathroom *scale*⟩

²scale *vb* **1 :** to weigh in scales **2 :** to have a specified weight

³scale *n* [MF *escale*, of Gmc origin; akin to E *shell*] **1 :** one of the small rigid flattened plates forming an outer covering on the body esp. of a fish or reptile **2 :** a small thin part or structure suggesting a fish scale: as **a :** a modified leaf covering a bud of a seed plant **b :** a small dry flake of skin ⟨dandruff *scales*⟩ **3 :** SCALE INSECT **4 :** a thin layer, coating, or incrustation forming esp. on metal (as iron) ⟨boiler *scale*⟩ — **scaled** \'skāld\ *adj* — **scale·less** \'skāl-ləs\ *adj* — **scale·like** \'skāl-ˌlīk\ *adj*

⁴scale *vb* **1 :** to remove scale or the scales from ⟨*scale* a boiler⟩ ⟨*scale* fish⟩ **2 :** to take off in scales or thin layers **3 :** to form scale on **4 :** to come off in scales or shed scales **:** FLAKE **5 :** to become encrusted with scale **6 :** to throw a flat object so as to sail in air or skip on water ⟨*scaling* cards into a hat⟩

⁵scale *n* [LL *scala* ladder, staircase, fr. L *scalae*, pl., stairs, ladder, fr. *scandere* to climb] **1** : something graduated esp. when used as a measure or rule: as **a** : a series of spaces marked by lines and used to measure distances or to register something (as the height of the mercury in a thermometer) **b** : a divided line on a map or chart indicating the length (as an inch) used to represent a larger unit of measure (as a mile) **c** : an instrument consisting of a strip (as of wood, plastic, or metal) with one or more sets of spaces graduated and numbered on its surface for measuring or laying off distances or dimensions **2** : a basis for a system of numbering ⟨the decimal *scale*⟩ **3** : a graduated series ⟨the *scale* of prices⟩ **4** : the size of a picture, plan, or model of a thing in proportion to the size of the thing itself **5** : a relative size or degree ⟨do things on a large *scale*⟩ **6** : a standard by which something can be measured or judged **7** : a graduated series of tones going up or down in pitch according to a specified scheme of intervals

⁶**scale** *vb* **1** : to climb by or as if by means of a ladder : SURMOUNT **2 a** : to arrange in a graduated series ⟨*scale* a test⟩ **b** : to measure by or as if by a scale **c** : to make, regulate, or estimate according to a rate or standard ⟨*scale* down a budget⟩ **syn** see ASCEND

scale armor *n* : armor made of small metallic scales on leather or cloth

scale–down \'skāl-,daůn\ *n* : a reduction according to a fixed ratio ⟨a *scale-down* of debts⟩

scale insect *n* : any of numerous small insects that are related to the plant lice, include many destructive plant pests, and have winged males, degenerated scale-covered females attached to the host plant, and young that suck the juices of plants

scale leaf *n* : a modified usu. small and scaly leaf (as of a cypress)

sca·lene \'skā-,lēn, skā-'\ *adj* [Gk *skalēnos*, lit., uneven] : having the sides unequal — see TRIANGLE illustration

scale·pan \'skāl-,pan\ *n* : a pan of a scale for weighing

scal·er \'skā-lər\ *n* : one that scales

scale–up \'skāl-,əp\ *n* : an increase according to a fixed ratio ⟨a *scale-up* of wages⟩

scal·lion \'skal-yən\ *n* [AF *scalun*, fr. L *ascalonia caepa* onion of Ascalon (a seaport in Palestine)] **1** : SHALLOT **2** : LEEK **3** : an onion without an enlarged bulb

¹**scal·lop** \'skäl-əp, 'skal-\ *n* [MF *escalope* shell, of Gmc origin] **1 a** : any of a family of marine bivalve mollusks with the shell radially ribbed **b** : the adductor muscle of a scallop as an article of food **2** : a scallop-shell valve or a similarly shaped dish used for baking **3** : one of a continuous series of circle segments or angular projections forming a border

²**scallop** *vt* **1** : to bake in a sauce usu. covered with seasoned bread or cracker crumbs ⟨*scalloped* potatoes⟩ **2 a** : to shape, cut, or finish in scallops **b** : to form scallops in — **scal·lop·er** *n*

scallop shell

scal·ly·wag *var of* SCALAWAG

¹**scalp** \'skalp\ *n* [of Scand origin] **1** : the part of the skin and flesh of the head usu. covered with hair **2** : a part of the human scalp cut or torn from an enemy as a token of victory by Indian warriors of No. America

²**scalp** *vb* **1 a** : to deprive of the scalp **b** : to remove an upper or better part from **2 a** : to buy and sell so as to make small quick profits **b** : to obtain speculatively and resell at greatly increased prices ⟨*scalp* theater tickets⟩ — **scalp·er** *n*

scal·pel \'skal-pəl, skal-'pel\ *n* [L *scalpellum*, dim. of *scalprum* chisel, knife, fr. *scalpere, sculpere* to carve] : a small straight thin-bladed knife used esp. in surgery

scalp lock *n* : a long tuft of hair on the crown of the otherwise shaved head of a warrior of some American Indian tribes

scaly \'skā-lē\ *adj* **scal·i·er; -est 1 a** : covered with, composed of, or rich in scale or scales **b** : FLAKY **2** : DESPICABLE, POOR **3** : infested with scale insects ⟨*scaly* fruit⟩ — **scal·i·ness** *n*

¹**scamp** \'skamp\ *n* **1** : RASCAL, ROGUE **2** : an impish or playful young person

²**scamp** *vt* : to perform in a hasty, neglectful, or imperfect manner : SKIMP ⟨*scamp* one's work⟩

scam·per \'skam-pər\ *vi* **scam·pered; scam·per·ing** \-p(ə-)riŋ\ : to run nimbly and playfully about — **scamper** *n*

scan \'skan\ *vb* **scanned; scan·ning** [LL *scandere*, fr. L, to climb] **1 a** : to read or mark verses so as to show metrical structure **b** : to conform to a metrical pattern **2 a** : to examine intensively **b** : to make a wide sweeping search of **c** : to look through or over hastily **3 a** : to bring under a moving electron beam for conversion of light and dark image values into corresponding electrical values to be transmitted by television; *also* : to move across in successive lines in reproducing a television image ⟨the electron beam *scans* the face of the picture tube⟩ **b** : to direct a succession of radar beams over in searching for a target **syn** see SCRUTINIZE — **scan** *n*

scan·dal \'skan-d⁰l\ *n* [Gk *skandalon* trap, stumbling block, offense] **1** : an offense against faith or morals that causes another to sin **2** : loss of or damage to reputation caused by actual or apparent violation of morality or propriety : DISGRACE ⟨to the *scandal* of the school⟩ **3 a** : a circumstance or action that offends propriety or established moral conceptions or disgraces those associated with it ⟨the slum is a *scandal*⟩ **b** : a person whose conduct offends propriety or morality **4** : malicious or defamatory gossip ⟨untouched by *scandal*⟩

scan·dal·i·za·tion \,skan-də-lə-'zā-shən\ *n* : the act of scandalizing : the state of being scandalized

scan·dal·ize \'skan-də-,līz\ *vt* **1** : to speak falsely or maliciously of : MALIGN **2** : to offend the moral sense of : SHOCK ⟨her actions *scandalized* the neighbors⟩ — **scan·dal·iz·er** *n*

scan·dal·mon·ger \'skan-d⁰l-,məŋ-gər, -,mäŋ-\ *n* : a person who spreads scandal

scan·dal·ous \'skan-d(ə-)ləs\ *adj* **1** : DEFAMATORY, LIBELOUS ⟨a *scandalous* story⟩ **2** : offensive to propriety or morality : SHOCKING ⟨*scandalous* behavior⟩ — **scan·dal·ous·ly** *adv* — **scan·dal·ous·ness** *n*

scandal sheet *n* : a newspaper or periodical dealing to a large extent in scandal and gossip

scan·dent \'skan-dənt\ *adj* [L *scandere* to climb] : CLIMBING ⟨*scandent* stems⟩

Scan·di·na·vi·an \,skan-də-'nā-vē-ən\ *n* **1 a** : a native or inhabitant of Scandinavia **b** : a person of Scandinavian descent **2** : the Germanic languages of the Scandinavian peoples including Icelandic, Norwegian, Swedish, and Danish — **Scandinavian** *adj*

scan·di·um \'skan-dē-əm\ *n* [NL, fr. L *Scandia*, southern part of the Scandinavian peninsula] : a white metallic chemical element — see ELEMENT table

scan·ner \'skan-ər\ *n* : one that scans

scan·sion \'skan-chən\ *n* [LL *scans-, scandere* to scan] : the analysis of verse to show its meter

scan·so·ri·al \skan-'sōr-ē-əl, -'sȯr-\ *adj* : relating to, capable of, or adapted for climbing

¹**scant** \'skant\ *adj* [ON *skamt*, neut. of *skammr* short] **1** *dial* : excessively frugal : PARSIMONIOUS **2 a** : barely or scarcely sufficient; *esp* : not quite coming up to a stated measure ⟨a *scant* cup of milk⟩ **b** : lacking in amplitude or quantity : MEAGER, SCANTY **3** : having a small or insufficient supply ⟨*scant* of breath⟩ — **scant·ly** *adv* — **scant·ness** *n*

²**scant** *adv, dial* : SCARCELY, HARDLY

³**scant** *vt* **1** : to provide with a meager or inadequate portion or allowance : STINT **2** : to make small, narrow, or meager : SKIMP **3** : to provide an incomplete supply of : WITHHOLD **4** : to give scant attention to : SLIGHT ⟨a subject *scanted* in textbooks⟩

scant·ling \'skant-liŋ, -lən\ *n* [alter. of ME *scantilon*, lit., mason's or carpenter's gauge, fr. ONF *escantillon*] : a small piece of lumber; *esp* : one of the upright pieces in the frame of a house

scanty \'skant-ē\ *adj* **scant·i·er; -est 1** : barely enough : lacking size or extent **2** : less than is needed : INSUFFICIENT **syn** see MEAGER — **scant·i·ly** \'skant-⁰l-ē\ *adv* — **scant·i·ness** \'skant-ē-nəs\ *n*

¹**scape** \'skāp\ *vb* : ESCAPE

²**scape** *n* [L *scapus* stalk] **1** : a leafless flower stalk (as in the tulip) that begins at or beneath the surface of the ground **2** : the shaft of a column **3** : the shaft of an

animal part (as an antenna or a feather) — **sca·pi·form**
\'skā-pə-ˌform\ *adj*

-scape \ˌskāp\ *n comb form* [*landscape*] **:** a (specified) type
of scene; *also* **:** a pictorial representation of (such a scene)
⟨moon*scape*⟩

scape·goat \'skāp-ˌgōt\ *n* **1 :** a goat upon whose head
are symbolically placed the sins of the people after which
he is sent into the wilderness in the biblical ceremony for
Yom Kippur **2 :** a person or thing bearing the blame for
others

scape·grace \-ˌgrās\ *n* **:** an incorrigible rascal

scaph·o·pod \'skaf-ə-ˌpäd\ *n* **:** TOOTH SHELL

sca·pose \'skā-ˌpōs\ *adj* **:** bearing, resembling, or being a
scape

scap·u·la \'skap-yə-lə\ *n, pl* **-lae** \-ˌlē, -ˌlī\ *or* **-las** [L,
shoulder, shoulder blade] **:** a large triangular flat bone of the
dorsal part of the shoulder that is the principal bone of the
corresponding half of the shoulder girdle and articulates
with the corresponding clavicle or coracoid to form a
socket for the humerus of the arm — called also *shoulder
blade*

1scap·u·lar \'skap-yə-lər\ *n* **1 a :** a long wide band of
cloth with an opening for the head worn front and back
over the shoulders as part of a monastic habit **b :** a pair of
small cloth squares joined by shoulder tapes and worn
under the clothing on the breast and back as a sacramental
and often also as a badge of a third order or confraternity
2 : one of the feathers covering the base of a bird's wing
— see BIRD illustration

2scapular *adj* **:** of or relating to the shoulder or the scapula

scapular medal *n* **:** a medal worn in place of a sacramental
scapular

1scar \'skär\ *n* [ON *sker* skerry] **1 :** an isolated or protruding rock **2 :** a steep rocky eminence **:** a bare place
on the side of a mountain

2scar *n* [MF *escare* scab, fr. LL *eschara*, fr. Gk, hearth,
scab] **1 a :** a mark remaining after injured tissue has
healed **b :** a mark resembling a scar and usu. marking
the former point of attachment of some other structure;
esp **:** one on a stem where a leaf or fruit has separated
2 : a lasting moral or emotional injury — **scar·less** \-ləs\
adj

3scar *vb* **scarred; scar·ring** *vb* **1 :** to mark with or form
a scar **2 :** to do lasting injury to **3 :** to become scarred

scar·ab \'skar-əb\ *n* [L *scarabaeus*] **1 :** a large black or
nearly black dung beetle regarded by the ancient Egyptians
as symbolic of resurrection and immortality; *also* **:** any of
various related beetles **2 :** an ornament or a gem made to
represent this beetle

scar·a·bae·us \ˌskar-ə-'bē-əs\ *n, pl* **-bae·us·es** *or* **-baei**
\-'bē-ˌī\ **:** SCARAB

scar·a·mouch *or* **scar·a·mouche** \'skar-ə-ˌmüsh, -ˌmüch,
-ˌmauch\ *n* **1 :** a cowardly buffoon **2 :** RASCAL, SCAMP

1scarce \'ske(ə)rs, 'ska(ə)rs\ *adj* [ONF *escars*, fr. (assumed) VL *excarpsus*, pp. of *excarpere* to pluck out, fr. L
ex- + *carpere* to pluck] **1 :** deficient in quantity or number **:** not plentiful or abundant ⟨food is *scarce*⟩ **2 :** not
provided in sufficient abundance to be free **:** UNCOMMON,
RARE — **scarce·ly** *adv* — **scarce·ness** *n*

2scarce *adv* **:** SCARCELY, HARDLY

scar·ci·ty \'sker-sət-ē, 'skar-\ *n, pl* **-ties :** the quality or
condition of being scarce **:** a very small supply

1scare \'ske(ə)r, 'ska(ə)r\ *vb* [ME *skerren*, fr. ON *skirra*,
fr. *skjarr* shy, timid] **1 :** to frighten suddenly **:** ALARM
2 : to become scared ⟨she *scared* easily⟩

2scare *n* **1 :** a sudden fright **2 :** a widespread state of
alarm **:** PANIC

scare·crow \'ske(ə)r-ˌkrō, 'ska(ə)r-\ *n* **1 a :** an object
usu. suggesting a human figure that is set up to scare birds
away from crops **b :** something frightening but harmless
2 : a skinny or ragged person

scare·head \-ˌhed\ *n* **:** a big, sensational, or alarming
newspaper headline

scare·mon·ger \-ˌmən-gər, -ˌmäŋ-\ *n* **:** ALARMIST

scar·er \'sker-ər, 'skar-\ *n* **:** one that scares

scare up *vt* **:** to bring to light or get together with considerable labor or difficulty ⟨managed to *scare up* the
necessary money⟩

1scarf \'skärf\ *n, pl* **scarves** \'skärvz\ *or* **scarfs**
\'skärfs\ [ONF *escarpe*] **1 :** a broad band (as of cloth)

worn about the shoulders, around the neck, over the head,
or about the waist **2 :** TIPPET 3 **3 :** RUNNER 6b

2scarf *n* [ME *skarf*] **1 :** either of the ends that fit together
to form a scarf joint **2 :** a joint made by beveling, halving,
or notching two pieces to correspond and lapping and
bolting them

3scarf *or* **scarph** \'skärf\ *vt* **:** to unite by a scarf joint

scarf·pin \'skärf-ˌpin\ *n* **:** TIEPIN

scarf·skin \'skärf-ˌskin\ *n* **:** CUTICLE, EPIDERMIS; *esp* **:** that
about the base of a nail

scar·i·fy \'skar-ə-ˌfī, 'sker-\ *vt* **-fied; -fy·ing** [MF *scarifier*, fr. LL *scarificare*, alter. of L *scarifare*, fr. Gk *skariphasthai* to scratch an outline, sketch] **1 :** to make
scratches or small cuts in **:** wound superficially ⟨*scarify*
skin for vaccination⟩⟨*scarify* seeds to help them germinate⟩
2 : to lacerate the feelings of **:** FLAY — **scar·i·fi·ca·tion**
\ˌskar-ə-fə-'kā-shən, ˌsker-\ *n* — **scar·i·fi·er** \'skar-ə-
ˌfī(-ə)r, 'sker-\ *n*

scar·i·ous \'sker-ē-əs, 'skar-\ *adj* **:** dry and membranous
in texture ⟨a *scarious* bract⟩

scar·la·ti·na \ˌskär-lə-'tē-nə\ *n* **:** a usu. mild scarlet
fever — **scar·la·ti·nal** \-'tēn-ᵊl\ *adj*

1scar·let \'skär-lət\ *n* [ML *scarlatum*, fr. Per *saqalāt*, a
kind of rich cloth] **1 :** scarlet cloth or clothes **2 :** a bright
red

2scarlet *adj* **:** of the color scarlet

scarlet fever *n* **:** an acute contagious disease caused by a
streptococcus and marked by fever, inflammation of the
nose, throat, and mouth, toxemia, and a red rash

scarlet runner *n* **:** a tropical American high-climbing bean
with large bright red flowers and red-and-black seeds
grown widely as an ornamental and in Great Britain as a
preferred table bean

scarlet sage *n* **:** any of several red-flowered salvias

scarlet tanager *n* **:** a common American tanager of which
the male is scarlet with black wings

1scarp \'skärp\ *n* [It *scarpa*] **1 :** the inner side of a ditch
below the parapet of a fortification **2 a :** a line of cliffs
produced by faulting or erosion **b :** a low steep slope
along a beach caused by wave erosion

2scarp *vt* **:** to cut down vertically or to a steep slope

scary *also* **scar·ey** \'ske(ə)r-ē, 'ska(ə)r-\ *adj* **scar·i·er;
-est 1 :** causing fright **:** ALARMING ⟨a *scary* movie⟩
2 : easily scared **:** TIMID **3 :** SCARED, FRIGHTENED ⟨*scary*
feeling⟩

1scat \'skat\ *vi* **scat·ted; scat·ting 1 :** to go away
quickly — often used interjectionally to drive away an
animal (as a cat) **2 :** to move fast **:** SCOOT

2scat *n* **:** jazz singing with nonsense syllables

3scat *vi* **scat·ted; scat·ting :** to improvise nonsense syllables to an instrumental accompaniment **:** sing scat

1scathe \'skāth\ *n* [ON *skathi*] **:** HARM, INJURY — **scathe·
less** \-ləs\ *adj*

2scathe *vt* **1 :** to do harm to **:** INJURE; *esp* **:** SCORCH, SEAR
2 : to assail with withering denunciation

scath·ing \'skā-thiŋ\ *adj* **:** bitterly severe ⟨*scathing* rebuke⟩
— **scath·ing·ly** \-thiŋ-lē\ *adv*

sca·tol·o·gy \skə-'täl-ə-jē, ska-\ *n* [Gk *skat-, skōr* dung]
: interest in or treatment of obscene matters esp. in literature — **scat·o·log·i·cal** \ˌskat-ᵊl-'äj-i-kəl\ *adj*

scat·ter \'skat-ər\ *vb* [ME *scateren*] **1 :** to cause to
separate widely **2 :** to distribute irregularly **3 :** to sow
broadcast **:** STREW **4 :** to diffuse or disperse (a beam of
radiation) in a random manner **5 :** to separate from each
other and go in various directions **6 :** to occur or fall irregularly or at random — **scat·ter·er** \-ər-ər\ *n*

syn SCATTER, DISPERSE, DISPEL, DISSIPATE mean to cause to
separate or break up. SCATTER implies forcefully driving
parts or units irregularly in many directions; DISPERSE
implies a wider separation and complete breaking up of
mass or group; DISPEL stresses a driving away or getting
rid of as if by scattering; DISSIPATE stresses complete disintegration or dissolution and final disappearance

scat·ter·brain \-ˌbrān\ *n* **:** a giddy heedless person incapable of concentration **:** FLIBBERTIGIBBET — **scat·ter·
brained** \-ˌbrānd\ *adj*

1scat·ter·ing *n* **1 :** an act or process in which something
scatters or is scattered **2 :** something scattered; *esp* **:** a
small number or quantity interspersed here and there ⟨a
scattering of visitors⟩

2scattering *adj* **1 :** going in various directions **2 :** found or placed far apart and in no order — **scat·ter·ing·ly** \-ə-riŋ-lē\ *adv*

scatter pin *n* : a small pin used as jewelry and worn usu. in groups of two or more on a woman's dress

scatter rug *n* : a rug of such a size that several can be used (as) to fill vacant places) in a room

scaup \'skóp\ *n, pl* **scaup** *or* **scaups** : any of several diving ducks

scav·enge \'skav-inj\ *vb* **1** : to remove dirt or refuse from an area **2** : to salvage usable material from what has been discarded

scav·en·ger \'skav-ən-jər\ *n* **1** *chiefly Brit* : a person employed to remove dirt and refuse from streets **2** : one that scavenges **3** : an organism that feeds habitually on refuse or carrion

sce·nar·io \sə-'nar-ē-,ō, -'ner-, -'när-\ *n, pl* **-i·os 1 a** : an outline or synopsis of a play **b** : the libretto of an opera **2 a** : SCREENPLAY **b** : SHOOTING SCRIPT

sce·nar·ist \-'nar-əst, -'ner-, -'när-\ *n* : a writer of scenarios

¹scend \'send\ *vi* : to rise or heave upward under the influence of a natural force (as on a wave)

²scend *n* **1** : the upward movement of a pitching ship **2** : the lift of a wave

scene \'sēn\ *n* [MF, stage, fr. L *scena*, fr. Gk *skēnē* temporary shelter, tent, building forming the background for a dramatic performance, stage] **1** : one of the subdivisions of a play: as **a** : a division of an act presenting continuous action in one place **b** : a single situation or unit of dialogue in a play **c** : a motion picture or television episode or sequence **2 a** : a stage setting ⟨change *scenes*⟩ **b** : a view or sight having pictorial quality ⟨a winter *scene*⟩ **3** : the place of an occurrence or action : LOCALE ⟨*scene* of a riot⟩ **4** : an exhibition of anger or indecorous behavior ⟨create a *scene*⟩ — **behind the scenes 1** : out of public view : in secret **2** : in a position to see or control the hidden workings ⟨the man *behind the scenes*⟩

scen·ery \'sēn-(ə-)rē\ *n* **1** : the painted scenes or hangings and accessories used on a theater stage **2** : a picturesque view or landscape ⟨mountain *scenery*⟩

scene·shift·er \'sēn-,shif-tər\ *n* : a worker who moves the scenes in a theater

scene·steal·er \-,stē-lər\ *n* : an actor who skillfully or ostentatiously diverts attention to himself when he is not intended to be the center of attraction

sce·nic \'sē-nik\ *adj* **1** : of or relating to the stage, a stage setting, or stage representation ⟨*scenic* effects⟩ **2** : of or relating to natural scenery ⟨a *scenic* route⟩ **3** : representing graphically an action, event, or episode ⟨a *scenic* frieze⟩ — **sce·ni·cal** \-ni-kəl\ *adj* — **sce·ni·cal·ly** \-ni-k(ə-)lē\ *adv*

scenic railway *n* : a miniature railway (as in an amusement park) with artificial scenery along the way

¹scent \'sent\ *vb* [ME *senten*, fr. MF *sentir* to feel, smell, fr. L *sentire* to perceive, feel] **1 a** : SMELL ⟨the dog *scented* a rabbit⟩ **b** : to get or have an inkling of ⟨*scent* trouble⟩ **2** : to imbue or fill with odor ⟨*scent* a handkerchief⟩

²scent *n* **1 a** : an odor left by an animal on a surface passed over; *also* : a course of pursuit or discovery ⟨throw one off the *scent*⟩ **b** : a characteristic or particular and usu. agreeable odor **2 a** : sense of smell ⟨a keen *scent*⟩ **b** : power of detection ⟨a *scent* for heresy⟩ : NOSE **3** : INKLING, INTIMATION ⟨a *scent* of trouble⟩ **4** : PERFUME 2 **5** : bits of paper dropped in the game of hare and hounds **6** : an odorous lure for an animal *syn see* SMELL

scent·ed *adj* : having scent; *esp* : PERFUMED

scent·less \'sent-ləs\ *adj* : lacking scent; *esp* : ODORLESS — **scent·less·ness** *n*

scep·ter \'sep-tər\ *n* [Gk *skēptron*; akin to E *shaft*] **1** : a staff or baton borne by a sovereign as an emblem of authority **2** : royal or imperial authority : SOVEREIGNTY — **scep·tered** \-tərd\ *adj*

scep·tic \'skep-tik\ *var of* SKEPTIC

¹sched·ule \'skej-ül, -əl, *Canad also* 'shej-, *Brit usu* 'shed-yül\ *n* [LL *schedula* slip of paper, dim. of L *scheda* sheet of papyrus] **1 a** : a written or printed list, catalog, or inventory **b** : TIMETABLE **2** : PROGRAM, AGENDA

²schedule *vt* **1** : to place in or as if in a schedule ⟨*schedule* a meeting⟩ **2** : to make a schedule of

schee·lite \'shā-,līt\ *n* : a mineral CaWO₄ that is a source of tungsten and its compounds

Sche·her·a·zade \shə-,her-ə-'zäd-(ə)\ *n* : the wife of the sultan of India and narrator of the tales in the *Arabian Nights' Entertainments*

sche·mat·ic \ski-'mat-ik\ *adj* : of, relating to, or forming a scheme, plan, or diagram : DIAGRAMMATIC — **schematic** *n* — **sche·mat·i·cal·ly** \-'mat-i-k(ə-)lē\ *adv*

sche·ma·tize \'skē-mə-,tīz\ *vt* **1** : to form or form into a scheme or systematic arrangement **2** : to express or depict schematically — **sche·ma·ti·za·tion** \,skē-mət-ə-'zā-shən\ *n*

¹scheme \'skēm\ *n* [Gk *schēmat-, schēma* arrangement, figure, fr. *schē-, echein* to have, hold, be in (such) a condition] **1** : a graphic sketch or outline **2** : a concise statement or table : EPITOME **3** : a plan or program of action; *esp* : a crafty or secret one **4** : a systematic or organized design ⟨color *scheme* of a room⟩ ⟨his whole *scheme* of life⟩ *syn see* PLAN

scheme *vb* **1** : to form a scheme for **2** : to form plans; *also* : to engage in intrigue : PLOT — **schem·er** *n*

schem·ing *adj* : given to forming schemes; *esp* : shrewdly devious and intriguing

scher·zan·do \skert-'sän-dō\ *adv (or adj)* [It, fr. *scherzare* to joke, of Gmc origin] : in sportive manner : PLAYFULLY — used as a direction in music indicating style and tempo ⟨allegretto *scherzando*⟩

scher·zo \'skert-sō\ *n, pl* **scherzos** *or* **scher·zi** \-(,)sē\ [It, lit., joke, fr. *scherzare* to joke] : a sprightly humorous instrumental musical composition or movement commonly in quick triple time

Schick test \'shik-\ *n* [after Béla *Schick* b1877 American pediatrician] : a serological test to determine whether an individual is susceptible to diphtheria

schil·ler \'shil-ər\ *n* : a bronzy iridescent luster (as of a mineral)

schil·ling \'shil-iŋ\ *n* [G; akin to E *shilling*] **1** : the basic monetary unit of Austria **2** : a coin representing one schilling

schism \'siz-əm, 'skiz-\ *n* [Gk *schismat-, schisma*, fr. *schizein* to split] **1** : DIVISION, SEPARATION; *also* : lack of harmony : DISCORD **2 a** : formal division in or separation from a church or religious body **b** : the offense of promoting schism

¹schis·mat·ic \s(k)iz-'mat-ik\ *n* : one who creates or takes part in schism

²schismatic *adj* : of, relating to, or guilty of schism — **schis·mat·i·cal** \-'mat-i-kəl\ *adj* — **schis·mat·i·cal·ly** \-i-k(ə-)lē\ *adv*

schis·ma·tist \'s(k)iz-mət-əst\ *n* : SCHISMATIC

schis·ma·tize \-mə-,tīz\ *vb* : to take part in or induce into schism

schist \'shist\ *n* [Gk *schistos* that may be split, fr. *schizein* to split] : any of various metamorphic crystalline rocks that can be split along approximately parallel planes — **schis·tose** \'shis-,tōs\ *adj*

schis·to·some \'shis-tə-,sōm, 'skis-\ *n* : any of various elongated trematode worms with the sexes separate that mostly parasitize the blood vessels of birds and mammals and in man cause serious diseases — **schistosome** *adj*

schis·to·so·mi·a·sis \,shis-tə-sə-'mī-ə-səs, ,skis-\ *n, pl* **-a·ses** \-ə-,sēz\ : infestation with or disease caused by schistosomes

schiz- *or* **schizo-** *comb form* [Gk *schizein* to split] **1** : split : cleft ⟨*schizocarp*⟩ **2** : characterized by or involving cleavage ⟨*schizogony*⟩

schizo \'skit-sō\ *n, pl* **schiz·os** : a schizophrenic individual

schiz·o·carp \'skiz-ə-,kärp, 'skit-sə-\ *n* : a dry compound fruit that splits at maturity into several closed one-seeded carpels — **schiz·o·car·pous** \,skiz-ə-'kär-pəs, ,skit-sə-\ *adj*

schi·zog·o·ny \skiz-'äg-ə-nē, skit-'säg-\ *n* : reproduction by multiple segmentation characteristic of sporozoans (as the malaria parasite) — **schi·zog·o·nous** \-nəs\ *adj*

schiz·oid \'skit-,sóid\ *adj* : characterized by, resulting from, or suggestive of a split personality — **schizoid** *n*

schiz·o·my·cete \,skiz-ə-'mī-,sēt, ,skit-sə-, -mī-'\ *n* : BACTERIUM — **schiz·o·my·ce·tous** \-mī-'sēt-əs\ *adj*

schiz·o·phrene \'skit-sə-,frēn\ *n* : SCHIZOPHRENIC

schiz·o·phre·nia \,skit-sə-'frē-nē-ə\ *n* [NL, fr. Gk *schizein* to split + *phrēn* mind] : a mental disorder marked by loss

scep·ter

of contact with environment and by personality disintegration — **schiz·o·phren·ic** \-'fren-ik\ *adj or n*

schiz·o·phyte \'skiz-ə-,fīt, 'skit-sə-\ *n* : any of a division (Schizophyta) of plants comprising the blue-green algae and bacteria — **schiz·o·phyt·ic** \,skiz-ə-'fit-ik, ,skit-sə-\ *adj*

schle·miel \shlə-'mēl\ *n* [Yiddish *shlumiel*] *slang* : an unlucky bungler : CHUMP

schmaltz *or* **schmalz** \'shmolts\ *n* [Yiddish *shmalts*, lit., rendered fat; akin to E *smelt*] : sentimental or florid music or art — **schmaltzy** \'shmolt-sē\ *adj*

schnapps \'shnaps\ *n, pl* **schnapps** [G *schnaps*] : any of various distilled liquors; *esp* : strong Holland gin

schnau·zer \'shnaut-sər\ *n* [G, fr. *schnauze* snout; akin to E *snout*] : any of an old German breed of terriers with a long head, small ears, and wiry coat

schnit·zel \'s(h)nit-səl\ *n* [G] : a veal cutlet variously seasoned and garnished

schnoz·zle \'s(h)näz-əl\ *n, slang* : NOSE

scho·la can·to·rum \,skō-lə-,kan-'tōr-əm, -'tor-\ *n, pl* **scho·lae can·torum** \-,lē-, -,lā-, -,lī-\ [ML, school of singers] : a liturgical choir or choir school

schol·ar \'skäl-ər\ *n* [L *schola* school] **1** : one who attends a school or studies under a teacher : PUPIL **2 a** : one who has done advanced study in a special field **b** : a learned person **3** : a holder of a scholarship
  syn SCHOLAR, PUPIL, STUDENT mean one who studies under a teacher. SCHOLAR stresses enrollment and instruction in a school; PUPIL stresses being under a teacher's personal care and oversight; STUDENT commonly applies to one attending an institution of higher learning

schol·ar·ly \-ər-lē\ *adj* : characteristic of or suitable to learned persons : LEARNED, ACADEMIC

schol·ar·ship \-ər-,ship\ *n* **1** : a grant-in-aid to a student (as by a college or foundation) **2** : the character, qualities, or attainments of a scholar : LEARNING

¹scho·las·tic \skə-'las-tik\ *adj* **1 a** *often cap* : of or relating to Scholasticism 〈*scholastic* theology〉 〈*scholastic* philosophy〉 **b** : excessively subtle : PEDANTIC **2** : of or relating to schools or scholars — **scho·las·ti·cal·ly** \-ti-k(ə-)lē\ *adv*

²scholastic *n* **1** *cap* : a Scholastic philosopher **2** : a person who prefers or uses scholastic or traditional methods (as in art)

scho·las·ti·cism \skə-'las-tə-,siz-əm\ *n* **1** *cap* : a dominant movement in medieval thought typically using methods of reasoning adapted from Aristotle to interpret systematically the dogmas of faith **2** : close adherence to traditional teachings or methods (as of a school or sect)

scho·li·ast \'skō-lē-,ast, -lē-əst\ *n* : a maker of scholia : COMMENTATOR, ANNOTATOR — **scho·li·as·tic** \,skō-lē-'as-tik\ *adj*

scho·li·um \'skō-lē-əm\ *n, pl* **-lia** \-lē-ə\ *or* **-li·ums** [NL, fr. Gk *scholion* comment, scholium, fr. dim. of *scholē* lecture] **1** : a marginal annotation or comment (as on the text of a classic by an early grammarian) **2** : explanatory or elaborative matter appended to but not essential to a demonstration or a train of reasoning

¹school \'skül\ *n* [OE *scōl*, fr. L *schola*, fr. Gk *scholē* leisure, discussion, lecture, school] **1 a** : a place or establishment for teaching and learning 〈public *schools*〉 〈a music *school*〉; *also* : SCHOOLHOUSE **b** : the students or students and teachers of a school 〈a *school* outing〉 〈the whole *school* was sick〉 **c** : a session of school 〈missed *school* yesterday〉 **2** : persons holding the same opinions and beliefs or accepting the same intellectual methods or leadership 〈the radical *school* of economists〉 〈architecture after the classical *school*〉 **3** : a faculty or division within an institution of higher learning devoted to teaching, study, and research in a particular field of knowledge : COLLEGE 〈the *school* of law〉 〈a graduate *school*〉 〈the *school* of business administration〉

²school *vt* : TEACH, TRAIN; *esp* : to drill in or habituate to something 〈*school* himself in patience〉

³school *n* [MD *schole;* akin to E **⁴***shoal*] : a large number of aquatic animals of one kind (as bass) swimming together

⁴school *vi* : to swim or feed in a school 〈bluefish are *schooling*〉

school age *n* : the period of life during which a child is considered mentally and physically fit to attend school and is commonly required to do so by law

school·bag \'skül-,bag\ *n* : a bag for carrying schoolbooks and school supplies

school board *n* : a board in charge of local public schools

school·book \'skül-,buk\ *n* : a school textbook

school·boy \-,boi\ *n* : a boy attending school

school bus *n* : a vehicle used for transporting children to or from school or on activities connected with school

school·child \'skül-,chīld\ *n* : a child attending school

school·fel·low \-,fel-ō\ *n* : SCHOOLMATE

school·girl \-,gərl\ *n* : a girl attending school

school·house \-,haus\ *n* : a building used as a school

school·ing **1** : instruction in school : EDUCATION **2** : the cost of instruction and maintenance at school **3** : the training of an animal and esp. a horse to service

School·man \'skül-mən, -,man\ *n* : SCHOLASTIC

school·marm \-,mä(r)m\ *or* **school·ma'am** \-,mäm\ *n* **1** : a woman schoolteacher esp. in an old-type rural or small-town school **2** : a person who exhibits characteristics (as pedantry and priggishness) attributed to schoolteachers

school·mas·ter \-,mas-tər\ *n* : a male schoolteacher

school·mate \-,māt\ *n* : a school companion

school·mis·tress \-,mis-trəs\ *n* : a woman schoolteacher

school·room \-,rüm, -,rum\ *n* : CLASSROOM

school·teach·er \-,tē-chər\ *n* : a person who teaches in a school

school·time \-,tīm\ *n* **1** : the time for beginning a session of school or during which school is held **2** : the period of life spent in school or in study — usu. used in pl.

school·work \-,wərk\ *n* : lessons done in classes at school or assigned to be done at home

school·yard \-,yärd\ *n* : the playground of a school

schoo·ner \'skü-nər\ *n* **1** : a fore-and-aft rigged ship with two or more masts **2** : a large tall glass (as for beer) **3** : PRAIRIE SCHOONER

schot·tische \'shät-ish, shä-'tēsh\ *n* [G, fr. *schottisch* Scottish] **1** : a round dance similar to the polka but slower **2** : music for the schottische

schuss \'shus, 'shüs\ *n* [G, lit., shot] **1** : a straight high-speed run on skis **2** : a straightaway downhill skiing course — **schuss** *vb*

schwa \'shwä\ *n* [G, fr. Heb *shěwā*] **1** : an unstressed vowel that is the usual sound of the first and last vowels of the English word *America* **2** : the symbol ə commonly used for a schwa and sometimes also for a similarly articulated stressed vowel (as in *cut*)

sci·at·ic \sī-'at-ik\ *adj* [MF *sciatique*, fr. LL *sciaticus* of sciatica, modif. of Gk *ischiadikos*, fr. *ischiad-, ischias* sciatica, fr. *ischion* ischium] **1** : of, relating to, or situated near the hip **2** : of, relating to, or caused by sciatica

sci·at·i·ca \sī-'at-i-kə\ *n* : pain along the course of a sciatic nerve esp. in the back of the thigh; *also* : pain in or near the hips

sci·ence \'sī-ən(t)s\ *n* [L *scientia*, fr. *scient-, sciens* having knowledge, fr. prp. of *scire* to know] **1 a** : a department of systematized knowledge that is an object of study 〈the *science* of theology〉; *esp* : one of the natural sciences 〈chemistry is a *science*〉 **b** : something (as a sport or technique) that may be studied or learned like systematized knowledge **2** : knowledge covering general truths or the operation of general laws esp. as obtained and tested through the scientific method 〈application of the laws of *science* to a study of atomic nuclei〉

science fiction *n* : fiction involving the impact of actual or imagined science upon society or individuals

sci·ent \'sī-ənt\ *adj* : KNOWING, SKILLFUL

sci·en·tial \sī-'en-chəl\ *adj* **1** : relating to or producing knowledge or science **2** : having efficient knowledge : CAPABLE

sci·en·tif·ic \,sī-ən-'tif-ik\ *adj* : of, relating to, or exhibiting the methods or principles of science — **sci·en·tif·i·cal·ly** \-'tif-i-k(ə-)lē\ *adv*

scientific method *n* : principles and procedures for the systematic pursuit of knowledge involving the recognition and formulation of a problem, the collection of data through observation and experiment, and the formulation and testing of hypotheses

scientific notation *n* : the representation of numbers as the product of a decimal between 1 and 10 and a power of 10

sci·en·tism \'sī-ən-,tiz-əm\ *n* **1** : methods and attitudes

---

j joke; ŋ sing; ō flow; ȯ flaw; ȯi coin; th thin; th this; ü loot; u̇ foot; y yet; yü few; yu̇ furious; zh vision

typical of or attributed to the natural scientist **2** : the proposition that only scientific and esp. materialistic methods can be used effectively in the pursuit of knowledge (as in philosophy or the social sciences)

sci·en·tist \'sī-ən-təst\ *n* **1** : one learned in science and esp. natural science : a scientific investigator **2** *cap* : CHRISTIAN SCIENTIST

sci·en·tis·tic \,sī-ən-'tis-tik\ *adj* **1** : devoted to scientific methods **2** : relating to or characterized by scientism

sci·li·cet \'skē-li-,ket, 'sī-lə-,set\ *adv* [L, surely, to wit, fr. *scire* to know + *licet* it is permitted, fr. *licēre* to be permitted] : to wit : NAMELY

scil·la \'s(k)il-ə\ *n* [L, squill] : any of a genus of Old World bulbous herbs of the lily family often grown for their clusters of pink, blue, or white flowers

scim·i·tar \'sim-ət-ər, -ə-,tär\ *n* [It *scimitarra*] : a saber that has a curved blade with the edge on the convex side and is used esp. by Arabs and Turks

scimitar

scin·til·la \sin-'til-ə\ *n* [L] : IOTA, TRACE

scin·til·late \'sint-ᵊl-,āt\ *vi* **1** : to give off sparks : SPARK **2 a** : to emit quick flashes as if throwing off sparks **b** : SPARKLE, TWINKLE **3** : to perform with dazzling brilliance **syn** see GLISTEN — **scin·til·lant** \-ᵊl-ənt\ *adj* — **scin·til·lant·ly** *adv* — **scin·til·la·tion** \,sint-ᵊl-'ā-shən\ *n* — **scin·til·la·tor** \'sint-ᵊl-,āt-ər\ *n*

scintillation counter *n* : a device for detecting and registering individual scintillations (as in radioactive emission)

sci·o·lism \'sī-ə-,liz-əm\ *n* [LL *sciolus* smatterer, fr. L *scire* to know] : a superficial show of learning — **sci·o·list** \-ləst\ *n* — **sci·o·lis·tic** \,sī-ə-'lis-tik\ *adj*

sci·on \'sī-ən\ *n* [MF *cion*] **1** : a detached living portion of a plant joined to a stock in grafting and usu. supplying solely aerial parts to a graft **2** : DESCENDANT, CHILD ⟨a *scion* of a royal stock⟩

scir·rhous \'s(k)ir-əs\ *adj* : hard or indurated with or as if with fibrous tissue

scis·sile \'sis-əl, -,īl\ *adj* : capable of being cut smoothly or split easily

scis·sion \'sizh-ən\ *n* : a dividing of or split in a group or union

¹scis·sor \'siz-ər\ *n* : SCISSORS

²scissor *vt* : to cut, cut up, or cut off with scissors or shears

scis·sors \'siz-ərz\ *n sing or pl* [ME *sisoures*, fr. MF *cisoires*, fr. LL *cisorium* cutting instrument, irreg. fr. L *caes-, caedere* to cut] **1** : a cutting instrument having two blades so fastened together that the sharp edges slide past each other **2** : a gymnastic or wrestling feat in which the leg movements suggest the action of scissors

scissors kick *n* : a swimming kick used in trudgen strokes and sidestrokes in which the legs move like scissors

scler- *or* **sclero-** *comb form* [Gk *sklēros*] **1** : hard ⟨*scler*ite⟩ ⟨*sclero*derma⟩ **2** : hardness ⟨*sclero*meter⟩

scle·ra \'sklir-ə\ *n* : the dense fibrous white or bluish white tissue that covers that portion of the eyeball not covered by the cornea

scle·re·id \'sklir-ē-əd\ *n* : a supporting cell of a plant that is lignified and often mineralized — called also *stone cell*

scle·ren·chy·ma \sklə-'reŋ-kə-mə\ *n* : a protective or supporting tissue in higher plants composed of cells with walls thickened and lignified and often mineralized — compare COLLENCHYMA — **scle·ren·chym·a·tous** \,sklir-ən-'kim-ət-əs, ,skler-\ *adj*

scle·rite \'skli(ə)r-,īt, 'skle(ə)r-\ *n* : a hard chitinous or calcareous plate or piece (as of the arthropod skeleton)

scle·roid \'skli(ə)r-,óid, 'skle(ə)r-\ *adj* : HARD, INDURATED ⟨*scleroid* tissue⟩

scle·ro·pro·tein \,sklir-ō-'prō-,tēn, ,skler-, -'prōt-ē-ən\ *n* : any of various fibrous proteins esp. from connective and skeletal tissues

scle·rose \sklə-'rōs\ *vb* **1** : to cause sclerosis in **2** : to undergo sclerosis

scle·ro·sis \sklə-'rō-səs\ *n* : a usu. pathological hardening of tissue esp. from increase of connective tissue

¹scle·rot·ic \sklə-'rät-ik\ *adj* **1** : being or relating to the sclera **2** : of, relating to, or affected with sclerosis

²sclerotic *n* : SCLERA

¹scoff \'skäf, 'skóf\ *n* [ME *scof*] : an expression of scorn, derision, or contempt : GIBE

²scoff *vb* : to show or treat with contempt by derisive acts or language : MOCK — **scoff·er** *n*

syn SNEER: SCOFF implies insolent or irreverent mockery or derision ⟨*scoffed* at the coach's training rules⟩ SNEER implies an ill-natured contempt often half concealed and conveyed only in the tone of voice or facial expression

scoff·law \-,ló\ *n* : a contemptuous law violator

¹scold \'skōld\ *n* [ME *scald, scold*] **1** : one addicted to abusive ribald speech **2** : one that scolds habitually or persistently

²scold *vb* **1** : to find fault noisily **2** : to rebuke severely or angrily — **scold·er** *n*

sco·lex \'skō-,leks\ *n, pl* **sco·li·ces** *also* **sco·le·ces** \-lə-,sēz\ *or* **sco·lex·es** \-,lek-səz\ [NL *scolic-, scolex*, fr. Gk *skōlēk-, skōlēx* worm] : the head of a tapeworm

sco·li·o·sis \,skō-lē-'ō-səs, ,skäl-ē-\ *n* : a lateral curvature of the spine — compare KYPHOSIS, LORDOSIS — **sco·li·ot·ic** \-'ät-ik\ *adj*

scom·broid \'skäm-,bróid\ *n* [Gk *skombros* mackerel] : any of a group (Scombroidea) of marine spiny-finned fishes (as mackerels, tunas, albacores, bonitos, and swordfishes) of great economic importance as food fishes — **scombroid** *adj*

sconce \'skän(t)s\ *n* [MF *esconse* screened lantern, fr. *escondre* to hide, fr. L *abscondere*] : a candlestick or group of candlesticks mounted on a plaque and fastened to a wall

scone \'skōn, 'skän\ *n* : a quick bread usu. made with oatmeal or barley flour and baked on a griddle

¹scoop \'sküp\ *n* [MD *schope*] **1 a** : a large shovel (as for shoveling coal) **b** : a tool or utensil shaped like a shovel for digging into a soft substance and lifting out a portion ⟨a *flour scoop*⟩ **c** : a small tool of similar shape for cutting or gouging **2** : an act or the action of scooping : a motion made with or as if with a scoop **3 a** : the amount held by a scoop ⟨a *scoop* of sugar⟩ **b** : a hole made by scooping **4** : information of immediate interest; *also* : BEAT 5b — **scoop·ful** \-,fúl\ *n*

²scoop *vt* **1** : to take out or up or empty with or as if with a scoop **2** : to make hollow : dig out **3** : BEAT 5a(2) — **scoop·er** *n*

scoot \'sküt\ *vi* : to go suddenly and swiftly : DART — **scoot** *n*

scoot·er \'sküt-ər\ *n* **1** : a child's foot-operated vehicle consisting of a narrow board mounted between two wheels tandem with an upright steering handle attached to the front wheel **2** : MOTOR SCOOTER

scop \'skäp\ *n* [OE] : an Old English bard or poet

¹scope \'skōp\ *n* [It *scopo* purpose, goal, fr. Gk *skopos*, fr. *skeptesthai* to look at] **1** : space or opportunity for unhampered action or thought : chance to develop **2** : extent covered, reached, or viewed : RANGE ⟨a subject broad in *scope*⟩

²scope *n* : any of various instruments for viewing: as **a** : MICROSCOPE **b** : TELESCOPE **c** : OSCILLOSCOPE **d** : RADARSCOPE

-scope \,skōp\ *n comb form* [Gk *-skopion*, fr. *skeptesthai* to look at; akin to E *spy*] : means (as an instrument) for viewing or observing ⟨micro*scope*⟩

sco·pol·amine \skō-'päl-ə-,mēn\ *n* : a poisonous alkaloid found in some plants of the nightshade family and used as a truth serum or esp. with morphine as a sedative

scop·u·la \'skäp-yə-lə\ *n* [LL, dim. of L *scopa* broom] : a bushy tuft of hairs (as on a bee) — **scop·u·late** \-,lāt\ *adj*

-s·co·py \s-kə-pē\ *n comb form, pl* **-pies** : viewing : observation ⟨radio*scopy*⟩

scor·bu·tic \skór-'byüt-ik\ *adj* [NL *scorbutus* scurvy] : of, relating to, or resembling scurvy; *also* : diseased with scurvy — **scor·bu·ti·cal·ly** \-'byüt-i-k(ə-)lē\ *adv*

¹scorch \'skórch\ *vb* [ME *scorchen*] **1 a** : to burn superficially usu. to the point of changing color, texture, or flavor ⟨shoes *scorching* on the hearth⟩ ⟨*scorch* a roast⟩ **b** : to parch and discolor with or as if with intense heat ⟨lawns *scorched* by summer suns⟩ **2** : to distress or embarrass with usu. sarcastic censure **3** : to travel at great and usu. excessive speed ⟨he went *scorching* by on his motorcycle⟩

²scorch *n* **1** : a result of scorching **2** : a browning of plant tissues usu. from disease or heat

scorched earth *n* : land stripped of anything that could be of use to an invading enemy force

---

ə abut; ᵊ kitten; ər further; a back; ā bake; ä cot, cart; aú out; ch chin; e less; ē easy; g gift; i trip; ī life

scorch·er \\'skȯr-chər\\ *n* : one that scorches; *esp* : a very hot day

¹score \\'skō(ə)r, 'skȯ(ə)r\\ *n, pl* **scores** *or* **score** [ON *skor* notch, tally, twenty; akin to E *shear*] **1 a** : TWENTY **b** : a group of 20 things — often used in combination with a cardinal number ⟨five*score*⟩ **c** *pl* : an indefinite large number **2 a** : a line made with or as if with a sharp instrument **b** : a mark used as a starting point or goal or for keeping account **3 a** : a reckoning kept by making marks on a tally **b** : ACCOUNT **c** : amount due : INDEBTEDNESS **4** : an obligation or injury kept in mind for requital **5 a** : REASON, GROUND **b** : SUBJECT, TOPIC **6** : a musical composition in written or printed notation **7** : a number expressing accomplishment (as in a game or test) or quality (as of a product) ⟨had a *score* of 80 out of a possible 100⟩; *also* : RATING ⟨the highest *score* was 83⟩ **8** : the stark inescapable facts of a situation ⟨we won't know what the *score* is until the laboratory results are in⟩ — **score·less** \\'skō(ə)r-ləs, 'skȯ(ə)r-\\ *adj*

²score *vb* **1 a** : to record by or as if by notches on a tally **b** : to keep score in a game or contest **2** : to mark with lines, grooves, scratches, or notches **3** : BERATE, SCOLD **4 a** : to make a score in or as if in a game : TALLY ⟨*score* a run⟩ **b** : to enable (a base runner) to make a score ⟨*scored* the man on second base with a single⟩ **c** : to have as a value in a game or contest : COUNT ⟨a touchdown *scores* six points⟩ **d** : ACHIEVE, WIN **5** : to determine the merit of : GRADE **6 a** : to write or arrange (music) for specific instruments or voices **b** : to make an orchestration of **7 a** : to gain or have the advantage **b** : to be successful — **scor·er** *n*

score·board \\'skōr-,bȯrd, 'skȯr-,bȯrd\\ *n* : a large board for displaying the score of a game or match

score·card \\-,kärd\\ *n* : a card for recording the score (as of a game)

score·keep·er \\-,kē-pər\\ *n* : one chosen or appointed to record the score during the progress of a game or contest

sco·ria \\'skȯr-ē-ə, 'skōr-\\ *n, pl* **-ri·ae** \\-ē-,ē, -ē-,ī\\ [Gk *skōria*, fr. *skōr* excrement] **1** : the refuse from melting of metals or reduction of ores : SLAG **2** : rough vesicular cindery lava — **sco·ri·a·ceous** \\,skōr-ē-'ā-shəs, ,skȯr-\\ *adj*

¹scorn \\'skȯrn\\ *n* [OF *escarn*, of Gmc origin] **1** : an emotion involving both anger and disgust : vigorous contempt **2** : an object of extreme disdain, contempt, or derision

²scorn *vb* **1** : to reject with bitter or angry contempt ⟨*scorn* a bribe⟩ **2** : to refuse because of scorn : DISDAIN ⟨*scorned* to reply to the charge⟩ **syn** see DESPISE — **scorn·er** *n*

scorn·ful \\'skȯrn-fəl\\ *adj* : full of scorn : CONTEMPTUOUS — **scorn·ful·ly** \\-fə-lē\\ *adv* — **scorn·ful·ness** *n*

Scor·pio \\'skȯr-pē-,ō\\ *n* [L, lit., scorpion] **1** : SCORPIUS **2** : the 8th sign of the zodiac — see ZODIAC table

scor·pi·oid \\-pē-,ȯid\\ *adj* **1** : of, relating to, or resembling the scorpion **2** : curved at the end like a scorpion's tail : CIRCINATE ⟨a *scorpioid* inflorescence⟩

scor·pi·on \\'skȯr-pē-ən\\ *n* [L *scorpion-, scorpio*, modif. of Gk *skorpios*] **1** : any of an order (Scorpionida) of arachnids having an elongated body and a narrow segmented tail with a venomous sting at the tip **2** : something that incites to action like a sting

scorpion fish *n* : any of a family of large-headed spiny-finned sea fishes including some with poisonous spines and others esteemed as food

Scor·pi·us \\'skȯr-pē-əs\\ *n* [L, fr. Gk *Skorpios*, lit., scorpion] : a southern constellation that is located partly in the Milky Way and adjoins Libra

scorpion

scot \\'skät\\ *n* [ME, fr. ON *skot* shot, contribution; akin to E *shot*] : money assessed or paid

Scot \\'skät\\ *n* **1** : one of a Gaelic people of northern Ireland settling in Scotland about A.D. 500 **2 a** : a native or inhabitant of Scotland **b** : a person of Scotch descent

scotch \\'skäch\\ *vt* [ME *scocchen* to gash] **1** : to injure so as to make temporarily harmless **2** : to stamp out : CRUSH ⟨*scotch* a rebellion⟩; *esp* : to end decisively by demonstrating the falsity of ⟨*scotch* a rumor⟩

¹Scotch \\'skäch\\ *adj* **1** : of, relating to, or characteristic of Scotland, the Scotch, or Scots **2** : FRUGAL

²Scotch *n* **1** : SCOTS **2 Scotch** *pl* : the people of Scotland **3** : whiskey distilled in Scotland esp. from barley

Scotch broth *n* : a soup made from beef or mutton and vegetables and thickened with barley

Scotch-Irish *adj* : of, relating to, or characteristic of the population of northern Ireland that is descended from Scotch settlers or of their descendants emigrating to the U.S. before 1846 — **Scotch-Irish** *n*

Scotch·man \\'skäch-mən\\ *n* : a man of Scotch descent : a male Scot — **Scotch·wom·an** \\-,wu̇m-ən\\ *n*

Scotch terrier *n* : SCOTTISH TERRIER

sco·ter \\'skōt-ər\\ *n, pl* **scoters** *or* **scoter** : any of several sea ducks of northern coasts of Europe and No. America

scot-free \\'skät-'frē\\ *adj* : completely free from obligation, harm, or penalty

sco·to·pia \\skə-'tō-pē-ə\\ *n* [Gk *skotos* darkness] : vision in dim light believed to be mediated by the retinal rods — **sco·to·pic** \\-'tō-pik\\ *adj*

¹Scots \\'skäts\\ *adj* : SCOTCH 1

²Scots *n* : the English language of Scotland

Scots·man \\'skäts-mən\\ *n* : SCOTCHMAN

scot·tie \\'skät-ē\\ *n* **1** *cap* : SCOTCHMAN **2** : SCOTTISH TERRIER

¹Scot·tish \\'skät-ish\\ *adj* : SCOTCH 1

²Scottish *n* : SCOTS

Scottish Gaelic *n* : the Gaelic language of Scotland

Scottish terrier *n* : any of an old Scottish breed of terrier with short legs, large head, small erect ears, broad deep chest, and a thick harsh coat

scoun·drel \\'skaun-drəl\\ *n* : a mean worthless fellow : VILLAIN — **scoundrel** *adj* — **scoun·drel·ly** \\-drə-lē\\ *adj*

¹scour \\'skau̇(ə)r\\ *vb* [ME *scuren*] **1** : to move about or through quickly esp. in search **2** : to examine minutely and rapidly — **scour·er** *n*

²scour *vb* [ME *scouren*] **1 a** : to rub hard for the purpose of cleansing **b** : to remove by rubbing hard and washing ⟨*scour* spots from the stove⟩ **2** : to free from foreign matter or impurities by or as if by washing ⟨*scour* wool⟩ **3 a** : to clear, dig, or remove by a powerful current of water **b** : to wear away (as by water) : ERODE ⟨a stream *scouring* its banks⟩ **4** : to suffer from diarrhea or dysentery **5** : to become clean and bright by rubbing — **scour·er** *n*

³scour *n* **1** : an action or result of scouring **2** *pl* : DIARRHEA, DYSENTERY

¹scourge \\'skərj\\ *n* [AF *escorge*, fr. (assumed) OF *escorgie* to whip, fr. OF *es-* ex- + L *corrigia* whip] **1** : WHIP, LASH **2 a** : an instrument of punishment or criticism **b** : a cause of widespread or great affliction ⟨the *scourge* of widespread unemployment⟩

²scourge *vt* **1** : to whip severely : FLOG **2** : to subject to affliction : DEVASTATE ⟨a region *scourged* by malaria⟩ — **scourg·er** *n*

scouring rush *n* : EQUISETUM; *esp* : one with strongly siliceous stems formerly used for scouring

¹scout \\'skaut\\ *vb* [MF *escouter* to listen, fr. L *auscultare*] **1** : to go about and observe in search of information : RECONNOITER, SPY ⟨*scout* an area for minerals⟩ ⟨*scouted* around the enemy position⟩ **2 a** : to make a search ⟨*scout* about for firewood⟩ **b** : to find by searching ⟨*scouted* up the necessary materials⟩

²scout *n* **1** : the act or an instance of scouting : RECONNAISSANCE **2 a** : one sent to obtain information and esp. to reconnoiter in war **b** : WATCHMAN, LOOKOUT **c** : a person who searches for talented newcomers (as to acting or a sport) **3 a** : BOY SCOUT **b** : GIRL SCOUT **4** : FELLOW, GUY

³scout *vb* [of Scand origin] **1** : to make fun of : MOCK **2** : to reject scornfully as absurd : SCOFF ⟨*scout* a theory⟩

scout car *n* : a fast armored military reconnaissance vehicle with four-wheel drive and open top

scout·craft \\-,kraft\\ *n* : the craft, skill, or practice of a scout

scout·er \\-ər\\ *n* **1** : one that scouts **2** : a member of the Boy Scouts of America over 18 years of age

scout·ing \\'skaut-iŋ\\ *n* **1** : the action of one that scouts **2** : the activities of the various boy scout and girl scout movements

scout·mas·ter \\'skaut-,mas-tər\\ *n* : the leader of a band of scouts and esp. of a troop of boy scouts

---

j joke; **ŋ** sing; **ō** flow; **ȯ** flaw; **ȯi** coin; **th** thin; **th** this; **ü** loot; **u̇** foot; **y** yet; **yü** few; **yu̇** furious; **zh** vision

scow \'skaú\ *n* [D *schouw*] : a large flat-bottomed boat with broad square ends used chiefly for transporting sand, gravel, or refuse

¹**scowl** \'skaúl\ *vb* [ME *skoulen*] **1** : to draw down the forehead in a frowning expression of displeasure **2** : to exhibit or express with a threatening aspect — **scowl·er** *n*

²**scowl** *n* : a facial expression of displeasure : FROWN

scow·man \'skaú-mən\ *n* : one who works on a scow

¹**scrab·ble** \'skrab-əl\ *vb* **scrab·bled; scrab·bling** \'skrab-(ə-)liŋ\ [D *schrabbelen* to scratch] **1** : SCRAWL, SCRIBBLE **2** : to scratch or scrape with hands or paws; *also* : SCRAMBLE **3** : to struggle by or as if by scraping or scratching ⟨*scrabble* for a living⟩ — **scrab·bler** \-(ə-)lər\ *n*

²**scrabble** *n* : an act or instance of scrabbling

scrab·bly \'skrab-(ə-)lē\ *adj* **scrab·bli·er; -est 1** : SCRATCHY, RASPY **2** : SPARSE, SCRUBBY

¹**scrag** \'skrag\ *n* **1** : a rawboned or scrawny person or animal **2** : the lean bony end of a neck of mutton or veal

²**scrag** *vt* **scragged; scrag·ging** : to wring the neck of

scrag·gly \'skrag-lē\ *adj* **scrag·gli·er; -est** : IR-REGULAR; *also* : RAGGED, UNKEMPT

scrag·gy \'skrag-ē\ *adj* **scrag·gi·er; -est 1** : ROUGH, JAGGED **2** : being lean and long : SCRAWNY

scram \'skram\ *vi* **scrammed; scram·ming** : to go away at once ⟨*scram*, you're not wanted⟩

scram·ble \'skram-bəl\ *vb* **scram·bled; scram·bling** \-b(ə-)liŋ\ **1** : to move or climb hastily on all fours **2** : to move or act urgently or unceremoniously in trying to win or escape something ⟨*scramble* for front seats⟩ ⟨*scrambled* out of the path of the bear⟩ **3** : SPRAWL, STRAGGLE **4 a** : to toss or mix together : JUMBLE **b** : to prepare (eggs) by stirring during cooking — **scramble** *n* — **scram·bler** \-b(ə-)lər\ *n*

scran·nel \'skran-ᵊl\ *adj* : HARSH, UNMELODIOUS

¹**scrap** \'skrap\ *n* [ON *skrap* scraps, trifles] **1** *pl* : fragments of discarded or leftover food **2** : a small bit : FRAGMENT ⟨*scraps* of cloth⟩ ⟨not a *scrap* of truth in the story⟩ **3** : discarded or waste metal for reprocessing ⟨buy *scrap*⟩

²**scrap** *vt* **scrapped; scrap·ping 1** : to break up into scrap ⟨*scrap* a battleship⟩ **2** : to discard as worthless ⟨*scrap* outworn methods⟩

³**scrap** *adj* : made up of odds and ends ⟨a *scrap* meal⟩; *also* : constituting scrap ⟨*scrap* metal⟩

⁴**scrap** *n* : QUARREL, FIGHT

⁵**scrap** *vi* **scrapped; scrap·ping** : QUARREL, FIGHT — **scrap·per** *n*

scrap·book \'skrap-,búk\ *n* : a blank book for mementos (as clippings and pictures)

¹**scrape** \'skrāp\ *vb* [ON *skrapa*] **1 a** : to remove by repeated strokes of an edged tool ⟨*scrape* off rust⟩ **b** : to clean or smooth by rubbing with an edged tool or abrasive **2** : to move along or over something with a grating noise : GRATE ⟨*scrape* the curb with a car⟩; *also* : to damage by such an action ⟨*scrape* a fender⟩ **3 a** : to gather with difficulty and little by little ⟨*scrape* together a few dollars⟩ **b** : to barely get by ⟨*scraped* through heavy traffic⟩ ⟨had just enough meat to *scrape* by at dinner⟩ ⟨*scraped* through with low marks⟩ — **scrap·er** *n*

²**scrape** *n* **1 a** : the act or process of scraping **b** : a sound, mark, or injury made by scraping ⟨a *scrape* on his leg⟩ **2** : a bow made by drawing back the foot **3** : a disagreeable predicament

scrap heap *n* **1** : a pile of discarded metal **2** : the place to which useless things are relegated : DISCARD

scrap·ple \'skrap-əl\ *n* : a seasoned mush of meat scraps and cornmeal set in a mold and served sliced and fried

¹**scrap·py** \'skrap-ē\ *adj* **scrap·pi·er; -est** : consisting of scraps : FRAGMENTARY

²**scrappy** *adj* **scrap·pi·er; -est 1** : QUARRELSOME **2** : aggressive and determined in spirit — **scrap·pi·ness** *n*

¹**scratch** \'skrach\ *vb* [blend of E dial. *scrat* to scratch and obs. E *cratch* to scratch] **1** : to dig, rub, or mar with or as if with the claws or nails **2 a** : SCRAPE 3 **b** : to make a living by hard work and saving **3** : to write or draw on a surface esp. hastily or carelessly : SCRAWL **4 a** : to erase by or as if by scraping away ⟨*scratch* a name from a list⟩ **b** : to withdraw (an entry) from competition **5 a** : to use the claws or nails in digging, tearing, or wounding **b** : to scrape or rub oneself (as to relieve itching) **6** : to make a thin grating sound ⟨this pen *scratches*⟩ — **scratch·er** *n*

²**scratch** *n* **1 a** : an act or sound of scratching **b** : a mark (as a line) or injury made by scratching **2 a** : the line from which contestants start in a race **b** : NOTHING ⟨start from *scratch*⟩ **3** : satisfactory condition or performance ⟨not up to *scratch*⟩

³**scratch** *adj* : intended for chance or casual action or use and usu. of less than the best quality ⟨*scratch* team⟩

scratch hit *n* : a batted ball not solidly hit or cleanly played yet credited to the batter as a base hit

scratch line *n* : a starting or restraining line in any of several track-and-field events

scratch paper *n* : paper that may be used for casual writing (as jottings or memoranda)

scratch test *n* : a test for allergic susceptibility made by rubbing an extract of an allergy-producing substance into small breaks or scratches in the skin

scratchy \'skrach-ē\ *adj* **scratch·i·er; -est 1** : likely to scratch or irritate : PRICKLY ⟨*scratchy* undergrowth⟩ ⟨*scratchy* woolens⟩ **2** : making a scratching noise **3** : marked or made with scratches ⟨a *scratchy* surface⟩ ⟨*scratchy* handwriting⟩ **4** : uneven in quality : RAGGED — **scratch·i·ly** \'skrach-ə-lē\ *adv* — **scratch·i·ness** \'skrach-ē-nəs\ *n*

scrawl \'skról\ *vb* : to write or draw awkwardly, hastily, or carelessly : SCRIBBLE — **scrawl** *n* — **scrawl·er** *n* — **scrawl·i·ness** \'skró-lē-nəs\ *n* — **scrawly** \'skró-lē\ *adj*

scraw·ny \'skró-nē\ *adj* **scraw·ni·er; -est** : ill-nourished : SKINNY ⟨*scrawny* cattle⟩ — **scraw·ni·ness** *n*

¹**scream** \'skrēm\ *vb* [ME *scremen*] **1** : to cry out, sound, or utter loudly and shrilly ⟨*screaming* with rage⟩ ⟨the saw *screamed* through the wood⟩ ⟨*screamed* a curse at his enemy⟩ **2** : to produce or give a vivid, startling, or alarming effect or expression ⟨a *screaming* red⟩ ⟨headlines that *screamed* the news⟩

²**scream** *n* **1** : a loud shrill prolonged cry or noise ⟨*screams* of terror⟩ **2** : one that provokes screams of laughter ⟨she's a *scream* when she gets going⟩

syn SHRIEK, SCREECH: SCREAM is the general term for utterance that is sharpened and prolonged by intensity of feeling. SHRIEK may imply an intensified scream or suggest a degree of wildness or lack of control ⟨*shrieks* of dismay⟩ ⟨hysterical *shrieks* of laughter⟩ SCREECH implies a harsh shrillness painful to the hearer and suggesting an unearthly or, often, a comic effect

scream·er \'skrē-mər\ *n* **1** : one that screams **2** : any of several large So. American birds with spurs on the wings **3** : a sensationally startling headline

scream·ing·ly \'skrē-miŋ-lē\ *adv* : to an extreme degree

¹**screech** \'skrēch\ *vb* [ME *scrichen*] **1** : to utter or utter with a shrill harsh cry : make an outcry usu. in terror or pain **2** : to make a sound like a screech — **screech·er** *n*

²**screech** *n* **1** : a shrill harsh cry usu. expressing pain or terror **2** : a sound like a screech ⟨*screech* of brakes⟩ **syn** see SCREAM

screed \'skrēd\ *n* [OE *scrēade* fragment, shred] : a lengthy discourse

¹**screen** \'skrēn\ *n* [MF *escren*, fr. MD *scherm*] **1** : a device or partition used to hide, restrain, protect, or decorate ⟨a wire-mesh window *screen*⟩; *also* : something that serves to shelter, protect, or conceal ⟨a *screen* of fighter planes⟩ ⟨used the store as a *screen* for his illegal activities⟩ **2** : a sieve or perforated material set in a frame and used for separating finer parts from coarser parts (as of sand) **3 a** : flat surface upon which a picture or series of pictures is projected; *also* : the surface upon which the image appears in a television or radar receiver **b** : the motion-picture industry

²**screen** *vb* **1** : to guard from injury or danger **2 a** : to shelter, protect, or separate with or as if with a screen **b** : to pass (as coal, gravel, or ashes) through a screen to separate the fine part from the coarse; *also* : to remove by or as if by a screen **c** : to examine systematically in order to separate into groups; *also* : to select or eliminate by such means **3** : to provide with a screen and esp. with screening to keep out insects ⟨*screen* a porch⟩ **4 a** : to project (as a motion-picture film) on a screen **b** : to present in a motion picture **c** : to appear on a motion-picture screen — **screen·a·ble** \'skrē-nə-bəl\ *adj* — **screen·er** *n*

screen·ing \'skrē-niŋ\ *n* **1** *pl* : material (as fine coal)

separated out by passage through or retention on a screen **2** : a mesh (as of metal or plastic) used esp. for screens
screen pass *n* : a forward pass in football in which the receiver is protected by a screen of blockers
screen·play \'skrēn-,plā\ *n* : the written form of a story prepared for film production and including description of characters, details of scenes and settings, dialogue, and stage directions
screen test *n* : a short film sequence testing the ability of a prospective motion-picture actor — **screen–test** *vt*
screen·writ·er \-,rīt-ər\ *n* : a writer of screenplays
¹screw \'skrü\ *n* [MF *escroe* screw nut] **1 a** : a simple machine consisting of a spirally grooved solid cylinder and a correspondingly grooved cylindrical hollow part into which it fits **b** : a nail-shaped or rod-shaped metal piece with a spiral groove and a slotted or recessed head used for fastening pieces of solid material together **2 a** : a screw-shaped form : SPIRAL **b** : a turn of a screw; *also* : a twist like the turn of a screw **c** : a screw-shaped device (as a corkscrew) **3** *chiefly Brit* : a small packet (as of tobacco or pepper) **4** : a sharp bargainer **5** : SCREW PROPELLER **6** : THUMBSCREW 2 — **screw·like** \-,līk\ *adj*

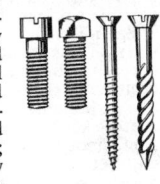

screws 1b

²screw *vb* **1 a** (1) : to attach, fasten, or close by means of a screw ⟨*screw* a hinge to a door⟩ (2) : to operate, tighten, or adjust by means of a screw ⟨*screw* up a sagging beam with a jack⟩ **b** : to move or cause to move spirally as a screw does; *also* : to close or set in position by such an action ⟨*screw* on a lid⟩⟨*screw* a jar shut⟩ **2 a** : to twist out of shape ⟨a face *screwed* up in pain⟩ **b** : SQUINT **3** : to increase in amount or capability ⟨*screwed* himself up to the point of asking for help⟩ ⟨*screwed* up his nerve⟩ — **screw·er** *n*
¹screw·ball \'skrü-,bȯl\ *n* **1** : a baseball pitch having reverse spin and a break in opposite direction to a curve **2** : a whimsical, eccentric, or crazy person
²screwball *adj* : crazily eccentric or whimsical
screw·driv·er \'skrü-,drī-vər\ *n* : a tool for turning screws
screw eye *n* : a screw having a head in the form of a loop
screw·fly \'skrü-,flī\ *n* : the adult of a screwworm
screw pine *n* : any of a genus of tropical monocotyledonous plants with slender palmlike stems, often huge prop roots, and terminal crowns of swordlike leaves — called also *pandanus*
screw propeller *n* : a device consisting of a hub with twisted radiating blades that is used for propelling airplanes or ships
screw thread *n* : the projecting spiral rib of a screw between the grooves
screw·worm \'skrü-,wərm\ *n* : the grub of a two-winged fly of warm parts of America that develops esp. in sores or wounds of mammals
screwy \'skrü-ē\ *adj* **screw·i·er; -est 1** : crazily absurd, eccentric, or unusual **2** : CRAZY, INSANE
scrib·al \'skrī-bəl\ *adj* : of, relating to, or due to a scribe ⟨*scribal* error⟩
scrib·ble \'skrib-əl\ *vb* **scrib·bled; scrib·bling** \'skrib-(ə-)liŋ\ [ML *scribillare*, fr. L *scribere* to write] : to write or draw hastily or carelessly — **scribble** *n*
scrib·bler \'skrib-lər\ *n* **1** : one that scribbles **2** : a minor or inferior author
¹scribe \'skrīb\ *n* [L *scriba* official or public secretary, fr. *scribere* to write] **1** : a scholar of the Jewish law in New Testament times **2 a** : an official or public secretary or clerk **b** : a copier of manuscripts **3** : AUTHOR; *esp* : JOURNALIST
²scribe *vt* : to mark or make by cutting or scratching with a pointed instrument ⟨*scribe* a line on metal⟩
scrib·er \'skrī-bər\ *n* : a sharp-pointed tool for marking off material (as wood or metal) to be cut
scrim \'skrim\ *n* : a light coarse usu. cotton fabric of open weave
¹scrim·mage \'skrim-ij\ *n* [alter. of ¹*skirmish*] **1** : a confused fight : SCUFFLE **2 a** : the interplay between two football teams that begins with the snap of the ball and continues until the ball is dead **b** : practice play between a team's squads (as in football)

²scrimmage *vi* : to take part in a scrimmage — **scrim·mag·er** *n*
scrimp \'skrimp\ *vb* **1** : to make too small, short, or scanty : SKIMP **2** : to be frugal : ECONOMIZE — **scrimpy** \'skrim-pē\ *adj*
scrim·shaw \'skrim-,shȯ\ *n* : carved or engraved articles made esp. by American whalers and from whale ivory — **scrimshaw** *vb*
¹scrip \'skrip\ *n* [ML *scrippum* pilgrim's knapsack] *archaic* : a small bag or wallet
²scrip *n* [short for *script*] **1** : a document showing that the holder or bearer is entitled to something (as stock or land) **2** : paper currency or a token issued for temporary use in an emergency
script \'skript\ *n* [L *scriptum*, fr. neut. of *scriptus*, pp. of *scribere* to write] **1 a** : something written **b** : an original or principal instrument or document **c** (1) : MANUSCRIPT 1 (2) : the written text of a stage play, screenplay, or broadcast **2 a** : printed lettering resembling handwriting **b** : letters and figures written by hand : HANDWRITING **c** : ALPHABET
scrip·to·ri·um \skrip-'tōr-ē-əm, -'tȯr-\ *n, pl* **-ria** \-ē-ə\ : a copying room in a medieval monastery set apart for the scribes
scrip·tur·al \'skrip-chə-rəl, 'skrip-shrəl\ *adj* : of, relating to, or being in accordance with a sacred writing; *esp* : BIBLICAL — **scrip·tur·al·ly** \-ē\ *adv*
scrip·ture \'skrip-chər\ *n* [L *scriptura* writing, fr. *script-, scribere* to write] **1 a** *cap* : the books of the Old and New Testaments or of either of them : BIBLE — often used in pl. **b** *often cap* : a passage from the Bible **c** : the sacred writings of a religion **2** : a body of writings considered as authoritative
script·writ·er \'skript-,rīt-ər\ *n* : one that writes scripts for motion pictures or for radio or television programs
scriv·e·ner \'skriv-(ə-)nər\ *n* : a professional copyist or writer : SCRIBE
scrod \'skräd\ *n* : a young fish (as a cod or haddock); *esp* : one split and boned for cooking
scrof·u·la \'skrȯf-yə-lə, 'skräf-\ *n* [ML, fr. LL *scrofulae*, pl., swellings of the lymph glands of the neck] : tuberculosis of the lymph glands esp. in the neck — **scrof·u·lous** \-ləs\ *adj*
scroll \'skrōl\ *n* [ME *scrowle*, alter. of *scrowe*, fr. MF *escroue* scrap, roll, of Gmc origin; akin to E *shred, screed*] **1** : a roll (as of paper or parchment) providing a writing surface; *also* : one on which something is written or engraved **2** : a spiral or coiled ornamental form suggesting a loosely or partly rolled scroll
scroll saw *n* : a thin handsaw for cutting curves or irregular designs
scroll·work \'skrōl-,wərk\ *n* : ornamental work (as in metal or wood) having a scroll or scrolls as its chief feature
scrooge \'skrüj\ *n, often cap* [Ebenezer *Scrooge*, character in *A Christmas Carol* by Charles Dickens] : a miserly person
scro·tum \'skrōt-əm\ *n, pl* **scro·ta** \'skrōt-ə\ *or* **scro·tums** [L] : the external pouch that in most mammals contains the testes — **scro·tal** \'skrōt-ᵊl\ *adj*
scrounge \'skraùnj\ *vb* **1** : to engage in or collect by or as if by foraging ⟨*scrounge* around for firewood⟩ **2** : CADGE, WHEEDLE ⟨*scrounge* a dollar from a friend⟩ — **scroung·er** *n*
¹scrub \'skrəb\ *n* [OE *scrybb* brushwood] **1 a** : a stunted tree or shrub **b** : vegetation consisting chiefly of or a tract covered with scrubs **2** : a usu. inferior domestic animal of mixed or unknown parentage **3 a** : a person of insignificant size or standing **b** : a player not belonging to the first team — **scrub** *adj*
²scrub *vb* **scrubbed; scrub·bing** [of LG or Scand origin] **1 a** : to rub hard in cleaning or washing ⟨*scrub* clothes⟩; *also* : to wash thoroughly ⟨*scrub* a floor⟩ **b** : to remove by or as if by scrubbing ⟨*scrub* out a spot⟩ **2** : to subject to friction : RUB — **scrub·ber** *n*
³scrub *n* **1** : an act or instance of scrubbing **2** : one that scrubs
scrub brush *n* : a brush with hard bristles for heavy cleaning
scrub·by \'skrəb-ē\ *adj* **scrub·bi·er; -est 1** : inferior in size or quality : STUNTED ⟨*scrubby* cattle⟩ **2** : covered with

or consisting of vegetational scrub **3** : lacking distinction : SHABBY

scrub typhus *n* : TSUTSUGAMUSHI DISEASE

scrub·wom·an \'skrəb-ˌwùm-ən\ *n* : a woman who hires herself out for cleaning : CHARWOMAN

scruff \'skrəf\ *n* : the loose skin of the back of the neck : NAPE

scruffy \-ē\ *adj* **scruff·i·er; -est** : SHABBY, CONTEMPTIBLE

scrump·tious \'skrəm(p)-shəs\ *adj* : DELIGHTFUL, EXCELLENT — **scrump·tious·ly** *adv*

¹scrunch \'skrənch\ *vb* **1 a** : CRUNCH, CRUSH, CRUMPLE **b** : to make or move with a crunching sound **2** : CROUCH, SQUEEZE

²scrunch *n* : a crunching sound

¹scru·ple \'skrü-pəl\ *n* [L *scrupulus*, a unit of weight, fr. *scrupulus* small sharp stone] **1** — see MEASURE table **2** : a tiny part or quantity

²scruple *n* [L *scrupulus*, lit., small sharp stone] **1** : an ethical consideration or principle that makes one uneasy or inhibits action **2** : SCRUPULOUSNESS syn see QUALM

³scruple *vi* **scru·pled; scru·pling** \-p(ə-)liŋ\ : to have scruples

scru·pu·los·i·ty \ˌskrü-pyə-'läs-ət-ē\ *n, pl* **-ties 1** : the quality or state of being scrupulous **2** : SCRUPLE

scru·pu·lous \'skrü-pyə-ləs\ *adj* : full of or having scruples : STRICT, PUNCTILIOUS syn see CAREFUL — **scru·pu·lous·ly** *adv* — **scru·pu·lous·ness** *n*

scru·ta·ble \'skrüt-ə-bəl\ *adj* : capable of being deciphered : COMPREHENSIBLE

scru·ti·nize \'skrüt-ᵊn-ˌīz\ *vb* : to examine very closely or critically : INSPECT — **scru·ti·niz·er** *n*

syn SCRUTINIZE, SCAN, EXAMINE mean to look at searchingly and critically. SCRUTINIZE stresses close attention to minute detail ⟨*scrutinized* every line of the contract⟩ SCAN suggests a rapid but thorough covering of an entire surface or body of printed matter ⟨*scanned* several newspapers each morning⟩ EXAMINE suggests scrutinizing in order to determine the nature, condition, or quality of a thing

scru·ti·ny \'skrüt-ᵊn-ē, 'skrüt-nē\ *n, pl* **-nies** [L *scrutinium*, fr. *scrutari* to search, fr. *scruta* trash] **1** : a searching study, inquiry, or inspection : EXAMINATION **2** : a searching look

scu·ba \'sk(y)ü-bə\ *n* [*self-contained underwater breathing apparatus*] : an apparatus used for breathing while swimming under water

¹scud \'skəd\ *vi* **scud·ded; scud·ding** : to move or run swiftly esp. as if driven forward

²scud *n* **1** : the act of scudding **2** : loose vapory clouds driven by wind

¹scuff \'skəf\ *vb* **1** : to scrape the feet in walking : SHUFFLE ⟨*scuffed* his feet on the ground⟩⟨*scuffed* along the path⟩ **2** : to become rough or scratched through wear ⟨*soft leather cuffs* easily⟩

²scuff *n* **1** : a noise or act of scuffing **2** : a flat-soled house slipper

scuf·fle \'skəf-əl\ *vb* **scuf·fled; scuf·fling** \'skəf-(ə-)liŋ\ **1** : to struggle in a confused way at close quarters **2** : to move with a quick shuffling gait; *also* : SCUFF — **scuffle** *n* — **scuf·fler** \-(ə-)lər\ *n*

¹scull \'skəl\ *n* [ME *sculle*] **1 a** : an oar used at the stern of a boat to propel it forward with a crosswise motion **b** : one of a pair of short oars for use by one person **2 a** : boat usu. for racing propelled by one or more pairs of sculls

²scull *vb* : to propel a boat by sculls — **scull·er** *n*

scul·lery \'skəl-(ə-)rē\ *n, pl* **-ler·ies** [MF *escuelerie*, fr. *escuelle* bowl, dish, fr. L *scutella*, dim. of *scutra* platter] : a room for cleaning and storing dishes and culinary utensils, washing vegetables, and similar domestic work

scul·lion \'skəl-yən\ *n* [MF *escouillon* mop for washing dishes, fr. *escouve* broom, fr. L *scopa*] : a kitchen helper

scul·pin \'skəl-pən\ *n, pl* **sculpins** *also* **sculpin** : any of numerous spiny large-headed broad-mouthed usu. scaleless scorpion fishes; *esp* : one of the southern California coast esteemed for food and sport

sculpt \'skəlpt\ *vb* : CARVE, SCULPTURE

sculp·tor \'skəlp-tər\ *n* [L, fr. *sculpere, scalpere* to carve] : one that sculptures — **sculp·tress** \-trəs\ *n*

sculp·tur·al \'skəlp-chə-rəl, 'skəlp-shrəl\ *adj* : of, relating to, or resembling sculpture — **sculp·tur·al·ly** \-ē\ *adv*

¹sculp·ture \'skəlp-chər\ *n* **1 a** : the act, process, or art of carving or cutting hard materials or modeling plastic materials into works of art **b** : work produced by sculpture; *also* : a piece of such work **2** : impressed or raised markings or the pattern of such markings on the surface of a plant or animal part

²sculpture *vb* **1** : to represent or produce by or subject to sculpture ⟨*sculpture* a model's head⟩ ⟨*sculpture* a statue⟩ ⟨*sculpture* marble⟩; *also* : to adorn with sculpture ⟨*sculpture* a tomb⟩ **2** : to work as a sculptor

¹scum \'skəm\ *n* [MD *schum*] **1 a** : extraneous matter or impurities risen to or formed on the surface of a liquid **b** : a slimy coating esp. on stagnant water **2 a** : foul or worthless things **b** : the lowest class : RABBLE — **scum·my** \'skəm-ē\ *adj*

²scum *vi* **scummed; scum·ming** : to form or become covered with or as if with scum

scun·ner \'skən-ər\ *n* : an unreasonable or extreme dislike or prejudice

scup \'skəp\ *n, pl* **scup** *also* **scups** [of AmerInd origin] : either of two porgies of the Atlantic coast of the U.S.

scup·per \'skəp-ər\ *n* [ME *skopper*] : an opening in the bulwarks of a boat through which water drains overboard

scup·per·nong \-ˌnòŋ, -ˌnäŋ\ *n* [*Scuppernong*, river and lake in No. Carolina] **1** : MUSCADINE; *esp* : a cultivated muscadine with yellowish green plum-flavored fruits **2** : a wine made from scuppernongs

scurf \'skərf\ *n* [of Scand origin] **1** : thin dry scales given off by the skin esp. in an abnormal skin condition **2** : a substance that sticks to a surface in flakes; *also* : a scaly deposit or covering (as on a plant surface) — **scurfy** \'skər-fē\ *adj*

scur·ri·lous \'skər-ə-ləs, 'skə-rə-\ *adj* [L *scurrilis*, fr. *scurra* wit, buffoon] **1 a** : using or given to the language of low buffoonery **b** : being vulgar and evil : LOW **2** : containing low obscenities or coarse abuse — **scur·ril·i·ty** \skə-'ril-ət-ē\ *n* — **scur·ri·lous·ly** \'skər-ə-ləs-lē, 'skə-rə-\ *adv* — **scur·ri·lous·ness** *n*

scur·ry \'skər-ē, 'skə-rē\ *vi* **scur·ried; scur·ry·ing** : to move briskly : SCAMPER — **scurry** *n*

¹scur·vy \'skər-vē\ *adj* **scur·vi·er; -est** [*scurf*] : MEAN, DESPICABLE ⟨*scurvy* tricks⟩ — **scur·vi·ly** \-və-lē\ *adv* — **scur·vi·ness** \-vē-nəs\ *n*

²scurvy *n* : a deficiency disease caused by lack of ascorbic acid and marked by spongy gums, loosened teeth, and bleeding into the skin and mucous membranes

scut \'skət\ *n* : a short erect tail (as of a rabbit)

scu·tate \'sk(y)ü-ˌtāt\ *or* **scu·tat·ed** \-ˌtāt-əd\ *adj* **1** : PELTATE **2** : covered by bony or horny plates or large scales

¹scutch \'skəch\ *vt* : to separate the woody fiber from (flax or hemp) by beating

²scutch *n* : SCUTCHER

scutch·eon \'skəch-ən\ *n* : ESCUTCHEON

scutch·er \'skəch-ər\ *n* : an implement or machine for scutching

scute \'sk(y)üt\ *n* [L *scutum* shield] : an external bony or horny plate or large scale

scu·tel·lum \sk(y)ü-'tel-əm\ *n, pl* **-tel·la** \-'tel-ə\ **1** : any of several small shield-shaped plant structures **2** : a hard plate or scale (as on the thorax of an insect) — **scu·tel·late** \-'tel-ət\ *adj*

scut·ter \'skət-ər\ *vi* : SCURRY, SCUTTLE

¹scut·tle \'skət-ᵊl\ *n* [L *scutella* flat dish, dim. of *scutra* platter] **1** : a shallow open basket (as for grain or garden produce) **2** : a metal pail for carrying coal

²scuttle *n* [ME *skottell*] : a small opening (as in the side or deck of a ship or the roof of a house) furnished with a lid; *also* : its lid

³scuttle *vt* **scut·tled; scut·tling** \'skət-liŋ, -ᵊl-iŋ\ : to sink (a boat) intentionally by cutting holes or by opening valves to let in water; *also* : to injure or end by a deliberate act ⟨*scuttle* a conference⟩

⁴scuttle *vi* **scut·tled; scut·tling** \'skət-liŋ, -ᵊl-iŋ\ : SCURRY

⁵scuttle *n* **1** : a quick shuffling pace : SCURRY **2** : a short swift run

scut·tle·butt \'skət-ᵊl-ˌbət\ *n* [*scuttlebutt* cask fitted with a spigot to provide drinking water on shipboard, drinking fountain on a ship] : RUMOR, GOSSIP

Scyl·la \'sil-ə\ *n* : a rock on the coast of Italy personified by the ancients as a female monster — **between Scylla**

and **Charybdis** : between two equally hazardous alternatives

scy·pha \'sī-fə\ n : any of various small mostly cup-shaped calcareous sponges

scy·phis·to·ma \sī-'fis-tə-mə\ n, pl **-mae** \-(,)mē\ also **-mas** [NL, fr. L scyphus cup + Gk stoma mouth] : a sexually produced scyphozoan larva that repeatedly constricts transversely to form free-swimming medusae

scy·pho·zo·an \,sī-fə-'zō-ən\ n : any of a class (Scyphozoa) of coelenterates comprising mostly large jellyfishes that lack a true polyp stage — **scyphozoan** adj

¹scythe \'sīth\ n [OE sīthe] : an implement used for mowing (as grass) and composed of a long curving blade fastened at an angle to a long handle; also : its blade

²scythe vt : to cut with or as if with a scythe : MOW

sea \'sē\ n [OE sǣ] **1 a** : a great body of salty water that covers much of the earth; also : the waters of the earth as distinguished from the land and air **b** : a body of salt water less extensive than an ocean ⟨the Mediterranean sea⟩ **c** : OCEAN **d** : an inland body of water either salt or fresh ⟨the Sea of Galilee⟩ **2 a** : surface motion on a large body of water or its direction ⟨a following sea⟩ **b** : rough water : a heavy swell or wave ⟨a high sea swept the deck⟩ **3** : something suggesting the sea (as in vastness) ⟨a golden sea of wheat⟩ **4** : the seafaring life — **sea** adj — **at sea 1** : on the sea; esp : on a sea voyage **2** : LOST, BEWILDERED — **to sea** : to or upon the open waters of the sea

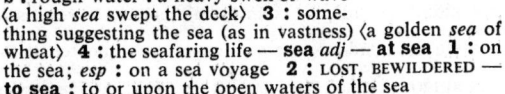

scythe

sea anchor n : a drag typically of canvas thrown overboard to retard the drifting of a ship or seaplane and to keep its head to the wind

sea anemone n : any of numerous usu. solitary polyps (order Actiniaria) that in form, bright and varied colors, and cluster of tentacles superficially resemble a flower

sea·bag \'sē-,bag\ n : a cylindrical canvas bag used esp. by a sailor for gear (as clothes)

sea bass n **1** : any of numerous marine fishes related to but usu. smaller and more active than the groupers; esp : a food and sport fish of the Atlantic coast of the U.S. **2** : any of numerous croakers or drums including noted sport and food fishes

sea·beach \'sē-,bēch\ n : a beach lying along the sea

sea·bed \-,bed\ n : the floor of a sea or ocean

Sea·bee \'sē-(,)bē\ n [alter. of cee + bee; fr. the initials of construction battalion] : a member of a construction battalion of the U.S. Navy

sea·bird \'sē-,bərd\ n : a bird (as a gull or albatross) frequenting the open ocean

sea biscuit n : hard biscuit or loaf bread prepared for use on shipboard : HARDTACK

sea·board \'sē-,bōrd, -,bórd\ n : SEACOAST; also : the country bordering a seacoast — **seaboard** adj

sea·boot \'sē-,büt\ n : a very high waterproof boot used esp. by sailors and fishermen

sea·borne \-,bōrn, -,bórn\ adj **1** : borne over or upon the sea ⟨a seaborne invasion⟩ **2** : engaged in or carried on by overseas shipping ⟨seaborne trade⟩

sea bread n : HARDTACK

sea bream n : any of numerous sea fishes related to the perches

sea breeze n : a breeze blowing inland from the sea

sea cabin n : an emergency cabin near a ship's bridge for the use of captain and officers

sea card n : the card of a mariner's compass

sea change n **1** : a change brought about by the sea **2** : TRANSFORMATION

sea chest n : a sailor's storage chest for personal property

sea·coast \'sē-,kōst\ n : the shore or border of the land adjacent to the sea

sea cow n **1** : SIRENIAN **2** : WALRUS **3** : HIPPOPOTAMUS

sea·craft \'sē-,kraft\ n **1** : seagoing ships **2** : skill in navigation

sea cucumber n : HOLOTHURIAN; esp : one whose contracted body suggests a cucumber in form

sea dog n **1 a** : any of several seals **b** : DOGFISH **2** : a veteran sailor

sea duty n : duty in the U.S. Navy performed outside the continental U.S. or specified dependencies thereof

sea fan n : a coelenterate with a fan-shaped skeleton that is related to the corals and sea anemones

sea·far·er \'sē-,far-ər, -,fer-\ n : MARINER

sea·far·ing \-,far-iŋ, -,fer-\ n **1** : traveling over the sea **2** : the occupation of a sailor — **seafaring** adj

sea·folk \-,fōk\ n : seafaring people : MARINERS

sea·food \'sē-,füd\ n : edible marine fish and shellfish

sea·fowl \-,faùl\ n : SEABIRD

sea·front \-,frənt\ n : the waterfront of a seaside place

sea gate n : a gate, beach, or channel that gives access to the sea

sea·girt \-,gərt\ adj : surrounded by the sea

sea·go·er \-,gō-(ə)r\ n : one that travels by sea : SEAFARER

sea·go·ing \-,gō-iŋ\ adj : adapted or used for sea travel ⟨seagoing ships⟩; also : SEAFARING ⟨a seagoing nation⟩

sea green n **1** : a moderate green or bluish green **2** : a moderate yellow green

sea gull n : GULL; esp : one frequenting the sea

sea hare n : any of various large naked sea mollusks with arched backs and anterior tentacles that project like ears

sea horse n **1** : a fabulous animal half horse and half fish **2 a** : WALRUS **b** : a small long-snouted fish that is covered with bony plates and has a head suggestive of a horse's head

sea horse

sea is·land cotton \,sē-,ī-lən(d)-\ n, often cap S&I : a cotton with esp. long silky fiber

sea king n : a Viking pirate chief

¹seal \'sēl\ n, pl **seals** also **seal** [OE seolh] **1** : any of numerous marine carnivorous mammals chiefly of cold regions with limbs modified into webbed flippers adapted primarily to swimming **2 a** : the pelt of a seal **b** : leather made from the skin of a seal

²seal vi : to hunt seals — **seal·er** n

³seal n [OF seel, fr. L sigillum, fr. dim. of signum sign, seal] **1** : a device with an identifying design or words cut into or raised on its surface that can be pressed or stamped (as into paper or wax) to form a mark (as for certifying a signature or authenticating a document); also : a piece of wax or a wafer bearing such an impressed mark or the mark itself **2** : a usu. ornamental adhesive stamp that may be used to close a letter or package; esp : one sold in a fund-raising campaign **3 a** : something (as a pledge) that makes safe or secure ⟨under seal of secrecy⟩ **b** : a closure that can be opened only by breaking or tearing **c** : a tight and perfect closure ⟨test the seal of the jars⟩; also : a device or an arrangement of material designed to produce such a closure ⟨covered the joint with a thick seal of rosin⟩ ⟨the water seal of a toilet⟩ — **under seal** : with an authenticating seal affixed

⁴seal vt **1** : to mark with or certify or authenticate by or as if by a seal ⟨seal a deed⟩ **2** : to close or make fast with or as if with a seal often to prevent or disclose tampering ⟨the sheriff sealed the premises⟩ ⟨seal a letter with glue⟩ ⟨ice sealed the ships into the harbor⟩ **3** : to determine finally and irrevocably ⟨this answer sealed our fate⟩ — **seal·er** n

sea ladder n **1** : a rope ladder or set of steps to be lowered over a ship's side for use in coming aboard (as at sea) **2** : SEA STEPS

sea lamprey n : a large lamprey sometimes used as food that is a pest destructive of native fish fauna in the Great Lakes

sea-lane \'sē-,lān\ n : an established sea route

seal·ant \'sē-lənt\ n : a sealing agent ⟨radiator sealant⟩

sea legs n : bodily adjustment to the motion of a ship at sea indicated esp. by ability to walk steadily and by freedom from seasickness

seal·ery \'sē-lə-rē\ n, pl **-er·ies** : a seal fishery

sea lettuce n : ULVA

sea level n : the height of the surface of the sea midway between the average high and low tides

sea lily n : CRINOID; esp : a stalked crinoid

sealing wax n : a resinous composition that is plastic when warm and is used for sealing (as letters, dry cells, or cans)

sea lion n : any of several large Pacific eared seals

seal ring n : a finger ring engraved with a seal : SIGNET RING

seal·skin \'sēl-ˌskin\ *n* **1** : the fur or pelt of a fur seal **2** : a garment (as a coat) of sealskin — **sealskin** *adj*

¹**seam** \'sēm\ *n* [OE *sēam;* akin to E *sew*] **1** : the joining or the mark made by the joining of two pieces or edges of material by sewing **2** : the space between adjacent planks of a ship **3 a** : a raised or depressed line (as of scarring) : GROOVE, FURROW, WRINKLE **b** : a layer or stratum (as of mineral) between distinctive layers ⟨coal *seams*⟩ — **seam·less** \-ləs\ *adj* — **seam·like** \-ˌlīk\ *adj*

²**seam** *vt* **1** : to join by or as if by sewing **2** : to mark with lines suggesting seams : FURROW ⟨creeks *seam* the valley⟩ — **seam·er** *n*

sea·man \'sē-mən\ *n* **1** : SAILOR, MARINER **2** : an enlisted man in the navy ranking above a seaman apprentice and below a petty officer third class

seaman apprentice *n* : an enlisted man in the navy ranking above a seaman recruit and below a seaman

sea·man·like \'sē-mən-ˌlīk\ *adj* : characteristic of or befitting a competent seaman

sea·man·ly \-lē\ *adj* : characteristic of or befitting a competent seaman

seaman recruit *n* : an enlisted man in the navy of the lowest rank

sea·man·ship \'sē-mən-ˌship\ *n* : the art or skill of handling, working, and navigating a ship

sea·mark \-ˌmärk\ *n* **1** : a line on a coast marking the tidal limit **2** : an elevated object serving as a beacon to mariners

sea mew *n* : SEA GULL

sea mile *n* : MILE 2

sea·most \-ˌmōst\ *adj* : situated nearest the sea

sea·mount \'sē-ˌmaunt\ *n* : a submarine mountain

seam·stress \'sēm(p)-strəs\ *n* : a woman who sews esp. for a living

seamy \'sē-mē\ *adj* **seam·i·er; -est** **1** : having or showing seams ⟨*seamy* ledges⟩ **2** : less pleasing or presentable : WORSE ⟨the *seamy* side of life⟩ — **seam·i·ness** *n*

sé·ance \'sā-ˌän(t)s, -ˌäⁿs\ *n* [F, lit., sitting, fr. *seoir* to sit, fr. L *sedēre*] **1** : a meeting for discussion : SESSION **2** : a spiritualist meeting

sea nettle *n* : a stinging jellyfish

sea otter *n* : a large marine otter of northern Pacific coasts nearly exterminated for its valuable fur

sea-ot·ter's-cab·bage \ˌsē-ˌät-ərz-'kab-ij\ *n* : a very large Pacific kelp among fronds of which sea otters congregate

sea pen *n* : any of numerous coelenterates that are related to the corals and have colonies of a feathery form

sea·piece \'sē-ˌpēs\ *n* : SEASCAPE 2

sea·plane \'sē-ˌplān\ *n* : an airplane designed to take off from and land on the water

sea·port \-ˌpōrt, -ˌpȯrt\ *n* : a port, harbor, or town accessible to seagoing ships

sea power *n* **1** : a nation having formidable naval strength **2** : naval strength

sea purse *n* : the horny egg case of a skate or of some sharks

¹**sear** \'si(ə)r\ *vb* [OE *sēarian*, fr. *sēar* sere] **1** : to cause withering or drying : PARCH, SHRIVEL ⟨harsh winds that *sear* and burn⟩ **2** : to burn, scorch, or injure with or as if with sudden application of intense heat; *also* : to brown the surface of quickly in cooking ⟨*sear* a pot roast⟩

²**sear** *n* : a mark or scar left by searing

¹**search** \'sərch\ *vb* [MF *cerchier*, fr. LL *circare* to go about, fr. L *circum* round about, fr. *circus* circle] **1 a** : to go through or look carefully and thoroughly in an effort to find or discover ⟨*search* a room⟩⟨*search* for a lost child⟩; *also* : to examine for articles concealed on the person ⟨*search* an arrested man⟩ **b** : to examine or explore with painstaking care often with a particular objective in view : PROBE ⟨*searching* for an escape from his problems⟩ ⟨*search* a wound for a bullet⟩ **2** : to find or come to know by or as if by careful investigation or scrutiny ⟨*searching* out every weakness in his adversary's argument⟩⟨the wind *searched* out every crack and crevice⟩ — **search·a·ble** \'sər-chə-bəl\ *adj* — **search·er** \-chər\ *n* — **search·ing·ly** \-chiŋ-lē\ *adv*

²**search** *n* **1 a** : an act of searching **b** : an act of boarding and inspecting a ship on the high seas (as by a belligerent seeking contraband goods) **2** : a person or party that searches

search·light \'sərch-ˌlīt\ *n* **1** : an apparatus for project-

ing a beam of light; *also* : a beam of light projected by it **2** : FLASHLIGHT 3

search warrant *n* : a warrant authorizing a search of a specified place (as a house) for stolen goods or unlawful possessions (as burglars' tools)

sea robin *n* : any of several gurnards

sea room *n* : room for maneuver at sea

sea rover *n* : one that roves the sea; *esp* : PIRATE

sea-run \ˌsē-ˌrən\ *adj* : ANADROMOUS ⟨a *sea-run* salmon⟩

sea·scape \'sē-ˌskāp\ *n* **1** : a view of the sea **2** : a picture representing a scene at sea

sea scorpion *n* : SCULPIN

sea scout *n* : one enrolled in the Boy Scouts of America program that provides training for older boys in seamanship and water activities

sea serpent *n* : a large marine animal resembling a snake often reported to have been seen but never proved to exist

sea·shell \'sē-ˌshel\ *n* : the shell of a marine animal and esp. a mollusk

sea·shine \-ˌshīn\ *n* : the shine of the sea; *esp* : light reflected off the sea

sea·shore \-ˌshōr, -ˌshȯr\ *n* : land adjacent to the sea : SEACOAST; *esp* : the ground between the ordinary high= water and low-water marks

sea·sick \-ˌsik\ *adj* : affected with or suggestive of seasickness

sea·sick·ness \-nəs\ *n* : motion sickness experienced on the water

sea·side \'sē-ˌsīd\ *n* : country adjacent to the sea : SEA-SHORE

sea·sid·er \-ˌsīd-ər\ *n* : a resident or frequenter of the seaside

sea slug *n* **1** : HOLOTHURIAN **2** : a naked marine gastropod mollusk

sea snake *n* **1** : any of numerous venomous aquatic snakes of warm seas **2** : SEA SERPENT

¹**sea·son** \'sēz-ᵊn\ *n* [OF *saison*, fr. L *sation-, satio* act of sowing, fr. *sat-, serere* to sow; akin to E *seed, sow*] **1 a** : a suitable or natural time or occasion ⟨your mother will explain at the proper *season*⟩ **b** : a usu. brief period of time ⟨willing to wait a *season*⟩; *also* : a particular point in a period or in the course of events ⟨visitors at all *seasons*⟩ **2 a** : a period of the year associated with some recurrent phenomenon or activity ⟨the growing *season*⟩ ⟨a long breeding *season*⟩ ⟨the strawberry *season*⟩ **b** : a period characterized by a particular kind of weather ⟨a long dry *season*⟩ ⟨during the rainy *season*⟩ **c** : one of the four quarters into which the year is commonly divided — compare AUTUMN, SPRING, SUMMER, WINTER **d** : a period of the year associated with a particular event (as a holiday) or phase of human activity (as agriculture, sport, or business) ⟨the Christmas *season*⟩ ⟨the baseball *season*⟩ — **in season 1** : at the right or fitting time **2** : in a state or at the stage of greatest fitness (as for eating) ⟨peaches are *in season*⟩; *also* : proper or legal to take by hunting or fishing — **out of season** : not in season ⟨fined for hunting *out of season*⟩; *esp* : available at other than the usual local season ⟨*out of season* delicacies⟩

²**season** *vb* **sea·soned; sea·son·ing** \'sēz-niŋ, -ᵊn-iŋ\ [MF *assaisoner* to ripen, season, fr. *saison* season] **1** : to give food better flavor or more zest by adding seasoning ⟨a perfectly *seasoned* stew⟩; *also* : to add seasoning ⟨*season* to taste⟩ **2 a** : to treat so as to be fit for use; *esp* : to prepare (lumber) for use by controlled drying **b** : to make fit by experience ⟨*seasoned* veterans⟩ **3** : to become seasoned — **sea·son·er** \'sēz-nər, -ᵊn-ər\ *n*

sea·son·a·ble \'sēz-nə-bəl, -ᵊn-ə-bəl\ *adj* **1** : occurring in good or proper time : OPPORTUNE ⟨*seasonable* advice⟩ **2** : suitable to the season or circumstances : TIMELY ⟨a *seasonable* frost⟩ — **sea·son·a·ble·ness** *n* — **sea·son·a·bly** \-blē\ *adv*

sea·son·al \'sēz-nəl, -ᵊn-əl\ *adj* : of, relating to, or restricted to a particular season ⟨*seasonal* industries⟩ ⟨*seasonal* activity⟩ — **sea·son·al·ly** \-ē\ *adv*

sea·son·ing \'sēz-niŋ, -ᵊn-iŋ\ *n* : something that serves to season; *esp* : an ingredient (as a condiment, spice, or herb) added to food primarily for savor

season ticket *n* : a ticket (as to all of a club's games or for specified daily transportation) valid during a specified time

sea spider *n* : any of a class (Pycnogonida) of small

long-legged marine arthropods superficially resembling spiders

sea squirt *n* : any of various simple pouched tunicates

sea star *n* : STARFISH

sea steps *n pl* : projecting metal plates or bars attached to the side of a ship by which it may be boarded

sea stores *n pl* : supplies (as of foodstuffs) laid in before starting on a sea voyage

sea·strand \'sē-ˌstrand\ *n* : SEASHORE

¹seat \'sēt\ *n* [ON *sæti*; akin to E *sit*] **1 a** : something (as a chair) intended to be sat in or on; *also* : the particular part of something on which one rests in sitting ⟨*seat* of the trousers⟩ ⟨a chair *seat*⟩ **b** : the part of the body that bears the weight in sitting : BUTTOCKS **2 a** : a seating accommodation ⟨his *seat* at table⟩ ⟨had three *seats* for the game⟩ **b** : a right of sitting usu. as a member ⟨a *seat* in the senate⟩; *also* : MEMBERSHIP ⟨a *seat* on the stock exchange⟩ **3** : a place or area where something is situated or centered ⟨the *seat* of the pain⟩ ⟨*seats* of higher learning⟩; *esp* : a place (as a capital city) from which authority is exercised ⟨the new *seat* of the government⟩ **4** : posture in or way of sitting esp. on horseback **5** : a part or surface on which another part or surface rests ⟨valve *seat*⟩ — **seat·ed** \-əd\ *adj*

²seat *vb* **1 a** : to cause to sit or assist in finding a seat ⟨*seat* a guest⟩ **b** : to provide seats for ⟨a theater *seating* 1000 persons⟩ **c** : to put in a sitting position ⟨*seated* himself at table⟩ **2** : to repair the seat of or provide a new seat for **3** : to fit to, on, or with a seat ⟨*seat* a valve⟩ — **seat·er** *n*

seat belt *n* : straps designed to hold a person steady in a seat (as during the takeoff of an airplane)

seat·mate \'sēt-ˌmāt\ *n* : one with whom one shares a seat (as in a vehicle equipped with double or paired seats)

sea train *n* **1** : a seagoing ship equipped for carrying a train of railroad cars **2** : several army or navy transports forming a convoy at sea

sea trout *n* **1** : a trout or char that as an adult inhabits the sea but ascends rivers to spawn **2** : any of various sea fishes (as a weakfish or greenling) resembling trouts

sea urchin *n* : any of a class (Echinoidea) of echinoderms enclosed in shells that are usu. flattened and globular and covered with movable spines

sea·wall \'sē-ˌwȯl\ *n* : a wall or embankment to protect the shore from erosion or to act as a breakwater

sea walnut *n* : CTENOPHORE

¹sea·ward \'sē-wərd\ *also* **sea·wards** \-wərdz\ *adv (or adj)* : toward the sea

²seaward *n* : the direction or side away from land and toward the open sea

sea·wa·ter \'sē-ˌwȯt-ər, -ˌwät-\ *n* : water in or from the sea

sea·way \-ˌwā\ *n* **1** : a moderate or rough sea ⟨caught in a *seaway*⟩ **2** : a ship's headway **3** : a route for travel on the sea; *also* : an ocean traffic lane **4** : a deep inland waterway that admits ocean shipping

sea·weed \-ˌwēd\ *n* : a plant growing in the sea; *esp* : a marine alga (as a kelp)

sea·worn \-ˌwȯrn, -ˌwȯrn\ *adj* **1** : impaired or eaten away by the sea ⟨*seaworn* shores⟩ **2** : worn out by sea voyaging

sea·wor·thy \-ˌwər-t͟hē\ *adj* : fit or safe for a sea voyage ⟨a *seaworthy* ship⟩ — **sea·wor·thi·ness** *n*

sea wrack *n* : SEAWEED; *esp* : that cast ashore in masses

se·ba·ceous \si-'bā-shəs\ *adj* : of, relating to, or secreting fatty material ⟨a *sebaceous* exudate⟩

sebaceous gland *n* : one of the skin glands that secrete an oily lubricating substance into the hair follicles

seb·or·rhea \ˌseb-ə-'rē-ə\ *n* : excessive secretion and discharge of sebum — **seb·or·rhe·ic** \-'rē-ik\ *adj*

se·bum \'sē-bəm\ *n* [L, tallow, grease] : the secretion of the sebaceous glands

se·cant \'sē-ˌkant, -kənt\ *n* [L *secant-, secans*, prp. of *secare* to cut] **1** : a straight line cutting a curve at two or more points **2** : a trigonometric function that for an acute angle in a right triangle is the ratio of the hypotenuse to the side adjacent to the angle

sec·a·teur \'sek-ə-ˌtər\ *n* [F *sécateur*, fr. L *secare* to cut] *chiefly Brit* : pruning shears — usu. used in pl.

se·cede \si-'sēd\ *vi* [L *secess-, secedere*, fr. *se-* apart + *cedere* to go] : to withdraw from an organization or com-

munion (as a nation, church, or political party) — **se·ced·er** *n*

se·ces·sion \si-'sesh-ən\ *n* **1** : the act of seceding : a formal withdrawal **2** *often cap* : the withdrawal of the 11 southern states from the Union at the start of the Civil War — **se·ces·sion·ism** \-'sesh-ə-ˌniz-əm\ *n* — **se·ces·sion·ist** \-'sesh-(ə-)nəst\ *n*

se·clude \si-'klüd\ *vt* [L *seclus-, secludere*, fr. *se-* apart + *claudere* to close] **1** : to withhold from free intercourse : make inaccessible ⟨*secluded* themselves with a few old friends⟩ **2** : to shut away : SCREEN, ISOLATE ⟨a cottage *secluded* by dense forests⟩

se·clud·ed *adj* **1** : screened or hidden from view : SEQUESTERED **2** : living in seclusion : SOLITARY — **se·clud·ed·ly** *adv* — **se·clud·ed·ness** *n*

se·clu·sion \si-'klü-zhən\ *n* **1** : the act of secluding : the condition of being secluded **2** : a secluded or isolated place — **se·clu·sive** \-'klü-siv, -ziv\ *adj* — **se·clu·sive·ly** *adv* — **se·clu·sive·ness** *n*

¹sec·ond \'sek-ənd\ *adj* [OF, fr. L *secundus* following, second, fr. *sequi* to follow] **1** — see NUMBER table **2** : next to the first in time, order, or importance ⟨*second* violin⟩ ⟨*second* place⟩ **3** : ALTERNATE, OTHER ⟨elects a mayor every *second* year⟩ **4** : resembling or suggesting a prototype : ANOTHER ⟨a *second* Cato⟩ — **second** *adv* — **sec·ond·ly** *adv*

²second *n* **1 a** — see NUMBER table **b** : one next after the first in time, order, or importance **2** : one who assists or supports another (as in a duel or prizefight) **3 a** : the musical interval embracing two diatonic degrees or a tone at this interval **b** : the harmonic combination of two tones a second apart **4** : an inferior or flawed article (as of merchandise) **5** : the act of seconding a motion **6** : the second gear or speed in an automotive vehicle

³second *n* [so called fr. its being the second sexagesimal division of a unit, as a minute is the first] **1** : the 60th part of a minute of time or of a degree **2** : an instant of time : MOMENT ⟨said he'd be back in a *second*⟩

⁴second *vt* **1** : to give support or encouragement to : ASSIST **2** : to endorse (a motion or a nomination) so that it may be debated or voted on — **sec·ond·er** *n*

¹sec·ond·ary \'sek-ən-ˌder-ē\ *adj* **1 a** : of second rank, importance, or value ⟨*secondary* streams⟩ **b** : of, relating to, or constituting the second strongest of the three or four degrees of stress ⟨the fourth syllable of *basketball team* carries *secondary* stress⟩ **c** : expressive of past time ⟨*secondary* tense⟩ **2 a** : derived from something original, primary, or basic **b** : of or relating to the induced current or its circuit in an induction coil or transformer ⟨a *secondary* coil⟩ ⟨*secondary* voltage⟩ **3 a** : of, relating to, or being a second order or stage in a sequence or series **b** : intermediate between elementary and collegiate ⟨*secondary* school⟩ — **sec·ond·ar·i·ly** \ˌsek-ən-'der-ə-lē\ *adv* — **sec·ond·ar·i·ness** \'sek-ən-ˌder-ē-nəs\ *n*

²secondary *n, pl* **-ar·ies** : one that is secondary: as **a** : a defensive football backfield **b** : any of the quill feathers of the forearm of a bird

secondary cell *n* : STORAGE CELL

secondary emission *n* : the emission of electrons from a surface that is bombarded by charged particles

secondary road *n* **1** : a road not of primary importance **2** : a road that feeds traffic to a more important road (as a turnpike)

secondary sex characteristic *n* : a bodily or mental peculiarity that appears in members of one sex at puberty or in seasonal breeders at the breeding season and is not directly concerned with reproduction

second base *n* **1** : the base that must be touched second by a base runner in baseball **2** : the position of the player defending the area on the first-base side of second base — **second baseman** *n*

sec·ond-best \ˌsek-ən-'best\ *adj* : next to the best ⟨wore his *second-best* suit⟩

second childhood *n* : DOTAGE

second class *n* **1** : the second and usu. next to highest group in a classification **2** : a class of U.S. or Canadian mail comprising newspapers and periodicals sent to regular subscribers

sec·ond-class \ˌsek-ˀn-'klas, -ən(d)-\ *adj* **1** : of or relating to a second class **2 a** : INFERIOR, MEDIOCRE **b** : socially or economically deprived

---

j joke; ŋ sing; ō flow; ȯ flaw; ȯi coin; th thin; t͟h this; ü loot; u̇ foot; y yet; yü few; yu̇ furious; zh vision

Second Coming *n* : the coming of Christ on Judgment Day

second-degree burn *n* : a burn marked by pain, blistering, and superficial destruction of the skin with fluid infiltration and reddening of the tissues beneath the burn

second fiddle *n* : one who fills a subordinate or secondary role or function — usu. used in the phrase *to play second fiddle*

second growth *n* : forest trees that come up naturally after removal of the first growth by cutting or by fire

sec·ond-guess \,sek-ən-'ges\ *vt* : to think out alternative strategies or explanations for after the event — **sec·ond-guess·er** *n*

second hand \'sek-ən(d)-,hand\ *n* : the hand marking seconds on a timepiece

¹**sec·ond·hand** \,sek-ən(d)-'hand\ *adj* **1** : not original : taken from someone else *(secondhand* information) **2** : not new : having had a previous owner *(a secondhand* car) **3** : selling used goods *(a secondhand* store)

²**secondhand** *adv* : in a secondhand condition; *esp* : INDIRECTLY

second lieutenant *n* : a commissioned officer (as in the army) of the lowest rank

second person *n* : a set of words or forms (as verb forms or pronouns) referring to the person or thing addressed in the utterance in which they occur; *also* : a word or form belonging to such a set

sec·ond-rate \,sek-ən-'(d)rāt\ *adj* : of second or inferior quality or value : MEDIOCRE — **sec·ond-rate·ness** *n* — **sec·ond-rat·er** \-'(d)rāt-ər\ *n*

Second Reader *n* : a member of a Christian Science church or society chosen to assist the First Reader

second sight *n* : a purported capacity to see remote or future objects or events : CLAIRVOYANCE

second-story man *n* : a burglar who enters a house by an upstairs window

se·cre·cy \'sē-krə-sē\ *n, pl* **-cies** **1** : the habit or practice of keeping secrets : SECRETIVENESS **2** : the quality or state of being hidden or concealed

¹**se·cret** \'sē-krət\ *adj* [L *secretus*, fr. pp. of *secernere* to separate, set apart, fr. *se-* apart + *cernere* to sift] **1 a** : hidden or kept from knowledge or view **b** : working in secret as a spy or detective : UNDERCOVER *(a secret* agent) **2** : remote from human resort or notice : SECLUDED **3** : revealed only to the initiated : ESOTERIC — **se·cret·ly** *adv*

syn SECRET, COVERT, CLANDESTINE, SURREPTITIOUS mean done without attracting observation. SECRET may imply concealment on any grounds or for any motive *(secret* diplomatic negotiations) COVERT stresses the mere fact of not being open or declared *(covert* envy of his brother) CLANDESTINE implies secrecy usu. of a forbidden act *(clandestine* drug trade) SURREPTITIOUS stresses the careful and skillful avoidance of detection as in violating a law or custom or right *(surreptitiously* copying from notes)

²**secret** *n* [L *secretum*, fr. neut. of *secretus*, adj., secret] **1 a** : something kept hidden or unexplained : MYSTERY **b** : something kept from the knowledge of others or shared only confidentially with a few **c** *often cap* : a prayer said inaudibly by the celebrant just before the preface of the mass **2** : a secret condition or place : SECRECY *(conspired in secret)* **3** : something taken to be a specific or key to a desired end *(the secret* of longevity)

se·cre·ta·gogue \si-'krēt-ə-,gäg\ *n* [*secretion* + Gk *-agōgos* promoting the expulsion of, fr. *agein* to lead, drive] : a substance stimulating secretion

sec·re·tar·i·at \,sek-rə-'ter-ē-ət\ *n* [F *secrétariat*, fr. ML *secretariatus*, fr. *secretarius* secretary] **1** : the office of a secretary **2 a** : an office housing a clerical staff **b** : the clerical staff of an organization **3** : the administrative department of a governmental organization *(the United Nations secretariat)*

sec·re·tary \'sek-rə-,ter-ē\ *n, pl* **-tar·ies** [ML *secretarius*, fr. L *secretum* secret] **1** : a person employed to handle correspondence and routine or detail work for a superior : a confidential clerk **2** : an officer of a business corporation or society who has charge of the correspondence and records **3** : a government official in charge of the affairs of a department *(Secretary* of State) **4** : a writing desk with a top section for books — **sec·re·tar·i·al** \,sek-rə-'ter-ē-əl\ *adj* — **sec·re·tary·ship** \'sek-rə-,ter-ē-,ship\ *n*

secretary-general *n, pl* **secretaries-general** : a principal administrative officer

secret ballot *n* : AUSTRALIAN BALLOT

¹**se·crete** \si-'krēt\ *vb* [back-formation fr. *secretion*] : to produce and give off a secretion *(glands that secrete* intermittently)

²**se·crete** \si-'krēt, 'sē-krət\ *vt* [¹*secret*] : to deposit or conceal in a hiding place *(will try to secrete* a small piece of metal about his person)

se·cre·tin \si-'krēt-ᵊn\ *n* : an intestinal hormone capable of stimulating the pancreas and liver to secrete

se·cre·tion \si-'krē-shən\ *n* [L *secret-*, *secernere* to separate, set apart, fr. *se-* apart + *cernere* to sift] **1** : a concealing or hiding of something **2 a** : the act or process of secreting **b** : a product of glandular activity; *esp* : one (as a hormone or enzyme) that performs a specific useful function in the organism — **se·cre·tion·ary** \-shə-,ner-ē\ *adj*

se·cre·tive \'sē-krət-iv, si-'krēt-\ *adj* : disposed to secrecy or concealment : not frank or open — **se·cre·tive·ly** *adv* — **se·cre·tive·ness** *n*

se·cre·to·ry \si-'krēt-ə-rē\ *adj* : of, relating to, or active in secretion

secret police *n* : a police organization operating for the most part in secrecy and esp. for the political purposes of its government often with terroristic methods

Secret Service *n* : a division of the U.S. Treasury Department charged chiefly with the suppression of counterfeiting and the protection of the president

secret society *n* : any of various oath-bound societies often devoted to purposes of brotherhood, moral discipline, and mutual assistance

sect \'sekt\ *n* [L *secta* path of life, doctrine, school, faction, fr. *sequi* to follow] **1 a** : a dissenting or schismatic religious body; *esp* : one regarded as extreme or heretical **b** : a religious denomination **2 a** : a group adhering to a distinctive doctrine or to a leader **b** : PARTY **c** : FACTION

¹**sec·tar·i·an** \sek-'ter-ē-ən\ *adj* **1** : of, relating to, or characteristic of a sect or sectarian **2** : limited in character or scope : PAROCHIAL — **sec·tar·i·an·ism** \-ē-ə-,niz-əm\ *n*

²**sectarian** *n* **1** : a member of a sect **2** : a narrow or bigoted person

sec·tar·i·an·ize \sek-'ter-ē-ə-,nīz\ *vb* **1** : to act as sectarians **2** : to make sectarian

sec·ta·ry \'sek-tə-rē\ *n, pl* **-ries** : a member of a sect

sec·tile \'sek-t°l, -,tīl\ *adj* **1** : capable of being severed by a knife with a smooth cut **2** : cut into small divisions *(a sectile* leaf) — **sec·til·i·ty** \sek-'til-ət-ē\ *n*

¹**sec·tion** \'sek-shən\ *n* [L *sect-*, *secare* to cut; akin to E ²*saw*] **1 a** : the action or an instance of cutting or separating by cutting **b** : a part set off by or as if by cutting : PORTION, SLICE **2** : a distinct part or portion of a writing: as **a** : a subdivision of a chapter **b** : a distinct component part of a newspaper *(sports section)* **3** : the profile of something as it would appear if cut through by an intersecting plane **4** : a character § used chiefly as a reference mark or to show the beginning of a section **5** : a piece of land one square mile in area forming one of the 36 subdivisions of a township **6** : a distinct part of an area, community, or group of people **7 a** : a division of a railroad sleeping car with an upper and a lower berth **b** : a part of a permanent railroad way under the care of a particular set of men **c** : one of two or more vehicles that run on the same schedule **8** : one of several component parts (as of a bookcase) that may be assembled or reassembled **9** : a division of an orchestra composed of one class of instruments *(brass section)*

²**section** *vb* **sec·tioned**; **sec·tion·ing** \-sh(ə-)niŋ\ **1** : to cut or separate into or become cut or separated into parts or sections **2** : to represent in sections (as by a drawing)

sec·tion·al \'sek-shnəl, -shən-°l\ *adj* **1 a** : of or relating to a section **b** : local or regional rather than general in character *(sectional* interests) **2** : consisting of or divided into sections *(sectional* furniture) — **sec·tion·al·ly** \-ē\ *adv*

sec·tion·al·ism \'sek-shnə-,liz-əm, -shən-°l-,iz-\ *n* : an exaggerated devotion to the interests of a region

section gang *n* : a gang or crew of track workers employed to maintain a railroad section

section hand *n* : a laborer belonging to a section gang

sec·tor \'sek-tər\ *n* [L, cutter, fr. *sect-*, *secare* to cut] **1** : the part of a circle included between two radii **2** : an area assigned to a military commander to defend **3** : a distinctive part (as of an economy) ⟨the industrial *sector*⟩

sec·to·ri·al \sek-'tōr-ē-əl, -'tòr-\ *adj* **1** : of, relating to, or constituting a sector **2** : having a variant sector in an otherwise normal body of tissue ⟨a *sectorial* plant hybrid⟩

¹sec·u·lar \'sek-yə-lər\ *adj* [LL *saeculum* the world, fr. L, generation, age, century] **1 a** : of or relating to the worldly or temporal ⟨*secular* concerns⟩ **b** : not overtly or specif. religious ⟨*secular* music⟩ **c** : not ecclesiastical or clerical ⟨*secular* courts⟩ ⟨*secular* landowners⟩ **2** : of or relating to clergy not belonging to a religious order ⟨a *secular* priest⟩ **3 a** : occurring once in an age or a century **b** : existing or continuing through ages or centuries ⟨*secular* enmities⟩ — **sec·u·lar·ly** *adv*

²secular *n* **1** : a secular ecclesiastic (as a parish priest) **2** : LAYMAN

sec·u·lar·ism \-lə-,riz-əm\ *n* : indifference to or rejection or exclusion of religion and religious considerations — **sec·u·lar·ist** \-rəst\ *n* — **secularist** *or* **sec·u·lar·is·tic** \,sek-yə-lə-'ris-tik\ *adj*

sec·u·lar·ize \'sek-yə-lə-,rīz\ *vt* **1** : to make secular **2** : to transfer from ecclesiastical to civil or lay use, possession, or control — **sec·u·lar·i·za·tion** \,sek-yə-lə-rə-'zā-shən\ *n* — **sec·u·lar·iz·er** \'sek-yə-lə-,rī-zər\ *n*

se·cur·ance \si-'kyùr-ən(t)s\ *n* : the act of making secure

¹se·cure \si-'kyù(ə)r\ *adj* [L *securus* carefree, safe, fr. *se* without + *cura* care] **1 a** : easy in mind : CONFIDENT **b** : assured in opinion or expectation : having no doubt **2 a** : free from danger **b** : free from risk of loss **c** : affording safety : INVIOLABLE ⟨*secure* hideaway⟩ **d** : TRUSTWORTHY, DEPENDABLE ⟨*secure* foundation⟩ **3** : ASSURED, CERTAIN ⟨*secure* victory⟩ **syn** see SAFE — **se·cure·ly** *adv* — **se·cure·ness** *n*

²secure *vb* **1 a** : to relieve from exposure to danger : make safe : GUARD, SHIELD ⟨*secure* a supply line from enemy raids⟩ **b** : to put beyond hazard of losing or of not receiving : GUARANTEE **c** : to give pledge of payment to (a creditor) or of (an obligation) ⟨*secure* a note by a collateral security⟩ **2 a** : to take (a person) into custody : hold fast : PINION **b** : to make fast : SEAL ⟨*secure* a door⟩ **c** : to tie up : BERTH ⟨the ship *secured* for the night⟩ **3 a** : to get secure possession of : PROCURE ⟨*secure* employment⟩ **b** : to bring about : EFFECT **4** : to release (naval personnel) from work or duty : EXCUSE; *also* : to stop work — **se·cur·er** *n*

se·cure·ment \si-'kyù(ə)r-mənt\ *n* : the act or process of making secure

se·cu·ri·ty \si-'kyùr-ət-ē\ *n*, *pl* **-ties** **1** : the quality or state of being secure: as **a** : freedom from danger : SAFETY **b** : freedom from fear or anxiety **2 a** : something given, deposited, or pledged to make certain the fulfillment of an obligation ⟨a poor *security*⟩ **b** : SURETY **3** : an evidence of debt or of property (as a stock certificate or bond) ⟨government *securities*⟩ **4 a** : something that secures : PROTECTION **b** : measures taken esp. to guard against espionage or sabotage ⟨a senate committee concerned with internal *security*⟩

Security Council *n* : a permanent council of the United Nations having primary responsibility for the maintenance of peace and security

se·dan \si-'dan\ *n* **1** : a portable often covered chair that is designed to carry one person and is borne on poles by two men **2 a** : an enclosed automobile that seats four to seven persons including the driver in a single compartment and has a permanent top **b** : a motorboat with one passenger compartment

se·date \si-'dāt\ *adj* [L *sedatus*, fr. pp. of *sedare* to calm, caus. of *sedēre* to sit] : QUIET, STAID, SOBER ⟨*sedate* manners⟩ ⟨too *sedate* for her age⟩ — **se·date·ly** *adv* — **se·date·ness** *n*

se·da·tion \si-'dā-shən\ *n* **1** : the inducing of a relaxed easy state esp. by the use of sedatives **2** : a state resulting from or like that resulting from sedation

¹sed·a·tive \'sed-ət-iv\ *adj* : tending to calm, moderate, or relieve tension or irritability

²sedative *n* : a sedative agent or drug

sed·en·tary \'sed-°n-,ter-ē\ *adj* [L *sedentarius* of one that sits, fr. *sedent-*, *sedens*, prp. of *sedēre* to sit] **1** : not migratory : SETTLED ⟨*sedentary* birds⟩ **2** : doing or requiring much sitting ⟨a *sedentary* job⟩ **3** : permanently attached ⟨*sedentary* barnacles⟩

se·der \'säd-ər\ *n*, *pl* **se·da·rim** \si-'där-əm\ *or* **seders** *often cap* [Heb *sēdher* order] : a Jewish home or community service and ceremonial dinner held on the first and by Orthodox Jews outside Israel on the second evening of the Passover in commemoration of the exodus from Egypt

sedge \'sej\ *n* [OE *secg*] : any of a family of usu. tufted marsh plants differing from the related grasses in having achenes and solid stems — **sedgy** \'sej-ē\ *adj*

se·di·lia \sə-'dē-lē-ə\ *n pl* [L, pl. of *sedile* seat, fr. *sedēre* to sit] : seats in the chancel for the celebrant, deacon, and subdeacon

sed·i·ment \'sed-ə-mənt\ *n* [L *sedimentum* settling, fr. *sedēre* to sit, sink down] **1** : the matter that settles to the bottom of a liquid : DREGS **2** : material (as stones and sand) deposited by water, wind, or glaciers — **sed·i·ment** \-,ment\ *vb*

sed·i·men·ta·ry \,sed-ə-'ment-ə-rē, -'men-trē\ *adj* **1** : of, relating to, or containing sediment ⟨*sedimentary* deposits⟩ **2** : formed by or from deposits of sediment ⟨limestone and sandstone are *sedimentary* rocks⟩

sed·i·men·ta·tion \,sed-ə-mən-'tā-shən, -,men-\ *n* : the action or process of depositing sediment : SETTLING

se·di·tion \si-'dish-ən\ *n* [L *sedition-*, *seditio* insurrection, fr. *sed-*, *se-* apart + *itio* act of going, fr. *ire* to go] : incitement of resistance to or of insurrection against lawful authority

syn SEDITION, TREASON mean a serious breach of allegiance. SEDITION implies acts leading to or exciting commotion or resistance to authority but not including overt acts of violence or betrayal; TREASON implies an overt act aiming at overthrow of government or betrayal to the enemy

se·di·tion·ary \si-'dish-ə-,ner-ē\ *n*, *pl* **-ar·ies** : an inciter or promoter of sedition

se·di·tious \si-'dish-əs\ *adj* **1** : disposed to arouse, take part in, or be guilty of sedition ⟨a *seditious* agitator⟩ **2** : of or relating to sedition ⟨*seditious* statements⟩ — **se·di·tious·ly** *adv* — **se·di·tious·ness** *n*

se·duce \si-'d(y)üs\ *vt* [L *seducere* to lead away, fr. *se-* apart + *ducere* to lead] **1** : to persuade to disobedience or disloyalty **2** : to lead astray ⟨*seduced* into crime⟩ **3** : to entice (a female) into unchastity **4** : ATTRACT — **se·duc·er** *n* — **se·duc·tion** \-'dək-shən\ *n*

se·duce·ment \si-'d(y)üs-mənt\ *n* **1** : SEDUCTION **2** : something that serves to seduce

se·duc·tive \si-'dək-tiv\ *adj* : ALLURING, TEMPTING — **se·duc·tive·ly** *adv* — **se·duc·tive·ness** *n*

se·duc·tress \-trəs\ *n* : a female seducer

sed·u·lous \'sej-ə-ləs\ *adj* [L *sedulus*, fr. *sedulo* sincerely, diligently, fr. *se dolo* without guile] : diligent in application or pursuit : ASSIDUOUS — **sed·u·lous·ly** *adv* — **sed·u·lous·ness** *n*

se·dum \'sēd-əm\ *n* : any of a genus of fleshy-leaved herbs including the orpine : STONECROP

¹see \'sē\ *vb* **saw** \'sò\; **seen** \'sēn\; **see·ing** \'sē-iŋ\ [OE *sēon*] **1 a** : to perceive by the eye or have the power of sight ⟨*see* a bird⟩ ⟨a person who cannot *see*⟩ **b** : to give or pay attention ⟨*see*, the bus is coming⟩ **c** : to look about **2 a** : to have experience of : UNDERGO ⟨*see* army service⟩ **b** : to come to know : DISCOVER **3 a** : to form a mental picture of : VISUALIZE **b** : to perceive the meaning or importance of : UNDERSTAND **c** : to be aware of : RECOGNIZE **d** : to imagine as a possibility : SUPPOSE ⟨couldn't *see* him as a crook⟩ **4 a** : to make investigation or inquiry : EXAMINE, WATCH ⟨want to *see* how he handles the problem⟩ **b (1)** : READ **(2)** : to read of **c** : to attend as a spectator ⟨*see* a play⟩ **5 a** : to take care of : provide for ⟨*see* him through⟩ **b** : to make sure ⟨*see* that order is kept⟩ **6 a** : to regard as : JUDGE **b** : to prefer to have ⟨I'll *see* him hanged first⟩ ⟨I'll *see* you dead before I accept your terms⟩ **c** : to find acceptable or attractive ⟨still can't *see* the design⟩ **7 a** : to call on : VISIT ⟨*see* a sick friend⟩ **b (1)** : to keep company with esp. in courtship or dating ⟨had been *seeing* each other for a year⟩ **(2)** : to grant an interview to : RECEIVE ⟨the president will *see* you⟩ **8** : AC-

COMPANY, ESCORT ⟨*see* the girls home⟩ **9** : to meet (a bet) in poker or to equal the bet of (a player) : CALL
²see *n* [OF *se*, fr. L *sedes* seat, fr. *sedēre* to sit] **1** : the city in which a bishop's church is located **2** : the jurisdiction of a bishop : DIOCESE
see·a·ble \'sē-ə-bəl\ *adj* : capable of being seen
¹seed \'sēd\ *n, pl* **seed** *or* **seeds** [OE *sǣd*; akin to E *sow*] **1 a** : the grains or ripened ovules of plants used for sowing **b** : the fertilized ripened ovule of a flowering plant containing an embryo and capable normally of germination to produce a new plant; *also* : a propagative plant structure (as a spore or small dry fruit) **2 a** : MILT, SEMEN **b** : a small egg (as of an insect) **c** : a developmental form of a lower animal suitable for transplanting; *esp* : SPAT **3** : PROGENY, DESCENDANTS ⟨the *seed* of David⟩ **4** : a source of development or growth : GERM ⟨sowed the *seeds* of discord⟩ **5** : something (as a small bubble in glass) that resembles a seed in shape or size — **seed** *adj* — **seed·ed** \-əd\ *adj* — **seed·like** \-,līk\ *adj*
²seed *vb* **1 a** : PLANT, SOW ⟨*seed* land to grass⟩ **b** : to bear or shed seeds ⟨weeds that *seed* freely⟩ **c** : to remove seeds from ⟨*seed* raisins⟩ **2 a** : INOCULATE **b** : to supply with nuclei (as of crystallization or condensation); *esp* : to treat (a cloud) with solid particles to convert water droplets into ice crystals in an attempt to produce rain **3** : to schedule (tournament players or teams) so that superior ones will not meet in early rounds
seed·bed \'sēd-,bed\ *n* : soil or a bed of soil prepared for planting seed
seed·case \-,kās\ *n* : a dry hollow fruit (as a pod) enclosing seeds
seed coat *n* : the hardened integuments of a ripened plant ovule forming an outer protective cover on a seed
seed·eat·er \'sēd-,ēt-ər\ *n* : a bird (as a finch) whose diet consists basically of seeds
seed·er \'sēd-ər\ *n* **1** : a machine for planting or sowing seeds **2** : a device for seeding fruit
seed fern *n* : any of an order (Cycadofilicales) of extinct plants with fronds like ferns and naked seeds
seed·ful \'sēd-fəl\ *adj* : full of seed : GENERATIVE
seed leaf *n* : COTYLEDON 2
seed·less \'sēd-ləs\ *adj* : having no seeds ⟨*seedless* grapes⟩
seed·ling \-liŋ\ *n* **1** : a plant grown from seed **2** : a young plant; *esp* : a tree smaller than a sapling — **seedling** *adj*
seed oyster *n* : a young oyster esp. of a size for transplantation
seed pearl *n* : a very small and often irregular pearl
seed plant *n* : a plant that bears seeds : SPERMATOPHYTE
seed·pod \'sēd-,päd\ *n* : POD 1
seeds·man \'sēdz-mən\ *n* **1** : SOWER **2** : a dealer in seeds
seed stock *n* : a supply (as of seed) for planting
seed·time \'sēd-,tīm\ *n* : the season of sowing
seedy \'sēd-ē\ *adj* **seed·i·er; -est 1 a** : containing or full of seeds ⟨a *seedy* fruit⟩ **b** : containing many small similar inclusions ⟨glass *seedy* with air bubbles⟩ **2** : inferior in condition or quality: as **a** : SHABBY, RUN-DOWN ⟨*seedy* clothes⟩ ⟨a *seedy* settlement⟩ **b** : somewhat disreputable : SQUALID ⟨a *seedy* district⟩ ⟨*seedy* entertainment⟩ **c** : slightly unwell : DEBILITATED ⟨felt *seedy* and went home early⟩ — **seed·i·ly** \'sēd-°l-ē\ *adv* — **seed·i·ness** \'sēd-ē-nəs\ *n*
see·ing \'sē-iŋ\ *conj* [prp. of *see*] : in view of the fact that
seek \'sēk\ *vb* **sought** \'sȯt\; **seek·ing** [OE *sēcan*] **1** : to resort to : go to ⟨*seek* the shade on a sunny day⟩ **2 a** : to go in search of : look for ⟨*seek* out the culprit⟩ **b** : to make a search or inquiry **c** : to try to discover **3** : to ask for : REQUEST ⟨*seeks* advice⟩ **4** : to try to acquire or gain : aim at ⟨*seek* one's fortune⟩ **5** : to make an attempt : TRY ⟨*seek* to find a way⟩ — **seek·er** *n*
seel \'sēl\ *vt* [MF *siller*, fr. ML *ciliare*, fr. L *cilium* eyelid] : to close the eyes of (as a hawk) by drawing threads through the eyelids
seem \'sēm\ *vi* [of Scand origin] **1 a** (1) : to give the impression of being : APPEAR ⟨*seem* reasonable⟩ (2) : to pretend to be : FEIGN **b** : to appear to the observation or understanding ⟨*seemed* to know⟩ **c** : to appear to one's own mind or opinion ⟨*seem* to feel no pain⟩ **2** : to give evidence of existing or being present ⟨there *seems* no reason for worry⟩

¹seem·ing \'sē-miŋ\ *n* : external appearance as distinguished from true character : LOOK
²seeming *adj* : apparent on superficial view : OSTENSIBLE ⟨*seeming* enthusiasm⟩ — **seem·ing·ly** \'sē-miŋ-lē\ *adv*
seem·ly \'sēm-lē\ *adj* **seem·li·er; -est 1** : good-looking : HANDSOME, ATTRACTIVE **2** : conventionally proper : DECOROUS ⟨*seemly* behavior⟩ **3** : suited to the occasion, purpose, or person : FIT ⟨a *seemly* reply⟩ — **seem·li·ness** *n* — **seemly** *adv*
see out *vt* : to continue with until the end : FINISH ⟨*see out* one's education⟩
seep \'sēp\ *vi* [OE *sipian*] : to flow or pass slowly through fine pores or small openings : OOZE ⟨water had *seeped* in through a crack in the ceiling⟩
seep·age \'sē-pij\ *n* **1** : the process of seeping : OOZING **2** : a quantity of fluid that has seeped through porous material
seer \'si(ə)r, *esp for 1 also* 'sē-ər\ *n* **1** : one that sees **2 a** : one that predicts events or developments : PROPHET **b** : a person credited with extraordinary moral and spiritual insight
seer·ess \'si(ə)r-əs\ *n* : a female seer : PROPHETESS
seer·suck·er \'si(ə)r-,sək-ər\ *n* [Hindi *śīrśaker*, fr. Per *shīr-o-shakar*, lit., milk and sugar] : a light fabric of linen, cotton, or rayon usu. striped and slightly puckered
¹see·saw \'sē-,sȯ\ *n* **1** : an alternating up-and-down or backward-and-forward motion or movement; *also* : a contest or struggle in which now one side now the other has the lead **2 a** : a game in which two children or groups of children ride on opposite ends of a plank balanced in the middle so that one end goes up as the other goes down **b** : the plank or apparatus so used — **seesaw** *adj*
²seesaw *vb* **see·sawed; see·saw·ing 1 a** : to move backward and forward or up and down **b** : to play at seesaw **2** : ALTERNATE
seethe \'sēth\ *vb* [OE *sēothan*] **1** : BOIL, STEW **2** : to soak or saturate in a liquid **3 a** : to be in a state of rapid agitated movement **b** : to churn or foam as if boiling ⟨the river rapids *seethed*⟩ **4** : to suffer violent internal excitement ⟨*seethed* with rage⟩

segment

¹seg·ment \'seg-mənt\ *n* [L *segmentum*, fr. *secare* to cut] **1** : any of the parts into which a thing is divided or naturally separates : SECTION, DIVISION **2 a** : a part cut off from a geometrical figure (as a circle or sphere) by a line or plane; *esp* : the part of a circle bounded by a chord and an arc of that circle **b** : a part of a straight line included between two points **syn** see PART — **seg·men·tary** \'seg-mən-,ter-ē\ *adj*
²seg·ment \'seg-,ment\ *vb* : to separate into segments : give off as segments
seg·men·tal \seg-'ment-°l\ *adj* **1** : of, relating to, or having the form of the segment or sector of a circle ⟨*segmental* fanlight⟩ ⟨*segmental* pediment⟩ **2** : METAMERIC **3** : of, relating to, or resulting from segmentation : SUBSIDIARY ⟨*segmental* data⟩ — **seg·men·tal·ly** \-°l-ē\ *adv*
seg·men·ta·tion \,seg-mən-'tā-shən, -,men-\ *n* : the process of dividing into segments; *esp* : the formation of many cells from a single cell (as in a developing egg)
se·go \'sē-gō\ *n, pl* **segos** [of AmerInd origin] : the bulb of the sego lily
sego lily *n* : a western No. American perennial herb of the lily family with bell-shaped flowers white within and largely green without and an edible bulb
¹seg·re·gate \'seg-ri-,gāt\ *vb* [L *segregare*, fr. *se-* apart + *greg-, grex* herd] **1** : to separate or set apart from others : ISOLATE; *esp* : to separate by races **2** : to separate from the general mass and collect together (as in crystallization) **3** : to separate during meiosis **syn** see AGGREGATE — **seg·re·ga·tive** \-,gāt-iv\ *adj*
²seg·re·gate \-gət, -,gāt\ *n* : a segregated individual or class of individuals
seg·re·ga·tion \,seg-ri-'gā-shən\ *n* **1** : the act or process of segregating : the state of being segregated **2** : the separation or isolation of a race, class, or ethnic group by discriminatory means (as restriction to an area, barriers to social intercourse, or separate educational facilities)
seg·re·ga·tion·ist \-sh(ə-)nəst\ *n* : an advocate of segregation esp. of races
se·gue \'sāg-wā, 'seg-\ *imperative verb* [It, there follows]

: proceed to what follows without pause — used as a direction in music

sei·del \'sīd-ᵊl\ *n* [G, fr. L *situla* bucket] **:** a large glass for beer

Seid·litz powders \'sed-ləts-\ *n pl* [*Sedlitz*, Czechoslovakia] **:** effervescing salts consisting of one powder of sodium bicarbonate and Rochelle salt and another of tartaric acid that are mixed in water and drunk as a mild cathartic

sei·gneur \sān-'yər\ *n, often cap* [MF, fr. ML *senior*, fr. L, adj., senior] **:** LORD, SEIGNIOR — **sei·gneur·i·al** \-ē-əl\ *adj*

sei·gnior \sān-'yó(ə)r\ *n* [MF *seigneur*] **:** a man of rank or authority; *esp* **:** the feudal lord of a manor

sei·gniory *or* **sei·gnory** \'sān-yə-rē\ *n, pl* **-gnior·ies** *or* **-gnor·ies :** the territory of a lord **:** DOMAIN

sei·gno·ri·al \sān-'yór-ē-əl, -'yór-\ *adj* **:** of, relating to, or befitting a seignior **:** MANORIAL

¹seine \'sān\ *n* [OE *segne*, fr. L *sagena*] **:** a large fishing net kept hanging vertically in the water by weights and floats

²seine *vb* **:** to fish with or catch with a seine — **sein·er** *n*

seism \'sī-zəm\ *n* [Gk *seismos*] **:** EARTHQUAKE

seis·mic \'sīz-mik, 'sīs-\ *adj* **:** of, subject to, or caused by an earthquake or an artificially produced earth vibration — **seis·mi·cal·ly** \-mi-k(ə-)lē\ *adv*

seismo- *comb form* [Gk *seismos*, fr. *seiein* to shake] **:** earthquake **:** vibration ⟨*seismograph*⟩

seis·mo·gram \'sīz-mə-,gram, 'sīs-\ *n* **:** the record of an earth tremor made by a seismograph

seis·mo·graph \-,graf\ *n* **:** an apparatus for recording the intensity, direction, and duration of earthquakes or similar vibrations of the ground — **seis·mo·graph·ic** \,sīz-mə-'graf-ik, ,sīs-\ *adj* — **seis·mog·ra·phy** \sīz-'mäg-rə-fē, sīs-\ *n*

seis·mol·o·gy \sīz-'mäl-ə-jē, sīs-\ *n* **:** a science that deals with earthquakes and with artificially produced vibrations of the earth — **seis·mo·log·i·cal** \,sīz-mə-'läj-i-kəl, ,sīs-\ *adj* — **seis·mo·log·i·cal·ly** \-k(ə-)lē\ *adv* — **seis·mol·o·gist** \sīz-'mäl-ə-jəst, sīs-\ *n*

seize \'sēz\ *vb* [OF *saisir* to put in possession, fr. ML *sacire*] **1 :** to take possession of by force ⟨*seize* a fortress⟩ **2 :** to take hold of suddenly or with force **:** CLUTCH **3 :** UNDERSTAND, COMPREHEND ⟨*seize* an idea quickly⟩ **4 :** to take prisoner **:** ARREST **5 :** to bind together by lashing (as with small cord) ⟨*seize* two ropes⟩ **6 :** to attack or overwhelm suddenly (as with fever) **7 :** to stick fast to a relatively moving part (as a bearing or piston) **syn** see TAKE — **seiz·er** *n* — **seize on** *or* **seize upon :** to take immediate advantage or make immediate use of **:** CLUTCH

seiz·ing \'sē-ziŋ\ *n* **1 :** the operation of fastening together or lashing with small rope or cord **2 a :** the cord used in seizing **b :** the fastening so made

sei·zure \'sē-zhər\ *n* **1 :** the act or process of seizing **:** the state of being seized **2 :** a sudden attack (as of disease) **:** FIT

se·la·chi·an \sə-'lā-kē-ən\ *n* [Gk *selachos*] **:** any of a variously limited group (Selachii) of elasmobranch fishes comprising the true sharks and often related forms — **selachian** *adj*

se·lag·i·nel·la \sə-,laj-ə-'nel-ə\ *n* **:** any of a genus of mossy lower vascular plants

se·lah \'sē-lə, -,lä\ *interj* — a biblical term found in the Psalms and in Habakkuk and believed to have been an exclamation or musical direction

sel·dom \'sel-dəm\ *adv* [OE *seldan*] **:** in few instances **:** RARELY, INFREQUENTLY

¹se·lect \sə-'lekt\ *adj* [L *selectus*, pp. of *seligere* to select, fr. *se-* apart + *legere* to gather, pick] **1 :** chosen from a number or group by fitness or preference **2 a :** of special value or excellence **:** SUPERIOR, CHOICE ⟨a *select* chorus⟩ **b :** exclusively or fastidiously chosen often with regard to social, economic, or cultural characteristics ⟨*select* membership⟩ **3 :** judicious or restrictive in choice **:** DISCRIMINATING — **se·lect·ness** *n*

²select *vb* **:** to take by preference from a number or group **:** pick out **:** CHOOSE

se·lect·ee \sə-,lek-'tē\ *n* **:** one inducted into military service under selective service

se·lec·tion \sə-'lek-shən\ *n* **1 :** the act or process of selecting **:** the state of being selected **2 :** one that is selected **:** CHOICE; *also* **:** a collection of selected things **3 :** a natural or artificial process that prevents or tends to prevent some individuals or groups of organisms from surviving and propagating and allows others to do so

se·lec·tive \sə-'lek-tiv\ *adj* **1 :** of, relating to, or characterized by selection **:** selecting or tending to select **2 :** of, relating to, or constituting the ability of a radio circuit or apparatus to respond to a specific frequency without interference — **se·lec·tive·ly** *adv* — **se·lec·tive·ness** *n* — **se·lec·tiv·i·ty** \si-,lek-'tiv-ət-ē, ,sē-\ *n*

selective service *n* **:** the military service of a person inducted into the armed forces under a governmental act or decree

se·lect·man \sə-'lek(t)-,man, -mən; -,lek(t)-'man\ *n* **:** one of a board of town officials elected annually in some of the New England states

se·lec·tor \sə-'lek-tər\ *n* **:** one that selects

Se·le·ne \sə-'lē-nē\ *n* **:** the goddess of the moon in Greek mythology

sel·e·nite \'sel-ə-,nīt\ *n* [Gk *selēnē* moon; fr. the belief that it waxed and waned with the moon] **:** a variety of gypsum occurring in transparent crystals or crystalline masses

se·le·ni·um \sə-'lē-nē-əm\ *n* [NL, fr. Gk *selēnē* moon] **:** a nonmetallic chemical element that varies in electrical conductivity with the intensity of its illumination and is used in electronic devices — see ELEMENT table

sel·e·nog·ra·pher \,sel-ə-'näg-rə-fər\ *n* **:** a specialist in selenography

sel·e·nog·ra·phy \,sel-ə-'näg-rə-fē\ *n* [Gk *selēnē* moon] **1 :** the science of the physical features of the moon **2 :** the physical features of the moon — **se·le·no·graph·ic** \sə-,lē-nə-'graf-ik\ *adj*

¹self \'self\ *pron* [OE, intensive pron.] **:** MYSELF, HIMSELF, HERSELF ⟨check payable to *self*⟩ ⟨accommodations for *self* and wife⟩

²self *adj* **1 :** having a single character or quality throughout; *esp* **:** having one color only ⟨a *self* flower⟩ **2 :** of the same kind (as in color, material, or pattern) as something with which it is used ⟨a *self* belt⟩⟨*self* trimming⟩

³self \'self\ *n, pl* **selves** \'selvz\ **1 :** a person regarded as an individual apart from everyone else ⟨a man's *self*⟩ **2 :** a particular side of a person's character ⟨his better *self*⟩ **3 :** personal interest or advantage ⟨without thought of *self*⟩

⁴self *vb* **1 :** INBREED **2 :** SELF-POLLINATE

self- \'self *before* '-stressed syllable, ,self *before* ,-stressed *or* unstressed syllable\ *comb form* **1 a :** oneself or itself ⟨*self*-loving⟩ **b :** of oneself or itself ⟨*self*-abasement⟩ **c :** by oneself or itself ⟨*self*-propelled⟩ **2 a :** to, with, for, or toward oneself or itself ⟨*self*-consistent⟩ ⟨*self*-addressed⟩ ⟨*self*-satisfaction⟩ **b :** of or in oneself or itself inherently ⟨*self*-evident⟩ **c :** from or by means of oneself or itself ⟨*self*-fertile⟩

self-aban·doned \,self-ə-'ban-dənd\ *adj* **:** abandoned by oneself; *esp* **:** given up to one's impulses

self-abase·ment \,self-ə-'bās-mənt\ *n* **:** humiliation of oneself based on feelings of inferiority, guilt, or shame

self-ab·ne·gat·ing \'self-'ab-ni-,gāt-iŋ\ *adj* **:** SELF-DENYING

self-ab·ne·ga·tion \,self-,ab-ni-'gā-shən\ *n* **:** SELF-DENIAL

self-ab·sorbed \,self-əb-'sórbd, -'zórbd\ *adj* **:** absorbed in one's own thoughts, activities, or interests

self-ab·sorp·tion \-'sórp-shən, -'zórp-\ *n* **:** preoccupation with oneself

self-abuse \,self-ə-'byüs\ *n* **1 :** reproach of oneself **2 :** MASTURBATION

self-ac·cu·sa·tion \,self-,ak-yə-'zā-shən\ *n* **:** the act or an instance of accusing oneself

self-ac·quired \,self-ə-'kwīrd\ *adj* **:** acquired by oneself or for one's own use and benefit

self-act·ing \'self-'ak-tiŋ\ *adj* **:** acting or capable of acting of or by itself **:** AUTOMATIC

self-ad·dressed \,self-ə-'drest, 'self-'ad-,rest\ *adj* **:** addressed for return to the sender ⟨*self-addressed* envelope⟩

self-ad·just·ing \,self-ə-'jəs-tiŋ\ *adj* **:** adjusting by itself ⟨*self-adjusting* wrench⟩

self-ad·min·is·tered \'self-əd-'min-ə-stərd\ *adj* **:** administered, managed, or dispensed by oneself

self-ad·mi·ra·tion \,self-,ad-mə-'rā-shən\ *n* **:** SELF-CONCEIT

self-ad·vance·ment \,self-əd-'van(t)s-mənt\ *n* **:** the act of advancing oneself

self-af·fect·ed \,self-ə-'fek-təd\ *adj* : SELF-LOVING, CONCEITED

self-ag·gran·dize·ment \,self-ə-'gran-dəz-mənt, -,dīz-; ,self-,ag-rən-'dīz-\ *n* : the act or process of making oneself greater (as in power or influence)

self-ag·gran·diz·ing \,self-ə-'gran-,dī-ziŋ, 'self-'ag-rən-\ *adj* : acting or seeking to make oneself greater

self-anal·y·sis \,self-ə-'nal-ə-səs\ *n* : a systematic attempt by an individual to understand his own personality without the aid of another person — **self-an·a·lyt·i·cal** \,self-,an-ᵊl-'it-i-kəl\ *adj*

self-ap·plause \,self-ə-'plòz\ *n* : an expression or feeling of approval of oneself

self-ap·point·ed \,self-ə-'pòint-əd\ *adj* : appointed by oneself usu. without warrant or qualifications ⟨a *self≠ appointed* censor⟩

self-ap·pro·ba·tion \,self-,ap-rə-'bā-shən\ *n* : satisfaction with one's actions and achievements

self-as·sert·ing \,self-ə-'sərt-iŋ\ *adj* 1 : asserting oneself or one's own rights or claims 2 : putting oneself forward in a confident or arrogant manner

self-as·ser·tion \,self-ə-'sər-shən\ *n* 1 : the act of asserting oneself or one's own rights or claims 2 : the act of asserting one's superiority over others

self-as·ser·tive \-'sərt-iv\ *adj* : given to or characterized by self-assertion — **self-as·sert·ive·ly** *adv* — **self-as·sert·ive·ness** *n*

self-as·sur·ance \,self-ə-'shùr-ən(t)s\ *n* : SELF-CONFIDENCE

self-as·sured \-'shùrd\ *adj* : SELF-CONFIDENT — **self-as·sured·ness** \-'shùr-əd-nəs, -'shùrd-\ *n*

self-aware·ness \,self-ə-'wa(ə)r-nəs, -'we(ə)r-\ *n* : an awareness of one's own personality or individuality

self-blind·ed \'self-'blīn-dəd\ *adj* : blinded or misled by oneself — **self-blind·ed·ness** *n*

self-born \'self-'bòrn\ *adj* 1 : arising within the self ⟨*self-born* sorrows⟩ 2 : springing from a prior self ⟨phoenix rising *self-born* from the fire⟩

self-cen·tered \'self-'sent-ərd\ *adj* : interested chiefly in one's own self : SELFISH — **self-cen·tered·ly** *adv* — **self-cen·tered·ness** *n*

self-charg·ing \-'chär-jiŋ\ *adj* : that charges itself

self-clos·ing \-'klō-ziŋ\ *adj* : closing or shutting automatically after being opened

self-col·ored \-'kəl-ərd\ *adj* : of a single color ⟨a *self≠ colored* flower⟩

self-com·mand \,self-kə-'mand\ *n* : control of one's own behavior and emotions : SELF-CONTROL

self-com·pat·i·ble \,self-kəm-'pat-ə-bəl\ *adj* : capable of effective self-pollination — compare SELF-INCOMPATIBLE

self-com·pla·cen·cy \,self-kəm-'plās-ᵊn-sē\ *n* : SELF≠ SATISFACTION

self-com·pla·cent \-ᵊnt\ *adj* : SELF-SATISFIED — **self-com·pla·cent·ly** *adv*

self-com·posed \,self-kəm-'pōzd\ *adj* : having control over one's emotions : CALM — **self-com·pos·ed·ly** \-'pō-zəd-lē\ *adv*

self-con·ceit \,self-kən-'sēt\ *n* : an exaggerated opinion of one's own qualities or abilities : VANITY — **self-con·ceit·ed** \-əd\ *adj*

self-con·cern \,self-kən-'sərn\ *n* : a selfish or morbid concern for oneself — **self-con·cerned** *adj*

self-con·dem·na·tion \,self-,kän-,dem-'nā-shən, -dəm-\ *n* : condemnation of one's own character or actions

self-con·demned \,self-kən-'demd\ *adj* : condemned by oneself

self-con·fessed \-'fest\ *adj* : openly acknowledged

self-con·fi·dence \'self-'kän-fəd-ən(t)s, -fə-,den(t)s\ *n* : confidence in oneself and in one's powers and abilities — **self-con·fi·dent** \-fəd-ənt, -fə-,dent\ *adj* — **self-con·fi·dent·ly** *adv*

self-con·scious \'self-'kän-chəs\ *adj* 1 : aware of oneself as an individual 2 : uncomfortably conscious of oneself as an object of the observation of others : ill at ease — **self-con·scious·ly** *adv* — **self-con·scious·ness** *n*

self-con·sis·tent \,self-kən-'sis-tənt\ *adj* : having each part logically consistent with the rest — **self-con·sist·en·cy** \-tən-sē\ *n*

self-con·sti·tut·ed \'self-'kän(t)-stə-,t(y)üt-əd\ *adj* : constituted by oneself

self-con·tained \,self-kən-'tānd\ *adj* 1 : sufficient in itself 2 a : showing self-command b : formal and reserved in manner 3 : complete in itself ⟨a *self-contained* machine⟩ — **self-con·tained·ly** \-'tā-nəd-lē, -'tān-dlē\ *adv* — **self-con·tained·ness** \-'tā-nəd-nəs, -'tān(d)-nəs\ *n* — **self-con·tain·ment** \-'tān-mənt\ *n*

self-con·tempt \,self-kən-'tem(p)t\ *n* : contempt for oneself

self-con·tent \-'tent\ *n* : SELF-SATISFACTION

self-con·tent·ed \-'tent-əd\ *adj* : SELF-SATISFIED — **self-con·tent·ed·ly** *adv* — **self-con·tent·ed·ness** *n*

self-con·tent·ment \-'tent-mənt\ *n* : SELF-SATISFACTION

self-con·tra·dic·to·ry \,self-,kän-trə-'dik-t(ə-)rē\ *adj* : consisting of two contradictory members or parts ⟨a *self≠ contradictory* statement⟩

self-con·trol \,self-kən-'trōl\ *n* : control over one's own impulses, emotions, or acts — **self-con·trolled** \-'trōld\ *adj*

self-cor·rect·ing \,self-kə-'rek-tiŋ\ *adj* : acting automatically to correct or compensate for errors or weaknesses

self-cre·at·ed \,self-krē-'āt-əd\ *adj* : created or appointed by oneself

self-crit·i·cism \'self-'krit-ə-,siz-əm\ *n* : the act or capacity of criticizing one's own faults or shortcomings

self-de·ceiv·ing \,self-di-'sē-viŋ\ *adj* 1 : given to self≠ deception ⟨a *self-deceiving* hypocrite⟩ 2 : serving to deceive oneself ⟨*self-deceiving* excuses⟩

self-de·cep·tion \,self-di-'sep-shən\ *n* : the act of deceiving oneself : the state of being deceived by oneself — **self-de·cep·tive** \-'sep-tiv\ *adj*

self-ded·i·ca·tion \,self-,ded-i-'kā-shən\ *n* : dedication of oneself to a cause or ideal

self-de·feat·ing \,self-di-'fēt-iŋ\ *adj* : acting to defeat its own purpose

self-de·fense \,self-di-'fen(t)s\ *n* : the act of defending oneself, one's property, or a close relative

self-de·ni·al \,self-di-'nī-(ə)l\ *n* : the act of refraining from gratifying one's own desires : a going without something that one wants or needs — **self-de·ny·ing** \-'nī-iŋ\ *adj*

self-de·pend·ence \,self-di-'pen-dən(t)s\ *n* : dependence on one's own resources or exertions : SELF-RELIANCE — **self-de·pend·ent** \-dənt\ *adj*

self-de·pre·ci·a·tion \,self-di-,prē-shē-'ā-shən\ *n* : disparagement or undervaluation of oneself

self-de·spair \,self-di-'spa(ə)r, -'spe(ə)r\ *n* : despair of oneself : HOPELESSNESS

self-de·struc·tion \,self-di-'strək-shən\ *n* : destruction of oneself; *esp* : SUICIDE — **self-de·struc·tive** \-'strək-tiv\ *adj*

self-de·ter·mi·na·tion \,self-di-,tər-mə-'nā-shən\ *n* 1 : the act or power of deciding things for oneself 2 : determination by the people of a territorial unit of their own future political status — **self-de·ter·min·ing** \-'tər-mə-niŋ\ *adj*

self-de·ter·mined \-'tər-mənd\ *adj* : determined by oneself

self-de·vel·op·ment \,self-di-'vel-əp-mənt\ *n* : development of the capabilities or possibilities of oneself

self-de·vo·tion \,self-di-'vō-shən\ *n* : devotion of oneself esp. in service or sacrifice

self-de·vour·ing \,self-di-'vaù(ə)r-iŋ\ *adj* : devouring itself

self-di·rect·ed \,self-də-'rek-təd, -dī-\ *adj* : directed by oneself; *esp* : not guided or impelled by an outside force or agency ⟨a *self-directed* personality⟩

self-dis·ci·pline \'self-'dis-ə-plən\ *n* : correction or regulation of oneself for the sake of improvement — **self-dis·ci·plined** \-plənd\ *adj*

self-dis·cov·ery \,self-dis-'kəv-(ə-)rē\ *n* : the act or process of achieving self-knowledge

self-dis·trust \,self-dis-'trəst\ *n* : a lack of confidence in oneself : DIFFIDENCE — **self-dis·trust·ful** \-fəl\ *adj*

self-doubt \'self-'daùt\ *n* : a lack of faith in oneself — **self-doubt·ing** \-iŋ\ *adj*

self-driv·en \-'driv-ən\ *adj* : driven by itself : AUTOMOTIVE

self-ed·u·cat·ed \-'ej-ə-,kāt-əd\ *adj* : educated by one's own efforts without formal instruction — **self-ed·u·ca·tion** \,self-,ej-ə-'kā-shən\ *n*

self-ef·face·ment \,self-ə-'fās-mənt\ *n* : the placing or keeping of oneself in the background

self-ef·fac·ing \,-'fā-siŋ\ *adj* : RETIRING — **self-ef·fac·ing·ly** \-siŋ-lē\ *adv*

self-em·ployed \,self-im-'plȯid\ *adj* : earning income directly from one's own business, trade, or profession rather than as salary or wages from an employer — **self-em·ploy·ment** \-'plȯi-mənt\ *n*

self-es·teem \,self-ə-'stēm\ *n* **1** : SELF-RESPECT **2** : SELF-CONCEIT

self-ev·i·dent \'self-'ev-əd-ənt, -ə-,dent\ *adj* : evident without proof or argument — **self-ev·i·dent·ly** *adv*

self-ex·am·i·na·tion \,self-ig-,zam-ə-'nā-shən\ *n* : INTROSPECTION

self-ex·e·cut·ing \'self-'ek-sə-,kyüt-iŋ\ *adj* : taking effect immediately without implementing legislation ⟨*self-executing* treaty⟩

self-ex·plain·ing \,self-ik-'splā-niŋ\ *adj* : SELF-EXPLANATORY

self-ex·plan·a·to·ry \-'splan-ə-,tōr-ē, -,tȯr-\ *adj* : understandable without explanation

self-ex·pres·sion \,self-ik-'spresh-ən\ *n* : the expression of one's own personality : assertion of one's individual traits — **self-ex·pres·sive** \-'spres-iv\ *adj*

self-feed \'self-'fēd\ *vt* : to provide (animals) with rations in bulk so as to permit individual selection of kind and quantity of food — **self-feed·er** *n*

self-fer·tile \'self-'fərt-ᵊl\ *adj* : fertile by means of its own pollen or sperm — **self-fer·til·i·ty** \,self-(,)fər-'til-ət-ē\ *n*

self-fer·til·i·za·tion \,self-,fərt-ᵊl-ə-'zā-shən\ *n* : fertilization effected by pollen or sperm from the same individual — **self-fer·til·ize** \'self-'fərt-ᵊl-,īz\ *vb*

self-flat·tery \'self-'flat-ə-rē\ *n* : the glossing over of one's own weaknesses or mistakes and the exaggeration of one's own good qualities and achievements

self-for·get·ful \'self-fər-'get-fəl\ *adj* : having or showing no thought of self or selfish interests — **self-for·get·ful·ly** \-fə-lē\ *adv* — **self-for·get·ful·ness** *n*

self-formed \'self-'fȯrmd\ *adj* : formed or developed by one's own efforts

self-fruit·ful \'self-'früt-fəl\ *adj* : capable of setting a crop of self-pollinated fruit — **self-fruit·ful·ness** *n*

self-ful·fill·ing \,self-fül-'fil-iŋ\ *adj* : marked by or achieving self-fulfillment

self-ful·fill·ment \-'fil-mənt\ *n* : fulfillment of oneself

self-giv·ing \'self-'giv-iŋ\ *adj* : SELF-SACRIFICING, UNSELFISH

self-glo·ri·fi·ca·tion \,self-,glȯr-ə-fə-'kā-shən, -,glȯr-\ *n* : a feeling or expression of one's superiority to others

self-glo·ry \'self-'glȯr-ē, -'glȯr-\ *n* : personal vanity : PRIDE

self-gov·ern·ment \'self-'gəv-ər(n)-mənt, -'gəv-ᵊm-ənt\ *n* **1** : SELF-CONTROL **2** : government of a political unit by action of its own people; *esp* : democratic government — **self-gov·erned** \-'gəv-ərnd\ *adj* — **self-gov·ern·ing** \-ər-niŋ\ *adj*

self-grat·i·fi·ca·tion \,self-,grat-ə-fə-'kā-shən\ *n* : the act of pleasing oneself or of satisfying one's desires

self-hard·en·ing \'self-'härd-niŋ, -ᵊn-iŋ\ *adj* : hardening by itself without quenching after heating ⟨*self-hardening* steel⟩

self-heal \'self-,hēl\ *n* : any of several plants held to possess healing properties; *esp* : a low-growing blue-flowered mint

self-help \'self-'help\ *n* : the act or an instance of providing for or helping oneself without dependence on others

self-hyp·no·sis \,self-hip-'nō-səs\ *n* : hypnosis of oneself

self-ig·nite \,self-ig-'nīt\ *vi* : to become ignited without flame or spark (as under high compression) — **self-ig·ni·tion** \-'nish-ən\ *n*

self-im·mo·la·tion \,self-,im-ə-'lā-shən\ *n* : a deliberate and willing sacrifice of oneself

self-im·por·tance \,self-ᵊm-'pȯrt-ᵊn(t)s, -ən(t)s\ *n* **1** : an exaggerated estimate of one's own importance : SELF-CONCEIT **2** : arrogant or pompous bearing or behavior — **self-im·por·tant** \-ᵊnt, -ənt\ *adj* — **self-im·por·tant·ly** *adv*

self-im·posed \,self-ᵊm-'pōzd\ *adj* : imposed on one by oneself : voluntarily assumed ⟨went into a *self-imposed* exile in his later years⟩

self-im·prove·ment \,self-ᵊm-'prüv-mənt\ *n* : improvement of oneself by one's own action

self-in·clu·sive \,self-in-'klü-siv, -ziv\ *adj* : complete in itself

self-in·com·pat·i·ble \,self-,in-kəm-'pat-ə-bəl\ *adj* : incapable of effective self-pollination — compare SELF-COMPATIBLE

self-in·crim·i·na·tion \,self-in-,krim-ə-'nā-shən\ *n* : incrimination of oneself; *esp* : the giving of evidence or answering of questions the tendency of which would be to subject one to criminal prosecution — **self-in·crim·i·nat·ing** \-'krim-ə-,nāt-iŋ\ *adj*

self-in·duced \,self-in-'d(y)üst\ *adj* **1** : induced by oneself **2** : produced by self-induction ⟨a *self-induced* voltage⟩

self-in·duc·tance \-'dək-tən(t)s\ *n* : inductance that induces an electromotive force in the same circuit as the one in which the current varies

self-in·duc·tion \-'dək-shən\ *n* : induction of an electromotive force in a circuit by a varying current in the same circuit

self-in·dul·gence \,self-in-'dəl-jən(t)s\ *n* : indulgence of one's own appetites, desires, or whims — **self-in·dul·gent** \-jənt\ *adj* — **self-in·dul·gent·ly** *adv*

self-in·flict·ed \,self-in-'flik-təd\ *adj* : inflicted by oneself or by one's own hand ⟨a *self-inflicted* wound⟩

self-ini·ti·at·ed \,self-in-'ish-ē-,āt-əd\ *adj* : initiated by oneself

self-in·struct·ed \,self-in-'strək-təd\ *adj* : SELF-TAUGHT

self-in·ter·est \'self-'in-trəst, -'int-ə-rəst\ *n* **1** : one's own interest or advantage **2** : a concern for one's own advantage and well-being — **self-in·ter·est·ed** \-əd\ *adj* — **self-in·ter·est·ed·ness** *n*

self-in·volved \,self-in-'välvd, -'vȯlvd\ *adj* : SELF-ABSORBED

self·ish \'sel-fish\ *adj* **1** : concerned excessively or exclusively with oneself : seeking or concentrating on one's own advantage, pleasure, or well-being without regard for others **2** : arising from concern with one's own welfare or advantage in disregard of others ⟨a *selfish* act⟩ — **self·ish·ly** *adv* — **self·ish·ness** *n*

self-jus·ti·fi·ca·tion \,self-,jəs-tə-fə-'kā-shən\ *n* : the act or an instance of making excuses for oneself

self-knowl·edge \'self-'näl-ij\ *n* : knowledge or understanding of one's own capabilities, character, feelings, or motivations

self·less \'self-ləs\ *adj* : having or showing no concern for self : UNSELFISH — **self·less·ly** *adv* — **self·less·ness** *n*

self-lim·it·ing \'self-'lim-ət-iŋ\ *adj* : limiting oneself or itself

self-liq·ui·dat·ing \'self-'lik-wə-,dāt-iŋ\ *adj* **1** : of or relating to a commercial transaction in which goods are converted into cash in a short time **2** : generating funds from its own operations to repay the investment made to create it ⟨a *self-liquidating* housing project⟩

self-lock·ing \'self-'läk-iŋ\ *adj* : locking by its own action

self-love \'self-'ləv\ *n* : love of self: **a** : VANITY **b** : regard for one's own happiness or advantage — **self-lov·ing** \-'ləv-iŋ\ *adj*

self-lu·bri·cat·ing \'self-'lü-brə-,kāt-iŋ\ *adj* : lubricating itself

self-lu·mi·nous \'self-'lü-mə-nəs\ *adj* : having in itself the property of emitting light

self-made \'self-'mād\ *adj* **1** : made by oneself or itself **2** : raised from poverty or obscurity by one's own efforts ⟨*self-made* man⟩

self-mas·tery \'self-'mas-t(ə-)rē\ *n* : SELF-COMMAND, SELF-CONTROL

self-mov·ing \'self-'mü-viŋ\ *adj* : capable of moving by itself

self-ob·ser·va·tion \,self-,äb-sər-'vā-shən, -zər-\ *n* **1** : observation of one's own appearance **2** : INTROSPECTION

self-op·er·at·ing \'self-'äp-ə-,rāt-iŋ\ *or* **self-op·er·a·tive** \-'äp-(ə-)rət-iv, -'äp-ə-,rāt-\ *adj* : SELF-ACTING

self-opin·ion·at·ed \,self-ə-'pin-yə-,nāt-əd\ *adj* **1** : CONCEITED **2** : stubbornly holding to one's own opinion : OPINIONATED

self-orig·i·nat·ed \,self-ə-'rij-ə-,nāt-əd\ *adj* : originated by oneself

self-per·pet·u·at·ing \,self-pər-'pech-ə-,wāt-iŋ\ *adj* : capable of continuing or renewing itself indefinitely ⟨*self-perpetuating* board of trustees⟩

self-pity \'self-'pit-ē\ *n* : pity for oneself — **self-pity·ing** \-ē-iŋ\ *adj* — **self-pity·ing·ly** \-iŋ-lē\ *adv*

self-poised \'self-'pòizd\ *adj* **1** : balanced without support **2** : having poise through self-command

self-pol·li·nate \'self-'päl-ə-,nāt\ *vb* : to undergo or cause to undergo self-pollination

self-pol·li·na·tion \,self-,päl-ə-'nā-shən\ *n* : pollination in which the pollen transferred is from the same flower or sometimes from a genetically identical flower (as of the same plant or clone)

self-por·trait \'self-'pōr-trət, -'pȯr-, -,trāt\ *n* : a portrait of oneself done by oneself

self-pos·sessed \,self-pə-'zest\ *adj* : having or showing self-possession : composed in mind or manner : CALM — **self-pos·sessed·ly** \-'zes-əd-lē, -'zest-lē\ *adv*

self-pos·ses·sion \,self-pə-'zesh-ən\ *n* : control of one's emotions or reactions : PRESENCE OF MIND, COMPOSURE

self-praise \'self-'prāz\ *n* : praise of oneself

self-pres·er·va·tion \,self-,prez-ər-'vā-shən\ *n* : the keeping of oneself from destruction, injury, or loss

self-pride \'self-'prīd\ *n* : pride in oneself or in that which relates to oneself

self-pro·claimed \,self-prō-'klāmd\ *adj* : based on one's own say-so ⟨a *self-proclaimed* genius⟩

self-pro·duced \,self-prə-'d(y)üst\ *adj* : produced by oneself

self-pro·pelled \,self-prə-'peld\ *adj* : containing within itself the means for its own propulsion

self-pro·pel·ling \-'pel-iŋ\ *adj* : SELF-PROPELLED

self-pro·tec·tion \,self-prə-'tek-shən\ *n* : protection of oneself : SELF-DEFENSE

self-pun·ish·ment \'self-'pən-ish-mənt\ *n* : punishment of oneself

self-pu·ri·fi·ca·tion \,self-,pyur-ə-fə-'kā-shən\ *n* : purification of oneself ⟨moral *self-purification*⟩

self-ques·tion·ing \'self-'kwes-chə-niŋ\ *n* : examination of one's own actions and motives

self-re·al·i·za·tion \,self-,rē-ə-lə-'zā-shən\ *n* : fulfillment by oneself of the possibilities of one's character or personality

self-re·cord·ing \,self-ri-'kȯrd-iŋ\ *adj* : making a record automatically ⟨*self-recording* instruments⟩

self-re·gard \,self-ri-'gärd\ *n* **1** : regard for or consideration of oneself or one's own interests **2** : SELF-RESPECT — **self-re·gard·ing** \-iŋ\ *adj*

self-reg·is·ter·ing \'self-'rej-ə-st(ə-)riŋ *adj* : registering automatically ⟨a *self-registering* barometer⟩

self-reg·u·lat·ing \'self-'reg-yə-,lāt-iŋ\ *adj* : regulating oneself; *esp* : AUTOMATIC ⟨a *self-regulating* mechanism⟩ — **self-reg·u·la·tion** \,self-,reg-yə-'lā-shən\ *n*

self-re·li·ance \,self-ri-'lī-ənts\ *n* : reliance upon one's own efforts and abilities — **self-re·li·ant** \-ənt\ *adj*

self-re·nun·ci·a·tion \,self-ri-,nən(t)-sē-'ā-shən\ *n* : renunciation of one's own desires or ambitions

self-re·pres·sion \,self-ri-'presh-ən\ *n* : the keeping to oneself of one's thoughts, wishes, or feelings

self-re·proach \,self-ri-'prōch\ *n* : the act of blaming or accusing oneself — **self-re·proach·ful** \-fəl\ *adj*

self-re·proach·ing \-'prō-chiŋ\ *adj* : reproaching oneself

self-re·spect \,self-ri-'spekt\ *n* **1** : a proper respect for oneself as a human being **2** : regard for one's own standing or position — **self-re·spect·ing** \-'spek-tiŋ\ *adj*

self-re·straint \,self-ri-'strānt\ *n* : restraint imposed on oneself : SELF-CONTROL

self-re·veal·ing \,self-ri-'vē-liŋ\ *adj* : marked by self-revelation

self-rev·e·la·tion \,self-,rev-ə-'lā-shən\ *n* : revelation of one's own thoughts, feelings, and attitudes esp. without deliberate intent

self-re·ward·ing \,self-ri-'wȯrd-iŋ\ *adj* : containing or producing its own reward ⟨a *self-rewarding* virtue⟩

self-righ·teous \'self-'rī-chəs\ *adj* : convinced of one's own righteousness esp. in contrast with the actions and beliefs of others — **self-righ·teous·ly** *adv* — **self-righ·teous·ness** *n*

self-right·ing \'self-'rīt-iŋ\ *adj* : capable of righting itself when capsized ⟨a *self-righting* boat⟩

self-ris·ing \'self-'rī-ziŋ\ *adj* : rising without the use of leaven ⟨*self-rising* flour⟩

self-sac·ri·fice \'self-'sak-rə-,fīs, -fəs\ *n* : sacrifice of oneself of one's interest for others or for a cause or ideal — **self-sac·ri·fic·ing** \-,fī-siŋ\ *adj* — **self-sac·ri·fic·ing·ly** \-siŋ-lē\ *adv*

self-same \'self-,sām\ *adj* : precisely the same : IDENTICAL — **self·same·ness** *n*

self-sat·is·fac·tion \,self-,sat-əs-'fak-shən\ *n* : a usu. smug satisfaction with oneself or one's position or achievements

self-sat·is·fied \'self-'sat-əs-,fīd\ *adj* : feeling or showing self-satisfaction

self-sat·is·fy·ing \-,fī-iŋ\ *adj* : giving satisfaction to oneself

self-seal·ing \'self-'sē-liŋ\ *adj* : capable of sealing itself (as after puncture) ⟨a *self-sealing* tire⟩

self-search·ing \'self-'sər-chiŋ\ *adj* : SELF-QUESTIONING

self-seek·er \'self-'sē-kər\ *n* : one that seeks only or mainly his own advantage or pleasure — **self-seek·ing** \-kiŋ\ *n or adj*

self-ser·vice \'self-'sər-vəs\ *n* : the serving of oneself (as in a cafeteria or supermarket) with things to be paid for at a cashier's desk usu. upon leaving — **self-service** *adj*

self-slaugh·ter \'self-'slȯt-ər\ *n* : SUICIDE

self-sow \'self-'sō\ *vi* : to sow itself by dropping seeds or by natural action (as of wind or water)

self-start·er \'self-'stärt-ər\ *n* : a more or less automatic attachment for starting an internal-combustion engine

self-start·ing \-'stärt-iŋ\ *adj* : capable of starting by itself

self-ster·ile \'self-'ster-əl\ *adj* : sterile to its own pollen or sperm — **self-ste·ril·i·ty** \,self-stə-'ril-ət-ē\ *n*

self-styled \'self-'stīld\ *adj* : called by oneself ⟨*self-styled* experts⟩

self-suf·fi·cient \,self-sə-'fish-ənt\ *adj* **1** : able to maintain oneself without outside aid : capable of providing for one's own needs **2** : having an extreme confidence in one's own ability or worth : HAUGHTY, OVERBEARING — **self-suf·fi·cien·cy** \-ən-sē\ *n*

self-suf·fic·ing \,self-sə-'fī-siŋ\ *adj* : SELF-SUFFICIENT — **self-suf·fic·ing·ly** \-'fī-siŋ-lē\ *adv* — **self-suf·fic·ing·ness** *n*

self-sup·port \,self-sə-'pōrt, -'pȯrt\ *n* : independent support of oneself or itself — **self-sup·port·ed** \-əd\ *adj* — **self-sup·port·ing** \-iŋ\ *adj*

self-sus·tained \,self-sə-'stānd\ *adj* : sustained by oneself

self-sus·tain·ing \-'stā-niŋ\ *adj* **1** : maintaining or able to maintain oneself by independent effort : SELF-SUPPORTING **2** : maintaining or able to maintain itself once commenced ⟨a *self-sustaining* nuclear reaction⟩

self-taught \'self-'tȯt\ *adj* **1** : having knowledge or skills acquired by one's own efforts without formal instruction **2** : learned by oneself ⟨*self-taught* knowledge⟩

self-treat·ment \'self-'trēt-mənt\ *n* : medication of oneself or treatment of one's ailment without medical supervision

self-trust \'self-'trəst\ *n* : SELF-CONFIDENCE

self-un·der·stand·ing \,self-,ən-dər-'stan-diŋ\ *n* : SELF-KNOWLEDGE

self-will \'self-'wil\ *n* : stubborn or willful adherence to one's own desires or ideas : OBSTINACY — **self-willed** \-'wild\ *adj*

self-wind·ing \'self-'wīn-diŋ\ *adj* : not needing to be wound by hand : winding by itself ⟨a *self-winding* watch⟩

Sel·juk \'sel-,jük, sel-'\ *or* **Sel·ju·ki·an** \sel-'jü-kē-ən\ *adj* **1** : of or relating to any of several Turkish dynasties ruling in western Asia in the 11th, 12th, and 13th centuries **2** : of, relating to, or characteristic of a Turkish people ruled over by a Seljuk dynasty — **Seljuk** *or* **Seljukian** *n*

¹**sell** \'sel\ *vb* **sold** \'sōld\; **sell·ing** [OE *sellan* to give, sell] **1** : to deliver up in violation of duty, trust, or loyalty : BETRAY ⟨the traitors *sold* their king to the enemy⟩ **2 a** : to give in exchange esp. for money ⟨he *sold* me his car⟩ ⟨*sells* his services to the highest bidder⟩; *also* : to give in exchange foolishly or dishonorably ⟨*sold* his birthright for a mess of pottage⟩ **b** : to work at or deal in the sale of : have or offer for sale ⟨he *sells* insurance⟩ ⟨that store *sells* only foreign foods⟩; *also* : to achieve the sale of ⟨tried *selling* encyclopedias for a while⟩ **3 a** : to find buyers : be bought ⟨that model didn't *sell* very well⟩ ⟨this item will really *sell*⟩ **b** : to be for sale ⟨they *sell* for $15 apiece⟩ **4 a** : to make acceptable, believable, or desirable by persuasion ⟨the President couldn't *sell* his program to Congress⟩ **b** : to bring around to a favorable way of thinking ⟨tried to *sell* me on his idea⟩ **c** : to gain acceptance or approval ⟨your idea won't *sell* with them⟩ — **sell-**

a·ble \'sel-ə-bəl\ *adj* — **sell short** : to underestimate the ability, strength, or importance of ⟨made the mistake of *selling* his rival *short*⟩

²sell *n* **1** : a deliberate deception : HOAX **2** : the act or a type of selling : SALESMANSHIP ⟨the hard *sell*⟩

sell·er \'sel-ər\ *n* **1** : one that offers for sale or makes a sale **2** : a product selling well or to a specified extent ⟨a good *seller*⟩

selling race *n* : a race in which the winning horse is put up for auction

sell out \(')sel-'aut\ *vb* **1** : to dispose of all of one's goods by sale **2** : to betray one's cause or associates

sell·out \'sel-ˌaut\ *n* **1** : the act or an instance of selling out **2** : a performance or exhibition for which all seats are sold

selt·zer \'selt-sər\ *n* [G *Selterser wasser* water of Selters, fr. *Nieder Selters*, Germany] : an artificially prepared water containing carbon dioxide

sel·vage *or* **sel·vedge** \'sel-vij\ *n* [ME *selvage*] : the edge of cloth so woven that it will not ravel

selves *pl of* SELF

se·man·tic \si-'mant-ik\ *adj* [Gk *sēmainein* to signify, mean, fr. *sēma* sign, token] **1** : of or relating to meaning in language **2** : of or relating to semantics — **se·man·ti·cal·ly** \-'mant-i-k(ə-)lē\ *adv*

se·man·ti·cist \si-'mant-ə-səst\ *n* : a specialist in semantics

se·man·tics \si-'mant-iks\ *n* : the study of meanings; *esp* : the historical and psychological study and the classification of changes in the meaning of words or forms viewed as factors in linguistic development

¹sem·a·phore \'sem-ə-ˌfōr, -ˌfór\ *n* [Gk *sēma* sign] **1** : an apparatus for visual signaling (as by the position of one or more movable arms) **2** : a system of visual signaling by two flags held one in each hand

²semaphore *vb* : to signal by or as if by semaphore

se·mat·ic \si-'mat-ik\ *adj* [Gk *sēmat-*, *sēma* sign] : serving as a warning of danger ⟨the conspicuous *sematic* colors of the skunk⟩

sem·blance \'sem-blən(t)s\ *n* [MF, fr. *sembler* to be like, seem, fr. L *similare* to copy, fr. *similis* similar] **1** : outward appearance **2** : LIKENESS, IMAGE

semaphore; indicating stop

se·men \'sē-mən\ *n*, *pl* **sem·i·na** \'sem-ə-nə\ *or* **semens** [L *semin-*, *semen* seed; akin to E ²*sow*] : a viscid whitish fluid of the male reproductive tract consisting of spermatozoa suspended in secretions of accessory glands

se·mes·ter \sə-'mes-tər\ *n* [G, fr. L *semestris* half-yearly, fr. *sex* six + *mensis* month] : one of two usu. 18-week terms into which an academic year is usu. divided — **se·mes·tral** \-trəl\ *or* **se·mes·tri·al** \-trē-əl\ *adj*

semi- \'sem-i, 'sem-, -ˌī\ *prefix* [L] **1 a** : precisely half of; *also* : being a usu. vertically bisected form of (a specified architectural feature) ⟨*semi*arch⟩ ⟨*semi*dome⟩ **b** : half in quantity or value : half of or occurring halfway through a specified period of time ⟨*semi*annual⟩ ⟨*semi*centenary⟩ — compare BI- **2** : to some extent : partly : incompletely ⟨*semi*plastic⟩ — compare DEMI-, HEMI- **3 a** : partial : incomplete ⟨*semi*education⟩ **b** : having some of the characteristics of ⟨*semi*porcelain⟩ **c** : quasi ⟨*semi*judicial⟩

semi·ab·strac·tion \ˌsem-ē-ab-'strak-shən, ˌsem-ˌī-\ *n* : a composition or creation (as in painting or sculpture) in which the subject matter is easily recognizable though the form is stylized according to an abstract system or device — **semi·ab·stract** \-ab-'strakt, -'ab-ˌ\ *adj*

semi·an·nu·al \ˌsem-ē-'an-y(ə-w)əl, ˌsem-ˌī-\ *adj* : occurring twice a year ⟨*semiannual* dividend on stock⟩ — **semi·an·nu·al·ly** \-ē\ *adv*

semi·aquat·ic \-ə-'kwät-ik, -'kwat-\ *adj* : growing indifferently in or adjacent to water; *also* : frequenting but not living wholly in water

semi·ar·bo·re·al \-ˌär-'bōr-ē-əl, -'bór-\ *adj* : often inhabiting and frequenting trees

semi·ar·id \-'ar-əd\ *adj* : characterized by light rainfall; *esp* : having from about 10 to 20 inches of annual precipitation

semi·au·to·mat·ic \-ˌȯt-ə-'mat-ik\ *adj* : not fully auto-

matic — **semiautomatic** *n* — **semi·au·to·mat·i·cal·ly** \-'mat-i-k(ə-)lē\ *adv*

semi·au·ton·o·mous \-ȯ-'tän-ə-məs\ *adj* : chiefly self-governing within a larger political or organizational entity

semi·base·ment \ˌsem-i-'bās-mənt, ˌsem-ˌī-\ *n* : a basement that is below ground level for only part of its depth

semi·breve \'sem-i-ˌbrēv, 'sem-ˌī-, -ˌbrev\ *n* : WHOLE NOTE

semi·cen·ten·a·ry \ˌsem-i-,sen-'ten-ə-rē, ˌsem-ˌī-, -'sent-°n-ˌer-ē\ *n or adj* : SEMICENTENNIAL

semi·cen·ten·ni·al \-ˌsen-'ten-ē-əl\ *n* : a 50th anniversary or its celebration — **semicentennial** *adj*

semi·cir·cle \'sem-i-ˌsər-kəl\ *n* : one of two halves of a circle formed by a diameter — **semi·cir·cu·lar** \ˌsem-i-'sər-kyə-lər\ *adj*

semicircular canal *n* : any of the loop-shaped tubular parts in the inner ear of vertebrates that together constitute a sensory organ concerned with the maintenance of bodily equilibrium

semi·civ·i·lized \ˌsem-i-'siv-ə-ˌlīzd, ˌsem-ˌī-\ *adj* : partly civilized

semi·clas·si·cal \-'klas-i-kəl\ *adj* **1** : having some of the characteristics of the classical: as **a** : of, relating to, or being a musical composition that acts as a bridge between classical and popular music **b** : of, relating to, or being a classical composition that has developed popular appeal **2** : inferior to the classical in importance or quality ⟨a *semiclassical* theory in physics⟩

semi·co·lon \'sem-i-ˌkō-lən\ *n* : a punctuation mark ; used chiefly to separate independent clauses not joined by a conjunction, to separate independent clauses the second of which begins with a conjunctive adverb, or to separate phrases and clauses containing commas

semi·con·duc·tor \ˌsem-i-kən-'dək-tər, ˌsem-ˌī-\ *n* : any of a class of solids (as germanium) whose electrical conductivity is between that of a conductor and that of an insulator in being nearly metallic at high temperatures and nearly absent at low temperatures — **semi·con·duct·ing** \-tiŋ\ *adj* — **semi·con·duc·tive** \-tiv\ *adj*

semi·con·scious \-'kän-chəs\ *adj* : incompletely conscious — **semi·con·scious·ly** *adv* — **semi·con·scious·ness** *n*

semi·crus·ta·ceous \-ˌkrəs-'tā-shəs\ *adj* : tending to form a somewhat crisp or brittle layer

semi·crys·tal·line \-'kris-tə-lən\ *adj* : partly crystalline

semi·dark·ness \-'därk-nəs\ *n* : partial darkness

semi·des·ert \-'dez-ərt\ *n* : an area having some of the characteristics of a desert and often lying between a desert and grassland or woodland

semi·de·tached \-di-'tacht\ *adj* : forming one of a pair of residences joined into one building by a common sidewall

semi·di·vine \-də-'vīn\ *adj* : more than mortal but not fully divine

semi·do·mes·ti·cat·ed \-də-'mes-ti-ˌkāt-əd\ *adj* : of, relating to, or living in semidomestication

semi·do·mes·ti·ca·tion \-də-ˌmes-ti-'kā-shən\ *n* : a captive state (as in a zoo) of a wild animal in which its living conditions and often its breeding are controlled by man

semi·dry \ˌsem-i-'drī\ *adj* : moderately dry

semi·dry·ing \ˌsem-i-'drī-iŋ\ *adj* : that dries imperfectly or slowly ⟨cottonseed oil is a *semidrying* oil⟩

semi·erect \ˌsem-ē-ə-'rekt, ˌsem-ˌī-ə-\ *adj* : imperfectly erect ⟨*semierect* primates⟩

semi·ev·er·green \-'ev-ər-ˌgrēn\ *adj* : HALF-EVERGREEN

¹semi·fi·nal \ˌsem-i-'fīn-°l\ *adj* **1** : being next to the last in an elimination tournament ⟨*semifinal* pairings⟩ **2** : of or participating in a semifinal

²semi·fi·nal \'sem-i-ˌfīn-°l\ *n* : a semifinal match or round — **semi·fi·nal·ist** \ˌsem-i-'fīn-°l-əst\ *n*

semi·fit·ted \ˌsem-i-'fit-əd, ˌsem-ˌī-\ *adj* : partly fitted

semi·flex·i·ble \-'flek-sə-bəl\ *adj* **1** : somewhat flexible **2** : consisting of a heavy flexible board under the covering material ⟨*semiflexible* book covers⟩

semi·flu·id \ˌsem-i-'flü-əd, ˌsem-ˌī-\ *adj* : having the qualities of both a fluid and a solid : VISCOUS ⟨fluid and *semifluid* greases⟩ — **semifluid** *n*

semi·for·mal \-'fȯr-məl\ *adj* : being or suitable for an occasion of moderate formality ⟨a *semiformal* dinner⟩ ⟨*semiformal* dress⟩

semi·glob·u·lar \-'gläb-yə-lər\ *adj* : having the form of half a sphere

semi·gloss \'sem-i-ˌgläs, 'sem-ˌī-, -ˌglós\ *adj* : having a low luster

semi·gov·ern·men·tal \ˌsem-i-ˌgəv-ər(n)-'ment-ᵊl, ˌsem-ˌī-\ *adj* : having some governmental functions and powers

semi·hard \-'härd\ *adj* : moderately hard; *esp* : that can be cut with little difficulty

semi·hol·i·day \ˌsem-i-'häl-ə-ˌdā, ˌsem-ˌī-\ *n* : a weekday during a religious festival (as the Passover) on which ceremonial observances continue but activities prohibited on full festival days are permitted though discouraged

semi·in·de·pend·ent \ˌsem-ē-ˌin-də-'pen-dənt, ˌsem-ˌī-\ *adj* : partially independent; *esp* : SEMIAUTONOMOUS

semi·in·di·rect \ˌsem-ē-ˌin-də-'rəkt, ˌsem-ˌī-, -ˌdī-\ *adj* : using a translucent reflector that transmits some light while reflecting most of it ⟨*semi-indirect* lighting⟩

semi·leg·end·ary \ˌsem-i-'lej-ən-ˌder-ē, ˌsem-ˌī-\ *adj* : elaborated in legend but having a dubious historical existence

semi·liq·uid \ˌsem-i-'lik-wəd, ˌsem-ˌī-\ *adj* : having the qualities of both a liquid and a solid : SEMIFLUID ⟨*semiliquid* ice cream⟩ — **semiliquid** *n*

semi·lit·er·ate \-'lit-ə-rət, -'li-trət\ *adj* **1** : able to read and write on an elementary level **2** : able to read but unable to write

semi·log·a·rith·mic \-,lóg-ə-'rith-mik, -,läg-\ *also* **semi·log** \'sem-i-,lóg, 'sem-,ī-, -,läg\ *adj* : having one scale logarithmic and the other arithmetic ⟨*semilogarithmic* graph paper⟩

semi·lu·nar \ˌsem-i-'lü-nər, ˌsem-ˌī-\ *adj* : shaped like a crescent

semilunar valve *n* : any of the crescentic valvular cusps that occur as a set of three between the heart and the aorta and another of three between the heart and the pulmonary artery

semi·lus·trous \-'ləs-trəs\ *adj* : slightly lustrous

semi·mat *or* **semi·matt** *or* **semi·matte** \ˌsem-i-'mat, ˌsem-ˌī-\ *adj* : having a slight luster

semi·moist \-'móist\ *adj* : slightly moist

semi·mo·nas·tic \-mə-'nas-tik\ *adj* : having some features characteristic of a monastic order

¹semi·month·ly \-'mən(t)th-lē\ *adj* : occurring twice a month

²semimonthly *n* : a semimonthly publication

³semimonthly *adv* : twice a month

semi·mys·ti·cal \-'mis-ti-kəl\ *adj* : having some of the qualities of mysticism

sem·i·nal \'sem-ən-ᵊl\ *adj* [L *semin-, semen* seed] **1** : of, relating to, or consisting of seed or semen **2** : having the character of a creative power, principle, or source : containing or contributing the seeds of later development : GERMINATIVE, ORIGINAL — **sem·i·nal·ly** \-ᵊl-ē\ *adv*

sem·i·nar \'sem-ə-ˌnär\ *n* [G, fr. L *seminarium* seedbed] **1** : a course of study pursued by a group of advanced students doing original research under a professor and exchanging results and discussions **2** : a meeting of a seminar or a room for such meetings

sem·i·nar·i·an \ˌsem-ə-'ner-ē-ən\ *n* : a student in a seminary esp. of the Roman Catholic Church

sem·i·nary \'sem-ə-ˌner-ē\ *n, pl* **-nar·ies** [ME, seedbed, fr. L *seminarium*, fr. *semin-, semen* seed] **1** : an institution of secondary education; *esp* : an academy for girls **2** : an institution for training clergymen

sem·i·nif·er·ous \ˌsem-ə-'nif-(ə-)rəs\ *adj* : producing or bearing seed or semen

sem·i·niv·o·rous \-'niv-ə-rəs\ *adj* : feeding on seeds

Sem·i·nole \'sem-ə-ˌnōl\ *n* : a member of an Indian people of Florida

semi·no·mad \ˌsem-i-'nō-ˌmad, ˌsem-ˌī-\ *n* : a member of a people living usu. in portable or temporary dwellings and practicing seasonal migration but having a base camp at which some crops are cultivated — **semi·no·mad·ic** \-nō-'mad-ik\ *adj*

semi·of·fi·cial \ˌsem-ē-ə-'fish-əl, ˌsem-ˌī-\ *adj* : having some official authority or standing ⟨a *semiofficial* statement⟩ — **semi·of·fi·cial·ly** \-'fish-(ə-)lē\ *adv*

semi·opaque \-ō-'pāk\ *adj* : nearly opaque

semi·pal·mate \ˌsem-i-'pal-ˌmāt, ˌsem-ˌī-, -'pä(l)m-ˌāt\ *or* **semi·pal·mat·ed** \-əd\ *adj* : having the anterior toes joined only part way down with a web

semi·per·ma·nent \-'pər-mə-nənt\ *adj* **1** : permanent in some respects **2** : lasting for an indefinite time

semi·per·me·a·ble \-'pər-mē-ə-bəl\ *adj* : partially but not freely or wholly permeable; *esp* : permeable to some usu. small molecules but not to other usu. larger particles ⟨a *semipermeable* membrane⟩ — **semi·per·me·a·bil·i·ty** \-ˌpər-mē-ə-'bil-ət-ē\ *n*

semi·po·lit·i·cal \-pə-'lit-i-kəl\ *adj* : of, relating to, or involving some political features or activity

semi·post·al \-'pōst-ᵊl\ *n* : a postage stamp sold (as for various humanitarian purposes) at a premium over its postal value

semi·pre·cious \-'presh-əs\ *adj* : of less commercial value than precious ⟨*semiprecious* gemstones⟩

semi·pri·vate \-'prī-vət\ *adj* : shared with only one or a few others ⟨a *semiprivate* room in a hospital⟩

semi·pro \'sem-i-ˌprō, 'sem-ˌī-\ *adj or n* : SEMIPROFESSIONAL

semi·pro·fes·sion·al \ˌsem-i-prə-'fesh-nəl, -ən-ᵊl, ˌsem-ˌī-\ *adj* **1** : engaging in an activity for pay or gain but not as a full-time occupation **2** : engaged in by semiprofessional players ⟨*semiprofessional* baseball⟩ — **semiprofessional** *n* — **semi·pro·fes·sion·al·ly** \-ē\ *adv*

semi·pub·lic \-'pəb-lik\ *adj* **1** : having some features of a public institution; *esp* : maintained as a public service by a private nonprofit organization **2** : open to some persons outside the regular constituency

semi·qua·ver \'sem-i-ˌkwā-vər, 'sem-ˌī-\ *n* : SIXTEENTH NOTE

semi·re·li·gious \-ri-'lij-əs\ *adj* : somewhat religious in character

semi·rig·id \-'rij-əd\ *adj* **1** : rigid to some degree or in some parts **2** : having a flexible cylindrical gas container with an attached stiffening keel that carries the load ⟨*semirigid* airships⟩

semi·sa·cred \-'sā-krəd\ *adj* : SEMIRELIGIOUS

semi·skilled \ˌsem-i-'skild, ˌsem-ˌī-\ *adj* : having or requiring less training than skilled labor and more than unskilled labor

semi·soft \-'sóft\ *adj* : moderately soft; *esp* : firm but easily cut ⟨*semisoft* cheese⟩

semi·sol·id \-'säl-əd\ *adj* : having the qualities of both a solid and a liquid ⟨jelly and paste are *semisolid*⟩ — **semisolid** *n*

semi·sweet \-'swēt\ *adj* : slightly sweetened ⟨*semisweet* chocolate⟩

Sem·ite \'sem-ˌīt\ *n* [LL *Sem* Shem, eldest son of Noah, fr. Heb *Shēm*] **1** : a member of any of the peoples descended from Shem **2** : a member of any of a group of peoples of southwestern Asia chiefly represented by the Jews and Arabs

semi·ter·res·tri·al \ˌsem-i-tə-'res-t(r)ē-əl, ˌsem-ˌī-\ *adj* **1** : growing on boggy ground **2** : frequenting but not living wholly on land

¹Se·mit·ic \sə-'mit-ik\ *adj* **1** : of, relating to, or characteristic of the Semites; *esp* : JEWISH **2** : of, relating to, or constituting a branch of the Afro-Asiatic language family that includes Hebrew, Aramaic, Arabic, and Ethiopic

²Semitic *n* : any or all of the Semitic languages

Sem·i·tism \'sem-ə-ˌtiz-əm\ *n* **1 a** : Semitic character or qualities **b** : a Semitic idiom or expression **2** : policy favorable to Jews : predisposition in favor of Jews

semi·ton·al \ˌsem-i-'tōn-ᵊl, ˌsem-ˌī-\ *adj* : CHROMATIC 2, SEMITONIC — **semi·ton·al·ly** \-ᵊl-ē\ *adv*

semi·tone \'sem-i-ˌtōn, 'sem-ˌī-\ *n* : the tone at a half step; *also* : HALF STEP — **semi·ton·ic** \ˌsem-i-'tän-ik, ˌsem-ˌī-\ *adj* — **semi·ton·i·cal·ly** \-'tän-i-k(ə-)lē\ *adv*

semi·trail·er \'sem-i-ˌtrā-lər, 'sem-ˌī-\ *n* : a freight trailer that when attached is supported at its forward end by the truck tractor; *also* : a semitrailer with attached tractor

semi·trans·lu·cent \ˌsem-i-ˌtran(t)s-'lüs-ᵊnt, ˌsem-ˌī-, -ˌtranz-\ *adj* : partly translucent

semi·trans·par·ent \-'par-ənt, -'per-\ *adj* : imperfectly transparent — **semi·trans·par·en·cy** \-ən-sē\ *n*

semi·trop·ic \ˌsem-i-'träp-ik, ˌsem-ˌī-\ *adj* : SUBTROPICAL — **semi·trop·i·cal** \-i-kəl\ *adj*

semi·trop·ics \-iks\ *n pl* : SUBTROPICS

¹semi·week·ly \-'wē-klē\ *adj* : occurring twice a week — **semiweekly** *adv*

²semiweekly *n* : a semiweekly publication

semi·woody \-'wùd-ē\ *adj* : somewhat woody

semi·works \'sem-i-ˌwərks, 'sem-ˌī-\ *n pl* : a manufacturing plant operating on a limited commercial scale to provide final tests of a new product or process

semi·year·ly \ˌsem-i-'yi(ə)r-lē, ˌsem-ˌī-\ *adj* : occurring twice a year

sem·o·li·na \ˌsem-ə-'lē-nə\ *n* [It *semolino*] : the purified middlings of hard wheat (as durum) used for macaroni, spaghetti, or vermicelli

sem·per·vi·vum \ˌsem-pər-'vī-vəm\ *n* [NL, fr. L, neut. of *sempervivus* ever-living, fr. *semper* ever + *vivus* living] : any of a large genus of Old World fleshy herbs of the orpine family often grown as ornamentals

sem·pi·ter·nal \ˌsem-pi-'tərn-ᵊl\ *adj* [L *sempiternus*, fr. *semper* ever, always] : of never-ending duration : EVERLASTING, ETERNAL — **sem·pi·ter·nal·ly** \-ᵊl-ē\ *adv* — **sem·pi·ter·ni·ty** \-'tər-nət-ē\ *n*

sem·pre \'sem-prā\ *adv* [It, fr. L *semper*] : ALWAYS — used to qualify an adverb or adjective used as a direction in music

semp·stress \'sem(p)-strəs\ *var of* SEAMSTRESS

sen \'sen\ *n*, *pl* **sen** [Jap] **1** : a unit of value equal to ¹⁄₁₀₀ yen **2** : a coin representing one sen

sen·ate \'sen-ət\ *n* [L *senatus*, fr. *sen-*, *senex* old, old man] **1 a** : the supreme council of the ancient Roman republic and empire **b** : the higher chamber in some bicameral legislatures **2** : the hall or chamber in which a senate meets **3** : a governing body of some universities charged with maintaining academic standards and regulations

sen·a·tor \'sen-ət-ər\ *n* : a member of a senate — **sen·a·tor·ship** \-ˌship\ *n*

sen·a·to·ri·al \ˌsen-ə-'tōr-ē-əl, -'tȯr-\ *adj* : of, relating to, or befitting a senator or a senate ⟨*senatorial* office⟩ ⟨*senatorial* rank⟩

senatorial courtesy *n* : a custom of the U.S. Senate of refusing to confirm a presidential appointment of an official in or from a state when the appointment is opposed by the senators or senior senator of the president's party from that state

send \'send\ *vb* **sent** \'sent\; **send·ing** [OE *sendan*] **1** : to cause to go : DISPATCH ⟨*sent* the pupil home⟩ ⟨*send* a message⟩; *esp* : to drive or propel physically ⟨*sent* the ball into right field⟩ ⟨*send* a rocket to the moon⟩ **2** : to cause to happen or occur ⟨asked the Lord to *send* some rain⟩ **3** : to have an agent, order, or request go or be transmitted ⟨*send* out for coffee⟩ ⟨*sent* away for a pair of skates⟩ ⟨*sent* for their price list⟩; *esp* : to transmit an order or request to come or return ⟨the principal *sent* for the boy⟩ **4** : to put or bring into a certain condition ⟨her request *sent* him into a tizzy⟩ — **send·er** *n* — **send packing** : to send off roughly or in disgrace ⟨if he comes in here just to fool around, I'll *send* him *packing*⟩

sen·dal \'sen-dᵊl\ *n* : a thin medieval silk of oriental origin used for fine clothing and church vestments

send-off \'send-ˌȯf\ *n* : a demonstration of goodwill and enthusiasm for the beginning of a new venture (as a trip or a new business)

Sen·e·ca \'sen-i-kə\ *n* : a member of an Iroquoian people of western New York

se·nec·ti·tude \si-'nek-tə-ˌt(y)üd\ *n* : the final stage of the normal life span

se·nesce \si-'nes\ *vi* [L *senescere*, fr. *sen-*, *senex* old] : to grow old — **se·nes·cence** \-'nes-ᵊn(t)s\ *n* — **se·nes·cent** \-ᵊnt\ *adj*

sen·e·schal \'sen-ə-shəl\ *n* [MF, of Gmc origin] : an agent or bailiff who managed a lord's estate in feudal times

se·nile \'sēn-ˌīl, 'sen-\ *adj* [L *sen-*, *senex* old man] : of or relating to old age : resulting from old age ⟨*senile* weaknesses⟩; *also* : having infirmities associated with old age ⟨a *senile* woman⟩ — **se·nile·ly** *adv*

se·nil·i·ty \si-'nil-ət-ē\ *n* : the quality or state of being senile; *esp* : the physical and mental infirmity of old age

¹se·nior \'sē-nyər\ *n* **1** : a person who is older or of higher rank than another **2** : a student in his last year before graduating from an educational institution of secondary or higher level

²senior *adj* [L, compar. of *sen-*, *senex* old] **1 a** : OLDER — used chiefly to distinguish a father with the same given name as his son **b** : earliest in date of origin **2** : higher in standing or rank ⟨*senior* partner⟩ **3** : of or relating to seniors in an educational institution

senior chief petty officer *n* : a petty officer in the navy ranking above a chief petty officer and below a master chief petty officer

senior high school *n* : a school usu. including the last three years of high school

se·nior·i·ty \ˌsēn-'yȯr-ət-ē, -'yär-\ *n* **1** : the quality or state of being senior : PRIORITY **2** : a privileged status attained by length of service

senior master sergeant *n* : a noncommissioned officer in the air force ranking above a master sergeant and below a chief master sergeant

sen·na \'sen-ə\ *n* [Ar *sanā*] **1** : CASSIA 2; *esp* : one used medicinally **2** : the dried leaflets of various cassias used as a purgative

sen·net \'sen-ət\ *n* : a signal call on a trumpet or cornet for entrance or exit on the stage

sen·night *also* **se'n·night** \'sen-ˌīt\ *n* [OE *seofon nihta* seven nights] *archaic* : the space of seven nights and days : WEEK

sen·nit \'sen-ət\ *n* **1** : a braided cord or fabric of plaited rope yarns or other small stuff **2** : a straw or grass braid for hats

se·nor *or* **se·ñor** \sān-'yȯ(ə)r\ *n*, *pl* **senors** *or* **se·ño·res** \-'yȯr-ˌās, -'yȯr-\ [Sp *señor*, fr. ML *senior* lord, fr. L, adj., senior] — used for or by a Spanish speaker as a title equivalent to *Mister*

se·no·ra *or* **se·ño·ra** \sān-'yȯr-ə, -'yȯr-\ *n* — used for or by a Spanish speaker as a title equivalent to *Mrs.*

se·no·ri·ta *or* **se·ño·ri·ta** \ˌsān-yə-'rēt-ə\ *n* — used for or by a Spanish speaker as a title equivalent to *Miss*

sen·sa·tion \sen-'sā-shən, sən-\ *n* **1 a** : awareness (as of noise or heat) or a mental process (as seeing, hearing, or smelling) due to stimulation of a sense organ **b** : an indefinite bodily feeling ⟨a *sensation* of buoyancy⟩ **c** : something that causes or is the object of sensation **2 a** : a state of excited interest or feeling **b** : a cause of such excitement ⟨the play was a *sensation*⟩

sen·sa·tion·al \-shnəl, -shən-ᵊl\ *adj* **1** : of or relating to sensation or the senses **2** : arousing or tending to arouse (as by lurid details) a quick, intense, and usu. superficial interest, curiosity, or emotional reaction ⟨*sensational* news⟩ **3** : exceedingly or unexpectedly excellent or great ⟨he made a *sensational* diving catch⟩ — **sen·sa·tion·al·ly** \-ē\ *adv*

sen·sa·tion·al·ism \-ˌiz-əm\ *n* : the use or effect of sensational subject matter or treatment — **sen·sa·tion·al·ist** \-əst\ *n* — **sen·sa·tion·al·is·tic** \-ˌsā-shnəl-'is-tik, -shən-ᵊl-\ *adj*

¹sense \'sen(t)s\ *n* [L *sensus*, lit., feeling, fr. *sens-*, *sentire* to feel] **1 a** : the faculty of perceiving by means of sense organs ⟨creatures dependent on *sense* for orientation⟩ **b** : a specialized animal function or mechanism (as sight, hearing, smell, taste, or touch) basically involving interaction of a stimulus and a sense organ ⟨the pain *sense*⟩ **2** : a particular sensation or kind or quality of sensation ⟨a good *sense* of balance⟩ **3** : AWARENESS, CONSCIOUSNESS ⟨a *sense* of danger⟩ **4** : intellectual appreciation ⟨a *sense* of humor⟩ **5** : INTELLIGENCE, JUDGMENT; *esp* : good judgment **6** : good reason or excuse ⟨no *sense* in waiting⟩ **7** : MEANING; *esp* : one of the meanings a word may bear **8** : IMPORT, INTENTION ⟨get the *sense* of the speaker's words⟩ **9** : one of two opposite directions describable by the motion of a point, line, or surface **syn** *see* MEANING

²sense *vt* **1 a** : to perceive by the senses **b** : to be or become conscious of ⟨*sense* danger⟩ **2** : GRASP, COMPREHEND **3** : to detect (as a symbol or radiation) automatically

sense·ful \'sen(t)s-fəl\ *adj* : full of sense or reason : JUDICIOUS

sense·less \'sen(t)s-ləs\ *adj* : destitute of, deficient in, or contrary to sense: as **a** : UNCONSCIOUS ⟨knocked *senseless*⟩ **b** : FOOLISH, STUPID **c** : PURPOSELESS, MEANINGLESS ⟨a *senseless* act⟩ — **sense·less·ly** *adv* — **sense·less·ness** *n*

sense organ *n* : a bodily structure affected by a stimulus (as heat or sound waves) in such a manner as to activate associated sensory nerve fibers to convey impulses to the central nervous system where they are interpreted as corresponding sensations

sen·si·bil·i·ty \ˌsen(t)-sə-'bil-ət-ē\ *n*, *pl* **-ties 1** : ability to receive sensations : SENSITIVENESS ⟨tactile *sensibility*⟩ **2** : peculiar susceptibility to a pleasurable or painful impression (as a slight or unkindness) — often used in pl.

3 : awareness of and responsiveness toward something (as emotion in another) **4** : refined sensitiveness in emotion and taste

sen·si·ble \'sen(t)-sə-bəl\ *adj* **1 a** : capable of being perceived by the senses or by reason or understanding **b** : of a significant size, amount, or degree ⟨a *sensible* error⟩ **2** : capable of receiving sense impressions ⟨*sensible* to pain⟩ **3** : COGNIZANT, AWARE **4** : having or containing good sense or reason : REASONABLE ⟨a *sensible* arrangement⟩ — **sen·si·ble·ness** *n* — **sen·si·bly** \-blē\ *adv*

sen·si·tive \'sen(t)-sət-iv, 'sen(t)-stiv\ *adj* [ML *sensitivus,* irreg. fr. L *sens-, sentire* to feel] **1** : subject to excitation by or responsive to stimuli **2** : easily or strongly affected or hurt ⟨a *sensitive* child⟩ : *esp* : HYPERSENSITIVE ⟨*sensitive* to egg protein⟩ **3 a** : capable of indicating minute differences : DELICATE ⟨*sensitive* scales⟩ **b** : readily affected or changed by various agents or causes (as light or mechanical shock) **c** : high in radio sensitivity **4** : concerned with or involving highly classified government information ⟨held a *sensitive* government post⟩ — **sen·si·tive·ly** *adv* — **sen·si·tive·ness** *n*

sensitive fern *n* : a common American fern with fronds very susceptible to frost injury

sensitive plant *n* : any of several mimosas having leaves that fold or droop when touched

sen·si·tiv·i·ty \,sen(t)-sə-'tiv-ət-ē\ *n, pl* **-ties** : the quality or state of being sensitive: as **a** : the capacity of an organism or sense organ to respond to stimulation : IRRITABILITY **b** : HYPERSENSITIVITY **c** : the degree to which a radio receiving set responds to incoming waves

sen·si·tize \'sen(t)-sə-,tīz\ *vb* : to make or become sensitive or hypersensitive — **sen·si·ti·za·tion** \,sen(t)-sət-ə-'zā-shən\ *n* — **sen·si·tiz·er** \'sen(t)-sə-,tī-zər\ *n*

sen·si·tom·e·ter \,sen(t)-sə-'täm-ət-ər\ *n* : an instrument for measuring sensitivity of photographic material — **sen·si·to·met·ric** \,sen(t)-sət-ə-'me-trik\ *adj* — **sen·si·tom·e·try** \,sen(t)-sə-'täm-ə-trē\ *n*

sen·sor \'sen-,sȯr, 'sen(t)-sər\ *n* : a device that responds to a physical stimulus (as heat, light, or a particular motion) and transmits a resulting impulse (as for operating a control)

sen·so·ri·al \sen-'sȯr-ē-əl, -'sȯr-\ *adj* : SENSORY — **sen·so·ri·al·ly** \-ē-ə-lē\ *adv*

sen·so·ri·mo·tor \,sen(t)s-(ə-)rē-'mōt-ər\ *adj* : of, relating to, or functioning in both sensory and motor aspects of bodily activity

sen·so·ry \'sen(t)s-(ə-)rē\ *adj* [L *sens-, sentire* to feel, perceive] **1** : of or relating to sensation or to the senses **2** : conveying nerve impulses from the sense organs : AFFERENT

sen·su·al \'sench-(ə-)wəl\ *adj* [L *sensus* sense] **1** : SENSORY **2** : relating to or consisting in the gratification of the senses or the indulgence of appetite : FLESHLY **3 a** : devoted to or preoccupied with the senses or appetites **b** : VOLUPTUOUS **c** : deficient in moral, spiritual, or intellectual interests : WORLDLY; *esp* : IRRELIGIOUS — **sen·su·al·i·ty** \,sen-chə-'wal-ət-ē\ *n* — **sen·su·al·ly** \'sench-(ə-)wə-lē\ *adv*

sen·su·al·ism \'sench-(ə-)wə-,liz-əm\ *n* : SENSUALITY — **sen·su·al·ist** \-ləst\ *n* — **sen·su·al·is·tic** \,sench-(ə-)wə-'lis-tik\ *adj*

sen·su·al·ize \'sench-(ə-)wə-,līz\ *vt* : to make sensual — **sen·su·al·i·za·tion** \,sench-(ə-)wə-lə-'zā-shən\ *n*

sen·su·ous \'sench-(ə-)wəs\ *adj* **1** : having to do with the senses or with things perceived by the senses ⟨*sensuous* pleasure⟩ **2** : characterized by sense impressions or imagery addressing the senses ⟨*sensuous* description⟩ **3** : highly susceptible to influence through the senses — **sen·su·ous·ly** *adv* — **sen·su·ous·ness** *n*

sent *past of* SEND

¹sen·tence \'sent-ᵊn(t)s, -ᵊnz\ *n* [L *sententia,* lit., feeling, opinion, irreg. fr. *sentire* to feel] **1 a** : JUDGMENT 2a; *esp* : one formally pronounced by a court in a criminal proceeding and specifying the punishment to be inflicted **b** : the punishment so imposed ⟨serve a *sentence* for robbery⟩ **2** : AXIOM, MAXIM **3** : a grammatically self-contained speech unit that expresses an assertion, a question, a command, a wish, or an exclamation, that in writing usu. begins with a capital letter and concludes with appropriate end punctuation, and that in speaking is phonetically distinguished by various patterns of stress, pitch, and

pauses — **sen·ten·tial** \sen-'ten-chəl\ *adj* — **sen·ten·tial·ly** \-chə-lē\ *adv*

²sentence *vt* **1** : to pronounce sentence on **2** : to condemn to a specified punishment

sentence fragment *n* : a word, phrase, or clause that lacks the grammatically self-contained structure of a sentence but has in speech the intonation of a sentence and is written and punctuated as if it were a complete sentence

sentence stress *n* : the manner in which stresses are distributed on the syllables of words assembled into sentences — called also *sentence accent*

sen·ten·tious \sen-'ten-chəs\ *adj* [L *sententia* feeling, maxim] **1** : being concise and forceful : PITHY **2** : containing, using, or inclined to use high-sounding empty phrases or pompous sayings — **sen·ten·tious·ly** *adv* — **sen·ten·tious·ness** *n*

sen·tient \'sen-ch(ē-)ənt\ *adj* [L *sentire* to feel] : capable of feeling : conscious of sense impressions ⟨the lowest of *sentient* creatures⟩ — **sen·tience** \-ch(ē-)ən(t)s\ *n* — **sen·tient·ly** *adv*

sen·ti·ment \'sent-ə-mənt\ *n* [L *sentire* to feel] **1 a** : an attitude, thought, or judgment prompted by feeling **b** : OPINION **2 a** : EMOTION **b** : refined feeling : delicate sensibility **c** : emotional idealism **d** : a romantic or nostalgic feeling **syn** *see* FEELING

sen·ti·men·tal \,sent-ə-'ment-ᵊl\ *adj* **1 a** : marked by or governed by feeling, sensibility, or emotional idealism **b** : resulting from feeling rather than reason or thought **2** : having an excess or affectation of sentiment or sensibility — **sen·ti·men·tal·ly** \-ᵊl-ē\ *adv*

sen·ti·men·tal·ism \-ᵊl-,iz-əm\ *n* **1** : the disposition to favor or indulge in sentiment **2** : an excessively sentimental conception or statement — **sen·ti·men·tal·ist** \-ᵊləst\ *n*

sen·ti·men·tal·i·ty \,sent-ə-,men-'tal-ət-ē, -mən-\ *n, pl* **-ties** **1** : the quality or state of being sentimental esp. to excess or in affectation **2** : a sentimental idea or its expression

sen·ti·men·tal·ize \-'ment-ᵊl-,īz\ *vb* **1** : to indulge in sentiment **2** : to look upon or imbue with sentiment — **sen·ti·men·tal·i·za·tion** \-,ment-ᵊl-ə-'zā-shən\ *n*

¹sen·ti·nel \'sent-nəl, -ᵊn-əl\ *n* [MF *sentinelle,* fr. It *sentinella,* fr. *sentina* vigilance, fr. *sentire* to perceive, fr. L] : one that watches or guards : SENTRY

²sentinel *vt* **-neled** *or* **-nelled; -nel·ing** *or* **-nel·ling** **1** : to watch over as a sentinel **2** : to furnish with a sentinel **3** : to post as sentinel

sen·try \'sen-trē\ *n, pl* **sen·tries** : GUARD, WATCH; *esp* : a soldier standing guard at a point of passage

sentry box *n* : a shelter for a sentry on his post

se·pal \'sēp-əl, 'sep-\ *n* [NL *sepalum,* irreg. fr. Gk *skepē* covering + NL *-lum* (as in *petalum* petal)] : one of the modified leaves comprising a flower calyx — see CARPEL illustration — **se·paled** *or* **se·palled** \-əld\ *adj* — **se·pal·oid** \-ə-,lȯid\ *adj*

sep·a·ra·ble \'sep-(ə-)rə-bəl\ *adj* : capable of being separated or distinguished — **sep·a·ra·bil·i·ty** \,sep-(ə-)rə-'bil-ət-ē\ *n* — **sep·a·ra·ble·ness** \'sep-(ə-)rə-bəl-nəs\ *n* — **sep·a·ra·bly** \-blē\ *adv*

¹sep·a·rate \'sep-ə-,rāt\ *vb* [L *separare,* fr. *se-* apart + *parare* to prepare, procure] **1 a** : to set or keep apart : DISCONNECT, DISUNITE **b** : to make a distinction between : DISTINGUISH ⟨*separate* religion from magic⟩ **c** : SORT ⟨*separate* mail⟩ **d** : to disperse in space or time : SCATTER ⟨widely *separated* homesteads⟩ **2** : to sever contractual relations with : DISCHARGE ⟨*separated* from the army⟩ **3** : to block off : SEGREGATE **4** : to isolate from a mixture ⟨*separate* cream from milk⟩ **5** : to become divided or detached : come apart **6 a** : to break off an association : WITHDRAW **b** : to cease to be or live together **7** : to go in different directions **8** : to become isolated from a mixture

syn SEPARATE, DIVIDE, SEVER mean to break or keep apart. SEPARATE may imply any one of several ways or causes such as dispersion, removal of one from others, or presence of an intervening thing; DIVIDE implies separating by cutting or breaking into pieces or sections; SEVER implies violence esp. in the removal of a part or member

²sep·a·rate \'sep-(ə-)rət\ *adj* **1** : not connected : not united or associated ⟨two *separate* apartments⟩ **2** : divided from another or others **3** : being apart from others : ISO-

LATED **4 :** relating to one only **:** not shared ⟨live in *separate* rooms⟩ **5 :** SINGLE, PARTICULAR ⟨the *separate* pieces of a puzzle⟩ — **sep·a·rate·ly** *adv* — **sep·a·rate·ness** *n*

³**sep·a·rate** \'sep-(ə-)rət\ *n* **:** an article of dress designed to be worn interchangeably with others to form various costume combinations — usu. used in pl.

sep·a·ra·tion \,sep-ə-'rā-shən\ *n* **1 :** the act or process of separating **:** the state of being separated **2 a :** a point, line, or means of division **b :** an intervening space **:** GAP **3 a :** a formal separating of husband and wife by agreement but without divorce **b :** termination of a contractual relationship (as employment or military service)

sep·a·rat·ist \'sep(-ə)-rət-əst\ *n, often cap* **:** one that favors separation: as **a** *cap* **:** one of a group of 16th and 17th century English Protestants preferring to separate from rather than to reform the Church of England **b :** an advocate of independence or autonomy for a part of a nation — **sep·a·rat·ism** \-,rə-,tiz-əm\ *n* — **separatist** *adj, often cap* — **sep·a·ra·tis·tic** \,sep(-ə)-rə-'tis-tik\ *adj*

sep·a·ra·tive \'sep-ə-,rāt-iv, 'sep-(ə-)rət-\ *adj* **:** tending toward, causing, or expressing separation

sep·a·ra·tor \'sep-ə-,rāt-ər\ *n* **:** one that separates; *esp* **:** a device for separating liquids (as cream from milk) of different specific gravities or liquids from solids — compare CENTRIFUGE

Se·phar·di \sə-'färd-ē\ *n, pl* **Se·phar·dim** \-'färd-əm\ [LHeb *sĕphāradhī*, fr. *Sĕphārad* Spain, fr. Heb, region where Jews were once exiled (Obadiah 1 : 20)] **:** a member of the occidental branch of European Jews settling in Spain and Portugal or one of their descendants — **Se·phar·dic** \-'färd-ik\ *adj*

¹**se·pia** \'sē-pē-ə\ *n* [Gk *sēpia* cuttlefish] **1 :** a brown melanin-containing pigment from the ink of cuttlefishes **2 :** a brownish gray to dark olive brown

²**sepia** *adj* **1 :** of the color sepia **2 :** made of or done in sepia ⟨*sepia* print⟩

se·poy \'sē-,pȯi\ *n* [Pg *sipai*, fr. Hindi *sipāhī*, fr. Per, cavalryman] **:** a native of India employed as a soldier in the service of a European power

sep·sis \'sep-səs\ *n, pl* **sep·ses** \'sep-,sēz\ [Gk *sēpsis* decay, fr. *sēpein* to make putrid] **:** a poisoned condition resulting from the spread of bacteria or their poisonous products from a center of infection

sept \'sept\ *n* **:** a branch of a family; *esp* **:** CLAN

sep·tate \'sep-,tāt\ *adj* **:** divided by or having a septum

Sep·tem·ber \sep-'tem-bər, səp-\ *n* [L, fr. *septem* seven; akin to *E seven;* fr. its having been orig. the seventh month of the Roman calendar] **:** the 9th month of the year

sep·ten·ni·al \sep-'ten-ē-əl\ *adj* **1 :** consisting of or lasting for seven years **2 :** occurring or being done every seven years — **sep·ten·ni·al·ly** \-ē-ə-lē\ *adv*

sep·ten·tri·o·nal \sep-'ten-trē-ən-ᵊl\ *adj* **:** NORTHERN

sep·tet *also* **sep·tette** \sep-'tet\ *n* [G *septett*, fr. L *septem* seven] **1 :** a musical composition for seven instruments or voices **2 :** a group or set of seven; *esp* **:** the musicians that perform a septet

sep·tic \'sep-tik\ *adj* [Gk *sēptikos*, fr. *sēpein* to make putrid] **1 :** PUTREFACTIVE **2 :** relating to or characteristic of sepsis

sep·ti·ce·mia \,sep-tə-'sē-mē-ə\ *n* **:** invasion of the bloodstream by virulent microorganisms from a focus of infection accompanied esp. by chills, fever, and prostration — called also *blood poisoning;* compare SEPSIS — **sep·ti·ce·mic** \-'sē-mik\ *adj*

sep·ti·cid·al \,sep-tə-'sīd-ᵊl\ *adj* **:** splitting longitudinally at or along a septum ⟨*septicidal* fruits⟩

septic sore throat *n* **:** a severe sore throat caused by streptococci and accompanied by fever, prostration, and toxemia

septic tank *n* **:** a tank in which the solid matter of continuously flowing sewage is disintegrated by bacteria

sep·til·lion \sep-'til-yən\ *n* — see NUMBER table

sep·tu·a·ge·nar·i·an \,sep-,t(y)ü-ə-jə-'ner-ē-ən, ,sep-tə-wə-jə-\ *n* [L *septuageni* 70 each, fr. *septuaginta* 70] **:** a person who is 70 or more but less than 80 years old — **sep·tuagenarian** *adj*

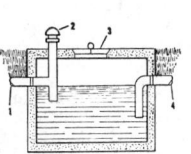

septic tank: *1* inlet, *2* vent cap, *3* manhole, *4* outlet

Sep·tu·a·ges·i·ma \,sep-tə-wə-'jes-ə-mə\ *n* **:** the 3d Sunday before Lent

Sep·tu·a·gint \sep-'t(y)ü-ə-jənt, 'sep-tə-wə-,jint\ *n* [L *septuaginta* 70, irreg. fr. *septem* seven; fr. the approximate number of its translators] **:** a pre-Christian Greek version of the Old Testament used by Greek-speaking Christians

sep·tum \'sep-təm\ *n, pl* **sep·ta** \-tə\ *also* **septums** [NL, fr. L *saeptum* enclosure, wall, fr. *saepire* to fence in, fr. *saepes* fence] **:** a dividing wall or membrane esp. between bodily spaces or masses of soft tissue — **sep·tal** \'sep-tᵊl\ *adj*

¹**sep·ul·cher** *or* **sep·ul·chre** \'sep-əl-kər\ *n* [L *sepulcrum, sepulchrum,* fr. *sepelire* to bury] **1 :** a place of burial **:** TOMB **2 :** a receptacle for religious relics esp. in an altar

²**sepulcher** *or* **sepulchre** *vt* **-chered** *or* **-chred; -cher·ing** *or* **-chring** \-k(ə-)riŋ\ **:** to place or receive in a sepulcher **:** BURY, ENTOMB

se·pul·chral \sə-'pəl-krəl\ *adj* **1 :** of or relating to burial, the grave, or monuments to the dead ⟨a *sepulchral* stone⟩ **2 :** DISMAL, GLOOMY — **se·pul·chral·ly** \-krə-lē\ *adv*

sep·ul·ture \'sep-əl-,chùr\ *n* [L *sepult-, sepelire* to bury] **1 :** BURIAL **2 :** SEPULCHER

se·qua·cious \si-'kwā-shəs\ *adj* **1** *archaic* **:** SUBSERVIENT, TRACTABLE **2 :** intellectually servile — **se·qua·cious·ly** *adv* — **se·quac·i·ty** \-'kwas-ət-ē\ *n*

se·quel \'sē-kwəl\ *n* [L *sequela,* fr. *sequi* to follow] **1 :** an event that follows or comes afterward **:** RESULT **2 :** a book that continues a story begun in another

se·que·la \si-'kwel-ə, -'kwē-lə\ *n, pl* **-que·lae** \-'kwel-(,)ē, -,ī; -'kwē-(,)lē\ [NL, fr. L, sequel] **1 :** an aftereffect of disease or injury **2 :** a secondary result **:** CONSEQUENCE

¹**se·quence** \'sē-kwən(t)s, -,kwen(t)s\ *n* [LL *sequentia* sequel, fr. L *sequi* to follow] **1 :** a continuous or connected series: as **a :** an extended series of poems united by a single theme ⟨sonnet *sequence*⟩ **b :** three or more playing cards usu. of the same suit in consecutive order of rank **c :** a succession of repetitions of a melodic phrase each in a new position **d :** a set of numbers having a definite order fixed by a rule **e :** a succession of related shots or scenes developing a single subject or phase of a film story **2 :** order of succession **3 a :** CONSEQUENCE, RESULT **b :** subsequent development **4 :** continuity of progression **syn** see SUCCESSION

²**sequence** *vt* **:** to arrange in a sequence

se·quenc·er \'sē-kwən-sər, -,kwen(t)-sər\ *n* **:** a device that determines a sequence

se·quen·cy \-kwən-sē\ *n, pl* **-cies :** SEQUENCE

se·quent \'sē-kwənt\ *adj* **:** following in time or as an effect — **sequent** *n*

se·quen·tial \si-'kwen-chəl\ *adj* **:** SEQUENT — **se·quen·tial·ly** \-chə-lē\ *adv*

se·ques·ter \si-'kwes-tər\ *vt* **se·ques·tered; se·ques·ter·ing** \-t(ə-)riŋ\ [LL *sequestrare,* lit., to surrender for safekeeping, fr. L *sequester* agent, depositary] **1 :** to set apart **:** SEGREGATE, WITHDRAW **2 :** to take custody of (as personal property) until a demand is satisfied

se·ques·trate \si-'kwes-,trāt\ *vt* **:** CONFISCATE

se·ques·tra·tion \,sē-kwəs-'trā-shən, si-,kwes-\ *n* **:** the act of sequestering **:** the state of being sequestered

se·quin \'sē-kwən\ *n* [F, fr. It *zecchino*] **1 :** an old gold coin of Italy and Turkey **2 :** a spangle used as an ornament on clothes

se·quined *or* **se·quinned** \-kwənd\ *adj* **:** ornamented with or as if with sequins

se·quoia \si-'kwȯi-ə\ *n* [NL, genus name, fr. *Sequoya* (George Guess) *d*1843 American Indian scholar] **:** either of two huge coniferous California trees of the pine family that reach a height of over 300 feet: **a :** BIG TREE **b :** REDWOOD 2

sera *pl of* SERUM

se·rac \sə-'rak\ *n* [F *serac,* lit., a kind of white cheese, fr. ML *seracium* whey, fr. L *serum* whey] **:** a pinnacle, sharp ridge, or block of ice among the crevasses of a glacier

se·ra·glio \sə-'ral-yō\ *n, pl* **-glios** *also* **-gli** \-(,)yē\ [It *serraglio,* fr. Turk *saray* palace] **:** HAREM 1a

serape *var of* SARAPE

ser·aph \'ser-əf\ *n, pl* **ser·a·phim** \-ə-,fim\ *or* **seraphs** [Heb *šĕrāphīm,* pl., seraphs] **:** an angel of a very high order — **seraph** *or* **se·raph·ic** \sə-'raf-ik\ *adj* — **se·raph·i·cal·ly** \-'raf-i-k(ə-)lē\ *adv*

Serb \'sərb\ *n* **:** a native or inhabitant of the former kingdom of Serbia or of the federal republic of Serbia in Yugoslavia — **Serb** *adj*

Ser·bi·an \'sər-bē-ən\ *n* **1** : SERB **2 a** : the Serbo-Croatian language as spoken in Serbia **b** : a literary form of Serbo-Croatian using the Cyrillic alphabet — **Serbian** *adj*

Ser·bo-Cro·a·tian \,sər-bō-krō-'ā-shən\ *n* **1** : the Slavic language of the Serbs and Croats consisting of Serbian written in the Cyrillic alphabet and Croatian written in the Roman alphabet **2** : one whose native language is Serbo-Croatian — **Serbo-Croatian** *adj*

¹sere \'si(ə)r\ *adj* [OE *sēar* dry] : dried up : WITHERED ⟨*sere* deserts⟩

²sere *n* : a series of communities that succeed one another in the ecological development of an area or formation — **ser·al** \'sir-əl\ *adj*

¹ser·e·nade \,ser-ə-'nād\ *n* [F *sérénade,* fr. It *serenata,* fr. *sereno* clear, calm (of weather), fr. L *serenus*] **1 a** : a complimentary vocal or instrumental performance; *esp* : one given outdoors at night for a woman **b** : a work so performed **2** : a work for chamber orchestra resembling a suite

²serenade *vb* : to entertain with or perform a serenade — **ser·e·nad·er** *n*

ser·en·dip·i·tous \,ser-ən-'dip-ət-əs\ *adj* : obtained by or characterized by serendipity ⟨*serendipitous* discoveries⟩

ser·en·dip·i·ty \,ser-ən-'dip-ət-ē\ *n* [fr. its possession by the heroes of the Persian fairy tale *The Three Princes of Serendip*] : the gift of finding valuable or agreeable things not sought for

¹se·rene \sə-'rēn\ *adj* [L *serenus*] **1 a** : being clear and free of storms ⟨*serene* skies⟩ **b** : shining bright and steady **2** : marked by utter calm : TRANQUIL **3** : AUGUST — used as part of a title ⟨His *Serene* Highness⟩ **syn** see CALM — **se·rene·ly** *adv* — **se·rene·ness** \-'rēn-nəs\ *n*

²serene *n* **1** : a serene condition or expanse (as of sky, sea, or light) **2** : SERENITY, TRANQUILLITY

se·ren·i·ty \sə-'ren-ət-ē\ *n* : the quality or state of being serene : PEACEFULNESS, REPOSE

serf \'sərf\ *n* [F, fr. L *servus* slave, servant, serf] : a member of a servile feudal class bound to the soil and more or less subject to the will of his lord — **serf·age** \'sər-fij\ *n* — **serf·dom** \'sərf-dəm\ *n* — **serf·hood** \-,hud\ *n* — **serf·ish** \'sər-fish\ *adj* — **serf·ism** \-,fiz-əm\ *n*

serge \'sərj\ *n* [MF *sarge,* fr. (assumed) VL *sarica,* fr. L *serica,* fr. fem. of *sericus* of silk, fr. Gk *sērikos,* fr. *Sēres,* an eastern Asiatic people producing silk in ancient times] : a durable twilled fabric having a smooth clear face and a diagonal rib on the front and the back

ser·gean·cy \'sär-jən-sē\ *n* : the function, office, or rank of a sergeant

ser·geant \'sär-jənt\ *n* [ME, lit., servant, fr. OF *sergent,* fr. L *servient-, serviens,* prp. of *servire* to serve] **1** : a police officer ranking in the U.S. just below captain or sometimes lieutenant and in England just below inspector **2** : a noncommissioned officer in the army ranking above a corporal and below a staff sergeant

sergeant at arms *n* : an officer of a court of law or a lawmaking body appointed to keep order

sergeant first class *n* : a noncommissioned officer in the army ranking above a staff sergeant and below a master sergeant

sergeant major *n, pl* **sergeants major** *or* **sergeant majors 1** : a noncommissioned officer (as in the army) serving as chief enlisted assistant in a headquarters **2** : a noncommissioned officer in the army of the highest enlisted rank

¹se·ri·al \'sir-ē-əl\ *adj* **1** : of, consisting of, or arranged in a series, rank, or row ⟨*serial* order⟩ **2** : appearing in parts or numbers that follow regularly ⟨a *serial* story⟩ — **se·ri·al·ly** \-ē-ə-lē\ *adv*

²serial *n* **1** : a work appearing (as in a magazine or on television) in parts at intervals **2** : one part of a serial work : INSTALLMENT — **se·ri·al·ist** \-ē-ə-ləst\ *n*

se·ri·al·ize \'sir-ē-ə-,līz\ *vt* : to arrange or publish in serial form — **se·ri·al·i·za·tion** \,sir-ē-ə-lə-'zā-shən\ *n*

se·ri·a·tim \,sir-ē-'āt-əm, -'ät-\ *adv* [ML, fr. L *series*] : in a series : SERIALLY

se·ri·ceous \sə-'rish-əs\ *adj* [L *sericum* silk garment, silk] **1** : of, relating to, or consisting of silk : SILKY **2** : finely pubescent ⟨*sericeous* leaf⟩

seri·cul·ture \'ser-ə-,kəl-chər\ *n* [L *sericum* silk + E *culture*] : the raising of silkworms for silk production — **seri·cul·tur·al** \,ser-ə-'kəlch-(ə-)rəl\ *adj*

se·ries \'si(ə)r-(,)ēz\ *n, pl* **series** [L, fr. *serere* to join, link together] **1 a** : a number of things or events of the same class coming one after another **b** : a group with an order of arrangement exhibiting progression **2** : the indicated sum of a sequence of numbers **3** : a succession of volumes or issues published with related subjects or authors, similar format and price, or continuous numbering **4** : a division of rock formations smaller than a system comprising rocks deposited during an epoch **5** : an arrangement of the parts of or elements in an electric circuit whereby the whole current passes through each part or element without branching **6** : a group of chemical compounds related in composition and structure **7** : a group of successive coordinate sentence elements joined together ⟨an a, b, and c *series*⟩ **syn** see SUCCESSION — **in series** : in a serial arrangement

series winding *n* : a winding in which the armature coil and the field-magnet coil are in series with the external circuit — **se·ries-wound** \,sir-ēz-'waund\ *adj*

ser·if \'ser-əf\ *n* [prob. fr. D *schreef* stroke, line, fr. MD *schriven* to write, fr. L *scribere*] : any of the short lines stemming from and at an angle to the upper and lower ends of the strokes of a printed letter

seri·graph \'ser-ə-,graf\ *n* [L *sericum* silk] : an original color print made by pressing pigments through a silk screen with a stencil design — **se·rig·ra·pher** \sə-'rig-rə-fər\ *n* — **se·rig·ra·phy** \-fē\ *n*

se·rio·com·ic \,sir-ē-ō-'käm-ik\ *adj* : having a mixture of the serious and the comic — **se·rio·com·i·cal·ly** \-'käm-i-k(ə-)lē\ *adv*

se·ri·ous \'sir-ē-əs\ *adj* [L *serius*] **1** : thoughtful or subdued in appearance or manner : SOBER **2 a** : requiring much thought or work ⟨*serious* study⟩ **b** : of or relating to a matter of importance ⟨a *serious* play⟩ **3** : not joking or trifling : EARNEST **4 a** : not easily answered or solved ⟨*serious* objections⟩ **b** : having important or dangerous possible consequences ⟨a *serious* injury⟩ — **se·ri·ous·ly** *adv* — **se·ri·ous·ness** *n*

syn EARNEST, SOLEMN : SERIOUS implies showing or having a concern for what really matters; EARNEST adds an implication of sincerity or intensity of purpose; SOLEMN suggests an impressive gravity utterly free from gaiety

se·ri·ous-mind·ed \,sir-ē-əs-'mīn-dəd\ *adj* : having a serious disposition or trend of thought — **se·ri·ous-mind·ed·ly** *adv* — **se·ri·ous-mind·ed·ness** *n*

ser·jeant *var of* SERGEANT

serjeant-at-law *n, pl* **serjeants-at-law** : a barrister of the highest rank

ser·mon \'sər-mən\ *n* [ML *sermon-, sermo,* fr. L, conversation, talk, fr. *serere* to join, link together] **1** : a public speech usu. by a clergyman giving religious instruction or exhortation **2 a** : a lecture on conduct or duty **b** : an annoying harangue — **ser·mon·ic** \,sər-'män-ik\ *adj*

ser·mon·ize \'sər-mə-,nīz\ *vb* **1** : to compose or deliver a sermon : PREACH **2** : to discourse didactically or dogmatically — **ser·mon·iz·er** *n*

Sermon on the Mount *n* : a talk by Jesus recorded in Matthew 5–7 and Luke 6: 20–49

se·rol·o·gy \sə-'räl-ə-jē\ *n* : a science dealing with serums and esp. their reactions and properties — **se·ro·log·ic** \,sir-ə-'läj-ik\ *or* **se·ro·log·i·cal** \-'läj-i-kəl\ *adj* — **se·ro·log·i·cal·ly** \-i-k(ə-)lē\ *adv* — **se·rol·o·gist** \sə-'räl-ə-jəst\ *n*

se·ro·pu·ru·lent \,sir-ō-'pyúr-(y)ə-lənt\ *adj* : consisting of a mixture of serum and pus ⟨*seropurulent* discharge⟩

se·ro·sa \sə-'rō-sə\ *n* [NL, fr. fem. of *serosus* serous, fr. L *serum*] : a usu. enclosing serous membrane — **se·ro·sal** \-'rō-səl, -zəl\ *adj*

se·rous \'sir-əs\ *adj* : of, relating to, resembling, or producing serum; *esp* : of thin watery constitution ⟨a *serous* exudate⟩

serous membrane *n* : a thin membrane (as the peritoneum) with cells that secrete a serous fluid : SEROSA

ser·pent \'sər-pənt\ *n* [L *serpent-, serpens,* fr. prp. of *serpere* to creep] **1** : SNAKE; *esp* : a large snake **2** : DEVIL **3** : a subtle treacherous malicious person

¹ser·pen·tine \'sər-pən-,tēn, -,tīn\ *adj* **1** : of or resembling a serpent **2** : subtly wily or tempting : DIABOLIC

---

3 : winding or turning one way and another **:** SINUOUS ⟨a *serpentine* path⟩
²serpentine *n* **:** something that winds sinuously
³serpentine *n* **:** a mineral consisting essentially of a hydrous silicate of magnesium usu. having a dull green color and often a mottled appearance
ser·pen·tine·ly *adv* **:** in a serpentine manner
serpent star *n* **:** BRITTLE STAR
ser·pig·i·nous \(,)sər-'pij-ə-nəs\ *adj* [ML *serpigin-, serpigo* creeping skin disease, fr. L *serpere* to creep] **:** SPREADING, CREEPING ⟨a *serpiginous* rash⟩
¹ser·rate \sə-'rāt, 'ser-,āt\ *vt* **:** to mark with serrations **:** NOTCH
²serrate *or* **ser·rat·ed** \sə-'rāt-əd, 'ser-,āt-\ *adj* [L *serratus*, fr. *serra* saw] **:** having a saw-toothed edge ⟨a *serrate* leaf⟩
ser·ra·tion \sə-'rā-shən, se-\ *n* **1 :** a serrate condition or formation **2 :** one of the teeth in a serrate margin
ser·ried \'ser-ēd\ *adj* **:** crowded or pressed together **:** COMPACT ⟨*serried* ranks of soldiers⟩ — **ser·ried·ly** *adv* — **ser·ried·ness** *n*
ser·ru·late \'ser-(y)ə-lət, -,lāt\ *also* **ser·ru·lat·ed** \-,lāt-əd\ *adj* **:** finely serrate — **ser·ru·la·tion** \,ser-(y)ə-'lā-shən\ *n*
ser·ry \'ser-ē\ *vb* **ser·ried; ser·ry·ing** [F *serré*, pp. of *serrer* to press, squeeze, fr. LL *serare* to bolt] **:** to crowd together
se·rum \'sir-əm\ *n, pl* **serums** *or* **se·ra** \'sir-ə\ [L] **:** the watery portion of an animal fluid (as blood) remaining after coagulation; *esp* **:** immune blood serum that contains specific immune bodies (as antitoxins or agglutinins) ⟨antitoxin *serum*⟩ — **se·ral** \'sir-əl\ *adj*
serum albumin *n* **:** an albumin or mixture of albumins normally constituting more than half of the blood serum protein and serving to maintain the blood osmotic pressure
serum globulin *n* **:** a globulin or mixture of globulins occurring in blood serum and containing most of the antibodies of the blood
ser·val \'sər-vəl\ *n* [F, fr. Pg *lobo serval* lynx, fr. ML *lupus cervalis*, lit., cervine wolf] **:** a tawny black-spotted African wildcat with large ears and long legs
ser·vant \'sər-vənt\ *n* [OF, fr. prp. of *servir* to serve] **:** one that serves others; *esp* **:** one that performs household or personal services
¹serve \'sərv\ *vb* [OF *servir*, fr. L *servire* to be a slave, serve, fr. *servus* slave, servant] **1 a :** to be a servant **:** ATTEND **b :** to give the service and respect due to (a superior); *also* **:** WORSHIP ⟨*serve* God⟩ **c :** to comply with the commands or demands of **:** GRATIFY **d** (1) **:** to work through or perform a term of service esp. in the army or navy (2) **:** to put in **:** SPEND ⟨*serve* a jail sentence⟩ **2 a :** to officiate as a clergyman or priest **b :** to assist as server at mass **3 a :** to be of use **:** answer a purpose ⟨the tree *serves* as shelter⟩ **b :** BENEFIT **c :** to be favorable, opportune, or convenient ⟨when the time *serves*⟩ **d :** to prove adequate or satisfactory **:** SUFFICE ⟨a pie that will *serve* eight people⟩ **e :** to hold an office **:** discharge a duty or function ⟨*serve* on a jury⟩ **4 a :** to help persons to foods (as at a table or counter) **b :** to set out portions of food or drink **5 a :** to furnish or supply with something (as heat or light) needed or desired **b :** to wait on customers **c :** to furnish professional services to **6 :** to make a serve (as in tennis) **7 :** to treat or act toward in a specified way **:** REQUITE ⟨he *served* me ill⟩ **8 a :** to bring to notice, deliver, or execute as required by law **b :** to make legal service on (a person named in a writ)
²serve *n* **:** the act of putting the ball or shuttlecock in play (as in tennis or badminton)
serv·er \'sər-vər\ *n* **1 :** one that serves food or drink **2 :** the player who puts a ball in play **3 :** the celebrant's assistant at low mass **4 :** something (as a tray) used in serving food or drink
¹ser·vice \'sər-vəs\ *n* [OF, fr. L *servitium* condition of a slave] **1 :** the occupation or function of serving ⟨in active *service*⟩; *esp* **:** employment as a servant ⟨entered his *service*⟩ **2 a :** the work or action performed by one that serves

⟨gives good and quick *service*⟩ **b :** HELP, USE, BENEFIT ⟨be of *service* to them⟩ **c :** contribution to the welfare of others **d :** disposal for use ⟨at your *service*⟩ **3 a :** a form followed in worship or in a religious ceremony ⟨the burial *service*⟩ **b :** a meeting for worship ⟨held an evening *service*⟩ **4 :** the act of serving: as **a :** a helpful act **:** good turn ⟨did him a *service*⟩ **b :** useful labor that does not produce a tangible commodity — usu. used in pl. ⟨charge for professional *services*⟩ **c :** SERVE **5 :** a set of articles for a particular use ⟨a coffee *service*⟩ **6 a :** an administrative division (as of a government) ⟨the consular *service*⟩ **b :** a nation's military forces or one of these forces ⟨called into the *service*⟩ **7 :** a facility supplying some public demand ⟨bus *service*⟩; *esp* **:** one providing maintenance and repair ⟨television *service*⟩
²service *adj* **1 a :** of or relating to the armed services **b :** of, relating to, or constituting a branch of an army that provides service and supplies **2 :** used in serving or supplying **3 :** intended for everyday use **:** DURABLE **4 :** providing services (as repairs or maintenance)
³service *vt* **:** to perform services for **:** repair or provide maintenance for
⁴ser·vice \'sär-vəs, 'sər-\ *n* **:** SERVICE TREE
ser·vice·a·ble \'sər-və-sə-bəl\ *adj* **1 :** HELPFUL, USEFUL **2 :** wearing well in use — **ser·vice·a·bil·i·ty** \,sər-və-sə-'bil-ət-ē\ *n* — **ser·vice·a·bly** \-blē\ *adv*
ser·vice·ber·ry \'sär-vəs-,ber-ē, 'sər-\ *n* **:** the fruit of a service tree
service book *n* **:** a book setting forth forms of worship used in religious services
service box *n* **:** the area in which a player stands while serving in various wall and net games
service charge *n* **:** a fee charged for a particular service often in addition to a standard or basic fee
service club *n* **1 :** a club of business or professional men or women organized for their common benefit and active in community service **2 :** a recreation center for enlisted men provided by one of the armed services
service court *n* **:** a part of the court into which the ball must be served (as in tennis)
ser·vice·man \'sər-vəs-,man, -mən\ *n* **1 :** a male member of the armed forces **2 :** a man employed to repair or maintain equipment
service mark *n* **:** a mark or device used to identify a service (as transportation or insurance) offered to customers
service medal *n* **:** a medal awarded to an individual who does military service in a specified war or campaign
service module *n* **:** a space vehicle module that contains propellant tanks, fuel cells, and the main rocket engine
service station *n* **:** FILLING STATION
service stripe *n* **:** a stripe worn on an enlisted man's left sleeve to indicate three years of service in the army or air force or four years in the navy
ser·vice tree \'sär-vəs-, 'sər-\ *n* [ME *serves*, pl. of *serve* serviceberry, service tree, fr. OE *syrfe*, fr. L *sorbus* service tree] **1 a :** an Old World tree resembling the related mountain ashes but having larger edible fruit **b :** MOUNTAIN ASH **2 :** JUNEBERRY
ser·vi·ette \,sər-vē-'et\ *n* [F, fr. *servir* to serve] *chiefly Brit* **:** a table napkin
ser·vile \'sər-vəl, -,vīl\ *adj* [L *servus* slave] **1 :** of or befitting a slave or an enslaved or menial class ⟨*servile* work⟩ ⟨*servile* flattery⟩ **2 :** lacking spirit or independence **:** SUBMISSIVE ⟨*servile* to authority⟩ — **ser·vile·ly** \-və(l)-lē, -,vīl-lē\ *adv* — **ser·vile·ness** \-vəl-nəs, -,vīl-\ *n* — **ser·vil·i·ty** \(,)sər-'vil-ət-ē\ *n*
serv·ing \'sər-vin\ *n* **:** a helping of food or drink ⟨another *serving* of meat⟩
Ser·vite \'sər-,vīt\ *n* **:** a member of the mendicant Order of Servants of Mary founded at Florence in 1233
ser·vi·tor \'sər-vət-ər\ *n* **:** a male servant
ser·vi·tude \'sər-və-,t(y)üd\ *n* [L *servitudo*, fr. *servus* slave] **:** the state of subjection to another that constitutes or resembles slavery or serfdom
ser·vo \'sər-vō\ *n, pl* **servos 1 :** SERVOMOTOR **2 :** SERVOMECHANISM
ser·vo·mech·a·nism \'sər-vō-,mek-ə-,niz-əm\ *n* **:** an automatic device for controlling large amounts of power by means of very small amounts of power and automatically correcting performance of a mechanism
ser·vo·mo·tor \'sər-vō-,mōt-ər\ *n* **:** a power-driven

service 5

mechanism that supplements a primary control operated by a comparatively feeble force (as in a servomechanism)

ses·a·me \'ses-ə-mē\ *n* [Gk *sēsamē*] **1 :** an East Indian annual erect hairy herb; *also* **:** its small somewhat flat seeds used as a source of oil and a flavoring agent **2 :** OPEN SESAME

sesqui- *comb form* [L, one and a half, lit., and a half, fr. *semis* half + *-que* and] **:** one and a half times ⟨*sesqui*centennial⟩

ses·qui·cen·ten·ni·al \ˌses-kwi-sen-'ten-ē-əl\ *n* **:** a 150th anniversary or its celebration — **sesquicentennial** *adj*

ses·qui·pe·da·lian \ˌses-kwə-pə-'dāl-yən\ *adj* [L *sesquipedalis*, lit., a foot and a half long, fr. *sesqui-* + *ped-*, *pes* foot] **1 :** having many syllables **:** LONG **2 :** given to or characterized by the use of long words

ses·sile \'ses-əl, -ˌīl\ *adj* [L *sessilis* of or fit for sitting, low, fr. *sess-*, *sedēre* to sit] **1 :** attached directly by the base and not raised upon a stalk or peduncle ⟨a *sessile* leaf⟩ **2 :** permanently attached and not free to move about **:** SEDENTARY ⟨*sessile* polyps⟩ — **ses·sil·i·ty** \se-'sil-ət-ē\ *n*

ses·sion \'sesh-ən\ *n* [L *session-*, *sessio*, lit., act of sitting, fr. *sess-*, *sedēre* to sit; akin to E *sit*] **1 :** a meeting or series of meetings of a body (as a court or legislature) for the transaction of business **2 :** the period between the first and last of a series of meetings of a legislative or judicial body **3 :** the ruling body of a Presbyterian congregation **4 :** the period during the year or day in which a school conducts classes **5 :** a meeting or period devoted to a particular activity ⟨recording *session*⟩ — **ses·sion·al** \'sesh-nəl, -ən-°l\ *adj*

ses·terce \'ses-ˌtərs\ *n* [L *sestertius*] **:** an ancient Roman coin equal to ¼ denarius

ses·tet \se-'stet\ *n* [It *sestetto*, fr. *sesto* sixth, fr. L *sextus*] **:** a stanza or poem of six lines; *esp* **:** the last six lines of an Italian sonnet — compare OCTAVE

¹set \'set\ *vb* **set**; **set·ting** [OE *settan*; akin to E *sit*] **1 a :** to cause to sit **b :** to place in or on a seat ⟨*set* a king on a throne⟩ **2 :** to give (a fowl) eggs to hatch or provide (eggs) with suitable conditions for hatching **3 a :** to put or fix in any place, condition, or position ⟨*set* a dish on the table⟩ ⟨*set* seedlings in the ground⟩ ⟨*set* a trap⟩ ⟨*set* an alarm clock⟩ ⟨*set* a watch⟩ ⟨*set* down opinions on paper⟩; *also* **:** to arrange or put into a desired and esp. a normal position ⟨*set* a broken bone⟩ ⟨*set* the sails⟩ **b :** to put (dough) aside to rise **4 :** to direct with fixed attention ⟨had *set* his heart on going home⟩ **5 :** to cause to assume a specified condition, relation, or occupation ⟨slaves were *set* free⟩ **6 :** to appoint or assign an office or duty **:** POST, STATION ⟨*set* pickets around the camp⟩ **7 :** APPLY ⟨*set* pen to paper⟩ ⟨*set* a match to kindling⟩ **8 :** FIX, SETTLE ⟨*set* a price⟩ ⟨*set* a wedding day⟩ **9 a :** to establish as the highest level or best performance ⟨*set* a record for a half-mile race⟩ **b :** to furnish as a pattern or model ⟨*set* an example of generosity⟩ ⟨*set* the pace⟩ **c :** to allot or appoint as a task or as work ⟨he was *set* the job of cleaning the windows⟩ **10 a :** to put in order for immediate use ⟨*set* the table⟩ **b :** to provide (as words or verses) with melody and instrumental accompaniment **c :** to make scenically ready for a performance ⟨*set* the stage⟩ **d :** to compose (type) for printing **:** put into type **11 :** to wave, curl, or arrange (hair) by wetting and drying **12 a :** to adorn with something affixed or infixed **:** STUD, DOT ⟨a clear sky *set* with stars⟩ **b :** to fix in a setting or frame ⟨*set* diamonds in a ring⟩ **13 a :** to place in a relative rank or category ⟨*set* duty before pleasure⟩ **b :** VALUE, RATE, ESTIMATE ⟨*set* the loss at $2000⟩ **14 a :** to direct to action **b :** to incite to attack or antagonism ⟨war *sets* brother against brother⟩ **15 :** to put and fix in a direction ⟨*set* our faces toward home once more⟩ **16 a :** to fix firmly **:** make immobile ⟨*set* his jaw in determination⟩ **b :** to make unyielding or obstinate ⟨*set* his mind against all appeals⟩ **17 :** to become or cause to become firm or solid ⟨the jelly is *setting*⟩ ⟨*set* cement⟩ **18 :** to form and bring (fruit or seed) to maturity **19** *chiefly dial* **:** SIT **20 :** to be becoming **:** be suitable ⟨his behavior does not *set* well with his years⟩ **21 :** to cover and warm eggs to hatch ⟨*setting* hens⟩ **22 :** to become lodged or fixed ⟨the pudding *sets* heavily on his stomach⟩ **23 :** to pass below the horizon **:** go down ⟨the sun *sets*⟩ **24 :** to apply oneself to some activity ⟨*set* to work⟩ **25 :** to have a specified direction in motion **:** FLOW, TEND **26 :** to dance face to face with another in

a square dance ⟨*set* to your partner and turn⟩ **27 :** to become permanent ⟨a dye that will not *set*⟩ **28 :** to become whole by knitting ⟨the bone has not *set*⟩ **29 :** to defeat (a contract) esp. in bridge — **set about :** to begin to do — **set aside 1 :** DISCARD **2 :** RESERVE, SAVE **3 :** DISMISS **4 :** ANNUL, OVERRULE ⟨the verdict was *set aside* by the court⟩ — **set at :** ATTACK, ASSAIL — **set forth 1 :** PUBLISH **2 :** to give an account or statement of **3 :** to start out on a journey **:** set out — **set forward 1 :** FURTHER **2 :** to set out on a journey **:** START — **set upon :** to attack with violence **:** ASSAULT

²set *adj* [fr. pp. of **¹set**] **1 :** INTENT, DETERMINED ⟨*set* upon going⟩ **2 :** PITCHED ⟨*set* battle⟩ **3 :** PRESCRIBED, SPECIFIED ⟨*set* hours of study⟩ **4 :** INTENTIONAL, PREMEDITATED ⟨did it of *set* purpose⟩ **5 :** reluctant to change **:** OBSTINATE ⟨an old man very *set* in his ways⟩ **6 a :** IMMOVABLE, RIGID ⟨a *set* frown⟩ **b :** BUILT-IN ⟨a *set* tub for washing⟩ **7 :** SETTLED, PERSISTENT ⟨*set* defiance⟩ **8 a :** PREPARED, READY **b :** poised to start running or to dive in at the instant the signal is given ⟨ready, set, go⟩

³set *n* **1 :** the act or action of setting **:** the condition of being set **2 :** inclination to an action or course **3 :** a number of persons or things of the same kind that belong, are associated, or are used together ⟨the social *set*⟩ ⟨a *set* of dishes⟩ **4 :** DIRECTION, COURSE ⟨*set* of the wind⟩ **5 :** form or carriage of the body or of its parts ⟨the *set* of his shoulders⟩ **6 :** the manner of fitting or of being placed or suspended ⟨the *set* of a coat⟩ **7 :** amount of deflection from a straight line **8 :** permanent change of form (as of metal) due to repeated or excessive stress **9 :** a young plant or a plant part (as a corm or a piece of tuber) suitable for planting or transplanting **10 :** an artificial setting for a scene of a play or motion picture **11 :** a group of tennis games in which one side wins six to opponent's four or less or in case of a deuced score wins two consecutive games **12 :** SETTING 6 **13 :** the basic formation in a country-dance or square dance **14 :** a collection of mathematical elements (as numbers or points) that are actually listed or are identified by a common characteristic or by a rule of formation **15 :** an electronic apparatus ⟨a radio *set*⟩ ⟨a television *set*⟩

se·ta \'sēt-ə\ *n*, *pl* **se·tae** \'sē-ˌtē\ [NL, fr. L *saeta*, *seta* bristle] **:** a slender usu. rigid or bristly and springy organ or part of an animal or plant — **se·tal** \'sēt-°l\ *adj*

se·ta·ceous \si-'tā-shəs\ *adj* **:** resembling a bristle **:** BRISTLY — **se·ta·ceous·ly** *adv*

set·back \'set-ˌbak\ *n* **1 :** a checking of progress **2 :** an unexpected reverse **3 :** a withdrawal of the face of a building to a line some distance to the rear of a particular line or of the wall below

set chisel *n* **:** a chisel or punch with a broad flat end

set down *vt* **1 :** to cause to sit down **:** SEAT **2 :** to place at rest on a surface or on the ground **3 :** to cause or allow to get off a vehicle **:** DELIVER **4 :** to land (an airplane) on the ground or water **5 :** to put in writing **6 a :** REGARD, CONSIDER ⟨*set* him *down* as a liar⟩ **b :** ATTRIBUTE ⟨*set down* his success to perseverance⟩

set in *vb* **1 :** INSERT; *esp* **:** to stitch (a small part) within a large article **2 :** to enter upon a particular state ⟨winter *set in* early⟩ **3 :** to set to work **:** begin to function

¹set-in \ˌset-ˌin\ *adj* **1 :** placed, located, or built as a part of some other construction ⟨*set-in* bookcase⟩ ⟨*set-in* washbasin⟩ **2 :** cut separately and stitched in ⟨*set-in* sleeves⟩

²set-in \'set-ˌin\ *n* **1 :** an instance or time of something setting in ⟨early *set-in* of frosty nights⟩ **2 :** INSERT

set·line \'set-ˌlīn\ *n* **:** a long heavy fishing line to which several hooks are attached in series

set off \(')set-'óf\ *vb* **1 a :** to show up by contrast ⟨her pale face *sets off* her dark eyes⟩ **b :** ADORN, EMBELLISH **c :** to set apart **:** make distinct or outstanding ⟨commas used to *set off* words in a series⟩ **2 a :** OFFSET, COMPENSATE **b :** to make a setoff of **3 a :** to set in motion **:** cause to begin ⟨that story *sets her off* laughing⟩ **b :** to cause to explode **4 :** to measure off on a surface **:** lay off **5 :** to start out on a course or a journey ⟨*set off* for home⟩

set·off \'set-ˌóf\ *n* **1 :** something that is set off against another thing **: a :** DECORATION, ORNAMENT **b :** COMPENSATION, COUNTERBALANCE **2 :** the discharge of a debt by setting against it a distinct claim in favor of the debtor; *also* **:** the claim itself

set on *vb* **1** : ATTACK **2 a** : to urge (as a dog) to attack or pursue **b** : to incite to action : INSTIGATE ⟨*set on* to rebellion by their leaders⟩ **c** : to set to work **3** : to go on : ADVANCE

se·tose \'sē-ˌtōs\ *adj* : BRISTLY, SETACEOUS

set out *vb* **1** : to recite, describe, or state at large **2 a** : to arrange and present graphically or systematically **b** : to mark out (as a design) : lay out the plan of **3** : to begin with the purpose of achieving : INTEND, UNDERTAKE ⟨deliberately *set out* to win⟩ **4** : to start out on a course, a journey, or a career

set·over \'set-ˌō-vər\ *n* : distance or amount set over

set piece *n* **1** : a realistic piece of stage scenery standing by itself **2** : a composition (as in literature) executed in a fixed or ideal form often with studied artistry and brilliant effect

set point *n* : a point that decides a tennis set if won by the side having an advantage in the score

set·screw \'set-ˌskrü\ *n* **1** : a screw screwed through one part tightly upon or into another part to prevent relative movement **2** : a screw for regulating a valve opening or a spring tension

set·tee \se-'tē\ *n* [alter. of *settle*] **1** : a long seat with a back **2** : a medium-sized sofa with arms and a back

set·ter \'set-ər\ *n* **1** : one that sets — often used in combination ⟨brick*setter*⟩ **2** : a large long-coated bird dog of a type formerly trained to crouch on finding game but now to point

set theory *n* : a branch of mathematics that deals with the nature and relations of sets — **set–theoretic** *adj*

set·ting \'set-iŋ\ *n* **1** : the manner, position, or direction in which something is set **2** : the frame or bed in which a gem is set **3 a** : BACKGROUND, ENVIRONMENT **b** : the time and place within which a scene of a play or motion picture is enacted **4** : the music composed for a poem or other text **5** : the articles of tableware required for setting a place at table **6** : a batch of eggs for incubation

¹**set·tle** \'set-ᵊl\ *n* [OE *setl* seat, chair] : a wooden bench with arms, a high solid back, and an enclosed foundation

²**settle** *vb* **set·tled**; **set·tling** \'set-liŋ, -ᵊl-iŋ\ [OE *setlan*, lit., to seat, fr. *setl* seat] **1** : to place so as to stay **2 a** : to establish residence in : COLONIZE ⟨*settled* the West⟩ **b** : to make one's home ⟨*settle* in the country⟩ **3 a** : to cause to pack down or to become compact by sinking : sink gradually or to the bottom **b** : to clarify by causing dregs or impurities to sink **c** : to become clear by depositing a constituent as sediment **4 a** : to make or become quiet or orderly ⟨crocheting *settles* her nerves⟩ **b** : to take up an ordered or stable life ⟨marry and *settle* down⟩ **5 a** : to fix or resolve conclusively ⟨*settle* the question⟩ **b** : to establish or secure permanently **6** : to arrange in a desired position **7 a** : to make or arrange for final disposition of ⟨*settle* an estate⟩ **b** : to bestow or give possession of legally ⟨*settled* property on his wife⟩ **c** : to pay in full ⟨*settle* a bill⟩ **8** : to adjust differences or accounts

settle

set·tle·ment \'set-ᵊl-mənt\ *n* **1** : the act or process of settling **2** : an amount bestowed by a settlement **3 a** : a place or region newly settled **b** : a small village **4** : an institution providing various community services to people in a crowded part of a city — called also *settlement house* **5** : an agreement composing differences

set·tler \'set-lər, -ᵊl-ər\ *n* : a person who settles in a new region : COLONIST

set·tling \'set-liŋ, -ᵊl-iŋ\ *n* : something that settles at the bottom of a liquid : SEDIMENT — usu. used in pl.

set·tlor \'set-lər, -ᵊl-ər\ *n* : one that makes a settlement or creates a trust of property

set to \(')set-'tü\ *vi* **1** : to begin actively and earnestly ⟨*set to* on the food with a will⟩ **2** : to begin fighting

set-to \'set-ˌtü\ *n*, *pl* **set-tos** \-ˌtüz\ : a usu. brief and vigorous contest (as a bout or an argument)

set up \(')set-'əp\ *vb* **1** : to raise to and place in a high position **2** : to make (a loud noise) with the voice ⟨*set up* a howl⟩ **3 a** : ELATE, GRATIFY **b** : to make proud or vain **4 a** : to put forward or extol as a model **b** : to claim (oneself) to be ⟨*sets* himself *up* as an authority⟩ **5 a** : to place upright : ERECT **b** : to assemble the parts of and

erect ⟨*set up* a printing press⟩ **c** : to put (a machine) in readiness or adjustment for a tooling operation **6 a** : FOUND, INAUGURATE **b** : to put in operation as a way of living ⟨*set up* housekeeping⟩ or a means of livelihood ⟨*set up* shop in a new neighborhood⟩ **c** : to come into active operation or use **7** : to bring or restore to normal health and strength **8** : to make carefully worked out plans for ⟨*set up* a bank robbery⟩ **9 a** : to treat to (drinks) **b** : to treat (someone) to something **10** : to make pretensions ⟨*setting up* for a wit⟩

set·up \'set-ˌəp\ *n* : the way in which something is set up : ORGANIZATION, ARRANGEMENT

sev·en \'sev-ən\ *n* [OE *seofon*] **1** — see NUMBER table **2** : the seventh in a set or series ⟨the *seven* of hearts⟩ **3** : something having seven units or members — **seven** *adj or pron*

Seven against Thebes \-'thēbz\ : an expedition undertaken by seven heroes of Greek legend to help Polynices recover a share in the kingship of Thebes

seven seas *n pl* : all the waters or oceans of the world ⟨*seven seas* is often applied collectively to the Arctic, Antarctic, North and South Atlantic, North and South Pacific, and Indian oceans⟩

sev·en·teen \ˌsev-ən-'tēn\ *n* — see NUMBER table — **seventeen** *adj or pron* — **sev·en·teenth** \-'tēn(t)th\ *adj or n*

seventeen–year locust *n* : a cicada of the U.S. with a life of seventeen years in the North and of thirteen years in the South of which the greatest part is spent as a wingless underground nymph that feeds on roots and finally emerges from the soil to become a short-lived winged adult

sev·enth \'sev-ən(t)th\ *n*, *pl* **sev·enths** \'sev-ən(t)s, -ən(t)ths\ **1** — see NUMBER table **2 a** : a musical interval embracing seven degrees **b** : LEADING TONE **c** : the harmonic combination of two tones a seventh apart — **seventh** *adj or adv*

sev·enth–day *adj* : advocating or practicing observance of Saturday as the Sabbath

Seventh Day Adventist *n* : a member of an evangelical Protestant denomination organized in the U.S. in 1863 and marked by emphasis on preparation for Christ's Second Coming

seventh heaven *n* : a state of extreme joy ⟨she was in *seventh heaven* when she won the prize⟩

sev·en·ty \'sev-ən-tē\ *n*, *pl* **-ties** — see NUMBER table — **sev·en·ti·eth** \-tē-əth\ *adj or n* — **seventy** *adj or pron*

sev·en·ty–eight \ˌsev-ən-tē-'āt\ *n* : a phonograph record for play at 78 revolutions per minute

Seven Wonders of the World : seven remarkable objects of the ancient world usu. listed as the pyramids of Egypt, the lighthouse of Alexandria, the walls and hanging gardens of Babylon, the temple of Artemis (Diana) at Ephesus, the statue of the Olympian Zeus (Jupiter) by Phidias, the mausoleum erected by Queen Artemisia at Halicarnassus, and the Colossus of Rhodes

sev·er \'sev-ər\ *vb* **sev·ered**; **sev·er·ing** \'sev-(ə-)riŋ\ [MF *severer*, fr. L *separare*] **1** : to put or keep apart : DIVIDE; *esp* : to part by violence (as by cutting) **2** : to come or break apart **syn** see SEPARATE — **sev·er·a·bil·i·ty** \ˌsev-(ə-)rə-'bil-ət-ē\ *n* — **sev·er·a·ble** \'sev-(ə-)rə-bəl\ *adj*

¹**sev·er·al** \'sev-(ə-)rəl\ *adj* [AF, fr. ML *separalis*, fr. L *separare* to separate] **1 a** : separate or distinct from others : DIFFERENT ⟨federal union of the *several* states⟩ **b** : PARTICULAR, RESPECTIVE ⟨specialists in their *several* fields⟩ **2 a** : more than one ⟨*several* pieces⟩ **b** : more than two but fewer than many ⟨moved *several* inches⟩ — **sev·er·al·ly** \-ē\ *adv*

²**several** *pron* : an indefinite number more than two and fewer than many ⟨*several* of the guests⟩

sev·er·al·fold \ˌsev-(ə-)rəl-'fōld\ *adj* **1** : having several parts or aspects **2** : being several times as large, as great, or as many as some understood size, degree, or amount ⟨a *severalfold* increase⟩ — **severalfold** *adv*

sev·er·al·ty \'sev-(ə-)rəl-tē\ *n* : the quality or state of being several : DISTINCTNESS, SEPARATENESS

sev·er·ance \'sev-(ə-)rən(t)s\ *n* : the act or process of severing : the state of being severed

se·vere \sə-'vi(ə)r\ *adj* [L *severus*] **1 a** : strict in judgment, discipline, or government **b** : of a strict or stern bearing or manner : AUSTERE **2** : rigorous in restraint, punishment, or requirement : STRINGENT **3** : sober or restrained in decoration or manner : PLAIN **4 a** : inflicting physical discomfort or hardship : HARSH ⟨*severe* winter⟩ **b** : inflicting pain or distress : GRIEVOUS ⟨*severe* wound⟩ **5** : requiring great effort : ARDUOUS ⟨*severe* test⟩ **6** : of a great degree : MARKED, SERIOUS ⟨*severe* economic depression⟩ — **se·vere·ly** *adv* — **se·vere·ness** *n*

syn SEVERE, STERN, AUSTERE mean showing or requiring discipline or restraint. SEVERE implies enforcing standards without indulgence or laxity and may suggest harshness; STERN stresses inflexibility and inexorability of temper or character; AUSTERE suggests absence of warmth, color, or feeling and may apply to rigorous simplicity or self-denial

se·ver·i·ty \sə-'ver-ət-ē\ *n, pl* **-ties** : the quality or state of being severe ⟨*severity* of the winter⟩ ⟨*severity* of his illness⟩

sè·vres \'sevr°\ *n* [*Sèvres*, France] : a fine often elaborately decorated French porcelain

sew \'sō\ *vb* **sewed**; **sewn** \'sōn\ *or* **sewed**; **sew·ing** [OE *sīwian, sēowan*] **1** : to unite or fasten by stitches made with a flexible thread or filament ⟨*sews* on the button⟩ **2** : to close or enclose by sewing ⟨*sew* the money in a bag⟩ **3** : to practice or engage in working with needle and thread

sew·age \'sü-ij\ *n* : refuse liquids or waste matter carried off by sewers

¹**sew·er** \'sō(-ə)r\ *n* : one that sews

²**sew·er** \'sü-ər, 'sù(-ə)r\ *n* [MF *esseweur, seweur,* fr. *es-sewer* to drain, fr. L *ex-* + *aqua* water] : a covered usu. underground passage to carry off water and sewage

sew·er·age \'sü-ə-rij, 'sù(-ə)r-ij\ *n* **1** : SEWAGE **2** : the removal and disposal of sewage and surface water by sewers **3** : a system of sewers

sew·ing \'sō-iŋ\ *n* **1** : the act, method, or occupation of one that sews **2** : material that has been or is to be sewed

sew up *vt* **1** : to get exclusive use or control of : MONOPO-LIZE **2** : to make certain of : ASSURE ⟨*sew up* most of the delegates⟩

sex \'seks\ *n* [L *sexus*] **1** : either of two divisions of organisms distinguished respectively as male and female **2** : the sum of the structural, functional, and behavioral peculiarities of living beings that are ultimately related to reproduction by two interacting parents and that serve to distinguish males and females **3** : sexual activity or intercourse

sex- *or* **sexi-** *comb form* [L *sex*; akin to E *six*] : six ⟨*sexi-*valent⟩ ⟨*sex*partite⟩

sex·a·ge·nar·i·an \,sek-sə-jə-'ner-ē-ən\ *n* [L *sexageni* 60 each, fr. *sexaginta* 60, fr. *sex* six] : a person who is 60 or more but less than 70 years old — **sexagenarian** *adj*

Sex·a·ges·i·ma \,sek-sə-'jes-ə-mə\ *n* : the second Sunday before Lent

sex·a·ges·i·mal \-məl\ *adj* [L *sexagesimus* sixtieth, fr. *sex* six] : of, relating to, or based on the number 60 ⟨*sexagesimal* measurement of angles⟩

sex appeal *n* : personal appeal or physical attractiveness for members of the opposite sex

sex cell *n* : GAMETE

sex chromosome *n* : a chromosome inherited differently in the two sexes that is or is held to be concerned directly with the inheritance of sex

sexed \'sekst\ *adj* : having sex or sexual instincts

sex gland *n* : GONAD

sex hormone *n* : a hormone that affects the growth or function of the reproductive organs or the development of secondary sex characteristics

sex hygiene *n* : a division of hygiene that deals with sex and sexual conduct as bearing on the health of the individual and the community

sex·less \'seks-ləs\ *adj* : lacking sex : NEUTER — **sex·less·ness** *n*

sex-link·age \'seks-,liŋ-kij\ *n* : the quality or state of being sex-linked

sex-linked \'seks-,liŋ(k)t\ *adj* **1** : located in a sex chromosome and heterozygous in one sex but homozygous in the other ⟨a *sex-linked* gene⟩ **2** : mediated by a sex-linked gene ⟨a *sex-linked* character⟩

sext \'sekst\ *n, often cap* [L *sexta* sixth hour of the day] : the fourth of the canonical hours

sex·tant \'sek-stənt\ *n* [NL *sextant-, sextans* sixth part of a circle, fr. L, sixth part, fr. *sextus* sixth] : an instrument

for measuring altitudes of celestial bodies from a moving ship or airplane

sex·tet *also* **sex·tette** \sek-'stet\ *n* [L *sextus* sixth, fr. *sex* six] **1** : a musical composition for six instruments or voices **2** : a group or set of six

sex·til·lion \sek-'stil-yən\ *n* — see NUMBER table

sex·ton \'sek-stən\ *n* [ME *secresteyn,* fr. MF *secrestain,* fr. ML *sacristanus* sacristan] : a church officer or employee whose duties include care of the buildings and property and the ringing of the bell for services and sometimes the digging of graves

¹**sex·tu·ple** \sek-'st(y)üp-əl, -'stəp-; 'sek-stəp-\ *adj* **1** : having six units or members **2** : being six times as great or as many — **sextuple** *n*

²**sextuple** *vb* **sex·tu·pled**; **sex·tu·pling** \-(ə-)liŋ\ : to make or become six times as much or as many

sex·tup·let \sek-'stəp-lət, -'st(y)üp-; 'sek-stəp-\ *n* **1** : a combination of six of a kind **2** : one of six offspring born at one birth

sex·u·al \'sek-sh(ə-w)əl\ *adj* **1** : of, relating to, or associated with sex or the sexes ⟨*sexual* differentiation⟩ ⟨*sexual* conflict⟩ **2** : having or involving sex ⟨*sexual* reproduction⟩ ⟨*sexual* spores⟩ — **sex·u·al·i·ty** \,sek-shə-'wal-ət-ē\ *n* — **sex·u·al·ly** \'sek-shə-wə-lē, 'seksh-(ə-)lē\ *adv*

sexy \'sek-sē\ *adj* **sex·i·er; -est** : sexually suggestive or stimulating : EROTIC — **sex·i·ness** *n*

sfer·ics \'sfi(ə)r-iks, 'sfer-\ *n pl* : ATMOSPHERICS

¹**sfor·zan·do** \sfòrt-'sän-dō\ *adj* [It, lit., forcing] : AC-CENTED — used of a single note or chord as a direction in music

²**sforzando** *n, pl* **-dos** *or* **-di** \-(,)dē\ : an accented tone or chord

sgraf·fi·to \zgra-'fē-,tō, skra-\ *n, pl* **sgraf·fi·ti** \-,tē\ [It, fr. pp. of *sgraffire* to scratch] : decoration (as of pottery) produced by scratching through a surface layer to reveal a differently colored background

sh \sh *often prolonged*\ *interj* — used often in prolonged or reduplicated form to enjoin silence

shab·by \'shab-ē\ *adj* **shab·bi·er; -est** [obs. *shab* scab, fr. OE *sceabb*] **1 a** : threadbare and faded from wear **b** : ill kept : DILAPIDATED **2** : clothed with worn or seedy garments **3 a** : MEAN, DESPICABLE **b** : UNGENEROUS, UN-FAIR **c** : inferior in quality — **shab·bi·ly** \'shab-ə-lē\ *adv* — **shab·bi·ness** \'shab-ē-nəs\ *n*

Sha·bu·oth \shə-'vü-,ōt(h), -,ōs\ *n* [Heb *shābhu'ōth,* lit., weeks] : a Jewish holiday celebrated in May or June to commemorate the revelation of the Ten Commandments at Mt. Sinai and in biblical times as a harvest festival

¹**shack** \'shak\ *n* **1** : HUT, SHANTY **2** : a room or similar enclosed structure for a particular person or use ⟨radio *shack*⟩ ⟨ammunition *shack*⟩

²**shack** *vi* : LIVE, STAY — often used with *up*

¹**shack·le** \'shak-əl\ *n* [OE *sceacul*] **1** : something (as a manacle or fetter) that confines the legs or arms **2** : something that checks or prevents free action as if by fetters — usu. used in pl. **3** : a device (as a clevis) for making something fast

²**shackle** *vt* **shack·led; shack·ling** \'shak-(ə-)liŋ\ **1 a** : to bind with shackles **b** : to make fast with a shackle **2** : to deprive of freedom of action by means of restrictions or handicaps : HINDER, IMPEDE

syn see HAMPER — **shack·ler** \-(ə-)lər\ *n*

shackle 3

shad \'shad\ *n, pl* **shad** [OE *sceadd*] : any of several deep-bodied food fishes that are closely related to the herrings but ascend rivers in the spring to spawn

shad·bush \-,bùsh\ *n* : JUNEBERRY — called also *shad-blow* \-,blō\

shad·dock \'shad-ək\ *n* [after Captain *Shaddock,* 17th cent. English ship commander] : a large thick-rinded usu. pear-shaped citrus fruit closely related to the grapefruit but often having coarse dry pulp; *also* : the tree that bears it

¹**shade** \'shād\ *n* [OE *sceadu*] **1 a** : partial darkness caused by interception of the rays of light **b** : relative obscurity or retirement **2 a** : shelter (as by foliage) from the heat and glare of sunlight **b** : a place sheltered from the sun **3** : an evanescent or unreal appearance **4** *pl* : the shadows that gather as darkness comes on **b** : NETH-ERWORLD, HADES **5** : a disembodied spirit : GHOST **6**

: something that intercepts or shelters from light, sun, or heat: as **a :** a device partially covering a lamp so as to reduce glare **b :** a screen usu. on a roller for regulating the light or the view through a window **7 a :** the representation of the effect of shade in painting or drawing **b :** a subdued or somber feature **8 a :** a color produced by a pigment or dye mixture having some black in it **b :** a color slightly different from the one under consideration **9 :** a minute difference or variation **:** NUANCE **10 :** a facial expression of sadness or displeasure **syn** see COLOR — **shade·less** \-ləs\ *adj*

²**shade** *vb* **1 a :** to shelter or screen by intercepting radiated light or heat **b :** to cover with a shade **2 :** to hide partly by or as if by a shadow **3 :** to darken with or as if with a shadow **4 :** to cast into the shade **:** OBSCURE **5 a :** to represent the effect of shade or shadow on **b :** to add shading to **c :** to color so that the shades pass gradually from one to another **6 :** to change by gradual transition or qualification **7 :** to reduce slightly (as a price) — **shad·er** *n*

shad·ing \'shād-iŋ\ *n* **:** the filling up within outlines that represents the effect of more or less darkness in a picture or drawing

sha·doof \shə-'düf\ *n* [Ar *shādūf*] **:** a counterbalanced sweep used since ancient times esp. in Egypt for raising water (as for irrigation)

¹**shad·ow** \'shad-ō\ *n* [OE *sceaduw-, sceadu* shade, shadow] **1 :** shade within defined bounds **2 :** a reflected image **3 :** shelter from danger or observation **4 a :** an imperfect and faint representation **b :** IMITATION, COPY **5 :** the image made by an obscured space on a surface that cuts across it usu. representing in silhouette the form of the interposed body **6 :** PHANTOM **7** *pl* **:** DARKNESS **8 :** a shaded or darker portion of a picture **9 :** a form without substance **:** REMNANT, VESTIGE (was only a *shadow* of his former self) **10 a :** an inseparable companion or follower **b :** one that shadows as a spy or detective **11 : a** small degree or portion **:** TRACE (not a *shadow* of a doubt) **12 :** a gloomy influence — **shad·ow·less** \-ləs\ *adj* — **shad·ow·like** \-ˌlīk\ *adj*

²**shadow** *vb* **1 a :** to cast a shadow upon **b :** to cast a gloom over **:** CLOUD **2 :** to represent or indicate obscurely or faintly **3 :** to follow esp. secretly **:** TRAIL **4** *archaic* **:** SHADE 5 **5 :** to shade off **6 :** to become overcast with or as if with shadows — **shad·ow·er** \'shad-ə-wər\ *n*

³**shadow** *adj* **1 :** having form without substance (*shadow* government) **2 :** having an indistinct pattern (*shadow* plaid)

shadow box *n* **:** a shallow enclosing case usu. with a glass front in which something is set for protection and display

shad·ow·box \'shad-ō-ˌbäks\ *vi* **:** to box with an imaginary opponent esp. as a form of training — **shad·ow·box·ing** *n*

shadow dance *n* **:** a dance shown by throwing the shadows of invisible dancers on a screen

shadow play *n* **:** a drama exhibited by throwing shadows of puppets or actors on a screen

shad·owy \'shad-ə-wē\ *adj* **1 a :** of the nature of or resembling a shadow **:** UNSUBSTANTIAL **b :** INDISTINCT, VAGUE **2 :** being in or obscured by shadow **3 :** SHADY 1

shady \'shād-ē\ *adj* **shad·i·er; -est** **1 :** producing or affording shade **2 :** sheltered from the sun's rays **3 a :** of questionable merit **b :** DISREPUTABLE — **shad·i·ly** \'shād-ᵊl-ē\ *adv* — **shad·i·ness** \'shād-ē-nəs\ *n*

¹**shaft** \'shaft\ *n, pl* **shafts** \'shaf(t)s, *in sense 3 also* 'shavz\ [OE *sceaft*] **1 a :** the long handle of a weapon (as a spear) **b :** SPEAR, LANCE **2 a :** the slender stem of an arrow — see ARROW illustration **b :** ARROW **3 :** POLE; *esp* **:** one of two poles between which a horse is hitched to pull a vehicle **4 :** a narrow beam of light **5 :** something suggestive of the shaft of an arrow or spear **:** a long slender part esp. when round (the *shaft* or trunk of a tree) **6 :** the handle of a tool **7 :** a tall monument (as a column) **8 :** a vertical opening or passage through the floors of a building (an air *shaft*) **9 :** a commonly cylindrical bar used to support rotating pieces or to transmit power or motion by rotation **10 :** a vertical or inclined opening of uniform and limited cross section made for finding or mining ore, raising water, or ventilating underground workings **11 :** the midrib of a feather **12 a :** a projectile

thrown like a spear or shot like an arrow **b :** a scornful or satirical remark **:** BARB

²**shaft** *vt* **:** to fit with a shaft

¹**shag** \'shag\ *n* [OE *sceacga*] **1 a :** a shaggy tangled mass or covering **b :** long coarse or matted fiber or nap **2 :** a strong coarse tobacco cut into fine shreds **3 :** CORMORANT

²**shag** *vb* **shagged; shag·ging** **1 :** to fall or hang in shaggy masses **2 :** to make rough or shaggy

³**shag** *vt* **shagged; shag·ging** **1 :** to chase after (as a ball) **2 :** to chase away

shag·bark \'shag-ˌbärk\ *n* **:** a hickory with a gray shaggy outer bark that peels off in long strips

shag·gy \'shag-ē\ *adj* **shag·gi·er; -est** **1 a :** covered with or consisting of long, coarse, or matted hair or thick, tangled, or unkempt vegetation **b :** having a rough or hairy nap, texture, or surface **2 a :** UNKEMPT **b :** RUDE, UNPOLISHED **c :** CONFUSED — **shag·gi·ly** \'shag-ə-lē\ *adv* — **shag·gi·ness** \'shag-ē-nəs\ *n*

sha·green \sha-'grēn, shə-\ *n* [F *chagrin*, fr. Turk *çağrı, sağrı*] **1 :** an untanned leather covered with small round granulations and usu. dyed green **2 :** the rough skin of various sharks and rays — **shagreen** *adj*

shah \'shä, 'shò\ *n* [Per *shāh* king] **:** the sovereign of Iran — **shah·dom** \'shäd-əm, 'shòd-\ *n*

¹**shake** \'shāk\ *vb* **shook** \'shuk\; **shak·en** \'shā-kən\; **shak·ing** [OE *sceacan*] **1 :** to move irregularly to and fro **:** QUIVER, TREMBLE (*shaking* with cold) **2 :** to become unsteady **:** TOTTER **3 :** to brandish, wave, or flourish often in a threatening manner **4 :** to cause to move in a quick jerky manner **5 :** to free oneself from (*shake* off a cold) **6 :** to cause to waver **:** WEAKEN (*shake* one's faith) **7 :** to dislodge or eject by quick jerky movements (*shake* the dust from a blanket) **8 :** to clasp (hands) in greeting or as a sign of goodwill or agreement **9 :** to stir the feelings of **:** UPSET (*shook* her up) — **shak·a·ble** *or* **shake·a·ble** \'shā-kə-bəl\ *adj*

syn SHAKE, AGITATE, ROCK mean to move up and down or back and forth with some violence. SHAKE applies to short, rapid movements often for a particular purpose; AGITATE suggests more violent and irregular tossing or stirring; ROCK implies a swinging or swaying motion resulting from violent impact or upheaval

— **shake a leg 1 :** DANCE **2 :** to hurry up

²**shake** *n* **1 :** an act of shaking: as **a :** an act of shaking hands **b :** an act of shaking oneself **2 a :** a blow or shock that upsets the equilibrium or disturbs the balance of something **b :** EARTHQUAKE **3** *pl* **a :** a condition of trembling (as from chill) **b :** MALARIA **4 :** something produced by shaking: as **a :** a fissure in strata **b :** MILK SHAKE **5 :** a wavering, quivering, or alternating motion caused by a blow or shock **6 :** TRILL **7 :** a very brief period of time **:** INSTANT (ready in two *shakes*) **8 :** ³DEAL 2 (a fair *shake*) **9 :** a shingle split from a piece of log usu. three to four feet long (cedar *shakes*) — **no great shakes :** of no great importance or ability **:** not extraordinary

¹**shake·down** \'shāk-ˌdaůn\ *n* **1 :** an improvised bed (as made up on the floor) **2 :** a boisterous dance **3 :** an act or instance of shaking someone down; *esp* **:** EXTORTION **4 :** a process or period of adjustment

²**shakedown** *adj* **:** designed to test a new ship or airplane under operating conditions and to familiarize the crew with it (*shakedown* cruise)

shake down \(ʼ)shāk-'daůn\ *vb* **1 a :** to take up temporary quarters **b :** to occupy a makeshift bed **2 a :** to become accustomed esp. to new surroundings or duties **b :** to settle down **c :** to test on a shakedown cruise **3 :** to obtain money from in a dishonest or illegal manner **4 :** to bring about a reduction of

shake·out \'shāk-ˌaůt\ *n* **:** a moderate stock market or business recession usu. corrective of an inflationary condition

shak·er \'shā-kər\ *n* **1 :** one that shakes; *esp* **:** any of various utensils or machines used in shaking **2** *cap* **:** a member of a millenarian sect originating in England in 1747 — **Shaker** *adj*

Shake·spear·ean *or* **Shake·spear·i·an** \shāk-'spir-ē-ən\ *adj* **:** of, relating to, or characteristic of Shakespeare or his writings

Shakespearean sonnet *n* **:** ENGLISH SONNET

shake up \(ʼ)shāk-'əp\ *vt* **1 :** to jar by or as if by a physical shock ⟨collision *shook* both drivers *up*⟩ **2** : to effect an extensive and often drastic reorganization of ⟨the new president *shook* things *up* in the office⟩

shake-up \'shāk-,əp\ *n* : an act or instance of shaking up; *esp* : an extensive and often drastic reorganization ⟨lost his job in an office *shake-up*⟩

shako \'shak-ō, 'shāk-\ *n, pl* **shak·os** *or* **shak·oes** [Hung *csákó*] : a stiff military cap with a high crown and plume

shaky \'shā-kē\ *adj* **shak·i·er; -est** **1 a** : lacking stability **b** : lacking in firmness **c** : lacking in authority or reliability : QUESTIONABLE **2 a** : somewhat unsound in health **b** : characterized by shaking : TREMBLING **3** : easily shaken : RICKETY — **shak·i·ly** \-kə-lē\ *adv* — **shak·i·ness** \-kē-nəs\ *n*

shale \'shāl\ *n* [ME, shell, scale, fr. OE *scealu*] : a rock that is formed by the consolidation of clay, mud, or silt, has a finely layered structure, and splits easily

shako

shall \shəl, (')shal\ *auxiliary verb, past* **should** \shəd, (')shu̇d\ *pres sing & pl* **shall** [OE *sceal* owe, owes, ought to, must] **1 a** — used to express a command or exhortation ⟨you *shall* go⟩ **b** — used in laws, regulations, or directives to express what is mandatory ⟨it *shall* be unlawful to carry firearms⟩ **2 a** — used to express what is inevitable or likely to happen in the future ⟨we *shall* have to be ready⟩ ⟨we *shall* see⟩ **b** — used to express simple futurity ⟨when *shall* we expect you⟩ **3** — used to express determination ⟨they *shall* not pass⟩

shal·lop \'shal-əp\ *n* [MF *chaloupe*] : a small open boat propelled by oars or sails and used chiefly in shallow waters

shal·lot \shə-'lät\ *n* [F *échalote*] : a bulbous perennial herb that resembles the related onion and produces small clustered bulbs used in seasoning

1shal·low \'shal-ō\ *adj* [ME *schalowe*] **1** : having little depth **2** : lacking intellectual depth — **shal·low·ly** *adv* — **shal·low·ness** *n*

2shallow *vb* : to make or become shallow

3shallow *n* : a shallow place or area in a body of water — usu. used in pl.

sha·lom \shä-'lōm\ *interj* — used as a Jewish greeting and farewell

sha·lom alei·chem \,shȯ-ləm-ə-'lā-kəm\ *interj* [Heb *shālōm 'alēkhem* peace unto you] — used as a traditional Jewish greeting

shalt \shəlt, (')shalt\ *archaic pres 2d sing of* SHALL

1sham \'sham\ *n* **1** : HOAX **2** : cheap falseness : HYPOCRISY **3** : a decorative piece of cloth simulating an article of personal or household linen and used in place of or over it **4** : an imitation or counterfeit purporting to be genuine **5** : a person who shams

2sham *vb* **shammed; sham·ming** : to act intentionally so as to give a false impression of being : COUNTERFEIT, FEIGN

3sham *adj* : FALSE: as **a** : FEIGNED, PRETENDED ⟨*sham* battle⟩ ⟨*sham* indignation⟩ **b** : made or used as an imitation ⟨*sham* jewelry⟩

sha·man \'shäm-ən, 'shā-mən\ *n* [Russ, of Altaic origin] : a priest who uses magic to cure the sick, to divine the hidden, and to control events

sha·man·ism \-,iz-əm\ *n* : a religion of the Ural-Altaic peoples of northern Asia and Europe characterized by belief in a world of gods, demons, and ancestral spirits responsive only to the shamans; *also* : a similar religion — **sha·man·ist** \-əst\ *n or adj* — **sha·man·is·tic** \,shäm-ən-'is-tik, ,shā-mən-\ *adj*

1sham·ble \'sham-bəl\ *vi* **sham·bled; sham·bling** \-b(ə)liŋ\ [*shamble legs* malformed legs, fr. *shamble* table for exhibition of meat for sale, fr. OE *sceamul* footstool, table] : to walk awkwardly with dragging feet : SHUFFLE

2shamble *n* : a shambling gait

sham·bles \'sham-bəlz\ *n sing or pl* [pl. of *shamble* table for exhibition of meat for sale, meat market] : a place or scene of slaughter or destruction

sham·bling *adj* : characterized by slow awkward movement ⟨a *shambling* gait⟩

1shame \'shām\ *n* [OE *scamu*] **1 a** : a painful emotion caused by consciousness of guilt, shortcoming, impropriety, or disgrace **b** : the susceptibility to such emotion **2** : DISHONOR, DISGRACE **3 a** : something that brings strong regret, censure, or reproach **b** : a cause of feeling shame

2shame *vt* **1** : to bring shame to : DISGRACE **2** : to put to shame by outdoing **3** : to cause to feel shame **4** : to force by causing to feel guilty ⟨they were *shamed* into confessing⟩

shame-faced \'shām-'fāst\ *adj* **1** : showing modesty : MODEST, SHY, BASHFUL **2** : ASHAMED — **shame·fac·ed·ly** \-'fā-səd-lē, -'fāst-lē\ *adv* — **shame·fac·ed·ness** \-'fā-səd-nəs, -'fās(t)-nəs\ *n*

shame·ful \'shām-fəl\ *adj* **1** : bringing shame : DISGRACEFUL **2** : arousing the feeling of shame : INDECENT — **shame·ful·ly** \-fə-lē\ *adv* — **shame·ful·ness** *n*

shame·less \'shām-ləs\ *adj* **1** : having no shame : BRAZEN **2** : showing lack of shame : DISGRACEFUL — **shame·less·ly** *adv* — **shame·less·ness** *n*

sham·mer \'sham-ər\ *n* : one that shams

sham·my \'sham-ē\ *var of* CHAMOIS

1sham·poo \sham-'pü\ *vt* [Hindi *cāpo*, imper. of *cāpnā* to press, shampoo] **1** *archaic* : MASSAGE **2 a** : to wash (as the hair) with soap and water or with a special preparation **b** : to wash the hair of **c** : to wash or clean (as a rug or upholstery) with soap or a dry-cleaning preparation — **sham·poo·er** *n*

2shampoo *n, pl* **shampoos** **1** : an act or instance of shampooing **2** : a preparation used in shampooing

sham·rock \'sham-,räk\ *n* [IrGael *seamrōg*] : any of several leguminous plants (as a wood sorrel or some clovers) having leaves with three leaflets and used as a floral emblem by the Irish

sha·mus \'shäm-əs, 'shā-məs\ *n* **1** *slang* : POLICEMAN **2** *slang* : a private detective

shan·dy·gaff \'shan-dē-,gaf\ *n* : a drink consisting of beer and ginger beer or ginger ale — called also *shandy*

shang·hai \shaŋ-'hī\ *vt* **shang·haied; shang·hai·ing** [*Shanghai*, China] **1** : to make helpless (as by drugs or alcohol) and put on a ship as a sailor **2** : to put by deceit or force into a place of detention — **shang·hai·er** \-'hī-(ə)r\ *n*

Shan·gri-la \,shaŋ-gri-'lä\ *n* [*Shangri-La*, imaginary community depicted in the novel *Lost Horizon* by James Hilton] **1** : a remote beautiful imaginary place where life approaches perfection : UTOPIA **2** : a remote usu. idyllic hideaway

shank \'shaŋk\ *n* [OE *scanca*] **1 a** : the part of the leg between the knee and the ankle in man or the corresponding part in various other vertebrates **b** : a cut of meat from usu. the upper part of a leg **2** : a straight narrow usu. essential part of an object: as **a** : the straight shaft of a nail, pin, or fishhook **b** : the stem of a tobacco pipe or the part between the stem and the bowl **c** : the narrow part of the sole of a shoe beneath the instep **3** : a part of a tool that connects the acting part with a part (as a handle) by which it is held or moved ⟨the *shank* of a drill⟩ ⟨the *shank* of a key⟩ **4 a** : the latter part of a period of time ⟨*shank* of the afternoon⟩ **b** : the early or main part of a period of time ⟨*shank* of the evening⟩

shan't \(')shant, (')shȧnt\ : shall not

shantey *or* **shanty** *var of* CHANTEY

shan·tung \(')shan-'təŋ\ *n* [*Shantung*, China] : a fabric in plain weave having a slightly irregular surface

shan·ty \'shant-ē\ *n, pl* **shanties** [CanF *chantier*, fr. F, frame for supporting barrels, fr. L *cantherius* trellis] : a small roughly built shelter or dwelling : HUT

shan·ty·man \-mən, -,man\ *n* : one (as a logger) who lives in a shanty

shan·ty·town \-,tau̇n\ *n* : a town or section of a town consisting mostly of shanties

shap·a·ble *or* **shape·a·ble** \'shā-pə-bəl\ *adj* **1** : capable of being shaped **2** : SHAPELY

1shape \'shāp\ *vb* [OE *scieppan*] **1** : FORM, CREATE; *esp* : to give a particular form or shape to **2** : to fashion (as a garment) by a pattern **3** : DEVISE, PLAN **4** : to embody in definite form ⟨*shaping* a folktale into an epic⟩ **5** : to make fit for : ADAPT, ADJUST ⟨learned to *shape* his aims to his abilities⟩ **6** : to determine or direct the course of (as a person's life) **7** : to take on or approach a definite form : DEVELOP — often used with *up* — **shap·er** *n*

²shape *n* **1 a :** the visible characteristic of a particular thing **b :** spatial form **c :** a standard or universally recognized spatial form **2 :** bodily contour esp. of the trunk : FIGURE **3 a :** PHANTOM, APPARITION **b :** assumed appearance : GUISE **4 :** form of embodiment **5 :** definite form and arrangement ⟨a plan now taking *shape*⟩ **6 :** something having a particular form **7 :** the condition in which someone or something exists at a particular time ⟨in excellent *shape* for his age⟩ **syn** see FORM — **shaped** \ˌshāpt\ *adj*

shape·less \ˈshāp-ləs\ *adj* **1 :** having no definite shape **2 a :** deprived of usual or normal shape : MISSHAPEN **b :** not shapely — **shape·less·ly** *adv* — **shape·less·ness** *n*

shape·ly \ˈshāp-lē\ *adj* **shape·li·er; -est :** having a regular or pleasing shape — **shape·li·ness** *n*

shap·en \ˈshā-pən\ *adj* **:** fashioned in or provided with a definite shape — usu. used in combination ⟨an ill≈ *shapen* body⟩

shard \ˈshärd\ *n* [OE *sceard*; akin to E *shear*] **1 :** a piece or fragment of something brittle (as pottery) **2 :** a small piece : FRAGMENT

¹share \ˈshe(ə)r, ˈsha(ə)r\ *n* [OE *scearu* cutting, tonsure; akin to E *shear*] **1 a :** a portion belonging to, due to, or contributed by an individual **b :** a fair portion **2 :** the part allotted or belonging to one of a number owning something together **3 :** any of the equal portions or interests into which the property of a corporation is divided

²share *vb* **1 :** to divide and distribute in shares : APPORTION — usu. used with *out* **2 :** to partake of, use, experience, or enjoy with others **3 a :** to give or be given a share in **b :** to take a share : PARTAKE — used with *in* — **shar·er** *n*

³share *n* [OE *scear*] **:** PLOWSHARE

share·crop \ˈshe(ə)r-ˌkräp, ˈsha(ə)r-\ *vb* **:** to farm or produce as a sharecropper

share·crop·per \-ˌkräp-ər\ *n* **:** a farmer who works land for a landlord in return for a share of the value of the crop — compare TENANT FARMER

share·hold·er \-ˌhōl-dər\ *n* **:** one that owns a share in a joint fund or property; *esp* : STOCKHOLDER

¹shark \ˈshärk\ *n* **:** any of numerous mostly rather large and typically gray marine elasmobranch fishes that are mostly active, voracious, and rapacious predators and are of economic importance esp. for their large livers which are a source of oil and for their hides from which leather is made

²shark *n* **1 :** a greedy crafty person who takes advantage of the needs of others ⟨a loan *shark*⟩ **2 :** a person who excels esp. in a particular line ⟨a *shark* at arithmetic⟩

³shark *vi* **:** to play the shark; *also* : to live by shifts and stratagems

shark·skin \-ˌskin\ *n* **1 :** the hide of a shark or leather made from it **2 a :** a smooth durable woolen or worsted suiting in twill or basket weave with small woven designs **b :** a smooth crisp fabric with a dull finish made usu. of rayon in basket weave

shark sucker *n* **:** REMORA

¹sharp \ˈshärp\ *adj* [OE *scearp*; akin to E *shear*] **1 :** adapted to cutting or piercing: as **a :** having a thin keen edge or fine point **b :** briskly cold : NIPPING **2 a :** keen in intellect : QUICK-WITTED **b :** keen in perception : ACUTE, VIGILANT **c :** keen in attention to one's own interest sometimes to the point of being unethical **3 :** keen in spirit or action: as **a :** EAGER, BRISK **b :** capable of acting or reacting strongly; *esp* : CAUSTIC **4 :** SEVERE, HARSH: as **a :** inclined to or marked by irritability or anger **b :** causing intense mental or physical distress **c :** cutting in language or import ⟨*sharp* retort⟩ **5 a :** having a strong odor or flavor ⟨*sharp* cheese⟩ **b :** ACRID **c :** having a strong piercing sound **6 a :** terminating in a point or edge ⟨*sharp* features⟩ **b :** involving an abrupt change in direction ⟨a *sharp* turn⟩ **c :** clear in outline or detail : DISTINCT **d :** set forth with clarity and distinctness ⟨*sharp* contrast⟩ **7 a :** higher by a half step ⟨tone of G *sharp*⟩ **b :** higher than the true pitch **c :** having a sharp in the signature ⟨key of F *sharp*⟩ **8 :** STYLISH, DRESSY — **sharp·ly** *adv* — **sharp·ness** *n*

syn KEEN, ACUTE: SHARP applies to things having an edge or point making cutting or piercing easy; applied to persons it implies quick perception, clever resourcefulness, or questionable trickiness ⟨*sharp* trader⟩ KEEN applies to

a very sharp edge and may suggest quickness and zest ⟨*keen* student of history⟩ ACUTE implies a power to penetrate and may suggest subtlety and sharpness of discrimination ⟨*acute* mathematical reasoning⟩

²sharp *vb* **1 :** to raise in pitch esp. by a half step **2 :** to sing or play above the true pitch

³sharp *adv* **1 :** in a sharp manner : SHARPLY **2 :** PRECISELY, EXACTLY ⟨4 o'clock *sharp*⟩

⁴sharp *n* **1 :** a musical note or tone one half step higher than a specified note or tone; *also* : a character ♯ on a line or space of the staff indicating such a note or tone **2 :** a real or self-styled expert; *also* : SHARPER

sharp·en \ˈshär-pən\ *vb* **sharp·ened; sharp·en·ing** \ˈshärp-(ə-)niŋ\ **:** to make or become sharp or sharper — **sharp·en·er** \-(ə-)nər\ *n*

sharp·er \ˈshär-pər\ *n* **:** CHEAT, SWINDLER

sharp-eyed \ˈshärp-ˈīd\ *adj* **:** having keen sight; *also* **:** keen in observing or penetrating

sharp-fanged \-ˈfaŋd\ *adj* **:** having sharp teeth; *also* **:** SARCASTIC

sharp-freeze \-ˈfrēz\ *vt* **:** QUICK-FREEZE

sharp·ie *or* **sharpy** \ˈshär-pē\ *n, pl* **sharp·ies 1 :** a long narrow shallow-draft boat with flat or slightly V-shaped bottom and one or two masts that bear a triangular sail **2 a :** SHARPER **b :** a person who is exceptionally keen or alert

sharp-nosed \ˈshärp-ˈnōzd\ *adj* **:** keen of scent

sharp practice *n* **:** dealing in which advantage is taken or sought unscrupulously

sharp-set \ˈshärp-ˈset\ *adj* **1 :** set at a sharp angle or so as to present a sharp edge **2 :** eager in appetite or desire — **sharp-set·ness** *n*

sharp·shoot·er \ˈshärp-ˌshüt-ər\ *n* **:** one skilled in shooting : a good marksman — **sharp·shoot·ing** \-ˌshüt-iŋ\ *n*

sharp-sight·ed \-ˈsīt-əd\ *adj* **1 :** having acute sight **2 :** mentally keen or alert

sharp-tongued \-ˈtəŋd\ *adj* **:** having a sharp tongue : bitter of speech

sharp-wit·ted \-ˈwit-əd\ *adj* **:** having or showing a quick keen mind

¹shat·ter \ˈshat-ər\ *vb* [ME *schateren*] **1 :** to dash, burst, or part violently into fragments **:** break at once into pieces **2 :** to damage badly : RUIN, WRECK ⟨his health had been *shattered*⟩ ⟨a ship *shattered* by a storm⟩ ⟨*shattered* hopes⟩ **3 :** to drop or scatter parts (as leaves, petals, or fruit)

²shatter *n* **:** FRAGMENT, SHRED ⟨an armful of dishes lay in *shatters*⟩

shat·ter·proof \ˌshat-ər-ˈprüf\ *adj* **:** made so as not to shatter ⟨*shatterproof* glass⟩

¹shave \ˈshāv\ *vb* **shaved; shaved** *or* **shav·en** \ˈshā-vən\; **shav·ing** [OE *scafan*] **1 :** to cut or pare off by means of an edged instrument (as a razor); *esp* : to remove hair close to the skin with a razor **2 :** to make bare or smooth by cutting the hair from ⟨had his head *shaved*⟩ **3 :** to cut off closely ⟨a lawn *shaven* close⟩ **4 :** to cut off thin slices from (as a board with a plane) **5 :** to pass close to : skim along or near the surface of with or without touching

²shave *n* **1 :** any of various tools for shaving or cutting thin slices **2 :** a thin slice : SHAVING **3 :** an act or process of shaving esp. the beard **4 :** an act of passing very near to so as almost to graze

shave·ling \ˈshāv-liŋ\ *n* **1 :** a tonsured clergyman : PRIEST — usu. used disparagingly **2 :** STRIPLING

shav·er \ˈshā-vər\ *n* **1 :** one that shaves; *esp* : an electric≈ powered razor **2 :** BOY, YOUNGSTER

shave-tail \ˈshāv-ˌtāl\ *n* **1 :** an untrained mule **2 :** a newly appointed second lieutenant — usu. used disparagingly

Sha·vi·an \ˈshā-vē-ən\ *n* **:** an admirer or devotee of G. B. Shaw, his writings, or his social and political theories — **Shavian** *adj*

shav·ing \ˈshā-viŋ\ *n* **1 :** the act of one that shaves **2 :** something shaved off ⟨wood *shavings*⟩

shaw \ˈshȯ\ *n* [OE *sceaga*] *dial* **:** COPPICE, THICKET

¹shawl \ˈshȯl\ *n* [Per *shāl*] **:** a square or oblong piece of woven or knitted fabric used esp. by women as a loose covering for the head or shoulders

²shawl *vt* **:** to wrap in or as if in a shawl

shawm \ˈshȯm\ *n* [ME *schalme*, fr. MF *chalemie*, modif.

---

j joke; ŋ sing; ō flow; ȯ flaw; ȯi coin; th thin; t̲h̲ this; ü loot; u̇ foot; y yet; yü few; yu̇ furious; zh vision

of LL *calamellus*, dim. of L *calamus* reed, fr. Gk *kalamos*] : a medieval double-reed woodwind instrument

Shaw·nee \shȯ-ˈnē, shä-\ *n* : a member of an Algonquian people ranging through most of the states east of the Mississippi and south of the Great Lakes

shay \ˈshā\ *n* [back-formation fr. *chaise*, taken as pl.] *chiefly dial* : CHAISE 1

¹she \(ˈ)shē\ *pron* [ME] : that female one ⟨*she* is my wife⟩ — compare HE, HER, HERS, IT, THEY

²she \ˈshē\ *n* : a female person or animal ⟨*she*-cat⟩ ⟨*she*-cousin⟩

sheaf \ˈshēf\ *n, pl* **sheaves** \ˈshēvz\ *also* **sheafs** \ˈshēfs\ [OE *scēaf*] **1** : a bundle of stalks and ears of grain **2** : something resembling or suggesting a sheaf of grain ⟨*sheaf* of arrows⟩ ⟨*sheaf* of papers⟩ — **sheaf·like** \ˈshēf-ˌlīk\ *adj*

¹shear \ˈshi(ə)r\ *vb* **sheared**; **sheared** *or* **shorn** \ˈshȯrn, ˈshȯrn\; **shear·ing** [OE *scieran*] **1** : to cut the hair or wool from : CLIP, SHAVE ⟨*shearing* sheep⟩ **2** : to deprive of by or as if by cutting off ⟨*shorn* of his power⟩ **3** : to cut or cut through with or as if with shears ⟨*shear* a metal sheet in two⟩ **4** : to become divided under the action of a shear ⟨bolt may *shear* off⟩ — **shear·er** *n*

²shear *n* **1 a** : a cutting implement similar or identical to a pair of scissors but typically larger — usu. used in pl.; *also* : one blade of a pair of shears **b** : any of various cutting machines operating by the action of opposed cutting edges of metal — usu. used in pl. **2** : an action or force that causes or tends to cause two parts of a body to slide on each other in a direction parallel to their plane of contact

sheared \ˈshi(ə)rd\ *adj* : formed or finished by shearing; *esp* : cut to uniform length ⟨*sheared* beaver coat⟩

shear·wa·ter \ˈshi(ə)r-ˌwȯt-ər, -ˌwät-\ *n* : any of numerous oceanic birds related to the petrels and albatrosses that in flight usu. skim close to the waves

sheath \ˈshēth\ *n, pl* **sheaths** \ˈshēthz, ˈshēths\ [OE *scēath*] **1** : a case for a blade (as of a knife) **2** : a covering esp. of an anatomical structure suggesting a sheath in form or use

sheathe \ˈshēth\ *vt* **1** : to put into or as if into a sheath **2** : to encase or cover with something (as thin boards or sheets of metal) that protects — **sheath·er** \ˈshē-thər, -thər\ *n*

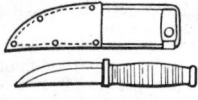
sheath and knife

sheath·ing \ˈshē-thiŋ, -thiŋ\ *n* : material used to sheathe something; *esp* : the first covering of boards or of waterproof material on the outside wall of a frame house or on a timber roof

sheath knife *n* : a knife having a fixed blade and designed to be carried in a sheath

¹sheave \ˈshiv, ˈshēv\ *n* [ME *sheve*] : a grooved wheel : PULLEY

²sheave \ˈshēv\ *vt* : to gather and bind into a sheaf

³sheave \ˈshēv\ *vi* : to reverse the action of the oars in rowing a boat

she·bang \shi-ˈbaŋ\ *n* : CONTRIVANCE, AFFAIR, CONCERN ⟨blew up the whole *shebang*⟩

¹shed \ˈshed\ *vb* **shed**; **shed·ding** [OE *scēadan* to divide, separate] **1** : to pour forth or down esp. in drops ⟨*shed* tears⟩ **2** : to cause to flow from a cut or wound ⟨*shed* blood⟩ **3** : to spread abroad : DIFFUSE ⟨the sun *sheds* light and heat⟩ **4** : to throw off ⟨the duck's plumage *sheds* water⟩ **5 a** : to cast aside or let fall ⟨some natural covering⟩ ⟨a snake *sheds* its skin⟩ ⟨the cat is *shedding*⟩ **b** : to rid oneself of : DISCARD ⟨*shed* excess weight⟩ ⟨*shed* inhibitions⟩ — **shed·der** *n*

²shed *n* **1** : a slight structure built for shelter or storage ⟨tool *shed*⟩ **2** : a single-storied building with one or more sides unenclosed ⟨customs *shed*⟩

³shed *vt* **shed·ded**; **shed·ding** : to put or house in a shed

she'd \(ˌ)shēd\ : she had : she would

sheen \ˈshēn\ *n* [OE *scīene*] **1** : subdued shininess of surface : LUSTER ⟨the *sheen* of satin⟩ **2** : GLOSS, GLITTER ⟨the *sheen* of worldly success⟩

sheeny \ˈshē-nē\ *adj* : lustrous with sheen : SHINING, RADIANT

sheep \ˈshēp\ *n, pl* **sheep** [OE *scēap*] **1** : any of a genus of ruminant mammals related to the goats but stockier and lacking a beard in the male; *esp* : one long domesticated for its flesh, wool, and other products **2** : one that is like a sheep (as in being timid, defenseless, or easily led) **3** : SHEEPSKIN — **sheep** *adj*

sheep·cote \-ˌkōt, -ˌkät\ *n, chiefly Brit* : SHEEPFOLD

sheep–dip \-ˌdip\ *n* : a liquid preparation of toxic chemicals into which sheep are plunged esp. to destroy parasitic arthropods

sheep dog *n* : a dog used or trained to tend, drive, or guard sheep

sheep·fold \ˈshēp-ˌfōld\ *n* : a pen or shelter for sheep

sheep·herd·er \ˈshēp-ˌhərd-ər\ *n* : a worker in charge of sheep esp. on open range — **sheep·herd·ing** \-ˌhərd-iŋ\ *n*

sheep·ish \ˈshē-pish\ *adj* **1** : resembling a sheep in meekness, stupidity, or timidity **2** : embarrassed by consciousness of a fault — **sheep·ish·ly** *adv* — **sheep·ish·ness** *n*

sheep's eye *n* : a shy, longing, and usu. amorous glance — usu. used in pl.

sheeps·head \ˈshēps-ˌhed\ *n* : any of several fishes; *esp* : a food fish of the Atlantic and Gulf coasts of the U.S. with broad incisor teeth

sheep·shear·er \ˈshēp-ˌshir-ər\ *n* : one that shears sheep

sheep·shear·ing \-ˌshi(ə)r-iŋ\ *n* **1** : the act of shearing sheep **2** : the time or season for shearing sheep

sheep·skin \ˈshēp-ˌskin\ *n* **1** : the skin of a sheep or leather prepared from it; *also* : PARCHMENT **2** : DIPLOMA

sheep·walk \-ˌwȯk\ *n, chiefly Brit* : a pasture for sheep

¹sheer \ˈshi(ə)r\ *adj* [ME *schere* free from guilt] **1** : very thin or transparent ⟨*sheer* stockings⟩ **2 a** : UNQUALIFIED, UTTER ⟨*sheer* nonsense⟩ **b** : taken or acting apart from everything else ⟨by *sheer* force⟩ **3** : very steep : being almost straight up and down ⟨a *sheer* drop to the sea⟩ **syn** see STEEP — **sheer·ly** *adv* — **sheer·ness** *n*

²sheer *adv* **1** : ALTOGETHER, COMPLETELY **2** : PERPENDICULARLY

³sheer *vi* : to deviate from a course : SWERVE

⁴sheer *n* **1** : a turn, deviation, or change in the course of a ship **2** : the position of a ship riding to a single anchor and heading toward it

⁵sheer *n* : the fore-and-aft curvature from bow to stern of a ship's deck as shown in side elevation

¹sheet \ˈshēt\ *n* [OE *scŷte, scēte*] **1** : a broad piece of cloth; *esp* : an oblong of usu. linen or cotton cloth used as an article of bedding next to the person **2 a** : a usu. rectangular piece of paper (as for writing or printing) **b** *pl* : the unbound pages of a book **c** : a newspaper, periodical, or occasional publication **d** : the unseparated postage stamps printed by one impression of a plate on a single piece of paper **3** : a broad expanse or surface of something ⟨*sheet* of ice⟩ **4** : a portion of something that is thin in comparison to its length and breadth ⟨a *sheet* of iron⟩

²sheet *vt* **1** : to cover with a sheet : SHROUD **2** : to furnish with sheets

³sheet *n* [OE *scēata* lower corner of a sail] **1** : a rope or chain that regulates the angle at which a sail is set in relation to the wind **2** *pl* : the spaces at either end of an open boat not occupied by thwarts

sheet anchor *n* **1** : a large strong anchor carried in the waist of a ship **2** : something that constitutes a main support or dependence in danger

sheet·ing \ˈshēt-iŋ\ *n* : material in the form of sheets or suitable for forming into sheets

sheet lightning *n* : lightning in diffused or sheet form

sheet metal *n* : metal in the form of a sheet

sheet music *n* : music printed on large unbound sheets of paper

sheikh *or* **sheik** \ˈshēk, *for 1 also* ˈshāk & ˈshīk\ *n* [Ar *shaykh*] **1** : an Arab chief **2** *usu* **sheik** : a man supposed to be irresistibly attractive to romantic young women — **sheik·dom** \-dəm\ *n*

shek·el \ˈshek-əl\ *n* [Heb *sheqel*] **1** : an ancient unit of weight or value; *esp* : a Hebrew unit equal to about 252 grains troy **2** : a coin weighing one shekel

shel·drake \ˈshel-ˌdrāk\ *n* **1** : any of several Old World ducks; *esp* : a common mostly black-and-white European duck slightly larger than the mallard **2** : MERGANSER

shelf \ˈshelf\ *n, pl* **shelves** \ˈshelvz\ [ME] **1 a** : a thin flat usu. long and narrow piece of material (as of wood or glass) fastened horizontally (as on a wall) at a distance from the floor to hold objects **b** : the contents of a shelf **2** : something resembling a shelf: as **a** : a sandbank or ledge of rocks usu. partially submerged **b** : a flat projecting layer of rock — **shelf·like** \'shelf-,līk\ *adj* — **on the shelf** : in a state of inactivity or uselessness

¹shell \'shel\ *n [OE sciell]* **1 a** : a hard rigid usu. largely calcareous covering of an animal (as a turtle, oyster, or beetle) **b** : the outer covering of an egg and esp. of a bird's egg **c** : the outer covering of a nut, fruit, or seed esp. when hard or toughly fibrous **2** : shell material or shells esp. of mollusks; *also* : a shell-bearing mollusk **3** : something that resembles a shell: as **a** : a framework or exterior structure **b** : a casing without substance ⟨the *shell* of his former self⟩ **c** : an edible case for holding a filling ⟨a pastry *shell*⟩ **d** : a reinforced concrete arched or domed roof used primarily over large unpartitioned areas **4** : an impersonal manner that conceals the presence or absence of feeling **5** : a narrow light racing boat propelled by one or more oarsmen **6** : any of the spaces occupied by the orbits of a group of electrons of approximately equal energy surrounding the nucleus of an atom **7 a** : a hollow projectile for cannon containing an explosive bursting charge **b** : a metal or paper case which holds the charge of powder and shot or bullet used with breech-loading small arms — **shell** *adj* — **shelled** \'sheld\ *adj* — **shell·work** \'shel-,wərk\ *n* — **shelly** \'shel-ē\ *adj*

shell for shotgun: *1* powder, *2* shot, *3*, *3* wads

²shell *vb* **1 a** : to remove from a natural enclosing cover (as a shell or husk) : SHUCK ⟨*shell* peas⟩ **b** : to remove the grains from (as an ear of Indian corn) **2** : to throw or shoot shells at, upon, or into : BOMBARD **3** : fall out of the pod or husk

she'll \(,)shēl, shil\ : she shall : she will

¹shel·lac \shə-'lak\ *n [shell + lac]* **1** : purified lac **2** : a preparation of lac dissolved in alcohol and used in filling wood or as a varnish

²shellac *vt* **shel·lacked; shel·lack·ing 1** : to coat or treat with shellac **2** : to defeat decisively

shel·lack·ing \shə-'lak-iŋ\ *n* : a sound drubbing ⟨took a *shellacking* in last year's election⟩

shell·back \'shel-,bak\ *n* : an old or veteran sailor : old salt

shell·bark \'shel-,bärk\ *n* : SHAGBARK

shell bean *n* : a bean grown primarily for its edible seeds; *also* : these seeds — compare SNAP BEAN

shell·fire \'shel-,fī(ə)r\ *n* : firing or shooting of shells

shell·fish \-,fish\ *n* : an aquatic invertebrate animal with a shell; *esp* : an edible mollusk or crustacean

shell out *vb* : PAY

shell pink *n* : a variable color averaging a light yellowish pink

shell·proof \'shel-'prüf\ *adj* : capable of resisting shells or bombs

shell shock *n* : a psychoneurotic condition appearing in soldiers exposed to modern warfare — **shell–shock** \'shel-,shäk\ *vt*

¹shel·ter \'shel-tər\ *n* **1** : something that covers or affords protection : a means or place of protection ⟨fallout *shelter*⟩ **2** : the state of being covered and protected ⟨take *shelter* from a storm⟩ — **shel·ter·less** \-ləs\ *adj*

²shelter *vb* **shel·tered; shel·ter·ing** \-t(ə-)riŋ\ **1** : to constitute or provide a shelter for : PROTECT **2** : to place under shelter or protection **3** : to take shelter — **shel·ter·er** \-tər-ər\ *n*

shel·ter·belt \-tər-,belt\ *n* : a barrier of trees and shrubs that protects (as soil and crops) from wind and storm and lessens erosion

shelter half *n* : one of the halves of a small two-man tent that consists of two interchangeable pieces of waterproof cotton duck fixed for buttoning or tying

shelter tent *n* : a small tent usu. consisting of two interchangeable pieces of waterproof cotton duck fixed for buttoning or tying

shel·ty *or* **shel·tie** \'shel-tē\ *n, pl* **shelties 1** : SHETLAND PONY **2** : SHETLAND SHEEPDOG

shelve \'shelv\ *vb* **1** : to furnish with shelves ⟨*shelve* a closet⟩ **2** : to place on a shelf ⟨*shelve* books⟩ **3 a** : to

put on the shelf : DISMISS **b** : to put aside temporarily or permanently ⟨*shelve* a bill⟩ **4** : to slope in a formation like a shelf : INCLINE — **shelv·er** *n*

shelv·ing \'shel-viŋ\ *n* **1** : material for shelves **2** : SHELVES

She·ma \shə-'mä\ *n [Heb shĕma' hear, first word of Deuteronomy 6:4]* : the central creed of Judaism comprising Deuteronomy 6:4–9 and 11:13–21 and Numbers 15:37–41

she·nan·i·gan \shə-'nan-i-gən\ *n* **1** : an underhand trick **2 a** : tricky or questionable conduct **b** : high-spirited or mischievous activity — usu. used in pl.

She·ol \shē-'ōl, 'shē-,\ *n* **1** : an underworld where according to ancient Hebrew belief the dead have a shadowy existence **2** : HELL

¹shep·herd \'shep-ərd\ *n* **1** : a man who tends and guards sheep **2** : PASTOR

²shepherd *vt* **1** : to tend as a shepherd **2** : to guide or guard in the manner of a shepherd ⟨*shepherd* tourists through a museum⟩

shepherd dog *n* : SHEEP DOG

shep·herd·ess \'shep-ərd-əs\ *n* : a woman or girl who tends sheep

shepherd's check *n* : a pattern of small even black and white checks; *also* : a fabric woven in this pattern — called also *shepherd's plaid*

shepherd's pie *n* : a meat pie with a mashed potato crust

Sher·a·ton \'sher-ət-²n\ *adj [after Thomas Sheraton d1806 English furniture maker]* : of or relating to an early 19th century English furniture style characterized by delicate construction, graceful proportions, and the use of straight lines

sher·bet \'shər-bət\ *n [Turk & Per; Turk şerbet, fr. Per sharbat, fr. Ar sharbah drink]* **1** : a cooling drink of sweetened and diluted fruit juice **2** : a water ice with milk, egg white, or gelatin added

sherd \'shərd\ *var of* SHARD

sher·iff \'sher-əf\ *n [OE scīrgerēfa, fr. scīr shire + gerēfa reeve]* : an important official of a county charged primarily with judicial duties (as executing the processes and orders of courts)

sher·lock \'shər-,läk\ *n, often cap [after Sherlock Holmes, detective in stories by Sir Arthur Conan Doyle]* : DETECTIVE

Sher·pa \'she(ə)r-pə, 'shər-\ *n* : a member of a Tibetan people living on the high southern slopes of the Himalayas and skilled in mountain climbing

sher·ry \'sher-ē\ *n, pl* **sherries** *[Jerez, Spain]* : a fortified wine with a distinctive nutty flavor

she's \(,)shēz\ : she is : she has

Shet·land \'shet-lənd\ *n* **1 a** : SHETLAND PONY **b** : SHETLAND SHEEPDOG **2** *often not cap* **a** : a lightweight loosely twisted yarn of Shetland wool used for knitting and weaving **b** : a fabric of Shetland wool

Shetland pony *n* : any of a breed of small stocky shaggy hardy ponies originating in the Shetland islands

Shetland sheepdog *n* : any of a breed of dogs resembling miniature collies with a profuse long coat developed in the Shetland islands

Shetland wool *n* : fine wool plucked by hand from sheep raised in the Shetland islands; *also* : yarn spun from this wool

shew \'shō\ *archaic var of* SHOW

shib·bo·leth \'shib-ə-ləth, -,leth\ *n [Heb shibbōleth stream; fr. the use of this word as a test to distinguish Gileadites from Ephraimites, who pronounced it sibbōleth (Judges 12:5, 6)]* **1 a** : CATCHWORD, SLOGAN **b** : a use of language that is distinctive of a particular group **2** : a custom or usage that is a criterion for distinguishing members of one group

¹shield \'shēld\ *n [OE scield]* **1** : a broad piece of defensive armor carried on the arm **2** : one that protects or defends : DEFENSE **3** : ESCUTCHEON **4 a** : a device or part that serves as a protective cover or barrier **b** : a protective structure (as a carapace) of some animals **5** : something shaped like or resembling a shield: as **a** : a policeman's badge **b** : a decorative or identifying emblem

²shield *vt* **1** : to cover with or as if with a shield **2** : to cut off from observation : HIDE **syn** see DEFEND

¹shift \'shift\ *vb [OE sciftan to divide, arrange]* **1** : to exchange for or replace by another : CHANGE **2 a** : to

---

j joke;   **ŋ** sing;   **ō** flow;   **ò** flaw;   **òi** coin;   **th** thin;   **th̲** this;   **ü** loot;   **ù** foot;   **y** yet;   **yü** few;   **yù** furious;   **zh** vision

change the place, position, or direction of : MOVE **b** : to make a change in place, position, or direction **c** : to change the gear rotating the transmission shaft of an automobile **3** : to change phonetically **4** : to get along : MANAGE ⟨left the others to *shift* for themselves⟩ — **shift·er** *n*

²shift *n* **1 a** : a means or device for effecting an end **b** : a deceitful scheme : DODGE **c** : an expedient tried in difficult circumstances : EXTREMITY **2** : a woman's slip or chemise **3** : a change in direction ⟨a *shift* in the wind⟩ **4** : a change in place or position **5** : a group who work together in alternation with other groups; *also* : the period during which one such group works **6** : a removal from one person or thing to another : TRANSFER ⟨a *shift* of responsibility⟩ **7** : GEARSHIFT

shift·less \'shift-ləs\ *adj* **1** : lacking in resourcefulness : INEFFICIENT **2** : lacking in ambition or incentive : LAZY — **shift·less·ly** *adv* — **shift·less·ness** *n*

shifty \'shif-tē\ *adj* **shift·i·er; -est 1 a** : given to deception, evasion, or fraud : TRICKY **b** : capable of evasive movement : ELUSIVE ⟨a *shifty* boxer⟩ **2** : indicative of a tricky nature ⟨*shifty* eyes⟩ — **shift·i·ly** \-tə-lē\ *adv* — **shift·i·ness** \-tē-nəs\ *n*

shill \'shil\ *n* : one who acts as a decoy (as for a pitchman or gambler) — **shill** *vi*

shil·le·lagh *also* **shil·la·lah** \shə-'lā-lē\ *n* [*Shillelagh*, Ireland] : CUDGEL, CLUB

shil·ling \'shil-iŋ\ *n* [OE *scilling*] **1 a** : a British monetary unit equal to 12 pence or ¹⁄₂₀ pound **b** : a coin representing this unit **2** : a unit of value equal to ¹⁄₂₀ pound and a corresponding coin in any of several countries in or formerly in the British Commonwealth **3** : any of several early American coins **4 a** : the basic monetary unit of British East Africa **b** : a coin representing this unit

¹shil·ly-shal·ly \'shil-ē-,shal-ē\ *adj* : IRRESOLUTE, VACILLATING

²shilly-shally *n* : INDECISION, IRRESOLUTION

³shilly-shally *vi* **shil·ly-shal·lied; shil·ly-shal·ly·ing 1** : to show hesitation or lack of decisiveness : VACILLATE **2** : to waste time : DAWDLE

¹shim \'shim\ *n* : a thin often tapered piece of wood, metal, or stone used (as in leveling a stone in a building) to fill in

²shim *vt* **shimmed; shim·ming** : to fill out or level up by the use of a shim

¹shim·mer \'shim-ər\ *vi* **shim·mered; shim·mer·ing** \'shim-(ə-)riŋ\ [OE *scimerian*] **1** : to shine with a wavering light : GLIMMER ⟨leaves *shimmering* in the sunshine⟩ **2** : to appear in a constantly changing wavy form ⟨the *shimmering* heat from the pavement⟩

²shimmer *n* **1** : a wavering light : subdued sparkle or sheen : GLIMMER **2** : a wavering image or effect esp. when produced by heat waves — **shim·mery** \'shim-(ə-)rē\ *adj*

¹shim·my \'shim-ē\ *n, pl* **shimmies** [short for *shimmy-shake*, fr. *shimmy*, alter. of *chemise*] **1** : a jazz dance characterized by a shaking of the body from the shoulders down **2** : an abnormal vibration esp. in the front wheels of an automobile

²shimmy *vi* **shim·mied; shim·my·ing 1** : to shake or quiver in or as if in dancing a shimmy **2** : to vibrate abnormally

¹shin \'shin\ *n* [OE *scinu*] : the front part of the leg below the knee

²shin *vb* **shinned; shin·ning 1** : to climb by moving oneself along alternately with the arms or hands and legs ⟨*shin* up a tree⟩ **2** : to move forward rapidly on foot

shin·bone \'shin-'bōn, -,bōn\ *n* : TIBIA 1a

shin·dig \'shin-,dig\ *n* : a festive occasion: as **a** : a social gathering with dancing **b** : a usu. large or lavish party

shin·dy \'shin-dē\ *n, pl* **shindys** *or* **shindies 1** : SHINDIG **2** : FRACAS, UPROAR

¹shine \'shīn\ *vb* **shone** \'shōn\ *or* **shined; shin·ing** [OE *scinan*] **1** : to send out rays of light **2** : to be bright by reflection of light : GLEAM **3** : to show brilliance : be eminent or distinguished ⟨*shine* in conversation⟩ **4** : to have a bright glowing appearance **5** : to be conspicuously evident or clear ⟨human sympathy *shone* through all her actions⟩ **6** : to throw or flash the light of **7** : to make bright by polishing ⟨*shined* his shoes every day⟩

²shine *n* **1** : brightness caused by the emission of light

2 : brightness caused by the reflection of light : LUSTER **3** : BRILLIANCE, SPLENDOR **4** : fair weather : SUNSHINE ⟨will go, rain or *shine*⟩ **5** : TRICK, CAPER — usu. used in pl. **6** : LIKING, FANCY ⟨took a *shine* to him⟩ **7** : a polish given to shoes

shin·er \'shī-nər\ *n* **1** : one that shines **2** : a silvery fish : *esp* : any of numerous small freshwater American fishes related to the carp **3** : a black eye

¹shin·gle \'shiŋ-gəl\ *n* [ME *schingel*] **1** : a small thin piece of building material (as of wood or a composition of asbestos) for laying in overlapping rows as a covering for the roof or sides of a building **2** : a small signboard **3** : a woman's haircut with the hair trimmed short from the back of the head to the nape

²shingle *vt* **shin·gled; shin·gling** \-g(ə-)liŋ\ **1** : to cover with or as if with shingles **2** : to bob and shape (the hair) in a shingle

³shingle *n* **1** : coarse pebbly gravel on the seashore **2** : a place (as a beach) strewn with shingle

shin·gler \'shiŋ-g(ə-)lər\ *n* : one that shingles

shin·gles \'shiŋ-gəlz\ *n* [ML *cingulus*, fr. L *cingulum* girdle, fr. *cingere* to gird] : a virus disease marked by inflammation of sensory ganglia with neuralgic pain and skin eruption usu. along the course of a single nerve

shin·gly \'shiŋ-g(ə-)lē\ *adj* : composed of or abounding in shingle ⟨a *shingly* beach⟩

shin·ing *adj* **1** : giving forth or reflecting light : GLOWING, RADIANT **2** : BRIGHT, RESPLENDENT ⟨a *shining* occasion⟩ **3** : having a distinguished quality : ILLUSTRIOUS ⟨a *shining* example of integrity⟩ — **shin·ing·ly** \'shī-niŋ-lē\ *adv*

shin·nery \'shin-ə-rē\ *n* [modif. of LaF *chénière*, fr. F *chêne* oak] : a dense growth of small trees (as scrubby oaks); *also* : an area of such growth

¹shin·ny \'shin-ē\ *n* : the game of hockey as informally played with a curved stick and a ball or block of wood by schoolboys

²shinny *vi* **shin·nied; shin·ny·ing** : SHIN 1

shin·plas·ter \'shin-,plas-tər\ *n* : a piece of privately issued paper currency; *esp* : one poorly secured and depreciated in value

Shin·to \'shin-,tō\ *n* [Jap *shintō*] : a religious cult of Japan consisting chiefly in the reverence of the spirits of natural forces, emperors, and heroes — **Shin·to·ism** \-,iz-əm\ *n* — **Shin·to·ist** \-əst\ *n or adj*

shiny \'shī-nē\ *adj* **shin·i·er; -est 1** : bright in appearance : GLITTERING, POLISHED ⟨*shiny* kitchenware⟩ **2** : rubbed or worn smooth ⟨*shiny* old clothes⟩ — **shin·i·ness** *n*

¹ship \'ship\ *n* [OE *scip*] **1 a** : a large seagoing boat **b** : a sailing boat having a bowsprit and usu. three square-rigged masts **2** : BOAT; *esp* : one propelled by power or sail **3** : a ship's crew **4** : AIRSHIP, AIRPLANE

²ship *vb* **shipped; ship·ping 1 a** : to place or receive on board a ship for transportation by water **b** : to cause to be transported ⟨*ship* grain by rail⟩ **2** : to put in place for use ⟨*ship* the tiller⟩ **3** : to take into a ship or boat ⟨*ship* oars⟩ **4** : to take (as water) over the side **5** : to engage to serve on shipboard

-ship \,ship\ *n suffix* [OE *-scipe*; akin to E *shape*] **1** : state : condition : quality ⟨friend*ship*⟩ **2** : office : dignity : profession ⟨clerk*ship*⟩ ⟨lord*ship*⟩ ⟨author*ship*⟩ **3** : art : skill ⟨horseman*ship*⟩ **4** : something showing, exhibiting, or embodying a quality or state ⟨town*ship*⟩ **5** : one entitled to a (specified) rank, title, or appellation ⟨his Lord*ship*⟩

ship biscuit *n* : HARDTACK — called also *ship bread*

ship·board \'ship-,bōrd, -,bord\ *n* **1** : the side of a ship **2** : SHIP ⟨met on *shipboard*⟩

ship·build·er \'ship-,bil-dər\ *n* : one who designs or builds ships — **ship·build·ing** \-diŋ\ *n*

ship canal *n* : a canal large enough for seagoing ships to use

ship chandler *n* : a dealer in supplies and equipment for ships

ship fever *n* : TYPHUS

ship·lap \'ship-,lap\ *n* : wooden sheathing in which the boards are rabbeted so that the edges of each board lap over the edges of adjacent boards to make a flush joint

ship·man \'ship-mən\ *n* **1** : SEAMAN, SAILOR **2** : SHIP-MASTER

---

ship·mas·ter \-ˌmas-tər\ *n* : the master or commander of a ship other than a warship

ship·mate \-ˌmāt\ *n* : a fellow sailor

ship·ment \'ship-mənt\ *n* **1** : the act or process of shipping **2** : the goods shipped

ship of the line : a ship of war large enough to have a place in the line of battle

ship·own·er \'ship-ˌō-nər\ *n* : the owner of a ship

ship·pa·ble \'ship-ə-bəl\ *adj* : suitable for shipping

ship·per \'ship-ər\ *n* : one that sends goods by any form of conveyance

ship·ping \'ship-iŋ\ *n* **1** : the body of ships in one place or belonging to one port or country **2** : the act or business of one that ships

shipping clerk *n* : one who is employed in a shipping room to assemble, pack, and send out or receive goods

ship·shape \'ship-ˌshāp\ *adj* : TRIM, TIDY

ship·side \-ˌsīd\ *n* : the area adjacent to shipping that is used for storage and loading of freight and passengers : DOCK

ship's papers *n pl* : the papers with which a ship is legally required to be provided for due inspection to show the character of the ship and cargo

ship's service *n* : a ship or navy post exchange — called also *navy exchange*

ship·way \'ship-ˌwā\ *n* **1** : the ways on which a ship is built **2** : a ship canal

ship·worm \'ship-ˌwərm\ *n* : any of various long-bodied marine clams that resemble worms, burrow in submerged wood, and damage wharf piles and wooden ships

¹ship·wreck \-ˌrek\ *n* **1** : a wrecked ship or its parts : WRECKAGE **2** : the destruction or loss of a ship **3** : total loss or failure : RUIN

²shipwreck *vt* **1 a** : to cause to experience shipwreck **b** : RUIN **2** : to destroy (a ship) by grounding or foundering

ship·wright \-ˌrīt\ *n* : a carpenter skilled in ship construction and repair

ship·yard \-ˌyärd\ *n* : a place where ships are built or repaired

shire \'shī(ə)r, *in place-name compounds* ˌshi(ə)r, shər\ *n* [OE *scīr*] : a territorial division of England usu. identical with a county

shirk \'shərk\ *vb* **1** : to evade the performance of an obligation ⟨some worked, others *shirked*⟩ **2** : AVOID ⟨*shirked* telling her the truth⟩ — **shirk·er** *n*

Shir·ley poppy \ˌshər-lē-\ *n* [*Shirley* vicarage, Croydon, England] : an annual garden poppy with bright solitary flowers

shirr \'shər\ *vt* **1** : to draw (as cloth) together in a shirring **2** : to bake (eggs removed from the shell) until set

shirr·ing \'shər-iŋ\ *n* : a decorative gathering (as of cloth) made by drawing up the material along two or more parallel lines of stitching

shirt \'shərt\ *n* [OE *scyrte;* akin to E *short*] : a garment for the upper part of the body: as **a** : a loose cloth garment usu. having a collar, sleeves, a front opening, and a tail long enough to be tucked inside trousers or a skirt **b** : UNDERSHIRT

shirt·front \-ˌfrənt\ *n* : the front of a shirt; *esp* : DICKEY

shirt·ing \'shərt-iŋ\ *n* : fabric suitable for shirts

shirt·mak·er \'shərt-ˌmā-kər\ *n* : one that makes shirts

shirt·tail \'shərt-ˌtāl\ *n* : the part of a shirt that reaches below the waist esp. in the back

shirt·waist \'shərt-ˌwāst\ *n* : a woman's tailored garment (as a dress or blouse) with details copied from men's shirts

shish ke·bab \'shish-kə-ˌbäb\ *n* [Arm *shish kabab*] : kabob cooked on skewers

Shi·va \'shē-və\ *var of* SIVA

shiv·a·ree \ˌshiv-ə-'rē, 'shiv-ə-ˌrē\ *n* [F *charivari*] : a noisy mock serenade to a newly married couple — **shivaree** *vt*

¹shiv·er \'shiv-ər\ *n* [ME] : one of the small pieces into which a brittle thing is broken by sudden violence

²shiver *vb* **shiv·ered; shiv·er·ing** \'shiv-(ə-)riŋ\ : to break into many small pieces : SHATTER

³shiver *vi* **shiv·ered; shiv·er·ing** \'shiv-(ə-)riŋ\ [ME *chiveren*] : to undergo trembling (as from cold or fear) : QUIVER

⁴shiver *n* : an instance of shivering : TREMBLE

shiv·ery \'shiv-(ə-)rē\ *adj* **1** : characterized by shivers

: TREMULOUS ⟨felt *shivery* before the interview⟩ **2** : causing shivers ⟨a *shivery* winter's day⟩ ⟨*shivery* ghost stories⟩

¹shoal \'shōl\ *adj* [OE *sceald*] : SHALLOW ⟨*shoal* water⟩

²shoal *n* **1** : a shallow place in a body of water (as the sea or a river) **2** : a sandbank or sandbar that makes the water shallow

³shoal *vi* : to become shallow

⁴shoal *n* [OE *scolu* multitude] : a large group (as of fish) : SCHOOL, CROWD

⁵shoal *vi* : THRONG, SCHOOL

shoat \'shōt\ *n* [ME *shote*] : a young hog usu. less than one year old

¹shock \'shäk\ *n* [ME] : a pile of sheaves of grain or stalks of Indian corn set up in a field with the butt ends down

²shock *vt* : to collect into shocks

³shock *n* [MF *choc*, fr. *choquer* to strike against] **1** : the impact or encounter of individuals or groups in combat **2** : a violent shake or jar : CONCUSSION ⟨an earthquake *shock*⟩ **3 a** : a disturbance in the equilibrium or permanence of something **b** : a sudden or violent disturbance in the mental or emotional faculties **4** : a state of profound bodily depression associated with reduced blood volume and pressure and caused usu. by severe esp. crushing injuries, hemorrhage, or burns **5** : sudden stimulation of the nerves and convulsive contraction of the muscles caused by the discharge of electricity through the animal body **6 a** : APOPLEXY **b** : CORONARY THROMBOSIS

⁴shock *vt* **1 a** : to strike with surprise, terror, horror, or disgust ⟨visitors were *shocked* by the city's slums⟩ **b** : to subject to the action of an electrical discharge **2** : to drive into or out of by or as if by a shock ⟨*shocked* the public into action⟩

⁵shock *n* : a thick bushy mass (as of hair)

shock absorber *n* : a device for absorbing the energy of sudden impulses or shocks in machinery or structures (as springs of automobiles)

shock·er \'shäk-ər\ *n* : one that shocks; *esp* : a sensational work of fiction or drama

shock·ing *adj* : extremely startling and offensive ⟨a *shocking* crime⟩ — **shock·ing·ly** \-iŋ-lē\ *adv*

shock troops *n pl* : troops esp. suited and chosen for offensive work because of their high morale, training, and discipline

shock wave *n* **1** : BLAST 5c **2** : a compressional wave formed whenever the speed of a body relative to a medium exceeds that at which the medium can transmit sound

shod \'shäd\ *adj* **1 a** : wearing shoes **b** : equipped with tires **2** : furnished or equipped with a shoe

¹shod·dy \'shäd-ē\ *n* **1** : a fabric often of inferior quality manufactured wholly or partly from reclaimed wool **2** : inferior, imitation, or pretentious articles or matter

²shoddy *adj* **shod·di·er; -est 1** : made of shoddy **2 a** : cheaply imitative : vulgarly pretentious **b** : hastily or poorly done : INFERIOR **c** : SHABBY — **shod·di·ly** \'shäd-ᵊl-ē\ *adv* — **shod·di·ness** \'shäd-ē-nəs\ *n*

¹shoe \'shü\ *n* [OE *scōh*] **1** : an outer covering for the human foot usu. made of leather with a thick or stiff sole and an attached heel **2** : something that resembles a shoe in appearance or use: as **a** : HORSESHOE **b** : the runner of a sled **c** : the part of a brake that presses on the wheel of a vehicle **3** : the outside casing of an automobile tire

²shoe *vt* **shod** \'shäd\ *also* **shoed** \'shüd\; **shoe·ing 1** : to furnish with a shoe or shoes **2** : to cover for protection, strength, or ornament

shoe·black \'shü-ˌblak\ *n* : BOOTBLACK

shoe·horn \-ˌhorn\ *n* : a curved piece (as of horn, wood, or metal) to aid in slipping on a shoe

shoe·lace \-ˌlās\ *n* : a lace or string for fastening a shoe

shoe·mak·er \-ˌmā-kər\ *n* : one whose business is selling or repairing shoes

shoehorn

shoe·string \-ˌstriŋ\ *n* **1** : SHOELACE **2** [fr. shoestrings' being a typical item sold by itinerant vendors] : a small or barely adequate amount of money or capital ⟨start a business on a *shoestring*⟩

shoe tree *n* : a foot-shaped device for inserting in a shoe to preserve its shape

sho·far \'shō-ˌfär, -fər\ *n, pl* **sho·froth** \shō-'frōt(h),

-'frōs\ [Heb *shōphār*] : a ram's-horn trumpet used in some synagogue observances

sho·gun \'shō-gən, -,gün\ *n* [Jap *shōgun* general] : one of a line of military governors ruling Japan until the revolution of 1867–68 — **sho·gun·ate** \-ət\ *n*

shone *past of* SHINE

shoo \'shü\ *vt* : to scare, drive, or send away by or as if by crying *shoo*

¹**shook** *past or chiefly dial past part of* SHAKE

²**shook** \'shuk\ *n* **1 a** : a set of staves and headings for one hogshead, cask, or barrel **b** : a bundle of parts (as of boxes) ready to be put together **2** : ¹SHOCK

shoon \'shün\ *chiefly dial pl of* SHOE

¹**shoot** \'shüt\ *vb* **shot** \'shät\; **shoot·ing** [OE *scēotan*] **1 a** : to let fly or cause to be driven forward with force ⟨*shoot* an arrow⟩ **b** : to cause a missile to be driven forth from : DISCHARGE ⟨*shoot* off a gun⟩ **c** : to cause an engine or weapon to discharge a missile ⟨*shoot* at a target⟩ **d** : to carry when discharged ⟨guns that *shoot* many miles⟩ **e** : to send forth with suddenness or intensity : DART ⟨*shot* him a meaningful look⟩ **f** : to propel (as a ball or puck) toward a goal; *also* : to score by so doing ⟨*shoot* a basket⟩ **g** : PLAY ⟨*shoot* a round of golf⟩ ⟨*shoot* craps⟩ **2 a** : to strike with a missile esp. from a bow or gun; *esp* : to wound or kill with a missile discharged from a firearm ⟨*shoot* deer⟩ ⟨*shot* a fleeing burglar⟩ **b** : to remove or destroy by use of firearms ⟨*shoot* off a lock⟩ **3** : to push or slide into or out of a fastening ⟨*shot* the door bolt⟩ **4** : to throw or cast esp. suddenly or with force ⟨*shoot* flour into bins⟩ **5** : to set off : DETONATE, IGNITE ⟨*shoot* off fireworks⟩ **6 a** : to push or thrust forward usu. abruptly or swiftly ⟨lizards *shooting* out their tongues⟩ **b** : to grow or sprout by or as if by putting forth shoots **c** : DEVELOP, MATURE **d** : to put forth in growing **7** : to utter or emit rapidly, suddenly, or with force ⟨*shot* out his answers⟩ **8** : to send or carry in haste or swiftly : DISPATCH ⟨*shoot* over a repairman⟩ **9 a** : to go or pass rapidly and precipitately ⟨*shot* out of his office⟩ ⟨the pain *shot* down his arm⟩ **b** : to pass swiftly along ⟨*shoot* the rapids in a canoe⟩ **c** : to stream out suddenly : SPURT **10 a** : to take the altitude of ⟨*shoot* the sun with a sextant⟩ **b** : to take a picture of : PHOTOGRAPH **c** : to film a scene ⟨the director is ready to *shoot*⟩ — **shoot·er** *n* — **shoot at** *or* **shoot for** : to aim at : strive for — **shoot one's bolt** : to exhaust one's capabilities and resources — **shoot the works 1** : to venture all one's capital on one play **2** : to put forth all one's efforts

²**shoot** *n* **1 a** : the aerial part of a plant : a stem with its leaves and appendages; *also* : a branch or part of a plant developed from a single bud **b** : OFFSHOOT **2 a** : an act or the action of shooting **b** : a hunting trip or party ⟨a duck *shoot*⟩ **c** : a shooting match ⟨skeet *shoot*⟩ **3 a** : a motion or movement of rapid thrusting **b** : a momentary darting sensation **4** : TWINGE **4** : CHUTE 2

shooting gallery *n* : a range usu. covered and equipped with targets for practice with firearms

shooting iron *n* : FIREARM

shooting script *n* **1** : a motion-picture script in which scenes are grouped in the order most convenient for shooting and without regard to plot sequence **2** : the final version of a television script used in the production of a program

shooting star *n* **1** : a meteor appearing as a temporary streak of light in the night sky **2** : a No. American perennial herb of the primrose family with entire oblong leaves and showy flowers

shooting stick *n* : a spiked stick with a top that opens into a seat

shoot-the-chutes \,shüt-thə-'shüts\ *n sing or pl* : an amusement ride consisting of a steep incline down which toboggans or boats with flat bottoms slide usu. to continue across a body of water at the bottom

¹**shop** \'shäp\ *n* [OE *sceoppa* booth] **1** : a handicraft establishment : ATELIER **2** : a building or room stocked with merchandise for sale : STORE **3** : FACTORY, MILL **4 a** : a school laboratory equipped for instruction in manual arts **b** : the art or science of working with tools and machinery **5 a** : a business establishment **b** : SHOP-TALK

²**shop** *vb* **shopped**; **shop·ping 1** : to examine goods or services with intent to buy or in search of the best buy

2 : to make a search : HUNT ⟨*shopped* around for the best-qualified man⟩

shop·keep·er \'shäp-,kē-pər\ *n* : STOREKEEPER

shop·lift·er \'shäp-,lif-tər\ *n* : a thief who steals merchandise on display in stores — **shop·lift·ing** \-tiŋ\ *n*

shop·per \'shäp-ər\ *n* **1** : one that shops **2** : one whose occupation is shopping as an agent for customers or for an employer

shopping center *n* : a group of retail and service stores located in a suburban area and provided with extensive parking space

shop steward *n* : a union member elected as the union representative of a shop or department in dealings with the management

shop·talk \'shäp-,tok\ *n* : the jargon or subject matter peculiar to an occupation or a special area of interest

shop·worn \-,wōrn, -,wórn\ *adj* **1** : faded, soiled, or impaired by remaining too long in a store ⟨sells *shopworn* merchandise at a discount⟩ **2** : BEDRAGGLED, JADED ⟨a speech full of *shopworn* clichés⟩

sho·ran \'shōr-,an, 'shór-\ *n* : a system of short-range navigation in which two radar signals transmitted by an airplane and intercepted and rebroadcast to the airplane by two ground stations of known position are used to determine the position of the airplane

¹**shore** \'shō(ə)r, 'shó(ə)r\ *n* [ME; akin to OE *scieran* to cut, shear] : the land bordering a usu. large body of water; *esp* : COAST

²**shore** *vt* [ME *shoren*] : to give support to : BRACE

³**shore** *n* : a prop or support placed beneath or against something to support it

shore·bird \-,bərd\ *n* : any of a group (Charadrii) of birds that frequent the seashore

shore dinner *n* : a complete dinner consisting chiefly of seafoods

shore leave *n* : a leave of absence to go on shore granted to a sailor or naval officer

shore·line \-,līn\ *n* : the line where a body of water touches the shore

shore patrol *n* : a branch of a navy that exercises guard and police functions

shor·ing \'shōr-iŋ, 'shór-\ *n* : a group of shores ⟨the *shoring* for a wall⟩

shorn *past part of* SHEAR

¹**short** \'short\ *adj* [OE *scort;* akin to E *shear*] **1 a** : having little length : not tall : LOW **2 a** : not extended in time : BRIEF ⟨a *short* life⟩ **b** : not retentive ⟨a *short* memory⟩ **c** : EXPEDITIOUS, QUICK **d** : seeming to pass quickly **3 a** : being a syllable or speech sound of relatively little duration **b** : being the member of a pair of similarly spelled vowel or vowel-containing sounds that is descended from a vowel short in duration ⟨*short a* in *fat*⟩ ⟨*short i* in *sin*⟩ **4** : limited in distance ⟨a *short* walk⟩ **5 a** : not coming up to a measure or requirement : INSUFFICIENT ⟨in *short* supply⟩ **b** : not reaching far enough **c** : enduring privation **d** : inherently or basically weak ⟨*short* on brains⟩ **6 a** : ABRUPT, CURT **b** : quickly provoked ⟨*short* tempers⟩ **7** : containing or cooked with shortening : CRISP, FRIABLE ⟨*short* piecrust⟩ **8 a** : not lengthy or drawn out **b** : ABBREVIATED ⟨*doc* is *short* for *doctor*⟩ **9** : consisting of or relating to the sale of securities or commodities that the seller does not possess or has not contracted for at the time of the sale ⟨*short* sale⟩ — **short·ish** \-ish\ *adj*

²**short** *adv* **1** : in a curt manner **2** : BRIEFLY ⟨*short-*lasting⟩ **3** : at a disadvantage : UNAWARES ⟨caught *short*⟩ **4** : so as to interrupt ⟨took him up *short*⟩ **5** : ABRUPTLY, SUDDENLY ⟨he stopped *short*⟩ **6** : at some point before a goal or limit aimed at ⟨the arrow fell *short*⟩ **7** : by or as if by a short sale

³**short** *n* **1** : the sum and substance : UPSHOT ⟨the *short* of it⟩ **2 a** : a short syllable **b** : a short sound or signal **3** *pl* **a** : a by-product of wheat milling that includes the germ, fine bran, and some flour **b** : refuse, clippings, or trimmings discarded in various manufacturing processes **4** : something that is shorter than the usual or regular length **5** *pl* **a** : knee-length or less than knee-length trousers **b** : short underpants **6** *pl* : DEFICIENCIES **7** : SHORT CIRCUIT **8** : SHORTSTOP 1 — **in short** : by way of summary : BRIEFLY

⁴**short** *vt* : SHORT-CIRCUIT

---

short·age \'short-ij\ *n* : a lack in the amount needed : DEFICIT ⟨a *shortage* in the accounts⟩

short·bread \'short-,bred\ *n* : a thick cookie made of flour, sugar, and much shortening

short·cake \-,kāk\ *n* **1** : a crisp and often unsweetened biscuit or cookie **2** : a dessert made of usu. very short baking-powder-biscuit dough baked· and spread with sweetened fruit

short·change \-'chānj\ *vt* **1** : to give less than the correct amount of change to **2** : to deprive of something due : CHEAT ⟨said that he was *shortchanged* during his first years in school⟩ — **short·chang·er** *n*

short circuit *n* : a connection of comparatively low resistance accidentally or intentionally made between points in an electric circuit between which the resistance is normally much greater

short-cir·cuit \'short-'sər-kət\ *vb* : to make a short circuit in or have a short circuit

short·com·ing \-'kəm-iŋ\ *n* : DEFICIENCY, DEFECT, FAULT

short·cut \-,kət\ *n* **1** : a route more direct than that usu. taken **2** : a quicker way of doing something

short division *n* : mathematical division in which the successive steps are performed without writing out the remainders

short·en \'short-°n\ *vb* **short·ened**; **short·en·ing** \'short-niŋ. -°n-iŋ\ : to make or become short or shorter — **short·en·er** \'short-nər, -°n-ər\ *n*
  syn CURTAIL, ABBREVIATE: SHORTEN may imply reduction either in extent or duration; CURTAIL adds an implication of a cutting off that deprives of completeness or adequacy ⟨rain *curtailed* the ceremony⟩ ABBREVIATE applies chiefly to the shortening of the written form of a word or phrase by omission of parts ⟨*Doctor* is commonly *abbreviated* to *Dr.*⟩

short·en·ing \'short-niŋ, -°n-iŋ\ *n* **1** : a making or becoming short or shorter **2** : an edible fat (as butter or lard) used for cooking (as in making biscuit or pastry)

short·hand \'short-,hand\ *n* : a method of writing rapidly by substituting characters, abbreviations, or symbols for letters, words, or phrases : STENOGRAPHY — **shorthand** *adj*

short·hand·ed \-'han-dəd\ *adj* : short of the regular or necessary number of people

short·horn \'short-,hórn\ *n* : any of a breed of red, roan, or white beef cattle originating in the north of England and including good milk-producing strains from which a distinct breed has been evolved — called also *Durham*

short-horned \-'hórnd\ *adj* : having short horns or antennae

short-horned grasshopper *n* : any of a family of grasshoppers with short antennae — called also *locust*

short-lived \'short-'līvd, -'livd\ *adj* : not living or lasting long ⟨*short-lived* happiness⟩ ⟨came from a *short-lived* family⟩ — **short-lived·ness** \-'līv(d)-nəs, -'liv(d)-\ *n*

short·ly \'short-lē\ *adv* **1 a** : in a few words : BRIEFLY ⟨put it *shortly*⟩ **b** : in an abrupt manner : CURTLY **2 a** : in a short time : SOON ⟨will arrive *shortly*⟩ **b** : at a short interval ⟨*shortly* after⟩

short·ness \'short-nəs\ *n* : the quality or state of being short ⟨*shortness* of breath⟩

short order *n* : an order for food that can be quickly cooked

short ribs *n pl* : a cut of beef consisting of rib ends between the rib roast and the plate

short shrift *n* **1** : a brief respite from death **2** : little consideration ⟨gave the matter *short shrift*⟩

short sight *n* : MYOPIA

short·sight·ed \'short-'sīt-əd\ *adj* **1** : NEARSIGHTED, MYOPIC **2** : characterized by lack of foresight — **shortsight·ed·ly** *adv* — **short·sight·ed·ness** *n*

short-spo·ken \-'spō-kən\ *adj* : CURT

short·stop \'short-,stäp\ *n* **1** : the position of the baseball player defending the area on the third-base side of second base **2** : the player stationed in the shortstop position

short story *n* : an invented prose narrative usu. dealing with a few characters and aiming at developing a single episode or creating a single mood

short-tem·pered \'short-'tem-pərd\ *adj* : having a quick temper : easily angered

short-term \-'tərm\ *adj* **1** : occurring over or involving a relatively short period of time **2** : of or relating to a

financial transaction based on a term usu. of less than a year

short·wave \-'wāv\ *n* : a radio wave of 60-meter wavelength or less used esp. in long-distance broadcasting

short-wind·ed \-'win-dəd\ *adj* : affected with or characterized by shortness of breath

Sho·sho·ni *also* **Sho·sho·ne** \shə-'shō-nē\ *n* : a member of a group of Indian peoples in California, Colorado, Idaho, Nevada, Utah, and Wyoming

¹shot \'shät\ *n* [OE *scot*] **1 a** : an action of shooting **b** : a directed propelling of a missile (as an arrow, stone, or rocket); *esp* : a directed discharge of a gun or cannon **c** : a stroke or throw in a game **d** : a setting off of an explosive ⟨a nuclear *shot*⟩ **e** : an injection of something (as a medicine or antibody) into the body ⟨penicillin *shots*⟩ ⟨typhoid *shots*⟩ **2 a** *pl* **shot** : something propelled by shooting; *esp* : small lead or steel pellets esp. forming a charge for a shotgun — see SHELL illustration **b** : a metal sphere of iron or brass that is put for distance **3 a** : the distance that a missile is or can be thrown **b** : RANGE, REACH **4** : a charge to be paid : SCOT **5** : one that shoots : MARKSMAN **6 a** : ATTEMPT, TRY ⟨take another *shot* at the puzzle⟩ **b** : GUESS, CONJECTURE **c** : CHANCE ⟨the horse was a 10 to 1 *shot*⟩ **7** : a remark so directed as to have telling effect **8 a** : PHOTOGRAPH **b** : a single sequence of a motion picture or a television program shot by one camera without interruption **9 a** : a single drink of liquor **b** : a portion (as of medicine) taken at one time

²shot *adj* **1 a** : having contrasting and changeable color effects that react varyingly to dyes : IRIDESCENT ⟨blue silk *shot* with silver⟩ **b** : suffused or streaked with a color ⟨hair *shot* with gray⟩ **c** : PERMEATED ⟨*shot* through with wit⟩ **2** : reduced to a state of ruin, prostration, or uselessness ⟨his nerves were *shot*⟩

shot·gun \'shät-,gən\ *n* : a gun with a smooth bore used to fire small shot at short range — see SHELL illustration

shot hole *n* **1** : a drilled hole in which a charge of dynamite is exploded **2** : a hole made usu. by a boring insect

shot put *n* : a field event consisting in putting the shot for distance — **shot-put·ter** \-,put-ər\ *n* — **shot-put·ting** \-,put-iŋ\ *n*

should \shəd, (')shud\ *past of* SHALL — used as an auxiliary verb to express (1) condition or possibility ⟨if you *should* see him, tell him this⟩, (2) obligation or propriety ⟨you *should* brush your teeth regularly⟩, (3) futurity from the point of view in the past ⟨thought I *should* soon be released⟩, (4) what is probable or expected ⟨they started early and *should* be here soon⟩, and (5) politeness in softening a request or assertion ⟨I *should* like some coffee⟩⟨so it *should* seem⟩

¹shoul·der \'shōl-dər\ *n* [OE *sculdor*] **1 a** : the laterally projecting part of the human body formed of the bones and joints by which the arm is connected with the trunk together with the muscles covering these **b** : the corresponding but usu. less projecting part of a lower vertebrate **2** : a cut of meat including the upper joint of the foreleg and adjacent parts **3** : the part of a garment at the wearer's shoulder **4** : a part or projection resembling a human shoulder ⟨*shoulder* of a hill⟩ **5** : the flat top of the body of a piece of printing type from which the bevel rises to join the face **6** : either edge of a road; *esp* : the part of a road outside of the traveled way

²shoulder *vb* **shoul·dered**; **shoul·der·ing** \-d(ə-)riŋ\ **1** : to push or thrust with the shoulder : JOSTLE ⟨*shouldered* his way through the crowd⟩ **2 a** : to place or bear on the shoulder ⟨*shouldered* the knapsack⟩ **b** : to assume the burden or responsibility of ⟨*shoulder* the blame⟩

shoulder blade *n* : SCAPULA

shoulder board *n* : one of a pair of broad pieces of stiffened cloth worn on the shoulders of a military uniform and carrying insignia of rank

shoulder girdle *n* : PECTORAL GIRDLE

shoulder knot *n* : a detachable ornament of braided wire cord worn on the shoulders of a uniform of ceremony by a commissioned officer

shoulder mark *n* : one of a pair of rectangular pieces of cloth worn parallel to the shoulder of some uniforms of U.S. Navy officers bearing insignia of rank and line or corps devices

shoulder patch *n* : a cloth patch bearing an identifying

j joke; **ŋ** sing; **ō** flow; **ó** flaw; **ói** coin; **th** thin; **th** this; **ü** loot; **ú** foot; **y** yet; **yü** few; **yú** furious; **zh** vision

mark and worn on one sleeve of a uniform below the shoulder

shoulder strap *n* **1** : a strap worn over the shoulder to hold up a garment **2** : a strip worn on the shoulder of a military uniform to show rank

should·est \'shud-əst\ *archaic past 2d sing of* SHALL

shouldn't \'shud-ᵊnt\ : should not

shouldst \(')shudst\ *archaic past 2d sing of* SHALL

¹shout \'shaut\ *vb* [ME *shouten*] **1** : to utter a sudden loud cry ⟨*shouted* with delight⟩ **2** : to utter in a loud voice ⟨*shouted* insults at each other⟩ — **shout·er** *n*

²shout *n* : a loud cry or call

shouting distance *n* : easy reach ⟨lived within *shouting distance* of his cousins⟩

¹shove \'shəv\ *vb* [OE *scūfan*] **1** : to push with steady force **2** : to push carelessly or rudely ⟨*shove* a person out of the way⟩ **syn** see PUSH — **shov·er** *n* — **shove off** **1** : to move away from shore by pushing **2** : to set out : DEPART

²shove *n* : an act or instance of shoving

¹shov·el \'shəv-əl\ *n* [OE *scofl*] **1** : an implement consisting of a plate or scoop attached to a long handle used for lifting and throwing loose material (as snow, earth, grain, or coal) **2** : SHOVELFUL ⟨toss up a *shovel* of earth⟩

²shovel *vb* **-eled** *or* **-elled**; **-el·ing** *or* **-el·ling** \'shəv-(ə-)liŋ\ **1** : to take up and throw with a shovel **2** : to dig or clean out with a shovel **3** : to throw or convey roughly or in the mass as if with a shovel ⟨*shovels* food into his mouth⟩

shov·el·er *or* **shov·el·ler** \'shəv-(ə-)lər\ *n* **1** : one that shovels **2** : any of several river ducks having a large and very broad bill

shov·el·ful \'shəv-əl-,ful\ *n, pl* **shovelfuls** \-,fulz\ *or* **shov·els·ful** \-əlz-,ful\ : the amount held by a shovel

shov·el·man \-,man\ *n* : one who works with a hand or power shovel

shov·el-nosed \,shəv-əl-'nōzd\ *adj* : having a broad flat head, nose, or beak

¹show \'shō\ *vb* **showed**; **shown** \'shōn\ *or* **showed**; **show·ing** [OE *scēawian* to look at, show] **1** : to place in sight : DISPLAY **2** : REVEAL ⟨*showed* himself a coward⟩ **3** : GRANT, BESTOW ⟨the king *showed* no mercy⟩ **4** : TEACH, INSTRUCT ⟨*showed* her how to knit⟩ **5** : PROVE ⟨the result *showed* that he was right⟩ **6** : DIRECT, USHER, GUIDE ⟨*show* a visitor to the door⟩ **7** : APPEAR ⟨anger *showed* in his face⟩ **8** : to be noticeable ⟨the patch hardly *shows*⟩ **9** : to be third or at least third in a horse race

syn SHOW, EXHIBIT, DISPLAY mean to present so as to invite notice or attention. SHOW implies enabling another to see or examine ⟨*showed* me a picture of his family⟩ EXHIBIT implies putting forward openly or publicly; DISPLAY stresses putting in position where others may see to advantage

²show *n* **1** : a demonstrative display ⟨a *show* of strength⟩ **2 a** : a false semblance : PRETENSE ⟨he made a *show* of friendship⟩ **b** : a more or less true appearance of something ⟨a *show* of reason⟩ **c** : an impressive display **d** : OSTENTATION **3** : CHANCE ⟨gave him a *show* in spite of his background⟩ **4** : something exhibited esp. for wonder or ridicule : SPECTACLE **5** : a public presentation: as **a** : a theatrical presentation **b** : a radio or television program **c** : ENTERTAINMENT 3 **6** : ENTERPRISE, AFFAIR ⟨he ran the whole *show*⟩ **7** : third place at the finish of a horse race

show bill *n* : an advertising poster

show·boat \'shō-,bōt\ *n* : a river steamboat containing a theater and carrying a troupe of actors to give plays at river communities

show·case \-,kās\ *n* : a glass case or box to display and protect wares in a store or articles in a museum

show·down \-,daun\ *n* : the final settlement of a contested issue; *also* : the test of strength by which a contested issue is resolved ⟨came hoping for a *showdown*⟩

¹show·er \'shau(-ə)r\ *n* [OE *scūr*] **1 a** : a fall of rain of short duration **b** : a like fall of sleet, hail, or snow **2** : something resembling a rain shower ⟨a *shower* of sparks from a bonfire⟩ ⟨a *shower* of tears⟩ **3** : a party given by friends who bring gifts often of a particular

kind ⟨attended a linen *shower* for the bride⟩ **4** : SHOWER BATH — **show·ery** \-ē\ *adj*

²shower *vb* **1** : to rain or fall in or as if in a shower **2** : to bathe in a shower bath **3** : to wet copiously (as with water) in a spray, fine stream, or drops **4** : to give in abundance ⟨*showered* her with gifts⟩

³show·er \'shō(-ə)r\ *n* : one that shows : EXHIBITOR

shower bath \,shau(-ə)r-'bath, -'bàth\ *n* : a bath in which water is sprayed on the person; *also* : the apparatus that provides such a bath

show·ing \'shō-iŋ\ *n* **1** : an act of putting something on view : DISPLAY, EXHIBITION ⟨a *showing* of fall millinery⟩ ⟨continuous *showings* of a feature picture⟩ **2** : PERFORMANCE, RECORD ⟨the team made a good *showing* in the meet⟩

show·man \'shō-mən\ *n* **1** : the producer of a theatrical show **2** : a person having a sense or knack for dramatization or visual effectiveness — **show·man·ship** \-,ship\ *n*

show off \(')shō-'of\ *vb* **1** : to display proudly **2** : to seek to attract attention by conspicuous behavior

show-off \'shō-,of\ *n* **1** : the act of showing off **2** : one that shows off

show·piece \-,pēs\ *n* : a prime or outstanding example used for exhibition

show·place \-,plās\ *n* : a place (as an estate or building) that is frequently exhibited or is regarded as an example of beauty or excellence

show·room \-,rüm, -,rum\ *n* : a room used for the display of merchandise or of samples

show up *vb* **1** : to reveal the true nature of : EXPOSE ⟨*showed up* her ignorance⟩ **2** : ARRIVE ⟨he *showed up* late⟩

showy \'shō-ē\ *adj* **show·i·er**; **-est** **1** : making an attractive show : STRIKING ⟨*showy* blossoms⟩ **2** : OSTENTATIOUS, GAUDY — **show·i·ly** \'shō-ə-lē\ *adv* — **show·i·ness** \'shō-ē-nəs\ *n*

shrap·nel \'shrap-nᵊl\ *n, pl* **shrapnel** [after Henry *Shrapnel* d1842 English artillery officer] **1** : a projectile that consists of a case provided with a powder charge and a large number of usu. lead balls and is exploded in flight **2** : bomb, mine, or shell fragments

¹shred \'shred\ *n* [OE *scrēade*] : a long narrow strip cut or torn off : PARTICLE, SCRAP ⟨*shreds* of cloth⟩

²shred *vb* **shred·ded**; **shred·ding** **1** : to cut or tear into shreds **2** : to break up into shreds — **shred·der** *n*

shrew \'shrü\ *n* [OE *scrēawa*] **1** : any of numerous small chiefly nocturnal mammals related to the moles, somewhat resembling mice, but having a long pointed snout, small eyes, and velvety fur **2** : a woman who scolds or quarrels constantly

shrewd \'shrüd\ *adj* [ME *shrewed* shrewish, evil, severe, fr. *shrewe* + -*ed*] **1 a** : SEVERE, HARD ⟨*shrewd* knock⟩ **b** : BITING, PIERCING ⟨*shrewd* wind⟩ **2** : marked by cleverness, discernment, or sagacity : ASTUTE ⟨*shrewd* observer⟩ — **shrewd·ly** *adv* — **shrewd·ness** *n*

syn ASTUTE, SAGACIOUS: SHREWD implies native cleverness, stubbornness, and an ability to see beneath the surface; ASTUTE stresses shrewdness in practical affairs and esp. connotes an ability to act successfully in one's own interests; SAGACIOUS suggests native shrewdness matured by experience into practical wisdom and farsightedness

shrew·ish \'shrü-ish\ *adj* : ILL-TEMPERED, SCOLDING, INTRACTABLE — **shrew·ish·ly** *adv* — **shrew·ish·ness** *n*

shrew·mouse \'shrü-,maus\ *n* : SHREW 1

¹shriek \'shrēk\ *vb* **1** : to utter a loud shrill sound **2** : to cry out in a high-pitched voice : SCREECH **3** : to utter with a shriek or sharply and shrilly

²shriek *n* **1** : a shrill usu. wild or involuntary cry **2** : a sound like a shriek ⟨a *shriek* of escaping steam⟩ **syn** see SCREAM

shrie·val \'shrē-vəl\ *adj* [obs. *shrieve* sheriff, fr. OE *scīrgerēfa*] : of or relating to a sheriff — **shrie·val·ty** \-tē\ *n*

shrift \'shrift\ *n* [OE *scrift*, fr. *scrīfan* to shrive] *archaic* : the confession of sins to a priest or the hearing of a confession by a priest

shrike \'shrīk\ *n* : any of numerous usu. largely gray or brownish singing birds that have a strong notched bill hooked at the tip, feed chiefly on insects, and often impale their prey on thorns

¹shrill \'shril\ *vb* [ME *shrillen*] : to utter or emit an acute piercing sound : SCREAM

shovels

²shrill *adj* **1** : having or emitting a sharp high-pitched tone or sound : PIERCING ⟨a *shrill* whistle⟩ **2** : accompanied by sharp high-pitched sounds or cries ⟨*shrill* gaiety⟩ **3** : having an intense or vivid effect on the senses — **shrill** *adv* — **shrill·ness** *n* — **shril·ly** \'shril-lē\ *adv*

³shrill *n* : a shrill sound

¹shrimp \'shrimp\ *n, pl* **shrimp** *or* **shrimps** [ME *shrimpe*] **1** : any of numerous small mostly marine crustaceans related to the lobsters and having a long slender body, compressed abdomen, and long legs; *also* : any small crustacean resembling a true shrimp **2** : a very small or puny person or thing

²shrimp *vi* : to fish for or catch shrimp

¹shrine \'shrīn\ *n* [OE *scrīn*, fr. L *scrinium* case, chest] **1** : a case or box for sacred relics (as the bones of a saint) **2 a** : the tomb of a saint **b** : a place in which devotion is paid to a saint or deity : SANCTUARY **c** : a niche containing a religious image **3** : a place or object hallowed because of its associations ⟨Westminster Abbey is a *shrine* for tourists⟩ **4** : something that enshrines

shrimp

²shrine *vt* : ENSHRINE

¹shrink \'shriŋk\ *vb* **shrank** \'shraŋk\ *also* **shrunk** \'shrəŋk\; **shrunk**; **shrink·ing** [OE *scrincan*] **1** : to contract or curl up the body or part of it : HUDDLE, COWER ⟨*shrink* in horror⟩ **2 a** : to contract or cause to contract to a less extent or compass **b** : to become or cause to become smaller or more compacted (as from heat or melting) ⟨the sweater *shrank* when it was washed⟩ ⟨the tailor *shrank* the material before he made the suit⟩ **c** : to lose substance or weight ⟨meat *shrinks* in cooking⟩ **d** : to lessen in value : DWINDLE ⟨their fortune *shrank* during the depression⟩ **3** : to draw back ⟨*shrink* from a quarrel⟩ — **shrink·a·ble** \'shriŋ-kə-bəl\ *adj* — **shrink·er** *n*

²shrink *n* : the act of shrinking

shrink·age \'shriŋ-kij\ *n* **1** : the act or process of shrinking **2** : the amount lost by shrinkage

shrinking violet *n* : a bashful or retiring person; *esp* : one who shrinks from public recognition of his merit

shrive \'shrīv\ *vb* **shrived** *or* **shrove** \'shrōv\; **shriv·en** \'shriv-ən\ *or* **shrived**; **shriv·ing** \'shrī-viŋ\ [OE *scrīfan* to prescribe, shrive, fr. L *scribere* to write] **1** : to hear the confession of and administer the sacrament of penance to : PARDON **2** : to confess one's sins esp. to a priest

shriv·el \'shriv-əl\ *vb* **-eled** *or* **-elled**; **-el·ing** *or* **-el·ling** \'shriv-(ə-)liŋ\ **1** : to draw into wrinkles esp. with a loss of moisture **2** : to reduce or become reduced to inanition, helplessness, or inefficiency **syn** see WITHER

Shrop·shire \'shräp-,shi(ə)r, -shər, *esp US* -,shī(ə)r\ *n* [*Shropshire*, England] : any of an English breed of dark-faced hornless mutton-type sheep that yield a heavy fleece

¹shroud \'shraud\ *n* [OE *scrūd* garment] **1** : burial garment : WINDING-SHEET **2** : something that covers, screens, or guards ⟨a *shroud* of secrecy⟩ **3 a** : one of the ropes leading usu. in pairs from a ship's masthead to give lateral support to the mast — see RATLINE illustration **b** : one of the cords that suspend the harness of a parachute from the canopy

²shroud *vt* **1 a** : to cut off from view : SCREEN ⟨trees *shrouded* in heavy mist⟩ **b** : to veil under another appearance ⟨*shrouded* in mystery⟩ **2** : to dress for burial

Shrove·tide \'shrōv-,tīd\ *n* [ME *schroftide;* akin to E *shrive*] : the period of three days immediately preceding Ash Wednesday

Shrove Tuesday \'shrōv-\ *n* : the Tuesday before Ash Wednesday

¹shrub \'shrəb\ *n* [OE *scrybb* brushwood] : a low usu. several-stemmed woody plant — compare HERB, TREE

²shrub *n* **1** : a beverage that consists of an alcoholic liquor, fruit juice, fruit rind, and sugar **2** : a beverage made by adding acidulated fruit juice to iced water

shrub·bery \'shrəb-(ə-)rē\ *n, pl* **-ber·ies** : a planting or growth of shrubs

shrub·by \'shrəb-ē\ *adj* **shrub·bi·er; -est** **1** : consisting of or covered with shrubs **2** : resembling a shrub

¹shrug \'shrəg\ *vb* **shrugged; shrug·ging** [ME *schruggen*]

: to raise or draw in the shoulders esp. to express lack of interest or dislike

²shrug *n* **1** : an act of shrugging **2** : a woman's small waist-length or shorter jacket

shrug off *vt* **1** : to brush aside : MINIMIZE **2** : to shake off **3** : to remove (a garment) by wriggling out

shrunk·en \'shrəŋ-kən\ *adj* **1** : that has diminished or contracted esp. in size or value ⟨*shrunken* dollar⟩ **2** : that has been subjected to a shrinking process ⟨*shrunken* human heads⟩

¹shuck \'shək\ *n* : SHELL, HUSK: as **a** : the outer covering of a nut or of Indian corn **b** : the shell of an oyster or clam

²shuck *vt* **1** : to strip of shucks **2** : to peel off ⟨*shucked* off his clothes⟩

¹shud·der \'shəd-ər\ *vi* **shud·dered; shud·der·ing** \'shəd-(ə-)riŋ\ [ME *shoddren*] **1** : to tremble convulsively (as with fear, horror, or aversion) : SHIVER ⟨*shuddered* to think of the accident⟩ ⟨*shudder* from cold⟩ **2** : QUIVER ⟨the train slowed up and *shuddered* to a halt⟩

²shudder *n* : an act of shuddering : TREMOR — **shud·dery** \-ə-rē\ *adj*

¹shuf·fle \'shəf-əl\ *vb* **shuf·fled; shuf·fling** \'shəf-(ə-)liŋ\ **1** : to mix in a mass confusedly : JUMBLE **2** : to put or thrust aside or under cover **3 a** : to mix or manipulate (as a pack of cards) with the real or ostensible purpose of causing a later appearance in random order **b** : to move about, back and forth, or from one place to another : SHIFT **4 a** : to move (as the feet) by sliding along or dragging back and forth without lifting **b** : to perform (as a dance) with a dragging sliding step **c** : to execute in a perfunctory or clumsy manner **5** : to work into or out of trickily : WORM ⟨*shuffle* out of a difficulty⟩ **6** : to act or speak in a shifty or evasive manner — **shuf·fler** \-(ə-)lər\ *n*

²shuffle *n* **1** : an evasion of the issue : EQUIVOCATION **2 a** : an act of shuffling **b** : a right or turn to shuffle **c** : JUMBLE **3 a** : a dragging sliding movement; *esp* : a sliding or scraping step in dancing **b** : a dance characterized by such a step

shuf·fle·board \'shəf-əl-,bōrd, -,bȯrd\ *n* [alter. of obs. *shove-board*] **1** : a game in which players use long-handled cues to shove wooden disks into scoring beds of a diagram marked on a smooth surface **2** : the diagram on which shuffleboard is played

shun \'shən\ *vt* **shunned; shun·ning** [OE *scunian*] : to avoid deliberately and esp. habitually — **shun·ner** *n*

shun·pike \'shən-,pīk\ *n* : a side road used to avoid toll on a turnpike

¹shunt \'shənt\ *vb* [ME *shunten* to flinch] **1** : to turn off to one side : SHIFT; *esp* : to switch (as a train) from one track to another **2** : to provide with or divert by means of an electrical shunt **3** : to travel back and forth — **shunt·er** *n*

²shunt *n* : a means or mechanism for turning or thrusting aside: as **a** *chiefly Brit* : a railroad switch **b** : a conductor joining two points in an electrical circuit so as to form a parallel or alternative path through which a portion of the current may pass

shush \'shəsh\ *n* : a sibilant sound uttered to demand silence — **shush** *vt*

shut \'shət\ *vb* **shut; shut·ting** [OE *scyttan*] **1** : to close or become closed by bringing openings or covering parts together ⟨*shut* the door⟩ ⟨*shut* his eyes⟩ **2** : to forbid entrance to or passage to or from : BAR **3** : to hold within limits by or as if by enclosure : hem in : IMPRISON ⟨*shut* up in a stalled elevator⟩ **4** : to cease or cause to cease or suspend operation ⟨the epidemic *shut* down the school⟩

shut·down \'shət-,daun\ *n* : a temporary or permanent ending of an activity (as work in a factory)

shute *var of* CHUTE

shut-in \'shət-,in\ *adj* : confined by illness or incapacity — **shut-in** \'shət-,in\ *n*

shut·off \'shət-,ȯf\ *n* **1** : something that shuts off **2** : INTERRUPTION, STOPPAGE

shut out \'shət-'aut, ,shət-\ *vt* **1** : to keep out : EXCLUDE **2** : to prevent (an opponent) from scoring in a game or contest

shut·out \'shət-,aut\ *n* : a game or contest in which one side fails to score

¹shut·ter \'shət-ər\ *n* **1** : one that shuts **2** : a usu.

movable cover or screen for a window or door **3** : the part of a camera that opens and closes to expose the film
²shutter *vt* : to close with or by shutters
shut·ter·bug \-,bəg\ *n* : a photography enthusiast
¹shut·tle \'shət-ᵊl\ *n* [ME *shittle*, *schutylle*] **1 a** : an instrument used in weaving to carry the thread back and forth from side to side through the threads that run lengthwise **b** : a spindle-shaped device holding the thread in tatting or netting **c** : any of various sliding thread holders for the lower thread of a sewing machine that carry the lower thread through a loop of the upper thread to make a stitch **2 a** : a going back and forth regularly over a specified and often short route by a vehicle **b** : a vehicle used in a shuttle ⟨a *shuttle* bus⟩ ⟨a *shuttle* train⟩
²shuttle *vb* **shut·tled; shut·tling** \'shət-liŋ, -ᵊl-iŋ\ **1** : to move or travel back and forth frequently **2** : to move by or as if by a shuttle
¹shut·tle·cock \'shət-ᵊl-,käk\ *n* : a feathered cork that is struck with rackets and played back and forth (as in badminton)
²shuttlecock *vt* : to send or toss to and fro : BANDY
shut up *vb* **1** : to cause (a person) to stop talking **2** : to cease writing or speaking
¹shy \'shī\ *adj* **shi·er** *or* **shy·er** \'shī(-ə)r\; **shi·est** *or* **shy·est** \'shī-əst\ [OE *scēoh*] **1** : easily frightened : TIMID **2** : disposed to avoid a person or thing : DISTRUSTFUL **3** : hesitant in committing oneself : CHARY **4** : marked by sensitive diffidence : BASHFUL **5 a** : very light : SCANT **b** : DEFICIENT, LACKING
  syn BASHFUL, MODEST, COY: SHY implies a timid shrinking from contact or familiarity with others; BASHFUL implies a hesitant shyness characteristic of childhood; MODEST suggests an absence of undue confidence or conceit; COY implies deliberately assumed or affected shyness
²shy *vi* **shied; shy·ing 1** : to draw back in sudden dislike or distaste : RECOIL ⟨*shied* from publicity⟩ **2** : to start suddenly aside through fright or alarm ⟨the horse *shied* at a blowing paper⟩
³shy *n, pl* **shies** : a sudden start aside (as of a horse)
⁴shy *vt* **shied; shy·ing** : to throw with a jerk : FLING
⁵shy *n, pl* **shies** : the act of shying : TOSS, THROW
shy·ly \'shī-lē\ *adv* : in a shy manner
shy·ness \'shī-nəs\ *n* : the quality or state of being shy
shy·ster \'shī-stər\ *n* : an unscrupulous lawyer or politician
si \'sē\ *n* [It] : the 7th note of the diatonic scale : TI
¹Si·a·mese \,sī-ə-'mēz, -'mēs\ *adj* **1** : of, relating to, or characteristic of Thailand, the Thais, or their language **2** [*Siamese twin*] : exhibiting great resemblance : very like
²Siamese *n, pl* **Siamese 1** : THAI 1 **2** : THAI 2
Siamese cat *n* : a slender blue-eyed short-haired domestic cat of a breed of oriental origin with pale body and darker ears, paws, tail, and face
Siamese twin *n* [after Chang *d*1874 and Eng *d*1874 congenitally united twins born in Siam] : either of a pair of congenitally united twins in man or lower animals
sib \'sib\ *n* [OE *sibb* related by blood] **1** : KINDRED, RELATIVES; *also* : a group of persons descended from the same real or supposed ancestor **2** : one closely related to another : a blood relation — **sib** *adj*
Si·be·ri·an husky \sī-,bir-ē-ən-\ *n* : any of a breed of medium-sized compact dogs developed as sled dogs in northeastern Siberia that in general resemble the Alaskan malamutes
¹sib·i·lant \'sib-ə-lənt\ *adj* [L *sibilare* to hiss] : having, containing, or producing the sound of or a sound resembling that of the *s* or the *sh* in *sash*
²sibilant *n* : a sibilant speech sound (as English \s\, \z\, \sh\, \ch (=tsh)\, or \j (=dzh)\)
sib·ling \'sib-liŋ\ *n* : one of the offspring of a pair of parents : a brother or sister without regard to sex
sib·yl \'sib-əl\ *n, often cap* [L *sibylla*, fr. Gk] **1** : any of several ancient prophetesses **2 a** : a female prophet **b** : FORTUNE-TELLER — **si·byl·ic** *or* **si·byl·lic** \sə-'bil-ik\ *adj* — **sib·yl·line** \'sib-ə-,līn\ *adj*
¹sic *or* **sick** \'sik\ *vt* **sicced** *or* **sicked** \'sikt\; **sic·cing** *or* **sick·ing** \'sik-iŋ\ [alter. of *seek*] : CHASE, ATTACK — usu. used as a command to a dog ⟨*sic* 'em⟩
²sic \'sik, 'sēk\ *adv* [L, so, thus] : intentionally so written — used after a printed word or passage to indicate that it exactly reproduces an original ⟨said he seed [*sic*] it all⟩

sic·ca·tive \'sik-ət-iv\ *n* [L *siccare* to dry, fr. *siccus* dry] : DRIER
sick \'sik\ *adj* [OE *sēoc*] **1 a** (1) : affected with disease or ill health : AILING (2) : of, relating to, or intended for use in sickness ⟨*sick* pay⟩ ⟨a *sick* ward⟩ **b** : NAUSEATED, QUEASY ⟨*sick* at his stomach⟩ **c** : MENSTRUATING **2** : spiritually or morally unsound or corrupt **3 a** : sickened by strong emotion (as shame or fear) **b** : SATIATED, SURFEITED ⟨*sick* of flattery⟩ **c** : depressed and longing for something ⟨*sick* at heart⟩ **4** : mentally or emotionally unsound or disordered : MORBID ⟨*sick* thoughts⟩ **5** : deficient or declining in vigor or condition ⟨*sick* crops⟩ ⟨a *sick* market⟩
  syn SICK, ILL mean not being in good health. SICK is the common general term in American use but not in British use where ILL is preferred and SICK usu. restricted to mean violently nauseated
sick bay *n* : a compartment in a ship used as a dispensary and hospital
sick·bed \'sik-,bed\ *n* : the bed of a sick person
sick call *n* **1** : a usu. daily formation at which individuals report as sick to the medical officer **2** : the period during which sick call is held
sick·en \'sik-ən\ *vb* **sick·ened; sick·en·ing** \'sik-(ə-)niŋ\ : to make or become sick
sick·en·er \'sik-(ə-)nər\ *n* : something that sickens, disgusts, or overwhelms
sick·en·ing *adj* : causing sickness : NAUSEATING — **sick·en·ing·ly** \'sik-(ə-)niŋ-lē\ *adv*
sick headache *n* : MIGRAINE
sick·ish \'sik-ish\ *adj* **1** : somewhat nauseated : QUEASY **2** : somewhat sickening ⟨a *sickish* odor⟩ — **sick·ish·ly** *adv* — **sick·ish·ness** *n*
sick·le \'sik-əl\ *n* [OE *sicol*, fr. L *secula*] **1 a** : an agricultural implement consisting of a curved metal blade with a short handle **b** : a cutting mechanism (as of a combine) consisting of a bar with a series of cutting elements **2** *cap* : a group of six stars in the constellation Leo — **sickle** *adj*
sick leave *n* **1** : an absence from duty or work permitted because of illness **2** : the number of days per year allowed an employee for sickness
sickle cell *n* : an abnormal red blood cell of crescent shape

sickle 1a

sickle-cell anemia *n* : a chronic familial anemia that occurs esp. in Negroes and is characterized by sickle cells in the circulating blood
sickle feather *n* : one of the long curved tail feathers of a cock
sick·ly \'sik-lē\ *adj* **sick·li·er; -est 1** : somewhat unwell; *also* : habitually or often ailing **2** : produced by or associated with sickness ⟨a *sickly* complexion⟩ ⟨a *sickly* appetite⟩ **3** : producing or tending to sickness ⟨a *sickly* climate⟩ **4** : appearing as if sick: **a** : LANGUID, PALE ⟨a *sickly* flame⟩ **b** : WRETCHED, UNEASY ⟨a *sickly* smile⟩ **c** : lacking in vigor : WEAK ⟨a *sickly* plant⟩ **5** : MAWKISH — **sick·li·ly** \'sik-lə-lē\ *adv* — **sick·li·ness** \'sik-lē-nəs\ *n* — **sickly** *adv*
sick·ness \'sik-nəs\ *n* **1** : ill health : ILLNESS **2** : a specific disease : MALADY **3** : NAUSEA
sick·room \'sik-,rüm, -,rum\ *n* : a room in which a person is confined by sickness
sid·dur \'sid-,ur, 'sid-ər\ *n, pl* **sid·du·rim** \sə-'dur-əm\ [LHeb *siddūr*] : a Jewish prayer book containing Hebrew and Aramaic prayers used in the daily liturgy
¹side \'sīd\ *n* [OE *sīde*] **1** : the right or left part of the trunk or wall of the body; *also* : the entire right or left half of the animal body ⟨a *side* of beef⟩ **2** : a place, space, or direction with respect to a center line (as of an aisle, river, or street) **3** : a surface forming a border or face of an object **4** : an outer portion of a thing considered as facing in a particular direction ⟨the upper *side*⟩ **5** : a slope or declivity of a hill or ridge **6 a** : a bounding line of a geometrical figure ⟨*side* of a square⟩ **b** : one of the surfaces that delimit a solid; *esp* : one of the longer surfaces **c** : either surface of a thin object ⟨one *side* of a record⟩ **7** : the space beside one **8** : the attitude or activity of one person or group with respect to another : PART

9 : a body of partisans or contestants ⟨victory for neither *side*⟩ **10 :** a line of descent traced through either parent **11 :** an aspect or part of something held to be contrasted with some other aspect or part ⟨the better *side* of his nature⟩ — **on the side 1 :** in addition to the main portion **2 :** in addition to a principal occupation ⟨selling insurance *on the side*⟩

²side *adj* **1 :** of, relating to, or situated on the side ⟨*side* window⟩ **2 a :** directed toward or from the side ⟨*side* thrust⟩ ⟨*side* wind⟩ **b :** in addition to or secondary to something primary **:** INCIDENTAL, INDIRECT ⟨*side* issue⟩ ⟨*side* payment⟩ **c :** additional to the main portion ⟨*side* order of french fries⟩

³side *vb* **1 :** to take sides **:** join or form sides ⟨*sided* with the rebels⟩ **2 :** to furnish with sides or siding ⟨*side* a house⟩

⁴side *n* **:** swaggering or arrogant manner **:** PRETENTIOUSNESS

side arm *n* **:** a weapon (as a sword, revolver, or bayonet) worn at the side or in the belt

side·board \'sīd-ˌbōrd, -ˌbòrd\ *n* **:** a piece of dining-room furniture with drawers and compartments for dishes, silverware, and table linen

side·burns \'sīd-ˌbərnz\ *n pl* [anagram of *burnsides*] **:** short side-whiskers worn with a smooth chin

side·car \'sīd-ˌkär\ *n* **:** a one-wheeled car attached to the side of a motorcycle

sid·ed \'sīd-əd\ *adj* **:** having sides often of a specified number or kind ⟨one-*sided*⟩ ⟨glass-*sided*⟩

side dish *n* **:** food served in addition to the main course in a separate dish

side effect *n* **:** a secondary and usu. adverse effect (as of a drug) — called also *side reaction*

side–glance \'sīd-ˌglan(t)s\ *n* **1 :** a glance directed to the side **2 :** a passing allusion **:** an indirect or slight reference

side issue *n* **:** an issue apart from the main point

side·kick \'sīd-ˌkik\ *n* **:** a person closely associated with another as subordinate or partner

side·light \-ˌlīt\ *n* **1 a :** light from the side **b :** incidental or additional information **2 :** the red light on the port bow or the green light on the starboard bow carried by ships under way at night

side·line \-ˌlīn\ *n* **1 :** a line at right angles to a goal line or end line and marking a side of a field of play **2 a :** a line of goods sold in addition to one's principal line **b :** a business or activity pursued in addition to one's regular occupation **3 a :** the space immediately outside the lines along either side of a playing area **b :** the standpoint of persons not immediately participating or concerned — usu. used in pl.

side·lin·er \-ˌlī-nər\ *n* **:** one that remains on the sidelines during an activity **:** one that does not participate

¹side·ling *or* **si·dling** \'sīd-liŋ\ *adv* **:** in a sidelong direction **:** SIDEWAYS

²sideling *or* **sidling** *adj* **1 :** directed toward one side **:** OBLIQUE **2 :** having an inclination **:** SLOPING ⟨*sideling* ground⟩

¹side·long \'sīd-ˌlòŋ\ *adv* [alter. of earlier *sideling*] **1 :** OBLIQUELY, SIDEWAYS **2 :** on the side

²sidelong *adj* **1 :** lying or inclining to one side **:** SLANTING **2 a :** directed to one side ⟨*sidelong* looks⟩ **b :** indirect rather than straightforward

side·man \'sīd-ˌman\ *n* **:** a member of a band or orchestra and esp. a jazz or swing band or orchestra

side·piece \-ˌpēs\ *n* **:** a piece contained in or forming the side of something

si·de·re·al \sī-'dir-ē-əl\ *adj* [L *sidereus*, fr. *sider-*, *sidus* star, constellation] **1 :** of or relating to the stars or constellations **2 :** measured by the apparent motion of fixed stars ⟨*sidereal* time⟩ ⟨a *sidereal* day⟩

sid·er·ite \'sid-ə-ˌrīt\ *n* [Gk *sidēros* iron] **:** a natural carbonate of iron $FeCO_3$ that is a valuable iron ore

side·sad·dle \'sīd-ˌsad-ᵊl\ *n* **:** a saddle for women in which the rider sits with both legs on the same side of the horse — **sidesaddle** *adv*

side·show \-ˌshō\ *n* **1 :** a minor show offered in addition to a main exhibition (as of a circus) **2 :** an incidental diversion

side·slip \-ˌslip\ *vi* **1 :** to skid sideways — used esp. of an automobile **2 :** to slide sideways through the air in a downward direction in an airplane — **sideslip** *n*

side·spin \-ˌspin\ *n* **:** a rotary motion that causes a ball to revolve horizontally

side·split·ting \-ˌsplit-iŋ\ *adj* **:** extremely funny **:** HILARIOUS

side step *n* **1 :** a step aside (as in boxing to avoid a blow) **2 :** a step taken sideways (as in climbing on skis)

side·step \'sīd-ˌstep\ *vb* **1 :** to take a side step **2 :** to avoid by a step to the side **3 :** to avoid meeting issues **:** EVADE ⟨adept at *sidestepping* awkward questions⟩

side·stroke \-ˌstrōk\ *n* **:** a stroke made by a swimmer while lying on his side in which the arms are moved without breaking water while the legs do a scissors kick

side·swipe \-ˌswīp\ *vt* **:** to strike with a glancing blow along the side ⟨*sideswiped* a parked car⟩

¹side·track \-ˌtrak\ *n* **1 :** SIDING **2 :** a position or condition of secondary importance to which one may be diverted

²sidetrack *vt* **1 :** to transfer from a main railroad line to a siding ⟨*sidetrack* a train⟩ **2 :** to turn aside from a main purpose or use ⟨*sidetrack* the conversation⟩; *also* **:** to divert to a subordinate position

side·walk \'sīd-ˌwók\ *n* **:** a usu. paved walk for pedestrians at the side of a street

sidewalk superintendent *n* **:** a spectator at a building or demolition job

side·wall \-ˌwól\ *n* **1 :** a wall forming the side of something **2 :** the side of an automotive tire between the tread shoulder and the rim bead

side·ward \-wərd\ *or* **side·wards** \-wərdz\ *adv* (*or adj*) **:** toward the side

side·way \-ˌwā\ *adv* (*or adj*) **:** SIDEWAYS

side·ways \-ˌwāz\ *adv* (*or adj*) **1 :** from one side **2 :** with one side forward **3 :** toward one side; *also* **:** ASKANCE

side–wheel \ˌsīd-ˌhwēl\ *adj* **:** being a steamer having a paddle wheel on each side — **side–wheel·er** \'sīd-ˌhwē-lər\ *n*

side–whis·kers \'sīd-ˌhwis-kərz\ *n pl* **:** whiskers on the side of the face usu. worn long with the chin shaven

side·wind·er \'sīd-ˌwīn-dər\ *n* **1 :** a heavy swinging blow from the side **2 :** a small rattlesnake of the southwestern U.S. that moves over sand by thrusting its body diagonally forward in flat loops using its neck as an anchor

side·wise \-ˌwīz\ *adv* (*or adj*) **:** SIDEWAYS

sid·ing \'sīd-iŋ\ *n* **1 :** a short railroad track connected with the main track by switches at one or more places — called also *sidetrack* **2 :** material (as boards or metal pieces) used to cover the outside walls of frame buildings

si·dle \'sīd-ᵊl\ *vb* **si·dled; si·dling** \'sīd-liŋ, -ᵊl-iŋ\ [prob. back-formation fr. *sideling* sidelong] **1 :** to go or move with one side foremost esp. in a furtive advance **2 :** to cause to move or turn sideways — **sidle** *n*

siege \'sēj\ *n* [OF, seat, blockade, fr. (assumed) VL *sedicum*, fr. L *sedēre* to sit] **1 :** a military blockade of a fortified place **2 :** a continued attempt to gain possession of something **3 :** a persistent attack (as of illness) ⟨a *siege* of the flu⟩

Sieg·fried \'sig-ˌfrēd, 'sēg-\ *n* **:** a hero in Germanic legend noted esp. for winning the hoard of the Nibelungs and for slaying a dragon

Siegfried line *n* **:** a line of German defensive fortifications facing the Maginot Line

si·en·na \sē-'en-ə\ *n* [It *terra di Siena*, lit., Siena earth, fr. *Siena*, Italy] **:** an earthy substance containing oxides of iron and usu. of manganese that is brownish yellow when raw and orange red or reddish brown when burnt and is used as a pigment

si·er·ra \sē-'er-ə\ *n* [Sp, lit., saw, fr. L *serra*] **1 a :** a range of mountains esp. with jagged peaks **b :** the country about a sierra **2 :** any of various large fishes that resemble the mackerels

si·es·ta \sē-'es-tə\ *n* [Sp, fr. L *sexta hora* noon, lit., sixth hour] **:** an afternoon nap or rest

sie·va bean \'sē-və-, 'siv-ē-\ *n* **:** any of several small-seeded beans closely related to and sometimes classed as lima beans

¹sieve \'siv\ *n* [OE *sife*] **:** a device with meshes or perforations through which finer particles of a mixture (as of ashes, flour, or sand) of various sizes are passed to separate them from coarser ones, through which the liquid is drained from liquid-containing material, or through

---

j joke; **ŋ** sing; **ō** flow; **ò** flaw; **òi** coin; **th** thin; **t͟h** this; **ü** loot; **ù** foot; **y** yet; **yü** few; **yù** furious; **zh** vision

which soft materials are forced for reduction to fine particles

²**sieve** vb : to put through a sieve : SIFT

sieve plate n **1** : a perforated body through which water passes into the body of a starfish or other echinoderm **2** : an area in the end wall of a sieve tube pierced by fine pores

sieve tube n : a tube that consists of an end-to-end series of thin-walled living cells, is the characteristic element of the phloem, and is held to function chiefly in translocation of organic solutes

sift \'sift\ vb [OE *siftan*] **1 a** : to put through a sieve ⟨*sift* flour⟩ **b** : to separate by putting through a sieve **2 a** : to screen out the valuable or good : SELECT **b** : to study or investigate thoroughly : PROBE **3** : to scatter by or as if by sifting **4** : to pass through or as if through a sieve — **sift·er** n

sift·ing n **1** : the act or process of sifting **2** pl : sifted material ⟨bran mixed with *siftings*⟩

sigh \'sī\ vb [OE *sīcan*] **1** : to take a deep audible breath (as in weariness or grief) **2** : to make a sound like sighing ⟨wind *sighing* in the branches⟩ **3** : GRIEVE, YEARN ⟨*sighing* for the days of his youth⟩ **4** : to express by sighs — **sigh** n — **sigh·er** \'sī-(ə)r\ n

¹**sight** \'sīt\ n [OE *gesiht* faculty or act of sight, thing seen; akin to E *see*] **1** : something that is seen : SPECTACLE **2 a** : a thing that is worth seeing **b** : something ludicrous or disorderly in appearance **3 a** : the process, power, or function of seeing; *esp* : the animal sense of which the eye is the receptor organ and by which the position, shape, and color of objects are perceived **b** : mental or spiritual perception **c** : mental view; *esp* : JUDGMENT **4 a** : the act of looking at or beholding **b** : INSPECTION, PERUSAL ⟨this letter is for your *sight* only⟩ **c** : VIEW, GLIMPSE **d** : an observation to determine direction or position (as by a navigator) **5 a** : a perceiving of an object by the eye **b** : the range of vision **6 a** : a device (as a small metal bead on a gun barrel) that aids the eye in aiming or in determining the direction of an object **b** : an aim or observation taken by means of such a device

²**sight** adj **1** : based on recognition or comprehension without previous study ⟨*sight* translation⟩ **2** : payable on presentation ⟨*sight* draft⟩

³**sight** vb **1** : to get sight of **2** : to look at through or as if through a sight **3** : to aim by means of sights **4** : to look carefully in a particular direction ⟨*sight* along the edge of a board⟩

sight·ed \'sīt-əd\ adj : having sight ⟨clear-*sighted*⟩

sight·less \'sīt-ləs\ adj : lacking sight : BLIND — **sight·less·ness** n

sight·ly \'sīt-lē\ adj **1** : pleasing to the sight : HANDSOME **2** : affording a good view ⟨a *sightly* location overlooking the valley⟩ — **sight·li·ness** n

sight-read \'sīt-ˌrēd\ vb **sight-read** \-ˌred\; **sight-read·ing** \-ˌrēd-iŋ\ : to read a foreign language or perform music without previous preparation or study — **sight reader** \-ˌrēd-ər\ n

¹**sight-see·ing** \'sīt-ˌsē-iŋ\ adj : engaged in, devoted to, or used for seeing things and places of interest

²**sight-seeing** n : the act or pastime of seeing places of interest — **sight-se·er** \'sīt-ˌsē-ər, -ˌsi(-ə)r\ n

sight unseen adv : without inspection or appraisal ⟨bought it *sight unseen*⟩

sig·il \'sij-əl, 'sig-ˌil\ n [L *sigillum*, fr. dim. of *signum* sign, seal] **1** : SEAL, SIGNET **2** : a sign, word, or device of supposed occult power in astrology or magic

sig·ma \'sig-mə\ n : the 18th letter of the Greek alphabet — Σ or σ or ς

sig·moid \'sig-ˌmȯid\ adj [Gk *sigmoeidēs*, fr. *sigma*; fr. a common form of sigma shaped like the Roman letter C] **1 a** : curved like the letter C **b** : curved in two directions like the letter S **2** : of, relating to, or being the sigmoid flexure of the intestine — **sig·moi·dal·ly** \sig-'mȯid-°l-ē\ adv

sigmoid flexure n : the contracted and crooked part of the colon immediately above the rectum — called also *sigmoid colon*

¹**sign** \'sīn\ n [L *signum* mark, sign, image, seal] **1 a** : a motion or gesture by which a thought is expressed or a command made known ⟨make the *sign* of the cross⟩ **b** : SIGNAL 1a **2** : a mark having a conventional meaning

and used in place of words or to represent a complex notion **3** : one of the 12 divisions of the zodiac **4 a** : a character (as a flat or sharp) used in musical notation **b** : a character (as ÷ or √‾) indicating a mathematical operation; *also* : one of two characters + and − characterizing a number as positive or negative **c** : the condition of being electrically positive or negative ⟨check the *sign* of the charge on the rod⟩ **5 a** : a lettered board or other display used to identify or advertise a place of business **b** : a posted command, warning, or direction **c** : SIGNBOARD **6 a** : something that serves to indicate the presence or existence of something : TOKEN **b** : PRESAGE, PORTENT **c** : an objective evidence of plant or animal disease — compare SYMPTOM

²**sign** vb [L *signare*, fr. *signum* sign] **1 a** : to place a sign upon **b** : to represent or indicate by a sign **2** : to affix a signature to : write one's name on something in token of assent, responsibility, or obligation **3** : to communicate by making a sign **4** : to hire by securing the signature of ⟨*sign* him on⟩ — **sign·er** n

¹**sig·nal** \'sig-n°l\ n **1 a** : an act, event, or watchword that serves to start some action **b** : something that incites to action **2** : a sound or gesture made to give warning or command **3** : an object placed to convey notice or warning **4 a** : the message, sound, or effect transmitted in electronic communication (as radio or television) **b** : a radio wave or electric current that transmits a message or effect (as in radio, television, or telephony)

²**signal** vb -**naled** or -**nalled**; -**nal·ing** or -**nal·ling** **1** : to notify by a signal **2** : to communicate by signals **3** : to make or send a signal — **sig·nal·er** n

³**signal** adj **1** : distinguished from the ordinary : OUTSTANDING ⟨*signal* achievement⟩ **2** : used in signaling ⟨*signal* beacon⟩ — **sig·nal·ly** \-n°l-ē\ adv

sig·nal·ize \'sig-n°l-ˌīz\ vt **1** : to make conspicuous : DISTINGUISH **2** : to point out carefully or distinctly **3** : to make signals to : SIGNAL; *also* : INDICATE — **sig·nal·i·za·tion** \ˌsig-n°l-ə-'zā-shən\ n

sig·nal·man \'sig-n°l-mən, -ˌman\ n : one who signals or works with signals

sig·nal·ment \-mənt\ n : description by peculiar, appropriate, or characteristic marks

sig·na·to·ry \'sig-nə-ˌtōr-ē, -ˌtȯr-\ n, pl -**ries** : a signer with another or others; *esp* : a government bound with others by a signed convention — **signatory** adj

sig·na·ture \'sig-nə-ˌchu̇r, -chər\ n **1** : the name of a person written with his own hand **2** : a letter at the bottom of the first page of a sheet of printed pages (as of a book) to ensure placement in the right order in binding; *also* : the sheet itself which when folded becomes one unit of the book **3 a** : KEY SIGNATURE **b** : TIME SIGNATURE **4** : a tune, musical number, or sound effect or in television a characteristic title or picture used to identify a program, entertainer, or orchestra

sign·board \'sīn-ˌbōrd, -ˌbȯrd\ n : a board bearing a notice or sign

¹**sig·net** \'sig-nət\ n [MF, dim. of *signe* sign, seal, fr. L *signum*] **1** : a seal used in place of a signature on a document **2** : the impression made by or as if by a signet **3** : a small intaglio seal (as in a finger ring)

²**signet** vt : to stamp or authenticate with a signet

signet ring n : a finger ring engraved with a signet

sig·ni·fi·a·ble \'sig-nə-ˌfī-ə-bəl\ adj : capable of being represented by a sign or symbol

sig·nif·i·cance \sig-'nif-i-kən(t)s\ n **1 a** : something signified **b** : SUGGESTIVENESS **2** : IMPORTANCE, CONSEQUENCE syn see MEANING

sig·nif·i·can·cy \-kən-sē\ n : SIGNIFICANCE

sig·nif·i·cant \-kənt\ adj [L *significare* to signify] **1** : having meaning : SUGGESTIVE, EXPRESSIVE **2** : suggesting or containing a disguised or special meaning **3 a** : IMPORTANT, WEIGHTY **b** : probably caused by something other than mere chance ⟨statistically *significant* correlation between vitamin deficiency and disease⟩ **c** : DISTINCTIVE ⟨the difference between the initial sounds of *keel* and *cool* is not *significant* in English⟩ — **sig·nif·i·cant·ly** adv

significant figures n pl : the figures of a number beginning with the first figure to the left that is not zero and ending with the last figure to the right that is not zero or is a zero that is considered to be exact

---

ə abut; ᵊ kitten; ər further; a back; ā bake; ä cot, cart; au̇ out; ch chin; e less; ē easy; g gift; i trip; ī life

sig·ni·fi·ca·tion \,sig-nə-fə-'kā-shən\ *n* **1** : a signifying by signs esp. to convey meaning **2** : IMPORT **syn** see MEANING

sig·nif·i·ca·tive \sig-'nif-ə-,kāt-iv\ *adj* **1** : INDICATIVE **2** : SIGNIFICANT, SUGGESTIVE — **sig·nif·i·ca·tive·ly** *adv* — **sig·nif·i·ca·tive·ness** *n*

sig·ni·fi·er \'sig-nə-,fī-(-ə)r\ *n* : one that signifies : SIGN

sig·ni·fy \'sig-nə-,fī\ *vb* **-fied; -fy·ing** [OF *signifier*, fr. L *significare*, fr. *signum* sign, token] **1** : MEAN, DENOTE **2** : to show esp. by a conventional token (as word, signal, or gesture) **3** : to have significance or importance

sign language *n* : a system of hand gestures used for communication by the deaf or by people speaking different languages

sign off *vi* : to announce the end of a message, program, or broadcast and discontinue radio or television transmitting

sign of the cross : a gesture of the hand forming a cross esp. on forehead, shoulders, and breast to profess Christian faith or invoke divine protection or blessing

si·gnor \sēn-'yȯ(ə)r, -'yō(ə)r\ *n, pl* **signors** *or* **si·gno·ri** \-'yȯr-(,)ē, -'yȯr-\ [It *signore*, *signor*, fr. ML *senior* lord, fr. L, adj., senior] : an Italian man of rank or gentility — used as a title equivalent to *Mister*

si·gno·ra \sēn-'yȯr-ə, -'yȯr-\ *n, pl* **-gnoras** *or* **-gno·re** \-'yȯr-(,)ā, -'yȯr-\ [It, fem. of *signore*, *signor*] : an Italian married woman usu. of rank or gentility — used as a title equivalent to *Mrs.*

si·gno·ri·na \,sē-nyə-'rē-nə\ *n, pl* **-nas** *or* **-ne** \-(,)nā\ [It, fr. dim. of *signora*] : an unmarried Italian woman — used as a title equivalent to *Miss*

sign·post \'sīn-,pōst\ *n* : a post with a sign on it to direct travelers

Sig·urd \'sig-,ùrd, 'sig-ərd\ *n* : a hero in Norse mythology who slays the dragon Fafnir

Sikh \'sēk\ *n* [Hindi, lit., disciple] : an adherent of a monotheistic religion of India founded about 1500 by a Hindu under Islamic influence and marked by rejection of idolatry and caste — **Sikh** *adj* — **Sikh·ism** \-,iz-əm\ *n*

si·lage \'sī-lij\ *n* [short for *ensilage*] : fodder converted into succulent feed for livestock through processes of anaerobic acid fermentation (as in a silo)

sild \'sild\ *n* [Norw] : a young herring other than a brisling canned as a sardine in Norway

¹si·lence \'sī-lən(t)s\ *n* **1** : forbearance from speech or noise — often used interjectionally **2** : absence of sound or noise : STILLNESS **3** : absence of mention : **a** : OBLIVION, OBSCURITY **b** : SECRECY

²silence *vt* **1** : to stop the noise or speech of : reduce to silence **2** : to restrain from expression : SUPPRESS **3** : to cause to cease hostile firing by return fire or by destroying

si·lenc·er \'sī-lən-sər\ *n* : one that silences; *esp* : a silencing device for small arms

si·lent \'sī-lənt\ *adj* [L *silēre* to be silent] **1** : making no utterance: **a** : MUTE, SPEECHLESS ⟨stood *silent* before his accusers⟩ **b** : indisposed to speak : TACITURN **2** : free from sound or noise : STILL **3** : performed or borne without utterance : UNSPOKEN ⟨*silent* disapproval⟩ ⟨*silent* grief⟩ **4 a** : making no mention ⟨history is *silent* about this man⟩ **b** : INACTIVE; *esp* : taking no active part in the conduct of a business ⟨*silent* partner⟩ **5** : UNPRONOUNCED ⟨*silent* b in *doubt*⟩ — **si·lent·ly** *adv*

syn TACITURN, RETICENT: SILENT implies a habit of saying no more than is necessary and often less than expected; TACITURN suggests a temperamental disinclination to talk and a sullen avoidance of sociability; RETICENT implies a reluctance to speak out plainly esp. about one's personal affairs

silent butler *n* : a receptacle with hinged lid for collecting table crumbs and the contents of ash trays

si·lex \'sī-,leks\ *n* [L, flint, quartz] : SILICA

Si·lex \'sī-,leks\ *trademark* — used for a vacuum coffee maker

¹sil·hou·ette \,sil-ə-'wet\ *n* [F, after Étienne de *Silhouette* d1767 French controller general of finances; fr. his petty economies] **1** : a drawing or cutout of the outline of an object filled in with black; *esp* : a profile portrait of this kind **2** : characteristic shape of an object (as an airplane) seen or as if seen against the light

²silhouette *vt* : to represent by a silhouette; *also* : to project upon a background like a silhouette

sil·i·ca \'sil-i-kə\ *n* [NL, fr. L *silic-*, *silex* flint, quartz] : the dioxide of silicon SiO_2 occurring in crystalline, amorphous, and impure forms (as in quartz, opal, and sand)

silica gel *n* : colloidal silica resembling coarse white sand in appearance but possessing many fine pores and therefore extremely adsorbent

sil·i·cate \'sil-i-kət, 'sil-ə-,kāt\ *n* : a compound regarded as derived from silica and any of various oxides of metals

si·li·ceous *or* **si·li·cious** \sə-'lish-əs\ *adj* : of, relating to, or containing silica or a silicate ⟨*siliceous* limestone⟩

si·lic·ic \sə-'lis-ik\ *adj* : of, relating to, or derived from silica or silicon

silicic acid *n* : any of various weakly acid substances obtained as gelatinous masses by treating silicates with acids

silicified wood *n* : chalcedony in the form of petrified wood

si·lic·i·fy \sə-'lis-ə-,fī\ *vt* **-fied; -fy·ing** : to convert into or impregnate with silica — **si·lic·i·fi·ca·tion** \-,lis-ə-fə-'kā-shən\ *n*

sil·i·con \'sil-i-kən, 'sil-ə-,kän\ *n* [*silica* + *-on* (as in *carbon*)] : a tetravalent nonmetallic chemical element that occurs combined as the most abundant element next to oxygen in the earth's crust and is used esp. in alloys — see ELEMENT table

silicon carbide *n* : a hard brittle crystalline compound SiC of silicon and carbon used as an abrasive

silicon dioxide *n* : SILICA

sil·i·cone \'sil-ə-,kōn\ *n* : any of various polymeric organic silicon compounds obtained as oils, greases, or plastics and used esp. for water-resistant and heat-resistant lubricants, varnishes, binders, and electric insulators

sil·i·co·sis \,sil-ə-'kō-səs\ *n* : a disease of the lungs marked by fibrosis and shortness of breath and caused by prolonged inhaling of silica dusts — **sil·i·cot·ic** \-'kät-ik\ *adj or n*

si·lique \sə-'lēk\ *n* [F, fr. L *siliqua* pod, husk] : a long narrow 2-valved usu. many-seeded capsule characteristic of the mustard family — **sil·i·quose** \'sil-ə-,kwōs\ *or* **sil·i·quous** \-kwəs\ *adj*

¹silk \'silk\ *n* [OE *seolc*] **1** : a fine continuous protein fiber produced by various insect larvae usu. for cocoons; *esp* : a lustrous tough elastic fiber produced by silkworms and used for textiles **2 a** : thread, yarn, or fabric made from silk **b** : a garment of silk **3** : a silky material or filament (as that produced by a spider) ⟨milkweed *silk*⟩; *esp* : the styles of an ear of Indian corn — **silk** *adj*

²silk *vi* : to develop the silk ⟨the corn is *silking*⟩

silk cotton *n* : the silky or cottony covering of seeds of a silk-cotton tree; *esp* : KAPOK

silk-cotton tree *n* : any of various tropical trees with palmate leaves and large fruits with the seeds enveloped by silk cotton

silk·en \'sil-kən\ *adj* **1** : made or consisting of silk **2 a** : resembling silk esp. in soft lustrous smoothness **b** : smoothly agreeable : HARMONIOUS ⟨*silken* voices⟩; *also* : INGRATIATING **3 a** : dressed in silk ⟨*silken* ankles⟩ **b** : LUXURIOUS

silk hat *n* : a hat with a tall elastic crown and a silk-plush finish worn by men as a dress hat

silk moth *n* : the silkworm moth

silk-screen process *n* : a stencil process in which coloring matter is forced onto the material to be printed through the meshes of a silk or organdy screen

silk-stocking *adj* **1** : fashionably dressed ⟨a *silk-stocking* audience⟩ **2** : ARISTOCRATIC, WEALTHY ⟨the *silk-stocking* districts of a city⟩

silk·worm \'silk-,wərm\ *n* : a moth larva that spins a large amount of strong silk in constructing its cocoon; *esp* : the rough wrinkled hairless yellowish caterpillar of an Asiatic moth long grown as a source of silk

silky \'sil-kē\ *adj* **silk·i·er; -est** **1** : SILKEN **2** : having or covered with fine soft hairs, plumes, or scales — **silk·i·ly** \-kə-lē\ *adv* — **silk·i·ness** \-kē-nəs\ *n*

sill \'sil\ *n* [OE *syll*] **1** : a horizontal piece (as a timber) that forms the lowest member of a

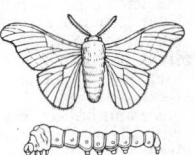

silkworm: adult
female and larva

framework or supporting structure (as of a house or bridge): as **a** : the horizontal member at the base of a window **b** : the timber or stone at the foot of a door : THRESHOLD **2** : a flat mass of igneous rock injected while molten between other rocks

sillabub var of SYLLABUB

sil·li·man·ite \'sil-ə-mə-,nīt\ n [Benjamin *Silliman* d1864 American geologist] : a brown, grayish, or pale green crystalline mineral that consists of an aluminum silicate

sil·ly \'sil-ē\ adj **sil·li·er; -est** [ME *sely* happy, innocent, pitiable, feeble, fr. OE *sæl* happiness] **1** : weak in intellect : FOOLISH **2** : contrary to reason : ABSURD **3** : TRIFLING, FRIVOLOUS — **sil·li·ly** \'sil-ə-lē\ adv — **sil·li·ness** \'sil-ē-nəs\ n — **silly** n or adv

si·lo \'sī-lō\ n, pl **silos** [Sp] **1** : a trench, pit, or esp. a tall cylinder (as of wood or concrete) usu. sealed to exclude air and used for making and storing silage **2** : a deep bin for housing a missile underground

¹silt \'silt\ n [ME *cylte*] **1** : loose sedimentary material with rock particles usu. ¹⁄₂₀ millimeter or less in diameter; *also* : soil containing 80 percent or more of such silt and less than 12 percent of clay **2** : a deposit of sediment (as by a river) — **silty** \'sil-tē\ adj

²silt vb : to become or make choked, obstructed, or covered with silt — **silt·a·tion** \sil-'tā-shən\ n

Si·lu·ri·an \sī-'lúr-ē-ən, sə-\ n [L *Silures*, a people of ancient Britain] : the period of the Paleozoic era between the Ordovician and Devonian marked by the beginning of coral-reef building and the appearance of very large crustaceans; *also* : the corresponding system of rocks — **Silurian** adj

silvan var of SYLVAN

¹sil·ver \'sil-vər\ n [OE *seolfor*] **1** : a white ductile and malleable metallic chemical element that takes a high polish, is usu. univalent in compounds, and has the highest thermal and electric conductivity of any substance — see ELEMENT table **2 a** : coin made of silver **b** : articles (as tableware) made of or plated with silver **3** : a nearly neutral slightly brownish medium gray

²silver adj **1** : relating to, made of, or yielding silver ⟨*silver* jewelry⟩ ⟨*silver* ore⟩ **2** : SILVERY 1

³silver vt **sil·vered; sil·ver·ing** \'silv-(ə-)riŋ\ **1 a** : to cover with silver (as by electroplating) **b** : to coat with a substance (as a metal) resembling silver ⟨*silver* a glass with an amalgam⟩ **2** : to give a silvery appearance to — **sil·ver·er** \'sil-vər-ər\ n

silver bromide n : a compound AgBr that is extremely sensitive to light and is much used in the preparation of photographic emulsions

silver chloride n : a compound AgCl sensitive to light and used esp. for photographic emulsions

silver cord n [fr. *The Silver Cord*, play by Sidney Howard] : the emotional tie between mother and child

sil·ver·fish \'sil-vər-,fish\ n **1** : any of various silvery fishes (as a tarpon or silversides) **2** : any of various small wingless insects (order Thysanura); *esp* : one found in houses and sometimes injurious to sized papers or starched clothes

silver fox n : a color phase of the common red fox in which the pelt is black tipped with white and which is a genetic variant that can breed true

silver iodide n : a compound AgI that is sensitive to light and is used in photography, rainmaking, and medicine

silver lining n **1** : a white edge on a cloud **2** : a consoling or hopeful prospect

sil·vern \'sil-vərn\ adj **1** : made of silver **2** : resembling or characteristic of silver : SILVERY

silver nitrate n : an irritant compound AgNO₃ that is used as a chemical reagent, in photography, and in medicine esp. as an antiseptic

silver paper n : a metallic paper with a coating or lamination resembling silver

silver perch n : any of various somewhat silvery fishes that resemble perch

silver plate n **1** : a plating of silver **2** : domestic flatware and hollow ware of silver or of a base metal plated with silver

silver protein n : a colloidal light-sensitive preparation of silver and protein used as an antiseptic

silver screen n **1** : a motion-picture screen **2** : MOTION PICTURES

sil·ver·sides \'sil-vər-,sīdz\ n sing or pl : any of a family of small fishes that have a silvery stripe along each side of the body and are related to the gray mullets

sil·ver·smith \-,smith\ n : a person who makes articles of silver

silver spoon n : WEALTH; *esp* : inherited wealth ⟨born with a *silver spoon* in his mouth⟩

silver standard n : a monetary standard under which the currency unit is defined by a stated quantity of silver

sil·ver·tongued \,sil-vər-'təŋd\ adj : ELOQUENT ⟨a *silver= tongued* orator⟩

sil·ver·ware \'sil-vər-,wa(ə)r, -,we(ə)r\ n : SILVER PLATE 2; *also* : FLATWARE

sil·very \'silv-(ə-)rē\ adj **1 a** : having a soft clear ring like that of struck silver **b** : having the white lustrous sheen of silver **2** : containing or consisting of silver — **sil·ver·i·ness** n

sil·vic·o·lous \sil-'vik-ə-ləs\ adj : living in woodlands

sil·vi·cul·ture \'sil-və-,kəl-chər\ n [F, fr. L *silva* forest] : a phase of forestry dealing with the development and care of forests — **sil·vi·cul·tur·al** \,sil-və-'kəlch-(ə-)rəl\ adj — **sil·vi·cul·tur·al·ly** \-ē\ adv — **sil·vi·cul·tur·ist** \-'kəlch-(ə-)rəst\ n

Sim·chas To·rah \,sim-käs-'tōr-ə, -'tor-\ n : a Jewish holiday observed in October or November in celebration of the completion of the annual reading of the Torah

¹sim·i·an \'sim-ē-ən\ adj [L *simia* ape, fr. *simus* snub-nosed, fr. Gk *simos*] : of, relating to, or resembling monkeys or apes

²simian n : MONKEY, APE

sim·i·lar \'sim-ə-lər\ adj [F *similaire*, fr. L *similis* like, similar] **1** : marked by correspondence or resemblance **2** : not differing in shape but only in size or position ⟨*similar* triangles⟩ — **sim·i·lar·ly** adv

syn SIMILAR, ANALOGOUS, PARALLEL mean closely resembling each other. SIMILAR implies the possibility of being mistaken for each other; ANALOGOUS applies to things belonging in essentially different categories but nevertheless having many similarities; PARALLEL suggests a marked likeness in the development of two things

sim·i·lar·i·ty \,sim-ə-'lar-ət-ē\ n, pl **-ties** **1** : the quality or state of being similar : RESEMBLANCE **2** : a point in which things are similar : CORRESPONDENCE **syn** see LIKENESS

sim·i·le \'sim-ə-(,)lē\ n [L, comparison, fr. neut. of *similis* like] : a figure of speech in which things different in kind or quality are compared by the use of the word *like* or *as* (as in *cheeks like roses*) — compare METAPHOR

si·mil·i·tude \sə-'mil-ə-,t(y)üd\ n **1 a** : COUNTERPART, DOUBLE **b** : a visible likeness : IMAGE **2** : an imaginative comparison **3** : SIMILARITY

sim·mer \'sim-ər\ vb **sim·mered; sim·mer·ing** \'sim-(ə-)riŋ\ [alter. of ME *simperen*] **1** : to stew gently below or just at the boiling point **2 a** : to be in a state of incipient development : FERMENT ⟨an idea *simmering* in the back of his mind⟩ **b** : to be in inward turmoil ⟨*simmered* with fury at the insult⟩ — **simmer** n

Si·mon \'sī-mən\ n **1** : PETER — called also *Simon Peter* **2** : one of the twelve disciples of Jesus — called also *Simon the Zealot* **3** : a Samaritan sorcerer converted by the evangelist Philip — called also *Simon Ma·gus* \,sī-mən-'mā-gəs\

si·mo·ni·ac \sī-'mō-nē-,ak, sə-\ n : one who practices simony — **simoniac** or **si·mo·ni·a·cal** \,sī-mə-'nī-ə-kəl, ,sim-ə-\ adj — **si·mo·ni·a·cal·ly** \-'nī-ə-k(ə-)lē\ adv

si·mo·nize \'sī-mə-,nīz\ vt [fr. *Simoniz*, a trademark] : to polish with or as if with wax

si·mon–pure \,sī-mən-'pyü(ə)r\ adj : of untainted purity or integrity; *also* : pretentiously or hypocritically pure

si·mo·ny \'sī-mə-nē, 'sim-ə-\ n [LL *simonia*, fr. *Simon Magus* (Acts 8:9–24)] : the buying or selling of a church office

si·moom \sə-'müm, sī-\ or **si·moon** \-'mün\ n [Ar *samūm*] : a hot dry violent wind laden with dust from Asian and African deserts

sim·pa·ti·co \sim-'pät-i-,kō, -'pat-\ adj [It, fr. *simpatia* sympathy, congeniality] : CONGENIAL, LIKABLE

¹sim·per \'sim-pər\ vi **sim·pered; sim·per·ing** \-p(ə-)riŋ\ : to smile in a foolish affected manner — **sim·per·er** \-pər-ər\ n

²simper n : a simpered smile : SMIRK

ə abut; ⁹ kitten; ər further; a back; ā bake; ä cot, cart; aù out; ch chin; e less; ē easy; g gift; i trip; ī life

¹sim·ple \'sim-pəl\ *adj* **sim·pler** \-p(ə-)lər\; **sim·plest** \-p(ə-)ləst\ [OF, plain, uncomplicated, artless, fr. L *simplus, simplex*] **1** : free from guile or vanity **2 a** : of humble origin **b** : deficient in education, experience, or intelligence **3** : free from complexity or complications: as **a** : free from elaboration or showiness ⟨a *simple* melody⟩ ⟨neat *simple* clothing⟩ **b** : not mixed or compounded with anything else ⟨a *simple* substance⟩ **c** : consisting of only one main clause and no subordinate clauses ⟨*simple* sentence⟩ **d** : not compound ⟨the *simple* noun "boat"⟩ ⟨a *simple* eye⟩ ⟨*simple* interest⟩ **e** (1) : not subdivided into branches or leaflets (2) : MONOCARPELLARY (3) : developing from a single ovary ⟨*simple* fruits⟩ **4 a** : UNMIXED, SHEER ⟨the *simple* truth⟩ **b** : unlikely to cause difficulty because of complexity or obscurity : STRAIGHT-FORWARD, EASY ⟨a *simple* explanation⟩ ⟨a *simple* text for young children⟩ — **sim·ple·ness** \-pəl-nəs\ *n*

syn SIMPLE, EASY mean not demanding great effort or involving difficulty. SIMPLE stresses lack of complexity or subtlety ⟨a *simple* case of theft⟩ EASY implies offering little resistance to being understood or accomplished or dealt with ⟨an *easy* problem⟩ ⟨an *easy* victory⟩

²simple *n* **1 a** : a person of humble station **b** : an ignorant or mentally retarded person **2 a** : a medicinal plant **b** : a vegetable drug having only one ingredient **3** : something incapable of further subdivision : a simple component

simple fraction *n* : a fraction having whole numbers for the numerator and denominator — compare COMPLEX FRACTION

simple fracture *n* : a breaking of a bone in such a way that the skin is not broken and bone fragments do not protrude

simple machine *n* : any of six elementary mechanisms having the elements of which all machines are composed and comprising the lever, the wheel and axle, the pulley, the inclined plane, the wedge, and the screw

sim·ple-mind·ed \,sim-pəl-'mīn-dəd\ *adj* : devoid of subtlety; *also* : FOOLISH — **sim·ple-mind·ed·ly** *adv* — **sim·ple-mind·ed·ness** *n*

simple sugar *n* : MONOSACCHARIDE

sim·ple·ton \'sim-pəl-tən\ *n* : a person lacking in common sense

simple vow *n* : a public vow taken by a religious in the Roman Catholic Church under which retention of property by the individual is permitted and marriage though regarded as a sin is valid under canon law

¹sim·plex \'sim-,pleks\ *adj* [L *simplic-, simplex*] : SIMPLE, SINGLE

²simplex *n, pl* **sim·pli·cia** \sim-'plish-(ē-)ə\ *or* **sim·pli·ces** \'sim-plə-,sēz\ : a word that is not a compound — **sim·pli·cial** \sim-'plish-əl\ *adj*

sim·plic·i·ty \sim-'plis-ət-ē\ *n, pl* **-ties** [L *simplic-, simplex* simple] **1** : the quality or state of being simple and esp. not compounded **2** : lack of subtlety : freedom from pretense or guile : HONESTY, STRAIGHTFORWARDNESS **3 a** : directness or clarity of expression **b** : restraint in ornamentation : PLAINNESS **4** : FOLLY, SILLINESS

sim·pli·fy \'sim-plə-,fī\ *vt* **-fied; -fy·ing** : to make simple or simpler — **sim·pli·fi·ca·tion** \,sim-plə-fə-'kā-shən\ *n* — **sim·pli·fi·er** \'sim-plə-,fī(-ə)r\ *n*

sim·ply \'sim-plē\ *adv* **1 a** : without ambiguity : CLEARLY ⟨stated the directions *simply*⟩ **b** : without embellishment : PLAINLY ⟨*simply* dressed⟩ **c** : DIRECTLY, CANDIDLY ⟨told the story as *simply* as a child would⟩ **2 a** : MERELY, SOLELY ⟨eats *simply* to keep alive⟩ **b** : LITERALLY, REALLY ⟨*simply* marvelous⟩

sim·u·la·crum \,sim-yə-'lāk-rəm, -'lak-\ *n, pl* **-cra** \-rə\ *also* **-crums** [L, fr. *simulare* to represent] **1** : IMAGE, REPRESENTATION **2** : an insubstantial form or semblance of something : SHADOW; *also* : TRACE

sim·u·late \'sim-yə-,lāt\ *vt* [L *simulare* to copy, represent, feign, fr. *similis* like] : to give the appearance or effect of : FEIGN, IMITATE — **sim·u·la·tive** \-,lāt-iv\ *adj* — **sim·u·la·tor** \-,lāt-ər\ *n*

simulated rank *n* : a civilian status equivalent to a military rank ⟨the head of research had the *simulated rank* of colonel⟩

sim·u·la·tion \,sim-yə-'lā-shən\ *n* **1** : the act or process of simulating **2** : a sham object : COUNTERFEIT

si·mul·cast \'sī-məl-,kast\ *vb* : to broadcast simulta-

neously by AM and FM radio or by radio and television — **simulcast** *n*

si·mul·ta·ne·ous \,sī-məl-'tā-nē-əs\ *adj* [(assumed) ML *simultaneus*, fr. L *simul* at the same time] **1** : existing or occurring at the same time : COINCIDENT **2** : satisfied by the same values of the variables ⟨*simultaneous* equations⟩ **syn** see CONTEMPORARY — **si·mul·ta·ne·i·ty** \-tə-'nē-ət-ē\ *n* — **si·mul·ta·ne·ous·ly** \-'tā-nē-əs-lē\ *adv* — **si·mul·ta·ne·ous·ness** *n*

¹sin \'sin\ *n* [OE *synn*] **1 a** : an offense against God **b** : a weakened state of human nature in which the self is estranged from God **2** : MISDEED, FAULT

²sin *vi* **sinned; sin·ning** : to commit a sin

Sin·an·thro·pus \sī-'nan(t)-thrə-pəs, ,sī-,nan-'thrō-\ *n* : PEKING MAN

¹since \(')sin(t)s\ *adv* [ME *sithens, sins*, fr. *sithen*, fr. OE *siththan*, fr. *sith tham* since that] **1** : from a definite past time until now ⟨has stayed there ever *since*⟩ **2** : before the present time : AGO ⟨long *since* dead⟩ **3** : after a time in the past : SUBSEQUENTLY ⟨has *since* become rich⟩

²since *prep* : from or after a specified time in the past ⟨improvements made *since* 1928⟩ ⟨happy *since* then⟩

³since *conj* **1** : at a time or times in the past after or later than ⟨has held two jobs *since* he graduated⟩ **2** : from the time in the past when ⟨ever *since* he was a child⟩ **3** : in view of the fact that : BECAUSE ⟨*since* it was raining he wore a hat⟩ **syn** see BECAUSE

sin·cere \sin-'si(ə)r\ *adj* [L *sincerus*] : being the same in fact as in appearance: as **a** : free from dissimulation : HONEST ⟨a *sincere* friend⟩ ⟨a *sincere* interest in study⟩ **b** : free from adulteration : PURE ⟨*sincere* doctrine⟩ **c** : true to self or nature : GENUINE ⟨a *sincere* work of art⟩ — **sin·cere·ly** *adv* — **sin·cere·ness** *n* — **sin·cer·i·ty** \-'ser-ət-ē, -'sir-\ *n*

sin·ci·put \'sin(t)-sə-(,)pət\ *n, pl* **sinciputs** *or* **sin·cip·i·ta** \sin-'sip-ət-ə\ [L *sincipit-, sinciput* half a head, fr. *semi-* + *caput* head] **1** : FOREHEAD **2** : the upper half of the skull — **sin·cip·i·tal** \sin-'sip-ət-°l\ *adj*

Sind·bad the Sailor \'sin-,bad-\ *n* : a citizen of Baghdad whose adventures are narrated in the *Arabian Nights' Entertainments*

sine \'sīn\ *n* [ML *sinus*, fr. L, curve, bosom] : a trigonometric function that for an acute angle in a right triangle is the ratio of the side opposite the angle to the hypotenuse

si·ne·cure \'sī-ni-kyúr, 'sin-i-\ *n* [ML *sine cura* without cure of souls] : an office or position that requires little or no work

si·ne die \,sī-ni-'dī-,ē, ,sin-ē-'dē-,ā\ *adv* [L, without a (fixed) day] : INDEFINITELY ⟨the meeting adjourned *sine die*⟩

si·ne qua non \,sin-ē-,kwä-'nōn, ,sī-nē-,kwä-'nän\ *n* [LL, without which not] : something absolutely essential or indispensable

sin·ew \'sin-yü, 'sin-ü\ *n* [OE *seono*] **1** : TENDON; *esp* : one dressed for use as a cord or thread **2** *obs* : NERVE **3 a** : solid resilient strength : POWER **b** : the chief supporting force — usu. used in pl.

sine wave *n* : a wave form that represents periodic oscillations in which the amplitude of displacement at each point is proportional to the sine of the phase angle of the displacement

sin·ewy \'sin-(y)ə-wē\ *adj* **1** : full of sinews : TOUGH, STRINGY ⟨*sinewy* meat⟩ **2** : STRONG ⟨*sinewy* arms⟩

sin·fo·nia \,sin-fə-'nē-ə\ *n, pl* **-nie** \-'nē-,ā\ [It, fr. L *symphonia* symphony] **1** : an orchestral musical composition found in 18th century opera **2** : SYMPHONY 2

sin·fo·niet·ta \,sin-fən-'yet-ə\ *n* **1** : a symphony of less than standard length or for fewer instruments **2** : a small symphony orchestra; *esp* : an orchestra of strings only

sin·ful \'sin-fəl\ *adj* : marked by or full of sin : WICKED — **sin·ful·ly** \-fə-lē\ *adv* — **sin·ful·ness** *n*

¹sing \'sin\ *vb* **sang** \'san\ *or* **sung** \'sən\; **sung; sing·ing** \'sin-in\ [OE *singan*] **1 a** : to produce musical sounds by means of the voice ⟨*sing* for joy⟩ **b** : to utter with musical sounds ⟨*sing* a song⟩; *also* : CHANT, INTONE ⟨*sing* mass⟩ **2** : to make pleasing musical sounds ⟨birds *singing* at dawn⟩ **3** : to make a slight shrill sound ⟨a kettle *singing* on the stove⟩ **4 a** : to tell a story in poetry : relate in verse **b** : to express vividly and enthusiastically ⟨*sing* her praises⟩ **5** : HUM, BUZZ, RING ⟨ears *singing* from the sudden descent⟩ **6** : to act on or affect by singing ⟨*sing* a baby to sleep⟩ ⟨*sing* the blues away⟩ **7 a** : to call aloud

: cry out ⟨*sing* out when you find them⟩ **b** : to divulge information or give evidence — **sing·a·ble** \'sin-ə-bəl\ *adj*

²sing *n* : a singing esp. in company

¹singe \'sinj\ *vb* **singed** \'sinjd\; **singe·ing** \'sin-jiŋ\ [OE *sengan*] : to burn superficially or lightly : SCORCH; *esp* : to remove hair, down, or fuzz from usu. by passing briefly over a flame

²singe *n* : a slight burn : SCORCH

¹sing·er \'siŋ-ər\ *n* : one that sings

²sing·er \'sin-jər\ *n* : one that singes

singing bird *n* **1** : SONGBIRD 1 **2** : a passerine bird

¹sin·gle \'siŋ-gəl\ *adj* [L *singulus* one only] **1** : UNMARRIED **2** : being alone : being the only one **3 a** (1) : having only one part or feature ⟨*single* consonant⟩ (2) : of or relating to one of two or more aspects or parts (3) : consisting of one ⟨*single* standard⟩ ⟨holds to a *single* ideal⟩ **b** : having but one whorl of petals or ray flowers ⟨a *single* rose⟩ **4 a** : consisting of a separate unique whole : INDIVIDUAL ⟨each *single* citizen⟩ **b** : of, relating to, or involving only one person **5** : FRANK, HONEST ⟨a *single* devotion⟩ **6** : UNBROKEN, UNDIVIDED **7** : engaged in man to man ⟨fight in *single* combat⟩ **8** : having no equal or like : SINGULAR **9** : designed for the use of one person or family only ⟨a *single* house⟩ — **sin·gle·ness** *n*

syn SOLITARY, SOLE, UNIQUE: SINGLE implies being unaccompanied or unassisted by any other ⟨operated by a *single* worker⟩ ⟨a *single* line of trees⟩ SOLITARY implies being both single and isolated ⟨*solitary* oak in a field⟩ SOLE implies being the only one existing or acting ⟨*sole* reason for refusing⟩ ⟨*sole* survivor of the wreck⟩ UNIQUE implies being the only one of its kind or character in existence ⟨*unique* specimen of a coin issue⟩

²single *n* **1** : a separate individual person or thing **2** : ONE-BASE HIT **3** *pl* : a game (as of tennis or golf) between two players

³single *vb* **sin·gled; sin·gling** \'siŋ-g(ə-)liŋ\ **1** : to select or distinguish (a person or thing) from a number or group ⟨*single* out the runt of the litter⟩ **2** : to make a one-base hit in baseball

sin·gle-breast·ed \,siŋ-gəl-'bres-təd\ *adj* : having a center closing with one row of buttons and no lap ⟨*single-breasted* coat⟩

single combat *n* : combat between two persons

single entry *n* : a method of bookkeeping that shows only one side of a business transaction and usu. consists only of a record of accounts with debtors and creditors

single file *n* : a line of persons or things arranged one behind another — **single file** *adv*

¹sin·gle-foot \'siŋ-gəl-,fut\ *n, pl* **single-foots** : ⁴RACK b

²single-foot *vi* : to go at a rack — **sin·gle-foot·er** *n*

sin·gle-hand·ed \,siŋ-gəl-'han-dəd\ *adj* **1** : managed or done by one person or with one hand **2** : working alone : lacking help — **sin·gle-hand·ed·ly** *adv* — **sin·gle-hand·ed·ness** *n*

sin·gle-heart·ed \-'härt-əd\ *adj* : characterized by sincerity and unity of purpose — **sin·gle-heart·ed·ly** *adv* — **sin·gle-heart·ed·ness** *n*

sin·gle-mind·ed \-'mīn-dəd\ *adj* **1** : SINCERE, SINGLEHEARTED **2** : having one overriding purpose — **sin·gle-mind·ed·ly** *adv* — **sin·gle-mind·ed·ness** *n*

sin·gle-space \-'spās\ *vt* : to type or print with no blank lines between lines of copy

sin·gle·stick \'siŋ-gəl-,stik\ *n* : fighting or fencing with a one-handed wooden stick or sword; *also* : the weapon used

sin·glet \'siŋ-glət\ *n, chiefly Brit* : an athletic jersey : UNDERSHIRT

single tax *n* : a tax to be levied on a single object as the sole source of public revenue

sin·gle·ton \'siŋ-gəl-tən\ *n* [F, fr. E *single*] **1** : a playing card that is the only one of its suit orig. held in a hand **2** : an individual distinct from others grouped with it

sin·gle·tree \-(,)trē\ *n* : WHIFFLETREE

sin·gly \'siŋ-g(ə-)lē\ *adv* **1** : by or with oneself **2** : INDIVIDUALLY **2** : SINGLE-HANDEDLY

¹sing·song \'siŋ-,soŋ\ *n* : a monotonous rhythm or a monotonous rise and fall of pitch; *also* : speech or voice marked by this

²singsong *adj* : having a monotonous cadence or rhythm

¹sin·gu·lar \'siŋ-gyə-lər\ *adj* [L *singularis*, fr. *singulus*

only one] **1 a** : of or relating to a separate person or thing : INDIVIDUAL **b** : of, relating to, or constituting a word form denoting one person, thing, or instance **c** : of or relating to a single instance or to something considered by itself **2 a** : distinguished by superiority : EXCEPTIONAL **b** : of unusual quality : UNIQUE **3** : being at variance with others : PECULIAR ⟨holding *singular* views of civic responsibility⟩ — **sin·gu·lar·ly** *adv*

²singular *n* : something that is singular; *esp* : the singular number, the inflectional form denoting it, or a word in that form

sin·gu·lar·i·ty \,siŋ-gyə-'lar-ət-ē\ *n, pl* **-ties** **1** : the quality or state of being singular **2** : something that is singular : PECULIARITY, ECCENTRICITY

sin·gu·lar·ize \'siŋ-gyə-lə-,rīz\ *vt* : to make singular

Sin·ha·lese \,sin-(h)ə-'lēz, -'lēs\ *or* **Sin·gha·lese** \,siŋ-gə-\ *n* **1** : a member of a people forming a major part of the population of Ceylon **2** : the Indic language of the Sinhalese people — **Sinhalese** *adj*

sin·is·ter \'sin-ə-stər\ *adj* [L, being on the left side, inauspicious] **1** : singularly evil or productive of evil : BAD, CORRUPTIVE **2** : of, relating to, or situated to the left or on the left side of something **3** : presaging or leading to ill fortune or trouble : OMINOUS — **sin·is·ter·ly** *adv* — **sin·is·ter·ness** *n*

sin·is·tral \'sin-ə-strəl\ *adj* : of, relating to, or inclined to the left; *esp* : LEFT-HANDED — **sin·is·tral·ly** \-strə-lē\ *adv*

sin·is·trorse \'sin-ə-,strórs\ *adj* [L *sinistrorsus* toward the left side, fr. *sinister* left + *versus*, pp. of *vertere* to turn] : twining spirally upward around an axis from right to left — used of a plant axis; compare DEXTRORSE — **sin·is·trorse·ly** *adv*

¹sink \'siŋk\ *vb* **sank** \'saŋk\ *or* **sunk** \'səŋk\; **sunk; sink·ing** [OE *sincan*] **1 a** : to move or cause to move downward usu. so as to be submerged or swallowed up ⟨feet *sinking* into deep mud⟩ **b** : to descend gradually lower and lower ⟨the sun *sank* behind the hills⟩ **c** : to fall to a lower level ⟨the lake *sank* during the drought⟩ **2** : to lessen in amount or intensity: as **a** : to make or become less active or vigorous ⟨*sank* his voice to a whisper⟩ ⟨the fire *sank* into ashes⟩ **b** : to fall to or into an inferior status (as of quality, worth, or number) : RETROGRESS, DECLINE ⟨*sink* into decay⟩ ⟨the population *sank* through war and famine⟩ **c** : to fail in strength, spirits, or health esp. from some burdening pressure ⟨his heart *sank* as he viewed the wreckage⟩ ⟨the old man was *sinking* fast⟩ **d** : RESTRAIN, SUBORDINATE ⟨*sinking* her pride she apologized⟩ **3 a** : to penetrate or cause to penetrate ⟨*sank* his ax into the tree⟩ ⟨the pile *sank* into the earth⟩ **b** : to become absorbed ⟨the water *sank* into the dry ground⟩; *also* : to be taken in so as to be apprehended and retained ⟨such a lesson will *sink* in⟩ **4** : to form by digging or boring usu. in the earth ⟨*sink* a well⟩ **5 a** : INVEST **b** : to spend or invest unwisely or without expectation of a return — **sink·a·ble** \'siŋ-kə-bəl\ *adj*

²sink *n* **1 a** : CESSPOOL **b** : SEWER **c** : a stationary basin for washing (as in a kitchen) connected with a drain and usu. a water supply **2** : a place where vice, corruption, or evil collect **3** : a depression in the land surface; *esp* : one having a saline lake with no outlet

sink·age \'siŋ-kij\ *n* : the act, process, or degree of sinking

sink·er \'siŋ-kər\ *n* **1** : one that sinks; *esp* : a weight for sinking a line or net **2** : DOUGHNUT

sink·hole \'siŋk-,hōl\ *n* : a hollow place in which drainage collects

sinking fund *n* : a fund set up and accumulated by usu. regular deposits for paying off the principal of a debt when it falls due

sin·less \'sin-ləs\ *adj* : free from sin : IMPECCABLE, HOLY — **sin·less·ly** *adv* — **sin·less·ness** *n*

sin·ner \'sin-ər\ *n* : one that sins

Si·no- \'sī-nō\ *comb form* [Gk *Sinai*, pl., the Chinese] **1** : Chinese ⟨*Sino*phile⟩ **2** : Chinese and ⟨*Sino*-Tibetan⟩

sin·ter \'sint-ər\ *vt* [G *sintern*, fr. *sinter* slag] : to cause to become a coherent nonporous mass by heating without melting

sin·u·ate \'sin-yə-wət, -,wāt\ *adj* : having the margin wavy with strong indentations ⟨*sinuate* leaves⟩ — **sin·u·ate·ly** *adv*

sin·u·os·i·ty \,sin-yə-'wäs-ət-ē\ *n, pl* **-ties** **1** : the quality or state of being sinuous **2 :** something that is sinuous **:** winding turn

sin·u·ous \'sin-yə-wəs\ *adj* [L *sinus* curve] **1 a :** of a serpentine or wavy form **:** WINDING   **b :** marked by strong lithe movements **2 :** INTRICATE, COMPLEX   **3 :** SINUATE — **sin·u·ous·ly** *adv* — **sin·u·ous·ness** *n*

si·nus \'sī-nəs\ *n* [NL, fr. L, curve, hollow, bosom] **:** CAVITY, HOLLOW: as   **a :** a narrow passage by which pus is discharged   **b :** any of several cavities in the skull mostly communicating with the nostrils   **c :** a dilatation in a bodily canal or vessel; *also* **:** a space forming a channel (as for the passage of blood)   **d :** a cleft or indentation between adjoining lobes (as of a leaf)

si·nus·i·tis \ˌsī-nə-'sīt-əs\ *n* **:** inflammation of a sinus esp. of the skull

si·nus ve·no·sus \ˌsī-nəs-vi-'nō-səs\ *n* [NL, venous sinus] **:** an enlarged pouch which adjoins the heart and through which venous blood enters the heart in lower vertebrates and embryos

Si·on \'sī-ən\ *var of* ZION

Siou·an \'sü-ən\ *n* **1 :** a language stock of central and eastern No. America **2 :** a member of a group of peoples speaking Siouan languages

Sioux \'sü\ *n, pl* **Sioux** \'sü(z)\ **1 :** DAKOTA   **2 :** SIOUAN

¹sip \'sip\ *vb* **sipped; sip·ping** [ME *sippen*] **1 :** to drink in small quantities or little by little **2 :** to take sips from **:** TASTE — **sip·per** *n*

²sip *n* **1 :** the act of sipping **2 :** a small amount taken by sipping

¹si·phon \'sī-fən\ *n* [Gk *siphōn* tube, siphon] **1 a :** a tube bent to form two legs of unequal length by which a liquid can be transferred to a lower level over an intermediate elevation by the pressure of the atmosphere in forcing the liquid up the shorter branch of the tube immersed in it while the excess of weight of the liquid in the longer branch when once filled causes a continuous flow   **b** *usu* **sy·phon :** a bottle for holding carbonated water that is driven out through a bent tube in its neck by the pressure of the gas when a valve in the tube is opened **2 :** any of various tubular organs in animals and esp. mollusks or arthropods used for drawing in or ejecting fluids

a siphon, b vessel

²siphon *vb* **si·phoned; si·phon·ing** \'sīf-(ə-)niŋ\ **:** to draw off or pass off by or as if by a siphon

si·phon·o·phore \sī-'fän-ə-ˌfōr, -ˌfór\ *n* **:** any of an order (Siphonophora) of mostly delicate, transparent, and colored compound hydrozoans

sir \(')sər\ *n* [ME, fr. *sire*] **1 :** a man entitled to be addressed as *sir* — used as a title before the given name of a knight or baronet **2 a :** used as a usu. respectful form of address   **b** *cap* — used as a conventional form of address in the salutation of a letter

sir·dar \'sər-,där\ *n* [Hindi *sardār*, fr. Per] **:** a person of high rank or holding a position of responsibility esp. in India

¹si·re \'sī(ə)r\ *n* [OF, fr. L *senior*, adj., senior] **1 a :** FATHER   **b** *archaic* **:** FOREFATHER   **c :** ORIGINATOR, AUTHOR **2** *archaic* **:** a man of rank or authority; *esp* **:** LORD — used formerly as a form of address and as a title **3 :** the male parent of an animal and esp. of a domestic animal

²sire *vt* **1 :** BEGET, PROCREATE — used esp. of domestic animals **2 :** to bring into being **:** ORIGINATE

¹si·ren \'sī-rən, *for 3 also* sī-'rēn\ *n* [Gk *seirēn*] **1** *often cap* **:** one of a group of creatures in Greek mythology depicted as birds with the heads and sometimes the breasts and arms of women that lured mariners to destruction by their singing **2 :** a woman who is insidiously seductive **:** TEMPTRESS **3 a :** an apparatus producing musical tones by the rapid interruption of a current (as of air or steam) by a perforated rotating disk   **b :** a device often electrically operated for producing a penetrating warning sound ⟨ambulance *siren*⟩ ⟨air-raid *siren*⟩ **4 a :** any of a genus of eel-shaped amphibians with small forelimbs but neither hind legs nor pelvis and with permanent external gills as well as lungs   **b :** SIRENIAN

²si·ren \'sī-rən\ *also* **si·ren·ic** \sī-'ren-ik, -'rēn-\ *adj* **:** of or relating to a siren **:** ENTICING, BEWITCHING ⟨a *siren* song⟩

si·re·ni·an \sī-'rē-nē-ən\ *n* **:** any of an order (Sirenia) of aquatic herbivorous mammals including the manatee and dugong

siren song *n* **:** an alluring utterance or appeal; *esp* **:** one that is seductive or dangerous

Sir·i·us \'sir-ē-əs\ *n* [L, fr. Gk *Seirios*] **:** a star of the constellation Canis Major constituting the brightest star in the heavens — called also *Dog Star*

sir·loin \'sər-,lóin\ *n* [MF *surlonge*, fr. *sur* over (fr. L *super*) + *loigne, longe* loin] **:** a cut of meat and esp. of beef from the part of the hindquarter just in front of the round

si·roc·co \sə-'räk-ō\ *n, pl* **-cos** [It, fr. Ar *sharq* east] **1 a :** a hot dust-laden wind from the Libyan desert that blows on the northern Mediterranean coast chiefly in Italy, Malta, and Sicily   **b :** a warm moist oppressive southeast wind in the same regions **2 :** a hot or warm wind of cyclonic origin from an arid or heated region

sir·rah *also* **sir·ra** \'sir-ə\ *n, obs* — used as a form of address implying inferiority and often in anger or contempt

sir·ree *also* **sir·ee** \(ˌ)sər-'ē\ *n* **:** SIR — used as an emphatic form usu. after *yes* or *no*

Sir Rog·er de Cov·er·ley \sə(r)-ˌräj-ərd-i-'kəv-ər-lē\ *n* **:** an English country-dance performed in two straight lines by an indefinite number

sirup, sirupy *var of* SYRUP, SYRUPY

si·sal \'sī-səl, -zəl\ *n* [*Sisal*, Mexico] **1 :** a strong durable white fiber used for cordage **2 :** a widely grown West Indian agave whose leaves yield sisal

sis·kin \'sis-kən\ *n* [G dial. *sisschen*] **:** a small chiefly greenish and yellowish Old World finch related to the goldfinch

sis·si·fied \'sis-i-,fīd\ *adj* **:** SISSY

sis·sy \'sis-ē\ *n, pl* **sissies** [*sis*, short for *sister*] **:** an effeminate man or boy; *also* **:** a timid or cowardly person — **sissy** *adj*

¹sis·ter \'sis-tər\ *n* [ME *suster* (fr. OE *sweostor*) & *sister*, fr. ON *systir*] **1 a :** a female person or lower animal viewed in relation to another person or animal having one or both parents in common   **b :** SISTER-IN-LAW   **c :** a kinswoman by blood **2** *often cap* **:** a member of a religious society of women; *esp* **:** one of a Roman Catholic congregation under simple vows **3 a :** a woman related to another by a common tie or interest   **b :** one having similar characteristics to another **4** *chiefly Brit* **:** NURSE

²sister *adj* **:** having or suggesting the relationship of a sister ⟨*sister* ships⟩

sis·ter·hood \-,hùd\ *n* **1 a :** the state of being a sister   **b :** sisterly relationship **2 :** a community or society of sisters; *esp* **:** a society of women religious

sis·ter–in–law \'sis-t(ə-)rən-,lò, -tərn-,lò\ *n, pl* **sis·ters–in–law** \-tər-zən-\ **1 :** the sister of one's spouse **2 a :** the wife of one's brother   **b :** the wife of one's spouse's brother

sis·ter·ly \'sis-tər-lē\ *adj* **:** of, relating to, or having the characteristics of a sister — **sisterly** *adv*

Sis·tine \'sis-,tēn, sis-'\ *adj* [It *sistino*, fr. NL *sixtinus*, fr. *Sixtus*] **1 :** of or relating to any of the popes named Sixtus **2 :** of or relating to the Sistine chapel in the Vatican

sis·trum \'sis-trəm\ *n* [Gk *seistron*, fr. *seiein* to shake] **:** an ancient Egyptian percussion instrument consisting of a thin metal frame with transverse metal rods that jingle when shaken

Sis·y·phus \'sis-i-fəs\ *n* **:** a legendary King of Corinth condemned to roll a heavy stone up a steep hill in Hades only to have it roll down again as it neared the top — **Sis·y·phe·an** \ˌsis-i-'fē-ən\ *adj*

¹sit \'sit\ *vb* **sat** \'sat\; **sit·ting** [OE *sittan*] **1 a :** to rest upon the buttocks or haunches ⟨*sit* in a chair⟩; *also* **:** to cause (as oneself) thus to rest **:** SEAT ⟨*sat* him down to write a letter⟩   **b :** PERCH, ROOST   **c :** to keep one's seat upon ⟨*sit* a horse⟩   **d :** to provide seats or seating room for ⟨car will *sit* six people⟩ **2 :** to occupy a place as a member of an official body ⟨*sit* in Congress⟩ **3 :** to hold a session **4 :** to cover eggs for hatching **:** BROOD   **5 a :** to pose for a portrait or photograph   **b :** to serve as a model **6 :** to lie or hang relative to a wearer ⟨the collar *sits* awkwardly⟩ **7 :** to lie or rest in any condition **8 a :** to have a location ⟨house *sits* well back from the road⟩   **b :** to blow from a certain direction ⟨the wind *sits* in the west⟩ **9 :** to remain inactive ⟨the car *sits* in the garage⟩ **10 :** BABY-SIT — **sit**

on 1 : to hold deliberations concerning **2** : REPRESS, SQUELCH **3** : to delay action or decision concerning : SUPPRESS — **sit on one's hands 1** : to withhold applause **2** : to fail to take action — **sit pretty** : to be in a highly favorable situation — **sit tight** : to maintain one's position without change — **sit under** : to attend the classes or lectures of (a teacher)

²**sit** n **1** : an act or period of sitting **2** : the manner in which a garment fits

sit-down \'sit-,daún\ n : a strike in which the workers stop work and refuse to leave their places of employment — called also *sit-down strike*

¹**site** \'sīt\ n [L *situs* place, position, fr. *sit-, sinere* to leave, place, lay] **1 a** : local position (as of a building, town, or monument) **b** : a space of ground occupied or to be occupied by a building **2** : the place or scene of something (as a significant event) ⟨famous battle *sites*⟩

²**site** vt : to place on a site or in position : LOCATE

sith \'(')sith\ adv *archaic var of* SINCE

sit-in \'sit-,in\ n **1** : SIT-DOWN **2** : an act of occupying seats in a racially segregated establishment in organized protest against discrimination

sit·ter \'sit-ər\ n : one that sits; *esp* : BABY-SITTER

¹**sit·ting** \'sit-iŋ\ n **1** : an act of one that sits; *esp* : a single occasion of continuous sitting **2 a** : a brooding over eggs for hatching **b** : SETTING 6 **3** : SESSION ⟨*sitting* of the legislature⟩

²**sitting** adj **1** : that is setting ⟨*sitting* hen⟩ **2** : easily hit ⟨*sitting* target⟩ **3 a** : used in or for sitting ⟨a *sitting* position⟩ **b** : performed while sitting ⟨a *sitting* shot⟩

sitting duck n : an easy or defenseless target (as for attack or criticism)

sitting room n : LIVING ROOM

¹**sit·u·ate** \'sich-ə-,wāt, -,wāt\ adj [ML *situatus*, pp. of *situare* to place, fr. L *situs* site] : having its site : LOCATED

²**sit·u·ate** \'sich-ə-,wāt\ vt : to place in a site or situation : LOCATE

sit·u·at·ed \-,wāt-əd\ adj **1** : LOCATED **2** : CIRCUM-STANCED, FIXED ⟨not rich but comfortably *situated*⟩

sit·u·a·tion \,sich-ə-'wā-shən\ n **1 a** : the way in which something is placed in relation to its surroundings **b** : SITE **2 a** : position or place of employment : POST, JOB **b** : position in life : STATUS **3** : position with respect to conditions and circumstances ⟨military *situation*⟩ **4 a** : relative position or combination of circumstances at a certain moment ⟨the *situation* seemed to call for a general retreat⟩ **b** : a particular or striking complex of affairs at a stage in the action of a narrative or drama — **sit·u·a·tion·al** \-shnəl, -shən-⁹l\ adj — **sit·u·a·tion·al·ly** \-ē\ adv

si·tus \'sīt-əs\ n [L, site] : the place where something exists or originates

sitz bath \'sits-\ n [part trans. of G *sitzbad*, fr. *sitz* act of sitting + *bad* bath] : a tub in which one bathes in a sitting posture; *also* : a bath so taken esp. therapeutically

sitz·mark \'sits-,märk\ n [G *sitzmarke*, fr. *sitzen* to sit + *marke* mark] : a depression left in the snow by a skier falling backward

Si·va \'s(h)ē-və\ n : a Hindu god who represents the principle of destruction in the sacred triad and in a major cult is worshiped as the gracious creator and sustainer of the world — compare BRAHMA, VISHNU — **Si·va·ism** \-,iz-əm\ n

Si·wash \'sī-,wȯsh, -,wäsh\ n [*Siwash*, fictional college in stories by George Fitch] : a small rus. inland college that is notably provincial in outlook ⟨cheer for dear old *Siwash*⟩

six \'siks\ n [OE *siex*] **1** — see NUMBER table **2** : the sixth in a set or series **3** : something having six units or members; *esp* : a 6-cylinder engine or automobile — **six** adj or pron — **at sixes and sevens** : in disorder : CON-FUSED

six-gun \'siks-,gən\ n : a 6-chambered revolver — called also *six-shoot·er* \'sik(s)-'shüt-ər\

six-o-six or **606** \,siks-,ō-'siks\ n : ARSPHENAMINE

six-pack \'siks-,pak\ n : an open paperboard carton containing six bottles or cans (as of a beverage) and usu. having a handle for carrying

six·pence \'siks-pən(t)s, US also -,pen(t)s\ n : the sum of six pence; *also* : a coin representing six pence or half a shilling

six·pen·ny \-pə-nē, US also -,pen-ē\ adj **1** : of the value

of or costing sixpence **2** : of trifling worth : CHEAP, TRASHY

six·teen \(')siks-'tēn\ n — see NUMBER table — **sixteen** adj or pron — **six·teenth** \-'tēn(t)th\ adj or n

sixteenth note n : a musical note with the time value of one sixteenth of a whole note

sixth \'siks(t)th, 'sikst\ n — see NUMBER table — **sixth** adj or adv — **sixth·ly** \-lē\ adv

sixth sense n : a keen intuitive power

Six·tine \'sik-,stīn, -,stēn\ var of SISTINE

six·ty \'sik-stē\ n — see NUMBER table — **six-ti·eth** \-stē-əth\ adj or n — **sixty** adj or pron

six·ty-fourth note \,sik-stē-'fȯrth-, -'fȯrth-\ n : a musical note with half the time value of a thirty-second note

siz·a·ble or **size·a·ble** \'sī-zə-bəl\ adj : fairly large : CONSIDERABLE — **siz·a·ble·ness** n — **siz·a·bly** \-blē\ adv

siz·ar also **siz·er** \'sī-zər\ n : a student (as in the universities of Cambridge and Dublin) who receives an allowance toward his college expenses

¹**size** \'sīz\ n [ME *sise* assize, regulation, fixed standard, fr. OF, short for *assise* assize] **1 a** : physical magnitude, extent, or bulk : relative or proportionate dimensions **b** : BIGNESS **2** : one of a series of graduated measures esp. of manufactured articles (as of clothing) conventionally identified by numbers or letters ⟨a *size* 7 hat⟩ **3** : character or status of a person or thing esp. with reference to importance, merit, or correspondence to needs **4** : actual state of affairs : true condition ⟨that's about the *size* of it⟩

²**size** vb **1** : to make a particular size : bring to proper or suitable size **2** : to arrange, grade, or classify according to size or bulk

³**size** n [ME *sise*] : a gluey material (as a preparation of glue, flour, varnish, or resins) used for filling the pores in a surface (as of plaster), as a stiffener (as of fabric), or as an adhesive for applying color or leaf to book edges or covers

⁴**size** vt : to apply size to

⁵**size** adj : SIZED ⟨medium-*size*⟩

sized \'sīzd\ adj **1** : having a specified size or bulk ⟨a small-*sized* house⟩ **2** : arranged or adjusted according to size

size up vb **1** : to form a judgment of ⟨*size up* a situation⟩ **2** : to equal in size or some particular : measure up : COMPARE — often used with *to* or *with*

siz·ing \'sī-ziŋ\ n : ³SIZE

¹**siz·zle** \'siz-əl\ vb **siz·zled; siz·zling** \'siz-(ə-)liŋ\ **1** : to burn up or sear with a hissing sound **2** : to make a hissing sound in or as if in burning or frying **3** : to seethe with deeply felt anger or resentment — **siz·zler** \-(ə-)lər\ n

²**sizzle** n : a hissing sound (as of something frying over a fire)

skald \'skȯld, 'skäld\ n [ON *skāld*] : an ancient Scandinavian poet or writer of history — **skald·ic** \-ik\ adj

¹**skate** \'skāt\ n [ON *skata*] : any of numerous rays with broadly developed pectoral fins

²**skate** n [D *schaats* stilt, skate] **1 a** : a metallic runner that has a frame usu. shaped to fit the sole of a shoe to which it is attached and that is used for gliding on ice **2** : ROLLER SKATE

³**skate** vi **1** : to glide along on skates propelled by the alternate action of the legs **2** : to slip or glide as if on skates — **skat·er** n

⁴**skate** n **1** : a thin awkward-looking or decrepit horse : NAG **2** : FELLOW

ske·dad·dle \ski-'dad-⁹l\ vi -**dad·dled; -dad·dling** \-'dad-liŋ, -⁹l-iŋ\ : to run away; *esp* : to flee in a panic

skeet \'skēt\ n [ON *skjōta* to shoot] : trapshooting in which clay targets are thrown in such a way as to simulate the angle of flight of a flushed game bird

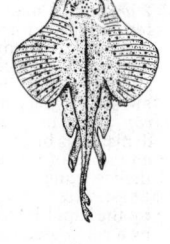

skate

¹**skein** \'skān\ n [MF *escaigne*] **1** or **skean** or **skeane** \'skān\ : a looped length of yarn or thread put up in a loose twist after it is taken from the reel **2** : something suggesting the twists or coils of a skein : TANGLE

²**skein** vt : to wind into skeins ⟨*skein* yarn⟩

skel·e·tal \'skel-ət-⁹l\ adj : of, relating or attached to, forming, or resembling a skeleton ⟨*skeletal* muscles⟩ ⟨the *skeletal* system⟩ — **skel·e·tal·ly** \-°l-ē\ *adv*

¹**skel·e·ton** \'skel-ət-°n\ *n* [Gk, neut. of *skeletos* dried up] **1** : a usu. rigid supporting or protecting structure or framework of an organism; *esp* : the bony or sometimes cartilaginous framework supporting the soft tissues and protecting the internal organs of a vertebrate (as a fish or man) **2** : something reduced to its minimum form or essential parts **3** : an emaciated person or animal **4** : something forming a structural framework **5** : something shameful and kept secret (as in a family)

²**skeleton** *adj* : of, consisting of, or resembling a skeleton ⟨a *skeleton* hand⟩ ⟨a *skeleton* crew⟩ ⟨*skeleton* essays⟩

skel·e·ton·ize \'skel-ət-°n-,īz\ *vt* : to produce in or reduce to skeleton form

skel·e·ton·iz·er \-,ī-zər\ *n* : a moth or butterfly larva that feeds on the parenchyma of leaves reducing them to a skeleton of veins

skeleton key *n* : a key made to open many locks

skel·ter \'skel-tər\ *vi* : SCURRY

skep \'skep\ *n* [ME *skeppe* basket, skep, fr. OE *sceppe* basketful] : a domed beehive made of twisted straw

skep·tic \'skep-tik\ *n* [Gk *skeptikos*, fr. *skeptesthai* to look, consider] **1** : an adherent or advocate of skepticism **2** : a person disposed to skepticism esp. regarding religion or religious principles

skep·ti·cal \-ti-kəl\ *adj* : relating to, characteristic of, or marked by skepticism — **skep·ti·cal·ly** \-k(ə-)lē\ *adv*

skep·ti·cism \'skep-tə-,siz-əm\ *n* **1** **a** : the doctrine that true knowledge or knowledge in a particular area is uncertain **b** : the method of suspended judgment, systematic doubt, or criticism characteristic of skeptics **2** : an attitude of doubt esp. concerning basic religious principles (as immortality, revelation)

sker·ry \'sker-ē\ *n, pl* **skerries** : a rocky isle : REEF

¹**sketch** \'skech\ *n* [D *schets*, fr. It *schizzo*, lit., splash, fr. *schizzare* to splash] **1** **a** : a rough drawing representing the chief features of an object or scene and often made as a preliminary study **b** : a tentative draft (as for a literary work) **2** : a brief description or outline **3** **a** : a short literary composition somewhat resembling the short story and the essay but intentionally slight in treatment and familiar in tone **b** : a short instrumental composition **c** : a slight theatrical piece having a single scene; *esp* : a comic vaudeville act

²**sketch** *vb* **1** : to make a sketch, rough draft, or outline of **2** : to draw or paint sketches — **sketch·er** *n*

sketch·book \'skech-,bùk\ *n* : a book of or for sketches

sketchy \'skech-ē\ *adj* **sketch·i·er; -est** **1** : of the nature of a sketch : roughly outlined **2** : wanting in completeness, clearness, or substance : SLIGHT, VAGUE — **sketch·i·ly** \'skech-ə-lē\ *adv* — **sketch·i·ness** \'skech-ē-nəs\ *n*

¹**skew** \'skyü\ *vb* [ONF *escuer* to shun, fr. Gmc origin; akin to E *shy*] **1** : to take an oblique course : move or turn aside : TWIST, SWERVE **2** : to make, set, or cut on the skew **3** : to distort from a true value or symmetrical form

²**skew** *adj* **1** **a** : set, placed, or running obliquely to something else **b** : neither parallel nor intersecting ⟨*skew* lines⟩ **2** : ASYMMETRICAL

³**skew** *n* : a deviation from a straight line : SLANT

skew·bald \'skyü-,bóld\ *adj* : marked with spots and patches of white and some other color ⟨a *skewbald* horse⟩

¹**skew·er** \'skyü-ər, 'skyù-(-ə)r\ *n* **1** : a pin for keeping meat in form while roasting or for holding small pieces of meat and vegetables for broiling **2** : something shaped or used like a meat skewer

²**skewer** *vt* : to fasten or pierce with or as if with a skewer

skew·ness \'skyü-nəs\ *n* : lack of straightness or symmetry

¹**ski** \'skē\ *n, pl* **skis** *or* **ski** [Norw, fr. ON *skīth*, lit., stick] : one of a pair of narrow strips of wood, metal, or plastic curving upward in front that are worn by people for gliding over snow or water

²**ski** *vi* **skied; ski·ing** : to glide on skis — **ski·er** *n*

ski boot *n* : a heavy usu. reinforced leather shoe for use with skis that extends just above the ankle and is provided usu. with a thick stiff sole and a heel grooved to accommodate bindings and is often padded around the ankles

¹**skid** \'skid\ *n* **1** : a log or plank for supporting something (as above the ground) ⟨put a boat on *skids*⟩ **2** : one

of the logs, planks, or rails along or on which something heavy is rolled or slid **3** : a device placed under a carriage wheel to prevent its turning : DRAG **4** : a runner used as part of the landing gear of an airplane or helicopter **5** : the act of skidding : SLIDE

²**skid** *vb* **skid·ded; skid·ding** **1** : to slow or halt by a skid **2** : to haul along, slide, hoist, or store on skids **3** : to slide without rotating ⟨the wheels *skidded* as we went down the hill⟩ **4** **a** : to fail to grip the roadway; *esp* : to slip sideways on the road ⟨the car *skidded* on an icy road⟩ **b** : to slide sideways away from the center of curvature when turning ⟨a *skidding* airplane⟩ **c** : SLIDE, SLIP ⟨*skid* across ice⟩ **5** : to fall rapidly, steeply, or far ⟨the temperature *skidded* to zero⟩

skid·der \'skid-ər\ *n* : one that skids or uses a skid

skid·doo *or* **skid·do** \skid-'ü\ *vi* : to go away : DEPART

skid row \-'rō\ *n* : a district of cheap saloons, cheap rooming houses, and employment agencies frequented by migrant workers, vagrants, and alcoholics

skiff \'skif\ *n* [It *schifo*, of Gmc origin; akin to E *ship*] **1** : a small light sailing ship **2** : a light rowboat **3** : a boat with centerboard and spritsail light enough to be rowed **4** : a small fast powerboat

ski·ing *n* : the art or sport of sliding and jumping on skis

ski jump *n* : a jump made by a person wearing skis; *also* : a course or track esp. prepared for such jumping — **ski jump** *vi*

ski lift *n* : a power-driven conveyor for transporting skiers or sightseers up a long slope or mountainside

skill \'skil\ *n* [ON *skil* discernment] **1** : ability or dexterity that comes from training or practice **2** **a** : a particular art or science ⟨achievements of medical *skill*⟩ **b** : a developed or acquired ability : ACCOMPLISHMENT ⟨*skills* of swimming and diving⟩ **syn** see ART

skilled \'skild\ *adj* **1** : having skill : EXPERT ⟨a *skilled* mason⟩ **2** : requiring skill and training ⟨a *skilled* trade⟩ **syn** SKILLFUL: SKILLED applies to one who has mastered the details and technique of a trade, art, or profession; SKILLFUL stresses adeptness and dexterity as individual qualities rather than standards ⟨a daring *skillful* driver⟩ ⟨*skillful* performance of a concerto⟩

skil·let \'skil-ət\ *n* [ME *skelet*] **1** *chiefly Brit* : a kettle or pot having feet and used for cooking on a hearth **2** : a frying pan

skill·ful *or* **skil·ful** \'skil-fəl\ *adj* **1** : having or displaying skill : EXPERT, DEXTEROUS ⟨*skillful* debater⟩ **2** : accomplished with skill ⟨*skillful* defense⟩ **syn** see PROFICIENT, SKILLED — **skill·ful·ly** \-fə-lē\ *adv* — **skill·ful·ness** *n*

skill·less *or* **skil·less** \'skil-ləs\ *adj* : having no skill — **skill·less·ness** *n*

¹**skim** \'skim\ *vb* **skimmed; skim·ming** [ME *skimmen*] **1** **a** : to clear (a liquid) of scum or floating substance : remove (as film or scum) from the surface of a liquid **b** : to remove cream from by skimming **2** : to read, study, or examine superficially and rapidly; *esp* : to glance through (as a book) for the chief ideas or the plot **3** : to throw in a gliding path; *esp* : to throw so as to ricochet along the surface of water **4** : to cover or become covered with or as if with a film, scum, or coat **5** : to pass swiftly or lightly over : glide or skip along, above, or near a surface

²**skim** *n* **1** : a thin layer, coating, or film **2** : the act of skimming **3** : something skimmed; *esp* : SKIM MILK

³**skim** *adj* **1** : SKIMMED **2** : made of skim milk ⟨*skim* cheese⟩

skim·mer \'skim-ər\ *n* **1** : one that skims; *esp* : a flat perforated scoop or spoon used for skimming **2** : any of several long-winged sea birds related to the terns that fly low over the water

skim milk *also* **skimmed milk** *n* : milk from which the cream has been taken

skim·ming \'skim-iŋ\ *n* : that which is skimmed from a liquid

skimp \'skimp\ *vb* **1** : to give insufficient or barely sufficient attention or effort to or funds for : SCAMP **2** : to save by or as if by skimping : SCRIMP

skimpy \'skim-pē\ *adj* **skimp·i·er; -est** : deficient (as in supply) esp. through skimping : SCANTY — **skimp·i·ly** \-pə-lē\ *adv* — **skimp·i·ness** \-pē-nəs\ *n*

¹**skin** \'skin\ *n* [ON *skinn*] **1** **a** : the integument of an animal and esp. of a small animal or furbearer when

separated from the body — compare HIDE **b** : a sheet of parchment or vellum made from a hide **c** : BOTTLE 1b **2 a** : the external limiting layer of an animal body esp. when forming a tough but flexible cover; *also* : the 2-layered tissue of which this is formed in a vertebrate — compare DERMIS, EPIDERMIS **b** : an outer or surface layer (as a rind) ⟨a sausage *skin*⟩ ⟨apple *skins*⟩ **3** : the life or physical well-being of a person ⟨made sure to save his *skin*⟩ **4** : a sheathing or casing forming the outside surface of a structure (as a ship or airplane) — **skin·less** \-ləs\ *adj* — **skinned** \'skind\ *adj*

²**skin** *vb* **skinned**; **skin·ning 1** : to cover or become covered with or as if with skin **2 a** : to strip, scrape, or rub off the skin of ⟨*skin* a fruit⟩ ⟨*skinned* his knee⟩ **b** : to strip or peel off **3 a** : CHEAT, FLEECE **b** : DEFEAT **c** : CENSURE, REPRIMAND **4 a** : to climb or descend ⟨*skin* up and down a rope⟩ **b** : to pass or get by with scant room to spare

skin-deep \'skin-'dēp\ *adj* **1** : as deep as the skin **2** : not thorough or lasting in impression : SUPERFICIAL

skin dive *vi* : to swim deep below the surface of water with a face mask and flippers and with or without a portable breathing device — **skin diver** *n*

skin·flint \'skin-ˌflint\ *n* : a person who is very hard and grasping in money matters

skin·ful \-ˌfu̇l\ *n* **1** : the contents of a skin bottle **2 a** : large or satisfying quantity esp. of liquor

skin game *n* : a swindling game or trick

skin graft *n* : a piece of skin transferred from a donor area to grow new skin at a place denuded (as by burning)

skink \'skiŋk\ *n* [Gk *skinkos*] : any of a family of mostly small lizards with small scales

skin·ner \'skin-ər\ *n* **1 a** : one that deals in skins, pelts, or hides **b** : one that removes, cures, or dresses skins **2** : a driver of draft animals and esp. of mules

skin·ny \'skin-ē\ *adj* **skin·ni·er**; **-est 1** : resembling skin : MEMBRANOUS ⟨a *skinny* layer⟩ **2** : very thin : LEAN, EMACIATED — **skin·ni·ness** *n*

skin test *n* : a test (as a scratch test) performed on the skin and used in detecting allergic hypersensitivity

skin·tight \'skin-'tīt\ *adj* : closely fitted to the figure

¹**skip** \'skip\ *vb* **skipped**; **skip·ping** [ME *skippen*] **1 a** : to move or proceed with leaps and bounds : CAPER **b** : to bound or cause to bound off one point after another : RICOCHET **c** : to leap over lightly and nimbly **2** : to leave or leave from hurriedly or secretly **3 a** : to pass over or omit (as an interval, item, or step) **b** : to omit or cause to omit a grade in school in advancing to the next **c** : to pass over without notice or mention **d** : to fail to attend ⟨*skipped* the meeting⟩ **e** : MISFIRE 1

²**skip** *n* **1 a** : a light bounding step **b** : a gait composed of alternating hops and steps **2** : an act of omission or the thing omitted

³**skip** *n* : the captain of a side in some games (as curling or lawn bowling)

⁴**skip** *vt* **skipped**; **skip·ping** : to act as skipper of

ski pants *n pl* : pants for skiing that are ribbed or close-fitted at the ankle

skip·jack \'skip-ˌjak\ *n, pl* **skipjacks** *or* **skipjack** : any of various fishes (as a bonito or bluefish) that jump above or play at the surface of the water

ski pole *n* : a metal-pointed pole or stick of steel or cane fitted with a strap for the hand at the top and an encircling disk set a little above the point and used as an aid in skiing

¹**skip·per** \'skip-ər\ *n* **1** : one that skips **2 a** : any of numerous small stout-bodied insects of swift erratic flight that differ from the typical butterflies in wing venation and the form of the antennae **b** : any of several small leaping insects ⟨cheese *skippers*⟩

²**skipper** *n* [MD *schipper*, fr. *schip* ship; akin to E *ship*] : the master of a ship; *esp* : the master of a fishing, small trading, or pleasure boat

¹**skirl** \'skərl, 'skirl\ *vb* : to sound the high shrill tone of the bagpipe

²**skirl** *n* : the high shrill sound of a bagpipe

¹**skir·mish** \'skər-mish\ *n* [MF *escarmouche*, fr. It *scaramuccia*] **1** : a minor fight in war usu. incidental to larger movements **2** : a brisk preliminary conflict

²**skirmish** *vi* **1** : to engage in a skirmish **2** : to search about (as for supplies) — **skir·mish·er** *n*

¹**skirr** \'skər\ *vb* **1** : to leave hurriedly : FLEE; *also* : to

move rapidly **2** : to pass rapidly over esp. in search of something

²**skirr** *n* : WHIR, ROAR

¹**skirt** \'skərt\ *n* [ON *skyrta* shirt, kirtle; akin to E *shirt*] **1 a** : a free hanging part of a garment extending from the waist down **b** : a separate free hanging garment for women and girls covering the body from the waist down **c** : either of two flaps on a saddle covering the bars on which the stirrups are hung **2** *pl* : the outlying parts of a town or city : OUTSKIRTS **3** : a part or attachment serving as a rim, border, or edging **4** *slang* : GIRL, WOMAN

²**skirt** *vb* **1** : to form or run along the edge of : BORDER **2** : to provide a skirt or border for **3 a** : to go or pass around or about; *esp* : to go around or keep away from in order to avoid danger or discovery **b** : to evade or miss by a narrow margin **4** : to be, lie, or move along an edge, border, or margin — **skirt·er** *n*

skirt·ing \-iŋ\ *n* **1** : something that skirts: as **a** : BORDER, EDGING **b** *Brit* : BASEBOARD **2** : fabric (as wool) suitable for skirts

ski run *n* : a slope or trail suitable for skiing

ski suit *n* : a warm outfit for winter sports made in one-piece or two-piece style with a jacket top and pants usu. having ribbed cuffs

skit \'skit\ *n* **1** : a satirical or humorous story or sketch; *esp* : a sketch included in a dramatic performance (as a review) **2** : a short serious dramatic piece; *esp* : one done by amateurs

ski tow *n* **1** : a power-driven conveyor for pulling skiers to the top of a slope that consists usu. of an endless motor-driven moving rope which the skier grasps **2** : SKI LIFT

skit·ter \'skit-ər\ *vb* : to glide or skip lightly or quickly : skim along a surface

skit·tish \'skit-ish\ *adj* [ME] **1** : lively or frisky in action : CAPRICIOUS **2** : easily frightened : RESTIVE ⟨a *skittish* horse⟩ **3** : COY, BASHFUL — **skit·tish·ly** *adv* — **skit·tish·ness** *n*

skit·tle \'skit-ᵊl\ *n* **1** *pl* : a form of ninepins that sometimes uses wooden disks instead of balls **2** : one of the pins used in skittles

¹**skiv·vy** \'skiv-ē\ *n, pl* **skivvies** *Brit* : a female domestic servant

²**skivvy** *n, pl* **skivvies** : underwear consisting of shorts and a collarless short-sleeved pullover — usu. used in pl.

skoal \'skōl\ *n* [Dan *skaal*, lit., cup; akin to E ¹*scale*] : TOAST, HEALTH — often used interjectionally

skua \'skyü-ə\ *n* [NL, of Scand origin] : JAEGER; *esp* : a large No. Atlantic jaeger

skul·dug·gery *or* **skull·dug·gery** \ˌskəl-'dəg-(ə-)rē\ *n, pl* **-ger·ies** : underhanded or unscrupulous behavior : DISHONESTY, TRICKERY

¹**skulk** \'skəlk\ *vi* [of Scand origin] **1** : to move in a stealthy or furtive manner : SNEAK **2** : to hide or conceal oneself from cowardice or fear or with treacherous intent — **skulk·er** *n*

syn SKULK, SLINK, SNEAK mean to go or act so as to escape attention. SKULK may imply shyness or cowardice but often suggests an intent to spy or waylay; SLINK stresses a moving so as to avoid notice rather than keeping actually out of sight; SNEAK may add an implication of furtively entering or leaving a place or of accomplishing a purpose by indirect and underhanded methods

²**skulk** *n* : SKULKER

skull \'skəl\ *n* [of Scand origin] **1** : the vertebrate head skeleton that forms a bony or cartilaginous case enclosing the brain and chief sense organs and supporting the jaws **2** : the seat of understanding or intelligence : MIND

skull and cross·bones \-'krȯs-ˌbōnz\ *n* : a representation of a human skull over crossbones usu. used as a warning of danger to life

skull·cap \'skəl-ˌkap\ *n* : a close-fitting cap; *esp* : a light cap without brim for indoor wear

skull practice *n* : a strategy class for an athletic team

¹**skunk** \'skəŋk\ *n, pl* **skunks** *also* **skunk** [of Algonquian origin] **1** : any of various common omnivorous black-and-white New World mammals related to the weasels and having glands near the anus from which a secretion of pungent and offensive odor is ejected when the animal is startled **2** : an obnoxious person

²skunk *vt* **:** to defeat decisively; *esp* **:** to shut out in a game
skunk cabbage *n* **:** an American perennial marsh herb of the arum family that sends up in early spring a cowl= shaped ill-smelling brownish purple spathe
¹sky \'skī\ *n, pl* **skies** [ON *skȳ* cloud] **1 :** the upper atmosphere that constitutes an apparent great vault or arch over the earth **:** FIRMAMENT **2 :** HEAVEN **2 3 :** WEATH- ER, CLIMATE ⟨the weatherman predicts sunny *skies*⟩
²sky *vb* **skied** *or* **skyed; sky·ing 1 :** to hit (as a ball) high into the air **2 :** to rise sharply **:** SKYROCKET
sky blue *n* **:** a variable color averaging a pale to light blue
sky·borne \'skī-ˌbȯrn, -ˌbȯrn\ *adj* **:** AIRBORNE ⟨*skyborne* troops⟩
sky·cap \-ˌkap\ *n* [¹*sky* + -*cap* (as in *redcap*)] **:** one em- ployed to carry hand luggage at an airport
sky·coach \-ˌkōch\ *n* **:** a commercial airplane that pro- vides low-cost transportation without special services (as sleeping accommodations)
sky·ey \'skī-ē\ *adj* **:** of or resembling the sky **:** ETHEREAL
sky-high \'skī-'hī\ *adv* (*or adj*) **1 a :** high into the air **b :** to a high level or degree **2 :** in an enthusiastic manner **3 :** to bits **:** APART **4 :** EXORBITANTLY
sky·jack·er \-ˌjak-ər\ *n* [*sky* + -*jacker* (as in *hijacker*)] **:** one who commandeers a flying airplane (as by coercing the pilot at gunpoint) — **sky·jack·ing** \-ˌjak-iŋ\ *n*
¹sky·lark \'skī-ˌlärk\ *n* **:** a common Old World lark that sings as it rises in almost perpendicular flight
²skylark *vi* **:** to play wild boisterous pranks **:** FROLIC — **sky·lark·er** *n*
sky·light \'skī-ˌlīt\ *n* **:** a window or group of windows in a roof or ceiling
sky·line \-ˌlīn\ *n* **1 :** the line where earth and sky or water and sky seem to meet **:** HORIZON **2 :** an outline against the sky ⟨a *skyline* of tall buildings⟩
sky pilot *n* **:** CLERGYMAN; *esp* **:** CHAPLAIN
¹sky·rock·et \'skī-ˌräk-ət\ *n* **:** ¹ROCKET 1
²skyrocket *vb* **1 :** to shoot up abruptly **2 :** to cause to rise or increase abruptly and rapidly
sky·sail \'skī-ˌsāl, -səl\ *n* **:** the sail above the royal
sky·scrap·er \'skī-ˌskrā-pər\ *n* **:** a very tall building
sky·ward \'skī-wərd\ *adv* (*or adj*) **1 :** toward the sky ⟨gaze *skyward*⟩ **2 :** UPWARD
sky·way \'skī-ˌwā\ *n* **1 :** a route used by airplanes **:** AIR LANE **2 :** an elevated highway
sky·writ·ing \'skī-ˌrīt-iŋ\ *n* **:** writing formed in the sky by means of a visible substance (as smoke) emitted from an airplane — **sky·writ·er** \-ˌrīt-ər\ *n*
slab \'slab\ *n* [ME *slabbe*] **1 :** a thick plate or slice (as of stone, wood, or bread) **2 :** the outside piece cut from a log in squaring it
slab·ber \'slab-ər\ *vb* **slab·bered; slab·ber·ing** \'slab- (ə-)riŋ\ **:** SLOBBER, DROOL — **slabber** *n*
slab-sid·ed \'slab-'sīd-əd\ *adj* **:** having flat sides; *also* **:** being tall or long and lank
¹slack \'slak\ *adj* [OE *sleac*] **1 :** not using due diligence, care, or dispatch **:** NEGLECT **2 a :** characterized by slowness, sluggishness, or lack of energy ⟨*slack* pace⟩ **b :** moderate in some quality; *esp* **:** moderately warm ⟨*slack* oven⟩ **3 a :** not tight **:** not tense or taut **:** RELAXED ⟨*slack* rope⟩ **b :** lacking in firmness **:** WEAK, SOFT ⟨*slack* control⟩ **4 :** wanting in activity **:** DULL ⟨*slack* season⟩ — **slack·ly** *adv* — **slack·ness** *n*
²slack *vb* **1 a :** to be or become slack or negligent in performing or doing **b :** LESSEN, MODERATE **2 :** to shirk or evade work or duty **3 :** LOOSEN **4 a :** to cause to abate **b :** SLAKE 4
³slack *n* **1 :** cessation in movement or flow **2 :** a part of something that hangs loose without strain ⟨take up the *slack* of a rope⟩ **3** *pl* **:** trousers esp. for casual wear **4 :** a dull season or period **:** LULL
⁴slack *n* [ME *sleck*] **:** the finest screenings of coal pro- duced at a mine unusable as fuel unless cleaned
slack·en \'slak-ən\ *vb* **slack·ened; slack·en·ing** \'slak- (ə-)niŋ\ **1 :** to make or become less active **:** slow up **:** MODERATE, RETARD ⟨*slacken* speed⟩ **2 :** to make less taut **:** LOOSEN ⟨*slacken* sail⟩ **3 :** to become negligent
slack·er \'slak-ər\ *n* **:** one who shirks work or evades an obligation esp. for military service in time of war
slack suit *n* **:** a suit for casual wear consisting of slacks and jacket top or sport shirt often of the same material and color

slack water *n* **:** the period at the turn of the tide when there is little or no horizontal motion of tidal water
slag \'slag\ *n* [MLG *slagge*] **1 :** waste left after the melt- ing of ores and the separation of the metal from them **2 :** volcanic lava resembling cinders — **slag·gy** \'slag-ē\ *adj*
slain *past part of* SLAY
slake \'slāk, 3 & 4 *are also* 'slak\ *vb* [OE *slacian*, fr. *sleac* slack] **1** *archaic* **:** to make or become less violent, intense, or severe **:** ABATE, MODERATE **2 :** to relieve or satisfy with water or liquid **:** QUENCH ⟨*slaked* his thirst⟩ **3 :** to become slaked ⟨lime may *slake* spontaneously in moist air⟩ **4 a :** to cause (lime) to heat and crumble by treatment with water **:** HYDRATE **b :** to alter (lime) by exposure to air with conversion at least in part to a carbonate
slaked lime *n* **:** a white powder consisting essentially of calcium hydroxide formed by treating lime with water
sla·lom \'släl-əm\ *n* [Norw, lit., sloping track] **:** skiing in a zigzag or wavy course between upright obstacles (as flags); *also* **:** a race against time over such a course
¹slam \'slam\ *n* **:** the winning of all or all but one of the tricks of a deal in bridge
²slam *vb* **slammed; slam·ming** [of Scand origin] **1 :** to strike or beat hard **2 :** to shut forcibly and noisily **:** BANG **3 :** to set or slap down violently or noisily **4 :** to make a banging noise **5 :** to criticize harshly
³slam *n* **1 :** a heavy impact **2 a :** a noisy violent closing **b :** a banging noise esp. from the slamming of a door **3 :** a cutting or violent criticism
slam-bang \'slam-'baŋ\ *adv* (*or adj*) **1 :** with noisy violence **2 :** HEADLONG, RECKLESSLY
¹slan·der \'slan-dər\ *n* [OF *esclandre*, fr. LL *scandalum* stumbling block, offense, fr. Gk *skandalon*] **1 :** the utter- ance of false charges or misrepresentations which defame and damage another's reputation **2 :** a false and defama- tory oral statement about a person — compare LIBEL — **slan·der·ous** \-d(ə-)rəs\ *adj* — **slan·der·ous·ly** *adv* — **slan·der·ous·ness** *n*
²slander *vt* **slan·dered; slan·der·ing** \-d(ə-)riŋ\ **:** to utter slander against **:** DEFAME — **slan·der·er** \-dər-ər\ *n*
syn SLANDER, DEFAME, MALIGN mean to injure by speak- ing ill of. SLANDER stresses the suffering of the victim regardless of the intent of the slanderer ⟨*slandered* by thoughtless tongues⟩ DEFAME stresses the actual loss of or injury to one's good name and repute; MALIGN usu. suggests the operation of hatred, prejudice, or bigotry often by subtle misrepresentation rather than direct ac- cusation ⟨*maligned* and persecuted in his own lifetime⟩
¹slang \'slaŋ\ *n* **1 :** language peculiar to a particular group, trade, or pursuit ⟨baseball *slang*⟩ **2 :** an informal nonstandard vocabulary composed typically of coinages, arbitrarily changed words, and extravagant, forced, or facetious figures of speech **syn** see DIALECT — **slang** *adj*
²slang *vb* **1** *chiefly Brit* **:** to abuse with harsh or coarse language **2 :** to use slang or vulgar abuse
slangy \'slaŋ-ē\ *adj* **slang·i·er; -est 1 :** of, relating to, or constituting slang **:** containing slang **2 :** addicted to the use of slang — **slang·i·ly** \'slaŋ-ə-lē\ *adv* — **slang·i· ness** \'slaŋ-ē-nəs\ *n*
¹slant \'slant\ *vb* [of Scand origin] **1 :** to turn or incline from a straight line or a level **:** SLOPE **2 :** to interpret or present in accordance with a special viewpoint ⟨*slanted* news⟩
²slant *n* **1 :** a slanting direction, line, or plane **:** SLOPE **2 a :** something that slants **b :** DIAGONAL 3 **3 :** a way of looking at something **:** a peculiar or personal point of view, attitude, or opinion ⟨considered the problem from a new *slant*⟩ **4 :** GLANCE, LOOK — **slant** *adj*
slant height *n* **1 :** the length of an element of a right circular cone **2 :** the altitude of a lateral face of a regular pyramid
slant·ways \'slant-ˌwāz\ *adv* **:** SLANTWISE
slant·wise \-ˌwīz\ *adv* (*or adj*) **:** so as to slant **:** at a slant **:** in a slanting direction or position
¹slap \'slap\ *n* [LG *slapp*] **1 :** a quick sharp blow esp. with the open hand; *also* **:** a noise suggesting that of a slap **2 :** REBUFF, INSULT
²slap *vb* **slapped; slap·ping 1 a :** to strike with or as if with the open hand **b :** to make a sound like that of slapping **2 :** to put, place, or throw with careless haste

or force ⟨*slapped* down his paper⟩ **3 :** to assail verbally
: INSULT
³slap *adv* **:** DIRECTLY, SMACK
slap·dash \'slap-ˌdash, -'dash\ *adv (or adj)* **:** in a slipshod
manner **:** HAPHAZARD; *also* **:** HASTILY
slap down *vt* **1 :** to prohibit or restrain usu. abruptly
and with censure from acting in a specified way **:** SQUELCH
2 : to put an abrupt stop to **:** SUPPRESS
slap·jack \'slap-ˌjak\ *n* **1 :** GRIDDLE CAKE **2 :** a card
game
slap·stick \'slap-ˌstik\ *n* **1 :** a device made of two flat
sticks so fastened as to make a loud noise when used to
strike a person **2 :** comedy stressing farce and horseplay
— **slapstick** *adj*
¹slash \'slash\ *vb* [ME *slaschen*] **1 :** to cut by sweeping
and aimless blows **:** GASH **2 :** to whip or strike with or
as if with a cane **3 :** to criticize without mercy **4 :** to
cut slits in (as a skirt) to reveal a color beneath **5 :** to
reduce sharply **:** CUT ⟨*slash* prices⟩ — **slash·er** *n*
²slash *n* **1 :** an act or result of slashing: as **a :** a long
cut or stroke made by slashing **b :** an ornamental slit
in a garment **c :** a sharp reduction ⟨budget *slash*⟩ **2 :** an
open debris-strewn tract in a forest; *also* **:** the debris in
such a tract
³slash *n* **:** a low swampy area often overgrown with brush
slash pine *n* **:** a southern pine important as a source of
turpentine and lumber
slash pocket *n* **:** a pocket suspended on the wrong side
of a garment from a finished slit on the right side that
serves as its opening
slat \'slat\ *n* [MF *esclat* splinter] **:** a thin narrow flat
strip of wood, plastic, or metal ⟨the *slats* of a blind⟩ —
slat·ted \'slat-əd\ *adj*
¹slate \'slāt\ *n* [MF *esclat* splinter] **1 :** a fine-grained
and usu. bluish gray rock that is formed by compression
of shales or other rocks and that splits readily into thin
layers or plates and is used esp. for roofing and black-
boards; *also* **:** a piece of this (as a shingle) dressed for use
2 : a tablet of material (as slate) used for writing on
3 : something (as deeds, events, or a list of candidates)
recorded or made public as if written on a slate **4 a :** a
dark purplish gray **b :** a gray similar in color to common
roofing slate — **slate** *adj* — **slate·like** \-ˌlīk\ *adj*
²slate *vt* **1 :** to cover with slate or a slatelike substance
⟨*slate* a roof⟩ **2 :** to register or schedule on or as if on a
slate ⟨*slate* a meeting⟩
slat·er \'slāt-ər\ *n* **1 :** one that slates **2 :** WOOD LOUSE
slath·er \'slath-ər\ *vt* **slath·ered; slath·er·ing** \'slath-
(ə-)riŋ\ **:** to spread with or on thickly or lavishly
slat·tern \'slat-ərn\ *n* **:** an untidy slovenly woman —
slat·tern·li·ness \-lē-nəs\ *n* — **slat·tern·ly** \-lē\ *adj
or adv*
slaty \'slāt-ē\ *adj* **:** of, containing, or characteristic of
slate; *also* **:** gray like slate
¹slaugh·ter \'slot-ər\ *n* [of Scand origin; akin to E *slay*]
1 : the act of killing; *esp* **:** the butchering of livestock for
market **2 :** destruction of human lives in battle **:** CARNAGE
²slaughter *vt* **1 :** to kill (an animal) for food **:** BUTCHER
2 : to kill ruthlessly or in large numbers **:** MASSACRE —
slaugh·ter·er \'slot-ər-ər\ *n*
slaugh·ter·house \'slot-ər-ˌhaus\ *n* **:** an establishment
where animals are butchered
slaugh·ter·ous \'slot-ə-rəs\ *adj* **:** of or relating to
slaughter **:** MURDEROUS — **slaugh·ter·ous·ly** *adv*
Slav \'släv, 'slav\ *n* **:** a person speaking a Slavic language
as his native tongue
¹slave \'slāv\ *n* [ML *sclavus*, fr. *Sclavus* Slav; fr. the reduction to slavery of many Slavic peoples of central
Europe] **1 :** a person held in servitude as the property
of another **2 :** a person who has lost control of himself
and is dominated by something or someone ⟨a *slave* to
drink⟩ **3 :** DRUDGE, TOILER — **slave** *adj*
²slave *vi* **:** to work like a slave **:** DRUDGE
slave driver *n* **1 :** a supervisor of slaves at work **2 :** a
harsh taskmaster
slave·hold·er \'slāv-ˌhōl-dər\ *n* **:** an owner of slaves —
slave·hold·ing \-diŋ\ *adj or n*
¹slav·er \'slav-ər, 'släv-\ *vi* **slav·ered; slav·er·ing**
\-(ə-)riŋ\ [of Scand origin] **:** DROOL, SLOBBER — **slaver** *n*
²slav·er \'slā-vər\ *n* **:** a person or ship engaged in the
slave trade

slav·ery \'slāv-(ə-)rē\ *n* **1 :** DRUDGERY, TOIL **2 a :** the
state of being a slave **:** SERVITUDE **b :** the practice of
slaveholding
slave state *n* **:** a state of the U.S. in which Negro slavery
was legal until the Civil War
slave trade *n* **:** traffic in slaves; *esp* **:** the buying and selling
of Negroes for profit prior to the American Civil War
slav·ey \'slā-vē\ *n, pl* **slaveys :** DRUDGE; *esp* **:** a maid of
all work
¹Slav·ic \'slav-ik, 'släv-\ *adj* **:** of, relating to, or characteristic of the Slavs or their languages
²Slavic *n* **:** a branch of the Indo-European language
family including Bulgarian, Czech, Polish, Serbo-
Croatian, Slovene, Russian, and Slovak
slav·ish \'slā-vish\ *adj* **1 :** of or characteristic of a slave
: SERVILE **2 :** lacking in independence or originality esp.
of thought ⟨*slavish* dependence on customary ways⟩
⟨*slavish* imitators⟩ — **slav·ish·ly** *adv* — **slav·ish·ness** *n*
¹Sla·von·ic \slə-'vän-ik\ *adj* **:** SLAVIC
²Slavonic *n* **1 :** SLAVIC **2 :** OLD CHURCH SLAVONIC
slaw \'slo\ *n* **:** COLESLAW
slay \'slā\ *vb* **slew** \'slü\; **slain** \'slān\; **slay·ing** [OE
slēan to strike, slay] **:** to put to death violently **:** KILL
syn see KILL — **slay·er** *n*
sleave \'slēv\ *n* **:** THREAD
slea·zy \'slē-zē, 'slā-\ *adj* **slea·zi·er; -est 1 :** not firmly
or closely woven **:** FLIMSY **2 :** made carelessly of inferior
material **:** SHODDY — **slea·zi·ly** \-zə-lē\ *adv* — **slea·zi·
ness** \-zē-nəs\ *n*
¹sled \'sled\ *n* [MD *sledde*] **1 :** a vehicle on runners for
conveying loads esp. over snow or ice **:** SLEDGE **2 :** a
sled used by children for coasting on snow-covered slopes
²sled *vb* **sled·ded; sled·ding :** to ride or carry on a sled
or sleigh — **sled·der** *n*
sled·ding *n* **1 :** the use of a sled; *also* **:** the conditions
under which a sled is used **2 :** GOING 3
sled dog *n* **:** a dog trained to draw a sledge esp. in the
Arctic regions — called also *sledge dog*
¹sledge \'slej\ *n* [OE *slecg*] **:** SLEDGEHAMMER
²sledge *n* [D dial. *sleedse*, fr. D *slede, slee* sleigh] **:** a
vehicle with low runners that is used for transporting
loads esp. over snow or ice
³sledge *vb* **:** to travel with or transport on a sledge
sledge·ham·mer \'slej-ˌham-ər\ *n* **:** a large heavy
hammer usu. wielded with both hands
— **sledgehammer** *adj or vb*
¹sleek \'slēk\ *vb* **1 :** to make or become sleek **2 :** to cover up **:** gloss over
²sleek *adj* **1 a :** smooth and glossy as
if polished ⟨*sleek* dark hair⟩ **b :** having
a smooth healthy well-groomed look
⟨*sleek* cattle grazing⟩ **2 :** having a
prosperous air **:** THRIVING — **sleek·ly**
adv — **sleek·ness** *n*

sledgehammer

¹sleep \'slēp\ *n* [OE *slǣp*] **1 :** the
natural periodic suspension of consciousness during which
the powers of the body are restored **2 :** a state resembling
sleep: as **a :** a state of torpid inactivity **b :** DEATH; *also*
: TRANCE, COMA — **sleep·like** \-ˌlīk\ *adj*
syn SLUMBER: SLEEP is the ordinary term applying to
men or animals and to states resembling or suggesting
actual sleeping ⟨the long *sleep* of the dead⟩ SLUMBER may
be merely a poetic substitute or it may call particular
attention to the fact of being asleep or in a specific kind
of sleep ⟨uneasy *slumber*⟩⟨wrapped in heavy *slumber*⟩
²sleep *vb* **slept** \'slept\; **sleep·ing 1 :** to rest or be in a
state of sleep **2 :** to have sexual relations **3 :** to get rid
of or spend in or by sleep ⟨*slept* away his cares⟩ **4 :** to
provide sleeping space for ⟨the boat *sleeps* six⟩
sleep·er \'slē-pər\ *n* **1 :** one that sleeps **2 :** a piece of
timber, stone, or steel on or near the ground to support
a superstructure, keep railroad rails in place, or receive
floor joists **3 :** SLEEPING CAR **4 :** something unpromising
or unnoticed that suddenly attains prominence or value
sleeping bag *n* **:** a bag usu. waterproof and warmly lined
or padded to sleep in outdoors
sleeping car *n* **:** a railroad passenger car having berths for
sleeping
sleeping porch *n* **:** a porch or room having open sides or
many windows arranged to permit sleeping in the open air
sleeping sickness *n* **1 :** a serious disease found in much

ə abut; ⁰ kitten; ər further; a back; ā bake; ä cot, cart; au̇ out; ch chin; e less; ē easy; g gift; i trip; ī life

of tropical Africa, marked by fever, protracted lethargy, tremors, and loss of weight, caused by either of two trypanosomes, and transmitted by tsetse flies **2** : any of various virus diseases of which lethargy or somnolence is a prominent feature

sleep·less \'slēp-ləs\ *adj* **1** : not able to sleep : INSOMNIAC **2** : affording no sleep **3** : unceasingly alert or active — **sleep·less·ly** *adv* — **sleep·less·ness** *n*

sleep out *vi* **1** : to sleep outdoors **2** : to go home at night from one's place of employment ⟨a cook who *sleeps out*⟩ **3** : to sleep away from home

sleep·walk·er \'slēp-,wȯ-kər\ *n* : one that walks in his sleep : SOMNAMBULIST — **sleep·walk·ing** \-kiŋ\ *n*

sleepy \'slē-pē\ *adj* **sleep·i·er; -est** **1** : ready to fall asleep : DROWSY **2** : quietly inactive : DULL, LETHARGIC ⟨a *sleepy* village⟩— **sleep·i·ly** \-pə-lē\ *adv* — **sleep·i·ness** \-pē-nəs\ *n*

sleepy·head \'slē-pē-,hed\ *n* : a sleepy person

¹sleet \'slēt\ *n* [ME *slete*] **1** : partly frozen rain : a mixture of rain and snow **2** : the icy coating formed by freezing rain : GLAZE — **sleety** \'slēt-ē\ *adj*

²sleet *vi* : to shower sleet

sleeve \'slēv\ *n* [OE *slīefe*] **1** : the part of a garment covering the arm **2** : something like a sleeve in shape or use; *esp* : a tubular part fitting over another part — **sleeved** \'slēvd\ *adj* — **sleeve·less** \'slēv-ləs\ *adj*

sleeve·let \'slēv-lət\ *n* : a covering for the forearm to protect clothing from wear or dirt

sleeve target *n* : a tubular cloth target towed by an airplane for use in air and ground antiaircraft gunnery practice

¹sleigh \'slā\ *n* [D *slede, slee* sleigh, sled; akin to E *slide*] : a vehicle on runners used for transporting persons or goods on snow or ice

²sleigh *vi* : to drive or travel in a sleigh

sleigh bell *n* : any of various bells commonly attached to a sleigh or to the harness of a horse drawing a sleigh

sleight \'slīt\ *n* [ON *slœgth*, fr. *slœgr* sly] **1** : deceitful craftiness : CUNNING; *also* : STRATAGEM **2** : DEXTERITY, SKILL

sleight of hand **1** : skill and dexterity esp. in juggling or conjuring tricks **2** : a conjuring or juggling trick requiring sleight of hand

slen·der \'slen-dər\ *adj* [ME *sclendre, slendre*] **1 a** : spare in frame or flesh; *esp* : gracefully slight **b** : small in circumference in proportion to length or height **2** : limited or inadequate in amount : MEAGER **syn** see THIN — **slen·der·ly** *adv* — **slen·der·ness** *n*

slen·der·ize \-,īz\ *vt* : to make slender

¹sleuth \'slüth\ *n* [short for *sleuthhound*] : DETECTIVE

²sleuth *vi* : to act as a detective

sleuth·hound \-,haůnd\ *n* [ON *slōth* track, trail] : a dog that tracks by scent; *esp* : BLOODHOUND

¹slew \'slü\ *past of* SLAY

²slew *var of* SLUE

³slew *n* [IrGael *sluagh*] : a large number : LOT

¹slice \'slīs\ *n* [MF *esclice* splinter, of Gmc origin; akin to E *slit*] **1** : a thin flat piece cut from something ⟨a *slice* of bread⟩ **2** : a spatula or knife with wedge-shaped blade ⟨fish *slice*⟩ **3** : a flight of a ball (as in golf) that deviates from a straight course and curves to the right of a right-handed player and to the left of a left-handed player

²slice *vb* **1 a** : to cut with or as if with a knife **b** : to cut into slices **2** : to hit (a ball) so that a slice results — **slic·er** *n*

¹slick \'slik\ *vt* [ME *sliken*] : to make sleek or smooth

²slick *adj* **1 a** : having a smooth surface : SLIPPERY **b** : GLIB, TRITE **2 a** : characterized by subtlety or nimble wit : CLEVER; *esp* : WILY **b** : DEFT, SKILLFUL — **slick·ly** *adv* — **slick·ness** *n*

³slick *n* **1** : something that is smooth or slippery; *esp* : a smooth patch of water covered with a film of oil **2** : a popular magazine printed on coated stock

slick·er \'slik-ər\ *n* **1** : a long loose raincoat often of oilskin or plastic **2** : a sly clever tricky person ⟨a city *slicker*⟩

¹slide \'slīd\ *vb* **slid** \'slid\; **slid·ing** \'slīd-iŋ\ [OE *slīdan*] **1 a** : to move or cause to move smoothly over a surface : GLIDE, SLIP ⟨*slide* a dish across the table⟩⟨the pen *slides* smoothly over the paper⟩ **b** : to coast on snow or

ice **2** : to slip and fall by a loss of footing, balance, or support ⟨the package *slid* from the heap⟩ **3 a** : to move or pass smoothly and easily ⟨the dog *slid* through the brush⟩ **b** : to move, pass, or put unobtrusively, stealthily, or imperceptibly ⟨*slid* quietly into his seat⟩ ⟨time *slid* by⟩⟨*slide* the note into his hand⟩

²slide *n* **1** : the act or motion of sliding **2** : a loosened mass that slides ⟨a rock *slide*⟩ **3 a** : a surface down which a person or thing slides **b** : something (as a cover for an opening) that operates or adjusts by sliding **4 a** : a transparent picture or image that can be thrown on a screen by means of a projecting device **b** : a glass plate on which is placed an object to be examined under a microscope

slide fastener *n* : ZIPPER

slid·er \'slīd-ər\ *n* **1** : one that slides or operates a slide **2** : any of several freshwater edible American turtles

slide rule *n* : an instrument consisting in its simple form

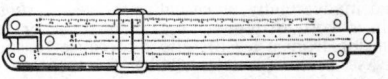

slide rule

of a ruler and a medial slide graduated with similar logarithmic scales labeled with the corresponding antilogarithms and used for rapid calculation

slide·way \'slīd-,wā\ *n* : a way along which something slides

sliding board *n* : a playground slide

¹slight \'slīt\ *adj* [ME, smooth, slight; akin to E *slick*] **1 a** : having a slim or delicate build : not stout or massive in body **b** : lacking in strength or substance : FLIMSY, FRAIL **c** : deficient in weight, solidity, or importance : TRIVIAL **2** : small of its kind or in amount : SCANTY, MEAGER **syn** see THIN — **slight·ly** *adv* — **slight·ness** *n*

²slight *vt* : to treat as slight or unimportant: as **a** : to treat with disdain or discourteous indifference **b** : to perform or attend to carelessly and inadequately

³slight *n* **1** : an act or an instance of slighting **2** : a humiliating discourtesy

slight·ing *adj* : characterized by disregard or disrespect : DISPARAGING ⟨a *slighting* remark⟩ — **slight·ing·ly** \-iŋ-lē\ *adv*

sli·ly *var of* SLYLY

¹slim \'slim\ *adj* **slim·mer; slim·mest** [D, bad, inferior] **1** : of small diameter or thickness in proportion to the height or length : SLENDER **2 a** : inferior in quality or amount : SLIGHT **b** : SCANTY, SMALL **syn** see THIN — **slim·ly** *adv* — **slim·ness** *n*

²slim *vb* **slimmed; slim·ming** : to make or become slender

slime \'slīm\ *n* [OE *slīm*] **1** : soft moist earth or clay; *esp* : sticky slippery mud **2** : a soft slippery substance; *esp* : a skin secretion (as of a slug or catfish)

slime mold *n* : any of a group (Myxomycetes or Mycetozoa) of organisms usu. held to be lower fungi but sometimes considered protozoans that live vegetatively as mobile plasmodia and reproduce by spores

slim-jim \'slim-'jim\ *n* : one that is notably slender

slimy \'slī-mē\ *adj* **slim·i·er; -est** **1** : of, relating to, or resembling slime : VISCOUS; *also* : covered with or yielding slime **2** : VILE, OFFENSIVE — **slim·i·ly** \-mə-lē\ *adv* — **slim·i·ness** \-mē-nəs\ *n*

¹sling \'sliŋ\ *vt* **slung** \'sləŋ\; **sling·ing** \'sliŋ-iŋ\ [ME *slingen*] **1** : to toss casually or forcibly : FLING **2** : to throw with a sling — **sling·er** \'sliŋ-ər\ *n*

²sling *n* : a slinging or hurling of or as if a missile

³sling *n* **1 a** : a device for throwing something (as stones) that usu. consists of a short strap with strings fastened to its ends and is whirled round to discharge its missile **b** : SLINGSHOT **2 a** : a usu. looped line (as of rope) used to hoist, lower, support, or carry something; *esp* : a hanging bandage suspended from the neck to support an arm or hand **b** : a chain or rope attached to a lower yard at the middle and passing around a mast near the masthead to support a yard **c** : a device (as a rope net) for enclosing material to be hoisted by a tackle or crane

⁴sling *vt* **slung** \'sləŋ\; **sling·ing** \'sliŋ-iŋ\ **1** : to put in or move or support with a sling ⟨*sling* cargo from a ship's hold⟩ **2** : to cause to become suspended ⟨*sling* a hammock⟩

sling·shot \'sliŋ-ˌshät\ *n* : a forked stick with an elastic band attached for shooting small stones

slink \'sliŋk\ *vb* **slunk** \'sləŋk\; **slink·ing** [OE *slincan* to creep] : to move or go stealthily : creep along (as in fear or shame) **syn** see SKULK

slinky \'sliŋ-kē\ *adj* **slink·i·er; -est 1** : stealthily quiet ⟨*slinky* movements⟩ **2** : sleek and sinuous in outline ⟨a *slinky* evening gown⟩

¹**slip** \'slip\ *vb* **slipped; slip·ping** [ME *slippen*] **1 a** : to move easily and smoothly : SLIDE ⟨the bolt *slipped* back⟩ ⟨*slip* the knife into its sheath⟩ **b** : to move or place quietly or stealthily : STEAL ⟨*slipped* from the room⟩ ⟨*slip* the note into her hand⟩ **c** : to pass without being noted or used ⟨time *slipped* by⟩⟨let the opportunity *slip*⟩ **2 a** : to get away from : ELUDE ⟨*slipped* his pursuers⟩; *also* : to free from : SHED ⟨the dog *slipped* his collar⟩ **b** : to escape the attention of ⟨*slipped* his mind⟩; *also* : to utter or become uttered inadvertently or casually ⟨the secret *slipped* out⟩ ⟨*slip* in a word of praise⟩ **c** : to let loose or let go of ⟨*slip* a dog from a leash⟩; *also* : to cause to slide open : RELEASE, DISENGAGE ⟨*slip* a bolt⟩ **d** : to let (a knitting stitch) pass from one needle to another without working a new stitch **3 a** : to slide out of place, away from a support, or from one's grasp ⟨the dish *slipped* to the floor⟩; *also* : to slide so as to fall or lose balance ⟨*slip* on a grease spot⟩ **b** : to cause to slide easp. in putting, passing, or inserting easily or quickly ⟨*slip* into a coat⟩ ⟨*slip* a foot into a shoe⟩ ⟨*slipped* a dress over her head⟩ **c** : to move sideways or aside; *also* : DISLOCATE **d** : to fail to progress or hold normally from or as if from sliding ⟨the loose belt continued to *slip*⟩ **4** : to fall from some level or standard (as of conduct or activity) usu. gradually or by degrees ⟨the market *slipped* from an earlier high⟩ ⟨his judgment *slipped*⟩ — **slip something over** : to foist something on another : get the better of another by trickery

²**slip** *n* **1 a** : a sloping ramp that extends out into the water and serves for landing or repairing ships **b** : a ship's berth between two piers **2** : the act or an instance of departing secretly or hurriedly **3** : a mistake in judgment, policy, or procedure : BLUNDER, MISSTEP **4** : the act or an instance of slipping down or out of place ⟨a *slip* on the ice⟩: as **a** : a sudden mishap ⟨many a *slip* between the cup and the lip⟩ **b** : a fall from some level or standard : DECLINE ⟨*slip* in stock prices⟩ **5 a** : an undergarment made in dress length with shoulder straps **b** : PILLOWCASE **6** : SIDESLIP

³**slip** *n* [ME *slippe*] **1** : a small shoot or twig cut for planting or grafting : CUTTING **2 a** : a long narrow strip of material **b** : a piece of paper used for a memorandum or record ⟨sales *slip*⟩ **3** : a young and slender person ⟨*slip* of a girl⟩

⁴**slip** *vt* **slipped; slip·ping** : to take cuttings from (a plant)

⁵**slip** *n* [OE *slypa* slime paste] : a mixture of fine clay and water used in pottery for casting, for decoration, or as a cement

slip·case \'slip-ˌkās\ *n* : a protective container with one open end for books

slip·cov·er \'slip-ˌkəv-ər\ *n* : a cover that may be slipped off and on: as **a** : a removable protective covering for an article of furniture **b** : a protective cover for a book : JACKET

slip·knot \'slip-ˌnät\ *n* : a knot that slips along a line around which it is made; *esp* : on ng an overhand knot around a rope to fo stable loop

slip noose *n* : a noose with a slipknot

slip-on \'slip-ˌón, -ˌän\ *n* : an article of clothing (as a glove, shoe, or girdle) that is easily slipped on or off

slip·over \-ˌō-vər\ *n* : SLIP-ON; *esp* : a pullover sweater

slip·page \'slip-ij\ *n* **1** : an act, instance, or process of slipping **2** : a loss in transmission of power; *also* : the difference between theoretical and actual output (as of power)

slipped disk *n* : a protrusion of one of the cartilage disks between vertebrae with pressure on spinal nerves resulting in low back pain

slip·per \'slip-ər\ *n* : a light low shoe without laces that is easily slipped on or off — **slip·pered** \-ərd\ *adj*

slip·pery \'slip-(ə-)rē\ *adj* **slip·per·i·er; -est 1** : having

a surface smooth enough to cause one to slide or lose one's hold : deficient in friction ⟨a *slippery* floor⟩ **2** : not worthy of trust : TRICKY, UNRELIABLE — **slip·per·i·ness** *n*

slippery elm *n* : a No. American elm with hard wood and fragrant mucilaginous inner bark; *also* : its wood or bark

slip·py \'slip-ē\ *adj* **slip·pi·er; -est** : SLIPPERY

slip sheet *n* : a sheet of paper placed between newly printed sheets to prevent offset — **slip-sheet** \'slip-ˌshēt\ *vt*

slip·shod \'slip-'shäd\ *adj* : very careless : SLOVENLY ⟨contempt for makeshift methods and *slipshod* work⟩

slip·slop \-ˌsläp\ *n* : shallow talk or writing : TWADDLE

slip·stick \'slip-ˌstik\ *n* : SLIDE RULE

slip stitch *n* : a concealed stitch for sewing folded edges (as hems) made by alternately running the needle inside the fold and picking up a thread or two from the body of the article

slip·stream \'slip-ˌstrēm\ *n* : the stream of air driven aft by the propeller of an aircraft

slip up \(')slip-'əp\ *vi* : to make a mistake : BLUNDER ⟨*slipped up* in his calculations⟩

slip-up \'slip-ˌəp\ *n* **1** : MISTAKE **2** : MISCHANCE

¹**slit** \'slit\ *vt* **slit; slit·ting** [ME *slitten*] **1 a** : to make a slit in : SLASH **b** : to cut off or away : SEVER **2** : to cut into long narrow strips — **slit·ter** *n*

²**slit** *n* : a long narrow cut or opening — **slit** *adj* — **slit·like** \-ˌlīk\ *adj*

slith·er \'slith-ər\ *vb* **slith·ered; slith·er·ing** \'slith-(ə-)riŋ\ [OE *slidrian*, freq. of *slīdan* to slide] **1** : to slide or cause to slide on or as if on a loose gravelly surface **2** : to slip or slide like a snake

slith·ery \-(ə-)rē\ *adj* : having a slippery surface, texture, or quality

slit trench *n* : a narrow trench for shelter in battle from bomb and shell fragments

¹**sliv·er** \'sliv-ər, *2 is usu* 'slīv-\ *n* [ME *slivere*, fr. *sliven* to slice off, fr. OE *-slīfan*] **1** : a long slender piece cut or torn off : SPLINTER **2** : an untwisted strand of textile fiber as it comes from a carding or combing machine

²**sliv·er** \'sliv-ər\ *vb* **sliv·ered; sliv·er·ing** \'sliv-(ə-)riŋ\ : to cut or form into slivers : SPLINTER

slob \'släb\ *n* : a slovenly or boorish person

¹**slob·ber** \'släb-ər\ *vb* **slob·bered; slob·ber·ing** \'släb-(ə-)riŋ\ [ME *sloberen*] **1** : to let saliva or liquid dribble from the mouth : DROOL **2** : to show feeling to excess : GUSH — **slob·ber·er** \'släb-ər-ər\ *n*

²**slobber** *n* **1** : dripping saliva **2** : silly excessive show of feeling — **slob·bery** \'släb-(ə-)rē\ *adj*

sloe \'slō\ *n* [OE *slāh*] : the tart bluish black globular fruit of the blackthorn; *also* : BLACKTHORN 1

sloe-eyed \'slō-'īd\ *adj* **1** : having soft dark bluish or purplish black eyes **2** : having slanted eyes

sloe gin *n* : a sweet reddish liqueur consisting of grain spirits flavored chiefly with sloes

slog \'släg\ *vb* **slogged; slog·ging 1** : to hit hard : BEAT **2** : to plod or work doggedly on — **slog·ger** *n*

slo·gan \'slō-gən\ *n* [ScGael *sluagh-ghairm* army cry] **1** : a word or phrase that calls to battle : WAR CRY **2** : a word or phrase used by a party, a group, or a business to attract attention

slo·gan·eer \ˌslō-gə-'ni(ə)r\ *n* : a coiner or user of slogans — **sloganeer** *vi*

slo·gan·ize \'slō-gə-ˌnīz\ *vt* : to express as a slogan

sloop \'slüp\ *n* [D *sloep*] : a sailing boat with one mast and a fore-and-aft mainsail and jib

¹**slop** \'släp\ *n* [ME *sloppe*] **1** : soft mud : SLUSH **2** : thin tasteless drink or liquid food — usu. used in pl. **3** : liquid spilled or splashed **4 a** : food waste (as garbage) or a thin gruel fed to animals **b** : excreted body waste — usu. used in pl.

²**slop** *vb* **slopped; slop·ping 1** : to spill on or over ⟨*slop* milk from a glass⟩ ⟨*slopped* her dress with gravy⟩ **2** : to feed slop to ⟨*slop* the pigs⟩ **3** : to behave or deal with in a sloppy manner ⟨*slop* about the house⟩

slop chest *n* [*slops* articles sold to sailors] : a store of clothing and personal requisites (as tobacco) carried on merchant ships for issue to the crew usu. as a charge against their wages

¹**slope** \'slōp\ *adj* [ME, adv., obliquely] : SLANTING, SLOPING

²slope *vb* **:** to take a slanting direction **:** give a slant to **:** INCLINE — **slop·er** *n*

³slope *n* **1 :** ground that forms a natural or artificial incline **2 :** upward or downward slant or inclination or degree of slant **3 :** the part of a continent draining to a particular ocean **4 :** the tangent of the angle made by a straight line with the horizontal reference line of a co-ordinate system

slop jar *n* **:** a large pail used as a chamber pot or to receive waste water from a washbowl

slop·py \'släp-ē\ *adj* **slop·pi·er; -est 1 a :** wet so as to spatter easily **:** SLUSHY **b :** wet with or as if with some-thing slopped over **2 :** SLOVENLY, CARELESS **3 :** dis-agreeably effusive — **slop·pi·ly** \'släp-ə-lē\ *adv* — **slop·pi·ness** \'släp-ē-nəs\ *n*

¹slosh \'släsh\ *n* **1 :** SLUSH **2 :** the slap or splash of liquid

²slosh *vb* **1 :** to flounder through or splash about in or with water, mud, or slush **2 :** to move with a splashing motion

¹slot \'slät\ *n* [ME, hollow running down the middle of the breast, fr. MF *esclot*] **:** a long narrow opening, groove, or passage **:** SLIT, NOTCH

²slot *vt* **slot·ted; slot·ting :** to cut a slot in

³slot *n, pl* **slot** [MF *esclot*] **:** the track of an animal and esp. a deer

sloth \'slóth, 'slōth\ *n* [ME *slouthe*, fr. *slow*] **1 :** IN-DOLENCE, LAZINESS **2 :** any of several slow-moving mam-mals of Central and So. America that are related to the armadillos and live in trees where they hang back down-ward and feed on leaves, shoots, and fruits

sloth·ful \-fəl\ *adj* **:** LAZY, SLUGGISH, INDOLENT — **sloth-ful·ly** \-fə-lē\ *adv* — **sloth·ful·ness** *n*

slot machine *n* **:** a machine whose operation is begun when a coin is dropped into a slot

¹slouch \'slaúch\ *n* **1 :** an awkward, lazy, or incompe-tent person **2 :** a gait or posture characterized by ungainly stooping of head and shoulders

²slouch *vi* **:** to walk with or assume a slouch — **slouch·er** *n*

slouch hat *n* **:** a soft usu. felt hat with a wide flexible brim

slouchy \'slaú-chē\ *adj* **slouch·i·er; -est :** slouching or slovenly esp. in appearance — **slouch·i·ly** \-chə-lē\ *adv* — **slouch·i·ness** \-chē-nəs\ *n*

¹slough *n* [OE *slōh*] **1** \'slü *also* 'slaú\ **:** a wet and marshy or muddy place (as a swamp or backwater) **2** \'slaú *also* 'slü\ **:** a discouraged, degraded, or dejected state

²slough *or* **sluff** \'sləf\ *n* [ME *slughe*] **1 :** the cast-off skin of a snake **2 :** a mass of dead tissue separating from an ulcer **3 :** something that may be shed or cast off

³slough *or* **sluff** \'sləf\ *vb* **1 :** to cast off or become cast off**:** as **a :** to cast off one's skin or dead tissue from living tissue **b :** to get rid of or discard as irksome, objection-able, or disadvantageous **2 :** to crumble slowly and fall away

slough of de·spond \,slaú-əv-di-'spänd *also* ,slü-\ [fr. the *Slough of Despond*, deep bog into which Christian falls in the allegory *Pilgrim's Progress*] **:** a state of extreme de-pression

slough over \,sləf-\ *vt* **:** to treat as slight or unimportant ⟨*sloughed over* certain aspects of the plan⟩

sloughy \'slü-ē *also* 'slaú-ē\ *adj* **:** full of sloughs **:** MIRY ⟨a *sloughy* creek⟩

Slo·vak \'slō-,väk, -,vak\ *n* **1 :** a member of a Slavic people of eastern Czechoslovakia **2 :** the Slavic language of the Slovak people — **Slovak** *adj* — **Slo·vak·i·an** \slō-'väk-ē-ən, -'vak-\ *adj or n*

¹slov·en \'sləv-ən\ *n* [ME *sloveyn* rascal] **:** one habitually negligent of neatness or cleanliness esp. in dress or person

²sloven *adj* **:** SLOVENLY

Slo·vene \'slō-,vēn\ *n* **1 a :** a member of a southern Slavic group of people usu. classed with the Serbs and Croats and living in Yugoslavia **b :** a native or inhabitant of Slovenia **2 :** the language of the Slovenes — **Slovene** *adj* — **Slo·ve·ni·an** \slō-'vē-nē-ən\ *adj or n*

slov·en·ly \'sləv-ən-lē\ *adj* **1 a :** untidy esp. in dress or person **b :** lazily slipshod **2 :** characteristic of a sloven — **slov·en·li·ness** *n* — **slovenly** *adv*

¹slow \'slō\ *adj* [OE *slāw*] **1 a :** mentally dull **:** STUPID **b :** naturally inert or sluggish **2 a :** lacking in readiness, promptness, or willingness **b :** not hasty or precipitate

3 a : moving, flowing, or proceeding without speed or at less than usual speed ⟨*slow* traffic⟩⟨a *slow* stream⟩ **b :** not vigorous or active ⟨a *slow* fire⟩; *also* **:** taking place at a low rate or over a considerable period of time ⟨*slow* growth⟩⟨a *slow* convalescence⟩ **4 :** having qualities that hinder or stop rapid progress or action ⟨a *slow* filter⟩ **5 a :** register-ing behind or below what is correct ⟨the clock is *slow*⟩ **b :** that is behind the time at a specified time or place **6 :** lacking in activity or liveliness ⟨a *slow* market⟩ ⟨a *slow* party⟩ — **slow·ly** *adv* — **slow·ness** *n*

²slow *adv* **:** SLOWLY

³slow *vb* **:** to make or go slow or slower

slow·down \'slō-,daún\ *n* **:** a slowing down

slow-foot·ed \'slō-'fút-əd\ *adj* **:** moving at a very slow pace **:** PLODDING — **slow-foot·ed·ness** *n*

slow·ish \'slō-ish\ *adj* **:** somewhat slow ⟨a *slowish* reader⟩

slow match *n* **:** a match or fuse made so as to burn slowly and evenly and used for firing (as of blasting charges)

slow motion *n* **:** action in a projected motion picture ap-parently taking place at a speed much slower than that of the photographed action

slow-poke \'slō-,pōk\ *n* **:** a very slow person

slow-wit·ted \-'wit-əd\ *adj* **:** SLOW 1 a

slow-worm \-,wərm\ *n* **:** BLINDWORM

sludge \'sləj\ *n* **1 :** MUD, MIRE **2 :** a muddy or slushy mass, deposit, or sediment; *esp* **:** precipitated solid matter produced by water and sewage treatment processes — **sludgy** \'sləj-ē\ *adj*

¹slue \'slü\ *var of* SLOUGH

²slue *vb* **:** to turn, twist, or swing about esp. out of a course **:** VEER

³slue *n* **:** an act or instance of or the position attained by sluing

⁴slue *var of* SLEW

¹slug \'sləg\ *n* [ME *slugge*, of Scand origin] **1 :** SLUG-GARD **2 :** any of numerous chiefly terrestrial mollusks that are closely related to the land snails but long and wormlike and with only a rudimentary shell or none **3 :** a smooth soft larva of a sawfly or moth that creeps like a snail

²slug *n* **1 :** a small piece of shaped metal**:** as **a :** a musket ball or bullet **b :** a metal disk for insertion in a slot ma-chine in place of a coin **2 a :** a strip of metal used like but thicker than a printer's lead **b :** a line of type cast as one piece **3 :** a single drink of liquor **:** SHOT **4 :** the gravitational unit of mass in the fps system to which a pound force can impart an acceleration of one foot per second per second

³slug *n* **:** a heavy blow esp. with the fist

⁴slug *vb* **slugged; slug·ging :** to strike heavily with or as if with the fist or a bat

slug·abed \'sləg-ə-,bed\ *n* **:** one who stays in bed after his usual or obligated time of getting up

slug·fest \'sləg-,fest\ *n* **:** a fight marked by exchange of heavy blows

slug·gard \'sləg-ərd\ *n* **:** an habitually lazy person — **sluggard** *adj*

slug·gard·ly \-lē\ *adj* **:** lazily inactive

slug·gard·ness *n* **:** the quality or state of being sluggardly **:** INDOLENCE

slug·ger \'sləg-ər\ *n* **:** one (as a batter or prizefighter) that strikes hard or with heavy blows

slug·gish \'sləg-ish\ *adj* **:** slow and inactive in movement or reaction by habit or condition — **slug·gish·ly** *adv* — **slug·gish·ness** *n*

¹sluice \'slüs\ *n* [MF *escluse*, fr. LL *exclusa*, fr. L, fem. of *exclusus*, pp. of *excludere* to shut off, exclude] **1 :** an artificial passage for water with a gate for controlling its flow or changing its direction **2 :** a body of water held back by a gate or a stream flowing through a gate **3 :** a device (as a water gate) for controlling the flow of water **4 :** a channel that carries off surplus water **5 :** a long inclined trough (as for washing gold-bearing earth or for floating logs to a sawmill)

²sluice *vt* **1 :** to draw off by or through a sluice **2 a :** to wash with or in water running through or from a sluice **b :** DRENCH, FLUSH

sluice·way \-,wā\ *n* **:** an artificial channel into which water is let by a sluice

¹slum \'sləm\ *n* **:** a thickly populated section esp. of a city marked by crowding, dirty run-down housing, and generally wretched living conditions

²slum *vi* **slummed; slum·ming** : to visit slums esp. out of curiosity or for pleasure — **slum·mer** *n*

¹slum·ber \'sləm-bər\ *vi* **slum·bered; slum·ber·ing** \-b(ə-)riŋ\ [ME *slumberen*, freq. of *slumen* to doze] **1** : to sleep usu. lightly **2** : to lie dormant or latent ⟨a *slumbering* volcano⟩ — **slum·ber·er** \-bər-ər\ *n*

²slumber *n* **1 a** : act of slumbering : SLEEP **b** : light sleep : DOZE **2** : LETHARGY, TORPOR **syn** see SLEEP

slum·ber·ous *or* **slum·brous** \'sləm-b(ə-)rəs\ *adj* **1** : SLEEPY, SOMNOLENT **2** : inviting slumber : SOPORIFIC

slumber party *n* : an overnight gathering of teen-age girls usu. at one of their homes at which they dress in nightclothes but pass the night more in talking than sleeping

slum·bery \'sləm-b(ə-)rē\ *adj* : SLUMBEROUS

slum·gul·lion \'sləm-ˌgəl-yən\ *n* : a meat stew

¹slump \'sləmp\ *vi* **1** : to drop or slide down suddenly : COLLAPSE **2** : to assume a drooping posture or carriage : SLOUCH **3** : to fall off sharply

²slump *n* : a marked or sustained decline esp. in economic activity or prices

slung *past of* SLING

slung·shot \'sləŋ-ˌshät\ *n* : a striking weapon consisting of a small mass of metal or stone fixed on a flexible handle or strap

slunk *past of* SLINK

¹slur \'slər\ *vb* **slurred; slur·ring 1 a** : to slide or slip over without due mention, consideration, or emphasis **b** : to perform hurriedly : SKIMP **2** : to perform (successive musical notes of different pitch) in a smooth or connected manner **3** : to speak indistinctly usu. as a result of carelessness or haste : enunciate obscurely **4** : DRAG, SHUFFLE

²slur *n* **1 a** : a curved line ⌣ or ⌒ connecting notes to be sung or performed without a break **b** : the combination of two or more slurred tones **2** : a slurring manner of speech

³slur *vb* **slurred; slur·ring** [ME *sloor* thin mud] **1** : to cast aspersions upon : DISPARAGE **2** : to make indistinct : OBSCURE **3** : to slip so as to cause a slur

⁴slur *n* **1 a** : ASPERSION, CALUMNY **b** : REPROACH, STIGMA **2** : a blurred spot in printed matter : SMUDGE

slurp \'slərp\ *vb* [D *slurpen*] : to eat or drink noisily or with a sucking sound — **slurp** *n*

slur·ry \'slər-ē, 'slə-rē\ *n, pl* **slurries** : a watery mixture of insoluble matter (as mud, lime, or pulverized ore)

slush \'sləsh\ *n* **1** : partly melted or watery snow **2** : soft mud : MIRE **3** : RUBBISH, DRIVEL

slush fund *n* **1** : a fund raised from the sale of refuse to obtain small luxuries or pleasures for a warship's crew **2** : a fund for bribing public officials or carrying on corruptive propaganda

slushy \'sləsh-ē\ *adj* **slush·i·er; -est** : full of or resembling slush ⟨a *slushy* road⟩ ⟨soft *slushy* ice⟩ — **slush·i·ness** *n*

slut \'slət\ *n* [ME *slutte*] **1** : a slovenly woman : SLATTERN **2** : a lewd woman; *esp* : PROSTITUTE — **slut·tish** \'slət-ish\ *adj* — **slut·tish·ly** *adv* — **slut·tish·ness** *n*

sly \'slī\ *adj* **sli·er** *also* **sly·er** \'slī-(ə-)r\; **sli·est** *also* **sly·est** \-slī-əst\ [ON *slægr*] **1 a** : artfully cunning : CRAFTY **b** : SECRETIVE, FURTIVE **2** : lightly mischievous : ROGUISH — **sly·ly** *adv* — **sly·ness** *n*

syn SLY, CRAFTY, WILY mean apt to attain an end by devious means. SLY stresses lack of forthrightness in behavior or speech ⟨*sly* insinuations⟩ CRAFTY suggests skill in deception acquired by experience ⟨*crafty* trial lawyer⟩ WILY stresses cleverness in setting or avoiding traps ⟨*wily* fox⟩

— on the sly : FURTIVELY

¹smack \'smak\ *n* [OE *smæc*] **1** : characteristic or perceptible taste or flavor **2** : a small quantity

²smack *vi* **1** : to have a flavor, trace, or suggestion ⟨the roast *smacks* of thyme⟩ ⟨such actions *smack* of treachery⟩

³smack *vb* **1** : to close and open (lips) noisily esp. in eating **2** : to kiss usu. loudly or boisterously **3** : to make or give a smack ⟨*smacked* the cat from the table⟩

⁴smack *n* **1** : a quick sharp noise made by rapidly compressing and opening the lips **2** : a loud kiss **3** : a sharp slap or blow

⁵smack *adv* : in a square and sharp manner : DIRECTLY ⟨it hit him *smack* in the face⟩

⁶smack *n* [D *smak* or LG *smack*] : a sailing ship (as a sloop or cutter) used chiefly in coasting and fishing

smack–dab \'smak-'dab\ *adv, dial* : SQUARELY, EXACTLY

smack·er \'smak-ər\ *n* **1** : one that smacks **2** *slang* : DOLLAR

smack·ing \'smak-iŋ\ *adj* : BRISK, LIVELY ⟨a *smacking* breeze⟩

¹small \'smȯl\ *adj* [OE *smæl*] **1** : little in size **2** : few in numbers or members ⟨a *small* crowd⟩ **3** : little in amount ⟨a *small* supply⟩ **4** : not very much ⟨*small* success⟩ **5** : UNIMPORTANT ⟨a *small* matter⟩ **6** : operating on a limited scale ⟨*small* dealers⟩ **7** : GENTLE, SOFT ⟨a *small* voice⟩ **8** : not generous : MEAN ⟨a *small* nature⟩ **9** : made up of small units **10** : HUMBLE, MODEST ⟨a *small* beginning⟩ **11** : HUMILIATED, HUMBLED ⟨felt very *small* to be caught cheating⟩ **12** : LOWERCASE — **small·ness** *n*

syn LITTLE: SMALL and LITTLE are often interchangeable but SMALL, contrasting with *large* or *great*, applies more to relative size determined by capacity, value, number ⟨a *small* mouth⟩ ⟨a *small* quantity of salt⟩ LITTLE, contrasting with *big* or *much*, is more absolute in implication and may suggest pettiness, peteteness, insignificance, immaturity ⟨*little* girl⟩ ⟨*little* hope of success⟩

²small *adv* **1** : in or into small pieces ⟨cut the meat *small*⟩ **2** : without force or loudness ⟨speak *small*⟩ **3** : in a small manner ⟨most businesses begin *small*⟩

³small *n* **1** : a part smaller and esp. narrower than the remainder ⟨the *small* of the back⟩ **2 a** *pl* : small-sized products **b** *pl, Brit* : SMALLCLOTHES

smal·lage \'smȯ-lij\ *n* [ME *smalache*, fr. *smal* small + *ache* wild celery, fr. OF, fr. L *apium*] : a strong-scented herb that is the wild form of celery

small arm *n* : a firearm fired while held in the hands

small beer *n* **1** : a weak or inferior beer **2** : something of small importance : TRIVIA

small change *n* **1** : coins of low denominations **2** : something trifling or petty

small circle *n* : a circle on the surface of a sphere whose plane does not pass through the center of the sphere; *esp* : such a circle on the surface of the earth — compare GREAT CIRCLE

small·clothes \'smȯl-ˌklō(th)z\ *n pl* : close-fitting knee breeches worn esp. in the 18th century

small–fry \-ˌfrī\ *adj* **1** : MINOR, UNIMPORTANT **2** : of or relating to children : CHILDISH

small game *n* : birds and small mammals (as rabbits) hunted for sport

small hours *n pl* : the early morning hours

small intestine *n* : the part of the intestine that lies between the stomach and colon, consists of duodenum, jejunum, and ileum, secretes digestive enzymes, and is the chief seat of the absorption of digested nutrients

small·ish \'smȯ-lish\ *adj* : somewhat small

small–mind·ed \'smȯl-'mīn-dəd\ *adj* : having narrow interests, sympathies, or outlook; *also* : typical of a smallminded person — **small–mind·ed·ly** *adv* — **small–mind·ed·ness** *n*

small potatoes *n* : someone or something of trivial importance or worth

small·pox \'smȯl-ˌpäks\ *n* : an acute contagious virus disease marked by fever and skin eruption with pustules, sloughing, and scar formation

small–scale \-'skāl\ *adj* **1** : small in scope; *esp* : small in output or operation **2** : having a scale (as one inch to 25 miles) that permits plotting of comparatively little detail ⟨a *small-scale* map⟩

small stores *n pl* : articles of clothing sold by a naval supply officer to naval personnel

small talk *n* : light or casual conversation

small–time \'smȯl-'tīm\ *adj* : insignificant in performance and standing : SMALL-SCALE, MINOR — **small–tim·er** \-'tī-mər\ *n*

¹smart \'smärt\ *vi* [OE *smeortan*] **1** : to cause or feel a sharp stinging pain **2** : to feel or endure distress, remorse, or embarrassment ⟨*smart* under criticism⟩

²smart *adj* **1** : causing smarting : STINGING **2** : marked by forceful activity or vigorous strength **3** : BRISK, SPIRITED **4 a** : mentally alert : BRIGHT **b** : sharp in scheming : SHREWD **5 a** : WITTY, CLEVER **b** : PERT, SAUCY **6 a** : stylish or elegant in dress or appearance **b** : SOPHISTICATED **c** : FASHIONABLE **syn** see CLEVER — **smart·ly** *adv* — **smart·ness** *n*

³smart *adv* : SMARTLY

⁴smart n **1** : a smarting pain; esp : a stinging local pain **2** : poignant grief or remorse

smart al·eck \'smärt-ˌal-ik, -ˌel-\ n : an offensively conceited and bumptious person — **smart-al·ecky** \-ˌal-ə-kē, -ˌel-\ or **smart-aleck** adj

smart·en \'smärt-ᵊn\ vb **smart·ened; smart·en·ing** \'smärt-niŋ, -ᵊn-iŋ\ **1** : to make smart or smarter : SPRUCE, FRESHEN ⟨smarten up an old dress with a new collar⟩ ⟨smartened himself for the party⟩ **2** : to make or become more alert ⟨smarten up, young man, if you don't want to get into trouble⟩

smart set n : ultrafashionable society

smart·weed \'smärt-ˌwēd\ n : any of various weedy plants with strong acrid juice that are related to the buckwheats

smarty or **smart·ie** \'smärt-ē\ n, pl **smart·ies** : SMART ALECK

¹smash \'smash\ vb **1** : to break in pieces by violence : SHATTER ⟨smash down a door⟩ ⟨the dish smashed on the floor⟩ **2** : to drive, throw, or move violently esp. with a destructive effect ⟨the ball smashed through the window⟩ **3** : to destroy utterly : WRECK **4** : to go to pieces suddenly : COLLAPSE — **smash·er** n

²smash n **1 a** : a smashing blow or attack **b** : a hard overhand stroke (as in tennis) **2** : the condition of being smashed **3 a** : the action or sound of smashing; esp : a wreck due to collision : CRASH **b** : utter collapse : RUIN; esp : BANKRUPTCY **4** : a striking success : HIT ⟨the new play is a smash⟩

smash·up \'smash-ˌəp\ n **1** : a complete collapse **2** : a destructive collision of motor vehicles

smat·ter \'smat-ər\ n : SMATTERING

smat·ter·ing \'smat-ə-riŋ\ n [fr. gerund of ME smateren to chatter, talk ignorantly] **1** : superficial piecemeal knowledge **2** : a small scattered number

smaze \'smāz\ n [smoke + haze] : a combination of haze and smoke similar to smog in appearance but less damp in consistency

¹smear \'smi(ə)r\ n [OE smeoru] **1** : a spot made by or as if by an oily or sticky substance : SMUDGE **2** : material smeared on a surface; esp : material prepared for microscopic examination by smearing on a slide **3** : a usu. unsubstantiated charge or accusation

²smear vt **1 a** : to spread or daub with something oily or sticky **b** : to spread over a surface **2** : to stain, smudge, or dirty by or as if by smearing; also : to blacken the reputation of **3** : to obliterate or blur by or as if by smearing — **smear·er** n

smear·case or **smier·case** \'smi(ə)r-ˌkās\ n [modif. of G schmierkäse, fr. schmieren to smear + käse cheese] chiefly Midland : COTTAGE CHEESE

smear word n : an epithet intended to smear a person or group

smeary \'smi(ə)r-ē\ adj **smear·i·er; -est 1** : SMEARED **2** : liable to cause smears

¹smell \'smel\ vb **smelled** \'smeld\ or **smelt** \'smelt\; **smell·ing** [ME smellen] **1** : to get the odor or scent of through stimuli affecting the olfactory sense organs of the nose **2** : to detect or become aware of as if by the sense of smell **3** : to exercise the sense of smell **4 a** : to have or give forth an odor **b** : to give off a suggestion of something and esp. of something unwholesome or evil ⟨the plan smells of trickery⟩ — **smell·er** n — **smell a rat** : to have a suspicion of something wrong

²smell n **1 a** : the process or power of smelling **b** : the special sense concerned with the perception of odor **2** : the property of a thing that affects the olfactory organs : ODOR **3** : a pervading quality : AURA **4** : an act of smelling

syn ODOR, SCENT, AROMA: SMELL and ODOR may imply either a pleasant or unpleasant sensation though SMELL may cover a wider range of quality, intensity, or source; SCENT implies less strength and suggests a substance, an animal, or a plant giving off a characteristic smell; AROMA suggests a pungent, pervasive, usu. pleasant smell ⟨aroma of fresh coffee⟩

smelling salts n pl : a usu. scented aromatic preparation of ammonium carbonate and ammonia water used to relieve faintness

smelly \'smel-ē\ adj **smell·i·er; -est** : having a smell and esp. a bad smell

¹smelt \'smelt\ n, pl **smelts** or **smelt** [OE] : any of several very small food fishes of coastal or fresh waters that resemble and are related to the trout

²smelt vt [D or LG smelten; akin to E melt] : to melt or fuse (as ore) usu. in order to separate the metal : REFINE, REDUCE

smelt·er \'smel-tər\ n : one that smelts: **a** : a worker in or an owner of a smeltery **b** or **smelt·ery** \-t(ə-)rē\ : an establishment for smelting

smidg·en or **smidg·eon** or **smidg·in** \'smij-ən\ n : a small amount : BIT

smi·lax \'smī-ˌlaks\ n [Gk, bindweed, yew] **1** : GREENBRIER **2** : a delicate greenhouse twining plant related to the garden asparagus and having ovate bright green terminal branches in place of leaves

¹smile \'smīl\ vb [ME smilen] **1** : to have, produce, or exhibit a smile **2 a** : to look with amusement or ridicule **b** : to be propitious or agreeable ⟨the weather smiled on our plans⟩ **3** : to express by a smile — **smil·er** n — **smil·ing·ly** \'smī-liŋ-lē\ adv

²smile n : a change of facial expression in which the eyes brighten and the lips curve slightly upward esp. in expression of amusement, pleasure, approval, or sometimes scorn — **smile·less** \'smīl-ləs\ adj — **smile·less·ly** adv

smirch \'smərch\ vt [ME smorchen] **1** : to make dirty, stained, or discolored esp. by smearing with something that soils **2** : to bring disrepute or disgrace on — **smirch** n

smirk \'smərk\ vi [OE smearcian to smile] : to smile in an affected manner : SIMPER — **smirk** n

smirky \'smər-kē\ adj : SMIRKING

smite \'smīt\ vb **smote** \'smōt\; **smit·ten** \'smit-ᵊn\ or **smote; smit·ing** \'smīt-iŋ\ [OE smītan] **1** : to strike sharply or heavily esp. with the hand or a hand weapon **2 a** : to kill or injure by smiting **b** : to attack or afflict suddenly and injuriously ⟨smitten by disease⟩ **3** : to affect like a sudden hard blow ⟨smitten with terror⟩ — **smit·er** \'smīt-ər\ n

smith \'smith\ n [OE] **1** : a worker in metals : BLACKSMITH **2** : MAKER — often used in combination ⟨gunsmith⟩ ⟨tunesmith⟩

smith·er·eens \ˌsmith-ə-'rēnz\ n pl [IrGael smidirín small fragment] : FRAGMENTS, BITS

smith·ery \'smith-ə-rē\ n **1** : the work, art, or trade of a smith **2** : SMITHY

smith·son·ite \'smith-sə-ˌnīt\ n [James Smithson d1829 British chemist] : a usu. white or nearly white native zinc carbonate $ZnCO_3$

smithy \'smith-ē, 'smith-\ n, pl **smith·ies** : the workshop of a smith

¹smock \'smäk\ n [OE smoc] **1** archaic : a woman's undergarment : CHEMISE **2** : a light loose garment worn usu. over regular clothing for protection from dirt

²smock vt : to embroider or shirr with smocking

smock·ing \'smäk-iŋ\ n : a decorative embroidery or shirring made by gathering cloth in regularly spaced round tucks

smog \'smäg\ n [blend of smoke and fog] : a fog made heavier and darker by smoke and chemical fumes — **smog·gy** \'smäg-ē\ adj

smock 2

smok·a·ble or **smoke·a·ble** \'smō-kə-bəl\ adj : fit for smoking

¹smoke \'smōk\ n [OE smoca] **1 a** : the gas of burning organic materials (as coal, wood, or tobacco) made visible by small particles of carbon **b** : a suspension of solid or liquid particles in a gas **2** : a mass or column of smoke **3** : fume or vapor often resulting from the action of heat on moisture **4** : something of little substance, permanence, or value **5** : something that obscures **6** : something to smoke (as a cigarette); also : the smoking of this — **smoke·like** \-ˌlīk\ adj

²smoke vb **1 a** : to emit or exhale smoke **b** : to emit excessive smoke **2** : to inhale and exhale the fumes of burning tobacco or something like tobacco; also : to use in smoking ⟨smoke a pipe⟩ ⟨smoke a cigar⟩ **3** : to act on with smoke: as **a** : to drive away by smoke **b** : to blacken or discolor with smoke **c** : to cure by exposure to smoke ⟨smoked meat⟩ ⟨smoked cheese⟩ **d** : to stupefy (as bees) by smoke

smoke·chas·er \-ˌchā-sər\ *n* : a forest-fire fighter

smoke–filled room \ˌsmōk-ˌfild-\ *n* : a room (as in a hotel) in which a small group of politicians carry on negotiations

smoke·house \ˈsmōk-ˌhaủs\ *n* : a building where meat or fish is cured by means of dense smoke

smoke jumper *n* : a forest-fire fighter who parachutes to locations otherwise difficult to reach

smoke·less \ˈsmōk-ləs\ *adj* : producing or containing little or no smoke ⟨*smokeless* powder⟩ ⟨a clean *smokeless* sky⟩

smoke out *vt* **1** : to drive out by or as if by smoke **2** : to bring to public knowledge

smok·er \ˈsmō-kər\ *n* **1** : one that smokes **2** : a railroad car or compartment in which smoking is allowed **3** : an informal social gathering for men

smoke screen *n* : a screen of or as if of smoke to hinder observation or detection esp. of a military force, area, or activity

smoke·stack \ˈsmōk-ˌstak\ *n* : a chimney or funnel through which smoke and gases are discharged (as from a ship or factory)

smoke tree *n* : a small shrubby tree of the sumac family often grown for its large panicles of tiny flowers suggesting a cloud of smoke

smoking jacket *n* : a man's soft jacket for wear at home

smoking lamp *n* : a lamp on a ship kept lighted during the hours when smoking is allowed

smoking room *n* : a room (as in a hotel or club) set apart for smokers

smoky \ˈsmō-kē\ *adj* **smok·i·er; -est** **1** : emitting smoke esp. in large quantities ⟨*smoky* stoves⟩ **2** : resembling or suggestive of smoke ⟨a *smoky* flavor⟩ ⟨a vague *smoky* outline⟩ **3** : filled with or darkened by smoke ⟨a *smoky* room⟩ ⟨*smoky* ceilings⟩ — **smok·i·ly** \-kə-lē\ *adv* — **smok·i·ness** \-kē-nəs\ *n*

smoky quartz *n* : CAIRNGORM

¹smol·der *or* **smoul·der** \ˈsmōl-dər\ *n* [ME *smolder*] : a slow smoky fire

²smolder *or* **smoulder** *vi* **smol·dered** *or* **smoul·dered; smol·der·ing** *or* **smoul·der·ing** \-d(ə-)riŋ\ **1** : to burn sluggishly with smoke and usu. without flame ⟨fire was *smoldering* in the grate⟩ **2** : to exist in a state of suppressed activity ⟨a *smoldering* rebellion⟩; *also* : to indicate a suppressed emotion ⟨eyes *smoldering* with anger⟩

smolt \ˈsmōlt\ *n* [ME (Sc)] : a salmon or sea trout when it is about two years old and silvery and first descends to the sea

smooch \ˈsmüch\ *vi* : KISS, PET — **smooch** *n*

¹smooth \ˈsmüth\ *adj* [OE *smōth*] **1 a** : having a continuous even surface : not rough ⟨a *smooth* skin⟩ **b** : being without hairs or projections : GLABROUS **c** : causing no resistance to sliding **2** : free from obstacles or difficulties ⟨a *smooth* path⟩ **3** : even and uninterrupted in flow or flight **4** : plausibly flattering : INGRATIATING ⟨a *smooth* salesman⟩ **5 a** : SERENE, EQUABLE **b** : AMIABLE, COURTEOUS **6** : not sharp or acid : BLAND ⟨a *smooth* sherry⟩ **syn** see SUAVE — **smooth·ly** *adv* — **smooth·ness** *n*

²smooth *vt* **1** : to make smooth **2 a** : to free from what is harsh or disagreeable : POLISH ⟨*smoothed* out his style⟩ **b** : SOOTHE **3** : to minimize (as a fault) in order to allay ill will : PALLIATE ⟨*smoothed* things over with apologies⟩ **4** : to free from obstruction or difficulty **5** : to cause to lie evenly and in order : PREEN ⟨*smooths* down her hair⟩ — **smooth·er** *n*

smooth·bore \-ˈbō(ə)r, -ˈbó(ə)r\ *adj* : having a smooth⸗ surfaced bore ⟨*smoothbore* firearms⟩ — **smooth·bore** \ˈsmüth-, \ *n*

smooth·en \ˈsmü-thən\ *vb* : to make or become smooth

smooth muscle *n* : muscle made up of spindle-shaped cells with single nuclei and no cross striations that is typical of visceral organs, occurs esp. in sheets and rings, and is not under voluntary control — called also *involuntary muscle;* compare STRIATED MUSCLE

smooth–tongued \ˈsmüth-ˈtəŋd\ *adj* : ingratiating in speech

smoothy *or* **smooth·ie** \ˈsmü-thē\ *n, pl* **smooth·ies** **1 a** : a person with polished manners **b** : a man with an ingratiating manner toward women **2** : a smooth-tongued person

smor·gas·bord \ˈsmór-gəs-ˌbórd, -ˌbōrd\ *n* [Sw *smörgås-*

bord, fr. smörgås buttered bread + *bord* table] : a luncheon or supper buffet offering a large variety of foods and dishes

smote *past of* SMITE

¹smoth·er \ˈsməth-ər\ *n* [ME *smorther* dense smoke, fr. *smoren* to smother, fr. OE *smorian*] **1** : a dense cloud (as of fog, foam, or dust) **2** : a confused multitude of things : WELTER

²smother *vb* **smoth·ered; smoth·er·ing** \ˈsməth-(ə-)riŋ\ **1 a** : to overcome by depriving of air or exposing to smoke or fumes : SUFFOCATE **b** : to prevent the development or activity of ⟨*smother* a child with too much care⟩ **2** : to become suffocated **3 a** : to cover up : SUPPRESS ⟨*smother* a yawn⟩ ⟨*smother* a revolt⟩ **b** : to overlay thickly : BLANKET ⟨broiled steak *smothered* with mushrooms⟩ **c** : OVERWHELM **d** : CONQUER

¹smudge \ˈsməj\ *vb* [ME *smogen*] **1 a** : to make a smudge on **b** : to soil as if by smudging **2** : to smoke or protect by a smudge **3** : to make a smudge or become smudged

²smudge *n* **1 a** : a blurry spot or streak : SMEAR **b** : STAIN **2** : a fire made to smoke (as for driving away mosquitoes or protecting fruit from frost) — **smudg·i·ly** \ˈsməj-ə-lē\ *adv* — **smudg·i·ness** \ˈsməj-ē-nəs\ *n* — **smudgy** \ˈsməj-ē\ *adj*

smug \ˈsməg\ *adj* **smug·ger; smug·gest** : highly self-satisfied : COMPLACENT — **smug·ly** *adv* — **smug·ness** *n*

smug·gle \ˈsməg-əl\ *vb* **smug·gled; smug·gling** \-(ə-)liŋ\ [LG *smuggeln*] **1** : to export or import secretly and unlawfully esp. to avoid paying duty ⟨*smuggle* jewels⟩ **2** : to take, bring, or introduce secretly or stealthily — **smug·gler** \ˈsməg-lər\ *n*

¹smut \ˈsmət\ *vb* **smut·ted; smut·ting** **1** : to stain, taint, or affect with smut **2** : to become affected by smut

²smut *n* **1** : matter that soils or blackens; *esp* : a particle of soot **2** : any of various destructive diseases of plants and esp. of cereal grasses caused by parasitic fungi that transform plant organs (as seeds) into dark masses of spores; *also* : a fungus causing a smut **3** : obscene or indecent language or matter

smut·ty \ˈsmət-ē\ *adj* **smut·ti·er; -est** **1** : soiled or tainted with smut ⟨a *smutty* face⟩ **2** : affected with smut fungus **3** : OBSCENE, INDECENT ⟨*smutty* jokes⟩ — **smut·ti·ly** \ˈsmət-ᵊl-ē\ *adv* — **smut·ti·ness** \ˈsmət-ē-nəs\ *n*

snack \ˈsnak\ *n* [ME *snake* bite] : a light meal : LUNCH

snack bar *n* : a public eating place where snacks are served usu. at a counter

snaf·fle \ˈsnaf-əl\ *n* : a simple jointed bit for a bridle — **snaffle** *vt*

¹snag \ˈsnag\ *n* [of Scand origin] **1** : a stump or stub of a tree branch esp. when embedded under water and not visible from the surface **2** : an uneven or broken projection from a smooth or finished surface **3** : a concealed or unexpected difficulty or hindrance — **snag·gy** \ˈsnag-ē\ *adj*

²snag *vt* **snagged; snag·ging** **1 a** : to catch and usu. damage on or as if on a snag ⟨*snagged* her new nylons⟩ **b** : to halt or impede as if by catching on a snag ⟨the bill was *snagged* in committee⟩ **2** : to catch or obtain by quick action ⟨*snagged* two tickets for the big game⟩

snag·gle·tooth \ˈsnag-əl-ˌtüth\ *n* : an irregular, broken, or projecting tooth — **snag·gle·toothed** \ˌsnag-əl-ˈtütht\ *adj*

snail \ˈsnāl\ *n* [OE *snægl*] **1** : a gastropod mollusk esp. when having an external enclosing spiral shell **2** : a slow-moving person or thing

¹snake \ˈsnāk\ *n* [OE *snaca*] **1** : any of numerous limbless reptiles (suborder Serpentes or Ophidia) with a long tapering body and often salivary glands modified to produce venom which is injected through grooved or tubular fangs **2** : a despicable or treacherous person — **snake·like** \-ˌlīk\ *adj*

snail

²snake *vb* **1** : to crawl or move sinuously, silently, or secretly **2** : to move (as logs) by dragging

snake·bird \ˈsnāk-ˌbərd\ *n* : any of several fish-eating birds related to the cormorants but distinguished by a long slender neck and sharp-pointed bill

snake·bite \-ˌbīt\ *n* : the bite of a snake and esp. a venomous snake

ə **abut;** ᵊ **kitten;** ər **further;** a **back;** ā **bake;** ä **cot, cart;** aủ **out;** ch **chin;** e **less;** ē **easy;** g **gift;** i **trip;** ī **life**

snake charmer *n* : an entertainer who exhibits his professed power to charm or fascinate venomous snakes

snake dance *n* **1 :** a ceremonial dance in which snakes or their images are handled, invoked, or symbolically imitated by individual sinuous actions **2 :** a group progression in a single-file serpentine path (as in celebration of an athletic victory)

snake doctor *n* : DRAGONFLY

snake fence *n* : WORM FENCE

snake in the grass 1 : a lurking or unsuspected danger **2 :** a secretly faithless friend

snake oil *n* : any of various substances or mixtures sold (as by a traveling medicine show) as medicine usu. without regard to their medical worth or properties

snake·root \'snāk-,rüt\ *n* : any of various plants mostly with roots reputed to cure snakebites

snake·skin \-,skin\ *n* : the skin of a snake or leather made from it

snaky \'snā-kē\ *adj* **snak·i·er; -est 1 :** of or resembling a snake **2 :** abounding in snakes — **snak·i·ly** \-kə-lē\ *adv*

¹snap \'snap\ *vb* **snapped; snap·ping** [D or LG *snappen*] **1 a :** to make a sudden closing of the jaws : seize something sharply with the mouth ⟨fish *snapping* at the bait⟩ **b :** to grasp at something eagerly ⟨*snapped* at the chance to travel⟩ **c :** to take possession of promptly and decisively ⟨*snap* up a bargain⟩ **2 :** to speak or utter sharply or irritably ⟨*snap* at a questioner⟩⟨*snap* out an answer⟩ **3 a :** to break or break apart suddenly esp. with a sharp sound ⟨the twig *snapped*⟩ ⟨*snapped* the bone in two⟩ **b :** to give way or cause to give way suddenly under stress ⟨his nerve *snapped* at the crucial moment⟩ **c :** to bring to a sudden end ⟨*snapped* the opposing team's winning streak⟩ **4 :** to make or cause to make a sharp or crackling sound ⟨*snap* a whip⟩ **5 a :** to close or fit in place with an abrupt movement ⟨the lid *snapped* shut⟩ **b :** to put into or remove from a position by a sudden movement or with a snapping sound ⟨*snap* a lock⟩ ⟨*snap* off a switch⟩ **c :** to close by means of snaps or fasteners ⟨*snapped* up the back of her dress⟩ **6 :** FLASH ⟨her eyes *snapped* in anger⟩ **7 a :** to act or be acted upon with snap ⟨*snapped* to attention⟩⟨*snapped* him out of his reverie⟩ **b :** to put (a football) in play esp. by passing or handing backward between the legs **c :** to take a snapshot of

²snap *n* **1 :** an abrupt closing (as of the mouth in biting or of scissors in cutting); *esp* : a biting or snatching with the teeth or jaws **2 :** something that is easy and presents no problems : CINCH **3 :** a small amount : BIT ⟨don't care a *snap*⟩ **4 a :** a sudden snatching at something **b :** a quick short movement **c :** a sudden sharp breaking **5 :** a sound made by snapping something ⟨shut the book with a *snap*⟩ **6 :** a sudden interval of harsh weather ⟨cold *snap*⟩ **7 :** a catch or fastening that closes or locks with a click ⟨*snap* of a bracelet⟩ **8 :** a thin brittle cookie **9 :** SNAPSHOT **10 a :** ENERGY **b :** SMARTNESS, SNAPPINESS **c :** RESILIENCE **11 :** an act or instance of snapping a football

³snap *adj* **1 :** made suddenly or without deliberation ⟨*snap* judgment⟩ **2 :** shutting or fastening with a click or by means of a device that snaps ⟨*snap* lock⟩ **3 :** unusually easy ⟨*snap* course⟩

snap back \(')snap-'bak\ *vi* : to make a quick or vigorous recovery ⟨*snap back* after an illness⟩

snap-back \'snap-,bak\ *n* **1 :** a football snap **2 :** a sudden rebound or recovery

snap bean *n* : a bean grown primarily for its young pods usu. used broken in pieces as a cooked vegetable — compare SHELL BEAN

snap·drag·on \'snap-,drag-ən\ *n* : any of several garden plants of the figwort family having showy white, crimson, or yellow 2-lipped flowers likened to the face of a dragon

snap·per \'snap-ər\ *n, pl* **snappers** *also* **snapper 1 a :** something that snaps **b :** SNAPPING TURTLE **2 a :** any of a large family of active carnivorous fishes of warm seas important as food and sport fishes **b :** any of several immature fishes (as the young of the bluefish) that resemble a snapper

snapping turtle *n* : any of several large edible American aquatic turtles with powerful jaws and a strong musky odor

snap·pish \'snap-ish\ *adj* **1 :** marked by snapping irritable speech : IRASCIBLE ⟨a *snappish* disposition⟩ **2 :** in-

clined to bite ⟨a *snappish* dog⟩ — **snap·pish·ly** *adv* — **snap·pish·ness** *n*

snap·py \'snap-ē\ *adj* **snap·pi·er; -est 1 :** SNAPPISH **2 a :** LIVELY **b :** briskly cold **c :** STYLISH, SMART — **snap·pi·ly** \'snap-ə-lē\ *adv* — **snap·pi·ness** \'snap-ē-nəs\ *n*

snap·shot \'snap-,shät\ *n* : a casual photograph made by rapid exposure usu. with a small hand-held camera

¹snare \'sna(ə)r, 'sne(ə)r\ *n* [ON *snara*] **1 :** a trap often consisting of a noose for catching small animals or birds **2 :** something by which one is entangled, trapped, or deceived **3 :** one of the catgut strings or metal spirals of a snare drum

²snare *vt* **1 :** to capture or entangle by or as if by use of a snare **2 :** to win or attain by skillful or deceptive maneuvers *syn* see CATCH — **snar·er** *n*

snare drum *n* : a small double-headed drum with one or more snares stretched across its lower head

¹snarl \'snärl\ *n* [ME] **1 :** a tangle esp. of hairs or thread : KNOT **2 :** a tangled situation : COMPLICATION ⟨a traffic *snarl*⟩

²snarl *vb* : to get into a tangle

³snarl *vb* [freq. of obs. *snar* to growl; akin to E *snore*] **1 :** to growl with a snapping or gnashing of teeth **2 :** to give vent to anger in surly language **3 :** to utter with a snarl — **snarl·er** *n*

⁴snarl *n* : a surly angry growl

¹snatch \'snach\ *vb* [ME *snacchen*] **1 :** to seize or try to seize something quickly or suddenly **2 :** to grasp or take suddenly or hastily : GRAB *syn* see TAKE — **snatch·er** *n*

²snatch *n* **1 :** a snatching at or of something **2 :** a brief opportune period ⟨slept in *snatches*⟩ **3 :** something brief, fragmentary, or hurried ⟨*snatches* of old tunes⟩

snatchy \'snach-ē\ *adj* : done in or by snatches

snath \'snath, 'sneth\ *or* **snathe** \'snāth, 'snath\ *n* [OE *snæd*] : the handle of a scythe

snaz·zy \'snaz-ē\ *adj* **snaz·zi·er; -est :** conspicuously or flashily attractive

¹sneak \'snēk\ *vb* **1 :** to go stealthily or furtively : SLINK **2 :** to put, bring, or take in a furtive or sly manner *syn* see SKULK

²sneak *n* **1 :** a person who acts in a stealthy, furtive, or sly manner **2 :** the act or an instance of sneaking

³sneak *adj* **1 :** carried on secretly : CLANDESTINE **2 :** SURPRISE ⟨a *sneak* attack⟩

sneak·er \'snē-kər\ *n* **1 :** one that sneaks **2 :** a usu. canvas sports shoe with a pliable rubber sole

sneak·ing \-kiŋ\ *adj* **1 :** FURTIVE, UNDERHAND **2 :** not openly expressed as if something to be ashamed of ⟨a *sneaking* sympathy⟩ ⟨a *sneaking* suspicion⟩ — **sneak·ing·ly** \-kiŋ-lē\ *adv*

sneaky \'snē-kē\ *adj* **sneak·i·er; -est :** marked by stealth, furtiveness, or slyness — **sneak·i·ly** \-kə-lē\ *adv* — **sneak·i·ness** \-kē-nəs\ *n*

¹sneer \'sni(ə)r\ *vi* **1 :** to smile or laugh with facial contortions that express scorn or contempt **2 :** to speak or write in a scornfully jeering manner *syn* see SCOFF — **sneer·er** *n*

²sneer *n* : a sneering expression or remark

¹sneeze \'snēz\ *vi* [ME *snesen*, alter. of *fnesen*, fr. OE *fnēosan*] : to make a sudden violent spasmodic audible expiration of breath — **sneez·er** *n* — **sneeze at :** to treat lightly : DESPISE

²sneeze *n* : an act or fact of sneezing

sneeze·weed \'snēz-,wēd\ *n* : a No. American yellow‑flowered perennial herb whose odor is said to cause sneezing

sneezy \'snē-zē\ *adj* : given to or causing sneezing

snell \'snel\ *n* : a short line (as of gut) by which a fish-hook is attached to a longer line

¹snick \'snik\ *vt* : to cut slightly : NICK

²snick *n* : a cutting or clicking noise

¹snick·er \'snik-ər\ *or* **snig·ger** \'snig-ər\ *vi* **snick·ered** *or* **snig·gered; snick·er·ing** *or* **snig·ger·ing** \-(ə-)riŋ\ : to laugh in a slight, covert, or partly suppressed manner : TITTER

²snicker *or* **snigger** *n* : an act or sound of snickering

snide \'snīd\ *adj* **1 :** MEAN, LOW ⟨a *snide* trick⟩ **2 :** slyly disparaging ⟨*snide* remarks⟩

sniff \'snif\ *vb* [ME *sniffen*] **1 :** to draw air audibly up the nose **2 :** to show or express disdain or scorn ⟨*sniffed* at laboring jobs⟩ **3 :** to smell or take by inhalation through the nose : INHALE ⟨*sniff* perfume⟩ **4** : to detect by or as if by smelling ⟨*sniff* out trouble⟩ — **sniff** *n* — **sniff·er** *n*

sniff·ish \'snif-ish\ *adj* : DISDAINFUL, SUPERCILIOUS — **sniff·ish·ly** *adv* — **sniff·ish·ness** *n*

¹snif·fle \'snif-əl\ *vi* **snif·fled; snif·fling** \'snif-(ə-)liŋ\ [freq. of *sniff*] **1** : to sniff repeatedly : SNUFFLE **2** : to speak with or as if with sniffling — **snif·fler** \-(ə-)lər\ *n*

²sniffle *n* **1** : an act or sound of sniffling **2** *pl* : a head cold marked by nasal discharge

sniffy \'snif-ē\ *adj* : inclined to sniff haughtily : SUPERCILIOUS — **sniff·i·ly** \'snif-ə-lē\ *adv* — **sniff·i·ness** \'snif-ē-nəs\ *n*

¹snip \'snip\ *n* [D or LG] **1** : a small piece that is snipped off; *also* : FRAGMENT **2** : an act or sound of snipping **3** : an impertinent person : MINX

²snip *vb* **snipped; snip·ping** : to cut or cut off with or as if with shears or scissors; *esp* : to clip suddenly or by bits

¹snipe \'snīp\ *n, pl* **snipes** *or* **snipe** [of Scand origin] : any of several game birds esp. of marshy areas that resemble the related woodcocks

²snipe *vi* **1** : to shoot at exposed individuals of an enemy's forces esp. when not in action from a usu. concealed point of vantage **2** : to aim a carping or snide attack — **snip·er** *n*

snip·pet \'snip-ət\ *n* : a small part, piece, or thing

snip·py \'snip-ē\ *adj* **snip·pi·er; -est 1** : SHORT-TEMPERED, SNAPPISH **2** : unduly brief or curt **3** : putting on airs — **snip·pi·ness** *n*

snips \'snips\ *n pl* : hand shears used esp. for cutting sheet metal ⟨tin *snips*⟩

snitch \'snich\ *vb* **1** : INFORM, TATTLE ⟨always *snitching* on someone⟩ **2** : to take by stealth; *esp* : PILFER ⟨*snitched* a dime from his sister⟩ — **snitch·er** *n*

sniv·el \'sniv-əl\ *vi* **-eled** *or* **-elled; -el·ing** *or* **-el·ling** \'sniv-(ə-)liŋ\ [ME *snivelen*] **1** : to run at the nose **2** : to snuff mucus up the nose audibly : SNUFFLE **3** : to cry or whine with snuffling **4** : to speak or act in a whining or weakly emotional manner — **sniv·el·er** \-(ə-)lər\ *n*

snob \'snäb\ *n* [obs. *snob* member of the lower classes, fr. E dial., shoemaker] **1** : one who blatantly imitates, fawningly admires, or vulgarly seeks association with those of higher status than himself **2** : one who looks down upon those he regards as inferior to himself

snob appeal *n* : attractiveness (as for a purchaser) based on expensiveness (as from high price, rarity, or foreign origin)

snob·bery \'snäb-(ə-)rē\ *n* : snobbish conduct : SNOBBISHNESS

snob·bish \'snäb-ish\ *adj* : characteristic of or befitting a snob — **snob·bish·ly** *adv* — **snob·bish·ness** *n* — **snob·bism** \'snäb-iz-əm\ *n*

snob·by \'snäb-ē\ *adj* : SNOBBISH

snood \'snüd\ *n* [OE *snōd* hair band] : a net or fabric bag for confining a woman's hair pinned or tied on at the back of the head

snook \'snuk, 'snük\ *n, pl* **snook** *or* **snooks** [D *snoek*] : a large vigorous sport and food fish of warm seas related to the perches but resembling a pike

snook·er \'snuk-ər\ *n* : pool played with 15 red balls and 6 variously colored balls

¹snoop \'snüp\ *vi* [D *snoepen* to buy or eat on the sly] : to look or pry esp. in a sneaking or meddlesome manner

²snoop *or* **snoop·er** \'snü-pər\ *n* : one that snoops

snoop·er·scope \'snü-pər-ˌskōp\ *n* : a device utilizing infrared radiation for enabling a person to see an object obscured (as by darkness)

snoopy \'snü-pē\ *adj* : given to snooping esp. for personal information about others

snoot \'snüt\ *n* **1** : SNOUT **2** : NOSE

snooty \'snüt-ē\ *adj* **snoot·i·er; -est** : haughtily contemptuous : SNOBBISH — **snoot·i·ly** \'snüt-ᵊl-ē\ *adv* — **snoot·i·ness** \'snüt-ē-nəs\ *n*

¹snooze \'snüz\ *vi* : to take a nap : DOZE — **snooz·er** *n*

²snooze *n* : a short sleep : NAP

snore \'snō(ə)r, 'snó(ə)r\ *vi* [ME *snoren*] : to breathe during sleep with a rough hoarse noise due to vibration of the soft palate — **snore** *n* — **snor·er** *n*

¹snor·kel \'snór-kəl\ *n* [G *schnorchel*] **1** : a tube or tubes that can be extended above the surface of the water to supply air to and remove exhaust from a submerged sub-

marine **2** : a tube used by swimmers for breathing with the head under water

²snorkel *vi* : to swim submerged using a snorkel

¹snort \'snórt\ *vb* [ME *snorten*] **1** : to force air violently through the nose with a rough harsh sound **2** : to express scorn, anger, indignation, or surprise by a snort — **snort·er** *n*

²snort *n* **1** : an act or sound of snorting **2** : a drink of usu. straight liquor taken in one draft

snout \'snaut\ *n* **1 a** : a long projecting nose or muzzle (as of a swine) **b** : an anterior prolongation of the head of an animal **c** : the human nose esp. when large or grotesque **2** : something resembling a snout — **snout·ed** \-əd\ *adj*

snout beetle *n* : WEEVIL

¹snow \'snō\ *n* [OE *snāw*] **1 a** : small white crystals of frozen water formed directly from the water vapor of the air **b** : a fall of snow crystals : a mass of snow crystals fallen to earth **2** : something resembling snow: as **a** : a congealed or crystallized substance resembling snow in appearance ⟨carbon dioxide *snow*⟩ **b** : small transient light or dark spots on a television or radar screen

²snow *vb* **1** : to fall or cause to fall in or as snow ⟨it's *snowing* out⟩ ⟨*snowed* messages on their congressmen⟩ **2** : to cover, shut in, or imprison with or as if with snow

¹snow·ball \-ˌból\ *n* **1** : a round mass of snow pressed or rolled together **2** : a viburnum widely grown for its showy clusters of white sterile flowers

²snowball *vb* **1** : to throw snowballs at **2** : to increase or expand at a rapidly accelerating rate

snow·bird \-ˌbərd\ *n* : any of several small birds (as a junco) seen chiefly in winter

snow-blind \-ˌblīnd\ *or* **snow-blind·ed** \-ˈblīn-dəd\ *adj* : affected with snow blindness

snow blindness *n* : inflammation and inability to tolerate light caused by exposure of the eyes to ultraviolet rays reflected from snow or ice

snow boot *n* : a boot reaching to the ankle or above for wear in snow

snow·bound \'snō-ˈbaund\ *adj* : shut in or blockaded by snow

snow·cap \-ˌkap\ *n* : a covering cap of snow (as on a mountain peak) — **snow·capped** \-ˌkapt\ *adj*

snow·drift \-ˌdrift\ *n* : a bank of drifted snow

snow·drop \-ˌdräp\ *n* : an early-blooming European plant of the amaryllis family that bears nodding white flowers

snow·fall \-ˌfól\ *n* **1** : a fall of snow **2** : the amount of snow that falls in a single storm or in a given period

snow·field \-ˌfēld\ *n* : a broad level expanse of snow; *esp* : a mass of perennial snow (as at the head of a glacier)

snow·flake \-ˌflāk\ *n* : a flake or crystal of snow

snow leopard *n* : a large cat of central Asia with a long heavy pelt blotched with brownish black in summer and almost pure white in winter

snow·man \'snō-ˌman\ *n* : snow shaped to resemble a person

snow·mo·bile \'snō-mō-ˌbēl\ *n* : any of various automotive vehicles for travel on snow

snow-on-the-mountain *n* : a showy white-bracted spurge native to the western U.S.

snow·plow \'snō-ˌplau\ *n* : any of various devices used for clearing away snow

¹snow·shoe \-ˌshü\ *n* : a light oval wooden frame strung with thongs that is attached to the foot to enable a person to walk on soft snow without sinking

snowshoe (without harness)

²snowshoe *vi* **snow·shoed; snow·shoe·ing** : to travel on snowshoes

snow·slide \'snō-ˌslīd\ *n* : the slipping down of a mass of snow (as on a mountain slope)

snow·storm \-ˌstórm\ *n* : a storm of falling snow

snow·suit \-ˌsüt\ *n* : a one-piece or two-piece lined garment worn by children

snow tire *n* : an automobile tire with a tread designed to give added traction on snow

snow train *n* : a special train to a place (as a ski resort) suitable for winter sports

snow under *vt* **1** : to overwhelm esp. in excess of capacity to absorb or deal with something **2** : to defeat by a large margin

snow-white \'snō-'hwīt\ *adj* : white as snow

snowy \'snō-ē\ *adj* **snow·i·er**; **-est** **1 a** : marked by snow ⟨a *snowy* day⟩ **b** : covered with snow ⟨*snowy* mountaintops⟩ **2** : whitened by or as if by snow ⟨an orchard *snowy* with apple blossoms⟩ **3** : SNOW-WHITE — **snow·i·ly** \'snō-ə-lē\ *adv* — **snow·i·ness** \'snō-ē-nəs\ *n*

snowy owl *n* : a large chiefly arctic owl that is white or white spotted with brown

¹snub \'snəb\ *vt* **snubbed**; **snub·bing** [of Scand origin] **1** : to check or stop with a cutting reply : REBUKE **2** : to check (as a line) suddenly while running out esp. by turning around a fixed object (as a post); *also* : to check the motion of by snubbing a line **3** : to treat with contempt or neglect : slight deliberately **4** : to extinguish by stubbing ⟨*snub* out a cigarette⟩

²snub *n* : an act or an instance of snubbing; *esp* : REBUFF

³snub *or* **snubbed** \'snəbd\ *adj* : BLUNT, STUBBY — **snub·ness** *n*

snub·ber \'snəb-ər\ *n* **1** : one that snubs **2** : SHOCK ABSORBER

snub·by \'snəb-ē\ *adj* **snub·bi·er**; **-est** : SNUB-NOSED

snub-nosed \'snəb-'nōzd\ *adj* : having a stubby and usu. slightly turned-up nose

¹snuff \'snəf\ *n* [ME *snoffe*] : the charred part of a candlewick

²snuff *vt* **1** : to cut or pinch off the snuff of (a candle) so as to brighten the light **2** : EXTINGUISH ⟨*snuff* out a candle⟩ ⟨*snuff* out a life⟩

³snuff *vb* [akin to E *sniff*] **1** : to draw forcibly through or into the nostrils **2** : to sniff inquiringly

⁴snuff *n* : the act of snuffing : SNIFF

⁵snuff *n* [D *snuf*, short for *snuftabak*, fr. *snuffen* to snuff + *tabak* tobacco] : a preparation of pulverized tobacco to be chewed, placed against the gums, or inhaled through the nostrils — **up to snuff** : in good shape

snuff·box \'snəf-,bäks\ *n* : a small box for holding snuff usu. carried about the person

¹snuff·er \'snəf-ər\ *n* **1** : a device somewhat like a pair of scissors for cropping and holding the snuff of a candle — usu. used in pl. **2** : a device for extinguishing candles

²snuffer *n* : one that snuffs or sniffs

¹snuf·fle \'snəf-əl\ *vb* **snuf·fled**; **snuf·fling** \'snəf-(ə-)liŋ\ **1** : to snuff or sniff usu. audibly and repeatedly **2** : to breathe through an obstructed nose with a sniffing sound **3** : WHINE — **snuf·fler** \-(ə-)lər\ *n*

²snuffle *n* : the sound made in snuffling

¹snug \'snəg\ *adj* **snug·ger**; **snug·gest** **1 a** : SEAWORTHY **b** : TRIM, NEAT **c** : fitting closely and comfortably ⟨a *snug* coat⟩ **2** : enjoying or affording warm secure shelter and comfort : COZY ⟨a *snug* little alcove⟩ **3** : fairly large : AMPLE ⟨a *snug* fortune⟩ **4** : SECRETED, CONCEALED — **snug** *adv* — **snug·ly** *adv* — **snug·ness** *n*

²snug *vb* **snugged**; **snug·ging** **1** : SNUGGLE **2** : to make snug

snug·gery \'snəg-(ə-)rē\ *n, pl* **-ger·ies** : a snug place; *esp* : DEN

snug·gle \'snəg-əl\ *vb* **snug·gled**; **snug·gling** \'snəg-(ə-)liŋ\ **1** : to curl up comfortably or cozily : CUDDLE **2** : to draw close esp. for comfort or in affection : NESTLE

¹so \(')sō, *esp before adj or adv & "that"* sə\ *adv* [OE *swā*] **1 a** : in a manner or way that is indicated or suggested ⟨said he'd attend and did *so*⟩ ⟨it *so* happened that all were wrong⟩ **b** : in the same manner or way : ALSO ⟨worked hard and *so* did she⟩ **c** : SUBSEQUENTLY, THEN ⟨and *so* home and to bed⟩ **2 a** : to an indicated or suggested extent or degree or way ⟨had never been *so* happy⟩ **b** : to a great extent or degree : VERY, EXTREMELY ⟨left her because he loved her *so*⟩ **c** : to a definite but unspecified extent or degree ⟨can only do *so* much in a day⟩ **d** : most certainly : INDEED ⟨you did *so* do it⟩ **3** : for a reason that has just been stated : THEREFORE ⟨the witness is biased and *so* unreliable⟩

²so \(')sō\ *conj* **1 a** : with the result that ⟨her diction is good, *so* every word is clear⟩ **b** : in order that ⟨be quiet *so* he can sleep⟩ — often followed by *that* **2** : provided that — often preceded by *just* **3** : for that reason : THEREFORE ⟨don't want to go, *so* I won't⟩

³so \'sō\ *adj* **1** : conforming with actual facts : TRUE

⟨said things that were not *so*⟩ **2** : marked by a definite order ⟨his books are always just *so*⟩

⁴so \,sō, 'sō\ *pron* **1** : such as has been specified : the same ⟨became chairman and remained *so*⟩ **2** : approximately that ⟨20 years or *so*⟩

⁵so \'sō\ *n, pl* **sos** : SOL

¹soak \'sōk\ *vb* [OE *socian*] **1 a** : to remain steeping in liquid (as water) **b** : to place in a medium (as liquid) to wet or as if to wet thoroughly : SUBMERGE, STEEP **2 a** : to enter or pass through something by or as if by pores or interstices : PERMEATE, SATURATE **b** : to penetrate or affect the mind or feelings **3 a** : to extract by or as if by steeping ⟨*soak* the dirt out⟩ **b** : to levy an exorbitant charge against ⟨*soaked* the taxpayers⟩ **4** : to draw in by or as if by suction or absorption ⟨*soaked* up the sunshine⟩ — **soak·er** *n*

²soak *n* **1** : the act or process of soaking : the state of being soaked **2** : DRUNKARD

soak·age \'sō-kij\ *n* **1** : liquid gained by absorption or lost by seepage **2** : the act or process of soaking : the state of being soaked

so-and-so \'sō-ən-,sō\ *n, pl* **so-and-sos** \-ən-,sōz\ : an unnamed or unspecified person or thing

¹soap \'sōp\ *n* [OE *sāpe*] **1** : a substance that is usu. made by the action of alkali on fat, dissolves in water, and is used for washing **2** : a salt of a fatty acid — **soap·less** \-ləs\ *adj* — **soap·mak·ing** \-,mā-kiŋ\ *n*

²soap *vt* : to rub soap over or into

soap·box \-,bäks\ *n* **1** : a box for soap **2** : an improvised platform used by a spontaneous or informal orator — **soapbox** *adj*

soap bubble *n* : a hollow iridescent globe formed by blowing a film of soapsuds from a pipe

soap·less \'sōp-ləs\ *adj* **1** : lacking soap **2** : UNWASHED, DIRTY

soap opera *n* [fr. its frequently being sponsored by soap manufacturers] : a radio or television serial drama performed usu. on a daytime commercial program

soap plant *n* : a plant with a part (as leaves or root) that can be used as a soap substitute

soap·stone \'sōp-,stōn\ *n* : a soft stone having a soapy feel and composed essentially of talc, chlorite, and often some magnetite

soap·suds \-,sədz\ *n pl* : SUDS 1

soap·wort \-,wərt, -,wȯrt\ *n* : a European herb of the pink family naturalized in the U.S. that has pink or white flowers and leaves with a detergent action when bruised

soapy \'sō-pē\ *adj* **soap·i·er**; **-est** **1** : smeared with or full of soap ⟨a *soapy* face⟩ **2** : containing or combined with soap ⟨*soapy* ammonia⟩ **3 a** : resembling or having the qualities of soap **3** : UNCTUOUS, SUAVE — **soap·i·ly** \-pə-lē\ *adv* — **soap·i·ness** \-pē-nəs\ *n*

¹soar \'sō(ə)r, 'sȯ(ə)r\ *vi* [MF *essorer* to air, soar, fr. L *ex-* + *aura* air] **1 a** : to fly aloft or about **b** : to sail or hover in the air often at a great height : GLIDE **2 a** : to move upward in position or status : RISE **b** : to ascend to a higher or more exalted level **3** : to rise to majestic stature : TOWER ⟨*soaring* cloud-draped peaks⟩ — **soar·er** *n*

²soar *n* : the act of soaring : upward flight

¹sob \'säb\ *vb* **sobbed**; **sob·bing** [ME *sobben*] **1** : to weep with heavings of the chest or with catching in the throat **2** : to bring about by sobbing ⟨*sobbed* himself to sleep⟩ **3** : to make a sound like that of sobbing ⟨the wind *sobbed* through the trees⟩; *also* : to utter with sobs ⟨*sobbed* out her story⟩

²sob *n* **1** : an act of sobbing **2** : a sound of or like that of sobbing

¹so·ber \'sō-bər\ *adj* **so·ber·er** \-bər-ər\; **so·ber·est** \-b(ə-)rəst\ [MF *sobre*, fr. L *sobrius*] **1 a** : sparing or temperate esp. in the use of food and drink **b** : not drunk **2** : being gravely or earnestly thoughtful in character or demeanor : SERIOUS, SOLEMN **3** : subdued in tone or color **4** : not fanciful or emotional : not prejudiced : well balanced ⟨*sober* decision⟩ — **so·ber·ly** \-bər-lē\ *adv* — **so·ber·ness** *n*

²sober *vb* **so·bered**; **so·ber·ing** \-b(ə-)riŋ\ : to make or become sober

so·ber·sid·ed \,sō-bər-'sīd-əd\ *adj* : EARNEST, SOLEMN ⟨a long *sobersided* report on the meetings⟩

so·ber·sides \'sō-bər-,sīdz\ *n sing or pl* : one who is sobersided

---

j joke; ŋ sing; ō flow; ȯ flaw; ȯi coin; th thin; th this; ü loot;   u̇ foot; y yet; yü few; yu̇ furious; zh vision

so·bri·e·ty \sə-'brī-ət-ē\ n [L *sobrietas,* fr. *sobrius* sober] : the quality or state of being sober

so·bri·quet \'sō-bri-ˌkā, -ˌket\ n [F] : a fanciful name or epithet : NICKNAME

sob sister n : a journalist who specializes in sentimental material

sob story n : a sentimental story or account designed chiefly to evoke emotional response

so-called \'sō-'kōld\ adj : commonly or popularly but often inaccurately so termed ⟨the *so-called* pocket veto⟩ ⟨his *so-called* friend⟩

soc·cer \'säk-ər\ n [by shortening & alter. fr. *association football,* fr. the *Football Association,* formed in England in 1863 to standardize the rules of football] : a football game with 11 players on a side in which a round ball is advanced by kicking or by propelling it with any part of the body except the hands and arms

so·cia·bil·i·ty \ˌsō-shə-'bil-ət-ē\ n, pl **-ties** : the quality or state of being sociable : AFFABILITY; *also* : the act or an instance of being sociable

¹so·cia·ble \'sō-shə-bəl\ adj [MF, fr. L *sociabilis,* fr. *sociare* to join, associate, fr. *socius* companion] **1** : inclined to seek or enjoy companionship : AFFABLE, FRIENDLY ⟨*sociable* people⟩ **2** : conducive to friendliness or pleasant social relations — **so·cia·ble·ness** n — **so·cia·bly** \-blē\ adv

²sociable n : an informal gathering for sociability and frequently a special activity or interest

¹so·cial \'sō-shəl\ adj [L *socius* companion, associate] **1 a** : marked by, devoted to, or engaged in for sociability ⟨*social* events⟩⟨her *social* life⟩⟨a *social* drinker⟩ **b** : SOCIABLE **2 a** : naturally living or growing in groups or communities ⟨bees are *social* insects⟩ **b** : tending to form cooperative and interdependent relationships with one's fellows ⟨man is a *social* being⟩ **3** : of or relating to human society, the interaction of the group and its members, and the welfare of these members ⟨*social* institutions⟩ ⟨*social* behavior⟩⟨*social* legislation⟩ **4** : of, relating to, or based on rank in a particular society ⟨different *social* circles⟩; *also* : of or relating to fashionable society ⟨a *social* leader⟩ **5** : SOCIALIST

²social n : SOCIABLE

social climber n : one who attempts to gain a higher social position or acceptance in fashionable society

social democracy n : a socialist movement; *esp* : one advocating a gradual and peaceful transition from capitalism to socialism by democratic means — **social democrat** n — **social democratic** adj

social disease n **1** : VENEREAL DISEASE **2** : a disease (as tuberculosis) whose incidence is directly related to social and economic factors

so·cial·ism \'sō-shə-ˌliz-əm\ n **1** : any of various economic and political theories or social systems based on collective or governmental ownership and administration of the means of production and distribution of goods **2** : a stage of society in Marxist theory transitional between capitalism and communism and distinguished by unequal distribution of goods and pay according to work done — **so·cial·ist** \'sōsh-(ə-)ləst\ n — **socialist** *or* **so·cial·is·tic** \ˌsō-shə-'lis-tik\ adj — **so·cial·is·ti·cal·ly** \-ti-k(ə-)lē\ adv

so·cial·ite \'sō-shə-ˌlīt\ n : a person prominent in fashionable society

so·ci·al·i·ty \ˌsō-shē-'al-ət-ē\ n, pl **-ties 1** : SOCIABILITY **2** : the tendency to associate with one's fellows or to form social groups

so·cial·ize \'sō-shə-ˌlīz\ vb **1** : to make social; *esp* : to train so as to develop the qualities essential to group living **2** : to adapt to social needs and uses **3** : to regulate according to the theory or practice of socialism : place under social control **4** : to take part in the social life around one — **so·cial·i·za·tion** \ˌsō-shə-lə-'zā-shən\ n — **so·cial·iz·er** \'sō-shə-ˌlī-zər\ n

socialized medicine n : medical and hospital services for the members of a class or population administered by an organized group (as a state agency) and paid for from funds obtained usu. by assessments, philanthropy, or taxation

so·cial·ly \'sōsh-(ə-)lē\ adv **1** : in a social manner ⟨*socially* popular⟩ **2** : with respect to society ⟨*socially* inferior⟩ **3** : by society ⟨*socially* prescribed values⟩

so·cial-mind·ed \ˌsō-shəl-'mīn-dəd\ adj : having an interest in society; *esp* : actively interested in social welfare or the well-being of society as a whole

social science n **1** : a science that deals with the institutions and functioning of human society and with the interrelationships of individuals as members of society **2** : a science (as economics or political science) dealing with a particular phase or aspect of human society — **social scientist** n

social secretary n : a personal secretary employed to handle social correspondence and appointments

social security n **1** : the principle or practice of public provision for the economic security and social welfare of the individual and his family **2** *often cap* : a U.S. government program established in 1935 to include old-age and survivors insurance, contributions to state unemployment insurance, and old-age assistance

social service n : an activity designed to promote social welfare

social studies n pl : the studies dealing with human relationships and the functioning of society (as history, civics, economics, and geography)

social welfare n : organized public or private social services for the assistance of disadvantaged classes or groups

social work n : the art, practice, or profession of extending the benefits of organized society esp. through assistance of the economically underprivileged and the socially maladjusted — **social worker** n

¹so·ci·e·ty \sə-'sī-ət-ē\ n, pl **-ties** [L *societas,* fr. *socius* companion] **1** : companionship with one's fellows : COMPANY **2** : the social order or community life considered as a system within which the individual lives ⟨rural *society*⟩ **3** : people in general ⟨the benefit of *society*⟩ **4** : an association of persons for some purpose ⟨a mutual benefit *society*⟩ **5** : a part of a community regarded as a unit distinguished by common interests or standards; *esp* : the group or set of fashionable persons **6** : a system of interdependent organisms or biological units; *also* : an assemblage of plants usu. of a single species or habit within a larger ecological community — **so·ci·e·tal** \-ət-ᵊl\ adj

²society adj : of, relating to, or characteristic of fashionable society

so·cio·ec·o·nom·ic \ˌsō-s(h)ē-ō-ˌek-ə-'näm-ik, -ˌē-kə-\ adj : of, relating to, or involving a combination of social and economic factors

so·ci·ol·o·gy \ˌsō-sē-'äl-ə-jē, -shē-\ n [F *sociologie,* fr. L *socius* companion] : the science of society, social institutions, and social relationships — **so·ci·o·log·ic** \-ə-'läj-ik\ *or* **so·ci·o·log·i·cal** \-ə-'läj-i-kəl\ adj — **so·ci·o·log·i·cal·ly** \-ə-'läj-i-k(ə-)lē\ adv — **so·ci·ol·o·gist** \-'äl-ə-jəst\ n

so·cio·po·lit·i·cal \ˌsō-s(h)ē-ō-pə-'lit-i-kəl\ adj : of, relating to, or involving a combination of social and political factors

¹sock \'säk\ n, pl **socks** [OE *socc* low shoe, fr. L *soccus*] **1** *or* pl **sox** \'säks\ : a knitted or woven covering for the foot usu. extending above the ankle and sometimes to the knee **2 a** : a shoe worn by actors in Greek and Roman comedy **b** : comic drama

²sock vb : to hit, strike, or apply forcefully : deliver a blow

³sock n : a vigorous or violent blow : PUNCH

sock·dol·a·ger *or* **sock·dol·o·ger** \säk-'däl-i-jər\ n **1** : a decisive blow or answer : FINISHER **2** : something outstanding or exceptional

sock·et \'säk-ət\ n [ME *soket* spearhead shaped like a plowshare, support of a spear, socket, fr. AF, spearhead, fr. dim. of OF *soc* plowshare] : an opening or hollow that receives and holds something ⟨the eye *socket*⟩

sock·eye \'säk-ˌī\ n : a small but commercially important Pacific salmon that spawns in spring — called also *red salmon*

So·crat·ic \sə-'krat-ik\ adj : of or relating to Socrates, his followers, or his philosophical method of systematic doubt and questioning of another

¹sod \'säd\ n [MD or MLG *sode*] **1 a** : TURF 1 **b** : the grass and forb covered surface of the ground **2** : one's native land

²sod vt **sod·ded; sod·ding** : to cover with sod or turfs

so·da \'sōd-ə\ n [It] **1 a** : SODIUM CARBONATE **b** : SODIUM

BICARBONATE **c :** SODIUM HYDROXIDE **d :** sodium oxide Na_2O **e :** SODIUM — used in combination ⟨*soda* alum⟩ **2 a :** SODA WATER **b :** a sweet drink consisting of soda water, flavoring, and often ice cream

soda ash *n* : anhydrous sodium carbonate

soda biscuit *n* **1 :** a biscuit leavened with baking soda and sour milk or buttermilk **2 :** SODA CRACKER

soda cracker *n* : a cracker leavened with bicarbonate of soda and cream of tartar

soda fountain *n* **1 :** an apparatus for drawing soda water **2 :** the equipment and counter for the preparation and serving of sodas, sundaes, and ice cream

soda jerk *n* : a counterman who dispenses carbonated drinks and ice cream at a soda fountain

soda lime *n* : a mixture of sodium hydroxide and slaked lime used esp. to absorb moisture and gases

so·da·list \'sōd-ᵊl-əst, sō-'dal-\ *n* : a sodality member

so·dal·i·ty \sō-'dal-ət-ē\ *n, pl* **-ties** [L *sodalis* comrade] **:** an organized society or fellowship; *esp* : a devotional or charitable association of Roman Catholic laity

soda pop *n* : a bottled soft drink consisting of soda water with added flavoring and a sweet syrup

soda water *n* **1 :** a beverage consisting of water highly charged with carbonic acid gas **2 :** SODA POP

¹sod·den \'säd-ᵊn\ *adj* [ME *soden*, fr. pp. of *sethen* to seethe] **1** *archaic* **:** cooked by stewing **:** BOILED **2 :** dull or lacking in expression ⟨*sodden* features⟩; *also* **:** TORPID, UNIMAGINATIVE ⟨*sodden* minds⟩ **3 a :** heavy with moisture **:** SOAKED, SATURATED ⟨*sodden* ground⟩ **b :** heavy or doughy because of imperfect cooking ⟨*sodden* biscuits⟩ — **sod·den·ly** *adv* — **sod·den·ness** \-ᵊn-(n)əs\ *n*

²sodden *vb* **:** to make or become sodden

sod·dy \'säd-ē\ *n, pl* **soddies :** SOD HOUSE

sod house *n* : a house of turfs in horizontal layers

so·di·um \'sōd-ē-əm\ *n* [NL, fr. E *soda*] **:** a soft waxy silver-white metallic element chemically very active and found abundantly in nature always in combination — see ELEMENT table

sodium benzoate *n* : a crystalline or granular sodium salt $NaC_7H_5O_2$ used chiefly as a food preservative

sodium bicarbonate *n* : a white crystalline weakly alkaline salt $NaHCO_3$ used esp. in baking powders, fire extinguishers, and medicine

sodium carbonate *n* : a sodium salt of carbonic acid: as **a :** a strongly alkaline compound Na_2CO_3 used in making glass, soaps, and chemicals **b :** SAL SODA

sodium chloride *n* : SALT 1a

sodium cyanide *n* : a white poisonous salt NaCN used esp. in electroplating, fumigating, and treating steel

sodium hydroxide *n* : a white brittle solid NaOH that is a strong caustic base used esp. in making soap, rayon, and paper and in bleaching

sodium hypochlorite *n* : an unstable salt NaOCl used as a bleaching agent and disinfectant

sodium hyposulfite *n* **1 :** SODIUM THIOSULFATE **2 :** a crystalline water-soluble salt $Na_2S_2O_4$ used esp. in dyeing and bleaching

sodium nitrate *n* : a deliquescent crystalline salt $NaNO_3$ found in crude form in Chile and used as a fertilizer and an oxidizing agent and in curing meat

sodium silicate *n* : WATER GLASS

sodium thiosulfate *n* : a hygroscopic crystalline salt $Na_2S_2O_3$ used esp. as a photographic fixing agent and a reducing or bleaching agent — called also *hypo*

sodium-vapor lamp *n* : an electric lamp that contains sodium vapor and electrodes between which a luminous discharge takes place

Sod·om \'säd-əm\ *n* [*Sodom*, city of ancient Palestine destroyed by God for its wickedness (Genesis 18:20, 21; 19:24–28)] **:** a place notorious for vice or corruption

so·ev·er \sō-'ev-ər\ *adv* **1 :** to any possible or known extent ⟨how fair *soever* she may be⟩ **2 :** of any or every kind that may be specified — used after a noun modified as by *any, no,* or *what* ⟨he gives no information *soever*⟩

so·fa \'sō-fə\ *n* [Ar *suffah* long bench] **:** a long upholstered seat usu. with arms and a back and often convertible into a bed

sofa bed *n* : an upholstered sofa that can be made to serve as a double bed by lowering its hinged upholstered back to horizontal position

so far as *conj* : insofar as

sof·fit \'säf-ət\ *n* [It *soffitto*, fr. pp. of obs. *soffiggere* to fasten underneath, fr. L *suffigere*] **:** the underside of a part or member of a building and esp. of an arch

soft \'sȯft\ *adj* [OE *sēfte, sōfte*] **1 :** having a pleasing, comfortable, or soothing quality or effect: as **a :** causing little distress or anguish **:** MILD ⟨a *soft* master⟩ **b :** not harsh or inclement **:** gentle in action ⟨*soft* breezes⟩ ⟨*soft* spring weather⟩ **c :** pleasing to the ear **:** melodious and quiet in pitch or volume ⟨*soft* voices⟩ **d :** not bright or glaring **:** subdued and with little contrast ⟨*soft* lighting⟩ **e :** demanding little effort **:** EASY ⟨a *soft* job⟩ **f :** smooth or delicate in appearance or texture ⟨a *soft* silk⟩ ⟨*soft* flowing lines⟩ **g :** pleasingly mild in taste or odor; *esp* **:** free from excessive pungency, acidity, or acridity **2 a :** having a mild gentle nature **:** DOCILE **b :** lacking in strength or vigor **:** unfit for prolonged exertion or severe stress **:** FEEBLE ⟨*soft* from good living⟩ **c :** weak or deficient mentally **d :** defective in firmness or resolution ⟨*soft* and uncertain in his dealings⟩ **e :** advocating or being a moderate or conciliatory policy ⟨took a *soft* stand toward the rebels⟩ **3 :** yielding to physical pressure **:** COMPRESSIBLE, MALLEABLE ⟨a *soft* mattress⟩ ⟨*soft* metals such as lead⟩; *also* **:** relatively lacking in hardness ⟨*soft* iron⟩ ⟨*soft* wood⟩ **4 :** gently or gradually curved or rounded **:** not harsh or jagged ⟨a range of *soft* hills⟩ **5 :** sounding as in *ace* and *gem* respectively — used of *c* and *g* **6 a :** deficient in or free from substances (as calcium and magnesium salts) that prevent lathering of soap ⟨*soft* water⟩ **b :** containing no alcohol ⟨*soft* drinks⟩ **7 :** having relatively low penetrating power ⟨*soft* X rays⟩ — **soft·ly** *or* **soft** *adv* — **soft·ness** \'sȯf(t)-nəs\ *n*

soft·ball \'sȯf(t)-,bȯl\ *n* **:** a game resembling baseball but played on a smaller diamond with a ball larger and softer than a baseball; *also* **:** the ball used in this game

soft-boiled \-'bȯild\ *adj* **:** lightly boiled so that the contents are only partly coagulated ⟨*soft-boiled* eggs⟩

soft coal *n* : BITUMINOUS COAL

soft·en \'sȯ-fən\ *vb* **soft·ened; soft·en·ing** \'sȯf-(ə-)niŋ\ **1 :** to make or become soft or softer **2 :** to impair the strength or resistance of ⟨*soften* up a sales prospect⟩ — **soft·en·er** \'sȯf-(ə-)nər\ *n*

soft-finned \'sȯf(t)-'find\ *adj* **:** having fins in which the membrane is supported entirely or mostly by soft or jointed rays — compare SPINY-FINNED

soft-head·ed \'sȯft-'hed-əd\ *adj* **:** having a weak, unrealistic, or uncritical mind **:** IMPRACTICAL — **soft·head·ed·ly** *adv* — **soft·head·ed·ness** *n*

soft-heart·ed \'sȯft-'härt-əd\ *adj* **:** emotionally responsive **:** SYMPATHETIC, TENDER — **soft·heart·ed·ly** *adv* — **soft·heart·ed·ness** *n*

soft palate *n* : a fold at the back of the hard palate that partially separates the mouth and pharynx

soft pedal *n* **1 :** a foot pedal on a piano that reduces the volume of sound **2 :** something that muffles, deadens, or reduces effect

soft-ped·al \'sȯf(t)-'ped-ᵊl\ *vt* **1 :** to use the soft pedal in playing **2 :** to play down **:** OBSCURE, MUFFLE

soft-rayed \'sȯft-'rād\ *adj* **1 :** having soft articulated rays ⟨*soft-rayed* fins⟩ **2 :** SOFT-FINNED

soft rot *n* : a mushy, watery, or slimy decayed state of a plant or plant part usu. caused by bacteria or fungi

soft scale *n* : a scale insect more or less active in all stages

soft sell *n* : the use of suggestion or persuasion in selling rather than aggressive pressure

soft-shell \'sȯf(t)-,shel\ *or* **soft-shelled** \-'sheld\ *adj* **:** having a soft or fragile shell esp. as a result of recent shedding

soft-shoe \'sȯf(t)-'shü\ *adj* **:** of or relating to tap dancing done in soft-soled shoes without metal taps

soft soap *n* **1 :** a semifluid soap **2 :** FLATTERY

soft-soap \'sȯf(t)-'sōp\ *vb* **:** to soothe or coax with flattery or blarney — **soft-soap·er** *n*

soft-spo·ken \'sȯf(t)-'spō-kən\ *adj* **:** speaking softly **:** having a mild or gentle voice **:** SUAVE

soft·ware \'sȯft-,wa(ə)r, -,we(ə)r\ *n* **:** the entire set of programs, procedures, and related documentation associated with a system and esp. a computer system; *specif* **:** computer programs

soft wheat *n* : a wheat with soft starchy kernels high in starch but usu. low in gluten

¹soft·wood \'sȯft-,wud\ *n* **1 :** the wood of a coniferous tree including both soft and hard woods **2** : a tree that yields softwood

²softwood *adj* **1** : having or made of softwood **2** : consisting of immature still pliable tissue ⟨*softwood* cuttings for propagating plants⟩

soft-wood-ed \-'wu̇d-əd\ *adj* **1** : having soft wood that is easy to work or finish **2** : SOFTWOOD 1

softy \'sȯf-tē\ *n, pl* **soft·ies 1** : a silly or sentimental person **2** : WEAKLING

sog·gy \'säg-ē\ *adj* **sog·gi·er; -est** [E dial. *sog* to soak] **1** : saturated or heavy with water or moisture : SOAKED, SODDEN ⟨*soggy* bread⟩ **2** : heavily dull : PONDEROUS ⟨*soggy* prose⟩ — **sog·gi·ly** \'säg-ə-lē\ *adv* — **sog·gi·ness** \'säg-ē-nəs\ *n*

soi-di-sant \ˌswäd-ē-'zäⁿ\ *adj* [F, lit., saying oneself] : SELF-STYLED, SO-CALLED — usu. used disparagingly ⟨a *soi-disant* artist⟩

soi-gné *or* **soi-gnée** \swän-'yā\ *adj* [F, fr. pp. of *soigner* to take care of] : elegantly maintained; *esp* : WELL-GROOMED

¹soil \'sȯil\ *vb* [OF *soiller* to wallow, soil, fr. *soil* pigsty, fr. L *sus* pig] : to make or become dirty or corrupt

²soil *n* **1 a** : SOILAGE, STAIN **b** : moral defilement : CORRUPTION **2** : something that soils or pollutes

³soil *n* [AF, fr. L *solium* seat] **1** : firm land : EARTH **2** : the loose surface material of the earth in which plants grow **3** : COUNTRY, LAND **4** : the agricultural life or calling **5** : a medium in which something may take root and grow ⟨slums are fertile *soil* for crime⟩

soil·age \'sȯi-lij\ *n* : the act of soiling : the condition of being soiled

soil bank *n* : acreage retired from crop cultivation and planted with soil-building crops under a federally sponsored plan that provides subsidies to farmers for the retired land

soil conservation *n* : management of soil designed to obtain optimum yields while improving and protecting the soil

soil·less \'sȯil-ləs\ *adj* : carried on without soil ⟨*soilless* agriculture⟩

soil·ure \'sȯil-yər\ *n* **1** : the act of soiling : the condition of being soiled **2** : STAIN, SMUDGE

soi·ree *or* **soi·rée** \swä-'rā\ *n* [F *soirée* evening period, evening party, fr. *soir* evening, fr. L *sero* at a late hour, fr. *serus* late] : an evening party or reception

¹so·journ \'sō-ˌjərn, sō-'\ *n* [OF *sojorn*, fr. *sojorner* to sojourn, fr. L *sub* under, during + LL *diurnum* day] : a temporary stay

²sojourn *vi* **1** : to stay as a temporary resident : STOP ⟨*sojourned* for a month at a resort⟩ — **so·journ·er** *n*

¹sol \'sōl\ *n* [ML] : the 5th note of the diatonic scale — called also *so*

²sol \'säl, 'sȯl\ *n, pl* **so·les** \'sō-ˌlās\ [AmerSp, fr. Sp, sun, fr. L] **1** : the basic monetary unit of Peru **2** : a coin or note representing one sol

³sol \'säl, 'sȯl\ *n* [*solution*] : a fluid colloidal system

Sol \'säl\ *n* [L] **1** : SUN **2** : the sun-god of the ancient Romans

¹sol·ace \'säl-əs\ *n* [L *solacium*, fr. *solari* to console] : alleviation of grief or anxiety or a source of this

²solace *vt* **1** : to give solace to : CONSOLE **2** : to make cheerful : DIVERT **3** : ALLAY, SOOTHE **syn** see COMFORT — **sol·ac·er** *n*

so·lan goose \ˌsō-lən-\ *n* [ME *soland*, fr. ON *sūla* gannet + * önd* duck] : a very large white gannet with black wing tips

so·la·num \sə-'lā-nəm\ *n* [L, nightshade] : any of a large genus of herbs, shrubs, and trees of the nightshade family that includes several economically important plants (as the potato and eggplant)

so·lar \'sō-lər\ *adj* [L *sol* sun] **1** : of, derived from, or relating to the sun **2** : measured by the earth's course in relation to the sun ⟨*solar* time⟩ ⟨*solar* year⟩ **3** : produced or operated by the action of the sun's light or heat ⟨a *solar* battery⟩ ⟨a *solar* furnace⟩; *also* : utilizing the sun's rays

solar flare *n* : a sudden temporary outburst of energy from a small area of the sun's surface

solar house *n* : a house equipped with glass areas and so planned as to utilize the sun's rays extensively in heating

so·lar·i·um \sō-'lar-ē-əm, -'ler-\ *n, pl* **-ia** \-ē-ə\ *also*

-i·ums : a room exposed to the sun (as for treatment of illness)

solar plexus *n* **1** : a nerve plexus in the abdomen behind the stomach and in front of the aorta that contains ganglia distributing nerve fibers to the viscera **2** : the pit of the stomach

solar system *n* : the sun and the planets, asteroids, comets, and meteors that revolve around it

sol·ate \'säl-ˌāt, 'sȯl-\ *vi* : to change into a colloidal sol

sold *past of* SELL

¹sol·der \'säd-ər, 'sȯd-\ *n* [MF *soudure*, fr. *souder* to solder, fr. L *solidare* to make solid, fr. *solidus* solid] **1** : a metal or metallic alloy used when melted to join metallic surfaces; *esp* : an alloy of lead and tin so used **2** : something that unites or cements

²solder *vb* **sol·dered; sol·der·ing** \-(ə-)riŋ\ **1** : to unite or repair with solder ⟨*solder* wires together⟩⟨*solder* a leak⟩ **2** : to bring into or restore to firm union **3** : to become joined or renewed by or as if by the use of solder — **sol·der·er** \-ər-ər\ *n*

soldering iron *n* : a metal device for applying heat in soldering

¹sol·dier \'sōl-jər\ *n* [OF *soudier*, fr. *soulde* pay, fr. LL *solidus* solidus] **1** : a person in military service usu. as an enlisted man or woman **2** : a worker in a cause **3** : a member of a caste of wingless individuals with large heads and jaws among termites and some ants **4** : SHIRKER, LOAFER — **sol·dier·ly** \-lē\ *adj* — **sol·dier·ship** \-ˌship\ *n*

²soldier *vi* **sol·diered; sol·dier·ing** \'sōlj-(ə-)riŋ\ **1** : to serve as or act like a soldier **2** : to make a show of activity while really loafing

sol·dier·ing *n* : the life, service, or practice of one who soldiers

soldier of fortune : one who follows a military career wherever there is promise of profit, adventure, or pleasure

soldiers' home *n* : an institution maintained (as by the federal or a state government) for the care and relief of military veterans

sol·diery \'sōlj-(ə-)rē\ *n, pl* **-dier·ies 1 a** : a body of soldiers **b** : SOLDIERS, MILITARY **2** : the profession or technique of soldiering

¹sole \'sōl\ *n* [L *solea* sandal] **1** : the undersurface of a foot **2** : the part of footwear on which the sole of the foot rests **3** : the bottom or lower part of something : the base on which something rests — **soled** \'sōld\ *adj*

²sole *vt* : to furnish with a sole ⟨*sole* shoes⟩

³sole *n* [L *solea* sandal, a flatfish] : any of a family of small-mouthed flatfishes having reduced fins and small closely set eyes and including valued food fishes; *also* : any of several other market flatfishes

⁴sole *adj* [L *solus*] **1** : having no companion : ALONE **2 a** : having no sharer ⟨*sole* owner⟩ **b** : being the only one **3** : functioning independently and without assistance or interference ⟨the *sole* judge⟩ **4** : belonging exclusively or otherwise limited to the one person, unit, or group named ⟨given *sole* authority⟩ **syn** see SINGLE — **sole·ness** *n*

sol·e·cism \'säl-ə-ˌsiz-əm, 'sō-lə-\ *n* [Gk *soloikos* speaking incorrectly, lit., inhabitant of Soloi, fr. *Soloi*, city in ancient Cilicia where a substandard form of Greek was spoken] **1** : an ungrammatical combination of words in a sentence **2** : something deviating from the proper, normal, or accepted; *esp* : a breach of etiquette or decorum — **sol·e·cis·tic** \ˌsäl-ə-'sis-tik, ˌsō-lə-\ *adj*

sole·ly \'sō(l)-lē\ *adv* **1** : without another : SINGLY, ALONE **2** : EXCLUSIVELY, ENTIRELY ⟨done *solely* for money⟩

sol·emn \'säl-əm\ *adj* [L *sollemnis* regularly appointed, solemn] **1** : celebrated with religious rites or ceremony : SACRED **2** : FORMAL, STATELY ⟨*solemn* procession⟩ **3** : done or made seriously and thoughtfully ⟨*solemn* promise⟩ **4** : GRAVE, SOBER ⟨*solemn* faces⟩ **5** : SOMBER ⟨robe of *solemn* black⟩ **syn** see SERIOUS — **so·lem·ni·ty** \sə-'lem-nət-ē\ *n* — **sol·emn·ly** \'säl-əm-lē\ *adv* — **sol·emn·ness** \-əm-nəs\ *n*

sol·em·nize \'säl-əm-ˌnīz\ *vt* **1** : to observe or honor with solemnity **2** : to perform with pomp or ceremony; *esp* : to celebrate (a marriage) with religious rites **3** : to make solemn : DIGNIFY — **sol·em·ni·za·tion** \ˌsäl-əm-nə-'zā-shən\ *n*

solemn vow *n* : an absolute and irrevocable public vow

taken by a religious in the Roman Catholic Church under which ownership of property by the individual is prohibited and marriage is invalid under canon law

so·le·noid \'sō-lə-ˌnȯid\ *n* [Gk *sōlēn* pipe] : a coil of wire commonly in the form of a long cylinder that when carrying a current resembles a bar magnet so that a movable core is drawn into the coil when a current flows — **so·le·noi·dal** \ˌsō-lə-'nȯid-ᵊl\ *adj*

sole·plate \'sōl-ˌplāt\ *n* : the undersurface of a flatiron

sole·print \-ˌprint\ *n* : a print of the sole of the foot; *esp* : one made in the manner of a fingerprint and used for the identification of an infant

soles *pl of* SOL *or of* SOLE

¹sol-fa \(')sōl-'fä\ *n* **1** : SOL-FA SYLLABLES **2** : SOLMIZATION; *also* : an exercise thus sung

²sol-fa *vb* **1** : to sing the sol-fa syllables **2** : to sing (as a melody) to sol-fa syllables

sol-fa syllables *n pl* : the syllables *do, re, mi, fa, sol, la, ti* used in singing the tones of the scale

soli *pl of* SOLO

so·lic·it \sə-'lis-ət\ *vb* [L *sollicitare* to disturb, fr. *sollicitus* solicitous] **1** : BEG, ENTREAT; *esp* : to approach with a request or plea **2** : to appeal for ⟨*solicited* the help of his neighbors⟩ **3 a** : to entice or lure esp. into evil **b** : to accost a man for immoral purposes **syn** see INVITE — **so·lic·i·ta·tion** \-ˌlis-ə-'tā-shən\ *n*

so·lic·i·tant \sə-'lis-ət-ənt\ *n* : one who solicits

so·lic·i·tor \sə-'lis-ət-ər\ *n* **1** : one that solicits; *esp* : an agent that solicits (as contributions to charity) **2** : a British lawyer who advises clients, represents them in the lower courts, and prepares cases for barristers to plead in the higher courts **3** : the chief law officer of a municipality, county, or government department — **so·lic·i·tor·ship** *n*

solicitor general *n, pl* **solicitors general** : a law officer appointed primarily to assist an attorney general

so·lic·i·tous \sə-'lis-ət-əs\ *adj* [L *sollicitus*, fr. *sollus* whole + *citus*, pp. of *ciēre* to move] **1** : full of concern or fears : APPREHENSIVE **2** : anxiously willing : EAGER **3** : meticulously careful **syn** see THOUGHTFUL — **so·lic·i·tous·ly** *adv* — **so·lic·i·tous·ness** *n*

so·lic·i·tude \sə-'lis-ə-ˌt(y)üd\ *n* : the state of being solicitous : ANXIETY; *also* : excessive care or attention

¹sol·id \'säl-əd\ *adj* [L *solidus*] **1 a** : having an interior filled with matter : not hollow **b** : written as one word without a hyphen ⟨a *solid* compound⟩ **c** : not interrupted ⟨for three *solid* hours⟩ **2** : having, involving, or dealing with three dimensions or with solids ⟨*solid* geometry⟩ **3 a** : not loose or spongy : COMPACT ⟨a *solid* mass of rock⟩ **b** : neither gaseous nor liquid : HARD, RIGID ⟨*solid* ice⟩ **4** : of good substantial quality or kind ⟨*solid* comfort⟩: as **a** : SOUND ⟨*solid* reasons⟩ **b** : STURDY **c** : musically excellent **5** : UNANIMOUS, UNITED ⟨*solid* for pay increases⟩ **6 a** : thoroughly dependable : RELIABLE ⟨a *solid* citizen⟩; *also* : well established financially **b** : serious in purpose or character ⟨*solid* reading⟩ **7** : of one substance or character: as **a** : entirely of one metal or containing the minimum of alloy necessary to impart hardness ⟨*solid* gold⟩ **b** : of a single color or tone — **solid** *adv* — **sol·id·ly** *adv* — **sol·id·ness** *n*

²solid *n* **1** : a geometrical figure or element (as a cube or sphere) having three dimensions **2** : a solid substance : a substance that does not flow perceptibly under moderate stress

sol·i·dar·i·ty \ˌsäl-ə-'dar-ət-ē\ *n, pl* **-ties** : community of interests, objectives, or standards in a group **syn** see UNITY

solid geometry *n* : a branch of geometry that deals with figures of three-dimensional space

so·lid·i·fi·ca·tion \sə-ˌlid-ə-fə-'kā-shən\ *n* : an act or instance of solidifying : the condition of being solidified

so·lid·i·fy \sə-'lid-ə-ˌfī\ *vb* **-fied; -fy·ing** : to make or become solid, compact, or hard

so·lid·i·ty \sə-'lid-ət-ē\ *n, pl* **-ties** **1** : the quality or state of being solid **2** : moral, mental, or financial soundness

solid–state *adj* **1** : relating to the properties, structure, or reactivity of solid material **2** : utilizing the electric, magnetic, or photic properties of solid materials : not utilizing electron tubes

sol·i·dus \'säl-əd-əs\ *n, pl* **sol·i·di** \-ə-ˌdī, -ˌdē\ [LL, fr.

L, solid] **1** : an ancient Roman gold coin introduced by Constantine and used to the fall of the Byzantine Empire **2** [ML, shilling, fr. LL; fr. its use as a symbol for shillings] : DIAGONAL 3

so·lil·o·quist \sə-'lil-ə-kwəst\ *n* : one who soliloquizes

so·lil·o·quize \sə-'lil-ə-ˌkwīz\ *vi* : to utter a soliloquy : talk to oneself — **so·lil·o·quiz·er** *n*

so·lil·o·quy \sə-'lil-ə-kwē\ *n, pl* **-quies** [LL *soliloquium*, fr. L *solus* alone + *loqui* to speak] **1** : the act of talking to oneself **2** : a dramatic monologue that gives the illusion of being a series of unspoken thoughts

sol·i·taire \'säl-ə-ˌta(ə)r, -ˌte(ə)r\ *n* [F, fr. *solitaire*, adj., solitary, fr. L *solitarius*] **1** : a single gem (as a diamond) set alone **2** : a card game played by one person alone

¹sol·i·tary \'säl-ə-ˌter-ē\ *adj* [L *solitarius*, fr. *solitas* solitude, fr. *solus* alone] **1** : all alone ⟨a *solitary* traveler⟩ **2** : seldom visited : LONELY **3** : being the only one : SOLE ⟨*solitary* example⟩ **4** : growing or living alone : not forming part of a group or cluster ⟨flowers terminal and *solitary*⟩ ⟨the *solitary* bees⟩ — **sol·i·tar·i·ly** \ˌsäl-ə-'ter-ə-lē\ *adv* — **sol·i·tar·i·ness** \ˈsäl-ə-ˌter-ē-nəs\ *n*

syn FORLORN, DESOLATE: SOLITARY implies the absence of any others of the same kind; FORLORN and DESOLATE imply absence or loss of friends and family; applied to places they suggest dreariness and desertion by former inhabitants; DESOLATE may also imply a sense of final and irreparable loss and loneliness **syn** see in addition SINGLE

²solitary *n, pl* **-tar·ies** : RECLUSE, HERMIT

sol·i·tude \'säl-ə-ˌt(y)üd\ *n* **1** : the quality or state of being alone or remote from society **2** : a lonely place

sol·mi·za·tion \ˌsäl-mə-'zā-shən\ *n* [F *solmiser* to sol-fa, fr. *sol* + *mi* + *-iser* -ize] : the act, practice, or system of using a set of syllables to denote the tones of a musical scale

¹so·lo \'sō-lō\ *n, pl* **solos** [It, fr. *solo* alone, fr. L *solus*] **1** *or pl* **so·li** \'sō-(ˌ)lē\ **a** : a musical composition for a single voice or instrument with or without accompaniment **b** : the featured part of a concerto or similar work **2** : an action in which there is only one performer (as in a dance or airplane flight)

²solo *adv* (*or adj*) : without a companion : ALONE

³solo *vi* : to perform by oneself; *esp* : to fly solo in an airplane

so·lo·ist \'sō-lō-wəst, -ˌlō-əst\ *n* : one who performs a solo

Sol·o·mon \'säl-ə-mən\ *n* : a son of David and 10th century B.C. king of Israel noted for his wisdom

Solomon's seal *n* **1** : an emblem consisting of two triangles forming a 6-pointed star and formerly used as an amulet esp. against fever **2** : any of a genus of perennial herbs of the lily family with gnarled rhizomes

so·lon \'sō-lən, -ˌlän\ *n* [*Solon d ab559*B.C. Athenian lawgiver] **1** : a wise and skillful lawgiver **2** : a member of a legislative body

so long \sō-'lȯŋ\ *interj* — used to express good-bye or farewell

so long as *conj* **1** : during and up to the end of the time that : WHILE **2** : provided that

sol·stice \'säl-stəs, 'sōl-, 'sȯl-\ *n* [OF, fr. L *solstitium*, fr. *sol* sun + *stat-, sistere* to come to a stop, cause to stand] **1** : the point in the apparent path of the sun at which the sun is farthest from the equator either north or south **2** : the time of the sun's passing a solstice which occurs on June 22d to begin summer in the northern hemisphere and on December 22d to begin winter in the northern hemisphere — **sol·sti·tial** \säl-'stish-əl, sōl-, sȯl-\ *adj*

sol·u·bil·i·ty \ˌsäl-yə-'bil-ət-ē\ *n, pl* **-ties** **1** : the quality or state of being soluble **2** : the amount of a substance that will dissolve in a given amount of another substance

sol·u·bi·lize \'säl-yə-bə-ˌlīz\ *vt* : to make soluble or increase the solubility of

sol·u·ble \'säl-yə-bəl\ *adj* [LL *solubilis*, fr. L *solvere* to loosen, solve, dissolve] **1 a** : capable of being dissolved in a fluid ⟨sugar is *soluble* in water⟩ **b** : EMULSIFIABLE ⟨a *soluble* oil⟩ **2** : capable of being solved or explained — **sol·u·ble·ness** *n* — **sol·u·bly** \-blē\ *adv*

sol·ute \'säl-ˌyüt\ *n* [L *solutus*, pp. of *solvere* to dissolve] : a dissolved substance

so·lu·tion \sə-'lü-shən\ *n* [L *solut-, solvere* to loosen, solve, dissolve] **1 a** : an act or process of solving **b** : an act or process of finding the unknown parts of a triangle from given parts **c** (1) : an answer to a problem : EX-

PLANATION (2) **:** SOLUTION SET; *also* **:** a member of a solution set **2 a :** an act or the process by which a solid, liquid, or gaseous substance is uniformly mixed with a liquid or sometimes a gas or solid **b :** a typically liquid uniform mixture formed by the process of solution **c :** the condition of being dissolved **d :** a liquid containing a dissolved substance **3 :** a bringing or coming to an end or into a state of discontinuity

solution set *n* **:** a set of values that satisfy an equation
solv·a·ble \'säl-və-bəl, 'sól-\ *adj* **:** capable of being solved — **solv·a·bil·i·ty** \,säl-və-'bil-ət-ē, ,sól-\ *n*
¹sol·vate \'säl-,vāt, 'sól-\ *n* **:** a combination of a solute with a solvent or of a dispersed phase with a dispersion medium
²solvate *vt* **:** to convert into a solvate — **sol·va·tion** \säl-'vā-shən, sól-\ *n*
solve \'sälv, 'sólv\ *vt* [L *solvere* to loosen, solve, dissolve, fr. *sed-, se-* apart + *luere* to release] **1 :** to find a solution for **2 :** to discover the unknown parts of (a triangle) from known parts
sol·ven·cy \'säl-vən-sē, 'sól-\ *n, pl* **-cies :** the quality or state of being solvent
¹sol·vent \-vənt\ *adj* [L *solvent-, solvens,* prp. of *solvere* to dissolve, pay] **1 :** able to pay all legal debts **2 :** dissolving or able to dissolve 〈*solvent* fluids〉〈*solvent* action of water〉 — **sol·vent·ly** *adv*
²solvent *n* **1 :** a usu. liquid substance capable of dissolving or dispersing one or more other substances **2 :** something that provides a solution
so·ma \'sō-mə\ *n* [Gk *sōma* body] **:** all of an organism except the germ cells
So·ma·li \sō-'mäl-ē\ *n* **:** a member of a Cushitic-speaking people chiefly of Somaliland and apparently of mixed Mediterranean and negroid stock — **Somali** *adj*
somat- *or* **somato-** *comb form* [Gk *sōmat-, sōma*] **1 :** body 〈*somatology*〉 **2 :** soma 〈*somatoplasm*〉
so·mat·ic \sō-'mat-ik\ *adj* **1 :** of, relating to, or affecting the body esp. as distinguished from the germ plasm or the psyche 〈*somatic* cells〉 **2 :** of or relating to the wall of the body **:** PARIETAL — **so·mat·i·cal·ly** \-'mat-i-k(ə-)lē\ *adv*
somatic mutation *n* **:** a mutation occurring in a somatic cell and inducing a chimera
so·ma·to·gen·ic \,sō-mət-ə-'jen-ik, sō-,mat-\ *adj* **:** originating in, affecting, or acting through the body or its cells esp. as distinguished from the mind — compare PSYCHOGENIC
so·ma·to·plasm \'sō-mət-ə-,plaz-əm, sō-'mat-\ *n* **:** somatic cells as distinguished from germ cells — **so·ma·to·plas·tic** \,sō-mət-ə-'plas-tik, sō-,mat-\ *adj*
so·ma·to·trop·ic \,sō-mət-ə-'träp-ik, sō-,mat-\ *adj* **:** growth promoting 〈a *somatotropic* hormone〉
so·ma·to·type \'sō-mət-ə-,tīp, sō-'mat-\ *n* **:** body type **:** PHYSIQUE — **so·ma·to·typ·ic** \,sō-mət-ə-'tip-ik, sō-,mat-\ *adj* — **so·ma·to·typ·i·cal·ly** \-'tip-i-k(ə-)lē\ *adv*
som·ber *or* **som·bre** \'säm-bər\ *adj* [F *sombre*] **1 :** so shaded as to be dark and gloomy **2 :** GRAVE, MELANCHOLY 〈a *somber* mood〉 **3 :** dull or dark colored — **som·ber·ly** *or* **som·bre·ly** *adv* — **som·ber·ness** *or* **som·bre·ness** *n*
som·bre·ro \səm-'bre(ə)r-ō, säm-\ *n, pl* **-ros** [Sp] **:** a high-crowned hat of felt or straw with a very wide brim worn esp. in the Southwest and Mexico

¹some \'səm *or, for 2b, without stress*\ *adj* [OE *sum*] **1 :** being one unknown, undetermined, or unspecified unit or thing 〈*some* person knocked〉 **2 a :** being one, a part, or an unspecified number of something (as a class or group) named or implied 〈*some* gems are hard〉 **b :** being of an unspecified amount or number 〈give me *some* water〉 〈have *some* apples〉 **3 :** worthy of notice or consideration 〈that was *some* party〉 **4 :** being at least one and sometimes all of

sombrero

²some \'səm\ *pron* **1 :** some one among a number 〈*some* of these days〉 **2 :** one indeterminate quantity, portion, or number as distinguished from the rest 〈*some* of the milk〉〈*some* of the apples〉
³some \'səm, ,səm\ *adv* **1 :** ABOUT 〈*some* eighty houses〉 **2 :** SOMEWHAT 〈felt *some* better〉
¹-some \səm\ *adj suffix* [OE *-sum*] **:** characterized by a

(specified) thing, quality, state, or action 〈awe*some*〉 〈burden*some*〉
²-some \səm\ *n suffix* [ME *sum,* pron., some] **:** group of (so many) members and esp. persons 〈four*some*〉
³-some \,sōm\ *n comb form* [Gk *sōma*] **:** body 〈chromo*some*〉
¹some·body \'səm-,bäd-ē, -bəd-\ *pron* **:** one or some person of no certain or known identity 〈*somebody* will come in〉
²somebody *n* **:** a person of position or importance
some·day \'səm-,dā\ *adv* **:** at some future time
some·how \'səm-,haù\ *adv* **:** in one way or another not known or designated **:** by some means
some·one \-(,)wən\ *pron* **:** SOMEBODY
some·place \-,plās\ *adv* **:** SOMEWHERE
som·er·sault \'səm-ər-,sólt\ *n* [MF *sombresaut* leap, fr. L *super* over + *saltus* leap, fr. *salire* to jump] **:** a leap or roll in which a person turns his heels over his head — **somersault** *vi*
som·er·set \-,set\ *n or vi* **:** SOMERSAULT
¹some·thing \'səm(p)-thiŋ\ *pron* **1 a :** some undetermined or unspecified thing **b :** some thing not remembered or immaterial 〈the twelve *something* train〉 **2 :** some definite but not specified thing 〈*something* to live for〉 **3 :** a person or thing of consequence
²something *adv* **1 :** in some degree **:** SOMEWHAT **2 :** EXTREMELY 〈swears *something* awful〉
¹some·time \'səm-,tīm\ *adv* **1 :** at some time in the future 〈I'll do it *sometime*〉 **2 :** at some not specified or definitely known point of time 〈*sometime* last night〉
²sometime *adj* **:** FORMER, LATE 〈*sometime* mayor of the city〉
some·times \'səm-,tīmz, (,)səm-'\ *adv* **:** at times **:** now and then **:** OCCASIONALLY
some·way \'səm-,wā\ *also* **some·ways** \-,wāz\ *adv* **:** in some way **:** SOMEHOW
¹some·what \-,hwät, -,hwət, (,)səm-'\ *pron* **1 :** something (as an amount or degree) indefinite or unspecified **2 :** some unspecified or indeterminate thing **:** SOMETHING **3 :** one having a character, quality, or nature to some extent 〈*somewhat* of a connoisseur〉 **4 :** an important or noteworthy person or thing
²somewhat *adv* **:** in some degree or measure **:** SLIGHTLY 〈*somewhat* relieved〉
¹some·where \'səm-,hwe(ə)r, -,hwa(ə)r, -hwər\ *adv* **1 :** in, at, or to a place unknown or unspecified **2 :** APPROXIMATELY 〈*somewhere* about nine o'clock〉
²somewhere *n* **:** an undetermined or unnamed place
some·wheres \-,hwe(ə)rz, -,hwa(ə)rz, -hwərz\ *adv, chiefly dial* **:** SOMEWHERE
so·mite \'sō-,mīt\ *n* **:** one segment of the longitudinal series of segments into which the body of vertebrates and many other animals is divided **:** METAMERE — **so·mit·ic** \sō-'mit-ik\ *adj*
som·me·lier \,səm-əl-'yā\ *n, pl* **sommeliers** \-'yā(z)\ [F, fr. MF, court official charged with transportation of supplies, fr. OProv *saumalier* pack animal driver, fr. *sauma* pack animal, fr. L *sagma* packsaddle] **:** a waiter in a restaurant who has charge of wines and their service
som·nam·bu·lant \säm-'nam-byə-lənt\ *adj* **:** walking or addicted to walking while asleep
som·nam·bu·lar \-lər\ *adj* **:** of, relating to, or characterized by somnambulism
som·nam·bu·late \-,lāt\ *vi* **:** to walk when asleep — **som·nam·bu·la·tion** \(,)säm-,nam-byə-'lā-shən\ *n* — **som·nam·bu·la·tor** \säm-'nam-byə-,lāt-ər\ *n*
som·nam·bu·lism \säm-'nam-byə-,liz-əm\ *n* [L *somnus* sleep + *ambulare* to walk] **:** a sleep or somnolent state in which motor acts (as walking) are performed; *also* **:** actions characteristic of this state — **som·nam·bu·list** \-ləst\ *n* — **som·nam·bu·lis·tic** \(,)säm-,nam-byə-'lis-tik\ *adj* — **som·nam·bu·lis·ti·cal·ly** \-ti-k(ə-)lē\ *adv*
som·nif·er·ous \säm-'nif-(ə-)rəs\ *adj* **:** SOPORIFIC — **som·nif·er·ous·ly** *adv*
som·no·lence \'säm-nə-lən(t)s\ *also* **som·no·len·cy** \-lən-sē\ *n* **:** DROWSINESS, SLEEPINESS
som·no·lent \-lənt\ *adj* [L *somnolentus,* fr. *somnus* sleep] **:** inclined to or heavy with sleep **:** DROWSY 〈a *somnolent* village〉 — **som·no·lent·ly** *adv*
son \'sən\ *n* [OE *sunu*] **1 a :** a male offspring esp. of human beings **b :** a male adopted child **c :** a male de-

ə abut; ə kitten; ər further; a back; ā bake; ä cot, cart; aù out; ch chin; e less; ē easy; g gift; i trip; ī life

scendant — usu. used in pl. **2** *cap* **:** the second person of the Trinity **3 :** a person closely associated with or deriving from a formative agent (as a nation, school, or race) ⟨hardy *sons* of the soil⟩

so·nance \'sō-nən(t)s\ *n* **:** SOUND

so·nant \'sō-nənt\ *adj* [L *sonare* to sound] **:** VOICED — used of speech sounds — **sonant** *n*

so·nar \'sō-,när\ *n* [*sound navigation ranging*] **:** an apparatus that detects the presence and location of submerged objects (as submarines) by reflected vibrations

so·na·ta \sə-'nät-ə\ *n* [It, fr. *sonare* to sound, fr. L] **:** an instrumental musical composition typically of three or four movements in contrasting rhythms and keys

sonata form *n* **:** a musical form consisting basically of an exposition, a development, and a recapitulation used esp. for the first movement of a sonata

son·a·ti·na \,sän-ə-'tē-nə\ *also* **son·a·tine** \-'tēn\ *n, pl* **sonatinas** *or* **son·a·ti·ne** \-'tē-,nä\ *also* **son·a·tines** \-'tēnz\ **:** a short usu. simplified sonata

song \'sóŋ\ *n* [OE *sang*] **1 :** the act or art of singing **2 :** poetical composition **:** POETRY **3 a :** a short musical composition of words and music **b :** a collection of such compositions **4 a :** a melody for a lyric poem or ballad **b :** a poem easily set to music **5 :** a small amount ⟨can be bought for a *song*⟩ — **song·book** \-,bùk\ *n*

song·bird \-,bərd\ *n* **1 :** a bird that utters a succession of musical tones **2 :** SINGING BIRD 2

song·fest \-,fest\ *n* **:** an informal session of group singing of popular or folk songs

song·ful \-fəl\ *adj* **:** given to singing **:** MELODIOUS — **song·ful·ly** \-fə-lē\ *adv* — **song·ful·ness** *n*

song·less \'sóŋ-ləs\ *adj* **:** lacking in, incapable of, or not given to song — **song·less·ly** *adv*

Song of Sol·o·mon \-'säl-ə-mən\ — see BIBLE table

song·smith \'sóŋ-,smith\ *n* **:** a composer of songs

song sparrow *n* **:** a common sparrow of eastern No. America noted for its sweet cheerful song

song·ster \'sóŋ(k)-stər\ *n* **:** one skilled in song **:** a man that sings — **song·stress** \-strəs\ *n*

song thrush *n* **1 :** a largely olive-brown Old World thrush noted for its song — called also *mavis*, *throstle* **2 :** WOOD THRUSH 1

song·writ·er \'sóŋ-,rīt-ər\ *n* **:** a person who composes words or music or both esp. for popular songs

son·ic \'sän-ik\ *adj* [L *sonus* sound] **1 :** having a frequency within the audibility range of the human ear — used of waves and vibrations **2 :** utilizing, produced by, or relating to sound waves ⟨*sonic* altimeter⟩ **3 :** of, relating to, or being the speed of sound in air that is about 741 miles per hour at sea level — **son·i·cal·ly** \'sän-i-k(ə-)lē\ *adv*

sonic boom *n* **:** a sound resembling an explosion produced when a pressure wave formed at the nose of an aircraft traveling at supersonic speed reaches the ground

sonic depth finder *n* **:** an instrument for determining the depth of a body of water or of an object below the surface by means of sound waves

son-in-law \'sən-ən-,lò\ *n, pl* **sons-in-law** \'sən-zən-\ **:** the husband of one's daughter

son·less \'sən-ləs\ *adj* **:** not possessing or never having had a son

son·ly \'sən-lē\ *adj* **:** FILIAL

son·net \'sän-ət\ *n* [It *sonetto*, fr. Prov *sonet* little song, fr. *son* sound, song, fr. L *sonus* sound] **:** a poem of 14 lines usu. in iambic pentameter rhyming according to a prescribed scheme — compare ENGLISH SONNET, ITALIAN SONNET

son·ne·teer \,sän-ə-'ti(ə)r\ *n* **:** a writer of sonnets

sonnet sequence *n* **:** a series of sonnets often having a unifying theme

son·ny \'sən-ē\ *n, pl* **sonnies** **:** a young boy — used chiefly as a term of address

so·nom·e·ter \sə-'näm-ət-ər\ *n* **:** an instrument for demonstrating the mathematical relations of musical tones that consists of a single string stretched on a board and a movable bridge

so·no·rant \sə-'nòr-ənt, -'nór-; 'sän-ə-rənt\ *n* **:** a resonant sound

so·nor·i·ty \sə-'nór-ət-ē, -'när-\ *n, pl* **-ties** **1 :** the quality or state of being sonorous **:** RESONANCE **2 :** a sonorous tone or speech

so·no·rous \sə-'nòr-əs, -'nór-; 'sän-ə-rəs\ *adj* [L *sonorus*, fr. *sonare* to sound] **1 :** producing sound (as when struck) **2 :** full or loud in sound **:** RESONANT **3 :** imposing or impressive in effect or style — **so·no·rous·ly** *adv* — **so·no·rous·ness** *n*

son·ship \'sən-,ship\ *n* **:** the relationship of son to father

soon \'sün\ *adv* [OE *sōna*] **1 :** before long **:** without undue time lapse ⟨*soon* after sunrise⟩ **2 :** PROMPTLY, SPEEDILY ⟨as *soon* as possible⟩ **3 :** before the usual time **4 :** READILY, WILLINGLY ⟨he would as *soon* do it now as later⟩

soot \'sùt, 'sət, 'süt\ *n* [OE *sōt*] **:** a black substance that is formed by combustion, rises in fine particles, and adheres to the sides of the chimney or pipe conveying the smoke; *esp* **:** the fine powder consisting chiefly of carbon that colors smoke

¹sooth \'süth\ *adj* [ME, fr. OE *sōth*; akin to E *is*] **1** *archaic* **:** TRUE **2** *archaic* **:** SOFT, SWEET

²sooth *n, archaic* **:** TRUTH, REALITY

soothe \'süth\ *vb* [OE *sōthian* to prove true, fr. *sōth* true] **1 a :** to please by or as if by attention or concern **:** PLACATE **b :** RELIEVE, ALLEVIATE **2 :** to bring comfort, solace, or reassurance

sooth·ing \'sü-thiŋ\ *adj* **:** tending to calm or allay; *also* **:** having a sedative effect ⟨*soothing* syrup⟩ — **sooth·ing·ly** \-thiŋ-lē\ *adv* — **sooth·ing·ness** *n*

sooth·ly \'süth-lē\ *adv, archaic* **:** in truth **:** TRULY

sooth·say·er \'süth-,sā-ər\ *n* **:** a person who claims to foretell events — **sooth·say·ing** \-,sā-iŋ\ *n*

soot·i·ness \'sùt-ē-nəs, 'sət-, 'süt-\ *n* **:** the quality or state of being sooty

sooty \'sùt-ē, 'sət-, 'süt-\ *adj* **soot·i·er; -est** **1 a :** of, relating to, or producing soot **b :** soiled with soot **2 :** of the color of soot — **soot·i·ly** \-ʲl-ē\ *adv*

sooty mold *n* **:** a dark layer of fungus mycelium growing in insect honeydew on the leaves of plants; *also* **:** a fungus producing this

¹sop \'säp\ *n* [OE *sopp*; akin to E *sup*] **1** *chiefly dial* **:** a piece of food dipped or steeped in a liquid (as bread dipped in milk or gravy) **2 :** a bribe, gift, or gesture for pacifying or winning favor

²sop *vt* **sopped; sop·ping** **1 a :** to steep or dip in or as if in liquid **b :** to wet thoroughly **:** SOAK ⟨*sop* a floor with soapy water⟩ **2 :** to mop up (as water) **3 :** to give a bribe or conciliatory gift to

soph·ism \'säf,iz-əm\ *n* **:** an unsound misleading argument that on the surface seems reasonable

soph·ist \'säf-əst\ *n* [L *sophista*, fr. Gk *sophistēs*, lit., expert, wise man, fr. *sophizesthai* to be wise, fr. *sophos* wise] **1** *cap* **:** one of a class of ancient Greek teachers of rhetoric, philosophy, and the art of successful living noted for their adroit subtle often specious reasoning **2 :** one who argues by the use of sophisms

so·phis·tic \sə-'fis-tik\ *or* **so·phis·ti·cal** \-ti-kəl\ *adj* **:** being clever and subtle but misleading — **so·phis·ti·cal·ly** \-ti-k(ə-)lē\ *adv*

¹so·phis·ti·cate \sə-'fis-tə-,kāt\ *vt* **1 :** to alter deceptively; *esp* **:** ADULTERATE **2 :** to deprive of genuineness, naturalness, or simplicity; *esp* **:** to deprive of naïveté and make worldly-wise **:** DISILLUSION — **so·phis·ti·ca·tion** \-,fis-tə-'kā-shən\ *n*

²so·phis·ti·cate \-'fis-ti-kət, -tə-,kāt\ *n* **:** a sophisticated person

so·phis·ti·cat·ed \-tə-,kāt-əd\ *adj* **1 :** not in a natural, pure, or original state **:** ADULTERATED ⟨a *sophisticated* oil⟩ **2 :** deprived of native or original simplicity: as **a :** highly complicated **:** COMPLEX ⟨*sophisticated* instruments⟩ **b :** WORLDLY-WISE, KNOWING ⟨a *sophisticated* adolescent⟩ **3 :** devoid of grossness **:** SUBTLE: as **a :** finely experienced and aware ⟨a *sophisticated* columnist⟩ **b :** intellectually appealing ⟨a *sophisticated* novel⟩ — **so·phis·ti·cat·ed·ly** *adv*

soph·ist·ry \'säf-ə-strē\ *n, pl* **-ries** **:** deceptively subtle reasoning or argumentation

soph·o·more \'säf-ʲm-,ōr, -ȯr; 'säf,mōr, -,mȯr\ *n* [prob. fr. Gk *sophos* wise + *mōros* foolish] **:** a student in his second year at a college or secondary school

soph·o·mor·ic \,säf-ə-'mōr-ik, -'mȯr-\ *adj* **1 :** of, relating to, or characteristic of a sophomore **2 :** being conceited and overconfident of knowledge but poorly informed and immature

---

j **joke;** ŋ **sing;** ō **flow;** ó **flaw;** ói **coin;** th **thin;** th̲ **this;** ü **loot;** ù **foot;** y **yet;** yü **few;** yù **furious;** zh **vision**

sop·o·rif·er·ous \ˌsäp-ə-ˈrif-(ə-)rəs, ˌsō-pə-\ *adj* : SOPO-RIFIC — **sop·o·rif·er·ous·ly** *adv* — **sop·o·rif·er·ous·ness** *n*

¹sop·o·rif·ic \-ˈrif-ik\ *adj* [L *sopor* deep sleep] **1 a** : causing or tending to cause sleep **b** : tending to dull awareness or alertness **2** : of, relating to, or characterized by sleepiness or lethargy ⟨*soporific* old men⟩

²soporific *n* : a soporific agent or drug

sop·ping \ˈsäp-iŋ\ *adj* [L *sordidus*, fr. *sordes* dirt; akin to wet through : SOAKING

sop·py \ˈsäp-ē\ *adj* **sop·pi·er; -est 1** : soaked through : SATURATED **2** : very wet

¹so·pra·no \sə-ˈpran-ō, -ˈprän-\ *n, pl* **-pran·os** [It, fr. *sopra* above, fr. L *supra*] **1** : the highest voice part in 4-part mixed harmony **2** : the highest singing voice **3** : a singer with a soprano voice

²soprano *adj* **1** : relating to the soprano voice or part **2** : having a high range ⟨*soprano* sax⟩

so·ra \ˈsōr-ə, ˈsȯr-\ *n* : a small short-billed No. American rail common in marshes

¹sorb \ˈsȯrb\ *n* [F *sorbe* fruit of the service tree, fr. L *sorbum*] : any of several Old World trees (as a rowan tree) related to the apples; *also* : the fruit of a sorb

²sorb *vt* [back-formation fr. *absorb* & *adsorb*] : to take up and hold by either adsorption or absorption

sor·cer·er \ˈsȯrs(-ə)-rər\ *n* : a person who practices sorcery : WIZARD — **sor·cer·ess** \-rəs\ *n*

sor·cer·ous \ˈsȯrs-(ə-)rəs\ *adj* : of or relating to sorcery : MAGICAL

sor·cery \ˈsȯrs-(ə-)rē\ *n, pl* **-cer·ies** [OF *sorcerie*, fr. *sorcier*, sorcerer, fr. L *sort-*, *sors* chance, lot] : the use of power gained from the assistance or control of evil spirits esp. for divining : WITCHCRAFT

sor·did \ˈsȯrd-əd\ *adj* [L *sordidus*, fr. *sordes* dirt; akin to E *swart*] **1** : DIRTY, FILTHY ⟨*sordid* surroundings⟩ **2** : marked by baseness or grossness : VILE ⟨*sordid* motives⟩ **3** : MISERLY, NIGGARDLY, COVETOUS **4** : of a dull or muddy color — **sor·did·ly** *adv* — **sor·did·ness** *n*

sor·di·no \sȯr-ˈdē-nō\ *n, pl* **-ni** \-(ˌ)nē\ [It, fr. *sordo* silent, fr. L *surdus*] : MUTE **2**

¹sore \ˈsō(ə)r, ˈsȯ(ə)r\ *adj* [OE *sār*] **1 a** : causing pain or distress ⟨*sore* news⟩ **b** : painfully sensitive : TENDER ⟨*sore* muscles⟩ **c** : hurt or inflamed so as to be or seem painful ⟨*sore* runny eyes⟩ **2** : attended by difficulties, hardship, or exertion ⟨a *sore* subject⟩ **3** : ANGERED, VEXED ⟨*sore* over a remark⟩ — **sore·ness** *n*

²sore *n* **1** : a localized sore spot on the body; *esp* : one (as an ulcer) with the tissues broken and usu. infected **2** : a source of pain or vexation : AFFLICTION

³sore *adv* : SORELY

sore·head \-ˌhed\ *n* : a person easily angered or disgruntled — **sorehead** *or* **sore·head·ed** \-ˈhed-əd\ *adj*

sore·ly \-lē\ *adv* : in a sore manner : PAINFULLY, SEVERELY, EXTREMELY

sore throat *n* : painful throat due to inflammation of the fauces and pharynx

sor·ghum \ˈsȯr-gəm\ *n* [NL, fr. It *sorgo*] **1** : any of an economically important genus of Old World tropical grasses similar to Indian corn in habit but with the spikelets in pairs on a hairy axis; *esp* : one cultivated for grain, forage, or syrup — compare SORGO **2** : syrup from sorgo

sor·go \ˈsȯr-gō\ *n, pl* **sorgos** [It] : a sorghum grown primarily for its sweet juice from which syrup is made but also used for fodder and silage

so·ro·ral \sə-ˈrōr-əl, -ˈrȯr-\ *adj* [L *soror* sister] : of, relating to, or characteristic of a sister : SISTERLY

so·ror·i·ty \sə-ˈrȯr-ət-ē, -ˈrär-\ *n, pl* **-ties** [L *soror* sister; akin to E *sister*] : a club of girls or women esp. at a college

so·rose \ˈsōr-ˌōs, ˈsȯr-\ *adj* : bearing or producing sori ⟨a *sorose* frond of a fern⟩

sorp·tion \ˈsȯrp-shən\ *n* [back-formation fr. *absorption* & *adsorption*] : the process of sorbing : the state of being sorbed

¹sor·rel \ˈsȯr-əl, ˈsär-\ *n* [MF *sorel*, fr. *sor* reddish brown] **1** : an animal (as a horse) of a sorrel color **2** : a brownish orange to light brown

²sorrel *n* [MF *surele*, fr. *sur* sour, of Gmc origin] : any of various plants with sour juice: as **a** : ¹DOCK **b** : WOOD SORREL

¹sor·row \ˈsär-ō, ˈsȯr-\ *n* [OE *sorg*] **1 a** : sadness or anguish due to loss (as of something loved) **b** : a cause of grief or sadness **2** : CONTRITION, REPENTANCE

syn SORROW, GRIEF, ANGUISH mean distress of mind. SORROW implies a sense of loss often with feelings of guilt and remorse; GRIEF implies a sharp feeling of distress for a definite and immediate cause; ANGUISH implies a torturing grief or dread

²sorrow *vi* : to feel or express sorrow : GRIEVE

sor·row·ful \-fəl\ *adj* **1** : full of or marked by sorrow **2** : expressive of or inducing sorrow — **sor·row·ful·ly** \-fə-lē\ *adv* — **sor·row·ful·ness** *n*

sor·ry \ˈsär-ē, ˈsȯr-\ *adj* **sor·ri·er; -est** [OE *sārig*, fr. *sār* sore] **1** : feeling sorrow, regret, or penitence **2** : MOURNFUL, SAD **3** : inspiring sorrow, pity, scorn, or ridicule : WRETCHED — **sor·ri·ly** \ˈsär-ə-lē, ˈsȯr-\ *adv* — **sor·ri·ness** \ˈsär-ē-nəs, ˈsȯr-\ *n*

¹sort \ˈsȯrt\ *n* [MF *sorte*, fr. L *sort-*, *sors* chance, lot] **1** : a group set up on the basis of any characteristic in common : CLASS **2** : a number of things used together : SET, SUIT **3** : method or manner of acting : WAY, MANNER **4** : general character or disposition; *also* : PERSON, INDIVIDUAL ⟨he's not a bad *sort* at heart⟩ **syn** see KIND — **after a sort** : in a rough or haphazard way — **of sorts** *or* **of a sort** : of an inconsequential or mediocre quality ⟨a poet *of sorts*⟩ — **out of sorts 1** : out of temper : IRRITABLE **2** : not well

²sort *vb* **1** : to put in a certain place or rank according to kind, class, or nature : CLASSIFY ⟨*sort* mail⟩ ⟨*sort* out colors⟩ **2** *archaic* : SUIT, HARMONIZE, AGREE — **sort·a·ble** \ˈsȯrt-ə-bəl\ *adj* — **sort·er** *n*

sor·tie \ˈsȯrt-ē, sȯr-ˈtē\ *n* [F, fr. *sortir* to go out] **1** : a sudden issuing of troops from a defensive position against the enemy : SALLY **2** : one mission or attack by a single plane — **sortie** *vi*

sort of *adv* : to a moderate degree : RATHER

so·rus \ˈsōr-əs, ˈsȯr-\ *n, pl* **so·ri** \ˈsōr-ˌī, ˈsȯr-, -(ˌ)ē\ [NL, fr. Gk *sōros* heap] : a cluster of plant reproductive bodies; *esp* : one of the dots on the underside of a fertile fern frond consisting of a cluster of spores

SOS \ˌes-(ˌ)ō-ˈes\ *n* **1** : an internationally recognized signal of distress in radio code · · · — — — · · · used esp. by ships calling for help **2** : a call or request for help or rescue

¹so-so \ˈsō-ˈsō\ *adv* : TOLERABLY, PASSABLY

²so-so *adj* : neither very good nor very bad : MIDDLING

so·ste·nu·to \ˌsō-stə-ˈnüt-ō, ˌsȯ-\ *adv* (*or adj*) [It] : SUSTAINED, PROLONGED — used as a direction in music

sot \ˈsät\ *n* [ME, fool, fr. OE *sott*] : a habitual drunkard

sot·ted \ˈsät-əd\ *adj* : BESOTTED

sot·tish \ˈsät-ish\ *adj* : resembling a sot : STUPID; *also* : DRUNKEN — **sot·tish·ly** *adv* — **sot·tish·ness** *n*

sot·to vo·ce \ˌsät-ō-ˈvō-chē\ *adv* (*or adj*) [It *sottovoce*, fr. *sotto* under + *voce* voice] **1** : under the breath : in an undertone; *also* : PRIVATELY **2** : very softly

sou \ˈsü\ *n* [F, fr. LL *solidus* solidus] : a French bronze coin of the period before 1914 worth 5 centimes or one twentieth of a franc

sou·brette \sü-ˈbret\ *n* [F] **1 a** : a coquettish maid or frivolous young woman in comedies **b** : an actress who plays such a part **2** : a soprano who sings supporting roles in comic opera

sou·bri·quet \ˈsō-bri-ˌkā, ˈsü-, -ˌket\ *var of* SOBRIQUET

¹souf·flé \sü-ˈflā\ *n* [F, fr. pp. of *souffler* to puff up, fr. L *sufflare*, fr. *sub-* + *flare* to blow] : a delicate spongy hot dish lightened in baking by stiffly beaten egg whites

²soufflé *or* **souf·fléed** \-ˈflād\ *adj* : puffed by or in cooking ⟨*soufflé* omelet⟩

sough \ˈsəf, ˈsaú\ *vi* [OE *swōgan*] : to make a moaning or sighing sound — **sough** *n*

sought *past of* SEEK

¹soul \ˈsōl\ *n* [OE *sāwol*] **1** : the spiritual part of man believed to give life to his body and in many religions regarded as immortal **2 a** : man's moral and emotional nature ⟨felt his *soul* rebel against cruelty⟩ **b** : spiritual force : FERVOR **3** : the essential part of something **4** : the moving spirit : LEADER ⟨the *soul* of an enterprise⟩ **5** : EMBODIMENT ⟨he was the *soul* of honor⟩ **6** : a human being : PERSON ⟨a kind *soul*⟩ **7** : a disembodied spirit **8** : a strong positive feeling (as of intense sensitivity and emotional fervor) typified by black American performers

syn SOUL, SPIRIT mean an immaterial entity distinguishable from and superior to the body. SOUL is preferred when the entity is considered as having functions, responsibilities,

ə abut; ᵉ kitten; ər further; a back; ā bake; ä cot, cart; aú out; ch chin; e less; ē easy; g gift; i trip; ī life

or a certain destiny ⟨to save his *soul*⟩ ⟨sold his *soul* to the devil⟩ SPIRIT is preferred when the quality, movement, activity is stressed ⟨their *spirits* were refreshed⟩ or opposition to the material part is intended ⟨the *spirit* is willing but the flesh is weak⟩

²**soul** *adj* **1** : of, relating to, or characteristic of black Americans or their culture **2** : designed for or controlled by blacks

soul·ful \-fəl\ *adj* : full of or expressing feeling or emotion — **soul·ful·ly** \-fə-lē\ *adv* — **soul·ful·ness** *n*

soul·less \'sōl-ləs\ *adj* : having no soul or no greatness or nobleness of mind or feeling — **soul·less·ly** *adv*

soul-search·ing \'sōl-,sər-chiŋ\ *n* : examination of one's conscience esp. with regard to motives and values

¹**sound** \'saund\ *adj* [OE *gesund*] **1** : free from flaw, defect, or decay **2** : not diseased or weak **a** : *sound* mind in a *sound* body **3** : SOLID, FIRM ⟨a building of *sound* construction⟩ **4** : STABLE **5** : not faulty : VALID, RIGHT ⟨a *sound* argument⟩ **6** : showing good sense : WISE ⟨*sound* advice⟩ **7** : HONORABLE, HONEST ⟨*sound* principles⟩ **8** : THOROUGH ⟨a *sound* beating⟩ **9** : UNDISTURBED, DEEP ⟨a *sound* sleep⟩ **syn** see HEALTHY, VALID — **sound·ly** *adv* — **sound·ness** \'saun(d)-nəs\ *n*

²**sound** *adv* : SOUNDLY ⟨*sound* asleep⟩

³**sound** *n* [OF *son*, fr. L *sonus*] **1 a** : the sensation experienced through the sense of hearing **b** : a particular auditory impression : NOISE, TONE **c** : mechanical energy that is transmitted by longitudinal pressure waves in a material medium (as air) and is the objective cause of hearing **2 a** : one of the noises that together make up human speech ⟨the *sound* of th in *this*⟩ **b** : a sequence of spoken noises ⟨*-cher* of *teacher* and *-ture* of *creature* have the same *sound*⟩ **3 a** : meaningless noise **b** : impression conveyed : IMPORT, IMPLICATION ⟨the excuse has a suspicious *sound*⟩ **4** : hearing distance : EARSHOT

⁴**sound** *vb* **1 a** : to make or cause to make a sound **b** : RESOUND **c** : to give a summons by sound **2** : to put into words : VOICE **3 a** : to make known : PROCLAIM **b** : to order, signal, or indicate by a sound **4** : to make or convey an impression : SEEM ⟨*sounds* incredible⟩ **5** : to examine by causing to emit sounds ⟨*sound* the lungs⟩ — **sound·a·ble** \'saun-də-bəl\ *adj*

⁵**sound** *n* [OE *sund* sea & ON *sund* strait] **1** : a long passage of water that is wider than a strait and often connects two larger bodies of water or forms a channel between the mainland and an island **2** : the air bladder of a fish

⁶**sound** *vb* [MF *sonder*, fr. *sonde* sounding line] **1 a** : to measure the depth of (as with a sounding line) : FATHOM **b** : to look into or investigate the possibility **2** : to try to find out the views or intentions of : PROBE **3** : to dive down suddenly ⟨a *sounding* whale⟩

sound barrier *n* : the sudden large increase in resistance that the air offers to an airplane whose speed nears the speed of sound

sound·board \'saun(d)-,bōrd, -,bord\ *n* **1** : a thin resonant board so placed in a musical instrument as to reinforce its tones by sympathetic vibration **2** : SOUNDING BOARD 1a

sound effects *n pl* : effects that are imitative of sounds called for in the script of a play, radio or television program, or motion picture and are produced by various means

sound·er \'saun-dər\ *n* : one that sounds; *esp* : an electromagnetic device in a telegraph receiver that makes clicking sounds from which the message can be interpreted

¹**sound·ing** \'saun-diŋ\ *n* **1 a** : measurement by sounding **b** : the depth so ascertained **2** : measurement of atmospheric conditions at various heights **3** : a probe, test, or sampling of opinion or intention

²**sounding** *adj* **1** : RESONANT, SONOROUS **2** : HIGH-SOUNDING — **sound·ing·ly** \-diŋ-lē\ *adv*

sounding board *n* **1 a** : a structure behind or over a pulpit, rostrum, or platform to give distinctness and sonority to sound uttered from it **b** : a device or agency that helps spread opinions or utterances **2** : SOUNDBOARD 1

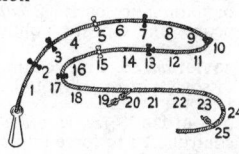

sounding line: *1, 4, 6, 8, 9, 11, 12, 14, 16, 18, 19, 21, 22, 23, 24,* deeps; *2, 3, 5, 7, 10, 13, 15, 17, 20, 25,* marks

sounding line *n* : a line, wire, or cord weighted at one end for sounding

¹**sound·less** \'saun-dləs\ *adj* : incapable of being sounded : UNFATHOMABLE

²**soundless** *adj* : making no sound : SILENT — **sound·less·ly** *adv*

sound off *vi* **1** : to count cadence while marching **2 a** : to speak up in a loud voice **b** : to voice one's opinions freely and vigorously

¹**sound·proof** \'saun(d)-'prüf\ *adj* : impervious to sound ⟨a *soundproof* room⟩

²**soundproof** *vt* : to insulate so as to obstruct the passage of sound

sound track *n* : the area on a motion-picture film that carries the sound record

sound truck *n* : a truck equipped with a loudspeaker

sound waves *n pl* : longitudinal pressure waves in a material medium regardless of whether they constitute audible sound

¹**soup** \'süp\ *n* [F *soupe* sop, soup, of Gmc origin; akin to E *sop*] **1** : a liquid food with a meat, fish, or vegetable stock as a base and often containing pieces of solid food **2** : something having or suggesting the consistency of soup (as a heavy fog or nitroglycerin) **3** : an unfortunate predicament ⟨in the *soup*⟩

²**soup** *vt* [E slang *soup* dope injected into a racehorse to change its speed] : to increase the power or efficiency of ⟨*souped* up the engine of his car⟩ — **souped–up** \'süpt-'əp\ *adj*

soup·çon \süp-'sōⁿ, 'süp-,sän\ *n* [F, lit., suspicion] : a little bit : TRACE ⟨detected a *soupçon* of ridicule in his words⟩

soup kitchen *n* : an establishment dispensing minimum dietary essentials (as soup and bread) to the needy

soupy \'sü-pē\ *adj* **soup·i·er; -est** **1** : having the consistency of soup **2** : densely foggy or cloudy

¹**sour** \'sau(ə)r\ *adj* [OE *sūr*] **1** : having an acid or tart taste ⟨*sour* as vinegar⟩ **2 a** : having undergone a usu. acid fermentation ⟨*sour* milk⟩ **b** : indicative of decay : PUTRID ⟨a *sour* odor⟩ **3** : UNPLEASANT, DISAGREEABLE ⟨a *sour* look⟩ ⟨played a *sour* note⟩ **4** : acid in reaction ⟨*sour* soil⟩ — **sour·ish** \-ish\ *adj* — **sour·ly** *adv* — **sour·ness** *n*

syn ACID, TART: SOUR usu. implies having lost sweetness or freshness through fermentation or spoiling ⟨*sour* cream⟩ ACID applies to things having naturally or normally a biting or stinging taste ⟨*acid* fruits like lemons⟩ TART suggests a sharp but agreeable acidity ⟨*tart* applesauce⟩

²**sour** *n* **1 a** : something sour **b** : the primary taste sensation produced by acid stimuli **2** : a cocktail made with spirituous liquor, lemon or lime juice, sugar, and sometimes soda water

³**sour** *vb* : to become or make sour

sour ball *n* : a spherical piece of hard candy having a tart flavor

source \'sōrs, 'sors\ *n* [MF *sourse*, fr. *sourdre* to rise, spring forth, fr. L *surgere*] **1** : the point of origin of a stream of water : FOUNTAINHEAD **2 a** : a generative force : CAUSE **b** (1) : a point of origin (2) : one that initiates : AUTHOR; *also* : PROTOTYPE, MODEL (3) : one that supplies information **3** : a firsthand document or primary reference work **syn** see ORIGIN

source book *n* : a fundamental document or record (as of history) on which subsequent writings, beliefs, or practices are based; *also* : a collection of such documents

sour cherry *n* : a small Old World cherry tree widely grown for its soft tart bright red to nearly black fruits; *also* : its fruit

sour·dough \'sau(ə)r-,dō\ *n* **1** : a leaven of dough in which fermentation is active **2** [fr. the use of sourdough for making bread in prospectors' camps] : an old-time prospector in Alaska or northwestern Canada

sour grapes *n pl* [fr. the fable ascribed to Aesop of the fox who being unable to reach some grapes he had desired disparaged them as sour] : disparagement of something that has proven unattainable

sour gum *n* : a timber tree of the eastern U.S. with blue-black fruits and close-grained grayish wood

sour·sop \'sau(ə)r-,säp\ *n* : a small tropical American tree related to the custard apple; *also* : its large edible fruit with fleshy spines and a slightly acid fibrous pulp

sou·sa·phone \'sü-zə-,fōn\ *n* [John P. *Sousa* d1932

American bandmaster and composer] : a large circular tuba with a flaring adjustable bell

¹souse \'saús\ *vb* [MF *souce* pickling solution, of Gmc origin; akin to E *salt*] **1** : PICKLE **2 a** : to plunge in liquid : IMMERSE **b** : DRENCH, SATURATE **3** : to make or become drunk : INEBRIATE

²souse *n* **1** : something pickled; *esp* : seasoned and chopped pork trimmings, fish, or shellfish **2** : an act of sousing : WETTING **3** : an habitual drunkard

sou·tache \sü-'tash\ *n* [F, fr. Hung *sujtás*] : a narrow braid with herringbone pattern used as trimming

sou·tane \sü-'tän, -'tan\ *n* [F, fr. It *sottana*, lit., under-garment] : CASSOCK

¹south \'saúth; *in compounds, as* "*southwest*", *also* (')saú *esp by seamen*\ *adv* [OE *sūth*] : to or toward the south

²south *adj* **1** : situated toward or at the south **2** : coming from the south

³south *n* **1 a** : the direction to the right of one facing east **b** : the compass point directly opposite to north — see COMPASS CARD **2** *cap* : regions or countries south of a specified or implied point

South African *n* : a native or inhabitant of the Republic of So. Africa; *esp* : AFRIKANER — **South African** *adj*

south·bound \'saúth-,baúnd\ *adj* : headed south

south by east : one point east of due south : S 11° 15′ E

south by west : one point west of due south : S 11° 15′ W

¹south·east \saúth-'ēst\ *adv* : to or toward the southeast

²southeast *n* **1 a** : the general direction between south and east **b** : the compass point midway between south and east — see COMPASS CARD **2** *cap* : regions or countries southeast of a specified or implied point

³southeast *adj* **1** : situated toward or at the southeast **2** : coming from the southeast

southeast by east : one point east of due southeast : S 56° 15′ E

southeast by south : one point south of due southeast : S 33° 45′ E

south·east·er \saúth-'ē-stər\ *n* **1** : a strong southeast wind **2** : a storm with southeast winds

south·east·er·ly \-lē\ *adv (or adj)* **1** : from the southeast **2** : toward the southeast

south·east·ern \saúth-'ē-stərn\ *adj* **1** *often cap* : of, relating to, or characteristic of a region conventionally designated Southeast **2** : lying toward or coming from the southeast — **south·east·ern·most** \-,mōst\ *adj*

South·east·ern·er \-stə(r)-nər\ *n* : a native or inhabitant of a southeastern region (as of the U.S.)

¹south·east·ward \saúth-'ēs-twərd\ *adv (or adj)* : toward the southeast — **south·east·wards** \-twərdz\ *adv*

²southeastward *n* : SOUTHEAST

south·er \'saú-thər\ *n* : a southerly wind

south·er·ly \'səth-ər-lē\ *adv (or adj)* **1** : from the south **2** : toward the south

south·ern \'səth-ərn\ *adj* **1** *often cap* : of, relating to, or characteristic of a region conventionally designated South **2** : lying toward or coming from the south — **south·ern·most** \-,mōst\ *adj*

Southern Cross *n* : four bright stars in the southern hemisphere situated as if at the extremities of a Latin cross; *also* : the constellation of which these four stars are the brightest

South·ern·er \'səth-ə(r)-nər\ *n* : a native or inhabitant of the South (as of the U.S.)

southern hemisphere *n* : the half of the earth that lies south of the equator

southern lights *n pl* : AURORA AUSTRALIS

south·ern·ly \'səth-ərn-lē\ *adj* **1** : coming from the south **2** : headed south

south·ing \'saú-thiŋ, -thiŋ\ *n* **1** : difference in latitude to the south from the last preceding point of reckoning **2** : southerly progress

south·land \'saúth-,land, -lənd\ *n, often cap* : land in the south : the south of a country or region

south·paw \'saúth-,pò\ *n* : LEFT-HANDER; *esp* : a left-handed baseball pitcher — **southpaw** *adj*

south pole *n* **1** *often cap S & P* : the southernmost point of the earth : the southern end of the earth's axis **2** : the pole of a magnet that points toward the south

South·ron \'səth-rən\ *n* : SOUTHERNER: as **a** *chiefly Scot* : ENGLISHMAN **b** *chiefly South* : a native or inhabitant of the southern states of the U.S.

south–southeast *n* — see COMPASS CARD

south–southwest *n* — see COMPASS CARD

¹south·ward \'saúth-wərd\ *adv (or adj)* : toward the south — **south·wards** \-wərdz\ *adv*

²southward *n* : southward direction or part ⟨sail to the *southward*⟩

¹south·west \saúth-'west\ *adv* **1** : to or toward the southwest

²southwest *n* **1 a** : the general direction between south and west **b** : the compass point midway between south and west — see COMPASS CARD **2** *cap* : regions or countries southwest of a specified or implied point

³southwest *adj* **1** : situated toward or at the southwest **2** : coming from the southwest

southwest by south : one point south of due southwest : S 33° 45′ W

southwest by west : one point west of due southwest : S 56° 15′ W

south·west·er \saúth-'wes-tər\ *n* : a storm or wind from the southwest

south·west·er·ly \-lē\ *adv (or adj)* **1** : from the southwest **2** : toward the southwest

south·west·ern \saúth-'wes-tərn\ *adj* **1** *often cap* : of, relating to, or characteristic of a region conventionally designated Southwest **2** : lying toward or coming from the southwest — **south·west·ern·most** \-,mōst\ *adj*

South·west·ern·er \-tə(r)-nər\ *n* : a native or inhabitant of a southwestern region (as of the U.S.)

¹south·west·ward \saúth-'wes-twərd\ *adv (or adj)* : toward the southwest — **south·west·wards** \-twərdz\ *adv*

²southwestward *n* : SOUTHWEST

sou·ve·nir \'sü-və-,ni(ə)r, ,sü-və-'\ *n* [F, lit., act of remembering, fr. *se souvenir* to remember, fr. L *subvenire* to come up, come to mind, fr. *sub-* up + *venire* to come] : something that serves as a reminder : MEMENTO, REMEMBRANCE

sou'·west·er \saú-'wes-tər\ *n* **1** : SOUTHWESTER **2 a** : a long oilskin coat worn esp. at sea during stormy weather **b** : a waterproof hat with wide slanting brim longer in back than in front

sou'wester 2b

¹sov·er·eign *also* **sov·ran** \'säv-(ə-)rən, 'säv-ərn, 'səv-\ *n* **1 a** : a person, body of persons, or a state possessing sovereignty; *esp* : a monarch exercising supreme authority in a state **b** : one that exercises supreme authority within a limited sphere **c** : an acknowledged leader : ARBITER **2** : a British gold coin no longer issued worth 1 pound sterling

²sovereign *also* **sovran** *adj* [MF *soverain*, fr. (assumed) VL *superanus*, fr. L *super* over, above] **1** : CHIEF, HIGHEST ⟨our *sovereign* interest⟩ ⟨a citizen's *sovereign* duty⟩ **2** : supreme in power or authority ⟨a *sovereign* prince⟩ **3** : having independent authority ⟨a *sovereign* state⟩ **4** : EFFECTUAL, EXCELLENT ⟨a *sovereign* remedy for colds⟩ **syn** see FREE — **sov·er·eign·ly** *adv*

sov·er·eign·ty \-tē\ *n, pl* **-ties 1** : the condition of being sovereign or a sovereign **2 a** : supreme power esp. over a politically organized unit : DOMINION **b** : freedom from external control : AUTONOMY **3** : one that is sovereign; *esp* : an autonomous state

¹so·vi·et \'sō-vē-,et, -ət, 'säv-ē-\ *n* [Russ *sovet*] **1 a** : one of the representative councils of workers, peasants, or soldiers formed chiefly on occupational lines during the Russian revolution of 1905 or 1917 that during the Bolshevik revolution of 1917 took over or acquired various governmental functions **b** : one of a hierarchy of governing councils in the U.S.S.R. elected on a territorial or nationality basis **2** *cap* **a** : the U.S.S.R. **b** *pl* : the people and esp. the political and military leaders of the U.S.S.R.

²soviet *adj* **1** : of, relating to, or organized on the basis of soviets ⟨a *soviet* republic⟩ **2** *cap* : of or relating to the U.S.S.R.

so·vi·et·ize \-,īz\ *vt, often cap* **1** : to bring under Soviet control **2** : to force into conformity with Soviet cultural patterns or governmental policies — **so·vi·et·i·za·tion** \,sō-vē-,et-ə-'zā-shən, ,säv-ē-, -ət-\ *n, often cap*

sov·khoz \säf-'kòz\ *n, pl* **sov·kho·zy** \-'kò-zē\ *or* **sov·khoz·es** [Russ, short for *sovetskoe khozyaĭstvo* soviet farm] **:** a state-owned farm of the U.S.S.R. paying wages to the workers — compare KOLKHOZ

¹sow \'saủ\ *n* [OE *sugu*] **:** an adult female swine

²sow \'sō\ *vb* **sowed; sown** \'sōn\ *or* **sowed; sow·ing** [OE *sāwan*] **1 a :** to plant seed for growth esp. by scattering **b :** PLANT 1a **c :** to strew with or as if with seed **d :** to introduce into a selected environment **:** IMPLANT **2 :** to set in motion **:** FOMENT ⟨*sow* suspicion⟩ **3 :** to spread abroad **:** DISPERSE, DISSEMINATE — **sow·er** \'sō(-ə)r\ *n*

sow·bel·ly \'saủ-ˌbel-ē\ *n* **:** fat salt pork or bacon

sow bug \'saủ-\ *n* **:** WOOD LOUSE

sow thistle \'saủ-\ *n* **:** any of a genus of spiny weedy European composite herbs widely naturalized (as in No. America)

sox *pl of* SOCK

soy \'sói\ *n* [Jap *shōyu,* fr. Chin (Cant) *shī-yaū,* lit., soybean oil] **1 :** a Chinese and Japanese sauce made from soybeans fermented in brine **2 :** SOYBEAN

soya \'sói-(y)ə\ *n* [D *soja,* fr. Jap *shōyu* soy] **:** SOYBEAN

soy·bean \'sói-ˌbēn, -ˌbēn\ *n* **:** a hairy annual Asiatic legume widely grown for its oil-rich and protein-rich edible seeds and for forage and soil improvement; *also* **:** its seed

spa \'spä, 'spó\ *n* [*Spa,* watering place in Belgium] **1 a :** a mineral spring **b :** a resort with mineral springs **2 :** a fashionable resort or hotel

¹space \'spās\ *n* [OF *espace,* fr. L *spatium* area, room, interval of space or time] **1 :** a period of time; *also* **:** its duration **2 a :** a limited extent in one, two, or three dimensions **:** DISTANCE, AREA, VOLUME **b :** an extent set apart or available ⟨parking *space*⟩ ⟨floor *space*⟩ **3 :** one of the degrees between or above or below the lines of a musical staff **4 :** a boundless three-dimensional extent in which objects and events occur and have relative position and direction **5 :** the region beyond the earth's atmosphere **6 a :** a blank area separating words or lines **b :** material used to produce such blank area; *esp* **:** a piece of type less than one en in width **7 :** a set of mathematical points each defined by one or more coordinates **8 :** an interval in operation during which a telegraph key is not in contact **9 a :** LINAGE 1 **b :** broadcast time available esp. to advertisers **10 :** accommodations on a public vehicle

²space *vt* **:** to place at intervals or arrange with space between

space charge *n* **:** an electric charge (as the electrons in the region near the filament of a vacuum tube) distributed throughout a three-dimensional region

space·craft \'spās-ˌkraft\ *n* **:** SPACESHIP

space·flight \-ˌflīt\ *n* **:** flight beyond the earth's atmosphere

space heater *n* **:** a device for heating an enclosed space; *esp* **:** an often portable device that heats the space in which it is located and has no external heating ducts

space·less \'spās-ləs\ *adj* **1 :** having no limits **:** BOUNDLESS **2 :** occupying no space

space·man \'spās-ˌman\ *n* **1 :** one who travels outside the earth's atmosphere **2 :** a person engaged in any of various fields bearing on flight through outer space

space medicine *n* **:** a branch of medicine that deals with the physiologic and biologic effects on the human body of flight beyond the earth's atmosphere

space·port \'spās-ˌpōrt, -ˌpȯrt\ *n* **:** an installation for testing and launching rockets, missiles, and satellites

space·ship \'spās(h)-ˌship\ *n* **:** a vehicle designed to operate outside the earth's atmosphere

space shuttle *n* **:** a usu. two-stage vehicle that is designed to serve as transportation between the earth and an orbiting space station

space station *n* **:** a manned artificial satellite designed for a fixed orbit about the earth and to serve as a base (as for scientific observation)

space suit *n* **:** a suit with air supply and provisions to make life in free space possible for its wearer

space writer *n* **:** a writer paid according to the space his matter fills in print

spa·cial *var of* SPATIAL

spac·ing *n* **1 :** an arrangement in space **2 a :** SPACE **b :** the distance between any two objects in a usu. regularly arranged series

spa·cious \'spā-shəs\ *adj* **1 :** vast or ample in extent

: ROOMY ⟨a *spacious* hall⟩ **2 :** large or magnificent in scale **:** EXPANSIVE — **spa·cious·ly** *adv* — **spa·cious·ness** *n*

¹spade \'spād\ *n* [OE *spadu*] **1 :** an implement for turning soil that resembles a shovel, is adapted for being pushed into the ground with the foot, and has a heavy usu. flat blade **2 :** a spade-shaped instrument — **call a spade a spade 1 :** to call a thing by its right name however coarse **2 :** to speak frankly

²spade *vb* **:** to dig with or use a spade — **spad·er** *n*

³spade *n* [It *spada* or Sp *espada* broad sword; both fr. L *spatha,* fr. Gk *spathē* blade; akin to E ¹*spade*] **:** a black figure resembling an inverted heart with a short stem at the bottom used to distinguish a suit of playing cards; *also* **:** a card of the suit bearing spades

spade·foot \'spād-ˌfůt\ *n, pl* **spadefoots :** any of several burrowing toads with the feet modified for digging — called also *spadefoot toad*

spade·ful \-ˌfůl\ *n, pl* **spadefuls** \-ˌfůlz\ *or* **spades·ful** \'spādz-ˌfůl\ **:** the amount held by a spade

spade·work \'spād-ˌwərk\ *n* **1 :** work done with the spade **2 :** the hard plain preliminary drudgery in any undertaking

spa·dix \'spād-iks\ *n, pl* **spa·di·ces** \'spād-ə-ˌsēz\ [NL *spadic-, spadix,* fr. L, frond torn from a palm tree, fr. Gk *spadik-, spadix*] **:** a floral spike (as in the arums) with a fleshy or succulent axis usu. enclosed in a spathe

spa·ghet·ti \spə-'get-ē\ *n* [It, fr. pl. of *spaghetto,* dim. of *spago* string] **:** a food made chiefly of semolina paste dried in the form of solid strings of small diameter

spake \'spāk\ *archaic past of* SPEAK

¹span \'span\ *archaic past of* SPIN

²span *n* [OE *spann*] **1 :** the distance from the end of the thumb to the end of the little finger of a spread hand; *also* **:** an English unit of length equal to 9 inches **2 :** an extent, stretch, reach, or spread between two limits: as **a :** a limited space of time ⟨*span* of life⟩ **b :** the spread of an arch, beam, truss, or girder from one support to another; *also* **:** the portion thus extended **3 :** the amount grasped in a single manual performance ⟨memory *span*⟩

³span *vt* **spanned; span·ning 1 a :** to measure by or as if by the hand with fingers and thumb extended **b :** MEASURE **2 a :** to reach or extend across ⟨a bridge *spans* the river⟩ **b :** to place or construct a span over **:** BRIDGE

⁴span *n* [D] **:** a pair of animals (as mules) driven together

span·drel *or* **span·dril** \'span-drəl\ *n* [ME *spandrell,* fr. OF *espandre* to spread out, expand, fr. L *expandere*] **:** the sometimes ornamented space between the right or left exterior curve of an arch and an enclosing right angle

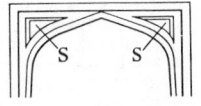

spandrels, *S, S*

¹span·gle \'span-gəl\ *n* [ME *spangel*] **1 :** a small piece of shining metal or plastic used for ornamentation esp. on dresses **2 :** a small glittering object

²spangle *vb* **span·gled; span·gling** \'span-g(ə-)lin\ **1 :** to set or sprinkle with or as if with spangles **2 :** to glitter as if covered with spangles **:** SPARKLE

Span·iard \'span-yərd\ *n* **:** a native or inhabitant of Spain

span·iel \'span-yəl\ *n* [MF *espaignol,* lit., Spaniard] **1 :** any of numerous small or medium-sized mostly short-legged dogs usu. having long wavy hair, feathered legs and tail, and large drooping ears **2 :** a cringing fawning person

Span·ish \'span-ish\ *n* **1 :** the Romance language of the largest part of Spain and of the countries colonized by Spaniards **2 Spanish** *pl* **:** the people of Spain — **Spanish** *adj*

Spanish American *n* **1 :** a native or inhabitant of one of the countries of America in which Spanish is the national language **2 :** a resident of the U.S. whose native language is Spanish and whose culture is of Spanish origin — **Spanish–American** *adj*

Spanish fly *n* **:** a green blister beetle of southern Europe; *also* **:** a dried preparation of these

Spanish mackerel *n* **:** any of various usu. large fishes chiefly of warm seas that resemble or are related to the common mackerel

Spanish moss *n* **:** an epiphytic plant related to the pineapple that forms pendent tufts of grayish green filaments on trees in the southern U.S. and the West Indies

Spanish omelet n : an omelet served with a sauce containing chopped green pepper, onion, and tomato

Spanish rice n : rice cooked with onions, green pepper, and tomatoes

spank \'spaŋk\ vt : to strike esp. on the buttocks usu. with the open hand — **spank** n

spank·er \'spaŋ-kər\ n 1 : the fore-and-aft sail on the mast nearest the stern of a square-rigged ship 2 : the sail on the sternmost mast in a schooner of four or more masts

spank·ing \'spaŋ-kiŋ\ adj 1 : remarkable of its kind 2 : moving with a quick, lively pace : BRISK, LIVELY ⟨a spanking team of horses⟩ ⟨a spanking wind⟩

span·ner \'span-ər\ n [G, instrument for winding springs, fr. spannen to stretch; akin to E span] 1 chiefly Brit : WRENCH 2 : a wrench having a jaw or socket to fit a nut or head of a bolt, a pipe, or hose coupling; esp : one having a tooth or pin in its jaw to fit a hole or slot in an object

span-new \'span-'n(y)ü\ adj : BRAND-NEW

span·worm \'span-ˌwərm\ n : LOOPER 1

¹spar \'spär\ n [ME sparre] 1 : a stout rounded wood or metal piece (as a mast, boom, or yard) used to support sail rigging 2 : one of the main longitudinal members of the wing of an airplane that carry the ribs

²spar vi **sparred; spar·ring** 1 : to strike or fight with the feet or spurs like a gamecock 2 a : BOX; esp : to gesture without landing a blow to draw one's opponent or create an opening b : to engage in a practice or exhibition bout of boxing 3 : SKIRMISH, WRANGLE

³spar n 1 : a movement of offense or defense in boxing 2 : a sparring match or session

⁴spar n [LG] : any of various nonmetallic somewhat lustrous minerals usu. able to be split readily in certain directions

¹spare \'spa(ə)r, 'spe(ə)r\ vb [OE sparian] 1 : to forbear to destroy, punish, or harm : be lenient ⟨spare a prisoner⟩ 2 : to refrain from attacking or reprimanding with necessary or salutary severity 3 : to relieve of the necessity of doing or undergoing something : EXEMPT ⟨be spared the labor⟩ 4 : to refrain from : AVOID ⟨spare no cost⟩ 5 : to use frugally ⟨spare the rod and spoil the child⟩ 6 a : to give up as not strictly needed ⟨unable to spare a dollar⟩ b : to have left over or as margin ⟨time to spare⟩

²spare adj [OE spær] 1 : not being used; esp : held for emergency use ⟨a spare tire⟩ 2 : being over and above what is needed : SUPERFLUOUS ⟨spare time⟩ 3 : not liberal or profuse : SPARING ⟨a spare diet⟩ 4 : somewhat thin ⟨of spare build⟩ 5 : not abundant or plentiful : SCANTY — **spare·ly** adv — **spare·ness** n

³spare n 1 : a spare or duplicate piece or part (as an automobile tire) 2 : the knocking down of all 10 pins with the first 2 bowls of a frame in bowling or the score made by this action

spare·a·ble \'spar-ə-bəl, 'sper-\ adj : that can be spared

spare·ribs \'spa(ə)r-ˌ(r)ibz, 'spe(ə)r-\ n pl [by folk etymology fr. LG ribbesper pickled pork ribs roasted on a spit, fr. ribbe rib + sper spear, spit] : a cut of pork ribs separated from the bacon strip

spar·ing \'spa(ə)r-iŋ, 'spe(ə)r-\ adj 1 : tending to save; esp : FRUGAL 2 : MEAGER, SCANTY — **spar·ing·ly** \-iŋ-lē\ adv

¹spark \'spärk\ n [OE spearca] 1 a : a small particle of a burning substance b : a hot glowing particle struck from a larger mass; esp : one heated by friction ⟨produce a spark by striking steel on flint⟩ 2 a : a luminous electrical discharge of very short duration between two conductors b : the electrical discharge in a spark plug c : the mechanism controlling the discharge in a spark plug 3 : SPARKLE, FLASH 4 : something that sets off a sudden force ⟨the spark that set off the rebellion⟩ 5 : a latent particle capable of growth or developing : GERM ⟨not a spark of life was found on the island⟩

²spark vb 1 a : to throw out or produce sparks : SPARKLE b : to flash or fall like sparks ⟨fireflies sparked in the darkness⟩ 2 : to respond with enthusiasm 3 : to set off in a burst of activity : ACTIVATE 4 : to stir to activity : INCITE, STIMULATE ⟨the captain sparked his team to victory⟩ — **spark·er** n

³spark n 1 : a foppish young man : GALLANT 2 : LOVER, BEAU

⁴spark vb : WOO, COURT — **spark·er** n

spark arrester n : a device for preventing the escape of sparks (as from a smokestack)

spark coil n : an induction coil for producing a spark discharge of electricity

sparking plug n, Brit : SPARK PLUG

¹spar·kle \'spär-kəl\ vi **spar·kled; spar·kling** \-k(ə-)liŋ\ 1 a : to throw out sparks b : to shine as if throwing out sparks : GLISTEN 2 : to perform brilliantly 3 : EFFERVESCE ⟨sparkling wine⟩ 4 : to become lively or animated syn see FLASH

²sparkle n 1 : a little spark : SCINTILLATION ⟨the sparkle of a diamond⟩ 2 : the quality of sparkling 3 a : ANIMATION, LIVELINESS ⟨the sparkle of a witty play⟩ b : EFFERVESCENCE

spar·kler \'spär-klər\ n : one that sparkles: as a : DIAMOND b : a firework that throws off brilliant sparks on burning

spark plug n 1 : a part that fits into the cylinder head of an internal-combustion engine and produces the spark for combustion 2 : one that initiates or gives impetus to an undertaking — **spark·plug** \'spärk-ˌpləg\ vt

sparring partner n : one with whom a boxer spars for practice during training

spar·row \'spar-ō\ n [OE spearwa] 1 : any of several small dull singing birds related to the finches; esp : HOUSE SPARROW 2 : any of various finches resembling the true sparrows

spar·row·grass \'spar-ə-ˌgras\ n, chiefly dial : ASPARAGUS

sparrow hawk n : any of various small hawks or falcons

sparse \'spärs\ adj [L sparsus spread out, fr. pp. of spargere to scatter] : not thickly grown or settled syn see MEAGER — **sparse·ly** adv — **sparse·ness** n — **spar·si·ty** \'spär-sət-ē\ n

¹Spar·tan \'spärt-ᵊn\ n 1 : a native or inhabitant of ancient Sparta 2 : a person of great courage and fortitude

²Spartan adj 1 : of or relating to Sparta in ancient Greece 2 a : marked by strict self-discipline and avoidance of comfort and luxury ⟨Spartan simplicity⟩ b : undaunted by pain or danger ⟨Spartan courage⟩

spar varnish n : an exterior waterproof varnish

spasm \'spaz-əm\ n [Gk spasmos, fr. span to draw, pull] 1 : an involuntary and abnormal muscular contraction 2 : a sudden violent and temporary effort or emotion

spas·mod·ic \spaz-'mäd-ik\ adj [Gk spasmōdēs, fr. spasmos spasm] 1 : relating to or affected or characterized by spasm ⟨spasmodic movements⟩ 2 : acting or proceeding fitfully : INTERMITTENT ⟨spasmodic interest⟩ 3 : subject to outbursts of emotional excitement : EXCITABLE — **spas·mod·i·cal·ly** \-'mäd-i-k(ə-)lē\ adv

¹spas·tic \'spas-tik\ adj 1 : of, relating to, or characterized by spasm ⟨spastic colon⟩ 2 : suffering from spastic paralysis ⟨spastic child⟩ — **spas·ti·cal·ly** \-ti-k(ə-)lē\ adv — **spas·tic·i·ty** \spa-'stis-ət-ē\ n

²spastic n : one suffering from spastic paralysis

spastic paralysis n : paralysis with rigidly contracted muscles and increased tendon reflexes — compare CEREBRAL PALSY

¹spat \'spat\ past of SPIT

²spat n, pl **spat** or **spats** : a young bivalve mollusk (as an oyster) — usu. used collectively

³spat n [short for spatterdash, a kind of legging] : a cloth or leather gaiter covering the instep and ankle

⁴spat n 1 : a brief petty quarrel : DISPUTE 2 chiefly dial : SLAP 3 : a sound like that of rain falling in large drops ⟨spat of bullets⟩

⁵spat vb **spat·ted; spat·ting** 1 chiefly dial : SLAP 2 : to quarrel pettily or briefly : DISPUTE 3 : to strike with a sound like that of rain falling in large drops

spate \'spāt\ n [ME] 1 : FRESHET, FLOOD 2 a : a large number or amount b : a sudden or strong outburst : RUSH

spa·tha·ceous \spā-'thā-shəs\ adj : having or resembling a spathe

spathe \'spāth\ n [L spatha broad sword, fr. Gk spathē blade] : a sheathing bract or pair of bracts enclosing an inflorescence and esp. a spadix — **spathed** \'spāthd\ adj

spa·tial \'spā-shəl\ adj [L spatium space] : relating to, occupying, or of the nature of space — **spa·ti·al·i·ty** \ˌspā-shē-'al-ət-ē\ n — **spa·tial·ly** \'spāsh-(ə-)lē\ adv

¹spat·ter \'spat-ər\ vb 1 : to splash with or as if with a liquid; also : to soil or spot in this way 2 : to scatter by splashing ⟨*spatter* mud⟩ **3 :** to injure by aspersion **:** DE-FAME ⟨*spatter* a good reputation⟩ **4 a :** to spurt forth in scattered drops **b :** to drop with a sound like rain

²spatter *n* **1 :** the act or noise of spattering **:** the state of being spattered **2 a :** a drop or splash spattered on something **:** a spot or stain due to spattering **b :** a small number or quantity **:** SPRINKLE ⟨a *spatter* of rain⟩⟨a *spatter* of applause⟩

spat·ter·dock \'spat-ər-ˌdäk\ *n* **:** a common yellow No. American water lily

spat·u·la \'spach-ə-lə\ *n* [LL, dim. of L *spatha* sword, spatula, fr. Gk *spathē*] **:** a flat thin usu. metal implement that resembles a knife and is used esp. for spreading or mixing soft substances, scooping, or lifting

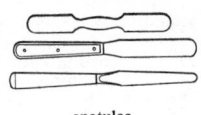

spatulas

spat·u·late \'spach-ə-lət\ *adj* **:** shaped like a spatula

spav·in \'spav-ən\ *n* [MF *espavain*] **:** a bony enlargement of the hock of a horse associated with strain — **spav·ined** \-ənd\ *adj*

¹spawn \'spȯn, 'spän\ *vb* [OF *espandre* to spread out, expand, fr. L *expandere*] **1 a :** to produce or deposit eggs or spawn — used of an aquatic animal **b :** to induce (fish) to spawn **2 :** to bring forth **:** GENERATE **3 :** to produce young esp. in large numbers — **spawn·er** *n*

²spawn *n* **1 :** the eggs of aquatic animals (as fishes or oysters) that lay many small eggs **2 :** PRODUCT, OFF-SPRING; *also* **:** offspring produced in large quantities **3 :** the seed, germ, or source of something **4 :** mycelium esp. prepared (as in bricks) for propagating mushrooms

spay \'spā\ *vt* [MF *espeer* to cut with a sword, fr. *espee* sword, fr. L *spatha*] **:** to remove the ovaries of (a female animal)

speak \'spēk\ *vb* **spoke** \'spōk\; **spo·ken** \'spō-kən\; **speak·ing** [OE *sprecan, specan*] **1 :** to utter words with the ordinary voice **:** TALK **2 :** to utter by means of words ⟨*speak* the truth⟩ **3 :** to address a gathering **4 :** to mention in speech or writing **5 :** to carry a meaning as if by speech ⟨his clothes *spoke* of poverty⟩ **6 :** to make a natural or characteristic sound ⟨the big gun *spoke*⟩ **7 :** to use in talking ⟨*speak* French⟩ — **speak·a·ble** \'spē-kə-bəl\ *adj* **syn** TALK: SPEAK may apply to any articulated sounds ranging from the least to the most coherent; TALK is less technical and less formal and implies a listener and connected discourse or exchange of thoughts —**speak for 1 :** to speak in behalf of **:** represent the opinions of **2 :** to apply for **:** CLAIM — **speak out 1 :** to speak loudly and distinctly **2 :** to speak freely — **speak to :** REPROVE, REBUKE — **speak up :** to speak out — **speak well for :** to be evidence in favor of — **speak with :** to talk to

speak·eas·y \'spēk-ˌē-zē\ *n* **:** a place where alcoholic drinks are illegally sold

speak·er \'spē-kər\ *n* **1 a :** one that speaks **b :** one who makes a public speech **c :** one who acts as a spokesman **2 :** the presiding officer of a deliberative assembly ⟨*Speaker* of the House of Representatives⟩ **3 :** LOUDSPEAKER

speak·er·ship \-ˌship\ *n* **:** the position of speaker esp. of a legislative body

speak·ing \'spē-kiŋ\ *adj* **1 :** highly significant or expressive **:** ELOQUENT ⟨*speaking* eyes⟩ **2 :** STRIKING, FAITHFUL ⟨a *speaking* resemblance⟩

speaking tube *n* **:** a pipe through which conversation may be conducted (as between different parts of a building)

¹spear \'spi(ə)r\ *n* [OE *spere*] **1 :** a thrusting or throwing weapon with long shaft and sharp head or blade **2 :** a sharp-pointed instrument with barbs used in spearing fish **3 :** SPEARMAN

²spear *adj* **:** PATERNAL, MALE ⟨the *spear* side of the family⟩

³spear *vb* **1 :** to pierce or strike with or as if with a spear ⟨*spear* salmon⟩ **2 :** to thrust with or as if with a spear — **spear·er** *n*

⁴spear *n* [alter. of **¹spire**] **:** a usu. young blade, shoot, or sprout (as of grass)

spear·fish \'spi(ə)r-ˌfish\ *n* **:** any of several large sea fishes related to the marlins and sailfishes

¹spear·head \'spi(ə)r-ˌhed\ *n* **1 :** the sharp-pointed head of a spear **2 :** a leading element, force, or influence (as in an attack, drive, or enterprise)

²spearhead *vt* **:** to serve as leader or leading element of ⟨*spearhead* the attack⟩

spear·man \'spi(ə)r-mən\ *n* **:** one (as a soldier) armed with a spear

spear·mint \-ˌmint, -mənt\ *n* **:** a common mint grown for flavoring and esp. for its aromatic oil

spe·cial \'spesh-əl\ *adj* [L *specialis* individual, particular, fr. *species* species] **1 a :** distinguished by some unusual quality ⟨a *special* occasion⟩ **b :** regarded with particular favor ⟨a *special* friend⟩ **2 a :** PECULIAR, UNIQUE ⟨a *special* case⟩ **b :** of, relating to, or constituting a species **:** SPECIFIC ⟨a *special* concept⟩ **3 :** ADDITIONAL, EXTRA ⟨a *special* edition⟩ **4 :** designed for a particular purpose or occasion ⟨a *special* diet⟩ — **special** *n* — **spe·cial·ly** \'spesh-(ə-)lē\ *adv*

special delivery *n* **:** messenger delivery of mail matter made ahead of the regular carrier delivery for an extra fee

spe·cial·ist \'spesh-(ə-)ləst\ *n* **1 :** one who devotes himself to a special occupation or branch of learning ⟨eye *specialist*⟩ **2 :** any of six enlisted ranks in the army corresponding to the ranks of corporal through sergeant major — **specialist** *or* **spe·cial·is·tic** \,spesh-ə-'lis-tik\ *adj*

spe·ci·al·i·ty \,spesh-ē-'al-ət-ē\ *n, pl* **-ties 1 :** a special mark or quality **2 :** a special object or class of objects **3 a :** a special aptitude or skill **b :** a particular occupation or branch of learning

spe·cial·i·za·tion \,spesh-(ə-)lə-'zā-shən\ *n* **1 :** a making or becoming specialized **2 a :** structural adaptation of a body part to a particular function or of an organism for life in a particular environment **b :** a body part or an organism adapted by specialization

spe·cial·ize \'spesh-ə-ˌlīz\ *vb* **1 :** to make particular mention of **:** PARTICULARIZE **2 :** to apply or direct to a specific end or use ⟨*specialized* study⟩ **3 :** to concentrate one's efforts in a special activity or field ⟨*specialize* in French⟩ **4 :** to undergo specialization; *esp* **:** to change adaptively

spe·cial·ty \'spesh-əl-tē\ *n, pl* **-ties 1 :** a distinctive mark or quality **2 a :** a special object or class of objects; *esp* **:** a product of a special kind or of special excellence ⟨a dealer in *specialties*⟩ ⟨pancakes were the cook's *specialty*⟩ **b :** the state of being special, distinctive, or peculiar **3 :** something in which one specializes or has special knowledge

spe·ci·ate \'spē-s(h)ē-ˌāt\ *vi* **:** to differentiate into new biological species — **spe·ci·a·tion** \,spē-s(h)ē-'ā-shən\ *n* — **spe·ci·a·tion·al** \-shnəl, -shən-ᵊl\ *adj*

spe·cie \'spē-shē, -sē\ *n* [fr. *in specie* in kind, in coin, fr. L, in kind] **:** money in coin esp. of gold or silver — **in specie :** in the same or like form or kind; *also* **:** in coin

¹spe·cies \'spē-(ˌ)shēz, -(ˌ)sēz\ *n, pl* **species** [L, appearance, kind, species] **1 a :** a class of individuals with common qualities and a common name **:** KIND, SORT **b (1) :** a category of biological classification ranking below the genus, comprising related organisms or populations potentially capable of interbreeding, and being designated by a binomial that consists of the name of its genus followed by a Latin or latinized uncapitalized noun or adjective agreeing grammatically with the genus name **(2) :** an individual or kind belonging to such a species **2 :** the consecrated eucharistic elements

²species *adj* **:** belonging to a biological species as distinguished from a horticultural variety ⟨a *species* rose⟩

spec·i·fi·a·ble \'spes-ə-ˌfī-ə-bəl\ *adj* **:** capable of being specified

¹spe·cif·ic \spi-'sif-ik\ *adj* [LL *specificus*, fr. *species*] **1 :** of, relating to, or constituting a species **2 :** PAR-TICULAR, ACTUAL, EXACT ⟨a *specific* date⟩ ⟨*specific* directions for assembling a machine⟩ **3 :** having a unique relation to something ⟨*specific* antibodies⟩; *esp* **:** exerting a distinctive and usu. a causative or curative influence ⟨quinine is *specific* for malaria⟩ **syn** see EXPLICIT — **spe·cif·i·cal·ly** \-'sif-i-k(ə-)lē\ *adv* — **spec·i·fic·i·ty** \,spes-ə-'fis-ət-ē\ *n*

²specific *n* **1 a :** something peculiarly adapted to a purpose or use **b :** a drug or remedy specific for a particular disease **2 a :** a characteristic quality or trait **b :** DETAILS, PARTICULARS **c :** SPECIFICATION 2a

spec·i·fi·ca·tion \,spes-(ə-)fə-'kā-shən\ *n* **1 :** the act or process of specifying **2 a (1) :** a detailed precise presentation of something or of a plan or proposal for something — often used in pl. ⟨the architect's *specifications* for a new building⟩ (2) **:** a written description of an invention for which a patent is sought **b :** a single item in such a detailed presentation

specific gravity *n* **:** the ratio of the weight of a volume of a substance to the weight of an equal volume of some other substance taken as the standard which is water for solids and liquids and air or hydrogen for gases

specific heat *n* **1 :** the ratio of the quantity of heat required to raise the temperature of a body one degree to that required to raise the temperature of an equal mass of water one degree **2 :** the heat in calories required to raise the temperature of one gram of a substance one degree centigrade

spec·i·fy \'spes-ə-ˌfī\ *vt* **-fied; -fy·ing** [LL *specificare*, fr. *specificus* specific] **1 :** to name or state explicitly or in detail ⟨*specify* the reason for absence⟩ **2 :** to include as an item in a specification ⟨*specify* oak flooring⟩ — **spec·i·fi·er** \-ˌfī(-ə)r\ *n*

spec·i·men \'spes-ə-mən\ *n* [L, fr. *specere* to look at] **1 :** an item or part typical of a group or whole **:** SAMPLE **2 :** SORT, INDIVIDUAL ⟨a tough *specimen*⟩

spe·ci·os·i·ty \ˌspē-shē-'äs-ət-ē\ *n* **:** SPECIOUSNESS

spe·cious \'spē-shəs\ *adj* [L *speciosus* beautiful, plausible, fr. *species* appearance, kind] **:** apparently but not really fair, just, or right **:** appearing well at first view **syn** see PLAUSIBLE — **spe·cious·ly** *adv* — **spe·cious·ness** *n*

¹speck \'spek\ *n* [OE *specca*] **1 :** a small discoloration or spot esp. from dirt or decay **2 :** BIT, PARTICLE **3 :** something marked or marred with specks

²speck *vt* **:** to produce specks on or in

¹speck·le \'spek-əl\ *n* **:** a little speck

²speckle *vt* **speck·led; speck·ling** \'spek-(ə-)liŋ\ **1 :** to mark with speckles **2 :** to be distributed in or on like speckles ⟨small lakes *speckled* the land⟩

specs \'speks\ *n pl* [contr. of *spectacles*] **:** GLASS 2b

spec·ta·cle \'spek-ti-kəl\ *n* [L *spectaculum*, fr. *spectare* to watch, freq. of *specere* to look at] **1 a :** something exhibited to view as unusual, notable, or entertaining; *esp* **:** an eye-catching or dramatic public display **b :** an object of curiosity or contempt ⟨made a *spectacle* of herself at the party⟩ **2** pl **:** GLASS 2b

spec·ta·cled \-kəld\ *adj* **1 :** having or wearing spectacles **2 :** having markings suggesting a pair of spectacles

¹spec·tac·u·lar \spek-'tak-yə-lər, spək-\ *adj* **:** of, relating to, or constituting a spectacle **:** STRIKING, SENSATIONAL — **spec·tac·u·lar·ly** *adv*

²spectacular *n* **:** something (as an elaborate television show) that is spectacular

spec·ta·tor \'spek-ˌtāt-ər, spek-'\ *n* [L *spectare* to watch] **:** one who looks on or watches **:** ONLOOKER — **spectator** *adj*

spec·ter *or* **spec·tre** \'spek-tər\ *n* [L *spectrum* appearance, specter, fr. *specere* to look, look at] **1 :** a visible disembodied spirit **:** GHOST **2 :** something that haunts or perturbs the mind

spec·tral \'spek-trəl\ *adj* **1 :** of, relating to, or suggesting a specter **:** GHOSTLY **2 :** of, relating to, or made by a spectrum ⟨*spectral* color⟩ — **spec·tral·ly** \-trə-lē\ *adv* — **spec·tral·ness** *n*

spec·tro·gram \'spek-trə-ˌgram\ *n* **:** a photograph or diagram of a spectrum

spec·tro·graph \'spek-trə-ˌgraf\ *n* **:** an apparatus for dispersing radiation into a spectrum and photographing or mapping the spectrum — **spec·tro·graph·ic** \ˌspek-trə-'graf-ik\ *adj* — **spec·tro·graph·i·cal·ly** \-'graf-i-k(ə-)lē\ *adv*

spec·trom·e·ter \spek-'träm-ət-ər\ *n* **1 :** an instrument used in determining the index of refraction **2 :** a spectroscope fitted for measurements of the spectra observed with it — **spec·tro·met·ric** \ˌspek-trə-'me-trik\ *adj* — **spec·trom·e·try** \spek-'träm-ə-trē\ *n*

spec·tro·scope \'spek-trə-ˌskōp\ *n* **:** any of various instruments for forming and examining spectra — **spec·tro·scop·ic** \ˌspek-trə-'skäp-ik\ *adj* — **spec·tro·scop·i·cal·ly** \-'skäp-i-k(ə-)lē\ *adv* — **spec·tros·co·pist** \spek-'träs-kə-pəst\ *n* — **spec·tros·co·py** \-pē\ *n*

spec·trum \'spek-trəm\ *n, pl* **spec·tra** \-trə\ *or* **spec·trums** [L, appearance, specter] **1 a :** a series of colors formed when a beam of white light is dispersed (as by

passing through a prism) so that the component waves are arranged in the order of their wavelengths from red continuing through orange, yellow, green, blue, indigo, and violet **b :** a series of radiations arranged in regular order according to some varying characteristic esp. wavelength — compare ELECTROMAGNETIC SPECTRUM **2 :** a continuous sequence or range ⟨a wide *spectrum* of political opinions⟩

spec·u·lar \'spek-yə-lər\ *adj* [L *speculum* mirror] **:** of, relating to, or having the qualities of a mirror — **spec·u·lar·ly** *adv*

spec·u·late \'spek-yə-ˌlāt\ *vi* [L *speculari* to spy out, examine, fr. *specula* watchtower, fr. *specere* to look] **1 a :** to meditate on or ponder a subject **:** REFLECT **b :** to think or theorize about something in which evidence is too slight for certainty to be reached **2 :** to assume a business risk in hope of gain; *esp* **:** to buy or sell in expectation of profiting from market fluctuations **syn** see THINK — **spec·u·la·tion** \ˌspek-yə-'lā-shən\ *n* — **spec·u·la·tive** \'spek-yə-ˌlāt-iv, -lət-\ *adj* — **spec·u·la·tive·ly** *adv* — **spec·u·la·tor** \-ˌlāt-ər\ *n*

spec·u·lum \'spek-yə-ləm\ *n, pl* **spec·u·la** \-lə\ *also* **speculums** [L, mirror, fr. *specere* to look at] **1 :** a tubular instrument inserted into a body passage for inspection or medication **2 :** a reflector in an optical instrument **3 :** a medieval compendium of all knowledge **4 :** a patch of color on the wing of a bird

speech \'spēch\ *n* [OE *sprǣc, spǣc;* akin to E *speak*] **1 a :** the communication or expression of thoughts in spoken words **b :** CONVERSATION **2 a :** something that is spoken **b :** a public discourse **3 a :** LANGUAGE, DIALECT **b :** an individual manner or style of speaking **4 :** the power of expressing or communicating thoughts by speaking

speech community *n* **:** a group of people sharing characteristic patterns of vocabulary, grammar, and pronunciation

speech·i·fy \'spē-chə-ˌfī\ *vi* **-fied; -fy·ing :** to make a speech **:** HARANGUE

speech·less \'spēch-ləs\ *adj* **1 :** lacking or deprived of the power of speaking **2 :** not speaking for a time **:** SILENT ⟨*speechless* with surprise⟩ **syn** see DUMB — **speech·less·ly** *adv* — **speech·less·ness** *n*

¹speed \'spēd\ *n* [OE *spēd*] **1** *archaic* **:** prosperity in an undertaking **:** SUCCESS **2 a :** the act or state of moving swiftly **:** SWIFTNESS **b :** rate of motion **:** VELOCITY **3 :** swiftness or rate of performance or action **:** QUICKNESS **4 a :** the sensitivity of a photographic film, plate, or paper **b :** the light gathering power of a lens expressed as relative aperture **5 :** a transmission gear in automotive vehicles ⟨shift to low *speed*⟩ **6 :** a drug used as a stimulant of the central nervous system; *also* **:** a related drug **syn** see HASTE

²speed *vb* **sped** \'sped\ *or* **speed·ed; speed·ing 1** *archaic* **a :** to prosper in an undertaking **b :** to help to succeed **:** AID **2 a :** to make haste **b :** to go or drive at excessive or illegal speed **3 :** to move, work, or take place faster **:** ACCELERATE **4 a :** to cause to move quickly **:** HASTEN **b :** to wish Godspeed to **c :** to increase the speed of **:** ACCELERATE ⟨*speeded* up the engine⟩ — **speed·er** *n*

³speed *adj* **:** of, relating to, or regulating speed

speed·boat \'spēd-ˌbōt\ *n* **:** a fast launch or motorboat

speed·i·ly \'spēd-ᵊl-ē\ *adv* **1 :** RAPIDLY, QUICKLY **2 :** PROMPTLY, SOON

speed limit *n* **:** the maximum speed permitted by law in a given area under specified circumstances

speed·om·e·ter \spi-'däm-ət-ər\ *n* **1 :** an instrument that measures speed **2 :** an instrument that both measures speed and records distance traveled

speed·ster \'spēd-stər\ *n* **:** one that speeds or is capable of great speed

speed trap *n* **:** a stretch of road policed by concealed officers or devices (as radar) to catch speeders

speed·up \'spēd-ˌəp\ *n* **:** ACCELERATION; *esp* **:** an employer's demand for accelerated output without increased pay

speed·way \'spēd-ˌwā\ *n* **1 :** a road on which more than ordinary speed is allowed **2 :** a racecourse for motor vehicles

speed·well \'spēd-ˌwel\ *n* **:** any of a genus of herbs of the figwort family; *esp* **:** a creeping perennial European herb with small bluish flowers

ə abut; ᵊ kitten; ər further; a back; ā bake; ä cot, cart; au̇ out; ch chin; e less; ē easy; g gift; i trip; ī life

speedy \'spēd-ē\ *adj* **speed·i·er; -est** : rapid in motion : FAST, SWIFT **syn** see QUICK — **speed·i·ness** *n*

spe·le·ol·o·gy \,spē-lē-'äl-ə-jē, ,spel-ē-\ *n* [Gk *spēlaion* cave] : the scientific study or exploration of caves — **spe·le·o·log·i·cal** \,spē-lē-ə-'läj-i-kəl, ,spel-ē-\ *adj* — **spe·le·ol·o·gist** \-'äl-ə-jəst\ *n*

¹spell \'spel\ *n* [OE, talk, tale] **1 a** : a spoken word or form of words believed to have magic power : INCANTATION **b** : a state of enchantment **2** : a strong compelling influence or attraction

²spell *vt* : to put under a spell : BEWITCH

³spell *vb* **spelled** \'speld, 'spelt\; **spell·ing** [OF *espeller*, of Gmc origin; akin to E **¹spell**] **1** : to read or discern slowly and with difficulty **2 a** : to name, write, or print the letters of in order **b** : to constitute the letters of ⟨*c-a-t* spells "cat"⟩ **3** : MEAN, SIGNIFY ⟨another drought may *spell* famine⟩ **4** : to form words with letters

⁴spell *vb* **spelled** \'speld\; **spell·ing** [OE *spelian*] **1** : to take the place of for a time : RELIEVE ⟨if we can *spell* each other we won't get tired⟩ **2** : to allow an interval of rest to : REST

⁵spell *n* **1** : one's turn at work **2** : a period spent in a job or occupation **3 a** : a short period of time **b** : a stretch of a specified type of weather **4** : a period of bodily or mental distress or disorder : ATTACK, FIT ⟨a *spell* of coughing⟩ ⟨fainting *spell*⟩

spell·bind \'spel-,bīnd\ *vt* **-bound** \-,baund\; **-bind·ing** : to hold by or as if by a spell : FASCINATE

spell·bind·er \-,bīn-dər\ *n* : a speaker of compelling eloquence

spell·bound \-'baund\ *adj* : ENTRANCED, FASCINATED

spell·down \'spel-,daun\ *n* : a spelling contest that proceeds by the elimination of each contestant who misspells a word

spell·er \'spel-ər\ *n* **1** : one who spells words **2** : a book with exercises for teaching spelling

spell·ing \'spel-iŋ\ *n* : the forming of words from letters according to accepted usage; *also* : the letters composing a word

spelling bee *n* : SPELLDOWN

spell out *vt* : to make very explicit or emphatic

¹spelt \'spelt\ *n* [OE, fr. LL *spelta*, of Gmc origin] : a wheat with loose spikes and spikelets containing two light-red kernels

²spelt \'spelt\ *chiefly Brit past of* SPELL

spel·ter \'spel-tər\ *n* : ZINC; *esp* : zinc cast in slabs for commercial use

spe·lunk·er \spi-'ləŋ-kər, 'spē-\ *n* [obs. *spelunk* cave, fr. L *spelunca*, fr. Gk *spēlynx*] : one who makes a hobby of exploring caves

spe·lunk·ing \-kiŋ\ *n* : the hobby or practice of exploring caves

spend \'spend\ *vb* **spent** \'spent\; **spend·ing** [partly fr. OE *spendan*, fr. L *expendere* to expend; partly fr. OF *despendre*, fr. L *dispendere* to weigh out, fr. *dis-* + *pendere* to weigh] **1** : to use up or pay out : EXPEND **2 a** : to wear out : EXHAUST **b** : to consume wastefully : SQUANDER **3** : to cause or permit to elapse : PASS **4** : to make use of : EMPLOY, OCCUPY — **spend·er** *n*

spend·a·ble \'spen-də-bəl\ *adj* : available for spending

spending money *n* : money for small personal expenses

spend·thrift \'spen(d)-,thrift\ *n* : one who spends lavishly or wastefully — **spendthrift** *adj*

Spen·se·ri·an \spen-'sir-ē-ən\ *adj* : of, relating to, or characteristic of Edmund Spenser or his writings

Spenserian stanza *n* [after Edmund *Spenser* d1599 English poet] : a stanza consisting of eight lines of iambic pentameter and an alexandrine with a rhyme scheme *ababbcbcc*

spent \'spent\ *adj* [ME, fr. pp. of *spenden* to spend] **1** : used up : CONSUMED **2** : drained of energy or effectiveness : EXHAUSTED

sperm \'spərm\ *n, pl* **sperm** *or* **sperms** [Gk *spermat-, sperma*, lit., seed, fr. *speirein* to sow] **1 a** : SEMEN **b** : a male gamete **2** : a product (as oil) of the sperm whale

sperm- *or* **spermo-** *or* **sperma-** *or* **spermi-** *comb form* [Gk *sperma*] : seed : germ : sperm ⟨*spermo*phile⟩ ⟨*sperma*theca⟩ ⟨*spermi*cidal⟩

sper·ma·ce·ti \,spər-mə-'sēt-ē, -'set-\ *n* [ML *sperma ceti* whale sperm] : a waxy solid obtained from the oil of cetaceans and esp. the sperm whale and used in ointments, cosmetics, and candles

sper·ma·ry \'spərm-(ə-)rē\ *n, pl* **-ries** : an organ in which male gametes are developed

spermat- *or* **spermato-** *comb form* [Gk *spermat-, sperma* seed, sperm] : seed : spermatozoon ⟨*spermat*id⟩ ⟨*spermato*cyte⟩

sper·ma·the·ca \,spər-mə-'thē-kə\ *n* : a sac for sperm storage in the female reproductive tract of many lower animals — **sper·ma·the·cal** \-kəl\ *adj*

sper·mat·ic \(,)spər-'mat-ik\ *adj* : of or relating to sperm or the male gonad

sper·ma·tid \'spər-mət-əd\ *n* : one of the cells produced in meiosis that differentiate into spermatozoa

sper·ma·ti·um \,spər-'mā-shē-əm\ *n, pl* **-tia** \-shē-ə\ : a nonmotile cell functioning or held to function as a male gamete in some lower plants — **sper·ma·tial** \-sh(ē-)əl\ *adj*

sper·mat·o·cid·al \(,)spər-,mat-ə-'sīd-ᵊl, ,spər-mət-\ *or* **sper·mi·cid·al** \,spər-mə-'sīd-ᵊl\ *adj* : able or used to kill sperm — **sper·mat·o·cide** \(,)spər-'mat-ə-,sīd, 'spər-mət-\ *n*

sper·mat·o·cyte \(,)spər-'mat-ə-,sīt, 'spər-mət-\ *n* : a cell giving rise to sperm cells; *esp* : a cell of the last generation or next to the last generation preceding the spermatozoon

sper·ma·to·gen·e·sis \,spər-mət-ə-'jen-ə-səs, (,)spər-,mat-\ *n, pl* **-gen·e·ses** \-ə-,sēz\ : the process of male gamete formation including meiosis and transformation of the four resulting spermatids into spermatozoa — **sper·mat·o·ge·net·ic** \(,)spər-,mat-ə-jə-'net-ik, ,spər-mət-ō-\ *adj*

sper·ma·to·go·ni·um \,spər-mət-ə-'gō-nē-əm, (,)spər-,mat-\ *n, pl* **-nia** \-nē-ə\ : a primitive male germ cell — **sper·ma·to·go·ni·al** \-nē-əl\ *adj*

sper·mat·o·phore \(,)spər-'mat-ə-,fōr, 'spər-mət-, -,fȯr\ *n* : a capsule, packet, or mass enclosing spermatozoa extruded by the male and conveyed to the female in the insemination of various lower animals

sper·mat·o·phyte \-,fīt\ *n* : any of a group (Spermatophyta) of higher plants comprising those that produce seeds and including the gymnosperms and angiosperms — **sper·mat·o·phyt·ic** \(,)spər-,mat-ə-'fit-ik, ,spər-mət-\ *adj*

sper·ma·to·zo·id \,spər-mət-ə-'zō-əd, (,)spər-,mat-\ *n* : a male gamete of a plant motile by anterior cilia and usu. produced in an antheridium

sper·ma·to·zo·on \-'zō-,än, -'zō-ən\ *n, pl* **-zoa** \-'zō-ə\ [Gk *zōion* animal] **1** : a motile male gamete of an animal usu. with rounded or elongate head and a long posterior flagellum — called also **sperm cell 2** : SPERMATOZOID — **sper·ma·to·zo·al** \-'zō-əl\ *adj*

sper·mi·o·gen·e·sis \,spər-mē-ō-'jen-ə-səs\ *n, pl* **-gen·e·ses** \-ə-,sēz\ **1** : transformation of a spermatid into a spermatozoon **2** : SPERMATOGENESIS

sperm nucleus *n* : either of two nuclei derived from the generative nucleus of a pollen grain that function in the double fertilization of a seed plant

sperm oil *n* : a pale yellow oil from the sperm whale used esp. as a lubricant

sper·mo·phile \'spər-mə-,fīl\ *n* : GROUND SQUIRREL

sperm whale \'spərm-\ *n* : a large toothed whale with a closed cavity in the head containing a fluid mixture of spermaceti and oil

¹spew \'spyü\ *vb* [OE *spīwan*] : to pour forth : VOMIT — **spew·er** *n*

²spew *n* : matter that is spewed

sphag·nic·o·lous \sfag-'nik-ə-ləs\ *adj* : living or growing in sphagnum

sphag·num \'sfag-nəm\ *n* [Gk *sphagnos*, a moss] **1** : any of a large genus of atypical mosses that grow only in wet acid areas where their remains become compacted with other plant debris to form peat **2** : a mass of sphagnum plants — **sphag·nous** \-nəs\ *adj*

sphal·er·ite \'sfal-ə-,rīt\ *n* [Gk *sphaleros* deceitful; so called fr. its being easily mistaken for galena] : a widely distributed ore of zinc composed essentially of zinc sulfide

sphe·no·don \'sfē-nə-,dän, 'sfen-ə-\ *n* : TUATARA — **sphe·no·dont** \-,dänt\ *adj*

¹sphe·noid \'sfē-,nȯid\ *or* **sphe·noi·dal** \sfi-'nȯid-ᵊl\ *adj* [Gk *sphēnoeidēs* wedge-shaped, fr. *sphēn* wedge] : of, relating to, or being a winged bone of the base of the cranium

²sphenoid *n* : a sphenoid bone

sphe·nop·sid \sfi-'näp-səd\ *n* : any of a major group

(Sphenopsida) of primitive, jointed, and mostly extinct vascular plants including the equisetums

sphere \'sfi(ə)r\ *n* [Gk *sphaira*, ball, globe, celestial sphere] **1 a** (1) : the apparent surface of the heavens of which half forms the dome of the visible sky (2) : one of the concentric and eccentric revolving spherical transparent shells in which according to ancient astronomy stars, sun, planets, and moon are set **b** : a globe representing the earth **2 a** : a globular body : BALL **b** : a surface all points of which are equally distant from a center; *also* : the space enclosed by such a surface **3** : natural, normal, or proper place; *esp* : social order or rank **4** : a field or range of influence or significance : PROVINCE — **spher·ic** \'sfi(ə)r-ik, 'sfer-\ *adj* — **sphe·ric·i·ty** \sfir-'is-ət-ē\ *n*

sphere 1b

sphere of influence *n* : a territorial area within which the political influence or the interests of one nation are held to be more or less paramount

spher·i·cal \'sfir-i-kəl, 'sfer-\ *adj* **1** : having the form of a sphere or of one of its segments **2** : relating to or dealing with a sphere or its properties — **spher·i·cal·ly** \-k(ə-)lē\ *adv*

spherical aberration *n* : aberration caused by the spherical form of a lens or mirror that gives different foci for central and marginal rays

spherical angle *n* : the angle between two intersecting arcs of great circles of a sphere

spherical triangle *n* : a figure analogous to a plane triangle formed by three intersecting arcs of great circles of a sphere

sphe·roid \'sfi(ə)r-,óid, 'sfe(ə)r-\ *n* : a figure resembling a flattened sphere — **sphe·roi·dal** \sfir-'óid-ºl\ *adj* — **sphe·roi·dal·ly** \-'óid-ºl-ē\ *adv*

spher·ule \'sfi(ə)r-(y)ül, 'sfe(ə)r-\ *n* : a little sphere or spherical body

spher·u·lite \'sfir-(y)ə-,līt, 'sfer-\ *n* : a usu. spherical crystalline body of radiating crystal fibers found in vitreous volcanic rocks — **spher·u·lit·ic** \,sfir-(y)ə-'lit-ik, ,sfer-\ *adj*

sphery \'sfi(ə)r-ē\ *adj* **1** : SPHERICAL, STARLIKE **2** : of or relating to the spheres

sphinc·ter \'sfiŋ(k)-tər\ *n* [Gk *sphinktēr*, fr. *sphingein* to bind tight] : a muscular ring surrounding and able to contract or close a bodily opening — **sphinc·ter·al** \-t(ə-)rəl\ *adj*

sphinx \'sfiŋ(k)s\ *n* **1 a** : a monster in ancient Greek mythology having typically a lion's body, wings, and the head and bust of a woman **b** : a person whose character, motives, or feelings are enigmatic **2** : an ancient Egyptian image in the form of a recumbent lion having a man's head, a ram's head, or a hawk's head **3** : HAWKMOTH

sphyg·mo·ma·nom·e·ter \,sfig-mō-mə-'nam-ət-ər\ *n* [Gk *sphygmos* pulse] : an instrument for measuring blood pressure and esp. arterial blood pressure — **sphyg·mo·man·o·met·ric** \-,man-ə-'me-trik\ *adj* — **sphyg·mo·man·o·met·ri·cal·ly** \-tri-k(ə-)lē\ *adv* — **sphyg·mo·ma·nom·e·try** \-mə-'nam-ə-trē\ *n*

Spi·ca \'spī-kə\ *n* [L, lit., spike of grain] : a star of the first magnitude in the constellation Virgo

spi·cate \'spī-,kāt\ *adj* [L *spicatus*, pp. of *spicare* to arrange in a spike, fr. *spica* spike] : POINTED, SPIKED; *esp* : arranged in the form of a spike ⟨a *spicate* inflorescence⟩

¹spice \'spīs\ *n* [OF *espice*, fr. LL *species* species, fr. L, species] **1** : any of various aromatic plant products (as pepper or nutmeg) used to season or flavor foods **2** : something that gives zest or relish **3** : a pungent or fragrant odor : PERFUME

²spice *vt* : to season with or as if with spices

spice box *n* : a box holding or designed to hold spices; *esp* : a box fitted with smaller boxes for holding spices

spice·bush \-,bùsh\ *n* **1** : an aromatic shrub of the laurel family with small early yellow flowers **2** : a tall upright strawberry shrub with slightly fragrant brown flowers

spi·ci·form \'spī-kə-,fórm, -sə-\ *adj* : shaped like a spike : SPICATE

spick-and-span \,spik-ən-'span\ *adj* **1** : FRESH, BRAND-NEW **2** : spotlessly clean and neat

spic·ule \'spik-yül\ *n* [L *spiculum* point] : a minute slender pointed usu. hard body; *esp* : one of the minute calcareous or siliceous bodies that support the tissues of various invertebrates — **spic·u·late** \'spik-yə-lət\ *adj* — **spic·u·la·tion** \,spik-yə-'lā-shən\ *n* — **spic·u·lif·er·ous** \,spik-yə-'lif-(ə-)rəs\ *adj*

spicy \'spī-sē\ *adj* **spic·i·er; -est** **1** : having the quality, flavor, or fragrance of spice **2** : producing or abounding in spices **3** : KEEN, ZESTFUL **4** : PIQUANT, RACY; *esp* : somewhat scandalous or salacious — **spic·i·ly** \-sə-lē\ *adv* — **spic·i·ness** \-sē-nəs\ *n*

spi·der \'spīd-ər\ *n* [ME *spithre*; akin to E *spin*] **1** : any of an order (Araneida) of arachnids having a body with two main divisions, four pairs of walking legs, and two or more pairs of abdominal organs for spinning threads of silk used in making cocoons for their eggs, nests for themselves, or webs for entangling their prey **2** : a cast-iron frying pan orig. made with short feet to stand among coals on the hearth

spider crab *n* : any of numerous crabs with extremely long legs and nearly triangular bodies

spider mite *n* : RED SPIDER

spider monkey *n* : any of a genus of New World monkeys with long slender limbs, the thumb absent or rudimentary, and a very long prehensile tail

spi·der·web \'spīd-ər-,web\ *n* **1** : the silken web spun by most spiders and used as a resting place and a trap for small prey **2** : something like a spiderweb in appearance or function

spi·der·wort \-,wərt, -,wórt\ *n* : any of a genus of monocotyledonous plants with short-lived usu. blue or violet flowers

spi·dery \'spīd-ə-rē\ *adj* **1** : resembling a spider; *also* : long and thin like the legs of a spider **2** : resembling a spiderweb **3** : full of spiders

spie·gel·ei·sen \'spē-gə-,līz-ºn\ *also* **spie·gel** \'spē-gəl\ *n* [G *spiegeleisen*, lit., mirror iron] : a pig iron containing 15 to 30 percent manganese and 4.5 to 6.5 percent carbon

¹spiel \'spēl\ *vb* [G *spielen* to play] : to talk volubly or perfunctorily — **spiel·er** *n*

²spiel *n* : voluble mechanical often extravagant talk ⟨advertising *spiel*⟩

spi·er \'spī(-ə)r\ *n* : SPY

spif·fy \'spif-ē\ *adj* **spiff·i·er; -est** : fine looking : SMART

spig·ot \'spig-ət, 'spik-ət\ *n* [ME] **1** : a pin or peg used to stop the vent in a cask **2** : FAUCET

¹spike \'spīk\ *n* [ME] **1** : a very large nail **2 a** : one of a row of pointed irons placed (as on the top of a wall) to prevent passage **b** : one of several metal projections set in the sole and heel of a shoe to improve traction in sports **3** : an unbranched antler of a young deer **4** : a spike-heeled shoe **5** : a pointed element (as in a graph)

²spike *vt* **1** : to fasten or furnish with spikes **2 a** : to disable (a muzzle-loading cannon) temporarily by driving a spike into the vent **b** : to suppress or block completely : QUASH **3** : to pierce or impale with or on a spike **4** : to add alcohol or liquor to (a drink)

³spike *n* [L *spica*] **1** : an ear of grain **2** : a long usu. rather narrow flower cluster like a raceme but having the flowers sessile on the axis

spiked \'spīkt\ *adj* **1 a** : bearing ears **b** : having a spiky inflorescence ⟨*spiked* flowers⟩ **2** : SPIKY

spike heel *n* : a very high tapering heel used on women's shoes

spike lavender *n* : a European mint related to and used like the true lavender

spike·let \'spīk-lət\ *n* : a small or secondary spike; *esp* : one of the small few-flowered bracted spikes that make up the compound inflorescence of a grass or sedge

spike·like \'spīk-,līk\ *adj* : resembling a spike

spike·nard \'spīk-,närd\ *n* [ML *spica nardi*, lit., spike of nard] **1 a** : a fragrant ointment of the ancients **b** : an East Indian aromatic plant of the valerian family from which the ointment may have been derived **2** : an American herb of the ginseng family with aromatic root and panicled umbels

spiky \'spī-kē\ *adj* **spik·i·er; -est** **1** : resembling a spike : POINTED **2** : furnished or armed with spikes

spile \'spīl\ *n* **1** : a large stake driven into the ground to support a superstructure : PILE **2** : a small plug used to

ə abut; ᵊ kitten; ər further; a back; ā bake; ä cot, cart; au̇ out; ch chin; e less; ē easy; g gift; i trip; ī life

stop the vent of a cask : BUNG **3** : a spout inserted in a tree to draw off sap — **spile** *vt*

spil·ing \'spī-liŋ\ *n* : a set of piles : PILING

¹spill \'spil\ *vb* **spilled** \'spild, 'spilt\ *also* **spilt** \'spilt\; **spill·ing** [OE *spillan* to kill, spill] **1** : to cause (blood) to flow **2 a** : to cause or allow accidentally or unintentionally to fall, flow, or run out **b** : to fall or run out so as to be lost or wasted **3** : to relieve (a sail) from the pressure of the wind **4** : to throw off or out ⟨a horse *spilled* him⟩ **5** : to let out : DIVULGE **6** : to fall from one's place — **spill·a·ble** \'spil-ə-bəl\ *adj*

²spill *n* **1** : an act or instance of spilling; *esp* : a fall from a horse or vehicle **2** : something spilled **3** : SPILLWAY

³spill *n* [ME *spille*] : a slender piece: as **a** : a metallic rod or pin **b** : a small roll or twist of paper or slip of wood for lighting a fire **c** : a roll or cone of paper serving as a container **d** : a peg for plugging a hole : SPILE

spill·age \'spil-ij\ *n* **1** : the act or process of spilling **2** : the quantity that spills

spil·li·kin \'spil-i-kən\ *n* : JACKSTRAW

spill·way \'spil-ˌwā\ *n* : a passage for surplus water to run over or around a dam or similar obstruction

spilth \'spilth\ *n* **1** : an act or instance of spilling **2 a** : something spilled **b** : REFUSE, RUBBISH

¹spin \'spin\ *vb* **spun** \'spən\; **spin·ning** [OE *spinnan*] **1** : to draw out and twist into yarn or thread ⟨*spin* flax⟩ **2 a** : to produce by drawing out and twisting fibers ⟨*spin* thread⟩ **b** : to form threads or a web or cocoon by extruding a viscous rapidly hardening fluid **3 a** : to revolve rapidly : GYRATE **b** : to be dizzy : feel as if turning rapidly **4** : to cause to whirl : TWIRL ⟨*spin* a top⟩ **5 a** : to extend to great length : PROLONG **b** : to make up with the imagination **6** : to move swiftly on wheels or in a vehicle **7** : to shape into threadlike form in manufacture; *also* : to manufacture by a whirling process

²spin *n* **1 a** : the act of spinning or twirling something **b** : whirling motion imparted by spinning : rapid rotation **c** : an excursion in a vehicle esp. on wheels **2 a** : an aerial maneuver in which an airplane moves downward in a somewhat corkscrew path **b** : a plunging descent or downward spiral **c** : a state of mental confusion

spin·ach \'spin-ich\ *n* [MF *espinache*, fr. Sp *espinaca*, fr. Ar *isfānākh*] : a potherb of the goosefoot family widely grown for its edible leaves

¹spi·nal \'spīn-ᵊl\ *adj* **1** : of, relating to, or situated near the backbone **2** : of, relating to, or affecting the spinal cord — **spi·nal·ly** \-ᵊl-ē\ *adv*

²spinal *n* : a spinal anesthetic

spinal column *n* : the axial skeleton of the trunk and tail of a vertebrate that consists of a jointed series of vertebrae enclosing and protecting the spinal cord — called also *backbone*

spinal cord *n* : the cord of nervous tissue that extends from the brain along the back in the cavity of the spinal column, gives off the spinal nerves, and not only carries impulses to and from the brain but also serves as a center for initiating and coordinating many reflex acts

spinal nerve *n* : any of the paired nerves which arise from the spinal cord and pass to various parts of the trunk and limbs and of which there are normally 31 pairs in man

¹spin·dle \'spin-dᵊl\ *n* [OE *spinel*] **1 a** : a round stick with tapered ends used to form and twist the yarn in hand spinning **b** : a rod holding a bobbin in a textile machine **2** : something shaped like a spindle (as a figure along which the chromosomes are distributed during mitosis) **3 a** : the bar that actuates the bolt of a lock **b** (1) : a turned often decorative piece of furniture or woodwork ⟨*spindles* of a chair⟩ (2) : NEWEL **c** : a revolving piece usu. smaller than a shaft; *also* : SHAFT **d** : the part of an axle on which a vehicle wheel turns

²spindle *vi* **spin·dled**; **spin·dling** \-(d)liŋ, -dᵊl-iŋ\ : to form a long slender stalk usu. without flower or fruit

spin·dle–legged \ˌspin-dᵊl-'(l)eg-əd, -'(l)egd\ *adj* : having long slender legs

spin·dle–shanked \ˌspin-dᵊl-'shaŋ(k)t\ *adj* : SPINDLE-LEGGED

spin·dling \'spin-(d)liŋ, 'spin-dᵊl-iŋ\ *adj* : being long or tall and thin and usu. feeble or frail ⟨*spindling* stems⟩

spin·dly \'spin-(d)lē, 'spin-dᵊl-ē\ *adj* **spin·dli·er**; **-est** : SPINDLING

spin·drift \'spin-ˌdrift\ *n* : spray blown from waves

spine \'spīn\ *n* [L *spina* thorn, spinal column] **1 a** : SPINAL COLUMN **b** : something resembling a spinal column or constituting a central axis or chief support **c** : the back of a book usu. lettered with the title and the author's and publisher's names **2** : a stiff pointed process; *esp* : one on a plant that is a modified leaf or leaf part

spi·nel \spə-'nel\ *n* **1** : a hard crystalline mineral consisting of an oxide of magnesium and aluminum that varies from colorless to ruby-red to black and is used as a gem **2** : any of a group of minerals that are essentially oxides of magnesium, ferrous iron, zinc, or manganese

spine·less \'spīn-ləs\ *adj* **1** : free from spines, thorns, or prickles **2 a** : having no spinal column : INVERTEBRATE **b** : lacking courage or strength of character : WEAK — **spine·less·ly** *adv* — **spine·less·ness** *n*

spi·nes·cent \spī-'nes-ᵊnt\ *adj* : somewhat spiny

spin·et \'spin-ət\ *n* [It *spinetta*] **1** : a small harpsichord similar to the virginal **2 a** : a small upright piano **b** : a small electronic organ

spin·na·ker \'spin-i-kər\ *n* : a large triangular sail set on a long light pole and used when running before the wind

spin·ner \'spin-ər\ *n* **1** : one that spins **2** : a fishing lure that revolves when drawn through the water

spin·ner·et \ˌspin-ə-'ret\ *n* **1** : an organ esp. of a spider or caterpillar for producing threads of silk from the secretion of silk glands **2** *or* **spin·ner·ette** : a small metal plate, thimble, or cap with fine holes through which a cellulose or chemical solution is forced in the spinning of man-made filaments (as rayon or nylon)

spinner play *n* : a football play in which the ballcarrier spins around in an attempt to deceive opposing players

spin·ney \'spin-ē\ *n*, *pl* **spinneys** [MF *espinaye* thorny thicket, fr. L *spinetum*, fr. *spina* thorn] *Brit* : a small wood with undergrowth : COPSE

spinning frame *n* : a machine that draws, twists, and winds yarn

spinning jen·ny \'spin-iŋ-ˌjen-ē\ *n* : an early multiple-spindle machine for spinning wool or cotton

spinning wheel *n* : a small domestic hand-driven or foot-driven machine for spinning yarn or thread in which a wheel drives a single spindle

spin–off \'spin-ˌȯf\ *n* : a collateral or derived product or effect : BY-PRODUCT ⟨household products that are *spin-offs* of missile research⟩

spinning wheel

spi·nose \'spī-ˌnōs\ *adj* : SPINY **1** — **spi·nose·ly** *adv*

spi·nous \'spī-nəs\ *adj* : SPINY

spin·ster \'spin(t)-stər\ *n* **1** : a woman whose occupation is to spin **2** : an unmarried woman; *esp* : a woman past the common age for marrying or one who seems unlikely to marry — **spin·ster·hood** \-ˌhu̇d\ *n* — **spin·ster·ish** \-st(ə-)rish\ *adj*

spin·thar·i·scope \spin-'thar-ə-ˌskōp\ *n* [Gk *spintharis* spark] : an instrument consisting of a fluorescent screen and a magnifying lens system for visual detection of alpha rays

spi·nule \'spī-nyu̇l\ *n* : a minute spine — **spi·nu·lose** \-nyə-ˌlōs\ *adj*

spiny \'spī-nē\ *adj* **spin·i·er**; **-est** **1** : covered or armed with spines or sometimes with prickles or thorns **2** : abounding with difficulties, obstacles, or annoyances : THORNY **3** : resembling a spine esp. in slender pointed form — **spin·i·ness** *n*

spiny anteater *n* : ECHIDNA

spiny–finned \ˌspī-nē-'find\ *adj* : having fins with one or more stiff unbranched rays without transverse segmentation — compare SOFT-FINNED

spiny–head·ed worm \ˌspī-nē-ˌhed-əd-\ *n* : any of a small phylum (Acanthocephala) of unsegmented parasitic worms with hooked proboscides by which they attach to the intestinal wall of the host

spiny lobster *n* : an edible crustacean distinguished from the related true lobster by the simple unenlarged first pair of legs and by the spiny carapace

spiny–rayed \ˌspī-nē-'rād\ *adj* **1** *of a fin* : having stiff unarticulated rays **2** : SPINY-FINNED

spir·a·cle \'spir-i-kəl, 'spī-ri-\ *n* [L *spiraculum*, fr. *spirare* to breathe] : a breathing orifice (as a blowhole of a whale or a tracheal opening of an insect) — **spi·rac·u·lar** \spə-'rak-yə-lər, spī-\ *adj*

¹spi·ral \'spī-rəl\ *adj* [L *spira* coil] **1 a** : winding around a center or pole and gradually receding from or approaching it ⟨*spiral* curve of a watch spring⟩ **b** : HELICAL ⟨*spiral* form of the thread of a screw⟩ **c** : of, relating to, or resembling a spiral ⟨a flat *spiral* coil of rope⟩ ⟨a *spiral* staircase⟩ **2** : advancing to higher levels through a series of cyclical movements — **spi·ral·ly** \-rə-lē\ *adv*

²spiral *n* **1 a** : the path of a point in a plane moving around a central point while continuously receding from or approaching it **b** : a three-dimensional curve (as a helix) turning about an axis **2** : a single turn or coil in a spiral object **3** : something having a spiral form **4** : a continuously spreading and accelerating increase or decrease ⟨wage *spiral*⟩

³spiral *vb* **-raled** *or* **-ralled; -ral·ing** *or* **-ral·ling** **1** : to move in a spiral course **2** : to form into a spiral

spi·rant \'spī-rənt\ *n* [L *spirant-, spirans*, prp. of *spirare* to breathe] : a consonant (as \f\, \s\, \sh\) uttered with decided friction of the breath against some part of the oral passage — **spirant** *adj*

¹spire \'spī(ə)r\ *n* [OE *spīr*] **1** : a slender tapering blade or stalk (as of grass) **2** : a sharp pointed tip (as of a tree or antler) **3 a** : a pointed roof esp. of a tower **b** : STEEPLE

²spire *vi* : to shoot up like a spire

³spire *n* [L *spira* coil, fr. Gk *speira*] **1 a** : SPIRAL **b** : COIL **2** : the upper part of a spiral mollusk shell

⁴spire *vi* : to rise upward in a spiral

spi·rea *or* **spi·raea** \spī-'rē-ə\ *n* [L, a plant, fr. Gk *speiraia*] : any of a genus of shrubs of the rose family with small perfect white or pink flowers in dense clusters

spired \'spī(ə)rd\ *adj* : having a spire ⟨*spired* shell⟩

spi·reme \'spī(ə)r-,ēm\ *n* [Gk *speirēma* twisted thread, fr. *speira* coil] : a continuous thread observed in fixed preparations of the prophase of mitosis that appears to be a strand of chromatin but is generally held to be artificial

spi·ril·lum \spī-'ril-əm\ *n, pl* **-ril·la** \-'ril-ə\ : any of a genus of long curved flagellate bacteria; *also* : any spiral filamentous bacterium (as a spirochete)

¹spir·it \'spir-ət\ *n* [L *spiritus*, lit., breath] **1** : a life≈ giving force; *esp* : a force within man held to endow his body with life, energy, and power : SOUL **2 a** *cap* : HOLY SPIRIT **b** : a supernatural being : GHOST, DEVIL **c** : a supernatural being that enters into and controls a person **d** : a bodiless being inhabiting a place or thing **3** : MOOD, DISPOSITION ⟨in good *spirits*⟩ **4** : mental vigor or animation : VIVACITY **5** : real meaning or intention ⟨the *spirit* of the law⟩ **6** : an emotion, frame of mind, or inclination governing one's actions ⟨said in a *spirit* of fun⟩ ⟨school *spirit*⟩ **7** : PERSON ⟨a bold *spirit*⟩ **8 a** : a distilled alcoholic liquor — usu. used in pl. **b** : an alcoholic solution of a volatile substance ⟨*spirit* of camphor⟩ — often used in pl. **syn** see SOUL

²spirit *vt* **1** : ANIMATE, ENCOURAGE **2** : to carry off or convey secretly or mysteriously

spir·it·ed \'spir-ət-əd\ *adj* : full of spirit, courage, or energy : LIVELY, ANIMATED — **spir·it·ed·ly** *adv* — **spir·it·ed·ness** *n*

spirit gum *n* : a solution (as of gum arabic in ether) used esp. for attaching false hair to the skin

spir·it·ism \'spir-ət-,iz-əm\ *n* : SPIRITUALISM 2a — **spir·it·ist** \-ət-əst\ *n* — **spir·it·is·tic** \,spir-ət-'is-tik\ *adj*

spirit lamp *n* : a lamp in which a volatile liquid fuel (as alcohol) is burned

spir·it·less \'spir-ət-ləs\ *adj* : lacking animation, cheerfulness, or courage — **spir·it·less·ly** *adv* — **spir·it·less·ness** *n*

spirit level *n* : a level using a bubble in alcohol as an indicator

spirits of turpentine *or* **spirit of turpentine** : TURPENTINE 2a

¹spir·i·tu·al \'spir-ich-(ə-w)əl\ *adj* **1** : of, relating to, or consisting of spirit : not bodily or material ⟨man's *spiritual* needs⟩ **2 a** : RELIGIOUS ⟨*spiritual* songs⟩ **b** : ecclesiastical rather than lay or temporal ⟨lords *spiritual*⟩ **3** : related or joined in spirit : having a spiritual rather than physical relationship ⟨*spiritual* home⟩ ⟨*spiritual* heir⟩ **4 a** : of or relating to supernatural beings **b** : SPIRITUALISTIC — **spir·i·tu·al·ly** \-ē\ *adv* — **spir·i·tu·al·ness** *n*

²spiritual *n* : a Negro religious song esp. of the southern U.S. usu. of a deeply emotional character

spiritual bouquet *n* : an offering by a Roman Catholic of devotional acts on behalf of another person (as on an anniversary or after a death)

spir·i·tu·al·ism \'spir-ich-(ə-w)ə-,liz-əm\ *n* **1** : the view that spirit is a prime element of reality **2 a** : a belief that the spirits of the dead communicate with the living **b** *cap* : a movement comprising religious organizations emphasizing spiritualism — **spir·i·tu·al·ist** \-ləst\ *n, often cap* — **spir·i·tu·al·is·tic** \,spir-ich-(ə-w)ə-'lis-tik\ *adj*

spir·i·tu·al·i·ty \,spir-ich-ə-'wal-ət-ē\ *n* **1** : sensitivity or attachment to religious values **2** : the quality or state of being spiritual

spir·i·tu·al·ize \'spir-ich-(ə-w)ə-,līz\ *vt* **1** : to make spiritual esp. by freeing from worldly influences **2** : to give a spiritual meaning to or understand in a spiritual sense — **spir·i·tu·al·i·za·tion** \,spir-ich-(ə-w)ə-lə-'zā-shən\ *n*

spi·ri·tu·el *or* **spi·ri·tu·elle** \,spir-i-chə-'wel\ *adj* [F *spirituel* (masc.), *spirituelle* (fem.), lit., spiritual] : of refined and usu. sprightly or witty nature

spir·i·tu·ous \'spir-ich-(ə-w)əs\ *adj* : containing or impregnated with distilled alcohol ⟨*spirituous* liquors⟩ — **spir·i·tu·os·i·ty** \,spir-ich-ə-'wäs-ət-ē\ *n*

spi·ro·chete *or* **spi·ro·chaete** \'spī-rə-,kēt\ *n* [Gk *speira* coil + *chaitē* long hair] : any of an order (Spirochaetales) of slender spirally undulating bacteria including those causing syphilis and relapsing fever — **spi·ro·che·tal** \,spī-rə-'kēt-°l\ *adj*

spi·ro·gy·ra \,spī-rə-'jī-rə\ *n* [NL, fr. Gk *speira* coil + *gyros* ring] : any of a genus of freshwater green algae with spiral chlorophyll bands

spi·rom·e·ter \spī-'räm-ət-ər\ *n* : an instrument for measuring the air entering and leaving the lungs — **spi·ro·met·ric** \,spī-rə-'me-trik\ *adj* — **spi·rom·e·try** \spī-'räm-ə-trē\ *n*

spirt *var of* SPURT

spiry \'spī(ə)r-ē\ *adj* : resembling a spire esp. in slender tapering form; *also* : having spires

¹spit \'spit\ *n* [OE *spitu*] **1** : a slender pointed rod for holding meat over a fire **2** : a small point of land esp. of sand or gravel running into a body of water

²spit *vt* **spit·ted; spit·ting** : to fix on or as if on a spit

³spit *vb* **spit** *or* **spat** \'spat\; **spit·ting** [OE *spittan*] **1 a** : to eject saliva from the mouth : EXPECTORATE **b** : to express by or as if by spitting or make a spitting sound ⟨the cat *spat* angrily⟩ ⟨*spitting* a contemptuous reply⟩ ⟨the wire *spat* and crackled⟩ **2 a** : to give off usu. briskly or vigorously : EMIT ⟨the fire *spat* sparks⟩ **b** : to rain or snow in flurries — **spit·ter** *n*

⁴spit *n* **1 a** : SALIVA **b** : the act of spitting **2** : a frothy secretion produced by spittlebugs **3** : perfect likeness ⟨the boy was the *spit* of his father⟩

spit and polish *n* [fr. the practice of polishing objects such as shoes by spitting on them and then rubbing them with a cloth] : extreme attention to cleanliness, orderliness, smartness of appearance, and ceremonial esp. at the expense of operational efficiency

spit·ball \'spit-,bȯl\ *n* **1** : paper chewed and rolled into a ball to be thrown as a missile **2** : a baseball pitch delivered after the ball has been moistened with saliva or sweat

spit curl *n* : a spiral curl that is usu. plastered on the forehead, temple, or cheek

¹spite \'spīt\ *n* [ME, short for *despite*] : petty ill will or malice with the disposition to irritate, annoy, or thwart — **in spite of** : in defiance or contempt of : NOTWITHSTANDING

²spite *vt* **1** : to treat maliciously (as by shaming or thwarting) **2** : ANNOY, OFFEND ⟨did it to *spite* me⟩

spite·ful \'spīt-fəl\ *adj* : filled with or showing spite : MALICIOUS — **spite·ful·ly** \-fə-lē\ *adv* — **spite·ful·ness** *n*

spit·fire \'spit-,fī(ə)r\ *n* : a quick-tempered or highly emotional person

spit·tle \'spit-°l\ *n* [OE *spǣtl*] **1** : SALIVA **2** : SPIT 2

spit·tle·bug \-,bəg\ *n* : any of numerous leaping insects whose larvae secrete froth

spittle insect *n* : SPITTLEBUG

spit·toon \spi-'tün\ *n* : a receptacle for spit — called also *cuspidor*

---

spitz \'spits\ *n* [G, fr. *spitz* pointed] : any of several stocky heavy-coated dogs of northern origin with erect ears and a heavily furred tail tightly recurved over the back

splanch·nic \'splaŋk-nik\ *adj* [Gk *splanchna* viscera] : of or relating to the viscera : VISCERAL

¹splash \'splash\ *vb* **1 a** : to strike or move through a liquid or semifluid substance and cause it to move and scatter roughly ⟨*splash* water⟩⟨*splash* through mud⟩ **b** : to wet or soil by dashing water or mud on : SPATTER ⟨*splashed* by a passing car⟩; *also* : to cause to soil something by splashing ⟨*splashed* mud on her shoes⟩ **2** : to make a splashing sound (as in falling or moving) ⟨a brook *splashing* over rocks⟩ **3 a** : to spread or scatter like a splashed liquid ⟨a painting *splashed* with color⟩⟨sunbeams *splashed* through the curtain⟩ **b** : to display prominently ⟨a scandal *splashed* all over the newspaper⟩ — **splash·er** *n*

²splash *n* **1** : splashed material; *also* : a spot or daub from or as if from splashed liquid **2** : the sound or action of splashing **3** : a vivid impression created esp. by ostentatious activity or appearance; *also* : an ostentatious display — **splash·i·ly** \'splash-ə-lē\ *adv* — **splash·i·ness** \'splash-ē-nəs\ *n* — **splashy** \'splash-ē\ *adj*

splash·down \'splash-,daún\ *n* : the landing of a manned spacecraft in the ocean — **splash down** \(')splash-'daún\ *vi*

splash guard *n* : a flap suspended behind a rear wheel to prevent tire splash from muddying windshields of following vehicles

splat \'splat\ *n* [obs. *splat* to spread flat] : a single flat thin usu. vertical member of a back of a chair

splat·ter \'splat-ər\ *vb* : SPATTER — **splatter** *n*

¹splay \'splā\ *vb* [ME *splayen*, short for *displayen* to display] **1** : to spread out **2** : to make or become slanting

²splay *n* **1** : a slope or bevel esp. of the sides of a door or window **2** : SPREAD, EXPANSION

³splay *adj* **1** : turned outward **2** : AWKWARD, UNGAINLY

splay·foot \'splā-,fút, -'fút\ *n* : a foot abnormally flattened and spread out : FLATFOOT — **splayfoot** *or* **splay-foot·ed** \-'fút-əd\ *adj*

spleen \'splēn\ *n* [Gk *splēn*] **1** : a very vascular ductless organ near the stomach or intestine of most vertebrates concerned with final destruction of blood cells, storage of blood, and production of lymphocytes **2** : ANGER, MALICE

spleen·ful \-fəl\ *adj* : SPLENETIC 2

spleen·wort \-,wərt, -,wórt\ *n* : any of a genus of ferns having linear or oblong sori borne obliquely on the upper side of the frond

spleeny \'splē-nē\ *adj* : full of or displaying spleen

splen·dent \'splen-dənt\ *adj* **1** : SHINING, GLOSSY **2** : ILLUSTRIOUS, BRILLIANT

splen·did \'splen-dəd\ *adj* [L *splendidus*, fr. *splendēre* to shine] **1** : possessing or displaying splendor: as **a** : SHINING, BRILLIANT **b** : SHOWY, MAGNIFICENT **2** : ILLUSTRIOUS, GRAND **3** : EXCELLENT — **splen·did·ly** *adv* — **splen·did·ness** *n*

syn SPLENDID, GLORIOUS, GORGEOUS mean extraordinarily impressive. SPLENDID implies outshining the usual in brilliance or excellence; GLORIOUS suggests beauty and distinction heightened by radiance; GORGEOUS implies a rich splendor esp. in display of color

splen·dif·er·ous \splen-'dif-(ə-)rəs\ *adj* **1** : SPLENDID **2** : deceptively splendid — **splen·dif·er·ous·ly** *adv* — **splen·dif·er·ous·ness** *n*

splen·dor \'splen-dər\ *n* [L, fr. *splendēre* to shine] **1 a** : great brightness or luster : BRILLIANCY ⟨the *splendor* of the sun⟩ **b** : sumptuous display or ceremonial : MAGNIFICENCE, POMP ⟨an affair of great *splendor*⟩ **2** : something splendid or contributing to splendor ⟨surrounded by *splendors* and luxuries⟩ — **splen·dor·ous** *also* **splen-drous** \-d(ə-)rəs\ *adj*

sple·net·ic \spli-'net-ik\ *adj* **1** : SPLENIC **2** : marked by bad temper, malevolence, or spite — **sple·net·i·cal·ly** \spli-'net-i-k(ə-)lē\ *adv*

sple·nic \'splen-ik\ *adj* : of, relating to, or located in the spleen

¹splice \'splīs\ *vt* [obs. D *splissen*] **1** : to unite (as two ropes) by weaving the strands together **2** : to unite (as rails or timbers) by lapping the ends together and making them fast — **splic·er** *n*

splice

²splice *n* : a joining or joint made by splicing

spline \'splīn\ *n* **1** : a thin wood or metal strip used in building construction **2** : a key that is fixed to one of two connected mechanical parts and fits into a keyway in the other; *also* : a keyway for such a key — **spline** *vb*

¹splint \'splint\ *or* **splent** \'splent\ *n* [MLG *splinte*, *splente*] **1 a** : a thin strip of wood interwoven with others in caning **b** : SPLINTER **c** : material or a device used to protect and immobilize a body part (as a broken arm) **2** : a bony enlargement on the cannon bone of a horse

²splint *vt* : to support and immobilize with or as if with a splint or splints

splint bone *n* : one of the slender rudimentary bones on each side of the cannon bone in the limb of a horse

¹splin·ter \'splint-ər\ *n* [MD] **1 a** : a thin piece split or torn off lengthwise : SLIVER **b** : a small jagged particle **2** : a group or faction broken away from a parent body — **splinter** *adj* — **splin·tery** \'splint-ə-rē\ *adj*

²splinter *vb* : to divide or break into splinters ⟨a *splintered* board⟩ ⟨the party *splintered* into quarreling factions⟩

¹split \'split\ *vb* **split**; **split·ting** [D *splitten*] **1 a** : to divide lengthwise usu. along a grain or seam or by layers : CLEAVE ⟨wood that *splits* easily⟩⟨*split* slate into shingles⟩ **b** : to separate the parts of by interposing something ⟨*split* an infinitive⟩⟨the river *split* the town⟩ **2 a** : to tear or break apart : BURST **b** : to subject (an atom or atomic nucleus) to artificial disintegration esp. by fission **c** : to affect as if by breaking up or tearing apart : SHATTER **3** : to divide into parts or portions: as **a** : to divide between individuals : SHARE ⟨the winning team *split* the prize⟩ **b** : to divide into factions, parties, or groups **c** : to mark (a ballot) or cast (a vote) for candidates of different parties **d** : to break down (a chemical compound) into constituents ⟨*split* a fat into glycerol and fatty acids⟩; *also* : to remove by such separation ⟨*split* off carbon dioxide⟩ **e** : to divide (stock) by issuing a larger number of shares to existing shareholders usu. without increase in total par value — **split·ter** *n* — **split hairs** : to make oversubtle or trivial distinctions

²split *n* **1** : a product or result of splitting: as **a** : a narrow break made by or as if by splitting : CRACK **b** : a part split off or made thin by splitting **c** : a group or faction formed by splitting **2** : the act or process of splitting : DIVISION ⟨a stock *split*⟩; *esp* : a dividing into divergent or antagonistic elements **3** : the feat of lowering oneself to the floor or leaping into the air with the legs extended in a straight line and in opposite directions

³split *adj* **1** : divided by or as if by splitting ⟨a *split* lip⟩ ⟨*split* families⟩; *also* : prepared for use by splitting ⟨*split* hides⟩ **2** : HETEROZYGOUS

split decision *n* : a decision in a boxing match reflecting a division of opinion among the referee and judges

split infinitive *n* : an infinitive having a modifier between the *to* and the verbal (as in "to really start")

split–lev·el \'split-'lev-əl\ *adj* : divided vertically so that the floor level of rooms in one part is approximately midway between the levels of two successive stories in an adjoining part ⟨*split-level* house⟩— **split–lev·el** \-,lev-əl\ *n*

split personality *n* : a personality structure composed of two or more internally consistent groups of behavior tendencies and attitudes each acting independently

split rail *n* : a fence rail split from a log

split second *n* : a fractional part of a second : FLASH ⟨happened in a *split second*⟩

split shift *n* : a shift of working hours divided into two or more working periods at times (as morning and evening) separated by more than normal periods of time off (as for lunch or rest)

split ticket *n* : a ballot cast by a voter who votes for candidates of more than one party

splotch \'spläch\ *n* : BLOTCH, SPOT — **splotch** *vt* — **splotchy** \'spläch-ē\ *adj*

¹splurge \'splərj\ *n* : a showy display

²splurge *vi* **1** : to make a splurge **2** : to indulge oneself extravagantly

¹splut·ter \'splət-ər\ *n* **1** : a confused noise (as of hasty speaking) **2** : a splashing or sputtering sound — **spluttery** \'splət-ə-rē\ *adj*

²splutter *vb* **1** : to make a noise as if spitting **2** : to speak or utter hastily and confusedly — **splut·ter·er** \'splət-ər-ər\ *n*

---

j joke; ŋ sing; ō flow; ó flaw; ói coin; th thin; th̲ this; ü loot; ú foot; y yet; yü few; yú furious; zh vision

¹spoil \'spȯil\ *n* [MF *espoille,* fr. L *spolia,* pl.] **1 a** : plunder taken from an enemy in war or a victim in robbery : LOOT **b** : public offices made the property of a successful party — usu. used in pl. **c** : something won usu. by effort or skill : PREY ⟨the *spoils* of the chase⟩ ⟨displayed the *spoils* from their ramble⟩ **2** : PLUNDERING, SPOLIATION **3** : earth and rock excavated or dredged **4** : an object damaged or flawed in the making

²spoil *vb* **spoiled** \'spȯild, 'spȯilt\; **spoilt** \'spȯilt\; **spoil·ing** **1** : DESPOIL, PILLAGE, ROB **2 a** : to damage seriously : RUIN ⟨a crop *spoiled* by floods⟩ **b** : to impair the quality or effect of ⟨a quarrel *spoiled* the celebration⟩ **c** : to decay or lose freshness, value, or usefulness usu. through being kept too long **3** : to damage the disposition or character of by pampering **4** : to have an eager desire ⟨*spoiling* for a fight⟩ — **spoil·a·ble** \'spȯi-lə-bəl\ *adj* — **spoil·er** *n*

spoil·age \'spȯi-lij\ *n* **1** : the act or process of spoiling **2** : something spoiled or wasted **3** : loss by spoilage

spoils·man \'spȯilz-mən\ *n* : one who serves a party for a share of the spoils; *also* : one who sanctions such practice

spoil·sport \'spȯil-spȯrt, -,spȯrt\ *n* : one who spoils the sport or pleasure of others

spoils system *n* : the practice of distributing public offices and their emoluments as plunder to members of the victorious party

¹spoke \'spōk\ *past & archaic past part of* SPEAK

²spoke *n* [OE *spāca*] **1 a** : one of the small radiating bars inserted in the hub of a wheel to support the rim **b** : something resembling the spoke of a wheel **2** : a rung of a ladder

³spoke *vt* : to furnish with or as if with spokes

spo·ken \'spō-kən\ *adj* **1 a** : delivered by word of mouth : ORAL **b** : used in speaking : UTTERED ⟨the *spoken* word⟩ **2** : speaking in (such) a manner — used in combination ⟨soft-*spoken*⟩ ⟨plain*spoken*⟩

spoke·shave \'spōk-,shāv\ *n* : a two-handled tool that is used for planing curved pieces of wood

spokes·man \'spōks-mən\ *n* : a person who speaks as a representative of another person or of a group

spo·li·a·tion \,spō-lē-'ā-shən\ *n* [L *spoliare* to plunder, fr. *spolia* spoils] : the act of plundering : the state of being plundered esp. in war — **spo·li·a·tor** \'spō-lē-,āt-ər\ *n*

spon·dee \'spän-,dē\ *n* [MF, fr. L *spondeum* foot of two long syllables, fr. Gk *spondeios,* fr. *spondē* libation; fr. its use in music accompanying libations] : a metrical foot consisting of two accented syllables (as in *tom-tom*) — **spon·da·ic** \spän-'dā-ik\ *adj*

¹sponge \'spənj\ *n* [OE, fr. L *spongia,* fr. Gk] **1 a** : an elastic porous mass of interlacing horny fibers that forms the internal skeleton of various marine animals (phylum Porifera) and is able when wetted to absorb water; *also* : a piece of this material or of a porous rubber or cellulose product of similar properties used esp. for cleaning **b** : any of a phylum (Porifera) of lowly aquatic animals that are essentially double-walled cell colonies and permanently attached as adults **2** : a pad (as of folded gauze) used in surgery and medicine (as to remove discharges or apply medication) **3** : one who lives upon others : SPONGER **4 a** : raised dough **b** : a whipped dessert usu. containing whites of eggs or gelatin **c** : a metal (as platinum) obtained in porous form usu. by reduction without fusion ⟨titanium *sponge*⟩

²sponge *vb* **1 a** : to cleanse, wipe, or moisten with or as if with a sponge **b** : to erase or destroy with or as if with a sponge **2** : to absorb with or as if with or like a sponge **3** : to get something from or live on another by imposing on hospitality or good nature **4** : to dive or dredge for sponges — **spong·er** *n*

sponge cake *n* : a cake made without shortening

sponge rubber *n* : cellular rubber resembling a natural sponge in structure used esp. for cushions and in weather= stripping

spon·gin \'spən-jən\ *n* : a scleroprotein that is the chief constituent of flexible fibers in sponge skeletons

spongy \'spən-jē\ *adj* **spong·i·er; -est** : resembling a sponge in appearance or absorbency : soft and full of holes or moisture : not firm or solid — **spong·i·ness** *n*

spongy parenchyma *n* : a spongy layer of irregular chlorophyll-bearing cells interspersed with air spaces

that fills the part of a leaf between the palisade parenchyma and the lower epidermis

spon·son \'spän(t)-sən\ *n* **1** : a projection (as a gun platform) from the side of a ship or a tank **2** : an air chamber along a canoe or seaplane to increase stability and buoyancy on water

¹spon·sor \'spän(t)-sər\ *n* [L *spons-, spondēre* to promise] **1** : a person who takes the responsibility for some other person or thing ⟨agreed to be his *sponsor* at the club⟩ **2** : GODPARENT **3** : a person or an organization that pays for or plans and carries out a project or activity; *esp* : one that pays the cost of a radio or television program usu. in return for limited advertising time during its course — **spon·so·ri·al** \spän-'sōr-ē-əl, -'sȯr-\ *adj* — **spon·sor·ship** \'spän(t)-sər-,ship\ *n*

²sponsor *vt* **spon·sored; spon·sor·ing** \'spän(t)s-(ə-)riŋ\ : to be or stand sponsor for

spon·ta·ne·i·ty \,spänt-ə-'nē-ət-ē, -'nā-\ *n* **1** : the quality or state of being spontaneous **2** : spontaneous action or movement

spon·ta·ne·ous \spän-'tā-nē-əs\ *adj* [L *spontaneus,* fr. *sponte* of one's free will] **1** : done, said, or produced freely and naturally ⟨*spontaneous* laughter⟩ **2** : acting or taking place without external force, cause, or influence ⟨*spontaneous* rebellion⟩ ⟨*spontaneous* recovery from illness⟩ — **spon·ta·ne·ous·ly** *adv* — **spon·ta·ne·ous·ness** *n*

syn SPONTANEOUS, IMPULSIVE, INSTINCTIVE, AUTOMATIC mean acting or activated without deliberation. SPONTANEOUS implies lack of prompting and connotes genuineness ⟨*spontaneous* expression of admiration⟩ IMPULSIVE implies acting under immediate stress of emotion or spirit of the moment ⟨*impulsive* act of generosity⟩ INSTINCTIVE stresses spontaneous action involving neither judgment nor conscious intention ⟨*instinctive* shrinking from snakes⟩ AUTOMATIC implies action engaging neither the mind nor the emotions and connotes a predictable response ⟨a soldier's *automatic* obedience to commands⟩

spontaneous combustion *n* : a bursting into flame of combustible material through heat produced within itself by chemical action (as oxidation)

spontaneous generation *n* : ABIOGENESIS

¹spoof \'spüf\ *vt* [fr. *Spoof,* a hoaxing game] **1** : DECEIVE, HOAX **2** : to make good-natured fun of ⟨a skit *spoofing* big business⟩

²spoof *n* **1** : HOAX, DECEPTION **2** : a light amiable takeoff (as on customs or manners)

¹spook \'spük\ *n* [D] : GHOST, SPECTER — **spook·ish** \'spü-kish\ *adj*

²spook *vb* : to make or become frightened or frantic : SCARE

spooky \'spü-kē\ *adj* **spook·i·er; -est** **1** : relating to, resembling, or suggesting spooks ⟨a very *spooky* movie⟩ ⟨*spooky* houses⟩ **2** : NERVOUS, SKITTISH ⟨a *spooky* horse⟩ — **spook·i·ness** *n*

spool \'spül\ *n* [MD *spoele*] **1** : a cylinder which has a rim or ridge at each end and usu. a hollow center and on which thread, wire, or tape is wound **2** : material wound on a spool — **spool** *vb*

¹spoon \'spün\ *n* [OE *spōn* splinter, chip] **1** : an implement that consists of a small shallow bowl with a handle and is used esp. in eating and cooking **2** : something that resembles a spoon in shape (as a usu. metal or shell fishing lure) **3** : a wooden-headed golf club with more loft than a brassie — called also *number three wood*

²spoon *vb* **1** : to take up and usu. transfer in or as if in a spoon **2** : to make love esp. in a silly demonstrative way

spoon·bill \'spün-,bil\ *n* **1** : any of several wading birds related to the ibises that have the bill broad and flat at the tip **2** : any of several broad-billed ducks

spoon–billed \'spün-'bild\ *adj* : having a bill or snout with a broad spoon-shaped tip

spoon bread *n, chiefly South & Midland* : soft bread made of cornmeal mixed with milk, eggs, shortening, and leavening and served with a spoon

spoon·drift \'spün-,drift\ *n* : spray blown from waves during a gale at sea

spoo·ner·ism \'spü-nə-,riz-əm\ *n* [William A. *Spooner* d1930 English clergyman and educator] : a transposition of usu. initial sounds of two or more words (as in *tons of soil* for *sons of toil*)

spoon–feed \'spün-,fēd\ *vt* **-fed; -feeding** **1** : to feed by means of a spoon **2** : to present information to in so complete a manner as to preclude independent thought

spoon·ful \'spün-ˌfůl\ *n, pl* **spoonfuls** \-ˌfůlz\ *or* **spoonsful** \'spünz-ˌfůl\ : as much as a spoon can hold; *esp* : TEASPOONFUL

¹spoor \'spů(ə)r, 'spō(ə)r, 'spó(ə)r\ *n* [Afrik] : a track or trail esp. of a wild animal

²spoor *vb* : to track something by a spoor

spor- *or* **sporo-** *comb form* [NL *spora*] : seed : spore ⟨*sporocyst*⟩ ⟨*sporangium*⟩

spo·rad·ic \spə-'rad-ik\ *adj* [Gk *sporadēn* here and there, fr. *sporad-, sporas* scattered, fr. *spor-, speirein* to sow] : occurring occasionally, singly, or in scattered instances : SEPARATE, ISOLATED ⟨*sporadic* outbreaks of disease⟩ **syn** see INFREQUENT — **spo·rad·i·cal·ly** \-'rad-i-k(ə-)lē\ *adv*

spo·ran·gi·o·phore \spə-'ran-jē-ə-ˌfōr, -ˌfór\ *n* : a stalk (as a fungal hypha) that bears sporangia

spo·ran·gi·um \spə-'ran-jē-əm\ *n, pl* **-gia** \-jē-ə\ [NL, fr. Gk *angeion* vessel] : a sac or case within which usu. asexual spores are produced — **spo·ran·gial** \-j(ē-)əl\ *adj*

¹spore \'spō(ə)r, 'spó(ə)r\ *n* [NL *spora* seed, spore, fr. Gk, act of sowing, seed, fr. *speirein* to sow] : a primitive usu. one-celled resistant or reproductive body produced by plants and some lower animals and capable of developing either directly or after fusion with another spore into a new individual in some cases unlike the parent — **spored** \'spōrd, 'spórd\ *adj* — **spo·rif·er·ous** \spə-'rif-(ə-)rəs\ *adj*

²spore *vi* : to produce or reproduce by spores

spore case *n* : SPORANGIUM

spore fruit *n* : a complex sporangium : FRUITING BODY

spore mother cell *n* : a cell whose final divisions produce spores usu. in tetrads

spo·ro·cyst \'spōr-ə-ˌsist, 'spór-\ *n* **1** : a resting cell (as in a slime mold) that may give rise to asexual spores **2** : a sac that is the first asexual reproductive form of a digenetic trematode and buds off cells from its inner surface which develop into rediae — **spo·ro·cys·tic** \ˌspōr-ə-'sis-tik, ˌspór-\ *adj*

spo·ro·cyte \'spōr-ə-ˌsīt, 'spór-\ *n* : SPORE MOTHER CELL

spo·ro·gen·e·sis \ˌspōr-ə-'jen-ə-səs, ˌspór-\ *n* **1** : reproduction by spores **2** : spore formation — **spo·ro·gen·ic** \-'jen-ik\ *adj* — **spo·rog·e·nous** \spə-'räj-ə-nəs\ *adj*

spo·ro·go·ni·um \ˌspōr-ə-'gō-nē-əm, ˌspór-\ *n, pl* **-nia** \-nē-ə\ : the sporophyte of a moss or liverwort having usu. the form of a capsule-bearing stalk and remaining permanently attached to the gametophyte

spo·rog·o·ny \spə-'räg-ə-nē\ *n* : reproduction by spores; *also* : spore formation in a sporozoan by encystment and subsequent division of a zygote — **spo·rog·o·nous** \-nəs\ *adj*

spo·ro·phore \'spōr-ə-ˌfōr, 'spór-ə-ˌfór\ *n* : the part or organ of a sporophyte that actually produces spores

spo·ro·phyll *or* **spo·ro·phyl** \'spōr-ə-ˌfil, 'spór-\ *n* : a spore-bearing and usu. greatly modified leaf (as a stamen or carpel)

spo·ro·phyte \-ˌfīt\ *n* : the individual or generation of a plant exhibiting alternation of generations that bears asexual spores — compare GAMETOPHYTE — **spo·ro·phyt·ic** \ˌspōr-ə-'fit-ik, ˌspór-\ *adj*

spo·ro·zo·an \ˌspōr-ə-'zō-ən, ˌspór-\ *n* : any of a large class (Sporozoa) of strictly parasitic protozoans that have a complicated life cycle usu. involving both asexual and sexual generations often in different hosts and include important pathogens (as the malaria parasites) — **spo·ro·zo·al** \-'zō-əl\ *adj* — **sporozoan** *adj* — **spo·ro·zo·on** \-'zō-ˌän\ *n*

spo·ro·zo·ite \-'zō-ˌīt\ *n* : a usu. motile infective form of some sporozoans that is formed by division of a zygote and initiates an asexual cycle in the new host

spor·ran \'spór-ən, 'spär-\ *n* [ScGael *sporan*] : a pouch of skin with the hair or fur on that is worn in front of the kilt by Highlanders in full dress

¹sport \'spōrt, 'spórt\ *vb* [ME *sporten*, short for *disporten* to disport] **1 a** : to amuse oneself : FROLIC **b** : to engage in a sport **2** : to speak or act in jest or mockingly : TRIFLE **3** : to make usu. ostentatious display of : show off ⟨*sport* a new hat⟩ **4** : to deviate or vary abruptly from type : MUTATE

²sport *n* **1 a** : a source of diversion : RECREATION **b** : physical activity engaged in for pleasure; *esp* : a particu-

lar activity (as hunting or an athletic game) so engaged in **2 a** : PLEASANTRY, JEST **b** : MOCKERY, DERISION **3 a** : something tossed or driven about in or as if in play ⟨the battered boat became the *sport* of wind and waves⟩ **b** : LAUGHINGSTOCK, BUTT **4 a** : SPORTSMAN **b** : a person devoted to a gay easy life; *also* : one inclined to be venturesome **5** : an individual exhibiting a sudden deviation from type usu. as a result of mutation esp. of somatic tissue

³sport *or* **sports** \'spōrts, 'spórts\ *adj* : of, relating to, or suitable for sport ⟨*sport* fish⟩ ⟨*sport* coats⟩

sport·ful \'spōrt-fəl, 'spórt-\ *adj* **1** : PLAYFUL, FROLICSOME **2** : done in sport — **sport·ful·ly** \-fə-lē\ *adv* — **sport·ful·ness** *n*

sport·ing \'spōrt-iŋ, 'spórt-\ *adj* **1 a** : used or suitable for sport **b** : marked by or calling for sportsmanship **c** : involving such risk as a sports contender may expect to take or encounter ⟨a *sporting* chance⟩ **2** : of or relating to dissipation and esp. gambling

sport·ive \'spōrt-iv, 'spórt-\ *adj* : PLAYFUL, FROLICSOME, MERRY — **sport·ive·ly** *adv* — **sport·ive·ness** *n*

sports car *also* **sport car** *n* : a low fast usu. two-seat open automobile

sports·cast \'spōrts-ˌkast, 'spórts-\ *n* : a broadcast dealing with sports events — **sports·cast·er** *n*

sport shirt *n* : a soft shirt for casual wear with open neck

sports·man \'spōrts-mən, 'spórts-\ *n* **1** : a person who engages in or is interested in sports and esp. outdoor sports **2** : a person who is fair and generous and a good loser and a graceful winner — **sports·man·like** \-ˌlīk\ *adj* — **sports·man·ly** \-lē\ *adj* — **sports·wom·an** \-ˌwům-ən\ *n*

sports·man·ship \-mən-ˌship\ *n* : skill in or devotion to sports; *esp* : conduct befitting a good sportsman

sports·wear \-ˌwa(ə)r, -ˌwe(ə)r\ *n* : clothes suitable for engaging in or watching sports

sports·writ·er \-ˌrīt-ər\ *n* : one who writes about sports esp. for a newspaper

sporty \'spōrt-ē, 'spórt-\ *adj* **sport·i·er; -est 1** : characteristic of a sportsman : SPORTSMANLIKE **2 a** : notably gay or dissipated : FAST **b** : FLASHY, SHOWY **3** : SPORT **sport·i·ly** \'spōrt-ᵊl-ē, 'spórt-\ *adv* — **sport·i·ness** \-ē-nəs, 'spórt-\ *n*

spor·u·la·tion \ˌspōr-yə-'lā-shən, ˌspór-\ *n* : formation of or division into spores — **spor·u·late** \'spōr-yə-ˌlāt, 'spór-\ *vi* — **spor·u·la·tive** \-ˌlāt-iv\ *adj*

¹spot \'spät\ *n* [ME] **1** : a blemish or stain on character or reputation : FAULT **2 a** : a small area visibly different (as in color, finish, or material) from the surrounding area **b** : an area marred or marked (as by dirt); *also* : a circumscribed surface lesion of disease (as measles) **3 a** : a small quantity or amount **b** : a small or particular place or extent of space ⟨a good *spot* for a picnic⟩ ⟨a sore *spot* in his throat⟩ **4 a** : a particular position (as in an organization or on a program) **b** : a position usu. of difficulty or embarrassment — **on the spot 1** : at once : IMMEDIATELY **2** : at the place of action **3 a** : in a responsible or accountable position **b** : in difficulty or danger

²spot *vb* **spot·ted; spot·ting 1** : to mark or mar with or as if with spots : STAIN, BLEMISH ⟨a *spotted* reputation⟩ ⟨white spots so easily⟩ **2** : to single out : IDENTIFY, DETECT ⟨*spot* a friend⟩ ⟨*spot* an opportunity⟩; *also* : to locate precisely ⟨*spot* an enemy's position⟩ **3 a** : to lie or occur at intervals in or on ⟨slopes *spotted* with plowed fields⟩ **b** : to place at intervals in a desired spot ⟨*spot* a picture on the wall⟩ **4** : to remove spots from — **spot·ta·ble** \'spät-ə-bəl\ *adj*

³spot *adj* **1** : being, originating, or done on the spot or in or for a particular spot ⟨*spot* coverage of the news⟩ **2 a** : paid out upon delivery ⟨*spot* cash⟩ **b** : broadcast between scheduled programs ⟨*spot* announcements⟩ **3** : made at random or restricted to a few places or instances ⟨a *spot* check⟩

spot–check \'spät-ˌchek\ *vb* : to sample or investigate quickly or at random : make a spot check

spot·less \'spät-ləs\ *adj* : free from spot or blemish : immaculately clean or pure — **spot·less·ly** *adv* — **spot·less·ness** *n*

¹spot·light \'spät-ˌlīt\ *n* **1 a** : a projected spot of light used to illuminate something (as a person on the stage) brilliantly **b** : conspicuous public notice **2** : a light designed to direct a narrow intense beam of light on a small area

²spotlight vt : to illuminate with or as if with a spotlight

spot pass n : a pass (as in football) made to a predetermined spot on the field or court rather than directly to a player

spot·ted \'spät-əd\ adj **1 a** : marked with spots **b** : SULLIED, TARNISHED **2** : accompanied by an eruption ⟨a spotted fever⟩ **3** : SPOTTY 2

spot·ter \'spät-ər\ n **1** : one that makes, applies, or removes spots **2** : one that keeps watch : OBSERVER; esp : a civilian watcher whose duty is to report all approaching airplanes

spot·ty \'spät-ē\ adj **spot·ti·er; -est 1** : marked with spots : SPOTTED **2** : lacking uniformity esp. in quality : UNEVEN ⟨spotty attendance⟩ — **spot·ti·ly** \'spät-ʰl-ē\ adv — **spot·ti·ness** \'spät-ē-nəs\ n

spou·sal \'spau̇-zəl, -səl\ adj : of, relating to, or celebrating marriage : NUPTIAL

spouse \'spau̇s, 'spau̇z\ n [OF espous, fr. L sponsus betrothed, newly married, fr. pp. of spondēre to promise, betroth] : a married person : HUSBAND, WIFE

¹spout \'spau̇t\ vb [ME spouten] **1** : to eject (as liquid) in a stream or jet ⟨wells spouting oil⟩; also : to release material in this manner ⟨whales spouting⟩ **2** : to speak or utter readily, volubly, and at length **3** : to issue with force or in a jet : SPURT ⟨blood spouted from the wound⟩ — **spout·er** n

²spout n **1** : a tube, pipe, or hole through which something (as rainwater) spouts **2** : a jet of liquid; esp : WATERSPOUT

¹sprain \'sprān\ n **1** : a sudden or violent twist or wrench of a joint with stretching or tearing of ligaments **2** : a sprained condition **syn** see STRAIN

²sprain vt : to subject to sprain

sprat \'sprat\ n [alter. of OE sprott] : a small European herring closely related to the common herring; also : a small or young herring or similar fish (as an anchovy)

sprawl \'sprȯl\ vb [ME sprawlen, fr. OE sprēawlian to thrash about] **1** : to creep or clamber awkwardly **2** : to lie or sit with arms and legs spread out **3** : to spread or cause to spread out irregularly or awkwardly ⟨the auto plant sprawls over a vast area⟩ — **sprawl** n

¹spray \'sprā\ n [ME] **1** : a usu. flowering branch or shoot or an arrangement of these **2** : something (as an ornament) resembling a spray

²spray n [obs. spray to sprinkle, fr. MD sprayen] **1** : water flying in small drops or particles blown from waves or thrown up by a waterfall **2 a** : a jet of vapor or finely divided liquid (as from an atomizer) **b** : a device (as an atomizer or sprayer) by which a spray is dispersed or applied ⟨paint sprays⟩

³spray vb **1** : to scatter or let fall in a spray **2** : to project spray on or into ⟨the waves sprayed us with salt water⟩ — **spray·er** n

spray gun n : a device for spraying paints and insecticides

¹spread \'spred\ vb **spread; spread·ing** [OE sprǣdan] **1 a** : to open or expand over a larger area ⟨spread out a map⟩ **b** : to stretch out : EXTEND ⟨spread her arms wide⟩ **2 a** : SCATTER, STREW ⟨spread fertilizer⟩ **b** : to distribute over a period or among a group ⟨spread the work to be done⟩ **c** : to apply on a surface ⟨spread butter on bread⟩ **d** : COVER, OVERLAY ⟨spread a floor with carpet⟩ **e (1)** : to prepare or furnish for dining : SET ⟨spread a table⟩ **(2)** : SERVE **3 a** : to become or cause to become disseminated or widely known ⟨the news spread rapidly⟩ **b** : to extend the range or incidence of ⟨spread a disease⟩ **4** : to stretch or move apart ⟨spreads his fingers⟩ — **spread·er** n

²spread n **1 a** : the act or process of spreading ⟨the spread of education⟩ **b** : extent of spreading ⟨the spread of a bird's wings⟩ **2** : something spread out: as **a** : EXPANSE **b** : a prominent display in a periodical **3** : something spread on or over a surface: as **a** : a food to be spread on bread or crackers **b** : a sumptuous meal : FEAST **c** : a cloth cover for a table or bed **4** : distance between two points : GAP

spread eagle n **1** : a representation of an eagle with wings raised and legs extended **2** : something resembling or suggestive of a spread eagle

spread–ea·gle \'spred-ˌē-gəl\ vb **spread-ea·gled; spread-**

ea·gling \-g(ə-)liŋ\ **1** : to stand, move, or stretch out in the position of a spread eagle **2** : STRADDLE

spreading adder n : HOGNOSE SNAKE

spree \'sprē\ n : an unrestrained indulgence in or outburst of an activity ⟨went on a buying spree⟩; esp : a drunken revel

¹sprig \'sprig\ n [ME sprigge] **1** : a small shoot : TWIG **2** : an ornament resembling a sprig, stemmed flower, or leaf **3** : a small headless nail : BRAD

²sprig vt **sprigged; sprig·ging** : to drive sprigs into

spright·ful \'sprīt-fəl\ adj : full of life or spirit : SPRIGHTLY — **spright·ful·ly** \-fə-lē\ adv — **spright·ful·ness** n

spright·ly \'sprīt-lē\ adj **spright·li·er; -est** [obs. spright sprite, alter. of sprite] : marked by a gay lightness and liveliness — **spright·li·ness** n

¹spring \'spriŋ\ vb **sprang** \'spraŋ\ or **sprung** \'sprəŋ\; **sprung; spring·ing** \'spriŋ-iŋ\ [OE springan] **1 a (1)** : DART, SHOOT **(2)** : to be resilient or elastic; also : to move by elastic force ⟨the lid sprang shut⟩ **b** : to become warped **2** : to issue with speed and force or as a stream **3 a** : to grow as a plant **b** : to issue by birth or descent **c** : to come into being : ARISE ⟨hope springs eternal⟩ **4 a** : to make a leap or series of leaps **b** : to jump up suddenly **5** : to stretch out in height : RISE ⟨new structures sprang from the ruins⟩ **6 a** : SPLIT, CRACK ⟨wind sprang the mast⟩ **b** : to undergo the opening of (a leak) **7** : to cause to operate suddenly ⟨spring a trap⟩ **8** : to produce or disclose suddenly or unexpectedly ⟨the prosecutor sprang an unknown eyewitness⟩ — **spring·er** \'spriŋ-ər\ n

²spring n **1 a** : a source of supply; esp : a source of water issuing from the ground **b** : an ultimate source esp. of action or motion **2 a** : the season between winter and summer comprising in the northern hemisphere usu. the months of March, April, and May or as reckoned astronomically extending from the March equinox to the June solstice **b** : a time or season of growth or development **3** : an elastic body or device that recovers its original shape when released after being distorted **4 a** : the act or an instance of leaping up or forward : BOUND **b** : capacity for springing : RESILIENCE, BOUNCE

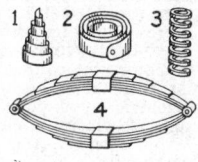

springs: 1, 3 spiral, 2 coil, 4 leaf

spring·board \'spriŋ-ˌbȯrd, -ˌbōrd\ n **1** : a flexible board usu. secured at one end and used for gymnastic stunts or diving **2** : a point of departure ⟨a springboard to political success⟩

spring–clean·ing \-'klē-niŋ\ n : the act or process of doing a thorough cleaning (as of a house)

springe \'sprinj\ n [ME] : SNARE, TRAP

spring·er spaniel \ˌspriŋ-ər-\ n : a medium-sized largely white sporting dog of English or Welsh origin used chiefly for finding and flushing small game

spring fever n : a lazy or restless feeling often associated with the onset of spring

spring–house \'spriŋ-ˌhau̇s\ n : a small building over a spring used for cool storage (as of dairy products or meat)

spring·let \'spriŋ-lət\ n : a little spring : STREAMLET

spring peeper n : a small brown tree toad of the eastern U.S. and Canada with a shrill piping call

spring·tail \'spriŋ-ˌtāl\ n : any of an order (Collembola) of small primitive wingless arthropods, related to or classed among the insects

spring·tide \'spriŋ-ˌtīd\ n : SPRINGTIME

spring tide n : a greater than usual tide occurring at each new moon and full moon

spring·time \'spriŋ-ˌtīm\ n : the season of spring

spring wagon n : a light wagon equipped with springs

spring·wood \'spriŋ-ˌwu̇d\ n : the softer more porous portion of an annual ring of wood that develops early in the growing season — compare SUMMERWOOD

springy \'spriŋ-ē\ adj **spring·i·er; -est** : having an elastic quality : RESILIENT ⟨a springy step⟩ — **spring·i·ly** \'spriŋ-ə-lē\ adv — **spring·i·ness** \'spriŋ-ē-nəs\ n

¹sprin·kle \'spriŋ-kəl\ vb **sprin·kled; sprin·kling** \-k(ə-)liŋ\ [ME sprinclen] **1** : to scatter in drops or particles **2** : to scatter over or at intervals in or among **b** : to wet lightly **3** : to rain lightly in scattered drops — **sprin·kler** \-k(ə-)lər\ n

²**sprinkle** *n* **1** : the act or an instance of sprinkling; *esp* : a light rain **2** : SPRINKLING

sprinkler system *n* : a system for protection against fire in which pipes are distributed for conveying an extinguishing fluid (as water) to outlets

sprin·kling \'sprin̄-klin̄\ *n* : a limited quantity or amount; *esp* : SCATTERING

¹**sprint** \'sprint\ *vi* [of Scand origin] : to run at top speed esp. for a short distance — **sprint·er** *n*

²**sprint** *n* **1** : the act or an instance of sprinting **2** : DASH 6b

sprit \'sprit\ *n* [OE *sprēot* pole, spear] : a spar that crosses a fore-and-aft sail diagonally

sprite \'sprīt\ *n* [OF *esprit* spirit, fr. L *spiritus*] **1** : a disembodied spirit **2 a** : ELF, FAIRY **b** : an elfish person

sprit·sail \'sprit-,sāl, -səl\ *n* : a sail extended by a sprit

sprock·et \'spräk-ət\ *n* **1** : a projection on the rim of a wheel shaped so as to interlock with the links of a chain **2** : a wheel having sprockets

¹**sprout** \'spraút\ *vb* [OE *-sprūtan*] **1** : to send out new growth **2** : to grow rapidly **3** : to cause to sprout ⟨*sprout* oats⟩

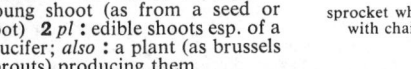

sprocket wheels with chain

²**sprout** *n* **1** : SHOOT 1a; *esp* : a young shoot (as from a seed or root) **2** *pl* : edible shoots esp. of a crucifer; *also* : a plant (as brussels sprouts) producing them

¹**spruce** \'sprüs\ *n* [obs. *Spruce* Prussia, fr. ME, alter. of *Pruce*, fr. OF] : any of a genus of evergreen trees of the pine family with a conical head of dense foliage and with soft light wood; *also* : its wood

²**spruce** *adj* : neat or smart in appearance : TRIM — **spruce·ly** *adv* — **spruce·ness** *n*

³**spruce** *vb* : to make or make oneself spruce ⟨*spruce* up a room⟩ ⟨*spruce* up a bit before an interview⟩

sprue \'sprü\ *n* [D *spruw*] : a chronic disease marked esp. by fatty diarrhea and dietary deficiency symptoms

sprung *past of* SPRING

spry \'sprī\ *adj* **spri·er** *or* **spry·er** \'sprī(-ə)r\; **spri·est** *or* **spry·est** \'sprī-əst\ : vigorously active : CHIPPER, NIMBLE, BRISK ⟨a *spry* old gentleman⟩ — **spry·ly** *adv* — **spry·ness** *n*

¹**spud** \'spəd\ *n* [ME *spudde* dagger] **1** : a tool or device (as for digging, lifting, or cutting) combining the characteristics of spade and chisel **2** : POTATO

²**spud** *vb* **spud·ded; spud·ding** : to dig with a spud

¹**spume** \'spyüm\ *n* [L *spuma*; akin to E *foam*] : frothy matter on liquids : FOAM, SCUM — **spu·mous** \'spyü-məs\ *adj* — **spumy** \'spyü-mē\ *adj*

²**spume** *vi* : FROTH, FOAM

spu·mo·ni *or* **spu·mo·ne** \spú-'mō-nē\ *n* [It *spumone*, fr. aug. of *spuma* foam, fr. L] : ice cream in layers of different colors, flavors, and textures often with candied fruits and nuts

spun *past of* SPIN

spun glass *n* : FIBER GLASS

spunk \'spənk\ *n* [*spunk* tinder, fr. ScGael *spong* sponge, tinder, fr. L *spongia* sponge] : SPIRIT, PLUCK

spunky \'spən-kē\ *adj* **spunk·i·er; -est** : full of spunk : SPIRITED — **spunk·i·ly** \-kə-lē\ *adv* — **spunk·i·ness** \-kē-nəs\ *n*

spun sugar *n* : a confection or garnish made from boiled sugar syrup drawn out into fine threads (as on a revolving spindle)

¹**spur** \'spər\ *n* [OE *spura*] **1 a** : a pointed device secured to a rider's heel and used to urge the horse **b** *pl* : recognition for achievement **2** : a goad to action : STIMULUS **3** : something projecting like or suggesting a spur: as **a** : a stiff sharp projecting part (as a broken branch of a tree or a horny process on a cock's leg) **b** : a hollow projecting appendage of a corolla or calyx (as in larkspur or columbine) **4** : a ridge that extends laterally from a mountain **5** : a short wooden brace of a post **6** : a railroad track diverging from a main line — **on the spur of the moment** : on hasty impulse

²**spur** *vb* **spurred; spur·ring** **1** : to urge a horse on with spurs **2** : INCITE, STIMULATE

spurge \'spərj\ *n* [MF, lit., purge, fr. *espurgier* to purge, fr. L *expurgare*] : any of a family of mostly shrubby

plants with a bitter milky juice and often showy bracts surrounding insignificant flowers — compare POINSETTIA

spur gear *n* : a gear wheel with radial teeth parallel to its axis

spu·ri·ous \'spyúr-ē-əs\ *adj* [LL *spurius*, fr. L, bastard] : not genuine or authentic : FALSE, COUNTERFEIT — **spu·ri·ous·ly** *adv* — **spu·ri·ous·ness** *n*

¹**spurn** \'spərn\ *vt* [OE *spurnan;* akin to E *spur*] **1** : to kick aside **2** : to reject or thrust aside with disdain or contempt **syn** see REJECT — **spurn·er** *n*

²**spurn** *n* **1** : KICK **2** : disdainful rejection

spur-of-the-moment *adj* : occurring or developing without premeditation ⟨a *spur-of-the-moment* decision⟩

spurred \'spərd\ *adj* **1** : wearing spurs **2** : having one or more spurs ⟨a *spurred* violet⟩

spur·ri·er \'spər-ē-ər\ *n* : one who makes spurs

¹**spurt** \'spərt\ *n* : a brief burst of increased effort or activity

²**spurt** *vi* : to make a spurt

³**spurt** *vb* **1** : to gush forth : SPOUT **2** : SQUIRT

⁴**spurt** *n* : a sudden gush : JET

spur track *n* : a track that diverges from a main line

sput·nik \'spút-nik, 'spət-\ *n* [Russ, lit., traveling companion, fr. *s* with + *put'* path] : SATELLITE 2b

¹**sput·ter** \'spət-ər\ *vb* **1** : to spit or squirt particles of food or saliva noisily from the mouth **2** : to speak or utter hastily or explosively in confusion or excitement ⟨*sputtered* out his protests⟩ **3** : to make explosive popping sounds ⟨the motor *sputtered* and died⟩ — **sput·ter·er** \-ər-ər\ *n*

²**sputter** *n* : the act or sound of sputtering

spu·tum \'sp(y)üt-əm\ *n, pl* **spu·ta** \-ə\ [L, fr. neut. of *sputus*, pp. of *spuere* to spit; akin to E *spew*] : material expectorated and made up of saliva and mucous discharges from the respiratory passages

¹**spy** \'spī\ *vb* **spied; spy·ing** [OF *espier*, of Gmc origin] **1** : to watch, inspect, or examine secretly : act as a spy ⟨*spied* on the neighbors⟩ ⟨*spied* for an intelligence agency⟩ **2** : to catch sight of : SEE ⟨*spies* a friend in the crowd⟩ **3** : to discover by intensive search or examination ⟨*spied* out the secrets of the atom⟩

²**spy** *n, pl* **spies** **1** : one that watches the conduct of others esp. in secret **2** : a person who tries secretly to obtain information for one country in the territory of another usu. hostile country

spy·glass \'spī-,glas\ *n* : a small telescope

squab \'skwäb\ *n, pl* **squabs** *or* **squab** : a fledgling bird; *esp* : a fledgling pigeon about four weeks old

¹**squab·ble** \'skwäb-əl\ *n* : a noisy quarrel usu. over trifles

²**squabble** *vi* **squab·bled; squab·bling** \'skwäb-(ə-)lin̄\ : to quarrel noisily and to no purpose : WRANGLE — **squab·bler** \-(ə-)lər\ *n*

squad \'skwäd\ *n* [MF *esquade*, fr. Sp *escuadra* & It *squadra*, fr. (assumed) VL *exquadrare* to make square] **1** : a small organized group of military personnel; *esp* : a tactical unit that can be easily directed in the field **2** : a small group engaged in a common effort or occupation ⟨a football *squad*⟩

squad car *n* : a police automobile connected by shortwave radiophone with headquarters — called also *cruiser, prowl car*

squad·ron \'skwäd-rən\ *n* [It *squadrone*, aug. of *squadra* squad] : any of several units of military organization

squad room *n* **1** : a room in a barracks used to billet soldiers **2** : a room in a police station where members of the force assemble (as for roll call or the assignment of duties)

squal·id \'skwäl-əd\ *adj* [L *squalidus*] **1** : marked by filthiness and degradation from neglect or poverty **2** : morally debased : SORDID — **squal·id·ly** *adv* — **squal·id·ness** *n*

¹**squall** \'skwól\ *vb* [of Scand origin] : to cry out raucously : SCREAM — **squall·er** *n*

²**squall** *n* **1** : a raucous cry **2** : SQUAWK

³**squall** *n* **1** : a sudden violent wind often with rain or snow **2** : a short-lived commotion

⁴**squall** *vi* : to blow a squall

squally \'skwó-lē\ *adj* **squall·i·er; -est** : marked by squalls : GUSTY, STORMY

squa·loid \'skwä-,lóid\ *adj* [NL *Squalus*, genus of sharks, fr. L, a sea fish] **:** being or resembling a typical shark — **squaloid** n

squal·or \'skwäl-ər\ n [L] **:** the quality or state of being squalid

squam- or **squamo-** comb form [L squama scale] **:** scale ⟨squamation⟩

squa·ma \'skwä-mə\ n, pl **squa·mae** \-ˌmē\ [L] **:** SCALE — **squa·mate** \-ˌmāt\ adj

squa·ma·tion \skwə-'mā-shən\ n **1 :** the state of being scaly **2 :** the arrangement of scales on an animal

squa·mo·sal \skwə-'mō-səl\ adj **1 :** SQUAMOUS **2 :** of, relating to, or being a bone of the skull of many vertebrates corresponding to the squamous portion of the temporal bone of man

squa·mous \'skwä-məs, 'skwä-\ also **squa·mose** \-ˌmōs\ adj **1 :** covered with or consisting of scales **:** SCALY **2 :** of, relating to, or being the anterior upper portion of the temporal bone of man and various mammals — **squa·mous·ly** adv

squan·der \'skwän-dər\ vb **squan·dered; squan·der·ing** \-d(ə-)riŋ\ **:** to spend extravagantly or wastefully — **squan·der·er** \-dər-ər\ n

¹square \'skwa(ə)r, 'skwe(ə)r\ n [MF esquarre, fr. (assumed) VL exquadra, fr. exquadrare to square, fr. L ex- + quadrare to square] **1 :** an instrument having at least one right angle and two straight edges used to lay out or test right angles **2 :** a rectangle with all four sides equal **3 :** any of the quadrilateral spaces marked out on a board for playing games **4 :** the product of a number multiplied by itself **5 a :** an open place or area formed at the meeting of two or more streets **b :** BLOCK 5b, 5c — **on the square 1 :** at right angles **2 :** in a fair open manner **:** HONESTLY — **out of square :** not at an exact right angle

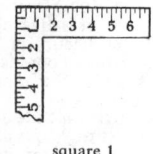

square 1

²square adj **1 a :** having four equal sides and four right angles **b :** forming a right angle ⟨square corner⟩ **2 :** raised to the second power **3 a :** of a shape suggesting strength and solidity ⟨square jaw⟩ ⟨square shoulders⟩ **b :** rectangular and equilateral in section ⟨square tower⟩ **c :** having a rectangular rather than curving outline **4 a :** converted from a linear unit into a square unit of area having the same length of side **:** SQUARED ⟨a square foot is the area of a square each side of which is a foot⟩ **b :** being of a specified length in each of two equal dimensions ⟨10 feet square⟩ **5 a :** exactly adjusted **:** well made **b :** JUST, FAIR **c :** leaving no balance **:** SETTLED **d :** TIED ⟨the golfers were all square at the end of the 6th hole⟩ **e :** SUBSTANTIAL, SATISFYING ⟨square meal⟩ — **square·ly** adv — **square·ness** n

³square vb **1 :** to make square **:** form with four equal sides and right angles or with right angles and straight lines or with flat surfaces ⟨square a timber⟩ **2 :** to bring to a right angle ⟨squared his shoulders⟩ **3 a :** to multiply (a number) by itself **b :** to find a square equal in area to ⟨square a circle⟩ **4 :** to agree or make agree **:** HARMONIZE ⟨his story does not square with the facts⟩ **5 :** BALANCE, SETTLE ⟨square an account⟩ **6 :** to mark off into squares **7 :** BRIBE, FIX **8 :** to take a fighting stance ⟨the two squared off playfully⟩

square away vb **:** to put in order or readiness

square bracket n **:** BRACKET 3a

square dance n **:** a dance for four couples who form a hollow square — **square dancer** n — **square dancing** n

square deal n **1 :** an honest and fair transaction or trade **2 :** the legislative and administrative program of President Theodore Roosevelt

square knot n **:** a knot made of two reverse half-knots and typically used to join the ends of two cords

square measure n **:** a unit or system of units for measuring area — see MEASURE table, METRIC SYSTEM table

square–rigged \'skwa(ə)r-'rigd, 'skwe(ə)r-\ adj **:** having the principal sails extended on yards fastened to the masts horizontally and at their center

square–rig·ger \-'rig-ər\ n **:** a square-rigged ship

square root n **:** a factor of a number that when squared gives the number ⟨the square root of 9 is ±3⟩

square sail \-ˌsāl, -səl\ n **:** a 4-sided sail extended on a yard suspended at the middle from a mast

square shooter n **:** a just or honest person

square–shoul·dered \-'shōl-dərd\ adj **:** having the shoulders high and well braced back

squar·ish \'skwa(ə)r-ish, 'skwe(ə)r-\ adj **:** somewhat square in form or appearance — **squar·ish·ly** adv

squar·rose \'skwär-ˌōs\ adj [L squarrosus] **:** rough with divergent scales or processes; esp **:** having stiff spreading bracts ⟨a squarrose involucre⟩ — **squar·rose·ly** adv

¹squash \'skwäsh\ vb [MF esquasser] **1 :** to press or beat into a pulp or a flat mass **:** CRUSH ⟨squash a beetle⟩ **2 :** to put down **:** SUPPRESS, SQUELCH **3 :** to proceed with a splashing or squelching sound ⟨squashed through the ooze⟩ **4 :** SQUEEZE, PRESS ⟨squashed into the seat⟩ — **squash·er** n

²squash n **1 :** the sudden fall of a heavy soft body or the sound of such a fall **2 :** a squelching sound made by walking on oozy ground or in water-soaked boots **3 :** a crushed mass **4** Brit **:** a drink of the sweetened juice of a citrus fruit usu. with added soda water **5 :** SQUASH RACQUETS

³squash n, pl **squash·es** or **squash** [of Algonquian origin] **:** a fruit of any of various widely grown plants of the gourd family that are used esp. as vegetables and for livestock feed; also **:** a plant that bears squashes

squash bug n **:** a large black American bug injurious to squash vines

squash racquets n **:** a game played in a 4-wall court with a racket and a rubber ball

squash tennis n **:** a racket game resembling squash racquets played with an inflated ball the size of a tennis ball

squashy \'skwäsh-ē\ adj **squash·i·er; -est :** easily squashed **:** SOFT — **squash·i·ly** \'skwäsh-ə-lē\ adv — **squash·i·ness** \'skwäsh-ē-nəs\ n

¹squat \'skwät\ vb **squat·ted; squat·ting** [MF esquatir] **1 :** to sit or cause (oneself) to sit on one's haunches or heels **2 :** to occupy land as a squatter **3 :** CROUCH, COWER ⟨squatting hare⟩

²squat n **1 :** the act of squatting **2 :** a squatting posture

³squat adj **squat·ter; squat·test 1 :** CROUCHING **2 :** low to the ground; also **:** being short and thick — **squat·ly** adv — **squat·ness** n

squat·ter \'skwät-ər\ n **1 :** one that squats **2 a :** one that settles on land without right or title or payment of rent **b :** one that settles on public land under government regulation with the purpose of acquiring title

squat·ty \'skwät-ē\ adj **squat·ti·er; -est :** SQUAT, THICKSET

squaw \'skwo\ n [of Algonquian origin] **:** an American Indian woman

squaw·fish \-ˌfish\ n **:** any of several mostly freshwater fishes of western No. America

¹squawk \'skwok\ vi **1 :** to utter a harsh abrupt scream **2 :** to complain or protest loudly or vehemently — **squawk·er** n

²squawk n **1 :** a harsh abrupt scream **2 :** a noisy complaint

squawk box n **:** an intercom speaker

squaw man n **:** a white man married to an Indian woman and usu. living as one of her tribe

¹squeak \'skwēk\ vb [ME squeken] **1 :** to make a short shrill cry or noise **2 :** to pass, succeed, or win by a narrow margin ⟨barely squeaked by⟩ **3 :** to utter in a shrill piping tone

²squeak n **1 :** a sharp shrill cry or sound **2 :** ESCAPE ⟨a close squeak⟩ — **squeaky** \'skwē-kē\ adj

¹squeal \'skwēl\ vb [ME squelen] **1 :** to make a shrill cry or noise **2 a :** to turn informer **b :** COMPLAIN, PROTEST **3 :** to utter with or as if with a squeal — **squeal·er** n

²squeal n **:** a shrill sharp cry or noise

squea·mish \'skwē-mish\ adj [modif. of AF escoymous] **1 a :** easily nauseated **:** QUEASY **b :** affected with nausea **:** NAUSEATED **2 a :** easily shocked or disgusted **:** PRUDISH **b :** excessively fastidious or scrupulous in conduct or belief — **squea·mish·ly** adv — **squea·mish·ness** n

squee·gee \'skwē-ˌjē\ n **:** a blade of leather or rubber set on a handle and used for spreading or wiping liquid material on, across, or off a surface (as a window) — **squeegee** vt

¹squeeze \'skwēz\ vb [alter. of OE cwȳsan] **1 a :** to

exert pressure esp. on opposite sides of : COMPRESS **b** : to extract or emit under pressure ⟨*squeeze* juice from a lemon⟩ ⟨*squeeze* information from a person⟩ **c** : to force or thrust by compression : CROWD ⟨two more *squeezed* into the car⟩ **2 a** : to extort money, goods, or services from ⟨*squeezed* their tenants mercilessly⟩ **b** : to cause hardship to : OPPRESS **c** : to reduce the amount of ⟨rising costs *squeezed* profits⟩ **3** : to gain or win by a narrow margin — **squeez·er** *n*

²squeeze *n* **1 a** : an act or instance of squeezing : COMPRESSION **b** : HANDCLASP; *also* : EMBRACE **2** : financial pressure caused by narrowing margins (as between costs and selling price) or by shortages

squeeze bottle *n* : a bottle of flexible plastic that dispenses its contents by being pressed

squeeze play *n* : a baseball play in which a batter attempts to score a runner from third base by bunting

¹squelch \'skwelch\ *n* **1** : a sound of or as if of semi-liquid matter under suction ⟨the *squelch* of mud⟩ **2 a** : a retort that silences an opponent

²squelch *vb* **1 a** : to fall or stamp on so as to crush **b** : to completely suppress : QUELL, SILENCE **2** : to emit or cause to emit a sucking sound **3** : to splash through water, slush, or mire — **squelch·er** *n*

sque·teague \skwi-'tēg\ *n, pl* **squeteague** [of Algonquian origin] : any of various weakfishes

squib \'skwib\ *n* **1 a** : a small firecracker **b** : a broken firecracker that burns out with a fizz **2** : a short humorous or satiric writing or speech

¹squid \'skwid\ *n, pl* **squid** *or* **squids** : any of numerous 10-armed cephalopod mollusks with a long tapered body, a fin on each side, and usu. a slender internal chitinous support

²squid *vi* **squid·ded; squid·ding** : to fish with or for squid

squig·gle \'skwig-əl\ *n* [*squiggle* to wriggle, blend of *squirm* and *wriggle*] : a short wavy twist or line : CURLICUE

squill \'skwil\ *n* [L *squilla*, fr. Gk *skilla*] **1** : a Mediterranean bulbous herb of the lily family with narrow leaves and white flowers; *also* : its bulb used in medicine and in rat poisons **2** : SCILLA

¹squint \'skwint\ *adj* : affected with cross-eye

²squint *vi* **1 a** : to look in a squint-eyed manner **b** : to be cross-eyed **2** : to look or peer with eyes partly closed — **squint·er** *n*

³squint *n* : STRABISMUS; *also* : SQUINTING — **squinty** \'skwint-ē\ *adj*

squint-eyed \'skwint-'īd\ *adj* **1** : having eyes that squint **2** : looking askance (as in envy or malice)

squinting construction *n* : an ambiguous grammatical construction that contains a word or phrase (as *often* in "getting dressed often is a nuisance") interpretable as modifying either what precedes or what follows

¹squire \'skwī(ə)r\ *n* [MF *esquier*, fr. LL *scutarius* guard armed with a shield, fr. L *scutum* shield] **1** : one who bears the shield or armor of a knight **2 a** : a male attendant on a great personage **b** : GALLANT, ESCORT **3 a** : a member of the British gentry ranking below a knight and above a gentleman **b** : an owner of a country estate **c** : JUSTICE OF THE PEACE

²squire *vt* : to attend as a squire or escort ⟨*squired* the ladies around town⟩

squire·archy *or* **squir·archy** \'skwī(ə)r-,är-kē\ *n* **1** : the gentry or landed-proprietor class **2** : government by a landed gentry

squir·ish \'skwī(ə)r-ish\ *adj* : of, relating to, or having the characteristics of a squire

squirm \'skwərm\ *vi* **1** : to twist about like an eel or a worm **2** : to feel acutely embarrassed ⟨undeserved praise made him *squirm*⟩ — **squirmy** \'skwər-mē\ *adj*

squir·rel \'skwər(-ə)l, 'skwə-rəl\ *n, pl* **squirrels** *also* **squirrel** [MF *esquireul*, modif. of L *sciurus*, fr. Gk *skiouros*, fr. *skia* shadow + *oura* tail] **1** : any of various small or medium-sized rodents (family Sciuridae); *esp* : one with a long bushy tail and strong hind legs adapted to leaping from branch to branch **2** : the fur of a squirrel

¹squirt \'skwərt\ *vb* [ME *squirten*] **1** : to come forth, drive, or eject in a sudden rapid stream : SPURT ⟨water *squirted* from the nozzle⟩ ⟨*squirted* tobacco juice out of his mouth⟩

²squirt *n* **1 a** : an instrument (as a syringe) for squirting a liquid **b** : a small quick stream : JET **c** : the action of squirting **2** : an impudent youngster

squishy \'skwish-ē\ *adj* : being soft, yielding, and damp

SST *abbr* supersonic transport

-st — see -EST

¹stab \'stab\ *n* [ME *stabbe*] **1** : a wound produced by a pointed weapon **2** : a thrust of a pointed weapon **3** : EFFORT, TRY

²stab *vb* **stabbed; stab·bing** **1** : to wound or pierce by the thrust of a pointed weapon **2** : THRUST, DRIVE **3** : to thrust or give a wound with or as if with a pointed weapon — **stab·ber** *n*

¹sta·bile \'stā-,bīl, -,bil\ *adj* : not moving or fluctuating

²sta·bile \-,bēl\ *n* : a stable abstract sculpture or construction typically made of sheet metal, wire, and wood

sta·bil·i·ty \stə-'bil-ət-ē\ *n, pl* **-ties** : the quality, state, or degree of being stable: as **a** : the property of a body that causes it to return to its original condition when disturbed (as in balance) **b** : resistance to chemical change or to physical disintegration

sta·bi·lize \'stā-bə-,līz\ *vb* : to make or become stable, steadfast, or firm; *also* : to hold steady (as by means of a stabilizer) — **sta·bi·li·za·tion** \,stā-bə-lə-'zā-shən\ *n*

sta·bi·liz·er \'stā-bə-,lī-zər\ *n* : one (as a chemical or a device) that stabilizes something; *esp* : a fixed surface for stabilizing the motion of an airplane

¹sta·ble \'stā-bəl\ *n* [OF *estable*, fr. L *stabulum*, fr. *stare* to stand] **1** : a building in which domestic animals are sheltered and fed; *esp* : such a building having stalls or compartments ⟨horse *stable*⟩ **2 a** : the racehorses of one owner **b** : a group of athletes (as boxers) under one management — **sta·ble·man** \-mən, -,man\ *n*

²stable *vb* **sta·bled; sta·bling** \-b(ə-)liŋ\ : to put, keep, or live in or as if in a stable

³stable *adj* **sta·bler** \-b(ə-)lər\; **sta·blest** \-b(ə-)ləst\ [L *stabilis*, fr. *stare* to stand] **1 a** : firmly established : FIXED, STEADFAST ⟨a *stable* community⟩ **b** : not changing or fluctuating : UNVARYING ⟨a *stable* income⟩ **c** : ENDURING, PERMANENT ⟨*stable* institutions⟩ **2** : steady in purpose : CONSTANT ⟨*stable* personalities⟩ **3 a** : designed so as to develop forces that restore the original condition when disturbed from a condition of equilibrium or steady motion ⟨a *stable* airplane⟩ **b** : able to resist alteration in chemical, physical, or biological properties ⟨a *stable* compound⟩ ⟨*stable* emulsions⟩ — **sta·bly** \-b(ə-)lē\ *adv*

sta·ble·ness \'stā-bəl-nəs\ *n* : STABILITY

sta·bler \-b(ə-)lər\ *n* : one that keeps a stable

sta·bling *n* : accommodation for animals in a building ⟨*stabling* for six horses⟩

stab·lish \'stab-lish\ *vb, archaic* : ESTABLISH — **stab·lish·ment** \-mənt\ *n, archaic*

stac·ca·to \stə-'kät-ō\ *adj* [It, lit., detached] **1 a** : cut short or apart in performing : DISCONNECTED ⟨*staccato* notes⟩ **b** : marked by short clear-cut playing or singing of tones or chords ⟨a *staccato* style⟩ **2** : ABRUPT, DISJOINTED ⟨the *staccato* noises of a skipping motor⟩ — **staccato** *adv* — **staccato** *n*

¹stack \'stak\ *n* [ON *stakkr*] **1** : a large usu. conical pile (as of hay, straw, or grain) **2** : an orderly pile of objects usu. one on top of the other ⟨a *stack* of dishes⟩ **3** : a vertical pipe for carrying off smoke or vapor : CHIMNEY, SMOKESTACK **4 a** : a rack with shelves for storing books **b** *pl* : the part of a library in which books are stored in racks **5** : three or more rifles arranged together to stand in the form of a pyramid

²stack *vb* : to arrange in or form a stack : PILE ⟨*stacked* the dishes on the table⟩ — **stack·er** *n*

stack up *vi* : to measure up : COMPARE ⟨see how one dictionary *stacks up* with another⟩

sta·dia \'stād-ē-ə\ *n* : a surveying method for determination of distances and differences of elevation that uses a telescopic instrument having two horizontal lines through which the marks on a graduated rod are observed; *also* : the instrument or the rod used in this method

sta·di·um \'stād-ē-əm\ *n, pl* **-dia** \-ē-ə\ *or* **-di·ums** [L, fr. Gk *stadion*] **1** : an ancient Greek or Roman unit of length ranging from 607 to 738 feet **2 a** : a course for footraces in ancient Greece orig. one stadium in length; *also* : associated tiers of seats for spectators **b** *pl usu* **stadiums** : a large usu. unroofed building with tiers of seats for spectators at modern sports events

¹staff \'staf\ *n, pl* **staffs** \'stafs\ *or* **staves** \'stavz, 'stāvz\ [OE *stæf*] **1 a** : a pole, stick, rod, or bar used as a support or as a sign of authority ⟨a flag hanging limp on its *staff*⟩ ⟨a bishop's *staff*⟩; *also* : the long handle of a weapon (as a lance or pike) **b** : CLUB, CUDGEL **2** : something that props or sustains ⟨bread is the *staff* of life⟩ **3** : the five horizontal lines with their spaces on which music is written **4** *pl* **staffs** **a** : a group of persons serving as assistants to or employees under a chief ⟨a hospital *staff*⟩ **b** : a group of officers or aides appointed to assist a civil executive or commanding officer **c** : military officers not eligible for operational command but having administrative duties — **staff** *adj*

staff 3 with clef

²**staff** *vt* : to supply with a staff or with workers
staff·er \'staf-ər\ *n* : a member of a staff and esp. a newspaper staff
staff sergeant *n* : a noncommissioned officer ranking in the army above a sergeant and below a sergeant first class and in the air force above an airman first class and below a technical sergeant
¹**stag** \'stag\ *n, pl* **stag** *or* **stags** [OE *stagga*] **1** : an adult male red deer : the male of various large deer **2** : a male animal castrated after maturity **3 a** : a social gathering of men only **b** : a man who attends a dance or party unaccompanied by a woman
²**stag** *adj* : restricted to men : intended or suitable for a gathering of men only ⟨gave him a *stag* party⟩⟨*stag* movies⟩ — **stag** *adv*
stag beetle *n* : any of numerous mostly large beetles whose males have long and often branched mandibles
¹**stage** \'stāj\ *n* [OF *estage*, fr. (assumed) VL *staticum*, fr. L *stare* to stand] **1** : one of the horizontal levels into which a structure is divisible: as **a** : a floor of a building **b** : a shelf or layer esp. as one of a series **c** : any of the levels attained by a river above an arbitrary zero point ⟨flood *stage*⟩ **2** : a raised platform (as a scaffold or landing stage): as **a** : a part of a theater including the acting area **b** : the small platform on which an object is placed for microscopic examination **3 a** : a center of attention : scene of action **b** : the theatrical profession or art **4** : a division or a dividing point: as **a** : a stopping place esp. for a stagecoach providing fresh horses and refreshments **b** : the distance between stopping places in a journey ⟨planned a short *stage* for the next day⟩ **c** : a degree of advance attained (as in a process or undertaking) ⟨reached a *stage* in the lesson where he needed help⟩ ⟨an early *stage* of a disease⟩ **d** : one of the distinguishable periods of the growth and development of a plant or animal ⟨the larval *stage* of a beetle⟩; *also* : an individual in such a stage **e** : one complete process or step in a sequential or recurrent activity **5** : STAGECOACH **6** : a propulsion unit in a rocket with its own fuel and containers ⟨a three-*stage* missile⟩ — **on the stage** : in or into the acting profession
²**stage** *vt* : to produce or show publicly on or as if on the stage ⟨*stages* two plays each year⟩ ⟨*stage* a track meet⟩ ⟨*stage* a fake accident⟩
stage·coach \-,kōch\ *n* : a horse-drawn passenger and mail coach running on a regular schedule between established stops
stage·craft \-,kraft\ *n* : the effective management of theatrical devices or techniques
stage direction *n* : a description or direction written or printed in a play
stage fright *n* : nervousness felt at appearing before an audience
stage·hand \'stāj-,hand\ *n* : a stage worker who handles scenery, properties, or lights
stage manager *n* : a person who is in charge of the stage and physical aspects of a theatrical production
stag·er \'stā-jər\ *n* : an experienced person : VETERAN ⟨old *stager*⟩
stage·struck \'stāj-,strək\ *adj* : fascinated by the stage; *esp* : urgently desirous of becoming an actor
stage whisper *n* : a loud whisper by an actor audible to the spectators but supposed not to be heard by persons on the stage; *also* : any similar whisper
¹**stag·ger** \'stag-ər\ *vb* **stag·gered**; **stag·ger·ing** \'stag-(ə-)riŋ\ [ON *stakra*] **1 a** : to move unsteadily from side to side as if about to fall : REEL **b** : to cause to reel or totter **2 a** : to begin to doubt and waver : become less

confident **b** : to cause to doubt, waver, or hesitate **3** : to place or arrange in a zigzag or alternate but regular way — **stag·ger·er** \'stag-ər-ər\ *n*
²**stagger** *n* **1** *pl* : an abnormal condition of domestic mammals and birds associated with damage to the central nervous system and marked by incoordination and a reeling unsteady gait **2** : a reeling or unsteady gait or stance
stag·ger·ing *adj* : serving to stagger : ASTONISHING, OVERWHELMING — **stag·ger·ing·ly** \'stag-(ə-)riŋ-lē\ *adv*
stag·hound \'stag-,haund\ *n* : a hound formerly used in hunting large animals (as the stag)
stag·ing \'stā-jiŋ\ *n* **1** : SCAFFOLDING **2** : the putting of a play on the stage **3** : the assembling of troops or supplies in a particular place
stag·nant \'stag-nənt\ *adj* **1** : not flowing in a current or stream : MOTIONLESS; *also* : STALE **2** : DULL, INACTIVE ⟨*stagnant* business⟩ — **stag·nan·cy** \-nən-sē\ *n* — **stag·nant·ly** *adv*
stag·nate \'stag-,nāt\ *vi* [L *stagnare*, fr. *stagnum* body of standing water] : to be or become stagnant — **stag·na·tion** \stag-'nā-shən\ *n*
stagy \'stā-jē\ *adj* **stag·i·er**; **-est** : of or resembling the stage; *esp* : theatrical or artificial in manner — **stag·i·ly** \-jə-lē\ *adv* — **stag·i·ness** \-jē-nəs\ *n*
¹**staid** \'stād\ *adj* [fr. pp. of ³*stay*] **1** : SETTLED, FIXED **2** : GRAVE, SEDATE — **staid·ly** *adv* — **staid·ness** *n*
²**staid** *past of* STAY
¹**stain** \'stān\ *vb* [MF *desteindre* to discolor, lose color, fr. *des-* dis- + *teindre* to dye, fr. L *tingere*] **1** : to soil or discolor esp. in spots **2** : to suffuse with color (as by dyeing) : TINGE **3 a** : to taint with guilt, vice, or corruption **b** : to bring reproach on — **stain·a·ble** \'stā-nə-bəl\ *adj* — **stain·er** *n*
²**stain** *n* **1** : a soiled or discolored spot **2** : a taint of guilt : STIGMA **3** : a preparation (as of dye or pigment) used in staining; *esp* : one capable of penetrating the pores of wood — **stain·less** \'stān-ləs\ *adj* — **stain·less·ly** *adv*
stained glass *n* : glass colored or stained for use in windows
stainless steel *n* : steel alloyed with chromium and highly resistant to stain, rust, and corrosion
stair \'sta(ə)r, 'ste(ə)r\ *n* [OE *stæger*] **1** : a series of steps or flights of steps for passing from one level to another — often used in pl. ⟨ran down the *stairs*⟩ **2** : one step of a stairway
stair·case \-,kās\ *n* : a flight of stairs with the supporting framework, casing, and balusters
stair·way \-,wā\ *n* : one or more flights of stairs usu. with landings to pass from one level to another
stair·well \-,wel\ *n* : a vertical shaft around which stairs are located
¹**stake** \'stāk\ *n* [OE *staca*] **1** : a pointed piece (as of wood) driven or to be driven into the ground esp. as a marker or support; *also* : a similar upright support (as for the load of a vehicle) **2 a** : a post to which a person is bound for execution by burning **b** : execution by burning at a stake **3 a** : something that is staked for gain or loss **b** : the prize in a contest **c** : an interest or share in a commercial venture **4** : a Mormon territorial unit comprising a number of wards **5** : GRUBSTAKE — **at stake** : at issue : in jeopardy
²**stake** *vt* **1 a** : to mark the limits of by stakes ⟨*stake* out a mining claim⟩ **b** : to tether to a stake **c** : to fasten up or support (as plants) with stakes **2 a** : BET, HAZARD **b** : to back financially; *esp* : GRUBSTAKE
stake·hold·er \'stāk-,hōl-dər\ *n* : a person entrusted with the stakes of two or more bettors
Sta·kha·nov·ite \stə-'kän-ə-,vīt\ *n* [Alexei G. *Stakhanov* b1905 Russian miner] : a Soviet worker given an award for high output
sta·lac·tite \stə-'lak-,tīt\ *n* [Gk *stalaktos*, adj., dripping, fr. *stalassein* to let drip] : a deposit of calcium carbonate resembling an icicle hanging from the roof or sides of a cavern — **stal·ac·tit·ic** \,stal-,ak-'tit-ik\ *adj*
sta·lag·mite \stə-'lag-,mīt\ *n* [Gk *stalagmos*, n., dripping, fr. *stalassein* to let drip] : a deposit like an inverted stalactite found on the floor of a cave — **stal·ag·mit·ic** \,stal-,ag-'mit-ik\ *adj*
¹**stale** \'stāl\ *adj* [ME, aged (of ale)] **1** : tasteless, unpleasant, or unwholesome from age ⟨*stale* food⟩ **2** : tedious from familiarity ⟨*stale* news⟩ **3** : impaired in vigor or

ə abut; ə kitten; ər further; a back; ā bake; ä cot, cart; aù out; ch chin; e less; ē easy; g gift; i trip; ī life

effectiveness ⟨felt *stale* and listless after his illness⟩ —
stale·ly \'stāl-lē\ *adv* — **stale·ness** *n*
²stale *vb* : to make or become stale
¹stale·mate \'stāl-ˌmāt\ *n* [obs. *stale* stalemate (fr. AF *estale*) + E *mate*] **1** : a drawing position in chess in which only the king can move and although not in check can move only into check **2** : a drawn contest : DEADLOCK
²stalemate *vt* : to bring into a stalemate
Sta·lin·ism \'stäl-ə-ˌniz-əm, 'stal-\ *n* : the political, economic, and social principles and policies associated with Stalin; *esp* : the theory and practice of communism developed by Stalin from Marxism-Leninism and characterized esp. by rigid authoritarianism, widespread use of terror, and often by Russian nationalism — **Sta·lin·ist** \-nəst\ *n or adj*
¹stalk \'stȯk\ *vb* [OE *-stealcian;* akin to E *steal*] **1** : to hunt stealthily ⟨a *stalking* cat⟩ ⟨*stalk* deer⟩; *also* : to cover (an area) in stalking prey **2** : to walk with haughty or pompous bearing **3** : to move through or follow usu. in a persistent or furtive way ⟨famine *stalked* the land⟩ ⟨*stalk* a criminal⟩ — **stalk·er** *n*
²stalk *n* **1** : the act of stalking **2** : a stalking gait
³stalk *n* [ME *stalke*] **1** : a plant stem (as a petiole or stipe); *esp* : the main stem of an herbaceous plant **2** : a slender upright or supporting or connecting structure : PEDUNCLE ⟨the *stalk* of a crinoid⟩ — **stalked** \'stȯkt\ *adj* — **stalk·less** \'stȯk-ləs\ *adj* — **stalky** \'stȯ-kē\ *adj*
stalk·ing–horse \'stȯ-kiŋ-ˌhȯrs\ *n* **1** : a horse or a figure like a horse behind which a hunter stalks game **2** : something used to mask a purpose
¹stall \'stȯl\ *n* [OE *steall*] **1 a** : a compartment for a domestic animal in a stable or barn **b** : a space set off (as for parking a motor vehicle) **2 a** : a seat in the chancel of a church with back and sides wholly or partly enclosed **b** *Brit* : a front orchestra seat in a theater **3** : a booth, stand, or counter at which articles are displayed for sale **4** : a protective sheath for a finger or toe
²stall *vb* **1** : to put into or keep in a stall **2** : to bring or come to a standstill: as **a** : MIRE **b** : to cause (an engine) to stop usu. inadvertently **c** : to cause (an airplane or airfoil) to go into a stall
³stall *n* : the condition of an airfoil or airplane operating so that there is a breakdown of airflow and loss of lift with a tendency to drop
⁴stall *n* [alter. of E dial. *stale* lure] : a ruse to deceive or delay
⁵stall *vb* : to hold off, divert, or delay by evasion or deception
stal·lion \'stal-yən\ *n* [MF *estalon,* of Gmc origin; akin to E ¹*stall*] : a male horse; *esp* : one kept primarily as a stud
¹stal·wart \'stȯl-wərt\ *adj* [OE *stælwierthe* serviceable] **1** : STOUT, STURDY **2** : VALIANT, RESOLUTE — **stal·wart·ly** *adv* — **stal·wart·ness** *n*
²stalwart *n* **1** : a stalwart person **2** : an unwavering partisan (as in politics)
sta·men \'stā-mən\ *n, pl* **stamens** *also* **sta·mi·na** \'stā-mə-nə, 'stam-ə-\ [L *stamin-, stamen* warp, thread] : an organ of a flower that produces male gametes, consists of an anther and a filament, and is morphologically a sporophyll
stam·i·na \'stam-ə-nə\ *n* [L, pl. of *stamen* warp, thread, thread of life] : VIGOR, ENDURANCE
stam·i·nal \'stam-ən-ᵊl\ *adj* **1** : of, relating to, or constituting stamina **2** \'stā-mən-ᵊl, 'stam-ən-\ : of, relating to, or consisting of a stamen
sta·mi·nate \'stā-mə-nət, 'stam-ə-, -ˌnāt\ *adj* : having stamens; *esp* : having stamens but no pistils
¹stam·mer \'stam-ər\ *vb* **stam·mered; stam·mer·ing** \'stam-(ə-)riŋ\ [OE *stamerian*] : to make or utter with involuntary stops and repetitions in speaking — **stam·mer·er** \-ər-ər\ *n*
syn STAMMER, STUTTER mean to speak haltingly or stumblingly. STAMMER often suggests a temporary inhibition through fear, embarrassment, or shock ⟨breathlessly *stammered* out his thanks⟩ STUTTER suggests an habitual defect of speech although it may imply merely the effect of haste or excitement
²stammer *n* : an act or instance of stammering
¹stamp \'stamp; 1b & 2 are also 'stämp\ *vb* [ME *stampen*]

1 a : to pound or crush with a heavy instrument **b** : to strike or beat forcibly with the bottom of the foot **c** : to extinguish or destroy by or as if by stamping with the foot **2** : to walk heavily or noisily **3 a** : IMPRESS, IMPRINT ⟨*stamp* the bill *paid*⟩ **b** : to attach a stamp to ⟨*stamp* a letter⟩ **4** : to form with a stamp or die **5** : CHARACTERIZE — **stamp·er** *n*
²stamp *n* **1** : a device or instrument for stamping **2** : the impression or mark made by stamping **3** : a distinctive character, indication, or mark **4** : the act of stamping **5** : a stamped or printed paper affixed in evidence that a tax has been paid; *also* : POSTAGE STAMP
¹stam·pede \stam-'pēd\ *n* [AmerSp *estampida*] **1** : a wild headlong rush or flight of frightened animals **2** : a mass movement of people at a common impulse
²stampede *vb* **1** : to run away or cause (as cattle) to run away in panic **2** : to act together or cause to act together suddenly and without thought
stamping ground *n* : a favorite or habitual resort
stance \'stan(t)s\ *n* [MF *estance* position, posture, stay, fr. (assumed) VL *stantia,* fr. L *stant-, stans,* prp. of *stare* to stand] **1** : way of standing or being placed : POSTURE **2** : intellectual or emotional attitude
¹stanch \'stȯnch, 'stänch\ *vt* [MF *estancher*] : to stop the flowing of; *also* : to stop the flow of blood from (a wound) — **stanch·er** *n*
²stanch *var of* STAUNCH
¹stan·chion \'stan-chən, 2 is often -chəl\ *n* [MF *estanchon,* aug. of *estance* stance, stay, prop] **1** : an upright bar, post, or support **2** : a device that fits loosely around an animal's neck and limits forward and backward motion (as in a stall)
²stanchion *vt* : to provide with stanchions or support or secure with or as if with a stanchion

stanchion 2

¹stand \'stand\ *vb* **stood** \'stud\; **standing** [OE *standan*] **1 a** : to support oneself on the feet in an erect position **b** : to be a specified height when fully erect **c** : to rise to one's feet **2 a** : to take up or maintain a usu. specified position or posture ⟨*stand* aside⟩ ⟨*stands* first in his class⟩ ⟨where do we *stand* on this question⟩ **b** : to maintain one's position **3 a** : to be firm and steadfast in support or opposition **b** : to be in a particular state or situation ⟨*stands* accused⟩ **4** : to hold a course at sea ⟨*standing* away from the shore⟩ **5** *chiefly Brit* : to be a candidate : RUN **6 a** : to rest, remain, or set upright on a base or lower end ⟨the spade *stood* in the sod⟩ **b** : to occupy a place or location ⟨a house *standing* on a knoll⟩ **7 a** : to remain stationary or inactive ⟨the car *stood* in the garage for a week⟩ ⟨rainwater *standing* in stagnant pools⟩ **b** : to remain in effect ⟨the order still *stands*⟩ **8** : to exist in a definite form ⟨you must take or leave his offer as it *stands*⟩ **9 a** : to endure or undergo successfully : BEAR, WITHSTAND ⟨*stand* pain⟩ ⟨able to *stand* an operation⟩ ⟨the building *stood* the pressure of the storm⟩ **b** : to submit to ⟨*stand* trial⟩ **10** : to perform the duty of ⟨*stand* guard⟩ **11** : to pay for ⟨*stand* drinks⟩ — **stand·er** *n* — **stand by 1** : to be or remain present, available, or loyal to — **stand for 1** : to be a symbol for : REPRESENT **2** : to put up with : PERMIT — **stand on 1** : to depend upon **2** : to insist on — **stand one's ground** : to maintain one's position — **stand pat** : to oppose or resist change
²stand *n* **1** : an act or instance of stopping or staying in one place: as **a** : a halt for defense or resistance **b** : a stop made to give a theatrical performance **2 a** : a place or post where one stands **b** : a position esp. with respect to an issue **3 a** : the place occupied by a witness testifying in court **b** : a tier of seats for spectators of an outdoor sport or spectacle **c** : a raised platform (as for a speaker) **4** : a small often open-air structure for a small retail business **5** : a support (as a rack or table) on or in which something may be placed ⟨umbrella *stands*⟩ **6** : a group of plants growing in a continuous area ⟨a good *stand* of wheat⟩
¹stan·dard \'stan-dərd\ *n* [MF *estandard* rallying point, standard, of Gmc origin; akin to E *stand*] **1 a** : a figure adopted as an emblem by an organized body of people ⟨the eagle was the Roman legion's *standard*⟩ **b** : the per-

sonal flag of the ruler of a state **2 a :** something set up by authority or by general consent as a rule for measuring or as a model ⟨a *standard* of weight⟩ ⟨*standards* of good manners⟩ **b :** the basis of value in a monetary system **3 :** a structure that serves as a support ⟨a lamp *standard*⟩ **4 a :** an enlarged upper petal of a flower; *esp* : one of the three inner usu. erect and incurved petals of an iris **b :** an herb or shrub grown with a single erect stem crowned with a head of foliage

syn STANDARD, GAUGE, CRITERION denote a means of determining what a thing should be. STANDARD applies to any definite rule, principle, or measure established by authority or custom; GAUGE applies to a means of testing a particular dimension (as thickness, depth, or diameter) or a particular quality or aspect; CRITERION may apply to anything used as a test of quality whether or not it is formulated as a rule or principle

²standard *adj* **1 a :** constituting or conforming to a standard established by law or custom ⟨*standard* weight⟩ ⟨*standard* silver⟩ **b :** being sound and usable but not of special or the highest quality ⟨*standard* beef⟩ **2 :** regularly and widely used ⟨*standard* practice in the trade⟩ **3 :** having recognized and permanent value ⟨*standard* reference work⟩ **4 :** substantially uniform and well established by usage in the speech and writing of the educated and widely recognized as acceptable and authoritative

stan·dard-bear·er \-,bar-ər, -,ber-\ *n* **1 :** one that bears a standard or banner **2 :** the leader of an organization or movement

stan·dard·bred \-,bred\ *n* : any of an American breed of light trotting and pacing horses bred for speed and noted for endurance

standard conditions *n pl* : a temperature of 0°C and a pressure of 760 millimeters of mercury employed esp. in comparison of gas volumes

Standard English *n* : the English that with respect to spelling, grammar, pronunciation, and vocabulary is substantially uniform though not devoid of regional differences, that is well established by usage in the formal and informal speech and writing of the educated, and that is widely recognized as acceptable wherever English is spoken and understood

stan·dard·ize \'stan-dər-,dīz\ *vt* : to compare with or bring into conformity with a standard — **stan·dard·i·za·tion** \,stan-dərd-ə-'zā-shən\ *n*

standard of living : the necessities, comforts, and luxuries that a person or group is accustomed to

standard time *n* : the time established by law or by general usage over a region or country — compare

ALASKA STANDARD TIME, ATLANTIC STANDARD TIME, BERING STANDARD TIME, CENTRAL STANDARD TIME, EASTERN STANDARD TIME, HAWAII STANDARD TIME, MOUNTAIN STANDARD TIME, PACIFIC STANDARD TIME, YUKON STANDARD TIME

stand by \(')stan(d)-'bī\ *vi* **1 :** to be present; *also* : to remain apart or aloof **2 :** to be or to get ready to act **stand·by** \'stan(d)-,bī\ *n* : one available or to be relied upon esp. in emergencies

stand down *vi* : to leave the witness stand

stand·ee \stan-'dē\ *n* : one who occupies standing room

stand in \(')stan-'din\ *vi* : to act as a stand-in — **stand in with** : to be in a specially favored position with

stand-in \'stan-,din\ *n* **1 :** someone employed to occupy an actor's place while lights and camera are readied **2 :** SUBSTITUTE

¹stand·ing \'stan-diŋ\ *adj* **1 :** upright on the feet or base : ERECT ⟨*standing* grain⟩ **2 a :** not flowing : STAGNANT **b :** remaining at the same level, degree, or amount for an indeterminate period ⟨*standing* offer⟩ **c :** continuing in existence or use indefinitely : PERMANENT ⟨a *standing* army⟩ ⟨*standing* committees⟩ **3 :** done from a standing position ⟨*standing* jump⟩

²standing *n* **1 :** the action or position of one that stands **2 :** DURATION ⟨a quarrel of long *standing*⟩; *esp* : length of service or experience esp. as determining status ⟨postgraduate *standing*⟩ **3 :** position or comparative rank (as in society, a profession, or a competitive activity) ⟨had the highest *standing* on the test⟩ ⟨a man of little *standing* in his profession⟩; *also* : good reputation ⟨people of *standing* in the community⟩

standing room *n* : space for standing; *esp* : accommodation available for spectators or passengers after all seats are filled

standing wave *n* : a vibration of a body or physical system in which the amplitude varies from place to place, is constantly zero at fixed points, and has maxima at other points

stand off \(')stan-'dȯf\ *vb* : to keep or hold at a distance (as in social intercourse)

stand·off \'stan-,dȯf\ *n* **1 :** a standing off; *esp* : ALOOFNESS **2 a :** a counterbalancing effect **b :** TIE, DRAW, DEADLOCK

stand·off·ish \stan-'dȯ-fish\ *adj* : lacking cordiality

stand out \(')stan-'daȯt\ *vi* **1 a :** to appear as if in relief : PROJECT **b :** to be prominent or conspicuous **2 :** to be stubborn in resolution or resistance

stand·out \'stan-,daȯt\ *n* : one that is prominent or conspicuous esp. because of excellence

STANDARD TIME IN 50 PLACES THROUGHOUT THE WORLD WHEN IT IS 12:00 NOON IN NEW YORK

CITY	TIME	CITY	TIME
¹Amsterdam, Netherlands	6:00 P.M.	Montreal, Quebec	12:00 NOON
Anchorage, Alaska	7:00 A.M.	¹Moscow, U.S.S.R.	8:00 P.M.
Bangkok, Thailand	12:00 MIDNIGHT	Ottawa, Ontario	12:00 NOON
Berlin, Germany	6:00 P.M.	¹Paris, France	6:00 P.M.
Bombay, India	10:30 P.M.	Peking, China	1:00 A.M. next day
¹Brussels, Belgium	6:00 P.M.	Perth, Australia	1:00 A.M. next day
²Buenos Aires, Argentina	2:00 P.M.	Rio de Janeiro, Brazil	2:00 P.M.
Calcutta, India	10:30 P.M.	Rome, Italy	6:00 P.M.
Cape Town, So. Africa	7:00 P.M.	Saint John's, Newfoundland	1:30 P.M.
Chicago, Ill.	11:00 A.M.	Salt Lake City, Utah	10:00 A.M.
Delhi, India	10:30 P.M.	San Francisco, Calif.	9:00 A.M.
Denver, Colo.	10:00 A.M.	San Juan, Puerto Rico	1:00 P.M.
Djakarta, Indonesia	12:30 A.M. next day	Santiago, Chile	1:00 P.M.
Halifax, Nova Scotia	1:00 P.M.	Shanghai, China	1:00 A.M. next day
Hong Kong	1:00 A.M. next day	Singapore	12:30 A.M. next day
Honolulu, Hawaii	7:00 A.M.	Stockholm, Sweden	6:00 P.M.
Istanbul, Turkey	7:00 P.M.	Sydney, Australia	3:00 A.M. next day
Juneau, Alaska	9:00 A.M.	Tehran, Iran	8:30 P.M.
Karachi, Pakistan	10:00 P.M.	Tokyo, Japan	2:00 A.M. next day
London, England	5:00 P.M.	Toronto, Ontario	12:00 NOON
Los Angeles, Calif.	9:00 A.M.	Vancouver, British Columbia	9:00 A.M.
¹Madrid, Spain	6:00 P.M.	¹Vladivostok, U.S.S.R.	3:00 A.M. next day
Manila, Philippines	1:00 A.M. next day	Washington, D.C.	12:00 NOON
Mexico City, Mexico	11:00 A.M.	Wellington, New Zealand	5:00 A.M. next day
²Montevideo, Uruguay	2:00 P.M.	Winnipeg, Manitoba	11:00 A.M.

¹Time in France, Spain, Netherlands, Belgium, and the U.S.S.R. is one hour in advance of the standard meridians.
²Time in Argentina and Uruguay is one hour in advance of the standard meridian.

ə abut; ᵊ kitten; ər further; a back; ā bake; ä cot, cart; aú out; ch chin; e less; ē easy; g gift; i trip; ī life

stand·pat \'stan(d)-ˌpat\ *adj* : stubbornly conservative — **stand·pat·ter** \-ˌpat-ər\ *n*

stand·pipe \'stan(d)-ˌpīp\ *n* : a high vertical pipe or reservoir for water used to deliver water at uniform pressure

stand·point \-ˌpóint\ *n* : a position from which objects or principles are viewed and according to which they are compared and judged

stand·still \-ˌstil\ *n* : a state marked by absence of motion or activity : STOP ⟨business was at a *standstill*⟩

stand up *vb* **1** : to remain sound and intact **2** : to fail to keep an appointment with — **stand up for** : DEFEND — **stand up to** **1** : to meet fairly and fully **2** : to face boldly

stank *past of* STINK

stan·nic \'stan-ik\ *adj* [LL *stannum* tin] : of, relating to, or containing tin esp. with a valence of four

stannic chloride *n* : a liquid compound SnCL₄ that fumes in moist air and is used esp. as a mordant

stan·nous \'stan-əs\ *adj* : of, relating to, or containing tin esp. when bivalent

stan·za \'stan-zə\ *n* [It, a staying, abode, room, stanza, fr. (assumed) VL *stantia* stance] : a division of a poem consisting of a series of lines arranged together in a usu. recurring pattern of meter and rhyme — **stan·za·ic** \stan-'zā-ik\ *adj*

sta·pes \'stā-ˌpēz\ *n, pl* **stapes** *or* **sta·pe·des** \'stā-pə-ˌdēz\ [ML *staped-*, *stapes* stirrup] : the innermost ossicle of the ear of a mammal — compare INCUS, MALLEUS — **sta·pe·di·al** \stā-'pēd-ē-əl, stə-\ *adj*

staph \'staf\ *n* : STAPHYLOCOCCUS

staph·y·lo·coc·cus \ˌstaf-ə-lō-'käk-əs\ *n, pl* **-coc·ci** \-'käk-ˌ(s)ī, -(ˌ)(s)ē\ [Gk *staphylē* bunch of grapes] : any of various nonmotile spherical bacteria that occur esp. in irregular clusters and include parasites of skin and mucous membranes — **staph·y·lo·coc·cal** \-'käk-əl\ *adj* — **staph·y·lo·coc·cic** \-'käk-(s)ik\ *adj*

¹sta·ple \'stā-pəl\ *n* [OE *stapol* post] **1** : a U-shaped piece of metal usu. with sharp points to be driven into a surface to hold something (as a hook, rope, or wire) **2** : a U-shaped piece of thin wire to be driven through papers and bent over at the ends to fasten them together or to be driven through thin material to fasten it to something else ⟨fasten insulation to rafters with *staples*⟩

²staple *vt* **sta·pled; sta·pling** \-p(ə-)liŋ\ : to fasten with staples

³staple *n* [MD *stapel* emporium] **1** : a town established as a center for the sale or exportation of commodities in bulk **2** : a place of supply : SOURCE **3** : a chief commodity or product of a place **4 a** : something in widespread and constant use or demand **b** : the sustaining or principal element : SUBSTANCE **5** : RAW MATERIAL **6** : textile fiber (as wool or rayon) of relatively short length that when spun and twisted forms a yarn rather than a filament

⁴staple *adj* **1** : used, needed, or enjoyed constantly usu. by many individuals **2** : produced regularly or in large quantities **3** : PRINCIPAL, CHIEF ⟨*staple* crop⟩

sta·pler \'stā-plər\ *n* : a device that staples

¹star \'stär\ *n* [OE *steorra*] **1** : any natural luminous body visible in the sky except a planet, satellite, comet, or meteor; *esp* : a self-luminous gaseous celestial body (as the sun) of great mass whose shape is usu. spheroidal and whose size may be as small as the earth or larger than the earth's orbit **2 a** : a planet or a configuration of the planets that is held in astrology to influence one's destiny or fortune — usu. used in pl. **b** : FORTUNE, FAME; *also, obs* : DESTINY **3 a** : a conventional figure with five or more points that represents or resembles a star; *esp* : ASTERISK **b** : an often star-shaped ornament or medal worn as a badge of honor, authority, or rank or as the insignia of an order **4 a** : the principal member of a theatrical or operatic company **b** : an outstandingly talented performer **c** : a person who stands out among his fellows ⟨one of the brightest *stars* in the legal profession⟩ — **star·like** \-ˌlīk\ *adj*

²star *vb* **starred; star·ring** **1** : to sprinkle or adorn with stars **2 a** : to mark with a star as being superior **b** : to mark with an asterisk **3** : to present in the role of a star **4** : to play the most prominent or important role ⟨will produce and *star* in a new play⟩ **5** : to perform outstandingly ⟨*starred* at shortstop in the series⟩

³star *adj* **1** : of, relating to, or being a star **2** : being of outstanding excellence : PREEMINENT ⟨*star* athlete⟩

¹star·board \'stär-bərd\ *n* [OE *stēorbord*, fr. *stēor*-steering oar + *bord* ship's side] : the right side of a ship or airplane looking forward — compare PORT

²starboard *vt* : to turn or put (a helm or rudder) to the right

³starboard *adj* : of, relating to, or situated to starboard

¹starch \'stärch\ *vt* [ME *sterchen*; akin to E *stark*] : to stiffen with or as if with starch

²starch *n* **1** : a white odorless tasteless granular or powdery complex carbohydrate $(C_6H_{10}O_5)_x$ that is the chief storage form of carbohydrate in plants, is an important foodstuff, and is used also in adhesives and sizes, in laundering, and in pharmacy and medicine **2** : a stiff formal manner : FORMALITY **3** : resolute vigor : ENERGY

Star Chamber *n* : a court existing in England from the 15th century until 1641 with wide civil and criminal jurisdiction and marked by secret often arbitrary and oppressive procedures

starchy \'stär-chē\ *adj* **starch·i·er; -est 1** : containing, consisting of, or resembling starch **2** : marked by formality or stiffness — **starch·i·ness** *n*

star–crossed \'stär-ˌkróst\ *adj* : not favored by the stars : ILL-FATED

star·dom \'stärd-əm\ *n* **1** : the status or position of a star **2** : a body of stars

star·dust \'stär-ˌdəst\ *n* : a feeling or impression of romance, magic, or ethereality

¹stare \'sta(ə)r, 'ste(ə)r\ *vb* [OE *starian*] **1** : to look fixedly often with wide-open eyes ⟨*stare* at a stranger⟩ **2** : to show oneself conspicuously **3** : to have an effect upon by looking fixedly at a person — **star·er** *n*

²stare *n* : the act or an instance of staring

stare down *vt* : to cause to waver or submit by or as if by staring ⟨*stare down* a dog⟩

star·fish \'stär-ˌfish\ *n* : any of a class (Asteroidea) of echinoderms having a body of usu. five arms radially arranged about a central disk and feeding largely on mollusks (as oysters)

star·flow·er \-ˌflaù(-ə)r\ *n* : any of several plants (as a star-of-Bethlehem) having star-shaped 5-petaled flowers

star·gaze \-ˌgāz\ *vi* **1** : to gaze at stars **2** : to stare absentmindedly : DAYDREAM

starfish

star·gaz·er \-ˌgā-zər\ *n* : one that gazes at the stars: as **a** : ASTROLOGER **b** : ASTRONOMER

¹stark \'stärk\ *adj* [OE *stearc* stiff, strong] **1** : STRONG, ROBUST **2 a** : rigid in or as if in death **b** : UNBENDING, STRICT ⟨*stark* discipline⟩ **3** : SHEER, UTTER ⟨*stark* nonsense⟩ **4 a** : BARREN, DESOLATE ⟨a *stark* landscape⟩ **b** (1) : having few or no ornaments : BARE (2) : HARSH, UNADORNED ⟨*stark* realism⟩ **5** : sharply delineated — **stark·ly** *adv* — **stark·ness** *n*

²stark *adv* **1** : STARKLY **2** : WHOLLY, ABSOLUTELY ⟨*stark* mad⟩

star·less \'stär-ləs\ *adj* : being without stars and esp. visible stars

star·let \-lət\ *n* : a young movie actress being coached and publicized for starring roles

star·light \-ˌlīt\ *n* : the light given by the stars

star·ling \'stär-liŋ\ *n* [OE *stærlinc*, fr. *stær* starling] : any of a family of usu. dark gregarious passerine birds; *esp* : a dark brown or in summer glossy greenish black European bird naturalized and often a pest in the U.S.

star·lit \'stär-ˌlit\ *adj* : lighted by the stars

star of Beth·le·hem \-'beth-li-ˌhem, -lē-(h)əm\ : a star held to have guided the Magi to the infant Jesus in Bethlehem

star-of–Bethlehem *n* : any of a genus of plants of the lily family with 5-petaled usu. greenish white flowers

Star of Da·vid \-'dā-vəd\ : a hexagram used as a symbol of Judaism

starred \'stärd\ *adj* **1** : adorned with or as if with stars **2** : marked with or having the shape of a star **3** : affected in fortune by the stars

star·ry \'stär-ē\ *adj* **star·ri·er; -est 1** : adorned with stars ⟨*starry* heavens⟩ **2** : of, relating to, or consisting of the stars : STELLAR ⟨*starry* light⟩ **3** : shining like stars : SPARKLING ⟨*starry* eyes⟩ **4** : having parts arranged like the rays of a star : STELLATE

star·ry-eyed \,stär-ē-'īd\ *adj* : regarding an object or a prospect in an overly favorable light

Stars and Bars *n sing or pl* : the first flag of the Confederate States of America having three bars of red, white, and red respectively and a blue union with white stars in a circle representing the seceded states

Stars and Stripes *n sing or pl* : the flag of the United States having 13 alternately red and white horizontal stripes and a blue union with white stars representing the states

star-span·gled \'stär-,spaŋ-gəld\ *adj* : studded with stars

Star-Spangled Banner *n* : STARS AND STRIPES

¹start \'stärt\ *vb* [ME *sterten*] **1** : to move suddenly and sharply : react with a quick involuntary movement **2 a** : to issue with sudden force ⟨blood *starting* from the wound⟩ **b** : to come into being, activity, or operation : BEGIN **3** : to seem to protrude : PROTRUDE ⟨his eyes *started* from their sockets⟩ **4** : to become or cause to become loosened or forced out of place **5 a** : to begin a course or journey **b** : to range from a specified initial point ⟨the rates *start* at ten dollars⟩ **6** : to be or cause to be a participant in a game or contest **7** : to cause to leave a place of concealment : FLUSH **8** *archaic* : STARTLE, ALARM **9** : to bring up for consideration or discussion **10** : to bring into being ⟨*start* a rumor⟩ **11** : to begin the use or employment of ⟨*started* him at $75 a week⟩ **12 a** : to cause to move, act, or operate ⟨*start* the motor⟩ **b** : to care for during early stages ⟨well-*started* seedlings⟩ **13** : to perform the first stages or actions of ⟨*started* studying music⟩

²start *n* **1 a** : a quick involuntary bodily reaction **b** : a brief and sudden action or movement **c** : a sudden capricious impulse or outburst **2** : a beginning of movement, activity, or development **3** : a lead or handicap at the beginning of a race or competition **4** : a place of beginning **5** : the act or an instance of being a competitor in a race or a member of a starting lineup in a game

start·er \'stärt-ər\ *n* **1** : one who initiates or sets going: as **a** : an official who gives the signal to begin a race **b** : one who dispatches vehicles **2 a** : one that enters a competition **b** : one that begins to engage in an activity or process **3** : one that causes something to begin operating: as **a** : SELF-STARTER **b** : material containing microorganisms used to induce a desired fermentation **4** : something that is the beginning of a process, activity, or series

¹star·tle \'stärt-ᵊl\ *vb* **star·tled; star·tling** \'stärt-liŋ, -ᵊl-iŋ\ [ME *stertlen*, freq. of *sterten* to start] **1** : to move or jump suddenly as in surprise or alarm **2** : to frighten suddenly and usu. not seriously **3** : to cause to start

²startle *n* : a sudden mild shock (as of surprise or alarm) : START

star·tling *adj* : causing a momentary fright, surprise, or astonishment — **star·tling·ly** \'stärt-liŋ-lē, -ᵊl-iŋ-\ *adv*

star·va·tion \stär-'vā-shən\ *n* : the act or an instance of starving : the state of being starved

starve \'stärv\ *vb* [OE *steorfan* to die] **1** : to die or suffer greatly from lack of food **2** *archaic* : to die of or suffer greatly from cold **b** : to kill with cold **3** : to suffer or perish or cause to suffer or perish from deprivation ⟨a child *starving* for affection⟩ **4 a** : to kill or subdue with hunger **b** : to deprive of nourishment **c** : to cause to capitulate as if by depriving of nourishment

starve·ling \-liŋ\ *n* : one thin and weakened by or as if by lack of food

¹stash \'stash\ *vt* : to store in a usu. secret place for future use

²stash *n* **1** : hiding place : CACHE **2** : something stored or hidden away

sta·sis \'stā-səs, 'stas-əs\ *n, pl* **sta·ses** \'stā-,sēz, 'stas-,ēz\ [Gk, act or condition of standing, stopping, fr. *histasthai* to stand] **1** : a slowing or stoppage of a normal bodily flow (as of blood) or rhythmic movement (as of the intestine) **2** : a state of static balance or equilibrium among opposing tendencies or forces : STAGNATION

stat·a·ble *or* **state·a·ble** \'stāt-ə-bəl\ *adj* : capable of being stated

¹state \'stāt\ *n* [L *status* position, condition, state, fr.

stat-, stare to stand] **1 a** : mode or condition of being ⟨water in the gaseous *state*⟩ ⟨*state* of readiness⟩ **b** (1) : condition of mind or temperament ⟨in a highly nervous *state*⟩ (2) : a condition of abnormal tension or excitement **2 a** : social position; *esp* : high rank **b** (1) : elaborate or luxurious style of living (2) : formal dignity : POMP ⟨travel in *state*⟩ **3 a** : ESTATE 3 **b** *obs* : a person of high rank : NOBLE **4 a** : a politically organized body of people usu. occupying a definite territory; *esp* : one that is sovereign **b** : the political organization of such a body of people **5** : the operations or concerns of the government of a country **6** : one of the constituent units of a nation having a federal government ⟨the United *States* of America⟩ **7** : the territory of a state — **state·less** \-ləs\ *adj* — **state·less·ness** *n*

²state *adj* **1** : suitable or used for ceremonial or formal occasions ⟨*state* robes⟩ **2** : of or relating to a national state or to a constituent state of a federal government ⟨a *state* church⟩ **3** : GOVERNMENTAL ⟨*state* secrets⟩

³state *vt* **1** : to set by regulation or authority ⟨at *stated* times⟩ **2** : to express the particulars of esp. in words : REPORT; *also* : to express in words ⟨*state* an opinion⟩

state bank *n* **1** : NATIONAL BANK 1 **2** : a bank chartered by and operating under the laws of a state esp. of the U.S.

state capitalism *n* : an economic system in which capital is largely under government ownership and control while other economic relations are little changed from capitalism

state church *n, often cap S & C* : ESTABLISHED CHURCH

state college *n* : a college that is financially supported by a state government, often specializes in a branch of technical or professional education, and often forms part of the state university

state·craft \'stāt-,kraft\ *n* : the art of conducting state affairs : STATESMANSHIP

stated clerk *n* : an executive officer of a Presbyterian governing body (as a synod) ranking below the moderator

State flower *n* : a flowering plant selected as the floral emblem of a state of the U.S.

state·hood \'stāt-,hùd\ *n* : the condition of being a state; *esp* : the condition or status of one of the states of the U.S.

state·house \-,haùs\ *n* : the building in which a state legislature sits

state·ly \'stāt-lē\ *adj* **state·li·er; -est** **1 a** : HAUGHTY, UNAPPROACHABLE **b** : marked by lofty or imposing dignity **2** : impressive in size or proportions — **state·li·ness** *n* — **stately** *adv*

state·ment \'stāt-mənt\ *n* **1** : the act or process of stating or presenting orally or on paper **2** : something stated: as **a** : a report of facts or opinions **b** : a single declaration or remark : ASSERTION **3** : a brief summarized record of a financial account ⟨a monthly bank *statement*⟩

state·room \'stāt-,rüm, -,rùm\ *n* : a private room on a ship or on a railroad car

state's evidence *n, often cap S* **1** : one who gives evidence for the prosecution in U.S. state or federal criminal proceedings **2** : evidence for the prosecution in a criminal proceeding

States General *n* : ESTATES GENERAL

¹state·side \'stāt-,sīd\ *adj* : of or relating to the United States as regarded from outside its conterminous limits ⟨*stateside* mail⟩

²stateside *adv* : in or to the conterminous U.S.

states·man \'stāts-mən\ *n* : a person engaged in fixing the policies and conducting the affairs of a government; *esp* : one having unusual wisdom in such matters — **states·man·like** \-,līk\ *adj* — **states·man·ly** \-lē\ *adj* — **states·man·ship** \-,ship\ *n*

state socialism *n* : an economic system with limited socialist characteristics introduced by usu. gradual political action

states' rights *n pl* : all rights not vested by the Constitution of the U.S. in the federal government nor forbidden by it to the separate states

state·wide \'stāt-'wīd\ *adj* : including all parts of a state ⟨a *statewide* spelling contest⟩

¹stat·ic \'stat-ik\ *adj* [Gk *statikos* causing to stand, fr. *histanai* to cause to stand, weigh; akin to E *stand*] **1** : exerting force by reason of weight alone without motion ⟨*static* load⟩ **2** : of or relating to bodies at rest or forces in equilibrium **3** : showing little change **4 a** : characterized by a lack of movement, animation, or progres-

sion **b** : producing an effect of repose or quiescence **5** : STATIONARY ⟨a *static* gun⟩ **6** : of, relating to, producing, or being stationary charges of electricity (as those produced by friction or induction) **7** : of, relating to, or caused by radio static — **stat·i·cal·ly** \'stat-i-k(ə-)lē\ *adv*
²static *n* [*static electricity*] **:** disturbing effects produced in a radio or television receiver by atmospheric or electrical disturbances; *also* : the electrical disturbances producing these effects
stat·ics \'stat-iks\ *n* : a branch of mechanics dealing with the relations of forces that produce equilibrium among material bodies
¹sta·tion \'stā-shən\ *n* [L *station-, statio,* fr. *stare* to stand] **1** : the place or position in which something or someone stands or is assigned to stand or remain **2** : the act or manner of standing : POSTURE **3** : a stopping place: as **a** : a regular stopping place in a transportation route **b** : a building at such a stopping place : DEPOT **4 a** : a post or sphere of duty or occupation **b** : a stock farm or ranch of Australia or New Zealand **5** : STANDING, RANK ⟨a woman of high *station*⟩ **6** : a place for specialized observation and study of scientific phenomena ⟨a biological *station*⟩ ⟨a weather *station*⟩ **7 a** : a place established to provide a public service ⟨police *station*⟩ ⟨fire *station*⟩ ⟨power *station*⟩ **b** : a branch post office **8 a** : a complete assemblage of radio or television equipment for transmitting or receiving **b** : the place in which such a station is located
²station *vt* **sta·tioned; sta·tion·ing** \'stā-sh(ə-)niŋ\ **:** to assign to or set in a station or position : POST
sta·tion·ary \'stā-shə-,ner-ē\ *adj* **1** : fixed in a station, course, or mode : IMMOBILE ⟨a *stationary* laundry tub⟩ **2** : unchanging in condition : STABLE ⟨a *stationary* population⟩
station break *n* : a pause in a radio or television broadcast for announcement of the identity of the network or station
sta·tion·er \'stā-sh(ə-)nər\ *n* [ML *stationarius,* fr. *station-, statio* shop, fr. L, station] **1** *archaic* **a** : BOOKSELLER **b** : PUBLISHER **2** : one that sells stationery
sta·tion·ery \'stā-shə-,ner-ē\ *n* [*stationer*] **1** : materials (as paper, pens, and ink) for writing or typing **2** : letter paper usu. accompanied with matching envelopes
station house *n* : a police station
sta·tion·mas·ter \'stā-shən-,mas-tər\ *n* : an official in charge of the operation of a railroad station
stations of the cross *often cap S & C* **1** : a series of usu. 14 images or pictures esp. in a church that represent the stages of Christ's passion **2** : a devotion involving commemorative meditation before the stations of the cross
station wagon *n* : an automobile that has an interior longer than a sedan's, has one or more rear seats readily lifted out or folded to facilitate light trucking, has no separate luggage compartment, and often has a door at the rear end
sta·tis·tic \stə-'tis-tik\ *n* [back-formation fr. *statistics*] **:** a single term or datum in a collection of statistics
stat·is·ti·cian \,stat-ə-'stish-ən\ *n* : one versed in or engaged in compiling statistics
sta·tis·tics \stə-'tis-tiks\ *n sing or pl* [G *statistik* study of political data, fr. L *status* state] **:** a branch of mathematics dealing with the collection, analysis, interpretation, and presentation of masses of numerical data; *also* : a collection of such numerical data — **sta·tis·ti·cal** \-'tis-ti-kəl\ *adj* — **sta·tis·ti·cal·ly** \-ti-k(ə-)lē\ *adv*
stato- *comb form* [Gk *statos* stationary, fr. *histasthai* to stand] **1** : resting ⟨*stat*oblast⟩ **2** : equilibrium ⟨*stato*cyst⟩
stat·o·blast \'stat-ə-,blast\ *n* [Gk *blastos* bud] **:** a bud of a freshwater bryozoan that passes the winter in a chitinous envelope and develops into a new individual in spring
stat·o·cyst \-,sist\ *n* : an organ of equilibrium occurring esp. in invertebrate animals and consisting usu. of a fluid-filled vesicle in which are suspended calcareous particles
stat·o·lith \'stat-ᵊl-,ith\ *n* : a calcareous body in a statocyst — **stat·o·lith·ic** \,stat-ᵊl-'ith-ik\ *adj*
sta·tor \'stā-tər\ *n* [L, one that stands, fr. *stare* to stand] **:** a stationary part in a machine or about which a rotor revolves
stat·u·ary \'stach-ə-,wer-ē\ *n, pl* **-ar·ies** **1 a** : a branch of sculpture treating of figures in the round **b** : a collection of statues **2** : SCULPTOR — **statuary** *adj*
stat·ue \'stach-ü\ *n* [L *statua,* fr. *statuere* to set up, fr.

status position, state] **:** a likeness (as of a person or animal) sculptured, modeled, or cast in a solid substance (as marble or bronze)
Statue of Liberty **:** a large copper statue of a woman holding a torch aloft in her right hand located on Liberty Island in New York harbor
stat·u·esque \,stach-ə-'wesk\ *adj* : resembling a statue esp. in well-proportioned or massive dignity — **stat·u·esque·ly** *adv* — **stat·u·esque·ness** *n*
stat·u·ette \,stach-ə-'wet\ *n* : a small statue
stat·ure \'stach-ər\ *n* [L *statura,* fr. *stare* to stand] **1** : natural height (as of a person) in an upright position ⟨a man of average *stature*⟩ **2** : quality or status gained by growth, development, or achievement ⟨reached man's *stature*⟩
sta·tus \'stāt-əs, 'stat-\ *n* [L, fr. *stare* to stand] **1** : position or rank in relation to others : STANDING **2** : CONDITION, SITUATION ⟨the economic *status* of a country⟩
sta·tus quo \,stāt-əs-'kwō, ,stat-\ *n* [L, state in which] **:** the existing state of affairs
stat·ute \'stach-üt, -ət\ *n* [LL *statutum* law, regulation, fr. L, neut. of *statutus,* pp. of *statuere* to set up, fr. *status* position, state] **:** a law enacted by the legislative branch of a government **syn** see LAW
statute mile *n* : MILE 1
statute of limitations **:** a statute assigning a certain time after which rights cannot be enforced by legal action
stat·u·to·ry \'stach-ə-,tōr-ē, -,tȯr-\ *adj* **1** : of, relating to, or of the nature of a statute **2** : fixed by statute **3** : punishable by statute
¹staunch *var of* STANCH
²staunch \'stȯnch, 'stänch\ *adj* [MF *estanche,* fem. of *estanc,* fr. *estancher* to stanch] **1 a** : WATERTIGHT, SOUND ⟨a *staunch* ship⟩ **b** : strongly built : SUBSTANTIAL ⟨*staunch* foundations⟩ **2** : steadfast in loyalty or principle ⟨a *staunch* friend⟩ — **staunch·ly** *adv* — **staunch·ness** *n*
¹stave \'stāv\ *n* [back-formation fr. *staves*] **1** : a wooden stick **2** : one of the narrow strips of wood or narrow iron plates placed edge to edge to form the sides, covering, or lining of a vessel (as a barrel) or structure **3** : STANZA **4** : STAFF 3
²stave *vb* **staved** *or* **stove** \'stōv\; **stav·ing** **1** : to break in the staves of (a cask) **2** : to smash a hole in ⟨*stave* in a boat⟩; *also* : to crush or break inward ⟨*staved* in several ribs⟩ **3** : to drive or thrust away **4** : to become stove in— used of a boat or ship
stave off *vt* : to ward or fend off ⟨*stave off* trouble⟩
staves *pl of* STAFF
¹stay \'stā\ *n* [OE *stæg*] **:** a strong rope or wire used to steady or brace something (as a mast)
²stay *vb* **1** : to fasten (as a smokestack) with stays **2** : to go about : TACK
³stay *vb* **stayed** \'stād\ *or* **staid** \'stād\; **stay·ing** [MF *ester* to stand, stay, fr. L *stare*] **1** : to stop going forward **1** : PAUSE **2** : to continue in a place or condition : REMAIN **3** : to stand firm **4** : to take up residence : LODGE **5** : WAIT, DELAY **6** : to last out (as a race) **7** : CHECK, HALT ⟨*stay* an execution⟩ **8** : ALLAY, PACIFY
  syn STAY, REMAIN, ABIDE, LINGER mean to continue in a place. STAY often implies the status of a guest or visitor; REMAIN suggests a continuing after others have gone; ABIDE may imply either continuing indefinitely in a residence or waiting patiently for an outcome; LINGER implies failing to depart when it is time to do so
⁴stay *n* **1** : the action of halting : the state of being stopped **2** : a residence or sojourn in a place
⁵stay *n* [MF *estaie,* of Gmc origin; akin to E *stand*] **1 a** : something that serves as a prop : SUPPORT **b** : a thin firm strip (as of whalebone, steel, or plastic) used for stiffening a garment (as a corset) or part (as a shirt collar) **2** : a corset stiffened with stays — usu. used in pl.
⁶stay *vt* **1** : to provide physical or moral support for : SUSTAIN ⟨a helping hand to *stay* him from falling⟩ **2** : to fix on as a foundation : GROUND, REST
stay-at-home \'stā-ət-,hōm\ *n* : one not given to wandering or travel : HOMEBODY
staying power *n* : capacity for endurance : STAMINA
stay·sail \'stā-,sāl, -səl\ *n* : a fore-and-aft sail hoisted on a stay
stead \'sted\ *n* [OE *stede* place, position; akin to E *stand*] **1** : ADVANTAGE, SERVICE ⟨his knowledge of French stood

j joke; ŋ sing; ō flow; ȯ flaw; ȯi coin; th thin; th this; ü loot; u̇ foot; y yet; yü few; yu̇ furious; zh vision

him in good *stead*⟩ **2** : the office, place, or function ordinarily occupied or carried out by someone or something else ⟨acted in his brother's *stead*⟩
stead·fast \'sted-,fast\ *adj* [OE *stedefæst*, fr. *stede* place + *fæst* fixed, fast] **1 a** : firmly fixed in place **b** : not subject to change ⟨a *steadfast* purpose⟩ **2** : firm in belief, determination, or adherence : LOYAL ⟨*steadfast* friends⟩ — **stead·fast·ly** *adv* — **stead·fast·ness** \-,fas(t)-nəs\ *n*
stead·ing \'sted-iŋ\ *n* [ME *steding*, fr. *stede* place, farm] : a small farm or homestead
¹steady \'sted-ē\ *adj* **stead·i·er**; **-est** [obs. *stead* position, fr. OE *stede*] **1 a** : firm in position : FIXED **b** : direct or sure in movement : UNFALTERING **2 a** : REGULAR, UNIFORM **b** : not fluctuating or varying widely **3 a** : not easily moved or upset : RESOLUTE **b** : constant in feeling, principle, purpose, or attachment : DEPENDABLE **c** : not given to dissipation or disorderly behavior : SOBER — **stead·i·ly** \'sted-ᵊl-ē\ *adv* — **stead·i·ness** \'sted-ē-nəs\ *n*
syn STEADY, EVEN, UNIFORM mean not varying throughout its course or extent. STEADY implies lack of fluctuation or interruption of movement; EVEN suggests an absence of variation in quality or character; UNIFORM stresses the sameness or alikeness of all the elements of an aggregate, a series or a set
²steady *vb* **stead·ied**; **steady·ing** : to make, keep, or become steady
³steady *adv* **1** : in a steady manner : STEADILY **2** : on the course set — used as a direction to the helmsman of a ship
⁴steady *n, pl* **stead·ies** : one that is steady; *esp* : a boyfriend or girl friend with whom one goes steady
steady state *n* : a dynamically balanced condition of a system or process that when once established tends to persist
steady state theory *n* : a theory in astronomy: the universe has always existed and has always been expanding with hydrogen being created continuously — compare BIG BANG THEORY
steak \'stāk\ *n* [ON *steik*] **1 a** : a slice of meat cut from a fleshy part of a beef carcass **b** : a similar slice of a specified meat other than beef **2** : a cross-section slice of a large fish (as salmon)
steak knife *n* : a table knife having a steel blade often with a serrated edge
¹steal \'stēl\ *vb* **stole** \'stōl\; **sto·len** \'stō-lən\; **steal·ing** [OE *stelan*] **1** : to come or go secretly, unobtrusively, gradually, or unexpectedly ⟨*stole* out of the room⟩ **2 a** : to take and carry away without right and with intent to keep the property of another : ROB **b** : to appropriate entirely to oneself or beyond one's proper share ⟨*steal* the show⟩ **3 a** : to move, convey, or introduce secretly : SMUGGLE **b** : to accomplish or get in a concealed or unobserved manner ⟨*steal* a nap⟩ **4 a** : to seize, gain, or win by trickery, skill, or daring ⟨*stole* the ball from his opponent⟩ **b** : to gain a base in baseball by running without the aid of a hit or an error — **steal·er** *n*
²steal *n* **1** : the act or an instance of stealing **2** : something offered or purchased at a low price : BARGAIN
stealth \'stelth\ *n* [ME *stelthe*; akin to E *steal*] **1** : the act or action of going or proceeding furtively, secretly, or imperceptibly **2** : FURTIVENESS, SLYNESS
stealthy \'stel-thē\ *adj* **stealth·i·er**; **-est** **1** : slow, deliberate, and secret in action or character **2** : intended to escape observation : FURTIVE ⟨*stealthy* glances⟩ — **stealth·i·ly** \-thə-lē\ *adv* — **stealth·i·ness** \-thē-nəs\ *n*
¹steam \'stēm\ *n* [OE *stēam*] **1 a** : the invisible vapor into which water is converted when heated to the boiling point **b** : the mist formed by the condensation on cooling of water vapor **2 a** : water vapor kept under pressure so as to supply energy for heating, cooking, or mechanical work; *also* : the power so generated **b** : driving force : POWER ⟨arrived under their own *steam*⟩ **c** : emotional tension ⟨needed to let off a little *steam* after his exams⟩ **3 a** : STEAMER 2a **b** : travel by or a trip in a steamer
²steam *vb* **1** : to rise or pass off as vapor **2** : to give off steam or vapor **3** : to move or travel by or as if by the agency of steam **4** : to be angry : BOIL **5** : to expose to the action of steam (as for softening or cooking)
steam·boat \-,bōt\ *n* : a boat propelled by steam power
steam engine *n* : an engine driven by steam; *esp* : a reciprocating engine having a piston driven in a closed cylinder by steam

steam·er \'stē-mər\ *n* **1** : a vessel in which something is steamed **2 a** : a ship propelled by steam **b** : an engine, machine, or vehicle operated by steam
steamer rug *n* : a warm covering for the lap and feet esp. of a person sitting on a ship's deck
steamer trunk *n* : a trunk suitable for use in a stateroom of a steamer
steam fitter *n* : one that installs or repairs equipment (as steam pipes) for heating, ventilating, or refrigerating systems — **steam fitting** *n*
steam heating *n* : a system of heating in which steam generated in a boiler is piped to radiators
steam iron *n* : a pressing iron with a compartment holding water that is converted to steam by the iron's heat and emitted through the bottom onto the fabric being pressed
¹steam·roll·er \'stēm-'rō-lər\ *n* **1** : a steam-driven road roller **2** : a power or force that crushes opposition
²steamroller *also* **steam·roll** \-'rōl\ *vb* **1** : to crush with a steamroller **2 a** : to overwhelm by greatly superior force **b** : to exert crushing force or pressure with respect to **3** : to move or proceed with irresistible force
steam·ship \'stēm-,ship\ *n* : STEAMER 2a
steam shovel *n* : a power shovel operated by steam
steam table *n* : a table having openings to hold containers of cooked food over steam or hot water circulating beneath them
steam turbine *n* : a turbine that is driven by the pressure of steam discharged at high velocity against the turbine vanes
steamy \'stē-mē\ *adj* **steam·i·er**; **-est** : consisting of, characterized by, or full of steam — **steam·i·ly** \-mə-lē\ *adv* — **steam·i·ness** \-mē-nəs\ *n*
ste·ap·sin \stē-'ap-sən\ *n* [Gk *stear* fat + E *-psin* (as in *pepsin*)] : the lipase in pancreatic juice
ste·a·rate \'stē-ə-,rāt\ *n* : a salt or ester of stearic acid
ste·ar·ic acid \stē-,ar-ik-\ *n* [Gk *stear* hard fat, suet] : a white crystalline acid obtained by saponifying tallow or other hard fats containing stearin
ste·a·rin \'stē-ə-rən\ *n* **1** : an ester of glycerol and stearic acid **2** *also* **ste·a·rine** \-rən, -,rēn\ : the solid portion of a fat
ste·a·tite \'stē-ə-,tīt\ *n* [Gk *steatitis*, a precious stone, fr. *steat-, stear* fat] : a massive talc having a grayish green or brown color : SOAPSTONE
stedfast *var of* STEADFAST
steed \'stēd\ *n* [OE *stēda* stallion] : HORSE; *esp* : a spirited horse
¹steel \'stēl\ *n* [OE *style, stēle*] **1** : commercial iron that contains carbon in any amount up to about 1.7 percent as an essential alloying constituent and is distinguished from cast iron by its malleability and lower carbon content **2** : an instrument or implement of or characteristically of steel: as **a** : a thrusting or cutting weapon **b** : an instrument (as a fluted round rod with a handle) for sharpening knives **c** : a piece of steel for striking sparks from flint **3** : a hard cold quality characteristic of steel ⟨a man of *steel*⟩
²steel *vt* **1** : to overlay, point, or edge with steel **2 a** : to cause to resemble steel **b** : to fill with resolution or determination
³steel *adj* **1** : made of or resembling steel **2** : of or relating to the production of steel
steel guitar *n* : HAWAIIAN GUITAR
steel·head \'stēl-,hed\ *n* : a large silvery western No. American anadromous trout usu. held to be a race of the rainbow trout
steel wool *n* : an abrasive material composed of long fine steel shavings and used esp. for scouring and burnishing
steel·work \'stēl-,wərk\ *n* **1** : work in steel **2** *pl* : an establishment where steel is made — **steel·work·er** \-,wər-kər\ *n*
steely \'stē-lē\ *adj* **steel·i·er**; **-est** **1** : made of steel **2** : resembling steel — **steel·i·ness** *n*
steel·yard \'stēl-,yärd\ *n* : a balance on which something to be weighed is hung from the shorter arm of a lever and is balanced by a weight that slides along the longer arm which is marked with a scale

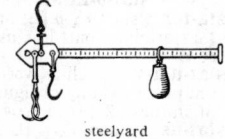

steelyard

¹steep \'stēp\ *adj* [OE *stēap*

high, deep] **1 :** making a large angle with the plane of the horizon **:** almost perpendicular **2 :** being or characterized by a very rapid decline or increase **3 :** difficult to accept, meet, or perform **:** EXCESSIVE ⟨*steep* prices⟩ — **steep·ly** *adv* — **steep·ness** *n*

syn PRECIPITOUS, SHEER: STEEP implies such sharpness of pitch that ascent or descent is very difficult ⟨*steep* hill⟩ ⟨*steep* roof⟩ PRECIPITOUS suggests an incline closely approaching the vertical ⟨*precipitous* canyon walls⟩ SHEER implies an unbroken perpendicular expanse ⟨*sheer* cliff⟩

²steep *n* **:** a precipitous place

³steep *vb* [ME *stepen*] **1 a :** to soak in a liquid (as for softening, bleaching, or extracting a flavor) at a temperature under the boiling point ⟨*steep* tea⟩ **b :** to undergo the process of soaking in a liquid **2 :** BATHE, WET **3 :** to saturate with or subject thoroughly to (some strong or pervading influence) ⟨*steeped* in learning⟩ — **steep·er** *n*

steep·en \'stē-pən\ *vb* **steep·ened; steep·en·ing** \'stēp-(ə-)niŋ\ **:** to make or become steeper

stee·ple \'stē-pəl\ *n* [OE *stēpel* tower] **:** a tall structure usu. having a small spire at the top and surmounting a church tower; *also* **:** a church tower — **stee·pled** \-pəld\ *adj*

stee·ple·chase \'stē-pəl-,chās\ *n* **:** a cross-country race by horsemen; *also* **:** a race over a course obstructed by obstacles (as hedges, walls, or hurdles) — **stee·ple·chas·er** \-,chā-sər\ *n*

stee·ple·jack \-,jak\ *n* **:** one whose work is building smokestacks, towers, or steeples or climbing up the outside of such structures to paint and make repairs

¹steer \'sti(ə)r\ *n* [OE *stēor*] **:** a domestic bull castrated before sexual maturity; *esp* **:** a young ox being raised for beef

²steer *vb* [OE *stīeran*] **1 :** to direct the course or the course of **:** GUIDE ⟨*steer* by the stars⟩ ⟨*steer* a boat⟩ ⟨*steer* a conversation⟩ **2 :** to set and hold to (a course) **3 :** to pursue a course of action **4 :** to be subject to guidance ⟨an automobile that *steers* well⟩ — **steer·a·ble** \'stir-ə-bəl\ *adj* — **steer·er** \'stir-ər\ *n* — **steer clear :** to keep entirely away ⟨*steer clear* of arguments⟩

³steer *n* **:** a hint as to procedure **:** TIP ⟨gave us a friendly *steer*⟩

steer·age \'sti(ə)r-ij\ *n* **1 :** the act or practice of steering; *also* **:** DIRECTION **2** [fr. its orig. being located near the rudder] **:** a section in a passenger ship for passengers paying the lowest fares

steering committee *n* **:** a managing or directing committee

steering gear *n* **:** a mechanism by which something is steered

steering wheel *n* **:** a handwheel by means of which one steers

steers·man \'sti(ə)rz-mən\ *n* **:** one who steers **:** HELMSMAN

steg·o·sau·rus \,steg-ə-'sȯr-əs\ *n* [NL, fr. Gk *stegos* roof + *sauros* lizard] **:** any of a genus of large armored dinosaurs of the Upper Jurassic rocks of Colorado and Wyoming

stein \'stīn\ *n* [prob. fr. G *steingut* stoneware, fr. *stein* stone + *gut* goods] **:** an earthenware mug esp. for beer commonly holding about a pint; *also* **:** the quantity of beer that a stein holds

stele \'stēl, 'stē-lē\ *n* [Gk *stēlē* pillar] **:** the usu. cylindrical central vascular portion of the axis of a vascular plant — **ste·lar** \'stē-lər\ *adj*

stel·lar \'stel-ər\ *adj* [L *stella* star; akin to E *star*] **1 a :** of or relating to the stars **:** ASTRAL ⟨*stellar* light⟩ **b :** composed of stars **2 :** of or relating to a theatrical or film star **3 a :** LEADING, PRINCIPAL ⟨a *stellar* role⟩ **b :** OUTSTANDING ⟨a *stellar* production⟩

stel·late \'stel-,āt\ *adj* **:** resembling a star esp. in shape ⟨a *stellate* leaf⟩ — **stel·late·ly** *adv*

stel·li·form \'stel-ə-,fȯrm\ *adj* **:** shaped like a star

stel·lu·lar \'stel-yə-lər\ *adj* [LL *stellula*, dim. of L *stella* star] **1 :** having the shape of a small star **2 :** radiating like a star

¹stem \'stem\ *n* [OE *stefn, stemn*] **1 a :** the main axis of a plant that develops buds and shoots instead of roots **b :** a plant part (as a petiole or stipe) that supports another **2 :** the bow or prow of a ship **3 :** a line of ancestry **:** STOCK; *esp* **:** a fundamental line from which others have arisen **4 :** the part of an inflected word that remains unchanged throughout an inflection **5 :** something felt to

resemble a plant stem **:** as **a :** a main or heavy stroke of a letter **b :** the short perpendicular line extending from the head of a musical note **c :** the part of a tobacco pipe from the bowl outward **d :** the cylindrical support of a piece of stemware (as a goblet) **e :** a shaft of a watch — **stem·less** \-ləs\ *adj* — **from stem to stern :** THROUGHOUT, THOROUGHLY

²stem *vt* **stemmed; stem·ming 1 :** to make headway against (as an adverse tide, current, or wind) **2 :** to go counter to (something adverse) ⟨*stemming* the tide of public opinion⟩

³stem *vb* **stemmed; stem·ming 1 :** to have or trace an origin or development **:** DERIVE ⟨illness that *stems* from an accident⟩ **2 :** to remove the stem from — **stem·mer** *n*

⁴stem *vb* **stemmed; stem·ming** [ON *stemma* to dam up] **1 :** to stop, check, or restrain by or as if by damming; *also* **:** to become checked or stanched **2 a :** to turn (skis) in stemming **b :** to retard oneself by forcing the heel of one ski or of both skis outward from the line of progress

⁵stem *n* **:** an act or instance of stemming on skis

¹stemmed \'stemd\ *adj* [¹*stem* + -*ed*] **:** having a stem

²stemmed *adj* [fr. pp. of ³*stem*] **:** having the stem removed ⟨*stemmed* berries⟩

stem·my \'stem-ē\ *adj* **:** abounding in stems ⟨*stemmy* hay⟩

stem·ware \'stem-,wa(ə)r, -,we(ə)r\ *n* **:** glass hollow ware mounted on a stem

stem–wind·ing \-'wīn-diŋ\ *adj* **:** wound by an inside mechanism turned by the knurled knob at the outside end of the stem ⟨a *stem-winding* watch⟩ — **stem–wind·er** \-dər\ *n*

stench \'stench\ *n* [OE *stenc*] **:** an extremely disagreeable smell **:** STINK

¹sten·cil \'sten(t)-səl\ *n* [MF *estanceler* to ornament with sparkling colors, fr. *estancele* spark, modif. of L *scintilla*] **1 :** an impervious material (as a sheet of paper, thin wax, or woven fabric) perforated with lettering or a design through which a substance (as ink, paint, or metallic powder) is forced onto a surface to be printed **2 :** a pattern, design, or print produced by means of a stencil **3 :** a printing process that uses a stencil

²stencil *vt* **-ciled** *or* **-cilled; -cil·ing** *or* **-cil·ling** \-s(ə-)liŋ\ **1 :** to produce by stencil **2 :** to mark or paint with a stencil

stencil paper *n* **:** strong tissue paper impregnated or coated (as with paraffin) for stencils

steno \'sten-ō\ *n, pl* **sten·os :** STENOGRAPHER

ste·nog·ra·pher \stə-'näg-rə-fər\ *n* **1 :** a writer of shorthand **2 :** one employed chiefly to take and transcribe dictation

ste·nog·ra·phy \-fē\ *n* [Gk *stenos* narrow] **1 :** the art or process of writing in shorthand **2 :** shorthand esp. written from dictation or oral discourse **3 :** the making of shorthand notes and subsequent transcription of them — **sten·o·graph·ic** \,sten-ə-'graf-ik\ *adj* — **sten·o·graph·i·cal·ly** \-'graf-i-k(ə-)lē\ *adv*

ste·no·sis \stə-'nō-səs\ *n, pl* **-no·ses** \-'nō-,sēz\ [Gk *stenoun* to narrow, fr. *stenos* narrow] **:** a narrowing or constriction of a bodily passage or orifice — **ste·nosed** \-'nōst\ *adj* — **ste·not·ic** \-'nät-ik\ *adj*

sten·tor \'sten-,tȯr, 'stent-ər\ *n* **1** *cap* **:** a Greek herald in the Trojan War noted for his loud voice **2 :** a person having a loud voice **3 :** any of a genus of trumpet-shaped ciliated protozoans

sten·to·ri·an \sten-'tȯr-ē-ən, -'tȯr-\ *adj* **:** extremely loud ⟨a *stentorian* voice⟩

¹step \'step\ *n* [OE *stæpe*] **1 :** a rest for the foot in ascending or descending: as **a :** STAIR **b :** a ladder rung **2 a** (1) **:** an advance or movement made by raising the foot and bringing it down elsewhere (2) **:** a combination of foot or foot and body movements constituting a unit or a repeated pattern (3) **:** manner of walking **:** STRIDE ⟨know a man by his *step*⟩ **b :** FOOTPRINT **c :** the sound of a footstep **3 a :** the space passed over in one step **b :** a short distance ⟨only a *step* away⟩ **c :** the height of one stair **4** *pl* **:** COURSE, WAY **5 a :** a degree, grade, or rank in a scale ⟨one *step* nearer graduation⟩ **b :** a stage in a process **6 :** a block supporting the heel of a mast **7 :** an action, proceeding, or measure often occurring as one in a series **8 :** pace with another **9 :** a steplike offset or part usu. occurring in a series **10 :** a musical scale degree — **step·like** \-,līk\ *adj* — **stepped** \'stept\ *adj*

²step *vb* **stepped; step·ping 1 a :** to move or take by raising the foot and bringing it down elsewhere or by moving each foot in succession ⟨*step* three paces⟩ ⟨*stepped* ashore⟩ **b :** DANCE   **2 a :** to go or traverse on foot ⟨WALK ⟨*step* outside⟩   **b :** to move briskly ⟨the horse *stepped* along⟩⟨kept us *stepping*⟩   **3 :** to press down with the foot ⟨*step* on a nail⟩   **4 :** to come as if at a single step ⟨*step* into a good job⟩   **5 :** to erect by fixing the lower end in a step   **6 :** to measure by steps ⟨*step* off 50 yards⟩   **7 :** to make steps in   **8 :** to construct or arrange in or as if in steps

step- *comb form* [OE *stēop-*] **:** related by virtue of a remarriage (as of a parent) and not by blood ⟨*step*parent⟩ ⟨*step*sister⟩

step·broth·er \'step-,brə<u>th</u>-ər\ *n* **:** a son of one's stepparent by a former marriage

step-by-step \,step-bə-'step\ *adj* **:** marked by successive degrees usu. of limited extent **:** GRADUAL

step·child \'step-,chīld\ *n* **:** a child of one's wife or husband by a former marriage

step·daugh·ter \-,dȯt-ər\ *n* **:** a daughter of one's wife or husband by a former marriage

step down \(')step-'daủn\ *vb* **1 :** to give up a position   **2 :** to lower the voltage of (a current) by means of a transformer — **step-down** \'step-,daủn\ *adj*

step·fa·ther \'step-,fä<u>th</u>-ər\ *n* **:** the husband of one's mother by a subsequent marriage

step-in \'step-,in\ *n* **1 :** an article of clothing that is put on by being stepped into   **2** *pl* **:** a woman's brief panties

step·lad·der \'step-,lad-ər\ *n* **:** a portable set of steps with a hinged frame for steadying

step·moth·er \-,mə<u>th</u>-ər\ *n* **:** the wife of one's father by a subsequent marriage

step out *vi* **1 :** to go away from a place usu. for a short distance and for a short time   **2 :** to go or march at a vigorous or increased pace   **3 :** to lead an active social life

step·par·ent \'step-,par-ənt, -,per-\ *n* **:** the husband or wife of one's mother or father by a subsequent marriage

steppe \'step\ *n* [Russ *step'*] **:** dry usu. rather level predominantly grass-covered land in regions of wide temperature range (as in southeastern Europe and parts of Asia)

stepladder

stepped-up \'stept-'əp\ *adj* **:** ACCELERATED, INTENSIFIED ⟨a *stepped-up* advertising program⟩

step·per \'step-ər\ *n* **:** one that steps (as a fast horse or a dancer)

step·ping-off place \,step-iŋ-'ȯf-\ *n* **1 :** the outbound end of a transportation line   **2 :** a place from which one departs

step·ping-stone \'step-iŋ-,stōn\ *n* **1 :** a stone on which to step (as in crossing a stream)   **2 :** a means of progress or advancement ⟨a *stepping-stone* to success⟩

step rocket *n* **:** a multistage rocket whose sections are fired successively

step·sis·ter \'step-,sis-tər\ *n* **:** a daughter of one's stepparent by a former marriage

step·son \-,sən\ *n* **:** a son of one's husband or wife by a former marriage

step stool *n* **:** a stool with one or two steps that often fold away beneath the seat

step up \(')step-'əp\ *vb* **1 :** to increase the voltage of (a current) by means of a transformer   **2 :** to increase, augment, or advance ⟨*step up* production⟩   **3 :** to come forward   **4 :** to receive a promotion — **step-up** \'step-,əp\ *adj*

step·wise \'step-,wīz\ *adj* **:** marked by steps **:** GRADUAL

-ster \stər\ *n comb form* [OE *-estre* female agent] **1 :** one that does or handles or operates ⟨spin*ster*⟩ ⟨tap*ster*⟩ ⟨team*ster*⟩   **2 :** one that makes or uses ⟨song*ster*⟩ ⟨pun*ster*⟩   **3 :** one that is associated with or participates in ⟨game*ster*⟩ ⟨gang*ster*⟩   **4 :** one that is ⟨young*ster*⟩

stere \'sti(ə)r, 'ste(ə)r\ *n* [F *stère*, fr. Gk *stereos* solid] — see METRIC SYSTEM table

stere- *or* **stereo-** *comb form* [Gk *stereos*] **1 :** solid ⟨*stereo*scope⟩   **2 :** stereoscopic ⟨*stereo*microscope⟩ ⟨*stereo*photograph⟩

ster·eo \'ster-ē-,ō, 'stir-\ *n* **1 :** STEREOTYPE   **2 a :** a stereoscopic method, system, or effect   **b :** a stereoscopic photograph   **3 a :** stereophonic reproduction   **b :** a stereophonic sound system — **stereo** *adj*

ster·e·og·ra·phy \,ster-ē-'äg-rə-fē, ,stir-\ *n* **:** stereoscopic

photography — **ster·eo·graph·ic** \,ster-ē-ə-'graf-ik, ,stir-\ *adj*

ster·eo·iso·mer \,ster-ē-ō-'ī-sə-mər, ,stir-\ *n* **:** any isomer in an example of stereoisomerism

ster·eo·iso·mer·ic \-,ī-sə-'mer-ik\ *adj* **:** of, relating to, or exhibiting stereoisomerism

ster·eo·isom·er·ism \-ī-'säm-ə-,riz-əm\ *n* **:** isomerism in which atoms are linked in the same order but differ in their spatial arrangement

ster·eo·mi·cro·scope \-'mī-krə-,skōp\ *n* **:** a microscope having a set of lenses for each eye to make an object appear in three dimensions

ster·e·o·phon·ic \,ster-ē-ə-'fän-ik, ,stir-\ *adj* **:** giving, relating to, or constituting a three-dimensional effect of reproduced sound

ster·e·op·ti·con \-ē-'äp-ti-kən\ *n* **:** a projector for transparent slides

ster·e·o·scope \'ster-ē-ə-,skōp, 'stir-\ *n* **:** an optical instrument with two eyeglasses for helping the observer to combine the images of two pictures taken from points of view a little way apart and thus to get the effect of solidity or depth

ster·e·o·scop·ic \,ster-ē-ə-'skäp-ik, ,stir-\ *adj* **1 :** of or relating to the stereoscope   **2 :** characterized by stereoscopy ⟨*stereoscopic* vision⟩ — **ster·e·o·scop·i·cal·ly** \-'skäp-i-k(ə-)lē\ *adv*

ster·e·os·co·py \,ster-ē-'äs-kə-pē, ,stir-\ *n* **:** the seeing of objects in three dimensions

ster·e·o·tax·is \,ster-ē-ə-'tak-səs, ,stir-\ *n* **:** a taxis in which contact esp. with a solid or rigid surface is the orienting factor

¹ster·e·o·type \'ster-ē-ə-,tīp, 'stir-\ *n* **1 :** a plate made by molding a matrix of a printing surface and making from this a cast in type metal   **2 :** something conforming to a fixed or general pattern and lacking individual distinguishing marks or qualities

²stereotype *vt* **1 :** to make a stereotype from   **2 a :** to repeat without variation   **b :** to develop a mental stereotype about — **ster·e·o·typ·er** *n*

ster·e·o·typed \-,tīpt\ *adj* **:** repeated by rote or without variation **:** lacking originality ⟨*stereotyped* response⟩ **syn** see TRITE

ster·e·o·ty·py \-,tī-pē\ *n* **:** the art or process of making or of printing from stereotype plates

ste·rig·ma \stə-'rig-mə\ *n, pl* **-ma·ta** \-mət-ə\ [Gk *stērigmat-*, *stērigma* prop, support] **:** a filament that supports a spore or chain of spores

ster·ile \'ster-əl\ *adj* [L *sterilis*] **1 :** not able to bear fruit, crops, or offspring **:** not fertile **:** BARREN ⟨*sterile* soil⟩   **2 :** free from living organisms and esp. microorganisms ⟨*sterile* dressing for a wound⟩   **3 :** deficient in ideas or originality — **ste·ril·i·ty** \stə-'ril-ət-ē\ *n*

  syn STERILE, BARREN mean lacking the power to produce offspring or bear fruit. STERILE implies inability through an organic defect; BARREN stresses lack of result or return for effort expended ⟨*barren* conquest⟩

ster·il·ize \'ster-ə-,līz\ *vt* **:** to make sterile: as   **a :** to deprive of the power of reproducing or germinating   **b :** to make powerless or useless   **c :** to free from living organisms (as bacteria) — **ster·il·i·za·tion** \,ster-ə-lə-'zā-shən\ *n* — **ster·il·iz·er** \'ster-ə-,lī-zər\ *n*

¹ster·ling \'stər-liŋ\ *n* [ME, silver penny] **1 :** British money   **2 :** sterling silver or articles of it

²sterling *adj* **1 :** of, relating to, or calculated in terms of British sterling   **2 a :** having a fixed standard of purity usu. defined legally as represented by an alloy of 925 parts of silver with 75 parts of copper ⟨*sterling* silver⟩   **b :** made of sterling silver   **3 :** conforming to the highest standard ⟨a man of *sterling* quality⟩ — **ster·ling·ly** \-liŋ-lē\ *adv* — **ster·ling·ness** *n*

sterling area *n* **:** a group of countries whose currencies are tied to the British pound sterling — called also *sterling bloc*

¹stern \'stərn\ *adj* [OE *styrne*] **1 :** hard and severe in nature or manner ⟨a *stern* judge⟩   **2 :** not inviting or attractive **:** FORBIDDING, GRIM   **3 :** showing severity **:** HARSH   **4 :** STOUT, RESOLUTE ⟨*stern* resolve⟩ **syn** see SEVERE — **stern·ly** *adv* — **stern·ness** \'stərn-nəs\ *n*

²stern *n* [ME, stern, rudder; akin to E ²*steer*] **1 :** the rear end of a boat   **2 :** a hinder or rear part

stern·most \'stərn-,mōst\ *adj* **:** farthest astern

stern·post \'stərn-ˌpōst\ *n* : the principal member at the stern of a ship extending from keel to deck

ster·num \'stər-nəm\ *n, pl* **sternums** *or* **ster·na** \-nə\ [Gk *sternon* chest, breastbone] : a compound ventral bone or cartilage connecting the ribs or the shoulder girdle or both — called also *breastbone* — **ster·nal** \'stərn-ᵊl\ *adj*

stern·ward \'stərn-wərd\ *or* **stern·wards** \-wərdz\ *adv (or adj)* : AFT, ASTERN

stern-wheel·er \-'hwē-lər\ *n* : a paddle-wheel steamer having a stern wheel instead of side wheels

ste·roid \'sti(ə)r-ˌóid, 'ste(ə)r-\ *n* : any of numerous compounds containing the carbon ring system of the sterols and including the sterols and various hormones and glycosides

ste·rol \'sti(ə)r-ˌól, 'ste(ə)r-, -ˌōl\ *n* [*cholesterol*] : any of various solid alcohols (as cholesterol) widely distributed in animal and plant lipides

ster·to·rous \'stərt-ə-rəs\ *adj* [NL *stertor* snoring sound, fr. L *stertere* to snore] : characterized by a harsh snoring or gasping sound ⟨*stertorous* breathing⟩ — **ster·to·rous·ly** *adv* — **ster·to·rous·ness** *n*

stet \'stet\ *vt* **stet·ted; stet·ting** [L, let it stand, fr. *stare* to stand] : to annotate (a word or passage) with or as if with the word *stet* in order to nullify a previous order to delete or omit from a manuscript or printer's proof

steth·o·scope \'steth-ə-ˌskōp, 'steth-\ *n* [Gk *stēthos* chest] : an instrument used for listening to sounds produced in the body and esp. in the chest — **steth·o·scop·ic** \ˌsteth-ə-'skäp-ik, ˌsteth-\ *or* **steth·o·scop·i·cal** \-'skäp-i-kəl\ *adj* — **steth·o·scop·i·cal·ly** \-i-k(ə-)lē\ *adv*

ste·ve·dore \'stē-və-ˌdōr, -ˌdór\ *n* [Sp *estibador*, fr. *estibar* to pack, fr. L *stipare* to press together] : a person whose work is to load and unload boats in port — **stevedore** *vb*

¹stew \'st(y)ü\ *vb* [MF *estuver* to steam] **1** : to boil slowly : cook in liquid over a low heat : SIMMER **2** : to become agitated or worried : FRET

²stew *n* **1** : food (as meat with vegetables) prepared by slow boiling **2** : a state of excitement, worry, or confusion

stew·ard \'st(y)ü-ərd, 'st(y)ü-(ə)rd\ *n* [OE *stīweard*, fr. *stig* hall, sty + *weard* ward] **1 a** : a person appointed to manage the domestic and business affairs of a large household or estate **b** : one actively concerned with the direction of the affairs of an organization (as a church or club) **2 a** : a person employed to supervise the provision and distribution of food (as on a ship) **b** : a worker who serves and attends the needs of passengers (as on a train or ship) — **stew·ard·ess** \-əs\ *n*

stew·ard·ship \-ˌship\ *n* : the office, duties, and obligations of a steward; *also* : the individual's responsibility to manage his life and property with proper regard to the rights of others

stew·pan \'st(y)ü-ˌpan\ *n* : a saucepan used for stewing

stib·nite \'stib-ˌnīt\ *n* [F *stibine* stibnite, fr. L *stibium* antimony, fr. Gk *stibi*, fr. Egypt *sṭm*] : a mineral Sb_2S_3 consisting of a sulfide of antimony occurring in lead-gray crystals of metallic luster and also massive

¹stick \'stik\ *n* [OE *sticca*] **1** : a cut or broken branch or twig esp. when dry and dead **2** : a long slender piece of wood: as **a** : a club or staff used as a weapon **b** : something suitable for use in compelling **c** : WALKING STICK **d** : an implement used for striking or propelling an object in a game **3** : something like a stick in shape, origin, or use ⟨a *stick* of dynamite⟩; *esp* : an airplane lever operating the elevators and ailerons **4** : a person who is dull, stiff, and lifeless **5** *pl* : remote or rural districts ⟨way out in the *sticks*⟩

²stick *vb* **stuck** \'stək\; **stick·ing** [OE *stician*] **1 a** : PIERCE, STAB **b** : to kill by piercing **2** : to cause (as a pointed instrument) to penetrate — used with *in, into,* or *through* ⟨*stuck* a needle in her finger⟩ **3 a** : to fasten by thrusting in **b** : IMPALE **c** : to push out, up, or under ⟨*stuck* out his hand⟩ **4** : to put or set in a specified place or position **5** : to attach by or as if by causing to adhere to a surface **6** : to halt the movement or action of **7** : BAFFLE, STUMP **8 a** : CHEAT, DEFRAUD **b** : to saddle with something disadvantageous or disagreeable **9** : to hold to something firmly by or as if by adhesion ⟨car *stuck* in the mud⟩ **10 a** : to remain in a place, situation, or environment **b** : to hold fast or adhere resolutely : CLING **c** : to keep close in a chase or competition **11 a** : to be unable

to proceed through fear or scruple **12** : PROJECT, PROTRUDE

syn STICK, ADHERE, COHERE mean to become or remain closely attached. STICK implies being embedded, glued, or cemented in or on something, and figuratively connotes obstinacy or persistence; ADHERE implies a growing together or a process like it, or figuratively a deliberate accepting and following; COHERE suggests a sticking together of parts so as to form a unified mass or whole

³stick *n* **1** : a thrust with a pointed instrument : STAB **2** : adhesive quality or substance

stick·a·bil·i·ty \ˌstik-ə-'bil-ət-ē\ *n* : ability to endure or persevere

stick around *vi* : to stay or wait about : LINGER

stick·er \'stik-ər\ *n* **1** : one (as a brier or knife) that pierces with a point **2 a** : one that adheres (as a bur) or causes adhesion (as glue) **b** : a slip of paper with gummed back that when moistened adheres to a surface

sticking plaster *n* : an adhesive plaster esp. for closing superficial wounds

stick insect *n* : any of various usu. wingless insects that are distantly related to the mantises and have a long round body resembling a stick

stick-in-the-mud \'stik-ən-thə-ˌməd\ *n* : one who is slow, old-fashioned, or unprogressive; *esp* : an old fogy

stick·le \'stik-əl\ *vi* **stick·led; stick·ling** \'stik-(ə-)liŋ\ [ME *stightlen,* freq. of *stighten* to arrange, fr. OE *stihtan*] **1** : to contend esp. stubbornly and usu. on insufficient grounds **2** : to feel often excessive scruples

stick·le·back \'stik-əl-ˌbak\ *n* [OE *sticel* goad; akin to E *stick*] : any of numerous small scaleless fishes having two or more free spines in front of the dorsal fin

stick·ler \'stik-(ə-)lər\ *n* : one who insists on exactitude or rigid propriety (as of conduct or dress)

stick·man \'stik-ˌman, -mən\ *n* : one who handles a stick: as **a** : one who supervises the play at a dice table, calls the decisions, and retrieves the dice **b** : a player in any of various games (as lacrosse) played with a stick

stick out *vb* **1 a** : PROJECT **b** : to be conspicuous **2** : to be persistent ⟨*stuck out* for higher wages⟩ **3** : to put up with : ENDURE

stick·pin \'stik-ˌpin\ *n* : an ornamental pin worn in a necktie

stick shift *n* : a manually operated gearshift mounted on the steering column or floor of an automobile

stick·tight \'stik-ˌtīt\ *n* : BUR MARIGOLD

stick-to-it·ive·ness \ˌstik-'tü-ət-iv-nəs\ *n* : dogged perseverance : TENACITY

stick up \(')stik-'əp\ *vt* : to rob at the point of a gun — **stick·up** \'stik-ˌəp\ *n*

stick·work \'stik-ˌwərk\ *n* **1** : the use (as in lacrosse) of one's stick in offensive and defensive techniques **2** : batting ability in baseball

sticky \'stik-ē\ *adj* **stick·i·er; -est 1 a** : ADHESIVE, GLUEY, VISCOUS **b** : coated with a sticky substance **2** : HUMID, MUGGY **3** : tending to stick ⟨*sticky* valve⟩ **4 a** : DISAGREEABLE, PAINFUL **b** : AWKWARD, STIFF — **stick·i·ly** \'stik-ə-lē\ *adv* — **stick·i·ness** \'stik-ē-nəs\ *n*

¹stiff \'stif\ *adj* [OE *stīf*] **1 a** : not easily bent : RIGID **b** : lacking in normal or usual suppleness or mobility ⟨*stiff* muscles⟩ ⟨a *stiff* glue⟩ ⟨*stiff* valves⟩ **2 a** : FIRM, RESOLUTE **b** : STUBBORN, UNYIELDING **c** : PROUD **d** : formally reserved in manner; *also* : lacking in ease or grace **3** : hard fought **4 a** : exerting great force : STRONG, VIGOROUS ⟨*stiff* wind⟩ **b** : POTENT ⟨a *stiff* dose⟩ **5 a** : HARSH, SEVERE ⟨a *stiff* penalty⟩ **b** : difficult to do or cope with ⟨a *stiff* task⟩; *also* : RUGGED ⟨*stiff* terrain⟩ **6** : EXPENSIVE, STEEP — **stiff·ly** *adv* — **stiff·ness** *n*

²stiff *adv* **1** : STIFFLY **2** : to an extreme degree : INTENSELY ⟨bored *stiff*⟩

³stiff *n* **1** : CORPSE **2** : PERSON, FELLOW, MAN ⟨lucky *stiff*⟩

stiff-arm \'stif-ˌärm\ *vb* : STRAIGHT-ARM — **stiff-arm** *n*

stiff·en \'stif-ən\ *vb* **stiff·ened; stiff·en·ing** \'stif-(ə-)niŋ\ : to make or become stiff or stiffer — **stiff·en·er** \-(ə-)nər\ *n*

stiff-necked \'stif-'nekt\ *adj* : arrogantly stubborn

¹sti·fle \'stī-fəl\ *n* [ME] : the joint next above the hock in the hind leg of a quadruped (as a horse) corresponding to the knee in man

²stifle *vb* **sti·fled; sti·fling** \-f(ə-)liŋ\ [ME *stuflen*] **1 a** : to kill by depriving of or die from lack of oxygen or air **b :** to smother by or as if by depriving of air ⟨*stifle* a fire⟩ ⟨a *stifling* room⟩ **2 a :** to keep in check by deliberate effort **:** REPRESS ⟨*stifle* his anger⟩ **b :** to restrain firmly or forcibly **:** DETER ⟨*stifled* the freedom of the press⟩ — **sti·fling·ly** \-f(ə-)liŋ-lē\ *adv*

stig·ma \'stig-mə\ *n, pl* **stig·ma·ta** \stig-'mät-ə, 'stig-mət-ə\ *or* **stigmas** [Gk *stigmat-, stigma* mark, brand, fr. *stizein* to tattoo] **1 a :** a mark of shame or discredit **:** STAIN **b :** an identifying mark or characteristic; *esp* **:** a specific diagnostic sign of a disease **2** *pl* **:** bodily marks or pains resembling the wounds of the crucified Christ **3 a :** a small spot, scar, or opening on a plant or animal **b :** the part of the pistil of a flower which receives the pollen grains and on which they germinate — see FLOWER illustration — **stig·mal** \'stig-məl\ *adj* — **stig·mat·ic** \stig-'mat-ik\ *adj* — **stig·mat·i·cal·ly** \-'mat-i-k(ə-)lē\ *adv*

stig·mat·ic \stig-'mat-ik\ *n* **:** one marked with stigmata

stig·ma·tize \'stig-mə-,tīz\ *vt* **:** to mark with a stigma; *esp* **:** to describe or identify in opprobrious terms — **stig·ma·ti·za·tion** \,stig-mət-ə-'zā-shən\ *n*

¹stile \'stīl\ *n* [OE *stigel;* akin to E *stair*] **:** a step or set of steps for passing over a fence or wall; *also* **:** TURNSTILE

²stile *n* **:** one of the vertical members in a frame or panel (as of a window or door) into which the secondary members are fitted

sti·let·to \stə-'let-ō\ *n, pl* **-tos** *or* **-toes** [It] **1 :** a slender dagger with a blade thick in proportion to its breadth **2 :** a pointed instrument for piercing holes for eyelets or embroidery

¹still \'stil\ *adj* [OE *stille*] **1 a :** MOTIONLESS **b :** not carbonated ⟨*still* wine⟩ **c :** of, relating to, or being an ordinary photograph as distinguished from a motion picture **2 a :** uttering no sound **:** QUIET **b :** SUBDUED, MUTED **3 a :** CALM, TRANQUIL **b :** free from noise or turbulence **:** PEACEFUL — **still·ness** *n*

sti-letto 1

²still *vb* **1 a :** ALLAY, CALM **b :** SETTLE **2 :** to make or become motionless or silent **:** QUIET

³still *adv* **1 :** without motion ⟨sit *still*⟩ **2** *archaic* **:** ALWAYS, CONTINUALLY **3** — used as a function word to indicate the continuance of an action or condition ⟨*still* lived there⟩ ⟨drink it while it's *still* hot⟩ **4 :** in spite of that **:** NEVERTHELESS ⟨those who take the greatest care *still* make mistakes⟩ ⟨the book is not perfect; *still,* it is very good⟩ **5 a :** EVEN ⟨a *still* more difficult problem⟩ **b :** in addition **:** YET ⟨won *still* another tournament⟩ **syn** see BUT

⁴still *n* **1 :** QUIET, SILENCE **2 :** a still photograph; *esp* **:** one of actors or scenes of a motion picture for publicity or documentary purposes

⁵still *n* [ME *stillen* to distill, short for *distillen*] **1 :** DISTILLERY **2 :** apparatus used in distillation

still alarm *n* **:** a fire alarm transmitted (as by telephone call) without sounding the signal apparatus

still·birth \'stil-,bərth\ *n* **:** the birth of a dead fetus

still·born \-'bórn\ *adj* **1 :** dead at birth **2 :** failing from the start **:** ABORTIVE — **still·born** \-,bórn\ *n*

still hunt *n* **:** a quiet pursuing or ambushing (as of game) — **still–hunt** \'stil-,hənt\ *vb*

still life *n, pl* **still lifes :** a picture consisting predominantly of inanimate objects

still·man \'stil-mən\ *n* **1 :** one who runs or operates a still **2 :** one who tends distillation equipment (as in an oil refinery)

¹still·ly \'stil-lē\ *adv* **:** CALMLY, QUIETLY

²stilly \'stil-ē\ *adj* **still·i·er; -est :** STILL

¹stilt \'stilt\ *n* [ME *stilte*] **1 a :** one of two poles each with a rest or strap for the foot used to elevate the wearer above the ground in walking **b :** a pile or post serving as one of the supports of a structure above ground or water level **2** *pl* **also stilt :** any of various long-legged three-toed birds related to the avocets that frequent inland ponds and marshes and nest in small colonies

²stilt *vt* **:** to raise on or as if on stilts

stilt·ed \'stil-təd\ *adj* **1 :** raised on or as if on stilts ⟨a *stilted* arch⟩ **2 :** stiffly formal **:** not easy and natural ⟨a *stilted* speech⟩ — **stilt·ed·ly** *adv* — **stilt·ed·ness** *n*

Stil·ton \'stilt-°n\ *n* [*Stilton,* England] **:** a blue-veined cheese with wrinkled rind made of whole cows' milk enriched with cream

stim·u·lant \'stim-yə-lənt\ *n* **1 :** an agent (as a drug)

that temporarily increases the functional activity or efficiency of a tissue or organ **2 :** STIMULUS ⟨a *stimulant* to trade⟩ **3 :** an alcoholic beverage — **stimulant** *adj*

s·tim·u·late \-,lāt\ *vb* [L *stimulare,* fr. *stimulus*] **1 :** to make active or more active **:** ANIMATE, AROUSE ⟨stimulate industry⟩ **2 :** to act toward as a physiological stimulus or stimulant **syn** see PROVOKE — **stim·u·la·tion** \,stim-yə-'lā-shən\ *n* — **stim·u·la·tive** \'stim-yə-,lāt-iv\ *adj* — **stim·u·la·tor** \-,lāt-ər\ *n* — **stim·u·la·to·ry** \-lə-,tōr-ē, -,tór-\ *adj*

stim·u·lus \'stim-yə-ləs\ *n, pl* **-li** \-,lī, -,lē\ [L, lit., goad] **1 :** something that rouses or incites to activity **:** INCENTIVE ⟨new *stimuli* to commerce and agriculture⟩ **2 :** an agent (as an environmental change) that directly influences the activity of living protoplasm (as by inducing a tropism or exciting a sensory organ)

¹sting \'stiŋ\ *vb* **stung** \'stəŋ\; **sting·ing** \'stiŋ-iŋ\ [OE *stingan*] **1 a :** to prick painfully esp. with a sharp or poisonous process **b :** to affect with or feel sharp, quick, and usu. burning pain or smart ⟨hail *stung* their faces⟩ **2 :** to cause to suffer acutely ⟨*stung* with remorse⟩ **3 :** OVERCHARGE, CHEAT ⟨got *stung* when he bought the gold-mine stock⟩ **4 :** to use a stinger

²sting *n* **1 a :** the act of stinging **b :** a wound or pain caused by or as if by stinging **2 :** STINGER **2 3 :** a stinging element, force, or quality — **sting·less** \'stiŋ-ləs\ *adj*

sting·a·ree \'stiŋ-ə-rē\ *n* **:** STINGRAY

sting·er \'stiŋ-ər\ *n* **1 :** one that stings; *esp* **:** a sharp blow or remark **2 :** a sharp organ of offense and defense (as of a bee or scorpion) usu. adapted to wound by piercing and injecting a poisonous secretion

stinging cell *n* **:** NEMATOCYST

stinging hair *n* **:** a glandular hair (as of a nettle) whose base secretes a stinging fluid

sting·ray \'stiŋ-,rā\ *n* **:** any of numerous rays with one or more large sharp barbed spines near the base of the whiplike tail capable of inflicting severe wounds

stin·gy \'stin-jē\ *adj* **stin·gi·er; -est 1 :** not generous or liberal **:** sparing or scant in giving or spending **2 :** SCANTY, MEAGER ⟨*stingy* portion⟩ — **stin·gi·ly** \-jə-lē\ *adv* — **stin·gi·ness** \-jē-nəs\ *n*

syn MISERLY: STINGY implies an unwillingness to spend, give, or share freely and a marked lack of generosity; MISERLY suggests a sordid avariciousness and a morbid pleasure in hoarding

¹stink \'stiŋk\ *vb* **stank** \'staŋk\ *or* **stunk** \'stəŋk\; **stunk; stink·ing** [OE *stincan*] **1 :** to give forth or cause to have a strong and offensive smell ⟨*stink* up a room⟩ **2 :** to be offensive or have something to an offensive degree **3 :** to be of wretchedly poor quality — **stink·er** *n*

²stink *n* **1 :** a strong offensive odor **:** STENCH **2 :** a public outcry against something offensive ⟨raised a *stink* about gambling⟩ — **stinky** \'stiŋ-kē\ *adj*

stink·bug \'stiŋk-,bəg\ *n* **:** any of various true bugs that emit a disagreeable odor

stink·horn \-,hórn\ *n* **:** an ill-smelling usu. erect fungus

¹stint \'stint\ *vb* [OE *styntan* to blunt, dull] **1 :** to limit in share or portion **:** cut short in amount ⟨*stint* the children's milk⟩ **2 :** to be sparing or frugal — **stint·er** *n*

²stint *n* **1 :** RESTRAINT, LIMITATION **2 :** a definite quantity of work assigned

³stint *n, pl* **stints** *also* **stint :** any of several small sandpipers

stipe \'stīp\ *n* [L *stipes* tree trunk, branch] **:** a short plant stalk; *esp* **:** one supporting a fern frond or the cap of a mushroom — **stiped** \'stīpt\ *adj*

sti·pend \'stī-,pend, -pənd\ *n* [L *stipendium,* fr. *stips* gift + *pendere* to pay] **:** a fixed sum of money paid periodically for services or to defray expenses **syn** see WAGE

¹sti·pen·di·ary \stī-'pen-dē-,er-ē\ *adj* **:** receiving or compensated by wages or salary ⟨a *stipendiary* curate⟩

²stipendiary *n, pl* **-ar·ies :** one who receives a stipend

¹stip·ple \'stip-əl\ *vt* **stip·pled; stip·pling** \'stip-(ə-)liŋ\ [D *stippelen* to spot, dot] **1 :** to engrave by means of dots and flicks **2 a :** to depict (as in paint or ink) by small short touches that together produce an even or softly graded shadow **b :** to apply (as paint) by repeated small touches **3 :** SPECKLE, FLECK — **stip·pler** \-(ə-)lər\ *n*

²stipple *n* **:** production of gradation of light and shade in graphic art by stippling; *also* **:** the effect produced

stip·u·late \'stip-yə-,lāt\ *vb* [L *stipulari*] **:** to make an agreement or arrange as part of an agreement; *esp* : to demand or insist on as a condition in an agreement — **stip·u·la·tor** \-,lāt-ər\ *n* — **stip·u·la·to·ry** \-lə-,tōr-ē, -,tȯr-\ *adj*

stip·u·la·tion \,stip-yə-'lā-shən\ *n* **1** : an act of stipulating **2** : something stipulated; *esp* : a condition required as part of an agreement

stip·ule \'stip-yül\ *n* [L *stipula* stalk, stubble] : either of a pair of small appendages at the base of the leaf in many plants — **stip·u·lar** \-yə-lər\ *adj* — **stip·u·late** \-yə-lət\ *or* **stip·uled** \-yüld\ *adj*

¹stir \'stər\ *vb* **stirred; stir·ring** [OE *styrian*] **1 a** : to make or cause to make an esp. slight movement or change of position **b** : to disturb the quiet of **2 a** : to disturb the relative position of the particles or parts of esp. by a continued circular movement; *also* : to treat something thus **b** : to mix by or as if by stirring **3** : BESTIR, EXERT **4** : to bring into notice or debate : RAISE ⟨the answer *stirred* our hopes⟩ **5 a** : to rouse to activity : INCITE, QUICKEN ⟨his emotions *stirred*⟩ ⟨had an easily *stirred* temper⟩ **b** : to call forth (as a memory) : EVOKE ⟨*stirring* thoughts of home⟩ **6** : to be active or busy — **stir·rer** *n*

²stir *n* **1 a** : a state of disturbance, agitation, or activity **b** : widespread notice and discussion : IMPRESSION **2 a** : a slight movement **b** : a stirring movement

stirp \'stərp\ *n* : a line descending from a common ancestor : STOCK, LINEAGE

stirps \'sti(ə)rps, 'stərps\ *n, pl* **stir·pes** \'sti(ə)r-,pās, 'stər-(,)pēz\ [L, lit., stem, stock] **1** : a branch of a family or the person from whom it is descended **2** : a group of related plants or animals

stir·ring \'stər-iŋ\ *adj* **1** : ACTIVE, BUSTLING **2** : ROUSING, INSPIRING

stir·rup \'stər-əp, 'stə-rəp\ *n* [OE *stigrāp*, lit., mounting rope] **1** : either of a pair of small light frames often of metal hung by straps from a saddle and used as a support for the foot of a horseback rider **2 a** : something (as a support or clamp) resembling or functioning like a stirrup **b** : STAPES

stirrup cup *n* **1** : a cup of drink (as wine) taken by a rider about to depart **2** : a farewell cup

¹stitch \'stich\ *n* [OE *stice;* akin to E *stick*] **1** : a local sharp and sudden pain esp. in the side **2 a** : one in-and-out movement of a threaded needle in sewing, embroidering, or suturing **b** : a portion of thread left in the material after one stitch **3** : a single loop of thread or yarn around an implement (as a knitting needle or crochet hook) **4** : a series of stitches **5** : a method of stitching — **in stitches** : in a state of uncontrollable laughter

²stitch *vb* **1 a** : to join with or as if with stitches **b** : to make, mend, or decorate with or as if with stitches **2** : to unite by means of staples **3** : to do needlework : SEW — **stitch·er** *n*

stithy \'stith-ē, 'stith-\ *n, pl* **stith·ies** [ON *stethi*] **1** : ANVIL **2** : SMITHY

sti·ver \'stī-vər\ *n* [D *stuiver*] **1 a** : a unit of value of the Netherlands equal to ½₀ gulden **b** : a coin representing one stiver **2** : something of little value

stoat \'stōt\ *n* [ME *stote*] : the European ermine esp. in its brown summer coat

stob \'stäb\ *n* [ME, stump] *chiefly dial* : STAKE, POST

¹stock \'stäk\ *n* [OE *stocc*] **1 a** : STUMP *archaic* : a log or block of wood **c** (1) : something without life or consciousness (2) : a dull, stupid, or lifeless person **2** : a supporting framework or part: as **a** *pl* : a timber frame with holes to contain the feet or feet and hands of an offender undergoing public punishment — compare PILLORY **b** : the wooden part by which a rifle or shotgun is held during firing **c** : the butt of an implement **3 a** : the main stem of a plant : TRUNK **b** : a plant or plant part united with a scion in grafting and supplying mostly underground parts to a graft **4** : the crosspiece of an anchor — see ANCHOR illustration **5 a** : the original (as a man, race, or language) from which others derive : SOURCE **b** : individuals or a group of common ancestry : FAMILY, LINEAGE,

stocks

STRAIN **6 a** (1) : the equipment of an establishment (2) : farm animals : LIVESTOCK **b** : a store or supply accumulated; *esp* : the inventory of goods of a merchant or manufacturer **7 a** : the capital that a firm employs in the conduct of business **b** : the proprietorship element in a corporation divided into shares giving to the owners an interest in its assets and earnings and usu. voting power **8** : any of a genus of herbs or subshrubs of the mustard family with racemes of usu. sweet-scented flowers **9** : a wide band or scarf worn about the neck esp. by some clergymen **10 a** : liquid in which meat, fish, or vegetables are simmered used as a basis for soup, stew, gravy, or sauce **b** : RAW MATERIAL **11 a** : the estimation in which one is held **b** : confidence placed in one **12** : the production and presentation of plays by a stock company

²stock *vb* **1** : to fit to or with a stock **2 a** : to provide with or acquire stock or a stock ⟨*stock* a family with linens⟩ **b** : to procure or keep a stock of ⟨a store that *stocks* only the finest goods⟩ **3** : to use (land) for pasture or put ⟨livestock⟩ on land to graze

³stock *adv* : COMPLETELY ⟨stood *stock* upright⟩ — usu. used in combination

⁴stock *adj* **1 a** : kept regularly in stock ⟨comes in *stock* sizes⟩ ⟨a *stock* model⟩ **b** : commonly used or brought forward : STANDARD ⟨the *stock* answer⟩ **2 a** : kept for breeding purposes ⟨a *stock* mare⟩ **b** : devoted to or used or intended for livestock ⟨*stock* train⟩ ⟨*stock* farm⟩

¹stock·ade \stä-'kād\ *n* [Sp *estacada,* fr. *estaca* stake, of Gmc origin; akin to E *stake*] **1** : a line of stout posts set firmly to form a defense **2 a** : an enclosure or pen made with posts and stakes **b** : an enclosure in which prisoners are kept

²stockade *vt* : to fortify or surround with a stockade

stock·bro·ker \'stäk-,brō-kər\ *n* : one that executes orders to buy and sell securities — **stock·brok·ing** \-,brō-kiŋ\ *or* **stock·bro·ker·age** \-k(ə-)rij\ *n*

stock car *n* **1** : an automotive vehicle of a model and type kept in stock for regular sales **2** : a racing car having the basic chassis of a commercially produced assembly-line model

stock clerk *n* : one that receives and handles merchandise and supplies in a stockroom

stock company *n* **1** : a corporation or joint-stock company whose capital is represented by stock **2** : a theatrical company attached to a repertory theater; *esp* : one without outstanding stars

stock exchange *n* **1** : a place where organized trading in securities is conducted **2** : an association of people organized to provide a market among themselves for the purchase and sale of securities

stock·fish \'stäk-,fish\ *n* : fish (as cod, haddock, or hake) dried hard in the open air without salt

stock·hold·er \-,hōl-dər\ *n* : an owner of stocks : SHAREHOLDER

stock·i·nette *or* **stock·i·net** \,stäk-ə-'net\ *n* [alter. of earlier *stocking net*] : a soft elastic usu. cotton fabric used esp. for bandages and infants' wear

stock·ing \'stäk-iŋ\ *n* [obs. *stock* to cover with a stocking, fr. E dial. *stock* stocking] **1 a** : a usu. knit close-fitting covering for the foot and leg **b** : SOCK **2** : something resembling a stocking; *esp* : a ring of distinctive color on the lower part of the leg of an animal — **stock·inged** \-iŋd\ *adj*

stocking cap *n* : a long knitted cone-shaped cap usu. with a tassel or pompon worn esp. for winter sports or play

stock-in-trade \,stäk-ən-'trād\ *n* **1** : the equipment necessary to or used in a trade or business **2** : something held to resemble the standard equipment of a tradesman or business

stock·man \'stäk-mən, -,man\ *n* : one occupied as an owner or worker in the raising of livestock

stock market *n* **1** : STOCK EXCHANGE 1 **2** : a market for stocks or for a particular stock

stock·pile \'stäk-,pīl\ *n* : a reserve supply esp. of something essential accumulated within a country for use during a shortage — **stockpile** *vb*

stock·pot \-,pät\ *n* : a pot in which soup stock is prepared

stock·room \-,rüm, -,rům\ *n* : a storage place for supplies or goods used in a business

stock-still \-'stil\ *adj* : very still : MOTIONLESS

stocky \'stäk-ē\ *adj* **stock·i·er; -est** : compact, sturdy, and relatively thick in build : THICKSET — **stock·i·ly** \'stäk-ə-lē\ adv — **stock·i·ness** \'stäk-ē-nəs\ n

stock·yard \'stäk-ˌyärd\ n : a yard for stock; esp : one in which livestock are kept temporarily for slaughter, market, or shipping

stodgy \'stäj-ē\ adj **stodg·i·er; -est** [stodge to stuff with food] **1** : having a thick gluey consistency : HEAVY ⟨stodgy bread⟩ **2** : moving in a slow plodding way esp. as a result of physical bulkiness **3** : having no excitement or interest : PROSAIC, DULL, COMMONPLACE **4** : extremely old-fashioned in attitude or outlook **5** : DRAB, DOWDY — **stodg·i·ly** \'stäj-ə-lē\ adv — **stodg·i·ness** \'stäj-ē-nəs\ n

sto·gie or **sto·gy** \'stō-gē\ n, pl **stogies** [by shortening & alter. fr. Conestoga, Pa.] : an inexpensive slender cylindrical cigar

¹sto·ic \'stō-ik\ n [Gk stōïkos, fr. Stoa Poikilē the Painted Portico, portico at Athens where Zeno, founder of the school, taught] **1** cap : a member of an ancient Greek school of philosophy holding that the wise man should be free from passion, unmoved by joy or grief, and submissive to natural law **2** : one who appears or claims to be indifferent to pleasure or pain

²stoic adj **1** cap : of or relating to the Stoics or their doctrines **2** : indifferent to pleasure or pain — **sto·i·cal** \'stō-i-kəl\ adj — **sto·i·cal·ly** \-i-k(ə-)lē\ adv

sto·i·cism \'stō-ə-ˌsiz-əm\ n **1** cap : the philosophy of the Stoics **2** : indifference to pleasure or pain : IM-PASSIVENESS

stoke \'stōk\ vb [D stoken] **1** : to stir up or tend (as a fire) : supply (as a furnace) with fuel **2** : to stir up a fire : tend the fires of furnaces **3** : to feed (as oneself) abundantly

stoke·hold \-ˌhōld\ n **1** : the space in front of the boilers of a ship from which the furnaces are fed **2** : a room containing a ship's boilers — called also fire·room \'fī(ə)r-ˌrüm, -ˌrum\

stoke·hole \'stōk-ˌhōl\ n **1** : the mouth to the grate of a furnace **2** : STOKEHOLD

stok·er \'stō-kər\ n **1** : one that tends a furnace; esp : one that tends a ship's steam boiler **2** : a machine for feeding a fire

sto·ke·sia \stō-'kē-zh(ē-)ə, 'stōk-sē-ə\ n [NL, fr. Jonathan Stokes d1831 English botanist] : an erect perennial herb widely grown for its showy usu. bluish flower heads — called also Stokes' aster \ˌstōks-(əz-)\

¹stole past of STEAL

²stole \'stōl\ n [OE, fr. L stola, fr. Gk stolē] **1** : a long loose garment : ROBE **2** : a long narrow band worn around the neck by bishops and priests and over the left shoulder by deacons in ceremonies **3** : a long wide scarf or similar covering worn by women usu. across the shoulders

stolen past part of STEAL

stol·id \'stäl-əd\ adj [L stolidus dull, stupid] : having or expressing little or no sensibility : not easily aroused or excited : UNEMOTIONAL **syn** see IMPASSIVE — **sto·lid·i·ty** \stä-'lid-ət-ē\ n — **stol·id·ly** \'stäl-əd-lē\ adv

sto·lon \'stō-lən, -ˌlän\ n [L stolon-, stolo branch, sucker] **1 a** : a horizontal branch from the base of a plant that produces new plants from buds at its tip or nodes (as in the strawberry) — called also runner **b** : a branch of fungus mycelium spreading over the surface of the medium on which it is growing **2** : an extension of the body wall (as of a hydrozoan) that develops buds giving rise to new zooids — **sto·lon·ate** \-lə-ˌnāt\ adj — **sto·lon·if·er·ous** \ˌstō-lə-'nif-(ə-)rəs\ adj

sto·ma \'stō-mə\ n, pl **sto·ma·ta** \-mət-ə\ also **stomas** [Gk stomat-, stoma mouth] : a small opening like a mouth in form or function; esp : one of those giving passage to moisture and gases through the epidermis of a leaf — **sto·ma·tal** \'stō-mət-ᵊl\ adj

¹stom·ach \'stəm-ək, -ik\ n [Gk stomachos gullet, esophagus, stomach, fr. stoma mouth] **1 a** : a pouch of the vertebrate alimentary canal into which food goes for further mixing and digestion after passing from the mouth by way of the esophagus and which communicates posteriorly with the duodenum **b** : an analogous cavity in an invertebrate animal **c** : the part of the body that contains the stomach : BELLY, ABDOMEN **2 a** : desire for food caused by hunger : APPETITE **b** : INCLINATION,

DESIRE **3** obs **a** : SPIRIT, VALOR **b** : PRIDE **c** : SPLEEN, RESENTMENT — **stomach** adj

²stomach vt **1** archaic : to take offense at **2** : to bear without overt reaction or resentment : put up with : BROOK

stom·ach·ache \-ˌāk\ n : pain in or in the region of the stomach

stom·ach·er \'stəm-ə-kər, -i-kər, -chər\ n : the front of a bodice usu. appearing between the laces of an outer garment (as in 16th century costume); also : a jeweled ornament for the front of a bodice

¹sto·mach·ic \stə-'mak-ik\ adj **1** : of or relating to the stomach ⟨stomachic vessels⟩ **2** : strengthening or stimulating to the stomach — **sto·mach·i·cal·ly** \-'mak-i-k(ə-)lē\ adv

²stomachic n : a stomachic medicine

sto·mate \'stō-ˌmāt\ n : a leaf stoma usu. together with its guard cells

sto·ma·tous \'stōm-ət-əs, 'stäm-\ adj : having stomata : being a stoma

sto·mo·dae·um or **sto·mo·de·um** \ˌstō-mə-'dē-əm\ n, pl **-daea** \-'dē-ə\ also **-dae·ums** or **-dea** also **-de·ums** : the anterior ectodermal part of the alimentary canal — **sto·mo·dae·al** \-'dē-əl\ adj

¹stomp \'stämp\ vb : STAMP — **stomp·er** n

²stomp n **1** : STAMP 4 **2** : a jazz dance characterized by heavy stamping

¹stone \'stōn\ n [OE stān] **1** : earth or mineral matter hardened in a mass **2** : a piece of rock not as fine as gravel ⟨throw stones⟩ **3** : rock used as a material esp. for building **4** : a piece of rock used for some special purpose (as for a monument at a grave) **5** : JEWEL, GEM ⟨precious stones⟩ **6** : CALCULUS 1 **7** : a hard stony seed or one (as of a plum) enclosed in a stony cover **8** pl usu **stone** : any of various units of weight; esp : an official British unit equal to 14 pounds

²stone vt **1** : to hurl stones at; esp : to kill by hitting with stones **2** : to remove the stones of (a fruit) **3 a** : to rub, scour, or polish (as leather or machined metal) with a stone **b** : to sharpen with a whetstone — **ston·er** n

³stone adj : of, relating to, or made of stone

Stone Age n : the first known period of prehistoric human culture characterized by the use of stone tools

stone-blind \'stōn-'blīnd\ adj : totally blind — **stone-blind·ness** \-'blīn(d)-nəs\ n

stone-broke \-'brōk\ adj : completely broke : lacking funds

stone cell n : SCLEREID

stone·chat \'stōn-ˌchat\ n : a common European singing bird related to the whinchat

stone·crop \-ˌkräp\ n : SEDUM; esp : a mossy evergreen creeping sedum with pungent leaves

stone·cut·ter \-ˌkət-ər\ n **1** : one that cuts, carves, or dresses stone **2** : a machine for dressing stone — **stone·cut·ting** \-ˌkət-iŋ\ n

stone-deaf \-'def\ adj : totally deaf — **stone-deaf·ness** n

stone fly n : any of an order (Plecoptera) of 4-winged insects with aquatic gilled carnivorous nymphs used by anglers for bait

stone fruit n : DRUPE

stone lily n : a fossil crinoid

stone·ma·son \'stōn-ˌmās-ᵊn\ n : a mason who builds with stone — **stone·ma·son·ry** \-rē\ n

stone wall n **1** chiefly North : a fence made of stones; esp : one built of rough stones without mortar to enclose a field **2** : an immovable block or obstruction (as in public affairs)

stone·ware \-ˌwa(ə)r, -ˌwe(ə)r\ n : an opaque glazed or unglazed pottery that is well vitrified and nonporous and that is commonly made from a single clay

stone·work \-ˌwərk\ n **1** : a structure or part built of stone : MASONRY **2** : the shaping, preparation, or setting of stone

stone·work·er \-ˌwər-kər\ n : STONECUTTER 1

stone·wort \-ˌwərt, -ˌwort\ n : any of a family of fresh-water green algae that resemble the horsetails and are often encrusted with calcareous deposits

stony also **ston·ey** \'stō-nē\ adj **ston·i·er; -est** **1** : abounding in or having the nature of stone : ROCKY **2 a** : insensitive as stone : PITILESS, HARDHEARTED **b** : manifesting no movement or reaction : DUMB, EX-

PRESSIONLESS **3** : STONE-BROKE — **ston·i·ly** \'stōn-ᵊl-ē\ *adv* — **ston·i·ness** \'stō-nē-nəs\ *n*

stood *past of* STAND

stooge \'stüj\ *n* **1** : an actor who usu. by asking questions prepares the way for a principal comedian's jokes **2** : one who slavishly follows or serves another — **stooge** *vi*

¹stool \'stül\ *n* [OE *stōl*] **1 a** : a seat without back or arms supported by three or four legs or by a central pedestal **b** : FOOTSTOOL **2 a** : a seat used while defecating or urinating **b** : a discharge of fecal matter **3 a** : a stump or plant crown from which shoots grow out **b** : a shoot or growth from a stool

²stool *vi* : to throw out shoots in the manner of a stool

stool pigeon *n* **1** : a pigeon used as a decoy to draw others within a net **2** : a person acting as a spy or informer for the police

¹stoop \'stüp\ *vb* [OE *stūpian*] **1** : to bend down or over **2** : to carry the head and shoulders or the upper part of the body bent forward **3** : to descend to doing something that is beneath one : degrade or debase oneself ⟨*stoop* to lying⟩ **4** : to descend swiftly on prey : SWOOP ⟨a hawk *stooping* after a mouse⟩

syn STOOP, CONDESCEND, DEIGN mean to descend from one's real or pretended level of dignity. STOOP may imply a descent from a relatively high plane to a much lower one morally or socially; CONDESCEND implies an unbending by one of high position to meet a social inferior on the same level; DEIGN suggests a haughty or reluctant condescension; CONDESCEND and DEIGN are used chiefly in irony or mild derision

²stoop *n* **1 a** : an act of bending the body forward **b** : a temporary or habitual forward bend of the back and shoulders **2** : the descent of a bird esp. on its prey **3** : a lowering of oneself either in condescension or in submission

³stoop *n* [D *stoep;* akin to E *step*] : a porch, platform, entrance stairway, or small veranda at a house door

¹stop \'stäp\ *vb* **stopped**; **stop·ping** [OE -*stoppian*, fr. L *stuppa* oakum, tow] **1** : to close an opening by filling or blocking it : PLUG ⟨nose *stopped* up by a cold⟩ ⟨*stopped* her ears with cotton⟩ **2** : CHECK, RESTRAIN ⟨*stop* a person from going⟩ **3** : to halt the movement or progress of ⟨*stop* the car⟩ **4** : to instruct one's banker not to honor or pay ⟨*stop* payment on a check⟩ **5** : to regulate the pitch of ⟨as a violin string⟩ by pressing with the finger **6** : to come to an end : cease activity or operation **7** : to make a visit : break one's journey ⟨*stopping* with friends for a week⟩

syn CEASE, DESIST, QUIT : STOP applies to action or progress or to what is operating or progressing and may imply suddenness or definiteness ⟨*stopped* at the red signal⟩ CEASE applies to states, conditions, or existence and may add a suggestion of gradualness and a degree of finality ⟨*ceased* raining during the night⟩ DESIST implies forbearance or restraint as a motive for stopping or ceasing ⟨*desisted* from further efforts to persuade him⟩ QUIT may stress either finality or abruptness in stopping or ceasing ⟨the engine faltered, sputtered, then *quit* altogether⟩

²stop *n* **1 a** : CESSATION, END **b** : a pause or breaking off in speech **2 a** : a graduated set of organ pipes of like kind and tone quality **b** : STOP KNOB **3 a** : something that impedes, obstructs, or brings to a halt : IMPEDIMENT, OBSTACLE **b** : the aperture of a camera lens **c** : STOPPER **4** : a device for arresting or limiting motion **5** : the act of stopping : the state of being stopped : CHECK **6 a** : a halt in a journey : STAY **b** : a stopping place **7 a** *chiefly Brit* : any of several punctuation marks **b** — used in telegrams and cables to indicate a period **8** : a consonant in the articulation of which there is a stage ⟨as in the *p* of *apt* or the *g* of *tiger*⟩ when the breath passage is completely closed

³stop *adj* : serving to stop : designed to stop ⟨*stop* line⟩ ⟨*stop* signal⟩ ⟨*stop* valve⟩

stop·cock \'stäp-,käk\ *n* : a cock for stopping or regulating flow ⟨as through a pipe⟩

stop down *vt* : to reduce the aperture of (a lens) by means of a diaphragm

¹stope \'stōp\ *n* : a usu. steplike excavation underground for the removal of ore

²stope *vb* : to mine by means of a stope

stop·gap \'stäp-,gap\ *n* : something that fills a gap : a temporary substitute or expedient : MAKESHIFT

stop knob *n* : one of the handles by which an organist draws or shuts off a particular stop

stop·light \'stäp-,līt\ *n* **1** : a light on the rear of a motor vehicle that is illuminated when the driver presses the brake pedal **2** : TRAFFIC SIGNAL

stop·over \'stäp-,ō-vər\ *n* **1** : a stop at an intermediate point in one's journey **2** : a stopping place on a journey

stop·page \'stäp-ij\ *n* : the act of stopping : the state of being stopped : HALT, OBSTRUCTION

¹stop·per \'stäp-ər\ *n* **1** : one that brings to a halt : CHECK **2** : one that closes, shuts, or fills up; *esp* : something (as a bung or cork) used to plug an opening

²stopper *vt* : to close or secure with or as if with a stopper

stop·ple \'stäp-əl\ *n* : something that closes an aperture : STOPPER, PLUG — **stopple** *vt*

stop street *n* : a street on which a vehicle must stop just before entering a through street

stop·watch \'stäp-,wäch\ *n* : a watch having a hand that can be started and stopped at will for exact timing (as of a race)

stor·a·ble \'stōr-ə-bəl, 'stȯr-\ *adj* : that may be stored ⟨*storable* commodities⟩ — **storable** *n*

stor·age \'stōr-ij, 'stȯr-\ *n* **1 a** : space or a place for storing **b** : an amount stored **2 a** : the act of storing : the state of being stored **b** : the price charged for storing something

storage cell *n* : a cell or connected group of cells that converts chemical energy into electrical energy by reversible chemical reactions and that may be recharged by passing a current through it in the direction opposite to that of its discharge — called also *storage battery*

sto·rax \'stōr-,aks, 'stȯr-\ *n* [LL, alter. of L *styrax*, fr. Gk] **1** : a resin related to benzoin and formerly used in incense **2** : a fragrant balsam from trees of the witch-hazel family

¹store \'stō(ə)r, 'stȯ(ə)r\ *vt* [OF *estorer* to construct, restore, store, fr. L *instaurare* to renew, restore] **1** : FURNISH, SUPPLY ⟨*store* a ship with provisions⟩ **2** : to lay away : ACCUMULATE ⟨*store* vegetables for winter use⟩ **3** : to deposit in a place (as a warehouse) for safekeeping or disposal ⟨*stored* her furniture until she found a new apartment⟩ **4** : to provide storage room for : HOLD

²store *n* **1** *pl* : accumulated supplies (as of food) ⟨a ship's *stores*⟩ **2** : something stored : STOCK ⟨a *store* of good jokes⟩ **3** : a place where goods are sold : SHOP **4** : VALUE, IMPORTANCE ⟨a family that set great *store* by tradition⟩ — **in store** : in a state of accumulation : in readiness for use

³store *adj* : purchased from a store : not made to order or homemade : READY-MADE ⟨*store* clothes⟩ ⟨*store* bread⟩

store cheese *n* : CHEDDAR

store·house \'stō(ə)r-,haủs, 'stȯ(ə)r-\ *n* **1** : a building for storing goods **2** : an abundant supply or source : REPOSITORY

store·keep·er \-,kē-pər\ *n* **1** : one who is in charge of stores **2** : one who keeps a store or shop

store·room \-,rüm, -,rùm\ *n* : a room for the storing of goods or supplies

store·wide \-'wīd\ *adj* : including all or most merchandise in a store ⟨a *storewide* sale⟩

¹sto·ried \'stōr-ēd, 'stȯr-\ *adj* **1** : decorated with designs representing scenes from story or history ⟨a *storied* tapestry⟩ **2** : having an interesting history : celebrated in story or history ⟨a *storied* castle⟩

²storied *or* **sto·reyed** *adj* : having stories ⟨a two-*storied* house⟩

stork \'stȯrk\ *n* [OE *storc*] : any of various large mostly Old World wading birds having a long stout bill and being related to the herons

stork's-bill \'stȯrks-,bil\ *n* : any of several plants of the geranium family with long beaked fruits

¹storm \'stȯrm\ *n* [OE; akin to E *stir*] **1 a** : a disturbance of the atmosphere attended by wind and usu. by rain, snow, hail, sleet, or thunder and lightning **b** : a heavy fall of rain, snow, or hail **c** : wind having a speed of 64 to 72 miles per hour **d** : a serious disturbance of an element of nature **2** : a disturbed or agitated state : a sudden or violent commotion **3 a** : PAROXYSM, CRISIS **b** : a sudden heavy influx or onset **4** : a heavy discharge

---

j joke;   **ŋ** sing;   **ō** flow;   **ȯ** flaw;   **ȯi** coin;   **th** thin;   **th̲** this;   **ü** loot;   **ù** foot;   **y** yet;   **yü** few;   **yù** furious;   **zh** vision

of objects (as missiles) or actions (as blows) **5 :** a tumultuous outburst **6 :** a violent assault on a defended position

²**storm** *vb* **1 a :** to blow with violence **b :** to rain, hail, snow, or sleet heavily **2 :** to attack by storm ⟨*stormed* ashore at zero hour⟩⟨*storm* the fort⟩ **3 :** to show violent emotion **:** RAGE ⟨*storming* at the unusual delay⟩ **4 :** to rush about violently ⟨the mob *stormed* through the streets⟩ **syn** see ATTACK

storm·bound \-,baund\ *adj* **:** cut off from outside communication by a storm or its effects **:** stopped or delayed by storms

storm door *n* **:** an additional door placed outside an ordinary outside door for protection against severe weather

storm petrel *n* **:** any of various small petrels; *esp* **:** a small sooty black white-marked petrel frequenting the north Atlantic and Mediterranean — called also *stormy petrel*

storm trooper *n* **:** a member of a private Nazi army notorious for aggressiveness, violence, and brutality

storm window *n* **:** a framed glass placed outside an ordinary window as a protection against severe weather — called also *storm sash*

stormy \'stór-mē\ *adj* **storm·i·er; -est 1 :** relating to, characterized by, or indicative of a storm ⟨a *stormy* day⟩ ⟨*stormy* skies⟩ **2 :** marked by turmoil or fury **:** PASSIONATE, TURBULENT ⟨a *stormy* life⟩ ⟨a *stormy* conference⟩ — **storm·i·ly** \-mə-lē\ *adv* — **storm·i·ness** \-mē-nəs\ *n*

stormy petrel *n* **1 :** STORM PETREL **2 :** one fond of strife **:** a harbinger of trouble

¹**sto·ry** \'stōr-ē, 'stór-\ *n, pl* **stories** [OF *estorie*, fr. L *historia* history] **1 a :** an account of incidents or events **b :** ANECDOTE **2 a :** a fictional narrative shorter than a novel; *esp* **:** SHORT STORY **b :** the plot of a narrative or dramatic work **3 :** a widely circulated rumor **4 :** LIE, FALSEHOOD **5 :** LEGEND, ROMANCE **6 :** a news article or broadcast

²**story** *vt* **sto·ried; sto·ry·ing 1** *archaic* **:** to narrate or describe in story **2 :** to adorn with a story or a scene from history

³**story** *or* **sto·rey** *n, pl* **stories** *or* **storeys** [ML *historia* picture, story of a building, fr. L, history; prob. fr. pictures adorning the windows of medieval buildings] **1 :** a set of rooms on one floor level of a building **2 :** a horizontal division of a building's exterior not necessarily corresponding exactly with the stories within

sto·ry·book \'stōr-ē-,búk, 'stór-\ *n* **:** a book of stories (as for children)

sto·ry·tell·er \-,tel-ər\ *n* **:** a teller of stories: as **a :** a relator of anecdotes **b :** a reciter of tales (as in a children's library) **c :** FIBBER, LIAR **d :** a writer of stories — **sto·ry·tell·ing** \-,tel-iŋ\ *adj or n*

stoup \'stüp\ *n* [ME *stowp*] **1 :** a container for beverages (as a large glass or a tankard) **2 :** a basin for holy water at the entrance of a church

¹**stout** \'staut\ *adj* [OF *estout*, of Gmc origin] **1 :** strong of character: as **a :** BRAVE, BOLD **b :** FIRM, DETERMINED **2 :** physically or materially strong: **a :** STURDY, VIGOROUS **b :** STAUNCH, ENDURING **c :** SOLID, SUBSTANTIAL **3 :** FORCEFUL **4 a :** bulky in body **:** THICKSET **b :** CORPULENT, FAT, FLESHY — **stout·ish** \-ish\ *adj* — **stout·ly** *adv* — **stout·ness** *n*

stoup 2

²**stout** *n* **1 :** a heavy-bodied dark brew made with roasted malt and a relatively high percentage of hops **2 a :** a fat person **b :** a clothing size designed for the large figure

stout·en \'staut-°n\ *vb* **stout·ened; stout·en·ing** \'staut-niŋ, -°n-iŋ\ **:** to make or become stout

stout·heart·ed \'staut-'härt-əd\ *adj* **:** COURAGEOUS, BOLD, VALIANT, BRAVE — **stout·heart·ed·ly** *adv* — **stout·heart·ed·ness** *n*

¹**stove** \'stōv\ *n* [MD or MLG, heated room] **1 :** an apparatus that burns fuel or uses electricity to provide heat (as for cooking or heating) **2 :** KILN

²**stove** *past of* STAVE

stove·pipe \'stōv-,pīp\ *n* **1 :** a metal pipe for carrying off smoke from a stove **2 :** a tall silk hat

sto·ver \'stō-vər\ *n* [AF *estovers* necessary supplies, fr. OF *estoveir* to be necessary, fr. L *est opus* there is need]

: dried stalks of grain from which the ears have been removed used as fodder

stow \'stō\ *vt* [ME *stowen* to place, fr. *stowe* place, fr. OE *stōw*] **1 :** HOUSE, LODGE **2 :** to put away **:** STORE **3 a :** to dispose in an orderly fashion **:** ARRANGE, PACK **b :** LOAD **4** *slang* **:** to put aside **:** STOP **5 :** to cram in (food)

stow·age \'stō-ij\ *n* **1 a :** an act or process of stowing **b :** goods stowed or to be stowed **2 a :** storage capacity **b :** a place for storage **3 :** STORAGE

stow away \,stō-ə-'wā, 'stō-ə-,\ *vi* **:** to secrete oneself aboard a vehicle as a means of obtaining transportation

stow·away \'stō-ə-,wā\ *n* **:** one who stows away **:** an unregistered passenger

stra·bis·mus \strə-'biz-məs\ *n* [Gk *strabismos*] **:** a visual disorder marked by inability to direct both eyes to the same object due to a fault of the muscles of the eyeball — **stra·bis·mic** \-mik\ *adj*

¹**strad·dle** \'strad-°l\ *vb* **strad·dled; strad·dling** \'strad-liŋ, -°l-iŋ\ [akin to E *stride*] **1 :** to part the legs wide **:** stand, sit, or walk with the legs wide apart; *esp* **:** to sit astride **2 :** to stand, sit, or be astride of **3 :** SPRAWL **4 :** to be noncommittal **:** favor or seem to favor two apparently opposite sides ⟨*straddle* an issue⟩ — **strad·dler** \'strad-lər, -°l-ər\ *n*

²**straddle** *n* **1 :** the act or position of one that straddles **2 :** a noncommittal or equivocal position

strafe \'strāf\ *vt* [G *Gott strafe England* God punish England, slogan of the Germans in World War I] **:** to fire upon (as ground troops) at close range and esp. with machine guns from low-flying airplanes — **straf·er** *n*

strag·gle \'strag-əl\ *vi* **strag·gled; strag·gling** \'strag-(ə-)liŋ\ [ME *straglen*] **1 :** to wander from the direct course or way **:** ROVE, STRAY **2 :** to trail off from others of its kind **:** spread out irregularly or scatteringly — **strag·gler** \-(ə-)lər\ *n*

strag·gly \'strag-(ə-)lē\ *adj* **strag·gli·er; -est :** spread out or scattered irregularly **:** STRAGGLING ⟨a *straggly* beard⟩

¹**straight** \'strāt\ *adj* [ME, fr. pp. of *strecchen* to stretch] **1 a :** free from curves, bends, angles, or irregularities ⟨*straight* hair⟩ ⟨*straight* timber⟩ ⟨*straight* stream⟩ **b :** generated by a point moving continuously in the same direction ⟨*straight* line⟩ **2 :** DIRECT, UNINTERRUPTED: as **a :** lying along or holding to a direct or proper course or method ⟨the *straighter* path there⟩ ⟨*straight* thinker⟩ **b :** CANDID, FRANK ⟨*straight* speech⟩ ⟨a *straight* answer⟩ **c :** coming directly from a trustworthy source ⟨a *straight* tip on the horses⟩ **d :** having the elements in an order ⟨the *straight* sequence of events⟩ **e :** UPRIGHT, VERTICAL **3 a :** JUST, VIRTUOUS ⟨*straight* dealings⟩ **b :** properly ordered or arranged ⟨set the kitchen *straight*⟩ **4 a :** not modified **:** UNMIXED, UNDILUTED ⟨*straight* whiskey⟩ **b :** not varying or modified ⟨*straight* pay⟩⟨works on *straight* time⟩ **5 :** making no exceptions in one's support of a party ⟨vote a *straight* ticket⟩ **6 :** not deviating from the general norm or prescribed pattern ⟨a *straight* part⟩ — **straight·ness** *n*

²**straight** *adv* **:** in a straight manner, course, or line

³**straight** *n* **1 :** something that is straight: as **a :** a straight line or arrangement **b :** STRAIGHTAWAY; *esp* **:** HOMESTRETCH **c :** a true or honest report or course **2 a :** a sequence (as of shots, strokes, or moves) resulting in a perfect score in a game or contest **b :** first place at the finish of a horse race **:** WIN **3 :** a combination of five cards in sequence in a poker hand

straight angle *n* **:** an angle whose sides lie in the same straight line and that equals two right angles

straight-arm \'strāt-,ärm\ *vb* **:** to ward off an opponent with the arm held straight — **straight-arm** *n*

¹**straight·away** \'strāt-ə-,wā\ *adj* **1 :** proceeding in a straight line **:** continuous in direction **:** STRAIGHTFORWARD **2 :** IMMEDIATE ⟨made a *straightaway* reply⟩

²**straightaway** *n* **:** a straight course: as **a :** the straight part of a closed racecourse **:** STRETCH **b :** a straight and unimpeded stretch of road or way

³**straight·away** \,strāt-ə-'wā\ *adv* **:** without hesitation or delay **:** IMMEDIATELY

straight·edge \'strāt-,ej\ *n* **:** a bar or piece of wood, metal, or plastic with a straight edge for testing straight lines and surfaces or drawing straight lines

straight·en \'strāt-°n\ *vb* **straight·ened; straight·en·ing** \'strāt-niŋ, -°n-iŋ\ **1 :** to make or become straight **2**

: to put in order ⟨*straighten* up a room⟩ ⟨*straightened* out my accounts⟩ — **straight·en·er** \ˈstrāt-nər, -ᵊn-ər\ *n*

straight face *n* **:** a face giving no evidence of emotion and esp. of merriment — **straight–faced** \ˈstrāt-ˈfāst\ *adj*

¹**straight·for·ward** \(ˈ)strāt-ˈfȯr-wərd\ *also* **straight·for·wards** \-wərdz\ *adv* **:** in a straightforward manner

²**straightforward** *adj* **1 :** proceeding in a straight course or manner **:** DIRECT, UNDEVIATING **2 a :** OUTSPOKEN, CANDID ⟨a *straightforward* reply⟩ **b :** CLEAR-CUT, PRECISE — **straight·for·ward·ly** *adv* — **straight·for·ward·ness** *n*

straight man *n* **:** an entertainer who feeds lines to a comedian

straight off *adv* **:** IMMEDIATELY

straight razor *n* **:** a razor with a rigid steel cutting blade hinged to a case that forms a handle when the razor is open for use

straight·way \ˈstrāt-ˌwā, -ˈwā\ *adv* **1 :** in a direct course **:** DIRECTLY **2 :** IMMEDIATELY, FORTHWITH

¹**strain** \ˈstrān\ *n* [ME *streen* progeny, lineage, fr. OE *strēon* gain, acquisition] **1 a :** LINEAGE, ANCESTRY **b :** a group of presumed common ancestry that is physiologically but usu. not morphologically distinct ⟨a high-yielding *strain* of winter wheat⟩ **c :** KIND, SORT **2 a :** inherited or inherent character, quality, or disposition ⟨a *strain* of madness in the family⟩ **b :** TRACE, STREAK ⟨a *strain* of sadness⟩ **3 a :** TUNE, AIR **b :** a passage of verbal or musical expression **4 a :** the general tone of an utterance (as a song or speech) or of a course of action or conduct **b :** MOOD, TEMPER

²**strain** *vb* [MF *estraindre*, fr. L *stringere*] **1 a :** to draw tight **:** cause to clasp firmly **b :** to stretch to maximum extension and tautness **2 a :** to exert (as oneself) to the utmost **:** STRIVE **b :** to injure or undergo injury by overuse, misuse, or excessive pressure ⟨*strained* his heart by overwork⟩ **c :** to cause a change of form or size in (a body) by application of external force **3 :** to squeeze or clasp tightly: as **a :** HUG **b :** CONSTRICT **4 a :** to pass or cause to pass through or as if through a strainer **:** FILTER **b :** to remove by straining ⟨*strain* lumps out of the gravy⟩ **5 :** to stretch beyond a proper limit ⟨*strain* the truth⟩ **6 :** to make great difficulty or resistance **:** BALK ⟨a horse *straining* at the lead⟩

³**strain** *n* **1 :** an act of straining or the condition of being strained: as **a :** excessive physical or mental tension **b :** bodily injury from excessive tension, effort, or use ⟨heart *strain*⟩; *esp* **:** one resulting from a wrench or twist and involving undue stretching of muscles or ligaments ⟨back *strain*⟩ **c :** deformation of a material body under the action of applied forces **2 :** a degree or intensity reached only by straining

syn STRAIN, SPRAIN mean damage to muscles or tendons through overstretching or overexertion. STRAIN may apply to any part of the body; SPRAIN applies chiefly to the tearing of ligaments at a joint by sharp wrenching or twisting

strained \ˈstrānd\ *adj* **1 :** FORCED ⟨a *strained* smile⟩ **2 :** pushed by antagonism near to open conflict ⟨*strained* relations between countries⟩

strain·er \ˈstrā-nər\ *n* **:** one that strains; *esp* **:** a device (as a screen, sieve, or filter) to retain solid pieces while a liquid passes through

¹**strait** \ˈstrāt\ *adj* [OF *estreit*, fr. L *strictus*, fr. pp. of *stringere* to bind tight] **1** *archaic* **a :** NARROW **b :** RESTRICTED **c :** closely fitting **:** CONSTRICTED, TIGHT **2** *archaic* **:** STRICT, RIGOROUS **3 a :** DISTRESSFUL, DIFFICULT **b :** LIMITED, STRAITENED — **strait·ly** *adv* — **strait·ness** *n*

²**strait** *n* **1 a** *archaic* **:** a narrow space or passage **b :** a comparatively narrow passageway connecting two large bodies of water — often used in pl. **c :** ISTHMUS **2 a :** a situation of perplexity or distress **:** DIFFICULTY, NEED ⟨in dire *straits*⟩

strait·en \ˈstrāt-ᵊn\ *vt* **strait·ened; strait·en·ing** \ˈstrāt-niŋ, -ᵊn-iŋ\ **1 a :** to make strait or narrow **b :** to hem in **:** squeeze together **:** CONFINE **2** *archaic* **:** to restrict in freedom or scope **:** HAMPER **3 :** to subject to distress, privation, or deficiency **:** limit or restrict esp. in resources ⟨in *straitened* circumstances⟩

strait·jack·et *or* **straight·jack·et** \ˈstrāt-ˌjak-ət\ *n* **:** a cover or overgarment of strong material (as canvas) used to bind the body and esp. the arms closely in restraining a violent prisoner or patient

strait·laced *or* **straight·laced** \ˈstrāt-ˈlāst\ *adj* **:** exces-

sively strict in manners, morals, or opinion — **strait·laced·ly** *adv* — **strait·laced·ness** *n*

strake \ˈstrāk\ *n* [ME; akin to E *stretch*] **:** a continuous band of hull planking or plates on a ship; *also* **:** the width of such a band

stra·mo·ni·um \strə-ˈmō-nē-əm\ *n* **:** the dried leaves of the jimsonweed used in medicine similarly to belladonna esp. in asthma

¹**strand** \ˈstrand\ *n* [OE] **:** the land bordering a body of water **:** SHORE, BEACH

²**strand** *vb* **1 :** to run, drive, or cause to drift onto a strand **:** run aground **:** BEACH **2 :** to leave in a strange or an unfavorable place esp. without funds or means to depart ⟨*stranded* in a strange city⟩

³**strand** *n* [ME *strond*] **1 :** one of the threads, strings, or wires twisted to make a cord, rope, or cable; *also* **:** the rope, cord, or cable into which these strands are twisted **2 :** an elongated or twisted and plaited body resembling a rope ⟨a *strand* of pearls⟩ ⟨a *strand* of hair⟩ **3 :** one of the elements interwoven in a complex whole ⟨the *strands* of a legal argument⟩

⁴**strand** *vt* **1 :** to form (as a rope) from strands **2 :** to play out, twist, or arrange in a strand

strange \ˈstrānj\ *adj* [OF *estrange*, fr. L *extraneus*, lit., external, fr. *extra* outside] **1** *archaic* **:** FOREIGN **2 :** of or relating to some other person or place ⟨the cuckoo lays her eggs in a *strange* nest⟩ **3 :** exciting surprise or wonder because not usual **:** UNACCOUNTABLE, QUEER ⟨*strange* clothes⟩ **4 :** UNFAMILIAR ⟨*strange* surroundings⟩ **5 :** ill at ease **:** SHY ⟨feels *strange* on his first day in school⟩ — **strange·ly** *adv* — **strange·ness** *n*

syn QUEER, PECULIAR, OUTLANDISH: STRANGE emphasizes unfamiliarity and may apply to what is foreign or unnatural or unaccountable; QUEER suggests a dubious, unexpected, often sinister strangeness ⟨a *queer* taste⟩; PECULIAR implies a marked difference from the usual ⟨a *peculiar* hobbling gait⟩ OUTLANDISH implies an uncouth or barbaric strangeness ⟨*outlandish* clothes⟩ ⟨*outlandish* customs⟩

strang·er \ˈstrān-jər\ *n* **1 :** one who is strange: as **a :** FOREIGNER **b :** GUEST, VISITOR, INTRUDER **c :** a person or thing that is unknown or with whom one is unacquainted **d :** one who does not belong to or is kept from the activities of a group **2 :** one ignorant of or unacquainted with someone or something ⟨a *stranger* to good manners⟩

stran·gle \ˈstraŋ-gəl\ *vb* **stran·gled; stran·gling** \-g(ə-)liŋ\ [MF *estrangler*, fr. L *strangulare*, fr. Gk *strangalan*, fr. *strangalē* halter] **1 :** to choke to death by squeezing the throat **2 :** to cause (someone or something) to stifle, choke, or suffocate **3 :** to become strangled — **stran·gler** \-g(ə-)lər\ *n*

stran·gle·hold \ˈstraŋ-gəl-ˌhōld\ *n* **1 :** a wrestling hold by which one's opponent is choked **2 :** a force or influence that chokes or suppresses freedom of movement or expression

stran·gu·late \ˈstraŋ-gyə-ˌlāt\ *vb* **1 :** STRANGLE, CONSTRICT **2 :** to become constricted so as to stop circulation ⟨a hernia may *strangulate*⟩

stran·gu·la·tion \ˌstraŋ-gyə-ˈlā-shən\ *n* **1 :** an act or process of strangling or strangulating **2 :** the state of being strangled or strangulated

stran·gu·ry \ˈstraŋ-gyə-rē\ *n* [Gk *strangouria*, fr. *strang-, stranx* drop squeezed out + *ourein* to urinate] **:** a slow and painful discharge of urine

¹**strap** \ˈstrap\ *n* [alter. of *strop*] **1 :** a band, plate, or loop of metal for binding objects together or for clamping an object in position **2 a :** a narrow usu. flat strip or thong of a flexible material and esp. leather used variously (as for securing, holding together, or wrapping) **b :** something made of a strap forming a loop ⟨boot *strap*⟩ **c :** a strip of leather used for flogging **2 :** STROP

²**strap** *vt* **strapped; strap·ping** **1 a :** to secure with or attach by means of a strap **b :** BIND, CONSTRICT; *also* **:** to support (as a sprained joint) with strips of adhesive plaster **2 :** to beat or punish with a strap **3 :** STROP

strap·hang·er \ˈstrap-ˌhaŋ-ər\ *n* **:** a passenger in a subway, streetcar, bus, or train who clings for support while standing to one of the short straps or similar devices running along the aisle

strap·less \-ləs\ *adj* **:** having no strap; *esp* **:** made or worn without shoulder straps ⟨*strapless* evening gown⟩

---

j joke; **ŋ** sing; **ō** flow; **ȯ** flaw; **ȯi** coin; **th** thin; **th** this; **ü** loot; **u̇** foot; **y** yet; **yü** few; **yu̇** furious; **zh** vision

strap·per \'strap-ər\ *n* : one that is unusually large or robust

strap·ping \'strap-iŋ\ *adj* : having a vigorously sturdy constitution : ROBUST

strat·a·gem \'strat-ə-jəm\ *n* [It *stratagemma,* fr. Gk *stratēgēma,* fr. *stratēgein* to be a general, maneuver, fr. *stratēgos* general] **1 a** : an artifice or trick in war for deceiving and outwitting the enemy **b** : a cleverly contrived trick or scheme for gaining an end **2** : skill in ruses or trickery **syn** see TRICK

stra·te·gic \strə-'tē-jik\ *adj* **1** : of, relating to, or marked by strategy ⟨*strategic* value of the position⟩ ⟨a *strategic* retreat⟩ **2 a** : important in strategy **b** : required for the conduct of war ⟨*strategic* materials⟩ **c** : of great importance within an integrated whole or to a planned effect ⟨emphasized *strategic* points⟩ **3** : designed or trained to strike an enemy at the sources of his power ⟨*strategic* bomber⟩ — **stra·te·gi·cal** \-ji-kəl\ *adj* — **stra·te·gi·cal·ly** \-k(ə-)lē\ *adv*

strat·e·gist \'strat-ə-jəst\ *n* : one skilled in strategy

strat·e·gy \'strat-ə-jē\ *n, pl* **-gies** [Gk *stratēgia* generalship, fr. *stratēgos* general, fr. *stratos* army + *agein* to lead] **1 a** (1) : the science and art of employing the political, economic, psychological, and military forces of a country so as to support adopted policies in peace or war (2) : the science and art of military command exercised to meet the enemy in combat under advantageous conditions — compare TACTICS **b** : a variety of or instance of the use of strategy **2 a** : a careful plan or method : a clever stratagem **b** : the art of devising or employing plans or stratagems toward a goal

syn TACTICS: STRATEGY applies to the devising of a general plan of attack, defense, or action so as to achieve an end with the forces or means available ⟨attempting to trade blows at close range with a stronger hitter is a mistake in *strategy*⟩ TACTICS applies to the technique of utilizing forces properly or skillfully in action or combat ⟨failing to protect the jaw is poor boxing *tactics*⟩

strath \'strath\ *n* [ScGael *srath*] : a flat wide river valley or the low-lying grassland along it

stra·tic·u·late \strə-'tik-yə-lət\ *adj* : characterized by thin parallel strata

strat·i·fy \'strat-ə-ˌfī\ *vb* **-fied; -fy·ing** **1** : to form, deposit, or arrange in strata ⟨*stratified* epithelium⟩ ⟨a society *stratified* by custom⟩ **2** : to become arranged in strata — **strat·i·fi·ca·tion** \ˌstrat-ə-fə-'kā-shən\ *n*

stra·tig·ra·phy \strə-'tig-rə-fē\ *n* **1** : the arrangement of strata **2** : geology that deals with the origin, composition, distribution, and succession of strata — **strat·i·graph·ic** \ˌstrat-ə-'graf-ik\ *adj*

stra·to·cu·mu·lus \ˌstrāt-ō-'kyü-myə-ləs, ˌstrat-\ *n* : stratified cumulus consisting of large balls or rolls of dark cloud which often cover the whole sky esp. in winter

strato·sphere \'strat-ə-ˌsfi(ə)r\ *n* [NL *stratum*] : an upper portion of the atmosphere above seven miles more or less depending on latitude, season, and weather in which temperature changes but little with altitude and clouds of water are rare — **strato·spher·ic** \ˌstrat-ə-'sfi(ə)r-ik, -'sfer-\ *adj*

stra·tum \'strāt-əm, 'strat-\ *n, pl* **stra·ta** \-ə\ *also* **stra·tums** \-əmz\ [NL, fr. L, spread, bed, fr. neut. of *stratus,* pp. of *sternere* to spread out] **1** : a layer of a substance; *esp* : one having parallel layers of other kinds lying above or below or both above and below it ⟨a rock *stratum*⟩ ⟨a *stratum* of earth⟩⟨a cold *stratum* in a lake⟩ **2 a** : a layer of tissue ⟨deep *stratum* of the skin⟩ **b** : one of the layers indicative of cultural sequences in which archaeological material is found **3 a** : a stage of historical or cultural development **b** : a level of society comprised of persons of the same or similar social, economic, or cultural status

stra·tus \'strāt-əs, 'strat-\ *n, pl* **stra·ti** \'strāt-ˌī, 'strat-\ [NL, fr. L, pp. of *sternere* to spread out] : a cloud form extending horizontally over a relatively large area at an altitude of from 2000 to 7000 feet

¹straw \'stro\ *n* [OE *strēaw;* akin to E *strew*] **1 a** : stalks of grain after threshing; *also* : any dry stalky plant residue ⟨pea *straw*⟩ ⟨pine *straw*⟩ **b** : a natural or artificial heavy fiber used for weaving, plaiting, or braiding **2** : a dry coarse stem esp. of a cereal grass **3 a** (1) : something of small worth or significance : TRIFLE ⟨not worth a *straw*⟩ (2) : something too insubstantial to provide support or

help in a desperate situation ⟨clutch at any *straw* in a crisis⟩ (3) : a slight fact that is an indication of a coming event **b** : CHAFF **2** **4** : a prepared tube for sucking up a beverage — **strawy** \'stro(-)ē\ *adj*

²straw *adj* **1 a** : made of straw ⟨a *straw* rug⟩ **b** : of, relating to, or used for straw ⟨a *straw* barn⟩ **2** : of the pale yellow color of straw **3** : of little or no value : WORTHLESS

straw·ber·ry \'stro-ˌber-ē, -b(ə-)rē\ *n* [so called fr. the appearance of the achenes on the surface] : an edible juicy red pulpy fruit of a low herb of the rose family with white flowers and long slender runners; *also* : this plant — **strawberry** *adj*

strawberry mark *n* : a usu. red and elevated birthmark that is a small vascular tumor

strawberry roan *n* : a roan horse with a decidedly red ground color

strawberry shrub *n* : any of a genus of American shrubs with fragrant brownish red flowers

straw·board \'stro-ˌbord, -ˌbord\ *n* : board made of straw pulp and used esp. for packing

straw boss *n* : a foreman of a small gang of workmen

straw·flow·er \'stro-ˌflau̇(-ə)r\ *n* : any of several everlasting flowers

straw·hat theater \ˌstro-ˌhat-\ *n* [fr. the former fashion of men's wearing straw hats in summer] : a summer theater

straw man *n* **1** : a weak or imaginary argument or adversary set up only to be easily confuted **2** : a person set up to serve as a cover for a questionable transaction

straw vote *n* : an unofficial vote (as taken at a chance gathering) to indicate the relative strength of opposing candidates or issues

straw·worm \'stro-ˌwərm\ *n* **1** : CADDISWORM **2** : any of several insect grubs that develop in the stalks of cereal grasses (as wheat)

¹stray \'strā\ *vi* [MF *estraier,* fr. (assumed) VL *extragare,* fr. L *extra-* outside + *vagari* to wander] **1** : to wander from company, restraint, or proper limits : ROAM **2 a** : to wander from a direct course or at random : DEVIATE, MEANDER **b** : ERR, SIN — **stray·er** *n*

²stray *n* **1 a** : a domestic animal wandering at large or lost **b** : a person or thing that strays : a detached individual : STRAGGLER, WAIF **2** : a disturbing electrical effect in radio reception not produced by a transmitting station

³stray *adj* **1** : WANDERING ⟨a *stray* cow⟩ ⟨*stray* survivors⟩ **2** : occurring at random or as detached individuals : SCATTERED, OCCASIONAL, INCIDENTAL ⟨a few *stray* hairs⟩ ⟨*stray* remarks⟩

¹streak \'strēk\ *n* [OE *strica*] **1** : a line or mark of a different color or texture from the ground : STRIPE **2** : the color of the fine powder of a mineral obtained by scratching or rubbing against a hard white surface **3 a** : a narrow band of light **b** : a lightning bolt **4 a** : TRACE, STRAIN ⟨*streak* of stubbornness⟩ **b** : a brief run (as of luck) **c** : a consecutive series ⟨winning *streak*⟩ **5** : a narrow layer ⟨a *streak* of fat in bacon⟩⟨a *streak* of ore⟩

²streak *vb* **1** : to make streaks on or in **2** : to move swiftly : RUSH ⟨*streaked* through the streets⟩

streaked \'strēkt, 'strē-kəd\ *adj* : marked with stripes or linear discolorations

streaky \'strē-kē\ *adj* **streak·i·er; -est** **1** : marked with streaks **2** : VARIABLE, UNRELIABLE ⟨a *streaky* hitter in baseball⟩ — **streak·i·ness** *n*

¹stream \'strēm\ *n* [OE *strēam*] **1** : a body of running water (as a river or brook) flowing on the earth; *also* : a body of flowing fluid (as water or gas) **2 a** : a steady succession **b** : a constantly renewed supply **c** : a continuous moving procession **3** : an unbroken flow (as of gas or particles of matter) **4** : a ray or beam of light **5** : a dominant attitude, group, or line of development

²stream *vb* **1** : to flow or cause to flow in or as if in a stream **b** : to leave a bright trail **2 a** : to exude a bodily fluid profusely **b** : to become saturated **3** : to trail out at full length **4** : to pour in large numbers **5** : to display fully extended

stream·er \'strē-mər\ *n* **1 a** : a flag that streams in the wind; *esp* : PENNANT **b** : a long narrow wavy strip like or suggesting a banner floating in the wind **c** : BANNER **2** **2** *pl* : AURORA BOREALIS

stream·let \'strēm-lət\ *n* : a small stream

stream·line \-'līn, -ˌlīn\ *vt* **1** : to design or construct with a contour for decreasing resistance to motion through water or air or as if for this purpose **2** : to bring up to date : MODERNIZE **3** : to make simpler or more efficient

stream·lined \-'līnd, -,līnd\ *also* **stream·line** *adj* **1 a** : contoured to reduce resistance to motion through water or air or as if for this purpose **b** : stripped of nonessentials : SIMPLIFIED, COMPACT **2** : MODERNIZED

stream of consciousness : individual conscious experience considered as a series of processes or experiences continuously moving forward in time

street \'strēt\ *n* [OE *strǣt*, fr. LL *strata* paved road, fr. L, fem. of *stratus*, pp. of *sternere* to spread out] **1 a** : a thoroughfare esp. in a city, town, or village usu. including sidewalks and being wider than an alley or lane **b** : the part of a street reserved for vehicles **c** : a thoroughfare with abutting property ⟨lived on Maple *Street*⟩ **2** : the people occupying property on a street ⟨the whole *street* was excited⟩

street ar·ab \-'ar-əb, -'ā-,rab\ *n, often cap A* : a homeless vagabond and esp. an outcast boy or girl in the streets of a city : GAMIN

street·car \'strēt-,kär\ *n* : a vehicle on rails used primarily for transporting passengers and typically operating on city streets

street railway *n* : a line operating streetcars or buses

street virus *n* : virulent or natural virus (as of rabies) as distinguished from virus attenuated in the laboratory

strength \'stren(k)th\ *n* [OE *strengthu*; akin to E *strong*] **1** : the quality or state of being strong : inherent power **2** : power to resist force : SOLIDITY, TOUGHNESS **3** : power of resisting attack : IMPREGNABILITY **4** : legal, logical, or moral force **5 a** : degree of potency of effect or of concentration **b** : intensity of light, color, sound, or odor **6** : force as measured in numbers ⟨army at full *strength*⟩ **7** : one regarded as embodying or affording force or firmness : SUPPORT ⟨has enough *strength* in the senate to pass the bill⟩ **syn** see POWER

strength·en \'stren(k)-thən\ *vb* **strength·ened; strength·en·ing** \'stren(k)th-(ə-)niŋ\ : to make or become stronger — **strength·en·er** \'stren(k)th-(ə-)nər\ *n*

strength·less \'stren(k)th-ləs\ *adj* : having no strength — **strength·less·ness** *n*

stren·u·os·i·ty \,stren-yə-'wäs-ət-ē\ *n* : the quality or state of being strenuous

stren·u·ous \'stren-yə-wəs\ *adj* [L *strenuus*] **1 a** : vigorously active : ENERGETIC **b** : FERVENT, ZEALOUS ⟨*strenuous* protest⟩ **2** : marked by or calling for energy or stamina : ARDUOUS **syn** see VIGOROUS — **stren·u·ous·ly** *adv* — **stren·u·ous·ness** *n*

strep \'strep\ *n* : STREPTOCOCCUS

strep throat *n* : SEPTIC SORE THROAT

strep·to·coc·cus \,strep-tə-'käk-əs\ *n, pl* **strep·to·coc·ci** \-'käk-,(s)ī, -,(,)(s)ē\ [NL, fr. Gk *streptos* twisted chain, fr. *strephein* to twist] : any of various nonmotile mostly parasitic spherical bacteria that occur in pairs or chains and include important pathogens of man and domestic animals — **strep·to·coc·cal** \-'käk-əl\ *or* **strep·to·coc·cic** \-'käk-(s)ik\ *adj*

strep·to·my·ces \,strep-tə-'mī-,sēz\ *n, pl* **streptomyces** *or* **strep·to·my·cetes** \-'mī-,sēts, -mī-'; -mī-'sēt-(,)ēz\ [NL, fr. Gk *streptos* twisted chain + *mykēt-, mykēs* fungus] : any of a genus of mostly soil actinomycetes including some that form antibiotics as by-products of their metabolism

strep·to·my·cin \,strep-tə-'mīs-ən\ *n* : an antibiotic base produced by a soil streptomyces and used esp. in the treatment of tuberculosis

¹stress \'stres\ *n* [ME *stresse* stress, distress, fr. *destresse*, fr. OF] **1** : constraining force or influence: as **a** : mutual force or action between contiguous surfaces of bodies caused by external force (as tension or shear) **b** : a force that tends to distort a body **c** : a factor that induces bodily or mental tension and may be a factor in disease causation; *also* : a state of tension resulting from a stress **2** : EMPHASIS, WEIGHT ⟨lay *stress* on a point⟩ **3** : intensity of utterance given to a speech sound, syllable, or word **4** : relative force or prominence of sound in verse; *also* : a syllable having this stress **5** : ACCENT 6a — **stress·less** \-ləs\ *adj* — **stress·less·ness** *n*

²stress *vt* **1** : ACCENT ⟨*stress* the first syllable⟩ **2** : to subject to physical stress **3** : to lay stress on : EMPHASIZE

stress·ful \-fəl\ *adj* : full of or subject to stress —**stress·ful·ly** \-fə-lē\ *adv*

stress mark *n* : a mark used with (as before, after, or over) a written syllable in the respelling of a word to show that this syllable is to be stressed when spoken : ACCENT MARK

¹stretch \'strech\ *vb* [ME *strecchen*, fr. OE *streccan*] **1** : to extend (as one's limbs or body) in a reclining position ⟨*stretched* himself out on the bed⟩ **2** : to reach out ⟨*stretched* forth his arm⟩ **3 a** : to extend in length or breadth or both : SPREAD **b** : to extend over a continuous period **4** : to cause the limbs of (a person) to be pulled esp. in torture **5** : to draw up (one's body) from a cramped, stooping, or relaxed position ⟨awoke and *stretched* himself⟩ **6** : to pull taut **7 a** : to enlarge or distend esp. by force **b** : STRAIN **8** : to cause to reach or continue ⟨*stretch* a wire between two posts⟩ **9** : to extend often unduly the scope or meaning of ⟨*stretch* the truth⟩ **10** : to become extended without breaking — **stretch·a·bil·i·ty** \,strech-ə-'bil-ət-ē\ *n* — **stretch·a·ble** \'strech-ə-bəl\ *adj*

²stretch *n* **1 a** : an exercise of something (as the imagination or understanding) beyond ordinary or normal limits **b** : an extension of the scope or application of something **2** : the extent to which something may be stretched **3** : the act of stretching : the state of being stretched **4 a** : an extent in length or area **b** : a continuous period of time ⟨silent for a *stretch*⟩ **5** : a walk to relieve fatigue **6** : a term of imprisonment **7 a** : either of the straight sides of a racecourse; *esp* : HOMESTRETCH **b** : a final stage **8** : the capacity for being stretched : ELASTICITY

³stretch *adj* : easily stretched : ELASTIC ⟨*stretch* hosiery⟩ ⟨*stretch* ski pants⟩

stretch·er \'strech-ər\ *n* **1** : one that stretches; *esp* : a device or machine for stretching or expanding something (as curtains) **2** : a litter (as of canvas) for carrying a disabled or dead person **3** : a rod or bar extending between two legs of a chair or table

stretch·er–bear·er \-,bar-ər, -,ber-\ *n* : one who carries one end of a stretcher

strew \'strü\ *vt* **strewed; strewed** *or* **strewn** \'strün\; **strew·ing** [OE *strewian*] **1** : to spread (as seeds or flowers) by scattering **2** : to cover by or as if by scattering something over or on **3** : to become dispersed over **4** : to spread abroad : DISSEMINATE

stria \'strī-ə\ *n, pl* **stri·ae** \'strī-,ē\ [L, furrow, channel] **1** : a minute groove or channel **2** : a narrow line or band (as of color) esp. when one of a series of parallel grooves or lines

stri·at·ed \'strī-,āt-əd\ *adj* : marked with lines, bands, or grooves — **stri·a·tion** \strī-'ā-shən\ *n*

striated muscle *n* : muscle that is made up of usu. elongated and multinucleate cells with alternate light and dark cross striations, is typical of the muscles which move the vertebrate skeleton, and is mostly under voluntary control — compare CARDIAC MUSCLE, SMOOTH MUSCLE

strick·en \'strik-ən\ *adj* [fr. pp. of *strike*] **1** : hit or wounded by or as if by a missile **2** : afflicted with disease, misfortune, or sorrow

strict \'strikt\ *adj* [L *strictus*, fr. pp. of *stringere* to bind tight] **1** : permitting no evasion or escape ⟨under *strict* orders⟩ **2 a** : inflexibly maintained or adhered to : COMPLETE, ABSOLUTE ⟨*strict* secrecy⟩ **b** (1) : rigorously conforming to principle or to a norm ⟨a *strict* Catholic⟩ (2) : severe in discipline **3** : EXACT, PRECISE **syn** see RIGID — **strict·ly** *adv* — **strict·ness** \'strik(t)-nəs\ *n*

strict constructionist *n* : one favoring a conservative interpretation of the U.S. Constitution as strictly limiting the powers of the federal government to those expressly granted

stric·ture \'strik-chər\ *n* [LL *strictura*, fr. L *strict-, stringere* to bind tight] **1** : an abnormal narrowing of a bodily passage; *also* : the narrowed part **2** : something that closely restrains or limits : RESTRICTION **3** : an adverse criticism : CENSURE

¹stride \'strīd\ *vb* **strode** \'strōd\; **strid·den** \'strid-ən\; **strid·ing** \'strīd-iŋ\ [OE *strīdan*] **1** : to move over, through, or along with or as if with long measured steps **2** : to take a very long step **3** : BESTRIDE, STRADDLE **4** : to step over — **strid·er** \'strīd-ər\ *n*

²stride *n* **1 a** : a step or the distance covered by a step ⟨measured out the boundary with long *strides*⟩ **b** : a cycle of locomotor movements of a quadruped completed when the feet regain their initial relative positions; *also* : the distance covered by this **2** : an act or manner of progressing on foot : way of striding ⟨a mannish *stride*⟩ **3** : a stage of progress : ADVANCE ⟨the *strides* made in the control of tuberculosis⟩

stri·dent \'strīd-ᵊnt\ *adj* [L *stridere, stridēre* to make a harsh noise] : harsh sounding : GRATING; *also* : SHRILL — **stri·den·cy** \-ᵊn-sē\ *n* — **stri·dent·ly** *adv*

stri·dor \'strīd-ər, 'strī-ˌdȯr\ *n* [L, fr. *stridere, stridēre* to make a harsh, shrill, or creaking noise]

strid·u·late \'strij-ə-ˌlāt\ *vi* : to make a shrill creaking noise by rubbing together special bodily structures — used esp. of male insects (as crickets or grasshoppers) — **strid·u·la·tion** \ˌstrij-ə-'lā-shən\ *n* — **strid·u·la·to·ry** \'strij-ə-lə-ˌtōr-ē, -ˌtȯr-\ *adj*

strid·u·lous \'strij-ə-ləs\ *adj* : making a shrill creaking sound — **strid·u·lous·ly** *adv*

strife \'strīf\ *n* [OF *estrif*] **1** : bitter sometimes violent conflict or dissension ⟨political *strife*⟩ **2** : an act of contention : FIGHT, STRUGGLE

strife·less \-ləs\ *adj* : free from strife

stri·gose \'strī-ˌgōs\ *adj* [NL *striga* bristle, fr. L, windrow, furrow] **1** : having bristles or scales that lie flat ⟨a *strigose* leaf⟩ **2** : marked with fine closely set grooves

¹strike \'strīk\ *vb* **struck** \'strək\; **struck** *also* **strick·en** \'strik-ən\; **strik·ing** \'strī-kiŋ\ [OE *strīcan* to stroke, go] **1** : to take a course : GO ⟨*strike* across the field⟩ **2 a** : to deliver a stroke, blow, or thrust : HIT **b** : to drive or remove by or as if by a blow ⟨*struck* the knife from his hand⟩ **c** : to attack or seize esp. with fangs or claws ⟨*struck* by a snake⟩ **3** : to come into contact or collision with : COLLIDE **4** : to remove or cancel with or as if with a stroke of the pen ⟨*struck* out a word in the text⟩ **5** : to lower, take down, or take apart ⟨*strike* a flag⟩⟨*strike* the tents⟩ **6 a** : to indicate or become indicated by a clock, bell, or chime **b** : to indicate by sounding **7** : to pierce or penetrate or to cause to pierce or penetrate **8** : to make a military attack : FIGHT ⟨*strike* for freedom⟩ **9** : to seize the bait ⟨a fish *struck*⟩ **10** : to begin or cause to grow : take root or cause to take root : GERMINATE ⟨some plant cuttings *strike* quickly⟩ **11** : to stop work in order to force an employer to comply with demands **12** : to make a beginning : LAUNCH ⟨the orchestra *struck* into another waltz⟩ **13** : to afflict suddenly : lay low ⟨*struck* down at the height of his career⟩ **14 a** : to bring into forceful contact **b** : to thrust suddenly **c** : to fall on ⟨sunlight *strikes* his face⟩ **d** : to become audible to ⟨a loud sound *struck* him⟩ **15 a** : to affect with a mental or emotional state or a strong emotion **b** : to affect a person with (a strong emotion) **c** : to cause to become by or as if by a sudden blow ⟨*struck* him dead⟩ **d** : to produce by stamping with a die or punch ⟨*strike* a medal⟩ **e** : to produce (as fire) by or as if by striking or rubbing **f** : to cause to ignite by friction ⟨*strike* a match⟩ **16** : to agree on the terms of ⟨*strike* a bargain⟩ **17 a** : to play by strokes on the keys or strings **b** : to produce by or as if by playing a musical instrument ⟨*strike* a chord on the piano⟩ **18 a** : to occur to : to appear to **c** : to make a strong impression on : IMPRESS **19** : to arrive at by computation ⟨*strike* an average⟩ **20 a** : to come to ⟨*strike* the main road⟩ **b** : to run across ⟨the best story I ever *struck*⟩ **21** : to take on : ASSUME ⟨*strike* a pose⟩

²strike *n* **1** : an act or instance of striking **2 a** : a work stoppage by a body of workers to force an employer to comply with demands **b** : a temporary stoppage of activities in protest against an act or condition **3** : the direction of the line of intersection of a horizontal plane with an uptilted geological stratum **4** : a pull on a line by a fish in striking **5** : a stroke of good luck; *esp* : a discovery of a valuable mineral deposit **6 a** : a pitched baseball recorded against a batter **b** : DISADVANTAGE, HANDICAP **7** : an act or instance of knocking down all the bowling pins with the first bowl **8** : infestation of the tissues by fly larvae ⟨body *strike* of sheep⟩ **9 a** : a military attack; *esp* : an air attack on a single objective **b** : a group of airplanes taking part in such an attack

strike·bound \'strīk-ˌbaund\ *adj* : subjected to a strike ⟨a *strikebound* factory⟩

strike·break·er \'strīk-ˌbrā-kər\ *n* : a person hired to help break up a strike of workmen

strike·break·ing \-kiŋ\ *n* : action designed to break up a strike

strike·less \'strīk-ləs\ *adj* : marked by the absence of strikes

strike off *vt* **1** : to produce in an effortless manner ⟨*strike off* a poem for the occasion⟩ **2** : to depict clearly and exactly

strike out \(')strīk-'aut\ *vb* **1** : to retire or be retired by a strikeout **2** : to enter upon a course of action ⟨*struck out* on his own after graduation⟩ **3** : to set out vigorously ⟨*struck out* for home⟩

strike·out \'strīk-ˌaut\ *n* : an out in baseball resulting from a batter's being charged with three strikes

strike·over \'strīk-ˌō-vər\ *n* : an act or instance of striking a typewriter character on a spot already occupied by another character

strik·er \'strī-kər\ *n* : one that strikes: as **a** : a player in any of several games who strikes **b** : the hammer of the striking mechanism of a clock or watch **c** : a worker on strike

strike up *vb* **1** : to begin or cause to begin to sing or play or to be sung or played ⟨a march *struck up* and the parade began⟩⟨*strike up* the band⟩ **2** : to cause to begin ⟨*strike up* a conversation⟩

strike zone *n* : the area (as between the knees and shoulders of a batter in his natural stance) over home plate through which a pitched baseball must pass to be called a strike

strik·ing \'strī-kiŋ\ *adj* : REMARKABLE, IMPRESSIVE ⟨a *striking* costume⟩ ⟨a *striking* resemblance⟩ — **strik·ing·ly** \-kiŋ-lē\ *adv*

¹string \'striŋ\ *n* [OE *streng*] **1** : a small cord used to bind, fasten, or tie **2** : a thin tough plant structure; *esp* : the fiber connecting the halves of a bean pod **3 a** : the gut or wire cord of a musical instrument **b** *pl* (1) : the stringed instruments of an orchestra (2) : the players of such instruments **4 a** : a group of objects threaded on a string **b** : a series of things arranged in or as if in a line ⟨a *string* of automobiles⟩ **c** : the animals and esp. horses belonging to or used by one individual **5** : a group of players ranked according to skill or proficiency ⟨third *string* of a football squad⟩ **6** : SUCCESSION, SEQUENCE **7** : LINE 14 **8** *pl* : contingent conditions or obligations ⟨an agreement with no *strings* attached⟩ **b** : CONTROL, DOMINATION — **string·less** \'striŋ-ləs\ *adj* — **on the string** : subject to one's pleasure or influence ⟨kept a potential buyer *on the string* for weeks before deciding not to sell the house⟩

²string *vb* **strung** \'strəŋ\; **string·ing** \'striŋ-iŋ\ **1 a** : to equip with strings ⟨*string* a tennis racket⟩ **b** : to tune the strings of **2** : to make tense ⟨her nerves were *strung* up⟩ **3 a** : to thread on or as if on a string ⟨*string* beads⟩ **b** : to thread with objects **c** : to tie, hang, or fasten with string **4** : to hang by the neck ⟨*strung* up from a high tree⟩ **5** : to remove the strings of ⟨*string* beans⟩ **6 a** : to extend or stretch like a string ⟨*string* wires from tree to tree⟩ **b** : to set out in a line or series **c** : to move, progress, or lie in a string **d** : to form into strings **7** : FOOL, HOAX

string along *vb* **1** : to go along : AGREE ⟨*string along* with the majority⟩ **2** : to keep dangling or waiting **3** : DECEIVE, FOOL ⟨would *string* him *along* with false promises⟩

string bass *n* : DOUBLE BASS

string bean *n* : SNAP BEAN

string·course \'striŋ-ˌkōrs, -ˌkȯrs\ *n* : a horizontal band (as of bricks) in a building forming a part of the design

stringed instrument \'striŋd-\ *n* : a musical instrument (as a violin, harp, or piano) sounded by plucking or striking or by drawing a bow across tense strings

strin·gent \'strin-jənt\ *adj* [L *stringent-, stringens*, prp. of *stringere* to bind tight] **1** : TIGHT, CONSTRICTED **2** : marked by rigor, strictness, or severity esp. with regard to rule or standard **syn** see RIGID — **strin·gen·cy** \-jən-sē\ *n* — **strin·gent·ly** *adv*

string·er \'striŋ-ər\ *n* **1** : one that strings **2 a** : a long horizontal member in a framed structure or a bridge **b** : one of the inclined sides of a stair supporting the treads and risers **c** : a longitudinal member (as in an airplane fuselage or wing) to reinforce the skin **3** : one estimated to be of specified excellence or quality or efficiency — usu. used in combination ⟨first-*stringer*⟩ ⟨second-*stringer*⟩

string·halt \'striŋ-ˌhȯlt\ *n* : lameness of the hind legs of a horse due to muscular spasm — **string·halt·ed** \-,hȯl·təd\ *adj*

string·ing \'striŋ-iŋ\ *n* : the gut, silk, or nylon with which a racket is strung

string quartet *n* **1** : a quartet of performers on stringed instruments usu. including a first and second violin, a viola, and a cello **2** : a composition for string quartet

string tie *n* : a narrow necktie

stringy \'striŋ-ē\ *adj* **string·i·er; -est 1 a** : containing, consisting of, or resembling fibrous matter or a string ⟨*stringy* root⟩ ⟨*stringy* hair⟩ **b** : lean and sinewy in build : WIRY **2** : capable of being drawn out to form a string : ROPY ⟨a *stringy* precipitate⟩ **3** : not compact ⟨a *stringy* sentence⟩ — **string·i·ness** *n*

¹strip \'strip\ *vb* **stripped** \'stript\ *also* **stript; strip·ping** [OE -*strīpan* to plunder] **1 a** : to remove clothing, covering, or surface matter from **b** : to remove (as clothing) from a person : UNDRESS **c** : SKIN, PEEL ⟨*strip* bark from a tree⟩ **2** : to divest of honors, privileges, or functions **3 a** : to remove extraneous or superficial matter from ⟨a prose style *stripped* to the bones⟩ **b** : to remove furniture, equipment, or accessories from ⟨*strip* a ship for action⟩ **4** : PLUNDER, SPOIL ⟨troops *stripped* the captured town⟩ **5** : to make bare or clear (as by cutting or grazing) **6** : DISMANTLE, DISASSEMBLE **7** : to tear or damage the screw thread of (as a bolt or nut) **8** : to separate (components) from a mixture or solution — **strip·per** *n*

²strip *n* [alter. of ME *stripe*] **1** : a long narrow piece or area ⟨*strips* of bacon⟩ ⟨*strip* of land⟩ **2** : AIRSTRIP

strip–crop·ping \'strip-,kräp-iŋ\ *n* : the growing of a cultivated crop (as corn) in strips alternating with strips of a sod-forming crop (as hay) arranged to follow land contours and minimize erosion — **strip-crop** \-,kräp\ *vb*

¹stripe \'strīp\ *n* [ME] : a stroke or blow with a rod or lash

²stripe *n* [ME, fr. MD] **1** : a line or long narrow section differing in color or texture from parts adjoining **2 a** : a piece of braid (as on the sleeve) to indicate military rank or length of service **b** : CHEVRON **3** : a distinct variety or sort : TYPE ⟨men of the same political *stripe*⟩ — **stripe·less** \'strīp-ləs\ *adj*

³stripe *vt* : to make stripes on or variegate with stripes

striped \'strīpt, 'strī-pəd\ *adj* : having stripes or streaks

striped bass *n* : a large sea bass of the Atlantic coast of the U.S. highly esteemed for sport and food

strip·ling \'strip-liŋ\ *n* : a youth just passing from boyhood to manhood

strive \'strīv\ *vi* **strove** \'strōv\ *also* **strived** \'strīvd\; **striv·en** \'striv-ən\ *or* **strived; striv·ing** \'strī-viŋ\ [OF *estriver*, of Gmc origin] **1** : to struggle in opposition : CONTEND **2** : to devote serious effort or energy : ENDEAVOR ⟨*strive* to win⟩ — **striv·er** \'strī-vər\ *n*

stro·bi·la \strō-'bī-lə\ *n, pl* -**lae** \-(,)lē\ *also* -**las** : a linear series of similar animal structures (as the segmented body of a tapeworm) produced by budding — **stro·bi·lar** \-lər\ *adj* — **stro·bi·la·tion** \,strō-,bī-'lā-shən\ *n*

strob·ile \'sträb-,īl, 'strōb-, -əl\ *n* **1** : STROBILUS **2** : a spike with persistent overlapping bracts that resembles a cone and is the pistillate inflorescence of the hop — **strob·i·lif·er·ous** \,sträb-,ī-'lif-(ə-)rəs, ,sträb-ə-, ,strōb-\ *adj*

stro·bi·lus \strō-'bī-ləs\ *n, pl* -**li** \-,lī, -,lī\ [NL, fr. Gk *strobilos* top, pinecone, fr. *strobos* whirl] **1 a** : an aggregation of sporophylls resembling a cone (as in a club moss or equisetum) **b** : the cone of a gymnosperm **2** : STROBILE **2 3** : STROBILA

stro·bo·scope \'strō-bə-,skōp\ *n* [Gk *strobos* whirl] : an instrument for determining speeds of rotation or frequencies of vibration by means of a rapidly flashing light that illuminates an object intermittently — **stro·bo·scop·ic** \,strō-bə-'skäp-ik\ *adj* — **stro·bo·scop·i·cal·ly** \-'skäp-i-k(ə-)lē\ *adv*

strode *past of* STRIDE

¹stroke \'strōk\ *vt* [OE *strācian*] **1** : to rub gently in one direction; *also* : CARESS — **strok·er** *n*

²stroke *n* **1** : the act of striking; *esp* : a blow with a weapon or implement **2** : a single unbroken movement; *esp* : one of a series of repeated or to-and-fro movements **3** : a striking of the ball in a game; *esp* : a striking or attempt to strike the ball that constitutes the scoring unit in golf **4** : a sudden action or process producing an impact ⟨*stroke* of lightning⟩ or unexpected result ⟨*stroke* of

luck⟩ **5** : APOPLEXY **6 a** : one of a series of propelling movements against a resisting medium ⟨*stroke* of an oar⟩ **b** : an oarsman who sets the tempo for a crew **7 a** : a vigorous or energetic effort **b** : a delicate or clever touch in a narrative, description, or construction **8** : the movement or the distance of the movement in either direction of a mechanical part (as a piston rod) having a reciprocating motion **9 a** : the sound of a bell being struck **b** : PULSATION, BEAT **10 a** : a mark made by a single movement of a tool **b** : one of the lines of a letter of the alphabet **syn** see BLOW

³stroke *vt* **1** : to mark or cancel with a line ⟨*stroked* out his name⟩ **2** : to set the rowing stroke for (a crew or boat) **3** : HIT

stroll \'strōl\ *vb* **1** : to walk in a leisurely or idle manner : RAMBLE **2** : to walk at leisure along or about — **stroll** *n*

stroll·er \'strō-lər\ *n* **1** : one that strolls **2** : a wheeled seat in which a baby may be pushed

stro·ma \'strō-mə\ *n, pl* **stro·ma·ta** \-mət-ə\ [Gk *strōmat-*, *strōma* bedspread, fr. *stornynai* to strew, spread] : a supporting framework in or of an organism: as **a** : the network of connective tissue that supports an animal organ **b** : an irregular mass of fungal hyphae supporting and enclosing spore-bearing structures

strong \'strȯŋ\ *adj* **strong·er** \'strȯŋ-gər\; **strong·est** \'strȯŋ-gəst\ [OE *strang*] **1** : having or marked by great physical power : ROBUST **2** : having moral or intellectual power **3** : having great resources (as of wealth) **4** : of a specified number ⟨an army ten thousand *strong*⟩ **5** : effective or efficient esp. in a specified direction **6** : FORCEFUL, COGENT ⟨*strong* arguments⟩ **7** : not mild or weak : INTENSE: as **a** : rich in some active agent (as a flavor or extract) ⟨*strong* beer⟩ **b** : high in saturation and medium in lightness ⟨a *strong* red⟩ **c** : ionizing freely in solution ⟨*strong* acids and bases⟩ **d** : magnifying by refracting greatly ⟨*strong* lens⟩ **8** : moving with rapidity or force ⟨*strong* wind⟩ **9** : ARDENT, ZEALOUS ⟨*strong* advocates of peace⟩ **10 a** : able to withstand stress : not easily injured : SOLID **b** : not easily subdued or taken ⟨a *strong* fort⟩ **11** : well established : FIRM **12** : having an offensive or intense odor or flavor : RANK **13** : of, relating to, or constituting a verb or verb conjugation that forms the past tense by a change in the root vowel and the past participle usu. by the addition of -*en* with or without change of the root vowel (as *strive, strove, striven* or *drink, drank, drunk*) — **strong** *adv* — **strong·ly** \'strȯŋ-lē\ *adv*

strong–arm \'strȯŋ-'ärm\ *adj* : having or using undue force : VIOLENT ⟨*strong-arm* methods⟩

strong–box \-,bäks\ *n* : a strongly made container for money or valuables

strong·hold \-,hōld\ *n* : a fortified place : FORTRESS

strong–mind·ed \-'mīn-dəd\ *adj* : markedly independent in thought and judgment — **strong–mind·ed·ly** *adv* — **strong–mind·ed·ness** *n*

strong room *n* : a room for money or valuables specially constructed to be fireproof and burglar-proof

strong suit *n* **1** : a long suit containing high cards **2** : something in which one excels : FORTE

stron·tium \'strän-ch(ē-)əm, 'stränt-ē-əm\ *n* [NL, fr. *strontia* strontium monoxide, fr. *Strontian*, village in Scotland] : a soft malleable ductile metallic element occurring only in combination — see ELEMENT table

strontium 90 *n* : a heavy radioactive isotope of strontium having the mass number 90 that is present in the fallout from nuclear explosions

¹strop \'sträp\ *n* [OE, thong for securing an oar, fr. L *stroppus* band, strap, fr. Gk *strophos*] : STRAP; *esp* : a usu. leather band for sharpening a razor

²strop *vt* **stropped; strop·ping** : to sharpen (a razor) on a strop

stro·phe \'strō-fē\ *n* [Gk *strophē*, lit., turn, fr. *strephein* to twist, turn] : a division of a poem : STANZA — **stroph·ic** \'sträf-ik, 'strō-fik\ *adj*

strove *past & chiefly dial past part of* STRIVE

struck \'strək\ *adj* : closed or affected by a labor strike ⟨a *struck* factory⟩ ⟨a *struck* employer⟩

struc·tur·al \'strək-chə-rəl, 'strək-shrəl\ *adj* **1** : of, relating to, or affecting structure ⟨*structural* defects⟩ ⟨*structural* principles⟩ **2** : used or formed for use in construction ⟨*structural* steel⟩ — **struc·tur·al·ly** \-ē\ *adv*

---

j joke; ŋ sing; ō flow; ȯ flaw; ȯi coin; th thin; th this; ü loot;   u̇ foot; y yet; yü few; yu̇ furious; zh vision

structural formula *n* : an expanded molecular formula showing the arrangement within the molecule of atoms and of bonds

¹**struc·ture** \'strək-chər\ *n* [L *struct-*, *struere* to heap up, build] **1** : the action of building : CONSTRUCTION **2 a** : something constructed **b** : something made up of interdependent parts in a definite pattern of organization **3** : manner of construction : MAKEUP **4** : the arrangement or relationship of elements (as particles, parts, or organs) in a substance, body, or system ⟨soil *structure*⟩ ⟨the *structure* of a plant⟩ ⟨molecular *structure*⟩ ⟨social *structure*⟩ ⟨the *structure* of a language⟩ — **struc·ture·less** \-ləs\ *adj*

²**structure** *vt* **struc·tured; struc·tur·ing** \'strək-chə-riŋ, 'strək-shriŋ\ : to form into a structure : ORGANIZE

stru·del \'s(h)trüd-ᵊl\ *n* [G] : a sheet of thin dough rolled up with filling and baked

¹**strug·gle** \'strəg-əl\ *vi* **strug·gled; strug·gling** \'strəg-(ə-)liŋ\ [ME *struglen*] **1** : to make violent strenuous efforts against opposition : STRIVE **2** : to proceed with difficulty or with great effort ⟨*struggled* through the snow⟩ — **strug·gler** \-(ə-)lər\ *n*

²**struggle** *n* **1** : a violent effort or exertion **2** : CONTEST, STRIFE

struggle for existence : the automatic competition (as for food, space, or light) of members of a natural population that tends to eliminate less efficient individuals and thereby to increase the chance of the more efficient to pass on their adaptive traits

strum \'strəm\ *vb* **strummed; strum·ming** : to play on a stringed instrument usu. idly or unskillfully — **strum·mer** *n*

stru·mose \'strü-,mōs\ *adj* [L *struma* scrofulous tumor] : SWOLLEN; *esp* : having many small surface swellings

strum·pet \'strəm-pət\ *n* [ME] : PROSTITUTE, HARLOT

strung *past of* STRING

¹**strut** \'strət\ *vb* **strut·ted; strut·ting** [OE *strūtian* to exert oneself] **1** : to walk with a stiff proud gait **2** : to parade (as clothes) with a show of pride — **strut·ter** *n* **syn** STRUT, SWAGGER mean to assume an air of importance. STRUT emphasizes pompous dignity and vanity; SWAGGER suggests ostentatiousness and insolence or boastfulness

²**strut** *n* **1** : a bar or brace to resist pressure in the direction of its length **2** : a pompous step or walk

strych·nine \'strik-,nīn, -nən, -,nēn\ *n* [F, fr. Gk *strychnos* nightshade] : a bitter poisonous alkaloid obtained from nux vomica and related plants and used as an economic poison (as for rodents) and medicinally as a tonic and stimulant

Stu·art \'st(y)ü-ərt, 'st(y)ù-(ə)rt\ *n* : a member of a British royal house furnishing rulers of Scotland from 1371 to 1603 and of Great Britain during most of the period from 1603 to 1714 — **Stuart** *adj*

¹**stub** \'stəb\ *n* [OE *stybb*] **1** : STUMP 1b **2** : something having or worn to a short or blunt shape: as **a** : a pen with a short blunt nib **b** : a short part left after a larger part has been broken off or used up ⟨pencil *stub*⟩ **3 a** : a small part of a check kept as a record of the contents of the check **b** : the part of a ticket returned to the user

²**stub** *vt* **stubbed; stub·bing** **1** : to pull by the roots ⟨*stub* out brush⟩ or to clear (land) by stubbing plants **2** : to extinguish (as a cigarette) by crushing **3** : to strike (as one's toe) against an object

stub·ble \'stəb-əl\ *n* [L *stipula, stupula*] **1** : the stem ends of herbaceous plants and esp. cereal grasses remaining attached to the soil after harvest **2** : a rough surface or growth resembling stubble; *esp* : a short growth of beard — **stub·bly** \'stəb-(ə-)lē\ *adj*

stub·born \'stəb-ərn\ *adj* [ME *stuborn*] **1 a** : having a firm idea or purpose : DETERMINED **b** : hard to convince, persuade, or move to action : OBSTINATE ⟨*stubborn* as a mule⟩ **2** : done or continued in an obstinate or persistent manner ⟨*stubborn* refusal⟩ **3** : difficult to handle, manage, or treat ⟨*stubborn* hair⟩ **syn** see OBSTINATE — **stub·born·ly** *adv* — **stub·born·ness** \-ərn-nəs\ *n*

stub·by \'stəb-ē\ *adj* **stub·bi·er; -est** **1** : resembling a stub esp. in shortness and broadness ⟨*stubby* fingers⟩ **2** : abounding with stubs : BRISTLY — **stub·bi·ness** *n*

¹**stuc·co** \'stək-ō\ *n, pl* **stuccos** *or* **stuccoes** [It, of Gmc origin] : a plaster made of portland cement, sand, and lime) used to cover exterior walls or ornament interior walls

²**stucco** *vt* : to coat or decorate with stucco

stuc·co·work \'stək-ō-,wərk\ *n* : work done in stucco

stuck *past of* STICK

stuck-up \'stək-'əp\ *adj* : CONCEITED, SELF-IMPORTANT

¹**stud** \'stəd\ *n* [OE *stōd*] : a group of animals and esp. horses kept primarily for breeding; *also* : the place where they are kept **2** : a male animal (as a stallion) kept for breeding — **at stud** : for breeding as a stud

²**stud** *n* [OE *studu* post] **1** : one of the smaller uprights in the framing of the walls of a building to which sheathing, paneling, or laths are fastened : SCANTLING **2 a** : a boss, rivet, or nail with a large head used for ornament or protection **b** : a solid button with a shank or eye on the back inserted through an eyelet in a garment as a fastener or ornament **3** : a piece (as a rod or pin) projecting from a machine and serving chiefly as a support or axis

³**stud** *vt* **stud·ded; stud·ding** **1** : to furnish (a building or wall) with studs **2** : to adorn, cover, or protect with studs **3** : to set (a place or thing) with a number of prominent objects ⟨water *studded* with islands⟩

stud·book \'stəd-,bùk\ *n* : an official record of the pedigree of purebred animals (as horses or dogs)

stud·ding \'stəd-iŋ\ *n* **1** : material for studs **2** : STUDS

stud·ding sail \'stəd-iŋ-,sāl, 'stən(t)-səl\ *n* : a light sail set at the side of a principal square sail of a ship in light winds

stu·dent \'st(y)üd-ᵊnt, *esp South* -ənt\ *n* [L *student-, studens,* fr. prp. of *studēre* to be zealous, study] **1** : LEARNER, SCHOLAR; *esp* : one who attends a school or college **2** : one who studies : an attentive and systematic observer ⟨a *student* of life⟩ **syn** see SCHOLAR

student government *n* : the organization and management of student life, activities, or discipline by various student organizations in a school or college

student teacher *n* : a student who is engaged in practice teaching

stud·horse \'stəd-,hòrs\ *n* : a stallion kept esp. for breeding

stud·ied \'stəd-ēd\ *adj* **1** : KNOWLEDGEABLE, LEARNED **2** : carefully considered or prepared : THOUGHTFUL **3** : produced or marked by conscious design or premeditation ⟨*studied* indifference⟩ — **stud·ied·ly** *adv* — **stud·ied·ness** *n*

stu·dio \'st(y)üd-ē-,ō\ *n, pl* **-di·os** [It, lit., study, fr. L *studium*] **1 a** : the working place of an artist **b** : a place for the study of an art **2** : a place where motion pictures are made **3** : a place maintained and equipped for the transmission of radio or television programs

studio couch *n* : an upholstered usu. backless couch that can be made to serve as a double bed by sliding from underneath it the frame of a single cot

stu·di·ous \'st(y)üd-ē-əs\ *adj* **1** : given to or concerned with study ⟨a *studious* boy⟩ ⟨*studious* habits⟩ **2** : marked by purposeful diligence : EARNEST ⟨made a *studious* effort to obey the rules⟩ — **stu·di·ous·ly** *adv* — **stu·di·ous·ness** *n*

¹**study** \'stəd-ē\ *n, pl* **stud·ies** [OF *estudie,* fr. L *studium* zeal, study] **1** : a state of contemplation : REVERIE **2 a** : application of the mind to the acquisition of knowledge often about a particular field or topic **b** : a careful examination or analysis of something; *also* : a report or publication on such a study **3** : a building or room devoted to study or literary pursuits **4** : PURPOSE, INTENT **5 a** : a branch or department of learning : SUBJECT **b** : the activity or work of a student **6** : a usu. preliminary or elementary artistic production concerned esp. with problems of technique ⟨a series of *studies* of classic heads⟩

²**study** *vb* **stud·ied; stud·y·ing** **1** : to engage in study or the study of ⟨*studied* hard⟩ ⟨liked to *study* literature⟩ **2** : ENDEAVOR, TRY ⟨*studied* to please his employer⟩ **3** : to develop a plan for : DESIGN ⟨*studied* out a better power system⟩ **4** : to consider attentively or in detail esp. with the intent of fixing in the mind or of appraising ⟨*study* a part in a play⟩ ⟨*studied* the question carefully⟩

study hall *n* **1** : a room in a school set aside for study **2** : a period in a student's day set aside for study and homework

¹**stuff** \'stəf\ *n* [MF *estoffe*] **1** : materials, supplies, or equipment used in various activities: as **a** : a person's or a family's movable possessions (as household goods or baggage) **b** : material to be manufactured, wrought, or used in construction **c** : a finished textile suitable for

clothing; *esp* : wool or worsted material   **2 a** : writing, discourse, or ideas often of little or transitory worth   **b** : actions or talk of a particular and often objectionable kind ⟨how do they get away with such *stuff*⟩   **3 a** : an aggregate of matter ⟨volcanic rock is curious *stuff*⟩   **b** : matter of a particular kind often unspecified ⟨sold tons of the *stuff*⟩   **4 a** : fundamental material : SUBSTANCE ⟨*stuff* of greatness⟩ ⟨*stuff* of manhood⟩   **b** : subject matter   **5** : special knowledge or capability ⟨a person who has the *stuff* will do well here⟩

²stuff *vb*   **1 a** : to fill by or as if by packing things in : CRAM   **b** : to eat gluttonously : GORGE, SURFEIT   **c** : to fill with a stuffing   **d** : to stop up : PLUG   **e** : to fill with ideas or information   **2** : to put or push into something esp. carelessly or casually : cause to enter or fill : THRUST, PRESS ⟨*stuffed* the clothes into the drawer⟩ ⟨*stuffed* a letter behind the clock⟩   **3** : to fill (a ballot box) with fraudulent votes — **stuff·er** *n*

stuffed shirt *n* : a smug, conceited, and usu. pompous and inflexibly conservative person

stuff·ing \ˈstəf-iŋ\ *n* : material used to stuff something; *esp* : a seasoned mixture used to stuff meat, vegetables, eggs, or poultry

stuffy \ˈstəf-ē\ *adj* **stuff·i·er; -est**   **1** : SULLEN, ILL= HUMORED   **2 a** : oppressive to the breathing : CLOSE   **b** : stuffed or choked up   **3** : DULL, STODGY   **4** : narrowly inflexible in standards of conduct : SELF-RIGHTEOUS — **stuff·i·ly** \ˈstəf-ə-lē\ *adv* — **stuff·i·ness** \ˈstəf-ē-nəs\ *n*

stul·ti·fy \ˈstəl-tə-ˌfī\ *vt* **-fied; -fy·ing** [L *stultus* foolish]   **1** : to cause to appear or be stupid, foolish, or absurdly illogical   **2** : to make futile or useless esp. through weakening or repressive influences ⟨*stultify* initiative⟩ ⟨the *stulti-fying* effect of a rigid caste system⟩ — **stul·ti·fi·ca·tion** \ˌstəl-tə-fə-ˈkā-shən\ *n*

stum·ble \ˈstəm-bəl\ *vi* **stum·bled; stum·bling** \-b(ə-)liŋ\ [ME *stumblen*]   **1** : to trip in walking or run-ning; *also* : to walk unsteadily   **2 a** : to blunder morally   **b** : to speak or act in a blundering or clumsy manner   **3** : to come or happen unexpectedly or by chance ⟨*stum-bled* on a discovery⟩ ⟨*stumbled* onto the ruins of an old fort⟩ — **stumble** *n* — **stum·bler** \-b(ə-)lər\ *n* — **stum·bling·ly** \-b(ə-)liŋ-lē\ *adv*

stum·bling block \ˈstəm-bliŋ-\ *n*   **1** : an impediment to belief or understanding : PERPLEXITY   **2** : an obstacle to progress

¹stump \ˈstəmp\ *n* [ME *stumpe*]   **1 a** : the base of a bodily part (as an arm or leg) remaining after the rest is removed   **b** : the part of a plant and esp. a tree remaining attached to the root after the top is cut off   **2** : a part (as of a tooth or pencil) remaining after the rest is worn away or lost : STUB   **3** : a place or occasion for political public speaking

²stump *vb*   **1 a** : STUB 3   **b** : to walk or walk over heavily or clumsily   **2 a** : CHALLENGE, DARE   **b** : PERPLEX, CON-FOUND   **3** : to clear (land) of stumps   **4** : to go about making political speeches or supporting a cause ⟨*stump* the state for the reform candidate⟩ — **stump·er** *n*

³stump *n* : a pointed roll of leather or paper used for shading a drawing by rubbing

stump·age \ˈstəm-pij\ *n* : the value of standing timber; *also* : uncut timber or the right to cut it

stump speaking *n* : speaking addressed to the general public esp. during a political campaign

stumpy \ˈstəm-pē\ *adj* **stump·i·er; -est**   **1** : full of stumps   **2** : being short and thick : SQUAT

stun \ˈstən\ *vt* **stunned; stun·ning** [OF *estoner* to aston-ish, fr. L *ex-* + *tonare* to thunder]   **1** : to make senseless or dizzy or as if by a blow   **2** : BEWILDER, STUPEFY ⟨*stunned* by the news⟩ — **stun** *n*

stung *past of* STING

stunk *past of* STINK

stun·ner \ˈstən-ər\ *n* : one that stuns; *esp* : an unusually attractive person

stun·ning \ˈstən-iŋ\ *adj*   **1** : tending or able to stupefy or bewilder ⟨a *stunning* blow⟩   **2** : strikingly lovely or pleasing ⟨a *stunning* dress⟩ — **stun·ning·ly** \-iŋ-lē\ *adv*

¹stunt \ˈstənt\ *vt* [E dial. *stunt* stunted, abrupt] : to hinder the normal growth of : DWARF

²stunt *n* : a plant disease in which dwarfing occurs

³stunt *n* : an unusual or difficult feat performed or under-taken usu. to gain attention or publicity

⁴stunt *vi* : to perform stunts

stu·pa \ˈstü-pə\ *n* [Skt *stūpa*] : a hemispherical or cylindri-cal mound or tower serving as a Buddhist shrine

stupe \ˈst(y)üp\ *n* : a hot wet often medicated cloth applied externally (as to stimulate circulation)

stu·pe·fa·cient \ˌst(y)ü-pə-ˈfā-shənt\ *adj* : bringing about a stupor : STUPEFYING, NARCOTIC — **stupefacient** *n*

stu·pe·fy \ˈst(y)ü-pə-ˌfī\ *vt* **-fied; -fy·ing** [MF *stupefier*, fr. L *stupefacere*, fr. *stupēre* to be astonished]   **1** : to make stupid, dull, or numb by or as if by drugs   **2** : ASTONISH, BEWILDER — **stu·pe·fac·tion** \ˌst(y)ü-pə-ˈfak-shən\ *n* — **stu·pe·fi·er** \ˈst(y)ü-pə-ˌfī(-ə)r\ *n*

stu·pen·dous \st(y)ü-ˈpen-dəs\ *adj* [L *stupendus* to be wondered at, fr. *stupēre* to be astonished] : stupefying or amazing esp. because of great size or height ⟨*stupendous* gorges⟩ **syn** see MONSTROUS — **stu·pen·dous·ly** *adv* — **stu·pen·dous·ness** *n*

stu·pid \ˈst(y)ü-pəd\ *adj* [L *stupidus*, fr. *stupēre* to be benumbed, be astonished]   **1 a** : slow of mind : OBTUSE   **b** : UNTHINKING, IRRATIONAL   **2 a** : dulled in feeling or sensation : TORPID   **b** : incapable of feeling or sensation   **3** : marked by or resulting from dullness : SENSELESS ⟨a *stupid* mistake⟩   **4** : DREARY, BORING ⟨a *stupid* plot⟩ — **stu·pid·ly** *adv* — **stu·pid·ness** *n*

syn STUPID, DULL, DENSE mean lacking in power to take in ideas or impressions. STUPID implies a slow-witted or dazed state of mind that may be either congenital or temporary; DULL suggests a slow or sluggish mind such as results from disease, depression, or shock; DENSE im-plies a relative imperviousness to new or complex ideas

stu·pid·i·ty \st(y)ü-ˈpid-ət-ē\ *n, pl* **-ties**   **1** : the quality or state of being stupid   **2** : something (as an idea or act) that is stupid

stu·por \ˈst(y)ü-pər\ *n* [L, fr. *stupēre* to be benumbed]   **1** : a condition characterized by great dulling or suspen-sion of sense or feeling ⟨drunken *stupor*⟩   **2** : a state of extreme apathy or torpor resulting often from stress or shock **syn** see LETHARGY — **stu·por·ous** \-p(ə-)rəs\ *adj*

stur·dy \ˈstərd-ē\ *adj* **stur·di·er; -est** [ME, brave, stub-born, fr. OF *estourdi* stunned, fr. pp. of *estourdir* to stun, fr. (assumed) VL *exturdire* to be dizzy as a thrush that is drunk from eating grapes, fr. L *ex-* + *turdus* thrush]   **1 a** : firmly built or made : STOUT   **b** : HARDY   **c** : sound in design or execution : SUBSTANTIAL   **2 a** : marked by or reflecting physical strength or vigor : ROBUST   **b** : FIRM, RESOLUTE — **stur·di·ly** \ˈstərd-°l-ē\ *adj* — **stur·di·ness** \ˈstərd-ē-nəs\ *n*

stur·geon \ˈstər-jən\ *n* [OF *estourjon*] : any of various usu. large long-bodied fishes that have a thick skin with rows of bony plates and are valued for their flesh and esp. for their roe which is made into caviar

¹stut·ter \ˈstət-ər\ *vb* : to speak or utter with spasmodic repetition as a result of excitement or impediment **syn** see STAMMER — **stut·ter·er** \ˈstət-ər-ər\ *n*

²stutter *n*   **1** : an act or instance of stuttering   **2** : a speech impediment involving stuttering

¹sty \ˈstī\ *n, pl* **sties** *also* **styes** \ˈstīz\ [OE *stig*]   **1** : a pen or enclosed housing for swine   **2** : a filthy, low, or vicious place

²sty *or* **stye** \ˈstī\ *n, pl* **sties** *or* **styes** \ˈstīz\ [short for earlier *styan*, fr. OE *stigend*, fr. *stīgan* to rise] : an inflamed swelling of a skin gland on the edge of an eyelid

sty·gian \ˈstij-(ē-)ən\ *adj, often cap* [Gk *Styg-*, *Styx* Styx]   **1** : of or relating to the river Styx   **2** : INFERNAL, GLOOMY

sty·lar \ˈstī-lər\ *adj* : STYLIFORM

sty·late \ˈstī-ˌlāt\ *adj* : bearing or resembling a style or stylet ⟨*stylate* insects⟩

¹style \ˈstīl\ *n* [L *stilus* stake, stylus, style of writing]   **1 a** : an instrument used by the ancients in writing on waxed tablets   **b** : the shadow-producing pin of a sundial   **c** : GRAVER   **d** : a phonograph needle   **e** : a slender pro-longation of a plant ovary bearing a stigma at its apex   **f** : a slender bodily process of an animal   **2** : mode of expressing thought in language; *esp* : one characteristic of an individual, period, school, or nation ⟨ornate *style*⟩   **3** : the custom or plan followed in spelling, capitalization, punctuation, and typographic arrangement and display   **4** : mode of address : TITLE   **5 a** (1) : manner or method of acting or performing esp. as sanctioned by some standard   (2) : a distinctive or characteristic manner   **b** : a fashion-able manner or mode ⟨dining in *style*⟩ ⟨her dress is out of *style*⟩ **c** : overall excellence, skill, or grace in performance, manner, or appearance **syn** see DICTION, FASHION — **style-less** \'stīl-ləs\ *adj*

²**style** *vt* **1** : NAME, CALL ⟨*styles* himself a scientist⟩ **2 a** : to cause to conform to a customary style **b** : to design and make in accord with the prevailing mode — **styl·er** *n*

style·book \'stīl-,búk\ *n* : a book explaining, describing, or illustrating the prevailing, accepted, or authorized style ⟨a *stylebook* for printers⟩

sty·let \'stī-lət\ *n* **1** : a slender surgical probe **2** : a style on an animal

sty·li·form \'stī-lə-,fórm\ *adj* : resembling a style : bristle-shaped

styl·ish \'stī-lish\ *adj* : having style; *esp* : conforming to current fashion — **styl·ish·ly** *adv* — **styl·ish·ness** *n*

styl·ist \'stī-ləst\ *n* **1** : a master or model of style; *esp* : a writer or speaker eminent in matters of style **2** : one who develops, designs, or advises on styles — **sty·lis·tic** \stī-'lis-tik\ *also* **sty·lis·ti·cal** \-ti-kəl\ *adj* — **sty·lis·ti·cal·ly** \-ti-k(ə-)lē\ *adv*

styl·ize \'stīl-,īz\ *vt* : to conform to a style : CONVENTIONALIZE; *esp* : to represent or design according to a style or stylistic pattern rather than according to nature — **styl·i·za·tion** \,stī-lə-'zā-shən\ *n* — **styl·iz·er** \'stīl-,ī-zər\ *n*

sty·lo·bate \'stī-lə-,bāt\ *n* [Gk *stylobatēs*, fr. *stylos* pillar + *bainein* to walk, go] : a continuous flat coping or pavement on which a row of architectural columns is supported

sty·loid \'stī-,lóid\ *adj* : resembling a style ⟨the slender pointed *styloid* process of the ulna⟩

sty·lus \'stī-ləs\ *n, pl* **sty·li** \'stī-,lī\ *also* **sty·lus·es** \'stī-lə-səz\ [NL, alter. of L *stilus* stake, stylus] **1** : STYLE 1e **2** : an instrument for writing or marking **3** : a phonograph needle

¹**sty·mie** \'stī-mē\ *n* **1** : a condition existing on a golf putting green when the ball nearer the hole lies in the line of play of another ball **2** : OBSTACLE

²**stymie** *vt* **sty·mied; sty·mie·ing** : BLOCK, CHECK ⟨an intercepted pass *stymied* our drive for a touchdown⟩

styp·tic \'stip-tik\ *adj* [Gk *styptikos*, fr. *styphein* to contract] : tending to contract or bind : ASTRINGENT; *esp* : tending to check bleeding ⟨*styptic* effect of cold⟩ — **styptic** *n* — **styp·tic·i·ty** \stip-'tis-ət-ē\ *n*

sty·rene \'stī(ə)r-,ēn\ *n* [L *styrax*, a resin from trees] : a fragrant liquid hydrocarbon used chiefly in making synthetic rubber, resins, and plastics

Styx \'stiks\ *n* : the chief river of the lower world in Greek mythology

sua·sion \'swā-zhən\ *n* [L *suas-, suadēre* to urge; akin to E *sweet*] : the act of influencing or persuading — **sua·sive** \'swā-siv, -ziv\ *adj* — **sua·sive·ly** *adv* — **sua·sive·ness** *n*

suave \'swäv\ *adj* [L *suavis*; akin to E *sweet*] : persuasively pleasing : smoothly polite and agreeable — **suave·ly** *adv* — **suave·ness** *n* — **suav·i·ty** \'swäv-ət-ē\ *n*

syn SUAVE, URBANE, BLAND, SMOOTH mean pleasingly tactful and well-mannered. SUAVE implies a specific ability to deal with others easily and without friction ⟨*suave* headwaiter⟩ URBANE suggests courtesy and poise developed by wide social experience ⟨*urbane* toastmaster⟩ BLAND emphasizes mildness of manner and absence of irritating qualities ⟨*bland*, kindly old gentleman⟩ SMOOTH usu. suggests a deliberately assumed suavity ⟨a *smooth* liar⟩

¹**sub** \'səb\ *n* : SUBSTITUTE

²**sub** *vi* **subbed; sub·bing** : to act as a substitute

³**sub** *n* : SUBMARINE

sub- \'səb, ,səb\ *prefix* [L, under, below, secretly, from below, up, near; akin to E *up*] **1** : under : beneath : below ⟨*subsoil*⟩ ⟨*subaqueous*⟩ **2 a** : subordinate : secondary ⟨*substation*⟩ **b** : subordinate portion of : subdivision of ⟨*subcommittee*⟩ ⟨*subtopic*⟩ ⟨*subspecies*⟩ **3** : with repetition of a process described in a simple verb so as to form, stress, or deal with subordinate parts or relations ⟨*sublet*⟩ ⟨*subcontract*⟩ **4 a** : less than completely, perfectly, or typically : somewhat ⟨*subdominant*⟩ ⟨*subovate*⟩ ⟨*subclinical*⟩

b : falling nearly in the category of and often adjoining : bordering upon ⟨*subarctic*⟩

sub·aer·i·al \,səb-'ar-ē-əl, 'səb-, -'er-; ,səb-ā-'ir-ē-əl\ *adj* : situated or occurring on or close to the surface of the earth ⟨*subaerial* habitat⟩ ⟨*subaerial* roots⟩ — **sub·aer·i·al·ly** \-ē-ə-lē\ *adv*

sub·al·pine \,səb-'al-,pīn, 'səb-\ *adj* **1** : of or relating to the region about the foot and lower slopes of the Alps **2** *cap* : of, relating to, or growing on upland slopes near timberline

¹**sub·al·tern** \sə-'bòl-tərn, *Brit* 'səb-əl-tərn\ *adj* [LL *subalternus*, fr. *sub-* + *alternus* alternate] : of low or lower rank : SUBORDINATE

²**subaltern** *n* : SUBORDINATE; *esp* : a commissioned officer in the British army below the rank of captain

sub·aque·ous \,səb-'ā-kwē-əs, 'səb-, -'ak-wē-\ *adj* [L *aqua* water] : formed, occurring, or existing in or under water

sub·arc·tic \-'ärk-tik, -'ärt-ik\ *adj* : of, relating to, or being regions immediately outside of the arctic circle or regions similar to these in climate or conditions of life

sub·as·sem·bly \,səb-ə-'sem-blē\ *n* : an assembled unit designed to be incorporated with other units in a finished product

sub·atom·ic \,səb-ə-'täm-ik\ *adj* : of or relating to the inside of the atom or particles smaller than atoms

sub·car·ti·lag·i·nous \,səb-,kärt-ᵊl-'aj-ə-nəs\ *adj* **1** : partially cartilaginous **2** : situated under a cartilage

sub·class \'səb-,klas\ *n* : a primary division of a class (as in taxonomy)

¹**sub·cla·vi·an** \,səb-'klā-vē-ən\ *adj* **1** : located under the clavicle **2** : of, relating to, or being a subclavian part

²**subclavian** *n* : a subclavian part (as an artery, vein, or nerve)

sub·clin·i·cal \,səb-'klin-i-kəl, 'səb-\ *adj* : not severe enough to be detectable by the usual clinical tests ⟨*subclinical* infection⟩ — **sub·clin·i·cal·ly** \-k(ə-)lē\ *adv*

sub·com·mit·tee \'səb-kə-,mit-ē\ *n* : a subdivision of a committee usu. organized for a specific purpose

sub·com·pact \'səb-'käm-,pakt\ *n* : an automobile smaller than a compact

¹**sub·con·scious** \,səb-'kän-chəs, 'səb-\ *adj* **1** : existing in the mind but not immediately available to consciousness **2** : imperfectly conscious ⟨a *subconscious* state⟩ — **sub·con·scious·ly** *adv* — **sub·con·scious·ness** *n*

²**subconscious** *n* : the mental activities just below the threshold of consciousness

sub·con·ti·nent \'səb-'känt-ᵊn-ənt, -'känt-nənt\ *n* : a large landmass (as Greenland) smaller than any of the usu. recognized continents; *also* : a major subdivision of a continent — **sub·con·ti·nen·tal** \,səb-,känt-ᵊn-'ent-ᵊl\ *adj*

sub·con·tract \'səb-'kän-,trakt\ *n* : a contract between a party to an original contract and a third party who usu. agrees to supply work or materials required in the original contract — **sub·con·tract** \,səb-'kän-,trakt, 'səb-'; ,səb-kən-'trakt\ *vb* — **sub·con·trac·tor** \,səb-'kän-,trak-tər, 'səb-; ,səb-kən-'trak-tər\ *n*

sub·crit·i·cal \,səb-'krit-i-kəl, 'səb-\ *adj* **1** : less or lower than critical **2** : of insufficient size to sustain a chain reaction ⟨*subcritical* mass of fissionable material⟩

sub·cul·ture \'səb-,kəl-chər\ *n* **1** : a culture (as of bacteria) derived from another culture; *also* : the producing of a subculture **2** : a distinguishable subdivision of a culture or society

sub·cu·ta·ne·ous \,səb-kyu̇-'tā-nē-əs\ *adj* : being, living, used, or made under the skin ⟨*subcutaneous* fat⟩ ⟨a *subcutaneous* needle⟩ ⟨*subcutaneous* parasite⟩ — **sub·cu·ta·ne·ous·ly** *adv*

sub·dea·con \,səb-'dē-kən, 'səb-\ *n* : a cleric ranking below a deacon; *esp* : a candidate for the Roman Catholic priesthood admitted to the lowest of the major orders — **sub·di·ac·o·nate** \-'ak-ə-nət\ *n*

sub·deb \'səb-,deb\ *n* : SUBDEBUTANTE

sub·deb·u·tante \,səb-'deb-yu̇-,tänt, 'səb-\ *n* : a young

See *sub-* and 2d element			
subacid	subapical	subcaliber	subcircular	subconic
subacute	subappressed	subcampanulate	subcivilized	subcordate
subadult	subaquatic	subcaption	subclassification	subcortical
subagency	subarachnoid	subcarcinogenic	subclause	subcostal
subagent	subatmospheric	subcaste	subcollegiate	subcrescentic
subalkaline	subaverage	subcategory	subcolumnar	subcrystalline
subangular	subbasement	subcaudal	subcommission	subcylindric
	subbituminous	subcentral		

girl who is about to become a society debutante; *also* : a girl in her middle teens ⟨*subdebutante* styles⟩

sub·di·vid·a·ble \ˌsəb-də-ˈvīd-ə-bəl\ *adj* : capable of being further divided : suitable for subdividing

sub·di·vide \ˌsəb-də-ˈvīd\ *vb* **1** : to divide the parts of into more parts **2** : to divide into several parts; *esp* : to divide (a tract of land) into building lots — **sub·di·vi·sion** \ˌsəb-də-ˈvizh-ən, ˈsəb-də-ˌ\ *n*

sub·dom·i·nant \ˌsəb-ˈdäm-ə-nənt, ˈsəb-\ *n* **1** : something dominant to an inferior or partial degree **2** : the 4th tone of the major or minor scale (as F in the scale of C) — **subdominant** *adj*

sub·due \səb-ˈd(y)ü\ *vt* [ME *sodewen, subduen* (influenced in form and meaning by L *subdere* to subject), fr. MF *soduire* to seduce (influenced in meaning by L *seducere* to seduce), fr. L *subducere* to withdraw, fr. *sub-* + *ducere* to lead, draw] **1** : to conquer and bring into subjection : VANQUISH **2** : to bring under control or into order : CURB **3** : to reduce the intensity or degree of ⟨*subdued* light⟩ **syn** see CONQUER — **sub·du·er** *n*

su·ber \ˈsü-bər\ *n* [L, cork tree, cork] : corky plant tissue

su·ber·in \ˈsü-bə-rən\ *n* [L *suber* cork] : a complex fatty substance that is the basis of cork

su·ber·ize \ˈsü-bə-ˌrīz\ *vt* : to convert to or infiltrate with suberin — **su·ber·i·za·tion** \ˌsü-bə-rə-ˈzā-shən\ *n*

sub·fam·i·ly \ˈsəb-ˌfam-(ə-)lē\ *n* : a taxonomic category next below a family

sub·freez·ing \ˈsəb-ˈfrē-ziŋ\ *adj* : lower than is required to produce freezing

sub·fusc \ˌsəb-ˈfəsk\ *adj* [L *subfuscus*, lit., brownish, fr. *sub-* + *fuscus* dark brown] : DRAB, DUSKY

sub·grade \ˈsəb-ˌgrād\ *n* : a surface of earth or rock leveled off to receive a foundation (as of a road)

sub·head \ˈsəb-ˌhed\ *or* **sub·head·ing** \-iŋ\ *n* **1** : a heading of a subdivision (as in an outline) **2** : a subordinate caption or title

sub·ja·cent \ˌsəb-ˈjās-ᵊnt\ *adj* [L *subjacēre* to lie under, fr. *sub-* + *jacēre* to lie] : lying under or below; *also* : lower than though not directly below ⟨hills and *subjacent* valleys⟩ — **sub·ja·cen·cy** \-ᵊn-sē\ *n* — **sub·ja·cent·ly** *adv*

¹sub·ject \ˈsəb-jikt\ *n* [L *subjectus* one under authority & *subjectum* subject of a proposition, fr. masc. & neut. respectively of *subjectus*, pp. of *subicere* to throw under, subject, fr. *sub-* + *jacere* to throw] **1** : one that is placed under authority or control: as **a** : one subject to a monarch and governed by his law **b** : one who lives in the territory of, enjoys the protection of, and owes allegiance to a sovereign power or state **2** : the thing or person of which a quality, attribute, or relation is affirmed **3 a** : a department of knowledge or learning **b** : an individual (as a person or plant) that is studied or experimented on; *esp* : a dead body for anatomical dissection **c** (1) : something concerning which something is said or done (2) : something represented or indicated in a work of art **4** : a noun or noun equivalent about which something is stated by the predicate **5** : the principal melodic phrase on which a musical composition or movement is based **syn** see CITIZEN

²subject *adj* **1** : owing obedience or allegiance to the dominion of another **2 a** : EXPOSED, LIABLE **b** : PRONE, DISPOSED **3** : CONDITIONAL, CONTINGENT ⟨*subject* to approval⟩

³sub·ject \səb-ˈjekt\ *vt* **1 a** : to bring under control or dominion : SUBJUGATE **b** : to make amenable to the discipline and control of a superior **2 a** : to make liable : PREDISPOSE **b** : to make accountable : SUBMIT **3** : to cause to undergo or submit to : EXPOSE — **sub·jec·tion** \səb-ˈjek-shən\ *n*

sub·jec·tive \səb-ˈjek-tiv\ *adj* **1** : of, relating to, or being a subject **2** : of, relating to, or arising within one's self or mind in contrast to what is outside : PERSONAL ⟨*subjective* experience⟩ ⟨*subjective* symptoms of disease⟩ — **sub·jec·tive·ly** *adv* — **sub·jec·tiv·i·ty** \ˌ(ˌ)səb-ˌjek-ˈtiv-ət-ē\ *n*

subjective complement *n* : a grammatical complement relating to the subject of an intransitive verb ⟨in "he had fallen sick" *sick* is a *subjective complement*⟩

subject matter *n* : matter presented for consideration in discussion, thought, or study; *also* : the substance as distinguished from the form of a literary or artistic production

sub·join \(ˌ)səb-ˈjóin\ *vt* : ANNEX, APPEND

sub·ju·gate \ˈsəb-jə-ˌgāt\ *vt* [L *subjugare*, lit., to bring under the yoke, fr. *sub jugum* under the yoke] **1** : to force to submit to control and governance : MASTER **2** : to bring into servitude : ENSLAVE **syn** see CONQUER — **sub·ju·ga·tion** \ˌsəb-jə-ˈgā-shən\ *n* — **sub·ju·ga·tor** \ˈsəb-jə-ˌgāt-ər\ *n*

¹sub·junc·tive \səb-ˈjəŋ(k)-tiv\ *adj* [L *subjunct-, subjungere* to subordinate, fr. *sub-* + *jungere* to join] : of, relating to, or constituting the grammatical mood that represents a denoted act or state not as fact but as contingent or possible or viewed emotionally (as with doubt or desire) ⟨the *subjunctive* mood⟩

²subjunctive *n* : the subjunctive mood of a verb or a verb in this mood

sub·lease \ˈsəb-ˈlēs\ *n* : a lease by a tenant of part or all of leased premises to another person — **sublease** *vb*

sub·let \ˈsəb-ˈlet\ *vb* **sub·let**; **sub·let·ting** **1** : to lease or rent all or part of a leased or rented property **2** : SUBCONTRACT

¹sub·li·mate \ˈsəb-lə-ˌmāt\ *vt* **1** : to cause to sublime ⟨*sublimate* sulfur⟩ **2** : to direct the energy of (desires and impulses) from a lower to a higher level — **sub·li·ma·tion** \ˌsəb-lə-ˈmā-shən\ *n*

²sub·li·mate \ˈsəb-lə-ˌmāt, -mət\ *n* : a chemical product obtained by sublimation

¹sub·lime \sə-ˈblīm\ *vb* [L *sublimare* to lift up, elevate, fr. *sublimis* raised on high] **1** : to pass from a solid to a gaseous state on heating and back to solid form on cooling without apparently passing through a liquid state ⟨*sublime* mercury⟩; *also* : to release or purify by such action ⟨*sublime* sulfur from a mixture⟩ **2** : to make finer or more worthy : convert into something better ⟨selfishness *sublimed* into care for the public welfare⟩ — **sub·lim·er** *n*

²sublime *adj* [L *sublimis*, lit., raised on high, fr. *sub* under, up to + *limen* threshold, lintel] **1 a** : lofty, grand, or exalted in thought, expression, or manner ⟨the *sublimest* lines in English prose⟩ **b** : of outstanding spiritual, intellectual, or moral worth ⟨*sublime* devotion to duty⟩ **2** : inspiring awe : SOLEMN ⟨*sublime* scenery⟩ ⟨a *sublime* occasion⟩ — **sub·lime·ly** *adv* — **sub·lime·ness** *n*

sub·lim·i·nal \(ˌ)səb-ˈlim-ən-ᵊl, ˈsəb-\ *adj* [L *limin-, limen* threshold] **1** : inadequate to produce a sensation or a perception ⟨*subliminal* stimuli⟩ **2** : existing or functioning outside the area of conscious awareness ⟨the *subliminal* mind⟩ ⟨*subliminal* techniques in advertising⟩ — **sub·lim·i·nal·ly** \-ᵊl-ē\ *adv*

sub·lim·i·ty \sə-ˈblim-ət-ē\ *n, pl* **-ties** **1** : something sublime or exalted **2** : the quality or state of being sublime

sub·lux·a·tion \ˌsəb-ˌlək-ˈsā-shən\ *n* [LL *luxation-, luxatio* dislocation, fr. L *luxare* to dislocate] : a partial dislocation of a bone or joint

sub·ma·chine gun \ˌsəb-mə-ˈshēn-ˌgən\ *n* : a lightweight automatic or semiautomatic portable firearm fired from the shoulder or hip

sub·mar·gin·al \ˌsəb-ˈmärj-nəl, ˈsəb-, -ən-ᵊl\ *adj* **1** : located near or beneath a margin or a marginal structure **2** : less than marginal; *esp* : inadequate for some end or use ⟨farming *submarginal* land⟩ ⟨a *submarginal* income⟩ — **sub·mar·gin·al·ly** \-ē\ *adv*

¹sub·ma·rine \ˈsəb-mə-ˌrēn, ˌsəb-mə-ˈ\ *adj* : being, acting, or growing under water esp. in the sea ⟨*submarine* plants⟩ ⟨*submarine* cameras⟩

²submarine *n* : something (as an explosive mine) that functions or operates underwater; *esp* : a naval vessel designed for undersea operations

See *sub-* and 2d element				
subdentate	subentry	subflora	subhuman	sublabial
subdepot	subepidermal	subfossil	subhumid	sublateral
subdermal	subequal	subfunctional	subindex	sublethal
subdimension	subequatorial	subgenus	subinterval	sublingual
subdorsal	suberect	subglobose	subintestinal	subliterate
subeffective	subesophageal	subgroup	subirrigate	sublunar
subelliptic	subessential	subhorizontal	subkingdom	sublunary
	subfauna			

³submarine *vt* : to make an attack upon or to sink by means of a submarine

sub·ma·rin·er \'səb-mə-ˌrē-nər, ˌsəb-mə-'; ˌsəb-'mar-ə-\ *n* : a crewman of a submarine

¹sub·max·il·lary \ˌsəb-'mak-sə-ˌler-ē, 'səb-\ *adj* : of, relating to, or situated below the lower jaw

²submaxillary *n, pl* **-lar·ies** : a submaxillary part (as an artery or gland)

sub·me·di·ant \-'mēd-ē-ənt\ *n* : the 6th tone above the tonic

sub·merge \səb-'mərj\ *vb* [L *submers-, submergere*, fr. *sub-* + *mergere* to plunge] **1** : to put under or plunge into water ⟨the whale *submerged*⟩ **2** : to cover or become covered with or as if with water : INUNDATE ⟨floods *submerged* the town⟩ ⟨memories *submerged* by time⟩ — **sub·mer·gence** \-'mər-jən(t)s\ *n* — **sub·merg·i·ble** \-'mər-jə-bəl\ *adj*

sub·merse \-'mərs\ *vt* : SUBMERGE — **sub·mer·sion** \-'mər-zhən\ *n*

sub·mersed *adj* : growing or adapted to grow under water

¹sub·mers·i·ble \səb-'mər-sə-bəl\ *adj* : SUBMERGIBLE

²submersible *n* : a boat capable of submerging : SUBMARINE

sub·mi·cro·scop·ic \ˌsəb-ˌmī-krə-'skäp-ik\ *adj* : too small to be seen in an ordinary light microscope

sub·min·i·a·ture \ˌsəb-'min-ē-ə-ˌchur, 'səb-, -'min-i-ˌchur, -chər\ *adj* : very small ⟨*subminiature* electronic equipment⟩

sub·mis·sion \səb-'mish-ən\ *n* [L *submiss-, submittere* to submit] **1** : an act of submitting something (as for consideration, inspection, or comment) **2** : the condition of being submissive, humble, or compliant **3** : an act of submitting to the authority or control of another

sub·mis·sive \-'mis-iv\ *adj* : inclined or willing to submit to others : YIELDING, MEEK — **sub·mis·sive·ly** *adv*

sub·mit \səb-'mit\ *vb* **sub·mit·ted; sub·mit·ting** [L *submittere* to send to, moderate, fr. *sub-* under, up + *mittere* to send] **1** : to give over or leave to the judgment or approval of someone else : REFER ⟨*submit* an issue for arbitration⟩ **2** : to subject to a process or practice **3** : to put forward as an opinion, reason, or statement : AFFIRM **4** : to yield to power or authority : SURRENDER **syn** see YIELD

sub·mu·co·sa \ˌsəb-myü-'kō-sə\ *n* : a supporting layer of loose connective tissue just under a mucous membrane — **sub·mu·co·sal** \-səl\ *adj* — **sub·mu·cous** \ˌsəb-'myü-kəs, 'səb-\ *adj*

¹sub·nor·mal \ˌsəb-'nor-məl, 'səb-\ *adj* : falling below what is normal — **sub·nor·mal·i·ty** \ˌsəb-nor-'mal-ət-ē\ *n* — **sub·nor·mal·ly** \ˌsəb-'nor-mə-lē, 'səb-\ *adv*

²subnormal *n* : one that is below normal; *esp* : a person of subnormal intelligence

sub·or·bit·al \ˌsəb-'or-bət-ᵊl, 'səb-\ *adj* **1** : situated beneath the eye or its orbit **2** : not being in orbit

sub·or·der \'səb-ˌord-ər\ *n* : a subdivision of an order ⟨a soil *suborder*⟩; *esp* : a taxonomic category ranking between an order and a family

¹sub·or·di·nate \sə-'bord-ᵊn-ət, -'bord-nət\ *adj* [ML *subordinatus*, pp. of *subordinare* to subordinate, fr. L *sub-* + *ordinare* to order] **1** : placed in or occupying a lower class or rank : INFERIOR **2** : submissive to or controlled by authority **3 a** : of, relating to, or constituting a clause that functions as a noun, adjective, or adverb **b** : grammatically subordinating — **sub·or·di·nate·ly** *adv* — **sub·or·di·nate·ness** *n*

²subordinate *n* : one that is subordinate

³sub·or·di·nate \sə-'bord-ᵊn-ˌāt\ *vt* : to make subordinate — **sub·or·di·na·tion** \sə-ˌbord-ᵊn-'ā-shən\ *n* — **sub·or·di·na·tive** \-'bord-ᵊn-ˌāt-iv\ *adj*

sub·orn \sə-'born\ *vt* [L *subornare*, fr. *sub-* secretly + *ornare* to furnish, equip] : to induce secretly to do an improper or unlawful thing and esp. to commit perjury ⟨*suborn* a witness⟩ — **sub·or·na·tion** \ˌsəb-ˌor-'nā-shən\ *n* — **sub·orn·er** \sə-'bor-nər\ *n*

sub·phy·lum \'səb-ˌfī-ləm\ *n* : a primary division of a phylum

sub·plot \-ˌplät\ *n* : a subordinate plot in fiction or drama

¹sub·poe·na \sə-'pē-nə\ *n* [L *sub poena* under penalty] : a writ commanding a person designated in it to appear in court under a penalty for failure to appear

²subpoena *vt* **-naed; -na·ing** : to serve with or summon by a writ of subpoena

sub ro·sa \ˌsəb-'rō-zə\ *adv* [NL, lit., under the rose; fr. the traditional custom of hanging a rose over the council table to indicate that all present were sworn to secrecy] : in confidence : SECRETLY

sub·scribe \səb-'skrīb\ *vb* [L *subscript-, subscribere*, lit., to write beneath, fr. *sub-* + *scribere* to write] **1 a** : to sign (one's name or a document) usu. to indicate consent to, obligation by, or approval or awareness of something written **b** : to signify adherence or approval by or as if by signing one's name ⟨we fully *subscribe* to your view of the situation⟩ **2 a** : to pledge payment of (as a sum of money) over one's signature ⟨*subscribed* 100 dollars to the building fund⟩ **b** : to agree to contribute to something; *also* : to make an agreed contribution **3 a** : to enter one's name for a publication or service; *also* : to receive a periodical or service regularly on order ⟨*subscribe* to several newspapers⟩ **b** : to make a signed application for securities of a new offering ⟨*subscribed* for 1000 shares⟩ — **sub·scrib·er** *n*

sub·script \'səb-ˌskript\ *n* [L *subscriptus*, pp. of *subscribere* to write beneath] : a distinguishing symbol or letter immediately below or below and to the right or left of another written character — **subscript** *adj*

sub·scrip·tion \səb-'skrip-shən\ *n* **1** : an act or instance of subscribing **2 a** : something that is subscribed **b** : an amount obtained by subscription

sub·se·quent \'səb-si-kwənt, -sə-ˌkwent\ *adj* [L *subsequi* to follow close, fr. *sub-* near + *sequi* to follow] : following in time, order, or place : SUCCEEDING — **sub·se·quence** \-sə-ˌkwen(t)s, -si-kwən(t)s\ *n* — **subsequent** *n* — **sub·se·quent·ly** \-ˌkwent-lē, -kwənt-\ *adv* — **sub·se·quent·ness** \-ˌkwent-, -kwənt-\ *n*

sub·serve \səb-'sərv\ *vt* [L *subservire*, fr. *sub-* + *servire* to serve] **1** : to serve as an instrument or means of **2** : to promote the welfare or purposes of

sub·ser·vi·ence \səb-'sər-vē-ən(t)s\ *also* **sub·ser·vi·en·cy** \-ən-sē\ *n, pl* **-enc·es** *also* **-en·cies** **1** : a subservient or subordinate place or function **2** : obsequious servility

sub·ser·vi·ent \-ənt\ *adj* [L *subservient-, subserviens*, prp. of *subservire* to subserve] **1** : useful in an inferior capacity : SUBORDINATE **2** : obsequiously servile — **sub·ser·vi·ent·ly** *adv*

sub·set \'səb-ˌset\ *n* : a mathematical set each of whose elements is also an element of a more inclusive set

sub·shrub \'səb-ˌshrəb\ *n* **1** : a perennial plant having stems woody toward the base **2** : UNDERSHRUB 2 — **sub·shrub·by** \-ˌshrəb-ē\ *adj*

sub·side \səb-'sīd\ *vi* [L *subsidere*, fr. *sub-* + *sidere* to sit down, sink; akin to E *sit*] **1** : to sink or fall to the bottom : SETTLE **2** : to tend downward : DESCEND, SINK ⟨the flood *subsided* slowly⟩ ⟨the fill *subsided* over the old dump⟩ **3** : to let oneself settle down : SINK ⟨*subside* into a chair⟩ **4** : to become quiet or less : ABATE ⟨as the fever *subsides*⟩ ⟨his anger *subsided*⟩ — **sub·sid·ence** \səb-'sīd-ᵊn(t)s, 'səb-səd-ən(t)s\ *n*

¹sub·sid·i·ary \səb-'sid-ē-ˌer-ē\ *adj* [L *subsidium* reserve troops] **1 a** : furnishing aid or support : AUXILIARY ⟨*subsidiary* details⟩ **b** : of secondary importance : TRIBUTARY ⟨*subsidiary* streams⟩ **2** : of, relating to, affected by, or constituting a subsidy ⟨*subsidiary* payments⟩ — **sub·sid·i·ar·i·ly** \-ˌsid-ē-'er-ə-lē\ *adv*

²subsidiary *n, pl* **-ar·ies** : one that is subsidiary; *esp* : a company wholly controlled by another

sub·si·dize \'səb-sə-ˌdīz, -zə-\ *vt* : to aid or furnish with a subsidy — **sub·si·di·za·tion** \ˌsəb-səd-ə-'zā-shən, ˌsəb-zəd-\ *n*

sub·si·dy \'səb-səd-ē, -zəd-\ *n, pl* **-dies** [L *subsidium* reserve troops, support, assistance, fr. *sub-* near + *sedēre*

See *sub-* and 2d element				
submature	suboceanic	subparagraph	subrational	subscapular
submaximal	subocular	subparallel	subrecent	subscience
submetallic	subopaque	subpermanent	subregion	subsense
subminimal	subopposite	subpolar	subrigid	subseptate
subneural	suboptimal	subpotent	subroutine	subserous
subnutrition	suborbicular	subprincipal	subsaline	subsexual
suboblique	subovate	subprofessional	subsaturated	subshining
	subovoid			

to sit] **:** a grant or gift esp. of money; *esp* **:** a grant by a government to a private person or company or to another government to assist an enterprise advantageous to the public

sub·sist \səb-'sist\ *vi* [LL *subsistere*, fr. L, to halt, remain, fr. *sub-* + *sistere* to come to a stand] **1 :** to have or continue to have existence **:** BE, PERSIST **2 :** to receive maintenance (as food and clothing) **:** LIVE

sub·sist·ence \səb-'sis-tən(t)s\ *n* **1 a :** real being **:** EXISTENCE **b :** CONTINUATION, PERSISTENCE **2 a :** means of subsisting **b :** the minimum (as of food and shelter) necessary to support life — **sub·sist·ent** \-tənt\ *adj*

¹sub·soil \'səb-,soil\ *n* **:** a layer of weathered material that lies just under the surface soil

²subsoil *vt* **:** to turn, break, or stir the subsoil of

sub·son·ic \,səb-'sän-ik, 'səb-\ *adj* **1 :** of, relating to, or being a speed less than that of sound in air **2 :** moving, capable of moving, or utilizing air currents moving at a subsonic speed **3 :** INFRASONIC 1

sub·spe·cies \'səb-,spē-shēz, -sēz\ *n* **:** a subdivision of a species: as **a :** a taxonomic category that ranks immediately below a species and designates a physically distinguishable and geographically isolated group whose members interbreed with those of other subspecies of the same species where their ranges overlap **b :** a named subdivision (as a race or variety) of a taxonomic species — **sub·spe·cif·ic** \,səb-spi-'sif-ik\ *adj*

sub·stance \'səb-stən(t)s\ *n* [OF, fr. L *substantia*, fr. *substare* to stand under, fr. *sub-* + *stare* to stand] **1 a :** essential nature **:** ESSENCE ⟨divine *substance*⟩ **b :** the fundamental or essential part, quality, or import ⟨the *substance* of his speech⟩⟨mistaking shadow for *substance*⟩ **2 a :** physical material from which something is made or which has discrete existence **b :** matter of particular or definite chemical constitution **3 :** material possessions **:** PROPERTY, WEALTH ⟨a man of *substance*⟩

sub·stan·dard \,səb-'stan-dərd, 'səb-\ *adj* **1 :** deviating from or falling short of a standard or norm **2 :** conforming to a pattern of linguistic usage existing within a speech community but not that of the prestige group in that community

sub·stan·tial \səb-'stan-chəl\ *adj* **1 a :** existing as or in substance **:** MATERIAL ⟨*substantial* life⟩ ⟨the *substantial* realities⟩ **b :** not illusory **:** REAL ⟨the *substantial* world⟩ **c :** IMPORTANT, ESSENTIAL ⟨a *substantial* difference in their stories⟩⟨sharing is a *substantial* part of happiness⟩ **2 :** having substance: as **a :** ample to satisfy and nourish ⟨a *substantial* diet⟩ **b :** possessed of means **:** WELL-TO-DO ⟨a *substantial* farmer⟩ **c :** considerable in quantity **:** significantly large ⟨earned a *substantial* wage⟩⟨sent *substantial* reinforcements⟩ **d :** well and sturdily built ⟨a *substantial* frame⟩ ⟨*substantial* buildings⟩ **3 :** being largely but not wholly that specified ⟨the opening night was a *substantial* success⟩ — **sub·stan·ti·al·i·ty** \-,stan-chē-'al-ət-ē\ *n* — **sub·stan·tial·ly** \-'stanch-(ə-)lē\ *adv*

sub·stan·ti·ate \səb-'stan-chē-,āt\ *vt* **1 :** to provide evidence for **:** PROVE ⟨*substantiated* his claims in court⟩ **2 :** to give substance or body to **:** EMBODY — **sub·stan·ti·a·tion** \-,stan-chē-'ā-shən\ *n*

¹sub·stan·tive \'səb-stən-tiv\ *n* [LL *substantivus* having or expressing substance] **:** a word or word group functioning syntactically as a noun — **sub·stan·ti·val** \,səb-stən-'tī-vəl\ *adj* — **sub·stan·ti·val·ly** \-'və-lē\ *adv*

²substantive *adj* [LL *substantivus* having or expressing substance, fr. L *substantia* substance] **1 a :** of, relating to, or constituting something real or independent **b :** belonging to the substance of a thing **:** not external, derivative, or accidental **:** ESSENTIAL ⟨*substantive* rights⟩ **c :** expressing existence ⟨the *substantive* verb is the verb *to be*⟩ **2 :** having the function of a grammatical substantive ⟨a *substantive* clause⟩ **3 :** considerable in amount or numbers **:** SUBSTANTIAL **4 :** creating and defining rights and duties ⟨*substantive* law⟩ — **sub·stan·tive·ly** *adv* — **sub·stan·tive·ness** *n*

sub·sta·tion \'səb-,stā-shən\ *n* **:** a station subordinate to another station (as a post-office branch)

¹sub·sti·tute \'səb-stə-,t(y)üt\ *n* [L *substitutus*, pp. of *substituere* to put in place of, fr. *sub-* + *statuere* to set up,

place] **:** a person or thing that takes the place of another — **substitute** *adj*

²substitute *vb* **1 :** to put in the place of another **:** EXCHANGE **2 :** to serve as a substitute **:** REPLACE — **sub·sti·tu·tion** \,səb-stə-'t(y)ü-shən\ *n* — **sub·sti·tu·tion·al** \-shnəl, -shən-°l\ *adj* — **sub·sti·tu·tion·al·ly** \-ē\ *adv* — **sub·sti·tu·tion·ary** \-shə-,ner-ē\ *adj*

sub·strate \'səb-,strāt\ *n* **1 :** the base on which an organism lives or over which it moves ⟨the soil is the *substrate* of most seed plants⟩ **2 :** a substance acted upon (as by an enzyme)

sub·stra·tum \'səb-,strāt-əm, -,strat-\ *n* [ML, fr. L, neut. of *substratus*, pp. of *substernere* to spread under, fr. *sub-* + *sternere* to spread] **:** an underlying support **:** FOUNDATION: as **a :** the material of which something is made and from which it derives its special qualities **b :** a layer beneath the surface soil **:** SUBSOIL **c :** SUBSTRATE

sub·struc·ture \'səb-,strək-chər\ *n* **:** FOUNDATION, GROUNDWORK

sub·sume \səb-'süm\ *vt* [NL *subsumere*, fr. L *sub-* + *sumere* to take] **:** to classify within a larger category or under a general principle — **sub·sump·tion** \səb-'səm(p)-shən\ *n*

sub·sur·face \'səb-,sər-fəs\ *adj* **:** of, relating to, or involving an area or material beneath a surface (as of the earth) ⟨*subsurface* water⟩

sub·teen \'səb-'tēn\ *n* **:** one of less than teen age; *esp* **:** a girl under 13 years of age for whom clothing in sizes 8–14 is designed

sub·ten·ant \,səb-'ten-ənt, 'səb-\ *n* **:** one who subleases from a tenant

sub·tend \səb-'tend\ *vt* [L *subtendere* to stretch beneath, fr. *sub-* + *tendere* to stretch] **1 a :** to be opposite to ⟨hypotenuse *subtends* a right angle⟩ **b :** to extend under and mark off ⟨a chord *subtends* an arc⟩ **2 :** to underlie so as to include

sub·ter·fuge \'səb-tər-,fyüj\ *n* [LL *subterfugium*, fr. L *subterfugere* to evade, fr. *subter-* beneath, secretly + *fugere* to flee] **:** a device (as a plan or trick) used to avoid some unpleasant circumstance (as to escape blame) **:** a deceptive evasion

sub·ter·ra·ne·an \,səb-tə-'rā-nē-ən\ *or* **sub·ter·ra·ne·ous** \-nē-əs\ *adj* [L *subterraneus*, fr. *sub terra* under the earth] **1 :** being, living, or operating under the surface of the earth **2 :** existing or working in secret **:** HIDDEN — **sub·ter·ra·ne·an·ly** *adv*

sub·tile \'sət-°l, 'səb-t°l\ *adj* **sub·til·er** \'sət-lər, -°l-ər; 'səb-tə-lər\; **sub·til·est** \'sət-ləst, -°l-əst; 'səb-tə-ləst\ **1 :** SUBTLE, ELUSIVE ⟨a *subtile* aroma⟩ **2 :** CUNNING, CRAFTY — **sub·tile·ly** \'sət-lē, -°l-(l)ē; 'səb-tə-lē\ *adv* — **sub·tile·ness** \'sət-°l-nəs, 'səb-t°l-\ *n*

sub·til·ty \'sət-°l-tē, 'səb-t°l-\ *n, pl* **-ties** **:** SUBTLETY

sub·ti·tle \'səb-,tīt-°l\ *n* **1 :** a secondary or explanatory title **2 :** a printed statement or fragment of dialogue appearing on the screen between the scenes of a silent motion picture or appearing as a translation at the bottom of the screen during the scenes — **subtitle** *vt*

sub·tle \'sət-°l\ *adj* **sub·tler** \'sət-lər, -°l-ər\; **sub·tlest** \'sət-ləst, -°l-əst\ [L *subtilis*, lit., finely woven] **1 a :** DELICATE, ELUSIVE ⟨a *subtle* fragrance⟩ **b :** difficult to understand or distinguish **:** OBSCURE ⟨*subtle* differences in vowel sounds⟩ **2 a :** marked by insight and sensitivity **:** PERCEPTIVE ⟨a *subtle* mind⟩ ⟨*subtle* characterizations of his friends⟩ **b :** SKILLFUL, EXPERT ⟨*subtle* workmanship⟩; *also* **:** cleverly made or contrived ⟨a *subtle* mechanism⟩ **3 a :** WILY, DEVIOUS, ARTFUL ⟨*subtle* flattery⟩ ⟨a *subtle* scheme⟩ **b :** INSIDIOUS ⟨*subtle* poison⟩ — **sub·tle·ness** \'sət-°l-nəs\ *n* — **sub·tly** \'sət-lē, -°l-(l)ē\ *adv*

sub·tle·ty \'sət-°l-tē\ *n, pl* **-ties** **1 :** the quality or state of being subtle **2 :** something subtle; *esp* **:** a fine distinction

sub·ton·ic \,səb-'tän-ik, 'səb-\ *n* **:** the 7th tone of the musical scale **:** LEADING TONE

sub·top·ic \'səb-,täp-ik\ *n* **:** a secondary topic (as in a composition or speech) **:** one of the subdivisions into which a topic may be divided

sub·tract \səb-'trakt\ *vb* [L *subtract-, subtrahere* to draw from beneath, withdraw, fr. *sub-* + *trahere* to draw]

See *sub-* and 2d element	subspace	subterete	subthreshold
subsize	subspecialty	subsystem	subterminal	subtidal
subsocial	subspherical	subtemperate	subtetanic	subtotal

: to take away by deducting : perform a subtraction ⟨*subtract* 5 from 9⟩ — **sub·tract·er** *n*

sub·trac·tion \səb-'trak-shən\ *n* **1** : an act or instance of subtracting **2** : the operation of deducting one number from another

sub·trac·tive \-'trak-tiv\ *adj* **1** : tending to subtract **2** : constituting or involving subtraction ⟨a *subtractive* error in spelling⟩ ⟨a *subtractive* correction⟩

sub·tra·hend \'səb-trə-,hend\ *n* [L *subtrahendus* to be withdrawn, fr. *subtrahere* to withdraw] : a number that is to be subtracted from a minuend

sub·trop·i·cal \,səb-'träp-i-kəl, 'səb-\ *also* **sub·trop·ic** \-'träp-ik\ *adj* : of, relating to, or being the regions bordering on the tropical zone

sub·trop·ics \-'träp-iks\ *n pl* : subtropical regions

su·bu·late \'sü-byə-lət, -,lāt\ *adj* [L *subula* awl] : being linear and tapering to a fine point ⟨a *subulate* leaf⟩

sub·um·brel·la \,səb-(,)əm-'brel-ə\ *n* : the concave under-surface of a jellyfish — **sub·um·brel·lar** \-'brel-ər\ *adj*

sub·urb \'səb-,ərb\ *n* [L *suburbium*, fr. *sub urbe* near the city] **1 a** : an outlying part of a city or town **b** : a smaller community adjacent to a city **2** *pl* : the residential area adjacent to a city or large town; *also* : ENVIRONS — **sub·ur·ban** \sə-'bər-bən\ *adj or n*

sub·ur·ban·ite \sə-'bər-bə-,nīt\ *n* : a dweller in the suburbs

sub·ven·tion \səb-'ven-chən\ *n* [L *subvenire* to come up, come to the rescue, fr. *sub*- up + *venire* to come] : financial support esp. in the form of an endowment or a subsidy

sub·ver·sion \səb-'vər-zhən\ *n* : the act of subverting : the state of being subverted; *esp* : a systematic attempt to overthrow or undermine a government or political system by persons working secretly within the country involved — **sub·ver·sive** \-'vər-siv, -ziv\ *adj or n* — **sub·ver·sive·ly** *adv*

sub·vert \səb-'vərt\ *vt* [L *subvers-, subvertere*, lit., to turn from beneath, fr. *sub*- + *vertere* to turn] **1** : to overturn or overthrow from the foundation : RUIN **2** : to undermine the morals, allegiance, or faith of : CORRUPT — **sub·vert·er** *n*

sub·way \'səb-,wā\ *n* : an underground way; *also* : a usu. electric underground railway

suc·ce·dent \sək-'sēd-ᵊnt\ *adj* : SUCCEEDING, SUBSEQUENT

suc·ceed \sək-'sēd\ *vb* [L *success-, succedere*, fr. *sub*-near + *cedere* to go] **1 a** : to come next after another in possession of an office or estate; *esp* : to inherit sovereignty **b** : to follow after another in order **2** : to turn out well : be successful ⟨his advertising campaign *succeeded*⟩ ⟨he *succeeded* in getting enough votes to win⟩ **syn** see FOLLOW — **suc·ceed·er** *n*

suc·cess \sək-'ses\ *n* [L *successus*, fr. *succedere* to succeed] **1 a** : degree or measure of succeeding **b** : a favorable termination of a venture **c** : the gaining of wealth, favor, or eminence **2** : one that succeeds

suc·cess·ful \-fəl\ *adj* **1** : resulting or terminating in success **2** : gaining or having gained success — **suc·cess·ful·ly** \-fə-lē\ *adv* — **suc·cess·ful·ness** *n*

suc·ces·sion \sək-'sesh-ən\ *n* **1** : the order, action, or right of succeeding to a throne, title, or property **2 a** : a repeated following of one person or thing after another **b** : a process of ecological development in which organisms of one kind are replaced by those of another kind **3** : a number of persons or things that follow one after another — **suc·ces·sion·al** \-'sesh-nəl, -ən-ᵊl\ *adj* — **suc·ces·sion·al·ly** \-ē\ *adv*

syn SEQUENCE, SERIES: SUCCESSION may apply to things of any sort that follow in order of time or place; SEQUENCE suggests a uniform, logical, or regular succession; SERIES implies that the objects are of a similar nature or stand in similar relation to each other

suc·ces·sive \sək-'ses-iv\ *adj* : following in succession or serial order : following each other without interruption ⟨failed in three *successive* tries⟩ **syn** see CONSECUTIVE — **suc·ces·sive·ly** *adv* — **suc·ces·sive·ness** *n*

suc·ces·sor \sək-'ses-ər\ *n* : one that follows; *esp* : one who succeeds to a throne, title, estate, or office

suc·cinct \(,)sək-'siŋ(k)t, sə-'siŋ(k)t\ *adj* [L *succinctus*, fr. pp. of *succingere* to gird up, tuck up, fr. *sub*- up + *cingere*

to gird] **1** *archaic* **a** : GIRDED **b** : close-fitting **2** : compressed into a narrow compass : CONCISE, TERSE — **suc·cinct·ly** *adv* — **suc·cinct·ness** *n*

¹suc·cor \'sək-ər\ *n* [OF *sucors*, fr. ML *succursus*, fr. L *succurrere* to run up, run to help, fr. *sub*- up + *currere* to run] : AID, HELP, RELIEF

²succor *vt* : to go to the aid of (one in want or distress) : RELIEVE — **suc·cor·er** *n*

suc·co·ry \'sək-(ə-)rē\ *n, pl* **-ries** : CHICORY

suc·co·tash \'sək-ə-,tash\ *n* [of Algonquian origin] : lima or shell beans and green corn cooked together

suc·cu·lence \'sək-yə-lən(t)s\ *n* : the state of being succulent

¹suc·cu·lent \-lənt\ *adj* [L *suculentus*, fr. *sucus* juice] **1 a** : full of juice : JUICY **b** : having fleshy tissues designed to conserve moisture ⟨*succulent* plants⟩ **2** : full of vitality, freshness, or richness — **suc·cu·lent·ly** *adv*

²succulent *n* : a succulent plant (as a cactus)

suc·cumb \sə-'kəm\ *vi* [L *succumbere*, fr. *sub*- + *-cumbere* to lie down] **1** : to yield to superior strength or force or overpowering appeal or desire **2** : to cease to exist : DIE

¹such \(')səch, (,)sich\ *adj* [OE *swilc, swylc*; akin to E *so* & to E *like*] **1 a** : of a kind or character to be indicated or suggested ⟨bag *such* as a doctor carries⟩ **b** : having a quality to a degree to be indicated ⟨his excitement was *such* that he shouted⟩ **2** : having a quality already specified ⟨deeply moved by *such* acts of kindness⟩ **3** : of the same class, type, or sort : SIMILAR ⟨established 20 *such* clinics throughout the state⟩ **4** : so great : so remarkable ⟨*such* a storm⟩ ⟨*such* courage⟩ — **such and such 1** : not named or specified ⟨if I go to *such and such* a place⟩ **2** : something unspecified ⟨charged with doing *such and such*⟩

²such *pron* **1** : such a person or thing ⟨he had a plan if it may be called *such*⟩ **2** : someone or something stated, implied, or exemplified ⟨*such* was the result⟩ ⟨*such* were the Romans⟩ **3** : someone or something of the same kind ⟨ships and planes and *such*⟩ — **as such** : in itself ⟨*as such* the gift was worth little⟩

³such *adv* **1** : to such a degree : SO ⟨*such* tall buildings⟩ ⟨*such* a fine person⟩ **2** : ESPECIALLY, VERY ⟨hasn't been in *such* good spirits lately⟩

¹such·like \'səch-,līk\ *adj* : of like kind : SIMILAR

²suchlike *pron* : someone or something of the same sort : a similar person or thing

¹suck \'sək\ *vb* [OE *sūcan*] **1 a** : to draw in (liquid) or draw liquid from by movements of the mouth ⟨*suck* venom from a snakebite⟩ **b** : to draw milk from a breast or udder with the mouth ⟨young pigs *sucking* well⟩ **c** (1) : to consume by applying the lips or tongue to ⟨*suck* a lollipop⟩ (2) : to apply the mouth to in the manner of a child sucking the breast ⟨*sucked* his bruised finger⟩ **2** : to take something in or up or remove something from by or as if by suction ⟨plants *sucking* moisture from the soil⟩ ⟨a well *sucked* dry by constant pumping⟩ **3** : to make or cause to make a sound or motion like that of sucking ⟨*suck* in your stomach⟩ ⟨his pipe *sucked* at each puff⟩ **4** : to act in an obsequious manner ⟨*sucking* up to his boss⟩

²suck *n* **1** : the act of sucking **2** : a sucking movement or force

¹suck·er \'sək-ər\ *n* **1** : one that sucks **2** : a person who is easily deceived or tricked **3** : a part of an animal's body used for sucking or for clinging by suction **4** : any of numerous freshwater fishes related to the carps but having usu. thick soft lips for sucking in food **5** : a secondary shoot from the roots or lower part of a plant **6** : LOLLIPOP

²sucker *vb* **suck·ered; suck·er·ing** \'sək-(ə-)riŋ\ **1** : to remove suckers from **2** : to have or send out suckers

suck·ing *adj* : not yet weaned : very young

sucking louse *n* : any of an order (Anoplura) of wingless insects comprising the true lice with mouthparts adapted to sucking body fluids

suck·le \'sək-əl\ *vt* **suck·led; suck·ling** \'sək-(ə-)liŋ\ [prob. back-formation fr. *suckling*] **1 a** : to give milk to from the breast or udder ⟨a mother *suckling* her child⟩ **b** : to bring up : NOURISH **2** : to draw milk from the breast or udder of ⟨lambs *suckling* the ewes⟩

suck·ling \'sək-liŋ\ *n* : a young unweaned mammal

su·crase \'sü-,krās\ *n* [F *sucre* sugar] : INVERTASE

See *sub-* and 2d element	subtype	subvisible		subvocal	
subtreasury	subunit				subzone

ə abut; ᵊ kitten; ər further; a back; ā bake; ä cot, cart; au̇ out; ch chin; e less; ē easy; g gift; i trip; ī life

su·cre \'sü-(,)krā\ *n* **1** : the basic monetary unit of Ecuador **2** : a coin representing one sucre

su·crose \'sü-,krōs\ *n* [F *sucre* sugar] : a sweet crystalline disaccharide sugar $C_{12}H_{22}O_{11}$ that occurs naturally in most land plants and is the sugar obtained from sugarcane or sugar beets

suc·tion \'sək-shən\ *n* [L *suct-, sugere* to suck; akin to E *suck*] **1** : the act or process of sucking **2 a** : the action of exerting a force upon something by means of reduced air pressure over part of its surface so that the normal air pressure on another part of its surface pushes or tends to push it toward the region of reduced pressure **b** : force so exerted

suc·to·ri·al \,sək-'tōr-ē-əl, -'tôr-\ *adj* : adapted for or feeding by sucking ⟨*suctorial* mouth⟩; *also* : having suctorial organs

Su·dan grass \sü-'dan-\ *n* : a vigorous tall-growing annual sorghum widely grown for hay and fodder

Su·dan·ic \sü-'dan-ik\ *n* : the languages neither Bantu nor Hamitic spoken in a belt extending from Senegal to southern Sudan — **Sudanic** *adj*

¹sud·den \'səd-ᵊn\ *adj* [MF *sodain*, fr. L *subitaneus*, fr. *subitus* sudden, fr. pp. of *subire* to come up, fr. *sub-* up + *ire* to go] **1 a** : happening or coming quickly and unexpectedly ⟨*sudden* shower⟩ **b** : come upon unexpectedly ⟨*sudden* turn in the road⟩ **c** : ABRUPT, STEEP ⟨*sudden* descent to the sea⟩ **2** : marked by or showing hastiness : RASH ⟨*sudden* decision⟩ **3** : made or brought about in a short time : PROMPT ⟨*sudden* cure⟩ — **sud·den·ly** *adv* — **sud·den·ness** \'səd-ᵊn-(n)əs\ *n*

²sudden *n, obs* : an unexpected occurrence : EMERGENCY — **all of a sudden** *or* **on a sudden** : sooner than was expected : at once : SUDDENLY

sudden death *n* **1** : a single full game played to break a tie **2** : a period of play to break a tie that terminates a game the moment one side scores

su·do·rif·er·ous \,süd-ə-'rif-(ə-)rəs\ *adj* [L *sudor* sweat; akin to E *sweat*] : producing or conveying sweat ⟨*sudoriferous* glands⟩

su·do·rif·ic \-'rif-ik\ *adj* : causing or inducing sweat ⟨*sudorific* herbs⟩ — **sudorific** *n*

¹suds \'sədz\ *n pl* **1** : soapy water esp. when frothy; *also* : the froth on soapy water **2** *slang* : BEER

²suds *vb* **1** : to wash in suds **2** : to form suds

sudsy \'səd-zē\ *adj* **suds·i·er; -est** : full of suds : FROTHY, FOAMY

sue \'sü\ *vb* [ME *suen*, fr. OF *suivre*, fr. (assumed) VL *sequere*, fr. L *sequi* to follow] **1** : to pay court or suit to : WOO **2** : to seek justice from a person by bringing a legal action **3** : to make a request or application : PLEAD — usu. used with *for* or *to* ⟨the weaker nation *sued* for peace⟩ — **su·er** *n*

suede *or* **suède** \'swād\ *n* [F *gants de Suède* Swedish gloves] **1** : leather with a napped surface **2** : a cloth fabric finished with a nap to simulate suede

su·et \'sü-ət\ *n* [AF *sue*, fr. L *sebum* tallow, suet] : the hard fat about the kidneys and loins in beef and mutton that yields tallow

suf·fer \'səf-ər\ *vb* **suf·fered; suf·fer·ing** \'səf-(ə-)riŋ\ [L *sufferre*, fr. *sub-* up + *ferre* to bear] **1** : to feel or endure pain **2** : EXPERIENCE, UNDERGO ⟨*suffer* a defeat⟩ **3** : to bear loss or damage ⟨his business *suffered* during his illness⟩ **4** : ALLOW, PERMIT — **suf·fer·a·ble** \'səf-(ə-)rə-bəl\ *adj* — **suf·fer·a·ble·ness** *n* — **suf·fer·a·bly** \-blē\ *adv* — **suf·fer·er** \'səf-ər-ər\ *n*

suf·fer·ance \'səf-(ə-)rən(t)s\ *n* **1** : consent or sanction implied by a lack of interference or failure to enforce a prohibition **2** : power or ability to endure ⟨it is beyond *sufferance*⟩

suf·fer·ing *n* **1** : the state or experience of one that suffers **2** : PAIN, HARDSHIP **syn** see DISTRESS

suf·fice \sə-'fīs\ *vb* [MF *suffis-, suffire*, fr. L *sufficere*, lit., to put under, fr. *sub-* + *facere* to make, do] **1** : to meet or satisfy a need : be sufficient **2** : to be competent or capable **3** : to be enough for

suf·fi·cien·cy \sə-'fish-ən-sē\ *n, pl* **-cies** **1** : sufficient means to meet one's needs : COMPETENCY **2** : the quality or state of being sufficient : ADEQUACY ⟨doubts the *sufficiency* of the equipment⟩

suf·fi·cient \sə-'fish-ənt\ *adj* [ME, fr. L *sufficient-, sufficiens*, fr. prp. of *sufficere* to suffice] : enough to meet the needs of a situation or a proposed end — **suf·fi·cient·ly** *adv*

syn ENOUGH, ADEQUATE: SUFFICIENT suggests a fairly exact meeting of a need; ENOUGH is less exact or less formal than SUFFICIENT; ADEQUATE may imply barely meeting a requirement or a moderate standard

¹suf·fix \'səf-,iks\ *n* [L *suffixus*, pp. of *suffigere* to fasten underneath, fr. *sub-* + *figere* to fasten] **1** : an affix occurring at the end of a word **2** : a mathematical subscript — **suf·fix·al** \-,ik-səl\ *adj* — **suf·fix·less** \-,iks-ləs\ *adj*

²suf·fix \'səf-,iks, (,)sə-'fiks\ *vt* : to attach as a suffix — **suf·fix·a·tion** \,səf-,ik-'sā-shən\ *n*

suf·fo·cate \'səf-ə-,kāt\ *vb* [L *suffocare*, fr. *sub-* + *fauces* throat] **1 a** : to stop the breath of (as by strangling or asphyxiation) **b** : to deprive of oxygen : distress by want of cool fresh air **2** : to impede or stop the development of **3** : to be or become suffocated; *esp* : to die or suffer from lack of breathable air — **suf·fo·cat·ing·ly** \-,kāt-iŋ-lē\ *adv* — **suf·fo·ca·tion** \,səf-ə-'kā-shən\ *n* — **suf·fo·ca·tive** \'səf-ə-,kāt-iv\ *adj*

¹suf·fra·gan \'səf-ri-gən\ *n* [ML *suffraganeus*, fr. L *suffragium* support] **1** : a diocesan bishop (as in the Roman Catholic Church and the Church of England) subordinate to a metropolitan **2** : an Anglican bishop assisting a diocesan bishop and not having the right of succession

²suffragan *adj* **1** : of or being a suffragan **2** : subordinate to a metropolitan or archiepiscopal see

suf·frage \'səf-rij\ *n* [ML *suffragium*, fr. L, vote, support] **1** : an intercessory prayer : SUPPLICATION **2** : a vote given in deciding a controverted question or in electing a person to office **3** : the right of voting : FRANCHISE; *also* : the exercise of such right

suf·frag·ette \,səf-ri-'jet\ *n* : a woman who advocates suffrage for her sex

suf·frag·ist \'səf-ri-jəst\ *n* : one who advocates extension of suffrage esp. to women

suf·fru·ti·cose \,sə-'früt-i-,kōs\ *adj* : woody and perennial at the base but remaining herbaceous above ⟨a low *suffruticose* perennial⟩

suf·fuse \sə-'fyüz\ *vt* [L *suffus-, suffundere*, lit., to pour beneath, fr. *sub-* + *fundere* to pour] : to spread over or through in the manner of fluid or light : FLUSH, FILL — **suf·fu·sion** \-'fyü-zhən\ *n* — **suf·fu·sive** \-'fyü-siv, -ziv\ *adj*

Su·fi \'sü-(,)fē\ *n* [Ar *ṣūfīy*] : a Muslim mystic — **Sufi** *adj* — **Su·fic** \-fik\ *adj* — **Su·fism** \-,fiz-əm\ *n*

¹sug·ar \'shúg-ər\ *n* [MF *sucre*, fr. ML *zuccarum*, fr. Al *zucchero*, fr. Ar *sukkar*, fr. Per *shakar*, fr. Skt *śarkarā*] **1** : a sweet crystallizable material that consists wholly or essentially of sucrose, is colorless or white when pure, is obtained commercially from sugarcane or sugar beet and less extensively from sorghum, maples, and palms, and is nutritionally important as a source of dietary carbohydrate and as a sweetener and preservative of other foods **2** : any of various water-soluble compounds that vary widely in sweetness and comprise the simpler carbohydrates

²sugar *vb* **sug·ared; sug·ar·ing** \'shúg-(ə-)riŋ\ **1** : to mix, cover, or sprinkle with sugar **2** : to make something less hard to take or bear : SWEETEN ⟨*sugar* advice with flattery⟩ **3** : to change to crystals of sugar ⟨candy or icing *sugars* when cooked too long⟩

sugar beet *n* : a white-rooted beet grown for the sugar in its roots

sugar bush *n* : woods in which sugar maples predominate

sug·ar·cane \'shúg-ər-,kān\ *n* : a stout tall perennial grass that has broad leaves and a large terminal panicle and is widely grown in warm regions as a source of sugar

sug·ar·coat \,shúg-ər-'kōt\ *vt* **1** : to coat with sugar **2** : to make attractive or agreeable on the surface ⟨*sugarcoat* an unpleasant truth⟩

sug·ar·house \'shúg-ər-,haús\ *n* : a building where sugar is made or refined; *esp* : one where maple sap is boiled in the making of maple syrup and maple sugar

sug·ar·loaf \-,lōf\ *n* **1** : refined sugar molded into a cone **2** : a hill or mountain shaped like a sugarloaf — **sugarloaf** *adj*

sugar maple *n* : a maple of eastern No. America with 3-lobed to 5-lobed leaves, hard close-grained wood much used for cabinetwork, and sap that is the chief source of maple syrup and maple sugar

sugar of lead n : LEAD ACETATE

sugar orchard n, *chiefly New Eng* : SUGAR BUSH

sug·ar·plum \'shug-ər-,pləm\ n : a round piece of candy : BONBON

sug·ary \'shug-(ə-)rē\ *adj* 1 : containing, resembling, or tasting of sugar 2 : cloyingly sweet : SENTIMENTAL

sug·gest \sə(g)-'jest\ *vt* [L *suggest-, suggerere* to put under, furnish, suggest, fr. *sub-* + *gerere* to carry] 1 a : to put (as a thought, plan, or desire) into a person's mind b : to propose as an idea or possibility ⟨*suggest* going for a walk⟩ 2 : to call to mind through close connection or association ⟨that smoke *suggests* a forest fire⟩ — **sug·gest·er** n

sug·gest·i·ble \sə(g)-'jes-tə-bəl\ *adj* : easily influenced by suggestion — **sug·gest·i·bil·i·ty** \-,jes-tə-'bil-ət-ē\ n

sug·ges·tion \sə(g)-'jes-chən\ n 1 a : the act or process of suggesting b : something suggested 2 a : the process by which one thought leads to another esp. through association of ideas b : a means or process of influencing attitudes and behavior hypnotically 3 : a slight indication : TRACE

syn HINT: a SUGGESTION is something put into the mind in some way other than direct statement or offered for consideration without commanding or requesting; a HINT is a suggestion intentionally but indirectly conveyed

sug·ges·tive \sə(g)-'jes-tiv\ *adj* 1 a : giving a suggestion : INDICATIVE b : full of suggestions : PROVOCATIVE ⟨*suggestive* commentary⟩ c : stirring mental associations : EVOCATIVE 2 : suggesting or tending to suggest something improper or indecent : RISQUÉ — **sug·ges·tive·ly** *adv* — **sug·ges·tive·ness** n

su·i·cid·al \,sü-ə-'sīd-ʾl\ *adj* 1 : relating to or of the nature of suicide 2 : marked by an impulse to commit suicide 3 a : very dangerous to life ⟨*suicidal* risks⟩ b : destructive of one's own interests — **su·i·cid·al·ly** \-ʾl-ē\ *adv*

su·i·cide \'sü-ə-,sīd\ n [L *sui* (gen.) of oneself + E *-cide*] 1 a : the act of taking one's own life voluntarily b : ruin of one's own interests ⟨risking scandal and political *suicide*⟩ 2 : one that commits or attempts suicide

sui ge·ner·is \,sü-,ī-'jen-ə-rəs\ *adj* [L, of its own kind] : constituting a class alone : UNIQUE, PECULIAR

¹suit \'süt\ n [OF *siute* act of following, suite, fr. (assumed) VL *sequita*, fr. L *sequi* to follow] 1 : an action or process in a court for enforcing a right or claim 2 : an act or instance of suing or seeking by entreaty : APPEAL; *esp* : COURTSHIP 3 : a number of things used together : SET 4 : a set of garments: as a : an outer costume of two or more pieces b : a costume to be worn for a special purpose or under particular conditions ⟨gym *suit*⟩ 5 a : all the playing cards of one kind (as spades or hearts) in a pack b : all the dominoes bearing the same number

suit 5a: sequence of 4 diamonds

²suit *vb* 1 : ACCORD, AGREE ⟨position *suits* with his abilities⟩ 2 : to be appropriate or satisfactory 3 : to outfit with clothes : DRESS 4 : ACCOMMODATE, ADAPT ⟨*suit* the action to the word⟩ 5 a : to be proper for : BEFIT b : to be becoming to 6 : to meet the needs or desires of

suit·a·ble \'süt-ə-bəl\ *adj* 1 : adapted to a use or purpose 2 : satisfying propriety : PROPER 3 : CAPABLE, QUALIFIED **syn** see FIT — **suit·a·bil·i·ty** \,süt-ə-'bil-ət-ē\ n — **suit·a·ble·ness** \'süt-ə-bəl-nəs\ n — **suit·a·bly** \-blē\ *adv*

suit·case \'süt-,kās\ n : TRAVELING BAG; *esp* : a rigid flat rectangular case

suite \'swēt, 2c is also 'süt\ n [F, alter. of OF *siute*] 1 : RETINUE; *esp* : the personal staff accompanying a ruler, diplomat, or dignitary on official business 2 : a group of things forming a unit or constituting a collection : SET: as a : a group of rooms occupied as a unit : APARTMENT b (1) : a 17th and 18th century instrumental musical form consisting of a series of dances in the same or related keys (2) : a modern instrumental composition in a number of usu. descriptive movements (3) : an orchestral concert arrangement in suite form of material drawn from a longer work (as a ballet) c : a set of matched furniture for a room

suit·ing \'süt-iŋ\ n : fabric for suits of clothes

suit·or \'süt-ər\ n 1 : one that petitions or entreats : PLEADER 2 : a party to a suit at law 3 : one who courts a woman or seeks to marry

su·ki·ya·ki \skē-'(y)äk-ē, ,sük-ē-'(y)äk-ē\ n [Jap] : a dish prepared from meat, soybean curd, and vegetables (as onions, celery, bamboo sprouts, and mushrooms) cooked in soy sauce, sake, and sugar

Suk·koth \'suk-,ōt(h), -,ōs\ n [Heb *hag has-sukkōth* feast of the tabernacles] : a Jewish holiday celebrated in September or October as a harvest festival of thanksgiving and to commemorate the temporary shelters used by the Jews during their wanderings in the wilderness

sul·cus \'səl-kəs\ n, pl **sul·ci** \-,kī, -,kē\ [L] : FURROW, GROOVE; *esp* : a shallow furrow on the surface of the brain separating adjacent convolutions — **sul·cate** \-,kāt\ *adj*

sulf- *comb form* [L *sulfur*] : sulfur : containing sulfur ⟨*sulfanilic*⟩

sul·fa \'səl-fə\ *adj* 1 : related chemically to sulfanilamide 2 : of, relating to, or employing sulfa drugs

sul·fa·di·a·zine \,səl-fə-'dī-ə-,zēn\ n : a sulfa drug used esp. in the treatment of meningitis, pneumonia, and intestinal infections

sulfa drug n : any of various synthetic organic bacteria-inhibiting drugs that are sulfonamides closely related chemically to sulfanilamide

sul·fa·nil·a·mide \,səl-fə-'nil-ə-,mīd, -məd\ n : a crystalline compound that is the amide of sulfanilic acid and the parent compound of most of the sulfa drugs

sul·fa·nil·ic acid \,səl-fə-,nil-ik-\ n [*sulf-* + *ani*line] : a crystalline acid obtained from aniline and used esp. in making dyes

sul·fate \'səl-,fāt\ n : a salt or ester of sulfuric acid

sul·fide *or* **sul·phide** \'səl-,fīd\ n : a compound of sulfur with one or more other elements : a salt or ester of hydrogen sulfide

sul·fite *or* **sul·phite** \'səl-,fīt\ n : a salt or ester of sulfurous acid — **sul·fit·ic** \,səl-'fit-ik\ *adj*

sul·fon·a·mide \,səl-'fän-ə-,mīd, -məd\ n : the amide (as sulfanilamide) of a sulfonic acid; *also* : SULFA DRUG

sul·fon·ic acid \,səl-,fän-ik-\ n : any of numerous acids that may be derived from sulfuric acid by replacement of a hydroxyl group by either an inorganic anion or a univalent organic radical

sul·fur *or* **sul·phur** \'səl-fər\ n [L] : a nonmetallic element that occurs either free or combined esp. in nature, is a constituent of proteins, exists in several forms including yellow crystals, and is used esp. in the chemical and paper industries, in rubber vulcanization, and in medicine for treating skin diseases — see ELEMENT table

sulfur dioxide n : a heavy strong-smelling gas SO_2 used esp. in making sulfuric acid, in bleaching, as a preservative, and as a refrigerant

sul·fu·re·ous \,səl-'fyur-ē-əs\ *adj* : SULFUROUS — **sul·fu·re·ous·ly** *adv* — **sul·fu·re·ous·ness** n

sul·fu·ric *or* **sul·phu·ric** \,səl-'fyu(ə)r-ik\ *adj* : of, relating to, or containing sulfur esp. in a higher valence

sulfuric acid n : a heavy corrosive oily strong acid H_2SO_4 that is colorless when pure and is a vigorous oxidizing and dehydrating agent

sul·fu·rous *or* **sul·phu·rous** \'səl-f(y)ə-rəs, *also esp for 1* ,səl-'fyur-əs\ *adj* 1 : of, relating to, or containing sulfur esp. in a lower valence 2 a : of, relating to, or dealing with the fire of hell : INFERNAL b : FIERY, INFLAMED ⟨*sulfurous* sermon⟩ c : PROFANE, BLASPHEMOUS — **sul·fu·rous·ly** *adv* — **sul·fu·rous·ness** n

sulfurous acid n : a weak unstable acid H_2SO_3 known in solution and through its salts and used as a reducing and bleaching agent

sulfur trioxide n : a compound SO_3 that is a heavy corrosive liquid when first produced but that changes into a solid form and is a powerful oxidizing agent

¹sulk \'səlk\ *vi* : to be moodily silent or ill-humored : nurse a grievance

²sulk n 1 : the state of one sulking — often used in pl. ⟨had a case of the *sulks*⟩ 2 : a sulky mood or spell ⟨was in a *sulk*⟩

¹sulky \'səl-kē\ *adj* **sulk·i·er; -est** 1 : inclined to sulk : given to fits of sulking 2 : DISCONTENTED, GLOOMY ⟨a *sulky* voice⟩ **syn** see SULLEN — **sulk·i·ly** \-kə-lē\ *adv* — **sulk·i·ness** \-kē-nəs\ n

²sulky *n, pl* **sulk·ies** : a light 2-wheeled vehicle having a seat for the driver only and usu. no body

sul·len \'səl-ən\ *adj* [ME *solein* solitary, sullen] **1 a** : gloomily or resentfully silent or repressed : not sociable **b** : suggesting a sullen state : LOWERING ⟨*sullen* refusal⟩ **2** : dull or somber in sound or color **3** : DISMAL, GLOOMY — **sul·len·ly** *adv* — **sul·len·ness** \'səl-ən-nəs\ *n*
syn SURLY, SULKY: SULLEN implies a gloomy silent bad humor and a refusal to be sociable; SURLY implies rudeness and gruffness esp. in response to requests or questions; SULKY suggests childish resentment expressed in fits of peevish sullenness

sul·ly \'səl-ē\ *vb* **sul·lied**; **sul·ly·ing** [prob. fr. MF *soiller* to soil] : to make or become soiled or tarnished : SMIRCH

sul·phur butterfly \,səl-fər-\ *n* : any of numerous rather small butterflies having usu. yellow or orange wings with a black border

sulphur yellow *n* : a variable color averaging a brilliant greenish yellow

sul·tan \'səlt-°n\ *n* [Ar *sulṭān*] : a king or sovereign esp. of a Muslim state

sul·tana \,səl-'tan-ə\ *n* [It] **1** : a female member of a sultan's family; *esp* : a sultan's wife **2 a** : a pale yellow seedless grape grown for raisins and wine **b** : the raisin of this grape

sul·tan·ate \'səlt-°n-,āt\ *n* **1** : the office, dignity, or power of a sultan **2** : a state or country governed by a sultan

sul·try \'səl-trē\ *adj* **sul·tri·er**; **-est** [obs. *sulter* to swelter, alter. of E *swelter*] **1** : very hot and humid **2** : burning hot ⟨*sultry* sun⟩ **3** : SENSUAL, VOLUPTUOUS ⟨*sultry* glances⟩ — **sul·tri·ly** \-trə-lē\ *adv* — **sul·tri·ness** \-trē-nəs\ *n*

¹sum \'səm\ *n* [L *summa*, fr. fem. of *summus* highest] **1** : an indefinite or specified amount of money **2** : the whole amount : AGGREGATE **3 a** : EPITOME, SUMMARY **b** : GIST **4 a** : the result of adding numbers ⟨*sum* of 5 and 7 is 12⟩ **b** : the limit of the sum of the first *n* terms of an infinite series as *n* increases indefinitely **c** : a problem in arithmetic
syn AMOUNT, AGGREGATE, TOTAL: SUM indicates the result of simple addition of numbers or particulars; AMOUNT implies the result of accumulating or successive additions; AGGREGATE stresses the notion of the grouping or massing together of distinct individuals; TOTAL stresses completeness or inclusiveness or adding or reckoning

²sum *vb* **summed**; **sum·ming** **1** : to calculate the sum of : COUNT **2** : to reach a sum : AMOUNT — usu. used with *to* **3** : SUMMARIZE — usu. used with *up*

su·mac *or* **su·mach** \'s(h)ü-,mak\ *n* [MF *sumac*, fr. Ar *summāq*] **1** : any of a genus of trees, shrubs, and woody vines with feathery compound leaves turning to brilliant red in autumn and spikes or loose clusters of red or whitish berries — compare POISON IVY, POISON OAK **2** : a material used in tanning and dyeing made of the leaves and other parts of sumac

Su·mer·i·an \sü-'mer-ē-ən, -'mir-\ *n* **1** : a native of Sumer **2** : the language of the Sumerians surviving as a literary language after the rise of Akkadian — **Sumerian** *adj*

sum·ma cum lau·de \,sù·m-ə-,kùm-'laùd-ə, -'laùd-ē; ,səm-ə-,kəm-'lôd-ē\ *adv* (*or adj*) [L, with highest praise] : with highest academic distinction ⟨graduated *summa cum laude*⟩

sum·ma·rize \'səm-ə-,rīz\ *vb* **1** : to tell in or reduce to a summary **2** : to make a summary — **sum·ma·ri·za·tion** \,səm-ə-rə-'zā-shən\ *n* — **sum·ma·riz·er** \'səm-ə-,rī-zər\ *n*

¹sum·ma·ry \'səm-ə-rē\ *adj* [L *summa* sum] **1** : expressing or covering the main points briefly : CONCISE ⟨a *summary* account⟩ **2** : done without delay or formality : quickly carried out ⟨a *summary* procedure⟩ — **sum·mar·i·ly** \(,)sə-'mer-ə-lē, 'səm-ə-rə-lē\ *adv*

²summary *n, pl* **-ries** : an abstract, abridgment, or compendium esp. of a preceding discourse : RECAPITULATION

sum·ma·tion \(,)sə-'mā-shən\ *n* **1** : the act or process of forming a sum : ADDITION **2** : SUM, TOTAL **3** : a final part of an argument reviewing points made and expressing conclusions — **sum·ma·tion·al** \-shnəl, -shən-°l\ *adj*

¹sum·mer \'səm-ər\ *n* [OE *sumor*] **1 a** : the season between spring and autumn comprising usu. the months of June, July, and August or as reckoned astronomically extending from the June solstice to the September equinox **b** : the warmer half of the year **2** : YEAR ⟨a girl of 16 *summers*⟩ **3** : a time or season of fulfillment

²summer *vb* **sum·mered**; **sum·mer·ing** \'səm-(ə-)riŋ\ **1** : to pass the summer **2** : to keep or carry through the summer; *esp* : to provide with pasture during the summer

³summer *n* [MF *somier* packhorse, beam, fr. LL *sagma* packsaddle, fr. Gk] : a large horizontal beam or stone used esp. in building (as for the lintel of a door or window)

sum·mer·house \'səm-ər-,haùs\ *n* : a rustic covered structure in a garden or park to provide a cool shady retreat in summer

summer kitchen *n* : a small building or shed built adjacent to a house and used as a kitchen in warm weather

sum·mer·sault *var of* SOMERSAULT

summer school *n* : a school or school session conducted in summer enabling students to accelerate progress toward a degree, to make up credits lost through absence or failure, or to round out professional education

summer squash *n* : any of various garden squashes closely related to the typical pumpkins and used as a vegetable while immature and before hardening of the seeds and rind

sum·mer·time \'səm-ər-,tīm\ *n* : the summer season or a period like summer

summer time *n, chiefly Brit* : DAYLIGHT SAVING TIME

sum·mer·wood \'səm-ər-,wùd\ *n* : the harder less porous portion of an annual ring of wood that develops late in the growing season — compare SPRINGWOOD

sum·mery \'səm-ə-rē\ *adj* : of, resembling, or fit for summer

sum·mit \'səm-ət\ *n* [MF *somete*, fr. dim. of *sum* top, fr. L *summus* highest] **1** : TOP, APEX; *esp* : the highest point (as of a mountain) **2** : the highest degree : PINNACLE **3** : the highest level (as of officials)
syn SUMMIT, PEAK, PINNACLE, APEX mean the highest point attained or attainable. SUMMIT implies the topmost level attainable ⟨a view from the *summit*⟩ PEAK suggests the highest among other high points ⟨*peak* of excitement⟩ PINNACLE suggests a dizzying often insecure height ⟨reach a *pinnacle* of success on the stage⟩ APEX implies the point at which all ascending lines converge and contrasts with base ⟨*apex* of cultural achievement⟩

sum·mon \'səm-ən\ *vt* [OF *somondre*, fr. L *summonēre* to remind secretly, fr. *sub-* secretly + *monēre* to warn] **1** : to issue a call to convene : CONVOKE **2** : to command by service of a summons to appear in court **3** : to send for : CALL ⟨*summon* a physician⟩ **4** : to call forth or arouse ⟨*summon* up enough courage to act⟩ — **sum·mon·er** *n*

¹sum·mons \'səm-ənz\ *n, pl* **sum·mons·es** **1** : the act of summoning; *esp* : a call by authority to appear at a place named or to attend to some duty **2** : a warning or notice to appear in court **3** : a call, signal, or knock that summons

²summons *vt* : SUMMON 2

sum·mum bo·num \,sùm-əm-'bō-nəm, ,səm-\ *n* [L] : the supreme or greatest good

sump \'səmp\ *n* [ME *sompe* swamp] : a pit or reservoir serving as a receptacle or as a drain for fluids

sump·ter \'səm(p)-tər\ *n* [MF *sometier*, fr. LL *sagmat-*, *sagma* packsaddle] : a pack animal

sump·tu·ary \'səm(p)-chə-,wer-ē\ *adj* [L *sumptus* expense, fr. *sumere* to take, spend] **1** : designed to regulate personal expenditures and esp. to prevent extravagance and luxury ⟨*sumptuary* laws⟩ **2** : designed to regulate habits on moral or religious grounds

sump·tu·ous \'səm(p)-chə-wəs, -chəs\ *adj* [L *sumptus* expense] : involving large expense : LAVISH, LUXURIOUS ⟨a *sumptuous* feast⟩ — **sump·tu·ous·ly** *adv* — **sump·tu·ous·ness** *n*

sum total **1** : a total arrived at through the counting of sums **2** : total result : TOTALITY ⟨the *sum total* of weeks of discussion was a deadlock⟩

¹sun \'sən\ *n* [OE *sunne*] **1 a** : the luminous celestial body around which the planets revolve, from which they receive heat and light, and which has a mean distance from the earth of 93,000,000 miles and a diameter of 864,000 miles **b** : a celestial body like the sun **2** : the heat or light radiated from the sun : SUNSHINE **3** : one

---

j joke; **ŋ** sing; **ō** flow; **ȯ** flaw; **ȯi** coin; **th** thin; **th** this; **ü** loot; **u̇** foot; **y** yet; **yü** few; **yu̇** furious; **zh** vision

resembling the sun usu. in brilliance **4** : the rising or setting of the sun ⟨from *sun* to *sun*⟩ — **in the sun** : in the public eye

²**sun** *vb* **sunned; sun·ning** **1** : to expose to or as if to the rays of the sun **2** : to sun oneself

sun·baked \'sən-,bākt\ *adj* **1** : baked by exposure to sunshine ⟨*sunbaked* bricks⟩ **2** : heated, parched, or compacted esp. by excessive sunlight

sun·bath \'sən-,bath, -,båth\ *n* : exposure to sunlight or a sunlamp

sun·bathe \-,bāth\ *vi* : to take a sunbath — **sun·bath·er** \-,bā-thər\ *n*

sun·beam \-,bēm\ *n* : a ray of sunlight

sun·bird \-,bərd\ *n* : any of a family of brightly colored Old World birds suggesting hummingbirds

sun·bon·net \-,bän-ət\ *n* : a woman's bonnet with a wide brim framing the face and usu. a ruffle at the back to protect the neck from the sun

¹**sun·burn** \-,bərn\ *vb* **1** : to burn or discolor by the sun **2** : to cause or undergo sunburn

²**sunburn** *n* : a skin inflammation caused by excessive exposure to sunlight

sun·burst \'sən-,bərst\ *n* **1** : a burst of sunlight esp. through a break in the clouds **2** : a representation of a sun surrounded by rays

sun·dae \'sən-dē\ *n* : a portion of ice cream served with topping (as crushed fruit, syrup, or nuts)

sun dance *n* : a solo or group solstice rite of American Indians

¹**Sun·day** \'sən-dē\ *n* [OE *sunnandæg*, lit., day of the sun] : the 1st day of the week : the Christian Sabbath
syn SABBATH: SUNDAY is the name of the first day of the week; SABBATH is the institution of observing one day of the week as a period of rest and worship, the day being Sunday for most Christians, Saturday for Jews and some Christians

²**Sunday** *adj* **1** : of, relating to, or associated with Sunday **2** : BEST ⟨*Sunday* suit⟩ **3** : AMATEUR, DILETTANTE ⟨*Sunday* painters⟩

³**Sunday** *vi* : to spend Sunday ⟨was *Sundaying* in the country⟩

Sunday best *n* : one's best clothes

Sunday punch *n* : a blow in boxing intended to knock out an opponent

Sunday school *n* : a school held on Sunday for religious education

sun deck *n* : a ship's deck or a roof or terrace used for sunning

sun·der \'sən-dər\ *vt* **sun·dered; sun·der·ing** \-d(ə-)riŋ\ [OE *gesundrian;* akin to E *sundry*] : to break or force apart or in two : sever esp. with violence

sun·dew \'sən-,d(y)ü\ *n* : any of a genus of insectivorous bog herbs that trap insects with their hairy glandular leaves

sun·di·al \-,dī(-ə)l\ *n* : a device to show the time of day by the position of the shadow cast on a plate or disk typically by an upright pin

sun dog *n* : PARHELION

sun·down \'sən-,daun\ *n* : SUNSET

sun·down·er \-,daú-nər\ *n, Austral* : TRAMP, HOBO

sun·dries \'sən-drēz\ *n pl* : miscellaneous small articles or items

sun·drops \-,dräps\ *n sing or pl* : a day-flowering herb similar to the related evening primrose

¹**sun·dry** \'sən-drē\ *adj* [OE *syndrig* separate, distinct] : MISCELLANEOUS, SEVERAL, VARIOUS ⟨for *sundry* reasons⟩

²**sundry** *pron* : an indeterminate number

sun·fast \'sən-,fast\ *adj* : resistant to fading by sunlight ⟨*sunfast* dyes⟩

sun·fish \-,fish\ *n* **1** : a large sea fish with a very deep, short, and flat body, high fins, and a small mouth **2** : any of a family of American freshwater fishes that are related to the perches and usu. have a deep compressed body and metallic luster

sun·flow·er \-,flaù(-ə)r\ *n* : any of a genus of tall herbs related to the daisies that are often grown for their showy yellow-rayed flower heads and for their oil-rich seeds

sung *past of* SING

sunfish 1

Sung \'sùŋ\ *n* : a Chinese dynasty dated A.D. 960–1280 and marked by cultural refinement and achievements in philosophy, literature, and art

sun·glass·es \'sən-,glas-əz\ *n pl* : glasses to protect the eyes from the sun

sun-god \'sən-,gäd\ *n* : a god in various religions that represents or personifies the sun

sunk *past of* SINK

sunk·en \'sən-kən\ *adj* **1** : SUBMERGED ⟨*sunken* ships⟩ **2** : fallen in : HOLLOW ⟨*sunken* cheeks⟩ **3 a** : lying in a depression ⟨*sunken* garden⟩ ⟨a *sunken* lane⟩ **b** : constructed below the general floor level ⟨*sunken* living room⟩

sun·lamp \'sən-,lamp\ *n* : an electric lamp designed to emit radiation of wavelengths from ultraviolet to infrared

sun·less \'sən-ləs\ *adj* : lacking sunshine : CHEERLESS, DARK

sun·light \-,līt\ *n* : the light of the sun : SUNSHINE

sun·lit \-,lit\ *adj* : lighted by or as if by the sun

sun·ny \'sən-ē\ *adj* **sun·ni·er; -est** **1** : bright with sunshine ⟨*sunny* day⟩ ⟨*sunny* room⟩ **2** : MERRY, BRIGHT, CHEERFUL ⟨*sunny* smile⟩ ⟨*sunny* disposition⟩ — **sun·ni·ly** \'sən-°l-ē\ *adv* — **sun·ni·ness** \'sən-ē-nəs\ *n*

sun parlor *n* : a glass-enclosed porch or living room with a sunny exposure — called also *sun porch, sun-room*

sun·rise \'sən-,rīz\ *n* **1** : the apparent rising of the sun above the horizon; *also* : the accompanying atmospheric effects **2** : the time at which the sun rises

sun·set \-,set\ *n* **1** : the apparent descent of the sun below the horizon; *also* : the accompanying atmospheric effects **2** : the time at which the sun sets **3** : a period of decline; *esp* : old age

sun·shade \-,shād\ *n* : something used as a protection from the sun's rays: as **a** : PARASOL **b** : AWNING

sun·shine \-,shīn\ *n* **1 a** : the sun's light or direct rays **b** : the warmth and light given by the sun's rays **c** : a spot or surface on which the sun's light shines **2** : something that radiates warmth, cheer, or happiness — **sun·shiny** \-,shī-nē\ *adj*

sun·spot \-,spät\ *n* : one of the dark spots that appear from time to time on the sun's surface consisting commonly of a blue-black umbra with a surrounding penumbra of lighter shade and usu. visible only with the telescope

sun·stroke \-,strōk\ *n* : heatstroke caused by direct exposure to the sun

sun·struck \-,strək\ *adj* : affected or touched by the sun

sun·suit \-,süt\ *n* : an outfit (as of halter and shorts) worn usu. for sunbathing and play

sun·tan \-,tan\ *n* **1** : a browning of the skin from exposure to the rays of the sun **2** *pl* : a tan-colored summer uniform

sun·tanned \-,tand\ *adj* : browned by exposure to the sun

sun time *n* : the time of day reckoned by the daily motion of the sun or by a sundial

sun-up \'sən-,əp\ *n* : SUNRISE

¹**sun·ward** \-wərd\ *or* **sun·wards** \-wərdz\ *adv* : toward the sun

²**sunward** *adj* : facing the sun

sun·wise \-,wīz\ *adv* : CLOCKWISE

¹**sup** \'səp\ *vb* **supped; sup·ping** [OE *sūpan, suppan*] **1** : to take or drink in swallows or gulps **2** *chiefly dial* : to take food and esp. liquid food into the mouth a little at a time (as from a spoon)

²**sup** *n* : a mouthful esp. of liquor or broth : SIP; *also* : a small quantity of liquid ⟨a *sup* of tea⟩

³**sup** *vi* **supped; sup·ping** [OF *souper*, fr. *soupe* sop, soup] **1** : to eat the evening meal **2** : to make one's supper — used with *on* or *off* ⟨*supped* on roast beef⟩

¹**su·per** \'sü-pər\ *n* **1 a** : a supernumerary actor **b** : SUPERINTENDENT, SUPERVISOR **2** : a removable upper story of a beehive **3** : a superfine grade or extra large size

²**super** *adj* [short for *superfine*] **1** : very good **2** : very large or powerful : GREAT — **super** *adv*

super- *prefix* [L, over, above, in addition; akin to E *over*] **1 a** : over and above : higher in quantity, quality, or degree than : more than ⟨*superhuman*⟩ **b** : in addition : extra ⟨*supertax*⟩ **c** : exceeding or so as to exceed a norm ⟨*superheat*⟩ **d** : in excessive degree or intensity ⟨*supersubtle*⟩ **e** : surpassing all or most others of its kind ⟨*superhighway*⟩ **2 a** : situated or placed above, on, or at the top of ⟨*supertower*⟩ **b** : next above or higher ⟨*supertonic*⟩ **3** : constituting a more inclusive category than that specified

⟨**super**family⟩   **4** : superior in status, title, or position ⟨**super**state⟩

su·per·a·ble \'sü-p(ə-)rə-bəl\ *adj* [L *superare* to surmount, fr. *super* over] : capable of being overcome or conquered : SURMOUNTABLE — **su·per·a·ble·ness** *n* — **su·per·a·bly** \-blē\ *adv*

su·per·abound \,sü-pər-ə-'baúnd\ *vi* : to abound or prevail greatly or to excess

su·per·abun·dant \-'bən-dənt\ *adj* : more than ample : EXCESSIVE — **su·per·abun·dance** \-dən(t)s\ *n* — **super·abun·dant·ly** *adv*

su·per·add \,sü-pər-'ad\ *vt* : to add over and above something or in extra or superfluous amount — **su·per·ad·di·tion** \-pər-ə-'dish-ən\ *n*

su·per·an·nu·ate \,sü-pər-'an-yə-,wāt\ *vb* [back-formation fr. *superannuated*] **1 a** : to make or declare obsolete or out-of-date **b** : to retire and pension because of age or infirmity **2** : to become retired or antiquated — **su·per·an·nu·a·tion** \-,an-yə-'wā-shən\ *n*

su·per·an·nu·at·ed *adj* [L *super-* + *annus* year] **1** : too old or outmoded for work or use **2** : retired on a pension

su·perb \sù-'pərb\ *adj* [L *superbus* excellent, proud, fr. *super* above] **1** : MAJESTIC, NOBLE **2** : RICH, SUMPTUOUS **3** : of supreme excellence or beauty — **su·perb·ly** *adv* — **su·perb·ness** *n*

su·per·car·go \,sü-pər-'kär-gō\ *n* : an officer on a merchant ship in charge of the commercial concerns of the voyage

su·per·charge \'sü-pər-,chärj\ *vt* **1** : to supply a charge to the intake of (as an engine) at a pressure higher than that of the surrounding atmosphere **2** : PRESSURIZE 1

su·per·charg·er \-,chär-jər\ *n* : a device (as a blower or compressor) for increasing the volume air charge of an internal-combustion engine or for pressurizing the cabin of an airplane

su·per·cil·i·ary \,sü-pər-'sil-ē-,er-ē\ *adj* [L *supercilium* eyebrow] : of, relating to, or adjoining the eyebrow

su·per·cil·i·ous \-'sil-ē-əs\ *adj* [L *supercilium* eyebrow, haughtiness, fr. *super-* + *-cilium* (akin to *celare* to hide)] : haughtily contemptuous — **su·per·cil·i·ous·ly** *adv* — **su·per·cil·i·ous·ness** *n*

su·per·con·duc·tiv·i·ty \,sü-pər-,kän-,dək-'tiv-ət-ē\ *n* : a complete disappearance of electrical resistance in various metals at temperatures near absolute zero — **su·per·con·duc·tive** \-kən-'dək-tiv\ *adj* — **su·per·con·duc·tor** \-kən-'dək-tər\ *n*

su·per·cool \,sü-pər-'kül\ *vt* : to cool below the freezing point without solidification or crystallization

su·per·ego \,sü-pər-'ē-gō\ *n* : a largely unconscious part of the psyche that aids in character formation by reflecting parental conscience and the rules of society

su·per·em·i·nent \-'em-ə-nənt\ *adj* : extremely high, distinguished, or conspicuous — **su·per·em·i·nence** \-nən(t)s\ *n* — **su·per·em·i·nent·ly** *adv*

su·per·er·o·ga·tion \,sü-pər-,er-ə-'gā-shən\ *n* [LL *supererogare* to expend in addition] : the act of performing more than is required by duty, obligation, or need

su·per·e·rog·a·to·ry \,sü-pər-i-'räg-ə-,tōr-ē-, -,tòr-\ *adj* **1** : observed or performed to an extent not demanded or needed **2** : SUPERFLUOUS, NONESSENTIAL

su·per·fi·cial \,sü-pər-'fish-əl\ *adj* [L *superficies* surface] **1 a** : of or relating to a surface **b** : situated on or near or affecting only the surface **2** : concerned only with the obvious or apparent : not profound or thorough : SHALLOW — **su·per·fi·ci·al·i·ty** \-,fish-ē-'al-ət-ē\ *n* — **su·per·fi·cial·ly** \-'fish-(ə-)lē\ *adv* — **su·per·fi·cial·ness** \-'fish-əl-nəs\ *n*

  syn SUPERFICIAL, CURSORY mean lacking in depth or solidity. SUPERFICIAL implies a concern only with what appears at the surface or first glance; CURSORY suggests a neglect of details through haste or indifference

su·per·fi·cies \-'fish-(,)ēz, -ē-,ēz\ *n, pl* superficies [L, surface, fr. *super-* + *facies* face] **1** : a surface of a body or a region of space **2** : the external aspects or appearance of a thing

su·per·fine \,sü-pər-'fīn\ *adj* **1** : overly refined or nice **2** : extremely fine **3** : of high quality or grade

su·per·flu·i·ty \,sü-pər-'flü-ət-ē\ *n, pl* **-ties** **1** : EXCESS,

OVERSUPPLY **2** : something unnecessary or more than enough

su·per·flu·ous \sù-'pər-flə-wəs\ *adj* [L *superfluus*, fr. *superfluere* to overflow, fr. *super-* + *fluere* to flow] : exceeding what is sufficient or necessary : EXTRA — **su·per·flu·ous·ly** *adv* — **su·per·flu·ous·ness** *n*

su·per·gi·ant \'sü-pər-,jī-ənt\ *n* : a star of very great luminosity and enormous size

su·per·heat \,sü-pər-'hēt\ *vt* **1 a** : to heat (a liquid) above the boiling point without converting into vapor **b** : to heat (steam) to a higher temperature than the normal boiling point of water **2** : to heat very much or excessively — **su·per·heat·er** *n*

su·per·het·er·o·dyne \,sü-pər-'het-ə-rə-,dīn\ *adj* : of or relating to a form of radio reception in which beats are produced of a frequency above audibility but below that of the received signals and the current of the beat frequency is then rectified, amplified, and finally rectified again so as to reproduce the sound — **superheterodyne** *n*

su·per·high frequency \,sü-pər-,hī-\ *n* : a radio frequency in the range between 3000 and 30,000 megacycles — abbr. *shf*

su·per·high·way \,sü-pər-'hī-,wā\ *n* : a broad highway designed for high-speed traffic

su·per·hu·man \-'hyü-mən, -'yü-\ *adj* **1** : being above the human : DIVINE **2** : exceeding normal human power, size, or capability : HERCULEAN ⟨*superhuman* effort⟩ — **su·per·hu·man·ly** *adv*

su·per·im·pose \,sü-pər-im-'pōz\ *vt* : to place or lay over or above something — **su·per·im·pos·a·ble** \-'pō-zə-bəl\ *adj* — **su·per·im·po·si·tion** \-,im-pə-'zish-ən\ *n*

su·per·in·cum·bent \-in-'kəm-bənt\ *adj* [L *superincumbere* to lie on top of, fr. *super-* + *incumbere* to lie down on] : lying or resting and usu. exerting pressure on something else — **su·per·in·cum·bent·ly** *adv*

su·per·in·duce \-in-'d(y)üs\ *vt* : to introduce as an addition over or above something already existing — **su·per·in·duc·tion** \-'dək-shən\ *n*

su·per·in·tend \,sü-p(ə-)rin-'tend\ *vt* [LL *superintendere*, fr. L *super-* + *intendere* to attend, direct attention to] : to have or exercise the charge and oversight of : DIRECT

su·per·in·tend·ence \-'ten-dən(t)s\ *or* **su·per·in·tend·en·cy** \-dən-sē\ *n, pl* **-enc·es** *or* **-en·cies** : the act, duty, or office of superintending or overseeing

su·per·in·tend·ent \-'ten-dənt\ *n* : a person who oversees or manages something ⟨a building *superintendent*⟩ ⟨*superintendent* of schools⟩

¹su·pe·ri·or \sù-'pir-ē-ər\ *adj* [L, compar. of *superus* being above, fr. *super* over, above] **1** : situated higher up or sometimes anterior or dorsal to something else : UPPER **2 a** : of higher rank, quality, or importance **b** : greater in quantity or numbers **3** : courageously or serenely indifferent ⟨rose *superior* to his distress⟩ **4 a** : excellent of its kind : BETTER **b** : affecting or assuming an air of superiority : SUPERCILIOUS **5** : more comprehensive ⟨a genus is *superior* to a species⟩ — **su·pe·ri·or·i·ty** \-,pir-ē-'òr-ət-ē, -'är-\ *n* — **su·pe·ri·or·ly** \-'pir-ē-ər-lē\ *adv*

²superior *n* **1** : one who is above another in rank, station, or office; *esp* : the head of a religious house or order **2** : one that surpasses another in quality or merit

superior court *n* **1** : a court intermediate between inferior courts and higher appellate courts **2** : a court with juries having original jurisdiction

superiority complex *n* **1** : an exaggerated opinion of oneself **2** : an excessive striving for or pretense of superiority to compensate for supposed inferiority

su·per·ja·cent \,sü-pər-'jās-ᵊnt\ *adj* [L *superjacēre* to lie over, fr. *super-* + *jacēre* to lie] : lying above or upon : OVERLYING ⟨*superjacent* rocks⟩

su·per·jet \'sü-pər-,jet\ *n* : a supersonic jet airplane

¹su·per·la·tive \sù-'pər-lət-iv\ *adj* [L *superlat-*, used as stem of *superferre* to carry over, raise high, fr. *super-* + *ferre* to carry] **1** : of, relating to, or constituting the degree of grammatical comparison that denotes an extreme or unsurpassed level or extent **2** : surpassing all others : SUPREME **3** : EXAGGERATED, EXCESSIVE — **su·per·la·tive·ly** *adv* — **su·per·la·tive·ness** *n*

²**su·per·la·tive** *n* **1** : the superlative degree or a superlative form in a language **2** : the superlative or utmost degree of something : ACME; *also* : something that is superlative

su·per·man \'sü-pər-ˌman\ *n* : a man with superhuman physical, mental, or spiritual powers

su·per·mar·ket \-ˌmär-kət\ *n* : a self-service retail market selling foods and household merchandise

su·per·nal \sú-'pərn-°l\ *adj* [L *supernus*, fr. *super* over, above] **1 a** : being or coming from on high : HEAVENLY **b** : LOFTY, ETHEREAL ⟨*supernal* strains of melody⟩ **2** : located or originating in the sky — **su·per·nal·ly** \-°l-ē\ *adv*

su·per·na·tant \ˌsü-pər-'nāt-°nt\ *adj* : floating on the surface — **supernatant** *n*

su·per·nat·u·ral \ˌsü-pər-'nach-(ə-)rəl\ *adj* **1** : of or relating to an order of existence beyond the visible observable universe; *esp* : of or relating to God or a god, demigod, spirit, or infernal being **2 a** : departing from what is usual or normal esp. so as to appear to transcend the laws of nature **b** : attributed to a supernormal agency (as a ghost or spirit) — **supernatural** *n* — **su·per·nat·u·ral·ly** \-'nach-(ə-)rə-lē, -'nach-ər-lē\ *adv* — **su·per·nat·u·ral·ness** \-'nach-(ə-)rəl-nəs\ *n*

su·per·nat·u·ral·ism \-'nach-(ə-)rə-ˌliz-əm\ *n* **1** : the quality or state of being supernatural **2** : belief in a supernatural power and order of existence — **su·per·nat·u·ral·ist** \-ləst\ *n or adj* — **su·per·nat·u·ral·is·tic** \-ˌnach-(ə-)rə-'lis-tik\ *adj*

su·per·nor·mal \-'nor-məl\ *adj* **1** : exceeding the normal or average **2** : being beyond natural human powers — **su·per·nor·mal·ly** \-mə-lē\ *adv*

su·per·no·va \-'nō-və\ *n* : a star that is a nova in which the maximum luminosity may reach 100 million times that of the sun

¹**su·per·nu·mer·ary** \ˌsü-pər-'n(y)ü-mə-ˌrer-ē\ *adj* [L *numerus* number] **1** : exceeding the stated or prescribed number **2** : SUPERFLUOUS

²**supernumerary** *n, pl* **-ar·ies** **1** : a supernumerary person or thing **2** : an actor employed to play a small usu. nonspeaking part (as in a mob scene or spectacle)

su·per·phos·phate \ˌsü-pər-'fäs-ˌfāt\ *n* : a soluble mixture of phosphates used as fertilizer

su·per·pose \ˌsü-pər-'pōz\ *vt* : to place or lay over or above another esp. so as to coincide ⟨congruent triangles can be *superposed*⟩ — **su·per·po·si·tion** \-pə-'zish-ən\ *n*

su·per·sat·u·rate \ˌsü-pər-'sach-ə-ˌrāt\ *vt* : to add to beyond saturation — **su·per·sat·u·ra·tion** \-ˌsach-ə-'rā-shən\ *n*

su·per·scribe \'sü-pər-ˌskrīb\ *vt* [L *superscript-, superscribere*, fr. *super-* + *scribere* to write] : to write or engrave on the top or outside; *esp* : to write (as a name or address) on the outside or cover of

su·per·script \'sü-pər-ˌskript\ *n* [L *superscriptus*, pp. of *superscribere* to superscribe] : a distinguishing symbol or letter written immediately above or above and to the right or left of another character — **superscript** *adj*

su·per·scrip·tion \ˌsü-pər-'skrip-shən\ *n* **1** : the act of superscribing **2** : something superscribed on something else : INSCRIPTION; *esp* : ADDRESS

su·per·sede \ˌsü-pər-'sēd\ *vt* [L *supersess-, supersedēre* to be superior to, refrain from, fr. *super-* + *sedēre* to sit] **1** : to force out of use as inferior **2** : to take the place, room, or position of **3** : to displace in favor of another : SUPPLANT syn see REPLACE — **su·per·sed·er** *n* — **su·per·se·dure** \-'sē-jər\ *n*

su·per·sen·si·tive \-'sen(t)-sət-iv, -'sen(t)-stiv\ *adj* : HYPERSENSITIVE — **su·per·sen·si·tive·ness** *n*

su·per·ses·sion \ˌsü-pər-'sesh-ən\ *n* : the act of superseding : the state of being superseded : SUPERSEDURE — **su·per·ses·sive** \-'ses-iv\ *adj*

su·per·son·ic \-'sän-ik\ *adj* [L *super-* + *sonus* sound] **1** : having a frequency above the human ear's audibility limit of about 20,000 cycles per second ⟨*supersonic* vibrations⟩ **2** : utilizing, produced by, or relating to supersonic waves or vibrations ⟨*supersonic* disintegration of a substance⟩ **3** : of, being, or relating to speeds from one to five times the speed of sound in air **4** : moving, capable of moving, or utilizing air currents moving at supersonic speed ⟨a *supersonic* airplane⟩ — **su·per·son·i·cal·ly** \-'sän-i-k(ə-)lē\ *adv*

su·per·son·ics \-'sän-iks\ *n* : the science of supersonic phenomena

su·per·star \'sü-pər-ˌstär\ *n* : a star (as in sports or the movies) who is considered extremely talented, has great public appeal, and who can usu. command a high salary

su·per·sti·tion \ˌsü-pər-'stish-ən\ *n* [L *superstit-, superstes* standing over (as witness or survivor), fr. *super-* + *stare* to stand] **1** : beliefs or practices resulting from ignorance, fear of the unknown, or trust in magic or chance **2** : an irrationally abject attitude of mind toward nature, the unknown, or God resulting from superstition — **su·per·sti·tious** \-'stish-əs\ *adj* — **su·per·sti·tious·ly** *adv* — **su·per·sti·tious·ness** *n*

su·per·struc·ture \'sü-pər-ˌstrək-chər\ *n* : something (as the part of a building above the basement or of a ship above the main deck) built upon an underlying or more fundamental base ⟨the social *superstructure*⟩ — **su·per·struc·tur·al** \-ˌstrək-chə-rəl, -ˌstrək-shrəl\ *adj*

su·per·ton·ic \ˌsü-pər-'tän-ik\ *n* : the second tone of the musical scale

su·per·vene \ˌsü-pər-'vēn\ *vi* [L *supervenire*, fr. *super-* + *venire* to come] : to take place as an additional, adventitious, or unlooked-for development — **su·per·ve·nience** \-'vē-nyən(t)s\ *n* — **su·per·ve·nient** \-nyənt\ *adj* — **su·per·ven·tion** \-'ven-chən\ *n*

su·per·vise \'sü-pər-ˌvīz\ *vt* [ML *supervis-, supervidēre*, fr. L *super-* + *vidēre* to see] : SUPERINTEND, OVERSEE — **su·per·vi·sion** \ˌsü-pər-'vizh-ən\ *n*

su·per·vi·sor \'sü-pər-ˌvī-zər\ *n* : one that supervises; *esp* : an administrative officer in charge of a business, government, or school unit or operation — **su·per·vi·so·ry** \ˌsü-pər-'vīz-(ə-)rē\ *adj*

su·pi·nate \'sü-pə-ˌnāt\ *vb* [L *supinare* to lay on the back, fr. *supinus* supine] **1** : to rotate (the hand or forearm) so as to bring the palm facing upward or forward; *also* : to rotate (a joint or part) backward and away from the midline — **su·pi·na·tion** \ˌsü-pə-'nā-shən\ *n*

su·pi·na·tor \'sü-pə-ˌnāt-ər\ *n* : a muscle that produces the motion of supination

¹**su·pine** \sú-'pīn\ *adj* [L *supinus*] **1 a** : lying on the back or with the face upward **b** : marked by supination **2** : showing mental or moral slackness syn see PRONE — **su·pine·ly** *adv* — **su·pine·ness** \-'pīn-nəs\ *n*

²**su·pine** \'sü-ˌpīn\ *n* : a Latin verbal noun having an accusative of purpose in -*um* and an ablative of specification in -*u*

sup·per \'səp-ər\ *n* [OF *souper*, fr. *souper* to sup] **1** : the evening meal when dinner is taken at midday **2** : refreshments served late in the evening esp. at a social gathering

sup·plant \sə-'plant\ *vt* [L *supplantare* to overthrow by tripping up, fr. *sub-* + *planta* sole of the foot] **1** : to take the place of (another) esp. by force or treachery **2 a** : to root out and supply a substitute for ⟨efforts to *supplant* the vernacular⟩ **b** : to gain the place of esp. by reason of superior excellence or power syn see REPLACE — **sup·plan·ta·tion** \ˌsə-ˌplan-'tā-shən\ *n* — **sup·plant·er** \sə-'plant-ər\ *n*

¹**sup·ple** \'səp-əl\ *adj* **sup·pler** \'səp-(ə-)lər\; **sup·plest** \'səp-(ə-)ləst\ [OF *souple*, fr. L *supplic-, supplex* bending under, submissive, suppliant, fr. *sub-* + *plicare* to fold] **1 a** : adapting easily and often obsequiously to the wishes of others **b** : readily adaptable to new situations **2 a** : capable of being bent or folded without creases or breaks : PLIANT ⟨*supple* leather⟩ **b** : able to bend or twist with ease and grace : LIMBER ⟨*supple* legs of a dancer⟩ — **sup·ple·ness** \-əl-nəs\ *n*

²**supple** *vt* **sup·pled**; **sup·pling** \'səp-(ə-)liŋ\ : to make supple

¹**sup·ple·ment** \'səp-lə-mənt\ *n* [L *supplementum*, fr.

ə abut; ° kitten; ər further; a back; ā bake; ä cot, cart; aú out; ch chin; e less; ē easy; g gift; i trip; ī life

supplēre to fill up, fr. *sub-* up + *plēre* to fill] **1** : something that supplies a want or makes an addition ⟨diet *supplements*⟩ ⟨the *supplement* at the back of the book⟩ **2** : the amount by which an arc or an angle falls short of 180 degrees — **sup·ple·men·tal** \ˌsəp-lə-'ment-ᵊl\ *adj* — **sup·ple·men·ta·tion** \ˌsəp-lə-ˌmen-'tā-shən\ *n*

²**sup·ple·ment** \'səp-lə-ˌment\ *vt* : to add to : COMPLETE ⟨*supplements* his income by doing odd jobs⟩

sup·ple·men·ta·ry \ˌsəp-lə-'ment-ə-rē, -'men-trē\ *adj* : added as a supplement : ADDITIONAL

supplementary angles *n pl* : two angles whose sum is 180 degrees

sup·ple·to·ry \sə-'plēt-ə-rē\ *adj* : supplying deficiencies : SUPPLEMENTARY

sup·pli·ance \'səp-lē-ə(n)ts\ *n* : SUPPLICATION, ENTREATY

¹**sup·pli·ant** \'səp-lē-ənt\ *n* [MF, fr. prp. of *supplier* to supplicate, fr. L *supplicare*] : one who supplicates

²**suppliant** *adj* : BESEECHING, IMPLORING — **sup·pli·ant·ly** *adv*

sup·pli·cant \'səp-li-kənt\ *n* : one who supplicates : SUPPLIANT — **supplicant** *adj* — **sup·pli·cant·ly** *adv*

sup·pli·cate \'səp-lə-ˌkāt\ *vb* [L *supplicare*, fr. *supplic-, supplex* submissive, suppliant, fr. *sub-* + *plicare* to fold] **1** : to make a humble entreaty; *esp* : to pray to God **2** : to ask earnestly and humbly : BESEECH ⟨*supplicates* a morsel of bread⟩ ⟨*supplicated* him not to leave her⟩ — **sup·pli·ca·tion** \ˌsəp-lə-'kā-shən\ *n* — **sup·pli·ca·to·ry** \'səp-li-kə-ˌtōr-ē, -ˌtȯr-\ *adj*

¹**sup·ply** \sə-'plī\ *vt* **sup·plied**; **sup·ply·ing** [MF *soupleier*, fr. L *supplēre* to fill up, supplement, supply, fr. *sub-* up + *plēre* to fill] **1** : to add as a supplement **2 a** : to provide for : SATISFY **b** : to provide or furnish with : AFFORD **c** : to satisfy the needs or wishes of — **sup·pli·er** \-'plī(-ə)r\ *n*

²**supply** *n, pl* **supplies** **1 a** : the quantity or amount (as of a commodity) needed or available **b** : PROVISIONS, STORES — usu. used in pl. **2** : the act or process of filling a want or need : PROVISION **3** : the quantities of goods or services offered for sale at a particular time or at one price

¹**sup·port** \sə-'pōrt, -'pȯrt\ *vt* [LL *supportare*, fr. L, to carry, fr. *sub-* + *portare* to carry] **1** : to endure bravely or quietly : BEAR **2 a** (1) : to promote the interests or cause of (2) : to uphold or defend as valid or right : ADVOCATE (3) : to argue or vote for **b** : ASSIST, HELP **c** : to act with (a star actor) **d** : SUBSTANTIATE, VERIFY **3** : to pay the costs of : MAINTAIN **4 a** : to hold up or in position or serve as a foundation or prop for **b** : to maintain (the price of a commodity) at a high level by purchases or loans **5** : to keep (something) going : SUSTAIN — **sup·port·a·ble** \-ə-bəl\ *adj* — **sup·port·a·ble·ness** *n* — **sup·port·a·bly** \-blē\ *adv*

²**support** *n* **1** : the act or process of supporting : the condition of being supported **2** : one that supports

sup·port·er \sə-'pōrt-ər, -'pȯrt-\ *n* : one that supports; *esp* : ADHERENT, ADVOCATE

sup·port·ive \sə-'pōrt-iv, -'pȯrt-\ *adj* : furnishing or intended to furnish support

sup·pos·a·ble \sə-'pō-zə-bəl\ *adj* : capable of being supposed : CONCEIVABLE — **sup·pos·a·bly** \-blē\ *adv*

sup·pose \sə-'pōz\ *vb* [MF *supposer*, irreg. fr. ML *supponere*, fr. L, to put under, substitute, fr. *sub-* + *ponere* to put] **1** : to take as true or as a fact for the sake of argument : lay down as a hypothesis ⟨*suppose* a fire should break out⟩ **2** : to hold as an opinion : BELIEVE ⟨they *supposed* they were on the right bus⟩ **3** : CONJECTURE, OPINE ⟨who do you *suppose* will win⟩

sup·posed \sə-'pōzd\ *adj* **1** : BELIEVED; *also* : mistakenly believed : IMAGINED **2** : EXPECTED — used in the phrase *be supposed to* ⟨knew she was *supposed* to practice two hours daily⟩ — **sup·pos·ed·ly** \-'pō-zəd-lē\ *adv*

sup·po·si·tion \ˌsəp-ə-'zish-ən\ *n* **1** : something that is supposed : HYPOTHESIS **2** : the act of supposing — **sup·po·si·tion·al** \-'zish-nəl, -ən-ᵊl\ *adj* — **sup·po·si·tion·al·ly** \-ē\ *adv*

sup·po·si·tious \-'zish-əs\ *adj* : SUPPOSITITIOUS

sup·po·si·ti·tious \sə-ˌpäz-ə-'tish-əs\ *adj* [L *supposititius*, fr. *supposit-, supponere* to put under, substitute] **1** : fraudulently substituted : SPURIOUS **2** : of the nature of a supposition : HYPOTHETICAL — **sup·po·si·ti·tious·ly** *adv* — **sup·po·si·ti·tious·ness** *n*

sup·pos·i·tive \sə-'päz-ət-iv\ *adj* : SUPPOSED — **sup·pos·i·tive·ly** *adv*

sup·pos·i·to·ry \sə-'päz-ə-ˌtōr-ē, -ˌtȯr-\ *n, pl* **-ries** [L *supposit-, supponere* to put under] : a solid but readily meltable cone or cylinder of usu. medicated material for insertion into a bodily passage or cavity (as the rectum)

sup·press \sə-'pres\ *vt* [L *suppress-, supprimere*, fr. *sub-* + *premere* to press] **1** : to put down by authority or force : SUBDUE **2 a** : to keep from being known **b** : to stop the publication or circulation of **3 a** : to exclude from consciousness **b** : to keep from giving vent to : CHECK **4 a** : to restrain from a usual course or action : HALT ⟨*suppress* a hemorrhage⟩ **b** : to inhibit the growth or development of : STUNT — **sup·press·i·ble** \-ə-bəl\ *adj* — **sup·pres·sion** \-'presh-ən\ *n* — **sup·pres·sive** \-'pres-iv\ *adj* — **sup·pres·sor** \-'pres-ər\ *n*

sup·pu·rate \'səp-yə-ˌrāt\ *vi* [L *suppurare*, fr. *sub-* + *pur-, pus* pus] : to form or give off pus — **sup·pu·ra·tion** \ˌsəp-yə-'rā-shən\ *n* — **sup·pu·ra·tive** \'səp-yə-ˌrāt-iv\ *adj*

supra- *prefix* [L, fr. *supra* above, beyond] **1** : SUPER- 2a ⟨*supra*orbital⟩ **2** : transcending ⟨*supra*molecular⟩

su·pra·na·tion·al \ˌsü-prə-'nash-nəl, -ən-ᵊl\ *adj* : transcending national boundaries or authority

su·pra·or·bit·al \ˌsü-prə-'ȯr-bət-ᵊl\ *adj* : situated or occurring above the orbit of the eye

su·pra·or·ga·nism \-'ȯr-gə-ˌniz-əm\ *n* : an organized society (as of a social insect) that functions as an organic whole

¹**su·pra·re·nal** \-'rēn-ᵊl\ *adj* [L *renes* kidneys] : situated above or anterior to the kidneys; *esp* : ADRENAL

²**suprarenal** *n* : a suprarenal part; *esp* : ADRENAL GLAND

su·prem·a·cist \sü-'prem-ə-səst\ *n* : an advocate of group supremacy ⟨a white *supremacist*⟩

su·prem·a·cy \sü-'prem-ə-sē\ *n, pl* **-cies** : the quality or state of being supreme; *also* : supreme authority or power

syn SUPREMACY, ASCENDANCY mean a being first in rank, power, or influence. SUPREMACY implies definite superiority over all others ⟨*supremacy* in steel production⟩ ASCENDANCY implies domination of one by another which may or may not involve supremacy ⟨seeking to keep her *ascendancy* over her old rival⟩

su·preme \sù-'prēm\ *adj* [L *supremus*, superl. of *superus* being above, fr. *super* over, above] **1** : highest in rank or authority **2** : highest in degree or quality **3** : ULTIMATE, FINAL ⟨*supreme* sacrifice⟩ — **su·preme·ly** *adv* — **su·preme·ness** *n*

Supreme Being *n* : ²GOD

supreme court *n* **1** : the highest court of the U.S. consisting of a chief justice and eight associate justices; *also* : a similar body in many states **2** : a subordinate court in New York state

sur- *prefix* [OF, fr. L *super-*] : over : SUPER- ⟨*sur*print⟩ ⟨*sur*tax⟩

sur·cease \sər-ˌsēs, (ˌ)sər-'\ *n* [ME *sursesen* to desist, take a respite, fr. MF *sursis*, pp. of *surseoir*, fr. L *supersedēre* to be superior to, refrain from, fr. *super-* + *sedēre* to sit] : CESSATION; *esp* : a temporary respite or end

¹**sur·charge** \'sər-ˌchärj\ *vt* **1 a** : OVERCHARGE **b** : to charge an extra fee **2** : OVERLOAD **3** : to mark a new denomination figure or a surcharge on (a stamp)

²**surcharge** *n* **1** : an additional tax or charge **2** : an excessive load or burden **3 a** : an overprint on a stamp; *esp* : one that alters the denomination **b** : a stamp bearing such an overprint

sur·cin·gle \'sər-ˌsiŋ-gəl\ *n* [MF *surcengle*, fr. *sur-* + *cengle* girdle, fr. L *cingulum*] : a belt, band, or girth passing around the body of a horse to bind a saddle or pack fast to the horse's back

sur·coat \'sər-ˌkōt\ *n* : an outer coat or cloak; *esp* : a tunic worn over armor

¹**surd** \'sərd\ *adj* [L *surdus* deaf, silent, stupid] **1** : IRRATIONAL **2** : VOICELESS — used of speech sounds

²**surd** *n* **1** : an irrational root (as √3) **2** : a surd speech sound

¹**sure** \'shù(ə)r\ *adj* [MF *sur*, fr. L *securus* secure] **1** : firmly established : STEADFAST **2** : RELIABLE, TRUSTWORTHY **3** : ASSURED, CONFIDENT **4** : admitting of no doubt : CERTAIN **5 a** : bound to happen : INEVITABLE ⟨*sure* disaster⟩ **b** : DESTINED, BOUND ⟨he is *sure* to win⟩ — **sure·ness** *n*

---

j joke;   ŋ sing;   ō flow;   ȯ flaw;   ȯi coin;   th thin;   t̲h̲ this;   ü loot;   u̇ foot;   y yet;   yü few;   yu̇ furious;   zh vision

syn SURE, CERTAIN, POSITIVE mean having no doubt of one's opinion or conclusion. SURE usu. stresses the subjective or intuitive feeling of assurance ⟨*sure* he had seen that face before⟩ CERTAIN implies basing a conclusion on definite grounds or indubitable evidence; POSITIVE intensifies sureness and may imply opinionated conviction or forceful expression of it
— **for sure** : without doubt : with certainty — **to be sure** **1** : SURELY, CERTAINLY **2** : ADMITTEDLY

²**sure** *adv* : SURELY

sure·fire \-'fī(ə)r\ *adj* : certain to get results : DEPENDABLE

sure·foot·ed \-'fút-əd\ *adj* : not liable to stumble or fall — **sure·foot·ed·ness** *n*

sure·ly \'shù(ə)r-lē\ *adv* **1 a** : with assurance : CONFIDENTLY **b** : without doubt : CERTAINLY ⟨slowly but *surely*⟩ **2** : INDEED, REALLY — often used as an intensive ⟨I *surely* am tired this afternoon⟩

sure·ty \'shúr-ət-ē, 'shù)rt-ē\ *n, pl* **sureties** **1** : sure knowledge : CERTAINTY **2** : a formal engagement (as a pledge) for the fulfillment of an undertaking : GUARANTEE **3** : one who assumes legal liability for the debt, default, or failure in duty of another — **sure·ty·ship** \-ē-,ship\ *n*

surf \'sərf\ *n* **1** : the swell of the sea that breaks upon the shore **2** : the foam, splash, and sound of breaking waves

¹**sur·face** \'sər-fəs\ *n* [F, fr. *sur-* + *face*] **1** : the outside of an object or body **2** : a plane or curved two-dimensional locus of points ⟨*surface* of a sphere⟩ **3** : the external or superficial aspect of something **4** : a complete airfoil — **surface** *adj*

²**surface** *vb* **1** : to give a surface to: as **a** : to plane or make smooth (as lumber) **b** : to apply the surface layer to **2** : to come to the surface ⟨the submarine *surfaced*⟩ — **sur·fac·er** *n*

surface tension *n* : a condition that exists at the free surface of a liquid by reason of intermolecular forces about the individual surface molecules and is manifested by properties resembling those of an elastic skin under tension

sur·fac·ing \'sər-fə-sin\ *n* : material forming or used to form a surface

surf·board \'sərf-,bōrd, -,bȯrd\ *n* : a buoyant board used in the sport of riding the surf — **surfboard** *vi* — **surf·board·er** *n*

surf·boat \-,bōt\ *n* : a boat for use in heavy surf

surf casting *n* : the technique or act of casting artificial or natural bait into the open ocean or in a bay where waves break on a beach — **surf caster** *n*

¹**sur·feit** \'sər-fət\ *n* [MF *surfait*, fr. *surfaire* to overdo, fr. *sur-* + *faire* to do, fr. L *facere*] **1** : an overabundant supply : EXCESS **2** : an intemperate indulgence in something (as food or drink) **3** : disgust caused by excess : SATIETY

²**surfeit** *vb* : to feed, supply, or indulge to the point of surfeit : CLOY

surf·rid·ing \'sərf-,rīd-in\ *n* : the sport of riding the surf on a surfboard

¹**surge** \'sərj\ *vi* [MF *sourge-, sourdre*, fr. L *surgere* to go straight up, rise, fr. *sub-* up + *regere* to lead straight] **1** : to rise and fall actively : TOSS **2** : to rise and move or roll forward in or as if in waves or billows : SWELL **3** : to rise suddenly to an abnormal value — used esp. of current or voltage

²**surge** *n* **1** : a swelling, rolling, or sweeping forward like that of a wave **2** : a large wave or billow : SWELL **3** : a transient sudden rise of current in an electrical circuit

sur·geon \'sər-jən\ *n* [OF *cirurgien*, fr. *cirurgie* surgery] : a physician who specializes in surgery

sur·gery \'sərj-(ə-)rē\ *n, pl* **-ger·ies** [OF *cirurgie, cirurgerie*, fr. L *chirurgia*, fr. Gk *cheirourgia*, fr. *cheir* hand + *-o-* + *ergon* work] **1** : a branch of medicine concerned with the correction of physical defects, the repair and healing of injuries, and the treatment of diseased conditions esp. through instrumental procedures **2** : work done by a surgeon : OPERATION **3 a** *Brit* : a physician's or dentist's office **b** : a room or area where surgery is performed

sur·gi·cal \'sər-ji-kəl\ *adj* : of, relating to, or associated with surgeons or surgery ⟨*surgical* skills⟩ ⟨*surgical* implements⟩ ⟨*surgical* fevers⟩ — **sur·gi·cal·ly** \-k(ə-)lē\ *adv*

sur·ly \'sər-lē\ *adj* **sur·li·er; -est** [ME *sirly* lordly, imperious, fr. *sir*] : ILL-NATURED, CRABBED, DISAGREEABLE **syn** see SULLEN — **sur·li·ness** *n*

¹**sur·mise** \sər-'mīz\ *vb* [ME *surmisen* to accuse, fr. MF

surmis, pp. of *surmetre*, fr. L *supermittere* to throw on, fr. *super-* + *mittere* to send] : to imagine or infer on slight grounds : GUESS **syn** see CONJECTURE

²**sur·mise** \sər-'mīz, 'sər-\ *n* : a thought or idea based on scanty evidence : CONJECTURE

sur·mount \sər-'maunt\ *vt* **1** : to rise superior to : OVERCOME ⟨*surmount* an obstacle⟩ **2** : to get to the top of : CLIMB **3** : to stand or lie at the top of : CROWN — **sur·mount·a·ble** \-ə-bəl\ *adj*

¹**sur·name** \'sər-,nām\ *n* **1** : an added name : NICKNAME **2** : the name borne in common by members of a family

²**surname** *vt* : to give a surname to

sur·pass \sər-'pas\ *vt* **1** : to be greater, better, or stronger than : EXCEED **2** : to go beyond the reach, powers, or capacity of **syn** see EXCEED — **sur·pass·a·ble** \-ə-bəl\ *adj*

sur·plice \'sər-pləs\ *n* [OF *surpliz*, fr. ML *superpellicium*, fr. *super-* + *pellicium* coat of skins, fr. L *pellis* skin] : a loose white tunic worn at service by a clergyman or choir member

sur·plus \'sər-(,)pləs\ *n* [MF, fr. ML *superplus*, fr. L *super-* + *plus* more] **1** : the amount that remains when use or need is satisfied : EXCESS **2** : an excess of receipts over disbursements — **surplus** *adj*

sur·plus·age \-ij\ *n* **1** : SURPLUS 1 **2** : excessive or nonessential matter

surplus value *n* : the difference in Marxist theory between the value of work done by labor and the wages paid by the employer

¹**sur·prise** \sə(r)-'prīz\ *n* [MF, fr. *surprendre* to take over, surprise, fr. *sur-* + *prendre* to take] **1 a** : an attack made without warning **b** : a taking unawares **2** : something that surprises **3** : the state of being surprised : ASTONISHMENT

²**surprise** *also* **sur·prize** *vt* **1** : to attack unexpectedly; *also* : to capture by an unexpected attack **2** : to take unawares : come upon unexpectedly **3** : to bring about or obtain by a taking unawares **4** : to strike with wonder or amazement because unexpected

syn SURPRISE, ASTONISH, ASTOUND mean to impress strongly through unexpectedness. SURPRISE stresses causing an effect through being unexpected at a particular time or place rather than by being essentially unusual or novel; ASTONISH implies surprising so greatly as to seem incredible; ASTOUND stresses the shock of astonishment

sur·pris·ing *adj* : ASTONISHING, AMAZING — **sur·pris·ing·ly** \-'prī-zin-lē\ *adv*

sur·re·al·ism \sə-'rē-ə-,liz-əm\ *n* : a modern movement in art and literature that purports to express subconscious mental activities through fantastic or incongruous imagery or unnatural juxtapositions and combinations — **sur·re·al·ist** \-ləst\ *n or adj* — **sur·re·al·is·tic** \-,rē-ə-'lis-tik\ *adj* — **sur·re·al·is·ti·cal·ly** \-ti-k(ə-)lē\ *adv*

¹**sur·ren·der** \sə-'ren-dər\ *vb* **sur·ren·dered; sur·ren·der·ing** \-d(ə-)rin\ [MF *surrendre* fr. *sur-* + *rendre* to yield] **1** : to give over to the power, control, or possession of another esp. under compulsion ⟨*surrendered* the fort⟩ **2 a** : to give oneself up into the power of another esp. as a prisoner **b** : to give oneself over to something (as an influence or course of action)

²**surrender** *n* : the giving of oneself or something into the power of another person or thing

sur·rep·ti·tious \,sər-əp-'tish-əs, ,sə-rəp-\ *adj* [L *surrepticius, surreptus, surripere* to snatch secretly, fr. *sub-* + *rapere* to seize] : done, made, or acquired by stealth : CLANDESTINE, STEALTHY **syn** see SECRET — **sur·rep·ti·tious·ly** *adv* — **sur·rep·ti·tious·ness** *n*

sur·rey \'sər-ē, 'sə-rē\ *n, pl* **surreys** [fr. *Surrey*, county of England] : a four-wheel two-seated horse-drawn pleasure carriage

sur·ro·gate \'sər-ə-,gāt, 'sə-rə-, -gət\ *n* [L *surrogatus*, pp. of *surrogare* to substitute, fr. *sub-* + *rogare* to ask] **1** : DEPUTY, SUBSTITUTE **2** : a local judicial officer in some states having probate jurisdiction

¹**sur·round** \sə-'raund\ *vt* [MF *suronder* to overflow, fr. LL *superun-*

surrey

dare, fr. L *super-* + *unda* wave] **:** to enclose on all sides **:** ENCIRCLE, ENCOMPASS

²surround *n* **:** something (as a border or edging) that surrounds

sur·round·ings \-'raún-diŋz\ *n pl* **:** the circumstances, conditions, or objects by which one is surrounded **:** ENVIRONMENT

sur·sum cor·da \,su(ə)r-səm-'kórd-ə\ *n* [LL, (lift) up (your) hearts] **1** *often cap S&C* **:** a versicle exhorting thanksgiving to God **2 :** something inspiriting

sur·tax \'sər-,taks\ *n* **:** an additional tax over and above a general tax

sur·tout \(,)sər-'tü\ *n* [F, fr. *sur tout* over all] **:** a man's long close-fitting overcoat

sur·veil·lance \sər-'vā-lən(t)s, -'vāl-yən(t)s\ *n* [F, fr. *surveiller* to watch over, fr. *sur-* + *veiller* to watch, fr. L *vigilare,* fr. *vigil* watchful] **:** close watch ⟨kept under constant *surveillance*⟩

sur·veil·lant \-'vā-lənt, -'vāl-yənt\ *n* **:** one that exercises surveillance

¹sur·vey \sər-'vā, 'sər-,\ *vt* **sur·veyed; sur·vey·ing** [MF *surveeir,* fr. *sur-* + *veeir* to see, fr. L *videre*] **1 :** to look over and examine closely **2 :** to determine the form, extent, and position of (a piece of land) **3 :** to view or study as a whole **:** make a survey of

²sur·vey \'sər-,vā, sər-'\ *n, pl* **surveys 1 :** the action or an instance of surveying **2 :** something that is surveyed **3 :** a careful examination to learn certain facts ⟨a *survey* of the school system⟩ **4 :** a history or description that covers much material by bare outlines ⟨a *survey* of world history⟩ **5 a :** the process of determining and making a record of the outline, measurements, and position of any part of the earth's surface esp. by use of geometry and trigonometry **b :** an organization engaged in surveying **6 :** a measured plan and description (as of a portion of land or of a road)

sur·vey·ing \sər-'vā-iŋ\ *n* **:** the occupation of a surveyor; *esp* **:** the branch of mathematics that teaches the art of measuring and representing the earth's surface accurately

sur·vey·or \sər-'vā-ər\ *n* **:** one that surveys; *esp* **:** one whose occupation is surveying land

sur·viv·al \sər-'vī-vəl\ *n* **1 :** a living or continuing longer than another or beyond something **2 :** one that survives

survival of the fittest : NATURAL SELECTION

sur·vive \sər-'vīv\ *vb* [MF *survivre* to outlive, fr. L *super-vivere,* fr. *super-* + *vivere* to live] **1 :** to remain alive or in existence **:** live on **2 :** to remain alive after the death of ⟨his son *survived* him⟩ **3 :** to continue to exist or live after ⟨*survived* the flood⟩ — **sur·vi·vor** \-'vī-vər\ *n*

sus·cep·ti·bil·i·ty \sə-,sep-tə-'bil-ət-ē\ *n, pl* **-ties 1 :** the quality or state of being susceptible; *esp* **:** lack of ability to resist some extraneous agent (as a pathogen or drug) **:** SENSITIVITY **2 a :** a susceptible temperament or constitution **b** *pl* **:** FEELINGS, SENSIBILITIES

sus·cep·ti·ble \sə-'sep-tə-bəl\ *adj* [L *suscept-, suscipere* to take up, fr. *sub-, sus-* up + *capere* to take] **1 :** capable of submitting to an action, process, or operation ⟨a theory *susceptible* to proof⟩ **2 :** open, subject, or unresistant to some stimulus, influence, or agency ⟨persons *susceptible* to colds⟩ **3 :** IMPRESSIONABLE — **sus·cep·ti·ble·ness** *n* — **sus·cep·ti·bly** \-blē\ *adv*

sus·cep·tive \sə-'sep-tiv\ *adj* **1 :** RECEPTIVE **2 :** SUSCEPTIBLE — **sus·cep·tive·ness** *n* — **sus·cep·tiv·i·ty** \sə-,sep-'tiv-ət-ē\ *n*

¹sus·pect \'səs-,pekt, sə-'spekt\ *adj* [L *suspectus,* fr. pp. of *suspicere* to suspect] **:** regarded with suspicion **:** SUSPECTED

²sus·pect \'səs-,pekt\ *n* **:** one who is suspected

³sus·pect \sə-'spekt\ *vb* [L *suspect-, suspicere* to look up at, regard with awe, suspect, fr. *sub-* up + *specere* to look at] **1 :** to have doubts of **:** DISTRUST **2 :** to believe it possible or likely that a person is guilty on slight evidence or without proof **3 :** to imagine to be or to be true, likely, or probable **:** SURMISE **4 :** to be suspicious

sus·pend \sə-'spend\ *vb* [L *suspendere, fr. sub-, sus-* up + *pendere* to cause to hang, weigh] **1 :** to bar temporarily from any privilege or office ⟨*suspend* a student from school⟩ **2 a :** to stop or do away with for a time **:** WITHHOLD ⟨*suspend* publication⟩ **b :** to defer on specified conditions ⟨*suspend* sentence on an offender⟩ ⟨*suspend* judgment⟩ **3 :** to cease for a time from operation or activity **4 a**

: HANG; *esp* **:** to hang so as to be free on all sides except at the point of support ⟨*suspend* a ball by a thread⟩ **b :** to keep from falling or sinking through the action of some force (as buoyancy) that opposes gravity ⟨dust *suspended* in the air⟩ **syn** see DEFER

suspended animation *n* **:** temporary suspension of the vital functions

sus·pend·er \sə-'spen-dər\ *n* **1 :** one that suspends **2 :** a device by which something may be suspended: as **a :** one of two supporting bands worn across the shoulders to support trousers, skirt, or belt — usu. used in pl. ⟨a pair of *suspenders*⟩ **b** *Brit* **:** GARTER

sus·pense \sə-'spen(t)s\ *n* [MF, fr. *suspendre* to suspend, fr. L *suspendere*] **1 :** temporary cessation **:** SUSPENSION **2 :** mental uncertainty: **a :** ANXIETY **b :** a pleasurable excitement produced by a story or play as to its outcome **3 :** the state of being undecided **:** lack of certainty **:** INDECISIVENESS ⟨our next move was still in *suspense*⟩ — **sus·pense·ful** \-fəl\ *adj*

sus·pen·sion \sə-'spen-chən\ *n* [L *suspens-, suspendere* to suspend] **1 :** the act of suspending or the state or period of being suspended: as **a :** temporary removal from office or privileges **b :** temporary withholding (as of belief or decision) **c :** temporary abrogation of a law or rule **2 :** the act of hanging **:** the state of being hung **3 a :** the state of a substance when its particles are mixed with but undissolved in a fluid or solid; *also* **:** a substance in this state **b :** a system consisting of a solid dispersed in a solid, liquid, or gas usu. in particles of larger than colloidal size **4 :** something suspended **5 a :** a device by which something is suspended **b :** the system of devices (as springs) supporting the upper part of a vehicle on the axles

suspension bridge *n* **:** a bridge that has its roadway suspended from two or more cables usu. passing over towers and securely anchored at the ends — see BRIDGE illustration

suspension points *n pl* **:** usu. three spaced periods used to show the omission of a word or word group

sus·pen·sive \sə-'spen(t)-siv\ *adj* **1 :** stopping temporarily **:** SUSPENDING **2 :** characterized by suspense, suspended judgment, or indecisiveness **3 :** characterized by suspension — **sus·pen·sive·ly** *adv*

sus·pen·sor \sə-'spen(t)-sər\ *n* **:** a suspending part or structure; *esp* **:** a group of cells supporting a plant embryo or zygospore

¹sus·pen·so·ry \sə-'spen(t)s-(ə-)rē\ *adj* **1 a :** SUSPENDED **b :** fitted or serving to suspend something **2 :** temporarily leaving undetermined **:** SUSPENSIVE 1

²suspensory *n, pl* **-ries :** something that suspends or holds up

¹sus·pi·cion \sə-'spish-ən\ *n* [L *suspicion-, suspicio,* fr. *suspicere* to suspect] **1 :** the act or an instance of suspecting or being suspected **2 :** a feeling that something is wrong without definite evidence **3 :** a slight touch or trace **:** SUGGESTION ⟨just a *suspicion* of garlic⟩ **syn** see DOUBT

²suspicion *vt* **sus·pi·cioned; sus·pi·cion·ing** \-'spish-(ə-)niŋ\ *chiefly substand* **:** SUSPECT

sus·pi·cious \sə-'spish-əs\ *adj* **1 :** tending to arouse suspicion **:** QUESTIONABLE **2 :** disposed to suspect **:** DISTRUSTFUL **3 :** indicative of suspicion ⟨a *suspicious* glance⟩ — **sus·pi·cious·ly** *adv* — **sus·pi·cious·ness** *n*

sus·pire \sə-'spī(ə)r\ *vi* [L *suspirare,* fr. *sub-* + *spirare* to breathe] **:** to draw a long deep breath **:** SIGH — **sus·pi·ra·tion** \,səs-pə-'rā-shən\ *n*

sus·tain \sə-'stān\ *vt* [OF *sustenir,* fr. L *sustinēre,* fr. *sub-, sus-* up + *tenēre* to hold] **1 :** to give support or relief to **2 :** to supply with sustenance **:** NOURISH **3 :** to keep up **:** PROLONG **4 :** to support the weight of **:** CARRY **5 :** to buoy up **6 a :** to bear up under **:** ENDURE **b :** RECEIVE, UNDERGO ⟨*sustained* a serious wound⟩ **7 a :** to support as true, legal, or just **b :** to allow or admit as valid ⟨the court *sustained* the motion⟩ **8 :** PROVE, CONFIRM — **sus·tain·a·ble** \-'stā-nə-bəl\ *adj* — **sus·tain·er** *n*

sustaining program *n* **:** a radio or television program that is paid for by a station or network and has no commercial sponsor

sus·te·nance \'səs-tə-nən(t)s\ *n* **1 a :** means of support, maintenance, or subsistence **b :** FOOD; *also* **:** NOURISHMENT **2 :** the act of sustaining **:** the state of being sus-

---

j joke; ŋ sing; ō flow; ȯ flaw; ȯi coin; th thin; th̲ this; ü loot; u̇ foot; y yet; yü few; yu̇ furious; zh vision

tained; *esp* : a supplying with the necessaries of life
3 : something that gives support, endurance, or strength
sus·ten·tac·u·lar \,səs-tən-'tak-yə-lər\ *adj* [L *sustentaculum* support, fr. *sustentare*, freq. of *sustinere* to sustain]
: serving to support or hold in place ⟨a *sustentacular* ligament⟩
su·sur·ra·tion \,sü-sə-'rā-shən\ *n* [L *susurrare* to whisper] : WHISPERING, MURMUR
sut·ler \'sət-lər\ *n* [obs. D *soeteler*, fr. LG *suteler* sloppy worker, camp cook] : a victualler to an army post often established in a shop on the post
sut·tee \(,)sə-'tē\ *n* [Skt *satī* wife who performs suttee, lit., good woman, fr. fem. of *sat* true, good; akin to E *sooth*] : the act or custom of a Hindu widow cremating herself or being cremated on the funeral pile of her husband; *also* : a woman cremated in this way
¹**su·ture** \'sü-chər\ *n* [L *sutura* seam, suture, fr. *suere* to sew; akin to E *sew*] **1 a** : a strand or fiber used to sew parts of the living body; *also* : a stitch made with this **b** : the act or process of sewing with sutures **2** : a seam or line along which two things or parts are joined by or as if by sewing: as **a** : the line of union in an immovable joint (as between the bones of the skull); *also* : such a joint **b** : a furrow at the junction of adjacent bodily parts; *esp* : a line along which a fruit dehisces — **su·tur·al** \'süch-(ə-)rəl\ *adj* — **su·tur·al·ly** \-ē\ *adv*
²**suture** *vt* **su·tured; su·tur·ing** \'süch-(ə-)riŋ\ : to unite, close, or secure with sutures ⟨*suture* a wound⟩
su·zer·ain \'süz-(ə-)rən, 'süz-ə-,rān\ *n* [F, fr. MF *sus* up + *-erain* (as in *soverain* sovereign)] **1** : a feudal lord : OVERLORD **2** : a state controlling the foreign relations of another but allowing it internal sovereignty — **su·zer·ain·ty** \-tē\ *n*
svelte \'svelt\ *adj* [F, fr. It *svelto*, lit., plucked] **1 a** : SLENDER, LITHE **b** : having clean lines : SLEEK **2** : URBANE, SUAVE — **svelte·ly** *adv* — **svelte·ness** *n*
Sven·ga·li \sven-'gäl-ē\ *n* [*Svengali*, maleficent hypnotist in the novel *Trilby* by George du Maurier] : one who attempts usu. with evil intentions to persuade or force another to do his bidding
¹**swab** \'swäb\ *n* **1 a** : MOP; *esp* : a yarn mop **b** : a wad of absorbent material usu. wound around one end of a small stick and used for applying medication or for removing material (as from a wound or lesion); *also* : a specimen taken with a swab **c** : a sponge attached to a long handle for cleaning the bore of a firearm **2 a** : a useless or contemptible person **b** : SAILOR, GOB
²**swab** *vt* **swabbed; swab·bing** : to use a swab on
swab·ber \'swäb-ər\ *n* **1** : one that swabs **2** : SWAB
swad·dle \'swäd-ªl\ *vt* **swad·dled; swad·dling** \'swäd-liŋ, -ªl-iŋ\ [ME *swadelen*] **1 a** : to wrap (an infant) with swaddling clothes **b** : SWATHE, ENVELOP **2** : RESTRAIN, RESTRICT
swaddling clothes *n pl* **1** : narrow strips of cloth wrapped around an infant to restrict movement **2** : limitations or restrictions imposed upon the immature or inexperienced
swag \'swag\ *n* **1 a** : something hanging in a curve between two points : FESTOON **b** : a suspended cluster **2 a** : goods acquired by unlawful means : LOOT **b** : SPOILS, PROFITS **3** *chiefly Austral* : a pack of personal belongings
¹**swage** \'swāj, 'swej\ *n* : a tool used by workers in metals for shaping their work by holding it on the work or the work on it and striking with a hammer
²**swage** *vt* : to shape by means of a swage
¹**swag·ger** \'swag-ər\ *vi* **swag·gered; swag·ger·ing** \'swag-(ə-)riŋ\ **1** : to conduct oneself in an arrogant or superciliously pompous manner; *esp* : to walk with an air of overbearing self-confidence **2** : BOAST, BRAG **syn** see STRUT — **swag·ger·er** \'swag-ər-ər\ *n* — **swag·ger·ing·ly** \-(ə-)riŋ-lē\ *adv*
²**swagger** *n* : an act or instance of swaggering
³**swagger** *adj* **1** : marked by elegance or showiness : SMART, STYLISH **2** : flaring from the shoulder so as to hang loose and full ⟨coat cut on *swagger* lines⟩
swagger stick *n* : a short light stick usu. covered with leather and tipped with metal at each end
swag·man \'swag-mən\ *n, chiefly Austral* : VAGRANT; *esp* : one who carries a swag when traveling
Swa·hi·li \swä-'hē-lē\ *n* **1** : a member of a Bantu-speaking people of Zanzibar and the adjacent coast of Africa

2 : a Bantu language that is a trade and governmental language over much of East Africa and in the Congo region
swain \'swān\ *n* [ON *sveinn* boy, servant] **1** : RUSTIC, PEASANT; *esp* : SHEPHERD **2** : a male admirer or suitor
swale \'swāl\ *n* [ME, shade] : a small, low-lying, and usu. wet stretch of land
¹**swal·low** \'swäl-ō\ *n* [OE *swealwe*] **1** : any of a family of small long-winged migratory passerine birds that are noted for their graceful flight and have usu. a deeply forked tail **2** : any of several swifts that superficially resemble swallows
²**swallow** *vb* [OE *swelgan*] **1 a** : to take into the stomach through the mouth and throat **b** : to perform the actions used in swallowing something ⟨cleared his throat and *swallowed* before answering⟩ **2** : to envelop or take in as if by swallowing **3** : to accept without question, protest, or resentment ⟨*swallow* an insult⟩ ⟨a hard story to *swallow*⟩ **4** : to take back : RETRACT ⟨had to *swallow* his words⟩ **5** : to keep from expressing or showing : REPRESS ⟨*swallowed* his anger⟩ ⟨tried to *swallow* a smile and keep a straight face⟩ **6** : to utter (as words) indistinctly — **swal·low·er** \'swäl-ə-wər\ *n*
³**swallow** *n* **1** : an act of swallowing **2** : an amount that can be swallowed at one time
swal·low·tail \'swäl-ō-,tāl\ *n* **1** : a deeply forked and tapering tail (as of a swallow) **2** : TAILCOAT **3** : any of various large butterflies with the border of the hind wing drawn out into a process resembling a tail — **swal·low·tailed** \,swäl-ō-'tāld\ *adj*
swam *past of* SWIM
swa·mi \'swäm-ē\ *n* [Hindi *svāmī*, fr. Skt *svāmin* owner, lord, fr. *sva* one's own] **1** : a Hindu ascetic or religious teacher — used as a title **2** : PUNDIT
¹**swamp** \'swämp, 'swómp\ *n* [alter. of ME *sompe*, fr. MD *somp* morass] : wet spongy land or a tract of this often partially or intermittently covered with water and usu. overgrown with shrubs and trees — compare MARSH — **swamp·land** \-,land\ *n*
²**swamp** *vb* **1 a** : to cause to capsize in water or fill with water and sink **b** : to fill with or as if with water : SUBMERGE **2** : to open by removing underbrush and debris **3** : OVERWHELM ⟨was *swamped* with work⟩
swamp buggy *n* : a vehicle used to negotiate swampy terrain: as **a** : an amphibious tractor **b** : a flat-bottomed boat driven by an airplane propeller
swampy \-ē\ *adj* : of, relating to, or resembling a swamp — **swamp·i·ness** *n*
swan \'swän\ *n, pl* **swans** *also* **swan** [OE] **1** : any of various heavy-bodied long-necked mostly pure white aquatic birds related to but larger than the geese **2** : one suggesting a swan (as in grace, whiteness, or fabled power of melody when dying)
swan dive *n* : a dive executed with the head back, back arched, and arms spread sideways and then brought together above the head to form a straight line with the body as the diver enters the water
¹**swank** \'swaŋk\ *vi* : to show off : SWAGGER
²**swank** *n* **1** : PRETENTIOUSNESS, SWAGGER **2** : ELEGANCE
³**swank** *or* **swanky** \'swaŋ-kē\ *adj* **swank·er** *or* **swank·i·er; -est** **1** : characterized by showy display : OSTENTATIOUS **2** : fashionably elegant : SMART — **swank·i·ly** \'swaŋ-kə-lē\ *adv* — **swank·i·ness** \-kē-nəs\ *n*
swans·down \'swänz-,daun\ *n* **1** : the very soft white down of the swan **2** : a heavy cotton flannel with a thick nap on the face
swan·skin \'swän-,skin\ *n* : any of various fabrics resembling flannel and having a soft nap or surface
swan song *n* **1** : a song that a dying swan is said to sing **2** : a farewell appearance or final act or pronouncement
¹**swap** \'swäp\ *vb* **swapped; swap·ping** [ME *swappen* to strike; fr. the practice of striking hands in closing a business deal] : to give in exchange : make an exchange : BARTER
²**swap** *n* : EXCHANGE, TRADE
sward \'sword\ *n* [OE *sweard* skin, rind] : the grassy surface of land : TURF
¹**swarm** \'sworm\ *n* [OE *swearm*] **1** : a great number of honeybees emigrating together from a hive in company with a queen to start a new colony elsewhere; *also* : a colony of honeybees settled in a hive **2** : an extremely

large number massed together and usu. in motion : MULTITUDE

²swarm vb **1** : to form and depart from a hive in a swarm **2** : to migrate, move, or gather in a swarm : THRONG **3** : to contain or fill with a swarm ⟨the picnic area was *swarming* with ants⟩ — **swarm·er** n

³swarm vb : to climb with the hands and feet; esp : SHIN ⟨*swarm* up a pole⟩

swarm spore n : a tiny motile spore; esp : ZOOSPORE

swart \'swórt\ adj [OE *sweart*] : SWARTHY — **swart·ness** n

swarthy \'swór-the͞, -the͞\ adj **swarth·i·er; -est** [alter. of obs. *swarty*, fr. *swart*] : of a dark color, complexion, or cast : DUSKY — **swarth·i·ness** n

¹swash \'swäsh\ n **1 a** : a body of splashing water **b** : a narrow channel of water lying within a sandbank or between a sandbank and the shore **2** : a dashing of water against or upon something **3** : a bar over which the sea washes **4** : SWAGGER

²swash vb **1** : BLUSTER, SWAGGER **2** : to make violent noisy movements **3** : to move with a splashing sound

swash·buck·ler \-,bək-lər\ n [²*swash* + *buckler*] : a boasting soldier or blustering daredevil : BRAVO — **swash·buck·le** \-,bək-əl\ vi — **swash·buck·ling** \-,bək-liŋ\ adj or n

swas·ti·ka \'swäs-ti-kə, swä-'stē-kə\ n [Skt *svastika*, fr. *svasti* welfare, fr. *su-* well + *asti* being (akin to E *is*); fr. its being regarded as a good luck symbol] : a symbol or ornament in the form of a Greek cross with the ends of the arms extended at right angles all in the same rotary direction

swastika

swat \'swät\ vb **swat·ted; swat·ting** : to hit with a quick hard blow — **swat** n — **swat·ter** n

swatch \'swäch\ n **1 a** : a sample piece (as of fabric) or a collection of samples **b** : a characteristic specimen **2** : PATCH **3** : a small collection

swath \'swäth, 'swóth\ *or* **swathe** \'swäth, 'swóth, 'swäth\ n [OE *swæth* footstep, trace] **1 a** : the sweep of a scythe or machine in mowing or the path cut in one course **b** : a row of cut grain or grass **2** : a long broad strip or belt **3** : a space devastated as if by a scythe

¹swathe \'swäth, 'swóth, 'swäth\ vt [OE *swathian*] **1** : to bind, wrap, or swaddle with or as if with a bandage **2** : ENVELOP — **swath·er** n

²swathe \'swäth, 'swóth, 'swäth\ *or* **swath** \'swäth, 'swäth, 'swóth, 'swóth\ n **1** : a band used in swathing **2** : an enveloping medium

¹sway \'swā\ vb [ME *sweyen* to fall, swoon] **1 a** : to swing or cause to swing slowly back and forth from a base or pivot **b** : to move gently from an upright to a leaning position **2** : to hold sway : act as ruler or governor **3** : to fluctuate or veer between one point, position, or opinion and another **4** : to cause to turn aside : DEFLECT, DIVERT **5** : to exert a guiding or controlling influence upon — **sway·er** n

syn SWAY, OSCILLATE, VIBRATE, WAVER mean to move back and forth. SWAY implies a slow swinging or teetering movement as of something large and heavy; OSCILLATE suggests a relatively rapid and rhythmic alternation of direction; VIBRATE applies esp. to the very rapid oscillation of an elastic body under stress or impact; WAVER stresses irregular movement suggestive of reeling or tottering **syn** see in addition INFLUENCE

²sway n **1** : the action or an instance of swaying or of being swayed : an oscillating, fluctuating, or sweeping motion **2** : an inclination or deflection caused by or as if by swaying **3 a** : a controlling force or influence **b** : sovereign power : DOMINION, RULE

sway·back \'swā-'bak\ n : a sagging or abnormally hollow back (as of a horse) — **sway·backed** \-'bakt\ adj

swear \'swa(ə)r, 'swe(ə)r\ vb **swore** \'swō(ə)r, 'swó(ə)r\; **sworn** \'swórn, 'swórn\; **swear·ing** [OE *swerian*] **1** : to utter or take solemnly (an oath) **2 a** : to assert as true or promise under oath **b** : to assert or promise emphatically or earnestly **3 a** : to administer an oath to ⟨the witness was *sworn*⟩ **b** : to bind by an oath ⟨*swore* him to secrecy⟩ **4** : to bring into a specified state by swearing ⟨*swore* his life away⟩ **5** : to take an oath **6** : to use profane or obscene language : CURSE — **swear·er** n — **swear by 1** : to take an oath by ⟨*swear by* Apollo⟩ **2** : to place great confidence in — **swear for** : to answer for : GUARANTEE

— **swear off** : to vow to abstain from : RENOUNCE ⟨*swear off* smoking⟩

swear in vt : to induct into office by administration of an oath

swear out vt : to procure (a warrant for arrest) by making a sworn accusation

swear·word \'swa(ə)r-,wərd, 'swe(ə)r-\ n : a profane or obscene word

¹sweat \'swet\ vb **sweat** *or* **sweat·ed; sweat·ing** [OE *swǣtan*, fr. *swāt* sweat] **1** : to give off perceptible salty moisture through the openings of the sweat glands : PERSPIRE **2** : to give off or cause to give off moisture **3** : to collect drops of moisture ⟨stones *sweat* at night⟩ **4 a** : to work so hard that one perspires : TOIL ⟨*sweat* over a lesson⟩ **b** : to undergo anxiety or mental distress **5** : to soak with sweat ⟨*sweat* a collar⟩ **6** : to get rid of or lose by perspiring ⟨*sweat* off weight⟩ ⟨*sweat* out a fever⟩ **7** : to drive hard : OVERWORK; esp : to force to work hard at low wages and under bad conditions ⟨a factory that *sweats* its employees⟩ **8** : to heat (as solder) so as to melt and cause to run esp. between surfaces to unite them; also : to unite by such means ⟨*sweat* a pipe joint⟩ — **sweat blood** : to work or worry intensely

²sweat n **1** : hard work : DRUDGERY **2** : fluid excreted from the sweat glands of the skin : PERSPIRATION **3** : moisture issuing from or gathering in drops on a surface **4** : the condition of one sweating or sweated **5** : a state of anxiety or impatience

sweat·band \'swet-,band\ n : a usu. leather band lining the inner edge of a hat or cap to prevent sweat damage

sweat·er \'swet-ər\ n **1** : one that sweats or causes sweating **2** : a knitted or crocheted jacket or pullover

sweat gland n : a gland of the skin that secretes perspiration and opens by a minute pore in the skin

sweat out vt **1** : to endure or wait through the course of **2** : to work one's way painfully through or to

sweat pants n pl : pants having a drawstring waist and elastic cuffs at the ankle that are worn esp. by athletes in warming up

sweat shirt n : a loose collarless long-sleeved pullover of heavy cotton jersey

sweat·shop \'swet-,shäp\ n : a shop or factory in which workers are employed for long hours at low wages and under unhealthy conditions

sweaty \'swet-ē\ adj **sweat·i·er; -est 1** : wet or stained with or smelling of sweat **2** : causing sweat ⟨a *sweaty* day⟩ ⟨*sweaty* work⟩ — **sweat·i·ly** \'swet-ᵊl-ē\ adv — **sweat·i·ness** \'swet-ē-nəs\ n

swede \'swēd\ n **1** cap a : a native or inhabitant of Sweden **b** : a person of Swedish descent **2** : RUTABAGA

Swed·ish \'swēd-ish\ n **1** : the Germanic language spoken in Sweden and a part of Finland **2 Swedish** pl : the people of Sweden — **Swedish** adj

¹sweep \'swēp\ vb **swept** \'swept\; **sweep·ing** [ME *swepen*] **1 a** : to remove from a surface with or as if with a broom or brush **b** : to remove or take with a single continuous forceful action **c** : to drive or carry along with irresistible force **2 a** : to clean with or as if with a broom or brush **b** : to clear by repeated and forcible action **c** : to move across or along swiftly, violently, or overwhelmingly **d** : to win an overwhelming victory in or on ⟨*sweep* the elections⟩ **3** : to touch in passing with a swift continuous movement **4** : to go with stately or sweeping movements **5** : to trace the outline of (a curve) **6** : to cover the entire range of **7** : to move or extend in a wide curve or range — **sweep·er** n

²sweep n **1** : something that sweeps or works with a sweeping motion: as **a** : a long pole pivoted on a post and used to raise and lower a bucket (as in a well) **b** : a long oar **c** : a windmill sail **2 a** : an act or instance of sweeping; esp : a clearing out or away with or as if with a broom **b** : an overwhelming victory (as the winning of all the contests or prizes in a competition) **3 a** : a movement of great range and force **b** : a curving or circular course or line **c** : the compass of a sweeping movement : SCOPE **d** : a broad extent **4** : CHIMNEY SWEEP **5** : SWEEPSTAKES

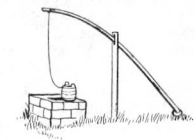

sweep 1a

sweep·back \'swēp-,bak\ *n* : the backward slant of an airplane wing in which the outer portion of the wing is downstream from the inner portion

sweep hand *n* : SWEEP-SECOND

¹sweep·ing *n* **1** : the act or action of one that sweeps ⟨gave the room a good *sweeping*⟩ **2** *pl* : things collected by sweeping : REFUSE

²sweeping *adj* **1 a** : moving or extending in a wide curve or over a wide area **b** : having a curving line or form **2 a** : EXTENSIVE ⟨*sweeping* reforms⟩ **b** : INDISCRIMINATE ⟨*sweeping* generalizations⟩ — **sweep·ing·ly** \'swē-piŋ-lē\ *adv*

sweep–sec·ond \'swēp-,sek-ənd\ *n* : a hand marking seconds on a timepiece mounted concentrically with the other hands and read on the minute dial

sweep·stakes \-,stāks\ *also* **sweep·stake** \-,stāk\ *n, pl* **sweepstakes** [ME *swepestake* one who wins all the stakes in a game, fr. *swepen* to sweep] **1 a** : a race or contest in which the entire prize may be awarded to the winner; *esp* : a horse race in which the stakes are made up at least in part of the entry fees or money contributed by the owners of the horses **b** : CONTEST, COMPETITION **2** : any of various lotteries

¹sweet \'swēt\ *adj* [OE *swēte*] **1 a** : pleasing to the taste **b** : being or inducing the one of the four basic taste sensations that is typically induced by table sugar and is mediated esp. by receptors at the front of the tongue **c** : having a relatively large sugar content **2 a** : pleasing to the mind or feelings : AGREEABLE **b** : marked by gentle good humor or kindliness **c** : FRAGRANT **d** : delicately pleasing to the ear or eye **c** : CLOYING, SACCHARINE **3** : much loved : DEAR **4 a** : not sour or rancid : not decaying or stale : WHOLESOME ⟨*sweet* milk⟩ **b** : not salt or salted : FRESH ⟨*sweet* water⟩ **c** : free from excessive acidity ⟨*sweet* soil⟩ **d** : free from noxious gases and odors — **sweet·ly** *adv* — **sweet·ness** *n* — **sweet on** : in love with

²sweet *adv* : SWEETLY

³sweet *n* **1** : something that is sweet to the taste: as **a** : a food (as a candy or preserve) having a high sugar content **b** *Brit* : DESSERT **c** *Brit* : CANDY **2** : a sweet taste sensation **3** : a pleasant or gratifying experience, possession, or state **4** : DARLING

sweet alyssum *n* : a perennial European herb of the mustard family often grown for its clusters of small fragrant usu. white flowers

sweet·bread \'swēt-,bred\ *n* : the thymus or pancreas esp. of a young animal used as food

sweet·bri·er \-,brī-(-ə)r\ *n* : an Old World rose with stout recurved prickles and white to deep rosy pink single flowers — called also *eglantine*

sweet cherry *n* : a white-flowered Eurasian cherry widely grown for its large sweet-flavored fruits; *also* : its fruit

sweet clover *n* : any of a genus of tall erect legumes widely grown for soil improvement or hay

sweet corn *n* : an Indian corn with kernels containing much sugar and adapted for table use when immature

sweet·en \'swēt-ⁿn\ *vb* **sweet·ened**; **sweet·en·ing** \'swēt-niŋ, -ⁿn-iŋ\ : to make or become sweet — **sweet·en·er** \'swēt-nər, -ⁿn-ər\ *n*

sweet·en·ing *n* **1** : the act or process of making sweet **2** : something that sweetens

sweet fern *n* : a small No. American shrub of the wax-myrtle family with sweet-scented or aromatic leaves

sweet flag *n* : a perennial marsh herb of the arum family with long leaves and a pungent rootstock

sweet gum *n* : RED GUM

sweet·heart \'swēt-,härt\ *n* **1** : DARLING **2** : LOVER

sweet·ing \'swēt-iŋ\ *n* **1** *archaic* : SWEETHEART **2** : a sweet apple

sweet·ish \'swēt-ish\ *adj* : somewhat and often unpleasantly sweet — **sweet·ish·ly** *adv*

sweet·meat \'swēt-,mēt\ *n* : a food rich in sugar: as **a** : a candied or crystallized fruit **b** : CANDY

sweet pea *n* : a garden plant with slender climbing stems and large fragrant flowers; *also* : its flower

sweet pepper *n* : a large mild-flavored thick-walled capsicum fruit; *also* : a plant bearing this — see PEPPER illustration

sweet potato *n* **1** : a tropical vine related to the morning glory with variously shaped leaves and purplish flowers;

also : its large sweet mealy tuberous root that is cooked and eaten as a vegetable **2** : OCARINA

sweet·shop \'swēt-,shäp\ *n, chiefly Brit* : a candy store

sweet sorghum *n* : SORGO

sweet tooth *n* : a craving or fondness for sweet food

sweet wil·liam \swēt-'wil-yəm\ *n, often cap W* : a widely grown Eurasian pink with small white to deep red or purple flowers often showily spotted, banded, or mottled and borne in flat clusters on erect stalks

¹swell \'swel\ *vb* **swelled**; **swelled** *or* **swol·len** \'swō-lən\; **swell·ing** [OE *swellan*] **1 a** : to expand or distend abnormally esp. by internal pressure or growth ⟨a *swollen* tree trunk⟩ ⟨the sprained ankle *swelled* badly⟩ **b** : to increase in size, number, or intensity **c** : to form a bulge or rounded elevation **2** : to fill or become filled with pride and arrogance **3** : to fill or become filled with emotion

²swell *n* **1 a** : the condition of being protuberant **b** : a rounded elevation **2** : a long often massive crestless wave or succession of waves **3 a** : a gradual increase and decrease of the loudness of a musical sound; *also* : a sign ⟨⟩ indicating a swell **b** : a device used in an organ for governing loudness **4 a** : a person dressed in the height of fashion **b** : a person of high social position or outstanding competence

³swell *adj* **1** : STYLISH, FASHIONABLE **2** : EXCELLENT, FIRST-RATE

swell box *n* : a chamber in an organ containing a set of pipes and having shutters that open or shut to regulate the volume of tone

swelled head *n* : an exaggerated opinion of oneself : SELF-CONCEIT — **swelled–head·ed** \'sweld-'hed-əd\ *adj* — **swelled–head·ed·ness** *n*

swell·ing \'swel-iŋ\ *n* **1** : something that is swollen; *esp* : an abnormal bodily protuberance or localized enlargement **2** : the condition of being swollen

¹swel·ter \'swel-tər\ *vb* **swel·tered**; **swel·ter·ing** \'swel-t(ə-)riŋ\ [ME *sweltren*, freq. of *swelten* to die, be overcome by heat, fr. OE *sweltan* to die] **1** : to suffer, sweat, or be faint from heat **2** : to oppress with heat

²swelter *n* **1** : a state of oppressive heat **2** : an excited or overwrought state of mind ⟨in a *swelter*⟩

swel·ter·ing *adj* : oppressively hot — **swel·ter·ing·ly** \-t(ə-)riŋ-lē\ *adv*

swept *past of* SWEEP

swept–back \'swep(t)-'bak\ *adj* : slanting toward the tail of an airplane to form an acute angle with the body ⟨*swept-back* wings⟩

¹swerve \'swərv\ *vb* [OE *sweorfan* to wipe, grind away] : to turn aside suddenly from a straight line or course ⟨*swerved* to avoid an oncoming car⟩

syn SWERVE, VEER mean to turn aside from a straight course. SWERVE may suggest a physical, mental, or moral turning away or aside that may be small in degree but is usu. sudden or sharp; VEER implies a considerable change in direction

²swerve *n* : an act or instance of swerving

¹swift \'swift\ *adj* [OE] **1** : moving or capable of moving with great speed **2** : occurring suddenly or within a very short time **3** : quick to respond ⟨*swift* to doubt⟩ **syn** see FAST — **swift·ly** *adv* — **swift·ness** \'swif(t)-nəs\ *n*

²swift *adv* : SWIFTLY ⟨*swift-flowing*⟩

³swift *n* **1** : any of several lizards that run swiftly **2** : any of numerous small and usu. sooty black birds that are related to the hummingbirds but superficially resemble swallows

¹swig \'swig\ *n* : a quantity drunk at one time : DRAFT

²swig *vb* **swigged**; **swig·ging** : to drink in gulps ⟨*swig* cider⟩ — **swig·ger** *n*

¹swill \'swil\ *vb* [OE *swillan*] **1** : WASH, DRENCH **2** : to drink great drafts of : consume freely, greedily, or to excess **3** : to feed (as a pig) with swill — **swill·er** *n*

²swill *n* **1** : food for animals (as swine) composed of edible refuse mixed with liquid **2** : GARBAGE, REFUSE **3** : a draft of liquor

¹swim \'swim\ *vb* **swam** \'swam\; **swum** \'swəm\; **swim·ming** [OE *swimman*] **1 a** : to move through water by natural means (as the action of limbs, fins, or tail) **b** : to move quietly and smoothly : GLIDE **2 a** : to float on or in or be covered with or as if with a liquid ⟨toy boats *swimming* in the tub⟩ ⟨meat that *swam* in fat⟩ **b** : to experience or suffer from or as if from vertigo ⟨his head *swam* in the stuffy room⟩ **3 :** to surmount difficulties **4 :** to cross by propelling oneself through water ⟨*swim* a stream⟩ — **swim·ma·ble** \'swim-ə-bəl\ *adj* — **swim·mer** *n*

²swim *n* **1 :** an act or period of swimming **2 :** a temporary dizziness or unconsciousness **3 :** the main current of activity ⟨be in the *swim*⟩

swim bladder *n* **:** the air bladder of a fish

swim·mer·et \,swim-ə-'ret\ *n* **:** one of a series of small appendages under the abdomen of many crustaceans that are used esp. for swimming or for carrying eggs

swimmer's itch *n* **:** an itchy skin inflammation caused by invasion of the skin by larval trematode worms that are not normally parasites of man

swim·ming *adj* **:** marked by, adapted to, or used in or for swimming

swim·ming·ly \-iŋ-lē\ *adv* **:** very well **: SPLENDIDLY**

swim·my \'swim-ē\ *adj* **:** verging on, causing, or affected by dizziness — **swim·mi·ly** \'swim-ə-lē\ *adv* — **swim·mi·ness** \'swim-ē-nəs\ *n*

swim·suit \'swim-,süt\ *n* **:** a suit for swimming or bathing

¹swin·dle \'swin-d�ᵊl\ *vb* **swin·dled; swin·dling** \-dliŋ, -d⁰l-iŋ\ [back-formation fr. *swindler*, fr. G *schwindler* giddy person, fantastic schemer, fr. *schwindeln* to be dizzy] **:** to obtain money or property from by fraud or deceit **: DEFRAUD syn** see CHEAT — **swin·dler** \-dlər, -d⁰l-ər\ *n*

²swindle *n* **:** an act or instance of swindling **: FRAUD**

swine \'swīn\ *n, pl* **swine** [OE *swīn;* akin to E **¹sow**] **1 :** any of a family of stout-bodied short-legged omnivorous hoofed mammals with a thick bristly skin and a long mobile snout; *esp* **:** a domesticated animal derived from the European wild boar and widely raised for meat **2 :** a contemptible person

swine·herd \-,hərd\ *n* **:** one who tends swine

¹swing \'swiŋ\ *vb* **swung** \'swəŋ\; **swing·ing** \'swiŋ-iŋ\ [OE *swingan* to beat, fling oneself, rush] **1 a :** to wield with a sweep or flourish ⟨*swing* an axe⟩ **b :** to cause to sway to and fro or turn on an axis; *also* **:** to face or move in another direction **2 a :** to hang or be hung so as to permit swaying or turning **b :** to die by hanging **c :** to move freely to and fro from or rotate about a point of suspension ⟨the door *swung* open⟩ **d :** to hang freely from a support **e :** to shift or fluctuate between extremes ⟨the market *swung* sharply downward⟩ **3 :** to handle successfully **: MANAGE 4 :** to play or sing (as a melody) in the style of swing music **:** perform swing music **5 a :** to move along rhythmically **b :** to start up in a smooth vigorous manner **c :** to hit at something with a sweeping movement — **swing·a·ble** \'swiŋ-ə-bəl\ *adj* — **swing·a·bly** \-blē\ *adv* — **swing·er** \'swiŋ-ər\ *n*

²swing *n* **1 :** an act of swinging **2 :** a swinging movement, blow, or rhythm: as **a :** a regular to-and-fro movement of or as if of a suspended body **b :** a steady pulsing rhythm (as in poetry or music); *also* **:** dancing to swing music **c :** a repeated shifting from one condition, form, or position to another **3 :** the distance through which something swings ⟨a pendulum with a 12-inch *swing*⟩ **4 a :** swinging seat usu. hung by overhead ropes **5 :** a curving course or outline or one beginning and ending at the same point ⟨took a *swing* through the hills⟩ **6 :** a style of jazz in which the melody is freely interpreted and improvised on by the individual players within a steadily maintained and usu. lively rhythm — called also *swing music* — **swing** *adj*

swin·gle·tree \'swiŋ-gəl-,trē\ *n* [*swingle* instrument for beating flax, cudgel] **: WHIFFLETREE**

swing shift *n* **:** the work shift between the day and night shifts (as from 4 p.m. to midnight)

swin·ish \'swī-nish\ *adj* **:** of, suggesting, or befitting swine **: BEASTLY** — **swin·ish·ly** *adv* — **swin·ish·ness** *n*

¹swipe \'swīp\ *n* **:** a strong sweeping blow

²swipe *vb* **1 :** to strike or wipe with a sweeping motion **2 : SNATCH, PILFER**

¹swirl \'swərl\ *n* [Sc, fr. ME] **1 :** a whirling mass or motion **2 :** whirling confusion **3 :** a twisting shape or mark

²swirl *vb* **1 :** to move with or pass in a swirl **2 :** to be marked with or arranged in swirls **3 :** to cause to swirl — **swirl·ing·ly** \'swər-liŋ-lē\ *adv*

¹swish \'swish\ *vb* **:** to make, move, or strike with a rustling or hissing sound — **swish·ly** \-iŋ-lē\ *adv*

²swish *n* **1 :** a prolonged hissing sound (as of a whip

cutting the air) or a light sweeping or rustling sound (as of silk in friction) **2 :** a swishing movement — **swishy** \-ē\ *adj*

Swiss \'swis\ *n* **1** *pl* **Swiss a :** a native or inhabitant of Switzerland **b :** a person of Swiss descent **2** *often not cap* **:** a fine sheer cotton fabric often with raised dots orig. made in Switzerland **3 :** a mild elastic hard cheese with large holes — **Swiss** *adj*

Swiss chard *n* **: CHARD**

¹switch \'swich\ *n* **1 :** a slender flexible whip, rod, or twig **2 :** an act of switching: as **a :** a blow with a switch **b :** a shift from one to another **3 :** a tuft of long hairs at the end of the tail of an animal (as a cow) **4 a :** a device made usu. of two movable rails and necessary connections and designed to turn a locomotive or train from one track to another **b :** a railroad siding **5 :** a device for making, breaking, or changing the connections in an electrical circuit **6 :** a strand of added or artificial hair used in some coiffures

²switch *vb* **1 :** to strike or whip with or as if with a switch **2 :** to lash from side to side **: WHISK** ⟨a cat *switching* his tail⟩ **3 :** to turn, shift, or change by operating a switch ⟨*switch* a train onto a siding⟩ ⟨*switch* off the light⟩ **4 :** to change one for another **: EXCHANGE** ⟨*switched* methods to improve production⟩ ⟨*switched* to a new barber⟩ — **switch·er** *n*

switch·back \'swich-,bak\ *n* **:** a zigzag road or arrangement of tracks for overcoming a steep grade

switch·blade knife \,swich-,blād-\ *n* **:** a pocketknife having the blade spring-operated so that pressure on a release catch causes it to fly open

switch·board \'swich-,bōrd, -,bord\ *n* **:** an apparatus (as in a telephone exchange) consisting of a panel on which are mounted electric switches so arranged that a number of circuits may be connected, combined, and controlled

switch-hit·ter \'swich-'hit-ər\ *n* **:** a baseball player who can bat either left-handed or right-handed

switch·man \'swich-mən\ *n* **:** one who attends a railroad switch

switch·yard \-,yärd\ *n* **:** a place where railroad cars are switched from one track to another and trains are made up

Swit·zer \'swit-sər\ *n* [MHG *Swīzer*] **: SWISS**

¹swiv·el \'swiv-əl\ *n* [ME] **:** a device joining two parts so that one or both can pivot freely (as on a bolt or pin)

²swivel *vb* **-eled** *or* **-elled; -el·ing** *or* **-el·ling** \'swiv-(ə-)liŋ\ **:** to turn on or as if on a swivel

swivel in chain

swivel chair *n* **:** a chair that swivels on its base

swiv·et \'swiv-ət\ *n* **:** a state of extreme agitation ⟨in a *swivet*⟩

swiz·zle stick \'swiz-əl-\ *n* **:** a stick used to stir mixed drinks

swob *var of* SWAB

swollen *past part of* SWELL

¹swoon \'swün\ *vi* [ME *swounen*] **1 : FAINT 2 :** to drift or fade imperceptibly — **swoon·er** *n* — **swoon·ing·ly** \'swü-niŋ-lē\ *adv*

²swoon *n* **1 :** a partial or total loss of consciousness; *also* **:** a dazed enraptured state **2 :** a languorous drift

¹swoop \'swüp\ *vb* [alter. of ME *swopen* to sweep, fr. OE *swāpan*] **1 :** to descend or pounce suddenly like a hawk attacking its prey **2 : SNATCH**

²swoop *n* **:** an act or instance of swooping

swoosh \'swüsh, 'swùsh\ *vb* **:** to make, move, or discharge with a rushing sound — **swoosh** *n*

swop *var of* SWAP

sword \'sōrd, 'sord\ *n* [OE *sweord*] **1 :** a weapon having a long usu. sharp-pointed and sharp-edged blade **2 :** something that kills or punishes as effectively as a sword **3 :** military power or the use of it **: WAR** — **sword·like** \-,līk\ *adj* — **at swords' points :** mutually antagonistic

sword cane *n* **:** a cane that conceals a sword or dagger blade

sword dance *n* **1 :** a dance executed by men holding swords in a ring **2 :** a dance performed over or around swords — **sword dancer** *n*

sword·fish \'sōrd-,fish, 'sord-\ *n* **:** a very large sea food fish having a long swordlike beak formed by the bones of the upper jaw

---

j joke;   ŋ sing;   ō flow;   ȯ flaw;   ȯi coin;   th thin;   t̲h̲ this;   ü loot;   u̇ foot;   y yet;   yü few;   yu̇ furious;   zh vision

sword grass *n* : a grass or sedge having leaves with a sharp or toothed edge

sword knot *n* : an ornamental cord or tassel tied to the hilt of a sword

sword·play \-,plā\ *n* : the art or skill of using a sword esp. in fencing

swords·man \'sōrdz-mən, 'sórdz-\ *n* **1** : one who fights with a sword **2** : one skilled in the use of the sword : FENCER

swords·man·ship \-,ship\ *n* : SWORDPLAY

sword·tail \'sōrd-,tāl, 'sórd-\ *n* : a small brightly marked Central American topminnow often kept in the tropical aquarium and bred in many colors

swore *past of* SWEAR

sworn *past part of* SWEAR

swum *past part of* SWIM

swung *past of* SWING

syb·a·rite \'sib-ə-,rīt\ *n* [Gk *Sybaritēs*, lit., inhabitant of Sybaris, Greek colony in Italy whose inhabitants were reputed to live luxuriously] : VOLUPTUARY, SENSUALIST — **syb·a·rit·ic** \,sib-ə-'rit-ik\ *adj* — **syb·a·rit·i·cal·ly** \-'rit-i-k(ə-)lē\ *adv*

syc·a·more \'sik-ə-,mōr, -,mór\ *n* [Gk *sykomoros*] **1** : a common fig tree of Egypt and Asia Minor **2** : a Eurasian maple with yellow flowers in long clusters **3** : a large spreading American plane tree with light-brown flaky bark and round fruits like buttons

syce \'sīs\ *n* [Hindi *sā'is*, fr. Ar] : an attendant esp. in India

syc·o·phant \'sik-ə-fənt\ *n* [L *sycophanta* informer, swindler, sycophant, fr. Gk *sykophantēs* informer] : a servile self-seeking flatterer : PARASITE — **syc·o·phan·cy** \-fən-sē\ *n* — **syc·o·phan·tic** \,sik-ə-'fant-ik\ *adj* — **syc·o·phan·ti·cal·ly** \-'fant-i-k(ə-)lē\ *adv*

sy·e·nite \'sī-ə-,nīt\ *n* [L *syenites lapis* stone of Syene, fr. *Syene*, ancient city in Egypt] : an igneous rock composed chiefly of feldspar — **sy·e·nit·ic** \,sī-ə-'nit-ik\ *adj*

syl·la·bary \'sil-ə-,ber-ē\ *n*, *pl* **-bar·ies** : a series or set of written characters each one of which is used to represent a syllable

syl·lab·ic \sə-'lab-ik\ *adj* [Gk *syllabikos*, fr. *syllabē* syllable] **1** : of, relating to, or denoting syllables 〈syllabic accent〉 **2** *of a consonant* : not accompanied in the same syllable by a vowel 〈\n\ is *syllabic* in \'fat-ᵊn-iŋ\ *fattening* and \'fat-ᵊnd\ *fattened*, nonsyllabic in \'fat-niŋ\ *fattening*〉 **3** : characterized by distinct enunciation or separation of syllables **4** : of, relating to, or constituting a type of verse distinguished primarily by count of syllables rather than by rhythmical arrangement (as of accents) — **syl·lab·i·cal·ly** \-'lab-i-k(ə-)lē\ *adv*

syl·lab·i·ca·tion \sə-,lab-ə-'kā-shən\ *n* : the forming of syllables : the division of words into syllables — **syl·lab·i·cate** \-'lab-ə-,kāt\ *vb*

syl·lab·i·fi·ca·tion \sə-,lab-ə-fə-'kā-shən\ *n* : SYLLABICA- TION

syl·lab·i·fy \sə-'lab-ə-,fī\ *vt* **-fied; -fy·ing** : to form or divide into syllables

¹syl·la·ble \'sil-ə-bəl\ *n* [Gk *syllabē*, fr. *syllambanein* to combine, fr. *syn-* + *lambanein* to take] **1** : a unit of spoken language that consists of one or more vowel sounds alone or of a syllabic consonant alone or of either with one or more consonant sounds preceding or following **2** : one or more letters (as *syl*, *la*, and *ble*) in a word (as *syl·la·ble*) usu. set off from the rest of the word by a centered dot or a hyphen and treated as guides to hyphenation at the end of a line **3** : the smallest conceivable expression or unit of something

²syllable *vt* **syl·la·bled; syl·la·bling** \-b(ə-)liŋ\ : to express or utter in syllables

syl·la·bub \'sil-ə-,bəb\ *n* **1** : a drink or dessert made by curdling milk or cream usu. with wine **2** : a dessert of sweetened milk or cream beaten to a froth and flavored with wine or liquor

syl·la·bus \-bəs\ *n*, *pl* **-bi** \-,bī, -,bē\ *or* **-bus·es** [LL, modif. of Gk *sillybos* label for a book] : a summary out- line (as of a discourse or course of study)

syl·lo·gism \'sil-ə-,jiz-əm\ *n* [Gk *syllogismos*, fr. *syllo- gizesthai* to reason deductively, fr. *syn-* + *logos* reckoning, reason, word] **1** : a brief form for stating an argument from the general to the particular that consists of two statements and a conclusion that must be true if

these two statements are true 〈"all lawbreakers deserve punishment; the man is a lawbreaker; therefore the man deserves punishment" is a *syllogism*〉 **2** : deductive reason- ing — **syl·lo·gis·tic** \,sil-ə-'jis-tik\ *adj* — **syl·lo·gis·ti- cal·ly** \-ti-k(ə-)lē\ *adv*

syl·lo·gize \'sil-ə-,jīz\ *vb* : to reason by means of syl- logisms : deduce by syllogism

sylph \'silf\ *n* [NL *sylphus*] **1** : an imaginary aerial spirit **2** : a slender graceful woman — **sylph·like** \-,līk\ *adj*

syl·van \'sil-vən\ *adj* [L *silva, sylva* woods] **1 a** : living or located in the woods or forest **b** : of, relating to, or characteristic of the woods or forest **2** : abounding in woods or trees : WOODED

syl·vat·ic \sil-'vat-ik\ *adj* [L *silvaticus* of the woods, wild, fr. *silva* woods] : occurring in or affecting wild animals

sylviculture *var of* SILVICULTURE

sym·bi·on \'sim-,bī-,än, -bē-\ *n* : SYMBIONT — **sym·bi- on·ic** \,sim-,bī-'än-ik, -bē-\ *adj*

sym·bi·ont \'sim-,bī-,änt, -bē-\ *n* [modif. of Gk *sym- biount-, symbiōn*, prp. of *symbioun* to live together] : an organism living in symbiosis; *esp* : the smaller member of a symbiotic pair — **sym·bi·on·tic** \,sim-,bī-'änt-ik, -bē-\ *adj*

sym·bi·o·sis \,sim-,bī-'ō-səs, -bē-\ *n*, *pl* **-o·ses** \-'ō-,sēz\ [Gk *symbiōsis* state of living together, fr. *symbioun* to live together, fr. *syn-* + *bios* life] : the living together in intimate association or close union of two dissimilar organisms esp. when mutually beneficial — **sym·bi·ot·ic** \-'ät-ik\ *adj* — **sym·bi·ot·i·cal·ly** \-'ät-i-k(ə-)lē\ *adv*

sym·bol \'sim-bəl\ *n* [Gk *symbolon* token of identity to be verified by matching it with its other half, symbol, fr. *symballein* to throw together, compare, fr. *syn-* + *ballein* to throw] **1** : something that stands for something else; *esp* : something concrete that represents or suggests another thing that cannot in itself be represented or visualized : EMBLEM 〈the cross is the *symbol* of Christianity〉 **2** : a letter, character, or sign used (as to represent a quantity, position, relationship, direction, or something to be done) instead of a word or group of words 〈the sign + is the *symbol* for addition〉

sym·bol·ic \sim-'bäl-ik\ *or* **sym·bol·i·cal** \-'bäl-i-kəl\ *adj* **1** : of, relating to, or using symbols or symbolism 〈a *symbolic* meaning〉 〈*symbolic* art〉 **2** : having the func- tion or significance of a symbol — **sym·bol·i·cal·ly** \-i-k(ə-)lē\ *adv*

sym·bol·ism \'sim-bə-,liz-əm\ *n* **1** : the art or practice of using symbols or indicating symbolically (as in art or literature) esp. by means of visible or sensuous representa- tions **2** : a system of symbols or representations

sym·bol·ist \-ləst\ *n* **1** : a user of symbols or symbolism (as in artistic expression) **2** : an expert in the interpreta- tion or explication of symbols — **symbolist** *or* **sym·bol- is·tic** \,sim-bə-'lis-tik\ *adj*

sym·bol·ize \'sim-bə-,līz\ *vb* **1** : to serve as a symbol of : TYPIFY 〈a lion *symbolizes* courage〉 **2** : to use symbols : represent by a symbol or set of symbols — **sym·bol·i·za- tion** \,sim-bə-lə-'zā-shən\ *n* — **sym·bol·iz·er** \'sim-bə- ,lī-zər\ *n*

sym·met·ri·cal \sə-'me-tri-kəl\ *or* **sym·met·ric** \-trik\ *adj* : having, involving, or exhibiting symmetry: as **a** : hav- ing corresponding points whose connecting lines are bisected by a given point or perpendicularly bisected by a given line or plane 〈*symmetrical* curves〉 **b** : capable of division by a longitudinal plane into similar halves 〈a *symmetrical* leaf〉 **c** : having the same number of members in each whorl of floral leaves 〈*symmetrical* flowers〉 — **sym·met·ri·cal·ly** \-tri-k(ə-)lē\ *adv* — **sym·met·ri·cal- ness** \-kəl-nəs\ *n*

sym·me·try \'sim-ə-trē\ *n*, *pl* **-tries** [Gk *symmetria*, fr. *syn-* + *metron* measure] **1** : balanced proportions; *also* : beauty of form arising from balanced proportions **2** : correspondence in size, shape, and relative position of parts on opposite sides of a dividing line or median plane or about a center or axis

sym·pa·thet·ic \,sim-pə-'thet-ik\ *adj* **1** : existing or operating through an affinity, interdependence, or mutual association **2** : not discordant or antagonistic: as **a** : ap- propriate to one's mood or disposition : CONGENIAL 〈a *sympathetic* environment〉 **b** : favorably impressed or in-

---

ə abut; ᵊ kitten; ər further; a back; ā bake; ä cot, cart; aů out; ch chin; e less; ē easy; g gift; i trip; ī life

clined ⟨*sympathetic* with their aims⟩ **c :** marked by kindly or pleased appreciation **3 :** given to or arising from sympathy, compassion, friendliness, and sensitivity to others ⟨a *sympathetic* personality⟩ ⟨*sympathetic* strikes⟩ **4 a :** of or relating to the sympathetic nervous system **b :** mediated by or acting on the sympathetic nerves — **sym·pa·thet·i·cal·ly** \-'thet-i-k(ə-)lē\ *adv*

sympathetic nervous system *n* **:** the part of the autonomic nervous system that contains chiefly adrenergic fibers and tends to depress secretion, decrease the tone and contractility of smooth muscle, and cause the contraction of blood vessels — compare PARASYMPATHETIC NERVOUS SYSTEM

sympathetic vibration *n* **:** a vibration produced in one body by vibrations of exactly the same period in a neighboring body

sym·pa·thin \'sim-pə-thən\ *n* **:** a substance that is secreted by sympathetic nerve endings and functions in impulse transmission

sym·pa·thize \'sim-pə-,thīz\ *vi* **1 :** to react or respond in sympathy **2 a :** to share in some distress, suffering, or grief **b :** to express sympathy **3 :** to be in accord with something; *also* **:** to approve and foster the policies of a group without total commitment ⟨*sympathize* with a subversive party⟩ — **sym·pa·thiz·er** *n*

sym·pa·tho·mi·met·ic \,sim-pə-thō-mə-'met-ik, -mī-\ *adj* **:** resembling sympathetic nervous action in physiological effect ⟨*sympathomimetic* drugs⟩

sym·pa·thy \'sim-pə-thē\ *n, pl* **-thies** [Gk *sympatheia,* fr. *syn-* + *pathos* feelings, experience] **1 :** a relationship between persons or things wherein whatever affects one similarly affects the other **2 a :** inclination to think or feel alike **:** emotional or intellectual accord forming a bond of goodwill **b :** tendency to favor or support ⟨republican *sympathies*⟩ **3 :** the act of or capacity for entering into or sharing the feelings or interests of another **4 :** the correlation existing between bodies capable of communicating their vibrational energy to one another through some medium

sym·pat·ric \sim-'pa-trik\ *adj* [Gk *syn-* + *patra* fatherland, fr. *patēr* father] **:** occurring in the same area or region ⟨*sympatric* species of birds⟩

sym·phon·ic \sim-'fän-ik\ *adj* **1 :** HARMONIOUS **2 :** of, relating to, or suggesting a symphony or symphony orchestra — **sym·phon·i·cal·ly** \-'fän-i-k(ə-)lē\ *adv*

sym·pho·ny \'sim(p)-fə-nē\ *n, pl* **-nies** [Gk *symphōnia* harmony of sounds, fr. *syn-* + *phōnē* voice, sound] **1 :** harmonious arrangement (as of sound or color) **2 a :** a usu. long and complex sonata for symphony orchestra **b :** something resembling a symphony in complexity or variety **3 a :** SYMPHONY ORCHESTRA **b :** a symphony orchestra concert

symphony orchestra *n* **:** a large orchestra of winds, strings, and percussion that plays symphonic works

sym·phy·sis \'sim(p)-fə-səs\ *n, pl* **-phy·ses** \-fə-,sēz\ [Gk, state of growing together, fr. *symphyesthai* to grow together, fr. *syn-* + *phyein* to make grow, bring forth] **:** a largely or completely immovable joint between bones esp. with the surfaces connected by pads of cartilage without a joint membrane — **sym·phy·se·al** \,sim(p)-fə-'sē-əl\ *adj*

sym·po·di·al \sim-'pōd-ē-əl\ *adj* [Gk *syn-* + *podion* base] **:** having an apparent main axis formed from successive secondary axes ⟨a *sympodial* inflorescence⟩ — **sym·po·di·al·ly** \-ē-ə-lē\ *adv*

sym·po·si·um \sim-'pō-zē-əm, -zh(ē-)əm\ *n, pl* **-sia** \-zē-ə, -zh(ē-)ə\ *or* **-si·ums** [L, drinking party after a banquet, fr. Gk *symposion,* fr. *sympinein* to drink together, fr. *syn-* + *pinein* to drink] **1 :** a meeting at which several speakers deliver short addresses on a topic or on related topics and which may be followed by group discussion **2 a :** a collection of opinions on a subject **b :** DISCUSSION

symp·tom \'sim(p)-təm\ *n* [Gk *symptōmat-, symptōma* occurrence, attribute, symptom, fr. *sympiptein* to occur, fr. *syn-* + *piptein* to fall] **1 :** a change in an organism indicative of disease or physical abnormality; *esp* **:** one (as headache) that is directly perceptible only to the individual affected — compare SIGN **2 :** INDICATION, SIGN, TRACE — **symp·tom·less** \-ləs\ *adj*

symp·tom·at·ic \,sim(p)-tə-'mat-ik\ *adj* **1 a :** being a symptom (as of disease) ⟨*symptomatic* of smallpox⟩

b : concerned with or affecting symptoms ⟨*symptomatic* medicine⟩ **2 :** CHARACTERISTIC, INDICATIVE — **symp·tom·at·i·cal·ly** \-'mat-i-k(ə-)lē\ *adv*

syn- *prefix* [Gk] **:** with **:** along with **:** together ⟨*syn*clinal⟩ ⟨*syn*karyon⟩

syn·a·gogue *or* **syn·a·gog** \'sin-ə-,gäg\ *n* [Gk *synagōgē* assembly, synagogue, fr. *synagein* to bring together, fr. *syn-* + *agein* to lead] **1 :** a Jewish congregation **2 :** the house of worship and communal center of a Jewish congregation — **syn·a·gog·al** \,sin-ə-'gäg-əl\ *adj*

¹syn·apse \'sin-,aps\ *n* [Gk *synapsis* juncture, fr. *synaptein* to fasten together, fr. *syn-* + *haptein* to fasten] **:** the point at which a nervous impulse passes from one neuron to another

²synapse *vi* **:** to form a synapse or come together in synapsis

syn·ap·sis \sə-'nap-səs\ *n* [NL, fr. Gk, juncture] **:** the association of homologous chromosomes that occurs in the first meiotic prophase and is the mechanism for crossing over — **syn·ap·tic** \-'nap-tik\ *adj*

¹sync \'siŋk\ *n* **:** SYNCHRONIZATION, SYNCHRONISM — **sync** *adj*

²sync *vb* **synced** \'siŋ(k)t\; **sync·ing** \'siŋ-kiŋ\ **:** SYNCHRONIZE

synchro- *comb form* **:** synchronized **:** synchronous ⟨*syn*chroflash⟩ ⟨*synchro*mesh⟩

syn·chro·cy·clo·tron \,siŋ-krō-'sī-klə-,trän, ,sin-\ *n* **:** a modified cyclotron that achieves greater energies for the charged particles

syn·chro·flash \'siŋ-krō-,flash, 'sin-\ *adj* **:** employing or produced with a mechanism that fires a flash lamp the instant the camera shutter opens

syn·chro·mesh \-,mesh\ *adj* **:** designed for effecting synchronized shifting of gears — **synchromesh** *n*

syn·chro·nism \'siŋ-krə-,niz-əm, 'sin-\ *n* **1 :** the quality or state of being synchronous **2 :** chronological arrangement of historical events and personages so as to indicate coincidence or coexistence — **syn·chro·nis·tic** \,siŋ-krə-'nis-tik, ,sin-\ *adj*

syn·chro·nize \'siŋ-krə-,nīz, 'sin-\ *vb* **1 :** to happen at the same time **:** agree in time **2 :** to cause to agree in time **:** represent, arrange, or tabulate according to dates or time ⟨*synchronize* the events of European history⟩ **3 :** to make (as two gears) synchronous in operation — **syn·chro·ni·za·tion** \,siŋ-krə-nə-'zā-shən, ,sin-\ *n* — **syn·chro·niz·er** \'siŋ-krə-,nī-zər, 'sin-\ *n*

syn·chro·nous \'siŋ-krə-nəs, 'sin-\ *adj* [Gk *synchronos,* fr. *syn-* + *chronos* time] **1 :** happening or existing at the same time **:** SIMULTANEOUS ⟨*synchronous* meetings⟩ **2 :** working, moving, or occurring together at the same rate and at the proper time with respect to each other ⟨*synchronous* beat of a bird's wings⟩; *esp* **:** having the same period and phase ⟨*synchronous* vibration⟩ — **syn·chro·nous·ly** *adv* — **syn·chro·nous·ness** *n*

synchronous motor *n* **:** an electric motor having a speed strictly proportional to the frequency of the operating current

syn·chro·tron \'siŋ-krə-,trän, 'sin-\ *n* **:** an apparatus for imparting very high speeds to charged particles

syn·cline \'sin-,klīn\ *n* [back-formation fr. *synclinal,* fr. Gk *syn-* + *klinein* to lean] **:** a trough of stratified rock in which the beds dip toward each other from either side — compare ANTICLINE — **syn·cli·nal** \sin-'klīn-ᵊl\ *adj*

syn·co·pate \'siŋ-kə-,pāt, 'sin-\ *vt* [ML *syncopare,* fr. Gk *synkopē* syncope] **1 a :** to shorten or produce by syncope **b :** to cut short **:** CLIP, ABBREVIATE **2 :** to modify or affect (musical rhythm) by syncopation — **syn·co·pa·tor** \-,pāt-ər\ *n*

syn·co·pa·tion \,siŋ-kə-'pā-shən, ,sin-\ *n* **1 :** a temporary displacement of the regular metrical accent in music caused typically by stressing the weak beat **2 :** a syncopated rhythm, passage, or dance step — **syn·co·pa·tive** \'siŋ-kə-,pāt-iv, 'sin-\ *adj*

syn·co·pe \'siŋ-kə-(,)pē, 'sin-\ *n* [Gk *synkopē,* fr. *synkoptein* to shorten, fr. *syn-* + *koptein* to cut] **1 :** FAINT, SWOON **2 :** the loss of one or more sounds or letters in the interior of a word (as *fo'c'sle* from *forecastle*)

syn·cy·tium \sin-'sish-(ē-)əm\ *n, pl* **-tia** \-(ē-)ə\ **:** a multinucleate mass of protoplasm usu. resulting from fusion of cells — **syn·cy·tial** \-'sish-əl\ *adj*

syn·dic \'sin-dik\ *n* [F, fr. LL *syndicus* representative of

---

j joke;   **ŋ** sing;   **ō** flow;   **ȯ** flaw;   **ȯi** coin;   **th** thin;   **t͟h** this;   **ü** loot;   **u̇** foot;   **y** yet;   **yü** few;   **yu̇** furious;   **zh** vision

a corporation, fr. Gk *syndikos* advocate, representative of a state, fr. *syn-* + *dikē* judgment, case at law] **1** : a municipal magistrate in some countries **2** : an agent of a corporation (as a university)
syn·di·cal \-di-kəl\ *adj* : of or relating to a syndic or to syndicalism
syn·di·cal·ism \'sin-di-kə-,liz-əm\ *n* [F *syndicalisme*, fr. *chambre syndicale* trade union] **1** : a revolutionary doctrine advocating seizure of control of the economy and the government by workers through use of direct means (as the general strike) **2** : a system of economic organization in which industries are owned and managed by the workers — **syn·di·cal·ist** \-ləst\ *adj or n*
¹syn·di·cate \'sin-di-kət\ *n* [F *syndicat*, fr. *syndic*] **1** : an association of persons officially authorized to undertake some duty or negotiate some business **2 a** : a group of persons or concerns who combine to carry out a particular transaction **b** : CARTEL **c** : a loose association of racketeers in control of organized crime **d** : a European labor union **3** : a business concern that sells materials for publication in a number of newspapers or periodicals simultaneously **4** : a group of newspapers under one management **syn** see MONOPOLY
²syn·di·cate \'sin-də-,kāt\ *vb* **1** : to subject to or manage as a syndicate **2** : to sell (as a cartoon) to a publication syndicate **3** : to unite to form a syndicate — **syn·di·ca·tion** \,sin-də-'kā-shən\ *n* — **syn·di·ca·tor** \'sin-də-,kāt-ər\ *n*
syn·drome \'sin-,drōm\ *n* [Gk *syndromē*, fr. *syn-* + *dramein* to run] : a group of signs and symptoms that occur together and characterize a particular abnormality
¹syne \('ˌ)sīn\ *adv, chiefly Scot* : since then : AGO
²syne *conj, Scot* : SINCE
³syne *prep, Scot* : SINCE
syn·ec·do·che \sə-'nek-də-(ˌ)kē\ *n* [Gk *synekdochē*] : a figure of speech in which a part is used for the whole (as *fifty sail* for *fifty ships*), the whole for a part (as *the smiling year* for *spring*), the species for the genus (as *cutthroat* for *assassin*), the genus for the species (as *a creature* for *a man*), or the name of the material for the thing made (as *willow* for *bat*)
syn·ecol·o·gy \,sin-i-'käl-ə-jē\ *n* : a branch of ecology that deals with ecological communities — **syn·ec·o·log·ic** \,sin-ek-ə-'läj-ik, -,ē-kə-\ *or* **syn·ec·o·log·i·cal** \-'läj-i-kəl\ *adj* — **syn·ec·o·log·i·cal·ly** \-i-k(ə-)lē\ *adv*
syn·er·gid \sə-'nər-jəd\ *n* : either of two small cells lying near the micropyle of the embryo sac of a seed plant
syn·er·gism \'sin-ər-,jiz-əm\ *n* [Gk *syn-* + *ergon* work] : cooperative action of discrete agencies such that the total effect is greater than the sum of the effects taken independently — **syn·er·gist** \-jəst\ *n*
syn·er·gis·tic \,sin-ər-'jis-tik\ *adj* : of, relating to, or able to function in synergism (a *synergistic* reaction) (*synergistic* drugs) — **syn·er·gis·ti·cal·ly** \-ti-k(ə-)lē\ *adv*
syn·ga·my \'siŋ-gə-mē\ *n* : sexual reproduction — **syn·gam·ic** \sin-'gam-ik\ *adj*
syn·kary·on \sin-'kar-ē-,än, -ē-ən\ *n* [Gk *karyon* nut] : a cell nucleus formed by the fusion of two preexisting nuclei — **syn·kary·on·ic** \,sin-,kar-ē-'än-ik\ *adj*
syn·od \'sin-əd\ *n* [Gk *synodos* meeting, fr. *syn-* + *hodos* way, journey] **1** : an ecclesiastical assembly or council: as **a** : the governing assembly of an Episcopal province **b** : a Presbyterian governing body ranking above the presbytery **c** : a regional or national organization of Lutheran congregations **2** : a group assembled (as for consultation) : MEETING, CONVENTION (a *synod* of cooks) — **syn·od·al** \-əd-ᵊl\ *adj*
syn·od·i·cal \sə-'näd-i-kəl\ *or* **syn·od·ic** \-'näd-ik\ *adj* **1** : SYNODAL **2** [Gk *synodikos*, fr. *synodos* meeting, conjunction] : relating to conjunction; *esp* : relating to the period between two successive conjunctions of the same celestial bodies
syn·o·nym \'sin-ə-,nim\ *n* [Gk *synōnymon*, fr. *syn-* + *onyma* name] **1** : one of two or more words of the same language that have the same or nearly the same meaning in some or all senses **2** : a symbolic or figurative name **3** : a taxonomic name rejected as being incorrectly applied or incorrect in form — **syn·o·nym·i·ty** \,sin-ə-'nim-ət-ē\ *n*
syn·on·y·mist \sə-'nän-ə-məst\ *n* : one who studies synonyms

syn·on·y·mize \-,mīz\ *vt* : to give or analyze the synonyms of (a word)
syn·on·y·mous \-məs\ *adj* : having the character of a synonym; *also* : alike in meaning or significance — **syn·on·y·mous·ly** *adv*
syn·on·y·my \-mē\ *n, pl* **-mies** **1 a** : the study or discrimination of synonyms **b** : a list or collection of synonyms often defined and discriminated from each other **2** : the quality or state of being synonymous
syn·op·sis \sə-'näp-səs\ *n, pl* **-op·ses** \-'äp-,sēz\ [Gk, lit., comprehensive view, fr. *synop-*, used as stem of *synoran* to see together, fr. *syn-* + *horan* to see] : a condensed statement or outline (as of a narrative or treatise) : SUMMARY, ABSTRACT
syn·op·tic \sə-'näp-tik\ *adj* **1** : affording a general view of a whole (a daily *synoptic* weather chart of Canada) **2** : manifesting or characterized by comprehensiveness or breadth of view (a *synoptic* genius) **a** : affording or sharing the same or a common view **b** *often cap* : of or relating to the first three Gospels of the New Testament — **syn·op·ti·cal** \-ti-kəl\ *adj* — **syn·op·ti·cal·ly** \-ti-k(ə-)lē\ *adv*
syn·o·vi·al \sə-'nō-vē-əl\ *adj* : of or relating to the connective tissue membrane that lines joint capsules and secretes a mucinous fluid
syn·tac·tic \sin-'tak-tik\ *adj* : of, relating to, or according to the rules of syntax — **syn·tac·ti·cal** \-ti-kəl\ *adj* — **syn·tac·ti·cal·ly** \-ti-k(ə-)lē\ *adv*
syn·tax \'sin-,taks\ *n* [Gk *syntaxis*, fr. *syntassein* to arrange together, fr. *syn-* + *tassein* to arrange] **1** : connected or orderly system or arrangement **2 a** : the way in which words are put together to form phrases, clauses, or sentences **b** : the part of grammar that deals with this
syn·the·sis \'sin(t)-thə-səs\ *n, pl* **-the·ses** \-thə-,sēz\ [Gk, fr. *syntithenai* to put together, fr. *syn-* + *tithenai* to put, place] **1** : the composition or combination of parts or elements so as to form a whole; *esp* : the production of a substance by union of chemically simpler substances **2 a** : the combining of often diverse conceptions into a coherent whole; *also* : the complex so formed **b** : deductive reasoning from general principles or causes to particular effects **c** : the final stage of a dialectic process combining thesis and antithesis into a new whole — **syn·the·sist** \-səst\ *n*
syn·the·size \-,sīz\ *vt* : to combine or produce by synthesis — **syn·the·siz·er** *n*
¹syn·thet·ic \sin-'thet-ik\ *adj* **1** : of or relating to synthesis **2** : produced artificially : MAN-MADE (*synthetic* rubber): **a** : produced only by chemical means : not found in nature (*synthetic* fibers such as rayon) **b** : made to substitute for or imitate a natural substance (*synthetic* milk) **syn** see ARTIFICIAL — **syn·thet·i·cal·ly** \-'thet-i-k(ə-)lē\ *adv*
²synthetic *n* : a product of chemical synthesis
syph·i·lis \'sif-(ə-)ləs\ *n* [NL, fr. *Syphilus*, hero of *Syphilis* (1530), epic poem by Girolamo Fracastoro] : a chronic contagious usu. venereal and sometimes congenital disease caused by a spirochete and marked by a clinical course in three stages extending over many years — **syph·i·lit·ic** \,sif-ə-'lit-ik\ *adj or n*
sy·phon *var of* SIPHON
Syr·i·ac \'sir-ē-,ak\ *n* [Gk *syriakos* of Syria] **1** : a literary language based on an eastern Aramaic dialect and used as the literary and liturgical language by several eastern Christian churches **2** : Aramaic spoken by Christian communities — **Syriac** *adj*
sy·rin·ga \sə-'riŋ-gə\ *n* [NL, fr. Gk *syring-, syrinx* panpipe] : PHILADELPHUS
¹sy·ringe \sə-'rinj, 'sir-inj\ *n* [Gk *syring-, syrinx* panpipe, tube] : a device used to inject fluids into or withdraw them from the body or its cavities
²syringe *vt* : to irrigate or cleanse with or as if with a syringe
syr·inx \'sir-iŋ(k)s\ *n, pl* **sy·rin·ges** \sə-'rin-,gēz, -'rin-,jēz\ *or* **syr·inx·es** \'sir-iŋ(k)-səz\ **1** [Gk *syring-, syrinx*] : PANPIPE **2** : the vocal organ of birds that is a special modification of the lower part of the trachea or of the bronchi or of both — **sy·rin·ge·al** \sə-'riŋ-gē-əl, -'rin-jē-\ *adj*
syr·up \'sər-əp, 'sir-əp, 'sə-rəp\ *n* [ML *syrupus*, fr. Ar

syringe

sharāb] **1** : a thick sticky solution of sugar and water often flavored or medicated **2** : the concentrated juice of a fruit or plant — **syr·upy** \-ē\ *adj*

sys·tem \'sis-təm\ *n* [Gk *systēmat-, systēma,* fr. *synistanai* to combine, fr. *syn-* + *histanai* to cause to stand] **1 a** : a group of objects or units so combined as to form a whole and work, function, or move interdependently and harmoniously ⟨railroad *system*⟩ ⟨steam heating *systems*⟩ ⟨a park *system*⟩ **b** (1) : a body that functions as a whole ⟨a *system* weakened by disease⟩ (2) : a group of bodily organs that together carry on one or more vital functions ⟨the nervous *system*⟩ **c** : a particular form of societal organization ⟨the capitalist *system*⟩ **d** : a major division of rocks usu. greater than a series **2 a** : an organized set of doctrines or principles usu. designed to explain the ordering or functioning of some whole **b** : a scheme or method of governing or arranging : a method of procedure or classification ⟨a decimal *system* of numbers⟩ ⟨taxonomic *systems*⟩ **3** : regular method or order ⟨it takes *system* to run a school⟩ — **sys·tem·less** \-ləs\ *adj*

sys·tem·at·ic \,sis-tə-'mat-ik\ *adj* **1** : relating to or forming a system ⟨*systematic* error⟩ ⟨*systematic* thought⟩ **2** : presented or formulated as a system : SYSTEMATIZED **3 a** : methodical in procedure or plan ⟨*systematic* investigation⟩ ⟨*systematic* scholar⟩ **b** : carried on or acting with thoroughness or persistency ⟨*systematic* attacks on his credibility⟩ **4** : of, relating to, or concerned with classification : TAXONOMIC — **sys·tem·at·i·cal** \-'mat-i-kəl\ *adj* — **sys·tem·at·i·cal·ly** \-i-k(ə-)lē\ *adv* — **sys·tem·at·ic·ness** *n*

sys·tem·at·ics \-'mat-iks\ *n sing or pl* **1** : the science of classification **2** : a system of classification **3** : the classification and study of organisms with regard to their natural relationships : TAXONOMY

sys·tem·a·tist \'sis-tə-mət-əst, sis-'tem-ət-\ *n* **1** : a maker or follower of a system **2** : TAXONOMIST

sys·tem·a·tize \'sis-tə-mə-,tīz\ *vt* : to make into or arrange according to a system — **sys·tem·a·ti·za·tion** \,sis-tə-mət-ə-'zā-shən\ *n* — **sys·tem·a·tiz·er** \'sis-tə-mə-,tī-zər\ *n*

sys·tem·ic \sis-'tem-ik\ *adj* : of, relating to, or common to a system; *esp* : of or relating to the body as a whole ⟨a *systemic* disease⟩ — **sys·tem·i·cal·ly** \-'tem-i-k(ə-)lē\ *adv*

systemic circulation *n* : the part of the blood circulation concerned with distribution of blood to the tissues as distinguished from the part concerned with gaseous exchange in the lungs

sys·tem·ize \'sis-tə-,mīz\ *vt* : SYSTEMATIZE — **sys·tem·i·za·tion** \,sis-tə-mə-'zā-shən\ *n*

sys·to·le \'sis-tə-(,)lē\ *n* [Gk *systolē,* fr. *systellein* to contract, fr. *syn-* + *stellein* to send] : a rhythmically recurrent contraction; *esp* : the contraction of the heart by which the blood is forced onward and the circulation kept up — **sys·tol·ic** \sis-'täl-ik\ *adj*

t \'tē\ *n, often cap* : the 20th letter of the English alphabet — **to a T** : PRECISELY, EXACTLY

't \t\ *pron* : IT ⟨'twill do⟩

¹tab \'tab\ *n* **1 a** : a short projecting device: as (1) : a small hand grip (2) : a projection from a card used as an aid in filing **b** : a small insert, addition, or remnant ⟨license plate *tab*⟩ **c** : APPENDAGE, EXTENSION; *esp* : one of a series of small pendants forming a decorative border or edge of a garment **d** : a small auxiliary airfoil hinged to a control surface (as a trailing edge) to help stabilize an airplane in flight **2 a** : SURVEILLANCE, WATCH ⟨keep *tab* on the situation⟩ **b** : a creditor's statement : BILL, CHECK

²tab *vt* **tabbed; tab·bing 1** : to furnish or ornament with tabs **2** : to single out : DESIGNATE ⟨*tabbed* as a bright prospect by pro football scouts⟩

tab·ard \'tab-ərd\ *n* [OF *tabart*] **1** : a tunic worn by a knight over his armor and emblazoned with his arms **2** : a herald's official cape or coat emblazoned with his lord's arms

¹tab·by \'tab-ē\ *n, pl* **tabbies** [F *tabis,* fr. ML *attabi,* fr. Ar *'attābī*] **1** : a plain silk taffeta esp. with moiré finish **2 a** : a domestic cat with a gray or tawny coat striped and mottled with black **b** : a female cat

²tabby *adj* **1** : relating to or made of tabby **2** : striped and mottled with darker color ⟨*tabby* fur⟩

tab·er·na·cle \'tab-ər-,nak-əl\ *n* [L *tabernaculum* tent, dim. of *taberna* hut, tavern] **1 a** *often cap* : a tent sanctuary used by the Israelites during the Exodus **b** : a dwelling place **c** *archaic* : a temporary shelter : TENT **2** : an ornamental locked box fixed to the middle of the altar and used for reserving bread consecrated at Mass **3** : a house of worship; *esp* : a building or shelter used for evangelistic services

ta·bes \'tā-,bēz\ *n, pl* **tabes** [L] : wasting accompanying a chronic disease — **ta·bet·ic** \tə-'bet-ik\ *adj*

¹ta·ble \'tā-bəl\ *n* [OE *tabule* & OF *table,* both fr. L *tabula* board, tablet, list] **1** : TABLET **2 a** : a piece of furniture consisting of a smooth flat slab fixed on legs **b** (1) : FOOD, FARE ⟨sets a good *table*⟩ (2) : an act of assembling to eat : MEAL **c** : a group of people assembled at or as if at a table **3 a** : a systematic arrangement of data in rows or columns for ready reference ⟨*table* of weights⟩ **b** : a condensed enumeration : LIST ⟨*table* of contents⟩ **4 a** : TABLELAND **b** : a horizontal stratum

²table *vt* **ta·bled; ta·bling** \-b(ə-)liŋ\ **1** : TABULATE **2** : to remove (a parliamentary motion) from consideration indefinitely **3** : to put on a table

tab·leau \'tab-,lō, tab-'lō\ *n, pl* **tableaus** *or* **tab·leaux** \-,lōz, -'lōz\ [F, fr. MF *tablel,* dim. of *table*] : a lifelike representation of a scene or event by an appropriate grouping of persons who remain silent and motionless

tableau curtain *n* : a stage curtain that opens in the center and has its sections drawn upward as well as to the side in order to produce a draped effect

ta·ble·cloth \'tā-bəl-,klöth\ *n* : a covering spread over a dining table before the places are set

ta·ble d'hôte \,täb-əl-'dōt, ,tab-\ *n* [F, lit., host's table] **1** : a meal served to all guests of a hotel at a stated hour and fixed price **2** : a complete meal of several courses offered in a restaurant or hotel at a fixed price — compare A LA CARTE

ta·ble·land \'tā-bə(l)-,land\ *n* : a broad level elevated area : PLATEAU

table linen *n* : linen (as tablecloths and napkins) for the table

table salt *n* : salt for use at the table and in cooking : SALT **1**

ta·ble·spoon \'tā-bəl-,spün\ *n* **1** : a spoon of a size convenient for serving rather than eating food **2** : TABLESPOONFUL

ta·ble·spoon·ful \,tā-bəl-'spün-,ful, 'tā-bəl-,\ *n, pl* **-spoonfuls** \-,fùlz\ *or* **-spoons·ful** \-'spünz-,ful, -,spünz-\ **1** : as much as a tablespoon can hold **2** : a unit of measure used esp. in cookery equal to one half fluidounce or three teaspoonfuls

table sugar *n* : SUCROSE

tab·let \'tab-lət\ *n* [MF *tablete,* dim. of *table*] **1 a** : a flat slab or plaque suited for or bearing an inscription **b** : a collection of sheets of writing paper glued together at one edge **2 a** : a compressed or molded block of a solid material : CAKE **b** : a small mass of medicated material usu. in the shape of a disk

table talk *n* : informal conversation at or as if at a dining table

table tennis *n* : a table game resembling lawn tennis played with wooden paddles and a small hollow plastic ball

ta·ble·top \'tā-bəl-,täp\ *n* **1** : the top of a table **2 a** : a photograph of small objects or a miniature scene arranged on a table — **tabletop** *adj*

ta·ble·ware \'tā-bəl-,wa(ə)r, -,we(ə)r\ *n* : utensils (as of china, glass, or silver) for table use

table wine *n* : a still wine of not more than 14 percent alcohol by volume usu. served with food

¹tab·loid \'tab-,lóid\ *adj* [fr. *Tabloid,* a trademark applied to a concentrated form of drugs and chemicals] : compressed or condensed into small scope ⟨*tabloid* information⟩

---

j joke; ŋ sing; ō flow; ò flaw; òi coin; th thin; th̲ this; ü loot; ů foot; y yet; yü few; yů furious; zh vision

²tabloid *n* : a newspaper about half the page size of an ordinary newspaper that contains news esp. of a sensational nature and much photographic matter

¹ta·boo *or* **ta·bu** \ta-'bü, tə-\ *adj* [Tongan *tabu*] : prohibited by a taboo

²taboo *or* **tabu** *n, pl* **taboos** *or* **tabus** **1** : a prohibition against touching, saying, or doing something on pain of immediate harm from a mysterious superhuman force **2** : a prohibition imposed by social custom

³taboo *or* **tabu** *vt* : to place under a taboo

ta·bor \'tā-bər\ *n* [OF] : a small drum with one head used to accompany a pipe played by the same person

ta·bor·er \-bər-ər\ *n* : one that plays on the tabor

tab·o·ret *or* **tab·ou·ret** \,tab-ə-'ret, -'rā\ *n* [F *tabouret*, fr. MF, dim. of *tabor, tabour* drum] **1** : a low stool without arms or back **2** : a small ornamental stand (as for a plant)

tab·u·lar \'tab-yə-lər\ *adj* [L *tabula* board, tablet] **1** : having a flat surface **2 a** : arranged or entered in a table **b** : computed by means of a table — **tab·u·lar·ly** *adv*

ta·bu·la ra·sa \,tab-yə-lə-'räz-ə\ *n, pl* **ta·bu·lae ra·sae** \-,lī-'räz-,ī\ [L, smoothed (wax) tablet] : the mind in its hypothetical primary blank or empty state before receiving outside impressions

tab·u·late \'tab-yə-,lāt\ *vt* : to put into tabular form — **tab·u·la·tion** \,tab-yə-'lā-shən\ *n*

tab·u·la·tor \'tab-yə-,lāt-ər\ *n* : one that tabulates: as **a** : a business machine that sorts and selects information from marked or perforated cards **b** : a device on a typewriter or biller for arranging data in columns

tac·a·ma·hac \'tak-ə-mə-,hak\ *n* [Sp *tacamahaca*, fr. Nahuatl *tecamaca*] **1** : any of several aromatic oleoresins used in ointments and plasters and for incense **2** : a tree yielding tacamahac; *esp* : a No. American poplar with resin-coated buds — called also *balsam poplar*

tach·i·na fly \,tak-ə-nə-\ *n* [NL *Tachina*, genus of flies, fr. Gk *tachinos* swift] : any of a family of bristly usu. grayish or black flies with parasitic larvae important in the biological control of pest insects

ta·chis·to·scope \tə-'kis-tə-,skōp\ *n* [Gk *tachistos*, superl. of *tachys* swift] : an apparatus for the brief exposure of visual stimuli

ta·chom·e·ter \tə-'käm-ət-ər\ *n* [Gk *tachos* speed] : a device for indicating speed of rotation

tach·y·car·dia \,tak-i-'kärd-ē-ə\ *n* [NL, fr. Gk *tachys* swift + *kardia* heart] : rapid heart action

ta·chym·e·ter \ta-'kim-ət-ər, tə-\ *n* : a surveying instrument (as a transit) for determining quickly the distances, bearings, and elevations of distant objects

tac·it \'tas-ət\ *adj* [L *tacitus* silent, fr. pp. of *tacēre* to be silent] **1** : expressed or carried on without words or speech **2** : implied or indicated but not actually expressed ⟨*tacit* consent⟩ — **tac·it·ly** *adv* — **tac·it·ness** *n*

tac·i·turn \'tas-ə-,tərn\ *adj* [L *taciturnus*, fr. *tacitus* silent] : habitually or temperamentally disinclined to talk **syn** see SILENT — **tac·i·tur·ni·ty** \,tas-ə-'tər-nət-ē\ *n* — **tac·i·turn·ly** \'tas-ə-,tərn-lē\ *adv*

¹tack \'tak\ *n* [ME *tak* fastener] **1** : a small short sharppointed nail usu. with a broad flat head for fastening some light object or material to a solid surface ⟨carpet *tack*⟩ **2 a** : a rope used to hold in place the forward lower corner of the lowest sail on any square-rigged mast of a ship **b** : the lower forward corner of a fore-and-aft sail **3 a** : the direction a ship is sailing as shown by the way the sails are trimmed; *also* : the run of a ship as trimmed in one way ⟨on the port *tack*⟩ **b** : a change of course from one tack to another **4** : a zigzag movement on land **5** : a course or method of action ⟨he is on the wrong *tack*⟩ **6** : a slight or temporary sewing or fastening

²tack *vb* **1** : ATTACH; *esp* : to fasten or affix with tacks **2** : to join in a slight or hasty manner **3** : to add as a supplement **4** : to change the direction of a sailing ship when sailing close-hauled by putting the helm alee and shifting the sails **5 a** : to sail in a different direction by a tack **b** : to follow a zigzag course **c** : to modify one's policy or an attitude abruptly — **tack·er** *n*

³tack *n* : STUFF; *esp* : FOODSTUFF

⁴tack *n* [short for *tackle*] : equipment for riding horses : stable gear

tack board *n* : a usu. cork board for tacking up notices and display materials

tack hammer *n* : a lightweight hammer often having one magnetized face for holding and driving tacks

tack·i·ness \'tak-ē-nəs\ *n* : the quality or state of being tacky

¹tack·le \'tak-əl, *by seamen often* 'tāk-\ *n* [ME *takel*] **1** : a set of the equipment used in a particular activity : GEAR ⟨fishing *tackle*⟩ **2 a** : a ship's rigging **b** : an assemblage of ropes and pulleys arranged to gain mechanical advantage for hoisting and pulling **3 a** : the act or an instance of tackling **b** : a football lineman who lines up inside the end

²tackle *vb* **tack·led**; **tack·ling** \'tak-(ə-)liŋ\ **1** : HARNESS ⟨*tackle* up the horses⟩ **2 a** : to seize, take hold of, or grapple with esp. with the intention of stopping or subduing **b** : to seize and throw down or stop in football **3** : to set about dealing with — **tack·ler** \-(ə-)lər\ *n*

¹tacky \'tak-ē\ *adj* **tack·i·er; -est** : barely sticky to the touch ⟨ADHESIVE ⟨*tacky* varnish⟩

²tacky *adj* **tack·i·er; -est 1 a** : characteristic of or suitable for a low-class person **b** : SHABBY, SEEDY **2** : marked by lack of style or good taste : DOWDY

ta·co \'täk-ō\ *n, pl* **tacos** \-ōz, -ōs\ [MexSp] : a sandwich made of a tortilla rolled up with or folded over a filling

tac·o·nite \'tak-ə-,nīt\ *n* [*Taconic* mountain range, U.S.] : a flinty rock high enough in iron content to become commercially valuable as an ore

tact \'takt\ *n* [F, sense of touch, fr. L *tactus*, fr. *tangere* to touch] : a keen understanding of how to act in getting along with others; *esp* : the ability to deal with others without offending them

tact·ful \'takt-fəl\ *adj* : having or showing tact — **tact·ful·ly** \-fə-lē\ *adv* — **tact·ful·ness** *n*

¹tac·tic \'tak-tik\ *adj* : of, relating to, or showing biological taxis

²tactic *n* **1** : a method of employing forces in combat **2** : a planned action or maneuver for accomplishing an end

tac·ti·cal \'tak-ti-kəl\ *adj* **1 a** : of or relating to combat tactics **b** : of, relating to, or designed for air attack in close support of friendly ground forces ⟨*tactical* air force⟩ **2 a** : of or relating to small-scale actions serving a larger purpose **b** : adroit in planning or maneuvering — **tac·ti·cal·ly** \-k(ə-)lē\ *adv*

tac·ti·cian \tak-'tish-ən\ *n* : one skilled in tactics

tac·tics \'tak-tiks\ *n sing or pl* [Gk *taktika*, pl., fr. *tassein* to arrange, marshal] **1 a** : the science and art of disposing and maneuvering forces in combat **b** : the art or skill of employing available means to accomplish an end **2** : a system or mode of procedure **syn** see STRATEGY

tac·tile \'tak-t'l, -,tīl\ *adj* [L *tact-, tangere* to touch] : of, relating to, or perceptible through the sense of touch — **tac·til·i·ty** \tak-'til-ət-ē\ *n*

tact·less \'takt-ləs\ *adj* : having or showing no tact — **tact·less·ly** *adv* — **tact·less·ness** *n*

tac·tu·al \'tak-chə-wəl\ *adj* [L *tactus* sense of touch, fr. *tangere* to touch] : TACTILE — **tac·tu·al·ly** \-wə-lē\ *adv*

tad \'tad\ *n* : BOY

tad·pole \'tad-,pōl\ *n* [ME *tad-depol*, fr. *tadde* toad + *pol* head, poll] : a larval aquatic frog or toad typically having a long tail, rounded body, and gills

tael \'tāl\ *n* [Pg, fr. Malay *tahil*] **1** : any of various units of weight of eastern Asia **2** : any of various Chinese units of value based on the value of a tael weight of silver

tae·nia \'tē-nē-ə\ *n, pl* **-ni·ae** \-nē-,ē\ *or* **-ni·as** [L, fr. Gk *tainia*] **1** : an ancient Greek fillet **2** : a band on a Doric order separating the frieze from the architrave **3** : a band of nervous tissue or muscle **4** : TAPEWORM

tae·ni·a·sis \tē-'nī-ə-səs\ *n, pl* **-a·ses** \-ə-,sēz\ : infestation with or disease caused by tapeworms

taf·fe·ta \'taf-ət-ə\ *n* [It *taffettà*, fr. Per *tāftah* woven] : a crisp plain-woven lustrous fabric of various fibers used esp. for women's clothing

taff·rail \'taf-,rāl, -rəl\ *n* : the rail around the stern of a ship

taf·fy \'taf-ē\ *n, pl* **taffies** **1** : a candy usu. of molasses

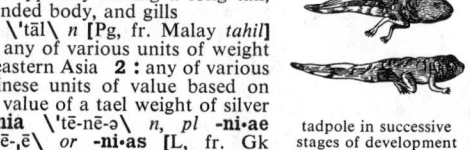

tadpole in successive stages of development

or brown sugar boiled and pulled until porous and light-colored **2** : insincere flattery

taffy pull *n* : a social gathering at which taffy is made

¹tag \\'tag\\ *n* [ME *tagge*] **1** : a loose hanging piece of cloth : TATTER **2** : a metal or plastic binding on an end of a shoelace **3** : a piece of hanging or attached material **4 a** : a brief quotation used for rhetorical emphasis or sententious effect **b** : a hackneyed saying : CLICHÉ **c** : TAG LINE **5 a** : a marker used for identification or classification ⟨price *tag*⟩ **b** : a descriptive or identifying phrase or epithet

²tag *vb* **tagged; tag·ging** **1** : to provide or mark with or as if with a tag **2** : to attach as an addition : APPEND **3** : to follow closely and persistently **4** : LABEL 3

³tag *n* **1** : a children's game in which one player is it and chases the others and tries to make one of them it by touching him **2** : an act or instance of touching a runner with the ball in baseball

⁴tag *vt* **tagged; tag·ging** **1 a** : to touch in or as if in a game of tag **b** : to put out (a runner in baseball) by touching with the ball **2** : to hit solidly : catch with a blow

Ta·ga·log \\tə-'gäl-əg, -,ȯg\\ *n* **1** : a member of a people of central Luzon **2** : an Austronesian language of the Tagalog people that is the official national language of the Philippines

tag·along \\'tag-ə-,lȯn\\ *n* : one that persistently and often annoyingly follows the lead of another

tag day *n* : a day on which contributions are solicited (as for a charity) and small tags are given in return

tag end *n* **1** : the last part **2** : a miscellaneous or random fragment

tag line *n* **1** : a final line (as in a play or joke); *esp* : one that serves to clarify a point or create a dramatic effect **2** : a reiterated phrase identified with an individual, group, or product : SLOGAN

tag, rag, and bob·tail *or* **tagrag and bobtail** \\,tag-,rag-ən-'bäb-,tāl\\ *n* : RABBLE

tag up *vi* : to touch a base in baseball before running after a fly ball is caught

Ta·hi·tian \\tə-'hē-shən, -'hēt-ē-ən\\ *n* **1** : a native or inhabitant of Tahiti **2** : the Polynesian language of the Tahitians — **Tahitian** *adj*

Tai \\'tī\\ *n, pl* **Tai** : a member of a group of peoples of southeast Asia

tai·ga \\'tī-'gä\\ *n* [Russ *taĭga*] : swampy coniferous northern forest (as of Siberia) beginning where the tundra ends

¹tail \\'tāl\\ *n* [OE *tægel*] **1** : the rear end or a process or prolongation of the rear end of the body of an animal **2** : something resembling an animal's tail ⟨*tail* of a kite⟩ **3** *pl* **a** : TAILCOAT **b** : full evening dress for men **4** : the back, last, lower, or inferior part of something; *esp* : the reverse of a coin **5** : a spy (as a detective) who follows someone **6** : the rear part of an airplane consisting of horizontal and vertical stabilizing surfaces with attached control surfaces **7** : the trail of a fugitive in flight ⟨posse on his *tail*⟩ — **tailed** \\'tāld\\ *adj* — **tail·less** \\'tāl-ləs\\ *adj* — **tail·like** \\'tāl-,līk\\ *adj*

²tail *adj* **1** : being at the rear ⟨*tail* gunner⟩ **2** : coming from the rear ⟨*tail* wind⟩

³tail *vb* **1 a** : to fasten by or at the tail, stern, or rear **b** : to connect end to end **2** : ³DOCK 1 **3** : to make or furnish with a tail **b** : to follow or be drawn behind like a tail **4** : to place the end of (as a rafter) in a wall or other support **5** : to follow closely for purposes of observation : SHADOW **6** : to grow progressively smaller, fainter, or more scattered : SUBSIDE

tail·back \\'tāl-,bak\\ *n* : the offensive football halfback farther from the line of scrimmage

tail·board \\-,bōrd, -,bȯrd\\ *n* : TAILGATE

tail·bone \\-'bōn, -,bōn\\ *n* : a caudal vertebra; *also* : COCCYX

tail·coat \\-'kōt\\ *n* : a man's full-dress coat with two long tapering skirts at the back

tail end *n* **1** : the hindmost end ⟨the *tail end* of the line⟩ **2** : the concluding period

tail fin *n* **1** : CAUDAL FIN **2** : an automobile fin

¹tail·gate \\'tāl-,gāt\\ *n* : a board at the back end of a vehicle (as a station wagon) that can be let down for loading and unloading

²tailgate *vb* : to drive dangerously close behind another vehicle : follow too close for safety

tail·ing \\'tā-lin\\ *n* **1** *pl* : refuse material separated as residue in the preparation of various products (as grain or ores) **2** : the part of a projecting stone or brick inserted in a wall

tail lamp *n* : TAILLIGHT

taille \\'tä-yə, 'täl\\ *n* [F, fr. OF, fr. *taillier* to cut, tax] : a tax formerly levied by a French king or lord on his subjects or on lands held of him

tail·light \\'tāl-,līt\\ *n* : a red warning light mounted at the rear of a vehicle

¹tai·lor \\'tā-lər\\ *n* [OF *tailleur*, fr. *taillier* to cut, fr. LL *taliare*] : one whose occupation is making or altering men's or women's outer garments

²tailor *vt* **1 a** : to make or fashion as the work of a tailor **b** : to make or adapt to suit a special need or purpose **2** : to fit with clothes **3** : to style (as women's garments) with trim lines and hand finishing like that of a tailor's work on men's garments

tai·lor·bird \\'tā-lər-,bərd\\ *n* : any of numerous tropical Old World warblers that stitch leaves together to support and hide their nests

tai·lored \\-lərd\\ *adj* **1** : made by a tailor **2** : fashioned or fitted to resemble a tailor's work **3** : CUSTOM-MADE

tai·lor·ing *n* **1 a** : the business or occupation of a tailor **b** : the work or workmanship of a tailor **2** : the making or adapting of something to suit a particular purpose

tai·lor-made \\,tā-lər-'mād\\ *adj* **1** : made by or as if by a tailor; *esp* : characterized by precise fit and simplicity of style **2** : made or seeming to have been made to suit a particular need

tail·piece \\'tāl-,pēs\\ *n* **1** : a piece added at the end : APPENDAGE **2** : a triangular piece to which the strings of a stringed instrument are fastened **3** : an ornament placed below the text matter of a page (as at the end of a chapter) **4** : a beam tailed in a wall and supported by a header — see HEADER illustration

tail pipe *n* **1** : the pipe discharging the exhaust gases from the muffler of an automotive engine **2** : the part of a jet engine that carries the exhaust gases rearward

tail plane *n* : the horizontal tail surfaces of an airplane

tail·race \\'tāl-,rās\\ *n* : the part of a millrace below the water wheel or turbine

tail·spin \\-,spin\\ *n* **1** : SPIN 2a **2** : a collapse into depression or confusion : DEMORALIZATION

tail·stock \\-,stäk\\ *n* : the adjustable or sliding head of a lathe containing the dead center

tail wind *n* : a wind having the same general direction as the course of a moving airplane or ship

¹taint \\'tānt\\ *vt* [ME *taynten* to affect by attainder, fr. MF *ataint*, pp. of *ataindre* to affect by attainder, attain] **1** : to touch or affect slightly with something bad **2** : to affect with putrefaction : SPOIL, DECAY **3** : to contaminate morally : CORRUPT

²taint *n* **1** : a trace of decay : STAIN, BLEMISH **2** : a contaminating influence — **taint·less** \\-ləs\\ *adj*

Tai·ping \\'tī-'pin\\ *n* : a Chinese insurgent taking part in a rebellion (1848–65) against the Manchu dynasty

Ta·jik \\tä-'jik\\ *n* : a member of a people of Iranian blood and speech who resemble Europeans and are dispersed among the populations of Afghanistan and Turkestan

¹take \\'tāk\\ *vb* **took** \\'tuk\\; **tak·en** \\'tā-kən\\; **tak·ing** [ON *taka*] **1** : to lay hold of : GRASP ⟨*take* my hand⟩ **2** : CAPTURE ⟨*take* a fort⟩ **3** : WIN ⟨*take* first prize⟩ **4** : to get possession of (as by buying or capturing) ⟨*take* a house⟩ ⟨*took* several trout with hook and line⟩ **5** : to seize and affect suddenly ⟨*taken* with a fever⟩ **6** : CHARM, DELIGHT ⟨was much *taken* with his new acquaintance⟩ **7** : EXTRACT ⟨*take* material from an encyclopedia⟩ **8** : REMOVE, SUBTRACT ⟨*take* 78 from 112⟩; *also* : to put an end to (as life) **9** : to find out by testing or examining ⟨*take* a patient's temperature⟩ **10** : SELECT, CHOOSE **11** : ASSUME ⟨*take* office⟩ **12** : ABSORB ⟨this cloth *takes* dye well⟩ **13** : to be affected by : CONTRACT ⟨*took* a fit⟩ ⟨*took* cold⟩ **14** : ACCEPT, FOLLOW ⟨*take* my advice⟩ **15** : to introduce into the body ⟨*take* medicine⟩ **16 a** : to submit to ⟨*took* his punishment like a man⟩ **b** : WITHSTAND ⟨*takes* a punch well⟩ **17** : to subscribe for **18** : UNDERSTAND ⟨*take* a nod to mean *yes*⟩ **19** : FEEL ⟨*take* pride in one's work⟩ ⟨*take* offense⟩ **20** : to be formed or used with ⟨a noun that *takes* an *s* in the plural⟩⟨this verb *takes* an object⟩ **21** : CONVEY, CONDUCT, CARRY ⟨*take* a parcel to the post office⟩ **22 a** : to avail oneself of ⟨*take* a vacation⟩ **b** : to proceed to occupy ⟨*take* a chair⟩ **23** : NEED, REQUIRE ⟨this job *takes* a lot of time⟩ **24** : to obtain an image or copy of ⟨*take* a photograph⟩ ⟨*take* fingerprints⟩ **25** : to set out to make, do, or perform ⟨*take* a walk⟩ — often used with *on* ⟨*took* on a new assignment⟩ **26** : to have effect (as by adherence or absorption) ⟨a dye that *takes* well⟩; *also* : to establish a take ⟨the vaccination *took*⟩ **27** : to betake oneself ⟨*take* to the hills⟩

syn SEIZE, GRASP, SNATCH: TAKE applies to any manner of getting something into one's possession or control; SEIZE suggests sudden forcible taking of something tangible ⟨*seized* the thief in the act of taking the money⟩ or apprehending some fleeting or elusive intangible ⟨*seize* an opportunity⟩ GRASP stresses a laying hold so as to have firmly in possession ⟨*grasped* his arm⟩ ⟨failed to *grasp* the idea⟩ SNATCH suggests more suddenness but less force than SEIZE **syn** see in addition BRING, RECEIVE — **take advantage of 1** : to use to advantage : profit by **2** : to impose upon : EXPLOIT — **take after 1** : to take as an example : FOLLOW **2** : to look like : RESEMBLE — **take amiss** : to impute a bad meaning or intention to : be offended by — **take care** : to be careful : exercise caution or prudence — **take care of** : to attend to or provide for the needs, operation, or treatment of — **take effect 1** : to become operative **2** : to produce a result as expected or intended : be effective — **take for** : to suppose to be; *esp* : to suppose mistakenly to be — **take for granted 1** : to assume as true, real, or expected **2** : to value too lightly — **take hold** : to become attached or established : take effect — **take into account** : to make allowance for — **take in vain** : to use (a name) profanely or without proper respect — **take issue** : to take up the opposite side — **take part** : JOIN, PARTICIPATE, SHARE — **take place** : HAPPEN, OCCUR — **take stock** : INVENTORY, ASSESS — **take the cake** : to carry off the prize : rank first — **take the count 1** : to be knocked out in a boxing match **2** : to go down in defeat — **take the floor** : to rise (as in a meeting) to make an address — **take to 1** : to take in hand : take care of **2** : to apply or devote oneself to (as a practice, habit, or occupation) ⟨*take* to begging⟩ **3** : to adapt oneself to : respond to **4** : to conceive a liking for — **take to task** : to call to account for a shortcoming : REPROVE

²**take** *n* **1** : an act or the action of taking (as by seizing, accepting, or coming into possession) **2** : something that is taken: **a** : money received : PROCEEDS, RECEIPTS **b** : SHARE, CUT **c** : the quantity (as of game) taken at one time : CATCH **d** (1) : a scene filmed or televised at one time without stopping the camera (2) : a sound recording made during a single recording period (3) : a trial recording **3 a** : a bodily reaction that indicates a successful immunization esp. against smallpox **b** : a successful union of a graft **4** : mental response or reaction ⟨delayed *take*⟩

take back *vt* : RETRACT, WITHDRAW ⟨would not *take back* what he had said⟩

take down \(')tāk-'daùn\ *vb* **1 a** : to pull to pieces **b** : DISASSEMBLE **2** : to lower the spirit or vanity of : HUMBLE **3 a** : to write down **b** : to record by mechanical means **4** : to become seized or attacked esp. by illness ⟨*took down* with the mumps⟩

¹**take-down** \'tāk-,daùn\ *adj* : constructed so as to be readily taken apart ⟨*takedown* rifle⟩

²**takedown** *n* : the action or an act of taking down: as **a** : the action of humiliating **b** : the action of taking apart **c** : the act of bringing one's opponent in amateur wrestling under control to the mat from a standing position

take–home pay \'tāk-,hōm-\ *n* : the part of gross salary or wages after deductions (as of income-tax withholding, retirement insurance payments, or union dues)

take in *vt* **1** : to draw into a smaller compass ⟨*take in* a slack line⟩: **a** : FURL **b** : to make (a garment) smaller by enlarging seams or tucks **2 a** : to receive as a guest or inmate **b** : to give shelter to **3** : to receive (work) into one's house to be done for pay ⟨*take in* washing⟩ **4** : to encompass within fixed limits : COMPRISE, INCLUDE

5 : ATTEND ⟨*take in* a movie⟩ **6** : to receive into the mind : PERCEIVE, COMPREHEND ⟨paused to *take* the situation *in*⟩ **7** : to impose upon : CHEAT, DECEIVE ⟨*taken in* by a hard luck story⟩

taken *past part of* TAKE

take off \(')tāk-'óf\ *vb* **1** : REMOVE **2** : RELEASE ⟨*take* the brake *off*⟩ **3** : to omit or withhold from service owed or from time being spent (as at one's occupation) ⟨*took* two weeks *off* in August⟩ **4 a** : to copy from an original : REPRODUCE **b** : MIMIC **5** : to take away : DETRACT **6 a** : to start off or away : set out ⟨*took off* without delay⟩ **b** : to branch off (as from a main stream or stem) **c** : to begin a leap or spring **d** : to leave the surface : begin flight

take-off \'tāk-,óf\ *n* **1** : an imitation esp. in the way of caricature **2 a** : a rise or leap from a surface in making a jump or flight or an ascent in an airplane **b** : an action of starting out or setting out **3** : a spot at which one takes off **4** : a mechanism for transmission of the power of an engine or vehicle to operate some other mechanism

take on *vb* **1** : to engage with as an opponent **2** : ENGAGE, HIRE **3** : to assume or acquire (as an appearance or quality) as or as if one's own **4** : to show one's feelings esp. of grief or anger in a demonstrative way

take out \(')tāk-'aùt\ *vb* **1** : to remove by cleansing **2** : to find release for : EXPEND **3** : to conduct or escort into the open or to a public entertainment **4** : to take as an equivalent in another form ⟨*took* the debt *out* in goods⟩ **5** : to obtain from the proper authority ⟨*take out* a charter⟩ **6** : to start on a course : set out — **take it out on** : to expend anger, vexation, or frustration in harassment of

take-out \'tāk-,aùt\ *n* : the action or an act of taking out

take over \(')tāk-'ō-vər\ *vb* : to assume control or possession of or responsibility for something ⟨*took over* the government⟩

take-over \'tāk-,ō-vər\ *n* : the action or an act of taking over

take up \(')tāk-'əp\ *vb* **1** : to remove by lifting or pulling up **2** : to accept or adopt for the purpose of assisting **3** : to take or accept (as a belief, idea, or practice) as one's own **4** : to pull up or pull in so as to tighten or to shorten **5** : to respond favorably to (as a bet, challenge, or proposal) **6** : to make a beginning where another has left off — **take up for** : to take the part or side of — **take up with** : to begin to associate with

take-up \'tāk-,əp\ *n* **1** : the action of taking up (as by gathering, contraction, absorption, or adjustment) **2** : a device for tightening or drawing in

¹**tak-ing** \'tā-kiŋ\ *n* **1** : a state of violent agitation and distress **2** *pl* : receipts esp. of money : PROFIT

²**taking** *adj* **1** : ATTRACTIVE, CAPTIVATING **2** : CONTAGIOUS

ta-lar-ia \tə-'lar-ē-ə, -'ler-\ *n pl* [L, fr. *talus* ankle, heel] : the winged shoes of the god Mercury

talc \'talk\ *n* [MF, mica, fr. ML *talk*, fr. Ar *ṭalq*] : a soft mineral consisting of a basic silicate of magnesium that is usu. whitish, greenish, or grayish with a soapy feel and occurs in flaky, granular, or fibrous masses

tal-cum powder \'tal-kəm-\ *n* [ML *talcum* mica, fr. Ar *ṭalq*] : a toilet powder composed of perfumed talc or talc and a mild antiseptic

tale \'tāl\ *n* [OE *talu*] **1** : an oral relation or recital ⟨a *tale* of woe⟩ **2** : a story about an imaginary event ⟨a fairy *tale*⟩ **3** : a false story : LIE **4** : a piece of harmful gossip ⟨all sorts of *tales* were going around about him⟩ **5 a** : COUNT, TALLY **b** : a number of things taken together : TOTAL

tale-bear-er \-,bar-ər, -,ber-\ *n* : one that spreads gossip, scandal, or idle rumors : GOSSIP — **tale-bear-ing** \-iŋ\ *adj or n*

tal-ent \'tal-ənt\ *n* [L *talentum*, fr. Gk *talanton*; in senses 2–4, fr. the parable of the talents in Matthew 25:14–30] **1** : any of several ancient units of weight and money value (as a unit of Palestine and Syria equal to 3000 shekels or a Greek unit equal to 6000 drachmas) **2** : the natural endowments of a person **3 a** : a special often creative or artistic aptitude **b** : general intelligence or mental power : ABILITY **4** : persons of talent in a field or activity — **tal-ent-ed** \-ən-təd\ *adj*

syn GENIUS: TALENT suggests a marked special ability without implying a mind of extraordinary power; GENIUS

ə abut; ᵊ kitten; ər further; a back; ā bake; ä cot, cart; aù out; ch chin; e less; ē easy; g gift; i trip; ī life

may also imply marked talent but suggests more commonly an inborn creative intelligence far above ordinary

talent scout *n* **:** a person engaged in discovering and recruiting people of talent for a specialized field or activity

talent show *n* **:** a show consisting of a series of individual performances (as singing) by amateurs who may be selected for special recognition as performing talent

ta·ler \'täl-ər\ *n* [G *thaler, taler,* short for *joachimsthaler,* fr. Sankt *Joachimsthal,* Bohemia, where the first talers were made] **:** any of numerous silver coins issued by various German states from the 15th to the 19th centuries

tales·man \'tālz-mən\ *n* **:** a person added to a jury usu. from among bystanders to make up a deficiency in the available number of jurors

tale-tell·er \'tāl-ˌtel-ər\ *n* **1 :** one who tells tales or stories **2 :** TALEBEARER — **tale-tell·ing** \-iŋ\ *adj or n*

tal·i·pes \'tal-ə-ˌpēz\ *n* [NL, fr. L *talus* ankle + *pes* foot] **:** CLUBFOOT

tal·is·man \'tal-əs-mən, -əz-\ *n, pl* **talismans** [F, fr. Ar *ṭilsam,* fr. MGk *telesma,* fr. Gk, consecration] **:** a ring or stone carved with symbols and believed to have magical powers **:** CHARM — **tal·is·man·ic** \ˌtal-əs-'man-ik, -əz-\ *adj* — **tal·is·man·i·cal·ly** \-'man-i-k(ə-)lē\ *adv*

¹talk \'tȯk\ *vb* [ME *talken;* akin to E *tale*] **1 :** to deliver or express in speech **:** UTTER (*talk* sense) **2 :** to make the subject of conversation or discourse **:** DISCUSS (*talk* business) **3 :** to influence, affect, or cause by talking (*talked* them into agreeing) **4 :** to use (a language) for conversing or communicating **:** SPEAK **5 a :** to express or exchange ideas by means of spoken words **:** CONVERSE **b :** to convey information or communicate in any way (as with signs or sounds) **c :** to use speech **:** SPEAK **6 a :** to speak idly **:** PRATE **b :** GOSSIP **c :** to reveal secret or confidential information **7 :** to give a talk **:** LECTURE **syn** see SPEAK — **talk·er** *n* — **talk back :** to answer impertinently — **talk turkey :** to speak frankly or bluntly

²talk *n* **1 :** the act or an instance of talking **:** SPEECH **2 :** a way of speaking **:** LANGUAGE **3 :** pointless or fruitless discussion **:** VERBIAGE **4 :** a formal discussion, negotiation, or exchange of views **:** CONFERENCE **5 :** RUMOR, GOSSIP **6 :** the topic of interested comment, conversation, or gossip (she is the *talk* of the village) **7 :** an analysis or discussion presented in an informal or conversational manner

talk·a·tive \'tȯ-kət-iv\ *adj* **:** fond of talking — **talk·a·tive·ness** *n*

syn TALKATIVE, GARRULOUS, VOLUBLE mean given to talk or talking. TALKATIVE implies a readiness to talk and engage in conversation; GARRULOUS suggests wordy, rambling, or tedious talkativeness; VOLUBLE suggests keeping up an uninterrupted seemingly endless flow of talk

talk down *vb* **1 :** to overcome or silence by argument or by loud talking **2 :** to speak in a condescending or oversimplified fashion on the assumption that the listener is ignorant of the matter involved

talk·ie \'tȯ-kē\ *n* **:** a motion picture with synchronized sound effects

talking book *n* **:** a phonograph recording of a reading of a book or magazine designed chiefly for the use of the blind

talking machine *n* **:** PHONOGRAPH

talking point *n* **:** something that lends support for an argument or proposal

talk·ing-to \'tȯ-kiŋ-ˌtü\ *n* **:** SCOLDING (her father gave her a severe *talking-to* last week)

talk out *vt* **:** to clarify or settle by oral discussion (*talk out* their differences)

talk over *vt* **:** to review or consider in conversation **:** DISCUSS

talk up *vt* **:** to discuss favorably **:** ADVOCATE

talky \'tȯ-kē\ *adj* **talk·i·er; -est** **1 :** given to talking **:** TALKATIVE **2 :** containing too much talk

tall \'tȯl\ *adj* [ME, brave, handsome] **1 :** great in stature or height **b :** of a specified height (five feet *tall*) **2 a :** large or formidable in amount, extent, or degree (*tall* order to fill) **b :** GRANDILOQUENT, HIGH-FLOWN (*tall* talk) **c :** INCREDIBLE, IMPROBABLE (*tall* story) — **tall** *adv* — **tall·ness** *n*

tall·boy \-ˌbȯi\ *n* **1 :** HIGHBOY **2 :** a double chest of drawers

tall·ish \'tȯ-lish\ *adj* **:** rather tall

tal·lith \'täl-əs, -ət(h)\ *n, pl* **tal·li·thim** \ˌtäl-ə-'sēm, -'t(h)ēm\ [Heb *tallīth* cover, cloak] **:** a shawl with fringed corners traditionally worn over the head or shoulders by Jewish men during morning prayers

tall oil \'täl-, 'tȯl-\ *n* [Sw *tallolja,* fr. *tall* pine + *olja* oil] **:** a resinous by-product from the manufacture of chemical wood pulp used esp. in making soaps, coatings, and oils

tal·low \'tal-ō\ *n* [ME *talgh, talow*] **:** the white nearly tasteless solid rendered fat of cattle and sheep used chiefly in soap, margarine, candles, and lubricants — **tal·lowy** \'tal-ə-wē\ *adj*

¹tal·ly \'tal-ē\ *n, pl* **tallies** [ML *talea,* fr. L, twig] **1 :** a device for recording business transactions; *esp* **:** a rod notched with marks representing numbers that serves as a record of a transaction and of the amount due or paid **2 a :** a reckoning or recorded account; *also* **:** a total recorded **b :** a score or point made (as in a game) **3 a :** a part that corresponds to an opposite or companion member **:** COMPLEMENT **b :** CORRESPONDENCE, AGREEMENT

²tally *vb* **tal·lied; tal·ly·ing** **1 :** to keep a reckoning of **:** COUNT **2 :** to make a tally **:** SCORE **3 :** MATCH, AGREE

tal·ly·ho \ˌtal-ē-'hō\ *n, pl* **tallyhos** **1 :** a call of a huntsman at sight of the fox **2 :** a four-in-hand coach

tal·ly·man \'tal-ē-mən\ *n* **1** *Brit* **:** one who sells goods on the installment plan **2 :** one who tallies, checks, or keeps an account or record (as of a receipt of goods)

Tal·mud \'täl-ˌmu̇d, 'tal-məd\ *n* [LHeb *talmūdh,* lit., instruction] **:** the authoritative body of Jewish tradition — **tal·mu·dic** \tal-'m(y)üd-ik, -'məd-\ *also* **tal·mu·di·cal** \-i-kəl\ *adj, often cap* — **tal·mud·ism** \'täl-ˌmu̇d,iz-əm, 'tal-məd-\ *n, often cap* — **tal·mud·ist** \-əst\ *n, often cap*

tal·on \'tal-ən\ *n* [MF, heel, spur, fr. (assumed) VL *talon-, talo,* fr. L *talus* ankle, anklebone] **1 :** the claw of an animal and esp. of a bird of prey **2 :** a part or object shaped like or suggestive of a heel or claw — **tal·oned** \-ənd\ *adj*

¹ta·lus \'tā-ləs\ *n* [F, sloping ground, fr. L *talutium* slope indicating presence of gold under the soil] **:** rock debris at the base of a cliff

²talus *n, pl* **ta·li** \'tā-ˌlī\ [L] **1 :** the bone that in man bears the weight of the body and with the tibia and fibula forms the ankle joint **2 :** the entire ankle

talon

tam \'tam\ *n* **:** TAM-O'-SHANTER

tam·a·ble *or* **tame·a·ble** \'tā-mə-bəl\ *adj* **:** capable of being tamed

ta·ma·le \tə-'mäl-ē\ *n* [MexSp *tamales,* pl. of *tamal* tamale, fr. Nahuatl *tamalli*] **:** ground meat seasoned usu. with chili, rolled in cornmeal dough, wrapped in corn husks, and steamed

tam·a·rack \'tam-ə-ˌrak\ *n* **:** any of several American larches; *also* **:** their wood

tam·a·rind \'tam-ə-ˌrind, -rənd\ *n* [Ar *tamr hindī,* lit., Indian date] **:** a tropical leguminous tree with hard yellowish wood, feathery pinnate leaves, and red-striped yellow flowers; *also* **:** its pod which has an acid pulp used for preserves or in drinks

tam·a·risk \'tam-ə-ˌrisk\ *n* [LL *tamariscus*] **:** any of a genus of chiefly desert shrubs having tiny narrow leaves and masses of minute flowers

¹tam·bour \'tam-ˌbu̇r\ *n* [F, fr. Ar *ṭanbūr*] **1 :** ¹DRUM 1 **2 a :** an embroidery frame; *esp* **:** a set of two interlocking hoops between which cloth is stretched before stitching **b :** embroidery made on a tambour frame **3 :** a rolling top or front (as of a desk) of narrow strips of wood glued on canvas

²tambour *vb* **1 :** to embroider (cloth) with tambour **2 :** to work at a tambour frame — **tam·bour·er** *n*

tam·bou·rine \ˌtam-bə-'rēn\ *n* **:** a small drum; *esp* **:** a shallow one-headed drum with loose metallic disks at the sides played by shaking, striking with the hand, or rubbing with the thumb

¹tame \'tām\ *adj* [OE *tam*] **1 :** reduced from a state of native wildness esp. so as to be tractable and useful to man **:** DOMESTICATED **2 :** made docile and submissive **:** SUBDUED **3 :** lacking spirit, zest, or interest **:** INSIPID — **tame·ly** *adv* — **tame·ness** *n*

²tame *vb* **1 a :** to make or become tame **b :** to subject to cultivation **2** : HUMBLE, SUBDUE **3** : to tone down : SOFTEN — **tam·er** *n*

tame·less \'tām-ləs\ *adj* : not tamed or tamable

Tam·il \'tam-əl\ *n* **1** : a Dravidian language of Madras state and of northern and eastern Ceylon **2** : a Tamil‑speaking person

Tam·ma·ny \'tam-ə-nē\ *adj* [after the *Tammany* Society, Democratic political organization in New York City] : of, relating to, or constituting a group exercising or seeking municipal political control by methods often associated with corruption and bossism

tam-o'-shan·ter \'tam-ə-,shant-ər\ *n* [after *Tam o' Shanter*, hero of the poem *Tam o' Shanter* by Robert Burns] : a cap of Scottish origin with a tight headband, wide flat circular crown, and usu. a pompon in the center

tamp \'tamp\ *vt* **1** : to fill up (a drill hole) above a blasting charge with material (as sand) **2** : to drive in or down by a succession of light or medium blows : COMPACT ⟨*tamp* wet concrete⟩ — **tamp·er** *n*

tam·pala \tam-'pal-ə\ *n* : an annual amaranth sometimes grown as a potherb

tam·per \'tam-pər\ *vi* **tam·pered; tam·per·ing** \-p(ə-)riŋ\ **1** : to use underhand or improper methods (as bribery) **2 a** : to interfere so as to cause a weakening or change for the worse **b** : to try foolish or dangerous experiments : MEDDLE — **tam·per·er** \-pər-ər\ *n*

tam·pi·on \'tam-pē-ən, 'täm-\ *n* : a wooden plug or a metal or canvas cover for the muzzle of a gun

¹**tam·pon** \'tam-,pän\ *n* [F] : a plug (as of cotton) introduced into a cavity usu. to check bleeding or absorb secretions

²**tampon** *vt* : to plug with a tampon

tam-tam \'tam-,tam, 'täm-,täm\ *n* [Hindi *ṭamṭam*] **1** : TOM-TOM **2** : GONG

¹**tan** \'tan\ *vb* **tanned; tan·ning** [MF *tanner*, fr. ML *tannare*, fr. *tannum* tanbark] **1** : to convert (hide) into leather esp. by treatment with an infusion of tannin‑rich bark **2** : to make or become tan or brown esp. by exposure to the sun ⟨a well-*tanned* skin⟩ **3** : THRASH, WHIP

²**tan** *n* **1** : TANBARK 1 **2** : a tanning material or its active agent (as tannin) **3** : a brown color imparted to the skin by exposure to the sun or weather **4** : a variable color averaging a light yellowish brown

³**tan** *adj* **tan·ner; -nest** : of the color tan

tan·a·ger \'tan-i-jər\ *n* [NL *tanagra*, fr. Pg *tangará*, of AmerInd origin] : any of a family of American birds related to the finches that have brightly colored males and inferior songs

tan·bark \'tan-,bärk\ *n* **1** : bark rich in tannin that is used in tanning **2** : a surface (as a circus ring) covered with spent tanbark

¹**tan·dem** \'tan-dəm\ *n* [L, at last, at length (taken to mean "lengthwise")] **1 a** : a 2-seated carriage drawn by horses harnessed one before the other; *also* : a team so harnessed **b** : TANDEM BICYCLE **2** : a group of two or more arranged one behind the other or used or acting in conjunction

²**tandem** *adv* (*or adj*) : one after or behind another

tandem bicycle *n* : a bicycle for two or more persons sitting tandem

tandem cart *n* : a 2-wheeled vehicle having seats back to back with the front one somewhat elevated

¹**tang** \'taŋ\ *n* [of Scand origin] **1** : a projecting part (as on a knife, file, or sword) to connect with the handle **2 a** : a sharp distinctive often lingering flavor **b** : a pungent odor **3 a** : a faint suggestion : TRACE **b** : a distinguishing characteristic that sets apart or gives a special individuality — **tanged** \'taŋd\ *adj*

²**tang** *n* [of Scand origin] : any of various large coarse seaweeds (as a rockweed)

³**tang** *vb* : CLANG, RING

⁴**tang** *n* : a sharp twanging sound

Tang \'täŋ\ *n* : a Chinese dynasty dated A.D. 618–907 and marked by wide contacts with other cultures and by the development of printing and the flourishing of poetry and art

tan·ge·lo \'tan-jə-,lō\ *n*, *pl* **-los** [blend of *tangerine* and *pomelo* grapefruit] : a hybrid between a tangerine and a grapefruit; *also* : its fruit

tan·gen·cy \'tan-jən-sē\ *n*, *pl* **-cies** : the quality or state of being tangent

¹**tan·gent** \-jənt\ *adj* [L *tangere* to touch] **1 a** : touching a curve or surface at only one point in the given location ⟨straight line *tangent* to a curve⟩ **b** (1) : having a common tangent line at a point ⟨*tangent* curves⟩ (2) : having a common tangent plane at a point ⟨*tangent* surfaces⟩ **2** : diverging from an original purpose or course : IRRELEVANT ⟨*tangent* remarks⟩

²**tangent** *n* **1** : the trigonometric function that for an acute angle in a right triangle is the ratio of the side opposite to the side adjacent **2 a** : a line tangent to a curve — see CIRCLE illustration **b** : the part of a tangent to a plane curve between the point of tangency and the horizontal axis **3** : an abrupt change of course : DIGRESSION ⟨went off on a *tangent* and never got to the point⟩

tan·gen·tial \tan-'jen-chəl\ *adj* **1** : TANGENT **2** : acting along or lying in a tangent ⟨*tangential* forces⟩ **3** : DIVERGENT, DIGRESSIVE ⟨*tangential* comment⟩ — **tan·gen·tial·ly** \-'jench-(ə-)lē\ *adv*

tan·ger·ine \'tan-jə-,rēn\ *n* [F *Tanger* Tangier, Morocco] **1** : MANDARIN 3; *esp* : one grown for its deep orange loose-skinned fruit esp. in the U.S. and southern Africa **2** : the fruit of the tangerine

tan·gi·bil·i·ty \,tan-jə-'bil-ət-ē\ *n*, *pl* **-ties** : the quality or state of being tangible

¹**tan·gi·ble** \'tan-jə-bəl\ *adj* [L *tangere* to touch] **1 a** : capable of being perceived esp. by the sense of touch : PALPABLE **b** : substantially real : MATERIAL **2** : capable of being appraised at an actual or approximate value ⟨*tangible* assets⟩ — **tan·gi·ble·ness** *n* — **tan·gi·bly** \-blē\ *adv*

²**tangible** *n* : something tangible; *esp* : a tangible asset

¹**tan·gle** \'taŋ-gəl\ *vb* **tan·gled; tan·gling** \-g(ə-)liŋ\ [ME *tangilen*] **1** : to make or become involved so as to hamper or embarrass : be or become entangled ⟨hopelessly *tangled* in argument⟩ **2** : to twist or become twisted together into a mass hard to straighten out again : ENTANGLE

²**tangle** *n* **1** : a tangled twisted mass (as of vines) confusedly interwoven : SNARL **2** : a complicated or confused state or condition **3** : DISPUTE, ARGUMENT

tan·gle·ment \'taŋ-gəl-mənt\ *n* : ENTANGLEMENT

tan·gly \'taŋ-g(ə-)lē\ *adj* **tan·gli·er; -est** : full of tangles or knots : INTRICATE

¹**tan·go** \'taŋ-gō\ *n*, *pl* **tangos** [AmerSp] **1** : a ballroom dance of Spanish-American origin marked by posturing, frequent pointing positions, and a variety of steps **2** : music for the tango in moderate duple time with dotted and syncopated rhythm

²**tango** *vi* : to dance the tango

tangy \'taŋ-ē\ *adj*, *sometimes* **tang·i·er; -est** : having or suggestive of a tang ⟨a *tangy* smell⟩

¹**tank** \'taŋk\ *n* [Pg *tanque*, alter. of *estanque*, fr. *estancar* to stanch] **1** : a pond built as a water supply **2** : a usu. large receptacle for holding, transporting, or storing liquids **3** : an enclosed heavily armed and armored combat vehicle supported and steered by endless-belt treads

²**tank** *vt* : to place, store, or treat in a tank

tank·age \'taŋ-kij\ *n* **1** : the capacity or contents of a tank **2** : dried animal residues usu. freed from the fat and gelatin and used as fertilizer and in feeds **3** : fees charged for storage in tanks

tan·kard \'taŋ-kərd\ *n* [ME] : a tall one-handled drinking vessel; *esp* : a silver or pewter mug with a lid

tank·er \'taŋ-kər\ *n* **1 a** : a boat fitted with tanks for carrying liquid in bulk **b** : a vehicle (as a truck or trailer) on which a tank is mounted to carry liquids **2** : a cargo airplane for transporting fuel

tank farm *n* : an area with tanks for storage of oil

tank town *n* **1** : a town at which trains stop for water **2** : a small town

tank trailer *n* : a truck-drawn trailer equipped as a tanker

tankard

tan·nage \'tan-ij\ *n* : the act, process, or result of tanning

tan·nate \'tan-,āt\ *n* : a compound (as a salt) of a tannin

tan·ner \'tan-ər\ *n* : one that tans hides

tan·nery \'tan-(ə-)rē\ *n*, *pl* **tan·ner·ies** : a place where tanning is carried on

Tann·häu·ser \'tän-,hȯi-zər\ *n* : a knight and minnesinger of Germanic legend noted for his stay with Venus in the Venusberg cavern and his subsequent repentance

tan·nic \'tan-ik\ *adj* : of, resembling, or derived from tan or a tannin

tannic acid *n* : TANNIN

tan·nin \'tan-ən\ *n* [F, fr. *tanner* to tan] : any of various substances of plant origin used in tanning and dyeing, in inks, and as an astringent

tan·ning *n* 1 : the art or process by which a skin is tanned 2 : a browning of the skin by exposure to sun 3 : WHIPPING, FLOGGING

tan·nish \'tan-ish\ *adj* : somewhat tan

tan·sy \'tan-zē\ *n, pl* **tansies** [OF *tanesie*, fr. ML *athanasia*, fr. Gk, immortality] : any of a genus of mostly weedy herbs related to the daisies; *esp* : one with finely cut leaves, aromatic odor, and very bitter taste

tan·ta·lize \'tant-ᵊl-ˌīz\ *vb* [*Tantalus*] : to tease or torment by or as if by presenting something desirable to the view but continually keeping it out of reach — **tan·ta·liz·er** *n*

tan·ta·liz·ing *adj* : possessing a quality that arouses or stimulates desire or interest : mockingly out of reach — **tan·ta·liz·ing·ly** \-ˌī-ziŋ-lē\ *adv*

tan·ta·lum \'tant-ᵊl-əm\ *n* [NL, fr. L *Tantalus*; fr. its inability to absorb acid] : a hard ductile gray-white acid-resisting metallic chemical element found combined in rare minerals — see ELEMENT table

Tan·ta·lus \'tant-ᵊl-əs\ *n* : a wealthy king and son of Zeus punished in the lower world by being condemned to stand in water up to the chin and beneath fruit-laden branches with water and fruit receding at each attempt to drink or eat

tan·ta·mount \'tant-ə-ˌmaunt\ *adj* [obs. *tantamount*, n., equivalent, fr. AF *tant amunter* to amount to as much] : equal in value, meaning, or effect

tan·tara \tan-'tar-ə, -'tär-\ *n* : the blare of a trumpet or horn

¹tan·tivy \tan-'tiv-ē\ *adv (or adj)* : at a gallop : HEADLONG

²tantivy *n* : a rapid gallop or ride : headlong rush

tan·trum \'tan-trəm\ *n* : a fit of bad temper

tan·yard \'tan-ˌyärd\ *n* : the section or part of a tannery housing tanning vats

Tao \'tau, 'dau\ *n* [Chin (Pek) *tao⁴*, lit., way] : the ultimate principle of the universe in Taoism

Tao·ism \-ˌiz-əm\ *n* 1 : a Chinese mystical philosophy traditionally founded by Lao-tzu in the 6th century B.C. that teaches conformity to the Tao by unassertive action and simplicity 2 : a religion developed from Taoist philosophy and folk and Buddhist religion and concerned with obtaining long life and good fortune often by magical means — **Tao·ist** \-əst\ *adj or n* — **Tao·is·tic** \tau-'is-tik, dau-\ *adj*

¹tap \'tap\ *n* [OE *tæppa* tap of a cask] 1 a : FAUCET, COCK, SPIGOT b : liquor drawn through a tap 2 : the procedure of removing fluid from a container or cavity by tapping 3 : a tool for forming an internal screw thread 4 : an intermediate point in an electric circuit where a connection may be made — **on tap** 1 : ready to be drawn ⟨ale *on tap*⟩ 2 : on hand : AVAILABLE

²tap *vt* **tapped; tap·ping** 1 : to release or cause to flow by piercing or by drawing a plug from the containing vessel or cavity ⟨*tap* wine from a cask⟩ 2 a : to pierce so as to let out or draw off a fluid ⟨*tap* maple trees⟩ b : to draw from or upon ⟨*tap* the nation's resources⟩ c : to connect into (a telephone or telegraph wire) to get information or to connect into (an electrical circuit) 3 : to form a female screw in by means of a tap — **tap·per** *n*

³tap *vb* **tapped; tap·ping** [MF *taper* to strike with the flat of the hand] 1 : to strike or cause to strike lightly esp. with a slight sound ⟨*tapping* the desk with his pencil⟩ 2 : to make or produce by repeated light blows ⟨a woodpecker *tapped* a hole in the tree⟩ 3 : to repair by putting a half sole on 4 : SELECT, DESIGNATE; *esp* : to elect to membership (as in a fraternity) — **tap·per** *n*

⁴tap *n* 1 : a light tap. audible blow; *also* : its sound 2 : HALF SOLE 3 : a small metal plate for the sole or heel of a shoe (as for tap dancing)

ta·pa \'täp-ə, 'tap-\ *n* : the bark of a tree pounded in the Pacific islands to make a coarse cloth usu. decorated with geometric patterns; *also* : this cloth

tap dance *n* : a step dance tapped out audibly with the feet — **tap-dance** \'tap-ˌdan(t)s\ *vi* — **tap dancer** *n* — **tap dancing** *n*

¹tape \'tāp\ *n* [OE *tæppe*] 1 : a narrow band of woven fabric 2 : a string stretched breast-high above the finishing line of a race 3 : a narrow flexible strip or band 4 : MAGNETIC TAPE

²tape *vt* 1 : to fasten, tie, bind, cover, or support with tape 2 : to measure with a tape measure 3 : to record on magnetic tape

tape deck *n* 1 a : a mechanism that moves a tape past a head (as for magnetic recording) b : a device that contains such a mechanism, that provides usu. for the recording as well as the playback of magnetic tapes, and that usu. has to be connected to a separate audio system 2 : a self-contained device for the playback of recorded magnetic tapes

tape·line \'tāp-ˌlīn\ *n* : TAPE MEASURE

tape measure *n* : a tape marked off usu. in inches and used for measuring

¹ta·per \'tā-pər\ *n* [OE] 1 a : a long waxed wick used esp. for lighting lamps, pipes, or fires; *also* : a slender candle b : a feeble light 2 a : a tapering form or figure b : gradual diminution of thickness, diameter, or width in an elongated object c : a gradual decrease

²taper *vb* **ta·pered; ta·per·ing** \-p(ə-)riŋ\ 1 : to make or become gradually smaller toward one end 2 : to diminish gradually

tape-re·cord \ˌtāp-ri-'kord\ *vt* : to make a recording of (as sounds) on magnetic tape — **tape recorder** *n* — **tape recording** *n*

taper off *vb* : to stop gradually

tap·es·try \'tap-ə-strē\ *n, pl* **-tries** [MF *tapisserie*, fr. *tapisser* to carpet, fr. *tapis* rug, carpet, fr. Gk *tapēs*] : a heavy decorative fabric used esp. as a wall hanging or furniture covering — **tap·es·tried** \-strēd\ *adj*

tapestry carpet *n* : a carpet in which the designs are printed in colors on the threads before the fabric is woven

ta·pe·tum \tə-'pēt-əm\ *n, pl* **ta·pe·ta** \-'pēt-ə\ [NL, fr. Gk *tapēt-, tapēs* rug, carpet] : a membranous layer; *esp* : one of nutritive cells about the sporogenous tissue in the sporangium of higher plants

tape·worm \'tāp-ˌwərm\ *n* : a flatworm with a segmented body that is parasitic when adult in the intestine of vertebrates : CESTODE

tap·hole \'tap-ˌhōl\ *n* : a hole for a tap; *esp* : a hole at or near the bottom of a furnace or ladle through which molten metal or slag can be tapped

tap·i·o·ca \ˌtap-ē-'ō-kə\ *n* [Sp & Pg, of AmerInd origin] : a usu. granular preparation of cassava starch used esp. in puddings and as a thickening in liquid foods

ta·pir \'tā-pər\ *n, pl* **tapir** *or* **tapirs** [of AmerInd origin] : any of several large inoffensive chiefly nocturnal hoofed mammals of tropical America, Malaya, and Sumatra that have long flexible snouts and are related to the horses and rhinoceroses

ta·pis \ta-'pē\ *n, obs* : material (as tapestry) used for hangings and floor and table coverings — **on the tapis** : under consideration

tap·pet \'tap-ət\ *n* [³*tap*] : a lever or projection moved by some other piece (as a cam) or intended to tap or touch something else to cause a particular motion (as in forms of internal-combustion-engine valve gear)

tap·room \'tap-ˌrüm, -ˌrum\ *n* : BARROOM

tap·root \-ˌrüt, -ˌrut\ *n* : a large strong root that grows vertically downward and gives off small lateral roots — compare FIBROUS ROOT

taps \'taps\ *n sing or pl* [prob. alter. of earlier *taptoo* tattoo] : the last bugle call at night blown as a signal that lights are to be put out; *also* : a similar call blown at military funerals and memorial services

tap·ster \'tap-stər\ *n* : one employed to dispense liquors in a barroom

¹tar \'tär\ *n* [OE *teoru*; akin to E *tree*] : a dark usu. odorous viscous liquid obtained by destructive distillation of organic material (as wood, coal, or peat)

²tar *vt* **tarred; tar·ring** : to treat or smear with or as if with tar

³tar *n* [by shortening fr. *tarpaulin*] : SEAMAN, SAILOR ⟨salt *tars*⟩

tar·an·tel·la \ˌtar-ən-'tel-ə\ *n* [It, fr. *Taranto*, Italy] : a vivacious folk dance of southern Italy in ⁶/₈ time

ta·ran·tu·la \tə-'ranch-(ə-)lə, -'rant-ᵊl-ə\ *n* [ML, fr. It *tarantola*, fr. *Taranto*, Italy] 1 : a large European spider whose bite was once thought to cause an uncontrollable desire to dance **2 :** any of a family of large hairy American spiders that are mostly rather sluggish and essentially harmless to man

tar·boosh also **tar·bush** \tär-'büsh\ n [Ar ṭarbūsh] : a usu. red hat similar to the fez used alone or as part of a turban and worn esp. by Muslim men

tar·dy \'tärd-ē\ adj **tar·di·er; -est** [alter. of earlier tardif, fr. MF, fr. L tardus] **1 :** moving slowly : SLUGGISH **2 :** LATE; also : DILATORY — **tar·di·ly** \'tärd-ᵊl-ē\ adv — **tar·di·ness** \'tärd-ē-nəs\ n

1tare \'ta(ə)r, 'te(ə)r\ n [ME] **1 a :** VETCH; also : its seed **b :** a weed of grainfields mentioned in the Bible **2** pl : an undesirable element

2tare n [MF, fr. Ar ṭarha] : a deduction of weight made to allow for the weight of a container or vehicle — **tare** vt

targe \'tärj\ n [OF, of Gmc origin] archaic : a light shield

tar·get \'tär-gət\ n [MF targette small shield, dim. of targe] **1 a :** a mark to shoot at **b :** an object of ridicule or criticism **c :** a goal to be achieved : OBJECTIVE **2 :** the surface usu. of platinum or tungsten upon which the cathode rays within an X-ray tube are focused and from which the X rays are emitted

target date n : the date set for an event or for the completion of a project, goal, or quota

tar·iff \'tar-əf\ n [It tariffa, fr. Ar ta'rīf notification] **1 a :** a schedule of duties imposed by a government on imported or in some countries exported goods **b :** a duty or rate of duty imposed in such a schedule **2 :** a schedule of rates or charges of a business or public utility

tar·la·tan \'tär-lət-ᵊn\ n [F tarlatane] : a sheer cotton fabric in open plain weave usu. heavily sized

tar·mac \'tär-,mak\ n [fr. Tarmac, a trademark] : a tarmacadam road, apron, or runway

Tar·mac \'tär-,mak\ trademark — used for a bituminous binder for surfacing roads

tar·mac·ad·am \,tär-mə-'kad-əm\ n **1 :** a pavement made by putting tar over courses of crushed stone and then rolling **2 :** a material of tar and aggregates mixed in a plant and shaped on the roadway

tarn \'tärn\ n [of Scand origin] : a small mountain lake or pool

1tar·nish \'tär-nish\ vb [MF terniss-, ternir] **1 :** to make or become dull, dim, or discolored ⟨silver tarnishes⟩ **2 :** IMPAIR, SULLY ⟨a tarnished reputation⟩ — **tar·nish·a·ble** \-ə-bəl\ adj

2tarnish n **1 :** tarnished condition **2 :** a surface film (as of oxide or sulfide) formed or deposited in tarnishing ⟨hard to get all the tarnish off silver⟩

ta·ro \'tär-ō, 'tar-, 'ter-\ n, pl **taros** [Tahitian & Maori] : a plant of the arum family grown throughout the tropics for its edible starchy tuberous rootstocks; also : this rootstock

tarp \'tärp\ n : TARPAULIN

tar paper n : a building felt coated or impregnated with tar or asphalt

tar·pau·lin \tär-'pó-lən, 'tär-pə-\ n : waterproofed material and esp. canvas used in sheets for protecting exposed objects

tar·pon \'tär-pən\ n, pl **tarpon** or **tarpons** : a large silvery sport fish common off the Florida coast

tar·ra·gon \'tar-ə-,gän, -gən\ n [MF targon, fr. Ar ṭarkhūn] : a small European wormwood grown for its pungent aromatic foliage used esp. in pickles and vinegar

1tar·ry \'tar-ē\ vi **tar·ried; tar·ry·ing** [ME tarien] **1 :** to be tardy : DELAY, LINGER **2 :** to abide or stay in or at a place : SOJOURN

2tar·ry \'tär-ē\ adj : of, resembling, or covered with tar

1tar·sal \'tär-səl\ adj : of or relating to the tarsus

2tarsal n : a tarsal part (as a bone or cartilage)

tar·si·er \'tär-sē-,ā, -sē-ər\ n [F, fr. tarse tarsus, fr. NL tarsus] : any of several small nocturnal arboreal East Indian mammals related to the lemurs — **tar·si·oid** \-sē-,óid\ adj or n

tar·sus \'tär-səs\ n, pl **tar·si** \-,sī, -,sē\ [NL, fr. Gk tarsos wickerwork mat, flat of the foot, ankle] **1 :** the part of the foot of a vertebrate between the metatarsus and the leg; also : the small bones that support this part of the limb **2 :** the shank of a bird's leg **3 :** the distal part of the limb of an arthropod

1tart \'tärt\ adj [OE teart sharp, severe] **1 :** agreeably

sharp to the taste : pleasantly acid **2 :** BITING, CAUSTIC **syn** see SOUR — **tart·ly** adv — **tart·ness** n

2tart n [MF tarte] **1 :** a small pie or pastry shell containing jelly, custard, or fruit **2 :** PROSTITUTE

1tar·tan \'tärt-ᵊn\ n **1 :** a plaid textile design of Scottish origin usu. distinctively patterned to designate a clan **2 :** a fabric or garment with tartan design

2tar·tan \'tärt-ᵊn, tär-'tan\ n : a Mediterranean coasting vessel with one mast carrying a large lateen sail

1tar·tar \'tärt-ər\ n [ML tartarum] **1 :** a substance consisting essentially of cream of tartar found in the juice of grapes and deposited in wine casks as a reddish crust or sediment **2 :** an incrustation on the teeth consisting of saliva, food residue, and various calcium salts

tartan

2tartar n **1** cap : a native or inhabitant of Tatary **2 :** a bad-tempered or unexpectedly formidable person — **Tartar** adj — **Tar·tar·i·an** \tär-'tar-ē-ən, -'ter-\ adj

tartar emetic n : a poisonous salt of sweetish metallic taste that is used in dyeing and in medicine esp. in the treatment of amebic dysentery

tar·tar·ic acid \tär-,tar-ik-\ n : a strong organic acid $C_4H_6O_6$ that occurs in four forms, is usu. obtained from grape tartar, and is used esp. in food and medicines and in photography

tar·tar sauce or **tar·tare sauce** \,tärt-ər-\ n : mayonnaise with chopped pickles, olives, capers, and parsley

Tar·ta·rus \'tärt-ə-rəs\ n : the infernal regions of ancient classical mythology

tart·ish \'tärt-ish\ adj : somewhat tart — **tart·ish·ly** adv

tart·let \'tärt-lət\ n : a small tart

tar·trate \'tär-,trāt\ n : a salt or ester of tartaric acid

Tar·via \'tär-vē-ə\ trademark — used for a viscid surfacing and binding material for roads that is made from coal tar

Tar·zan \'tärz-ᵊn, 'tär-,zan\ n [Tarzan, hero of adventure stories by Edgar Rice Burroughs] : a strong agile person of heroic proportions and bearing

task \'task\ n [ONF tasque, fr. ML tasca tax or service imposed by a feudal superior, fr. ML taxare to tax] : a piece of work esp. as assigned by another : DUTY, FUNCTION

syn TASK, DUTY, ASSIGNMENT, JOB mean a piece of work to be done. TASK implies work imposed by one in authority or by circumstance ⟨every child in the household had his task to perform daily⟩ DUTY implies an obligation to perform or responsibility for performance ⟨the limits of his duties as guardian⟩ ASSIGNMENT implies a definite limited task assigned by one in authority; JOB applies to a piece of work one is asked to do or agrees to do voluntarily ⟨a man to do jobs around the house⟩ and often stresses quality or difficulty of performance ⟨did a good job on his research project⟩

task force n : a temporary grouping esp. of armed forces units to accomplish a particular objective

task·mas·ter \'task-,mas-tər\ n : one that imposes a task or burdens another with labor — **task·mis·tress** \-,mis-trəs\ n

task·work \-,wərk\ n **1 :** PIECEWORK **2 :** hard work

Tas·ma·ni·an devil \taz-,mā-nē-ən-\ n : a powerful stocky burrowing carnivorous marsupial of Tasmania

Tasmanian wolf n : a carnivorous marsupial formerly common in Australia that somewhat resembles a dog

1tas·sel \'tas-əl also esp of corn 'täs-, 'tós-\ n [OF, clasp, tassel, fr. L taxillus small die] **1 :** a hanging ornament made of a bunch of cords of even length fastened at one end **2 :** something resembling a tassel; esp : the terminal male inflorescence of Indian corn

2tassel vb **-seled** or **-selled; -sel·ing** or **-sel·ling** \-(ə-)liŋ\ : to adorn with or put forth tassels

1taste \'tāst\ vb [OF taster to touch, taste, fr. (assumed) VL taxitare, freq. of L taxare to touch] **1 :** EXPERIENCE, UNDERGO **2 :** to try or determine the flavor of something by taking a little into the mouth **3 a :** to eat or drink esp. in small quantities **b :** to experience slightly **4 :** to perceive or recognize as if by the sense of taste **5 :** to have a specific flavor — **tast·er** n

2taste n **1 a :** a small amount tasted **b :** a small sample of experience ⟨first *taste* of battle⟩ **2** : the one of the special senses that perceives and distinguishes the sweet, sour, bitter, or salty quality of a dissolved substance and is mediated by receptors in the taste buds of the tongue **3 a** : the objective quality of a dissolved substance perceptible to the sense of taste **b** : a complex sensation resulting from usu. combined stimulation of the senses of taste, smell, and touch : FLAVOR **4** : the distinctive quality of an experience **5** : individual preference : INCLINATION **6 a** : critical judgment, discernment, or appreciation **b** : manner or aesthetic quality indicative of discernment or appreciation

syn TASTE, RELISH, GUSTO mean a liking for something that gives pleasure. TASTE may imply a natural or acquired specific liking or interest; RELISH suggests a capability for keen gratification of appetite or other senses; GUSTO implies a heartiness in relishing that goes with vitality or high spirits

taste bud *n* : any of the sensory organs by which taste is perceived and which lie chiefly in the epithelium of the tongue
taste·ful \'tāst-fəl\ *adj* : having, showing, or conforming to good taste — **taste·ful·ly** \-fə-lē\ *adv* — **taste·ful·ness** *n*
taste·less \'tāst-ləs\ *adj* **1** : lacking flavor : FLAT, INSIPID **2** : not having or showing good taste ⟨*tasteless* decorations⟩ — **taste·less·ly** *adv* — **taste·less·ness** *n*
tasty \'tā-stē\ *adj* **tast·i·er; -est 1** : pleasing to the taste : SAVORY **2** : TASTEFUL — **tast·i·ly** \-stə-lē\ *adv* — **tast·i·ness** \-stē-nəs\ *n*
tat \'tat\ *vb* **tat·ted; tat·ting** : to work at or make by tatting
Ta·tar \'tät-ər\ *n* : a member of any of numerous chiefly Turkic peoples found mainly in the Tatar Republic of the U.S.S.R., the north Caucasus, Crimea, and parts of Siberia
¹tat·ter \'tat-ər\ *n* [of Scand origin] **1** : a part torn and left hanging : SHRED **2** *pl* : tattered clothing : RAGS
²tatter *vb* : to make or become ragged
tat·ter·de·ma·lion \,tat-ərd-i-'māl-yən\ *n* : a person dressed in ragged clothing : RAGAMUFFIN
tat·tered \'tat-ərd\ *adj* **1** : wearing ragged clothes ⟨a *tattered* barefoot boy⟩ **2** : torn in shreds : RAGGED ⟨*tattered* flag⟩; *also* : DILAPIDATED
tat·ter·sall \'tat-ər-,sól\ *n* [*Tattersall's* horse market, London, England] **1** : a pattern of colored lines forming squares of solid background **2** : a fabric woven or printed in a tattersall pattern
tat·ting \'tat-iŋ\ *n* **1** : a delicate handmade lace formed usu. by looping and knotting with a single thread and a small shuttle **2** : the act or process of making tatting
¹tat·tle \'tat-ªl\ *vb* **tat·tled; tat·tling** \'tat-liŋ, -ªl-iŋ\ [MD *tatelen*] **1** : CHATTER, PRATTLE **2** : to tell secrets : BLAB
²tattle *n* **1** : idle talk : CHATTER **2** : GOSSIP, TALEBEARING
tat·tler \'tat-lər, -ªl-ər\ *n* **1** : TATTLETALE **2** : any of various slender long-legged shorebirds (as the willet and yellowlegs) with a loud and frequent call
tat·tle·tale \'tat-ªl-,tāl\ *n* : one that tattles : INFORMER
¹tat·too \ta-'tü\ *n, pl* **tattoos** [D *taptoe*, fr. the phrase *tap toe!* taps shut!] **1 a** : a call sounded shortly before taps as notice to go to quarters **b** : outdoor military exercise given by troops as evening entertainment **2** : a rapid rhythmic rapping ⟨the horse's hoofs beat a *tattoo* on the road⟩
²tattoo *n* [Tahitian *tatau*] : an indelible mark or figure fixed upon the body by insertion of pigment under the skin or by production of scars
³tattoo *vt* **1** : to mark or color (the skin) with tattoos **2** : to mark the skin with (a tattoo) ⟨*tattooed* a flag on his chest⟩ — **tat·too·er** *n*
tau \'taú, 'tó\ *n* : the 19th letter of the Greek alphabet— T or τ
taught *past of* TEACH
¹taunt \'tónt, 'tänt\ *vt* : to reproach or challenge in a mocking or insulting manner : jeer at — **taunt·er** *n* — **taunt·ing·ly** \-iŋ-lē\ *adv*
²taunt *n* : a sarcastic or jeering challenge or insult
taupe \'tōp\ *n* [F, lit., mole] : a brownish gray
tau·rine \'tór-,īn\ *adj* [L *taurus* bull] **1** : of, relating to, or befitting a bull ⟨*taurine* moral standards⟩ **2** : of or

relating to the common domestic cattle as distinguished from Indian humped cattle
Tau·rus \'tór-əs\ *n* [L, lit., bull] **1** : a zodiacal constellation that contains the Pleiades and Hyades and is represented pictorially by a bull's forequarters **2** : the 2d sign of the zodiac — see ZODIAC table
taut \'tót\ *adj* [ME *tought*] **1 a** : tightly drawn : not slack ⟨*taut* rope⟩ **b** : HIGH-STRUNG, TENSE ⟨*taut* nerves⟩ **2 a** : kept in proper order or condition ⟨a *taut* ship⟩ **b** : not loose or flabby : FIRM syn see TIGHT — **taut·ly** *adv* — **taut·ness** *n*
taut·en \'tót-ªn\ *vb* **taut·ened; taut·en·ing** \'tót-niŋ, -ªn-iŋ\ : to make or become taut
tau·tog \tó-'tóg\ *n* [of Algonquian origin] : an edible fish related to the wrasses and found along the Atlantic coast of the U.S. — called also *blackfish*
tau·tol·o·gy \tó-'täl-ə-jē\ *n, pl* **-gies** [Gk *tauto* the same, contr. of *to auto*] **1** : needless repetition of an idea, statement, or word; *also* : an instance of such repetition **2** : a statement true by virtue of its logical form alone — **tau·to·log·i·cal** \,tót-ªl-'äj-i-kəl\ *adj* — **tau·to·log·i·cal·ly** \-k(ə-)lē\ *adv* — **tau·tol·o·gous** \tó-'täl-ə-gəs\ *adj* — **tau·tol·o·gous·ly** *adv*
tav·ern \'tav-ərn\ *n* [OF *taverne*, fr. L *taberna*, lit., shed, hut] **1** : an establishment where alcoholic liquors are sold to be drunk on the premises **2** : INN
tav·ern·er \'tav-ə(r)-nər\ *n* : one who keeps a tavern
taw \'tó\ *n* **1** : a marble used as a shooter **2** : the line from which players shoot at marbles
taw·dry \'tód-rē, 'täd-\ *adj* **taw·dri·er; -est** [*tawdry lace* tie of lace for the neck, fr. *St. Audrey* (Etheldreda) *d*679 queen of Northumbria] : cheap and gaudy in appearance and quality — **taw·dri·ly** \-rə-lē\ *adv* — **taw·dri·ness** \-rē-nəs\ *n*
¹taw·ny \'tó-nē, 'tän-ē\ *adj* **taw·ni·er; -est** [MF *tanné*, pp. of *tanner* to tan] : of the color tawny — **taw·ni·ness** *n*
²tawny *n, pl* **tawnies** : a brownish orange to light brown color
¹tax \'taks\ *vt* [ML *taxare*, fr. L, to feel, estimate, censure, freq. of *tangere* to touch] **1** : to levy a tax on **2** : to call to account for something : CENSURE ⟨*taxed* him with neglect of his duty⟩ **3** : to make onerous and rigorous demands upon : subject to excessive stress ⟨*tax* one's strength⟩ — **tax·a·bil·i·ty** \,tak-sə-'bil-ət-ē\ *n* — **tax·a·ble** \'tak-sə-bəl\ *adj* — **tax·er** *n*
²tax *n* **1 a** : a charge usu. of money imposed by authority upon persons or property for public purposes **b** : a sum levied on members of an organization to defray expenses **2** : something (as an effort or duty) that makes heavy demands : STRAIN
tax·a·tion \tak-'sā-shən\ *n* **1** : the action of taxing; *esp* : the imposition of taxes **2** : revenue obtained from taxes
tax-ex·empt \,taks-ig-'zem(p)t\ *adj* : exempted from a tax; *also* : bearing interest free from federal or state income tax ⟨*tax-exempt* securities⟩
¹taxi \'tak-sē\ *n, pl* **tax·is** \-sēz\ *also* **tax·ies** : TAXICAB; *also* : a similarly operated boat or airplane
²taxi *vb* **tax·ied; taxi·ing** *or* **taxy·ing; tax·is** \-sēz\ *or* **tax·ies 1 a** : to ride in a taxicab **b** : to transport by taxi **2** : to go at low speed along the surface of the ground ⟨the plane *taxied* into the wind⟩ ⟨*taxied* the plane over to the hangar⟩
taxi·cab \'tak-sē-,kab\ *n* [fr. earlier *taximeter cab*, fr. *taximeter* instrument for automatically determining the fare of a hired vehicle, fr. ML *taxa* tax, charge, fr. *taxare* to tax] : an automobile that carries passengers for a fare usu. determined by the distance traveled and often shown by a meter
taxi dancer *n* : a girl employed by a dance hall, café, or cabaret to dance with patrons who pay a certain amount for each dance
tax·i·der·my \'tak-sə-,dər-mē\ *n* [Gk *taxis* arrangement + *derma* skin] : the art of preparing, stuffing, and mounting skins of animals — **tax·i·der·mic** \,tak-sə-'dər-mik\ *adj* — **tax·i·der·mist** \'tak-sə-,dər-məst\ *n*
taxi·me·ter \'tak-sē-,mēt-ər\ *n* : an instrument for use in a hired vehicle (as a taxicab) for automatically showing the fare due
tax·is \'tak-səs\ *n, pl* **tax·es** \'tak-,sēz\ [Gk, arrangement, fr. *tassein* to arrange] : reflex movement by a freely motile organism in relation to a source of stimulation (as a light or a temperature or chemical gradient); *also* : a

reflex reaction involving such movement — compare TROPISM

taxi stand *n* : a place where taxis may park awaiting hire

tax·on \'tak-,sän\ *n, pl* **taxa** \-sə\ *also* **tax·ons** [NL, back-formation fr. *taxonomia* taxonomy] : a taxonomic group or entity; *also* : its name in a formal system of nomenclature

tax·on·o·my \tak-'sän-ə-mē\ *n* [F *taxonomie*, fr. Gk *taxis* arrangement + *nom-, nemein* to control, distribute] **1** : the study of scientific classification : SYSTEMATICS **2** : CLASSIFICATION; *esp* : orderly classification of plants and animals according to their presumed natural relationships — **tax·o·nom·ic** \,tak-sə-'näm-ik\ *adj* — **tax·o·nom·i·cal·ly** \-'näm-i-k(ə-)lē\ *adv* — **tax·on·o·mist** \tak-'sän-ə-məst\ *n*

tax·pay·er \'taks-,pā-ər\ *n* : one that pays or is liable for a tax

tax·us \'tak-səs\ *n, pl* **tax·us** \-səs\ [L] : YEW 1a

TB \(')tē-'bē\ *n* [*TB* (abbr. for *tubercle bacillus*)] : TUBERCULOSIS

tea \'tē\ *n* [Chin (Amoy dial.) *t'e*] **1 a** : a shrub related to the camellia that has lance-shaped leaves and fragrant white flowers and is grown mainly in China, Japan, India, and Ceylon   **b** : the leaves and leaf buds of this plant prepared for use in beverages usu. by immediate curing by heat or by such curing following a period of fermentation — called also respectively *green tea, black tea;* compare OOLONG   **c** : an aromatic beverage prepared from tea by steeping in boiling water   **2** : any of various plants used like tea; *also* : an infusion from their leaves used medicinally or as a beverage   **3 a** : a late afternoon serving of tea and a light meal   **b** : a party or reception at which tea is served

tea bag *n* : a cloth or filter-paper bag holding enough tea for an individual serving

tea ball *n* : a perforated metal ball for making tea in cups or in a teapot

tea·ber·ry \'tē-,ber-ē\ *n* : CHECKERBERRY

tea biscuit *n, Brit* : CRACKER, COOKIE

teach \'tēch\ *vb* **taught** \'tȯt\; **teach·ing** [OE *tæcan*] **1** : to assist in learning how to do something : show how ⟨*teach* a child to read⟩   **2** : to guide the studies of : INSTRUCT ⟨*teach* the senior class⟩   **3** : to give lessons in : instruct pupils in ⟨*teach* music⟩   **4** : to be a teacher   **5** : to cause to learn : cause to know the consequences of an action ⟨*taught* by experience⟩

syn INSTRUCT, EDUCATE, TRAIN: TEACH applies to any manner of imparting information or skill so that others may learn; INSTRUCT suggests methodical or formal teaching ⟨*instructed* him in swimming⟩ EDUCATE suggests providing formal schooling for fostering mental, moral, and physical growth and maturity and usu. stresses book learning; TRAIN stresses instruction and drill with a specific end in view ⟨athletic *training*⟩ ⟨*trained* singers in operatic roles⟩ **syn** see in addition LEARN

teach·a·ble \'tē-chə-bəl\ *adj* **1** : capable of being taught; *esp* : apt and willing to learn   **2** : well adapted for use in teaching ⟨a *teachable* textbook⟩ — **teach·a·bil·i·ty** \,tē-chə-'bil-ət-ē\ *n*

teach·er \'tē-chər\ *n* : one that teaches; *esp* : one whose occupation is to instruct

teachers college *n* : a college for the training of teachers usu. offering a full 4-year course and granting a bachelor's degree

teach·ing *n* **1** : the act, practice, or profession of a teacher   **2** : something taught; *esp* : DOCTRINE

tea·cup \'tē-,kəp\ *n* : a cup usu. of less than 8-oz. capacity used with a saucer for hot beverages

tea·cup·ful \-,ful\ *n, pl* **-cupfuls** \-,fulz\ *or* **-cups·ful** \-,kəps-,ful\ : as much as a teacup can hold

tea dance *n* : a dance held in the late afternoon

tea garden *n* **1** : a public garden where tea and other refreshments are served   **2** : a tea plantation

tea·house \'tē-,haus\ *n* : a public house or restaurant where tea and light refreshments are sold

teak \'tēk\ *n* [Pg *teca*, of Dravidian origin] : a tall East Indian timber tree of the vervain family; *also* : its hard durable yellowish brown wood

tea·ket·tle \'tē-,ket-ᵊl\ *n* : a covered kettle with a handle and spout for boiling water

teak·wood \'tēk-,wud\ *n* : TEAK

teal \'tēl\ *n, pl* **teal** *or* **teals** [ME *tele*] : any of several small short-necked river ducks of Europe and America

¹team \'tēm\ *n* [OE *tēam* group of draft animals; akin to E **¹tow**] **1** : a group of animals: as   **a** : two or more draft animals harnessed to the same vehicle or implement; *also* : one or more animals with harness and attached vehicle   **b** : a brood esp. of young pigs or ducks   **c** : a matched group of animals for exhibition   **2** : a number of persons associated together in work or activity: as   **a** : a group on one side in a match   **b** : CREW, GANG

²team *vb* **1** : to yoke or join in a team   **2** : to haul with or drive a team   **3** : to form a team ⟨*team* up together⟩

team·mate \'tēm-,māt\ *n* : a fellow member of a team

team·ster \'tēm(p)-stər\ *n* : one who drives a team or motortruck esp. as an occupation

team·work \'tēm-,wərk\ *n* : the work or activity of a number of persons acting in close association as members of a unit ⟨*teamwork* won the game⟩

tea·pot \'tē-,pät\ *n* : a vessel with a spout for brewing and serving tea

tea·poy \'tē-,pȯi\ *n* [Hindi *tipaī*] **1** : a three-legged ornamental stand   **2** : a stand for a tea service

¹tear \'ti(ə)r\ *n* [OE *tæhher, tēar*] **1** : a drop of the salty liquid that keeps the eye and the inner eyelids moist   **2** : a transparent drop of fluid or hardened fluid matter (as resin) — **teary** \'ti(ə)r-ē\ *adj*

²tear *vi* : to shed tears

³tear \'ta(ə)r, 'te(ə)r\ *vb* **tore** \'tō(ə)r, 'tȯ(ə)r\; **torn** \'tōrn, 'tȯrn\; **tear·ing** [OE *teran*] **1** : to separate or pull apart by force : REND; *also* : LACERATE ⟨*tear* the skin⟩   **2** : to divide or disrupt by the pull of contrary forces ⟨a mind *torn* with doubts⟩   **3** : to remove by force : WRENCH ⟨children *torn* away from their mothers⟩   **4** : to effect by force or violent means ⟨the raging waters *tore* a hole in the wall⟩   **5** : to move or act with violence, haste, or force ⟨went *tearing* down the street⟩⟨*tore* through his homework in an hour⟩ — **tear·er** *n*

⁴tear \'ta(ə)r, 'te(ə)r\ *n* **1 a** : the act of tearing   **b** : damage from being torn; *esp* : a torn place : RENT   **2 a** : a hurried pace : HURRY   **b** : SPREE ⟨go on a *tear*⟩

tear down *vt* **1 a** : to cause to decompose or disintegrate : DESTROY   **b** : VILIFY, DENIGRATE   **2** : to take apart : DISASSEMBLE

tear·drop \'ti(ə)r-,dräp\ *n* **1** : ¹TEAR 1   **2** : something shaped like a dropping tear; *esp* : a pendent gem on an earring or necklace

tear·ful \'ti(ə)r-fəl\ *adj* : flowing with, accompanied by, or causing tears — **tear·ful·ly** \-fə-lē\ *adv* — **tear·ful·ness** *n*

tear gas *n* : a solid, liquid, or gaseous substance that on dispersion in the atmosphere blinds the eyes with tears

tear·jerk·er \'ti(ə)r-,jər-kər\ *n* : an extravagantly pathetic story, play, film, or broadcast — **tear·jerk·ing** \-,kiŋ\ *adj*

tea·room \'tē-,rüm, -,rum\ *n* : a small restaurant serving light meals

tear·stain \'ti(ə)r-,stān\ *n* : a spot or streak left by tears — **tear·stained** \-,stānd\ *adj*

¹tease \'tēz\ *vt* [OE *tǣsan*] **1 a** : to disentangle and lay parallel by combing or carding ⟨*tease* wool⟩   **b** : TEASEL   **2 a** : to annoy persistently : PESTER, TORMENT   **b** : TANTALIZE — **teas·er** *n*

²tease *n* **1** : the act of teasing : the state of being teased   **2** : one that teases

¹tea·sel *or* **tea·zel** *or* **tea·zle** \'tē-zəl\ *n* [OE *tǣsel*, fr. *tǣsan* to tease] **1** : any of a genus of Old World prickly herbs; *esp* : one with flower heads covered with stiff hooked bracts — called also *fuller's teasel*   **2 a** : a dried flower head of the fuller's teasel used to raise a nap on woolen cloth   **b** : a wire substitute for the fuller's teasel

²teasel *vt* **tea·seled** *or* **tea·selled**; **tea·sel·ing** *or* **tea·sel·ling** \'tēz-(ə-)liŋ\ : to raise a nap on (cloth) with teasels

tea·spoon \'tē-,spün, -'spün\ *n* **1** : a small spoon used esp. for eating soft foods and stirring beverages   **2** : TEASPOONFUL

teasel

tea·spoon·ful \-,ful\ *n, pl* **-spoonfuls** \-,fulz\ *or* **-spoons·ful** \-,spünz-,ful, -'spünz-\ **1** : as much as a teaspoon can hold **2** : a unit of measure used esp. in cookery equal to 1⅓ fluidrams or one third of a tablespoonful

teat \'tit, 'tēt\ *n* [OF *tete*, of Gmc origin; akin to E *tit*] **1** : the protuberance through which milk is drawn from an udder or breast : NIPPLE **2** : a small projection (as on a mechanical part) — **teat·ed** \-əd\ *adj*

tea time \'tē-,tīm\ *n* : the customary time for tea : late afternoon or early evening

tea wagon *n* : a small table on wheels used in serving tea and light refreshments

tech·ne·tium \tek-'nē-sh(ē-)əm\ *n* [NL, fr. Gk *technētos* artificial, fr. *technē* art] : a metallic chemical element obtained by bombarding molybdenum and in the fission of uranium — see ELEMENT table

tech·nic \'tek-nik, *for 1 also* tek-'nēk\ *n* **1** : TECHNIQUE 1 **2** *pl* : TECHNOLOGY 1a

tech·ni·cal \'tek-ni-kəl\ *adj* [Gk *technē* art, skill] **1 a** : having special usu. practical knowledge esp. of a mechanical or scientific subject 〈*technical* experts〉 **b** : marked by or characteristic of specialization 〈*technical* language〉 **2** : of or relating to a particular subject; *esp* : of or relating to a practical subject organized on scientific principles 〈*technical* training〉 **3** : existing by application of the laws or rules 〈a *technical* knockout〉 **4** : of or relating to technique 〈shows *technical* virtuosity but no creative artistry〉 **5** : of, relating to, or produced by commercial processes 〈*technical* sulfuric acid〉 — **tech·ni·cal·ly** \-k(ə-)lē\ *adv*

tech·ni·cal·i·ty \,tek-nə-'kal-ət-ē\ *n, pl* **-ties** **1** : the quality or state of being technical **2** : something technical; *esp* : a detail meaningful only to a specialist

technical sergeant *n* : a noncommissioned officer in the air force ranking above a staff sergeant and below a master sergeant

tech·ni·cian \tek-'nish-ən\ *n* : a person skilled in the technical details or in the technique of a subject, art, or occupation

tech·nique \tek-'nēk\ *n* [F, fr. *technique* technical] **1** : the manner in which technical details are treated (as by a writer) or basic physical movements are used (as by a dancer); *also* : ability in such treatment or use 〈faultless piano *technique*〉 **2 a** : technical methods esp. in scientific research 〈laboratory *technique*〉 **b** : a method of accomplishing a desired aim 〈a *technique* for handling complaints〉

tech·noc·ra·cy \tek-'näk-rə-sē\ *n* : management of society by technical experts

tech·no·log·i·cal \,tek-nə-'läj-i-kəl\ *or* **tech·no·log·ic** \-'läj-ik\ *adj* : of, relating to, or characterized or caused by technology 〈*technological* advance〉 〈*technological* unemployment〉 — **tech·no·log·i·cal·ly** \-'läj-i-k(ə-)lē\ *adv*

tech·nol·o·gist \tek-'näl-ə-jəst\ *n* : a specialist in technology

tech·nol·o·gy \-jē\ *n, pl* **-gies** [Gk *technē* art, skill] **1 a** : applied science **b** : a technical method of achieving a practical purpose **2** : the means employed to provide objects for human sustenance and comfort

ted \'ted\ *vt* **ted·ded; ted·ding** : to spread or turn and scatter (as new-mown grass) for drying — **ted·der** *n*

ted·dy bear \'ted-ē-\ *n* [*Teddy*, nickname of President Theodore Roosevelt; fr. a cartoon showing him sparing the life of a bear cub while hunting] : a stuffed toy bear

Te De·um \(')tā-'dā-əm, (')tē-'dē-\ *n, pl* **Te Deums** [LL *Te Deum laudamus* Thee, God, we praise] : an ancient liturgical hymn of praise to God

te·dious \'tēd-ē-əs, 'tē-jəs\ *adj* : tiresome because of length or dullness : BORING — **te·dious·ly** *adv* — **te·dious·ness** *n*

te·di·um \'tēd-ē-əm\ *n* [L *taedium* disgust, irksomeness, fr. *taedēre* to disgust, weary] : the quality or state of being tedious : TEDIOUSNESS; *also* : BOREDOM

¹tee \'tē\ *n* : the area from which a golf ball is struck in starting play on a hole; *also* : a tiny mound or a small peg with concave top on which the ball is set to be struck

²tee *vb* **teed; tee·ing** **1** : to place (a ball) on a tee — often used with *up* **2** : to drive a golf ball from a tee; *also* : BEGIN, START — usu. used with *off*

teem \'tēm\ *vi* [OE *tieman* to bring forth, give birth to] **1** : to become filled to overflowing : ABOUND 〈lakes *teem* with fish〉 **2** : to be present in large quantity

teen \'tēn\ *adj* : TEEN-AGE

teen·age \'tēn-,āj\ *or* **teen·aged** \-,ājd\ *adj* : of, being, or relating to people in their teens

teen·ag·er \-,ā-jər\ *n* : a person in his teens.

teens \'tēnz\ *n pl* **1** : the numbers 13 through 19; *esp* : the years 13 through 19 in a lifetime or century **2** : TEEN-AGERS

tee·ny \'tē-nē\ *adj* **tee·ni·er; -est** : TINY

tee·pee *var of* TEPEE

tee shirt *var of* T-SHIRT

tee·ter \'tēt-ər\ *vi* [ME *titeren*] **1 a** : to move unsteadily : WOBBLE 〈*teetered* on the edge and fell over the side〉 **b** : WAVER, VACILLATE **2** : SEESAW — **teeter** *n*

tee·ter·board \-,bōrd, -,bȯrd\ *n* **1** : SEESAW 2b **2** : a board placed on a raised support in such a way that a person standing on one end of the board is thrown into the air if another person jumps on the opposite end

teeth *pl of* TOOTH

teethe \'tēth\ *vi* : to cut one's teeth : grow teeth

teeth·ridge \'tēth-,rij\ *n* : the inner surface of the gums of the upper front teeth

tee·to·tal·er *or* **tee·to·tal·ler** \'tē-'tōt-ᵊl-ər\ *n* [*total* + *total* (abstinence)] : a person who completely abstains from alcoholic liquor

tee·to·tal·ism \-ᵊl-,iz-əm\ *n* : the principle or practice of complete abstinence from alcoholic drinks

teg·u·ment \'teg-yə-mənt\ *n* [L *tegumentum* covering, fr. *tegere* to cover] : INTEGUMENT — **teg·u·men·ta·ry** \,teg-yə-'ment-ə-rē, -'men-trē\ *adj*

tek·tite \'tek-,tīt\ *n* [Gk *tēktos* molten, fr. *tēkein* to melt] : a glassy body of probably meteoric origin and of rounded but indefinite shape

Tel-Au·to·graph \tel-'ȯt-ə-,graf\ *trademark* — used for a telegraph for reproducing graphic matter (as writing or pictures) by means of a pen whose movements are the same as those of a pen at the sending station

tele- *or* **tel-** *comb form* [Gk *tēle* far off] **1** : at a distance 〈*telegram*〉 〈*telepathy*〉 **2** : television 〈*telecast*〉

tele·cam·era \'tel-i-,kam-(ə-)rə\ *n* : a television camera

tele·cast \'tel-i-,kast\ *vb* **telecast** *also* **tele·cast·ed; tele·cast·ing** [*tele-* + broad*cast*] : to broadcast by television — **telecast** *n* — **tele·cast·er** *n*

tele·com·mu·ni·ca·tion \,tel-i-kə-,myü-nə-'kā-shən\ *n* : communication at a distance (as by cable, radio, telegraph, telephone, or television)

tele·course \'tel-i-,kōrs, -,kȯrs\ *n* : a course of study conducted over television

tel·e·gen·ic \,tel-ə-'jen-ik, -'jēn-\ *adj* : suitable for television broadcast — **tel·e·gen·i·cal·ly** \-i-k(ə-)lē\ *adv*

tel·e·gram \'tel-ə-,gram, *South also* -grəm\ *n* : a message sent by telegraph

¹tel·e·graph \-,graf\ *n* : an apparatus for communication at a distance by coded signals; *esp* : an apparatus, system, or process for communication at a distance by electric transmission of such signals over wire — **tel·e·graph·ic** \,tel-ə-'graf-ik\ *adj* — **tel·e·graph·i·cal·ly** \-'graf-i-k(ə-)lē\ *adv*

²telegraph *vt* **1 a** : to send by or as if by telegraph **b** : to send a telegram to **c** : to send (as flowers or money) by means of a telegraphic order **2** : to make known by signs esp. unknowingly and in advance 〈*telegraph* a punch〉 — **te·leg·ra·pher** \tə-'leg-rə-fər\ *n* — **te·leg·ra·phist** \-fəst\ *n*

te·leg·ra·phy \tə-'leg-rə-fē\ *n* : the use or operation of a telegraph apparatus or system

tele·lens \'tel-i-,lenz\ *n* : a telephoto lens

Te·lem·a·chus \tə-'lem-ə-kəs\ *n* : a son of Odysseus and Penelope who after failing to find his father returns home in time to help slay his mother's suitors

¹tel·e·me·ter \'tel-ə-,mēt-ər\ *n* : an electrical apparatus for measuring something (as pressure, speed, or temperature), transmitting the result esp. by radio to a distant station, and there indicating the measurement — **tel·e·met·ric** \,tel-ə-'me-trik\ *adj* — **tel·e·met·ri·cal·ly** \-tri-k(ə-)lē\ *adv* — **te·lem·e·try** \tə-'lem-ə-trē\ *n*

²telemeter *vt* : to transmit (the measurement of something) by telemeter 〈data *telemetered* from a rocket〉

tel·e·ol·o·gist \,tel-ē-'äl-ə-jəst, ,tē-lē-\ *n* : a specialist or believer in teleology

tel·e·ol·o·gy \,tel-ē-'äl-ə-jē, ,tē-lē-\ *n* [Gk *tele-, telos* end, purpose] : a doctrine that attributes a purpose to nature or that explains natural phenomena as directed toward some goal — **tel·e·o·log·i·cal** \,tel-ē-ə-'läj-i-kəl, ,tē-lē-\ *adj*

tel·e·ost \'tel-ē-,äst, 'tē-lē-\ *n* [Gk *teleios* complete, perfect (fr. *telos* end) + *osteon* bone] : any of a group (Teleostei or Teleostomi) of fishes comprising those with a bony rather than a cartilaginous skeleton and including all jawed fishes with the exception of the elasmobranchs and sometimes of the ganoids and dipnoans — **teleost** *adj* —
tel·e·os·te·an \,tel-ē-'äs-tē-ən, ,tē-lē-\ *adj or n*
tel·e·o·stome \'tel-ē-ə-,stōm, 'tē-lē-\ *n or adj* [Gk *teleios* complete + *stoma* mouth] : TELEOST

te·lep·a·thy \tə-'lep-ə-thē\ *n* : apparent communication from one mind to another otherwise than through the channels of sense — **tel·e·path·ic** \,tel-ə-'path-ik\ *adj* —
tel·e·path·i·cal·ly \-'path-i-k(ə-)lē\ *adv*

¹tel·e·phone \'tel-ə-,fōn\ *n* : an instrument for reproducing sounds at a distance; *esp* : an instrument for receiving and reproducing the sound of the human voice transmitted from a distance over wires by means of electricity

²telephone *vb* **1** : to communicate by telephone **2** : to send by telephone **3** : to speak to by telephone — **tel·e·phon·er** *n*

tel·e·phon·ic \,tel-ə-'fän-ik\ *adj* **1** : conveying sound to a distance **2** : of, relating to, or conveyed by telephone

te·leph·o·ny \tə-'lef-ə-nē, 'tel-ə-,fō-\ *n* : the use or operation of an apparatus for transmission of sounds between widely removed points with or without connecting wires

¹tele·pho·to \,tel-ə-'fōt-ō\ *adj* : TELEPHOTOGRAPHIC; *esp* : being a camera lens designed to give a large image of a distant object

²telephoto *n* : a telephoto lens

Telephoto *trademark* — used for an apparatus for transmitting photographs electrically or for a photograph so transmitted

tele·pho·tog·ra·phy \,tel-ə-fə-'täg-rə-fē\ *n* **1** : FACSIMILE 2 **2** : the photography of distant objects usu. by a camera provided with a telephoto lens or mounted in place of the eyepiece of a telescope — **tele·pho·to·graph·ic** \-,fōt-ə-'graf-ik\ *adj*

tele·play \'tel-ē-ə-,plā\ *n* : a play written for television
tele·print·er \'tel-ē-,print-ər\ *n* : TELETYPEWRITER
Tele·Promp·Ter \-,präm(p)-tər\ *trademark* — used for a device for unrolling a magnified script in front of a speaker on television

¹tel·e·scope \'tel-ə-,skōp\ *n* **1** : a usu. tubular optical instrument for viewing distant objects and esp. the heavenly bodies by means of the refraction of light rays through a lens or the reflection of light rays by a concave mirror — compare REFLECTOR, REFRACTOR **2** : any of various tubular magnifying optical instruments **3** : RADIO TELESCOPE

²telescope *vb* **1** : to slide or pass or cause to slide or pass one within another like the cylindrical sections of a hand telescope **2** : to force a way into or enter another lengthwise as the result of collision **3** : to run together in order to shorten or simplify : COMPRESS, CONDENSE

telescope box *n* : a 2-piece box in which the sides of one part fit over those of the other

tel·e·scop·ic \,tel-ə-'skäp-ik\ *adj* **1 a** : of, with, or relating to a telescope **b** : suitable for seeing or magnifying distant objects **2** : seen or discoverable only by a telescope ⟨*telescopic* stars⟩ **3** : able to discern objects at a distance : FARSEEING **4** : having parts that telescope — **tel·e·scop·i·cal·ly** \-'skäp-i-k(ə-)lē\ *adv*

tel·e·thon \'tel-ə-,thän\ *n* [*tele-* + *-thon* (as in *marathon*)] : a long television program usu. to solicit funds for a charity

Tele·type \'tel-ə-,tīp\ *trademark* **1** — used for a teletypewriter **2** : a message sent by a Teletype machine
tele·type·writ·er \,tel-ə-'tīp-,rīt-ər\ *n* : a printing telegraph recording like a typewriter
tele·typ·ist \'tel-ə-,tī-pəst\ *n* : one that operates a teletypewriter

tele·view \'tel-ə-,vyü\ *vi* : to observe or watch by means of a television receiver — **tele·view·er** *n*

tel·e·vise \'tel-ə-,vīz\ *vt* [back-formation fr. *television*] : to pick up and usu. to broadcast (as a baseball game) by television

tel·e·vi·sion \'tel-ə-,vizh-ən\ *n* **1** : an electronic system of transmitting transient images of fixed or moving objects together with sound over a wire or through space by apparatus that converts light and sound into electrical waves and reconverts them into visible light rays and audible sound **2** : a television receiving set **3 a** : the television broadcasting industry **b** : television as a medium of communication

television tube *n* : KINESCOPE 1
te·li·o·spore \'tē-lē-ə-,spōr, -,spȯr\ *n* [Gk *teleios* complete, fr. *telos* end] : a thick-walled spore forming the final stage in the life cycle of a rust fungus and giving rise to a basidium — **te·li·o·spor·ic** \,tē-lē-ə-'spōr-ik, -'spȯr-\ *adj*

tell \'tel\ *vb* told \'tōld\; **tell·ing** [OE *tellan*; akin to E *tale*] **1** : COUNT, ENUMERATE **2 a** : to relate in detail : NARRATE ⟨*tell* a story⟩ **b** : SAY, UTTER ⟨*tell* a lie⟩ **3 a** : to make known : DIVULGE, REVEAL ⟨*tell* a secret⟩ **b** : to express in words ⟨can't *tell* you how pleased we are⟩ **4** : to report to : INFORM **5** : ORDER, DIRECT ⟨*told* her to wait⟩ **6** : to ascertain by observing : find out ⟨can *tell* the man's honest⟩ **7** : to act as a talebearer ⟨*tell* on a cheater⟩ **8** : to have a marked effect ⟨the pressure began to *tell* on him⟩ **9** : EVIDENCE, INDICATE

tell·er \'tel-ər\ *n* **1** : one that relates or communicates ⟨a *teller* of tales⟩ **2** : a person who counts votes (as in a legislative body) **3** : a bank employee who receives and pays out money

tell·ing \'tel-iŋ\ *adj* : producing a marked effect : EFFECTIVE, STRIKING ⟨a *telling* argument⟩ — **tell·ing·ly** \-iŋ-lē\ *adv*

tell off *vt* **1** : to number and set apart; *esp* : to detail for special duty **2** : REPRIMAND, SCOLD

¹tell·tale \'tel-,tāl\ *n* **1 a** : TALEBEARER, INFORMER **b** : an outward sign : INDICATION **2** : a device for indicating or recording something: as **a** : a device that shows the position of the helm or rudder **b** : a railroad warning device (as a row of long strips hanging over tracks near the approach to a low overhead bridge)

²telltale *adj* : INFORMING, REVEALING ⟨*telltale* fingerprints⟩
tel·lu·ride \'tel-yə-,rīd\ *n* : a binary compound of tellurium with another element or a radical

tel·lu·ri·um \tə-'lur-ē-əm\ *n* [NL, fr. L *tellur-*, *tellus* the earth] : a chemical element that resembles selenium and sulfur in properties and that occurs in crystalline form, in a dark amorphous form, or combined with metals — see ELEMENT table

tel·ly \'tel-ē\ *n, chiefly Brit* : TELEVISION
te·lome \'tē-,lōm\ *n* [G *telom*, fr. Gk *telos* end] : a basic structural unit of a vascular plant — **te·lo·mic** \tē-'lōm-ik, -'läm-\ *adj*

te·lo·phase \'tē-lə-,fāz, 'tel-ə-\ *n* [Gk *telos* end] : a final stage of mitosis in which new nuclei differentiate — **te·lo·pha·sic** \,tē-lə-'fā-zik, ,tel-ə-\ *adj*

tel·son \'tel-sən\ *n* [Gk, end of a plowed field] : the terminal segment of the body of an arthropod or segmented worm; *esp* : that of a crustacean forming the middle lobe of the tail

tem·blor \'tem-blər, -,blȯr, -,blōr\ *n* [Sp, lit., trembling, fr. *temblar* to tremble, fr. ML *tremulare*] : EARTHQUAKE
tem·er·ar·i·ous \,tem-ə-'rar-ē-əs, -'rer-\ *adj* : marked by temerity : rashly or presumptuously daring : RECKLESS, BRASH — **tem·er·ar·i·ous·ly** *adv*

te·mer·i·ty \tə-'mer-ət-ē\ *n* [L *temeritas*, fr. *temere* at random, rashly] : unreasonable or foolhardy contempt of danger or opposition : RASHNESS

syn AUDACITY : TEMERITY suggests boldness arising from rashness and contempt of danger ⟨had the *temerity* to challenge the dictatorial order⟩ AUDACITY implies a disregard of restraints imposed by prudence or convention ⟨had the *audacity* to come to the party uninvited⟩

¹tem·per \'tem-pər\ *vb* **tem·pered; tem·per·ing** \'tem-p(ə-)riŋ\ [L *temperare* to moderate, mix] **1** : MODERATE, SOFTEN ⟨the mountains *temper* the wind⟩ **2** : to control by reducing : SUBDUE ⟨*temper* one's anger⟩ **3** : to bring to the desired consistency or texture ⟨*temper* modeling clay⟩ **4** : to bring (as steel) to the desired hardness by heating and cooling **5** : to be or become tempered — **tem·per·a·ble** \-p(ə-)rə-bəl\ *adj*

²temper *n* **1** : characteristic tone : TREND, TENDENCY ⟨the *temper* of the times⟩ **2** : high quality of mind or spirit : COURAGE, METTLE **3** : the state of a substance with respect to certain desired qualities (as hardness, elasticity, or workability) ⟨*temper* of a knife blade⟩

4 a : a characteristic cast of mind or state of feeling **:** DISPOSITION **b :** calmness of mind **:** COMPOSURE ⟨lost his *temper*⟩ **c :** state of feeling or frame of mind at a particular time **d :** a state of anger **e :** a proneness to anger ⟨he has a hot *temper*⟩ **syn** see MOOD

tem·pera *also* **tem·po·ra** \'tem-pə-rə\ *n* [It *tempera*, lit., temper] **:** a process of painting in which an albuminous or colloidal medium is employed as a vehicle instead of oil

tem·per·a·ment \'tem-p(ə-)rə-mənt\ *n* [L *temperamentum* mixture, makeup, constitution, fr. *temperare* to mix, temper] **1 :** characteristic or habitual inclination or mode of emotional response ⟨nervous *temperament*⟩ **2 :** excessive sensitiveness or irritability

tem·per·a·men·tal \,tem-p(ə-)rə-'ment-°l\ *adj* **1 :** of, relating to, or arising from temperament ⟨*temperamental* peculiarities⟩ **2 a :** marked by excessive sensitivity and impulsive changes of mood **:** HIGH-STRUNG, EXCITABLE ⟨a *temperamental* opera singer⟩ **b :** UNPREDICTABLE, CAPRICIOUS — **tem·per·a·men·tal·ly** \-°l-ē\ *adv*

tem·per·ance \'tem-p(ə-)rən(t)s\ *n* [L *temperantia*, fr. *temperare* to moderate, be moderate] **1 :** moderation in action, thought, or feeling **:** RESTRAINT **2 :** habitual moderation in the indulgence of the appetites or passions; *esp* **:** moderation in or abstinence from the use of intoxicating drink

tem·per·ate \'tem-p(ə-)rət\ *adj* **1 :** marked by moderation: as **a :** not excessive or extreme **b :** moderate in satisfying one's needs or desires **c :** moderate in the use of liquor **d :** marked by self-control **:** RESTRAINED ⟨*temperate* speech⟩ **2 :** having, found in, or associated with a moderate climate ⟨*temperate* heat⟩ **syn** see MODERATE — **tem·per·ate·ly** *adv* — **tem·per·ate·ness** *n*

temperate zone *n, often cap T&Z* **:** the area or region between the tropic of Cancer and the arctic circle or between the tropic of Capricorn and the antarctic circle — see ZONE illustration

tem·per·a·ture \'tem-pər-,chùr, 'tem-p(ə-)rə-,chùr, -chər\ *n* **1 :** the degree of hotness or coldness of something (as air, water, or the body) as shown by a thermometer **2 :** FEVER ⟨have a *temperature*⟩

tem·pered \'tem-pərd\ *adj* **1 :** having a particular kind of temper ⟨a bad-*tempered* boy⟩ **2 :** brought to the desired state (as of hardness, toughness, or flexibility) ⟨*tempered* steel⟩ ⟨*tempered* glass⟩ **3 :** qualified, lessened, or diluted by the mixture or influence of an additional ingredient **:** MODERATED ⟨justice *tempered* with mercy⟩

tem·pest \'tem-pəst\ *n* [L *tempestas* season, weather, storm, fr. *tempus* time] **1 :** an extensive violent wind; *esp* **:** one accompanied by rain, hail, or snow **2 :** a violent commotion **:** TUMULT, UPROAR

tem·pes·tu·ous \tem-'pes-chə-wəs\ *adj* **:** VIOLENT, STORMY — **tem·pes·tu·ous·ly** *adv* — **tem·pes·tu·ous·ness** *n*

Tem·plar \'tem-plər\ *n* [L *templum* temple] **1 :** a knight of a religious military order established in 1118 in Jerusalem to protect pilgrims and the Holy Sepulcher **2 :** KNIGHT TEMPLAR 2

tem·plate *or* **tem·plet** \'tem-plət\ *n* **:** a gauge, pattern, or mold (as a thin plate or board) used as a guide to the form of a piece being made

¹tem·ple \'tem-pəl\ *n* [L *templum*] **1 :** a building for the worship of a deity **2** *often cap* **:** one of three successive national sanctuaries in ancient Jerusalem **3 :** a building for Mormon sacred ordinances **4 :** a Reform or Conservative synagogue — **tem·pled** \-pəld\ *adj*

²temple *n* [MF, modif. of L *tempora*, pl., temples] **:** the flattened space on each side of the forehead of man and some other mammals

temple (Chinese)

tem·po \'tem-pō\ *n, pl* **tem·pi** \-(,)pē\ *or* **tempos** [It, lit., time, fr. L *tempus*] **1 :** the rate of speed of a musical piece or passage indicated by one of a series of directions (as largo, presto, or allegro) and often by an exact metronome marking **2 :** rate of motion or activity **:** PACE

¹tem·po·ral \'tem-p(ə-)rəl\ *adj* [L *tempor-, tempus* time] **1 :** of or relating to time as opposed to eternity **:** TEMPORARY **2 a :** of or relating to earthly life **b :** of or

relating to lay or secular concerns — **tem·po·ral·ly** \-ē\ *adv*

²temporal *adj* [L *tempora* temples] **:** of or relating to the temples or to the sides of the skull behind the orbits — **tem·po·ral·ly** \-ē\ *adv*

temporal bone *n* **:** a compound bone of the side of the human skull

tem·po·ral·i·ty \,tem-pə-'ral-ət-ē\ *n, pl* **-ties 1 a :** civil or political as distinguished from spiritual or ecclesiastical power or authority **b :** an ecclesiastical property or revenue — often used in pl. **2 :** the quality or state of being temporal

tem·po·rary \'tem-pə-,rer-ē\ *adj* **:** lasting for a time only **:** IMPERMANENT — **tem·po·rar·i·ly** \,tem-pə-'rer-ə-lē\ *adv* — **tem·po·rar·i·ness** \'tem-pə-,rer-ē-nəs\ *n*

temporary duty *n* **:** temporary military service away from one's unit

tem·po·rize \'tem-pə-,rīz\ *vi* **1 :** to act to suit the time or occasion **:** yield to current or dominant opinion **:** COMPROMISE **2 :** to draw out negotiations so as to gain time — **tem·po·ri·za·tion** \,tem-pə-rə-'zā-shən\ *n* — **tem·po·riz·er** \'tem-pə-,rī-zər\ *n*

tempt \'tem(p)t\ *vt* [L *tentare, temptare* to feel, try, tempt] **1 :** to entice to do wrong by promise of pleasure or gain **:** allure into evil **:** SEDUCE **2 a** *obs* **:** to make trial of **:** TEST **b :** to try presumptuously **:** PROVOKE **c :** to risk the dangers of **3 a :** to induce to do something **:** INCITE ⟨*tempted* him into a rash act⟩ **b :** to cause to be strongly inclined **:** almost move or persuade ⟨was *tempted* to call it quits⟩ — **tempt·a·ble** \'tem(p)t-ə-bəl\ *adj*

temp·ta·tion \tem(p)-'tā-shən\ *n* **1 :** the act of tempting **:** the state of being tempted esp. to evil **:** ENTICEMENT **2 :** something tempting

tempt·er \'tem(p)-tər\ *n* **:** one that tempts or entices — **tempt·ress** \-trəs\ *n*

tempt·ing *adj* **:** ALLURING, ENTICING — **tempt·ing·ly** \'tem(p)-tiŋ-lē\ *adv*

ten \'ten\ *n* [OE *tiene*] **1** — see NUMBER table **2 :** the tenth in a set or series ⟨the *ten* of hearts⟩ **3 :** something having ten units or members **4 :** a ten-dollar bill **5 :** the number in the second decimal place to the left of the decimal point in arabic numerals — **ten** *adj or pron*

ten·a·bil·i·ty \,ten-ə-'bil-ət-ē\ *n* **:** the quality or state of being tenable

ten·a·ble \'ten-ə-bəl\ *adj* [F, fr. *tenir* to hold, fr. L *tenēre*] **:** capable of being held, maintained, or defended **:** DEFENSIBLE, REASONABLE ⟨a *tenable* argument⟩ ⟨retreated when the position became no longer *tenable*⟩ — **ten·a·ble·ness** *n* — **ten·a·bly** \-blē\ *adv*

te·na·cious \tə-'nā-shəs\ *adj* [L *tenac-, tenax* tending to hold fast, fr. *tenēre* to hold] **1 a :** not easily pulled apart **:** COHESIVE, TOUGH ⟨a *tenacious* metal⟩ **b :** tending to adhere to another substance **:** STICKY ⟨*tenacious* burs⟩ **2 a :** holding fast or tending to hold fast **:** PERSISTENT, STUBBORN ⟨*tenacious* of his rights⟩ **b :** RETENTIVE ⟨a *tenacious* memory⟩ — **te·na·cious·ly** *adv* — **te·na·cious·ness** *n*

te·nac·i·ty \tə-'nas-ət-ē\ *n* **:** the quality or state of being tenacious

ten·an·cy \'ten-ən-sē\ *n, pl* **-cies 1 :** the temporary possession or occupancy of property that belongs to another; *also* **:** the period of such occupancy or possession **2 :** the ownership of property

¹ten·ant \'ten-ənt\ *n* [MF, fr. prp. of *tenir* to hold] **1 a :** the owner or possessor of property **b :** one who occupies or has temporary possession of property of another; *esp* **:** one who rents or leases (as a house) from a landlord **2 :** DWELLER, OCCUPANT

²tenant *vt* **:** to hold or occupy as a tenant **:** INHABIT — **ten·ant·a·ble** \-ən-tə-bəl\ *adj*

tenant farmer *n* **:** a farmer who works land owned by another and pays rent either in cash or in shares of produce — compare SHARECROPPER

ten·ant·less \'ten-ənt-ləs\ *adj* **:** having no tenants **:** UNOCCUPIED

ten·ant·ry \'ten-ən-trē\ *n* **1 :** the condition of being a tenant **2 :** a group of tenants (as on an estate)

ten-cent store \'ten-'sent-\ *n* **:** FIVE-AND-TEN

tench \'tench\ *n, pl* **tench** *or* **tench·es** [MF *tenche*, fr. LL *tinca*] **:** a Eurasian freshwater fish related to the dace and noted for its ability to survive outside water

Ten Commandments *n pl* : the commandments of God given to Moses on Mount Sinai

¹tend \'tend\ *vb* [ME *tenden*, short for *attenden*] **1** : to pay attention ⟨*tend* strictly to business⟩ **2** : to take care of : attend to (as plants) : CULTIVATE **3** : to have charge of as caretaker or overseer **4** : to manage or superintend the operation of ⟨*tend* a machine⟩

²tend *vi* [L *tendere* to stretch, tend] **1** : to move or turn in a certain direction : LEAD ⟨the road *tends* to the right⟩ **2** : to have a tendency : be likely ⟨a boy who *tends* to slouch⟩

ten·dance \'ten-dən(t)s\ *n* : watchful care : ATTENDANCE

tend·en·cy \'ten-dən-sē\ *n, pl* **-cies** **1 a** : direction or approach toward a place, object, effect, or limit **b** : IN-CLINATION, BENT **c** : a proneness to a particular kind of thought or action : PROPENSITY **2** : the purposeful trend of something written or said : AIM

syn TENDENCY, TREND, DRIFT mean movement in a particular direction. TENDENCY implies an ever-present inclination or force sending a person or thing in a particular direction ⟨had a *tendency* to exaggerate⟩ ⟨counteracts the *tendency* of engines to knock⟩ TREND implies a general direction maintained in spite of irregularities and more often subject to change than TENDENCY ⟨*trends* of current fiction⟩ DRIFT suggests a tendency determined by external influences ⟨the present *drift* toward centralization⟩ or it may apply to an underlying trend of a discourse ⟨lost the *drift* of the conversation⟩

ten·den·tious *also* **ten·den·cious** \ten-'den-chəs\ *adj* : marked by a tendency in favor of a particular point of view : BIASED — **ten·den·tious·ly** *adv* — **ten·den·tious·ness** *n*

¹ten·der \'ten-dər\ *adj* [OF *tendre*, fr. L *tener*] **1 a** : having a soft or yielding texture : easily broken, cut, or damaged : DELICATE, FRAGILE **b** : easily chewed : SUC-CULENT **2 a** : physically weak : not able to endure hardship **b** : IMMATURE, YOUNG ⟨children of *tender* years⟩ **c** : incapable of resisting cold ⟨*tender* shrubs⟩ **3** : marked by, responding to, or expressing the softer emotions : FOND, LOVING ⟨a *tender* lover⟩ **4 a** : showing care : CONSIDERATE, SOLICITOUS **b** : highly susceptible to impressions or emotions : IMPRESSIONABLE ⟨a *tender* conscience⟩ **5 a** : appropriate or conducive to a delicate or sensitive constitution or character : GENTLE, MILD ⟨*tender* breeding⟩ ⟨*tender* irony⟩ **b** : delicate or soft in quality or tone **6 a** : sensitive to touch : easily hurt ⟨a *tender* scar⟩ **b** : sensitive to injury or insult : TOUCHY **c** : demanding careful and sensitive handling : TICKLISH — **ten·der·ly** *adv* — **ten·der·ness** *n*

²tend·er \'ten-dər\ *n* : one that tends or takes care: as **a** : a ship employed (as to supply provisions) to attend other ships **b** : a boat that carries passengers or freight between shore and a larger ship **c** : a vehicle attached to a locomotive for carrying a supply of fuel and water

³ten·der *n* [MF *tendre* to stretch, stretch out, offer, fr. L *tendere*] **1** : an offer of money in satisfaction of a debt **2** : an offer or proposal made for acceptance; *esp* : an offer of a bid for a contract **3** : something that may by law be offered in payment; *esp* : MONEY

⁴ten·der *vt* **ten·dered; ten·der·ing** \-d(ə-)riŋ\ **1** : to make a tender of ⟨*tender* the amount of rent⟩ **2** : to present for acceptance : PROFFER ⟨*tendered* his resignation⟩ ⟨*tendered* his advice⟩

ten·der·foot \'ten-dər-,fůt\ *n, pl* **-feet** \-,fēt\ *also* **-foots** **1** : a person who is not hardened to a rough out-of-door life; *esp* : a newcomer in a recent settlement (as on a frontier) **2** : a boy scout or girl scout of the beginning class **3** : an inexperienced beginner : NEOPHYTE, GREEN-HORN

ten·der·heart·ed \,ten-dər-'härt-əd\ *adj* : easily moved to love, pity, or sorrow : COMPASSIONATE, IMPRESSIONABLE — **ten·der·heart·ed·ly** *adv* — **ten·der·heart·ed·ness** *n*

ten·der·ize \'ten-də-,rīz\ *vt* : to make (meat) tender — **ten·der·i·za·tion** \,ten-də-rə-'zā-shən\ *n* — **ten·der·iz·er** \'ten-də-,rī-zər\ *n*

ten·der·loin \'ten-dər-,lȯin\ *n* **1** : a strip of tender meat on each side of the backbone : a fillet of beef or pork **2** : a district of a city largely devoted to vice and other forms of lawbreaking that encourage political or police corruption

ten·di·nous \'ten-də-nəs\ *adj* [NL *tendin-, tendo* tendon,

alter. of ML *tendon-, tendo*] **1** : of, relating to, or re-sembling a tendon **2** : consisting of tendons : SINEWY

ten·don \'ten-dən\ *n* [ML *tendon-, tendo,* fr. L *tendere* to stretch] : a tough cord or band of fibrous tissue connecting a muscle to some other part (as a bone) and transmitting the force exerted by the muscle

tendon of Achil·les \-ə-'kil-ēz\ [so called fr. the legend that the heel was Achilles' one vulnerable spot] : the strong tendon by which the large muscles of the lower leg are connected to the bone of the heel

ten·dril \'ten-drəl\ *n* **1** : a leaf, stipule, or stem modified into a slender spirally coiling sensitive organ serving to attach a plant to its support **2** : something that curls like a tendril ⟨*tendrils* of hair⟩ — **ten·driled** *or* **ten·drilled** \-drəld\ *adj* — **ten·dril·ly** \-drə-lē\ *adj* — **ten·dril·ous** \-drə-ləs\ *adj*

Ten·e·brae \'ten-ə-,brā, -,brī, -,brē\ *n sing or pl* [ML, fr. L, darkness] : the office of matins and lauds for the three days before Easter commemorating the sufferings and death of Christ with a progressive extinguishing of candles

te·neb·ri·ous \tə-'neb-rē-əs\ *adj* : TENEBROUS

ten·e·brous \'ten-ə-brəs\ *adj* [L *tenebrae* darkness] : shut off from the light : GLOOMY, OBSCURE

1080 *also* **ten-eighty** \ten-'āt-ē\ *n* [fr. its laboratory serial number] : a poisonous substance that is chemically sodium fluoroacetate and is used to kill rodents

ten·e·ment \'ten-ə-mənt\ *n* [ML *tenementum,* fr. L *tenēre* to hold] **1** : land or property treated in law like land that is held by one person from another : HOLDING **2 a** : a house used as a dwelling : RESIDENCE **b** : APARTMENT, FLAT **c** : TENEMENT HOUSE **3** : DWELLING, HABITATION

tenement house *n* : APARTMENT BUILDING; *esp* : one barely meeting minimum standards of sanitation, safety, and comfort and housing poorer families

ten·et \'ten-ət\ *n* [L, he holds, fr. *tenēre* to hold] : a princi-ple, belief, or doctrine generally held to be true; *esp* : one held in common by members of an organization, group, or profession **syn** see DOCTRINE

ten·fold \'ten-,fōld, -'fōld\ *adj* **1** : having 10 units or members **2** : of or amounting to 1000 percent — **tenfold** *adv*

ten·nis \'ten-əs\ *n* [ME *tenetz, tenys*] **1** : COURT TENNIS **2** : a game that is played with rackets and a light elastic ball by two players or pairs of players on a level court divided by a low net

tennis shoe *n* : SNEAKER

Ten·ny·so·ni·an \,ten-ə-'sō-nē-ən\ *adj* : of, relating to, or characteristic of the poet Tennyson or his writings

¹ten·on \'ten-ən\ *n* [OF, fr. *tenir* to hold] : a projecting part in a piece of material (as wood) for insertion into a mortise to make a joint

²tenon *vt* **1** : to unite by a tenon **2** : to cut or fit for in-sertion in a mortise

¹ten·or \'ten-ər\ *n* [OF, fr. L *tenor* uninterrupted course, fr. *tenēre* to hold] **1** : the general drift of something spoken or written : PURPORT **2 a** : the voice part next to the lowest in 4-part harmony **b** : the highest natural adult male voice **c** : one that performs a tenor part **3** : a continuance in a course, movement, or activity : TREND

²tenor *adj* **1** : of or relating to the tenor in music **2** : close in range to a tenor voice ⟨*tenor* sax⟩

ten·pen·ny \,ten-,pen-ē\ *adj* : amounting to, worth, or costing ten pennies

tenpenny nail *n* [fr. its original price per hundred] : a nail 3 inches long

ten·pin \'ten-,pin\ *n* **1** : a bottle-shaped bowling pin 15 inches high **2** *pl* : a bowling game using 10 tenpins and a large ball and allowing each player to bowl 2 balls in each of 10 frames

ten·pound·er \'ten-'paůn-dər\ *n* : a large silvery food and sport fish that somewhat resembles a herring but is related to the tarpon

¹tense \'ten(t)s\ *n* [MF *tens* time, tense, fr. L *tempus*] **1** : a distinction of form in a verb to express distinctions of time **2** : a particular inflectional form or set of inflectional forms of a verb expressing a specific time distinction

²tense *adj* [L *tensus,* fr. pp. of *tendere* to stretch; akin to E *thin*] **1** : stretched tight : made taut : RIGID **2 a** : feeling or showing nervous tension : HIGH-STRUNG **b** : marked by strain or suspense **3** : produced with the speech muscles in a relatively tense state ⟨the *tense* vowels \ē\

and \ü\〉— compare LAX **syn** see TIGHT — **tense·ly** *adv* — **tense·ness** *n*

³tense *vb* **:** to make or become tense 〈he *tensed* up and played a poor game〉

ten·sile \'ten(t)-səl, 'ten-ˌsīl\ *adj* **1 :** capable of tension **:** DUCTILE **2 :** of or relating to tension

tensile strength *n* **:** the greatest longitudinal stress (as pounds per square inch) a substance can bear without tearing apart

¹ten·sion \'ten-chən\ *n* **1 a :** the act or action of stretching or the condition or degree of being stretched to stiffness **:** TAUTNESS 〈*tension* of a muscle〉 **b :** STRESS 1c **2 a :** either of two balancing forces causing or tending to cause extension of a body **b :** the condition in an elastic body resulting from elongation **c :** PRESSURE 〈oxygen *tension* in lake water〉 **3 a :** a state of mental unrest often with signs of physiological stress **b :** a state of latent hostility or opposition between individuals or groups **c :** a balance maintained in an artistic work between opposing forces or elements **4 :** VOLTAGE 〈a high-*tension* wire〉 **5 :** a device to produce a desired tension (as in a loom) — **ten·sion·al** \'tench-nəl, -ən-ᵊl\ *adj*

²tension *vt* **:** to subject to tension

ten·sion·less \'ten-chən-ləs\ *adj* **:** free from tension

ten·si·ty \'ten(t)-sət-ē\ *n* **:** TENSENESS

ten·sor \'ten(t)-sər, 'ten-ˌsȯr\ *n* **:** a muscle that stretches a part — **ten·so·ri·al** \ten-'sōr-ē-əl, -'sȯr-\ *adj*

ten·strike \'ten-ˌstrīk\ *n* **1 :** a strike in tenpins **2 :** a highly successful stroke or achievement

¹tent \'tent\ *n* [OF *tente*, fr. L *tenta*, fem. of *tentus*, pp. of *tendere* to stretch] **1 :** a collapsible shelter (as of canvas) stretched and sustained by poles and used esp. (as by campers) as temporary housing **2 :** something that resembles a tent or that serves as a shelter; *esp* **:** a canopy or enclosure placed over the head and shoulders to retain medicinal vapors or oxygen administered

²tent *vb* **1 :** to live or lodge in a tent **2 :** to cover with or as if with a tent

ten·ta·cle \'tent-i-kəl\ *n* [NL *tentaculum*, fr. L *tentare* to feel, touch] **1 :** one of the long flexible processes usu. about the head or mouth of an animal (as a worm or fish) used esp. for feeling, grasping, or handling **2 :** something suggesting a tentacle; *esp* **:** a sensitive hair on a plant — **ten·ta·cled** \-kəld\ *adj* — **ten·tac·u·lar** \ten-'tak-yə-lər\ *adj*

ten·ta·tive \'tent-ət-iv\ *adj* [L *tentare, temptare* to feel, try] **1 :** not fully worked out or developed **:** not final **:** PROVISIONAL, TEMPORARY 〈*tentative* plans〉 〈a *tentative* hypothesis〉 **2 :** HESITANT, UNCERTAIN 〈a *tentative* smile〉 — **ten·ta·tive·ly** *adv* — **ten·ta·tive·ness** *n*

tent caterpillar *n* **:** any of several destructive gregarious caterpillars that construct large silken webs on trees

ten·ter \'tent-ər\ *n* [ME *teyntur*] **:** a frame or endless track with hooks or clips along two sides that is used for drying and stretching cloth

ten·ter·hook \'tent-ər-ˌhùk\ *n* **:** a sharp hooked nail used esp. for fastening cloth on a tenter — **on tenterhooks :** in a state of uneasiness, strain, or suspense

tenth \'ten(t)th\ *n* **1** — see NUMBER table **2 :** one of 10 equal parts of something **3 :** the one numbered 10 in a countable series — **tenth** *adj or adv*

tent·mak·er \'tent-ˌmā-kər\ *n* **:** one that makes tents

tent stitch *n* **:** a short stitch slanting to the right that is used (as in embroidery) to form even lines of solid background

ten·u·ous \'ten-yə-wəs\ *adj* [L *tenuis* thin, tenuous; akin to E *thin*] **1 :** not dense **:** RARE 〈a *tenuous* fluid〉 **2 :** not thick **:** SLENDER 〈a *tenuous* rope〉 **3 :** having little substance or strength **:** FLIMSY, WEAK 〈*tenuous* influences〉 〈a *tenuous* hold on reality〉— **te·nu·i·ty** \te-'n(y)ü-ət-ē, tə-\ *n* — **ten·u·ous·ly** *adv* — **ten·u·ous·ness** *n*

ten·ure \'ten-yər\ *n* [OF, fr. ML *tenitura*, fr. L *tenēre* to hold] **1 :** the act, right, manner, or term of holding something (as real property, a position, or an office) **2 :** GRASP, HOLD — **ten·ur·i·al** \te-'nyùr-ē-əl\ *adj* — **ten·ur·i·al·ly** \-ē-ə-lē\ *adv*

te·nu·to \tā-'nüt-ō\ *adv* (*or adj*) [It, lit., held] **:** in a manner so as to hold a tone or chord firmly to its full value — used as a direction in music

te·o·sin·te \ˌtā-ə-'sint-ē\ *n* **:** a large annual fodder grass of Mexico and Central America closely related to and possibly ancestral to maize

te·pee \'tē-(ˌ)pē\ *n* [of AmerInd origin] **:** a conical tent usu. of skins used by some American Indians

tep·id \'tep-əd\ *adj* [L *tepidus*, fr. *tepēre* to be moderately warm] **1 :** moderately warm **:** LUKEWARM 〈a *tepid* bath〉 **2 :** lacking enthusiasm or conviction **:** HALFHEARTED 〈a *tepid* interest〉 — **te·pid·i·ty** \tə-'pid-ət-ē, te-\ *n* — **tep·id·ly** \'tep-əd-lē\ *adv* — **tep·id·ness** *n*

te·qui·la \tə-'kē-lə\ *n* [MexSp, fr. *Tequila*, Mexico] **:** a Mexican liquor made by redistilling mescal

tera- \'ter-ə\ *comb form* [Gk *teras* monster] **:** trillion 〈*terawatt*〉

tepee

te·rai \tə-'rī\ *n* [*Tarai*, lowland belt of India] **:** a wide-brimmed double felt sun hat worn esp. in subtropical regions

ter·a·tol·o·gy \ˌter-ə-'täl-ə-jē\ *n* [Gk *terat-, teras* monster] **:** the study of malformations, monstrosities, and major deviation from normality in the development of organisms — **ter·a·to·log·i·cal** \ˌter-ət-ᵊl-'äj-i-kəl\ *adj*

ter·bi·um \'tər-bē-əm\ *n* [NL, fr. *Ytterby*, Sweden] **:** a usu. trivalent metallic chemical element — see ELEMENT table

terce \'tərs\ *n, often cap* [ML *tertia*, fr. L, fem. of *tertius* third] **:** the third of the canonical hours

ter·cen·te·na·ry \ˌtər-ˌsen-'ten-ə-rē, (ˌ)tər-'sent-ᵊn-ˌer-ē\ *n, pl* **-ries** [L *ter* three times; akin to E *three*] **:** a 300th anniversary or its celebration — **tercentenary** *adj*

ter·cen·ten·ni·al \ˌtər-ˌsen-'ten-ē-əl\ *adj or n* **:** TERCENTENARY

ter·cet \'tər-sət\ *n* [It *terzetto*] **:** a unit or group of three lines of verse

ter·e·binth \'ter-ə-ˌbin(t)th\ *n* [Gk *terebinthos*] **:** a small European tree related to the sumac that yields an oleoresin

te·re·do \tə-'rēd-ō\ *n, pl* **-dos** *or* **-di·nes** \-'red-ᵊn-ˌēz\ [L *teredin-, teredo*, fr. Gk *terēdōn*] **:** SHIPWORM

te·rete \tə-'rēt\ *adj* [L *teret-, teres* well turned, rounded] **:** approximately cylindrical but usu. tapering at both ends 〈a *terete* seedpod〉

ter·gal \'tər-gəl\ *adj* **:** of or relating to a tergum; *esp* **:** DORSAL

ter·gi·ver·sate \'tər-ji-(ˌ)vər-ˌsāt\ *vi* [L *tergiversari*, fr. *tergum* back + *versare* to turn, freq. of *vertere*] **1 :** to change one's mind about or desert something (as a cause or party) **2 :** to use subterfuges **:** EQUIVOCATE — **ter·gi·ver·sa·tion** \ˌtər-ji-(ˌ)vər-'sā-shən\ *n* — **ter·gi·ver·sa·tor** \'tər-ji-(ˌ)vər-ˌsāt-ər\ *n*

ter·gum \'tər-gəm\ *n, pl* **ter·ga** \-gə\ [L] **:** the back of an animal; *also* **:** a plate on the back of an arthropod

¹term \'tərm\ *n* [OF *terme* boundary, end, fr. L *terminus*] **1 a :** a time or date that is a boundary between periods or is assigned to a particular purpose (as payment of rent or interest) **b :** END, LIMIT **2 :** a limited or definite extent of time esp. as fixed by law, custom, or some recurrent phenomenon: as **a :** one for which an estate is granted **b :** one during which a court is in session **c :** a division in a school year in which instruction is given **3 :** the time for which something lasts **:** DURATION **4** *pl* **:** provisions determining the nature and scope of something esp. of an agreement **5 a :** a word or expression that has a precise meaning in some uses or is peculiar to a particular field 〈legal *terms*〉 **b** *pl* **:** diction of a specified kind 〈spoke in glowing *terms* of their prospects〉 **c :** one of the three words or groups of words each of which appears twice in the subject or predicate of a syllogism **6 a :** a mathematical expression connected with another by a plus or minus sign **b :** an element of a fraction or proportion or of a series or sequence **7** *pl* **a :** mutual relationship **:** FOOTING 〈on good *terms*〉 **b :** AGREEMENT, CONCORD 〈came to *terms* with his father〉 — **in terms of :** with respect to 〈considered *in terms of* today's wages〉〈measured *in terms of* footage produced〉

²term *vt* **:** to apply a term to **:** CALL, NAME

¹ter·ma·gant \'tər-mə-gənt\ *n* **:** an overbearing quarrelsome woman **:** SHREW

²termagant *adj* **:** noisily quarrelsome

¹ter·mi·nal \'tər-mən-ᵊl\ *adj* **1 a :** of or relating to an end, extremity, boundary, or terminus 〈*terminal* pillar〉 **b :** growing at the end of a branch or stem 〈*terminal* bud〉

2 : of, relating to, or occurring in a term or each term **3 a :** occurring at or constituting the end of a period or series : CONCLUDING   **b :** limited but complete in itself — **ter·mi·nal·ly** \-ⁿl-ē\ adv

²**terminal** n   **1 :** a part that forms the end   **2 :** a terminating usu. ornamental detail : FINIAL   **3 :** a device attached to the end (as of a wire) for convenience in making electrical connections   **4 a :** either end of a carrier line (as a railroad or shipping line) with its handling and storage facilities, offices, and stations; also : a usu. major freight or passenger station   **b :** a town at the end of a carrier line : TERMINUS

   syn TERMINAL, TERMINUS mean end, finishing point, boundary, or limit. In transportation TERMINAL and TERMINUS are interchangeable in referring to either end of a carrier line. TERMINAL applies also to the specific building ⟨bus *terminal*⟩ TERMINUS applies generally to the place ⟨New York City is the *terminus* of many lines⟩

terminal leave n : a final leave consisting of accumulated unused leave granted to a member of the armed forces just prior to his separation or discharge from service

terminal side n : a straight line that rotates about a point on another line in generating an angle

ter·mi·nate \'tər-mə-ˌnāt\ vb **1 a :** to bring to or come to an end : CLOSE   **b :** to form the conclusion of : form an ending   **2 :** to serve as a limit to : BOUND   **3 :** to extend only to a limit (as a point or line); esp : to reach a terminus **syn** see CLOSE — **ter·mi·na·ble** \-mə-nə-bəl\ adj — **ter·mi·na·tive** \-ˌnāt-iv\ adj

ter·mi·na·tion \ˌtər-mə-'nā-shən\ n **1 :** end in time or existence : CONCLUSION ⟨*termination* of life⟩   **2 :** a limit in space or extent : BOUND   **3 :** the last part of a word : SUFFIX; esp : an inflectional ending   **4 :** the act of terminating **syn** see END — **ter·mi·na·tion·al** \-shnəl, -shən-ⁿl\ adj

ter·mi·na·tor \'tər-mə-ˌnāt-ər\ n **1 :** one that terminates **2 :** the dividing line between the illuminated and the unilluminated part of the moon's or a planet's disk

ter·mi·nol·o·gy \ˌtər-mə-'näl-ə-jē\ n, pl **-gies** [ML *terminus* term, expression, fr. L, boundary, limit] : the technical or special terms or expressions used in a business, art, science, or special subject ⟨the *terminology* of law⟩ — **ter·mi·no·log·i·cal** \ˌtərm-nə-'läj-i-kəl, ˌtərm-ən-ⁿl-'äj-\ adj

term insurance n : insurance for a specified period providing for no payment to the insured except for losses during the period and becoming void upon the expiration of the period

ter·mi·nus \'tər-mə-nəs\ n, pl **-ni** \-ˌnī, -ˌnē\ or **-nus·es** [L, boundary, end] **1 :** final goal : finishing point   **2 :** a post or stone marking a boundary   **3 a :** either end of a transportation line or travel route   **b :** the station or the town or city at such a place : TERMINAL   **4 :** EXTREMITY, TIP ⟨*terminus* of a glacier⟩ **syn** see END

ter·mite \'tər-ˌmīt\ n [LL *termit-, termes*, a worm that eats wood] : any of an order (Isoptera) of pale-colored soft-bodied social insects that have winged sexual forms, wingless sterile workers, and often soldiers, feed on wood, and include some very destructive to wooden structures and trees — called also *white ant*

term paper n : a major written assignment in a school or college course representative of a student's achievement during a term — called also *term report*

term·time \'tərm-ˌtīm\ n : the time during an academic or legal term

tern \'tərn\ n [of Scand origin] : any of numerous sea gulls that are smaller and slenderer in body and bill than typical gulls and have narrower wings, often forked tails, black cap, and white body

ter·na·ry \'tər-nə-rē\ adj [L *terni* three each; akin to E *three*] **1 a :** of, relating to, or proceeding by threes **b :** having three elements or parts   **2 :** third in order or rank

ter·nate \'tər-ˌnāt\ adj : arranged in threes or having subdivisions so arranged — **ter·nate·ly** adv

ter·pene \'tər-ˌpēn\ n [G *terpentin* turpentine] : any of various hydrocarbons (C_5H_8)ₙ found esp. in essential oils, resins, and balsams and used esp. as solvents and in organic synthesis

Terp·sich·o·re \ˌtərp-'sik-ə-(ˌ)rē\ n : the Greek Muse of dancing and choral song

terp·si·cho·re·an \ˌtərp-(ˌ)sik-ə-'rē-ən\ adj : of or relating to dancing

¹**ter·race** \'ter-əs\ n [MF, pile of earth, terrace, fr. OProv *terrassa*, fr. *terra* earth, fr. L] **1 a :** a flat roof or open platform : BALCONY, DECK   **b :** a relatively level paved or planted area adjoining a building   **2 :** a raised embankment with the top leveled; also : one of a series of banks or ridges formed in a slope to conserve moisture and soil for agriculture   **3 a** (1) : a row of houses on raised ground or a sloping site   (2) : a group of such houses   **b :** a strip of park in the middle of a street   **c :** STREET

²**terrace** vt : to make into a terrace or supply with terraces

ter·rac·er \'ter-ə-sər\ n : a machine used for constructing terraces or wide channels for surface drainage

ter·ra-cot·ta \ˌter-ə-'kät-ə\ n, pl **terra-cottas** [It *terra cotta*, lit., baked earth] **1 :** a glazed or unglazed fired earthenware   **2 :** a brownish orange

ter·ra fir·ma \-'fər-mə\ n [NL, lit., solid land] : dry land : solid ground

ter·rain \tə-'rān, te-\ n [F, land, ground, fr. L *terrenum*, fr. *terra* earth, land] : the surface features of a tract of land ⟨a rough *terrain*⟩

ter·ra in·cog·ni·ta \'ter-ə-ˌin-ˌkäg-'nēt-ə, -in-'käg-nət-ə\ n, pl **ter·rae in·cog·ni·tae** \'ter-ˌī-in-ˌkäg-'nē-ˌtī, -in-'käg-nə-ˌtī\ [L, unknown land] : an unexplored region (as of the earth or of knowledge)

Ter·ra·my·cin \ˌter-ə-'mīs-ⁿn\ trademark — used for an antibiotic produced by a soil bacterium

ter·ra·pin \'ter-ə-pən, 'tar-\ n [of Algonquian origin] : any of various edible No. American turtles living in fresh or brackish water

ter·rar·i·um \tə-'rar-ē-əm, -'rer-\ n, pl **-ia** \-ē-ə\ or **-iums :** a vivarium without standing water

ter·raz·zo \tə-'raz-ō, -'rät-sō\ n [It, lit., terrace] : a mosaic flooring made by embedding small pieces of marble or granite in mortar

ter·res·tri·al \tə-'res-t(r)ē-əl\ adj [L *terrestris*, fr. *terra* earth] **1 a :** of or relating to the earth or its inhabitants ⟨*terrestrial* magnetism⟩   **b :** mundane in scope or character : PROSAIC   **2 :** of or relating to land as distinct from air or water ⟨*terrestrial* transportation⟩   **3 a :** living on or in or growing from land ⟨*terrestrial* plants⟩ ⟨*terrestrial* birds⟩ **b :** of or relating to terrestrial organisms ⟨*terrestrial* habits⟩ — **terrestrial** n — **ter·res·tri·al·ly** \-ē\ adv

ter·ri·ble \'ter-ə-bəl\ adj [L *terribilis*, fr. *terrēre* to frighten] **1 :** causing terror or awe : FEARFUL, DREADFUL ⟨a *terrible* disaster⟩   **2 a :** hard to bear usu. because of excess of some quality ⟨*terrible* cold⟩   **b :** very bad or extremely unpleasant ⟨had a *terrible* time⟩   **c :** of notably inferior quality ⟨did a *terrible* job on the painting⟩ — **ter·ri·bly** \-blē\ adv

ter·ric·o·lous \te-'rik-ə-ləs\ adj [L *terra* earth] : living on or in the ground

ter·ri·er \'ter-ē-ər\ n [F *chien terrier*, lit., earth dog] : any

terriers: *1* Airedale,
2 wirehaired fox terrier

of various usu. small dogs orig. used by hunters to dig for small game and engage the quarry underground or drive it out

ter·rif·ic \tə-'rif-ik\ adj **1 :** TERRIBLE, FRIGHTFUL ⟨*terrific* destruction⟩   **2 :** EXTRAORDINARY, ASTOUNDING ⟨*terrific* speed⟩; esp : TREMENDOUS ⟨a *terrific* explosion⟩   **3 :** unusually fine : MAGNIFICENT ⟨the party was *terrific*⟩ — **ter·rif·i·cal·ly** \-'rif-i-k(ə-)lē\ adv

ter·ri·fy \'ter-ə-ˌfī\ vb **-fied; -fy·ing :** to fill with or move to some action by terror — **ter·ri·fy·ing·ly** \-ˌfī-iŋ-lē\ adv

¹ter·ri·to·ri·al \,ter-ə-'tōr-ē-əl, -'tȯr-\ *adj* **1 a :** of or relating to territory ⟨*territorial* claims⟩ **b** *often cap* **:** of or relating to all or any of the territories of the U.S. ⟨a *territorial* government⟩ **2 :** organized primarily for territorial defense ⟨a *territorial* army⟩ **3 :** of, relating to, or exhibiting territoriality ⟨*territorial* birds⟩ — **ter·ri·to·ri·al·ly** \-ē-ə-lē\ *adv*

²territorial *n* **:** a member of a territorial military unit

ter·ri·to·ri·al·i·ty \,ter-ə-,tōr-ē-'al-ət-ē, -,tȯr-\ *n* **:** the pattern of behavior associated with the defense of a male animal's territory

ter·ri·to·ri·al·ize \-'tōr-ē-ə-,līz, -'tȯr-\ *vt* **:** to organize on a territorial basis — **ter·ri·to·ri·al·i·za·tion** \-,tōr-ē-ə-lə-'zā-shən, -,tȯr-\ *n*

territorial waters *n pl* **:** the waters under the sovereign jurisdiction of a nation or state including both marginal sea and inland waters

ter·ri·to·ry \'ter-ə-,tōr-ē, -,tȯr-\ *n, pl* **-ries** [L *territorium,* fr. *terra* land] **1 a :** a geographical area belonging to or under the jurisdiction of a government **b :** an administrative subdivision of a country (as the U.S.S.R.) **c :** a part of the U.S. not included within any state but organized with a separate legislature **d :** a geographical area dependent upon an external government but having some degree of autonomy **2 a :** an indeterminate geographical area **b :** a field of knowledge or interest **3 a :** an assigned area ⟨a salesman's *territory*⟩ **b :** an area usu. including the nesting or denning site and foraging range that is preempted and defended by a male bird or mammal

ter·ror \'ter-ər\ *n* [L, fr. *terrēre* to frighten] **1 :** a state of intense fear **2 a :** a cause of fear or anxiety **b :** an appalling person or thing; *esp* **:** BRAT **3 a :** REIGN OF TERROR **b :** the deliberate use of violence and brutality esp. as a political weapon

ter·ror·ism \'ter-ər-,iz-əm\ *n* **:** systematic use of terror esp. as a means of keeping or gaining control of a government — **ter·ror·ist** \-ər-əst\ *adj or n* — **ter·ror·is·tic** \,ter-ər-'is-tik\ *adj*

ter·ror·ize \'ter-ər-,īz\ *vt* **1 :** to fill with terror or anxiety **2 :** to coerce by threat or violence — **ter·ror·i·za·tion** \,ter-ər-ə-'zā-shən\ *n*

ter·ry \'ter-ē\ *n, pl* **terries :** an absorbent fabric with a loose pile of uncut loops

terse \'tərs\ *adj* [L *tersus* clean, neat, fr. pp. of *tergēre* to wipe off] **:** using as few words as possible without loss of force or clearness **:** being brief and effective **:** SUCCINCT — **terse·ly** *adv* — **terse·ness** *n*

¹ter·tian \'tər-shən\ *adj* **:** occurring every third day reckoning inclusively ⟨a *tertian* fever⟩

²tertian *n* **:** an intermittent fever that recurs at approximately 48-hour intervals; *esp* **:** a tertian malaria

¹ter·ti·ary \'tər-shē-,er-ē\ *n, pl* **-ar·ies 1 :** a member of a monastic third order esp. of lay people **2** *cap* **:** the Tertiary period or system of rocks

²tertiary *adj* [L *tertiarius,* fr. *tertius* third; akin to E *three*] **1 a :** of 3d rank, importance, or value **b :** of, relating to, or constituting the 3d strongest of three or four degrees of stress ⟨the 3d syllable of *basketball team* carries *tertiary* stress⟩ **2** *cap* **:** of, relating to, or being the first period of the Cenozoic era or the corresponding system of rocks marked by the formation of high mountains (as the Alps and Himalayas) and the dominance of mammals on land **3 :** formed by the substitution of three atoms or groups ⟨a *tertiary* salt⟩ **4 :** occurring in or being a 3d stage

ter·za ri·ma \,tert-sə-'rē-mə\ *n* [It, lit., third rhyme] **:** a verse form consisting of tercets usu. in iambic pentameter with an interlaced rhyme scheme (as *aba, bcb, cdc*)

tes·sel·late \'tes-ə-,lāt\ *vt* [LL *tessellare* to pave with tesserae, fr. L *tessella,* dim. of *tessera*] **:** to form into or adorn with mosaic — **tes·sel·la·tion** \,tes-ə-'lā-shən\ *n*

tes·sel·lat·ed \'tes-ə-,lāt-əd\ *adj* **:** made of or resembling mosaic; *esp* **:** having a checkered appearance

tes·sera \'tes-ə-rə\ *n, pl* **-ser·ae** \-,rē, -,rī\ [L] **1 :** a small tablet (as of wood, bone, or ivory) used by the ancient Romans as a ticket, tally, voucher, or means of identification **2 :** a small piece (as of marble, glass, or tile) used in mosaic work

¹test \'test\ *n* [ME, vessel in which metals were assayed, cupel, fr. L *testum* earthen vessel] **1 a :** a critical examination, observation, or evaluation **:** TRIAL ⟨put his courage to the *test*⟩ **b :** something that tries quality or resistance

⟨ideas that can only be judged by the *test* of time⟩ **2 :** a means of testing: as **a :** a procedure, reaction, or reagent used to identify or differentiate something ⟨a *test* for starch⟩⟨a series of allergy *tests*⟩ **b :** an examination (as in a school) intended to determine factual knowledge or acquired skill or sometimes intelligence, capacities, or aptitudes **3 :** a result of or rating based on a test ⟨a boiler of 300 pounds *test*⟩

²test *vb* **1 :** to put to test or proof **:** TRY **2 a :** to undergo a test **b :** to achieve a rating on the basis of tests **3 :** to use tests as a means of analysis or diagnosis ⟨*test* for copper⟩ ⟨*test* for allergens⟩ — **test·a·ble** \'tes-tə-bəl\ *adj*

³test *n* **:** a firm or rigid outer covering (as a shell) of many invertebrates

tes·ta \'tes-tə\ *n, pl* **tes·tae** \-,tē, -,tī\ [L, shell] **:** the hard outer coat of a seed

tes·ta·ceous \te-'stā-shəs\ *adj* [L *testa* shell, earthen pot, brick] **1 a :** having a shell ⟨a *testaceous* animal⟩ **b :** consisting of or resembling shell ⟨*testaceous* material⟩ **2 :** of reddish to yellowish brown

tes·ta·cy \'tes-tə-sē\ *n* **:** the state or circumstance of being testate

tes·ta·ment \'tes-tə-mənt\ *n* [LL *testamentum* covenant, holy scripture & L *testamentum* last will, fr. *testari* to call to witness, make a will, fr. *testis* witness] **1 a** *archaic* **:** a covenant between God and man **b** *cap* **:** either of two chief divisions of the Bible; *esp* **:** NEW TESTAMENT **2 a :** a tangible proof or tribute **b :** an expression of conviction **:** CREDO **3 :** a legal instrument by which a person determines the disposition of his property after his death — **tes·ta·men·ta·ry** \,tes-tə-'ment-ə-rē, -'men-trē\ *adj*

¹tes·tate \'tes-,tāt, -tət\ *adj* **:** having left a will ⟨a person dying *testate*⟩

²tes·tate \-,tāt\ *adj* **:** having a firm outer covering (as a test or testa)

tes·ta·tor \'tes-,tāt-ər, te-'stāt-\ *n* **:** a person who leaves a will in force at his death — **tes·ta·trix** \te-'stā-triks\ *n*

test case *n* **1 :** a representative case whose outcome is likely to serve as a precedent **2 :** a proceeding brought by agreement or on an understanding of the parties to obtain a decision as to the constitutionality of a statute

test·cross \'test-,krȯs\ *n* **:** a cross made between a homozygous recessive and a corresponding dominant to determine whether or not the latter is also homozygous

test·ed \'tes-təd\ *adj* **:** subjected to or qualified through testing ⟨time-*tested* principles⟩ ⟨tuberculin-*tested* cattle⟩

¹tes·ter \'tēs-tər, 'tes-\ *n* [MF *testiere* head covering, fr. *teste* head, fr. LL *testa* skull, fr. L, shell] **:** a canopy over a bed, pulpit, or altar

²test·er \'tes-tər\ *n* **:** one that tests

tes·ti·cle \'tes-ti-kəl\ *n* [L *testiculus,* dim. of *testis*] **:** TESTIS — **tes·tic·u·lar** \te-'stik-yə-lər\ *adj*

tes·ti·fy \'tes-tə-,fī\ *vb* **-fied; -fy·ing** [L *testificari* fr. *testis* witness] **1 :** to make a solemn statement of what is personally known or believed to be true **:** give evidence **:** declare solemnly (as under oath) ⟨*testify* in court⟩ **2 :** to give outward proof **:** serve as a sign of ⟨smiles *testifying* contentment⟩ — **tes·ti·fi·er** \-,fī-(ə)r\ *n*

¹tes·ti·mo·ni·al \,tes-tə-'mō-nē-əl\ *adj* **:** being a testimonial; *also* **:** expressive of appreciation or esteem ⟨*testimonial* dinner⟩

²testimonial *n* **1 :** an indication of worth or quality ⟨the agreement is a *testimonial* to the negotiators' devoted care⟩: as **a :** an endorsement of a product or service ⟨writing *testimonials* for patent medicines⟩ **b :** a character reference **:** letter of recommendation **2 :** an expression of appreciation **:** TRIBUTE

tes·ti·mo·ny \'tes-tə-,mō-nē\ *n, pl* **-nies** [L *testi█* evidence, witness, fr. *testis* witness] **1 a :** the ▒ inscribed with the Mosaic law or the ark containing ▒ **b :** a divine decree attested in the Scriptures **2 a :** evi█ based on observation or knowledge **:** authoritativ ▒ dence ⟨according to the *testimony* of historians⟩ ⟨h█ is *testimony* of his worth⟩ **b :** a solemn declaration █. made orally by a witness under oath in respons█ to interrogation by a lawyer or authorized public off █l **3 :** an open acknowledgment or profession (as of relig ▒s experience)

tes·tis \'tes-təs\ *n, pl* **tes·tes** \'tes-,tēz\ [L, witn█ss, testis] **:** a male reproductive gland

tes·tos·ter·one \te-'stäs-tə-ˌrōn\ *n* : a potent androgen that is produced by special cells of the testis or made synthetically

test paper *n* : paper saturated with a reagent that changes color in testing for various substances

test pilot *n* : a pilot employed to put new airplanes through severe tests

test tube *n* : a usu. plain tube of thin glass closed at one end and used esp. in chemistry and biology

tes·tu·do \te-'st(y)üd-ō\ *n* [L, lit., tortoise, tortoise shell] : a cover of overlapping shields or a shed wheeled up to a wall used by the ancient Romans to protect an attacking force

tes·ty \'tes-tē\ *adj* **tes·ti·er; -est** [AF *testif* headstrong, fr. OF *teste* head] **1** : easily annoyed ▪ IRRITABLE **2** : marked by impatience or ill humor ▪ EXASPERATED ⟨a *testy* remark⟩ **syn** see IRASCIBLE — **tes·ti·ly** \-tə-lē\ *adv* — **tes·ti·ness** \-tē-nəs\ *n*

te·tan·ic \te-'tan-ik\ *adj* : of, relating to, or being tetanus or tetany — **te·tan·i·cal·ly** \-'tan-i-k(ə-)lē\ *adv*

tet·a·nize \'tet-ᵊn-ˌīz\ *vt* : to induce tetanus in ⟨*tetanize* a muscle⟩

tet·a·nus \'tet-ᵊn-əs\ *n* [Gk *tetanos*, fr. *tetanos* stretched, rigid; akin to E *thin*] **1** : an acute infectious disease characterized by tonic spasm of voluntary muscles esp. of the jaw and caused by the toxin of a clostridium bacillus which usu. enters a wound and multiplies in damaged tissue **2** : prolonged contraction of a muscle resulting from rapidly repeated motor impulses

tet·a·ny \'tet-ᵊn-ē\ *n* : a condition marked by tonic spasm of muscles and associated usu. with deficient parathyroid secretion and faulty mineral balance

tetchy \'tech-ē\ *adj* : irritably or peevishly sensitive ▪ TOUCHY

¹tête-à-tête \ˌtāt-ə-'tāt\ *adv* [F, lit., head to head] : face to face ▪ PRIVATELY

²tête-à-tête *n* **1** : a private conversation between two persons **2** : a seat for two persons facing each other

³tête-à-tête *adj* : being face to face ▪ PRIVATE

¹teth·er \'teth-ər\ *n* [ME *tethir*] **1** : a line (as of rope or chain) by which an animal is fastened so as to restrict its range **2** : the limit of one's strength or resources ▪ SCOPE ⟨the end of his *tether*⟩

²tether *vt* **teth·ered; teth·er·ing** \'teth-(ə-)riŋ\ : to fasten or restrain by or as if by a tether

tet·ra \'te-trə\ *n* : any of various small brightly colored So. American fishes often bred in the tropical aquarium

tetra- *or* **tetr-** *comb form* [Gk; akin to E *four*] : four : having four : having four parts ⟨*tetratomic*⟩

tet·ra·chlo·ride \ˌte-trə-'klōr-ˌīd, -'klòr-\ *n* : a chloride containing four atoms of chlorine

tet·ra·chord \'te-trə-ˌkòrd\ *n* : a diatonic series of four tones : half an octave

tet·ra·cy·cline \ˌte-trə-'sī-ˌklēn\ *n* : a yellow crystalline broad-spectrum antibiotic produced by a soil actinomycete or synthetically

tet·rad \'te-ˌtrad\ *n* : a group or arrangement of four: as **a** : a group of four cells produced by the successive divisions of a mother cell **b** : an arrangement of chromosomes by fours in the first meiotic prophase due to early splitting of paired chromosomes — **te·trad·ic** \te-'trad-ik\ *adj*

tet·ra·eth·yl lead \ˌte-trə-ˌeth-əl-\ *n* : a heavy oily poisonous liquid Pb(C_2H_5)$_4$ used as an antiknock agent

tet·ra·he·dron \ˌte-trə-'hē-drən\ *n, pl* **-drons** *or* **-dra** \-drə\ : a polyhedron of four faces — **tet·ra·he·dral** \-drəl\ *adj*

te·tral·o·gy \te-'träl-ə-jē, -'tral-\ *n, pl* **-gies** : a series of four connected works (as operas or novels)

te·tram·er·ous \te-'tram-ə-rəs\ *adj* : having or characterized by the presence of four parts or by parts arranged in sets or multiples of four

te·tram·e·ter \te-'tram-ət-ər\ *n* : a line consisting of four metrical feet

tet·ra·ploid \'te-trə-ˌplòid\ *adj* : fourfold in appearance or arrangement; *esp* : having or being a chromosome number four times the monoploid number ⟨a *tetraploid* cell⟩ — **tetraploid** *n* — **tet·ra·ploi·dy** \-ˌplòid-ē\ *n*

tet·ra·pod \'te-trə-ˌpäd\ *n* [Gk *pod-, pous* foot] : a vertebrate (as a frog, bird, or cat) with two pairs of limbs

tet·rarch \'te-ˌträrk, 'tē-\ *n* : a governor of a part and esp. of the 4th part of a province (as of ancient Rome) — **te-**

trar·chic \te-'trär-kik, tē-\ *adj* — **tet·rar·chy** \'te-ˌträr-kē, 'tē-\ *n*

tet·ra·va·lent \ˌte-trə-'vā-lənt\ *adj* **1** : having a valence of four **2** ▪ QUADRUPLE ⟨homologous chromosomes become *tetravalent* during synapsis⟩

tet·rode \'te-ˌtrōd\ *n* : a vacuum tube with four electrodes

te·trox·ide \te-'träk-ˌsīd\ *n* : a compound of an element or radical with four atoms of oxygen

tet·ter \'tet-ər\ *n* : any of various skin diseases (as ringworm or eczema) marked by sore itching eruptions

Teu·ton \'t(y)üt-ᵊn\ *n* **1** : a member of an ancient prob. Germanic or Celtic people **2** : a member of a people speaking a language of the Germanic branch of the Indo-European language family; *esp* ▪ GERMAN

¹Teu·ton·ic \t(y)ü-'tän-ik\ *adj* : of, relating to, or characteristic of the Teutons — **Teu·ton·i·cal·ly** \-'tän-i-k(ə-)lē\ *adv*

²Teutonic *n* ▪ GERMANIC

tex·as \'tek-səs, -siz\ *n* [*Texas*, state of U.S.; fr. the naming of cabins on Mississippi steamboats after states, the officers' cabins being the largest] : a structure on an upper deck of a steamer containing the officers' cabins and having the pilothouse in front or on top

Texas fever *n* : an infectious disease of cattle transmitted by a tick and caused by a protozoan that multiplies in the blood and destroys the red blood cells

Texas Ranger *n* : a member of a mounted police force in Texas

Texas tower *n* [fr. the resemblance to Texas offshore oil derricks] : a radar-equipped platform supported on caissons sunk in the ocean floor

text \'tekst\ *n* [L *textus* texture, context, fr. *texere* to weave] **1 a** : the original written or printed words and form of a literary work **b** : an edited or emended copy of an original work ⟨several *texts* of the play are in print⟩ **2 a** : the main body of printed or written matter on a page **b** : the principal part of a book exclusive of front and back matter **3 a** : a passage of Scripture chosen for the subject of a sermon; *also* : a passage providing a basis (as for a speech) **b** : a source of information or authority **c** : a subject on which one writes or speaks ▪ THEME, TOPIC **4** ▪ TEXTBOOK ⟨a history *text* written with the high-school student in mind⟩

text·book \'teks(t)-ˌbúk\ *n* : a book used in the study of a subject; *esp* : one that presents the principles of a subject and is used as a basis of instruction

tex·tile \'tek-ˌstīl, 'teks-tᵊl\ *n* [L *texere* to weave] **1** ▪ CLOTH 1; *esp* : a woven or knit cloth **2** : a fiber, filament, or yarn used in making cloth — **textile** *adj*

tex·tu·al \'teks-ch(ə-w)əl\ *adj* : of, relating to, or based on a text — **tex·tu·al·ly** \-ē\ *adv*

textual criticism *n* **1** : the study of a literary work that aims to establish the original text **2** : a critical study of literature emphasizing a close reading and analysis of the text — **textual critic** *n*

¹tex·ture \'teks-chər\ *n* **1** : something (as cloth or a web) formed by or as if by weaving **2 a** : the structure, feel, and appearance of a textile that result from the kind and arrangement of its threads ⟨the harsh *texture* of burlap⟩ ⟨a silk with a smooth lustrous *texture*⟩ **b** : similar qualities dependent on the nature and arrangement of the constituent particles of a substance ⟨a gritty *texture*⟩⟨rock with a very fine *texture*⟩ **3** : an essential or identifying part or quality ⟨the truly American *texture* of the experience⟩⟨the unmistakable *texture* of his writing⟩ — **tex·tur·al** \-chə-rəl\ *adj*

²texture *vt* : to give a particular and esp. a rough texture to ⟨*texture* a ceiling⟩

¹-th — see -ETH

²-th *or* **-eth** *adj suffix* [OE *-tha*] — used in forming ordinal numbers ⟨hundred*th*⟩ ⟨fortie*th*⟩

³-th *n suffix* [OE] **1** : act or process ⟨spil*th*⟩ **2** : state or condition ⟨dear*th*⟩

Thai \'tī\ *n* **1** : a native or inhabitant of Thailand **2** : the official language of Thailand — **Thai** *adj*

thal·a·mus \'thal-ə-məs\ *n, pl* **-mi** \-ˌmī, -ˌmē\ [NL, fr. Gk *thalamos* chamber] : the largest subdivision of the diencephalon forming a coordinating center through which afferent nerve impulses are directed to appropriate parts of the brain cortex — **tha·lam·ic** \thə-'lam-ik\ *adj*

tha·las·sic \thə-'las-ik\ *adj* [Gk *thalassa* sea] **1** : of or relating to the sea or ocean **2 :** of or relating to seas or gulfs as distinguished from oceans

tha·ler \'täl-ər\ *var of* TALER

Tha·lia \thə-'lī-ə\ *n* **1 :** the Greek Muse of comedy and pastoral poetry **2 :** one of the three Graces

thal·lic \'thal-ik\ *adj* **:** of, relating to, or containing thallium esp. with a valence of three

thal·li·um \'thal-ē-əm\ *n* [NL, fr. Gk *thallos* young shoot; fr. the green line in its spectrum] **:** a poisonous metallic chemical element resembling lead in physical properties — see ELEMENT table

thal·lo·phyte \'thal-ə-ˌfīt\ *n* **:** any of a primary division (Thallophyta) of the plant kingdom comprising plants with single-celled sex organs or with sex organs of which all cells give rise to gametes, including the algae, fungi, and lichens, and usu. held to be a heterogeneous assemblage — **thal·lo·phyt·ic** \ˌthal-ə-'fit-ik\ *adj*

thal·lous \'thal-əs\ *adj* **:** of, relating to, or containing thallium with a valence of one

thal·lus \'thal-əs\ *n*, *pl* **thal·li** \'thal-ˌī, -ˌē\ *also* **thal·lus·es** [Gk *thallos* young shoot, fr. *thallein* to sprout] **:** the thallophytic plant body characterized by failure to differentiate into distinct members (as stem, leaves, or roots) and by growth that is not confined to an apical point — **thal·loid** \'thal-ˌȯid\ *adj*

than \thən, (ˌ)than\ *conj* [OE *thonne*, fr. *thonne* then] **1** — used after a comparative adjective or adverb to introduce the second part of a comparison expressing inequality ⟨older *than* I am⟩⟨easier said *than* done⟩ **2** — used after *other* or a word of similar meaning to express a difference of kind, manner, or identity ⟨adults other *than* parents⟩ ⟨anywhere else *than* at home⟩

thane \'thān\ *n* **1 :** THEGN **2 :** a Scottish feudal lord

thane·ship \-ˌship\ *n* **:** the office or position of a thane

¹thank \'thaŋk\ *n* [OE *thanc* thought, gratitude] **1** *pl* **:** kindly or grateful thoughts **:** GRATITUDE ⟨express my *thanks* for their kindness⟩ **2 :** an expression of gratitude — usu. used in pl. ⟨return *thanks* before the meal⟩; often used in an utterance containing no verb and serving as an ordinarily courteous and somewhat informal expression of gratitude ⟨many *thanks*⟩

²thank *vt* **1 :** to express gratitude to ⟨*thanked* her for the present⟩ ⟨*thank* you for the loan⟩ **2 :** to hold responsible ⟨had only himself to *thank* for his loss⟩

thank·ful \'thaŋk-fəl\ *adj* **1 :** conscious of benefit received **2 :** expressive of thanks **3 :** well pleased **:** GLAD **syn** see GRATEFUL — **thank·ful·ly** \-fə-lē\ *adv* — **thank·ful·ness** *n*

thank·less \'thaŋk-ləs\ *adj* **1 :** not expressing or feeling gratitude **:** UNGRATEFUL **2 :** not likely to obtain thanks **:** UNAPPRECIATED — **thank·less·ly** *adv* — **thank·less·ness** *n*

thanks·giv·ing \thaŋ(k)s-'giv-iŋ\ *n* **1 :** the act of giving thanks **2 :** a prayer expressing gratitude **3** *cap* **:** THANKS-GIVING DAY

Thanksgiving Day *n* **:** the 4th Thursday in November observed as a legal holiday for public thanksgiving to God

thank·wor·thy \'thaŋk-ˌwər-thē\ *adj* **:** worthy of thanks or gratitude **:** MERITORIOUS

thank-you-ma'am \-yù-ˌmam, -(y)ē-ˌmam\ *n* [prob. fr. its causing a nodding of the head] **:** a bump or depression in a road

¹that \(ˌ)that\ *pron*, *pl* **those** \(ˌ)thōz\ [OE *thæt* neut. demonstrative pron. & definite article] **1 a :** the person, thing, or idea indicated, mentioned, or understood from the situation ⟨*that* is my father⟩ **b :** the one, kind, or thing specified as follows ⟨the purest water is *that* produced by distillation⟩ **2 a :** the one farther away or less immediately under observation ⟨*those* are elms and these are maples⟩ **b :** the former one

²that *adj*, *pl* **those** **1 :** being the one specified or understood ⟨*that* boy did it⟩ **2 :** the farther away or less immediately under observation or discussion ⟨this chair or *that* one⟩

³that \thət, (ˌ)that\ *conj* **1 a** (1) — used to introduce a noun clause serving esp. as the subject or object of a verb or as a predicate nominative ⟨*that* he has succeeded is undeniable⟩ ⟨said *that* he was afraid⟩ ⟨the reason for his absence is *that* he is ill⟩ (2) — used to introduce a subordinate clause that modifies a noun or adjective or is in apposition with a noun ⟨certain *that* this is true⟩ ⟨the

certainty *that* this is true⟩ ⟨the fact *that* you are here⟩ **b** — used to introduce an exclamatory clause expressing surprise, sorrow, or indignation ⟨*that* it should come to this⟩ **2 a** — used alone or after *so* or *in order* to introduce a subordinate clause expressing purpose ⟨saved money so *that* he could buy a bicycle⟩ **b** — used to introduce an exclamatory clause expressing a wish ⟨oh, *that* she were here⟩ **3** — used to introduce a subordinate clause expressing a reason ⟨delighted *that* you could come⟩ **4** — used esp. after an expression including the word *so* or *such* to introduce a subordinate clause expressing result ⟨worked so hard *that* he became exhausted⟩

⁴that \that, (ˌ)that\ *pron* **1** — used to introduce a relative clause and to serve as a substitute within that clause for the substantive modified by that clause ⟨the house *that* Jack built⟩ **2 :** at which **:** in which **:** on which **:** by which **:** with which **:** to which ⟨each year *that* the lectures are given⟩ **syn** see WHO

⁵that \'that\ *adv* **:** to such an extent ⟨need a nail about *that* long⟩

¹thatch \'thach\ *vt* [OE *theccan* to cover] **:** to cover with or as if with thatch — **thatch·er** *n*

²thatch *n* **:** a plant material (as straw) for use as roofing (as for a house); *also* **:** a cover (as a roof) of thatch or as if of thatch ⟨a *thatch* of white hair⟩

thau·ma·tur·gy \'thȯ-mə-ˌtər-jē\ *n* [Gk *thaumatourgia*, fr. *thaumat-*, *thauma* wonder + *-o-* + *ergon* work] **:** the performance of miracles or wonders; *also* **:** MAGIC — **thau·ma·tur·gic** \ˌthȯ-mə-'tər-jik\ *adj* — **thau·ma·tur·gist** \'thȯ-mə-ˌtər-jəst\ *n*

¹thaw \'thȯ\ *vb* [OE *thawian*] **1 :** to melt or cause to melt **:** reverse the effect of freezing ⟨ice on the pond is *thawing*⟩ **2 a :** to become so warm or mild as to melt ice or snow **b :** to recover from chilling ⟨the skiers *thawed* out in front of the fire⟩ **3 :** to grow less cold or reserved in manner **:** become more friendly

²thaw *n* **1 :** the action, fact, or process of thawing **2 :** a warmth of weather sufficient to thaw ice

¹the \thə (*esp before consonant sounds*), thē (*before vowel sounds*); 1g is often 'thē\ *definite article* [OE *thē*, masc. demonstrative pron. & definite article, alter. of *sē*] **1 a :** that (one) or those (ones) previously mentioned or clearly understood from the context or situation ⟨put *the* cat out⟩ **b :** that unique (one) **:** that (one) existing as only one at a time ⟨*the* Lord⟩ ⟨*the* Pope⟩ **c :** that (one) or those (ones) near in space, time, or thought ⟨news of *the* day⟩ **d :** that (one) or those (ones) best known to the speaker or writer or to the hearer or reader ⟨*the* President⟩ ⟨*the* courts will decide⟩ **e :** MY, YOUR, HIS, HER, ITS, OUR, THEIR, ONE'S ⟨grabbed him by *the* collar⟩ ⟨how's *the* family⟩ ⟨the ankle is better today⟩ **f** (1) **:** in, to, or for each ⟨a dollar *the* bottle⟩ (2) **:** EACH, EVERY ⟨eighty crackers to *the* box⟩ **g :** that (one) or those (ones) considered best, most typical, or most worth singling out ⟨*the* poet of his day⟩ ⟨a young man named Einstein, not related to *the* Einstein⟩ ⟨my friend Adams is not one of *the* Adamses⟩ **2 a :** any (one) typical of or standing for an entire class so named ⟨courtesy distinguishes *the* gentleman⟩ ⟨good for *the* soul⟩ **b :** that which is ⟨an essay on *the* sublime⟩ **3 :** all those that are ⟨*the* Greeks⟩ ⟨*the* wise⟩ ⟨*the* aristocracy⟩

²the *adv* [OE *thȳ* by that, instrumental of *thæt* that] **1 :** than before **:** than otherwise — used before a comparative ⟨none *the* wiser for attending⟩ **2 a :** to what extent ⟨*the* sooner the better⟩ **b :** to that extent ⟨the sooner *the* better⟩

the- *or* **theo-** *comb form* [Gk *theos*] **:** god **:** God ⟨theism⟩ ⟨theocentric⟩

the·a·ter *or* **the·a·tre** \'thē-ət-ər\ *n* [Gk *theatron*, fr. *theasthai* to view] **1 :** a building or area for dramatic performances or for showing motion pictures **2 :** a place resembling a theater in form or use; *esp* **:** a room often with rising tiers of seats for assemblies (as for a lecture) **3 :** a place of enactment of significant events or action ⟨a *theater* of war⟩ **4 a :** dramatic literature or performance **b :** dramatic effectiveness

the·a·ter·go·er \-ˌgō(-ə)r\ *n* **:** a person who frequently goes to the theater — **the·a·ter·go·ing** \-ˌgō-iŋ\ *n*

theater-in-the-round *n* **:** ARENA THEATER

The·a·tine \'thē-ə-ˌtīn, -ˌtēn\ *n* **:** a priest of the Order of Clerks Regular established in 1524 in Italy to reform morality and combat Lutheranism — **Theatine** *adj*

ȷ joke; ŋ sing; ō flow; ȯ flaw; ȯi coin; th thin; th̠ this; ü loot; u̇ foot; y yet; yü few; yu̇ furious; zh vision

the·at·ri·cal \thē-'a-tri-kəl\ *adj* **1 :** of or relating to the theater or the presentation of plays ⟨*theatrical* costume⟩ **2 :** marked by pretense or artificiality of emotion **:** not natural and simple **:** SHOWY ⟨*theatrical* acceptance speech⟩ *syn* see DRAMATIC — **the·at·ri·cal·ism** \-kə-‚liz-əm\ *n* — **the·at·ri·cal·i·ty** \-‚a-trə-'kal-ət-ē\ *n* — **the·at·ri·cal·ly** \-'a-tri-k(ə-)lē\ *adv*

the·at·ri·cals \the-'a-tri-kəlz\ *n pl* **:** the performance of plays ⟨amateur *theatricals*⟩; *also* **:** the arts of acting and stagecraft

the·at·rics \-triks\ *n pl* **1 :** THEATRICALS **2 :** staged or contrived effects

the·ca \'thē-kə\ *n, pl* **the·cae** \'thē-‚sē, -‚kē\ [NL, fr. Gk *thēkē*, fr. *tithenai* to put] **:** an envelope or sheath enclosing an organism or one of its parts **:** CAPSULE, TEST — **the·cal** \'thē-kəl\ *or* **the·cate** \-‚kāt\ *adj*

the·co·dont \'thē-kə-‚dänt\ *n* **:** any of an order (Thecodontia) of generalized Triassic reptiles held to be ancestral to the dinosaurs, crocodiles, and birds — **thecodont** *adj*

thé dan·sant \tā-dän°-sän°\ *n, pl* **thés dansants** \same\ [F] **:** TEA DANCE

thee \('))thē\ *pron, objective case of* THOU

theft \'theft\ *n* [OE *thiefth*; akin to E *thief*] **:** the act of stealing: as **a :** LARCENY **b :** unlawful acquisition (as by embezzlement or burglary) of property

thegn \'thān\ *n* [OE] **:** a free retainer of an Anglo-Saxon lord; *esp* **:** one holding lands of the king and performing military service

their \thər, (‚)the(ə)r, (‚)tha(ə)r\ *adj* **:** of or relating to them or themselves esp. as possessors, agents, or objects of an action ⟨*their* clothes⟩ ⟨*their* deeds⟩ ⟨*their* being seen⟩

theirs \'the(ə)rz, 'tha(ə)rz\ *pron* **:** their one **:** their ones — used without a following noun as a pronoun equivalent in meaning to the adjective *their*

the·ism \'thē-‚iz-əm\ *n* **:** belief in the existence of a god or gods; *esp* **:** belief in the existence of God as creator and ruler of the universe — **the·ist** \'thē-əst\ *n* — **the·is·tic** \thē-'is-tik\ *adj* — **the·is·ti·cal** \-'is-ti-kəl\ *adj* — **the·is·ti·cal·ly** \-ti-k(ə-)lē\ *adv*

-theism *n comb form* **:** belief in (such) a god or (such or so many) gods ⟨monotheism⟩

-theist *n comb form* **:** believer in (such) a god or (such or so many) gods ⟨pantheist⟩

them \(th)əm, (‚)them, *after* p, b, v, f *also* °m\ *pron, objective case of* THEY

theme \'thēm\ *n* [Gk *themat-*, *thema*, lit., something laid down, fr. *tithenai* to put] **1 :** a subject of discourse, of artistic representation, or of musical composition **2 :** a written exercise **:** COMPOSITION — **the·mat·ic** \thi-'mat-ik\ *adj* — **the·mat·i·cal·ly** \-'mat-i-k(ə-)lē\ *adv*

theme song *n* **1 :** a melody recurring so often in a musical play that it characterizes the production or one of its characters **2 :** SIGNATURE 4

them·selves \thəm-'selvz, them-\ *pron* **1 :** those identical ones that are they — compare THEY 1; used reflexively, for emphasis, or in absolute constructions ⟨nations that govern *themselves*⟩ ⟨they *themselves* were present⟩ ⟨*themselves* busy, they disliked idleness in others⟩ **2 :** their normal, healthy, or sane condition or selves ⟨it was more than a week before they were *themselves* again⟩

¹then \(')then\ *adv* [OE *thonne, thænne;* akin to E *that*] **1 :** at that time **2 :** soon after that ⟨walked to the door, *then* turned⟩ **3 a :** following next after in order **b :** in addition **:** BESIDES **4 a :** in that case **b :** according to that ⟨your mind is made up, *then*⟩ **c :** as it appears ⟨the cause, *then*, is established⟩ **d :** as a necessary consequence ⟨if you were there, *then* you saw him⟩

²then \'then\ *n* **:** that time ⟨wait until *then*⟩

³then \'then\ *adj* **:** existing or acting at or belonging to the time mentioned ⟨the *then* king⟩

the·nar \'thē-‚när, -nər\ *n* [Gk] **1 :** the ball of the thumb **2 a :** the palm of the hand **b :** the sole of the foot — **thenar** *adj*

thence \'then(t)s, 'then(t)s\ *adv* [ME *thanne, thannes*, fr. OE *thanon;* akin to E *that*] **1 :** from that place **2** *archaic* **:** from that time **:** THENCEFORTH **3 :** from that fact or circumstance **:** THEREFROM

thence·forth \-‚fōrth, -‚fôrth\ *adv* **:** from that time forward **:** THEREAFTER

thence·for·ward \then(t)s-'fôr-wərd, then(t)s-\ *also*

thence·for·wards \-wərdz\ *adv* **:** onward from that place or time **:** THENCEFORTH

theo- — see THE-

the·oc·ra·cy \thē-'äk-rə-sē\ *n, pl* **-cies 1 :** government of a country by officials regarded as divinely guided **2 :** a country governed by a theocracy — **theo·crat** \'thē-ə-‚krat\ *n* — **the·o·crat·ic** \‚thē-ə-'krat-ik\ *adj* — **the·o·crat·i·cal·ly** \-'krat-i-k(ə-)lē\ *adv*

the·od·o·lite \thē-'äd-°l-‚īt\ *n* **:** a surveyor's instrument for measuring horizontal and usu. also vertical angles — **the·od·o·lit·ic** \-‚äd-°l-'it-ik\ *adj*

the·o·lo·gian \‚thē-ə-'lō-jən\ *n* **:** a specialist in theology

the·o·log·i·cal \‚thē-ə-'läj-i-kəl\ *adj* **:** of or relating to theology — **the·o·log·i·cal·ly** \-k(ə-)lē\ *adv*

theological virtue *n* **:** a spiritual grace (as faith, hope, or charity) held to perfect the natural virtues

the·o·logue *or* **the·o·log** \'thē-ə-‚lóg\ *n* **:** a theological student or specialist

the·ol·o·gy \thē-'äl-ə-jē\ *n, pl* **-gies 1 :** the study and interpretation of religious faith, practice, and experience; *esp* **:** thought about God and his relation to the world **2 :** a course of professional religious training

the·o·rem \'thē-ə-rəm, 'thi(ə)r-əm\ *n* [Gk *theōrēma*, fr. *theōrein* to look at, consider, fr. *thea* sight, view] **1 :** a formula, proposition, or statement (as in logic) that has been or is to be proved from other formulas or propositions **2 :** an idea accepted or proposed as a demonstrable truth **:** PROPOSITION ⟨the *theorem* that the best defense is offense⟩

the·o·ret·i·cal \‚thē-ə-'ret-i-kəl\ *also* **the·o·ret·ic** \-'ret-ik\ *adj* **1 a :** relating to or having the character of theory **:** ABSTRACT **b :** confined to theory or speculation **:** SPECULATIVE ⟨*theoretical* mechanics⟩ **2 :** given to or skilled in theorizing **3 :** existing only in theory **:** HYPOTHETICAL — **the·o·ret·i·cal·ly** \-i-k(ə-)lē\ *adv*

the·o·re·ti·cian \‚thē-ə-rə-'tish-ən\ *n* **:** THEORIST

the·o·rist \'thē-ə-rəst, 'thi(ə)r-əst\ *n* **:** a person that theorizes

the·o·rize \'thē-ə-‚rīz\ *vi* **:** to form a theory **:** SPECULATE — **the·o·ri·za·tion** \‚thē-ə-rə-'zā-shən\ *n* — **the·o·riz·er** \'thē-ə-‚rī-zər\ *n*

the·o·ry \'thē-ə-rē, 'thi(ə)r-ē\ *n, pl* **-ries** [Gk *theōria* speculation, theory, fr. *theōrein* to look at, consider, fr. *thea* sight, view] **1 :** the general or abstract principles of a body of fact, a science, or an art ⟨music *theory*⟩ — compare PRACTICE **2 :** a plausible or scientifically acceptable general principle or body of principles offered to explain phenomena ⟨wave *theory* of light⟩ **3 a :** a hypothesis assumed for the sake of argument or investigation **b :** SUPPOSITION, CONJECTURE **4 :** abstract thought **:** SPECULATION *syn* see HYPOTHESIS

the·os·o·phy \thē-'äs-ə-fē\ *n* [Gk *sophia* wisdom] **1 :** belief about God and the world held to be based on mystical insight **2** *often cap* **:** the beliefs of a modern movement originating in the U.S. in 1875 and following chiefly Buddhist and Brahmanic theories esp. of pantheistic evolution and reincarnation — **the·o·soph·i·cal** \‚thē-ə-'säf-i-kəl\ *adj* — **the·o·soph·i·cal·ly** \-'säf-i-k(ə-)lē\ *adv* — **the·os·o·phist** \thē-'äs-ə-fəst\ *n*

ther·a·peu·tic \‚ther-ə-'pyüt-ik\ *adj* [Gk *therapeuein* to attend, treat, fr. *theraps* attendant] **:** of, relating to, or dealing with healing and esp. with remedies for diseases **:** MEDICINAL ⟨a *therapeutic* dose of arsenic⟩ ⟨*therapeutic* studies⟩ — **ther·a·peu·ti·cal·ly** \-'pyüt-i-k(ə-)lē\ *adv*

ther·a·peu·tics \-'pyüt-iks\ *n* **:** a branch of medical science dealing with the use of remedies

ther·a·pist \'ther-ə-pəst\ *n* **:** one specializing in therapy; *esp* **:** a person trained in methods of treatment and rehabilitation other than the use of drugs or surgery ⟨a speech *therapist*⟩

the·rap·sid \thə-'rap-səd\ *n* [Gk *theraps* attendant] **:** any of an order (Therapsida) of Permian and Triassic reptiles held to be ancestral to the mammals

ther·a·py \'ther-ə-pē\ *n, pl* **-pies** [Gk *therapeia*, fr. *therapeuein* to treat] **:** therapeutic treatment of bodily, mental, or social disorders or maladjustment

¹there \'tha(ə)r, 'the(ə)r\ *adv* [OE *thēr;* akin to E *that*] **1 :** in or at that place ⟨stand over *there*⟩ — often used interjectionally **2 :** to or into that place **:** THITHER **3 :** at that point or stage ⟨*there* the plot thickens⟩ **4 :** in that matter, respect, or relation ⟨*there* you have a choice⟩ **5** — used interjectionally to express satisfaction, approval, soothing, or defiance ⟨*there*, I'm through⟩

²**there** \(,)tha(ə)r, (,)the(ə)r, *I* is also thər\ *pron* **1** — used as a function word to introduce a sentence or clause esp. when the verb has no complement ⟨*there* shall come a time⟩ **2** — used as an indefinite substitute for a name ⟨hi *there*⟩

³**there** *like*¹\ *n* **1** : that place or position **2** : that point ⟨you take it from *there*⟩

⁴**there** *like*¹\ *adj* — used for emphasis esp. after a demonstrative pronoun or a noun modified by a demonstrative adjective ⟨those men *there* can tell you⟩

there·abouts *or* **there·about** \,thar-ə-'baut(s), ,ther-\ *adv* **1** : near that place or time **2** : near that number, degree, or quantity ⟨fifty people or *thereabouts*⟩

there·af·ter \thar-'af-tər, ther-\ *adv* **1** : after that **2** *archaic* : according to that : ACCORDINGLY

there·at \-'at\ *adv* **1** : at that place **2** : at that occurrence : on that account

there·by \tha(ə)r-'bī, the(ə)r-\ *adv* **1** : by that : by that means ⟨made a friend *thereby*⟩ **2** : connected with or with reference to that ⟨*thereby* hangs a tale⟩

there·for \-'fó(ə)r\ *adv* : for or in return for that ⟨issued bonds *therefor*⟩

there·fore \'tha(ə)r-,fór, 'the(ə)r-, -,fór\ *adv* **1 a** : for that reason : CONSEQUENTLY **b** : because of that **c** : on that ground **2** : to that end

there·from \tha(ə)r-'frəm, the(ə)r-, -'främ\ *adv* : from that or it ⟨learned much *therefrom*⟩

there·in \thar-'in, ther-\ *adv* **1** : in or into that place, time, or thing ⟨the world and all *therein*⟩ **2** : in that particular or respect ⟨*therein* they disagreed⟩

there·in·af·ter \,thar-in-'af-tər, ,ther-\ *adv* : in the following part of that matter (as writing, document, or speech)

there·in·to \thar-'in-tü, ther-\ *adv, archaic* : into that or it

there·of \-'əv, -'äv\ *adv* **1** : of that or it ⟨took the bread and ate *thereof*⟩ **2** : from that cause or particular : THEREFROM ⟨a wound so deep that he died *thereof*⟩

there·on \-'ón, -'än\ *adv* **1** : on that ⟨a table with a vase set *thereon*⟩ **2** *archaic* : THEREUPON

there·to \tha(ə)r-'tü, the(ə)r-\ *adv* : to that ⟨signed his name *thereto*⟩

there·to·fore \'thart-ə-,fór, 'thert-, -,fór\ *adv* : up to that time

there·un·der \thar-'ən-dər, ther-\ *adv* : under that

there·un·to \-'ən-tü\ *adv, archaic* : THERETO

there·upon \'thar-ə-,pón, 'ther-, -,pän\ *adv* **1** : on that matter : THEREON ⟨they disagreed *thereupon*⟩ **2** : THEREFORE **3** : immediately after that : at once

there·with \tha(ə)r-'with, the(ə)r-, -'with\ *adv* **1** : with that ⟨led a simple life and was happy *therewith*⟩ **2** *archaic* : THEREUPON, FORTHWITH

there·with·al \'tha(ə)r-wə-,thól, 'the(ə)r-, -,thól\ *adv* **1** *archaic* : BESIDES **2** : THEREWITH

the·ri·ac \'thir-ē-,ak\ *n* **1** : THERIACA **2** : CURE-ALL

the·ri·a·ca \thir-'ī-ə-kə\ *n* [L, fr. Gk *thēriakē* antidote against a poisonous bite, fr. *thērion* wild animal] : a mixture of many drugs with honey formerly valued as an antidote to poison — **the·ri·a·cal** \-kəl\ *adj*

therm- *or* **thermo-** *comb form* [Gk, fr. *thermē*, fr. *thermos* hot; akin to E *warm*] : heat ⟨*thermion*⟩ ⟨*thermostat*⟩

¹**ther·mal** \'thər-məl\ *adj* : of, relating to, or caused by heat : WARM, HOT — **ther·mal·ly** \-mə-lē\ *adv*

²**thermal** *n* : a rising body of warm air

therm·ion \'thərm-,ī-ən, -,ī-,än\ *n* : an electrically charged particle emitted by an incandescent substance — **therm·ion·ic** \,thərm-ī-'än-ik\ *adj*

therm·is·tor \'thər-,mis-tər\ *n* [*therm*al res*istor*] : an electrical resistor made of a material whose resistance varies sharply in a known manner with the temperature

Ther·mit \'thər-mət\ *trademark* — used for a mixture of aluminum powder and iron oxide that when ignited evolves a great deal of heat and is used in welding and in incendiary bombs

ther·mo·cou·ple \'thər-mə-,kəp-əl\ *n* : a thermoelectric couple used to measure temperature differences

ther·mo·du·ric \,thər-mō-'d(y)ü(ə)r-ik\ *adj* [L *durare* to last, endure] : able to survive high temperatures esp. of pasteurization ⟨*thermoduric* bacteria⟩

ther·mo·dy·nam·ics \,thər-mə-dī-'nam-iks\ *n* : physics that deals with the mechanical action or relations of heat

— **ther·mo·dy·nam·ic** \-ik\ *adj* — **ther·mo·dy·nam·i·cal·ly** \-'nam-i-k(ə-)lē\ *adv*

ther·mo·elec·tric \,thər-mō-i-'lek-trik\ *adj* : of or relating to phenomena involving relations between the temperature and the electrical condition in a metal or in contacting metals

thermoelectric couple *n* : a union of two conductors (as bars or wires of dissimilar metals joined at their extremities) for producing a thermoelectric current

ther·mo·elec·tric·i·ty \,thər-mō-i-,lek-'tris-ət-ē, -'tris-tē\ *n* : electricity produced by the direct action of heat (as by the unequal heating of a circuit composed of two dissimilar metals)

ther·mo·graph \'thər-mə-,graf\ *n* : a self-recording thermometer

ther·mo·la·bile \,thər-mō-'lā-,bīl, -bəl\ *adj* : unstable when heated; *esp* : losing characteristic properties on being heated to or above 55°C ⟨many immune bodies, enzymes, and vitamins are *thermolabile*⟩ — compare THERMOSTABLE — **ther·mo·la·bil·i·ty** \-,lā-'bil-ət-ē\ *n*

ther·mom·e·ter \thə(r)-'mäm-ət-ər\ *n* : an instrument for measuring temperature commonly by means of the expansion or contraction of mercury or alcohol as indicated by its rise or fall in a thin glass tube alongside a numbered scale — **ther·mo·met·ric** \,thər-mə-'me-trik\ *adj* — **ther·mo·met·ri·cal·ly** \-tri-k(ə-)lē\ *adv*

ther·mom·e·try \thə(r)-'mäm-ə-trē\ *n* : the measurement of temperature

ther·mo·nu·cle·ar \,thər-mō-'n(y)ü-klē-ər\ *adj* **1** : of or relating to the transformations in the nucleus of atoms of low atomic weight (as hydrogen) that require a very high temperature (as in the hydrogen bomb or the sun) ⟨*thermonuclear* reaction⟩ ⟨*thermonuclear* weapon⟩ **2** : of, utilizing, or relating to a thermonuclear bomb ⟨*thermonuclear* war⟩

ther·mo·phile \'thər-mə-,fīl\ *n* : an organism growing at a high temperature — **thermophile** *or* **ther·mo·phil·ic** \,thər-mə-'fil-ik\ *adj*

ther·mo·pile \'thər-mə-,pīl\ *n* : an apparatus consisting of a number of thermoelectric couples combined so as to multiply the effect and used for generating electric currents or for determining intensities of radiation

ther·mo·plas·tic \,thər-mə-'plas-tik\ *adj* : having the property of softening or fusing when heated and of hardening again when cooled ⟨*thermoplastic* synthetic resins⟩ — **thermoplastic** *n*

ther·mo·reg·u·la·tor \,thər-mō-'reg-yə-,lāt-ər\ *n* : a device for the regulation of temperature : THERMOSTAT

Ther·mos \'thər-məs\ *trademark* — used for a vacuum bottle

ther·mo·set·ting \'thər-mō-,set-iŋ\ *adj* : having the property of becoming permanently rigid when heated or cured ⟨a *thermosetting* synthetic resin⟩

ther·mo·sta·ble \,thər-mō-'stā-bəl\ *adj* : stable when heated; *esp* : retaining characteristic properties on being moderately heated — compare THERMOLABILE

ther·mo·stat \'thər-mə-,stat\ *n* [Gk *statēs* one that stops or steadies, fr. *histanai* to cause to stand] : an automatic device for regulating temperature (as of a heating system); *also* : a device for actuating fire alarms or for controlling automatic sprinklers — **ther·mo·stat·ic** \,thər-mə-'stat-ik\ *adj* — **ther·mo·stat·i·cal·ly** \-'stat-i-k(ə-)lē\ *adv*

ther·mo·tax·is \,thər-mə-'tak-səs\ *n* : a taxis in which a temperature gradient constitutes the directive factor — **ther·mo·tac·tic** \-'tak-tik\ *adj*

ther·mot·ro·pism \(,)thər-'mä-trə-,piz-əm\ *n* : a tropism in which a temperature gradient determines the orientation — **ther·mo·trop·ic** \,thər-mə-'träp-ik\ *adj*

the·sau·rus \thi-'sór-əs\ *n, pl* **-sau·ri** \-'sór-,ī, -,ē\ *or* **-sau·rus·es** \-əz\ [L, treasure, collection, fr. Gk *thēsauros* treasure, treasury] **1** : a book of words or of information about a particular field; *esp* : a dictionary of synonyms **2** : TREASURY, STOREHOUSE

these *pl of* THIS

The·seus \'thē-,süs, -sē-əs\ *n* : a Greek hero held to have slain Procrustes and the Minotaur and to have conquered the Amazons and married their queen

the·sis \'thē-səs\ *n, pl* **the·ses** \'thē-,sēz\ [Gk, lit., act of laying down, fr. *tithenai* to put] **1** : a proposition to be proved or advanced without proof : HYPOTHESIS **2** : the first stage of a dialectic process — compare SYNTHESIS **3** : a dissertation embodying results of original research and esp. substantiating a specific view; *esp* : one written by a candidate for an academic degree

¹thes·pi·an \'thes-pē-ən\ *adj, often cap* [*Thespis*, 6th cent. B.C. Greek poet, traditional originator of the actor's role] : relating to the drama : DRAMATIC

²thespian *n* : ACTOR

Thes·sa·lo·nians \,thes-ə-'lō-nyənz\ *n* — see BIBLE table

the·ta \'thāt-ə, 'thet-\ *n* : the 8th letter of the Greek alphabet — θ or θ

The·tis \'thēt-əs\ *n* : a Nereid and mother of Achilles

thew \'th(y)ü\ *n* [OE *thēaw* habit, virtue] **1** : MUSCLE, SINEW — usu. used in pl. **2 a** : muscular power or development : STRENGTH

they \(')thā\ *pron* [ON *their*; akin to E *that*] **1** : those ones — used as 3d person pronoun serving as the plural of *he, she,* or *it* or referring to a group of two or more individuals not all of the same sex ⟨*they* dance well⟩ **2** : PEOPLE **1** ⟨curiosity killed a cat, *they* say⟩

they'd \(,)thād\ : they had : they would

they'll \(,)thā(ə)l, thel\ : they shall : they will

they're \thər, (,)the(ə)r, ,thā-ər\ : they are

they've \(,)thāv\ : they have

thi- *or* **thio-** *comb form* [Gk *theion*] : sulfur ⟨*thiamin*⟩ ⟨*thiourea*⟩

thi·am·i·nase \thī-'am-ə-,nās, 'thī-ə-mə-\ *n* : an enzyme that promotes the breakdown of thiamine

thi·a·mine \'thī-ə-mēn, -mən\ *or* **thi·a·min** \-mən\ *n* : a vitamin of the B complex essential to normal metabolism and nerve function and widely distributed in plants and animals — called also *vitamin B₁*

¹thick \'thik\ *adj* [OE *thicce*] **1 a** : having or being of relatively great depth or extent from one surface to its opposite ⟨*thick* plank⟩ **b** : heavily built : THICKSET **2 a** : close-packed : DENSE ⟨*thick* forest⟩ **b** : occurring in large numbers : NUMEROUS **c** : viscous in consistency ⟨*thick* syrup⟩ **d** : SULTRY, STUFFY ⟨the air is *thick* with tobacco smoke⟩ **e** : marked by haze, fog, or mist ⟨*thick* weather⟩ **f** : impenetrable to the eye : PROFOUND ⟨*thick* darkness⟩ **g** : extremely intense ⟨*thick* silence⟩ **3** : measuring in thickness ⟨12 inches *thick*⟩ **4 a** : imperfectly articulated : INDISTINCT ⟨*thick* speech⟩ **b** : PRONOUNCED ⟨*thick* French accent⟩ **c** : producing inarticulate speech ⟨*thick* tongue⟩ **5** : OBTUSE, STUPID **6** : associated on close terms : INTIMATE **7** : exceeding bounds of propriety or fitness : EXCESSIVE — **thick·ish** \-ish\ *adj* — **thick·ly** *adv*

²thick *n* **1** : the most crowded or active part ⟨in the *thick* of battle⟩ **2** : the part of greatest thickness

³thick *adv* : THICKLY

thick and thin *n* : every difficulty and obstacle ⟨stood by his friend through *thick and thin*⟩

thick·en \'thik-ən\ *vb* **thick·ened; thick·en·ing** \'thik-(ə-)niŋ\ **1 a** : to make or become thick, dense, or viscous in consistency **b** : to make or become close or compact **2** : to add to the depth or diameter of **3 a** : to make inarticulate : BLUR ⟨alcohol *thickened* his speech⟩ **b** : to grow blurred or obscure **4** : to grow broader or bulkier **5** : to grow complicated or keen ⟨the plot *thickens*⟩ — **thick·en·er** \-(ə-)nər\ *n*

thick·en·ing *n* **1** : the act of making or becoming thick **2** : something used to thicken (as flour in a gravy) **3** : a thickened part or place

thick·et \'thik-ət\ *n* **1** : a thick usu. circumscribed growth of shrubbery, small trees, or underbrush **2** : something resembling a thicket in density or impenetrability : TANGLE — **thick·et·ed** \-ət-əd\ *adj*

thick·head·ed \'thik-'hed-əd\ *adj* **1** : having a thick head **2** : STUPID

thick·ness \'thik-nəs\ *n* **1** : the quality or state of being thick **2** : the smallest of three dimensions ⟨length, width, and *thickness*⟩ **3** : viscous consistency **4** : the thick part of something **5** : CONCENTRATION, DENSITY **6** : DULLNESS, STUPIDITY **7** : LAYER, PLY, SHEET ⟨a single *thickness* of canvas⟩

thick·set \'thik-'set\ *adj* **1** : closely placed or planted **2** : of short stout build : STOCKY

thick-skinned \-'skind\ *adj* **1** : having a thick skin **2** : CALLOUS, INSENSITIVE

thick-wit·ted \-'wit-əd\ *adj* : dull or slow of mind : STUPID

thief \'thēf\ *n, pl* **thieves** \'thēvz\ [OE *thēof*] : one that steals — **thiev·ish** \'thē-vish\ *adj* — **thiev·ish·ly** *adv* — **thiev·ish·ness** *n*

thieve \'thēv\ *vb* : STEAL, ROB

thiev·ery \'thēv-(ə-)rē\ *n, pl* **-er·ies** : the action of stealing : THEFT

thigh \'thī\ *n* [OE *thēoh*] **1 a** : the segment of the vertebrate hind limb extending from the hip to the knee and supported by a single large bone; *also* : the next outer segment in a bird or in a quadruped in which the true thigh is obscured **b** : the femur of an insect **2** : something resembling or covering a thigh

thigh·bone \-'bōn, -,bōn\ *n* : FEMUR

thig·mo·tax·is \,thig-mə-'tak-səs\ *n* [Gk *thigma* contact] : a taxis in which contact (as with a rigid surface) is the directive factor

thig·mot·ro·pism \thig-'mä-trə-,piz-əm\ *n* [Gk *thigma* contact, fr. *thinganein* to touch] : a tropism in which contact (as with a rigid surface) is the orienting factor

thim·ble \'thim-bəl\ *n* [ME *thymbyl*, prob. fr. OE *thȳmel* covering for the thumb, fr. *thūma* thumb] **1** : a cap or cover used in sewing to protect the finger that pushes the needle **2** : a grooved ring of thin metal used to fit in a loop in a wire or rope **3** : a ring or lining in a hole or a short tube put around or through something

thim·ble·ber·ry \-,ber-ē\ *n* : any of several American raspberries or blackberries with thimble-shaped fruit

thimble 1

thim·ble·ful \-,fúl\ *n* **1** : as much as a thimble will hold **2** : a very small quantity

¹thim·ble·rig \'thim-bəl-,rig\ *n* **1** : a swindling trick in which a small ball or pea is quickly shifted from under one to another of three small cups to fool a spectator guessing its location **2** : THIMBLERIGGER

²thimblerig *vt* **1** : to swindle by thimblerig **2** : to cheat by trickery — **thim·ble·rig·ger** *n*

¹thin \'thin\ *adj* **thin·ner; thin·nest** [OE *thynne*] **1 a** : having little extent from one surface to its opposite ⟨*thin* paper⟩ **b** : measuring little in cross section or diameter ⟨*thin* rope⟩ **2** : not dense in arrangement or distribution ⟨*thin* hair⟩ **3** : not well fleshed : LEAN **4 a** : more fluid or rarefied than normal ⟨*thin* air⟩ **b** : having less than the usual number : SCANTY ⟨*thin* attendance⟩ **5** : lacking substance or strength ⟨*thin* broth⟩ ⟨*thin* excuse⟩ **6** : somewhat feeble, shrill, and lacking in resonance ⟨*thin* voice⟩ — **thin·ly** *adv* — **thin·ness** \'thin-nəs\ *n* — **thin·nish** \'thin-ish\ *adj*

syn THIN, SLENDER, SLIM, SLIGHT mean not thick, broad, abundant, or dense. THIN implies comparatively little extension between surfaces or in diameter ⟨*thin* layer of ice⟩⟨*thin* wire⟩ or it may imply lack of substance, richness, or abundance ⟨*thin* soup⟩ ⟨*thin* hedge⟩ SLENDER implies leanness often with graceful proportions ⟨*slender* columns⟩ SLIM suggests scantiness or fragile slenderness ⟨*slim* paycheck⟩ SLIGHT implies thinness and smallness ⟨a man of *slight* build⟩ or lack of weight or seriousness ⟨of *slight* importance⟩

²thin *adv* **thin·ner; thin·nest** : THINLY ⟨*thin*-clad⟩

³thin *vb* **thinned; thin·ning** : to make or become thin or thinner: **a** : to reduce in thickness or depth : ATTENUATE **b** : to make less dense or viscous **c** : DILUTE, WEAKEN **d** : to cause to lose flesh **e** : to reduce in number or bulk

¹thine \(')thīn\ *adj* [OE *thīn*] *archaic* : THY — used esp. before a word beginning with a vowel or *h*

²thine \'thīn\ *pron, archaic* : thy one : thy ones — used without a following noun as a pronoun equivalent in meaning to the adjective *thy*

thing \'thiŋ\ *n* [OE] **1 a** : a matter of concern : AFFAIR ⟨many *things* to do⟩ **b** *pl* : state of affairs in general or within a specified or implied sphere ⟨*things* are improving⟩ **c** : a particular state of affairs : SITUATION ⟨look at this *thing* another way⟩ **d** : EVENT, CIRCUMSTANCE ⟨that shooting was a terrible *thing*⟩ **2 a** : DEED, ACT, ACCOMPLISHMENT ⟨do great *things*⟩ **b** : a product of work or activity ⟨likes to build *things*⟩ **c** : the aim of effort or activity ⟨the *thing* is to get well⟩ **3 a** : a separate and distinct item or object : ENTITY; *esp* : a tangible object **b** : an

ə abut; **ᵊ kitten;** **ər further;** **a back;** **ā bake;** **ä cot, cart;** **aú out;** **ch chin;** **e less;** **ē easy;** **g gift;** **i trip;** **ī life**

inanimate object distinguished from a living being **4 a** *pl* : POSSESSIONS, EFFECTS ⟨pack your *things*⟩ **b** : an article of clothing ⟨not a *thing* to wear⟩ **c** *pl* : equipment or utensils esp. for a particular purpose ⟨bring the tea *things*⟩ **5** : an object or entity not precisely designated or capable of being designated ⟨use this *thing*⟩ **6 a** : DETAIL, POINT ⟨checks every little *thing*⟩ **b** : a material or substance of a specified kind ⟨avoid starchy *things*⟩ **7 a** : a spoken or written observation or point **b** : IDEA, NOTION ⟨says the first *thing* he thinks of⟩ **c** : a piece of news or information ⟨couldn't get a *thing* out of him⟩ **8** : INDIVIDUAL; *esp* : PERSON **9** : the proper or fashionable way of behaving, talking, or dressing ⟨it is the *thing* to do⟩

thing·ama·jig *or* **thing·um·a·jig** \'thiŋ-ə-mə-ˌjig\ *n* : something which is hard to classify or whose name is unknown or forgotten — called also *thing·ama·bob* \-mə-ˌbäb\

T hinge \'tē-\ *n* : a hinge having the shape of a letter T when opened

thing·um·my \'thiŋ-ə-mē\ *n, pl* **-mies** : THINGAMAJIG

¹think \'thiŋk\ *vb* **thought** \'thȯt\; **think·ing** [OE *thencan*] **1** : to form or have in the mind **2** : INTEND, PLAN ⟨*thought* to return early⟩ **3 a** : to have as an opinion : BELIEVE ⟨*think* it's so⟩ **b** : to regard as : CONSIDER ⟨*think* the rule unfair⟩ **4** : to reflect on : PONDER ⟨*think* the matter over⟩ **5** : to call to mind : REMEMBER ⟨never *thought* to ask⟩ **6** : to form a mental picture of **7** : to subject to the processes of logical thought ⟨*think* things out⟩ **8** : to exercise the powers of judgment, conception, or inference : REASON **9 a** : to have the mind engaged in reflection : MEDITATE **b** : to consider the suitability ⟨*thought* of him for president⟩ **10** : to have a view or opinion ⟨*thinks* of himself as a poet⟩ **11** : to have concern ⟨*think* of just yourself⟩ **12** : EXPECT, SUSPECT — **think·a·ble** \'thiŋ-kə-bəl\ *adj* — **think·er** *n*

syn THINK, REFLECT, REASON, SPECULATE mean to use one's powers of conception, judgment, or inference. THINK may apply to any mental activity but often suggests attainment of clear ideas or conclusions; REFLECT suggests unhurried consideration of something recalled to mind; REASON stresses consecutive logical thinking; SPECULATE implies reasoning but stresses the uncertain, theoretical, or problematic character of the conclusions ⟨*speculated* on the probable consequences of a nuclear war⟩

²think *n* : an act of thinking ⟨has another *think* coming⟩

¹think·ing *n* **1** : the action of using one's mind to produce thoughts **2 a** : OPINION, JUDGMENT **b** : THOUGHT

²thinking *adj* : marked by use of the intellect : RATIONAL ⟨a *thinking* man⟩ — **think·ing·ly** \'thiŋ-kiŋ-lē\ *adv* — **think·ing·ness** *n*

thinking cap *n* : a state or mood in which one thinks ⟨put on your *thinking cap*⟩

think piece *n* : a news article consisting chiefly of background material and personal opinion and analysis

thin·ner \'thin-ər\ *n* : one that thins; *esp* : a volatile liquid (as turpentine) used to thin paint

thin–skinned \'thin-'skind\ *adj* **1** : having a thin skin or rind **2** : unduly susceptible to criticism or insult : TOUCHY

thio- — see THI-

thi·o·pen·tal \ˌthī-ō-'pen-ˌtal, -ˌtȯl\ *n* : a barbiturate used in intravenous anesthesia and psychotherapy

thio·sul·fate \-'səl-ˌfāt\ *n* : a salt or ester of thiosulfuric acid

thio·sul·fu·ric acid \-ˌsəl-ˌfyu̇r-ik-\ *n* : an unstable acid $H_2S_2O_3$ derived from sulfuric acid and known only in solution

thio·urea \-yu̇-'rē-ə, -'yu̇r-ē-ə\ *n* : a colorless crystalline bitter compound $CS(NH_2)_2$ analogous to and resembling urea that is used esp. as a photographic and organic chemical reagent

thi·ram \'thī-ˌram\ *n* : a sulfur-containing fungicide and seed disinfectant

¹third \'thərd\ *adj* [OE *thridda;* akin to E *three*] **1 a** — see NUMBER table **b** : next after the second in time, order, or importance **2** : being one of three equal parts of something — **third** *adv* — **third·ly** *adv*

²third *n* **1** — see NUMBER table **2** : one of three equal parts of something **3 a** : a musical interval of three degrees or a tone at this interval **b** : the harmonic combination of two tones a third apart **4** : the third gear

or speed of an automotive vehicle **5** : one next after a second in time, order, or importance

third base *n* **1** : the base that must be touched third by a base runner in baseball **2** : the position of the player defending the area around third base — **third baseman** *n*

third class *n* : the class next below second class in a classification ⟨travel by *third class* to Europe⟩; *esp* : a class of U.S. mail including various printed matter and merchandise that weighs less than 16 ounces and is open to inspection — **third–class** *adj or adv*

third degree *n* : severe or brutal treatment of a prisoner by the police in order to get an admission

third-degree burn *n* : a burn in which there is destruction of the whole thickness of the skin and sometimes of deeper tissues with loss of fluid and often shock

third dimension *n* **1** : thickness, depth, or apparent thickness or depth that confers solidity on an object **2** : a quality that confers reality or lifelikeness — **third-di·men·sion·al** *adj*

third estate *n* : the third of the traditional political orders : COMMON 3a; *also* : MIDDLE CLASS

third force *n* : a grouping (as of political parties or international powers) intermediate between two opposing political forces

third order *n, often cap T & O* **1** : an organization composed of lay people living in secular society under a religious rule and directed by a religious order **2** : a congregation esp. of teaching or nursing sisters affiliated with a religious order

third party *n* **1** : a person other than the principals ⟨a *third party* to a divorce proceeding⟩ **2** : a political party operating usu. for a limited time in addition to the two major parties in a 2-party system

third person *n* : a set of words or forms (as verb forms or pronouns) referring to someone or something that is neither the speaker or writer of the utterance in which they occur nor the one to whom that utterance is addressed; *also* : a word or form belonging to such a set

third rail *n* : a metal rail through which electric current is led to the motors of an electric locomotive

third–rate \'thərd-'rāt\ *adj* : of third quality or value; *esp* : worse than second-rate — **third–rat·er** \-'rāt-ər\ *n*

¹thirst \'thərst\ *n* [OE *thurst*] **1** : a feeling of dryness in the mouth and throat associated with a desire for liquids; *also* : the bodily condition (as of dehydration) that induces this **2** : an ardent desire : CRAVING, LONGING

²thirst *vi* **1** : to feel thirsty : suffer thirst **2** : to have a vehement desire : CRAVE

thirsty \'thər-stē\ *adj* **thirst·i·er; -est 1 a** : feeling thirst **b** : deficient in moisture : PARCHED ⟨*thirsty* land⟩ **c** : highly absorbent ⟨*thirsty* towels⟩ **2** : having a strong desire : AVID ⟨*thirsty* for knowledge⟩ — **thirst·i·ly** \-stə-lē\ *adv* — **thirst·i·ness** \-stē-nəs\ *n*

thir·teen \ˌthər(t)-'tēn, 'thər(t)-\ *n* [OE *thrēotīne;* akin to E *three* & to E *ten*] — see NUMBER table — **thirteen** *adj or pron* — **thir·teenth** \-'tēn(t)th\ *adj or n*

thir·ty \'thərt-ē\ *n, pl* **thirties** [OE *thrītig;* akin to E *three*] **1** — see NUMBER table **2** *pl* : the numbers 30 to 39; *esp* : the years 30 to 39 in a lifetime or century **3** : a mark or sign of completion **4** : the 2d point scored by a side in a game of tennis **5** : a 30 caliber machine gun — usu. written .30 — **thir·ti·eth** \-ē-əth\ *n or adj* — **thirty** *adj or pron*

thir·ty–eight \ˌthərt-ē-'āt\ *n* : a 38 caliber pistol — usu. written .38

thirty–second note *n* : a musical note having the time value of one thirty-second of a whole note

thir·ty–thir·ty \ˌthərt-ē-'thərt-ē\ *n* : a rifle that fires a 30 caliber cartridge having a 30 grain powder charge

thir·ty–three \-'thrē\ *n* : a phonograph record for play at 33⅓ revolutions per minute

thir·ty–two \-'tü\ *n* : a 32 caliber pistol — usu. written .32

¹this \(')this, thəs\ *pron, pl* **these** \(')thēz\ [OE *thes* (masc.), *this* (neut.); akin to E *that*] **1** : the person, thing, or idea present or near in place, time, or thought, or just mentioned ⟨*these* are my hands⟩ **2 a** : the one nearer or more immediately under observation ⟨*this* is iron and that is tin⟩ **b** : the latter one

²this *adj, pl* **these 1** : being the one present or near in place, time, or thought, or just mentioned ⟨*this* book is

mine⟩⟨early *this* morning⟩⟨friends all *these* years⟩ **2** : the nearer at hand or more immediately under observation or discussion ⟨*this* car or that one⟩ ⟨considers *these* colors preferable to those⟩
³**this** \'this\ *adv* : to the degree or extent indicated by something immediately present ⟨didn't expect to wait *this* long⟩
This·be \'thiz-bē\ *n* :. a legendary young woman of Babylon loved by Pyramus
this·tle \'this-əl\ *n* [OE *thistel*] : any of various prickly plants related to the daisies but distinguished by often showy heads of mostly tubular flowers — **this·tly** \'this-(ə-)lē\ *adj*
this·tle–down \-,daůn\ *n* : the down from the ripe flower head of a thistle
thistle tube *n* : a funnel tube usu. of glass with a bulging top and flaring mouth
¹**thith·er** \'thith-ər, 'thith-\ *adv* [OE *thider;* akin to E *that*] : to that place : THERE
²**thither** *adj* : being on the other and farther side : more remote
thith·er·to \-,tü\ *adv* : until that time
thith·er·ward \-wərd\ *also* **thith·er·wards** \-wərdz\ *adv* : toward that place : THITHER
tho *var of* THOUGH
thole \'thōl\ *also* **thole·pin** \-,pin\ *n* [OE *thol*] : a pin set in the gunwale of a boat as a pivot for an oar
Thom·as \'täm-əs\ *n* : an apostle who demanded proof of Christ's resurrection
Tho·mism \'tō-,miz-əm\ *n* : the scholastic philosophical and theological system of St. Thomas Aquinas — **Tho·mist** \-məst\ *n or adj* — **Tho·mis·tic** \tō-'mis-tik\ *adj*
Thomp·son submachine gun \'täm(p)-sən-\ *n* [John T. *Thompson* d1940 American army officer] : a portable automatic weapon with a pistol grip and buttstock for firing from the shoulder
thong \'thóŋ\ *n* [OE *thwong*] : a strip of leather used esp. for fastening something
Thor \'thó(ə)r\ *n* : the god of thunder in Norse mythology represented as armed with a hammer
thoracic duct *n* : the chief lymphatic vessel carrying lymph back to the bloodstream esp. from the abdomen and lower limbs, lying along the front of the spinal column, and opening into the left subclavian vein
tho·rax \'thōr-,aks, 'thór-\ *n, pl* **tho·rax·es** *or* **tho·ra·ces** \thə-'rā-,sēz\ [L *thorac-, thorax,* fr. Gk *thōrak-, thōrax,* lit., breastplate] **1** : the part of the body of a mammal between the neck and the abdomen; *also* : its cavity in which the heart and lungs lie **2** : the middle of the three chief divisions of the body of an insect — **tho·rac·ic** \thə-'ras-ik\ *adj*
tho·ria \'thōr-ē-ə, 'thór-\ *n* [NL, fr. *thorium* + *-a* (as in *magnesia*)] : a powdery white oxide of thorium used esp. in crucibles and optical glass
tho·ri·um \'thōr-ē-əm, 'thór-\ *n* [NL, fr. ON *Thōrr* Thor, god of thunder] : a radioactive metallic chemical element that occurs combined in minerals — see ELEMENT table
thorn \'thórn\ *n* [OE] **1** : a woody plant bearing sharp processes (as briers, prickles, or spines); *esp* : HAWTHORN **2 a** : a sharp rigid process on a plant; *esp* : one that is a short, rigid, sharp-pointed, and leafless branch **b** : a sharp rigid process on an animal **3** : something that causes distress or irritation — **thorned** \'thórnd\ *adj* — **thorn·less** \'thórn-ləs\ *adj* — **thorn·like** \-,līk\ *adj*
thorn apple *n* **1** : the fruit of a hawthorn **2** : JIMSONWEED
thorn·bush \'thórn-,bůsh\ *n* **1** : any of various spiny or thorny shrubs or small trees **2** : a low growth of thorny shrubs esp. of dry tropical regions
thorny \'thór-nē\ *adj* **thorn·i·er; -est 1** : full of or covered with thorns : SPINY **2** : DIFFICULT, TRYING ⟨a *thorny* problem⟩ — **thorn·i·ness** *n*
thoro *nonstand var of* THOROUGH
tho·ron \'thōr-,än, 'thór-\ *n* : a gaseous radioactive chemical element formed from thorium
thor·ough \'thər-ō, 'thə-rō\ *adj* [ME *thorow,* fr. *thorow, through,* adv. & prep., through] **1** : being such to the fullest degree : EXHAUSTIVE, DETAILED, COMPLETE ⟨a *thorough* search⟩ ⟨*thorough* study⟩ ⟨*thorough* success⟩ **2** : careful about detail : PAINSTAKING ⟨a *thorough* workman⟩ — **thor·ough·ly** *adv* — **thor·ough·ness** *n*
thorough bass *n* : the representation of chords by figures

under the bass notes; *also* : the technique of writing or reading this
¹**thor·ough·bred** \-,bred\ *adj* **1** : thoroughly trained or skilled **2** : bred from the best blood through a long line : PUREBRED ⟨*thoroughbred* dogs⟩ **3** *cap* : of, relating to, or being a member of the Thoroughbred breed of horses **4 a** : marked by high-spirited grace and elegance ⟨a *thoroughbred* lady⟩ **b** : of the best quality or highest worth : FIRST-CLASS ⟨*thoroughbred* sports car⟩
²**thoroughbred** *n* **1** *cap* : any of an English breed of light speedy horses kept chiefly for racing and originating from crosses between English mares of uncertain ancestry and Arab stallions **2** : a purebred or pedigreed animal **3** : a person of sterling qualities
thor·ough·fare \-,fa(ə)r, -,fe(ə)r\ *n* [ME *thoruhfare,* fr. *thoruh, through* through + *faren* to fare] **1** : a public way connecting two streets : a street or road open at both ends **2** : a main road : a busy street
thor·ough·go·ing \,thər-ə-'gō-iŋ, ,thə-rə-\ *adj* : marked by thoroughness or zeal
thor·ough–paced \-'pāst\ *adj* : THOROUGH, COMPLETE
thorp \'thórp\ *n* [OE] *archaic* : VILLAGE, HAMLET
those *pl of* THAT
thou \(')thaů\ *pron* [OE *thū*] *archaic* : the one spoken to — used as 2d person singular pronoun esp. in biblical or poetic language; compare THEE, THINE, THY, YE, YOU
¹**though** \'thō\ *adv* [of Scand origin] : HOWEVER, NEVERTHELESS ⟨not for long, *though*⟩
²**though** \(,)thō\ *conj* **1** : in spite of the fact that ⟨*though* it was raining, he went for a walk⟩ **2** : even if : even supposing ⟨determined to tell the truth *though* he should die for it⟩
¹**thought** *past of* THINK
²**thought** \'thót\ *n* [OE *thōht;* akin to E *think*] **1 a** : the act or process of thinking **b** : serious consideration : careful attention ⟨give *thought* to the future⟩ **2 a** : power of thinking and esp. of reasoning and judging **b** : power of imagining or comprehending ⟨beauty beyond *thought*⟩ **3 a** : a product of thinking (as an idea, fancy, or invention) ⟨idle *thoughts*⟩ ⟨a pleasing *thought*⟩ **b** : the intellectual product or the organized views and principles of a period, place, group, or individual ⟨modern scientific *thought*⟩ **4** : a slight amount : BIT ⟨add just a *thought* more salt to the stew⟩
thought·ful \'thót-fəl\ *adj* **1 a** : absorbed in thought : MEDITATIVE **b** : characterized by careful reasoned thinking **2** : MINDFUL, HEEDFUL; *esp* : attentive to the needs of others — **thought·ful·ly** \-fə-lē\ *adv* — **thought·ful·ness** *n* **syn** THOUGHTFUL, CONSIDERATE, SOLICITOUS mean mindful of others. THOUGHTFUL implies unselfish concern and ability to anticipate another's needs; CONSIDERATE implies kind concern for the feelings of others; SOLICITOUS implies deep concern and suggests anxiety for the welfare of another ⟨*solicitous* about his wife's health⟩
thought·less \'thót-ləs\ *adj* **1 a** : insufficiently alert : CARELESS **b** : RECKLESS, RASH **2** : devoid of thought : INSENSATE **3** : lacking concern for others : INCONSIDERATE — **thought·less·ly** *adv* — **thought·less·ness** *n*
thought–out \-'aůt\ *adj* : produced or arrived at through careful and thorough consideration
thou·sand \'thaůz-ⁿn(d)\ *n, pl* **thousands** *or* **thousand** [OE *thūsend*] **1** — see NUMBER table **2** : the number in the 4th decimal place to the left of the decimal point in arabic numerals **3** : a very large or indefinitely great number ⟨had a *thousand* of them on hand⟩ ⟨a show with a cast of *thousands*⟩ — **thousand** *adj*
thou·sand–head·ed kale \,thaůz-ⁿn-,hed-əd-\ *n* : a tall branched leafy kale grown as green feed for livestock
thou·sand–leg·ger \,thaůz-ⁿn-'leg-ər\ *n* : MILLIPEDE
thou·sandth \'thaůz-ⁿn(t)th\ *n* **1** : one of 1000 equal parts of something **2** : the one numbered 1000 in a countable series — see NUMBER table — **thousandth** *adj*
thrall \'thról\ *n* [ON *thrǽll*] **1** : SLAVE; *also* : SERF **2** : the condition of a thrall : SLAVERY — **thrall·dom** *or* **thral·dom** \-dəm\ *n*
¹**thrash** \'thrash\ *vb* [alter. of *thresh*] **1** : THRESH **1 2** : to beat soundly or strike about with or as if with a stick or whip : FLOG; *also* : DEFEAT **3** : to swing, beat, or stir about in the manner of a rapidly moving flail ⟨*thrashing* his arms⟩ **4** : to go over again and again ⟨*thrash* the matter over in his mind⟩ ⟨*thrash* out a plan⟩

ə abut; ᵊ kitten; ər further; a back; ā bake; ä cot, cart; aů out; ch chin; e less; ē easy; g gift; i trip; ī life

²thrash n : an act of thrashing esp. of the legs in swimming

¹thrash·er \'thrash-ər\ n : one that thrashes or threshes

²thrasher n : any of numerous long-tailed American singing birds that resemble thrushes and include notable singers and mimics

¹thread \'thred\ n [OE *thrǣd*] **1** : a thin continuous filament ⟨the spider's sticky *thread*⟩; esp : a textile cord made by twisting together strands of spun fiber (as cotton, flax, or silk) **2 a** : something (as a streak or slender stream) suggesting a filament ⟨a *thread* of light⟩ **b** : SCREW THREAD **c** : a tenuous or feeble support **3** : a line of reasoning or train of thought that connects the parts in a sequence of ideas or events ⟨lost the *thread* of his story⟩ — **thread·like** \-,līk\ adj

²thread vb **1** : to put a thread in working position in (as a needle) **2 a** : to pass through in the manner of a thread ⟨*thread* a pipe with wire⟩ **b** : to make one's way through or between : wind a way ⟨*threading* narrow alleys⟩ **3** : to put together on or as if on a thread : STRING ⟨*thread* beads⟩ **4** : to interweave with or as if with threads : INTERSPERSE ⟨dark hair *threaded* with silver⟩ **5** : to form a screw thread on or in **6** : to draw out into a thread when dripped from a spoon — **thread·er** n

thread·bare \'thred-,ba(ə)r, -,be(ə)r\ adj **1** : having the nap worn off so that the thread shows : SHABBY **2** : HACKNEYED — **thread·bare·ness** n

thread·worm \-,wərm\ n : a slender nematode worm (as a pinworm)

thready \'thred-ē\ adj **thread·i·er; -est 1** : consisting of or bearing fibers or filaments ⟨a *thready* bark⟩ **2** : FILAMENTOUS **3** : lacking in fullness, body, or vigor : THIN ⟨a *thready* voice⟩ ⟨a *thready* pulse⟩ — **thread·i·ness** n

threat \'thret\ n [OE *thrēat* coercion] **1** : an expression of an intent to do harm or something wrong or foolish **2** : something that threatens

threat·en \'thret-ⁿn\ vb **threat·ened; threat·en·ing** \'thret-niŋ, -ⁿn-iŋ\ **1** : to utter threats : make threats against ⟨*threaten* trespassers⟩ **2** : to give warning of by a threat or sign ⟨clouds *threatening* rain⟩ **3** : to give signs of trouble to come — **threat·en·er** \'thret-nər, -ⁿn-ər\ n — **threat·en·ing·ly** \'thret-niŋ-lē, -ⁿn-iŋ-lē\ adv

syn MENACE: THREATEN applies to a probable occurrence of evil or affliction; it may imply an impersonal warning of trouble, punishment, or retribution ⟨forgot to punish as he had *threatened*⟩ MENACE implies alarming by a hostile or fearful aspect or character ⟨nuclear arms that *menace* humanity⟩

three \'thrē\ n [OE *thrīe* (masc.), *thrēo* (fem. & neut.)] **1** — see NUMBER table **2** : the third in a set or series **3** : something having three units or members — **three** adj or pron

three–base hit n : a base hit that enables a batter to reach third base safely — called also **three-bag·ger** \'thrē-'bag-ər\, **triple**

3–D \'thrē-'dē\ n : the three-dimensional form or a picture produced in it

three–deck·er \'thrē-'dek-ər\ n **1** : a ship having three decks; also : a warship carrying guns on three decks **2** : something having three floors, tiers, or layers; esp : a sandwich with three slices of bread and two layers of filling

three–di·men·sion·al adj **1** : of, relating to, or having three dimensions **2** : giving the illusion of depth or varying distances — used of a pictorial representation (as a moving-picture image)

three·fold \'thrē-,fōld, -'fōld\ adj **1** : having three units or members **2** : of or amounting to 300 percent — **threefold** adv

three–gait·ed \-'gāt-əd\ adj : trained to use the walk, trot, and canter ⟨*three-gaited* saddle horses⟩

three–hand·ed \-'han-dəd\ adj : played or to be played by three players ⟨*three-handed* bridge⟩

Three Hours n : a service of devotion between noon and three o'clock on Good Friday

three–legged \'thrē-'leg(-ə)d\ adj : having three legs ⟨a *three-legged* stool⟩

three–mile limit n : the limit of the marginal sea of three miles included in the territorial waters of a state

three·pence \'threp-ən(t)s, 'thrip-, 'thrɔp-, US also 'thrē-,pen(t)s\ n, pl **threepence** or **three·penc·es 1** : the sum of three usu. British pennies **2** : a coin worth three pennies

three–pen·ny \'threp-(ə-)nē, 'thrip-, 'thrɔp-, US also 'thrē-,pen-ē\ adj **1** : costing or worth threepence **2** : of little value : POOR

three–ply \'thrē-'plī\ adj : consisting of three distinct strands, veneers, or interwoven layers

three–point landing n : an airplane landing in which the two main wheels of the landing gear and the tail wheel or skid or nose wheel touch the ground simultaneously

three–ring circus n **1** : a circus with simultaneous performances in three rings **2** : something confusing, engrossing, or entertaining

three R's n pl [fr. the playful phrase *reading, 'riting, and 'rithmetic*] : the fundamentals taught in elementary school; esp : reading, writing, and arithmetic

three–score \'thrē-'skō(ə)r, -'skô(ə)r\ adj : SIXTY

three·some \'thrē-səm\ n : a group of three persons or things

thren·o·dy \'thren-əd-ē\ n, pl **-dies** [Gk *thrēnōidia*, fr. *thrēnos* dirge + *ōid-, aidein* to sing] : a song of lamentation or sorrow : DIRGE

thre·o·nine \'thrē-ə-,nēn\ n : an amino acid held essential to normal nutrition

thresh \'thrash, 'thresh\ vb [OE *threscan*] **1** : to separate seed from (a harvested plant) mechanically : beat out (grain) from straw **2** : THRASH ⟨*thresh* over a problem⟩ ⟨*threshed* about in his bed⟩

thresh·er \-ər\ n **1** : one that threshes; esp : THRESHING MACHINE **2** : a large common shark having a long curved upper lobe on its tail with which it is said to thresh the water to round up the fish on which it feeds — called also *fox shark, thresher shark*

threshing machine n : a machine for separating grain or seeds from straw

thresh·old \'thresh-,(h)ōld\ n [OE *threscwald*] **1** : the sill of a door **2 a** : GATE, DOOR, ENTRANCE **b** : a place of beginning : OUTSET ⟨at the *threshold* of an adventure⟩ **3** : the point or level at which a physiological or psychological effect begins to be produced ⟨below the *threshold* of consciousness⟩ — **threshold** adj

threw past of THROW

thrice \'thrīs\ adv [ME *thrie, thries*, fr. OE *thriga;* akin to E *three*] **1** : three times **2** : to a high degree

thrift \'thrift\ n [ON, prosperity, fr. *thrīfask* to thrive] **1** : economical management : FRUGALITY **2** : healthy vigorous growth (as of a plant) **3** : a tufted stemless herb having heads of pink or white flowers growing on mountains and seacoasts

thrift·less \'thrift-ləs\ adj **1** : lacking usefulness or worth **2** : wasteful of money or resources : IMPROVIDENT — **thrift·less·ness** n

thrifty \'thrif-tē\ adj **thrift·i·er; -est 1** : inclined to save : SAVING **2** : thriving through industry and frugality : PROSPEROUS **3** : thriving in health and growth ⟨*thrifty* cattle⟩ — **thrift·i·ly** \-tə-lē\ adv — **thrift·i·ness** \-tē-nəs\ n

thrill \'thril\ vb [OE *thyrlian* to pierce; akin to E *through*] **1 a** : to experience or cause to experience a sudden sharp feeling of excitement **b** : to have or cause to have a shivering or tingling sensation **c** : to feel an intense emotional response ⟨*thrill* to splendid sights⟩ **2** : VIBRATE, TREMBLE ⟨voice *thrilling* with emotion⟩ — **thrill** n

thrill·er \-ər\ n : one that produces thrills; esp : a work of fiction or drama designed to hold the interest by the use of a high degree of action, intrigue, adventure, or suspense

thrips \'thrips\ n, pl **thrips** [Gk, worm that bores in wood] : any of an order (Thysanoptera) of small to tiny sucking insects most of which feed often destructively on plant juices

thrive \'thrīv\ vi **throve** \'thrōv\ or **thrived; thriv·en** \'thriv-ən\ also **thrived; thriv·ing** \'thrī-viŋ\ [ON *thrīfask*] **1** : to grow vigorously : do well **2** : to gain in wealth or possessions : PROSPER, FLOURISH — **thriv·er** \'thrī-vər\ n — **thriv·ing·ly** \-viŋ-lē\ adv

throat \'thrōt\ n [OE *throte*] **1** : the part of the neck in front of the spinal column; also : the passage through it to the stomach and lungs **2** : something resembling the throat esp. in being an entrance, a passageway, a constriction, or a narrowed part — **throat·ed** \-əd\ adj

throat·latch \-,lach\ n : a strap of a bridle or halter passing under a horse's throat

throaty \'thrōt-ē\ *adj* **throat·i·er; -est** **1** : uttered or produced from low in the throat ⟨a *throaty* voice⟩ **2** : heavy, thick, and deep as if from the throat ⟨*throaty* notes of a horn⟩ — **throat·i·ly** \'thrōt-ᵊl-ē\ *adv* — **throat·i·ness** \'thrōt-ē-nəs\ *n*

¹throb \'thräb\ *vi* **throbbed; throb·bing** [ME *throbben*] **1** : to pulsate or pound with abnormal force or rapidity : PALPITATE **2** : to beat or vibrate rhythmically

²throb *n* : BEAT, PULSE

throe \'thrō\ *n* [OE *thrawu*] **1** : PANG, SPASM ⟨death *throes*⟩ ⟨*throes* of childbirth⟩ **2** *pl* : a hard or painful struggle

thromb- *or* **thrombo-** *comb form* [Gk *thrombos*] : blood clot : clotting of blood ⟨*thrombin*⟩ ⟨*thromboplastic*⟩

throm·base \'thräm-ˌbās\ *n* : THROMBIN

throm·bin \'thräm-bən\ *n* : a proteolytic enzyme that is formed from prothrombin and assists the clotting of blood by promoting conversion of fibrinogen to fibrin

throm·bo·cyte \-bə-ˌsīt\ *n* : BLOOD PLATELET; *also* : an invertebrate cell with similar function — **throm·bo·cyt·ic** \ˌthräm-bə-'sit-ik\ *adj*

throm·bo·em·bo·lism \ˌthräm-bō-'em-bə-ˌliz-əm\ *n* : a blocking of a blood vessel by an embolus that has broken away from a thrombus and become lodged elsewhere

throm·bo·ki·nase \-'kīn-ˌās, -'kin-\ *n* [Gk *kinein* to move + E *-ase*] : THROMBOPLASTIN

throm·bo·plas·tic \ˌthräm-bō-'plas-tik\ *adj* **1** : initiating or accelerating the clotting of blood **2** : of, relating to, or being thromboplastin — **throm·bo·plas·ti·cal·ly** \-ti-k(ə-)lē\ *adv*

throm·bo·plas·tin \-'plas-tən\ *n* : a complex protein substance found esp. in blood platelets that functions in the clotting of blood

throm·bo·sis \thräm-'bō-səs\ *n, pl* **-bo·ses** \-'bō-ˌsēz\ : the formation or presence of a blood clot within a blood vessel during life — **throm·bot·ic** \-'bät-ik\ *adj*

throm·bus \'thräm-bəs\ *n, pl* **throm·bi** \-ˌbī, -ˌbē\ [NL, fr. Gk *thrombos* clot] : a clot of blood formed within a blood vessel and remaining attached to its place of origin — compare EMBOLUS

¹throne \'thrōn\ *n* [Gk *thronos*] **1 a** : the chair of state of a high dignitary (as a king or bishop) **b** : the seat of a deity or devil **2** : royal power and dignity : SOVEREIGNTY

²throne *vt* : to seat on a throne : ENTHRONE

throne room *n* : a formal audience room containing the throne of a sovereign

¹throng \'thrȯŋ\ *n* [OE *thrang*] **1 a** : a multitude of assembled persons **b** : a large number : CROWD **2 a** : crowding together of many individuals **syn** SEE MULTITUDE

²throng *vb* **thronged; throng·ing** \'thrȯŋ-iŋ\ **1** : to crowd upon or into ⟨*throng* a stadium⟩ **2** : to crowd together in great numbers

thros·tle \'thräs-əl\ *n* [OE] : ¹THRUSH

¹throt·tle \'thrät-ᵊl\ *vb* **throt·tled; throt·tling** \'thrät-liŋ, -ᵊl-iŋ\ [ME *throtlen*, fr. *throte* throat] **1 a** : CHOKE, STRANGLE **b** : to prevent or check expression or activity of : SUPPRESS **2 a** : to obstruct the flow of (as fuel to an engine) by closing a valve **b** : to reduce the speed of (an engine) by such means — often used with *down* — **throt·tler** \'thrät-lər, -ᵊl-ər\ *n*

²throttle *n* **1 a** : THROAT 1 **b** : TRACHEA 1 **2 a** : a valve controlling the volume of steam or of fuel (as gasoline) delivered to the cylinders of an engine **b** : a lever controlling this valve

throt·tle·hold \'thrät-ᵊl-ˌhōld\ *n* : a vicious, strangling, or stultifying control

¹through *also* **thru** \(')thrü\ *prep* [ME *through, thorow*, fr. OE *thurh, thuruh*] **1 a** : in at one side and out at the opposite side of ⟨drove *through* the town⟩ **b** : by way of ⟨left *through* the window⟩ **c** : in the midst of : AMONG ⟨highway *through* the trees⟩ **2 a** : by means of ⟨succeeded *through* perseverance⟩ **b** : because of ⟨failed *through* ignorance⟩ **3** : over the whole surface or extent of ⟨all *through* the country⟩ **4 a** : from the beginning to the end of : DURING ⟨*through* the summer⟩ **b** : to and including ⟨Monday *through* Friday⟩ **syn** SEE BY

²through *also* **thru** \'thrü\ *adv* **1 a** : from one end or side to the other ⟨his arm was pierced *through*⟩ **b** : over the whole distance ⟨shipped *through* to Boston⟩ **2 a** : from beginning to end ⟨read the book *through* at one sitting⟩ **b** : to completion, conclusion, or accomplishment ⟨see it

through⟩ **3** : to the core : COMPLETELY ⟨he was wet *through*⟩ **4** : into the open : OUT ⟨break *through*⟩

³through *also* **thru** \'thrü\ *adj* **1 a** : extending from one surface to another ⟨a *through* mortise⟩ **b** : admitting free or continuous passage : DIRECT ⟨a *through* road⟩ **2 a** (1) : going from point of origin to destination without change or reshipment ⟨a *through* train⟩ (2) : of or relating to such movement ⟨a *through* ticket⟩ **b** : initiated at and destined for points outside a local zone ⟨*through* traffic⟩ **3 a** : arrived at completion or accomplishment ⟨he is *through* with the job⟩ **b** : WASHED-UP, FINISHED ⟨you're *through* — that was your last chance⟩

¹through·out \thrü-'aùt\ *adv* **1** : in or to every part : EVERYWHERE ⟨of one color *throughout*⟩ **2** : during the whole time or action : from beginning to end ⟨remained loyal *throughout*⟩

²throughout *prep* **1** : in or to every part of ⟨*throughout* the house⟩ **2** : during the whole time of ⟨*throughout* the evening⟩

through street *n* : a street on which the through movement of traffic is given preference

through·way *var of* THRUWAY

throve *past of* THRIVE

¹throw \'thrō\ *vb* **threw** \'thrü\; **thrown** \'thrōn\; **throw·ing** [OE *thrāwan* to cause to twist or turn] **1** : to twist two or more fibers of (as silk) to form one thread **2** : to hurl or cast esp. with a quick forward motion of the arm **3** : to propel through the air in any way **4** : to cause to fall ⟨the wrestler *threw* his opponent⟩ ⟨a horse shied and *threw* his rider⟩ **5** : to put suddenly in a certain condition or position ⟨was suddenly *thrown* out of work⟩; *also* : to form or shape on a potter's wheel **6** : to put on or take off hastily ⟨*throw* on a coat⟩ **7** : SHED ⟨a snake *throws* its skin⟩ **8** : to move quickly ⟨*throw* in reinforcements⟩ **9** : to move (as a switch or a lever) to an open or closed position **10** *slang* : to act as host for : put on ⟨*throw* a party⟩ **11** : to lose (a game or contest) intentionally ⟨paid to *throw* the fight⟩ **12** : to make a cast of or at dice — **throw·er** \'thrō(-ə)r\ *n*

syn FLING, HURL, TOSS: THROW is interchangeable with the other terms but may imply a movement of the arm propelling an object through the air or in any direction; FLING stresses force in throwing and may suggest an emotional aimlessness in the action ⟨rushed to the window and *flung* it open⟩ HURL implies power as in throwing a massive weight ⟨ocean waves *hurling* their weight upon the shore⟩ TOSS suggests a light or aimless upward throwing ⟨leaves *tossed* by the wind⟩

²throw *n* **1** : an act of throwing, hurling, or flinging **b** : an act of throwing dice; *also* : the number thrown with a cast of dice **c** : a method of throwing an opponent in wrestling or judo **2** : the distance a missile is or may be thrown **3** : an undertaking involving chance or danger **4 a** : a light coverlet **b** : a woman's scarf or light wrap

throw away \ˌthrō-ə-'wā\ *vt* **1** : to get rid of : DISCARD **2** : SQUANDER, WASTE

throw·away \'thrō-ə-ˌwā\ *n* : a handbill or circular distributed free

throw back \(')thrō-'bak\ *vb* **1** : to delay the progress or advance of : CHECK **2** : to cause to rely : make dependent **3** : REFLECT **4** : to revert to an earlier type or phase

throw·back \'thrō-ˌbak\ *n* : reversion to an earlier type or phase; *also* : an instance or product of such reversion

throw in *vt* : to contribute to or introduce into a larger whole

throw off *vt* **1 a** : to free oneself from **b** : to cast off often in a hurried or vigorous manner **c** : to shake off : DIVERT **2** : to give off : EMIT **3** : to produce in an offhand manner **4 a** : to cause to depart from an expected or desired course **b** : to cause to make a mistake : MISLEAD

throw out *vt* **1 a** : to remove from a place, office, or employment usu. in a sudden or unexpected manner **b** : to reject or get rid of as worthless or unnecessary **2** : to give expression to : UTTER **3** : to give forth from within : EMIT **4 a** : to send out **b** : to cause to project : EXTEND **5** : to cause to stand out : make prominent **6** : to make a throw that enables a teammate in baseball to put out (a base runner) **7** : DISENGAGE ⟨*throw out* the clutch⟩

throw over *vt* **1 :** to forsake despite bonds of attachment or duty **2 :** to refuse to accept **:** REJECT
throw rug *n* **:** SCATTER RUG
throw up *vb* **1 :** to raise quickly **2 :** to give up **:** QUIT **3 :** to build hurriedly **4 :** VOMIT **5 :** to bring forth **6 :** to cause to stand out **7 :** to mention repeatedly by way of reproach ⟨*throw up* a past mistake⟩
thru *var of* THROUGH
¹thrum \'thrəm\ *n* **:** PARTICLE, FILAMENT — **thrum** *adj*
²thrum *vb* **thrummed; thrum·ming** *vb* **1 :** to play or pluck a stringed instrument idly **:** STRUM **2 :** to sound with a monotonous hum **:** recite tiresomely or monotonously
³thrum *n* **:** the monotonous sound of thrumming
¹thrush \'thrəsh\ *n* [OE *thrysce*] **:** any of a large family of small or medium-sized passerine birds that are mostly of a plain color often with spotted underparts and include many excellent singers
²thrush *n* **1 :** a fungal disease esp. of infants marked by white patches in the mouth **2 :** a suppurative disorder of the feet in various animals
¹thrust \'thrəst\ *vb* **thrust; thrust·ing** [ON *thr̄ysta*] **1 :** to push or drive with force **:** SHOVE **2 :** to cause to enter or pierce something by or as if by pushing **3 :** STAB, PIERCE **4 :** to push forth **:** EXTEND ⟨*thrust* out roots⟩ **5 :** INTERJECT, INTERPOLATE **6 :** to press or force the acceptance of upon someone **7 :** to make a thrust, stab, or lunge with or as if with a pointed weapon **syn** see PUSH
²thrust *n* **1 a :** a push or lunge with a pointed weapon **b :** a verbal attack **c :** a military assault **2 a :** a strong continued pressure **b :** the sideways pressure of one part of a structure against another part (as of an arch against an abutment) **c** (1) **:** the force exerted endwise through a propeller shaft to give forward motion (2) **:** the forwardly directed reaction force produced by a high-speed jet of fluid discharged rearward from a nozzle (as in a jet airplane or a rocket) **3 a :** a forward or upward push **b :** a movement (as by a group of people) in a specified direction
thru·way *or* **through·way** \'thrü-,wā\ *n* **:** EXPRESSWAY
¹thud \'thəd\ *vi* **thud·ded; thud·ding :** to move or strike so as to make a thud
²thud *n* **1 :** BLOW **2 :** a dull sound **:** THUMP
thug \'thəg\ *n* [Hindi *thag*, lit., thief] **:** a brutal ruffian or assassin **:** GANGSTER, KILLER — **thug·gery** \'thəg-ə-rē\ *n* — **thug·gish** \'thəg-ish\ *adj*
thug·gee \'thəg-,ē\ *n* [Hindi *thagi* robbery, fr. *thag* thief] **:** the practice of murder and robbery by thugs
Thu·le \'th(y)ü-lē\ *n* [L, fr. Gk *Thoulē*, land reported to exist far north of Britain] **:** the northernmost part of the habitable ancient world
thu·li·um \'th(y)ü-lē-əm\ *n* [NL, fr. L *Thule*] **:** a rare metallic chemical element — see ELEMENT table
¹thumb \'thəm\ *n* [OE *thūma*] **1 :** the short thick first digit of the human hand opposable to the other fingers; *also* **:** the corresponding digit in lower animals **2 :** the part of a glove or mitten that covers the thumb
²thumb *vt* **1 a :** to leaf through with the thumb **:** TURN ⟨*thumb* the pages of a book⟩ **b :** to soil or wear by or as if by repeated thumbing ⟨a well-*thumbed* book⟩ **2 :** to request or obtain (a ride) in a passing automobile by signaling with the thumb
thumb index *n* **:** an index consisting of rounded thumb notches cut symmetrically on the fore edge of a book and tabs denoting the letters (as in a dictionary) or sections referred to
¹thumb·nail \'thəm-,nāl, -'nāl\ *n* **:** the nail of the thumb
²thumb·nail \,thəm-,nāl\ *adj* **:** CONCISE, BRIEF ⟨a *thumbnail* sketch⟩
thumb·print \'thəm-,print\ *n* **:** an impression made by the thumb; *esp* **:** a print made by the inside of the first joint
thumb·screw \'thəm-,skrü\ *n* **1 :** a screw having a flat-sided or knurled head so that it may be turned by the thumb and forefinger **2 :** an instrument of torture for compressing the thumb by a screw
thumb·tack \-,tak\ *n* **:** a tack with a broad flat head for pressing into a board or wall with the thumb
¹thump \'thəmp\ *vb* **1 :** to strike or beat with or as if with something thick or heavy so as to cause a dull sound

2 : POUND, KNOCK **3 :** CUDGEL, THRASH **4 :** to inflict or emit a thump
²thump *n* **:** a blow or knock with or as if with something blunt or heavy; *also* **:** the sound made by such a blow
thump·ing *adj* **:** impressively large, great, or excellent ⟨a *thumping* majority⟩
¹thun·der \'thən-dər\ *n* [OE *thunor*] **1 a :** the loud sound that follows a flash of lightning and is caused by sudden expansion of the air in the path of the electrical discharge **b** *archaic* **:** a discharge of lightning **:** THUNDERBOLT **2 :** a loud utterance or threat **3 :** BANG, RUMBLE ⟨the *thunder* of guns⟩
²thunder *vb* **thun·dered; thun·der·ing** \-d(ə-)riŋ\ **1 a :** to produce thunder ⟨it *thundered*⟩ **b :** to give forth or strike with a sound likened to thunder ⟨horses *thundered* down the road⟩ **2 :** ROAR, SHOUT — **thun·der·er** \-dər-ər\ *n*
thun·der·bolt \'thən-dər-,bōlt\ *n* **1 :** a single discharge of lightning with the accompanying thunder **2 a :** a person or thing likened to lightning in suddenness, effectiveness, or destructive power **b :** vehement threatening or censure
thun·der·clap \-,klap\ *n* **1 :** a crash of thunder **2 :** something sharp, loud, or sudden like a clap of thunder
thun·der·cloud \-,klaůd\ *n* **:** a dark storm cloud that produces lightning and thunder
thun·der·head \-,hed\ *n* **:** a rounded mass of cumulus cloud often appearing before a thunderstorm
thun·der·ing *adj* **:** awesomely great, intense, or unusual ⟨and has been a *thundering* success ever since⟩ — **thun·der·ing·ly** \-d(ə-)riŋ-lē\ *adv*
thunder lizard *n* **:** BRONTOSAURUS
thun·der·ous \'thən-d(ə-)rəs\ *adj* **:** producing thunder; *also* **:** making or accompanied by a noise like thunder ⟨*thunderous* applause⟩ — **thun·der·ous·ly** *adv*
thun·der·show·er \'thən-dər-,shaů(-ə)r\ *n* **:** a shower accompanied by lightning and thunder
thun·der·storm \-,storm\ *n* **:** a storm accompanied by lightning and thunder
thun·der·struck \-,strək\ *adj* **:** stunned as if struck by a thunderbolt **:** struck dumb **:** ASTONISHED ⟨*thunderstruck* when he heard the news⟩
thu·ri·ble \'th(y)ůr-ə-bəl, 'thər-\ *n* [L *thuribulum*, fr. *thur-*, *thus* incense, fr. Gk *thyos*, fr. *thyein* to sacrifice] **:** CENSER
thu·ri·fer \-ə-fər\ *n* [L *thur-*, *thus* incense + *ferre* to carry] **:** one who carries a censer
Thurs·day \'thərz-dē\ *n* [ON *thōrsdagr*, lit., day of Thor (god of thunder)] **:** the 5th day of the week
thus \'thəs\ *adv* [OE; akin to E *that*] **1 :** in this or that manner or way **2 :** to this degree or extent **:** so ⟨a mild winter *thus* far⟩ **3 :** because of this or that **:** HENCE **4 :** as an example
thwack \'thwak\ *vt* **:** to strike with or as if with something flat or heavy **:** WHACK — **thwack** *n*
¹thwart \'thwort, *naut often* 'thort\ *adv* [ON *thvert*, fr. neut. of *thverr* transverse, oblique] **:** ATHWART
²thwart *adj* **:** situated or placed across something else **:** TRANSVERSE, OBLIQUE
³thwart *vt* **1 :** OPPOSE, BAFFLE **2 :** BLOCK, DEFEAT **syn** see FRUSTRATE — **thwart·er** *n*
⁴thwart *n* **:** a rower's seat extending athwart a boat
thwart·wise \-,wīz\ *adv* (*or adj*) **:** CROSSWISE
thy \(,)thī\ *adj* [OE *thīn*] *archaic* **:** of or relating to thee or thyself esp. as possessor or agent or as object of an action — used esp. in biblical or poetic language
thy·la·cine \'thī-lə-,sīn\ *n* [NL *Thylacinus*, genus of marsupials, fr. Gk *thylakos* pouch] **:** TASMANIAN WOLF
thyme \'tīm, 'thīm\ *n* [Gk *thymon*] **:** any of a genus of mints with small pungent aromatic leaves; *esp* **:** one grown for use in seasoning and formerly in medicine
thy·mine \'thī-,mēn\ *n* [Gk *thymos* thymus; fr. its being derived from an acid found in the thymus] **:** a pyrimidine base regularly present in the polynucleotide chain of deoxyribonucleic acid
thy·mol \-,mól, -,mōl\ *n* [*thyme*] **:** a crystalline compound C₁₀H₁₄O of aromatic odor and antiseptic properties used as a fungicide and preservative
thy·mus \'thī-məs\ *n, pl* **thy·mus·es** *or* **thy·mi** \-,mī\ [Gk *thymos*] **:** a largely lymphoid glandular structure of uncertain function that is present in most young vertebrates typically at the base of the neck and tends to dis-

appear or become rudimentary in the adult — **thy·mic** \-mik\ *adj*

thymy *or* **thym·ey** \'tī-mē, 'thī-\ *adj* : abounding in or fragrant with thyme

¹**thy·roid** \'thī-ˌroid\ *adj* [Gk *thyreoeidēs* shield-shaped, thyroid, fr. *thyreos* oblong shield, fr. *thyra* door; akin to E *door*] **1** : of, relating to, or being a large endocrine gland of most vertebrates that lies at the base of the neck and produces an iodine-containing hormone which affects esp. growth, development, and metabolic rate **2** : of, relating to, or being the chief cartilage of the larynx

²**thyroid** *n* **1** : a thyroid gland or cartilage; *also* : a part (as an artery or nerve) associated with either of these **2** : a preparation of mammalian thyroid gland used medicinally

thy·ro·trop·ic \ˌthī-rō-'träp-ik\ *adj* : stimulating the thyroid gland ⟨the *thyrotropic* hormone of the anterior pituitary⟩

thy·rox·in *also* **thy·rox·ine** \thī-'räk-sən, -ˌsēn\ *n* : the hormone of the thyroid gland or a preparation or derivative of this used to treat thyroid disorders

thyrse \'thərs\ *n* [Gk *thyrsos* staff wreathed with leaves and tipped with a pinecone] : an inflorescence (as of a lilac) in which the main axis is racemose and secondary axes are cymose — **thyr·soid** \'thər-ˌsoid\ *adj*

thy·sa·nop·ter·an \ˌthī-sə-'näp-tə-rən\ *n* [Gk *thysanos* tassel + *pteron* wing] : THRIPS — **thysanopteran** *adj* — **thy·sa·nop·ter·ous** \-rəs\ *adj*

thy·sa·nu·ran \-'n(y)ùr-ən\ *n* [Gk *thysanos* tassel + *oura* tail] : BRISTLETAIL — **thysanuran** *adj* — **thy·sa·nu·rous** \-əs\ *adj*

thy·self \thī-'self\ *pron, archaic* : YOURSELF — used esp. in biblical or poetic language

ti \'tē\ *n* [alter. of *si*] : the 7th note of the diatonic scale

ti·ara \tē-'ar-ə, -'er-, -'är-\ *n* [Gk, royal Persian headdress] **1** : a 3-tiered crown worn by the pope **2** : a decorative band or semicircular ornament for the head for formal wear by women

Ti·bet·an \tə-'bet-ᵊn\ *n* **1** : a member of the Mongoloid native race of Tibet modified in the wes. and south by intermixture with Indian peoples and in the east with Chinese **2** : the language of the Tibetan people — **Tibetan** *adj*

tib·ia \'tib-ē-ə\ *n, pl* **-i·ae** \-ē-ˌē, -ē-ˌī\ *also* **-i·as** [L] **1 a** : the inner and usu. larger of the two bones of the vertebrate hind limb between the knee and ankle **b** : the fourth joint of the leg of an insect between the femur and tarsus **2** : an ancient flute orig. fashioned from an animal's leg bone — **tib·i·al** \-ē-əl\ *adj*

tib·io·fib·u·la \ˌtib-ē-ō-'fib-yə-lə\ *n* : a single bone that replaces the tibia and fibula in a frog or toad

tic \'tik\ *n* [F] : local and habitual twitching of particular muscles esp. of the face

¹**tick** \'tik\ *n* [ME *tyke*] **1** : any of numerous bloodsucking arachnids that are larger than the related mites, attach themselves to warm-blooded vertebrates to feed, and include important vectors of infectious diseases **2** : any of several usu. wingless bloodsucking parasitic dipterous insects

²**tick** *n* **1** : a light rhythmic audible tap or beat (as of a clock); *also* : a series of such ticks **2** : a small spot or mark; *esp* : one used to direct attention to something, to check an item on a list, or to represent a point on a scale

³**tick** *vb* **1 a** : to make the sound of a tick or a series of ticks **b** : to mark, count, or announce by or as if by ticking beats ⟨a meter *ticking* off his cab fare⟩ **2** : to operate as or in the manner of a functioning mechanism : RUN ⟨tried to understand what made him *tick*⟩ **3** : to mark with a written tick : CHECK ⟨*ticking* off each name on the list⟩

⁴**tick** *n* [ME *tike*, prob. fr. MD, fr. L *theca* cover, fr. Gk *thēkē* case] **1** : the fabric case of a mattress, pillow, or bolster; *also* : a mattress consisting of a tick and its filling **2** : TICKING

⁵**tick** *n* [short for *ticket*] : CREDIT, TRUST; *also* : a credit account ⟨bought on *tick*⟩

ticked \'tikt\ *adj* **1** : marked with ticks : FLECKED **2** : banded with two or more colors ⟨*ticked* hairs in the coat of a rabbit⟩

tick·er \'tik-ər\ *n* : something that ticks or produces a ticking sound: as **a** : WATCH **b** : a telegraphic receiving instrument that automatically prints off stock quotations or news on a paper ribbon **c** *slang* : HEART

ticker tape *n* : the paper ribbon on which a telegraphic ticker prints off its information

¹**tick·et** \'tik-ət\ *n* [F *étiquette* label, fr. MF *estiquette*, fr. *estiquier* to attach, fr. MD *steken* to stick; akin to E *stick*] **1 a** : a document that serves as a certificate, license, or permit; *esp* : a mariner's or airman's certificate **b** : TAG, LABEL ⟨price *ticket*⟩ **2** : a summons or warning issued to a traffic offender **3** : a document or token showing that a fare or admission fee has been paid **4** : a list of candidates for nomination or election **5** : a slip or card recording a transaction or undertaking or giving instructions ⟨sales *ticket*⟩ ⟨a driver's trip *ticket*⟩ ⟨repair *ticket*⟩

²**ticket** *vt* **1** : to attach a ticket to : LABEL; *also* : DESIGNATE **2** : to serve with a traffic ticket

ticket agent *n* : one who acts as an agent of a transportation company to sell tickets for travel by train, boat, airplane, or bus; *also* : one who sells theater and entertainment tickets — **ticket agency** *n*

ticket-of-leave *n, pl* **tickets-of-leave** : a license or permit formerly given in the United Kingdom and the British Commonwealth to a convict under imprisonment to go at large and to labor for himself subject to certain specific conditions

tick·ing \'tik-iŋ\ *n* : a strong linen or cotton fabric used in upholstering and as a covering for mattresses and pillows

¹**tick·le** \'tik-əl\ *vb* **tick·led**; **tick·ling** \'tik-(ə-)liŋ\ [ME *tikelen*] **1** : to have a tingling or prickling sensation ⟨my back *tickles*⟩ **2 a** : to excite or stir up agreeably : PLEASE ⟨food that *tickles* the palate⟩ **b** : to provoke to laughter or merriment : AMUSE **3** : to touch a body part lightly so as to excite the surface nerves and cause uneasiness, laughter, or spasmodic movements

²**tickle** *n* **1** : something that tickles **2** : a tickling sensation **3** : the act of tickling

tick·ler \'tik-(ə-)lər\ *n* **1** : a person or device that tickles **2** : a device for jogging the memory; *esp* : a file arranged to bring matters to timely attention

tick·lish \'tik-(ə-)lish\ *adj* **1** : sensitive to tickling **2 a** : TOUCHY, OVERSENSITIVE ⟨*ticklish* about his baldness⟩ **b** : easily overturned : UNSTABLE ⟨a canoe is *ticklish* to handle⟩ **3** : requiring delicate handling : CRITICAL ⟨a *ticklish* subject⟩ ⟨a *ticklish* international situation⟩ — **tick·lish·ly** *adv* — **tick·lish·ness** *n*

tick·seed \'tik-ˌsēd\ *n* : TICK TREFOIL

tick·tack·toe *also* **tic-tac-toe** \ˌtik-ˌtak-'tō\ *n* : a game in which two players alternately put crosses and ciphers in compartments of a figure formed by two vertical lines crossing two horizontal lines and each tries to get a row of three crosses or three ciphers before the opponent does

tick·tock \'tik-ˌtäk\ *n* : the ticking sound of a large clock

tick trefoil *n* : any of various leguminous plants having leaves with three leaflets and rough sticky fruits

tid·al \'tīd-ᵊl\ *adj* **1** : of or relating to tides : periodically rising and falling or flowing and ebbing ⟨*tidal* waters⟩ **2** : dependent (as to the time of arrival or departure) on the state of the tide ⟨*tidal* steamer⟩ — **tid·al·ly** \-ᵊl-ē\ *adv*

tidal wave *n* **1 a** : an unusually high sea wave that sometimes follows an earthquake **b** : an unusual rise of water alongshore due to strong winds **2** : something overwhelming (as a sweeping majority vote or an irresistible impulse)

tid·bit \'tid-ˌbit\ *n* **1** : a choice morsel of food **2** : a choice or pleasing bit (as of news)

tid·dle·dy·winks *or* **tid·dly·winks** \'tid-ᵊl-(d)ē-ˌwiŋ(k)s, 'tid-lē-ˌwiŋ(k)s\ *n* : a game the object of which is to snap small disks from a flat surface into a small container

¹**tide** \'tīd\ *n* [OE *tīd* time] **1 a** *obs* : a space of time : PERIOD **b** : a fit or opportune time : OPPORTUNITY **c** : an ecclesiastical anniversary or festival; *also* : its season **2 a** (1) : the alternate rising and falling of the surface of the ocean that occurs twice a day and is caused by the gravitational attraction of the sun and moon occurring unequally on different parts of the earth (2) : a less marked rising and falling of an inland body of water **b** : FLOOD TIDE **3** : something that fluctuates like the tides of the sea : VICISSITUDE ⟨the *tides* of fortune⟩ **4 a** : a flowing stream : CURRENT **b** : FLOOD WATERS

²**tide** *vb* **1** : to drift or cause to drift with the tide **2** : to

enable to surmount or endure a difficulty ⟨the gift *tided* him over⟩ ⟨money to *tide* him over the emergency⟩

tide·land \-ˌland, -lənd\ *n* **1** : land overflowed during flood tide **2** : land underlying the ocean beyond the low-water limit of the tide but within a nation's territorial waters — often used in pl.

tide·mark \ˈtīd-ˌmärk\ *n* **1 a** : a high-water or sometimes low-water mark left by tidal water or a flood **b** : a mark placed to indicate this point **2** : the point to which something has attained or below which it has receded

tide·wait·er \-ˌwāt-ər\ *n* : a customs inspector working on the docks or aboard ships

tide·wa·ter \-ˌwȯt-ər, -ˌwät-\ *n* **1** : water overflowing land at flood tide **2** : low-lying coastal land

tid·ing \ˈtīd-iŋ\ *n* [OE *tīdung*, fr. *tīdan* to happen; akin to E *tide*] : a piece of news — usu. used in pl. ⟨good *tidings*⟩

¹ti·dy \ˈtīd-ē\ *adj* **ti·di·er; -est** [ME, lit., timely, fr. *tide* time] **1** : properly filled out : PLUMP **2** : ADEQUATE, SATISFACTORY; *also* : DECENT, FAIR ⟨a *tidy* arrangement⟩ **3 a** : neat and orderly in appearance or habits : well ordered and cared for **b** : METHODICAL, PRECISE ⟨a *tidy* mind⟩ **4** : LARGE, SUBSTANTIAL ⟨a *tidy* price⟩ — **ti·di·ly** \ˈtīd-ᵊl-ē\ *adv* — **ti·di·ness** \ˈtīd-ē-nəs\ *n*

²tidy *vb* **ti·died; ti·dy·ing 1** : to put in order ⟨*tidy* up a room⟩ **2** : to make things tidy ⟨*tidying* up after supper⟩

³tidy *n, pl* **tidies** : a piece of fancywork used to protect the back, arms, or headrest of a chair or sofa from wear or soiling

¹tie \ˈtī\ *n* [OE *tēag*; akin to E **¹tow**] **1 a** : a line, ribbon, or cord used for fastening, uniting, or drawing something closed; *esp* : SHOELACE **b** (1) : a structural element (as a beam or angle iron) holding two pieces together : a tension member in a construction (2) : one of the transverse supports to which railroad rails are fastened **2** : something that serves as a connecting link: as **a** : a moral or legal obligation to someone or something **b** : a bond of kinship or affection **3** : a curved line that joins two musical notes indicating the same pitch used to denote a single tone sustained through the time value of the two **4 a** : an equality in number (as of votes or scores) **b** : equality in a contest; *also* : a contest that ends in a draw **5** : a method or style of tying or knotting **6** : something that is knotted or is to be knotted when worn: as **a** : NECKTIE **b** : a low laced shoe : OXFORD

²tie *vb* **tied; ty·ing** \ˈtī-iŋ\ *or* **tie·ing 1 a** : to fasten, attach, or close by means of a tie **b** : to form a knot or bow in ⟨*tie* your scarf⟩ **c** : to make by tying constituent elements ⟨*tied* a wreath⟩ ⟨*tie* a fishing fly⟩ **2 a** : to unite in marriage **b** : to unite (musical notes) by a tie **3** : to restrain or constrain the acts of **4 a** : to make or have an equal score with in a contest **b** : to come up with something equal to : EQUAL **5** : to make a tie: as **a** : to make a bond or connection **b** : to make an equal score **c** : AT-TACH

tie in \(ˈ)tī-ˈin\ *vb* **1** : to bring into connection or coordination with something relevant **2** : to become tied in ⟨that *ties in* with the facts⟩ ⟨the illustrations were cleverly *tied in* with the text⟩

tie-in \ˈtī-ˌin\ *n* : something that ties in, relates, or connects

tie·pin \-ˌpin\ *n* : an ornamental straight pin that has usu. a jeweled head and a sheath for the point and is used to hold the ends of a necktie in place

¹tier \ˈti(ə)r\ *n* [MF *tire* rank, of Gmc origin] : a row, rank, or layer of articles; *esp* : one of two or more rows arranged one above another

²tier *vb* **1** : to place or arrange in tiers **2** : to rise in tiers

³ti·er \ˈtī-(ə)r\ *n* : a person or thing that ties

¹tierce \ˈti(ə)rs\ *var of* TERCE

²tierce *n* [MF, fr. fem. of *tierz*, adj., third, fr. L *tertius*] **1** *obs* : THIRD 1 **2** : a unit of capacity equal to 42 U.S. gallons **3** : a sequence of three playing cards of the same suit **4** : the third of the eight defensive positions in fencing

tier·cel \ˈti(ə)r-səl\ *n* : a male hawk — compare FALCON

tiered \ˈti(ə)rd\ *adj* : having or arranged in tiers, rows, or layers ⟨triple-*tiered*⟩

tie up \(ˈ)tī-ˈəp\ *vt* **1** : to attach, fasten, or bind securely; *also* : to wrap up and fasten **2 a** : to use in such a manner as to make unavailable for other purposes **b** : to restrain from operation or progress ⟨traffic was *tied up* for miles⟩ **3** : DOCK ⟨the ferry *ties up* at the south slip⟩ **4** : to place in

or assume a relationship with something else ⟨this *ties up* with what was said before⟩

tie-up \ˈtī-ˌəp\ *n* **1** : a suspension of traffic or business (as by a strike or lockout or a mechanical breakdown) **2** : CONNECTION, ASSOCIATION ⟨looking for a helpful financial *tie-up*⟩

¹tiff \ˈtif\ *n* : a petty quarrel

²tiff *vi* : to have a minor quarrel

tif·fin \ˈtif-ən\ *n* : a midday meal : LUNCHEON

ti·ger \ˈtī-gər\ *n, pl* **tigers** *also* **tiger** [L *tigris*, fr. Gk] **1 a** : a large Asiatic carnivorous mammal of the cat family having a tawny coat transversely striped with black **b** : any of several large wildcats (as the jaguar or cougar) **c** : TIGER CAT 2 **2** : a fierce and bloodthirsty person or quality ⟨aroused the *tiger* in him⟩ **3** : a yell often of the word *tiger* at the end of a round of cheering

tiger

tiger beetle *n* : any of numerous active carnivorous beetles having larvae that tunnel in the soil

tiger cat *n* **1** : any of various wildcats (as the serval, ocelot, or margay) of moderate size and variegated coloration **2** : a striped or sometimes blotched tabby cat

ti·ger·ish \ˈtī-g(ə-)rish\ *adj* : of, relating to, or resembling a tiger — **ti·ger·ish·ly** *adv* — **ti·ger·ish·ness** *n*

ti·ger·like \ˈtī-gər-ˌlīk\ *adj* : having the ways or appearance of a tiger

tiger lily *n* : a common Asiatic lily widely grown for its nodding orange-colored flowers densely spotted with black

tiger moth *n* : any of a family of stout-bodied moths usu. with broad striped or spotted wings

tiger salamander *n* : a common black or brown yellow-blotched No. American salamander

tiger shark *n* : a large brown or gray shark of warm seas that is often a man-eater

¹tight \ˈtīt\ *adj* [of Scand origin] **1** : so close in structure as not to permit passage of a fluid or light ⟨a *tight* roof⟩ **2 a** : fixed very firmly in place ⟨loosen a *tight* jar cover⟩ **b** : not slack or loose : TAUT ⟨*tight* drumhead⟩ **c** : fitting too closely for comfort or free movement **3** : neat and orderly in arrangement or design : SNUG **4** : difficult to get through or out of : TRYING, EXACTING ⟨in a *tight* corner⟩ **5 a** : firm in control ⟨kept a *tight* hand on all his affairs⟩ **b** : STINGY, MISERLY **6** : packed or compressed to the limit : entirely full **7** : DRUNK **8** : scantily supplied : SCARCE ⟨*tight* loan money⟩ **9** : sound and free from checks ⟨*tight* lumber⟩ — **tight·ly** *adv* — **tight·ness** *n*

syn TIGHT, TAUT, TENSE mean drawn or stretched to the limit. TIGHT may imply a binding, constricting, or jamming encirclement, or the removal of the smallest opening or looseness; TAUT suggests the pulling of a rope or fabric until there is no give or slack; TENSE adds to TAUT the suggestion of strain impairing normal functioning

²tight *adv* **1** : TIGHTLY, FIRMLY, HARD ⟨door was shut *tight*⟩ **2** : SOUNDLY ⟨sleep *tight*⟩

tight·en \ˈtīt-ᵊn\ *vb* **tight·ened; tight·en·ing** \ˈtīt-niŋ, -ᵊn-iŋ\ : to make or become tight or tighter — **tight·en·er** \ˈtīt-nər, -ᵊn-ər\ *n*

tight·fist·ed \ˈtīt-ˈfis-təd\ *adj* : MISERLY, STINGY

tight-lipped \-ˈlipt\ *adj* **1** : having the lips closed tight (as in determination) **2** : TACITURN, SILENT

tight-mouthed \-ˈmau̇thd, -ˈmau̇tht\ *adj* : CLOSE-MOUTHED

tight·rope \ˈtīt-ˌrōp\ *n* : a rope or wire stretched taut for acrobats to perform on

tights \ˈtīts\ *n pl* : a skintight garment covering the body from the neck down or from the waist down

tight·wad \ˈtīt-ˌwäd\ *n* : a stingy person

tight·wire \-ˌwī(ə)r\ *n* : a tightrope made of wire

ti·gon \ˈtī-gən\ *n* [*tiger* + *lion*] : a hybrid between a male tiger and a female lion

ti·gress \ˈtī-grəs\ *n* : a female tiger

tike *var of* TYKE

til·bury \ˈtil-ˌber-ē, -b(ə-)rē\ *n, pl* **-bur·ies** [*Tilbury*, 19th cent. English coach builder] : a light 2-wheeled carriage : GIG

til·de \ˈtil-də\ *n* [Sp, fr. L *titulus* label, title] : a mark ~ placed esp. over the letter *n* (as in Spanish *señor* sir) to denote the sound \n^y\ or over vowels (as in Portuguese *irmã* sister) to indicate nasality

¹tile \'tīl\ *n* [OE *tigele,* fr. L *tegula;* akin to E *thatch*]
1 *pl* **tiles** *or* **tile a :** a flat or curved piece of fired clay, stone, or concrete used esp. for roofs, floors, or walls **b :** a hollow or a concave earthenware or concrete piece

tile roof

used for a drain **2 :** TILING 2b **3 :** a thin piece of resilient material (as linoleum or rubber) for covering floors or walls
²tile *vt* **1 :** to cover with tiles **2 :** to install drainage tile in — **til·er** *n*
til·ing \'tī-liŋ\ *n* **1 :** the act of one who tiles **2 a :** TILES **b :** a surface of tiles
¹till \t^ə l, təl, (,)til\ *prep or conj* [OE *til*] : UNTIL
²till \'til\ *vt* [OE *tilian*] : to work by plowing, sowing, and raising crops from : CULTIVATE — **till·a·ble** \-ə-bəl\ *adj*
³till \'til\ *n* [AF *tylle*] : a receptacle (as a drawer) for money
⁴till \'til\ *n* : unstratified glacial drift consisting of clay, sand, gravel, and boulders intermingled
till·age \'til-ij\ *n* **1 :** the operation of tilling land **2 :** cultivated land
¹till·er \'til-ər\ *n* : one that tills : CULTIVATOR
²til·ler \'til-ər\ *n* [ME *tiler* stock of a crossbow, fr. MF *telier,* lit., beam of a loom, fr. ML *telarium,* fr. L *tela* web] **1 :** a lever used to turn the rudder of a boat from side to side **2 :** a steering wheel for the rear wheels or trailer section of a vehicle (as a fire truck) — called also *tiller wheel*
³til·ler *n* [OE *telgor, telgra* twig, shoot] : SPROUT, STALK; *esp* : one from the base of a cereal grass
⁴til·ler *vi* : to put forth tillers ⟨cereal grasses *tiller*⟩
til·ler·man \'til-ər-mən\ *n* : one in charge of a tiller esp. on a fire truck
¹tilt \'tilt\ *vb* [ME *tilten*] **1 :** to cause to slope : INCLINE **2 :** to move or shift so as to lean or incline : SLANT **3 a :** to point or thrust in or as if in a tilt ⟨*tilt* a lance⟩ **b :** to charge against ⟨*tilt* an adversary⟩ **4 a :** to engage in a combat with lances : JOUST **b :** to make an impetuous attack ⟨*tilt* at wrongs⟩ — **tilt·er** *n*
²tilt *n* **1 :** an exercise on horseback in which two combatants charging with lances try to unhorse each other : JOUST **2 a :** an encounter (as with words) bringing about a sharp collision : ALTERCATION, QUARREL **b :** SPEED — used in the phrase *at full tilt* **3 a :** the act of tilting : the state or position of being tilted **b :** a sloping surface **4 :** a sport resembling or suggesting tilting with lances; *esp* : a water sport in which the contestants stand on logs or in canoes or boats and thrust with poles
³tilt *n* [OE *teld* tent, canopy] : a canopy for a wagon, boat, or stall
⁴tilt *vt* : to cover or provide with a tilt
tilth \'tilth\ *n* [OE, fr. *tilian* to till] **1 :** cultivation of the soil **2 :** cultivated land : TILLAGE **3 :** the state of being tilled
tilt·yard \'tilt-,yärd\ *n* : a yard or place for tilting
tim·bal \'tim-bəl\ *n* [F *timbale,* modif. of Sp *atabal,* fr. Ar *aṭ-ṭabl* the drum] : KETTLEDRUM
tim·bale \'tim-bəl; tim-'bäl, tam-\ *n* [F, lit., timbal] **1 :** a creamy mixture (as of chicken, lobster, cheese, or fish) cooked in a drum-shaped mold **2 :** a small pastry shell filled with a cooked timbale mixture
¹tim·ber \'tim-bər\ *n* [OE, building, wood] **1 :** wood for use in making something **2 :** a squared or dressed and usu. large piece of wood **3 :** wooded land or growing trees constituting a source of timber **4 :** a curving frame branching outward from the keel of a ship that is usu. composed of several pieces united : RIB — **timber** *adj*
²timber *vt* **tim·bered; tim·ber·ing** \-b(ə-)riŋ\ : to frame, cover, or support with timbers
tim·bered \'tim-bərd\ *adj* **1 :** furnished with, made of, or covered with timber **2 :** having walls framed by exposed timbers
timber hitch *n* : a knot used to secure a line to a log or spar
tim·ber·ing \'tim-b(ə-)riŋ\ *n* : a set of timbers : timber construction

tim·ber·land \'tim-bər-,land\ *n* : wooded land esp. with marketable timber
tim·ber·line \-,līn\ *n* : the upper limit of tree growth in mountains or high latitudes
timber wolf *n* : a large usu. gray No. American wolf extinct over much of the eastern and southern parts of its range
tim·ber·work \'tim-bər-,wərk\ *n* : a timber construction
tim·bre \'tam-bər, 'tim-\ *n* [F, fr. MF, bell struck by a hammer, fr. OF, drum, fr. Gk *tympanon*] : the quality given to a sound by its overtones: as **a :** the resonance by which the ear recognizes and identifies a voiced speech sound **b :** the tone distinctive of a singing voice or a musical instrument
tim·brel \'tim-brəl\ *n* [dim. of ME *timbre* tambourine, fr. OF, drum] : a small hand drum or tambourine — **tim·brelled** \-brəld\ *adj*
¹time \'tīm\ *n* [OE *tīma*] **1 a :** the measured or measurable period during which an action, process, or condition exists or continues : DURATION **b :** LEISURE ⟨*time* for reading⟩ **2 :** the point or period when something occurs : OCCASION **3 :** an appointed, fixed, or customary moment or hour for something to happen, begin, or end ⟨arrived on *time*⟩ **4 a :** an historical period : AGE **b :** a division of geologic chronology **c :** conditions at present or at some specified period ⟨*times* are hard⟩ ⟨move with the *times*⟩ **d :** the present time ⟨issues of the *time*⟩ **5 a :** LIFETIME **b :** a period or term esp. of military service **c :** a prison sentence **6 :** SEASON **7 a :** rate of speed : TEMPO **b :** the grouping of the beats of music : RHYTHM **8 a :** a moment, hour, day, or year as indicated by a clock or calendar ⟨what *time* is it⟩ **b :** any of various systems (as sidereal or solar) of reckoning time **9 a :** one of a series of recurring instances or repeated actions ⟨told him many *times*⟩ **b** *pl* : multiplied instances ⟨five *times* greater⟩ **c :** TURN ⟨three *times* at bat⟩ **10 :** finite as contrasted with infinite duration **11 :** a person's experience during a specified period or on a particular occasion ⟨a good *time*⟩ **12 a :** the period of one's work ⟨make up *time*⟩ **b :** an hourly pay rate **13 a :** the playing time of a game **b :** TIME-OUT — **at the same time :** HOWEVER, NEVERTHELESS — **at times :** now and then — **from time to time :** OCCASIONALLY — **in time 1 :** early enough **2 :** in the course of time : EVENTUALLY **3 :** in correct rhythm or tempo — **on time 1 :** PUNCTUAL, PUNCTUALLY **2 :** on an installment payment plan : on credit
²time *vt* **1 a :** to arrange or set the time of : SCHEDULE **b :** to regulate (a watch) to keep correct time **2 :** to set the tempo, speed, or duration of **3 :** to cause to keep time with something **4 :** to determine or record the time, duration, or rate of **5 :** to dispose (as a mechanical part) so that an action occurs at a desired instant
³time *adj* **1 a :** of or relating to time **b :** recording time **2 :** timed to ignite or explode at a specific moment ⟨*time* charge⟩ **3 a :** payable on a specified future day or a certain length of time after presentation **b :** based on installment payments ⟨*time* sale⟩
time and a half *n* : payment of a worker (as for overtime) at one and a half times his regular wage rate
time capsule *n* : a container holding historical records or objects representative of current culture that is deposited (as in a cornerstone) for preservation until discovery by some future age
time card *n* : a card used with a time clock to record an employee's starting and quitting times each day or on each job
time clock *n* : a clock that mechanically records the times of arrival and departure of workers
timed \'tīmd\ *adj* **1 :** made to occur at or in a set time ⟨a *timed* explosion⟩ **2 :** done or taking place at a time of a specified sort ⟨an ill-*timed* arrival⟩
time deposit *n* : a bank deposit payable a specified number of days after deposit or upon advance notice to the bank
time draft *n* : a draft payable a specified number of days after date of the draft or presentation to the drawee
time exposure *n* : exposure of a photographic film for a definite time usu. of more than one half second; *also* : a photograph taken by such exposure
time-hon·ored \'tīm-,än-ərd\ *adj* : honored or respected because of age or long-established usage
time·keep·er \'tīm-,kē-pər\ *n* **1 :** TIMEPIECE **2 :** a clerk

---

ə abut; ᵊ kitten; ər further; a back; ā bake; ä cot, cart; au̇ out; ch chin; e less; ē easy; g gift; i trip; ī life

who keeps records of the time worked by employees **3** : one appointed to mark and announce the time in an athletic game or contest — **time·keep·ing** \-piŋ\ n

time·less \'tīm-ləs\ adj **1 a** : having no beginning or end : UNENDING **b** : not restricted to a particular time or date **2** : not affected by time : AGELESS — **time·less·ly** adv — **time·less·ness** n

time lock n : a lock controlled by clockwork to prevent its being opened before a set time

time·ly \'tīm-lē\ adj **time·li·er; -est 1** : coming early or at the right time : OPPORTUNE **2** : appropriate or adapted to the times or the occasion ⟨a timely book⟩ — **time·li·ness** n

time-out \'tīm-'aùt\ n : a suspension of play in an athletic game

time·piece \'tīm-,pēs\ n : a device (as a clock or watch) to measure the passage of time

tim·er \'tī-mər\ n : one that times: as **a** : TIMEPIECE **b** : a device in the ignition system of an internal-combustion engine that causes the spark to be produced in the cylinder at the correct time **c** : a device (as a clock) that indicates by an audible signal the end of an interval of time or that automatically starts or stops a device

times \,tīmz\ prep : multiplied by ⟨two times seven is fourteen⟩

time-sav·er \'tīm-,sā-vər\ n : something that saves time

time·sav·ing \'tīm-,sā-viŋ\ adj : intended or serving to expedite something ⟨a timesaving device⟩

time-serv·er \-,sər-vər\ n : a person who fits his behavior and ideas to the pattern of his times or his superiors — **time-serv·ing** \-viŋ\ adj or n

time signature n : a fractional sign placed just after the key signature whose denominator indicates the kind of note (as a quarter note) taken as the time unit for the beat and whose numerator indicates the number of these to the measure

time·ta·ble \'tīm-,tā-bəl\ n **1** : a table of departure and arrival times of trains, buses, or airplanes **2** : a schedule showing a planned order or sequence

time·worn \-,wōrn, -,wòrn\ adj **1** : worn or impaired by time **2 a** : AGE-OLD, ANCIENT **b** : HACKNEYED, STALE ⟨a timeworn joke⟩

time zone n : a geographical region within which the same standard time is used

tim·id \'tim-əd\ adj [L timidus, fr. timēre to fear] : feeling or showing a lack of courage or self-confidence : FEARFUL, SHY — **ti·mid·i·ty** \tə-'mid-ət-ē\ n — **tim·id·ly** \'tim-əd-lē\ adv

tim·ing n **1** : selection for maximum effect of the precise moment for beginning or doing something **2** : observation and recording (as by a stopwatch) of the elapsed time of an act, action, or process

tim·o·rous \'tim-(ə-)rəs\ adj [L timor fear, fr. timēre to fear] **1** : of a timid disposition : AFRAID **2** : expressing or suggesting timidity ⟨a somewhat timorous bearing⟩ — **tim·o·rous·ly** adv — **tim·o·rous·ness** n

tim·o·thy \'tim-ə-thē\ n [prob. after Timothy Hanson, 18th cent. American farmer said to have introduced it from New England to the southern states] : a European grass with long cylindrical spikes widely grown for hay

Tim·o·thy \'tim-ə-thē\ n **1** : a disciple of the apostle Paul **2** — see BIBLE table

tim·pa·ni \'tim-pə-nē\ n pl [It, pl. of timpano kettledrum, fr. L tympanum drum]· : a set of two or three kettledrums played by one performer — **tim·pa·nist** \-nəst\ n

1tin \'tin\ n [OE] **1** : a soft bluish white lustrous crystalline metallic chemical element that is malleable and ductile at ordinary temperatures and that is used as a protective coating in tinfoil and in soft solders and alloys — see ELEMENT table **2 a** : a box, can, pan, vessel, or a sheet made of tinplate **b** chiefly Brit : a sealed can holding food — **tin** adj

2tin vt **tinned; tin·ning 1** : to cover or plate with tin or an alloy of tin **2** chiefly Brit : to put up or pack in tins : CAN

tin can n, slang : DESTROYER 2

1tinct \'tiŋ(k)t\ adj : TINGED, TINTED

2tinct n : TINCTURE, TINGE

1tinc·ture \'tiŋ(k)-chər\ n [L tinctura act of dyeing, fr. tingere to tinge] **1 a** : a substance that colors, dyes, or stains **b** : COLOR, TINT **2 a** : a characteristic quality

: CAST **b** : a slight admixture : TRACE **3** : an alcoholic solution of a medicinal substance

2tincture vt **1** : to tint or stain with a color : TINGE **2** : to infuse or instill with a property or quality : IMPREGNATE

tin·der \'tin-dər\ n [OE tynder] : a very flammable substance that can be used as kindling — **tin·dery** \-d(ə-)rē\ adj

tin·der·box \-,bäks\ n **1 a** : a metal box for holding tinder and usu. a flint and steel for striking a spark **b** : a highly flammable object or place **2** : a person, place, or situation likely to erupt into strife or conflict

tine \'tīn\ n [OE tind] : a slender pointed projecting part : PRONG ⟨the tines of a fork⟩

tin·ea \'tin-ē-ə\ n [L, worm, moth] : any of several fungous diseases of the skin; esp : RINGWORM — **tin·e·al** \-ē-əl\ adj

tin fish n, slang : TORPEDO

tin·foil \'tin-,fòil\ n : a thin metal sheeting usu. of aluminum or tin-lead alloy

1ting \'tiŋ\ vb : to sound or cause to sound with a ting

2ting n : a high-pitched sound (as from a light stroke on a glass)

1tinge \'tinj\ vt **tinged; tinge·ing** or **ting·ing** \'tin-jiŋ\ [L tingere to dip, tinge] **1 a** : to color slightly : TINT **b** : to affect or modify with a slight odor or taste **2** : to modify in character ⟨respect tinged with envy⟩

2tinge n **1** : a slight staining or suffusing shade or color **2** : a modifying property or influence : TOUCH

1tin·gle \'tin-gəl\ vi **tin·gled; tin·gling** \-g(ə-)liŋ\ [ME tinglen, alter. of tinklen to tinkle, tingle] **1 a** : to feel a ringing, stinging, prickling, or thrilling sensation **b** : to cause such a sensation **2** : TINKLE

2tingle n **1** : a tingling sensation or condition **2** : a tinkling sound — **tin·gly** \'tin-g(ə-)lē\ adj

tin hat n : a metal helmet

tin·horn \'tin-,hòrn\ n : a pretentious or boastful person or gambler with little money, power, or ability

1tin·ker \'tin-kər\ n [ME tinkere] **1 a** : a usu. itinerant mender of household utensils (as pots and pans) **b** : an unskilled mender : BUNGLER **2** : any of several small fishes; esp : a young mackerel

2tinker vb **tin·kered; tin·ker·ing** \-k(ə-)riŋ\ : to work in the manner of a tinker; esp : to repair or adjust something in an unskilled or experimental manner — **tin·ker·er** \-kər-ər\ n

tinker's damn or **tinker's dam** n : something absolutely worthless

1tin·kle \'tiŋ-kəl\ vb **tin·kled; tin·kling** \-k(ə-)liŋ\ [ME tinklen, freq. of tinken to tinkle] **1** : to make or emit a tinkle **2 a** : to cause to make a tinkle **b** : to produce by tinkling ⟨tinkle a tune⟩

2tinkle n : a series of short high ringing or clinking sounds — **tin·kly** \-k(ə-)lē\ adj

tin·man \'tin-mən\ n : TINSMITH

tin·ni·tus \'tin-ə-təs\ n [L, ringing, tinnitus, fr. tinnire to ring] : a subjective sensation of noise (as a ringing or roaring)

tin·ny \'tin-ē\ adj **tin·ni·er; -est 1** : of, abounding in, or yielding tin **2** : resembling or suggestive of tin: as **a** : LIGHT, CHEAP **b** : thin in tone : METALLIC ⟨a tinny voice⟩ — **tin·ni·ly** \'tin-ᵊl-ē\ adv — **tin·ni·ness** \'tin-ē-nəs\ n

Tin Pan Alley n : a district occupied chiefly by composers or publishers of popular music; also : the body of such composers or publishers

tin·plate \'tin-'plāt\ n : thin sheet iron or steel coated with tin

tin-plate vt : to plate or coat (as a metal sheet) with tin

1tin·sel \'tin(t)-səl\ n [MF estincelle, etincelle spark, spangle, fr. L scintilla spark] **1** : a thread, strip, or sheet of metal, paper, or plastic used to produce a glittering and sparkling appearance (as in fabrics, yarns, or decorations) **2** : something superficially attractive or glamorous but of little real worth

2tinsel adj **1** : made of or covered with tinsel **2** : cheaply gaudy : TAWDRY

3tinsel vt **tin·seled** or **tin·selled; tin·sel·ing** or **tin·sel·ling** \-s(ə-)liŋ\ **1** : to interweave, overlay, or adorn with or as if with tinsel **2** : to impart a specious brightness to — **tin·sel·ly** \'tin(t)-s(ə-)lē\ adj : TINSELED

tin·smith \'tin-,smith\ n : a worker who makes or repairs things of metal (as tin)

¹**tint** \'tint\ *n* [L *tinctus* act of dyeing, fr. *tingere* to tinge] **1** : a slight or pale coloring : TINGE ⟨white without a *tint* of yellow⟩ **2** : a light color or shade ⟨pale *tints* of red⟩ **3** : a usu. slight modifying quality or characteristic **4** : dye for the hair **syn** see COLOR — **tint·er** *n*

²**tint** *vt* : to impart or apply a tint to : COLOR

tin·tin·nab·u·la·tion \ˌtin-tə-ˌnab-yə-'lā-shən\ *n* [L *tin-tinnabulum* bell, fr. *tintinnare* to jingle] **1** : the ringing or sounding of bells **2** : a jingling or tinkling sound as if of bells

tin·type \'tin-ˌtīp\ *n* : a photograph made on a thin iron plate having a darkened surface

tin·ware \-ˌwa(ə)r, -ˌwe(ə)r\ *n* : articles made of tinplate

tin·work \-ˌwərk\ *n* **1** : work in tin *pl* : an establishment where tin is smelted, rolled, or otherwise worked

ti·ny \'tī-nē\ *adj* **ti·ni·er; -est** [alter. of ME *tine*] : very small or diminutive : MINUTE — **ti·ni·ness** *n*

¹**tip** \'tip\ *n* [ME] **1** : the pointed or rounded end of something : END **2** : a small piece or part serving as an end, cap, or point

²**tip** *vt* **tipped; tip·ping 1 a** : to furnish with a tip **b** : to cover or adorn the tip of **2** : to affix (an insert) in a book — often used with *in* **3** : to remove the ends of ⟨*tip* raspberries⟩

³**tip** *vb* **tipped; tip·ping** [ME *tipen*] **1** : OVERTURN, UPSET **2** : LEAN, SLANT, TILT **3** : to raise and tilt forward in salute ⟨*tipped* his hat⟩

⁴**tip** *n* : the act or an instance of tipping : TILT

⁵**tip** *n* [ME *tippe*] : a light touch or blow : TAP

⁶**tip** *vt* **tipped; tip·ping 1** : to strike lightly : TAP **2** : to hit (as a baseball) a glancing blow with the edge of a bat ⟨*tipped* the first pitch⟩

⁷**tip** *vb* **tipped; tip·ping 1** : to give a gratuity to ⟨*tip* a waitress⟩ **2** : to give gratuities ⟨was miserly about *tipping*⟩

⁸**tip** *n* : a gift or small sum of money tendered for a service performed or anticipated : GRATUITY

⁹**tip** *n* : an item of authoritative or confidential information ⟨a *tip* on a sure winner in a horse race⟩

¹⁰**tip** *vt* **tipped; tip·ping** : to give information or advice about or to often in a secret or confidential manner ⟨*tipped* off as to what would happen⟩

tip·cart \'tip-ˌkärt\ *n* : a cart whose body can be tipped on the frame to empty its contents

tip·cat \-ˌkat\ *n* : a game in which one player using a bat strikes lightly a tapered wooden peg and as it flies up strikes it again to drive it as far as possible while fielders try to recover it; *also* : the peg used in this game

ti·pi \'tē-(ˌ)pē\ *var of* TEPEE

tip-off \'tip-ˌof\ *n* : WARNING, TIP

tip·per \'tip-ər\ *n* : one that tips

tip·pet \'tip-ət\ *n* [ME *tipet*] **1** : a long hanging part of a garment (as on a sleeve or cape) **2** : a shoulder cape usu. with hanging ends **3** : a long black scarf worn over the robe by Anglican clergymen

¹**tip·ple** \'tip-əl\ *vb* **tip·pled; tip·pling** \'tip-(ə-)liŋ\ [back-formation fr. obs. *tippler* barkeeper, fr. ME *tipeler*] : to drink intoxicating liquor esp. continuously in small amounts — **tip·pler** \-(ə-)lər\ *n*

²**tipple** *n* : an intoxicating beverage : DRINK

³**tipple** *n* **1** : an apparatus by which loaded cars are emptied by tipping **2** : the place where tipping is done; *esp* : a coal-screening plant

tip·staff \'tip-ˌstaf\ *n, pl* **tip·staves** \-ˌstavz, -ˌstāvz\ : an officer (as a constable or bailiff) who bears a staff

tip·ster \'tip-stər\ *n* : one who gives or sells tips esp. for gambling or speculation

tip·sy \'tip-sē\ *adj* **tip·si·er; -est 1** : unsteady, staggering, or foolish from the effects of alcohol : somewhat drunk **2** : UNSTEADY, ASKEW ⟨a *tipsy* angle⟩ — **tip·si·ly** \-sə-lē\ *adv* — **tip·si·ness** \-sē-nəs\ *n*

¹**tip·toe** \'tip-ˌtō, -'tō\ *n* : the tip of a toe; *also* : the ends of the toes — **on tiptoe** : ALERT, EXPECTANT

²**tiptoe** *adv* : on or as if on tiptoe ⟨walk *tiptoe*⟩

³**tiptoe** *adj* **1** : characterized by standing or walking on tiptoe **2** : CAUTIOUS, STEALTHY ⟨a *tiptoe* approach⟩

⁴**tiptoe** *vi* : to stand, raise oneself, or walk on or as if on tiptoe

¹**tip-top** \'tip-ˌtäp, -ˌtäp\ *n* : the highest point : SUMMIT

²**tip-top** *adj* : EXCELLENT, FIRST-RATE — **tip-top** *adv*

ti·rade \tī-'rād, 'tī-ˌ\ *n* [F, lit., shot, fr. It *tirata*, fr. *tirare* to draw, shoot] : a long violent usu. abusive speech

¹**tire** \'tī(ə)r\ *vb* [OE *tēorian, tȳrian*] **1** : to become weary **2** : to exhaust or greatly decrease the physical strength of : FATIGUE **3** : to wear out the patience or attention of : BORE

²**tire** *n* **1** : a metal hoop forming the tread of a wheel **2 a** : a rubber cushion that encircles a wheel and usu. consists of a rubber-and-fabric covering containing a cavity or a separate inner tube that is filled with compressed air **b** : the external rubber-and-fabric covering of a pneumatic tire that uses an inner tube

tired \'tī(ə)rd\ *adj* : FATIGUED, WEARY — **tired·ly** *adv* — **tired·ness** *n*

tire·less \'tī(ə)r-ləs\ *adj* : UNTIRING, INDEFATIGABLE — **tire·less·ly** *adv* — **tire·less·ness** *n*

tire·some \'tī(ə)r-səm\ *adj* : WEARISOME, TEDIOUS — **tire·some·ly** *adv* — **tire·some·ness** *n*

tire·wom·an \-ˌwùm-ən\ *n* [obs. *tire* to attire] : a lady's maid

tir·ing-room \'tī-riŋ-ˌrüm, -ˌrùm\ *n* [fr. gerund of obs. *tire* to attire, short for *attire*] : a dressing room esp. in a theater

ti·ro *var of* TYRO

tis·sue \'tish-(ˌ)ü\ *n* [OF *tissu*, a rich fabric, fr. pp. of *tistre* to weave, fr. L *texere*] **1 a** : a fine lightweight often sheer fabric **b** : MESH, NETWORK, WEB ⟨a *tissue* of lies⟩ **2 a** : a piece of soft absorbent paper used esp. as a handkerchief or for removing cosmetics **3** : a mass or layer of cells usu. of one kind that together with their intercellular substance form the basic structural materials of a plant or an animal — compare ORGAN; CONNECTIVE TISSUE, EPITHELIUM, PARENCHYMA

tissue paper *n* : a thin gauzy paper used variously (as to protect engravings in books or to wrap delicate articles)

¹**tit** \'tit\ *n* [OE] : TEAT

²**tit** *n* : TITMOUSE; *also* : any of various small plump often long-tailed birds

ti·tan \'tīt-ᵊn\ *n* **1** *cap* : one of a family of giants overthrown by the Olympian gods **2** : one of gigantic size, power, or achievement

Titan *adj* : TITANIC

ti·ta·nate \'tīt-ᵊn-ˌāt\ *n* **1** : any of various oxides of titanium and another metal **2** : a titanium ester

ti·tan·ess \'tīt-ᵊn-əs\ *n, often cap* : a female titan

ti·tan·ic \tī-'tan-ik\ *adj* **1** *cap* : of, relating to, or resembling the Titans **2** : of great magnitude, force, or power : COLOSSAL

ti·ta·ni·um \tī-'tā-nē-əm, tə-\ *n* [NL, fr. Gk *Titan* Titan] : a silvery gray light strong metallic chemical element found combined in various minerals and used in alloys (as steel) — see ELEMENT table

titanium dioxide *n* : an oxide TiO_2 of titanium used esp. as a white pigment

titanium white *n* : a titanium dioxide used as a pigment

ti·tan·o·saur \tī-'tan-ə-ˌsor\ *n* [Gk *sauros* lizard] : a large herbivorous Cretaceous dinosaur

ti·tan·o·there \tī-'tan-ə-ˌthi(ə)r\ *n* [Gk *thērion* wild animal] : any of various large often horned extinct mammals distantly related to the horses

tit·bit \'tit-ˌbit\ *var of* TIDBIT

tit for tat \ˌtit-fər-'tat\ : an equivalent given in return (as for an injury) : RETALIATION

¹**tithe** \'tīth\ *vb* [OE *teogothian*, fr. *teogotha* tenth; akin to E *ten*] **1** : to pay or give a tithe **2** : to levy a tithe on — **tith·er** *n*

²**tithe** *n* **1** : a tenth part paid in kind or money as a voluntary contribution or as a tax esp. for the support of a religious establishment **2 a** : TENTH **b** : a small part

ti·tian \'tish-ən\ *adj, often cap* [after *Titian* d1576 Italian painter] : of a brownish orange color

tit·il·late \'tit-ᵊl-ˌāt\ *vt* [L *titillare*] **1** : TICKLE **2** : to excite pleasurably — **tit·il·la·tion** \ˌtit-ᵊl-'ā-shən\ *n* — **tit·il·la·tive** \'tit-ᵊl-ˌāt-iv\ *adj*

tit·i·vate *or* **tit·ti·vate** \'tit-ə-ˌvāt\ *vb* : to dress up : spruce up : SMARTEN — **tit·i·va·tion** \ˌtit-ə-'vā-shən\ *n*

¹**ti·tle** \'tīt-ᵊl\ *n* [L *titulus* inscription, label, title] **1 a** : RIGHT, PRIVILEGE; *esp* : the elements constituting legal ownership **b** : the instrument (as a deed) that is evidence of a right **2** : something that justifies or substantiates a claim **3 a** : a descriptive or general heading (as of a chapter in a book) **b** : the heading of an act or statute or of a

legal action or proceeding **4** : the distinguishing name of a written, printed, or filmed production or of a musical composition or a work of art **5** : a division of an instrument, book, or bill; *esp* : one larger than a section or article **6** : an appellation of dignity or honor attached to a person or family (as by hereditary right) ⟨a *title* of nobility⟩ **7** : CHAMPIONSHIP 2a ⟨won the batting *title*⟩

²**title** *vt* **ti·tled; ti·tling** \'tīt-liŋ, -ᵊl-iŋ\ : to designate or call by a title : TERM, STYLE

ti·tled \'tīt-ᵊld\ *adj* : having a title esp. of nobility

title deed *n* : the deed constituting the evidence of a person's legal account

ti·tle·hold·er \'tit-ᵊl-,hōl-dər\ *n* : one that holds a title; *esp* : CHAMPION

title page *n* : a page of a book bearing the title and usu. the names of the author and publisher and the place of publication

title role *n* : a part or character that gives a play its name

ti·tlist \'tīt-ᵊl-əst, 'tīt-ləst\ *n* : TITLEHOLDER

tit·mouse \'tit-,maús\ *n, pl* **tit·mice** \-,mīs\ [ME *titmose* fr. (assumed) ME *tit* small object or creature + ME *mose* titmouse, fr. OE *māse*] : any of numerous small arboreal and insectivorous birds related to the nuthatches but longer tailed

Ti·to·ism \'tēt-ō-,iz-əm\ *n* : nationalistic policies and practices followed by a communist state independently of the U.S.S.R. esp. as practiced in Yugoslavia by Marshal Tito

ti·trate \'tī-,trāt\ *vb* : to subject to titration

ti·tra·tion \tī-'trā-shən\ *n* [F *titre* title, proportion of gold or silver in a coin, fr. OF *title* label, title, fr. L *titulus*] : the process of determining the strength of a solution or the concentration of a substance in solution in terms of the smallest amount of a reagent of known concentration required to bring about a given effect in reaction with a known volume of the test solution

ti·tri·met·ric \,tī-trə-'me-trik\ *adj* : determined by titration — **ti·tri·met·ri·cal·ly** \-tri-k(ə-)lē\ *adv*

tit·tat·toe \,ti-,ta(t)-'tō\ *var of* TICKTACKTOE

tit·ter \'tit-ər\ *vi* **1** : to give vent to partly suppressed laughter **2** : to laugh in a nervous manner esp. at a high pitch — **titter** *n*

tit·tle \'tit-ᵊl\ *n* [ML *titulus*, fr. L, label, title] **1** : a point or small sign used as a diacritical mark in writing or printing **2** : a very small part

tit·tle-tat·tle \'tit-ᵊl-,tat-ᵊl\ *n* : GOSSIP, PRATTLE — **tittle-tattle** *vi*

tit·u·lar \'tich-(ə-)lər\ *adj* [L *titulus* title] **1 a** : existing in title only : NOMINAL **b** : having the title belonging to an office or dignity without its duties or responsibilities **2** : bearing a title **3** : of, relating to, or constituting a title — **tit·u·lar·ly** *adv*

titular bishop *n* : a Roman Catholic bishop with the title of but without jurisdiction in a defunct see (as in Christian lands under Muslim control)

Ti·tus \'tīt-əs\ *n* **1** : an associate of the apostle Paul **2** — see BIBLE table

tiz·zy \'tiz-ē\ *n, pl* **tizzies** : a highly excited and distracted state of mind

TNT \,tē-,en-'tē\ *n* [*trinitrotoluene*] : TRINITROTOLUENE

¹**to** \tə, tü, (')tü\ *prep* [OE *tō*] **1 a** : in the direction of and reaching ⟨walked *to* school⟩ **b** : in the direction of : so as to approach ⟨broke down while driving *to* town⟩ ⟨tendency *to* silliness⟩ **c** : close against : ON ⟨applied polish *to* the table⟩ **d** : as far as ⟨stripped *to* the waist⟩ **2 a** : for the purpose of : FOR ⟨came *to* our aid⟩ **b** : in honor of ⟨a toast *to* the bride⟩ **c** : so as to become or bring about ⟨broken *to* pieces⟩ ⟨beaten *to* death⟩ **3 a** : BEFORE ⟨ten minutes *to* five⟩ **b** : UNTIL ⟨from eight *to* five⟩ **4 a** : being a part or accessory of ⟨the trousers *to* this suit⟩ ⟨a key *to* the door⟩ **b** : with the accompaniment of : in harmony with ⟨sang *to* his guitar⟩ **5 a** : in a relation of likeness or unlikeness with ⟨similar *to* that one⟩ ⟨inferior *to* the other⟩ **b** (1) : in accordance with ⟨add salt *to* taste⟩ (2) : within the range of ⟨*to* my knowledge⟩ **c** : contained, occurring, or included in ⟨400 *to* the box⟩ ⟨five strokes *to* a second⟩ **6 a** : as regards ⟨agreeable *to* everyone⟩ ⟨attitude *to* our friends⟩ **b** : affecting as the receiver or beneficiary of an action ⟨spoke *to* his father⟩ ⟨gave it *to* me⟩ **c** : for no one except ⟨had a room *to* himself⟩ **7** — used to indicate that the following verb is an infinitive ⟨wants

to go⟩ ⟨something *to* do⟩ and often used by itself at the end of a clause to stand for an infinitive ⟨knows more than he seems *to*⟩ ⟨don't want *to*⟩

²**to** \'tü\ *adv* **1** — used as a function word to indicate direction toward ⟨feathers wrong end *to*⟩ ⟨run *to* and fro⟩ **2** : into contact, position, or attachment esp. with a frame (as of a door) ⟨snapped her purse *to*⟩ **3** : to the matter or business at hand esp. with vigorous concentration ⟨the boxers set *to* with a flurry of blows⟩ ⟨if we all fall *to* the job we will soon be done⟩ **4** : to a state of consciousness or awareness ⟨brings her *to* with smelling salts⟩ **5** : at hand : BY ⟨saw the moose close *to*⟩

toad \'tōd\ *n* [OE *tāde*] : any of numerous tailless leaping amphibians that as compared with the related frogs are generally more terrestrial in habit, squatter and shorter in build and with weaker hind limbs, and rough, dry, and warty rather than smooth and moist of skin

toad·eat·er \-,ēt-ər\ *n* : TOADY

toad·fish \-,fish\ *n* : any of various marine fishes with a large thick head, a wide mouth, and scaleless slimy skin

toad·flax \-,flaks\ *n* : a common European perennial herb of the figwort family that has showy yellow and orange flowers and is a widely naturalized weed in No. America

toad spit *n* : CUCKOO SPIT 1 — called also *toad spittle*

toad·stone \'tōd-,stōn\ *n* : a stone or similar object held to have formed in the head or body of a toad and formerly often worn as a charm or antidote to poison

toad·stool \'tōd-,stül\ *n* : a fungus having an umbrella-shaped cap : MUSHROOM; *esp* : one that is poisonous or inedible

¹**toady** \'tōd-ē\ *n, pl* **toad·ies** : a person who flatters or fawns upon another in the hope of receiving favors

²**toady** *vi* **toad·ied; toad·y·ing** : to behave as a toady — **toad·y·ism** \-ē-,iz-əm\ *n*

to-and-fro \,tü-ən-'frō\ *adj* : forward and backward ⟨*to-and-fro* motion⟩ ⟨*to-and-fro* visiting⟩

¹**toast** \'tōst\ *vb* [MF *toster*, fr. LL *tostare* to roast, intens. of L *torrēre* to dry, parch] **1** : to make (as bread) crisp, hot, and brown by heat **2** : to warm thoroughly : become toasted

²**toast** *n* **1** : sliced toasted bread browned on both sides by heat **2** [fr. the use of pieces of spiced toast to flavor drinks] **a** : a person whose health is drunk or something in honor of which persons drink **b** : a highly admired person **3** : an act of proposing or of drinking in honor of a toast

³**toast** *vt* : to propose or drink to as a toast ⟨*toasting* each other's health⟩

toast·er \'tō-stər\ *n* : one that toasts; *esp* : an electrical appliance for toasting

toast·mas·ter \'tōs(t)-,mas-tər\ *n* : one that presides at a banquet and introduces the after-dinner speakers — **toast·mis·tress** \-,mis-trəs\ *n*

to·bac·co \tə-'bak-ō\ *n, pl* **-cos** [Sp *tabaco*, of AmerInd origin] **1** : any of a genus of chiefly American plants of the nightshade family with sticky foliage and tubular flowers; *esp* : a tall erect annual So. American herb grown for its leaves **2** : the leaves of cultivated tobacco prepared for use in smoking or chewing or as snuff **3** : manufactured products of tobacco (as cigars or cigarettes); *also* : smoking as a practice

tobacco heart *n* : a functional disorder of the heart marked by irregularity of action and caused by excessive use of tobacco

tobacco mosaic *n* : any of a complex of virus diseases of tobacco and related plants

to·bac·co·nist \tə-'bak-ə-nəst\ *n* : a dealer in tobacco esp. at retail

to-be \tə-'bē\ *adj* : that is to be : FUTURE ⟨a pretty bride-*to-be*⟩

¹**to·bog·gan** \tə-'bäg-ən\ *n* [CanF *tobogan*, of Algonquian origin] **1** : a long flat-bottomed light sled made without runners and curved up at the front **2** : a downward course or a sharp decline

²**toboggan** *vi* **1** : to coast on a toboggan **2** : to decline suddenly and sharply (as in value) — **to·bog·gan·er** *n* — **to·bog·gan·ist** \-'bäg-ə-nəst\ *n*

to·by \'tō-bē\ *n, pl* **tobies** *often cap* [*Toby*, nickname fr. the name *Tobias*] : a small jug, pitcher, or mug (as for ale) modeled in the form of a stout man with a cocked hat for the brim

toc·ca·ta \tə-'kät-ə\ *n* [It, fr. *toccare* to touch] : a brilliant

---

j joke; **ŋ** sing; **ō** flow; **ȯ** flaw; **ȯi** coin; **th** thin; **t͟h** this; **ü** loot; ** u̇** foot; **y** yet; **yü** few; **yu̇** furious; **zh** vision

musical composition usu. for organ or harpsichord in a free style

to·coph·er·ol \tō-ˈkäf-ə-ˌról, -ˌról\ *n* [Gk *tokos* childbirth, offspring + *pherein* to carry, bear] : any of various fat-soluble phenolic compounds with varying degrees of antioxidant and vitamin E activity

toc·sin \ˈtäk-sən\ *n* [MF *toquassen*, fr. OProv *tocasenh*, fr. *tocar* to touch, ring + *senh* sign, bell, fr. L *signum* sign] **1** : an alarm bell or the ringing of it **2** : a warning signal

¹to·day \tə-ˈdā\ *adv* **1** : on or for this day **2** : at the present time : NOWADAYS

²today *n* : the present day, time, or age

tod·dle \ˈtäd-ᵊl\ *vi* **tod·dled**; **tod·dling** \ˈtäd-liŋ, -ᵊl-iŋ\ : to walk with short tottering steps in the manner of a young child — **toddle** *n* — **tod·dler** \ˈtäd-lər, -ᵊl-ər\ *n*

tod·dy \ˈtäd-ē\ *n*, *pl* **toddies** [Hindi *tāṛī*] **1** : the sap of various mostly East Indian palms often fermented to form an alcoholic liquor **2** : a hot drink consisting of an alcoholic liquor, water, sugar, and spices

to–do \tə-ˈdü\ *n*, *pl* **to–dos** \-ˈdüz\ : BUSTLE, STIR

¹toe \ˈtō\ *n* [OE *tā*] **1 a** : one of the jointed members that make up the front end of a vertebrate foot **b** : the front end or part of a foot or hoof **c** : the forepart of something (as a shoe) worn on the foot **2** : something that resembles the toe of a foot esp. in form or position ⟨the *toe* of a golf club or of a hockey stick⟩ — **toe·less** \-ləs\ *adj*

²toe *vb* **toed**; **toe·ing** **1** : to furnish with a toe ⟨*toe* off a sock in knitting⟩ **2** : to touch, reach, or drive with the toe ⟨*toe* a line⟩ **3** : to drive (as a nail) slantwise; *also* : to fasten by nails so driven **4** : to stand or walk so that the toes assume an indicated position or direction ⟨*toe* in⟩ — **toe the line** : to conform rigorously to a rule or standard

toed \ˈtōd\ *adj* **1** : having a toe or such or so many toes — used esp. in combination ⟨5-*toed*⟩ **2** : driven obliquely ⟨a *toed* nail⟩; *also* : secured by toed nails

toe dance *n* : a dance executed on the tips of the toes — **toe–dance** \ˈtō-ˌdan(t)s\ *vi* — **toe dancer** *n*

toe·hold \ˈtō-ˌhōld\ *n* **1** : a small foothold or a slight footing **2** : a hold in which the offensive wrestler bends or twists his opponent's foot

¹toe·nail \ˈtō-ˌnāl, -ˈnāl\ *n* : a nail of a toe

²toenail *vt* : to fasten by toed nails : TOE

tof·fee *or* **tof·fy** \ˈtäf-ē\ *n*, *pl* **toffees** *or* **toffies** [alter. of *taffy*] : candy of brittle but tender texture made by boiling sugar and butter together

tog \ˈtäg\ *vt* **togged**; **tog·ging** : to put togs on : DRESS ⟨*togged* out in the latest fashion⟩

to·ga \ˈtō-gə\ *n* [L; akin to E *thatch*] : the loose outer garment worn in public by citizens of ancient Rome; *also* : a similar loose wrap or a professional, official, or academic gown — **to·gaed** \-gəd\ *adj*

to·geth·er \tə-ˈgeth-ər\ *adv* [OE *togædere*, fr. *tō* to + *gædere* together; akin to E *gather*] **1** : in or into one group, body, or place ⟨gathered *together*⟩ **2** : in or into association, union, or contact with each other ⟨in business *together*⟩ ⟨the doors banged *together*⟩ **3 a** : at one time ⟨they all cheered *together*⟩ **b** : in succession : without intermission ⟨work for hours *together*⟩ **4 a** : in or by combined effort ⟨worked *together* to clear the road⟩ **b** : in or into agreement ⟨get *together* on a plan⟩ **c** : so as to form an integrated or coherent whole ⟨his story hangs *together*⟩ ⟨put words *together* in sentences⟩ **5** : considered as a whole : in the aggregate ⟨gave more than all the others *together*⟩ — **to·geth·er·ness** *n*

tog·gery \ˈtäg-(ə-)rē\ *n*, *pl* **-ger·ies** : CLOTHING

¹tog·gle \ˈtäg-əl\ *n* **1** : a crosspiece attached to the end of or to a loop in a rope, chain, or belt to prevent slipping or to serve as a fastening or as a grip for tightening **2** : TOGGLE JOINT; *also* : a device with a toggle joint

²toggle *vt* **tog·gled**; **tog·gling** \ˈtäg-(ə-)liŋ\ **1** : to fasten with or as if with a toggle **2** : to furnish with a toggle

toggle joint *n* : a device consisting of two bars jointed together end to end but not in line so that when a force is applied to the joint tending to straighten it pressure will be exerted on the parts fixed at the ends of the bars

toggle switch *n* : an electric switch depending on a toggle joint with a spring to open or close the circuit when a projecting lever is pushed through a small arc

togs \ˈtägz\ *n pl* : CLOTHING; *esp* : a set of clothes and accessories for a specified use ⟨riding *togs*⟩

¹toil \ˈtói(ə)l\ *n* [OF *toeil* confusion, battle] : long hard tiring labor : DRUDGERY — **toil·ful** \-fəl\ *adj* — **toil·ful·ly** \-fə-lē\ *adv*

²toil *vi* **1** : to work hard and long : LABOR **2** : to proceed with laborious effort : PLOD ⟨*toiling* up a steep hill⟩ — **toil·er** *n*

³toil *n* [MF *toile* cloth, net, fr. L *tela* web, fr. *texere* to weave] : something that involves or holds one fast : SNARE, TRAP — usu. used in pl.

¹toi·let \ˈtói-lət\ *n* [MF *toilette* cloth put over the shoulders while dressing the hair or shaving, dim. of *toile* cloth, fr. L *tela* web] **1** : the act or process of dressing and grooming oneself **2 a** : BATHROOM **b** : a fixture for defecation and urination; *esp* : WATER CLOSET

²toilet *vb* **1** : to make one's toilet **2** : to train (a child) to the use of the toilet

toilet paper *n* : a thin soft sanitary absorbent paper for bathroom use chiefly after evacuation

toilet powder *n* : a fine powder usu. with soothing or antiseptic ingredients for sprinkling or rubbing (as after bathing) over the skin

toi·let·ry \ˈtói-lə-trē\ *n*, *pl* **-ries** : an article or preparation used in making one's toilet — usu. used in pl.

toilet soap *n* : a mild soap of high quality that is often perfumed and colored and is used for washing one's person

toi·lette \twä-ˈlet\ *n* [F] **1** : TOILET 1 **2 a** : formal or fashionable attire or style of dressing **b** : a particular costume or outfit

toilet water *n* : a perfumed largely alcoholic liquid for use in or after a bath or as a skin freshener

toil·some \ˈtói(ə)l-səm\ *adj* : attended with toil or fatigue : LABORIOUS — **toil·some·ly** *adv* — **toil·some·ness** *n*

toil·worn \-ˌwórn, -ˌwórn\ *adj* : showing the effects of or worn out by long hard work

To·kay \tō-ˈkā\ *n* : a sweet usu. dark gold dessert wine made near Tokaj, Hungary; *also* : a similar wine made elsewhere

toke \ˈtōk\ *n*, *slang* : a puff on a marijuana cigarette

¹to·ken \ˈtō-kən\ *n* [OE *tācen*; akin to E *teach*] **1** : an outward sign ⟨*tokens* of his grief⟩ **2** : SYMBOL, EMBLEM ⟨a white flag is a *token* of surrender⟩ **3 a** : SOUVENIR, KEEPSAKE **b** : an indication or reminder of something ⟨a mere *token* of future benefits⟩ **4 a** : something used or shown as a symbol of identity, right, or authority ⟨the box contained no *token* of the sender⟩ **b** : a piece resembling a coin issued as money or a particular use (as for a ticket on a public conveyance)

²token *adj* : done or given in partial fulfillment of an obligation or undertaking ⟨a *token* payment⟩ **2** : SIMULATED, MINIMAL, PERFUNCTORY ⟨*token* resistance⟩

token money *n* **1** : money of regular government issue having a greater face value than intrinsic value **2** : privately issued tokens for use as money

tol·booth \ˈtōl-ˌbüth, ˈtäl-\ *n* [ME *tolbothe* tollbooth, town hall, jail] **1** *Scot* : a town or market hall **2** *Scot* : JAIL, PRISON

tol·bu·ta·mide \täl-ˈbyüt-ə-ˌmīd\ *n* : a sulfonamide that lowers blood sugar level and is used in the treatment of diabetes

told *past of* TELL

tole \ˈtōl\ *n* [F *tôle* sheet metal, fr. F dial., table, slab, fr. L *tabula* board, tablet] : usu. japanned or painted sheet metal (as tinplate) used mostly for decorative objects (as trays or boxes) and finished in various colors often with stenciled designs

To·le·do \tə-ˈlēd-ō\ *n*, *pl* **-dos** : a finely tempered sword or blade of a kind made in Toledo, Spain

tol·er·a·ble \ˈtäl-(ə-)rə-bəl, ˈtäl-ər-bəl\ *adj* **1** : capable of being borne or endured **2** : moderately good or agreeable : PASSABLE — **tol·er·a·bil·i·ty** \ˌtäl-(ə-)rə-ˈbil-ət-ē\ *n* — **tol·er·a·bly** \ˈtäl-(ə-)rə-blē, ˈtäl-ər-blē\ *adv*

tol·er·ance \ˈtäl-(ə-)rən(t)s\ *n* **1** : relative capacity to endure or adapt physiologically to an unfavorable environmental factor **2 a** : sympathy or indulgence for beliefs or practices differing from one's own **b** : the act of allowing something : TOLERATION **3** : the allowable deviation from a standard — **tol·er·ant** \-rənt\ *adj* — **tol·er·ant·ly** *adv*

tol·er·ate \ˈtäl-ə-ˌrāt\ *vt* [L *tolerare*] **1** : to allow something to be done or to exist without making a move to stop it : put up with : ENDURE **2** : to show tolerance toward

⟨plants that *tolerate* drought⟩ ⟨*tolerate* a drug⟩ — **tol·er·a·tion** \,täl-ə-'rā-shən\ *n* — **tol·er·a·tive** \'täl-ə-,rāt-iv\ *adj* — **tol·er·a·tor** \-,rāt-ər\ *n*

¹toll \'tōl\ *n* [OE] **1** : a tax paid for a privilege (as the use of a highway or bridge) **2** : a charge paid for a service (as placing a long-distance telephone call) **3** : a grievous or ruinous price; *esp* : cost in life or health

²toll *vt* : to take as toll or take a toll from (someone)

³toll *or* **tole** \'tōl\ *vt* [ME *tollen, tolen*] : ATTRACT, ENTICE

⁴toll *vb* [ME *tollen*] **1 a** : to announce (as a death) or summon (as defenders) by the sounding of a bell **b** : to announce (the time) by striking ⟨the clock *tolled* six⟩ **2** : to sound (a bell) usu. with slow measured strokes **3** : to sound with slow measured strokes

⁵toll *n* : the sound of a tolling bell

toll·booth \'tōl-,büth\ *n* : a booth where tolls are paid

toll call *n* : a long-distance telephone call at charges above a local rate

toll·gate \'tōl-,gāt\ *n* : a point where vehicles stop to pay toll

toll·house \-,haús\ *n* : a house or booth where tolls are taken

toll·man \-mən\ *n* : a collector of tolls (as on a highway or bridge)

Tol·tec \'tōl-,tek, 'täl-\ *n* : a member of a Nahuatlan people of central and southern Mexico — **Tol·tec·an** \-ən\ *adj*

tol·u·ene \'täl-yə-,wēn\ *n* [NL *tolu*, a balsam from which it was distilled] : a hydrocarbon similar to benzene but less volatile, flammable, and toxic that is used esp. as a solvent and in organic synthesis

tom \'täm\ *n* : the male of various animals ⟨a *tom* swan⟩: as **a** : TOMCAT **b** : a male turkey : TURKEY-COCK

¹tom·a·hawk \'täm-i-,hók\ *n* [of Algonquian origin] : a light ax used as a weapon by No. American Indians

²tomahawk *vt* : to cut, strike, or kill with a tomahawk

to·ma·to \tə-'māt-ō, -'mät-\ *n, pl* **-toes** [Sp *tomate*, fr. Nahuatl *tomatl*] **1** : any of a genus of So. American herbs of the nightshade family; *esp* : one widely grown for its edible fruits **2** : the usu. large, rounded, and red or yellow pulpy berry of a tomato

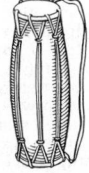

tomahawk

tomb \'tüm\ *n* [LL *tumba* sepulchral mound, fr. Gk *tymbos*] **1 a** : GRAVE **b** : a place of interment **2** : a house, chamber, or vault for the dead

tom·boy \'täm-,bói\ *n* : a girl of boyish behavior : HOYDEN — **tom·boy·ish** \-ish\ *adj* — **tom·boy·ish·ness** *n*

tomb·stone \'tüm-,stōn\ *n* : GRAVESTONE

tom·cat \'täm-,kat\ *n* : a male cat

tom·cod \-,käd\ *n* : any of several small fishes resembling the related common codfish

Tom, Dick, and Har·ry \,täm-,dik-ən-'har-ē\ *n* : the common run of humanity : EVERYONE

tome \'tōm\ *n* [Gk *tomos* section, tome, fr. *temnein* to cut] : a usu. large or scholarly book

to·men·tose \tō-'men-,tōs, 'tō-mən-\ *adj* [*tomentum* cushion stuffing] : covered with densely matted hairs ⟨a *tomentose* leaf⟩

tom·fool \'täm-'fül\ *n* : a great fool : BLOCKHEAD, DOLT — **tomfool** *adj* — **tom·fool·ery** \,täm-'fül-(ə-)rē\ *n*

Tom·my \'täm-ē\ *n, pl* **Tommies** : a British soldier — called also *Tommy At·kins* \,täm-ē-'at-kənz\

tom·my gun \'täm-ē-,gən\ *n* : SUBMACHINE GUN

¹to·mor·row \tə-'mär-ō, -'mór-\ *adv* [OE *tō morgen*, fr. *tō* to + *morgen* morrow, morning] : on or for the day after today

²tomorrow *n* **1** : the day after the present **2** : FUTURE 1a ⟨the world of *tomorrow*⟩

Tom Thumb \'täm-'thəm\ *n* : a legendary English dwarf

tom·tit \(')täm-'tit\ *n* : any of various small active birds

tom-tom \'täm-,täm, 'təm-,təm\ *n* [Hindi *tamtam*] : a small-headed drum commonly beaten with the hands

-t·o·my \t-ə-mē\ *n comb form, pl* **-tomies** [Gk *tom-, temnein* to cut] : cutting : incision ⟨tracheo*tomy*⟩

tom-tom

ton \'tən\ *n, pl* **tons** *also* **ton** [ME *tunne*, a unit of weight or capacity, fr. *tunne* tun] **1** : any of various units of weight: **a** — see MEASURE table **b** : METRIC TON **2 a** : a unit of internal capacity for ships equal to 100 cubic feet **b** : a unit approximately equal to the volume of a long ton weight of seawater used in reckoning the displacement of ships and equal to 35 cubic feet **c** : a unit of volume for cargo freight usu. reckoned at 40 cubic feet **3** : a great quantity : LOT — used chiefly in pl.

ton·al \'tōn-°l\ *adj* **1** : of, relating to, or having tonality **2** : of or relating to tone or tonicity — **ton·al·ly** \-°l-ē\ *adv*

to·nal·i·ty \tō-'nal-ət-ē\ *n, pl* **-ties** : tonal quality: as **a** : the character of a musical composition dependent on its key or on the relation of its tones and chords to a keynote **b** : the arrangement or interrelation of color tones (as of a picture)

¹tone \'tōn\ *n* [Gk *tonos* tension, pitch, tone, fr. *ton-, teinein* to stretch; akin to E *thin*] **1 a** : quality of vocal or musical sound **b** : a sound of definite pitch or vibration **c** : pitch, inflection, or modulation of voice esp. as an individual characteristic, a mode of emotional expression, or a linguistic device ⟨a shrill *tone*⟩ ⟨in *tones* of wrath⟩ **2** : a style or manner of speaking or writing ⟨reply in a friendly *tone*⟩ **3** : general character, quality, or trend ⟨a school noted for its studious *tone*⟩ ⟨the depressing *tone* of his thoughts⟩ **4 a** : color quality or value : a tint or shade of color ⟨decorated in soft *tones*⟩ **b** : a color that modifies another ⟨gray with a blue *tone*⟩ **5 a** : a healthy state of the body or any of its parts; *also* : a state of normal tension and responsiveness to stimulation **b** : RESILIENCY **6** : the general usu. harmonious effect in painting of light and shade with color ⟨a picture that has *tone*⟩

²tone *vb* **1** : to give a particular intonation or inflection to **2** : to impart tone to : STRENGTHEN ⟨medicine to *tone* up the system⟩ **3** : to soften, blend, or harmonize in color, appearance, or sound — **ton·er** *n*

tone arm *n* : the movable part of a phonograph that carries the pickup and permits the needle to follow the record groove

tone-deaf \'tōn-,def\ *adj* : relatively insensitive to differences in musical pitch

tone language *n* : a language (as Chinese) in which variations in tone distinguish words of different meaning that otherwise would sound alike

¹tong \'täŋ, 'tóŋ\ *vb* **1** : to take, hold, or handle with tongs **2** : to use tongs esp. in taking or handling something — **tong·er** \'täŋ-ər, 'tóŋ-\ *n*

²tong *n* [Chin (Cant) *t'ong* hall] : a secret society of Chinese in the U.S.

tongs \'täŋz, 'tóŋz\ *n pl* [ME *tonges*, pl. of *tonge*, fr. OE *tang*] : any of numerous grasping devices consisting commonly of two pieces joined at one end by a pivot or hinged like scissors

¹tongue \'təŋ\ *n* [OE *tunge*] **1 a** : a fleshy movable process of the floor of the mouth in most vertebrates that bears sensory organs and small glands and functions esp. in taking and swallowing food and in man as a speech organ **b** : an analogous part of various invertebrate animals **2** : the flesh of a tongue (as of the ox or sheep) used as food **3** : the power of communication through speech **4 a** : LANGUAGE; *esp* : a spoken language **b** : manner or quality of utterance with respect to tone or sound, the sense of what is expressed, or the intention of the speaker **c** : ecstatic usu. unintelligible utterance accompanying religious excitement — usu. used in pl. **5** : something resembling an animal's tongue in being elongated and fastened at one end only: as **a** : a movable pin in a buckle **b** : a swinging inner part that strikes the sides as a bell is swung **c** : the flap under the lacing of a shoe **6** : a projecting ridge or rib (as on one edge of a board) — **tongue·less** \-ləs\ *adj* — **tongue·like** \-,līk\ *adj*

²tongue *vb* **tongued; tongu·ing** \'təŋ-iŋ\ **1** : to touch or lick with or as if with the tongue **2** : to cut a tongue on ⟨*tongue* a board⟩ **3** : to articulate notes on a wind instrument by means of the tongue

tongue and groove *n* : a joint made by a tongue on one edge of a board fitting into a corresponding groove in the edge of another board

tongue in cheek *adv* (*or adj*) : with insincerity, irony, or whimsical exaggeration

tongue–lash \'tǝŋ-,lash\ vb : CHIDE, REPROVE — **tongue–lash·ing** n

tongue–tied \-,tīd\ adj : unable to speak clearly or freely usu. from abnormal shortness of the membrane under the tongue or from shyness

tongue twister n : an utterance difficult to articulate because of a succession of similar consonants

¹**ton·ic** \'tän-ik\ adj [Gk tonos tension, tone, accent] **1 a** : of, relating to, or characterized by tension and esp. muscular tension : exhibiting tonus **b** : producing or tending to produce healthy muscular condition and reaction **c** : being or marked by excessive and prolonged muscular contraction ⟨tonic convulsions⟩ **2 a** : improving physical or mental tone : INVIGORATING **b** : yielding a tonic substance **3** : relating to or based on the first tone of a scale ⟨tonic harmony⟩ **4 a** : VOICED 2 **b** of a syllable : bearing a principal stress or accent — **ton·i·cal·ly** \'tän-i-k(ǝ-)lē\ adv

²**tonic** n **1** : a tonic agent (as a drug) **2** : the first degree of a major or minor scale **3** : a voiced sound

to·nic·i·ty \tō-'nis-ǝt-ē\ n : the quality of having tone and esp. healthy vigor of body or mind

¹**to·night** \tǝ-'nīt\ adv : on this present night or the night following this present day

²**tonight** n : the present or the coming night

ton·nage \'tǝn-ij\ n **1 a** : a duty on ships based on cargo capacity **b** : a duty on goods per ton transported **2** : ships in terms of the total number of tons registered or carried or of their carrying capacity **3 a** : the cubical content of a merchant ship in units of 100 cubic feet **b** : the displacement of a warship **4** : total weight in tons shipped, carried, or mined

ton·neau \tǝ-'nō\ n [F, lit., tun, fr. OF tonnel, dim. of tonne tun] : the rear seating compartment of an automobile

ton·sil \'tän(t)-sǝl\ n [L tonsillae, pl., tonsils] : either of a pair of masses of lymphoid tissue that lie one on each side of the throat at the back of the mouth — **ton·sil·lar** \-sǝ-lǝr\

ton·sil·lec·to·my \,tän(t)-sǝ-'lek-tǝ-mē\ n, pl -mies : the surgical removal of the tonsils

ton·sil·li·tis \-'līt-ǝs\ n : inflammation of the tonsils

ton·sil·lot·o·my \-'lät-ǝ-mē\ n, pl -mies : incision of a tonsil; also : partial or total tonsillectomy

ton·so·ri·al \tän-'sōr-ē-ǝl, -'sor-\ adj [L tonsor barber, fr. tons-, tondēre to shear] : of or relating to a barber or his work ⟨tonsorial parlor⟩

ton·sure \'tän-chǝr\ n [ML tonsura, fr. L, act of shearing, fr. tons-, tondēre to shear] **1 a** : the Roman Catholic or Eastern rite of admission to the clerical state by the clipping or shaving of the head **b** : the shaven crown or patch worn by monks and many clerics **2** : a bald spot resembling a tonsure; also : a clipped or shaven state (as of a dog or hedge) — **ton·sured** \-chǝrd\ adj

to·nus \'tō-nǝs\ n [NL, fr. Gk tonos tension, tone] : TONE 5a; esp : the state of partial contraction characteristic of normal muscle

too \('|)tü\ adv [OE tō to, too] **1** : ALSO, BESIDES ⟨sell the house and furniture too⟩ **2 a** : EXCESSIVELY ⟨the dress was too short⟩ **b** : to such a degree as to be regrettable ⟨this has gone too far⟩ **c** : VERY ⟨said he would be only too glad to help⟩

took past of TAKE

¹**tool** \'tül\ n [OE tōl] **1** : an instrument (as a hammer, saw, wrench) used or worked by hand or by a machine; also : a machine that operates tools for shaping work **2 a** : an instrument or apparatus used in performing an operation or necessary in the practice of a vocation or profession ⟨a scholar's books are tools⟩ **b** : a means to an end **3** : a person used or manipulated by another : DUPE **syn** see IMPLEMENT

²**tool** vb **1** : DRIVE **2** : to shape, form, or finish with a tool; esp : to letter or ornament (as a book cover) by means of hand tools **3** : to equip a plant or industry with machines and tools for production

tool·box \'tül-,bäks\ n : a chest for tools

tool·head \'tül-,hed\ n : a part of a machine in which a tool or toolholder is clamped and which is provided with adjustments to bring the tool into the desired position

tool·hold·er \-,hōl-dǝr\ n : a short steel bar having a shank at one end to fit into the toolhead of a machine and a clamp at the other end to hold small interchangeable cutting bits

tool·house \-,haus\ n : a building (as in a garden) for storing tools — called also tool·shed \-,shed\

tool·mak·er \'tül-,mā-kǝr\ n : a machinist who specializes in the construction, repair, maintenance, and calibration of the tools, jigs, fixtures, and instruments of a machine shop

tool·room \-,rüm, -,rüm\ n : a room where tools are kept; esp : a room in a machine shop in which tools are made, stored, or loaned out to the workmen

¹**toot** \'tüt\ vb **1** : to sound a short blast ⟨a horn tooted⟩ **2** : to blow or sound an instrument (as a horn) esp. so as to produce short blasts ⟨the trumpeter tooted in many bands⟩ ⟨toot a whistle⟩ — **toot·er** n

²**toot** n : a short blast (as on a horn); also : a sound resembling such a blast

³**toot** n : a drinking bout : SPREE ⟨he went on a toot⟩

tooth \'tüth\ n, pl **teeth** \'tēth\ [OE tōth] **1 a** : one of the hard bony structures borne esp. on the jaws of vertebrates and used for seizing and chewing food and as weapons **b** : any of various usu. hard and sharp processes esp. about the mouth of an invertebrate **2** : TASTE, LIKING ⟨a tooth for sweets⟩ **3** : a projection resembling or suggesting the tooth of an animal in shape, arrangement, or action ⟨the tooth of a saw⟩ **4** : one of the projections on the rim of a cogwheel : COG **5 a** : something that injures, tortures, devours, or destroys ⟨in the teeth of a wind⟩ **b** pl : effective means of enforcement **6** : a roughness of surface produced by mechanical or artificial means — **tooth·less** \-lǝs\ adj — **tooth·like** \-,līk\ adj

teeth: m molars, b bicuspids, c canine, i incisors

tooth·ache \-,āk\ n : pain in or about a tooth

tooth and nail adv : with every available means : all out ⟨fight tooth and nail⟩

tooth·brush \'tüth-,brǝsh\ n : a brush for cleaning the teeth

toothed \'tütht\ adj **1** : provided with teeth or such or so many teeth **2** : NOTCHED, JAGGED

toothed whale n : any of a group (Odontoceti) of whales with numerous simple conical teeth

tooth·paste \'tüth-,pāst\ n : a paste dentifrice

tooth·pick \-,pik\ n : a pointed instrument (as a small flat tapering splinter) used for clearing the teeth of substances lodged between them

tooth powder n : a dentifrice in powder form

tooth shell n : any of a class (Scaphopoda) of marine mollusks with a tapering tubular shell; also : this shell

tooth·some \'tüth-sǝm\ adj **1** : pleasing to the taste : DELICIOUS ⟨toothsome delicacies⟩ **2** : ATTRACTIVE, LUSCIOUS — **tooth·some·ly** adv — **tooth·some·ness** n

toothy \'tü-thē\ adj **tooth·i·er; -est** : having or showing prominent teeth ⟨a toothy grin⟩ — **tooth·i·ly** \-thǝ-lē\ adv

¹**top** \'täp\ n [OE] **1 a** : the highest point, level, or part of something ⟨the top of the head⟩ ⟨walked to the top of the hill⟩ **b** : the upper end, edge, or surface ⟨the top of the page⟩ ⟨filled the glass to the top⟩ **2** : the stalk and leaves of a plant and esp. of one with edible roots ⟨beet tops⟩ **3** : an integral part serving as an upper piece, lid, or covering ⟨pajama top⟩ ⟨put the top on the jar⟩ **4** : a platform high up on the lower mast of a ship serving to spread the topmost rigging **5** : the highest position or rank : ACME ⟨reached the top of his profession⟩; also : one in such a position ⟨secrets known only to the top⟩ **6** : a forward spin given to a ball by striking it on or near the top — **topped** \'täpt\ adj

²**top** vt **topped; top·ping 1** : to remove or cut the top of ⟨top a tree⟩ **2 a** : to cover with a top or on the top : provide, form, or serve as a top : CROWN, CAP **b** : to supply with a decorative or protective finish or a final touch ⟨topped off the sundae with nuts⟩ ⟨a meal topped off with coffee⟩ **3 a** : to be or become higher than ⟨tops the previous record⟩ **b** : to be superior to : EXCEL, SURPASS ⟨topped his own record⟩ **c** : to gain ascendancy over : DOMINATE **4 a** : to rise to, reach, or be at the top of

---

ǝ abut; ᵉ kitten; ǝr further; a back; ā bake; ä cot, cart; au̇ out; ch chin; e less; ē easy; g gift; i trip; ī life

b : to go over the top of **:** CLEAR, SURMOUNT **5 a :** to strike above the center ⟨*top* a golf ball⟩ **b :** to make (as a stroke) by hitting the ball in this way

³top *adj* **:** of, relating to, or at the top **:** HIGHEST, UPPERMOST

⁴top *n* [OE] **:** a commonly cylindrical or conoidal child's toy that has a point on which it is made to spin

to·paz \'tō-ˌpaz\ *n* [L *topazus*, fr. Gk *topazos*] **1 :** a hard mineral consisting of a silicate of aluminum and occurring in crystals of various colors with the yellow variety being the one usu. cut and prized as a gem **2 :** a gem (as a yellow sapphire) resembling the true topaz

top billing *n* **1 :** the position at the top of a theatrical bill usu. featuring the star's name **2 :** prominent emphasis, featuring, or advertising

top boot *n* **:** a high boot often with light-colored leather bands around the upper part

top·coat \'täp-ˌkōt\ *n* **:** a lightweight overcoat

top·cross \'täp-ˌkrös\ *n* **:** a cross between a superior or purebred male and inferior female stock to improve the average quality of the progeny; *also* **:** an offspring from such a cross

top drawer *n* **:** the highest level of society, authority, or excellence

tope \'tōp\ *n* **:** a widely distributed small shark with a liver rich in vitamin A

to·pee *or* **to·pi** \tō-'pē, 'tō-(ˌ)pē\ *n* [Hindi *ṭopī*] **:** a lightweight helmet-shaped hat made of pith or cork

top·er \'tō-pər\ *n* **:** a heavy drinker; *esp* **:** DRUNKARD

top flight *n* **:** the highest level of achievement, excellence, or eminence **:** TOP DRAWER — **top·flight** \'täp-'flīt\ *adj*

¹top·gal·lant \(')täp-'gal-ənt, tə-'gal-\ *adj* **1 :** of, relating to, or being a part next above the topmast and below the royal mast ⟨*topgallant* sail⟩ ⟨*topgallant* mast⟩ **2 :** raised above the adjoining portions ⟨*topgallant* rail⟩

²topgallant *n* **:** a topgallant mast or sail

top hat *n* **:** a man's tall-crowned hat usu. of beaver or silk

top–heavy \'täp-ˌhev-ē\ *adj* **:** having the top part too heavy for the lower part **:** lacking in stability

To·phet \'tō-fət\ *n* [Heb *tōpheth*, shrine south of ancient Jerusalem where human sacrifices were performed to Moloch (Jeremiah 7:31)] **:** HELL

top–hole \'täp-'hōl\ *adj, chiefly Brit* **:** EXCELLENT

¹to·pi·ary \'tō-pē-ˌer-ē\ *adj* [L *topia* ornamental gardening, fr. Gk *topos* place] **:** of, relating to, or being the training and trimming of woody plants into odd or ornamental shapes; *also* **:** characterized by such work

²topiary *n, pl* **-ar·ies :** topiary art or gardening; *also* **:** a topiary garden

top·ic \'täp-ik\ *n* [Gk *Topika*, a work by Aristotle on the general forms of argument employed in probable reasoning, fr. *topos* place, commonplace] **1 :** a heading in an outlined argument or exposition **2 :** the subject of a discourse or a section of it **:** THEME

top·i·cal \'täp-i-kəl\ *adj* [Gk *topos* place] **1 a :** of or relating to a place **b :** local or designed for local application ⟨a *topical* remedy⟩ ⟨a *topical* anesthetic⟩ **2 a :** of, relating to, or arranged by topics ⟨set down in *topical* form⟩ **b :** referring to the topics of the day or place ⟨*topical* allusions⟩ — **top·i·cal·i·ty** \ˌtäp-ə-'kal-ət-ē\ *n* — **top·i·cal·ly** \'täp-i-k(ə-)lē\ *adv*

topic sentence *n* **:** a sentence that states the main thought of a paragraph or of a larger unit of discourse

top·kick \'täp-ˌkik\ *n* **:** FIRST SERGEANT 1

top·knot \'täp-ˌnät\ *n* **1 :** an ornament (as a knot of ribbons or a pompon) forming a headdress or worn as part of a coiffure **2 :** a crest of feathers or hair on the top of the head

top·less \-ləs\ *adj* **1 :** being without a top **2 a :** wearing no clothing on the upper body **b :** featuring topless waitresses or entertainers

top·lofty \-ˌlóf-tē\ *also* **top·loft·i·cal** \täp-'lóf-ti-kəl\ *adj* **:** very superior in air or attitude **:** SUPERCILIOUS, HAUGHTY — **top·loft·i·ness** \-ˌlóf-tē-nəs\ *n*

top·mast \-ˌmast, -məst\ *n* **:** the mast that is next above the lower mast and topmost in a fore-and-aft rig

top milk *n* **:** the cream-rich upper layer of milk that has stood in a container

top·min·now \'täp-ˌmin-ō\ *n* **:** any of a large family of small viviparous surface-feeding fishes

top·most \-ˌmōst\ *adj* **:** highest of all **:** UPPERMOST

top·notch \-'näch\ *adj* **:** of the highest quality **:** FIRST=

RATE — **top·notch** *n* — **top·notch·er** \-'näch-ər\ *n*

to·pog·ra·pher \tə-'päg-rə-fər\ *n* **:** one skilled in topography

top·o·graph·ic \ˌtäp-ə-'graf-ik, ˌtō-pə-\ *adj* **:** TOPO-GRAPHICAL 1

top·o·graph·i·cal \-'graf-i-kəl\ *adj* **1 :** of, relating to, or concerned with topography ⟨*topographical* engineer⟩ **2 :** of, relating to, or concerned with the artistic representation of a particular locality ⟨a *topographical* poem⟩ — **top·o·graph·i·cal·ly** \-k(ə-)lē\ *adv*

to·pog·ra·phy \tə-'päg-rə-fē\ *n* [Gk *topos* place] **1 :** the art or practice of detailing on maps or charts natural and man-made features of a place or region esp. so as to show elevations **2 :** the configuration of a surface including its relief and the position of its natural and man-made features ⟨a map showing *topography*⟩

to·pol·o·gy \tə-'päl-ə-jē\ *n* **1 :** topographical study of a particular place; *esp* **:** the history of a region as indicated by its topography **2 :** the anatomy of a particular region of the body **3 :** a branch of mathematics that investigates the properties of geometric figures that do not change when the shape of the figure is subjected to continuous change — **top·o·log·i·cal** \ˌtäp-ə-'läj-i-kəl, ˌtō-pə-\ *adj* — **to·pol·o·gist** \tə-'päl-ə-jəst\ *n*

top·per \'täp-ər\ *n* **1 :** one that is at or on the top **2 a :** SILK HAT **b :** OPERA HAT **3 :** something (as a joke) that caps everything preceding **4 :** a woman's usu. short and loose-fitting lightweight outer coat

¹top·ping \'täp-iŋ\ *n* **:** something that forms a top: as **a :** GARNISH **b :** a flavorful addition (as of sauce or nuts) served on top of a dessert

²topping *adj* **1 :** highest in rank or eminence **2** *chiefly Brit* **:** EXCELLENT

top·ple \'täp-əl\ *vb* **top·pled; top·pling** \'täp-(ə-)liŋ\ **1 :** to fall or cause to fall from or as if from being topheavy **:** OVERTURN **2 :** to be or seem unsteady **:** TOTTER **3 :** OVERTHROW ⟨*topple* a government⟩

top·sail \'täp-ˌsāl, -səl\ *also* **top·s'l** \-səl\ *n* **1 :** the sail next above the lowermost sail on a mast in a square-rigged ship **2 :** the sail set above and sometimes on the gaff in a fore-and-aft rigged ship

top secret *adj* **:** demanding inviolate secrecy among top officials or a select few

top sergeant *n* **:** FIRST SERGEANT 1

top·side \'täp-ˌsīd\ *adv* **1** *also* **top·sides** \-'sīdz\ **:** on deck **2 :** to or on the top or surface

top·sides \-ˌsīdz\ *n pl* **:** the top portion of the outer surface of a ship on each side above the waterline

top·soil \-ˌsóil\ *n* **:** surface soil; *esp* **:** the organic layer in which plants have most of their roots and which the farmer turns over in plowing

top·sy–tur·vi·ness \ˌtäp-sē-'tər-vē-nəs\ *n* **:** the quality or state of being topsy-turvy

¹top·sy–tur·vy \ˌtäp-sē-'tər-vē\ *adv* **1 :** upside down **2 :** in utter confusion or disorder

²topsy–turvy *adj* **:** turned topsy-turvy **:** totally disordered

³topsy–turvy *n* **:** TOPSY-TURVINESS — **top·sy–tur·vy·dom** \-vēd-əm\ *n*

toque \'tōk\ *n* [MF, soft round hat with a narrow brim or no brim] **:** a woman's small hat usu. without a brim made in any of various soft close-fitting shapes

tor \'tó(ə)r\ *n* [OE *torr*] **:** a high craggy hill

To·rah \'tōr-ə, 'tór-\ *n* [Heb *tōrāh*] **1 :** LAW 5b, PENTATEUCH **2 :** the body of divine knowledge and law found in the Jewish scriptures and oral tradition

torch \'tórch\ *n* [OF *torche* bundle of twisted straw or tow, fr. L *torquēre* to twist] **1 :** a flaming light made of something that burns brightly (as resinous wood) and usu. carried in the hand **2 :** something (as wisdom or knowledge) likened to a torch as giving light or guidance **3 :** any of various portable devices for producing a hot flame — compare BLOWTORCH **4** *chiefly Brit* **:** FLASHLIGHT — **torch·bear·er** \-ˌbar-ər, -ˌber-\ *n* — **torch·light** \-ˌlīt\ *n*

torch singer *n* **:** a singer of torch songs

torch song *n* **:** a popular sentimental song of unrequited love

tore past of TEAR

tor·e·a·dor \'tór-ē-ə-ˌdór\ *n* [Sp, fr. *torear* to fight bulls, fr. *toro* bull, fr. L *taurus*] **:** BULLFIGHTER

to·re·ro \tə-'re(ə)r-ō\ *n, pl* **-ros** [Sp, fr. L *taurarius*, fr. *taurus* bull] **:** BULLFIGHTER

tori *pl of* TORUS

to·rii \'tōr-ē-ē, 'tōr-\ *n, pl* **torii** [Jap] : a Japanese gateway of light construction built at the approach to a Shinto temple

¹**tor·ment** \'tȯr-,ment\ *n* [L *tormentum* torture, fr. *torquēre* to twist, torture] **1** : the infliction of torture (as by rack or wheel) **2** : extreme pain or anguish of body or mind : AGONY **3** : a source of vexation or pain

²**tor·ment** \tȯr-'ment, 'tȯr-,\ *vt* **1 a** : to cause severe suffering of body or mind to : DISTRESS **b** : to cause worry or vexation to : HARASS **2** : DISTORT, TWIST *syn see* AFFLICT — **tor·men·tor** \-ǝr\ *n*

torn *past part of* TEAR

tor·na·dic \tȯr-'nad-ik, -'nād-\ *adj* : relating to, characteristic of, or constituting a tornado

tor·na·do \tȯr-'nād-ō\ *n, pl* **-does** *or* **-dos** [modif. of Sp *tronada* thunderstorm, fr. *tronar* to thunder, fr. L *tonare*] : a violent destructive whirling wind accompanied by a funnel-shaped cloud that progresses in a narrow path over the land

¹**tor·pe·do** \tȯr-'pēd-ō\ *n, pl* **-does** [L, lit., numbness, fr. *torpēre* to be numb] **1** : ELECTRIC RAY **2 a** : a submarine mine **b** : a self-propelling cigar-shaped submarine projectile filled with an explosive charge that is released from a ship against another **3 a** : a charge of explosive enclosed in a container or case **b** : a small firework that explodes when thrown against a hard object

²**torpedo** *vt* **1** : to hit with or destroy by a torpedo **2** : to destroy or nullify altogether : WRECK ⟨*torpedo* a plan⟩

torpedo boat *n* : a small very fast thinly plated boat for discharging torpedoes

torpedo–boat destroyer *n* : a large, swift, and powerful armed torpedo boat orig. intended principally for the destruction of torpedo boats but later used also as a formidable torpedo boat

tor·pid \'tȯr-pǝd\ *adj* [L *torpidus*, fr. *torpēre* to be numb] **1 a** : having lost motion or the power of exertion or feeling : DORMANT ⟨a bear *torpid* in his winter sleep⟩ **b** : sluggish in functioning or acting ⟨a *torpid* mind⟩ **2** : lacking in energy or vigor : APATHETIC, DULL — **tor·pid·i·ty** \tȯr-'pid-ǝt-ē\ *n* — **tor·pid·ly** \'tȯr-pǝd-lē\ *adv*

tor·por \'tȯr-pǝr\ *n* [L, fr. *torpēre* to be numb] **1** : temporary loss or suspension of motion or feeling : extreme sluggishness ⟨the *torpor* of bears in winter⟩ **2** : DULLNESS, APATHY *syn see* LETHARGY

torque \'tȯrk\ *n* [L *torquēre* to twist] : a force which produces or tends to produce rotation or torsion and whose effectiveness is measured by the product of the force and the perpendicular distance from the line of action of the force to the axis of rotation

tor·rent \'tȯr-ǝnt, 'tär-\ *n* [L *torrent-, torrens*, fr. *torrens* burning, seething, rushing, fr. prp. of *torrēre* to parch, burn; akin to E *thirst*] **1** : a violent or rushing stream of a liquid (as water or lava) **2** : a raging flood : a tumultuous outpouring : FLUX, RUSH ⟨a *torrent* of abuse⟩

tor·ren·tial \tȯ-'ren-chǝl, tǝ-\ *adj* **1 a** : relating to or having the character of a torrent ⟨*torrential* rains⟩ **b** : caused by or resulting from action of rapid streams ⟨*torrential* gravel⟩ **2** : resembling a torrent in violence or rapidity of flow ⟨his *torrential* speeches⟩ — **tor·ren·tial·ly** \-'rench-(ǝ-)lē\ *adv*

tor·rid \'tȯr-ǝd, 'tär-\ *adj* [L *torridus*, fr. *torrēre* to parch] **1 a** : parched with heat esp. of the sun : HOT ⟨*torrid* sands⟩ **b** : giving off intense heat : SCORCHING **2** : ARDENT, PASSIONATE ⟨*torrid* love letters⟩ — **tor·rid·i·ty** \tȯ-'rid-ǝt-ē\ *n* — **tor·rid·ly** \'tȯr-ǝd-lē, 'tär-\ *adv* — **tor·rid·ness** *n*

torrid zone *n* : the belt of the earth between the tropics over which the sun is vertical at some period of the year — see ZONE illustration

tor·sion \'tȯr-shǝn\ *n* [*tors-, torquēre* to twist] **1** : the act or process of turning or twisting **2** : the state of being twisted — **tor·sion·al** \-shnǝl, -shǝn-ᵊl\ *adj* — **tor·sion·al·ly** \-ē\ *adv*

tor·so \'tȯr-sō\ *n, pl* **torsos** *or* **tor·si** \-,sē\ [It, lit., stalk, fr. L *thyrsus*, fr. Gk *thyrsos*] **1** : the trunk of a sculptured representation of a human body; *esp* : the trunk of a statue whose head and limbs are mutilated **2** : something that is mutilated or left unfinished **3** : the human trunk

tort \'tȯrt\ *n* [MF, fr. ML *tortum*, fr. L, neut. of *tortus*, pp. of *torquēre* to twist] : a wrongful act except one involving a breach of contract for which the injured party can recover damages in a civil action

torte \'tȯrt(-ǝ)\ *n, pl* **tor·ten** \'tȯrt-ᵊn\ *or* **tortes** \'tȯrt-ǝz, 'tȯrts\ [G] : a cake made of many eggs, sugar, and often grated nuts or dry bread crumbs and usu. covered with a rich frosting

tor·ti·lla \tȯr-'tē-(y)ǝ\ *n* [AmerSp, dim. of Sp *torta* cake, fr. LL, round loaf of bread] : a round flat cake of unleavened cornmeal bread with a topping or filling of ground meat or cheese

tor·toise \'tȯrt-ǝs\ *n* [ME *tortu, tortuce*, fr. MF *tortue*] : any of an order (Testudinata) of reptiles : TURTLE; *esp* : a land turtle

¹**tor·toise-shell** \'tȯrt-ǝs(h)-,shel\ *n* **1** : a mottled horny substance that covers the bony shell of some sea turtles and is used in inlaying and in making various ornamental articles **2** : any of several showy butterflies

²**tortoiseshell** *adj* : made of or resembling tortoiseshell esp. in spotted brown and yellow coloring

tor·to·ni \tȯr-'tō-nē\ *n* : ice cream made of heavy cream sometimes with minced almonds, chopped maraschino cherries, or various flavoring ingredients

tor·tu·ous \'tȯrch-(ǝ-)wǝs\ *adj* [L *tortus* twist, fr. *torquēre* to twist] **1** : marked by repeated twists, bends, or turns : WINDING ⟨a *tortuous* stream⟩ **2 a** : marked by devious or indirect tactics : CROOKED, TRICKY **b** : CIRCUITOUS, INVOLVED ⟨the *tortuous* workings of government⟩ — **tor·tu·ous·ly** *adv* — **tor·tu·ous·ness** *n*

¹**tor·ture** \'tȯr-chǝr\ *n* [L *tort-, torquēre* to twist, torture] **1** : the infliction of intense pain (as from burning, crushing, or wounding) esp. to punish or obtain a confession **2 a** : anguish of body or mind : AGONY **b** : something that causes agony or pain

²**torture** *vt* **tor·tured; tor·tur·ing** \'tȯrch-(ǝ-)riŋ\ **1** : to punish or coerce by inflicting excruciating pain **2** : to cause intense suffering to : TORMENT **3** : to twist or wrench out of shape : DISTORT *syn see* AFFLICT — **tor·tur·er** \'tȯr-chǝr-ǝr\ *n*

tor·tur·ous \'tȯrch-(ǝ-)rǝs\ *adj* : causing torture : cruelly painful — **tor·tur·ous·ly** *adv*

to·rus \'tōr-ǝs, 'tȯr-\ *n, pl* **to·ri** \'tōr-,ī, 'tȯr-, -,ē\ [NL, L, protuberance, bulge, fr. L *torus* molding] **1** : a smooth rounded anatomical protuberance **2** : a large molding of convex profile commonly occurring as the lowest molding in the base of a column **3** : RECEPTACLE 2 **4** : a doughnut-shaped surface generated by a circle rotated about an axis in its plane that does not intersect the circle

To·ry \'tōr-ē, 'tȯr-\ *n, pl* **Tories** [IrGael *tōraidhe* pursued man; fr. Irish royalists outlawed in the 17th century] **1 a** : a member of a British political group of the 18th and early 19th centuries favoring royal authority and the established church and seeking to preserve the traditional political structure — compare WHIG **b** : CONSERVATIVE 1b **2** : an American upholding the cause of the British Crown during the American Revolution : LOYALIST **3** *often not cap* : an extreme conservative esp. in politics and economics — **Tory** *adj*

¹**toss** \'tȯs, 'täs\ *vb* **1** : to keep throwing here and there or backward and forward : cause to pitch or roll ⟨waves *tossed* the ship about⟩ **2** : to throw with a quick light motion ⟨*toss* a ball into the air⟩ **3** : to lift with a sudden motion ⟨*toss* the head⟩ **4** : to pitch or bob about rapidly ⟨the light canoe is *tossing* on the waves⟩ **5** : to be restless : fling oneself about ⟨*tossed* in his sleep⟩ **6** : to stir or mix lightly ⟨*toss* a salad⟩ *syn see* THROW

²**toss** *n* **1** : the state or fact of being tossed **2 a** : an act or instance of tossing **b** : a deciding by chance and esp. by flipping a coin

toss·pot \-,pät\ *n* : DRUNKARD

toss–up \-,ǝp\ *n* **1** : TOSS 2b **2** : an even chance

¹**tot** \'tät\ *n* **1** : a small child : TODDLER **2** : a small drink or allowance of liquor

²**tot** *vb* **tot·ted; tot·ting** [*tot.*, abbr. of *total*] : to add together : SUMMARIZE, TOTAL

¹**to·tal** \'tōt-ᵊl\ *adj* [L *totus*, adj., whole] **1** : of or relating to the whole of something ⟨a *total* eclipse of the sun⟩ **2** : making up the whole : ENTIRE **3** : COMPLETE, UTTER ⟨*total* ruin⟩ **4** : making use of every means to carry out a planned program ⟨*total* war⟩

²**total** *n* **1** : a product of addition : SUM **2** : an entire quantity : AMOUNT *syn see* SUM

³**total** *vt* **to·taled** *or* **to·talled; to·tal·ing** *or* **to·tal·ling**
1 : to add up **:** COMPUTE **2 :** to amount to **:** NUMBER

total eclipse *n* **:** an eclipse in which one celestial body is completely obscured by the shadow or body of another

to·tal·i·tar·i·an \(,)tō-,tal-ə-'ter-ē-ən\ *adj* **:** of or relating to a political regime based on subordination of the individual to the state and strict control of all aspects of life esp. by coercive measures; *also* **:** advocating, constituting, or characteristic of such a regime — **totalitarian** *n* — **to·tal·i·tar·i·an·ism** \-ē-ə,niz-əm\ *n*

to·tal·i·ty \tō-'tal-ət-ē\ *n, pl* **-ties 1 :** an aggregate amount **:** SUM, WHOLE **2 :** the quality or state of being total **:** ENTIRETY

to·tal·ize \'tōt-ᵊl-,īz\ *vt* **1 :** to add up **:** TOTAL **2 :** to express as a whole **:** SUMMARIZE

to·tal·ly \'tōt-ᵊl-ē\ *adv* **1 :** in a total manner **:** WHOLLY **2 :** as a whole **:** in toto

tote \'tōt\ *vt* **:** to carry by hand; *also* **:** PACK, HAUL — **tot·er** *n*

to·tem \'tōt-əm\ *n* [of AmerInd origin] **:** an object (as an animal or plant) serving as the emblem of a family or clan and often as a reminder of its ancestry; *also* **:** a usu. carved or painted representation of such an object — **to·tem·ic** \tō-'tem-ik\ *adj*

totem pole *n* **:** a pole carved and painted with totemic symbols representing family lineage that is erected before the houses of some northwest coast Indians

to·tip·o·tent \tō-'tip-ət-ənt\ *adj* [L *totus* whole + *potent-, potens* powerful, potent] **:** capable of development along any of the lines inherently possible to its kind ⟨*totipotent* cells equally able to develop into gland or muscle⟩

¹**tot·ter** \'tät-ər\ *vi* [ME *toteren*] **1 a :** to tremble or rock as if about to fall **:** SWAY **b :** to become unstable **:** threaten to collapse **2 :** to move unsteadily **:** STAGGER, WOBBLE — **tot·tery** \-ə-rē\ *adj*

²**totter** *n* **:** an unsteady gait **:** WOBBLE

tot·ter·ing *adj* **1 a :** unstable in condition ⟨a *tottering* building⟩ **b :** walking unsteadily **2 :** lacking firmness or stability **:** INSECURE ⟨a *tottering* regime⟩ — **tot·ter·ing·ly** \-ə-riŋ-lē\ *adv*

tou·can \'tü-,kan, tü-'\ *n* [F, fr. Pg *tucano*, of AmerInd origin] **:** any of a family of fruit-eating birds of tropical America with brilliant coloring and a very large but light and thin-walled bill

¹**touch** \'təch\ *vb* [OF *tuchier*, fr. (assumed) VL *toccare* to knock, strike a bell, touch] **1 :** to feel or handle (as with fingers or hands) esp. so as to perceive through the tactile sense ⟨*touching* and stroking the soft silk⟩ **2 a :** to bring or come into or be in contact with something ⟨*touch* a match to the kindling⟩ ⟨waves *touching* the shore⟩ ⟨glazed wares must not *touch* in the kiln⟩ **b :** to come near to or have a common boundary with something **:** ADJOIN ⟨New Hampshire just *touches* on the ocean⟩ **c :** to come near to being something mentioned ⟨his acts *touched* on treason⟩ **3 a :** to hit lightly ⟨*touch* a horse with the spur⟩ **b :** to affect physically by some contact or agent ⟨the strongest file will not *touch* this alloy⟩ ⟨no bleach would *touch* the stain⟩; *also* **:** to have a usu. slight injurious physical effect on ⟨plants *touched* by frost⟩ **4 a :** to lay hands on (as in taking, using, or examining) ⟨wouldn't *touch* the legacy⟩ ⟨don't *touch* the exhibits⟩ **b :** to act on or tamper with so as to damage in some way or degree ⟨a gray old building *touched* and warped by sun and wind⟩; *esp* **:** to commit violence upon ⟨swore he hadn't *touched* the child⟩ **c :** to make use of esp. as food or drink ⟨never *touches* meat⟩ **5 :** to speak or write of something briefly or casually **:** mention in passing ⟨barely *touched* on domestic politics⟩ **6 :** to relate or be of concern to **:** affect the interest of ⟨a matter that *touches* every parent⟩ **7 a :** to affect the mind or spirit of **:** IMBUE ⟨*touched* by the creative fire⟩; *also* **:** to be or become disordered in mind ⟨the old fellow is *touched* but quite harmless⟩ **b :** to move emotionally ⟨*touched* by his friend's regard⟩ **8 a :** to reach as a limit **:** ATTAIN **b :** to come close **:** APPROACH **9 :** to make a usu. brief or incidental stop in port ⟨*touched* at several coastal towns⟩ **10 :** to rival in quality or value **:** stand comparison with ⟨the new mattress doesn't *touch* the old for comfort⟩ **11 a :** to receive (as money) for a purpose

totem pole

or as a recompense **b :** to induce to give or lend **12 a :** to improve or alter with or as if with slight strokes of a brush or pencil ⟨*touch* up a painting⟩ **b :** to mark or change slightly (as in color or aspect) ⟨lips *touched* with a smile⟩ ⟨moonlight *touching* the still sea⟩ — **touch·a·ble** \-ə-bəl\ *adj* — **touch·er** *n*

²**touch** *n* **1 :** a light stroke, tap, or blow **2 :** the act or fact of touching or being touched **3 a :** the special sense by which light pressure or traction is perceived ⟨soft to the *touch*⟩ **b :** a particular sensation conveyed by this sense ⟨the soft *touch* of silk⟩ **4 :** a state of contact or communication **:** close relationship ⟨keeping in *touch* with friends⟩ **5 :** quality or kind esp. as attested by authority; *also* **:** an attesting mark (as on silver) **6 a :** manner of touching or striking esp. the keys of a keyboard ⟨a firm *touch* on the piano⟩; *also* **:** the character of response of such keys to being struck ⟨a typewriter with a very stiff *touch*⟩ **b :** an individual productive act or its product (as a line or dash of color) esp. in an artistic production ⟨giving a *touch* here and there to bring out the main figures⟩ ⟨*touches* of rose⟩ **c :** skillful or distinctive manner or method (as in artistic production) ⟨the *touch* of a master⟩ **7 :** a characteristic or distinguishing trait or quality ⟨a classic *touch* distinguishes his writing⟩ **8 :** a small amount **:** TRACE ⟨a *touch* of spring in the air⟩; *esp* **:** a trivial or transitory attack (as of fever) ⟨a *touch* of conscience⟩

touch and go *n* **:** a highly uncertain or precarious situation — **touch-and-go** *adj*

touch·back \'təch-,bak\ *n* **:** an act or instance in football of having possession of the ball behind one's own goal line when the ball is declared dead after it has crossed the goal line as a result of impetus given by an opponent — compare SAFETY

touch·down \-,daun\ *n* **1 :** the act of touching a football to the ground behind an opponent's goal; *esp* **:** the act of scoring six points in American football by being lawfully in possession of the ball on, above, or behind an opponent's goal line when the ball is declared dead **2 :** the act or moment of touching down with an airplane

tou·ché \tü-'shā\ *interj* [F, lit., touched] — used to acknowledge a hit in fencing or the success of an argument

touch football *n* **:** football played informally and chiefly characterized by the substitution of touching for tackling

touch·hole \'təch-,hōl\ *n* **:** the vent in old-time cannons or firearms through which the charge was ignited

¹**touch·ing** *prep* **:** in reference to **:** CONCERNING

²**touching** *adj* **:** arousing tenderness or compassion **:** PATHETIC — **touch·ing·ly** \-iŋ-lē\ *adv*

touch-me-not \'təch-mē-,nät\ *n* **:** IMPATIENS

touch off *vt* **1 :** to describe or characterize to a nicety **2 a :** to cause to explode by or as if by touching with fire **b :** to release or initiate with sudden violence ⟨*touched off* a new wave of violence⟩

touch·stone \'təch-,stōn\ *n* **1 :** a black stone formerly used to test the purity of gold and silver by the streak left on the stone when rubbed by the metal **2 :** a test or criterion for judging something

touch system *n* **:** a method of typewriting that assigns a particular finger to each key and makes it possible to type without looking at the keyboard

touch up *vt* **1 :** to improve or perfect by small additional strokes or alterations **2 :** to stimulate by or as if by a flick of a whip

touch·wood \'təch-,wud\ *n* **:** ³PUNK

touchy \'təch-ē\ *adj* **touch·i·er; -est 1 :** marked by readiness to take offense on slight provocation **2 :** acutely sensitive or irritable ⟨a *touchy* swelling⟩ **3 :** calling for tact, care, or caution in treatment ⟨a *touchy* subject among the members of his family⟩ **syn** see IRASCIBLE — **touch·i·ly** \'təch-ə-lē\ *adv* — **touch·i·ness** \'təch-ē-nəs\ *n*

¹**tough** \'təf\ *adj* [OE *tōh*] **1 :** able to undergo great strain **:** flexible and not brittle ⟨*tough* fibers⟩ **2 :** not easily chewed ⟨*tough* meat⟩ **3 :** able to stand hard work and hardship **:** ROBUST ⟨a *tough* body⟩ **4 a :** hard to influence **:** STUBBORN ⟨a *tough* bargainer⟩ **b :** very difficult ⟨a *tough* problem⟩ **5 :** hardened in vice **:** ROWDY, LAWLESS ⟨a *tough* neighborhood⟩ **6 :** free from softness or sentimentality ⟨a *tough* approach to delinquency⟩; *esp* **:** marked by firm uncompromising determination ⟨a *tough* foreign policy⟩ — **tough·ly** *adv* — **tough·ness** *n*

²**tough** *n* **:** a tough person; *esp* **:** ROWDY

tough·en \'təf-ən\ *vb* **tough·ened; tough·en·ing** \'təf-(ə-)niŋ\ : to make or become tough

tough–mind·ed \'təf-'mīn-dəd\ *adj* : realistic or unsentimental in temper or habitual point of view

tou·pee \tü-'pā\ *n* [F *toupet*] : a small wig for a bald spot

¹tour \'tu̇(ə)r, *1 is also* 'tau̇(ə)r\ *n* [MF, fr. OF *tourn, tour* lathe, circuit, turn, fr. L *tornus* lathe] **1** : a period (as of duty) under some orderly schedule **2** : a trip or excursion usu. ending at the point of beginning ⟨a *tour* of the city⟩

²tour *vb* : to make a tour of : travel as a tourist

tour de force \,tü(ə)rd-ə-'fȯrs, -'fȯrs\ *n, pl* **tours de force** *same*\ [F] : a feat of strength, skill, or ingenuity

touring car *n* : an open automobile with two cross seats, usu. four doors, and a folding top

tour·ist \'tu̇r-əst\ *n* : one who travels for pleasure — **tourist** *adj*

tourist class *n* : economy accommodation on a ship, airplane, or train

tourist court *n* : MOTEL

tourist home *n* : a house in which rooms are available for rent to transients

tour·ma·line \'tu̇r-mə-lən, -,lēn\ *n* [Sinhalese *toramalli* carnelian] : a mineral of variable color that is a complex silicate and makes a gem of great beauty when transparent and cut

tour·na·ment \'tu̇r-nə-mənt, 'tər-\ *n* [modif. of OF *torneiement*, fr. *torneier* to engage in a tourney] **1 a** : a contest of skill and courage between armored knights fighting with blunted lances or swords **b** : a series of knightly contests occurring at one time and place **2** : a series of athletic contests, sports events, or games for a championship ⟨a tennis *tournament*⟩

tour·ney \'tu̇(ə)r-nē\ *n, pl* **tourneys** [MF *tornei*, fr. *torneier* to engage in a tourney, fr. *tourn, torn* turn] : TOURNAMENT

tour·ni·quet \'tu̇r-ni-kət, 'tər-\ *n* [F, fr. *tourner* to turn] : a device (as a bandage twisted tight with a stick) to check bleeding or blood flow

¹tou·sle \'tau̇-zəl\ *vt* **tou·sled; tou·sling** \'tau̇z-(ə-)liŋ\ [ME *touselen*] : DISHEVEL, RUMPLE

²tousle *n* : a tangled mass or condition

¹tout \'tau̇t\ *vb* [ME *tuten* to peer] **1** : to solicit or canvass for patronage, trade, votes, or support **2 a** *chiefly Brit* : to spy about at racing stables and tracks to get information to be used in betting **b** : to provide tips on racehorses

²tout *n* : one who touts: as **a** : one who solicits custom **b** : one who gives tips or solicits bets on a racehorse

³tout *vt* [alter. of ¹*toot*] : to praise or publicize insistently or excessively

tout·er \'tau̇t-ər\ *n* : TOUT

¹tow \'tō\ *vt* [OE *togian*] : to draw or pull along behind : HAUL

²tow *n* **1** : an act or instance of towing or the fact or condition of being towed **2** : a line or rope for towing **3** : something (as a tugboat or barge) that tows or is towed — **in tow 1** : in the state or course of being towed **2** : under guidance or protection : in the position of a follower

³tow *n* [OE *tow-* spinning] **1** : short broken fiber from flax, hemp, or jute used for yarn, twine, or stuffing **2** : yarn or cloth made of tow

tow·age \'tō-ij\ *n* **1** : the act of towing **2** : the price paid for towing

¹to·ward \'tō-(ə)rd, 'tȯ(ə)rd\ *adj* [OE *tōweard* facing, imminent, fr. *tō* to + *-weard* -ward] **1** *also* **to·wards** \'tō-(ə)rdz, 'tȯ(ə)rdz\ [ME *towardes*, fr. OE *tōweardes*, prep., toward, fr. *tōweard*, adj.] **a** : coming soon : IMMINENT **b** : happening at the moment : AFOOT **2 a** *obs* : quick to learn : APT **b** : FAVORING, PROPITIOUS ⟨a *toward* breeze⟩

²to·ward *or* **to·wards** \(')tō-(ə)rd(z), (')tȯ-(ə)rd(z), tə-'wȯrd(z), (')twȯrd(z)\ *prep* **1** : in the direction of ⟨driving *toward* town⟩ **2 a** : along a course leading to ⟨efforts *toward* reconciliation⟩ **b** : in relation to ⟨attitude *toward* life⟩ **3** : so as to face ⟨his back was *toward* me⟩ **4** : not long before ⟨*toward* noon⟩ **5** : to provide part of the payment for ⟨save *toward* his education⟩

tow·boat \'tō-,bōt\ *n* **1** : TUGBOAT **2** : a compact shallow-draft boat for pushing tows of barges on inland waterways

¹tow·el \'tau̇(-ə)l\ *n* [OF *toaille*, of Gmc origin] : a cloth or piece of absorbent paper for wiping or drying

²towel *vb* **-eled** *or* **-elled; -el·ing** *or* **-el·ling** : to rub or dry with or use a towel

tow·el·ing *or* **tow·el·ling** \'tau̇-(ə-)liŋ\ *n* : material for towels

¹tow·er \'tau̇(-ə)r\ *n* [OE *torr* & OF *tur*, fr. L *turris*, fr. Gk *tyrsis, tyrrhis*] **1** : a building or structure typically higher than its diameter and high relative to its surroundings that may stand apart (as a campanile) or be attached (as a church belfry) to a larger structure and that may be of skeleton framework (as an observation or transmission tower) **2** : a towering citadel : FORTRESS — **tow·ered** \'tau̇(-ə)rd\ *adj*

²tower *vi* : to reach or rise to a great height

tow·er·ing *adj* **1** : impressively high or great : IMPOSING **2** : reaching a high point of intensity : OVERWHELMING ⟨a *towering* rage⟩ **3** : going beyond proper bounds : EXCESSIVE ⟨*towering* ambitions⟩

tower

tower wagon *n* : a wagon or motortruck with a high adjustable platform on which workmen can stand

tow·head \'tō-,hed\ *n* : a person having soft whitish hair — **tow·head·ed** \-'hed-əd\ *adj*

to·whee \tō-'(h)ē, -'hwē; 'tō-,hē, 'tō-(,)ē\ *n* : any of numerous American finches; *esp* : one of eastern No. America having the male black, white, and rufous — called also *chewink*

to wit \tə-'wit\ *adv* [ME *to witen*, lit., to know] : that is to say : NAMELY

tow·line \'tō-,līn\ *n* : a line used in towing

town \'tau̇n\ *n* [OE *tūn* enclosure, village, town] **1 a** : a compactly settled area as distinguished from surrounding rural territory; *esp* : one larger than a village but smaller than a city **b** : CITY **c** : an English village having a periodic fair or market **2 a** : the city or urban life as contrasted with the country **b** : TOWNSPEOPLE **3** : a New England territorial and political unit usu. containing both rural and urban areas under a single town government — called also *township* — **town** *adj*

town clerk *n* : an official who keeps the town records

town crier *n* : a town officer who makes public proclamations

town hall *n* : a public building used for town-government offices and meetings

town house *n* : the city residence of one having a country-seat or a chief residence elsewhere

town meeting *n* : a meeting of inhabitants or taxpayers constituting the legislative authority of a town

towns·folk \'tau̇nz-,fōk\ *n pl* : TOWNSPEOPLE

town·ship \'tau̇n-,ship\ *n* **1 a** : TOWN 3 **b** : a unit of local government in some northeastern and north central states **c** : a subdivision of the county esp. in the southern U.S. **2** : a division of territory in surveys of U.S. public land containing 36 sections or 36 square miles

towns·man \'tau̇nz-mən\ *n* **1** : a native or resident of a town or city **2** : a fellow citizen of a town — **towns·wom·an** \-,wu̇m-ən\ *n*

towns·peo·ple \-,pē-pəl\ *n pl* **1** : the inhabitants of a town or city : TOWNSMEN **2** : town-dwelling or town-bred persons

tow·path \'tō-,path, -,pȧth\ *or* **towing path** *n* : a path (as along a canal) traveled by men or animals towing boats

tow·rope \'tō-,rōp\ *n* : a line used in towing

tow truck *n* : WRECKER 4 — called also *tow car*

tox- *or* **toxo-** *comb form* [L *toxicum* poison] : poisonous : poison ⟨*toxemia*⟩

tox·a·phene \'täk-sə-,fēn\ *n* [fr. *Toxaphene*, a trademark] : a chlorine-containing insecticide

tox·e·mia \täk-'sē-mē-ə\ *n* : an abnormal condition associated with the presence of toxic substances in the blood — **tox·e·mic** \-mik\ *adj*

tox·ic \'täk-sik\ *adj* [LL *toxicus*, fr. L *toxicum* poison, fr. Gk *toxikon* arrow poison, fr. *toxon* bow, *toxa*, pl., bow and arrows] **1** : of, relating to, or caused by a poison or toxin **2** : POISONOUS — **tox·ic·i·ty** \täk-'sis-ət-ē\ *n*

tox·i·cant \'täk-si-kənt\ *n* [L *toxicare* to poison, fr.

toxicum poison] **:** a poisonous agent (as for killing vermin) — **toxicant** *adj*

tox·i·col·o·gy \ˌtäk-sə-'käl-ə-jē\ *n* [L *toxicum* poison] **:** a science that deals with poisonous materials and their effect and with the problems involved in their use and control — **tox·i·co·log·ic** \ˌtäk-si-kə-'läj-ik\ *adj* — **tox·i·co·log·i·cal·ly** \-'läj-i-k(ə-)lē\ *adv* — **tox·i·col·o·gist** \ˌtäk-sə-'käl-ə-jəst\ *n*

tox·in \'täk-sən\ *n* **:** a complex usu. unstable substance that is a metabolic product of a living organism (as a bacterium), that is very poisonous when introduced directly into the tissues but is usu. destroyed by the digestive process when taken by mouth, and that typically induces antibody formation ⟨tetanus *toxin*⟩ — compare ANTITOXIN, TOXOID

tox·in-an·ti·tox·in \'täk-sən-'ant-i-ˌtäk-sən\ *n* **:** a mixture of a toxin and its antitoxin used esp. formerly in immunizing against a disease (as diphtheria)

tox·oid \'täk-ˌsȯid\ *n* **:** a toxin (as of tetanus) treated so as to destroy its poisonous effects while leaving it still capable of causing the formation of antibodies when injected into the body

¹**toy** \'tȯi\ *n* [ME *toye* dalliance] **1 :** something (as a trinket) of small or no real value or importance **:** TRIFLE **2 :** something for a child to play with **3 :** something tiny; *esp* **:** an animal of a breed or variety characterized by exceptionally small size — **toy** *adj* — **toy·like** \-ˌlīk\ *adj*

²**toy** *vi* **:** to amuse oneself as if with a toy **:** PLAY, TRIFLE ⟨*toy* with an idea⟩ — **toy·er** *n*

toy·on \'tȯi-ˌän\ *n* [AmerSp *tollon*] **:** an ornamental evergreen shrub of the No. American Pacific coast that is related to the rose and has white flowers succeeded by persistent bright red berries

tra·bec·u·la \trə-'bek-yə-lə\ *n, pl* **-lae** \-ˌlē, -ˌlī\ *also* **-las** [NL, fr. L dim. of *trabs, trabes* beam] **:** a small anatomical bar, rod, or septum often bridging a gap or forming part of a framework ⟨spleen *trabeculae*⟩ — **tra·bec·u·lar** \-lər\ *adj* — **tra·bec·u·late** \-lət\ *adj*

¹**trace** \'trās\ *n* [MF, fr. *tracier* to trace] **1 :** a mark or line left by something that has passed **:** TRAIL, TRACK; *also* **:** FOOTPRINT **2 :** a sign or evidence of some past thing **:** VESTIGE **3 :** something traced or drawn (as a line); *esp* **:** the marking made by a recording instrument (as a seismograph or kymograph) **4 :** a minute amount or indication ⟨a *trace* of red⟩; *esp* **:** an amount of a chemical constituent not quantitatively determined because of minuteness

syn TRACE, VESTIGE, TRACK mean a sign left by something that has passed. TRACE may suggest any line or mark or discernible effect ⟨*traces* of a deer in the snow⟩⟨*traces* of her native dialect in her speech⟩ VESTIGE applies to tangible remains, as a fragment, remnant, or relic ⟨*vestiges* of a primitive society⟩ TRACK suggests a continuous line that can be followed ⟨hounds on the *track* of a fox⟩

²**trace** *vb* [MF *tracier*, fr. (assumed) VL *tractiare* to drag, draw, fr. L *tract-, trahere* to pull, draw] **1 a :** DELINEATE, SKETCH **b :** to form (as letters or figures) carefully or painstakingly **c :** to copy (as a drawing) by following the lines or letters as seen through a transparent superimposed sheet **d :** to make a graphic instrumental record of ⟨*trace* the heart action⟩ **e :** to adorn with linear ornamentation (as tracery or chasing) **2 a :** to follow the footprints, track, or trail of **b :** to study out or follow the development and progress of in detail or step by step **3 :** to be traceable historically ⟨a family that *traces* to the Norman conquest⟩

³**trace** *n* [ME *trais*, pl., traces, fr. MF, pl. of *trait* pull, draft, trace, fr. L *tractus* act of drawing, fr. *trahere* to draw] **1 :** either of two straps, chains, or lines of a harness for attaching a horse to something (as a vehicle) to be drawn **2 :** one or more vascular bundles supplying a leaf or twig

trace·a·ble \'trā-sə-bəl\ *adj* **1 :** capable of being traced **2 :** ATTRIBUTABLE, DUE ⟨a failure *traceable* to laziness⟩ — **trace·a·bly** \-blē\ *adv*

trace element *n* **:** a chemical element used by organisms in minute quantities and held essential to their physiology

trace·less \'trās-ləs\ *adj* **:** having or leaving no trace — **trace·less·ly** *adv*

trac·er \'trā-sər\ *n* **1 a :** a person who traces missing persons or property **b :** an inquiry sent out in tracing a

shipment lost in transit **2 :** a draftsman who traces designs, patterns, or markings **3 :** a device (as a stylus) used in tracing **4 a :** ammunition containing a chemical composition to mark the flight of projectiles by a trail of smoke or fire **b :** a substance and esp. a labeled element or atom used to trace the course of a chemical or biological process

trac·ery \'trās(-ə)-rē\ *n, pl* **-er·ies 1 :** architectural ornamental work with branching lines; *esp* **:** decorative openwork in the head of a Gothic window **2 :** a decorative interlacing of lines suggestive of Gothic tracery — **trac·er·ied** \-rēd\ *adj*

tracery

tra·chea \'trā-kē-ə\ *n, pl* **-che·ae** \-kē-ˌē, -kē-ˌī\ *also* **-che·as** [ML, fr. LL *trachia*, fr. Gk *tracheia artēria*, lit., rough artery] **1 :** the main trunk of the system of tubes by which air passes to and from the lungs in vertebrates **2 :** a xylem element or series of elements in a vascular plant **3 :** one of the air-conveying tubules forming the respiratory system of most insects and many other arthropods — **tra·che·al** \-kē-əl\ *adj* — **tra·che·ate** \-kē-ˌāt\ *adj*

tracheal gill *n* **:** one of the external gills that connect with the tracheae of some aquatic insect larvae or nymphs

tra·che·id \'trā-kē-əd, -ˌkēd\ *n* **:** a long tubular xylem cell that functions in conduction and support and has tapering closed ends and thickened lignified walls — **tra·che·i·dal** \trā-'kē-əd-ᵊl\ *adj*

tra·che·o·phyte \'trā-kē-ə-ˌfīt\ *n* **:** any of a division (Tracheophyta) comprising green plants with a vascular system that contains tracheids or tracheal elements and including ferns and related plants and the seed plants

tra·che·ot·o·my \ˌtrā-kē-'ät-ə-mē\ *n, pl* **-mies :** the surgical operation of cutting into the trachea esp. through the skin

tra·cho·ma \trə-'kō-mə\ *n* [Gk *trachōmat-, trachōma*, fr. *trachys* rough] **:** a chronic contagious eye disease marked by inflammation of the conjunctiva, caused by a rickettsia, and sometimes causing blindness — **tra·chom·a·tous** \-'käm-ət-əs, -'kōm-\ *adj*

trac·ing *n* **1 :** the act of one that traces **2 :** something that is traced

¹**track** \'trak\ *n* [MF *trac*] **1 a :** detectable evidence (as the wake of a ship, a line of footprints, or a wheel rut) that something has passed **b :** a path made by repeated footfalls **:** TRAIL **c** (1) **:** a course laid out esp. for racing (2) **:** the parallel rails of a railroad **2 :** the course along which something moves **3 a :** a sequence of events **:** a train of ideas **:** SUCCESSION **b :** awareness of a fact or progression ⟨lose *track* of the time⟩ **4 a :** the width of a wheeled vehicle from wheel to wheel **b :** either of two endless metal belts on which a vehicle (as a tractor) travels **5 :** track-and-field sports; *esp* **:** those performed on a racing track **syn** see TRACE — **in one's tracks :** where one is at the moment **:** on the spot **:** INSTANTLY ⟨dropped the deer *in its tracks*⟩

²**track** *vb* **1 :** to follow the tracks or traces of **:** TRAIL **2 :** to trace by following the signs or course of ⟨*track* a missile with radar⟩ **3 :** to pass over **:** TRAVERSE **4 :** to make tracks upon or with ⟨*track* up the floor with muddy feet⟩⟨*track* mud all over the floor⟩ **5 a** *of a pair of wheels* **:** to maintain a constant distance apart on the straightaway **b** *of a rear wheel of a vehicle* **:** to accurately follow the corresponding fore wheel on a straightaway — **track·er** *n*

track·age \'trak-ij\ *n* **1 :** lines of railway track **2 a :** a right to use the tracks of another road **b :** the charge for such right

track-and-field \ˌtrak-ən-'fēld\ *adj* **:** of or relating to a sport performed on a racing track or on the adjacent field

track·lay·ing \'trak-ˌlā-iŋ\ *adj* **:** of, relating to, or being a vehicle that travels on two endless metal belts

track·less \'trak-ləs\ *adj* **:** having no track **:** UNTROD — **track·less·ly** *adv* — **track·less·ness** *n*

¹**tract** \'trakt\ *n, often cap* [ML *tractus*, fr. L, action of drawing, extension; fr. its being sung without a break by one voice] **:** the verses of Scripture replacing the alleluia verse after the gradual in penitential and requiem masses

²**tract** n [ME, modif. of L *tractatus* treatise] **:** a pamphlet or leaflet intended to draw attention or gain support for something (as a political or religious movement)

³**tract** n [L *tractus* action of drawing, extension, fr. *trahere* to pull, draw] **1 a :** an indefinite stretch esp. of land ⟨broad *tracts* of prairie⟩ **b :** a defined area esp. of land ⟨garden *tract*⟩ **2 :** a system of body parts or organs that collectively serve some special purpose ⟨the digestive *tract* of man⟩

trac·ta·ble \'trak-tə-bəl\ adj [L *tractare* to handle, treat, freq. of *trahere* to draw] **1 :** easily led, taught, or controlled **:** DOCILE ⟨*tractable* horse⟩ **2 :** easily handled, managed, or wrought **:** MALLEABLE — **trac·ta·bil·i·ty** \,trak-tə-'bil-ət-ē\ n — **trac·ta·ble·ness** \'trak-tə-bəl-nəs\ n — **trac·ta·bly** \-blē\ adv

trac·tile \'trak-t°l, -,tīl\ adj [L *tract-*, *trahere* to draw] **:** capable of being drawn out in length **:** TENSILE, DUCTILE — **trac·til·i·ty** \trak-'til-ət-ē\ n

trac·tion \'trak-shən\ n [L *tract-*, *trahere* to draw] **1 :** the act of drawing **:** the state of being drawn; *also* **:** the force exerted in drawing **2 :** the drawing of a vehicle by motive power; *also* **:** the motive power employed **3 :** the adhesive friction of a body on a surface on which it moves (as of a wheel on a rail) — **trac·tion·al** \-shnəl, -shən-°l\ adj

traction engine n **:** a locomotive for drawing vehicles on highways or in the fields

trac·tive \'trak-tiv\ adj **:** serving to pull **:** used in pulling

trac·tor \'trak-tər\ n **1 :** TRACTION ENGINE **2 a :** a 4-wheeled or tracklaying rider-controlled automotive vehicle used esp. for drawing implements (as agricultural) or for bearing and propelling such implements **b :** a smaller 2-wheeled apparatus controlled through handlebars by a walking operator **c :** a truck with short chassis and no body used in combination with a trailer for the highway hauling of freight

¹**trade** \'trād\ n [ME, path, track, course of action, fr. MLG, path; akin to E *tread*] **1 :** a customary course of action **:** PRACTICE **2 a :** the business or work in which one engages regularly **:** OCCUPATION **b :** an occupation requiring manual or mechanical skill **:** CRAFT **c :** the persons engaged in an occupation, business, or industry **3 :** the business of buying and selling or bartering commodities **:** COMMERCE; *also* **:** TRAFFIC, MARKET **4 a :** an act or instance of trading **:** TRANSACTION; *esp* **:** an exchange of property without use of money **b :** a firm's customers **:** CLIENTELE **c :** the concerns engaged in a business or industry **syn** see BUSINESS

²**trade** vb **1 a :** to give in exchange for another commodity **:** BARTER; *also* **:** to make an exchange of **b :** to buy and sell (as stock) regularly **2 a :** to engage in the exchange, purchase, or sale of goods **b :** to make one's purchases **:** SHOP

³**trade** adj **1 :** of, relating to, or used in trade **2 :** intended for persons in a business or industry ⟨a *trade* journal⟩ **3 :** of, composed of, or representing the trades or trade unions **4 :** of or associated with a trade wind ⟨the *trade* belts⟩

trade acceptance n **:** a time draft for the amount of a purchase drawn by the seller on the buyer and bearing the buyer's acceptance

trade dollar n **:** a U.S. silver dollar weighing 420 grains .900 fine issued 1873–85 for use in oriental trade

trade in \'(')trād-'in\ vt **:** to turn in as usu. part payment for a purchase ⟨*trade* an old car *in* on a new one⟩

trade-in \'trād-,in\ n **:** something given in trade usu. as part payment of the price of another

trade-last \-,last\ n **:** a complimentary remark by a third person that a hearer offers to repeat to the person complimented if he will first report a compliment made about the hearer

¹**trade·mark** \-,märk\ n **:** a device (as a word) pointing distinctly to the origin or ownership of merchandise to which it is applied and legally reserved to the exclusive use of the owner as maker or seller

²**trademark** vt **:** to secure trademark rights for **:** register the trademark of

trade name n **1 :** the name by which an article is called in its own trade **2 :** a name that is given by a manufacturer or merchant to a product to distinguish it as made or sold by him and that may be used and protected as a

trademark 3 : the name under which a firm does business

trad·er \'trād-ər\ n **1 :** a person who trades **2 :** a ship engaged in trade

trade school n **:** a secondary school teaching the skilled trades

trades·man \'trādz-mən\ n **1 :** one who runs a retail store **:** SHOPKEEPER **2 :** a workman in a skilled trade **:** CRAFTSMAN

trades·peo·ple \-,pē-pəl\ n pl **:** TRADESMEN 1

trade union n **:** LABOR UNION; *esp* **:** CRAFT UNION — **trade unionism** n — **trade unionist** n

trade wind n **:** a wind blowing almost continually in the same course, from northeast to southwest in a belt north of the equator and from southeast to northwest in one south of the equator

trading post n **:** a station or store of a trader or trading company established in a sparsely settled region

trading stamp n **:** a printed stamp of value given as a premium to a retail customer to be accumulated and redeemed in merchandise

tra·di·tion \trə-'dish-ən\ n [L *tradere* to hand over, hand down, fr. *trans-* + *dare* to give] **:** the handing down of information, beliefs, or customs from one generation to another; *also* **:** something thus handed down — **tra·di·tion·al** \-'dish-nəl, -ən-°l\ adj — **tra·di·tion·al·ly** \-ē\ adv

tra·di·tion·al·ism \-'dish-nə-,liz-əm, -ən-°l-,iz-\ n **:** the doctrines or practices of those who follow or accept tradition — **tra·di·tion·al·ist** \-nə-ləst, -ən-°l-əst\ n or adj — **tra·di·tion·al·is·tic** \-,dish-nə-'lis-tik, -ən-°l-'is-\ adj

tra·duce \trə-'d(y)üs\ vt [L *traducere* to transfer, degrade, fr. *trans-* + *ducere* to lead] **1 :** to injure the reputation of by falsehood or misrepresentation **:** DEFAME **2 :** to make a mock of **:** BETRAY — **tra·duce·ment** \-mənt\ n — **tra·duc·er** n

¹**traf·fic** \'traf-ik\ n [MF *trafique*, fr. It *traffico*] **1 :** the business of carrying passengers or goods ⟨the tourist *traffic*⟩ **2 :** the business of buying and selling **:** TRADE, COMMERCE **3 :** DEALINGS, FAMILIARITY ⟨*traffic* with the enemy⟩ **4 :** the persons or goods carried by train, boat, or airplane or passing along a road, river, or air route; *also* **:** the motions or activity of such persons or carriers ⟨heavy holiday *traffic*⟩

²**traffic** vi **traf·ficked**; **traf·fick·ing :** to carry on traffic **:** TRADE, DEAL — **traf·fick·er** n

traffic circle n **:** ROTARY 2

traffic court n **:** a minor court for disposition of petty prosecutions for violations of statutes, ordinances, and local regulations governing the use of highways and motor vehicles

traffic island n **:** a paved or planted island in a roadway designed to guide the flow of traffic

traffic signal n **:** an electrically operated signal (as a system of colored lights) for controlling traffic — called also *traffic light*

trag·a·canth \'traj-ə-,kan(t)th, 'trag-\ n [Gk *tragakantha*, a shrub producing tragacanth, fr. *tragos* goat + *akantha* thorn] **:** a gum from various Old World plants related to the American locoweeds that swells in water and is used in the arts and in pharmacy

tra·ge·di·an \trə-'jēd-ē-ən\ n **1 :** a writer of tragedies **2 :** an actor of tragic roles

tra·ge·di·enne \trə-,jēd-ē-'en\ n [F *tragédienne*] **:** an actress who plays tragic roles

trag·e·dy \'traj-əd-ē\ n, pl **-dies** [L *tragoedia*, fr. Gk *tragōidia*, fr. *tragos* goat + *aidein* to sing; prob. fr. the satyrs represented by the original chorus] **1 :** a serious drama typically describing a conflict between the protagonist and a superior force (as destiny) and having a sorrowful or disastrous conclusion that excites pity or terror **2 a :** a disastrous event **:** CALAMITY **b :** MISFORTUNE **3 :** tragic quality or element

trag·ic \'traj-ik\ adj **1 :** of, marked by, or expressive of tragedy **2 a :** dealing with or treated in tragedy ⟨the *tragic* hero⟩ **b :** appropriate to or typical of tragedy **3 a :** DEPLORABLE, LAMENTABLE **b :** marked by a sense of tragedy — **trag·i·cal** \-i-kəl\ adj — **trag·i·cal·ly** \-i-k(ə-)lē\ adv — **trag·i·cal·ness** \-i-kəl-nəs\ n

tragic flaw n **:** a flaw in the character of the hero of a tragedy that brings about his downfall

tragi·com·e·dy \,traj-i-'käm-əd-ē\ n **:** a drama or a situation blending tragic and comic elements — **tragi·com·ic** \-'käm-ik\ *or* **tragi·com·i·cal** \-'käm-i-kəl\ *adj*

tra·gus \'trā-gəs\ *n, pl* **tra·gi** \-,gī, -,jī\ [Gk *tragos*, lit., goat] **:** the prominence in front of the external opening of the ear

¹trail \'trāl\ *vb* [MF *trailler* to tow, fr. L *tragula* sledge, dragnet] **1 :** to drag or draw along behind ⟨the horse *trailed* its reins⟩ **2 :** to lag behind ⟨the horse *trailed* in the race⟩ **3 :** to carry or bring along as a burden or bother ⟨disliked to *trail* his sister around with him⟩ **4 :** to follow in the tracks of **:** PURSUE ⟨dogs *trailing* a fox⟩ **5 :** to hang or let hang so as to touch the ground ⟨a *trailing* skirt⟩ **6 :** to grow to such a length as to hang down or rest on or creep over the ground ⟨*trailing* vines⟩ **7 :** to form a trail **:** STRAGGLE ⟨smoke *trailed* from the chimney⟩ **8 :** DWINDLE ⟨the sound *trailed* off⟩ *syn* see CHASE

²trail *n* **1 :** something that trails or is trailed: as **a :** the train of a gown **b :** a trailing arrangement (as of flowers) **:** SPRAY **c :** the part of a gun carriage that rests on the ground when the piece is ready for action **2 a :** something that follows or moves along as if being drawn along **:** TRAIN **b** (1) **:** the streak produced by a meteor (2) **:** a line produced photographically by the moving image of a celestial body ⟨star *trails*⟩ **c :** a chain of consequences **:** AFTERMATH **3 a :** a trace or mark left by something that has passed or been drawn along ⟨a *trail* of blood⟩ **b** (1) **:** a track made by passage through a wilderness **:** a beaten path (2) **:** a marked path through a forest or mountainous region

trail·blaz·er \-,blā-zər\ *n* **1 :** one that marks or points out a trail to guide others **:** PATHFINDER **2 :** PIONEER — **trail·blaz·ing** \-ziŋ\ *adj*

trail·er \'trā-lər\ *n* **1 :** a trailing plant **2 a :** a vehicle designed to be hauled (as by a tractor) **b :** a vehicle designed to serve wherever parked as a dwelling or as a place of business

trailer camp *n* **:** an area where house trailers are congregated — called also *trailer court, trailer park*

trail·er·ite \'trā-lə-,rīt\ *n* **:** a person living or accustomed to live in a trailer

trailing arbutus *n* **:** the common No. American arbutus

trailing edge *n* **:** the rearmost edge of an airfoil

¹train \'trān\ *n* [MF, fr. *trainer* to draw, drag] **1 :** a part of a gown that trails behind the wearer **2 :** RETINUE **3 :** a moving file of persons, vehicles, or animals **4 a :** regular or proper order designed to lead to some result **b :** a connected series ⟨*train* of thought⟩ **c :** accompanying circumstances **:** AFTERMATH **5 :** a line of gunpowder laid to lead fire to a charge **6 :** a series of moving machine parts (as gears) for transmitting and modifying motion **7 a :** a connected line of railroad cars with or without a locomotive **b :** an automotive tractor with one or more trailer units

²train *vb* [MF *trainer* to draw, drag] **1 :** to direct the growth of (a plant) usu. by bending, pruning, and tying **2 :** to teach in an art, profession, or trade ⟨*trained* him in the law⟩ ⟨*trained* several generations of long-distance runners⟩ **3 :** to make ready (as by exercise) for a test of skill **4 :** to aim (as a gun) at a target **:** bring to bear **5 :** to undergo instruction, discipline, or drill *syn* see TEACH — **train·a·ble** \'trā-nə-bəl\ *adj* — **train·ee** \trā-'nē\ *n* — **train·er** \'trā-nər\ *n*

train·ing \'trā-niŋ\ *n* **1 :** the course followed by one who trains or is being trained ⟨take nursing *training*⟩ **2 :** the condition of one who has trained for a test or contest *syn* see EDUCATION

train·load \'trān-'lōd\ *n* **:** the full freight or passenger capacity of a railroad train

train·man \'trān-mən, -,man\ *n* **:** a member of a railroad train crew supervised by a conductor

train oil \'trān-\ *n* [MD *trane* or MLG *trān*, lit., tear; akin to E **¹tear**] **:** oil from a marine animal (as a whale)

train·sick \'trān-,sik\ *adj* **:** affected with motion sickness induced by riding on a train — **train sickness** *n*

traipse \'trāps\ *vi* **:** to walk or trudge about — **traipse** *n*

trait \'trāt\ *n* [MF, lit., act of drawing, fr. L *tractus*, fr. *trahere* to draw] **:** a distinguishing quality (as of personality or physical makeup) **:** PECULIARITY, CHARACTERISTIC

trai·tor \'trāt-ər\ *n* [OF *traitre*, fr. L *traditor*, fr. *tradere* to hand over, betray, fr. *trans-* + *dare* to give] **1 :** one who betrays another's trust or is false to an obligation or

duty **2 :** one who commits treason — **trai·tress** \'trā-trəs\ *n*

trai·tor·ous \'trāt-ə-rəs, 'trā-trəs\ *adj* **1 :** guilty or capable of treason **2 :** constituting treason — **trai·tor·ous·ly** *adv*

tra·jec·to·ry \trə-'jek-t(ə-)rē\ *n, pl* **-ries** [L *traject-, traicere* to cause to cross, cross, fr. *trans-* + *jacere* to throw] **:** the curve that a body (as a planet in its orbit, a projectile, or a rocket) describes in space

tram \'tram\ *n* **1 :** a cart or wagon running on rails (as in a mine) **2** *chiefly Brit* **:** STREETCAR **3 :** the carriage of an overhead conveyor

tram·car \-,kär\ *n* **1** *chiefly Brit* **:** STREETCAR **2 :** TRAM 1

tram·line \-,līn\ *n, Brit* **:** a streetcar line

¹tram·mel \'tram-əl\ *n* [MF *tremail*, fr. LL *tremaculum*, fr. L *tres* three + *macula* mesh, spot] **1 :** a net for catching birds or fish **2 :** something impeding activity, progress, or freedom **:** RESTRAINT — usu. used in pl. **3 :** an adjustable pothook for a fireplace crane

²trammel *vt* **-meled** *or* **-melled; -mel·ing** *or* **-mel·ling** \'tram-(ə-)liŋ\ **1 :** to catch or hold in or as if in a net **:** ENMESH **2 :** to prevent or impede the free play of **:** CONFINE

¹tramp \'tramp, *1 & 2 are also* 'trämp\ *vb* [ME *trampen*] **1 :** to walk heavily **2 :** to tread on forcibly and repeatedly **:** TRAMPLE **3 a :** to travel or wander through on foot **b :** to travel as a tramp — **tramp·er** *n*

²tramp \'tramp, *3 & 4 are also* 'trämp\ *n* **1 :** a begging or thieving vagrant **2 :** a walking trip **:** HIKE **3 :** the succession of sounds made by the beating of marching feet **4 :** an iron plate to protect the sole of a shoe **5 :** a ship not making regular trips but taking cargo to any port

¹tram·ple \'tram-pəl\ *vb* **tram·pled; tram·pling** \-p(ə-)liŋ\ [ME *tramplen*, freq. of *trampen* to tramp] **1 :** to tramp or tread heavily so as to bruise, crush, or injure **2 :** to tread underfoot **:** stamp on **3 :** to inflict pain, injury, or loss by ruthless or heartless treatment ⟨*trampled* on his feelings⟩ ⟨*trampled* over their weaker rivals⟩ — **tram·pler** \-p(ə-)lər\ *n*

²trample *n* **:** the act or sound of trampling

tram·po·line \,tram-pə-'lēn\ *n* [Sp *trampolín*, fr. It *trampolino*, of Gmc origin] **:** a resilient canvas sheet or web supported by springs in a metal frame used as a springboard in tumbling — **tram·po·lin·er** \-'lē-nər\ *n* — **tram·po·lin·ist** \-nəst\ *n*

tram·way \'tram-,wā\ *n* **1 :** a road or way for trams **2** *Brit* **:** a streetcar line

trance \'tran(t)s\ *n* [MF *transe*, fr. *transir* to pass away, swoon, fr. L *transire* to cross over, pass away, fr. *trans-* + *ire* to go] **1 :** a state of partly suspended animation or inability to function **:** STUPOR **2 :** a somnolent state (as of deep hypnosis) **3 :** a state of profound abstraction or absorption **:** ECSTASY

tran·quil \'traŋ-kwəl, 'tran-\ *adj* [L *tranquillus*] **1 a :** free from agitation **:** SERENE **b :** free from disturbance or turmoil **:** QUIET **2 :** STEADY, STABLE — **tran·quil·ly** \-kwə-lē\ *adv* — **tran·quil·ness** *n*

tran·quil·ize *or* **tran·quil·lize** \-kwə-,līz\ *vb* **:** to make or become tranquil or relaxed; *esp* **:** to ease the mental tension and anxiety of usu. by means of drugs

tran·quil·iz·er \-,lī-zər\ *n* **:** one that tranquilizes; *esp* **:** a drug used to reduce anxiety and tension

tran·quil·li·ty *or* **tran·quil·i·ty** \tran-'kwil-ət-ē, traŋ-\ *n* **:** the quality or state of being tranquil

trans- *prefix* [L *trans-, tra-;* akin to E *through*] **1 :** on or to the other side of **:** across **:** beyond ⟨*transatlantic*⟩ **2 :** through ⟨*transcutaneous*⟩ **3 :** so or such as to change or transfer ⟨*transliterate*⟩ ⟨*translocation*⟩ ⟨*transship*⟩

trans·act \tran(t)s-'akt, tranz-\ *vb* [L *transact-, transigere*, lit., to drive across, fr. *trans-* + *agere* to drive] **1 :** to carry through **:** bring about **:** NEGOTIATE ⟨*transact* a sale of property⟩ **2 :** to carry on **:** CONDUCT ⟨*transact* business⟩ — **trans·ac·tor** \-'ak-tər\ *n*

trans·ac·tion \-'ak-shən\ *n* **1 :** an act, process, or instance of transacting **2 a :** something transacted; *esp* **:** a business deal **b** *pl* **:** the record of the meeting of a society **:** PROCEEDINGS — **trans·ac·tion·al** \-shnəl, -shən-ᵊl\ *adj*

trans·al·pine \-'al-,pīn\ *adj* **1 :** situated on the farther

trammel 3

side of the Alps **2 :** of, relating to, or characteristic of the region or peoples beyond the Alps — **transalpine** n

trans·at·lan·tic \ˌtran(t)s-ət-'lant-ik, ˌtranz-\ adj **:** extending across or situated beyond the Atlantic ocean

trans·ceiv·er \tran(t)s-'ē-vər, tranz-\ n [transmitter + receiver] **:** a radio transmitter-receiver that uses some of the same components for transmission and reception

tran·scend \tran-'send\ vb [L transcendere, fr. trans- + scandere to climb] **1 a :** to rise above or go beyond the limits of **:** EXCEED **b :** to be prior to, beyond, and above (the universe or material existence) **2 :** SURPASS **syn** see EXCEED

tran·scend·ence \-'sen-dən(t)s\ also **tran·scend·en·cy** \-dən-sē\ n **:** the quality or state of being transcendent

tran·scend·ent \-dənt\ adj **1 :** exceeding usual limits **:** SURPASSING **2 :** extending or lying beyond the limits of ordinary experience **3 :** transcending the universe or material existence — **tran·scend·ent·ly** adv

tran·scen·den·tal \ˌtran-ˌsen-'dent-ᵊl, ˌtran(t)-sən-\ adj **1 :** TRANSCENDENT **2 :** incapable of being the root of an algebraic equation with integral rational coefficients ⟨π is a transcendental number⟩ **3 :** of or relating to transcendentalism — **tran·scen·den·tal·ly** \-'ᵊl-ē\ adv

tran·scen·den·tal·ism \-'ᵊl-ˌiz-əm\ n **:** a philosophy holding that ultimate reality is unknowable and asserting the primacy of the spiritual over the material and empirical — **tran·scen·den·tal·ist** \-'ᵊl-əst\ adj or n

trans·con·ti·nen·tal \ˌtran(t)s-ˌkänt-ᵊn-'ent-ᵊl\ adj **1 :** extending or going across a continent ⟨transcontinental railroad⟩ **2 :** situated on the farther side of a continent

tran·scribe \tran-'skrīb\ vt [L transcript-, transcribere, fr. trans- + scribere to write] **1 a :** to make a written copy of **b :** to make a copy of (dictated or recorded matter) in longhand or on a typewriter **2 a :** to represent (speech sounds) by means of phonetic symbols **b :** to transfer (data) from one recording form to another **c :** to record (as on magnetic tape) for later broadcast **3 :** to make a musical transcription of **4 :** to broadcast by electrical transcription — **tran·scrib·er** n

tran·script \'tran-ˌskript\ n **1 a :** a written, printed, or typed copy **b :** an official copy (as of a student's educational record) **2 :** a copy or rendering (as of experience) in an art form

tran·scrip·tion \tran-'skrip-shən\ n **1 :** an act, process, or instance of transcribing **2 :** COPY, TRANSCRIPT: as **a :** an arrangement of a musical composition for some instrument or voice other than the original **b :** ELECTRICAL TRANSCRIPTION — **tran·scrip·tion·al** \-shnəl, -shən-ᵊl\ adj — **tran·scrip·tion·al·ly** \-ē\ adv

trans·duc·er \tran(t)s-'d(y)ü-sər, tranz-\ n [L transducere to lead across, fr. trans- + ducere to lead] **:** a device that is actuated by power from one system and supplies power in any other form to a second system

¹tran·sect \tran-'sekt\ vt [trans- + L sect-, secare to cut] **:** to cut transversely — **tran·sec·tion** \-'sek-shən\ n

²tran·sect \'tran-ˌsekt\ n **:** a sample area (as of vegetation) usu. in the form of a long continuous strip

tran·sept \'tran-ˌsept\ n [NL transeptum, fr. L trans- + saeptum enclosure, wall, fr. saeptus, pp. of saepire to fence in, fr. saepes fence] **:** the part forming the arms of a cross-shaped church

¹trans·fer \tran(t)s-'fər, 'tran(t)s-\ vb trans·ferred; trans·fer·ring [L transferre, fr. trans- + ferre to carry] **1 a :** to convey from one person, place, or situation to another **:** TRANSPORT **b :** to cause to pass from one to another **:** TRANSMIT **2 :** to make over the possession or ownership of **:** CONVEY **3 :** to print or otherwise copy from one surface to another by contact **4 :** to move to a different place, region, or situation; esp **:** to withdraw from one educational institution to enroll at another **5 :** to change from one vehicle or transportation line to another — **trans·fer·a·bil·i·ty** \(ˌ)tran(t)s-ˌfər-ə-'bil-ət-ē\ n — **trans·fer·a·ble** \tran(t)s-'fər-ə-bəl\ adj — **trans·fer·al** \-'fər-əl\ n — **trans·fer·rer** \-'fər-ər\ n

²trans·fer \'tran(t)s-ˌfər\ n **1 :** conveyance of right, title, or interest in real or personal property from one person to another **2 :** an act, process, or instance of transferring **:** TRANSFERENCE **3 :** one that transfers or is transferred; esp **:** a graphic image transferred by contact from one surface to another **4 :** a place where a transfer is made

(as of trains to ferries) **5 :** a ticket entitling a passenger on a public conveyance to continue his journey on another route

trans·fer·ase \-(ˌ)fər-ˌās\ n **:** an enzyme that promotes transfer of a group from one molecule to another

trans·fer·ee \ˌtran(t)s-(ˌ)fər-'ē\ n **1 :** a person to whom a conveyance is made **2 :** one transferred

trans·fer·ence \tran(t)s-'fər-ən(t)s\ n **:** an act, process, or instance of transferring **:** TRANSFER

trans·fer·or \tran(t)s-'fər-ər\ n **:** one that conveys a title, right, or property

trans·fig·u·ra·tion \(ˌ)tran(t)s-ˌfig-(y)ə-'rā-shən\ n **1 :** a change of form or appearance; esp **:** a glorifying or exalting change **2** cap **a :** the supernatural change in the appearance of Jesus on the mountain **b :** a church festival on August 6 commemorating this

trans·fig·ure \tran(t)s-'fig-yər, esp Brit -'fig-ər\ vt **1 :** to change the form or appearance of **:** METAMORPHOSE **2 :** to make bright or radiant **:** EXALT, GLORIFY **syn** see TRANSFORM

trans·fix \tran(t)s-'fiks\ vt **1 :** to pierce through with or as if with a pointed weapon **:** IMPALE **2 :** to hold motionless by or as if by piercing — **trans·fix·ion** \-'fik-shən\ n

trans·form \tran(t)s-'form\ vb **1 a :** to change in composition, structure, or character **:** CONVERT **b :** to change in outward appearance **2 :** to change in mathematical form without altering value or meaning **3 :** to change (a current) in potential (as from high voltage to low) or in type (as from alternating to direct) — **trans·form·a·tive** \-'for-mət-iv\ adj

syn TRANSFORM, METAMORPHOSE, TRANSMUTE, TRANSFIGURE mean to change something into a different thing. TRANSFORM implies a change in form, nature, or function ⟨transformed a desert into a fertile plain⟩ METAMORPHOSE suggests an abrupt or striking alteration induced as if supernaturally or by chemical or other natural agencies ⟨the ugly duckling metamorphosed into a swan⟩ TRANSMUTE implies a change from a lower to a higher element or thing ⟨believed base metals could be transmuted into gold⟩ TRANSFIGURE implies a change that exalts and glorifies

trans·form·a·ble \-'for-mə-bəl\ adj **:** capable of being transformed

trans·for·ma·tion \ˌtran(t)s-fər-'mā-shən\ n **1 :** an act, process, or instance of transforming or being transformed **2 :** false hair esp. as worn by a woman **3 :** the operation of changing one configuration or expression into another in accordance with a mathematical rule

trans·form·er \tran(t)s-'for-mər\ n **:** one that transforms; esp **:** a device without moving parts for changing an electric current into one of higher or lower voltage by electromagnetic induction without changing the current energy

trans·fuse \tran(t)s-'fyüz\ vt [L transfus-, transfundere, fr. trans- + fundere to pour] **1 a :** to cause to pass from one to another **:** TRANSMIT **b :** to diffuse into or through **:** PERMEATE **2 a :** to transfer (as blood or saline) into a vein of a man or animal **b :** to subject (a patient) to transfusion — **trans·fus·i·ble** or **trans·fus·a·ble** \-'fyü-zə-bəl\ adj — **trans·fu·sion** \-'fyü-zhən\ n

trans·gress \tran(t)s-'gres, tranz-\ vb [L transgress-, transgredi, fr. trans- + gradi to step] **1 :** to go beyond limits set by **:** VIOLATE ⟨transgress the divine law⟩ **2 :** to pass beyond or go over a limit or boundary **3 :** to violate a command or law **:** SIN — **trans·gres·sor** \-'gres-ər\ n

trans·gres·sion \-'gresh-ən\ n **:** an act, process, or instance of transgressing; esp **:** violation of a law, command, or duty

tran·ship var of TRANSSHIP

tran·sience \'tran-chən(t)s\ n **:** the quality or state of being transient

¹tran·sient \-chənt\ adj [L transeunt-, transiens, prp. of transire to cross, pass, fr. trans- + ire to go] **1 :** not lasting or staying long ⟨a hotel accepts transient guests⟩ **2 :** changing in form or appearance **:** SHIFTING ⟨a transient scene⟩ — **tran·sient·ly** adv

syn TRANSITORY: TRANSIENT applies to what is short in duration and passes quickly ⟨transient guests⟩ ⟨transient as music⟩ TRANSITORY stresses the inevitability of changing, ending, or dying out ⟨transitory fads and fashions⟩

ə **abut;** ᵊ **kitten;** ər **further;** a **back;** ā **bake;** ä **cot, cart;** au **out;** ch **chin;** e **less;** ē **easy;** g **gift;** i **trip;** ī **life**

²**transient** *n* **:** one that is transient: as **a :** a transient guest **b :** a person traveling about usu. in search of work

tran·sis·tor \tran-'zis-tər, -'sis-\ *n* [¹*transfer* + *resistor;* fr. its transferring an electrical signal across a resistor] **:** an electronic device similar to the electron tube in use (as amplification and rectification) consisting of a small block of a semiconductor (as germanium) that has at least three electrodes

tran·sis·tor·ize \-tə-,rīz\ *vt* **:** to equip (a device) with transistors

¹**tran·sit** \'tran(t)s-ət, 'tranz-\ *n* [L *transitus,* fr. *transire* to cross, pass, fr. *trans-* + *ire* to go] **1 a :** an act, process, or instance of passing through or over **:** PASSAGE **b** (1) **:** conveyance of persons or things from one place to another ⟨goods lost in *transit*⟩ (2) **:** local transportation of people by public conveyance or a system of such transportation **2 a :** passage of a celestial body over the meridian of a place or through the field of a telescope **b :** passage of a smaller body (as Venus) across the disk of a larger (as the sun) **3 :** a theodolite with the telescope mounted so that it can be transited

²**transit** *vb* **1 :** to make a transit **2 a :** to pass or cause to pass over or through **b :** to pass across **3 :** to turn (a telescope) about the horizontal transverse axis in surveying

transit instrument *n* **1 :** a telescope mounted at right angles to a horizontal east-west axis and used with a clock and chronograph for observing the time of transit of a celestial body over the meridian of a place **2 :** TRANSIT 3

tran·si·tion \tran(t)s-'ish-ən, tranz-\ *n* **1 :** a passing from one state, stage, place, or subject to another **:** CHANGE ⟨*transition* from war to peacetime⟩ **2 a :** a musical modulation **b :** a musical passage leading from one section of a piece to another — **tran·si·tion·al** \-'ish-nəl, -ən-ᵊl\ *adj* — **tran·si·tion·al·ly** \-ē\ *adv*

tran·si·tive \'tran(t)s-ət-iv, 'tranz-\ *adj* **1 :** characterized by having or containing a direct object ⟨a *transitive* verb⟩ **2 :** being a relation such that if *A* is so related to *B* and *B* is so related to *C,* then *A* is so related to *C* ⟨equality is a *transitive* relation⟩ **3 :** TRANSITIONAL — **tran·si·tive·ly** *adv* — **tran·si·tive·ness** *n* — **tran·si·tiv·i·ty** \,tran(t)s-ə-'tiv-ət-ē, ,tranz-\ *n*

tran·si·to·ry \'tran(t)s-ə-,tōr-ē, 'tranz-, -,tȯr-\ *adj* **:** lasting only a short time **:** SHORT-LIVED, TEMPORARY **syn** see TRANSIENT — **tran·si·to·ri·ly** \,tran(t)s-ə-'tōr-ə-lē, ,tranz-, -'tȯr-\ *adv* — **tran·si·to·ri·ness** \'tran(t)s-ə-,tōr-ē-nəs, 'tranz-, -,tȯr-\ *n*

trans·late \tran(t)s-'lāt, tranz-\ *vb* [L *translat-,* used as stem of *transferre* to transfer, translate] **1 a :** to bear or change from one place, state, form, or appearance to another **:** TRANSFER, TRANSFORM ⟨*translate* plans into action⟩ **b :** to convey to heaven or to a nontemporal condition without death **2 a :** to turn from one language into another **b :** to transfer or turn from one set of symbols into another **:** TRANSCRIBE **c :** PARAPHRASE, EXPLAIN — **trans·lat·a·bil·i·ty** \-,lāt-ə-'bil-ət-ē\ *n* — **trans·lat·a·ble** \-'lāt-ə-bəl\ *adj* — **trans·la·tor** \-'lāt-ər\ *n*

trans·la·tion \tran(t)s-'lā-shən, tranz-\ *n* **:** an act, process, or instance of translating: as **a :** a rendering from one language into another; *also* **:** the product of such a rendering **b :** CONVERSION, TRANSFORMATION — **trans·la·tion·al** \-shnəl, -shən-ᵊl\ *adj*

trans·la·tive \-'lāt-iv\ *adj* **1 :** of, relating to, or involving removal or transference from one person or place to another **2 :** of, relating to, or serving to translate from one language or system into another

trans·lit·er·ate \tran(t)s-'lit-ə-,rāt, tranz-\ *vt* [L *littera* letter] **:** to represent or spell in the characters of another alphabet — **trans·lit·er·a·tion** \-,lit-ə-'rā-shən\ *n*

trans·lo·cate \'tran(t)s-lō-,kāt, 'tranz-, tran(t)s-'-, tranz-'\ *vt* **:** to transfer by translocation

trans·lo·ca·tion \,tran(t)s-lō-'kā-shən, ,tranz-\ *n* **:** a changing of location **:** DISPLACEMENT: as **a :** the conducting of soluble material from one part of a plant to another **b :** exchange of parts between nonhomologous chromosomes

trans·lu·cence \tran(t)s-'lüs-ᵊn(t)s, tranz-\ *or* **trans·lu·cen·cy** \-ᵊn-sē\ *n* **:** the quality or state of being translucent

trans·lu·cent \-ᵊnt\ *adj* [L *translucēre* to shine through,

fr. *trans-* + *lucēre* to shine, fr. *luc-, lux* light] **1 :** shining or glowing through **:** LUMINOUS **2 :** admitting and diffusing light so that objects beyond cannot be clearly distinguished ⟨frosted glass is *translucent*⟩ **syn** see CLEAR — **trans·lu·cent·ly** *adv*

trans·mi·gra·tion \,tran(t)s-,mī-'grā-shən, ,tranz-\ *n* **1 :** the changing of one's home from one country to another **:** MIGRATION **2 :** the passing of a soul into another body after death — **trans·mi·grate** \tran(t)s-'mī-,grāt, tranz-\ *vi* — **trans·mi·gra·to·ry** \-'mī-grə-,tōr-ē, -,tȯr-\ *adj*

trans·mis·si·ble \tran(t)s-'mis-ə-bəl, tranz-\ *adj* **:** capable of being transmitted ⟨*transmissible* diseases⟩ — **trans·mis·si·bil·i·ty** \-,mis-ə-'bil-ət-ē\ *n*

trans·mis·sion \-'mish-ən\ *n* **1 :** an act, process, or instance of transmitting something **2 :** the passage of radio waves in the space between transmitting and receiving stations; *also* **:** the act or process of transmitting by radio or television **3 :** the gear including the change gear and the propeller shaft by which power is transmitted from an automobile engine to the live axle **4 :** something transmitted — **trans·mis·sive** \-'mis-iv\ *adj* — **trans·mis·siv·i·ty** \,tran(t)s-mis-'iv-ət-ē, ,tranz-\ *n*

trans·mit \tran(t)s-'mit, tranz-\ *vb* **trans·mit·ted; trans·mit·ting** [L *transmiss-, transmittere,* fr. *trans-* + *mittere* to send] **1 a :** to send or transfer from one person or place to another **:** FORWARD **b :** to convey by or as if by inheritance **c :** to convey (infection) abroad or to another **2 a** (1) **:** to cause (as light or force) to pass or be conveyed through space or a medium (2) **:** to admit the passage of ⟨glass *transmits* light⟩ **b :** to send out a signal either by radio waves or over a wire — **trans·mit·ta·ble** \-'mit-ə-bəl\ *adj* — **trans·mit·tal** \-'mit-ᵊl\ *n*

trans·mit·ter \-'mit-ər\ *n* **1 :** one that transmits ⟨a *transmitter* of disease⟩ **2 :** the instrument in a telegraph system that sends out messages **3 :** the part of a telephone that includes the mouthpiece and a mechanism that picks up sound waves and sends them over the wire **4 :** the apparatus that sends out radio or television signals or the building in which it is housed

trans·mog·ri·fy \tran(t)s-'mäg-rə-,fī, tranz-\ *vt* **-fied; -fy·ing :** to change or alter often with grotesque or humorous effect — **trans·mog·ri·fi·ca·tion** \-,mäg-rə-fə-'kā-shən\ *n*

trans·mu·ta·tion \,tran(t)s-myü-'tā-shən, ,tranz-\ *n* **:** an act or instance of transmuting or being transmuted: as **a :** the conversion of base metals into gold or silver **b :** the conversion of one element or nuclide into another either naturally or artificially — **trans·mut·a·tive** \tran(t)s-'myüt-ət-iv, tranz-\ *adj*

trans·mute \tran(t)s-'myüt, tranz-\ *vb* [L *transmutare,* fr. *trans-* + *mutare* to change] **1 :** to change or alter in form, appearance, or nature **:** CONVERT **2 :** to subject (as an element or base metal) to transmutation **3 :** to undergo transmutation **syn** see TRANSFORM — **trans·mut·a·ble** \-'myüt-ə-bəl\ *adj*

trans·na·tion·al \(')tran(t)s-'nash-nəl, (')tranz-, -ən-ᵊl\ *adj* **:** extending beyond national boundaries

trans·oce·an·ic \(,)tran(t)s-,ō-shē-'an-ik, (,)tranz-\ *adj* **1 :** lying or dwelling beyond the ocean **2 :** crossing or extending across the ocean ⟨*transoceanic* cables⟩

tran·som \'tran(t)-səm\ *n* [prob. fr. L *transtrum,* fr. *trans* across] **1 :** a transverse piece in a structure **:** CROSSPIECE: as **a :** LINTEL **b :** a horizontal crossbar in a window, over a door, or between a door and a window or fanlight above it **c :** any of several transverse timbers or beams secured to the sternpost of a boat **2 :** a window above a door or other window built on and commonly hinged to a transom

tran·son·ic *also* **trans·son·ic** \tran(t)s-'sän-ik, tran-'sän-\ *adj* [*trans-* + *-sonic* (as in *supersonic*)] **1 :** being or relating to a speed approximating the speed of sound in air — often used of aeronautical speeds between 600 and 900 miles per hour **2 :** moving, capable of moving, or utilizing air currents moving at a transonic speed ⟨*transonic* bomber⟩

trans·pa·cif·ic \,tran(t)s-pə-'sif-ik\ *adj* **:** crossing or extending across or situated beyond the Pacific ocean

trans·par·ence \-'par-ən(t)s, -'per-\ *n* **:** TRANSPARENCY 1

trans·par·en·cy \-ən-sē\ *n, pl* **-cies 1 :** the quality or state of being transparent **2 :** a picture or design on glass, thin cloth, paper, or film viewed by light shining through it or by projection

trans·par·ent \-ənt\ *adj* [ML *transparēre* to show through, fr. L *trans-* + *parēre* to show oneself, appear] **1 a** (1) : having the property of transmitting light so that bodies lying beyond are entirely visible (2) : pervious to any specified form of radiation (as X rays or ultraviolet light) **b** : fine or sheer enough to be seen through ⟨*transparent* gauze⟩ **2 a** : FRANK, GUILELESS **b** : easily detected or seen through : OBVIOUS ⟨*transparent* falsehood⟩ **syn** see CLEAR — **trans·par·ent·ly** *adv* — **trans·par·ent·ness** *n*

tran·spi·ra·tion \ˌtran(t)s-pə-ˈrā-shən\ *n* : the act or process or an instance of transpiring; *esp* : the passage of watery vapor from a living body through a membrane or pores — compare PERSPIRATION

tran·spire \tran(t)s-ˈpī(ə)r\ *vb* [MF *transpirer*, fr. L *trans-* + *spirare* to breathe] **1 a** : to pass off or give passage to (a fluid) through pores or interstices; *esp* : to excrete watery vapor through a membrane or pores ⟨a large tree may *transpire* tons of water in a season⟩ **b** : to escape in the form of a vapor esp. from a living body **2** : to give off vaporous material **3** : to pass in the form of a vapor from a living body **4** : to become known or apparent : come to light **5** : to come to pass : OCCUR **syn** see HAPPEN

¹trans·plant \tran(t)s-ˈplant\ *vb* **1** : to lift and reset (a plant) in another soil or situation **2** : to remove from one place and settle or introduce elsewhere : TRANSPORT **3** : to transfer (an organ or tissue) from one part or individual to another **4** : to admit of being transplanted — **trans·plant·a·ble** \-ə-bəl\ *adj* — **trans·plan·ta·tion** \ˌtran(t)s-ˌplan-ˈtā-shən\ *n* — **trans·plant·er** \tran(t)s-ˈplant-ər\ *n*

²trans·plant \ˈtran(t)s-ˌplant\ *n* **1** : the act or process of transplanting **2** : something transplanted

trans·po·lar \(ˈ)tran(t)s-ˈpō-lər\ *adj* : going or extending across either of the polar regions

¹trans·port \tran(t)s-ˈpōrt, -ˈpȯrt\ *vt* [L *transportare*, fr. *trans-* + *portare* to carry] **1** : to convey from one place to another : CARRY **2** : ENRAPTURE ⟨*transported* with delight⟩ **3** : to send to a penal colony overseas — **trans·port·a·bil·i·ty** \-ˌpōrt-ə-ˈbil-ət-ē, -ˌpȯrt-\ *n* — **trans·port·a·ble** \-ˈpōrt-ə-bəl, -ˈpȯrt-\ *adj* — **trans·port·er** *n*

²trans·port \ˈtran(t)s-ˌpōrt, -ˌpȯrt\ *n* **1** : the act of transporting : TRANSPORTATION **2** : strong or intensely pleasurable emotion : ECSTASY, RAPTURE ⟨*transports* of joy⟩ **3 a** : a ship for carrying soldiers or military equipment **b** : a vehicle (as a truck or plane) used to transport persons or goods **c** : a system of public conveyance : TRANSIT **4** : that which is transported

trans·por·ta·tion \ˌtran(t)s-pər-ˈtā-shən\ *n* **1** : an act, process, or instance of transporting or being transported **2** : banishment to a penal colony **3 a** : means of conveyance or travel from one place to another **b** : public conveyance of passengers or goods esp. as a commercial enterprise

trans·pose \tran(t)s-ˈpōz\ *vt* [MF *transposer*, irreg. fr. L *transponere* to change the position of, fr. *trans-* + *ponere* to put, place] **1** : TRANSFORM, TRANSMUTE **2** : TRANSLATE **3** : to transfer from one place or period to another : SHIFT **4** : to change the relative place or normal order of : alter the sequence of ⟨*transpose* letters to change the spelling⟩ **5** : to write or perform (a musical composition) in a different key **6** : to bring (a term) from one side of an algebraic equation to the other with change of sign — **trans·pos·a·ble** \-ˈpō-zə-bəl\ *adj* — **trans·po·si·tion** \ˌtran(t)s-pə-ˈzish-ən\ *n*

trans·ship \tran-ˈship, tran(t)s-\ *vb* : to transfer for further transportation from one ship or conveyance to another — **trans·ship·ment** \-mənt\ *n*

tran·sub·stan·ti·ate \ˌtran(t)-səb-ˈstan-chē-ˌāt\ *vb* : to change into another substance : TRANSMUTE

tran·sub·stan·ti·a·tion \-ˌstan-chē-ˈā-shən\ *n* **1** : an act or instance of transubstantiating or being transubstantiated **2** : the change in the consecrated bread and wine at Mass in substance but not in appearance to the body and blood of Christ

tran·sude \tran(t)s-ˈ(y)üd, tranz-\ *vb* [L *trans-* + *sudare* to sweat] : to pass or allow to pass through a membrane or permeable substance : EXUDE — **tran·su·da·tion** \ˌtran(t)s-(y)ü-ˈdā-shən, ˌtranz-\ *n* — **tran·su·da·tion** \ˌtran(t)s-(y)ü-ˈdā-shən, ˌtranz-\ *n*

trans·ura·ni·um \ˌtran-shə-ˈrā-nē-əm, ˌtran-zhə-\ *or*

trans·uran·ic \-ˈran-ik, -ˈrā-nik\ *adj* : having an atomic number greater than that of uranium

¹trans·ver·sal \tran(t)s-ˈvər-səl, tranz-\ *adj* : TRANSVERSE ⟨*transversal* line⟩ — **trans·ver·sal·ly** \-sə-lē\ *adv*

²transversal *n* : a line that intersects a system of lines

¹trans·verse \tran(t)s-ˈvərs, tranz-ˈ, ˈtran(t)s-ˌ, ˈtranz-\ *adj* [L *transversus*, fr. pp. of *transvertere* to turn across, fr. *trans-* + *vertere* to turn] : lying or being across : set crosswise ⟨the *transverse* pieces in a window frame⟩ — **trans·verse·ly** *adv*

²trans·verse \ˈtran(t)s-ˌvərs, ˈtranz-\ *n* : something transverse (as a piece, muscle, or part)

¹trap \ˈtrap\ *n* [OE *treppe* & OF *trape* (of Gmc origin)] **1** : a device (as a snare or pitfall) for catching animals; *esp* : one that holds by springing shut suddenly **2** : something by which one is caught or stopped unawares **3 a** : a device for hurling clay pigeons into the air **b** : a hazard on a golf course consisting of a depression containing sand **4** : a light usu. one-horse carriage with springs **5** : any of various devices for preventing passage of something often while allowing other matter to proceed **6** : a device for drains or sewers consisting of a bend or partitioned chamber in which the liquid forms a seal to prevent the passage of sewer gas **7** *pl* : PERCUSSION INSTRUMENTS

²trap *vb* **trapped**; **trap·ping** **1 a** : to catch in or as if in a trap : ENSNARE **b** : to place in a restricted position : CONFINE **2** : to provide with a trap **3** : to separate out (as water from steam) **4** : to engage in trapping animals (as for fur) **syn** see CATCH — **trap·per** *n*

³trap *vt* **trapped**; **trap·ping** [ME *trappen*, fr. *trappe* cloth, modif. of MF *drap*] : to adorn with or as if with trappings

⁴trap *also* **trap·rock** \ˈtrap-ˌräk\ *n* [Sw *trapp*] : any of various dark-colored fine-grained igneous rocks used esp. in road making

trap·door \ˈtrap-ˈdō(ə)r, -ˈdȯ(ə)r\ *n* : a lifting or sliding door covering an opening in a roof, ceiling, or floor

trap·door spider *n* : any of various spiders that build silk-lined underground nests topped with a hinged lid

tra·peze \tra-ˈpēz\ *n* [F *trapèze*, fr. NL *trapezium*] : a gymnastic or acrobatic apparatus consisting of a short horizontal bar suspended at a height by two parallel ropes

tra·pez·ist \-ˈpē-zəst\ *n* : a performer on the trapeze

tra·pe·zi·um \trə-ˈpē-zē-əm\ *n*, *pl* **-zi·ums** *or* **-zia** \-zē-ə\ [NL, fr. Gk *trapezion*, lit., small table, dim. of *trapeza* table, fr. *tra-* four (akin to E *four*) + *peza* foot (akin to E *foot*)] **1** : a quadrilateral having no two sides parallel **2** *Brit* : TRAPEZOID 2

tra·pe·zi·us \-zē-əs\ *n* [NL, fr. *trapezium*; fr. the figure formed by the pair] : a large flat triangular superficial muscle of each side of the back

trapezium

trap·e·zoid \ˈtrap-ə-ˌzȯid\ *n* **1** *Brit* : TRAPEZIUM 1 **2** : a quadrilateral having only two sides parallel — **trap·e·zoi·dal** \ˌtrap-ə-ˈzȯid-ᵊl\ *adj*

trap·nest \ˈtrap-ˌnest\ *n* : a nest with a hinged door designed to close on and confine an entering hen so that individual egg production can be determined — **trap·nest** *vt*

trap·ping \ˈtrap-iŋ\ *n* **1** : CAPARISON 1 — usu. used in pl. **2** *pl* : outward decoration or dress : ORNAMENTS

Trap·pist \ˈtrap-əst\ *n* [F *trappiste*, fr. La *Trappe*, French monastery] : a monk of an austere branch of the Cistercian Order — **Trappist** *adj*

traps \ˈtraps\ *n pl* : personal belongings : LUGGAGE

trap·shoot·ing \ˈtrap-ˌshüt-iŋ\ *n* : shooting at clay pigeons sprung into the air from a trap — **trap·shoot·er** \-ˌshüt-ər\ *n*

trash \ˈtrash\ *n* [of Scand origin] **1** : something worth little or nothing: as **a** : JUNK, RUBBISH **b** : NONSENSE **c** : inferior or worthless artistic matter **2** : something in a crumbled or broken condition or mass; *esp* : debris from pruning or processing plant material **3** : a worthless person; *also* : RIFFRAFF

trash farming *n* : a method of cultivation in which the soil is loosened by methods that leave vegetational residues (as stubble) on or near the surface to check erosion and serve as a mulch

trashy \ˈtrash-ē\ *adj* **trash·i·er**; **-est** : resembling trash : WORTHLESS — **trash·i·ness** *n*

trat·to·ria \ˌträt-ə-ˈrē-ə\ *n* [It, fr. *trattore* restaurant owner, fr. F *traiteur*, fr. *traiter* to treat, entertain] **:** an eating house **:** RESTAURANT

trau·ma \'traù-mə, 'trò-\ *n, pl* **trau·ma·ta** \-mət-ə\ *or* **traumas** [Gk *traumat-, trauma* wound; akin to E *throe*] **1 a :** a bodily injury caused by a physical force applied from without ⟨surgical *trauma*⟩ **b :** a disordered psychic or behavioral state resulting from stress or injury **2 :** a cause of trauma — **trau·mat·ic** \trə-'mat-ik, trò-, traù-\ *adj* — **trau·mat·i·cal·ly** \-'mat-i-k(ə-)lē\ *adv*

¹tra·vail \trə-'vāl, 'trav-,āl\ *n* [OF, fr. *travaillier* to torture, travail, fr. LL *tripalium* instrument of torture, fr. L *tripalis* having three stakes, fr. *tri-* + *palus* stake] **1 a :** work esp. of a painful or laborious nature **:** TOIL **b :** a piece of work **:** TASK **c :** AGONY, TORMENT **2 :** LABOR, PARTURITION

²travail *vi* **:** to labor hard **:** TOIL

¹trav·el \'trav-əl\ *vb* **-eled** *or* **-elled; -el·ing** *or* **-el·ling** \'trav-(ə-)liŋ\ [OF *travaillier* to travail] **1 :** to journey from place to place or to a distant place **2 :** to journey from place to place selling or taking orders **3 a :** to move or advance from one place to another **b :** to undergo transportation **4 :** to journey through or over **:** TRAVERSE ⟨this road can be *traveled* only on horseback⟩

²travel *n* **1 a :** the act of traveling **:** PASSAGE **b :** JOURNEY, TRIP — often used in pl. **2** *pl* **:** an account of one's travels **3 :** the number traveling **:** TRAFFIC **4 a :** MOVEMENT, PROGRESSION **b :** the motion of a piece of machinery; *esp* **:** reciprocating motion

travel agency *n* **:** an agency engaged in selling, arranging, or furnishing information about personal transportation or travel — called also *travel bureau* — **travel agent** *n*

trav·eled *or* **trav·elled** \'trav-əld\ *adj* **1 :** experienced in travel **2 :** used by travelers ⟨a *traveled* road⟩

trav·el·er *or* **trav·el·ler** \'trav-(ə-)lər\ *n* **:** one that travels

traveler's check *n* **:** a draft purchased from a bank or express company and signed by the purchaser at the time of purchase and again at the time of cashing as a precaution against forgery

traveling bag *n* **:** a bag carried by hand and designed to hold a traveler's clothing and personal articles

traveling salesman *n* **:** a traveling representative of a business concern who solicits orders

trav·el·ogue *also* **trav·el·og** \'trav-ə-,lòg\ *n* **:** a usu. illustrated lecture on travel

tra·ver·sal \trə-'vər-səl\ *n* **:** the act or an instance of traversing

¹trav·erse \'trav-ərs, *esp for 5 also* trə-'vərs\ *n* [MF, fr. *traverser* to cross, fr. LL *transversare*, fr. L *transversus* transverse] **1 :** something that crosses or lies across **2 :** OBSTACLE, ADVERSITY **3 :** a gallery of communication from side to side in a large building **4 :** a route or way across or over (as a zigzag course) **5 :** the act or an instance of traversing **:** CROSSING **6 :** a protective projecting wall or bank of earth in a trench **7 :** a line surveyed across a plot of ground

²tra·verse \trə-'vərs\ *vb* **1 :** to go against or act in opposition to **:** OPPOSE, THWART **2 :** to pass through, across, or over **3 :** to make a study of **:** EXAMINE **4 :** to ascend, descend, or cross (a slope or gap) at an angle **5 :** to move back and forth or from side to side **6 :** to move or turn laterally **:** SWIVEL **7 :** to climb or ski at an angle or in a zigzag course — **tra·vers·a·ble** \-'vər-sə-bəl\ *adj* — **tra·vers·er** *n*

³trav·erse \'trav-(,)ərs, trə-'vərs\ *adj* **:** lying across **:** TRANSVERSE

trav·erse jury \'trav-ərs-\ *n* **:** PETIT JURY

trav·er·tine *also* **trav·er·tin** \'trav-ər-,tēn, -tən\ *n* [F *travertin*, fr. It *tivertino, travertino*, fr. L *tiburtinus* of Tivoli, fr. *Tibur* Tivoli] **:** a massive usu. layered calcium carbonate formed by deposition from spring waters or esp. from hot springs

¹trav·es·ty \'trav-ə-stē\ *n, pl* **-ties** [obs. *travesty* disguised, parodied, fr. F *travesti*, pp. of *travestir* to disguise, fr. It *travestire*, fr. *tra-* trans- + *vestire* to dress, fr. L, fr. *vestis* clothing] **1 :** a burlesque and usu. grotesque translation or imitation **2 :** an inferior imitation or likeness ⟨a *travesty* of justice⟩ **syn** see CARICATURE

²travesty *vt* **-tied; -ty·ing :** to make a travesty of **:** PARODY

tra·vois \trə-'vòi, 'trav-,òi\ *also* **tra·voise** \-'vòiz, -,òiz\ *n, pl* **tra·vois** \-'vòiz, -,òiz\ *also* **tra·vois·es** \-'vòi-zəz, -,òi-zəz\ [CanF *travois*] **:** a vehicle used by Plains Indians

consisting of two trailing poles serving as shafts and bearing a platform or net for the load

¹trawl \'tròl\ *vb* **:** to fish or catch with a trawl — **trawl·er** *n*

²trawl *n* **1 :** a large conical net dragged along the sea bottom in fishing **2 :** SETLINE

tray \'trā\ *n* [OE *trīg, trēg*] **:** an open receptacle with flat bottom and low rim for holding, carrying, or exhibiting articles ⟨a waiter's *tray*⟩ ⟨the *trays* of a trunk⟩

treach·er·ous \'trech-(ə-)rəs\ *adj* **1 :** guilty of or inclined to treachery **2 a :** UNRELIABLE ⟨a *treacherous* memory⟩ **b :** giving a false appearance of safety ⟨*treacherous* quicksand⟩ — **treach·er·ous·ly** *adv* — **treach·er·ous·ness** *n*

treach·ery \'trech-(ə-)rē\ *n, pl* **-er·ies** [OF *trecherie*, fr. *trechier* to deceive] **1 :** violation of allegiance or of faith and confidence **:** TREASON **2 :** an act of perfidy or treason

trea·cle \'trē-kəl\ *n* [MF *triacle*, an antidote against poison, fr. L *theriaca*, fr. Gk *thēriakē* antidote against a poisonous bite, fr. *thērion*, dim. of *thēr* wild animal] **1** *chiefly Brit* **:** MOLASSES **2 :** something (as a tone of voice) heavily sweet and cloying — **trea·cly** \-k(ə-)lē\ *adj*

¹tread \'tred\ *vb* **trod** \'träd\; **trod·den** \'träd-ᵊn\ *or* **trod; tread·ing** [OE *tredan*] **1 a :** to step or walk on or over **b :** to walk along **:** FOLLOW **2 a :** to beat or press with the feet **:** TRAMPLE **b :** to subdue or repress as if by trampling **:** CRUSH **3 a :** to form by treading **:** BEAT ⟨*tread* a path⟩ **b :** to execute by stepping or dancing ⟨*tread* a measure⟩ **4 a :** to set foot **b :** to put one's foot **:** STEP — **tread·er** *n* — **tread water :** to keep the body nearly upright in the water and the head above water by a treading motion of the feet usu. aided by the hands

²tread *n* **1 :** a mark made by or as if by treading **2 :** the action, manner, or sound of treading or stepping **3 a :** the part of a sole that touches the ground **b :** the part of a wheel that bears on a road or rail; *esp* **:** the thickened face of an automobile tire **4 :** the distance between the points of contact with the ground of the two front wheels or the two rear wheels of a vehicle **5 :** the horizontal part of a step

¹trea·dle \'tred-ᵊl\ *n* [OE *tredel* step of a stair, fr. *tredan* to tread] **:** a lever or other device pressed by the foot to drive a machine

²treadle *vb* **trea·dled; trea·dling** \'tred-liŋ, -ᵊl-iŋ\ **:** to operate a treadle on a machine

tread·mill \'tred-,mil\ *n* **1 :** a device moved by persons treading on steps set around the rim of a wide wheel or by animals walking on an endless belt **2 :** a wearisome or monotonous routine

trea·son \'trēz-ᵊn\ *n* [ME *tresoun*, fr. OF *traison*, fr. ML *tradition-, traditio*, fr. L *tradere* to hand over, betray, fr. *trans-* + *dare* to give] **1 :** the betrayal of a trust **:** PERFIDY, TREACHERY **2 :** the offense of attempting by overt acts to overthrow the government of the state to which one owes allegiance or to bring about its defeat in war **syn** see SEDITION

trea·son·a·ble \'trēz-nə-bəl, -ᵊn-ə-bəl\ *adj* **:** relating to, consisting of, or involving treason — **trea·son·a·bly** \-blē\ *adv*

trea·son·ous \'trēz-nəs, -ᵊn-əs\ *adj* **:** TREASONABLE

¹trea·sure \'trezh-ər, 'trāzh-\ *n* [OF *tresor*, fr. L *thesaurus*, fr. Gk *thēsauros*] **1 a** (1) **:** wealth (as money, jewels, or precious metals) stored up or hoarded ⟨buried *treasure*⟩ (2) **:** RICHES **b :** a store of money in reserve **2 :** something of great worth or value; *also* **:** a person esteemed as rare or precious

²treasure *vt* **trea·sured; trea·sur·ing** \-(ə-)riŋ\ **1 :** to collect and store up (something of value) for future use **:** HOARD **2 :** to hold or keep as precious **:** CHERISH — **trea·sur·a·ble** \-(ə-)rə-bəl\ *adj*

treasure hunt *n* **:** a game in which each player or team tries to be first to find whatever has been hidden

trea·sur·er \'trezh-rər, 'trāzh-ər-ər, 'trāzh-\ *n* **:** a person trusted with charge of a treasure or a treasury; *esp* **:** an officer of a club, business, or government who has charge of money taken in and paid out — **trea·sur·er·ship** \-,ship\ *n*

treasure trove \'trezh-ər-,trōv, 'trāzh-\ *n* [AF *tresor trové*, fr. L, found treasure] **1 :** treasure found buried in the ground or hidden away and of unknown ownership **2 :** a discovery or something discovered that is full of things to be treasured

---

j joke; **ŋ** sing; **ō** flow; **ò** flaw; **òi** coin; **th** thin; **th̲** this; **ü** loot; **u̇** foot; **y** yet; **yü** few; **yu̇** furious; **zh** vision

trea·sury \'trezh-(ə-)rē, 'trāzh-\ *n, pl* **trea·sur·ies** **1 a** : a place in which stores of wealth are kept **b** : the place of deposit and disbursement of collected funds; *esp* : one where public revenues are deposited, kept, and disbursed **c** : funds kept in a place of deposit **2** *cap* : a governmental department in charge of finances **3** : a repository for treasures ⟨a *treasury* of poems⟩

treasury note *n* : a currency note issued by the U.S. Treasury in payment for silver bullion purchased under the Sherman Silver Purchase Act of 1890

¹treat \'trēt\ *vb* [OF *traitier*, fr. L *tractare* to handle, deal with, freq. of *trahere* to draw] **1** : to discuss terms of accommodation or settlement : NEGOTIATE **2 a** : to deal with a matter esp. in writing : DISCOURSE ⟨books *treating* of crime⟩ **b** : to present or represent artistically : to deal with : HANDLE **3 a** : to bear the expense of another's entertainment **b** : to provide with free food, entertainment, or enjoyment **4 a** : to behave or act toward : USE ⟨*treat* a horse cruelly⟩ **b** : to regard and deal with in a specified manner ⟨*treat* as confidential⟩ **5** : to care for or deal with medically or surgically **6** : to subject to some action (as of a chemical) ⟨*treat* soil with lime⟩ — **treat·er** *n*

²treat *n* **1** : an entertainment given without expense to those invited **2** : an esp. unexpected source of pleasure or amusement ⟨the *treat* of seeing him again⟩

trea·tise \'trēt-əs\ *n* : a book or an article treating a subject systematically ⟨a *treatise* on war⟩

treat·ment \'trēt-mənt\ *n* **1** : the act or manner or an instance of treating someone or something : HANDLING, USAGE **2** : a substance or technique used in treating

trea·ty \'trēt-ē\ *n, pl* **treaties** [MF *traité*, fr. ML *tractatus*, fr. L, treatment, fr. *tractare* to treat] **1** : the action of treating and esp. of negotiating **2** : an agreement or arrangement made by negotiation; *esp* : a contract between two or more states or sovereigns

treaty port *n* : one of a number of ports and inland cities in China, Japan, and Korea formerly open by treaty to foreign commerce

¹tre·ble \'treb-əl\ *n* [ME] **1 a** : the highest of the four voice parts in vocal music : SOPRANO **b** : a singer or instrument taking this part **c** : a high-pitched or shrill voice, tone, or sound **d** : the upper half of the musical pitch range **2** : something treble in construction, uses, amount, number, or value

²treble *adj* [MF, fr. L *triplus* triple] **1 a** : having three parts **b** : triple in number or amount **2 a** : relating to or having the range of a musical treble ⟨*treble* voice⟩ **b** : high-pitched : SHRILL — **tre·bly** \'treb-(ə-)lē\ *adv*

³treble *vb* **tre·bled; tre·bling** \'treb-(ə-)liŋ\ **1** : to make or become three times the size, amount, or number ⟨*treble* its weight⟩ **2** : to sing treble

treble clef *n* [fr. its use for the notation of treble parts] **1** : a clef that places G above middle C on the second line of the staff **2** : TREBLE STAFF

treble staff *n* : the musical staff carrying the treble clef

¹tree \'trē\ *n* [OE *trēow*] **1 a** : a woody perennial plant having a single usu. tall main stem with few or no branches on its lower part **b** : a shrub or herb of arborescent form ⟨rose *trees*⟩ ⟨a banana *tree*⟩ **2** : a piece of wood (as a post or pole) usu. adapted to a particular use or forming part of a structure or implement **3** : something in the form of or felt to resemble a tree: as **a** : a diagram that depicts a branching from an original stem ⟨genealogical *tree*⟩ **b** : a much-branched system of channels esp. in an animal body ⟨the vascular *tree*⟩ — **tree·less** \-ləs\ *adj* — **trææ·like** \-,līk\ *adj*

²tree *vt* **treed; tree·ing** **1 a** : to drive to or up a tree ⟨*treed* by a bull⟩ ⟨dogs *treeing* game⟩ **b** : to bring to bay : CORNER **2** : to furnish or fit with a tree ⟨*tree* an axle⟩

tree farm *n* : an area of forest land managed to ensure continuous commercial production

tree fern *n* : a tropical fern with a woody stalk and a crown of large often feathery fronds

tree house *n* : a structure (as a playhouse) built among the branches of a tree

tree of heaven *n* : an ailanthus widely grown as a shade and ornamental tree

tree surgery *n* : the profession of caring for specimen and shade trees; *also* : the practices (as operative treatment of disease or decay) belonging to this profession — **tree surgeon** *n*

tree toad *n* : any of numerous tailless amphibians that live in trees and usu. have adhesive disks on the toes — called also *tree frog;* compare SPRING PEEPER

tree·top \'trē-,täp\ *n* **1** : the topmost part of a tree **2** *pl* : the height or line marked by the tops of a group of trees

tref \'trāf\ *adj* [Yiddish *treyfe, treyf*, fr. Heb *ṭĕrēphāh* animal torn by wild beasts] : ritually unclean according to Jewish law

tre·foil \'trē-,fȯil, 'tref-,ȯil\ *n* [MF *trefeuil*, fr. L *trifolium*, fr. *tri-* + *folium* leaf] **1 a** : CLOVER; *also* : any of several leguminous herbs having leaves with three leaflets **b** : a trifoliolate leaf **2** : an ornament or symbol in the form of a 3-parted leaf

trefoil 2

¹trek \'trek\ *n* **1** *chiefly southern Africa* : an organized migration of a group of settlers by ox wagon **2** : a slow or difficult journey or migration

²trek *vi* **trekked; trek·king** [Afrik, fr. MD *trecken* to pull, haul, migrate] **1** *chiefly southern Africa* : to migrate by ox wagon or in a train of such wagons **2** : to make one's way arduously — **trek·ker** *n*

¹trel·lis \'trel-əs\ *n* [MF *treliz* fabric of coarse weave, trellis] : a frame of latticework used esp. as a screen or a support for climbing plants

²trellis *vt* **1** : to provide with or train on a trellis ⟨*trellis* a vine⟩ **2** : to cross or interlace on or through : INTERWEAVE

trel·lis·work \-,wərk\ *n* : LATTICEWORK

trem·a·tode \'trem-ə-,tōd\ *n* [Gk *trēmatōdēs* pierced with holes, fr. *trēmat-, trēma* hole] : any of a class (Trematoda) of parasitic flatworms including the flukes — **trematode** *adj*

¹trem·ble \'trem-bəl\ *vi* **trem·bled; trem·bling** \-b(ə-)liŋ\ [MF *trembler*, fr. ML *tremulare*, fr. L *tremulus* tremulous] **1** : to shake involuntarily (as with fear or cold) : SHIVER **2** : to move, sound, pass, or come to pass as if shaken or tremulous **3** : to be affected with fear or doubt ⟨*tremble* for the safety of a friend⟩ — **trem·bler** \-b(ə-)lər\ *n*

²tremble *n* **1** : a fit or spell of involuntary shaking or quivering **2** : a tremor or series of tremors

trem·bly \'trem-b(ə-)lē\ *adj* : TREMBLING, TREMULOUS

tre·men·dous \tri-'men-dəs\ *adj* [L *tremendus*, fr. *tremere* to tremble] **1** : such as may excite trembling or arouse dread, awe, or terror : DREADFUL **2** : astonishing by reason of extreme size, power, greatness, or excellence **syn** see MONSTROUS — **tre·men·dous·ly** *adv* — **tre·men·dous·ness** *n*

trem·o·lo \'trem-ə-,lō\ *n, pl* **-los** [It, fr. *tremolo* tremulous, fr. L *tremulus*] **1 a** : the rapid reiteration of a musical tone or of alternating tones to produce a tremulous effect **b** : a perceptible rapid variation of pitch in singing similar to the vibrato of a stringed instrument **2** : a mechanical device in an organ for causing a tremulous effect

trem·or \'trem-ər\ *n* [L, fr. *tremere* to tremble] **1** : a trembling or shaking usu. from weakness or disease **2** : a quivering or vibratory motion (as of the earth or a leaf) **3** : a feeling of uncertainty or insecurity

trem·u·lant \'trem-yə-lənt\ *adj* : TREMULOUS, TREMBLING

trem·u·lous \'trem-yə-ləs\ *adj* [L *tremulus*, fr. *tremere* to tremble] **1** : characterized by or affected with trembling or tremors ⟨*tremulous* hands⟩ **2** : affected with timidity : TIMOROUS ⟨a shy *tremulous* girl⟩ **3** : such as is caused by a tremulous state ⟨a *tremulous* smile⟩ **4** : exceedingly sensitive — **trem·u·lous·ly** *adv* — **trem·u·lous·ness** *n*

¹trench \'trench\ *n* [MF *trenche* act of cutting, fr. *trenchier* to cut] **1** : a long narrow cut in land : DITCH; *also* : a similar depression in an ocean floor **2** : a long ditch protected by a bank of earth thrown before it that is used to shelter soldiers

²trench *vb* **1** : to protect with or as if with a trench **2** : to cut a trench in : DITCH **3** : to come close : VERGE ⟨his answer *trenched* on impudence⟩

tren·chan·cy \'tren-chən-sē\ *n* : the quality of being trenchant

tren·chant \'tren-chənt\ *adj* [MF, prp. of *trenchier* to cut] **1** : having a sharp edge or point : CUTTING ⟨a *trenchant* blade⟩ ⟨*trenchant* sarcasm⟩ **2** : sharply clear : PENETRATING ⟨a *trenchant* analysis of a situation⟩ **3** : mentally energetic **syn** see INCISIVE — **tren·chant·ly** *adv*

ə abut; ə kitten; ər further; a back; ā bake; ä cot, cart; au̇ out; ch chin; e less; ē easy; g gift; i trip; ī life

trench coat n **1** : a waterproof overcoat with a removable lining designed for wear in trenches **2** : a loose double-breasted raincoat with deep pockets, belt, and straps on the shoulders

¹tren·cher \'tren-chər\ n [ME, fr. MF *trencheoir* platter for carving, fr. *trenchier* to cut] : a usu. wooden platter for serving food

²trench·er n : one that digs trenches

tren·cher·man \-mən\ n **1** : a hearty eater **2** *archaic* : HANGER-ON, SPONGER

trench fever n : a rickettsial disease marked by fever and pain (as in joints) and transmitted by the body louse

trench foot n : a painful foot disorder resembling frostbite and resulting from exposure to cold and wet

trench knife n : a knife with a strong double-edged 8-inch blade suited for hand-to-hand fighting

trench mouth n **1** : VINCENT'S ANGINA **2** : VINCENT'S INFECTION

¹trend \'trend\ vi [OE *trendan* to turn, revolve] **1 a** : to extend in a general direction **b** : to veer in a new direction : BEND **2 a** : to show a tendency : INCLINE **b** : SHIFT

²trend n **1** : general direction taken ⟨easterly *trend* of the shoreline⟩ **2 a** : a prevailing tendency or inclination : DRIFT **b** : a general movement : SWING **c** : a current style or preference ⟨ : a line of development **syn** see TENDENCY

¹tre·pan \tri-'pan\ n [ML *trepanum*, fr. Gk *trypanon* auger] : TREPHINE

²trepan vt **tre·panned**; **tre·pan·ning** : to remove a disk from (the skull) — **trep·a·na·tion** \,trep-ə-'nā-shən\ n

tre·pang \tri-'paŋ\ n [Malay *tĕripang*] : any of several large Pacific sea cucumbers that are used dried esp. by the Chinese for making soup — called also *bêche-de-mer*

tre·phine \'trē-,fīn\ n [F *tréphine*, fr. obs. E *trafine*, fr. L *tres fines* three ends] : a surgical instrument for cutting out circular sections (as of bone or corneal tissue)

trep·i·da·tion \,trep-ə-'dā-shən\ n [L *trepidare* to tremble, fr. *trepidus* agitated] **1** *archaic* : a tremulous motion **2** : a state of alarm : FEAR

trep·o·ne·ma \,trep-ə-'nē-mə\ n, pl **-ma·ta** \-mət-ə\ or **-mas** [NL, fr. Gk *trepein* to turn + *nēma* thread] : any of a genus of spirochetes that parasitize warm-blooded animals and include organisms causing syphilis and yaws — **trep·o·ne·mal** \-məl\ or **trep·o·nem·a·tous** \-'nem-ət-əs, -'nēm-\ adj

¹tres·pass \'tres-pəs, -,pas\ n [OF *trespas*, fr. *trespasser* to go beyond, trespass, fr. *tres-* trans- + *passer* to pass] **1 a** : a violation of morals : TRANSGRESSION; *esp* : SIN **b** : an unwarranted infringement **2 a** (1) : an unlawful act committed on the person, property, or rights of another (2) : the action for injuries done by such an act **b** : the tort of wrongful entry on real property

²trespass vi **1** : ERR, SIN **2** : to commit a trespass; *esp* : to enter unlawfully upon the land of another — **tres·pass·er** n

tress \'tres\ n [OF *trece*] **1** *archaic* : a plait of hair : BRAID **2 a** : a long lock of hair **b** *pl* : the long unbound hair of a woman

tres·tle \'tres-əl\ n [MF *trestel*, fr. L *transtillum*, dim. of *transtrum* traverse beam, fr. *trans* across] **1** : a braced frame consisting usu. of a horizontal piece with spreading legs at each end that supports something (as a tabletop or drawing board) **2** : a braced framework of timbers or steel for carrying a road or railroad over a depression

tres·tle·work \-,wərk\ n : a system of connected trestles supporting a structure (as a bridge)

trews \'trüz\ n pl [ScGael *triubhas*] : tight-fitting trousers usu. of tartan; *esp* : close-cut tartan trunk hose worn under the kilt in Highland dress

trey \'trā\ n, pl **treys** [MF *treis*, *treie*, fr. L *tres* three] : a card or die with three spots

tri- comb form [L (fr. *tri-*, *tres*) & Gk, fr. *tri-*, *treis*; akin to E *three*] **1** : three ⟨*tricostate*⟩ : having three elements or parts ⟨*trigraph*⟩ **2** : into three ⟨*trisect*⟩ **3** : thrice ⟨*tri-weekly*⟩ : every third ⟨*trimonthly*⟩

tri·a·ble \'trī-ə-bəl\ adj : liable or subject to judicial or quasi-judicial examination or trial ⟨a case *triable* without a jury⟩ — **tri·a·ble·ness** n

tri·ad \'trī-,ad, -əd\ n **1** : a union or group of three usu. closely related persons or things **2** : a chord of three

tones consisting of a root with its third and fifth and constituting the harmonic basis of tonal music — called also *common chord* — **tri·ad·ic** \trī-'ad-ik\ adj — **tri·ad·i·cal·ly** \-'ad-i-k(ə-)lē\ adv

¹tri·al \'trī(-ə)l\ n [AF, fr. *trier* to try] **1** : the action or process of trying or putting to the proof : TEST **2** : formal examination before a competent tribunal of the matter in issue in a civil or criminal case **3** : a test of faith, patience, or stamina **4** : a tryout or experiment to test quality, value, or usefulness **5** : ATTEMPT, EFFORT

²trial adj **1** : of, relating to, or used in a trial **2** : made or done as a test or experiment **3** : used or tried out in a test or experiment

trial and error n : a finding out of the best way to reach a desired result or a correct solution by trying out one or more ways or means and by noting and eliminating errors or causes of failure; *also* : the trying of this and that until something succeeds

trial balance n : a list of the debit and credit balances of accounts in a ledger at a given date made primarily to verify their equality

trial balloon n **1** : a balloon sent up to test air currents and wind velocity **2** : a project or scheme tentatively announced in order to test public opinion

trial run n : a testing exercise : EXPERIMENT

tri·an·gle \'trī-,aŋ-gəl\ n **1** : a polygon having three

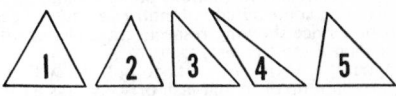

triangles: *1* equilateral, *2* isosceles, *3* right-angled, *4* obtuse, *5* scalene

sides **2 a** : a musical percussion instrument made of a rod of steel bent into the form of a triangle open at one angle **b** : a drafting instrument consisting of a thin flat right-angled triangle with acute angles of 45 degrees or of 30 degrees and 60 degrees

tri·an·gu·lar \trī-'aŋ-gyə-lər\ adj **1 a** : of, relating to, or having the form of a triangle **b** : having a triangular base or principal surface ⟨*triangular* table⟩ ⟨*triangular* pyramid⟩ **2** : of, relating to, or involving three parts or persons ⟨a *triangular* business deal⟩ ⟨a *triangular* love affair⟩ — **tri·an·gu·lar·i·ty** \(,)trī-,aŋ-gyə-'lar-ət-ē\ n — **tri·an·gu·lar·ly** \trī-'aŋ-gyə-lər-lē\ adv

¹tri·an·gu·late \trī-'aŋ-gyə-lət\ adj : consisting of or marked with triangles

²tri·an·gu·late \-,lāt\ vt **1** : to divide into triangles **2** : to survey, map, or determine by triangulation

tri·an·gu·la·tion \(,)trī-,aŋ-gyə-'lā-shən\ n : the measurement of the elements necessary to determine the network of triangles into which any part of the earth's surface is divided in surveying

Tri·as·sic \trī-'as-ik\ n [L *trias* triad; fr. the three subdivisions of the European Triassic] : the earliest period of the Mesozoic era; *also* : the corresponding system of rocks — **Triassic** adj

tri·atom·ic \,trī-ə-'täm-ik\ adj : having three atoms in the molecule

tri·ax·i·al \(')trī-'ak-sē-əl\ adj : having or involving three axes

trib·al \'trī-bəl\ adj : of, relating to, or characteristic of a tribe ⟨*tribal* customs⟩ — **trib·al·ly** \-bə-lē\ adv

trib·al·ism \-bə-,liz-əm\ n **1** : tribal consciousness and loyalty; *esp* : exaltation of the tribe above other groups **2** : strong loyalty within a social group

tribe \'trīb\ n [L *tribus*, a division of the Roman people, tribe] **1** : a usu. primitive social group comprising numerous families, clans, or generations **2** : a group of persons having a common character, occupation, or interest **3 a** : a taxonomic category of variable rank; *also* : a natural group irrespective of taxonomic rank ⟨the cat *tribe*⟩ **b** : a group of closely related animals or strains within a breed

tribes·man \'trībz-mən\ n : a member of a tribe

trib·u·la·tion \,trib-yə-'lā-shən\ n [L *tribulare* to press, oppress, fr. *tribulum* nail-studded board used in threshing, fr. *terere* to rub] : distress or suffering resulting from oppression, persecution, or affliction; *also* : a trying experience

---

j joke; **ŋ** sing; **ō** flow; **ȯ** flaw; **ȯi** coin; **th** thin; **t̲h̲** this; **ü** loot; **u̇** foot; **y** yet; **yü** few; **yu̇** furious; **zh** vision

tri·bu·nal \trī-'byün-ᵊl, trib-'yün-\ *n* [L, platform for magistrates, fr. *tribunus* tribune] **1** : the seat of a judge : TRIBUNE **2** : a court of justice **3** : something that decides or determines ⟨the *tribunal* of public opinion⟩
trib·u·nate \'trib-yə-ˌnāt, trib-'yü-nət\ *n* : the office, function, or term of office of a tribune : TRIBUNESHIP
¹trib·une \'trib-ˌyün, trib-'yün\ *n* [L *tribunus*, fr. *tribus* tribe] **1 a** : one of six officers of a Roman legion who orig. functioned in turn as its commander **b** : a Roman official under the monarchy and the republic with the function of protecting the plebeian citizen from arbitrary action by patrician magistrates **2** : a defender of the people esp. against arbitrary abuse of authority — **trib·une·ship** \-ˌship\ *n*
²tribune *n* [F, fr. It *tribuna*, fr. L *tribunal*] : a platform from which an assembly is addressed
¹trib·u·tary \'trib-yə-ˌter-ē\ *adj* **1** : paying tribute to another : SUBJECT **2** : paid or owed as tribute **3** : CONTRIBUTORY **4** : flowing into a larger stream or a lake
²tributary *n, pl* **-tar·ies** **1** : a ruler or state that pays tribute **2** : a stream feeding a larger stream or a lake
trib·ute \'trib-ˌyüt, -yət\ *n* [L *tributum* payment to the state, fr. neut. of *tributus*, pp. of *tribuere* to allot, pay, fr. *tribus* tribe] **1 a** : a payment made by one ruler or nation to another to show submission or to secure peace or protection **b** : a tax to raise money for this payment **c** : the obligation to pay tribute ⟨nations under *tribute*⟩ **2** : something given or contributed voluntarily as due or deserved : a gift or service showing respect, gratitude, or affection ⟨floral *tribute*⟩; *esp* : PRAISE, CREDIT
¹trice \'trīs\ *vt* [ME *trisen*, lit., to pull, fr. MD *trisen* to hoist] : to haul up or in and lash or secure (as a sail) with a small rope
²trice *n* [ME *trise*, lit., pull, fr. *trisen* to pull] : a brief space of time : INSTANT — used chiefly in the phrase *in a trice*
tri·ceps \'trī-ˌseps\ *n, pl* **tri·ceps·es** *also* **triceps** [NL *tricipit-, triceps*, fr. L, 3-headed, fr. *tri-* + *capit-, caput* head] : a muscle that arises from three heads; *esp* : the great extensor muscle along the back of the upper arm
tri·cer·a·tops \trī-'ser-ə-ˌtäps\ *n* [Gk *tri-* + *kerat-, keras* horn + *ōps* face] : a large herbivorous Cretaceous dinosaur with three horns, a bony hood or crest on the neck, and hoofed toes
-trices *pl of* -TRIX
tri·chi·na \trə-'kī-nə\ *n, pl* **-nae** \-(ˌ)nē\ *also* **-nas** [NL, fr. Gk *trichinos* made of hair, fr. *trich-, thrix* hair] **1** : a small slender nematode worm that in the larval state is parasitic in the voluntary muscles of flesh-eating mammals (as man and hog) **2** : TRICHINOSIS — **tri·chi·nal** \-'kīn-ᵊl\ *adj* — **trich·i·nous** \'trik-ə-nəs, trə-'kī-nəs\ *adj*
trich·i·nize \'trik-ə-ˌnīz\ *vt* : to infest with trichinae
trich·i·no·sis \ˌtrik-ə-'nō-səs\ *n, pl* **-no·ses** \-'nō-ˌsēz\ : a disease caused by trichinae and marked esp. by muscular pain, dyspnea, fever, and edema
trich·o·cyst \'trik-ə-ˌsist\ *n* [Gk *trich-, thrix* hair] : any of the minute lassoing or stinging organs of a protozoan — **trich·o·cys·tic** \ˌtrik-ə-'sis-tik\ *adj*
trich·ome \'trik-ˌōm\ *n* [G *trichom*, fr. Gk *trichōma* growth of hair, fr. *trich-, thrix* hair] : a filamentous outgrowth; *esp* : an epidermal filament on a plant — **tri·chom·ic** \trik-'äm-ik, -'ōm-\ *adj*
trich·o·mon·ad \ˌtrik-ə-'män-ˌad, -'mō-ˌnad\ *n* : any of a genus of flagellated protozoans parasitic in various animals including man
trich·o·mo·ni·a·sis \ˌtrik-ə-mə-'nī-ə-səs\ *n, pl* **-a·ses** \-ə-ˌsēz\ : infection with or disease caused by trichomonads; *esp* : a human vaginal inflammation with a persistent discharge
tri·chop·ter·an \trik-'äp-tə-rən\ *n* [Gk *trich-, thrix* hair + *pteron* wing] : any of an order (Trichoptera) of insects consisting of the caddis flies — **trichopteran** *or* **tri·chop·ter·ous** \-rəs\ *adj*
tri·chot·o·mous \trī-'kät-ə-məs\ *adj* [Gk *tricha* in three + *tom-, temnein* to cut] : divided or dividing into three parts or into threes : THREEFOLD ⟨*trichotomous* branching⟩ — **tri·chot·o·mous·ly** *adv* — **tri·chot·o·my** \-mē\ *n*
-tri·chous \tri-kəs\ *adj comb form* [Gk *trich-, thrix* hair] : having (such) hair : -haired ⟨peri*trichous*⟩
¹trick \'trik\ *n* [ONF *trique*, fr. *trikier* to deceive] **1 a** : a crafty procedure or practice meant to deceive or defraud **b** : a mischievous act : PRANK **c** : an indiscreet or childish

action **d** : a dexterous or ingenious feat designed to puzzle or amuse ⟨a juggler's *tricks*⟩ **2 a** : an habitual peculiarity of behavior or manner **b** : a characteristic and identifying feature ⟨a *trick* of speech⟩ **c** : an optical illusion ⟨a mere *trick* of the light⟩ **3 a** : a quick or artful way of getting a result : KNACK **b** : a technical device (as of an art or craft) ⟨the *tricks* of stage technique⟩ **4** : the cards played in one round of a card game often used as a scoring unit **5 a** : a turn of duty at the helm usu. lasting for two hours **b** : a working shift
syn TRICK, RUSE, STRATAGEM mean an indirect means to gain an end. TRICK may imply deception, roguishness, or illusion and either an evil or harmless end; RUSE stresses an attempt to mislead by a false impression; STRATAGEM implies a ruse to entrap or outwit and suggests a more or less carefully laid-out plan
²trick *adj* **1** : of or relating to or involving tricks or trickery ⟨*trick* photography⟩ ⟨*trick* dice⟩ **2** : TRIG **3** : somewhat defective and unreliable
³trick *vt* **1** : to deceive by cunning or artifice : CHEAT **2** : to dress or adorn esp. fancifully or ornately ⟨*tricked* out in a gaudy uniform⟩
trick·ery \'trik-(ə-)rē\ *n, pl* **-er·ies** : the use of tricks to deceive or defraud **syn** see DECEPTION
¹trick·le \'trik-əl\ *vi* **trick·led**; **trick·ling** \'trik-(ə-)liŋ\ [ME *triklen*] **1** : to issue or fall in drops **2** : to flow in a thin gentle stream
²trickle *n* : a trickling stream : DRIBBLE, DRIP
trick·let \'trik-lət\ *n* : a thin stream
trick or treat *n* : a Halloween pastime of asking for goodies from door to door under threat of playing tricks on householders who refuse
trick·ster \'trik-stər\ *n* : one who tricks or cheats
tricksy \'trik-sē\ *adj* **tricks·i·er**; **-est** **1** *archaic* : smartly attired : SPRUCE **2** : full of tricks : PRANKISH **3** : TRICKY — **tricks·i·ness** *n*
tricky \'trik-ē\ *adj* **trick·i·er**; **-est** **1** : of or characteristic of a trickster : SLY **2** : requiring skill, aptitude, or caution : DELICATE **3** : TRICK 3 — **trick·i·ly** \'trik-ə-lē\ *adv* — **trick·i·ness** \-ē-nəs\ *n*
tri·clin·ic \(')trī-'klin-ik\ *adj* : being a crystal in which there are three unequal axes intersecting at oblique angles
tric·o·lette \ˌtrik-ə-'let\ *n* [*tricot* + *-lette* (as in *flannelette*)] : a usu. silk or rayon knitted fabric used esp. for women's clothing
¹tri·col·or \'trī-ˌkəl-ər\ *n* : a flag of three colors ⟨the French *tricolor*⟩
²tricolor *or* **tri·col·ored** \'trī-ˌkəl-ərd\ *adj* : having or using three colors
tri·corn \'trī-ˌkȯrn\ *adj* [L *cornu* horn] : having three horns or corners
tri·corne *or* **tri·corn** \'trī-ˌkȯrn\ *n* : COCKED HAT
tri·cor·nered \'trī-'kȯr-nərd\ *adj* : having three corners
tri·cot \'trē-ˌkō, 'trī-ˌkət\ *n* [F, fr. *tricoter* to knit] **1** : a plain warp-knitted fabric (as for underwear) of nylon, wool, rayon, silk, or cotton **2** : a twilled clothing fabric of wool or wool and cotton
tric·o·tine \ˌtrik-ə-'tēn\ *n* : a sturdy suiting woven of tightly twisted yarns in a double twill
¹tri·cus·pid \(')trī-'kəs-pəd\ *adj* : having three cusps
²tricuspid *n* : a tricuspid anatomical structure; *esp* : a tooth having three cusps
tricuspid valve *n* : a valve of three flaps that prevents return of blood from the right ventricle to the right auricle
tri·cy·cle \'trī-ˌsik-əl\ *n* : a 3-wheeled vehicle propelled by pedals, hand levers, or a motor
¹tri·dent \'trīd-ᵊnt\ *n* [L *trident-, tridens*, fr. *tri-* + *dent-, dens* tooth] : a 3-pronged spear
²trident *adj* : TRIDENTATE
tri·den·tate \(')trī-'den-ˌtāt\ *adj* : having three teeth, processes, or points ⟨a *tridentate* leaf⟩
Tri·den·tine \trī-'dent-ᵊn, -'den-ˌtēn\ *adj* [L *Tridentum* Trent] : of or relating to Trent, Italy, or to a Roman Catholic church council held there from 1545 to 1563
tri·di·men·sion·al \ˌtrīd-ə-'mench-nəl, -ən-ᵊl\ *adj* : of or relating to three dimensions
trid·u·um \'trij-ə-wəm\ *n* [L, period of three days] : a period of three days of prayer usu. preceding a Roman Catholic feast
tried \'trīd\ *adj* [fr. pp. of *try*] : found good, faithful, or trustworthy through experience or testing

ə abut; ᵊ kitten; ər further; a back; ā bake; ä cot, cart; aù out; ch chin; e less; ē easy; g gift; i trip; ī life

tri·en·ni·al \(')trī-'en-ē-əl\ *adj* **1** : consisting of or lasting for three years **2** : occurring or being done every three years — **triennial** *n* — **tri·en·ni·al·ly** \-ē-ə-lē\ *adv*

tri·en·ni·um \trī-'en-ē-əm\ *n, pl* **-ni·ums** *or* **-nia** \-ē-ə\ [L, fr. *annus* year] : a period of three years

tri·er \'trī-(ə)r\ *n* : someone or something that tries

tri·fa·cial \(')trī-'fā-shəl\ *adj or n* : TRIGEMINAL

tri·fid \'trī-,fid, -fəd\ *adj* [L *trifidus* split into three, fr. *findere* to split] : deeply and narrowly tridentate

¹tri·fle \'trī-fəl\ *n* [OF *trufe, trufle* mockery] **1** : something of little value or importance; *esp* : an insignificant amount (as of money) **2** : a dessert of sponge cake spread with jam or jelly covered with custard and whipped cream

²trifle *vb* **tri·fled; tri·fling** \-f(ə-)liŋ\ **1 a** : to talk in a jesting or mocking manner with intent to delude or mislead **b** : to act heedlessly or frivolously : PLAY **2** : to waste time : DALLY **3** : to spend or waste in trifling or on trifles ⟨*trifle* away money⟩ **4** : to handle something idly : TOY — **tri·fler** \-f(ə-)lər\ *n*

tri·fling \'trī-fliŋ\ *adj* : lacking in significance or solid worth: as **a** : FRIVOLOUS ⟨*trifling* talk⟩ **b** : TRIVIAL ⟨a *trifling* gift⟩

¹tri·fo·cal \(')trī-'fō-kəl\ *adj* : having three focal lengths

²trifocal *n* : a trifocal glass or lens

tri·fo·li·ate \(')trī-'fō-lē-ət\ *adj* **1** *or* **tri·fo·li·at·ed** \-lē-,āt-əd\ : having three leaves ⟨a *trifoliate* plant⟩ **2** : TRIFOLIOLATE

tri·fo·li·o·late \(')trī-'fō-lē-ə-,lāt\ *adj* : having three leaflets ⟨a *trifoliolate* leaf⟩

tri·fo·ri·um \trī-'fōr-ē-əm, -'fôr-\ *n, pl* **-ria** \-ē-ə\ : a gallery forming an upper story to the aisle of a church

tri·fur·cate \(')trī-'fər-kət, -,kāt; 'trī-fər-,kāt\ *adj* [L *trifurcus*, fr. *tri-* + *furca* fork] : TRICHOTOMOUS — **tri·fur·cate** \-,kāt, trī-'fər-\ *vi* — **tri·fur·ca·tion** \,trī-(,)fər-'kā-shən\ *n*

¹trig \'trig\ *adj* [ME, trusty, nimble, of Scand origin; akin to E *true*] **1** : stylishly trim : SMART, NEAT **2** : extremely precise : PRIM

²trig *n* : TRIGONOMETRY

tri·gem·i·nal \trī-'jem-ən-ᵊl\ *adj* [L *trigeminus* threefold, fr. *tri-* + *geminus* twin] : of, relating to, or being a pair of large mixed cranial nerves that supply motor and sensory fibers mostly to the face — **trigeminal** *n*

¹trig·ger \'trig-ər\ *n* [D *trekker*, fr. *trekken* to pull, draw] : a movable lever attached to a catch that when released by pressure allows a mechanism to go into action; *esp* : the part of the lock of a firearm that releases the hammer and so fires the gun — **trigger** *adj* — **trig·gered** \-ərd\ *adj*

²trigger *vb* **trig·gered; trig·ger·ing** \'trig-(ə-)riŋ\ **1** : to fire by pulling a mechanical trigger ⟨*trigger* a rifle⟩; *also* : to cause the explosion of (as a missile) **2** : to initiate, actuate, or set in motion as if by pulling a trigger

trig·ger–hap·py \'trig-ər-,hap-ē\ *adj* **1** : irresponsible in the use of firearms; *esp* : inclined to shoot before clearly identifying the target **2** : inclined to be irresponsible in matters that might precipitate war ⟨*trigger-happy* border guards⟩ **3** : aggressively belligerent in attitude ⟨*trigger-happy* in dealing with reporters⟩

tri·glyph \'trī-,glif\ *n* [Gk *triglyphos*, fr. *tri-* + *glyphein* to carve] : a slightly projecting rectangular tablet in a Doric frieze with two vertical channels and two corresponding half channels on the vertical sides

trig·o·no·met·ric \,trig-ə-nə-'me-trik\ *adj* : of, relating to, or in accordance with trigonometry — **trig·o·no·met·ri·cal** \-tri-kəl\ *adj* — **trig·o·no·met·ri·cal·ly** \-tri-k(ə-)lē\ *adv*

trigonometric function *n* : one of a group of functions based on ratios between pairs of sides of a right-angled triangle

trig·o·nom·e·try \,trig-ə-'näm-ə-trē\ *n* [Gk *trigōnon* triangle, fr. *tri-* + *gōnia* angle] : the study of the properties of triangles and trigonometric functions and of their applications

tri·graph \'trī-,graf\ *n* : a group of three successive letters representing a single sound or a complex sound which is not a combination of the sounds ordinarily represented by each in other occurrences ⟨"eau" in "beau" is a *trigraph*⟩ — **tri·graph·ic** \trī-'graf-ik\ *adj*

tri·he·dral \(')trī-'hē-drəl\ *adj* **1** : having three faces ⟨*trihedral* angle⟩ **2** : of or relating to a trihedral angle — **trihedral** *n*

tri·lat·er·al \(')trī-'lat-ə-rəl, -'la-trəl\ *adj* : having three sides — **tri·lat·er·al·i·ty** \,trī-,lat-ə-'ral-ət-ē\ *n* — **tri·lat·er·al·ly** \(')trī-'lat-ə-rə-lē, -'la-trə-\ *adv*

tri·lin·gual \(')trī-'liŋ-gwəl\ *adj* **1** : of, containing, or expressed in three languages **2** : using or able to use three languages esp. with the fluency characteristic of a native speaker — **tri·lin·gual·ly** \-gwə-lē\ *adv*

¹trill \'tril\ *n* [It *trillo*] **1 a** : the alternation of two musical tones a scale degree apart — called also *shake* **b** : VIBRATO **c** : a rapid reiteration of the same tone esp. on a percussion instrument **2** : a sound felt to resemble a musical trill : WARBLE **3** : the rapid vibration of one speech organ against another (as of the tip of the tongue against the teethridge); *also* : a speech sound so made

²trill *vb* **1** : to utter as or with a trill **2** : to play or sing with a trill : QUAVER — **trill·er** *n*

tril·lion \'tril-yən\ *n* **1** — see NUMBER table **2** : a very large number — **trillion** *adj* — **tril·lionth** \-yən(t)th\ *adj* — **trillionth** *n*

tril·li·um \'tril-ē-əm\ *n* : any of a genus of herbs of the lily family with short rootstocks and an erect stem bearing a whorl of three leaves and a large solitary 3-petaled flower

tri·lo·bate \(')trī-'lō-,bāt\ *or* **tri·lo·bat·ed** \-,bāt-əd\ *or* **tri·lobed** \'trī-'lōbd\ *adj* : having three lobes ⟨a *trilobate* leaf⟩ — **tri·lo·ba·tion** \,trī-lō-'bā-shən\ *n*

tri·lo·bite \'trī-lə-,bīt\ *n* : any of a group (Trilobita) of extinct Paleozoic marine arthropods having a segmented body divided by longitudinal furrows on the back into three lobes — **trilobite** *or* **tri·lo·bit·ic** \,trī-lə-'bit-ik\ *adj*

tri·loc·u·lar \(')trī-'läk-yə-lər\ *or* **tri·loc·u·late** \-lət\ *adj* : having three cells or cavities

tril·o·gy \'tril-ə-jē\ *n, pl* **-gies** : a series of three dramas or sometimes three literary or musical compositions that although each is in one sense complete are closely related and develop a single theme

¹trim \'trim\ *vb* **trimmed; trim·ming** [OE *trymian* to strengthen, arrange, fr. *trum* strong, firm] **1 a** : to embellish with ribbons, lace, or ornaments : ADORN **b** : to arrange a display of goods in (a shop window) **2 a** : to administer a beating to : THRASH; *also* : to defeat resoundingly **b** : to worst in a bargain **3 a** : to make trim and neat esp. by cutting or clipping **b** : to free of excess or extraneous matter by or as if by cutting ⟨*trim* a budget⟩ **4 a** : to cause (a ship or boat) to assume a desirable position in the water by arrangement of ballast, cargo, or passengers; *also* : to adjust (as an airplane, blimp, or submarine) for horizontal movement or for motion upward or downward **b** : to adjust (as a sail) to a desired position **5 a** : to maintain neutrality between opposing parties **b** : to change one's views for reasons of expediency

²trim *adj* **trim·mer; trim·mest 1** *archaic* : suitably adjusted, equipped, or prepared for service or use **2** : neat, orderly, and compact in line or structure ⟨*trim* houses⟩ ⟨a *trim* figure⟩ — **trim·ly** *adv* — **trim·ness** *n*

³trim *adv* : TRIMLY

⁴trim *n* **1 a** : the readiness of a ship for sailing **b** : the readiness of a person or thing for action or use : FITNESS **2 a** : material used for ornament or trimming **b** : the woodwork in the finish of a building esp. around openings **c** : the interior furnishings of an automobile **3 a** : the position of a ship or boat esp. with reference to the horizontal **b** : the relation between the plane of a sail and the direction of the ship **4** : something that is trimmed off or cut out

trim·er·ous \'trim-ə-rəs\ *adj* : having the parts in threes ⟨a *trimerous* flower⟩

tri·mes·ter \(')trī-'mes-tər, 'trī-,\ *n* [L *trimestris* of three months, fr. *tri-* + *mensis* month] **1** : a period of three or about three months **2** : one of three terms into which an academic year is sometimes divided — **tri·mes·tral** \trī-'mes-trəl\ *adj* — **tri·mes·tri·al** \trī-'mes-trē-əl\ *adj*

trim·e·ter \'trim-ət-ər\ *n* : a line consisting of three metrical feet

trim·mer \'trim-ər\ *n* **1 a** : one that trims articles **b** : an instrument or machine with which trimming is done **2 a** : a beam that holds the end of a header in floor framing — see HEADER illustration **3** : a person who modifies his opinions out of expediency

trim·ming \'trim-iŋ\ *n* **1** : the action of one that trims **2** : BEATING, DEFEAT **3** : something that trims, ornaments, or completes ⟨the *trimming* on a hat⟩ ⟨roast turkey and all the *trimmings*⟩ **4** *pl* : parts removed by trimming

tri·month·ly \(')trī-'mon(t)th-lē\ *adj* : occurring every three months

tri·mor·phic \(')trī-'mȯr-fik\ *or* **tri·mor·phous** \-fəs\ *adj* : occurring in or having three distinct forms — **tri·mor·phism** \-,fiz-əm\ *n*

tri·mo·tor \'trī-,mōt-ər\ *n* : an airplane powered with three engines

tri·nal \'trīn-l\ *adj* : THREEFOLD

trine \'trīn\ *adj* [L *trinus*, fr. *tres* three] : THREEFOLD, TRIPLE

trine immersion *n* : the practice of immersing a candidate for baptism three times in the names in turn of the Trinity

trin·i·tar·i·an \,trin-ə-'ter-ē-ən\ *adj* **1** *cap* : of or relating to the Trinity, the doctrine of the Trinity, or adherents to that doctrine **2** : having three parts or aspects **Trinitarian** *n* : one who subscribes to the doctrine of the Trinity — **Trin·i·tar·i·an·ism** \-ē-ə-,niz-əm\ *n*

tri·ni·tro·tol·u·ene \,trī-,nī-trō-'täl-yə-,wēn\ *n* : a flammable toxic compound obtained by nitrating toluene and used as a high explosive and in chemical synthesis — called also *TNT*

Trin·i·ty \'trin-ət-ē\ *n, pl* **-ties** [L *trinus* trine] **1** : the unity of Father, Son, and Holy Spirit as three persons in one Godhead **2** *not cap* : TRIAD **3** : TRINITY SUNDAY

Trinity Sunday *n* : the 8th Sunday after Easter

Trin·i·ty·tide \'trin-ət-ē-,tīd\ *n* : the season of the church year between Trinity Sunday and Advent

trin·ket \'trin-kət\ *n* **1** : a small ornament (as a jewel or ring) **2** : a thing of little value : TRIFLE

trin·ket·ry \-kə-trē\ *n* : small items of personal ornament

¹tri·no·mi·al \trī-'nō-mē-əl\ *n* [*tri-* + *-nomial* (as in *binomial*)] **1** : a polynomial of three terms **2** : a biological taxonomic name consisting of three terms of which the first denotes the genus, the second the species, and the third the particular variety or subspecies named in full by the combination

²trinomial *adj* **1** : consisting of three terms **2** : of or relating to trinomials

trio \'trē-ō\ *n, pl* **tri·os** [F, fr. It, fr. L *tri-*, *tres* three] **1 a** : a musical composition for three voice parts or three instruments **b** : a dance by three people **c** : the performers of a musical or dance trio **2** : a group or set of three

tri·ode \'trī-,ōd\ *n* : a vacuum tube with three electrodes

tri·oe·cious \trī-'ē-shəs\ *adj* [Gk *oikos* house] : having male, female, and hermaphroditic flowers on different plants — **tri·oe·cious·ly** *adv*

tri·o·let \,trī-ə-'lā, 'trī-ə-lət\ *n* : a poem or stanza of eight lines in which the first line is repeated as the fourth and seventh and the second line as the eighth with a rhyme scheme of *ABaAabAB*

tri·ose \'trī-,ōs\ *n* : either of two simple sugars containing three carbon atoms

tri·ox·ide \(')trī-'äk-,sīd\ *n* : an oxide containing three atoms of oxygen

¹trip \'trip\ *vb* **tripped**; **trip·ping** [MF *triper*, of Gmc origin] **1 a** : to move (as in dancing or walking) with light quick steps **b** : to perform (as a dance) lightly or nimbly **2** : to catch one's foot while walking or running : cause to stumble **3 a** : to make or cause to make a mistake : SLIP, BLUNDER **b** : to catch in a misstep, fault, or blunder; *also* : EXPOSE **4** : to put (as a mechanism) into operation usu. by release of a catch or detent; *also* : to become operative

²trip *n* **1** : an act of causing another (as a wrestler) to lose footing **2 a** : VOYAGE, JOURNEY ⟨a *trip* to Europe⟩ **b** : a brief round having a specific aim or recurring regularly (as in one's occupation) ⟨a *trip* to the dentist's⟩ ⟨the milkman's daily *trip*⟩ **3** : ERROR, MISSTEP **4** : a quick light step **5** : a false step : STUMBLE **6 a** : the action of tripping mechanically **b** : a device (as a catch or detent) for tripping a mechanism **7** : an intense visionary experience undergone by a person who has taken a psychedelic drug (as LSD)

tri·par·tite \(')trī-'pär-,tīt\ *adj* **1** : having three parts **2** : having three corresponding parts or copies **3** : made between or involving three parties — **tri·par·tite·ly** *adv*

tripe \'trīp\ *n* [OF] **1** : stomach tissue of a ruminant and esp. of the ox for use as food **2** : TRASH

trip–ham·mer \'trip-,ham-ər\ *n* : a massive hammer raised by machinery and then tripped to fall on the work below

triph·thong \'trif-,thȯŋ, 'trip-\ *n* [Gk *phthongos* voice, sound] **1** : a 3-element speech sound **2** : TRIGRAPH

¹tri·ple \'trip-əl\ *vb* **tri·pled**; **tri·pling** \'trip-(ə-)liŋ\ **1** : to make or become three times as great or as many : multiply by three **2** : to make a three-base hit

²triple *n* **1 a** : a triple sum, quantity, or number **b** : a combination, group, or series of three **2** : THREE-BASE HIT

³triple *adj* [L *triplus*, fr. *tri-* + *-plus* fold] **1** : having three units or members **2** : being three times as great or as many **3** : having a threefold relation or character **4** : three times repeated

triple play *n* : a play in baseball by which three base runners are put out

tri·ple–space \,trip-əl-'spās\ *vb* **1** : to type (copy) leaving two blank lines between lines of copy **2** : to type on every third line

tri·plet \'trip-lət\ *n* **1** : a unit of three lines of verse **2** : a combination, set, or group of three **3** : one of three offspring born at one birth **4** : a group of three notes played in the time of two of the same value

triple threat *n* : a football player adept at running, kicking, and passing

¹tri·plex \'trip-,leks, 'trī-,pleks\ *adj* [L *triplic-*, *triplex*, fr. *tri-* + *-plic-*, *-plex* -fold] : TRIPLE

²triplex *n* : something that is triplex

¹trip·li·cate \'trip-li-kət\ *adj* [L *triplicatus*, pp. of *triplicare* to triple, fr. *triplic-*, *triplex* triplex] **1** : repeated three times **2** : THIRD

²triplicate *n* **1** : one of three like things **2** : three copies all alike ⟨typed in *triplicate*⟩

³trip·li·cate \-lə-,kāt\ *vt* : to make triple or provide in triplicate — **trip·li·ca·tion** \,trip-lə-'kā-shən\ *n*

trip·lo·blas·tic \,trip-lō-'blas-tik\ *adj* : having three primary germ layers

trip·loid \'trip-,lȯid\ *adj* : having or being a chromosome number three times the monoploid number — **triploid** *n* — **trip·loi·dy** \-,lȯid-ē\ *n*

tri·ply \'trip-(ə)lē\ *adv* : in a triple degree, amount, or manner

tri·pod \'trī-,päd\ *n* [Gk *tripod-*, *tripous*, fr. *tri-* + *pod-*, *pous* foot] **1** : something (as a container or stool) resting on three legs **2** : a three-legged stand (as for a camera) — **tripod** *or* **trip·o·dal** \'trip-əd-l, 'trī-,päd-\ *adj*

trip·per \'trip-ər\ *n* **1** *chiefly Brit* : EXCURSIONIST **2** : a tripping device or mechanism

trip·ping·ly \'trip-iŋ-lē\ *adv* : NIMBLY; *also* : FLUENTLY

trip·tych \'trip-(,)tik\ *n* [Gk *triptychos* having three folds, fr. *tri-* + *ptychē* fold] **1** : an ancient Roman writing tablet with three waxed leaves hinged together **2** : a picture or carving in three panels side by side

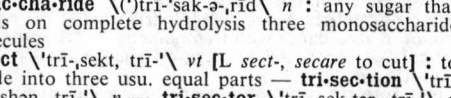
tripod 2

tri·ra·di·ate \(')trī-'rād-ē-ət, -ē-,āt\ *adj* : having three rays or radiating branches — **triradiate** — **tri·ra·di·ate·ly** *adv*

tri·reme \'trī-,rēm\ *n* [L *triremis*, fr. *tri-* + *remus* oar; akin to E **¹row**] : an ancient galley having three banks of oars

tri·sac·cha·ride \(')trī-'sak-ə-,rīd\ *n* : any sugar that yields on complete hydrolysis three monosaccharide molecules

tri·sect \'trī-,sekt, trī-'\ *vt* [L *sect-*, *secare* to cut] : to divide into three usu. equal parts — **tri·sec·tion** \'trī-,sek-shən, trī-'\ *n* — **tri·sec·tor** \'trī-,sek-tər, trī-'\ *n*

tri·so·di·um \,trī-'sōd-ē-əm\ *adj* : containing three atoms of sodium in the molecule

tri·so·mic \(')trī-'sō-mik\ *adj* : having one or a few chromosomes triploid in an otherwise diploid set — **trisomic** *n*

Tris·tan \'tris-tən, -,tän, -,tan\ *n* : TRISTRAM

triste \'trēst\ *adj* : SAD, MOURNFUL; *also* : WISTFUL

Tris·tram \'tris-trəm\ *n* : a hero of medieval romance held to have drunk a love potion and ultimately to have died with the Irish princess Isolde

tri·syl·lab·ic \,trī-sə-'lab-ik\ *adj* : having three syllables — **tri·syl·lab·i·cal·ly** \-'lab-i-k(ə-)lē\ *adv* — **tri·syl·la·ble** \'trī-,sil-ə-bəl, (')trī-'\ *n*

trite \'trīt\ *adj* [L *tritus*, fr. pp. of *terere* to rub, wear away]

: so common that the novelty has worn off : STALE, HACKNEYED ⟨a *trite* remark⟩ — **trite·ly** *adv* — **trite·ness** *n*
syn TRITE, HACKNEYED, STEREOTYPED mean lacking freshness and power to interest or compel attention. TRITE applies to a once effective phrase or idea spoiled by long familiarity; HACKNEYED stresses being worn out by overuse so as to become dull and meaningless; STEREOTYPED implies falling invariably into the same pattern or form
tri·the·ism \'trī-thē-ˌiz-əm\ *n* : a belief in three gods — **tri·the·ist** \-(ˌ)thē-əst\ *n or adj* — **tri·the·is·tic** \ˌtrī-thē-'is-tik\ *adj* — **tri·the·is·ti·cal** \-'is-ti-kəl\ *adj*
trit·i·um \'trit-ē-əm, 'trish-ē-\ *n* [NL, fr. Gk *tritos* third] : a radioactive isotope of hydrogen with atoms of three times the mass of ordinary light hydrogen atoms
trit·o·ma \'trit-ə-mə\ *n* : any of a genus of African herbs of the lily family often grown for their spikes of showy red or yellow flowers
tri·ton \'trīt-ᵊn\ *n* **1** *cap* : a son of Poseidon and Amphitrite described as a demigod of the sea with the lower part of his body like that of a fish **2 a** : any of various large sea snails with a heavy conical shell; *also* : this shell **b** : NEWT, EFT
trit·u·ra·ble \'trich-ə-rə-bəl\ *adj* : capable of being triturated
¹trit·u·rate \'trich-ə-ˌrāt\ *vt* [LL *triturare* to thresh, fr. L *tritura* act of rubbing, threshing, fr. *trit-, terere* to rub] **1** : CRUSH, GRIND **2** : to reduce to a fine powder by rubbing or grinding — **trit·u·ra·tion** \ˌtrich-ə-'rā-shən\ *n* — **trit·u·ra·tor** \'trich-ə-ˌrāt-ər\ *n*
²trit·u·rate \'trich-ə-rət\ *n* : a triturated substance
¹tri·umph \'trī-əm(p)f\ *n* [L *triumphus*] **1** : an ancient Roman ceremonial honoring a general for a decisive victory over a foreign enemy **2** : joy or exultation of victory or success **3** : a military victory or conquest; *also* : any notable success **syn** see VICTORY
²triumph *vi* **1** : to celebrate victory or success often boastfully or exultingly **2** : to obtain victory : PREVAIL, WIN
tri·um·phal \trī-'əm(p)-fəl\ *adj* : of, relating to, or used in a triumph
tri·um·phant \trī-'əm(p)-fənt\ *adj* **1** : CONQUERING, VICTORIOUS **2** : rejoicing for or celebrating victory : EXULTANT — **tri·um·phant·ly** *adv*
tri·um·vir \trī-'əm-vər\ *n* [L, back-formation fr. *triumviri,* pl., commission of three men, fr. *trium virum* of three men] : one of a commission or ruling body of three esp. in ancient Rome
tri·um·vi·rate \-və-rət\ *n* **1** : the office or term of office of a triumvir **2** : government by three persons who share authority and responsibility **3** : a group of three persons who share power or office
tri·une \'trī-ˌ(y)ün\ *adj* [L *tri-* + *unus* one] : three in one; *esp* : of or relating to the Trinity ⟨the *triune* God⟩
tri·va·lent \(ˈ)trī-'vā-lənt\ *adj* : having a valence of three — **tri·va·lence** \-lən(t)s\ *or* **tri·va·len·cy** \-lən-sē\ *n*
triv·et \'triv-ət\ *n* [OE *trefet*] **1** : a three-legged stand or support; *esp* : one for holding a kettle near the fire **2** : an ornamental metal plate on very short legs used under a hot dish to protect the table
triv·ia \'triv-ē-ə\ *n sing or pl* : unimportant matters : TRIFLES
triv·i·al \'triv-ē-əl\ *adj* [L *trivialis* found everywhere, commonplace, trivial, fr. *trivium* crossroads, fr. *tri-* + *via* way] **1** : ORDINARY, COMMONPLACE **2** : of little worth or importance : INSIGNIFICANT — **triv·i·al·ly** \-ē-ə-lē\ *adv*
triv·i·al·i·ty \ˌtriv-ē-'al-ət-ē\ *n, pl* **-ties 1** : the quality or state of being trivial **2** : something trivial : TRIFLE
trivial name *n* **1** : the second term of a taxonomic binomial **2** : a common or vernacular name of an organism or chemical
triv·i·um \'triv-ē-əm\ *n, pl* **triv·ia** \-ē-ə\ [ML, fr. L, meeting of three ways, crossroads] : the three liberal arts of grammar, rhetoric, and logic forming the elementary division of the seven liberal arts in medieval schools
¹tri·week·ly \(ˈ)trī-'wē-klē\ *adj* **1** : occurring or appearing three times a week **2** : occurring or appearing every three weeks — **triweekly** *adv*
²triweekly *n* : a triweekly publication
-trix \(ˌ)triks\ *n suffix, pl* **-tri·ces** \trə-ˌsēz, 'trī-(ˌ)sēz\ *or* **-trix·es** \(ˌ)trik-səz\ [ME, fr. L *-tric-, -trix,* fem. of *-tor,* suffix denoting an agent] **1** : female that does or is associ-

ated with a (specified) thing ⟨avia*trix*⟩ **2** : geometric line, point, or surface ⟨genera*trix*⟩
tro·chan·ter \trō-'kant-ər\ *n* [Gk *trochantēr*] **1** : a rough prominence at the upper part of the femur of many vertebrates **2** : a small segment immediately external to the coxa of the leg of an insect — **tro·chan·ter·al** \-'kant-ə-rəl\ *or* **tro·chan·ter·ic** \ˌtrō-ˌkan-'ter-ik\ *adj*
tro·che \'trō-kē, Brit also* 'trōsh\ *n* [alter. of earlier *trochisk,* fr. Gk *trochiskos,* fr. dim. of *trochos* wheel, fr. *trechein* to run] : a usu. circular medicinal tablet or lozenge used esp. as a demulcent
tro·chee \'trō-(ˌ)kē\ *n* [F *trochée,* fr. L *trochaeus,* fr. Gk *trochaios,* fr. *trochē* run, course, fr. *trechein* to run] : a metrical foot consisting of one accented syllable followed by one unaccented syllable (as in *hungry*) — **tro·cha·ic** \trō-'kā-ik\ *adj*
troch·lea \'träk-lē-ə\ *n* [L, block of pulleys, fr. Gk *trochileia*] : an anatomical structure resembling a pulley; *esp* : one on the humerus that articulates with the ulna
troch·le·ar \-lē-ər\ *adj* **1** : of, relating to, or being a trochlea **2** : of, relating to, or being either of the 4th pair of cranial nerves which control movements of some of the eye muscles
troch·o·phore \'träk-ə-ˌfōr, -ˌfȯr\ *n* [Gk *trochos* wheel] : a free-swimming ciliated larva typical of marine annelid worms but occurring also in several other invertebrate groups
trod *past of* TREAD
trod·den *past part of* TREAD
trog·lo·dyte \'träg-lə-ˌdīt\ *n* [Gk *trōglodytēs,* fr. *trōglē* hole, cave + *dyein* to enter] : CAVEMAN 1; *also* : a person resembling a troglodyte esp. in seclusive habits — **trog·lo·dyt·ic** \ˌträg-lə-'dit-ik\ *adj*
troi·ka \'troi-kə\ *n* [Russ *troĭka,* fr. *troe* three; akin to E *three*] **1** : a Russian vehicle drawn by three horses abreast; *also* : a team for such a vehicle **2** : a group of three
Troi·lus \'troi-ləs, 'trō-ə-ləs\ *n* : a son of Priam and lover of Cressida
Tro·jan \'trō-jən\ *n* **1** : a native or inhabitant of Troy **2** : one who shows pluck, endurance, or determined energy — **Trojan** *adj*
Trojan horse *n* **1** : a large hollow wooden horse filled with Greek soldiers and introduced within the walls of Troy by a stratagem during the Trojan War **2** : someone or something intended to undermine or subvert from within
Trojan War *n* : a 10-year war between the Greeks and Trojans brought on by the abduction of Helen by Paris and ended with the destruction of Troy
¹troll \'trōl\ *vb* [ME *trollen* to roll] **1 a** : to sing the parts of (as a round or catch) in succession **b** : to sing loudly or in a jovial manner **2** : to speak or recite in a rolling voice **3** : to angle or angle for with a hook and line drawn through the water — **troll·er** *n*
²troll *n* **1** : a lure or a line with its lure and hook used in trolling **2** : a song sung in parts successively : ROUND
³troll *n* [Norw *troll* & Dan *trold,* fr. ON *troll* giant, demon] : a fabled dwarf or giant of Teutonic folklore inhabiting caves or hills
trol·ley *or* **trol·ly** \'träl-ē\ *n, pl* **trolleys** *or* **trollies 1 a** : a device for carrying current from a wire to an electrically driven vehicle **b** : TROLLEY CAR **2** : a wheeled carriage running on an overhead rail or track
trolley bus *n* : a bus powered by electric power from two overhead wires
trolley car *n* : a streetcar that runs on tracks and gets its electric power through a trolley
trol·lop \'träl-əp\ *n* **1** : a slovenly woman : SLATTERN **2** : a loose woman : WANTON
trom·bone \träm-'bōn, (ˌ)träm-\ *n* [It, aug. of *tromba* trumpet] : a brass wind instrument that has a cupped mouthpiece, that consists of a long cylindrical metal tube bent twice upon itself and ending in a bell, and that has a movable slide with which to vary the pitch — **trom·bon·ist** \-'bō-nəst\ *n*

trombone

-tron \ˌträn\ *n suffix* [Gk, suffix denoting an instrument]

1 : vacuum tube ⟨mega*tron*⟩ **2** : device for the manipulation of subatomic particles ⟨cyclo*tron*⟩

¹**troop** \'trüp\ *n* [MF *troupe* company, herd, of Gmc origin] **1 a** : a group of soldiers **b** : a cavalry unit corresponding to an infantry company **c** : armed forces : SOLDIERS — usu. used in pl. **2** : a collection of beings or things : COMPANY **3** : a unit of boy or girl scouts under a leader

²**troop** *vi* **1** : to move or gather in crowds **2** : to consort in company : ASSOCIATE

troop carrier *n* : a transport airplane used to carry troops

troop·er \'trü-pər\ *n* **1** : CAVALRYMAN **2 a** : a mounted policeman **b** : a state policeman

troop·ship \'trüp-,ship\ *n* : a ship for carrying troops : TRANSPORT

trop- *or* **tropo-** *comb form* [Gk *tropos*, fr. *trepein* to turn] **1** : turn : turning : change ⟨*tropo*sphere⟩ **2** : tropism ⟨*tropic*⟩

trope \'trōp\ *n* [Gk *tropos* turn, way, trope] : the use of a word or expression in a figurative sense : FIGURE OF SPEECH

troph·ic \'träf-ik, 'trō-fik\ *adj* [Gk *trophē* nourishment] **1** : of or relating to nutrition : NUTRITIONAL ⟨*trophic* disorders⟩ **2** : ³TROPIC — **troph·i·cal·ly** \-(ə-)lē\ *adv*

troph·o·zo·ite \,träf-ə-'zō-,īt\ *n* [Gk *trophē* nourishment + *zōion* animal] : a protozoan in an actively feeding and growing phase as distinguished from a resting or reproductive form

tro·phy \'trō-fē\ *n, pl* **trophies** [MF *trophee*, fr. L *tropaeum*, *trophaeum*, fr. Gk *tropaion*, fr. *trepein* to turn, put to flight] **1 a** : a memorial of an ancient Greek or Roman victory raised on the field of battle **b** : a representation of such a memorial (as on a medal) **2** : something taken in battle or conquest esp. as a memorial ⟨Indians took scalps as *trophies*⟩ **3** : something (as a loving cup) given to commemorate a victory or as an award for achievement **4** : SOUVENIR, MEMENTO — **tro·phied** \-fēd\ *adj*

-tro·phy \trə-fē\ *n comb form, pl* **-trophies** [Gk *troph-*, *trephein* to nourish] : nutrition : nurture : growth ⟨hyper*trophy*⟩

¹**trop·ic** \'träp-ik\ *n* [Gk *tropikos* of the solstice, fr. *tropē* turn; so called because their projections on the celestial sphere mark the sun's declination at the solstices] **1** : either of the two parallels of the earth's latitude that are approximately 23½ degrees north of the equator and approximately 23½ degrees south of the equator **2** *pl, often cap* : the region lying between the two tropics

²**tropic** *adj* : of, relating to, or occurring in the tropics : TROPICAL

³**tropic** *adj* **1** : of, relating to, or characteristic of tropism or of a tropism **2** : influencing the activity of a specified gland ⟨*tropic* hormones⟩

trop·i·cal \'träp-i-kəl\ *adj* **1** : of, located in, or used in the tropics **2** \'trō-pi-kəl, 'träp-i-\ [Gk *tropos* trope] : FIGURATIVE, METAPHORICAL — **trop·i·cal·ly** \-k(ə-)lē\ *adv*

tropical aquarium *n* : an aquarium kept at a uniform warmth and used esp. for tropical fish

tropical cyclone *n* : a cyclone in the tropics characterized by winds rotating at the rate of 75 miles an hour or more

tropical fish *n* : any of various small usu. showy fishes of exotic origin often kept in the tropical aquarium

tropical storm *n* : a tropical cyclone with strong winds of less than hurricane intensity

tropic bird *n* : any of several web-footed oceanic birds related to the gannets that are mostly white with a little black and a very long central pair of tail feathers

tropic of Cancer [fr. the sign of the zodiac which its celestial projection intersects] : the parallel of latitude that is 23½ degrees north of the equator and is the northernmost latitude reached by the overhead sun — see ZONE illustration

tropic of Capricorn [fr. the sign of the zodiac which its celestial projection intersects] : the parallel of latitude that is 23½ degrees south of the equator and is the southernmost latitude reached by the overhead sun — see ZONE illustration

tro·pism \'trō-,piz-əm, 'träp-,iz-\ *n* [Gk *trop-*, *trepein* to turn] : involuntary orientation by an organism or one of its parts that involves turning or curving and is a positive

or negative response to a source of stimulation; *also* : a reflex reaction involving such movement — **tro·pis·tic** \trō-'pis-tik, trä-\ *adj*

tro·po·sphere \'trō-pə-,sfi(ə)r, 'träp-ə-\ *n* : the portion of the atmosphere which is below the stratosphere, which extends outward about 7 to 10 miles from the earth's surface, and in which generally temperature decreases rapidly with altitude and clouds form — **tro·po·spher·ic** \,trō-pə-'sfi(ə)r-ik, ,träp-ə-, -'sfer-\ *adj*

¹**trot** \'trät\ *n* [MF, fr. *troter* to trot, of Gmc origin; akin to E *tread*] **1 a** (1) : a moderately fast gait of a quadruped (as a horse) in which the legs move in diagonal pairs (2) : a jogging gait of man that falls between a walk and a run **b** : a ride on horseback **2** : PONY 3

²**trot** *vb* **trot·ted; trot·ting 1 a** : to ride, drive, or go at a trot **b** : to cause to go at a trot **2** : to proceed briskly : HURRY

¹**troth** \'trōth, 'träth, 'trȯth\ *n* [OE *trēowth*, fr. *trēowe* faithful, true] **1** : loyal or pledged faithfulness : FIDELITY **2** : one's pledged word; *also* : BETROTHAL

²**troth** \'träth, 'trōth, 'trȯth\ *vt* : PLEDGE, BETROTH

Trots·ky·ism \'trät-skē-,iz-əm, 'trȯt-\ *n* : the Communist principles associated with Trotsky usu. including adherence to the concept of worldwide revolution as opposed to socialism in one country — **Trots·ky·ist** \-skē-əst\ *n or adj* — **Trots·ky·ite** \-skē-,īt\ *n or adj*

trot·ter \'trät-ər\ *n* : one that trots; *esp* : a standardbred horse trained for harness racing

trou·ba·dour \'trü-bə-,dōr, -,dȯr, -,du̇r\ *n* [F, fr. OProv *trobador*, fr. *trobar* to compose] : one of a class of lyric poets and poet-musicians often of knightly rank who flourished from the 11th to the end of the 13th century chiefly in Provence, the south of France, and the north of Italy

¹**trou·ble** \'trəb-əl\ *vb* **trou·bled; trou·bling** \'trəb-(ə-)liŋ\ [OF *tourbler*, *troubler*, modif. of L *turbidare*, fr. *turbidus* turbid, troubled] **1 a** : to agitate or become agitated mentally or spiritually : WORRY, DISTURB **b** : to produce physical disorder in : AFFLICT ⟨*troubled* with deafness⟩ **c** : to put to exertion or inconvenience ⟨*trouble* you for the salt⟩ **2** : to put into confused motion ⟨wind *troubled* the sea⟩ **3** : to make an effort : take pains ⟨do not *trouble* to come⟩

²**trouble** *n* **1 a** : the quality or state of being troubled : MISFORTUNE ⟨help people in *trouble*⟩ **b** : an instance of distress, annoyance, or perturbation **2 a** : civil disorder or agitation ⟨labor *trouble*⟩ **b** : EXERTION, PAINS ⟨took the *trouble* to call⟩ **c** (1) : a condition of physical distress (2) : DISEASE, AILMENT (3) : MALFUNCTION ⟨engine *trouble*⟩ ⟨*trouble* with the plumbing⟩ **d** : a personal characteristic that is a handicap or a source of distress — **trou·ble·mak·er** \-,mā-kər\ *n*

trou·ble·shoot·er \-,shüt-ər\ *n* **1** : a skilled workman employed to locate trouble and make repairs in machinery and technical equipment **2** : a man expert in resolving disputes or problems — **trou·ble·shoot** \-,shüt\ *vi*

trou·ble·some \'trəb-əl-səm\ *adj* **1** : giving trouble or anxiety : VEXATIOUS ⟨a *troublesome* infection⟩ **2** : DIFFICULT, BURDENSOME — **trou·ble·some·ly** *adv* — **trou·ble·some·ness** *n*

trou·blous \'trəb-ləs\ *adj* **1** : full of trouble : AFFLICTED; *also* : AGITATED, STORMY **2** : causing trouble : TURBULENT — **trou·blous·ly** *adv* — **trou·blous·ness** *n*

trough \'trȯf\ *n, pl* **troughs** \'trȯfs, 'trȯvz\ [OE *trog*] **1 a** : a long shallow often V-shaped receptacle for the drinking water or feed of domestic animals **b** : any of various domestic or industrial containers **2 a** : a conduit, drain, or channel for water; *esp* : a gutter along the eaves **b** : a long narrow or shallow depression (as between waves or hills) **3** : the low point in a cycle; *esp* : an elongated area of low barometric pressure

trounce \'trau̇n(t)s\ *vt* : to thrash or punish severely: as **a** : FLOG, CUDGEL **b** : to defeat decisively

¹**troupe** \'trüp\ *n* [MF, of Gmc origin] : COMPANY, TROOP; *esp* : a group of performers on the stage

²**troupe** *vi* : to travel in a troupe; *also* : to perform as a member of a theatrical troupe — **troup·er** *n*

trou·pi·al \'trü-pē-əl\ *n* [F *troupiale*, fr. *troupe*; fr. its living in flocks] : a large showy oriole of tropical America

trou·ser \'trau̇-zər\ *adj* : of, relating to, or designed for trousers ⟨*trouser* pockets⟩

trou·sers \ˈtraù-zərz\ *n pl* [alter. of earlier *trouse*, fr. ScGael *triubhas*] : an outer garment extending from the waist to the ankle or sometimes only to the knee, covering each leg separately, and worn typically by men and boys

trous·seau \ˈtrü-ˌsō\ *n, pl* **trous·seaux** \-ˌsōz\ *or* **trous·seaus** [F, fr. dim. of *trousse* bundle, fr. *trousser* to truss] : the personal possessions of a bride usu. including clothes, accessories, and household linens and wares

trout \ˈtraùt\ *n, pl* **trout** *also* **trouts** [OE *trūht*, fr. LL *trocta, tructa*, a fish with sharp teeth, fr. Gk *trōktēs*, lit., gnawer] **1** : any of various fishes mostly smaller than the related salmons, restricted to cool clear fresh waters, and highly regarded as table and game fish **2** : any of various fishes felt to resemble the true trouts — compare SEA TROUT

trout lily *n* : DOGTOOTH VIOLET

trove \ˈtrōv\ *n* [short for *treasure trove*] **1** : DISCOVERY, FIND **2** : a valuable collection : TREASURE; *also* : HAUL

trow \ˈtrō\ *vb* [OE *trēowan*; akin to E *true*] **1** *obs* : BELIEVE, TRUST **2** *archaic* : THINK, SUPPOSE

¹trow·el \ˈtraù(-ə)l\ *n* [MF *truelle*, fr. LL *truella*, dim. of L *trua* ladle] **1** : a small hand tool consisting of a flat blade with a handle used for spreading and smoothing mortar or plaster **2** : a small hand tool with a curved blade used by gardeners

²trowel *vt* **-eled** *or* **-elled; -el·ing** *or* **-el·ling** : to smooth, mix, or apply with a trowel

troy \ˈtroi\ *adj* : expressed in troy weight

troy weight *n* [fr. *Troyes*, France] : a series of units of weight based on a pound of 12 ounces and the ounce of 20 pennyweights or 480 grains — see MEASURE table

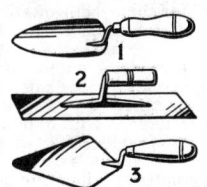

trowels: 1 gardener's, 2 plasterer's, 3 bricklayer's

tru·ant \ˈtrü-ənt\ *n* [OF, vagrant, of Celt origin] : one who shirks duty; *esp* : one who stays out of school without permission — **tru·an·cy** \-ən-sē\ *n* — **truant** *adj*

truant officer *n* : a school officer whose duty is to investigate and deal with cases of truancy

truce \ˈtrüs\ *n* [ME *trewes*, pl. of *trewe* agreement, fr. OE *trēow* fidelity; akin to E *true*] **1** : an interruption of warfare by mutual agreement : ARMISTICE **2** : a temporary rest : RESPITE

Truce of God : a truce enforced by the medieval church during part of the week and at various holy seasons

¹truck \ˈtrək\ *vb* [OF *troquer*] : to exchange goods : BARTER

²truck *n* **1** : BARTER **2** : goods for barter or for small trade **3** : close association : DEALINGS **4** : payment of wages in goods instead of cash **5** : vegetables grown for market **6** : small articles of little value; *also* : RUBBISH

³truck *n* **1** : a small wooden cap at the top of a flagpole or mast **2** : a vehicle (as a small flat-topped car on wheels, a two-wheeled barrow with long handles, or a strong heavy wagon or automobile) for carrying heavy articles **3** : a swiveling carriage with springs and one or more pairs of wheels used to carry an end of a railroad car or a locomotive; *also* : an automotive vehicle equipped with a swiveling device for hauling a trailer

⁴truck *vb* **1** : to transport on or by truck **2** : to be employed as a truck driver

truck·age \ˈtrək-ij\ *n* **1** : money paid for conveying on a truck **2** : conveyance by truck

truck·er \ˈtrək-ər\ *n* **1** : one whose business is transporting goods by truck **2** : a truck driver

truck farm *n* : a farm growing vegetables for market — **truck farmer** *n*

truck·ing \ˈtrək-iŋ\ *n* : the process or business of transporting goods on trucks

truck·le \ˈtrək-əl\ *vi* **truck·led; truck·ling** \ˈtrək-(ə-)liŋ\ : to act in a subservient manner : yield to the will of another : SUBMIT ⟨*truckle* to a conqueror⟩ — **truck·ler** \-(ə-)lər\ *n*

truckle bed *n* : TRUNDLE BED

truck·line \ˈtrək-ˌlīn\ *n* : a carrier using trucks and related freight vehicles

truck·man \ˈtrək-mən\ *n* **1** : TRUCKER **2** : a member of a fire department unit that operates a ladder truck

truck system *n* : the system of paying wages in goods instead of cash

truck trail·er *n* **1** \ˈtrək-ˌtrā-lər\ : a freight vehicle to be drawn by a motortruck **2** *usu* **truck–trail·er** \-ˈtrā-lər\ : a combination of a truck trailer and its motortruck

truc·u·lence \ˈtrək-yə-lən(t)s, ˈtrük-\ *also* **truc·u·len·cy** \-lən-sē\ *n* : the quality or state of being truculent

truc·u·lent \-lənt\ *adj* [L *truculentus*, fr. *truc-, trux* fierce] **1** : feeling or displaying ferocity : CRUEL, FIERCE, SAVAGE **2** : DEADLY, DESTRUCTIVE **3** : scathingly harsh **4** : BELLIGERENT, PUGNACIOUS — **truc·u·lent·ly** *adv*

¹trudge \ˈtrəj\ *vb* **1** : to walk or march steadily and usu. laboriously **2** : to walk or march along or over — **trudg·er** *n*

²trudge *n* : a long tiring walk : TRAMP

trud·gen stroke \ˈtrəj-ən-\ *n* [after John *Trudgen*, 19th cent. English swimmer] : a swimming stroke in which a double overarm motion is combined with a scissors kick

¹true \ˈtrü\ *adj* [OE *trēowe*] **1** : FAITHFUL, LOYAL **2** *archaic* : TRUTHFUL **3** : that can be relied on : CERTAIN **4 a** : corresponding to fact or actuality : ACCURATE, CORRECT **b** : logically necessary **5** : SINCERE ⟨*true* friendship⟩ **6** : properly so called : GENUINE ⟨lichens have no *true* stems⟩⟨whales are *true* but not typical mammals⟩; *also* : TYPICAL ⟨the *true* cats⟩ **7** : placed or formed accurately ⟨a *true* square⟩ **8** : RIGHTFUL, LEGITIMATE ⟨the *true* owner⟩ ⟨our *true* king⟩ **syn** see REAL — **true·ness** *n*

²true *n* **1** : TRUTH, REALITY — usu. used with *the* **2** : the quality or state of being accurate (as in alignment or adjustment) — used in the phrases *in true* and *out of true*

³true *vt* **trued; tru·ing** *also* **tru·ing** : to make level, square, balanced, or concentric : bring to desired mechanical accuracy or form

⁴true *adv* **1** : TRUTHFULLY **2 a** : ACCURATELY ⟨the bullet flew straight and *true*⟩ **b** : without variation from type ⟨breed *true*⟩

true bill *n* : a bill of indictment endorsed by a grand jury as warranting prosecution of the accused

true–blue \ˈtrü-ˈblü\ *adj* : marked by unswerving loyalty (as to a party) : highly faithful

true–born \-ˌbȯrn\ *adj* : genuinely such by birth ⟨a *trueborn* Englishman⟩

true discount *n* : the interest discounted in advance on a note and computed on the principal of the note — compare BANK DISCOUNT

true–false test *n* : a test consisting of a series of statements to be marked as true or false

true–heart·ed \ˈtrü-ˈhärt-əd\ *adj* : FAITHFUL, STEADFAST, LOYAL

true–life \ˌtrü-ˌlīf\ *adj* : true to life ⟨a *true-life* story⟩

true·love \ˈtrü-ˌləv\ *n* : one truly beloved or loving : SWEETHEART

true lover's knot *n* : a complicated ornamental knot not readily untying and emblematic of mutual love — called also *truelove knot*

true rib *n* : one of the ribs connected directly with the sternum by cartilages and in man constituting the first seven pairs

truf·fle \ˈtrəf-əl, ˈtrüf-\ *n* [modif. of MF *truffe*, fr. OProv *trufa*, modif. of L *tuber* tuber, truffle] : the usu. dark wrinkled edible subterranean fruiting body of a European fungus; *also* : this fungus

tru·ism \ˈtrü-ˌiz-əm\ *n* : an obvious truth — **tru·is·tic** \ˈtrü-ˈis-tik\ *adj*

trull \ˈtrəl\ *n* : TROLLOP, STRUMPET

tru·ly \ˈtrü-lē\ *adv* **1** : SINCERELY — often used as a complimentary close after *yours* **2** : TRUTHFULLY **3** : ACCURATELY **4 a** : INDEED — often used as an intensive ⟨*truly*, she is fair⟩ or interjectionally to express astonishment or doubt **b** : GENUINELY **5** : PROPERLY, RIGHTFULLY

¹trump \ˈtrəmp\ *n* [OF *trompe*, of Gmc origin] : TRUMPET : the sound of a trumpet ⟨till the last *trump* blows⟩

²trump *n* [alter. of **³triumph**] **1 a** : a card of a suit any of whose cards will win over a card that is not a trump **b** : the suit whose cards are trumps for a particular hand — often used in pl. **2** : a dependable and exemplary person

³trump *vb* **1** : to take with a trump ⟨*trump* a trick⟩ **2** : to play a trump **3** : to get the better of : OUTDO

trumped–up \ˈtrəm(p)t-ˈəp\ *adj* : fraudulently concocted : SPURIOUS ⟨*trumped-up* charges⟩

ȷ joke; ŋ sing; ō flow; ȯ flaw; ȯi coin; th thin; t̲h̲ this; ü loot; u̇ foot; y yet; yü few; yu̇ furious; zh vision

trum·pery \'trəm-p(ə-)rē\ *n, pl* **-per·ies** [MF *tromperie* deceit, fr. *tromper* to deceive] **1 a :** trivial or useless articles : things of no value : RUBBISH, JUNK **b :** worthless nonsense **2** *archaic :* tawdry finery — **trumpery** *adj*

¹**trum·pet** \'trəm-pət\ *n* [MF *trompette*, dim. of *trompe* trump] **1 :** a wind instrument consist-ing of a long cylin-drical metal tube commonly once or twice curved and ending in a bell **2 :** a trumpet player **3 :** something that resembles a trumpet

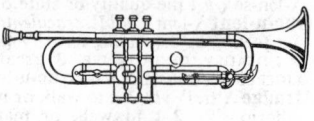

trumpet

or its tonal quality: as **a :** a funnel-shaped instrument (as a megaphone or a diaphragm horn) for collecting, direct-ing, or intensifying sound ⟨an ear *trumpet*⟩ **b :** a stentorian voice **c :** a penetrating cry (as of an elephant) — **trum·pet-like** \-,līk\ *adj*

²**trumpet** *vb* **1 :** to blow a trumpet **2 :** to sound or proclaim on or as if on a trumpet ⟨*trumpeted* the news⟩ **3 :** to make a sound suggestive of that of a trumpet

trumpet creeper *n* : a No. American woody vine with pinnate leaves and large red trumpet-shaped flowers — called also *trumpet vine*

trum·pet·er \'trəm-pət-ər\ *n* **1 :** a trumpet player; *esp* : one that gives signals with a trumpet **2 a :** any of several large gregarious long-legged long-necked So. American birds related to the cranes and often kept to protect poultry **b :** a rare pure white No. American wild swan noted for its sonorous voice **c :** any of an Asiatic breed of pigeons with a rounded crest and heavily feathered feet

trump up *vt* **1 :** to concoct esp. with intent to deceive : FABRICATE, INVENT ⟨*trump up* false charges⟩ **2** *archaic* : to cite as support for an action or claim : ALLEGE

¹**trun·cate** \'trəŋ-,kāt, 'trən-\ *vt* [L *truncare*, fr. *truncus* mutilated, lopped] : to shorten by or as if by cutting off : LOP — **trun·ca·tion** \,trəŋ-'kā-shən, ,trən-\ *n*

²**trun·cate** \'trəŋ-,kāt, 'trən-\ *adj* : having the end square or blunt ⟨a *truncate* leaf⟩

trun·cat·ed \-,kāt-əd\ *adj* **1 :** having the apex replaced by a plane section and esp. by one parallel to the base ⟨*truncated* cone⟩ **2 a :** cut short : CURTAILED **b :** lacking an expected or normal element (as a syllable) at beginning or end **3 :** TRUNCATE

¹**trun·cheon** \'trən-chən\ *n* [MF *tronchon*, fr. L *truncus* mutilated, lopped] **1 :** a shattered spear or lance **2 a** *obs* : CLUB, BLUDGEON **b :** BATON 1 **c :** a policeman's billy

²**truncheon** *vt, archaic* : to beat with a truncheon

¹**trun·dle** \'trən-dºl\ *n* [ME *trendle* circle, ring, wheel, fr. OE *trendel*, fr. *trendan* to turn] **1 a :** a small wheel or roller **b :** CIRCLET, HOOP **2 :** a low-wheeled cart or truck

²**trundle** *vb* **trun·dled; trun·dling** \'trən-dliŋ, -dºl-iŋ\ **1 a :** to propel by causing to rotate : ROLL ⟨*trundled* a wheelbarrow⟩ **b :** to progress by revolving **2 :** to trans-port in a wheeled vehicle : HAUL, WHEEL — **trun·dler** \-dlər, -dºl-ər\ *n*

trundle bed *n* : a low bed usu. on casters that can be slid under a higher bed — called also *truckle bed*

¹**trunk** \'trəŋk\ *n* [MF *tronc*, fr. L *truncus* tree trunk, torso, fr. *truncus* lopped, deprived of branches] **1 a :** the main stem of a tree apart from branches or roots **b :** the body of a person or lower animal apart from the head and limbs **c :** the main or basal part of something ⟨*trunk* of an artery⟩ **d :** a trunk line **2 a :** a box or chest for holding clothes or other goods esp. for traveling **b :** the enclosed space usu. in the rear of an automobile for carrying articles (as luggage) **3 :** the long versatile muscular nose of an elephant; *also :* PROBOSCIS **4** *pl :* men's shorts worn chiefly for sports

²**trunk** *adj* **1 :** being or relating to a main line of a system (as of a railroad, pipeline, or canal) **2 :** being or relating to the circuit between two telephone exchanges ⟨*trunk* call⟩ ⟨*trunk* operator⟩

trunk hose *n pl* : short full breeches reaching about half-way down the thigh worn chiefly in the late 16th and early 17th centuries

trunk line *n* **1 :** a system handling long-distance through traffic **2 a :** a main supply channel **b :** a direct link

trun·nion \'trən-yən\ *n* [F *trognon* core, stump] : PIN, PIVOT; *esp* : either of two opposite projections on which a cannon is swiveled

¹**truss** \'trəs\ *vt* [OF *trousser*] **1 a :** to secure tightly : BIND ⟨they *trussed* up their victim⟩ **b :** to arrange for cooking by binding close the wings or legs of ⟨*truss* a turkey⟩ **2 :** to support, strengthen, or stiffen by a truss — **truss·er** *n*

²**truss** *n* **1 a :** BUNDLE, PACK **b** *Brit* : a bundle of hay or straw **2 :** a rigid framework of beams, bars, or rods ⟨a *truss* for a roof⟩ **3 :** a device worn to hold a hernia in place **4 :** a compact flower or fruit cluster

truss bridge *n* : a bridge supported mainly by trusses — see BRIDGE illustration

¹**trust** \'trəst\ *n* [ME; akin to E *true*] **1 a :** assured re-liance on the character, ability, strength, or truth of some-one or something **b :** one in which confidence is placed **2 a :** dependence on something future or contingent : HOPE **b :** reliance on future payment for goods delivered : CREDIT **3 a :** a legal right or interest in property that one does not actually own ⟨income received under a *trust* established by his father⟩ **b :** property held or managed by one person or concern (as a bank or trust company) for the benefit of another **c :** a combination of firms or corporations formed by a legal agreement; *esp* : one that reduces or threatens to reduce competition **4 a :** some-thing (as a public office) committed to one to be used or cared for in the interest of another **b :** responsible charge or office **c :** CARE, CUSTODY **syn** see MONOPOLY

²**trust** *vb* **1 a :** to place confidence : DEPEND ⟨*trust* in God⟩ ⟨*trust* to luck⟩ **b :** to be confident : HOPE **2 :** to commit or place in one's care or keeping : ENTRUST **3 a :** to rely on the truthfulness or accuracy of : BELIEVE **b :** to place confidence in : rely on **c :** to hope or expect confidently ⟨*trusted* to find oil on the land⟩ **4 :** to sell to in confidence of later payment : extend credit to — **trust·er** *n*

trust-bust·er \'trəst-,bəs-tər\ *n* : one who seeks to break up business trusts; *esp* : a federal official who prosecutes trusts under the antitrust laws — **trust-bust·ing** \-tiŋ\ *n*

trust company *n* : a corporation and esp. a bank organized to perform fiduciary functions

trust·ee \,trəs-'tē\ *n* : one to whom something is entrusted: as **a :** a person to whom property is legally committed in trust **b :** a country charged with the supervision of a trust territory

trust·ee·ship \-,ship\ *n* **1 :** the office or function of a trustee **2 :** supervisory control by one or more countries over a trust territory

trust·ful \'trəst-fəl\ *adj* : full of trust : CONFIDING — **trust·ful·ly** \-fə-lē\ *adv* — **trust·ful·ness** *n*

trust fund *n* : money, securities, or similar property settled or held in trust

trust·ing \'trəs-tiŋ\ *adj* : having trust, faith, or confidence : TRUSTFUL — **trust·ing·ly** \-tiŋ-lē\ *adv*

trust territory *n* : a non-self-governing territory placed under an administrative authority by the Trusteeship Council of the United Nations

trust·wor·thy \'trəst-,wər-thē\ *adj* : worthy of confidence : DEPENDABLE — **trust·wor·thi·ly** \-thə-lē\ *adv* — **trust·wor·thi·ness** *n*

¹**trusty** \'trəs-tē\ *adj* **trust·i·er; -est :** TRUSTWORTHY

²**trusty** \'trəs-tē, ,trəs-'tē\ *n, pl* **trust·ies :** a trusty or trusted person; *esp* : a convict considered trustworthy and allowed special privileges

truth \'trüth\ *n, pl* **truths** \'trüthz, 'trüths\ [OE *trēowth*, fr. *trēowe* faithful, true] **1 a** *archaic :* FIDELITY, CONSTANCY **b :** TRUTHFULNESS, HONESTY; *esp* : conformity (as in art) with what is natural, substantial, or convincing **2 :** some-thing that is real or true: as **a** (1) : a judgment, proposi-tion, idea, or statement that is or is accepted as true ⟨the *truths* of science⟩ (2) : the body of such truths **b** (1) : the real state of things : FACT (2) : the body of real things, events, and facts : ACTUALITY **3 :** agreement with fact or among propositions : the property of being in accord with what is, has been, or must be — **in truth :** in fact : AC-TUALLY, REALLY

truth·ful \'trüth-fəl\ *adj* : telling or disposed to tell the truth — **truth·ful·ly** \-fə-lē\ *adv* — **truth·ful·ness** *n*

truth serum *n* : a hypnotic or anesthetic held to induce a subject under questioning to talk freely

truth set *n* : a set of the elements that can be substituted to make an open sentence true

¹try \'trī\ *vb* **tried; try·ing** [AF *trier*, fr. OF, to pick out, sift] **1 a :** to examine or investigate judicially **b :** to conduct the trial of **2 a :** to put to test or trial **b :** to test to the limit or breaking point : STRAIN ⟨*tries* his patience⟩ **3 :** to melt down and procure in a pure state : RENDER ⟨*try* out whale oil from blubber⟩ **4 :** to make an effort to do : ENDEAVOR

    syn ATTEMPT: TRY suggests effort or experiment made in the hope of ascertaining facts or of testing or proving something ⟨*tried* various occupations⟩ ATTEMPT suggests a beginning or venturing upon and often implies failure ⟨*attempted* to break through the enemy lines⟩

²try *n, pl* **tries :** an experimental trial : ATTEMPT

try for point : an attempt made after scoring a touchdown in football to kick a goal so as to score an additional point or to again carry the ball across the opponents' goal line or complete a forward pass in the opponents' end zone so as to score two additional points

try·ing \'trī-iŋ\ *adj* **:** causing distress or annoyance : hard to bear or endure ⟨a *trying* experience⟩

try on \(')trī-'ón, -'än\ *vt* **:** to put on (a garment) in order to test the fit — **try-on** \'trī-,ón, -,än\ *n*

try·out \'trī-,aut\ *n* **:** an experimental performance or demonstration: as **a :** a testing of one's ability to perform esp. as an athlete or actor **b :** a test performance of a play prior to its formal opening

try·pan·o·so·ma \trip-,an-ə-'sō-mə, ,trip-ə-nə-\ *n* **:** TRYPANOSOME

try·pan·o·some \trip-'an-ə-,sōm, 'trip-ə-nə-\ *n* [NL *Trypanosoma*, genus name, fr. Gk *trypanon* auger + *sōma* body] **:** any of a genus of parasitic flagellate protozoans that invade the blood of various vertebrates including man, are usu. transmitted by the bite of an insect, and include causers of serious disease (as sleeping sickness)

try·pan·o·so·mi·a·sis \trip-,an-ə-sə-'mī-ə-səs\ *n, pl* **-a·ses** \-ə-,sēz\ **:** infection with or disease caused by trypanosomes

tryp·sin \'trip-sən\ *n* [Gk *tryein* to wear down + E *-psin* (as in *pepsin*)] **:** an enzyme from pancreatic juice that breaks down protein in an alkaline medium — **tryp·tic** \'trip-tik\ *adj*

tryp·sin·o·gen \trip-'sin-ə-jən\ *n* **:** the inactive form of trypsin present in the pancreas

tryp·to·phan \'trip-tə-,fan\ *or* **tryp·to·phane** \-,fān\ *n* **:** a crystalline amino acid obtained esp. from casein and fibrin that is essential to animal life

try square *n* **:** an instrument used for laying off right angles and testing whether work is square

tryst \'trist, 'trīst\ *n* [OF *triste* watch post] **1 :** an agreement (as between lovers) to meet **2 :** an appointed meeting or meeting place

tsar \'zär, '(t)sär\ *var of* CZAR

tset·se \'(t)set-sē, 'tet-, '(t)sēt-, 'tēt-\ *n, pl* **tsetse** *or* **tseses** [Afrik, of Bantu origin] **:** any of a genus of two-winged flies mostly of Africa south of the Sahara desert that include vectors of human and animal trypanosomes — called also *tsetse fly*

T-shirt \'tē-,shərt\ *n* **:** a collarless short-sleeved cotton undershirt for men; *also* **:** a cotton or wool jersey outer shirt of similar design

T square *n* **:** a ruler with a crosspiece or head at one end used in making parallel lines

tsu·na·mi \(t)sü-'näm-ē\ *n* [Jap] **:** a great sea wave produced by submarine earth movement or volcanic eruption — **tsu·na·mic** \-'näm-ik\ *adj*

tsu·tsu·ga·mu·shi disease \,(t)süt-sə-gə-'mü-shē-\ *n* [Jap *tsutsugamushi* scrub typhus mite, fr. *tsutsuga* sickness + *mushi* insect] **:** an acute rickettsial disease of the western Pacific area that resembles typhus and is transmitted by larval mites — called also *scrub typhus*

Tua·reg \'twä-,reg\ *n* **:** a member of the dominant nomadic people of the central and western Sahara and the Middle Niger

tu·a·ta·ra \,tü-ə-'tär-ə\ *n* [Maori *tuatàra*] **:** a large spiny four-footed reptile of islands off the coast of New Zealand that has a vestigial third eye and is the only survivor of a once widely distributed order

¹tub \'təb\ *n* [MD *tubbe*] **1 :** a wide low vessel orig. formed with wooden staves, round bottom, and hoops **2 :** an old or slow boat **3 :** BATHTUB; *also* **:** BATH **4 :** the amount that a tub will hold

²tub *vb* **tubbed; tub·bing :** to wash or bathe in a tub — **tub·ba·ble** \'təb-ə-bəl\ *adj*

tu·ba \'t(y)ü-bə\ *n* [It, fr. L, trumpet] **:** a large low-pitched brass wind instrument; *esp* **:** one with a conical bore and cup-shaped mouthpiece

tub·al \'t(y)ü-bəl\ *adj* **:** of, relating to, or involving a tube

tub·by \'təb-ē\ *adj* **tub·bi·er; -est :** PUDGY, FAT

tube \'t(y)üb\ *n* [L *tubus*] **1 a :** a hollow elongated cylinder; *esp* **:** one to convey fluids **b :** a slender channel within a plant or animal body : DUCT **2 :** any of various usu. cylindrical structures or devices: as **a :** a round metal container from which a paste is dispensed by squeezing **b :** TUNNEL **c :** the basically cylindrical part connecting the mouthpiece and bell of a wind instrument **d :** INNER TUBE **e :** ELECTRON TUBE **f :** VACUUM TUBE — **tubed** \'t(y)übd\ *adj* — **tube·like** \'t(y)üb-,līk\ *adj*

tuba

tube foot *n* **:** one of the small flexible tubular processes of most echinoderms that are extensions of the water-vascular system used esp. in locomotion and grasping

tube·less \'t(y)üb-ləs\ *adj* **:** lacking a tube; *esp* **:** being a pneumatic tire that does not depend on an inner tube for airtightness

tube nucleus *n* **:** the nucleus of a pollen grain that is held to control growth of the pollen tube — compare GENERATIVE NUCLEUS

tu·ber \'t(y)ü-bər\ *n* [L, lump, tuber] **1 a :** a plant underground resting stage consisting of a short fleshy stem bearing minute scale leaves each with a bud in its axil potentially able to produce a new plant — compare BULB, CORM **b :** a fleshy root or rhizome resembling a tuber **2 :** an anatomical prominence : TUBEROSITY

tu·ber·cle \'t(y)ü-bər-kəl\ *n* [L *tuberculum*, dim. of *tuber* lump, tuber] **1 :** a small knobby prominence or outgrowth esp. on a plant or animal : NODULE **2 :** a small abnormal lump in the substance of an organ or in the skin; *esp* **:** one caused by tuberculosis — **tu·ber·cled** \-kəld\ *adj*

tubercle bacillus *n* **:** the bacterium that causes tuberculosis

tu·ber·cu·lar \t(y)u̇-'bər-kyə-lər\ *adj* **1 :** relating to, resembling, or constituting a tubercle : TUBERCULATE **2 :** characterized by tubercular lesions ⟨*tubercular* leprosy⟩ **3 :** of, relating to, or affected with tuberculosis : TUBERCULOUS ⟨*tubercular* meningitis⟩ — **tu·ber·cu·lar·ly** *adv*

tu·ber·cu·late \t(y)u̇-'bər-kyə-lət\ *or* **tu·ber·cu·lat·ed** \-,lāt-əd\ *adj* **1 :** having or beset with tubercles **2 :** TUBERCULAR — **tu·ber·cu·late·ly** *adv* — **tu·ber·cu·la·tion** \-,bər-kyə-'lā-shən\ *n*

tu·ber·cu·lin \t(y)u̇-'bər-kyə-lən\ *n* **:** a sterile liquid containing substances from the tubercle bacillus that is used in the diagnosis of tuberculosis

tuberculin test *n* **:** a test for hypersensitivity to tuberculin as an indication of past or present tubercular infection

tu·ber·cu·loid \t(y)u̇-'bər-kyə-,lȯid\ *adj* **:** suggesting tuberculosis esp. by the presence of tubercles ⟨*tuberculoid* leprosy⟩

tu·ber·cu·lo·sis \t(y)u̇-,bər-kyə-'lō-səs\ *n* [L *tuberculum* tubercle] **:** a communicable disease of some vertebrates caused by the tubercle bacillus and typically marked by wasting, fever, and formation of cheesy tubercles that in man primarily occur in the lungs

tu·ber·cu·lous \t(y)u̇-'bər-kyə-ləs\ *adj* **1 :** TUBERCULAR 1, TUBERCULATE **2 :** being or affected or associated with tuberculosis ⟨a *tuberculous* process⟩ ⟨*tuberculous* peritonitis⟩ — **tu·ber·cu·lous·ly** *adv*

tube·rose \'t(y)üb-,rōz; 't(y)ü-bə-,rōz, -bə-,rōs\ *n* [L *tuberosus* tuberous, fr. *tuber*] **:** a Mexican bulbous herb of the amaryllis family grown for its spike of fragrant white flowers

tu·ber·os·i·ty \,t(y)ü-bə-'räs-ət-ē\ *n, pl* **-ties :** a rounded prominence; *esp* **:** one on a bone usu. serving for the attachment of muscles or ligaments

tu·ber·ous \'t(y)ü-b(ə-)rəs\ *adj* **1 a :** consisting of or resembling a tuber **b :** bearing tubers **2 :** of, relating to, or being a plant tuber or tuberous root — **tu·ber·ous·ly** *adv*

tuberous root *n* **:** a thick fleshy storage root like a tuber but lacking buds or scale leaves — **tu·ber·ous–root·ed** \‚t(y)ü-b(ə-)rəs-'rüt-əd, -'rüt-\ *adj*

tu·bi·fex \'t(y)ü-bə-‚feks\ *n, pl* **-fex** *or* **-fex·es** : any of a genus of slender reddish oligochaete worms that live in tubes in fresh or brackish water and are widely used as food for aquarium fish

tub·ing \'t(y)ü-biŋ\ *n* **1** : material in the form of a tube; *also* : a length or piece of tube **2** : a series or system of tubes

tu·bu·lar \'t(y)ü-byə-lər\ *adj* **1** : having the form of or consisting of a tube **2** : made or provided with tubes — **tu·bu·lar·i·ty** \‚t(y)ü-byə-'lar-ət-ē\ *n* — **tu·bu·lar·ly** \'t(y)ü-byə-lər-lē\ *adv*

tu·bule \'t(y)ü-byül\ *n* [L *tubulus*, dim. of *tubus* tube] : a small tube; *esp* : a long slender anatomical channel

tu·bu·lif·er·ous \‚t(y)ü-byə-'lif-(ə-)rəs\ *adj* : having or made up of tubules

¹tuck \'tək\ *vb* [ME *tukken*] **1 a** : to pull up or draw together into folds **b** : to make a tuck in **2** : to put or fit into a snug position or place ⟨cottage *tucked* away in the hill⟩ ⟨*tuck* your legs out of the way⟩ **3 a** : to push in the loose end of so as to hold tightly ⟨*tuck* in your shirt⟩ **b** : to cover by tucking in bedclothes ⟨a child *tucked* in for the night⟩

²tuck *n* **1** : a stitched fold (as in a garment) **2 a** : an act or instance of tucking **b** : a tucked position or piece

³tuck *n* : VIGOR, ENERGY

¹tuck·er \'tək-ər\ *n* **1** : one that tucks **2** : a piece of lace or cloth in the neckline of a dress

²tucker *vt* **tuck·ered; tuck·er·ing** \'tək-(ə-)riŋ\ : EXHAUST

-tude \‚t(y)üd\ *n suffix* [L *-tudin-, -tudo*] : -NESS ⟨omni*tude*⟩

Tu·dor \'t(y)üd-ər\ *adj* **1** : of or relating to an English royal family reigning from 1485 to 1603 **2** : of, relating to, or characteristic of the Tudor period — **Tudor** *n*

Tues·day \'t(y)üz-dē\ *n* [OE *tīwesdæg*, lit., day of Tiu (god of war)] : the 3d day of the week

tu·fa \'t(y)ü-fə\ *n* [It *tufo*, fr. L *tophus*] **1** : TUFF **2 a** : a porous rock formed as a deposit from springs or streams — **tu·fa·ceous** \t(y)ü-'fā-shəs\ *adj*

tuff \'təf\ *n* : a rock composed of the finer kinds of volcanic detritus — **tuff·a·ceous** \‚tə-'fā-shəs\ *adj*

tuf·fet \'təf-ət\ *n* **1** : TUFT 1a **2** : a low seat

¹tuft \'təft\ *n* [modif. of MF *tufe*] **1 a** : a small cluster of long flexible outgrowths (as hairs or feathers) **b** : a bunch of soft fluffy threads cut off short and used as ornament **2** : CLUMP, CLUSTER ⟨a *tuft* of grass⟩ **3** : MOUND — **tufty** \'təf-tē\ *adj*

²tuft *vt* **1** : to provide or adorn with a tuft **2** : to make (as a mattress) firm by stitching at intervals and sewing on tufts

¹tug \'təg\ *vb* **tugged; tug·ging** [ME *tuggen;* akin to E *¹tow*] **1 a** : to pull hard **b** : to move by pulling hard : DRAG, HAUL; *also* : to carry with difficulty **2** : to struggle in opposition : CONTEND **3** : to tow with a tugboat — **tug·ger** *n*

²tug *n* **1 a** : a harness trace **b** : a rope or chain used for pulling **2 a** : an act or instance of tugging : PULL **b** : a struggle between opposing individuals or forces **3** : a strong pulling force or straining effort **4** : TUGBOAT

tug·boat \'təg-‚bōt\ *n* : a strongly built powerful boat used for towing and pushing

tug–of–war \‚təg-ə(v)-'wò(ə)r\ *n, pl* **tugs–of–war 1** : a struggle for supremacy **2** : an athletic contest in which two teams pull against each other at opposite ends of a rope

tu·i·tion \t(y)ù-'ish-ən\ *n* [L *tuition-, tuitio* guardianship, fr. *tueri* to look at, guard] **1** : the act or profession of teaching : INSTRUCTION **2** : the price of or payment for instruction — **tu·i·tion·al** \-'ish-nəl, -ən-°l\ *adj*

tu·la·re·mia \‚t(y)ü-lə-'rē-mē-ə\ *n* [NL, fr. *Tulare* county, Calif.] : an infectious bacterial disease of rodents, man, and some domestic animals transmitted esp. by the bites of insects and in man marked by symptoms (as fever) of toxemia — **tu·la·re·mic** \-mik\ *adj*

tu·le \'tü-lē\ *n* [Sp, fr. Nahuatl *tullin*] : either of two large coarse sedges growing on wet land of the southwestern U.S.

tu·lip \'t(y)ü-ləp\ *n* [NL *tulipa*, fr. Turk *tülbend* turban] : any of a genus of Eurasian bulbous herbs of the lily family that have linear or broadly lanceolate leaves and are widely grown for their showy flowers; *also* : the flower or bulb of a tulip

tulip tree *n* : a tall No. American timber tree of the magnolia family with large greenish yellow tulip-shaped flowers and soft white wood used esp. for cabinetwork and woodenware; *also* : its wood

tulle \'tül\ *n* [F, fr. *Tulle*, France] : a sheer often stiffened silk, rayon, or nylon net used chiefly for veils, evening dresses, or ballet costumes

tul·li·bee \'təl-ə-bē\ *n* : any of several American whitefishes; *esp* : a common cisco that is a commercially important food fish

¹tum·ble \'təm-bəl\ *vb* **tum·bled; tum·bling** \-b(ə-)liŋ\ [ME *tumblen*, freq. of *tumben* to dance, fr. OE *tumbian*] **1 a** : to perform gymnastic feats of rolling and turning **b** : to turn end over end in falling or flight **2 a** : to fall suddenly and helplessly **b** : to suffer a sudden decline, downfall, or defeat : COLLAPSE **3** : to move or go hurriedly and confusedly **4** : to come to understand **5 a** : to throw or push and cause to topple or tumble **b** : to toss about or together into a confused mass **c** : RUMPLE, DISORDER

²tumble *n* **1** : a disorderly state or collection **2** : an act or instance of tumbling

tum·ble·bug \'təm-bəl-‚bəg\ *n* : a large stout-bodied beetle that rolls dung into small balls, buries them in the ground, and lays its eggs in them

tum·ble·down \‚təm-bəl-‚daùn\ *adj* : DILAPIDATED, RAMSHACKLE

tum·bler \'təm-blər\ *n* **1** : one that tumbles: as **a** : GYMNAST, ACROBAT **b** : a pigeon that habitually somersaults backward in flight **2** : a drinking glass without foot or stem and orig. with pointed or convex base — compare GOBLET **3** : a movable part in a lock that must be adjusted (as by a key) before the bolt can be thrown **4** : a device or mechanism for tumbling (as a revolving cage in which clothes are dried)

tum·ble·weed \'təm-bəl-‚wēd\ *n* : a plant that breaks away from its roots in autumn and is blown about by the wind

tum·bling *n* : the skill, practice, or sport of executing gymnastic tumbles

tum·brel *or* **tum·bril** \'təm-brəl\ *n* [OF *tumberel* tipcart, fr. *tomber* to fall, of Gmc origin; akin to E *tumble*] : a farmer's cart used during the French Revolution to carry condemned persons to the guillotine

tu·me·fac·tion \‚t(y)ü-mə-'fak-shən\ *n* : a swelling or becoming tumorous or the resulting state or lesion — **tu·me·fac·tive** \-'fak-tiv\ *adj* — **tu·me·fied** \'t(y)ü-mə-‚fīd\ *adj*

tu·mes·cence \t(y)ü-'mes-°n(t)s\ *n* : a swelling or becoming swollen or the resulting state — **tu·mes·cent** \-°nt\ *adj*

tu·mid \'t(y)ü-məd\ *adj* [L *tumidus*, fr. *tumēre* to be swollen] **1** : marked by swelling : SWOLLEN, ENLARGED **2** : BOMBASTIC, TURGID — **tu·mid·i·ty** \t(y)ü-'mid-ət-ē\ *n*

tum·my \'təm-ē\ *n, pl* **tummies** : STOMACH 1c

tu·mor \'t(y)ü-mər\ *n* [L *tumor*, fr. *tumēre* to be swollen] : a swollen or distended part; *esp* : an abnormal mass of tissue that is not inflammatory, arises without obvious cause from cells of preexistent tissue, and possesses no physiologic function — **tu·mor·like** \-‚līk\ *adj* — **tu·mor·ous** \'t(y)üm-(ə-)rəs\ *adj*

tump·line \'təmp-‚līn\ *n* : a sling formed by a strap slung over the forehead or chest used for carrying a pack on the back or in hauling loads

tu·mult \'t(y)ü-‚məlt\ *n* [L *tumultus*] **1** : violent and disorderly commotion or disturbance (as of a crowd of people) with uproar and confusion ⟨the *tumult* of the sea⟩ **2** : violent agitation of mind

tu·mul·tu·ous \t(y)ü-'məl-chə-wəs, -chəs\ *adj* : marked by tumult and esp. by violent or overwhelming turbulence or upheaval — **tu·mul·tu·ous·ly** *adv* — **tu·mul·tu·ous·ness** *n*

tu·mu·lus \'t(y)ü-myə-ləs\ *n, pl* **-li** \-‚lī, -‚lē\ [L] : an artificial hillock or mound usu. over an ancient grave : BARROW

tun \'tən\ *n* [OE *tunne*] **1** : a large cask for liquids and esp. wine **2** : the capacity of a tun as a varying liquid measure; *esp* : a measure of 252 gallons

---

ə abut; ᵊ kitten; ər further; a back; ā bake; ä cot, cart; aù out; ch chin; e less; ē easy; g gift; i trip; ī life

¹tu·na \'tü-nə\ *n* [Sp, of AmerInd origin] **:** any of several flat-jointed prickly pears; *also* **:** the edible fruit of a tuna

²tu·na \'t(y)ü-nə\ *n, pl* **tuna** *or* **tunas** [AmerSp, alter. of Sp *atún,* fr. Ar *at-tūn* the tunny, fr. L *thunnus* tunny] **:** any of several mostly large active sea fishes (as an albacore or bonito) related to the mackerels and valued for food and sport

tun·a·ble *also* **tune·a·ble** \'t(y)ü-nə-bəl\ *adj* **1** *archaic* **a :** TUNEFUL **b :** sounding in tune **:** CONCORDANT **2 :** capable of being tuned — **tun·a·ble·ness** *n* — **tun·a·bly** \-blē\ *adv*

tun·dra \'tən-drə, 'tün-\ *n* [Russ, of Finno-Ugric origin] **:** a treeless plain of arctic and subarctic regions

¹tune \'t(y)ün\ *n* [ME, alter. of *tone*] **1 a :** a succession of pleasing musical tones **:** MELODY **b :** the musical setting of a song ⟨a hymn *tune*⟩ **2 :** correct musical pitch or consonance ⟨the piano was not in *tune*⟩ **3 a :** AGREEMENT, HARMONY ⟨in *tune* with the times⟩ **b :** general attitude ⟨changed his *tune* after reading the report⟩ **4 :** AMOUNT, EXTENT ⟨a subsidy to the *tune* of $5,000,000⟩

²tune *vb* **1 :** to come or bring into harmony **:** ATTUNE **2 :** TUNE IN ⟨*tune* a radio⟩ **3 :** to adjust in musical pitch **4 :** to adjust for precise functioning ⟨*tune* a motor⟩

tune·ful \'t(y)ün-fəl\ *adj* **:** MELODIOUS, MUSICAL — **tune·ful·ly** \-fə-lē\ *adv* — **tune·ful·ness** *n*

tune in *vb* **:** to adjust a radio or television receiver to respond to waves of a particular frequency so as to receive the material that is broadcast ⟨*tune* in a radio⟩⟨*tune in* a station⟩ ⟨*tune* in to a program⟩

tune out *vt* **:** to adjust a radio or television receiver so as not to receive (an unwanted signal) ⟨*tune out* a program⟩

tun·er \'t(y)ü-nər\ *n* **1 :** one that tunes ⟨piano *tuner*⟩ **2 :** something used for tuning; *esp* **:** the part of a receiving set consisting of the circuit used to adjust resonance

tune-up \'t(y)ün-,əp\ *n* **1 :** a general adjustment to ensure efficient functioning ⟨a motor *tune-up*⟩ **2 :** a preliminary trial **:** WARM-UP

tung \'təŋ\ *n* [Chin (Pek) *t'ung²*] **:** any of several trees of the spurge family whose seeds yield a drying oil; *esp* **:** a Chinese tree widely grown in warm regions

tung·sten \'təŋ(k)-stən\ *n* [Sw, fr. *tung* heavy + *sten* stone] **:** a gray-white heavy ductile hard metallic chemical element that is used esp. for electrical purposes and in hardening alloys (as steel) — called also *wolfram;* see ELEMENT table

tung tree *n* **:** TUNG

Tun·gu·sic \tún-'gü-zik\ *n* **:** a subfamily of Altaic languages spoken in Manchuria and northward — **Tungusic** *adj*

tu·nic \'t(y)ü-nik\ *n* [L *tunica*] **1 a :** a simple belted knee≈length or longer slip-on garment worn by ancient Greeks and Romans **b :** a long usu. plain and close-fitting jacket with high collar worn esp. as part of a uniform **c :** a blouse or jacket reaching to or just below the hips **2 :** an enclosing or covering anatomical structure **:** TUNICA

tu·ni·ca \'t(y)ü-ni-kə\ *n, pl* **-cae** \-nə-,kē, -,kī\ [L, tunic, membrane] **:** an enveloping integument, membrane, or layer of animal or plant tissue

¹tu·ni·cate \'t(y)ü-ni-kət, -nə-,kāt\ *also* **tu·ni·cat·ed** \-nə-,kāt-əd\ *adj* **1 :** having or covered with a tunic or tunica; *also* **:** made up of concentric layers ⟨a *tunicate* bulb⟩ **2 :** of or relating to the tunicates

²tunicate *n* **:** any of a major group (Tunicata) of lowly marine chordates with a reduced nervous system and an outer cuticular covering **:** SEA SQUIRT

tuning fork *n* **:** a 2-pronged metal instrument that gives a fixed tone when struck and is useful for tuning musical instruments and ascertaining standard pitch

tuning fork

¹tun·nel \'tən-ᵊl\ *n* [MF *tonnel,* dim. of *tonne* tun, of Celt origin] **:** an enclosed passage (as a tube or conduit; *esp* **:** one underground (as under an obstruction or in a mine) — **tun·nel·like** \-ᵊl-,(l)īk\ *adj*

²tunnel *vb* **-neled** *or* **-nelled; -nel·ing** *or* **-nel·ling** \'tən-liŋ, -ᵊl-iŋ\ **:** to make or use a tunnel or form a tunnel in — **tun·nel·er** \'tən-lər, -ᵊl-ər\ *n*

tun·ny \'tən-ē\ *n, pl* **tunnies** *also* **tunny** [L *thunnus,* fr. Gk *thynnos*] **:** TUNA

tu·pe·lo \'t(y)ü-pə-,lō\ *n, pl* **-los** [of AmerInd origin] **1 :** any of a genus of mostly No. American trees of the

dogwood family; *esp* **:** BLACK GUM **2 :** the pale soft easily worked wood of a tupelo

Tu·pi \tü-'pē, 'tü-,\ *n* **1 :** a member of a group of peoples of the Amazon valley **2 :** the language of the Tupi people

tup·pence *var of* TWOPENCE

tuque \'t(y)ük\ *n* [CanF, alter. of F *toque*] **:** a warm knitted usu. pointed stocking cap

tur·ban \'tər-bən\ *n* [MF *turbant,* fr. Turk *tülbend,* fr. Per *dulband*] **1 :** a headdress worn chiefly in countries of the eastern Mediterranean and southern Asia esp. by Muslims and made of a cap around which is wound a long cloth **2 :** a woman's close-fitting hat without a brim — **tur·baned** *or* **tur·banned** \-bənd\ *adj*

tur·bel·lar·i·an \,tər-bə-'ler-ē-ən, -'lar-\ *n* **:** any of a class (Turbellaria) of mostly aquatic and free-living flatworms; *esp* **:** PLANARIAN — **turbellarian** *adj*

tur·bid \'tər-bəd\ *adj* [L *turbidus* confused, turbid, fr. *turba* confusion, crowd] **1 a :** thick or opaque with roiled sediment ⟨*turbid* stream⟩ **b :** heavy with smoke or mist **:** DENSE **2 :** CONFUSED, MUDDLED ⟨*turbid* thought⟩ — **tur·bid·i·ty** \,tər-'bid-ət-ē\ *n* — **tur·bid·ly** \'tər-bəd-lē\ *adv* — **tur·bid·ness** *n*

tur·bi·nal \'tər-bən-ᵊl\ *adj* **:** TURBINATE 2 — **turbinal** *n*

¹tur·bi·nate \'tər-bə-nət\ *adj* [L *turbin-, turbo* top, whirlwind] **1 :** shaped like an inverted cone or a child's top ⟨a *turbinate* shell⟩ **2 :** of, relating to, or being the thin bony or cartilaginous plates on the walls of the nasal passages — **tur·bi·nat·ed** \-,nāt-əd\ *adj*

²turbinate *n* **:** a turbinate bone or cartilage

tur·bine \'tər-bən, -,bīn\ *n* [F, fr. L *turbin-, turbo* top, whirlwind] **:** an engine whose central driving shaft is fitted with vanes whirled around by the pressure of water or hot gases (as steam or exhaust gases)

tur·bo \'tər-bō\ *n, pl* **turbos** **1 :** TURBINE **2 :** TURBO-SUPERCHARGER

turbo- *comb form* **1 :** coupled directly to a driving turbine ⟨*turbo*fan⟩ **2 :** consisting of or incorporating a turbine ⟨*turbo*jet engine⟩

tur·bo·jet \'tər-bō-,jet\ *n* **:** an airplane powered by turbojet engines

turbojet engine *n* **:** an airplane propulsion system in which the power developed by a turbine is used to drive a compressor that supplies air to a burner and hot gases from the burner pass through the burner and thence to a rearward-directed thrust-producing exhaust nozzle

tur·bo·prop \'tər-bō-,präp\ *n* **1 :** TURBO-PROPELLER ENGINE **2 :** an airplane powered by turbo-propeller engines

tur·bo·pro·pel·ler engine \,tər-bō-prə-'pel-ər-\ *n* **:** a jet engine having a turbine-driven propeller and designed to produce thrust principally by means of a propeller although additional thrust is usu. obtained from the hot exhaust gases which issue in a jet

tur·bo·su·per·charg·er \-'sü-pər-,chär-jər\ *n* **:** a turbine compressor driven by hot exhaust gases of an airplane engine for feeding rarefied air at high altitudes into the carburetor of the engine at sea-level pressure so as to increase engine power

tur·bot \'tər-bət\ *n, pl* **turbot** *also* **turbots** [OF *tourbot*] **:** a large brownish European flatfish highly esteemed as a food fish; *also* **:** any of various flatfishes resembling this

tur·bu·lence \'tər-byə-lən(t)s\ *also* **tur·bu·len·cy** \-lən-sē\ *n* **:** the quality or state of being turbulent: as **a :** wild commotion **b :** irregular atmospheric motion esp. when characterized by up and down currents **c :** departure in a fluid from a smooth flow

tur·bu·lent \-lənt\ *adj* [L *turbulentus,* fr. *turba* confusion, crowd] **1 :** causing unrest, violence, or disturbance **2 :** characterized by agitation or tumult **:** TEMPESTUOUS — **tur·bu·lent·ly** *adv*

turbulent flow *n* **:** a fluid flow in which the velocity at a given point varies erratically in magnitude and direction

Tur·co- *or* **Tur·ko-** \'tər-kō\ *comb form* **1 :** Turkic **:** Turkish **:** Turk ⟨*Turco*phil⟩ **2 :** Turkish and ⟨*Turco*≈Greek⟩

tu·reen \tə-'rēn, tyü-\ *n* [F *terrine,* fr. fem. of *terrin* earthen, fr. *terre* earth, fr. L *terra*] **:** a deep bowl from which food (as soup) is served at table

¹turf \'tərf\ *n, pl* **turfs** \'tərfs\ *or* **turves** \'tərvz\ [OE] **1 :** the upper layer of soil bound by grass and plant roots into a thick mat; *also* **:** a piece of this — called also *sod*

---

j joke;   **ŋ** sing;   **ō** flow;   **ȯ** flaw;   **ȯi** coin;   **th** thin;   **t̲h̲** this;   **ü** loot;   **u̇** foot;   **y** yet;   **yü** few;   **yu̇** furious;   **zh** vision

2 a : PEAT **b :** a piece of peat dried for fuel **3 a :** a track or course for horse racing **b :** the sport or business of horse racing — **turfy** \'tər-fē\ *adj*

²turf *vt* : to cover with turf

turf·man \'tərf-mən\ *n* : a devotee of horse racing; *esp* : one who owns and races horses

tur·ges·cent \,tər-'jes-°nt\ *adj* [L *turgescere* to swell, inchoative of *turgēre* to be swollen] : becoming turgid, distended, or inflated : SWELLING — **tur·ges·cence** \-°n(t)s\ *n*

tur·gid \'tər-jəd\ *adj* [L *turgidus*, fr. *turgēre* to be swollen] **1 :** being in a state of distension : SWOLLEN ⟨*turgid* limbs⟩; *esp* : exhibiting turgor **2 :** excessively embellished in style or language : BOMBASTIC, POMPOUS — **tur·gid·i·ty** \,tər-'jid-ət-ē\ *n* — **tur·gid·ly** \'tər-jəd-lē\ *adv* — **tur·gid·ness** *n*

tur·gor \'tər-gər, -,gȯr\ *n* [LL, turgidity, fr. L *turgēre* to be swollen] : the normal state of firmness and tension typical of living cells

Turk \'tərk\ *n* **1 :** a member of any of numerous Asian peoples speaking Turkic languages who live in the region ranging from the Adriatic to the Sea of Okhotsk **2 :** a native or inhabitant of Turkey

tur·key \'tər-kē\ *n* [fr. *Turkey;* fr. confusion with the guinea fowl, supposed to be imported from Turkish territory] **1 :** a large American bird which is related to the common fowl, is of wide range in No. America, and is domesticated in most parts of the world **2 :** FAILURE, FLOP

turkey buzzard *n* : an American vulture common in So. and Central America and in the southern U.S. — called also *turkey vulture*

tur·key-cock \'tər-kē-,käk\ *n* **1 :** a male turkey — called also *tom, turkey-gob·bler* \,tər-kē-'gäb-lər\ **2 :** a strutting pompous person

turkey shoot *n* : a contest of marksmanship with a gun at a moving target and with a turkey as a prize

Tur·ki \'tər-,kē, 'tür-\ *n* : any central Asian Turkic language

Turk·ic \'tər-kik\ *n* : a subfamily of Altaic languages including Turkish — **Turkic** *adj*

¹Turk·ish \'tər-kish\ *adj* **1 :** of, relating to, or characteristic of Turkey, the Turks, or Turkish **2 :** TURKIC

²Turkish *n* : the Turkic language of Turkey

Turkish bath *n* : a bath in which the bather passes through a series of rooms heated to increasingly extreme temperatures by steam and then receives a rubdown, massage, and cold shower

Turkish coffee *n* : a sweetened decoction of pulverized coffee

Turkish delight *n* : a jellylike or gummy confection usu. cut in cubes and dusted with sugar — called also *Turkish paste*

Turkish tobacco *n* : a very aromatic tobacco of small leaf size grown chiefly in Turkey and Greece and adjoining territories and used esp. in cigarettes

Turkish towel *n* : a towel made of cotton terry cloth

Tur·ko·man *or* **Tur·co·man** \'tər-kə-mən\ *n, pl* **Turkomans** *or* **Turcomans** : a member of a group of peoples living chiefly in the Turkmen, Uzbek, and Kazakh republics of the U.S.S.R.

tur·mer·ic \'tərm-(ə-)rik, 'tüm-\ *n* [modif. of MF *terre merite*, fr. ML *terra merita*, lit., deserving or deserved earth] **1 :** an East Indian herb of the ginger family; *also* : its aromatic rootstock powdered for use as a condiment, yellow dye, or stimulant **2 :** any of several plants resembling turmeric

tur·moil \'tər-,mȯil\ *n* : an utterly confused or extremely agitated state or condition

¹turn \'tərn\ *vb* [OE *turnian, tyrnan* & OF *torner, tourner,* both fr. ML *tornare,* fr. L, to turn on a lathe, fr. *tornus* lathe, fr. Gk *tornos*] **1 a :** to move or cause to move around an axis or center : ROTATE, REVOLVE ⟨wheels *turning* slowly⟩⟨*turn* a crank⟩; *also* : to operate or cause to operate by so turning ⟨*turn* a key in a lock⟩ **b :** to whirl giddily : become dizzy ⟨his head *turned* at the height⟩ **c :** to have as a center (as of interest) or a decisive factor ⟨his decision must *turn* on circumstances⟩⟨the story *turns* about the adventures of a poor boy⟩ **d :** to execute by revolving ⟨*turn* handsprings⟩ **e :** to revolve mentally : PONDER **2 a :** to alter or reverse in position usu. by moving through an arc ⟨*turned* toward his companion⟩

⟨*turned* the paper over⟩: as **(1) :** to delve in or plow so as to turn ⟨*turn* the soil⟩ **(2) :** to make over by reversing the material and refastening ⟨*turn* a collar⟩ **b :** to disturb or upset the order or state or balance of ⟨everything *turned* topsy-turvy⟩⟨praise had *turned* his head⟩⟨a sight to *turn* her stomach⟩ **c :** to injure by a sudden twist : WRENCH ⟨*turned* her ankle⟩; *also* : to fold or cause to fold back ⟨*turn* the edge of a knife⟩ **3 a :** to take or cause to take or move in another, an opposite, or a particular direction ⟨*turned* the flood into an old stream bed⟩⟨the road *turns* to the left⟩⟨*turned* his car around⟩⟨when the tide *turns*⟩; *also* : to pass with a change of direction ⟨*turn* a corner⟩ **b :** to alter from a previous or anticipated course ⟨these few votes *turned* the election⟩ **c (1) :** to change one's attitude or reverse one's course of action to one of opposition or hostility ⟨felt his friends had *turned* against him⟩; *also* : DEFECT **(2) :** to attack suddenly and usu. unexpectedly and violently ⟨the dog *turned* on his master⟩ **d :** to bring to bear : TRAIN ⟨*turn* a weapon on an enemy⟩; *also* : to direct or point usu. toward or away from something ⟨the light *turned* toward the gate⟩⟨*turned* his thoughts homeward⟩ **e :** to influence toward a change (as in one's way of life) **f :** DEVOTE, APPLY ⟨*turned* his skills to the service of mankind⟩ **g :** to cause to recoil ⟨*turn* an opponent's argument against him⟩ **h :** to drive or send from or to a specified place or condition ⟨*turn* cattle into a field⟩ ⟨*turn* mutineers adrift⟩ **i :** to seek out as a source of something ⟨*turn* to a friend for help⟩ **4 :** to change or cause to change ⟨water *turned* to ice⟩: as **a :** TRANSFORM, BECOME ⟨*turn* wild land into fruitful farms⟩⟨*turn* traitor⟩ **b :** to cause to spoil : SOUR ⟨*turned* milk⟩ **c :** to change in color ⟨leaves *turning* in the fall⟩ **d :** to give a particular nature or appearance to ⟨hair *turned* white by sorrow⟩ **e :** TRANSLATE, PARAPHRASE **f :** to exchange for something else ⟨*turn* property into cash⟩ **g :** to be inconstant : VARY **5 a :** to give a rounded form to by means of a lathe and cutting tool **b :** to give a well-rounded or graceful shape or form to ⟨*turn* the heel of a sock⟩⟨*turned* a phrase⟩ **c :** to become or cause to become bent or curved **6 a :** to stock and dispose of (as money or goods) : change or cause to change hands **b :** to gain in the course of business ⟨*turning* a quick profit⟩ — **turn a hair :** to be or become upset or frightened — **turn one's hand** *or* **turn a hand :** to set to work : apply oneself usefully — **turn tail :** to run away : FLEE — **turn the scale :** to prove decisive — **turn the trick :** to bring about the desired result or effect — **turn turtle :** CAPSIZE, OVERTURN

²turn *n* **1 :** the action or an act of turning about a center or axis ⟨each *turn* of the wheel⟩ **2 a :** a change or changing of direction, course, or position ⟨an illegal left *turn*⟩⟨*turn* of the tide⟩ **b :** a place where something turns : BEND, CURVE ⟨at the *turn* of the road⟩ **c (1) :** a change or changing of condition or trend ⟨took a *turn* for the better⟩⟨a *turn* in the weather⟩ **(2) :** a usu. sudden and brief spell of disorder of body or spirits; *esp* : a state of nervous shock or faintness ⟨gave him a *turn*⟩ **d :** a musical ornament consisting of a group of notes including the one next above and next below the principal note **3 :** a short walk or ride ⟨took a *turn* through the park⟩ **4 :** an act affecting another ⟨did me a very bad *turn*⟩ **5 a :** a period of action or activity : SPELL ⟨each took a *turn* at the job⟩⟨a *turn* as guard⟩ **b :** place or appointed time in a succession or scheduled order ⟨waited his *turn* at the dentist's⟩ ⟨take *turns*⟩ **6 :** special purpose or need ⟨it served his *turn*⟩ **7 a :** distinctive quality or character ⟨a neat *turn* of phrase⟩ **b :** the form in accord with which something is fashioned : CAST ⟨a peculiar *turn* of mind⟩ **c :** manner of arrangement esp. in being coiled or twisted; *also* : a single round (as of a rope) ⟨took a *turn* around a post to hold the steer⟩ **d :** a special adaptive twist or interpretation ⟨gave the old tale a new *turn*⟩ **8 :** particular or special aptitude or skill : BENT ⟨a *turn* for languages⟩ — **at every turn :** CONSTANTLY, CONTINUOUSLY — **to a turn :** precisely right : PERFECTLY

turn·about \'tərn-ə-,baut\ *n* : a change or reversal of direction, trend, policy, or role

turn·around \-,raund\ *n* : a space permitting the turning around of a vehicle

turn away *vb* **1 :** DEFLECT, AVERT **2 a :** to send away : REJECT, DISMISS **b :** REPEL **c :** to refuse admittance or acceptance to **3 :** to start to go away : DEPART

turn back *vb* **1 a :** to stop going forward **b :** to go in the reverse direction : RETURN **2 :** to refer to an earlier time or place **3 :** to drive back or away **4 :** to stop the advance of : CHECK **5 :** to fold back

turn·buck·le \'tərn-,bək-əl\ *n* : a link with a screw thread at one or both ends used for tightening a rod or stay by pulling together the ends that it connects

turn·coat \'tərn-,kōt\ *n* : one who forsakes his party or principles : TRAITOR

turn down \'tərn-'daùn, ,tərn-\ *vt* **1 :** to fold or double down **2 :** to turn upside down : INVERT **3 :** to reduce in height or intensity by turning a control ⟨*turn down* the lights⟩ **4 :** REJECT — **turn·down** \'tərn-,daùn\ *adj or n*

turn·er \'tər-nər\ *n* : one that turns or is used for turning ⟨cake *turner*⟩; *esp* : one that forms articles with a lathe

turn·ery \'tər-nə-rē\ *n, pl* **-er·ies :** the work, products, or shop of a turner

turn in *vb* **1 a :** to give up or hand over ⟨*turn in* extra supplies⟩ **b :** to inform on : BETRAY **c :** to acquit oneself of ⟨*turn in* a good job⟩ **2 :** to turn from a road or path so as to enter ⟨*turn in* at the gate⟩ **3 :** to go to bed

turning point *n* : a point at which a significant change occurs

tur·nip \'tər-nəp\ *n* : either of two biennial herbs of the mustard family with thick roots eaten as a vegetable or fed to stock: **a :** one with hairy leaves and usu. white and flattened roots **b :** RUTABAGA

turn·key \'tərn-,kē\ *n* : one who has charge of a prison's keys : JAILER

turn off \'tərn-'óf, ,tərn-\ *vt* **1 :** DISMISS, DISCHARGE ⟨*turn off* a bad servant⟩ **2 :** to turn aside or aside from something ⟨*turn off* a puzzling question⟩ ⟨*turned off* into a side road⟩ **3 :** to stop the functioning or flow of by or as if by turning a control **4 :** to evoke a negative feeling in

turn-off \'tərn-,óf\ *n* **1 :** a turning off **2 :** a place where one turns off

turn on *vt* **1 :** to cause to function or flow by or as if by turning a control ⟨*turn* the water *on* full⟩ ⟨*turn on* the lights⟩ ⟨*turned on* all of her charm⟩ **2 a :** to undergo or cause to undergo an intense often visionary experience by taking a drug; *also* : to cause to get high **b :** to move pleasurably ⟨rock music *turns* her *on*⟩; *also* : to excite sexually

turn out \'tərn-'aùt, ,tərn-\ *vb* **1 :** to put out of some shelter : EVICT **2 :** to empty of contents; *also* : CLEAN **3 :** to make with rapidity or regularity **4 :** to equip, dress, or finish in a careful or elaborate way **5 :** to turn off (as a light) **6 a :** to call (as a guard) from rest or shelter **b :** to come out in answer to a summons **c :** to get out of bed **7 :** to prove ultimately to be

turn-out \'tərn-,aùt\ *n* **1 :** an act of turning out **2 :** a gathering of people for a special purpose **3 :** a widened space (as in a highway) for vehicles to pass or park **4 :** a clearing out for cleaning **5 a :** a carriage with its team and equipment **b :** an outfit of clothes : COSTUME **6 :** YIELD, OUTPUT

turn over \'tərn-'ō-vər, ,tərn-\ *vb* **1 :** to shift in position (as by overturning, rolling, or capsizing); *also* : ROTATE ⟨engines *turning over* slowly⟩ **2 a :** to examine or search by shifting item by item often slowly or idly ⟨*turning over* old letters⟩ **b :** to examine in the mind : meditate on ⟨*turned over* the problem in search of a solution⟩ **3 a :** to hand over : TRANSFER ⟨*turned over* his duties to an assistant⟩ **b :** to receive and dispose of esp. in the course of business ⟨*turned over* his stock several times in the course of a year⟩; *also* : to do business to the amount of ⟨expected to *turn over* $1000 a week⟩ **4 :** to heave with nausea ⟨his stomach *turned over* with shock⟩

¹turn·over \'tərn-,ō-vər\ *n* **1 :** an act or result of turning over; *esp* : UPSET **2 :** a shifting usu. in position or opinion **3 :** a reorganization esp. of personnel **4 :** a pie or tart with one half of the crust turned over the other **5 :** a part (as the flap of an envelope) turned or folded over **6 :** the amount of business done or work accomplished; *also* : the rate at which material is processed **7 :** the buying, selling, and replacing of goods considered as one complete process ⟨the annual *turnover* in shoes⟩ **8 :** the number of employees hired in a given time to replace those leaving or discharged

²turn·over \,tərn-,ō-vər\ *adj* : capable of being turned over : TURNDOWN ⟨*turnover* cuffs⟩

turn·pike \'tərn-,pīk\ *n* [ME *turnepike* revolving frame bearing spikes and serving as a barrier, fr. *turnen* to turn + *pike*] **1 :** a toll bar : TOLLGATE **2 a :** a toll road; *esp* : a toll expressway **b :** a main road

turn·spit \-,spit\ *n* **1 :** one that turns a spit **2 :** a rotatable spit

turn·stile \-,stīl\ *n* : a post with arms pivoted on the top set in a passageway so that persons can pass through only on foot one by one

turn·stone \-,stōn\ *n* : any of various widely distributed migratory shorebirds resembling the related plovers and sandpipers

turn·ta·ble \-,tā-bəl\ *n* : a revolvable platform: as **a :** a platform with a track for turning wheeled vehicles **b :** LAZY SUSAN **c :** a rotating platform that carries a phonograph record

turnstile

turn to \'tərn-'tü\ *vi* : to apply oneself to work : act vigorously

turn up \'tərn-'əp, ,tərn-\ *vb* **1 :** to bring or come to light usu. unexpectedly or after being lost ⟨the papers will *turn up*⟩ **2 :** to raise or increase by or as if by adjusting a control ⟨*turn up* the heat⟩ **3 a :** to turn out to be ⟨*turned up* missing⟩ : become evident ⟨name is always *turning up* in the newspapers⟩ **b :** to put in an appearance ⟨*turned up* half an hour late⟩ **4 :** to happen unexpectedly — **turn up one's nose** : to show scorn or disdain

turn-up \,tərn-,əp\ *adj* **1 :** turned up ⟨*turnup* nose⟩ **2 :** made or fitted to be turned up ⟨*turnup* collar⟩

turn·ver·ein \'tərn-və-,rīn, 'türn-\ *n* [G, fr. *turnen* to perform gymastic exercises + *verein* club] : an association of gymnasts and athletes : an athletic club

tur·pen·tine \'tər-pən-,tīn\ *n* [MF *tourbentine* oleoresin obtained from the terebinth, fr. L *terebinthus* terebinth, fr. Gk *terebinthos*] **1 :** an oleoresin obtained from various conifers (as some pines and firs) **2 a :** an essential oil obtained from turpentines by distillation and used esp. as a solvent and thinner — called also *gum turpentine* **b :** a similar oil obtained by distillation or carbonization of pinewood — called also *wood turpentine*

tur·pi·tude \'tər-pə-,t(y)üd\ *n* [L *turpitudo*, fr. *turpis* vile, base] : inherent baseness : DEPRAVITY ⟨moral *turpitude*⟩

turps \'tərps\ *n* : TURPENTINE

tur·quoise \'tər-,k(w)óiz\ *n* [MF *turquoyse*, fem. of *turquoys* Turkish] **1 :** a mineral that is a blue, bluish green, or greenish gray hydrous basic copper aluminum phosphate, takes a high polish, and sometimes is valued as a gem **2 :** a variable color averaging a light greenish blue

tur·ret \'tər-ət, 'tə-rət, 'tür-ət\ *n* [MF *toret*, dim. of *tor*, *tur* tower, fr. L *turris*] **1 :** a little tower often at a corner of a building **2 a :** a pivoted and revolvable holder in a machine tool **b :** a photographic or television camera device holding several lenses **3 a :** a gunner's fixed or movable enclosure in an airplane **b :** a revolving structure on a warship or on a tank in which guns are mounted — **tur·ret·ed** \-əd\ *adj*

¹tur·tle \'tərt-ᵊl\ *n* [OE *turtla*, fr. L *turtur*] *archaic* : TURTLEDOVE

²turtle *n, pl* **turtles** *also* **turtle** [prob. modif. of F *tortue*] : any of an order (Testudinata) of land, freshwater, and marine reptiles with a toothless horny beak and a bony shell which encloses the trunk and into which the head, limbs, and tail usu. may be withdrawn — compare TERRAPIN, TORTOISE

³turtle *vi* **tur·tled; tur·tling** \'tərt-liŋ, -ᵊl-iŋ\ : to catch turtles esp. as an occupation

tur·tle·back \'tərt-ᵊl-,bak\ *n* : a raised convex surface — **turtleback** *or* **tur·tle-backed** \,tərt-ᵊl-'bakt\ *adj*

tur·tle·dove \'tərt-ᵊl-,dəv\ *n* [¹*turtle*] : any of several small wild pigeons esp. of an Old World genus noted for plaintive cooing

tur·tle·neck \-,nek\ *n* : a high close-fitting turnover collar used esp. for sweaters; *also* : a sweater with a turtleneck

turves *pl of* TURF

¹Tus·can \'təs-kən\ *n* **1 :** a native or inhabitant of Tuscany **2 a :** the Italian language spoken in Tuscany **b :** the standard literary dialect of Italian

j joke; **ŋ** sing; **ō** flow; **ó** flaw; **ói** coin; **th** thin; **th** this; **ü** loot; **ù** foot; **y** yet; **yü** few; **yù** furious; **zh** vision

²Tuscan *adj* : of, relating to, or characteristic of Tuscany, the Tuscans, or Tuscan

Tus·ca·ro·ra \ˌtəs-kə-ˈrōr-ə, -ˈrór-\ *n* : a member of an Iroquoian people of No. Carolina and later of New York and Ontario

¹tush \ˈtəsh\ *n* [OE *tūsc*] : a long pointed tooth : TUSK — **tushed** \ˈtəsht\ *adj*

²tush *interj* — used to express disdain or reproach

¹tusk \ˈtəsk\ *n* [alter. of OE *tūx*] **1** : a long greatly enlarged tooth (as of an elephant, walrus, or boar) that projects when the mouth is closed and serves for digging food or as a weapon **2** : a tooth-shaped part — **tusked** \ˈtəskt\ *adj*

²tusk *vt* : to dig up or gash with a tusk

tusk·er \ˈtəs-kər\ *n* : an animal with tusks; *esp* : a male elephant with two normally developed tusks

¹tus·sle \ˈtəs-əl\ *vi* **tus·sled; tus·sling** \ˈtəs-(ə-)liŋ\ [ME *tussillen*] : to struggle roughly : SCUFFLE

²tussle *n* **1** : a physical contest or struggle : SCUFFLE **2** : a rough argument, controversy, or struggle against difficult odds

tus·sock \ˈtəs-ək\ *n* : a compact tuft esp. of grass or sedge; *also* : a hummock in marsh bound together by plant roots — **tus·socky** \ˈtəs-ə-kē\ *adj*

tussock moth *n* : any of numerous dull-colored moths commonly with wingless females

tut \a t-*sound made by suction rather than explosion; often read as* 'tət\ *or* **tut-tut** *interj* — used to express disapproval or disbelief

tu·tee \t(y)ü-ˈtē\ *n* : one who is being tutored

tu·te·lage \ˈt(y)üt-ºl-ij\ *n* [L *tutela* protection, guardian, fr. *tut-, tueri* to look at, guard] **1** : an act of guarding or protecting : GUARDIANSHIP **2** : the state of being under a guardian or tutor; *also* : the right, power, or influence of a tutor over his pupil **3** : INSTRUCTION

tu·te·lar \ˈt(y)üt-ºl-ər\ *adj* : TUTELARY

tu·te·lary \ˈt(y)üt-ºl-ˌer-ē\ *adj* **1** : having the guardianship of a person or a thing ⟨*tutelary* goddess⟩ **2** : of or relating to a guardian ⟨*tutelary* authority⟩

¹tu·tor \ˈt(y)üt-ər\ *n* [L, guardian, fr. *tut-, tueri* to look at, guard] : a person charged with the instruction and guidance of another: as **a** : a private teacher **b** : a college teacher esp. in a British university who guides the individual studies of undergraduates in his field **c** : a college or university teacher ranking below an instructor **d** : a college or university officer having administrative or counseling functions — **tu·tor·ship** \-ˌship\ *n*

²tutor *vb* : to teach usu. individually

¹tu·to·ri·al \t(y)ü-ˈtōr-ē-əl, -ˈtór-\ *adj* : of, relating to, or involving a tutor

²tutorial *n* : a class conducted by a tutor for one student or a small number of students

tut·ti-frut·ti \ˌtüt-ē-ˈfrüt-ē\ *n* [It *tutti frutti*, lit., all fruits] : a confection or ice cream containing chopped usu. candied fruits

tu·tu \ˈtü-tü\ *n* [F] : a very short projecting skirt worn by a ballerina

tu-whit tu-whoo \tə-ˌ(h)wit-tə-ˈ(h)wü\ *n* : the cry of an owl

tux \ˈtəks\ *n* : TUXEDO

tux·e·do \ˌtək-ˈsēd-ō\ *n, pl* **-dos** *or* **-does** [*Tuxedo* Park, N.Y.] **1** : a single-breasted or double-breasted usu. black or blackish blue jacket **2** : semiformal evening dress for men

tu·yere \twē-ˈe(ə)r\ *n* [F *tuyère*, fr. *tuyau* pipe] : a nozzle through which an air blast is delivered to a forge or blast furnace

TV \(ˈ)tē-ˈvē\ *n* : TELEVISION

twa \ˈtwå\ *or* **twae** \ˈtwå, ˈtwē\ *Scot var of* TWO

twad·dle \ˈtwäd-ºl\ *n* : silly idle talk : DRIVEL

twain \ˈtwān\ *n* [OE *twēgen*, adj. & pron., two] **1** : TWO **2** : COUPLE, PAIR

¹twang \ˈtwaŋ\ *n* **1** : a harsh quick ringing sound like that of a plucked bowstring **2 a** : nasal speech or resonance **b** : the characteristic speech of a region, locality, or group of people

²twang *vb* **twanged; twang·ing** \ˈtwaŋ-iŋ\ **1** : to sound or cause to sound with a twang **2** : to speak with a nasal intonation

¹tweak \ˈtwēk\ *vt* [ME *twikken*, fr. OE *twiccian* to pluck] : to pinch and pull with a sudden jerk and twist : TWITCH

²tweak *n* : an act of tweaking : PINCH

tweed \ˈtwēd\ *n* [alter. of Sc *tweel* twill, fr. ME *twyll*] **1** : a rough woolen fabric made usu. in twill weaves **2** *pl* : tweed clothing; *esp* : a tweed suit

tweedy \ˈtwēd-ē\ *adj* **tweed·i·er; -est 1** : of or resembling tweed **2 a** : given to wearing tweeds **b** : informal or suggestive of the outdoors in taste or habits

¹tweet \ˈtwēt\ *n* : a chirping note

²tweet *vb* : CHIRP

tweet·er \ˈtwēt-ər\ *n* : a small loudspeaker responsive only to the higher acoustic frequencies and reproducing sounds of high pitch

tweeze \ˈtwēz\ *vt* [back-formation fr. *tweezers*] : to pluck or remove with tweezers

tweez·ers \ˈtwē-zərz\ *n pl* [obs. *tweeze* case for small implements, alter. of obs. *etwee*, fr. F *étui*] : a small metal instrument that is usu. held between the thumb and forefinger, is used for plucking, holding, or manipulating, and consists of two legs joined at one end

twelfth \ˈtwelfth, ˈtwelft\ *n* — see NUMBER table — **twelfth** *adj or adv*

Twelfth Day *n* : EPIPHANY

Twelfth Night *n* **1** : the eve preceding Epiphany **2** : the evening of Epiphany

twelve \ˈtwelv\ *n* [OE *twelf*; akin to E *two*] **1** — see NUMBER table **2** *cap* : the twelve original disciples of Jesus **3** : the 12th in a set or series **4** : something having 12 units or members — **twelve** *adj or pron*

twelve·month \-ˌmən(t)th\ *n* : YEAR

twen·ti·eth \ˈtwent-ē-əth\ *n* — see NUMBER table — **twentieth** *adj*

twen·ty \ˈtwent-ē\ *n, pl* **twenties** [OE *twēntig*; akin to E *two* & to E *ten*] — see NUMBER table — **twenty** *adj or pron*

twen·ty-one *or* **21** \ˌtwent-ē-ˈwən\ *n* : a card game the object of which is to be dealt cards having a higher count than those of the dealer up to but not exceeding 21 — called also *blackjack, vingt-et-un*

twen·ty-twen·ty \ˌtwent-ē-ˈtwent-ē\ *adj* [fr. the custom of testing vision chiefly at a distance of 20 feet] : of normal acuity ⟨*twenty-twenty* vision⟩ — often written 20/20

twen·ty-two \ˌtwent-ē-ˈtü\ *n* : a 22-caliber rifle or pistol — usu. written .22

twerp \ˈtwərp\ *n* : a silly, insignificant, or contemptible person

twice \ˈtwīs\ *adv* [ME *twiges, twies*, fr. OE *twiga*; akin to E *two*] : two times ⟨*twice* absent⟩⟨*twice* two is four⟩

twice-born \-ˈbórn\ *adj* : having undergone a spiritual rebirth or regeneration through religious conversion or renewal or by an initiation ceremony

twice-laid \-ˈlād\ *adj* : made from the ends of rope and strands of used rope ⟨*twice-laid* rope⟩

twice-told \ˌtwīs-ˌtōld\ *adj* **1** : narrated twice **2** : HACKNEYED, TRITE — used chiefly in the phrase *a twice-told tale*

¹twid·dle \ˈtwid-ºl\ *vb* **twid·dled; twid·dling** \ˈtwid-liŋ, -ºl-iŋ\ **1** : to be busy with trifles : FIDDLE **2** : to rotate lightly or idly : TWIRL ⟨*twiddle* one's thumbs⟩

²twiddle *n* : an act of twiddling : TURN, TWIST

¹twig \ˈtwig\ *n* [OE *twigge*] : a small shoot or branch — **twigged** \ˈtwigd\ *adj* — **twig·gy** \ˈtwig-ē\ *adj*

²twig *vb* **twigged; twig·ging** : to catch on : NOTICE, UNDERSTAND

twi·light \ˈtwī-ˌlīt\ *n* **1** : the light from the sky between full night and sunrise or between sunset and full night **2** : a state of indistinctness or of deepening darkness or gloom — **twilight** *adj*

twilight sleep *n* : a state produced by injection of morphine and scopolamine in which awareness and memory of pain is dulled or effaced

¹twill \ˈtwil\ *n* [ME *twyll*, fr. OE *twilic* having a double thread, modif. of L *bilic-, bilix*, fr. *bi-* + *licium* thread] **1** : a fabric with a twill weave **2** : a textile weave that produces a pattern of diagonal lines or ribs

²twill *vt* : to make (cloth) with a twill weave

¹twin \ˈtwin\ *adj* [OE *twinn* twofold; akin to E *two*] **1** : born with one other or as a pair at one birth ⟨*twin* brother⟩⟨*twin* girls⟩ **2 a** : made up of two similar, related, or connected members or parts **b** : paired in a close or necessary relationship **c** : having or consisting of two identical units **d** : being one of a pair ⟨*twin* city⟩

²twin *n* **1** : either of two offspring produced at a birth

2 : one of two persons or things closely related to or resembling each other

³twin vb **twinned; twin·ning** **1** : to bring together in close association : COUPLE **2** : MATCH **3** : to bring forth twins

twin bill n : DOUBLEHEADER

twin·born \'twin-'bȯrn\ adj : born at the same birth

¹twine \'twīn\ n [OE twīn; akin to E two] **1** : a strong string of two or more strands twisted together **2 a** : an act of twining or interlacing **b** : TANGLE

²twine vb **1 a** : to twist together : WEAVE **b** : INTERLACE **2 a** : to coil or cause to coil about a support **b** : EMBRACE **3** : WIND, MEANDER

¹twinge \'twinj\ vb **twinged; twing·ing** or **twinge·ing** [OE twengan to pinch] : to affect with or feel a sudden sharp local pain

²twinge n **1** : a sudden sharp stab of pain **2** : a moral or emotional pang

¹twin·kle \'twiŋ-kəl\ vb **twin·kled; twin·kling** \'twiŋ-k(ə-)liŋ\ [OE twinclian] **1** : to shine or cause to shine with a flickering or sparkling light : SCINTILLATE **2** : to appear bright with merriment **3 a** : to move or flutter rapidly **b** : FLIT — **twin·kler** \-k(ə-)lər\ n

²twinkle n **1** : a wink of the eyelids **2** : the instant's duration of a wink : TWINKLING **3** : SPARKLE, FLICKER — **twin·kly** \-k(ə-)lē\ adj

twin·kling \'twiŋ-k(ə-)liŋ, for 1b -kliŋ\ n **1 a** : a winking of the eye **b** : INSTANT **2** : SCINTILLATION

twin-screw \'twin-'skrü\ adj : having a right-handed and a left-handed screw propeller parallel to each other on each side of the plane of the keel

¹twirl \'twərl\ vb **1** : to revolve or cause to revolve rapidly : SPIN, WHIRL ⟨twirl a baton⟩ **2** : to pitch in a baseball game **3** : CURL, TWIST ⟨twirled his moustache⟩ — **twirl·er** n

²twirl n **1** : an act of twirling **2** : COIL, WHORL

twirp var of TWERP

¹twist \'twist\ vb [ME twisten, fr. OE -twist rope] **1** : to unite by winding one thread, strand, or wire around another **2** : TWINE, COIL **3 a** : to turn so as to sprain or hurt ⟨twisted my ankle⟩ **b** : to alter the meaning of : PERVERT ⟨twisted the facts⟩ **c** : CONTORT ⟨twisted his face into a grin⟩ **d** : to pull off, rotate, or break by a turning force **e** : WARP, DEFORM **4** : to follow a winding course : SNAKE **5 a** : to turn or change shape under a turning force **b** : SQUIRM, WRITHE **6** : to turn around

²twist n **1** : something formed by twisting or winding: as **a** : a thread, yarn, or cord formed by twisting two or more strands together **b** : a baked piece of twisted dough **c** : tobacco leaves twisted into a thick roll **2** : an act of twisting : the state of being twisted **b** : the spin given the ball in any of various games (as baseball) **c** : a spiral turn or curve **3 a** : a turning aside : DEFLECTION **b** : ECCENTRICITY, BIAS **c** : DISTORTION, WRENCH **4 a** : an unexpected turn or development **b** : VARIATION **c** : DEVICE, GIMMICK

twist·er \'twis-tər\ n **1** : one that twists; esp : a ball with a forward and spinning motion **2** : a tornado, waterspout, or dust devil in which the rotatory ascending movement of a column of air is esp. apparent

twit \'twit\ vt **twit·ted; twit·ting** [OE ætwītan to reproach, fr. æt + wītan to blame] : to subject to light ridicule or reproach : RALLY ⟨twitted the girl on her vanity⟩

¹twitch \'twich\ vb [ME twicchen] **1** : to move or pull with a sudden motion : JERK **2** : PLUCK, SNATCH **3** : QUIVER

²twitch n **1** : an act of twitching **2 a** : a short sharp contraction of muscle fibers **b** : a slight jerk of a body part

¹twit·ter \'twit-ər\ vb [ME twiteren] **1** : to utter successive chirping noises **2 a** : to talk in a chattering fashion **b** : GIGGLE, TITTER **3** : to tremble or cause to tremble with agitation : FLUTTER

²twitter n **1** : a trembling agitation : QUIVER **2** : the chirping of birds **3** : a light chattering : GABBLE — **twit·tery** \-ə-rē\ adj

twixt \('t)wikst\ prep [ME twix, short for betwix, betwixt] : BETWEEN

two \'tü\ n [OE twā, adj. & pron. (fem. & neut.)] **1** — see NUMBER table **2** : the second in a set or series **3** : something having two units or members — **two** adj or pron

two-base hit n : a base hit that enables a batter to reach

second base safely — called also double, **two-bag·ger** \'tü-'bag-ər\

two-bit \,tü-'bit\ adj **1** : of the value of two bits **2** : PETTY, SMALL-TIME

two bits n sing or pl **1** : the value of a quarter of a dollar **2** : something of small worth or importance

¹two-by-four \,tü-bə-'fō(ə)r, -'fȯ(ə)r\ adj **1** : measuring two units (as inches) by four **2** : SMALL, CRAMPED

²two-by-four n : a piece of lumber approximately 2 by 4 inches as sawed and usu. 1⅝ by 3⅝ inches if dressed

two-dimensional adj **1** : having two dimensions **2** : lacking depth of characterization ⟨two-dimensional fiction⟩

two-faced \'tü-'fāst\ adj **1** : having two faces **2** : DOUBLE-DEALING, FALSE — **two-faced·ly** \-'fā-səd-lē, -'fāst-lē\ adv

two-fist·ed \'tü-'fis-təd\ adj : VIRILE, VIGOROUS

two·fold \'tü-,fōld, -'fōld\ adj **1** : having two units or members **2** : of or amounting to 200 percent — **twofold** adv

2,4-D \,tü-,fȯr-'dē, -,fȯr-\ n : a white crystalline organic compound used as a weed killer

two-hand·ed \'tü-'han-dəd\ adj **1** : used with both hands **2** : requiring two persons ⟨a two-handed saw⟩ **3** : having or efficient with two hands

two·pence \'təp-ən(t)s, US also 'tü-,pen(t)s\ n : the sum of two pence

two·pen·ny \'təp-(ə-)nē, US also 'tü-,pen-ē\ adj : of the value of or costing twopence

two-ply adj : consisting of two strands or thicknesses

two·some \'tü-səm\ n **1** : a group of two persons or things **2** : a golf single

two-star adj : being or having the rank of major general or rear admiral

two-step \'tü-,step\ n **1** : a ballroom dance executed in march or polka time **2** : a piece of music for the two-step — **two-step** vi

two-time \'tü-,tīm\ vt **1** : to betray (a spouse or lover) by secret lovemaking with another **2** : DOUBLE-CROSS

two-way adj : involving two elements or allowing movement or use in two directions or manners

two-winged fly \,tü-,wiŋd-\ n : any of a large order (Diptera) of insects including the true flies (as the housefly), mosquitoes, gnats, and related forms with the anterior wings functional and the posterior reduced to halteres and a few with no wings

ty·coon \tī-'kün\ n [Jap taikun, fr. Chin (Pek) ta⁴ great + chün¹ ruler] **1** : SHOGUN **2** : a businessman of exceptional wealth and power

tying pres part of TIE

tyke \'tīk\ n [ON tīk bitch] **1** : DOG, CUR **2** : a small child

tympani n pl : TIMPANI

tym·pan·ic \tim-'pan-ik\ adj **1** : of, relating to, or being a tympanum **2** : resembling a drum

tympanic membrane n : EARDRUM

tym·pa·nist \'tim-pə-nəst\ n : a member of an orchestra who plays the kettledrums

tym·pa·ni·tes \,tim-pə-'nīt-ēz\ n [Gk tympanitēs, fr. tympanon drum] : abdominal distension due to accumulation of gas (as in the intestine) — **tym·pa·nit·ic** \-'nit-ik\ adj

tym·pa·num \'tim-pə-nəm\ n, pl **-na** \-nə\ also **-nums** [L, drum, architectural panel, fr. Gk tympanon drum] **1 a** (1) : EARDRUM (2) : MIDDLE EAR **b** : a thin tense membrane covering an organ of hearing or of sound-production of an insect **2 a** : the recessed usu. triangular face of a pediment within the frame made by the upper and lower cornices **b** : the space within an arch and above a lintel or a subordinate arch

¹type \'tīp\ n [Gk typos blow, impression, model, fr. typtein to strike, beat] **1 a** : a person or thing believed to foreshadow or symbolize another **b** : one having qualities of a higher category : MODEL **2 a** : a rectangular block typically of metal or wood bearing a relief character from which an inked print is made **b** : a collection of such blocks or the letters printed from them **3 a** : general form or character common to a number of individuals that distinguishes them as

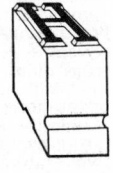

type 2a

an identifiable class ⟨horses of draft *type*⟩ **b** : a particular kind, class, or group ⟨a seedless *type* of orange⟩ **c** : something distinguishable as a variety : SORT ⟨reactions of this *type*⟩ **syn** see KIND

²type *vb* **1** : TYPIFY **2** : TYPEWRITE **3** : to identify as belonging to a type: as **a** : to determine the natural type of (as a blood sample) **b** : TYPECAST — **typ·a·ble** or **type·a·ble** \'tī-pə-bəl\ *adj*

type·cast \'tīp-ˌkast\ *vt* **1** : to cast (an actor) in a part calling for the same characteristics as those possessed by the actor himself **2** : to cast (an actor) repeatedly in the same type of role

type·face \'tīp-ˌfās\ *n* : all type of a single design

type·found·er \-ˌfaún-dər\ *n* : one engaged in the design and production of metal printing type for hand composition — **type·found·ing** \-diŋ\ *n* — **type·found·ry** \-drē\ *n*

type metal *n* : an alloy that consists essentially of lead, antimony, and tin and is used in making printing type

type·script \-ˌskript\ *n* [*type* + *-script* (as in *manuscript*)] : typewritten matter

type·set·ter \-ˌset-ər\ *n* : one (as a compositor) that sets printing type — **type·set·ting** \-ˌset-iŋ\ *adj or n*

type·write \'tīp-ˌrīt\ *vb* : to write with a typewriter

type·writ·er \-ˌrīt-ər\ *n* **1** : a machine for writing in characters similar to those produced by printer's type by means of keyboard-operated types striking through an inked ribbon **2** : TYPIST

type·writ·ing \-ˌrīt-iŋ\ *n* **1** : the act or study of or skill in using a typewriter **2** : the printing done with a typewriter

typh·lo·sole \'tif-lə-ˌsōl\ *n* [Gk *typhlos* blind + *sōlēn* pipe] : a fold of the wall that projects into the cavity of the intestine of some invertebrates (as the earthworm)

¹ty·phoid \'tī-ˌfóid, (')tī-'\ *adj* **1** : of, relating to, or suggestive of typhus **2** : of, relating to, or being typhoid

²typhoid *n* : a communicable bacterial disease marked esp. by fever, diarrhea, prostration, headache, and intestinal inflammation — called also *typhoid fever*

ty·phoon \tī-'fün\ *n* [Chin (Cant) *taai fung*, lit., great wind] : a tropical cyclone occurring in the region of the Philippines or the China sea

ty·phus \'tī-fəs\ *n* [Gk *typhos* fever] : a severe rickettsial disease marked by high fever, stupor alternating with delirium, intense headache, and a dark red rash and transmitted esp. by body lice

typ·i·cal \'tip-i-kəl\ *adj* **1** : being or having the nature of a type ⟨*typical* species⟩ **2** : SYMBOLIC **2** : combining or exhibiting the essential characteristics of a group ⟨*typical* suburban house⟩ **syn** see REGULAR — **typ·i·cal·i·ty** \ˌtip-ə-'kal-ət-ē\ *n* — **typ·i·cal·ly** \'tip-i-k(ə-)lē\ *adv* — **typ·i·cal·ness** \-kəl-nəs\ *n*

typ·i·fy \'tip-ə-ˌfī\ *vt* **-fied; -fy·ing** **1** : PREFIGURE, REPRESENT **2** : to have or embody the essential or main characteristics of

typ·ist \'tī-pəst\ *n* : one who typewrites

ty·po \'tī-pō\ *n, pl* **typos** : a typographical error

ty·pog·ra·pher \tī-'päg-rə-fər\ *n* **1** : COMPOSITOR **2** : PRINTER **3** : a specialist in the choice and arrangement of type matter

ty·pog·ra·phy \-fē\ *n* **1** : LETTERPRESS **2** : the art of letterpress printing **3** : the style, arrangement, or appearance of letterpress matter — **ty·po·graph·ic** \ˌtī-pə-'graf-ik\ *adj* — **ty·po·graph·i·cal** \-'graf-i-kəl\ *adj* — **ty·po·graph·i·cal·ly** \-i-k(ə-)lē\ *adv*

typy *or* **ty·pey** \'tī-pē\ *adj* **typ·i·er; -est** : of superior bodily conformation ⟨a *typy* steer⟩

ty·ran·ni·cal \tə-'ran-i-kəl, tī-\ *also* **ty·ran·nic** \-'ran-ik\ *adj* [Gk *tyrannos* tyrant] : of, relating to, or characteristic of a tyrant or tyranny : DESPOTIC — **ty·ran·ni·cal·ly** \-'ran-i-k(ə-)lē\ *adv*

tyr·an·nize \'tir-ə-ˌnīz\ *vb* **1** : to exercise arbitrary power **2** : to treat tyrannically — **tyr·an·niz·er** *n*

ty·ran·no·sau·rus \tə-ˌran-ə-'sór-əs, tī-\ *n* [Gk *tyrannos* tyrant + *sauros* lizard] : a very large American carnivorous dinosaur of the Cretaceous having small forelegs and walking on its hind legs

tyr·an·nous \'tir-ə-nəs\ *adj* : marked by tyranny; *esp* : unjustly severe — **tyr·an·nous·ly** *adv*

tyr·an·ny \'tir-ə-nē\ *n, pl* **-nies** **1 a** : a government in which absolute power is vested in a single ruler **b** : the office, authority, and administration of such a ruler **2**

: arbitrary and despotic government; *esp* : rigorous, cruel, and oppressive government **3** : SEVERITY, RIGOR ⟨the *tyranny* of the alarm clock⟩ **4** : a tyrannical act

ty·rant \'tī-rənt\ *n* [OF *tyran, tyrant*, fr. L *tyrannus*, fr. Gk *tyrannos*] **1** : an absolute ruler unrestrained by law or constitution **2 a** : a ruler who exercises absolute power oppressively or brutally **b** : one resembling such a tyrant in the harsh use of authority or power

tyrant flycatcher *n* : any of a family of large American flycatchers with a flattened bill usu. hooked at the tip

tyre *chiefly Brit var of* TIRE

Tyr·i·an purple \ˌtir-ē-ən-\ *n* [*Tyre*, Phoenicia] : a synthetic crimson or purple dye formerly obtained by the ancient Greeks and Romans from gastropod mollusks

ty·ro \'tī-rō\ *n, pl* **tyros** [L *tiro* recruit, tyro] : a beginner in learning **syn** see NOVICE

ty·ro·sine \'tī-rə-ˌsēn\ *n* [irreg. fr. Gk *tyros* cheese] : an amino acid obtained by hydrolysis of proteins

tzar \'zär, 'tsär\ *var of* CZAR

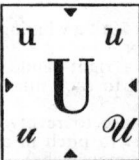

u \'yü\ *n, often cap* : the 21st letter of the English alphabet

ubiq·ui·tous \yü-'bik-wət-əs\ *adj* [*ubiquity*, fr. L *ubique* everywhere] : existing or being everywhere at the same time : widely or generally present — **ubiq·ui·tous·ly** *adv* — **ubiq·ui·tous·ness** *n* — **ubiq·ui·ty** \-wət-ē\ *n*

U-boat \'yü-ˌbōt\ *n* [trans. of G *u-boot*, short for *unterseeboot*, lit., undersea boat] : a German submarine

ud·der \'əd-ər\ *n* [OE *üder*] **1** : a large pendulous organ consisting of two or more mammary glands enclosed in a common envelope and each provided with a nipple **2** : a mammary gland

UFO \ˌyü-(ˌ)ef-'ō\ *n, pl* **UFO's** *or* **UFOs** \-'ōz\ [*unidentified flying object*] : an unidentified flying object; *esp* : FLYING SAUCER

ugh *often read as* 'əg *or* 'ək\ *interj* — used to indicate the sound of a cough or grunt or to express disgust or horror

ug·li·fy \'əg-li-ˌfī\ *vt* **-fied; -fy·ing** : to make ugly

ug·ly \'əg-lē\ *adj* **ug·li·er; -est** [ON *uggligr*, fr. *ugga* to fear] **1** : FRIGHTFUL, DIRE **2 a** : offensive to the sight : UNSIGHTLY, HIDEOUS **b** : offensive or unpleasing to any sense ⟨an *ugly* smell⟩ **3** : morally offensive or objectionable : REPULSIVE **4 a** : likely to cause inconvenience or discomfort : TROUBLESOME ⟨an *ugly* situation⟩ ⟨*ugly* wounds⟩ **b** : surly ⟨an *ugly* disposition⟩ — **ug·li·ness** *n*

ugly duckling *n* [fr. *The Ugly Duckling*, story by Hans Christian Andersen in which a supposed ugly duckling develops into a swan] : an unpromising child or thing actually capable of developing into a person or thing worthy of attention or respect

Ugri·an \'(y)ü-grē-ən\ *n* : a member of the eastern division of the Finno-Ugric peoples — **Ugrian** *adj*

uh·lan \'ü-ˌlän, '(y)ü-lən\ *n* [G, fr. Pol *ulan*, fr. Turk *oğlan* boy, servant] : one of a body of Prussian light cavalry orig. modeled on Tatar lancers

uin·ta·there \yù-'int-ə-ˌthi(ə)r\ *n* [*Uinta* county, Wyoming + Gk *thērion* beast] : any of a genus of extinct herbivorous ungulate mammals that somewhat resembled elephants

ukase \yü-'kās\ *n* [F, fr. Russ *ukaz*] : an edict esp. of a Russian emperor or government

Ukrai·ni·an \yü-'krā-nē-ən\ *n* **1** : a native or inhabitant of the Ukraine **2** : the Slavic language of the Ukrainian people — **Ukrainian** *adj*

uku·le·le \ˌyü-kə-'lā-lē\ *n* [Hawaiian, lit., flea] : a small guitar popularized in Hawaii, strung usu. with four strings, and played with the fingers or a pick

ul·cer \'əl-sər\ *n* [L *ulcer-, ulcus*] **1** : a necrotic or eroded sore that often discharges pus **2** : something that festers and corrupts like an open sore

ukulele

ul·cer·ate \'əl-sə-ˌrāt\ vb : to cause or become affected with an ulcer ⟨an *ulcerated* wound⟩ — **ul·cer·a·tion** \ˌəl-sə-'rā-shən\ n

ul·cer·ous \'əls-(ə-)rəs\ adj 1 : being or marked by ulceration ⟨*ulcerous* lesions⟩ 2 : affected with an ulcer : ULCERATED

-ule \(ˌ)yül\ n suffix [F & L; F, fr. L *-ulus, -ula, -ulum,* dim. suffix] : little one ⟨duc*tule*⟩

ul·lage \'əl-ij\ n [MF *eullage* act of filling a cask, fr. *eullier* to fill a cask, fr. OF *ouil* eye, bunghole, fr. L *oculus* eye] : the amount that a container (as a cask) lacks of being full

ul·na \'əl-nə\ n, pl **ulnas** or **ul·nae** \-ˌnē, -ˌnī\ [NL, fr. L, elbow; akin to E *ell,* elbow] : the inner of the two bones of the forearm or a corresponding part of the forelimb of vertebrates above fishes — **ul·nar** \-nər\ adj

ul·ster \'əl-stər\ n [*Ulster,* Ireland] : a long loose overcoat of heavy material

ul·te·ri·or \ˌəl-'tir-ē-ər\ adj [L, farther, further, compar. of (assumed) L *ulter* situated beyond] 1 : situated beyond or on the farther side 2 : lying farther away : more remote 3 : going beyond what is openly said or shown : HIDDEN ⟨*ulterior* motives⟩ — **ul·te·ri·or·ly** adv

ul·ti·ma \'əl-tə-mə\ n [L, fem. of *ultimus* last] : the last syllable of a word

¹ul·ti·mate \'əl-tə-mət\ adj [ML *ultimatus* last, fr. LL, pp. of *ultimare* to come to an end, fr. L *ultimus* last, superl. of (assumed) L *ulter* situated beyond] 1 a : most remote in space or time : FARTHEST b : last in a progression : FINAL c : EXTREME, UTMOST 2 : finally reckoned 3 a : FUNDAMENTAL, ABSOLUTE, SUPREME ⟨*ultimate* reality⟩ b : incapable of further analysis, division, or separation : ELEMENTAL 4 : MAXIMUM syn see LAST — **ul·ti·mate·ly** adv — **ul·ti·mate·ness** n

²ultimate n : something ultimate

Ultima Thu·le \-'th(y)ü-lē\ n [L, most distant Thule] : THULE

ul·ti·ma·tum \ˌəl-tə-'māt-əm, -'mät-\ n, pl **-tums** or **-ta** \-ə\ [NL, fr. ML, neut. of *ultimatus* last] : a final proposition, condition, or demand; esp : one whose rejection will bring about an end of negotiations and a resort to direct action (as by force)

ul·ti·mo \'əl-tə-ˌmō\ adj [L *ultimo mense* in the last month] : of or occurring the month preceding the present

¹ul·tra \'əl-trə\ adj [*ultra-*] : going beyond others or beyond due limit : EXTREME

²ultra n : EXTREMIST

ultra- prefix [L, fr. *ultra* beyond, adv. & prep., fr. (assumed) L *ulter* situated beyond] 1 : beyond in space : on the other side ⟨*ultra*violet⟩ 2 : beyond the range or limits of : transcending : SUPER- ⟨*ultra*microscopic⟩ ⟨*ultra*sonic⟩ 3 : beyond what is ordinary, proper, or moderate : excessively ⟨*ultra*modern⟩

ul·tra·cen·tri·fuge \ˌəl-trə-'sen-trə-ˌfyüj, -'sän-\ n : a high-speed centrifuge able to sediment small (as colloidal) particles — **ul·tra·cen·trif·u·gal** \-(ˌ)sen-'trif-yə-gəl, -(ˌ)sän-, -'trif-i-gəl\ adj — **ul·tra·cen·trif·u·ga·tion** \-ˌtrif-(y)ə-'gā-shən\ n

ul·tra·con·ser·va·tive \-kən-'sər-vət-iv\ adj : extremely conservative

ul·tra·fash·ion·a·ble \-'fash-(ə-)nə-bəl\ adj : extremely fashionable

ul·tra·high frequency \ˌəl-trə-ˌhī-\ n : any radio frequency in the range between 300 and 3000 megacycles — abbr. **uhf**

¹ul·tra·ma·rine \ˌəl-trə-mə-'rēn\ n 1 : a deep blue pigment 2 : a vivid blue

²ultramarine adj : situated beyond the sea

ul·tra·mi·cro \ˌəl-trə-'mī-krō\ adj : being or dealing with something smaller than micro

ul·tra·mi·cro·chem·is·try \-ˌmī-krō-'kem-ə-strē\ n : chemistry dealing with very minute quantities of substances

ul·tra·mi·cro·scope \ˌəl-trə-'mī-krə-ˌskōp\ n : an apparatus for making visible by scattered light particles too small to be perceived with an ordinary microscope

ul·tra·mi·cro·scop·ic \-ˌmī-krə-'skäp-ik\ adj 1 : too small to be seen with an ordinary microscope 2 : of or relating to an ultramicroscope — **ul·tra·mi·cro·scop·i·cal·ly** \-'skäp-i-k(ə-)lē\ adv

ul·tra·mod·ern \ˌəl-trə-'mäd-ərn\ adj : extreme or excessively modern in idea, style, or tendency — **ul·tra·mod·ern·ist** \-ər-nəst\ n

ul·tra·short \-'shȯrt\ adj : very short; esp : having a wavelength below 10 meters

¹ul·tra·son·ic \-'sän-ik\ adj : SUPERSONIC — **ul·tra·son·i·cal·ly** \-'sän-i-k(ə-)lē\ adv

²ultrasonic n : a supersonic wave or frequency

ul·tra·son·ics \-iks\ n : SUPERSONICS

ul·tra·sound \ˌəl-trə-'saund\ n : vibrations of the same physical nature as sound but with frequencies above the range of human hearing

ul·tra·vi·o·let \-'vī-ə-lət\ adj 1 : situated beyond the visible spectrum at its violet end and having a wavelength shorter than those of visible light but longer than those of X rays 2 : relating to, producing, or employing ultraviolet radiation — **ultraviolet** n

ultraviolet light n : ultraviolet radiation

ul·tra vi·res \ˌəl-trə-'vī-(ˌ)rēz\ adv (or adj) [NL, lit., beyond power] : beyond the scope of legal power or authority

ul·tra·vi·rus \'əl-trə-ˌvī-rəs\ n : VIRUS 1a — called also *ul·tra·mi·crobe* \-ˌmī-ˌkrōb\

ul·u·late \'əl-yə-ˌlāt, '(y)ül-\ vi [L *ululare*] : HOWL, WAIL — **ul·u·lant** \-lənt\ adj — **ul·u·la·tion** \ˌəl-yə-'lā-shən, ˌ(y)ül-yə-\ n

ul·va \'əl-və\ n [L, sedge] : any of a genus of green marine algae with a flat edible thallus — called also *sea lettuce*

Ulys·ses \yu̇-'lis-(ˌ)ēz\ n : ODYSSEUS

um·bel \'əm-bəl\ n [L *umbella* umbrella] : a racemose inflorescence typical of the carrot family in which the pedicels appear to spring from the same point to form a flat or rounded flower cluster — **um·beled** or **um·belled** \-bəld\ adj — **um·bel·late** \ˌəm-bə-ˌlāt, -lət, ˌəm-'bel-ət\ adj

um·bel·lule \'əm-bəl-(ˌ)yül\ n : a secondary umbel in a compound umbel — **um·bel·lu·late** \ˌəm-'bel-yə-lət\ adj

um·ber \'əm-bər\ n 1 : a brown earth valued as a pigment 2 a : a moderate to dark yellowish brown b : a moderate brown — **umber** adj

um·bil·i·cal \ˌəm-'bil-i-kəl\ adj : of, relating to, or adjacent to the navel

umbilical cord n : a cord arising from the navel that connects the fetus with the placenta

um·bil·i·cate \ˌəm-'bil-i-kət\ or **um·bil·i·cat·ed** \-'bil-ə-ˌkāt-əd\ adj : having or suggesting an umbilicus — **um·bil·i·ca·tion** \ˌəm-ˌbil-ə-'kā-shən\ n

um·bil·i·cus \ˌəm-'bil-i-kəs\ n, pl **-bil·i·ci** \-'bil-ə-ˌkī, -ˌkē, -ˌsī\ or **-bil·i·cus·es** [L; akin to E *navel*] 1 a : a depression in the abdominal wall at the point of attachment of the umbilical cord to the fetus b : any of several morphological depressions (as the hilum of a seed) 2 : a central point : CORE, HEART

um·bles \'əm-bəlz\ n pl [ME, alter. of *nombles,* fr. MF, pl. of *nomble* fillet of beef, pork loin, modif. of L *lumbulus,* dim. of *lumbus* loin] : the entrails of an animal and esp. of a deer used as food

um·bo \'əm-bō\ n, pl **um·bo·nes** \ˌəm-'bō-nēz\ or **umbos** [L *umbon-, umbo;* akin to E *navel*] 1 : the boss of a shield 2 : a rounded anatomical elevation; esp : one of the lateral prominences just above the hinge of a bivalve shell — **um·bo·nal** \'əm-bən-ᵊl, ˌəm-'bōn-\ adj — **um·bo·nate** \'əm-bə-ˌnāt\ adj

um·bra \'əm-brə\ n, pl **umbras** or **um·brae** \-(ˌ)brē, -ˌbrī\ [L, shade, shadow] 1 : a shaded area 2 : the conical part of the shadow of a celestial body excluding all light from the primary source 3 : the central dark part of a sunspot

um·brage \'əm-brij\ n 1 a : a growth (as of tangled branches) that gives shade b : SHADE 2 : RESENTMENT, OFFENSE ⟨take *umbrage* at a remark⟩ — **um·bra·geous** \ˌəm-'brā-jəs\ adj

um·brel·la \ˌəm-'brel-ə\ n [It *ombrella,* modif. of L *umbella,* dim. of *umbra* shade] 1 : a collapsible shade for protection against weather consisting of fabric stretched over hinged ribs radiating from a center pole; esp : a small one for carrying in the hand 2 : the bell-shaped or saucer-shaped largely gelatinous body proper of most jellyfishes

umbrella plant n : an African sedge that has large terminal whorls of slender leaves and is often grown as a houseplant

umbrella tree n 1 : an American magnolia having large leaves clustered at the ends of the branches 2 : any of various trees or shrubs resembling an umbrella esp. in the arrangement of leaves or the shape of the crown

Um·bri·an \'əm-brē-ən\ *n* **1 a** : a member of a people of ancient Italy occupying Umbria **b** : a native or inhabitant of the Italian province of Umbria **2** : the Italic language of ancient Umbria — **Umbrian** *adj*

umi·ak \'ü-mē-,ak\ *n* [Esk] : an open Eskimo boat made of a wooden frame covered with hide and usu. propelled with broad paddles

umiak

¹**um·laut** \'üm-,laut, 'üm-\ *n* [G, fr. *um-* around + *laut* sound] **1 a** : the change of a vowel caused by partial assimilation to a succeeding sound **b** : a vowel resulting from such partial assimilation **2** : a diacritical mark ¨ placed esp. over a German vowel to indicate umlaut

²**umlaut** *vt* **1** : to produce by umlaut **2** : to write or print an umlaut over

¹**um·pire** \'əm-,pī(ə)r\ *n* [ME *oumpere,* alter. of *noumpere* (the phrase *a noumpere* being understood as *an oumpere*), fr. MF *nomper* not equal, not paired, fr. *non-* + *per* equal, fr. L *par*] **1** : one having authority to decide finally a controversy or question between parties **2** : an official in a sport who rules on plays

²**umpire** *vb* : to supervise or act as umpire ⟨*umpire* a baseball game⟩

ump·teen \'əm(p)-'tēn, ,əm(p)-\ *adj* : very many : indefinitely numerous — **ump·teenth** \-'tēn(t)th\ *adj*

¹**un-** \,ən, 'ən\ *prefix* [OE; akin to E *no*] **1** : not : IN-, NON- — in adjectives formed from adjectives ⟨*un*strenuous⟩ ⟨*un*skilled⟩ or participles ⟨*un*dressed⟩ and in nouns formed from nouns ⟨*un*ostentation⟩ **2** : opposite of : contrary to — in adjectives formed from adjectives ⟨*un*constitutional⟩ or participles ⟨*un*believing⟩ and in nouns formed from nouns ⟨*un*rest⟩

²**un-** *prefix* [OE *on-, un-,* alter. of *and-* against] **1** : do the opposite of : reverse (a specified action) : DE-1a, DIS-1a — in verbs formed from verbs ⟨*un*bend⟩ ⟨*un*dress⟩ ⟨*un*fold⟩ **2 a** : deprive of, remove (a specified thing) from, or free or release from — in verbs formed from nouns ⟨*un*frock⟩ ⟨*un*sex⟩ ⟨*un*hand⟩ ⟨*un*bosom⟩ **b** : cause to cease to be — in verbs formed from nouns ⟨*un*man⟩ **3** : completely ⟨*un*loose⟩

un·abashed \,ən-ə-'basht\ *adj* : not abashed — **un·abash·ed·ly** \-'basht-lē, -'bash-əd-lē\ *adv*

un·abat·ed \,ən-ə-'bāt-əd\ *adj* : not abated : at full strength or force — **un·abat·ed·ly** *adv*

un·able \,ən-'ā-bəl, 'ən-\ *adj* : not able : INCAPABLE

un·abridged \,ən-ə-'brijd\ *adj* **1** : not abridged : COMPLETE ⟨an *unabridged* edition of Shakespeare⟩ **2** : complete of its class : not based on one larger ⟨an *unabridged* dictionary⟩

un·ac·com·mo·dat·ed \,ən-ə-'käm-ə-,dāt-əd\ *adj* : not accommodated : UNPROVIDED

un·ac·com·pa·nied \,ən-ə-'kəmp-(ə-)nēd\ *adj* : not accompanied; *esp* : being without instrumental accompaniment

un·ac·count·a·ble \,ən-ə-'kaunt-ə-bəl\ *adj* **1** : not to be accounted for : INEXPLICABLE, STRANGE, MYSTERIOUS **2** : not to be called to account : not responsible — **un·ac·count·a·bly** \-blē\ *adv*

un·ac·count·ed \-'kaunt-əd\ *adj* : not accounted : UNEXPLAINED — often used with *for*

un·ac·cus·tomed \,ən-ə-'kəs-təmd\ *adj* **1** : UNUSUAL, UNFAMILIAR ⟨*unaccustomed* scenes⟩ **2** : not used : not habituated ⟨*unaccustomed* to travel⟩

una cor·da \,ü-nə-'kȯr-dä\ *adv (or adj)* [It, lit., one string] : with soft pedal depressed — used as a direction in piano music

una corda pedal *n* : SOFT PEDAL

un·adorned \,ən-ə-'dȯrnd\ *adj* : not adorned : lacking embellishment or decoration : BARE, PLAIN, SIMPLE

un·adul·ter·at·ed \,ən-ə-'dəl-tə-,rāt-əd\ *adj* : PURE, UNMIXED — **un·adul·ter·at·ed·ly** *adv*

un·ad·vised \,ən-əd-'vīzd\ *adj* **1** : done without due consideration : RASH **2** : not prudent — **un·ad·vis·ed·ly** \-'vī-zəd-lē\ *adv*

un·af·fect·ed \,ən-ə-'fek-təd\ *adj* **1** : not influenced or changed mentally, physically, or chemically **2** : free from affectation : GENUINE — **un·af·fect·ed·ly** *adv* — **un·af·fect·ed·ness** *n*

un·alien·a·ble \,ən-'āl-yə-nə-bəl, 'ən-, -'ā-lē-ə-nə-\ *adj* : INALIENABLE

un·aligned \,ən-ə-'līnd\ *adj* : not associated with any one of competing international blocs ⟨*unaligned* nations⟩

un·al·loyed \,ən-ə-'lȯid\ *adj* : not alloyed : UNMIXED, UNQUALIFIED, PURE ⟨*unalloyed* metals⟩ ⟨*unalloyed* happiness⟩

un·al·ter·a·ble \,ən-'ȯl-t(ə-)rə-bəl, 'ən-\ *adj* : not capable of being altered or changed ⟨*unalterable* resolve⟩ ⟨*unalterable* hatred⟩ — **un·al·ter·a·ble·ness** *n* — **un·al·ter·a·bly** \-blē\ *adv*

un·Amer·i·can \,ən-ə-'mer-ə-kən\ *adj* : not American : not characteristic of or consistent with American customs, principles, or traditions — **un·Amer·i·can·ism** \-kə-,niz-əm\ *n*

un·an·chor \,ən-'aŋ-kər, 'ən-\ *vt* : to loosen from an anchor

un·aneled \,ən-ə-'nēld\ *adj, archaic* : not having received extreme unction

una·nim·i·ty \,yü-nə-'nim-ət-ē\ *n* : the quality or state of being unanimous

unan·i·mous \yu̇-'nan-ə-məs\ *adj* [L *unanimus,* fr. *unus* one + *animus* mind] **1** : being of one mind : agreeing completely **2** : assented to by all ⟨a *unanimous* vote⟩ — **unan·i·mous·ly** *adv*

un·an·swer·a·ble \,ən-'an(t)s-(ə-)rə-bəl, 'ən-\ *adj* : not answerable; *esp* : IRREFUTABLE ⟨admitted that their arguments were *unanswerable*⟩

un·ap·peal·a·ble \,ən-ə-'pē-lə-bəl\ *adj* : not appealable : not subject to appeal

un·ap·peal·ing \,ən-ə-'pē-liŋ\ *adj* : not appealing : UNATTRACTIVE

un·ap·peas·a·ble \,ən-ə-'pē-zə-bəl\ *adj* : not to be appeased : IMPLACABLE — **un·ap·peas·a·bly** \-blē\ *adv*

un·apt \,ən-'apt, 'ən-\ *adj* **1** : UNSUITABLE, INAPPROPRIATE **2** : not accustomed and not likely **3** : INAPT, DULL, BACKWARD — **un·apt·ly** *adv* — **un·apt·ness** \-'ap(t)-nəs\ *n*

un·arm \,ən-'ärm, 'ən-\ *vt* : DISARM

un·armed \-'ärmd\ *adj* : not armed or armored

un·ar·mored \,ən-,är-mərd-\ *n* : any of various scale insects without a substantial waxy covering

un·asked \,ən-'askt, 'ən-\ *adj* : not asked or asked for

un·as·sail·a·ble \,ən-ə-'sā-lə-bəl\ *adj* : not assailable : not liable to doubt, attack, or question — **un·as·sail·a·bly** \-blē\ *adv*

un·as·sert·ive \,ən-ə-'sərt-iv\ *adj* : not assertive : MODEST, SHY

un·as·sum·ing \,ən-ə-'sü-miŋ\ *adj* : not putting on airs : MODEST, RETIRING — **un·as·sum·ing·ly** \-miŋ-lē\ *adv* — **un·as·sum·ing·ness** *n*

un·at·tached \,ən-ə-'tacht\ *adj* **1** : not attached **2** : not married or engaged

un·avail·ing \ˌən-ə-'vā-liŋ\ adj : of no avail : not success-ful : VAIN — **un·avail·ing·ly** \-liŋ-lē\ adv

un·avoid·a·ble \ˌən-ə-'void-ə-bəl\ adj : not avoidable : INEVITABLE — **un·avoid·a·bly** \-blē\ adv

¹**un·aware** \ˌən-ə-'wa(ə)r, -'we(ə)r\ adv : UNAWARES

²**unaware** adj : not aware : IGNORANT — **un·aware·ness** n

un·awares \-'wa(ə)rz, -'we(ə)rz\ adv **1** : without warn-ing : by surprise ⟨taken *unawares*⟩ **2** : without knowing : UNINTENTIONALLY

un·backed \ˌən-'bakt, 'ən-\ adj **1** : never mounted by a rider : not broken **2** : not supported **3** : having no back

un·bal·ance \ˌən-'bal-ən(t)s, 'ən-\ vt : to put out of bal-ance

un·bal·anced \-ən(t)st\ adj **1** : not in equilibrium **2** : mentally disordered or deranged **3** : not adjusted so as to make credits equal to debits ⟨an *unbalanced* account⟩ **4** : having more players on one side of the center than on the other ⟨an *unbalanced* line in football⟩

un·bal·last·ed \ˌən-'bal-ə-stəd, 'ən-\ adj : not furnished with or steadied by ballast : UNSTEADY

un·bar \ˌən-'bär, 'ən-\ vt **-barred; -bar·ring** : to remove a bar from : UNBOLT, OPEN

un·barred \-'bärd\ adj **1** : not secured by a bar : UN-LOCKED **2** : not marked with bars

un·bear·a·ble \ˌən-'bar-ə-bəl, 'ən-, -'ber-\ adj : greater than can be borne ⟨*unbearable* pain⟩ — **un·bear·a·bly** \-blē\ adv

un·beat·a·ble \-'bēt-ə-bəl\ adj : not capable of being defeated

un·beat·en \-'bēt-ⁿn\ adj **1** : not pounded or beaten : not whipped **2** : UNTROD **3** : UNDEFEATED

un·be·com·ing \ˌən-bi-'kəm-iŋ\ adj : not becoming : UN-SUITABLE, IMPROPER — **un·be·com·ing·ly** \-iŋ-lē\ adv — **un·be·com·ing·ness** n

un·be·known \ˌən-bi-'nōn\ or **un·be·knownst** \-'nōn(t)st\ adj : happening without one's knowledge : UNKNOWN — usu. used with *to*

un·be·lief \ˌən-bə-'lēf\ n : the withholding or absence of belief : DOUBT

syn DISBELIEF, INCREDULITY: UNBELIEF suggests with-holding of belief ⟨warned against skepticism and *unbelief*⟩ DISBELIEF stresses rejection of what is asserted or stated ⟨*disbelief* in class struggle⟩ INCREDULITY implies a skeptical attitude ⟨received the news with *incredulity*⟩ and suggests rejection on general grounds rather than immediate evidence

un·be·liev·a·ble \ˌən-bə-'lē-və-bəl\ adj : too improbable for belief — **un·be·liev·a·bly** \-blē\ adv

un·be·liev·er \-'lē-vər\ n **1** : one who does not believe : DOUBTER **2** : one who does not believe in a particular religious faith : INFIDEL

un·be·liev·ing \-'lē-viŋ\ adj : marked by unbelief — **un·be·liev·ing·ly** \-viŋ-lē\ adv

un·bend \ˌən-'bend, 'ən-\ vb **-bent** \-'bent\; **-bend·ing** **1** : to free from being bent : make or become straight **2** : to unfasten (as sails) from the spars : UNTIE **3** : to make or become less stiff or more affable : RELAX

un·bend·ing \ˌən-'ben-diŋ, 'ən-\ adj : formal and distant in manner : INFLEXIBLE

un·be·seem·ing \ˌən-bi-'sē-miŋ\ adj : not befitting : UN-BECOMING

un·bi·ased \ˌən-'bī-əst, 'ən-\ adj : free from bias ⟨*unbiased* estimate⟩; esp : UNPREJUDICED, IMPARTIAL **syn** see FAIR

un·bid·den \-'bid-ⁿn\ also **un·bid** \-'bid\ adj : not bidden : UNASKED, UNINVITED

un·bind \-'bīnd\ vt **-bound** \-'baúnd\; **-bind·ing 1** : to remove a band from : free from fastenings : UNTIE, UNFASTEN, LOOSE **2** : to set free : RELEASE

un·bit·ted \-'bit-əd\ adj : UNBRIDLED, UNCONTROLLED

un·blenched \-'blencht\ adj : not disconcerted : UN-DAUNTED

un·blessed also **un·blest** \-'blest\ adj **1** : not blessed **2** : EVIL

un·blush·ing \-'bləsh-iŋ\ adj **1** : not blushing **2** : SHAMELESS, UNABASHED — **un·blush·ing·ly** \-iŋ-lē\ adv

un·bod·ied \-'bäd-ēd\ adj **1** : having no body : INCOR-POREAL; also : DISEMBODIED **2** : FORMLESS

un·bolt \ˌən-'bōlt, 'ən-\ vt : to open or unfasten by with-drawing a bolt

un·bolt·ed \-'bōl-təd\ adj : not sifted ⟨*unbolted* flour⟩; also : COARSE

un·bon·net \-'bän-ət\ vi : to remove one's bonnet esp. as a mark of respect

un·bon·net·ed \-'bän-ət-əd\ adj : BAREHEADED

un·born \-'bórn\ adj : not born : not brought into life; also : still to appear : FUTURE ⟨*unborn* generations⟩

un·bos·om \-'búz-əm\ vb **1** : to give expression to : DIS-CLOSE, REVEAL **2** : to disclose the thoughts or feelings of oneself

un·bound \-'baúnd\ adj : not bound: as **a** (1) : not fastened (2) : not confined **b** : not having the leaves fastened together ⟨an *unbound* book⟩

un·bound·ed \-'baún-dəd\ adj : having no bounds or limits ⟨*unbounded* space⟩ ⟨*unbounded* enthusiasm⟩

un·bowed \-'baúd\ adj **1** : not bowed down **2** : UN-SUBDUED

un·brace \-'brās\ vt **1** : to free or detach by or as if by untying or removing a brace or bond **2** : ENFEEBLE, WEAKEN

un·braid \-'brād\ vt : to separate the strands of : UNRAVEL

un·branched \ˌən-'brancht, 'ən-\ adj : free from or not divided into branches ⟨a straight *unbranched* trunk⟩ ⟨a leaf with *unbranched* veins⟩

un·bred \-'bred\ adj : not bred : never having been bred ⟨an *unbred* heifer⟩

un·bri·dled \-'brīd-ⁿld\ adj **1** : not confined by a bridle **2** : UNRESTRAINED, UNGOVERNED ⟨greeted the star's appear-ance with *unbridled* enthusiasm⟩

un·bro·ken \-'brō-kən\ adj **1** : not damaged : WHOLE **2** : not subdued or tamed ⟨an *unbroken* colt⟩ **3** : not inter-rupted : CONTINUOUS ⟨an *unbroken* row of trees⟩ ⟨*unbroken* sleep⟩

un·buck·le \ˌən-'bək-əl, 'ən-\ vt : to unfasten the buckle of (as a shoe or a belt)

un·build \-'bild\ vt : to pull down : DEMOLISH, RAZE

un·built \-'bilt\ adj **1** : not built : not yet constructed **2** : not built on ⟨an *unbuilt* plot⟩

un·bur·den \-'bərd-ⁿn\ vt **1** : to free or relieve from a burden **2** : to relieve oneself of (as cares, fears, or wor-ries) : cast off

un·but·ton \-'bət-ⁿn\ vt : to unfasten the buttons of (as a garment)

un·but·toned \-ⁿnd\ adj **1 a** : not buttoned **b** : not provided with buttons **2** : not under constraint

un·cage \-'kāj\ vt : to release from or as if from a cage

un·called-for \-'kóld-ˌfór\ adj : not called for : not needed or wanted : not proper ⟨an *uncalled-for* remark⟩

un·can·ny \-'kan-ē\ adj **1** : seeming to have a super-natural character or origin : MYSTERIOUS **2** : being beyond what is normal or expected : suggesting superhuman or supernatural powers ⟨an *uncanny* sense of direction⟩ **syn** see WEIRD — **un·can·ni·ly** \-'kan-ⁿl-ē\ adv

un·cap \-'kap\ vt **-capped; -cap·ping** : to remove a cap or covering from

un·caused \-'kózd\ adj : having no antecedent cause

un·ceas·ing \-'sē-siŋ\ adj : never ceasing : CONTINUOUS, INCESSANT — **un·ceas·ing·ly** \-'sē-siŋ-lē\ adv

un·cer·e·mo·ni·ous \ˌən-ˌser-ə-'mō-nē-əs\ adj : acting without or lacking ordinary courtesy — **un·cer·e·mo·ni·ous·ly** adv — **un·cer·e·mo·ni·ous·ness** n

un·cer·tain \ˌən-'sərt-ⁿn, 'ən-\ adj **1** : not determined or fixed ⟨an *uncertain* quantity⟩ **2** : subject to chance or change : not dependable ⟨an *uncertain* temper⟩ **3** : not

See ¹un- and 2d element			
unauspicious	unawed	unblenching	unbruised	uncanceled
unauthentic	unbaked	unblinking	unbrushed	uncanonical
unauthenticated	unbandage	unborrowed	unbudging	uncapitalized
unauthenticity	unbaptized	unbought	unburdened	uncared-for
unauthorized	unbeautiful	unbracketed	unburied	uncaring
unavailable	unbefitting	unbranded	unburned	uncastrated
unavenged	unblamable	unbreakable	unburnished	uncataloged
unavowed	unblamed	unbridgeable	unburnt	uncaught
unawakened	unbleached	unbridged	unbusinesslike	uncensored
	unblemished	unbrotherly	uncalled	uncensured

sure ⟨*uncertain* of the truth⟩ **4** : not definitely known —
un·cer·tain·ly *adv* — **un·cer·tain·ness** \-°n-(n)əs\ *n*
un·cer·tain·ty \-°n-tē\ *n* **1** : lack of certainty : DOUBT
2 : something that is uncertain
syn UNCERTAINTY, DOUBT mean lack of sureness about
someone or something. UNCERTAINTY may range from a
falling short of certainty to an almost complete lack of
knowledge about an outcome or result; DOUBT suggests
in addition the inability to reach a decision or arrive at
conviction
un·chain \‚ən-'chān, 'ən-\ *vt* : to free by or as if by removing a chain : set loose
un·chancy \-'chan(t)-sē\ *adj* **1** *chiefly Scot* : ILL-FATED
2 *chiefly Scot* : DANGEROUS
un·change·a·ble \-'chān-jə-bəl\ *adj* : not changing or to
be changed : IMMUTABLE — **un·change·a·ble·ness** *n* —
un·change·a·bly \-blē\ *adv*
un·charged \-'chärjd\ *adj* : having no electric charge
un·char·i·ta·ble \-'char-ət-ə-bəl\ *adj* : not charitable; *esp*
: severe in judging others — **un·char·i·ta·ble·ness** *n* —
un·char·i·ta·bly \-blē\ *adv*
un·chart·ed \-'chärt-əd\ *adj* : not recorded or plotted on
a map, chart, or plan : UNKNOWN
un·chaste \-'chāst\ *adj* : not chaste : lacking in chastity
— **un·chaste·ly** *adv* — **un·chaste·ness** \-'chās(t)-nəs\ *n*
— **un·chas·ti·ty** \-'chas-tət-ē\ *n*
un·chris·tian \-'kris-chən\ *adj* **1** : not of the Christian
faith **2 a** : contrary to the Christian spirit or character
b : BARBAROUS, UNCIVILIZED
un·church \-'chərch\ *vt* **1** : EXCOMMUNICATE **2** : to
deprive of a church or of status as a church
un·churched \-'chərcht\ *adj* : not belonging to or connected with a church
unci *pl of* UNCUS
¹un·cial \'ən-chəl, 'ən(t)-sē-əl\ *adj* [L *uncialis* inch-high,
fr. *uncia* twelfth part, ounce, inch] : written in the style or
size of uncials — **un·cial·ly** \-ē\ *adv*
²uncial *n* **1** : a handwriting used esp. in Greek and Latin
manuscripts of the 4th to the
8th centuries A.D. and made   ROMAN UNCIAL
with somewhat rounded sepa-
rated majuscules but having cur-
sive forms for some letters **2**   uncials
: an uncial letter
un·ci·form \'ən(t)-sə-‚fórm\ *adj* [L *uncus* hook] : shaped
like a hook : UNCINATE
un·ci·nar·ia \‚ən(t)-sə-'nar-ē-ə, -'ner-\ *n* : HOOKWORM
un·ci·nate \'ən(t)-sə-‚nāt\ *adj* [L *uncinus* hook] : bent at
the tip like a hook : HOOKED
un·ci·nus \‚ən-'sī-nəs\ *n, pl* **-ni** \-‚nī\ [L, hook] : a
small uncinate structure or process
un·cir·cum·cised \‚ən-'sər-kəm-‚sīzd, 'ən-\ *adj* : not circumcised; *also* : HEATHEN — **un·cir·cum·ci·sion** \‚ən-
‚sər-kəm-'sizh-ən\ *n*
un·civ·il \‚ən-'siv-əl, 'ən-\ *adj* **1** : not civilized : BAR-
BAROUS **2** : lacking in courtesy : ILL-MANNERED, IM-
POLITE
un·civ·i·lized \-'siv-ə-‚līzd\ *adj* **1** : not civilized : BAR-
BAROUS **2** : remote from civilization : WILD
un·clad \-'klad\ *adj* : not clothed : UNDRESSED, NAKED
un·clasp \-'klasp\ *vt* : to release from a clasp
un·clas·si·fied \-'klas-ə-‚fīd\ *adj* : not classified; *esp* : not
subject to a security classification
un·cle \'əŋ-kəl\ *n* [OF, fr. L *avunculus* mother's brother]
1 : the brother of one's father or mother **2** : the husband
of one's aunt
un·clean \‚ən-'klēn, 'ən-\ *adj* **1** : morally or spiritually
impure **2** : prohibited by ritual law for use or contact
3 : DIRTY, FILTHY — **un·clean·ness** \-'klēn-nəs\ *n*
¹un·clean·ly \-'klen-lē\ *adj* : morally or physically unclean — **un·clean·li·ness** *n*
²un·clean·ly \-'klēn-lē\ *adv* : in an unclean manner

un·clench \-'klench\ *vb* : to open from a clenched position : RELAX
Un·cle Sam \‚əŋ-kəl-'sam\ *n* [expansion of *U.S.*, abbr. of
United States] **1** : the U.S. government personified **2**
: the American nation or people
un·clinch \‚ən-'klinch, 'ən-\ *vt* : UNCLENCH
un·cloak \‚ən-'klōk, 'ən-\ *vb* **1** : to remove a cloak or
cover from **2** : REVEAL, UNMASK **3** : to take off a cloak
un·close \-'klōz\ *vb* : OPEN
un·clothe \-'klō̱th\ *vt* : to strip of clothes or a covering
¹un·co \'əŋ-kō̱, -kə\ *adj* [short for ME *uncouth*] **1** *chiefly
Scot* **a** : STRANGE, UNKNOWN **b** : UNCANNY, WEIRD
2 *chiefly Scot* : EXTRAORDINARY
²unco *adv* : EXTREMELY, REMARKABLY, UNCOMMONLY
un·coil \‚ən-'kóil, 'ən-\ *vb* : to release or become released
from a coiled state : UNWIND
un·coined \-'kóind\ *adj* **1** : not minted ⟨*uncoined* metal⟩
2 : not fabricated : NATURAL
un·com·fort·a·ble \-'kəm(p)(f)-tə-bəl, -'kəm(p)-fərt-ə-bəl\
adj **1** : causing discomfort ⟨an *uncomfortable* chair⟩
2 : feeling discomfort : UNEASY — **un·com·fort·a·bly**
\-blē\ *adv*
un·com·mit·ted \‚ən-kə-'mit-əd\ *adj* : not committed;
esp : not pledged to a particular belief, allegiance, or program
un·com·mon \‚ən-'käm-ən, 'ən-\ *adj* **1** : not ordinarily
encountered : UNUSUAL **2** : REMARKABLE, EXCEPTIONAL —
un·com·mon·ly *adv* — **un·com·mon·ness** \-ən-nəs\ *n*
un·com·mu·ni·ca·tive \‚ən-kə-'myü-nə-‚kāt-iv, -ni-kət-\
adj : not inclined to talk or impart information : RESERVED
un·com·pli·men·ta·ry \'ən-‚käm-plə-'ment-ə-rē, -'men-
trē\ *adj* : not complimentary : DEROGATORY
un·com·pro·mis·ing \‚ən-'käm-prə-‚mī-ziŋ, 'ən-\ *adj*
: not making or accepting a compromise : making no concessions : INFLEXIBLE, UNYIELDING — **un·com·pro·mis-
ing·ly** \-ziŋ-lē\ *adv*
un·con·cern \‚ən-kən-'sərn\ *n* **1** : lack of care or interest
: INDIFFERENCE **2** : freedom from excessive concern or
anxiety **syn** see INDIFFERENCE
un·con·cerned \-'sərnd\ *adj* **1** : not involved : not having any part or interest **2** : not anxious or upset : free of
worry — **un·con·cern·ed·ly** \-'sər-nəd-lē\ *adv* — **un-
con·cern·ed·ness** \-nəd-nəs\ *n*
un·con·di·tion·al \‚ən-kən-'dish-nəl, -'dish-ən-°l\ *adj*
: not limited : ABSOLUTE, UNQUALIFIED ⟨*unconditional* sur-
render⟩ — **un·con·di·tion·al·ly** \-ē\ *adv*
un·con·di·tioned \-'dish-ənd\ *adj* **1** : not subject to
conditions **2** : not dependent on conditioning or learning
: INHERENT
un·con·form·a·ble \‚ən-kən-'fór-mə-bəl\ *adj* : not conforming — **un·con·form·a·bly** \-blē\ *adv*
un·con·for·mi·ty \‚ən-kən-'fór-mət-ē\ *n* **1** : lack of
continuity in deposition between rock strata in contact
corresponding to a period of nondeposition, weathering, or
erosion **2** : the surface of contact between strata exhibiting unconformity
un·con·quer·a·ble \‚ən-'käŋ-k(ə-)rə-bəl, 'ən-\ *adj* : incapable of being conquered or overcome : INDOMITABLE
— **un·con·quer·a·bly** \-blē\ *adv*
un·con·scio·na·ble \-'känch-(ə-)nə-bəl\ *adj* [obs. *con-
scionable* conscientious] **1** : not being in accordance with
what is right or just : UNREASONABLE, EXCESSIVE **2** : not
guided or controlled by conscience — **un·con·scio·na·bly**
\-blē\ *adv*
¹un·con·scious \-'kän-chəs\ *adj* **1** : having lost consciousness ⟨knocked *unconscious* by a fall⟩ **2** : not aware
⟨*unconscious* of having made a mistake⟩ **3** : not realized
by oneself : not consciously done ⟨an *unconscious* mistake⟩
⟨*unconscious* humor⟩ — **un·con·scious·ly** *adv* — **un·con-
scious·ness** *n*
²unconscious *n* : the part of one's mental life that is not
ordinarily available to consciousness and is manifested in

See ¹*un-* and 2d element	uncluttered	uncoated	uncomforted	uncompanionable	unconcealed
unchallenged	unchristened	uncoated	uncompanionable	unconcealed
unchanged	unciliated	uncocked	uncompensated	unconfined
unchanging	unclaimed	uncoiled	uncomplaining	unconfirmed
unchaperoned	unclassifiable	uncollected	uncompleted	uncongealed
uncharacteristic	uncleaned	uncollectible	uncomplicated	uncongenial
unchary	unclear	uncolored	uncompounded	unconnected
unchastened	uncleared	uncombed	uncomprehended	unconquered
unchecked	unclosed	uncombined	uncomprehending	unconscientious
unchivalrous	unclothed	uncomely	uncomprehensible	unconsecrated
	unclouded			

spontaneous overt behavior (as slips of the tongue) or in dreams

un·con·sid·ered \ˌən-kən-'sid-ərd\ *adj* **1** : not considered or worth consideration **2** : not resulting from consideration or study

un·con·sti·tu·tion·al \'ən-ˌkän(t)-stə-'t(y)üsh-nəl, -ən-ᵊl\ *adj* : not according to or consistent with the constitution of a state or society — **un·con·sti·tu·tion·al·i·ty** \-ˌt(y)ü-shə-'nal-ət-ē\ *n* — **un·con·sti·tu·tion·al·ly** \-'t(y)üsh-nə-lē, -ən-ᵊl-ē\ *adv*

un·con·trol·la·ble \ˌən-kən-'trō-lə-bəl\ *adj* : incapable of being controlled : UNGOVERNABLE — **un·con·trol·la·bly** \-blē\ *adv*

un·con·ven·tion·al \ˌən-kən-'vench-nəl, -ən-ᵊl\ *adj* : not conventional : not bound by or in accordance with convention : being out of the ordinary — **un·con·ven·tion·al·i·ty** \-ˌven-chə-'nal-ət-ē\ *n* — **un·con·ven·tion·al·ly** \-'vench-nə-lē, -ən-ᵊl-ē\ *adv*

un·cork \ˌən-'kórk, 'ən-\ *vt* **1** : to draw a cork from **2 a** : to release from a sealed or pent-up state ⟨uncork a surprise⟩ **b** : to let go : RELEASE ⟨uncork a wild pitch⟩

un·count·ed \-'kaunt-əd\ *adj* **1** : not counted **2** : INNUMERABLE

un·cou·ple \-'kəp-əl\ *vt* **-cou·pled; -cou·pling** \-'kəp-(ə-)liŋ\ **1** : to loose (hunting dogs) to seek game **2** : DISCONNECT ⟨uncouple railroad cars⟩

un·couth \-'küth\ *adj* [ME, strange, unfamiliar, fr. OE *uncūth*, fr. ¹*un-* + *cūth* known; akin to E *can*] **1** : strange, awkward, and clumsy in shape or appearance **2** : vulgar in conduct or speech : RUDE

un·cov·er \-'kəv-ər\ *vb* **1** : to make known : bring to light : DISCLOSE, REVEAL **2** : to expose to view by removing some covering **3 a** : to take the cover from **b** : to remove the hat from; *also* : to take off the hat as a token of respect

un·cov·ered \-'kəv-ərd\ *adj* : not covered or supplied with a covering

un·cre·at·ed \ˌən-krē-'āt-əd\ *adj* **1** : not existing by creation : ETERNAL **2** : not yet created

un·crit·i·cal \ˌən-'krit-i-kəl, 'ən-\ *adj* **1** : not critical : lacking in discrimination **2** : showing lack or improper use of critical standards or procedures — **un·crit·i·cal·ly** \-k(ə-)lē\ *adv*

un·cross \-'krós\ *vt* : to change from a crossed position ⟨uncrossed his legs⟩

un·crown \-'kraun\ *vt* : to take the crown from : DEPOSE, DETHRONE

un·crys·tal·lized \-'kris-tə-ˌlīzd\ *adj* : not crystallized

unc·tion \'əŋ(k)-shən\ *n* [L *unct-, unguere* to anoint] **1** : the act of anointing as a rite of consecration or healing **2** : exaggerated, assumed, or superficial earnestness of language or manner

unc·tu·ous \'əŋ(k)-ch(ə-w)əs\ *adj* [L *unctus* act of anointing, fr. *unguere* to anoint] **1** : being like an ointment esp. in smooth greasy texture or appearance; *also* : OILY, FATTY **2** : full of unction in speech and manner; *esp* : insincerely smooth — **unc·tu·ous·ly** *adv* — **unc·tu·ous·ness** *n*

un·curl \ˌən-'kərl, 'ən-\ *vb* : to make or become straightened out from a curled or coiled position

un·cus \'əŋ-kəs\ *n, pl* **un·ci** \'əŋ-ˌkī, -ˌkē; 'ən-ˌsī\ [L, hook] : a hooked anatomical part or process

un·cut \ˌən-'kət, 'ən-\ *adj* **1** : not cut down or cut into **2** : not shaped by cutting ⟨an uncut diamond⟩ **3** : not having the folds of the leaves slit **4** : not abridged or curtailed

un·daunt·ed \-'dónt-əd, -'dänt-\ *adj* : not daunted : not discouraged or dismayed : FEARLESS — **un·daunt·ed·ly** *adv*

un·de·ceive \ˌən-di-'sēv\ *vt* : to free from deception, illusion, or error

un·de·cid·ed \ˌən-di-'sīd-əd\ *adj* **1** : not yet decided : not settled ⟨the question is still *undecided*⟩ **2** : not having decided : uncertain what to do ⟨still *undecided* about it⟩ — **un·de·cid·ed·ly** *adv*

un·de·mon·stra·tive \ˌən-di-'män(t)-strət-iv\ *adj* : restrained or reserved in expression of feeling : not effusive — **un·de·mon·stra·tive·ly** *adv* — **un·de·mon·stra·tiveness** *n*

un·de·ni·a·ble \ˌən-di-'nī-ə-bəl\ *adj* **1** : plainly true : INCONTESTABLE **2** : unquestionably excellent or genuine ⟨an applicant with *undeniable* references⟩ — **un·de·ni·able·ness** *n* — **un·de·ni·a·bly** \-blē\ *adv*

¹un·der \'ən-dər\ *adv* [OE] **1** : in or into a position below or beneath something ⟨the duck surfaced, then went *under* again⟩ **2** : below some quantity, level, or norm ⟨ten dollars or *under*⟩— often used in combination ⟨*under*played his part⟩ **3** : in or into a condition of subjection, subordination, or unconsciousness ⟨the ether put him *under*⟩ **4** : so as to be covered or hidden ⟨turned *under* by the plow⟩

²un·der \ˌən-dər, 'ən-\ *prep* **1 a** : lower than and overhung, surmounted, or sheltered by ⟨*under* sunny skies⟩ ⟨*under* a tree⟩ **b** : below the surface of ⟨swimming *under* water⟩ **c** : in or into such a position as to be covered or concealed by ⟨the moon went *under* a cloud⟩ ⟨wearing a sweater *under* his jacket⟩ **2 a** (1) : subject to the authority or guidance of ⟨served *under* the general⟩ (2) : with the guarantee of ⟨*under* the royal seal⟩ **b** : controlled, limited, or oppressed by ⟨*under* quarantine⟩ ⟨collapsed *under* the strain⟩ **c** : subject to the action or effect of ⟨*under* an anesthetic⟩ **3** : within the group or designation of ⟨*under* this heading⟩ **4 a** : less or lower than (as in size, amount, or rank) ⟨all weights *under* 12 ounces⟩ ⟨nobody *under* a colonel⟩ **b** : below the standard or required degree of ⟨*under* legal age⟩ **syn** see BELOW

³under \'ən-dər\ *adj* **1 a** : lying or placed below, beneath, or on the ventral side **b** : facing or protruding downward — often used in combination ⟨*under*surface of a leaf⟩ **2** : lower in rank or authority : SUBORDINATE **3** : lower than usual, proper, or desired in amount, quality, or degree

un·der·act \ˌən-dər-'akt\ *vb* : to perform feebly or with restraint: as **a** : to perform (a dramatic part) with less than the requisite skill or vigor **b** : to perform with restraint for greater dramatic impact or personal force

un·der·age \-'āj\ *adj* : of less than mature or legal age

¹un·der·arm \-'ärm\ *adj* **1** : placed under or on the underside of the arm ⟨*underarm* seams⟩ **2** : performed with the hand kept below the level of the shoulder : UNDERHAND ⟨an *underarm* toss⟩ — **underarm** *n*

²underarm *adv* : with an underarm motion

un·der·bel·ly \'ən-dər-ˌbel-ē\ *n* : the under surface of a body or mass; *also* : a vulnerable point

un·der·bid \ˌən-dər-'bid\ *vb* **-bid; -bid·ding** **1** : to bid less than (a competing bidder) **2** : to bid too low (as in cards) — **un·der·bid·der** *n*

un·der·body \'ən-dər-ˌbäd-ē\ *n* : the lower or ventral part of an animal's body

un·der·bred \ˌən-dər-'bred\ *adj* **1** : marked by lack of good breeding : ILL-BRED **2** : of inferior or mixed breed ⟨an *underbred* dog⟩

un·der·brush \'ən-dər-ˌbrəsh\ *n* : shrubs and small trees growing among large trees: UNDERGROWTH

un·der·car·riage \-ˌkar-ij\ *n* **1** : a supporting framework (as of an automobile) **2** : the landing gear of an airplane

un·der·charge \ˌən-dər-'chärj\ *vt* : to charge (as a person) too little — **un·der·charge** \'ən-dər-ˌchärj\ *n*

un·der·class·man \ˌən-dər-'klas-mən\ *n* : a member of the freshman or sophomore class

un·der·clothes \'ən-dər-ˌklō(th)z\ *n pl* : UNDERWEAR

un·der·cloth·ing \-ˌklō-thiŋ\ *n* : UNDERWEAR

un·der·coat \-ˌkōt\ *n* **1** : a coat or jacket formerly worn under another **2** : a growth of short hair or fur partly concealed by a longer growth ⟨a dog's *undercoat*⟩ **3** : a

unconsolidated	uncooked	uncrippled	uncurrent	undefeated
unconstrained	uncooperative	uncropped	uncurtained	undefended
unconsumed	uncoordinated	uncrossed	undamaged	undefiled
uncontaminated	uncordial	uncrowded	undamped	undefinable
uncontested	uncorked	uncrowned	undated	undefined
uncontradicted	uncorrected	uncultivable	undazzled	undelayed
uncontrolled	uncorroborated	uncultivated	undecipherable	undeliverable
unconverted	uncorrupted	uncultured	undecked	undemanding
unconvinced	uncountable	uncurbed	undeclared	undemocratic
unconvincing	uncourteous	uncured	undeclinable	undenominational
	uncredited	uncurious	undecorated	undependable

coat of paint under another **4** : UNDERCOATING — **under-coat** vb

un·der·coat·ing \-ˌkōt-iŋ\ n : a special waterproof coating applied to the undersurfaces of a vehicle

un·der·col·ored \ˌən-dər-ˈkəl-ərd\ adj : having less color than needed or proper

un·der·con·sump·tion \ˌən-dər-kən-ˈsəm(p)-shən\ n : too little consumption

un·der·cool \-ˈkül\ vt : SUPERCOOL

un·der·cov·er \-ˈkəv-ər\ adj : acting or executed in secret; esp : employed or engaged in spying or secret investigation

un·der·croft \ˈən-dər-ˌkróft\ n [ME, fr. under + crofte crypt, fr. MD, fr. L crypta] : a subterranean room; esp : a vaulted chamber under a church : CRYPT

un·der·cur·rent \-ˌkər-ənt, -ˌkə-rənt\ n **1** : a current below the upper currents or surface **2** : a hidden tendency of opinion or feeling often contrary to the one publicly shown

¹un·der·cut \ˌən-dər-ˈkət\ vb -cut; -cut·ting **1 a** : to cut away the under part of ⟨undercut a vein of ore⟩ **b** : to perform the action of cutting away beneath **2** : to cut away material from the underside of (an object) so as to leave an overhanging portion in relief **3** : to offer to sell at lower prices than or to work for lower wages than (a competitor) **4** : to strike (the ball) in golf or tennis obliquely downward so as to give a backspin or elevation to the shot

²un·der·cut \ˈən-dər-ˌkət\ n **1** : the action or result of cutting away from the underside of anything **2** : a notch cut in the base of a tree before felling esp. to determine the direction of fall

un·der·de·vel·op \ˌən-dər-di-ˈvel-əp\ vt : to develop to a point below that which is usual or required

un·der·de·vel·oped \-ˈvel-əpt\ adj **1** : not normally or adequately developed ⟨underdeveloped muscles⟩ **2** : failing to reach a potential level of economic development (as from lack of capital) ⟨the underdeveloped nations⟩

un·der·do \ˌən-dər-ˈdü\ vt -did \-ˈdid\; -done \-ˈdən\; -do·ing \-ˈdü-iŋ\ : to do less thoroughly than one can; esp : to cook (as meat) rare

un·der·dog \ˈən-dər-ˌdóg\ n : the loser or predicted loser in a struggle

un·der·done \ˌən-dər-ˈdən\ adj : not thoroughly done or cooked : RARE ⟨underdone steak⟩

un·der·draw·ers \ˈən-dər-ˌdró(-ə)rz\ n pl : an article of underwear covering the lower body and the legs

un·der·es·ti·mate \ˌən-dər-ˈes-tə-ˌmāt\ vt **1** : to estimate as being less than the actual size, quantity, or number **2** : to place too low a value on : UNDERRATE — **un·der·es·ti·mate** \-mət\ n — **un·der·es·ti·ma·tion** \-ˌes-tə-ˈmā-shən\ n

un·der·ex·pose \-ik-ˈspōz\ vt : to expose (a photographic plate or film) for less time than is needed — **un·der·ex·po·sure** \-ˈspō-zhər\ n

un·der·feed \-ˈfēd\ vt -fed \-ˈfed\; -feed·ing **1** : to feed with too little food **2** : to feed with fuel from the underside

un·der·foot \ˌən-dər-ˈfüt\ adv **1** : under the feet **2** : close about one's feet : in the way

un·der·fur \ˈən-dər-ˌfər\ n : the thick soft fur lying beneath the longer and coarser hair of a mammal

un·der·gar·ment \-ˌgär-mənt\ n : a garment to be worn under another

un·der·gird \ˌən-dər-ˈgərd\ vt **1** : to make secure underneath **2** : to brace up : STRENGTHEN

un·der·go \ˌən-dər-ˈgō\ vt -went \-ˈwent\; -gone \-ˈgón, -ˈgän\; -go·ing \-ˈgō-iŋ\ **1** : to submit or be subjected to : ENDURE ⟨undergo an operation⟩ **2** : to pass through : EXPERIENCE ⟨undergo a change⟩

un·der·grad·u·ate \-ˈgraj-ə-wət, -ˌwāt\ n : a student at a college or university who has not taken a first degree

¹un·der·ground \ˌən-dər-ˈgraúnd\ adv **1** : beneath the surface of the earth **2** : in or into hiding or secret operation ⟨the party went underground⟩

²un·der·ground \ˈən-dər-ˌgraúnd\ adj **1** : being, growing, operating, or situated below the surface of the ground ⟨underground stream⟩ **2** : conducted by secret means ⟨underground resistance movement⟩ **3** : produced or published outside the establishment esp. by the avant-garde ⟨underground newspapers⟩; also : of or relating to the avant-garde underground ⟨an underground theater⟩

³un·der·ground \ˈən-dər-ˌgraúnd\ n **1** : a space under the surface of the ground; esp : an underground railway **2** : a secret political movement or group; esp : an organized body working in secret to overthrow a government or an occupying power **3** : a usu. avant-garde group or movement that functions outside the establishment

Underground Railroad n : a system of cooperation among active antislavery people in the U.S. before 1863 by which fugitive slaves were secretly helped to reach the North or Canada

un·der·growth \ˈən-dər-ˌgröth\ n : low growth on the floor of a forest including seedlings and saplings, shrubs, and herbs

¹un·der·hand \ˈən-dər-ˌhand\ adv **1** : in an underhand or secret manner **2** : with an underhand motion ⟨bowl underhand⟩ ⟨pitch underhand⟩

²underhand adj **1** : marked by secrecy, chicanery, and deception : not honest and aboveboard : SLY **2** : performed with the hand kept below the level of the shoulder ⟨underhand pass in football⟩

un·der·hand·ed \ˌən-dər-ˈhan-dəd\ adj (or adv) : UNDERHAND — **un·der·hand·ed·ly** adv — **un·der·hand·ed·ness** n

¹un·der·lay \ˌən-dər-ˈlā\ vt -laid \-ˈlād\; -lay·ing **1** : to cover, line, or traverse the bottom of : give support to on the underside or below ⟨shingles underlaid with tar paper⟩ **2** : to raise or support by something laid under

²un·der·lay \ˈən-dər-ˌlā\ n : something that is laid under

un·der·let \ˌən-dər-ˈlet\ vt **1** : to let below the real value **2** : SUBLET

un·der·lie \ˌən-dər-ˈlī\ vt -lay \-ˈlā\; -lain \-ˈlān\; -ly·ing \-ˈlī-iŋ\ **1** : to lie or be situated under **2** : to be at the basis of : form the foundation of : SUPPORT ⟨ideas underlying the revolution⟩

un·der·line \ˈən-dər-ˌlīn, ˌən-dər-ˈ\ vt **1** : to draw a line under **2** : EMPHASIZE — **un·der·line** \ˈən-dər-ˌlīn\ n

un·der·ling \ˈən-dər-liŋ\ n : one who is under the orders of another : SUBORDINATE, INFERIOR

un·der·lip \ˈən-dər-ˌlip\ n : the lower lip

un·der·ly·ing \ˌən-dər-ˈlī-iŋ\ adj **1** : lying under or below ⟨the underlying rock is shale⟩ **2** : FUNDAMENTAL, BASIC ⟨underlying principles⟩

un·der·mine \ˌən-dər-ˈmīn\ vt **1** : to dig out or wear away the supporting earth beneath ⟨undermine a wall⟩ **2** : to weaken or wear away secretly or gradually ⟨undermine a government⟩

un·der·most \ˈən-dər-ˌmōst\ adj : lowest in relative position — **undermost** adv

¹un·der·neath \ˌən-dər-ˈnēth\ prep **1** : directly under **2** : under subjection to

²underneath adv **1** : under or below an object or a surface : BENEATH **2** : on the lower side

un·der·nour·ished \-ˈnər-isht, -ˈnə-risht\ adj : supplied with insufficient nourishment and esp. foods for sound health and growth — **un·der·nour·ish·ment** \-ˈnər-ish-mənt, -ˈnə-rish-\ n

un·der·pants \ˈən-dər-ˌpan(t)s\ n pl : short or long pants worn under an outer garment : DRAWERS

un·der·part \-ˌpärt\ n **1** : a part lying on the lower side esp. of a bird or mammal **2** : a subordinate or auxiliary part or role

un·der·pass \-ˌpas\ n : a passage underneath something (as for a road passing under a railroad or another road)

un·der·pay \ˌən-dər-ˈpā\ vt -paid \-ˈpād\; -pay·ing : to pay too little

un·der·pin \-ˈpin\ vt -pinned; -pin·ning **1** : to form part of, strengthen, or replace the foundation of ⟨underpin a structure⟩ **2** : SUPPORT, SUBSTANTIATE ⟨underpin a thesis with evidence⟩

un·der·pin·ning \ˈən-dər-ˌpin-iŋ\ n **1** : the material and construction (as a foundation) used for support of a structure **2** : SUPPORT, PROP **3** : a person's legs — usu. used in pl.

un·der·play \ˌən-dər-ˈplā\ vb : to treat or handle with restraint; esp : to play a role with subdued force

un·der·plot \ˈən-dər-ˌplät\ n : a dramatic plot that is subordinate to the main action

un·der·priv·i·leged \ˌən-dər-ˈpriv-(ə-)lijd\ adj : having fewer esp. economic and social privileges than others : POOR

un·der·pro·duc·tion \-prə-ˈdək-shən\ n : the production

of less than enough to satisfy the demand or of less than the usual supply

un·der·rate \,ən-də(r)-'rāt\ *vt* : to rate too low : UNDERVALUE

un·der·ripe \-'rīp\ *adj* : insufficiently ripe

un·der·run \-'rən\ *n* : the amount by which something produced falls below an estimate

un·der·score \'ən-dər-,skōr, -,skȯr\ *vt* **1** : to draw a line under : UNDERLINE **2** : EMPHASIZE — **underscore** *n*

¹un·der·sea \,ən-dər-,sē\ *adj* **1** : being or carried on under the sea or under the surface of the sea ⟨*undersea* fighting⟩ **2** : designed for use under the surface of the sea ⟨*undersea* fleet⟩

²un·der·sea \,ən-dər-'sē\ *or* **un·der·seas** \-'sēz\ *adv* : under the sea : beneath the surface of the sea ⟨photographs taken *undersea*⟩

un·der·sec·re·tary \,ən-dər-'sek-rə-,ter-ē\ *n* : a secretary immediately subordinate to a principal secretary ⟨*undersecretary* of state⟩

un·der·sell \-'sel\ *vt* **-sold** \-'sōld\; **-sell·ing** : to sell articles cheaper than ⟨*undersell* a competitor⟩

un·der·sexed \-'sekst\ *adj* : deficient in sexual desire

un·der·shirt \'ən-dər-,shərt\ *n* : a collarless undergarment with or without sleeves

un·der·shoot \,ən-dər-'shüt\ *vt* **-shot** \-'shät\; **-shoot·ing** **1** : to shoot short of or below (a target) **2** : to fall short of (a runway) in landing an airplane

un·der·shot \,ən-dər-'shät\ *adj* **1** : having the lower incisor teeth or lower jaw projecting beyond the upper when the mouth is closed **2** : moved by water passing beneath ⟨*undershot* wheel⟩

un·der·shrub \'ən-dər-,shrəb\ *n* **1** : SUBSHRUB 1 **2** : a small low-growing shrub — **un·der·shrub·by** \-,shrəb-ē\ *adj*

un·der·side \'ən-dər-,sīd, ,ən-dər-'\ *n* : the side or surface lying underneath

un·der·signed \'ən-dər-,sīnd\ *n, pl* **undersigned** : one who signs his name at the end of a document ⟨the *undersigned* testifies⟩ ⟨the *undersigned* all agree⟩

un·der·sized \,ən-dər-'sīzd\ *adj* : smaller than is usual or standard ⟨*undersized* fruit⟩

un·der·skirt \'ən-dər-,skərt\ *n* : a skirt worn under an outer skirt; *esp* : PETTICOAT

un·der·slung \,ən-dər-'sləŋ\ *adj* **1 a** : suspended so as to extend below the axles ⟨an *underslung* automobile frame⟩ **b** : having a low center of gravity **2** : UNDERSHOT 1

un·der·song \'ən-dər-,sȯŋ\ *n* : a subordinate melody or part

un·der·spin \-,spin\ *n* : BACKSPIN

un·der·stand \,ən-dər-'stand\ *vb* **-stood** \-'stu̇d\; **-stand·ing** **1** : to grasp the meaning of : COMPREHEND **2** : to have thorough acquaintance with ⟨*understand* the arts⟩ **3** : GATHER, INFER ⟨I *understand* that he will come today⟩ **4** : INTERPRET, EXPLAIN ⟨*understand* the letter to be a refusal⟩ **5** : to have a sympathetic attitude ⟨his wife doesn't *understand* about these things⟩ **6** : to accept as settled ⟨it is *understood* that I will pay⟩ **7** : to supply in thought as though expressed ⟨"to be married" is commonly *understood* after the word *engaged*⟩ — **un·der·stand·a·bil·i·ty** \-,stan-də-'bil-ət-ē\ *n* — **un·der·stand·a·ble** \-'stan-də-bəl\ *adj* — **un·der·stand·a·bly** \-blē\ *adv*

¹un·der·stand·ing \,ən-dər-'stan-diŋ\ *n* **1** : knowledge and ability to apply judgment : INTELLIGENCE ⟨act according to your *understanding* of your duty⟩ **2** : ability to comprehend and judge ⟨a man of *understanding*⟩ **3 a** : agreement of opinion or feeling **b** : a mutual agreement informally or tacitly entered into ⟨an *understanding* between two nations over trade⟩

²understanding *adj* : endowed with understanding : TOLERANT, SYMPATHETIC ⟨she seems very *understanding*⟩ — **un·der·stand·ing·ly** \-'stan-diŋ-lē\ *adv*

un·der·state \,ən-dər-'stāt\ *vt* **1** : to represent as less than is the case **2** : to state with restraint esp. for greater effect — **un·der·state·ment** \-mənt\ *n*

un·der·stood \,ən-dər-'stu̇d\ *adj* **1** : agreed upon **2** : IMPLICIT

¹un·der·study \'ən-dər-,stəd-ē\ *vb* **1** : to study another

actor's part in order to be his substitute in an emergency **2** : to prepare as understudy to (as an actor)

²understudy *n* : one who stands prepared to act another's part or take over another's duties

un·der·sur·face \'ən-dər-,sər-fəs\ *n* : UNDERSIDE

un·der·take \,ən-dər-'tāk\ *vt* **-took** \-'tu̇k\; **-tak·en** \-'tā-kən\ **1** : to take upon oneself as a task : enter upon ⟨*undertake* a journey⟩ **2** : to put oneself under obligation : AGREE, CONTRACT ⟨*undertake* to deliver a package⟩ **3** : GUARANTEE, PROMISE

un·der·tak·er \'ən-dər-,tā-kər\ *n* : a person whose business is to prepare the dead for burial and to take charge of funerals

un·der·tak·ing \2 *is* 'ən-dər-,tā-kiŋ, *other senses are also* ,ən-dər-'\ *n* **1** : the act of a person who undertakes something **2** : the business of an undertaker **3** : something undertaken **4** : PROMISE, GUARANTEE

un·der·ten·ant \'ən-dər-,ten-ənt\ *n* : one who holds lands or tenements by a sublease

un·der-the-count·er *adj* : UNLAWFUL, ILLICIT ⟨*under-the-counter* sale of drugs⟩

un·der·tone \'ən-dər-,tōn\ *n* **1** : a low or subdued tone **2** : a subdued color (as seen through and modifying another color)

un·der·tow \-,tō\ *n* : a current beneath the surface of the water that moves away from or along the shore while the surface water above it moves toward the shore

un·der·trick \-,trik\ *n* : a trick by which a declarer in bridge falls short of making his contract

un·der·val·ue \,ən-dər-'val-yü\ *vt* **1** : to value below the real worth **2** : to set little value on — **un·der·val·u·a·tion** \-,val-yə-'wā-shən\ *n*

un·der·waist \'ən-dər-,wāst\ *n* : a waist for wear under another garment

un·der·wa·ter \,ən-dər-,wȯt-ər, -,wät-\ *adj* : lying, growing, worn, or operating below the surface of the water — **un·der·wa·ter** \-'wȯt-, -'wät-\ *adv*

under way *adv* **1** : in motion; *also* : into motion from a standstill **2** : in progress : AFOOT

un·der·way \'ən-dər-,wā\ *adj* : occurring, performed, or used while traveling or in motion ⟨*underway* refueling⟩

un·der·wear \'ən-dər-,wa(ə)r, -,we(ə)r\ *n* : a garment worn next to the skin and under other clothing

¹un·der·weight \,ən-dər-'wāt\ *n* : weight below what is normal, average, or necessary

²underweight *adj* : weighing less than the normal or requisite amount

¹un·der·wing \'ən-dər-,wiŋ\ *n* : either of the posterior pair of wings of an insect

²underwing *adj* : located or growing beneath or on the under surface of a wing ⟨*underwing* coverts⟩

un·der·wood \'ən-dər-,wu̇d\ *n* : UNDERBRUSH, UNDERGROWTH

un·der·wool \-,wu̇l\ *n* : short woolly underfur

un·der·world \-,wərld\ *n* **1** *archaic* : EARTH **2** : the place of departed souls : HADES **3** : the side of the earth opposite to one **4** : a social sphere below the level of ordinary life; *esp* : the world of organized crime

un·der·write \'ən-də(r)-,rīt, ,ən-də(r)-'\ *vb* **-wrote** \-,rōt, -'rōt\; **-writ·ten** \-,rit-ᵊn, -'rit-\; **-writ·ing** \-,rīt-iŋ, -'rīt-\ **1** : to write under or at the end of something else **2** : to set one's name to (an insurance policy) and thereby become answerable to the insured for a designated loss or damage : insure life or property **3** : to subscribe to : agree to **4 a** : to undertake the sale of (a security issue) and agree to purchase on a fixed date any remaining unsold **b** : to guarantee financial support of — **un·der·writ·er** *n*

un·de·sign·ing \,ən-di-'zī-niŋ\ *adj* : having no artful, ulterior, or fraudulent purpose : SINCERE

un·de·sir·a·bil·i·ty \,ən-di-,zī-rə-'bil-ət-ē\ *n* : the quality or state of being undesirable

¹un·de·sir·a·ble \-'zī-rə-bəl\ *adj* : not desirable : UNWANTED — **un·de·sir·a·ble·ness** *n* — **un·de·sir·a·bly** \-blē\ *adv*

²undesirable *n* : one that is undesirable

un·de·vi·at·ing \,ən-'dē-vē-,āt-iŋ, 'ən-\ *adj* : keeping a true course : UNSWERVING — **un·de·vi·at·ing·ly** \-iŋ-lē\ *adv*

See ¹*un-* and 2d element	undeserving	undetachable	undeterminable	undeterred
undeserved	undesired	undetected	undetermined	undeveloped

un·dies \'ən-dēz\ *n pl* : UNDERWEAR; *esp* : women's underwear

un·dine \,ən-'dēn\ *n* [NL *undina,* fr. L *unda* wave] : a water nymph

un·di·rect·ed \,ən-də-'rek-təd, -,dī-\ *adj* : not directed ⟨*undirected* efforts⟩

un·do \,ən-'dü, 'ən-\ *vb* **-did** \-'did\; **-done** \-'dən\; **-do·ing 1** : to make or become unfastened or loosened : OPEN, UNTIE **2** : to make of no effect or as if not done : make null : REVERSE **3 a** : to ruin the worldly means, reputation, or hopes of **b** : to disturb the composure of : UPSET — **un·do·er** *n*

un·do·ing \-'dü-iŋ\ *n* **1** : LOOSING, UNFASTENING **2** : RUIN; *also* : a cause of ruin **3** : ANNULMENT, REVERSAL

un·done \,ən-'dən, 'ən-\ *adj* : not done : not performed or finished : NEGLECTED

un·dou·ble \-'dəb-əl\ *vb* : UNFOLD, UNCLENCH

un·doubt·ed \-'daut-əd\ *adj* : not doubted or called into question : CERTAIN ⟨*undoubted* proof of guilt⟩

un·doubt·ed·ly \-əd-lē\ *adv* : beyond doubt : CERTAINLY

un·drape \-'drāp\ *vt* : to strip of drapery : UNVEIL

un·draw \-'drȯ\ *vt* **-drew** \-'drü\; **-drawn** \-'drȯn\; **-draw·ing** : to draw (as a curtain) aside : OPEN

¹un·dress \,ən-'dres, 'ən-\ *vb* : to remove the clothes or covering of : STRIP, DISROBE

²undress *n* **1** : informal dress: as **a** : a loose robe or dressing gown **b** : ordinary dress **2** : NUDITY

un·dressed \-'drest\ *adj* : not dressed: as **a** : partially, improperly, or informally clothed **b** : not fully processed or finished ⟨*undressed* hides⟩ **c** : not cared for or tended ⟨an *undressed* wound⟩ ⟨*undressed* fields⟩

un·due \-'d(y)ü\ *adj* **1** : not due : not yet payable **2 a** : INAPPROPRIATE, UNSUITABLE **b** : exceeding or violating propriety or fitness

un·du·lant \'ən-jə-lənt, 'ən-d(y)ə-\ *adj* : UNDULATING

undulant fever *n* : a persistent human bacterial disease marked by remittent fever, pain and swelling in the joints, and great weakness and contracted by contact with infected domestic animals or consumption of their products

¹un·du·late \'ən-jə-lət, 'ən-d(y)ə-\ *or* **un·du·lat·ed** \-,lāt-əd\ *adj* [L *undulatus,* fr. (assumed) L *undula,* dim. of L *unda* wave; akin to E *water*] : having a wavy surface, margin, or markings

²un·du·late \-,lāt\ *vb* **1** : to form or move in waves : FLUCTUATE **2** : to rise and fall in volume, pitch, or cadence **3** : to present a wavy appearance

un·du·la·tion \,ən-jə-'lā-shən, ,ən-d(y)ə-\ *n* **1 a** : the action of undulating **b** : a wavelike motion to and fro in a fluid or elastic medium : VIBRATION **2** : a wavy appearance or form : WAVINESS

un·du·la·to·ry \'ən-jə-lə-,tōr-ē, 'ən-d(y)ə-, -,tȯr-\ *adj* : of or relating to undulation : UNDULATING

un·du·ly \,ən-'d(y)ü-lē, 'ən-\ *adv* : in an undue manner; *esp* : EXCESSIVELY

un·du·ti·ful \-'d(y)üt-i-fəl\ *adj* : not dutiful — **un·du·ti·ful·ly** \-fə-lē\ *adv* — **un·du·ti·ful·ness** *n*

un·dy·ing \-'dī-iŋ\ *adj* : not dying : IMMORTAL, PERPETUAL

un·earned \-'ərnd\ *adj* : not gained by labor, service, or skill ⟨*unearned* income⟩

un·earth \,ən-'ərth, 'ən-\ *vt* **1** : to drive or draw from the earth : dig up ⟨*unearth* buried treasure⟩ **2** : to bring (as a secret) to light : DISCOVER

un·earth·ly \-lē\ *adj* **1** : not of or belonging to the earth **2** : SUPERNATURAL, WEIRD, TERRIFYING — **un·earth·li·ness** *n*

un·easy \-'ē-zē\ *adj* **1** : not easy in manner : AWKWARD ⟨*uneasy* among strangers⟩ **2** : disturbed by pain or worry : RESTLESS ⟨rain made the crew *uneasy*⟩ — **un·eas·i·ly** \-'ēz-(ə-)lē\ *adv* — **un·eas·i·ness** \-'ē-zē-nəs\ *n*

un·em·ploy·a·ble \,ən-im-'plȯi-ə-bəl\ *adj* : not capable of being employed; *esp* : not capable of holding a job — **unemployable** *n*

un·em·ployed \-'plȯid\ *adj* : not employed: **a** : not being used **b** : not engaged in a gainful occupation

un·em·ploy·ment \,ən-im-'plȯi-mənt\ *n* : the state of being out of work : lack of employment

un·end·ing \,ən-'en-diŋ, 'ən-\ *adj* : having no ending : ENDLESS — **un·end·ing·ly** \-diŋ-lē\ *adv*

¹un·equal \-'ē-kwəl\ *adj* **1 a** : not of the same measurement, quantity, or number as another **b** : not like or not the same as another in degree, worth, or status **2** : not uniform : VARIABLE, UNEVEN **3** : badly balanced or matched **4** : INADEQUATE, INSUFFICIENT ⟨timber *unequal* to the strain⟩ — **un·equal·ly** \-kwə-lē\ *adv*

²unequal *n* : one that is not equal to another

un·equaled \-'ē-kwəld\ *adj* : not equaled : UNPARALLELED

un·equiv·o·cal \,ən-i-'kwiv-ə-kəl\ *adj* : leaving no doubt : CLEAR, UNAMBIGUOUS — **un·equiv·o·cal·ly** \-k(ə-)lē\ *adv*

un·err·ing \,ən-'e(ə)r-iŋ, -'ər-iŋ, 'ən-\ *adj* : making no errors : CERTAIN, UNFAILING — **un·err·ing·ly** \-iŋ-lē\ *adv*

un·es·sen·tial \,ən-ə-'sen-chəl\ *adj* : not essential : DISPENSABLE

un·even \,ən-'ē-vən, 'ən-\ *adj* **1** : ODD 2a **2 a** : not even : not level or smooth : RUGGED, RAGGED ⟨large *uneven* teeth⟩ ⟨*uneven* handwriting⟩ **b** : varying from the straight or parallel **c** : not uniform : IRREGULAR ⟨*uneven* combustion⟩ **d** : varying in quality ⟨an *uneven* performance⟩ — **un·even·ly** *adv* — **un·even·ness** \-vən-nəs\ *n*

un·event·ful \,ən-i-'vent-fəl\ *adj* : not eventful : lacking interesting or noteworthy happenings ⟨an *uneventful* vacation⟩ — **un·event·ful·ly** \-fə-lē\ *adv*

un·ex·am·pled \,ən-ig-'zam-pəld\ *adj* : having no example or parallel : UNPRECEDENTED

un·ex·cep·tion·a·ble \,ən-ik-'sep-sh(ə-)nə-bəl\ *adj* [*un-* + obs. *exception* to take exception, object] : not open to objection or criticism : beyond reproach : UNIMPEACHABLE — **un·ex·cep·tion·a·ble·ness** *n* — **un·ex·cep·tion·a·bly** \-blē\ *adv*

un·ex·pect·ed \,ən-ik-'spek-təd\ *adj* : not expected : UNFORESEEN ⟨an *unexpected* happening⟩ — **un·ex·pect·ed·ly** *adv* — **un·ex·pect·ed·ness** *n*

un·ex·pres·sive \-'spres-iv\ *adj* : INEXPRESSIVE

un·fad·a·ble \,ən-'fād-ə-bəl, 'ən-\ *adj* **1** : not subject to fading : FAST **2** : incapable of being forgotten

un·fail·ing \,ən-'fā-liŋ, 'ən-\ *adj* : not failing or liable to fail: **a** : CONSTANT, UNFLAGGING **b** : EVERLASTING, INEXHAUSTIBLE **c** : INFALLIBLE — **un·fail·ing·ly** \-liŋ-lē\ *adv* — **un·fail·ing·ness** *n*

un·fair \-'fa(ə)r, -'fe(ə)r\ *adj* **1** : marked by injustice, partiality, or deception : UNJUST, DISHONEST **2** : not equitable in business dealings — **un·fair·ly** *adv* — **un·fair·ness** *n*

un·faith \-'fāth\ *n* : absence of faith : DISBELIEF

un·faith·ful \-'fāth-fəl\ *adj* : not faithful: **a** : not adher-

---

See ¹*un-* and 2d element

undifferentiated	undissolved	uneager	unenforceable	unexchangeable
undigested	undistinguishable	unease	unenforced	unexcited
undignified	undistinguished	uneatable	unengaged	unexciting
undiluted	undistributed	uneaten	unenjoyable	unexecuted
undiminished	undisturbed	uneconomic	unenlarged	unexhausted
undiminishing	undiversified	uneconomical	unenlightened	unexpanded
undimmed	undivided	unedifying	unenrolled	unexpended
undiplomatic	undivulged	uneducable	unenterprising	unexperienced
undiplomatically	undogmatic	uneducated	unentertaining	unexpired
undiscerning	undomestic	unembarrassed	unenthusiastic	unexplainable
undischarged	undomesticated	unembellished	unenviable	unexplained
undisciplined	undoubled	unemotional	unenvied	unexploded
undisclosed	undoubting	unemphatic	unenvious	unexplored
undiscoverable	undrained	unemphatically	unequipped	unexposed
undiscovered	undramatic	unenclosed	unethical	unexpressed
undiscriminating	undreamed	unencumbered	unexaggerated	unexpurgated
undisguised	undreamt	unendorsed	unexamined	unextended
undismayed	undrinkable	unendurable	unexcelled	unextinguished
undisputed	undulled	unenduring	unexceptional	unfading
	undyed			

---

ing to vows, allegiance, or duty **:** DISLOYAL **b :** not faithful to marriage vows **c :** INACCURATE, UNTRUSTWORTHY — **un·faith·ful·ly** \-fə-lē\ *adv* — **un·faith·ful·ness** *n*

un·fa·mil·iar \ˌən-fə-'mil-yər\ *adj* **:** not familiar: **a :** not well known **:** STRANGE ⟨an *unfamiliar* place⟩ **b :** not well acquainted ⟨*unfamiliar* with the subject⟩ — **un·fa·mil·iar·i·ty** \-ˌmil-'yar-ət-ē, -ˌmil-ē-'ar-\ *n* — **un·fa·mil·iar·ly** \-'mil-yər-lē\ *adv*

un·fas·ten \ˌən-'fas-ᵊn, 'ən-\ *vb* **:** to make or become loose **:** UNDO, DETACH, UNTIE

un·fa·vor·a·ble \-'fāv-(ə-)rə-bəl, -'fā-vər-bəl\ *adj* **:** not favorable: as **a :** OPPOSED, NEGATIVE **b :** not propitious **:** DISADVANTAGEOUS — **un·fa·vor·a·ble·ness** *n* — **un·fa·vor·a·bly** \-blē\ *adv*

un·feath·ered \-'feth-ərd\ *adj* **:** UNFLEDGED

un·feel·ing \-'fē-liŋ\ *adj* **1 :** lacking feeling **:** INSENSATE **2 :** lacking kindness or sympathy **:** HARDHEARTED, CRUEL — **un·feel·ing·ly** \-liŋ-lē\ *adv* — **un·feel·ing·ness** *n*

un·feigned \ˌən-'fānd, 'ən-\ *adj* **:** not counterfeit **:** not hypocritical **:** GENUINE — **un·feign·ed·ly** \-'fā-nəd-lē, -'fān-dlē\ *adv*

un·fet·ter \-'fet-ər\ *vt* **1 :** to free from fetters **2 :** LIBERATE

un·fil·i·al \-'fil-ē-əl, -'fil-yəl\ *adj* **:** not observing the obligations of a child to a parent **:** UNDUTIFUL

un·fin·ished \-'fin-isht\ *adj* **:** not finished; *esp* **:** not brought to the final desired state

¹un·fit \-'fit\ *adj* **:** not fit: **a :** not adapted to a purpose **:** UNSUITABLE **b :** INCAPABLE, INCOMPETENT **c :** physically or mentally unsound — **un·fit·ly** *adv* — **un·fit·ness** *n*

²unfit *vt* **:** to make unfit **:** DISABLE, DISQUALIFY

un·fix \ˌən-'fiks, 'ən-\ *vt* **1 :** to loosen from a fastening **:** DETACH, DISENGAGE **2 :** to make unstable **:** UNSETTLE

un·fledged \-'flejd\ *adj* **1 :** not feathered or ready for flight **2 :** IMMATURE, CALLOW

un·flinch·ing \-'flin-chiŋ\ *adj* **:** not flinching or shrinking **:** STEADFAST — **un·flinch·ing·ly** \-chiŋ-lē\ *adv*

un·fold \-'fōld\ *vb* **1 a :** to open the folds of **:** spread or cause to spread or straighten out from a folded position or arrangement **b :** UNWRAP **2 a :** BLOSSOM **b :** DEVELOP **3 :** to open out or cause to open out gradually to the view or understanding

un·fold·ed \-'fōl-dəd\ *adj* **:** not folded

un·for·get·ta·ble \ˌən-fər-'get-ə-bəl\ *adj* **:** not to be forgotten **:** lasting in memory — **un·for·get·ta·bly** \-blē\ *adv*

un·formed \ˌən-'fórmd, 'ən-\ *adj* **:** not arranged in regular shape, order, or relations: **a :** UNDEVELOPED, IMMATURE **b :** INCHOATE, SHAPELESS

¹un·for·tu·nate \-'fórch-(ə-)nət\ *adj* **1 a :** not fortunate **:** UNLUCKY **b :** marked or accompanied by or resulting in misfortune **2 a :** UNSUITABLE, INFELICITOUS **b :** DEPLORABLE — **un·for·tu·nate·ly** *adv*

²unfortunate *n* **:** an unfortunate person

un·found·ed \-'faún-dəd\ *adj* **:** lacking a sound basis **:** GROUNDLESS ⟨an *unfounded* accusation⟩

un·fre·quent·ed \ˌən-frē-'kwent-əd; ˌən-'frē-kwənt-, 'ən-\ *adj* **:** not often visited or traveled over

un·friend·ed \ˌən-'fren-dəd, 'ən-\ *adj* **:** having no friends **:** not befriended

un·friend·ly \ˌən-'fren-dlē, 'ən-\ *adj* **1 :** not friendly **:** not kind **:** HOSTILE ⟨an *unfriendly* greeting⟩ **2 :** not favorable — **un·friend·li·ness** *n*

un·frock \-'fräk\ *vt* **1 :** to divest of a frock **2 :** to deprive (as a priest) of the right to exercise the functions of office

un·fruit·ful \-'früt-fəl\ *adj* **1 :** not bearing fruit or offspring **2 :** not producing a desired result **:** not resulting in gain ⟨*unfruitful* efforts⟩ — **un·fruit·ful·ly** \-fə-lē\ *adv* — **un·fruit·ful·ness** *n*

un·fund·ed \ˌən-'fən-dəd, 'ən-\ *adj* **:** not funded **:** FLOATING ⟨an *unfunded* debt⟩

un·furl \-'fərl\ *vb* **:** to loose from a furled state **:** open or spread **:** UNFOLD ⟨*unfurl* sails⟩ ⟨*unfurl* a flag⟩

un·gain·ly \-'gān-lē\ *adj* **:** CLUMSY, AWKWARD ⟨an *ungainly* walk⟩ — **un·gain·li·ness** *n*

un·gen·er·ous \-'jen-(ə-)rəs\ *adj* **:** not generous: **a :** PETTY, MEAN **b :** lacking in generosity **:** STINGY — **un·gen·er·ous·ly** *adv*

un·gird \ˌən-'gərd, 'ən-\ *vt* **:** to divest of a restraining band or girdle **:** UNBIND

un·girt \-'gərt\ *adj* **1 :** having the belt or girdle off or loose **2 :** LOOSE, SLACK

un·glue \-'glü\ *vt* **:** to separate by or as if by dissolving an adhesive

un·god·ly \-'gäd-lē, -'gód-\ *adj* **1 a :** IMPIOUS, IRRELIGIOUS **b :** SINFUL, WICKED **2 :** OUTRAGEOUS — **un·god·li·ness** *n*

un·gov·ern·a·ble \-'gəv-ər-nə-bəl\ *adj* **:** not capable of being governed, guided, or restrained **syn** see UNRULY — **un·gov·ern·a·bly** \-blē\ *adv*

un·grace·ful \-'grās-fəl\ *adj* **:** not graceful **:** AWKWARD — **un·grace·ful·ly** \-fə-lē\ *adv* — **un·grace·ful·ness** *n*

un·gra·cious \-'grā-shəs\ *adj* **1 :** not courteous **:** RUDE **2 :** not pleasing **:** DISAGREEABLE — **un·gra·cious·ly** *adv* — **un·gra·cious·ness** *n*

un·grate·ful \ˌən-'grāt-fəl, 'ən-\ *adj* **1 :** not thankful for favors **2 :** not pleasing **:** DISAGREEABLE — **un·grate·ful·ly** \-fə-lē\ *adv* — **un·grate·ful·ness** *n*

un·ground·ed \-'graún-dəd\ *adj* **1 :** UNFOUNDED, BASELESS **2 :** not instructed or informed

un·guard·ed \-'gärd-əd\ *adj* **1 :** vulnerable to attack **:** UNPROTECTED **2 :** free from guile or wariness **:** DIRECT, INCAUTIOUS — **un·guard·ed·ly** *adv*

un·guent \'əŋ-gwənt, 'ən-; 'ən-jənt\ *n* [L *unguentum*, fr. *unguere* to anoint] **:** a soothing or healing salve **:** OINTMENT

¹un·guic·u·late \ˌən-'gwik-yə-lət\ *adj* [fr. L *unguiculus*, dim. of *unguis* nail] **:** having nails or claws **:** CLAWED

²unguiculate *n* **:** a mammal having claws or nails as distinguished from an ungulate or cetacean

un·guis \'əŋ-gwəs\ *n*, *pl* **un·gues** \-ˌgwēz\ [L] **1 :** a nail, claw, or hoof esp. on a digit of a vertebrate **2 :** a narrow pointed base of a flower petal — **un·gual** \-gwəl\ *adj*

¹un·gu·late \'əŋ-gyə-lət\ *adj* [L *ungula* hoof, fr. *unguis* nail, hoof] **1 :** having hoofs **2 :** of or relating to the ungulates

²ungulate *n* **:** any of a group (Ungulata) consisting of the hoofed mammals and including the ruminants, swine, horses, tapirs, rhinoceroses, elephants, and hyraxes of which most are herbivorous and many horned

un·hal·lowed \ˌən-'hal-ōd, 'ən-\ *adj* **1 :** UNCONSECRATED, UNHOLY **2 a :** IMPIOUS, PROFANE **b :** IMMORAL

un·hand \ˌən-'hand, 'ən-\ *vt* **:** to remove the hand from **:** let go

un·hand·some \-'han(t)-səm\ *adj* **:** not handsome: as **a :** not beautiful **:** HOMELY **b :** UNBECOMING, UNSEEMLY **c :** lacking in courtesy or taste — **un·hand·some·ly** *adv*

un·handy \-'han-dē\ *adj* **1 :** hard to handle **:** INCONVENIENT **2 :** lacking in skill or dexterity **:** AWKWARD — **un·hand·i·ness** *n*

un·hap·py \-'hap-ē\ *adj* **1 :** not fortunate **:** UNLUCKY ⟨the result of an *unhappy* mistake⟩ **2 :** not cheerful **:** SAD, MISERABLE **3 :** INAPPROPRIATE — **un·hap·pi·ly** \-'hap-ə-lē\ *adv* — **un·hap·pi·ness** \-'hap-i-nəs\ *n*

un·har·ness \-'här-nəs\ *vt* **:** to divest of harness

un·healthy \-'hel-thē\ *adj* **1 :** not conducive to health ⟨an *unhealthy* climate⟩ **2 :** not in good health **:** SICKLY, DISEASED **3 a :** RISKY, UNSOUND **b :** BAD, INJURIOUS — **un·health·i·ly** \-thə-lē\ *adv* — **un·health·i·ness** \-thē-nəs\ *n*

See ¹*un-* and 2d element				
unfaltering	unfertilized	unforeseen	unfurnished	ungrudging
unfashionable	unfilled	unforested	ungallant	unguided
unfastened	unfiltered	unforgivable	ungarnished	unhackneyed
unfathomable	unfired	unforgiving	ungathered	unhampered
unfathomed	unfitted	unforked	ungentle	unhanged
unfeasible	unfitting	unformulated	ungentlemanly	unhardened
unfed	unflagging	unfortified	ungifted	unharmed
unfeminine	unflattering	unframed	unglazed	unharmonious
unfenced	unflavored	unfree	ungoverned	unharnessed
unfermentable	unflexed	unfrozen	ungraded	unhatched
unfermented	unforced	unfulfilled	ungrammatical	unhealthful
	unforeseeable			

---

un·heard \,ən-'hərd, 'ən-\ *adj* **1** : not perceived by the ear **2** : not given a hearing

un·heard–of \-,əv, -,äv\ *adj* : previously unknown : UNPRECEDENTED

un·hinge \,ən-'hinj, 'ən-\ *vt* **1** : to remove (as a door) from the hinges **2** : to make unstable : UNSETTLE, DISRUPT (a mind *unhinged* by grief)

un·hitch \-'hich\ *vt* : to free from or as if from being hitched

un·ho·ly \-'hō-lē\ *adj* : not holy : PROFANE, WICKED — **un·ho·li·ness** *n*

un·hood \-'hùd\ *vt* : to remove a hood or covering from

un·hook \-'hùk\ *vt* **1** : to remove from a hook **2** : to unfasten by disengaging a hook

un·horse \-'hórs\ *vt* : to dislodge from or as if from a horse : OVERTHROW, UNSEAT

un·hou·seled \-'haù-zəld\ *adj* [obs. *housel* to administer the Eucharist to] *archaic* : not having received the Eucharist

un·hur·ried \-'hər-ēd, -'hə-rēd\ *adj* : not hurried : LEISURELY

uni- *prefix* [L *unus;* akin to E *one*] : one : single (*uni*cellular)

Uni·ate \'(y)ü-nē-,at\ *or* **Uni·at** *n* [Russ *uniyat,* fr. Pol *uniat,* fr. *unja* union, fr. LL *unio*] : a Christian of one of the Eastern churches accepting the pope as head and having distinctive liturgies and laws — **Uniate** *adj*

uni·ax·i·al \,yü-nē-'ak-sē-əl\ *adj* **1** : having only one axis **2** : of or relating to only one axis — **uni·ax·i·al·ly** \-sē-ə-lē\ *adv*

uni·cam·er·al \,yü-ni-'kam(-ə)-rəl\ *adj* [L *camera* chamber] : having or consisting of a single legislative chamber — **uni·cam·er·al·ly** \-rə-lē\ *adv*

uni·cel·lu·lar \-'sel-yə-lər\ *adj* : having or consisting of a single cell — **uni·cel·lu·lar·i·ty** \-,sel-yə-'lar-ət-ē\ *n*

uni·corn \'yü-nə-,kórn\ *n* [LL *unicornis,* fr. L *unus* one + *cornu* horn] : a fabulous animal generally depicted with the body and head of a horse, the hind legs of a stag, the tail of a lion, and a single horn in the middle of the forehead

uni·cy·cle \'yü-ni-,sī-kəl\ *n* : a vehicle that has a single wheel and is usu. propelled by pedals

uni·di·rec·tion·al \,yü-ni-də-'rek-shnəl, -dī-, -shən-ᵊl\ *adj* : having, moving in, or responsive in a single direction (a *unidirectional* current) (a *unidirectional* microphone)

unicorn in British Royal Coat of Arms

uni·fac·to·ri·al \-fak-'tōr-ē-əl, -'tór-\ *adj* : relating to or controlled by a single gene

uni·fi·a·ble \'yü-nə-,fī-ə-bəl\ *adj* : capable of being unified

uni·fi·ca·tion \,yü-nə-fə-'kā-shən\ *n* : the act, process, or result of unifying : the state of being unified

uni·fi·er \'yü-nə-,fī(-ə)r\ *n* : one that unifies

¹uni·form \'yü-nə-,fórm\ *adj* **1** : having always the same form, manner, or degree : not varying or variable **2** : of the same form with others : conforming to one rule **syn** see STEADY — **uni·form·ly** *adv* — **uni·form·ness** *n*

²uniform *vt* : to clothe with a uniform

³uniform *n* : distinctive dress worn by members of a particular group (as an army or a police force)

uni·for·mi·tar·i·an·ism \,yü-nə-,fór-mə-'ter-ē-ə-,niz-əm\ *n* : a geological doctrine that existing processes acting in the same manner as at present are sufficient to account for all geological changes

uni·for·mi·ty \,yü-nə-'fór-mət-ē\ *n, pl* **-ties** : the quality or state or an instance of being uniform

uni·fy \'yü-nə-,fī\ *vt* **-fied; -fy·ing** : to make into a unit or a coherent whole : UNITE

uni·lat·er·al \,yü-ni-'lat-ə-rəl, -'la-trəl\ *adj* : of, relating to, having, or done by one side only (*unilateral* paralysis) (*unilateral* disarmament) — **uni·lat·er·al·ly** \-ē\ *adv*

uni·lin·e·ar \-'lin-ē-ər\ *adj* : developing in or involving a series of stages usu. from the primitive to the more advanced

uni·loc·u·lar \-'läk-yə-lər\ *adj* : containing a single cavity

un·im·peach·a·ble \,ən-im-'pē-chə-bəl\ *adj* : not impeachable : not to be called in question : not liable to accusation : IRREPROACHABLE, BLAMELESS — **un·im·peach·a·bly** \-blē\ *adv*

un·im·proved \-'prüvd\ *adj* : not improved: as **a** : not tilled, built upon, or otherwise improved for use (*unimproved* land) **b** : not used or employed advantageously **c** : not selectively bred for better quality or productiveness

un·in·hib·it·ed \,ən-in-'hib-ət-əd\ *adj* : free from inhibition; *esp* : boisterously informal — **un·in·hib·it·ed·ly** *adv*

un·in·tel·li·gent \,ən-in-'tel-ə-jənt\ *adj* : lacking intelligence : UNWISE, IGNORANT — **un·in·tel·li·gent·ly** *adv*

un·in·tel·li·gi·ble \-'tel-ə-jə-bəl\ *adj* : not intelligible : OBSCURE — **un·in·tel·li·gi·ble·ness** *n* — **un·in·tel·li·gi·bly** \-blē\ *adv*

un·in·ten·tion·al \,ən-in-'tench-nəl, -'ten-chən-ᵊl\ *adj* : not intentional — **un·in·ten·tion·al·ly** \-ē\ *adv*

un·in·ter·est·ed \,ən-'in-trəs-təd, 'ən-, -'int-ə-rəs-\ *adj* **1** : having no interest and esp. no property interest in **2** : not having the mind or feelings engaged : not having the curiosity or sympathy aroused

syn DISINTERESTED: UNINTERESTED usu. has only the negative implication of being indifferent to through lack of sympathy for or curiosity toward something; DISINTERESTED may imply the positive idea of a circumstantial freedom from concern for personal or financial advantage that enables one to judge, advise, or act without bias

un·in·ter·rupt·ed \,ən-,int-ə-'rəp-təd\ *adj* : not interrupted : CONTINUOUS — **un·in·ter·rupt·ed·ly** *adv* — **un·in·ter·rupt·ed·ness** *n*

uni·nu·cle·ate \,yü-ni-'n(y)ü-klē-ət\ *also* **uni·nu·cle·ar** \-klē-ər\ *adj* : having a single nucleus

union \'yü-nyən\ *n* [LL *union-, unio,* fr. L *unus* one] **1 a** : an act or instance of uniting two or more things into one: as (1) : the formation of a single political unit from two or more separate and independent units (2) : a uniting in marriage (3) : the growing together of severed parts **b** : a unified condition : COMBINATION, JUNCTION **2** : something formed by a combining of parts or members: as **a** : a confederation of independent individuals (as nations or persons) for some common purpose **b** : a political unit constituting an organic whole formed from several units that may have been previously independent **c** : LABOR UNION **d** *cap* : an organization on a college or university campus providing recreational, social, cultural, and sometimes dining facilities; *also* : the building housing it **e** : the set of all elements that belong to one or both of two sets **3 a** : a device emblematic of the union of two or more sovereignties borne on a national flag **b** : the upper inner corner of a flag **4 a** : a device for connecting parts (as of a machine) **b** : a coupling for pipes **syn** see UNITY

union 4b, partly cut away

Union *adj* : of, relating to, or being the side favoring the federal union in the U.S. Civil War (the *Union* army)

union card *n* : a card certifying personal membership in good standing in a labor union

union·ism \'yü-nyə-,niz-əm\ *n* : the principle or policy of forming or adhering to a union: as **a** *cap* : adherence to the policy of a firm federal union prior to or during the U.S. Civil War **b** : the principles, theory, or system of trade unions — **union·ist** \-yə-nəst\ *n, often cap*

ə abut; ᵊ kitten; ər further; a back; ā bake; ä cot, cart; aù out; ch chin; e less; ē easy; g gift; i trip; ī life

union·ize \'yü-nyə-ˌnīz\ vt : to cause to become a member of or subject to the rules of a labor union : form into a labor union — **union·i·za·tion** \ˌyü-nyə-nə-'zā-shən\ n

un·ion·ized \ˌən-'ī-ə-ˌnīzd, 'ən-\ adj : not ionized

union jack n 1 : a flag consisting of the part of a national flag that signifies union; esp : a U.S. flag consisting of a blue field with one white star for each state 2 cap U & J : the national flag of the United Kingdom

union shop n : an establishment in which the employer is free to hire nonunion workers but retains them on the payroll only on condition of their becoming members of the union within a specified time

union suit n : an undergarment with shirt and drawers in one piece

uni·pa·ren·tal \ˌyü-ni-pə-'rent-°l\ adj : having or involving a single parent; also : PARTHENOGENETIC — **uni·pa·ren·tal·ly** \-°l-ē\ adv

unip·a·rous \yü-'nip-ə-rəs\ adj [L parere to produce, bear] 1 : producing but one egg or offspring at a time 2 : having produced but one offspring

uni·pla·nar \ˌyü-ni-'plā-nər\ adj : lying or occurring in one plane : PLANAR

uni·po·lar \ˌyü-ni-'pō-lər\ adj 1 : having, produced by, or acting by a single magnetic or electrical pole 2 : having but one process ⟨unipolar ganglion cells⟩ — **uni·po·lar·i·ty** \-pō-'lar-ət-ē\ n

unip·o·tent \yü-'nip-ət-ənt, ˌyü-ni-'pōt-°nt\ adj : capable of development in but one direction or to one end product ⟨unipotent cells⟩ — compare TOTIPOTENT

unique \yu̇-'nēk\ adj [F, fr. L unicus, fr. unus one] 1 : being the only one of its kind 2 : very unusual : NOTABLE
syn see SINGLE — **unique·ly** adv — **unique·ness** n

un·i·ra·mous \ˌyü-ni-'rā-məs\ adj [L ramus branch] : UNBRANCHED

uni·sex \'yü-nə-ˌseks\ adj : not distinguishable as male or female ⟨unisex clothing⟩

uni·sex·u·al \ˌyü-ni-'sek-sh(ə-w)əl\ adj : of, relating to, or restricted to one sex : a : male or female but not hermaphroditic b : DICLINOUS ⟨a unisexual flower⟩ — **uni·sex·u·al·i·ty** \-ˌsek-shə-'wal-ət-ē\ n — **uni·sex·u·al·ly** \-'sek-sh(ə-w)ə-lē\ adv

uni·son \'yü-nə-sən, -zən\ n [MF, fr. ML unisonus having the same sound, fr. L unus one + sonus sound] 1 : sameness or identity in pitch 2 : the condition of being tuned or sounded at the same pitch or at an octave ⟨sing in unison rather than in harmony⟩ 3 : exact agreement : ACCORD ⟨all are in unison on the next move⟩

unit \'yü-nət\ n [back-formation fr. unity] 1 a (1) : the first and least natural number : ONE (2) : a single quantity regarded as a whole in calculation b : the number occupying the position immediately to the left of the decimal point in the Arabic system of numerals 2 : a definite quantity (as of length, time, or value) adopted as a standard of measurement; esp : an amount of work (as 120 hours in a completed course) used in calculating student credits 3 a : a single thing or person or group that is a constituent of a whole b : a part of a military establishment that has a prescribed organization c : a piece or complex of apparatus serving to perform one particular function d : a part of a school course focusing on a central theme and making use of resources from numerous subject areas and the pupils' own experience

uni·tar·i·an \ˌyü-nə-'ter-ē-ən\ n 1 a often cap : one who believes that the deity exists only in one person b cap : a member of a Christian denomination that stresses individual freedom of belief, the free use of reason in religion, a united world community, and liberal social action 2 : an advocate of unity or a unitary system — **unitarian** adj, often cap — **uni·tar·i·an·ism** \-ē-ə-ˌniz-əm\ n, often cap

uni·tary \'yü-nə-ˌter-ē\ adj 1 a : of or relating to a unit b : based on or characterized by unity or units 2 : having the character of a unit : UNDIVIDED, WHOLE

unit character n : a natural character inherited on an all-or-none basis; esp : one dependent on the presence or absence of a single gene

unite \yu̇-'nīt\ vb [LL unire, fr. L unus one] 1 a : to put or come together to form a single unit b : to cause to adhere c : to link by a legal or moral bond 2 : to become one or as if one 3 : to join in action : act as if one syn see JOIN — **unit·er** n

unit·ed \yu̇-'nīt-əd\ adj 1 : made one : COMBINED

2 : relating to or produced by joint action 3 : being in agreement : HARMONIOUS — **unit·ed·ly** adv

united front n 1 : a state or appearance of unity, common purpose, or general agreement 2 : a coalition of leftist and sometimes middle-of-the-road political parties

United Nations n pl : an international organization consisting orig. of 50 nations formed in 1945 to further international peace, security, and cooperation

unit·ize \'yü-nat-ˌīz\ vb : to convert into a unit

uni·ty \'yü-nat-ē\ n, pl -ties [L unus one] 1 : the quality or state of being one : SINGLENESS, ONENESS 2 : CONCORD, HARMONY 3 : continuity without change ⟨unity of purpose and effort⟩ 4 : a definite mathematical quantity or combination of quantities taken as one or for which 1 is made to stand in a calculation 5 : reference of all the parts of an artistic or literary composition to a single main idea : singleness of effect or style 6 : totality of related parts
syn UNITY, SOLIDARITY, UNION mean the character of a thing that is a whole composed of many parts. UNITY implies oneness gained by the interdependence of its varied parts; SOLIDARITY implies such unity in a group, class, or community that enables it to show undivided strength as through opinion or influence; UNION implies a thorough integration of parts and their harmonious cooperation ⟨the union of the thirteen states⟩

¹**uni·va·lent** \ˌyü-ni-'vā-lənt\ adj 1 : having a chemical valence of one 2 : not one of a pair ⟨a univalent chromosome⟩

²**univalent** n : a univalent chromosome

¹**uni·valve** \'yü-ni-ˌvalv\ adj : having or consisting of one valve

²**univalve** n : a univalve mollusk shell or a mollusk having such a shell

¹**uni·ver·sal** \ˌyü-nə-'vər-səl\ adj 1 : including or covering all or a whole without limit or exception 2 a : present or occurring everywhere b : existent or operative everywhere or under all conditions ⟨universal cultural patterns⟩ 3 a : embracing a major part or the greatest portion ⟨universal practices⟩ b : comprehensively broad and versatile ⟨a universal genius⟩ 4 : affirming or denying something of all members of a class ⟨"no man knows everything" is a universal negative⟩ 5 : adapted or adjustable to meet varied requirements (as of use, shape, or size) ⟨a universal wrench⟩ — **uni·ver·sal·ly** \-s(ə-)lē\ adv — **uni·ver·sal·ness** \-səl-nəs\ n
syn UNIVERSAL, GENERAL mean of all or of the whole. UNIVERSAL implies reference to everyone without exception in the class, category, or genus considered ⟨universal franchise⟩ GENERAL implies reference to all or nearly all ⟨the theory has general but not universal acceptance⟩

²**universal** n 1 : a universal proposition in logic 2 : a general concept or term or something in reality to which it corresponds

uni·ver·sal·ism \ˌyü-nə-'vər-sə-ˌliz-əm\ n, often cap 1 : a theological doctrine that all men will eventually be saved 2 : the principles and practices of a liberal Christian denomination founded in the 18th century to uphold belief in universal salvation and united with Unitarianism — **uni·ver·sal·ist** \-s(ə-)ləst\ n or adj, often cap

uni·ver·sal·i·ty \ˌyü-nə-(ˌ)vər-'sal-ət-ē\ n : the quality or state of being universal (as in range, occurrence, or appeal)

uni·ver·sal·ize \-'vər-sə-ˌlīz\ vt : to make universal — **uni·ver·sal·i·za·tion** \-ˌvər-sə-lə-'zā-shən\ n

universal joint n : a shaft coupling capable of transmitting rotation from one shaft to another not in a straight line with it

uni·verse \'yü-nə-ˌvərs\ n [L universum, fr. neut. of universus entire, whole, fr. unus one + versus turned toward, fr. pp. of vertere to turn] 1 : the whole body of things and phenomena observed or postulated : COSMOS 2 a : a systematic whole held to arise by and persist through the direct intervention of divine power b : the world of human experience 3 a : MILKY WAY GALAXY b : an aggregate of stars comparable to the Milky Way galaxy syn see EARTH

universal joint

uni·ver·si·ty \ˌyü-nə-'vər-sət-ē, -'vər-stē\ n, pl -ties : an institution of higher learning authorized to grant degrees in various special fields (as law, medicine, and theology) as well as in the arts and sciences generally

---

j joke; ŋ sing; ō flow; ȯ flaw; ȯi coin; th thin; th̲ this; ü loot; u̇ foot; y yet; yü few; yu̇ furious; zh vision

univ·o·cal \yü-'niv-ə-kəl\ *adj* [LL *univocus,* fr. *unus* one + *voc-, vox* voice] : having one meaning only — **univ·o·cal·ly** \-k(ə-)lē\ *adv*

un·just \,ən-'jəst, 'ən-\ *adj* : characterized by injustice : deficient in justice and fairness : WRONGFUL — **un·just·ly** *adv* — **un·just·ness** \-'jəs(t)-nəs\ *n*

un·kempt \-'kem(p)t\ *adj* [*un-* + *kempt,* pp. of E dial. *kemb* to comb, fr. OE *cemban;* akin to E *comb*] **1 a** : not combed ⟨*unkempt* hair⟩ **b** : deficient in order or neatness of person : DISHEVELED **2** : ROUGH, UNPOLISHED

un·ken·nel \-'ken-ᵊl\ *vt* **1 a** : to drive (as a fox) from a hiding place or den **b** : to free (dogs) from a kennel **2** : UNCOVER

un·kind \-'kīnd\ *adj* : deficient in kindness or sympathy : HARSH, CRUEL — **un·kind·ly** *adv* — **un·kind·ness** \-'kīn(d)-nəs\ *n*

un·kind·ly \-'kīn-dlē\ *adj* : UNKIND — **un·kind·li·ness** *n*

un·knit \,ən-'nit, 'ən-\ *vb* : UNDO, UNRAVEL

un·know·a·ble \,ən-'nō-ə-bəl, 'ən-\ *adj* : not knowable

un·know·ing \,ən-'nō-iŋ, 'ən-\ *adj* : not knowing — **un·know·ing·ly** \-iŋ-lē\ *adv*

¹un·known \,ən-'nōn, 'ən-\ *adj* : not known; *also* : having an unknown value ⟨*unknown* quantity⟩

²unknown *n* : something that is unknown and usu. to be discovered; *esp* : an unknown quantity usu. symbolized in mathematics by one of the last letters of the alphabet

Unknown Soldier *n* : an unidentified soldier whose body is selected to receive national honors as a representative of all of the same nation who died in a war

un·lace \,ən-'lās, 'ən-\ *vt* : to loose by undoing a lacing

un·lade \-'lād\ *vb* **1** : to take the load or cargo from **2** : DISCHARGE, UNLOAD

un·lash \-'lash\ *vt* : to untie the lashing of : LOOSE, UNDO

un·latch \-'lach\ *vb* **1** : to open or loose by lifting the latch **2** : to become loosed or opened

un·law·ful \-'lò-fəl\ *adj* **1** : not lawful : contrary to law : ILLEGAL **2** : ILLEGITIMATE — **un·law·ful·ly** \-f(ə-)lē\ *adv* — **un·law·ful·ness** \-fəl-nəs\ *n*

un·lay \-'lā\ *vt* **-laid** \-'lād\; **-lay·ing** : to untwist the strands of ⟨as of a rope⟩

un·lead·ed \-'led-əd\ *adj* **1** : stripped of lead **2** : not having leads between the lines in printing

un·learn \-'lərn\ *vt* : to put out of one's knowledge or memory

un·learned *adj* **1** \-'lər-nəd\ : not learned : UNEDUCATED, ILLITERATE ⟨a good but *unlearned* man⟩ **2** \-'lərnd\ : not learned by study : not known ⟨lessons *unlearned* by many⟩ **3** \-'lərnd\ : not learned by previous experience ⟨breathing is *unlearned* behavior⟩

un·leash \-'lēsh\ *vt* : to free from or as if from a leash ⟨*unleash* a dog⟩ ⟨the storm *unleashed* its fury on the mountain⟩

un·less \ən-'les, ,ən-\ *conj* [ME *onlesse,* fr. *on + lesse* less] : except on the condition that : if not ⟨will fail *unless* he works harder⟩

un·let·tered \,ən-'let-ərd, 'ən-\ *adj* **1** : not educated **2** : ILLITERATE

un·licked \-'likt\ *adj* : not licked dry : lacking proper form or shape

¹un·like \,ən-'līk, 'ən-\ *prep* **1** : different from ⟨feeling completely *unlike* a hero⟩ **2** : not characteristic of ⟨it was *unlike* him to be inquisitive⟩ **3** : in a different manner from ⟨behaving *unlike* his associates⟩

²unlike *adj* : not like: as **a** : marked by dissimilarity : DIFFERENT **b** : UNEQUAL — **un·like·ness** *n*

un·like·li·hood \-'lī-klē-,hud\ *n* : IMPROBABILITY

un·like·ly \-'lī-klē\ *adj* **1** : not likely : IMPROBABLE **2** : likely to fail : UNPROMISING — **un·like·li·ness** *n*

un·lim·ber \,ən-'lim-bər, 'ən-\ *vb* : to prepare for action

un·lim·it·ed \-'lim-ət-əd\ *adj* **1** : lacking any controls

2 : BOUNDLESS, INFINITE **3** : not bounded by exceptions : UNDEFINED

un·link \-'liŋk\ *vt* : to unfasten the links of : SEPARATE, DISCONNECT

un·list·ed \-'lis-təd\ *adj* : not appearing upon a list; *esp* : not listed on an organized securities exchange ⟨*unlisted* stocks⟩

un·live \-'liv\ *vt* : to live down : ANNUL, REVERSE

un·load \-'lōd\ *vb* **1 a** : to take away or off : REMOVE ⟨*unload* cargo from a hold⟩; *also* : to get rid of **b** : to take a load from ⟨*unload* a ship⟩; *also* : to relieve or set free : UNBURDEN ⟨*unload* your mind of worries⟩ **2** : to get rid of or be relieved of a load or burden ⟨the ship is *unloading* now⟩ **3** : to sell in volume : DUMP ⟨*unload* surplus goods⟩

un·lock \-'läk\ *vb* **1** : to open or unfasten through release of a lock ⟨*unlock* the door⟩ ⟨the chest won't *unlock*⟩ **2** : RELEASE ⟨*unlock* a flood of emotions⟩ **3** : DISCLOSE, REVEAL ⟨*unlock* the secrets of nature⟩

un·looked-for \-'lukt-,fór\ *adj* : UNEXPECTED

un·loose \,ən-'lüs, 'ən-\ *vt* **1** : to relax the strain of ⟨*unloose* a grip⟩ **2** : to release from or as if from restraints : set free **3** : UNTIE

un·loos·en \-'lüs-ᵊn\ *vt* : UNLOOSE

un·love·ly \-'ləv-lē\ *adj* : having no charm or appeal : not amiable : DISAGREEABLE ⟨an *unlovely* disposition⟩ — **un·love·li·ness** *n*

un·lucky \-'lək-ē\ *adj* **1** : marked by adversity or failure **2** : likely to bring misfortune **3** : producing dissatisfaction : REGRETTABLE — **un·luck·i·ly** \-'lək-ə-lē\ *adv* — **un·luck·i·ness** \-'lək-ē-nəs\ *n*

un·make \-'māk\ *vt* **-made** \-'mād\; **-mak·ing** **1** : to cause to disappear : DESTROY **2** : to deprive of rank or office : DEPOSE **3** : to deprive of essential characteristics : change the nature of

un·man \-'man\ *vt* **1** : to deprive of manly courage **2** : to deprive of men

un·man·ly \-'man-lē\ *adj* : not manly: as **a** : being of weak character : COWARDLY **b** : EFFEMINATE — **un·man·li·ness** *n*

un·manned \-'mand\ *adj* : having no men aboard ⟨*unmanned* airplanes⟩

un·man·nered \-'man-ərd\ *adj* **1** : lacking good manners : RUDE **2** : UNAFFECTED — **un·man·nered·ly** *adv*

¹un·man·ner·ly \-'man-ər-lē\ *adv* : in an unmannerly fashion

²unmannerly *adj* : RUDE, IMPOLITE — **un·man·ner·li·ness** *n*

un·mask \-'mask, 'ən-\ *vb* **1** : to strip of a mask or a disguise : EXPOSE ⟨*unmask* a traitor⟩ **2** : to take off one's own disguise (as at a masquerade)

un·mean·ing \-'mē-niŋ\ *adj* : having no meaning : SENSELESS

un·meant \-'ment\ *adj* : not meant : UNINTENTIONAL

un·meet \-'mēt\ *adj* : not meet : UNSUITABLE, IMPROPER

un·men·tion·a·ble \-'mench-(ə-)nə-bəl\ *adj* : not fit or proper to be talked about

un·mer·ci·ful \-'mər-si-fəl\ *adj* : not merciful : MERCILESS, CRUEL — **un·mer·ci·ful·ly** \-f(ə-)lē\ *adv*

un·mind·ful \-'mīn(d)-fəl\ *adj* : not mindful

un·mis·tak·a·ble \,ən-mə-'stā-kə-bəl\ *adj* : not capable of being mistaken or misunderstood : CLEAR, OBVIOUS — **un·mis·tak·a·bly** \-blē\ *adv*

un·mit·i·gat·ed \,ən-'mit-ə-,gāt-əd, 'ən-\ *adj* **1** : not softened or lessened **2** : ABSOLUTE, DOWNRIGHT ⟨an *unmitigated* liar⟩ ⟨*unmitigated* impudence⟩ — **un·mit·i·gat·ed·ly** *adv*

un·moor \-'mu(ə)r\ *vb* **1** : to loose from or as if from moorings **2** : to cast off moorings

un·mor·al \-'mór-əl, -'mär-\ *adj* : having no moral quality or relation : being neither moral nor immoral — **un·mor·al·ly** \-ə-lē\ *adv*

See ¹*un-* and 2d element				
unjoined	unleavened	unmagnified	unmated	unmilitary
unjointed	unlicensed	unmailable	unmeasurable	unmilled
unjustifiable	unlighted	unmalleable	unmeasured	unmingled
unjustified	unlikable	unmanageable	unmechanical	unmitigable
unkept	unlined	unmanufactured	unmeditated	unmixed
unknowledgeable	unlit	unmapped	unmelodious	unmodified
unlabeled	unlivable	unmarked	unmelted	unmodulated
unlabored	unlobed	unmarketable	unmentioned	unmolested
unladylike	unlovable	unmarred	unmerchantable	unmortgaged
unlaid	unloved	unmarried	unmerited	unmotivated
unlamented	unloving	unmastered	unmethodical	unmounted
	unmagnetized	unmatched	unmetrical	unmovable

un·moved \-'müvd\ *adj* **1** : not moved : remaining in the same place **2** : FIRM, RESOLUTE, UNSHAKEN ⟨*unmoved* in his purpose⟩ **3** : not disturbed emotionally ⟨seeming *unmoved* by the sad news⟩

un·muf·fle \-'məf-əl\ *vt* : to free from something that muffles

un·muz·zle \-'məz-əl\ *vt* : to remove a muzzle from

un·my·e·lin·at·ed \-'mī-ə-lə-ˌnāt-əd\ *adj* : lacking a myelin sheath

un·nail \ˌən-'nāl, 'ən-\ *vt* : to unfasten by removing nails

un·nat·u·ral \ˌən-'nach-(ə-)rəl, 'ən-\ *adj* **1** : not being in accordance with nature or consistent with a normal course of events **2 a** : not according with normal feelings or behavior : PERVERSE, ABNORMAL **b** : ARTIFICIAL, CONTRIVED **c** : STRANGE, IRREGULAR — **un·nat·u·ral·ly** \-'nach-(ə-)rə-lē, -'nach-ər-lē\ *adv* — **un·nat·u·ral·ness** \-'nach-(ə-)rəl-nəs\ *n*

un·nec·es·sar·i·ly \ˌən-ˌnes-ə-'ser-ə-lē\ *adv* **1** : not by necessity ⟨spent money *unnecessarily*⟩ **2** : to an unnecessary degree ⟨*unnecessarily* harsh⟩

un·nec·es·sary \ˌən-'nes-ə-ˌser-ē, 'ən-\ *adj* : not necessary

un·nerve \ˌən-'nərv, 'ən-\ *vt* : to deprive of nerve, courage, or self-control

un·num·bered \ˌən-'nəm-bərd, 'ən-\ *adj* **1** : INNUMERABLE **2** : not having an identifying number ⟨*unnumbered* page⟩

un·ob·tru·sive \ˌən-əb-'trü-siv, -ziv\ *adj* : not obtrusive : not blatant or aggressive : INCONSPICUOUS — **un·ob·tru·sive·ly** *adv* — **un·ob·tru·sive·ness** *n*

un·oc·cu·pied \ˌən-'äk-yə-ˌpīd, 'ən-\ *adj* **1** : not busy : UNEMPLOYED **2** : not occupied : EMPTY

un·of·fi·cial \ˌən-ə-'fish-əl\ *adj* : not official — **un·of·fi·cial·ly** \-'fish-(ə-)lē\ *adv*

un·or·ga·nized \ˌən-'ȯr-gə-ˌnīzd, 'ən-\ *adj* : not subjected to organization: as **a** : not formed or brought into an integrated or ordered whole **b** : not organized into unions ⟨*unorganized* labor⟩

un·or·tho·dox \-'ȯr-thə-ˌdäks\ *adj* : not orthodox

un·owned \-'ōnd\ *adj* : not owned : not belonging to anybody

un·pack \ˌən-'pak, 'ən-\ *vb* **1** : to separate and remove things packed **2** : to open and remove the contents of ⟨*unpack* a trunk⟩

un·paired \-'pa(ə)rd, -'pe(ə)rd\ *adj* **1** : not paired; *esp* : not matched or mated **2** : situated in the median plane of the body ⟨an *unpaired* fin⟩

un·par·al·leled \-'par-ə-ˌleld\ *adj* : having no parallel; *esp* : having no equal or match : UNSURPASSED

un·par·lia·men·ta·ry \ˌən-ˌpär-lə-'ment-ə-rē, -ˌpärl-yə-, -'men-trē\ *adj* : contrary to parliamentary practice

un·peg \-'peg\ *vt* : to remove a peg from : UNFASTEN

un·peo·ple \-'pē-pəl\ *vt* : DEPOPULATE

un·per·fect \-'pər-fikt\ *adj* : IMPERFECT

un·pile \-'pīl\ *vt* : to take or disentangle from a pile

un·pin \-'pin\ *vt* : to remove a pin from : UNFASTEN

un·pleas·ant \-'plez-°nt\ *adj* : not pleasant : not amiable or agreeable : DISPLEASING — **un·pleas·ant·ly** *adv*

un·pleas·ant·ness *n* **1** : the quality or state of being unpleasant **2** : an unpleasant situation, experience, or event

un·plumbed \ˌən-'pləmd, 'ən-\ *adj* **1** : not tested with a plumb line **2 a** : not measured with a plumb **b** : not explored in depth, intensity, or significance

un·po·lit·i·cal \ˌən-pə-'lit-i-kəl\ *adj* : not interested or engaged in politics

un·pop·u·lar \-'päp-yə-lər\ *adj* : not popular : viewed or received unfavorably : disliked by many people — **un·pop·u·lar·i·ty** \-ˌpäp-yə-'lar-ət-ē\ *n*

un·prec·e·dent·ed \-'pres-ə-ˌdent-əd\ *adj* : having no precedent : NOVEL, UNEXAMPLED — **un·prec·e·dent·ed·ly** *adv*

un·pre·dict·a·ble \ˌən-pri-'dik-tə-bəl\ *adj* : not predictable — **un·pre·dict·a·bil·i·ty** \-ˌdik-tə-'bil-ət-ē\ *n* — **un·pre·dict·a·bly** \-'dik-tə-blē\ *adv*

un·prej·u·diced \-'prej-əd-əst, 'ən-\ *adj* : not prejudiced : free from undue bias, warp, or prepossession : IMPARTIAL

un·pre·ten·tious \ˌən-pri-'ten-chəs\ *adj* : not pretentious : not showy or pompous : SIMPLE, MODEST — **un·pre·ten·tious·ly** *adv* — **un·pre·ten·tious·ness** *n*

un·prin·ci·pled \ˌən-'prin(t)-sə-pəld\ *adj* : lacking moral principles : UNSCRUPULOUS

un·print·a·ble \-'print-ə-bəl\ *adj* : unfit to be printed

un·pro·fessed \ˌən-prə-'fest\ *adj* : not professed ⟨an *unprofessed* aim⟩

un·pro·fes·sion·al \ˌən-prə-'fesh-nəl, -ən-°l\ *adj* : not professional; *esp* : not conforming to the standards of one's profession — **un·pro·fes·sion·al·ly** \-ē\ *adv*

un·prof·it·a·ble \ˌən-'präf-ət-ə-bəl, 'ən-, -'präf-tə-bəl\ *adj* : not profitable : USELESS — **un·prof·it·a·ble·ness** *n* — **un·prof·it·a·bly** \-blē\ *adv*

un·prom·is·ing \-'präm-ə-siŋ\ *adj* : appearing unlikely to prove worthwhile or result favorably — **un·prom·is·ing·ly** \-siŋ-lē\ *adv*

un·qual·i·fied \-'kwäl-ə-ˌfīd\ *adj* **1** : not fit : not having requisite qualifications **2** : not modified or restricted by reservations ⟨an *unqualified* denial⟩ — **un·qual·i·fied·ly** \-ˌfī(-ə)d-lē\ *adv*

un·ques·tion·a·ble \-'kwes-chə-nə-bəl\ *adj* **1** : acknowledged as beyond question or doubt ⟨*unquestionable* authority⟩ **2** : not questionable : INDISPUTABLE ⟨*unquestionable* evidence⟩ — **un·ques·tion·a·bly** \-blē\ *adv*

un·ques·tion·ing \-chə-niŋ\ *adj* : not questioning : accepting without examination or hesitation ⟨*unquestioning* obedience⟩ — **un·ques·tion·ing·ly** \-niŋ-lē\ *adv*

un·qui·et \-'kwī-ət\ *adj* **1** : not quiet : AGITATED, TURBULENT **2** : physically, emotionally, or mentally restless : UNEASY — **un·qui·et·ly** *adv* — **un·qui·et·ness** *n*

un·quote \'ən-ˌkwōt\ *vi* : to state that the matter preceding is quoted

un·rav·el \ˌən-'rav-əl, 'ən-\ *vb* **1** : to separate the threads of : DISENTANGLE ⟨*unravel* a snarl⟩ **2** : SOLVE ⟨*unravel* a mystery⟩ **3** : to become unraveled

un·read \-'red\ *adj* **1** : not read ⟨an *unread* book⟩ **2** : not well informed through reading : UNEDUCATED

un·read·a·ble \-'rēd-ə-bəl\ *adj* **1** : too dull or unattractive to read ⟨a long, *unreadable* dissertation⟩ **2** : not legible or decipherable : ILLEGIBLE — **un·read·a·bil·i·ty** \-ˌrēd-ə-'bil-ət-ē\ *n*

syn UNREADABLE, ILLEGIBLE mean difficult or impossible to read. ILLEGIBLE usu. implies a physical impossibility of making out letters or signs; UNREADABLE more often im-

See ¹**un-** and 2d element				
unmoving	unoriginal	unpersuasive	unpowered	unpropitious
unmusical	unostentatious	unperturbed	unpractical	unproportionate
unnameable	unoxygenated	unphilosophic	unpracticed	unproportioned
unnamed	unpaid	unphilosophical	unpremeditated	unprosperous
unnaturalized	unpainted	unphonetic	unprepared	unprotected
unnavigable	unpalatable	unpitied	unprepossessing	unprotesting
unneighborly	unpardonable	unpitying	unprescribed	unproved
unnoted	unpardoned	unplaced	unpresentable	unproven
unnoticeable	unparenthesized	unplanned	unpressed	unprovided
unnoticed	unpartisan	unplanted	unpretending	unprovoked
unobjectionable	unpartitioned	unplayable	unpretty	unpruned
unobliging	unpasteurized	unpleasing	unprevailing	unpublished
unobscured	unpastoral	unpledged	unpreventable	unpunctual
unobservant	unpatient	unplowed	unprinted	unpunished
unobserved	unpatriotic	unpoetic	unprivileged	unpurchasable
unobserving	unpaved	unpoetical	unprocessed	unpure
unobstructed	unpedigreed	unpointed	unproductive	unquenchable
unobtainable	unperceivable	unpolarized	unprofaned	unquenched
unoffending	unperceived	unpolished	unprofound	unquestioned
unopened	unperceiving	unpolled	unprogressive	unraised
unopposed	unperceptive	unpolluted	unprohibited	unransomed
unordained	unperformed	unpolymerized	unprompted	unrated
unordered	unperplex	unposed	unpronounceable	unratified
	unpersuadable	unpossessing	unpronounced	unravished

plies a psychological impossibility of continuing to read with interest or pleasure

un·ready \-'red-ē\ *adj* : not ready : UNPREPARED — **un·read·i·ness** *n*

un·re·al \-'rē(-ə)l\ *adj* : lacking in reality, substance, or genuineness : ARTIFICIAL

un·re·al·is·tic \'ən-,rē-ə-'lis-tik\ *adj* : not realistic : inappropriate to reality or fact — **un·re·al·is·ti·cal·ly** \-ti-k(ə-)lē\ *adv*

un·re·al·i·ty \,ən-rē-'al-ət-ē\ *n* **1 a** : the quality or state of being unreal : NONEXISTENCE **b** : something unreal, insubstantial, or visionary : FIGMENT **2** : ineptitude in dealing with reality

un·rea·son \,ən-'rēz-ᵊn, 'ən-\ *n* : the absence of reason or sanity : IRRATIONALITY

un·rea·son·a·ble \,ən-'rēz-nə-bəl, 'ən-, -ᵊn-ə-bəl\ *adj* **1 a** : not governed by or acting according to reason **b** : not conformable to reason : ABSURD **2** : exceeding the bounds of reason or moderation ⟨*unreasonable* suspicion⟩ **syn** see IRRATIONAL — **un·rea·son·a·ble·ness** *n* — **un·rea·son·a·bly** \-blē\ *adv*

un·rea·soned \-'rēz-ᵊnd\ *adj* : not based on reason or reasoning

un·rea·son·ing \-'rēz-niŋ, -ᵊn-iŋ\ *adj* : not reasoning; *esp* : not using or showing the use of reason as a guide or control ⟨*unreasoning* fear⟩ ⟨the *unreasoning* beasts⟩ — **un·rea·son·ing·ly** *adv*

un·re·con·struct·ed \,ən-,rē-kən-'strək-təd\ *adj* : not reconciled to some political, economic, or social change; *esp* : holding stubbornly to principles, beliefs, or views that are or are held to be outmoded

un·reel \,ən-'rēl, 'ən-\ *vb* : to unwind from or as if from a reel

un·re·gen·er·ate \,ən-ri-'jen-(ə-)rət\ *adj* : not reborn spiritually : not at peace with God : SINFUL, WICKED

un·re·lent·ing \,ən-ri-'lent-iŋ\ *adj* **1** : not softening or yielding in determination : HARD, STERN **2** : not letting up or weakening in vigor or pace — **un·re·lent·ing·ly** \-iŋ-lē\ *adv*

un·re·mit·ting \,ən-ri-'mit-iŋ\ *adj* : not stopping : UNCEASING, PERSEVERING — **un·re·mit·ting·ly** \-iŋ-lē\ *adv*

un·re·serve \,ən-ri-'zərv\ *n* : absence of reserve : FRANKNESS

un·re·served \,ən-ri-'zərvd\ *adj* **1** : not held in reserve : not kept back **2** : having or showing no reserve in manner or speech — **un·re·serv·ed·ly** \-'zər-vəd-lē\ *adv* — **un·re·served·ness** \-'zər-vəd-nəs, -'zərv(d)-nəs\ *n*

un·re·spon·sive \,ən-ri-'spän(t)-siv\ *adj* : not responsive — **un·re·spon·sive·ly** *adv* — **un·re·spon·sive·ness** *n*

un·rest \,ən-'rest, 'ən-\ *n* : want of rest : a disturbed or uneasy state : TURMOIL

un·re·strained \,ən-ri-'strānd\ *adj* **1** : not restrained : IMMODERATE, UNCONTROLLED **2** : free of constraint : SPONTANEOUS — **un·re·strain·ed·ly** \-'strā-nəd-lē\ *adv*

un·re·straint \-'strānt\ *n* : lack of restraint

un·rid·dle \,ən-'rid-ᵊl, 'ən-\ *vt* : to read the riddle of : SOLVE

un·rig \,ən-'rig, 'ən-\ *vt* : to strip of rigging ⟨*unrig* a ship⟩

un·righ·teous \-'rī-chəs\ *adj* **1** : not righteous : SINFUL, WICKED **2** : UNJUST, UNMERITED — **un·righ·teous·ly** *adv* — **un·righ·teous·ness** *n*

un·rip \-'rip\ *vt* : to rip or slit up : cut or tear open

un·ripe \-'rīp\ *adj* **1** : not ripe : IMMATURE **2** : UNREADY, UNSEASONABLE — **un·ripe·ness** *n*

un·ri·valed *or* **un·ri·valled** \-'rī-vəld\ *adj* : having no rival : INCOMPARABLE, UNEQUALED

un·robe \-'rōb\ *vb* : DISROBE, UNDRESS

un·roll \-'rōl\ *vb* **1** : to unwind a roll of : open out ⟨*unroll* a carpet⟩ **2** : DISPLAY, DISCLOSE **3** : to become unrolled or spread out : UNFOLD ⟨a great vista of lofty mountains *unrolled* before their eyes⟩

un·roof \-'rüf, -'rüf\ *vt* : to strip off the roof or covering of

un·root \-'rüt, -'rüt\ *vt* : to tear up by the roots : UPROOT

un·round \-'raund\ *vt* : to pronounce (a sound) without, or with decreased, rounding of the lips — **un·round·ed** *adj*

un·ruf·fled \-'rəf-əld\ *adj* **1** : not upset or agitated **2** : not ruffled : SMOOTH ⟨*unruffled* water⟩

un·ruly \,ən-'rü-lē, 'ən-\ *adj* : not yielding readily to rule or restraint : UNCONTROLLABLE ⟨an *unruly* temper⟩ ⟨an *unruly* horse⟩ — **un·rul·i·ness** *n*
syn UNGOVERNABLE: UNRULY implies lack of discipline or incapacity for discipline and often connotes waywardness or turbulence of behavior ⟨*unruly* children⟩ UNGOVERNABLE implies either an escape from control or guidance or a state of being unsubdued and incapable of controlling oneself or being controlled by others ⟨*ungovernable* rage⟩ ⟨*ungovernable* stampeding cattle⟩

un·sad·dle \-'sad-ᵊl\ *vb* **1** : to remove the saddle from a horse **2** : UNHORSE

un·sat·u·rate \-'sach-(ə-)rət\ *n* : an unsaturated chemical compound

un·sat·u·rat·ed \-'sach-ə-,rāt-əd\ *adj* **1** : capable of absorbing or dissolving more of something ⟨an *unsaturated* salt solution⟩ **2** : able to form a new product by direct chemical combination with another substance; *esp* : containing double or triple bonds between carbon atoms ⟨an *unsaturated* acid⟩ — **un·sat·u·ra·tion** \-,sach-ə-'rā-shən\ *n*

un·saved \-'sāvd\ *adj* : not saved; *esp* : not rescued from eternal punishment

un·sa·vory \-'sāv-(ə-)rē\ *adj* **1** : having little or no taste **2** : having a bad taste or smell **3** : morally offensive — **un·sa·vor·i·ly** \-rə-lē\ *adv*

un·say \-'sā\ *vt* **-said** \-'sed\; **-say·ing** \-'sā-iŋ\ : to take back (something said) : RETRACT, WITHDRAW

un·scathed \,ən-'skāthd, 'ən-\ *adj* : wholly unharmed : not injured

un·schooled \-'sküld\ *adj* : not schooled : UNTAUGHT, UNTRAINED

un·sci·en·tif·ic \,ən-,sī-ən-'tif-ik\ *adj* **1** : not used in scientific work **2** : not according with the principles and methods of science — **un·sci·en·tif·i·cal·ly** \-'tif-i-k(ə-)lē\ *adv*

un·scram·ble \,ən-'skram-bəl, 'ən-\ *vt* **1** : to separate (as a conglomeration or tangle) into original components : RESOLVE, CLARIFY **2** : to restore (as a radio message) to intelligible form

un·screw \-'skrü\ *vb* **1** : to draw the screws from **2** : to loosen or withdraw by turning

un·scru·pu·lous \-'skrü-pyə-ləs\ *adj* : not scrupulous : UNPRINCIPLED — **un·scru·pu·lous·ly** *adv* — **un·scru·pu·lous·ness** *n*

un·seal \-'sēl\ *vt* : to break or remove the seal of : OPEN

un·seam \-'sēm\ *vt* : to open the seams of

un·search·a·ble \-'sər-chə-bəl\ *adj* : not to be searched or explored : INSCRUTABLE — **un·search·a·bly** \-blē\ *adv*

un·sea·son·a·ble \-'sēz-nə-bəl, -ᵊn-ə-bəl\ *adj* : not seasonable : happening or coming at the wrong time : UN-

TIMELY — **un·sea·son·a·ble·ness** n — **un·sea·son·a·bly** \-blē\ adv

un·seat \ˌən-'sēt, 'ən-\ vt **1** : to dislodge from one's seat esp. on horseback **2** : to dislodge from a place or position; esp : to remove from political office

¹**un·seem·ly** \-'sēm-lē\ adj : not seemly : UNBECOMING, INDECENT ⟨unseemly bickering in public⟩ **syn** see INDECOROUS

²**unseemly** adv : in an unseemly manner

un·seen \-'sēn\ adj : not seen or perceived : INVISIBLE

un·seg·re·gat·ed \-'seg-ri-ˌgāt-əd\ adj : not segregated; esp : free from racial segregation

un·self·ish \-'sel-fish\ adj : not selfish : GENEROUS — **un·self·ish·ly** adv — **un·self·ish·ness** n

un·set·tle \ˌən-'set-ᵊl, 'ən-\ vb : to move or loosen from a settled state : make or become displaced or disturbed

un·set·tled \-ᵊld\ adj **1** : not settled : not fixed (as in position or character) ⟨unsettled weather⟩ **2** : not calm : DISTURBED ⟨unsettled waters⟩ **3** : not decided in mind : UNDETERMINED ⟨unsettled what to do⟩ **4** : not paid ⟨an unsettled account⟩; also : not disposed of according to law ⟨an unsettled estate⟩ **5** : not occupied by settlers ⟨an unsettled region⟩

un·sew \ˌən-'sō, 'ən-\ vt **-sewed**; **-sewn** \-'sōn\ or **-sewed**; **-sew·ing** : to undo the sewing of

un·sex \-'seks\ vt : to deprive of sex or of qualities typical of one's sex

un·shack·le \-'shak-əl\ vt : to loose from shackles

un·shaped \-'shāpt\ adj : not shaped : as **a** : not dressed or finished to final form ⟨an unshaped timber⟩ **b** : imperfect in form or formulation ⟨unshaped ideas⟩

un·shap·en \-'shā-pən\ adj : UNSHAPED

un·sheathe \-'shēth\ vt : to draw from or as if from a sheath or scabbard ⟨unsheathe a sword⟩

un·ship \ˌən-'ship, 'ən-\ vb **1** : to remove from a ship **2** : to remove or become removed from position ⟨unship an oar⟩

un·shod \-'shäd\ adj : lacking shoes

un·sight·ly \-'sīt-lē\ adj : unpleasant to the sight : UGLY ⟨an unsightly scar⟩ — **un·sight·li·ness** n

un·skilled \-'skild\ adj **1** : not skilled; esp : not skilled in a specified branch of work : lacking technical training **2** : not requiring skill ⟨unskilled jobs⟩ **3** : marked by lack of skill

un·skill·ful \-'skil-fəl\ adj : not skillful : lacking in skill or proficiency — **un·skill·ful·ly** \-fə-lē\ adv — **un·skill·ful·ness** n

un·sling \-'sliŋ\ vt **-slung** \-'sləŋ\; **-sling·ing** \-'sliŋ-iŋ\ **1** : to remove from being slung **2** : to take off the slings of esp. aboard ship : release from slings

un·snap \-'snap\ vt : to loosen or free by or as if by undoing a snap

un·snarl \-'snärl\ vt : to disentangle a snarl in

un·so·cia·bil·i·ty \ˌən-ˌsō-shə-'bil-ət-ē\ n : the quality or state of being unsociable

un·so·cia·ble \ˌən-'sō-shə-bəl, 'ən-\ adj **1** : having or showing a disinclination for society or conversation : SOLITARY, RESERVED **2** : not conducive to sociability — **un·so·cia·ble·ness** n — **un·so·cia·bly** \-blē\ adv

un·so·cial \-'sō-shəl\ adj **1** : not social : not seeking or given to association **2** : ANTISOCIAL — **un·so·cial·ly** \-'sōsh-(ə-)lē\ adv

un·so·phis·ti·cat·ed \ˌən(t)-sə-'fis-tə-ˌkāt-əd\ adj : not sophisticated: as **a** : not changed or corrupted : GENUINE

b (1) : not worldly-wise : lacking sophistication **(2)** : lacking adornment or complexity of structure : PLAIN, SIMPLE

un·so·phis·ti·ca·tion \-ˌfis-tə-'kā-shən\ n : lack of sophistication

un·sought \ˌən-'sót, 'ən-\ adj : not sought : not searched for or asked for : not obtained by effort ⟨unsought honors⟩

un·sound \-'saúnd\ adj : not sound: as **a** : not healthy or whole **b** : not mentally normal : not wholly sane **c** : not firmly made, placed, or fixed **d** : not valid or true : INVALID, SPECIOUS — **un·sound·ly** adv — **un·sound·ness** \-'saún(d)-nəs\ n

un·spar·ing \-'spa(ə)r-iŋ, -'spe(ə)r-\ adj **1** : not merciful or forbearing : HARD, RUTHLESS **2** : not frugal : LIBERAL, PROFUSE — **un·spar·ing·ly** \-iŋ-lē\ adv

un·speak·a·ble \-'spē-kə-bəl\ adj **1** : impossible to express in words **2** : extremely bad ⟨unspeakable conduct⟩ — **un·speak·a·bly** \-blē\ adv

un·sphere \-'sfi(ə)r\ vt : to remove (as a planet) from a sphere

un·spot·ted \ˌən-'spät-əd, 'ən-\ adj : not spotted : free from spot or stain; esp : free from moral stain

un·sprung \-'sprəŋ\ adj : not sprung; esp : not equipped with springs

un·sta·ble \-'stā-bəl\ adj : not stable : not firm or fixed : not constant: as **a** : FLUCTUATING, IRREGULAR **b** : FICKLE, VACILLATING ⟨unstable beliefs⟩; also : having defective emotional control ⟨an unstable person⟩ **c** : readily changing in chemical composition or physical state or properties ⟨an unstable emulsion⟩; esp : tending to decompose spontaneously ⟨an unstable atomic nucleus⟩ — **un·sta·ble·ness** n — **un·sta·bly** \-b(ə-)lē\ adv

un·state \-'stāt\ vt : to deprive of state, dignity, or rank

un·steady \-'sted-ē\ adj : not steady : UNSTABLE — **un·stead·i·ly** \-'sted-ᵊl-ē\ adv — **un·stead·i·ness** \-'sted-ē-nəs\ n

un·step \-'step\ vt : to remove (a mast) from a step

un·stick \-'stik\ vt **-stuck** \-'stək\; **-stick·ing** : to release from being stuck or bound

un·stint·ing·ly \-'stint-iŋ-lē\ adv : FREELY, GENEROUSLY ⟨gave unstintingly of his time⟩

un·stop \-'stäp\ vt **1** : to free from an obstruction : OPEN **2** : to remove a stopper from

un·strap \-'strap\ vt : to remove or loose a strap from

un·stressed \-'strest\ adj : not stressed; esp : not bearing a stress or accent

un·string \-'striŋ\ vt **-strung** \-'strəŋ\; **-string·ing** \-'striŋ-iŋ\ **1** : to loosen or remove the strings of **2** : to remove from a string **3** : to make weak, disordered, or unstable

un·stud·ied \-'stəd-ēd\ adj **1** : not acquired by study **2** : not studied or planned with a certain effect in mind : NATURAL, UNFORCED

un·sub·stan·tial \ˌən(t)-səb-'stan-chəl\ adj : lacking substance, firmness, or strength — **un·sub·stan·ti·al·i·ty** \-ˌstan-chē-'al-ət-ē\ n — **un·sub·stan·tial·ly** \-'stanch-(ə-)lē\ adv

un·suc·cess·ful \ˌən(t)-sək-'ses-fəl\ adj : not successful : not meeting with or producing success — **un·suc·cess·ful·ly** \-fə-lē\ adv

un·suit·a·ble \ˌən-'süt-ə-bəl, 'ən-\ adj : not suitable or fitting : UNBECOMING, INAPPROPRIATE — **un·suit·a·bly** \-blē\ adv

un·sung \-'səŋ\ adj **1** : not sung **2** : not celebrated in song or verse ⟨unsung heroes⟩

See ¹**un-** and 2d element

unseasoned	unshadowed	unsized	unspecified	unstructured
unseaworthy	unshakable	unslacked	unspent	unstuck
unseconded	unshaken	unslaked	unspiritual	unsubdued
unsecured	unshapely	unsmiling	unsplit	unsubstantiated
unseeded	unshared	unsnuffed	unspoiled	unsuggestive
unseeing	unsharp	unsoiled	unspoken	unsuited
unsegmented	unshaved	unsold	unsportsmanlike	unsullied
unselected	unshaven	unsoldierly	unspun	unsupervised
unselfconscious	unshed	unsolicited	unsquared	unsupportable
unsensitive	unsheltered	unsolicitous	unstained	unsupported
unsentimental	unshielded	unsolid	unstatesmanlike	unsuppressed
unseparated	unshorn	unsolvable	unsterilized	unsure
unserved	unshrinkable	unsolved	unstinted	unsurmountable
unserviceable	unshrinking	unsorted	unstinting	unsurpassable
unset	unshut	unsounded	unstopped	unsurpassed
unsettlement	unsifted	unsoured	unstrained	unsusceptible
unsexual	unsigned	unsown	unstratified	unsuspected
unshaded	unsingable	unspecialized	unstriated	unsuspecting
	unsinkable	unspecific	unstriped	unsuspicious

un·swathe \-'swäth, -'swȯth, -'swath\ *vt* : to free from something that swathes

un·swear \-'swa(ə)r, -'swe(ə)r\ *vb* **-swore** \-'swō(ə)r, -'swȯ(ə)r\; **-sworn** \-'swōrn, -'swȯrn\; **-swear·ing** **1** : to retract something sworn **2** : RECANT

un·swerv·ing \-'swər-viŋ\ *adj* **1** : not swerving or turning aside **2** : STEADY ⟨*unswerving* loyalty⟩

un·sym·met·ri·cal \,ən(t)-sə-'me-tri-kəl\ *also* **un·sym·met·ric** \-trik\ *adj* : not symmetrical : ASYMMETRIC — **un·sym·met·ri·cal·ly** \-tri-k(ə-)lē\ *adv*

un·tan·gle \,ən-'taŋ-gəl, 'ən-\ *vt* **1** : to remove a tangle from : DISENTANGLE **2** : to straighten (as something complex or confused) out : RESOLVE **syn** see EXTRICATE

un·taught \-'tȯt\ *adj* **1** : not instructed or trained : IGNORANT **2** : NATURAL, SPONTANEOUS

un·teth·er \-'teth-ər\ *vt* : to free from a tether

un·think·a·ble \-'thiŋ-kə-bəl\ *adj* : not to be thought of or considered as possible ⟨cruelty *unthinkable* in a decent human being⟩

un·think·ing \-'thiŋ-kiŋ\ *adj* **1** : not taking thought : HEEDLESS, UNMINDFUL **2** : not indicating thought or reflection **3** : not having the power of thought — **un·think·ing·ly** \-kiŋ-lē\ *adv*

un·thought-of \-'thȯt-,əv, -,äv\ *adj* : not thought of : not considered : not imagined

un·thread \-'thred\ *vt* **1** : to draw or take out a thread from **2** : to loosen the threads or connections of **3** : to make one's way through ⟨*unthread* a maze⟩

un·throne \-'thrōn\ *vt* : to remove from or as if from a throne

un·ti·dy \-'tīd-ē\ *adj* **1** : not neat : CARELESS, SLOVENLY **2 a** : not neatly organized or carried out **b** : conducive to a lack of neatness — **un·ti·di·ly** \-'tīd-°l-ē\ *adv* — **un·ti·di·ness** \-'tīd-ē-nəs\ *n*

un·tie \-'tī\ *vb* **-tied; -ty·ing** *or* **-tie·ing** **1** : to free from something that ties, fastens, or restrains : UNBIND **2 a** : to disengage the knotted parts of **b** : DISENTANGLE, RESOLVE **3** : to become loosened or unbound

¹un·til \ən-,til, ,ən-, -,t°l\ *prep* [ME, fr. *un-* to, until (akin to E *end*) + *til* till] : up to the time of ⟨stayed *until* morning⟩

²until *conj* **1** : up to the time that ⟨played *until* it got dark⟩ **2** : to the point or degree that ⟨ran *until* he was breathless⟩

¹un·time·ly \,ən-'tīm-lē, 'ən-\ *adv* **1** : at an inopportune time : UNSEASONABLY **2** : PREMATURELY

²untimely *adj* **1** : occurring or done before the due, natural, or proper time : too early : PREMATURE ⟨*untimely* death⟩ **2** : INOPPORTUNE, UNSEASONABLE ⟨an *untimely* joke⟩ ⟨*untimely* frost⟩ — **un·time·li·ness** *n*

un·ti·tled \-'tīt-°ld\ *adj* **1** : having no title esp. of nobility **2** : not named ⟨an *untitled* novel⟩

un·to \,ən-tə, -tü\ *prep* [ME, fr. *un-* to, until + *to*] : TO

un·told \,ən-'tōld, 'ən-\ *adj* **1** : not told : not revealed ⟨*untold* secrets⟩ ⟨a story yet *untold*⟩ **2** : not counted : VAST, NUMBERLESS ⟨*untold* resources⟩

¹un·touch·a·ble \-'təch-ə-bəl\ *adj* **1 a** : forbidden to the touch **b** : exempt from criticism or control **2** : lying beyond the reach **3** : disagreeable or defiling to the touch — **un·touch·a·bil·i·ty** \-,təch-ə-'bil-ət-ē\ *n*

²untouchable *n* : one that is untouchable; *esp* : a member of a large formerly segregated hereditary group in India having in traditional Hindu belief the quality of defiling by contact a member of a higher caste

un·to·ward \-'tō(ə)rd, -'tȯ(ə)rd\ *adj* **1** : difficult to manage : STUBBORN, WILLFUL ⟨an *untoward* child⟩ **2** : IN-CONVENIENT, TROUBLESOME, AWKWARD ⟨an *untoward* accident⟩ ⟨an *untoward* encounter⟩ — **un·to·ward·ly** *adv* — **un·to·ward·ness** *n*

un·tread \-'tred\ *vt* **-trod** \-'träd\; **-trod·den** \-'träd-°n\; **-tread·ing** : to tread back : RETRACE

un·tried \-'trīd\ *adj* **1** : not tested or proved by experience or trial ⟨*untried* soldiers⟩ **2** : not tried in court ⟨a backlog of *untried* cases⟩

un·true \-'trü\ *adj* **1** : not faithful : DISLOYAL **2** : not according with a standard of correctness : not level or exact **3** : not according with the facts : FALSE — **un·tru·ly** \-'trü-lē\ *adv*

un·truth \-'trüth\ *n* **1** : lack of truthfulness : FALSITY **2** : something that is untrue : FALSEHOOD

un·truth·ful \-'trüth-fəl\ *adj* : not containing or telling the truth : FALSE, INACCURATE ⟨*untruthful* report⟩ — **un·truth·ful·ly** \-fə-lē\ *adv* — **un·truth·ful·ness** *n*

un·tuck \-'tək\ *vt* : to release from a tuck or from being tucked up

un·tune \-'t(y)ün\ *vt* **1** : to put out of tune **2** : DIS-ARRANGE, DISCOMPOSE

un·tu·tored \,ən-'t(y)üt-ərd, 'ən-\ *adj* : UNTAUGHT, UN-LEARNED, IGNORANT

un·twine \-'twīn\ *vb* **1** : to unwind the twisted or tangled parts of : DISENTANGLE **2** : to remove by unwinding **3** : to become disentangled or unwound

un·twist \-'twist\ *vb* **1** : to separate the twisted parts of : UNTWINE **2** : to become untwined

un·used \-'yüzd, *in the phrase* "unused to" *usually* -'yüs(t)\ *adj* **1** : not habituated : UNACCUSTOMED **2** : not used : as **a** : FRESH, NEW **b** : not being in use : IDLE **c** : not consumed : ACCRUED

un·usu·al \-'yüzh-(ə-w)əl\ *adj* : not usual : UNCOMMON, RARE — **un·usu·al·ly** \-ē\ *adv* — **un·usu·al·ness** *n*

un·ut·ter·a·ble \-'ət-ə-rə-bəl\ *adj* **1** : not capable of being pronounced : UNPRONOUNCEABLE **2** : not capable of being put into words : INEXPRESSIBLE — **un·ut·ter·a·bly** \-blē\ *adv*

un·val·ued \-'val-yüd\ *adj* **1** : not important or prized : DISREGARDED **2** : not appraised

un·var·nished \,ən-'vär-nisht, 'ən-\ *adj* **1** : not varnished **2** : not heightened or exaggerated : not embellished : PLAIN ⟨the *unvarnished* truth⟩

un·veil \-'vāl\ *vb* **1** : to remove a veil or covering from : DISCLOSE ⟨*unveil* a statue⟩ **2** : to remove a veil : reveal oneself

un·vo·cal \-'vō-kəl\ *adj* : not eloquent or outspoken

un·voiced \-'vȯist\ *adj* **1** : not verbally expressed **2** : VOICELESS

un·war·rant·a·ble \-'wȯr-ənt-ə-bəl, -'wär-\ *adj* : not justifiable : INEXCUSABLE — **un·war·rant·a·bly** \-blē\ *adv*

un·wary \-'wa(ə)r-ē, -'we(ə)r-\ *adj* : not alert : easily fooled or surprised : HEEDLESS, GULLIBLE — **un·war·i·ly** \-'war-ə-lē, -'wer-\ *adv* — **un·war·i·ness** \-'war-ē-nəs, -'wer-\ *n*

un·wea·ried \-'wi(ə)r-ēd\ *adj* : not tired or jaded : FRESH

un·weave \,ən-'wēv, 'ən-\ *vt* **-wove** \-'wōv\; **-wo·ven** \-'wō-vən\; **-weav·ing** : DISENTANGLE, RAVEL

un·weet·ing \-'wēt-iŋ\ *adj, archaic* : UNWITTING — **un·weet·ing·ly** \-iŋ-lē\ *adv, archaic*

un·well \-'wel\ *adj* **1** : being in poor health : AILING, SICK **2** : MENSTRUATING

un·wept \-'wept\ *adj* : not mourned : UNLAMENTED ⟨died *unwept* and unsung⟩

See ¹*un-* and 2d element			
unsustained	untarnished	untillable	untroubled	unvulcanized
unswayed	untaxed	untilled	untrustworthy	unwalled
unsweetened	unteachable	untired	untufted	unwanted
unsworn	untechnical	untiring	untunable	unwarlike
unsympathetic	untempered	untouched	untwisted	unwarranted
unsympathizing	untenable	untraceable	untypical	unwashed
unsystematic	untenanted	untracked	unusable	unwatched
unsystematical	untended	untrained	unuttered	unwatered
unsystematized	unterrified	untrammeled	unvaried	unwavering
untactful	untested	untransferable	unvarying	unweaned
untainted	unthanked	untranslatable	unveiled	unwearable
untalented	unthankful	untranslated	unventilated	unwearying
untalked-of	unthatched	untraveled	unveracious	unweathered
untamable	unthawed	untraversed	unverifiable	unwed
untamed	untheatrical	untreated	unverified	unwedded
untanned	unthoughtful	untrimmed	unversed	unweeded
untapped	unthreaded	untrod	unvexed	unwelcome
	unthrifty	untrodden	unvisited	unwelded

un·whole·some \-'hōl-səm\ *adj* : detrimental to physical, mental, or moral well-being : UNHEALTHY

un·wieldy \-'wēl-dē\ *adj* : not easily handled or managed because of size or weight : AWKWARD, CLUMSY, CUMBERSOME ⟨an *unwieldy* tool⟩ — **un·wield·i·ness** *n*

un·willed \-'wild\ *adj* : not willed : INVOLUNTARY

un·will·ing \,ən-'wil-iŋ, 'ən-\ *adj* : not willing — **un·will·ing·ly** \-iŋ-lē\ *adv* — **un·will·ing·ness** *n*

un·wind \-'wīnd\ *vb* **-wound** \-'waȯnd\ *also* **-wind·ed**; **-wind·ing** **1 a** : to cause to uncoil : wind off **b** : to become uncoiled or disentangled **c** : to free from or as if from a binding or wrapping **2** : to make or become free of tension : RELAX

un·wise \-'wīz\ *adj* : not wise : FOOLISH — **un·wise·ly** *adv*

un·wit·ting \-'wit-iŋ\ *adj* **1** : not intended : INADVERTENT **2** : not knowing : UNAWARE — **un·wit·ting·ly** \-iŋ-lē\ *adv*

un·wont·ed \-'wȯnt-əd, -'wōnt-\ *adj* **1** : being out of the ordinary : RARE, UNUSUAL **2** *archaic* : not accustomed by experience — **un·wont·ed·ly** *adv* — **un·wont·ed·ness** *n*

un·world·ly \-'wərl-(d)lē\ *adj* **1** : not of this world; *esp* : SPIRITUAL **2 a** : not wise in the ways of the world : NAÏVE **b** : not swayed by mundane considerations — **un·world·li·ness** *n*

un·worn \-'wōrn, -'wȯrn\ *adj* **1** : unimpaired by use **2** : not worn : NEW

un·wor·thy \,ən-'wər-thē, 'ən-\ *adj* **1** : BASE, DISHONORABLE **2** : not meritorious : not worthy : UNDESERVING — **un·wor·thi·ly** \-thə-lē\ *adv* — **un·wor·thi·ness** \-thē-nəs\ *n*

un·wrap \-'rap\ *vt* : to remove the wrapping from : DISCLOSE

un·wreathe \-'rēth\ *vt* : UNCOIL, UNTWIST

un·writ·ten \-'rit-ᵊn\ *adj* **1** : not reduced to writing : ORAL, TRADITIONAL **2** : containing no writing : BLANK

un·yield·ing \-'yēl-diŋ\ *adj* **1** : characterized by lack of softness or flexibility **2** : characterized by firmness or obduracy

un·yoke \-'yōk\ *vt* **1** : to free (as oxen) from a yoke **2** : SEPARATE, DISCONNECT

un·zip \-'zip\ *vb* : to open by means of a zipper

¹up \'əp\ *adv* [OE] **1 a** : in or to a higher position or level **b** : away from the center of the earth **b** : from beneath a surface (as ground or water) **c** : from below the horizon **d** : in or into an upright position **e** : out of bed **2** : with greater intensity ⟨speak *up*⟩ **3 a** : in or into a better or more advanced state **b** : in or into a state of greater intensity or activity ⟨stir *up* a fire⟩ **4 a** : into existence, evidence, or knowledge ⟨the missing ring turned *up*⟩ **b** : into consideration ⟨brought the matter *up*⟩ **5** : into possession or custody ⟨gave himself *up*⟩ **6 a** : ENTIRELY, COMPLETELY ⟨eat it *up*⟩ ⟨house burned *up*⟩ **b** — used as a function word for emphasis ⟨clean *up* a room⟩ **7** : ASIDE, BY ⟨lay *up* supplies⟩ ⟨put his car *up* for the winter⟩ **8** : into a state of closure or confinement ⟨button *up*⟩ ⟨seal *up* a package⟩ **9 a** : so as to arrive or approach ⟨came *up* the drive⟩ **b** : in a direction conventionally opposite to down **c** : so as to be even with, overtake, or arrive at ⟨catch *up*⟩ ⟨keep *up* with the times⟩ **10** : in or into parts ⟨tear *up* paper⟩ ⟨blow *up* a bridge⟩ **11** : to a stop ⟨pull *up*⟩ ⟨drew *up* at the curb⟩ **12 a** : in advance ⟨went one *up* on his opponent⟩ **b** : for each side ⟨score was 15 *up*⟩

²up *adj* **1 a** : risen above the horizon **b** : being out of bed **c** : relatively high ⟨the river is *up*⟩⟨was well *up* in his class⟩ ⟨prices are *up*⟩ **d** : RAISED, LIFTED ⟨windows are *up*⟩ **e** : BUILT ⟨the house is *up* but not finished⟩ **f** : grown above a surface ⟨the corn is *up*⟩ **g** : moving, inclining, or directed upward or in a direction regarded as up ⟨an *up* grade⟩⟨the *up* escalator⟩ **2 a** : marked by agitation, excitement, or activity ⟨was eager to be *up* and doing⟩ ⟨passions were *up* and the situation looked grim⟩ **b** : READY; *esp* : highly prepared **c** : going on : taking place ⟨find out what is *up*⟩ **3** : EXPIRED, ENDED ⟨your time is *up*⟩ **4** : well informed ⟨always *up* on the news⟩ **5** : being ahead or in advance of an opponent ⟨was three games *up* in the series⟩ **6 a** : presented for or under consideration ⟨contracts *up* for negotiation⟩ **b** : charged before a court ⟨was *up* for robbery⟩

— up to **1** : capable of performing or dealing with ⟨feels *up to* her role⟩ **2** : engaged in ⟨what is he *up to*⟩ **3** : being the responsibility of ⟨it's *up to* me⟩

³up *vb* **upped** *or in 1* **up**; **up·ping**; **ups** *or in 1* **up** **1** : to act abruptly or surprisingly — usu. followed by *and* and another verb **2** : to rise from a lying or sitting position **3** : to move or cause to move upward : ASCEND, RAISE

⁴up \(,)əp, 'əp\ *prep* **1** : to, toward, or at a higher point of ⟨*up* the hill⟩ **2 a** (1) : toward the source of ⟨*up* the river⟩ (2) : toward the northern part of ⟨*up* the coast⟩ **b** : to, toward, or in the inner part of ⟨*up* country⟩ **3** : ALONG ⟨walking *up* the street⟩

⁵up \'əp\ *n* **1** : an upward course or slope **2** : a period or state of prosperity or success ⟨had had his *ups* and downs⟩

up-and-down \,əp-ᵊm-'daȯn, ,əp-ən-\ *adj* **1** : marked by alternate upward and downward movement, action, or surface **2** : PERPENDICULAR

Upa·ni·shad \ü-'pan-ə-,shad, 'ü-pə-ni-shəd\ *n* [Skt *upaniṣad*] : one of a class of Vedic philosophical treatises

upas \'yü-pəs\ *n* [Malay *pohon upas* poison tree] : either of two Asiatic and East Indian trees of the mulberry family with a poisonous juice used as an arrow poison; *also* : this juice or a concentrate of it

¹up·beat \'əp-,bēt\ *n* : an unaccented beat in a musical measure; *esp* : the last beat of the measure

²upbeat *adj* : OPTIMISTIC, CHEERFUL

up·braid \,əp-'brād\ *vt* [OE *upbregdan*] : to criticize, reproach, or scold severely or vehemently — **up·braid·er** *n*

up·bring·ing \'əp-,briŋ-iŋ\ *n* : the process of bringing up and training

up·chuck \'əp-,chək\ *vb* : VOMIT

up·com·ing \,əp-,kəm-iŋ\ *adj* : FORTHCOMING, APPROACHING

¹up·coun·try \,əp-,kən-trē\ *adj* : of or relating to the interior of a country or a region — **up·coun·try** \'əp-\ *n*

²up·coun·try \,əp-'kən-trē\ *adv* : to or in the interior of a country or a region

up·date \,əp-'dāt\ *vt* : to bring up to date

up·draft \'əp-,draft, -,dràft\ *n* : an upward movement of gas (as air)

up·end \,əp-'end\ *vb* : to set, stand, or rise on end

¹up·grade \'əp-,grād\ *n* **1** : an upward grade or slope **2 a** : INCREASE, RISE **b** : a rise toward a better state or position ⟨trade is on the *upgrade*⟩ — **up·grade** \-'grād\ *adv*

²up·grade \-,grād\ *vt* : to raise to a higher grade or position

up·growth \'əp-,grōth\ *n* : the process of growing up : upward growth : DEVELOPMENT; *also* : a product or result of this

up·heav·al \,əp-'hē-vəl\ *n* **1** : the action or an instance of upheaving esp. of part of the earth's crust **2** : an instance of violent agitation or change

up·heave \,əp-'hēv\ *vb* **-heaved**; **-heav·ing** : to heave or lift up from beneath — **up·heav·er** *n*

¹up·hill \'əp-'hil\ *adv* **1** : upward on a hill or incline **2** : against difficulties

²up·hill \,əp-,hil\ *adj* **1** : situated on elevated ground **2** : going up : ASCENDING **3** : DIFFICULT, LABORIOUS

up·hold \,əp-'hōld\ *vt* **-held** \-'held\; **-hold·ing** **1 a** : to give support to **b** : to support against an opponent **2 a** : to keep elevated **b** : to lift up — **up·hold·er** *n*

up·hol·ster \(,)əp-'hōl-stər\ *vt* **-stered**; **-ster·ing** \-st(ə-)riŋ\ [back-formation fr. *upholstery*] : to furnish with or as if with upholstery — **up·hol·ster·er** \-stər-ər, -strər\ *n*

up·hol·stery \-st(ə-)rē\ *n, pl* **-ster·ies** [ME *upholdester* upholsterer, fr. *upholden* to uphold, maintain] : materials (as fabric, padding, and springs) used to make a soft covering esp. for a seat

up·keep \'əp-,kēp\ *n* **1** : the act or cost of maintaining in good condition : MAINTENANCE **2** : the state of being maintained

up·land \'əp-lənd, -,land\ *n* : high land esp. at some distance from the sea — **upland** *adj*

See ¹*un*- and 2d element				
unwifely	unwitnessed	unworkable	unworn	unwoven
unwinking	unwomanly	unworked	unworried	unwrinkled
unwished	unwon	unworkmanlike	unwounded	unwrought
	unwooded			

j joke; **ŋ** sing; **ō** flow; **ȯ** flaw; **ȯi** coin; **th** thin; **th** this; **ü** loot; **u̇** foot; **y** yet; **yü** few; **yu̇** furious; **zh** vision

upland cotton *n, often cap U* : any of various usu. short-staple cottons cultivated esp. in the U.S.

upland plover *n* : a large sandpiper of eastern No. America that frequents fields and uplands

1up·lift \(,)əp-'lift\ *vb* **1** : to lift up : ELEVATE **2** : to improve the condition of esp. spiritually, socially, or intellectually **3** : RISE — **up·lift·er** *n*

2up·lift \'əp-,lift\ *n* : an act, process, or result of uplifting: as **a** : the uplifting of a part of the earth's surface **b** : moral or social improvement; *also* : a movement to make such improvement **c** : influences intended to uplift

up·most \'əp-,mōst\ *adj* : UPPERMOST

up·on \ə-'pȯn, -'pän, -pən\ *prep* : ON

1up·per \'əp-ər\ *adj* **1** : higher in physical position, rank, or order **2** : constituting the smaller and more restricted branch of a bicameral legislature **3** *cap* : of, relating to, or constituting a later geologic period or formation **4** : being toward the interior : further inland ⟨the *upper* Amazon⟩ **5** : NORTHERN ⟨*upper* New York state⟩

2upper *n* : one that is upper: as **a** : the parts of a shoe or boot above the sole **b** : an upper tooth or denture **c** : an upper berth

3upper *n* : a stimulant drug; *esp* : AMPHETAMINE

up·per·case \,əp-ər-'kās\ *adj* [fr. the printer's practice of keeping capitals in the upper of his two typecases] : CAPITAL — **uppercase** *n*

upper class *n* : a social class occupying a position above the middle class and having the highest status in a society — **upper-class** *adj*

up·per·class·man \,əp-ər-'klas-mən\ *n* : a junior or senior in a college or high school

upper crust *n* : the highest social class or group

up·per·cut \'əp-ər-,kət\ *n* : a swinging blow (as in boxing) directed upward with a bent arm — **uppercut** *vb*

upper hand *n* : MASTERY, ADVANTAGE

up·per·most \'əp-ər-,mōst\ *adv* : in or into the highest or most prominent position — **uppermost** *adj*

up·per·part \-,pärt\ *n* : a part lying on the upper side (as of a bird)

up·pish \'əp-ish\ *adj* : UPPITY — **up·pish·ness** *n*

up·pi·ty \'əp-ət-ē\ *adj* : putting on airs of superiority : ARROGANT — **up·pi·ty·ness** *n*

up·raise \,əp-'rāz\ *vt* : to raise or lift up : ELEVATE

up·rear \-'ri(ə)r\ *vb* **1** : to lift up : RAISE, ERECT **2** : RISE

1up·right \'əp-,rīt\ *adj* **1 a** : PERPENDICULAR, VERTICAL **b** : erect in carriage or posture **c** : having the main axis or a main part perpendicular **2** : morally correct : HONEST, HONORABLE — **up·right·ly** *adv* — **up·right·ness** *n*

2upright *n* **1** : the state of being upright : PERPENDICULAR ⟨a pillar out of *upright*⟩ **2** : something upright

upright piano *n* : a piano whose strings run vertically

1up·rise \,əp-'rīz\ *vi* **-rose** \-'rōz\ **-ris·en** \-'riz-ʰn\ **-ris·ing** \-'rī-ziŋ\ **1 a** : to rise to a higher position **b** : to get up (as from sleep or a sitting position) **c** : to come into view esp. from below the horizon **2** : to swell in sound : increase in size or volume — **up·ris·er** *n*

2up·rise \'əp-,rīz\ *n* **1** : an act or instance of uprising **2** : an upward slope

up·ris·ing \'əp-,rī-ziŋ\ *n* : an act or instance of rising up; *esp* : INSURRECTION, REVOLT

up·roar \'əp-,rȯr, -,rȯr\ *n* [by folk etymology fr. D *oproer*, fr. *op* up + *roer* motion] : a state of commotion, excitement, or violent disturbance

up·roar·i·ous \,əp-'rȯr-ē-əs, -'rȯr-\ *adj* **1** : marked by uproar **2** : extremely funny — **up·roar·i·ous·ly** *adv* — **up·roar·i·ous·ness** *n*

up·root \,əp-'rüt, -'rüt\ *vt* **1** : to remove by or as if by pulling up by the roots **2** : to displace from a country or traditional habitat — **up·root·er** *n*

1up·set \,əp-'set\ *vb* **-set; -set·ting** **1** : to thicken and shorten (as a heated bar of iron) by hammering on the end : SWAGE **2** : to force or be forced out of the usual upright, level, or proper position : OVERTURN, CAPSIZE **3 a** : to disturb emotionally **b** : to make somewhat ill **4 a** : to throw into disorder : DISARRANGE **b** : INVALIDATE **c** : to defeat unexpectedly — **up·set·ter** *n*

2up·set \'əp-,set\ *n* **1** : an act or result of upsetting : a state of being upset **2 a** : a minor physical disorder

⟨a stomach *upset*⟩ **b** : an emotional disturbance **3 a** : a part of a rod (as the head on a bolt) that is upset **b** : a swage used in upsetting

upset price \'əp-,set-\ *n* : a minimum price set for property offered at auction or public sale

up·shot \'əp-,shät\ *n* : final result : OUTCOME

up·side \'əp-,sīd\ *n* : the upper side or part

up·side down \,əp-,sīd-'daun\ *adv* **1** : with the upper and the lower parts reversed in position **2** : in or into great disorder — **upside-down** *adj*

up·si·lon \'yüp-sə-,län, 'əp-\ *n* : the 20th letter of the Greek alphabet — Υ or υ

1up·stage \'əp-'stāj\ *adv* : toward or at the rear of a stage

2upstage *adj* **1** : of or relating to the rear of a stage **2** : HAUGHTY

3up·stage \,əp-'stāj\ *vt* **1** : to force (an actor) to face away from the audience by staying upstage **2** : to treat snobbishly

1up·stairs \'əp-'sta(ə)rz, -'ste(ə)rz\ *adv* **1** : up the stairs : to or on a higher floor **2** : to or at a high altitude or higher position

2up·stairs \-,sta(ə)rz, -,ste(ə)rz\ *adj* **1** : situated above the stairs **2** : of or relating to the upper floors ⟨*upstairs* maid⟩

3up·stairs \'əp-', 'əp-,\ *n* : the part of a building above the ground floor

up·stand·ing \,əp-'stan-diŋ, 'əp-,\ *adj* **1** : ERECT **2** : HONEST, STRAIGHTFORWARD — **up·stand·ing·ness** *n*

1up·start \,əp-'stärt\ *vi* : to jump up suddenly

2up·start \'əp-,stärt\ *n* : one that has risen suddenly (as from a low position to wealth or power) : PARVENU; *esp* : one that claims more personal importance than he warrants — **up·start** \,əp-,\ *adj*

1up·state \'əp-,stāt\ *adj* : of, relating to, or characteristic of a part of a state away from a large city and esp. to the north

2upstate *n* : an upstate region — **up·stat·er** \-'stāt-ər\ *n*

up·stream \'əp-'strēm\ *adv* : at or toward the source of a stream — **upstream** *adj*

up·stroke \'əp-,strōk\ *n* : an upward stroke (as of a pen)

up·surge \'əp-,sərj\ *n* : a rapid or sudden rise

up·sweep \'əp-,swēp\ *vb* **-swept** \-,swept\ **-sweep·ing** : to sweep upward : curve or slope upward — **upsweep** *n*

up·swept \'əp-,swept\ *adj* : swept upward

up·swing \'əp-,swiŋ\ *n* : an upward swing; *esp* : a marked increase or rise (as in activity)

up·take \'əp-,tāk\ *n* **1** : UNDERSTANDING, COMPREHENSION ⟨quick on the *uptake*⟩ **2** : a flue leading upward **3** : an act or instance of absorbing and incorporating esp. into a living organism

up·throw \'əp-,thrō\ *n* : an upward displacement (as of a rock stratum) : UPHEAVAL

up·thrust \'əp-,thrəst\ *n* : an upward thrust; *esp* : an uplift of part of the earth's crust

up·tight \'əp-'tīt, (,)əp-', ,əp-,\ *adj* **1** : TENSE, UNEASY **2** : ANGRY, INDIGNANT **3** : rigidly conventional

up·tilt \,əp-'tilt\ *vt* : to tilt upward

up to *prep* **1** : as far as a designated part or place ⟨sank *up to* his hips⟩ **2** : to or in fulfillment of ⟨write *up to* the standard⟩ **3 a** : to the limit of ⟨guesses ran *up to* 1000⟩ **b** : as many or as much as ⟨carry *up to* 10 tons⟩ **4** : UNTIL, TILL ⟨from dawn *up to* dusk⟩

up-to-date \,əp-tə-'dāt\ *adj* **1** : extending up to the present time **2** : abreast of the times (as in style or technique) : MODERN — **up-to-date·ness** *n*

up·town \'əp-'taun\ *adv* : toward, to, or in the upper part of a town — **up·town** \-,taun\ *adj*

up·trend \'əp-,trend\ *n* : a tendency upward

1up·turn \'əp-,tərn, ,əp-'\ *vb* **1** : to turn up or over **2** : to turn or direct upward

2up·turn \'əp-,tərn\ *n* : an upward turn (as toward better conditions or higher prices)

1up·ward \'əp-wərd\ *or* **up·wards** \-wərdz\ *adv* **1** : in a direction from lower to higher **2** : toward a higher or better condition **3** : toward a greater amount or higher number, degree, or rate

2upward *adj* **1** : directed toward or situated in a higher place or level : ASCENDING **2** : ascending toward a head, origin, or source — **up·ward·ly** *adv* — **up·ward·ness** *n*

upwards of *also* **upward of** *adv* : more than : in excess of

up·well \,əp-'wel\ *vi* : to well up

up·wind \'əp-'wind\ *adv (or adj)* : in the direction from which the wind is blowing

ur- *or* **uro-** *comb form* [Gk *ouron*] **1** : urine ⟨*uric*⟩ **2** : urinary tract ⟨*urology*⟩ **3** : urinal and ⟨*urogenital*⟩ **4** : urea ⟨*uracil*⟩

ura·cil \'yùr-ə-ˌsil\ *n* : a pyrimidine base regularly present in the polynucleotide chain of ribonucleic acid

Ural–Al·ta·ic \ˌyùr-əl-al-'tā-ik\ *adj* : a language type showing agglutination and occurring esp. in languages of Eurasia — **Ural–Altaic** *adj*

Ural·ic \yù-'ral-ik\ *n* : a language family comprising the Finno-Ugric languages and some languages of northwest Siberia

Ura·nia \yù-'rā-nē-ə\ *n* : the Greek Muse of astronomy

uran·ic \yù-'ran-ik, -'rā-nik\ *adj* : of, relating to, or containing uranium

ura·nif·er·ous \ˌyùr-ə-'nif-(ə-)rəs\ *adj* : containing uranium

ura·ni·nite \yù-'rā-nə-ˌnīt\ *n* : a mineral that is a black oxide of uranium, contains also various metals (as thorium and lead), and is the chief ore of uranium

ura·ni·um \yù-'rā-nē-əm\ *n* [NL, fr. *Uranus*] : a silvery heavy radioactive metallic chemical element that is found esp. in pitchblende and uraninite and exists naturally as a mixture of three isotopes of mass number 234, 235, and 238 — see ELEMENT table

uranium 238 *n* : an isotope of uranium of mass number 238 that absorbs fast neutrons to form a uranium isotope of mass number 239 which then decays through neptunium to form plutonium of mass number 239

uranium 235 *n* : a light isotope of uranium of mass number 235 that when bombarded with slow neutrons undergoes rapid fission into smaller atoms with the release of neutrons and atomic energy

ura·nous \yù-'rā-nəs, 'yùr-ə-\ *adj* : of, relating to, or containing uranium esp. with a lower valence than in uranic compounds

Ura·nus \'yùr-ə-nəs, yù-'rā-\ *n* [Gk *Ouranos*, fr. *ouranos* heaven] **1** : heaven personified as a god in Greek mythology and father of the Titans **2** : the planet 7th in order from the sun — see PLANET table

urate \'yùr-ˌāt\ *n* : a salt of uric acid

ur·ban \'ər-bən\ *adj* [L *urbanus*, fr. *urbs* city] : of, relating to, characteristic of, or constituting a city

ur·bane \ˌər-'bān\ *adj* [L *urbanus* urban, urbane] : notably polite or finished in manner : POLISHED **syn** see SUAVE — **ur·bane·ly** *adv*

ur·ban·ite \'ər-bə-ˌnīt\ *n* : one living in a city

ur·ban·i·ty \ˌər-'ban-ət-ē\ *n, pl* **-ties 1** : the quality or state of being urbane **2** *pl* : urbane acts or conduct

ur·ban·ize \'ər-bə-ˌnīz\ *vt* **1** : to cause to take on urban characteristics ⟨*urbanized* areas⟩ **2** : to impart an urban way of life to — **ur·ban·i·za·tion** \ˌər-bə-nə-'zā-shən\ *n*

ur·ce·o·late \ˌər-'sē-ə-lət, 'ər-sē-ə-ˌlāt\ *adj* [L *urceolus*, dim. of *urceus* pitcher] : shaped like an urn

ur·chin \'ər-chən\ *n* [MF *herichon*, fr. L *ericius*] **1** : HEDGEHOG **2** : a pert or roguish youngster **3** : SEA URCHIN

Ur·du \'ù(ə)r-dü, 'ər-\ *n* : an Indic language that is an official literary language of Pakistan and is widely used in India

-ure *n suffix* [L *-ura*] **1** : act : process : being ⟨expos*ure*⟩ **2** : office : function; *also* : body performing (such) a function ⟨legislat*ure*⟩

urea \yù-'rē-ə\ *n* [NL, fr. F *urée*, fr. *urine*] : a soluble weakly basic nitrogenous compound that is the chief solid component of mammalian urine and an end product of protein decomposition — **ure·ic** \-'rē-ik\ *adj*

urea–formaldehyde resin *n* : a thermosetting synthetic resin made by condensing urea with formaldehyde

ure·ase \'yùr-ē-ˌās\ *n* : an enzyme that promotes the hydrolysis of urea

ure·din·i·um \ˌyùr-ə-'din-ē-əm\ *n, pl* **-din·ia** \-ē-ə\ [NL, fr. L *uredin-, uredo* burning, blight, fr. *urere* to burn] : a crowded usu. brownish mass of hyphae and spores of a rust fungus forming pustules that rupture the host's cuticle — **ure·din·i·al** \-ē-əl\ *adj*

ure·do·spore \'yù-'rēd-ə-ˌspōr, -ˌspȯr\ *or* **ure·dio·spore** \-'rēd-ē-ə-\ *n* : one of the one-celled vegetative spores of a rust fungus that are produced in a uredinium and follow the aeciospores

ure·mia \yù-'rē-mē-ə\ *n* [NL] : accumulation in the blood usu. in severe kidney disease of constituents normally eliminated in the urine resulting in a severe toxic condition — **ure·mic** \-mik\ *adj*

ure·ter \'yùr-ət-ər\ *n* [Gk *ourētēr*, fr. *ourein* to urinate] : a duct that carries urine from a kidney to the bladder or cloaca — **ure·ter·al** \yù-'rēt-ə-rəl\ *or* **ure·ter·ic** \ˌyùr-ə-'ter-ik\ *adj*

ure·thra \yù-'rē-thrə\ *n, pl* **-thras** *or* **-thrae** \-(ˌ)thrē\ [Gk *ourēthra*, fr. *ourein* to urinate] : the canal that in most mammals carries off the urine from the bladder and in the male serves also as a genital duct — **ure·thral** \-thrəl\ *adj*

¹urge \'ərj\ *vb* [L *urgēre*] **1** : to present, advocate, or demand something earnestly ⟨continually *urging* reform⟩ **2 a** : to try to persuade or sway ⟨*urge* a guest to stay longer⟩ **b** : to serve as a motive or reason for **3** : to press or impel to some course or activity (as greater speed) ⟨the dog *urged* the sheep toward the gate⟩ — **urg·er** *n*

²urge *n* **1** : the act or process of urging **2** : a force or impulse that urges; *esp* : a continuing impulse toward an activity or goal

ur·gent \'ər-jənt\ *adj* **1 a** : calling for immediate attention : PRESSING ⟨*urgent* appeals⟩ **b** : conveying a sense of urgency ⟨an *urgent* manner⟩ **2** : urging insistently : IMPORTUNATE — **ur·gen·cy** \-jən-sē\ *n* — **ur·gent·ly** *adv*

uric \'yùr-ik\ *adj* : of, relating to, or found in urine

uric acid *n* : a white odorless nearly insoluble nitrogenous acid that is present in small quantity in mammalian urine and is the chief nitrogenous excretion in birds and lower forms

Uri·el \'yùr-ē-əl\ *n* : one of the archangels

uri·nal \'yùr-ən-ᵊl\ *n* **1** : a receptacle for urine **2** : a place for urinating

uri·nal·y·sis \ˌyùr-ə-'nal-ə-səs\ *n, pl* **uri·nal·y·ses** \-ə-ˌsēz\ : the analysis of urine

uri·nary \'yùr-ə-ˌner-ē\ *adj* **1** : relating to, occurring in, or constituting the organs concerned with the formation and discharge of urine **2** : of, relating to, or used for urine **3** : excreted as or in urine

uri·nate \'yùr-ə-ˌnāt\ *vi* : to discharge urine — **uri·na·tion** \ˌyùr-ə-'nā-shən\ *n*

urine \'yùr-ən\ *n* [MF, fr. L *urina*] : waste material that is secreted by the kidney, is rich in end products of protein metabolism together with salts and pigments, and is usu. a yellowish liquid in mammals but semisolid in birds and reptiles — **urin·ous** \'yùr-ə-nəs\ *adj*

urn \'ərn\ *n* [L *urna*] **1** : a vessel that typically has the form of a vase on a pedestal and often is used for preserving the ashes of the dead **2** : a closed vessel usu. with a spigot for serving a hot beverage ⟨coffee *urn*⟩

urn 2

uro- — see UR-

uro·chord \'yùr-ə-ˌkȯrd\ *n* [Gk *oura* tail] **1** : the tunicate notochord typically restricted to the tail region of the larva **2** : TUNICATE

uro·dele \'yùr-ə-ˌdēl\ *n* [F *urodèle*, fr. Gk *oura* tail + *dēlos* evident, showing] : any of an order (Caudata) of amphibians (as newts) with a tail throughout life — **urodele** *adj*

uro·gen·i·tal \ˌyùr-ō-'jen-ə-tᵊl\ *adj* : of, relating to, or being the organs or functions of excretion and reproduction

urol·o·gy \yù-'räl-ə-jē\ *n* : a branch of medical science dealing with the urinary or urogenital tract and its disorders — **uro·log·ic** \ˌyùr-ə-'läj-ik\ *or* **uro·log·i·cal** \-'läj-i-kəl\ *adj* — **urol·o·gist** \yù-'räl-ə-jəst\ *n*

uro·pod \'yùr-ə-ˌpäd\ *n* [Gk *oura* tail] : either of the flat lateral appendages of the last abdominal segment of a crustacean — **urop·o·dal** \yù-'räp-əd-ᵊl\ *or* **urop·o·dous** \-əd-əs\ *adj*

uro·pyg·i·um \ˌyùr-ə-'pij-ē-əm\ *n* [NL, fr. Gk *ouropygion*, fr. *oura* tail + *pygē* rump] : the prominence at the rear end of a bird's body that supports the tail feathers — **uro·pyg·i·al** \-ē-əl\ *adj*

uro·style \'yùr-ə-ˌstīl\ *n* [Gk *oura* tail + *stylos* pillar] : a bony rod made of fused vertebrae that forms the end of the spinal column of a frog or toad

Ur·sa Ma·jor \ˌər-sə-'mā-jər\ *n* [L, lit., greater bear] : the most conspicuous of the northern constellations that is situated near the north pole of the heavens and contains the stars forming the Big Dipper two of which are in a line indicating the direction of the North Star — called also *Great Bear*

Ursa Mi·nor \-'mī-nər\ *n* [L, lit., lesser bear] **:** the constellation including the north pole of the heavens and the stars that form the Little Dipper with the North Star at the tip of the handle — called also *Little Bear*

ur·sine \'ər-,sīn\ *adj* [L *ursus, ursa* bear] **:** of, relating to, or resembling the bears

Ur·su·line \'ər-sə-lən\ *n* [fr. St. *Ursula*, legendary Christian martyr] **:** a member of a teaching order of nuns founded in Italy about 1537 — **Ursuline** *adj*

ur·ti·cant \'ərt-i-kənt\ *adj* **:** producing itching or stinging

ur·ti·car·ia \,ərt-ə-'kar-ē-ə, -'ker-\ *n* [NL, fr. L *urtica* nettle] **:** HIVES — **ur·ti·car·i·al** \-ē-əl\ *adj*

urus \'yúr-əs\ *n* [L, of Gmc origin] **:** an extinct large long-horned wild ox of the German forests held to be a wild ancestor of domestic cattle

us \(')əs\ *pron* [OE *ūs*] *objective case of* WE

us·a·ble \'yü-zə-bəl\ *adj* **:** suitable or fit for use ⟨*usable* waste⟩ — **us·a·bil·i·ty** \,yü-zə-'bil-ət-ē\ *n* — **us·a·bly** \'yü-zə-blē\ *adv*

us·age \'yü-sij, -zij\ *n* **1 a :** customary practice or procedure **b :** the way in which words and phrases are actually used in a language community **2 a :** the action or mode of using **:** USE **b :** manner of treating **syn** *see* HABIT

¹use \'yüs\ *n* [L *usus*, fr. *uti* to use] **1 a :** the act or practice of employing something **:** EMPLOYMENT, APPLICATION ⟨put knowledge to *use*⟩ **b :** the fact or state of being used ⟨a dish in daily *use*⟩ **c :** way of using ⟨the proper *use* of tools⟩ **d :** USAGE, CUSTOM ⟨had long been our family *use* to sing in the evening⟩ **2 a :** the privilege or benefit of using something **b :** the ability or power to use something (as a limb or faculty) **c (1) :** the legal enjoyment of property; *esp* **:** the physical occupation of real property that constitutes an element of ownership **(2) :** a legal arrangement resembling a trust whereby one person is invested with the legal possession or occupation of real property for the benefit of another party; *also* **:** the benefit or profit conferred **3 a :** a particular service or end **:** OBJECT, FUNCTION **b :** the quality of being suitable for employment **:** USEFULNESS, UTILITY **c :** the occasion or need to employ **4 :** ESTEEM, LIKING ⟨had no *use* for modern art⟩

²use \'yüz\ *vb* **used** \'yüzd, *in the phrase "used to" usually* \'yüs(t)\; **us·ing** \'yü-ziŋ\ **1 :** ACCUSTOM, HABITUATE **2 :** to put into action or service **:** EMPLOY **3 :** to consume or take (as liquor or drugs) regularly **4 :** to carry out a purpose or action by means of **:** UTILIZE ⟨*use* tact⟩ **5 :** to expend or consume by putting to use **6 :** to behave toward **:** TREAT ⟨*used* the prisoners cruelly⟩ **7 —** used in the past with *to* to indicate a former practice, fact, or state ⟨claims winters *used* to be harder⟩⟨how they *used* to quarrel as children⟩ — **us·er** \'yü-zər\ *n*

syn EMPLOY, UTILIZE: USE implies availing oneself of something as a means or instrument to an end; EMPLOY suggests the use of a person or thing that is available because idle, inactive, or disengaged; UTILIZE suggests the discovery of a new, profitable, or practical use for something ⟨how to *utilize* scrap metal⟩

used \'yüzd, *in the phrase "used to" usually* \'yüs(t)\ *adj* **1 :** employed in accomplishing something **2 :** that has endured use; *esp* **:** SECONDHAND ⟨*used* car⟩ **3 :** ACCUSTOMED, HABITUATED

use·ful \'yüs-fəl\ *adj* **:** capable of being put to use **:** USABLE ⟨a rock makes a *useful* substitute for a hammer⟩ ⟨*useful* scraps of material⟩; *also* **:** of a kind to be valuable or productive ⟨a *useful* invention⟩⟨*useful* ideas⟩⟨*useful* arts⟩ — **use·ful·ly** \-fə-lē\ *adv* — **use·ful·ness** *n*

use·less \'yüs-ləs\ *adj* **:** having or being of no use **:** UNSERVICEABLE, WORTHLESS — **use·less·ly** *adv* — **use·less·ness** *n*

¹ush·er \'əsh-ər\ *n* [MF *ussier*, lit., doorkeeper, fr. L *ostiarius*, fr. *ostium* door, fr. *os* mouth] **1 :** an officer who walks before a person of rank **2 :** one who escorts persons to seats (as in a theater)

²usher *vt* **ush·ered; ush·er·ing** \'əsh-(ə-)riŋ\ **1 :** to conduct to a place **2 :** to precede as an usher, forerunner, or harbinger **3 :** INAUGURATE, INTRODUCE ⟨*usher* in a new era⟩

usu·al \'yüzh-(ə-w)əl\ *adj* [L *usus* use, usage] **1 :** accordant with usage, custom, or habit **:** NORMAL **2 :** commonly or ordinarily used **3 :** found in ordinary practice or in the ordinary course of events **:** ORDINARY — **usu·al·ly** \-ē\ *adv* — **usu·al·ness** *n*

syn CUSTOMARY, HABITUAL, ACCUSTOMED: USUAL stresses the absence of strangeness or unexpectedness; CUSTOMARY applies to what accords with the practices, conventions, or usages of an individual or community ⟨their *customary* dress for dinner⟩ HABITUAL suggests a practice settled or established by much repetition ⟨*habitual* frown⟩ ACCUSTOMED is less emphatic than HABITUAL and suggests something that is noticed or expected by others ⟨*accustomed* graciousness⟩

usu·fruct \'yü-zə-,frəkt\ *n* [L *ususfructus*, fr. *usus et fructus* use and enjoyment] **:** the legal right of using and enjoying the fruits or profits of something belonging to another

usu·rer \'yü-zhər-ər\ *n* **:** one that lends money esp. at an excessively high rate of interest

usu·ri·ous \yù-'zhùr-ē-əs\ *adj* **:** practicing, involving, or constituting usury ⟨*usurious* interest⟩ — **usu·ri·ous·ly** *adv* — **usu·ri·ous·ness** *n*

usurp \yù-'sərp, -'zərp\ *vt* [L *usurpare*, fr. *usu* by use + *rapere* to seize] **:** to seize and hold by force or without right ⟨*usurp* a throne⟩ — **usur·pa·tion** \,yü-sər-'pā-shən, ,yü-zər-\ *n* — **usurp·er** \yù-'sər-pər, -'zər-\ *n*

usu·ry \'yüzh-(ə-)rē\ *n, pl* **usuries** [ML *usuria*, alter. of L *usura*, fr. *us-, uti* to use] **1 :** the lending of money with an interest charge for its use **2 :** an excessive rate or amount of interest charged; *esp* **:** interest above an established legal rate

Ute \'yüt\ *n* **:** a member of any of a group of Indian peoples of Colorado, Utah, and New Mexico

uten·sil \yù-'ten(t)-səl\ *n* [ME, vessels for domestic use, fr. L *utensilia*, fr. neut. pl. of *utensilis* useful, fr. *uti* to use] **1 :** an instrument or vessel used in a household and esp. a kitchen **2 :** an article serving a useful purpose **syn** *see* IMPLEMENT

uter·us \'yüt-ə-rəs\ *n, pl* **uteri** \-,rī, -,rē\ *also* **uter·us·es** [L] **1 :** an organ of the female mammal for containing and usu. for nourishing the young during development previous to birth — called also *womb* **2 :** an analogous structure in some lower animals in which eggs or young develop — **uter·ine** \-rən, -,rīn\ *adj*

Uther \'yü-thər\ *n* **:** a legendary king of Britain and father of Arthur — called also *Uther Pen·drag·on* \-pen-'drag-ən\

utile \'yüt-°l, 'yü-,tīl\ *adj* [L *utilis*] **:** USEFUL

¹util·i·tar·i·an \yù-,til-ə-'ter-ē-ən, ,yü-\ *n* **:** an advocate or adherent of utilitarianism

²utilitarian *adj* **1 :** of or relating to utilitarianism **2 a :** of or relating to utility **b :** aiming at usefulness rather than beauty **c :** serving a useful purpose

util·i·tar·i·an·ism \-ē-ə,niz-əm\ *n* **:** a doctrine that one's conduct should be determined by the usefulness of its consequences; *esp* **:** a theory that the aim of action should be the greatest happiness of the greatest number

¹util·i·ty \yù-'til-ət-ē\ *n, pl* **-ties** [L *utilis* useful, fr. *uti* to use] **1 a :** the quality or state of being useful **:** USEFULNESS **b :** capacity to satisfy human wants **2 :** something useful or designed for use **3 a :** PUBLIC UTILITY **b (1) :** a public service or a commodity provided by a public utility **(2) :** equipment or a piece of equipment (as plumbing in a house) to provide such or a similar service

²utility *adj* **1 :** capable of serving as a substitute in various roles or positions ⟨*utility* infielder⟩ **2 :** being of a usable but inferior grade ⟨*utility* beef⟩ **3 :** serving primarily for usefulness rather than beauty **:** UTILITARIAN **4 :** designed for general use

uti·lize \'yüt-°l-,īz\ *vt* **:** to make use of **:** convert to use **syn** *see* USE — **uti·liz·a·ble** \-,ī-zə-bəl\ *adj* — **uti·li·za·tion** \,yüt-°l-ə-'zā-shən\ *n* — **uti·liz·er** *n*

ut·most \'ət-,mōst\ *adj* [ME, alter. of *utmest*, fr. OE *ūtmest*, superl. adj., fr. *ut*, adv., out] **1 :** situated at the farthest or most distant point **:** EXTREME **2 :** of the greatest or highest degree, quantity, number, or amount — **utmost** *n*

uto·pia \yù-'tō-pē-ə\ *n* [fr. *Utopia*, imaginary ideal country in *Utopia* by Sir Thomas More, fr. Gk *ou* not, no + *topos* place] **1** *often cap* **:** a place of ideal perfection esp. in laws, government, and social conditions **2 :** an impractical scheme for social improvement

¹uto·pi·an \-pē-ən\ *adj, often cap* **1** : of, relating to, or having the characteristics of a utopia **2** : proposing or advocating ideal social and political schemes that are impractical : VISIONARY

²utopian *n* **1** : a believer in the perfectibility of human society **2** : one that proposes or advocates utopian schemes — **uto·pi·an·ism** \-pē-ə-ˌniz-əm\ *n*

utopian socialism *n* : socialism based on a belief that owners of the means of production will voluntarily and peacefully surrender their holdings to society — **utopian socialist** *n*

utri·cle \'yü-tri-kəl\ *n* [L *utriculus*, dim. of *uter* leather bag] : a small pouched part of an animal or plant body; *esp* : the larger chamber of the membranous labyrinth of the ear into which the semicircular canals open — compare SACCULE — **utric·u·lar** \yù-'trik-yə-lər\ *adj*

utric·u·lus \yù-'trik-yə-ləs\ *n* : UTRICLE

¹ut·ter \'ət-ər\ *adj* [OE *ūtera* outer, compar. adj. fr. *ūt* out] : ABSOLUTE, TOTAL ⟨an *utter* impossibility⟩ ⟨*utter* strangers⟩ — **ut·ter·ly** *adv*

²utter *vt* [ME *uttren*, fr. *utter*, adv., outside, fr. OE *ūtor*, compar. of *ūt* out] **1 a** : to send forth usu. as a sound **b** : to express in usu. spoken words **2** : to put (as currency) into circulation — **ut·ter·a·ble** \'ət-ə-rə-bəl\ *adj* — **ut·ter·er** \'ət-ər-ər\ *n*

ut·ter·ance \'ət-ə-rən(t)s\ *n* **1** : something uttered; *esp* : an oral or written statement **2** : the action of uttering with the voice : SPEECH **3** : power, style, or manner of speaking

ut·ter·most \'ət-ər-ˌmōst\ *adj* : EXTREME, UTMOST — **uttermost** *n*

uvea \'yü-vē-ə\ *n* [ML, fr. L *uva* grape] : the posterior pigmented part of the iris of the eye — **uve·al** \-əl\ *adj*

uvu·la \'yü-vyə-lə\ *n, pl* **-las** *or* **-lae** \-ˌlē, -ˌlī\ [ML, dim. of L *uva* grape, uvula] : the pendent fleshy lobe in the middle of the posterior border of the soft palate

uvu·lar \-lər\ *adj* **1** : of or relating to the uvula ⟨*uvular* glands⟩ **2** : produced with the aid of the uvula ⟨*uvular* r⟩

ux·o·ri·ous \ˌək-'sōr-ē-əs, -'sòr-; ˌəg-'zōr-, -'zòr-\ *adj* [L *uxorius*, fr. *uxor* wife] : excessively fond of or submissive to a wife — **ux·o·ri·ous·ly** *adv* — **ux·o·ri·ous·ness** *n*

Uz·bek \'üz-ˌbek, 'əz-\ *n* : a member of a people of Turkestan and esp. of the Uzbek Republic of the U.S.S.R.

v \'vē\ *n, often cap* **1** : the 22d letter of the English alphabet **2** : the roman numeral 5

va·can·cy \'vā-kən-sē\ *n, pl* **-cies** **1 a** : a vacating of an office, post, or property **b** : the time such office or property is vacant **2** : a vacant office, post, or tenancy ⟨two *vacancies* in a building⟩ **3** : empty space ⟨stare into *vacancy*⟩ **4** : the state of being vacant : VACUITY

va·cant \'vā-kənt\ *adj* [L *vacant-, vacans*, prp. of *vacare* to be empty, be free] **1** : being without an occupant : not used ⟨*vacant* room⟩ ⟨*vacant* chair⟩ **2** : free from business or care : LEISURE ⟨a few *vacant* hours⟩ **3** : BRAINLESS, FOOLISH ⟨a *vacant* laugh⟩ syn see EMPTY — **va·cant·ly** *adv* — **va·cant·ness** *n*

va·cate \'vā-ˌkāt, vā-'\ *vt* [L *vacare* to be free] **1** : to make void : ANNUL ⟨*vacate* an agreement⟩ **2** : to make vacant : leave empty ⟨*vacate* a building⟩ ⟨*vacate* a position⟩

¹va·ca·tion \vā-'kā-shən, və-\ *n* **1** : a respite or a time of respite from something : INTERMISSION **2 a** : a period during which activity (as of a school) is suspended **b** : a period of exemption from work granted to an employee for rest and relaxation **3** : a period spent away from home or business in travel or recreation ⟨had a restful *vacation* at the beach⟩ **4** : an act or an instance of vacating

²vacation *vi* **-tioned; -tion·ing** \-sh(ə-)niŋ\ : to take or spend a vacation ⟨*vacation* in July⟩

va·ca·tion·er \-sh(ə-)nər\ *n* : VACATIONIST

va·ca·tion·ist \-sh(ə-)nəst\ *n* : a person taking a vacation

va·ca·tion·land \-shən-ˌland\ *n* : an area with recreational attractions and facilities for vacationists

vac·ci·nal \'vak-sən-°l, vak-'sēn-\ *adj* : of or relating to vaccine or vaccination

vac·ci·nate \'vak-sə-ˌnāt\ *vb* : to inoculate (a person) with cowpox virus in order to produce immunity to smallpox; *also* : to administer a vaccine to usu. by injection — **vac·ci·na·tor** \-ˌnāt-ər\ *n*

vac·ci·na·tion \ˌvak-sə-'nā-shən\ *n* **1** : the act of vaccinating **2** : the scar left by vaccinating

vac·cine \vak-'sēn, 'vak-, \ *n* [L *vaccinus* of cows, fr. *vacca* cow] : material (as a preparation of killed or modified virus or bacteria) used in vaccinating — **vaccine** *adj*

vac·cin·ia \vak-'sin-ē-ə\ *n* : COWPOX — **vac·cin·i·al** \-ē-əl\ *adj*

vac·il·lant \'vas-ə-lənt\ *adj* : WAVERING, UNCERTAIN

vac·il·late \'vas-ə-ˌlāt\ *vi* [L *vacillare* to sway, waver] **1** : FLUCTUATE, OSCILLATE ⟨a *vacillating* stock market⟩ **2** : to incline first to one course or opinion and then to another : WAVER syn see HESITATE — **vac·il·la·tion** \ˌvas-ə-'lā-shən\ *n* — **vac·il·la·tor** \'vas-ə-ˌlāt-ər\ *n* — **vac·il·la·to·ry** \-lə-ˌtōr-ē, -ˌtór-\ *adj*

vac·il·lat·ing·ly \'vas-ə-ˌlāt-iŋ-lē\ *adv* : in a vacillating manner

va·cu·i·ty \va-'kyü-ət-ē, və-\ *n, pl* **-ties** **1** : an empty space **2 a** : the state, fact, or quality of being vacuous : EMPTINESS, HOLLOWNESS **b** : vacancy of mind **3** : a vacuous or inane thing ⟨a speech filled with *vacuities*⟩

vac·u·o·late \'vak-yə-(ˌ)wō-ˌlāt\ *or* **vac·u·o·lat·ed** \-ˌlāt-əd\ *adj* : containing one or more vacuoles — **vac·u·o·la·tion** \ˌvak-yə-(ˌ)wō-'lā-shən\ *n*

vac·u·ole \'vak-yə-ˌwōl\ *n* [F, lit., small vacuum, fr. L *vacuum*] : a usu. fluid-filled cavity in tissues or in the protoplasm of an individual cell — see AMOEBA illustration — **vac·u·o·lar** \ˌvak-yə-'wō-lər\ *adj*

vac·u·ous \'vak-yə-wəs\ *adj* [L *vacuus*] **1** : EMPTY **2** : marked by lack of ideas or intelligence : STUPID, INANE ⟨*vacuous* mind⟩ ⟨*vacuous* expression⟩ **3** : devoid of serious occupation : IDLE — **vac·u·ous·ly** *adv* — **vac·u·ous·ness** *n*

¹vac·u·um \'vak-yə(-wə)m, -yüm\ *n, pl* **-ums** *or* **-ua** \-yə-wə\ [L, fr. neut. of *vacuus* empty] **1 a** : a space absolutely devoid of matter **b** : a space partially exhausted (as to the highest degree possible) by artificial means (as an air pump) **c** : a degree of rarefaction below atmospheric pressure **2 a** : a vacant space : VOID **b** : a state of isolation from outside influences **3** : a device creating or utilizing a partial vacuum; *esp* : VACUUM CLEANER

²vacuum *adj* : of, containing, producing, or utilizing a partial vacuum

³vacuum *vt* : to use a vacuum device (as a cleaner) upon

vacuum bottle *n* : a cylindrical container with a vacuum between an inner and an outer wall used to keep liquids either hot or cold

vacuum cleaner *n* : an electrical appliance for cleaning (as floors, carpets, tapestry, or upholstered work) by suction

vac·u·um·ize \'vak-yə-(wə-),mīz\ *vt* **1** : to produce a vacuum in **2** : to clean, dry, or pack by a vacuum mechanism or in a vacuum container

vac·u·um-packed \ˌvak-yə(-wə)m-'pakt, -yüm-\ *adj* : having much of the air removed before being sealed ⟨*vacuum-packed* can of coffee⟩

vacuum pump *n* : a pump for exhausting gas from an enclosed space

vacuum tube *n* : an electron tube evacuated to a high degree of vacuum

va·de me·cum \ˌvād-ē-'mē-kəm\ *n, pl* **vade mecums** [L, go with me] **1** : a book for ready reference : MANUAL **2** : something regularly carried about by a person

¹vag·a·bond \'vag-ə-ˌbänd\ *adj* [MF, fr. L *vagabundus*, fr. *vagari* to wander] **1** : moving from place to place without a fixed home : WANDERING ⟨*vagabond* minstrels⟩ **2 a** : of, relating to, or characteristic of a wanderer **b** : leading an unsettled, irresponsible, or disreputable life

²vagabond *n* : one who leads a vagabond life; *esp* : TRAMP — **vag·a·bond·age** \-ˌbän-dij\ *n* — **vag·a·bond·ism** \-ˌbän-ˌdiz-əm\ *n*

vag·a·bond·ish \-ˌbän-dish\ *adj* : of, relating to, or characteristic of a vagabond

va·gar·i·ous \vā-'ger-ē-əs, və-, -'gar-\ *adj* : marked by vagaries : CAPRICIOUS — **va·gar·i·ous·ly** *adv*

va·ga·ry \'vā-gə-rē; və-'ge(ə)r-ē, -'ga(ə)r-\ *n, pl* **-ries** : an eccentric or unpredictable manifestation, action, or notion **syn** see CAPRICE

va·gi·na \və-'jī-nə\ *n, pl* **-nae** \-(,)nē\ *or* **-nas** [L, lit., sheath] **1** : a canal that leads from the uterus to the external opening of the genital canal **2** : SHEATH; *esp* : an ensheathing leaf base — **vag·i·nal** \'vaj-ən-°l\ *adj*

vag·i·nate \'vaj-ə-,nāt\ *or* **vag·i·nat·ed** \-,nāt-əd\ *adj* : invested with or as if with a sheath

va·gran·cy \'vā-grən-sē\ *n, pl* **-cies** **1** : VAGARY **2** : the state or action of being vagrant

¹va·grant \'vā-grənt\ *n* **1 a** : one who wanders idly from place to place without a home or apparent means of support **b** : a person classed as a vagrant by statute **2** : WANDERER, ROVER

²vagrant *adj* **1** : wandering about from place to place usu. with no means of support **2 a** : having a fleeting, wayward, or inconstant quality **b** : having no fixed course : RANDOM ⟨*vagrant* thoughts⟩

vague \'vāg\ *adj* [MF, fr. L *vagus*, lit., wandering] **1 a** : not clearly expressed : stated in indefinite terms ⟨*vague* accusations⟩ **b** : not having a precise meaning ⟨*vague* term of abuse⟩ **2** : not clearly felt, grasped, or understood : INDISTINCT ⟨*vague* idea⟩ ⟨a *vague* longing⟩ **3** : not thinking or expressing one's thoughts clearly or precisely ⟨*vague* about dates and places⟩ **4** : not sharply outlined : HAZY, SHADOWY **syn** see OBSCURE — **vague·ly** *adv* — **vague·ness** *n*

va·gus \'vā-gəs\ *n, pl* **va·gi** \-,gī, -,jī\ [NL *vagus nervus*, lit., wandering nerve] : either of a pair of nerves that are the tenth cranial nerves, arise from the medulla, and supply autonomic sensory and motor fibers mostly to the viscera — **va·gal** \-gəl\ *adj*

vail \'vāl\ *vt* [MF *valer*, short for *avaler*, fr. *a* to + *val* valley] : to lower esp. as a sign of respect or submission

vain \'vān\ *adj* [OF, fr. L *vanus* empty, vain; akin to E *wane*] **1** : WORTHLESS ⟨*vain* promises⟩ **2** : not succeeding : FUTILE ⟨a *vain* attempt⟩ **3** : proud of one's looks or abilities : CONCEITED — **vain·ly** *adv* — **vain·ness** \'vān-nəs\ *n*

syn VAIN, FUTILE, IDLE mean producing no result. VAIN usu. implies simple failure to achieve a purpose or succeed in an attempt; FUTILE may suggest completeness of failure or folly of undertaking; IDLE may stress the uselessness or inadequacy of the means employed or cast doubt on the seriousness of the attempt

— **in vain** **1** : to no purpose : without success **2** : IRREVERENTLY, BLASPHEMOUSLY

vain·glo·ri·ous \(')vān-'glōr-ē-əs, -'glór-\ *adj* : marked by vainglory : BOASTFUL — **vain·glo·ri·ous·ly** *adv* — **vain·glo·ri·ous·ness** *n*

vain·glo·ry \'vān-,glōr-ē, -,glór-\ *n* **1** : excessive or ostentatious pride esp. in one's achievements **2** : vain display or show : VANITY

vair \'va(ə)r, 've(ə)r\ *n* [OF, fr. *vair*, adj., variegated, fr. L *varius* variegated, various] : the bluish gray and white fur of a squirrel prized for ornament in medieval times

val·ance \'val-ən(t)s, 'vāl-\ *n* **1** : a drapery hung along the edge of a bed, table, altar, canopy, or shelf **2** : a short drapery or wood or metal frame used as a decorative heading to conceal the top of curtains and fixtures

¹vale \'vāl\ *n* [OF *val*, fr. L *valles, vallis*] : VALLEY, DALE

²va·le \'väl-(,)ā, 'wäl-\ *n* [L, farewell, interj., fr. imper. of *valēre* to be strong, be well] : a salutation of leave-taking

val·e·dic·tion \,val-ə-'dik-shən\ *n* [L *valedicere* to say farewell, fr. *vale* farewell + *dicere* to say] : an act or utterance of leave-taking : FAREWELL

val·e·dic·to·ri·an \,val-ə-,dik-'tōr-ē-ən, -'tòr-\ *n* : the student usu. of the highest rank in a graduating class who delivers the valedictory oration at the commencement exercises

¹val·e·dic·to·ry \-'dik-t(ə-)rē\ *adj* : of or relating to leave-taking : FAREWELL; *esp* : given at a leave-taking ceremony (as school commencement exercises)

²valedictory *n, pl* **-ries** : a valedictory oration or statement

va·lence \'vā-lən(t)s\ *n* [LL *valentia* power, capacity, fr. L *valent-, valens*, prp. of *valēre* to be strong] **1 a** : the de-

gree of combining power of an element or radical as shown by the number of atomic weights of a univalent element (as hydrogen) with which the atomic weight of the element will combine or for which it can be substituted **b** : a unit of valence ⟨the four *valences* of carbon⟩ **2** : relative capacity to unite, react, or interact (as with antigens or a biological substrate)

valence electron *n* : a single electron or one of two or more electrons contained in the outer shell of an atom and responsible for the chemical properties of the atom

Va·len·ci·ennes \və-,len(t)-sē-'en(z), ,val-ən-sē-\ *n* [*Valenciennes*, France] : a fine handmade lace

-va·lent \'vā-lənt\ *adj comb form* : having a (specified) valence or valences ⟨bivalent⟩ ⟨multivalent⟩

val·en·tine \'val-ən-,tīn\ *n* **1** : a sweetheart chosen or complimented on St. Valentine's Day **2** : a gift or greeting sent or given on St. Valentine's Day

Valentine Day *or* **Valentine's Day** *n* : SAINT VALENTINE'S DAY

va·le·ri·an \və-'lir-ē-ən\ *n* [ML *valeriana*] **1** : any of a genus of perennial herbs mostly with flat-topped clusters of flowers and roots and rootstock which have medicinal properties **2** : a drug consisting of the dried roots and rootstocks of the garden heliotrope

val·et \'val-ət, va-'lā\ *n* [MF *vaslet, varlet* page, domestic servant, fr. ML *vassus* servant, vassal] : a male servant or hotel employee who takes care of a man's clothes and performs personal services

val·e·tu·di·nar·i·an \,val-ə-,t(y)üd-°n-'er-ē-ən\ *n* [L *valetudin-, valetudo* state of health, sickness, fr. *valēre* to be strong, be well] : a person of a weak or sickly constitution; *esp* : one whose chief concern is his invalidism — **valetudinarian** *adj* — **val·e·tu·di·nar·i·an·ism** \-,iz-əm\ *n*

Val·hal·la \val-'hal-ə\ *n* [G *Walhalla*, fr. ON *Valhöll*, lit., hall of the slain] : the hall of Odin into which the souls of heroes slain in battle are received

val·iance \'val-yən(t)s\ *n* : VALOR

val·ian·cy \-yən-sē\ *n* : VALOR

¹val·iant \'val-yənt\ *adj* [MF *vaillant*, fr. prp. of *valoir* to be of worth, fr. L *valēre* to be strong] **1** : boldly brave : COURAGEOUS ⟨a *valiant* leader⟩ **2** : VALOROUS, HEROIC ⟨*valiant* fighting⟩ — **val·iant·ly** *adv* — **val·iant·ness** *n*

²valiant *n* : a valiant person

val·id \'val-əd\ *adj* [ML *validus*, fr. L, strong, fr. *valēre* to be strong] **1** : founded on truth or fact : WELL-GROUNDED ⟨*valid* reasons⟩ **2** : binding in law : SOUND ⟨a *valid* contract⟩ — **val·id·ly** *adv* — **val·id·ness** *n*

syn VALID, SOUND, COGENT mean having such force as to compel acceptance. VALID implies being supported by objective truth or generally accepted authority; SOUND implies being based on solid fact and reasoning; COGENT stresses soundness or lucidness that makes argument or evidence conclusive

val·i·date \'val-ə-,dāt\ *vi* **1** : to make valid **2** : CONFIRM, SUBSTANTIATE — **val·i·da·tion** \,val-ə-'dā-shən\ *n*

va·lid·i·ty \və-'lid-ət-ē\ *n* : the quality or state of being valid

val·ine \'val-,ēn, 'vā-,lēn\ *n* : a crystalline essential amino acid that occurs esp. in fibrous proteins

va·lise \və-'lēs\ *n* [F, fr. It *valigia*] : TRAVELING BAG

Val·kyr·ie \val-'kir-ē\ *n* [ON *valkyrja*, lit., chooser of the slain] : one of the maidens of Odin who choose the heroes to be slain in battle and conduct them to Valhalla

val·late \'val-,āt\ *adj* [L *vallum* wall, rampart] : having a raised edge surrounding a depression

val·ley \'val-ē\ *n, pl* **valleys** [OF *valee*, fr. *val* vale] **1** : an elongate depression of the earth's surface usu. between ranges of hills or mountains **2 a** : HOLLOW, DEPRESSION **b** : the place of meeting of two slopes of a roof forming a drainage channel

val·or \'val-ər\ *n* [LL, value, worth, fr. L *valēre* to be strong, have value] : personal bravery in combat **syn** see COURAGE

val·or·ous \'val-ə-rəs\ *adj* **1** : possessing or exhibiting valor : BRAVE ⟨*valorous* men⟩ **2** : characterized by or performed with valor ⟨*valorous* feats⟩ — **val·or·ous·ly** *adv*

valse \väls\ *n* [F, fr. G *walzer*] : WALTZ; *esp* : a concert waltz

¹val·u·a·ble \'val-yə(-wə)-bəl\ *adj* **1 a** : having monetary value **b** : worth a great deal of money **2** : having value

: of great use or service ⟨*valuable* friendship⟩ **syn** see COSTLY — **val·u·a·ble·ness** *n* — **val·u·a·bly** \-blē\ *adv*
²valuable *n* : a personal possession (as a jewel) of relatively great monetary value — usu. used in pl. ⟨stored *valuables* in the hotel safe⟩
val·u·ate \'val-yə-‚wāt\ *vt* : to place a value on : APPRAISE — **val·u·a·tor** \-‚wāt-ər\ *n*
val·u·a·tion \‚val-yə-'wā-shən\ *n* **1** : the act or process of valuing; *esp* : appraisal of property **2** : the estimated or determined value **3** : judgment or appreciation of worth or character — **val·u·a·tion·al** \-shnəl, -shən-ºl\ *adj* — **val·u·a·tion·al·ly** \-ē\ *adv*
¹val·ue \'val-yü\ *n* [MF, fr. pp. of *valoir* to be worth, fr. L *valēre*, lit., to be strong] **1** : a fair return or equivalent in goods, services, or money for something exchanged **2** : the amount of another commodity for which a given thing can be exchanged; *esp* : the amount of money that something will bring : monetary worth **3** : relative worth, utility, or importance : degree of excellence **4 a** : a numerical quantity assigned or computed **b** : the magnitude of a physical quantity **c** : precise signification **d** : the sound or sounds answering to a letter or orthographic item ⟨the *value* of *a* in *ate*⟩ **5** : the relative duration of a musical note **6 a** : relative lightness or darkness of a color : LUMINOSITY **b** : the relation of one part in a picture to another with respect to lightness and darkness **7** : something intrinsically valuable or desirable **8** : DENOMINATION 4 **syn** see WORTH
²value *vt* **1 a** : to estimate or assign the monetary worth of : APPRAISE ⟨*value* a necklace⟩ **b** : to rate or scale in usefulness, importance, or general worth : EVALUATE **2** : to consider or rate highly : PRIZE, ESTEEM ⟨*valued* friendship⟩ **syn** see ESTEEM — **val·u·er** \-yə-wər\ *n*
val·ued \-yüd\ *adj* : highly regarded : ESTEEMED
val·ue·less \'val-yü-ləs\ *adj* : of no value : WORTHLESS
val·vate \'val-‚vāt\ *adj* : having or opening by valves or parts resembling a valve
valve \'valv\ *n* [L *valva* leaf of a double door] **1** : a structure esp. in a bodily channel (as a vein) that closes temporarily to obstruct passage of material or permits movement of a fluid in one direction only **2 a** : a mechanical device by which the flow of liquid, gas, or loose material in bulk may be started, stopped, or regulated by a movable part; *also* : the movable part of such a device **b** : a device in a brass wind instrument for quickly varying the tube length in order to change the fundamental tone by some definite interval **c** *chiefly Brit* : ELECTRON TUBE **3** : one of the distinct and usu. movably jointed pieces of which the shell of some shell-bearing animals and esp. bivalve mollusks consists **4** : one of the segments or pieces into which a ripe seed capsule or pod separates — **valved** \'valvd\ *adj*
val·vu·lar \'val-vyə-lər\ *adj* **1** : resembling or functioning as a valve; *also* : opening by valves **2** : of or relating to a valve esp. of the heart
va·moose \va-'müs, və-\ *vi* [Sp *vamos* let us go] *slang* : to depart quickly : DECAMP
¹vamp \'vamp\ *n* [OF *avampié* sock, fr. *avant*- fore- + *pié* foot] : the part of a shoe upper or boot upper covering esp. the forepart of the foot and sometimes also extending forward over the toe or backward to the back seam of the upper
²vamp *vt* **1 a** : to provide (a shoe) with a new vamp **b** : to piece (something old) with a new part : PATCH ⟨*vamp* up old sermons⟩ **2** : INVENT, FABRICATE ⟨*vamp* up an excuse⟩
³vamp *n* [short for *vampire*] : a woman who uses her charm or wiles to seduce and exploit men
⁴vamp *vt* : to practice seductive wiles on
vam·pire \'vam-‚pī(ə)r\ *n* [F, fr. G *vampir*, of Slav origin] **1** : the body of a dead person believed to come from the grave at night and suck the blood of persons asleep **2 a** : one who lives by preying on others **b** : a woman who exploits and ruins her lover **3** : any of various bats reputed to feed on blood: as **a** : any of several large So. and Central American insectivorous bats **b** : any of various So. American bats that feed on blood and are dangerous to man and domestic animals esp. as vectors of disease (as rabies) **c** : a large harmless Old World bat (as a fruit bat) — **vam·pir·ism** \-‚pī(ə)r-‚iz-əm\ *n*
¹van \'van\ *n* : VANGUARD

²van *n* [short for *caravan*] **1** : a usu. enclosed wagon or motortruck used for transportation of goods or animals **2** *chiefly Brit* : an enclosed railroad freight or baggage car

van for livestock

va·na·di·um \və-'nād-ē-əm\ *n* [NL, fr. ON *Vanadīs* Freya, goddess of love and beauty] : a grayish malleable metallic chemical element found combined in minerals and used esp. to form alloys (as of steel) — see ELEMENT table
Van Al·len radiation belt \van-'al-ən-, vən-\ *n* [after James A. *Van Allen* b1914 American physicist] : a belt of intense ionizing radiation that surrounds the earth in the outer atmosphere
van·dal \'van-dºl\ *n* **1** *cap* : one of a Germanic people overrunning Gaul, Spain, and northern Africa in the 4th and 5th centuries A.D., and in 455 sacking Rome **2** : one who willfully destroys, damages, or defaces public or private property — **vandal** *adj, often cap*
van·dal·ism \'van-dºl-‚iz-əm\ *n* : willful or malicious destruction or defacement of public or private property
van·dal·is·tic \‚van-dºl-'is-tik\ *adj* : of, relating to, or perpetrating vandalism
van·dal·ize \'van-dºl-‚īz\ *vt* : to subject to vandalism : DAMAGE
Van de Graaff generator \‚van-də-‚graf-\ *n* [after Robert J. *Van de Graaff* d1967 American physicist] : a generator of high voltages in which electric charges on a moving belt are transferred to a hollow sphere
Van·dyke \van-'dīk\ *n* [after Sir Anthony *Vandyke* d1641 Flemish painter] : a trim pointed beard
vane \'vān\ *n* [OE *fana* banner] **1** : a movable device attached to an elevated object (as a spire) for showing the direction of the wind **2** : a flat or curved extended surface attached to an axis and moved by the wind or water ⟨the *vanes* of a windmill⟩; *also* : a device revolving in a manner resembling this and moving in water or air ⟨the *vanes* of a propeller⟩ **3 a** : the web or flat expanded part of a feather **b** : a feather fastened to the shaft near the nock of an arrow — **vaned** \'vānd\ *adj*

Vandyke

van·guard \'van-‚gärd\ *n* [MF *avant-garde*, lit., fore guard] **1** : the troops moving at the head of an army **2** : the forefront of an action or movement or those in the forefront
va·nil·la \və-'nil-ə\ *n* [NL, fr. Sp *vainilla*, fr. dim. of *vaina* sheath, fr. L *vagina*] **1** : any of a genus of tropical American climbing orchids **2** : the long pod of a vanilla that is an important article of commerce for the flavoring extract that it yields; *also* : this extract
va·nil·lin \və-'nil-ən, 'van-ºl-\ *n* : a compound that is the chief fragrant component of vanilla
van·ish \'van-ish\ *vi* [MF *evaniss-, evanir*, fr. L *evanescere* to dissipate like vapor, vanish, fr. *ex-* + *vanus* empty] **1** : to pass quickly from sight : DISAPPEAR **2** : to pass completely from existence — **van·ish·er** *n*
vanishing cream *n* : a cosmetic preparation that is less oily than cold cream and is used chiefly as a foundation for face powder
vanishing point *n* **1** : a point at which receding parallel lines seem to meet **2** : a point at which something disappears or ceases to exist
van·i·ty \'van-ət-ē\ *n, pl* **-ties** [L *vanus* empty, vain] **1** : something that is vain **2** : the quality or fact of being vain: as **a** : WORTHLESSNESS, EMPTINESS **b** : FUTILITY **c** : inflated pride in oneself or one's appearance : CONCEIT **3** : a fashionable article or knickknack **4 a** : ³COMPACT 1 **b** : DRESSING TABLE
vanity fair *n, often cap V&F* [*Vanity-Fair*, a fair held in the frivolous town of Vanity in *Pilgrim's Progress*] : a place of busy pride and empty ostentation
van·quish \'van-kwish, 'van-\ *vt* [MF *venquis*, preterit of *veintre* to conquer, fr. L *vincere*] **1** : to overcome in battle : subdue completely **2** : to gain mastery over (as an emotion or temptation or competitor) : DEFEAT — **van·quish·a·ble** \-ə-bəl\ *adj* — **van·quish·er** *n*
van·tage \'vant-ij\ *n* [AF, fr. MF *avantage* advantage] **1** : superiority in a contest **2** : a position giving a strategic

advantage, commanding perspective, or comprehensive view **3** : ADVANTAGE 3

van·ward \'van-wərd\ *adj* : located in the vanguard : ADVANCED — **vanward** *adv*

vap·id \'vap-əd\ *adj* [L *vapidus* flat tasting] : lacking liveliness, tang, briskness, or force : FLAT, UNINTERESTING ⟨*vapid* remark⟩⟨*vapid* smile⟩ **syn** see INSIPID — **va·pid·i·ty** \va-'pid-ət-ē\ *n* — **vap·id·ly** \'vap-əd-lē\ *adv* — **vap·id·ness** *n*

¹va·por \'vā-pər\ *n* [L, steam, vapor] **1** : fine particles of matter (as fog or smoke) floating in the air and clouding it **2** : a substance in a gaseous state; *esp* : such a substance that is liquid under ordinary conditions **3** : something insubstantial or fleeting

²vapor *vi* **va·pored**; **va·por·ing** \-p(ə-)riŋ\ **1 a** : to rise or pass off in vapor **b** : to emit vapor **2** : to indulge in bragging, blustering, or idle talk — **va·por·er** \-pər-ər\ *n*

va·por·if·ic \vā-pə-'rif-ik\ *adj* : producing or tending to pass into vapor : VAPOROUS

va·por·ing \'vā-p(ə-)riŋ\ *n* : the act or speech of one that vapors; *esp* : an idle, extravagant, or high-flown expression or speech — usu. used in pl.

va·por·ish \'vā-p(ə-)rish\ *adj* **1** : resembling or suggestive of vapor **2** : given to fits of depression or hysteria — **va·por·ish·ness** *n*

va·por·ize \'vā-pə-,rīz\ *vb* **1** : to turn from a liquid or solid into vapor **2** : to cause to become ethereal or dissipated — **va·por·iz·a·ble** \-,rī-zə-bəl\ *adj* — **va·por·i·za·tion** \,vā-pə-rə-'zā-shən\ *n*

va·por·iz·er \'vā-pə-,rī-zər\ *n* : a device that vaporizes something (as a fuel oil or a medicated liquid)

vapor lock *n* : a partial or complete interruption of fuel flow in an internal-combustion engine caused by the formation of bubbles of vapor in the fuel-feeding system

va·por·ous \'vā-p(ə-)rəs\ *adj* **1** : consisting of or characteristic of vapor **2** : containing or obscured by vapors : MISTY **3** : UNSUBSTANTIAL, VAGUE — **va·por·ous·ly** *adv* — **va·por·ous·ness** *n*

vapor pressure *n* : the pressure exerted by a vapor that is in equilibrium with its solid or liquid form — called also *vapor tension*

vapor trail *n* : CONTRAIL

va·pory \'vā-p(ə-)rē\ *adj* : VAPOROUS, VAGUE

va·que·ro \vä-'ke(ə)r-ō\ *n, pl* **-ros** [Sp, fr. *vaca* cow, fr. L *vacca*] : a ranch hand : COWBOY

var·ia \'ver-ē-ə, 'var-\ *n pl* [NL, fr. L, neut. pl. of *varius* various] : MISCELLANY; *esp* : a literary miscellany

¹var·i·a·ble \'ver-ē-ə-bəl, 'var-\ *adj* **1 a** : able or apt to vary : CHANGEABLE ⟨*variable* winds⟩ **b** : FICKLE, INCONSTANT **2 a** : characterized by variations : not true to type : ABERRANT ⟨a *variable* species of wheat⟩ **3** : having the characteristics of a variable — **var·i·a·bil·i·ty** \,ver-ē-ə-'bil-ət-ē, ,var-\ *n* — **var·i·a·ble·ness** \'ver-ē-ə-bəl-nəs, 'var-\ *n* — **var·i·a·bly** \-blē\ *adv*

²variable *n* **1** : something that is variable **2 a** : a quantity that may assume any one of a set of values **b** : a symbol in a mathematical formula representing a variable

variable star *n* : a star whose brightness changes usu. in more or less regular periods

var·i·ance \'ver-ē-ən(t)s, 'var-\ *n* **1** : the fact, quality, or state of being variable or variant : DIFFERENCE, DEVIATION ⟨yearly *variance* in crops⟩ **2** : the fact or state of being in disagreement : DISSENSION, DISPUTE — **at variance** : not in harmony or agreement

¹var·i·ant \'ver-ē-ənt, 'var-\ *adj* **1** : differing from others of its kind or class and esp. from others regarded as representing a norm, standard, or type **2** : being one of two or more similar but not identical forms with the same meaning ⟨a *variant* spelling⟩

²variant *n* : one of two or more individuals exhibiting usu. slight differences: as **a** : one that exhibits variation from a type or norm **b** : one of two or more different spellings or pronunciations of the same word

var·i·a·tion \,ver-ē-'ā-shən, ,var-\ *n* **1 a** : the act or process of varying : the state or fact of being varied **b** : an instance of varying **c** : the extent to which or range in which a thing varies **2** : DECLINATION 5 **3** : the repetition of a musical theme with modifications in rhythm, tune, harmony, or key **4 a** : divergence in qualities of an organism or biotype from those typical or usual to its group **b** : an individual or group exhibiting variation

— var·i·a·tion·al \-shnəl, -shən-ᵊl\ *adj* — **var·i·a·tion·al·ly** \-ē\ *adv*

var·i·cel·la \,var-ə-'sel-ə\ *n* : CHICKEN POX — **var·i·cel·lar** \-'sel-ər\ *adj*

vari·col·ored \'ver-i-,kəl-ərd, 'var-\ *adj* : having various colors : VARIEGATED ⟨*varicolored* marble⟩

var·i·cose \'var-ə-,kōs\ *adj* [L *varic-, varix* dilated vein] : abnormally swollen or dilated ⟨*varicose* veins⟩

var·i·cos·i·ty \,var-ə-'käs-ət-ē\ *n, pl* **-ties** **1** : the quality or state of being varicose **2** : a varicose part or lesion (as of a vein)

var·ied \'ve(ə)r-ēd, 'va(ə)r-\ *adj* **1** : CHANGED, ALTERED **2** : having numerous forms or types : DIVERSE **3** : VARIEGATED — **var·ied·ly** *adv*

var·ie·gate \'ver-(ē-)ə-,gāt, 'var-\ *vt* [L *variegare*, fr. *varius* various] **1** : to diversify in external appearance esp. with different colors **2** : to enliven by variety — **var·ie·ga·tion** \,ver-(ē-)ə-'gā-shən, ,var-\ *n* — **var·ie·ga·tor** \'ver-(ē-)ə-,gāt-ər, 'var-\ *n*

var·ie·gat·ed *adj* **1** : having patches, stripes, or marks of different colors ⟨*variegated* flowers⟩ **2** : full of variety ⟨a *variegated* career⟩

va·ri·e·ty \və-'rī-ət-ē\ *n, pl* **-ties** [L *varietas*, fr. *varius* various] **1** : the quality or state of having different forms or types **2** : a number or collection of different things : ASSORTMENT ⟨the store stocked a large *variety* of goods⟩ **3 a** : something differing from others of the same general kind **b** : any of various groups of plants or animals of less than specific rank **4** : entertainment consisting of successive unrelated performances (as dances, skits, or acrobatic feats) — **va·ri·e·tal** \-ət-ᵊl\ *adj* — **va·ri·e·tal·ly** \-ᵊl-ē\ *adv*

variety store *n* : a retail establishment dealing in a large variety of merchandise esp. of low unit value

var·i·form \'ver-ə-,fórm, 'var-\ *adj* : having various forms

var·i·o·la \,ver-ē-'ō-lə, ,var-\ *n* [LL, pustule] : any of several virus diseases (as smallpox or cowpox) marked by a pustular eruption

var·i·o·rum \,ver-ē-'ōr-əm, ,var-, -'ór-\ *n* [L *cum notis variorum* with the notes of various persons] : an edition or text esp. of a classical author with notes by different persons and often with variant readings of the text

var·i·ous \'ver-ē-əs, 'var-\ *adj* [L *varius*] **1** : marked by variation or variety (as in appearance or properties) : of differing kinds : DIVERSIFIED ⟨*various* enterprises use metals⟩ ⟨his *various* responsibilities⟩ **2 a** : differing one from another : UNLIKE ⟨animals as *various* as cat and mouse⟩ **b** : VARIANT ⟨*various* readings are known⟩ **3** : consisting of an indefinite number greater than one : SUNDRY, DIVERS ⟨*various* schemes⟩ ⟨stop at *various* towns⟩ — **var·i·ous·ly** *adv* — **var·i·ous·ness** *n*

vari·sized \'ver-i-,sīzd, 'var-\ *adj* : of various sizes

va·ris·tor \və-'ris-tər, ve-\ *n* [*vary* + *resistor*] : an electrical resistor whose resistance depends on the applied voltage

var·ix \'var-iks\ *n, pl* **var·i·ces** \'var-ə-,sēz\ [L *varic-, varix*] **1** : a dilated tortuous blood or lymph vessel **2** : a prominent ridge across each whorl of a gastropod shell

var·let \'vär-lət\ *n* [MF, young nobleman, page] **1** *archaic* : ATTENDANT **2** : a low fellow

¹var·nish \'vär-nish\ *n* [MF *vernis*] **1 a** : a liquid preparation that is spread like paint and dries to a hard lustrous typically transparent coating **b** : the covering or glaze given by the application of varnish **2** : outside show : GLOSS — **var·nishy** \-ni-shē\ *adj*

²varnish *vt* : to cover with or as if with varnish — **var·nish·er** *n*

var·si·ty \'vär-sət-ē, -stē\ *n, pl* **-ties** [by shortening & alter. fr. *university*] : a first team representing a university, college, school, or club — **varsity** *adj*

varve \'värv\ *n* [Sw *varv* turn, layer] : a pair of layers of alternately finer and coarser silt or clay believed to comprise an annual cycle of deposition in a body of still water

vary \'ve(ə)r-ē, 'va(ə)r-\ *vb* **var·ied**; **var·y·ing** [L *variare*, fr. *varius* various] : to differ or cause to differ: as **a** : to make a usu. minor or partial change in ⟨the rule must not be *varied*⟩ **b** : to give variety to : DIVERSIFY ⟨*vary* a diet⟩ ⟨a program *varied* to avoid monotony⟩ **c** : to exhibit or undergo change ⟨*varying* skies⟩⟨the accuracy of the several

chapters *varies* greatly⟩; *also* **:** to be different ⟨laws *vary* from state to state⟩ **d :** to take on successive values ⟨*y varies* inversely with *x*⟩ **e :** to diverge structurally or physiologically from typical members of a group **syn** see CHANGE — **var·y·ing·ly** \-iŋ-lē\ *adv*
varying hare *n* **:** any of several hares having white fur in winter
vas \'vas\ *n, pl* **vasa** \'vas-ə\ [L, vessel] **:** an anatomical vessel **:** DUCT — **vas·sal** \'vā-səl\ *adj*
vas·cu·lar \'vas-kyə-lər\ *adj* [L *vasculum* small vessel, dim. of *vas*] **:** of, relating to, or being an anatomical vessel or a system of these; *also* **:** supplied with or made up of such vessels and esp. blood vessels ⟨a *vascular* tumor⟩ — **vas·cu·lar·i·ty** \ˌvas-kyə-'lar-ət-ē\ *n*
vascular bundle *n* **:** a unit of the vascular system of a higher plant consisting usu. of xylem and phloem together with parenchyma cells and fibers
vascular plant *n* **:** a plant having a specialized conducting system that includes xylem and phloem **:** TRACHEOPHYTE
vascular tissue *n* **:** a specialized conducting tissue of higher plants that consists essentially of phloem and xylem and forms a continuous system throughout the body
vas·cu·lum \'vas-kyə-ləm\ *n, pl* **-la** \-lə\ [L, small vessel] **:** a usu. metal and commonly cylindrical covered box used in collecting botanical specimens
vas def·er·ens \'vas-'def-ə-rənz\ *n, pl* **va·sa def·er·en·tia** \ˌvas-ə-ˌdef-ə-'ren-ch(ē-)ə\ [NL, lit., vessel that brings down] **:** a spermatic duct esp. of a higher vertebrate
vase \'vās, 'vāz\ *n* [F, fr. L *vas* vessel] **:** a usu. round vessel of greater depth than width used chiefly for ornament or for flowers
Vas·e·line \'vas-ə-ˌlēn\ *trademark* — used for petrolatum
vaso·con·stric·tion \ˌvas-ō-kən-'strik-shən\ *n* **:** narrowing of the diameter of blood vessels — **vaso·con·stric·tive** \-'strik-tiv\ *adj*
vaso·con·stric·tor \-'strik-tər\ *n* **:** an agent (as a sympathetic nerve fiber or a drug) that induces or initiates vasoconstriction
vaso·di·la·ta·tion \ˌvas-ō-ˌdil-ə-'tā-shən, -ˌdī-lə-\ *or* **vaso·di·la·tion** \-dī-'lā-shən\ *n* **:** widening of the diameter of blood vessels
vaso·di·la·tor \-dī-'lāt-ər, -'dī-,\ *n* **:** an agent (as a parasympathetic nerve fiber or a drug) that induces or initiates vasodilation
vaso·in·hib·i·tor \-in-'hib-ət-ər\ *n* **:** an agent (as a drug) that depresses or inhibits vasomotor and esp. vasoconstrictor activity — **vaso·in·hib·i·to·ry** \-'hib-ə-ˌtōr-ē, -ˌtȯr-\ *adj*
vaso·mo·tor \-'mōt-ər\ *adj* **:** of, relating to, or being nerves or centers controlling the size of blood vessels
vaso·pres·sin \-'pres-ᵊn\ *n* [fr. *Vasopressin*, a trademark] **:** a polypeptide hormone secreted by the posterior lobe of the pituitary that increases blood pressure and decreases urine flow
vaso·pres·sor \-'pres-ər\ *adj* **:** raising blood pressure through a vasoconstrictor effect
vas·sal \'vas-əl\ *n* [ML *vassallus*, fr. *vassus* servant, vassal, of Celt origin] **1 :** a person under the protection of another who is his feudal lord and to whom he has vowed homage and fealty **:** a feudal tenant **2 :** one in a subservient or subordinate position — **vassal** *adj*
vas·sal·age \-ə-lij\ *n* **1 :** the condition of being a vassal **2 :** homage and loyalty due a lord from his vassal **3 :** a politically dependent territory
¹vast \'vast\ *adj* [L *vastus*] **:** very great in size, amount, degree, intensity, or esp. in extent **syn** see ENORMOUS — **vast·ly** *adv* — **vast·ness** \'vas(t)-nəs\ *n*
²vast *n* **:** a boundless space **:** IMMENSITY
vasty \'vas-tē\ *adj* **vast·i·er; -est :** VAST, IMMENSE
vat \'vat\ *n* [OE *fæt*] **:** a large vessel (as a cistern, tub, or barrel) esp. for liquids
vat dye *n* **:** a textile dye in a colorless reduced solution in which material to be dyed is steeped and which on exposure to air is oxidized and deposited in the fibers of the material — **vat-dyed** \'vat-'dīd\ *adj*
vat·ic \'vat-ik\ *adj* [L *vates* seer, prophet] **:** PROPHETIC, ORACULAR
Vat·i·can \'vat-i-kən\ *n* **1 :** the papal headquarters in Rome **2 :** the papal government
va·tic·i·nate \və-'tis-ᵊn-ˌāt\ *vb* [L *vaticinari*, fr. *vates* prophet + *canere* to sing] **:** PROPHESY, PREDICT — **va·**

tic·i·na·tion \-ˌtis-ᵊn-'ā-shən\ *n* — **va·tic·i·na·tor** \-'tis-ᵊn-ˌāt-ər\ *n*
vau·de·ville \'vȯd(-ə)-vəl, 'vōd-, -ˌvil\ *n* [F] **:** light theatrical entertainment featuring usu. unrelated variety acts (as songs, dances, and sketches) — **vau·de·vil·lian** \ˌvȯd-(ə-)'vil-yən, ˌvōd-\ *adj or n*
¹vault \'vȯlt\ *n* [MF *voute*] **1 a :** an arched structure of masonry usu. forming a ceiling or roof **b :** something suggesting a vault esp. in arched or domed structure ⟨the blue *vault* of the sky⟩ **2 a :** a space covered by an arched structure; *esp* **:** an underground passage or room **b :** an underground storage compartment **c :** a room or compartment for the safekeeping of valuables **3 a :** a burial chamber **b :** a case usu. of metal or concrete in which a casket is enclosed at burial

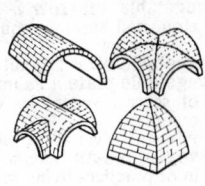
vaults 1a

²vault *vt* **:** to form or cover with or as if with a vault **:** ARCH
³vault *vb* [MF *volter*, fr. It *voltare*, fr. (assumed) VL *volvitare*, freq. of L *volvere* to roll] **:** to execute a leap using the hands or a pole; *also* **:** to leap over — **vault·er** *n*
⁴vault *n* **:** an act of vaulting **:** LEAP
vault·ed \'vȯl-təd\ *adj* **1 :** built in the form of a vault **:** ARCHED **2 :** covered with a vault
vault·ing \-tiŋ\ *adj* **1 :** leaping upwards ⟨*vaulting* sparks⟩ ⟨*vaulting* spirits⟩; *esp* **:** straining unreasonably or arrogantly toward the heights ⟨a *vaulting* ambition⟩ **2 :** used in gymnastics and esp. in vaulting ⟨a *vaulting* buck⟩
¹vaunt \'vȯnt, 'vänt\ *vb* [MF *vanter*, fr. LL *vanitare* to be vain, fr. L *vanitas* vanity] **:** BRAG, BOAST — **vaunt·er** *n* — **vaunt·ing·ly** \-iŋ-lē\ *adv*
²vaunt *n* **1 :** a vainglorious display (as of worth or accomplishment) **2 :** a bragging assertive speech
vaunt·ful \-fəl\ *adj* **:** BOASTFUL, VAINGLORIOUS
V-day \'vē-ˌdā\ *n* **:** a day of victory
've \v, əv\ *vb* **:** HAVE ⟨we've been there⟩
veal \'vēl\ *n* [MF *veel*, fr. L *vitellus*, dim. of *vitulus* calf; akin to E *wether*] **1 :** CALF; *esp* **:** VEALER **2 :** the flesh of a young calf
veal·er \'vē-lər\ *n* **:** a calf grown for or suitable for veal
vec·tor \'vek-tər\ *n* [L, carrier, fr. *vect-, vehere* to carry] **1 :** a quantity that has magnitude, direction, and sense **2 :** an organism (as an insect) that transmits a pathogen **3 :** DRIVE 5 — **vec·to·ri·al** \vek-'tōr-ē-əl, -'tȯr-\ *adj*
Ve·da \'vād-ə\ *n* [Skt, lit., knowledge; akin to E *wit*] **:** any of a primary class of Hindu sacred writings; *esp* **:** any of four canonical collections of hymns, prayers, and liturgical formulas
ve·da·lia \və-'dāl-yə\ *n* **:** a predaceous Australian ladybug widely used in controlling scale insects
Ve·dan·ta \vā-'dänt-ə, -'dant-\ *n* [Skt *Vedānta*, lit., end of the Veda] **:** an orthodox system of Hindu philosophy — **Ve·dan·tic** \-ik\ *adj*
ve·dette \vi-'det\ *n* [F] **:** a mounted sentinel stationed in advance of pickets
Ve·dic \'vād-ik\ *adj* **:** of or relating to the Vedas, the language in which they are written, or Hindu history and culture between 2000 B.C. and 500 B.C.
veep \'vēp\ *n* [fr. *v.p.*, abbr. for *vice-president*] **:** VICE-PRESIDENT
¹veer \'vi(ə)r\ *vb* [MF *virer*] **:** to change direction or course **:** TURN; *esp* **:** to shift in a clockwise direction ⟨the wind *veered* from northwest to northeast⟩ **syn** see SWERVE — **veer·ing·ly** \-iŋ-lē\ *adv*
²veer *n* **:** a change in course or direction
vee·ry \'vi(ə)r-ē\ *n, pl* **veeries :** a tawny brown thrush common in woodlands of the eastern U.S.
Ve·ga \'vē-gə, 'vā-\ *n* [NL, fr. Ar *al-Nasr al-Wāqi*, lit., the falling vulture] **:** a star of the first magnitude that is the brightest in the constellation Lyra
¹veg·e·ta·ble \'vej-tə-bəl, 'vej-ə-tə-bəl\ *adj* [ML *vegetabilis*, fr. *vegetare* to grow, fr. L, to animate, freq. of *vegēre* to rouse; akin to E *wake*] **1 :** of, relating to, or made up of plants ⟨the *vegetable* kingdom⟩ ⟨*vegetable* growth⟩ **2 :** obtained from plants ⟨*vegetable* oils⟩ ⟨*vegetable* drugs⟩ **3 :** suggesting that of a plant (as in monotony) ⟨a *vegetable* existence⟩ — **veg·e·ta·bly** \-blē\ *adv*

---

j joke; **ŋ** sing; **ō** flow; **ȯ** flaw; **ȯi** coin; **th** thin; **th̲** this; **ü** loot; **u̇** foot; **y** yet; **yü** few; **yu̇** furious; **zh** vision

²**vegetable** n **1 a :** PLANT 1 **b :** a usu. herbaceous plant grown for an edible part that is usu. eaten with the principal course of a meal; *also :* such edible part **2 :** a human being having a dull or merely physical existence

vegetable ivory n **:** the hard white endosperm of the seed of a So. American palm that is used as a substitute for ivory

vegetable marrow n **:** any of various smooth-skinned elongated summer squashes with creamy white to deep green skins

vegetable oil n **:** an oil of plant origin

vegetable plate n **:** a main course without meat consisting of several vegetables cooked separately and served on one plate

veg·e·tal \'vej-ət-ᵊl\ adj **1 :** VEGETABLE **2 :** VEGETATIVE

¹**veg·e·tar·i·an** \,vej-ə-'ter-ē-ən\ n **1 :** one who believes in or practices living solely upon vegetables, fruits, grains, and nuts or excluding meat from the diet **2 :** HERBIVORE — **veg·e·tar·i·an·ism** \-ē-ə-,niz-əm\ n

²**vegetarian** adj **1 :** of or relating to vegetarians **2 :** consisting wholly of vegetables ⟨a *vegetarian* diet⟩

veg·e·tate \'vej-ə-,tāt\ vb **1 :** to live or grow in the manner of a plant: as **a :** to grow exuberantly or with formation of fleshy or warty outgrowths **b :** to lead a passive effortless existence **2 :** to establish vegetation in or on ⟨richly *vegetated* slopes⟩

veg·e·ta·tion \,vej-ə-'tā-shən\ n **1 :** the act or process of vegetating **2 :** inert existence **3 :** plant life or cover (as of an area) **4 :** an abnormal bodily outgrowth — **veg·e·ta·tion·al** \-shnəl, -shən-ᵊl\ adj

veg·e·ta·tive \'vej-ə-,tāt-iv\ adj **1 a :** of, relating to, or functioning in nutrition and growth as contrasted with reproduction ⟨a *vegetative* nucleus⟩ **b :** of, relating to, or involving propagation by other than sexual means **2 :** VEGETATIONAL ⟨*vegetative* cover⟩ **3 :** affecting, arising from, or relating to involuntary bodily functions : AUTONOMIC ⟨*vegetative* nerves⟩ **4 :** VEGETABLE 3 — **veg·e·ta·tive·ly** adv — **veg·e·ta·tive·ness** n

veg·e·tive \'vej-ət-iv\ adj **:** VEGETABLE, VEGETATIVE

ve·he·ment \'vē-ə-mənt\ adj [L *vehement-, vehemens*] **:** marked by forceful energy : POWERFUL ⟨a *vehement* wind⟩: as **a :** intensely emotional : IMPASSIONED, FERVID ⟨*vehement* patriotism⟩⟨*vehement* denunciations⟩ **b :** deeply felt and usu. of a kind to compel attention ⟨*vehement* suspicion⟩ — **ve·he·mence** \-mən(t)s\ n — **ve·he·ment·ly** adv

ve·hi·cle \'vē-,(h)ik-əl\ n [L *vehiculum* carriage, conveyance, fr. *vehere* to carry] **1 :** a medium through which something is administered, transmitted, expressed, achieved, or displayed ⟨newspapers are *vehicles* of ideas⟩ ⟨turpentine is a common *vehicle* for paint⟩ **2 :** something used to transport persons or goods : CONVEYANCE

ve·hic·u·lar \vē-'hik-yə-lər\ adj **1 :** of, relating to, or designed for vehicles esp. motor vehicles **2 :** serving as a vehicle

V-eight \'vē-'āt\ n [so called from the resemblance of the angle formed by the two banks to the letter V] **1 :** an internal-combustion engine having two banks of four cylinders each with the banks at an angle to each other; *also :* an automobile having such an engine

¹**veil** \'vāl\ n [ONF *veile*, fr. L *vela*, pl. of *velum* veil] **1 a :** a length of cloth or net worn esp. by women over the head and shoulders or attached to a hat or headdress and sometimes (as in eastern countries) drawn also over the face **b :** a concealing curtain or cover of cloth **c :** something (as darkness or a membrane) that covers or obscures like a veil ⟨the rest of the story was enclosed by a *veil* of secrecy⟩ **2 :** the vows or life of a nun ⟨take the *veil*⟩

²**veil** vt **:** to cover, provide, obscure, or conceal with or as if with a veil

veil·ing \'vā-liŋ\ n **1 :** VEIL **2 :** a light sheer fabric (as net or chiffon) suitable for veils

¹**vein** \'vān\ n [OF *veine*, fr. L *vena*] **1 :** a fissure in rock filled with mineral matter ⟨a *vein* of gold⟩ **2 a :** one of the tubular branching vessels that carry blood from the capillaries toward the heart **b :** one of the vascular bundles forming the framework of a leaf **c :** one of the thickened ribs that stiffen the wings of an insect **3 :** something like a vein usu. in irregular linear form or in forming a channel ⟨underground water *veins*⟩; *esp :* a wavy band or streak

(as of a different color or texture) ⟨a marble with greenish *veins*⟩ **4 a :** a distinctive mode of expression : STYLE ⟨writing in the classic *vein*⟩ **b :** a pervasive element or quality : STRAIN ⟨a *vein* of mysticism in her character⟩ **c :** MOOD — **vein·al** \-ᵊl\ adj — **veined** \'vānd\ adj — **veiny** \'vā-nē\ adj

²**vein** vt **:** to form veins in or mark with veins

vein·ing \'vā-niŋ\ n **:** a pattern of veins : VENATION

vein·let \'vān-lət\ n **:** a small vein esp. of a leaf

ve·lar \'vē-lər\ adj **1 :** of, relating to, or forming a velum and esp. the soft palate **2 :** formed with the back of the tongue touching or near the soft palate ⟨the *velar* \k\ of \'kül\ *cool*⟩ — **velar** n

ve·late \'vē-lət, -,lāt\ adj **:** having a veil or velum — **ve·la·tion** \vi-'lā-shən\ n

veld or **veldt** \'felt, 'velt\ n [Afrik *veld*, fr. MD, field; akin to E *field*] **:** open grassland esp. of southern Africa usu. with scattered shrubs or trees

vel·le·i·ty \ve-'lē-ət-ē\ n [NL *velleitas*, fr. L *velle* to wish, will] **1 :** the lowest degree of volition **2 :** a slight wish or tendency : INCLINATION

vel·lum \'vel-əm\ n [MF *veelin*, fr. *veel* calf] **1 :** a fine-grained unsplit lambskin, kidskin, or calfskin prepared esp. for writing on or for binding books **2 :** a strong cream-colored paper resembling vellum — **vellum** adj

ve·loc·i·pede \və-'läs-ə-,pēd\ n [F *vélocipède*, fr. L *veloc-, velox* quick + *ped-, pes* foot] **:** a light-weight wheeled vehicle propelled by the rider; *esp :* TRICYCLE

ve·loc·i·ty \və-'läs-ət-ē, -'läs-tē\ n, pl **-ties** [L *veloc-, velox* quick] **1 :** quickness of motion : SPEED ⟨the *velocity* of sound⟩ **2 :** time rate of linear motion in a given direction **3 :** rate of occurrence or action : RAPIDITY

velocipede

ve·lour or **ve·lours** \və-'lù(ə)r\ n, pl **velours** \-'lù(ə)rz\ [F *velours*, fr. OF *velous*, fr. L *villosus* shaggy, fr. *villus* shaggy hair] **1 :** a usu. heavy fabric with a pile or napped surface resembling velvet **2 :** a fur felt with a long velvety nap used esp. for hats

ve·lum \'vē-ləm\ n [NL, fr. L, curtain, veil] **:** a membrane or anatomical partition likened to a veil or curtain; *esp* **:** SOFT PALATE

ve·lu·ti·nous \və-'lüt-ᵊn-əs\ adj [NL *velutinus*, fr. ML *velutum* velvet] **:** having a silky pubescence : VELVETY

¹**vel·vet** \'vel-vət\ n [ME *veluet, velvet*, fr. MF *velu* shaggy, fr. (assumed) VL *villutus*, fr. L *villus* shaggy hair] **1 :** a usu. silk or synthetic fabric with a thick soft pile of short erect threads **2 :** something suggesting velvet (as in softness); *esp* **:** the soft vascular skin covering the developing antler of a deer **3 :** an unanticipated gain or profit

²**velvet** adj **1 :** made of or covered with velvet **2 :** resembling or suggesting velvet : VELVETY

velvet ant n **:** any of various solitary burrowing usu. brightly colored wasps with the females wingless

vel·ve·teen \,vel-və-'tēn\ n **:** a cotton fabric made in imitation of velvet

velvet sponge n **:** a Caribbean commercial sponge of fine soft texture

vel·vety \'vel-vət-ē\ adj **1 :** soft and smooth like velvet ⟨soft *velvety* fur⟩⟨a *velvety* singing voice⟩⟨*velvety* blackness⟩ **2 :** smooth to the taste : MILD

ven- or **veni-** comb form [L *vena*] **:** vein ⟨*venation*⟩ ⟨*veni*puncture⟩

ve·na ca·va \,vē-nə-'kā-və\ n, pl **ve·nae ca·vae** \,vē-nē-'kā-(,)vē\ [NL, lit., hollow vein] **:** one of the usu. three large veins by which the blood is returned to the right atrium of the heart in an air-breathing vertebrate

ve·nal \'vēn-ᵊl\ adj [L *venalis* for sale, fr. *venus* sale] **1 :** willing to take bribes : open to corrupt influences **2 :** influenced by bribery : CORRUPT ⟨*venal* conduct⟩⟨*venal* magistrates⟩ — **ve·nal·i·ty** \vi-'nal-ət-ē\ n — **ve·nal·ly** \'vēn-ᵊl-ē\ adv

ve·na·tion \vā-'nā-shən, vē-\ n **:** an arrangement or system of veins ⟨the *venation* of the hand⟩⟨the *venation* of a leaf⟩ — **ve·na·tion·al** \-shnəl, -shən-ᵊl\ adj

vend \'vend\ vb [L *vendere* to sell, contr. of *venum dare* to give for sale] **:** to sell or offer for sale esp. as a hawker or peddler ⟨*vend* fruit⟩ — **vend·er** \'ven-dər\ or **ven·dor**

\\'ven-dər, ven-'dȯ(ə)r\\ *n* — **vend·i·ble** *or* **vend·a·ble** \\'ven-də-bəl\\ *adj*

vend·ee \\ven-'dē\\ *n* : one to whom a thing is sold : BUYER

ven·det·ta \\ven-'det-ə\\ *n* [It., lit., revenge, fr. L *vindicta*] : a feud in which the relatives of a murdered man try to take vengeance by killing the murderer or his relatives

vending machine *n* : a slot machine for vending merchandise

ven·di·tion \\ven-'dish-ən\\ *n* : the act of selling : SALE

ven·due \\ven-'d(y)ü\\ *n* [obs. F, fr. MF, fr. *vendre* to sell, fr. L *vendere*] : a public sale at auction

¹ve·neer \\və-'ni(ə)r\\ *n* [G *furnier*, fr. *furnieren* to veneer, fr. F *fournir* to furnish] **1** : a thin sheet of a material: as **a** : a layer of a valuable or beautiful wood to be glued to an inferior wood **b** : any of the thin layers bonded together to form plywood **2** : a protective or ornamental facing (as of brick or stone) **3** : a superficial or false show : GLOSS ⟨a *veneer* of courtesy⟩

²veneer *vt* : to overlay with a veneer — **ve·neer·er** *n*

ven·er·a·ble \\'ven-ər-(ə-)bəl, 'ven-rə-bəl\\ *adj* **1** : deserving to be venerated — used as a title for an Anglican archdeacon or a Roman Catholic in the first stage of canonization **2** : made sacred by association (as religious or historic) **3 a** : calling forth respect through age, character, and attainments **b** : impressive by reason of age ⟨under *venerable* pines⟩ — **ven·er·a·bil·i·ty** \\,ven-(ə-)rə-'bil-ət-ē\\ *n* — **ven·er·a·ble·ness** \\'ven-ər-(ə-)bəl-nəs, 'ven-rə-bəl-\\ *n* — **ven·er·a·bly** \\-blē\\ *adv*

ven·er·ate \\'ven-ə-,rāt\\ *vt* [L *veneratus*, fr. *vener-, venus* love, charm; akin to E *win*] : to regard with reverential respect or with admiration and deference **syn** see REVERE — **ven·er·a·tor** \\-,rāt-ər\\ *n*

ven·er·a·tion \\,ven-ə-'rā-shən\\ *n* **1** : the act of venerating : the state of being venerated ⟨*veneration* of saints⟩ **2** : a feeling of reverence or deep respect : DEVOTION

ve·ne·re·al \\və-'nir-ē-əl\\ *adj* [L *venereus*, fr. *vener-, venus* love, sexual desire] : of or relating to sexual intercourse or to diseases transmitted by it ⟨a *venereal* infection⟩

venereal disease *n* : a contagious disease (as syphilis) that is typically acquired by sexual intercourse

¹ven·ery \\'ven-ə-rē\\ *n* [MF *venerie*, fr. *vener* to hunt, fr. L *venari*] **1** : the art, act, or practice of hunting **2** : animals that are hunted : GAME

²venery *n* [ML *veneria*, fr. L *vener-, venus* sexual desire] : the pursuit of sexual indulgence or pleasure; *also* : sexual intercourse

vene·sec·tion *or* **veni·sec·tion** \\'ven-ə-,sek-shən\\ *n* : the operation of opening a vein to draw off blood

ve·ne·tian blind \\və-,nē-shən-\\ *n* : a blind having thin horizontal slats that can be set to overlap to keep out light or tipped to let light come in between them

Venetian red *n* : an earthy hematite used as a pigment; *also* : a synthetic iron oxide pigment

ven·geance \\'ven-jən(t)s\\ *n* [OF, fr. *vengier* to avenge, fr. L *vindicare*, fr. *vindic-, vindex* avenger] : punishment inflicted in retaliation for an injury or offense : RETRIBUTION — **with a vengeance 1** : VIOLENTLY **2** : EXTREMELY

venge·ful \\'venj-fəl\\ *adj* : filled with a desire for revenge : VINDICTIVE — **venge·ful·ly** \\-fə-lē\\ *adv* — **venge·ful·ness** *n*

V-en·gine \\'vē-'en-jən\\ *n* : an internal-combustion engine the cylinders of which are arranged in two banks forming an acute angle

veni — see VEN-

ve·ni·al \\'vē-nē-əl, -nyəl\\ *adj* [L *venia* indulgence, pardon] : FORGIVABLE, EXCUSABLE; *esp* : committed in a minor matter or without reflection or full consent and held in Roman Catholicism to merit only temporal punishment ⟨*venial* sin⟩ — compare MORTAL — **ve·ni·al·ly** \\-ē\\ *adv* — **ve·ni·al·ness** *n*

ven·in \\'ven-ən\\ *n* : a toxic component of snake venom

veni·punc·ture \\'ven-ə-,pəŋ(k)-chər\\ *n* : a puncturing of a vein usu. to draw blood or to introduce medication

ve·ni·re \\və-'nī(ə)r-ē, -'ni(ə)r-\\ *n* [ML *venire facias* you are to cause to come (opening words of the writ)] **1** : a writ summoning persons to appear in court to serve as jurors **2** : a panel from which a jury is drawn

ve·ni·re·man \\-mən\\ *n* : a juror summoned by a venire

ven·i·son \\'ven-ə-sən, -ə-zən\\ *n, pl* **venisons** *also* **venison**

[OF *veneison* hunting, game, fr. L *venation-, venatio*, fr. *venari* to hunt; akin to E *win*] **1** : the edible flesh of a wild animal taken by hunting **2** : the flesh of a deer ⟨elk *venison*⟩

Ve·ni·te \\və-'nīt-ē, -'nē-,tä\\ *n* [L, O come] : a liturgical chant composed of parts of Psalms 95 and 96

ven·om \\'ven-əm\\ *n* [OF *venim*, modif. of L *venenum* magic charm, drug, poison] **1** : poisonous matter normally secreted by an animal (as a snake, scorpion, or bee) and communicated chiefly by biting or stinging **2** : something that embitters or blights the mind or spirit : MALIGNITY

ven·om·ous \\'ven-ə-məs\\ *adj* **1** : filled with venom: as **a** : POISONOUS **b** : SPITEFUL, MALIGNANT ⟨*venomous* words⟩ **2** : secreting and using venom ⟨*venomous* snakes⟩ — **ven·om·ous·ly** *adv* — **ven·om·ous·ness** *n*

ve·nous \\'vē-nəs\\ *adj* [L *vena* vein] **1** : of, relating to, or full of veins ⟨a *venous* rock⟩ ⟨a *venous* system⟩ **2** : being purplish red oxygen-deficient blood present in most veins — **ve·nous·ly** *adv*

¹vent \\'vent\\ *vt* [ME *venten*] **1 a** : to provide with an outlet **b** : to serve as an outlet for ⟨chimneys *vent* smoke⟩ **2** : to give expression to ⟨*vented* his anger⟩ **3** : to relieve by venting

²vent *n* : OUTLET; *esp* : an opening (as the anus, a flue, or a fumarole) for the escape of a gas or liquid or for the relief of pressure

³vent *n* [MF *fente*, fr. *fendre* to split, fr. L *findere*] : a slit in a garment and esp. in the lower part of a seam

ven·tail \\'ven-,tāl\\ *n* [MF *ventaille*, fr. *vent* wind] : the lower movable front of a medieval helmet

ven·ter \\'vent-ər\\ *n* [L, belly, womb] **1** : a wife or mother that is a source of offspring **2** : a protuberant and often hollow anatomical structure

ven·ti·fact \\'vent-ə-,fakt\\ *n* [L *ventus* wind + E *-ifact* (as in *artifact*)] : a stone worn, polished, or faceted by windblown sand — called also *rill-stone* \\'ril-,stōn\\

ven·ti·late \\'vent-ᵊl-,āt\\ *vt* [LL *ventilare*, fr. L, to fan, winnow, fr. *ventus* wind; akin to E *wind*] **1** : to discuss freely and openly : make public ⟨*ventilate* a complaint⟩ **2 a** : to expose to air and esp. to a current of fresh air **b** : to provide with ventilation ⟨*ventilated* by powerful fans⟩ — **ven·ti·la·tive** \\-,āt-iv\\ *adj*

ven·ti·la·tion \\,vent-ᵊl-'ā-shən\\ *n* **1** : the act or process of ventilating **2** : circulation of air ⟨a room with good *ventilation*⟩ **3** : a system or means of providing fresh air

ven·ti·la·tor \\'vent-ᵊl-,āt-ər\\ *n* : one that ventilates; *esp* : a contrivance for introducing fresh air or expelling foul or stagnant air

ven·trad \\'ven-,trad\\ *adv* : toward the ventral side

ven·tral \\'ven-trəl\\ *adj* [L *ventr-, venter* belly] **1** : of or relating to the belly : ABDOMINAL **2** : of or relating to or located on or near the surface of the body that in man is the front but in most other animals is the lower surface ⟨a fish's *ventral* fins⟩ — **ven·tral·ly** \\-trə-lē\\ *adv*

ven·tri·cle \\'ven-tri-kəl\\ *n* [L *ventriculus*, fr. dim. of *venter* belly] : a cavity of a bodily part or organ: as **a** : a chamber of the heart which receives blood from a corresponding atrium and from which blood is forced into the arteries **b** : one of the communicating cavities in the brain that are continuous with the central canal of the spinal cord

ven·tri·cose \\'ven-tri-,kōs\\ *adj* : DISTENDED, INFLATED; *esp* : markedly swollen on one side — **ven·tri·cos·i·ty** \\,ven-tri-'käs-ət-ē\\ *n*

ven·tric·u·lar \\ven-'trik-yə-lər\\ *adj* : of, relating to, or being a ventricle or ventriculus

ven·tric·u·lus \\-ləs\\ *n, pl* **-li** \\-,lī, -,lē\\ : a digestive cavity

ven·tril·o·quism \\ven-'tril-ə-,kwiz-əm\\ *n* [LL *ventriloquus* ventriloquist, fr. L *venter* belly + *loqui* to speak; fr. the belief that the voice is produced from the ventriloquist's stomach] : the production of the voice in such a manner that the sound appears to come from a source other than the vocal organs of the speaker — **ven·tri·lo·qui·al** \\,ven-trə-'lō-kwē-əl\\ *adj* — **ven·tri·lo·qui·al·ly** \\-kwē-ə-lē\\ *adv*

ven·tril·o·quist \\ven-'tril-ə-kwəst\\ *n* : one who uses or is skilled in ventriloquism; *esp* : a professional entertainer who holds a dummy and apparently carries on conversation with it — **ven·tril·o·quis·tic** \\(,)ven-,tril-ə-'kwis-tik\\ *adj*

venetian blind

ven·tril·o·quize \ven-'tril-ə-ˌkwīz\ *vb* : to use ventriloquism; *also* : to utter in the manner of a ventriloquist
ven·tril·o·quy \ven-'tril-ə-kwē\ *n* : VENTRILOQUISM
¹ven·ture \'ven-chər\ *vb* **ven·tured; ven·tur·ing** \'vench-(ə-)riŋ\ [ME *venteren*, alter. of *aventuren*, fr. *aventure* adventure] **1** : to expose to hazard : RISK ⟨*ventured* more than he could afford on the game⟩ **2** : to face the risks and dangers of : BRAVE ⟨unwilling to *venture* the stormy sea⟩ **3** : to offer at the risk of rebuff or censure ⟨*venture* an opinion⟩ ⟨*venture* to disagree⟩ **4** : to proceed despite danger : DARE — **ven·tur·er** \'vench-(ə-)rər\ *n*
²venture *n* **1** : an undertaking involving chance, risk, or danger; *esp* : a speculative business enterprise **2** : a venturesome act — **at a venture** : at hazard or random
ven·ture·some \'ven-chər-səm\ *adj* **1** : disposed to court danger or take risks : DARING ⟨*venturesome* hunter⟩ **2** : involving risk : HAZARDOUS ⟨*venturesome* journey⟩ **syn** see ADVENTUROUS — **ven·ture·some·ly** *adv* — **ven·ture·some·ness** *n*
ven·tur·ous \'vench-(ə-)rəs\ *adj* **1** : VENTURESOME ⟨*venturous* spirit⟩ **2** : HAZARDOUS ⟨*venturous* enterprise⟩ — **ven·tur·ous·ly** *adv* — **ven·tur·ous·ness** *n*
ven·ue \'ven-yü\ *n* [MF, action of coming, fr. *venir* to come, fr. L *venire*] **1** : the place in which alleged events from which a legal action arises take place **2** : the place from which the jury is drawn and in which trial is held in a venue action
ven·ule \'ven-yül\ *n* : a small vein; *esp* : one of the minute veins connecting blood capillaries with larger veins
Ve·nus \'vē-nəs\ *n* **1** : the goddess of love and beauty in Roman mythology **2** : the planet 2d in order from the sun — see PLANET table
Ve·nus·berg \-ˌbərg\ *n* : a mountain in central Germany containing a cavern in which according to medieval legend Venus held court
Venus flower basket *or* **Ve·nus's-flow·er-basket** \ˌvē-nə-səz-\ *n* : a tubular or cornucopia-shaped sponge with a delicate glassy siliceous skeleton
Ve·nus-hair \'vē-nəs-ˌha(ə)r, -ˌhe(ə)r\ *n* : a delicate maidenhair fern with black stalks
Ve·nu·sian \vi-'n(y)ü-zhən\ *adj* : of or relating to the planet Venus — **Venusian** *n*
Ve·nus's-fly-trap \ˌvē-nə-səz-'flī-ˌtrap\ *n* : an insectivorous plant of the sundew family that grows along the Carolina coast and has the leaf apex modified into an insect trap
ve·ra·cious \və-'rā-shəs\ *adj* [L *verac-, verax*, fr. *verus* true] **1** : TRUTHFUL, HONEST **2** : ACCURATE, TRUE — **ve·ra·cious·ly** *adv* — **ve·ra·cious·ness** *n*
ve·rac·i·ty \və-'ras-ət-ē\ *n, pl* **-ties** **1** : devotion to the truth : TRUTHFULNESS **2** : ACCURACY, CORRECTNESS **3** : something true
ve·ran·da *or* **ve·ran·dah** \və-'ran-də\ *n* [Hindi *varaṇḍā*] **1** : PORCH **2** : a long roofed gallery extending along one or more sides of a building
ver·a·trine \'ver-ə-ˌtrēn\ *n* : a poisonous irritant mixture of alkaloids from sabadilla seed that has been used esp. as a counterirritant and insecticide
verb \'vərb\ *n* [L *verbum* word, verb; akin to E *word*] : a word that characteristically is the grammatical center of a predicate and expresses an act, occurrence, or mode of being and that in various languages is inflected (as for agreement with the subject or for tense)
¹ver·bal \'vər-bəl\ *adj* **1 a** : of, relating to, or consisting of words **b** : of, relating to, or involving words only rather than meaning or substance or effective action **2** : of, relating to, or formed from a verb ⟨*verbal* adjective⟩ **3** : spoken rather than written ⟨*verbal* contract⟩ **4** : word-for-word : VERBATIM ⟨*verbal* translation⟩ **syn** see ORAL — **ver·bal·ly** \-bə-lē\ *adv*
²verbal *n* : a word that combines characteristics of a verb with those of a noun or adjective
ver·bal·ism \'vər-bə-ˌliz-əm\ *n* **1** : a verbal expression : TERM **2 a** : an association in one's mind between an item of experience and the words that describe it **b** : the confusion of a word with what it stands for **3 a** : an empty form of words **b** : VERBOSITY
ver·bal·ist \-ləst\ *n* **1** : one who stresses words above substance or reality **2** : a person skilled with words — **ver·bal·is·tic** \ˌvər-bə-'lis-tik\ *adj*
ver·bal·ize \'vər-bə-ˌlīz\ *vb* **1** : to speak, write, or ex-

press in wordy or empty fashion **2** : to express something in words : describe verbally **3** : to convert into a verb — **ver·bal·i·za·tion** \ˌvər-bə-lə-'zā-shən\ *n* — **ver·bal·iz·er** \'vər-bə-ˌlī-zər\ *n*
verbal noun *n* : a noun derived directly from a verb or verb stem and in some uses having the sense and constructions of a verb
ver·ba·tim \(ˌ)vər-'bāt-əm\ *adv (or adj)* [ML, fr. L *verbum* word] : word for word : in the same words : LITERAL ⟨a *verbatim* translation⟩⟨took down the governor's speech *verbatim*⟩
ver·be·na \(ˌ)vər-'bē-nə\ *n* [NL, genus of plants, fr. L, sing. of *verbenae* sacred boughs] : VERVAIN; *esp* : any of numerous garden plants of hybrid origin widely grown for their showy spikes of white, pink, red, or blue flowers which are borne in profusion over a long season
ver·bi·age \'vər-bē-ij\ *n* **1** : superfluity of words in proportion to sense or content : WORDINESS **2** : DICTION, WORDING ⟨concise military *verbiage*⟩
ver·bose \(ˌ)vər-'bōs\ *adj* : excessively wordy : PROLIX — **ver·bose·ly** *adv* — **ver·bose·ness** *n* — **ver·bos·i·ty** \-'bäs-ət-ē\ *n*
ver·bo·ten \vər-'bōt-ᵊn\ *adj* [G, forbidden] : forbidden usu. by authority and often unreasonably
ver·dant \'vərd-ᵊnt\ *adj* [MF *verd, vert* green, fr. L *viridis*, fr. *virēre* to be green] **1 a** : green in color ⟨*verdant* grass⟩ **b** : green with growing plants ⟨*verdant* fields⟩ **2** : unripe in experience or judgment — **ver·dan·cy** \-ᵊn-sē\ *n* — **ver·dant·ly** *adv*
ver·dict \'vər-(ˌ)dikt\ *n* [AF *verdit*, fr. OF *ver dit* true dictum] **1** : the finding or decision of a jury on the matter submitted to them in trial **2** : OPINION, JUDGMENT
ver·di·gris \'vərd-ə-ˌgrēs, -ˌgris\ *n* [OF *vert de Grice*, lit., green of Greece] : a green or greenish blue poisonous pigment produced by the action of acetic acid on copper or found on brass surfaces exposed to weather
ver·dure \'vər-jər\ *n* [MF, fr. *verd* green] : the greenness of growing vegetation; *also* : such vegetation itself — **ver·dured** \-jərd\ *adj* — **ver·dur·ous** \'vərj-(ə-)rəs\ *adj* — **ver·dur·ous·ness** *n*
¹verge \'vərj\ *n* [MF, fr. L *virga* rod, stripe] **1 a** : a staff carried as an emblem of authority or office **b** : an area around a place or within which jurisdiction is exercised **2 a** : something that borders, limits, or bounds : EDGE, BOUNDARY ⟨the *verge* of the sea⟩ **b** : BRINK, THRESHOLD ⟨on the *verge* of bankruptcy⟩
²verge *vi* **1** : to be contiguous **2** : to be on the verge ⟨conduct that *verges* on the absurd⟩
³verge *vi* [L *vergere* to bend, incline] **1** : to move or extend in some direction or toward some condition : INCLINE **2** : to be in transition or change
verg·er \'vər-jər\ *n* **1** *Brit* : an attendant that carries a verge (as before a bishop or justice) **2** : a church official who keeps order during services or serves as an usher or a sacristan
Ver·gil·i·an \(ˌ)vər-'jil-ē-ən\ *adj* : of, relating to, or characteristic of Vergil or his writings
ver·i·fi·a·ble \'ver-ə-ˌfī-ə-bəl\ *adj* : capable of being verified — **ver·i·fi·a·ble·ness** *n* — **ver·i·fi·a·bly** \-blē\ *adv*
ver·i·fy \'ver-ə-ˌfī\ *vt* **-fied; -fy·ing** [MF *verifier*, fr. ML *verificare*, fr. L *verus* true] **1** : to prove to be true or correct : CONFIRM **2** : to check or test the accuracy of — **ver·i·fi·ca·tion** \ˌver-ə-fə-'kā-shən\ *n* — **ver·i·fi·er** \'ver-ə-ˌfī(-ə)r\ *n*
ver·i·ly \'ver-ə-lē\ *adv* [ME *verraily*, fr. *verray* true, very] : in fact : CERTAINLY
veri·sim·i·lar \ˌver-ə-'sim-ə-lər\ *adj* [L *verisimilis*, fr. *veri similis* like the truth] : having the appearance of truth : PROBABLE — **veri·sim·i·lar·ly** *adv*
veri·si·mil·i·tude \-sə-'mil-ə-ˌt(y)üd\ *n* **1** : the quality or state of being verisimilar **2** : something verisimilar
ver·i·ta·ble \'ver-ət-ə-bəl\ *adj* : ACTUAL, TRUE — **ver·i·ta·ble·ness** *n* — **ver·i·ta·bly** \-blē\ *adv*
ver·i·ty \'ver-ət-ē\ *n, pl* **-ties** [L *verus* true] **1** : the quality or state of being true or real **2** : a true fact or statement **3** : HONESTY, VERACITY
ver·juice \'vər-ˌjüs\ *n* [MF *vert jus*, lit., green juice] **1** : the sour juice of crab apples or unripe fruit (as grapes) or an acid liquor made from this **2** : acidity of disposition or manner

---

ə abut; ᵊ kitten; ər further; a back; ā bake; ä cot, cart; aù out; ch chin; e less; ē easy; g gift; i trip; ī life

ver·meil *n* **1** \'vər-məl, -ˌmāl\ : VERMILION **2** \ve(ə)r-'mā\ : gilded silver, bronze, or copper — **vermeil** *adj*

vermi- *comb form* [L *vermis;* akin to E *worm*] : worm ⟨*vermiform*⟩

ver·mi·cel·li \ˌvər-mə-'chel-ē, -'sel-\ *n* [It, fr. pl. of *vermicello,* dim. of *verme* worm, fr. L *vermis*] : a food like spaghetti but of smaller diameter

ver·mi·cide \'vər-mə-ˌsīd\ *n* : an agent that destroys worms

ver·mic·u·lar \(ˌ)vər-'mik-yə-lər\ *adj* [L *vermiculus,* dim. of *vermis* worm] **1 a** : resembling a worm in form or motion **b** : VERMICULATE 1 **2** : of, relating to, or caused by worms

ver·mic·u·late \-lət\ *or* **ver·mic·u·lat·ed** \-ˌlāt-əd\ *adj* **1** : marked with irregular fine lines or with wavy impressed lines ⟨a *vermiculate* nut⟩ **2** : TORTUOUS, INVOLUTE — **ver·mic·u·la·tion** \-ˌmik-yə-'lā-shən\ *n*

ver·mic·u·lite \(ˌ)vər-'mik-yə-ˌlīt\ *n* : any of numerous minerals that are usu. altered micas whose granules expand greatly at high temperatures to give a lightweight absorbent heat-resistant material used esp. in seedbeds and as insulation

ver·mi·form \'vər-mə-ˌfórm\ *adj* : resembling a worm in shape

vermiform appendix *n* : the intestinal appendix

ver·mi·fuge \'vər-mə-ˌfyüj\ *adj* [L *fugare* to put to flight] : serving to destroy or expel parasitic worms — **vermifuge** *n*

ver·mil·ion *or* **ver·mil·lion** \vər-'mil-yən\ *n* [OF *vermeillon,* fr. *vermeil,* adj., bright red, vermilion, fr. LL *vermiculus* kermes, fr. L, dim. of *vermis* worm] **1** : a bright red pigment; *esp* : one consisting of mercuric sulfide **2** : a variable color averaging a vivid reddish orange

ver·min \'vər-mən\ *n, pl* **vermin** [MF, fr. L *vermis* worm] **1** : small common harmful or objectionable animals (as fleas or mice) that are difficult to control **2** : a noxious or offensive person

ver·min·ous \'vər-mə-nəs\ *adj* **1** : consisting of or full of vermin ⟨a *verminous* brood⟩ ⟨*verminous* houses⟩ **2** : caused by vermin ⟨*verminous* disease⟩ — **ver·min·ous·ly** *adv*

ver·miv·o·rous \(ˌ)vər-'miv-ə-rəs\ *adj* : feeding on worms ⟨*vermivorous* birds⟩

ver·mouth \vər-'müth\ *n* [F *vermout,* fr. G *wermut* wormwood; akin to E *wormwood*] : a white wine flavored with aromatic herbs and used as an aperitif or in mixed drinks

¹ver·nac·u·lar \və(r)-'nak-yə-lər\ *adj* [L *vernaculus* native, fr. *verna* slave born in his master's house, native] **1** : using a language or dialect native to a region or country rather than a literary, cultured, or foreign language **2** : of, relating to, or used in the normal spoken form of a language — **ver·nac·u·lar·ly** *adv*

²vernacular *n* **1** : a vernacular language **2** : the mode of expression of a group or class **3** : a common name of a plant or animal as distinguished from the latinized taxonomic name

ver·nal \'vərn-ᵊl\ *adj* [L *vernalis,* fr. *ver* spring] **1** : of, relating to, or occurring in the spring ⟨*vernal* equinox⟩ ⟨*vernal* sunshine⟩ **2** : fresh or new like the spring; *also* : YOUTHFUL — **ver·nal·ly** \-ᵊl-ē\ *adv*

ver·nal·ize \'vərn-ᵊl-ˌīz\ *vt* : to hasten the flowering and fruiting of (plants) by treating seeds, bulbs, or seedlings so as to shorten the vegetative period — **ver·nal·i·za·tion** \ˌvərn-ᵊl-ə-'zā-shən\ *n*

ver·na·tion \(ˌ)vər-'nā-shən\ *n* : the arrangement of foliage leaves within the bud

ver·ni·er \'vər-nē-ər\ *n* [after Pierre *Vernier* d1637 French mathematician] **1** : a short scale made to slide along the divisions of a graduated instrument for indicating parts of divisions **2** : a small auxiliary device used with a main device to obtain fine adjustment

vernier caliper *n* : a caliper gauge with a graduated beam and a sliding jaw having a vernier

Ver·o·nal \'ver-ə-ˌnól, -ən-ᵊl\ *trademark* — used for barbital

ve·ron·i·ca \və-'rän-i-kə\ *n* : SPEEDWELL

ver·ru·cose \və-'rü-ˌkōs\ *adj* : covered with warty elevations

ver·sa·tile \'vər-sət-ᵊl\ *adj* [L *versatilis* turning easily, fr.

versare, freq. of *vertere* to turn] **1** : changing or fluctuating readily : VARIABLE **2** : embracing a variety of subjects, fields, or skills; *also* : turning with ease from one thing or position to another **3** : having many uses or applications — **ver·sa·tile·ly** \-ᵊl-(l)ē\ *adv* — **ver·sa·tile·ness** \-ᵊl-nəs\ *n* — **ver·sa·til·i·ty** \ˌvər-sə-'til-ət-ē\ *n*

¹verse \'vərs\ *n* [L *versus* turning, row, verse, fr. *vers-, vertere* to turn] **1** : a line of metrical writing **2 a** : metrical writing distinguished from poetry esp. by its lower level of intensity **b** : POETRY ⟨Elizabethan *verse*⟩ ⟨has written both *verse* and prose⟩ **c** : POEM ⟨read the group some of her *verses*⟩ **3** : STANZA **4** : one of the short divisions into which a chapter of the Bible is traditionally divided

²verse *vb* : VERSIFY

versed \'vərst\ *adj* [L *versatus,* pp. of *versari* to be active, be occupied (in), pass. of *versare*] : made familiar by study or experience : SKILLED ⟨*versed* in science⟩

ver·si·cle \'vər-si-kəl\ *n* [L *versiculus,* dim. of *versus* verse] **1** : a short verse or sentence said or sung in public worship by a priest or minister and followed by a response from the people **2** : a little verse

ver·si·fi·ca·tion \ˌvər-sə-fə-'kā-shən\ *n* **1** : the making of verses **2** : metrical structure : PROSODY

ver·si·fy \'vər-sə-ˌfī\ *vb* **-fied; -fy·ing** **1** : to compose or turn into verse **2** : to relate or describe in verse — **ver·si·fi·er** \-ˌfī-(ə)r\ *n*

ver·sion \'vər-zhən\ *n* [L *vers-, vertere* to turn] **1 a** : a translation from another language; *esp* : a translation of the Bible or a part of it **2 a** : an account or description from a particular point of view esp. as contrasted with another account **b** : an adaptation of a literary or musical work ⟨a stage *version* of the novel⟩ **3** : a form or variant of an original ⟨an experimental *version* of the plane⟩ **4 a** : a condition in which an anatomical structure (as the uterus) is turned from its normal position **b** : manual turning of the fetus in the uterus to aid delivery — **ver·sion·al** \'vərzh-nəl, -ən-ᵊl\ *adj*

vers li·bre \ve(ə)r-'lēbr'\ *n, pl* **vers li·bres** \same\ [F] : FREE VERSE

ver·so \'vər-sō\ *n, pl* **versos** [NL *verso folio* the page being turned] : a left-hand page — compare RECTO

verst \'vərst\ *n* [Russ *versta*] : a Russian unit of distance equal to 0.6629 miles

ver·sus \'vər-səs, -səz\ *prep* [ML, towards, against, fr. L, adv., so as to face, fr. pp. of *vertere* to turn] **1** : AGAINST ⟨John Doe *versus* Richard Roe⟩ **2** : in contrast to or as the alternative of ⟨free trade *versus* protection⟩

ver·te·bra \'vərt-ə-brə\ *n, pl* **-brae** \-(ˌ)brē, -ˌbrā\ *or* **-bras** [L, joint, vertebra, fr. *vertere* to turn] : one of the bony or cartilaginous segments composing the spinal column that in higher vertebrates have a short nearly cylindrical body whose ends articulate by pads of strong tissue with those of adjacent vertebrae and a bony arch that encloses the spinal cord

ver·te·bral \(ˌ)vər-'tē-brəl\ *adj* : of, relating to, or made up of vertebrae : SPINAL — **ver·te·bral·ly** \-ē\ *adv*

vertebral column *n* : SPINAL COLUMN

¹ver·te·brate \'vərt-ə-brət, -ˌbrāt\ *adj* **1 a** : having a spinal column **b** : of or relating to the vertebrates **2** : having a strong framework suggesting vertebrae

²vertebrate *n* : any of a primary division (Vertebrata) of chordates comprising animals (as mammals, birds, reptiles, amphibians, or fishes) with a segmented spinal column together with a few primitive forms in which the backbone is represented by a notochord

ver·tex \'vər-ˌteks\ *n, pl* **ver·ti·ces** \'vərt-ə-ˌsēz\ *also* **ver·tex·es** [L *vertic-, vertex* whirlpool, top of the head, summit, fr. *vertere* to turn] **1 a** : the point opposite to and farthest from the base in a figure **b** : ZENITH 1 **2** : the top of the head **3** : a principal or highest point : SUMMIT, APEX ⟨a monument on the *vertex* of the hill⟩

ver·ti·cal \'vərt-i-kəl\ *adj* **1** : situated at the highest point : directly overhead or in the zenith **2** : perpendicular to the plane of the horizon or to a primary axis : UPRIGHT **3** : composed of economic units on different levels of production or distribution ⟨a *vertical* business organization⟩ — **vertical** *n* — **ver·ti·cal·i·ty** \ˌvərt-ə-'kal-ət-ē\ *n* — **ver·ti·cal·ly** \'vərt-i-k(ə-)lē\ *adv* — **ver·ti·cal·ness** \-kəl-nəs\ *n*

syn VERTICAL, PERPENDICULAR, PLUMB mean being at

right angles to a base line. VERTICAL suggests a line or direction rising straight upward toward a zenith; PERPENDICULAR may stress the stiff straightness of a line making a right angle with any other line, not necessarily a horizontal one; PLUMB stresses an exact verticality determined (as with a plumb line) by earth's gravity

vertical angle *n* : one of two angles having the same vertex and sides that are straight line extensions of each other

vertical circle *n* : a great circle of the celestial sphere whose plane is perpendicular to that of the horizon

vertical file *n* : a collection esp. of pamphlets and clippings that is maintained (as in a library) to answer questions quickly or to provide points of information not easy to locate elsewhere

ver·ti·cil \'vərt-ə-,sil\ *n* [NL *verticillus,* dim. of L *vertex* whirl] : a circle of similar parts (as leaves, flowers, or inflorescences) about the same point on an axis : WHORL — **ver·ti·cil·late** \,vərt-ə-'sil-ət\ *adj* — **ver·ti·cil·late·ly** *adv* — **ver·ti·cil·la·tion** \,vərt-ə-sil-'ā-shən\ *n*

ver·tig·i·nous \(,)vər-'tij-ə-nəs\ *adj* **1** : marked by, suffering from, or tending to cause dizziness **2** : marked by turning : ROTARY ⟨the *vertiginous* motion of the earth⟩ — **ver·tig·i·nous·ly** *adv*

ver·ti·go \'vərt-i-,gō\ *n, pl* **ver·ti·goes** *or* **ver·tig·i·nes** \(,)vər-'tij-ə-,nēz\ [L *vertigin-, vertigo,* fr. *vertere* to turn] : DIZZINESS, GIDDINESS

ver·tu \,vər-'tü, ve(ə)r-\ *var of* VIRTU

ver·vain \'vər-,vān\ *n* [MF *verveine,* fr. L *verbena,* sing. of *verbenae* sacred boughs] : any of a genus of mostly American herbs or subshrubs with often showy heads or spikes of 5-parted regular flowers — called also *verbena*

verve \'vərv\ *n* [F, fr. L *verba,* pl. of *verbum* word] **1** : the spirit and enthusiasm that animate artistic composition or performance : VIVACITY **2** : ENERGY, VITALITY

¹very \'ver-ē\ *adj* **ver·i·er; -est** [OF *verai,* fr. L *verac-, verax* truthful, fr. *verus* true] **1 a** : properly entitled to the name or designation : TRUE **b** : ACTUAL, REAL **2 a** : EXACT, PRECISE ⟨*very* heart of the city⟩ **b** : exactly suitable or necessary ⟨the *very* thing for the purpose⟩ **3** : ABSOLUTE, UTTER ⟨the *veriest* fool alive⟩ **4** : MERE, BARE ⟨the *very* thought terrified him⟩ **5** : SELFSAME, IDENTICAL ⟨the *very* man I saw⟩ **6** — used as an intensive ⟨the *very* dogs refused the food⟩

²very *adv* **1** : to a high degree : EXCEEDINGLY ⟨a *very* hot day⟩ ⟨*very* much better⟩ **2** : in actual fact : TRULY ⟨the *very* best store in town⟩ ⟨told the *very* same story⟩

very high frequency *n* : a radio frequency in the range between 30 and 300 megacycles — abbr. *vhf*

Very light \,ver-ē-, vi(ə)r-ē-\ *n* [after Edward W. *Very* d1910 American naval officer] : a pyrotechnic signal in a system of signaling using white or colored balls of fire projected from a special pistol

very low frequency *n* : a radio frequency in the range between 10 and 30 kilocycles — abbr. *vlf*

Very Reverend — used as a title for various ecclesiastical officials (as cathedral deans and canons and rectors of Roman Catholic colleges and seminaries)

ves·i·cant \'ves-i-kənt\ *n* [L *vesica* bladder, blister] : an agent (as a drug or a plant substance) that causes blistering — **vesicant** *adj*

ves·i·cate \'ves-ə-,kāt\ *vb* : BLISTER

ves·i·ca·to·ry \'ves-i-kə-,tōr-ē, -,tor-\ *adj or n* : VESICANT

ves·i·cle \'ves-i-kəl\ *n* [L *vesicula,* dim. of *vesica* bladder] **1 a** : a membranous and usu. fluid-filled pouch (as a cyst or vacuole) in a plant or animal; *also* : a small abnormal elevation of the outer layer of skin enclosing a watery liquid : BLISTER **b** : a pocket of embryonic tissue that is the beginning of an organ (the optic *vesicle*) **2** : a small cavity esp. in mineral or rock — **ve·sic·u·lar** \və-'sik-yə-lər\ *adj* — **ve·sic·u·lar·ly** *adv*

ve·sic·u·late \və-'sik-yə-,lāt\ *vb* : to make or become vesicular — **ve·sic·u·la·tion** \-,sik-yə-'lā-shən\ *n*

¹ves·per \'ves-pər\ *n* [ME, fr. L, evening star, evening] **1** *cap* : EVENING STAR **2** : a vesper bell **3** *archaic* : EVENING, EVENTIDE

²vesper *adj* : of or relating to vespers or the evening

ves·pers \'ves-pərz\ *n pl, often cap* **1** : the sixth of the canonical hours **2** : EVENING PRAYER **3** : a late afternoon or evening worship service

ves·per·til·i·an \,ves-pər-'til-ē-ən\ *adj* [L *vespertilio* bat, fr. *vesper* evening] : of or relating to bats

ves·per·tine \'ves-pər-,tīn\ *adj* **1 a** : of, relating to, or occurring in the evening **b** : resembling that of evening ⟨*vespertine* shadows⟩ **2** : active or flourishing in the evening : CREPUSCULAR

ves·pine \'ves-,pīn\ *adj* [L *vespa* wasp; akin to E *wasp*] : of, relating to, or resembling wasps and esp. the typical colonial wasps

ves·sel \'ves-əl\ *n* [OF *vaissel,* fr. LL *vascellum,* dim. of L *vas* vase, vessel] **1 a** : a hollow or concave utensil (as a hogshead, bottle, kettle, cup, or bowl) for holding something **b** : a person into whom some quality (as grace) is infused **2** : a craft bigger than a rowboat for navigation of the water **3 a** : a tube or canal (as an artery) in which a body fluid is contained and conveyed or circulated **b** : a conducting tube in a vascular plant formed by the fusion and loss of end walls of a series of cells

¹vest \'vest\ *vb* [MF *vestir* to clothe, invest, fr. L *vestire* to clothe, fr. *vestis* clothing, garment; akin to E *wear*] **1 a** : to place or give a right, authority, or title into the possession or discretion of some person or body ⟨powers *vested* in the presidency⟩ **b** : to become legally vested ⟨title *vests* in the purchaser⟩ **2** : to clothe with or as if with a garment; *esp* : to garb in ecclesiastical vestments **3** : to put on garments; *esp* : to robe in ecclesiastical vestments

²vest *n* **1 a** : a man's sleeveless garment worn under a suit coat **b** : a similar garment for women **c** : a protective garment worn on active military duty or in or on the water **2** : a knitted undershirt for women **3** : a plain or decorative piece used to fill in the front neckline of a woman's outer garment (as a waist, coat, or gown)

ves·ta \'ves-tə\ *n* **1** *cap* : the Roman goddess of the hearth and hearth fire **2** : a short match with a shank of wax; *also* : a short wooden match

¹ves·tal \'vest-°l\ *adj* **1** : of or relating to a   *vest 1a* vestal virgin **2** : CHASTE — **ves·tal·ly** *adv*

²vestal *n* **1** : a virgin consecrated to the Roman goddess Vesta and to the service of watching the sacred fire perpetually kept burning on her altar — called also *vestal virgin* **2** : a chaste woman

vested interest *n* **1** : an interest (as in an existing economic arrangement) in which the holder has a strong personal commitment **2** : one having a vested interest in something

vest·ee \ve-'stē\ *n* **1** : DICKEY; *esp* : one made to resemble a vest and worn under a coat **2** : VEST 3

ves·ti·ary \'ves-tē-,er-ē\ *n, pl* **-ar·ies** [OF *vestiarie* vestry] **1** : a room (as in a monastery) where clothing is kept **2** : CLOTHING; *esp* : a set of clerical vestments

ves·tib·u·lar \ve-'stib-yə-lər\ *adj* : of, relating to, or functioning as a vestibule

ves·ti·bule \'ves-tə-,byül\ *n* [L *vestibulum*] **1 a** : a passage, hall, or room between the outer door and the interior of a building : LOBBY **b** : an enclosed entrance at the end of a railway passenger car **2** : any of various bodily cavities mostly serving as or resembling an entrance to some other cavity or space; *esp* : the central cavity of the labyrinth of the ear

ves·tige \'ves-tij\ *n* [F, fr. L *vestigium* footprint, track, vestige] **1 a** : a visible sign left by something vanished or lost **b** : a minute remaining amount **2** : a small and imperfectly developed bodily part or organ that remains from one more fully developed in an earlier stage of the individual, in a past generation, or in closely related forms **syn** see TRACE — **ves·ti·gial** \ve-'stij-(ē-)əl\ *adj* — **ves·ti·gial·ly** \-ē\ *adv*

vest·ment \'ves(t)-mənt\ *n* **1 a** : an outer garment; *esp* : a robe of ceremony or office **b** *pl* : CLOTHING, GARB **2** : a covering resembling a garment ⟨the verdant *vestment* which spring spreads over the land⟩ **3** : a ceremonial garment worn by a person officiating or assisting at a religious service — **vest·ment·al** \ves(t)-'ment-°l\ *adj*

vest-pock·et \,vest-'päk-ət\ *adj* : adapted to fit into the vest pocket : of very small size or scope

ves·try \'ves-trē\ *n, pl* **vestries** [MF *vestiarie,* fr. ML *vestiarium,* fr. L *vestire* to clothe] **1 a** : a room in a church building for sacred furnishings (as vestments) **b** : a storage place for clothing **c** : a room used for church meetings and classes **2 a** : the business meeting of an

---

ə abut; ᵉ kitten; ər further; a back; ā bake; ä cot, cart; aù out; ch chin; e less; ē easy; g gift; i trip; ī life

English parish; *also* : the parishioners assembled for it **b** : an elective body administering the finances, property, and ministerial relations of an Episcopal parish

ves·try·man \-mən\ *n* : a member of a vestry

ves·ture \'ves-chər\ *n* **1 a** : a covering garment (as a robe or vestment) **b** : CLOTHING, APPAREL **2** : something that covers like a garment

¹vet \'vet\ *n* ▸VETERINARIAN, VETERINARY

²vet *vt* **vet·ted; vet·ting** **1** : to provide veterinary care for (an animal) or medical care for (a person) **2** : to subject to expert appraisal or correction

³vet *adj or n* : VETERAN

vetch \'vech\ *n* [ONF *veche*, fr. L *vicia*] : any of a genus of herbaceous twining plants related to the pea that include valuable fodder and soil-building plants

vet·er·an \'vet-ə-rən, 've-trən\ *n* [L *veteranus* soldier of long experience, fr. *veter-, vetus* old] **1** : a person who has had long experience in something and esp. in war **2** : a former member of the armed forces esp. in war — **veteran** *adj*

Veterans Day *n* : November 11 observed as a legal holiday in commemoration of the end of hostilities in 1918 and 1945

vet·er·i·nar·i·an \,vet-ə-rən-'er-ē-ən, ,ve-trən-, ,vet-ʰn-\ *n* : one qualified and authorized to treat diseases and injuries of animals

¹vet·er·i·nary \'vet-ə-rən-,er-ē, 've-trən-, 'vet-ʰn-\ *adj* [L *veterinus* of beasts of burden] : of, relating to, or being the medical care of animals and esp. domestic animals

²veterinary *n, pl* **-nar·ies** : VETERINARIAN

¹ve·to \'vēt-ō\ *n, pl* **vetoes** [L, I forbid, fr. *vetare* to forbid] **1** : an authoritative prohibition : INTERDICTION **2 a** : a power of one branch of a government to forbid or prohibit the carrying out of projects attempted by another department; *esp* : the power of a chief executive to prevent permanently or temporarily the enactment of measures passed by a legislature **b** : the exercise of such authority **c** : a power possessed by members of some bodies (as the U. N. Security Council) to prohibit action by the body

²veto *vt* : to refuse to admit or approve : PROHIBIT; *esp* : to refuse assent to (a legislative bill) so as to prevent enactment or cause reconsideration — **ve·to·er** *n*

vex \'veks\ *vt* **vexed** *also* **vext; vex·ing** [L *vexare*] **1 a** : to bring trouble, distress, or agitation to **b** : to irritate or annoy by petty provocations : HARASS **c** : PUZZLE, BAFFLE **2** : to debate or discuss at length ⟨a *vexed* question⟩ **3** : to shake or toss about : BATTER ⟨a coast *vexed* by waves⟩

vex·a·tion \vek-'sā-shən\ *n* **1** : the quality or state of being vexed : IRRITATION **2** : the act of harassing or vexing : TROUBLING **3** : a cause of trouble or worry : AFFLICTION

vex·a·tious \-shəs\ *adj* **1 a** : causing vexation : DISTRESSING **b** : intended to harass **2** : full of disorder or stress : TROUBLED — **vex·a·tious·ly** *adv* — **vex·a·tious·ness** *n*

via \,vī-ə, ,vē-ə\ *prep* [L, abl. of *via* way] : by way of ⟨go *via* the northern route⟩

vi·a·ble \'vī-ə-bəl\ *adj* [F, fr. *vie* life, fr. L *vita*] **1** : capable of living; *esp* : born alive with such form and development of organs as to be normally capable of living **2** : capable of growing or developing ⟨*viable* seeds⟩ ⟨*viable* eggs⟩ **3** : WORKABLE — **vi·a·bil·i·ty** \,vī-ə-'bil-ət-ē\ *n* — **vi·a·bly** \'vī-ə-blē\ *adv*

vi·a·duct \'vī-ə-,dəkt\ *n* [L *via* way, road + E *-duct* (as in *aqueduct*)] : a bridge with high supporting towers or piers for carrying a road or railroad over something (as a gorge or a highway)

viaduct

vi·al \'vī-(ə)l\ *n* [MF *fiole*, fr. OProv *fiola*, fr. L *phiala*, fr. Gk *phialē*] : a small vessel for liquids (as medicines or chemicals)

vi·and \'vī-ənd\ *n* [MF *viande*, fr. ML *vivanda* food, alter. of L *vivenda*, neut. pl. of *vivendus*, gerundive of *vivere* to live] **1** : an article of food **2** *pl* : PROVISIONS, FOOD

vi·at·i·cum \vī-'at-i-kəm, vē-\ *n, pl* **-cums** *or* **-ca** \-kə\ [L, fr. neut. of *viaticus* of a journey, fr. *via* way] **1 a** : an allowance (as of transportation or supplies and money) for traveling expenses **b** : provisions for a journey **2** : Communion given to a person in danger of death

vi·a·tor \vī-'āt-ər\ *n* [L, fr. *via* way] : TRAVELER, WAYFARER

vi·bran·cy \'vī-brən-sē\ *n, pl* **-cies** : the quality or state of being vibrant : VIBRATION

vi·brant \'vī-brənt\ *adj* **1 a** (1) : VIBRATING, PULSING (2) : pulsating with life, vigor, or activity ⟨a *vibrant* personality⟩ **b** (1) : readily set in vibration (2) : RESPONSIVE, SENSITIVE **2** : sounding as a result of vibration : RESONANT — **vi·brant·ly** *adv*

vi·bra·phone \'vī-brə-,fōn\ *n* : a percussion musical instrument resembling the xylophone but having metal bars and motor-driven resonators for sustaining the tone and producing a vibrato — **vi·bra·phon·ist** \-,fō-nəst\ *n*

vi·brate \'vī-,brāt\ *vb* [L *vibrare*; akin to E *wipe*] **1** : to swing or move back and forth ⟨*vibrating* pendulum⟩ **2** : to set in vibration **3** : to oscillate very rapidly so as to produce a quivering effect or sound : SHAKE, QUIVER ⟨mandolin strings *vibrate* when plucked⟩ **4** : THRILL ⟨hearts *vibrating* with joy⟩ **5** : FLUCTUATE ⟨*vibrating* between two choices⟩ **syn** see SWAY

vi·bra·tile \'vī-brət-ʰl, -brə-,tīl\ *adj* **1** : characterized by vibration **2** : adapted to or used in vibratory motion ⟨the *vibratile* organs of insects⟩ — **vi·bra·til·i·ty** \,vī-brə-'til-ət-ē\ *n*

vi·bra·tion \vī-'brā-shən\ *n* **1 a** : the action of vibrating : the state of being vibrated **b** : motion or a movement to and fro : OSCILLATION ⟨the *vibration* of a pendulum⟩ **c** : a periodic motion of the particles of an elastic body or medium rapidly to and fro (as when a stretched cord is pulled or struck and produces a musical tone or when particles of air transmit sounds to the ear) **d** : a quivering or trembling motion ⟨*vibration* of a house caused by a passing truck⟩ **2** : vacillation in opinion or action : WAVERING — **vi·bra·tion·al** \-shnəl, -shən-ʰl\ *adj* — **vi·bra·tion·less** \-shən-ləs\ *adj*

vi·bra·tive \'vī-,brāt-iv\ *adj* : VIBRATORY

vi·bra·to \vē-'brät-ō\ *n, pl* **-tos** [It, pp. of *vibrare* to vibrate, fr. L] **1** : a slightly tremulous effect imparted to vocal or instrumental tone for added warmth and expressiveness by slight and rapid variations in pitch **2** : TREMOLO 1b

vi·bra·tor \'vī-,brāt-ər\ *n* **1** : one that vibrates or causes vibration **2** : an electromagnetic device that converts low direct current to pulsating direct current or alternating current

vi·bra·to·ry \'vī-brə-,tōr-ē, -,tȯr-\ *adj* **1** : consisting in, capable of, or causing vibration **2** : VIBRANT, VIBRATING

vib·rio \'vib-rē-,ō\ *n, pl* **-ri·os** : any of a genus of short rigid motile bacteria that are typically shaped like a comma or an S and include serious pathogens (as of Asiatic cholera) — **vib·ri·on·ic** \,vib-rē-'än-ik\ *adj*

vi·bris·sa \vī-'bris-ə\ *n, pl* **-sae** \-'bris-(,)ē\ : one of the stiff mostly tactile hairs esp. about the face in many mammals — **vi·bris·sal** \-'bris-əl\ *adj*

vi·bur·num \vī-'bər-nəm\ *n* [L] : any of a genus of widely distributed shrubs or trees of the honeysuckle family with simple leaves and white or rarely pink flowers in broad clusters

vic·ar \'vik-ər\ *n* [L *vicarius*, fr. *vicarius* vicarious] **1** : SUBSTITUTE, AGENT; *esp* : an administrative deputy **2** : an Anglican parish priest who does not hold the right to the tithes **3** : an Episcopal clergyman having charge of a mission or of a dependent parish — **vic·ar·ship** \-,ship\ *n*

vic·ar·age \'vik-ə-rij\ *n* **1** : the benefice or house of a vicar **2** : VICARIATE

vicar apostolic *n, pl* **vicars apostolic** : a Roman Catholic titular bishop who governs a territory not yet organized as a diocese

vic·ar·ate \'vik-ə-rət, -,rāt\ *n* : VICARIATE

vicar fo·rane \-fȯ-'rān, -fə-; -'fȯr-ən, -'fär-\ *n, pl* **vicars forane** : DEAN 1b

vicar-general *n, pl* **vicars-general** : an administrative deputy of a Roman Catholic or Anglican bishop or of the head of a religious order

vi·car·i·al \vī-'kar-ē-əl, -'ker-\ *adj* **1** : DELEGATED, DEPUTED **2** : of or relating to a vicar

vi·car·i·ate \vī-'ker-ē-ət, -'kar-\ *n* : the office, jurisdiction, or tenure of a vicar

vi·car·i·ous \vī-'ker-ē-əs, -'kar-\ *adj* [L *vicarius*, fr. *vicis* change, alternation, stead] **1** : serving instead of or for another or something else **2** : performed or suffered by one person as a substitute for another or to the benefit or advantage of another : SUBSTITUTIONARY ⟨*vicarious* sacrifice⟩ **3** : experienced or realized through imaginative or sympathetic participation in the experience of another **4** : occurring in an unexpected or abnormal situation in the body — **vi·car·i·ous·ly** *adv* — **vi·car·i·ous·ness** *n*

Vicar of Christ : the Roman Catholic pope

¹vice \'vīs\ *n* [OF, fr. L *vitium* fault, vice] **1 a** : moral depravity or corruption : WICKEDNESS **b** : a moral fault or failing **c** : FOIBLE **2** : BLEMISH, DEFECT **3** : an abnormal behavior pattern in a domestic animal detrimental to its health or usefulness

²vice *n*, *chiefly Brit* : VISE

³vi·ce \'vī-sē\ *prep* [L, abl. of *vicis* change, alternation, stead] : in the place of

vice- \(')vīs, ‚vīs\ *prefix* : one that takes the place of ⟨*vice*-consul⟩

vice admiral *n* : a commissioned officer in the navy ranking above a rear admiral and below an admiral

vi·cen·ni·al \vī-'sen-ē-əl\ *adj* [LL *vicennium* period of 20 years, fr. L *vicies* 20 times + *annus* year] : occurring once every 20 years

vice-pres·i·dent \'vīs-'prez-əd-ənt, -'prez-dənt, -ə-,dent\ *n* : an official (as of a government) whose rank is next below that of the president and who takes the place of the president when necessary — **vice-pres·i·den·cy** \-'prez-əd-ən-sē, -'prez-dən-sē, -ə-,den-sē\ *n*

vice-re·gal \-'rē-gəl\ *adj* : of or relating to a viceroy or viceroyalty — **vice-re·gal·ly** \-gə-lē\ *adv*

vice-reine \'vīs-,rān\ *n* [F, fr. *vice-* + *reine* queen, fr. L *regina*] **1** : the wife of a viceroy **2** : a woman viceroy

vice·roy \'vīs-,rói\ *n* [MF *vice-roi*, fr. *vice-* + *roi* king, fr. L *reg-*, *rex*] **1** : the governor of a country or province who rules as the representative of his king or sovereign **2** : a showy American butterfly resembling but smaller than the monarch — **vice·roy·ship** \-,ship\ *n*

vice·roy·al·ty \'vīs-,rói(-ə)l-tē\ *n* : the office, jurisdiction, or term of service of a viceroy

vi·ce ver·sa \,vī-si-'vər-sə, (')vīs-'vər-\ *adv* [L] : with the alternation or order changed : CONVERSELY

vi·chys·soise \,vish-ē-'swäz\ *n* [F, fr. fem. of *vichyssois* of Vichy, fr. *Vichy*, France] : a soup of pureed leeks or onions and potatoes, cream, chicken stock, and seasoning and usu. served cold

Vi·chy water \'vish-ē-\ *n* : a natural sparkling mineral water from Vichy, France; *also* : an imitation of or substitute for this

vic·i·nage \'vis-ᵊn-ij\ *n* : a neighboring or surrounding district : VICINITY

vic·i·nal \'vis-ᵊn-əl\ *adj* : of or relating to a limited district : LOCAL

vi·cin·i·ty \və-'sin-ət-ē\ *n*, *pl* **-ties** [L *vicinus* neighboring, fr. *vicus* row of houses, village] **1** : the quality or state of being near : PROXIMITY **2** : a surrounding area or district

vi·cious \'vish-əs\ *adj* **1** : given to or constituting vice or immorality : DEPRAVED, WICKED **2** : DEFECTIVE, FAULTY; *also* : INVALID **3** : IMPURE, NOXIOUS **4** : dangerously aggressive ⟨a *vicious* dog⟩ **5** : MALICIOUS, SPITEFUL ⟨*vicious* slander⟩ — **vi·cious·ly** *adv* — **vi·cious·ness** *n*

vicious circle *n* **1** : a situation or condition that endlessly repeats itself (as when a cause produces an effect which in turn produces the original cause) **2** : a worthless argument or definition that assumes as true or as understood something that is to be proved or defined

vi·cis·si·tude \və-'sis-ə-,t(y)üd, vī-\ *n* [L *vicissitudo*, fr. *vicissim* in turn, fr. *vicis* change] : a change or succession from one thing to another; *esp* : an irregular, unexpected, or surprising change ⟨the *vicissitudes* of the weather⟩ — **vi·cis·si·tu·di·nous** \-,sis-ə-'t(y)üd-ᵊn-əs\ *adj*

vic·tim \'vik-təm\ *n* [L *victima*] **1** : a living being offered as a sacrifice in a religious rite **2** : an individual injured or killed (as by disease or accident) **3** : a person cheated, fooled, or damaged whether by someone else or by some impersonal force ⟨a *victim* of the economic system⟩

vic·tim·ize \'vik-tə-,mīz\ *vt* : to make a victim of esp. by

deception : CHEAT — **vic·tim·i·za·tion** \,vik-tə-mə-'zā-shən\ *n* — **vic·tim·iz·er** \'vik-tə-,mī-zər\ *n*

vic·tor \'vik-tər\ *n* [L, fr. *vict-*, *vincere* to conquer, win] : one that defeats an enemy or opponent : WINNER — **victor** *adj*

vic·to·ria \vik-'tōr-ē-ə, -'tór-\ *n* [after *Victoria* *d* 1901 queen of England] **1** : a low four-wheeled pleasure carriage for two with a calash top and a raised seat in front for the driver **2** : an open passenger automobile with a calash top that usu. extends over the rear seat only **3** : any of a genus of very large So. American water lilies with immense rose-white flowers

victoria 1

¹Vic·to·ri·an \vik-'tōr-ē-ən, -'tór-\ *adj* **1** : of or relating to the reign of Queen Victoria of England or the art, letters, or taste of her time **2** : typical of the moral standards or conduct of the age of Victoria esp. when regarded as stuffy or hypocritical — **Vic·to·ri·an·ism** \-ē-ə-,niz-əm\ *n*

²Victorian *n* : a person and esp. an author living during Queen Victoria's reign

vic·to·ri·an·ize \-ē-ə-,nīz\ *vt*, *often cap* : to make Victorian (as in style or taste)

vic·to·ri·ous \vik-'tōr-ē-əs, -'tór-\ *adj* : having won a victory : CONQUERING ⟨a *victorious* army⟩ ⟨*victorious* strategy⟩ — **vic·to·ri·ous·ly** *adv* — **vic·to·ri·ous·ness** *n*

vic·to·ry \'vik-t(ə-)rē\ *n*, *pl* **-ries** **1** : the overcoming of an enemy or opponent **2** : achievement of success in a struggle against odds or difficulties

syn VICTORY, CONQUEST, TRIUMPH mean a successful outcome in a contest or struggle. VICTORY stresses the fact of winning against an opponent or against odds; CONQUEST implies the subjugation of a defeated opponent ⟨the *conquest* of Mexico⟩ TRIUMPH suggests acclaim and personal satisfaction to the victor following a brilliant victory or achievement ⟨*triumphs* of the space flights⟩

¹vict·ual \'vit-ᵊl\ *n* [ME *vitaille*, fr. MF, fr. LL *victualia*, pl., victuals, fr. L *victus* nourishment, fr. *vict-*, *vivere* to live] **1** : food usable by man **2** *pl* : supplies of food : PROVISIONS

²victual *vb* **-ualed** *or* **-ualled; -ual·ing** *or* **-ual·ling** **1** : to supply with food **2** : EAT **3** : to lay in provisions

vict·ual·ler *or* **vict·ual·er** \'vit-ᵊl-ər\ *n* **1** : the keeper of a restaurant or tavern **2** : one that furnishes provisions (as to an army or a ship)

vi·cu·ña *or* **vi·cu·na** \vī-'k(y)ü-nə, vi-'kün-yə\ *n* [Sp *vicuña*, fr. Quechua *wikúña*] **1** : a wild ruminant of the Andes that is related to the domesticated llama and alpaca **2 a** : the wool from the vicuña's fine lustrous undercoat **b** : a fabric made of vicuña wool; *also* : a sheep's-wool imitation of this

vi·de \'vīd-ē, 'vē-,dā\ *v imper* [L, imper. of *vidēre* to see] : SEE — used to direct a reader to another item

vi·de·li·cet \və-'del-ə-,set, vī-\ *adv* [L, clearly, namely, fr. *vidēre* to see + *licet* it is permitted] : that is to say : NAMELY — abbr. *viz.*

¹vid·eo \'vid-ē-,ō\ *adj* [L *vidēre* to see + E *-o* (as in *audio*)] : relating to or used in the transmission or reception of the television image ⟨*video* channel⟩ ⟨*video* frequency⟩ — compare AUDIO

²video *n* : TELEVISION

vid·eo·gen·ic \,vid-ē-ō-'jen-ik, -'jēn-\ *adj* : TELEGENIC

vid·eo·tape \'vid-ē-ō-,tāp\ *vt* : to make a recording of (a television production) on magnetic tape — **videotape** *n*

vi·dette *var of* VEDETTE

vie \'vī\ *vi* **vied; vy·ing** \'vī-iŋ\ [modif. of MF *envier* to invite, challenge, wager, fr. L *invitare* to invite] : to strive for superiority : CONTEND — **vi·er** \'vī(-ə)r\ *n*

Vi·en·na sausage \vē-,en-ə-\ *n* : a short slender frankfurter in a thin casing usu. having the ends cut off

Viet·nam·ese \vē-,et-nə-'mēz, -'mēs, -,mēs\ *n*, *pl* **Vietnamese** **1** : a native or inhabitant of Vietnam **2** : the language of the largest group in Vietnam and the official language of the country — **Vietnamese** *adj*

¹view \'vyü\ *n* [MF *veue*, fr. *veeir*, *voir* to see, fr. L *vidēre*] **1** : the act of seeing or examining : INSPECTION; *also* : SURVEY **2** : manner of looking at or regarding something : OPINION, JUDGMENT ⟨state his *views*⟩ **3** : SCENE, PROSPECT **4** : extent or range of vision : SIGHT ⟨the planes passed out of *view*⟩ **5 a** : something that is looked toward or kept in sight : OBJECT ⟨studied hard with a *view* to winning honors⟩ **b** : something that is expected or anticipated ⟨no hope in *view*⟩ **6** : a pictorial representation : SKETCH — **in view of** : in regard to : in consideration of

²view *vt* **1** : SEE, BEHOLD **2** : to look at attentively : SCRUTINIZE **3** : to survey or examine mentally : CONSIDER ⟨*view* all sides of a question⟩

view·er \-ər\ *n* : one that views: as **a** : an optical device used in viewing ⟨a *viewer* for photographic transparencies⟩ **b** : a person who watches television

view·less \'vyü-ləs\ *adj* **1** : INVISIBLE, UNSEEN **2** : affording no view **3** : expressing no views or opinions — **view·less·ly** *adv*

view·point \'vyü-ˌpȯint\ *n* : POINT OF VIEW, STANDPOINT

vi·ges·i·mal \vī-'jes-ə-məl\ *adj* [L *vicesimus, vigesimus* twentieth] : based on the number 20

vig·il \'vij-əl\ *n* [L *vigilia* wakefulness, watch, fr. *vigil* awake, watchful] **1 a** : a watch formerly kept on the night before a religious feast with devotions (as prayer) **b** : the day before a religious feast observed as a day of spiritual preparation **c** : prayers or devotional services held in the evening or at night — usu. used in pl. **2** : the act of keeping awake at times when sleep is customary; *also* : a period of wakefulness **3** : an act of surveillance (as for protection) : WATCH ⟨the soldiers kept *vigil* all night⟩

vig·i·lance \'vij-ə-lən(t)s\ *n* : the quality or state of being vigilant : WATCHFULNESS

vig·i·lant \-lənt\ *adj* : alertly watchful esp. to avoid danger ⟨*vigilant* forest rangers⟩ **syn** see WATCHFUL — **vig·i·lant·ly** *adv*

vig·i·lan·te \ˌvij-ə-'lant-ē\ *n* [Sp, watchman, guard, fr. *vigilante* vigilant] : a member of a local volunteer committee organized to suppress and punish crime esp. where the processes of law seem inadequate

¹vi·gnette \vin-'yet\ *n* [F, fr. dim. of *vigne* vine] **1** : a running ornament (as of vine leaves, tendrils, and grapes) put on or just before a title page or at the beginning or end of a chapter; *also* : a small decorative design or picture so placed **2** : a picture (as an engraving or photograph) that shades off gradually into the surrounding ground **3** : a brief word picture : SKETCH

²vignette *vt* **1** : to finish (as a photograph) in the manner of a vignette **2** : to describe or sketch briefly — **vi·gnett·er** *or* **vi·gnett·ist** \-'yet-əst\ *n*

vig·or \'vig-ər\ *n* [L, fr. *vigēre* to be vigorous] **1** : active strength or energy of body or mind ⟨in the full *vigor* of youth⟩ **2** : INTENSITY, FORCE ⟨trees growing with *vigor*⟩ ⟨the *vigor* of their quarrel⟩

vi·go·ro·so \ˌvig-ə-'rō-sō\ *adj (or adv)* [It, lit., vigorous] : energetic in style — used as a direction in music

vig·or·ous \'vig-(ə-)rəs\ *adj* **1** : having vigor : ROBUST ⟨*vigorous* youth⟩ ⟨a *vigorous* plant⟩ **2** : done with vigor : carried out forcefully and energetically ⟨a *vigorous* protest⟩ ⟨*vigorous* exercise⟩ — **vig·or·ous·ly** *adv* — **vig·or·ous·ness** *n*

syn VIGOROUS, ENERGETIC, STRENUOUS mean having a great vitality and force. VIGOROUS suggests active strength and implies undiminishing freshness or robustness ⟨still *vigorous* in his old age⟩ ENERGETIC suggests a capacity for intense activity; STRENUOUS suggests a preference for coping with the arduous and challenging ⟨*strenuous* objections⟩ ⟨*strenuous* exercise⟩

vig·our \'vig-ər\ *chiefly Brit var of* VIGOR

Vi·king \'vī-kiŋ\ *n* : one of the pirate Northmen plundering the coasts of Europe in the 8th to 10th centuries

¹vile \'vīl\ *adj* [L *vilis*] **1** : of small worth or account : COMMON; *also* : MEAN **2** : morally base : WICKED ⟨*vile* deeds⟩ **b** : physically repulsive : FOUL ⟨*vile* living quarters⟩ **3** : DEGRADED, LOW **4** : DISGUSTING, CONTEMPTIBLE ⟨a *vile* temper⟩ — **vile·ly** \'vīl-lē\ *adv* — **vile·ness** *n*

²vile *adv* : in a vile manner : VILELY ⟨*vile*-smelling⟩

vil·i·fy \'vil-ə-ˌfī\ *vt* **-fied; -fy·ing 1** : to lower in estimation or importance : DEGRADE **2** : to utter slanderous and abusive statements against : DEFAME — **vil·i·fi·ca·tion** \ˌvil-ə-fə-'kā-shən\ *n* — **vil·i·fi·er** \'vil-ə-ˌfī(-ə)r\ *n*

vil·la \'vil-ə\ *n* [It, fr. L] **1** : a country estate **2** : the rural or suburban residence of a person of wealth

vil·lage \'vil-ij\ *n* [MF, fr. *ville* farm, village, fr. L *villa* country estate] **1** : a settlement usu. larger than a hamlet and smaller than a town **2** : the residents of a village

vil·lag·er \'vil-ij-ər\ *n* : an inhabitant of a village

vil·lain \'vil-ən\ *n* [ME *vilain, vilein*] **1** : VILLEIN **2** : a person of boorish mind and manners **3** : EVILDOER, CRIMINAL **4** : a scoundrel in a story or play — **vil·lain·ess** \'vil-ə-nəs\ *n*

vil·lain·ous \'vil-ə-nəs\ *adj* **1** : befitting a villain : DEPRAVED **2** : highly objectionable : WRETCHED — **vil·lain·ous·ly** *adv* — **vil·lain·ous·ness** *n*

vil·lainy \'vil-ə-nē\ *n, pl* **-lain·ies 1** : villainous conduct or a villainous act **2** : villainous character or nature : WICKEDNESS

vil·la·nelle \ˌvil-ə-'nel\ *n* [F, fr. It *villanella*] : a chiefly French verse form running on two rhymes and consisting typically of five tercets and a quatrain in which the first and third lines of the opening tercet recur alternately at the end of the other tercets and together as the last two lines of the quatrain

vil·lat·ic \vil-'at-ik\ *adj* : of or relating to a villa or a village : RURAL

vil·lein \'vil-ən, 'vil-ˌān, vil-'ān\ *n* [ME *vilain, vilein*, fr. MF, fr. ML *villanus*, fr. L *villa* country estate] **1** : a free peasant of any of various feudal classes **2** : an unfree peasant standing as the slave of his feudal lord but free in his legal relations with others

vil·len·age \'vil-ə-nij\ *n* **1** : tenure of land given by a feudal lord to a villein **2** : the status of a villein

vil·lous \'vil-əs\ *adj* **1** : covered or furnished with villi **2** : having soft long hairs ⟨leaves *villous* underneath⟩ — compare PUBESCENT — **vil·los·i·ty** \vil-'äs-ət-ē\ *n* — **vil·lous·ly** \'vil-əs-lē\ *adv*

vil·lus \'vil-əs\ *n, pl* **vil·li** \'vil-ˌī, -(ˌ)ē\ [NL, fr. L, shaggy hair] : a small slender usu. vascular process; *esp* : one of the tiny finger-shaped processes of the mucous membrane of the small intestine that function in the absorption of nutriments

vim \'vim\ *n* [L, accus. of *vis* strength] : robust energy and enthusiasm : VITALITY

vin·ai·grette \ˌvin-i-'gret\ *n* [F, fr. *vinaigre* vinegar] : a small ornamental box or bottle with perforated top used for holding an aromatic preparation (as smelling salts)

vi·nal \'vīn-ᵊl\ *adj* [L *vinum* wine] : of or relating to wine : VINOUS

vin·ca \'viŋ-kə\ *n* [NL, short for L *pervinca*] : **¹**PERIWINKLE

Vin·cen·tian \vin-'sen-chən\ *n* : a priest or brother of the Roman Catholic Congregation of the Mission founded in 1625 by St. Vincent de Paul and devoted to missions and clerical seminaries — **Vincentian** *adj*

Vin·cent's angina \ˌvin(t)-sən(t)s-, vaⁿ-ˌsäⁿz-\ *n* [after Jean Hyacinthe *Vincent d*1950 French bacteriologist] : a contagious disease marked by ulceration of the mucous membrane of the mouth and adjacent parts and caused by a bacterium often in association with a spirochete — compare VINCENT'S INFECTION

Vincent's infection *n* : a bacterial infection of the respiratory tract and mouth marked by destructive ulceration esp. of the mucous membranes — compare VINCENT'S ANGINA

vin·ci·ble \'vin(t)-sə-bəl\ *adj* [L *vincere* to conquer] : capable of being overcome or subdued : SURMOUNTABLE

vin·cu·lum \'viŋ-kyə-ləm\ *n, pl* **-lums** *or* **-la** \-lə\ [L, fr. *vincire* to bind] **1** : a unifying bond : LINK, TIE **2** : a straight horizontal mark placed over two or more members of a compound mathematical expression as a symbol of grouping (as in a − b — c = a − [b − c])

vin·di·cate \'vin-də-ˌkāt\ *vt* [L *vindicare* to lay claim to, avenge, fr. *vindic-, vindex* claimant, avenger] **1 a** : EXONERATE, ABSOLVE **b** (1) : CONFIRM, SUBSTANTIATE (2) : to provide justification or defense for : JUSTIFY **c** : to protect from attack or encroachment : DEFEND **2** : to maintain a right to : ASSERT **syn** see MAINTAIN — **vin·di·ca·tor** \-ˌkāt-ər\ *n* — **vin·di·ca·to·ry** \-di-kə-ˌtōr-ē, -ˌtȯr-\ *adj*

vin·di·ca·tion \ˌvin-də-'kā-shən\ *n* : the act of vindicating : the state of being vindicated; *esp* : justification against denial or censure : DEFENSE

vin·dic·tive \vin-'dik-tiv\ *adj* [L *vindicta* revenge, fr. *vindic-, vindex* avenger] **1 a** : disposed to seek revenge

: VENGEFUL   **b** : intended for or involving revenge   **2** : VICIOUS, SPITEFUL — **vin·dic·tive·ly** *adv* — **vin·dic·tive·ness** *n*

¹vine \'vīn\ *n* [OF *vigne*, fr. L *vinea* vine, vineyard, fr. *vinum* wine]   **1** : GRAPE 2   **2** : a plant whose stem requires support and which climbs by tendrils or twining or creeps along the ground; *also* : the stem of such a plant

²vine *vi* : to form or grow in the manner of a vine

vin·eal \'vin-ē-əl, 'vīn-\ *adj* [L *vinea* vine, fr. *vinum* wine] : of or relating to wine

vine·dress·er \'vīn-,dres-ər\ *n* : one that cultivates and prunes grapevines

vin·e·gar \'vin-i-gər\ *n* [OF *vinaigre*, fr. *vin* wine (fr. L *vinum*) + *aigre* sour, fr. L *acer* sharp] : a sour liquid obtained by the fermentation of cider, wine, or malt and used to flavor or preserve foods

vinegar eel *n* : a tiny roundworm often found in vinegar or acid fermenting vegetable matter

vin·e·gar·ish \'vin-i-g(ə-)rish\ *adj* : VINEGARY 2

vin·e·gary \-g(ə-)rē\ *adj*   **1** : resembling vinegar : SOUR   **2** : disagreeable, bitter, or irascible in character or manner : CRABBED ⟨a *vinegary* remark⟩

vin·ery \'vīn-(ə-)rē\ *n, pl* **-er·ies** : an area or building in which vines are grown

vine·yard \'vin-yərd\ *n* : a planting of grapevines — **vine·yard·ist** \-əst\ *n*

vingt-et-un \,van-,tā-'œn\ *n* [F] : TWENTY-ONE

vin·i·cul·ture \'vin-ə-,kəl-chər, 'vī-nə-\ *n* : VITICULTURE

vi·nif·er·ous \vī-'nif-(ə-)rəs\ *adj* : yielding or grown for the production of wine

vi·nos·i·ty \vī-'näs-ət-ē\ *n* : the characteristic body, flavor, and color of a wine

vi·nous \'vī-nəs\ *adj* [L *vinum* wine]   **1** : of, relating to, or made with wine ⟨*vinous* medications⟩   **2** : showing the effects of the use of wine

vin·tage \'vint-ij\ *n* [MF *vendenge*, fr. L *vindemia*, fr. *vinum* wine, grapes + *demere* to take off]   **1 a** (1) : the grapes or wine produced during one season   (2) : WINE; *esp* : a wine of a particular type, region, and year and usu. of superior quality   **b** : a collection of contemporaneous and similar persons or things : CROP   **2** : the act or time of gathering grapes or making wine   **3 a** : a period of origin or manufacture ⟨songs of the *vintage* of 1890⟩   **b** : length of existence : AGE — **vintage** *adj*

vint·ner \'vint-nər\ *n* : a wine merchant

viny \'vī-nē\ *adj* **vin·i·er; -est**   **1** : of, relating to, or resembling vines ⟨*viny* plants⟩   **2** : covered with or abounding in vines ⟨*viny* hillsides⟩

vi·nyl \'vīn-³l\ *n* [L *vinum* wine]   **1** : a univalent radical CH_2 = CH — derived from ethylene by removal of one hydrogen atom   **2** : a polymer of a vinyl compound or product made from one

vinyl resin *n* : any of a group of elastic resins that are resistant to chemical agents and are used for protective coatings and molded articles — called also *vinyl plastic*

vi·ol \'vī-(ə)l\ *n* [MF *viole*, fr. OProv *viola*] : a bowed stringed instrument like the violin but weaker in tone and simpler in construction and playing technique

¹vi·o·la \vē-'ō-lə\ *n* [It, fr. OProv, viol] : a stringed musical instrument like a violin but slightly larger and lower in pitch

²vi·o·la \vī-'ō-lə, vē-\ *n* [L] : VIOLET 1a; *esp* : any of various garden hybrids with solitary white, yellow, or purple often variegated flowers resembling but smaller than typical pansies

vi·o·la·ble \'vī-ə-lə-bəl\ *adj* : capable of being or likely to be violated — **vi·o·la·bil·i·ty** \,vī-ə-lə-'bil-ət-ē\ *n* — **vi·o·la·ble·ness** \'vī-ə-lə-bəl-nəs\ *n* — **vi·o·la·bly** \-blē\ *adv*

vi·o·late \'vī-ə-,lāt\ *vt* [L *violare*]   **1** : to fail to keep : BREAK, DISREGARD ⟨*violate* the law⟩   **2** : to do harm to the person or esp. the chastity of; *esp* : RAPE   **3** : PROFANE, DESECRATE   **4** : INTERRUPT, DISTURB — **vi·o·la·tor** \-,lāt-ər\ *n*

vi·o·la·tion \,vī-ə-'lā-shən\ *n* : the act of violating : the state of being violated: as   **a** : INFRINGEMENT, TRANSGRESSION   **b** : an act of irreverence or desecration : PROFANATION   **c** : INTERRUPTION, DISTURBANCE   : RAPE

vi·o·lence \'vī-ə-lən(t)s\ *n*   **1 a** : the use of physical force in a manner calculated to do harm to a person or his property ⟨the *violence* and bloodshed of war⟩ ⟨unlawful acts of *violence*⟩   **b** : injury esp. to something that merits respect or reverence : OUTRAGE ⟨such a requirement does *violence* to our principles⟩ ⟨the scandal did *violence* to his reputation⟩; *also* : improper or damaging treatment or interference (as by alteration of the wording or sense of a text) ⟨a translation that does *violence* to the spirit of the original⟩ ⟨avoiding *violence* to the customs of primitive people⟩   **2** : a violent act ⟨the *violences* and abuses of dictatorial government⟩   **3 a** : vigor in physical and esp. in destructive action : ENERGY ⟨knocked on the door with urgent *violence*⟩ ⟨the *violence* of the storm⟩   **b** : vehemence in feeling, behavior, or emotion : ARDOR, PASSION ⟨denied the charge with *violence*⟩

vi·o·lent \-lənt\ *adj* [L *violentus*]   **1** : marked by extreme force or sudden intense activity ⟨a *violent* attack⟩ ⟨*violent* storms⟩   **2 a** : notably furious or vehement ⟨a *violent* denunciation⟩; *also* : excited or mentally disordered to the point of loss of self-control ⟨the patient became *violent* and had to be restrained⟩   **b** : EXTREME, INTENSE ⟨*violent* pain⟩   **3** : caused by force : not natural ⟨a *violent* death⟩ — **vi·o·lent·ly** *adv*

vi·o·let \'vī-ə-lət\ *n* [MF *violete*, dim. of *viole* violet, fr. L *viola*]   **1 a** : any of a genus of herbs or subshrubs with alternate stipulate leaves and both aerial and underground flowers; *esp* : one with small usu. solid-colored flowers as distinguished from the usu. larger-flowered violas and pansies   **b** : any of several plants of other genera — compare DOGTOOTH VIOLET   **2** : any of a group of colors of reddish blue hue, low lightness, and medium saturation

violet ray *n* : an ultraviolet ray

vi·o·lin \,vī-ə-'lin\ *n* [It *violino*, dim. of *viola*]   **1** : a bowed stringed instrument with four strings tuned at intervals of a fifth distinguished from the viol in having a shallower body, shoulders at right angles with the neck, and a more curved bridge   **2** : VIOLINIST

vi·o·lin·ist \-'lin-əst\ *n* : one who plays the violin

vi·o·list \vē-'ō-ləst\ *n* : one who plays the viola

vi·o·lon·cel·list \,vī-ə-lən-'chel-əst, ,vē-\ *n* : CELLIST

vi·o·lon·cel·lo \-'chel-ō\ *n* [It, dim. of *violone*, aug. of *viola*] : CELLO

vi·os·ter·ol \vī-'äs-tə-,ról, -,rōl\ *n* [ultraviolet + *sterol*] : a vitamin D esp. when dissolved in an edible vegetable oil

violin

VIP \,vē-,ī-'pē\ *n* [*very important person*] : a person of great influence or prestige; *esp* : a high official with special privileges

vi·per *n* \'vī-pər\ *n* [L *vipera*]   **1 a** : any of a family of sluggish heavy-bodied broad-headed Old World venomous snakes with hollow tubular fangs   **b** : PIT VIPER   **c** : a venomous or reputedly venomous snake   **2** : a malignant or treacherous person — **vi·per·ine** \-pə-,rīn\ *adj*

vi·per·ish \'vī-p(ə-)rish\ *adj* : spitefully vituperative : VENOMOUS

vi·per·ous \'vī-p(ə-)rəs\ *adj*   **1** : of or relating to vipers   **2** : having the qualities attributed to vipers : MALIGNANT, VENOMOUS ⟨a *viperous* treachery⟩ — **vi·per·ous·ly** *adv*

vi·ra·go \və-'räg-ō, 'vir-ə,gō\ *n, pl* **-goes** *or* **-gos** [L *viragin-, virago*, fr. *vir* man]   **1** : a woman of great stature, strength, and courage   **2** : a loud overbearing woman : TERMAGANT — **vi·rag·i·nous** \və-'raj-ə-nəs\ *adj*

vi·ral \'vī-rəl\ *adj* : of, relating to, or caused by a virus

vir·eo \'vir-ē-,ō\ *n, pl* **-e·os** [L, a small bird, fr. *virēre* to be green] : any of a family of small insect-eating songbirds that are chiefly olive-green or grayish in color

vi·res·cence \və-'res-³n(t)s, vī-\ *n* : the state or condition of becoming green

vi·res·cent \-³nt\ *adj* [L *virescere* to become green, fr. *virēre* to be green] : beginning to be green : GREENISH

vir·ga \'vər-gə\ *n* [L, branch, streak in the sky suggesting rain] : trailing wisps of precipitation evaporating before reaching the ground

vir·gate \'vər-,gāt\ *adj* : shaped like a rod or wand

Vir·gil·i·an \(,)vər-'jil-ē-ən\ *adj* : VERGILIAN

¹vir·gin \'vər-jən\ *n* [L *virgin-, virgo* young woman, virgin]   **1** : an unmarried woman devoted to religion   **2** *cap* : VIRGIN MARY   **3** : a girl or woman who has not had sexual intercourse

²virgin *adj* **1** : being a virgin : CHASTE, MODEST **2** : PURE, FRESH, UNSOILED ⟨*virgin* snow⟩; *esp* : not altered by human activity ⟨*virgin* soil⟩ **3** : being used or worked for the first time or produced by a simple extractive process ⟨*virgin* wool⟩ ⟨*virgin* oil⟩

¹vir·gin·al \'vər-jən-°l\ *adj* : of, relating to, characteristic of, or suitable for a virgin or virginity; *esp* : CHASTE — **vir·gin·al·ly** \-°l-ē\ *adv*

²virginal *n* : a small rectangular spinet having no legs and only one wire to a note

virgin birth *n* **1** : birth from a virgin **2** *often cap V&B* : the theological doctrine that Jesus was miraculously begotten of God and born of a virgin mother

Vir·gin·ia creeper \vər-,jin-yə-\ *n* : a common No. American tendril-climbing vine of the grape family having leaves with five leaflets and bluish black berries — called also *woodbine*

Virginia reel *n* : a country-dance in which all couples in turn participate in a series of figures

vir·gin·i·ty \(,)vər-'jin-ət-ē\ *n, pl* **-ties** : the quality or state of being virgin : CHASTITY; *esp* : MAIDENHOOD

Virgin Mary *n* : the mother of Jesus

virgin's bower *n* : any of several usu. small-flowered and climbing clematises

Vir·go \'vər-gō\ *n* [L, lit., virgin] **1** : a zodiacal constellation due south of the handle of the Dipper pictured as a woman holding a spike of grain **2** : the 6th sign of the zodiac — see ZODIAC table

vir·gu·late \'vər-gyə-lət, -,lāt\ *adj* [L *virgula*, dim. of *virga* rod] : shaped like a rod

vir·gule \'vər-gyül\ *n* [F, fr. L *virgula*, a symbol used in MSS to mark suspected passages, fr. dim. of *virga* rod] : DIAGONAL 3

vi·ri·cide \'vī-rə-,sīd\ *n* : an agent that destroys or in-activates viruses — **vi·ri·cid·al** \,vī-rə-'sīd-°l\ *adj*

vir·i·des·cent \,vir-ə-'des-°nt\ *adj* [L *viridis* green] : slightly green : GREENISH

vir·ile \'vir-əl\ *adj* [L *virilis*, fr. *vir* man] **1** : having the nature, powers, or qualities of a man **2 a** : ENERGETIC, VIGOROUS **b** : MASTERFUL, FORCEFUL

vi·ril·i·ty \və-'ril-ət-ē\ *n* : the quality or state of being virile: **a** : MANHOOD **b** : manly vigor : MASCULINITY

vi·rol·o·gy \vī-'räl-ə-jē\ *n* : a branch of science that deals with viruses — **vi·ro·log·i·cal** \,vī-rə-'läj-i-kəl\ *adj* — **vi·rol·o·gist** \vī-'räl-ə-jəst\ *n*

vi·ro·sis \vī-'rō-səs\ *n, pl* **-ro·ses** \-'rō-,sēz\ : infection with or disease caused by a virus

vir·tu \,vər-'tü, lit., virtue, fr. L *virtut-*, *virtus*] **1** : a taste for or knowledge of curios or objets d'art **2** : productions of art esp. of a curious or antique nature

vir·tu·al \'vər-ch(ə-w)əl\ *adj* [ML *virtualis* possessed of powers or virtues, fr. L *virtus* strength, virtue] : being in essence or effect but not in fact or name ⟨the *virtual* ruler of the country⟩ — **vir·tu·al·i·ty** \,vər-chə-'wal-ət-ē\ *n* — **vir·tu·al·ly** \'vər-ch(ə-w)ə-lē, 'vərch-lē\ *adv*

virtual focus *n* : a point from which divergent rays (as of light) seem to emanate but do not actually do so (as in the image of a point source seen in a plane mirror)

virtual image *n* : an image (as seen in a plane mirror) formed of virtual foci

vir·tue \'vər-chü\ *n* [OF *virtu*, fr. L *virtut-*, *virtus* manli-ness, courage, virtue, fr. *vir* man] **1** : moral action or excellence : MORALITY; *esp* : CHASTITY **2** : a particular moral excellence ⟨justice and charity are *virtues*⟩ **3 a** : an active beneficial power ⟨quinine has *virtue* in the treatment of malaria⟩ **b** : a desirable or commendable quality or trait : MERIT ⟨the *virtues* of country life⟩⟨had the *virtue* of accepting correction graciously⟩ — **by virtue of** *or* **in virtue of** : through the force of : by authority of

vir·tue·less \'vər-chü-ləs\ *adj* **1** : devoid of excellence or worth **2** : lacking in moral goodness

vir·tu·os·i·ty \,vər-chə-'wäs-ət-ē\ *n, pl* **-ties** **1** : taste for or interest in virtu **2** : great technical skill in the practice of the fine arts

vir·tu·o·so \,vər-chə-'wō-sō, -zō\ *n, pl* **-sos** *or* **-si** \-(,)sē, -(,)zē\ [It, fr. *virtuoso* virtuous, skilled] **1** : an experi-menter or investigator esp. in the arts and sciences : SAVANT **2** : one skilled in or having a taste for the fine arts **3** : one who excels in the technique of an art; *esp* : a musical performer (as on the violin) — **virtuoso** *adj*

vir·tu·ous \'vər-chə-wəs\ *adj* : having virtue and esp. moral virtue; *esp* : CHASTE — **vir·tu·ous·ly** *adv* — **vir·tu·ous·ness** *n*

vi·ru·cide \'vī-rə-,sīd\ *n* : VIRICIDE

vir·u·lent \'vir-(y)ə-lənt\ *adj* [L *virulentus*, fr. *virus* poison] **1 a** : marked by a rapid, severe, and malignant course ⟨a *virulent* infection⟩ **b** : able to overcome bodily defensive mechanisms ⟨a *virulent* pathogen⟩ **2** : extremely poisonous or venomous : NOXIOUS **3** : full of malice : MALIGNANT **4** : objectionably harsh or strong — **vir·u·lence** \-lən(t)s\ *or* **vir·u·len·cy** \-lən-sē\ *n* — **vir·u·lent·ly** *adv*

vi·rus \'vī-rəs\ *n* [L, slimy liquid, poison] **1 a** : any of a large group of submicroscopic infective agents that are held by some to be living organisms and by others to be complex protein molecules containing nucleic acids and comparable to genes, that are capable of growth and multiplication only in living cells, and that cause various important diseases in man, lower animals, or plants; *also* : any of various infective agents (as a true virus or a rickettsia) that remain active after passing through a filter too fine for a bacterium to pass — called also *filter-able virus* **b** : a disease caused by a virus **2** : something (as a corrupting influence) that poisons the mind or spirit

¹vi·sa \'vē-zə\ *n* [F, fr. L, neut. pl. of *visus*, pp. of *vidēre* to see] **1** : an endorsement made on a passport by the proper authorities denoting that it has been examined and that the bearer may proceed **2** : a signature of formal approval by a superior upon a document

²visa *vt* **vi·saed** \-zəd\; **vi·sa·ing** \-zə-iŋ\ : to give a visa to

vis·age \'viz-ij\ *n* [OF, fr. *vis* face, fr. L *visus* sight, fr. *vidēre* to see] **1** : the face or countenance of a person or sometimes a lower animal **2** : ASPECT, APPEARANCE — **vis·aged** \-ijd\ *adj*

¹vis-à-vis \,vē-zə-'vē\ *n, pl* **vis-à-vis** \-zə-'vē(z)\ [F, lit., face to face] **1** : one that is face to face with another **2 a** : ESCORT, DATE **b** : COUNTERPART **3** : TÊTE-À-TÊTE

²vis-à-vis *prep* **1** : face to face with : OPPOSITE **2** : in relation to **3** : as compared with

³vis-à-vis *adv* : in company : TOGETHER

Vi·sa·yan \və-'sī-ən\ *var of* BISAYAN

viscera *pl of* VISCUS

vis·cer·al \'vis-ə-rəl\ *adj* **1 a** : felt in or as if in the viscera : DEEP ⟨*visceral* sensation⟩ **b** : of, relating to, or being the viscera : SPLANCHNIC **2** : not intellectual : INSTINCTIVE ⟨*visceral* drives⟩ — **vis·cer·al·ly** \-rə-lē\ *adv*

vis·cer·o·gen·ic \,vis-ə-rə-'jen-ik\ *adj* : arising within the body ⟨*viscerogenic* pain⟩

vis·cer·o·mo·tor \-'mōt-ər\ *adj* : causing or concerned in the functioning of the viscera ⟨*visceromotor* nerves⟩

vis·cid \'vis-əd\ *adj* **1** : STICKY, VISCOUS **2** : covered with a sticky layer — **vis·cid·i·ty** \vis-'id-ət-ē\ *n* — **vis·cid·ly** \'vis-əd-lē\ *adv*

vis·co·elas·tic \,vis-kō-i-'las-tik\ *adj* : having both viscous and elastic properties in appreciable degree

vis·com·e·ter \vis-'käm-ət-ər\ *n* : an instrument with which to measure viscosity — **vis·co·met·ric** \,vis-kə-'me-trik\ *adj*

¹vis·cose \'vis-,kōs\ *adj* **1** : VISCOUS **2** : of, relating to, or made from viscose

²viscose *n* **1** : a viscous golden-brown solution made by treating cellulose with caustic alkali solution and carbon disulfide and used in making rayon **2** : viscose rayon

vis·cos·i·ty \vis-'käs-ət-ē\ *n, pl* **-ties** : the quality of being viscous; *esp* : a tendency of a liquid to flow slowly result-ing from friction of its molecules ⟨an oil of high *viscosity*⟩

vis·count \'vī-,kaúnt\ *n* [MF *viscomte*, fr. ML *vicecomit-*, *vicecomes*, fr. LL *vice-* + *comes* count] : a member of the British peerage ranking below an earl and above a baron — **vis·count·cy** \-sē\ *n* — **vis·county** \-,kaúnt-ē\ *n*

vis·count·ess \-əs\ *n* **1** : the wife or widow of a viscount **2** : a woman who holds the rank of a viscount in her own right

vis·cous \'vis-kəs\ *adj* [L *viscum* birdlime] **1** : somewhat sticky or glutinous : ADHESIVE, VISCID **2** : having or char-acterized by viscosity — **vis·cous·ly** *adv* — **vis·cous·ness** *n*

vis·cus \'vis-kəs\ *n, pl* **vis·cera** \'vis-ə-rə\ [L *viscer-*, *viscus*] : an internal organ of the body; *esp* : one (as the heart, liver, or intestine) located in the great cavity of the trunk proper

---

j joke; ŋ sing; ō flow; ȯ flaw; ȯi coin; th thin; th this; ü loot; u̇ foot; y yet; yü few; yu̇ furious; zh vision

¹vise \'vīs\ n [MF vis something winding, fr. L vitis vine] : any of various tools having two jaws for holding work that operate usu. by a screw, lever, or cam

²vi·sé \'vē-,zā, vē-'\ vt **vi·séd** also **vi·séed; vi·sé·ing** [modif. of F viser, fr. visa, n.] : VISA

³visé n : VISA

Vish·nu \'vish-nü\ n : a Hindu god worshiped in the sacred triad as the Preserver and in a major cult in various incarnations — compare BRAHMA, SIVA

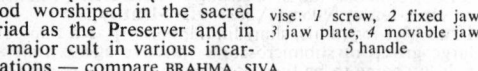

vise: 1 screw, 2 fixed jaw, 3 jaw plate, 4 movable jaw, 5 handle

vis·i·bil·i·ty \,viz-ə-'bil-ət-ē\ n 1 : the quality or state of being visible 2 : the degree of clearness of the atmosphere esp. as affording clear vision toward the horizon

vis·i·ble \'viz-ə-bəl\ adj [L vis-, vidēre to see] 1 : capable of being seen : apparent to the eye ⟨stars visible to the naked eye⟩ 2 : APPARENT, DISCOVERABLE ⟨visible means of support⟩ — **vis·i·ble·ness** n — **vis·i·bly** \-blē\ adv

Visi·goth \'viz-ə-,gäth\ n : a member of the western division of the Goths — called also West Goth; compare OSTROGOTH — **Visi·goth·ic** \,viz-ə-'gäth-ik\ adj

¹vi·sion \'vizh-ən\ n [L vis-, vidēre to see; akin to E wit] 1 a : something seen in a dream, trance, or ecstasy b : an object of imagination c : a manifestation to the senses of something immaterial 2 a : the act or power of imagination b : unusual discernment or foresight 3 a : the act or power of seeing : SIGHT b : the special sense by which the qualities of an object (as color, luminosity, or shape and size) constituting its appearance are perceived and which is mediated by the eye 4 : something seen; esp : a lovely or charming sight — **vi·sion·al** \'vizh-nəl, -ən-°l\ adj — **vi·sion·al·ly** \-ē\ adv — **vi·sion·less** \'vizh-ən-ləs\ adj

²vision vt **vi·sioned; vi·sion·ing** \'vizh-(ə-)niŋ\ : IMAGINE, ENVISION

¹vi·sion·ary \'vizh-ə-,ner-ē\ adj 1 : given to dreaming or imagining 2 : resembling a vision esp. in fanciful or impractical quality ⟨visionary schemes⟩ — **vi·sion·ari·ness** n

²visionary n, pl **-ar·ies** 1 : one who sees visions : SEER 2 : one whose ideas or projects are impractical : DREAMER

¹vis·it \'viz-ət\ vb **vis·it·ed** \'viz-ət-əd, 'viz-təd\; **vis·it·ing** \'viz-ət-iŋ, 'viz-tiŋ\ [L visitare, freq. of visere to go to see, freq. of vidēre to see] 1 : to go to see in order to comfort or help 2 a : to pay a call upon as an act of friendship or courtesy b : to go or come to see in an official or professional capacity c : to dwell with temporarily as a guest 3 a : to come to or upon as a reward, affliction, or punishment b : INFLICT 4 : to make a visit or frequent or regular visits 5 : CHAT, CONVERSE

²visit n 1 : a brief stay : CALL 2 : a stay as a guest or nonresident ⟨a weekend visit⟩ ⟨made a visit to the city⟩ 3 : an official or professional call

vis·it·a·ble \'viz-ət-ə-bəl\ adj 1 : subject to or allowing visitation or inspection 2 : socially eligible to receive visits

Vis·i·tan·dine \,viz-ə-'tan-,dēn\ n : a nun of the Roman Catholic Order of the Visitation of the Blessed Virgin Mary founded in France in 1610 and devoted to contemplation and education

vis·i·tant \'viz-ət-ənt, 'viz-tənt\ n 1 : VISITOR; esp : one thought to come from a spirit world 2 : a migratory bird that appears at intervals for a limited period — **visitant** adj

vis·i·ta·tion \,viz-ə-'tā-shən\ n 1 : VISIT; esp : an official visit (as for inspection) 2 a : a special dispensation of divine favor or wrath b : a severe trial : AFFLICTION 3 cap a : the visit of the Virgin Mary to Elisabeth before the birth of Elisabeth's son John the Baptist b : a church festival on July 2 commemorating this visit — **vis·i·ta·tion·al** \-shnəl, -shən-°l\ adj

visiting nurse n : a nurse employed to visit sick persons or perform public-health services in a community

visiting teacher n : an educational officer employed by a public school system to enforce attendance regulations or to instruct sick or handicapped pupils unable to attend school

vis·i·tor \'viz-ət-ər, 'viz-tər\ n : one that visits: as a : one

that makes formal visits of inspection b : TOURIST, TRAVELER

vi·sor \'vī-zər\ n [AF viser, fr. OF visiere, fr. vis face] 1 : the front piece of a helmet; esp : a movable upper piece 2 : a projecting part (as on a cap or an automobile windshield) to protect or shade the eyes — **vi·sored** \-zərd\ adj — **vi·sor·less** \-zər-ləs\ adj

visor (on a windshield)

vis·ta \'vis-tə\ n [It, sight, fr. vedere to see, fr. L vidēre] 1 : a distant view through or along an avenue or opening : PROSPECT 2 : an extensive mental view over a stretch of time or a series of events

vi·su·al \'vizh-(ə-w)əl\ adj [L visus sight, fr. vidēre to see] 1 : of, relating to, or used in vision ⟨visual organs⟩ 2 : attained or maintained by sight ⟨maintaining visual contact⟩ ⟨visual impressions⟩ 3 a : VISIBLE b : producing mental images : VIVID 4 : primarily appealing to the sense of sight or employing this as a medium (as of education) ⟨a visual lesson⟩⟨visual techniques in the elementary school⟩ — **vi·su·al·ly** \-ē\ adv

visual acuity n : the relative capacity of the visual organ to resolve detail

visual aid n : an instructional device (as a chart, map, or model) that appeals chiefly to vision; esp : an educational motion picture or filmstrip

vi·su·al·ize \'vizh-ə-(wə-),līz\ vb : to make visible; esp : to see or form a mental image : ENVISAGE — **vi·su·al·i·za·tion** \,vizh-ə-(wə-)lə-'zā-shən\ n — **vi·su·al·iz·er** \'vizh-ə-(wə-),lī-zər\ n

visual purple n : a photosensitive red or purple pigment in the retinal rods of various vertebrates; esp : RHODOPSIN

vi·ta \'vīt-ə, 'wē-,tä\ n, pl **vi·tae** \'vīt-ē, 'wē-,tī\ [L, lit., life] : a brief autobiographical sketch

vi·tal \'vīt-°l\ adj [L vita life; akin to E quick] 1 : of, relating to, or characteristic of life : showing the qualities of living things ⟨vital activities⟩ 2 : concerned with or necessary to the maintenance of life ⟨vital organs⟩ 3 : full of vitality : ANIMATED 4 : FATAL, MORTAL 5 : of first importance : BASIC syn see ESSENTIAL — **vi·tal·ly** \-°l-ē\ adv

vital capacity n : the breathing capacity of the lungs expressed as the number of cubic inches or cubic centimeters of air that can be forcibly exhaled after a full inspiration

vi·tal·ism \'vīt-°l-,iz-əm\ n : the doctrine that the life processes are not wholly explicable by the laws of physics and chemistry and that life is in some part self-determining — compare MECHANISM — **vi·tal·ist** \-°l-əst\ n — **vi·tal·is·tic** \,vīt-°l-'is-tik\ adj

vi·tal·i·ty \vī-'tal-ət-ē\ n, pl **-ties** 1 a : the peculiarity distinguishing the living from the nonliving b : capacity to live and develop; also : physical or mental vigor esp. when highly developed 2 a : power of enduring or continuing ⟨the vitality of bad habits⟩ b : lively and animated character : VIGOR

vi·tal·ize \'vīt-°l-,īz\ vt : to endow with vitality : ANIMATE — **vi·tal·i·za·tion** \,vīt-°l-ə-'zā-shən\ n

vi·tals \'vīt-°lz\ n pl 1 : vital organs 2 : essential parts

vital statistics n sing or pl : statistics relating to births, deaths, marriages, health, and disease

vi·ta·mer \'vīt-ə-mər\ n [vitamin + isomer] : any of two or more compounds that relieve a particular vitamin deficiency — **vi·ta·mer·ic** \,vīt-ə-'mer-ik\ adj

vi·ta·min \'vīt-ə-mən\ n [L vita life + E amine] : any of various organic substances that are essential in minute quantities to the nutrition of most animals and some plants, act in the regulation of metabolic processes but do not provide energy or serve as building units, and are present in natural foodstuffs or sometimes produced within the body

vitamin A n : a fat-soluble vitamin or vitamin mixture found esp. in animal products (as egg yolk, milk, or fish-liver oils) whose lack causes injury to epithelial tissues (as in the eye with resulting visual defects)

vitamin B n 1 : VITAMIN B COMPLEX 2 : THIAMINE — called also vitamin B₁ \-'bē-'wən\

vitamin B complex n : a group of water-soluble vitamins found widely in foods that include essential coenzymes and growth factors — called also B complex;

compare BIOTIN, CHOLINE, NICOTINIC ACID, PANTOTHENIC ACID, THIAMINE

vitamin B₆ \-'bē-'siks\ *n* : pyridoxine or a closely related compound

vitamin B₁₂ \-'bē-'twelv\ *n* : a complex cobalt-containing member of the vitamin B complex that occurs esp. in liver, is essential to normal blood formation, neural function, and growth, and is used esp. in treating pernicious anemia

vitamin B₂ \-'bē-'tü\ *n* : RIBOFLAVIN

vitamin C *n* : a water-soluble vitamin $C_6H_8O_6$ that is present esp. in fruits and leafy vegetables, apparently functions as an enzyme in certain bodily oxidations and syntheses, and is used medicinally in the prevention and treatment of scurvy

vitamin D *n* : any or all of several fat-soluble vitamins that are chemically related to steroids, are essential for normal bone and tooth structure, and are found esp. in fish-liver oils, egg yolk, and milk or produced by activation (as by ultraviolet irradiation) of sterols

vitamin E *n* : any of several tocopherols of which the lack in various mammals and birds is associated with infertility, muscular dystrophy, or vascular abnormalities and which occur esp. in leaves and in seed-germ oils

vitamin G *n* : RIBOFLAVIN

vi·ta·min·ize \'vīt-ə-mə-ˌnīz\ *vt* **1** : to provide or supplement with vitamins **2** : to make vigorous as if by the feeding of vitamins

vitamin K *n* : any of several fat-soluble vitamins essential for the clotting of blood because of their role in the production of prothrombin

vi·tel·line \vī-'tel-ən, və-\ *adj* [L *vitellus* yolk, lit., small calf] : of, relating to, resembling, or producing yolk

vi·ti·ate \'vish-ē-ˌāt\ *vt* [L *vitiare*, fr. *vitium* fault, vice] **1** : to injure the quality of : SPOIL, DEBASE **2** : to destroy the validity of (fraud *vitiates* a contract) — **vi·ti·a·tion** \ˌvish-ē-'ā-shən\ *n* — **vi·ti·a·tor** \'vish-ē-ˌāt-ər\ *n*

vit·i·cul·ture \'vit-ə-ˌkəl-chər\ *n* [L *vitis* vine] : the growing of grapes — **vit·i·cul·tur·al** \ˌvit-ə-'kəlch-(ə-)rəl\ *adj* — **vit·i·cul·tur·ist** \-'kəlch-(ə-)rəst\ *n*

vit·i·li·go \ˌvit-°l-'ī-gō\ *n* [L, tetter] : a skin disorder in which smooth white spots appear on the body

vit·re·ous \'vi-trē-əs\ *adj* [L *vitreus*, fr. *vitrum* glass] **1** : of, relating to, derived from, or resembling glass : GLASSY (*vitreous* rocks)(a *vitreous* luster) **2** : of, relating to, or being the vitreous humor — **vit·re·ous·ness** *n*

vitreous humor *n* : the clear colorless transparent jelly that fills the eyeball posterior to the lens

vit·ri·fy \'vi-trə-ˌfī\ *vb* **-fied; -fy·ing** : to change into glass or a glassy substance by heat and fusion — **vit·ri·fi·a·ble** \-ˌfī-ə-bəl\ *adj* — **vit·ri·fi·ca·tion** \ˌvi-trə-fə-'kā-shən\ *n*

vit·ri·ol \'vi-trē-əl\ *n* [ML *vitriolum*, fr. L *vitreus* vitreous] **1 a** : a sulfate of any of various metals (as copper, iron, or zinc) **b** : SULFURIC ACID **2** : something resembling vitriol in caustic quality; *esp* : virulence of feeling or of speech — **vit·ri·ol·ic** \ˌvi-trē-'äl-ik\ *adj*

vit·ta \'vit-ə\ *n, pl* **vit·tae** \'vit-ē\ [L, fillet] : STRIPE, STREAK — **vit·tate** \'vi-ˌtāt\ *adj*

vit·tle \'vit-°l\ *n* : VICTUAL

vi·tu·per·ate \vī-'t(y)ü-pə-ˌrāt, və-\ *vt* [L *vituperare*, fr. *vitium* fault + *parare* to make] : to abuse or censure severely or abusively : BERATE — **vi·tu·per·a·tive** \-'t(y)ü-p(ə-)rət-iv, -pə-ˌrāt-\ *adj* — **vi·tu·per·a·tive·ly** *adv* — **vi·tu·per·a·tor** \-pə-ˌrāt-ər\ *n* — **vi·tu·per·a·to·ry** \-rə-ˌtȯr-ē, -ˌtōr-ē, -ˌtȯr-\ *adj*

vi·tu·per·a·tion \-ˌt(y)ü-pə-'rā-shən\ *n* : sustained and bitter railing and condemnation **syn** see ABUSE

vi·va \'vē-və, -ˌvä\ *interj* [It, long live, fr. 3d pers. sing. pres. subj. of *vivere* to live, fr. L] — used to express goodwill or approval

vi·va·ce \vē-'väch-ā\ *adv (or adj)* [It, lit., vivacious] : in a brisk spirited manner — used as a direction in music

vi·va·cious \və-'vā-shəs, vī-\ *adj* [L *vivac-, vivax*, lit., long-lived, fr. *vivere* to live] : lively in temper or conduct : SPRIGHTLY **syn** see LIVELY — **vi·va·cious·ly** *adv* — **vi·va·cious·ness** *n*

vi·vac·i·ty \-'vas-ət-ē\ *n* : the quality or state of being vivacious

vi·var·i·um \vī-'ver-ē-əm\ *n, pl* **-ia** \-ē-ə\ *or* **-i·ums** : an enclosure for keeping or raising and observing

animals or plants indoors; *esp* : one for terrestrial animals — called also *terrarium*

¹vi·va vo·ce \ˌvī-və-'vō-sē\ *adv* [ML, with the living voice] : by word of mouth : ORALLY

²viva voce *adj* : expressed or conducted by word of mouth : ORAL

Viv·i·an *or* **Viv·i·en** \'viv-ē-ən\ *n* : the mistress of Merlin in Arthurian legend

viv·id \'viv-əd\ *adj* [L *vividus*, fr. *vivere* to live; akin to E *quick*] **1** : having the appearance of vigorous life or freshness : very lively (a *vivid* sketch) **2** : very strong or intense : of very high saturation (a *vivid* red) **3** : producing a strong or clear impression on the senses : SHARP; *esp* : producing distinct mental images (a *vivid* description) **4** : acting clearly and vigorously (a *vivid* imagination) **syn** see GRAPHIC — **viv·id·ly** *adv* — **viv·id·ness** *n*

viv·i·fy \'viv-ə-ˌfī\ *vt* **-fied; -fy·ing 1** : to endue with life : QUICKEN, ANIMATE **2** : to make vivid — **viv·i·fi·ca·tion** \ˌviv-ə-fə-'kā-shən\ *n* — **viv·i·fi·er** \'viv-ə-ˌfī-(ə)r\ *n*

vi·vip·a·rous \vī-'vip-(ə-)rəs\ *adj* [L *vivus* alive + *parere* to produce] : producing living young from within the body rather than from eggs — **vi·vi·par·i·ty** \ˌvī-və-'par-ət-ē\ *n* — **vi·vip·a·rous·ly** \vī-'vip-(ə-)rəs-lē\ *adv* — **vi·vip·a·rous·ness** *n*

vivi·sec·tion \ˌviv-ə-'sek-shən\ *n* [L *vivus* alive] : the cutting of or operation on a living animal usu. for scientific investigation; *also* : animal experimentation esp. if considered to cause distress to the subject — **vivi·sect** \'viv-ə-ˌsekt\ *vb* — **vivi·sec·tion·al** \ˌviv-ə-'sek-shnəl, -shən-°l\ *adj* — **vivi·sec·tion·al·ly** \-ē\ *adv* — **vivi·sec·tion·ist** \-'sek-sh(ə-)nəst\ *n* — **vivi·sec·tor** \'viv-ə-ˌsek-tər\ *n*

vix·en \'vik-sən\ *n* [alter. of ME *fixen*, fr. OE *fyxe*, fem. of *fox*] **1** : a female fox **2** : a shrewish ill-tempered woman — **vix·en·ish** \-s(ə-)nish\ *adj* — **vix·en·ish·ly** *adv*

viz·ard \'viz-ərd\ *n* [alter. of ME *viser* mask, visor] **1** : a mask for disguise or protection **2** : DISGUISE, GUISE

vi·zier \və-'zi(ə)r\ *n* [Turk *vezir*, fr. Ar *wazīr*] : a high executive officer of various Muslim countries and esp. of the former Ottoman Empire — **vi·zier·i·al** \-'zir-ē-əl\ *adj* — **vi·zier·ship** \-'zi(ə)r-ˌship\ *n*

vi·zor *var of* VISOR

vo·ca·ble \'vō-kə-bəl\ *n* [L *vocabulum* name, term] : a word composed of various sounds or letters without regard to its meaning

vo·cab·u·lary \vō-'kab-yə-ˌler-ē\ *n, pl* **-lar·ies** [ML *vocabularium*, fr. L *vocabulum* name, term, fr. *vocare* to call] **1** : a list or collection of words or of words and phrases usu. alphabetically arranged and explained or defined **2** : a sum or stock of words employed by a language, group, individual, or work or in a field of knowledge

vocabulary entry *n* : a word (as the noun *book*), hyphenated or open compound (as the verb *book-match* or the noun *book review*), word element (as the affix *pro-*), abbreviation (as *agt*), verbalized symbol (as *Na*), or term (as *man in the street*) entered alphabetically in a dictionary for the purpose of definition or identification or expressly included as an inflectional form (as the noun *mice* or the verb *saw*) or as a derived form (as the noun *godlessness* or the adverb *globally*) or related phrase (as *one for the book*) run on at its base word and usu. set in a type (as boldface) readily distinguishable from that of the lightface running text which defines, explains, or identifies the entry

¹vo·cal \'vō-kəl\ *adj* [L *vocalis*, fr. *voc-, vox* voice] **1 a** : uttered by the voice : ORAL **b** : produced in the larynx : uttered with voice **2** : relating to, composed or arranged for, or sung by the human voice (*vocal* music) **3** : VOCALIC **4 a** : having or exercising the power of producing voice, speech, or sound **b** : EXPRESSIVE **c** : full of voices : RESOUNDING **d** : given to expressing oneself freely or insistently : OUTSPOKEN **e** : expressed in words **5** : of, relating to, or resembling the voice — **vo·cal·ly** \-kə-lē\ *adv*

²vocal *n* **1** : a vocal sound **2** : the vocal solo in a dance or jazz number

vocal cords *n pl* : either of two pairs of elastic folds of mucous membrane that project into the cavity of the larynx and have free edges extending dorsoventrally toward the

---

j joke; ŋ sing; ō flow; ȯ flaw; ȯi coin; th thin; t͟h this; ü loot; u̇ foot; y yet; yü few; yu̇ furious; zh vision

middle line and that play a major role in the production of vocal sounds — called also *vocal folds*

vo·cal·ic \vō-'kal-ik\ *adj* [L *vocalis* vowel, fr. *vocalis* vocal] **1** : marked by or consisting of vowels **2** : of, relating to, or functioning as a vowel — **vo·cal·i·cal·ly** \-'kal-i-k(ə-)lē\ *adv*

vo·cal·ist \'vō-kə-ləst\ *n* : SINGER

vo·cal·i·za·tion \,vō-kə-lə-'zā-shən\ *n* : an act, process, or instance of vocalizing

vo·cal·ize \'vō-kə-,līz\ *vb* **1 a** : to give vocal expression to   **b** : SING; *esp* : to sing without words (as in practicing) **2 a** : VOICE **b** : to convert to a vowel — **vo·cal·iz·er** *n*

vo·ca·tion \vō-'kā-shən\ *n* [L *vocation-, vocatio* summons, fr. *vocare* to call, fr. *voc-, vox* voice] **1 a** : a summons or strong inclination to a particular state or course of action; *esp* : a divine call to the religious life   **b** : the special function of an individual or group **2 a** : the work in which a person is regularly employed : OCCUPATION **b** : the persons engaged in a particular occupation
   syn AVOCATION: VOCATION denotes one's livelihood; AVOCATION denotes a leisure occupation which may or may not bring remuneration

vo·ca·tion·al \-shnəl, -shən-ᵊl\ *adj* **1** : of, relating to, or concerned with a vocation   **2** : concerned with choice of or training in a skill or trade to be pursued as a career ⟨*vocational* guidance⟩ ⟨*vocational* school⟩ — **vo·ca·tion·al·ly** \-ē\ *adv*

vo·ca·tion·al·ism \-,iz-əm\ *n* : emphasis on vocational training in education

voc·a·tive \'väk-ət-iv\ *adj* : of, relating to, or constituting a grammatical case marking the one addressed — **vocative** *n* — **voc·a·tive·ly** *adv*

vo·cif·er·ant \vō-'sif-ə-rənt\ *adj* : CLAMOROUS, VOCIFEROUS — **vo·cif·er·ance** \-rən(t)s\ *n*

vo·cif·er·ate \vō-'sif-ə-,rāt\ *vb* [L *vociferari*, fr. *voc-, vox* voice + *ferre* to carry] : to cry out or utter loudly : CLAMOR, SHOUT — **vo·cif·er·a·tion** \-,sif-ə-'rā-shən\ *n* — **vo·cif·er·a·tor** \-'sif-ə-,rāt-ər\ *n*

vo·cif·er·ous \vō-'sif-(ə-)rəs\ *adj* : making a loud outcry : NOISY, CLAMOROUS — **vo·cif·er·ous·ly** *adv* — **vo·cif·er·ous·ness** *n*

vod·ka \'väd-kə\ *n* [Russ, fr. *voda* water; akin to E *water*] : a colorless and unaged alcoholic liquor distilled from a mash (as of rye or wheat)

vogue \'vōg\ *n* [MF, action of rowing, course, fashion, fr. It *voga*, fr. *vogare* to row] **1** : the leading place in popularity or acceptance **2 a** : popular acceptation or favor : POPULARITY   **b** : a period of popularity **3** : something or someone in fashion at a particular time   **syn** see FASHION — **vogue** *adj*

vogu·ish \'vō-gish\ *adj* **1** : FASHIONABLE, SMART **2** : suddenly or temporarily popular

¹voice \'vois\ *n* [OF *vois*, fr. L *voc-, vox*] **1 a** : sound produced by vertebrates by means of lungs, larynx, or syrinx; *esp* : sound so produced by human beings   **b** (1) : musical sound produced by the vocal cords and resonated by the cavities of head and throat   (2) : the power or ability to produce musical tones   (3) : SINGER   (4) : one of the melodic parts in a vocal or instrumental composition   (5) : condition of the vocal organs with respect to production of musical tones   **c** : expiration of air with the vocal cords drawn close so as to vibrate audibly (as in uttering vowels and some consonants)   **d** : the faculty of utterance : SPEECH   **2** : a sound resembling or suggesting vocal utterance **3** : a medium of expression **4 a** : wish, choice, or opinion openly or formally expressed   **b** : right of expression : SUFFRAGE **5** : distinction of form or a system of inflections of a verb to indicate the relation of the subject of the verb to the action which the verb expresses — **with one voice** : UNANIMOUSLY

²voice *vt* **1** : UTTER **2** : to regulate the tone of (as organ pipes) **3** : to pronounce (as a consonant) with voice

voice box *n* : LARYNX

voiced \'voist\ *adj* **1 a** : furnished with a voice ⟨soft-*voiced*⟩   **b** : expressed by the voice ⟨a frequently *voiced* opinion⟩ **2** : uttered with vocal cord vibration ⟨*voiced* consonant⟩ — **voiced·ness** \'vois(t)-nəs, 'voi-səd-nəs\ *n*

voice·less \'vois-ləs\ *adj* **1** : having no voice : MUTE **2** : not voiced ⟨*voiceless* consonant⟩ — **voice·less·ly** *adv* — **voice·less·ness** *n*

voice part *n* : VOICE 1b (4)

voice·print \'vois-,print\ *n* [*voice* + *-print* (as in *fingerprint*)] : an individually distinctive pattern of certain voice characteristics that is spectrographically produced

¹void \'void\ *adj* [OF *voide*, fr. (assumed) VL *vocitus*, fr. L *vacuus* empty] **1** : containing nothing ⟨*void* space⟩ **2** : IDLE, LEISURE **3 a** : UNOCCUPIED, VACANT ⟨*void* bishopric⟩   **b** : DESERTED **4 a** : WANTING, DEVOID   **b** : having no members or examples ⟨bid a *void* suit as a slam signal⟩ **5** : of no legal force or effect : **syn** see EMPTY

²void *n* **1 a** : empty space : EMPTINESS, VACUUM   **b** : OPENING, GAP **2** : LACK, ABSENCE **3** : a feeling of want or hollowness **4** : absence of cards of a particular suit in a hand as dealt

³void *vt* **1 a** : to make empty or vacant : CLEAR   **b** : VACATE, LEAVE **2** : DISCHARGE, EMIT ⟨*void* excrement⟩ **3** : NULLIFY, ANNUL ⟨*void* a contract⟩ — **void·er** *n*

void·a·ble \'void-ə-bəl\ *adj* : capable of being voided

voile \'voil\ *n* [F, veil, fr. L *velum*] : a soft sheer fabric of silk, cotton, rayon, or wool used esp. for curtains or women's summer clothing

vo·lant \'vō-lənt\ *adj* **1** : having the wings extended as if in flight — used of a heraldic bird **2** : FLYING : capable of flying **3** : QUICK, NIMBLE

vo·lan·te \vō-'län-tā\ *adj* [It, lit., flying] : moving with light rapidity — used as a direction in music

vo·lar \'vō-lər\ *adj* [L *vola* palm, sole] : relating to the palm of the hand or the sole of the foot

¹vol·a·tile \'väl-ət-ᵊl\ *adj* [L *volatilis* flying, fr. *volare* to fly] **1** : readily becoming a vapor at a relatively low temperature ⟨a *volatile* solvent⟩ **2 a** : LIGHTHEARTED, LIVELY   **b** : easily aroused   **c** : tending to erupt into violent action **3** : CHANGEABLE, FICKLE **4** : TRANSITORY — **vol·a·tile·ness** *n* — **vol·a·til·i·ty** \,väl-ə-'til-ət-ē\ *n*

²volatile *n* : a volatile substance

vol·a·til·ize \'väl-ət-ᵊl-,īz\ *vb* : to pass off or make pass off in vapor — **vol·a·til·i·za·tion** \,väl-ət-ᵊl-ə-'zā-shən\ *n*

¹vol·can·ic \väl-'kan-ik\ *adj* **1 a** : of or relating to a volcano ⟨a *volcanic* eruption⟩   **b** : having volcanoes ⟨a *volcanic* region⟩   **c** : made of materials from volcanoes ⟨*volcanic* dust⟩ **2** : explosively violent : VOLATILE — **vol·can·i·cal·ly** \-'kan-i-k(ə-)lē\ *adv*

²volcanic *n* : a volcanic rock

volcanic glass *n* : natural glass produced by the cooling of molten lava too rapidly to permit crystallization

vol·ca·nism \'väl-kə-,niz-əm\ *n* : volcanic power or action

vol·ca·nist \'väl-kə-nəst\ *n* : a specialist in the study of volcanic phenomena

vol·ca·no \väl-'kā-nō\ *n, pl* **-noes** *or* **-nos** [It *vulcano*, fr. L *Volcanus, Vulcanus* Vulcan] : a vent in the earth's crust from which molten or hot rock and steam issue; *also* : a hill or mountain composed wholly or in part of the ejected material

vol·ca·nol·o·gy \,väl-kə-'näl-ə-jē\ *n* : a branch of science that deals with volcanic phenomena — **vol·ca·no·log·i·cal** \,väl-kən-ᵊl-'äj-i-kəl\ *adj* — **vol·ca·nol·o·gist** \-kə-'näl-ə-jəst\ *n*

vole \'vōl\ *n* [of Scand origin] : any of various small rodents closely related to the lemmings and muskrats but in general resembling stocky mice or rats

vo·li·tion \vō-'lish-ən\ *n* [ML *volition-, volitio*, fr. L *vol-, velle* to will, wish] **1** : the act or power of making one's own choices or decisions : WILL **2** : the choice made or decision reached — **vo·li·tion·al** \-'lish-nəl, -ən-ᵊl\ *adj*

vol·i·tive \'väl-ət-iv\ *adj* **1** : of or relating to the will **2** : expressing a wish or permission

volks·lied \'fōks-,lēt\ *n, pl* **volks·lie·der** \-,slēd-ər\ [G] : FOLK SONG

¹vol·ley \'väl-ē\ *n, pl* **volleys** [MF *volee* flight, fr. *voler* to fly, fr. L *volare*] **1 a** : a flight of missiles (as arrows or bullets)   **b** : simultaneous discharge of a number of missile weapons (as rifles)   **c** : one round per gun in a battery fired as soon as each gun is ready   **d** (1) : the flight of the ball in tennis or its course before striking the ground; *also* : a return of the ball before it touches the ground   (2) : a kick of the ball in soccer before it rebounds   (3) : the exchange of the shuttlecock in badminton following the serve **2** : a bursting forth of many things at once ⟨a *volley* of bubbles⟩ ⟨a *volley* of curses⟩

²volley *vb* **vol·leyed; vol·ley·ing** **1** : to discharge in a volley **2** : to propel an object while in the air and before touching the ground; *esp* **:** to hit a tennis ball on the volley

vol·ley·ball \'väl-ē-,ból\ *n* **:** a game played by volleying a large inflated ball over a net

¹vol·plane \'väl-,plān\ *n* [F *vol plané*, lit., gliding flight] **:** a glide in an airplane

²volplane *vi* **:** to glide in or as if in an airplane

¹volt \'vōlt, 'vólt\ *n* **:** a leaping movement in fencing to avoid a thrust

²volt \'vōlt\ *n* [fr. Alessandro *Volta* d1827 Italian physicist] **:** the practical mks unit of electrical potential difference and electromotive force equal to the difference of potential between two points in a conducting wire carrying a constant current of one ampere when the power dissipated between these two points is equal to one watt and equivalent to the potential difference across a resistance of one ohm when one ampere is flowing through it

volt·age \'vōl-tij\ *n* **:** potential difference expressed in volts

voltage divider *n* **:** a resistor or series of resistors provided with taps at certain points and used to provide various potential differences from a single power source

vol·ta·ic \väl-'tā-ik, vōl-\ *adj* [fr. A. *Volta*] **:** of, relating to, or producing direct electric current by chemical action (as in a battery)

voltaic cell *n* **:** an apparatus for generating electricity through chemical action on two unlike metals in an electrolyte

voltaic pile *n* **:** ³PILE 3a

volt·am·e·ter \vōl-'tam-ət-ər, 'vōl-tə-,mēt-\ *n* **:** an apparatus for measuring the quantity of electricity passed through a conductor by the amount of electrolysis produced (as by measuring the gases generated or by weighing the metal deposited)

volt–am·pere \'vōlt-'am-,pi(ə)r\ *n* **:** a unit of electric measurement equal to the product of a volt and an ampere that for direct current constitutes a measure of power equivalent to a watt and for alternating current a measure of apparent power

volte–face \,vólt-(ə-)'fäs\ *n* [F, fr. It *voltafaccia*] **:** a facing about esp. in policy **:** ABOUT-FACE

volt·me·ter \'vōlt-,mēt-ər\ *n* **:** an instrument for measuring in volts the differences of potential between different points of an electrical circuit

vol·u·ble \'väl-yə-bəl\ *adj* [L *volubilis* rolling, fluent, fr. *volvere* to roll] **1 :** having the power or habit of twining ⟨*voluble* plant stem⟩ **2 :** characterized by ready or rapid speech **:** GLIB, FLUENT **syn** see TALKATIVE — **vol·u·bil·i·ty** \,väl-yə-'bil-ət-ē\ *n* — **vol·u·bly** \'väl-yə-blē\ *adv*

vol·u·ble·ness \'väl-yə-bəl-nəs\ *n* **:** VOLUBILITY

vol·ume \'väl-yəm\ *n* [MF, fr. L *volumen* roll, book in the form of a roll of papyrus, fr. *volvere* to roll] **1 :** BOOK ⟨a dozen *volumes* on the shelf⟩ **2 :** any of a series of books forming a complete work or collection ⟨the 5th *volume* of an encyclopedia⟩ **3 :** space occupied **:** bounded space as measured in cubic units ⟨the *volume* of a cylinder⟩ **4 a :** a large amount ⟨*volumes* of smoke⟩ **b :** the representation of mass (as in painting) **5 :** intensity or quantity of tone **:** LOUDNESS ⟨turn up the *volume* on the radio⟩ **syn** see BULK

vol·u·met·ric \,väl-yə-'me-trik\ *adj* **:** of or relating to the measurement of volume — **vol·u·met·ri·cal·ly** \-tri-k(ə-)lē\ *adv*

vo·lu·mi·nous \və-'lü-mə-nəs\ *adj* [L *volumin-, volumen* roll, volume] **1 :** consisting of many folds, coils, or convolutions **:** WINDING **2 a :** having or marked by great volume or bulk **:** LARGE; *esp* **:** FULL **b :** NUMEROUS **3 a :** filling or capable of filling a large volume or several volumes **b :** writing or speaking much or at great length — **vo·lu·mi·nous·ly** *adv* — **vo·lu·mi·nous·ness** *n*

vol·un·tar·i·ly \,väl-ən-'ter-ə-lē\ *adv* **:** of one's own free will

¹vol·un·tary \'väl-ən-,ter-ē\ *adj* [L *voluntarius*, fr. *voluntas* will, fr. *vol-, velle* to will, wish; akin to E *will*] **1 :** done, given, or made in accordance with one's own free will or choice ⟨*voluntary* assistance⟩ **2 :** not accidental **:** INTENTIONAL ⟨*voluntary* manslaughter⟩ **3 :** of or relating to the will **:** controlled by the will ⟨*voluntary* behavior⟩

syn VOLUNTARY, INTENTIONAL, DELIBERATE mean done or brought about of one's own accord. VOLUNTARY implies spontaneousness and freedom from compulsion ⟨*voluntary* contributions⟩ or stresses control of the will ⟨*voluntary* eye movements⟩ INTENTIONAL stresses consciousness of purpose ⟨an *intentional* oversight⟩ DELIBERATE implies full consciousness of the nature of an intended action ⟨a *deliberate* insult⟩

²voluntary *n, pl* **-tar·ies :** a prefatory often extemporized musical piece; *also* **:** an organ piece played before, during, or after a religious service

voluntary muscle *n* **:** muscle (as most striated muscle) under voluntary control

¹vol·un·teer \,väl-ən-'ti(ə)r\ *n* [F *volontaire*, fr. *volontaire* voluntary, fr. L *voluntarius*] **1 :** one who enters into or offers himself for any service of his own free will; *esp* **:** one who enters into military service voluntarily **2 :** a volunteer plant

²volunteer *adj* **1 :** of, relating to, or consisting of volunteers **:** VOLUNTARY ⟨a *volunteer* army⟩ **2 :** growing spontaneously without direct human care esp. from seeds lost from a previous crop

³volunteer *vb* **1 :** to offer or bestow voluntarily ⟨*volunteered* his services⟩ **2 :** to offer oneself as a volunteer

vo·lup·tu·ary \və-'ləp-chə-,wer-ē\ *n, pl* **-ar·ies :** one whose chief interest is luxury and the gratification of sensual appetites **:** SENSUALIST — **voluptuary** *adj*

vo·lup·tu·ate \-,wāt\ *vi* **:** LUXURIATE

vo·lup·tu·ous \və-'ləp-chə-wəs, -chəs\ *adj* [L *voluptuosus*, fr. *voluptas* pleasure] **1 :** giving pleasure to the senses **:** providing sensual or sensuous gratification ⟨*voluptuous* furnishings⟩ ⟨*voluptuous* dancers⟩ **2 :** being a voluptuary — **vo·lup·tu·ous·ly** *adv* — **vo·lup·tu·ous·ness** *n*

vo·lute \və-'lüt\ *n* [L *voluta*, fr. *volvere* to roll] **1 :** a spiral or scroll-shaped form **2 a :** a spiral scroll-shaped ornament forming the chief feature of the Ionic capital **b :** a turn of a spiral shell — **vo·lute** or **vo·lut·ed** \-'lüt-əd\ *adj*

vol·va \'väl-və\ *n* **:** a membranous sac or cup about the base of the stem in many mushrooms — **vol·vate** \-,vāt\ *adj*

volute 1

vol·vox \'väl-,väks\ *n* **:** any of a genus of green flagellates that form spherical colonies

vo·mer \'vō-mər\ *n* [L, plowshare] **:** a bone of the lower skull of most vertebrates that in man forms part of the nasal septum — **vo·mer·ine** \-mə-,rīn\ *adj*

¹vom·it \'väm-ət\ *n* [L *vomitus*, fr. *vomere* to vomit] **:** an act or instance of disgorging the contents of the stomach through the mouth; *also* **:** the disgorged matter

²vomit *vb* **1 :** to disgorge the contents of the stomach through the mouth **2 :** to spew forth **:** BELCH, GUSH ⟨lava *vomited* from the volcano⟩ — **vom·it·er** *n*

vom·i·tus \'väm-ət-əs\ *n* [L, fr. *vomere* to vomit] **:** material discharged by vomiting

¹voo·doo \'vüd-ü\ *n, pl* **voodoos** [LaF *voudou*, of African origin] **1 :** VOODOOISM **2 a :** one who deals in spells and necromancy **b** (1) **:** a sorcerer's spell (2) **:** a hexed object — **voodoo** *adj*

²voodoo *vt* **:** to bewitch by or as if by means of voodoo **:** HEX

voo·doo·ism \'vüd-ü-,iz-əm\ *n* **1 :** a religion derived from African ancestor worship, practiced chiefly by Negroes of Haiti, and consisting largely of magic and sorcery **2 :** the practice of witchcraft — **voo·doo·ist** \'vüd-,ü-əst\ *n* — **voo·doo·is·tic** \,vüd-ü-'is-tik\ *adj*

vo·ra·cious \vȯ-'rā-shəs, və-\ *adj* [L *vorac-, vorax*, fr. *vorare* to devour] **1 :** greedy in eating **:** RAVENOUS ⟨a *voracious* animal⟩ ⟨a *voracious* appetite⟩ **2 :** excessively eager **:** INSATIABLE — **vo·ra·cious·ly** *adv* — **vo·rac·i·ty** \-'ras-ət-ē\ *n*

vor·tex \'vȯr-,teks\ *n, pl* **vor·ti·ces** \-tə-,sēz\ *also* **vor·tex·es** [L *vertic-, vertex, vortic-, vortex* whirlpool, fr. *vertere* to turn] **1 :** a mass of fluid and esp. of a liquid having a whirling motion tending to form a cavity in the center and to draw things toward this cavity; *esp* **:** WHIRLPOOL, EDDY **2 :** a whirling mass (as a whirlwind, tornado, or waterspout); *also* **:** the eye of a cyclone

vor·ti·cal \'vȯrt-i-kəl\ *adj* **:** of, relating to, or resembling a vortex **:** SWIRLING

vor·ti·cel·la \,vȯrt-ə-'sel-ə\ *n, pl* **-cel·lae** \-'sel-(,)ē\ *or* **-cellas :** any of a genus of stalked bell-shaped ciliates

vor·tic·i·ty \vȯr-'tis-ət-ē\ *n* : the state of a fluid in vortical motion

vo·ta·rist \'vōt-ə-rəst\ *n* : VOTARY

vo·ta·ry \'vōt-ə-rē\ *n, pl* **-ries** [L *votum* vow] **1 a :** ENTHUSIAST, DEVOTEE **b :** a devoted adherent or admirer **2 :** a devout or zealous worshiper

¹vote \'vōt\ *n* [L *votum* vow, wish, fr. *vovēre* to vow] **1 a :** a formal expression of opinion or will; *esp* : one given as an indication of approval or disapproval of a proposal or a candidate for office **b :** the total number of such expressions of opinion made known at a single time (as at an election) **c :** BALLOT 1 **2 :** the collective opinion of a body of persons expressed by voting **3 :** the right to cast a vote : SUFFRAGE **4 a :** the act or process of voting (bring the issue to a *vote*) **b :** a method of voting **5 a :** VOTER **b :** a group of voters with common characteristics (the farm *vote*)

²vote *vb* **1 :** to express one's wish or choice by a vote : cast a vote **2 :** to make into law by a vote (*vote* an income tax) **3 :** ELECT (*vote* someone into office) **4 :** to declare by common consent **5 :** PROPOSE, SUGGEST

vote·less \'vōt-ləs\ *adj* : having no vote; *esp* : denied the political franchise

vot·er \'vōt-ər\ *n* : one that votes or has the legal right to vote

voting machine *n* : a mechanical device for recording and counting votes cast in an election

vo·tive \'vōt-iv\ *adj* [L *votum* vow] **1 :** offered or performed in fulfillment of a vow or in gratitude or devotion **2 :** consisting of or expressing a vow, wish, or desire (a *votive* prayer) — **vo·tive·ly** *adv* — **vo·tive·ness** *n*

votive mass *n* : a mass celebrated for a special intention in place of the mass of the day

vouch \'vaůch\ *vb* [ME *vouchen* to summon into court to give warranty, fr. MF *vocher*, fr. L *vocare* to call] **1** *archaic* **a :** ASSERT, AFFIRM **b :** ATTEST **2** *archaic* : to cite or refer to as authority or supporting evidence **3 :** PROVE, SUBSTANTIATE **4 :** to give a guarantee : become surety (I'll *vouch* for his honesty) **5 a :** to supply supporting evidence or testimony **b :** to give personal assurance (*vouch* for the truth of a story)

vouch·ee \vaů-'chē\ *n* : one for whom another vouches

vouch·er \'vaů-chər\ *n* **1 :** one who vouches for another **2 :** a document that serves to establish the truth of something; *esp* : a paper (as a receipt) showing payment of a bill or debt

vouch·safe \vaůch-'sāf\ *vt* : to grant in the manner of one doing a favor : condescend to give or grant

vous·soir \vü-'swär\ *n* [F] : one of the wedge-shaped pieces forming an arch or vault

¹vow \'vaů\ *n* [OF *vowe*, fr. L *votum*, fr. *vovēre* to vow] : a solemn promise or assertion; *esp* : one by which a person binds himself to an act, service, or condition

²vow *vb* **1 :** to make a vow or as a vow **2 :** to bind or consecrate by a vow

³vow *vb* : AVOW, DECLARE

vow·el \'vaů(-ə)l\ *n* [MF *vouel*, fr. L *vocalis*, fr. *vocalis* vocal] **1 :** a speech sound in the articulation of which the oral part of the breath channel is not blocked and is not constricted enough to cause audible friction **2 :** a letter representing a vowel; *esp* : any of the letters *a, e, i, o, u,* and sometimes *y* in English — **vow·el·like** \'vaů(-ə)l-‚līk\ *adj*

vox po·pu·li \'väks-'päp-yə-‚lī\ *n* [L, voice of the people] : popular sentiment

¹voy·age \'vȯi-ij\ *n* [OF *voiage* journey, fr. LL *viaticum*, fr. L *viaticus* of a journey, fr. *via* way] **1 :** a journey by water : CRUISE **2 :** a journey through air or space

²voyage *vb* **1 :** to take a trip : TRAVEL **2 :** SAIL, TRAVERSE — **voy·ag·er** *n*

voya·geur \‚vwä-‚yä-'zhər\ *n* [CanF, fr. F, traveler] : a man employed by a fur company to transport goods and men to and from remote stations in the Northwest

Vul·can \'vəl-kən\ *n* : the god of fire and of metalworking in Roman mythology

Vul·ca·ni·an \‚vəl-'kā-nē-ən\ *adj* : of or relating to Vulcan or to working in metals (as iron)

vul·can·ism \'vəl-kə-‚niz-əm\ *n* : VOLCANISM

vul·can·ite \-‚nīt\ *n* : a hard vulcanized rubber

vul·can·ize \'vəl-kə-‚nīz\ *vb* [L *Vulcanus* Vulcan, fire] : to treat rubber or similar plastic material chemically

in order to give it useful properties (as elasticity, strength, or stability) — **vul·can·i·za·tion** \‚vəl-kə-nə-'zā-shən\ *n* — **vul·can·iz·er** \'vəl-kə-‚nī-zər\ *n*

vul·gar \'vəl-gər\ *adj* [L *vulgaris* of the mob, vulgar, fr. *vulgus* mob, common people] **1 a :** generally used, applied, or accepted **b :** having or understanding in the ordinary sense **2 :** VERNACULAR **3 a :** of or relating to the common people : PLEBEIAN **b :** generally current : PUBLIC **c :** of the usual, typical, or ordinary kind **4 a :** lacking in cultivation, perception, or taste : COARSE **b :** morally crude or undeveloped : GROSS **c :** ostentatious or excessive in expenditure or display : PRETENTIOUS **5 a :** offensive in language : EARTHY **b :** OBSCENE, PROFANE — **vul·gar·ly** *adv*

vul·gar·i·an \‚vəl-'gar-ē-ən, -'ger-\ *n* : a vulgar person

vul·gar·ism \'vəl-gə-‚riz-əm\ *n* **1 a :** a word or expression originated or used chiefly by illiterate persons **b :** a coarse word or phrase **2 :** VULGARITY

vul·gar·i·ty \‚vəl-'gar-ət-ē\ *n, pl* **-ties** **1 :** the quality or state of being vulgar **2 :** something vulgar

vul·gar·ize \'vəl-gə-‚rīz\ *vt* **1 :** to diffuse generally : POPULARIZE **2 :** to make vulgar : COARSEN — **vul·gar·i·za·tion** \‚vəl-gə-rə-'zā-shən\ *n* — **vul·gar·iz·er** \'vəl-gə-‚rī-zər\ *n*

Vulgar Latin *n* : the nonliterary Latin of ancient Rome including the speech of plebeians and the informal speech of the educated established by comparative evidence as the chief source of the Romance languages

Vul·gate \'vəl-‚gāt\ *n* [LL *vulgata editio* edition in general circulation] : a Latin version of the Bible authorized and used by the Roman Catholic Church

vul·ner·a·ble \'vəln-(ə-)rə-bəl, 'vəl-nər-bəl\ *adj* [L *vulnerare* to wound, fr. *vulner-, vulnus* wound] **1 :** capable of being wounded **2 :** open to attack or damage : ASSAILABLE (a *vulnerable* fort) **3 :** liable to increased penalties but entitled to increased bonuses in a game of contract bridge — **vul·ner·a·bil·i·ty** \‚vəln-(ə-)rə-'bil-ət-ē\ *n* — **vul·ner·a·bly** \'vəln-(ə-)rə-blē, 'vəl-nər-blē\ *adv*

vul·pine \'vəl-‚pīn\ *adj* [L *vulpes* fox] : of, relating to, or resembling a fox esp. in cunning : CRAFTY

vul·ture \'vəl-chər\ *n* [L *vultur*] **1 :** any of various large birds that are related to the hawks and eagles but have weaker claws and the head usu. naked and that subsist chiefly or entirely on carrion **2 :** a greedy or predatory person

vul·va \'vəl-və\ *n* [L] : the external parts of the female genital organs; *also* : the opening between their projecting parts — **vul·val** \'vəl-vəl\ *or* **vul·var** \-vər\ *adj*

vying *pres part of* VIE

vulture

w \'dəb-əl-‚(‚)yü, -yə\ *n, often cap* : the 23d letter of the English alphabet

wab·ble \'wäb-əl\ *var of* WOBBLE

Wac \'wak\ *n* : a member of the Women's Army Corps established in the U.S. during World War II

wacky \'wak-ē\ *adj* **wack·i·er; -est** : absurdly or amusingly eccentric or irrational : CRAZY — **wack·i·ly** \'wak-ə-lē\ *adv* — **wack·i·ness** \'wak-ē-nəs\ *n*

¹wad \'wäd\ *n* **1 :** a small mass, bundle, or tuft (plugged the hole with *wads* of clay): as **a :** a soft mass of usu. light fibrous material **b :** a pliable pad or plug (as of felt) used to retain a powder charge in a gun or cartridge — see SHELL illustration **c :** a roll of paper money : a considerable amount (as of money)

²wad *vt* **wad·ded; wad·ding 1 :** to form into a wad (*wad* up a handkerchief) **2 :** to push a wad into (*wad* a gun) **3 :** to hold in by a wad (*wad* a bullet in a gun) **4 :** to stuff or line with a wad or padding

wad·a·ble *or* **wade·a·ble** \'wād-ə-bəl\ *adj* : capable of being waded (a *wadable* stream)

wad·ding \'wäd-iŋ\ *n* **1 :** wads or material for making

wads 2 : a soft mass or sheet of short loose fibers used for stuffing or padding

¹wad·dle \'wäd-°l\ *vi* **wad·dled; wad·dling** \'wäd-liŋ, -°l-iŋ\ [freq. of *wade*] : to walk with short steps swaying from side to side like a duck — **wad·dler** \'wäd-lər, -°l-ər\ *n*

²waddle *n* : an awkward clumsy swaying gait

¹wade \'wād\ *vb* [OE *wadan*] **1** : to step in or through a medium (as water) offering more resistance than air **2** : to move or proceed with difficulty or labor and often with determined vigor ⟨*wade* through a dull book⟩ ⟨*wade* into a task⟩ **3** : to pass or cross by wading

²wade *n* : an act of wading ⟨a *wade* in the brook⟩

wad·er \'wād-ər\ *n* **1** : one that wades **2** : WADING BIRD **3** *pl* : high waterproof boots or trousers for wading

wa·di \'wäd-ē\ *n* [Ar *wādiy*] : a stream bed or valley esp. of southwestern Asia and northern Africa that is usu. dry except during the rainy season

wading bird *n* : any of many long-legged birds including the shorebirds and various inland water birds (as cranes and herons) that wade in water in search of food

wading pool *n* : a shallow pool of portable or permanent construction used by children for wading

Waf \'waf\ *n* : a member of the women's component of the U.S. Air Force formed after World War II

wa·fer \'wā-fər\ *n* [ONF *waufre*, of Gmc origin; akin to E *weave*] **1 a** : a thin crisp cake or cracker **b** : a round thin piece of unleavened bread in the Eucharist **2** : something (as a piece of candy or an adhesive seal) resembling a wafer esp. in thin round form

waf·fle \'wäf-əl\ *n* [D *wafel*; akin to E *weave*] : a crisp cake of pancake batter baked in a waffle iron

waffle iron *n* : a cooking utensil with two hinged metal parts that shut upon each other and impress surface projections on a waffle

¹waft \'wäft, 'waft\ *vb* [(assumed) ME *waughten* to guard, convoy, convey, fr. MD or MLG *wachten* to watch, guard] : to cause to move or go lightly by or as if by the impulse of wind or waves — **waft·er** *n*

²waft *n* **1** : a slight breeze : PUFF **2** : the act of waving

waft·age \'wäf-tij, 'waf-\ *n* : the act of wafting : the state of being wafted; *also* : CONVEYANCE

¹wag \'wag\ *vb* **wagged; wag·ging** [ME *waggen*] : to swing to and fro or from side to side ⟨the dog *wagged* his tail⟩ — **wag·ger** *n*

²wag *n* **1** : WIT, JOKER **2** : an act of wagging : a wagging movement

¹wage \'wāj\ *vb* **wagen** to pledge, give as security, fr. ONF *wagier*, fr. *wage* pledge] **1** : to engage in or carry on ⟨*wage* war⟩ ⟨*wage* a campaign⟩ **2** : to be in process of being waged

²wage *n* [ME, pledge, wage, fr. ONF, of Gmc origin; akin to E *wed*] **1** : payment for labor or services usu. according to contract and on an hourly, daily, or piece-work basis **2** *pl* : RECOMPENSE, REWARD

syn WAGE, SALARY, STIPEND, FEE mean the price paid for labor or services. WAGE implies a regular amount paid daily or weekly esp. for chiefly physical labor; SALARY and STIPEND apply to a fixed amount paid usu. at longer intervals for services requiring training or special ability; STIPEND may also imply a grant or allowance rather than direct pay for work done; FEE applies to the sum asked for the services of a doctor, lawyer, artist, or other professional

wage earner *n* : one that works for wages or salary

wage·less \'wāj-ləs\ *adj* : having no wages : UNPAID

wage level *n* : the approximate position of wages at any given time in any occupation or trade or esp. in industry at large

¹wa·ger \'wā-jər\ *n* [ME, pledge, bet, fr. AF *wageure*, fr. ONF *wagier* to pledge] **1** : something risked on an uncertain event : STAKE **2** : an act of betting : GAMBLE

²wager *vb* **wa·gered; wa·ger·ing** \'wāj-(ə-)riŋ\ : to hazard on an issue : RISK, VENTURE; *esp* : GAMBLE, BET — **wa·ger·er** \'wā-jər-ər\ *n*

wage scale *n* **1** : a schedule of rates of wages paid for related tasks **2** : the level of wages paid by an employer

wag·gery \'wag-ə-rē\ *n*, *pl* **-ger·ies 1** : mischievous merriment : PLEASANTRY **2** : JEST; *esp* : PRACTICAL JOKE

wag·gish \'wag-ish\ *adj* **1** : resembling or characteristic of a wag : FROLICSOME **2** : done or made in waggery or

for sport : HUMOROUS ⟨a *waggish* trick⟩ — **wag·gish·ly** *adv* — **wag·gish·ness** *n*

wag·gle \'wag-əl\ *vb* **wag·gled; wag·gling** \'wag-(ə-)liŋ\ : to move backward and forward or from side to side : WAG — **waggle** *n* — **wag·gly** \-(ə-)lē\ *adj*

Wag·ne·ri·an \väg-'nir-ē-ən\ *adj* : of, relating to, or characteristic of Richard Wagner or his music

wag·on \'wag-ən\ *n* [D *wagen*; akin to E *wain*] **1** : a four-wheeled vehicle; *esp* : one drawn by animals and used for carrying goods **2** : a child's four-wheeled cart **3** : STATION WAGON **4** : PATROL WAGON — **wag·on·er** \'wag-ə-nər\ *n* — **on the wagon** : abstaining from alcoholic liquors

wagon

wag·on·ette \,wag-ə-'net\ *n* : a light wagon with two facing seats along the sides back of a transverse front seat

wa·gon-lit \vä-gōⁿ-lē\ *n*, *pl* **wagons-lits** *or* **wagon-lits** \-gōⁿ-lē\ [F, fr. *wagon* railroad car + *lit* bed] : a railroad sleeping car

wagon master *n* : a person in charge of one or more wagons esp. for transporting freight

wagon train *n* : a group of wagons (as of pioneers) traveling overland

wag·tail \'wag-ˌtāl\ *n* : any of numerous slender mostly Old World birds related to the pipits and having a very long tail that is habitually jerked up and down

Wah·ha·bi *or* **Wa·ha·bi** \wə-'häb-ē\ *n* : a member of a puritanical Muslim sect founded in Arabia in the 18th century — **Wah·ha·bism** \-'häb-ˌiz-əm\ *n* — **Wah·ha·bite** \-'häb-ˌīt\ *adj or n*

wa·hi·ne \wä-'hē-nā\ *n* [Maori & Hawaiian] : a Polynesian woman

¹wa·hoo \'wä-ˌhü\ *n*, *pl* **wahoos** [of AmerInd origin] : any of various American trees or shrubs; *esp* : either of two elms

²wahoo *n*, *pl* **wahoos** [of AmerInd origin] : either of two No. American shrubs or shrubby trees with very hard wood and bright autumn foliage

waif \'wāf\ *n* [ONF, lost, unclaimed] **1** : something found without an owner and esp. by chance **2** : a stray person or animal; *esp* : a homeless child

¹wail \'wāl\ *vb* [of Scand origin; akin to E *woe*] **1** : to express sorrow audibly : LAMENT **2** : to make a sound suggestive of a mournful cry **3** : to express dissatisfaction plaintively : COMPLAIN — **wail·er** *n*

²wail *n* **1 a** : a usu. prolonged cry or sound expressing grief or pain **b** : a sound suggestive of this ⟨the *wail* of an air-raid siren⟩ **2** : a querulous expression of grievance : COMPLAINT

wail·ful \'wāl-fəl\ *adj* : SORROWFUL, MOURNFUL ⟨the *wailful* sound of distant bagpipes⟩ — **wail·ful·ly** \-fə-lē\ *adv*

wain \'wān\ *n* [OE *wægn*] : a usu. large and heavy vehicle for farm use

¹wain·scot \'wānz-kət, -ˌkōt, -ˌkät\ *n* [MD *wagenschot*] **1** : a usu. paneled and wooden lining of an interior wall **2** : the lower three or four feet of an interior wall when finished differently from the remainder of the wall

²wainscot *vt* **-scot·ed** *or* **-scot·ted; -scot·ing** *or* **-scot·ting** : to line with or as if with boards or paneling

wain·scot·ing \-ˌkōt-iŋ, -ˌkät-, -kət-\ *or* **wain·scot·ting** \-ˌkät-, -kət-\ *n* : material for wainscot : WAINSCOT

wain·wright \'wān-ˌrīt\ *n* : a maker and repairer of wagons

waist \'wāst\ *n* [ME *wast*; akin to E ³*wax*] **1 a** : the narrowed part of the body between the chest and hips **b** : the greatly constricted front part of the abdomen of some insects (as a wasp) **2** : a part resembling the human waist esp. in narrowness or central position ⟨the *waist* of a ship⟩ ⟨the *waist* of a violin⟩ **3** : a garment or the part of a garment that covers the body from the neck to the waist

waist·band \'wās(t)-ˌband\ *n* : a band (as of trousers or a skirt) fitting around the waist

waist·coat \'wās(t)-ˌkōt, 'wes-kət\ *n*, *chiefly Brit* : VEST — **waist·coat·ed** \-əd\ *adj*

waist·line \'wāst-ˌlīn\ *n* **1** : a line surrounding the

waist at its narrowest part; *also* : the length of this line **2** : the line at which the waist and skirt of a dress meet
¹wait \'wāt\ *vb* [ONF *waitier* to watch, of Gmc origin; akin to E *watch*] **1** : to remain inactive in readiness (as for action) or expectation (as of a coming event) : AWAIT ⟨*wait* for sunrise⟩ ⟨*wait* your turn⟩ ⟨*wait* for orders⟩ **2** : POSTPONE, DELAY ⟨*wait* dinner for a guest⟩ **3** : to attend as a waiter : SERVE ⟨*wait* tables⟩ ⟨*wait* at a luncheon⟩ **4** : to be ready — **wait on** *or* **wait upon 1 a** : to attend as a servant **b** : to supply the wants of : SERVE ⟨*wait on* a customer⟩ **2** : to make a formal call on **3** : to follow as a consequence — **wait up** : to delay going to bed
²wait *n* **1 a** : a hidden or concealed position — used chiefly in the expression *lie in wait* **b** : a state or attitude of watchfulness and expectancy **2** : an act or period of waiting
wait·er \'wāt-ər\ *n* **1** : one that waits upon another; *esp* : a man who waits on table (as in a restaurant) **2** : a tray on which something is carried : SALVER
waiting game *n* : a strategy in which one or more participants withhold action temporarily in the hope of having a favorable opportunity for more effective action later
waiting list *n* : a list or roster of those waiting (as for election to a club or appointment to a position)
waiting room *n* : a room (as at a railroad station) for the use of persons waiting
wait·ress \'wā-trəs\ *n* : a woman who waits on table
waive \'wāv\ *vt* [ONF *weyver*, fr. *waif* lost, unclaimed] **1** : to give up claim to ⟨*waive* his right to answer⟩ **2** : to put off the consideration of : POSTPONE
waiv·er \'wā-vər\ *n* [AF *weyver*, fr. ONF *weyver* to waive] : the act of waiving a right, claim, or privilege or an instrument evidencing such an act
¹wake \'wāk\ *vb* **waked** \'wākt\ *or* **woke** \'wōk\; **waked** *or* **wo·ken** \'wō-kən\; **wak·ing** [OE *wacan* to awake & *wacian* to be awake] **1 a** : to be or remain awake **b** : to remain awake on watch esp. over a corpse **2** : AWAKE — often used with *up* — **wak·er** *n*
²wake *n* **1** : the state of being awake **2** : a watch held over the body of a dead person prior to burial and sometimes accompanied by festivity
³wake *n* [of Scand origin] : the track left by a moving body (as a ship) in the water; *also* : a track or path left
wake·ful \'wāk-fəl\ *adj* : not sleeping or able to sleep — **wake·ful·ly** \-fə-lē\ *adv* — **wake·ful·ness** *n*
wak·en \'wā-kən\ *vb* **wak·ened**; **wak·en·ing** \'wāk-(ə-)niŋ\ : AWAKE — often used with *up* — **wak·en·er** \-(ə-)nər\ *n*
wake–rob·in \'wāk-,räb-ən\ *n* : any of several plants: as **a** : TRILLIUM **b** : JACK-IN-THE-PULPIT
Wal·den·ses \wȯl-'den-,sēz\ *n pl* [ML, fr. Peter *Waldo*, 12th cent. French heretic] : a Christian sect arising in southern France in the 12th century, adopting Calvinist doctrines in the 16th century, and later living chiefly in Piedmont — **Wal·den·sian** \-'den-chən\ *adj or n*
Wal·dorf salad \,wȯl-,dȯrf-\ *n* [*Waldorf*-Astoria Hotel, New York City] : a salad made typically of diced apples, celery, and nuts and dressed with mayonnaise
wale \'wāl\ *n* [OE *walu*] **1 a** : a streak or ridge made on the skin usu. by a rod or whip : WHEAL **b** : a narrow raised surface or ridge (as on cloth) **2** : one of the extra-strong strakes on the sides of a wooden ship next above the waterline
¹walk \'wȯk\ *vb* [OE *wealcan* to roll, toss] **1 a** : to move or cause to move along on foot usu. at a natural unhurried gait ⟨*walk* to town⟩ ⟨*walk* a horse up a hill⟩ **b** : to pass over, through, or along by walking ⟨*walk* the streets⟩ **c** : to perform or affect by walking ⟨*walk* guard⟩ **2** : to follow a course of action or way of life ⟨*walk* humbly in the sight of God⟩ **3** : to take or cause to take first base with a base on balls **4** : to move or cause to move in a manner suggestive of walking ⟨*walked* his fingers across the table⟩ — **walk away from 1** : to outrun or get the better of without difficulty **2** : to survive (an accident) with little or no injury — **walk into 1 a** : ATTACK **b** : to reprimand or criticize severely **2** : to eat or drink greedily ⟨*walked* right *into* the pretzels⟩ — **walk off with 1** : STEAL **2** : to win or gain esp. by outdoing one's competitors without difficulty — **walk over** : to disregard the wishes or feelings of
²walk *n* **1** : a going on foot ⟨go for a *walk*⟩ **2** : a place,

path, or course for walking **3** : distance to be walked **4 a** : manner of living : CONDUCT, BEHAVIOR **b** : social or economic status ⟨various *walks* of life⟩ **5 a** : manner of walking **b** : a gait of a quadruped in which there are always at least two feet on the ground; *esp* : a slow 4-beat gait of a horse in which the feet strike the ground in the sequence left hind, left fore, right hind, right fore **6** : BASE ON BALLS
walk·away \-ə-,wā\ *n* : an easily won contest
walk·er \'wȯ-kər\ *n* : one that walks or is used in walking; *esp* : a framework with wheels designed to support one learning to walk
walk·ie-talk·ie \,wȯ-kē-'tȯ-kē\ *n* : a small portable radio set for receiving and sending messages
walk–in \'wȯk-,in\ *adj* : large enough to be walked into ⟨a *walk-in* refrigerator⟩
walking fern *n* : any of a genus of ferns that form new plants at the tips of the long fronds
walking papers *n pl* : DISMISSAL, DISCHARGE
walking stick *n* **1** : a stick used in walking **2** *usu* **walk·ing·stick** : STICK INSECT
walk–on \'wȯk-,ȯn, -,än\ *n* : a small usu. nonspeaking part in a dramatic production
walk out \(')wȯk-'aút\ *vi* **1** : to go on strike **2** : to leave suddenly often as an expression of disapproval — **walk out on** : to leave in the lurch : ABANDON, DESERT
walk·out \'wȯk-,aút\ *n* **1** : STRIKE 2a **2** : the leaving of a meeting or organization as an expression of disapproval
walk·over \'wȯk-,ō-vər\ *n* : a one-sided contest or an easy or uncontested victory
walk–up \-,əp\ *n* : a building or apartment house without an elevator — **walk–up** *adj*
walk·way \-,wā\ *n* : a passage for walking : WALK
¹wall \'wȯl\ *n* [OE *weall*, fr. L *vallum* rampart] **1 a** : a structure (as of brick or stone) raised to some height and meant to enclose or shut off a space; *esp* : a side of a room or building **2** : something like a wall; *esp* : something that acts as a barrier or defense ⟨a tariff *wall*⟩ **3** : a material layer enclosing space ⟨the heart *wall*⟩ ⟨the *walls* of a boiler⟩ — **walled** \'wȯld\ *adj* — **wall-like** \'wȯl-,līk\ *adj*
²wall *vt* **1** : to provide, separate, or surround with or as if with a wall ⟨*wall* in the garden⟩ **2** : to close (an opening) with or as if with a wall ⟨*wall* up a door⟩
wal·la·by \'wäl-ə-bē\ *n, pl* **-bies** *also* **-by** [*wolabā*, native name in New So. Wales, Australia] : any of various small or medium-sized usu. brightly colored kangaroos
wall·board \'wȯl-,bōrd, -,bȯrd\ *n* : a structural material (as of wood pulp, gypsum, or plastic) made in large rigid sheets and used esp. for sheathing interior walls and ceilings
wal·let \'wäl-ət\ *n* [ME *walet*] **1** : a bag or sack for carrying things on a journey **2 a** : BILLFOLD **b** : a pocketbook with compartments (as for change and cards)
wall·eye \'wȯl-,ī\ *n* [back-formation fr. *walleyed*, fr. ON *vagl* beam] **1 a** : an eye with a whitish iris or an opaque white cornea **b** : an eye that turns outward showing more than a normal amount of white; *also* : the condition of having such eyes : divergent strabismus **2** : a large vigorous American freshwater food and sport fish that has prominent eyes and is related to the perches but resembles the true pike — called also *walleyed pike* — **wall·eyed** \-'īd\ *adj*

wallet 2b

wall·flow·er \'wȯl-,flaú(-ə)r\ *n* **1** : any of several Old World herbaceous or subshrubby perennial plants of the mustard family; *esp* : one widely grown for its showy fragrant flowers **2** : a person who from shyness or unpopularity remains on the sidelines of a social activity (as a dance)
Wal·loon \wä-'lün\ *n* : a member of a chiefly Celtic people of southern and southeastern Belgium and adjacent parts of France — **Walloon** *adj*
¹wal·lop \'wäl-əp\ *n* [ME, gallop, fr. ONF *walop*, fr. *waloper* to gallop] **1** : a powerful blow or impact **2** : the ability (as of a boxer) to hit hard
²wallop *vt* **1** : to beat soundly : TROUNCE **2** : to hit with force : SOCK — **wal·lop·er** *n*

ə abut; ⁹ kitten; ər further; a back; ā bake; ä cot, cart; aú out; ch chin; e less; ē easy; g gift; i trip; ī life

wal·lop·ing \'wäl-ə-piŋ\ *adj* **1** : LARGE, WHOPPING **2** : exceptionally fine or impressive

¹wal·low \'wäl-ō\ *vi* [OE *wealwian* to roll] **1** : to roll oneself about in or as if in deep mud ⟨elephants *wallowing* in the river⟩ **2** : to live or be filled with excessive pleasure in some condition ⟨*wallow* in luxury⟩ **3** : to become or remain helpless ⟨allowed them to *wallow* in their ignorance⟩

²wallow *n* **1** : an act or instance of wallowing **2** : a muddy or dust-filled area used by animals for wallowing

wall painting *n* : FRESCO

wall·pa·per \'wȯl-ˌpā-pər\ *n* : decorative paper for the walls of a room — **wallpaper** *vb*

wall·plug *n* : an electric receptacle in a wall

Wall Street \'wȯl-\ *n* [*Wall Street*, site of the New York Stock Exchange] : the influential financial interests of the U.S. economy

wal·nut \'wȯl-ˌnət\ *n* [OE *wealhhnutu*, lit., foreign nut, fr. *wealh* Celt, Welshman, foreigner] **1 a** : an edible nut with a furrowed usu. rough shell and an adherent husk; *also* : any of a genus of trees related to the hickories that produce such nuts **b** : the usu. reddish to dark brown wood of a walnut widely used for cabinetwork and veneers **c** : a hickory nut or tree **2** : a moderate reddish brown that is a color of the heartwood of the black walnut

Wal·pur·gis Night \väl-ˈpu̇r-gəs-\ *n* [G *Walpurgis* St. Walburga *d* A.D.777 English saint whose feast day falls on May Day] : the eve of May Day on which witches are held to ride to a satanic rendezvous

wal·rus \'wȯl-rəs, 'wäl-\ *n, pl* **walrus** *or* **wal·rus·es** [D, of Scand origin] : either of two large mammals of northern seas related to the seals and hunted esp. for the hide, the ivory tusks of the males, and oil

¹waltz \'wȯl(t)s\ *n* [G *walzer*, fr. *walzen* to roll, dance] **1** : a round dance in ¾ time with strong accent on the first beat **2** : music for or suitable for waltzing

²waltz *vb* **1** : to dance a waltz **2** : to move or advance easily or conspicuously — **waltz·er** *n*

wam·ble \'wäm-bəl\ *vi* **wam·bled; wam·bling** \-b(ə-)liŋ\ [ME *wamlen*] **1** : to feel or become nauseated **2** : to progress unsteadily or with a lurching shambling gait

wam·pum \'wäm-pəm\ *n* [of Algonquian origin] **1** : beads of shells strung in strands, belts, or sashes and used by No. American Indians as money and ornaments **2** *slang* : MONEY

wan \'wän\ *adj* [OE *wann* dark, livid] **1 a** : SICKLY, PALLID **b** : FEEBLE **2** : DIM, FAINT **3** : LANGUID ⟨a *wan* smile⟩ — **wan·ly** *adv* — **wan·ness** \'wän-nəs\ *n*

wand \'wänd\ *n* [ON *vöndr* slender stick] **1** : a fairy's, diviner's, or magician's staff **2** : any of various light rods; *also* : the rigid tube between nozzle and hose of a vacuum cleaner

wan·der \'wän-dər\ *vb* **wan·dered; wan·der·ing** \-d(ə-)riŋ\ [OE *wandrian*] **1** : to move about aimlessly or without a fixed course or goal : RAMBLE **2 a** : to deviate (as from a course) : STRAY **b** : to go astray in conduct or thought; *esp* : to become delirious or mentally disoriented — **wander** *n* — **wan·der·er** \-dər-ər\ *n*

Wandering Jew *n* **1** : a Jew held in medieval legend to be condemned to wander the earth until Christ's second coming for having mocked at him on the day of the crucifixion **2** *not cap W* : any of several mostly creeping plants of the spiderwort family

wan·der·lust \'wän-dər-ˌləst\ *n* : strong or unconquerable longing for or impulse toward wandering

¹wane \'wän\ *vi* [OE *wanian*] **1** : to be diminished : grow smaller or less: as **a** : to undergo gradual diminution after being at the full ⟨as the moon *wanes*⟩ ⟨his strength *waned* with exhaustion⟩ **b** : to lose power, prosperity, or influence ⟨the nation *waned* as its commerce declined⟩ **c** : to draw toward an end ⟨summer *wanes* away⟩

²wane *n* **1** : the act or process of waning **2** : a period or time of waning; *esp* : the period from full phase of the moon to the new moon

wan·gle \'waŋ-gəl\ *vb* **wan·gled; wan·gling** \-g(ə-)liŋ\ **1 a** : to obtain by sly, roundabout, or underhand means **b** : to use trickery or devious or questionable means to achieve an end **2 a** : to work by skill or indirection : MANIPULATE **b** : to make (one's way) by devious or questionable means : FINAGLE — **wan·gler** \-g(ə-)lər\ *n*

wan·i·gan *or* **wan·ni·gan** \'wän-i-gən\ *n* [of Algonquian

origin] : a movable shelter often mounted on wheels or tracks or on a raft

Wan·kel engine \ˌväŋ-kəl-, ˌwäŋ-\ *n* [after Felix *Wankel* *b*1902 G engineer] : an internal-combustion rotary engine that has a rounded triangular rotor functioning as a piston and rotating in a space in the engine and that has only two major moving parts

¹want \'wȯnt, 'wänt\ *vb* [ON *vanta*; akin to E *wane*] **1** : to be without : LACK ⟨this coat is *wanting* a button⟩ **2** : to fall short by ⟨*wants* one year of being of full age⟩ **3** : to feel or suffer the need of ⟨cannot get the rest he *wants*⟩ **4** : NEED, REQUIRE ⟨our house *wants* painting⟩ **5** : to desire earnestly : WISH ⟨*wants* to go to college⟩ **syn** see DESIRE

²want *n* **1 a** : a lack of a required or usual amount **b** : dire need : DESTITUTION **2** : something wanted : NEED, DESIRE **3** : personal defect : FAULT

want ad *n* : a newspaper advertisement stating that something (as an employee or a specified item) is wanted

¹want·ing *adj* **1** : not present or in evidence : ABSENT **2 a** : falling below standards or expectations **b** : lacking in ability or capacity : DEFICIENT

²wanting *prep* **1** : WITHOUT ⟨a book *wanting* a cover⟩ **2** : LESS, MINUS ⟨a month *wanting* two days⟩

¹wan·ton \'wȯnt-ᵊn, 'wänt-\ *adj* [ME, lit., unruly, fr. *wan-* mis- (fr. OE *wan* deficient) + *towen*, pp. of *teen* to draw, train, discipline, fr. OE *tēon*] **1 a** : FROLICSOME **2** : UNCHASTE, LEWD; *also* : SENSUAL **3 a** : MERCILESS, INHUMANE ⟨*wanton* cruelty⟩ **b** : having no just cause : MALICIOUS ⟨a *wanton* attack⟩ **4** : UNRESTRAINED, EXTRAVAGANT, LUXURIANT — **wan·ton·ly** *adv* — **wan·ton·ness** \-ᵊn-(n)əs\ *n*

²wanton *n* : a wanton individual; *esp* : a lascivious person

³wanton *vb* **1** : to be wanton or act wantonly **2** : to pass or waste wantonly

wa·pi·ti \'wäp-ət-ē\ *n, pl* **-tis** *or* **-ti** [of Algonquian origin] : the American elk

wap·per·jawed \ˌwäp-ər-ˈjȯd, ˌwäp-ē-\ *adj* : having a crooked, undershot, or wry jaw

¹war \'wȯ(ə)r\ *n* [ONF *werre*, fr. OHG *werra* confusion, strife] **1 a** : a state or period of usu. open and declared armed hostile conflict between states or nations **b** : the art or science of warfare **2 a** : a state of hostility, conflict, or antagonism **b** : a struggle between opposing forces or for a particular end ⟨*war* against disease⟩

²war *vi* **warred; war·ring** **1** : to engage in warfare ⟨*warring* nations⟩ **2** : to be in conflict

¹war·ble \'wȯr-bəl\ *n* [ONF *werble* tune] **1** : a melodious succession of low pleasing sounds **2** : a musical trill **3** : the action of warbling

²warble *vb* **war·bled; war·bling** \-b(ə-)liŋ\ **1** : to sing or render in a trilling manner or with many turns and variations **2** : to express by or as if by warbling

³warble *n* : a swelling under the hide (as of the back of cattle) caused by the maggot of a warble fly; *also* : such a maggot — **war·bled** \-bəld\ *adj*

warble fly *n* : any of various two-winged flies whose larvae are warbles

war·bler \'wȯr-blər\ *n* **1** : one that warbles : SONGSTER **2 a** : any of numerous small Old World singing birds many of which are noted songsters and are closely related to the thrushes **b** : any of numerous small brightly colored American songbirds with a usu. weak and unmusical song — called also *wood warbler*

war·bon·net \'wȯr-ˌbän-ət\ *n* : an Indian ceremonial headdress with a feathered extension down the back

war chest *n* : a fund accumulated for a specific purpose, action, or campaign

war crime *n* : a crime (as genocide or maltreatment of prisoners) committed during or in connection with war — usu. used in pl.

war cry *n* **1** : a cry used by a body of fighters in war **2** : a slogan used esp. to rally people to a cause

¹ward \'wȯrd\ *n* [OE *weard*] **1 a** : a guarding or being under guard; *esp* : CUSTODY **b** : a body of guards **2 a** : a division (as a cell or block) of a prison **b** : a division in a hospital **3 a** : a division of a city for electoral or administrative purposes **b** : a local Mormon congregation **4** : a projecting ridge of metal in a lock casing or keyhole permitting only the insertion of a key with a corresponding notch; *also* : a corresponding notch in a key **5 a** : a

j joke; **ŋ** sing; **ō** flow; **ȯ** flaw; **ȯi** coin; **th** thin; **th** this; **ü** loot; **u̇** foot; **y** yet; **yü** few; **yu̇** furious; **zh** vision

person (as a child or lunatic) under the protection of a court or a guardian **b** : a person or body of persons under the protection or tutelage of a government — **ward·ed** \-əd\ *adj*

²**ward** *vt* **1** : to keep watch over : GUARD **2** : to turn aside : DEFLECT — usu. used with *off* ⟨*ward* off a cold⟩

¹**-ward** \wərd\ *also* **-wards** \wərdz\ *adj suffix* [OE *-weard*] **1** : that moves, tends, faces, or is directed toward ⟨wind*ward*⟩ **2** : that occurs or is situated in the direction of ⟨left*ward*⟩

²**-ward** *or* **-wards** *adv suffix* **1** : in a (specified) spatial or temporal direction ⟨up*wards*⟩⟨after*ward*⟩ **2** : toward a (specified) point, position, or area ⟨earth*ward*⟩

war dance *n* : a dance performed by primitive peoples as preparation for battle or in celebration of victory

war·den \'wȯrd-°n\ *n* [ONF *wardein*, fr. *warder* to guard, of Gmc origin; akin to E *ward*] **1** : GUARDIAN, KEEPER **2** : the governor of a town, district, or fortress **3 a** : an official charged with special supervisory duties or with the enforcement of specified laws or regulations ⟨game *warden*⟩⟨air raid *warden*⟩ **b** : an official in charge of the operation of a prison **c** : any of various British administrative officials ⟨*warden* of the mint⟩ **4 a** : one of two ranking lay officers of an Episcopal parish **b** : any of various British college officials — **war·den·ship** \-,ship\ *n*

ward·er \'wȯrd-ər\ *n* : a person who keeps guard : WATCHMAN, WARDEN

ward heeler *n* : a local worker for a political boss

ward·robe \'wȯrd-,rōb\ *n* **1 a** : a room or closet where clothes are kept **b** : CLOTHESPRESS **2** : a collection of wearing apparel (as of one person or for one activity)

ward·room \-,rüm, -,rùm\ *n* : the space in a warship allotted for living quarters to the commissioned officers excepting the captain; *esp* : the messroom assigned to these officers

ward·ship \-,ship\ *n* **1** : GUARDIANSHIP **2** : the state of being under a guardian

¹**ware** \'wa(ə)r, 'we(ə)r\ *adj* [OE *wær* careful, aware] : AWARE, CONSCIOUS

²**ware** *vt* : to beware of — used chiefly as a command to hunting animals ⟨*ware* chase⟩

³**ware** *n* [OE *waru*] **1 a** : manufactured articles or products of art or craft : GOODS ⟨*ware* whittled from wood⟩ — often used in combination ⟨tin*ware*⟩ **b** : an article of merchandise ⟨a peddler hawking his *wares*⟩ **2** : items (as dishes) of fired clay : POTTERY

¹**ware·house** \'wa(ə)r-,haùs, 'we(ə)r-\ *n* : a place for the storage of merchandise or commodities — **ware·house·man** \-mən\ *n*

²**ware·house** \-,haùz, -,haùs\ *vt* : to deposit, store, or stock in or as if in a warehouse

ware·room \-,rüm, -,rùm\ *n* : a room in which goods are exhibited for sale

war·fare \'wȯr-,fa(ə)r, -,fe(ə)r\ *n* **1** : military operations between enemies : WAR; *also* : an activity undertaken by one country to weaken or destroy another ⟨economic *warfare*⟩ **2** : STRUGGLE, CONFLICT ⟨industrial *warfare*⟩

war·fa·rin \'wȯr-fə-rən\ *n* [*Wisconsin Alumni Research Foundation* (its patentee) + *coumarin*, a chemical] : a crystalline compound that deters blood clotting and is used as a rodent poison and in medicine

war footing *n* : the condition of being prepared to undertake or maintain war

war·head \'wȯr-,hed\ *n* : the section of a missile (as a torpedo) containing the explosive, chemical, or incendiary charge

war-horse \-,hȯrs\ *n* **1** : a horse used in war : CHARGER **2** : a veteran soldier or public person (as a politician)

war·less \-ləs\ *adj* : free from war

war·like \-,līk\ *adj* **1** : fond of war ⟨*warlike* people⟩ **2** : of, relating to, or having to do with war ⟨*warlike* supplies⟩ **3** : threatening war : HOSTILE ⟨*warlike* attitudes⟩ **syn** see MARTIAL

war·lock \'wȯr-,läk\ *n* [OE *wærloga* one that breaks faith, the Devil, fr. *wær* faith, troth + *lēogan* to lie] : SORCERER, WIZARD

war·lord \-,lȯrd\ *n* **1** : a high military leader **2** : a military commander (as formerly in China) exercising local civil power by force

¹**warm** \'wȯrm\ *adj* [OE *wearm*] **1 a** : having or giving out heat to a moderate or adequate degree ⟨*warm* food⟩

⟨a *warm* stove⟩ **b** : serving to retain heat (as of the body) ⟨*warm* clothes⟩ **c** : feeling or inducing sensations of heat ⟨*warm* from exertion⟩⟨a long *warm* walk⟩ **2 a** : showing or marked by strong feeling : ARDENT ⟨a *warm* advocate of temperance⟩⟨a girl of *warm* nature⟩ **b** : marked by tense excitement or hot anger ⟨a *warm* political campaign⟩ ⟨made *warm* remarks about one another⟩ **3** : marked by or tending toward injury, distress, or pain ⟨gave the enemy a *warm* reception⟩ **4 a** : newly made : FRESH ⟨a *warm* scent⟩ **b** : near to a goal **5** : giving a pleasant impression of warmth, cheerfulness, or friendliness; *esp* : of a hue in the range yellow through orange to red — **warm·ly** *adv* — **warm·ness** *n*

²**warm** *vb* **1** : to make or become warm **2 a** : to give a feeling of warmth or vitality to **b** : to experience feelings of affection or pleasure ⟨*warmed* to her young guests⟩ **3** : to reheat (cooked food) for eating **4 a** : to make or become ready for operation or performance by preliminary exercise or operation — often used with *up* **b** : to become increasingly ardent, interested, or competent ⟨a speaker *warming* to his topic⟩

³**warm** *adv* : WARMLY — usu. used in combination ⟨*warm*-clad⟩⟨*warm*-tinted⟩

warm–blood·ed \'wȯrm-'bləd-əd\ *adj* **1** : having the capacity to maintain a relatively high and constant body temperature that is essentially independent of that of the surroundings **2** : warm in feeling : FERVENT, ARDENT — **warm–blood·ed·ness** *n*

warmed–over \'wȯrmd-'ō-vər\ *adj* **1** : REHEATED ⟨*warmed-over* cabbage⟩ **2** : not fresh or new : STALE ⟨*warmed-over* ideas⟩

warm·er \'wȯr-mər\ *n* : one that warms; *esp* : a device for keeping something warm ⟨foot *warmer*⟩

warm front *n* : an advancing edge of a warm air mass

warm·heart·ed \'wȯrm-'härt-əd\ *adj* : marked by warmth of feeling — **warm·heart·ed·ness** *n*

warming pan *n* : a long-handled covered pan filled with live coals and formerly used to warm a bed

warm·ish \'wȯr-mish\ *adj* : somewhat warm

war·mon·ger \'wȯr-,məŋ-gər, -,mäŋ-\ *n* : one who urges or attempts to stir up war : JINGO — **war·mon·ger·ing** \-g(ə-)riŋ\ *n*

warmth \'wȯrm(p)th\ *n* : the quality or state of being warm: as **a** : emotional intensity (as of enthusiasm, anger, or love) **b** : a glowing effect such as is produced by the use of warm colors

warm up \(')wȯrm-'əp\ *vi* **1** : to engage in exercise or practice esp. before entering a game or contest **2** : to approach a state of violence, conflict, or danger

warm–up \'wȯrm-,əp\ *n* : the act or an instance of warming up; *also* : a procedure (as a set of exercises) used in warming up

warn \'wȯrn\ *vb* [OE *warnian*] **1 a** : to give notice to beforehand esp. of danger or evil **b** : ADMONISH, COUNSEL **c** : to notify esp. in advance : INFORM **2** : to order to go or stay away — **warn·er** *n*
syn CAUTION: WARN may range from simple notification of something to be watched for to threats of violence or reprisal; CAUTION stresses giving advice that suggests the need of taking care or watching out

¹**warn·ing** \'wȯr-niŋ\ *n* **1** : the act of warning : state of being warned ⟨he had *warning* of his illness⟩ **2** : something that warns or serves to warn

²**warning** *adj* : serving as an alarm, signal, summons, or admonition ⟨*warning* bell⟩⟨*warning* shot⟩ — **warn·ing·ly** \-niŋ-lē\ *adv*

warning coloration *n* : a conspicuous coloration possessed by an animal otherwise defended ⟨the *warning coloration* of the skunk⟩

war of nerves *n* : a conflict characterized by psychological tactics (as bluff, threats, and intimidation) designed primarily to create confusion, indecision, or breakdown of morale

¹**warp** \'wȯrp\ *n* [OE *wearp*] **1 a** : a series of yarns extended lengthwise in a loom and crossed by the woof **b** : FOUNDATION, BASE **2 a** : a twist or curve that has developed in something orig. flat or straight ⟨a *warp* in a door⟩ **b** : a mental twist or aberration

²**warp** *vb* [OE *weorpan* to throw] **1 a** : to turn or twist out of shape and esp. out of a plane; *also* : to become so turned or twisted **b** : to cause to judge, choose, or act

---

ə abut; ᵊ kitten; ər further; a back; ā bake; ä cot, cärt; aù out; ch chin; e less; ē easy; g gift; i trip; I life

wrongly : PERVERT **c** : FALSIFY, DISTORT **2** : to arrange (yarns) so as to form a warp **3** : to move (as a ship) or become moved by hauling on a line attached to a fixed object — **warp·er** n

war paint n **1** : paint put on parts of the body (as the face) by American Indians on going to war **2** : ceremonial or fine dress; also : MAKEUP 2

war·path \'wòr-,path, -,päth\ n **1** : the route taken by a party of American Indians going on a warlike expedition **2** : a hostile course of action or frame of mind

war·plane \-,plān\ n : a military airplane; esp : one armed for combat

¹war·rant \'wòr-ənt, 'wär-\ n [ONF, protector, warrant, of Gmc origin] **1 a** : AUTHORIZATION **b** : JUSTIFICATION, GROUND **2** : evidence of authorization (as a document); esp : a legal writ authorizing an officer to make an arrest, seizure, or search **3** : a certificate of appointment issued to an officer of lower rank than a commissioned officer

²warrant vt **1 a** : to declare or maintain positively **b** : to assure (a person) of the truth of what is said **2** : to guarantee (something) to be as appears or as represented **3** : to guarantee security or immunity to : SECURE **4** : SANCTION, AUTHORIZE **5 a** : to give proof of : ATTEST **b** : GUARANTEE **6** : to serve as or give ground or reason for : JUSTIFY — **war·rant·a·ble** \-ənt-ə-bəl\ adj — **war·rant·a·ble·ness** n — **war·rant·a·bly** \-blē\ adv — **war·rant·er** \-ənt-ər\ or **war·ran·tor** \,wòr-ən-'tò(ə)r, ,wär-\ n

war·ran·tee \,wòr-ən-'tē, ,wär-\ n : the person to whom a warranty is made

warrant officer n : an officer (as in the army) ranking above a noncommissioned officer and below a commissioned officer

war·ran·ty \'wòr-ənt-ē, 'wär-\ n, pl **-ties** [ONF warantie, fr. fem. of waranti, pp. of warantir to guarantee, warrant] : an expressed or implied statement that some situation or thing is as it appears or is represented to be; esp : a usu. written guarantee of the integrity of a product and of the maker's responsibility for the repair or replacement of defective parts

war·ren \'wòr-ən, 'wär-\ n [ONF warenne] **1 a** : a place for keeping small game (as hare or pheasant) **b** : the right of hunting game in such a warren **2** : an area where rabbits breed **3** : a crowded tenement or district

war·rior \'wòr-yər, 'wòr-ē-ər, 'wär-ē-\ n : a man engaged or experienced in warfare

war·ship \'wòr-,ship\ n : a government ship employed for war purposes; esp : one armed for combat

wart \'wòrt\ n [OE wearte] **1 a** : a horny projection on the skin caused by a virus — called also ver·ru·ca vul·ga·ris \və-,rü-kə-,vəl-'gar-əs, -'ger-\ **b** : any of numerous similar skin lesions **2** : a protuberance (as on a plant) resembling a wart — **wart·ed** \'wòrt-əd\ adj — **warty** \-ē\ adj

wart·hog \'wòrt-,hòg, -,häg\ n : any of a genus of African wild hogs with two pairs of rough warty protuberances on the face and large protruding tusks

war·time \'wòr-,tīm\ n : a period during which a war is in progress

war whoop n : a war cry esp. of American Indians

wary \'wa(ə)r-ē, 'we(ə)r-\ adj **war·i·er; -est** [ME ware, fr. OE wær careful, aware] : marked by keen caution; esp : watchfully prudent in detecting and escaping danger — **war·i·ly** \'war-ə-lē, 'wer-\ adv — **war·i·ness** \'war-ē-nəs, 'wer-\ n

was [OE, 1st & 3d sing. past indic. of wesan to be] past 1st & 3d sing of BE

¹wash \'wòsh, 'wäsh\ vb [OE wascan; akin to E water] **1** : to cleanse with or as if with a liquid (as water) (wash clothes) (washed his face) **2** : to wet thoroughly with liquid **3** : to flow along the border of (waves wash the shore) **4** : to pour or flow in a stream or current (the river washes against its banks) **5** : to move or carry by the action of water (a man washed overboard) **6** : to cover or daub lightly with a liquid (as whitewash or varnish) **7** : to run water over in order to separate valuable matter from refuse (wash sand for gold) **8** : to bear washing without injury **9** : to stand a test or proof (that story won't wash) **10** : to be worn away by washing (the heavy rain caused the bridge to wash out)

²wash n **1 a** : the act or process or an instance of washing or being washed **b** : articles to be washed or being washed **2** : the surging action of waves or its sound **3 a** : a piece of ground washed by the sea or river **b** : BOG, MARSH **c** : a shallow body of water or creek **d** West : the dry bed of a stream — called also dry wash **4** : worthless esp. liquid waste : REFUSE **5 a** : a sweep or splash esp. of color made by or as if by a long stroke of a brush **b** : a thin coat of paint (as watercolor) **c** : a thin liquid used for coating a surface (as a wall) **6** : LOTION **7** : loose or eroded surface material of the earth (as rock debris) transported and deposited by running water **8 a** : BACKWASH 1 **b** : a disturbance in the air produced by the passage of an airfoil or propeller

³wash adj : WASHABLE

wash·a·ble \'wòsh-ə-bəl, 'wäsh-\ adj : capable of being washed without damage (a washable silk) — **wash·a·bil·i·ty** \,wòsh-ə-'bil-ət-ē, ,wäsh-\ n

wash and wear adj : of, relating to, or constituting a fabric or garment not needing to be ironed after washing

wash·ba·sin \'wòsh-,bās-'n, 'wäsh-\ n : WASHBOWL

wash·board \-,bòrd, -,bórd\ n : a grooved board to scrub clothes on

wash·bowl \-,bōl\ n : a large bowl for water to wash one's hands and face

wash·cloth \-,klòth\ n : a cloth for washing one's face and body — called also wash·rag \-,rag\

wash drawing n : watercolor painting in or chiefly in washes

washed–out \'wòsht-,aùt, 'wäsht-\ adj **1** : faded in color **2** : depleted in vigor or animation : EXHAUSTED

washed–up \-'əp\ adj **1** : left with no effective power and no capacity or opportunity for recovery **2** usu **washed up** : ready to quit esp. from disgust : THROUGH

wash·er \'wòsh-ər, 'wäsh-\ n **1** : one that washes; esp : WASHING MACHINE **2** : a ring (as of metal or leather) used to make something fit tightly or to prevent rubbing

wash·er·wom·an \-,wùm-ən\ n : a woman who works at washing clothes

wash·house \'wòsh-,haùs, 'wäsh-\ n : a house or building used or equipped for washing; esp : one for washing clothes

washers 2

wash·ing \'wòsh-iŋ, 'wäsh-\ n **1** : material obtained by washing **2** : a thin covering or coat (a washing of silver) **3** : articles washed or to be washed

washing machine n : a machine for washing; esp : one for washing clothes and household linen

washing soda n : SAL SODA

Wash·ing·ton pie \,wòsh-iŋ-tən-, ,wäsh-\ n : cake layers put together with a jam or jelly filling

Washington's Birthday n [George Washington d1799 first president of the U.S.] : February 22 observed as a legal holiday

wash out \(')wòsh-'aùt, (')wäsh-\ vb **1 a** : to drain the color from in laundering **b** : to deplete the strength or vitality of **c** : to eliminate or be eliminated as useless or unsatisfactory **2** : to become depleted of color or vitality : FADE

wash·out \'wòsh-,aùt, 'wäsh-\ n **1** : the washing out or away of earth esp. in a roadbed by a freshet; also : a place where earth is washed away **2** : one that fails to measure up : FAILURE; esp : one who fails in a course of training or study (as military flight training)

wash·room \-,rüm, -,rùm\ n : a room equipped with washing and toilet facilities : LAVATORY

wash·stand \-,stand\ n **1** : a stand holding articles needed for washing one's face and hands **2** : a washbowl permanently set in place and attached to water pipes and drainpipes

wash·tub \-,təb\ n : a tub for washing clothes or for soaking them prior to washing

wash up vt : ELIMINATE, FINISH (the scandal washed him up as a politician)

wash·wom·an \'wòsh-,wùm-ən, 'wäsh-\ n : WASHER-WOMAN

washy \'wòsh-ē, 'wäsh-\ adj **1** : WEAK, WATERY **2** : deficient in color : PALLID **3** : lacking in vigor, individuality, or definiteness

wasn't \'wəz-'nt, 'wäz-\ : was not

wasp \'wäsp, 'wòsp\ n [OE wæps, wæsp; akin to E weave]

: a winged insect related to the bees and ants that has a slender body with the abdomen attached by a narrow stalk and in females and workers a powerful sting

wasp·ish \'wäs-pish, 'wòs-\ *adj* **1 :** SNAPPISH, IRRITABLE **2 :** resembling a wasp in form; *esp* **:** slightly built — **wasp·ish·ly** *adv* — **wasp·ish·ness** *n*

wasp waist *n* **:** a very slender waist

1was·sail \'wäs-əl, wä-'sāl\ *n* [ON *ves heill* be well] **1 :** an early English toast to someone's health **2 :** a liquor formerly drunk in England on festive occasions (as at Christmas) and made of ale or wine with spices and other ingredients (as sugar, toast, or roasted apples) **3 :** riotous drinking **:** REVELRY

2wassail *vb* **1 :** to hold a wassail **:** CAROUSE **2 :** to drink to the health or thriving of

was·sail·er \'wäs-ə-lər, wä-'sā-lər\ *n* **1 :** one that carouses **:** REVELER **2** *archaic* **:** one who goes about singing carols

Was·ser·mann reaction \'wäs-ər-mən-, 'väs-\ *n* [after August von *Wassermann d*1925 German bacteriologist] **:** a complement-fixing reaction occurring with the serum of syphilitic patients and used as a test for syphilis

Wassermann test *n* **:** a test for the detection of syphilitic infection using the Wassermann reaction

wast \wəst, (')wäst\ *archaic past 2d sing of* BE

wast·age \'wā-stij\ *n* **:** loss by use, decay, erosion, or leakage or through wastefulness

1waste \'wāst\ *n* [ONF *wast*, fr. *wast*, adj., desolate, waste, fr. L *vastus*] **1 a :** a sparsely settled or barren region **:** DESERT **b :** uncultivated land **c :** a broad and empty expanse (as of water) **2 :** the act or an instance of wasting **:** the state of being wasted **3 :** gradual loss or decrease by use, wear, or decay **4 a :** damaged, defective, or superfluous material produced by a manufacturing process: as (1) **:** material rejected during a textile manufacturing process and used usu. for wiping away dirt and oil (2) **:** fluid (as steam) allowed to escape without being utilized **b** (1) **:** refuse (as garbage, sewage, or rubbish) that accumulates about habitations ⟨collection of city *wastes*⟩ (2) **:** material (as excrement) that is produced by a living body and is of no value to the organism that produces it

2waste *vb* **1 :** DEVASTATE **2 :** to wear away or diminish gradually **:** CONSUME **3 a :** to spend money or use property carelessly **:** SQUANDER **b :** to allow to be used inefficiently or become dissipated **4 :** to lose or cause to lose weight, strength, or vitality — often used with *away* **5 a :** to become diminished in bulk or substance **b :** to become consumed

3waste *adj* **1 :** being wild and uninhabited **:** DESOLATE, BARREN **2 :** RUINED, DEVASTATED **3 :** thrown away as worthless after being used **4 :** of no further use to a person, animal, or plant ⟨the *waste* matter of the body⟩

waste·bas·ket \'wās(t)-,bas-kət\ *n* **:** an open receptacle for wastepaper

waste·ful \'wāst-fəl\ *adj* **:** given to or marked by waste **:** LAVISH, PRODIGAL — **waste·ful·ly** \-fə-lē\ *adv* — **waste·ful·ness** *n*

waste·land \'wāst-,land\ *n* **:** barren or uncultivated land

waste·pa·per \'wās(t)-'pā-pər\ *n* **:** paper discarded as used, superfluous, or not fit for use

waste pipe *n* **:** a pipe for carrying off waste fluid

waste product *n* **:** material resulting from a process (as of metabolism or manufacture) that is of no further use to the system producing it

wast·er \'wā-stər\ *n* **:** one that wastes or squanders

wast·rel \'wā-strəl\ *n* **:** WASTER, SPENDTHRIFT

1watch \'wäch\ *vb* [OE *wæccan*; akin to E *wake*] **1 :** to stay awake intentionally (as at the bedside of a sick person or for purposes of religious devotion) **2 :** to be on the alert **:** be on one's guard **3 :** to be on the lookout **4 :** to keep guard ⟨*watch* outside the door⟩ **5 :** to keep one's eyes on **:** keep in view ⟨*watch* a game⟩ **6 :** to keep in view so as to prevent harm or warn of danger ⟨*watch* a brush fire carefully⟩ **7 :** to keep oneself informed about ⟨*watch* someone's career⟩ **8 :** to be on the alert for the chance to make use of ⟨*watched* his opportunity⟩ — **watch·er** *n*

2watch *n* **1 a :** the act of keeping awake to guard, protect, or attend **b :** a state of alert and continuous attention **c :** close observation **:** SURVEILLANCE **2 :** one of the indeterminate wakeful intervals marking the passage of night

— usu. used in pl. **3 :** one that watches **:** LOOKOUT, WATCHMAN **4 a :** a body of sentinels making up a guard **b :** a watchman or body of watchmen formerly assigned to patrol the streets **5 a :** a portion of time during which a part of a ship's company is on duty **b :** the part of a ship's company required to be on duty during a particular watch **6 :** a portable timepiece designed to be worn (as on the wrist) or carried in the pocket

watch·band \-,band\ *n* **:** the bracelet or strap of a wristwatch

watch·case \-,kās\ *n* **:** the outside metal covering of a watch

watch·dog \-,dòg\ *n* **1 :** a dog kept to guard property **2 :** one that guards against loss, waste, theft, or undesirable practices

watch·eye \-,ī\ *n* **:** a walleye esp. of a dog

watch·ful \-fəl\ *adj* **:** steadily attentive and alert esp. to danger — **watch·ful·ly** \-fə-lē\ *adv* — **watch·ful·ness** *n*
syn WATCHFUL, VIGILANT, ALERT mean being on the lookout esp. for opportunity or danger. WATCHFUL is the general and least explicit term for this; VIGILANT suggests maintaining a keen, unremitting watchfulness; ALERT stresses readiness or promptness in meeting danger or seizing opportunity

watch glass *n* **1 :** a glass that is usu. convex outwardly and used for covering a watch dial **2 :** a glass dish similar to a round watch-dial covering in shape **3 :** a small flat-bottomed circular thick-glass dish — called also *Syr·a·cuse watch glass* \'sir-ə-,kyüs-, -,kyüz-\

watch·mak·er \'wäch-,mā-kər\ *n* **:** one that makes or repairs watches or clocks — **watch·mak·ing** \-kiŋ\ *n*

watch·man \-mən\ *n* **:** a person assigned to watch **:** GUARD

watch night *n* **:** a devotional service lasting until after midnight esp. on New Year's Eve

watch out *vi* **:** to be vigilant — often used with *for*

watch·tow·er \'wäch-,taù-(-ə)r\ *n* **:** a tower for a lookout

watch·word \-,wərd\ *n* **1 :** a secret word used as a signal or sign of recognition **2 :** a motto used as a slogan or rallying cry

1wa·ter \'wòt-ər, 'wät-\ *n* [OE *wæter*] **1 a :** the liquid that descends from the clouds as rain, forms streams, lakes, and seas, and is a major constituent of all living matter and that is an odorless, tasteless, very slightly compressible oxide of hydrogen H_2O **b :** a natural mineral water — usu. used in pl. **2** *pl* **:** a band of seawater bordering on and under the control of a country ⟨sailing Canadian *waters*⟩ **3 :** travel or transportation on water ⟨came by *water*⟩ **4 :** the level of water at a particular state of the tide **:** TIDE **5 :** liquid containing or resembling water: as **a :** a pharmaceutical or cosmetic preparation made with water **b :** a watery fluid (as tears, urine, or sap) formed or circulating in a living body **6 a :** the limpidity and luster of a precious stone and esp. a diamond **b :** a wavy lustrous pattern (as of a textile) **7 :** capital stock not representing assets of the issuing company — **above water :** out of difficulty — **in deep water :** in serious difficulties

2water *vb* **1 :** to supply with or get or take water ⟨*water* horses⟩ ⟨the ship *watered* at each port⟩ **2 :** to treat with or as if with water; *esp* **:** to impart a lustrous appearance and wavy pattern to (cloth) by calendering **3 a :** to dilute by or as if by the addition of water **b :** to add to the total par value of (stocks) without adding to the assets represented **4 :** to form or secrete water or watery matter (as tears or saliva)

water ballet *n* **:** a synchronized sequence of evolutions performed by a group of swimmers

water bed *n* **:** a bed whose mattress is a plastic bag filled with water

water beetle *n* **:** any of numerous oval flattened aquatic beetles that swim by means of their fringed hind legs which act together as oars

water bird *n* **:** a swimming or wading bird — compare WATERFOWL

water blister *n* **:** a blister with a clear watery content

water bloom *n* **:** an accumulation of algae and esp. of blue-green algae at or near the surface of a body of water; *also* **:** an alga causing this

water boatman *n* **:** any of various aquatic bugs with one pair of legs modified into paddles

ə abut; ᵊ kitten; ər further; a back; ā bake; ä cot, cart; aù out; ch chin; e less; ē easy; g gift; i trip; ī life

wa·ter·borne \'wȯt-ər-,bōrn, 'wät-, -,bȯrn\ *adj* : supported or carried by water

water boy *n* : one who keeps a group (as of football players) supplied with drinking water

water brash \-,brash\ *n* [Sc *brash* eruption of liquid] : salivation accompanied by regurgitation of acid material from the stomach

wa·ter·buck \-,bək\ *n*, *pl* **waterbuck** *or* **waterbucks** : any of various Old World antelopes that commonly frequent streams or wet lands

water buffalo *n* : an often domesticated Asiatic buffalo somewhat resembling a large ox

water chestnut *n* : any of several aquatic herbs with edible fruits or tubers; *also* : the edible part

water clock *n* : a device or machine for measuring time by the fall or flow of water

water closet *n* : a compartment or room for defecation and excretion into a hopper : BATHROOM; *also* : the hopper together with its accessories

wa·ter·col·or \'wȯt-ər-,kəl-ər, 'wät-\ *n* 1 : a paint whose liquid part is water 2 : a picture painted with watercolor 3 : the art of painting with watercolor — **wa·ter·col·or·ist** \-,kəl-ə-rəst\ *n*

wa·ter-cooled \,wȯt-ər-'küld, ,wät-\ *adj* : cooled by means of water and esp. circulating water (as in a water jacket)

wa·ter·course \'wȯt-ər-,kōrs, -,kȯrs\ *n* 1 : a bed over which or channel through which water flows 2 : a stream of water (as a river, brook, or underground stream)

wa·ter·craft \-,kraft\ *n* 1 : skill in water activities (as managing boats) 2 : craft for water transport

wa·ter·cress \-,kres\ *n* : any of several water-loving cresses; *esp* : a perennial cress found chiefly in springs or running water and used in salads or as a potherb

water dog *n* : a large salamander; *esp* : MUD PUPPY

wa·ter·er \'wȯt-ər-ər, 'wät-\ *n* : one that waters

wa·ter·fall \'wȯt-ər-,fȯl, 'wät-\ *n* : a perpendicular or very steep descent of the water of a stream

water flea *n* : any of various small active dark or brightly colored freshwater crustaceans

wa·ter·fowl \-,faúl\ *n* 1 : a bird that frequents water; *esp* : a swimming bird 2 **waterfowl** *pl* : swimming game birds as distinguished from upland game birds and shorebirds

wa·ter·front \-,frənt\ *n* : land or a section of a town bordering on a body of water

water gap *n* : a pass in a mountain ridge through which a stream runs

water gas *n* : a poisonous flammable gaseous mixture that consists chiefly of carbon monoxide and hydrogen, is usu. made by blowing air and then steam over red-hot coke or coal, and is used as a fuel

water gate *n* 1 : a gate (as of a building) giving access to a body of water 2 : FLOODGATE

water glass *n* 1 : a glass vessel (as a drinking glass) for holding water 2 : an instrument consisting of an open box or tube with a glass bottom used for examining objects in or under water 3 : a water-soluble substance consisting usu. of sodium silicate $Na_2O.SiO_2$ of varying composition found in commerce as a glassy mass, a stony powder, or dissolved in water as a syrupy liquid and used as a protective coating and in preserving eggs

water gum *n* : a gum tree (as a tupelo) growing on wet land

water heater *n* : an apparatus for heating and usu. storing hot water (as for domestic use)

water hemlock *n* : any of a genus of poisonous plants of the carrot family; *esp* : a tall Eurasian perennial herb

water hen *n* : any of several birds of the rail group (as a coot or gallinule)

water hole *n* 1 : a natural hole or hollow containing water 2 : a hole in a surface of ice

water hyacinth *n* : a floating aquatic plant often clogging waterways in the southern U.S.

water ice *n* : a frozen dessert consisting of water, sugar, and flavoring

watering place *n* 1 : a place where water may be obtained; *esp* : one where animals and esp. livestock come to drink 2 : a health or recreational resort featuring mineral springs or water activities

watering pot *n* : a vessel usu. with a perforated spout

used to sprinkle water esp. on plants — called also *watering can*

wa·ter·ish \'wȯt-ə-rish, 'wät-\ *adj* : somewhat watery — **wa·ter·ish·ness** *n*

water jacket *n* : an outer casing which holds water or through which water circulates for cooling something

water jump *n* : an obstacle (as in a steeplechase) consisting of a pool, stream, or ditch of water

wa·ter·less \'wȯt-ər-ləs, 'wät-\ *adj* 1 : destitute of water : DRY 2 : not requiring water (as for cooling or cooking) — **wa·ter·less·ly** *adv* — **wa·ter·less·ness** *n*

water lily *n* : any of a family of aquatic monocotyledonous plants with rounded floating leaves and usu. showy flowers

wa·ter·line \-,līn\ *n* : any of several lines that are marked upon the outside of a ship and correspond with the surface of the water when it is afloat on an even keel

wa·ter·logged \-,lȯgd, -,lägd\ *adj* : so filled or soaked with water as to be heavy or hard to manage ⟨a *waterlogged* boat⟩

wa·ter·loo \,wȯt-ər-'lü, ,wät-\ *n* [*Waterloo*, Belgium, scene of Napoleon's defeat in 1815] : a decisive defeat

water main *n* : a pipe or conduit for conveying water (as from a reservoir)

wa·ter·man \'wȯt-ər-mən, 'wät-\ *n* : a man who lives and works mostly in or near water; *esp* : a boatman who plies for hire

¹wa·ter·mark \-,märk\ *n* 1 : a mark that indicates a line to which water has risen 2 : a mark (as the maker's name or trademark) made in paper during manufacture and visible when the paper is held up to the light

²watermark *vt* : to mark (paper) with a watermark

wa·ter·mel·on \-,mel-ən\ *n* 1 : a large oblong or rounded fruit with a hard green or white rind often striped or variegated, a sweet watery pink, yellowish, or red pulp, and many seeds 2 : a widely grown African vine of the gourd family whose fruits are watermelons

water meter *n* : an instrument for recording the quantity of water passing through a particular outlet

water milfoil *n* : any of a genus of aquatic plants with finely pinnate submersed leaves

water moccasin *n* : a venomous semiaquatic pit viper of the southern U.S. closely related to the copperhead

water mold *n* : an aquatic fungus

water nymph *n* : a goddess (as a naiad) associated with a body of water

water oak *n* : any of several American oaks that thrive in wet soil

water of crystallization : water of hydration present in many crystallized substances

water of hydration : water chemically combined with a substance to form a hydrate that can be expelled (as by heating) without essentially altering the composition of the substance

water ouzel *n* : any of several birds related to the thrushes that dive into swift mountain streams and walk on the bottom in search of food — called also *dipper*

water pipe *n* 1 : a pipe for conveying water 2 : a tobacco-smoking device so arranged that the smoke is drawn through water

water pistol *n* : a toy pistol designed to throw a jet of liquid — called also *water gun*

water polo *n* : a goal game played in water by teams of swimmers with a ball resembling a soccer ball

wa·ter·pow·er \'wȯt-ər-,paú(-ə)r, 'wät-\ *n* : the power of moving water used to run machinery (as for generating electricity)

¹wa·ter·proof \,wȯt-ər-'prüf, ,wät-\ *adj* : not letting water through; *also* : covered or treated with a material (as a solution of rubber) to prevent permeation by water — **wa·ter·proof·ness** *n*

²wa·ter·proof \'wȯt-ər-,, 'wät-\ *n* 1 : a waterproof fabric 2 *chiefly Brit* : RAINCOAT

³wa·ter·proof \,wȯt-ər-', 'wät-\ *vt* : to make waterproof — **wa·ter·proof·er** *n*

wa·ter·proof·ing *n* 1 **a** : the act or process of making something waterproof **b** : the condition of being made waterproof 2 : something (as a coating) capable of imparting waterproofness

water rat *n* 1 : a rodent that frequents water 2 : a waterfront loafer or petty thief

wa·ter-re·pel·lent \,wȯt-ə(r)-ri-'pel-ənt, ,wät-\ *adj*

---

j joke; **ŋ** sing; **ō** flow; **ȯ** flaw; **ȯi** coin; **th** thin; **th̲** this; **ü** loot; **ú** foot; **y** yet; **yü** few; **yú** furious; **zh** vision

: treated with a finish that is resistant but not impervious to penetration by water

wa·ter·re·sis·tant \-ri-'zis-tənt\ *adj* : resistant to but not wholly proof against the action or entry of water

water scorpion *n* : any of various large aquatic bugs with the end of the abdomen prolonged by a long breathing tube

wa·ter·shed \'wȯt-ər-ˌshed, 'wät-\ *n* 1 : a dividing ridge (as a mountain range) separating one drainage area from others 2 : the whole area that drains into a particular river or lake

wa·ter·side \-ˌsīd\ *n* : the land bordering a body of water

water ski *n* : a ski used on water

water-ski *vi* : to ski on water while towed by a speedboat

water snake *n* : any of numerous snakes frequenting or inhabiting fresh waters and feeding largely on aquatic animals

wa·ter·soak \'wȯt-ər-ˌsōk, 'wät-\ *vt* : to soak in water

water spaniel *n* : a rather large spaniel with a heavy curly coat used esp. for retrieving waterfowl

wa·ter·spout \'wȯt-ər-ˌspau̇t, 'wät-\ *n* 1 : a pipe for carrying off water from a roof 2 : a slender funnel-shaped cloud that extends down to a cloud of spray torn up from water by a whirlwind

water sprite *n* : a sprite supposed to inhabit or haunt water : WATER NYMPH

water sprout *n* : a vigorous but unproductive shoot arising usu. from the base of a tree (as an apple)

water strider *n* : any of various long-legged bugs that move about on the surface of the water

water table *n* : the upper limit of the ground wholly saturated with water

water thrush *n* 1 : any of several American warblers usu. living near streams 2 : a European water ouzel

wa·ter·tight \ˌwȯt-ər-'tīt, ˌwät-\ *adj* 1 : of such tight construction or fit as to be waterproof 2 : leaving no possibility of misconstruction or evasion — **wa·ter·tight·ness** *n*

water tower *n* 1 : a tower or standpipe serving as a reservoir to deliver water 2 : a fire apparatus having a vertical pipe that can be extended to various heights and supplied with water under high pressure

water vapor *n* : the vapor of water esp. when below the boiling temperature and in diffused form (as in the atmosphere)

water-vascular system *n* : a system of vessels in echinoderms containing a circulating water fluid that is used for the movement of tentacles and tube feet and may also function in excretion and respiration

water wave *n* : a method or style of setting hair by dampening with water and forming into waves — **wa·ter·waved** \'wȯt-ər-ˌwāvd, 'wät-\ *adj*

wa·ter·way \'wȯt-ər-ˌwā, 'wät-\ *n* : a channel or a body of water by which ships can travel

wa·ter·weed \-ˌwēd\ *n* : a weedy aquatic plant usu. with inconspicuous flowers — compare WATER LILY

wa·ter·wheel \-ˌhwēl\ *n* : a wheel made to turn by a flow of water against it

water wings *n pl* : an air-filled device to give support to the body of a person swimming or learning to swim

wa·ter·works \-ˌwərks\ *n pl* : the system of reservoirs, channels, mains, and pumping and purifying equipment by which a water supply is obtained and distributed (as to a city)

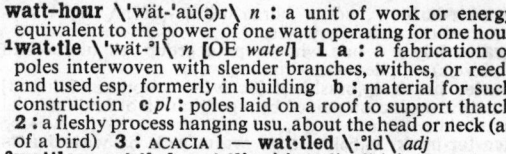

waterwheel

wa·ter·worn \-ˌwȯrn, -ˌwȯrn\ *adj* : worn, smoothed, or polished by the action of water

wa·tery \'wȯt-ə-rē, 'wät-\ *adj* 1 : of or having to do with water (a *watery* grave) 2 : containing, full of, or giving out water (*watery* clouds) 3 : being like water : THIN, WEAK (*watery* lemonade) 4 : being soft and soggy (*watery* turnips) — **wa·ter·i·ness** *n*

watt \'wät\ *n* [after James *Watt* d1819 Scottish engineer] : the mks unit of power equal to the work done at the rate of one joule per second or to the rate of work represented by a current of one ampere under a pressure of one volt

watt·age \-ij\ *n* : amount of power expressed in watts

watt-hour \'wät-ˌau̇(ə)r\ *n* : a unit of work or energy equivalent to the power of one watt operating for one hour

¹wat·tle \'wät-ᵊl\ *n* [OE *watel*] 1 a : a fabrication of poles interwoven with slender branches, withes, or reeds and used esp. formerly in building b : material for such construction c *pl* : poles laid on a roof to support thatch 2 : a fleshy process hanging usu. about the head or neck (as of a bird) 3 : ACACIA 1 — **wat·tled** \-ᵊld\ *adj*

²wattle *vt* **wat·tled; wat·tling** \'wät-liŋ, ᵊl-iŋ\ 1 : to form or build of or with wattle 2 a : to form into wattle : interlace to form wattle b : to unite or make solid by interweaving light flexible material

watt·me·ter \'wät-ˌmēt-ər\ *n* : an instrument for measuring electric power in watts

¹wave \'wāv\ *vb* [OE *wafian* to wave with the hands] 1 : to float, play, or shake in an air current : move or cause to move loosely to and fro : FLUTTER 2 : to motion with the hands or with something held in them in signal or salute 3 a : to become moved or brandished to and fro b : BRANDISH, FLOURISH (*waved* a pistol menacingly) 4 : to move before the wind with a wavelike motion (field of *waving* grain) 5 : to follow or cause to follow a curving line or take a wavy form : UNDULATE — **wav·er** *n*

²wave *n* 1 : a moving swell or crest on the surface of water 2 : a wavelike formation or shape (a *wave* in the hair) 3 : the action or process of making wavy or curly 4 : a waving motion (as of the hand or a flag) 5 : FLOW, GUSH (a *wave* of color swept the girl's face) 6 : a surge or rapid increase (a *wave* of buying) (a heat *wave*) 7 : a disturbance that transfers energy progressively from point to point and that may take the form of an elastic deformation or of a variation of pressure, electric or magnetic intensity, electric potential, or temperature (a light *wave*) — **wave·like** \-ˌlīk\ *adj*

Wave \'wāv\ *n* [*W*omen *A*ccepted for *V*olunteer *E*mergency *S*ervice] : a woman serving in the U.S. Navy

waved \'wāvd\ *adj* : having a wavelike form or outline: as a : UNDULATING, CURVING (the *waved* cutting edge of a bread knife) b : having wavy lines of color : WATERED (*waved* cloth)

wave·length \'wāv-ˌleŋ(k)th\ *n* : the distance (as from crest to crest) in the line of advance of a wave from any one point to the next corresponding point

wave·less \-ləs\ *adj* : having no waves : CALM

wave·let \-lət\ *n* : a little wave : RIPPLE

wave mechanics *n* : a theory of matter holding that elementary particles (as electrons, protons, or neutrons) have wave properties

¹wa·ver \'wā-vər\ *vi* **wa·vered; wa·ver·ing** \'wāv-(ə-)riŋ\ [ME *waveren*] 1 : to vacillate irresolutely between choices : fluctuate in opinion, allegiance, or direction 2 a : to weave or sway unsteadily to and fro : REEL, TOTTER b : QUIVER, FLICKER (*wavering* flames) c : FALTER 3 : to give an unsteady sound : QUAVER **syn** see HESITATE, SWAY — **wa·ver·er** \'wā-vər-ər\ *n* — **wa·ver·ing·ly** \'wāv-(ə-)riŋ-lē\ *adv*

²waver *n* : an act of wavering, quivering, or fluttering

wavy \'wā-vē\ *adj* **wav·i·er; wav·i·est** : having waves : moving in waves — **wav·i·ly** \-və-lē\ *adv* — **wav·i·ness** \-vē-nəs\ *n*

¹wax \'waks\ *n* [OE *weax*] 1 : a yellowish plastic substance secreted by bees and used by them for constructing the honeycomb — called also *beeswax* 2 : any of various substances resembling beeswax in physical or chemical properties: a : a plant or animal product that is harder and less greasy than a typical fat b : a solid mixture of higher hydrocarbons c : CERUMEN 3 : something likened to wax as soft, impressionable, or readily molded — **wax·like** \-ˌlīk\ *adj*

²wax *vt* : to treat or rub with wax

³wax *vi* [OE *weaxan*] 1 : to grow larger or greater: as a : to grow in volume or duration (a stream *waxing* with melting snows) b : to increase in apparent size and brightness (the moon *waxes* toward the full) 2 : to pass from one state to another : BECOME (the party *waxed* merry)

⁴wax *n* 1 : INCREASE, GROWTH 2 : the period from the new moon to the full phase of the moon

wax bean *n* : a kidney bean with pods that are yellow when fit for use as snap beans

waxed paper *n* : paper treated with wax to make it impervious to water and grease

wax·en \'wak-sən\ *adj* **1** : made of wax **2** : resembling wax (as in pliability, pallor, or lustrous smoothness)

wax myrtle *n* : any of a genus of trees or shrubs with aromatic foliage; *esp* : an American shrub having small hard berries with a thick coating of white wax used for candles

wax·wing \'waks-,wiŋ\ *n* : any of several American and Eurasian passerine birds that are mostly brown with a showy crest and velvety plumage

wax·work \-,wərk\ *n* **1** : an effigy in wax usu. of a person **2** *pl* : an exhibition of wax effigies

waxy \'wak-sē\ *adj* **wax·i·er; -est 1** : made of or full of or covered with wax (a *waxy* surface) (*waxy* berries) **2** : resembling wax : WAXEN — **wax·i·ness** *n*

¹way \'wā\ *n* [OE *weg*] **1 a** : a track for travel or passage : PATH, ROAD, STREET **b** : an opening for passage (as through a crowd or a gate) **2** : the course traveled from one place to another : ROUTE **3 a** : a course of action (chose the easy *way*) **b** : opportunity, capability, or fact of doing as one pleases (determined to have his *way*) **c** : POSSIBILITY (there are no two *ways* about it) **4 a** : manner in which something is done or happens : METHOD, MODE (this *way* of thinking) (a new *way* of painting) (the *way* the mind works) **b** : FEATURE, RESPECT (a good worker in many *ways*) **c** : the usual or characteristic state of affairs (as is the *way* with dreams) **d** : STATE, CONDITION (that's the *way* things are) (was in a bad *way* with rheumatism) **5 a** : a particular or characteristic mode or trick of behavior (it's just his *way*) (noticed the child's pretty *ways* with her pets) **b** : a regular continued course (as of life or action) (championing the American *way*) (people met in the *way* of business); *also* : a body of ethical or religious practice (as the Christian religion) **6 a** : the length of a course : DISTANCE (a short *way* down the road) (still a *way* from success) **b** : progress along a course (earning his *way* through school) (made their *way* through difficult terrain) **7** : something (as a locality) having direction as an attribute (come this *way*) (out our *way*) (stroking the fur the wrong *way*) **8 a** : room or chance to progress or advance (make *way* for the queen) **b** : place for something else (slums torn down to make *way* for parks) **9 a** : a guiding track that facilitates passage or movement **b** *pl* : an inclined support on which a ship is built and from which it is launched **10** : CATEGORY, KIND (get what you need in the *way* of supplies) **11** : motion or speed of a boat through the water (making slow *way* down the harbor) — **by way of 1** : for the purpose of (*by way of* illustration) **2** : by the route through : VIA — **out of the way 1** : WRONG, IMPROPER **2** : SECLUDED, REMOTE — **under way 1** : in motion through the water **2** : in progress

²way *adj* : of, connected with, or constituting an intermediate point on a route (*way* station)

³way *adv* : ¹AWAY 7

way·bill \'wā-,bil\ *n* : a document prepared by the carrier of a shipment of goods and containing details of the shipment, route, and charges

way·far·er \-,far-ər, -,fer-\ *n* : a traveler esp. on foot — **way·far·ing** \-,far-iŋ, -,fer-\ *adj*

way·lay \'wā-,lā\ *vt* **-laid** \-,lād\; **-lay·ing** : to lie in wait for often in order to seize, rob, or kill

Way of the Cross : STATIONS OF THE CROSS

-ways \,wāz\ *adv suffix* [ME, fr. *ways*, gen. of *way*] : in (such) a way, course, direction, or manner (side*ways*) (flat*ways*)

ways and means *n pl* : methods and resources for accomplishing something and esp. for raising revenues needed by a state; *also* : a legislative committee concerned with this function

way·side \'wā-,sīd\ *n* : the side of or land adjacent to a road or path — **wayside** *adj*

way station *n* : an intermediate station between principal stations on a line of travel (as a railroad)

way·ward \'wā-wərd\ *adj* [ME, short for *awayward* turned away] **1** : taking one's own and usu. irregular or improper way : DISOBEDIENT (*wayward* children) **2** : CONTRARY, PERVERSE (their *wayward* behavior) **3** : following no clear principle or law — **way·ward·ly** *adv* — **way·ward·ness** *n*

way·worn \-,wōrn, -,wȯrn\ *adj* : wearied by traveling

we \(')wē\ *pron* [OE *wē*] **1** : I and one or more others — used as pronoun of the 1st person plural; compare I, OUR,

OURS, US **2** : I — used by a sovereign or an editor or writer

weak \'wēk\ *adj* [ON *veikr*] **1** : lacking strength: as **a** : deficient in physical vigor : FEEBLE, DEBILITATED **b** : not able to sustain or resist much weight, pressure, or strain **c** : deficient in vigor of mind or character; *also* : resulting from or indicative of such deficiency (a *weak* policy) **d** : DILUTE (*weak* tea) **2** : not factually grounded or logically presented (a *weak* argument) **3 a** : not able to function properly **b** : lacking skill or proficiency : indicative of a lack of skill or aptitude **c** : wanting in vigor of expression or effect **4 a** : not having or exerting authority (*weak* government) **b** : INEFFECTIVE, IMPOTENT **5** : of, relating to, or constituting a verb or verb conjugation that forms the past tense and past participle by adding the suffix *-ed* or *-d* or *-t* **6** : bearing the minimal degree of stress occurring in the language (*weak* syllable) — **weak·ly** *adv*

weak·en \'wē-kən\ *vb* **weak·ened; weak·en·ing** \'wēk-(ə-)niŋ\ : to make or become weak or weaker

weak·fish \'wēk-,fish\ *n* : any of several marine food fishes related to the perches; *esp* : a common sport and market fish of the eastern coast of the U.S.

weak·heart·ed \-'härt-əd\ *adj* : lacking courage : FAINT-HEARTED

weak-kneed \'wēk-'nēd\ *adj* : lacking willpower or resolution : IRRESOLUTE

weak·ling \'wēk-liŋ\ *n* : one that is weak in body, character, or mind — **weakling** *adj*

weak·ly \'wēk-lē\ *adj* **weak·li·er; -est** : FEEBLE, WEAK — **weak·li·ness** *n*

weak-mind·ed \'wēk-'mīn-dəd\ *adj* **1** : lacking in judgment or good sense : FOOLISH **2** : FEEBLE-MINDED — **weak-mind·ed·ness** *n*

weak·ness \'wēk-nəs\ *n* **1** : the quality or state of being weak; *also* : an instance or period of being weak **2** : FAULT, DEFECT **3** : an object of special desire or fondness

¹weal \'wēl\ *n* [ME *wele*, fr. OE *wela*; akin to E ³*well*] : WELL-BEING, PROSPERITY

²weal *n* : WELT

weald \'wēld\ *n* [fr. the *Weald*, wooded district in southeastern England] **1** : a heavily wooded area : FOREST (*Weald* of Kent) **2** : a wild or uncultivated usu. upland region

wealth \'welth\ *n* [ME *welthe*, fr. *wele* weal] **1** : abundance of possessions or resources : AFFLUENCE **2** : abundant supply : PROFUSION (a *wealth* of detail) **3 a** : all property that has a money or an exchange value **b** : all material objects that have economic utility; *esp* : those in existence at any one time

wealthy \'wel-thē\ *adj* **wealth·i·er; -est 1** : having wealth : AFFLUENT **2** : characterized by abundance : AMPLE — **wealth·i·ly** \-thə-lē\ *adv* — **wealth·i·ness** \-thē-nəs\ *n*

wean \'wēn\ *vt* [OE *wenian* to accustom, wean] **1** : to accustom (as a child) to take food otherwise than by nursing **2** : to turn (one) away from something long desired or followed (*wean* a boy from a bad habit) — **wean·er** *n*

wean·ling \-liŋ\ *n* : one newly weaned — **weanling** *adj*

weap·on \'wep-ən\ *n* [OE *wǣpen*] **1** : something (as a gun, knife, or club) that may be used to fight with **2** : a means by which one contends against another

weap·on·less \-ləs\ *adj* : lacking weapons : UNARMED

weap·on·ry \-rē\ *n* : the science of designing and making weapons

¹wear \'wa(ə)r, 'we(ə)r\ *vb* **wore** \'wō(ə)r, 'wȯ(ə)r\; **worn** \'wōrn, 'wȯrn\; **wear·ing** [OE *werian*] **1 a** : to bear on the person or use habitually for clothing or adornment (*wears* a toupee) (*wore* a jacket) **b** : to carry on the person (*wear* a sword) **2** : to have or show an appearance of (*wore* a happy smile) **3 a** : to impair, diminish, or decay by use or attrition (the dress finally *wore* to bits) (letters on the stone *worn* away by weathering) **b** : to produce gradually by friction or attrition (*wear* a hole in the rug) **c** : to exhaust or lessen the strength of : WEARY, FATIGUE (*worn* by care and toil) **4** : to endure use : last under use or the passage of time (a silk that *wears* well) **5 a** : to diminish or fail with the passage of time (her nagging *wore* his patience away) (the day *wore* on) **b** : to grow or become by attrition or use (hair *worn* thin about the temples⟩ **6 :** to go or cause to go about by turning the stern to the wind — compare TACK — **wear·a·ble** \'war-ə-bəl, 'wer-\ *adj* — **wear·er** \-ər\ *n* — **wear on** **:** IRRITATE, FRAY

²**wear** *n* **1 :** the act of wearing **:** the state of being worn **:** USE ⟨clothes for everyday *wear*⟩ **2 :** clothing or an article of clothing usu. of a particular kind or for a special occasion or use **3 :** wearing quality **:** durability under use **4 :** the result of wearing or use **:** diminution or impairment due to use ⟨*wear*-resistant surface⟩

wear and tear *n* **:** the loss or injury to which something is subjected by or in the course of use; *esp* **:** normal depreciation

wear down *vt* **:** to weary and overcome by persistent resistance or pressure

wea·ri·less \'wir-ē-ləs\ *adj* **:** TIRELESS — **wea·ri·less·ly** *adv*

wear·ing \'wa(ə)r-iŋ, 'we(ə)r-\ *adj* **:** subjecting to or inflicting wear; *esp* **:** FATIGUING ⟨a *wearing* journey⟩ — **wear·ing·ly** \-iŋ-lē\ *adv*

wea·ri·some \'wir-ē-səm\ *adj* **:** causing weariness **:** TIRESOME — **wea·ri·some·ly** *adv* — **wea·ri·some·ness** *n*

wear off *vi* **:** to diminish gradually (as in effect)

wear out *vb* **1 :** to make or become useless by wear **2 :** TIRE, WEARY; *also* **:** EXHAUST

¹**wea·ry** \'wi(ə)r-ē\ *adj* **wea·ri·er; -est** [OE *wērig*] **1 :** worn out in strength, endurance, vigor, or freshness **2 :** expressing or characteristic of weariness **3 :** having one's patience, tolerance, or pleasure exhausted — used with *of* **4 :** TIRESOME — **wea·ri·ly** \'wir-ə-lē\ *adv* — **wea·ri·ness** \'wir-ē-nəs\ *n*

²**weary** *vb* **wea·ried; wea·ry·ing :** to become or make weary

wea·sand \'wēz-°nd\ *n* [ME *wesand*] **:** THROAT, GULLET; *also* **:** WINDPIPE

¹**wea·sel** \'wē-zəl\ *n, pl* **weasel** *or* **weasels** [OE *weosule*] **:** any of various small slender active carnivorous mammals related to the minks

²**weasel** *vi* **wea·seled; wea·sel·ing** \'wēz-(ə-)liŋ\ [*weasel word*] **1 :** to speak evasively **:** EQUIVOCATE **2 :** to escape from or evade a situation or obligation — often used with *out*

weasel word *n* [fr. the weasel's habit of sucking the contents out of an egg while leaving the shell superficially intact] **:** a word used in order to evade or retreat from a direct or forthright statement or position

¹**weath·er** \'weth-ər\ *n* [OE *weder*] **:** state of the atmosphere with respect to heat or cold, wetness or dryness, calm or storm, clearness or cloudiness **:** meteorological condition; *also* **:** a particular and esp. a disagreeable atmospheric state — **under the weather :** somewhat ill or drunk

²**weather** *adj* **:** WINDWARD — compare LEE

³**weather** *vb* **weath·ered; weath·er·ing** \'weth-(ə-)riŋ\ **1 a :** to expose to or endure the action of the elements **b :** to alter (as in color or texture) by exposure **2 :** to sail or pass to the windward of **3 :** to bear up against and come safely through ⟨*weather* a storm⟩

weath·er·a·bil·i·ty \,weth-(ə-)rə-'bil-ət-ē\ *n* **:** capability of withstanding weather ⟨*weatherability* of a plastic⟩

weath·er·beat·en \'weth-ər-,bēt-°n\ *adj* **:** worn or altered by exposure to weather

weath·er·board \-,bōrd, -,bórd\ *n* **:** CLAPBOARD, SIDING

weath·er·board·ing \-,bōrd-iŋ, -,bórd-\ *n* **:** CLAPBOARDS, SIDING

weath·er·bound \-,baùnd\ *adj* **:** kept in port or at anchor or from travel or sport by bad weather

weather bureau *n* **:** an organization that collects weather reports, formulates weather predictions and storm warnings, and compiles weather statistics

weath·er·cock \-,käk\ *n* **1 :** a vane often in the figure of a cock mounted so as to turn freely with the wind and show its direction **2 :** one that changes readily or often

weath·er·glass \-,glas\ *n* **:** a simple instrument for showing changes in atmospheric pressure by the changing level of liquid in a spout connected with a closed reservoir

weath·er·ing *n* **:** alteration of exposed

weathercock

objects by action of the elements; *esp* **:** physical disintegration and chemical decomposition of earth materials at or near the earth's surface

weath·er·man \'weth-ər-,man\ *n* **:** one who reports and forecasts the weather **:** METEOROLOGIST

weather map *n* **:** a chart showing the principal meteorological features at a given hour and over an extended region

weath·er·proof \,weth-ər-'prüf\ *adj* **:** able to withstand exposure to weather without damage or loss of function — **weatherproof** *vt* — **weath·er·proof·ness** *n*

weather station *n* **:** a station for taking, recording, and reporting meteorological observations

weather strip *n* **:** a strip of material used to make a seal where a door or window joins the sill or casing — **weather-strip** *vt*

weath·er·tight \,weth-ər-'tīt\ *adj* **:** proof against wind and rain ⟨*weathertight* storage bin⟩

weather vane *n* **:** VANE 1

weath·er·wise \'weth-ər-,wīz\ *adj* **:** skillful in forecasting changes in the weather

weath·er·worn \-,wōrn, -,wórn\ *adj* **:** worn by exposure to the weather

¹**weave** \'wēv\ *vb* **wove** \'wōv\; **wo·ven** \'wō-vən\; **weav·ing** [OE *wefan*] **1 a :** to form by interlacing strands of material; *esp* **:** to make (cloth) on a loom by interlacing warp and filling threads **b :** to interlace (as threads) into a fabric and esp. cloth **2 :** SPIN 2b **3 a :** to produce by elaborately combining elements **:** CONTRIVE **b :** to unite in a coherent whole **c :** to introduce as an appropriate element **:** work in ⟨*wove* the episodes into a story⟩ ⟨*weave* a moral into a tale⟩ **4 :** to direct or move in a winding or zigzag course esp. to avoid obstacles — **weav·er** *n*

²**weave** *n* **:** a pattern or method of weaving ⟨a coarse loose *weave*⟩

³**weave** *vi* **:** to move in a wavering manner from side to side **:** SWAY

weav·er·bird \'wē-vər-,bərd\ *n* **:** any of a family of Old World passerine birds that resemble finches and mostly construct elaborate nests of interlaced vegetation — called also *weaver finch*

¹**web** \'web\ *n* [OE; akin to E *weave*] **1 :** a fabric on a loom or in process of being removed from a loom **2 a :** COBWEB 1 **b :** SNARE, ENTANGLEMENT **3 :** a membrane of an animal or plant; *esp* **:** one uniting toes (as of many birds) **4 :** the plate connecting the upper and lower flanges of a girder or rail **5 :** NETWORK ⟨a *web* of highways⟩ **6 :** the series of barbs implanted on each side of the shaft of a feather **:** VANE **7 :** a continuous sheet of paper manufactured or undergoing manufacture or a reel of this for use in a rotary printing press — **web·by** \'web-ē\ *adj* — **web·like** \'web-,līk\ *adj*

²**web** *vb* **webbed; web·bing 1 :** to cover or provide with webs or a network **2 :** ENTANGLE, ENSNARE **3 :** to make a web

web·bing \'web-iŋ\ *n* **:** a strong closely woven tape used esp. for straps, harness, or upholstery

web·foot \'web-'fùt\ *n* **:** a foot having webbed toes — **web·foot·ed** \-əd\ *adj*

web spinner *n* **:** an insect that spins a web; *esp* **:** any of an order (Embiodea) of small slender insects with biting mouthparts that live in silken tunnels which they spin

web·worm \'web-,wərm\ *n* **:** any of various mostly gregarious caterpillars that spin large webs

wed \'wed\ *vb* **wed·ded** *also* **wed; wed·ding** [OE *weddian*, fr. *wedd* pledge] **1 :** to take, give, or join in marriage **:** enter into matrimony **:** MARRY **2 :** to unite firmly

we'd \(,)wēd\ **:** we had **:** we should **:** we would

wed·ding \'wed-iŋ\ *n* **1 :** a marriage ceremony usu. with accompanying festivities **:** NUPTIALS **2 :** a joining in close association **3 :** a wedding anniversary or its celebration — usu. used in combination

¹**wedge** \'wej\ *n* [OE *wecg*] **1 :** a piece of wood or metal tapered to a thin edge and used esp. to split wood or rocks and in lifting heavy weights — compare SIMPLE MACHINE **2 :** something (as a piece of pie or land or a flight of wild geese) shaped like a wedge **3 :** a thing that serves to make a gradual opening or cause

wedge 1

a change in something ⟨use every concession as an entering *wedge*⟩
²**wedge** *vt* **1** : to fasten or tighten by or as if by driving in a wedge **2** : to press or force (something) into a narrow space ⟨*wedged* paper around the loose window⟩ **3** : to separate or split with or as if with a wedge

wedged \'wejd\ *adj* : shaped like a wedge ⟨the *wedged* formation of flying geese⟩

Wedg·wood \'wej-ˌwu̇d\ *n* [after Josiah *Wedgwood* d1795 English potter] : pottery ware with a tinted body and applied white reliefs

wed·lock \'wed-ˌläk\ *n* [OE *wedlāc* marriage bond, fr. *wedd* pledge + *-lāc*, suffix denoting activity] : the state of being married : MARRIAGE — **out of wedlock** : with the natural parents not legally married to each other

Wednes·day \'wenz-dē\ *n* [OE *wōdnesdæg*, lit., day of Odin] : the 4th day of the week

wee \'wē\ *adj* [ME *we*, fr. *we* little bit, fr. OE *wǣge* weight] **1** : very small : TINY **2** : very early ⟨*wee* hours of the morning⟩

¹**weed** \'wēd\ *n* [OE *wēod*] **1** : a plant of no value and usu. of rank growth; *esp* : one that tends to overgrow or choke out more desirable plants **2** : something (as an obnoxious thing or person) like a weed — **weed·less** \-ləs\ *adj*

²**weed** *vb* **1** : to free from or remove weeds or something harmful, inferior, or superfluous **2** : to get rid of (weeds or unwanted items) ⟨*weed* out the loafers from the crew⟩ — **weed·er** *n*

³**weed** *n* [OE *wǣd*] **1** : GARMENT — often used in pl. **2** : dress worn (as by a widow) as a sign of mourning — usu. used in pl.

weed·i·cide \'wēd-ə-ˌsīd\ *n* : HERBICIDE

weedy \'wēd-ē\ *adj* **weed·i·er**; **-est** **1** : abounding with or consisting of weeds ⟨a *weedy* field⟩ **2** : resembling a weed esp. in rank growth or ready propagation **3** : noticeably lean and scrawny : LANKY ⟨*weedy* cattle⟩

week \'wēk\ *n* [OE *wicu*] **1 a** : seven successive days ⟨was sick for a *week*⟩ **b** : a calendar period of seven days beginning with Sunday and ending with Saturday ⟨the last *week* of the month⟩ **2** : the working or school days of the calendar week ⟨had a hard *week*⟩

week·day \-ˌdā\ *n* : a day of the week except Sunday or sometimes except Saturday and Sunday

week·days \-ˌdāz\ *adv* : on weekdays repeatedly : on any weekday ⟨takes a bus *weekdays*⟩

¹**week·end** \-ˌend\ *n* : the end of the week; *esp* : the period between the close of one working or school week and the beginning of the next

²**weekend** *vi* : to spend the weekend

week·ends \-ˌen(d)z\ *adv* : on weekends repeatedly : on any weekend ⟨travels *weekends*⟩

¹**week·ly** \'wē-klē\ *adj* **1** : occurring, done, produced, or issued every week **2** : computed in terms of one week — **weekly** *adv*

²**weekly** *n, pl* **weeklies** : a weekly publication

ween \'wēn\ *vt* [OE *wēnan*] *archaic* : IMAGINE, SUPPOSE

wee·ny \'wē-nē\ *adj* [*wee* + *tiny*] : exceptionally small

¹**weep** \'wēp\ *vb* **wept** \'wept\; **weep·ing** [OE *wēpan*] **1 a** : to express emotion and esp. sorrow by shedding tears : BEWAIL **b** : to pour forth (tears) : CRY **2** : to give off (liquid) slowly or in drops : OOZE

²**weep** *n* : LAPWING

weep·er \'wē-pər\ *n* **1** : one that weeps **2** : a professional mourner

weep·ing \'wē-piŋ\ *adj* **1** : TEARFUL; *also* : RAINY **2** : having slender pendent branches

weeping willow *n* : an Asiatic willow with weeping branches

weepy \'wē-pē\ *adj* **weep·i·er**; **-est** : inclined to weep : TEARFUL

wee·vil \'wē-vəl\ *n* [OE *wifel*] : any of a large group (Rhynchophora) of mostly small beetles having the head long and usu. curved downward to form a snout bearing the jaws at the tip and including many very injurious to plants or plant products — **wee·vily** *or* **wee·vil·ly** \'wēv-(ə-)lē\ *adj*

weft \'weft\ *n* [OE; akin to E *weave*] **1 a** : WOOF 1 **b** : yarn used for the woof **2** : WEB, FABRIC; *also* : an article of woven fabric

wei·ge·la \wī-'jē-lə\ *n* [NL, fr. Christian E. *Weigel* d1831

German physician] : any of a genus of showy shrubs of the honeysuckle family; *esp* : a Chinese shrub widely grown for its pink or red flowers

¹**weigh** \'wā\ *vb* [OE *wegan* to move, carry, weigh; akin to E *way*] **1 a** : to ascertain the heaviness of by or as if by a balance **b** : to have weight or a specified weight **2 a** : to consider carefully : PONDER **b** : to merit consideration as important : COUNT ⟨evidence will *weigh* heavily against him⟩ **3** : to heave up (an anchor) preparatory to sailing **4** : to measure or apportion (a definite quantity) on or as if on a scales **5 a** : to press down with or as if with a heavy weight **b** : to have a saddening or disheartening effect — **weigh·a·ble** \'wā-ə-bəl\ *adj* — **weigh·er** *n*

²**weigh** *n* : WAY — used in the phrase *under weigh*

weigh down *vt* **1** : OVERBURDEN **2** : OPPRESS, DEPRESS

weigh in *vi* : to have something weighed; *esp* : to have oneself weighed preliminary to participation in a sports event

¹**weight** \'wāt\ *n* [OE *wiht*] **1 a** : quantity as determined by weighing ⟨sold by *weight*⟩ **b** : the property of a body that is measurable by weighing and that depends on the interaction of its mass with a gravitational field **c** : the standard or established amount that something should weigh ⟨coin of full *weight*⟩ **d** : something with weight : material substance ⟨adding *weight* to the load⟩ **2 a** : a quantity or portion weighing a usu. specified amount ⟨take equal *weights* of flour and butter⟩ ⟨100 lbs. *weight* of iron⟩ **b** : the amount that something weighs ⟨worth his *weight* in gold⟩ **c** : relative heaviness (as of a textile) — usu. used in combination **3 a** : a unit (as a pound or kilogram) of weight or mass — see MEASURE table, METRIC SYSTEM table **b** : an integrated system of such units **4 a** : an object (as a piece of metal) of known weight for balancing a scale in weighing other objects **b** : a heavy object used to hold, press down, or counterbalance something else ⟨clock *weights*⟩ **c** : a heavy object (as a metal ball) used in athletic exercises **5 a** : something heavy : LOAD ⟨skill in handling *weights*⟩ **b** : an immaterial burden or pressure ⟨had a *weight* on his conscience⟩ **6 a** : overpowering forces (as of an onslaught) **b** : relative importance or claim to consideration : NOTE ⟨opinions that carry *weight*⟩ ⟨a man of *weight* in the community⟩ **c** : the greater or more impressive part ⟨the *weight* of the evidence was against this view⟩

²**weight** *vt* **1** : to load or make heavy with or as if with a weight **2** : to oppress with a burden ⟨*weighted* down with cares⟩ **3** : to assign a relative importance to (as in a statistical study)

weight·less \'wāt-ləs\ *adj* : having little weight : lacking apparent gravitational pull — **weight·less·ly** *adv* — **weight·less·ness** *n*

weight lifter *n* : one that lifts barbells in competition or as an exercise — **weight lifting** *n*

weighty \'wāt-ē\ *adj* **weight·i·er**; **-est** **1** : having much weight : HEAVY **2 a** : of much importance or consequence : SERIOUS, MOMENTOUS ⟨*weighty* problems⟩ **b** : expressing seriousness : SOLEMN ⟨a *weighty* manner⟩ **3** : exerting authority or influence ⟨*weighty* arguments⟩ — **weight·i·ly** \'wāt-°l-ē\ *adv* — **weight·i·ness** \'wāt-ē-nəs\ *n*

wei·ma·ra·ner \ˌvī-mə-'rän-ər, 'wī-mə-ˌ\ *n* [G, fr. *Weimar*, Germany] : any of a German breed of large gray short-haired sporting dogs

weir \'wa(ə)r, 'we(ə)r, 'wi(ə)r\ *n* [OE *wer*] **1** : a fence set in a stream to catch fish **2** : a dam in a stream to raise the water level or divert its flow

weird \'wi(ə)rd\ *adj* [ME *werd* of or relating to fate or the Fates, fr. *werd* fate, fr. OE *wyrd*] **1 a** : of, relating to, or caused by witchcraft or the supernatural : MAGICAL **b** : UNEARTHLY, MYSTERIOUS **2** : of strange or extraordinary character : ODD, FANTASTIC — **weird·ly** *adv* — **weird·ness** *n*

 syn WEIRD, EERIE, UNCANNY mean mysteriously strange or fantastic. WEIRD may imply unearthliness or simply extreme queerness or oddness; EERIE suggests an uneasy or fearful consciousness of the presence of mysterious and malign spirits; UNCANNY applies esp. to abilities or perceptions so remarkable as to seem magical

Weird Sisters *n pl* : FATES

Weis·mann·ism \'vīs-ˌmän-ˌiz-əm, 'wīs-mən-\ *n* : the theories of heredity proposed by August Weismann

stressing particularly the separation of the germ cells and somatic cells and the continuity of the germinal elements
Welch \'welch\ *var of* WELSH

¹wel·come \'wel-kəm\ *interj* [alter. of OE *wilcuma* desirable guest] — used to express a greeting to a guest or newcomer upon his arrival

²welcome *vt* **1** : to greet hospitably and with courteous cordiality **2** : to meet or face with pleasure ⟨*welcomed* criticism of his report⟩ — **wel·com·er** *n*

³welcome *adj* **1** : received gladly into one's presence or companionship ⟨a *welcome* visitor⟩ **2** : giving pleasure : PLEASING ⟨a *welcome* rainfall⟩ ⟨*welcome* news⟩ **3** : willingly permitted to do, have, or enjoy something ⟨anyone is *welcome* to use the swimming pool⟩

⁴welcome *n* : a cordial greeting or reception

¹weld \'weld\ *vb* [alter. of ME *wellen* to boil, well, weld] **1** : to join (pieces of metal or plastic) by heating and allowing the edges to flow together or by hammering or pressing together **2** : to join as if by welding ⟨*welded* together in friendship⟩ **3** : to become or be capable of being welded ⟨not all metals *weld* well⟩ — **weld·er** *n*

²weld *n* **1** : a welded joint **2** : union by welding

weld·ment \'weld-mənt\ *n* : a unit formed by welding together an assembly of pieces

wel·fare \'wel-,fa(ə)r, -,fe(ə)r\ *n* [ME, fr. *wel faren* to fare well] **1** : the state of doing well esp. in respect to happiness, well-being, or prosperity **2** : WELFARE WORK **3** : RELIEF 1b — **welfare** *adj*

welfare state *n* : a nation or state that assumes primary responsibility for the individual and social welfare of its citizens

welfare work *n* : organized efforts for the social betterment of a group in society — **welfare worker** *n*

wel·kin \'wel-kən\ *n* [ME, cloud, sky, fr. OE *wolcen*] **1** : SKY **2** : AIR

¹well \'wel\ *n* [OE *welle*] **1 a** : an issue of water from the earth : a pool fed by a spring **b** : a source of supply : WELLSPRING ⟨was a *well* of information⟩ **2** : a hole sunk into the earth to reach a natural deposit (as of water, oil, or gas) **3** : an enclosure in the middle of a ship's hold about the pumps **4** : an open space extending vertically through floors of a structure (as for a staircase) **5** : something (as a container or space) suggesting a well for water ⟨tears *welled* from her eyes⟩

²well *vb* : to rise to the surface and flow forth : RUN, GUSH ⟨tears *welled* from her eyes⟩

³well *adv* **bet·ter** \'bet-ər\; **best** \'best\ [OE *wel*] **1 a** : in a pleasing or desirable manner : SATISFACTORILY, FORTUNATELY ⟨the party turned out *well*⟩ **b** : in a good or proper manner : EXCELLENTLY, SKILLFULLY ⟨did his work *well*⟩ **2** : ABUNDANTLY, FULLY ⟨eat *well*⟩ ⟨the orchard bore *well*⟩ **3** : with reason or courtesy : PROPERLY ⟨the girl could not very *well* refuse the invitation⟩ **4** : COMPLETELY, THOROUGHLY ⟨received a *well*-deserved ovation⟩ **5** : INTIMATELY, CLOSELY ⟨know a person *well*⟩ **6** : CONSIDERABLY, FAR ⟨*well* ahead⟩ ⟨*well* over his quota⟩ **7** : without trouble or difficulty ⟨he could *well* have gone⟩ **8** : EXACTLY, DEFINITELY ⟨remember it *well*⟩ — **as well 1** : in addition : ALSO ⟨other features as well⟩ **2** : without real loss or gain : EQUALLY ⟨might as well stop here⟩ — **as well as** : and not only : and in addition ⟨skillful *as well as* strong⟩

⁴well *interj* **1** — used to express surprise or expostulation **2** — used to indicate resumption of a thread of discourse or to introduce a remark

⁵well *adj* **1** : SATISFACTORY, PLEASING ⟨all's *well* that ends well⟩ **2 a** : PROSPEROUS, WELL-OFF **b** : being in satisfactory condition or circumstances **3** : ADVISABLE, DESIRABLE ⟨not *well* to anger him⟩ **4 a** : free or recovered from infirmity or disease : HEALTHY **b** : CURED, HEALED ⟨the wound is nearly *well*⟩ **5** : being a cause for thankfulness : FORTUNATE ⟨it is *well* that this has happened⟩ **syn** see HEALTHY

we'll \(,)wēl\ : we shall : we will

well-ad·vised \,wel-əd-'vīzd\ *adj* : acting wisely or properly : based on wise counsel : DISCREET, PRUDENT ⟨he was *well-advised* in following his doctor's orders⟩ ⟨a *well-advised* restraint⟩

wel·la·way \,wel-ə-'wā\ *interj* [OE *weilāwei*, alter. of *wā lā wā* woe! lo! woe!] — used to express sorrow or lamentation

well-be·ing \'wel-'bē-iŋ\ *n* : the state of being happy, healthy, or prosperous : WELFARE

well-be·loved \,wel-bi-'ləvd\ *adj* **1** : sincerely and deeply loved ⟨my *well-beloved* wife⟩ **2** : sincerely respected — used in various ceremonial forms of address

well-born \'wel-'bórn\ *adj* : born of good stock either socially or genetically

well-bred \-'bred\ *adj* : having or displaying good breeding : REFINED

well-con·di·tioned \,wel-kən-'dish-ənd\ *adj* **1** : characterized by proper disposition, morals, or behavior **2** : having a good physical condition : SOUND ⟨a *well-conditioned* animal⟩

well-de·fined \,wel-di-'fīnd\ *adj* : having clearly distinguishable limits or boundaries ⟨in mathematics a *well-defined* collection is a set⟩ ⟨a *well-defined* scar⟩

well-dis·posed \-dis-'pōzd\ *adj* : disposed to be friendly, favorable, or sympathetic ⟨*well-disposed* to our plan⟩

well-done \'wel-'dən\ *adj* **1** : rightly or properly performed **2** : cooked thoroughly

well-fa·vored \'wel-'fā-vərd\ *adj* : good-looking : HANDSOME — **well-fa·vored·ness** *n*

well-fixed \-'fikst\ *adj* : well-off financially

well-found \-'faund\ *adj* : fully furnished : properly equipped ⟨a *well-found* ship⟩

well-found·ed \-'faun-dəd\ *adj* : based on sound reasoning, information, judgment, or grounds

well-groomed \-'grümd, -'grùmd\ *adj* **1** : well dressed and scrupulously neat ⟨*well-groomed* men⟩ **2** : made neat, tidy, and attractive down to the smallest details ⟨a *well-groomed* lawn⟩

well-ground·ed \-'graùn-dəd\ *adj* : having a firm foundation : WELL-FOUNDED

well·head \'wel-,hed\ *n* **1 a** : the source of a spring or a stream **b** : principal source **2** : the top of or a structure built over a well

well-heeled \'wel-'hēld\ *adj* : WELL-FIXED

well-knit \-'nit\ *adj* : well and firmly formed or framed ⟨a *well-knit* argument⟩

well-known \-'nōn\ *adj* : fully or widely known

well-mean·ing \-'mē-niŋ\ *adj* : having or based on good intentions

well-nigh \-'nī\ *adv* : ALMOST, NEARLY

well-off \'wel-'óf\ *adj* : being in good condition or circumstances; *esp* : WELL-TO-DO

well-or·dered \-'órd-ərd\ *adj* : having an orderly procedure or arrangement ⟨a *well-ordered* household⟩

well-read \-'red\ *adj* : well informed and deeply versed through reading ⟨*well-read* in history⟩

well-spoken \-'spō-kən\ *adj* **1** : having a good command of language : speaking well and esp. courteously **2** : spoken with propriety ⟨*well-spoken* words⟩

well·spring \'wel-,spriŋ\ *n* **1** : SPRING, FOUNTAINHEAD **2** : a source of continual supply

well-timed \'wel-'tīmd\ *adj* : occurring opportunely : TIMELY

well-to-do \,wel-tə-'dü\ *adj* : having more than adequate material resources : PROSPEROUS

well-turned \'wel-'tərnd\ *adj* **1** : pleasingly rounded : SHAPELY ⟨a *well-turned* ankle⟩ **2** : pleasingly and appropriately expressed ⟨a *well-turned* phrase⟩

well-wish·er \'wel-,wish-ər\ *n* : one that wishes well to another — **well-wish·ing** \-,wish-iŋ\ *adj or n*

well-worn \-'wórn, -'wórn\ *adj* **1 a** : worn by much use ⟨*well-worn* shoes⟩ **b** : made stale by overuse : TRITE ⟨a *well-worn* quotation⟩ **2** : worn well or properly ⟨*well-worn* honors⟩

Wels·bach \'welz-,bak\ *trademark* — used for a burner for producing gaslight by heating a gas mantle to incandescence through the combustion of a mixture of air and gas

welsh \'welsh, 'welch\ *vi* : to cheat by avoiding payment of bets — **welsh·er** *n*

Welsh \'welsh\ *n* **1 Welsh** *pl* : the natives or inhabitants of Wales **2** : the Celtic language of the Welsh people — **Welsh** *adj*

Welsh cor·gi \-'kór-gē\ *n* [W *corgi*, fr. *cor* dwarf + *ci* dog] : a short-legged long-backed Welsh dog with foxy head occurring in two varieties

Welsh·man \'welsh-mən\ *n* : one of the Welsh — **Welsh·wom·an** \-,wùm-ən\ *n*

Welsh rabbit *n* : melted often seasoned cheese poured over toast or crackers

ə abut; ᵊ kitten; ər further; a back; ā bake; ä cot, cart; aù out; ch chin; e less; ē easy; g gift; i trip; ī life

Welsh rare·bit \-'ra(ə)r-bət, -'re(ə)r-\ *n* [by alter.]
: WELSH RABBIT

¹**welt** \'welt\ *n* [ME *welte*] **1 a** : the narrow strip of leather between a shoe upper and sole to which other parts are stitched **b** : any of various distinguishable margins, inserts, or strips **2 a** : a ridge or lump raised on the skin usu. by a blow **b** : a heavy blow

²**welt** *vt* **1** : to furnish with a welt **2 a** : to raise a welt on ⟨mosquitoes *welted* his arms⟩ **b** : to hit hard

¹**wel·ter** \'wel-tər\ *vi* [ME *welteren*] **1 a** : to twist or roll one's body about : WALLOW **b** : to rise and fall or toss about in or with waves; *also* : to be in a turmoil of waves ⟨came safely through the *weltering* sea⟩ **2 a** : to lie soaked or drenched ⟨*weltering* in his gore⟩ **b** : to become deeply sunk or involved ⟨*weltered* in misery⟩

²**welter** *n* **1** : a state of wild disorder : TURMOIL **2** : a chaotic mass or jumble ⟨trying to understand a *welter* of conflicting regulations⟩

³**welter** *n* : WELTERWEIGHT

wel·ter·weight \-,wāt\ *n* : a boxer weighing more than 135 but not over 147 pounds

wen \'wen\ *n* [OE *wenn*] : a cyst formed by obstruction of a skin gland and filled with fatty material

wench \'wench\ *n* [ME *wenchel, wenche* child, fr. OE *wencel*] **1** : a young woman : GIRL **2** : a female servant

wend \'wend\ *vb* [OE *wendan;* akin to E ⁴*wind*] : to direct one's course : proceed on (one's way)

Wend \'wend\ *n* : a member of a Slavic people of eastern Germany — **Wend·ish** \'wen-dish\ *adj*

went [ME, fr. past of *wenden* to wend] *past of* GO

wen·tle·trap \'went-ᵊl-,trap\ *n* [D *wenteltrap* winding stair] : any of a family of marine snails with usu. tall-spired sculptured white shells; *also* : one of the shells

wept *past of* WEEP

were [OE *wæron,* past pl., & *wære,* past subj. sing., & *wæren,* past subj. pl.; akin to E *was*] *past 2d sing, past pl, or past subjunctive of* BE

we're \(,)wi(ə)r, (,)wər\ : we are

weren't \(')wərnt, 'wər-ənt\ : were not

were·wolf \'wi(ə)r-,wulf, 'wər-, 'we(ə)r-\ *n, pl* **were·wolves** \-,wulvz\ [OE *werwulf,* fr. *wer* man + *wulf* wolf] : a person held to be transformed or able to transform into a wolf

wert \(')wərt\ *archaic past 2d sing of* BE

wes·kit \'wes-kət\ *n* [alter. of *waistcoat*] : VEST 1a, 1b

Wes·ley·an \'wes-lē-ən, 'wez-\ *adj* **1** : of or relating to John or Charles Wesley **2** : of or relating to the Arminian Methodism taught by John Wesley — **Wesleyan** *n* — **Wes·ley·an·ism** \-lē-ə-,niz-əm\ *n*

¹**west** \'west\ *adv* [OE] : to or toward the west

²**west** *adj* **1** : situated toward or at the west **2** : coming from the west

³**west** *n* **1 a** : the general direction of sunset **b** : the compass point directly opposite to east — see COMPASS CARD **2** *cap* : regions or countries west of a specified or implied point **3** : the end of a church opposite the chancel

west·bound \'wes(t)-,baund\ *adj* : headed west

west by north : one point north of due west : N 78° 45' W

west by south : one point south of due west : S 78° 45' W

west·er \'wes-tər\ *vi* **wes·tered; wes·ter·ing** \-t(ə-)riŋ\ : to turn or move westward

¹**west·er·ly** \'wes-tər-lē\ *adv (or adj)* **1** : from the west **2** : toward the west

²**westerly** *n, pl* **-lies** : a wind blowing from the west

¹**west·ern** \'wes-tərn\ *adj* **1** *often cap* : of, relating to, or characteristic of a region conventionally designated West **2** : lying toward or coming from the west **3** *cap* : of or relating to the Roman Catholic or Protestant segment of Christianity ⟨*Western* liturgies⟩ — **west·ern·most** \-,mōst\ *adj*

²**western** *n* **1** : one that is produced in or characteristic of a western region and esp. the western U.S. **2** *often cap* : a novel, story, motion picture, or broadcast dealing with life in the western U.S. during the latter half of the 19th century

West·ern·er \'wes-tə(r)-nər\ *n* : a native or inhabitant of the West (as of the U.S.)

western hemisphere *n* : the half of the earth comprising No. and So. America and surrounding waters

west·ern·ize \'wes-tər-,nīz\ *vt* : to give western characteristics to — **west·ern·i·za·tion** \,wes-tər-nə-'zā-shən\ *n*

West Germanic *n* : a subdivision of the Germanic languages including English, Frisian, Dutch, and German

West Highland white terrier *n* : a small white long-coated dog of a breed developed in Scotland

west·ing \'wes-tiŋ\ *n* **1** : difference in longitude to the west from the last preceding point of reckoning **2** : westerly progress

west-northwest *n* — see COMPASS CARD

West·pha·lian ham \wes(t)-,fāl-yən-\ *n* : a ham of distinctive flavor produced by smoking with juniper brush

west-southwest *n* — see COMPASS CARD

¹**west·ward** \'wes-twərd\ *adv (or adj)* : toward the west — **west·wards** \-twərdz\ *adv*

²**westward** *n* : westward direction or part ⟨sail to the *westward*⟩

¹**wet** \'wet\ *adj* **wet·ter; wet·test** [ME, partly fr. pp. of *weten* to wet & partly fr. OE *wǣt* wet; akin to E *water*] **1 a** : consisting of, containing, covered with, or soaked with liquid (as water) **b** : RAINY **2** : still moist enough to smudge or smear ⟨*wet* paint⟩ **3** : permitting or advocating the manufacture and sale of alcoholic liquor **4** : involving the use or presence of liquid ⟨*wet* processes⟩ **5** : perversely wrong : MISGUIDED ⟨all *wet*⟩ — **wet·ly** *adv* — **wet·ness** *n*

²**wet** *n* **1** : WATER; *also* : WETNESS, MOISTURE **2** : rainy weather : RAIN **3** : an advocate of a wet liquor policy

³**wet** *vb* **wet** *or* **wet·ted; wet·ting** **1** : to make or become wet **2** : URINATE — **wet one's whistle** : to take a drink esp. of liquor

wet·back \'wet-,bak\ *n* : a Mexican who enters (as by wading the Rio Grande) the U.S. illegally

wet blanket *n* : one that quenches or dampens enthusiasm or pleasure — **wet-blanket** *vt*

wet down *vt* : to dampen by sprinkling with water

weth·er \'weth-ər\ *n* [OE] : a male sheep castrated before sexual maturity

wet·land \'wet-,land\ *n* : land containing much soil moisture : swampy or boggy land

wet nurse *n* : one that cares for and suckles young not her own

wet-nurse \'wet-,nərs\ *vt* **1** : to tend to as a wet nurse **2** : to devote unremitting or excessive care to

wet·ta·ble \'wet-ə-bəl\ *adj* : capable of being wetted — **wet·ta·bil·i·ty** \,wet-ə-'bil-ət-ē\ *n*

wetting agent *n* : a substance that when adsorbed on a surface reduces its tendency to repel a liquid

wet·tish \'wet-ish\ *adj* : somewhat wet : MOIST

wet wash *n* : laundry returned damp and not ironed

we've \(,)wēv\ : we have

¹**whack** \'hwak\ *vb* **1** : to strike with a smart or resounding blow **2** : to cut with or as if with a whack : CHOP **3** : to divide into shares ⟨*whack* up the profits⟩ — **whack·er** *n*

²**whack** *n* **1** : a smart or resounding blow; *also* : the sound of or as if of such a blow **2** : PORTION, SHARE **3** : CONDITION; *esp* : proper working order ⟨the machine is out of *whack*⟩ **4 a** : an opportunity or attempt to do something : CHANCE **b** : a single action or occasion : TIME ⟨marked a hundred papers at a *whack*⟩

whack up *vt* : to divide into shares

¹**whale** \'hwāl\ *n, pl* **whale** *or* **whales** [OE *hwæl*] **1** : an aquatic mammal (order Cetacea) that superficially resembles a large fish and is valued commercially for its oil, flesh, and sometimes whalebone; *esp* : one of the larger members of this group **2** : a person or thing impressive in size or qualities ⟨a *whale* of a story⟩

²**whale** *vi* : to engage in whale fishing

³**whale** *vt* **1** : THRASH **2** : to strike or hit vigorously

whale·boat \-,bōt\ *n* **1** : a long narrow rowboat made with both ends sharp and raking, often steered with an oar, and used by whalers for hunting whales **2** : a long narrow rowboat or motorboat resembling the original whaleboats that is often carried by warships and merchant ships

whale·bone \-,bōn\ *n* : a horny substance found in two rows of long plates attached along the upper jaw of whalebone whales

whalebone whale *n* : any of various usu. large whales having whalebone instead of teeth

whal·er \'hwā-lər\ *n* **1** : a person or ship engaged in whale fishing **2** : WHALEBOAT 2

whale shark *n* : a very large harmless shark of tropical seas

¹**wham** \'hwam\ *n* **1** : the loud sound of a hard impact **2** : a solid blow

²**wham** *vb* **whammed; wham·ming** : to propel, strike, or beat so as to produce a loud impact

wham·my \'hwam-ē\ *n, pl* **whammies** : JINX, HEX

¹**whang** \'hwaŋ\ *vb* **1** : to propel or strike with force **2** : to beat or work with force or violence

²**whang** *n* : a loud sharp vibrant or resonant sound

wharf \'hwȯrf\ *n, pl* **wharves** \'hwȯrvz\ *also* **wharfs** [OE *hwearf*] : a structure built along or at an angle from the shore of navigable waters so that ships may lie alongside to receive and discharge cargo and passengers

wharf·age \'hwȯr-fij\ *n* **1** : the provision or the use of a wharf **2** : the charge for the use of a wharf

wharf·in·ger \-fən-jər\ *n* : the operator or manager of a commercial wharf — called also *wharf·mas·ter* \'hwȯrf-,mas-tər\

¹**what** \(')hwät, (')hwət\ *pron* [OE *hwæt*, neut. of *hwā* who] **1** — used as an interrogative in asking about the identity or nature of a thing ⟨*what* is this⟩⟨*what* are those things on the table⟩⟨*what* is honor⟩ or about the character, occupation, or position of a person ⟨*what* do you think I am, a fool⟩ **2** : that which : the one or ones that ⟨no income but *what* he gets from his writings⟩ **3** : WHATEVER 1 ⟨say *what* you will⟩

²**what** *adv* **1 a** : in what respect : HOW **b** : how much ⟨*what* does he care⟩ **2** — used with *with* to introduce a prepositional phrase that expresses cause ⟨kept busy *what* with studies and extracurricular activities⟩

³**what** *adj* **1 a** — used as an interrogative expressing inquiry about the identity or nature of a person, object, or matter ⟨*what* minerals do we export⟩ **b** : how remarkable or surprising ⟨*what* a suggestion⟩⟨*what* a charming girl⟩ **2** : WHATEVER 1a

¹**what·ev·er** \hwät-'ev-ər, (,)hwət-\ *pron* **1** : anything or everything that ⟨take *whatever* is needed⟩ **2** : no matter what ⟨obey orders, *whatever* happens⟩

²**whatever** *adj* **1 a** : any . . . that : all . . . that ⟨take *whatever* action is needed⟩ **b** : no matter what **2** : of any kind at all ⟨no food *whatever*⟩

what·not \'hwät-,nät, 'hwət-\ *n* : a light open set of shelves for bric-a-brac

what·so·ev·er \,hwät-sə-'wev-ər, ,hwət-\ *pron or adj* : WHATEVER

wheal \'hwēl\ *n* [alter. of *wale*] : a suddenly formed elevation of the skin surface: as **a** : WELT **b** : a flat burning or itching eminence on the skin

wheat \'hwēt\ *n* [OE *hwǣte; akin to E *white*] **1** : a cereal grain that yields a fine white flour, is the chief breadstuff of temperate climates, and is important in animal feeds — compare BRAN, MIDDLINGS **2** : any of a genus of grasses grown in most temperate areas for the wheat they yield; *esp* : an annual cereal grass with long dense flower spikes and white to dark red grains that is the chief source of wheat and is known only in cultivation — **wheat·en** \-ˀn\ *adj*

wheat cake *n* : a griddle cake made of wheat flour

wheat·ear \'hwēt-,i(ə)r\ *n* : a small white-rumped northern bird related to the stonechat and whinchat

wheat germ *n* : the embryo of the wheat kernel separated in milling and used esp. as a source of vitamins

wheat rust *n* : a destructive disease of wheat caused by rust fungi; *also* : a fungus causing a wheat rust

whee \'hwē\ *interj* — used to express delight or general exuberance

whee·dle \'hwēd-ˀl\ *vb* **whee·dled; whee·dling** \'hwēd-liŋ, -ˀl-iŋ\ **1** : to coax or entice by soft words or flattery **2** : to gain or get by wheedling ⟨*wheedled* permission out of her mother⟩

¹**wheel** \'hwēl\ *n* [OE *hwēol*] **1** : a disk or circular frame capable of turning on a central axis **2** : something that is like a wheel (as in being round or in turning on an axis) **3** : a device the main part of which is a wheel **4** : BICYCLE **5** : a circular frame which when turned controls some apparatus **6 a** : a curving or circular movement **b** : a rotation or turn usu. about an axis or center; *esp* : a turning movement of troops or ships in line in which the units preserve alignment and relative positions as they change direction **7 a** : a moving power : MECHANISM ⟨the *wheels*

of government⟩ **b** : a person of importance esp. in an organization — **wheeled** \'hwēld\ *adj*

²**wheel** *vb* **1** : to carry or move on wheels or in a vehicle with wheels ⟨*wheel* a load into the barn⟩ **2** : to turn or cause to turn on an axis or in a circle : REVOLVE ⟨the earth *wheels* about the sun⟩ **3** : to change direction as if revolving on an axis ⟨*wheeled* about to face his antagonist⟩

wheel and axle *n* : a simple machine consisting of a grooved wheel turned by a cord or chain with a rigidly attached axle (as for winding up a weight) together with the supporting standards

wheel animal *n* : ROTIFER — called also *wheel animalcule*

wheel·bar·row \'hwēl-,bar-ō\ *n* : a small vehicle with handles and one or more wheels for carrying small loads

wheel·base \-,bās\ *n* : the distance in inches between the front and rear axles of an automotive vehicle

wheel·chair \-,che(ə)r, -,cha(ə)r\ *n* : a chair mounted on wheels esp. for the use of invalids

wheel·er \'hwē-lər\ *n* **1** : one that wheels **2** : WHEELHORSE **3** : something (as a vehicle or ship) that has wheels — used esp. in combinations ⟨side-*wheeler*⟩

wheel·horse \'hwēl-,hȯrs\ *n* **1** : a horse in a position nearest the wheels in a tandem or similar arrangement **2** : a steady and effective worker esp. in a political body

wheelchair

wheel·house \-,haus\ *n* : PILOTHOUSE

wheels·man \'hwēlz-mən\ *n* : one who steers with a wheel; *esp* : HELMSMAN

wheel·wright \'hwēl-,rīt\ *n* : a man whose occupation is to make or repair wheels and wheeled vehicles

¹**wheeze** \'hwēz\ *vi* [ME *whesen*] **1** : to breathe with difficulty usu. with a whistling sound **2** : to make a sound resembling that of wheezing

²**wheeze** *n* **1** : a sound of wheezing **2 a** : GAG, JOKE **b** : a trite saying

wheezy \'hwē-zē\ *adj* **wheez·i·er; -est** **1** : inclined to wheeze **2** : having a wheezing sound — **wheez·i·ly** \-zə-lē\ *adv* — **wheez·i·ness** \-zē-nəs\ *n*

whelk \'hwelk, 'wilk\ *n* [OE *weoloc*] : any of numerous large marine snails; *esp* : one much used as food in Europe

whelm \'hwelm\ *vb* [ME *whelmen*] : to overcome or engulf completely : OVERWHELM

¹**whelp** \'hwelp\ *n* [OE *hwelp*] **1** : one of the young of various carnivorous mammals and esp. of the dog **2** : CUR 2

²**whelp** *vb* **1** : to give birth to (whelps) **2** : to bring forth whelps

¹**when** \(')hwen, hwən\ *adv* [OE *hwanne, hwenne; akin to E *who*] **1** : at what time ⟨asked him *when* it happened⟩ ⟨*when* will he return⟩ **2** : at or during which time ⟨an era *when* the arts decayed⟩

²**when** *conj* **1 a** : at or during the time that : WHILE ⟨went fishing *when* he was a boy⟩ **b** : just after the time that ⟨left *when* the bell rang⟩ **c** : every time that ⟨*when* she hears that tune, she cries⟩ **2** : in the event that : IF ⟨the batter is out *when* he bunts foul with two strikes on him⟩ **3** : in spite of the fact that : THOUGH ⟨gave up politics *when* he might have made a great career in it⟩

³**when** \,hwen\ *pron* : what or which time ⟨he left in April, since *when* I have not seen him⟩

whence \(')hwen(t)s\ *adv* [ME *whenne, whennes*, fr. OE *hwanon; akin to E *who*] **1** : from what place, source, or cause ⟨*whence* come all these doubts⟩ **2** : from or out of which ⟨the stock *whence* he sprang⟩

¹**when·ev·er** \hwen-'ev-ər, hwən-\ *conj* : at any or every time that ⟨stop *whenever* you wish⟩

²**whenever** *adv* : at whatever time ⟨available *whenever* desired⟩

when·so·ev·er \'hwen(t)-sə-,wev-ər, 'wen(t)-\ *conj* : WHENEVER

¹**where** \(')hwe(ə)r, (')hwa(ə)r, (,)hwər\ *adv* [OE *hwǣr; akin to E *who*] **1** : at, in, or to which place, circumstances, or respect ⟨*where* are we going⟩ ⟨*where* is he wrong⟩ **2** : in, at, or to which ⟨the house *where* he was born⟩ **3** : from what place or source ⟨*where* did you get that idea⟩

²**where** *conj* **1 a** : at or in the place at or in which ⟨stay *where* you are⟩ **b** : to the place at, in, or to which ⟨went *where* he had promised to go⟩ **2** : WHEREVER ⟨sits *where* he

pleases⟩ **3** : in a case, situation, or respect in which ⟨outstanding *where* endurance is called for⟩
³**where** \'hwe(ə)r, 'hwa(ə)r\ *n* **1** : PLACE, LOCATION ⟨the *where* and the how of the accident⟩ **2** : what place, source, or cause ⟨*where* is he from⟩
¹**where·abouts** \-ə-,baůts\ *also* **where·about** \-,baůt\ *adv* : about where : near what place ⟨*whereabouts* is the house⟩
²**whereabouts** *n sing or pl* : the place or general locality where a person or thing is
where·as \hwer-'az, hwar-, (,)hwər-\ *conj* **1** : in view of the fact that : SINCE — used esp. to introduce a preamble **2** : while on the contrary ⟨water puts out fire, *whereas* alcohol burns⟩
where·at \-'at\ *conj* **1** : at or toward which **2** : in consequence of which : WHEREUPON
where·by \-'bī\ *conj* : by, through, or in accordance with which
¹**where·fore** \'hwe(ə)r-,fōr, 'hwa(ə)r-, -,fór\ *adv* **1** : for what reason or purpose : WHY **2** : THEREFORE
²**wherefore** *n* : a statement giving an explanation : REASON
where·from \-,frəm, -,främ\ *conj* : from which
¹**where·in** \hwer-'in, hwar-, (,)hwər-\ *adv* : in what : in what particular or respect ⟨*wherein* was he wrong⟩
²**wherein** *conj* **1** : in which : WHERE ⟨the city *wherein* he resides⟩ **2** : during which ⟨the epoch *wherein* feudalism arose⟩
where·of \-'əv, -'äv\ *conj* **1** : of what ⟨knows *whereof* she speaks⟩ **2** : of which or whom ⟨books *whereof* the best are lost⟩
where·on \-'ón, -'än\ *adv* : on which ⟨the base *whereon* it rests⟩
where·so·ev·er \'hwer-sə-,wev-ər, 'hwar-\ *conj, archaic* : WHEREVER
¹**where·to** \-,tü\ *adv* : to what place or purpose
²**whereto** *conj* : to which
where·un·to \hwer-'ən-tü, hwar-, (,)hwər-\ *adv or conj* : WHERETO
where·up·on \'hwer-ə-,pón, 'hwar-, -,pän\ *conj* **1** : on which **2** : closely following and in consequence of which
¹**wher·ev·er** \hwer-'ev-ər, hwar-, (,)hwər-\ *adv* : where in the world ⟨*wherever* did she get that hat⟩
²**wherever** *conj* **1** : at, in, or to whatever place ⟨thrives *wherever* he goes⟩ **2** : in any circumstance in which ⟨*wherever* it is possible, he tries to help⟩
where·with \'hwer-,with, 'hwa(ə)r-, -,with\ *adv* **1** *obs* : with what **2** : with or by means of which
where·with·al \'hwe(ə)r-with-,ól, 'hwa(ə)r-, -with-\ *n* : MEANS, RESOURCES; *esp* : MONEY
wher·ry \'hwer-ē\ *n, pl* **wherries** [ME *whery*] : any of various light boats; *esp* : a long light rowboat pointed at both ends
¹**whet** \'hwet\ *vt* **whet·ted; whet·ting** [OE *hwettan*] **1** : to sharpen by rubbing on or with something (as a stone) ⟨*whet* a knife⟩ **2** : to make keen : STIMULATE ⟨*whet* the appetite⟩
²**whet** *n* **1** : GOAD **2** : APPETIZER; *also* : a drink of liquor
wheth·er \'hweth-ər, (,)hwəth-ər\ *conj* [OE *hwæther, hwether,* fr. *hwæther, hwether,* pron., which of two; akin to E *who*] **1 a** (1) : if it is or was true that ⟨ask *whether* he is going⟩ (2) : if it is or was better ⟨uncertain *whether* to go or stay⟩ **b** : whichever is or was the case, namely, that ⟨*whether* we succeed or fail, we must try⟩ **2** : EITHER ⟨seated him next to her *whether* by accident or design⟩
whet·stone \'hwet-,stōn\ *n* : a stone for whetting sharp-edged tools
whew *often read as* 'hwü, 'hyü\ *n* **1** : a whistling sound **2** : a sound like a half-formed whistle uttered as an exclamation — used interjectionally chiefly to express amazement, discomfort, or relief
whey \'hwā\ *n* [OE *hwæg*] : the watery part of milk that separates after the milk sours and thickens — **whey·ey** \'hwā-ē\ *adj*
¹**which** \(')hwich\ *adj* [OE *hwilc*] of what kind, which; akin to E *who* & to E *-ly*] **1** : being what one or ones out of a group — used as an interrogative ⟨*which* tie should I wear⟩ ⟨knew *which* men were outsiders⟩ **2** : WHICHEVER ⟨it will not fit, turn it *which* way you like⟩
²**which** *pron* **1** : what one or ones out of a group — used as an interrogative ⟨*which* of those houses do you live in⟩ ⟨*which* of you want tea and *which* want lemonade⟩ ⟨he is

swimming or canoeing, I don't know *which*⟩ **2** : WHICHEVER ⟨take *which* you like⟩ **3** — used to introduce a relative clause and to serve as a substitute within that clause for the substantive modified by that clause; used in any grammatical relation except that of a possessive; used esp. in reference to animals, inanimate objects, groups, or ideas ⟨the records *which* he bought⟩ **syn** see WHO
¹**which·ev·er** \hwich-'ev-ər\ *pron* : whatever one or ones out of a group ⟨take two of the four elective subjects, *whichever* you prefer⟩
²**whichever** *adj* : being whatever one or ones out of a group : no matter which ⟨*whichever* way you go⟩
which·so·ev·er \,hwich-sə-'wev-ər\ *pron or adj* : WHICHEVER
whick·er \'hwik-ər\ *vi* **whick·ered; whick·er·ing** \'hwik-(ə-)riŋ\ : NEIGH, WHINNY — **whicker** *n*
¹**whiff** \'hwif\ *n* **1 a** : a quick puff or slight gust esp. of air, odor, gas, smoke, or spray **b** : an inhalation of odor, gas, or smoke **2** : a slight trace : HINT
²**whiff** *vb* **1 a** : to expel, puff out, or blow away in or as if in whiffs **b** : SMOKE **2** : to inhale an odor **3** : to strike out in baseball
whif·fle·tree \'hwif-əl-(,)trē\ *n* : the pivoted swinging bar to which the traces of a harness are fastened and by which a vehicle or implement is drawn
Whig \'hwig\ *n* [short for *Whiggamore* member of a Scottish anticourt movement in 1648] **1** : a member or supporter of a British political group of the 18th and early 19th centuries seeking to limit royal authority and increase parliamentary power — compare TORY **2** : an American favoring independence from Great Britain during the American Revolution **3** : a member or supporter of an American political party formed about 1834 in opposition to the Jacksonian Democrats, associated chiefly with manufacturing, commercial, and financial interests, and succeeded about 1854 by the Republican party — **Whig** *adj* — **Whig·gish** \-ish\ *adj*
¹**while** \'hwīl\ *n* [OE *hwīl*] **1** : a period of time ⟨stay here for a *while*⟩ **2** : the time and effort used (as in the performance of an action) : TROUBLE ⟨worth your *while*⟩
²**while** *conj* **1 a** : during the time that ⟨take a nap *while* I'm out⟩ **b** : as long as ⟨*while* there's life there's hope⟩ **2** : in spite of the fact that : THOUGH ⟨*while* respected, he is not liked⟩
³**while** *vt* : to cause to pass esp. without boredom or in a pleasant manner — usu. used with *away* ⟨*while* away the time⟩
¹**whi·lom** \'hwī-ləm\ *adv* [ME, lit., at times, fr. OE *hwīlum,* dat. pl. of *hwīl* time, while] *archaic* : FORMERLY
²**whilom** *adj* : FORMER ⟨his *whilom* friends⟩
whilst \'hwīlst\ *conj, chiefly Brit* : WHILE
whim \'hwim\ *n* : a sudden wish, desire, or change of mind : a sudden notion or fancy **syn** see CAPRICE
whim·brel \'hwim-brəl\ *n* : a small European curlew
¹**whim·per** \'hwim-pər\ *vi* **whim·pered; whim·per·ing** \-p(ə)riŋ\ **1** : to make a low whining plaintive or broken sound **2** : to complain with or as if with a whimper
²**whimper** *n* **1** : a whimpering cry or sound **2** : a whining complaint or protest
whim·si·cal \'hwim-zi-kəl\ *adj* **1** : full of whims : CAPRICIOUS ⟨a *whimsical* person⟩ **2** : resulting from or characterized by whim or caprice : ERRATIC ⟨*whimsical* behavior⟩ — **whim·si·cal·i·ty** \,hwim-zə-'kal-ət-ē\ *n* — **whim·si·cal·ly** \'hwim-zi-k(ə-)lē\ *adv* — **whim·si·cal·ness** \-kəl-nəs\ *n*
whim·sy *or* **whim·sey** \'hwim-zē\ *n, pl* **whimsies** *or* **whimseys** **1** : WHIM, CAPRICE **2** : a fanciful or fantastic device, object, or creation esp. in writing or art
whin \'hwin\ *n* [of Scand origin] : FURZE
whin·chat \'hwin-,chat\ *n* : a small brown and buff European singing bird of grassy meadows
¹**whine** \'hwīn\ *vi* [OE *hwīnan* to whiz] **1** : to utter a usu. high-pitched plaintive or distressed cry; *also* : to make a sound similar to such a cry **2** : to utter a complaint with or as if with a whine — **whin·er** *n* — **whin·ing·ly** \'hwī-niŋ-lē\ *adv*
²**whine** *n* **1** : a prolonged usu. high-pitched cry expressive of distress or pain; *also* : a sound resembling such a cry **2** : a complaint uttered with or as if with a whine — **whiny** *or* **whin·ey** \'hwī-nē\ *adj*

---

j joke; **ŋ** sing; **ō** flow; **ȯ** flaw; **ȯi** coin; **th** thin; **th** this; **ü** loot; **ů** foot; **y** yet; **yü** few; **yů** furious; **zh** vision

¹**whin·ny** \'hwin-ē\ *vi* **whin·nied; whin·ny·ing** : to neigh esp. in a low or gentle fashion

²**whinny** *n, pl* **whinnies** **1** : NEIGH **2** : a sound resembling a neigh

¹**whip** \'hwip\ *vb* **whipped; whip·ping** [ME *whippen;* akin to E *wipe*] **1** : to take, pull, snatch, jerk, or otherwise move very quickly and forcefully ⟨*whip* out a gun⟩ **2 a** : to strike with a slender lithe implement (as a lash or rod) esp. as a punishment; *also* : SPANK **b** : to drive or urge on by or as if by using a whip **3 a** : to bind or wrap (as a rope or fishing rod) with cord in order to protect and strengthen **b** : to wind or wrap around something **4** : to thoroughly overcome : DEFEAT **5** : to stir up : INCITE ⟨*whip* up enthusiasm for the job⟩ **6** : to produce in a hurry ⟨*whip* up a batch of cookies⟩ **7** : to beat (as eggs or cream) into a froth **8** : to gather together or hold together for united action ⟨*whipped* the doubtful members into line⟩ **9 a** : to move nimbly or briskly **b** : to thrash about flexibly in the manner of a whiplash — **whip·per** *n*

²**whip** *n* **1** : an instrument consisting usu. of a handle and lash forming a flexible rod that is used for whipping **2** : a stroke or cut with or as if with a whip **3 a** : a dessert made by whipping a portion of the ingredients **b** : a kitchen utensil (as of wire mesh) used in whipping **4** : one that handles a whip; *esp* : a driver of horses : COACHMAN **5** : a member of a legislative body appointed by his party to enforce discipline and to secure the attendance of party members at important sessions **6** : a whipping or thrashing motion — **whip·like** \-,līk\ *adj*

whip·cord \-,kȯrd\ *n* **1** : a thin tough cord made of braided or twisted hemp or catgut **2** : a cloth that is made of hard-twisted yarns and has fine diagonal cords or ribs

whip hand *n* : positive control : ADVANTAGE

whip·lash \'hwip-,lash\ *n* : the lash of a whip

whip·per·snap·per \'hwip-ər-,snap-ər\ *n* : a diminutive, insignificant, or presumptuous person

whip·pet \'hwip-ət\ *n* : a small swift slender dog of greyhound type that is often used for racing

whip·ping *n* : the act of one that whips; *esp* : a severe beating

whipping boy *n* [fr. the former practice of maintaining a boy to share the education of a prince and be punished in his stead] : SCAPEGOAT

whipping post *n* : a post to which offenders are tied to be whipped

whip·ple·tree \'hwip-əl-(,)trē\ *var of* WHIFFLETREE

whip·poor·will \,hwip-ər-'wil, 'hwip-ər-,\ *n* : a nocturnal goatsucker of the eastern U.S. and Canada related to the European nightjar

¹**whip·saw** \'hwip-,sȯ\ *n* **1** : a narrow saw tapering from butt to point and having hook teeth **2** : a 2-man crosscut saw

²**whipsaw** *vt* **whip·sawed; whip·saw·ing** **1** : to saw with a whipsaw **2** : to worst in two opposite ways at once, by a two-phase operation, or by the collusive action of two opponents

whip scorpion *n* : any of an order (Pedipalpida) of arachnids somewhat resembling true scorpions but having a long slender tail process and no sting

whip·worm \'hwip-,wərm\ *n* : any of a family of parasitic roundworms with a body thickened behind and very long and slender in front; *esp* : one of the human intestine

¹**whir** *also* **whirr** \'hwər\ *vb* **whirred; whir·ring** : to fly, revolve, or move rapidly with a whir

²**whir** *also* **whirr** *n* : a continuous fluttering or vibratory sound made by something in rapid motion

¹**whirl** \'hwərl\ *vb* [ME *whirlen*] **1** : to move or drive in a circle or similar curve esp. with force or speed **2 a** : to turn or cause to turn on or around an axis : SPIN **b** : to turn abruptly : WHEEL **3** : to pass, move, or go quickly **4** : to become giddy or dizzy : REEL — **whirl·er** *n*

²**whirl** *n* **1 a** : a rapid rotating or circling movement **b** : something undergoing a rotating movement : VORTEX **2 a** : a confused tumult : BUSTLE **b** : a confused or giddy mental state **3** : an experimental attempt : TRY

whirl·i·gig \'hwər-li-,gig\ *n* [ME *whirlegigg,* fr. *whirlen* to whirl + *gigg* top] **1** : a child's toy having a whirling motion **2** : something that continuously whirls or changes; *also* : a whirling course

whirligig beetle *n* : any of a family of swift-moving beetles that live mostly on the surface of water

whirl·pool \'hwərl-,pül\ *n* : water moving rapidly in a circle so as to produce a depression in the center into which floating objects may be drawn : EDDY, VORTEX

whirl·wind \-,wind\ *n* **1** : a small rotating windstorm marked by an inward and upward spiral motion of the lower air **2** : a confused rush : WHIRL

whirly·bird \'hwər-lē-,bərd\ *n* : HELICOPTER

¹**whish** \'hwish\ *vb* **1** : to urge on or cause to move with a rushing sound **2** : to make a sibilant sound **3** : to move with a whish esp. at high speed : WHIZ

²**whish** *n* : a rushing sound : SWISH

¹**whisk** \'hwisk\ *n* [ME *wisk*] **1** : a quick light brushing or whipping motion ⟨a *whisk* of the hand⟩ **2 a** : a small usu. wire kitchen implement used for hand beating of food **b** : a flexible bunch (as of twigs, feathers, or straw) attached to a handle for use as a brush

²**whisk** *vb* **1** : to move nimbly and quickly ⟨squirrels *whisked* up the trees⟩ **2** : to move or convey briskly ⟨*whisked* out a knife⟩ ⟨*whisked* the children off to bed⟩ **3** : to mix or fluff up by or as if by beating with a whisk ⟨*whisk* eggs⟩ **4** : to brush or wipe off lightly ⟨*whisk* crumbs from a table⟩

whisk 2a

whisk broom *n* : a small broom with a short handle used esp. as a clothes brush

whis·ker \'hwis-kər\ *n* **1 a** : a hair of the beard **b** *pl* : the part of the beard growing on the sides of the face or on the chin **2** : one of the long projecting hairs or bristles growing near the mouth of an animal (as a cat or bird) — **whis·kered** \-kərd\ *adj*

whis·kery \'hwis-k(ə-)rē\ *adj* : having or resembling whiskers ⟨*whiskery* eyebrows⟩

whis·key *or* **whis·ky** \'hwis-kē\ *n, pl* **whiskeys** *or* **whis·kies** [IrGael *uisce beathadh* & ScGael *uisge beatha,* lit., water of life] : a distilled alcoholic liquor made from fermented mash of grain (as rye, corn, barley, or wheat)

¹**whis·per** \'hwis-pər\ *vb* **whis·pered; whis·per·ing** \-p(ə-)riŋ\ [OE *hwisperian*] **1** : to speak very low or under the breath **2** : to tell or utter by whispering ⟨*whisper* a secret⟩ **3** : to make a low rustling sound ⟨*whispering* leaves⟩ — **whis·per·er** \-pər-ər\ *n*

²**whisper** *n* **1 a** : an act or instance of whispering; *esp* : speech without vibration of the vocal cords **b** : a sibilant sound that resembles whispered speech **2** : something communicated by or as if by whispering : HINT, RUMOR ⟨*whispers* of a scandal⟩

whispering campaign *n* : the systematic dissemination by word of mouth of derogatory rumors or charges esp. against a candidate for public office

whist \'hwist\ *n* [alter. of earlier *whisk*] : a card game for four players in two partnerships

¹**whis·tle** \'hwis-əl\ *n* [OE *hwistle*] **1** : a device by which a shrill sound is produced ⟨tin *whistle*⟩ ⟨steam *whistle*⟩ **2 a** : a shrill clear sound produced by forcing breath out or air in through the puckered lips **b** : the sound or signal produced by a whistle or as if by whistling; *esp* : the shrill clear note of a bird or other animal

²**whistle** *vb* **whis·tled; whis·tling** \'hwis-(ə-)liŋ\ **1 a** : to utter a shrill clear sound by blowing or drawing air through the puckered lips **b** : to utter a shrill note or call resembling a whistle **c** : to make a shrill clear sound esp. by rapid movement ⟨bullets *whistled* by⟩ **d** : to blow or sound a whistle **2** : to give a signal or issue an order or summons by or as if by whistling ⟨*whistle* to a dog⟩ **3** : to send, bring, signal, or call by or as if by whistling **4** : to produce, utter, or express by whistling ⟨*whistle* a tune⟩ — **whis·tler** \-(ə-)lər\ *n*

¹**whis·tle-stop** \'hwis-əl-,stäp\ *n* **1 a** : a small station at which trains stop only on signal **b** : a small community **2** : a brief personal appearance by a political candidate orig. on the rear platform of a touring train

²**whistle-stop** *vi* : to make a tour esp. in a political campaign with many brief personal appearances in small communities

whit \'hwit\ *n* [alter. of ME *wiht* creature, thing, bit, fr. OE] : the smallest part or particle imaginable : BIT ⟨cared not a *whit*⟩

¹**white** \'hwīt\ *adj* [OE *hwīt*] **1 a** : free from color **b** : of the color of new snow or milk; *esp* : of the color white

c : light or pallid in color ⟨*white* wine⟩⟨lips *white* with fear⟩ **d** : lustrous pale gray : SILVERY; *also* : made of silver **2 a** : of, relating to, or being a member of a group or race characterized by reduced pigmentation **b** *slang* : marked by upright fairness ⟨a *white* man if ever there was one⟩ **3** : free from spot or blemish: as **a** : free from moral impurity : INNOCENT **b** : unmarked by writing or printing **c** : not intended to cause harm ⟨*white* lie⟩ ⟨*white* magic⟩ **d** : FAVORABLE, FORTUNATE **4 a** : wearing or habited in white **b** : marked by the presence of snow : SNOWY ⟨*white* Christmas⟩ **5** : notably ardent : PASSIONATE ⟨*white* fury⟩ **6** : conservative or reactionary in political outlook and action

²**white** *n* **1** : the characteristic color of fresh snow **2** : a white or light-colored part of something: as **a** : a mass of albuminous material surrounding the yolk of an egg **b** : the white part of the ball of the eye **c** : the light-colored pieces in a two-handed board game or the player by whom these are played **3** : one that is or approaches the color white **4** : a person belonging to a light-skinned race **5** : a member of a conservative or reactionary political group (as one opposed to the Bolsheviks after the Russian revolution of 1917)

³**white** *vt, archaic* : WHITEN

white ant *n* : TERMITE

white·bait \'hwīt-,bāt\ *n* : the young of a European herring; *also* : any of various similar small fishes used as food

white bass *n* : a No. American freshwater food fish

white·beard \-,bi(ə)rd\ *n* : an old man : GRAYBEARD

white blood cell *n* : a blood cell that does not contain hemoglobin : LEUCOCYTE

white·cap \'hwīt-,kap\ *n* : a wave crest breaking into white foam

white cedar *n* : any of various No. American timber trees including true cedars, junipers, and cypress

white cell *n* : LEUCOCYTE

white clover *n* : any of various tall or low-growing clovers with white flowers

white-col·lar \'hwīt-'käl-ər\ *adj* : of, relating to, or constituting the class of salaried employees whose duties call for well-groomed appearance

white corpuscle *n* : LEUCOCYTE

white crappie *n* : a silvery No. American sunfish highly esteemed as a panfish and often used for stocking small ponds

white Dutch clover *n* : a Eurasian clover with round heads of white flowers that is widely used in lawns and pastures and is an important honey plant

white elephant *n* [so called fr. the fact that in parts of India pale-colored elephants are held sacred and are maintained without being required to work] **1** : something requiring much care and expense and yielding little profit **2** : an object no longer wanted by its owner though not without value to others

white-faced \'hwīt-'fāst\ *adj* **1** : having a wan pale face **2** : having the face white in whole or in part ⟨a *white-faced* steer⟩

white feather *n* [fr. the superstition that a white feather in the plumage of a gamecock is a mark of a poor fighter] : a mark or symbol of cowardice (show the *white feather*)

white·fish \'hwīt-,fish\ *n* : any of various freshwater food fishes related to the salmons and trouts and mostly greenish above and silvery white below

white flag *n* : a flag of plain white used as a flag of truce or as a token of surrender

white·fly \'hwīt-,flī\ *n* : any of various small white winged insects related to the scale insects and esp. destructive to greenhouse plants

white friar *n, often cap W & F* : CARMELITE

white gold *n* : a pale alloy of gold resembling platinum in appearance

white goods *n pl* **1** : white fabrics or articles (as sheets or towels) typically made of cotton or linen **2** : major household appliances (as stoves) typically finished in white enamel

white grub *n* : a grub that is the larva of a june beetle and a destructive pest of grass roots

White·hall \'hwīt-,hol\ *n* [fr. *Whitehall*, street of London in which are located the chief offices of British government] : the British government

white·head \'hwīt-,hed\ *n* : a small whitish lump in the skin

white-head·ed \-'hed-əd\ *adj* **1** : having the hair, fur, or plumage of the head white or very light **2** : highly favored : FORTUNATE ⟨society's *white-headed* boy⟩

white heat *n* **1** : a temperature at which a metallic body becomes brightly incandescent so as to appear white **2** : a state of intense mental or physical strain, emotion, or activity — **white-hot** *adj*

White Horde *n* : a Mongolian people powerful in Russia in the 14th century

White House *n* **1** : the presidential mansion in Washington **2** : the executive department of the U.S. government

white lead *n* : a heavy white poisonous carbonate of lead chiefly used as a pigment

white-liv·ered \'hwīt-'liv-ərd\ *adj* : COWARDLY, PUSILLANIMOUS

white matter *n* : whitish neural tissue that consists largely of medullated nerve fibers and underlies the gray matter of the brain and spinal cord or forms nerves

whit·en \'hwīt-°n\ *vb* **whit·ened**; **whit·en·ing** \'hwīt-niŋ, -°n-iŋ\ : to make or become white or whiter **syn** WHITEN, BLANCH, BLEACH mean to make or grow white. WHITEN implies making white usu. by the application or addition of a white substance; BLANCH implies the removal or withdrawal of color esp. from living tissue; BLEACH implies the action of sunlight or chemicals in removing color

whit·en·er \'hwīt-nər, -°n-ər\ *n* : one that whitens; *esp* : an agent (as a bleach) used to impart whiteness to something

white·ness \'hwīt-nəs\ *n* : the quality or state of being white

white oak *n* : any of various oaks with acorns that mature in one year and leaf veins that never extend beyond the margin of the leaf; *also* : the hard, strong, durable, and moisture-resistant wood of a white oak

white paper *n* : a government report on any subject

white perch *n* : a small silvery anadromous sea bass of the coast and coastal streams of the eastern U.S.

white pine *n* : a tall-growing pine of eastern No. America with leaves in clusters of five; *also* : its wood which is much used in building construction

white-pine blister rust *n* : a destructive disease of white pine caused by a rust fungus that passes part of its life on currant or gooseberry bushes; *also* : this fungus

white plague *n* : tuberculosis of the lungs

white rust *n* : any of various plant diseases caused by lower fungi and marked by production of masses of white spores that escape through ruptures in the host tissue; *also* : a fungus causing a white rust

white sale *n* : a sale of white goods

white sauce *n* : a sauce consisting essentially of milk, cream, or stock with flour and seasoning

white sea bass *n* : a large Pacific croaker closely related to the Atlantic weakfishes

white·tail \'hwīt-,tāl\ *n* : a No. American deer with a rather long tail white on the undersurface and forward-arching antlers — called also *white-tailed deer* \,hwīt-,tāl(d)-'di(ə)r\

white tie *n* : formal evening dress for men

white·wall \'hwīt-,wol\ *n* : an automobile tire having a white sidewall

¹**white·wash** \'hwīt-,wosh, -,wash\ *vt* **1** : to whiten with whitewash **2** : to clear of a charge of wrongdoing by offering excuses, hiding facts, or conducting a perfunctory investigation **3** : to hold (an opponent) scoreless — **white·wash·er** *n*

²**whitewash** *n* **1** : a composition (as of lime and water) for whitening structural surfaces **2 a** : a clearing by whitewashing **b** : a defeat in a contest in which the loser fails to score

white whale *n* : BELUGA 2

white·wood \'hwīt-,wud\ *n* **1** : any of various trees with pale or white wood: as **a** : BASSWOOD 1 **b** : COTTONWOOD **2** : the wood of a whitewood and esp. of the tulip tree

whith·er \'hwith-ər\ *adv* [OE *hwider*; akin to E *who*] **1** : to what place ⟨*whither* will they go⟩ **2** : to what situation, position, degree, or end ⟨*whither* will this abuse drive him⟩ **3 a :** to the place at, in, or to which **b :** to which place ⟨the village *whither* we had brought our horses⟩ **4 :** to whatever place

whith·er·so·ev·er \,hwi<u>th</u>-ər-sə-'wev-ər\ *conj* **:** to whatever place

whith·er·ward \'hwi<u>th</u>-ər-wərd\ *adv* **:** toward what or which place

¹**whit·ing** \'hwīt-iŋ\ *n, pl* **whiting** *or* **whitings** [MD *witinc*, fr. *wit* white] **:** any of several edible fishes (as the hake) found mostly near seacoasts

²**whiting** *n* **:** calcium carbonate prepared as fine powder and used esp. as a pigment and extender, in putty, and in rubber compounding

whit·ish \'hwīt-ish\ *adj* **:** somewhat white

whit·low \'hwit-,lō\ *n* [ME *whitflawe, whitlowe*] **:** ²FELON

Whit·sun \'hwit-sən\ *adj* **:** of, relating to, or observed on Whitsunday or at Whitsuntide

Whit·sun·day \'hwit-'sən-dē, -sən-,dā\ *n* [OE *hwīta sunnandæg*, lit., white Sunday] **:** PENTECOST 2

Whit·sun·tide \'hwit-sən-,tīd\ *n* **:** the week beginning with Whitsunday; *esp* **:** the first three days of this week

¹**whit·tle** \'hwit-ᵊl\ *n* [ME *thwitel, whittel*, fr. *thwiten* to whittle, fr. OE *thwītan*] **:** a large knife

²**whittle** *vb* **whit·tled; whit·tling** \'hwit-liŋ, -ᵊl-iŋ\ **1 a :** to pare or cut off chips from the surface of (wood) with a knife **b :** to shape or form by so paring or cutting **2 :** to reduce, remove, or destroy gradually as if by cutting off bits with a knife **:** PARE ⟨*whittle* down expenses⟩ — **whit·tler** \'hwit-lər, -ᵊl-ər\ *n*

¹**whiz** *or* **whizz** \'hwiz\ *vb* **whizzed; whiz·zing 1 :** to hum, whir, or hiss like a speeding object (as an arrow or ball) passing through air **2 :** to fly or move swiftly with a whiz **3 :** to rotate very rapidly — **whiz·zer** *n*

²**whiz** *or* **whizz** *n, pl* **whiz·zes 1 :** a hissing, buzzing, or whirring sound **2 :** a movement or passage of something accompanied by a whizzing sound

³**whiz** *n, pl* **whiz·zes :** WIZARD 2

whiz·bang *or* **whizz·bang** \'hwiz-,baŋ\ *n* **:** someone or something conspicuous for noise, speed, or startling effect

whiz–bang *adj* **:** EXCELLENT, NOTABLE

who *pron* [OE *hwā*] **1** \(')hü\ **:** what or which person or persons — used as an interrogative ⟨*who* was elected president⟩ ⟨find out *who* they are⟩; used by speakers on all educational levels and by many reputable writers as the object of a verb or a following preposition ⟨*who* did you meet⟩⟨*who* is it for⟩ **2** \(,)hü, ü\ — used to introduce a relative clause and to serve as a substitute within that clause for the substantive modified by that clause; used esp. in reference to persons ⟨my father, *who* was a lawyer⟩; used by speakers on all educational levels and by many reputable writers as the object of a verb ⟨a man *who* you all know well⟩

syn WHO, WHICH, THAT are relative pronouns. WHO is used only of persons ⟨my brother, *who* is older than I⟩ ⟨those *who* believe in miracles⟩ WHICH refers to animals, to inanimate objects, or to ideas or situations expressed but not named (replacing *and that*) ⟨you are in trouble, *which* is why I am here⟩ THAT may be used of persons, animals, or things in restrictive clauses ⟨the first man *that* spoke to me⟩⟨the car *that* just went by⟩ but not in descriptive (nonrestrictive) clauses referring to persons; WHICH is less usual than THAT in restrictive clauses referring to things except when it follows a preposition ⟨the chair on *which* he sat⟩

whoa \'wō, 'hō, 'hwō\ *imperative verb* — a command to a draft animal to stand still

who·dun·it \hü-'dən-ət\ *n* **:** a detective story or mystery story presented as a novel, play, or motion picture

who·ev·er \hü-'ev-ər\ *pron* **:** whatever person ⟨*whoever* he may be⟩ — used in any grammatical relation except that of a possessive

¹**whole** \'hōl\ *adj* [OE *hāl*] **1 :** being in healthy or sound condition **:** free from defect or damage **:** WELL, INTACT ⟨careful nursing made him *whole*⟩ ⟨every egg was *whole*⟩ **2 :** having all its proper parts or elements ⟨*whole* milk⟩ **3 a :** constituting the total sum of **:** INTEGRAL **b :** each or all of the ⟨the *whole* family⟩ **4 a :** constituting an undivided unit ⟨a *whole* roast suckling pig⟩ **b :** directed to one end **:** CONCENTRATED ⟨promised to give it his *whole* attention⟩ **5 :** seemingly complete or total ⟨the *whole* sky was red⟩

syn ENTIRE, PERFECT: WHOLE suggests a completeness or perfection that is normal and can be sought, gained, or regained; ENTIRE implies wholeness deriving from integrity, soundness, or completeness with nothing omitted or taken away; PERFECT implies the soundness and excellence of every part or element often as an unattainable or theoretical state

²**whole** *n* **1 :** a complete amount or sum **:** a number, aggregate, or totality lacking no part, member, or element **2 :** something constituting a complex unity **:** a coherent system or organization of parts fitting or working together as one — **on the whole 1 :** in view of all the circumstances or conditions **:** all things considered ⟨*on the whole* we shouldn't complain⟩ **2 :** in general **:** in most instances **:** TYPICALLY ⟨men, *on the whole*, approve the law⟩

whole·heart·ed \'hōl-'härt-əd\ *adj* **:** undivided in purpose, enthusiasm, or will **:** HEARTY, ZESTFUL ⟨*wholehearted* effort⟩ — **whole·heart·ed·ly** *adv* — **whole·heart·ed·ness** *n*

whole hog *n* **:** the whole way **:** farthest limit **:** ALL ⟨go the *whole hog*⟩

whole·ness \'hōl-nəs\ *n* **:** the quality or state of being whole

whole note *n* **:** a time unit of musical notation equal in value to four quarter notes or two half notes or one measure in common time

whole number *n* **:** INTEGER

¹**whole·sale** \'hōl-,sāl\ *n* **:** the sale of commodities in quantity usu. for resale by a retail merchant

²**wholesale** *adj* **1 :** of, relating to, or engaged in wholesaling ⟨a *wholesale* grocer⟩ ⟨*wholesale* prices⟩ **2 :** performed on a large scale esp. without discrimination ⟨*wholesale* slaughter⟩ — **wholesale** *adv*

³**wholesale** *vb* **:** to sell at wholesale — **whole·sal·er** *n*

whole·some \'hōl-səm\ *adj* **1 a :** promoting mental, spiritual, or bodily health or well-being ⟨*wholesome* advice⟩ ⟨a *wholesome* environment⟩ **b :** not detrimental to health or well-being; *esp* **:** fit for food ⟨some sausages are legally permitted to contain a percentage of *wholesome* filler as well as meat and seasoning⟩ **2 :** sound in body, mind, or morals **:** HEALTHY **3 :** based on well-grounded fear **:** PRUDENT ⟨*wholesome* respect for the champion's right hand⟩ syn see HEALTHFUL — **whole·some·ly** *adv* — **whole·some·ness** *n*

whole·souled \-'sōld\ *adj* **:** moved by ardent enthusiasm or single-minded devotion

whole step *n* **:** a musical interval comprising two half steps (as C–D or F♯–G♯) — called also *whole tone*

whole wheat *adj* **:** made of ground entire wheat kernels

whol·ly \'hō(l)-lē\ *adv* **1 :** to the full or entire extent **:** COMPLETELY, TOTALLY **2 :** to the exclusion of other things **:** SOLELY

whom *pron, objective case of* WHO — used as an interrogative \(')hüm\ *or relative* \(,)hüm, üm\; used as object of a verb or a preceding preposition ⟨to *whom* was it given⟩ or less frequently as the object of a following preposition ⟨the man *whom* you spoke to⟩ though now often considered stilted esp. as an interrogative and esp. in oral use

whom·ev·er \hü-'mev-ər\ *objective case of* WHOEVER

whom·so \'hüm-sō\ *objective case of* WHOSO

whom·so·ev·er \,hüm-sə-'wev-ər\ *objective case of* WHOSOEVER

¹**whoop** \'h(w)üp, 'h(w)ùp\ *vb* [MF *houpper*] **1 :** to shout or call loudly and vigorously esp. in expression of eagerness, enthusiasm, or enjoyment ⟨the boys *whooped* with joy⟩ **2 :** to make the sound that follows an attack of coughing in whooping cough **3 :** to go or pass with a loud noise **4 a :** to utter or express with a whoop **b :** to urge, drive, or cheer on with a whoop — **whoop it up 1 :** to celebrate riotously **:** CAROUSE **2 :** to stir up enthusiasm

²**whoop** *n* **1 :** a whooping sound or utterance: as **a :** a shout of hunters or of men in battle or pursuit **b :** a loud booming call of a bird (as an owl or crane) **:** HOOT **c :** a crowing sound accompanying the intake of breath after a coughing attack in whooping cough **2 :** the smallest bit ⟨not worth a *whoop*⟩

¹**whoop·ee** \'(h)wùp-(,)ē, '(h)wü-(,)pē\ *interj* — used to express exuberant delight

²**whoopee** *n* **:** boisterous convivial fun

whooping cough *n* **:** an infectious bacterial disease esp. of children marked by a convulsive spasmodic cough sometimes followed by a crowing intake of breath — called also *per·tus·sis* \pər-'təs-əs\

whooping crane *n* : a large white nearly extinct No. American crane

whoop·la \'h(w)üp-,lä, 'h(w)úp-\ *n* **1** : a noisy commotion **2** : boisterous merrymaking

¹**whoosh** \'hwüsh\ *vb* : to move with an explosive or sibilant rush

²**whoosh** *n* : a swift or explosive rush

whop·per \'hwäp-ər\ *n* **1** : something unusually large or extreme of its kind **2** : a monstrous lie

whop·ping \'hwäp-iŋ\ *adj* : extremely large

¹**whore** \'hō(ə)r, 'hó(ə)r\ *n* [OE *hōre*] : PROSTITUTE

²**whore** *vi* : to have unlawful sexual intercourse as or with a whore

whorl \'hwórl, 'hwərl\ *n* [ME *wharle, whorle*] **1** : a row of parts (as leaves or petals) encircling an axis and esp. a stem **2** : something that whirls, coils, or spirals or whose form suggests such movement : COIL, SPIRAL (the *whorl* of a rapid) **3** : one of the turns of a univalve shell — **whorled** \'hwórld, 'hwərld\ *adj*

whor·tle·ber·ry \'hwərt-ʾl-,ber-ē\ *n* [alter. of ME *hurtilberye,* irreg. fr. OE *horte* whortleberry] **1** : a European blueberry with a blackish berry : BILBERRY; *also* : its berry **2** : BLUEBERRY

¹**whose** \(')hüz, üz\ *adj* [ME *whos,* gen. of *who, what*] : of or relating to whom or which esp. as possessor, agent, or object of an action (asked *whose* bag it was) (*whose* plays are greater than Shakespeare's) (the book *whose* publication was announced)

²**whose** \(')hüz\ *pron* : whose one : whose ones — used without a following noun as a pronoun equivalent in meaning to the adjective *whose*

whose·so·ev·er \,hüz-sə-'wev-ər\ *adj* : of or relating to whomsoever

who·so \'hü-,sō\ *pron* : WHOEVER

who·so·ev·er \,hü-sə-'wev-ər\ *pron* : WHOEVER

¹**why** \(')hwī\ *adv* [OE *hwȳ,* instr. of *hwæt* what] : for what cause, reason, or purpose (*why* did you do it)

²**why** *conj* **1** : the cause, reason, or purpose for which (know *why* you did it)(that is *why* you did it) **2** : for which : on account of which (know the reason *why* you did it)

³**why** \'hwī\ *n, pl* **whys** : REASON, CAUSE (the *why* of race prejudice)

⁴**why** \(,)wī, (,)hwī\ *interj* — used to express surprise, hesitation, approval, disapproval, or impatience (*why,* here's what I was looking for)

whyd·ah \'hwid-ə\ *n* [alter. of *widow* (bird); so called fr. its long black tail feathers resembling a widow's veil] : any of various mostly black and white African weaverbirds often kept as cage birds

wick \'wik\ *n* [OE *wēoce*] : a cord, strip, or ring of loosely woven material through which a liquid (as melted tallow, wax, or oil) is drawn by capillary action to the top in a candle, lamp, or oil stove for burning

wick·ed \'wik-əd\ *adj* [ME, alter. of *wicke* wicked] **1** : morally bad : EVIL **2 a** : FIERCE, VICIOUS **b** : causing or likely to cause harm or trouble **c** : REPUGNANT, VILE (*wicked* odor)(*wicked* weather) **d** : disposed to mischief : ROGUISH (a *wicked* glance) — **wick·ed·ly** *adv* — **wick·ed·ness** *n*

wick·er \'wik-ər\ *n* [of Scand origin] **1** : a small pliant twig or osier : WITHE **2 a** : WICKERWORK **b** : something made of wicker — **wicker** *adj*

wick·er·work \-,wərk\ *n* : work of osiers, twigs, or rods : BASKETRY

wick·et \'wik-ət\ *n* [ONF *wiket,* of Gmc origin] **1** : a small gate or door; *esp* : one in or near a larger one **2** : a small window with a grille or grate (as at a ticket office) **3 a** : either of the 2 sets of 3 rods topped by 2 crosspieces at which the ball is bowled in cricket **b** : an area 10 feet wide bounded by these wickets **c** : one innings of a batsman; *esp* : one that is not completed or never begun (win by 3 *wickets*) **4** : an arch or hoop in croquet

wick·et·keep·er \-,kē-pər\ *n* : the player who fields immediately behind the wicket in cricket

wick·ing \'wik-iŋ\ *n* : material for wicks

wick·i·up \'wik-ē-,əp\ *n* [of AmerInd origin] : a hut used by nomadic Indians

wickiup

of the western and southwestern U.S. with a usu. oval base and a rough frame covered with reed mats, grass, or brushwood

Wi·dal test \wi-,dal-, -,däl-\ *n* [after Fernand *Widal* d1929 French physician] : a test for typhoid based on the ability of the serum of an infected person to agglutinate typhoid bacilli

¹**wide** \'wīd\ *adj* [OE *wīd*] **1** : covering a vast area : VAST (the *wide* world) **2** : measured across or at right angles to length (cloth 54 inches *wide*) **3** : having a generous measure across : BROAD **4** : opened as far as possible (eyes *wide* with wonder) **5** : not limited : EXTENSIVE (*wide* experience) **6** : far from the goal, mark, or truth (a *wide* guess) syn see BROAD — **wide·ly** *adv* — **wide·ness** *n*

²**wide** *adv* **1 a** : over a great distance or extent : WIDELY (searched far and *wide*) **b** : over a specified distance, area, or extent (expanded the business country*wide*) **2 a** : so as to leave much space or distance between (*wide* apart) **b** : so as to pass at or clear by a considerable distance (ran *wide* around left end) **3** : COMPLETELY, FULLY (opened her eyes *wide*) **4** : so as to diverge or miss : ASTRAY (the bullet went *wide*)

wide-awake \,wīd-ə-'wāk\ *adj* **1** : fully awake; *also* : KNOWING, ALERT — **wide-awake·ness** *n*

wide-eyed \'wīd-'īd\ *adj* **1** : having the eyes wide open **2** : struck with wonder or astonishment : AMAZED **3** : marked by unsophisticated or uncritical acceptance or admiration : NAÏVE (a *wide-eyed* belief in the goodness of everybody)

wide-mouthed \-'maúthd, -'maútht\ *adj* **1** : having a wide mouth (*widemouthed* jars) **2** : having one's mouth opened wide (as in awe)

wid·en \'wīd-ʾn\ *vb* **wid·ened; wid·en·ing** \'wīd-niŋ, -ʾn-iŋ\ : to make or become wide or wider : BROADEN — **wid·en·er** *n*

wide·spread \'wīd-'spred\ *adj* **1** : widely extended or spread out (*widespread* wings) **2** : widely diffused or prevalent (*widespread* dissatisfaction)

wid·geon *also* **wi·geon** \'wij-ən\ *n, pl* **widgeons** *or* **widgeons** : any of several freshwater ducks between the teal and the mallard in size

wid·ish \'wīd-ish\ *adj* : somewhat wide

¹**wid·ow** \'wid-ō\ *n* [OE *widuwe*] **1** : a woman who has lost her husband by death; *esp* : one who has not remarried **2** : GRASS WIDOW — **wid·ow·hood** \-,húd\ *n*

²**widow** *vt* : to cause to become a widow (*widowed* by war)

wid·ow·er \'wid-ə-wər\ *n* : a man who has lost his wife by death and has not married again

widow's mite *n* [fr. the widow who cast two mites into the Temple treasury (Mark 12:12)] : a small contribution that is willingly given and is all one can afford

widow's peak *n* : PEAK 7

widow's walk *n* : a railed observation platform atop a coastal house

width \'width\ *n* [¹*wide*] **1** : a distance from side to side : the measurement taken at right angles to the length : BREADTH, WIDENESS **2 a** : largeness of extent or scope; *also* : FULLNESS **b** : GENEROSITY, LIBERALITY **3** : a measured and cut piece of material (a *width* of calico) (a *width* of lumber)

width·ways \-,wāz\ *adv* : WIDTHWISE

width·wise \-,wīz\ *adv* : in the direction of the width : CROSSWISE

wield \'wēld\ *vt* [OE *wieldan*] **1** : to handle (as a tool) effectively (*wield* a broom) **2** : to exert one's authority by means of (*wield* influence) — **wield·er** *n*

wieldy \'wēl-dē\ *adj* : capable of wielding or being wielded

wie·ner \'wē-nər, -nē\ *n* [short for G *wienerwurst* Vienna sausage] : FRANKFURTER

Wie·ner schnit·zel \'vē-nər-,s(h)nit-səl, 'wē-nər-,snit-\ *n* [G, lit., Vienna cutlet] : a thin breaded veal cutlet served with a garnish

wife \'wīf\ *n, pl* **wives** \'wīvz\ [OE *wīf*] **1 a** *dial* : WOMAN **b** : a woman acting in a specified capacity — used in combination (fish*wife*) **2** : a married woman

wife·hood \'wīf-,húd\ *n* : the quality or state of being a wife

wife·less \-ləs\ *adj* : having no wife

wife·ly \'wī-flē\ *adj* **wife·li·er; -est** : of, relating to, or befitting a wife — **wife·li·ness** *n*

---

wig \'wig\ *n* [short for *periwig*] : a manufactured covering of hair for the head usu. made of human hair; *also* : TOUPEE

wigged \'wigd\ *adj* : wearing a wig ⟨the judge, all *wigged* and robed⟩

wig·gle \'wig-əl\ *vb* **wig·gled; wig·gling** \'wig-(ə-)liŋ\ [ME *wiglen*] **1** : to move to and fro with quick jerky or shaking motions : JIGGLE ⟨*wiggled* his toes⟩ **2** : to proceed with twisting and turning movements : WRIGGLE — **wiggle** *n*

wig·gler \'wig-(ə-)lər\ *n* **1** : one that wiggles **2** : a larval or pupal mosquito — called also *wriggler*

wig·gly \'wig-(ə-)lē\ *adj* **wig·gli·er; -est 1** : tending to wiggle ⟨a *wiggly* worm⟩ **2** : WAVY ⟨*wiggly* lines⟩

wight \'wīt\ *n* [OE *wiht* creature, thing] : a living being : CREATURE

¹wig·wag \'wig-,wag\ *vb* **wig·wagged; -wag·ging 1** : to signal by or as if by a flag or light waved according to a code **2** : to make or cause to make a signal (as with the hand or arm)

²wigwag *n* **1** : the art or practice of wigwagging **2** : a wigwagged message

wig·wam \'wig-,wäm\ *n* [of Algonquian origin] : a hut of the Indians of the eastern U.S. having typically an arched framework of poles overlaid with bark, rush mats, or hides

wigwam

wil·co \'wil-kō\ *interj* [*will comply*] — used esp. in radio and signaling to indicate that a message received will be complied with

¹wild \'wīld\ *adj* [OE] **1 a** : living in a state of nature and not ordinarily tame or domesticated ⟨*wild* duck⟩ **b** : growing or produced without the aid and care of man ⟨*wild* honey⟩; *also* : related to or resembling a corresponding cultivated or domesticated organism ⟨*wild* parsley⟩ **c** : of or relating to wild organisms ⟨the *wild* state⟩ **2** : not inhabited or cultivated : WASTE, DESOLATE ⟨*wild* land⟩ **3 a** : not subjected to restraint or regulation : UNCONTROLLED, UNRULY ⟨*wild* rage⟩ ⟨a *wild* young stallion⟩ **b** : TURBULENT, STORMY ⟨a *wild* night⟩ **c** : EXTRAVAGANT, FANTASTIC ⟨*wild* colors⟩⟨*wild* ideas⟩ **d** : indicative of strong passion, desire, or emotion ⟨a *wild* stare⟩ **4** : UNCIVILIZED, SAVAGE **5** : deviating from the natural or expected course ⟨a *wild* price increase⟩ **6** : having a denomination determined by the holder ⟨a round of poker with deuces *wild*⟩ — **wild·ly** *adv* — **wild·ness** \'wīl(d)-nəs\ *n*

²wild *n* **1** : WILDERNESS **2** : a natural uncultivated or undomesticated state or existence

³wild *adv* **1** : WILDLY **2** : without regulation or control ⟨running *wild*⟩

wild and woolly *adj* : marked by a boisterous and untamed lack of polish and refinement ⟨a *wild and woolly* town⟩

wild boar *n* : an Old World wild hog from which most domestic swine have been derived

wild carrot *n* : a widely naturalized white-flowered Eurasian weed that is prob. the original of the cultivated carrot — called also *Queen Anne's lace*

¹wild·cat \'wīl(d)-,kat\ *n, pl* **wildcats** *or* **wildcat 1** : any of various small or medium-sized cats (as the lynx or ocelot) **2** : a savage quick-tempered person

²wildcat *adj* **1 a** : financially irresponsible or unreliable ⟨*wildcat* banks⟩ **b** : issued by a wildcat bank ⟨*wildcat* currency⟩ **2** : operating, produced, or carried on outside the bounds of standard or legitimate business practices **3** : of, relating to, or being an oil or gas well drilled in territory not known to be productive **4** : begun by a group of workers without union approval or in violation of a contract ⟨*wildcat* strike⟩⟨*wildcat* work stoppage⟩

³wildcat *vi* **-cat·ted; -cat·ting** : to prospect and drill an experimental oil or gas well or mine shaft in territory not known to be productive — **wild·cat·ter** *n*

wil·de·beest \'wil-də-,bēst\ *n, pl* **wildebeests** *also* **wildebeest** [Afrik *wildebees*, lit., wild ox] : GNU

wil·der·ness \'wil-dər-nəs\ *n* [ME, fr. *wildern* wild, fr. OE *wilddēoren* of wild beasts] : an uncultivated and uninhabited region : wild or waste land

wilderness area *n* : an area (as of national forest land) set aside for preservation of natural conditions for scientific or recreational purposes

wild–eyed \'wīld-'īd\ *adj* **1** : appearing or being furious or raving ⟨haggard and *wild-eyed* men⟩ **2** : RADICAL, EXTREME ⟨*wild-eyed* reformers⟩

wild·fire \'wīl(d)-,fī(ə)r\ *n* **1** : a sweeping and destructive conflagration **2** : something of unquenchable intensity or all-inclusive action ⟨the news spread through the town like *wildfire*⟩

wild flower *n* : the flower of a wild or uncultivated plant or the plant bearing it

wild·fowl \'wīl(d)-,faul\ *n* : a game bird; *esp* : a game waterfowl (as a wild duck or goose) — **wild·fowl·er** \-,fau-lər\ *n* — **wild·fowl·ing** \-liŋ\ *n*

wild ginger *n* : a No. American perennial woodland herb with pungent creeping rootstock and bluntly heart-shaped leaves

wild–goose chase *n* : the pursuit of something unattainable

wild·ing \'wīl-diŋ\ *n* : a plant or animal growing or living in the wild — **wilding** *adj*

wild land *n* : WILDERNESS, WASTELAND

wild·life \'wīl-,(d)līf\ *n* : creatures that are neither human nor domesticated; *esp* : mammals, birds, and fishes hunted by man — **wildlife** *adj*

wild·ling \'wīl-(d)liŋ\ *n* : a wild plant or animal

wild oat *n* **1 a** : any of several wild grasses closely related to the cultivated oat **b** : any of a genus of small herbs of the lily family with drooping bell-shaped yellowish flowers **2** *pl* : offenses and indiscretions ascribed to youthful exuberance — usu. used in the phrase *sow one's wild oats*

wild pansy *n* : a common and long-cultivated European viola which has short-spurred flowers usu. blue or purple mixed with white and yellow and from which most of the garden pansies are derived — called also *heartsease, Johnny-jump-up*

wild parsley *n* : any of various wild plants of the carrot family with finely divided leaves

wild pitch *n* : a pitched ball that cannot be stopped by the catcher and that allows a base runner to advance

wild rice *n* : a tall aquatic No. American perennial grass yielding an edible grain

wild type *n* : the typical form of an organism as ordinarily encountered in nature as contrasted with mutant individuals

wild West *n* : the western U.S. in its frontier period

wild·wood \'wīl-,(d)wùd\ *n* : a wood unaltered or unfrequented by man

¹wile \'wīl\ *n* [ME *wil*] **1** : a trick or stratagem intended to ensnare or deceive; *also* : a beguiling or playful trick **2** : TRICKERY, GUILE

²wile *vt* : LURE, ENTICE ⟨the balmy weather *wiled* them from their work⟩

wil·i·ness \'wī-lē-nəs\ *n* : the quality or state of being wily

¹will \wəl, (ə)l, (')wil\ *vb, past* **would** \wəd, (ə)d, (')wùd\; *pres sing & pl* **will** [OE *wille*] **1** : DESIRE, WISH ⟨call it what you *will*⟩ **2** — used as an auxiliary verb (1) to express desire, willingness, or in negative contructions refusal ⟨*will* you have another helping⟩⟨could find no one who *would* take the job⟩⟨he *won't* stop pestering me⟩, (2) to express frequent, customary, or habitual action or natural tendency ⟨*will* get angry over nothing⟩, (3) to express simple futurity ⟨tomorrow we *will* go shopping⟩, (4) to express capability or sufficiency ⟨the back seat *will* hold three passengers⟩, (5) to express probability or recognition and often equivalent to the simple verb ⟨that *will* be the milkman ringing the doorbell⟩, (6) to express determination or willfulness ⟨I have made up my mind to go and I *will*⟩, and (7) to express a command ⟨you *will* do as I say⟩

²will \'wil\ *n* **1** : wish or desire often combined with determination ⟨the *will* to win⟩ **2** : something desired; *esp* : a choice or determination of one having authority or power **3** : the act, process, or experience of willing : VOLITION **4 a** : the mental powers manifested as wishing, choosing, desiring, intending **b** : a disposition to act according to principles or ends **5** : SELF-CONTROL ⟨a man of iron *will*⟩ **6** : a legal declaration in which a person states how he wishes his property to be disposed of after his death

³will \'wil\ *vb* **1** : to dispose of by or as if by a will : BEQUEATH **2 a** : to determine by an act of choice ⟨*willed*

herself to sleep⟩ **b** : DECREE, ORDAIN ⟨Providence *wills* it⟩ **c** : INTEND, PURPOSE ⟨he *willed* it so⟩ **3** : to exercise the will **4** : CHOOSE ⟨went wherever they *willed*⟩

willed \'wild\ *adj* : having a will esp. of a specified kind ⟨strong-*willed*⟩

wil·lem·ite \'wil-ə-,mīt\ *n* [G *willemit*, fr. *Willem* (William) I *d*1843 king of the Netherlands] : a mineral Zn₂SiO₄ consisting of zinc silicate, occurring in prisms and in massive or granular forms, and varying in color

wil·let \'wil-ət\ *n, pl* **willet** : a large shorebird of the eastern and Gulf coasts and the central parts of No. America

will·ful *or* **wil·ful** \'wil-fəl\ *adj* **1** : governed by will without regard to reason : OBSTINATE **2** : done deliberately : INTENTIONAL ⟨*willful* murder⟩ — **will·ful·ly** \-fə-lē\ *adv* — **will·ful·ness** *n*

Wil·liam Tell \,wil-yəm-'tel\ *n* : a legendary Swiss patriot sentenced to shoot an apple from his son's head

wil·lies \'wil-ēz\ *n pl* : a fit of nervousness : JITTERS ⟨acrobats give me the *willies*⟩

will·ing \'wil-iŋ\ *adj* **1** : inclined or favorably disposed in mind : READY ⟨*willing* to go⟩ **2** : prompt to act or respond ⟨*willing* workers⟩ **3** : done, borne, or accepted of choice or without reluctance : VOLUNTARY ⟨*willing* obedience⟩ **4** : of or relating to the will or power of choosing : VOLITIONAL — **will·ing·ly** \-iŋ-lē\ *adv* — **will·ing·ness** *n*

wil·li·waw \'wil-ē-,wȯ\ *n* **1** : a sudden violent gust of cold land air common along mountainous coasts of high latitudes **2** : a violent commotion or agitation

will·less \'wil-ləs\ *adj* **1** : involving no exercise of the will : INVOLUNTARY ⟨*will-less* obedience⟩ **2** : not exercising the will ⟨*will-less* human beings⟩

will-o'-the-wisp \,wil-ə-thə-'wisp\ *n* **1** : IGNIS FATUUS 1 **2** : a delusive goal or hope

wil·low \'wil-ō\ *n* [OE *welig*] **1** : any of a large genus of trees and shrubs bearing catkins of flowers without petals and including forms of value for wood, osiers, or tanbark and a few ornamentals **2** : an object made of willow wood; *esp* : a cricket bat — **willow** *adj* — **wil·low·like** \-,līk\ *adj*

willow herb *n* : a perennial herb of the evening-primrose family with tall spikes of pinkish purple flowers that is a locally important honey plant

willow oak *n* : an oak with lanceolate leaves

wil·low·ware \'wil-ō-,wa(ə)r, -,we(ə)r\ *n* : china that is usu. blue and white and that is decorated with a storytelling design featuring a large willow tree by a little bridge

wil·lowy \'wil-ə-wē\ *adj* **1** : abounding with willows **2 a** : resembling a willow : PLIANT **b** : gracefully tall and slender ⟨a *willowy* young woman⟩

will·pow·er \'wil-,pau̇(-ə)r\ *n* : energetic determination : RESOLUTENESS

wil·ly-nil·ly \,wil-ē-'nil-ē\ *adv* (*or adj*) [alter. of *will I nill* (archaic negative of *will*) *I or will ye nill ye or will he nill he*] : by compulsion : HELPLESSLY ⟨rushed us along *willy-nilly*⟩

¹**wilt** \'wəlt, (')wilt\ *archaic pres 2d sing of* WILL

²**wilt** \'wilt\ *vb* [alter. of earlier *welk*, fr. ME *welken*] **1** : to lose or cause to lose freshness and become limp : DROOP ⟨*wilting* roses⟩ **2** : to grow weak or faint : LANGUISH ⟨as the Roman Empire *wilted*⟩

³**wilt** \'wilt\ *n* **1** : an act or instance of wilting : the state of being wilted **2** : a plant disorder (as various fungus diseases) in which the soft tissues lose their turgor and droop and often shrivel

wily \'wī-lē\ *adj* **wil·i·er; -est** : full of guile : TRICKY **syn** see SLY

wim·ble \'wim-bəl\ *n* [AF, fr. MD *wimmel* auger] : any of various instruments for boring holes

¹**wim·ple** \'wim-pəl\ *n* [OE *wimpel*] : a cloth covering worn outdoors over the head and around the neck and chin by women esp. in the late medieval period and by some nuns

²**wimple** *vb* **wim·pled; wim·pling** \-p(ə-)liŋ\ **1** : to cover with or as if with a wimple : VEIL **2** : to cause to ripple : RIPPLE **3** : to fall or lie in folds

¹**win** \'win\ *vb* **won** \'wən\; **win·ning** [OE *winnan* to struggle] **1** : to gain the victory in or as if in a contest : SUCCEED **2** : to get possession of esp. by effort : GAIN **3 a** : to gain in or as if in battle or contest **b** : to be the victor in ⟨*won* the war⟩ **4** : to obtain by work : EARN

5 : to solicit and gain the favor of; *esp* : to induce to accept oneself in marriage

²**win** *n* : VICTORY; *esp* : first place at the finish of a horse race

wince \'win(t)s\ *vi* [ME *wenchen* to be impatient, dart about] : to shrink back involuntarily (as from pain) : FLINCH — **wince** *n*

winch \'winch\ *n* [OE *wince*] : a machine that has a roller on which rope is coiled for hauling or hoisting and is operated by a crank

winch

¹**wind** \'wind\ *n* [OE] **1** : a movement of the air of any velocity **2** : a force or agency that carries along or influences : TENDENCY, TREND **3 a** : BREATH 2a **b** : the pit of the stomach : SOLAR PLEXUS **4** : gas generated in the stomach or the intestines **5** : something insubstantial; *esp* : idle words **6 a** : air carrying a scent (as of a hunter or game) **b** : slight information esp. about something secret ⟨got *wind* of our plans⟩ **7 a** : wind instruments esp. as distinguished from strings and percussion **b** *pl* : players of wind instruments **8 a** : a direction from which the wind may blow : a point of the compass; *esp* : one of the cardinal points **b** : the direction from which the wind is blowing — **get the wind up** : to become excited or alarmed — **have in the wind** : to be on the scent of — **have the wind of 1** : to be to windward of **2** : to be on the scent of **3** : to have a superior position to — **in the wind** : about to happen : ASTIR, AFOOT — **near the wind 1** : CLOSE-HAULED **2** : close to a point of danger : near the permissible limit — **off the wind** : away from the direction from which the wind is blowing — **under the wind 1** : to leeward **2** : in a place protected from the wind : under the lee

²**wind** *vt* **1** : to get a scent of ⟨the dogs *winded* game⟩ **2** : to cause to be out of breath **3** : to allow (as a horse) to rest so as to recover breath

³**wind** \'wīnd, 'wind\ *vt* **wound** \'waund\; **wind·ing** : to sound by blowing ⟨*wind* a horn⟩

⁴**wind** \'wīnd\ *vb* **wound** \'waund\ *also* **wind·ed; wind·ing** [OE *windan* to twist, brandish] **1** : BEND, WARP **2** : to have a curving course or shape ⟨a river *winding* through the valley⟩ **3** : to move or lie so as to encircle **4** : to turn when lying at anchor **5 a** : ENTANGLE, INVOLVE **b** : to introduce sinuously or stealthily : INSINUATE **6 a** : to encircle or cover with something pliable **b** : to turn completely or repeatedly about an object : COIL, TWINE ⟨*wind* thread on a spool⟩ **c** (1) : to hoist or haul by means of a rope or chain and a windlass ⟨*wind* up a pail⟩ (2) : to move (a ship) by hauling on a capstan **d** (1) : to tighten the spring of ⟨*wind* a clock⟩ ⟨*wind* up a toy train⟩ (2) : CRANK ⟨*wound* down the car window⟩ **e** : to raise to a high level (as of excitement or tension) **7 a** : to cause to move in a curving line or path **b** (1) : to cause (as a ship) to change direction : TURN (2) : to turn (a ship) end for end **c** : to traverse on a curving course ⟨the river *winds* the valley⟩ — **wind·er** *n*

⁵**wind** \'wīnd\ *n* : COIL, TURN

wind·age \'win-dij\ *n* **1** : the influence of the wind in turning the course of a projectile **2** : the amount of deflection caused by the wind

wind·bag \'win(d)-,bag\ *n* : an idly talkative person

wind·blown \-,blōn\ *adj* : blown by the wind; *also* : having the appearance of being blown by the wind

wind·bound \-,baund\ *adj* : prevented from sailing by a contrary or a high wind

wind·break \-,brāk\ *n* : something (as a growth of trees or shrubs) serving to break the force of the wind

Wind·break·er \-,brā-kər\ *trademark* — used for a wind-resistant outer jacket with fitted cuffs and waistband

wind·bro·ken \-,brō-kən\ *adj* : having an impaired ability to breathe because of disease ⟨*wind-broken* horses⟩

wind·burn \-,bərn\ *n* : skin irritation caused by wind — **wind·burned** \-,bərnd\ *adj*

wind cone *n* : WIND SOCK

wind erosion *n* : dissipation of exposed topsoil by the action of wind

wind·fall \'win(d)-,fȯl\ *n* **1** : something (as a tree or fruit) blown down by the wind **2** : an unexpected or sudden gift, gain, or advantage

wind·flow·er \-ˌflau̇(-ə)r\ n : ANEMONE

wind gap n : a notch in the crest of a mountain ridge

wind·hov·er \'wind-ˌhəv-ər\ n, Brit : KESTREL

wind·ing \'wīn-diŋ\ n : material (as wire) wound or coiled about an object (as an armature); also : a single turn of the wound material

wind·ing-sheet \-ˌshēt\ n : a sheet used to wrap a corpse for burial : SHROUD

wind instrument n : a musical instrument (as a flute or horn) sounded by wind and esp. by the breath

wind·jam·mer \'win(d)-ˌjam-ər\ n : a sailing ship or one of its crew

wind·lass \'win-dləs\ n [ME wyndlas, alter. of wyndas, fr. ON vindāss, fr. vinda to wind + āss pole] : a winch used esp. on ships for hauling and hoisting

¹wind·mill \'win(d)-ˌmil\ n : a mill or a machine (as for pumping water) worked by the wind turning sails or vanes at the top of a tower

²windmill vb : to move or cause to move like a windmill

win·dow \'win-dō\ n [ON vindauga, fr. vindr wind + auga eye] 1 : an opening esp. in the wall of a building for admission of light and air usu. closed by casements or sashes containing glass 2 : WINDOWPANE 3 : something suggestive of or functioning like a window (as a shutter, opening, or valve)

window box n : a box designed to hold soil for growing plants on a windowsill

window dressing n 1 : display of merchandise in a store window 2 : a showing made to create a good but sometimes false impression

window envelope n : an envelope having a transparent panel through which the address on the enclosure is visible

win·dow·pane \-ˌpān\ n : a pane in a window

window seat n : a seat built into a window recess

window shade n : a shade or curtain for a window

win·dow-shop \-ˌshäp\ vi : to look at the displays in store windows without going inside the stores to make purchases — **win·dow-shop·per** n

win·dow·sill \-ˌsil\ n : the horizontal member at the bottom of a window opening

wind·pipe \'wind-ˌpīp\ n : a firm tubular passage connecting the pharynx and lungs : TRACHEA

wind·proof \-'prüf\ adj : proof against the wind ⟨a windproof jacket⟩

¹wind·row \'win-ˌ(d)rō\ n 1 : hay raked up into a row to dry 2 : a row of something (as sand or dry leaves) heaped up by or as if by the wind

²windrow vt : to put into windrows

wind·screen \'win(d)-ˌskrēn\ n, Brit : an automobile windshield

wind·shield \-ˌshēld\ n : a transparent screen (as of glass) in front of the occupants of a vehicle to protect them from the wind

wind sock n : a truncated cloth cone open at both ends and mounted in an elevated position to indicate the direction of the wind — called also wind sleeve

Wind·sor chair \ˌwin-zər-\ n [Windsor, England] : a wooden chair with spindle back, raking legs, and usu. a slightly concave seat

Windsor knot n : a knot used for tying four-in-hand ties that is wider than the usual four-in-hand knot

wind sprint n : a sprint performed as a training exercise to develop the wind

wind·storm \'win(d)-ˌstȯrm\ n : a storm marked by high wind with little or no precipitation

wind·swept \-ˌswept\ adj : swept by or as if by wind ⟨windswept plains⟩

wind tunnel n : an enclosed passage through which air is blown against structures (as airplanes) to test the effect of wind pressure on them

wind up \(ˈ)wīn-ˈdəp\ vb : to bring or come to a conclusion : END 2 : to put in order : SETTLE 3 : to arrive in a place, situation, or condition at the end or as a result of a course of action ⟨wound up as millionaires⟩ 4 : to give a preliminary swing to the arm (as before pitching a baseball)

¹wind·up \'wīn-ˌdəp\ n 1 a : the act of bringing to an end b : a concluding act or part : FINISH 2 : a preliminary swing of the arm before pitching a baseball ⟨here's the windup and the pitch⟩

²windup adj : having a spring wound up by hand for operation ⟨windup toy⟩

¹wind·ward \'win-(d)wərd\ adj : moving or situated toward the direction from which the wind is blowing — compare LEEWARD

²windward n : the side or direction from which the wind is blowing

wind-wing \'win-ˌ(d)wiŋ\ n : a small panel in an automobile window that can be turned outward for ventilation

windy \'win-dē\ adj wind·i·er; -est 1 : having wind : exposed to winds ⟨a windy day⟩ ⟨a windy prairie⟩ 2 : indulging in or characterized by useless talk ⟨a windy speaker⟩ — **wind·i·ly** \-də-lē\ adv — **wind·i·ness** \-dē-nəs\ n

¹wine \'wīn\ n [OE wīn, fr. L vinum] 1 : fermented grape juice containing varying percentages of alcohol 2 : the usu. fermented juice of a plant product (as a fruit) used as a beverage 3 : something that invigorates or intoxicates 4 : a variable color averaging a dark red

²wine vb 1 : to treat to wine ⟨wined and dined his friends⟩ 2 : to drink wine

wine cellar n : a room for storing wines; also : a stock of wines

wine-grower \'wīn-ˌgrō(-ə)r\ n : one that cultivates a vineyard and makes wine

wine-press \-ˌpres\ n : a vat in which juice is expressed from grapes by treading or by means of a plunger

win·ery \'wīn-(ə-)rē\ n, pl -er·ies : a wine-making establishment

wine·shop \'wīn-ˌshäp\ n : a tavern that specializes in serving wine

wine·skin \-ˌskin\ n : a bag made from the skin of an animal and used for holding wine

win·ey var of WINY

¹wing \'wiŋ\ n [of Scand origin] 1 : one of the movable feathered or membranous paired appendages by means of which a bird, bat, or insect is able to fly 2 : an appendage or part likened to a wing in shape, appearance, or position: as a : a flat or broadly expanded plant or animal part : ALA ⟨the wings of the nose⟩ ⟨a stem with woody wings⟩; esp : either lateral petal of a pealike flower b : a turned-back or extended edge on an article of clothing c : a sidepiece at the top of an armchair d : one of the airfoils that develop a major part of the lift which supports a heavier-than-air aircraft 3 : a means of flight or rapid progress 4 : the act or manner of flying : FLIGHT 5 : ARM; esp : a throwing or pitching arm 6 : a side or outlying region or district 7 : a part or feature usu. projecting from and subordinate to a main or central part ⟨the rear wing of the house⟩ 8 pl : the area at the side of the stage out of sight 9 a : a section of an army or fleet b : one of the positions or players on each side of a center position or line of a field, court, or rink; esp : such a position or player on the forward line of a team 10 a : either of two opposing groups in an organization : FACTION b : a section of a legislative chamber representing a distinct group or faction — **on the wing** : in flight : FLYING — **under one's wing** : under one's protection : in one's charge or care

²wing vb 1 : to pass through in flight : FLY 2 : to wound in the wing ⟨wing a bird⟩; also : to wound without killing

wing·back \-ˌbak\ n : an offensive football halfback who lines up outside the offensive end

wing case n : ELYTRON

wing chair n : an upholstered armchair with high solid back and sides that provide a rest for the head and protection from drafts

wing·ding \'wiŋ-ˌdiŋ\ n : a wild or lively or lavish party

winged \'wiŋd also except for "esp." sense 'wiŋ-əd\ adj 1 : having wings esp. of a specified character 2 a : soaring with or as if with wings : ELEVATED b : SWIFT, RAPID

wing chair

wing·less \'wiŋ-ləs\ adj : having no wings or very rudimentary wings — **wing·less·ness** n

wing·like \-ˌlīk\ adj : resembling a wing in form or lateral position

wing·man \-mən\ n : a pilot that flies back and outside the leader of a flying formation

wing nut *n* : a nut with wings affording a grip for the thumb and finger

wings \'wiŋz\ *n pl* : insignia consisting of an outspread pair of stylized bird's wings which are awarded on completion of prescribed training to a qualified crew member (as a pilot or navigator) or a balloon pilot in the armed services

wing·span \'wiŋ·ˌspan\ *n* : WINGSPREAD; *esp* : the distance between the tips of an airplane's wings

wing·spread \-ˌspred\ *n* : the spread of the wings; *esp* : the distance between the tips of the fully extended wings of a winged animal

¹**wink** \'wiŋk\ *vb* [OE *wincian*] **1** : to close and open the eyes quickly : BLINK **2** : to avoid seeing : pretend not to look : pay no attention ⟨*wink* at a violation of the law⟩ **3** : FLICKER, TWINKLE **4** : to close and open one eye quickly as a signal or hint

syn WINK, BLINK mean to close and open one's eyelids. WINK implies light, rapid, usu. involuntary motion; BLINK often implies a slower motion suggesting a dazzled or dazed state or a struggle against drowsiness; in figurative use WINK implies connivance or indulgence, BLINK suggests shirking or evasion

²**wink** *n* **1** : a brief period of sleep : NAP **2 a** : a hint or sign given by winking **b** : an act of winking **3** : the time of a wink : INSTANT

wink·er \'wiŋ·kər\ *n* **1** : one that winks **2** : EYELASH

win·kle \'wiŋ·kəl\ *n* **1** : ²PERIWINKLE **2** : any of various whelks that feed esp. on oysters and clams

win·na·ble \'win-ə-bəl\ *adj* : able to be won

win·ner \'win-ər\ *n* : one that wins

winner's circle *n* : an enclosure near a racetrack where the winning horse and jockey are brought for photographs and awards

¹**win·ning** \'win-iŋ\ *n* **1** : the act of one that wins : VICTORY. **2** : something won; *esp* : money won at gambling — often used in pl.

²**winning** *adj* : ATTRACTIVE, CHARMING — **win·ning·ly** \-iŋ-lē\ *adv*

win·now \'win-ō\ *vt* [OE *windwian*; akin to E ¹*wind*] **1 a** : to remove (as chaff from grain) by a current of air **b** : to subject (as grain) to a current of air to remove waste **2** : to get rid of (something unwanted) or to sort or separate (something) as if by winnowing

win·now·er \'win-ə-wər\ *n* : one that winnows; *esp* : a winnowing machine

wino \'wī-nō\ *n, pl* **win·os** : one who is chronically addicted to drinking wine

win·some \'win(t)-səm\ *adj* [OE *wynsum*, fr. *wynn* joy] **1** : causing joy or pleasure : WINNING, CHARMING **2** : CHEERFUL, GAY — **win·some·ly** *adv* — **win·some·ness** *n*

¹**win·ter** \'wint-ər\ *n* [OE] **1 a** : the season between autumn and spring comprising in the northern hemisphere usu. the months of December, January, and February or as reckoned astronomically extending from the December solstice to the March equinox **b** : the colder half of the year **2** : YEAR ⟨a man of 70 *winters*⟩ **3** : a time or season of inactivity or decay

²**winter** *vb* **win·tered; win·ter·ing** \'wint-ə-riŋ, 'win-triŋ\ **1** : to pass or live through the winter ⟨the cattle *wintered* on the range⟩ **2** : to keep, feed, or manage during the winter ⟨*winter* livestock⟩

³**winter** *adj* : occurring in or surviving the winter; *esp* : sown in autumn for harvesting in the following spring or summer ⟨*winter* wheat⟩ ⟨*winter* rye⟩

win·ter·ber·ry \'wint-ər-ˌber-ē\ *n* : any of various American hollies with bright red berries persistent through the winter

winter flounder *n* : a rusty brown flounder of the northwestern Atlantic important as a market fish esp. in winter

win·ter·green \'wint-ər-ˌgrēn\ *n* **1** : any of several low-growing evergreen plants related to the heaths; *esp* : one with white bell-shaped flowers followed by spicy red berries **2** : an essential oil from the common wintergreen or its flavor; *also* : something flavored with it

win·ter·ize \'wint-ə-ˌrīz\ *vt* : to make ready for winter or winter use and esp. resistant or proof against winter weather — **win·ter·i·za·tion** \ˌwint-ə-rə-'zā-shən\ *n*

win·ter·kill \'wint-ər-ˌkil\ *vb* : to kill (as a plant) by exposure to winter conditions; *also* : to die as a result of such exposure — **winterkill** *n*

winter melon *n* : a muskmelon with smooth rind and sweet white or greenish flesh that keeps well

winter quarters *n pl* : a winter residence or station (as of a military unit)

winter squash *n* : any of various squashes or pumpkins that keep well in storage

win·ter·tide \'wint-ər-ˌtīd\ *n* : the season of winter

win·ter·time \-ˌtīm\ *n* : the winter season

win through *vi* : to survive difficulties and reach a desired or satisfactory end

win·try \'win-trē\ *adj* **win·tri·er; -est** **1** : of or characteristic of winter : coming in winter : having to do with winter ⟨*wintry* weather⟩ **2** : CHILLING, COLD, CHEERLESS ⟨a *wintry* welcome⟩ — **win·tri·ly** \-trə-lē\ *adv* — **win·tri·ness** \-trē-nəs\ *n*

winy \'wī-nē\ *adj* **1** : having the taste or qualities of wine : VINOUS **2** : EXHILARATING ⟨*winy* autumn breezes⟩

¹**wipe** \'wīp\ *vt* [OE *wīpian*] **1** : to clean or dry by rubbing ⟨*wipe* dishes⟩ **2** : to remove by or as if by rubbing ⟨*wipe* away tears⟩ **3** : to erase completely : DESTROY ⟨the regiment was *wiped* out⟩ **4** : to pass or draw over a surface ⟨*wiped* his hand across his face⟩ — **wip·er** *n*

²**wipe** *n* **1** : an act or instance of wiping **2** : something used for wiping

wir·a·ble \'wī-rə-bəl\ *adj* : capable of being wired

¹**wire** \'wī(ə)r\ *n* [OE *wīr*] **1 a** : metal in the form of a usu. very flexible thread or slender rod **b** : a thread or rod of metal **2** *usu pl* **a** : a system of wires used to operate the puppets in a puppet show **b** : hidden or secret influences on a person or organization **3 a** : a line of wire for conducting electrical current — compare CORD 3b **b** : a telephone or telegraph wire or system **c** : TELEGRAM, CABLEGRAM — **wire·like** \-ˌlīk\ *adj* — **under the wire** **1** : at the finish line **2** : at the last moment

²**wire** *vb* **1** : to provide with wire; *also* : to provide with electricity ⟨*wire* a farm⟩ **2** : to send or send word to by telegraph **3** : to send a telegraphic message

wire cloth *n* : a fabric of woven metallic wire (as for strainers)

wire coat *n* : a wire-haired coat (as of a dog)

wired \'wī(ə)rd\ *adj* **1** : reinforced or bound with wire ⟨a *wired* container⟩ **2** : having a netting or fence of wire ⟨a *wired* enclosure for chickens⟩

wired radio *n* : a system for distributing radio programs over wire lines — called also *wired wireless, wire radio*

wire·draw·ing \'wī(ə)r-ˌdró-iŋ\ *n* : the act, process, or occupation of drawing metal into wire

wire·drawn \'wī(ə)r-ˌdrón\ *adj* : excessively minute and subtle ⟨*wiredrawn* distinctions⟩

wire gauge *n* : a gauge esp. for measuring the diameter of wire or thickness of sheet metal

wire·haired \'wī(ə)r-'ha(ə)rd, -'he(ə)rd\ *adj* : having a stiff wiry outer coat of hair

¹**wire·less** \'wī(ə)r-ləs\ *adj* **1** : having no wire or wires **2** *chiefly Brit* : of or relating to radiotelegraphy, radiotelephony, or radio

²**wireless** *n* **1** : WIRELESS TELEGRAPHY **2** : RADIOTELEPHONY **3** *chiefly Brit* : RADIO — **wireless** *vb*

wireless telegraphy *n* : telegraphy carried on by radio waves and without connecting wires

wire·man \'wī(ə)r-mən\ *n* : a maker of or worker with wire; *esp* : LINEMAN

wire netting *n* : a texture of woven wire coarser than wire gauze

Wire·pho·to \'wī(ə)r-'fōt-ō\ *trademark* — used for a photograph transmitted by electrical signals over telephone wires

wire–pull·er \-ˌpu̇l-ər\ *n* : one who uses secret or underhand means to influence the acts of a person or organization — **wire–pull·ing** \-ˌpu̇l-iŋ\ *n*

wire recorder *n* : a magnetic recorder using magnetic wire

wire recording *n* : magnetic recording on magnetic wire; *also* : the recording made by this process

wire rope *n* : a rope formed wholly or chiefly of wires

wire service *n* : a news agency that sends out syndicated news copy by wire to subscribers

¹**wire·tap** \'wī(ə)r-ˌtap\ *vi* : to tap a telephone or telegraph wire to get information — **wire·tap·per** *n*

²**wiretap** *n* : the act or an instance of wiretapping

wire·worm \-ˌwərm\ *n* : the slender hard-coated larva of various click beetles that is often destructive to roots

---

j joke;   ŋ sing;   ō flow;   ȯ flaw;   ȯi coin;   th thin;   th̲ this;   ü loot;   u̇ foot;   y yet;   yü few;   yu̇ furious;   zh vision

wir·i·ness \'wī-rē-nəs\ *n* : the quality or state of being wiry

wir·ing \'wī(ə)r-iŋ\ *n* **1** : the act of providing or using wire **2** : a system of wires; *esp* : an arrangement of wires used for electric distribution

wiry \'wī(ə)r-ē\ *adj* **wir·i·er; wir·i·est 1** : of, relating to, or resembling wire **2** : being slender yet strong and sinewy

wis \'wis\ *vb* [by incorrect division fr. *iwis* (understood as *I wis*, with *wis* taken to be an archaic pres. indic. of ¹*wit*)] *archaic* : KNOW

wis·dom \'wiz-dəm\ *n* **1 a** : accumulated learning : KNOWLEDGE **b** : ability to discern inner qualities and relationships **c** : good sense : JUDGMENT **2** : a wise attitude or course of action **3** : the teachings of the ancient wise men

wisdom tooth *n* [fr. being cut usu. in the late teens] : the last tooth of the full set on each half of each jaw in man

¹**wise** \'wīz\ *n* [OE *wīse*] : WAY, MANNER, FASHION — used in such phrases as *in any wise, in no wise, in this wise*

²**wise** *adj* [OE *wīs;* akin to E *wit*] **1** : having or showing wisdom, good sense, or good judgment : SENSIBLE **2** : aware of what is going on : INFORMED — **wise·ly** *adv*

³**wise** *vb* : to make or become informed or knowledgeable — used with *up*

-wise \ˌwīz\ *adv comb form* [OE *-wīsan,* fr. *wīse* ¹*wise*] **1 a** : in the manner of ⟨crab*wise*⟩⟨fan*wise*⟩ **b** : in the position or direction of ⟨slant*wise*⟩⟨clock*wise*⟩ **2** : with regard to : in respect of ⟨dollar*wise*⟩

wise·acre \'wī-ˌzā-kər\ *n* [MD *wijssegger* soothsayer] : one who pretends to knowledge or cleverness : SMART ALECK

¹**wise·crack** \'wīz-ˌkrak\ *n* : a clever, smart, or flippant remark **syn** see JEST

²**wisecrack** *vi* : to make a wisecrack — **wise·crack·er** *n*

wise guy \'wīz-ˌgī\ *n* : a cocky conceited fellow

wise·ness \'wīz-nəs\ *n* : the quality or state of being wise : WISDOM

wi·sen·hei·mer \'wīz-ᵊn-ˌhī-mər\ *n* [²*wise* + G *-enheimer* (as in G family names such as *Guggenheimer, Oppenheimer*)] : one who has the air of knowing all about something or everything : WISEACRE

wi·sent \'vē-ˌzent\ *n* [G] : a nearly extinct European bison

¹**wish** \'wish\ *vb* [OE *wȳscan*] **1** : to have a desire : long for : WANT ⟨*wish* you were here⟩⟨*wish* for a puppy⟩ **2** : to form or express a desire concerning ⟨*wished* him a merry Christmas⟩ **3** : to request by expressing a desire ⟨I *wish* you to go now⟩ — **wish·er** *n* **syn** see DESIRE

²**wish** *n* **1 a** : an act or instance of wishing or desire : WANT **b** : an object of desire : GOAL **2 a** : an expressed will or desire : MANDATE **b** : a request or command couched as a wish **3** : an invocation of good or evil fortune on someone

wish·bone \'wish-ˌbōn\ *n* [fr. the superstition that when two persons pull it apart the one getting the longer fragment will have his wish granted] : a forked bone in front of the breastbone of a bird consisting chiefly of the fused clavicles

wish·ful \'wish-fəl\ *adj* **1** : having a wish : DESIROUS **2** : according with wishes rather than fact ⟨*wishful* thinking⟩ — **wish·ful·ly** \-fə-lē\ *adv* — **wish·ful·ness** *n*

wishy-washy \'wish-ē-ˌwȯsh-ē, -ˌwäsh-\ *adj* : WEAK, INSIPID; *also* : morally feeble

wisp \'wisp\ *n* [ME] **1** : a small bunch of hay or straw **2 a** : a thin strip or fragment **b** : a thready streak ⟨a *wisp* of smoke⟩ **c** : something frail, slight, or fleeting ⟨a *wisp* of a girl⟩ ⟨a *wisp* of a smile⟩ — **wispy** \'wis-pē\ *adj*

wist \'wist\ *vt* [alter. of *wis*] *archaic* : KNOW

wis·tar·ia \wis-'tir-ē-ə, -'ter-\ *n* : WISTERIA

wis·te·ria \wis-'tir-ē-ə\ *n* [NL, fr. Caspar *Wistar* d1818 American physician] : any of a genus of chiefly Asiatic mostly woody leguminous vines having compound leaves and showy blue, white, purple, or rose pealike flowers in long hanging clusters

wist·ful \'wist-fəl\ *adj* [blend of *wishful* and obs. *wistly* intently] : full of unfulfilled longing or desire : YEARNING — **wist·ful·ly** \-fə-lē\ *adv* — **wist·ful·ness** *n*

¹**wit** \'wit\ *vb* **wist** \'wist\; **wit·ting;** *pres 1st & 3d sing* **wot** \'wät\ [OE *witan*] *archaic* : KNOW, LEARN

²**wit** *n* [OE] **1** : reasoning power : INTELLIGENCE **2 a** : mental soundness : SANITY — usu. used in pl. **b** : RESOURCEFULNESS, INGENUITY; *esp* : quickness and cleverness in handling words and ideas **3 a** : a talent for making clever remarks **b** : one noted for making witty remarks **syn** HUMOR: WIT is more purely intellectual than HUMOR and depends for its effect chiefly on verbal ingenuity or unexpectedness of turn or application; HUMOR implies an ability to perceive the ludicrous, the comical, and the absurd in human life and to express these sympathetically and without bitterness

— **at one's wit's end** *or* **at one's wits' end** : at a loss for a means of solving a problem

¹**witch** \'wich\ *n* [OE *wicca* (masc.) & *wicce* (fem.)] **1** : a person believed to have magic powers **2** : an ugly old woman : HAG **3** : a charming girl or woman

²**witch** *vb* **1** : BEWITCH **2** : DOWSE

witch·craft \'wich-ˌkraft\ *n* : the power or practices of a witch : SORCERY

witch doctor *n* : a professional worker of magic in a primitive society resembling a shaman or medicine man

witch·ery \'wich-(ə-)rē\ *n, pl* **-er·ies 1** : the practice of witchcraft : SORCERY **b** : an act of witchcraft **2** : an irresistible fascination : CHARM

witch·es'-broom \'wich-əz-ˌbrüm, -ˌbrüm\ *n* : an abnormal tufted growth of small branches on a tree or shrub caused esp. by fungi or viruses

witch·grass \'wich-ˌgras\ *n* : any of several weedy grasses most of which spread aggressively by underground rhizomes

witch ha·zel \'wich-ˌhā-zəl\ *n* [OE *wice,* a tree with pliant branches] **1** : any of a genus of shrubs with slender-petaled yellow flowers borne in late fall or early spring; *esp* : one of eastern No. America that blooms in the fall **2** : an alcoholic solution of material from the bark of the common witch hazel used as a soothing and mildly astringent lotion

witch-hunt \-ˌhənt\ *n* **1** : a searching out and persecution of persons accused of witchcraft **2** : the searching out and deliberate harassment of those (as political opponents) with unpopular views — **witch-hunt·er** *n*

witch·ing \'wich-iŋ\ *adj* **1** : of, relating to, or suitable for sorcery or supernatural occurrences **2** : BEWITCHING, FASCINATING

wi·te·na·ge·mot *or* **wi·te·na·ge·mote** \'wit-ᵊn-ə-gə-ˌmōt\ *n* [OE *witena gemōt,* fr. *witena* (gen. pl. of *wita* sage, adviser) + *gemōt* assembly] : an Anglo-Saxon council of nobles, prelates, and officials convened to advise the king on administrative and judicial matters — called also **wi·tan** \'wi-ˌtän\

with \(')with, (')with\ *prep* [OE] **1 a** : in opposition to : AGAINST ⟨fought *with* his brother⟩ **b** : so as to be separated from ⟨parting *with* his friends⟩ **2** : in mutual relation to ⟨talking *with* a friend⟩ ⟨trade *with* other countries⟩ **3** : as regards : TOWARD ⟨angry *with* her⟩ ⟨on friendly terms *with* all nations⟩ **4 a** : compared to : equal to ⟨on equal terms *with* the others⟩ ⟨a dress identical *with* hers⟩ **b** : on the side of : FAVORING ⟨voted *with* the majority⟩ **c** : as well as ⟨can pitch *with* the best of them⟩ **5 a** : in the judgment or estimation of ⟨in good standing *with* his classmates⟩ **b** : in the experience or practice of ⟨*with* him a promise is a real obligation⟩ **6 a** : by means of ⟨write *with* a pen⟩ **b** : because of ⟨danced *with* joy⟩ **7** : having or showing as manner of action or attendant circumstance ⟨spoke *with* ease⟩ ⟨stood there *with* his hat on⟩ **8 a** : in possession of : HAVING ⟨animals *with* horns⟩ **b** : characterized or distinguished by ⟨a person *with* a hot temper⟩ **9 a** : in the company of ⟨went to the movies *with* her⟩ : in addition to ⟨his money, *with* his wife's, comes to a million⟩ **b** : inclusive of ⟨costs five dollars *with* the tax⟩ : CONTAINING ⟨tea *with* sugar⟩ **10 a** : at the time of ⟨*with* the outbreak of war they went home⟩ : at the same time as ⟨rose *with* the sun⟩ **b** : in proportion to ⟨the pressure varies *with* the depth⟩ **11** : in the possession or care of ⟨left the money *with* his mother⟩ **12** : in spite of ⟨*with* all his cleverness, he failed⟩ **13** : in the direction of ⟨drift *with* the current⟩ **syn** see BY

¹**with·al** \with-'ȯl, with-\ *adv* [ME, fr. *with* + *all, al* all] **1** : together with this : BESIDES **2** *archaic* : THEREWITH **3** : on the other hand : NEVERTHELESS

²**withal** *prep, archaic* : WITH — used with a preceding relative or interrogative pronoun as its object

with·draw \with-'drȯ, with-\ *vb* **-drew** \-'drü\; **-drawn** \-'drȯn\; **-draw·ing** [ME *withdrawen,* fr. *with-* against,

---

ə abut; ᵊ kitten; ər further; a back; ā bake; ä cot, cart; au̇ out; ch chin; e less; ē easy; g gift; i trip; ī life

from (fr. OE) + *drawen* to draw] **1** : to take back or away usu. from a holder, a place, or a condition : draw away : REMOVE ⟨*withdrew* his money from the bank⟩ ⟨*withdrawing* a knife from his pocket⟩ ⟨the troops were *withdrawn* from combat⟩ ⟨*withdrew* his thoughts from his reading⟩ **2** : to call back (as from consideration) : RECALL, RESCIND ⟨*withdrew* the nomination⟩ ⟨*withdrew* his opposition to a plan⟩; *also* : RETRACT, RECANT ⟨*withdrew* his remarks and apologized⟩ **3 a** : to go away : RETREAT, LEAVE ⟨*withdrew* to the country⟩ ⟨the enemy *withdrew* from the field⟩ **b** : to terminate one's participation or involvement in something ⟨*withdrew* from society⟩ ⟨ready to *withdraw* from the firm⟩

with·draw·al \-'drô(-ə)l\ *n* : an act or instance of withdrawing (as a removal, a retreat, or a retraction)

with·drawn \-'drôn\ *adj* **1** : ISOLATED, SECLUDED ⟨*withdrawn* mountain communities⟩ **2** : socially detached and unresponsive ⟨a *withdrawn* manner⟩ — **with·drawn·ness** \-'drôn-nəs\ *n*

withe \'with\ *n* [OE *withthe*] : a slender flexible branch or twig; *esp* : one used as a band or rope

with·er \'with-ər\ *vb* **with·ered; with·er·ing** \'with-(ə-)riŋ\ [ME *widren*] **1** : to become dry and sapless; *esp* : to shrivel from or as if from loss of bodily moisture **2** : to lose vitality, force, or freshness **3** : to cause to wither **4** : to cause to feel shriveled or blighted ⟨*withered* him with a glance⟩

syn SHRIVEL : WITHER implies the loss of vital moisture with consequent fading, shrinking, and approaching death and decay; SHRIVEL stresses a wrinkling and shrinking as by drought or intense heat or blight

with·er·ing *adj* : acting or serving to cut down or destroy : DEVASTATING ⟨a *withering* fire from the enemy⟩

with·er·ite \'with-ə-,rīt\ *n* [G *witherit*, fr. William *Withering* d1799 English physician] : a mineral consisting of barium carbonate occurring as crystals and in masses

with·ers \'with-ərz\ *n pl* : the ridge between the shoulder bones of a horse; *also* : the corresponding part in other quadrupeds

with·hold \with-'hōld, with-\ *vt* **-held** \-'held\; **-hold·ing** [ME *withholden*, fr. *with-* against, from (fr. OE) + *holden* to hold] **1** : to hold back : RESTRAIN; *also* : RETAIN **2** : to refrain from granting, giving, or allowing ⟨*withhold* permission⟩ — **with·hold·er** *n*

withholding tax *n* : a tax on income withheld at the source

¹with·in \with-'in, with-\ *adv* [OE *withinnan*, fr. *with-* + *innan* inwardly, within, fr. *in*] **1** : in or into the interior : INSIDE **2** : inside oneself : INWARDLY ⟨calm without but furious *within*⟩

²within *prep* **1** : in or into the inner part of ⟨*within* the house⟩ **2** : in or into the limits or compass of: as **a** : not beyond the quantity or limitations of ⟨lives *within* his income⟩ **b** : in or into the range of ⟨*within* sight⟩

³within *n* : an inner place or area ⟨revolt from *within*⟩

¹with·out \with-'aůt, with-\ *prep* [OE *withūtan*, fr. *with-* + *ūtan* outside, fr. *ūt* out] **1** : OUTSIDE 1, 2 **2 a** : not having : LACKING ⟨*without* food⟩ **b** : with absence or omission of ⟨listened *without* answering⟩

²without *adv* **1** : on the outside : EXTERNALLY **2** : with something lacking or absent ⟨has learned to do *without*⟩

³without *n* : an outer place or area ⟨came from *without*⟩

with·stand \with-'stand, with-\ *vt* **-stood** \-'stůd\; **-stand·ing** [OE *withstandan*, fr. *with-* against + *standan* to stand] : to stand against : RESIST; *esp* : to oppose (as an attack or bad influence) successfully

withy \'with-ē\ *n, pl* **with·ies** [OE *wīthig*] **1** : OSIER **2** : WITHE

wit·less \'wit-ləs\ *adj* : lacking wit or understanding : mentally defective : FOOLISH — **wit·less·ly** *adv* — **wit·less·ness** *n*

wit·loof \'wit-,lôf\ *n* [D dial. *witloof* chicory, fr. D *wit* white + *loof* foliage] : CHICORY; *also* : ENDIVE 2

¹wit·ness \'wit-nəs\ *n* [OE *witnes* knowledge, testimony, one that gives testimony, fr. **²wit**] **1 a** : attestation of a fact or event : TESTIMONY **b** : public testimony to a religious faith **2** : one that gives evidence; *esp* : one who testifies in a cause or before a court **3 a** : one present at a transaction so as to be able to testify to its having taken place **b** : one who has personal knowledge or experience of something **4** : something serving as evidence or proof : SIGN **5** *cap* : JEHOVAH'S WITNESS

²witness *vb* **1** : to bear witness : ATTEST, TESTIFY **2** : to act as legal witness of **3** : to furnish proof of : BETOKEN **4** : to be a witness of

witness stand *n* : a stand or an enclosure from which a witness gives evidence in a court

wit·ted \'wit-əd\ *adj* : having wit or understanding — usu. used in combination ⟨dull-*witted*⟩

wit·ti·cism \'wit-ə-,siz-əm\ *n* [*witty* + *-cism* (as in *criticism*)] : a witty saying

wit·ting·ly \'wit-iŋ-lē\ *adv* : with knowledge or awareness of what one is doing : CONSCIOUSLY

wit·ty \'wit-ē\ *adj* **wit·ti·er; -est** : marked by or full of wit : AMUSING ⟨a *witty* writer⟩ ⟨a *witty* remark⟩ — **wit·ti·ly** \'wit-ʔl-ē\ *adv* — **wit·ti·ness** \'wit-ē-nəs\ *n*

wive \'wīv\ *vb* [OE *wīfian*, fr. *wīf* woman, wife] **1** : to marry a woman **2** : to take for a wife

wives *pl of* WIFE

wiz·ard \'wiz-ərd\ *n* [ME *wysard*, fr. *wys* wise] **1** : MAGICIAN, SORCERER **2** : a very clever or skillful person ⟨a *wizard* at chess⟩

wiz·ard·ry \'wiz-ər-drē\ *n, pl* **-ries** **1** : the art or practices of a wizard : SORCERY **2** : a seemingly magical transforming power or influence

wiz·en \'wiz-ʔn\ *vb* [OE *wisnian*] : WITHER, SHRIVEL

woad \'wōd\ *n* [OE *wād*] : a European herb of the mustard family formerly grown for the blue dyestuff yielded by its leaves; *also* : this dyestuff

¹wob·ble \'wäb-əl\ *vb* **wob·bled; wob·bling** \'wäb-(ə-)liŋ\ **1 a** : to move or cause to move with an irregular rocking or side-to-side motion **b** : TREMBLE, QUAVER **2** : WAVER, VACILLATE — **wob·bler** \-(ə-)lər\ *n* — **wob·bly** \-(ə-)lē\ *adj*

²wobble *n* : a wobbling action or movement ⟨the wheel had a bad *wobble*⟩

¹woe \'wō\ *interj* [OE *wā*] — used to express grief, regret, or distress

²woe *n* **1** : a condition of deep suffering from misfortune, affliction, or grief **2** : CALAMITY, MISFORTUNE ⟨economic *woes*⟩

woe·be·gone \'wō-bi-,gȯn, -,gän\ *adj* [ME *wo begon*, fr. *wo* woe + *begon*, pp. of *begon* to go about, beset, fr. OE *begān*, fr. *be-* + *gān* to go] **1** : exhibiting great woe, sorrow, or misery ⟨*woebegone* faces⟩ **2** : DISMAL, DESOLATE ⟨a *woebegone* village⟩ — **woe·be·gone·ness** \-,gȯn-nəs, -,gän-\ *n*

woe·ful *also* **wo·ful** \'wō-fəl\ *adj* **1** : full of woe : AFFLICTED **2** : involving, bringing, or relating to woe **3** : PALTRY, DEPLORABLE — **woe·ful·ly** \-f(ə-)lē\ *adv* — **woe·ful·ness** \-fəl-nəs\ *n*

woke *past of* WAKE

woken *past part of* WAKE

wold \'wōld\ *n* [OE *weald, wald* forest] : an upland plain or stretch of rolling country without woods

¹wolf \'wůlf\ *n, pl* **wolves** \'wůlvz\ *also* **wolf** [OE *wulf*] **1** : any of several large erect-eared bushy-tailed mammals that resemble the related dogs and are crafty, rapacious, and very destructive to game, sheep, and cattle — compare COYOTE, JACKAL **2 a** : a person resembling a wolf (as in ferocity or guile); *esp* : a man forward and zealous in attentions to women **b** : a destructive agency; *esp* : dire poverty — **wolf·ish** \'wůl-fish\ *adj* — **wolf·like** \'wůlf-,līk\ *adj* — **wolf in sheep's clothing** : one who cloaks a hostile intention with a friendly manner

wolf

²wolf *vt* : to eat greedily : DEVOUR

wolf dog *n* **1** : a large dog used in hunting wolves : WOLFHOUND **2** : the hybrid offspring of a wolf and a domestic dog **3** : a large wolflike domestic dog

wolf·hound \'wůlf-,haůnd\ *n* : any of several large dogs used in hunting large animals (as wolves)

wol·fram \'wůl-frəm\ *n* [G] : TUNGSTEN

wol·fram·ite \'wůl-frə-,mīt\ *n* : a brownish or grayish mineral that consists of an iron manganese tungstate, occurs in crystals and masses, and is a source of tungsten

wolfs·bane \'wůlfs-,bān\ *n* : ACONITE 1; *esp* : a highly variable yellow-flowered Eurasian herb

---

j joke; **ŋ** sing; **ō** flow; **ȯ** flaw; **ȯi** coin; **th** thin; **th** this; **ü** loot; **ů** foot; **y** yet; **yü** few; **yů** furious; **zh** vision

wolf spider n : any of various active wandering ground spiders

wol·ver·ine \ˌwu̇l-və-ˈrēn\ n : a blackish shaggy-furred carnivorous mammal of northern No. America that is related to the martens and sables and is noted for its cunning and gluttony

wom·an \ˈwu̇m-ən\ n, pl **wom·en** \ˈwim-ən\ [OE wīfman, fr. wīf woman, wife + man person, man] 1 : an adult female person 2 : WOMANKIND 3 : a female servant or attendant — **woman** adj

wom·an·hood \ˈwu̇m-ən-ˌhu̇d\ n 1 : the state of being a woman 2 : womanly qualities 3 : WOMEN

wom·an·ish \ˈwu̇m-ə-nish\ adj 1 : characteristic of a woman 2 : suitable to a woman rather than to a man — **wom·an·ish·ly** adv — **wom·an·ish·ness** n

wom·an·kind \ˈwu̇m-ən-ˌkīnd\ n : female human beings : WOMEN

wom·an·like \-ˌlīk\ adj : resembling or characteristic of a woman : WOMANLY

wom·an·ly \-lē\ adj : marked by qualities characteristic of a woman **syn** see FEMALE — **wom·an·li·ness** n — **womanly** adv

woman suffrage n : the possession and exercise of the suffrage by women

womb \ˈwüm\ n [OE] 1 : UTERUS 2 : a place where something is generated or developed — **wombed** \ˈwümd\ adj

wom·bat \ˈwäm-ˌbat\ n [of Australian origin] : any of several stocky burrowing Australian marsupials resembling small bears

wom·en·folk \ˈwim-ən-ˌfōk\ or **wom·en·folks** \-ˌfōks\ n pl : WOMEN

won past of WIN

¹won·der \ˈwən-dər\ n [OE wundor] 1 a : a cause of astonishment or surprise : MARVEL b : MIRACLE 2 a : a feeling (as of awed astonishment or of uncertainty) aroused by something extraordinary or affecting b : the quality of exciting wonder ⟨the charm and wonder of the scene⟩

²wonder vb **won·dered; won·der·ing** \-d(ə-)riŋ\ 1 : to feel surprise or amazement 2 : to feel curiosity or doubt — **won·der·er** \-dər-ər\ n

wonder drug n : a medicinal substance of outstanding effectiveness

won·der·ful \ˈwən-dər-fəl\ adj 1 : exciting wonder : MARVELOUS, ASTONISHING 2 : unusually good : ADMIRABLE — **won·der·ful·ly** \-f(ə-)lē\ adv — **won·der·ful·ness** \-fəl-nəs\ n

won·der·land \ˈwən-dər-ˌland, -lənd\ n 1 : a fairylike imaginary realm 2 : a place that excites admiration or wonder

won·der·ment \-mənt\ n 1 : ASTONISHMENT, SURPRISE 2 : curiosity about something

won·der·work·er \-ˌwər-kər\ n : one that performs wonders

won·drous \ˈwən-drəs\ adj : WONDERFUL, MARVELOUS — **wondrous** adv, archaic — **won·drous·ly** adv — **won·drous·ness** n

¹wont \ˈwȯnt, ˈwōnt\ adj [ME, fr. pp. of wonen to dwell, be accustomed, fr. OE wunian] : ACCUSTOMED, USED ⟨as he is wont to do⟩

²wont n : CUSTOM, USAGE ⟨according to his wont⟩

won't \(ˈ)wōnt, ˈwənt\ : will not

wont·ed \ˈwȯnt-əd, ˈwōnt-\ adj : ACCUSTOMED, USUAL ⟨took his wonted rest⟩ — **wont·ed·ly** adv — **wont·ed·ness** n

woo \ˈwü\ vb [OE wōgian] 1 : to try to gain the love of : make love : COURT 2 : to seek usu. urgently to gain or bring about ⟨a clever auctioneer wooing dollars from his audience⟩

¹wood \ˈwu̇d\ n [OE wudu] 1 a : a dense growth of trees usu. greater in extent than a grove and smaller than a forest — often used in pl. ⟨a thick woods runs along the ridge⟩ b : WOODLAND 2 : a hard fibrous substance that is basically xylem and makes up the greater part of the stems and branches of trees or shrubs beneath the bark; also : this material suitable or prepared for some use (as burning or building) 3 : something made of wood; esp : a golf club having a wooden head — **out of the woods** : escaped from peril or difficulty

²wood adj 1 : WOODEN 2 : suitable for cutting or working wood ⟨wood chisels⟩ 3 or **woods** \ˈwu̇dz\ : living or growing in woods

³wood vb 1 : to supply or load with wood esp. for fuel : take on wood ⟨wood up the stove⟩ ⟨the boat wooded up at night⟩ 2 : to cover with a growth of trees or plant with trees

wood alcohol n : METHANOL

wood anemone n : any of several anemones that grow in open woodlands

wood·bin \ˈwu̇d-ˌbin\ n : a bin for holding firewood

wood·bine \ˈwu̇d-ˌbīn\ n : any of several climbing vines of Europe and America (as a honeysuckle or the Virginia creeper)

wood block n 1 : a solid block of wood (as for paving) 2 : WOODCUT

wood–carv·er \ˈwu̇d-ˌkär-vər\ n : a person who carves usu. ornamental objects of wood — **wood carv·ing** \-viŋ\ n

wood–chop·per \-ˌchäp-ər\ n : one engaged esp. in chopping down trees

wood·chuck \ˈwu̇d-ˌchək\ n [by folk etymology fr. Ojibwa otchig fisher, marten, or Cree otcheck fisher] : a grizzled thickset marmot of the northeastern U.S. and Canada; also : a related rodent of mountainous western No. America

wood·cock \-ˌkäk\ n, pl **woodcocks** or **woodcock** : either of two long-billed mottled and usu. brown birds related to the snipe; esp : an American upland bird prized as a game bird

wood·craft \-ˌkraft\ n : knowledge about the woods and how to take care of oneself in them

wood·cut \-ˌkət\ n 1 : a printing surface consisting of a wooden block with a usu. pictorial design cut with the grain 2 : a print from a woodcut

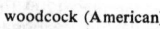

woodcock (American)

wood·cut·ter \-ˌkət-ər\ n : one that cuts wood esp. as an occupation

wood·ed \ˈwu̇d-əd\ adj : covered with trees

wood·en \ˈwu̇d-ᵊn\ adj 1 : made of wood 2 a : lacking resilience : STIFF b : lacking ease, interest, or zest ⟨written in a wooden style⟩ — **wood·en·ly** adv — **wood·en·ness** \-ᵊn-(n)əs\ n

wood engraving n 1 : the art or process of cutting a design upon wood and esp. upon the end grain of wood for use as a printing surface; also : such a printing surface 2 : a design printed from a wood engraving

wood·en·ware \ˈwu̇d-ᵊn-ˌwa(ə)r, -ˌwe(ə)r\ n : articles made of wood for domestic use

wood hyacinth n : a European squill with long clusters of drooping bell-shaped flowers — called also harebell

wood ibis n : a large wading bird closely related to the Old World storks that frequents wooded swamps of So. and Central America and the southern U.S.

¹wood·land \ˈwu̇d-lənd, -ˌland\ n : land covered with woody vegetation : FOREST — **wood·land·er** \-ər\ n

²woodland adj 1 : of, relating to, or being woodland 2 : growing or living in woodland

wood·lot \ˈwu̇d-ˌlät\ n : a relatively small area of trees kept usu. to meet fuel and timber needs ⟨a farm woodlot⟩

wood louse n : a small flat grayish crustacean that lives esp. under stones and bark — called also pill bug, sow bug

wood·man \ˈwu̇d-mən\ n : WOODSMAN

wood·note \-ˌnōt\ n : a sound or call (as of a bird) natural in a wood

wood nymph n : a nymph living in woods — called also dryad

wood·peck·er \ˈwu̇d-ˌpek-ər\ n : any of numerous usu. brightly marked birds with specialized feet and stiff spiny tail feathers used in climbing or resting on tree trunks and a very hard bill used to drill into trees for insect food or to excavate nesting cavities

wood·pile \-ˌpīl\ n : a pile of wood and esp. firewood

wood pulp n : pulp from wood used in making cellulose derivatives (as paper or rayon)

wood pussy n : SKUNK

wood rat n : any of numerous native voles of the southern and western U.S. with soft pale fur, well-furred tails, and large ears

wood·ruff \ˈwu̇d-(ˌ)rəf\ n [OE wudurofe] : a small European sweet-scented herb of the madder family used in perfumery and for flavoring wine

wood·shed \'wùd-ˌshed\ *n* : a shed for storing wood and esp. firewood

woods·man \'wùdz-mən\ *n* : one who frequents or works in the woods; *esp* : one skilled in woodcraft

wood sorrel *n* : any of a genus of herbs with acid sap, compound leaves, and regular 5-petaled flowers; *esp* : a stemless herb having leaves with three leaflets that is held to be the original shamrock

woodsy \'wùd-zē\ *adj* : relating to or suggestive of woods

wood thrush *n* **1** : a large thrush of eastern No. America noted for its loud clear song **2** : SONG THRUSH 1

wood turning *n* : the art or process of fashioning useful articles from wooden pieces or blocks by means of a lathe — **wood·turn·er** *n*

wood warbler *n* : any of various warblers that frequent woodlands

wood·wax·en \'wùd-ˌwak-sən\ *n* : a low bushy yellow-flowered Eurasian leguminous shrub grown for ornament or formerly as the source of a yellow dye

wood·wind \'wùd-ˌwind\ *n* **1** : one of a group of wind instruments including flutes, clarinets, oboes, bassoons, and sometimes saxophones **2** : the woodwind section of a band or orchestra — **woodwind** *adj*

wood·work \-ˌwərk\ *n* : work made of wood; *esp* : interior fittings (as moldings or stairways) of wood

wood·work·ing \-ˌwər-kiŋ\ *n* : the act, process, or occupation of working with wood — **wood·work·er** \-kər\ *n* — **woodworking** *adj*

woody \'wùd-ē\ *adj* **wood·i·er; -est 1** : abounding or overgrown with trees **2** : of or containing wood or wood fibers : LIGNEOUS **3** : characteristic of or resembling wood ⟨a *woody* texture⟩ — **wood·i·ness** *n*

wood·yard \'wùd-ˌyärd\ *n* : a yard for storing or sawing wood

woo·er \'wü-ər\ *n* : one that woos : SUITOR

woof \'wùf, 'wüf\ *n* [ME *oof*, fr. OE *ōwef*, fr. *on* + *wefan* to weave] **1** : the threads that cross the warp in a woven fabric **2** : a woven fabric or its texture

woof·er \'wùf-ər\ *n* : a loudspeaker that is usu. larger than a tweeter, is responsive only to the lower acoustic frequencies, and is used for reproducing sounds of low pitch

wool \'wùl\ *n* [OE *wull*] **1** : the heavy soft wavy or curly undercoat of various mammals and esp. the sheep **2** : a product of wool; *esp* : a woven fabric or garment of such fabric **3 a** : a dense felted pubescence esp. on a plant **b** : a filamentous mass (as of glass or metal) **c** : short thick often crisp curly hair on a human head — **wooled** \'wùld\ *adj*

¹**wool·en** *or* **wool·len** \'wùl-ən\ *adj* **1** : made of wool — compare WORSTED **2** : of or relating to the manufacture or sale of woolen products

²**woolen** *or* **woollen** *n* **1** : a fabric made of wool **2** : garments of woolen fabric — usu. used in pl.

wool·er \'wùl-ər\ *n* : an animal (as an Angora rabbit) bred or kept for its wool

wool-gath·er \'wùl-ˌgath-ər\ *vi* : to indulge in woolgathering — **wool·gath·er·er** \-ər-ər\ *n*

wool-gath·er·ing \-ˌgath-(ə-)riŋ\ *n* : the act of indulging in vagrant fancies

¹**wool·ly** *also* **wooly** \'wùl-ē\ *adj* **wool·li·er; -est 1 a** : of, relating to, or bearing wool **b** : resembling wool **2** : CONFUSED, BLURRY ⟨*woolly* thinking⟩ **3** : marked by a lack of order or restraint ⟨the wild and *woolly* West of frontier times⟩ — **wool·li·ness** *n*

²**wool·ly** *also* **wool·ie** *or* **wooly** \'wùl-ē\ *n, pl* **wool·lies** : a garment made from wool; *esp* : underclothing of knitted wool — usu. used in pl.

woolly aphid *n* : any of several plant lice that secrete a dense coating of woolly wax filaments

woolly bear *n* : any of various rather large very hairy caterpillars; *esp* : such a moth larva

wool·sack \'wùl-ˌsak\ *n* **1** : a sack for wool **2** : the official seat of the lord chancellor or of one of the judges of the High Court of Justice in the House of Lords

wool·skin \-ˌskin\ *n* : a sheepskin having the wool still on it

wool sponge *n* : a soft durable commercial sponge esp. from the Caribbean area

woo·zy \'wü-zē\ *adj* **woo·zi·er; -est 1** : BEFUDDLED **2** : affected with dizziness, mild nausea, or weakness : SICK — **woo·zi·ly** \-zə-lē\ *adv* — **woo·zi·ness** \-zē-nəs\ *n*

Worces·ter·shire sauce \ˌwùs-tə(r)-ˌshi(ə)r-, -shər-\ *n* : a pungent sauce orig. made in Worcester, England, of soy, vinegar, and many other ingredients

¹**word** \'wərd\ *n* [OE] **1 a** : something that is said **b** *pl* : TALK, DISCOURSE **c** : a brief remark or conversation **2 a** : a speech sound or series of speech sounds that symbolizes and communicates a meaning without being divisible into smaller units capable of independent use **b** : a written or printed character or combination of characters representing a spoken word **c** : a combination of electrical or magnetic impulses conveying a unit of information in communication and computer work **3** : ORDER, COMMAND **4** *often cap* **a** : the second person of the Trinity through whom all things were created **b** : GOSPEL 1a **c** : the expressed or manifested mind and will of God **5** : NEWS, INFORMATION **6** : PROMISE, DECLARATION **7** : a quarrelsome utterance or conversation — usu. used in pl. **8** : a verbal signal : PASSWORD — **word for word** : in the exact words : VERBATIM

²**word** *vt* : to express in words : PHRASE

word·age \'wərd-ij\ *n* **1** : WORDS **2** : number of words **3** : WORDING

word·book \'wərd-ˌbùk\ *n* : VOCABULARY, DICTIONARY

word class *n* : a linguistic form class whose members are words; *esp* : PART OF SPEECH

word-hoard \'wərd-ˌhōrd, -ˌhórd\ *n* : a supply of words : VOCABULARY

word·ing \'wərd-iŋ\ *n* : expression in words : PHRASING, PHRASEOLOGY

word·less \'wərd-ləs\ *adj* **1** : not expressed in or accompanied by words **2** : SILENT, INARTICULATE — **word·less·ly** *adv* — **word·less·ness** *n*

word of mouth *n* : oral communication

word order *n* : the order of arrangement of words in a phrase, clause, or sentence

word·play \'wərd-ˌplā\ *n* : verbal wit

word square *n* : ACROSTIC 3

word stress *n* : the manner in which stresses are distributed on the syllables of a word — called also *word accent*

wordy \'wərd-ē\ *adj* **word·i·er; -est** : using or containing many words : VERBOSE — **word·i·ly** \'wərd-ᵊl-ē\ *adv* — **word·i·ness** \'wərd-ē-nəs\ *n*

wore *past of* WEAR

¹**work** \'wərk\ *n* [OE *werc, weorc*] **1** : the use of one's strength or ability in order to get something done or to achieve some desired result : LABOR, TOIL; *esp* : such work undertaken as one's regular employment **2** : something that needs to be done : TASK, JOB ⟨have *work* to do⟩ **3** : DEED, ACHIEVEMENT ⟨good *works*⟩ **4** : the material on which effort is put in the process of making something **5** : something produced by mental exertion or physical labor; *esp* : an artistic production **6** *pl* : a place where industrial labor is carried on : PLANT, FACTORY ⟨a locomotive *works*⟩ **7** *pl* : the working or moving parts of a mechanical device ⟨the *works* of a watch⟩ **8** : manner of working : WORKMANSHIP ⟨careless *work*⟩ **9** : a fortified structure of any kind **10** : the transference of energy that is produced by the motion of the point of application of a force and is measured by multiplying the force and the distance through which the force acts **11** *pl* **a** : everything possessed, available, or belonging ⟨the whole *works*, rod, reel, tackle box, went overboard⟩ **b** : subjection to drastic treatment ⟨gave him the *works*⟩ — **at work 1** : engaged in working : BUSY; *esp* : engaged in one's regular occupation **2** : having effect : OPERATING, FUNCTIONING — **out of work** : without regular employment : JOBLESS

²**work** *adj* **1** : suitable or styled for wear while working ⟨*work* clothes⟩ **2** : used for work ⟨*work* elephant⟩

³**work** *vb* **worked** \'wərkt\ *or* **wrought** \'rót\; **work·ing 1** : to bring to pass : EFFECT **2** : to fashion or create by expending labor or exertion upon **3 a** : to prepare for use by stirring or kneading **b** : to bring into a desired form by a gradual process of cutting, hammering, scraping, pressing, or stretching ⟨*work* cold steel⟩ **4** : to set or keep in motion or operation ⟨a pump *worked* by hand⟩ **5** : to solve (a problem) by reasoning or calculation

6 a : to cause to toil or labor : get work out of **b :** to make use of : EXPLOIT **c :** to control or guide the operation of **7 :** to carry on an operation through or in or along **8 :** to pay for with labor or service ⟨*work* off a debt⟩ **9 a :** to get (as oneself or an object) into or out of a condition or position by stages **b :** CONTRIVE, ARRANGE ⟨if we can *work* it⟩ **10 a :** to practice trickery or cajolery on for some end ⟨*worked* the management for a free ticket⟩ **b :** EXCITE, PROVOKE ⟨*worked* himself into a rage⟩ **11 a :** to exert oneself physically or mentally esp. in sustained effort for a purpose or under compulsion or necessity **b :** to perform a task requiring sustained effort or repeated operations **c :** to perform work regularly for wages **12 :** to function or operate according to plan or design ⟨hinges *work* better with oil⟩ **13 :** to produce a desired effect : SUCCEED **14 :** to make way slowly and with difficulty : move or progress laboriously **15 :** to permit of being worked : react in a specified way to being worked ⟨this wood *works* easily⟩ **16 a :** to be in agitation or restless motion **b :** FERMENT 1 **c :** to move slightly in relation to another part **d :** to get into a specified condition by slow or imperceptible movements ⟨the knot *worked* loose⟩ — **work on 1 :** AFFECT ⟨*worked on* his sympathies⟩ **2 :** to strive to influence or persuade — **work upon :** to have effect upon : operate on : PERSUADE, INFLUENCE

work·a·ble \'wər-kə-bəl\ *adj* **1 :** capable of being worked **2 :** PRACTICABLE, FEASIBLE — **work·a·bil·i·ty** \,wər-kə-'bil-ət-ē\ *n* — **work·a·ble·ness** \'wər-kə-bəl-nəs\ *n*

work·a·day \'wər-kə-,dā\ *adj* **1 :** relating to or suited for working days **2 :** PROSAIC, ORDINARY

work·bag \'wərk-,bag\ *n* **:** a bag for implements or materials for work; *esp* **:** a bag for needlework

work·bas·ket \-,bas-kət\ *n* **:** a basket for needlework

work·bench \-,bench\ *n* **:** a bench on which work esp. of mechanics, machinists, and carpenters is performed

work·book \-,bük\ *n* **1 :** a booklet outlining a course of study **2 :** a workman's manual **3 :** a record book of work done **4 :** a student's individual book of problems to be solved directly on the pages

work·box \-,bäks\ *n* **:** a box for work instruments and materials

work·day \-,dā\ *n* **1 :** a day on which work is performed as distinguished from Sunday or a holiday **2 :** the period of time in a day during which work is performed — **workday** *adj*

worked \'wərkt\ *adj* **:** that has been subjected to some process of development, treatment, or manufacture

worked up *adj* **:** emotionally aroused : EXCITED ⟨all *worked up* over the coming wedding⟩

work·er \'wər-kər\ *n* **1 a :** one that works **b :** a member of the working class **2 :** one of the members of a colony of social ants, bees, wasps, or termites that are incompletely developed sexually and usu. sterile and that perform most of the labor and protective duties of the colony

work farm *n* **:** a farm on which minor offenders are confined and put to work

work force *n* **1 :** the workers engaged in a specific activity ⟨the factory's *work force*⟩ **2 :** the number of workers potentially assignable for any purpose ⟨the nation's *work force*⟩

work·horse \'wərk-,hórs\ *n* **1 :** a horse used chiefly for labor **2 a :** a person who undertakes arduous labor **b :** a markedly useful or durable vehicle, tool, or machine

work·house \-,haús\ *n* **1** *Brit* **:** POORHOUSE **2 :** an institution where persons who have committed a minor offense are confined

¹work·ing \'wər-kiŋ\ *adj* **1 a :** doing work esp. for a living ⟨*working* girl⟩ **b :** FUNCTIONING ⟨a *working* model⟩ **2 :** relating to work : taken up with work : used in or fitted for use in work **3 :** good enough to allow work or further work to be done ⟨a *working* majority⟩⟨a *working* arrangement⟩

²working *n* **:** an excavation or group of excavations made in mining, quarrying, or tunneling — usu. used in pl.

working class *n* **:** the class of people who are employed for wages usu. in manual labor — **working-class** *adj*

work·ing·man \'wər-kiŋ-,man\ *n* **:** one who works for wages usu. at manual labor or in industry

working papers *n pl* **:** official documents legalizing the employment of a minor

work·less \'wərk-ləs\ *adj* **:** being without work : UNEMPLOYED — **work·less·ness** *n*

work·man \'wərk-mən\ *n* **1 :** WORKINGMAN **2 :** ARTISAN, CRAFTSMAN

work·man·like \-,līk\ *or* **work·man·ly** \-lē\ *adj* **:** worthy of a good workman : SKILLFUL

work·man·ship \'wərk-mən-,ship\ *n* **1 :** the art or skill of a workman : CRAFTSMANSHIP **2 :** the quality or character of a piece of work ⟨the excellent *workmanship* of the desk⟩

workmen's compensation insurance *n* **:** insurance that reimburses an employer for damages that he is required to pay to an employee for injury occurring in the scope and course of his employment

work of art : a product of one of the fine arts; *esp* **:** a painting or sculpture of high artistic quality

work out \(')wərk-'aút\ *vb* **1 :** to effect by labor and exertion **2 a :** SOLVE **b :** to bring about esp. by resolving difficulties **c :** DEVELOP, ELABORATE **3 :** to discharge (as a debt) by labor **4 :** to exhaust (as a mine) by working **5 a :** to prove effective, practicable, or suitable **b :** to amount to a total or calculated figure — used with *at* **6 :** to go through a training session esp. in an athletic specialty

work·out \'wərk-,aút\ *n* **:** a practice or exercise to test or improve one's fitness esp. for athletic competition, ability, or performance

work·room \'wərk-,rüm, -,rùm\ *n* **:** a room used esp. for manual work

work·shop \-,shäp\ *n* **1 :** a small establishment where manufacturing or handicrafts are carried on **2 :** a seminar emphasizing free discussion, exchange of ideas, and practical methods and given mainly for adults already employed in the field

work·ta·ble \-,tā-bəl\ *n* **:** a table for holding working materials and implements (as for needlework)

work·week \-,wēk\ *n* **:** the hours or days of work in a calendar week ⟨40-hour *workweek*⟩⟨a 5-day *workweek*⟩

work·wom·an \,wùm-ən\ *n* **:** a woman who works esp. at manual labor or in industry

world \'wərld\ *n* [OE *woruld* human existence, this world, lit., age of man] **1 :** UNIVERSE, CREATION **2 :** the earth with its inhabitants and all things upon it **3 :** people in general : MANKIND **4 :** a state of existence : scene of life and action ⟨the *world* of the future⟩ **5 :** a great number or quantity ⟨a *world* of troubles⟩ **6 :** a part or section of the earth or its inhabitants by itself **7 :** the affairs of men ⟨withdraw from the *world*⟩ **8 :** a heavenly body esp. if inhabited **9 :** a distinctive class of persons or their sphere of interest ⟨the musical *world*⟩ syn see EARTH — **in the world :** among innumerable possibilities : EVER — used as an intensive ⟨what *in the world* is it⟩ — **out of this world :** of extraordinary excellence : SUPERB

world–beat·er \'wərld-,bēt-ər\ *n* **:** one that excels all others of its kind : CHAMPION

world·ling \'wərl-(d)liŋ\ *n* **:** a person engrossed in the concerns of this present world

world·ly \'wərl-(d)lē\ *adj* **world·li·er; -est 1 :** of, relating to, or devoted to this world and its pursuits rather than to spiritual affairs **2 :** WORLDLY-WISE syn see EARTHLY — **world·li·ness** *n*

world·ly–mind·ed \,wərl-(d)lē-'mīn-dəd\ *adj* **:** devoted to or engrossed in worldly interests — **world·ly–mind·ed·ness** *n*

world·ly–wise \'wərl-(d)lē-,wīz\ *adj* **:** wise as to things and ways of this world

world power *n* **:** a political unit (as a nation) powerful enough to affect the entire world by its influence or actions

world series *n, often cap W&S* **:** a series of baseball games played each fall between the pennant winners of the major leagues to decide the professional championship of the U.S.

world war *n* **:** a war involving all or most of the chief nations of the world; *esp, cap both Ws* **:** either of two such wars of the 20th century

world–wea·ri·ness \'wərld-,wir-ē-nəs\ *n* **:** fatigue from or boredom with the life of the world and esp. with material pleasures — **world–wea·ry** \-,wi(ə)r-ē\ *adj*

world–wide \'wərl-'dwīd\ *adj* **:** extended throughout the world ⟨*worldwide* fame⟩

¹worm \'wərm\ *n* [OE *wyrm* serpent, worm] **1 a :** EARTH-

WORM; *also* **:** an annelid worm **b :** any of various small long usu. naked and soft-bodied creeping animals (as a maggot or planarian) **2 a :** a human being who is an object of contempt, loathing, or pity **:** WRETCH **b :** something that inwardly torments or devours **3** *pl* **:** infestation with or disease caused by parasitic worms **4 :** something (as a mechanical device) spiral or vermiculate in form or appearance: as **a :** the thread of a screw **b :** a short revolving screw whose threads gear with the teeth of another mechanical part — **worm** *adj* — **worm·like** \-,līk\ *adj*
²worm *vb* **1 :** to move or cause to move or proceed sinuously or insidiously ⟨spies *worm* into important positions⟩⟨managed to *worm* out⟩ **2 :** to insinuate or introduce (oneself) by devious or subtle means **3 :** to free (as a dog) from worms **4 :** to obtain or extract by artful or insidious questioning or by pleading, asking, or persuading ⟨*wormed* the truth out of him⟩ — **worm·er** *n*
worm cast *n* **:** a cylindrical mass of earth voided by an earthworm
worm-eat·en \'wərm-,ēt-ᵊn\ *adj* **1 a :** eaten or burrowed by worms ⟨*worm-eaten* timber⟩ **b :** PITTED **2 :** WORN-OUT, ANTIQUATED
worm fence *n* **:** a zigzag fence consisting of interlocking rails supported by crossed poles — called also *snake fence*
worm gear *n* **1 :** WORM WHEEL **2 :** a gear of a worm and a worm wheel working together
worm·hole \'wərm-,hōl\ *n* **:** a hole or passage burrowed by a worm
worm·seed \-,sēd\ *n* **:** any of various plants whose seeds possess vermifuge properties (as ragweed or goosefoot)
worm snake *n* **:** a small harmless burrowing snake that suggests an earthworm
worm wheel *n* **:** a toothed wheel gearing with the thread of a worm

worm gear

worm·wood \'wərm-,wüd\ *n* [ME *wormwode*, by folk etymology fr. OE *wermōd*] **1 :** any of a genus of woody herbs related to the daisies; *esp* **:** a European plant yielding a bitter slightly aromatic dark green oil used in absinthe **2 :** something bitter or grievous **:** BITTERNESS
wormy \'wər-mē\ *adj* **worm·i·er; -est 1 :** containing, infested with, or damaged by worms ⟨*wormy* flour⟩ ⟨*wormy* timbers⟩ **2 :** resembling or suggestive of a worm
worn *past part of* WEAR
worn-out \'wōrn-'aut, 'wȯrn-\ *adj* **:** exhausted or used up by or as if by wear
wor·ri·ment \'wər-ē-mənt, 'wə-rē-\ *n* **:** an act or instance of worrying; *also* **:** TROUBLE, WORRY
wor·ri·some \-səm\ *adj* **1 :** causing distress or worry **2 :** inclined to worry or fret — **wor·ri·some·ly** *adv*
¹wor·ry \'wər-ē, 'wə-rē\ *vb* **wor·ried; wor·ry·ing** [OE *wyrgan* to strangle] **1 :** to shake and tear or mangle with the teeth ⟨a puppy *worrying* an old shoe⟩ **2 :** to torment with anxiety **:** FRET, TROUBLE ⟨his late hours *worried* his parents⟩ **3 :** to feel or express great anxiety **syn** *see* ANNOY — **wor·ri·er** *n*
²worry *n, pl* **worries 1 :** ANXIETY **2 :** a cause of anxiety **:** TROUBLE
wor·ry·wart \-,wȯrt\ *n* **:** one who is inclined to worry unduly
¹worse \'wərs\ *adj, comparative of* BAD *or of* ILL [OE *wyrsa*] **1 :** of more inferior quality, value, or condition **2 a :** more unfavorable, unpleasant, or painful; *esp* **:** more unwell **:** SICKER ⟨the boy was *worse* the next day⟩ **b :** more faulty, unsuitable, or incorrect **c :** less skillful or efficient **3 :** bad, evil, or corrupt in a greater degree **:** more reprehensible
²worse *n* **1 :** one that is worse **2 :** a greater degree of ill or badness
³worse *adv, comparative of* BAD *or of* ILL **:** in a worse manner **:** to a worse extent or degree
wors·en \'wərs-ᵊn\ *vb* **wors·ened; wors·en·ing** \'wərs-niŋ, -ᵊn-iŋ\ **:** to make or become worse
¹wor·ship \'wər-shəp\ *n* [OE *weorthscipe* worthiness, respect, reverence, fr. *weorth* worthy, worth + *-scipe* -ship] **1** *chiefly Brit* **:** a person of importance — used as a title for officials (as magistrates and some mayors) ⟨sent a petition to his *Worship*⟩ **2 :** reverence toward God, a god, or a sacred object; *also* **:** the expression of such reverence **3 :** extravagant respect or admiration for or devotion to an object of esteem ⟨*worship* of the dollar⟩

²worship *vb* **-shiped** *or* **-shipped; -ship·ing** *or* **-ship·ping 1 :** to honor or reverence as a divine being or supernatural power **2 :** to regard with extravagant respect, honor, or devotion **:** IDOLIZE **3 :** to perform or take part in worship or an act of worship **syn** *see* REVERE — **wor·ship·er** *or* **wor·ship·per** *n*
wor·ship·ful \-fəl\ *adj* **1 a** *archaic* **:** NOTABLE, DISTINGUISHED **b** *chiefly Brit* — used as a title for various persons or groups of rank or distinction **2 :** VENERATING, WORSHIPING — **wor·ship·ful·ly** \-fə-lē\ *adv* — **wor·ship·ful·ness** *n*
wor·ship·less \'wər-shəp-ləs\ *adj* **:** lacking worship or worshipers
¹worst \'wərst\ *adj, superlative of* BAD *or of* ILL [OE *wyrsta*] **1 :** most bad, evil, ill, or corrupt **2 a :** most unfavorable, unpleasant, or painful **b :** most unsuitable, faulty, unattractive, or ill-conceived **c :** least skillful or efficient **3 :** most wanting in quality, value, or condition
²worst *n* **1 :** one that is worst **2 :** the greatest degree of ill or badness
³worst *adv, superlative of* ILL *or of* BAD *or* BADLY **:** to the extreme degree of badness or inferiority **:** in the worst manner
⁴worst *vt* **:** to get the better of **:** DEFEAT
wor·sted \'wus-təd, 'wərs-\ *n* [*Worstead*, England] **1 :** a smooth compact yarn from long wool fibers used esp. for firm napless fabrics, carpeting, or knitting **2 :** a fabric made from worsted yarns — **worsted** *adj*
¹wort \'wərt, 'wȯrt\ *n* [OE *wyrt* root, herb, plant] **:** PLANT; *esp* **:** an herbaceous plant — usu. used in combination
²wort *n* [OE *wyrt*; akin to E **¹wort**] **:** a dilute solution of sugars obtained by infusion from malt and fermented to form beer
¹worth \'wərth\ *prep* [ME, fr. OE *weorth*, adj., having value, worthy] **1 a :** equal in value to **b :** having possessions or income equal to **2 :** deserving of ⟨well *worth* the effort⟩ **3 :** capable of ⟨ran for all he was *worth*⟩
²worth *n* **1 a :** monetary value **b :** the equivalent of a specified amount or figure **2 :** the value of something measured by its qualities or by the esteem in which it is held **3 a :** moral or personal value **b :** MERIT, EXCELLENCE **4 :** WEALTH, RICHES
syn VALUE, PRICE: WORTH applies to what is intrinsically excellent, admirable, useful, or desirable; VALUE may imply the immediate estimation of the worth of something to an individual or at a particular time or place; PRICE applies to what is actually exchanged for something else and may or may not imply an equivalent intrinsic worth
worth·ful \'wərth-fəl\ *adj* **1 :** full of merit **:** HONORABLE **2 :** having value **:** ESTEEMED — **worth·ful·ness** *n*
worth·less \'wərth-ləs\ *adj* **1 a :** lacking worth **:** VALUELESS **b :** USELESS **2 :** LOW, DESPICABLE — **worth·less·ly** *adv* — **worth·less·ness** *n*
worth·while \'wərth-'hwīl\ *adj* **:** being worth the time or effort spent — **worth·while·ness** *n*
¹wor·thy \'wər-thē\ *adj* **wor·thi·er; -est 1 a :** having worth or value **:** ESTIMABLE **b :** HONORABLE, MERITORIOUS **2 :** having sufficient worth ⟨a man *worthy* of the honor⟩ — **wor·thi·ly** \-thə-lē\ *adv* — **wor·thi·ness** \-thē-nəs\ *n*
²worthy *n, pl* **worthies :** a worthy person
wot *pres 1st & 3d sing of* WIT
would \wəd, (ə)d, (')wud\ *past of* WILL **1 a** *archaic* **:** WISHED, DESIRED **b** *archaic* **:** wish for **:** WANT ⟨he *would* a word with you⟩ **c :** strongly desire **:** WISH ⟨I *would* I were young again⟩ **2** — used as an auxiliary verb (1) with *rather* or *sooner* to express preference between alternatives ⟨he *would* sooner die than face them⟩, (2) to express wish, desire, or intent ⟨those who *would* forbid gambling⟩, (3) to express willingness or preference, (4) to express plan or intention ⟨said he *would* come⟩, (5) to express custom or habitual action ⟨we *would* meet often for lunch⟩, (6) to express consent or choice ⟨*would* put it off if he could⟩, (7) to express contingency or possibility ⟨if he were coming, he *would* be here now⟩, (8) to express completion of a statement of desire, request, or advice ⟨we wish that he *would* go⟩, and (9) to express probability or presumption in past or present time ⟨*would* have won it had he not tripped⟩ **3 :** COULD ⟨the barrel *would* hold 20 gallons⟩ **4** — used as an auxiliary verb (1) to express a request with which voluntary compliance is expected ⟨*would* you please help us⟩ and (2) to express doubt or

uncertainty ⟨the explanation *would* seem satisfactory⟩ **5** : SHOULD ⟨knew I *would* enjoy the trip⟩⟨*would* be glad to know the answer⟩
would-be \'wu̇d-,bē\ *adj* : desiring or professing to be ⟨a *would-be* poet⟩
would-est \'wu̇d-əst\ *archaic past 2d sing of* WILL
wouldn't \'wu̇d-ᵊnt\ : would not
wouldst \(')wu̇dst\ *archaic past 2d sing of* WILL
¹wound \'wünd\ *n* [OE *wund*] **1** : an injury involving cutting or breaking of bodily tissue (as by violence, accident, or surgery) **2** : an injury or hurt to feelings or reputation
²wound *vb* **1** : to cause a wound to or in **2** : to inflict a wound ⟨a *wounding* remark⟩
³wound \'waůnd\ *past of* WIND
wound·wort \'wünd-,wərt, -,wȯrt\ *n* : any of various plants whose downy leaves have been used to dress wounds
wove *past of* WEAVE
woven *past part of* WEAVE
¹wow \'waů\ *interj* — used to express pleasure, surprise, or strong feeling
²wow *n* : a distortion in reproduced sound consisting of a slow rise and fall of pitch caused by speed variation in the reproducing system
¹wrack \'rak\ *n* [OE *wræc* misery, punishment, something driven by the sea; akin to E *wreak*] **1** : RUIN, DESTRUCTION **2** : a remnant of something destroyed
²wrack *n* [MD or MLG *wrak*; akin to E ¹*wrack*] **1 a** : a wrecked ship **b** : WRECKAGE **c** : WRECK **2 a** : marine vegetation; *esp* : KELP **b** : dried seaweeds
³wrack *vt* : to utterly ruin : WRECK
⁴wrack *vb* : ²RACK
⁵wrack *n* : ¹RACK 2
wraith \'rāth\ *n* **1 a** : an apparition of a living person in his exact likeness seen usu. just before his death **b** : GHOST, SPECTER **2** : an insubstantial appearance of something : SHADOW
¹wran·gle \'raŋ-gəl\ *vb* **wran·gled**; **wran·gling** \-g(ə-)liŋ\ [ME *wranglen*] **1** : to dispute angrily or peevishly : BICKER **2** : ARGUE **3** : to obtain by persistent arguing **4** : to herd and care for (livestock and esp. horses) on the range
²wrangle *n* **1** : an angry, noisy, or prolonged dispute or quarrel **2** : CONTROVERSY
wran·gler \-g(ə-)lər\ *n* **1** : one that wrangles or bickers **2** : a ranch hand who takes care of the saddle horses
¹wrap \'rap\ *vb* **wrapped**; **wrap·ping** [ME *wrappen*] **1 a** : to cover esp. by winding or folding ⟨*wrap* a baby in a blanket⟩ **b** : to envelop and secure for transportation or storage : BUNDLE ⟨*wrap* groceries⟩ **c** : ENFOLD, EMBRACE **d** : to coil, fold, draw, or twine about something **2 a** : SURROUND, ENVELOP **b** : SUFFUSE **c** : to involve completely : ENGROSS ⟨*wrapped* up in a hobby⟩ **3** : to conceal or obscure as if by enveloping or enfolding ⟨a city *wrapped* in darkness⟩ **4** : to put on clothing : DRESS ⟨*wrapped* up warm⟩ **5** : to be subject to covering, enclosing, or packaging ⟨*wraps* up into a small package⟩
²wrap *n* **1 a** : WRAPPER, WRAPPING **b** : an article of clothing that may be wrapped round a person; *esp* : an outer garment (as a coat or shawl) **2** : a single turn or convolution of something wound round an object **3** *pl* **a** : RESTRAINT **b** : SECRECY, CENSORSHIP
wrap·around \'rap-ə-,raůnd\ *n* : a garment (as a dress or coat) made with a full-length opening and adjusted to the figure by wrapping around
wrap·per \'rap-ər\ *n* **1** : that in which something is wrapped: as **a** : a tobacco leaf used for the outside covering esp. of cigars **b** (1) : JACKET 2c (2) : the paper cover of a book not bound in boards **c** : a paper wrapped around a newspaper or magazine in the mail **2** : one that wraps **3** : an article of clothing worn wrapped around the body
wrap·ping \'rap-iŋ\ *n* : something used to wrap an object : WRAPPER
wrap up \(')rap-'əp\ *vt* **1** : END, CONCLUDE **2** : to make a single comprehensive report of
wrap-up \'rap-,əp\ *n* : a summarizing news report
wrasse \'ras\ *n* [Corn *gwragh*] : any of various usu. brilliantly colored spiny-finned fishes with a long deep narrow body that include important food fishes esp. of warm seas

wrath \'rath\ *n* [OE *wræththo*, fr. *wrāth* wroth] **1** : violent anger : RAGE **2** : retributory punishment for sin or crime **syn** see ANGER — **wrathy** \-ē\ *adj*
wrath·ful \'rath-fəl\ *adj* **1** : filled with wrath : IRATE **2** : arising from, marked by, or indicative of wrath ⟨a *wrathful* expression⟩ — **wrath·ful·ly** \-fə-lē\ *adv* — **wrath·ful·ness** *n*
wreak \'rēk\ *vt* [OE *wrecan* to drive, punish, avenge] **1** : to exact as a punishment : INFLICT ⟨*wreak* vengeance⟩ **2** : to give free scope or rein to ⟨*wreaked* his wrath⟩
wreath \'rēth\ *n, pl* **wreaths** \'rēthz, 'rēths\ [OE *writha*; akin to E *writhe*] : something intertwined into a circular shape; *esp* : GARLAND, CHAPLET ⟨a *wreath* of smoke⟩ ⟨a *wreath* of flowers⟩
wreathe \'rēth\ *vb* **1** : to twist or contort so as to show folds, coils, or creases ⟨a face *wreathed* in smiles⟩ **2 a** : to shape into a wreath **b** : to take on the shape of a wreath : move or extend in circles or spirals ⟨smoke *wreathed* upward⟩ **c** : to cause to coil about something **3** : to encircle or adorn with or as if with a wreath ⟨ivy *wreathed* the pole⟩
¹wreck \'rek\ *n* [AF *wrek*, of Scand origin; akin to E *wreak*] **1** : goods cast upon the land by the sea after a shipwreck **2** : broken remains (as of a ship or vehicle after heavy damage by storm, collision, or fire) **3** : something disabled or in a state of ruin or dilapidation; *also* : an individual broken in health or strength **4** : SHIPWRECK **5** : the action of breaking up or destroying something : WRECKING ⟨injured in the *wreck* of a train⟩
²wreck *vt* **1 a** : SHIPWRECK **b** : to damage or ruin by breaking up ⟨*wreck* a building⟩ ⟨*wreck* a friendship⟩ **c** : to involve in disaster or ruin **2** : WREAK 1
wreck·age \'rek-ij\ *n* **1** : the act of wrecking or state of being wrecked **2** : the remains of a wreck
wreck·er \'rek-ər\ *n* **1** : one that wrecks **2** : a person who searches for or works upon wrecks of vessels **3** : a ship used in salvaging wrecks **4** : a truck equipped to remove wrecked or disabled cars — called also *tow truck*
wrecking bar *n* : a small crowbar with a claw for pulling nails at one end and a slight bend for prying at the other end
wren \'ren\ *n* [OE *wrenna*] **1** : any of a large family of small mostly brown singing birds with short rounded wings and short erect tail **2** : any of various small singing birds resembling the true wrens in size and habits
¹wrench \'rench\ *vb* [OE *wrencan*] **1** : to move with a violent twist **2** : to pull, strain, or tighten with violent twisting or force **3** : to injure or disable by a violent twisting or straining **4** : to change (as the meaning of a word) violently **5** : to snatch forcibly : WREST **6** : to cause to suffer anguish : RACK
²wrench *n* **1 a** : a violent twisting or a pull with or as if with twisting **b** : a sharp twist or sudden jerk straining muscles or ligaments; *also* : the resultant injury (as of a joint) **c** : ALTERATION; *esp* : DISTORTION **d** : acute emotional distress

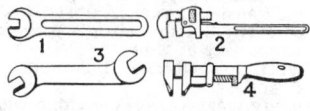

wrenches: *1* single-head, *2* pipe, *3* double-head, *4* monkey

: sudden violent mental change **2** : a hand or power tool for holding, twisting, or turning an object (as a bolt or nut)
¹wrest \'rest\ *vt* [OE *wrǣstan*; akin to E *writhe*] **1** : to pull, force, or move by violent wringing or twisting movements **2** : to gain with difficulty by or as if by force or violence ⟨*wrest* a living⟩ ⟨*wrest* the power from the king⟩ **3 a** : to divert to an unnatural or improper use **b** : DISTORT ⟨they *wrest* my every word⟩ — **wrest·er** *n*
²wrest *n* : a forcible twist : WRENCH
¹wres·tle \'res-əl\ *vb* **wres·tled**; **wres·tling** \'res-(ə-)liŋ\ [OE *wrǣstlian*, freq. of *wrǣstan* to wrest] **1** : to grapple with an opponent in an attempt to trip him or throw him down **2** : to contend against in wrestling **3** : to struggle for mastery (as with something difficult) ⟨*wrestle* with a problem⟩ ⟨*wrestle* with a heavy suitcase⟩ — **wres·tler** \'res-lər\ *n*
²wrestle *n* : the action or an instance of wrestling : STRUGGLE
wres·tling \'res-liŋ\ *n* : the sport of hand-to-hand combat

between two unarmed contestants who seek to throw each other

wrest pin *n* [²*wrest*] : a pin in a stringed instrument (as a harp or piano) around which the ends of the strings are coiled and by which the instrument is tuned

wretch \'rech\ *n* [OE *wrecca* outcast; akin to E *wreak*] **1** : a miserable unhappy person **2** : a base, despicable, or vile person

wretch·ed \'rech-əd\ *adj* **1** : deeply afflicted, dejected, or distressed : MISERABLE **2** : WOEFUL, GRIEVOUS ⟨a *wretched* accident⟩ **3** : hatefully contemptible : DESPICABLE ⟨a *wretched* trick⟩ **4** : very poor in quality or ability : INFERIOR ⟨*wretched* workmanship⟩ — **wretch·ed·ly** *adv* — **wretch·ed·ness** *n*

wrig·gle \'rig-əl\ *vb* **wrig·gled**; **wrig·gling** \'rig-(ə-)liŋ\ [ME *wrigglen*] **1** : to move to and fro with short writhing motions like a worm : SQUIRM ⟨*wriggled* in his chair⟩ ⟨*wriggled* her toes⟩; *also* : to progress by such movements ⟨a snake *wriggled* along the path⟩ **2** : to extricate or insinuate oneself or reach a goal by maneuvering, equivocation, or ingratiation ⟨*wriggle* out of a difficulty⟩ — **wriggle** *n* — **wrig·gly** \-(ə-)lē\ *adj*

wrig·gler \'rig-(ə-)lər\ *n* : one that wriggles; *esp* : WIGGLER 2

wright \'rīt\ *n* [OE *wyrhta,wryhta* worker, maker; akin to E *work*] : a workman in wood : CARPENTER — usu. used in combination ⟨ship*wright*⟩ ⟨wheel*wright*⟩

wring \'riŋ\ *vb* **wrung** \'rəŋ\; **wring·ing** \'riŋ-iŋ\ [OE *wringan*] **1** : to squeeze or twist esp. so as to make dry or to extract moisture or liquid ⟨*wring* wet clothes⟩ **2** : to get by or as if by twisting or pressing ⟨*wring* the truth out of him⟩ **3 a** : to twist so as to strain or sprain : CONTORT **b** : to twist together (clasped hands) as a sign of anguish **4** : to place or insert by a twisting movement **5** : to affect painfully as if by wringing : TORMENT ⟨her plight *wrung* our hearts⟩ **6** : to shake (a hand) vigorously in greeting — **wring** *n*

wring·er \'riŋ-ər\ *n* : one that wrings; *esp* : a machine or device for pressing out liquid or moisture ⟨clothes *wringer*⟩

¹wrin·kle \'riŋ-kəl\ *n* [ME] **1** : a crease or small fold on a surface (as in the skin or in cloth) **2 a** : METHOD, TECHNIQUE; *also* : information about a method : HINT **b** : an innovation in method, technique, or equipment : NOVELTY ⟨the latest *wrinkle* in hairdos⟩ — **wrin·kly** \-k(ə-)lē\ *adj*

²wrinkle *vb* **wrin·kled**; **wrin·kling** \-k(ə-)liŋ\ *vb* : to develop or cause to develop wrinkles

wrist \'rist\ *n* [OE] : the joint or the region of the joint between the human hand and the arm or a corresponding part on a lower animal

wrist·band \'ris(t)-,band\ *n* **1** : the part of a sleeve covering the wrist **2** : a band encircling the wrist

wrist·let \'ris(t)-lət\ *n* : a band encircling the wrist; *esp* : a close-fitting knitted band worn for warmth

wrist pin *n* : a stud or pin that forms a journal for a connecting rod

wrist·watch \'rist-,wäch\ *n* : a small watch attached to a bracelet or strap to fasten about the wrist

writ \'rit\ *n* [OE] **1** : something written : WRITING ⟨Holy *Writ*⟩ **2 a** : a legal order in writing issued under seal in the name of the sovereign or of a court or judicial officer commanding the person to whom it is directed to perform or refrain from performing a specified act **b** : a written order constituting a symbol of the power and authority of the issuer ⟨where the king's *writ* has no force⟩

writ·a·ble \'rīt-ə-bəl\ *adj* : capable of being put in writing

write \'rīt\ *vb* **wrote** \'rōt\; **writ·ten** \'rit-ⁿn\ *also* **writ** \'rit\; **writ·ing** \'rīt-iŋ\ [OE *wrītan*, lit., to scratch] **1** : to form letters or words with pen or pencil ⟨learn to read and *write*⟩ **2** : to form the letters or the words of (as on paper) : INSCRIBE ⟨*write* his name⟩ ⟨*write* a check⟩ **3** : to put down on paper : give expression to in writing ⟨*wrote* his impressions of the circus⟩ **4** : to make up and set down for others to read : COMPOSE ⟨*write* a book⟩ ⟨*wrote* music⟩ **5** : to pen, dictate, or typewrite a letter to ⟨*write* the president⟩ **6** : to communicate by letter : CORRESPOND **7** : to be fitted for writing ⟨this pen *writes* easily⟩

write down *vb* **1** : to record in written form **2 a** : to reduce in status, rank, or value **b** : to play down in

writing **3** : to write so as to appeal to a lower level of taste, comprehension, or intelligence ⟨*write down* to an audience of children⟩

write in *vt* : to insert (a name not listed) on a ballot in an appropriate space by writing or use of a printed sticker

write off *vt* **1** : to reduce the estimated value of : DEPRECIATE **2** : to take off the books : CANCEL ⟨*write off* a bad debt⟩

write out *vt* : to put in writing; *esp* : to put into a full and complete written form

writ·er \'rīt-ər\ *n* : one that writes esp. as a business or occupation : AUTHOR

writer's cramp *n* : a painful spasmodic cramp of muscles of the hand or fingers brought on by excessive use (as in writing)

write up \(')rīt-'əp\ *vt* **1 a** : to write an account of : DESCRIBE **b** : to put into finished written form **2** : to bring up to date the writing of **3** : to set down an unduly high value for

write-up \'rīt-,əp\ *n* : a written account (as in a newspaper); *esp* : a flattering article

writhe \'rīth\ *vb* [OE *wrīthan*] **1** : to twist and turn this way and that ⟨*writhe* in pain⟩ **2** : to suffer with shame or confusion : SQUIRM

writ·ing \'rīt-iŋ\ *n* **1 a** : the act or process of one that writes : the formation of letters to express words and ideas **b** : HANDWRITING **2 a** : something (as a letter, book, or document) that is written or printed **b** : INSCRIPTION **3** : a style or form of composition **4** : the occupation of a writer

writing desk *n* : a desk often with a sloping top for writing on

writing paper *n* : paper intended for writing on with ink and usu. finished with a smooth surface and sized

writ of assistance : a writ issued (as by British authorities in the American colonies) to an officer (as a sheriff) to aid in the search for smuggled or illegal goods

¹wrong \'roŋ\ *n* [of Scand origin] **1** : an injurious, unfair, or unjust act **2** : that which is wrong : principles, practices, or conduct contrary to justice, goodness, equity, or law ⟨know right from *wrong*⟩ **3 a** : the state, position, or fact of being or doing wrong **b** : the state of being guilty **4** : a violation of the legal rights of another; *esp* : TORT

²wrong *adj* **1** : not according to the moral standard : SINFUL, IMMORAL **2** : not right or proper according to a code, standard, or convention : IMPROPER **3** : not suitable or appropriate **4** : not according to truth or facts : INCORRECT **5** : not satisfactory (as in condition, results, health, or temper) **6** : constituting a side or part of something opposite to the principal one or one turned down, inward, or away, or least finished or polished ⟨the *wrong* side of a fabric⟩ — **wrong** *adv* — **wrong·ly** \'roŋ-lē\ *adv* — **wrong·ness** *n*

³wrong *vt* **wronged**; **wrong·ing** \'roŋ-iŋ\ **1** : to do wrong to : INJURE, HARM **2** : to make unjust remarks about : DISHONOR, MALIGN — **wrong·er** \'roŋ-ər\ *n*

wrong·do·er \'roŋ-'dü-ər\ *n* : a person who does wrong and esp. moral wrong — **wrong·do·ing** \-'dü-iŋ\ *n*

wrong·ful \'roŋ-fəl\ *adj* **1** : WRONG, UNJUST **2** : UNLAWFUL — **wrong·ful·ly** \-fə-lē\ *adv* — **wrong·ful·ness** *n*

wrong·head·ed \'roŋ-'hed-əd\ *adj* : stubborn in adherence to wrong opinion or principles : PERVERSE — **wrong·head·ed·ly** *adv* — **wrong·head·ed·ness** *n*

wroth \'roth, 'rōth\ *adj* [OE *wrāth*] : filled with wrath : ANGRY

wrought \'rot\ *adj* [ME, fr. pp. of *worken* to work] **1** : FASHIONED, FORMED **2** : ORNAMENTED **3** : MANUFACTURED **4** : beaten into shape by tools : HAMMERED ⟨*wrought* metals⟩ **5** : deeply stirred : EXCITED ⟨gets easily *wrought* up over nothing⟩

wrought iron *n* : a commercial form of iron that is tough, malleable, and relatively soft

wrung *past of* WRING

wry \'rī\ *adj* **wri·er** \'rī(-ə)r\; **wri·est** \'rī-əst\ [*wry* to twist, fr. OE *wrigian* to incline] **1** : turned abnormally to one side : CONTORTED **2** : made by distortion of the facial muscles ⟨a *wry* smile⟩ **3** : cleverly and often ironically or grimly humorous — **wry·ly** *adv* — **wry·ness** *n*

wry·neck \'rī-,nek\ *n* **1** : a disorder marked by a

twisting of the neck and an unnatural position of the head **2** : any of a genus of atypical woodpeckers with soft tail feathers and a peculiar way of twisting the neck
wurst \'wərst, 'wu̇rst\ *n* [G] : SAUSAGE
wy·an·dotte \'wī-ən-ˌdät\ *n* : any of an American breed of medium-sized domestic fowls

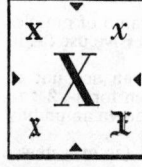

¹x \'eks\ *n, often cap* **1** : the 24th letter of the English alphabet **2** : the roman numeral 10 **3** : an unknown quantity
²x *vt* **x–ed** *also* **x'd** *or* **xed** \'ekst\ ; **x–ing** *or* **x'ing** \'ek-siŋ\ **1** : to mark with an x **2** : to cancel or obliterate with a series of x's — usu. used with *out*
xan·thic \'zan(t)-thik\ *adj* [Gk *xanthos* yellow, blond] : of, relating to, or tending toward a yellow color
Xan·thip·pe \zan-'t(h)ip-ē\ *or* **Xan·tip·pe** \-'tip-\ *n* [after *Xanthippe*, wife of Socrates] : an ill-tempered woman
xan·tho·phyll \'zan(t)-thə-ˌfil\ *n* [Gk *xanthos* yellow + *phyllon* leaf] : any of several neutral yellow carotenoid pigments that are usu. oxygen derivatives of carotenes — **xan·tho·phyl·lic** \ˌzan(t)-thə-'fil-ik\ *adj* — **xan·tho·phyl·lous** \-'fil-əs\ *adj*
x–ax·is \'eks-\ *n* : the axis of abscissas in a plane Cartesian coordinate system
X chromosome *n* : a sex chromosome that carries factors for femaleness and usu. occurs paired in each female zygote and cell and single in each male zygote and cell — compare Y CHROMOSOME
X–dis·ease \'eks-diz-ˌēz\ *n* : any of various usu. virus diseases of obscure etiology and relationships; *esp* : a viral encephalitis of man first detected in Australia
xe·bec \'zē-ˌbek\ *n* [Ar *shabbāk*] : a usu. 3-masted Mediterranean sailing ship with long overhanging bow and stern
xe·nia \'zē-nē-ə\ *n* [Gk, hospitality, fr. *xenos* stranger, guest, host] : the effect of genes introduced by a male nucleus on seed-plant structures (as endosperm or fruit) other than an embryo
xe·non \'zē-ˌnän\ *n* [Gk, neut. of *xenos* strange] : a heavy gaseous chemical element occurring in air in minute quantities — see ELEMENT table
xeno·pho·bia \ˌzen-ə-'fō-bē-ə\ *n* [Gk *xenos* strange, foreigner] : fear and hatred of strangers or foreigners or of anything that is strange or foreign — **xeno·phobe** \'zen-ə-ˌfōb\ *n* — **xeno·pho·bic** \ˌzen-ə-'fō-bik\ *adj*
xer– *or* **xero–** *comb form* [Gk *xēros*] : dry 〈*xeric*〉〈*xerophyte*〉〈*xerothermic*〉
xe·ric \'zi(ə)r-ik\ *adj* **1** : low or deficient in available moisture for the support of life **2** : XEROPHYTIC — **xe·ri·cal·ly** \'zir-i-k(ə-)lē\ *adv*
xe·rog·ra·phy \zə-'räg-rə-fē\ *n* : the formation of pictures or copies of graphic matter by the action of light on an electrically charged surface in which the latent image usu. is developed with powders — **xe·ro·graph·ic** \ˌzir-ə-'graf-ik\ *adj*
xe·roph·i·lous \zə-'räf-ə-ləs\ *or* **xe·ro·phile** \'zir-ə-ˌfīl\ *adj* : thriving in or tolerant or characteristic of a dry environment — **xe·roph·i·ly** \zə-'räf-ə-lē\ *n*
xe·roph·thal·mia \ˌzir-ˌäf-'thal-mē-ə, -ˌäp-'thal-\ *n* : a dry thickened lusterless condition of the eyeball resulting from a severe systemic deficiency of vitamin A — **xe·roph·thal·mic** \-mik\ *adj*
xe·ro·phyte \'zir-ə-ˌfīt\ *n* : a plant adapted for growth with a limited water supply esp. by means of mechanisms that limit transpiration or that provide for the storage of water — **xe·ro·phyt·ic** \ˌzir-ə-'fit-ik\ *adj* — **xe·ro·phyt·i·cal·ly** \-'fit-i-k(ə-)lē\ *adv* — **xe·ro·phyt·ism** \'zir-ə-ˌfīt-ˌiz-əm\ *n*
xe·ro·ther·mic \ˌzir-ə-'thər-mik\ *adj* **1** : marked by heat and dryness **2** : adapted to or thriving in a hot dry environment
xi \'zī\ *n* : the 14th letter of the Greek alphabet — Ξ or ξ
xiphi·ster·num \ˌzif-i-'stər-nəm\ *n, pl* **-na** \-nə\ [NL,

fr. Gk *xiphos* sword] : the posterior segment of the sternum — called also *xiphoid process*
xiph·oid \'zī-ˌfȯid, 'zif-ˌȯid\ *adj* [Gk *xiphos* sword] : shaped like a sword
xiph·os·uran \ˌzif-ə-'su̇r-ən\ *n* [Gk *xiphos* sword + *oura* tail] : any of an order (Xiphosura) of arthropods comprising the king crabs and extinct related forms — **xiph·osuran** *adj*
Xmas \'kris-məs, 'eks-məs\ *n* [fr. X, symbol for Christ, fr. the Gk letter chi (X), initial of *Christos* Christ] : CHRISTMAS
X–ra·di·a·tion \ˌeks-\ *n* **1** : exposure to X rays **2** : radiation consisting of X rays
X ray \'eks-ˌrā\ *n* **1** : any of the electromagnetic radiations of the same nature as light rays but of very short wavelength that are generated by a stream of electrons striking against a metal surface in vacuum and that are able to penetrate various thicknesses of solids and act on photographic film like light and to cause a fluorescent screen to emit light **2** : a photograph esp. of conditions inside the surface of a body taken by the use of X rays — **X-ray** *adj*
x–ray *vt, often cap X* : to examine, treat, or photograph with X rays
X–ray photograph *n* : a shadow picture made with X rays
X–ray therapy *n* : medical treatment (as of a cancer) by controlled application of X rays
X–ray tube *n* : a vacuum tube in which a concentrated stream of electrons strikes a metal target and produces X rays
xyl– *or* **xylo–** *comb form* [Gk *xylon*] : wood 〈*xylophone*〉
xy·lem \'zī-ləm, -ˌlem\ *n* [G, fr. Gk *xylon* wood] : a complex tissue of higher plants that transports water and dissolved materials upward, functions also in support and storage, lies internal to the phloem, and typically constitutes the woody element (as of a plant stem) — **xy·la·ry** \'zī-lə-rē\ *adj*
xy·lene \'zī-ˌlēn\ *n* : a colorless flammable liquid obtained from wood tar, coal tar, coke-oven gas, or petroleum and used chiefly as a solvent
xy·lol \'zī-ˌlȯl, -ˌlōl\ *n* : XYLENE
xy·loph·a·gous \zī-'läf-ə-gəs\ *adj* : feeding on or in wood
xy·loph·i·lous \zī-'läf-ə-ləs\ *adj* : growing or living on or in wood
xy·lo·phone \'zī-lə-ˌfōn\ *n* : a musical instrument consisting of a series of wooden bars graduated in length to sound the musical scale and played by striking with two wooden hammers — **xy·lo·phon·ist** \-ˌfō-nəst\ *n*
xy·lose \'zī-ˌlōs\ *n* : a crystalline sugar not fermentable by ordinary yeasts

xylophone

y \'wī\ *n, often cap* : the 25th letter of the English alphabet
¹-y *also* **-ey** \ē\ *adj suffix* **-i·er** ; **-i·est** [OE *-ig*] **1 a** : characterized by : full of 〈blossom*y*〉 〈dirt*y*〉 〈mudd*y*〉 〈clay*ey*〉 **b** : having the character of : composed of 〈ic*y*〉 〈wax*y*〉 **c** : like : like that of 〈home*y*〉 〈wintr*y*〉 〈stag*y*〉 **d** : devoted to : addicted to : enthusiastic over 〈hors*y*〉 **2 a** : tending or inclined to 〈sleep*y*〉 〈chatt*y*〉 **b** : giving occasion for (specified) action 〈tear*y*〉 **c** : performing (specified) action 〈curl*y*〉 **3 a** : somewhat : rather : -ISH〈chill*y*〉 **b** : having (such) characteristics to a marked degree or in an affected or superficial way 〈French*y*〉
²-y \ē\ *n suffix, pl* **-ies** [OF *-ie*, fr. L *-ia*] **1** : state : condition : quality 〈beggar*y*〉 **2** : activity, place of business, or goods dealt with 〈chandler*y*〉〈laundr*y*〉 **3** : whole body or group 〈soldier*y*〉
³-y *n suffix, pl* **-ies** [AF *-ie*, fr. L *-ium*] : instance of a (specified) action 〈entreat*y*〉 〈inquir*y*〉
⁴-y — see -IE
¹yacht \'yät\ *n* [obs. D *jaght*, fr. MLG *jacht*, short for

jachtschiff, lit., hunting ship] **:** any of various relatively small sailing or mechanically driven ships that usu. have a sharp prow and graceful lines and are used esp. for pleasure cruising or racing

²yacht *vi* **:** to race or cruise in a yacht

yacht·ing *n* **:** the action, fact, or pastime of racing or cruising in a yacht

yachts·man \'yäts-mən\ *n* **:** a person who owns or sails a yacht

ya·hoo \'yä-hü, 'yä-\ *n, pl* **yahoos** **1** *cap* **:** a member of a race of brutes in Swift's *Gulliver's Travels* who have the form and all the vices of man **2 :** an uncouth or rowdy person

Yah·weh \'yä-,wā, -,vā\ *also* **Yah·veh** *or* **Yah·vè** \-,vā\ *n* **:** the God of the Hebrews

¹yak \'yak\ *n, pl* **yaks** *also* **yak** [Tibetan *gyak*] **:** a large long-haired wild or domesticated ox of Tibet and adjacent elevated parts of central Asia

²yak *n* **:** persistent or voluble talk — **yak** *vi*

yam \'yam\ *n* [Pg *inhame* & Sp *ñame*, of African origin] **1 :** an edible starchy tuberous root that is a staple food in tropical areas; *also* **:** a monocotyledonous plant distantly related to the lilies that produces these **2 :** a moist-fleshed and usu. orange-fleshed sweet potato

yam·mer \'yam-ər\ *vi* **yam·mered**; **yam·mer·ing** \'yam-(ə-)riŋ\ [OE *geōmrian* to lament] **1 :** WHIMPER **2 :** CHATTER — **yammer** *n*

yang \'yäŋ\ *n* [Chin (Pek) *yang²*] **:** the masculine active principle (as of light, heat, or dryness) in nature that in Chinese cosmology combines with yin to produce all that comes to be

¹yank \'yaŋk\ *n* **:** a strong sudden pull **:** JERK

²yank *vb* **:** to pull or pull on or out with a quick vigorous movement ⟨*yank* a drawer open⟩

Yank \'yaŋk\ *n* **:** YANKEE

Yan·kee \'yaŋ-kē\ *n* **1 a :** a native or inhabitant of New England **b :** a native or inhabitant of the northern U.S. **2 :** a native or inhabitant of the U.S. — **Yankee** *adj*

yan·qui \'yäŋ-kē\ *n, often cap* [Sp, fr. E *Yankee*] **:** a citizen of the U.S. as distinguished from a Latin American

¹yap \'yap\ *vi* **yapped**; **yap·ping** **1 :** to bark in yaps **:** YELP **2 :** CHATTER, SCOLD

²yap *n* **1 :** a quick sharp bark **:** YELP **2 :** often complaining chatter **3** *slang* **:** MOUTH

¹yard \'yärd\ *n* [OE *gierd* twig, measure, yard] **1 :** any of various units of measure; *esp* **:** a unit of length equal in the U.S. to 0.9144 meter — see MEASURE table **2 :** a long spar tapered toward the ends that supports and spreads the head of a square sail, lateen, or lugsail

²yard *n* [OE *geard* enclosure, yard] **1 a :** a small usu. enclosed area open to the sky and adjacent to a building **b :** the grounds of a building or group of buildings **2 a :** an enclosure for livestock **b :** an area with its buildings and facilities set aside for a particular business or activity **c :** a system of railroad tracks for storage and maintenance of cars and making up trains **3 :** a locality in a forest where deer herd in winter

³yard *vb* **:** to drive into, gather, or confine in or as if in a yard

yard·age \'yärd-ij\ *n* **:** an aggregate number of yards; *also* **:** the length, extent, or volume of something as measured in yards

yard·arm \'yärd-,ärm\ *n* **:** either end of the yard of a square-rigged ship

yard goods *n pl* **:** fabrics sold by the yard

yard grass *n* **:** a coarse weedy annual grass with digitate spikes

yard·man \'yärd-mən, -,man\ *n* **:** a man employed in or about a yard

yard·mas·ter \-,mas-tər\ *n* **:** the man in charge of operations in a railroad yard

yard·stick \-,stik\ *n* **1 :** a measuring stick a yard long **2 :** a rule or standard by which something is measured or judged **:** CRITERION

¹yarn \'yärn\ *n* [OE *gearn*] **1 a :** textile fiber (as spun wool, cotton, flax, or silk) for use in weaving, knitting, or the manufacture of thread **b :** a strand of material (as metal, glass, or asbestos) for uses comparable to those of a textile yarn **2 :** an interesting or exciting story often told without regard for strict accuracy

²yarn *vi* **:** to tell a yarn

yarn–dye \-'dī\ *vt* **:** to dye before weaving or knitting

yar·row \'yar-ō\ *n* [OE *gearwe*] **:** a strong-scented herb related to the daisies that has finely divided leaves and white or rarely pink flowers in flat clusters

yat·a·ghan \'yat-ə-,gan\ *n* [Turk *yatağan*] **:** a long knife or short saber common among Muslims that is made without a cross guard and usu. with a double curve to the edge

yataghan

yau·pon \'yü-,pän, 'yō-, 'yo-\ *n* [of AmerInd origin] **:** a holly of the southern U.S. with smooth leaves used as a substitute for tea

yaw \'yo\ *vi* **1 :** to turn abruptly from a straight course **2 :** SWERVE, VEER ⟨a heavy sea made the ship *yaw*⟩ — **yaw** *n*

yawl \'yol\ *n* [LG *jolle*] **1 :** a ship's small boat **2 :** a fore-and-aft rigged sailboat carrying a mainsail and one or more jibs with a mizzenmast far aft

¹yawn \'yon, 'yän\ *vb* [OE *ginian, geonian*] **1 :** to open wide **:** GAPE **2 :** to open the mouth wide usu. as an involuntary reaction to fatigue or boredom **3 :** to utter with a yawn — **yawn·er** *n*

²yawn *n* **:** a deep usu. involuntary intake of breath through the wide-open mouth

yawn·ing *adj* **1 :** wide open **:** CAVERNOUS ⟨a *yawning* hole⟩ **2 :** showing fatigue or boredom by yawns ⟨a *yawning* congregation⟩

¹yawp *or* **yaup** \'yop\ *vi* [ME *yolpen*] **1 :** to make a raucous noise **:** SQUAWK **2 :** CLAMOR, COMPLAIN — **yawp·er** *n*

²yawp *also* **yaup** *n* **:** a raucous noise **:** SQUAWK

yaws \'yoz\ *n sing or pl* [of AmerInd origin] **:** a tropical disease caused by a spirochete and marked by ulcerating surface lesions with later bone involvement

y-ax·is \'wī-\ *n* **:** the axis of ordinates in a plane Cartesian coordinate system

Y chromosome *n* **:** a sex chromosome occurring in male zygotes and cells and formerly held to carry factors for maleness that are prob. actually in autosomes — compare X CHROMOSOME

yclept \i-'klept\ *or* **ycleped** \-'klēpt, -'klept\ *adj* [ME, fr. OE *geclipod*, pp. of *clipian* to cry out, name] *archaic* **:** NAMED, CALLED

¹ye \(')ē\ *pron* [OE *gē*] *archaic* **:** YOU **1** — used formerly only as a plural pronoun of the 2d person in the nominative case

²ye \yē, yə, or like THE\ *definite article* [alter. of OE *þe*; fr. the use by early printers of the letter *y* to represent *þ* (th) of manuscripts] *archaic* **:** THE ⟨*Ye* Olde Gifte Shoppe⟩

¹yea \'yā\ *adv* [OE *gēa*] **1 :** YES — used in oral voting **2** — used as a function word to introduce a more explicit or emphatic phrase

²yea *n* **1 :** AFFIRMATION, ASSENT **2 a :** an affirmative vote **b :** a person casting a yea vote

yean \'(y)ēn\ *vi* [ME *yenen*, fr. OE *ge-*, prefix denoting completed action + *ēanian* to yean] **:** to bring forth young — used of a sheep or goat

yean·ling \-liŋ\ *n* **:** LAMB, KID

year \'yi(ə)r\ *n* [OE *gēar*] **1 :** the period of one apparent revolution of the sun around the ecliptic or of the earth's revolution around the sun amounting to approximately 365¼ days **2 a :** a period of 365 days or in leap year 366 days beginning January 1 **b :** a period of time equal to this but beginning at a different time ⟨a fiscal *year*⟩ **3 :** a continuous period of time that constitutes the period of some event (as revolution of a planet about its sun) or activity whether greater or less than the calendar year ⟨a school *year* of less than six months⟩

year·book \-,bůk\ *n* **1 :** a book published yearly esp. as a report **:** ANNUAL **2 :** a school publication recording the history and activities of a graduating class

year·ling \-liŋ\ *n* **:** one that is a year old: as **a :** an animal in the second year of its age **b :** a racehorse between January 1st of the year after the year in which it was foaled and the next January 1st — **yearling** *adj*

year·long \-'loŋ\ *adj* **:** lasting through a year

year·ly \-lē\ *adj* **1 :** occurring, done, produced, or acted upon every year **:** ANNUAL **2 :** computed in terms of one year — **yearly** *adv*

yearn \'yərn\ *vi* [OE *giernan*] **1 :** to feel a longing or

---

j joke;   **ŋ** sing;   **ō** flow;   **ȯ** flaw;   **ȯi** coin;   **th** thin;   **th̲** this;   **ü** loot;   **ů** foot;   **y** yet;   **yü** few;   **yů** furious;   **zh** vision

craving **2** : to feel tenderness or compassion **syn** see LONG — **yearn·er** n

yearn·ing n : a tender or urgent longing

year of grace : a year of the Christian era ⟨the *year of grace* 1962⟩

year-round \'yi(ə)r-'raùnd\ adj : effective, employed, or operating for the full year : not seasonal ⟨a *year-round* resort⟩

yeast \'yēst\ n [OE *gist*] **1 a** : a surface froth or a sediment that occurs esp. in sweet liquids in which it promotes alcoholic fermentation, consists largely of cells of a tiny fungus, and is used esp. in the making of alcoholic liquors and as a leaven in baking **b** : a commercial product containing yeast plants in a moist or dry medium **c** : any of various tiny fungi that are usu. one-celled and reproduce by budding; *esp* : one present and functionally active in a yeast froth or sediment **2** : foam or spume esp. of waves **3** : something that causes ferment or activity — **yeasty** \'yē-stē\ adj

yegg \'yeg\ n : SAFECRACKER, ROBBER

1yell \'yel\ vb [OE *giellan*] **1** : to utter a loud cry, scream, or shout **2** : to give a cheer usu. in unison **3** : to utter or declare with or as if with a yell : SHOUT — **yell·er** n

2yell n **1** : SCREAM, SHOUT **2** : a usu. rhythmic cheer used esp. in schools or colleges to encourage athletic teams

1yel·low \'yel-ō\ adj [OE *geolu*] **1 a** : of the color yellow **b** : yellowish from age, disease, or discoloration **c** : having a yellow complexion or skin **2 a** : featuring sensational or scandalous items or ordinary news sensationally distorted ⟨*yellow* journalism⟩ **b** : COWARDLY

2yellow vb : to make or turn yellow

3yellow n **1 a** : a color whose hue resembles that of ripe lemons or sunflowers or is that of the portion of the spectrum lying between green and orange **b** : a pigment or dye that colors yellow **2** : something yellow or marked by a yellow color **3** pl **a** : JAUNDICE **b** : any of several plant virus diseases marked by yellowing of the foliage and stunting

yellow–dog contract n : an employment contract in which a worker agrees not to join a labor union during the period of his employment

yellow fever n : an acute destructive infectious disease of warm regions marked by sudden onset, prostration, fever, jaundice, and often hemorrhage and caused by a virus transmitted by a mosquito — called also *yellow jack*

yellow–fever mosquito n : a small dark-colored mosquito that is the usual vector of yellow fever

yellow–green alga n : any of a division (Chrysophyta) of algae with the chlorophyll masked by brown or yellow pigment

yel·low·ham·mer \'yel-ō-,ham-ər\ n [OE *amore* yellowhammer] **1** : a common European finch having the male largely bright yellow **2** : YELLOW-SHAFTED FLICKER

yel·low·ish \'yel-ə-wish\ adj : somewhat yellow

yellow jack n **1** : YELLOW FEVER **2** : a flag raised on ships in quarantine **3** : a silvery and golden food fish of Florida and the West Indies

yellow jacket n : any of various small yellow-marked social wasps that commonly nest in the ground

yellow jessamine n **1** : a true jasmine **2** : a twining evergreen shrub related to the nux vomica and grown in warm regions for its fragrant yellow flowers — called also *yellow jasmine*

yel·low·legs \'yel-ō-,legz\ n sing or pl : either of two American shorebirds with long yellow legs

yellow ocher n **1** : a yellow mixture of limonite usu. with clay and silica used as a pigment **2** : a moderate orange yellow

yellow perch n : a common American perch that is yellowish with broad green bars and is an excellent sport and table fish

yellow pine n : the yellowish resinous wood of any of several American pines; *also* : a pine (as the longleaf pine or ponderosa pine) that yields such wood

yel·low·shaft·ed flicker \,yel-ō-,shaf-təd-\ n : a common large woodpecker of eastern No. America with bright symmetrical markings among which are a black crescent on the breast, red nape, white rump, and yellow shafts to the tail and wing feathers — called also *yellowhammer*

yellow spot n : the most sensitive area on the human retina — called also *mac·u·la lu·tea* \,mak-yə-lə-'lüt-ē-ə\

yel·low·tail \'yel-ō-,tāl\ n, pl **-tail** or **-tails** : any of various fishes having a yellow or yellowish tail and including several esteemed for sport or food

yel·low·throat \-,thrōt\ n : a largely olive American warbler with yellow breast and throat

yellow warbler n : a small No. American warbler that is in the male bright yellow with brown streaks on the underparts

yel·low·wood \'yel-ō-,wùd\ n : any of various trees having yellowish wood or yielding a yellow extract; *also* : this wood

1yelp \'yelp\ vi [OE *gielpan* to boast, exult] : to utter a sharp quick shrill cry ⟨*yelping* dogs⟩ — **yelp·er** n

2yelp n : a sharp shrill bark or cry (as of a dog)

1yen \'yen\ n, pl **yen** [Jap *en*] **1** : the basic monetary unit of Japan **2** : a coin or note representing one yen

2yen n [Chin (Cant) *yăn* craving] : an intense desire : URGE, LONGING ⟨have a *yen* to travel⟩

yeo·man \'yō-mən\ n [ME *yoman*] **1 a** : an attendant or officer in a royal or noble household **b** : a naval petty officer who performs clerical duties **2** : a small farmer who cultivates his own land; *esp* : one of a class of English freeholders below the gentry

yeo·man·ly \-lē\ adj : becoming to a yeoman : STURDY, SELF-RELIANT, LOYAL

yeoman of the guard : a member of a military corps of the British royal household serving as ceremonial attendants of the sovereign

yeo·man·ry \'yō-mən-rē\ n **1** : the body of yeomen and esp. of small landed proprietors **2** : a British volunteer cavalry force created from yeomen in 1761 and incorporated in 1907 into the territorial force

yeoman's service or **yeoman service** n : great and loyal service, assistance, or support

-yer — see -ER

yer·ba ma·té \,yer-bə-'mä-,tā, ,yər-\ n [AmerSp *yerba mate*, fr. *yerba* herb + *mate* maté] : MATÉ

1yes \'yes\ adv [OE *gēse*] **1** — used as a function word to express assent or agreement ⟨are you ready? *Yes*, I am⟩ **2** — used as a function word to introduce correction or contradiction of a negative assertion, direction, or request ⟨don't say that! *Yes*, I will⟩ **3** — used as a function word to introduce a more emphatic or explicit phrase ⟨we are glad, *yes*, very glad to see you⟩ **4** — used as a function word to indicate interest or attentiveness ⟨*yes*, what is it you want⟩

2yes n : an affirmative reply

ye·shi·va or **ye·shi·vah** \yə-'shē-və\ n, pl **-shivas** or **-shivahs** or **-shi·voth** \-,shē-'vōt(h)\ [LHeb *yĕshībhāh*] **1** : a school for Talmudic study **2** : an Orthodox Jewish rabbinical seminary **3** : a Jewish day school providing secular and religious instruction

yes-man \'yes-,man\ n : a person who agrees with everything that is said to him; *esp* : one who endorses without criticism every opinion or proposal of a superior

1yes·ter·day \'yes-tərd-ē\ adv [OE *giestran dæg*, fr. *giestran* yesterday + *dæg* day] **1** : on the day preceding today **2** : at a time not long past : only a short time ago

2yesterday n **1** : the day next before the present **2** : recent time : time not long past ⟨fashions of *yesterday*⟩

yes·ter·year \'yes-tər-,yi(ə)r\ n **1** : last year **2** : the recent past

1yet \(')yet\ adv [OE *gīet*] **1 a** : in addition : BESIDES ⟨gives *yet* another reason⟩ **b** : EVEN 2b ⟨a *yet* higher speed⟩ **2 a** (1) : up to now : so far ⟨hasn't done much *yet*⟩ (2) : at this or that time : so soon as now ⟨not time to go *yet*⟩ **b** : continuously up to the present or a specified time : STILL ⟨is *yet* a new country⟩ **c** : at a future time : EVENTUALLY ⟨may *yet* see the light⟩ **3** : NEVERTHELESS, HOWEVER ⟨strong, *yet* not strong enough⟩

2yet conj : despite that fact : BUT

yew \'yü\ n [OE *īw*] **1 a** : any of a genus of evergreen trees and shrubs with stiff poisonous needles and fruits with a fleshy aril **b** : the wood of a yew; *esp* : the heavy fine-grained wood of an Old World yew that is used for bows and small articles **2** archaic : an archery bow made of yew

yew: twig with ripe fruits

Ygg·dra·sil \'ig-drə-,sil\ n [ON] : a

ə abut; ᵊ kitten; ər further; a back; ā bake; ä cot, cart; aù out; ch chin; e less; ē easy; g gift; i trip; ī life

huge ash tree in Norse mythology that overspreads the world and binds earth, hell, and heaven together

Yid·dish \'yid-ish\ n [Yiddish yidish, short for yidish daytsh, lit., Jewish German] : a High German language spoken by Jews chiefly in eastern Europe and areas to which Jews from eastern Europe have migrated and commonly written in Hebrew characters — **Yiddish** adj

¹yield \'yēld\ vb [OE gieldan] **1 :** to give up possession of on claim or demand : hand over possession of **2 :** to give (oneself) up to an inclination, temptation, or habit **3 a :** to bear or bring forth as a natural product esp. as a result of cultivation **b :** to furnish as return or result of expended effort **c :** to produce as return from an expenditure or investment : furnish as profit or interest **d :** to produce as revenue : bring in **4 :** to be fruitful or productive **5 :** to give up and cease resistance or contention **6 :** to give way to pressure or influence : submit to urging, persuasion, or entreaty **7 :** to give way under physical force so as to bend, stretch, or break **8 a :** to give place or precedence : acknowledge the superiority of someone else **b :** to give way to or become succeeded by someone or something else — **yield·er** n
syn SUBMIT: YIELD may apply to any sort or degree of giving way or giving in before force, argument, persuasion, or entreaty; SUBMIT suggests full surrendering after resistance or conflict to the will or control of another

²yield n : something yielded : PRODUCT; esp : the amount or quantity produced or returned ⟨yield of wheat per acre⟩

yield·ing adj **1 :** lacking rigidity or stiffness : FLEXIBLE ⟨a yielding mass⟩ **2 :** disposed to submit or comply ⟨a cheerful yielding nature⟩

yin \'yin\ n [Chin (Pek) yin¹] : the feminine passive principle (as of darkness, cold, or wetness) in nature that in Chinese cosmology combines with yang to produce all that comes to be

yip \'yip\ vi **yipped; yip·ping :** YELP — used chiefly of a dog — **yip** n

yip·pee \'yip-ē\ interj — used to express exuberant delight or triumph

-yl \əl, ⁐l, (,)il\ n comb form [Gk hylē matter, material, lit., wood] : chemical and usu. univalent radical ⟨ethyl⟩ ⟨hydroxyl⟩

¹yo·del \'yōd-⁐l\ vb **-deled** or **-delled; -del·ing** or **-del·ling** \'yōd-liŋ, -⁐l-iŋ\ [G jodeln] : to sing by suddenly changing from chest voice to falsetto and the reverse; also : to shout or call in this manner — **yo·del·er** \'yōd-lər, -⁐l-ər\ n

²yodel n : a song or refrain sung by yodeling; also : a yodeled shout

yo·ga \'yō-gə\ n [Skt, lit., yoking; akin to E yoke] **1** cap : a Hindu theistic philosophy teaching the suppression of all activity of body, mind, and will in order that the self may realize its distinction from them and attain liberation **2 :** a system of exercises for attaining bodily or mental control and well-being — **yo·gic** \-gik\ adj, often cap

yo·gi \'yō-gē\ or **yo·gin** \-gən\ n [Skt yogin, fr. yoga] **1 :** a person who practices yoga **2** cap : an adherent of Yoga philosophy

yo·gurt or **yo·ghurt** \'yō-gərt\ n [Turk yoğurt] : a fermented slightly acid semifluid milk food made of skimmed cow's milk and milk solids to which cultures of bacteria have been added

¹yoke \'yōk\ n, pl **yokes** [OE geoc] **1 a :** a wooden bar or frame by which two draft animals (as oxen) are coupled at the heads or necks for working together **b :** a frame fitted to a person's shoulders to carry a load in two equal portions **c :** a clamp or similar piece that embraces two parts to hold or unite them in position **2** pl usu **yoke :** two animals yoked together **3 a :** an oppressive agency **b :** SERVITUDE, BONDAGE **c :** TIE, LINK ⟨the yoke of matrimony⟩ **4 :** a fitted or shaped piece at the top of a skirt or at the shoulder of various garments

²yoke vb **1 a :** to put a yoke on or couple with a yoke **b :** to attach (a draft animal) to something **2 :** to join as if by a yoke **3 :** to put to work

yoke·fellow \-,fel-ō\ n : a close companion : MATE

yo·kel \'yō-kəl\ n : RUSTIC, BUMPKIN

yolk \'yōk, 'yōlk\ n [OE geoloca, fr. geolu yellow] **1 a :** the yellow inner mass of the egg of a bird or reptile **b :** the material stored in an ovum that supplies food material to the developing embryo **2 :** oily material in

raw sheep wool — **yolk** adj — **yolked** \'yō(l)kt\ adj — **yolky** \'yō(l)-kē\ adj

yolk sac n : a membranous sac that is attached to many embryos, encloses food yolk, and is continuous with the intestinal cavity

yolk stalk n : a narrow tubular stalk connecting the yolk sac with the embryo

Yom Kip·pur \,yōm-'kip-ər, ,yəm-, ,yōm-, -ki-'pu̇(ə)r\ n [Heb yōm kippūr day of atonement] : a Jewish holiday observed in September or October with fasting and prayer : a day of atonement

¹yon \'yän\ adj [OE geon] : YONDER

²yon adv **1 :** YONDER **2 :** THITHER ⟨ran hither and yon⟩

¹yond \'yänd\ adv [OE geond] archaic : YONDER

²yond adj, dial : YONDER

¹yon·der \'yän-dər\ adv [ME, fr. yond + -er (as in hither)] : at or to that place : over there

²yonder adj **1 :** farther removed : more distant ⟨the yonder side of the river⟩ **2 :** being at a distance within view ⟨yonder hills⟩

yore \'yō(ə)r, 'yȯ(ə)r\ n [OE geāra long ago] : time long past — usu. used in the phrase of yore

York·ist \'yȯr-kəst\ n : a member or supporter of the English royal house of York furnishing sovereigns from 1461 to 1485 — compare LANCASTRIAN — **Yorkist** adj

York·shire pudding \,yȯrk-,shi(ə)r-, -shər-\ n : a batter of eggs, flour, and milk baked in meat drippings

you \(')yü, yə, yē\ pron [OE ēow, dat. & acc. of gē ye] **1 :** the one or ones spoken to — used as the pronoun of the 2d person singular or plural in any grammatical relation except that of a possessive ⟨you are my friends⟩⟨can I pour you a cup of tea⟩; used formerly only as a plural pronoun of the 2d person in the objective case; compare THEE, THOU, YE, YOUR, YOURS **2 :** ²ONE 1b ⟨you never know what will happen⟩

you-all \(')yü-'ȯl, 'yȯl\ pron : YOU — usu. used in addressing two or more persons or sometimes one person as representing also another or others

you'd \(,)yüd, (,)yu̇d, yəd\ : you had : you would

you'll \(,)yül, (,)yu̇l, yəl\ : you shall : you will

¹young \'yəŋ\ adj **young·er** \'yəŋ-gər\; **young·est** \'yəŋ-gəst\ [OE geong] **1 a :** being in the first or an early stage of life, growth, or development **b :** JUNIOR 1a **2 :** having little experience **3 a :** recently come into being : NEW **b :** YOUTHFUL **4** ⟨young mountain⟩ **4 :** of, relating to, or having the characteristics of youth or a young person **5** cap : belonging to or representing a new or revived usu. political group or movement ⟨Young Turk⟩ ⟨Young England⟩ — **young·ness** \'yəŋ-nəs\ n

²young n, pl **young 1** pl : young persons : YOUTH **b :** immature offspring esp. of lower animals **2 :** a single recently born or hatched animal — **with young :** PREGNANT — used of animals

young·ber·ry \'yəŋ-,ber-ē\ n [B. M. Young, 20th cent. American fruit grower] : the large sweet reddish black fruit of a hybrid between a trailing blackberry and a southern dewberry grown in western and southern U.S.; also : the bramble that bears this fruit

young·er \'yəŋ-gər\ n : an inferior in age : JUNIOR — usu. used with a possessive pronoun ⟨is several years his younger⟩

young·est \'yəŋ-gəst\ n : one that is the least old esp. of a family

young·ish \'yəŋ-ish\ adj : somewhat young

young·ling \'yəŋ-liŋ\ n : one that is young : a young person or animal — **youngling** adj

Young Pioneer n : a member of a Communist youth group in the U.S.S.R. for children from age 9 to 15

young·ster \'yəŋ(k)-stər\ n **1 :** a young person : YOUTH **2 :** CHILD

Young Turk n [Young Turk, member of a 20th cent. revolutionary party in Turkey] : an insurgent or member of an insurgent group in a political party

youn·ker \'yəŋ-kər\ n [D jonker young nobleman] **1 :** a young man **2 :** CHILD, YOUNGSTER

your \yər, (')yu̇(ə)r, (')yō(ə)r, (')yȯ(ə)r\ adj [OE ēower] **1 :** of or relating to you esp. as possessor ⟨your house⟩, agent ⟨your contributions⟩, or object of an action ⟨your discharge⟩ **2 :** of or relating to one ⟨when you face the north, east is at your right⟩ **3 —** used before a title of honor in address ⟨your Majesty⟩⟨your Honor⟩

you're \yər, (,)yü(ə)r, (,)yō(ə)r, (,)yȯ(ə)r\ : you are
yours \'yu̇(ə)rz, 'yō(ə)rz, 'yȯ(ə)rz\ *pron* : your one : your ones — used without a following noun as a pronoun equivalent in meaning to the adjective *your*; often used esp. with an adverbial modifier in the complimentary close of a letter ⟨*yours* truly⟩
your·self \yər-'self\ *pron* **1 a** : that identical one that is you — used reflexively ⟨don't hurt *yourself*⟩, for emphasis ⟨carry them *yourself*⟩, or in absolute constructions **b** : your normal, healthy, or sane condition or self **2** : ONESELF
your·selves \-'selvz\ *pron* **1** : those identical ones that are you — used reflexively ⟨get *yourselves* a treat⟩, for emphasis, or in absolute constructions **2** : the normal, healthy, or sane conditions or selves of you persons
youth \'yüth\ *n, pl* **youths** \'yüthz, 'yüths\ [OE *geoguth*; akin to E *young*] **1** : the time of life marked by growth and development; *esp* : the period between childhood and maturity **2 a** : a young man **b** : young persons — usu. pl. in constr. **3** : YOUTHFULNESS
youth·ful \'yüth-fəl\ *adj* **1** : of, relating to, or appropriate to youth **2** : being young and not yet mature **3** : FRESH, VIGOROUS **4** : having accomplished or undergone little erosion ⟨a *youthful* valley⟩ — **youth·ful·ly** \-fə-lē\ *adv* — **youth·ful·ness** *n*
youth hostel *n* : HOSTEL 2
you've \(,)yüv, yəv\ : you have
¹yowl \'yau̇l\ *vi* [ME *yowlen*] : to utter a loud long often mournful cry : WAIL
²yowl *n* : a loud long mournful wail or howl (as of a cat)
yo-yo \'yō-,yō\ *n, pl* **yo-yos** *also* **yo-yoes** : a thick divided disk that is made to fall and rise to the hand by unwinding and rewinding on a string
yt·ter·bi·um \i-'tər-bē-əm, ə-\ *n* [NL, fr. *Ytterby*, Sweden] : a metallic chemical element that occurs in several minerals — see ELEMENT table
yt·tri·um \'i-trē-əm\ *n* [NL, fr. *yttria* yttrium oxide, fr. *Ytterby*, Sweden] : a metallic chemical element usu. included among the rare-earth metals with which it occurs in minerals — see ELEMENT table
yu·an \'yü-ən, yu̇-'än\ *n, pl* **yuan** [Chin (Pek) *yüan*²] **1** : the basic monetary unit of China **2** : a coin or note representing one yuan
yuc·ca \'yək-ə\ *n* [NL, fr. Sp *yuca*] : any of a genus of plants of the lily family growing in dry regions and having stiff sharp-pointed fibrous leaves mostly in a rosette at the base and whitish flowers usu. in erect clusters
Yu·kon standard time \'yü-,kän-\ *n* : the time of the 9th time zone west of Greenwich that includes the Yukon Territory and part of southern Alaska
yule \'yül\ *n, often cap* [OE *geōl*] : the feast of the nativity of Jesus Christ : CHRISTMAS
yule log *n, often cap* Y : a large log formerly put on the hearth on Christmas Eve as the foundation of the fire
yule·tide \'yül-,tīd\ *n, often cap* : the Christmas season : CHRISTMASTIDE
yum·my \'yəm-ē\ *adj* [*yum-yum*, interj. expressing pleasure in the taste of food] : highly attractive or pleasing : DELECTABLE
yurt \'yu̇(ə)rt\ *n* [Russ *yurta*, of Turkic origin] : a light round tent of skins or felt stretched over a lattice framework used by various nomadic tribes in Siberia

z \'zē\ *n, often cap* : the 26th letter of the English alphabet
¹za·ny \'zā-nē\ *n, pl* **zanies** [It *zanni*, fr. It dial. *Zanni*, nickname for It *Giovanni* John] **1** : CLOWN, MERRY-ANDREW **2** : BUFFOON; *also* : SIMPLETON
²zany *adj* **za·ni·er; -est 1** : being or having the characteristics of a zany **2** : fantastically or irrationally ludicrous : CRAZY — **za·ni·ly** \'zān-ᵊl-ē\ *adv* — **za·ni·ness** \'zā-nē-nəs\ *n*
zeal \'zēl\ *n* [Gk *zēlos*] : eagerness and ardent interest in pursuit of something : FERVOR

syn ENTHUSIASM: ZEAL implies energetic and unflagging pursuit of an aim or devotion to a cause; ENTHUSIASM suggests lively or eager interest in or admiration for a proposal or cause or activity
zeal·ot \'zel-ət\ *n* [Gk *zēlōtēs*, fr. *zēlos* zeal] **1** *cap* : one of a fanatical sect of ancient Judea bitterly opposing the Roman domination of Palestine **2** : a zealous person; *esp* : a fanatical partisan — **zealot** *adj* — **zeal·ot·ry** \'zel-ə-trē\ *n*
zeal·ous \'zel-əs\ *adj* : filled with, characterized by, or due to zeal — **zeal·ous·ly** *adv* — **zeal·ous·ness** *n*
ze·bra \'zē-brə\ *n, pl* **zebras** *also* **zebra** [It, fr. Sp *cebra*] : any of several fleet African mammals related to the horse but distinctively and conspicuously patterned in stripes of black or dark brown and white or buff — **ze·brine** \-,brīn\ *adj* — **ze·broid** \-,brȯid\ *adj*

zebra

ze·bu \'zē-b(y)ü\ *n* [F *zébu*] : an Asiatic ox domesticated and differentiated into many breeds and distinguished from European cattle with which it crosses freely by a large fleshy hump over the shoulders and a loose skin prolonged into dewlap and folds
Zech·a·ri·ah \,zek-ə-'rī-ə\ *n* **1** : a Hebrew prophet of the 6th century B.C. **2** — see BIBLE table
zed \'zed\ *n* [MF *zede*, fr. LL *zeta* zeta, fr. Gk *zēta*] *chiefly Brit* : the letter z
ze·in \'zē-ən\ *n* [NL *Zea*, genus including Indian corn] : a protein from Indian corn used esp. in making textile fibers, plastics, and adhesives
zeit·geist \'tsīt-,gīst, 'zīt-\ *n* [G, lit., time spirit] : the general intellectual, moral, and cultural state of an era
zemst·vo \'zem(p)st-vō, -və\ *n, pl* **zemstvos** [Russ, fr. *zemlya* earth] : one of the district and provincial assemblies established in Russia in 1864
Zen \'zen\ *n* [Jap, religious meditation, fr. Chin (Pek) *ch'an*², fr. Pali *jhāna*, fr. Skt *dhyāna*, fr. *dhyāti* he thinks] : a Japanese Buddhist sect that teaches self-discipline, meditation, and attainment of enlightenment by direct intuition and characteristically expresses its teachings by means of paradoxical and nonlogical statements
ze·na·na \zə-'nän-ə\ *n* [Hindi *zanāna*] : HAREM, SERAGLIO
Zend-Aves·ta \,zen-də-'ves-tə\ *n* : AVESTA
ze·nith \'zē-nəth\ *n* [ML *cenith*, fr. Sp *zenit, cenit*, fr. Ar *samt ar-ra*'s, lit., way of the head] **1** : the point in the heavens directly overhead **2** : the highest point : APEX, SUMMIT ⟨the *zenith* of a hero's glory⟩
ze·nith·al \-əl\ *adj* : of, relating to, or located at or near the zenith
ze·o·lite \'zē-ə-,līt\ *n* [Sw *zeolit*, fr. Gk *zein* to boil] : any of various silicates chemically related to the feldspars that are used esp. in water softening — **ze·o·lit·ic** \,zē-ə-'lit-ik\ *adj*
Zeph·a·ni·ah \,zef-ə-'nī-ə\ *n* **1** : a Hebrew prophet of the 7th century B.C. **2** — see BIBLE table
zeph·yr \'zef-ər\ *n* [Gk *Zephyros*, god of the west wind, west wind] **1 a** : a breeze from the west **b** : a gentle breeze **2 a** : a fine soft wool yarn **b** : any of various lightweight fabrics and articles of clothing
Zeph·y·rus \'zef-ə-rəs\ *n* [L, fr. Gk *Zephyros*] : the west wind personified
zep·pe·lin \'zep-(ə-)lən\ *n* [Count Ferdinand von *Zeppelin* d1917 German airship manufacturer] : a rigid airship consisting of a cylindrical trussed and covered frame supported by internal gas cells
¹ze·ro \'zē-rō, 'zi(ə)r-ō\ *n, pl* **zeros** *also* **zeroes** [It, fr. ML *zephirum*, fr. Ar *ṣifr*] **1 a** : the numerical symbol 0 **b** : the number represented by the symbol 0 — see NUMBER table **2 a** : the point of departure in reckoning; *also* : the point from which the graduation of a scale (as of a thermometer) commences **b** : a value or reading of zero; *esp* : the temperature represented by the zero mark on a thermometer **3** : a person or thing having no importance or independent existence : NONENTITY **4 a** : a state of total absence or neutrality : NOTHING. **b** : the lowest point : NADIR

²zero *adj* **1 a :** of, relating to, or being a zero **b (1) :** not existing **:** LACKING ⟨a *zero* change in value⟩ **(2) :** having no modified inflectional form ⟨*zero* plural⟩ **2 a :** limiting vision to 50 feet or less ⟨*zero* cloud ceiling⟩ **b :** limited to 165 feet or less ⟨*zero* visibility⟩

³zero *vb* **1 :** to concentrate firepower (as of artillery) on the exact range of — usu. used with *in* **2 :** to adjust fire on a specific target — usu. used with *in*

zero hour *n* **1 :** the hour at which a previously planned military movement is scheduled to start **2 :** the moment at which an ordeal is to begin **:** the moment of crisis

zero–zero *adj* **:** characterized by or being atmospheric conditions that reduce ceiling and visibility to zero ⟨*zero-zero* weather⟩

zest \'zest\ *n* [F, orange or lemon peel used as flavoring] **1 :** a quality of enhancing enjoyment **:** PIQUANCY **2 :** keen enjoyment **:** RELISH, GUSTO — **zest·ful** \-fəl\ *adj* — **zest·ful·ly** \-fə-lē\ *adv* — **zest·ful·ness** *n* — **zesty** \'zes-tē\ *adj*

ze·ta \'zāt-ə, 'zēt-ə\ *n* **:** the 6th letter of the Greek alphabet — Z or ζ

Zeus \'züs\ *n* **:** the chief of the Olympian gods and husband of Hera

¹zig \'zig\ *n* **:** one of the sharp turns or changes or a straight section of a zigzag course

²zig *vi* **zigged; zig·ging :** to execute a turn or follow a section of a zigzag course

zig·gu·rat \'zig-ə-,rat\ *n* [Akkadian *ziqqurratu* pinnacle] **:** an ancient Mesopotamian temple tower consisting of a lofty pyramidal structure built in successive stages with outside staircases and a shrine at the top

¹zig·zag \'zig-,zag\ *n* [F] **1 :** a line or course made up of sharp opposite angles or turns at short and rather regular intervals; *also* **:** something (as a road or path) that takes such a course **2 :** one of the units making up a zigzag **:** a sharp angle or turn with the lines enclosing it ⟨the road followed a *zigzag* around the obstruction⟩

²zigzag *adv* **:** in or by a zigzag path or course

³zigzag *adj* **:** having short sharp turns or angles

⁴zigzag *vi* **zig·zagged; zig·zag·ging :** to lie in, proceed along, or consist of a zigzag course

zil·lion \'zil-yən\ *n* [z + -illion (as in *million*)] **:** a large indeterminate number

zinc \'ziŋk\ *n* [G *zink*] **:** a bluish white metallic chemical element that tarnishes only slightly in moist air at ordinary temperatures and is used esp. as a protective coating for iron — see ELEMENT table

zinc blende *n* **:** SPHALERITE

zinc chloride *n* **:** a poisonous caustic deliquescent salt ZnCl₂ used esp. in fireproofing and preserving wood

zinc·ic \'ziŋ-kik\ *adj* **:** relating to, containing, or resembling zinc

zinc·ite \'ziŋ-,kīt\ *n* **:** a brittle deep-red to orange-yellow mineral consisting of zinc oxide that occurs in massive or granular form

zinc ointment *n* **:** an ointment containing about 20 percent of zinc oxide and used in treating skin diseases

zinc oxide *n* **:** an infusible white solid ZnO used esp. as a pigment, in compounding rubber, and in pharmaceutical and cosmetic preparations

zinc sulfate *n* **:** a crystalline salt ZnSO₄ used esp. in making a white paint pigment and in printing and dyeing

zinc sulfide *n* **:** a fluorescent compound ZnS used as a white pigment and as the light-producing substance in fluorescent lamps and television tubes

zinc white *n* **:** a white pigment used esp. in house paints and glazes that consists of zinc oxide

zing \'ziŋ\ *n* **1 :** a shrill humming noise **2 :** VITALITY, VIM — **zing** *vi*

zinj·an·thro·pus \zin-'jan(t)-thrə-pəs, ,zin-,jan-'thrō-\ *n, pl* **-pi** \-,pī, -,pē\ *or* **-pus·es** [NL, genus name, fr. Ar *Zinj* eastern Africa + Gk *anthrōpos* human being] **:** any of a genus of fossil hominids based on a skull found in eastern Africa, characterized by very low brow and large molars, and tentatively assigned to the Lower Pleistocene

zin·nia \'zin-ē-ə, 'zin-yə, 'zēn-\ *n* [NL, fr. Johann G. *Zinn* d1759 German physician] **:** any of a small genus of tropical American herbs related to the daisies and having showy flower heads with long-lasting ray flowers

Zi·on \'zī-ən\ *n* [Zion, citadel in Palestine which was the nucleus of Jerusalem] **1 a :** the Jewish people **:** ISRAEL

b : the Jewish homeland as a symbol of Judaism or of Jewish national aspiration **c :** the ideal nation or society envisaged by Judaism **2 :** HEAVEN **3 :** UTOPIA

Zi·on·ism \'zī-ə-,niz-əm\ *n* **:** a theory, plan, or movement for setting up a Jewish national or religious community in Palestine — **Zi·on·ist** \-nəst\ *adj or n* — **Zi·on·is·tic** \,zī-ə-'nis-tik\ *adj*

¹zip \'zip\ *vb* **zipped; zip·ping 1 :** to move or act with speed and vigor **2 :** to travel with a sharp hissing or humming sound **3 :** to add zest, interest, or life to — often used with *up*

²zip *n* **1 :** a sudden sharp hissing or sibilant sound **2 :** ENERGY, VIM

³zip *vb* **zipped; zip·ping** [back-formation fr. *zipper*] **:** to close or open or attach by means of a zipper

zip gun *n* **:** a gun that is made from a toy pistol or a length of pipe, is usu. powered by a rubber band, and fires a .22 caliber bullet

zip·per \'zip-ər\ *n* **:** a fastener consisting of two rows of metal or plastic teeth on strips of tape and a sliding piece that closes an opening by drawing the teeth together

zip·pered \-ərd\ *adj* **:** equipped with a zipper

zip·py \'zip-ē\ *adj* **zip·pi·er; -est :** full of zip **:** BRISK, SNAPPY

zi·ram \'zī-,ram\ *n* **:** an organic zinc salt used esp. as a fungicide

zir·con \'zər-,kän\ *n* [G *zirkon*, modif. of F *jargon*, fr. It *giargone*] **1 :** a crystalline mineral which is a silicate of zirconium and of which several transparent varieties are used as gemstones **2 :** a gem cut from zircon

zir·co·nia \,zər-'kō-nē-ə\ *n* **:** ZIRCONIUM OXIDE

zir·con·ic \,zər-'kän-ik\ *adj* **:** of, relating to, or containing zirconium

zir·co·ni·um \,zər-'kō-nē-əm\ *n* [NL, fr. E *zircon*] **:** a steel-gray strong ductile metallic chemical element with a high melting point that is highly resistant to corrosion and is used in alloys and in refractories and ceramics — see ELEMENT table

zirconium oxide *n* **:** a white crystalline compound ZrO₂ used esp. in refractories, in thermal and electric insulation, in abrasives, and in enamels and glazes

zith·er \'zith-ər, 'zith-\ *n* [G, fr. L *cithara* lyre, fr. Gk *kithara*] **:** a many-stringed musical instrument played with the tips of the fingers and a plectrum — **zith·er·ist** \-ə-rəst\ *n*

zlo·ty \'zlót-ē, zə-'lót-\ *n, pl* **zlo·tys** \-ēz\ *also* **zloty** [Pol *złoty*] **1 :** the basic monetary unit of Poland **2 :** a coin representing one zloty

zo- *or* **zoo-** *comb form* [Gk *zōion*, fr. *zōē* life; akin to E *quick*] **:** animal **:** animal kingdom or kind ⟨*zoology*⟩ ⟨*zooid*⟩

zo·an·thar·i·an \,zō-,an-'thar-ē-ən, -'ther-\ *n* **:** any of a large group (Zoantharia) of coelenterates including most of the recent corals and sea anemones — **zoantharian** *adj*

zo·ar·i·um \zō-'ar-ē-əm, -'er-\ *n, pl* **zo·ar·ia** \-ē-ə\ **:** a colony of colonial bryozoans — **zo·ar·i·al** \-ē-əl\ *adj*

zo·di·ac \'zōd-ē-,ak\ *n* [Gk *zōidiakos*, fr. *zōidion* carved figure, sign of the zodiac, fr. dim. of *zōion* animal, figure] **1 :** an imaginary belt in the heavens that encompasses the apparent paths of all the principal planets except Pluto, that has as its central line the apparent path of the sun, and that is divided into 12 constellations or signs each taken for astrological purposes to extend 30 degrees of longitude **2 :** a figure representing the signs of the zodiac and their symbols — **zo·di·a·cal** \zō-'dī-ə-kəl\ *adj*

THE SIGNS OF THE ZODIAC

NUMBER	NAME	SYMBOL	SUN ENTERS
1	Aries the Ram	♈	March 21
2	Taurus the Bull	♉	April 20
3	Gemini the Twins	♊	May 21
4	Cancer the Crab	♋	June 22
5	Leo the Lion	♌	July 23
6	Virgo the Virgin	♍	August 23
7	Libra the Balance	♎	September 23
8	Scorpio the Scorpion	♏	October 24
9	Sagittarius the Archer	♐	November 22
10	Capricorn the Goat	♑	December 22
11	Aquarius the Water Bearer	♒	January 20
12	Pisces the Fishes	♓	February 19

zo·ea \zō-'ē-ə\ *n, pl* **zo·eae** \-'ē-,ē\ *or* **zo·eas** \-'ē-əz\ : an early larval form of many decapod crustaceans and esp. crabs — **zo·e·al** \zō-'ē-əl\ *adj*

-zo·ic \'zō-ik\ *adj comb form* [Gk *zōē* life] : of, relating to, or being a (specified) geological era ⟨Archeo*zoic*⟩

zom·bi *or* **zom·bie** \'zäm-bē\ *n* [of African origin] : a will-less and speechless human in the West Indies capable only of automatic movement who is held to have died and been reanimated but often believed to have been drugged into catalepsy for the hours of interment

zon·al \'zōn-°l\ *adj* **1** : of, relating to, or having the form of a zone **2** : of, relating to, or being a soil or major soil group marked by well-developed characteristics that are determined primarily by the action of climate and organisms esp. vegetation — compare AZONAL, INTRAZONAL

zon·ate \'zō-,nāt\ *also* **zon·at·ed** \-,nāt-əd\ *adj* : marked with or arranged in zones — **zo·na·tion** \zō-'nā-shən\ *n*

¹zone \'zōn\ *n* [Gk *zōnē*, lit., belt, girdle] **1** : any of five great divisions of the earth's surface with respect to latitude and temperature — compare FRIGID ZONE, TEMPERATE ZONE, TORRID ZONE **2** *archaic* : GIRDLE, BELT **3 a** : an encircling anatomical structure **b** : a distinctive belt, layer, or series of layers of earth materials (as rock) **4** : a region or area set off as distinct from surrounding or adjoining parts or created for a particular purpose: as **a** : a zoned section (as of a city) **b** : any of the eight concentric bands

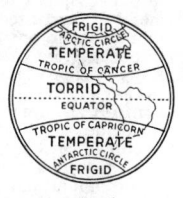

zones 1

of territory centered on a given U.S. parcel-post shipment point to which mail is charged at a single rate

²zone *vt* **1** : to surround with a zone : ENCIRCLE **2** : to arrange in or mark off into zones; *esp* : to divide (as a city) into sections reserved for different purposes

zoo \'zü\ *n, pl* **zoos** [short for *zoological garden*] : a zoological garden or collection of living animals

zoo·flag·el·late \,zō-ə-'flaj-ə-lət, -flə-'jel-ət\ *n* : a flagellate protozoan lacking plantlike characteristics (as photosynthesis) — compare PLANTLIKE FLAGELLATE

zoo·ge·og·ra·phy \-jē-'äg-rə-fē\ *n* : a branch of biogeography concerned with the geographical distribution of animals — **zoo·ge·og·ra·pher** \-fər\ *n* — **zoo·geo·graph·ic** \-,jē-ə-'graf-ik\ *or* **zoo·geo·graph·i·cal** \-'graf-i-kəl\ *adj* — **zoo·geo·graph·i·cal·ly** \-i-k(ə-)lē\ *adv*

zo·oid \'zō-,ȯid\ *n* : an entity (as a phagocyte) that resembles (as in independent motility) but is not wholly the same as a separate individual organism; *esp* : a more or less independent animal (as a polyp of a colonial coral) produced by other than direct sexual methods — **zo·oi·dal** \zō-'ȯid-°l\ *adj*

zo·o·log·i·cal \,zō-ə-'läj-i-kəl\ *adj* **1** : of, relating to, or occupied with zoology **2** : of, relating to, or affecting lower animals often as distinguished from man ⟨*zoological* infections⟩ — **zo·o·log·i·cal·ly** \-i-k(ə-)lē\ *adv*

zoological garden *n* : a garden or park where wild animals are kept for exhibition

zo·ol·o·gy \zō-'äl-ə-jē\ *n* **1** : a science that deals with animals and is the branch of biology concerned with the animal kingdom and animal life **2 a** : animal life : FAUNA **b** : the properties of vital phenomena exhibited by an animal, animal type, or group — **zo·ol·o·gist** \-jəst\ *n*

¹zoom \'züm\ *vb* **1** : to move with a loud low hum or buzz **2** : to climb for a short time at an angle greater than that which can be maintained in steady flight ⟨the airplane *zoomed* and vanished in the distance⟩ **3** : to move toward or away from an object being photographed or televised so that the image appears to come closer to or move away from an observer ⟨the camera *zoomed* closer and closer⟩ **4** : to cause to zoom

²zoom *n* **1** : an act or process of zooming **2** : a zooming sound

zoom lens *n* : a camera lens in which the image size can be varied continuously so that the image remains in focus at all times

zoo·mor·phic \,zō-ə-'mȯr-fik\ *adj* **1** : having the form of an animal **2** : of, relating to, or being a deity conceived of in animal form or with the attributes of an animal — **zoo·mor·phism** \-,fiz-əm\ *n*

zoo·par·a·site \'zō-ə-'par-ə-,sīt\ *n* : a parasitic animal — **zoo·par·a·sit·ic** \-,par-ə-'sit-ik\ *adj*

zoo·phyte \'zō-ə-,fīt\ *n* : any of numerous invertebrate animals (as a coral, sea anemone, or sponge) suggesting plants in appearance or mode of growth — **zoo·phyt·ic** \,zō-ə-'fit-ik\ *adj*

zoo·plank·ton \,zō-ə-'plaŋ(k)-tən, -,tän\ *n* : animal life of the plankton — **zoo·plank·ton·ic** \-,plaŋ(k)-'tän-ik\ *adj*

zoo·spore \'zō-ə-,spȯr, -,spȯr\ *n* : an independently motile spore; *esp* : a flagellated asexual spore of an alga or lower fungus

zoot suit \'züt-,süt\ *n* : a flashy suit of extreme cut typically consisting of a thigh-length jacket with wide padded shoulders and peg-top trousers tapering to narrow cuffs — **zoot-suit·er** \-ər\ *n*

Zo·ro·as·tri·an \,zōr-ə-'was-trē-ən, ,zȯr-\ *adj* : of or relating to the Persian prophet Zoroaster or the religion founded by him and marked by belief in a cosmic war between good and evil — **Zoroastrian** *n* — **Zo·ro·as·tri·an·ism** \-trē-ə-,niz-əm\ *n*

Zou·ave \zü-'äv\ *n* [F, fr. Berber *Zwāwa*, an Algerian tribe] **1** : a member of a French infantry unit orig. composed of Algerians wearing a brilliant uniform and conducting a quick spirited drill **2** : a member of a military unit modeled on the Algerian Zouaves

zounds \'zaün(d)z\ *interj* [euphemism for *God's wounds*] — used as a mild oath

zoy·sia \'zȯi-sē-ə\ *n* : any of a genus of creeping perennial grasses having fine wiry leaves and including some used as lawn grasses

ZPG *abbr* zero population growth

zuc·chet·to \zü-'ket-ō\ *n, pl* **-tos** [It, fr. *zucca* gourd, head, fr. LL *cucutia* gourd] : a small round skullcap worn by Roman Catholic ecclesiastics in colors that vary according to the rank of the wearer

zuc·chi·ni \zü-'kē-nē\ *n, pl* **-ni** *or* **-nis** [It, pl. of *zucchino*, dim. of *zucca* gourd] : a summer squash of bushy growth with smooth slender cylindrical dark green fruits

Zu·lu \'zü-lü\ *n* **1** : a member of a Bantu-speaking people of Natal **2** : a Bantu language of the Zulus — **Zulu** *adj*

zwie·back \'swē-,bak, 'swī-\ *n* [G, lit., twice baked] : a usu. sweetened bread enriched with eggs that is baked and then sliced and toasted until dry and crisp

Zwing·li·an \'zwiŋ-(g)lē-ən, 'swin-\ *adj* : of or relating to Ulrich Zwingli or his doctrine that in the Lord's Supper there is an influence of Christ upon the soul but that the true body of Christ is present by the contemplation of faith and not in essence or reality — **Zwinglian** *n*

zyg- *or* **zygo-** *comb form* [Gk *zygon*; akin to E *yoke*] **1** : yoke ⟨*zygo*morphic⟩ **2** : concerned with or produced in sexual reproduction ⟨*zygo*spore⟩

zy·go·dac·tyl \,zī-gə-'dak-t°l\ *or* **zy·go·dac·ty·lous** \-tə-ləs\ *adj* : having the toes arranged two in front and two behind — used of a bird — **zygodactyl** *n*

zy·go·mat·ic \,zī-gə-'mat-ik\ *adj* [Gk *zygōmat-, zygōma* zygomatic arch, fr. *zygoun* to yoke] : of, relating to, being, or situated in the region of the arched bony support of the part of the cheek below and to the side of the orbit

zy·go·mor·phic \-'mȯr-fik\ *adj* : bilaterally symmetrical in respect to but one axis

zy·go·spore \'zī-gə-,spȯr, -,spȯr\ *n* : a plant spore that is formed by conjugation of two similar sexual cells, usu. serves as a resting spore, and ultimately produces the sporophytic phase of the plant — compare OOSPORE

zy·gote \'zī-,gōt\ *n* [Gk *zygōtos* yoked, fr. *zygoun* to yoke, fr. *zygon* yoke] : a cell formed by the union of two gametes; *also* : the developing individual produced from such a cell — **zy·got·ic** \zī-'gät-ik\ *adj* — **zy·got·i·cal·ly** \-'gät-i-k(ə-)lē\ *adv*

-zy·gous \'zī-gəs, zī-gəs\ *adj comb form* : having (such) a zygotic constitution ⟨hetero*zygous*⟩

zym- *or* **zymo-** *comb form* [Gk *zymē* leaven] **1** : fermentation ⟨*zymase*⟩ **2** : enzyme ⟨*zymogen*⟩

zy·mase \'zī-,mās\ *n* : an enzyme or enzyme complex that promotes fermentation of simple sugars

zy·mo·gen \'zī-mə-jən\ *n* : an inactive precursor of an enzyme as secreted by glandular cells and requiring activation (as by an acid) before it can function — **zy·mo·gen·ic** \,zī-mə-'jen-ik\ *adj*

ə abut; ᵊ kitten; ər further; a back; ā bake; ä cot, cart; aú out; ch chin; e less; ē easy; g gift; i trip; ī life
j joke; ŋ sing; ō flow; ȯ flaw; ȯi coin; th thin; th this; ü loot; u̇ foot; y yet; yü few; yu̇ furious; zh vision

For a list of special abbreviations used in this dictionary see page 9a preceding the vocabulary. Most of these abbreviations have been normalized to one form. Variation in use of periods, in typeface, and in capitalization is frequent and widespread (as *mph, MPH, m.p.h., Mph*)

a acre, alto, answer, are
A ace, argon
Å angstrom
AA Alcoholics Anonymous, associate in arts
A and M agricultural and mechanical
AAR against all risks
AB able-bodied seaman, bachelor of arts
abbr abbreviation
abl ablative
abp archbishop
abs absolute
abstr abstract
ac account
Ac actinium
AC alternating current, ante Christum (L, before Christ)
acad academic, academy
acc, accus accusative
acct account
ack acknowledge, acknowledgment
act active, actual
ACT Australian Capital Territory
actg acting
ACTH adrenocorticotropic hormone
AD after date, anno Domini
ADC aide-de-camp
addn addition
ad int ad interim
adj adjective, adjutant
ad loc ad locum (L, to or at the place)
adm admiral
admin administration
ADP adenosine diphosphate
adv adverb, adverbial, advertisement
ad val ad valorem
advt advertisement
AEF American Expeditionary Force
aet, aetat aetatis (L, of age)
AF air force, audio frequency
AFB air force base
afft affidavit
AFL–CIO American Federation of Labor and Congress of Industrial Organizations
Afr Africa, African
Ag argentum (L, silver)
agcy agency
agric agricultural, agriculture
agt agent
AK Alaska
Al aluminum
AL, Ala Alabama
Alb Albanian
alc alcohol
ald alderman
alg algebra

alk alkaline
alt alternate, altitude
Alta Alberta
a.m. ante meridiem
Am America, American, americium
AM amplitude modulation, master of arts
amb ambassador
amdt amendment
Amer America, American
amp ampere
amt amount
AMU atomic mass unit
anal analogy, analysis, analytic
anat anatomy
anc ancient
ann annals, annual
anon anonymous
ans answer
ant antonym
anthrop anthropology
a/o account of
ap apothecaries'
AP additional premium, Associated Press
APO army post office
app apparatus, appendix
appl applied
approx approximate, approximately
Apr April
apt apartment
aq aqua, aqueous
ar arrival, arrive
Ar argon
AR Arkansas
Arab Arabian, Arabic
arch, archit architecture
archeol archeology
arith arithmetic
Ariz Arizona
Ark Arkansas
arr arranged, arrival, arrive
art article
As arsenic
AS Anglo-Saxon
assn association
assoc associate, association
asst assistant
astrol astrology
astron astronomer, astronomy
ASV American Standard Version
At astatine
Atl Atlantic
atm atmosphere, atmospheric
at no atomic number
ATP adenosine triphosphate
att attached, attention, attorney
attn attention
attrib attributive, attributively
atty attorney

at wt atomic weight
Au aurum (L, gold)
ÅU angstrom unit
Aug August
AUS Army of the United States
Austral Australian
auth authentic, author, authorized
aux auxiliary
av avenue, average, avoirdupois
AV audiovisual, Authorized Version
avdp avoirdupois
ave avenue
avg average
avn aviation
AZ Arizona

b bass, book, born
B bachelor, bishop, boron
Ba barium
BA bachelor of arts
bal balance
Bart baronet
BBC British Broadcasting Corporation
bbl barrel
BC before Christ, British Columbia
BCS bachelor of commercial science
bd board, bound
BD bachelor of divinity, bills discounted, brought down
bd ft board foot
bdl bundle
Be beryllium
BE bill of exchange
BEF British Expeditionary Force
Belg Belgian, Belgium
bet between
BeV billion electron volts
bf boldface
BF brought forward
bg bag
Bi bismuth
bib Bible, biblical
bibliog bibliographer, bibliography
BID bis in die (L, twice a day)
biog biographical, biography
biol biologic, biological, biology
bk bank, book
Bk berkelium
bkt basket
bl bale
B/L bill of lading
bldg building
blvd boulevard
BM board measure
BMR basal metabolic rate
BO body odor, box office,

branch office, buyer's option
BOD biochemical oxygen demand
BOQ bachelor officers' quarters
bor borough
bot botanical, botany
bp bishop, boiling point
BP bills payable
bpl birthplace
br branch
Br British, bromine
BR bills receivable
brig brigade, brigadier
Brit Britain, British
bro brother
bros brothers
BS bachelor of science, balance sheet, bill of sale
BSA Boy Scouts of America
BSc bachelor of science
bskt basket
Bt baronet
Btu British thermal unit
bu bushel
bull bulletin
bur bureau
bus business
BV Blessed Virgin
BWI British West Indies
bx box

c cape, carat, cent, centimeter, century, chapter, circa, copyright, cup
C carbon, centigrade
ca centare, circa
Ca calcium
CA California, chartered accountant, chief accountant, chronological age
CAF, C and F cost and freight
cal calendar, caliber, calorie
Cal large calorie
Calif, Cal California
Can, Canad Canada, Canadian
canc canceled
cap capacity, capital, capitalize, capitalized
caps capitals, capsule
capt captain
card cardinal
CARE Cooperative for American Relief to Everywhere
cat catalog
Cb columbium
CBC Canadian Broadcasting Corporation
CBD cash before delivery
cc cubic centimeter
CC carbon copy, common carrier
cd cord
Cd cadmium

1043

CD carried down
cdr commander
Ce cerium
CE chemical engineer, civil engineer
cen central
cent centigrade, central, centum, century
cert certificate, certification, certified, certify
cf confer (L, compare)
Cf californium
CF carried forward
CFI cost, freight, and insurance
cg, cgm centigram
CG coast guard
cgs centimeter-gram-second
ch chain, chapter, church
CH clearinghouse, courthouse, customhouse
chap chapter
chem chemical, chemist, chemistry
chg change, charge
Chin Chinese
chm, chmn chairman
chron chronicle, chronological, chronology
CI cost and insurance
CIF cost, insurance, and freight
C in C commander in chief
cir, circ circular
cit citation, cited, citizen
civ civil, civilian
ck cask, check
cl centiliter, class
Cl chlorine
CL carload
clk clerk
clo clothing
cm centimeter
Cm curium
CM Congregation of the Mission
cml commercial
CN credit note
CNO chief of naval operations
CNS central nervous system
co company, county
c/o care of
Co cobalt, coenzyme
CO cash order, Colorado, commanding officer, conscientious objector
COD cash on delivery, collect on delivery
C of C Chamber of Commerce
C of S chief of staff
cog cognate
col colonel, column
coll college
collat collateral
colloq colloquial
Colo Colorado
colog cologarithm
com commander, commerce, commissioner, committee, common
comb combination, combining
comdg commanding
comdr commander
comdt commandant
coml commercial
comm commission, commonwealth
comp comparative, com-

piled, compiler, composition, compound
comr commissioner
con consul
conc concentrated
cond conductivity
conf conference
Confed Confederate
cong congress
conj conjunction
Conn Connecticut
cons consonant
consol consolidated
const constant, constitution, constitutional
constr construction
cont containing, contents, continent, continental, continued, control
contd continued
contg containing
contr contract, contraction
contrib contribution, contributor
corp corporal, corporation
corr corrected, correction, correspondence, corresponding
cos companies, cosine, counties
COS cash on shipment, chief of staff
cosec cosecant
cot cotangent
cp compare, coupon
CP candlepower, chemically pure, communist party
CPA certified public accountant
cpd compound
cpl corporal
CPO chief petty officer
CPS cycles per second
CQ charge of quarters
cr credit, creditor, crown
Cr chromium
cresc crescendo
crit critical, criticism
cryst crystalline
cs case, cases
c/s cycles per second
Cs cesium
CS chief of staff, civil service
CSA Confederate States of America
csc cosecant
CSF cerebrospinal fluid
CSsR Congregatio Sanctissimi Redemptoris (L, Congregation of the Most Holy Redeemer)
CST Central standard time
ct carat, cent, count, court
CT Central time, Connecticut
ctn carton, cotangent
ctr center
cu cubic
Cu cuprum (L, copper)
cur currency, current
CV cardiovascular
CW continuous wave
CWO cash with order, chief warrant officer
cwt hundredweight
cyc, cycl cyclopedia
cyl cylinder
CZ Canal Zone

d date, daughter, day, degree, density, died, penny

D Democrat, Democratic, deuterium, diameter, doctor, dollar
DA days after acceptance, deposit account, district attorney
Dan Danish
DAR Daughters of the American Revolution
dat dative
db debenture, decibel
DBH diameter at breast height
dbl double
DC da capo, direct current, District of Columbia, double crochet
DD days after date, demand draft, doctor of divinity
DDS doctor of dental science, doctor of dental surgery
DE Delaware
deb debenture
dec decrease
Dec December
def definite, definition
deg degree
del delegate, delegation
Del Delaware
dely delivery
Dem Democrat, Democratic
Den Denmark
dent dental, dentistry
dep depart, departure, deposit, deputy
dept department
deriv derivation, derivative
det detached, detachment, detail
DEW distant early warning
DF damage free
DFC distinguished flying cross
DFM distinguished flying medal
dg decigram
DG Dei gratia (LL, by the grace of God), director general
dia, diam diameter
diag diagonal, diagram
dial dialect
dict dictionary
diff difference
dig digest
dil dilute
dim dimension, diminished, diminuendo, diminutive
dir director
disc discount
dist distance, district
distn distillation
distr distribute, distribution
div divided, dividend, division
dk dark
dkg dekagram
dkl dekaliter
dkm dekameter
dks dekastere
dl deciliter
DLitt, DLit doctor of letters, doctor of literature
DLO dead letter office
dm decimeter
dn down
do ditto
DOA dead on arrival
doc document
dol dollar

dom domestic, dominion
doz dozen
dpt department
dr debit, debtor, dram, drive
Dr doctor
ds decistere
DS dal segno, days after sight
DSC distinguished service cross
DSM distinguished service medal
DSO distinguished service order
dsp decessit sine prole (L, died without issue)
DST daylight saving time
Du Dutch
dup, dupl duplicate
DV Deo volente (L, God willing), Douay Version
DVM doctor of veterinary medicine
dwt pennyweight
DX distance
Dy dysprosium
dz dozen

E east, eastern, einsteinium, English, excellent
ea each
E and OE errors and omissions excepted
EB eastbound
eccl ecclesiastic, ecclesiastical
ECG electrocardiogram
ecol ecological, ecology
econ economics, economist, economy
Ecua Ecuador
ed edited, edition, editor, education
ED extra duty
EDT Eastern daylight time
educ education, educational
EEG electroencephalogram
e.g. exempli gratia (L, for example)
Eg Egypt, Egyptian
ehf extremely high frequency
el, elev elevation
elec electric, electrical, electricity
elem elementary
embryol embryology
emer emeritus
EMF electromotive force
emp emperor, empress
emu electromagnetic unit
enc, encl enclosure
ency, encyc encyclopedia
eng engine, engineer, engineering
Eng England, English
engr engineer, engraved, engraving
enl enlarged, enlisted
ens ensign
entom, entomol entomology
env envelope
EOM end of month
EP extended play
eq equation
equip equipment
equiv equivalent
Er erbium
Es einsteinium
esp especially
ESP extrasensory perception

esq esquire
est established, estimate, estimated
EST Eastern standard time
esu electrostatic unit
ET Eastern time
ETA estimated time of arrival
et al et alii (L, and others)
etc et cetera
ETD estimated time of departure
ethnol ethnology
et seq et sequens (L, and the following one), et sequentes *or* et sequentia (L, and those that follow)
Eu europium
Eur Europe, European
EV electron volt
evap evaporate
ex example, express, extra
exc excellent, except
exch exchange, exchanged
ex div without dividend
exec executive
exp expense, export, exported, express
expt experiment
exptl experimental
ext extension, exterior, external, extra, extract

f farad, female, feminine, focal length, folio, following, forte, frequency
F Fahrenheit, fair, fellow, filial generation, fluorine, French
fac facsimile, faculty
FAdm fleet admiral
Fahr Fahrenheit
FAO Food and Agricultural Organization of the United Nations
FAS free alongside ship
fath fathom
FB freight bill
FBI Federal Bureau of Investigation
fcp foolscap
fcy fancy
FDIC Federal Deposit Insurance Corporation
Fe ferrum (L, iron)
Feb February
fed federal, federation
fem feminine
FEPC Fair Employment Practices Commission
ff folios, following, fortissimo
FICA Federal Insurance Contributions Act
FIFO first in, first out
fig figurative, figuratively, figure
Finn Finnish
fl flourished, fluid
FL, Fla Florida
fl dr fluidram
Flem Flemish
fl oz fluidounce
fm fathom
Fm fermium
FM frequency modulation
fn footnote
fo, fol folio
FOB free on board
FOC free of charge

for foreign, forestry
FOR free on rail
FOS free on steamer
FOT free on truck
fp freezing point
fpm feet per minute
FPO fleet post office
fps feet per second, foot-pound-second
fr father, friar, from
Fr francium, French
freq frequent, frequentative, frequently
Fri Friday
front frontispiece
FRS Federal Reserve System
frt freight
frwy freeway
FSH follicle-stimulating hormone
ft feet, foot, fort
ft lb foot-pound
fur furlong
fut future
fwd forward
FYI for your information

g acceleration of gravity, gauge, gram, gravity
G German, good
ga gauge
Ga gallium, Georgia
GA general agent, general assembly, general average, Georgia
gal gallon
galv galvanized
gar garage
GAW guaranteed annual wage
gaz gazette, gazetteer
GB Great Britain
GCA ground-controlled approach
Gd gadolinium
gds goods
Ge germanium
gen general, genitive
genl general
geog geographic, geographical, geography
geol geologic, geological, geology
geom geometrical, geometry
ger gerund
Ger German, Germany
GHQ general headquarters
gi gill
GI gastrointestinal, general issue, government issue
Gk Greek
gm gram
GM general manager, grand master
GMT Greenwich mean time
GNP gross national product
GOP Grand Old Party (Republican)
Goth Gothic
gov governor
govt government
gp group
GP general practitioner
GPO general post office, Government Printing Office
GQ general quarters
gr grade, grain, gram, gravity, gross
grad graduate

gram grammar
gro gross
GSA Girl Scouts of America
gt great
Gt Brit Great Britain
GU genitourinary, Guam

h hard, hardness, henry, hour, husband
H hydrogen
ha hectare
handbk, hdbk handbook
Hb hemoglobin
HBM Her Britannic Majesty, His Britannic Majesty
HC House of Commons
HCF highest common factor
hd head
HD heavy-duty
hdkf handkerchief
hdwe hardware
He helium
HE high explosive, His Eminence, His Excellency
Heb Hebrew
hf half, high frequency
Hf hafnium
hg hectogram
Hg hydrargyrum (L, mercury)
hgt height
HH Her Highness, His Highness, His Holiness
hhd hogshead
HI Hawaii
hist historian, historical, history
hl hectoliter
HL House of Lords
hm hectometer
HM Her Majesty, His Majesty
HMS Her Majesty's Ship, His Majesty's Ship
Ho holmium
hon honorable, honorary
hor horizontal
hort horticultural, horticulture
hosp hospital
hp horsepower
HP high pressure
HQ headquarters
hr hour
HR House of Representatives
HRH Her Royal Highness, His Royal Highness
HS high school
ht height
HT high-tension
Hung Hungarian, Hungary
hwy highway
hy henry
hyp hypothesis, hypothetical

I iodine, island, isle
Ia, IA Iowa
ib, ibid ibidem
ICBM intercontinental ballistic missile
ICC Interstate Commerce Commission
ICJ International Court of Justice
id idem
ID Idaho, identification
i.e. id est (L, that is)
IF intermediate frequency
IGY International Geo-

physical Year
IL Illinois
ill, illus, illust illustrated, illustration
Ill Illinois
ILS instrument landing system
imit imitative
imp imperative, imperfect, imperial, import, imported
imperf imperfect
in inch
In indium
IN Indiana
inc incorporated, increase
incl including, inclusive
incog incognito
ind independent, index, industrial, industry
Ind Indiana
indef indefinite
indic indicative
infl influenced
INP International News Photo
INRI Iesus Nazarenus Rex Iudaeorum (L, Jesus of Nazareth, King of the Jews)
ins inches, insurance
insol insoluble
inst instant, institute, institution
instr instructor, instrument
int interest, interior, internal, international
interj interjection
interrog interrogative
intl international
intrans intransitive
introd introduction
inv invoice
IPA International Phonetic Alphabet
iq idem quod (L, the same as)
IQ intelligence quotient
Ir iridium, Irish
IRBM intermediate range ballistic missile
Ire Ireland
irreg irregular
is island
Isr Israel, Israeli
ISV International Scientific Vocabulary
It, Ital Italian
ital italic, italicized
IU international unit
IW Isle of Wight
IWW Industrial Workers of the World

J jack, joule
Jam Jamaica
Jan January
Jap Japan, Japanese
JCC Junior Chamber of Commerce
JCS joint chiefs of staff
jct junction
Je June
jg junior grade
jnt, jt joint
jour journal
JP jet propulsion, justice of the peace
jr, jun junior
JRC Junior Red Cross
junc junction
juv juvenile
JV junior varsity

k karat, knit
K kalium (L, potassium), Kelvin, king
Kans Kansas
kc kilocycle
KC King's Counsel
kcal kilocalorie
kc/s kilocycles per second
KD knocked down
kg, kgm kilogram
KG knight of the Garter
KKK Ku Klux Klan
kl kiloliter
km kilometer
KP kitchen police
Kr krypton
KS Kansas
kt karat, knight
kv kilovolt
kw kilowatt
kwh, kwhr kilowatt hour
Ky, KY Kentucky

l left, length, line, liter
L lake, large, Latin, libra (L, pound)
La lanthanum, Louisiana
LA law agent, Los Angeles, Louisiana
Lab Labrador
lang language
lat latitude
Lat Latin
lb pound
lc lowercase
LC letter of credit, Library of Congress
LCD lowest common denominator
LCL less-than-carload lot
LCM least common multiple
ld load, lord
LD lethal dose
ldg landing, loading
lect lecture
leg legal, legislative, legislature
legis legislative, legislature
lf lightface, low frequency
lg large
LH left hand, luteinizing hormone
li link
Li lithium
LI Long Island
lib liberal, librarian, library
lieut lieutenant
LIFO last in, first out
lin lineal, linear
liq liquid, liquor
lit liter, literal, literally, literary, literature
lith, litho lithography
LittD, LitD doctor of letters, doctor of literature
ll lines
LL Late Latin
LLD doctor of laws
loc cit loco citato (L, in the place cited)
log logarithm
Lond London
long longitude
loq loquitur·(L, he speaks, she speaks)
LP low pressure
LS left side, letter signed, locus sigilli (L, place of the seal)
lt lieutenant, light
LT long ton, low-tension

ltd limited
LTL less-than-truckload lot
ltr letter
Lu lutetium
lub lubricant, lubricating
lv leave

m male, married, masculine, meridian, meridies (L, noon), meter, mile, mill, minim, minute, month, moon
M mach, master, medium, mille (L, thousand), monsieur
ma milliampere
MA Massachusetts, master of arts, mental age
mach machine, machinery, machinist
mag magazine, magnetism, magneto, magnitude
maj major
man manual
Man Manitoba
manuf manufacture, manufacturing
mar maritime
Mar March
masc masculine
Mass Massachusetts
math mathematical, mathematician, mathematics
max maximum
mb millibar
mc megacycle
MC master of ceremonies
Md Maryland, mendelevium
MD doctor of medicine, Maryland, months after date
mdse merchandise
Me Maine
ME Maine, mechanical engineer, Middle English
meas measure
mech mechanical, mechanics
med medical, medicine, medieval, medium
meg megohm
mem member, memoir, memorial
mer meridian
met metropolitan
meteorol meteorology
MEV million electron volts
Mex Mexican, Mexico
mf medium frequency, mezzo forte, microfarad
mfd manufactured, microfarad
mfg manufacturing
mfr manufacture, manufacturer
mg milligram
Mg magnesium
mgr manager, monseigneur, monsignor
mgt management
mi mile, mill
MI, Mich Michigan
mid middle
mil military
min minim, minimum, mining, minor, minute
Minn Minnesota
misc miscellaneous
Miss Mississippi
mixt mixture
mk mark
mks meter-kilogram-second

ml milliliter
MLD minimum lethal dose
Mlle mademoiselle
mm millimeter
MM Maryknoll Missioners, messieurs
Mme madame
Mn manganese
MN Minnesota
mo month
Mo Missouri, molybdenum
MO mail order, medical officer, Missouri, money order
mod moderate, modern
modif modification
mol molecular, molecule
mol wt molecular weight
MOM middle of month
Mon Monday
Mont Montana
mos months
mp melting point
MP member of parliament, metropolitan police, military police, military policeman
mpg miles per gallon
mph miles per hour
MS manuscript, master of science, Mississippi, motor ship
msec millisecond
msgr monseigneur, monsignor
MSgt master sergeant
MSS manuscripts
MST Mountain standard time
mt mount, mountain
MT metric ton, Montana, Mountain time
mtg, mtge mortgage
mtn mountain
mun, munic municipal
mus museum, music
mv millivolt
Mv mendelevium
mym myriameter
mythol mythology

n net, neuter, new, noon, note, noun, number
N knight, nitrogen, normal, north, northern
Na natrium (L, sodium)
NA no account
NAS naval air station
nat national, native, natural
natl national
NATO North Atlantic Treaty Organization
naut nautical
nav naval, navigable, navigation
Nb niobium
NB Nebraska, New Brunswick, northbound, nota bene
NBS National Bureau of Standards
NC no charge, North Carolina
NCE New Catholic Edition
NCO noncommissioned officer
Nd neodymium
ND no date, North Dakota
N Dak North Dakota
Ne neon
NE New England, northeast

NEB New English Bible
Nebr, Neb Nebraska
NED New English Dictionary
neg negative
Neth Netherlands
neurol neurology
neut neuter
Nev Nevada
NF no funds
Nfld Newfoundland
NG national guard, no good
NH New Hampshire
Ni nickel
NJ New Jersey
NL New Latin, night letter
NM, N Mex New Mexico
no north, number
No nobelium
nol pros nolle prosequi (L, to be unwilling to prosecute)
nom nominative
non seq non sequitur
Norw Norway, Norwegian
NOS not otherwise specified
Nov November
Np neptunium
NP no protest, notary public
NPN nonprotein nitrogen
NS New Style, not specified, Nova Scotia
NSF not sufficient funds
NSW New South Wales
NT New Testament
NT Northern Territory
NTP normal temperature and pressure
nt wt net weight
numis numismatic, numismatics
NV Nevada
NW northwest
NWT Northwest Territories
NY New York
NYC New York City
NZ New Zealand

o ocean, ohm
O Ohio, oxygen
o/a on account
OAS Organization of American States
ob obiit (L, he died, she died)
obj object, objective
obl oblique, oblong
obs obsolete
obv obverse
OC overcharge
occas occasionally
OCS officer candidate school
oct octavo
Oct October
o/d on demand
OD officer of the day, olive drab, overdraft, overdrawn
OE Old English
OED Oxford English Dictionary
off office, officer, official
OFM Order of Friars Minor
OG original gum
OH Ohio
OK, Okla Oklahoma
Ont Ontario
op opus (L, work), out of print
OP Order of Preachers
op cit opere citato (L, in the work cited)

opp opposite
opt optical, optician, optional
OR Oregon, owner's risk
orch orchestra
ord order, ordnance
Oreg, Ore Oregon
org organization, organized
orig original, originally
ornith ornithology
o/s out of stock
Os osmium
OS Old Style, ordinary seaman
OS and D over, short, and damaged
OSB Order of St. Benedict
OT Old Testament, overtime
OTS officers' training school
oz ounce

p page, participle, past, penny, per, piano, pint, purl
P parental generation, pawn, phosphorus, pressure
pa per annum
Pa Pennsylvania, protactinium
PA passenger agent, Pennsylvania, power of attorney, press agent, private account, public address, purchasing agent
Pac Pacific
paleon paleontology
pam pamphlet
Pan Panama
P and L profit and loss
par paragraph, parallel, parish
part participial, participle, particular
pass passenger, passive
pat patent
path, pathol pathology
payt payment
Pb plumbum (L, lead)
pc percent, piece, postcard
PC petty cash, privy council, privy councillor
pd paid
Pd palladium
PD per diem (L, by the day), potential difference
PEI Prince Edward Island
penin peninsula
Penn, Penna Pennsylvania
per period
perf perfect, perforated
perh perhaps
perm permanent
perp perpendicular
pers person, personal
Pers Persia, Persian
pert pertaining
pf, pfd preferred
pfc private first class
pg page
PG postgraduate
pharm pharmaceutical, pharmacist, pharmacy
PhD doctor of philosophy
Phila Philadelphia
philos philosopher, philosophy
phon phonetics
photog photographic, photography
phr phrase
phys physical, physician, physics

physiol physiologist, physiology
pizz pizzicato
pk park, peak, peck
pkg package
pkt packet
pkwy parkway
pl place, plate, plural
pm premium
p.m. post meridiem
Pm promethium
PM paymaster, police magistrate, postmaster, postmortem, prime minister, provost marshal
pmk postmark
pmt payment
PN promissory note
Po polonium
PO petty officer, post office
POC port of call
POD pay on delivery
POE port of embarkation, port of entry
Pol Poland, Polish
polit political, politician
polytech polytechnic
pop popular, population
POR pay on return
Port Portugal, Portuguese
pos position, positive
poss possessive
POW prisoner of war
pp pages, pianissimo
PP parcel post, past participle, postpaid, prepaid
ppd postpaid, prepaid
PPS post postscriptum (L, an additional postscript)
ppt precipitate
pptn precipitation
PQ Province of Quebec
pr pair, price
Pr praseodymium
PR payroll, public relations, Puerto Rico
prec preceding
pred predicate
pref preface, preference, preferred, prefix
prelim preliminary
prem premium
prep preparatory, preposition
pres present, president
prev previous
prf proof
prim primary
prin principal
PRO public relations officer
prob probable, probably, problem
proc proceedings
prod production
prof professor
prom promontory
pron pronoun, pronounced, pronunciation
prop propeller, property, proposition, proprietor
pros prosody
Prot Protestant
prov province, provincial, provisional
prox proximo
PS postscriptum (L, postscript), public school
pseud pseudonym
psi pounds per square inch
PST Pacific standard time
psych psychology

psychol psychologist, psychology
pt part, payment, pint, point, port
Pt platinum
PT Pacific time, physical therapy, physical training
PTA Parent-Teacher Association
pte private (British)
ptg printing
PTO please turn over
Pu plutonium
pub public, publication, published, publisher, publishing
publ publication, published
pvt private
PW prisoner of war
pwt pennyweight
PX post exchange

q quart, quarto, query, question, quintal, quire
Q quartile, queen
QC Queen's Counsel
QED quod erat demonstrandum (L, which was to be demonstrated)
QEF quod erat faciendum (L, which was to be done)
QEI quod erat inveniendum (L, which was to be found out)
QID quater in die (L, four times a day)
Qld, Q'land Queensland
QM quartermaster
QMC quartermaster corps
QMG quartermaster general
qq v quae vide (L pl., which see)
qr quarter, quire
qt quart, quiet
qto quarto
qty quantity
quad quadrant
Que Quebec
quot quotation
qv quod vide (L, which see)
qy query

r rare, right, river, roentgen
R rabbi, radius, Republican, resistance, rook
Ra radium
RA regular army, royal academy
RAAF Royal Australian Air Force
rad radical, radio, radius
RAdm rear admiral
RAF Royal Air Force
Rb rubidium
RBC red blood cells, red blood count
RBI runs batted in
RC Red Cross, Roman Catholic
RCAF Royal Canadian Air Force
RCMP Royal Canadian Mounted Police
rd road, rod, round
RD rural delivery
re reference, regarding
Re rhenium
rec receipt, record, recording, recreation
recd received

recip reciprocal, reciprocity
rec sec recording secretary
rect rectangle, rectangular, receipt, rectified
ref referee, reference, referred, reformed, refunding
refl reflex, reflexive
refrig refrigerating, refrigeration
reg region, register, registered, regular, regulation
regt regiment
rel relating, relative
relig religion
rep report, reporter, representative, republic
Rep Republican
repl replace, replacement
rept report
req require, required, requisition
res research, reserve, residence, resolution
resp respective, respectively
ret retain, retired, return
retd retained, retired, returned
rev revenue, reverend, reverse, review, reviewed, revised, revision, revolution
RF radio frequency
RFD rural free delivery
Rh rhodium
RH right hand
RI Rhode Island
RIP requiescat in pace (L, may he [she] rest in peace)
rit ritardando
riv river
rm ream, room
RMA Royal Military Academy (Sandhurst)
Rn radon
RN registered nurse, Royal Navy
RNZAF Royal New Zealand Air Force
ROG receipt of goods
Rom Roman, Romance, Romania, Romanian
ROTC Reserve Officers' Training Corps
rpm revolutions per minute
RPO railway post office
rps revolutions per second
rpt repeat, report
RQ respiratory quotient
RR railroad, rural route
RS recording secretary, revised statutes, right side, Royal Society
RSV Revised Standard Version
RSVP répondez s'il vous plaît (Fr, please reply)
RSWC right side up with care
rt right
rte route
Ru ruthenium
Rum Rumania, Rumanian
Russ Russia, Russian
RW right worshipful, right worthy
ry railway

s second, section, semi, series, shilling, sine, singular, son, soprano, stere
S saint, senate, signor,

small, south, southern, sulfur
SA Salvation Army, sex appeal, sine anno (L, without date), South Africa, South Australia, subject to approval
SAC Strategic Air Command
sanit sanitary, sanitation
Sask Saskatchewan
sat saturate, saturated, saturation
Sat Saturday
S Aust South Australia
sb substantive
Sb stibium (L, antimony)
SB bachelor of science, southbound
sc scale, scene, science, scilicet, small capitals
Sc scandium, Scots
SC South Carolina
Scand Scandinavia, Scandinavian
ScD doctor of science
sch school
sci science, scientific
scil scilicet
Scot Scotland, Scottish
script scripture
SD sea-damaged, sight draft, sine die (L, without day), South Dakota, special delivery
S Dak South Dakota
Se selenium
SE southeast
SEATO Southeast Asia Treaty Organization
sec secant, second, secondary, secretary, section, secundum (L, according to)
sect section
secy secretary
sel select, selected, selection
sem seminary
sen senate, senator, senior
sep separate
sepn separation
Sept, Sep September
seq sequens (L, the following)
seqq sequentia (L pl., the following)
ser serial, series
serg, sergt sergeant
serv service
sf science fiction, sforzando
SF sinking fund
sfc sergeant first class
sfz sforzando
sg senior grade, singular
SG solicitor general, surgeon general
sgt sergeant
sh share
Shak Shakespeare
shf superhigh frequency
shpt, shipt shipment
sht sheet
shtg shortage
Si silicon
sig signal, signature, signor
sin sine
sing singular
SJ Society of Jesus
Skt Sanskrit
SL salvage loss
sm small
Sm samarium

SM master of science
Sn stannum (LL, tin)
so south
SO seller's option
soc social, society
sociol sociology
sol solicitor, soluble, solution
soln solution
sop soprano
soph sophomore
sp special, species, specimen, spelling, spirit
Sp Spain, Spanish
SP shore patrol, shore patrolman, sine prole (L, without issue)
Span Spanish
SPCA Society for the Prevention of Cruelty to Animals
SPCC Society for the Prevention of Cruelty to Children
spec special
specif specific, specifically
sp gr specific gravity
spp species (pl)
sq squadron, square
sr senior
Sr senor, sister, strontium
SR shipping receipt
Sra senora
Sres señores
SRO standing room only
Srta senorita
SS saints, steamship, Sunday school
SSgt staff sergeant
ssp subspecies
SSS Selective Service System
st saint, stanza, state, stitch, stone, strait, street
ST short ton
sta station
stat statute
stbd starboard
std standard
STD doctor of sacred theology
ste sainte
stg, ster sterling
stk stock
STP standard temperature and pressure
stud student
subj subject, subjunctive
suff sufficient, suffix
Sun Sunday
sup superior, supplement, supplementary, supply, supra (L, above)
superl superlative
supp, suppl supplement, supplementary
supt superintendent
surg surgeon, surgery, surgical
surv survey, surveying, surveyor
SV sub verbo or sub voce (L, under the word)
Sw, Swed Sweden, Swedish
SW shipper's weight, shortwave, southwest
SWA South-West Africa
Switz Switzerland
syll syllable
sym symbol, symmetrical
syn synonym, synonymous, synonymy

syst system

t teaspoon, temperature, tenor, ton, troy
T tablespoon
Ta tantalum
tan tangent
Tas, Tasm Tasmania
taxon taxonomy
Tb terbium
TB trial balance, tuberculosis
tbs, tbsp tablespoon
Tc technetium
TC teachers college
TD touchdown
TDN total digestible nutrients
Te tellurium
tech technical, technically, technician, technological, technology
tel telegram, telegraph, telephone
teleg telegraphy
temp temperature, temporary, tempore (L, in the time of)
Tenn Tennessee
ter terrace, territory
terr territory
Tex Texas
Th thorium, Thursday
ThD doctor of theology
theat theatrical
theol theologian, theological, theology
therm thermometer
thou thousand
Thurs, Thur, Thu Thursday
Ti titanium
TID ter in die (L, three times a day)
tinct tincture
TKO technical knockout
tkt ticket
Tl thallium
TL total loss
TLC tender loving care
Tm thulium
TM trademark
tn ton, town
TN Tennessee
tnpk turnpike
TO telegraph office, turn over
topog topography
tot total
tp title page, township
tpk turnpike
tr translated, translation, translator, transpose
trans transaction, transitive, translated, translation, translator, transportation, transverse
transl translated, translation
transp transportation
treas treasurer, treasury
trib tributary
trig trigonometry
TSgt technical sergeant
TSH thyroid-stimulating hormone
tsp teaspoon
TT teletypewriter, tuberculin tested
Tues, Tue Tuesday
Turk Turkey, Turkish
TV television

TVA Tennessee Valley Authority
TX Texas

u unit
U university, uranium
UAR United Arab Republic
uc upper case
UFO unidentified flying object
uhf ultrahigh frequency
UK United Kingdom
ult ultimate, ultimo
UMT Universal Military Training
UN United Nations
UNESCO United Nations Educational, Scientific, and Cultural Organization
UNICEF United Nations Children's Fund
univ universal, university
UNRWA United Nations Relief and Works Agency
UPI United Press International
US United States
USA United States Army, United States of America
USAF United States Air Force
USCG United States Coast Guard
USES United States Employment Service
USM United States mail
USMA United States Military Academy
USMC United States Marine Corps
USN United States Navy
USNA United States Naval Academy
USP United States Pharmacopeia
USS United States Ship
USSR Union of Soviet Socialist Republics
usu usual, usually
UT Utah
UV ultraviolet
UW underwriter

v vector, velocity, verb, verse, versus, vice, vide (L, see), voice, volume, vowel
V vanadium, victory, volt, voltage
Va Virginia
VA Veterans Administration, vice admiral, Virginia
VAdm vice admiral
val value
var variable, variant, variation, variety, various
vb verb
VC vice-chancellor, vice-consul, Victoria Cross
VD venereal disease
veg vegetable
vel vellum, velocity
ven venerable
vert vertical
vet veterinarian, veterinary
VFD volunteer fire department
VFW Veterans of Foreign Wars
vhf very high frequency
vi verb intransitive, vide infra (L, see below)

VI Virgin Islands
vic vicinity
Vic Victoria
vil village
vis visibility, visual
viz videlicet (L, namely)
vlf very low frequency
VNA Visiting Nurse Association
voc vocative
vocab vocabulary
vol volume, volunteer
VOR very-high-frequency omnirange
vou voucher
VP vice-president
vs verse, versus, vide supra (L, see above)
vss verses, versions
vt verb transitive
Vt, VT Vermont
VTOL vertical takeoff and landing
Vulg Vulgate

vv verses, vice versa
w water, watt, week, weight, wide, width, wife, with
W west, western, wolfram (G, tungsten)
WA Washington
war warrant
Wash Washington
W Aust Western Australia
WB water ballast, waybill, westbound
WBC white blood cells, white blood count
WC water closet, without charge
WCTU Women's Christian Temperance Union
Wed Wednesday
wh watt-hour, which
whf wharf
WHO World Health Organization
whr watt-hour

whs, whse warehouse
whsle wholesale
WI West Indies, Wisconsin
wid widow, widower
Wis. Wisc Wisconsin
wk week, work
WL wavelength
wmk watermark
w/o without
WO warrant officer
wpm words per minute
wrnt warrant
wt weight
WV, WVa West Virginia
WW World War
WY, Wyo Wyoming

xd, x div without dividend
Xe xenon
x in, x int without interest
XL extra large
Xn Christian
Xnty Christianity

y yard, year
Y YMCA, yttrium
Yb ytterbium
yd yard
YMCA Young Men's Christian Association
YMHA Young Men's Hebrew Association
yr year, your
yrbk yearbook
yrs years, yours
Yt yttrium
YT Yukon Territory
YWCA, YW Young Women's Christian Association
YWHA Young Women's Hebrew Association

z zero
Zn zinc
zool zoological, zoology
Zr zirconium

SIGNS AND SYMBOLS

BIOLOGY

① *or* ☉ annual plant
② *or* ☉ biennial plant
♃ perennial herb
♄ tree or shrub
♀ female
♂ male
♀ neuter
♀ *or* ☿ hermaphrodite
✕ crossed with; hybrid; magnified by
∞ indefinitely numerous
= equals; is merged in
‖ parallel to
⊥ at right angles to
·|· bilaterally symmetrical
⊕ radially symmetrical

BOOKS

f° folio
4° *or* 4to quarto
8° *or* 8vo octavo
18° *or* 18mo octodecimo; eighteenmo

BUSINESS

@ at; each ⟨4 apples @ 5¢ =20¢⟩
℔ per ⟨sheep $4 ℔ head⟩
number if it precedes a numeral ⟨track #3⟩; pounds if it follows ⟨a 5# sack of sugar⟩
℔ pound; pounds
% percent
‰ per thousand
$ dollars
¢ cents
£ pounds
/ shillings

© copyrighted
® registered trademark

CHEMISTRY

(For element symbols see ELEMENT table)
+ signifies "plus", "and", "together with", and is used between the symbols of substances brought together for, or produced by, a reaction; placed above a symbol or to its right above the line, it signifies a unit charge of positive electricity: Ca^{++} denotes the ion of calcium, which carries two positive charges
− signifies a single "bond", or unit of attractive force or affinity, and is used between the symbols of elements or groups which unite to form a compound: $H-Cl$ for HCl, $H-O-H$ for H_2O; placed above a symbol or to its right above the line, it signifies a unit charge of negative electricity: Cl^- denotes a chlorine ion carrying a negative charge
′ often indicates valence (as Fe^{II} denotes bivalent iron, Fe^{III}, trivalent iron) is often used: (1) to indicate a bond (as H.Cl for $H-Cl$) or (2) to denote a unit positive charge of electricity (as Ca.. denotes two positive charges) or (3) to separate parts of a compound regarded as loosely joined (as $Cu-SO_4.5H_2O$)
⬡ denotes the benzene ring

= indicates a double bond; placed above a symbol or to its right above the line, it signifies two unit charges of negative electricity (as $SO_4=$, the negative ion of sulfuric acid, carrying two negative charges)
: indicates a double bond
( ) mark groups or radicals within a compound [as in $C_6H_4(CH_3)_2$, the formula for xylene which contains two methyl radicals (CH_3)]
= give or form
→ give, pass over to, or lead to
⇄ forms and is formed from
↓ indicates precipitation of the substance
↑ indicates that the substance passes off as a gas
pH hydrogen-ion concentration

MATHEMATICS

+ plus; positive ⟨a+b=c⟩ —used also to indicate omitted figures or an approximation
− minus; negative
± plus or minus ⟨the square root of $4a^2$ is ± 2a⟩; more or less than ⟨a deviation of ±2⟩
✕ multiplied by; times ⟨6✕4=24⟩—also indicated by placing a dot between the factors ⟨6·4=24⟩ or by writing factors other than numerals without signs
÷ *or* : divided by ⟨24÷6 =4⟩ — also indicated by writing the divisor under the dividend with a line between ⟨$\frac{24}{6}$=4⟩ or by writing the divisor after the

dividend with a diagonal between ⟨3/8⟩
= equals ⟨6+2=8⟩
≠ *or* ≠ is not equal to
> is greater than ⟨6>5⟩
< is less than ⟨3<4⟩
≧ *or* ≥ is greater than or equal to
≦ *or* ≤ is less than or equal to
≯ is not greater than
≮ is not less than
≈ is approximately equal to
≡ is identical to
≃ equivalent; similar
≅ is congruent to
: is to; the ratio of
∴ therefore
∞ infinity
0 zero
∠ angle; the angle ⟨∠ABC⟩
∟ right angle ⟨∟ABC⟩
⊥ the perpendicular; is perpendicular to ⟨AB ⊥ CD⟩
‖ parallel; is parallel to ⟨AB ‖ CD⟩
⊙ *or* ○ circle
△ triangle
□ square
▭ rectangle
√ *or* √ root—used without a figure to indicate a square root ⟨as in √4=2⟩ or with an index above the sign to indicate another degree ⟨as in $\sqrt[3]{3}$, $\sqrt[5]{7}$⟩; also denoted by a fractional index at the right of a number whose denominator expresses the degree of the root ⟨$3^{1/3}=\sqrt[3]{3}$⟩

( ) parentheses ⎫
[ ] brackets ⎬ indicate that the quantities enclosed by them are to be taken together
{ } braces ⎭

π pi; the number 3.141-59265+; the ratio of the circumference of a circle to its diameter

! —used to indicate the product of all the whole numbers up to and including a given preceding number

e or ε (1) the number 2.7182818+; the base of the natural system of logarithms (2) the eccentricity of a conic section

° degree ⟨60°⟩

′ minute; foot ⟨30′⟩—

used also to distinguish between different values of the same variable or between different variables (as a', a'', a''', usu. read a prime, a double prime, a triple prime)

″ second, inch ⟨30″⟩

², ³, etc. —used as exponents placed above and at the right of an expression to indicate that it is raised to a power whose degree is indicated by the figure ⟨a^2, the square of a⟩

n —used as a constant denoting an unspecified degree, order, class, or power

i imaginary unit; $+\sqrt{-1}$

∪ union of two sets

∩ intersection of two sets

⊂ is included in, is a subset of

⊃ contains as a subset

∈ or ε is an element of

∉ is not an element of

Λ or 0 or φ or {} empty set, null set

MISCELLANEOUS

& and

&c etcetera; and so forth

< derived from ⎫
> whence derived ⎬ used in etymologies
+ and ⎭
* assumed

† died—used esp. in genealogies

✶ monogram from Greek XP signifying Jesus

LXX Septuagint

✡ Star of David

☥ ankh

℣ versicle

℟ response

✳ —used in Roman Catholic and Anglican service books to divide each verse of a psalm, indicating where the response begins

✠ or + —used in some service books to indicate where the sign of the cross is to be made; also used by certain Roman Catholic and Anglican prelates as a sign of the cross preceding their signatures

$f/$ or f: relative aperture of a photographic lens

☠ poison

℞ take—used on prescriptions

CD civil defense

(For Roman numerals see NUMBER table)